T0394702

2025
Harris
Ohio
Industrial Directory

MERGENT
Exclusive Provider of
Dun & Bradstreet Library Solutions

dun&bradstreet

 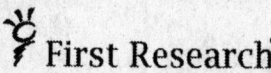 

Published July 2025 next update July 2026

Publisher

Mergent Inc.
444 Madison Ave
New York, NY 10022

©Mergent Inc All Rights Reserved
2025 Mergent Business Press
ISSN 1080-2614
ISBN 978-1-63053-065-5

MERGENT
BUSINESS PRESS
by FTSE Russell

TABLE OF CONTENTS

SUMMARY OF CONTENTS

Number of Companies 15,058

Number of Decision Makers 25,361

Minimum Number of Employees 6

EXPLANATORY NOTES

How to Cross-Reference in This Directory

Sequential Entry Numbers. Each establishment in the Geographic Section is numbered sequentially (G-0000). The number assigned to each establishment is referred to as its "entry number." To make cross-referencing easier, each listing in the Geographic, SIC, Alphabetic and Product Sections includes the establishment's entry number. To facilitate locating an entry in the Geographic Section, the entry numbers for the first listing on the left page and the last listing on the right page are printed at the top of the page next to the city name.

Source Suggestions Welcome

Although all known sources were used to compile this directory, it is possible that companies were inadvertently omitted. Your assistance in calling attention to such omissions would be greatly appreciated. A special form on the facing page will help you in the reporting process.

Analysis

Every effort has been made to contact all firms to verify their information. The one exception to this rule is the annual sales figure, which is considered by many companies to be confidential information. Therefore, estimated sales have been calculated by multiplying the nationwide average sales per employee for the firm's major SIC/NAICS code by the firm's number of employees. Nationwide averages for sales per employee by SIC/NAICS codes are provided by the U.S. Department of Commerce and are updated annually. All sales—sales (est)—have been estimated by this method. The exceptions are parent companies (PA), division headquarters (DH) and headquarter locations (HQ) which may include an actual corporate sales figure—sales (corporate-wide) if available.

Types of Companies

Descriptive and statistical data are included for companies in the entire state. These comprise manufacturers, machine shops, fabricators, assemblers and printers. Also identified are corporate offices in the state.

Employment Data

This directory contains companies with 6 or more employees. The employment figure shown in the Geographic Section includes male and female employees and embraces all levels of the company: administrative, clerical, sales and maintenance. This figure is for the facility listed and does not include other plants or offices. It should be recognized that these figures represent an approximate year-round average. These employment figures are broken into codes A through G and used in the Product and SIC Sections to further help you in qualifying a company. Be sure to check the footnotes on the bottom of pages for the code breakdowns.

Standard Industrial Classification (SIC)

The Standard Industrial Classification (SIC) system used in this directory was developed by the federal government for use in classifying establishments by the type of activity they are engaged in. The SIC classifications used in this directory are from the 1987 edition published by the U.S. Government's Office of Management and Budget. The SIC system separates all activities into broad industrial divisions (e.g., manufacturing, mining, retail trade). It further subdivides each division. The range of manufacturing industry classes extends from two-digit codes (major industry group) to four-digit codes (product).

For example:

Industry Breakdown	Code	Industry, Product, etc.
*Major industry group	20	Food and kindred products
Industry group	203	Canned and frozen foods
*Industry	2033	Fruits and vegetables, etc.

*Classifications used in this directory

Only two-digit and four-digit codes are used in this directory.

Arrangement

1. The **Geographic Section** contains complete in-depth corporate data. This section is sorted by cities listed in alphabetical order and companies listed alphabetically within each city. A County/City Index for referencing cities within counties precedes this section.

IMPORTANT NOTICE: It is a violation of both federal and state law to transmit an unsolicited advertisement to a facsimile machine. Any user of this product that violates such laws may be subject to civil and criminal penalties, which may exceed $500 for each transmission of an unsolicited facsimile. Mergent Inc. provides fax numbers for lawful purposes only and expressly forbids the use of these numbers in any unlawful manner.

2. The **Standard Industrial Classification (SIC) Section** lists companies under approximately 500 four-digit SIC codes. An alphabetical and a numerical index precedes this section. A company can be listed under several codes. The codes are in numerical order with companies listed alphabetically under each code.

3. The **Alphabetic Section** lists all companies with their full physical or mailing addresses and telephone number.

4. The **Product Section** lists companies under unique Harris categories. An index preceding this section lists all product categories in alphabetical order. Companies can be listed under several categories.

USER'S GUIDE TO LISTINGS

GEOGRAPHIC SECTION

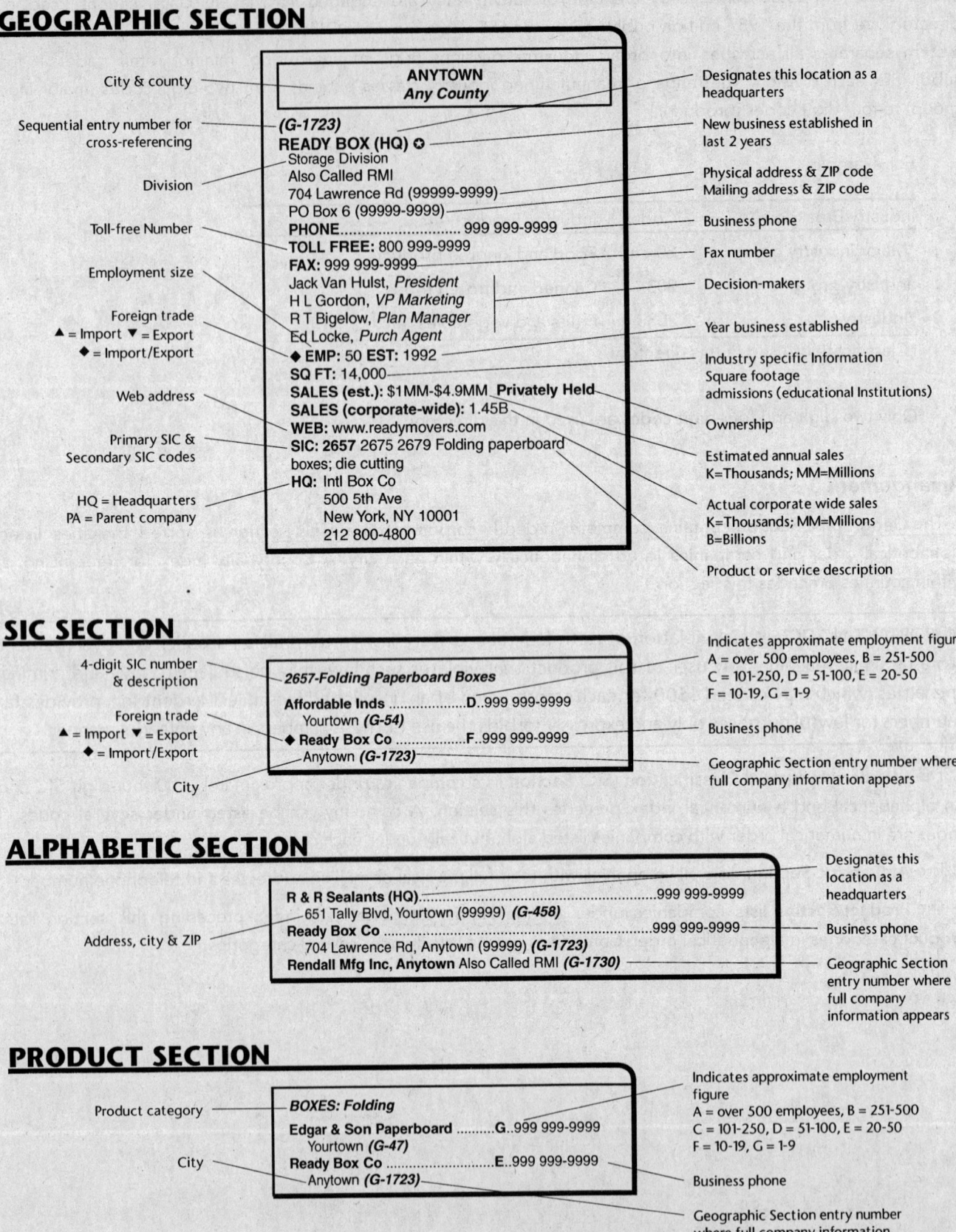

City & county

Sequential entry number for cross-referencing

Division

Toll-free Number

Employment size

Foreign trade
▲ = Import ▼ = Export
◆ = Import/Export

Web address

Primary SIC & Secondary SIC codes

HQ = Headquarters
PA = Parent company

ANYTOWN
Any County

(G-1723)
READY BOX (HQ) ✪
Storage Division
Also Called RMI
704 Lawrence Rd (99999-9999)
PO Box 6 (99999-9999)
PHONE............................ 999 999-9999
TOLL FREE: 800 999-9999
FAX: 999 999-9999
Jack Van Hulst, *President*
H L Gordon, *VP Marketing*
R T Bigelow, *Plan Manager*
Ed Locke, *Purch Agent*
◆ **EMP:** 50 **EST:** 1992
SQ FT: 14,000
SALES (est.): $1MM-$4.9MM **Privately Held**
SALES (corporate-wide): 1.45B
WEB: www.readymovers.com
SIC: 2657 2675 2679 Folding paperboard boxes; die cutting
HQ: Intl Box Co
500 5th Ave
New York, NY 10001
212 800-4800

Designates this location as a headquarters

New business established in last 2 years

Physical address & ZIP code
Mailing address & ZIP code

Business phone

Fax number

Decision-makers

Year business established

Industry specific Information
Square footage
admissions (educational Institutions)

Ownership

Estimated annual sales
K=Thousands; MM=Millions

Actual corporate wide sales
K=Thousands; MM=Millions
B=Billions

Product or service description

SIC SECTION

4-digit SIC number & description

Foreign trade
▲ = Import ▼ = Export
◆ = Import/Export

City

2657-Folding Paperboard Boxes

Affordable Inds ....**D**..999 999-9999
Yourtown **(G-54)**
◆ **Ready Box Co** ....**F**..999 999-9999
Anytown **(G-1723)**

Indicates approximate employment figure
A = over 500 employees, B = 251-500
C = 101-250, D = 51-100, E = 20-50
F = 10-19, G = 1-9

Business phone

Geographic Section entry number where full company information appears

ALPHABETIC SECTION

Address, city & ZIP

R & R Sealants (HQ)..................................999 999-9999
651 Tally Blvd, Yourtown (99999) **(G-458)**
Ready Box Co 999 999-9999
704 Lawrence Rd, Anytown (99999) **(G-1723)**
Rendall Mfg Inc, Anytown Also Called RMI **(G-1730)**

Designates this location as a headquarters

Business phone

Geographic Section entry number where full company information appears

PRODUCT SECTION

Product category

City

BOXES: Folding

Edgar & Son Paperboard ....**G**..999 999-9999
Yourtown **(G-47)**
Ready Box Co ....**E**..999 999-9999
Anytown **(G-1723)**

Indicates approximate employment figure
A = over 500 employees, B = 251-500
C = 101-250, D = 51-100, E = 20-50
F = 10-19, G = 1-9

Business phone

Geographic Section entry number where full company information appears

GEOGRAPHIC SECTION

Companies sorted by city in alphabetical order
In-depth company data listed

STANDARD INDUSTRIAL CLASSIFICATIONS

Alphabetical index of classification descriptions
Numerical index of classification descriptions
Companies sorted by SIC product groupings

ALPHABETIC SECTION

Company listings in alphabetical order

PRODUCT INDEX

Product categories listed in alphabetical order

PRODUCT SECTION

Companies sorted by product and manufacturing service classifications

GEOGRAPHIC

SIC

ALPHABETIC

PRDT INDEX

PRODUCT

COUNTY/CITY CROSS-REFERENCE INDEX

ENTRY #	ENTRY #	ENTRY #	ENTRY #	ENTRY #

Senecaville .... (G-11906)

Hamilton
Addyston .... (G-8)
Blue Ash .... (G-1241)
Cincinnati .... (G-2319)
Cleves .... (G-4532)
Harrison .... (G-7542)
Miamitown .... (G-9756)
Montgomery .... (G-10124)
Newtown .... (G-10583)
North Bend .... (G-10620)
Norwood .... (G-10866)
Sharonville .... (G-11945)
Springdale .... (G-12273)
West Chester ....(G-14096)

Hancock
Arcadia .... (G-482)
Findlay ....(G-6831)
Mc Comb .... (G-9352)
Mount Cory .... (G-10205)
Rawson .... (G-11551)
Van Buren ....(G-13524)
Vanlue ....(G-13585)

Hardin
Ada ....(G-2)
Alger .... (G-363)
Dunkirk .... (G-6375)
Forest .... (G-6938)
Kenton .... (G-8095)
Mount Victory .... (G-10269)

Harrison
Bowerston .... (G-1399)
Cadiz .... (G-1719)
Freeport .... (G-7089)
Jewett .... (G-7989)
Scio ....(G-11888)
Tippecanoe .... (G-12856)

Henry
Deshler .... (G-6222)
Liberty Center .... (G-8376)
Malinta .... (G-8742)
Mc Clure .... (G-9351)
Napoleon .... (G-10274)
Okolona .... (G-10932)
Ridgeville Corners ... (G-11615)

Highland
Greenfield ....(G-7324)
Hillsboro .... (G-7713)
Leesburg .... (G-8298)

Hocking
Laurelville .... (G-8237)
Logan ....(G-8508)

Holmes
Berlin .... (G-1198)
Big Prairie .... (G-1216)
Charm ....(G-2227)
Glenmont ....(G-7284)
Holmesville .... (G-7793)
Killbuck .... (G-8130)
Lakeville .... (G-8159)
Millersburg .... (G-9966)
Mount Hope .... (G-10213)
Walnut Creek .... (G-13693)

Huron
Bellevue .... (G-1117)
Collins .... (G-4587)
Greenwich .... (G-7361)
Monroeville .... (G-10117)
New London .... (G-10410)
Norwalk .... (G-10829)
Plymouth .... (G-11433)
Wakeman .... (G-13678)
Willard .... (G-14401)

Jackson
Jackson .... (G-7938)
Oak Hill .... (G-10887)
Wellston .... (G-13905)

Jefferson
Bergholz .... (G-1195)
Brilliant .... (G-1497)
Irondale .... (G-7927)
Mingo Junction .... (G-10050)
Rayland .... (G-11552)
Richmond .... (G-11604)
Steubenville .... (G-12399)
Tiltonsville .... (G-12809)
Toronto .... (G-13185)
Wintersville .... (G-14610)
Yorkville .... (G-14798)

Knox
Bladensburg .... (G-1232)
Centerburg .... (G-2128)
Danville ....(G-5598)
Fredericktown .... (G-7074)
Gambier .... (G-7211)
Mount Vernon .... (G-10232)

Lake
Concord Township .... (G-5385)
Eastlake .... (G-6414)
Fairport Harbor .... (G-6816)
Grand River .... (G-7310)
Kirtland .... (G-8144)
Madison .... (G-8723)
Mentor .... (G-9467)
Mentor On The Lake .. (G-9656)
Painesville .... (G-11066)
Perry ....(G-11190)
Wickliffe .... (G-14365)
Willoughby .... (G-14412)
Willoughby Hills ...... (G-14555)
Willowick .... (G-14565)

Lawrence
Chesapeake .... (G-2228)
Ironton .... (G-7928)
Kitts Hill .... (G-8147)
Proctorville .... (G-11499)
South Point .... (G-12221)

Licking
Croton ....(G-5514)
Etna ....(G-6635)
Granville .... (G-7313)
Heath .... (G-7592)
Hebron .... (G-7606)
Homer .... (G-7804)
Johnstown .... (G-7990)
Newark ....(G-10489)

Pataskala .... (G-11137)
Saint Louisville .... (G-11728)
Utica ....(G-13485)

Logan
Belle Center .... (G-1094)
Bellefontaine .... (G-1098)
De Graff .... (G-6091)
East Liberty .... (G-6383)
Huntsville .... (G-7863)
Lakeview .... (G-8158)
Lewistown .... (G-8365)
Rushsylvania .... (G-11665)
Russells Point .... (G-11667)
West Liberty .... (G-14175)
West Mansfield .... (G-14178)

Lorain
Amherst .... (G-444)
Avon ....(G-710)
Avon Lake .... (G-746)
Columbia Station .... (G-4588)
Elyria ....(G-6492)
Grafton .... (G-7299)
Lagrange .... (G-8148)
Lorain .... (G-8544)
North Ridgeville .... (G-10723)
Oberlin .... (G-10914)
Sheffield Lake .... (G-11953)
Sheffield Village .... (G-11955)
Wellington .... (G-13883)

Lucas
Holland .... (G-7743)
Maumee .... (G-9257)
Oregon .... (G-10955)
Sylvania .... (G-12700)
Toledo .... (G-12859)
Waterville .... (G-13830)
Whitehouse .... (G-14357)

Madison
London .... (G-8529)
Mount Sterling .... (G-10227)
Plain City .... (G-11389)
West Jefferson .... (G-14160)

Mahoning
Austintown .... (G-704)
Beloit .... (G-1144)
Berlin Center .... (G-1201)
Boardman .... (G-1368)
Campbell .... (G-1770)
Canfield .... (G-1801)
Lowellville .... (G-8657)
New Middletown ...... (G-10424)
New Springfield ...... (G-10472)
North Jackson .... (G-10682)
North Lima .... (G-10704)
Poland .... (G-11434)
Sebring .... (G-11890)
Struthers .... (G-12615)
Youngstown .... (G-14799)

Marion
Caledonia .... (G-1731)
Marion ....(G-8964)
Morral .... (G-10199)
Prospect .... (G-11501)
Waldo .... (G-13690)

Medina
Brunswick .... (G-1577)
Hinckley .... (G-7730)
Litchfield .... (G-8481)
Lodi .... (G-8495)
Medina .... (G-9369)
Seville .... (G-11908)
Sharon Center .... (G-11936)
Spencer .... (G-12233)
Valley City .... (G-13489)
Wadsworth .... (G-13625)

Meigs
Pomeroy .... (G-11437)
Portland .... (G-11462)
Racine .... (G-11504)
Tuppers Plains .... (G-13262)

Mercer
Burkettsville .... (G-1698)
Celina ....(G-2098)
Chickasaw .... (G-2240)
Coldwater .... (G-4567)
Fort Recovery .... (G-6961)
Maria Stein .... (G-8899)
Rockford .... (G-11630)
Saint Henry .... (G-11720)

Miami
Bradford .... (G-1451)
Casstown .... (G-2092)
Conover .... (G-5420)
Covington .... (G-5488)
Ludlow Falls .... (G-8672)
Piqua ....(G-11332)
Pleasant Hill .... (G-11431)
Tipp City .... (G-12811)
Troy ....(G-13198)
West Milton .... (G-14182)

Monroe
Clarington .... (G-3270)
Hannibal .... (G-7540)
Lewisville .... (G-8366)
Sardis ....(G-11887)
Woodsfield .... (G-14612)

Montgomery
Beavercreek .... (G-987)
Brookville .... (G-1561)
Centerville .... (G-2129)
Clayton .... (G-3271)
Dayton .... (G-5627)
Englewood .... (G-6605)
Farmersville .... (G-6823)
Germantown .... (G-7252)
Huber Heights .... (G-7820)
Kettering .... (G-8117)
Miamisburg .... (G-9659)
Moraine ....(G-10140)
New Lebanon .... (G-10399)
Oakwood .... (G-10895)
Trotwood .... (G-13195)
Union .... (G-13410)
Vandalia .... (G-13548)
West Carrollton .... (G-13926)

Morgan
Malta ....(G-8744)
Mcconnelsville .... (G-9362)

Morrow
Cardington .... (G-2053)
Fulton .... (G-7151)
Iberia .... (G-7883)
Marengo .... (G-8896)
Mount Gilead .... (G-10209)

Muskingum
Adamsville .... (G-7)
Frazeysburg .... (G-7059)
Nashport .... (G-10299)
New Concord .... (G-10384)
Norwich .... (G-10864)
Roseville .... (G-11653)
South Zanesville ...... (G-12232)
Zanesville .... (G-14980)

Noble
Caldwell .... (G-1722)
Dexter City .... (G-6223)
Sarahsville .... (G-11884)
Summerfield .... (G-12660)

Ottawa
Curtice .... (G-5517)
Elmore .... (G-6488)
Genoa .... (G-7247)
Gypsum .... (G-7460)
Lakeside .... (G-8157)
Marblehead .... (G-8895)
Oak Harbor .... (G-10881)
Port Clinton .... (G-11439)
Williston .... (G-14411)

Paulding
Antwerp .... (G-461)
Grover Hill .... (G-7459)
Haviland .... (G-7586)
Latty .... (G-8236)
Oakwood .... (G-10896)
Paulding .... (G-11153)
Payne .... (G-11163)

Perry
Corning .... (G-5440)
Crooksville .... (G-5508)
Junction City .... (G-8002)
Mount Perry .... (G-10225)
New Lexington .... (G-10401)
Shawnee .... (G-11952)
Somerset .... (G-12210)
Thornville .... (G-12765)

Pickaway
Ashville .... (G-624)
Circleville .... (G-3246)
New Holland .... (G-10397)
Orient .... (G-10970)

Pike
Beaver .... (G-960)
Latham .... (G-8235)
Piketon .... (G-11306)
Waverly .... (G-13863)

Portage
Atwater .... (G-658)
Aurora ....(G-659)
Deerfield .... (G-6093)
Diamond .... (G-6226)
Garrettsville .... (G-7217)

ENTRY #	ENTRY #	ENTRY #	ENTRY #	ENTRY #

Hiram .... (G-7737)
Kent .... (G-8012)
Mantua .... (G-8867)
Mogadore .... (G-10068)
North Benton .... (G-10623)
Randolph .... (G-11509)
Ravenna ....(G-11511)
Rootstown .... (G-11646)
Streetsboro .... (G-12484)
Windham .... (G-14600)

Preble

Camden .... (G-1767)
Eaton .... (G-6448)
Eldorado .... (G-6480)
Gratis .... (G-7321)
Lewisburg .... (G-8358)
New Paris .... (G-10425)
Verona .... (G-13591)
West Alexandria ...... (G-13916)
West Manchester ..... (G-14177)

Putnam

Cloverdale .... (G-4555)
Columbus Grove ...... (G-5382)
Continental .... (G-5422)
Gilboa .... (G-7261)
Glandorf .... (G-7283)
Kalida .... (G-8003)
Leipsic .... (G-8306)
Ottawa ....(G-11030)
Ottoville .... (G-11051)

Richland

Bellville .... (G-1137)
Lexington .... (G-8367)
Mansfield .... (G-8757)
Ontario .... (G-10947)
Shelby .... (G-11966)
Shiloh ....(G-11977)

Ross

Chillicothe .... (G-2241)
Frankfort .... (G-7004)
Richmond Dale .... (G-11606)

Sandusky

Clyde ....(G-4556)
Fremont .... (G-7090)
Gibsonburg .... (G-7258)
Millersville .... (G-10027)
Woodville .... (G-14616)

Scioto

Franklin Furnace .... (G-7058)
Haverhill .... (G-7585)
Lucasville .... (G-8666)
Mc Dermott ....(G-9356)
New Boston .... (G-10355)
Otway ....(G-11058)
Portsmouth .... (G-11463)
South Webster .... (G-12231)
Wheelersburg .... (G-14352)

Seneca

Alvada ....(G-420)
Attica .... (G-656)
Bettsville .... (G-1207)
Bloomville .... (G-1240)
Fostoria .... (G-6974)
New Riegel .... (G-10470)
Old Fort .... (G-10933)
Tiffin ....(G-12772)

Shelby

Anna .... (G-459)
Botkins .... (G-1396)
Fort Loramie .... (G-6944)
Jackson Center .... (G-7957)
Kettlersville .... (G-8125)
Port Jefferson .... (G-11454)
Russia .... (G-11672)
Sidney .... (G-11988)

Stark

Alliance ....(G-364)
Beach City .... (G-904)
Brewster .... (G-1490)
Canal Fulton .... (G-1772)
Canton .... (G-1819)
East Canton .... (G-6376)
East Sparta .... (G-6411)
Greentown .... (G-7332)
Hartville .... (G-7574)
Louisville .... (G-8598)
Magnolia .... (G-8735)
Massillon .... (G-9168)
Middlebranch .... (G-9765)
Minerva ....(G-10032)
Navarro .... (G 10302)
North Canton .... (G-10626)
North Lawrence .... (G-10701)
Uniontown .... (G-13416)
Waynesburg .... (G-13875)
Wilmot ....(G-14592)

Summit

Akron ....(G-9)
Barberton .... (G-790)
Bath .... (G-898)
Clinton ....(G-4553)
Copley .... (G-5427)
Coventry Township ... (G-5479)
Cuyahoga Falls .... (G-5519)
Fairlawn .... (G-6797)
Green ....(G-7323)
Hudson ....(G-7826)
Lakemore .... (G-8156)
Macedonia .... (G-8676)
Munroe Falls .... (G-10271)
New Franklin .... (G-10388)
Northfield .... (G-10791)
Norton ....(G-10816)
Peninsula .... (G-11179)
Richfield .... (G-11587)
Silver Lake .... (G-12063)
Stow ....(G-12414)
Tallmadge .... (G-12729)
Twinsburg .... (G-13264)

Trumbull

Bristolville .... (G-1498)
Brookfield .... (G-1514)
Burghill .... (G-1697)
Cortland ....(G-5442)
Girard ....(G-7262)
Hartford .... (G-7573)
Hubbard ....(G-7808)
Kinsman .... (G-8140)
Leavittsburg .... (G-8239)
Masury .... (G-9253)
Mc Donald .... (G-9357)
Mineral Ridge .... (G-10029)
Newton Falls .... (G-10576)
Niles ....(G-10584)
North Bloomfield ..... (G-10625)
Vienna .... (G-13607)
Warren .... (G-13731)
West Farmington ..... (G-14159)

Tuscarawas

Baltic ....(G-775)
Bolivar ....(G-1381)
Dennison .... (G-6216)
Dover ....(G-6228)
Dundee ....(G-6364)
Gnadenhutten .... (G-7291)
Midvale ....(G-9906)

Mineral City

Mineral City .... (G-10028)
New Philadelphia ..... (G-10428)
Newcomerstown ...... (G-10566)
Port Washington ...... (G-11455)
Strasburg .... (G-12475)
Sugarcreek .... (G-12631)
Uhrichsville .... (G-13401)

Union

Marysville .... (G-9014)
Milford Center .... (G-9956)
Raymond .... (G-11553)
Richwood .... (G-11614)

Van Wert

Convoy .... (G-5425)
Middle Point .... (G-9764)
Van Wert ....(G-13525)
Venedocia .... (G-13586)

Vinton

Hamden .... (G-7461)
Mc Arthur .... (G-9348)
Zaleski ....(G-14979)

Warren

Carlisle .... (G-2065)
Franklin .... (G-7006)
Kings Mills .... (G-8137)
Lebanon .... (G-8241)
Maineville .... (G-8737)
Mason ....(G-9056)
Morrow .... (G-10201)
Pleasant Plain .... (G-11432)
South Lebanon .... (G-12220)
Springboro .... (G-12244)
Waynesville .... (G-13879)

Washington

Belpre .... (G-1146)
Beverly .... (G-1208)
Graysville .... (G-7322)
Little Hocking .... (G-8485)
Lower Salem .... (G-8665)
Marietta .... (G-8901)
New Matamoras ...... (G-10423)
Vincent .... (G-13619)
Waterford .... (G-13825)
Whipple .... (G-14356)

Wayne

Apple Creek .... (G-465)
Creston .... (G-5505)
Dalton ....(G-5583)
Doylestown .... (G-6269)
Fredericksburg .... (G-7060)
Kidron ....(G-8126)
Marshallville .... (G-9007)
Mount Eaton .... (G-10206)
Orrville .... (G-10972)
Rittman .... (G-11621)
Shreve .... (G-11981)
Smithville .... (G-12064)
Sterling .... (G-12398)
West Salem .... (G-14186)
Wooster .... (G-14617)

Williams

Bryan .... (G-1625)
Edgerton .... (G-6464)
Edon .... (G-6472)
Holiday City .... (G-7742)
Montpelier .... (G-10126)
Pioneer .... (G-11317)
Stryker .... (G-12621)
West Unity .... (G-14191)

Wood

Bowling Green .... (G-1403)
Bradner .... (G-1454)
Grand Rapids .... (G-7307)
Luckey .... (G-8670)
Millbury .... (G-9959)
North Baltimore .... (G-10612)
Northwood .... (G-10801)
Pemberville .... (G-11174)
Perrysburg .... (G-11201)
Portage .... (G-11457)
Risingsun .... (G-11620)
Rossford .... (G-11656)
Walbridge .... (G-13683)
Weston .... (G-14347)

Wyandot

Carey .... (G-2056)
Mc Cutchenville .... (G-9355)
Nevada .... (G-10323)
Sycamore .... (G-12699)
Upper Sandusky ...... (G-13433)
Wharton ....(G-14351)

GEOGRAPHIC SECTION

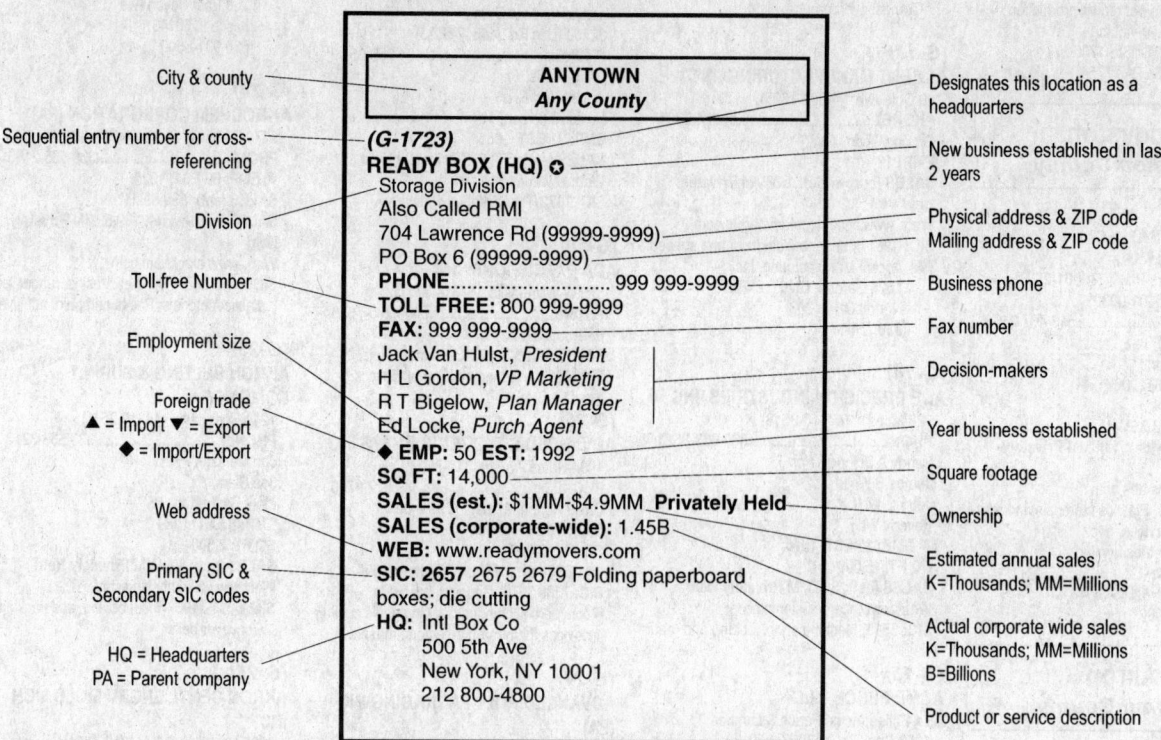

City & county →

Sequential entry number for cross-referencing →

Division →

Toll-free Number →

Employment size →

Foreign trade
▲ = Import ▼ = Export
◆ = Import/Export →

Web address →

Primary SIC & Secondary SIC codes →

HQ = Headquarters
PA = Parent company →

ANYTOWN
Any County

(G-1723)
READY BOX (HQ) ✿
Storage Division
Also Called RMI
704 Lawrence Rd (99999-9999)
PO Box 6 (99999-9999)
PHONE............................ 999 999-9999
TOLL FREE: 800 999-9999
FAX: 999 999-9999
Jack Van Hulst, *President*
H L Gordon, *VP Marketing*
R T Bigelow, *Plan Manager*
Ed Locke, *Purch Agent*
◆ **EMP:** 50 **EST:** 1992
SQ FT: 14,000
SALES (est.): $1MM-$4.9MM **Privately Held**
SALES (corporate-wide): 1.45B
WEB: www.readymovers.com
SIC: 2657 2675 2679 Folding paperboard boxes; die cutting
HQ: Intl Box Co
500 5th Ave
New York, NY 10001
212 800-4800

→ Designates this location as a headquarters

→ New business established in last 2 years

→ Physical address & ZIP code
→ Mailing address & ZIP code

→ Business phone

→ Fax number

→ Decision-makers

→ Year business established

→ Square footage

→ Ownership

→ Estimated annual sales
K=Thousands; MM=Millions

→ Actual corporate wide sales
K=Thousands; MM=Millions
B=Billions

→ Product or service description

G E O G R A P H I C

See footnotes for symbols and codes identification.
- This section is in alphabetical order by city.
- Companies are sorted alphabetically under their respective cities.
- To locate cities within a county refer to the County/City Cross Reference Index.

IMPORTANT NOTICE: It is a violation of both federal and state law to transmit an unsolicited advertisement to a facsimile machine. Any user of this product that violates such laws may be subject to civil and criminal penalties which may exceed $500 for each transmission of an unsolicited facsimile. Harris InfoSource provides fax numbers for lawful purposes only and expressly forbids the use of these numbers in any unlawful manner.

Aberdeen
Brown County

(G-1)
HILLTOP BASIC RESOURCES INC
Also Called: Maysville Ready Mix Con Co
8030 Rte 52 Us (45101)
PHONE.............................937 795-2020
John F Steele Junior, *CEO*
EMP: 10
SALES (corp-wide): 49.96MM **Privately Held**
Web: www.hilltopcompanies.com
SIC: 3273 Ready-mixed concrete
PA: Hilltop Basic Resources, Inc.
50 E Rvrcnter Blvd Ste 10
Covington KY 41011
513 651-5000

Ada
Hardin County

(G-2)
ADA TECHNOLOGIES INC (HQ)
805 E North Ave (45810-1809)

PHONE.............................419 634-7000
Noriyuki Suzuki, *Pr*
Keith Montgomery, *
Masakatsu Marui, *
▲ **EMP:** 240 **EST:** 1995
SQ FT: 156,000
SALES (est): 45.65MM **Privately Held**
Web: www.adatechinc.com
SIC: 3714 Motor vehicle transmissions, drive assemblies, and parts
PA: Motherson Atsumitec Automotive System Company Limited
4-6-1, Takaokanishi, Chuo-Ku
Hamamatsu SZO 433-8

(G-3)
ASSOCIATED PLASTICS CORP
502 Eric Wolber Dr (45810-1100)
PHONE.............................419 634-3910
Fred Wolber, *Pr*
George Wolber, *
Samuel W Diller, *
▲ **EMP:** 70 **EST:** 1976
SQ FT: 63,000
SALES (est): 8.41MM **Privately Held**
Web: www.associatedplasticscorp.com
SIC: 3089 Injection molding of plastics

(G-4)
NASG OHIO LLC
Also Called: North American Stamping Group
605 E Montford Ave (45810-1804)
P.O. Box 265 (45810-0265)
PHONE.............................419 634-3125
Michael Haughey, *Managing Member*
EMP: 11 **EST:** 2002
SALES (est): 5.08MM
SALES (corp-wide): 250.69MM **Privately Held**
Web: www.nasg.net
SIC: 3469 Stamping metal for the trade
PA: Nasg Realty, Llc
119 Kirby Dr
Portland TN 37148
615 323-0500

(G-5)
SAY SECURITY GROUP USA LLC (PA)
520 E Montford Ave (45810-1821)
PHONE.............................419 634-0004
Jason Szuch, *Managing Member*
▲ **EMP:** 18 **EST:** 2003
SQ FT: 10,000
SALES (est): 1.49MM
SALES (corp-wide): 1.49MM **Privately Held**

Web: www.saysecurity.com
SIC: 7382 3699 Security systems services, Security devices

(G-6)
WILSON SPORTING GOODS CO
217 Liberty St (45810-1135)
P.O. Box 116 (45810-0116)
PHONE.............................419 634-9901
Dan Riegle, *Mgr*
EMP: 208
SQ FT: 30,000
Web: www.wilson.com
SIC: 3949 Sporting and athletic goods, nec
HQ: Wilson Sporting Goods Co.
One Prdntial Plz 130 E Rn
Chicago IL 60601
773 714-6400

Adamsville
Muskingum County

(G-7)
EXCO RESOURCES (PA) LLC
4100 Valley Rd (43802)
PHONE.............................740 796-5231
EMP: 16

(PA)=Parent Co (HQ)=Headquarters
✿ = New Business established in last 2 years

2025 Harris Ohio
Industrial Directory

13

SALES (corp-wide): 394.03MM **Privately Held**
SIC: 1311 Crude petroleum production
HQ: Exco Resources, Llc
   12377 Merit Dr Ste 1700
   Montoursville PA 17754

Addyston
Hamilton County

(G-8)
INEOS ABS (USA) LLC
Also Called: Ineos
356 Three Rivers Pkwy (45001-2553)
P.O. Box 39 (45001-0039)
PHONE..........................513 467-2400
Clint Herring, *VP*
Rebecca Libourel, *
◆ **EMP:** 185 **EST:** 2007
SQ FT: 372,600
SALES (est): 48.31MM
SALES (corp-wide): 1.38MM **Privately Held**
Web: www.ineos-abs.com
SIC: 2821 7389 Plastics materials and resins ; Business services, nec
HQ: Ineos Industries Limited
   Hawkslease
   Lyndhurst HANTS SO43
   238 028-7000

Akron
Summit County

(G-9)
A BEST TRMT & PEST CTRL SUPS
Also Called: A-Best Termite and Pest Ctrl
891 Gorge Blvd (44310-3462)
PHONE..........................330 434-5555
Todd Anderson, *Pr*
EMP: 6 **EST:** 1995
SALES (est): 441.31K **Privately Held**
Web: www.abestpest.com
SIC: 7342 2879 5191 Pest control in structures; Insecticides and pesticides; Pesticides

(G-10)
A-A BLUEPRINT CO INC
2757 Gilchrist Rd (44305-4400)
PHONE..........................330 794-8803
Daisy Scalia, *Prin*
John Scalia, *
EMP: 32 **EST:** 1968
SQ FT: 30,000
SALES (est): 4.3MM **Privately Held**
Web: www.aablueprint.com
SIC: 2791 2759 7334 2789 Typesetting; Letterpress printing; Photocopying and duplicating services; Bookbinding and related work

(G-11)
ABATEMENT LEAD TSTG RISK ASSSS
404 Abbyshire Rd (44319-3806)
PHONE..........................330 785-6420
EMP: 6
SALES (est): 681.47K **Privately Held**
SIC: 1031 Lead and zinc ores

(G-12)
ACC AUTOMATION CO INC
475 Wolf Ledges Pkwy (44311-1199)
PHONE..........................330 928-3821
Frank Rzicznek, *VP*
EMP: 25 **EST:** 1962
SQ FT: 7,500

SALES (est): 284.44K **Privately Held**
SIC: 8711 3536 Consulting engineer; Cranes, overhead traveling

(G-13)
ACCENT MANUFACTURING INC
80 Cole Ave (44301-1605)
PHONE..........................330 724-7704
Gregory Todd, *Mgr*
EMP: 12
SALES (corp-wide): 1.38MM **Privately Held**
Web: www.accentcustommarble.com
SIC: 3281 Marble, building: cut and shaped
PA: Accent Manufacturing, Inc.
   1026 Gardner Blvd
   Norton OH 44203
   330 724-7704

(G-14)
ACE PRECISION INDUSTRIES INC
925 Moe Dr (44310-2518)
PHONE..........................330 633-8523
Sandy A Di Fiore, *Prin*
James S Wolf, *
Jerry S Wolf, *
Beverly Wolf, *
▲ **EMP:** 25 **EST:** 1974
SQ FT: 15,000
SALES (est): 5.87MM **Privately Held**
Web: www.aceprecisionind.com
SIC: 3599 Machine shop, jobbing and repair

(G-15)
ACME FENCE LLC
Also Called: Acme Fence & Lumber
1053 Bank St (44305-2507)
PHONE..........................330 784-0456
Donny Zigdon, *Owner*
Randy Lewis, *Pr*
EMP: 16 **EST:** 1939
SQ FT: 10,000
SALES (est): 2.86MM **Privately Held**
Web: www.acmefence.com
SIC: 3446 2499 3315 3089 Fences or posts, ornamental iron or steel; Fencing, wood; Chain link fencing; Fences, gates, and accessories: plastics

(G-16)
ACRO TOOL & DIE COMPANY
Also Called: Metalcraft Solutions
325 Morgan Ave (44311-2494)
PHONE..........................330 773-5173
Pamela Thielo, *Pr*
T T Thompson, *
Pamela Perrin, *
▲ **EMP:** 37 **EST:** 1951
SQ FT: 27,000
SALES (est): 6.02MM **Privately Held**
Web: www.metalcraftsolutions.com
SIC: 0781 0811 3541 3444 Landscape services; Christmas tree farm; Machine tools, metal cutting type; Sheet metalwork

(G-17)
ACU-SERVE CORP (PA)
121 S Main St Ste 102 (44308-1436)
PHONE..........................330 923-5258
Angie Barone, *Pr*
Timothy Barone, *VP*
EMP: 140 **EST:** 1993
SALES (est): 13.52MM **Privately Held**
Web: www.acuservecorp.com
SIC: 7372 6411 Prepackaged software; Medical insurance claim processing, contract or fee basis

(G-18)
AD COMPANY HOLDINGS INC
Also Called: Auto Data
3245 Pickle Rd (44312-5333)
PHONE..........................404 256-3544
Craig Harris, *Pr*
Jason Clift, *Sec*
David Andersen, *VP*
EMP: 21 **EST:** 1985
SALES (est): 579.86K **Privately Held**
Web: www.driverse.com
SIC: 7372 Prepackaged software

(G-19)
ADA EXTRUSIONS INC
505 W Wilbeth Rd (44314-3717)
PHONE..........................440 285-7653
EMP: 6 **EST:** 2014
SALES (est): 244.43K **Privately Held**
SIC: 3089 Injection molding of plastics

(G-20)
ADVANCED CRYOGENIC ENTPS INC
1034 Home Ave (44310-3502)
PHONE..........................330 922-0750
David Norton, *Managing Member*
EMP: 11 **EST:** 2006
SQ FT: 52,000
SALES (est): 1.08MM **Privately Held**
SIC: 7389 3679 Grinding, precision: commercial or industrial; Cryogenic cooling devices for infrared detectors, masers

(G-21)
ADVANCED POLY-PACKAGING INC (PA)
1331 Emmitt Rd (44306-3807)
P.O. Box 7040 (44306-0040)
PHONE..........................330 785-4000
▲ **EMP:** 116 **EST:** 1978
SALES (est): 20.59MM
SALES (corp-wide): 20.59MM **Privately Held**
Web: ecom.advancedpoly.com
SIC: 3565 5199 Packaging machinery; Packaging materials

(G-22)
AIR ENTERPRISES INC
735 Glaser Pkwy (44306-4160)
PHONE..........................330 794-9770
Dorothy Gaffney, *Ch Bd*
Ed Gaffney Junior, *CEO*
James Dowey, *Pr*
EMP: 925 **EST:** 1964
SQ FT: 100,000
SALES (est): 2.97MM
SALES (corp-wide): 97.71MM **Privately Held**
Web: www.airenterprises.com
SIC: 3822 3585 3564 Air conditioning and refrigeration controls; Air conditioning units, complete: domestic or industrial; Blowers and fans
PA: Resilience Capital Partners Llc
   25101 Chgrin Blvd Ste 350
   Cleveland OH 44122
   216 292-0200

(G-23)
AJINOMOTO HLTH NTRTN N AMER IN
Also Called: More Than Gourmet
929 Home Ave (44310-4107)
PHONE..........................330 762-6652
EMP: 73
Web: www.ajihealthandnutrition.com
SIC: 2032 Soups and broths, canned, jarred, etc.

HQ: Ajinomoto Health & Nutrition North America, Inc.
   250 East Devon Ave
   Itasca IL 60143
   630 931-6800

(G-24)
AKROCHEM CORPORATION (PA)
3770 Embassy Pkwy (44333-8367)
PHONE..........................330 535-2100
◆ **EMP:** 60 **EST:** 1929
SALES (est): 139.59MM
SALES (corp-wide): 139.59MM **Privately Held**
Web: www.akrochem.com
SIC: 5169 2851 Synthetic resins, rubber, and plastic materials; Paints and paint additives

(G-25)
AKRON BELTING & SUPPLY COMPANY
1244 Home Ave (44310-2511)
PHONE..........................330 633-8212
Joe Mentzer, *Pr*
Joe Clark, *Pr*
Mark Brotherton, *VP*
EMP: 8 **EST:** 1989
SQ FT: 2,500
SALES (est): 4.44MM **Privately Held**
Web: www.akronbelting.com
SIC: 5085 3496 Hose, belting, and packing; Conveyor belts

(G-26)
AKRON CENTL ENGRV MOLD MCH INC
1625 Massillon Rd (44312-4204)
PHONE..........................330 794-8704
Frank James Muhl, *Pr*
John Kaeberlein, *Pr*
Frank R Muhl, *Stockholder*
EMP: 20 **EST:** 1969
SQ FT: 15,000
SALES (est): 3.09MM **Privately Held**
Web: www.acemm.com
SIC: 3544 8742 4213 Industrial molds; New products and services consultants; Automobiles, transport and delivery

(G-27)
AKRON COCA-COLA BOTTLING CO
Also Called: Coca-Cola
1560 Triplett Blvd (44306-3306)
PHONE..........................330 784-2653
Matt Cartaglia, *Genl Mgr*
▲ **EMP:** 1300 **EST:** 1985
SALES (est): 5.66MM
SALES (corp-wide): 45.75B **Publicly Held**
Web: www.summit4success.com
SIC: 2086 Bottled and canned soft drinks
HQ: Coca-Cola Refreshments Usa, Llc
   1 Coca Cola Plz Nw
   Atlanta GA 30313
   770 989-3000

(G-28)
AKRON COTTON PRODUCTS INC
437 W Cedar St (44307-2321)
PHONE..........................330 434-7171
Michael Zwick, *Pr*
EMP: 9 **EST:** 1929
SQ FT: 26,000
SALES (est): 787.49K **Privately Held**
Web: www.akroncotton.com
SIC: 2211 5999 Scrub cloths; Cleaning equipment and supplies

(G-29)
AKRON EQUIPMENT COMPANY
3522 Manchester Rd Ste B (44319-1451)

PHONE..............................330 645-3780
Edward L Mc Cartt, *Ch Bd*
Gary A Hill, *
Andrea Friede, *
▼ **EMP:** 80 **EST:** 1917
SQ FT: 2,000
SALES (est): 981.82K **Privately Held**
SIC: 3599 Machine shop, jobbing and repair

(G-30)
AKRON FELT CHENILLE MFG CO INC
1671 E Market St (44305-4210)
PHONE..............................330 733-7778
Daniel J Fanelly, *Pr*
EMP: 10 **EST:** 1925
SALES (est): 751.12K **Privately Held**
Web: www.akronfeltoh.com
SIC: 2399 2396 5091 Emblems, badges,
and insignia: from purchased materials;
Printing and embossing on plastics fabric
articles; Sporting and recreation goods

(G-31)
AKRON FOUNDRY CO (PA)
2728 Wingate Ave (44314-1300)
P.O. Box 27028 (44319-7028)
PHONE..............................330 745-3101
George Ostich, *Pr*
Geraldine Ostich, *
Michael Ostich, *
Ronald C Allan, *
EMP: 175 **EST:** 1969
SQ FT: 100,000
SALES (est): 24.37MM
SALES (corp-wide): 24.37MM **Privately
Held**
Web: www.akronfoundry.com
SIC: 3369 5063 3365 3363 Castings, except
die-castings, precision; Boxes and fittings,
electrical; Aluminum foundries; Aluminum
die-castings

(G-32)
AKRON GEAR & ENGINEERING INC
501 Morgan Ave (44311-2431)
P.O. Box 269 (44309-0269)
PHONE..............................330 773-6608
W Thomas James Iii, *Pr*
Carl G James, *VP*
John A Neuman, *VP Fin*
Gary Davis, *Asst Tr*
William Moore, *CUST SVCS*
EMP: 21 **EST:** 1911
SQ FT: 25,000
SALES (est): 7.96MM
SALES (corp-wide): 1.51B **Privately Held**
Web: www.akrongear.com
SIC: 3568 3566 3545 3462 Sprockets
(power transmission equipment); Gears,
power transmission, except auto; Machine
tool accessories; Iron and steel forgings
PA: Forge Industries, Inc.
4450 Market St
Youngstown OH 44512
330 960-2468

(G-33)
AKRON LEGAL NEWS INC
60 S Summit St (44308-1775)
PHONE..............................330 296-7578
John L Burleson, *Pr*
EMP: 10 **EST:** 1922
SQ FT: 4,000
SALES (est): 414.08K **Privately Held**
Web: www.akronlegalnews.com
SIC: 2711 8111 Newspapers: publishing
only, not printed on site; Legal services

(G-34)
AKRON LITHO-PRINT COMPANY INC
1026 S Main St (44311-2346)

PHONE..............................330 434-3145
Pete P Ripplinger, *Pr*
Sharon Ripplinger, *Sec*
EMP: 13 **EST:** 1935
SQ FT: 5,500
SALES (est): 2.26MM **Privately Held**
Web: www.lithoprintco.com
SIC: 2752 2759 Lithographing on metal;
Letterpress printing

(G-35)
AKRON ORTHOTIC SOLUTIONS INC
582 W Market St (44303-1839)
PHONE..............................330 253-3002
Robert Mcinturff, *Pr*
EMP: 8 **EST:** 1995
SALES (est): 1.66MM **Privately Held**
SIC: 3842 5999 Braces, orthopedic;
Orthopedic and prosthesis applications

(G-36)
AKRON PAINT & VARNISH INC
Also Called: APV Engineered Coatings
1390 Firestone Pkwy (44301-1695)
PHONE..............................330 773-8911
Dave Venarge, *Pr*
Ed Apsega, *General Vice President*
Mike Summers, *Purchasing*
◆ **EMP:** 90 **EST:** 1878
SQ FT: 160,000
SALES (est): 22.49MM **Privately Held**
Web: www.apvcoatings.com
SIC: 2851 2891 3953 Paints and paint
additives; Adhesives and sealants; Marking
devices

(G-37)
AKRON PLATING CO INC
1774 Hackberry St (44301-2493)
PHONE..............................330 773-6878
Robert Ormsby Junior, *Pr*
Fred Beidle, *VP*
Jennifer Ormsby, *Sec*
EMP: 10 **EST:** 1948
SQ FT: 7,500
SALES (est): 1.01MM **Privately Held**
Web: www.akronplating.com
SIC: 3471 Electroplating of metals or formed
products

(G-38)
**AKRON POLYMER PRODUCTS INC
(PA)**
1471 Exeter Rd (44300-3050)
PHONE..............................330 628-5551
Greg C Anderson, *Pr*
Kevin Gandee, *
▲ **EMP:** 68 **EST:** 1986
SALES (est): 9.57MM
SALES (corp-wide): 9.57MM **Privately
Held**
Web: www.akronpolymer.com
SIC: 3089 3082 Extruded finished plastics
products, nec; Tubes, unsupported plastics

(G-39)
**AKRON PORCELAIN & PLASTICS
CO (PA)**
Also Called: Akron Porcelain & Plastic Co
2739 Cory Ave (44314-1308)
P.O. Box 15157 (44314-5157)
PHONE..............................330 745-2159
George H Lewis Junior, *Ch Bd*
Michael B Dunphy, *
Robert Briggs, *
▲ **EMP:** 140 **EST:** 1890
SQ FT: 120,000
SALES (est): 9.6MM
SALES (corp-wide): 9.6MM **Privately Held**
Web: www.akronporcelain.com

SIC: 3089 3264 Injection molded finished
plastics products, nec; Porcelain electrical
supplies

(G-40)
AKRON REBAR CO (PA)
Also Called: Cleveland Rebar
809 W Waterloo Rd (44314-1527)
P.O. Box 3710 (44314-0710)
PHONE..............................330 745-7100
Michael B Humphrey, *Prin*
Michael Humphrey Ii, *CEO*
▲ **EMP:** 32 **EST:** 1978
SQ FT: 32,600
SALES (est): 4.16MM
SALES (corp-wide): 4.16MM **Privately
Held**
Web: www.akronrebar.com
SIC: 3441 3449 Fabricated structural metal;
Bars, concrete reinforcing: fabricated steel

(G-41)
**AKRON SPECIAL MACHINERY INC
(PA)**
Also Called: Poling Group, The
2740 Cory Ave (44314-1396)
PHONE..............................330 753-1077
David Poling Senior, *Pr*
Marlene Poling, *
David Poling Junior, *CFO*
▼ **EMP:** 49 **EST:** 1978
SQ FT: 60,000
SALES (est): 11.7MM
SALES (corp-wide): 11.7MM **Privately
Held**
Web: www.polinggroup.com
SIC: 3599 Machine shop, jobbing and repair

(G-42)
AKRON STEEL FABRICATORS CO
Also Called: Poling Group
3291 Manchester Rd (44319-1495)
PHONE..............................330 644-0616
David Poling Senior, *Pr*
Keith Kline, *
Marlene M Poling, *
David Poling Junior, *CFO*
Carolyn Clay, *
▼ **EMP:** 30 **EST:** 1947
SQ FT: 28,000
SALES (est): 5.54MM **Privately Held**
Web: www.polinggroup.com
SIC: 3491 Process control regulator valves

(G-43)
AKRON STEEL TREATING CO
336 Morgan Ave (44311-2424)
P.O. Box 2290 (44309-2290)
PHONE..............................330 773-8211
Christopher Powell, *CEO*
Joseph A Powell, *
Jim Stewart, *
Rick Miller, *
EMP: 45 **EST:** 1943
SQ FT: 46,000
SALES (est): 9.58MM **Privately Held**
Web: www.akronsteeltreating.com
SIC: 3398 3479 Metal heat treating;
Painting, coating, and hot dipping

(G-44)
AKRON THERMOGRAPHY INC
Also Called: B C T
3406 Fortuna Dr (44312)
PHONE..............................330 896-9712
Randal S Teague, *Pr*
Lisa R Teague, *Sec*
EMP: 11 **EST:** 1995
SALES (est): 943.95K **Privately Held**
Web: www.evoprint.com

SIC: 2752 Commercial printing, lithographic

(G-45)
AKRON THERMOGRAPHY INC
Also Called: B C T
3506 Fortuna Dr (44312-5284)
PHONE..............................330 896-9712
Randal S Teague, *Pr*
EMP: 7 **EST:** 1995
SALES (est): 286.88K **Privately Held**
Web: www.evoprint.com
SIC: 2752 Offset printing

(G-46)
AKRON VAULT COMPANY INC
Also Called: Akron Crematory
2399 Gilchrist Rd (44305-4496)
PHONE..............................330 784-5475
Marty Ebie, *Pr*
Phil Kauffman, *Sec*
EMP: 11 **EST:** 1944
SQ FT: 11,000
SALES (est): 1.41MM **Privately Held**
SIC: 3272 Burial vaults, concrete or precast
terrazzo

(G-47)
ALCO-CHEM INC (PA)
Also Called: Alco
45 N Summit St (44308-1933)
PHONE..............................330 253-3535
Anthony Mandala Junior, *Pr*
Bart Mandala, *
Robert Mandala, *
▲ **EMP:** 34 **EST:** 1966
SQ FT: 22,000
SALES (est): 21.28MM
SALES (corp-wide): 21.28MM **Privately
Held**
Web: www.alco-chem.com
SIC: 5087 2869 2842 Janitors' supplies;
Industrial organic chemicals, nec; Polishes
and sanitation goods

(G-48)
ALCON TOOL COMPANY
Also Called: Alcon
565 Lafollette St (44311-1824)
PHONE..............................330 773-9171
Charles E Conner, *CEO*
▼ **EMP:** 50 **EST:** 1946
SQ FT: 100,000
SALES (est): 9.37MM **Privately Held**
Web: www.alcontool.com
SIC: 3541 Machine tools, metal cutting type

(G-49)
ALEXANDER PIERCE CORP
1874 Englewood Ave (44312-1002)
PHONE..............................330 798-9840
Kim Hocevar-claxon, *Prin*
EMP: 6 **EST:** 2019
SALES (est): 1.51MM **Privately Held**
Web:
www.alexanderpiercerestaurant.com
SIC: 3479 Coating of metals and formed
products

(G-50)
ALL-TECH MANUFACTURING LTD
1477 Industrial Pkwy (44310-2601)
PHONE..............................330 633-1095
Candace Presley, *CEO*
Joseph Manijak, *Managing Member*
Frank Manijak, *Managing Member*
EMP: 21 **EST:** 1996
SQ FT: 9,000
SALES (est): 4.97MM **Privately Held**
Web: www.all-techmfg.com
SIC: 3599 Machine shop, jobbing and repair

(G-51)
ALLEN RANDALL ENTERPRISES INC
70 E Miller Ave (44301-1324)
P.O. Box 1117 (44309-1117)
PHONE..............................330 374-9850
Jim Bradshaw, *Pr*
EMP: 10 **EST:** 1988
SQ FT: 12,500
SALES (est): 1.41MM **Privately Held**
Web: www.allen-randall.com
SIC: 3599 Machine shop, jobbing and repair

(G-52)
ALLIANCE FORGING GROUP LLC
847 Pier Dr # 1000 (44307-2267)
PHONE..............................330 680-4861
David Risher, *Managing Member*
EMP: 6 **EST:** 2013
SQ FT: 100,000
SALES (est): 758.55K **Privately Held**
SIC: 3462 Ornamental metal forgings, ferrous

(G-53)
ALTERRA ENERGY LLC
1200 E Waterloo Rd (44306-3806)
PHONE..............................800 569-6061
EMP: 7 **EST:** 2019
SALES (est): 20.39MM
SALES (corp-wide): 24.92B **Privately Held**
Web: www.alterraenergy.com
SIC: 2899 Chemical preparations, nec
PA: Neste Oyj
   Keilaranta 21
   Espoo 02150
   1045811

(G-54)
AMERI-KART CORP
1293 S Main St (44301-1302)
PHONE..............................800 232-0847
EMP: 88
SALES (corp-wide): 836.28MM **Publicly Held**
Web:
www.myersengineeredsolutions.com
SIC: 3089 Injection molding of plastics
HQ: Ameri-Kart Corp.
   1667 Commerce Dr
   Bristol IN 46507

(G-55)
AMERICAN BOTTLING COMPANY
1259 George Washington Blvd
(44312-3007)
PHONE..............................330 733-3830
Joe Laduto, *Mgr*
EMP: 27
Web: www.keurigdrpepper.com
SIC: 2086 Soft drinks: packaged in cans,
bottles, etc.
HQ: The American Bottling Company
   6425 Hall Of Fame Ln
   Frisco TX 75034

(G-56)
AMERICAN MADE BAGS LLC
999 Sweitzer Ave (44311-2359)
PHONE..............................330 475-1385
Thomas Armour, *Pr*
EMP: 19 **EST:** 2010
SALES (est): 2.46MM **Privately Held**
SIC: 2393 Canvas bags

(G-57)
**AMERICAN POLYMERS
CORPORATION (PA)**
231 Springside Dr Ste 145 (44333-2455)
PHONE..............................330 666-6048
Kevin Copeland, *Prin*
Phil Farensworth, *Sr VP*

EMP: 6 **EST:** 1999
SQ FT: 2,000
SALES (est): 566.77K
SALES (corp-wide): 566.77K **Privately Held**
SIC: 2821 Plastics materials and resins

(G-58)
AMERICAN PRINTING INC
1121 Tower Dr (44305-1089)
PHONE..............................330 630-1121
David Hall, *Pr*
Kim Krietz, *Sec*
EMP: 10 **EST:** 1928
SQ FT: 15,000
SALES (est): 999.6K **Privately Held**
Web: www.americanprintinginc.com
SIC: 2752 Offset printing

(G-59)
AMERICAN UTILITY PROC LLC
1246 Princeton St (44301-1168)
PHONE..............................330 535-3000
Richard K Kmiecik, *Managing Member*
EMP: 34 **EST:** 2003
SQ FT: 60,000
SALES (est): 4.63MM **Privately Held**
Web: www.aup10.com
SIC: 3471 Electroplating of metals or formed
products

(G-60)
ARIEL CORPORATION
3360 Miller Park Rd (44312-5342)
PHONE..............................330 896-2660
Karen Buchwald Wright, *Pr*
EMP: 62
SALES (corp-wide): 170.79MM **Privately Held**
Web: www.arielcorp.com
SIC: 3563 Air and gas compressors
including vacuum pumps
PA: Ariel Corporation
   35 Blackjack Rd
   Mount Vernon OH 43050
   740 397-0311

(G-61)
ASH SEWER & DRAIN SERVICE
451 E North St (44304-1217)
PHONE..............................330 376-9714
Greg Ash, *Prin*
EMP: 6 **EST:** 1987
SALES (est): 140.38K **Privately Held**
SIC: 3272 4959 Sewer pipe, concrete;
Sanitary services, nec

(G-62)
ASTER INDUSTRIES INC
275 N Arlington St Ste B (44305-1600)
PHONE..............................330 762-7965
Kimberly Oplinger, *Pr*
Michael J Oplinger, *
EMP: 26 **EST:** 1990
SQ FT: 14,500
SALES (est): 6.28MM **Privately Held**
Web: www.asterind.com
SIC: 3999 2599 Advertising display products
; Bar, restaurant and cafeteria furniture

(G-63)
ATCPC OF OHIO LLC
Also Called: Klutch Cannabis
1055 Home Ave (44310-3501)
PHONE..............................330 670-9900
Adam Thomarios, *Pr*
EMP: 48 **EST:** 2009
SALES (est): 5.37MM **Privately Held**
SIC: 3999

(G-64)
AURIS NOBLE LLC (PA)
160 E Voris St (44311-1514)
P.O. Box 522 (44309-0522)
PHONE..............................330 321-6649
Patrick Deeringer, *COO*
Lou Britton, *Manager*
EMP: 22 **EST:** 2011
SQ FT: 2,000
SALES (est): 3.66MM
SALES (corp-wide): 3.66MM **Privately Held**
Web: www.aurisnoble.com
SIC: 3341 4953 5093 Secondary precious
metals; Recycling, waste materials;
Nonferrous metals scrap

(G-65)
AUTO DEALER DESIGNS INC
303 W Bartges St (44307-2205)
P.O. Box 2379 (44224-1200)
PHONE..............................330 374-7666
John Volpe, *CEO*
David Volpe, *Pr*
Paul Volpe, *VP*
Paula Volpe, *Sec*
Marilyn Volpe, *Treas*
EMP: 22 **EST:** 1971
SQ FT: 16,152
SALES (est): 2.32MM **Privately Held**
Web: www.autodealerdesigns.com
SIC: 3993 5199 Signs and advertising
specialties; Advertising specialties

(G-66)
AXIOM INTERNATIONAL INC
3517 Embassy Pkwy Ste 150 (44333-8407)
PHONE..............................330 396-5942
Wayne Stair, *Pr*
Cinda Klatil, *Contrlr*
Mike Leidhty, *CFO*
EMP: 6 **EST:** 2011
SQ FT: 7,500
SALES (est): 183.09K **Privately Held**
Web: www.americasinternational.com
SIC: 2821 Plastics materials and resins

(G-67)
BABCOCK & WILCOX COMPANY (HQ)
1200 E Market St Ste 650 (44305-4067)
P.O. Box 351 (44203)
PHONE..............................330 753-4511
Mark Low, *Sr VP*
Jimmy Morgan, *
Louis Salamone, *
◆ **EMP:** 1000 **EST:** 1867
SQ FT: 16,000
SALES (est): 735.73MM
SALES (corp-wide): 717.33MM **Publicly Held**
Web: www.babcock.com
SIC: 1629 1711 3443 7699 Industrial plant
construction; Plumbing, heating, air-
conditioning; Fabricated plate work (boiler
shop); Boiler and heating repair services
PA: Babcock & Wilcox Enterprises, Inc.
   1200 E Market St Ste 650
   Akron OH 44305
   330 753-4511

(G-68)
BABCOCK & WILCOX ENTPS INC (PA)
1200 E Market St Ste 650 (44305-4067)
PHONE..............................330 753-4511
Kenneth M Young, *Ch Bd*
Cameron Frymyer, *Ex VP*
Jimmy B Morgan, *CCO*
John J Dziewisz, *Corporate Secretary*
Chris Riker, *Ex VP*

EMP: 106 **EST:** 1867
SALES (est): 717.33MM
SALES (corp-wide): 717.33MM **Publicly Held**
Web: www.babcock.com
SIC: 3621 3829 Power generators; Nuclear
instrument modules

(G-69)
BABCOCK & WILCOX HOLDINGS LLC
1200 E Market St Ste 650 (44305-4067)
PHONE..............................330 453-4511
Christopher S Riker, *Managing Member*
EMP: 2400 **EST:** 2017
SALES (est): 4.88MM **Privately Held**
Web: www.babcock.com
SIC: 3511 8711 Turbines and turbine
generator sets; Engineering services

(G-70)
BABCOX MEDIA INC
3550 Embassy Pkwy (44333-8318)
PHONE..............................330 670-1234
William E Babcox, *Pr*
Greg Cira, *
Lance Goeddel, *CAO*
EMP: 75 **EST:** 1913
SQ FT: 40,000
SALES (est): 23.2MM **Privately Held**
Web: www.babcox.com
SIC: 2721 Magazines: publishing only, not
printed on site

(G-71)
BAKER MEDIA GROUP LLC
Also Called: Akron Life
1653 Merriman Rd Ste 116 (44313-5293)
PHONE..............................330 253-0056
Don Baker Junior, *Managing Member*
Colin Baker Publ, *Prin*
EMP: 11 **EST:** 2004
SQ FT: 3,000
SALES (est): 386.46K **Privately Held**
Web: www.akronlife.com
SIC: 2721 Magazines: publishing only, not
printed on site

(G-72)
BANSAL ENTERPRISES INC
Also Called: Ink Well
1538 Home Ave (44310-1601)
PHONE..............................330 633-9355
Usha Bansal, *Pr*
EMP: 10 **EST:** 1988
SQ FT: 3,750
SALES (est): 991.94K **Privately Held**
Web: www.theinkwellusa.com
SIC: 2752 7389 Offset printing; Advertising,
promotional, and trade show services

(G-73)
BDU HOLDINGS INC
467 Dan St (44310-3906)
PHONE..............................330 374-1810
Tim Lowe, *Pr*
EMP: 10 **EST:** 1983
SQ FT: 20,000
SALES (est): 414.34K **Privately Held**
SIC: 3069 Custom compounding of rubber
materials

(G-74)
BEACON JOURNAL PUBLISHING CO
Also Called: Akron Beacon Journal
44 E Exchange St (44308-1510)
P.O. Box 640 (44309)
PHONE..............................330 996-3600
Christopher Hargreaves, *Prin*
Kirk Davis, *
EMP: 115 **EST:** 1859

SQ FT: 250,000
SALES (est): 8.82MM
SALES (corp-wide): 2.51B **Publicly Held**
Web: www.beaconjournal.com
SIC: **2711** Newspapers, publishing and printing
HQ: Gatehouse Media, Llc
175 Sllys Trl Fl 3 Corp C
Pittsford NY 14534
585 598-0030

(G-75)
BELAIRE PRODUCTS INC
763 S Broadway St (44311)
P.O. Box 189 (44309-0189)
PHONE..........................330 253-3116
Richard W Vogt, *Prin*
Richard Vogt, *
John C Beringer Senior, *CEO*
▲ EMP: 50 EST: 1985
SQ FT: 32,000
SALES (est): 694.36K **Privately Held**
Web: www.belaireproducts.com
SIC: **3949** 3161 7389 2393 Sporting and athletic goods, nec; Traveling bags; Sewing contractor; Textile bags

(G-76)
BERINGER PLATING INC
1211 Devalera St (44310-2488)
PHONE..........................330 633-8409
James Beringer Junior, *Pr*
Laura Beringer, *Sec*
EMP: 8 EST: 1953
SQ FT: 21,000
SALES (est): 3.08MM **Privately Held**
Web: www.beringerplating.com
SIC: **3471** 8711 Electroplating of metals or formed products; Engineering services

(G-77)
BERRAN INDUSTRIAL GROUP INC
570 Wolf Ledges Pkwy (44311-1022)
PHONE..........................330 253-5800
Randy P Adair, *Pr*
Don Schultz, *
EMP: 26 EST: 1980
SQ FT: 18,000
SALES (est): 7.75MM **Privately Held**
Web: www.berranindustrialgroup.com
SIC: **3599** 3441 3549 3444 Custom machinery; Fabricated structural metal; Metalworking machinery, nec; Sheet metalwork

(G-78)
BEST MOLD & MANUFACTURING INC
1546 E Turkeyfoot Lake Rd (44312-5350)
P.O. Box 544 (44685-0544)
PHONE..........................330 896-9988
Dave Miller, *Pr*
EMP: 45 EST: 2000
SQ FT: 26,000
SALES (est): 1.24MM **Privately Held**
Web: www.bestmmi.com
SIC: **3599** Machine shop, jobbing and repair

(G-79)
BIF CO LLC
Also Called: Bif, LLC
1405 Home Ave (44310-2514)
PHONE..........................330 564-0941
Mark Schoenbaechler, *Pr*
EMP: 10 EST: 2001
SQ FT: 150,000
SALES (est): 2.48MM
SALES (corp-wide): 9.63MM **Privately Held**
Web: www.bifwater.com

SIC: **3824** Impeller and counter driven flow meters
PA: Logan Machine Company
1405 Home Ave
Akron OH 44310
330 633-6163

(G-80)
BLINGED & BRONZED
2303 Manchester Rd (44314-3602)
PHONE..........................330 631-1255
Danielle Stoll, *Pr*
EMP: 10 EST: 2020
SALES (est): 171.36K **Privately Held**
SIC: **2869** Tanning agents, synthetic organic

(G-81)
BOGIE INDUSTRIES INC LTD
Also Called: Weaver Fab & Finishing
1100 Home Ave (44310-3504)
PHONE..........................330 745-3105
Jim Lauer, *Pr*
Fuzzy Helton, *
Marian Lauer, *
EMP: 38 EST: 1998
SQ FT: 40,000
SALES (est): 8.99MM **Privately Held**
Web: www.weaverfab.com
SIC: **3444** 1799 3399 Sheet metalwork; Coating of metal structures at construction site; Powder, metal

(G-82)
BONNOT COMPANY (PA)
1301 Home Ave (44310-2654)
PHONE..........................330 896-6544
George W Bain, *Pr*
John Negrelli, *
▼ EMP: 21 EST: 1891
SQ FT: 40,000
SALES (est): 4.46MM
SALES (corp-wide): 4.46MM **Privately Held**
Web: www.thebonnotco.com
SIC: **3599** Custom machinery

(G-83)
BRIDGSTONE AMRCAS TIRE OPRTONS
1670 Firestone Pkwy (44301-1659)
PHONE..........................330 379-3714
Paolo Ferrari, *Brnch Mgr*
EMP: 75
Web: www.bridgestoneamericas.com
SIC: **3011** Tires and inner tubes
HQ: Bridgestone Americas Tire Operations, Llc
200 4th Ave S Ste 100
Nashville TN 37201
615 937-1000

(G-84)
BRIGHT STAR BOOKS INC
1357 Home Ave (44310-2549)
PHONE..........................330 888-2156
Keith Seher, *Dir*
Nancy Baxter, *Dir*
Iriel Hopkins, *Dir*
Dave Plahuta, *Dir*
Christin Seher, *Dir*
EMP: 7 EST: 2017
SALES (est): 217.72K **Privately Held**
Web: www.brightstarbooks.org
SIC: **2731** Book publishing

(G-85)
BUCKEYE READY MIX CONCRETE
1562 Massillon Rd (44312-4203)
PHONE..........................330 798-5511
John Chafe, *Pr*
EMP: 6 EST: 1996

SALES (est): 178.39K **Privately Held**
SIC: **3273** Ready-mixed concrete

(G-86)
BURGHARDT MANUFACTURING INC
1524 Massillon Rd (44306-4162)
PHONE..........................330 253-7590
Adam Burghardt, *Pr*
EMP: 9 EST: 1987
SQ FT: 8,000
SALES (est): 2.93MM **Privately Held**
SIC: **3441** Fabricated structural metal for bridges

(G-87)
BURGHARDT METAL FABG INC
1638 Mcchesney Rd (44306-4396)
PHONE..........................330 794-1830
Craig Shuster, *Pr*
Cindy Archer, *Sec*
EMP: 18 EST: 1958
SQ FT: 22,000
SALES (est): 2.31MM **Privately Held**
Web: www.burgmetalfab.com
SIC: **3449** 3441 Miscellaneous metalwork; Fabricated structural metal

(G-88)
CALIBER MOLD AND MACHINE INC
2200 Massillon Rd (44312-4234)
P.O. Box 847 (45701-0847)
PHONE..........................330 633-8171
Jack Thornton, *Pr*
Thomas Thornton, *
EMP: 40 EST: 1986
SALES (est): 2.54MM **Privately Held**
Web: jax.tiremolds.com
SIC: **3544** Industrial molds

(G-89)
CARDINAL PRINTING INC
112 W Wilbeth Rd (44301-2415)
P.O. Box 678 (44232-0678)
PHONE..........................330 773-7300
Vince Rosnack, *Pr*
Pam Rosnack, *Sec*
EMP: 8 EST: 1980
SQ FT: 6,700
SALES (est): 122.09K **Privately Held**
Web: www.cardinalprinting.net
SIC: **2752** Offset printing

(G-90)
CARGILL INCORPORATED
Also Called: Cargill
2065 Manchester Rd (44314-1770)
PHONE..........................330 745-0031
Wayne A Brown, *Mgr*
EMP: 91
SALES (corp-wide): 159.59B **Privately Held**
Web: www.cargill.com
SIC: **2048** Prepared feeds, nec
PA: Cargill, Incorporated
15407 Mcginty Rd W
Wayzata MN 55391
800 227-4455

(G-91)
CCSI INC
1868 Akron Peninsula Rd (44313-4808)
PHONE..........................800 742-8535
Frank Orlando, *VP*
EMP: 7 EST: 2013
SALES (est): 1.91MM **Privately Held**
Web: www.ccsi-inc.com
SIC: **3829** Measuring and controlling devices, nec

(G-92)
CEC ELECTRONICS CORP
1739 Akron Peninsula Rd (44313-5157)
P.O. Box 3870 (44223)
PHONE..........................330 916-8100
Dan Lujan, *Pr*
EMP: 7 EST: 1981
SQ FT: 3,000
SALES (est): 2.76MM **Privately Held**
Web: www.cecelectronics.info
SIC: **3679** Electronic circuits

(G-93)
CECIL C PECK CO
1029 Arlington Cir (44306-3959)
PHONE..........................330 785-0781
Paul Stewart, *Pr*
▲ EMP: 10 EST: 1945
SQ FT: 8,350
SALES (est): 398.46K **Privately Held**
Web: www.summitmachinesolutions.com
SIC: **3699** 8711 Welding machines and equipment, ultrasonic; Designing: ship, boat, machine, and product

(G-94)
CED PROCESS MINERALS INC (PA)
863 N Cleveland Massillon Rd (44333-2167)
PHONE..........................330 666-5500
Leland D Cole, *VP*
William M Douglas, *Sec*
Nolan E Douglas, *Treas*
▼ EMP: 18 EST: 1981
SQ FT: 2,368
SALES (est): 2.03MM
SALES (corp-wide): 2.03MM **Privately Held**
Web: www.cedprocessminerals.com
SIC: **1446** Foundry sand mining

(G-95)
CENTRAL COCA-COLA BTLG CO INC
Also Called: Coca-Cola
1560 Triplett Blvd (44306-3306)
PHONE..........................330 875-1487
EMP: 31
SALES (corp-wide): 45.75B **Publicly Held**
Web: www.coca-cola.com
SIC: **2086** 8741 Bottled and canned soft drinks; Management services
HQ: Central Coca-Cola Bottling Company, Inc.
555 Taxter Rd Ste 550
Elmsford NY 10523
914 789-1100

(G-96)
CHARLES AUTO ELECTRIC CO INC
600 Grant St (44311-1502)
P.O. Box 2872 (44720-0872)
PHONE..........................330 535-6269
Daniel Ardelean, *Pr*
Erik S Ardelean, *VP*
Mary Ardelean, *Treas*
EMP: 8 EST: 1972
SQ FT: 8,000
SALES (est): 422.4K **Privately Held**
Web: www.charlesautoelectric.com
SIC: **3694** 3621 Generators, automotive and aircraft; Starters, for motors

(G-97)
CHARLES COSTA INC
Also Called: Costa Machine
924 Home Ave (44310-4108)
PHONE..........................330 376-3636
George Marino, *Pr*
Carl Prentiss, *VP*
EMP: 6 EST: 1972
SQ FT: 10,000

GEOGRAPHIC

SALES (est): 240.53K **Privately Held**
Web: www.costamachine.com
SIC: **3599** Machine shop, jobbing and repair

(G-98)
CHROME DEPOSIT CORPORATION
1566 Firestone Pkwy (44301-1626)
PHONE.....................330 773-7800
Philip Court, *Pr*
EMP: 29
SALES (corp-wide): 18.05B **Publicly Held**
Web: www.chromedeposit.com
SIC: **3471** Chromium plating of metals or
formed products
HQ: Chrome Deposit Corporation
6640 Melton Rd
Portage IN 46368
219 763-1571

(G-99)
CHUTE SOURCE LLC
525 Kennedy Rd (44305-4425)
PHONE.....................330 475-0377
Nello Decarli, *Managing Member*
EMP: 15
SQ FT: 13,000
SALES (est): 4.61MM **Privately Held**
Web: www.chutesourcellc.com
SIC: **3443** 3444 Chutes and troughs; Sheet
metalwork

(G-100)
CIMS INCORPORATED
2701 Gilchrist Rd (44305-4434)
P.O. Box 1610 (44309-1610)
PHONE.....................330 794-8102
Susan L Kruder, *Pr*
EMP: 7 EST: 1973
SQ FT: 7,200
SALES (est): 385.04K **Privately Held**
Web: www.cimstireregistration.com
SIC: **7534** Tire retreading and repair shops

(G-101)
CIOFFI HOLDINGS LLC
1001 Eastwood Ave (44305-1127)
P.O. Box 412 (44278-0412)
PHONE.....................330 794-9448
Jamie Stone, *Prin*
EMP: 7 EST: 2019
SALES (est): 3.04MM **Privately Held**
Web: www.libertyredimix.com
SIC: **3273** Ready-mixed concrete

(G-102)
CLASSIC COUNTERTOPS LLC
1519 Kenmore Blvd (44314-1661)
PHONE.....................330 882-4220
EMP: 6 EST: 2008
SQ FT: 4,700
SALES (est): 274.66K **Privately Held**
Web: www.classiccountertops.net
SIC: **3131** 1799 Counters; Counter top
installation

(G-103)
CLEARSONIC MANUFACTURING INC
1025 Evans Ave (44305-1020)
PHONE.....................828 772-9809
▲ EMP: 8 EST: 1995
SALES (est): 749.02K **Privately Held**
Web: www.clearsonic.com
SIC: **3999** Barber and beauty shop
equipment

(G-104)
COMBS MANUFACTURING INC
380 Kennedy Rd (44305-4422)
PHONE.....................330 784-3151
▲ EMP: 70

SIC: **3599** 7692 2421 Machine shop, jobbing
and repair; Welding repair; Sawmills and
planing mills, general

(G-105)
CONTITECH USA LLC (DH)
Also Called: Continental Contitech
703 S Cleveland Massillon Rd
(44333-3023)
PHONE.....................330 664-7000
Andreas Gerstenberger, *CEO*
James T Hill, *Pr*
Irshaid Zoubi, *VP*
Timothy P Rogers, *VP*
◆ EMP: 16 EST: 2007
SQ FT: 100,000
SALES (est): 468.18MM
SALES (corp-wide): 42B **Privately Held**
Web: www.continental-industry.com
SIC: **3069** Molded rubber products
HQ: Contitech North America, Inc.
703 S Clvlnd-Massillon Rd
Fairlawn OH 44333

(G-106)
CORPORATE CNSULTING SVC INSTRS
Also Called: CCS Instruments
1868 Akron Peninsula Rd (44313-4808)
▲ EMP: 10 EST: 1986
SALES (est): 1.85MM **Privately Held**
Web: www.ccsi-inc.com
SIC: **3829** Testing equipment: abrasion,
shearing strength, etc.

(G-107)
COS BLUEPRINT INC
590 N Main St (44310-3145)
P.O. Box 4931 (44310-0931)
PHONE.....................330 376-0022
Jim Scalia, *Pr*
Martin Hyatt, *
Linda Scalia, *
EMP: 24 EST: 1985
SQ FT: 12,000
SALES (est): 1.37MM **Privately Held**
Web: www.reprosinc.com
SIC: **2752** 5999 5712 5943 Offset printing;
Typewriters and business machines; Office
furniture; Office forms and supplies

(G-108)
COUNTRY PURE FOODS INC (PA)
222 S Main St Ste 401 (44308-1525)
PHONE.....................330 753-2293
Tony Muscato, *CEO*
◆ EMP: 120 EST: 1995
SALES (est): 521.7MM **Privately Held**
Web: www.countrypure.com
SIC: **2033** 2037 2086 Fruit juices: fresh; Fruit
juice concentrates, frozen; Fruit drinks (less
than 100% juice): packaged in cans, etc.

(G-109)
CRAWFORD AE LLC
Also Called: Hickok Ae LLC
735 Glaser Pkwy (44306-4166)
PHONE.....................330 794-9770
Brian Powers, *
◆ EMP: 95 EST: 2017
SALES (est): 25.82MM
SALES (corp-wide): 150.2MM **Publicly
Held**
SIC: **3585** Heating and air conditioning
combination units
PA: Crawford United Corporation
10514 Dupont Ave Ste 200
Cleveland OH 44108
216 243-2614

(G-110)
CURTIS STEEL & SUPPLY INC
1210 Curtis St (44301-1428)
PHONE.....................330 376-7141
Tom Poinar, *Pr*
Michael S Poinar, *VP*
EMP: 14 EST: 1947
SQ FT: 22,000
SALES (est): 682.99K **Privately Held**
SIC: **3599** 5051 Machine shop, jobbing and
repair; Ferrous metals

(G-111)
CUSTOM APPAREL LLC
1180 Brittain Rd (44305-1034)
PHONE.....................330 633-2626
EMP: 6 EST: 1988
SQ FT: 3,500
SALES (est): 235.26K **Privately Held**
Web: www.customappareletc.com
SIC: **2759** Screen printing

(G-112)
CUSTOM CRAFT CONTROLS INC
Also Called: Custom Craft
1620 Triplett Blvd (44306-3308)
P.O. Box 7363 (44306-0363)
PHONE.....................330 630-9599
Kenneth Mike Dunaway, *Pr*
Debbie Dunaway, *Pr*
EMP: 18 EST: 1986
SQ FT: 10,000
SALES (est): 2.1MM **Privately Held**
Web: www.customcraftcontrols.com
SIC: **3613** 8711 Control panels, electric;
Engineering services

(G-113)
D & L MACHINE CO INC
1029 Arlington Cir (44306-3959)
PHONE.....................330 785-0781
Charles Bell, *Pr*
Naaman Elliott, *
EMP: 25 EST: 1943
SQ FT: 18,100
SALES (est): 5.62MM **Privately Held**
Web: www.summitmachinesolutions.com
SIC: **3599** Machine shop, jobbing and repair

(G-114)
D AND D PLASTICS INC
581 E Tallmadge Ave (44310-2402)
P.O. Box 285 (44278-0285)
PHONE.....................330 376-0668
Charles Hay, *Pr*
Terri Hay, *Treas*
EMP: 10 EST: 1982
SQ FT: 8,000
SALES (est): 402.89K **Privately Held**
Web: www.d-dplastics.com
SIC: **3089** Extruded finished plastics
products, nec

(G-115)
DATAQ INSTRUMENTS INC
241 Springside Dr (44333-2432)
PHONE.....................330 668-1444
John J Bowers, *Pr*
Roger Lockhart, *VP*
Karen Bowers, *Sec*
EMP: 19 EST: 1984
SQ FT: 4,000
SALES (est): 5.32MM **Privately Held**
Web: www.dataq.com
SIC: **3577** Computer peripheral equipment,
nec

(G-116)
DAUPHIN HOLDINGS INC
Also Called: Arnold's Candies

931 High Grove Blvd (44312-3405)
PHONE.....................330 733-4022
Laurel Dauphin, *Pr*
EMP: 6 EST: 2011
SALES (est): 182.48K **Privately Held**
SIC: **2064** Candy and other confectionery
products

(G-117)
DAVID WOLFE DESIGN INC
829 Moe Dr (44310-2516)
PHONE.....................330 633-6124
David Wolfe Senior, *Pr*
Nancy C Wolfe, *Sec*
EMP: 15 EST: 1985
SALES (est): 2.49MM **Privately Held**
Web: www.davidwolfedesign.com
SIC: **7389** 3089 Design, commercial and
industrial; Plastics processing

(G-118)
DC LEGACY CORP
3300 Massillon Rd (44312-5361)
PHONE.....................330 896-4220
Michael Hochschwender, *CEO*
Albert Kungl, *
▲ EMP: 40 EST: 1971
SQ FT: 26,000
SALES (est): 4.99MM **Privately Held**
Web: www.delcollc.com
SIC: **3544** Special dies and tools

(G-119)
DIAMOND AMERICA CORPORATION (PA)
Also Called: Akron Tool and Die
96 E Miller Ave (44301-1325)
PHONE.....................330 762-9269
▲ EMP: 15 EST: 1950
SALES (est): 6.84MM
SALES (corp-wide): 6.84MM **Privately
Held**
Web: www.daextrusion.com
SIC: **3544** 3469 Extrusion dies; Machine
parts, stamped or pressed metal

(G-120)
DIAMOND DESIGNS INC
231 Springside Dr Ste 145 (44333-2455)
PHONE.....................330 434-6776
Philip H Gross, *Pr*
Bradley Gross, *VP*
EMP: 8 EST: 1980
SALES (est): 723.9K **Privately Held**
SIC: **3911** Jewelry, precious metal

(G-121)
DIAMOND POLYMERS INCORPORATED
1353 Exeter Rd (44306-3853)
PHONE.....................330 773-2700
◆ EMP: 66
SIC: **2821** 2295 Plastics materials and resins
; Resin or plastic coated fabrics

(G-122)
DIE-GEM CO INC
Also Called: Kel-Eez
394 Greenwood Ave (44320-1245)
PHONE.....................330 784-7400
James Adams, *Pr*
James Adams, *Pr*
Diane Adams, *VP*
EMP: 15 EST: 1971
SQ FT: 17,000
SALES (est): 1.04MM **Privately Held**
Web: www.die-gem.com
SIC: **3089** Injection molding of plastics

(G-123)
DIGITAL COLOR INTL LLC
Also Called: D C I
1653 Merriman Rd Ste 211 (44313-5276)
EMP: 19 **EST:** 2011
SQ FT: 38,000
SALES (est): 490.55K **Privately Held**
Web: www.digitalcolorinternational.com
SIC: 7336 2752 2653 7331 Creative services
to advertisers, except writers; Commercial
printing, lithographic; Display items, solid
fiber; made from purchased materials;
Direct mail advertising services

(G-124)
DLH ENTERPRISES LLC
Also Called: Hotcards of Akron
2086 Romig Rd Ste 2 (44320-3874)
PHONE................................330 253-6960
EMP: 6 **EST:** 2010
SALES (est): 104.38K **Privately Held**
SIC: 2759 Commercial printing, nec

(G-125)
DOWCO LLC
Also Called: Finite Fibers
1374 Markle St (44306-1801)
PHONE................................330 773-6654
▲ **EMP:** 22 **EST:** 2005
SQ FT: 1,500
SALES (est): 4.84MM **Privately Held**
Web: www.finitefiber.com
SIC: 2824 Nylon fibers

(G-126)
DOWNING ENTERPRISES INC
Also Called: Downing Exhibits
1287 Centerview Cir (44321-1632)
PHONE................................330 666-3888
William Downing Junior, *CEO*
Michael Carano, *
Karen Gallaher, *
Craig Marsall, *
◆ **EMP:** 100 **EST:** 1972
SQ FT: 144,000
SALES (est): 4.71MM **Privately Held**
Web: www.downingexhibits.com
SIC: 7389 3999 Trade show arrangement;
Barber and beauty shop equipment

(G-127)
DRB HOLDINGS LLC
3245 Pickle Rd (44312-5333)
PHONE................................330 645-3299
Bill Morgenstern, *CEO*
EMP: 285 **EST:** 2003
SALES (est): 1.64MM **Privately Held**
Web: www.drb.com
SIC: 7373 7371 7372 Systems software
development services; Custom computer
programming services; Prepackaged
software

(G-128)
DRB SYSTEMS LLC (HQ)
Also Called: Drb Tunnel Solutions
3245 Pickle Rd (44312-5333)
P.O. Box 550 (44685-0550)
PHONE................................330 645-3299
Dale Brott, *Pr*
Donald A Brott, *
Kenneth Brott, *
EMP: 240 **EST:** 1984
SALES (est): 24.47MM
SALES (corp-wide): 2.98B **Publicly Held**
Web: www.drb.com
SIC: 7373 7371 7372 Systems software
development services; Custom computer
programming services; Prepackaged
software
PA: Vontier Corporation

5438 Wade Pk Blvd Ste 600
Raleigh NC 27607
984 275-6000

(G-129)
EARTHQUAKER DEVICES LLC
Also Called: Earthquaker Devices
350 W Bowery St (44307-2538)
PHONE................................330 252-9220
Jamie Stillman, *Pt*
Jamie Stillman, *Managing Member*
▲ **EMP:** 41 **EST:** 2007
SALES (est): 5.71MM **Privately Held**
Web: www.earthquakerdevices.com
SIC: 3931 Guitars and parts, electric and
nonelectric

(G-130)
ELKHART PLASTICS LLC (HQ)
1293 S Main St (44301-1302)
PHONE................................888 605-2068
Jack Welter, *Pr*
EMP: 46 **EST:** 2020
SALES (est): 23.8MM
SALES (corp-wide): 836.28MM **Publicly
Held**
Web: www.epi-roto.com
SIC: 3089 7389 Injection molding of plastics;
Business services, nec
PA: Myers Industries, Inc.
1293 S Main St
Akron OH 44301
330 253-5592

(G-131)
ELLET NEON SALES & SERVICE INC
Also Called: E S C
3041 E Waterloo Rd (44312-4058)
P.O. Box 6063 (44312-0063)
PHONE................................330 628-9907
Gregory Peters, *Pr*
Claudia Peters, *
Mike Croston, *
Johnathan Webb, *
Amy Yelling, *
EMP: 50 **EST:** 1956
SQ FT: 7,000
SALES (est): 4.76MM **Privately Held**
Web: www.elletneon.com
SIC: 3993 Electric signs

(G-132)
ELLORAS CAVE PUBLISHING INC
1050 Home Ave (44310-3502)
P.O. Box 937 (44223-0937)
PHONE................................330 253-3521
Patty L Marks, *CEO*
Tina M Engler, *
Christina M Brashear, *
EMP: 9 **EST:** 2002
SQ FT: 12,960
SALES (est): 375.16K **Privately Held**
SIC: 2741 2731 Miscellaneous publishing;
Book publishing

(G-133)
ENDURANCE MANUFACTURING INC
1615 E Market St (44305-4210)
PHONE................................330 628-2600
Thomas J Turkalj, *Prin*
EMP: 7 **EST:** 2011
SALES (est): 1.3MM **Privately Held**
SIC: 2813 Industrial gases

(G-134)
**ENERGY HBR NCLEAR GNRATION
LLC**
168 E Market St (44308-2014)
PHONE................................888 254-6359
John Judge, *Pr*
EMP: 6 **EST:** 2007

SALES (est): 2.76MM
SALES (corp-wide): 17.22B **Publicly Held**
SIC: 3443 Nuclear reactors, military or
industrial
HQ: Energy Harbor Corp.
168 E Market St
Akron OH 44308
888 254-6359

(G-135)
ENGINEERED PLASTICS CORP
420 Kenmore Blvd (44301-1038)
PHONE................................330 376-7700
Jim Rauh, *Pr*
Joe Raugh, *
▲ **EMP:** 7 **EST:** 1994
SQ FT: 1,000,000
SALES (est): 421.07K **Privately Held**
SIC: 3052 Plastic belting

(G-136)
ENLARGING ARTS INC
161 Tarbell St (44303-2233)
PHONE................................330 434-3433
John Welsh Iii, *Pr*
Shirley Welsh, *VP*
EMP: 8 **EST:** 1994
SALES (est): 246.66K **Privately Held**
SIC: 2752 7384 3993 7336 Commercial
printing, lithographic; Photofinish
laboratories; Signs and advertising
specialties; Commercial art and graphic
design

(G-137)
EPIROC USA LLC
820 Glaser Pkwy (44306-4133)
PHONE................................717 552-8488
EMP: 11
SIC: 3532 Mining machinery
HQ: Epiroc Usa Llc
8001 Arista Pl Ste 400
Broomfield CO 80021
844 437-4762

(G-138)
ESI-EXTRUSION SERVICES INC
305 W North St (44303-2350)
PHONE................................330 374-3388
EMP: 35 **EST:** 1981
SALES (est): 7.27MM **Privately Held**
Web: www.esi-extrusion.com
SIC: 3544 3559 3549 3541 Special dies,
tools, jigs, and fixtures; Plastics working
machinery; Metalworking machinery, nec;
Machine tools, metal cutting type

(G-139)
ESP AKRON SUB LLC
240 W Emerling Ave (44301-1620)
PHONE................................330 374-2242
Thomas Holleran, *CEO*
EMP: 72 **EST:** 2020
SALES (est): 1.39MM **Privately Held**
SIC: 2899 Chemical preparations, nec

(G-140)
EVONIK CORPORATION
Also Called: Degussa
3500 Embassy Pkwy Ste 100 (44333-8327)
PHONE................................330 668-2235
Salena Wilson, *Prin*
EMP: 24
SALES (corp-wide): 16.03B **Privately Held**
Web: corporate.evonik.com
SIC: 2869 Industrial organic chemicals, nec
HQ: Evonik Corporation
2 Turner Pl
Piscataway NJ 08854
732 981-5060

(G-141)
EZURIO LLC (PA)
50 S Main St Ste 1100 (44308-1831)
PHONE................................330 434-7929
Bill Steinike, *CEO*
Bob Sallmann, *
EMP: 75 **EST:** 2019
SALES (est): 43.83MM
SALES (corp-wide): 43.83MM **Privately
Held**
Web: www.ezurio.com
SIC: 3674 Computer logic modules

(G-142)
F M MACHINE CO
1114 Triplett Blvd (44306-3098)
PHONE................................330 773-8237
Robert R Christian, *Pr*
Joel Christian, *
Shannon Adolph, *
Courtney Wagner, *
EMP: 45 **EST:** 1963
SQ FT: 36,000
SALES (est): 1MM **Privately Held**
Web: www.fmmachine.com
SIC: 3599 3441 Machine shop, jobbing and
repair; Fabricated structural metal

(G-143)
**FALLS MTAL FBRCTORS INDUS
SVCS**
380 Kennedy Rd (44305-4422)
PHONE................................330 253-7181
Daniel Pugh, *Pr*
Daniel R Pugh, *Pr*
Stephanie Pugh, *Treas*
EMP: 13 **EST:** 2014
SALES (est): 3.13MM **Privately Held**
Web: www.fmfis.com
SIC: 1542 1541 3542 Nonresidential
construction, nec; Factory construction;
Punching, shearing, and bending machines

(G-144)
FALLS TOOL AND DIE INC
1416 Piedmont Ave (44310-2614)
PHONE................................330 633-4884
Marvin Hardy, *Pr*
David Cunningham, *Contrlr*
EMP: 8 **EST:** 1964
SQ FT: 18,500
SALES (est): 944.45K **Privately Held**
SIC: 3469 3544 3465 Stamping metal for the
trade; Special dies and tools; Automotive
stampings

(G-145)
FAMOUS INDUSTRIES INC (DH)
Also Called: Johnson Contrls Authorized Dlr
2620 Ridgewood Rd Ste 200 (44313-3507)
PHONE................................330 535-1811
Pat Mccaffrey, *Pr*
EMP: 50 **EST:** 1948
SALES (est): 24.65MM
SALES (corp-wide): 3.97B **Privately Held**
Web: www.johnsoncontrols.com
SIC: 3444 5065 5074 Metal ventilating
equipment; Telephone equipment;
Plumbing and heating valves
HQ: Flex-Tek Group Llc
1473 Gould Dr
Cookeville TN 38501
931 432-7212

(G-146)
FENIX FABRICATION INC
2689 Wingate Ave (44314-1301)
PHONE................................330 745-8731
Christopher J Forgan, *Pr*
EMP: 19 **EST:** 2007
SALES (est): 2.83MM **Privately Held**

Web: www.fenixfab.com
SIC: 3441 Fabricated structural metal

(G-147)
FERRIOT INC
1000 Arlington Cir (44306-3973)
P.O. Box Po Box7670 (44306-0670)
PHONE..............................330 786-3000
Gordon Keeler, *CEO*
George D Grosso, *
David Ferriot, *
▲ **EMP:** 170 **EST:** 1929
SQ FT: 220,000
SALES (est): 27.22MM **Privately Held**
Web: www.ferriot.com
SIC: 3089 3544 Injection molding of plastics;
　Industrial molds

(G-148)
FIRESTONE POLYMERS LLC (DH)
Also Called: Polymer Engineering Pilot Ctr
381 W Wilbeth Rd (44301-2465)
P.O. Box 26611 (44319-6611)
PHONE..............................330 379-7000
Ryan Sullivan, *
◆ **EMP:** 73 **EST:** 2001
SALES (est): 97.1MM **Privately Held**
Web: www.firestonepolymers.com
SIC: 3069 Latex, foamed
HQ: Bridgestone Americas, Inc.
　200 4th Ave S Ste 100
　Nashville TN 37201
　615 937-1000

(G-149)
FIVE STAR HEALTHY VENDING LLC
388 S Main St Ste 440 (44311-1064)
PHONE..............................330 549-6011
EMP: 11
SALES (est): 1.56MM **Privately Held**
SIC: 3581 Automatic vending machines

(G-150)
FLEXSYS AMERICA LP (HQ)
Also Called: Flexsys America
260 Springside Dr (44333-4554)
PHONE..............................330 666-4111
Sandip Tyagi, *CEO*
Mark Schie, *CFO*
◆ **EMP:** 65 **EST:** 1995
SQ FT: 85,000
SALES (est): 36.72MM
SALES (corp-wide): 142.37MM **Privately
Held**
SIC: 3069 8731 2899 2823 Reclaimed
　rubber and specialty rubber compounds;
　Commercial physical research; Chemical
　preparations, nec; Cellulosic manmade
　fibers
PA: Flexsys Holdings, Inc.
　260 Springside Dr
　Akron OH 44333
　330 666-4111

(G-151)
FLEXSYS INC
260 Springside Dr (44333-4554)
PHONE..............................212 605-6000
Sandip Tyagi, *CEO*
Tony Lee, *Treas*
EMP: 500 **EST:** 2021
SALES (est): 360MM **Privately Held**
Web: www.flexsys.com
SIC: 2819 7389 Industrial inorganic
　chemicals, nec; Business Activities at Non-
　Commercial Site

(G-152)
FOUNDATION INDUSTRIES INC (PA)
Also Called: F I C
880 W Waterloo Rd Ste B (44314-1519)

PHONE..............................330 564-1250
Richard Huscroft, *Pr*
◆ **EMP:** 40 **EST:** 1991
SQ FT: 109,000
SALES (est): 9.88MM **Privately Held**
Web: www.foundationind.com
SIC: 3999 Barber and beauty shop
　equipment

(G-153)
G&O RESOURCES LTD
677 Kling St (44311-1767)
PHONE..............................330 253-2525
Robert Nelson, *CEO*
EMP: 6 **EST:** 1997
SALES (est): 1.23MM **Privately Held**
SIC: 1382 Oil and gas exploration services

(G-154)
GABRIEL PHENOXIES INC (PA)
240 W Emerling Ave (44301-1620)
PHONE..............................704 499-9801
Seth Tomasch, *CEO*
◆ **EMP:** 25 **EST:** 1993
SALES (est): 9.21MM
SALES (corp-wide): 9.21MM **Privately
Held**
SIC: 2821 Plastics materials and resins

(G-155)
GALENAS LLC
1956 S Main St (44301-2877)
PHONE..............................330 208-9423
Geoffrey Korff, *Managing Member*
EMP: 16 **EST:** 2016
SALES (est): 2.38MM **Privately Held**
Web: www.galenas.com
SIC: 2834 Pharmaceutical preparations

(G-156)
GARRO TREAD CORPORATION (PA)
Also Called: Ace Rubber Products Division
100 Beech St (44308-1916)
P.O. Box 4567 (44310-0567)
PHONE..............................330 376-3125
Charles Garro, *Pr*
Greg Garro, *VP*
EMP: 9 **EST:** 1980
SQ FT: 100,000
SALES (est): 4.17MM
SALES (corp-wide): 4.17MM **Privately
Held**
Web: www.acerubber.net
SIC: 3069 5531 Mats or matting, rubber, nec
　; Automotive tires

(G-157)
**GEAR STAR AMRCN PRFMCE
TRNSMSS**
Also Called: Gear Star
132 N Howard St (44308-1937)
PHONE..............................330 434-5216
Zack Farah, *Pr*
Derek Kriebel, *Prin*
◆ **EMP:** 20 **EST:** 2001
SALES (est): 2.37MM **Privately Held**
Web: www.gearstar.com
SIC: 5571 5013 3714 Motorcycle parts and
　accessories; Motor vehicle supplies and
　new parts; Motor vehicle transmissions,
　drive assemblies, and parts

(G-158)
GEHM & SONS LIMITED
825 S Arlington St (44306-2498)
PHONE..............................330 724-8423
Juanita Gehm, *Pr*
EMP: 6 **EST:** 1929
SQ FT: 5,780
SALES (est): 2.75MM **Privately Held**
Web: www.4dryice.com

SIC: 5145 2086 5169 Syrups, fountain;
　Carbonated beverages, nonalcoholic;
　pkged. in cans, bottles; Dry ice

(G-159)
GEN DIGITAL INC
Also Called: Symantec
159 S Main St (44308-1317)
PHONE..............................330 252-1171
Joe Cassner, *Brnch Mgr*
EMP: 8
SALES (corp-wide): 3.81B **Publicly Held**
Web: www.nortonlifelock.com
SIC: 3674 Semiconductors and related
　devices
PA: Gen Digital Inc.
　60 E Rio Slado Pkwy Ste 1
　Tempe AZ 85281
　650 527-8000

(G-160)
**GENERAL METALS POWDER CO
LLC (PA)**
Also Called: Gempco
1195 Home Ave (44310-2576)
PHONE..............................330 633-1226
Jerry Lynch, *Pr*
Louis L Cseko Junior, *VP*
Barry P Alvord, *
EMP: 43 **EST:** 1929
SQ FT: 30,000
SALES (est): 4.76MM
SALES (corp-wide): 4.76MM **Privately
Held**
Web: www.gmpfriction.com
SIC: 3499 3714 3568 Friction material, made
　from powdered metal; Motor vehicle parts
　and accessories; Power transmission
　equipment, nec

(G-161)
GENTZLER TOOL & DIE CORP (PA)
3903 Massillon Rd (44312)
P.O. Box 158 (44232-0158)
PHONE..............................330 896-1941
David W Gentzler, *Pr*
Geraldine Gentzler, *Pr*
David Gentzler, *VP*
EMP: 20 **EST:** 1953
SQ FT: 20,000
SALES (est): 2.21MM
SALES (corp-wide): 2.21MM **Privately
Held**
Web: www.gentzlertoolanddie.com
SIC: 3469 3544 Stamping metal for the trade
　; Special dies and tools

(G-162)
GOJO CANADA INC
1 Gojo Plz Ste 500 (44311-1085)
PHONE..............................330 255-6000
EMP: 11 **EST:** 2011
SALES (est): 282.59K **Privately Held**
Web: www.gojo.com
SIC: 2842 Polishes and sanitation goods

(G-163)
GOJO INDUSTRIES INC (PA)
Also Called: Gojo
1 Gojo Plz Ste 500 (44311-1085)
P.O. Box 991 (44311)
PHONE..............................330 255-6000
Joseph Kanfer, *Ch Bd*
Mark Lerner, *
◆ **EMP:** 200 **EST:** 1946
SQ FT: 500,000
SALES (est): 802.21MM
SALES (corp-wide): 802.21MM **Privately
Held**
Web: www.gojo.com

SIC: 2842 3586 2844 Polishes and
　sanitation goods; Measuring and
　dispensing pumps; Perfumes, cosmetics
　and other toilet preparations

(G-164)
**GOODYEAR TIRE & RUBBER
COMPANY (PA)**
Also Called: Goodyear
200 E Innovation Way (44316-0001)
PHONE..............................330 796-2121
Mark W Stewart, *Pr*
Laurette T Koellner, *
Christina L Zamarro, *Ex VP*
Nicole Gray, *Chief Human Resource Officer*
Laura P Duda, *CCO*
◆ **EMP:** 2602 **EST:** 1898
SALES (est): 18.88B
SALES (corp-wide): 18.88B **Publicly Held**
Web: www.goodyear.com
SIC: 3011 5531 7534 7538 Inner tubes, all
　types; Automotive tires; Tire retreading and
　repair shops; General automotive repair
　shops

(G-165)
GRADY MCCAULEY INC
Also Called: LSI Graphic Solutions Plus
5127 Boyer Pkwy (44312-4272)
PHONE..............................330 494-9444
David Mccauley, *Pr*
EMP: 100 **EST:** 1963
SALES (est): 5MM
SALES (corp-wide): 469.64MM **Publicly
Held**
SIC: 3993 2759 Electric signs; Screen
　printing
PA: Lsi Industries Inc.
　10000 Alliance Rd
　Cincinnati OH 45242
　513 793-3200

(G-166)
**GREAT LAKES POLYMER PROC INC
(PA)**
1210 Massillon Rd (44306-3327)
PHONE..............................313 655-4024
Alan Mitchell, *CEO*
EMP: 19 **EST:** 2020
SALES (est): 500K
SALES (corp-wide): 500K **Privately Held**
SIC: 2822 Ethylene-propylene rubbers,
　EPDM polymers

(G-167)
H & H MACHINE SHOP AKRON INC
955 Grant St (44311-2490)
PHONE..............................330 773-3327
Henry R Haas, *Pr*
Anna Haas, *Sec*
EMP: 21 **EST:** 1959
SQ FT: 24,000
SALES (est): 2.44MM **Privately Held**
Web: www.hhmachine.com
SIC: 3599 7692 Machine shop, jobbing and
　repair; Welding repair

(G-168)
H & M METAL PROCESSING CO (HQ)
1414 Kenmore Blvd (44314-1600)
PHONE..............................330 745-3075
Robert Mcmillen, *Pr*
Robert Mcmillen Iv, *Stockholder*
Ben Mcmillen, *Stockholder*
Alexandra Evanko, *Stockholder**
EMP: 43 **EST:** 1942
SQ FT: 7,000
SALES (est): 8.02MM **Privately Held**
Web: www.blacknitride.com
SIC: 3398 Metal heat treating
PA: Moore, Mc Millen Holdings, Inc

▲ = Import ▼ = Export
◆ = Import/Export

1850 Front St
Cuyahoga Falls OH 44221

(G-169)
HALLER ENTERPRISES INC
1621 E Market St (44305-4210)
PHONE..............................330 733-9693
TOLL FREE: 800
David Haller, *Pr*
Harriet Haller, *VP*
Daid Haller Junior, *VP*
EMP: 10 **EST:** 1966
SQ FT: 6,000
SALES (est): 988.66K **Privately Held**
SIC: 2097 5999 Manufactured ice; Ice

(G-170)
HAMLIN NEWCO LLC
2741 Wingate Ave (44314-1301)
PHONE..............................330 753-7791
Charles N Biehara, *
▲ **EMP:** 52 **EST:** 2007
SQ FT: 110
SALES (est): 9.82MM **Privately Held**
Web: www.hnmetalstamping.com
SIC: 3469 Stamping metal for the trade

(G-171)
HAMLIN STEEL PRODUCTS LLC
2741 Wingate Ave (44314-1301)
PHONE..............................330 753-7791
EMP: 10 **EST:** 1978
SQ FT: 110,000
SALES (est): 2.02MM **Privately Held**
Web: www.hnmetalstamping.com
SIC: 3469 Stamping metal for the trade

(G-172)
HARRY C LOBALZO & SONS INC
Also Called: Hobart Sales & Service
61 N Cleveland Massillon Rd Unit A
(44333-4556)
PHONE..............................330 666-6758
Mike Lobalzo, *Ch*
Joe Saporito, *
Rick Lobalzo, *Vice Chairman*
▲ **EMP:** 45 **EST:** 1956
SQ FT: 20,000
SALES (est): 9.07MM **Privately Held**
Web: www.retailfoodequip.com
SIC: 5046 7699 3556 Restaurant equipment
and supplies, nec; Restaurant equipment
repair; Food products machinery

(G-173)
HERBERT USA INC
1480 Industrial Pkwy (44310-2602)
PHONE..............................330 929-4297
Mathias Walter, *Pr*
Todd Jarvis, *
▲ **EMP:** 55 **EST:** 1974
SQ FT: 25,000
SALES (est): 4.18MM **Privately Held**
Web: www.herbert.eu
SIC: 3544 Industrial molds

(G-174)
HERITAGE INDUSTRIAL FINSHG INC
1874 Englewood Ave (44312-1002)
PHONE..............................330 798-9840
Agathonico Pamboukis, *Ch*
Nicholas Pamboukis, *
Russell Kemppel, *
Frank J Witschey, *
Marla Kay, *
▲ **EMP:** 58 **EST:** 1965
SQ FT: 35,000
SALES (est): 3.26MM **Privately Held**
Web:
www.heritageindustrialfinishing.com

SIC: 3479 Painting of metal products

(G-175)
HEXPOL COMPOUNDING LLC
Also Called: Hexpol Silicone
1497 Exeter Rd (44306-3856)
PHONE..............................440 682-4038
EMP: 121
SALES (corp-wide): 6.47MM **Privately
Held**
Web: www.hexpol.com
SIC: 3069 Medical and laboratory rubber
sundries and related products
HQ: Hexpol Compounding Llc
14330 Kinsman Rd
Burton OH 44021
440 834-4644

(G-176)
HEXPOL COMPOUNDING PC INC
115 W Bartges St (44311-1008)
PHONE..............................330 258-2016
EMP: 10
SALES (corp-wide): 6.47MM **Privately
Held**
Web: www.preferredperforms.com
SIC: 3089 Injection molding of plastics
HQ: Hexpol Compounding Pc, Inc.
1020 Lambert St
Barberton OH 44203

(G-177)
**HUNTSMAN ADVNCED MTLS
AMRCAS L**
240 W Emerling Ave (44301-1620)
PHONE..............................330 374-2424
EMP: 30
SALES (corp-wide): 6.04B **Publicly Held**
Web: www.huntsman.com
SIC: 2821 Plastics materials and resins
HQ: Huntsman Advanced Materials
Americas Llc
10003 Woodloch Forest Dr
The Woodlands TX 77380
281 719-6000

(G-178)
**HUNTSMAN ADVNCED MTLS
AMRCAS L**
Also Called: Gabriel Performance Products
240 W Emerling Ave (44301-1620)
PHONE..............................866 800-2436
EMP: 33
SALES (corp-wide): 6.04B **Publicly Held**
Web: www.huntsman.com
SIC: 2821 Plastics materials and resins
HQ: Huntsman Advanced Materials
Americas Llc
10003 Woodloch Forest Dr
The Woodlands TX 77380
281 719-6000

(G-179)
HUNTSMAN CORPORATION
Also Called: Cvc Thermoset Specialties
240 W Emerling Ave (44301-1620)
PHONE..............................330 374-2418
Jeffrey Michaels, *Prin*
EMP: 100
SALES (corp-wide): 6.04B **Publicly Held**
Web: www.huntsman.com
SIC: 2899 2821 Chemical preparations, nec;
Plastics materials and resins
PA: Huntsman Corporation
10003 Woodloch Forest Dr
The Woodlands TX 77380
281 719-6000

(G-180)
HYGENIC ACQUISITION CO
1245 Home Ave (44310-2510)
P.O. Box 1818 (44312)
PHONE..............................330 633-8460
Earl Decarli, *Pr*
Stewart Lorenzen, *
Niels Lichti, *
Kurt Marhoefer, *
Harold Baker, *
EMP: 125 **EST:** 2003
SQ FT: 135,000
SALES (est): 2.93MM **Privately Held**
Web: www.hygenic.com
SIC: 3069 3061 Mechanical rubber goods;
Medical and laboratory rubber sundries and
related products
HQ: Baird Capital Partners Management
Company, Iii Llc
777 E Wisconsin Ave
Milwaukee WI 53202
414 765-3500

(G-181)
HYGENIC COMPANY LLC
Also Called: Performance Health
1245 Home Ave (44310-2510)
PHONE..............................330 633-8460
Marshall Dahneke, *Pr*
Niels Lichti, *
Ralph Buster, *Corporate Vice President*
◆ **EMP:** 324 **EST:** 1925
SQ FT: 135,000
SALES (est): 32.77MM
SALES (corp-wide): 174.71MM **Privately
Held**
Web: www.hygenic.com
SIC: 3069 3061 Medical and laboratory
rubber sundries and related products;
Mechanical rubber goods
PA: Cogr, Inc.
140 E 45th St 43rd Fl
New York NY 10017
212 370-5600

(G-182)
INDUSTRIAL TECHNOLOGIES INC
1643 Massillon Rd (44312-4273)
PHONE..............................330 434-2033
Gregg Caprez, *Pr*
Michelle H Caprez, *VP*
EMP: 7 **EST:** 1997
SQ FT: 3,000
SALES (est): 870.71K **Privately Held**
Web: www.industrialtech.info
SIC: 3543 Industrial patterns

(G-183)
INTERGROUP INTERNATIONAL LTD
1653 Merriman Rd Ste 211 (44313-5276)
PHONE..............................216 965-0257
Neil Gloger, *Pt*
Sarah Gatanas, *Pt*
EMP: 70 **EST:** 1999
SQ FT: 130,000
SALES (est): 8.56MM **Privately Held**
Web: www.intergroupinternational.com
SIC: 2821 Plastics materials and resins

(G-184)
ITEM NA
925 Glaser Pkwy (44306-4161)
PHONE..............................216 271-7241
EMP: 7 **EST:** 2018
SALES (est): 696.8K **Privately Held**
Web: www.industrialprofile.com
SIC: 3999 Manufacturing industries, nec

(G-185)
JDA SOFTWARE GROUP INC
Also Called: JDA SOFTWARE GROUP, INC.
308 N Cleveland Massillon Rd
(44333-9302)
PHONE..............................480 308-3000
Kurt Thomiet, *Brnch Mgr*
EMP: 13
Web: www.blueyonder.com
SIC: 7372 Prepackaged software
HQ: Blue Yonder Group, Inc.
15059 N Scttsdale Rd Ste
Scottsdale AZ 85254

(G-186)
JILCO PRECISION MOLD MCH INC
Also Called: Jilco
1245 Devalera St (44310-2457)
PHONE..............................330 633-9645
John Shepherd, *Pr*
EMP: 6 **EST:** 1983
SQ FT: 3,300
SALES (est): 1.44MM **Privately Held**
Web: www.jilco.us
SIC: 3599 Machine shop, jobbing and repair

(G-187)
JORDANKELLY LLC
165 Ira Ave (44301-1117)
PHONE..............................216 855-8550
EMP: 11 **EST:** 2018
SALES (est): 1.25MM **Privately Held**
SIC: 3531 4231 Construction machinery;
Trucking terminal facilities

(G-188)
JRB ATTACHMENTS LLC (DH)
820 Glaser Pkwy (44306-4133)
PHONE..............................330 734-3000
Steve Andrews, *CEO*
Steve Klyn, *CFO*
Jeremy Wild, *Contrlr*
Michael Flannery, *VP*
Robert Hunt, *Contrlr*
▲ **EMP:** 7 **EST:** 1983
SALES (est): 9.99MM
SALES (corp-wide): 15.37B **Publicly Held**
Web: www.paladinattachments.com
SIC: 3531 Construction machinery
attachments
HQ: Paladin Brands Group, Inc.
2800 N Zeeb Rd
Dexter MI 48130
319 378-3696

(G-189)
JSC EMPLOYEE LEASING CORP (PA)
1560 Firestone Pkwy (44301-1626)
PHONE..............................330 773-8971
Jack Jeter, *Pr*
Nicholas George, *Sec*
Pam Love, *Ex VP*
EMP: 56 **EST:** 1971
SQ FT: 150,000
SALES (est): 4.47MM
SALES (corp-wide): 4.47MM **Privately
Held**
SIC: 2522 5021 Office cabinets and filing
drawers, except wood; Filing units

(G-190)
JSH INTERNATIONAL LLC
124 Darrow Rd Ste 5 (44305-3835)
PHONE..............................330 734-0251
Kevin Mulvihill, *Managing Member*
EMP: 6 **EST:** 2008
SALES (est): 189.56K **Privately Held**
Web: www.jshinternational.net
SIC: 5084 2836 Industrial machinery and
equipment; Biological products, except
diagnostic

(G-191)
KARMAN RUBBER COMPANY
2331 Copley Rd (44320-1499)
PHONE....................330 864-2161
David W Mann, *Pr*
G Jay Hearty, *
EMP: 90 **EST:** 1945
SQ FT: 55,000
SALES (est): 4.29MM **Privately Held**
Web: www.karman.com
SIC: 3069 3829 3822 3061 Molded rubber products; Measuring and controlling devices, nec; Environmental controls; Mechanical rubber goods

(G-192)
KAYLO ENTERPRISES LLC
540 S Main St Ste 115 (44311-1023)
PHONE....................330 535-1860
Thomas A Lovick, *Pr*
EMP: 7 **EST:** 2015
SALES (est): 1.4MM **Privately Held**
SIC: 2621 7389 3579 2262 Book, bond and printing papers; Advertising, promotional, and trade show services; Mailing, letter handling, and addressing machines; Screen printing: manmade fiber and silk broadwoven fabrics

(G-193)
KENMORE DEVELOPMENT & MCH CO
1395 Kenmore Blvd (44314-1658)
PHONE....................330 753-2274
Richard Roten, *Pr*
EMP: 10 **EST:** 1939
SQ FT: 20,000
SALES (est): 1.23MM **Privately Held**
Web: www.bdwlegal.com
SIC: 3599 Machine shop, jobbing and repair

(G-194)
KENMORE GEAR & MACHINE CO INC
2129 Jennifer St (44313-4763)
PHONE....................330 753-6671
David Ingham, *Pr*
Pamela S Ballinger, *VP*
Gary Ballinger, *Treas*
David Ingham Junior, *Sec*
EMP: 7 **EST:** 1926
SQ FT: 9,352
SALES (est): 428.04K **Privately Held**
SIC: 3566 Speed changers, drives, and gears

(G-195)
KILLBUCK OIL AND GAS LLC
52 Marvin Ave (44302-1048)
PHONE....................330 447-8423
Nathan Mcintyre, *Prin*
EMP: 6 **EST:** 2016
SALES (est): 154.54K **Privately Held**
SIC: 1389 Oil and gas field services, nec

(G-196)
KILLIAN LATEX INC
2064 Killian Rd (44312-4897)
PHONE....................330 644-6746
Timothy J Killian, *Pr*
Joan Killian Fisk, *
EMP: 30 **EST:** 1975
SQ FT: 65,000
SALES (est): 5.67MM **Privately Held**
Web: www.killianlatex.com
SIC: 3069 3087 Custom compounding of rubber materials; Custom compound purchased resins

(G-197)
KING MODEL COMPANY
Also Called: King Castings
365 Kenmore Blvd (44301-1053)
PHONE....................330 633-0491
Michael Wells, *Pr*
Gifford Wells, *
John Horrell, *
EMP: 31 **EST:** 1975
SQ FT: 15,000
SALES (est): 2.27MM **Privately Held**
Web: www.kingmachinemolds.com
SIC: 3999 Models, general, except toy

(G-198)
KOKI LABORATORIES INC
1081 Rosemary Blvd (44306-3727)
PHONE....................330 773-7669
John J Piscitelli, *Owner*
EMP: 20 **EST:** 2002
SALES (est): 2.39MM **Privately Held**
Web: www.kokilab.com
SIC: 2899 Chemical preparations, nec

(G-199)
KRUPP RUBBER MACHINERY
103 Western Ave (44313-6300)
PHONE....................330 864-0800
William Bradshaw, *Prin*
EMP: 6 **EST:** 2007
SALES (est): 565.28K **Privately Held**
SIC: 3069 5084 Fabricated rubber products, nec; Plastic products machinery

(G-200)
KURTZ BROS COMPOST SERVICES
2677 Riverview Rd (44313-4719)
PHONE....................330 864-2621
Thomas Kurtz, *Pr*
▲ **EMP:** 6 **EST:** 1990
SALES (est): 768.39K **Privately Held**
SIC: 2875 8741 Compost; Management services

(G-201)
LAIRD TECHNOLOGIES INC
50 S Main St Ste 1100 (44308-1831)
PHONE....................330 434-7929
EMP: 12
SALES (corp-wide): 12.39B **Publicly Held**
Web: www.lairdtech.com
SIC: 3679 Electronic circuits
HQ: Laird Technologies, Inc.
16401 Swngley Rdge Rd Ste
Chesterfield MO 63017
636 898-6000

(G-202)
LANCER DISPERSIONS INC
1680 E Market St (44305-4246)
EMP: 65
Web: www.akrondispersions.com
SIC: 3089 3087 2816 Coloring and finishing of plastics products; Custom compound purchased resins; Inorganic pigments

(G-203)
LANDMARK PLASTIC CORPORATION (PA)
1331 Kelly Ave (44306-3773)
PHONE....................330 785-2200
Robert G Merzweiler, *CEO*
◆ **EMP:** 190 **EST:** 1984
SQ FT: 200,000
SALES (est): 23.73MM
SALES (corp-wide): 23.73MM **Privately Held**
Web: www.landmarkplastic.com
SIC: 3089 Plastics containers, except foam

(G-204)
LEHNER SCREW MACHINE LLC
1169 Brittain Rd (44305-1004)
PHONE....................330 688-6616
Thomas Bader, *Pr*
John Bader, *VP*
EMP: 21 **EST:** 1950
SQ FT: 10,524
SALES (est): 1.46MM **Privately Held**
Web: www.ogsindustries.com
SIC: 3451 3599 Screw machine products; Machine shop, jobbing and repair

(G-205)
LELAND-GIFFORD INC
1029 Arlington Cir (44306-3959)
PHONE....................330 785-9730
Robert Hartford, *Pr*
EMP: 9 **EST:** 1984
SQ FT: 20,000
SALES (est): 722.17K **Privately Held**
Web: www.summitmachinesolutions.com
SIC: 3541 Drilling and boring machines

(G-206)
LIFESTYLE MEDIA GROUP LLC
3550 Embassy Pkwy (44333-8318)
PHONE....................954 377-9470
EMP: 16 **EST:** 2013
SALES (est): 217.38K **Privately Held**
Web: www.lmgfl.com
SIC: 2721 Magazines: publishing and printing

(G-207)
LIPPINCOTT AND PETO INC
Also Called: Rubber World Magazine
1741 Akron Peninsula Rd (44313-5157)
P.O. Box 5451 (44334-0451)
PHONE....................330 864-2122
Joe Lippincott, *Pr*
EMP: 6
SQ FT: 2,500
SALES (est): 26.68K **Privately Held**
Web: www.rubberworld.com
SIC: 2721 Trade journals: publishing only, not printed on site

(G-208)
LOCK 15 BREWING COMPANY LLC
21 W North St (44304-1035)
PHONE....................234 900-8277
EMP: 42 **EST:** 2015
SALES (est): 1.13MM **Privately Held**
Web: www.lock15brewing.com
SIC: 5813 2082 Bars and lounges; Malt beverages

(G-209)
LOCKHEED MRTIN INTGRTED SYSTEM
Also Called: Aerospace Simulations
1210 Massillon Rd (44315-0001)
PHONE....................330 796-2800
Dan Fiest, *Mgr*
EMP: 192
SIC: 3812 Search and navigation equipment
HQ: Lockheed Martin Integrated Systems, Llc
6801 Rockledge Dr
Bethesda MD 20817

(G-210)
LOGAN MACHINE COMPANY (PA)
Also Called: LMC
1405 Home Ave (44310-2586)
PHONE....................330 633-6163
Mark Schoenbaechler, *Pr*
Kenneth Schoenbaechler, *
▲ **EMP:** 64 **EST:** 1943
SQ FT: 96,000
SALES (est): 9.63MM
SALES (corp-wide): 9.63MM **Privately Held**
Web: www.loganmachine.com
SIC: 3599 3728 3544 3469 Custom machinery; Aircraft parts and equipment, nec; Special dies, tools, jigs, and fixtures; Metal stampings, nec

(G-211)
LOWRY FURNACE CO INC
Also Called: Hvac
663 Flora Ave (44314-1754)
PHONE....................330 745-4822
Gregory Shiflett, *Pr*
EMP: 6 **EST:** 1945
SQ FT: 3,000
SALES (est): 603.24K **Privately Held**
Web: www.lowryfurnace.com
SIC: 1711 3444 Warm air heating and air conditioning contractor; Sheet metalwork

(G-212)
LUND EQUIPMENT COMPANY
2400 N Cleveland Massillon Rd (44333-1251)
P.O. Box 213 (44210-0213)
PHONE....................330 659-4800
John Skeel, *Pr*
Raymond Smiley, *VP*
EMP: 20 **EST:** 1932
SQ FT: 5,000
SALES (est): 1.64MM **Privately Held**
Web: www.lundkey.com
SIC: 3444 Sheet metalwork

(G-213)
LYONDLLBSELL ADVNCED PLYMERS I
1353 Exeter Rd (44306-3853)
PHONE....................330 773-2700
EMP: 124
Web: www.lyondellbasell.com
SIC: 2821 Molding compounds, plastics
HQ: Lyondellbasell Advanced Polymers Inc.
1221 Mckinney St Ste 300
Houston TX 77010
713 309-7200

(G-214)
LYONDLLBSELL ADVNCED PLYMERS I
790 E Tallmadge Ave (44310-3564)
PHONE....................330 630-0308
Derold Hines, *Brnch Mgr*
EMP: 202
SQ FT: 104,823
Web: www.lyondellbasell.com
SIC: 2821 Molding compounds, plastics
HQ: Lyondellbasell Advanced Polymers Inc.
1221 Mckinney St Ste 300
Houston TX 77010
713 309-7200

(G-215)
LYONDLLBSELL ADVNCED PLYMERS I
1183 Home Ave (44310-2508)
PHONE....................330 630-3315
Joe Ocampo, *Brnch Mgr*
EMP: 93
SQ FT: 52,766
Web: www.lyondellbasell.com
SIC: 2821 Molding compounds, plastics
HQ: Lyondellbasell Advanced Polymers Inc.
1221 Mckinney St Ste 300
Houston TX 77010
713 309-7200

(G-216)
M & J MACHINE COMPANY
2420 Pickle Rd (44312-4227)
PHONE..........................330 645-0042
James Kuts, *Pr*
Charlene Kuts, *VP*
Jonathan Kuts, *Sec*
EMP: 10 **EST:** 1977
SQ FT: 15,000
SALES (est): 918.14K **Privately Held**
Web: www.mjmachine.net
SIC: 3599 Machine shop, jobbing and repair

(G-217)
M&MS AUTOSALES LLC
2203 Manchester Rd (44314-3723)
PHONE..........................234 334-7022
EMP: 10 **EST:** 2020
SALES (est): 486.42K **Privately Held**
SIC: 2396 Automotive and apparel trimmings

(G-218)
M7 HRP LLC
Also Called: Harwood Rubber Products
75 E Market St (44308-2010)
PHONE..........................330 923-3256
Ryan Smith, *Managing Member*
EMP: 17 **EST:** 1965
SALES (est): 1.15MM **Privately Held**
SIC: 3069 Fabricated rubber products, nec

(G-219)
MACK CONCRETE INDUSTRIES INC
Also Called: Mack Ready-Mix
124 Darrow Rd Ste 7 (44305-3835)
PHONE..........................330 784-7008
Ron Blanton, *Mgr*
EMP: 35
SALES (corp-wide): 86.93MM **Privately Held**
Web: www.mackconcrete.com
SIC: 3273 Ready-mixed concrete
HQ: Mack Concrete Industries, Inc.
201 Columbia Rd
Valley City OH 44280
330 483-3111

(G-220)
MARK-ALL ENTERPRISES LLC
Also Called: Excelsior Marking
888 W Waterloo Rd (44314-1528)
PHONE..........................800 433-3615
▲ **EMP:** 22 **EST:** 1905
SQ FT: 32,000
SALES (est): 5.95MM **Privately Held**
Web: www.excelsiormarking.com
SIC: 3953 2796 3999 Figures (marking devices), metal; Platemaking services; Badges, metal: policemen, firemen, etc.

(G-221)
MARKETHTCH INC D/B/A MH EYE CA
Also Called: J G Pads
91 E Voris St (44311-1507)
P.O. Box 1151 (44309)
PHONE..........................330 376-6363
Paul Joyce, *Pr*
EMP: 10 **EST:** 1993
SQ FT: 9,400
SALES (est): 855.6K **Privately Held**
Web: www.mheyecare.us
SIC: 3841 5047 Surgical and medical instruments; Medical equipment and supplies

(G-222)
MARKHAM MACHINE COMPANY INC
160 N Union St (44304-1355)
PHONE..........................330 762-7676
James M Markham, *Pr*

EMP: 18 **EST:** 1965
SQ FT: 13,000
SALES (est): 2.38MM **Privately Held**
SIC: 3599 Machine shop, jobbing and repair

(G-223)
MARTIN ALLEN TRAILER LLC
Also Called: AMG Trailer and Equipment
837 N Cleveland Massillon Rd
(44333-2167)
PHONE..........................330 942-0217
Dean Martin, *Pr*
EMP: 8 **EST:** 2014
SALES (est): 895.34K **Privately Held**
Web: www.peterbilt.com
SIC: 3715 5084 Truck trailers; Trailers, industrial

(G-224)
MAXION WHEELS SEDALIA LLC
428 Seiberling St (44306-3205)
PHONE..........................330 794-2300
Randy Arnst, *Brnch Mgr*
EMP: 2543
Web: www.maxionwheels.com
SIC: 3714 Motor vehicle parts and accessories
HQ: Hayes Lemmerz International-- Sedalia, Llc
3610 W Main St
Sedalia MO 65301
660 827-3640

(G-225)
MCNEIL & NRM INC (HQ)
96 E Crosier St (44311-2342)
PHONE..........................330 761-1855
Paul Yared, *CEO*
F H Yared, *
A Melek, *
A P Singh, *
◆ **EMP:** 65 **EST:** 1979
SQ FT: 35,000
SALES (est): 23.42MM
SALES (corp-wide): 23.42MM **Privately Held**
Web: www.mcneilnrm.com
SIC: 3559 3599 3542 Rubber working machinery, including tires; Custom machinery; Machine tools, metal forming type
PA: Mcneil & Nrm Intl., Inc.
96 E Crosier St
Akron OH 44311
330 253-2525

(G-226)
MCNEIL & NRM INTL INC (PA)
96 E Crosier St (44311-2342)
PHONE..........................330 253-2525
F H Yared, *Ch Bd*
Al M Melek, *
R A Nelson, *
Joel Siegfried, *
EMP: 75 **EST:** 1979
SQ FT: 35,000
SALES (est): 23.42MM
SALES (corp-wide): 23.42MM **Privately Held**
Web: www.mcneilnrm.com
SIC: 3559 3599 Rubber working machinery, including tires; Custom machinery

(G-227)
MEASUREMENT SPECIALTIES INC
2236 N Cleveland Massillon Rd Ste A
(44333-1288)
PHONE..........................330 659-3312
Robert Visger, *Brnch Mgr*
EMP: 118
SALES (corp-wide): 400.61MM **Privately Held**

Web: www.te.com
SIC: 3829 Measuring and controlling devices, nec
PA: Measurement Specialties, Inc.
1000 Lucas Way
Hampton VA 23666
757 766-1500

(G-228)
MEGGITT ARCFT BRKING SYSTEMS C (DH)
Also Called: Mabsc
1204 Massillon Rd (44306-4188)
P.O. Box 7670 (44306-0670)
PHONE..........................330 796-4400
Luke Duardogan, *Pr*
◆ **EMP:** 769 **EST:** 1989
SQ FT: 733,000
SALES (est): 286.11MM
SALES (corp-wide): 19.93B **Publicly Held**
Web: www.kfabsc.com
SIC: 3728 Brakes, aircraft
HQ: Meggitt Limited
Pilot Way
Coventry W MIDLANDS CV7 9
247 682-6900

(G-229)
METALICO AKRON INC (HQ)
Also Called: Metalico Annaco
943 Hazel St (44305-1609)
P.O. Box 1148 (44309-1148)
PHONE..........................330 376-1400
TOLL FREE: 800
Jeffery Bauer, *Genl Mgr*
EMP: 14 **EST:** 1930
SQ FT: 30,000
SALES (est): 17.7MM
SALES (corp-wide): 133.04MM **Privately Held**
Web: www.annaco.com
SIC: 5093 4953 3341 Ferrous metal scrap and waste; Refuse systems; Secondary nonferrous metals
PA: Metalico, Inc.
135 Dermody St
Cranford NJ 07016
908 497-9610

(G-230)
MEYER DESIGN INC
100 N High St (44308-1918)
PHONE..........................330 434-9176
TOLL FREE: 800
Christopher Meyer, *Pr*
EMP: 13 **EST:** 1974
SQ FT: 18,000
SALES (est): 1.26MM **Privately Held**
Web: www.meyerdesign.com
SIC: 3949 Playground equipment

(G-231)
MIKRON INDUSTRIES INC
388 S Main St Ste 700 (44311-1060)
PHONE..........................859 623-2643
Jeff Sandwith, *Mgr*
EMP: 160
Web: www.mikronvinyl.com
SIC: 3089 Extruded finished plastics products, nec
HQ: Mikron Industries, Inc.
388 S Main St Ste 700
Akron OH 44311
713 961-4600

(G-232)
MIKRON INDUSTRIES INC (HQ)
388 S Main St Ste 700 (44311-1060)
PHONE..........................713 961-4600
Scott Zuehlke, *CFO*
Paul Cornett, *Sec*

George Wilson, *CEO*
EMP: 54 **EST:** 1969
SALES (est): 12.62MM **Publicly Held**
Web: www.quanex.com
SIC: 3081 3089 Vinyl film and sheet; Extruded finished plastics products, nec
PA: Quanex Building Products Corporation
945 Bunker HI Rd Ste 900
Houston TX 77024

(G-233)
MILESTONE SERVICES CORP
551 Beacon St (44311-1805)
PHONE..........................330 374-9988
Richard Drillien, *Pr*
George Stanley, *Treas*
EMP: 6 **EST:** 1997
SQ FT: 200
SALES (est): 480.81K **Privately Held**
Web: www.milestoneservicescorp.com
SIC: 3471 Plating and polishing

(G-234)
MILLERS APLUS CMPT SVCS LLC
Also Called: Mapcs
1067 Mercer Ave (44320-3613)
P.O. Box 1901 (44309-1901)
PHONE..........................330 620-5288
Alisa Miller, *Prin*
EMP: 10 **EST:** 2020
SALES (est): 321.69K **Privately Held**
Web: www.millers.com
SIC: 8748 8243 8742 7373 Systems engineering consultant, ex. computer or professional; Operator training, computer; Management information systems consultant; Office computer automation systems integration

(G-235)
MOHICAN INDUSTRIES INC
1225 W Market St (44313-7107)
PHONE..........................330 869-0500
Judy Dipaola, *Pr*
EMP: 8 **EST:** 1980
SQ FT: 20,000
SALES (est): 1.45MM
SALES (corp-wide): 4.95MM **Privately Held**
SIC: 2822 Synthetic rubber
PA: Sovereign Chemical Company
4040 Embassy Pkwy Ste 190
Akron OH 44333
330 869-0500

(G-236)
MONTGOMERY & MONTGOMERY LLC
80 N Pershing Ave (44313-6258)
PHONE..........................330 858-9533
EMP: 7 **EST:** 2014
SALES (est): 117.35K **Privately Held**
SIC: 7692 Welding repair

(G-237)
MORE THAN GOURMET HOLDINGS INC
929 Home Ave (44310-4107)
PHONE..........................330 762-6652
Brad Sacks, *CEO*
▲ **EMP:** 50 **EST:** 1993
SALES (est): 21.29MM **Privately Held**
Web: www.morethangourmet.com
SIC: 5149 2032 Seasonings, sauces, and extracts; Soups and broths, canned, jarred, etc.
HQ: Ajinomoto Health & Nutrition North America, Inc.
250 East Devon Ave
Itasca IL 60143
630 931-6800

(G-238)
MT VERNON MOLD WORKS INC
2200 Massillon Rd (44312-4234)
PHONE.............................618 242-6040
Steve Zoumberakis, *Pr*
EMP: 21 **EST:** 1991
SALES (est): 2.49MM
SALES (corp-wide): 17.76MM **Privately Held**
SIC: 3544 7692 Special dies and tools; Welding repair
PA: Saehwa Imc Na, Inc.
2200 Massillon Rd
Akron OH 44312
330 645-6653

(G-239)
MUELLER ELECTRIC COMPANY INC (HQ)
2850 Gilchrist Rd Ste 5 (44305-4445)
P.O. Box 92922 (44194-2922)
PHONE.............................216 771-5225
Arnold Siemer, *Pr*
▲ **EMP:** 52 **EST:** 2011
SALES (est): 8.7MM
SALES (corp-wide): 90.88MM **Privately Held**
Web: www.mullerelectric.com
SIC: 3644 3643 3694 3496 Insulators and insulation materials, electrical; Current-carrying wiring services; Harness wiring sets, internal combustion engines; Miscellaneous fabricated wire products
PA: Desco Corporation
7795 Walton Pkwy Ste 175
New Albany OH 43054
614 888-8855

(G-240)
MULTIBASE INC
3835 Copley Rd (44321-1671)
PHONE.............................330 666-0505
Brian Schell, *Pr*
Gifford Shearer, *
Thomas G Tangney, *
Paul A Marcela, *
Joseph Rinaldi, *
▲ **EMP:** 85 **EST:** 1988
SQ FT: 160,000
SALES (est): 35.85MM
SALES (corp-wide): 12.39B **Publicly Held**
Web: multibase.lookchem.com
SIC: 2821 Plastics materials and resins
PA: Dupont De Nemours, Inc.
974 Centre Rd Bldg 730
Wilmington DE 19805
302 295-5783

(G-241)
MYE AUTOMOTIVE INC
1293 S Main St (44301-1302)
PHONE.............................330 253-5592
John C Orr, *Pr*
EMP: 7 **EST:** 1999
SALES (est): 1.02MM
SALES (corp-wide): 836.28MM **Publicly Held**
Web: www.myersindustries.com
SIC: 3089 Pallets, plastics
PA: Myers Industries, Inc.
1293 S Main St
Akron OH 44301
330 253-5592

(G-242)
MYERS INDUSTRIES INC
Akro-Mils Division
1293 S Main St (44301-1339)
P.O. Box 989 (44309-0989)
PHONE.............................330 253-5592
David Grider, *Genl Mgr*

EMP: 49
SALES (corp-wide): 836.28MM **Publicly Held**
Web: www.myersindustries.com
SIC: 3089 3443 Molding primary plastics; Fabricated plate work (boiler shop)
PA: Myers Industries, Inc.
1293 S Main St
Akron OH 44301
330 253-5592

(G-243)
MYERS INDUSTRIES INC (PA)
Also Called: MYERS INDUSTRIES
1293 S Main St (44301-1339)
PHONE.............................330 253-5592
Dave Basque, *Pr*
F Jack Liebau Junior, *Ch Bd*
Grant Fitz, *Ex VP*
Sue A Rilley Senior, *Corporate Counsel*
Lorelei Evans, *Senior Vice President Human Resources*
EMP: 50 **EST:** 1933
SQ FT: 129,000
SALES (est): 836.28MM
SALES (corp-wide): 836.28MM **Publicly Held**
Web: www.myersindustries.com
SIC: 3089 3086 3069 3052 Pallets, plastics; Plastics foam products; Rubber automotive products; Automobile hose, rubber

(G-244)
NETWORK POLYMERS INC
1353 Exeter Rd (44306-3853)
PHONE.............................330 773-2700
◆ **EMP:** 29
Web: www.networkpolymers.com
SIC: 2821 5162 Plastics materials and resins ; Plastics resins

(G-245)
NEW CASTINGS INC
Also Called: Quality Molded
2200 Massillon Rd (44312-4234)
PHONE.............................330 645-6653
Mike Cingel, *Pr*
EMP: 31 **EST:** 1994
SQ FT: 15,000
SALES (est): 963.68K
SALES (corp-wide): 17.76MM **Privately Held**
SIC: 3544 Industrial molds
PA: Saehwa Imc Na, Inc.
2200 Massillon Rd
Akron OH 44312
330 645-6653

(G-246)
NEWSOME & WORK METALIZING CO
258 Kenmore Blvd (44301-1000)
P.O. Box 27091 (44319-7091)
PHONE.............................330 376-7144
Michael Newsome, *Pr*
EMP: 7 **EST:** 1958
SQ FT: 10,000
SALES (est): 945.23K **Privately Held**
SIC: 3471 Sand blasting of metal parts

(G-247)
NORKAAM INDUSTRIES LLC
Also Called: Maple Valley Cleaners
1477 Copley Rd (44320-2656)
PHONE.............................330 873-9793
Eugene Norris, *Mgr*
EMP: 9 **EST:** 2016
SALES (est): 179.7K **Privately Held**
SIC: 3999 Manufacturing industries, nec

(G-248)
NORTH COAST THEATRICAL INC
2181 Killian Rd (44312-4887)
PHONE.............................330 762-1768
Richard Arconti, *Pr*
John Kramanak, *VP*
EMP: 9 **EST:** 1991
SALES (est): 995.32K **Privately Held**
Web: www.northcoasttheatrical.com
SIC: 3993 7922 Signs and advertising specialties; Theatrical production services

(G-249)
NORTH HILL MARBLE & GRANITE CO
448 N Howard St (44310-3185)
PHONE.............................330 253-2179
TOLL FREE: 800
Miles V Buzzi, *Pr*
Miles V Buzzi Ii, *VP*
Paul Buzzi, *Sec*
EMP: 10 **EST:** 1919
SQ FT: 4,000
SALES (est): 179.74K **Privately Held**
Web: www.northhillmarbleandgranite.com
SIC: 5999 1741 3993 3281 Monuments, finished to custom order; Masonry and other stonework; Signs, not made in custom sign painting shops; Cut stone and stone products

(G-250)
NORTHHILL T-SHIRT PRINT DSIGN
509 E Glenwood Ave (44310-3470)
PHONE.............................330 208-0338
EMP: 7 **EST:** 2021
SALES (est): 205.61K **Privately Held**
SIC: 3161 Clothing and apparel carrying cases

(G-251)
OHIO BEAUTY CUT STONE II INC
Also Called: Ohio Beauty Cut Stone
40 W Turkeyfoot Lake Rd (44319-4097)
PHONE.............................330 644-2241
Jason Berenyi, *Pr*
Frank J Berenyi Junior, *Pr*
Sirenna Berenyi, *VP*
EMP: 7 **EST:** 1947
SQ FT: 8,000
SALES (est): 877.55K **Privately Held**
Web: www.ohiobeautycutstone.net
SIC: 5032 3281 1411 Granite building stone; Cut stone and stone products; Dimension stone

(G-252)
OHIO GASKET AND SHIM CO INC (PA)
Also Called: Ogs Industries
976 Evans Ave (44305-1019)
PHONE.............................330 630-0626
John S Bader, *Pr*
Thomas Bader, *
◆ **EMP:** 45 **EST:** 1959
SQ FT: 84,000
SALES (est): 21.3MM
SALES (corp-wide): 21.3MM **Privately Held**
Web: www.ogsindustries.com
SIC: 3469 3053 3599 3499 Stamping metal for the trade; Gaskets, all materials; Machine shop, jobbing and repair; Shims, metal

(G-253)
OHIO HCKRY HRVEST BRND PDTS IN
Also Called: Hickory Harvest Foods

90 Logan Pkwy (44319-1177)
PHONE.............................330 644-6266
Joe Swiatkowski, *Pr*
Michael Swiatkowski, *
EMP: 32 **EST:** 1972
SQ FT: 32,000
SALES (est): 15.78MM **Privately Held**
Web: www.hickoryharvest.com
SIC: 5145 5149 2099 Nuts, salted or roasted ; Fruits, dried; Food preparations, nec

(G-254)
OHIO PURE FOODS INC (HQ)
681 W Waterloo Rd (44314-1547)
PHONE.............................330 753-2293
Kenny Sadai, *Ch Bd*
Thomas Kolb, *
▲ **EMP:** 89 **EST:** 1949
SQ FT: 100,000
SALES (est): 9.37MM **Privately Held**
Web: www.countrypure.com
SIC: 2033 2086 Fruit juices: fresh; Fruit drinks (less than 100% juice): packaged in cans, etc.
PA: Country Pure Foods, Inc.
222 S Main St Ste 401
Akron OH 44308

(G-255)
PALMER PRODUCTS INC
Also Called: Palmer Products
920 Moe Dr (44310-2519)
PHONE.............................330 630-9397
Leonard Palmer, *Pr*
Leonard Palmer Junior, *Pr*
Len Senior, *Pr*
EMP: 7 **EST:** 1973
SQ FT: 8,000
SALES (est): 1.09MM **Privately Held**
Web: www.palmerbearings.com
SIC: 3599 Machine shop, jobbing and repair

(G-256)
PARKER FABRICATING CO
20 E North St (44304-1203)
PHONE.............................330 379-0112
Scott Parker, *Pr*
Don Johnson, *
EMP: 30 **EST:** 1993
SQ FT: 52,000
SALES (est): 376.6K **Privately Held**
SIC: 3441 1791 Fabricated structural metal; Structural steel erection

(G-257)
PERFECT PRCISION MACHINING LTD
920 Clay St (44311-2214)
PHONE.............................330 475-0324
Margaret Habib, *Prin*
EMP: 9 **EST:** 2004
SALES (est): 3.19MM **Privately Held**
Web: www.ppm-ohio.com
SIC: 3599 Machine shop, jobbing and repair

(G-258)
PIN OAK ENERGY PARTNERS LLC (PA)
388 S Main St Ste 401b (44311-4407)
PHONE.............................888 748-0763
Christopher Halvorson, *CEO*
Mark Van Tyne, *Chief Business Development Officer*
Christine Shepard-dessai, *VP*
Heidi Ewing, *Accounting*
EMP: 11 **EST:** 2015
SALES (est): 8.46MM
SALES (corp-wide): 8.46MM **Privately Held**
Web: www.pinoakep.com
SIC: 1311 Crude petroleum and natural gas production

▲ = Import ▼ = Export
◆ = Import/Export

(G-259)
PIONEER PLASTICS CORPORATION
3330 Massillon Rd (44312-5397)
PHONE..............................330 896-2356
Ralph J Danesi Junior, *Pr*
Jakob Denzinger, *
EMP: 125 EST: 1975
SQ FT: 45,000
SALES (est): 13.24MM **Privately Held**
Web: www.pioneerplasticscorp.com
SIC: 3089 Injection molding of plastics

(G-260)
PLATE-ALL METAL COMPANY INC
1210 Devalera St (44310-2483)
PHONE..............................330 633-6166
John L Burg, *Pr*
Irene Burg, *Contrlr*
Charles Killinger, *Manager*
EMP: 8 EST: 1945
SQ FT: 6,660
SALES (est): 1.08MM **Privately Held**
Web: www.plateallmetal.com
SIC: 3471 8711 Chromium plating of metals
or formed products; Engineering services

(G-261)
PMBP LEGACY CO INC
219 E Miller Ave (44301-1326)
P.O. Box 3858 (44314-0858)
PHONE..............................330 253-8148
Paul Michalec, *Dir*
EMP: 15
SALES (corp-wide): 9.53MM **Privately
Held**
Web: www.ruscoe.com
SIC: 2865 Color pigments, organic
PA: Pmbp Legacy Co., Inc.
485 Kenmore Blvd
Akron OH 44301
330 253-8148

(G-262)
PMBP LEGACY CO INC (PA)
Also Called: Ruscoe
485 Kenmore Blvd (44301-1013)
P.O. Box 3858 (44314-0858)
PHONE..............................330 253-8148
Angel Esplin, *CEO*
Betty Pfaff, *
EMP: 49 EST: 1949
SQ FT: 24,000
SALES (est): 9.53MM
SALES (corp wide): 9.53MM **Privately
Held**
Web: www.ruscoe.com
SIC: 2891 3297 2851 Adhesives and
sealants; Nonclay refractories; Paints and
allied products

(G-263)
POLYMET RECOVERY LLC
1280 Devalera St (44310-2418)
PHONE..............................330 630-9006
Frank Moore, *Pr*
EMP: 6 EST: 2015
SALES (est): 2.75MM **Privately Held**
Web: www.polymetrecovery.com
SIC: 3471 Plating and polishing

(G-264)
PORTAGE MACHINE CONCEPTS INC
Also Called: Portage Knife Company
75 Skelton Rd (44312-1821)
P.O. Box 248 (44260-0248)
PHONE..............................330 628-2343
Jeannine Lizak, *Pr*
Christopher Michalec, *Treas*
W Duane Huff, *Sec*
▲ EMP: 16 EST: 1981
SQ FT: 6,500

SALES (est): 2.8MM **Privately Held**
Web: www.portageknife.com
SIC: 3541 Machine tools, metal cutting type

(G-265)
PREMIER SEALS MFG LLC
Also Called: Premier Seals Mfg
909 W Waterloo Rd (44314-1529)
PHONE..............................330 861-1060
▼ EMP: 8 EST: 2005
SALES (est): 537.6K **Privately Held**
Web: www.premiersealsmfg.com
SIC: 3999 Barber and beauty shop
equipment

(G-266)
PRESSLERS MEATS INC
2553 Pressler Rd (44312-5500)
PHONE..............................330 644-5636
Roger H Pressler, *Pr*
Richard Pressler, *VP*
EMP: 15 EST: 1944
SQ FT: 1,800
SALES (est): 1.75MM **Privately Held**
SIC: 2011 Meat packing plants

(G-267)
PRO-FAB INC
2570 Pressler Rd (44312-5554)
PHONE..............................330 644-0044
Anna Myers, *CEO*
Monroe W Townsend, *VP*
EMP: 9 EST: 1978
SQ FT: 15,000
SALES (est): 3.35MM **Privately Held**
Web: www.profabincorporated.net
SIC: 3441 1791 Fabricated structural metal;
Structural steel erection

(G-268)
PRO-GRAM ENGINEERING CORP
1680 Hampton Rd (44305-3575)
PHONE..............................330 745-1004
Kenneth Anderson, *Pr*
Dadan Anderson, *VP*
EMP: 9 EST: 1984
SALES (est): 192.13K **Privately Held**
Web: www.billetspeedworks.com
SIC: 3599 Machine shop, jobbing and repair

(G-269)
PROGRESSIVE MFG CO INC
Also Called: Progrssive Mtllizing Machining
300 Massillon Rd (44312-1914)
PHONE..............................330 784-4717
Doris Datsko, *Pr*
David Datsko, *VP*
George Datsko Junior, *Sec*
EMP: 8 EST: 1972
SQ FT: 18,000
SALES (est): 1.74MM **Privately Held**
Web: www.prorebuild.com
SIC: 3599 3479 5084 Machine shop, jobbing
and repair; Painting, coating, and hot
dipping; Industrial machinery and equipment

(G-270)
PUR HAIR EXTENSIONS LLC
1088 E Tallmadge Ave (44310-3516)
PHONE..............................330 786-5772
EMP: 6 EST: 2018
SALES (est): 86.29K **Privately Held**
Web: www.purhairextensions.com
SIC: 7231 3999 Cosmetology and personal
hygiene salons; Hair and hair-based
products

(G-271)
Q MODEL INC
3414 E Waterloo Rd (44312-4011)

P.O. Box 25 (44260-0025)
PHONE..............................330 733-6545
Todd Strohfus, *Pr*
Laverne Strohfus, *CFO*
EMP: 15 EST: 1989
SQ FT: 35,000
SALES (est): 4.64MM **Privately Held**
Web: www.qmodelinc.net
SIC: 3469 3069 Patterns on metal; Molded
rubber products

(G-272)
QT EQUIPMENT COMPANY (PA)
151 W Dartmore Ave (44301-2462)
PHONE..............................330 724-3055
Daniel Root, *Pr*
Dave Root, *
▼ EMP: 35 EST: 1992
SQ FT: 20,000
SALES (est): 4.18MM **Privately Held**
Web: www.qtequipment.com
SIC: 7532 5531 3713 Body shop, trucks;
Automotive tires; Utility truck bodies

(G-273)
QUANEX IG SYSTEMS INC (HQ)
Also Called: Quanex Building Products
388 S Main St Ste 700 (44311-1060)
PHONE..............................216 910-1500
Michael Hovan, *Pr*
Jim Hummel, *
Kevin Gray, *
David Gingrich, *
◆ EMP: 102 EST: 1994
SQ FT: 400,000
SALES (est): 103.54MM **Publicly Held**
Web: www.quanex.com
SIC: 3061 3053 Mechanical rubber goods;
Gaskets; packing and sealing devices
PA: Quanex Building Products Corporation
945 Bunker HI Rd Ste 900
Houston TX 77024

(G-274)
QUARRYMASTERS INC
1644 Berna Rd (44312-5434)
PHONE..............................330 612-0474
Joseph A Della, *Pr*
Jacalyn Tutthill, *VP*
▲ EMP: 9 EST: 2006
SALES (est): 93.55K **Privately Held**
SIC: 3281 8742 Granite, cut and shaped;
General management consultant

(G-275)
**QUIKEY MANUFACTURING CO INC
(PA)**
1500 Industrial Pkwy (44310-2600)
PHONE..............................330 633-8106
Michael W Burns, *Pr*
Thomas Stiller, *
Patrick P Burns, *
William B Stiller, *
Mary Lou Burns, *Stockholder*
▲ EMP: 125 EST: 1959
SQ FT: 50,000
SALES (est): 8.45MM
SALES (corp-wide): 8.45MM **Privately
Held**
Web: www.quikey.com
SIC: 3993 Advertising novelties

(G-276)
R C MUSSON RUBBER CO
1320 E Archwood Ave (44306-2825)
P.O. Box 7038 (44306-0038)
PHONE..............................330 773-7651
Bennie D Segers, *Ch Bd*
Frank W Rockhold, *VP*
Robert S Segers, *VP*
William J Segers, *VP*

Billie H Dreyer, *Sec*
EMP: 20 EST: 1945
SQ FT: 40,000
SALES (est): 4.05MM **Privately Held**
Web: www.mussonrubber.com
SIC: 3069 5085 Mats or matting, rubber, nec
; Rubber goods, mechanical

(G-277)
RAINBOW MASTER MIXING INC
467 Dan St (44310-3900)
PHONE..............................330 374-1810
Tim Lowe, *Managing Member*
EMP: 24 EST: 2007
SALES (est): 2.57MM **Privately Held**
Web: www.rainbowmastermixing.com
SIC: 3069 Medical and laboratory rubber
sundries and related products

(G-278)
RAUH POLYMERS INC
420 Kenmore Blvd (44301-1038)
PHONE..............................330 376-1120
Joseph M Rauh, *Pr*
James T Rauh, *VP*
▼ EMP: 15 EST: 2004
SALES (est): 17.23MM **Privately Held**
Web: www.rauhpolymers.com
SIC: 2821 Plastics materials and resins

(G-279)
RCM ENGINEERING COMPANY
2089 N Cleveland Massillon Rd
(44333-1258)
P.O. Box 517 (44210-0517)
PHONE..............................330 666-0575
Robert C Mc Dowell, *Owner*
EMP: 9 EST: 1903
SQ FT: 2,200
SALES (est): 408.22K **Privately Held**
SIC: 1311 1321 Natural gas production;
Natural gasoline production

(G-280)
REGENCY SEATING INC
Also Called: Regency Office Furniture
2375 Romig Rd (44320-3824)
PHONE..............................330 848-3700
John Summerville, *Pr*
Aaron Summerville, *
◆ EMP: 35 EST: 1941
SQ FT: 100,000
SALES (est): 6.42MM **Privately Held**
Web: www.regencyof.com
SIC: 2426 Furniture stock and parts,
hardwood

(G-281)
REPORTER NEWSPAPER INC
1088 S Main St (44301-1206)
P.O. Box 2042 (44309-2042)
PHONE..............................330 535-7061
William Ellis Junior, *Pr*
EMP: 10 EST: 1951
SALES (est): 149.73K **Privately Held**
Web:
www.thereporternewspaperonline.com
SIC: 2711 Newspapers: publishing only, not
printed on site

(G-282)
REVLIS CORPORATION (PA)
255 Fountain St (44304-1920)
PHONE..............................330 535-2100
▲ EMP: 38 EST: 1971
SALES (est): 14.39MM
SALES (corp-wide): 14.39MM **Privately
Held**
Web: www.akrochem.com
SIC: 2865 2869 Dyes and pigments;
Industrial organic chemicals, nec

(G-283)
REVVITY HEALTH SCIENCES INC
520 S Main St Ste 2423 (44311-1086)
PHONE..................................330 825-4525
Chritine Gradisher, *Mgr*
EMP: 63
SALES (corp-wide): 2.76B **Publicly Held**
Web: www.perkinelmer.com
SIC: **2835** 2836 5049 Diagnostic substances
; Biological products, except diagnostic;
Laboratory equipment, except medical or
dental
HQ: Revvity Health Sciences, Inc.
940 Winter St
Waltham MA 02451
781 663-6900

(G-284)
RICHARDS WHL FENCE CO INC
Also Called: Richard's Fence Company
1600 Firestone Pkwy (44301-1659)
PHONE..................................330 773-0423
Richard Peterson, *Pr*
Bill Peterson, *
▲ EMP: 30 EST: 1968
SQ FT: 235,000
SALES (est): 12.28MM **Privately Held**
Web: www.richardsfence.com
SIC: **3315** 5039 Chain link fencing; Wire
fence, gates, and accessories

(G-285)
RICKS GRAPHIC ACCENTS INC
3554 S Arlington Rd Unit B (44312-5223)
PHONE..................................330 896-4700
Rick Lange, *Pr*
Rick Lang, *Pr*
EMP: 6 EST: 1992
SALES (est): 372.49K **Privately Held**
Web: www.graphicaccents.net
SIC: **3993** Signs and advertising specialties

(G-286)
**RIVER VALLEY PAPER COMPANY
LLC**
Also Called: River Valley Paper
131 N Summit St (44304-1277)
P.O. Box 1191 (44309-1191)
PHONE..................................330 535-1001
Rick Torbeck, *Managing Member*
EMP: 11 EST: 2016
SALES (est): 772.07K **Privately Held**
Web: www.intfiber.com
SIC: **2611** Pulp manufactured from waste or
recycled paper

(G-287)
RJS CORPORATION
Also Called: Rjs
3400 Massillon Rd (44312-5392)
PHONE..................................330 896-2387
◆ EMP: 45 EST: 1948
SALES (est): 9.37MM **Privately Held**
Web: www.rjscorp.com
SIC: **3559** 3546 3496 Rubber working
machinery, including tires; Power-driven
handtools; Miscellaneous fabricated wire
products

(G-288)
ROCHLING AUTOMOTIVE USA LLP
2275 Picton Pkwy (44312-4270)
PHONE..................................330 400-5785
Robert Roach, *Manager*
EMP: 75
SALES (corp-wide): 2.96B **Privately Held**
Web: www.roechling.com
SIC: **3714** Motor vehicle engines and parts
HQ: Rochling Automotive Usa Llp
245 Parkway E 29334
Duncan SC 29334
864 486-0888

(G-289)
ROETMANS WELDING LLC
155 Beaver St (44304-1907)
PHONE..................................216 385-5938
Robert Roetman, *Pr*
EMP: 9 EST: 2013
SALES (est): 606.45K **Privately Held**
Web: www.roetmansweldingllc.com
SIC: **7692** Welding repair

(G-290)
**ROGERS INDUSTRIAL PRODUCTS
INC**
532 S Main St (44311-1018)
PHONE..................................330 535-3331
John Cole, *Pr*
◆ EMP: 35 EST: 1951
SQ FT: 239,000
SALES (est): 4.13MM **Privately Held**
Web: www.rogersusa.com
SIC: **3542** 3625 3491 3643 Presses:
hydraulic and pneumatic, mechanical and
manual; Industrial electrical relays and
switches; Pressure valves and regulators,
industrial; Current-carrying wiring services

(G-291)
ROTOCAST TECHNOLOGIES INC
1900 Englewood Ave (44312-1004)
PHONE..................................330 798-9091
Edward W Kissel, *Pr*
EMP: 30 EST: 1996
SQ FT: 25,000
SALES (est): 3.86MM **Privately Held**
Web: www.rotocastmold.com
SIC: **3365** 3544 Aluminum and aluminum-
based alloy castings; Special dies, tools,
jigs, and fixtures

(G-292)
ROYALTON MANUFACTURING INC
1169 Brittain Rd (44305-1004)
P.O. Box 33190 (44133-0190)
PHONE..................................440 237-2233
Kenneth Wesner, *Pr*
William Calfee, *VP*
Judith Wesner, *Treas*
EMP: 8 EST: 1978
SQ FT: 12,000
SALES (est): 749.43K **Privately Held**
SIC: **3599** Machine shop, jobbing and repair

(G-293)
RUBBER CITY MACHINERY CORP
Also Called: R C M
One Thousand Sweitzer Avenue (44311)
P.O. Box 2043 (44309-2043)
PHONE..................................330 434-3500
George B Sobieraj, *Pr*
Robert J Westfall, *
Bernie Sobieraj, *
Robert F Longano, *Prin*
▲ EMP: 32 EST: 1980
SQ FT: 100,000
SALES (est): 4.86MM **Privately Held**
Web: www.rcmc.com
SIC: **3559** 5084 7629 Rubber working
machinery, including tires; Industrial
machinery and equipment; Electrical repair
shops

(G-294)
RUBBER WORLD MAGAZINE INC
1741 Akron Peninsula Rd (44313-5157)
PHONE..................................330 864-2122
Job Lippincott, *Pr*
EMP: 8 EST: 1984
SALES (est): 177.37K **Privately Held**
Web: www.rubberworld.com
SIC: **2721** Periodicals

(G-295)
RUSCOE COMPANY
485 Kenmore Blvd (44301-1013)
PHONE..................................330 253-8148
Angel Esplin, *CFO*
EMP: 33 EST: 2020
SALES (est): 2.87MM **Privately Held**
SIC: **2891** Adhesives and sealants

(G-296)
RUSSELL PRODUCTS CO INC
De Valera Division
275 N Forge St Ste 1 (44304-1440)
PHONE..................................330 535-9246
Robert Evans, *Prin*
EMP: 10
SQ FT: 14,000
SALES (corp-wide): 4.28MM **Privately
Held**
Web: www.russprodco.com
SIC: **3479** 3471 Painting of metal products;
Anodizing (plating) of metals or formed
products
PA: Russell Products Co., Inc.
275 N Forge St
Akron OH 44304
330 535-9246

(G-297)
RUSSELL PRODUCTS CO INC
Also Called: Akron Anodizing & Coating Div
1066 Home Ave (44310-3502)
PHONE..................................330 535-3391
Daniel Dzurovcin, *VP*
EMP: 9
SALES (corp-wide): 4.28MM **Privately
Held**
Web: www.russprodco.com
SIC: **3471** Finishing, metals or formed
products
PA: Russell Products Co., Inc.
275 N Forge St
Akron OH 44304
330 535-9246

(G-298)
RUSSELL PRODUCTS CO INC (PA)
Also Called: Falholt Division
275 N Forge St (44304-1440)
PHONE..................................330 535-9246
◆ EMP: 10 EST: 1959
SALES (est): 4.28MM
SALES (corp-wide): 4.28MM **Privately
Held**
Web: www.russprodco.com
SIC: **3479** 3471 Painting of metal products;
Anodizing (plating) of metals or formed
products

(G-299)
**RUSSELL STANDARD
CORPORATION**
Also Called: Jasa Asphalt Russell Standard
990 Hazel St (44305-1610)
PHONE..................................330 733-9400
Robert Gunther, *Mgr*
EMP: 6
SALES (corp-wide): 97.54MM **Privately
Held**
Web: www.russellstandard.com
SIC: **5032** 2951 Asphalt mixture; Concrete,
bituminous
PA: Russell Standard Corporation
285 Kappa Dr Ste 300
Pittsburgh PA 15238
412 449-0700

(G-300)
S & A INDUSTRIES CORPORATION
1500 Exeter Rd (44306)
PHONE..................................330 733-6040

EMP: 22
Web: www.s-aindustries.com
SIC: **3086** Plastics foam products
HQ: S & A Industries Corporation
1471 Exeter Rd
Akron OH 44306

(G-301)
**S & A INDUSTRIES CORPORATION
(DH)**
1471 Exeter Rd (44306-3856)
PHONE..................................330 733-6040
Greg Anderson, *Pr*
▲ EMP: 66 EST: 2010
SQ FT: 42,000
SALES (est): 33.02MM **Privately Held**
Web: www.s-aindustries.com
SIC: **3086** Plastics foam products
HQ: Sekiso Corporation
1-3, Hinakitamachi
Okazaki AIC 444-0

(G-302)
S I T STRINGS CO INC
2493 Romig Rd (44320-4109)
PHONE..................................330 434-8010
Virgil Lay, *Pr*
Robert C Hird, *VP*
Edwin Speedy, *Ex VP*
EMP: 20 EST: 1980
SQ FT: 16,000
SALES (est): 2.45MM **Privately Held**
Web: www.sitstrings.com
SIC: **3931** 5736 Guitars and parts, electric
and nonelectric; Musical instrument stores

(G-303)
SACO LOWELL PARTS LLC
1395 Triplett Blvd (44306-3124)
PHONE..................................330 794-1535
Bruce Weick, *VP*
John Daenes, *Pr*
Russell Dunlap, *VP*
EMP: 7 EST: 2001
SALES (est): 518.39K **Privately Held**
Web: www.wwwilliams.com
SIC: **3469** Machine parts, stamped or
pressed metal

(G-304)
SAEHWA IMC NA INC (PA)
Also Called: Versitech Mold Div
2200 Massillon Rd (44312-4234)
PHONE..................................330 645-6653
Mike Cingel, *Pr*
Stanley B Migdal, *
Mike Politis, *
Jerry Candiliotis, *
Jim Finfield, *
▲ EMP: 100 EST: 1978
SQ FT: 83,821
SALES (est): 17.76MM
SALES (corp-wide): 17.76MM **Privately
Held**
SIC: **3544** Industrial molds

(G-305)
SAINT-GOBAIN PRFMCE PLAS CORP
2664 Gilchrist Rd (44305-4412)
PHONE..................................330 798-6981
Chris Mattern, *Manager*
EMP: 200
SQ FT: 100,000
SALES (corp-wide): 402.18MM **Privately
Held**
Web: plastics.saint-gobain.com
SIC: **3061** 3083 Medical and surgical rubber
tubing (extruded and lathe-cut); Laminated
plastics plate and sheet

▲ = Import ▼ = Export
◆ = Import/Export

HQ: Saint-Gobain Performance Plastics
Corporation
20 Moores Rd
Malvern PA 19355
440 836-6900

(G-306)
SCANDINAVIAN TOB GROUP LN LTD
Also Called: Stg Lane
1424 Diagonal Rd (44320-4016)
PHONE.....................770 934-4594
J Kelly Michols, *CEO*
W David Parrish, *Finance Treasurer*
Phil Gee, *Managing Director US Operations*
Daniel Mcgee, *Sec*
Elliot Fledz, *Asst Tr*
◆ **EMP:** 130 **EST:** 1975
SALES (est): 1.72MM **Privately Held**
Web: www.st-group.com
SIC: 2131 5194 Smoking tobacco; Tobacco
and tobacco products

(G-307)
**SCHOTT METAL PRODUCTS
COMPANY**
Also Called: Design Wheel and Hub
2225 Lee Dr (44306-4399)
PHONE.....................330 773-7873
Samuel Schott, *Pr*
F W Schott, *
Paul Graham, *
EMP: 6 **EST:** 1945
SQ FT: 90,000
SALES (est): 959.63K **Privately Held**
Web: www.schott.com
SIC: 3469 3714 Stamping metal for the trade
; Motor vehicle parts and accessories

(G-308)
SHIN-ETSU SILICONES AMER INC
963 Evans Ave (44305-1041)
PHONE.....................330 630-9860
EMP: 13 **EST:** 2010
SALES (est): 2.01MM **Privately Held**
Web: www.shinetsusilicones.com
SIC: 2869 Industrial organic chemicals, nec

(G-309)
**SHIN-ETSU SILICONES OF AMERICA
INC (HQ)**
1150 Damar Dr (44305-1066)
PHONE.....................330 630-9460
◆ **FMP:** 150 **EST:** 1985
SALES (est): 112.54MM **Privately Held**
Web: www.shinetsusilicones.com
SIC: 5169 2822 2869 Silicon lubricants;
Silicone rubbers; Industrial organic
chemicals, nec
PA: Shin-Etsu Chemical Co., Ltd.
1-4-1, Marunouchi
Chiyoda-Ku TKY 100-0

(G-310)
SHINCOR SILICONES INC
1030 Evans Ave (44305-1021)
PHONE.....................330 630-9460
▲ **EMP:** 50
Web: www.shinetsusilicones.com
SIC: 2822 2891 2869 Silicone rubbers;
Adhesives and sealants; Industrial organic
chemicals, nec

(G-311)
**SHOOK MANUFACTURED PDTS INC
(PA)**
1017 Kenmore Blvd (44314-2153)
P.O. Box 15058 (44314-5058)
PHONE.....................330 848-9780
Roy Knittle, *Pr*
Thomas Johns, *VP*

▲ **EMP:** 9 **EST:** 1968
SQ FT: 10,000
SALES: 976.14K
SALES (corp-wide): 976.14K **Privately
Held**
Web: www.shookmfg.com
SIC: 3545 5072 Chucks: drill, lathe, or
magnetic (machine tool accessories);
Hardware

(G-312)
SIGNET ENTERPRISES LLC (PA)
19 N High St (44308-1912)
PHONE.....................330 762-9102
Anthony S Manna, *Managing Member*
EMP: 24 **EST:** 2011
SQ FT: 26,000
SALES (est): 4.75MM
SALES (corp-wide): 4.75MM **Privately
Held**
Web: www.signetllc.com
SIC: 2899 Chemical preparations, nec

(G-313)
SLS MACHINING GROUP LLC
2642 Gilchrist Rd (44305-4412)
PHONE.....................330 428-2094
Sam Mitchell, *CEO*
Samuel Mitchel Junior, *VP*
Luke Mitchel, *VP*
EMP: 15 **EST:** 2013
SALES (est): 5.37MM **Privately Held**
SIC: 3599 Machine and other job shop work

(G-314)
SOUTH AKRON AWNING CO (PA)
763 Kenmore Blvd (44314-2196)
PHONE.....................330 848-7611
Ranell Minear, *Pr*
Kathleen Mueller, *Sec*
Michelle Halafa, *VP*
EMP: 14 **EST:** 1913
SQ FT: 19,000
SALES (est): 2.22MM
SALES (corp-wide): 2.22MM **Privately
Held**
Web: www.southakronawning.com
SIC: 2394 1799 7359 Awnings, fabric: made
from purchased materials; Awning
installation; Tent and tarpaulin rental

(G-315)
**STANDARD JIG BORING SVC LLC
(HQ)**
Also Called: Sjbs
3360 Miller Park Rd (44312-5388)
PHONE.....................330 896-9530
Ginger Townsend, *Managing Member*
Jeffrey R Wahl, *
▲ **EMP:** 20 **EST:** 2007
SQ FT: 30,000
SALES (corp-wide): 3.3MM
SALES (corp-wide): 170.79MM **Privately
Held**
SIC: 3599 Machine shop, jobbing and repair
PA: Ariel Corporation
35 Blackjack Rd
Mount Vernon OH 43050
740 397-0311

(G-316)
STANDARD JIG BORING SVC LLC
3194 Massillon Rd (44312-5363)
PHONE.....................330 644-5405
George Koberlein, *Brnch Mgr*
EMP: 79
SALES (corp-wide): 170.79MM **Privately
Held**
SIC: 3599 Machine shop, jobbing and repair
HQ: Standard Jig Boring Service, Llc
3360 Miller Park Rd

Akron OH 44312
330 896-9530

(G-317)
STAR PRINTING COMPANY INC
125 N Union St (44304-1390)
PHONE.....................330 376-0514
Vicki Lauck, *Pr*
Robert D Lauck Junior, *VP*
Paul M Lauck, *VP*
Lynda Moore, *Sec*
EMP: 22 **EST:** 1932
SQ FT: 20,000
SALES (est): 2.54MM **Privately Held**
Web: www.starptg.com
SIC: 2752 2759 2789 Offset printing;
Letterpress printing; Bookbinding and
related work

(G-318)
STERLING ASSOCIATES INC
Also Called: Fastsigns
1783 Brittain Rd (44310-1801)
PHONE.....................330 630-3500
Milton L Liming, *Pr*
Brent B Liming, *VP*
Elaine Liming, *Sec*
EMP: 8 **EST:** 1962
SQ FT: 2,000
SALES (est): 430.11K **Privately Held**
Web: www.fastsigns.com
SIC: 3993 2721 Signs, not made in custom
sign painting shops; Periodicals

(G-319)
SUMMIT COUNTY
Also Called: FA Sibrling Ntrelm Mtro Pk Smm
1828 Smith Rd (44313-5012)
PHONE.....................330 865-8065
Keith Shy, *Dir*
EMP: 9
SALES (corp-wide): 612.48MM **Privately
Held**
Web: www.summitcasagal.org
SIC: 2531 9111 Picnic tables or benches,
park; County supervisors' and executives'
office
PA: Summit County
650 Dan St
Akron OH 44310
330 643-2500

(G-320)
SUMMIT DESIGN AND TECH INC
Also Called: West Reserve Controls
1147 Sweitzer Ave (44301-1337)
PHONE.....................330 733-6662
Jay Mendpara, *CEO*
EMP: 18 **EST:** 2022
SALES (est): 2.94MM **Privately Held**
Web: www.anzer-usa.com
SIC: 3559 Electronic component making
machinery

(G-321)
SUMMIT MACHINE SOLUTIONS LLC
Also Called: Cecil Peck Co
1029 Arlington Cir (44306-3959)
PHONE.....................330 785-0781
Jay Hofner, *Managing Member*
EMP: 9 **EST:** 2010
SALES (est): 1.97MM **Privately Held**
Web: www.summitmachinesolutions.com
SIC: 3548 Welding apparatus

(G-322)
SUMMIT TOOL COMPANY (HQ)
Also Called: Ken-Tools
768 E North St (44305-1164)
P.O. Box 9320 (44305-0320)
PHONE.....................330 535-7177

Larry Sorles, *Dir*
Douglas Romstadt, *
▲ **EMP:** 65 **EST:** 1932
SQ FT: 70,000
SALES (est): 10.25MM **Privately Held**
Web: www.kentool.com
SIC: 3544 Special dies and tools
PA: North Coast Holdings Incorporated
768 E North St
Akron OH 44305

(G-323)
SYNTHOMER INC
1380 Tech Way (44306-2572)
PHONE.....................330 734-1237
EMP: 10
SALES (corp-wide): 2.52B **Privately Held**
Web: www.omnova.com
SIC: 2819 Industrial inorganic chemicals, nec
HQ: Synthomer Inc.
25435 Harvard Rd
Beachwood OH 44122
216 682-7000

(G-324)
SYSTEMS KIT LLC MB
Also Called: Industrial Profile Systems
925 Glaser Pkwy (44306-4161)
PHONE.....................330 945-4500
Rick Sabo, *VP*
EMP: 25 **EST:** 2019
SALES (est): 9.34MM
SALES (corp-wide): 77.71K **Privately Held**
Web: www.industrialprofile.com
SIC: 3354 8711 Shapes, extruded aluminum,
nec; Mechanical engineering
HQ: Weiss North America, Inc.
3860 Ben Hur Ave 2
Willoughby OH 44094
440 269-8031

(G-325)
T & CS REPAIRS & RETAIL LLC
1153 Marcy St (44301-1305)
PHONE.....................704 964-7325
EMP: 20 **EST:** 2020
SALES (est): 127.06K **Privately Held**
SIC: 3161 Clothing and apparel carrying
cases

(G-326)
T L SQUIRE AND COMPANY INC
4040 Embassy Pkwy Ste 300 (44333-8341)
PHONE.....................330 668-2604
Joseph Wozny, *Pr*
David Schierenbeck, *VP*
Ed Brodbeck, *VP*
EMP: 6 **EST:** 1982
SQ FT: 1,800
SALES (est): 43.9MM **Privately Held**
Web: www.tlsquire.com
SIC: 2822 Synthetic rubber

(G-327)
T W CORPORATION
99 S Seiberling St (44305-4216)
PHONE.....................440 461-3234
Thomas T Whims, *Pr*
Thomas T Whims, *Pr*
Thomas M Seger, *Sec*
EMP: 8 **EST:** 1994
SQ FT: 28,000
SALES (est): 482.78K **Privately Held**
Web: www.twdesignbuild.com
SIC: 3365 Aerospace castings, aluminum

(G-328)
TALLMADGE SPINNING & METAL CO
2783 Gilchrist Rd Unit A (44305-4406)
P.O. Box 58 (44278-0058)
PHONE.....................330 794-2277

John Sasanecki, *Pr*
Jacob Sasanecki, *VP*
Linda Sasanecki, *Treas*
EMP: 15 **EST:** 1947
SQ FT: 15,000
SALES (est): 2.47MM **Privately Held**
Web: www.tsm1947.com
SIC: 3444 Sheet metalwork

(G-329)
TB BACKSTOP INC
4478 Regal Dr (44321-1174)
PHONE..........................330 434-4442
Thomas Brennan, *Pr*
EMP: 14 **EST:** 1985
SALES (est): 930.4K **Privately Held**
Web: www.valleyrubber.com
SIC: 3069 Reclaimed rubber and specialty
rubber compounds

(G-330)
TEMPLE ISRAEL
Also Called: Jewish Synagogue
91 Springside Dr (44333-2428)
PHONE..........................330 762-8617
Pastor David Lipper, *Prin*
Milton I Wiskind, *Pr*
Doctor Davis Meckler, *VP*
Henry Nagel, *VP*
Fabian Velia, *Sec*
EMP: 9 **EST:** 1866
SALES (est): 210.4K **Privately Held**
Web: www.templeisraelakron.org
SIC: 8661 3625 Synagogue; Switches,
electric power

(G-331)
THE LUBRIZOL CORPORATION
1779 Marvo Dr (44306-4331)
PHONE..........................216 447-6212
EMP: 6
SALES (corp-wide): 424.23B **Publicly
Held**
Web: www.lubrizol.com
SIC: 2899 Chemical preparations, nec
HQ: The Lubrizol Corporation
29400 Lakeland Blvd
Wickliffe OH 44092
440 943-4200

(G-332)
THE PIONEER TOOL AND DIE CO
1363 Triplett Blvd (44306-3165)
PHONE..........................330 724-5572
EMP: 80 **EST:** 1944
SALES (est): 9.75MM **Privately Held**
Web: www.pioneertoolanddie.com
SIC: 3469 3544 Stamping metal for the trade
; Special dies and tools

(G-333)
THE R C A RUBBER COMPANY
1833 E Market St (44305-4214)
P.O. Box 9240 (44305-0240)
PHONE..........................330 784-1291
◆ **EMP:** 80
Web: www.rcarubber.com
SIC: 3069 Molded rubber products

(G-334)
THEKEN COMPANIES LLC
1800 Triplett Blvd (44306-3311)
PHONE..........................330 733-7600
EMP: 14 **EST:** 2013
SQ FT: 30,000
SALES (est): 1.71MM **Privately Held**
Web: www.nextsteparthropedix.com
SIC: 3841 Surgical and medical instruments

(G-335)
THEKEN PORT PARK LLC
1800 Triplett Blvd (44306-3311)
PHONE..........................330 733-7600
EMP: 57 **EST:** 2015
SALES (est): 2.72MM **Privately Held**
Web: www.nextsteparthropedix.com
SIC: 3313 Alloys, additive, except copper:
not made in blast furnaces

(G-336)
THERMO-RITE MFG COMPANY
Also Called: Star Fire Distributing
1355 Evans Ave (44305-1038)
PHONE..........................330 633-8680
Roy Allen, *CEO*
EMP: 20 **EST:** 1946
SQ FT: 120,000
SALES (est): 4.55MM **Privately Held**
Web: www.thermo-rite.com
SIC: 3429 Fireplace equipment, hardware:
andirons, grates, screens

(G-337)
THYME INC
3245 Pickle Rd (44312-5333)
PHONE..........................484 872-8430
Robert N Sampson, *Pr*
EMP: 10 **EST:** 1987
SALES (est): 357.37K **Privately Held**
SIC: 7371 7373 5734 3578 Computer
software development; Computer
integrated systems design; Software,
computer games; Calculating and
accounting equipment

(G-338)
TINYCIRCUITS
540 S Main St (44311-1079)
PHONE..........................330 329-5753
EMP: 8 **EST:** 2013
SALES (est): 3.99MM **Privately Held**
Web: www.tinycircuits.com
SIC: 3679 Electronic circuits

(G-339)
TLT-BABCOCK INC
260 Springside Dr (44333-2433)
PHONE..........................330 867-8540
▲ **EMP:** 92
SIC: 3564 3822 Blowers and fans; Damper
operators: pneumatic, thermostatic, electric

(G-340)
TLT-TURBO INC
2693 Wingate Ave (44314-1301)
P.O. Box 3830 (44314-0830)
PHONE..........................330 776-5115
John A Landis, *Dir*
▲ **EMP:** 6 **EST:** 2014
SALES (est): 5.77MM
SALES (corp-wide): 92.38B **Privately Held**
Web: northamerica.tlt-turbo.com
SIC: 3564 Ventilating fans: industrial or
commercial
HQ: Tlt-Turbo Gmbh
Gleiwitzstr. 7
Zweibrucken RP 66482
63328080

(G-341)
TOTAL CALL CENTER SOLUTIONS
1014 Margate Dr Ste 200 (44313-5808)
PHONE..........................330 869-9844
Mark Thorne, *Pr*
Gary Cooper, *VP*
Rhonda Thorne, *Stockholder*
EMP: 10 **EST:** 1990
SALES (est): 378.65K **Privately Held**

SIC: 3661 7389 Telephone dialing devices,
automatic; Telephone services

(G-342)
TRI CAST LIMITED PARTNERSHIP
2128 Killian Rd (44312-4898)
PHONE..........................330 733-8718
John Voight, *CEO*
EMP: 24 **EST:** 2000
SQ FT: 18,712
SALES (est): 417.37K **Privately Held**
Web: www.tri-cast.com
SIC: 3321 Gray iron castings, nec

(G-343)
TRI-CAST INC (PA)
2128 Killian Rd (44312-4898)
PHONE..........................330 733-8718
John Voight, *CEO*
EMP: 30 **EST:** 1967
SQ FT: 28,000
SALES (est): 4.42MM
SALES (corp-wide): 4.42MM **Privately
Held**
Web: www.tri-cast.com
SIC: 3321 Gray iron castings, nec

(G-344)
TRITON DURO WERKS INC
3475 W Bath Rd (44333-2183)
PHONE..........................407 497-9116
Victor G De Leon, *Prin*
EMP: 6 **EST:** 2016
SALES (est): 1.56MM **Privately Held**
Web: www.tritonduro.com
SIC: 3621 Motors and generators

(G-345)
TRUMBULL INDUSTRIES INC
209 Perkins St (44304-1298)
PHONE..........................330 434-6174
Joe Reguerio, *Brnch Mgr*
EMP: 54
SALES (corp-wide): 100.91MM **Privately
Held**
Web: www.trumbull.com
SIC: 5074 8711 2541 Plumbing fittings and
supplies; Engineering services; Wood
partitions and fixtures
PA: Trumbull Industries, Inc.
400 Dietz Rd Ne
Warren OH 44483
800 477-1799

(G-346)
TRUSEAL TECHNOLOGIES INC (HQ)
388 S Main St Ste 700 (44311-1060)
PHONE..........................216 910-1500
August J Coppola, *CEO*
Lee Burroughs, *
David Marlar, *
Joseph Stevenot, *
Joel Falck, *
◆ **EMP:** 35 **EST:** 1997
SQ FT: 80,000
SALES (est): 9.33MM **Publicly Held**
Web: www.truseal.com
SIC: 2891 Sealants
PA: Quanex Building Products Corporation
945 Bunker HI Rd Ste 900
Houston TX 77024

(G-347)
TS SALES LLC
Also Called: Top Shot Ammunition
847 Pier Dr (44307-2267)
PHONE..........................727 804-8060
Mark Schneider, *Managing Member*
EMP: 15 **EST:** 2014
SALES (est): 268.44K **Privately Held**

SIC: 5941 3484 Firearms; Guns (firearms) or
gun parts, 30 mm. and below

(G-348)
TUFFY MANUFACTURING
360 Massillon Rd (44312-2021)
PHONE..........................330 940-2356
Lewis Zimmerman, *Pr*
EMP: 16 **EST:** 2014
SALES (est): 992.7K **Privately Held**
Web: www.tuffymfg.com
SIC: 5521 5013 3999 Automobiles, used
cars only; Automotive servicing equipment;
Manufacturing industries, nec

(G-349)
UCAN TEST INSTRUMENTS LLC ✪
388 S Main St (44311-1064)
PHONE..........................330 696-6624
Kelly Hsieh, *CEO*
EMP: 9 **EST:** 2024
SALES (est): 1.34MM **Privately Held**
SIC: 3714 Motor vehicle parts and
accessories

(G-350)
UNINTERRUPTED LLC
3800 Embassy Pkwy Ste 360 (44333-8389)
PHONE..........................216 771-2323
Maverick Carter, *CEO*
EMP: 15 **EST:** 2014
SALES (est): 963.4K **Privately Held**
SIC: 7372 Application computer software

(G-351)
UNITED FEED SCREWS LTD
487 Wellington Ave (44305-2680)
PHONE..........................330 798-5532
Paul Norton, *Pr*
Joe Norton Senior, *Techl Dir*
▲ **EMP:** 10 **EST:** 1998
SQ FT: 14,500
SALES (est): 2.75MM **Privately Held**
Web: www.unitedfeedscrews.com
SIC: 3061 Oil and gas field machinery
rubber goods (mechanical)

(G-352)
V-I-S-C-E-R-O-T-O-N-I-C INC
118 W Market St (44303-2359)
PHONE..........................330 690-3355
Christopher Cook, *Pr*
Rich Cook, *VP*
EMP: 100 **EST:** 2021
SALES (est): 695.49K **Privately Held**
SIC: 2515 Mattresses and bedsprings

(G-353)
VERTICAL DATA LLC
Also Called: Medtrace
2169 Chuckery Ln (44333-4742)
P.O. Box 38 (44210-0038)
PHONE..........................330 289-0313
EMP: 15 **EST:** 2015
SALES (est): 572.82K **Privately Held**
Web: www.vertical-data.com
SIC: 7372 Application computer software

(G-354)
**VIRTUAL HOLD TECH SLUTIONS
LLC (DH)**
Also Called: Mindful
3875 Embassy Pkwy Ste 350 (44333-8343)
PHONE..........................330 670-2200
Matt Dimaria, *Pr*
Thomas Jameson, *
Kevin Shinseki, *
Ted Bray, *
EMP: 29 **EST:** 1995
SQ FT: 18,000

▲ = Import ▼ = Export
◆ = Import/Export

SALES (est): 23.35MM
SALES (corp-wide): 460.84MM **Privately Held**
Web: www.getmindful.com
SIC: **7371** 7372 Computer software development; Prepackaged software
HQ: Medallia, Inc.
6220 Stnrdge Mall Rd Fl 2
Pleasanton CA 94588
650 321-3000

(G-355)
VULCAN MACHINERY CORPORATION
20 N Case Ave (44305-2598)
PHONE..............................330 376-6025
David Jacobs, *Pr*
Bradley J Jacobs, *
EMP: 13 EST: 1966
SALES (est): 3.51MM **Privately Held**
Web: www.vulcanmachinery.com
SIC: **3559** 7299 Plastics working machinery; Banquet hall facilities

(G-356)
WHITE INDUSTRIAL TOOL INC
Also Called: White Tool
102 W Wilbeth Rd (44301-2415)
PHONE..............................330 773-6889
Ronald White Junior, *Pr*
Richard White, *VP*
Christopher White, *Treas*
Robert White, *Sec*
Ronald White Senior, *Stockholder*
EMP: 9 EST: 1965
SQ FT: 18,000
SALES (est): 939.79K **Privately Held**
Web: www.whiteindtool.com
SIC: **3423** Hand and edge tools, nec

(G-357)
WI INC
Also Called: Wek Industries, Inc.
1293 S Main St (44301-1302)
PHONE..............................440 576-6940
EMP: 125
SIC: **3089** Injection molding of plastics

(G-358)
WRC HOLDINGS INC
Also Called: Wrc
1485 Exeter Rd (44306-3856)
PHONE..............................330 733-6662
✿ **EMP:** 19 **EST:** 1990
SALES (est): 4.17MM **Privately Held**
Web: www.wrcakron.com
SIC: **3625** 8711 Relays and industrial controls; Designing: ship, boat, machine, and product

(G-359)
WSI SELLER INC
323 N Arlington St (44305-1601)
PHONE..............................330 379-0270
Carl Martin, *Brnch Mgr*
EMP: 12
SALES (corp-wide): 202.99MM **Privately Held**
Web: www.woodhillsupply.com
SIC: **7623** 5722 5074 3432 Air conditioning repair; Air conditioning room units, self-contained; Plumbing fittings and supplies; Plumbing fixture fittings and trim
HQ: Wsi Seller, Inc.
4665 Beidler Rd
Willoughby OH 44094
440 269-1100

(G-360)
YANKE BIONICS INC (PA)
303 W Exchange St (44302-1702)
PHONE..............................330 762-6411
Mark Yanke, *Pr*
Gary Charton, *
Jim Kraus, *
EMP: 44 **EST:** 1993
SQ FT: 15,000
SALES (est): 9.97MM
SALES (corp-wide): 9.97MM **Privately Held**
Web: www.yankebionics.com
SIC: **3842** Limbs, artificial

(G-361)
YOKOHAMA TWS NORTH AMERICA INC (DH)
Also Called: Interfit
1501 Exeter Rd (44306-3889)
PHONE..............................330 436-5168
Paolo Pompei, *Pr*
◆ **EMP:** 40 **EST:** 1991
SQ FT: 600,000
SALES (est): 49.4MM
SALES (corp-wide): 60.4MM **Privately Held**
SIC: **3011** 3061 Industrial tires, pneumatic; Appliance rubber goods (mechanical)
HQ: Trelleborg Corporation
200 Veterans Blvd Ste 3
South Haven MI 49090
269 639-9891

(G-362)
ZIEGLER TIRE AND SUPPLY CO
Also Called: Ziegler Tire Oil
547 Wolf Ledges Pkwy (44311-1091)
PHONE..............................330 434-7126
Mike Angle, *Mgr*
EMP: 9
SALES (corp-wide): 93.71MM **Privately Held**
Web: www.zieglertire.com
SIC: **5014** 5531 7534 Automobile tires and tubes; Automotive tires; Tire repair shop
PA: The Ziegler Tire And Supply Company
4150 Millennium Blvd Se
Massillon OH 44646
330 834-3332

Alger
Hardin County

(G-363)
WIWA LLC
107 N Main St (45812-8506)
P.O. Box 398 (45812-0398)
PHONE..............................419 757-0141
Jeffrey Wold, *Genl Mgr*
▲ **EMP:** 10 **EST:** 2001
SQ FT: 12,000
SALES (est): 5.86MM
SALES (corp-wide): 13.75MM **Privately Held**
Web: www.wiwausa.com
SIC: **3563** Spraying and dusting equipment
PA: Wiwa Wilhelm Wagner Gmbh & Co. Kg
Gewerbestr. 1-3
Lahnau HE 35633
64416090

Alliance
Stark County

(G-364)
A R SCHOPPS SONS INC
14536 Oyster Rd (44601-9243)

P.O. Box 2513 (44601-0513)
PHONE..............................330 821-8406
Robert Schopp, *Pr*
David Schopp, *
Mary Schopp, *
▲ **EMP:** 50 **EST:** 1898
SQ FT: 3,084
SALES (est): 2.19MM **Privately Held**
Web: www.arschopp.com
SIC: **3931** Organ parts and materials

(G-365)
ACME INDUSTRIAL GROUP INC
540 N Freedom Ave (44601-1816)
P.O. Box 2388 (44601-0388)
PHONE..............................330 821-3900
Richard Burton Junior, *Pr*
Deborah Burton, *VP*
EMP: 6 **EST:** 1952
SALES (est): 622.92K **Privately Held**
SIC: **3471** Electroplating of metals or formed products

(G-366)
ACME SURFACE DYNAMICS INC
555 N Freedom Ave (44601-1873)
P.O. Box 2388 (44601-0388)
PHONE..............................330 821-3900
EMP: 10 **EST:** 2012
SALES (est): 1.78MM **Privately Held**
Web: www.acmesdi.com
SIC: **3312** Stainless steel

(G-367)
ALL COATINGS CO INC
510 W Ely St (44601-1610)
PHONE..............................330 821-3806
Scott Brothers, *Pr*
Wanda Lou Brothers, *Sec*
EMP: 7 **EST:** 1998
SQ FT: 70,000
SALES (est): 148.65K **Privately Held**
Web: www.allcoatings.com
SIC: **2951** 2851 Asphalt paving mixtures and blocks; Paints and paint additives

(G-368)
ALLIANCE ABRASIVES LLC
23649 State Route 62 (44601-9027)
P.O. Box 3447 (44601-7447)
PHONE..............................330 823-7957
▲ **EMP:** 15
Web: www.allianceabrasives.com
SIC: **3291** Abrasive products

(G-369)
ALLIANCE CASTINGS COMPANY LLC
1001 E Broadway St (44601-2602)
PHONE..............................330 829-5600
▲ **EMP:** 20 **EST:** 2003
SALES (est): 2.5MM
SALES (corp-wide): 3.54B **Publicly Held**
SIC: **3743** Railroad equipment
PA: The Greenbrier Companies Inc
1 Centerpointe Dr Ste 200
Lake Oswego OR 97035
503 684-7000

(G-370)
ALLIANCE EQUIPMENT COMPANY INC
1000 N Union Ave (44601-1392)
PHONE..............................330 821-2291
Patricia Antonosanti, *Pr*
Matthew Antonosanti, *VP*
▲ **EMP:** 11 **EST:** 1982
SQ FT: 49,000
SALES (est): 3.8MM **Privately Held**
Web: www.alliance-equipment.com

SIC: **3089** Plastics and fiberglass tanks

(G-371)
ALLIANCE MACHINE COMPANY
1049 S Mahoning Ave (44601-3212)
PHONE..............................330 823-6120
Christopher Sause, *Prin*
EMP: 7
SALES (est): 601.84K **Privately Held**
Web: www.morganengineering.com
SIC: **3599** Machine shop, jobbing and repair

(G-372)
ALLIANCE PUBLISHING CO INC (HQ)
Also Called: Review, The
40 S Linden Ave (44601-2447)
P.O. Box 9901 (44711-0901)
PHONE..............................330 453-1304
Chuck Dix, *Pr*
R Victor Dix, *
Robert C Dix, *
David E Dix, *
Timothy Dix, *
EMP: 125 **EST:** 1888
SQ FT: 25,000
SALES (est): 46.01MM
SALES (corp-wide): 467.21MM **Privately Held**
Web: www.the-review.com
SIC: **2711** 2752 Newspapers, publishing and printing; Commercial printing, lithographic
PA: Dix 1898, Inc.
212 E Liberty St
Wooster OH
330 264-3511

(G-373)
BUCKEYE PACKAGING CO INC
12223 Marlboro Ave Ne (44601-9772)
PHONE..............................330 935-0301
EMP: 80 **EST:** 1952
SALES (est): 8.65MM **Privately Held**
Web: www.buckeyepackaging.com
SIC: **2673** 2759 3081 Bags: plastic, laminated, and coated; Commercial printing, nec; Packing materials, plastics sheet

(G-374)
C JS SIGNS
1670 Charl Ann Dr (44601-3688)
PHONE..............................330 821-7446
Christopher Liebhart, *Owner*
EMP: 6 **EST:** 1998
SALES (est): 236.63K **Privately Held**
Web: www.cjsigns.net
SIC: **3993** Signs and advertising specialties

(G-375)
CARNATION MACHINE AND TOOL INC
14632 Oyster Rd (44601-9244)
PHONE..............................330 823-5352
A Edgar Smith Junior, *Pr*
Carol Smith, *Sec*
EMP: 6 **EST:** 1965
SQ FT: 4,200
SALES (est): 701.78K **Privately Held**
Web: www.carnationmachine.com
SIC: **3599** Machine shop, jobbing and repair

(G-376)
CENTRAL COATED PRODUCTS LLC
2025 Mccrea St (44601-2794)
P.O. Box 3348 (44601-7348)
PHONE..............................330 821-9830
Thomas A Tormey, *Pr*
Steven T Porter, *
Pamela Porter, *Stockholder*
Anne Tormey, *Stockholder*
▲ **EMP:** 60 **EST:** 1976

SQ FT: 77,500
SALES (est): 455.01K **Privately Held**
Web: www.centralcoated.com
SIC: 2672 2671 Paper; coated and
laminated, nec; Paper, coated or laminated
for packaging

(G-377)
COASTAL PET PRODUCTS INC
911 Leadway Ave (44601-2792)
P.O. Box 2178 (44601-0178)
PHONE..............................330 821-7363
▲ EMP: 525 EST: 1969
SALES (est): 40.39MM **Privately Held**
Web: www.coastalpet.com
SIC: 2399 3199 Pet collars, leashes, etc.:
non-leather; Dog furnishings: collars,
leashes, muzzles, etc.: leather

(G-378)
CUSTOM POLY BAG LLC
9465 Edison St Ne (44601-9799)
PHONE..............................330 935-2408
EMP: 57 EST: 1969
SALES (est): 10.59MM
SALES (corp-wide): 496.77MM **Privately
Held**
Web: www.ppcflex.com
SIC: 2673 2759 Plastic bags: made
from purchased materials; Extruded
finished plastics products, nec;
Flexographic printing
PA: Ppc Flexible Packaging, Llc
1111 Busch Pkwy
Buffalo Grove IL 60089
847 541-0000

(G-379)
DAMON INDUSTRIES INC (PA)
12435 Rockhill Ave Ne (44601-1065)
P.O. Box 2120 (44601-0120)
PHONE..............................330 821-5310
TOLL FREE: 800
◆ EMP: 90 EST: 1938
SALES (est): 6.12MM
SALES (corp-wide): 6.12MM **Privately
Held**
Web: www.damonq.com
SIC: 2842 2899 3541 2879 Cleaning or
polishing preparations, nec; Water treating
compounds; Buffing and polishing machines
; Agricultural chemicals, nec

(G-380)
DAVIS TECHNOLOGIES INC
Also Called: Dti
837 W Main St (44601-2208)
P.O. Box 2475 (44601-0475)
PHONE..............................330 823-2544
EMP: 12 EST: 1987
SQ FT: 7,500
SALES (est): 781.56K **Privately Held**
Web: www.moretraction.com
SIC: 8711 3625 Electrical or electronic
engineering; Control equipment, electric

(G-381)
DOM TUBE CORP
640 Keystone St (44601-1886)
P.O. Box 2298 (44601-0298)
PHONE..............................412 299-2616
◆ EMP: 657
SIC: 3317 Seamless pipes and tubes

(G-382)
FILNOR INC (PA)
227 N Freedom Ave (44601-1897)
P.O. Box 2328 (44601-0328)
PHONE..............................330 821-8731
Ronald L Neely, *CEO*
James C Neely, *Pr*

Craig Clarke, *VP*
Daren Szekely, *VP*
Renee Shahaden, *Treas*
◆ EMP: 12 EST: 1970
SQ FT: 72,000
SALES (est): 8.63MM
SALES (corp-wide): 8.63MM **Privately
Held**
Web: www.filnor.com
SIC: 3625 5063 Electric controls and control
accessories, industrial; Electrical apparatus
and equipment

(G-383)
GNW ALUMINUM INC
1356 Beeson St Ne (44601-6201)
P.O. Box 2418 (44601-0418)
PHONE..............................330 821-7955
Nathan Hoopes, *Pr*
Adam Hoopes, *
Beatrice K Hoopes, *
EMP: 40 EST: 2002
SALES (est): 4.69MM **Privately Held**
SIC: 3341 Aluminum smelting and refining
(secondary)

(G-384)
HAISS FABRIPART LLC
22421 Lake Park Blvd (44601-3469)
PHONE..............................330 821-2028
EMP: 30 EST: 1998
SQ FT: 6,600
SALES (est): 5.57MM **Privately Held**
Web: www.haissfabripart.com
SIC: 3599 Machine shop, jobbing and repair

(G-385)
IML CONTAINERS OHIO INC
2455 W Main St (44601-2109)
PHONE..............................330 754-1066
John P Lacroix, *Pr*
EMP: 15 EST: 2018
SALES (est): 9.8MM
SALES (corp-wide): 355.83K **Privately
Held**
SIC: 3089 Plastics containers, except foam
HQ: Les Contenants I.M.L. D'amerique Du
Nord Inc
2625 Rte 344
Saint-Placide QC J0V 2
450 258-3130

(G-386)
JARMAN PRINTING LLC
350 S Union Ave (44601-2664)
P.O. Box 2505 (44601-0505)
PHONE..............................330 823-8585
Krista Jarvis, *Managing Member*
EMP: 6 EST: 1906
SQ FT: 6,500
SALES (est): 471.76K **Privately Held**
Web: www.jarmanprinting.com
SIC: 2752 2759 Lithographing on metal;
Letterpress printing

(G-387)
KEENER RUBBER COMPANY
14700 Commerce St Ne (44601-1035)
P.O. Box 2717 (44601-0717)
PHONE..............................330 821-1880
Richard A Michelson, *CEO*
EMP: 10 EST: 1956
SQ FT: 30,000
SALES (est): 1.96MM **Privately Held**
Web: www.keenerrubber.com
SIC: 3069 Rubber bands

(G-388)
MAC MANUFACTURING INC (HQ)
Also Called: Mac
14599 Commerce St Ne (44601-1003)

PHONE..............................330 823-9900
Michael Conny, *Prin*
Dan Tubbs, *
Jenny Conny, *
Steve Hallas, *Prin*
Bill Ogden, *Prin*
▲ EMP: 700 EST: 1995
SALES (est): 23.95MM **Privately Held**
Web: www.mactrailer.com
SIC: 3715 5012 Truck trailers; Trailers for
trucks, new and used
PA: Mac Trailer Manufacturing, Inc.
14599 Commerce St
Alliance OH 44601

(G-389)
MAC STEEL TRAILER LTD
14599 Commerce St Ne (44601-1003)
PHONE..............................330 823-9900
Michael A Conny, *Managing Member*
EMP: 6 EST: 1999
SALES (est): 1.59MM **Privately Held**
Web: www.mactrailer.com
SIC: 3715 Truck trailers

(G-390)
**MAC TRAILER MANUFACTURING
INC (PA)**
14599 Commerce St Ne (44601-1003)
PHONE..............................800 795-8454
Michael A Conny, *Pr*
Bill Ogden, *
◆ EMP: 1300 EST: 1992
SQ FT: 220,000
SALES (est): 182.08MM **Privately Held**
Web: www.mactrailer.com
SIC: 3715 5012 5013 5015 Truck trailers;
Trailers for trucks, new and used; Motor
vehicle supplies and new parts; Motor
vehicle parts, used

(G-391)
MAC TRAILER SERVICE INC
14504 Commerce St Ne (44601-1000)
PHONE..............................330 823-9190
Michael Conny, *Pr*
EMP: 40 EST: 1997
SALES (est): 9.61MM **Privately Held**
Web: www.mactrailer.com
SIC: 3715 Truck trailers

(G-392)
MARLBORO MANUFACTURING INC
11750 Marlboro Ave Ne (44601-9798)
PHONE..............................330 935-2221
Thomas Naughton, *Pr*
Renee Milliken, *
Daniel Lough, *
Patrick Whitaker, *
▲ EMP: 50 EST: 1960
SQ FT: 54,000
SALES (est): 4.72MM **Privately Held**
Web: www.marlborohinge.com
SIC: 3429 Piano hardware

(G-393)
**MORGAN ENGINEERING SYSTEMS
INC**
1182 E Summit St (44601-3224)
PHONE..............................330 821-4721
James Broch, *Brnch Mgr*
EMP: 130
SALES (corp-wide): 24.45MM **Privately
Held**
Web: www.morganengineering.com
SIC: 3536 Cranes, overhead traveling
PA: Morgan Engineering Systems, Inc.
1049 S Mahoning Ave
Alliance OH 44601
330 823-6130

(G-394)
**MORGAN ENGINEERING SYSTEMS
INC (PA)**
1049 S Mahoning Ave (44601-3212)
PHONE..............................330 823-6130
▼ EMP: 50 EST: 1868
SALES (est): 24.45MM
SALES (corp-wide): 24.45MM **Privately
Held**
Web: www.morganengineering.com
SIC: 3536 Cranes, overhead traveling

(G-395)
MORGAN SITE SERVICES INC
1049 S Mahoning Ave (44601-3212)
PHONE..............................330 823-6120
Brian Mertes, *CEO*
EMP: 25
SALES (est): 2.56MM **Privately Held**
Web: www.morganengineering.com
SIC: 3999 Manufacturing industries, nec

(G-396)
MYERS INDUSTRIES INC
Also Called: Trilogy Plastics
2290 W Main St (44601-2272)
PHONE..............................330 821-4700
Andrean Horton, *Pr*
EMP: 154
SALES (corp-wide): 836.28MM **Publicly
Held**
Web: www.myersindustries.com
SIC: 3089 Injection molding of plastics
PA: Myers Industries, Inc.
1293 S Main St
Akron OH 44301
330 253-5592

(G-397)
P&E SALES LTD
1595 W Main St (44601-2104)
P.O. Box 340 (44650-0340)
PHONE..............................330 829-0100
Paul J Tatulinski, *Pr*
Ellen Tatulinski, *VP*
EMP: 8 EST: 1984
SQ FT: 5,600
SALES (est): 457.53K **Privately Held**
Web: pesalesohio.wordpress.com
SIC: 3053 5085 Gaskets, all materials;
Gaskets and seals

(G-398)
PHILLIPS MFG & MCH CORP
118 1/2 E Ely St (44601-1809)
P.O. Box 2627 (44601-0627)
PHONE..............................330 823-9178
Deborah L Williamson, *Pr*
EMP: 9 EST: 1914
SQ FT: 20,000
SALES (est): 491.79K **Privately Held**
SIC: 3599 Machine shop, jobbing and repair

(G-399)
PITTMAN ENGINEERING INC
15835 Armour St Ne (44601-9349)
P.O. Box 3734 (44601-7734)
PHONE..............................330 821-4365
Michael Anstine, *Pr*
EMP: 18 EST: 1997
SQ FT: 23,000
SALES (est): 2.24MM **Privately Held**
Web: www.anstine.net
SIC: 3599 3441 Machine shop, jobbing and
repair; Fabricated structural metal

(G-400)
PREMIER BANDAG 8 INC
1469 W Main St (44601-2153)
PHONE..............................330 823-3822

Will Tollerton, *Pr*
EMP: 10 **EST:** 1998
SALES (est): 1.25MM **Privately Held**
SIC: 7534 Tire retreading and repair shops

(G-401)
PTC ALLIANCE LLC
640 Keystone St (44601-1886)
PHONE..............................330 821-5700
Peter Whiting, *Brnch Mgr*
EMP: 104
SALES (corp-wide): 48.69MM **Privately Held**
Web: www.ptcalliance.com
SIC: 3317 Steel pipe and tubes
HQ: Ptc Alliance Llc
6051 Wallace Road Ext # 200
Wexford PA 15090
412 299-7900

(G-402)
SAMS GRAPHIC INDUSTRIES
Also Called: Graphic Industries
611 Homeworth Rd (44601-9072)
PHONE..............................330 821-4710
Sam Schuette, *Owner*
EMP: 10 **EST:** 1966
SQ FT: 6,000
SALES (est): 83.27K **Privately Held**
SIC: 2796 2759 Engraving platemaking
services; Engraving, nec

(G-403)
SANCAP LINER TECHNOLOGY INC
16125 Armour St Ne (44601-9301)
PHONE..............................330 821-1166
EMP: 90
SIC: 3081 Unsupported plastics film and
sheet

(G-404)
SILMARILLION PARTNERS INC (PA)
2290 W Main St (44601-2272)
P.O. Box 2600 (44601-0600)
PHONE..............................330 821-4700
Stephen Osborn, *Pr*
Rex Roseberry, *
Bruce Frank, *
EMP: 152 **EST:** 1896
SQ FT: 90,000
SALES (est): 8.32MM
SALES (corp-wide): 8.32MM **Privately Held**
Web:
www.myersengineeredsolutions.com
SIC: 3089 Injection molding of plastics

(G-405)
SMITH MACHINE INC
20651 Lake Park Blvd (44601-3319)
PHONE..............................330 821-9898
David F Smith, *Pr*
Eileen R Smith, *VP*
Tim Smith, *Genl Mgr*
EMP: 7 **EST:** 1976
SALES (est): 772.91K **Privately Held**
SIC: 3599 Machine shop, jobbing and repair

(G-406)
STEEL EQP SPECIALISTS INC (PA)
Also Called: S.E.S. Engineering
1507 Beeson St Ne (44601-2142)
PHONE..............................330 823-8260
James R Boughton, *CEO*
T Virgil Huggett, *
Donald Watkins, *
Wayne W Weisenburger, *
Allan Wolfgang, *
▲ **EMP:** 72 **EST:** 1976
SQ FT: 32,000
SALES (est): 28.11MM

SALES (corp-wide): 28.11MM **Privately Held**
Web: www.seseng.com
SIC: 7699 3599 7629 3593 Industrial
machinery and equipment repair; Custom
machinery; Electrical repair shops; Fluid
power cylinders and actuators

(G-407)
STUCHELL PRODUCTS LLC
Also Called: Sare Plastics
12240 Rockhill Ave Ne (44601-1064)
PHONE..............................330 821-4299
EMP: 45 **EST:** 2005
SALES (est): 9.8MM **Privately Held**
Web: www.sareplastics.com
SIC: 3089 Injection molded finished plastics
products, nec

(G-408)
SUN AMERICA LLC
46 N Rockhill Ave (44601-2211)
PHONE..............................330 821-6300
Dwayne Robinson, *CFO*
EMP: 33 **EST:** 2015
SALES (est): 10.53MM **Privately Held**
Web: www.sun-america.com
SIC: 2671 Paper; coated and laminated
packaging

(G-409)
SUNAMERICACONVERTING LLC
46 N Rockhill Ave (44601-2211)
PHONE..............................330 821-6300
▲ **EMP:** 55 **EST:** 2004
SQ FT: 72,000
SALES (est): 8.47MM **Privately Held**
Web: www.sun-america.com
SIC: 2656 Paper cups, plates, dishes, and
utensils

(G-410)
T & W FORGE INC
Also Called: T & W Forge
562 W Ely St (44601-6409)
EMP: 60
Web: www.pair.com
SIC: 3462 Iron and steel forgings

(G-411)
TRAILSTAR INTERNATIONAL INC
14599 Commerce St Ne (44601-1003)
P.O. Box 2086 (44601-0086)
PHONE..............................330 823-9900
Tom Hahn, *Pr*
EMP: 39
SALES (corp-wide): 8.11MM **Privately Held**
Web: www.trailstarintl.com
SIC: 3715 Truck trailers
PA: Trailstar International, Inc.
20700 Hrrsburg Wstvlle Rd
Alliance OH 44601
330 821-9900

(G-412)
TRAILSTAR INTERNATIONAL INC (PA)
Also Called: Trailstar
20700 Harrisburg Westville Rd
(44601-8907)
P.O. Box 2086 (44601-0086)
PHONE..............................330 821-9900
Michael Conny, *CEO*
Tom Hahn, *Pr*
EMP: 37 **EST:** 2012
SALES (est): 8.11MM
SALES (corp-wide): 8.11MM **Privately Held**
Web: www.trailstarintl.com
SIC: 3715 Truck trailers

(G-413)
TRILOGY PLASTICS ALLIANCE INC
Also Called: Trilogy Plastics
2290 W Main St (44601-2272)
P.O. Box 2600 (44601-0600)
PHONE..............................330 821-4700
EMP: 10 **EST:** 2005
SALES (est): 2.18MM
SALES (corp-wide): 836.28MM **Publicly Held**
Web:
www.myersengineeredsolutions.com
SIC: 3089 Injection molding of plastics
PA: Myers Industries, Inc.
1293 S Main St
Akron OH 44301
330 253-5592

(G-414)
W J EGLI COMPANY INC (PA)
205 E Columbia St (44601-2563)
P.O. Box 2605 (44601-0605)
PHONE..............................330 823-3666
William J Egli, *Pr*
Garth Egli, *VP*
Cheryl A Stuffel, *Sec*
▼ **EMP:** 15 **EST:** 1968
SQ FT: 100,000
SALES (est): 1.59MM
SALES (corp-wide): 1.59MM **Privately Held**
Web: www.wjegli.com
SIC: 2541 3496 3498 3444 Display fixtures,
wood; Miscellaneous fabricated wire
products; Fabricated pipe and fittings;
Sheet metalwork

(G-415)
WEDGE HARDWOOD PRODUCTS
2137 Knox School Rd (44601-6923)
PHONE..............................330 525-7775
Michael Stahl, *Pt*
Jim Hahlen, *Pt*
EMP: 6 **EST:** 1985
SQ FT: 7,200
SALES (est): 273.36K **Privately Held**
SIC: 2431 Planing mill, millwork

(G-416)
WHITACRE GREER COMPANY (PA)
1400 S Mahoning Ave (44601-3433)
P.O. Box 2960 (44601-0960)
PHONE..............................330 823-1610
J R Whitacre Junior, *Ch Bd*
Janet Kaboth, *Vice Chairman**
L A Morrison, *
EMP: 38 **EST:** 1916
SALES (est): 5.84MM
SALES (corp-wide): 5.84MM **Privately Held**
Web: www.wgpaver.com
SIC: 3251 3255 Paving brick, clay; Clay
refractories

(G-417)
WIELAND METAL SVCS FOILS LLC
2081 Mccrea St (44601-2704)
PHONE..............................330 823-1700
Kevin Bense, *Pr*
Robert M James, *VP*
Marc R Bacon, *CFO*
Greg Keown, *Genl Mgr*
▲ **EMP:** 53 **EST:** 1986
SQ FT: 80,000
SALES (est): 8.96MM **Privately Held**
Web: www.wieland-metalservices.com
SIC: 3341 3353 3471 3497 Secondary
nonferrous metals; Aluminum sheet, plate,
and foil; Plating and polishing; Metal foil
and leaf
HQ: Wieland Metal Services, Llc

301 Mtro Ctr Blvd Ste 204
Warwick RI 02886
401 739-0800

(G-418)
WINKLE INDUSTRIES INC
2080 W Main St (44601-2187)
PHONE..............................330 823-9730
Joe Schatz, *CEO*
Beth A Felger, *
Christina M Schatz, *
▲ **EMP:** 55 **EST:** 1949
SQ FT: 85,000
SALES (est): 12.56MM **Privately Held**
Web: www.winkleindustries.com
SIC: 7699 3499 5063 Industrial machinery
and equipment repair; Magnets,
permanent: metallic; Control and signal
wire and cable, including coaxial

Alpha
Greene County

(G-419)
UNISON INDUSTRIES LLC
2070 Heller Rd (45301)
PHONE..............................937 426-0621
EMP: 10 **EST:** 1998
SALES (est): 568.94K **Privately Held**
Web: www.unisonindustries.com
SIC: 7699 3315 Typewriter repair, including
electric; Steel wire and related products

Alvada
Seneca County

(G-420)
BR PALLET INC
21395 County Road 7 (44802-9620)
P.O. Box 68 (44802-0068)
PHONE..............................419 427-2200
Carl Ruehle, *Ch*
Dwayne Hoschar, *
Bryan Ruhle, *
EMP: 36 **EST:** 1990
SQ FT: 1,500
SALES (est): 2.59MM **Privately Held**
SIC: 2448 Pallets, wood

(G-421)
CIRCUIT BOARD MINING LLC
23546 Us Highway 224 (44802-9641)
PHONE..............................419 348-1057
EMP: 6 **EST:** 2021
SALES (est): 230.56K **Privately Held**
SIC: 3341 Secondary nonferrous metals

(G-422)
MIDWEST LASER SYSTEMS INC
Also Called: MLS Systems
4777 S Us Highway 23 (44802-9702)
PHONE..............................419 424-0062
Chad Bouillon, *Pr*
William J Hunter, *
EMP: 25 **EST:** 1980
SALES (est): 2.93MM **Privately Held**
Web: www.mlssystems.com
SIC: 3599 3549 Custom machinery;
Metalworking machinery, nec

Amanda
Fairfield County

(G-423)
CLEAR CREEK SCREW MACHINE CO
4900 Julian Rd Sw (43102-9514)

PHONE..................................740 969-2113
George Bartrom, *Pr*
EMP: 8 **EST:** 1959
SQ FT: 15,000
SALES (est): 469.57K **Privately Held**
SIC: 3599 3451 Machine shop, jobbing and repair; Screw machine products

(G-424)
MID-WEST FABRICATING CO (PA)
Also Called: Mid West Fabricating Co
313 N Johns St (43102-9002)
PHONE..................................740 969-4411
Jennifer Johns Friel, *Pr*
Julia Johns, *
Ann Custer, *
◆ **EMP:** 125 **EST:** 1945
SQ FT: 280,000
SALES (est): 28.07MM
SALES (corp-wide): 28.07MM **Privately Held**
Web: www.midwestfab.com
SIC: 3496 Miscellaneous fabricated wire products

Amelia
Clermont County

(G-425)
A & A SAFETY INC (PA)
1126 Ferris Rd (45102-1892)
PHONE..................................513 943-6100
William N Luttmer, *Pr*
Francis Luttmer, *
EMP: 50 **EST:** 1979
SQ FT: 12,300
SALES (est): 22.88MM
SALES (corp-wide): 22.88MM **Privately Held**
Web: www.aasafetyinc.com
SIC: 7359 3993 5084 1721 Work zone traffic equipment (flags, cones, barrels, etc.); Signs and advertising specialties; Safety equipment; Painting and paper hanging

(G-426)
ACREO INC
3209 Marshall Dr (45102-9213)
P.O. Box 361 (45157-0361)
PHONE..................................513 734-3327
Roger Williams, *Pr*
EMP: 7 **EST:** 1994
SQ FT: 10,000
SALES (est): 246.27K **Privately Held**
SIC: 7389 3556 Design, commercial and industrial; Food products machinery

(G-427)
ALCON INC (HQ)
1132 Ferris Rd (45102-1020)
PHONE..................................513 722-1037
Michael Ball, *Ch*
EMP: 40 **EST:** 1967
SQ FT: 15,000
SALES (est): 1.31B **Privately Held**
Web: www.alcon-inc.net
SIC: 3643 Connectors and terminals for electrical devices
PA: Alcon Ag
0
Fribourg FR 1700

(G-428)
ALL WRITE RIBBON INC
3916 Bach Buxton Rd (45102-1014)
P.O. Box 67 (45102-0067)
PHONE..................................513 753-8300
William E Lyon, *Pr*
Harold Wolfe, *

▲ **EMP:** 10 **EST:** 1981
SQ FT: 20,000
SALES (est): 1.02MM **Privately Held**
Web: www.allwriteribbon.com
SIC: 3955 Print cartridges for laser and other computer printers

(G-429)
DEIMLING/JELIHO PLASTICS INC
4010 Bach Buxton Rd (45102-1048)
PHONE..................................513 752-6653
William Deimling, *Pr*
Mary Ann Deimling, *
▲ **EMP:** 83 **EST:** 1975
SQ FT: 60,000
SALES (est): 7.37MM **Privately Held**
Web: www.deimling-jeliho.com
SIC: 3089 3599 Injection molding of plastics; Machine shop, jobbing and repair

(G-430)
KOEBBE PRODUCTS INC (PA)
1132 Ferris Rd (45102-1020)
PHONE..................................513 753-4200
Dick Koebbe, *Pr*
EMP: 60 **EST:** 1969
SQ FT: 38,400
SALES (est): 9.82MM
SALES (corp-wide): 9.82MM **Privately Held**
Web: www.egerproducts.com
SIC: 3644 3544 5039 Insulators and insulation materials, electrical; Forms (molds), for foundry and plastics working machinery; Ceiling systems and products

(G-431)
LT MOSES WILLARD INC
3972 Bach Buxton Rd (45102-1099)
PHONE..................................513 248-5500
Christopher L Nordloh, *Pr*
EMP: 32 **EST:** 1965
SQ FT: 18,000
SALES (est): 337.9K **Privately Held**
SIC: 3645 Residential lighting fixtures

(G-432)
MARK J MYERS
Also Called: Heritage Tool & Manufacturing
80 W Main St (45102-1736)
PHONE..................................513 753-7300
Mark J Myers, *Owner*
EMP: 30 **EST:** 1981
SALES (est): 403.61K **Privately Held**
SIC: 3599 Machine shop, jobbing and repair

(G-433)
MCDONALDS
1261 W Ohio Pike (45102-1242)
PHONE..................................513 753-6100
EMP: 12 **EST:** 2019
SALES (est): 91.3K **Privately Held**
Web: www.mcdonalds.com
SIC: 5813 5812 5499 2038 Drinking places; Eating places; Miscellaneous food stores; Frozen specialties, nec

(G-434)
MOBILE CONVERSIONS INC
3354 State Route 132 (45102-2249)
PHONE..................................513 797-1991
Michael G Dobbins, *Pr*
EMP: 14 **EST:** 1994
SQ FT: 2,176
SALES (est): 807.75K **Privately Held**
Web: www.mobileconversions.com
SIC: 7532 2451 Van conversion; Mobile homes

(G-435)
PRINTINK INC
3976 Bach Buxton Rd (45102-1014)
PHONE..................................513 943-0599
Glenn Pearson, *Pr*
EMP: 9 **EST:** 2000
SQ FT: 25,000
SALES (est): 148.82K **Privately Held**
SIC: 2893 Printing ink

(G-436)
SANREED MANAGEMENT GROUP LLC
Also Called: Alcon Connectors
1132 Ferris Rd (45102-1020)
PHONE..................................513 722-1037
EMP: 4585 **EST:** 2019
SALES (est): 10.19MM **Privately Held**
SIC: 3643 Connectors and terminals for electrical devices

(G-437)
SOUTHERN OHIO MFG INC
3214 Marshall Dr (45102-9212)
PHONE..................................513 943-2555
Dave Rechtin, *Pr*
EMP: 10 **EST:** 1984
SALES (est): 785.06K **Privately Held**
Web: www.southernohiomfg.com
SIC: 3599 Machine shop, jobbing and repair

(G-438)
STEWART FILMSCREEN CORP
3919 Bach Buxton Rd (45102-1013)
PHONE..................................513 753-0800
Grant Stewart, *Pr*
EMP: 40
SALES (corp-wide): 24.61MM **Privately Held**
Web: www.stewartfilmscreen.com
SIC: 3861 Screens, projection
PA: Stewart Filmscreen Corp.
1161 Sepulveda Blvd
Torrance CA 90502
310 784-5300

(G-439)
SUN CHEMICAL CORPORATION
Colors Dispersion Division
3922 Bach Buxton Rd (45102-1098)
PHONE..................................513 753-9550
Edward Polaski, *Mgr*
EMP: 67
SQ FT: 7,200
Web: www.sunchemical.com
SIC: 2893 2865 Printing ink; Cyclic crudes and intermediates
HQ: Sun Chemical Corporation
35 Waterview Blvd
Parsippany NJ 07054
973 404-6000

(G-440)
TRI-STATE FABRICATORS INC
1146 Ferris Rd (45102-1020)
PHONE..................................513 752-5005
Richard Mark Vogt, *Pr*
Jeffrey G Vogt, *
Joanne Vogt, *
Jay Richard Vogt, *
EMP: 50 **EST:** 1983
SQ FT: 120,000
SALES (est): 10.84MM **Privately Held**
Web: www.tristatefabricators.com
SIC: 3441 3444 3471 3479 Fabricated structural metal; Sheet metalwork; Plating and polishing; Painting of metal products

(G-441)
WELLEX AMG
3214 Marshall Dr (45102-9212)
PHONE..................................513 734-1700
EMP: 6 **EST:** 2012
SALES (est): 126.33K **Privately Held**
Web: www.wellexmfg.com
SIC: 3599 Machine shop, jobbing and repair

(G-442)
WELLEX MANUFACTURING INC
3214 Marshall Dr (45102-9212)
PHONE..................................513 734-1700
John Born, *Pr*
David Uible, *Pr*
John Born, *Prin*
Marliese Born, *Prin*
EMP: 7 **EST:** 1963
SQ FT: 3,400
SALES (est): 1.54MM **Privately Held**
Web: www.wellexmfg.com
SIC: 3599 Machine shop, jobbing and repair

Amesville
Athens County

(G-443)
THIRD SALVO COMPANY
16355 Tick Ridge Rd (45711-9522)
PHONE..................................740 818-9669
Joseph Gillespie, *Prin*
EMP: 7 **EST:** 2017
SALES (est): 498.59K **Privately Held**
SIC: 1741 1521 1389 1542 Foundation and retaining wall construction; Single-family housing construction; Construction, repair, and dismantling services; Garage construction

Amherst
Lorain County

(G-444)
CLOVERVALE FARMS LLC (DH)
Also Called: Clovervale Foods
8133 Cooper Foster Park Rd (44001)
PHONE..................................440 960-0146
Richard Cawrse Junior, *Pr*
Suzanne Graham, *
Richard Cecil, *
EMP: 100 **EST:** 1920
SQ FT: 38,000
SALES (est): 24.36MM
SALES (corp-wide): 53.31B **Publicly Held**
Web: clovervalefarms.openfos.com
SIC: 2032 2033 2038 0191 Puddings, except meat: packaged in cans, jars, etc.; Fruits: packaged in cans, jars, etc.; Frozen specialties, nec; General farms, primarily crop
HQ: Advancepierre Foods, Inc.
9990 Prnceton Glendale Rd
West Chester OH 45246
513 874-8741

(G-445)
CURRIER RICHARD & JAMES
Also Called: Amherst Party Shop
540 Mcintosh Ln (44001-3108)
P.O. Box 500 (44001-0500)
PHONE..................................440 988-4132
Richard Currier, *Pr*
James Currier, *Pt*
EMP: 6 **EST:** 1954
SALES (est): 156.53K **Privately Held**
Web: www.amherstpartyshop.com
SIC: 5921 2086 Beer (packaged); Bottled and canned soft drinks

(G-446)
ECO FUEL SOLUTION LLC
779 Sunrise Dr (44001-1660)
PHONE..............................440 282-8592
James Bodnar, *Prin*
EMP: 6 **EST:** 2011
SALES (est): 110.92K **Privately Held**
SIC: 2869 Fuels

(G-447)
KTM NORTH AMERICA INC (PA)
Also Called: Gasgas North America
1119 Milan Ave (44001-1319)
PHONE..............................855 215-6360
Di Stefan Pierer, *CEO*
Rod Bush, *
Selvaraj Narayana, *
John S Harden, *
Jon-erik Burleson, *Treas*
▲ **EMP:** 87 **EST:** 1992
SQ FT: 5,000
SALES (est): 53.86MM **Privately Held**
Web: www.ktm.com
SIC: 5012 3751 Motorcycles; Motorcycles,
bicycles and parts

(G-448)
NORDSON CORPORATION
300 Nordson Dr (44001-2422)
PHONE..............................440 985-4496
Wendy Jordan, *Brnch Mgr*
EMP: 432
SALES (corp-wide): 2.69B **Publicly Held**
Web: www.nordson.com
SIC: 3563 Air and gas compressors
PA: Nordson Corporation
28601 Clemens Rd
Westlake OH 44145
440 892-1580

(G-449)
NORDSON CORPORATION
444 Gordon Ave Dock C1-C3 (44001)
PHONE..............................440 985-4458
EMP: 32
SALES (corp-wide): 2.69B **Publicly Held**
Web: www.nordson.com
SIC: 3563 Spraying outfits: metals, paints,
and chemicals (compressor)
PA: Nordson Corporation
28601 Clemens Rd
Westlake OH 44145
440 892-1580

(G-450)
NORDSON CORPORATION
100 Nordson Dr M 81 (44001-2454)
PHONE..............................440 985-4000
Michael Hilton, *Pr*
EMP: 500
SALES (corp-wide): 2.69B **Publicly Held**
Web: www.nordson.com
SIC: 3563 Spraying outfits: metals, paints,
and chemicals (compressor)
PA: Nordson Corporation
28601 Clemens Rd
Westlake OH 44145
440 892-1580

(G-451)
PAPA JOES PIES INC (PA)
Also Called: Mama Jo Homestyle Pies
1969 Cooper Foster Park Rd (44001-1207)
PHONE..............................440 960-7437
Johanna Mann, *Pr*
EMP: 11 **EST:** 1993
SALES (est): 1.22MM
SALES (corp-wide): 1.22MM **Privately
Held**
Web: www.mamajopies.com

SIC: 2051 Pies, bakery: except frozen

(G-452)
SKAGGS TRLR & TIRE REPR CO INC
516 W Main St (44001-9709)
PHONE..............................440 986-7470
Claude J Skaggs, *Owner*
EMP: 12 **EST:** 2002
SALES (est): 95.13K **Privately Held**
SIC: 5531 7538 7534 7539 Automotive tires;
General automotive repair shops; Tire
retreading and repair shops; Automotive
repair shops, nec

(G-453)
TYSON FOODS INC
1833 Cooper Foster Park Rd (44001-1206)
PHONE..............................440 960-0146
EMP: 6
SALES (corp-wide): 53.31B **Publicly Held**
Web: www.tyson.com
SIC: 2011 Meat packing plants
PA: Tyson Foods, Inc.
2200 W Don Tyson Pkwy
Springdale AR 72762
479 290-4000

Andover
Ashtabula County

(G-454)
ADVANCED TECHNOLOGY CORP
101 Parker Dr (44003-9456)
PHONE..............................440 293-4064
Seymour S Stein, *Ch Bd*
Anthony Stavole, *
Sherry Epstein, *
◆ **EMP:** 12 **EST:** 1951
SQ FT: 220,000
SALES (est): 4.99MM
SALES (corp-wide): 20.07MM **Privately
Held**
Web: www.atc-lighting-plastics.com
SIC: 3647 3469 Vehicular lighting equipment
; Metal stampings, nec
HQ: Atc Lighting & Plastics, Inc.
101 Parker Dr
Andover OH 44003

(G-455)
ATC GROUP INC (PA)
Also Called: Atc Lighting & Plastics
101 Parker Dr (44003-9456)
P.O. Box 1120 (44003-1120)
PHONE..............................440 293-4064
Seymour S Stein Ph.d., *Pr*
Sherry Epstein, *
▲ **EMP:** 100 **EST:** 1984
SQ FT: 50,000
SALES (est): 20.07MM
SALES (corp-wide): 20.07MM **Privately
Held**
Web: www.oneatlas.com
SIC: 3647 3089 3841 Vehicular lighting
equipment; Injection molded finished
plastics products, nec; Surgical and
medical instruments

(G-456)
ATC LIGHTING & PLASTICS INC (HQ)
Also Called: Kdlamp Company
101 Parker Dr (44003-9456)
P.O. Box 1120 (44003-1120)
PHONE..............................440 466-7670
Seymour S Stein Ph.d., *Ch Bd*
▲ **EMP:** 155 **EST:** 1991
SALES (est): 10.04MM
SALES (corp-wide): 20.07MM **Privately
Held**

Web: www.atc-lighting-plastics.com
SIC: 3647 3714 3713 3648 Motor vehicle
lighting equipment; Motor vehicle parts and
accessories; Truck and bus bodies;
Lighting equipment, nec
PA: Atc Group, Inc.
101 Parker Dr
Andover OH 44003
440 293-4064

(G-457)
K-D LAMP COMPANY
Also Called: Etc Lighting and Plastic
101 Parker Dr (44003-9456)
PHONE..............................440 293-4064
Seymour Stein, *Treas*
Doctor Seymour Stein, *Pr*
Sherry Epstein, *
▲ **EMP:** 49 **EST:** 2005
SALES (est): 8.95MM
SALES (corp-wide): 20.07MM **Privately
Held**
SIC: 3647 Headlights (fixtures), vehicular
PA: Atc Group, Inc.
101 Parker Dr
Andover OH 44003
440 293-4064

(G-458)
LIGHTING PRODUCTS INC
101 Parker Dr (44003-9456)
P.O. Box 1120 (44003-1120)
PHONE..............................440 293-4064
Seymour S Stein Ph.d., *Pr*
Seymour S Stein Ph.d., *Pr*
Anthony Stavole, *Sec*
Sherry Epstein, *Sec*
▲ **EMP:** 12 **EST:** 1994
SALES (est): 2.4MM
SALES (corp-wide): 20.07MM **Privately
Held**
Web: www.atc-lighting-plastics.com
SIC: 3647 Motor vehicle lighting equipment
HQ: Atc Lighting & Plastics, Inc.
101 Parker Dr
Andover OH 44003

Anna
Shelby County

(G-459)
AGRANA FRUIT US INC
1619T County Road 25a (45302-9490)
PHONE..............................937 693-3821
Jeff Elliot, *Mgr*
EMP: 150
SALES (corp-wide): 2.67MM **Privately
Held**
Web: us.agrana.com
SIC: 8734 2099 2087 Food testing service;
Food preparations, nec; Flavoring extracts
and syrups, nec
HQ: Agrana Fruit Us, Inc.
6850 Southpointe Pkwy
Brecksville OH 44141
440 546-1199

(G-460)
CHILLTEX LLC
Also Called: Honeywell Authorized Dealer
7440 Hoying Rd (45302-9616)
PHONE..............................937 710-3308
Matt Eilerman, *Prin*
EMP: 13 **EST:** 2005
SALES (est): 2.55MM **Privately Held**
Web: www.chilltexllc.com
SIC: 3585 Heating equipment, complete

Antwerp
Paulding County

(G-461)
ANTWERP TL DIE & ENGRG CO INC
3167 County Road 424 (45813-9416)
P.O. Box 712 (45813-0712)
PHONE..............................419 258-5271
Gerald A Snyder, *Pr*
EMP: 15 **EST:** 1985
SQ FT: 10,500
SALES (est): 1.69MM **Privately Held**
Web: www.antwerptool.com
SIC: 3544 3545 Special dies and tools;
Machine tool accessories

(G-462)
ATWOOD MOBILE PRODUCTS LLC
5406 County Road 424 (45813-9577)
PHONE..............................419 258-5531
Vincent Proaccina, *Prin*
EMP: 81
SALES (corp-wide): 2.26B **Privately Held**
Web: www.dometic.com
SIC: 3714 Motor vehicle parts and
accessories
HQ: Atwood Mobile Products Llc
1120 N Main St
Elkhart IN 46514

(G-463)
PARAGON TEMPERED GLASS LLC
5406 County Road 424 (45813-9577)
PHONE..............................419 258-5531
EMP: 125
Web: www.paragontemperedglass.com
SIC: 3231 Products of purchased glass
HQ: Paragon Tempered Glass, Llc
1830 Terminal Rd
Niles MI 49120
269 684-5060

(G-464)
WEST BEND PRINTING & PUBG INC
101 N Main St (45813-8406)
P.O. Box 1008 (45813-1008)
PHONE..............................419 258-2000
Bryce Steiner, *Pr*
EMP: 6 **EST:** 2005
SQ FT: 3,000
SALES (est): 191.79K **Privately Held**
Web: www.westbendprinting.com
SIC: 2752 Offset printing

Apple Creek
Wayne County

(G-465)
COBLENTZ BROTHERS INC
7101 S Kohler Rd (44606-9613)
PHONE..............................330 857-7211
Wayne Liechty, *Pr*
Jonas Coblentz, *
Ray Coblentz, *
EMP: 28 **EST:** 1961
SQ FT: 20,100
SALES (est): 1.62MM **Privately Held**
Web: www.coblentzpallet.com
SIC: 2448 2421 Pallets, wood; Sawmills and
planing mills, general

(G-466)
DUTCH LEGACY COMPANY LLC
Also Called: Pallet Solutions
9821 Harrison Rd (44606-9432)
PHONE..............................330 359-0270
Garrett M Roach, *Managing Member*
EMP: 8 **EST:** 2008

SQ FT: 20,000
SALES (est): 903.07K **Privately Held**
Web: www.amishfireplacedirect.com
SIC: 2511 Wood household furniture

(G-467)
ELDORADO STONE LLC
Stone Craft
167 Maple St (44606-9599)
PHONE....................................330 698-3931
Melanie Garcia, *Mgr*
EMP: 30
Web: www.eldoradostone.com
SIC: 3272 1771 Concrete products, precast, nec; Concrete work
HQ: Eldorado Stone Llc
   3817 Ocean Ranch Blvd
   Oceanside CA 92056
   800 925-1491

(G-468)
ELY ROAD REEL COMPANY LTD
9081 Ely Rd (44606-9320)
PHONE....................................330 683-1818
Marvin Weaver, *Pt*
Robert Weaver, *
EMP: 25 EST: 1987
SQ FT: 16,000
SALES (est): 2.19MM **Privately Held**
Web: www.elyroadreel.com
SIC: 2499 Spools, reels, and pulleys: wood

(G-469)
GROSS LUMBER INC
8848 Ely Rd (44606-9799)
PHONE....................................330 683-2055
Rick Grossniklaus, *Pr*
Don Grossniklaus, *
Rick Grossniklaus, *VP*
EMP: 7 EST: 1957
SQ FT: 30,000
SALES (est): 227.93K **Privately Held**
Web: www.jlgrosslumber.com
SIC: 2448 5031 5099 2426 Pallets, wood; Lumber: rough, dressed, and finished; Wood and wood by-products; Hardwood dimension and flooring mills

(G-470)
JAE TECH INC
32 Hunter St (44606-9600)
PHONE....................................330 698-2000
Ian Cameron, *Prin*
EMP: 55 EST: 2000
SQ FT: 37,500
SALES (est): 9.89MM **Privately Held**
Web: www.jaetechinc.com
SIC: 3714 Axle housings and shafts, motor vehicle

(G-471)
MILLWOOD INC
Also Called: Litco Wood Products
8208 S Kohler Rd (44606-9420)
PHONE....................................330 857-3075
Ely Miller, *Brnch Mgr*
EMP: 108
Web: www.millwoodinc.com
SIC: 2448 Pallets, wood
PA: Millwood, Inc.
   3708 International Blvd
   Vienna OH 44473

(G-472)
MILLWOOD INCORPORATED
13407 Dover Rd (44606-9387)
PHONE....................................330 704-6707
Lionel Trebilcock, *Pr*
EMP: 10 EST: 1998
SALES (est): 178.49K **Privately Held**
Web: www.millwoodinc.com

SIC: 2448 Pallets, wood

(G-473)
MOWHAWK LUMBER LTD
2931 S Carr Rd (44606-9306)
PHONE....................................330 698-5333
EMP: 20 EST: 2008
SALES (est): 446.14K **Privately Held**
Web: www.mohawklumber.com
SIC: 2421 Sawmills and planing mills, general

(G-474)
OMEGA CEMENTING CO
3776 S Millborne Rd (44606-9757)
P.O. Box 357 (44606-0357)
PHONE....................................330 695-7147
Donald Gaddis, *CEO*
EMP: 7 EST: 1986
SQ FT: 3,000
SALES (est): 926.95K **Privately Held**
SIC: 1389 1081 7349 Well plugging and abandoning, oil and gas; Metal mining exploration and development services; Cleaning service, industrial or commercial

(G-475)
PRECISION PRODUCTS GROUP INC
Also Called: Paramount Tube
339 Mill St (44606-9541)
PHONE....................................330 698-4711
EMP: 8
Web: www.paramounttube.com
SIC: 3082 3565 5113 7389 Tubes, unsupported plastics; Packaging machinery ; Paper tubes and cores; Packaging and labeling services
PA: Precision Products Group, Inc.
   8770 Guion Rd Ste A
   Indianapolis IN 46268

(G-476)
REBERLAND EQUIPMENT INC
Also Called: Firovac
5963 Fountain Nook Rd (44606-9677)
PHONE....................................330 698-5883
Larry Reber, *Pr*
Rebecca Reber, *Sec*
Valerie Lewis, *Treas*
▲ EMP: 18 EST: 1979
SQ FT: 10,000
SALES (est): 2.43MM **Privately Held**
Web: www.firovac.com
SIC: 7699 5083 3711 3713 Farm machinery repair; Agricultural machinery and equipment; Fire department vehicles (motor vehicles), assembly of; Tank truck bodies

(G-477)
ROCK DECOR COMPANY
Also Called: Casa Di Sassi
167 Maple St (44606-9599)
P.O. Box 148 (44606-0148)
PHONE....................................330 830-9760
Gary Miller, *Prin*
EMP: 35 EST: 2010
SALES (est): 5.62MM **Privately Held**
Web: www.rock-decor.com
SIC: 3272 Stone, cast concrete

(G-478)
STEIN-WAY EQUIPMENT
12335 Emerson Rd (44606-9798)
PHONE....................................330 857-8700
Oris Steiner, *Pt*
Oris Steiner, *Genl Pt*
EMP: 6 EST: 1976
SQ FT: 20,000
SALES (est): 875.19K **Privately Held**
Web: www.steinwayequipment.com

SIC: 3523 Barn, silo, poultry, dairy, and livestock machinery

(G-479)
VERSI-TECH INCORPORATED
Also Called: Versa Tech Technologies
32 Hunter St (44606-9600)
PHONE....................................586 944-2230
Ron Schroeder, *Prin*
EMP: 10 EST: 1973
SALES (est): 2.12MM
SALES (corp-wide): 21.82MM **Privately Held**
Web: www.versatechmi.com
SIC: 3599 Machine shop, jobbing and repair
PA: Mid-West Forge Corporation
   2778 S..M. Ctr Rd Ste 200
   Willoughby OH 44094
   216 481-3030

(G-480)
WAYNEDALE TRUSS AND PANEL CO
8971 Dover Rd (44606-9407)
PHONE....................................330 698-7373
James Fry, *Pr*
Diane Fry, *
EMP: 34 EST: 1978
SQ FT: 2,000
SALES (est): 297.05K **Privately Held**
Web: www.waynedaletruss.com
SIC: 2439 Trusses, wooden roof

(G-481)
WEAVER WOODCRAFT L L C
9652 Harrison Rd (44606-9623)
PHONE....................................330 695-2150
Dave Weaver, *Prin*
EMP: 9 EST: 2008
SALES (est): 225.16K **Privately Held**
SIC: 2511 Wood household furniture

Arcadia
Hancock County

(G-482)
MAASS MIDWEST MFG INC
Also Called: Dickens Foundry
19710 State Route 12 (44804-9503)
PHONE....................................419 894-6424
Mike Wedge, *Ltd Pt*
EMP: 9
SALES (corp-wide): 4.64MM **Privately Held**
Web: www.maassmidwest.com
SIC: 3366 3491 3432 Brass foundry, nec; Industrial valves; Plumbing fixture fittings and trim
PA: Maass - Midwest Mfg. Inc.
   11283 Dundee Rd
   Huntley IL 60142
   847 669-5135

(G-483)
RPM CARBIDE DIE INC
Also Called: RPM
202 E South St (44804-9773)
P.O. Box 278 (44804-0278)
PHONE....................................419 894-6426
Eric E Metcalfe, *CEO*
Joseph E Phillips, *
EMP: 38 EST: 1967
SQ FT: 18,500
SALES (est): 5.03MM **Privately Held**
Web: www.rpmcarbidedie.com
SIC: 3544 Special dies and tools

Arcanum
Darke County

(G-484)
HOFMANNS LURES INC
3937 Kilbourn Rd (45304-9732)
PHONE....................................937 684-0338
Denis Short, *Pr*
EMP: 8 EST: 1987
SALES (est): 146.57K **Privately Held**
Web: www.hofmannslures.com
SIC: 3949 Masks: hockey, baseball, football, etc.

Archbold
Fulton County

(G-485)
AMERICAN POWER PULL CORP
2022 S Defiance St (43502-9112)
P.O. Box 96 (43502-0096)
PHONE....................................419 335-7050
Edward S Kraemer, *Pr*
◆ EMP: 8 EST: 1919
SQ FT: 36,600
SALES (est): 2.45MM **Privately Held**
Web: www.americanpowerpull.com
SIC: 3423 3531 3536 Jacks: lifting, screw, or ratchet (hand tools); Winches; Hoists, cranes, and monorails

(G-486)
ARCHBOLD BUCKEYE INC
207 N Defiance St (43502-1187)
PHONE....................................419 445-4466
Ross William Taylor, *Pr*
Brent C Taylor, *VP*
Sharon S Taylor, *Sec*
EMP: 10 EST: 1905
SQ FT: 2,800
SALES (est): 259.79K **Privately Held**
Web: www.archboldbuckeye.com
SIC: 2711 Newspapers: publishing only, not printed on site

(G-487)
ARCHBOLD CONTAINER CORP
800 W Barre Rd (43502-9595)
P.O. Box 10 (43502-0010)
PHONE....................................800 446-2520
Lynn Aschliman, *Pr*
Lynn Aschliman, *Pr*
Elvin D Yoder, *
EMP: 150 EST: 1970
SQ FT: 230,000
SALES (est): 9.29MM
SALES (corp-wide): 1.87B **Privately Held**
Web: www.gbp.com
SIC: 2653 3086 Boxes, corrugated: made from purchased materials; Packaging and shipping materials, foamed plastics
PA: Green Bay Packaging Inc.
   1700 N Webster Ave
   Green Bay WI 54302
   920 433-5111

(G-488)
ARCHBOLD FURNITURE CO
733 W Barre Rd (43502-9304)
PHONE....................................567 444-4666
Pat Mcnamara, *Pr*
Pete Gstaldar, *
◆ EMP: 26 EST: 1978
SALES (est): 4.71MM **Privately Held**
Web: www.archboldfurniture.com
SIC: 5712 2511 Furniture stores; Unassembled or unfinished furniture, household: wood

(G-489)

ARROW TRU-LINE INC (PA)
2211 S Defiance St (43502-9151)
PHONE............................419 446-2785
Marvin Miller, *Pr*
Stacy Sauber, *
◆ **EMP:** 150 **EST:** 1959
SQ FT: 63,000
SALES (est): 46.8MM
SALES (corp-wide): 46.8MM **Privately Held**
Web: www.arrowtruline.com
SIC: 3469 Metal stampings, nec

(G-490)

BIL-JAX INC (DH)
Also Called: Biljax Scaffolding
125 Taylor Pkwy (43502-9123)
PHONE............................419 445-8915
◆ **EMP:** 13 **EST:** 1947
SALES (est): 24.7MM
SALES (corp-wide): 1.22MM **Privately Held**
Web: www.biljax.com
SIC: 3446 Scaffolds, mobile or stationary: metal
HQ: Haulotte Group
Rue Emile Zola
Lorette ARA 42420
477292424

(G-491)

CONAGRA BRANDS INC
La Choy Food Products Division
901 Stryker St (43502-1053)
PHONE............................419 445-8015
Ron Corkins, *Brnch Mgr*
EMP: 99
SALES (corp-wide): 12.05B **Publicly Held**
Web: www.conagrabrands.com
SIC: 2032 2099 Chinese foods, nec: packaged in cans, jars, etc.; Food preparations, nec
PA: Conagra Brands, Inc.
222 W Mdse Mart Plz Ste 1
Chicago IL 60654
312 549-5000

(G-492)

D & G WELDING INC
302 W Barre Rd (43502-1554)
PHONE............................419 445-5751
Dan Stuckey, *Pr*
Julie Stuckey, *VP*
EMP: 6 **EST:** 1956
SQ FT: 2,500
SALES (est): 512.46K **Privately Held**
Web: www.dgweldinginc.com
SIC: 7692 1796 Welding repair; Millwright

(G-493)

FM MANUFACTURING INC
300 E Mechanic St (43502-1425)
PHONE............................419 445-0700
Ron Rupp, *Pr*
EMP: 9 **EST:** 1985
SQ FT: 4,000
SALES (est): 1.34MM **Privately Held**
Web: www.fmmfg.com
SIC: 3699 Laser systems and equipment

(G-494)

FROZEN SPECIALTIES INC
Also Called: FSI
720 W Barre Rd (43502-9304)
P.O. Box 410 (43502-0410)
PHONE............................419 445-9015
Khun Anat Julintron, *CEO*
▼ **EMP:** 140 **EST:** 1969
SALES (est): 23.75MM **Privately Held**
Web: www.frozenspecialties.com

SIC: 2038 Pizza, frozen
HQ: Bellisio Foods, Inc
701 N Wash St Ste 400
Minneapolis MN 55401

(G-495)

GERALD GRAIN CENTER INC
3265 County Road 24 (43502-9415)
PHONE............................419 445-2451
Chet Phillips, *Brnch Mgr*
EMP: 15
SALES (corp-wide): 24.97MM **Privately Held**
Web: www.geraldgrain.com
SIC: 3523 5191 Elevators, farm; Animal feeds
PA: Gerald Grain Center, Inc.
14540 County Rd U
Napoleon OH 43545
419 598-8015

(G-496)

GGC FEEDS LLC
3265 County Road 24 (43502-9415)
PHONE............................419 445-2451
Todd Gerig, *Managing Member*
EMP: 22 **EST:** 2013
SALES (est): 948.52K **Privately Held**
Web: www.geraldgrain.com
SIC: 2048 Feed premixes

(G-497)

HAULOTTE NORTH AMERICA MFG LLC
125 Taylor Pkwy (43502-9122)
PHONE............................419 445-8915
Alexander Saubot, *CEO*
EMP: 6 **EST:** 2021
SALES (est): 2.66MM
SALES (corp-wide): 1.22MM **Privately Held**
Web: www.haulotte-usa.com
SIC: 3446 Scaffolds, mobile or stationary: metal
HQ: Haulotte Group
Rue Emile Zola
Lorette ARA 42420
477292424

(G-498)

HIT TROPHY INC
4989 State Route 66 (43502-9362)
PHONE............................419 445-5356
Tom Wyse, *Pr*
Abe Wyse, *Mktg Dir*
EMP: 6 **EST:** 1949
SALES (est): 792.56K **Privately Held**
Web: www.hittrophy.com
SIC: 3499 5999 2499 Trophies, metal, except silver; Trophies and plaques; Trophy bases, wood

(G-499)

LAUBER MANUFACTURING CO
3751 County Road 26 (43502-9434)
P.O. Box 175 (43502-0175)
PHONE............................419 446-2450
Bruce Lauber, *Pr*
Elizabeth Grime, *Sec*
Graeme O Lauber Junior, *Treas*
EMP: 7 **EST:** 1929
SQ FT: 43,000
SALES (est): 135.69K **Privately Held**
Web: www.lauberinsurance.org
SIC: 2511 Wood household furniture

(G-500)

LIECHTY SPECIALTIES INC
Also Called: Industrial WD Prts Fabrication
1901 S Defiance St (43502-9438)
P.O. Box 6 (43502-0006)

PHONE............................419 445-6696
Allen K Liechty, *Pr*
Virgina Liechty, *Sec*
EMP: 8 **EST:** 1965
SQ FT: 25,000
SALES (est): 438.02K **Privately Held**
Web: www.nefltd.com
SIC: 2431 Millwork

(G-501)

LOGO THIS
301 Ditto St Ste E (43502-1111)
PHONE............................419 445-1355
Dan Rychener, *Pr*
EMP: 6 **EST:** 2000
SALES (est): 166.3K **Privately Held**
Web: www.logothisohio.com
SIC: 2395 Embroidery products, except Schiffli machine

(G-502)

MERILLAT RACING LLC
22670 County Road H (43502-9757)
PHONE............................419 376-4833
Martin Merillat, *Admn*
EMP: 6 **EST:** 2014
SALES (est): 1.74MM **Privately Held**
Web: merillat-racing-llc.myshopify.com
SIC: 3714 Motor vehicle parts and accessories

(G-503)

MILLER BROS PAVING INC (HQ)
1613 S Defiance St (43502-9488)
P.O. Box 30 (43502-0030)
PHONE............................419 445-1015
Dean Miller, *Pr*
Robert Miller, *VP*
Steven A Everhart, *Sec*
Bradley Dmiller Pe, *Pr*
EMP: 10 **EST:** 1972
SQ FT: 48,000
SALES (est): 2.24MM **Privately Held**
Web: www.mbcholdings.com
SIC: 2951 Asphalt paving mixtures and blocks
PA: Mbc Holdings, Inc.
1613 S Defiance St
Archbold OH 43502

(G-504)

NAPOLEON SPRING WORKS INC (HQ)
111 Welres Dr (43502-9153)
P.O. Box 160 (43502-0160)
PHONE............................419 445-1010
Robert Shram Senior, *Pr*
◆ **EMP:** 143 **EST:** 1960
SALES (est): 25.14MM
SALES (corp-wide): 15.37MM **Privately Held**
Web: www.lynx-nsw.com
SIC: 3493 3429 Torsion bar springs; Builders' hardware
PA: Industries Lynx Inc
175 Rue Upper Edison
Saint-Lambert QC J4R 2
514 866-1068

(G-505)

NEF LTD
Also Called: Liechty Specialties
1901 S Defiance St (43502-9438)
P.O. Box 6 (43502)
PHONE............................419 445-6696
Nisha E Francis, *Pr*
EMP: 6 **EST:** 2017
SALES (est): 1.2MM **Privately Held**
Web: www.nef4u.com
SIC: 2452 Prefabricated buildings, wood

(G-506)

NOFZIGER DOOR SALES INC
111 Taylor Pkwy (43502-9309)
PHONE............................419 445-2961
Tom Rufenacht, *Mgr*
EMP: 13
SALES (corp-wide): 28.62MM **Privately Held**
Web: www.dublinohiogaragedoors.com
SIC: 3442 5211 Metal doors; Garage doors, sale and installation
PA: Nofziger Door Sales, Inc.
320 Sycamore St
Wauseon OH 43567
419 337-9900

(G-507)

P T I INC
100 Taylor Pkwy (43502-9309)
P.O. Box 53256 (43553-0256)
PHONE............................419 445-2800
Charles F Lantz, *Pr*
▲ **EMP:** 10 **EST:** 1998
SALES (est): 1.1MM **Privately Held**
Web: www.inplastech.com
SIC: 3089 Plastics processing

(G-508)

PROGRESSIVE FURNITURE INC (HQ)
Also Called: Progressive International
502 Middle St (43502-1559)
P.O. Box 308 (43502-0308)
PHONE............................419 446-4500
Dan Kendrick, *Ex VP*
John Boring, *VP Fin*
◆ **EMP:** 25 **EST:** 1985
SQ FT: 8,000
SALES (est): 23.25MM
SALES (corp-wide): 543.69MM **Privately Held**
Web: www.progressivefurniture.com
SIC: 2511 2517 5021 Bed frames, except water bed frames: wood; Home entertainment unit cabinets, wood; Tables, occasional
PA: Sauder Woodworking Co.
502 Middle St
Archbold OH 43502
419 446-2711

(G-509)

SAUDER MANUFACTURING CO (HQ)
Also Called: Wieland
930 W Barre Rd (43502-9320)
P.O. Box 230 (43502-0230)
PHONE............................419 445-7670
Virgil L Miller, *Pr*
William Ogden, *
Phil Bontrager, *
◆ **EMP:** 220 **EST:** 1945
SQ FT: 300,000
SALES (est): 44.61MM
SALES (corp-wide): 543.69MM **Privately Held**
Web: www.saudermfg.com
SIC: 2531 Church furniture
PA: Sauder Woodworking Co.
502 Middle St
Archbold OH 43502
419 446-2711

(G-510)

SAUDER WOODWORKING CO
330 N Clydes Way (43502-9170)
PHONE............................419 446-2711
EMP: 11
SALES (corp-wide): 543.69MM **Privately Held**
Web: www.sauder.com

SIC: 2519 5021 Fiberglass and plastic furniture; Furniture
PA: Sauder Woodworking Co.
502 Middle St
Archbold OH 43502
419 446-2711

(G-511)
SAUDER WOODWORKING CO (PA)
Also Called: Sauder
502 Middle St (43502-1500)
P.O. Box 156 (43502-0156)
PHONE.............................419 446-2711
Nolan Pike, *Pr*
Patrick Sauder, *
◆ **EMP:** 2100 **EST:** 1934
SQ FT: 5,000,000
SALES (est): 543.69MM
SALES (corp-wide): 543.69MM **Privately Held**
Web: www.sauder.com
SIC: 5021 2512 Household furniture; Upholstered household furniture

(G-512)
SYSTECH HANDLING INC
120 Taylor Pkwy (43502-9309)
PHONE.............................419 445-8226
Wendell Lantz, *Pr*
Mike Waidelich, *VP*
EMP: 12 **EST:** 1999
SQ FT: 12,500
SALES (est): 6.1MM **Privately Held**
Web: www.systechhandling.com
SIC: 3599 8711 7692 3444 Custom machinery; Engineering services; Welding repair; Sheet metalwork

(G-513)
YODER & FREY INC
3649 County Road 24 (43502-9317)
P.O. Box 155 (43502-0155)
PHONE.............................419 445-2070
Robert Frey, *Pr*
EMP: 8 **EST:** 1947
SQ FT: 12,000
SALES (est): 979.35K **Privately Held**
Web: www.yoderandfreyfarm.com
SIC: 5083 3523 Agricultural machinery and equipment; Farm machinery and equipment

Ashland
Ashland County

(G-514)
ACTIVE METAL AND MOLDS INC
2219 Cottage St (44805-1296)
PHONE.............................419 281-9623
▲ **EMP:** 12
Web: www.activemetalinc.com
SIC: 3444 3449 3599 7692 Sheet metalwork; Miscellaneous metalwork; Machine shop, jobbing and repair; Welding repair

(G-515)
ALTEC INDUSTRIES
1236 Township Road 1175 (44805-1979)
PHONE.............................419 289-6066
Bob Donaldson, *Prin*
EMP: 8 **EST:** 2005
SALES (est): 398.52K **Privately Held**
Web: www.kualerts.com
SIC: 3531 Construction machinery

(G-516)
ASHLAND PRECISION TOOLING LLC
1750 S Baney Rd (44805-3522)
P.O. Box 129 (44691-0129)
PHONE.............................419 289-1736

EMP: 21 **EST:** 2002
SQ FT: 56,000
SALES (est): 1.01MM **Privately Held**
Web: www.ashlandprecisiontooling.com
SIC: 3599 Machine shop, jobbing and repair

(G-517)
ASHLAND PUBLISHING CO
Also Called: Ashland Times Gazette
40 E 2nd St (44805-2304)
P.O. Box 693 (44805-0693)
PHONE.............................419 281-0581
Timothy Dix, *Sec*
G Charles Dix Ii, *Treas*
Troy Dix, *
EMP: 533 **EST:** 1850
SQ FT: 12,400
SALES (est): 1.3MM
SALES (corp-wide): 38.43MM **Privately Held**
Web: www.times-gazette.com
SIC: 2711 Newspapers, publishing and printing
PA: Dix 1898, Inc.
212 E Liberty St
Wooster OH
330 264-3511

(G-518)
ASHLAND WATER GROUP INC (PA)
1191 Commerce Pkwy (44805-8955)
PHONE.............................877 326-3561
Larry Donelson, *Pr*
Jody Bartter, *Treas*
▲ **EMP:** 7 **EST:** 2008
SALES (est): 8.16MM
SALES (corp-wide): 8.16MM **Privately Held**
Web: www.ashlandpump.com
SIC: 3561 Pumps and pumping equipment

(G-519)
ATLAS BOLT & SCREW COMPANY LLC (DH)
Also Called: Atlas Fasteners For Cnstr
1628 Troy Rd (44805-1398)
PHONE.............................419 289-6171
Robert W Moore, *Pr*
Robert C Gluth, *
Robert Webb, *
▲ **EMP:** 175 **EST:** 1986
SQ FT: 75,000
SALES (est): 47.18MM
SALES (corp-wide): 424.23B **Publicly Held**
Web: www.atlasfasteners.com
SIC: 3452 5085 5051 5072 Washers, metal; Fasteners, industrial: nuts, bolts, screws, etc.; Metals service centers and offices; Hardware
HQ: Marmon Group Llc
181 W Madison St Ste 3900
Chicago IL 60602
312 372-9500

(G-520)
BARBASOL LLC
2011 Ford Dr (44805-1277)
PHONE.............................419 903-0738
▲ **EMP:** 36 **EST:** 2009
SQ FT: 80,000
SALES (est): 34.57MM
SALES (corp-wide): 34.57MM **Privately Held**
Web: www.barbasol.com
SIC: 2844 Toilet preparations
PA: Perio, Inc.
6156 Wilcox Rd
Dublin OH 43016
614 791-1207

(G-521)
BENDON INC (PA)
1840 S Baney Rd (44805-3524)
PHONE.............................419 207-3600
Benjamin Ferguson, *CEO*
Benjamin Ferguson, *Pr*
Terry Gerwig, *
Jenny Hastings, *
David Swank, *
▲ **EMP:** 54 **EST:** 2001
SQ FT: 220,000
SALES (est): 25.02MM
SALES (corp-wide): 25.02MM **Privately Held**
Web: www.bendonpub.com
SIC: 5999 5961 5092 2731 Educational aids and electronic training materials; Educational supplies and equipment, mail order; Educational toys; Books, publishing only

(G-522)
BOOKMASTERS INC (HQ)
Also Called: Baker & Taylor Publisher Svcs
30 Amberwood Pkwy (44805-9765)
PHONE.............................419 281-1802
Raymond Sevin, *Pr*
Thomas Wurster, *
◆ **EMP:** 157 **EST:** 1972
SQ FT: 180,000
SALES (est): 20.99MM **Privately Held**
Web: www.btpubservices.com
SIC: 7389 2752 2731 2791 Printers' services: folding, collating, etc.; Commercial printing, lithographic; Book publishing; Typesetting
PA: Baker & Taylor, Llc
2810 Clseum Cntre Dr Ste
Charlotte NC 28217

(G-523)
BOR-IT MFG CO INC
1687 Cleveland Rd (44805-1929)
P.O. Box 789 (44805-0789)
PHONE.............................419 289-6639
Michael W Albers, *Pr*
Michelle Albers, *Sec*
▼ **EMP:** 20 **EST:** 1987
SQ FT: 12,500
SALES (est): 3.8MM **Privately Held**
Web: www.bor-it.com
SIC: 3541 Drilling and boring machines

(G-524)
BOSTIK INC
1745 Cottage St (44805-1237)
PHONE.............................419 289-9588
Barry Sheets, *Brnch Mgr*
EMP: 22
SALES (corp-wide): 134.78MM **Privately Held**
Web: www.bostik.com
SIC: 2891 Adhesives and sealants
HQ: Bostik, Inc.
11320 W Wtertown Plank Rd
Wauwatosa WI 53226
414 774-2250

(G-525)
CABINET RESTYLERS INC
Also Called: Cabinet Restylers
419 E 8th St (44805-1953)
PHONE.............................419 281-8449
Eric Thiel, *Pr*
Denise Appleby, *VP*
EMP: 56 **EST:** 1968
SQ FT: 50,000
SALES (est): 4.57MM **Privately Held**
Web: www.thiels.com

SIC: 1751 2541 5211 1799 Window and door (prefabricated) installation; Cabinets, lockers, and shelving; Cabinets, kitchen; Bathtub refinishing

(G-526)
CENTERRA CO-OP (PA)
813 Clark Ave (44805-1967)
PHONE.............................419 281-2153
Jean Bratton, *CEO*
William Bullock, *
EMP: 30 **EST:** 2003
SALES (est): 174.64MM
SALES (corp-wide): 174.64MM **Privately Held**
Web: www.centerracoop.com
SIC: 5983 5261 5999 2048 Fuel oil dealers; Fertilizer; Feed and farm supply; Bird food, prepared

(G-527)
CERTIFIED LABS & SERVICE INC
535 E 7th St (44805-2553)
PHONE.............................419 289-7462
Gary E Funkhouser, *Pr*
Michael C Huber, *VP*
Harret Funkhouser, *Treas*
Pam Huber, *Sec*
EMP: 6 **EST:** 1984
SQ FT: 5,000
SALES (est): 257.28K **Privately Held**
Web: www.certifiedlabsservice.com
SIC: 7699 3822 3561 Pumps and pumping equipment repair; Hydronic controls; Pumps, domestic: water or sump

(G-528)
CHANDLER SYSTEMS INCORPORATED
Also Called: Best Controls Company
710 Orange St (44805-1725)
PHONE.............................888 363-9434
William Chandler III, *Pr*
Polly Chandler, *
Bill Chandler, *
▲ **EMP:** 65 **EST:** 1993
SQ FT: 52,000
SALES (est): 20.61MM **Privately Held**
Web: www.chandlersystemsinc.com
SIC: 5074 3625 Water purification equipment ; Relays and industrial controls

(G-529)
CITY OF ASHLAND
City Services
310 W 12th St (44805-1756)
P.O. Box Remont Ave (44805)
PHONE.............................419 289-8728
Jerry Mack, *Dir*
EMP: 9
SALES (corp-wide): 35.24MM **Privately Held**
Web: www.ashland-ohio.com
SIC: 3589 Garbage disposers and compactors, commercial
PA: City Of Ashland
206 Claremont Ave
Ashland OH 44805
419 289-8170

(G-530)
CONERY MANUFACTURING INC
1380 Township Road 743 (44805-8926)
PHONE.............................419 289-1444
Scott Conery, *Pr*
Chris Shafer, *VP*
▲ **EMP:** 16 **EST:** 1979
SQ FT: 24,000
SALES (est): 3.41MM **Privately Held**
Web: www.conerymfg.com

SIC: **3822** Liquid level controls, residential or commercial heating

(G-531)
CRAZY MONKEY BAKING INC
1191 Commerce Pkwy (44805-8955)
PHONE.....................419 903-0403
David Vespor, *Pr*
David Vesper, *Pr*
Jody Bartter, *Treas*
▲ **EMP:** 8 **EST:** 2007
SALES (est): 8.01MM
SALES (corp-wide): 8.16MM **Privately Held**
Web: www.crazymonkeybaking.com
SIC: **2064** Candy and other confectionery products
PA: Ashland Water Group, Inc.
1191 Commerce Pkwy
Ashland OH 44805
877 326-3561

(G-532)
CUSTOM HOISTS INC (HQ)
771 County Road 30a (44805-9227)
PHONE.....................419 368-4721
Rick Hiltunen, *Pr*
▲ **EMP:** 165 **EST:** 1973
SQ FT: 110,000
SALES (est): 19.26MM
SALES (corp-wide): 720.63MM **Publicly Held**
Web: www.customhoists.com
SIC: **3593** Fluid power cylinders and actuators
PA: Standex International Corporation
23 Keewaydin Dr
Salem NH 03079
603 893-9701

(G-533)
DRAWNEAR INC
228 N Countryside Dr (44805-3934)
PHONE.....................567 215-5305
Robert Beer, *Pr*
EMP: 6 **EST:** 2002
SALES (est): 365.65K **Privately Held**
Web: www.drawnear.com
SIC: **2741** Miscellaneous publishing

(G-534)
FARR AUTOMATION INC
58 Sugarbush Ct (44805-9737)
PHONE.....................419 209-1000
Ross Farr, *Pr*
Karen Farr, *Sec*
EMP: 6 **EST:** 1999
SQ FT: 26,000
SALES (est): 995.77K **Privately Held**
Web: www.farrautomation.com
SIC: **3599** Custom machinery

(G-535)
FOLLETT HGHER EDCATN GROUP INC
Also Called: Baker & Taylor Publisher Svcs
30 Amberwood Pkwy (44805-9765)
PHONE.....................419 281-5100
Bob Gospodarek, *Sr VP*
EMP: 180
SALES (corp-wide): 906.01MM **Privately Held**
Web: www.btpubservices.com
SIC: **2731** Book publishing
PA: Follett Higher Education Group, Llc
3 Westbrook Corp Ctr Ste
Westchester IL 60154
800 365-5388

(G-536)
GENCO
1250 George Rd (44805-8916)
PHONE.....................419 207-7648
EMP: 6 **EST:** 2014
SALES (est): 822.48K **Privately Held**
Web: www.genco.us
SIC: **1389** Oil field services, nec

(G-537)
HARRIS WELDING AND MACHINE CO
2219 Cottage St (44805-1296)
P.O. Box 317 (44805-0317)
PHONE.....................419 281-8351
John Kochenderfer, *Pr*
Tracy Kochenderfer, *Sec*
EMP: 10 **EST:** 1964
SQ FT: 7,500
SALES (est): 1.73MM **Privately Held**
Web: www.machlev.com.br
SIC: **7692** 3599 Welding repair; Machine shop, jobbing and repair

(G-538)
HEDSTROM PLASTICS LLC
100 Hedstrom Dr (44805-3586)
PHONE.....................419 289-9310
Rod Mitchell, *
Scott Conery, *
EMP: 75 **EST:** 2020
SALES (est): 7.07MM **Privately Held**
Web: www.hedstromplastics.com
SIC: **3086** Plastics foam products

(G-539)
HERITAGE PRESS INC
Also Called: Northcoast Advertising
651 Sandusky St (44805-1524)
PHONE.....................419 289-9209
Ramon Dever, *Pr*
EMP: 20 **EST:** 1959
SQ FT: 6,000
SALES (est): 458.49K **Privately Held**
Web: www.heritagepressinc.com
SIC: **2752** 2791 Offset printing; Typesetting, computer controlled

(G-540)
HILLMAN PRECISION INC
462 E 9th St Ste 1 (44805-1923)
PHONE.....................419 289-1557
Geoff Hillman Senior, *CEO*
Geoff Hillman Junior, *Pr*
EMP: 16 **EST:** 1991
SQ FT: 37,000
SALES (est): 1.76MM **Privately Held**
Web: www.hillmanprecision.com
SIC: **3599** Machine shop, jobbing and repair

(G-541)
HYDROMATIC PUMPS INC
1101 Myers Pkwy (44805-1969)
PHONE.....................419 289-1144
Keith Lang, *Pr*
▼ **EMP:** 6 **EST:** 1959
SALES (est): 654.4K **Privately Held**
Web: www.hydromatic.com
SIC: **3561** Pumps and pumping equipment

(G-542)
JUST NAME IT INC
110 Hedstrom Dr (44805-3586)
PHONE.....................614 626-8662
Joe Grubbs, *Pr*
EMP: 7 **EST:** 2010
SALES (est): 107.08K **Privately Held**
Web: just-name-it.square.site
SIC: **2759** Screen printing

(G-543)
KAR-DEL PLASTICS INC
1177 Faultless Dr (44805-1250)
PHONE.....................419 289-9739
Scott Pay, *Pr*
Shari L Regan, *VP*
Teresa Pay, *Sec*
EMP: 8 **EST:** 1984
SQ FT: 14,000
SALES (est): 915.3K **Privately Held**
Web: www.kar-delplastics.com
SIC: **3089** Plastics and fiberglass tanks

(G-544)
KEEN PUMP COMPANY INC
Also Called: Keen Pump
471 E State Rte 250 E (44805)
PHONE.....................419 207-9400
Gregory W Keener, *Pr*
Frank Yuhafz, *
Suzzanne Keener, *
Jacob Studer, *
▲ **EMP:** 35 **EST:** 2007
SQ FT: 100,000
SALES (est): 5.06MM **Privately Held**
Web: www.keenpump.com
SIC: **3561** Pumps and pumping equipment

(G-545)
KEHL-KOLOR INC
824 Us Highway 42 (44805-9516)
P.O. Box 770 (44805-0770)
PHONE.....................419 281-3107
Jon B Kehl, *Pr*
Mark Kehl, *
▲ **EMP:** 32 **EST:** 1971
SQ FT: 60,000
SALES (est): 1.6MM **Privately Held**
Web: www.kehlkolor.com
SIC: **2752** 2796 2791 2789 Offset printing; Lithographic plates, positives or negatives; Typesetting; Bookbinding and related work

(G-546)
KENAG INC
101 E 7th St (44805-1702)
P.O. Box 326 (44805-0326)
PHONE.....................419 281-1204
Doug Patton, *Pr*
▲ **EMP:** 21 **EST:** 1997
SQ FT: 35,000
SALES (est): 4.81MM **Privately Held**
Web: www.kenag.com
SIC: **2621** 6086 Milk filter disks; Filters, industrial

(G-547)
KNOWLTON MACHINE INC
726 Virginia Ave (44805-1944)
P.O. Box 656 (44805-0656)
PHONE.....................419 281-6802
James Knowlton, *Pr*
EMP: 6 **EST:** 1988
SQ FT: 6,000
SALES (est): 688.29K **Privately Held**
Web: www.knowltonmachine.com
SIC: **3599** 1799 Machine shop, jobbing and repair; Welding on site

(G-548)
LAKE ERIE FROZEN FOODS MFG CO
1830 Orange Rd (44805-1335)
PHONE.....................419 289-9204
Mike Buckingham, *CEO*
William Buckingham, *
Mike Buckingham, *VP*
▲ **EMP:** 80 **EST:** 1962
SQ FT: 30,000
SALES (est): 9.12MM **Privately Held**
Web: www.leffco.net

SIC: **2038** 2037 2022 Snacks, incl. onion rings, cheese sticks, etc.; Vegetables, quick frozen & cold pack, excl. potato products; Cheese; natural and processed

(G-549)
LIQUI-BOX CORPORATION
Also Called: Bag & Bottle Manufacturing
1817 Masters Ave (44805-1291)
PHONE.....................419 289-9696
Sheff Sweet, *Brnch Mgr*
EMP: 46
SALES (corp-wide): 5.39B **Publicly Held**
Web: www.liquibox.com
SIC: **2673** 3089 3081 2671 Plastic bags: made from purchased materials; Plastics processing; Unsupported plastics film and sheet; Paper; coated and laminated packaging
HQ: Liqui-Box Corporation
2415 Cascade Pointe Blvd
Charlotte NC 28208
804 325-1400

(G-550)
MAVERICK INNVTIVE SLUTIONS LLC
Also Called: Mis
532 County Road 1600 (44805-9207)
PHONE.....................419 281-7944
James Dygert, *Rep*
Todd Meldrum, *Rep*
◆ **EMP:** 75 **EST:** 1937
SQ FT: 50,000
SALES (est): 2.92MM **Privately Held**
SIC: **3556** 3585 Food products machinery; Refrigeration and heating equipment

(G-551)
MCGRAW-HILL SCHL EDCATN HLDNGS
Also Called: Mc Graw-Hill Educational Pubg
1250 George Rd (44805-8916)
PHONE.....................419 207-7400
Maryellen Valaitis, *Prin*
EMP: 750
Web: www.mheducation.com
SIC: **2731** 5192 Books, publishing and printing; Books, periodicals, and newspapers
HQ: Mcgraw-Hill School Education Holdings, Llc
2 Penn Plz Fl 20
New York NY 10121
646 766-2000

(G-552)
MIDWEST CONVEYOR PRODUCTS INC
Also Called: Ashland Conveyor Products
1919 Cellar Dr (44805-1275)
PHONE.....................419 281-1235
William Waltz, *Pr*
Tim Swineford, *VP*
EMP: 23 **EST:** 1998
SQ FT: 50,000
SALES (est): 6.83MM **Privately Held**
Web: www.ashlandconveyor.com
SIC: **5084** 3535 Conveyor systems; Belt conveyor systems, general industrial use

(G-553)
MORITZ MATERIALS INC (PA)
859 Faultless Dr (44805-1274)
P.O. Box 392 (44805-0392)
PHONE.....................419 281-0575
James Moritz, *Pr*
Joseph Moritz, *VP*
EMP: 22 **EST:** 1985
SQ FT: 2,000
SALES (est): 2.45MM
SALES (corp-wide): 2.45MM **Privately Held**

Web: www.moritzmaterials.com
SIC: 3273 5032 Ready-mixed concrete;
   Concrete building products

(G-554)
MP TECHNOLOGIES INC
Also Called: Manufacturing Process Tech
532 County Road 1600 (44805-9207)
PHONE.............................440 838-4466
Paul Takacs, *Pr*
Laraine Takacs, *VP*
EMP: 17 **EST:** 1985
SALES (est): 3.9MM **Privately Held**
Web: www.mptechnologiesltd.com
SIC: 3463 Machinery forgings, nonferrous

(G-555)
NOVATEX NORTH AMERICA INC
1070 Faultless Dr (44805-1247)
PHONE.............................419 282-4264
Michael Donofrio, *Pr*
▲ **EMP:** 55 **EST:** 2006
SALES (est): 8.32MM
SALES (corp-wide): 448.67K **Privately
Held**
Web: www.novatex.us
SIC: 3069 3085 3089 Nipples, rubber;
   Plastics bottles; Injection molded finished
   plastics products, nec
HQ: Novatex Gmbh
   Werner-Von-Siemens-Str. 14
   Pattensen NI 30982
   510191950

(G-556)
OHIO CARBON INDUSTRIES INC
1201 Jacobson Ave (44805-1842)
PHONE.............................888 248-5029
Will Reineke, *Pr*
Will Reineke, *Owner*
EMP: 25 **EST:** 1988
SALES (est): 4.9MM **Privately Held**
Web: www.ohiocarbon.com
SIC: 3624 Carbon and graphite products

(G-557)
OHIO TOOL WORK LLC ✪
1374 Township Road 743 (44805-8926)
PHONE.............................419 281-3700
David Boliantz, *Genl Mgr*
EMP: 40 **EST:** 2024
SALES (est): 1.91MM **Privately Held**
SIC: 3541 Grinding, polishing, buffing,
   lapping, and honing machines

(G-558)
OHIO TOOL WORKS LLC
1374 Township Road 743 743
(44805-8926)
EMP: 59 **EST:** 2004
SQ FT: 45,000
SALES (est): 8.64MM **Privately Held**
Web: www.ohiotoolworks.com
SIC: 3599 Machine shop, jobbing and repair
HQ: Hardinge Inc.
   One Hardinge Dr
   Elmira NY 14902
   607 734-2281

(G-559)
**PACKAGING CORPORATION
AMERICA**
Also Called: Pca/Ashland 307
929 Faultless Dr (44805-1246)
P.O. Box 367 (44805-0367)
PHONE.............................419 282-5809
Jeff Kaser, *Brnch Mgr*
EMP: 110
SALES (corp-wide): 7.73B **Publicly Held**
Web: www.packagingcorp.com

SIC: 2653 Boxes, corrugated: made from
   purchased materials
PA: Packaging Corporation Of America
   1 N Field Ct
   Lake Forest IL 60045
   847 482-3000

(G-560)
PENTAIR PUMP GROUP INC
740 E 9th St (44805-1954)
PHONE.............................419 281-9918
EMP: 16 **EST:** 1985
SALES (est): 784.59K **Privately Held**
Web: www.pentair.com
SIC: 3561 Pumps and pumping equipment

(G-561)
PHILWAY PRODUCTS INC
521 E 7th St (44805-2553)
PHONE.............................419 281-7777
EMP: 195
Web: www.philway.com
SIC: 3672 Printed circuit boards

(G-562)
PIONEER NATIONAL LATEX INC
114 E 7th St (44805-1701)
PHONE.............................419 289-3300
Daniel Derick, *Brnch Mgr*
EMP: 70
SALES (corp-wide): 89.59MM **Privately
Held**
Web: www.pioneernational.com
SIC: 3069 Toys, rubber
HQ: Pioneer National Latex, Inc.
   246 E Fourth St
   Wichita KS 67220
   419 289-3300

(G-563)
PIONEER NATIONAL LATEX INC
Also Called: Packaging Department
244 Commercial Ave (44805)
PHONE.............................419 289-3300
Vernon Gilmore, *Brnch Mgr*
EMP: 20
SALES (corp-wide): 89.59MM **Privately
Held**
Web: www.pioneernational.com
SIC: 3069 3944 Toys, rubber; Games, toys,
   and children's vehicles
HQ: Pioneer National Latex, Inc.
   246 E Fourth St
   Wichita KS 67220
   419 289-3300

(G-564)
PLAID HAT GAMES
1172 State Route 96 (44805-1071)
PHONE.............................419 552-5490
Colby Dauch, *CEO*
EMP: 8 **EST:** 2020
SALES (est): 472.44K **Privately Held**
Web: www.plaidhatgames.com
SIC: 3944 Board games, puzzles, and
   models, except electronic

(G-565)
PLAID HAT GAMES LLC
1172 State Route 96 (44805-1071)
PHONE.............................419 552-5490
Colby Dauch, *CEO*
EMP: 8 **EST:** 2020
SALES (est): 465.54K **Privately Held**
Web: www.plaidhatgames.com
SIC: 3944 Board games, puzzles, and
   models, except electronic

(G-566)
PRECISION DESIGN INC
Also Called: Ohio Electric Control
2221 Ford Dr (44805-1280)
PHONE.............................419 289-1553
Robert Mcmullen, *Pr*
EMP: 6 **EST:** 1995
SALES (est): 2.45MM **Privately Held**
Web: www.ohioelectriccontrol.com
SIC: 3621 Control equipment for electric
   buses and locomotives

(G-567)
PWP INC
532 County Road 1600 (44805-9207)
PHONE.............................216 251-2181
Micheal Hooper, *CEO*
▲ **EMP:** 45 **EST:** 1953
SALES (est): 1.91MM
SALES (corp-wide): 16.97MM **Privately
Held**
Web: www.progresswire.com
SIC: 3496 Miscellaneous fabricated wire
   products
PA: Tahoma Enterprises, Inc.
   255 Wooster Rd N
   Barberton OH 44203
   330 745-9016

(G-568)
R & J AG MANUFACTURING INC
Also Called: All-Plant Liquid Plant Food
821 State Route 511 (44805-9562)
PHONE.............................419 962-4707
Roger D Shopbell, *Pr*
James Shopbell, *Treas*
Joan Shopbell, *VP*
Pam Tobias, *Sec*
EMP: 10 **EST:** 1982
SQ FT: 5,000
SALES (est): 861.22K **Privately Held**
SIC: 2873 5999 Nitrogenous fertilizers; Farm
   equipment and supplies

(G-569)
RAIN DROP PRODUCTS LLC
2121 Cottage St (44805-1245)
PHONE.............................419 207-1229
Mark Williams, *Pr*
Michael Hooper, *
James Cox, *
◆ **EMP:** 30 **EST:** 1999
SQ FT: 30,000
SALES (est): 7.25MM **Privately Held**
Web: www.rain-drop.com
SIC: 3949 Water sports equipment

(G-570)
RETURN POLYMERS INC
400 Westlake Dr (44805-1397)
PHONE.............................419 289-1998
David Foell, *Pr*
EMP: 65 **EST:** 1992
SQ FT: 26,000
SALES (est): 4.4MM
SALES (corp-wide): 1.44B **Publicly Held**
Web: www.returnpolymers.com
SIC: 2821 Plastics materials and resins
PA: The Azek Company Inc
   1330 W Fulton St Ste 350
   Chicago IL 60607
   877 275-2935

(G-571)
ROTOSOLUTIONS INC
1401 Jacobson Ave (44805-1846)
PHONE.............................419 903-0800
Ralph Kirkpatrick, *CEO*
EMP: 12 **EST:** 2013
SALES (est): 4.76MM **Privately Held**
Web: www.rotosolutions.com

SIC: 3089 Injection molding of plastics

(G-572)
SCHOONOVER INDUSTRIES INC
1440 Simonton Rd (44805-1906)
P.O. Box 69 (44805-0069)
PHONE.............................419 289-8332
Robert P Schoonover, *Pr*
EMP: 19 **EST:** 1983
SQ FT: 12,000
SALES (est): 3.56MM **Privately Held**
Web: www.schoonoveronline.com
SIC: 3441 3444 Fabricated structural metal;
   Sheet metalwork

(G-573)
SEPTIC PRODUCTS INC
1378 Township Road 743 (44805-8926)
PHONE.............................419 282-5933
Rod Mitchell, *Pr*
EMP: 8 **EST:** 2005
SALES (est): 2.49MM **Privately Held**
Web: www.septicproducts.com
SIC: 3272 Septic tanks, concrete

(G-574)
SJE RHOMBUS CONTROLS
2221 Ford Dr (44805-1280)
PHONE.............................419 281-5767
Vic Olivieri, *Prin*
EMP: 15 **EST:** 2018
SALES (est): 4.21MM **Privately Held**
Web: www.sjeinc.com
SIC: 3822 Environmental controls

(G-575)
STEEL CITY CORPORATION (PA)
100 Hedstrom Dr (44805-3586)
P.O. Box 1227 (44501-1227)
PHONE.............................330 792-7663
Chris Shafer, *Pr*
Rod Mitchell, *Prin*
Scott Conery, *Prin*
◆ **EMP:** 20 **EST:** 1939
SALES (est): 472.14K
SALES (corp-wide): 472.14K **Privately
Held**
Web: www.scity.com
SIC: 2678 Newsprint tablets and pads: made
   from purchased materials

(G-576)
STRAIGHTAWAY FABRICATIONS LTD
481us Highway 250 E (44805-9771)
PHONE.............................419 281-9440
David Bowles, *Pr*
EMP: 11 **EST:** 2004
SQ FT: 1,500
SALES (est): 4.12MM **Privately Held**
Web: www.straightawayfab.com
SIC: 3441 Fabricated structural metal

(G-577)
SUPPRESSOR CO LLC
Also Called: Hop Munitions
2004 State Route 60 (44805-9260)
PHONE.............................330 749-5234
Shawn Payne, *Managing Member*
EMP: 8 **EST:** 2022
SALES (est): 1.34MM **Privately Held**
SIC: 3999 Manufacturing industries, nec

(G-578)
**TAHOMA ENGINEERED SOLUTIONS
INC**
Also Called: Tahoma Engineered Solutions
532 County Road 1600 (44805-9207)
PHONE.............................330 345-6169
EMP: 29 **EST:** 1966
SALES (est): 5.11MM **Privately Held**

▲ = Import ▼ = Export
◆ = Import/Export

Web: www.waynemachineinc.com
SIC: 3599 Machine shop, jobbing and repair

(G-579)
TAHOMA RUBBER & PLASTICS INC (HQ)
Also Called: Rondy & Co.
532 County Road 1600 (44805-9207)
PHONE...............................330 745-9016
William P Herrington, *CEO*
◆ **EMP:** 100 **EST:** 1965
SALES (est): 8.41MM
SALES (corp-wide): 16.97MM **Privately Held**
Web: www.tahomarubberplastics.com
SIC: 3069 3089 5199 5162 Reclaimed rubber (reworked by manufacturing processes); Plastics processing; Foams and rubber; Plastics products, nec
PA: Tahoma Enterprises, Inc.
255 Wooster Rd N
Barberton OH 44203
330 745-9016

(G-580)
TREMCO CPG INC
1451 Jacobson Ave (44805-1865)
PHONE...............................419 289-2050
James Mongiardo, *Brnch Mgr*
EMP: 124
SALES (corp-wide): 7.34B **Publicly Held**
Web: www.tremcosealants.com
SIC: 2891 Adhesives and sealants
HQ: Tremco Cpg Inc.
3735 Green Rd
Beachwood OH 44122
216 292-5000

(G-581)
ZEPHYR INDUSTRIES INC
600 Township Road 1500 (44805-9759)
PHONE...............................419 281-4485
Vincent Richilano, *Pr*
David E Richilano, *Sec*
EMP: 8 **EST:** 1958
SQ FT: 20,000
SALES (est): 883.94K **Privately Held**
Web: www.zephyrindustries.com
SIC: 3365 3569 3599 Machinery castings, aluminum; Firefighting and related equipment; Machine shop, jobbing and repair

Ashley
Delaware County

(G-582)
IMPERIAL ON-PECE FIBRGLS POOLS
255 S Franklin St (43003-9749)
PHONE...............................740 747-2971
TOLL FREE: 800
Charles Levings Junior, *Pr*
Carol Mash, *VP*
Glen Mash, *Prin*
John Mash, *Prin*
EMP: 10 **EST:** 1969
SQ FT: 10,000
SALES (est): 175.57K **Privately Held**
SIC: 3949 1799 Swimming pools, except plastic; Swimming pool construction

(G-583)
ROTARY PRODUCTS INC
202 W High St (43003-9703)
P.O. Box 370 (43003-0370)
PHONE...............................740 747-2623
Chris Buechel, *Pr*
EMP: 15

SALES (corp-wide): 4.58MM **Privately Held**
Web: www.rotaryproductsinc.com
SIC: 3081 Unsupported plastics film and sheet
PA: Rotary Products, Inc.
117 E High St
Ashley OH 43003
740 747-2623

(G-584)
ROTARY PRODUCTS INC (PA)
117 E High St (43003)
P.O. Box 370 (43003-0370)
PHONE...............................740 747-2623
Christopher Buechel, *Pr*
EMP: 14 **EST:** 1958
SQ FT: 9,000
SALES (est): 4.58MM
SALES (corp-wide): 4.58MM **Privately Held**
Web: www.rotaryproductsinc.com
SIC: 3081 Vinyl film and sheet

Ashtabula
Ashtabula County

(G-585)
AAM MOLD AND MACHINE INC
1015 Westwood Dr (44004-2369)
PHONE...............................440 998-2040
Anthony Martino, *Pr*
EMP: 16 **EST:** 2010
SALES (est): 2.75MM **Privately Held**
Web: www.aammold.com
SIC: 3599 Machine shop, jobbing and repair

(G-586)
AKALINA ASSOCIATES INC
2751 West Ave (44004-3117)
P.O. Box 398 (44005-0398)
PHONE...............................440 992-2195
Nicholas J Jammal, *Pr*
▲ **EMP:** 200 **EST:** 1945
SQ FT: 72,000
SALES (est): 21.98MM **Privately Held**
Web: www.ashtabularubber.com
SIC: 3061 3069 3053 Mechanical rubber goods; Hard rubber and molded rubber products; Gaskets, all materials

(G-587)
CICOGNA ELECTRIC AND SIGN CO (PA)
Also Called: Cicogna
4330 N Bend Rd (44004-9797)
P.O. Box 234 (44005-0234)
PHONE...............................440 998-2637
Frank Cicogna, *Pr*
James M Timonere, *
EMP: 75 **EST:** 1975
SQ FT: 55,000
SALES (est): 4.6MM
SALES (corp-wide): 4.6MM **Privately Held**
Web: www.cicognasign.com
SIC: 3993 Neon signs

(G-588)
CREATIVE MILLWORK OHIO INC
1801 W 47th St (44004-5425)
P.O. Box 1157 (44005-1157)
PHONE...............................440 992-3566
Joseph J Lalli, *COO*
Brian A Estock, *
Cynthia Estock, *
Joann Andersen, *
EMP: 80 **EST:** 1987
SQ FT: 67,000
SALES (est): 14MM **Privately Held**

Web: www.creativemillwork.com
SIC: 3089 3442 Window frames and sash, plastics; Window and door frames

(G-589)
CUSTOM CRAFT COLLECTION INC
Also Called: Russel Upholstery
5422 Main Ave (44004-7058)
PHONE...............................440 998-3000
TOLL FREE: 888
Dusty Russell, *Pr*
EMP: 10 **EST:** 1994
SQ FT: 10,000
SALES (est): 86.64K **Privately Held**
Web: www.russellupholstery.com
SIC: 2512 7641 2522 Upholstered household furniture; Reupholstery and furniture repair; Office furniture, except wood

(G-590)
ELCO CORPORATION
Also Called: Elco Corporation
1100 State Rd (44004-3943)
PHONE...............................440 997-6131
Tom Steiv, *Mgr*
EMP: 28
Web: www.lubeperformanceadditives.com
SIC: 2869 2819 2899 Industrial organic chemicals, nec; Industrial inorganic chemicals, nec; Chemical preparations, nec
HQ: Elco Corporation
1000 Belt Line Ave
Cleveland OH 44109
800 321-0467

(G-591)
ESAB GROUP INCORPORATED
3325 Middle Rd (44004-3974)
P.O. Box 943 (44005-0943)
PHONE...............................440 813-2506
Cheri Houser, *Prin*
EMP: 6 **EST:** 2016
SALES (est): 396.78K **Privately Held**
SIC: 3356 Nonferrous rolling and drawing, nec

(G-592)
FREZERVE INC
1218 Lake Ave (44004-2932)
P.O. Box 890 (44005-0890)
PHONE...............................440 661-4037
David Hellmer, *Pr*
EMP: 0 **EST:** 2021
SALES (est): 500K **Privately Held**
SIC: 2034 2095 Fruits, freeze-dried; Freeze-dried coffee

(G-593)
G M R TECHNOLOGY INC
2131 Aetna Rd (44004-6291)
PHONE...............................440 992-6003
Connie J Speakman, *Prin*
Peter P Zawaly Junior, *Prin*
◆ **EMP:** 30 **EST:** 1984
SQ FT: 45,000
SALES (est): 2.13MM **Privately Held**
Web: www.zehrco-giancola.com
SIC: 3089 Injection molding of plastics

(G-594)
GRAND RIVER RUBBER & PLASTICS COMPANY
2029 Aetna Rd (44004-6298)
P.O. Box 477 (44005-0477)
PHONE...............................440 998-2900
◆ **EMP:** 200 **EST:** 1976
SALES (est): 24.35MM **Privately Held**
Web: www.grandriverrubber.com

SIC: 3069 3053 Washers, rubber; Gaskets, all materials

(G-595)
HONES HARBOR HOUSE GIFTS
720 E 6th St (44004-3520)
PHONE...............................216 334-9836
Lynn Homes, *Prin*
EMP: 6 **EST:** 2012
SALES (est): 71.95K **Privately Held**
SIC: 3291 Hones

(G-596)
INEOS KOH INC
3509 Middle Rd (44004-3915)
P.O. Box 858 (44005)
PHONE...............................440 997-5221
Ashley Reed, *CEO*
Lucie David, *
▲ **EMP:** 117 **EST:** 1989
SALES (est): 23.63MM
SALES (corp-wide): 1.38MM **Privately Held**
Web: www.ashtachemicals.com
SIC: 2812 Caustic potash, potassium hydroxide
HQ: Ineos Enterprises Us Holdco Llc
23425 W Amoco Rd
Channahon IL 60410
614 787-2058

(G-597)
INEOS PIGMENTS ASU LLC
2501 Middle Rd (44004-3917)
PHONE...............................440 994-1999
James Koutras, *Managing Member*
EMP: 10 **EST:** 2013
SQ FT: 30,000
SALES (est): 1.23MM
SALES (corp-wide): 1.38MM **Privately Held**
SIC: 2819 Industrial inorganic chemicals, nec
HQ: Ineos Enterprises Holdings Limited
15-19 Britten Street
London SW3 3
192 851-6948

(G-598)
INEOS PIGMENTS USA INC
Also Called: Millennium
2900 Middle Rd (44004-3925)
P.O. Box 160 (44005-0160)
PHONE...............................440 994-1400
Joseph Dozman, *Mgr*
EMP: 200
SALES (corp-wide): 1.38MM **Privately Held**
Web: www.ineos.com
SIC: 2819 Industrial inorganic chemicals, nec
HQ: Ineos Pigments Usa Inc.
6752 Baymeadow Dr
Glen Burnie MD 21060
410 762-1000

(G-599)
ITEN INDUSTRIES INC (PA)
Also Called: Plant 2
4602 Benefit Ave (44004-5455)
P.O. Box 2150 (44005-2150)
PHONE...............................440 997-6134
Peter D Huggins, *CEO*
Peter D Huggins, *Pr*
Bill Kane, *
Terry Warren, *
◆ **EMP:** 172 **EST:** 1922
SQ FT: 175,000
SALES (est): 23.97MM
SALES (corp-wide): 23.97MM **Privately Held**
Web: www.itenindustries.com

GEOGRAPHIC

SIC: **3089** Laminating of plastics

(G-600)
ITEN INDUSTRIES INC
3500 N Ridge Rd W (44004-6370)
PHONE..............................440 997-6134
EMP: 10
SALES (corp-wide): 23.97MM **Privately Held**
Web: www.itenindustries.com
SIC: **3089** Laminating of plastics
PA: Iten Industries, Inc.
    4602 Benefit Ave
    Ashtabula OH 44004
    440 997-6134

(G-601)
KOSKI CONSTRUCTION CO (PA)
5841 Woodman Ave (44004-7919)
P.O. Box 1038 (44005-1038)
PHONE..............................440 997-5337
Donald R Koski, *Pr*
Thomas Pope, *VP*
David C Sheldon, *Treas*
EMP: 6 **EST:** 1921
SQ FT: 3,500
SALES (est): 5.12MM
SALES (corp-wide): 5.12MM **Privately Held**
Web: www.koski-construction.com
SIC: **1611** 1794 1771 2951 Surfacing and paving; Excavation work; Concrete work; Asphalt and asphaltic paving mixtures (not from refineries)

(G-602)
LAKE CITY PLATING LLC (PA)
Also Called: Lake City Plating
1701 Lake Ave (44004-3099)
PHONE..............................440 964-3555
Todd Bendis, *CEO*
Ryan Carroll, *
EMP: 99 **EST:** 1949
SQ FT: 60,000
SALES (est): 22.53MM
SALES (corp-wide): 22.53MM **Privately Held**
Web: www.lakecityplating.com
SIC: **3471** Electroplating of metals or formed products

(G-603)
LINDE INC
Praxair
3102 Lake Rd E (44004-3829)
PHONE..............................440 994-1000
J J Redmond, *Brnch Mgr*
EMP: 12
Web: www.lindeus.com
SIC: **2813** Oxygen, compressed or liquefied
HQ: Linde Inc.
    10 Riverview Dr
    Danbury CT 06810
    203 837-2000

(G-604)
MEESE INC
Meese Orbitron Dunne
4920 State Rd (44004-6237)
P.O. Box 607 (44005-0607)
PHONE..............................440 998-1202
Robert W Dunne Junior, *Pr*
EMP: 13
Web: www.recyclingproductnews.com
SIC: **3429** 3089 3544 3444 Hardware, nec; Injection molded finished plastics products, nec; Special dies, tools, jigs, and fixtures; Sheet metalwork
HQ: Meese, Inc.
    1745 Cragmont St
    Madison IN 47250
    800 829-4535

(G-605)
MFG COMPOSITE SYSTEMS COMPANY
Also Called: Mfg CSC
2925 Mfg Pl (44004-9701)
P.O. Box 675 (44005-0675)
PHONE..............................440 997-5851
Richard Morrison, *Pr*
Andy Juhola, *
Alec Raffa, *
Keith Bihary, *
Dan Plona, *
◆ **EMP:** 350 **EST:** 1948
SALES (est): 24.36MM
SALES (corp-wide): 360.86MM **Privately Held**
Web: www.moldedfiberglass.com
SIC: **3229** 2823 Glass fiber products; Cellulosic manmade fibers
PA: Molded Fiber Glass Companies
    2925 Mfg Pl
    Ashtabula OH 44004
    440 997-5851

(G-606)
MODROTO
4920 State Rd (44004-6237)
PHONE..............................440 998-1202
Bob Dunne, *Pr*
EMP: 6 **EST:** 2015
SALES (est): 353.69K **Privately Held**
Web: www.meese-inc.com
SIC: **2655** 2599 5085 Fiber cans, drums, and containers; Carts, restaurant equipment ; Bins and containers, storage

(G-607)
MOLDED FIBER GLASS COMPANIES (PA)
2925 Mfg Pl (44004-9445)
P.O. Box 675 (44005-0675)
PHONE..............................440 997-5851
Richard Morrison, *CEO*
Dave Denny, *
Darren Schwede, *
Greg Tilton, *
Carl Lafrance, *CIO*
◆ **EMP:** 685 **EST:** 1946
SQ FT: 265,000
SALES (est): 360.86MM
SALES (corp-wide): 360.86MM **Privately Held**
Web: www.moldedfiberglass.com
SIC: **3089** Molding primary plastics

(G-608)
MOLDED FIBER GLASS COMPANIES
Also Called: Msg Premier Molded Fiber
4401 Benefit Ave (44004-5458)
P.O. Box 675 (44005-0675)
PHONE..............................440 997-5851
Richard Morrison, *CEO*
EMP: 72
SQ FT: 168,000
SALES (corp-wide): 360.86MM **Privately Held**
Web: www.moldedfiberglass.com
SIC: **3089** Molding primary plastics
PA: Molded Fiber Glass Companies
    2925 Mfg Pl
    Ashtabula OH 44004
    440 997-5851

(G-609)
MOLDED FIBER GLASS COMPANIES
1315 W 47th St (44004-5403)
PHONE..............................440 994-5100
Pete Emrich, *Brnch Mgr*
EMP: 51
SALES (corp-wide): 360.86MM **Privately Held**

Web: www.moldedfiberglass.com
SIC: **3089** Plastics containers, except foam
PA: Molded Fiber Glass Companies
    2925 Mfg Pl
    Ashtabula OH 44004
    440 997-5851

(G-610)
NEBC INC
1726 Griswold Ave (44004-9213)
P.O. Box 370 (44005-0370)
PHONE..............................440 992-5500
Ron Marchewka, *Pr*
EMP: 55 **EST:** 1978
SQ FT: 110,000
SALES (est): 10.28MM
SALES (corp-wide): 457.79MM **Privately Held**
Web: www.northeastbox.com
SIC: **2653** Boxes, corrugated: made from purchased materials
PA: Welch Packaging Group, Inc.
    1020 Herman St
    Elkhart IN 46516
    574 295-2460

(G-611)
PESKA INC (PA)
Also Called: Sports & Sports
3600 N Ridge Rd E (44004-4316)
PHONE..............................440 998-4664
Steve Reichert, *Pr*
Edith M Reichert, *Prin*
Paul A Reichert, *Prin*
EMP: 10 **EST:** 1983
SQ FT: 6,000
SALES (est): 919.58K
SALES (corp-wide): 919.58K **Privately Held**
Web: www.sportsnsports.com
SIC: **5941** 2396 Sporting goods and bicycle shops; Screen printing on fabric articles

(G-612)
PINNEY DOCK & TRANSPORT LLC
1149 E 5th St (44004-3513)
P.O. Box 41 (44005-0041)
PHONE..............................440 964-7186
◆ **EMP:** 11 **EST:** 1953
SQ FT: 20,000
SALES (est): 12.83MM **Publicly Held**
SIC: **3731** 4491 5032 Drydocks, floating; Docks, piers and terminals; Limestone
PA: Kinder Morgan Inc
    1001 La St Ste 1000
    Houston TX 77002

(G-613)
PROFESSIONAL MARINE REPAIR LLC
1453 Dover Cntr Rd (44004)
PHONE..............................440 409-9957
EMP: 8 **EST:** 2018
SALES (est): 311.9K **Privately Held**
SIC: **3731** Lighters, marine: building and repairing

(G-614)
REESE MACHINE COMPANY INC
2501 State Rd (44004-5235)
P.O. Box 1396 (44005-1396)
PHONE..............................440 992-3942
Dale Reese, *Pr*
EMP: 10 **EST:** 1965
SALES (est): 1.01MM **Privately Held**
Web: www.reesemc.com
SIC: **3599** Machine shop, jobbing and repair

(G-615)
REX INTERNATIONAL USA INC
Also Called: Wheeler Manufacturing
3744 Jefferson Rd (44004-9601)
P.O. Box 688 (44005-0688)
PHONE..............................800 321-7950
John Miyagawa, *CEO*
◆ **EMP:** 20 **EST:** 1988
SQ FT: 22,000
SALES (est): 9.99MM **Privately Held**
Web: www.wheelerrex.com
SIC: **3423** 3546 3545 3541 Hand and edge tools, nec; Power-driven handtools; Machine tool accessories; Pipe cutting and threading machines
HQ: Rex Industries Co., Ltd.
    1-9-3, Hishiyahigashi
    Higashi-Osaka OSK 578-0

(G-616)
SHORT RUN MACHINE PRODUCTS INC
4744 Kister Ct (44004-8974)
PHONE..............................440 969-1313
Scott Ray, *Pr*
EMP: 12 **EST:** 1989
SALES (est): 1.23MM **Privately Held**
Web: www.shortrunmachine.com
SIC: **3599** 3544 Machine shop, jobbing and repair; Special dies, tools, jigs, and fixtures

(G-617)
STAN-KELL LLC
2621 West Ave (44004-3115)
P.O. Box 429 (44005-0429)
PHONE..............................440 998-1116
Brian Lewis, *Pr*
Steve Berndt, *VP*
EMP: 10 **EST:** 1963
SQ FT: 18,450
SALES (est): 1.55MM **Privately Held**
Web: www.pencotool.com
SIC: **3544** 3599 7692 Industrial molds; Machine shop, jobbing and repair; Welding repair

(G-618)
ULTIMATE CHEM SOLUTIONS INC
1800 E 21st St (44004-4012)
P.O. Box 1768 (44005-1768)
PHONE..............................440 998-6751
Yogi V Chokshi, *Pr*
EMP: 14 **EST:** 2010
SALES (est): 2.42MM **Privately Held**
SIC: **2869** Industrial organic chemicals, nec

(G-619)
USALCO MICHIGAN CITY PLANT LLC
1741 W 47th St (44004-5423)
PHONE..............................440 992-7039
EMP: 97
SALES (corp-wide): 42.96MM **Privately Held**
Web: www.usalco.com
SIC: **2819** Industrial inorganic chemicals, nec
PA: Usalco Michigan City Plant, Llc
    2601 Cannery Ave
    Baltimore MD 21226
    410 918-2230

(G-620)
VEITSCH-RADEX AMERICA LLC
4741 Kister Ct (44004-8975)
PHONE..............................717 793-7122
David Lawrie, *Pr*
Carlo A D'amicis, *COO*
Craig Powell, *STEEL*
Giovanni Tancredo, *INDUSTRIAL*
Kelly L Myers, *Sec*
EMP: 65 **EST:** 2002
SALES (est): 8.13MM **Privately Held**

▲ = Import ▼ = Export
◆ = Import/Export

SIC: 3255 Brick, clay refractory
HQ: Veitsch-Radex Gmbh & Co Og
Kranichberggasse 6
Wien 1120
502130

(G-621)
VIBRANTZ COLOR SOLUTIONS INC (DH)
Also Called: Chromaflo
2600 Michigan Ave (44004-3140)
P.O. Box 816 (44005)
PHONE..................................440 997-5137
Scott Becker, *CEO*
Jim Hill, *
◆ **EMP:** 137 **EST:** 1970
SQ FT: 175,000
SALES (est): 96.44MM
SALES (corp-wide): 1.88B **Privately Held**
Web: www.vibrantz.com
SIC: 2816 3087 2865 Inorganic pigments; Custom compound purchased resins; Color pigments, organic
HQ: Vibrantz Technologies Inc.
16945 Nrthchase Dr Ste 20
Houston TX 77060
646 747-4222

(G-622)
WITT ENTERPRISES INC
2024 Aetna Rd (44004-6260)
PHONE..................................440 992-8333
Ron Kister Junior, *Pr*
EMP: 9 **EST:** 1986
SQ FT: 600
SALES (est): 1.06MM **Privately Held**
Web: www.cw2.com
SIC: 3471 Sand blasting of metal parts

(G-623)
ZEHRCO-GIANCOLA COMPOSITES INC (PA)
1501 W 47th St (44004-5419)
PHONE..................................440 994-6317
Anthony Giancola, *Pr*
▼ **EMP:** 105 **EST:** 2003
SQ FT: 150,000
SALES (est): 21.61MM
SALES (corp-wide): 21.61MM **Privately Held**
Web: www.zehrco-giancola.com
SIC: 3089 Injection molding of plastics

Ashville
Pickaway County

(G-624)
COLUMBUS INDUSTRIES INC (HQ)
2938 State Route 752 (43103-9543)
P.O. Box 257 (43103-0257)
PHONE..................................740 983-2552
Harold T Pontius, *Ch Bd*
Jeffrey Pontius, *
Eric Pontius, *
Wayne Vickers, *
Debbie Vickers, *
◆ **EMP:** 100 **EST:** 1965
SQ FT: 78,000
SALES (est): 103.8MM
SALES (corp-wide): 1.05B **Privately Held**
Web: www.columbusindustries.com
SIC: 3569 Filters
PA: Filtration Group Corporation
1 Tower Ln
Oakbrook Terrace IL 60181
630 968-1730

(G-625)
COLUMBUS INDUSTRIES ONE LLC
2938 State Route 752 (43103-9543)
P.O. Box 257 (43103-0257)
PHONE..................................740 983-2552
Wayne Vickers, *Managing Member*
EMP: 10 **EST:** 2000
SALES (est): 1.19MM **Privately Held**
SIC: 3569 Filters

(G-626)
INTERFACE LOGIC SYSTEMS INC
Also Called: Weighing Division
3368 State Route 752 Ste A (43103-9009)
P.O. Box 30772 (43230-0772)
PHONE..................................614 236-8388
James Gottliebson, *Pr*
Eli Sneward, *Pr*
EMP: 9 **EST:** 1986
SALES (est): 341.16K **Privately Held**
Web: www.interfacelogic.com
SIC: 7629 3596 Electrical measuring instrument repair and calibration; Scales and balances, except laboratory

(G-627)
NOVELIS ALR ROLLED PDTS LLC
1 Reynolds Rd (43103-9204)
PHONE..................................740 983-2571
EMP: 829
Web: www.novelis.com
SIC: 3355 Aluminum rolling and drawing, nec
HQ: Novelis Alr Rolled Products, Llc
25825 Scnce Pk Dr Ste 400
Beachwood OH 44122
216 910-3400

(G-628)
NOVELIS CORPORATION
1 Reynolds Rd (43103-9204)
P.O. Box 197 (43103-0197)
PHONE..................................740 983-2571
EMP: 156
Web: www.novelis.com
SIC: 3341 3444 Secondary nonferrous metals; Sheet metalwork
HQ: Novelis Corporation
3550 Pchtree Rd Ne Ste 11
Atlanta GA 30326
404 760-4000

(G-629)
OWENS CORNING SALES LLC
Also Called: Owens Corning
1 Reynolds Rd (43103-9204)
P.O. Box 197 (43103-0197)
PHONE..................................740 983-1300
Rodney Sawall, *Mgr*
EMP: 15
SIC: 3444 3354 Siding, sheet metal; Aluminum extruded products
HQ: Owens Corning Sales, Llc
1 Owens Corning Pkwy
Toledo OH 43659
419 248-8000

(G-630)
PRODUCTION PLUS CORP
Also Called: Magic Rack
101 S Business Pl (43103-6502)
PHONE..................................740 983-5178
Jeremy Davitz, *Pr*
EMP: 16 **EST:** 1979
SALES (est): 1.86MM **Privately Held**
Web: www.magicrack.com
SIC: 3496 Miscellaneous fabricated wire products

Athens
Athens County

(G-631)
AC GREEN LLC
6648 Hudnell Rd (45701-8952)
PHONE..................................740 292-2604
Claire Green, *Pr*
EMP: 12 **EST:** 2021
SALES (est): 4.45MM **Privately Held**
SIC: 3441 Fabricated structural metal

(G-632)
ALL POWER EQUIPMENT LLC (PA)
Also Called: Kubota Authorized Dealer
8880 United Ln (45701-3667)
PHONE..................................740 593-3279
EMP: 19 **EST:** 1997
SQ FT: 6,000
SALES (est): 2.33MM **Privately Held**
Web: www.cecturfandtractor.com
SIC: 5261 5561 3799 5083 Lawnmowers and tractors; Camper and travel trailer dealers; All terrain vehicles (ATV); Farm and garden machinery

(G-633)
ATHENS MOLD AND MACHINE INC
180 Mill St (45701-2627)
P.O. Box 847 (45701-0847)
PHONE..................................740 593-6613
Jack D Thornton, *Pr*
Mark Thornton, *
EMP: 81 **EST:** 1985
SQ FT: 70,000
SALES (est): 7.81MM **Privately Held**
Web: www.athensnews.com
SIC: 3544 3599 7692 Special dies and tools; Machine shop, jobbing and repair; Welding repair

(G-634)
ATHENS TECHNICAL SPECIALISTS
Also Called: Atsi
8157 Us Highway 50 (45701-9303)
PHONE..................................740 592-2874
Ted Gilfert, *VP*
James Gilfert, *Pr*
Una Gilfert, *Sec*
▲ **EMP:** 14 **EST:** 1982
SQ FT: 6,000
SALES (est): 3.73MM **Privately Held**
Web: www.bectactical.com
SIC: 3669 8748 Traffic signals, electric; Traffic consultant

(G-635)
BRIDGESTONE RET OPERATIONS LLC
Also Called: Firestone
820 E State St (45701-2112)
PHONE..................................740 592-3075
Greg Myers, *Mgr*
EMP: 8
Web: www.bridgestoneamericas.com
SIC: 5531 7534 Automotive tires; Rebuilding and retreading tires
HQ: Bridgestone Retail Operations, Llc
200 4th Ave S Ste 100
Nashville TN 37201
615 937-1000

(G-636)
CITY OF ATHENS
395 W State St (45701-1527)
PHONE..................................740 592-3344
Crystal Kynard, *Brnch Mgr*
EMP: 18
SALES (corp-wide): 28.15MM **Privately Held**

Web: ci.athens.oh.us
SIC: 3589 4941 Water treatment equipment, industrial; Water supply
PA: City Of Athens
8 E Washington St
Athens OH 45701
740 592-3338

(G-637)
CRUMBS INC
Also Called: Crumbs Bakery
94 Columbus Rd (45701-1312)
P.O. Box 315 (45701-0315)
PHONE..................................740 592-3803
Jeremy Bowman, *Pr*
EMP: 10 **EST:** 1986
SALES (est): 231.63K **Privately Held**
Web: crumbsbakery.a-zcompanies.com
SIC: 2051 5461 Bakery: wholesale or wholesale/retail combined; Retail bakeries

(G-638)
DIAGNOSTIC HYBRIDS INC
2005 E State St Ste 100 (45701-2125)
PHONE..................................740 593-1784
David R Scholl Ph.d., *Pr*
James L Brown, *
Geoff Morgan, *
Gail Pres-regulatory Goodrum V, *Quality AFFAIRS*
Paul D Olivo Ph.d., *Research Vice President*
EMP: 220 **EST:** 1982
SQ FT: 25,000
SALES (est): 10.42MM
SALES (corp-wide): 2.78B **Publicly Held**
Web: www.quidelortho.com
SIC: 2835 3841 Diagnostic substances; Diagnostic apparatus, medical
HQ: Quidel Corporation
9975 Summers Ridge Rd
San Diego CA 92121
858 552-1100

(G-639)
FUSION NOODLE COMPANY INC
30 E Union St (45701-2911)
PHONE..................................740 589-5511
EMP: 8 **EST:** 2013
SALES (est): 181.77K **Privately Held**
Web: www.fusionnoodleathens.com
SIC: 2098 Noodles (e.g. egg, plain, and water), dry

(G-640)
G & J PEPSI-COLA BOTTLERS INC
Also Called: Pepsi-Cola
2001 E State St (45701-2125)
PHONE..................................740 593-3366
Curt Allison, *Brnch Mgr*
EMP: 34
SALES (corp-wide): 404.54MM **Privately Held**
Web: www.gjpepsi.com
SIC: 2086 5149 Carbonated soft drinks, bottled and canned; Beverages, except coffee and tea
PA: G & J Pepsi-Cola Bottlers Inc
9435 Wtrstone Blvd Ste 39
Cincinnati OH 45249
513 785-6060

(G-641)
GLOBAL COOLING INC
Also Called: Stirling Ultracold
6000 Poston Rd (45701-9051)
PHONE..................................740 274-7900
Neill Lane, *Pr*
David Berchowitz, *
Yong-rak Kwon, *VP*
Phill Reynolds, *

GEOGRAPHIC

Tim Dannels, *
◆ **EMP:** 121 **EST:** 1993
SQ FT: 15,000
SALES (est): 23.6MM
SALES (corp-wide): 1.02B **Publicly Held**
Web: www.biolifesolutions.com
SIC: 3821 Freezers, laboratory
HQ: Gci Holdings, Llc
   100 Crescent Ct Fl 7
   Dallas TX 75205
   907 265-5600

(G-642)
HOCKING VALLEY CONCRETE INC
748 W Union St (45701-9408)
PHONE............................740 592-5335
EMP: 8 **EST:** 2008
SALES (est): 478.37K **Privately Held**
Web: www.hockingvalleyconcrete.com
SIC: 3273 Ready-mixed concrete

(G-643)
MCHAPPYS DNUTS PARKERSBURG INC
Also Called: Mc Happys Donuts
384 Richland Ave (45701-3204)
PHONE............................740 593-8744
Bonnie Boring, *Mgr*
EMP: 75
SALES (corp-wide): 29.21MM **Privately Held**
Web: www.mchappys.com
SIC: 5461 2051 Doughnuts; Doughnuts, except frozen
HQ: Mchappy's Donuts Of Parkersburg, Inc.
   2515 Washington Blvd
   Belpre OH 45714
   740 423-6351

(G-644)
MESSENGER PUBLISHING COMPANY
Also Called: Athens Messenger, The
9300 Johnson Hollow Rd (45701-9028)
P.O. Box 4210 (45701-4210)
PHONE............................740 592-6612
Mark Policinski, *Pr*
Clarence Brown Junior, *Ch Bd*
Joyce Brown, *
John Aston, *
EMP: 125 **EST:** 1825
SQ FT: 25,000
SALES (est): 3.11MM
SALES (corp-wide): 333.51MM **Privately Held**
Web: www.athensmessenger.com
SIC: 2711 2752 Newspapers, publishing and printing; Offset printing
HQ: Adams Publishing Group, Llc
   9300 Johnson Hollow Rd
   Athens OH 45701
   740 592-6612

(G-645)
PETRO QUEST INC (PA)
3 W Stimson Ave (45701-2679)
P.O. Box 268 (45701-0268)
PHONE............................740 593-3800
Paul J Gerig, *Pr*
Christian Gerig, *VP*
Debora Jarvis, *Sec*
EMP: 6 **EST:** 1983
SQ FT: 2,200
SALES (est): 874.3K
SALES (corp-wide): 874.3K **Privately Held**
SIC: 1381 8111 Drilling oil and gas wells; General practice attorney, lawyer

(G-646)
PRECISION IMPRINT
26 E State St (45701-2540)
PHONE............................740 592-5916
Randy Shoup, *Owner*
EMP: 8 **EST:** 1988
SQ FT: 5,000
SALES (est): 297.34K **Privately Held**
Web: www.precisionimprint.com
SIC: 2261 5136 5137 2759 Screen printing of cotton broadwoven fabrics; Sportswear, men's and boys'; Sportswear, women's and children's; Screen printing

(G-647)
PREMIER ENRGY SYSTEMS OHIO LLC ✪
2099 E State St Ste D (45701-2141)
PHONE............................304 252-1918
Jerry Priddy, *Prin*
EMP: 10 **EST:** 2024
SALES (est): 1.12MM **Privately Held**
SIC: 3822 Environmental controls

(G-648)
QUICK LOADZ CONTAINER SYS LLC
Also Called: Quickloadz
5850 Industrial Park Rd (45701-8736)
P.O. Box 272 (45780-0272)
PHONE............................888 304-3946
▲ **EMP:** 30 **EST:** 2013
SALES (est): 4.91MM **Privately Held**
Web: www.quickloadz.com
SIC: 3715 Trailer bodies

(G-649)
QUIDEL CORPORATION
2005 E State St # 100 (45701-2125)
PHONE............................858 552-1100
Scott Mccloud, *Brnch Mgr*
EMP: 23
SALES (corp-wide): 2.78B **Publicly Held**
Web: www.quidelortho.com
SIC: 2835 Diagnostic substances
HQ: Quidel Corporation
   9975 Summers Ridge Rd
   San Diego CA 92121
   858 552-1100

(G-650)
QUIDEL CORPORATION
1055 E State St Ste 100 (45701-7911)
PHONE............................740 589-3300
EMP: 8
SALES (corp-wide): 2.78B **Publicly Held**
Web: www.quidelortho.com
SIC: 2835 Diagnostic substances
HQ: Quidel Corporation
   9975 Summers Ridge Rd
   San Diego CA 92121
   858 552-1100

(G-651)
QUIDEL DHI
2005 E State St (45701-2125)
PHONE............................740 589-3300
Chris Ridgway, *Mgr*
EMP: 22 **EST:** 2013
SALES (est): 7.9MM
SALES (corp-wide): 2.78B **Publicly Held**
Web: www.quidelortho.com
SIC: 3829 Medical diagnostic systems, nuclear
HQ: Quidel Corporation
   9975 Summers Ridge Rd
   San Diego CA 92121
   858 552-1100

(G-652)
SMITH CONCRETE CO
5240 Hebbardsville Rd (45701-9359)
PHONE............................740 593-5633
Phil Parsons, *Mgr*
EMP: 8
SALES (corp-wide): 5.77MM **Privately Held**
Web: www.shellyco.com
SIC: 3273 Ready-mixed concrete
PA: Smith Concrete Co
   2301 Progress St
   Dover OH 44622
   740 373-7441

(G-653)
STEWART-MACDONALD MFG CO (PA)
Also Called: Stewart McDnalds Guitar Sp Sup
21 N Shafer St (45701-2304)
PHONE............................740 592-3021
Kay Tousley, *CEO*
Jay Hostetler, *
John A Woodrow, *
▲ **EMP:** 40 **EST:** 1969
SQ FT: 12,000
SALES (est): 4.98MM
SALES (corp-wide): 4.98MM **Privately Held**
Web: www.stewmac.com
SIC: 3931 5736 Banjos and parts; Musical instrument stores

(G-654)
SUNPOWER INC
2005 E State St Ste 104 (45701-2125)
PHONE............................740 594-2221
Jeffrey Hatfield, *VP*
EMP: 95 **EST:** 1974
SQ FT: 16,000
SALES (est): 20.87MM
SALES (corp-wide): 6.94B **Publicly Held**
Web: www.sunpowerinc.com
SIC: 8731 8711 8733 3769 Commercial physical research; Engineering services; Physical research, noncommercial; Space vehicle equipment, nec
HQ: Advanced Measurement Technology, Inc.
   801 S Illinois Ave
   Oak Ridge TN 37830
   865 482-4411

(G-655)
UPTOWN DOG THE INC
9 W Union St (45701-2819)
PHONE............................740 592-4600
Mary Swintek, *Pr*
EMP: 8 **EST:** 1987
SQ FT: 1,000
SALES (est): 195.75K **Privately Held**
Web: www.uptowndogtshirts.com
SIC: 5699 2261 2759 Sports apparel; Screen printing of cotton broadwoven fabrics; Screen printing

Attica
Seneca County

(G-656)
EITLE MACHINE TOOL INC
6036 Coder Rd (44807-9638)
PHONE............................419 935-8753
Jerrold Eitle, *Pr*
EMP: 7 **EST:** 1972
SALES (est): 1.42MM **Privately Held**
SIC: 3599 Machine shop, jobbing and repair

(G-657)
OMAR ASSOCIATES LLC
625 N State Route 4 (44807-9533)
PHONE............................419 426-0610
Eric J Wi, *Owner*
EMP: 8 **EST:** 2001
SALES (est): 4.36MM **Privately Held**
Web: www.omarassociates.net
SIC: 3556 Food products machinery

Atwater
Portage County

(G-658)
CURTIS HILBRUNER
Also Called: Acorn Rubber
1315 Bank St (44201-9302)
P.O. Box 126 (44201-0126)
PHONE............................330 947-3527
Curtis Hilbruner, *Owner*
EMP: 9 **EST:** 1977
SALES (est): 326.2K **Privately Held**
Web: www.acornrubber.co.uk
SIC: 3069 Hard rubber and molded rubber products

Aurora
Portage County

(G-659)
ADIDAS NORTH AMERICA INC
Also Called: Adidas Outlet Store Aurora
549 S Chillicothe Rd (44202-7848)
PHONE............................330 562-4689
EMP: 15
SALES (corp-wide): 25.04B **Privately Held**
SIC: 2329 Athletic clothing, except uniforms: men's, youths' and boys'
HQ: Adidas North America, Inc.
   3449 N Anchor St Ste 500
   Portland OR 97217
   971 234-2300

(G-660)
ADVANCED INNOVATIVE MFG INC
Also Called: A.I.M.
255 Campus Dr (44202-6663)
PHONE............................330 562-2468
Joseph Hawald, *Pr*
Joseph A Hawald, *
Mark J Hawald, *
EMP: 58 **EST:** 2014
SQ FT: 68,000
SALES (est): 8MM **Privately Held**
Web: www.a-i-mfg.com
SIC: 3541 Machine tools, metal cutting type

(G-661)
ATRIUM AT ANNA MARIA INC
849 N Aurora Rd (44202-9537)
PHONE............................330 562-7777
Aaron Baker, *Admn*
EMP: 11 **EST:** 2014
SALES (est): 538.43K **Privately Held**
Web: www.annamariaofaurora.com
SIC: 2711 Newspapers, publishing and printing

(G-662)
AUTOMATION PLASTICS CORP
150 Lena Dr (44202-9202)
PHONE............................330 562-5148
Harry Smith, *Pr*
EMP: 60 **EST:** 1978
SQ FT: 43,000
SALES (est): 14.6MM **Privately Held**
Web: www.automationplastics.com

▲ = Import ▼ = Export
◆ = Import/Export

SIC: **3089** 3544 Injection molding of plastics; Special dies, tools, jigs, and fixtures

(G-663)
BARRACUDA TECHNOLOGIES INC
2900 State Route 82 (44202-9395)
PHONE...............................216 469-1566
Kris Santin, *CEO*
EMP: 7 EST: 2011
SALES (est): 91.6K **Privately Held**
SIC: **3644** Noncurrent-carrying wiring devices

(G-664)
BERRY PLASTICS FILMCO INC
1450 S Chillicothe Rd (44202-9282)
PHONE...............................330 562-6111
David Meldren, *Pr*
Judy Ciocca, *Prin*
▲ **EMP: 15 EST**: 1997
SQ FT: 85,000
SALES (est): 9.49MM **Privately Held**
SIC: **3081** Plastics film and sheet
HQ: Berry Global, Inc.
    101 Oakley St
    Evansville IN 47710

(G-665)
CANTEX INC
11444 Chamberlain Rd # 1 (44202-9306)
PHONE...............................330 995-3665
Mike Schafer, *Brnch Mgr*
EMP: 83
Web: www.cantexinc.com
SIC: **3084** 3089 Plastics pipe; Fittings for pipe, plastics
HQ: Cantex Inc.
    301 Commerce St Ste 2700
    Fort Worth TX 76102

(G-666)
CUSTOM PULTRUSIONS INC (HQ)
1331 S Chillicothe Rd (44202-9218)
PHONE...............................330 562-5201
Jay Lund, *CEO*
EMP: 62 EST: 2009
SALES (est): 10.32MM
SALES (corp-wide): 1.78B **Privately Held**
Web: www.custompultrusions.com
SIC: **3089** Injection molding of plastics
PA: Andersen Corporation
    100 4th Ave N
    Bayport MN 55003
    651 264-5150

(G-667)
EATON CORPORATION
Synflex Division
115 Lena Dr (44202-9202)
PHONE...............................330 274-0743
Phil Corvo, *Mgr*
EMP: 20
SQ FT: 7,568
Web: www.dix-eaton.com
SIC: **3089** 3494 3429 3052 Plastics containers, except foam; Valves and pipe fittings, nec; Hardware, nec; Rubber and plastics hose and beltings
HQ: Eaton Corporation
    1000 Eaton Blvd
    Cleveland OH 44122
    440 523-5000

(G-668)
ELECTRIC SPEED INDICATOR CO
650 Cedar Bark Dr (44202-7750)
PHONE...............................216 251-2540
Robert P Riley, *Pr*
EMP: 10 EST: 1934
SALES (est): 127.58K **Privately Held**
Web: www.electricspeedindicator.com

(G-669)
EPG INC
500 Lena Dr (44202-9245)
PHONE...............................330 995-5125
Michael Orazen, *Mgr*
EMP: 64
SALES (corp-wide): 60.4MM **Privately Held**
SIC: **3053** 3061 Gaskets, all materials; Mechanical rubber goods
HQ: Epg, Inc.
    1780 Miller Pkwy
    Streetsboro OH 44241
    330 995-9725

(G-670)
FREEDOM HEALTH LLC
65 Aurora Industrial Pkwy (44202-8088)
PHONE...............................330 562-0888
Mark Yoho, *VP*
Patrick Warczak Junior, *VP*
Vincenzo Franco, *VP*
▲ **EMP: 20 EST**: 2004
SQ FT: 50,000
SALES (est): 5.03MM **Privately Held**
Web: www.succeed-equine.com
SIC: **2023** Dietary supplements, dairy and non-dairy based

(G-671)
GODFREY & WING INC (PA)
220 Campus Dr (44202-6663)
PHONE...............................330 562-1440
Alexander Alford, *CEO*
Christopher Gilmore, *
Karen Gilmore, *
Brad Welch, *
▲ **EMP: 50 EST**: 1947
SQ FT: 68,000
SALES (est): 10.26MM
SALES (corp-wide): 10.26MM **Privately Held**
Web: www.godfreywing.com
SIC: **3479** 8734 Coating of metals with plastic or resins; Testing laboratories

(G-672)
GUNNISON ASSOCIATES LLC
114 Barrington Town Square Dr # 11 (44202-7792)
PHONE...............................330 562-5230
EMP: 6 EST: 1998
SALES (est): 415.41K **Privately Held**
SIC: **3565** Packaging machinery

(G-673)
HEINENS INC
Also Called: Heinen's 8
115 N Chillicothe Rd (44202-7797)
PHONE...............................330 562-5297
Paul Otoole, *Mgr*
EMP: 143
SALES (corp-wide): 337.91MM **Privately Held**
Web: www.heinens.com
SIC: **5411** 2051 Supermarkets, chain; Bread, cake, and related products
PA: Heinen's, Inc.
    4540 Richmond Rd
    Warrensville Heights OH 44128
    216 475-2300

(G-674)
HF GROUP LLC (PA)
400 Aurora Commons Cir Unit 74 (44202-5304)
P.O. Box 74 (44202)
PHONE...............................440 729-2445
Jay B Fairfield, *Managing Member*
EMP: 10 EST: 2006
SQ FT: 6,000
SALES (est): 44.72MM **Privately Held**
Web: www.hfgroup.com
SIC: **2732** Book printing

(G-675)
INTEGRITY PARKING LLC ✪
Also Called: Consulting
400 Aurora Commons Cir Unit 438 (44202-5326)
PHONE...............................440 543-4123
Lee Shorts, *CEO*
Lee Shorts, *Managing Member*
EMP: 16 EST: 2023
SALES (est): 1.69MM **Privately Held**
Web: www.integrityparking.com
SIC: **3559** 8742 7521 Parking facility equipment and supplies; Transportation consultant; Parking structure

(G-676)
LAYERZERO POWER SYSTEMS INC (PA)
1500 Danner Dr (44202-9298)
PHONE...............................440 399-9000
Milind Bhanoo, *Pr*
James M Galm, *VP*
EMP: 19 EST: 2001
SALES (est): 14.11MM
SALES (corp-wide): 14.11MM **Privately Held**
Web: www.layerzero.com
SIC: **3613** Power switching equipment

(G-677)
LYNK PACKAGING INC (PA)
Also Called: Jit Milrob
1250 Page Rd (44202-6666)
PHONE...............................330 562-8080
David R Jones, *Ch*
Elaine Jones, *VP*
EMP: 22 EST: 1985
SQ FT: 60,000
SALES (est): 9.01MM
SALES (corp-wide): 9.01MM **Privately Held**
Web: www.lynkpkg.com
SIC: **2448** 5113 5085 2653 Pallets, wood; Corrugated and solid fiber boxes; Industrial supplies; Corrugated and solid fiber boxes

(G-678)
MERIDIAN LLC
Also Called: Meridian
325 Harris Dr (44202-7539)
PHONE...............................330 995-0371
EMP: 9 EST: 2010
SALES (est): 161.13K **Privately Held**
Web: www.meridianmed.net
SIC: **3841** Surgical and medical instruments

(G-679)
MERIDIENNE INTERNATIONAL INC
Also Called: Atlantic Water Gardens
125 Lena Dr (44202-9202)
PHONE...............................330 274-8317
William Lynne, *Pr*
▲ **EMP: 7 EST**: 1983
SALES (est): 9.03MM
SALES (corp-wide): 2.67MM **Privately Held**
Web: www.atlantic-oase.com
SIC: **3083** 1799 3271 0781 Laminated plastics plate and sheet; Fountain installation; Blocks, concrete: landscape or retaining wall; Landscape services
HQ: Oase Living Water Gmbh
    Tecklenburger Str. 161

Horstel NW 48477
5454800

(G-680)
NATURAL ESSENTIALS INC
115 Lena Dr (44202-9202)
PHONE...............................330 562-8022
EMP: 10
Web: www.naturalessentialsinc.com
SIC: **2844** Perfumes, cosmetics and other toilet preparations
PA: Natural Essentials Incorporated
    1830 Miller Pkwy
    Streetsboro OH 44241

(G-681)
NETWORK TECHNOLOGIES INC
1275 Danner Dr (44202-8054)
PHONE...............................330 562-7070
◆ **EMP: 96 EST**: 1984
SALES (est): 17.38MM **Privately Held**
Web: www.networktechinc.com
SIC: **3678** Electronic connectors

(G-682)
OASE NORTH AMERICA INC
125 Lena Dr (44202-9202)
PHONE...............................800 365-3880
Andreas Szabados, *CEO*
Birgit Kempe-heeger, *Sec*
Ansgar Paul, *Sec*
◆ **EMP: 6 EST**: 1994
SALES (est): 6.28MM
SALES (corp-wide): 2.67MM **Privately Held**
Web: www.atlantic-oase.com
SIC: **3594** 3524 5251 Fluid power pumps; Lawn and garden equipment; Pumps and pumping equipment
HQ: Oase International Holding Gmbh
    Tecklenburger Str. 161
    Horstel NW
    5454800

(G-683)
OMEGA POLYMER TECHNOLOGIES INC (PA)
Also Called: Opti
1331 S Chillicothe Rd (44202-8066)
PHONE...............................330 562-5201
Ronald Baker, *Pr*
Bob Jackson, *Sec*
EMP: 6 EST: 1994
SALES (est): 4.21MM **Privately Held**
SIC: **3089** Injection molding of plastics

(G-684)
OMEGA PULTRUSIONS INCORPORATED
1331 S Chillicothe Rd (44202-8066)
PHONE...............................330 562-5201
Donald F Borraccini, *Pr*
EMP: 182 EST: 1970
SQ FT: 95,000
SALES (est): 2.4MM **Privately Held**
SIC: **3089** Injection molding of plastics
PA: Omega Polymer Technologies, Inc.
    1331 S Chillicothe Rd
    Aurora OH 44202

(G-685)
PHILPOTT RUBBER LLC
Also Called: Philpott Rubber and Plastics
375 Gentry Dr (44202-7540)
PHONE...............................330 225-3344
EMP: 8
SALES (corp-wide): 28.02MM **Privately Held**
Web: www.philpottsolutions.com

SIC: **3069** Medical sundries, rubber
HQ: Philpott Rubber Llc
1010 Industrial Pkwy N
Brunswick OH 44212
330 225-3344

(G-686)
RADIX WIRE CO
350 Harris Dr (44202-7536)
PHONE.....................330 995-3677
Craig Hines, *Mgr*
EMP: 18
SQ FT: 10,000
SALES (corp-wide): 20.56MM **Privately Held**
Web: www.radix-wire.com
SIC: **3357** Nonferrous wiredrawing and insulating
PA: Radix Wire Co
30333 Emerald Valley Pkwy
Solon OH 44139
216 731-9191

(G-687)
ROBECK FLUID POWER CO
Also Called: Robeck
350 Lena Dr (44202-8098)
PHONE.....................330 562-1140
Peter Becker, *Pr*
Ken Traeger, *
Ida Becker, *
▲ EMP: 65 EST: 1983
SQ FT: 6,000
SALES (est): 29.77MM **Privately Held**
Web: www.robeckfluidpower.com
SIC: **5084 3593 3594 3494** Hydraulic systems equipment and supplies; Fluid power cylinders and actuators; Fluid power pumps and motors; Valves and pipe fittings, nec

(G-688)
SACO AEI POLYMERS INC
Also Called: Macro Meric
1395 Danner Dr (44202-9273)
PHONE.....................330 995-1600
Matt Mclaughlin, *Brnch Mgr*
EMP: 16
SQ FT: 28,829
SALES (corp-wide): 47.99MM **Privately Held**
Web: www.sacoaei.com
SIC: **2821** Plastics materials and resins
PA: Saco Aei Polymers, Inc.
3220 Crocker Ave
Sheboygan WI 53081
920 803-0778

(G-689)
THYSSNKRUPP ROTHE ERDE USA INC (DH)
Also Called: Rotek
1400 S Chillicothe Rd (44202-9282)
P.O. Box 312 (44202-0312)
PHONE.....................330 562-4000
Mark Girman, *Pr*
Jose Muzzi, *
Frank Kuepper, *SLS & ENGINEERING* *
▲ EMP: 160 EST: 1855
SQ FT: 132,000
SALES (est): 24.32MM
SALES (corp-wide): 39.13B **Privately Held**
Web: www.thyssenkrupp-rotheerde.com
SIC: **3562 3462 3463 3321** Ball bearings and parts; Iron and steel forgings; Nonferrous forgings; Gray and ductile iron foundries
HQ: Thyssenkrupp North America, Llc
111 W Jckson Blvd Ste 240
Chicago IL 60604
312 525-2800

(G-690)
TRELLBORG SLING PRFILES US INC
Also Called: Trelleborg
285 Lena Dr (44202-9247)
P.O. Box 639 (46507-0639)
PHONE.....................330 995-9725
Smitty Mckee, *Pr*
Gabe Orazen, *
Michael Scanlon, *
EMP: 130 EST: 2006
SALES (est): 16.76MM
SALES (corp-wide): 60.4MM **Privately Held**
SIC: **3465 3089** Body parts, automobile: stamped metal; Extruded finished plastics products, nec
HQ: Trelleborg Corporation
200 Veterans Blvd Ste 3
South Haven MI 49090
269 639-9891

(G-691)
UNIVERSAL HEAT TREATING INC
Also Called: Universal Black Oxiding
60 Samantha Dr (44202-9801)
PHONE.....................216 641-2000
Ernie D'amato, *CEO*
Michael D Amato, *
Kevin D'amato, *VP*
EMP: 32 EST: 1965
SALES (est): 2.44MM **Privately Held**
Web: www.glitznglamourcosmetics.com
SIC: **3398** Metal heat treating

(G-692)
USA INSTRUMENTS INC
Also Called: GE
1515 Danner Dr (44202-9273)
PHONE.....................330 562-1000
Eric Stahre, *Pr*
▲ EMP: 250 EST: 1993
SQ FT: 58,000
SALES (est): 48.44MM
SALES (corp-wide): 19.67B **Publicly Held**
SIC: **3677** Electronic coils and transformers
HQ: Ge Healthcare Inc.
3350 N Ridge Ave
Arlington Heights IL 60004
732 457-8667

(G-693)
VIDEO PRODUCTS INC
Also Called: VPI
1275 Danner Dr (44202-8054)
PHONE.....................330 562-2622
Carl Jagatich, *Pr*
EMP: 60 EST: 1977
SQ FT: 8,000
SALES (est): 1.72MM **Privately Held**
Web: www.vpi.us
SIC: **3577** Computer peripheral equipment, nec

(G-694)
WYATT INDUSTRIES LLC
965 Cascades Dr (44202-7799)
PHONE.....................330 954-1790
Beverly Clemens, *CEO*
EMP: 6 EST: 2011
SALES (est): 331.48K **Privately Held**
SIC: **3089** Plastics processing

Austinburg
Ashtabula County

(G-695)
AUSTINBURG MACHINE INC
2899 Industrial Park Dr (44010-9764)
PHONE.....................440 275-2001

Richard Pildner, *Pr*
John Pildner, *VP*
Lynetta Pildner, *Sec*
EMP: 8 EST: 1970
SQ FT: 8,200
SALES (est): 1.11MM **Privately Held**
SIC: **3599** Machine shop, jobbing and repair

(G-696)
BISMARK LAWNCARE LLC
4057 State Route 307 (44010-9705)
PHONE.....................440 361-5561
Robert W Bismark, *Pt*
EMP: 12 EST: 2013
SALES (est): 1.06MM **Privately Held**
SIC: **0782 1389** Lawn care services; Construction, repair, and dismantling services

(G-697)
ENCAPSULATION TECHNOLOGIES LLC
2937 Industrial Park Dr (44010-9763)
PHONE.....................419 819-6319
Canaima Technologies, *Prin*
EMP: 9 EST: 2017
SALES (est): 52.58K **Privately Held**
Web: www.salvona.com
SIC: **2834** Pharmaceutical preparations

(G-698)
EUCLID REFINISHING COMPNAY INC
Also Called: Surftech
2937 Industrial Park Dr (44010-9763)
PHONE.....................440 275-3356
Nicholas Cottone, *CEO*
EMP: 10 EST: 1988
SQ FT: 15,000
SALES (est): 1.46MM **Privately Held**
Web: www.euclidrefinishing.com
SIC: **3479** Coating of metals and formed products

(G-699)
FARIN INDUSTRIES INC
2844 Industrial Park Dr (44010-9764)
P.O. Box 185 (44010-0185)
PHONE.....................440 275-2755
Michael F Farinacci, *Pr*
EMP: 6 EST: 1984
SQ FT: 10,000
SALES (est): 942.27K **Privately Held**
Web: www.farin.us
SIC: **3714** Motor vehicle parts and accessories

(G-700)
FUTURE CONTROLS CORPORATION
1419 State Route 45 (44010-9749)
P.O. Box 130 (44010-0130)
PHONE.....................440 275-3191
John Williams, *Pr*
Jeremy Sutch, *
Philip Bunnell, *
EMP: 41 EST: 1985
SQ FT: 33,000
SALES (est): 2.05MM **Privately Held**
Web: www.futurecontrols.com
SIC: **3823 3625 3822** Temperature instruments: industrial process type; Relays and industrial controls; Environmental controls

(G-701)
PAINESVILLE PUBLISHING INC
2883 Industrial Park Dr (44010-9764)
P.O. Box 12 (44010-0012)
PHONE.....................440 354-4142
Don Tiknovnik, *Pr*
Marie Baker, *VP*
EMP: 7 EST: 1941

SQ FT: 3,000
SALES (est): 371.42K **Privately Held**
Web: www.painesvillepublishing.com
SIC: **2752 2791 2789** Offset printing; Typesetting; Bookbinding and related work

(G-702)
RTS COMPANIES (US) INC
2900 Industrial Park Dr (44010-9763)
PHONE.....................440 275-3077
Graham Lobban, *Pr*
◆ EMP: 40 EST: 2008
SALES (est): 11.04MM **Privately Held**
Web: www.rtscompaniesinc.com
SIC: **3089** Injection molding of plastics

(G-703)
SPRING TEAM INC
2851 Industrial Park Dr (44010-9764)
P.O. Box 215 (44010-0215)
PHONE.....................440 275-5981
Russ Bryer, *Pr*
Richard Kovach, *
Gary Van Buren, *
Nancy Sidley, *
Ed Hall, *
▼ EMP: 67 EST: 1968
SQ FT: 42,000
SALES (est): 2.53MM **Privately Held**
Web: www.springteam.com
SIC: **3496 3495** Miscellaneous fabricated wire products; Wire springs

Austintown
Mahoning County

(G-704)
COWLES INDUSTRIAL TOOL CO LLC
Also Called: Cowles Industrial Tool
185 N Four Mile Run Rd (44515-3006)
PHONE.....................330 799-9100
David Smith, *Pr*
EMP: 35 EST: 2012
SQ FT: 30,000
SALES (est): 5.17MM **Privately Held**
Web: www.cowles-tool.com
SIC: **3545** Tools and accessories for machine tools

(G-705)
HAZ-SAFE LLC
3850 Hendricks Rd (44515-1528)
P.O. Box 181 (26175-0181)
PHONE.....................330 793-0900
EMP: 15 EST: 2008
SALES (est): 1.01MM **Privately Held**
Web: www.hazsafe.com
SIC: **3448** Prefabricated metal buildings and components
PA: Precision, L.L.C.
843 N Cleveland Massillon
Akron OH 44333

(G-706)
L M ENGINEERING INC
Also Called: Lm Cases
3760 Oakwood Ave (44515-3041)
PHONE.....................330 270-2400
Joann Laguardia, *Pr*
William Laguardia, *
EMP: 25 EST: 1982
SQ FT: 40,000
SALES (est): 5.46MM **Privately Held**
Web: www.lmcases.com
SIC: **3161** Musical instrument cases

(G-707)
PRECISION FOAM FABRICATION INC
3760 Oakwood Ave Ste B (44515-3041)

PHONE...................330 270-2440
Joann Laguargia, *Pr*
EMP: 6 **EST:** 1998
SALES (est): 750.72K **Privately Held**
Web: www.precisionfoam.com
SIC: 3089 Injection molding of plastics

(G-708)
TRANSUE & WILLIAMS STAMPG CORP
207 N Four Mile Run Rd (44515-3008)
PHONE...................330 821-5777
John Staudt, *VP*
John Beringer, *Treas*
▲ **EMP:** 30 **EST:** 1986
SALES (est): 6.05MM **Privately Held**
Web: www.twstamping.com
SIC: 3469 Stamping metal for the trade

(G-709)
XALOY LLC (PA)
375 Victoria Rd Ste 1 (44515-2053)
PHONE...................330 726-4000
Kamal K Tiwari, *CEO*
Keith Young, *
◆ **EMP:** 190 **EST:** 2021
SALES (est): 91MM
SALES (corp-wide): 91MM **Privately Held**
Web: www.xaloy.com
SIC: 3089 8711 Automotive parts, plastic; Engineering services

---

Avon
Lorain County

(G-710)
A J ROSE MFG CO (PA)
38000 Chester Rd (44011-4022)
PHONE...................216 631-4645
Daniel T Pritchard, *Pr*
Douglas E Krzywicki, *
Dale A Pritchard, *
Terry J Sweeney, *
◆ **EMP:** 235 **EST:** 1922
SQ FT: 270,000
SALES (est): 74.13MM
SALES (corp-wide): 74.13MM **Privately Held**
Web: www.ajrose.com
SIC: 3469 Perforated metal, stamped

(G-711)
ACCEL CORPORATION (HQ)
Also Called: Accel Color
38620 Chester Rd (44011-1074)
PHONE...................440 934-7711
▲ **EMP:** 60 **EST:** 1998
SALES (est): 4.92MM
SALES (corp-wide): 184.58MM **Privately Held**
SIC: 3087 Custom compound purchased resins
PA: Techmer Pm, Llc
1 Quality Cir
Clinton TN 37716
865 457-6700

(G-712)
ADVANCED POLYMER COATINGS LTD
951 Jaycox Rd (44011-1396)
P.O. Box 269 (44011-0269)
PHONE...................440 937-6218
Donald Keehan, *Ch*
Denise Keehan, *
◆ **EMP:** 26 **EST:** 1987
SQ FT: 35,000
SALES (est): 9.98MM **Privately Held**
Web: www.adv-polymer.com

SIC: 3081 Plastics film and sheet

(G-713)
AIRCRAFT WHEEL & BRAKE LLC
1160 Center Rd (44011-1208)
PHONE...................440 937-6211
EMP: 99 **EST:** 2022
SALES (est): 2.41MM
SALES (corp-wide): 1.27B **Privately Held**
Web: www.kaman.com
SIC: 3728 Wheels, aircraft
HQ: Kaman Corporation
1332 Blue Hills Ave
Bloomfield CT 06002
860 243-7100

(G-714)
B3 FULFILLMENT
Also Called: B3
3450 Nagel Rd (44011-2504)
PHONE...................866 405-0910
Scott Raybuck, *Pr*
Scott Raybuck, *Prin*
Derek Rapkin, *Prin*
EMP: 22 **EST:** 2010
SALES (est): 2.47MM **Privately Held**
Web: www.b3fulfillment.com
SIC: 3565 Bottling machinery: filling, capping, labeling

(G-715)
BARENTZ N AMER INTRMDATE HLDNG
1390 Jaycox Rd (44011-1317)
PHONE...................440 937-1000
Jean-luc Joye, *Prin*
EMP: 6 **EST:** 2014
SALES (est): 1.16MM **Privately Held**
Web: www.barentz-na.com
SIC: 2869 5169 Industrial organic chemicals, nec; Chemicals and allied products, nec

(G-716)
BENDIX COML VHCL SYSTEMS LLC (DH)
Also Called: Bendix
35500 Chester Rd (44011-1215)
P.O. Box 4016 (44035)
PHONE...................440 329-9000
Piotr Sroka, *Pr*
Carlos Hungria, *
Dave Kralic, *
Berend Bracht, *
◆ **EMP:** 350 **EST:** 2001
SALES (est): 997.21MM
SALES (corp-wide): 144.19K **Privately Held**
Web: www.bendix.com
SIC: 3714 5013 5088 Motor vehicle brake systems and parts; Automotive supplies and parts; Combat vehicles
HQ: Knorr-Bremse Ag
Moosacher Str. 80
Munchen BY 80809
8935470

(G-717)
BRIMAR PACKAGING INC
37520 Colorado Ave (44011-1534)
PHONE...................440 934-3080
EMP: 40 **EST:** 1992
SALES (est): 1.62MM **Privately Held**
Web: www.brimarpackaging.com
SIC: 2449 2653 5085 2657 Wood containers, nec; Boxes, corrugated: made from purchased materials; Commercial containers; Folding paperboard boxes

(G-718)
CHALFANT MANUFACTURING COMPANY (DH)
1050 Jaycox Rd (44011-1312)
PHONE...................330 273-3510
Gloria Slaga, *CEO*
John Slaga, *Pr*
▼ **EMP:** 7 **EST:** 1945
SALES (est): 9.06MM **Privately Held**
Web: www.chalfant-obo.com
SIC: 3643 Current-carrying wiring services
HQ: Obo Bettermann Holding Gmbh & Co. Kg
Huingser Ring 52
Menden (Sauerland) NW
2373890

(G-719)
CLEAN REMEDIES LLC
1431 Lear Industrial Pkwy Ste A (44011-1359)
PHONE...................440 670-2112
Meredith Farrow, *CEO*
EMP: 13 **EST:** 2018
SALES (est): 966.41K **Privately Held**
Web: www.cleanremedies.com
SIC: 2833 Drugs and herbs: grading, grinding, and milling

(G-720)
COMPREHENSIVE LOGISTICS CO INC
1200a Chester Industrial Pkwy (44011-1081)
PHONE...................440 934-3517
Daryl Legg, *Brnch Mgr*
EMP: 30
Web: www.complog.com
SIC: 3714 Motor vehicle transmissions, drive assemblies, and parts
PA: Comprehensive Logistics, Co., Inc.
8200 Hlth Ctr Blvd Ste 10
Bonita Springs FL 34135

(G-721)
CORE TECHNOLOGY INC
1260 Moore Rd Ste E (44011-4021)
PHONE...................440 934-9935
Jack A Redilla, *Pr*
▲ **EMP:** 10 **EST:** 1995
SQ FT: 5,500
SALES (est): 1.6MM **Privately Held**
Web: www.coretechnology.com
SIC: 3629 Power conversion units, a.c. to d.c.: static-electric

(G-722)
CUTTING DYNAMICS LLC
35050 Avon Commerce Pkwy (44011-1374)
PHONE...................440 249-4666
Miles Arnone, *Brnch Mgr*
EMP: 94
SALES (corp-wide): 108.68MM **Privately Held**
Web: www.cuttingdynamics.com
SIC: 3599 Amusement park equipment
HQ: Cutting Dynamics, Llc
980 Jaycox Rd
Avon OH 44011
440 249-4150

(G-723)
CUTTING DYNAMICS LLC (HQ)
Also Called: CDI
980 Jaycox Rd (44011-1352)
PHONE...................440 249-4150
Miles Arnone, *CEO*
Marie Carson, *
▲ **EMP:** 30 **EST:** 1985
SQ FT: 50,000

SALES (est): 26.67MM
SALES (corp-wide): 108.68MM **Privately Held**
Web: www.cuttingdynamics.com
SIC: 3599 Machine shop, jobbing and repair
PA: Re Build Manufacturing, Llc
161 Worcester Rd Ste 606
Framingham MA 01701
774 777-5276

(G-724)
ECP CORPORATION
Also Called: Polycase Division
1305 Chester Industrial Pkwy (44011-1083)
PHONE...................440 934-0444
Steven Began, *Pr*
▲ **EMP:** 48 **EST:** 1951
SQ FT: 40,000
SALES (est): 9.34MM **Privately Held**
Web: www.polycase.com
SIC: 3469 Electronic enclosures, stamped or pressed metal

(G-725)
EIDP INC
Also Called: Dupont
38620 Chester Rd (44011-1074)
PHONE...................440 934-6444
Bob Langenderfer, *Mgr*
EMP: 10
SALES (corp-wide): 16.91B **Publicly Held**
Web: www.dupont.com
SIC: 2911 Petroleum refining
HQ: Eidp, Inc.
9330 Zionsville Rd
Indianapolis IN 46268
833 267-8382

(G-726)
FLAVORSEAL LLC
35179 Avon Commerce Pkwy (44011-1374)
PHONE...................440 937-3900
Chris Carroll, *Pr*
◆ **EMP:** 99 **EST:** 2010
SQ FT: 40,000
SALES (est): 30.6MM
SALES (corp-wide): 30.6MM **Privately Held**
Web: www.flavorseal.com
SIC: 2673 Bags: plastic, laminated, and coated
PA: M&Q Acquisition Llc
3 Earl Ave
Schuylkill Haven PA

(G-727)
FREEMAN MANUFACTURING & SUP CO (PA)
1101 Moore Rd (44011-4043)
PHONE...................440 934-1902
Lou Turco, *Pr*
Gerald W Rusk, *Ch Bd*
EMP: 50 **EST:** 1942
SQ FT: 110,000
SALES (est): 46.59MM
SALES (corp-wide): 46.59MM **Privately Held**
Web: www.freemansupply.com
SIC: 5084 3087 3543 2821 Industrial machinery and equipment; Custom compound purchased resins; Industrial patterns; Plastics materials and resins

(G-728)
GREEN ACQUISITION LLC
Also Called: Green Bearing Co
1141 Jaycox Rd (44011-1366)
PHONE...................440 930-7600
EMP: 10 **EST:** 1940
SALES (est): 2.69MM
SALES (corp-wide): 11.11MM **Privately Held**

SIC: 3714 Bearings, motor vehicle
PA: Bearing Technologies, Ltd.
33554 Pin Oak Pkwy
Avon Lake OH 44012
800 597-3486

(G-729)
KAYDON CORPORATION
1500 Nagel Rd (44011-1337)
PHONE..........................231 755-3741
◆ EMP: 71 EST: 1962
SALES (est): 5.05MM
SALES (corp-wide): 740.17MM **Privately
Held**
SIC: 3562 Ball bearings and parts
HQ: Kaydon Corporation
2723 S State St Ste 300
Ann Arbor MI 48104
734 747-7025

(G-730)
L & W INC
Also Called: L&W Cleveland
1190 Jaycox Rd (44011-1313)
PHONE..........................734 397-6300
Steve Schafer, *Mgr*
EMP: 54
SALES (corp-wide): 4.41B **Privately Held**
Web: www.autokiniton.com
SIC: 3469 3465 3441 3429 Stamping metal
for the trade; Automotive stampings;
Fabricated structural metal; Hardware, nec
HQ: L & W, Inc.
17757 Woodland Dr
New Boston MI 48164
734 397-6300

(G-731)
LEISURE TIME PDTS DESIGN CORP
1284 Miller Rd (44011-1004)
P.O. Box 276 (44011-0276)
PHONE..........................440 934-1032
Alan N Johnson, *Pr*
EMP: 6 EST: 1992
SALES (est): 232.45K **Privately Held**
Web: www.leisuretimecorp.com
SIC: 2326 3069 3844 3949 Aprons, work,
except rubberized and plastic: men's;
Aprons, vulcanized rubbed or rubberized
fabric; X-ray apparatus and tubes; Camping
equipment and supplies

(G-732)
LOGISYNC CORPORATION
Also Called: Logisync
1313 Lear Industrial Pkwy (44011-1360)
P.O. Box 368 (44011-0368)
PHONE..........................440 937-0388
▲ EMP: 7 EST: 1992
SALES (est): 216.73K **Privately Held**
Web: www.logisync.com
SIC: 7373 3672 3822 3625 Computer
integrated systems design; Printed circuit
boards; Environmental controls; Relays and
industrial controls

(G-733)
P M R INC
4661 Jaycox Rd (44011-2499)
PHONE..........................440 937-6241
Robert W Younglas, *Pr*
John Lucas, *VP*
Gay L Mcviegh, *Treas*
EMP: 6 EST: 1966
SQ FT: 25,000
SALES (est): 410.27K **Privately Held**
Web: www.pmr4ws.com
SIC: 3541 Machine tools, metal cutting type

(G-734)
PARKER-HANNIFIN CORPORATION
Parker Hannifin Corp
1160 Center Rd (44011-1297)
P.O. Box 158 (44011-0158)
PHONE..........................440 937-6211
EMP: 110
SALES (corp-wide): 14.35B **Publicly Held**
Web: www.parker.com
SIC: 3728 Wheels, aircraft
PA: Parker-Hannifin Corporation
6035 Parkland Blvd
Cleveland OH 44124
216 896-3000

(G-735)
PISTON AUTOMOTIVE LLC
37988 Avon Commerce Pkwy (44011-1389)
PHONE..........................313 541-8674
Brandon Tankefeley, *Mgr*
EMP: 89
SALES (corp-wide): 2.3B **Privately Held**
SIC: 3714 Motor vehicle parts and
accessories
HQ: Piston Automotive, L.L.C.
12723 Telegraph Rd
Redford MI 48239
313 541-8674

(G-736)
PRO-TEC INDUSTRIES INC
Also Called: Protech Industries
1384 Lear Industrial Pkwy (44011-1368)
PHONE..........................440 937-4142
Kurt F Van Luit, *Pr*
Jeff Leonard, *VP*
EMP: 6 EST: 1992
SQ FT: 6,000
SALES (est): 910.22K **Privately Held**
SIC: 3089 Plastics hardware and building
products

(G-737)
QUAL-FAB INC
34250 Mills Rd (44011-2471)
PHONE..........................440 327-5000
Gary Vanek, *Pr*
Craig Hartzell, *
Jeffrey Ogle, *
Kathy Bennett, *
David Peter, *
▼ EMP: 48 EST: 2000
SQ FT: 80,000
SALES (est): 9.71MM **Privately Held**
Web: www.qual-fab.net
SIC: 3312 3498 3433 Stainless steel;
Fabricated pipe and fittings; Heating
equipment, except electric

(G-738)
RICHTECH INDUSTRIES INC
34000 Lear Industrial Pkwy (44011-1375)
PHONE..........................440 937-4401
Kurt Van Luit, *CEO*
EMP: 9 EST: 1990
SALES (est): 958.7K **Privately Held**
Web: www.richtechindustries.com
SIC: 3299 1799 Moldings, architectural:
plaster of paris; Waterproofing

(G-739)
SOLAS LTD
Also Called: Solas Global Solutions
33587 Streamview Dr (44011-2598)
PHONE..........................650 501-0889
William Sammon, *Managing Member*
EMP: 21 EST: 2010
SALES (est): 354.56K **Privately Held**

SIC: 5113 2656 2653 2499 Disposable
plates, cups, napkins, and eating utensils;
Straws, drinking: made from purchased
material; Pallets, solid fiber: made from
purchased materials; Trays: wood, wicker,
and bagasse

(G-740)
TECHNIFAB INC (PA)
Also Called: Technifab Engineered Products
1355 Chester Industrial Pkwy (44011-1083)
PHONE..........................440 934-8324
Jeffrey L Petras, *Pr*
◆ EMP: 21 EST: 1994
SQ FT: 40,000
SALES (est): 8.2MM **Privately Held**
Web: www.technifabinc.com
SIC: 3086 Insulation or cushioning material,
foamed plastics

(G-741)
VALENSIL TECHNOLOGIES LLC
34910 Commerce Way (44011)
P.O. Box 388 (44011-0388)
PHONE..........................440 937-8181
Richard A West, *Prin*
EMP: 25 EST: 2014
SALES (est): 7.74MM **Privately Held**
Web: www.valensil.com
SIC: 3841 8733 Surgical and medical
instruments; Medical research

(G-742)
WESTLAKE TOOL & DIE MFG CO
1280 Moore Rd (44011-1014)
PHONE..........................440 934-5305
Seamus Walsh, *CEO*
EMP: 100 EST: 2017
SALES (est): 5.39MM **Privately Held**
Web: www.westlaketool.com
SIC: 3469 Stamping metal for the trade

(G-743)
WONDER MACHINE SERVICES INC
35340 Avon Commerce Pkwy (44011-1374)
PHONE..........................440 937-7500
George Woyansky, *Pr*
Jeanine Woyansky, *
Diane Woyansky, *
EMP: 30 EST: 1976
SQ FT: 22,500
SALES (est): 4.92MM **Privately Held**
Web: www.wondermachine.com
SIC: 3599 3541 Machine shop, jobbing and
repair; Machine tools, metal cutting type

(G-744)
WOODMAN AGITATOR INC
1404 Lear Industrial Pkwy (44011-1363)
PHONE..........................440 937-9865
James Bielozer, *Pr*
Mary Bielozer, *VP*
Keith M Bielozer, *VP*
◆ EMP: 17 EST: 1947
SALES (est): 3.47MM **Privately Held**
Web: www.woodmanagitator.com
SIC: 3559 Paint making machinery

(G-745)
WTD REAL ESTATE INC
1280 Moore Rd (44011-1014)
P.O. Box 240 (44011-0240)
PHONE..........................440 934-5305
Seamus E Walsh, *Pr*
Theresa Walsh, *VP*
EMP: 60 EST: 1968
SQ FT: 65,100
SALES (est): 2.41MM **Privately Held**
Web: www.westlaketool.com
SIC: 3469 Stamping metal for the trade

Avon Lake
Lorain County

(G-746)
APPLIED SPECIALTIES
INNOVATIONS LLC
Also Called: Asi Chemical Company
33555 Pin Oak Pkwy (44012-2319)
P.O. Box 307 (44012-0307)
PHONE..........................440 933-9442
◆ EMP: 30 EST: 1981
SALES (est): 12.42MM **Privately Held**
Web: www.appliedspecialties.com
SIC: 2899 8742 Water treating compounds;
Industry specialist consultants

(G-747)
AVIENT CORPORATION
33587 Walker Rd # Rdb-418 (44012-1145)
P.O. Box 31480 (44131-0480)
PHONE..........................440 930-3727
EMP: 34
Web: www.avient.com
SIC: 2821 Plastics materials and resins
PA: Avient Corporation
33587 Walker Rd
Avon Lake OH 44012

(G-748)
AVIENT CORPORATION (PA)
Also Called: Avient
33587 Walker Rd (44012-1145)
PHONE..........................440 930-1000
Ashish K Khandpur, *Pr*
Richard H Fearon, *Non-Executive
Chairman of the Board**
Jamie A Beggs, *Sr VP*
Philip G Clark Junior, *Sr VP*
Kristen A Gajewski, *Chief Human Resource
Officer*
◆ EMP: 73 EST: 1885
SALES (est): 3.24B **Publicly Held**
Web: www.avient.com
SIC: 2821 3087 5162 3081 Thermoplastic
materials; Custom compound purchased
resins; Resins; Unsupported plastics film
and sheet

(G-749)
AVON LAKE PRINTING
32908 Sorrento Ln (44012-2387)
PHONE..........................440 933-2078
Thomas Brock, *Owner*
EMP: 9 EST: 1985
SALES (est): 463.34K **Privately Held**
Web: www.minuteman.com
SIC: 2752 5943 Offset printing; Office forms
and supplies

(G-750)
AVON LAKE SHEET METAL CO
33574 Pin Oak Pkwy (44012-2320)
P.O. Box 64 (44012-0064)
PHONE..........................440 933-3505
Carl Wetzig Junior, *Pr*
Gary Wightman, *
EMP: 38 EST: 1953
SQ FT: 32,000
SALES (est): 4.28MM **Privately Held**
Web: www.avonlakesheetmetal.com
SIC: 3444 1761 Sheet metalwork; Sheet
metal work, nec

(G-751)
CATANIA MEDALLIC SPECIALTY INC
Also Called: Catania Medallic Specialities
668 Moore Rd (44012-2315)
PHONE..........................440 933-9595
Vince Frank, *Pr*

Trisha Frank, *
▲ **EMP:** 20 **EST:** 1971
SQ FT: 12,000
SALES (est): 2.53MM **Privately Held**
Web: www.cataniainc.com
SIC: 3469 3965 3369 2395 Ornamental metal stampings; Fasteners, buttons, needles, and pins; Nonferrous foundries, nec; Pleating and stitching

(G-752)
CUTTING DYNAMICS LLC
33597 Pin Oak Pkwy (44012-2319)
PHONE.................................440 930-2862
Miles Arnone, *CEO*
EMP: 94
SALES (corp-wide): 108.68MM **Privately Held**
Web: www.cuttingdynamics.com
SIC: 3599 Machine shop, jobbing and repair
HQ: Cutting Dynamics, Llc
980 Jaycox Rd
Avon OH 44011
440 249-4150

(G-753)
DANCO METAL PRODUCTS LLC
760 Moore Rd (44012-2317)
PHONE.................................440 871-2300
EMP: 95
Web: www.dancometal.com
SIC: 3444 3644 3469 3443 Metal housings, enclosures, casings, and other containers; Noncurrent-carrying wiring devices; Metal stampings, nec; Fabricated plate work (boiler shop)

(G-754)
ELECTRA SOUND INC (PA)
Also Called: Electrasound TV & Appl Svc
32483 English Turn (44012-3321)
PHONE.................................216 433-9600
TOLL FREE: 800
Robert C Masa Junior, *CEO*
Patricia Masa, *
Charles C Masa, *
EMP: 70 **EST:** 1968
SALES (est): 3.86MM
SALES (corp-wide): 3.86MM **Privately Held**
Web: www.techni-car.com
SIC: 3694 7622 5065 5731 Automotive electrical equipment, nec; Television repair shop; Sound equipment, electronic; Automotive sound equipment

(G-755)
EMPIRE SYSTEMS INC
33683 Walker Rd (44012-1044)
PHONE.................................440 653-9300
Jeffery Eagens, *CEO*
Cheryle Hayley, *CFO*
◆ **EMP:** 9 **EST:** 2003
SQ FT: 41,000
SALES (est): 3.94MM **Privately Held**
Web: www.empiresystemsinc.com
SIC: 8711 3559 Consulting engineer; Foundry machinery and equipment

(G-756)
FORD MOTOR COMPANY
Also Called: Ford
650 Miller Rd (44012-2398)
PHONE.................................440 933-1215
Deborah S Kent, *Engr*
EMP: 247
SALES (corp-wide): 184.99B **Publicly Held**
Web: www.ford.com
SIC: 5511 3711 Automobiles, new and used; Motor vehicles and car bodies

PA: Ford Motor Company
1 American Rd
Dearborn MI 48126
313 322-3000

(G-757)
GEON PERFORMANCE SOLUTIONS LLC
556 Moore Rd (44012-2313)
PHONE.................................440 930-1000
EMP: 75
Web: www.geon.com
SIC: 2821 Thermoplastic materials
HQ: Geon Performance Solutions, Llc
25777 Detroit Rd Ste 202
Westlake OH 44145
800 438-4366

(G-758)
HASHIER & HASHIER MFG
644 Moore Rd (44012-2315)
PHONE.................................440 933-4883
Frank Hashier, *Pr*
EMP: 6 **EST:** 1976
SQ FT: 6,000
SALES (est): 1.08MM **Privately Held**
Web: www.hashiermfg.com
SIC: 3469 Stamping metal for the trade

(G-759)
HELICAL LINE PRODUCTS CO
659 Miller Rd (44012-2306)
P.O. Box 217 (44012-0217)
PHONE.................................440 933-9263
Albert C Bonds, *Pr*
William T Bonds, *
Robert S Bonds, *
▼ **EMP:** 23 **EST:** 1964
SQ FT: 33,000
SALES (est): 2.72MM **Privately Held**
Web: www.helical-line.com
SIC: 3496 Miscellaneous fabricated wire products

(G-760)
HINKLEY LIGHTING INC (PA)
Also Called: Fredrick Ramond
33000 Pin Oak Pkwy (44012-2641)
PHONE.................................440 653-5500
Jess Wiedemer, *Pr*
Eric Wiedemer, *
◆ **EMP:** 45 **EST:** 1922
SQ FT: 100,000
SALES (est): 23.2MM
SALES (corp-wide): 23.2MM **Privately Held**
Web: www.hinkley.com
SIC: 3645 3646 3634 Residential lighting fixtures; Commercial lighting fixtures; Ceiling fans

(G-761)
JOHN CHRIST WINERY INC
32421 Walker Rd (44012-2226)
PHONE.................................440 933-9672
Dean Gunter, *Genl Mgr*
EMP: 8 **EST:** 2001
SALES (est): 285.9K **Privately Held**
Web: www.laughingbomb.com
SIC: 2084 Wines

(G-762)
KLINGSHIRN WINERY INC
33050 Webber Rd (44012-2330)
PHONE.................................440 933-6666
Lee Klingshirn, *Pr*
Lee Klingshirn, *Pr*
Nancy Klingshirn, *VP*
EMP: 8 **EST:** 1935
SQ FT: 3,850
SALES (est): 516.91K **Privately Held**

Web: www.klingshirnwine.com
SIC: 2084 Wines

(G-763)
LUBRIZOL GLOBAL MANAGEMENT INC
550 Moore Rd (44012-2313)
P.O. Box 134 (44012-0134)
PHONE.................................440 933-0400
Joseph Lazeunick, *Brnch Mgr*
EMP: 50
SALES (corp-wide): 424.23B **Publicly Held**
Web: www.lubrizol.com
SIC: 2899 2821 Chemical preparations, nec; Plastics materials and resins
HQ: Lubrizol Global Management, Inc.
9911 Brecksville Rd
Cleveland OH 44141
216 447-5000

(G-764)
MARKERS INC
33490 Pin Oak Pkwy (44012-2318)
PHONE.................................440 933-5927
Dale Hlavin, *Stockholder*
EMP: 6 **EST:** 1987
SALES (est): 247.28K **Privately Held**
Web: www.markersinc.com
SIC: 2399 5261 Banners, pennants, and flags; Lawn and garden supplies

(G-765)
MEXICHEM SPECIALTY RESINS INC (HQ)
33653 Walker Rd (44012-1044)
P.O. Box 277 (44012-0277)
PHONE.................................440 930-1435
Nicholas Peter Ballas, *CEO*
Jorge Alberto Barron Garcia, *
◆ **EMP:** 27 **EST:** 2013
SALES (est): 82.66MM **Privately Held**
Web: www.vestolit.com
SIC: 2822 2821 Ethylene-propylene rubbers, EPDM polymers; Polymethyl methacrylate resins, plexiglass
PA: Orbia Advance Corporation, S.A.B. De C.V.
Av. Paseo De La Reforma No. 483 Piso 47
Mexico CMX 06500

(G-766)
NATIONAL FLEET SVCS OHIO LLC
607 Miller Rd (44012-2306)
PHONE.................................440 930-5177
Tim Lariviere, *Pr*
EMP: 12 **EST:** 2008
SALES (est): 3.77MM **Privately Held**
Web: www.nationalfleetservices.com
SIC: 3089 7532 Automotive parts, plastic; Van conversion

(G-767)
NORTH AMERICAN COMPOSITES
33660 Pin Oak Pkwy (44012-2322)
PHONE.................................440 930-0602
EMP: 9 **EST:** 2019
SALES (est): 2.03MM **Privately Held**
Web: www.ip-corporation.com
SIC: 2821 Plastics materials and resins

(G-768)
POLYMER DIAGNOSTICS INC
33587 Walker Rd (44012-1145)
PHONE.................................440 930-1361
Tom Waltermire, *CEO*
EMP: 20 **EST:** 1998
SALES (est): 9.29MM **Publicly Held**
Web: www.polymerdiagnostics.com

SIC: 2869 Laboratory chemicals, organic
PA: Avient Corporation
33587 Walker Rd
Avon Lake OH 44012

(G-769)
POLYONE LLC
33587 Walker Rd (44012-1145)
PHONE.................................440 930-1000
Robert M Patterson, *Pr*
EMP: 10 **EST:** 2013
SALES (est): 8.53MM **Publicly Held**
Web: www.avient.com
SIC: 2821 Thermoplastic materials
PA: Avient Corporation
33587 Walker Rd
Avon Lake OH 44012

(G-770)
SPARTECH MEXICO HOLDING CO TWO
33587 Walker Rd (44012-1145)
PHONE.................................440 930-3619
Richard N Altice, *Pr*
EMP: 13 **EST:** 2015
SALES (est): 853.21K **Privately Held**
SIC: 2821 Plastics materials and resins

(G-771)
THOGUS PRODUCTS COMPANY
33490 Pin Oak Pkwy (44012-2318)
PHONE.................................440 933-8850
Helen Thompson, *CEO*
Matthew Grantson, *
◆ **EMP:** 96 **EST:** 1958
SQ FT: 50,000
SALES (est): 20.27MM **Privately Held**
Web: www.thogus.com
SIC: 3089 3494 3492 Injection molding of plastics; Valves and pipe fittings, nec; Fluid power valves and hose fittings

(G-772)
W R G INC
Also Called: Buckeye Metals
631 Parkside Dr (44012-4006)
PHONE.................................216 351-8494
EMP: 25
SIC: 5093 3341 Nonferrous metals scrap; Secondary nonferrous metals

(G-773)
WATTEREDGE LLC (DH)
Also Called: Watteredge
567 Miller Rd (44012-2304)
PHONE.................................440 933-6110
Joseph P Langhenry, *Pr*
◆ **EMP:** 64 **EST:** 1970
SQ FT: 65,000
SALES (est): 26.43MM
SALES (corp-wide): 584.3MM **Privately Held**
Web: www.watteredge.com
SIC: 5085 3643 5051 3052 Industrial supplies; Current-carrying wiring services; Metals service centers and offices; Rubber and plastics hose and beltings
HQ: Coleman Cable, Llc
1 Overlook Pt
Lincolnshire IL 60069
847 672-2300

(G-774)
WOLFF TOOL & MFG COMPANY INC
Also Called: O G Bell
139 Lear Rd (44012-1904)
PHONE.................................440 933-7797
Alan Wolff, *Pr*
Barbara Wolff, *VP*
EMP: 10 **EST:** 1946
SQ FT: 1,610

SALES (est): 749.62K **Privately Held**
Web: www.ogbell.com
SIC: **3599** Machine shop, jobbing and repair

Baltic
Tuscarawas County

(G-775)
ANDAL WOODWORKING
1411 Township Road 151 (43804-9627)
PHONE..............................330 897-8059
Andrew Yoder, *Prin*
Andrew Yoder, *Owner*
EMP: 10 EST: 2008
SALES (est): 353.98K **Privately Held**
SIC: **2511** Wood bedroom furniture

(G-776)
BALTIC COUNTRY MEATS
Also Called: Baltic Meats
3320 State Route 557 (43804-9609)
PHONE..............................330 897-7025
Susie Raber, *Owner*
Dan Miller, *Owner*
EMP: 6 EST: 1987
SALES (est): 483.17K **Privately Held**
SIC: **2011** 5411 Meat packing plants;
　Delicatessen stores

(G-777)
FLEX TECHNOLOGIES INC
Also Called: Poly Flex
3430 State Route 93 (43804-9705)
P.O. Box 300 (43804-0300)
PHONE..............................330 897-6311
Brian Harrison, *Mgr*
EMP: 53
SQ FT: 20,000
SALES (corp-wide): 6MM **Privately Held**
Web: www.flextechnologies.com
SIC: **2821** 5169 3087 Molding compounds,
　plastics; Synthetic resins, rubber, and
　plastic materials; Custom compound
　purchased resins
PA: Flex Technologies, Inc.
　5479 Gundy Dr
　Midvale OH 44653
　740 922-5992

(G-778)
GERBER & SONS INC (PA)
Also Called: Gerber & Sons
201 E Main St (43804-3516)
P.O. Box 248 (43804-0248)
PHONE..............................330 897-6201
Thomas Gerber, *Pr*
Michael Gerber, *
Douglas A Davis, *
Steven Gerber, *
EMP: 25 EST: 1905
SQ FT: 7,200
SALES (est): 11.13MM
SALES (corp-wide): 11.13MM **Privately Held**
Web: www.gerberandsons.com
SIC: **2048** 5999 Livestock feeds; Farm
　equipment and supplies

(G-779)
HOLMES PANEL LLC
3052 State Route 557 (43804-7504)
PHONE..............................330 897-5040
Junior Keim, *Pt*
Dan Hershberger, *Pt*
Wayne Hershberger, *Pt*
EMP: 9 EST: 2000
SQ FT: 600
SALES (est): 394.95K **Privately Held**

SIC: **5211** 2511 Lumber and other building
　materials; Wood household furniture

(G-780)
POLYNEW INC
3557 State Route 93 (43804-9705)
P.O. Box 318 (43804-0318)
PHONE..............................330 897-3202
Robert Burket, *Pr*
Gail Burket, *Sec*
EMP: 6 EST: 1988
SQ FT: 12,000
SALES (est): 475.56K **Privately Held**
Web: www.polynew.com
SIC: **2821** Plastics materials and resins

(G-781)
TBONE SALES LLC
Also Called: Tbone Sales
410 N Ray St (43804-8901)
P.O. Box 75 (43804-0075)
PHONE..............................330 897-6131
EMP: 7 EST: 1954
SQ FT: 7,500
SALES (est): 1.45MM **Privately Held**
Web: www.tbonesales.com
SIC: **5411** 7549 5531 5511 Convenience
　stores; Automotive maintenance services;
　Auto and truck equipment and parts;
　Trucks, tractors, and trailers: new and used

(G-782)
TRI STATE DAIRY LLC (PA)
Also Called: Es Steiner Dairy
9946 Fiat Rd Sw (43804-9049)
PHONE..............................330 897-5555
EMP: 6 EST: 2011
SALES (est): 1.19MM
SALES (corp-wide): 1.19MM **Privately Held**
SIC: **2022** Cheese; natural and processed

Baltimore
Fairfield County

(G-783)
BRIAN HOSHER BACKHOE PLUM
1053 W Market St (43105-1129)
PHONE..............................740 503-4434
EMP: 6 EST: 2017
SALES (est): 297.8K **Privately Held**
SIC: **3531** Backhoes

(G-784)
CARAUSTAR INDUSTRIES INC
Ohio Paperboard
310 W Water St (43105-1276)
PHONE..............................740 862-4167
Jeff Peters, *Mgr*
EMP: 56
SALES (corp-wide): 5.45B **Publicly Held**
Web: www.greif.com
SIC: **2631** 2611 Paperboard mills; Pulp mills
HQ: Caraustar Industries, Inc.
　5000 Astell Pwdr Sprng Rd
　Austell GA 30106
　770 948-3101

(G-785)
FILTER TECHNOLOGY INC
11885 Paddock View Ct Nw (43105-9556)
PHONE..............................614 921-9801
Ray Reisiger, *Prin*
EMP: 6 EST: 2011
SALES (est): 99.67K **Privately Held**
SIC: **3569** Filters

(G-786)
GREEN GOURMET FOODS LLC
515 N Main St (43105-1214)
PHONE..............................740 400-4212
EMP: 6 EST: 2011
SQ FT: 150,000
SALES (est): 421.55K **Privately Held**
Web: www.greengourmetfoods.net
SIC: **2034** Potato products, dried and
　dehydrated

(G-787)
SAW DUST LTD
4799 Refugee Rd Nw (43105-9424)
PHONE..............................740 862-0612
James Wagenbrenner, *Owner*
EMP: 8 EST: 1995
SALES (est): 101.55K **Privately Held**
Web: www.edrichlumber.com
SIC: **2431** Woodwork, interior and
　ornamental, nec

(G-788)
TRI-TECH LED SYSTEMS LLC
Also Called: Tri-Tech
600 W Market St (43105-1176)
PHONE..............................614 593-2868
Scott Graham, *CEO*
David Hanson, *CFO*
Timothy Bosick, *VP*
Terry Nicopolis, *VP*
Bill Mcguire, *Acctnt*
EMP: 7 EST: 2012
SQ FT: 2,000
SALES (est): 926.85K **Privately Held**
SIC: **3674** Light emitting diodes

(G-789)
WOODEN HORSE
204 N Main St (43105-1212)
PHONE..............................740 503-5243
Wade Messmer, *Owner*
Barbara Messmer, *Pt*
EMP: 6 EST: 1979
SQ FT: 2,400
SALES (est): 241.82K **Privately Held**
SIC: **5947** 5092 2426 8299 Gift, novelty, and
　souvenir shop; Toys and hobby goods and
　supplies; Hardwood dimension and flooring
　mills; Arts and crafts schools

Barberton
Summit County

(G-790)
AKAY HOLDINGS INC
1031 Lambert St (44203-1611)
PHONE..............................330 753-8458
Albert Kay, *Pr*
Charles Kay, *Marketing**
John Lindeman, *
EMP: 23 EST: 1946
SQ FT: 90,000
SALES (est): 4.26MM **Privately Held**
Web: www.asbindustries.com
SIC: **1799** 3599 3542 4215 Coating,
　caulking, and weather, water, and
　fireproofing; Machine shop, jobbing and
　repair; Presses: hydraulic and pneumatic,
　mechanical and manual; Courier services,
　except by air

(G-791)
AKRON FOUNDRY CO
Also Called: Akron Electric
1025 Eagon St (44203-1603)
PHONE..............................330 745-3101
Mike Pancoe, *Genl Mgr*
EMP: 9

SALES (corp-wide): 24.37MM **Privately Held**
Web: www.akronelectric.com
SIC: **1731** 3699 3644 3444 Electrical work;
　Electrical equipment and supplies, nec;
　Noncurrent-carrying wiring devices; Sheet
　metalwork
PA: Akron Foundry Co.
　2728 Wingate Ave
　Akron OH 44314
　330 745-3101

(G-792)
AMERICAN MOLDING COMPANY INC
711 Wooster Rd W (44203-2444)
PHONE..............................330 620-6799
EMP: 11 EST: 2014
SALES (est): 167.04K **Privately Held**
Web: www.americanmolding.us
SIC: **3089** Injection molding of plastics

(G-793)
ANDERSON GRAPHICS INC
711 Wooster Rd W (44203-2444)
PHONE..............................330 745-2165
John Anderson, *Pr*
Larry Okolish, *
EMP: 30 EST: 1979
SALES (est): 389.56K **Privately Held**
Web: www.anderson-graphics.com
SIC: **2752** 2759 2789 2791 Offset printing;
　Commercial printing, nec; Bookbinding and
　related work; Typesetting

(G-794)
B & C RESEARCH INC
Also Called: B & C Research
842 Norton Ave (44203-1750)
P.O. Box 70 (44203-0070)
PHONE..............................330 848-4000
Bob Clements, *Ch Bd*
Louis Bilinovich, *
▲ **EMP: 500 EST:** 1985
SQ FT: 100,000
SALES (est): 41.71MM
SALES (corp-wide): 7.43B **Publicly Held**
SIC: **3599** Machine shop, jobbing and repair
HQ: Howmet Securities Llc
　101 Cherry St Ste 400
　Burlington VT 05401
　802 658-2661

(G-795)
B & P POLISHING INC
123 9th St Nw (44203-2455)
P.O. Box 408 (44203-0408)
PHONE..............................330 753-4202
Louie Vilinovach, *Pr*
▲ **EMP: 11 EST:** 2001
SALES (est): 981.48K **Privately Held**
SIC: **3291** Buffing or polishing wheels,
　abrasive or nonabrasive

(G-796)
B&C MACHINE CO LLC
401 Newell St (44203-2018)
P.O. Box 345 (44203-0345)
PHONE..............................330 745-4013
EMP: 10 EST: 2002
SQ FT: 300,000
SALES (est): 829.04K **Privately Held**
SIC: **3599** 3714 3743 3398 Machine shop,
　jobbing and repair; Motor vehicle parts and
　accessories; Locomotives and parts; Metal
　heat treating

(G-797)
BABCOCK & WILCOX COMPANY
Also Called: Barberton Facility
91 Stirling Ave (44203-2600)
PHONE..............................330 753-4511

Doug Garlock, *Brnch Mgr*
EMP: 20
SALES (corp-wide): 717.33MM **Publicly Held**
Web: www.babcock.com
SIC: 3443 Fabricated plate work (boiler shop)
HQ: The Babcock & Wilcox Company
1200 E Market St Ste 650
Akron OH 44305
330 753-4511

(G-798)
BARBERTON STEEL INDUSTRIES INC
240 E Huston St (44203-3044)
P.O. Box 350 (44203-0350)
PHONE..........................330 745-6837
Jim Kotarski, *CEO*
Jim Cecconi, *
EMP: 48 **EST:** 2004
SALES (est): 5.35MM **Privately Held**
Web: www.barbertonsteel.net
SIC: 3321 Gray iron castings, nec

(G-799)
BUCKEYE ABRASIVE INC
1020 Eagon St (44203-1604)
PHONE..........................330 753-1041
Robert J Armour, *Pr*
EMP: 10 **EST:** 1954
SQ FT: 14,400
SALES (est): 978.29K **Privately Held**
Web: www.buckeyeabrasive.com
SIC: 3291 Wheels, abrasive

(G-800)
BWX TECHNOLOGIES INC
91 Stirling Ave (44203-2615)
PHONE..........................330 860-1692
EMP: 103
Web: www.bwxt.com
SIC: 3823 Process control instruments
PA: Bwx Technologies, Inc.
800 Main St Fl 4
Lynchburg VA 24504

(G-801)
CARDINAL RUBBER COMPANY
939 Wooster Rd N (44203-1698)
PHONE..........................330 745-2191
Diane Mcconnell, *Pr*
Thomas R Schnee, *
Robert F Schnee Junior, *Stockholder*
▲ **EMP:** 30 **EST:** 1944
SQ FT: 80,000
SALES (est): 1.88MM **Privately Held**
Web: www.cardinalrubbercompany.com
SIC: 3069 3061 3479 2891 Molded rubber products; Automotive rubber goods (mechanical); Bonderizing of metal or metal products; Adhesives and sealants

(G-802)
COMPASS SYSTEMS & SALES LLC
Also Called: Compass S&S
5185 New Haven Cir (44203-4672)
PHONE..........................330 733-2111
Robert S Sherrod, *Pr*
Mark Rubin, *
Phil Hart, *
Brenda Pavlantos, *
▼ **EMP:** 56 **EST:** 2014
SQ FT: 43,500
SALES (est): 11.48MM **Privately Held**
Web: www.compasssystems.com
SIC: 3542 0724 Mechanical (pneumatic or hydraulic) metal forming machines; Cotton ginning

(G-803)
DAVIS PRINTING COMPANY
Also Called: Davis Graphic Comm Solutions
101 Robinson Ave (44203-3502)
PHONE..........................330 745-3113
◆ **EMP:** 38 **EST:** 1906
SALES (est): 4.97MM **Privately Held**
Web: www.davisgcs.com
SIC: 2752 3993 2791 2789 Commercial printing, lithographic; Signs and advertising specialties; Typesetting; Bookbinding and related work

(G-804)
FLOHR MACHINE COMPANY INC
Also Called: Flohrmachine.com
1028 Coventry Rd (44203-1636)
PHONE..........................330 745-3030
Gerard Flohr, *Pr*
Ivan W Flohr, *
William Flohr, *
Joseph Flohr, *
Jude Flohr, *
EMP: 24 **EST:** 1966
SQ FT: 6,000
SALES (est): 3.47MM **Privately Held**
Web: www.flohrmachine.com
SIC: 3599 Machine shop, jobbing and repair

(G-805)
FLORENCE ALLOYS INC
Also Called: Hard Drive Co
121 Snyder Ave (44203-4007)
PHONE..........................330 745-9141
Jim Federan, *Pr*
EMP: 7 **EST:** 1984
SQ FT: 7,700
SALES (est): 613.22K **Privately Held**
Web: www.ifparty.com
SIC: 3714 5013 Transmissions, motor vehicle ; Automotive supplies and parts

(G-806)
GENERAL PLASTEX INC
35 Stuver Pl (44203-2417)
PHONE..........................330 745-7775
Renee Hershberger, *Pr*
EMP: 31 **EST:** 1985
SQ FT: 52,500
SALES (est): 1.93MM **Privately Held**
Web: www.generalplastex.com
SIC: 7699 3452 Industrial machinery and equipment repair; Screws, metal

(G-807)
GLAS ORNAMENTAL METALS INC
1559 Waterloo Rd (44203-1335)
PHONE..........................330 753-0215
John Glas, *Pr*
Rita Glas, *Ch Bd*
Karol Glas, *Sec*
EMP: 9 **EST:** 1961
SQ FT: 6,300
SALES (est): 972.58K **Privately Held**
Web: www.glasornamental.com
SIC: 3446 Railings, prefabricated metal

(G-808)
GLASS SURFACE SYSTEMS INC
Also Called: G S S
24 Brown St (44203-2315)
P.O. Box 311 (44203)
PHONE..........................330 745-8500
Barry Jacobs, *Pr*
EMP: 75 **EST:** 1970
SQ FT: 17,000
SALES (est): 2.38MM **Privately Held**
Web: www.glasscoat.com
SIC: 3231 Strengthened or reinforced glass

(G-809)
HANNECARD ROLLER COATINGS INC
1031 Lambert St (44203-1611)
PHONE..........................330 753-8458
Dirk Vidts, *CEO*
Charles Kay, *
Peter De Marre, *
EMP: 33 **EST:** 2020
SALES (est): 8.24MM **Privately Held**
Web: www.asbindustries.com
SIC: 3069 Top roll covering, for textile mill machinery: rubber

(G-810)
HEXPOL COMPOUNDING PC INC (HQ)
Also Called: Preferred Compounding
1020 Lambert St (44203-1612)
PHONE..........................330 798-4790
Mikael Fryklund, *Pr*
Joe Hudson, *
Scott Lieberman, *
Andrew Chan, *
Randy Niedermier, *
▲ **EMP:** 109 **EST:** 2002
SQ FT: 70,000
SALES (est): 98.21MM
SALES (corp-wide): 6.47MM **Privately Held**
Web: www.preferredperforms.com
SIC: 3069 Custom compounding of rubber materials
PA: Hexpol Ab
Skeppsbron 3
Malmo 211 2
40254660

(G-811)
HOWMET AEROSPACE INC
Also Called: HOWMET AEROSPACE INC
842 Norton Ave (44203-1715)
PHONE..........................330 848-4000
Tim Doyle, *Brnch Mgr*
EMP: 135
SALES (corp-wide): 7.43B **Publicly Held**
Web: www.howmet.com
SIC: 3353 Aluminum sheet and strip
PA: Howmet Aerospace Inc.
201 Isabella St Ste 200
Pittsburgh PA 15212
412 553-1950

(G-012)
HYCOM INC
374 5th St Nw (44203-2127)
PHONE..........................330 753-2330
Thomas J Bilinovich, *CEO*
Ralph Bowling, *
EMP: 45 **EST:** 1993
SQ FT: 126,684
SALES (est): 10.16MM **Privately Held**
Web: www.hycominc.com
SIC: 3498 Tube fabricating (contract bending and shaping)

(G-813)
IDEAL DRAPERY COMPANY INC
1024 Wooster Rd N (44203-1626)
PHONE..........................330 745-9873
FAX: 330 745-1504
EMP: 17
SQ FT: 4,000
SALES (est): 993.92K **Privately Held**
SIC: 2395 7389 Decorative and novelty stitching: for the trade; Sewing contractor

(G-814)
JCI JONES CHEMICALS INC
2500 Vanderhoof Rd (44203-4650)

PHONE..........................330 825-2531
Dan Casmey, *Mgr*
EMP: 19
SQ FT: 22,848
SALES (corp-wide): 105.12MM **Privately Held**
Web: www.jcichem.com
SIC: 2812 8734 Chlorine, compressed or liquefied; Testing laboratories
PA: Jci Jones Chemicals, Inc.
1765 Ringling Blvd
Sarasota FL 34236
941 330-1537

(G-815)
JOHNDOW INDUSTRIES INC
151 Snyder Ave (44203-4007)
PHONE..........................330 753-6895
Drew Dawson, *Pr*
Robert Christy, *
◆ **EMP:** 24 **EST:** 1981
SQ FT: 120,000
SALES (est): 11.48MM **Privately Held**
Web: www.johndow.com
SIC: 3559 Automotive maintenance equipment

(G-816)
KEM ADVERTISING AND PRTG LLC
564 W Tuscarawas Ave Ste 104 (44203-8213)
PHONE..........................330 818-5061
Kimberly Okolish, *Prin*
EMP: 6 **EST:** 2014
SALES (est): 224.43K **Privately Held**
SIC: 2752 Commercial printing, lithographic

(G-817)
LINDE INC
Also Called: Praxair
4805 Fairland Rd (44203-3913)
P.O. Box 509 (44203-0509)
PHONE..........................330 825-4449
Dave Corly, *Mgr*
EMP: 6
Web: www.lindeus.com
SIC: 2813 Industrial gases
HQ: Linde Inc.
10 Riverview Dr
Danbury CT 06810
203 837-2000

(G-818)
MAC RESOURCES LLC
711 Wooster Rd W (44203-2444)
P.O. Box 590 (44203-0590)
PHONE..........................330 294-0494
Michael Giovanini, *Managing Member*
Joseph Giovanini, *Managing Member*
▲ **EMP:** 16 **EST:** 2007
SQ FT: 3,300
SALES (est): 2.83MM **Privately Held**
Web: www.magresources.net
SIC: 5023 2431 2591 8742 Venetian blinds; Blinds (shutters), wood; Window blinds; Business planning and organizing services

(G-819)
MALCO PRODUCTS INC (PA)
Also Called: Malco Products
361 Fairview Ave (44203-2700)
P.O. Box 892 (44203-0892)
PHONE..........................330 753-0361
◆ **EMP:** 175 **EST:** 1953
SALES (est): 63.82MM
SALES (corp-wide): 63.82MM **Privately Held**
Web: www.malcopro.com

SIC: 2842 8742 2899 2841 Polishes and sanitation goods; Marketing consulting services; Chemical preparations, nec; Soap and other detergents

(G-820)
MAY LIN SILICONE PRODUCTS INC
955 Wooster Rd W (44203-7149)
P.O. Box 335 (44203-0335)
PHONE.................................330 825-9019
Linda Weaver, *Pr*
Dave Weaver, *VP*
EMP: 6 EST: 1958
SQ FT: 1,800
SALES (est): 229.61K **Privately Held**
Web: www.may-lin.com
SIC: 3069 3053 Molded rubber products; Gaskets, all materials

(G-821)
MCCOY GROUP INC
1020 Eagon St (44203-1604)
PHONE.................................330 753-1041
Penni Cooper, *Prin*
EMP: 6 EST: 2019
SALES (est): 819.02K **Privately Held**
Web: www.buckeyeabrasive.com
SIC: 2431 Millwork

(G-822)
MERRYWEATHER FOAM INC (PA)
Also Called: Merryweather
11 Brown St (44203-2300)
PHONE.................................330 753-0353
▲ **EMP: 35 EST:** 1944
SALES (est): 16.67MM
SALES (corp-wide): 16.67MM **Privately Held**
Web: www.merryweather.com
SIC: 3086 3069 3089 2891 Plastics foam products; Sponge rubber and sponge rubber products; Extruded finished plastics products, nec; Adhesives and sealants

(G-823)
MITCHELL PLASTICS INC
130 31st St Nw (44203-7238)
PHONE.................................330 825-2461
Mitchell E Volk, *Pr*
EMP: 22 EST: 1976
SQ FT: 15,000
SALES (est): 2.32MM **Privately Held**
Web: www.mpicase.com
SIC: 3069 3993 Laboratory sundries: cases, covers, funnels, cups, etc.; Signs and advertising specialties

(G-824)
NEIDERT FABRICATING INC
712 Wooster Rd W (44203-2420)
PHONE.................................330 753-3331
Paul Neidert, *Pr*
Carol Neidert, *Sec*
EMP: 8 EST: 1980
SQ FT: 9,000
SALES (est): 721.24K **Privately Held**
Web: www.neidertfabricating.com
SIC: 3599 3441 Machine shop, jobbing and repair; Fabricated structural metal

(G-825)
NOVATION SOLUTIONS LLC
25 Foundation Pl (44203-3520)
PHONE.................................330 620-6721
Thomas J Tupa, *Prin*
EMP: 13 EST: 2012
SALES (est): 5.12MM **Privately Held**
Web: www.novationsi.com
SIC: 2869 Industrial organic chemicals, nec

(G-826)
NOVEX OPERATING COMPANY LLC
74 Robinson Ave (44203-2630)
PHONE.................................330 335-2371
EMP: 14 EST: 2022
SALES (est): 1.12MM **Privately Held**
Web: www.novexinc.com
SIC: 3052 3069 Rubber belting; Sheets, hard rubber

(G-827)
OGONEK CUSTOM HARDWOOD INC (PA)
61 E State St (44203-2730)
PHONE.................................833 718-2531
Daniel Ogonek, *Pr*
EMP: 7 EST: 1985
SALES (est): 1.94MM
SALES (corp-wide): 1.94MM **Privately Held**
Web: www.ogonekhardwoods.com
SIC: 2431 2426 7389 Millwork; Furniture stock and parts, hardwood; Interior designer

(G-828)
OHIO PRECISION MOLDING INC
Also Called: Opm
122 E Tuscarawas Ave (44203-2628)
PHONE.................................330 745-9393
Bruce Vereecken, *Pr*
Joe Vereecken, *
David Vereecken, *
Karen Vereecken, *Stockholder**
▲ **EMP: 30 EST:** 1994
SQ FT: 30,000
SALES (est): 6.94MM **Privately Held**
Web: www.ohioprecisionmolding.com
SIC: 3089 Injection molding of plastics

(G-829)
OLSON SHEET METAL CNSTR CO
465 Glenn St (44203-1499)
PHONE.................................330 745-8225
John Sveda, *Pr*
Joanne Sveda, *Sec*
EMP: 6 EST: 1938
SALES (est): 578.36K **Privately Held**
SIC: 3441 Fabricated structural metal

(G-830)
PARATUS SUPPLY INC
30 2nd St Sw (44203-2620)
PHONE.................................330 745-3600
Craig Cutcher, *VP*
John Sesic, *Genl Mgr*
EMP: 10 EST: 2010
SALES (est): 973.22K **Privately Held**
Web: www.paratussupply.com
SIC: 3563 3086 Spraying and dusting equipment; Insulation or cushioning material, foamed plastics

(G-831)
PATHFINDER CMPT SYSTEMS INC
345 5th St Ne (44203-2863)
PHONE.................................330 928-1961
Rodney Starcher, *Pr*
Chuck Rainer, *VP*
EMP: 7 EST: 1990
SALES (est): 863.23K **Privately Held**
Web: www.pathfindercs.com
SIC: 7372 7371 Prepackaged software; Custom computer programming services

(G-832)
PEACEFUL FRUITS LLC
101 E Tuscarawas Ave (44203-2627)
PHONE.................................330 356-8515
Evan Delahanty, *CEO*
EMP: 12 EST: 2014

SALES (est): 1.74MM **Privately Held**
Web: www.peacefulfruits.com
SIC: 2034 Dried and dehydrated fruits

(G-833)
PLASTIC MOLD TECHNOLOGY INC
40 Stuver Pl (44203-2416)
PHONE.................................330 848-4921
Damir Petkovic, *Pr*
Robin Petkovic, *Sec*
EMP: 8 EST: 1994
SQ FT: 6,500
SALES (est): 774.79K **Privately Held**
SIC: 3544 Industrial molds

(G-834)
PPG INDUSTRIES INC
Also Called: South Plant
4829 Fairland Rd (44203-3905)
PHONE.................................330 825-0831
Carl E Johnson, *Brnch Mgr*
EMP: 24
SALES (corp-wide): 18.25B **Publicly Held**
Web: www.ppg.com
SIC: 2851 Paints and paint additives
PA: Ppg Industries, Inc.
1 Ppg Pl
Pittsburgh PA 15272
412 434-3131

(G-835)
REVLIS CORPORATION
Also Called: Revlon
2845 Newpark Dr (44203-1047)
PHONE.................................330 535-2108
Brad Wehman, *Mgr*
EMP: 18
SQ FT: 10,000
SALES (corp-wide): 14.39MM **Privately Held**
Web: www.akrochem.com
SIC: 2816 Inorganic pigments
PA: Revlis Corporation
255 Fountain St
Akron OH 44304
330 535-2100

(G-836)
RICHARDSON PUBLISHING COMPANY
Also Called: Barberton Herald
70 4th St Nw Ste 1 (44203-8283)
P.O. Box 830 (44203-0830)
PHONE.................................330 753-1068
Dave Richardson, *Pr*
Cathy Robertson, *VP*
EMP: 10 EST: 1923
SALES (est): 179.26K **Privately Held**
Web: www.barbertonherald.com
SIC: 2711 Newspapers: publishing only, not printed on site

(G-837)
ROTARY SMER SPCALIST GROUP LLC
Also Called: Rss Maclin
635 Wooster Rd W (44203-2440)
PHONE.................................330 299-8210
Anthony Ganni, *Managing Member*
Christopher Ganni, *Managing Member*
EMP: 10 EST: 2019
SALES (est): 2.55MM **Privately Held**
Web: www.rssmaclin.com
SIC: 3599 Machine and other job shop work

(G-838)
SPARTON ENTERPRISES LLC
3717 Clark Mill Rd (44203-1035)
PHONE.................................877 772-7866
James E Little Junior, *Pr*

Andy Little, *
▲ **EMP: 25 EST:** 1969
SQ FT: 110,000
SALES (est): 7.49MM **Privately Held**
Web: www.spartonenterprises.com
SIC: 3069 Reclaimed rubber (reworked by manufacturing processes)

(G-839)
SPECIFIED STRUCTURES INC
643 Holmes Ave (44203-2181)
PHONE.................................330 753-0693
Grant Senn, *Pr*
EMP: 8 EST: 1984
SQ FT: 10,000
SALES (est): 985.23K **Privately Held**
Web: www.specifiedstructures.com
SIC: 2434 Wood kitchen cabinets

(G-840)
TAHOMA ENTERPRISES INC (PA)
255 Wooster Rd N (44203-2560)
PHONE.................................330 745-9016
William P Herrington, *CEO*
EMP: 100 EST: 2007
SALES (est): 16.97MM
SALES (corp-wide): 16.97MM **Privately Held**
Web: www.tahomaenterprises.com
SIC: 3069 3089 5199 5162 Reclaimed rubber (reworked by manufacturing processes); Plastics processing; Foams and rubber; Plastics products, nec

(G-841)
WINERY AT WOLF CREEK
2637 S Cleveland Massillon Rd (44203-6417)
PHONE.................................330 666-9285
Andrew Troutman, *Owner*
EMP: 10 EST: 1981
SALES (est): 1.09MM **Privately Held**
Web: www.wineryatwolfcreek.com
SIC: 2084 Wines

(G-842)
WRIGHT TOOL COMPANY
1 Wright Pl (44203-2798)
P.O. Box 512 (44203-0512)
PHONE.................................330 848-0600
Richard Wright, *Ch Bd*
Terry G Taylor, *
Tom Futey, *
▲ **EMP: 160 EST:** 1927
SQ FT: 124,000
SALES (est): 24.46MM **Privately Held**
Web: www.wrighttool.com
SIC: 3462 3423 Iron and steel forgings; Wrenches, hand tools

Barnesville
Belmont County

(G-843)
ART WORKS
119 E Pike St (43713-1539)
PHONE.................................740 425-5765
Ann Hudson, *Owner*
Brad Hudson, *Owner*
EMP: 6 EST: 1995
SALES (est): 225.73K **Privately Held**
Web: www.artworks.biz
SIC: 2759 Screen printing

(G-844)
BUCKEYE STEEL INC
607 Watt Ave (43713-1272)
P.O. Box 458 (43713-0458)
PHONE.................................740 425-2306

▲ = Import ▼ = Export
◆ = Import/Export

Richard W Pryor, *Pr*
Douglas E Kriechbaum, *VP*
EMP: 10 **EST:** 1994
SQ FT: 34,000
SALES (est): 958.21K **Privately Held**
SIC: 3441 Fabricated structural metal

(G-845)
K & J MACHINE INC
326 Fairmont Ave (43713-9669)
PHONE..................740 425-3282
Homer Luyster, *Pr*
Martha L Luyster, *VP*
Sharon Lucas, *Sec*
EMP: 6 **EST:** 1971
SQ FT: 3,300
SALES (est): 383.48K **Privately Held**
SIC: 7699 3599 7692 Aircraft and heavy
   equipment repair services; Machine shop,
   jobbing and repair; Welding repair

(G-846)
RODNEY WELLS
Also Called: Rods Welding and Rebuilding
34225 Holland Rd (43713-9602)
PHONE..................740 425-2266
Rodney Wells, *Owner*
EMP: 7 **EST:** 1991
SALES (est): 963.46K **Privately Held**
Web: www.rodsweld.com
SIC: 7692 Welding repair

(G-847)
SUN SHINE AWARDS
36099 Bethesda Street Ext (43713-9619)
PHONE..................740 425-2504
Danny Kimble, *Owner*
EMP: 10 **EST:** 1987
SALES (est): 61.55K **Privately Held**
SIC: 5999 2395 Trophies and plaques;
   Embroidery and art needlework

Batavia
Clermont County

(G-848)
A-1 FABRICATORS FINISHERS LLC
4220 Curliss Ln (45103-3276)
PHONE..................513 724-0383
Dennis Doane, *Managing Member*
Joe Strack, *
Jamie Doane, *
EMP: 78 **EST:** 2003
SQ FT: 80,000
SALES (est): 8.6MM **Privately Held**
Web: www.a1fabricators.com
SIC: 3441 Fabricated structural metal

(G-849)
AAG GLASS LLC
760 Kent Rd (45103-1704)
PHONE..................513 286-8268
Frank Lauch, *Managing Member*
EMP: 20 **EST:** 2018
SALES (est): 5.02MM **Privately Held**
Web: www.aagglass.com
SIC: 3231 Windshields, glass: made from
   purchased glass

(G-850)
**AMERICAN MICRO PRODUCTS INC
(PA)**
4288 Armstrong Blvd (45103-1600)
PHONE..................513 732-2674
◆ **EMP:** 101 **EST:** 1957
SALES (est): 23.14MM
SALES (corp-wide): 23.14MM **Privately
Held**
Web: www.american-micro.com

SIC: 3451 3452 3678 Screw machine
   products; Bolts, nuts, rivets, and washers;
   Electronic connectors

(G-851)
AUTO TEMP INC
Also Called: ATI
950 Kent Rd (45103-1738)
P.O. Box 631690 (45263-1690)
PHONE..................513 732-6969
Frank Lauch, *CEO*
Matt Fassler, *
Doug Fassler, *
◆ **EMP:** 155 **EST:** 1991
SQ FT: 210,000
SALES (est): 24.96MM **Privately Held**
Web: www.autotempinc.com
SIC: 3231 Tempered glass: made from
   purchased glass

(G-852)
AVENUE FABRICATING INC
1281 Clough Pike (45103-2501)
PHONE..................513 752-1911
Gretchen Nichols, *Pr*
Robert Nichols, *
EMP: 41 **EST:** 1989
SQ FT: 17,800
SALES (est): 9.89MM **Privately Held**
Web: www.avenuefabricating.com
SIC: 3441 Fabricated structural metal

(G-853)
**BECKMAN ENVIRONMENTAL SVCS
INC**
Also Called: Besco
4259 Armstrong Blvd (45103-1697)
PHONE..................513 752-3570
Joan Beckman, *Pr*
John Beckman, *General Vice President*
EMP: 12 **EST:** 1973
SQ FT: 6,700
SALES (est): 2.92MM **Privately Held**
Web: www.besco.co
SIC: 3589 7699 Sewage treatment
   equipment; Sewer cleaning and rodding

(G-854)
BLACK MACHINING & TECH INC
4020 Bach Buxton Rd (45103-2525)
PHONE..................513 752-8625
Frank Black, *Pr*
Margaret Lynn Black, *VP*
Stephanie Standring, *Sec*
EMP: 10 **EST:** 1983
SALES (est): 2.06MM **Privately Held**
SIC: 3599 Machine shop, jobbing and repair

(G-855)
CINCHEMPRO INC
Also Called: Cincinnati Chemical Processing
458 W Main St (45103-1712)
PHONE..................513 724-6111
John Glass, *CEO*
EMP: 105 **EST:** 1970
SQ FT: 22,000
SALES (est): 4.8MM **Privately Held**
Web: www.cinchempro.com
SIC: 2899 Chemical preparations, nec

(G-856)
CINCINNATI MACHINES INC
4165 Half Acre Rd (45103-3247)
PHONE..................513 536-2432
Rose Acree, *Supervisor*
▲ **EMP:** 6 **EST:** 1998
SALES (est): 511.67K **Privately Held**
Web: www.cinmac.com
SIC: 3088 Plastics plumbing fixtures

(G-857)
**CLERMONT STEEL FABRICATORS
LLC**
2565 Old State Route 32 (45103-3205)
PHONE..................513 732-6033
Robert Mampe, *CEO*
Ken Miller, *
◆ **EMP:** 70 **EST:** 2004
SQ FT: 144,000
SALES (est): 9.94MM **Privately Held**
Web: www.clermontsteel.com
SIC: 3441 Fabricated structural metal

(G-858)
COLLOTYPE LABELS USA INC
4053 Clough Woods Dr (45103-2587)
PHONE..................513 381-1480
David Buse, *Pr*
EMP: 100 **EST:** 1903
SALES (est): 2.41MM
SALES (corp-wide): 14.54B **Privately Held**
SIC: 2759 Labels and seals: printing, nsk
HQ: Multi-Color Corporation
   6111 N River Rd Fl 8
   Rosemont IL 60018
   847 427-5354

(G-859)
**CORE COMPOSITES CINCINNATI
LLC**
4174 Half Acre Rd (45103-3250)
PHONE..................513 724-6111
John Glass, *Prin*
EMP: 20 **EST:** 2004
SALES (est): 7.8MM **Publicly Held**
Web: www.coremt.com
SIC: 3089 Injection molding of plastics
PA: Core Molding Technologies, Inc.
   800 Manor Park Dr
   Columbus OH 43228

(G-860)
D&D DESIGN CONCEPTS INC
Also Called: W.T.nickell Co.
4360 Winding Creek Blvd (45103-1729)
PHONE..................513 752-2191
Rick Meyer, *Pr*
EMP: 10 **EST:** 1960
SQ FT: 8,000
SALES (est): 2.44MM **Privately Held**
Web: www.wtnickell.com
SIC: 2759 Labels and seals: printing, nsk

(G-861)
DELTEC INCORPORATED
4230 Grissom Dr (45103-1669)
PHONE..................513 732-0800
Chris Dugle, *Ch*
Jason Dugle, *
EMP: 46 **EST:** 1970
SQ FT: 42,000
SALES (est): 4.73MM **Privately Held**
Web: www.deltec-inc.com
SIC: 3599 Machine shop, jobbing and repair

(G-862)
ELECTRODYNE COMPANY INC
4188 Taylor Rd (45103-9736)
P.O. Box 321 (45103-0321)
PHONE..................513 732-2822
Scott Blume, *Pr*
Cathy Brinkman, *VP*
▲ **EMP:** 14 **EST:** 1972
SQ FT: 22,000
SALES (est): 1.06MM **Privately Held**
Web: www.edyne.com
SIC: 3264 Porcelain electrical supplies

(G-863)
ELLIS & WATTS GLOBAL INDS INC
4400 Glen Willow Lake Ln (45103-2379)
PHONE..................513 752-9000
Gina Cottrell, *Pr*
EMP: 36 **EST:** 2014
SALES (est): 6.4MM
SALES (corp-wide): 424.23B **Publicly
Held**
Web: www.elliswatts.com
SIC: 3585 Refrigeration and heating
   equipment
HQ: Marmon Holdings, Inc.
   181 W Madison St Ste 3900
   Chicago IL 60602
   312 372-9500

(G-864)
ENGINEERED MBL SOLUTIONS INC
Also Called: E M S
4155 Taylor Rd (45103-9792)
PHONE..................513 724-0247
Bryce Johnson, *VP*
EMP: 15 **EST:** 2007
SALES (est): 4.44MM **Privately Held**
Web: www.engmobilesolutions.com
SIC: 3715 Truck trailers

(G-865)
**FREEMAN ENCLOSURE SYSTEMS
LLC**
4160 Half Acre Rd (45103-3250)
PHONE..................877 441-8555
Dale Freeman, *Pr*
EMP: 210 **EST:** 2010
SQ FT: 120,000
SALES (est): 48.23MM **Publicly Held**
Web: www.freemanenclosures.com
SIC: 3444 Sheet metalwork
HQ: Ies Infrastructure Solutions, Llc
   800 Nave Rd Se
   Massillon OH 44646
   330 830-3500

(G-866)
GUTTER TOPPER LTD
4111 Founders Blvd (45103-2534)
P.O. Box 349 (45102-0349)
PHONE..................513 797-5800
Anthony Iannelli, *Pt*
Phyllis Iannelli, *Pt*
EMP: 7 **EST:** 1994
SALES (est): 1.79MM **Privately Held**
Web: www.guttertopper.com
SIC: 3444 5033 1521 Gutters, sheet metal;
   Roofing, siding, and insulation; Single-
   family housing construction

(G-867)
HUHTAMAKI INC
1985 James E Sauls Sr Dr (45103-3246)
PHONE..................513 201-1525
EMP: 99
SALES (corp-wide): 4.36B **Privately Held**
Web: www.huhtamaki.com
SIC: 3565 2656 Labeling machines, industrial
   ; Ice cream containers: made from
   purchased material
HQ: Huhtamaki, Inc.
   9201 Packaging Dr
   De Soto KS 66018
   913 583-3025

(G-868)
INGREDIENT MASTERS INC
Also Called: Manufacturing Animal Food Phrm
4001 Borman Dr (45103-1684)
PHONE..................513 231-7432
Scott Culshaw, *Pr*
Cheryl Culshaw, *Sec*
▼ **EMP:** 7 **EST:** 1980

SALES (est): 2.75MM **Privately Held**
Web: www.ingredientmasters.com
SIC: 3556 3559 Bakery machinery; Refinery, chemical processing, and similar machinery

(G-869)
KEY RESIN COMPANY (DH)
4050 Clough Woods Dr (45103-2586)
PHONE..................................513 943-4225
Eric Borglum, *Pr*
◆ EMP: 16 EST: 1993
SQ FT: 18,000
SALES (est): 12.4MM
SALES (corp-wide): 7.34B **Publicly Held**
Web: www.keyresin.com
SIC: 2821 2822 Epoxy resins; Ethylene-propylene rubbers, EPDM polymers
HQ: The Euclid Chemical Company
19215 Redwood Rd
Cleveland OH 44110
800 321-7628

(G-870)
KOEBBE PRODUCTS INC
4226 Grissom Dr (45103-1669)
PHONE..................................513 735-1400
Scott Mclarin, *Brnch Mgr*
EMP: 90
SQ FT: 2,128
SALES (corp-wide): 9.82MM **Privately Held**
Web: www.egerproducts.com
SIC: 3089 Injection molding of plastics
PA: Koebbe Products, Inc.
1132 Ferris Rd
Amelia OH 45102
513 753-4200

(G-871)
MCC-NORWAY LLC
4053 Clough Woods Dr (45103-2587)
PHONE..................................513 381-1480
EMP: 6 EST: 2010
SALES (est): 2.4MM
SALES (corp-wide): 14.54B **Privately Held**
SIC: 2759 Labels and seals: printing, nsk
HQ: Multi-Color Corporation
6111 N River Rd Fl 8
Rosemont IL 60018
847 427-5354

(G-872)
MET FAB FABRICATION AND MCH
2974 Waitensburg Pike (45103)
P.O. Box 363 (45103-0363)
PHONE..................................513 724-3715
Rod Stouder, *Pr*
Debbie Stouder, *Treas*
EMP: 6 EST: 1984
SQ FT: 14,000
SALES (est): 2.4MM **Privately Held**
Web: www.met-fabinc.com
SIC: 3535 3599 Conveyors and conveying equipment; Machine and other job shop work

(G-873)
MIDWEST MOLD & TEXTURE CORP
4270 Armstrong Blvd (45103-1670)
PHONE..................................513 732-1300
Yoji Tatematsu, *Ch*
Katsumi Kawaguchi, *
Marico Cummings, *
▲ EMP: 38 EST: 1987
SQ FT: 20,000
SALES (est): 9.98MM **Privately Held**
Web: www.mmtcorp.com
SIC: 3544 Industrial molds
HQ: Tmw Co., Ltd.
27-1, Okudaosawacho
Inazawa AIC 492-8

(G-874)
MILACRON HOLDINGS CORP (HQ)
Also Called: Milacron
4165 Half Acre Rd (45103-3247)
PHONE..................................513 487-5000
Thomas Goeke, *Pr*
Bruce Chalmers, *
Mark Miller, *Chief Human Resources Officer*
Hugh O'donnell, *VP*
EMP: 285 EST: 1860
SALES (est): 1.24B **Publicly Held**
Web: www.milacron.com
SIC: 3544 Industrial molds
PA: Hillenbrand, Inc.
1 Batesville Blvd
Batesville IN 47006

(G-875)
MILACRON MARKETING COMPANY LLC (DH)
Also Called: Wear Technology
4165 Half Acre Rd (45103-3247)
PHONE..................................513 536-2000
◆ EMP: 46 EST: 2009
SQ FT: 275,000
SALES (est): 218.34MM **Publicly Held**
Web: www.milacron.com
SIC: 3541 Machine tools, metal cutting type
HQ: Milacron Llc
10200 Alliance Rd Ste 200
Cincinnati OH 45242

(G-876)
MILACRON PLAS TECH GROUP LLC (DH)
4165 Half Acre Rd (45103-3247)
PHONE..................................513 536-2000
Tom Goeke, *CEO*
Ron Krisanda, *COO*
Richard A Oleary, *VP*
▲ EMP: 156 EST: 2009
SALES (est): 51.95MM **Publicly Held**
Web: www.milacron.com
SIC: 3544 Forms (molds), for foundry and plastics working machinery
HQ: Milacron Llc
10200 Alliance Rd Ste 200
Cincinnati OH 45242

(G-877)
MULTI-COLOR AUSTRALIA LLC (DH)
4053 Clough Woods Dr (45103-2587)
PHONE..................................513 381-1480
Nigel A Vinecombe, *CEO*
Sharon E Birkett, *CAO*
Mary T Fetch, *
EMP: 58 EST: 2010
SALES (est): 1.4MM
SALES (corp-wide): 14.54B **Privately Held**
SIC: 2754 2752 2759 Commercial printing, gravure; Commercial printing, lithographic; Advertising literature: printing, nsk
HQ: Multi-Color Corporation
6111 N River Rd Fl 8
Rosemont IL 60018
847 427-5354

(G-878)
MULTI-COLOR CORPORATION
4053 Clough Woods Dr (45103-2587)
PHONE..................................513 381-1480
EMP: 119
SALES (corp-wide): 14.54B **Privately Held**
SIC: 2759 2679 2672 Labels and seals: printing, nsk; Labels, paper: made from purchased material; Labels (unprinted); gummed: made from purchased materials
HQ: Multi-Color Corporation
6111 N River Rd Fl 8
Rosemont IL 60018
847 427-5354

(G-879)
NEWACT INC
2084 James E Sauls Sr Dr (45103-3259)
PHONE..................................513 321-5177
Rodney J Newman, *Pr*
Tom Vale, *VP Mktg*
Ennes Ireton Iii, *VP Engg*
EMP: 17 EST: 1987
SQ FT: 16,000
SALES (est): 9.46MM **Privately Held**
Web: www.newactinc.com
SIC: 5085 3643 3069 Industrial supplies; Electric connectors; Molded rubber products

(G-880)
ON DISPLAY LTD
1250 Clough Pike (45103-2502)
PHONE..................................513 841-1600
EMP: 20 EST: 1996
SQ FT: 35,000
SALES (est): 7.02MM **Privately Held**
Web: www.ondisplay.net
SIC: 3999 Advertising display products

(G-881)
ORBIT MANUFACTURING INC
4291 Armstrong Blvd (45103-1697)
P.O. Box 144 (45103-0144)
PHONE..................................513 732-6097
James S Paul, *Pr*
Kathy Paul, *Sec*
EMP: 7 EST: 1984
SQ FT: 10,000
SALES (est): 470.99K **Privately Held**
Web: www.orbitman.com
SIC: 3089 Injection molding of plastics

(G-882)
PLASTIKOS CORPORATION
Also Called: Multi-Form Plastics
700 Kent Rd (45103-1704)
P.O. Box 138 (45103-0138)
PHONE..................................513 732-0961
Richard Bates, *Ch*
EMP: 22 EST: 1979
SQ FT: 48,000
SALES (est): 1.49MM **Privately Held**
Web: www.multiformplasticsinc.com
SIC: 3089 Thermoformed finished plastics products, nec

(G-883)
POWER SOURCE SERVICE LLC
5400 Belle Meade Dr (45103-8549)
PHONE..................................513 607-4555
EMP: 7 EST: 2006
SQ FT: 5,000
SALES (est): 743.08K **Privately Held**
Web: www.powersourceservice.com
SIC: 3629 3646 Electronic generation equipment; Commercial lighting fixtures

(G-884)
PRINTERS BINDERY SERVICES INC
Also Called: Printers Bindery
4564 Winners Cir (45103-9256)
PHONE..................................513 821-8039
Joyce Bowman, *Pr*
▲ EMP: 68 EST: 1985
SALES (est): 1.33MM **Privately Held**
Web: www.printersbinderyohio.com
SIC: 2789 2675 Binding only: books, pamphlets, magazines, etc.; Die-cut paper and board

(G-885)
PROCOAT PAINTING INC
601 W Main St (45103-1715)
PHONE..................................513 735-2500
Steve Hickey, *Prin*

EMP: 6 EST: 2014
SALES (est): 495.16K **Privately Held**
Web: www.procoatptg.com
SIC: 1721 3479 Painting and paper hanging; Painting of metal products

(G-886)
S & K METAL POLSG & BUFFING
4194 Taylor Rd (45103-9736)
PHONE..................................513 732-6662
Aldena Sons, *Pr*
Everett J Sons, *VP*
EMP: 7 EST: 1971
SQ FT: 17,500
SALES (est): 210.02K **Privately Held**
SIC: 3471 Electroplating of metals or formed products

(G-887)
SAVOR SEASONINGS LLC
4292 Armstrong Blvd (45103-1600)
PHONE..................................513 732-2333
Jeff Higgins, *Managing Member*
Shelly Higgins, *Pr*
EMP: 19 EST: 2002
SQ FT: 10,000
SALES (est): 4.66MM **Privately Held**
Web: www.savorseasonings.com
SIC: 2099 Seasonings and spices

(G-888)
SENECA ENTERPRISES INC
4053 Clough Woods Dr (45103-2587)
PHONE..................................814 432-7890
Randy L Hicks, *Pr*
Edward Mc Mullen, *Sec*
Joseph Schwabenbauer, *VP*
Dennis Pascarella, *CEO*
Robert Puleo, *VP Opers*
EMP: 8 EST: 1995
SALES (est): 221.29K **Privately Held**
SIC: 2752 Tickets, lithographed

(G-889)
SPECTRA-TECH MANUFACTURING INC
4013 Borman Dr (45103-1684)
PHONE..................................513 735-9300
Scott Reilman, *Pr*
Shirley Reilman, *
Jason Jasper, *
Craig Wilson, *
▲ EMP: 47 EST: 1998
SQ FT: 18,000
SALES (est): 18.81MM **Privately Held**
Web: www.4spectra.com
SIC: 3613 Panelboards and distribution boards, electric

(G-890)
SUPERIOR STEEL SERVICE LLC
2760 Old State Route 32 (45103-3210)
PHONE..................................513 724-7888
Jeffrey A Brewsaugh, *Managing Member*
EMP: 15 EST: 2004
SQ FT: 12,000
SALES (est): 4.08MM **Privately Held**
Web: www.superiorsteelservice.com
SIC: 3441 Fabricated structural metal

(G-891)
TIPTON ENVIRONMENTAL INTL INC
4446 State Route 132 (45103-1229)
PHONE..................................513 735-2777
Fred Tipton, *Pr*
Scott Tipton, *VP*
EMP: 10 EST: 1995
SQ FT: 3,600
SALES (est): 971.23K **Privately Held**
Web: www.fluencecorp.com

▲ = Import ▼ = Export
◆ = Import/Export

SIC: 3589 Water treatment equipment, industrial

(G-892)
TSP INC
2009 Glenn Pkwy (45103-1676)
PHONE..............................513 732-8900
J Stuart Newman, *Pr*
EMP: 10 EST: 1986
SQ FT: 30,000
SALES (est): 2.01MM Privately Held
Web: www.tspinc.com
SIC: 3479 3089 3081 Painting, coating, and hot dipping; Windows, plastics; Plastics film and sheet

(G-893)
UNILOY MILACRON INC
4165 Half Acre Rd (45103-3247)
PHONE..............................513 487-5000
John C Francy, *Pr*
◆ EMP: 25 EST: 1998
SALES (est): 18.74MM Publicly Held
Web: www.milacron.com
SIC: 2821 Plastics materials and resins
HQ: Milacron Llc
10200 Alliance Rd Ste 200
Cincinnati OH 45242

(G-894)
UNIVERSAL PACKG SYSTEMS INC
Also Called: Paklab
5055 State Route 276 (45103-1211)
PHONE..............................513 732-2000
Richard Burton, *Brnch Mgr*
EMP: 158
SALES (corp-wide): 379.38MM Privately Held
Web: www.paklab.com
SIC: 2844 7389 3565 2671 Cosmetic preparations; Packaging and labeling services; Bottling machinery: filling, capping, labeling; Plastic film, coated or laminated for packaging
PA: Universal Packaging Systems, Inc.
14570 Monte Vista Ave
Chino CA 91710
909 517-2442

(G-895)
UNIVERSAL PACKG SYSTEMS INC
5069 State Route 276 (45103-1211)
PHONE..............................513 735-4777
EMP: 158
SALES (corp-wide): 379.38MM Privately Held
Web: www.paklab.com
SIC: 2844 7389 3565 2671 Cosmetic preparations; Packaging and labeling services; Bottling machinery: filling, capping, labeling; Plastic film, coated or laminated for packaging
PA: Universal Packaging Systems, Inc.
14570 Monte Vista Ave
Chino CA 91710
909 517-2442

(G-896)
VERSTRETE IN MOLD LBELS USA IN
Also Called: Multi-Color
4101 Founders Blvd (45103-3616)
PHONE..............................513 943-0080
Mike Henry, *Pr*
Sharon Birkett, *CFO*
EMP: 15 EST: 2017
SQ FT: 115,000
SALES (est): 4.62MM
SALES (corp-wide): 14.54B Privately Held
SIC: 2759 2679 Labels and seals: printing, nsk; Labels, paper: made from purchased material

HQ: Multi-Color Corporation
6111 N River Rd Fl 8
Rosemont IL 60018
847 427-5354

(G-897)
WHITEWATER FOREST PRODUCTS LLC
Also Called: White Water Forest
1970 Clark Ln (45103-1752)
P.O. Box 429 (45103-0429)
PHONE..............................513 724-0157
Dan Shiels, *Managing Member*
EMP: 15 EST: 2013
SQ FT: 60,000
SALES (est): 5.38MM Privately Held
Web: www.whitewaterforest.com
SIC: 2421 Sawmills and planing mills, general

Bath
Summit County

(G-898)
WARMUS AND ASSOCIATES INC
Also Called: Smith Carl E Cnslting Engneers
2324 N Cleveland Massillon Rd (44210)
P.O. Box 807 (44210-0807)
PHONE..............................330 659-4440
Alfred T Warmus, *Pr*
Roy P Stype Iii, *VP*
Brain Warmus, *Sec*
EMP: 7 EST: 1935
SQ FT: 7,000
SALES (est): 711.5K Privately Held
SIC: 8711 3441 5063 Consulting engineer; Tower sections, radio and television transmission; Electrical apparatus and equipment

Bay Village
Cuyahoga County

(G-899)
ARCHER PUBLISHING LLC
27101 E Oviatt Rd (44140-3307)
PHONE..............................440 338-5233
Janelle Regotti, *Prin*
EMP: 7 EST: 2019
SALES (est): 310K Privately Held
SIC: 2741 Miscellaneous publishing

(G-900)
CLEARVUE PRODUCTS LLC
24620 Wolf Rd (44140-2767)
PHONE..............................440 871-4209
Thomas Hortel, *Prin*
EMP: 10 EST: 2016
SALES (est): 50.22K Privately Held
SIC: 3441 Fabricated structural metal

(G-901)
CONCENTRIC CORPORATION
27101 E Oviatt Rd Ste 8 (44140-3301)
PHONE..............................440 899-9090
Marc R Klecka, *Pr*
EMP: 10 EST: 1990
SALES (est): 1.52MM Privately Held
Web: www.citizenmachines.com
SIC: 3599 Machine shop, jobbing and repair

(G-902)
GENERATIONS ACE INC
Also Called: Super Suppers
29121 Inverness Dr (44140-1836)
PHONE..............................440 835-4872
James Bracken, *Pr*

Jody Bracken, *VP*
EMP: 8 EST: 2006
SALES (est): 389.94K Privately Held
SIC: 2099 Emulsifiers, food

(G-903)
SHI SHI EVENTS
26758 Russell Rd (44140-2226)
PHONE..............................440 623-3822
EMP: 6 EST: 2011
SALES (est): 80.13K Privately Held
Web: www.shi-shievents.com
SIC: 2335 Wedding gowns and dresses

Beach City
Stark County

(G-904)
MERIDIAN INDUSTRIES INC
Also Called: Kleen Test Products
9901 Chestnut Ridge Rd Nw (44608-9417)
PHONE..............................330 359-5809
Peter Morton, *Mgr*
EMP: 28
SQ FT: 15,000
SALES (corp-wide): 331.16MM Privately Held
Web: www.meridiancompanies.com
SIC: 2299 2844 Pads, fiber: henequen, sisal, istle; Perfumes, cosmetics and other toilet preparations
PA: Meridian Industries, Inc.
735 N Water St Ste 630
Milwaukee WI 53202
414 224-0610

(G-905)
MILLER CORE II INC
9823 Chestnut Ridge Rd Nw (44608-9480)
PHONE..............................330 359-0500
Joseph Miller, *Pr*
Reuben Miller, *VP*
Linda Miller, *Sec*
EMP: 8 EST: 2005
SALES (est): 2.34MM Privately Held
Web: www.millercore2.com
SIC: 3567 Core baking and mold drying ovens

(G-906)
PROGRESSIVE FOAM TECH INC
6753 Chestnut Ridge Rd Nw (44608-9464)
PHONE..............................330 756-3200
Patrick Culpepper, *Pr*
Richard Wilson, *
▲ EMP: 120 EST: 1990
SQ FT: 100,000
SALES (est): 24.71MM Privately Held
Web: www.progressivefoam.com
SIC: 2821 Polystyrene resins

(G-907)
STARK TRUSS COMPANY INC
Also Called: Stark Truss Beach City Lumber
6855 Chestnut Ridge Rd Nw (44608-9462)
PHONE..............................330 756-3050
EMP: 59
SALES (corp-wide): 99.05MM Privately Held
Web: www.starktruss.com
SIC: 2439 2421 Trusses, wooden roof; Sawmills and planing mills, general
PA: Stark Truss Company, Inc.
109 Miles Ave Sw
Canton OH 44710
330 478-2100

Beachwood
Cuyahoga County

(G-908)
ALCHEM ALUMINUM EUROPE INC
25825 Science Park Dr Ste 400 (44122-7323)
PHONE..............................216 910-3400
Sean Stack, *Pr*
EMP: 6 EST: 2009
SALES (est): 740.99K Privately Held
SIC: 3555 Printing trades machinery

(G-909)
ALERIS RM INC
25825 Science Park Dr Ste 400 (44122-7323)
PHONE..............................216 910-3400
EMP: 356 EST: 2015
SALES (est): 9.65MM Privately Held
SIC: 3355 Aluminum rolling and drawing, nec
HQ: Novelis Air Aluminum Holdings Corporation
3550 Peachtree Rd Ne
Atlanta GA 30326

(G-910)
BECHEM LUBRICATION TECH LLC
2000 Auburn Dr Ste 200-402 (44122-4314)
P.O. Box 23609 (44023-0609)
PHONE..............................440 543-9845
Steve Puffpaff, *Pr*
▲ EMP: 14 EST: 1999
SALES (est): 4.72MM
SALES (corp-wide): 145.39MM Privately Held
Web: www.bechem.de
SIC: 2992 Lubricating oils
PA: Carl Bechem Gmbh
Weststr. 120
Hagen NW 58089
23319350

(G-911)
CFO NTIC
23205 Mercantile Rd (44122-5911)
PHONE..............................216 450-5700
EMP: 8 EST: 2011
SALES (est): 360.06K Privately Held
Web: www.ntic.com
SIC: 2899 Chemical preparations, nec

(G-912)
CLEVELAND JEWISH PUBL CO FDN
23800 Commerce Park (44122-5828)
PHONE..............................216 454-8300
Barry Chesler, *Prin*
EMP: 11 EST: 1964
SALES (est): 210.66K Privately Held
Web: www.clevelandjewishnews.com
SIC: 2711 Newspapers, publishing and printing

(G-913)
COHESANT INC (PA)
3601 Green Rd Ste 308 (44122-5719)
PHONE..............................216 910-1700
EMP: 45
SALES (est): 20.9MM Privately Held
Web: www.cohesant.com
SIC: 3563 3559 3586 Spraying outfits: metals, paints, and chemicals (compressor); Paint making machinery; Measuring and dispensing pumps

(G-914)
DATATRAK INTERNATIONAL INC
3690 Orange Pl Ste 375 (44122-4466)
PHONE..............................440 443-0082

GEOGRAPHIC

James R Ward, *Pr*
Julia Henderson, *
Alex Tabatabai, *
EMP: 47 **EST:** 1991
SQ FT: 4,300
SALES (est): 7.16MM **Privately Held**
Web: www.fountayn.com
SIC: 7374 7372 Data processing and
preparation; Prepackaged software

(G-915)
EATON CORPORATION
Also Called: Fluid Power Plant
1000 Eaton Blvd (44122-6058)
PHONE..............................440 523-5000
Joy Davis, *Brnch Mgr*
EMP: 500
Web: www.dix-eaton.com
SIC: 3714 3824 Motor vehicle electrical
equipment; Mechanical and
electromechanical counters and devices
HQ: Eaton Corporation
1000 Eaton Blvd
Cleveland OH 44122
440 523-5000

(G-916)
EATON LEASING CORPORATION
1000 Eaton Blvd (44122-6058)
PHONE..............................216 382-2292
Richard Fearon, *Pr*
Billie Rawot, *VP*
EMP: 500 **EST:** 1981
SQ FT: 1,200
SALES (est): 4.07MM **Privately Held**
SIC: 7359 3612 3594 3593 Equipment rental
and leasing, nec; Transformers, except
electric; Fluid power pumps and motors;
Fluid power cylinders and actuators
HQ: Eaton Corporation
1000 Eaton Blvd
Cleveland OH 44122
440 523-5000

(G-917)
ETS SCHAEFER LLC (DH)
3700 Park East Dr Ste 300 (44122-4399)
PHONE..............................330 468-6600
Terrance Hogan, *CEO*
Michael Hobey, *CFO*
EMP: 27 **EST:** 2018
SALES (est): 18.88MM
SALES (corp-wide): 483.55MM **Publicly
Held**
Web: www.etsschaefer.com
SIC: 3297 3433 Nonclay refractories;
Heating equipment, except electric
HQ: Real Alloy Recycling, Llc
3700 Park E Dr Ste 300
Beachwood OH 44122
216 755-8900

(G-918)
EUCLID CHEMICAL COMPANY
3735 Green Rd (44122-5705)
PHONE..............................216 292-5000
Moorman L Scott Junior, *Pr*
EMP: 11
SALES (corp-wide): 7.34B **Publicly Held**
Web: www.euclidchemical.com
SIC: 2899 Chemical preparations, nec
HQ: The Euclid Chemical Company
19215 Redwood Rd
Cleveland OH 44110
800 321-7628

(G-919)
GENERAL ENVMTL SCIENCE CORP
3659 Green Rd Ste 306 (44122-5715)
PHONE..............................216 464-0680
Barton Gilbert, *Pr*

Elaine Gilbert, *VP*
EMP: 8 **EST:** 1974
SALES (est): 245.33K **Privately Held**
Web:
www.generalenvironmentalscience.com
SIC: 2836 Bacteriological media

(G-920)
HELIX LINEAR TECHNOLOGIES INC
23200 Commerce Park (44122-5802)
PHONE..............................216 485-2263
Jaseph Nook, *Prin*
EMP: 49 **EST:** 2013
SALES (est): 9.94MM **Privately Held**
Web: www.helixlinear.com
SIC: 3549 Screw driving machines

(G-921)
HELIX OPERATING COMPANY LLC
23200 Commerce Park (44122-5802)
PHONE..............................855 435-4958
Jaseph Nook, *Managing Member*
EMP: 8 **EST:** 2016
SALES (est): 1.68MM **Privately Held**
SIC: 3451 3549 Screw machine products;
Screw driving machines

(G-922)
IMCO RECYCLING OF INDIANA INC
25825 Science Park Dr Ste 400
(44122-7323)
PHONE..............................216 910-3400
Michael D Friday, *Pr*
EMP: 6 **EST:** 2009
SALES (est): 898.75K **Privately Held**
SIC: 3555 Printing trades machinery

(G-923)
ITL LLC
Also Called: Industrial Timber and Lumber
23925 Commerce Park Rd (44122-5821)
PHONE..............................216 831-3140
EMP: 7 **EST:** 2015
SALES (est): 846.82K **Privately Held**
SIC: 2426 Lumber, hardwood dimension
PA: Northwest Hardwoods, Inc.
2600 Network Blvd Ste 600
Frisco TX 75034

(G-924)
**KIRTLAND CAPITAL PARTNERS LP
(PA)**
Also Called: K C P
3201 Enterprise Pkwy Ste 200
(44122-7329)
PHONE..............................216 593-0100
John Nestor, *Prin*
Corrie Menary, *Pt*
◆ **EMP:** 46 **EST:** 1992
SQ FT: 4,031
SALES (est): 13.29MM **Privately Held**
Web: www.kirtlandcapital.com
SIC: 5051 3312 3498 3494 Metals service
centers and offices; Tubes, steel and iron;
Fabricated pipe and fittings; Valves and
pipe fittings, nec

(G-925)
LEWIS UNLIMITED INC
3690 Orange Pl Ste 340 (44122-4438)
PHONE..............................216 514-8282
Joseph Lewis, *Pr*
Nina Lewis, *VP*
EMP: 7 **EST:** 1993
SQ FT: 3,000
SALES (est): 919.17K **Privately Held**
Web: www.lewisunlimited.com
SIC: 3599 Machine shop, jobbing and repair

(G-926)
MAKERGEAR LLC
23632 Mercantile Rd Ste I (44122-5916)
PHONE..............................216 765-0030
▲ **EMP:** 6 **EST:** 2009
SALES (est): 973.38K **Privately Held**
Web: www.makergear.com
SIC: 3999 Education aids, devices and
supplies

(G-927)
**MASTER BLDRS SLTONS
ADMXTRES U (PA)**
Also Called: Mbcc Admixtures
23700 Chagrin Blvd (44122-5506)
PHONE..............................216 839-7500
Boris Gorella, *CEO*
Christian Hammel, *
Karsten Eller, *
EMP: 106 **EST:** 2019
SALES (est): 146.86MM
SALES (corp-wide): 146.86MM **Privately
Held**
Web:
www.master-builders-solutions.com
SIC: 2899 Concrete curing and hardening
compounds

(G-928)
MASTER BUILDERS LLC (HQ)
Also Called: Degussa Construction
23700 Chagrin Blvd (44122-5506)
PHONE..............................800 228-3318
Anthony Price, *CEO*
◆ **EMP:** 50 **EST:** 1911
SALES (est): 467.64MM **Privately Held**
Web:
www.master-builders-solutions.com
SIC: 2899 2851 1799 Concrete curing and
hardening compounds; Epoxy coatings;
Caulking (construction)
PA: Sika Ag
Zugerstrasse 50
Baar ZG 6340

(G-929)
MASTERBRAND INC (PA)
Also Called: Masterbrand
3300 Enterprise Pkwy Ste 300
(44122-7200)
PHONE..............................877 622-4782
R David Banyard Junior, *Pr*
David D Petratis, *Non-Executive Chairman
of the Board*
Andrea H Simon, *Ex VP*
Navi Grewal, *DIGITAL*
Andrean R Horton, *CLO*
EMP: 2252 **EST:** 1954
SALES (est): 2.7B
SALES (corp-wide): 2.7B **Publicly Held**
Web: www.masterbrand.com
SIC: 2434 Wood kitchen cabinets

(G-930)
MIM SOFTWARE INC (HQ)
25800 Science Park Dr Ste 180
(44122-7311)
PHONE..............................216 455-0600
Andrew Nelson, *CEO*
Jonathan Piper, *
Peter Simmelink, *
Jerimy Brockway, *
Mark Cain, *
EMP: 86 **EST:** 2003
SALES (est): 14.76MM
SALES (corp-wide): 19.67B **Publicly Held**
Web: www.mimsoftware.com
SIC: 7372 Application computer software
PA: Ge Healthcare Technologies Inc.
500 W Monroe St
Chicago IL 60661

833 735-1139

(G-931)
NATIONAL BIOLOGICAL CORP
23700 Mercantile Rd (44122-5900)
PHONE..............................216 831-0600
Kenneth Oif, *Pr*
Michael Kaufman, *
▲ **EMP:** 50 **EST:** 1965
SQ FT: 36,000
SALES (est): 8.16MM **Privately Held**
Web: www.natbiocorp.com
SIC: 3841 3648 Surgical and medical
instruments; Ultraviolet lamp fixtures

(G-932)
**NOVELIS ALR ALMNUM-ALABAMA
LLC**
25825 Science Park Dr Ste 400
(44122-7323)
PHONE..............................256 353-1550
EMP: 21 **EST:** 1993
SALES (est): 7.19MM **Privately Held**
Web: www.novelis.com
SIC: 3353 Aluminum sheet, plate, and foil

(G-933)
NOVELIS ALR ALUMINUM LLC
Also Called: Davenport Rolling Mill
25825 Science Park Dr Ste 400
(44122-7323)
PHONE..............................216 910-3400
EMP: 542 **EST:** 2007
SALES (est): 105.62MM **Privately Held**
Web: www.novelis.com
SIC: 3355 3354 Aluminum rolling and
drawing, nec; Shapes, extruded aluminum,
nec
HQ: Novelis Alr Rolled Products, Inc.
3550 Pchtree Rd Ne Ste 11
Atlanta GA 30326
216 910-3400

(G-934)
**NOVELIS ALR ROLLED PDTS LLC
(DH)**
25825 Science Park Dr Ste 400
(44122-7392)
PHONE..............................216 910-3400
Sean Stack, *Managing Member*
▲ **EMP:** 21 **EST:** 2000
SALES (est): 21.7MM **Privately Held**
Web: www.novelis.com
SIC: 3355 Aluminum rolling and drawing, nec
HQ: Novelis Alr Aluminum Holdings
Corporation
3550 Peachtree Rd Ne
Atlanta GA 30326

(G-935)
OHIO NITROGEN LLC
25800 Science Park Dr (44122-7339)
PHONE..............................216 839-5485
EMP: 12 **EST:** 2019
SALES (est): 614.22K **Privately Held**
SIC: 2813 Nitrogen

(G-936)
OLD RAR INC
3700 Park East Dr Ste 300 (44122-4399)
PHONE..............................216 545-7249
EMP: 1000 **EST:** 2009
SQ FT: 7,000
SALES (est): 136.73MM **Privately Held**
SIC: 3341 Secondary nonferrous metals

(G-937)
OMNOVA WALLCOVERING USA INC
25435 Harvard Rd (44122-6201)
PHONE..............................216 682-7000

▲ = Import ▼ = Export
◆ = Import/Export

Kevin Mc Mullin, *CEO*
EMP: 100 **EST:** 1998
SALES (est): 7MM
SALES (corp-wide): 2.52B **Privately Held**
Web: www.omnova.com
SIC: 2819 Industrial inorganic chemicals, nec
HQ: Synthomer Inc.
　25435 Harvard Rd
　Beachwood OH 44122
　216 682-7000

(G-938)
PCC AIRFOILS LLC (DH)
3401 Enterprise Pkwy Ste 200
(44122-7340)
PHONE..............................216 831-3590
Peter Waite, *Managing Member*
William Mc Cormick, *
William D Larsson, *
John O Neill, *
◆ **EMP:** 29 **EST:** 2002
SQ FT: 14,000
SALES (est): 839.5MM
SALES (corp-wide): 424.23B **Publicly Held**
Web: www.pccairfoils.com
SIC: 3369 Nonferrous foundries, nec
HQ: Precision Castparts Corp.
　5885 Meadows Rd Ste 620
　Lake Oswego OR 97035
　503 946-4800

(G-939)
PCC AIRFOILS LLC
25201 Chagrin Blvd Ste 290 (44122-5600)
PHONE..............................216 766-6206
EMP: 64 **EST:** 2017
SALES (est): 1MM **Privately Held**
Web: www.pccairfoils.com
SIC: 3369 Nonferrous foundries, nec

(G-940)
PHILIPS MED SYSTEMS CLVLAND IN
100 Park Ave Ste 300 (44122-8203)
PHONE..............................617 245-5510
EMP: 112
SALES (corp-wide): 18.51B **Privately Held**
Web: www.emergin.com
SIC: 3844 X-ray apparatus and tubes
HQ: Philips Medical Systems (Cleveland), Inc.
　595 Miner Rd
　Cleveland OH 44143
　440 483 3000

(G-941)
PRIME CONDUIT INC (PA)
23240 Chagrin Blvd Ste 405 (44122-5468)
P.O. Box 22897 (44122)
PHONE..............................216 464-3400
Jim Abel, *Pr*
Kay Condon, *Sec*
◆ **EMP:** 18 **EST:** 2008
SALES (est): 25.8MM **Privately Held**
Web: www.primeconduit.com
SIC: 2821 3312 Polyvinyl chloride resins, PVC; Pipes and tubes

(G-942)
REAL ALLOY RECYCLING LLC (DH)
3700 Park East Dr Ste 300 (44122-4399)
PHONE..............................216 755-8900
▲ **EMP:** 100 **EST:** 2018
SQ FT: 7,000
SALES (est): 345.81MM
SALES (corp-wide): 483.55MM **Publicly Held**
Web: www.realalloy.com
SIC: 3341 Secondary nonferrous metals
HQ: Real Alloy Holding, Llc
　3700 Park East Dr Ste 300

Beachwood OH 44122
216 755-8900

(G-943)
REAL ALLOY SPECIALTY PDTS LLC (DH)
3700 Park East Dr Ste 300 (44122-4399)
PHONE..............................844 732-5087
Terry Hogan, *Pr*
EMP: 100 **EST:** 2018
SALES (est): 20.66MM
SALES (corp-wide): 483.55MM **Publicly Held**
Web: www.realalloy.com
SIC: 3341 3334 3313 Secondary nonferrous metals; Pigs, aluminum; Ferromanganese, not made in blast furnaces
HQ: Real Alloy Recycling, Llc
　3700 Park E Dr Ste 300
　Beachwood OH 44122
　216 755-8900

(G-944)
RELIABLE WHEELCHAIR TRANS
28899 Harvard Rd (44122-4741)
PHONE..............................216 390-3999
Lapetha Ruffin, *Prin*
EMP: 6 **EST:** 2010
SALES (est): 81.88K **Privately Held**
SIC: 3842 Wheelchairs

(G-945)
REXON COMPONENTS INC
24500 Highpoint Rd (44122-6002)
PHONE..............................216 292-7373
M R Farukhi, *Pr*
Zaid H Farukhi, *VP*
Steve Fink, *Sec*
◆ **EMP:** 20 **EST:** 1983
SQ FT: 10,000
SALES (est): 2.36MM **Privately Held**
Web: www.rexon.com
SIC: 3674 Semiconductors and related devices

(G-946)
RSI COMPANY (PA)
Also Called: Worthington
24050 Commerce Park Ste 200
(44122-5831)
PHONE..............................216 360-9800
Steve Sords, *Pr*
Robert Sords, *CFO*
▼ **EMP:** 19 **EST:** 1990
SQ FT: 60,000
SALES (est): 1.93MM **Privately Held**
Web: www.rsi.com
SIC: 3559 3585 Recycling machinery; Refrigeration and heating equipment

(G-947)
SAMEGOAL INC
3401 Enterprise Pkwy Ste 340
(44122-7340)
PHONE..............................216 766-5713
Andrew Hochhaus, *Mgr*
EMP: 17 **EST:** 2016
SALES (est): 266.83K **Privately Held**
Web: www.samegoal.com
SIC: 7372 Prepackaged software

(G-948)
SEAFORTH MINERAL & ORE CO INC (PA)
3690 Orange Pl Ste 495 (44122-4465)
PHONE..............................216 292-5820
Gary Mcclurg, *Ch Bd*
James Mcclurg, *Pr*
▲ **EMP:** 15 **EST:** 1957
SQ FT: 3,500

SALES (est): 15.15MM
SALES (corp-wide): 15.15MM **Privately Held**
Web: www.seaforthinc.com
SIC: 5052 3295 Nonmetallic minerals and concentrate; Minerals, ground or treated

(G-949)
SHAQ INC
Also Called: Shaw Stainless
22901 Millcreek Blvd Ste 650 (44122-5732)
PHONE..............................770 427-0402
Richard Marabito, *CEO*
EMP: 70 **EST:** 2021
SALES (est): 2.79MM
SALES (corp-wide): 1.94B **Publicly Held**
SIC: 5085 5051 3312 Valves and fittings; Pipe and tubing, steel; Stainless steel
PA: Olympic Steel, Inc.
　22901 Mllcreek Blvd Ste 6
　Cleveland OH 44122
　216 292-3800

(G-950)
SYNTHOMER ADHESIVE TECH LLC
25435 Harvard Rd (44122-6201)
PHONE..............................216 682-7000
Stephan Lynen, *Pr*
EMP: 18 **EST:** 2021
SALES (est): 6.85MM **Privately Held**
SIC: 2891 Adhesives

(G-951)
SYNTHOMER INC (HQ)
25435 Harvard Rd (44122-6201)
PHONE..............................216 682-7000
Calum G Maclean, *Pr*
Stephen G Bennett, *
Richard Atkinson, *
Joseph Muska, *
◆ **EMP:** 140 **EST:** 1952
SALES (est): 306.32MM
SALES (corp-wide): 2.52B **Privately Held**
Web: www.omnova.com
SIC: 2819 2211 3069 3081 Industrial inorganic chemicals, nec; Decorative trim and specialty fabrics, including twist weave; Roofing, membrane rubber; Unsupported plastics film and sheet
PA: Synthomer Plc
　Temple Mead
　Harlow CM20
　127 943-6211

(G-952)
SYNTHOMER USA LLC (HQ)
25435 Harvard Rd (44122-6201)
PHONE..............................678 400-6655
Calum Maclean, *CEO*
Julia Harp, *Development PROD*
Richard Cochran, *CFO*
◆ **EMP:** 24 **EST:** 2016
SALES (est): 4.96MM
SALES (corp-wide): 2.52B **Privately Held**
SIC: 2891 3479 Adhesives; Painting, coating, and hot dipping
PA: Synthomer Plc
　Temple Mead
　Harlow CM20
　127 943-6211

(G-953)
THE CLEVELAND JEWISH PUBL CO
23880 Commerce Park Ste 1 (44122-5294)
PHONE..............................216 454-8300
Rob Certner, *Prin*
EMP: 33 **EST:** 2012
SALES (est): 448.95K **Privately Held**
Web: www.clevelandjewishnews.com
SIC: 2711 Newspapers, publishing and printing

(G-954)
TOA TECHNOLOGIES INC (PA)
3333 Richmond Rd Ste 420 (44122-4194)
PHONE..............................216 925-5950
Yuval Brisker, *Pr*
Irad Carmi, *
Brian Cook, *
Bruce Grainger, *
Michael Mcdonnell, *VP*
EMP: 216 **EST:** 2003
SALES (est): 10.17MM
SALES (corp-wide): 10.17MM **Privately Held**
Web: www.oracle.com
SIC: 7372 Prepackaged software

(G-955)
TREMCO CPG INC
23150 Commerce Park (44122-5807)
PHONE..............................216 514-7783
EMP: 22
SALES (corp-wide): 7.34B **Publicly Held**
Web: www.tremcosealants.com
SIC: 2891 Sealants
HQ: Tremco Cpg Inc.
　3735 Green Rd
　Beachwood OH 44122
　216 292-5000

(G-956)
TREMCO INCORPORATED (HQ)
3735 Green Rd (44122-5730)
PHONE..............................216 292-5000
Paul Hoogenboom, *CEO*
◆ **EMP:** 214 **EST:** 1980
SALES (est): 332.97MM
SALES (corp-wide): 7.34B **Publicly Held**
Web: www.tremcoroofing.com
SIC: 2891 2952 1761 1752 Sealants; Roofing materials; Roofing contractor; Floor laying and floor work, nec
PA: Rpm International Inc.
　2628 Pearl Rd
　Medina OH 44258
　330 273-5090

(G-957)
WALTER H DRANE CO INC
23811 Chagrin Blvd Ste 344 (44122-5525)
PHONE..............................216 514-1022
William Kenneweg, *Pr*
EMP: 8 **EST:** 1955
SALES (est): 242.55K **Privately Held**
SIC: 2741 Technical manual and paper publishing

(G-958)
XELLIA PHARMACEUTICALS INC (DH)
Also Called: Xellia Pharmaceuticals
2000 Auburn Dr Ste 200 (44122-4328)
PHONE..............................847 947-0200
Carl-aake Carlsson, *CEO*
Rich Zawadski, *Genl Mgr*
Mikkel L Olsen, *Sec*
Mads Bodenhoff, *CFO*
EMP: 9 **EST:** 2008
SALES (est): 79.85MM
SALES (corp-wide): 39.23B **Privately Held**
SIC: 5122 2834 Pharmaceuticals; Pharmaceutical preparations
HQ: Xellia Pharmaceuticals Aps
　Dalslandsgade 11
　Kobenhavn S 2300
　32645500

(G-959)
ZEKELMAN INDUSTRIES INC
3201 Entp Pkwy Ste 150 (44122)
PHONE..............................216 910-3700
Frank A Riddick Iii, *Brnch Mgr*

GEOGRAPHIC

EMP: 31
Web: www.zekelman.com
SIC: 3317 Steel pipe and tubes
PA: Zekelman Industries, Inc.
227 W Monroe St Ste 2600
Chicago IL 60606

Beaver
Pike County

(G-960)
BEAVER WOOD PRODUCTS
190 Buck Hollow Rd (45613-9498)
P.O. Box 404 (45613-0404)
PHONE..............................740 226-6211
Walter Thornsberry, *Pt*
Rick Thornsberry, *Pt*
EMP: 7 EST: 1988
SALES (est): 1.02MM **Privately Held**
SIC: 2421 2436 2435 2426 Sawmills and planing mills, general; Softwood veneer and plywood; Hardwood veneer and plywood; Hardwood dimension and flooring mills

(G-961)
WISEMAN BROS FABG & STL LTD
2598 Glade Rd (45613-9613)
P.O. Box 307 (45613-0307)
PHONE..............................740 988-5121
EMP: 10 EST: 1995
SQ FT: 8,000
SALES (est): 1.97MM **Privately Held**
Web: www.wisemanbrothers.com
SIC: 3441 Fabricated structural metal

Beavercreek
Greene County

(G-962)
A C HADLEY - PRINTING INC
Also Called: Hadley Printing
1530 Marsetta Dr (45432-2733)
PHONE..............................937 426-0952
Nancy Hadley, *Pr*
Scott Hadley, *VP*
Michael Hadley, *Sec*
EMP: 6 EST: 1959
SQ FT: 4,800
SALES (est): 185.98K **Privately Held**
SIC: 2396 2759 Automotive and apparel trimmings; Thermography

(G-963)
A SERVICE GLASS INC
1363 N Fairfield Rd (45432-2693)
PHONE..............................937 426-4920
Donald T Sullivan, *Pr*
Donald J Sullivan, *Pr*
William C Sullivan, *VP*
Glenn Sullivan, *Sec*
EMP: 15 EST: 1959
SQ FT: 8,000
SALES (est): 1.96MM **Privately Held**
Web: www.aserviceglass.com
SIC: 5231 3231 1793 5039 Glass; Doors, glass: made from purchased glass; Glass and glazing work; Glass construction materials

(G-964)
ADVANT-E CORPORATION (PA)
2434 Esquire Dr (45431-2573)
PHONE..............................937 429-4288
Jason K Wadzinski, *Ch Bd*
James E Lesch, *CFO*
EMP: 10 EST: 1994
SQ FT: 19,000
SALES (est): 11.97MM

SALES (corp-wide): 11.97MM **Privately Held**
Web: www.advant-e.com
SIC: 7372 7375 Application computer software; Information retrieval services

(G-965)
ARCTOS MISSION SOLUTIONS LLC
2601 Mission Point Blvd (45431-6600)
PHONE..............................813 609-5591
James Fugit, *CEO*
Steven Shugart, *
Todd J Schweitzer, *
Brian Overstreet, *
David Joseph, *
EMP: 40 EST: 2008
SALES (est): 1.83MM
SALES (corp-wide): 49.23MM **Privately Held**
Web: www.arctos-us.com
SIC: 7379 5045 3728 Computer related consulting services; Computers, peripherals, and software; Aircraft parts and equipment, nec
HQ: Arctos, Llc
2601 Mssion Pt Blvd Ste 3
Beavercreek OH 45431
478 923-9995

(G-966)
ASTRO INDUSTRIES INC
4403 Dayton Xenia Rd (45432-1805)
PHONE..............................937 429-5900
Kailash Mehta, *Pr*
EMP: 24 EST: 1967
SQ FT: 24,000
SALES (est): 8.68MM **Privately Held**
Web: www.astro-ind.com
SIC: 3678 3679 5063 3357 Electronic connectors; Electronic circuits; Wiring devices; Communication wire

(G-967)
CARBIDE PROBES INC
1328 Research Park Dr (45432-2897)
PHONE..............................937 429-9123
Greg Shellabarger, *Pr*
Dan Shellabarger, *Prin*
Roberta Lee Shellabarger, *VP*
Cheryl Terry, *Treas*
Jessica Ross, *Admn*
EMP: 22 EST: 1955
SQ FT: 10,000
SALES (est): 2.17MM **Privately Held**
Web: www.carbideprobes.com
SIC: 3545 Machine tool attachments and accessories

(G-968)
COMMUNICATION CONCEPTS INC
508 Mill Stone Dr (45434-5840)
PHONE..............................937 426-8600
Rodger L Southworth, *Pr*
Marlis Southworth, *Sec*
EMP: 6 EST: 1978
SALES (est): 1.23MM **Privately Held**
Web:
www.communication-concepts.com
SIC: 5961 3674 Mail order house, nec; Semiconductors and related devices

(G-969)
DECIBEL RESEARCH INC
Also Called: DECIBEL RESEARCH, INC
2661 Commons Blvd Ste 136 (45431-3704)
PHONE..............................256 705-3341
Bassem Mahafza, *Brnch Mgr*
EMP: 49
SALES (corp-wide): 13.17MM **Privately Held**
Web: www.decibelresearch.com

SIC: 3812 Radar systems and equipment
PA: Decibel Research, Inc.
325 Bob Heath
Huntsville AL 35806
256 716-0787

(G-970)
DRS ADVANCED ISR LLC (DH)
2601 Mission Point Blvd Ste 250
(45431-6600)
PHONE..............................937 429-7408
Angella Cowan, *
Sandra L Hodgkinson, *
Terence J Murphy, *
EMP: 150 EST: 2009
SQ FT: 25,000
SALES (est): 47.43MM
SALES (corp-wide): 16.62B **Publicly Held**
Web: www.leonardodrs.com
SIC: 3812 Navigational systems and instruments
HQ: Drs Defense Solutions, Llc
4910 Executive Ct S
Frederick MD 21703

(G-971)
DRS LEONARDO INC
Also Called: Leonardo Drs Arbr Intllgnce Sy
2601 Mission Point Blvd Ste 250
(45431-6600)
PHONE..............................937 429-7408
EMP: 49
SALES (corp-wide): 16.62B **Publicly Held**
Web: www.leonardodrs.com
SIC: 3812 Search and navigation equipment
HQ: Leonardo Drs, Inc.
2345 Crystal Dr Ste 1000
Arlington VA 22202
703 416-8000

(G-972)
DRS SIGNAL TECHNOLOGIES INC
4393 Dayton Xenia Rd (45432-1803)
PHONE..............................937 429-7470
Leo Torresani, *Pr*
EMP: 7 EST: 1990
SALES (est): 1.06MM
SALES (corp-wide): 16.62B **Publicly Held**
Web: www.leonardodrs.com
SIC: 3825 7371 Electrical energy measuring equipment; Custom computer programming services
HQ: Leonardo Drs, Inc.
2345 Crystal Dr Ste 1000
Arlington VA 22202
703 416-8000

(G-973)
EDICT SYSTEMS INC
2434 Esquire Dr (45431-2573)
PHONE..............................937 429-4288
Ason K Wadzinski, *Ch Bd*
EMP: 45 EST: 1989
SQ FT: 12,000
SALES (est): 11.71MM
SALES (corp-wide): 11.97MM **Privately Held**
Web: www.edictsystems.com
SIC: 7372 Prepackaged software
PA: Advant-E Corporation
2434 Esquire Dr
Beavercreek OH 45431
937 429-4288

(G-974)
EDL DISPLAYS INC
1304 Research Park Dr (45432-2818)
PHONE..............................937 429-7423
Charles W Mc Intire, *Pr*
Michael J Mc Ardle, *General Vice President*
EMP: 20 EST: 1993

SQ FT: 10,000
SALES (est): 1.01MM **Privately Held**
SIC: 3663 Television monitors

(G-975)
GENERAL DYNMICS MSSION SYSTEMS
2673 Commons Blvd Ste 200 (45431-3505)
PHONE..............................513 253-4770
Bob Kiley, *Mgr*
EMP: 11
SALES (corp-wide): 47.72B **Publicly Held**
Web: www.gdmissionsystems.com
SIC: 3669 3812 Transportation signaling devices; Search and navigation equipment
HQ: General Dynamics Mission Systems, Inc.
12450 Fair Lakes Cir
Fairfax VA 22033
877 449-0600

(G-976)
GREENTEC PRECISION INC
2280 Grange Hall Rd (45431-2350)
PHONE..............................937 431-1840
Hideki Onoda, *Pr*
Philip Rumme, *VP*
EMP: 9 EST: 1997
SALES (est): 2.35MM **Privately Held**
Web: www.greentec-precision.com
SIC: 3545 Machine tool accessories

(G-977)
LEIDOS INC
3745 Pentagon Blvd (45431-2369)
PHONE..............................937 656-8433
Dennis Anders, *Brnch Mgr*
EMP: 77
Web: www.leidos.com
SIC: 8731 7371 7373 8742 Commercial physical research; Computer software development; Systems engineering, computer related; Training and development consultant
HQ: Leidos, Inc.
1750 Presidents St
Reston VA 20190
855 953-4367

(G-978)
MONARCH WATER SYSTEMS INC
689 Greystone Dr (45434-4202)
PHONE..............................937 426-5773
TOLL FREE: 888
John Glaser, *VP*
Patricia A Glaser, *Pr*
EMP: 10 EST: 1918
SQ FT: 7,500
SALES (est): 438.47K **Privately Held**
SIC: 3589 Water filters and softeners, household type

(G-979)
NUCOR CORPORATION
Also Called: Vulcraft
3000 Presidential Dr Ste 110 (45324-6208)
PHONE..............................937 390-2300
Sean Murphy, *Mgr*
EMP: 8
SALES (corp-wide): 30.73B **Publicly Held**
Web: www.nucor.com
SIC: 3312 Blast furnaces and steel mills
PA: Nucor Corporation
1915 Rexford Rd
Charlotte NC 28211
704 366-7000

(G-980)
RAYTHEON COMPANY
Also Called: Raytheon
2970 Presidential Dr Ste 300 (45324-6752)

PHONE.....................937 429-5429
Mike Evans, *Brnch Mgr*
EMP: 10
SALES (corp-wide): 80.74B **Publicly Held**
Web: www.rtx.com
SIC: 3812 Sonar systems and equipment
HQ: Raytheon Company
870 Winter St
Waltham MA 02451
781 522-3000

(G-981)
RELIABLE HERMETIC SEALS LLC
Also Called: Rh Seals
4156 Dayton Xenia Rd (45432-1904)
PHONE.....................888 747-3250
Mark Nuttbrock, *Managing Member*
EMP: 12 **EST:** 2012
SALES (est): 2.29MM **Privately Held**
Web: www.rhseals.com
SIC: 3643 3679 Bus bars (electrical conductors); Hermetic seals, for electronic equipment

(G-982)
SHOPS BY TODD INC (PA)
Also Called: Occassionally Yours
2727 Fairfield Commons Blvd Spc W273 (45431-5748)
PHONE.....................937 458-3192
Todd Bettman, *Pr*
EMP: 9 **EST:** 1985
SQ FT: 1,750
SALES (est): 951.97K **Privately Held**
Web: www.occasionallyyoursgifts.com
SIC: 5947 2759 Gift shop; Invitation and stationery printing and engraving

(G-983)
SIERRA NEVADA CORPORATION
Also Called: SIERRA NEVADA CORPORATION
2611 Commons Blvd (45431-3704)
PHONE.....................937 431-2800
William Sullivan, *Prin*
EMP: 24
SALES (corp-wide): 2.38B **Privately Held**
Web: www.sncorp.com
SIC: 8731 3577 Electronic research; Computer peripheral equipment, nec
PA: Sierra Nevada Company, Llc
444 Salomon Cir
Sparks NV 89434
775 331 0222

(G-984)
SONALYSTS INC
2940 Presidential Dr Ste 160 (45324-6564)
PHONE.....................937 429-9711
EMP: 20
SALES (corp-wide): 21.69MM **Privately Held**
Web: www.sonalysts.com
SIC: 3211 Window glass, clear and colored
PA: Sonalysts, Inc.
215 Parkway N
Waterford CT 06385
860 442-4355

(G-985)
TERADYNE INC
Avionics Interface Tech
2689 Commons Blvd Ste 201 (45431-3822)
PHONE.....................937 427-1280
Andy Kragick, *Mgr*
EMP: 15
SALES (corp-wide): 2.82B **Publicly Held**
Web: www.teradyne.com
SIC: 3829 Measuring and controlling devices, nec
PA: Teradyne, Inc.

600 Riverpark Dr
North Reading MA 01864
978 370-2700

(G-986)
THREAD WORKS CUSTOM EMBROIDERY
Also Called: Thread Wrks EMB Screenprinting
2630 Colonel Glenn Hwy (45324-6559)
PHONE.....................937 478-5231
Toni Webb, *Owner*
Don Webb, *Genl Mgr*
▲ **EMP:** 6 **EST:** 1993
SQ FT: 1,700
SALES (est): 209.84K **Privately Held**
Web: www.twlogo.com
SIC: 2395 Embroidery and art needlework

Beavercreek
Montgomery County

(G-987)
A & A SAFETY INC
4080 Industrial Ln (45430-1017)
PHONE.....................937 567-9781
Tim Weeks, *Mgr*
EMP: 10
SALES (corp-wide): 22.88MM **Privately Held**
Web: www.aasafetyinc.com
SIC: 7359 1721 5084 1611 Work zone traffic equipment (flags, cones, barrels, etc.); Painting and paper hanging; Safety equipment; Highway and street sign installation
PA: A & A Safety, Inc.
1126 Ferris Rd
Amelia OH 45102
513 943-6100

(G-988)
ALEKTRONICS INC
4095 Executive Dr (45430-1062)
PHONE.....................937 429-2118
Alan Eakle, *CEO*
EMP: 16 **EST:** 1988
SQ FT: 4,800
SALES (est): 5.4MM **Privately Held**
Web: www.alekcompanies.com
SIC: 3672 Printed circuit boards

(G-989)
ATK SPACE SYSTEMS LLC
1365 Technology Ct (45430-2212)
PHONE.....................937 490-4121
Todd Henrich, *VP*
EMP: 131
Web: www.psi-pci.com
SIC: 3812 Search and navigation equipment
HQ: Atk Space Systems Llc
6033 E Bandini Blvd
Commerce CA 90040
323 722-0222

(G-990)
ATK SYSTEMS
1365 Technology Ct (45430-2212)
PHONE.....................937 429-8632
EMP: 9
SALES (est): 263.04K **Privately Held**
SIC: 3812 Search and navigation equipment

(G-991)
EXITO MANUFACTURING LLC
4120 Industrial Ln Ste B (45430-1004)
PHONE.....................937 291-9871
EMP: 7 **EST:** 2000
SALES (est): 577.78K **Privately Held**
Web: www.exitomfg.com

SIC: 3544 3542 3728 3714 Special dies, tools, jigs, and fixtures; Machine tools, metal forming type; Aircraft parts and equipment, nec; Motor vehicle parts and accessories

(G-992)
HII MISSION TECHNOLOGIES CORP
1430 Oak Ct (45430-1069)
PHONE.....................937 426-3421
Charlie Schwegman, *Brnch Mgr*
EMP: 8
Web: www.hii.com
SIC: 8711 3721 Engineering services; Aircraft
HQ: Hii Mission Technologies Corp.
8350 Broad St Ste 1400
Mclean VA 22102
703 918-4480

(G-993)
NORTHROP GRMMAN INNVTION SYSTE
1365 Technology Ct (45430-2212)
PHONE.....................937 429-9261
Don Hairston, *Prin*
EMP: 150
Web: www.northropgrumman.com
SIC: 3812 Search and navigation equipment
HQ: Northrop Grumman Innovation Systems, Inc.
2980 Fairview Park Dr
Falls Church VA 22042

(G-994)
NORTHROP GRUMMAN SYSTEMS CORP
Also Called: Aeronics Systems Arspc Strctr
1365 Technology Ct (45430-2212)
PHONE.....................937 490-4111
Richard Passmore, *Brnch Mgr*
EMP: 174
Web: www.northropgrumman.com
SIC: 3812 Search and navigation equipment
HQ: Northrop Grumman Systems Corporation
2980 Fairview Park Dr
Falls Church VA 22042
703 280-2900

(G-995)
PROGRAM MANAGERS INC
Also Called: World Digital Imaging
1138 Richfield Ctr (45430-1121)
PHONE.....................937 431-1982
Craig Howick, *Prin*
Jerry Warner, *Prin*
EMP: 7 **EST:** 1998
SALES (est): 436.01K **Privately Held**
Web: www.worlddigitalimaging.com
SIC: 2752 Offset printing

(G-996)
SUPERIOR SODA SERVICE LLC
3626 Napanee Dr (45430-1322)
P.O. Box 341450 (45434-1450)
PHONE.....................937 657-9700
EMP: 6 **EST:** 2010
SALES (est): 244.17K **Privately Held**
Web: www.superiorsodaservice.com
SIC: 7699 3441 Vending machine repair; Fabricated structural metal

(G-997)
THE SCHAEFER GROUP INC (PA)
1300 Grange Hall Rd (45430-1013)
PHONE.....................937 253-3342
▲ **EMP:** 50 **EST:** 1956
SALES (est): 20.24MM
SALES (corp-wide): 20.24MM **Privately Held**

Web: www.theschaefergroup.com
SIC: 3567 1741 Metal melting furnaces, industrial: electric; Refractory or acid brick masonry

Beavercreek Township
Greene County

(G-998)
FLUID APPLIED ROOFING LLC
Also Called: Manufacturing
830 Space Dr (45434-7163)
PHONE.....................855 860-2300
Sonny Arwood, *CEO*
EMP: 17 **EST:** 2012
SALES (est): 8.96MM **Privately Held**
Web: www.fluidappliedroofing.com
SIC: 2952 Roofing materials

(G-999)
MOSHER MACHINE & TOOL CO INC
2201 Valley Springs Rd (45434-6100)
PHONE.....................937 258-8070
Kevin Mosher, *Pr*
Michael Mosher, *VP*
EMP: 32 **EST:** 1973
SALES (est): 4.47MM **Privately Held**
Web: www.moshermachine.com
SIC: 3451 3599 Screw machine products; Machine shop, jobbing and repair

(G-1000)
NORTHROP GRMMAN TCHNCAL SVCS I
Also Called: Ngts
4065 Colonel Glenn Hwy (45431-1601)
PHONE.....................937 320-3100
Saju Kuruvilla, *Brnch Mgr*
EMP: 104
SIC: 3812 8711 7373 Search and navigation equipment; Engineering services; Computer integrated systems design
HQ: Northrop Grumman Technical Services, Inc.
7575 Colshire Dr
Mc Lean VA 22102
703 556-1144

(G-1001)
NORTHROP GRUMMAN SYSTEMS CORP
4005 Colonel Glenn Hwy (45431-1001)
PHONE.....................937 429-6450
Mel Meadows, *Brnch Mgr*
EMP: 88
Web: www.northropgrumman.com
SIC: 3812 Search and navigation equipment
HQ: Northrop Grumman Systems Corporation
2980 Fairview Park Dr
Falls Church VA 22042
703 280-2900

(G-1002)
OCULII CORP
829 Space Dr (45434-7162)
PHONE.....................937 912-9261
Feng-ming Wang, *CEO*
EMP: 25 **EST:** 2012
SALES (est): 2.96MM
SALES (corp-wide): 284.87MM **Publicly Held**
Web: www.oculii.com
SIC: 3812 Radar systems and equipment
PA: Ambarella, Inc.
3101 Jay Street
Santa Clara CA 95054
408 734-8888

GEOGRAPHIC

(G-1003)
PHILLIPS COMPANIES (PA)
620 Phillips Dr (45434-7230)
P.O. Box 187 (45301-0187)
PHONE.....................................937 426-5461
George E Phillips, *Ch*
Richard L Phillips Ii, *Pr*
Dennis Phillips, *Sec*
Bradley Phillips, *VP*
Jason Phillips, *Treas*
EMP: 20 **EST:** 1942
SQ FT: 2,000
SALES (est): 11.8MM **Privately Held**
SALES (corp-wide): 11.8MM **Privately Held**
Web: www.phillipscompanies.com
SIC: 1442 6552 1794 Sand mining;
   Subdividers and developers, nec;
   Excavation work

(G-1004)
QUALITY QUARTZ ENGINEERING INC
802 Orchard Ln (45434-7217)
PHONE.....................................937 236-3250
◆ **EMP:** 52 **EST:** 2007
SALES (est): 8.65MM **Privately Held**
Web: www.qqe.com
SIC: 3679 Quartz crystals, for electronic application
PA: Quality Quartz Engineering, Incorporated
   802 Orchard Ln
   Beavercreek Township OH 45434

(G-1005)
QUALITY QUARTZ ENGINEERING INC (PA)
802 Orchard Ln (45434-7217)
PHONE.....................................510 791-1013
Scott Moseley, *CEO*
Kevin Cordia, *
▲ **EMP:** 24 **EST:** 1995
SALES (est): 8.65MM **Privately Held**
Web: www.qqe.com
SIC: 3679 Quartz crystals, for electronic application

(G-1006)
SONOCO PRODUCTS COMPANY
Sonoco Consumer Products
761 Space Dr (45434-7171)
PHONE.....................................937 429-0040
Norwood Bizzell, *Mgr*
EMP: 45
SALES (corp-wide): 5.31B **Publicly Held**
Web: www.sonoco.com
SIC: 2655 5113 2891 Cans, fiber: made from purchased material; Paper tubes and cores; Adhesives and sealants
PA: Sonoco Products Company
   1 N 2nd St
   Hartsville SC 29550
   843 383-7000

(G-1007)
W&W AUTOMOTIVE & TOWING INC
Also Called: W & W Automotive
680 Orchard Ln (45434-7205)
PHONE.....................................937 429-1699
Regina White, *Pr*
EMP: 10 **EST:** 1981
SQ FT: 16,000
SALES (est): 999.12K **Privately Held**
Web: www.wandwautomotive.com
SIC: 3711 7532 Chassis, motor vehicle; Body shop, automotive

Beaverdam
Allen County

(G-1008)
GOODYEAR TIRE & RUBBER COMPANY
Also Called: Goodyear
415 E Main St (45808-9728)
PHONE.....................................419 643-8273
Paul Morton, *Brnch Mgr*
EMP: 10
SALES (corp-wide): 18.88B **Publicly Held**
Web: www.wingfootct.com
SIC: 7534 5531 Tire retreading and repair shops; Automotive tires
PA: The Goodyear Tire & Rubber Company
   200 Innovation Way
   Akron OH 44316
   330 796-2121

Bedford
Cuyahoga County

(G-1009)
277 NORTHFIELD INC
277 Northfield Rd (44146-4648)
PHONE.....................................440 439-1029
Guriqbal Multani, *Admn*
EMP: 7 **EST:** 2013
SALES (est): 1.69MM **Privately Held**
SIC: 3441 Fabricated structural metal

(G-1010)
ALS HIGH TECH INC (PA)
Also Called: Al's Electric Motor Service
135 Northfield Rd (44146-4606)
PHONE.....................................440 232-7090
Dale Ochwat, *Pr*
Elaine Ochwat, *CEO*
Lynn O Meffen, *Sec*
EMP: 11 **EST:** 1955
SQ FT: 45,000
SALES (est): 1.63MM
SALES (corp-wide): 1.63MM **Privately Held**
Web: www.alselectricmotorservice.com
SIC: 7694 5063 Electric motor repair; Electrical apparatus and equipment

(G-1011)
AM CASTLE & CO
Also Called: Oliver Steel Plate
26800 Miles Rd (44146-1405)
PHONE.....................................330 425-7000
Scott J Dolan, *Brnch Mgr*
EMP: 19
SALES (corp-wide): 2.37B **Privately Held**
Web: www.castlemetals.com
SIC: 5051 3444 3443 3398 Steel; Sheet metalwork; Fabricated plate work (boiler shop); Metal heat treating
HQ: A.M. Castle & Co.
   1420 Knsington Rd Ste 220
   Oak Brook IL 60523
   847 455-7111

(G-1012)
APEX WELDING INCORPORATED
Also Called: Apex Bulk Handlers
1 Industry Dr (44146-4413)
P.O. Box 46199 (44146-0199)
PHONE.....................................440 232-6770
D J Warner, *Pr*
B A Danna, *VP*
EMP: 15 **EST:** 1947
SQ FT: 15,200
SALES (est): 2.37MM **Privately Held**
Web: www.apexbulkhandlers.com

SIC: 3444 3443 Hoppers, sheet metal; Fabricated plate work (boiler shop)

(G-1013)
AUTOMATED PACKG SYSTEMS INC
Sidepouch
25900 Solon Rd (44146-4788)
PHONE.....................................330 342-2000
Bob Stinger, *Mgr*
EMP: 21
SQ FT: 59,780
SALES (corp-wide): 5.39B **Publicly Held**
Web: www.autobag.com
SIC: 3565 2673 Packaging machinery; Bags: plastic, laminated, and coated
HQ: Automated Packaging Systems, Llc
   10175 Philipp Pkwy
   Streetsboro OH 44241
   330 528-2000

(G-1014)
BASWA ACOUSTICS NORTH AMER LLC
Also Called: Sound Solutions Cnstr Svcs
21863 Aurora Rd (44146-1201)
P.O. Box 620 (44255-0620)
PHONE.....................................216 475-7197
Ed Sellers, *Mng Pt*
Matt Townsend, *Pt*
▲ **EMP:** 12 **EST:** 2006
SQ FT: 3,000
SALES (est): 5.51MM **Privately Held**
Web: www.baswana.com
SIC: 5082 3272 General construction machinery and equipment; Building materials, except block or brick: concrete

(G-1015)
BEAUTY CFT MET FABRICATORS INC
5439 Perkins Rd (44146-1856)
PHONE.....................................440 439-0710
Ronald Walnsch, *Pr*
Brian Walnsch, *VP*
Mary Walnsch, *Sec*
EMP: 10 **EST:** 1976
SQ FT: 7,000
SALES (est): 370.54K **Privately Held**
Web:
www.beautycraftmetalfabricators.com
SIC: 3441 Fabricated structural metal

(G-1016)
BEN VENUE LABORATORIES INC
Also Called: Bedford Laboratories
300 Northfield Rd (44146-4650)
P.O. Box 46568 (44146-0568)
PHONE.....................................800 989-3320
▲ **EMP:** 1336
Web: www.boehringer-ingelheim.com
SIC: 2834 Pharmaceutical preparations

(G-1017)
BEST RESULT MARKETING INC
Also Called: Cashman Kiosk
7730 First Pl Ste E (44146-6720)
PHONE.....................................234 212-1194
Nilu Patel, *CEO*
Janie Horsburgh, *Prin*
EMP: 6 **EST:** 2020
SALES (est): 121.98K **Privately Held**
SIC: 3581 Automatic vending machines

(G-1018)
BRAINMASTER TECHNOLOGIES INC
195 Willis St # 3 (44146-3508)
P.O. Box 46725 (44146-0725)
PHONE.....................................440 232-6000
Thomas F Collura, *Pr*
Terri Collura, *Ex VP*
William Mrklas, *VP Opers*

EMP: 9 **EST:** 1999
SALES (est): 1.51MM **Privately Held**
Web: www.brainmaster.com
SIC: 3845 7371 Electromedical equipment; Computer software development

(G-1019)
CANNON SALT & SUPPLY INC
26041 Cannon Rd (44146-1835)
PHONE.....................................440 232-1700
Robert Foster, *Pr*
EMP: 6 **EST:** 2010
SALES (est): 929.08K **Privately Held**
Web: www.cannonsaltandsupply.com
SIC: 3524 3423 Lawn and garden equipment ; Garden and farm tools, including shovels

(G-1020)
CARR BROS INC
7177 Northfield Rd (44146-5403)
P.O. Box 46387 (44146-0387)
PHONE.....................................440 232-3700
Mike Carr, *Owner*
EMP: 24 **EST:** 2015
SALES (est): 4.5MM **Privately Held**
Web: www.carrbros.net
SIC: 3273 Ready-mixed concrete

(G-1021)
CERTON TECHNOLOGIES INC (PA)
Also Called: Har Adhesive Technologies
60 S Park St (44146-3635)
PHONE.....................................440 786-7185
Joe Cerino, *Prin*
Joseph Cerino, *Pr*
Diane Cerino, *VP*
EMP: 14 **EST:** 1996
SQ FT: 30,000
SALES (est): 10.09MM
SALES (corp-wide): 10.09MM **Privately Held**
Web: www.haradhesive.com
SIC: 2891 2851 7699 7359 Adhesives; Paints and paint additives; Professional instrument repair services; Home cleaning and maintenance equipment rental services

(G-1022)
COMMAND PLASTIC CORPORATION
22475 Aurora Rd (44146-1270)
PHONE.....................................800 321-8001
Richard S Ames, *Pr*
Ann Ames, *Dir*
Ron Brengartner, *Pr*
▲ **EMP:** 19 **EST:** 1971
SALES (est): 2MM **Privately Held**
Web: www.commandplastic.com
SIC: 2671 3081 2673 Plastic film, coated or laminated for packaging; Unsupported plastics film and sheet; Bags: plastic, laminated, and coated

(G-1023)
CONTINENTAL BUSINESS ENTPS INC (PA)
Also Called: Ace Metal Stamping Company
7311 Northfield Rd (44146-6199)
PHONE.....................................440 439-4400
Louis P Trolli, *Pr*
Richard L Laribee, *Sec*
Lynn Di Geronimo House, *Sec*
EMP: 16 **EST:** 1966
SQ FT: 33,000
SALES (est): 912.49K
SALES (corp-wide): 912.49K **Privately Held**
Web: www.acemetalstamping.com
SIC: 3469 3544 Stamping metal for the trade ; Special dies, tools, jigs, and fixtures

(G-1024)
CUSTOM SURFACES INC
26185 Broadway Ave (44146-6512)
PHONE...................................440 439-2310
Tim Mcconnell, *Pr*
EMP: 9 EST: 1975
SQ FT: 9,000
SALES (est): 115.85K **Privately Held**
SIC: 2511 Wood household furniture

(G-1025)
DENGENSHA AMERICA CORPORATION
Also Called: Dengensha America
7647 First Pl (44146-6701)
PHONE...................................440 439-8081
Donald Grisez, *Pr*
▲ EMP: 13 EST: 1985
SALES (est): 6.5MM **Privately Held**
Web: www.dengensha.com
SIC: 3559 5084 Automotive related machinery; Industrial machinery and equipment
PA: Dengensha Toa Co., Ltd.
1-23-1, Masugata, Tama-Ku
Kawasaki KNG 214-0

(G-1026)
DEUFOL WORLDWIDE PACKAGING LLC
19800 Alexander Rd (44146-5346)
PHONE...................................440 232-1100
Rich Stillman, *Brnch Mgr*
EMP: 22
SIC: 5113 3412 3086 Boxes and containers; Metal barrels, drums, and pails; Plastics foam products
HQ: Deufol Worldwide Packaging Llc
924 S Meridian St
Sunman IN 47041
888 845-2843

(G-1027)
DIVERSIFIED BRANDS
26300 Fargo Ave (44146-1310)
PHONE...................................216 595-8777
Gayle Dlougon, *Prin*
EMP: 14 EST: 2010
SALES (est): 220.18K **Privately Held**
Web: www.sherwin-williams.com
SIC: 2819 Industrial inorganic chemicals, nec

(G-1028)
DONE-RITE BOWLING SERVICE CO (PA)
Also Called: Paragon Machine Company
20434 Krick Rd (44146-4422)
PHONE...................................440 232-3280
Robert W Gable, *CEO*
Glenn Gable, *Pr*
Dave Patz, *VP*
Gale Burns, *VP*
Ann Gable, *Stockholder*
▲ EMP: 22 EST: 1950
SQ FT: 20,000
SALES (est): 863.57K
SALES (corp-wide): 863.57K **Privately Held**
Web: www.donerite.com
SIC: 3949 1752 5091 Bowling equipment and supplies; Floor laying and floor work, nec; Bowling equipment

(G-1029)
DRIBBLE CREEK INC
Also Called: Kadee Industries
7160 Krick Rd Ste A (44146-4438)
PHONE...................................440 439-8650
Brian Mullins, *Pr*
Joseph Scott, *Ex VP*

Catherine Mullins, *Sec*
EMP: 10 EST: 1980
SALES (est): 1.71MM **Privately Held**
Web: www.kadeeindustries.com
SIC: 3496 2273 Mats and matting; Carpets and rugs

(G-1030)
E J SKOK INDUSTRIES (PA)
Also Called: Skok Industries
26901 Richmond Rd (44146-1416)
PHONE...................................216 292-7533
Edward J Skok, *Pr*
Richard Skok, *Sec*
EMP: 20 EST: 1974
SQ FT: 18,000
SALES (est): 741.87K
SALES (corp-wide): 741.87K **Privately Held**
Web: www.skokind.com
SIC: 2541 2434 Table or counter tops, plastic laminated; Wood kitchen cabinets

(G-1031)
FEDERAL METAL COMPANY (HQ)
Also Called: FM
7250 Division St (44146-5495)
PHONE...................................440 232-8700
David R Nagusky, *CEO*
Peter Nagusky, *
Chris Greenfield, *
Robert I Kohn, *
Mike Buyarski, *
EMP: 16 EST: 1913
SQ FT: 65,000
SALES (est): 7.14MM **Privately Held**
Web: www.federalmetal.com
SIC: 3351 3364 Copper and copper alloy sheet, strip, plate, and products; Copper and copper alloy die-castings
PA: Oakwood Industries Inc.
7250 Division St
Bedford OH 44146

(G-1032)
FERRO CORPORATION
FERRO CORPORATION
7050 Krick Rd (44146-4416)
PHONE...................................216 577-7144
Kent Lee, *Brnch Mgr*
EMP: 54
SALES (corp-wide): 1.88B **Privately Held**
Web: www.vibrantz.com
CIC: 2851 2860 2842 2836 Paint driers; Industrial organic chemicals, nec; Polishes and sanitation goods; Biological products, except diagnostic
HQ: Vibrantz Corporation
6060 Prkland Blvd Ste 250
Mayfield Heights OH 44124
216 875-5600

(G-1033)
GROUNDHOGS 2000 LLC
33 Industry Dr (44146-4413)
PHONE...................................440 653-1647
EMP: 6 EST: 2006
SALES (est): 1.12MM **Privately Held**
Web: www.groundhogs2000.com
SIC: 1381 1623 7389 Directional drilling oil and gas wells; Water, sewer, and utility lines ; Business Activities at Non-Commercial Site

(G-1034)
GUILD INTERNATIONAL INC
Also Called: Guild International
7273 Division St (44146-5490)
PHONE...................................440 232-5887
Joe Thomas, *Pr*
Bill Maruschak, *

Mark Wagner, *
◆ EMP: 46 EST: 1956
SQ FT: 12,000
SALES (est): 8.85MM **Privately Held**
Web: www.guildint.com
SIC: 3549 Coiling machinery

(G-1035)
HIKMA PHARMACEUTICALS USA INC
Also Called: Research & Development Div
300 Northfield Rd (44146-4650)
PHONE...................................732 542-1191
EMP: 24
SALES (corp-wide): 3.13B **Privately Held**
Web: www.hikma.com
SIC: 2834 Pharmaceutical preparations
HQ: Hikma Pharmaceuticals Usa Inc.
200 Connell Dr 4th Fl
Berkeley Heights NJ 07922
908 673-1030

(G-1036)
HOME CITY ICE COMPANY
20282 Hannan Pkwy (44146-5353)
PHONE...................................440 439-5001
Rick Wetterau, *Mgr*
EMP: 9
SQ FT: 15,947
SALES (corp-wide): 100.42MM **Privately Held**
Web: www.homecityice.com
SIC: 5999 2097 Ice; Manufactured ice
PA: The Home City Ice Company
6045 Bridgetown Rd Ste 1
Cincinnati OH 45248
513 574-1800

(G-1037)
HY-TECH CONTROLS INC
7411 First Pl (44146-6712)
PHONE...................................440 232-4040
EMP: 30 EST: 1983
SALES (est): 6.91MM **Privately Held**
Web: www.hy-techcontrols.com
SIC: 3613 Control panels, electric

(G-1038)
I SCHUMANN & CO LLC
Also Called: I Schumann & Co
22500 Alexander Rd (44146-5576)
PHONE...................................440 439-2300
Scott Schumann, *Managing Member*
David Schumann, *
Michael Schumann, *Managing Member*
Anthony Schumann, *
Don Robertson, *
◆ EMP: 104 EST: 1917
SQ FT: 150,000
SALES (est): 9.24MM **Privately Held**
Web: www.ischumann.com
SIC: 3341 Brass smelting and refining (secondary)

(G-1039)
ILLINOIS TOOL WORKS INC
Anchor Fasteners
26101 Fargo Ave (44146-1305)
PHONE...................................216 292-7161
Ray Belcher, *Brnch Mgr*
EMP: 35
SALES (corp-wide): 16.11B **Publicly Held**
Web: www.itw.com
SIC: 3496 Miscellaneous fabricated wire products
PA: Illinois Tool Works Inc.
155 Harlem Ave
Glenview IL 60025
847 724-7500

(G-1040)
IOPPOLO CONCRETE CORPORATION
10 Industry Dr (44146-4414)
PHONE...................................440 439-6606
Anthony Ioppolo Junior, *Pr*
EMP: 9 EST: 1958
SQ FT: 6,000
SALES (est): 858.13K **Privately Held**
Web: www.ioppoloconcrete.com
SIC: 3273 1711 7353 4959 Ready-mixed concrete; Plumbing, heating, air-conditioning; Heavy construction equipment rental; Snowplowing

(G-1041)
KCN TECHNOLOGIES LLC
Also Called: Ace Hydraulics
1 W Interstate St # 13 (44146-4215)
PHONE...................................440 439-4219
Gary Schuster, *Prin*
Brian Schuster, *Genl Mgr*
EMP: 8 EST: 1996
SALES (est): 279.62K **Privately Held**
SIC: 1799 7694 7629 Hydraulic equipment, installation and service; Armature rewinding shops; Electrical repair shops

(G-1042)
KOLTCZ CONCRETE BLOCK CO
7660 Oak Leaf Rd (44146-5554)
PHONE...................................440 232-3630
Stanley M Koltcz, *Pr*
EMP: 26 EST: 1938
SQ FT: 55,000
SALES (est): 7.36MM **Privately Held**
Web: www.koltczblock.com
SIC: 3271 5032 5211 Blocks, concrete or cinder: standard; Masons' materials; Masonry materials and supplies

(G-1043)
LAKE SHORE ELECTRIC CORP
205 Willis St (44146-3583)
PHONE...................................440 232-0200
Michael Shane, *Pr*
Wayne Bussard, *
◆ EMP: 25 EST: 1922
SQ FT: 40,000
SALES (est): 10.39MM **Privately Held**
Web: www.lake-shore-electric.com
SIC: 3625 3613 3643 3621 Control equipment, electric; Switches, electric power except snap, push button, etc.; Current-carrying wiring services; Motors and generators

(G-1044)
LOVEMAN STEEL CORPORATION
5455 Perkins Rd (44146-1856)
PHONE...................................440 232-6200
Anthony Murru, *CEO*
Robin Davis Ray, *Prin*
David Loveman, *
Rob Loveman, *
James Loveman, *
◆ EMP: 75 EST: 1928
SQ FT: 80,000
SALES (est): 10MM **Privately Held**
Web: www.lovemansteel.com
SIC: 5051 3443 Plates, metal; Weldments

(G-1045)
MAJESTIC FIREPLACE DISTR
7500 Northfield Rd (44146-6110)
PHONE...................................440 439-1040
EMP: 7 EST: 2018
SALES (est): 701.29K **Privately Held**
Web: www.masonsteel.com

SIC: 3462 Iron and steel forgings

(G-1046)
MARLEN MANUFACTURING & DEV CO (PA)
Also Called: Marlen
5150 Richmond Rd (44146-1331)
PHONE..................................216 292-7060
Gary Fenton, *Pr*
Michael Magar, *Treas*
▲ **EMP:** 6 **EST:** 1952
SQ FT: 45,000
SALES (est): 8.85MM
SALES (corp-wide): 8.85MM **Privately Held**
Web: www.marlenmfg.com
SIC: 3842 Surgical appliances and supplies

(G-1047)
MARLEN MANUFACTURING & DEV CO
Medco Coated Products
5156 Richmond Rd (44146-1331)
PHONE..................................216 292-7546
Mark Fenton, *Mgr*
EMP: 15
SALES (corp-wide): 8.85MM **Privately Held**
Web: www.marlenmfg.com
SIC: 2891 3842 2672 2671 Adhesives and sealants; Surgical appliances and supplies; Paper; coated and laminated, nec; Paper; coated and laminated packaging
PA: Marlen Manufacturing And Development Co.
5150 Richmond Rd
Bedford OH 44146
216 292-7060

(G-1048)
MOLDING DYNAMICS INC
7009 Krick Rd (44146-4415)
PHONE..................................440 786-8100
Charles F Connors Iii, *Pr*
EMP: 15 **EST:** 1979
SQ FT: 14,000
SALES (est): 4.15MM **Privately Held**
Web: www.moldingdynamics.net
SIC: 3089 Injection molding of plastics

(G-1049)
NEW YORK FROZEN FOODS INC (DH)
25900 Fargo Ave (44146-1302)
PHONE..................................216 292-5655
Bruce Rosa, *Pr*
Donald Penn, *
Larry R Linhart, *Prin*
EMP: 260 **EST:** 1978
SQ FT: 55,000
SALES (est): 22.17MM
SALES (corp-wide): 1.87B **Publicly Held**
SIC: 2051 Bread, all types (white, wheat, rye, etc); fresh or frozen
HQ: T.Marzetti Company
380 Polaris Pkwy Ste 400
Westerville OH 43082
614 846-2232

(G-1050)
NPK CONSTRUCTION EQUIPMENT INC (HQ)
7550 Independence Dr (44146-5541)
PHONE..................................440 232-7900
Dan Tyrell, *Pr*
Nick Shah, *
◆ **EMP:** 60 **EST:** 1985
SQ FT: 150,000
SALES (est): 46.27MM **Privately Held**
Web: www.npkce.com

SIC: 5082 3599 3546 3532 General construction machinery and equipment; Machine shop, jobbing and repair; Power-driven handtools; Mining machinery
PA: Nippon Pneumatic Manufacturing Co.,Ltd.
4-11-5, Kamiji, Higashinari-Ku
Osaka OSK 537-0

(G-1051)
OAKWOOD INDUSTRIES INC (PA)
Also Called: Federal Metal Co
7250 Division St (44146-5406)
PHONE..................................440 232-8700
David R Nagusky, *Pr*
Malvin E Bank, *
◆ **EMP:** 60 **EST:** 1986
SQ FT: 65,000
SALES (est): 34.55MM **Privately Held**
Web: www.federalmetal.com
SIC: 3341 3364 Brass smelting and refining (secondary); Nonferrous die-castings except aluminum

(G-1052)
ONE WISH LLC
Also Called: Audimute Sndprfing Mdic Bttrie
23700 Aurora Rd (44146-1796)
PHONE..................................800 505-6883
EMP: 18 **EST:** 2003
SALES (est): 6.63MM **Privately Held**
Web: www.audimute.com
SIC: 5063 5999 8742 1742 Batteries; Batteries, non-automotive; Marketing consulting services; Acoustical and insulation work

(G-1053)
OVERSEAS PACKING LLC
Also Called: United Packaging Supply Co Div
19800 Alexander Rd (44146-5346)
PHONE..................................440 232-2917
EMP: 8 **EST:** 1940
SQ FT: 52,000
SALES (est): 1.4MM **Privately Held**
SIC: 2449 3412 4783 Wood containers, nec; Metal barrels, drums, and pails; Packing goods for shipping

(G-1054)
PRECISION MCHNING SRFACING INC
20637 Krick Rd (44146-5412)
PHONE..................................440 439-9850
David Slifka, *Pr*
EMP: 6 **EST:** 2000
SALES (est): 2.06MM **Privately Held**
Web: www.pre-machining.com
SIC: 3599 Machine shop, jobbing and repair

(G-1055)
RELIANT WORTH CORP
20638 Krick Rd (44146-5409)
PHONE..................................440 232-1422
Don Shumay, *Pr*
EMP: 7 **EST:** 1967
SQ FT: 2,500
SALES (est): 704.03K **Privately Held**
Web: www.arconequipment.com
SIC: 3691 Storage batteries

(G-1056)
RESERVE MILLWORK LLC
26881 Cannon Rd (44146-1851)
PHONE..................................216 531-6982
Tony Azzolina, *Pr*
Virginia Azzolina, *VP*
EMP: 41 **EST:** 1980
SQ FT: 18,000
SALES (est): 4.54MM **Privately Held**
Web: www.reservemillwork.com

SIC: 2431 2434 2541 Ornamental woodwork: cornices, mantels, etc.; Wood kitchen cabinets; Wood partitions and fixtures

(G-1057)
RESIDEO LLC
Also Called: ADI Global Distribution
7710 First Pl Ste A (44146-6718)
PHONE..................................440 439-7002
Mark Blackburn, *Mgr*
EMP: 6
SALES (corp-wide): 6.76B **Publicly Held**
Web: www.adiglobaldistribution.us
SIC: 5063 3669 3822 Electrical apparatus and equipment; Emergency alarms; Environmental controls
HQ: Resideo Llc
275 Bradhollow Rd Ste 400
Melville NY 11747
631 692-1000

(G-1058)
S & H INDUSTRIES INC (PA)
5200 Richmond Rd (44146-1387)
PHONE..................................216 831-0550
Eric Turk, *CEO*
Steve Perney, *Treas*
EMP: 16 **EST:** 1978
SALES (est): 2.41MM
SALES (corp-wide): 2.41MM **Privately Held**
Web: www.shindustries.com
SIC: 3423 Mechanics' hand tools

(G-1059)
SWIFT FILTERS INC
24040 Forbes Rd (44146-5650)
PHONE..................................877 887-9438
Edwin C Swift Junior, *Pr*
Charles C Swift, *
EMP: 38 **EST:** 1995
SQ FT: 6,000
SALES (est): 10.91MM **Privately Held**
Web: www.swiftfilters.com
SIC: 3569 5075 Filters; Air filters

(G-1060)
TAVENS CONTAINER INC
Also Called: Tavens Packg Display Solutions
22475 Aurora Rd (44146-1270)
PHONE..................................216 883-3333
Richard Ames, *
Graham Klintworth, *
EMP: 60 **EST:** 1957
SQ FT: 87,000
SALES (est): 2.19MM **Privately Held**
Web: www.tavens.com
SIC: 2653 3412 Boxes, corrugated: made from purchased materials; Metal barrels, drums, and pails

(G-1061)
THERMO GAMMA-METRICS LLC (HQ)
1 Thermo Fisher Way (44146-6536)
PHONE..................................858 450-9811
Ken Berger, *Pr*
Sandra Lambert, *Sec*
▲ **EMP:** 20 **EST:** 1980
SALES (est): 2.91MM
SALES (corp-wide): 42.86B **Publicly Held**
SIC: 3824 3826 3812 3823 Controls, revolution and timing instruments; Environmental testing equipment; Search and detection systems and instruments; Process control instruments
PA: Thermo Fisher Scientific Inc.
168 3rd Ave
Waltham MA 02451
781 622-1000

(G-1062)
TOTH MOLD & DIE INC
380 Solon Rd Ste 6 (44146-3809)
PHONE..................................440 232-8530
Timothy Toth, *Pr*
Thomas Toth, *Sec*
EMP: 10 **EST:** 1982
SALES (est): 824.64K **Privately Held**
Web: www.tothmold.net
SIC: 3089 Injection molded finished plastics products, nec

(G-1063)
VITEC INC
26901 Cannon Rd (44146-1809)
PHONE..................................216 464-4670
Richard A Wynveen, *Pr*
Franz H Schubert, *Stockholder*
EMP: 7 **EST:** 1974
SQ FT: 15,000
SALES (est): 1.08MM **Privately Held**
Web: www.vitec-inc.com
SIC: 3823 Process control instruments

(G-1064)
WALTON PLASTICS INC
Also Called: Wal Plax
20493 Hannan Pkwy (44146-5356)
PHONE..................................440 786-7711
Steven Wake, *CEO*
Marvin Bollinger, *Stockholder*
Tim Bollinger, *Stockholder*
Marinko Milos, *CFO*
Larry Crystal, *Prin*
▲ **EMP:** 21 **EST:** 1992
SQ FT: 44,000
SALES (est): 4.41MM **Privately Held**
Web: www.waltonplastics.com
SIC: 3081 Vinyl film and sheet

(G-1065)
WAXMAN INDUSTRIES INC (PA)
5386 Majestic Pkwy (44146-1784)
PHONE..................................440 439-1830
Larry Waxman, *Pr*
Melvin Waxman, *Ch Bd*
Laurence Waxman, *Pr*
Mark Wester, *Sr VP*
◆ **EMP:** 110 **EST:** 1962
SALES (est): 47.75MM
SALES (corp-wide): 47.75MM **Privately Held**
Web: www.waxman.com
SIC: 5072 5074 3494 3491 Hardware; Plumbing and hydronic heating supplies; Valves and pipe fittings, nec; Industrial valves

(G-1066)
YOUNG REGULATOR COMPANY INC
7100 Krick Rd Ste A (44146-4443)
PHONE..................................440 232-9452
Michael E Mcguigan, *Pr*
EMP: 20 **EST:** 1930
SQ FT: 40,000
SALES (est): 1.9MM **Privately Held**
Web: www.youngregulator.com
SIC: 3822 1711 Air conditioning and refrigeration controls; Plumbing, heating, air-conditioning

(G-1067)
ZENEX INTERNATIONAL
7777 First Pl (44146-6733)
PHONE..................................440 232-4155
George Kniere, *Owner*
▲ **EMP:** 9 **EST:** 2006
SALES (est): 8.91MM **Privately Held**
Web: www.zenexint.com
SIC: 2813 Aerosols

▲ = Import ▼ = Export
◆ = Import/Export

Bedford Heights
Cuyahoga County

(G-1068)
AMERICAN SPRING WIRE CORP (PA)
Also Called: Asw
26300 Miles Rd (44146-1072)
PHONE..............................216 292-4620
Timothy W Selhorst, *CEO*
Timothy W Selhorst, *Pr*
Greg Bokar, *
◆ **EMP: 200 EST:** 1968
SQ FT: 360,500
SALES (est): 23.2MM
SALES (corp-wide): 23.2MM **Privately Held**
Web: www.americanspringwire.com
SIC: 3272 3315 3316 3339 Concrete products, nec; Wire products, ferrous/iron: made in wiredrawing plants; Wire, flat, cold-rolled strip: not made in hot-rolled mills; Primary nonferrous metals, nec

(G-1069)
ASWPENGG LLC
Also Called: Amrican Spring Wire
26300 Miles Rd (44146-1410)
PHONE..............................216 292-4620
Manish Ishwar, *CEO*
EMP: 19 EST: 2016
SALES (est): 5.06MM **Privately Held**
Web: www.wire-pengg.com
SIC: 3592 3495 Valves; Wire springs

(G-1070)
BRAND CASTLE LLC
5111 Richmond Rd (44146)
PHONE..............................216 292-7700
Carolyn Resar, *Pr*
Cristina Fritts, *
▲ **EMP: 36 EST:** 2003
SALES (est): 24.76MM
SALES (corp-wide): 1.37B **Privately Held**
Web: www.brandcastle.com
SIC: 2052 5149 Bakery products, dry; Crackers, cookies, and bakery products
HQ: Signature Brands, Llc
808 Sw 12th St
Ocala FL 34474
352 622-3134

(G-1071)
BRIDGE ANALYZERS INC
5198 Richmond Rd (44146-1331)
PHONE..............................216 332-0592
David Anderson, *Prin*
EMP: 18 EST: 2017
SALES (est): 3.49MM **Privately Held**
Web: www.bridgeanalyzers.com
SIC: 3826 Analytical instruments

(G-1072)
CARDINAL FSTENER SPECIALTY INC
Also Called: Cardinal Fastener
5185 Richmond Rd (44146-1330)
PHONE..............................216 831-3800
Bill Boak, *Pr*
Denise R Muha, *
Bill Walczak, *
Wendy L Brugmann, *
▲ **EMP: 50 EST:** 1983
SQ FT: 100,000
SALES (est): 1.16MM **Privately Held**
SIC: 3965 Fasteners

(G-1073)
CLEVELAND COCA-COLA BTLG INC
Also Called: Coca-Cola
25000 Miles Rd (44146-1319)

PHONE..............................216 690-2653
George M Gernhardt, *
H C Gram, *Prin*
William L Arnett, *Prin*
Peter E Benzino, *
Charles R Hanlon, *
EMP: 220 EST: 1911
SQ FT: 220,000
SALES (est): 10.37MM **Privately Held**
Web: www.abartacocacola.com
SIC: 2086 Bottled and canned soft drinks

(G-1074)
CLEVELAND STEEL SPECIALTY CO
26001 Richmond Rd (44146-1435)
P.O. Box 1687 (44224-0687)
PHONE..............................216 464-9400
Robert W Ehrhardt Senior, *Pr*
Robert W Ehrhardt Senior, *CEO*
Robert W Ehrhardt Junior, *Pr*
EMP: 30 EST: 1924
SQ FT: 24,000
SALES (est): 2.43MM **Privately Held**
Web: www.clevelandsteel.com
SIC: 3443 3429 3444 Metal parts; Builders' hardware; Sheet metalwork

(G-1075)
CWH GRAPHICS LLC
Also Called: Ink Well
23196 Miles Rd Ste A (44128-5490)
P.O. Box 22651 (44122-0651)
PHONE..............................866 241-8515
EMP: 7 EST: 2005
SQ FT: 4,000
SALES (est): 620.85K **Privately Held**
Web: www.shortstackprinting.com
SIC: 2752 Offset printing

(G-1076)
FOOD EQUIPMENT MFG CORP
Also Called: Femc
22201 Aurora Rd (44146-1273)
PHONE..............................216 672-5859
Robert Sauer, *Pr*
EMP: 20 EST: 1977
SQ FT: 65,000
SALES (est): 5.04MM **Privately Held**
Web: www.femc.com
SIC: 3565 Packaging machinery

(G-1077)
FROHN NORTH AMERICA INC
23800 Corbin Dr Ste B (44128-5402)
PHONE..............................770 819-0089
Peter Beckmerhagen, *Pr*
Peter Beckmerhagen, *Pr*
Herb Gray, *VP*
Sandra Schadwill, *Sec*
◆ **EMP: 8 EST:** 1994
SQ FT: 24,000
SALES (est): 2.25MM **Privately Held**
Web: www.frohnnorthamerica.com
SIC: 3369 Nonferrous foundries, nec

(G-1078)
HOIST EQUIPMENT CO INC (PA)
26161 Cannon Rd (44146-1896)
PHONE..............................440 232-0300
Nicholas Gambatesa, *CEO*
Jeffrey Sadar, *
EMP: 25 EST: 1953
SQ FT: 40,000
SALES (est): 5.24MM
SALES (corp-wide): 5.24MM **Privately Held**
Web: www.hoistequipment.com
SIC: 3537 3535 3536 Cranes, industrial truck ; Overhead conveyor systems; Hoists

(G-1079)
METRON INSTRUMENTS INC
5198 Richmond Rd (44146-1331)
P.O. Box 39325 (44139-0325)
PHONE..............................216 332-0592
David Anderson, *Pr*
EMP: 8 EST: 2003
SALES (est): 283.49K **Privately Held**
Web: www.bridgeanalyzers.com
SIC: 3826 Analytical instruments

(G-1080)
NATIONAL PEENING
23800 Corbin Dr Unit B (44128-5402)
PHONE..............................216 342-9155
Don Kvorka, *Pr*
EMP: 9 EST: 2013
SALES (est): 827.28K **Privately Held**
Web: www.sintoamerica.com
SIC: 3398 Shot peening (treating steel to reduce fatigue)

(G-1081)
SIGN GYPSIES CLEVELAND LLC
Also Called: Sign Gypsies
5940 Lehman Dr (44146-3131)
PHONE..............................216 202-2093
EMP: 12 EST: 2017
SALES (est): 590.14K **Privately Held**
Web: www.signgypsies.com
SIC: 3993 Signs and advertising specialties

(G-1082)
THE PERFECT SCORE COMPANY
Also Called: Perfect Score, The
25801 Solon Rd (44146-4759)
PHONE..............................440 439-9320
Ed Fraschetti, *Pr*
Megan Gross, *Sec*
EMP: 15 EST: 1996
SQ FT: 2,000
SALES (est): 1.59MM **Privately Held**
SIC: 3556 Bakery machinery

(G-1083)
UNITREX LTD
Also Called: Sparoom
5060 Taylor Dr Ste D (44128-6505)
PHONE..............................216 831-1900
Anthony Padrazo, *CEO*
▲ **EMP: 68 EST:** 2012
SALES (est): 60MM **Privately Held**
Web: www.sparoom.com
SIC: 2899 Oils and essential oils

(G-1084)
ZENA BABY SOAP COMPANY
6651 Hedgeline Dr (44146-4870)
PHONE..............................216 317-6433
Dawn Schwark, *CEO*
Dawn Schwark, *Pr*
Donnita Diggs-owens, *Pr*
Latonya Moore, *Pr*
Karen Teague, *Pr*
EMP: 6 EST: 2018
SALES (est): 173.05K **Privately Held**
SIC: 2844 Perfumes, cosmetics and other toilet preparations

Bellaire
Belmont County

(G-1085)
BELMONT COMMUNITY HOSPITAL
Also Called: Belmont Community Health Ctr
4697 Harrison St (43906-1303)
PHONE..............................740 671-1216
Garry Gould, *CEO*
EMP: 22

SALES (corp-wide): 6.01B **Privately Held**
Web: www.hospital-data.com
SIC: 2599 Hospital beds
HQ: Belmont Community Hospital
4697 Harrison St
Bellaire OH 43906
740 671-1200

(G-1086)
COUNTRY CLB RTRMENT CTR IV LLC
55801 Conno Mara Dr (43906-9698)
PHONE..............................740 676-2300
EMP: 7 EST: 2015
SALES (est): 4.52MM **Privately Held**
Web: www.countryclubretirementcampus.com
SIC: 3949 Indian clubs

(G-1087)
GERDAU AMERISTEEL US INC
5310 Guernsey St (43906-9516)
PHONE..............................740 671-9410
EMP: 7
Web: www.gerdau.com
SIC: 3499 3312 1771 Bank chests, metal; Blast furnaces and steel mills; Concrete work
HQ: Gerdau Ameristeel Us Inc.
4221 W Boy Scout Blvd Ste
Tampa FL 33607
813 286-8383

(G-1088)
GUMBYS LLC
2300 Belmont St (43906-1733)
PHONE..............................740 671-0818
Beau Lamotte, *Brnch Mgr*
EMP: 11
Web: www.gumbys.com
SIC: 3999 Cigarette and cigar products and accessories
PA: Gumby's, L.L.C.
98 E Cove Ave Ste 1
Wheeling WV 26003

(G-1089)
LION INDUSTRIES LLC
423 53rd St (43906-9514)
P.O. Box 455 (43950-0455)
PHONE..............................740 676-1100
David A Humphreys Junior, *Managing Member*
EMP: 20 EST: 2008
SALES (est): 5.02MM **Privately Held**
Web: www.lionind.com
SIC: 3443 3449 Fabricated plate work (boiler shop); Custom roll formed products

(G-1090)
XTO ENERGY INC
Also Called: Xto Energy
2358 W 23rd St (43906-9614)
PHONE..............................740 671-9901
EMP: 8
SALES (corp-wide): 349.58B **Publicly Held**
Web: www.xtoenergy.com
SIC: 1311 Crude petroleum production
HQ: Xto Energy Inc.
22777 Sprngwoods Vlg Pkwy
Spring TX 77389

Bellbrook
Greene County

(G-1091)
ERNST ENTERPRISES INC
Also Called: Sugarcreek Ready Mix

2181 Ferry Rd (45305-9728)
PHONE..............................937 848-6811
John Ernst Junior, *Pr*
EMP: 32
SQ FT: 5,000
SALES (corp-wide): 240.08MM **Privately Held**
Web: www.ernstconcrete.com
SIC: 3273 Ready-mixed concrete
PA: Ernst Enterprises, Inc.
　　993 Falls Creek Dr
　　Vandalia OH 45377
　　937 233-5555

(G-1092)
GOLDEN SPRING COMPANY INC
2143 Ferry Rd (45305-9728)
P.O. Box 244 (45305-0244)
PHONE..............................937 848-2513
Paul Smith, *Pr*
Rita Treser, *VP*
EMP: 10 **EST:** 1953
SQ FT: 5,100
SALES (est): 429.35K **Privately Held**
Web: www.golden-spring.com
SIC: 3493 Coiled flat springs

(G-1093)
SUPPLY ONE CORPORATION
4146 Woodedge Dr (45305-1617)
PHONE..............................937 297-1111
Allen Pippenger, *Pr*
▲ **EMP:** 14 **EST:** 1940
SQ FT: 128,000
SALES (est): 958K **Privately Held**
SIC: 2434 Wood kitchen cabinets

Belle Center
Logan County

(G-1094)
BELLE CENTER AIR TOOL CO INC
202 N Elizabeth St (43310-9684)
P.O. Box 37 (43310-0037)
PHONE..............................937 464-7474
Carroll Doty, *Pr*
Ruth Doty, *Sec*
▲ **EMP:** 9 **EST:** 1985
SQ FT: 9,500
SALES (est): 2.23MM **Privately Held**
Web: belle-corner.edan.io
SIC: 5084 3532 Pneumatic tools and
　　equipment; Drills, bits, and similar
　　equipment

(G-1095)
HEINTZ FARMS ENTERPRISE
PARTNR
4367 State Route 273 W (43310-9710)
PHONE..............................937 464-2535
William Heintz, *Pt*
EMP: 6 **EST:** 2017
SALES (est): 1.02MM **Privately Held**
SIC: 3523 Driers (farm): grain, hay, and seed

(G-1096)
HIGHS WELDING INC
3065 County Road 150 (43310-1107)
PHONE..............................937 464-3029
Nick S High, *Pr*
EMP: 6 **EST:** 1972
SALES (est): 320.11K **Privately Held**
SIC: 7692 Welding repair

(G-1097)
TROYERS CABINET SHOP LTD
9442 County Road 101 (43310-9589)
PHONE..............................937 464-7702
Leon H Troyer, *Pt*

Marcus Troyer, *Pt*
Nathan Troyer, *Pt*
EMP: 10 **EST:** 1979
SALES (est): 386.81K **Privately Held**
SIC: 2434 Wood kitchen cabinets

Bellefontaine
Logan County

(G-1098)
5 CORE INC
1221 W Sandusky Ave (43311-1046)
PHONE..............................951 386-6372
Amarjit Singh Karla, *Pr*
EMP: 17 **EST:** 2020
SQ FT: 24,000
SALES (est): 3.7MM **Privately Held**
Web: www.5core.com
SIC: 3651 Household audio and video
　　equipment

(G-1099)
ARDEN J NEER SR
Also Called: Neer's Engineering Labs
4859 Township Road 45 (43311-9624)
PHONE..............................937 585-6733
Arden J Neer Senior, *Owner*
EMP: 10 **EST:** 1927
SQ FT: 7,500
SALES (est): 1.72MM **Privately Held**
Web: www.neerssandandgravel.com
SIC: 1442 Construction sand mining

(G-1100)
AXIS CORPORATION
314 Water Ave (43311-1734)
P.O. Box 668 (43311-0668)
PHONE..............................937 592-1958
Matt Oldiges, *Pr*
Linda Luebke, *Sec*
Thomas Oldiges, *Stockholder*
EMP: 10 **EST:** 1969
SQ FT: 20,000
SALES (est): 3.37MM **Privately Held**
Web: www.axiscorporation.com
SIC: 3441 Fabricated structural metal

(G-1101)
CLAYTON HOMES
2720 Us Highway 68 S (43311-8900)
PHONE..............................937 592-3039
EMP: 10 **EST:** 2019
SALES (est): 144.08K **Privately Held**
Web:
www.claytonhomesofbellefontaine.com
SIC: 2451 Mobile homes

(G-1102)
COUNTY CLASSIFIEDS
Also Called: The County Classified's
117 E Patterson Ave (43311-1912)
P.O. Box 596 (43311-0596)
PHONE..............................937 592-8847
Leah Frank, *Pr*
EMP: 8 **EST:** 1987
SALES (est): 64.5K **Privately Held**
Web:
www.thecountyclassifiedsonline.com
SIC: 2711 2752 2741 Job printing and
　　newspaper publishing combined;
　　Commercial printing, lithographic;
　　Miscellaneous publishing

(G-1103)
D H S LLC
220 Reynolds Ave (43311-3003)
P.O. Box 3083 (43016-0040)
PHONE..............................937 599-2485
EMP: 15 **EST:** 1993

SQ FT: 3,500
SALES (est): 1.35MM **Privately Held**
SIC: 3679 Harness assemblies, for
　　electronic use: wire or cable

(G-1104)
DAIDO METAL BELLEFONTAINE LLC
1215 S Greenwood St (43311-1628)
PHONE..............................937 592-5010
▲ **EMP:** 17 **EST:** 1997
SQ FT: 224,000
SALES (est): 4.8MM **Privately Held**
Web: www.daidometal.com
SIC: 3714 Motor vehicle parts and
　　accessories
PA: Daido Metal Co., Ltd.
　　2-3-1, Sakae, Naka-Ku
　　Nagoya AIC 460-0

(G-1105)
DESIGNED HARNESS SYSTEMS INC
Also Called: Dhs Innovations
227 Water Ave (43311-1731)
P.O. Box 37 (43311-0037)
PHONE..............................937 599-2485
Craig Lingon, *Pr*
EMP: 10 **EST:** 2010
SALES (est): 911.58K **Privately Held**
SIC: 3714 Automotive wiring harness sets

(G-1106)
DMG TOOL & DIE LLC
1215 S Greenwood St (43311-1628)
PHONE..............................937 407-0810
Thomas D Moreland, *Managing Member*
EMP: 6 **EST:** 2009
SQ FT: 10,000
SALES (est): 1.68MM **Privately Held**
Web: www.dmgtool.com
SIC: 3544 Special dies and tools

(G-1107)
EWH SPECTRUM LLC
221 W Chillicothe Ave (43311-1467)
PHONE..............................937 593-8010
Robert L Robinson, *Pr*
Jean Robinson, *
EMP: 74 **EST:** 1992
SQ FT: 27,500
SALES (est): 9.17MM **Privately Held**
Web: www.ewhspectrum.com
SIC: 3679 3694 Harness assemblies, for
　　electronic use: wire or cable; Engine
　　electrical equipment

(G-1108)
HBD/THERMOID INC
Also Called: Thermoid
1301 W Sandusky Ave (43311-1082)
PHONE..............................800 543-8070
Randy Lady, *Genl Mgr*
▼ **EMP:** 250 **EST:** 2003
SALES (est): 39.34MM
SALES (corp-wide): 241.4MM **Privately
Held**
Web: www.thermoid.com
SIC: 3429 3052 Hardware, nec; Rubber and
　　plastics hose and beltings
PA: Hbd Industries, Inc.
　　565 Metro Pl S Ste 250
　　Dublin OH 43017
　　614 526-7000

(G-1109)
HI-POINT GRAPHICS LLC
127 E Chillicothe Ave (43311-1957)
PHONE..............................937 407-6524
Andrea Wrocklage, *Prin*
Rodney Wrocklage, *Prin*
EMP: 8 **EST:** 2013
SALES (est): 360.77K **Privately Held**

Web: www.hi-pointgraphics.com
SIC: 2752 Offset printing

(G-1110)
HUBBARD PUBLISHING CO
127 E Chillicothe Ave (43311-1957)
P.O. Box 40 (43311-0040)
PHONE..............................937 592-3060
Janet Hubbard, *Pr*
Jon B Hubbard, *
EMP: 9 **EST:** 1891
SQ FT: 13,000
SALES (est): 471.33K **Privately Held**
Web: www.examiner.org
SIC: 2711 2752 2791 Commercial printing
　　and newspaper publishing combined;
　　Offset printing; Typesetting

(G-1111)
IEG PLASTICS LLC
223 Lock And Load Rd (43311-2500)
PHONE..............................937 565-4211
Jim Moore, *Prin*
EMP: 22 **EST:** 2014
SALES (est): 7.83MM **Privately Held**
Web: www.ieg-llc.com
SIC: 3089 Injection molding of plastics

(G-1112)
MAJESTIC PLASTICS INC
811 N Main St (43311-2376)
P.O. Box 47 (43311-0047)
PHONE..............................937 593-9500
Sean Ammons, *Pr*
EMP: 61 **EST:** 2000
SQ FT: 7,800
SALES (est): 4.97MM **Privately Held**
SIC: 3089 Injection molding of plastics

(G-1113)
MCKNIGHT INDUSTRIES INC
Also Called: National Extrusion & Mfg Co
Orchard & Elm Street (43311)
P.O. Box 460 (43311-0460)
PHONE..............................937 592-9010
Christopher A Kerns, *Pr*
Craig Johnson, *
Carsten Lemkau, *
John D Bishop, *
▲ **EMP:** 15 **EST:** 1949
SQ FT: 41,942
SALES (est): 3.98MM **Privately Held**
SIC: 3354 Aluminum extruded products

(G-1114)
OHIO WIRE HARNESS LLC
225 Lincoln Ave (43311-1717)
P.O. Box 27 (43311-0027)
PHONE..............................937 292-7355
EMP: 10 **EST:** 2011
SALES (est): 1.01MM **Privately Held**
Web: www.theohiowireharness.com
SIC: 3679 Harness assemblies, for
　　electronic use: wire or cable

(G-1115)
POWERBILT MTL HDLG SLTIONS
LLC (PA)
230 Reynolds Ave (43311-3003)
PHONE..............................937 592-5660
Richard Hauck, *Managing Member*
Nathaniel Hauck, *
EMP: 75 **EST:** 2000
SQ FT: 3,200
SALES (est): 30MM
SALES (corp-wide): 30MM **Privately Held**
Web: www.powerbuilt.net

▲ = Import ▼ = Export
◆ = Import/Export

SIC: **3531** 5084 5063 Aerial work platforms: hydraulic/elec. truck/carrier mounted; Materials handling machinery; Lighting fixtures, commercial and industrial

(G-1116)
SIEMENS INDUSTRY INC
811 N Main St (43311-2300)
PHONE.............................937 593-6010
Larry Falk, *Mgr*
EMP: 44
SALES (corp-wide): 84.78B **Privately Held**
Web: www.siemens.com
SIC: **3612** 3613 3643 Transformers, except electric; Switchgear and switchboard apparatus; Current-carrying wiring services
HQ: Siemens Industry, Inc.
1000 Deerfield Pkwy
Buffalo Grove IL 60089
847 215-1000

Bellevue
Huron County

(G-1117)
ABC TECHNOLOGIES WMG USA INC (DH)
Also Called: Tenneplas Div Wndsor Mold USA
560 Goodrich Rd (44811-1139)
PHONE.............................419 483-0653
Brian K Moll, *Pr*
▲ **EMP:** 19 **EST:** 1992
SALES (est): 30.77MM
SALES (corp-wide): 26.11B **Publicly Held**
Web: www.windsormoldgroup.com
SIC: **3089** Injection molding of plastics
HQ: Abc Technologies Wmg Inc
4035 Malden Rd
Windsor ON N9C 2
519 972-9032

(G-1118)
AMCOR RIGID PACKAGING USA LLC
975 W Main St (44811-9011)
PHONE.............................419 483-4343
Dave Hoover, *BD*
EMP: 7
SALES (corp-wide): 14.69B **Privately Held**
SIC: **3089** Plastics containers, except foam
HQ: Amcor Rigid Packaging Usa, Llc
10621 Hwy M52
Manchester MI 48158

(G-1119)
AMERICAN BALER CO
800 E Center St (44811-1748)
P.O. Box 29 (44811-0029)
PHONE.............................419 483-5790
Dave Kowaleski, *Pr*
E E Moulton, *
Frank B Cameron, *
Richard R Hollington, *
Roger Williams, *
EMP: 65 **EST:** 1945
SQ FT: 80,133
SALES (est): 18.11MM
SALES (corp-wide): 474.53MM **Privately Held**
Web: www.americanbaler.com
SIC: **3569** 3523 Baling machines, for scrap metal, paper, or similar material; Farm machinery and equipment
PA: Avis Industrial Corporation
1909 S Main St
Upland IN 46989
765 998-8100

(G-1120)
BELLEVUE MANUFACTURING COMPANY (PA)
520 Goodrich Rd (44811-1139)
PHONE.............................419 483-3190
EMP: 88 **EST:** 1915
SQ FT: 150,000
SALES (est): 23.33MM
SALES (corp-wide): 23.33MM **Privately Held**
Web: www.tbmc.net
SIC: **3714** Filters: oil, fuel, and air, motor vehicle

(G-1121)
BUNGE NORTH AMERICA EAST LLC
605 Goodrich Rd (44811-1142)
P.O. Box 369 (44811-0369)
PHONE.............................419 483-5340
Ray Bowns, *Brnch Mgr*
EMP: 8
Web: www.bungeag.com
SIC: **2075** 2041 Soybean oil, cake or meal; Flour and other grain mill products
HQ: Bunge North America (East), L.L.C.
1391 Tmbrlake Mnor Pkwy S
Chesterfield MO 63017
314 292-2000

(G-1122)
CAPITOL ALUMINUM & GLASS CORP
1276 W Main St (44811-9424)
PHONE.............................800 331-8268
Robert C Wagner, *Ch Bd*
Gail P Coe, *
Tory J Woodard, *
Dean Kemp, *
EMP: 55 **EST:** 1955
SQ FT: 75,000
SALES (est): 9.7MM **Privately Held**
Web: www.capitol-windows.com
SIC: **3442** Metal doors

(G-1123)
DONALD E DIDION II
Also Called: Didion's Mechanical
1027b County Road 308 (44811-9497)
PHONE.............................419 483-2226
Donald E Didion Ii, *Owner*
EMP: 25 **EST:** 1977
SQ FT: 20,000
SALES (est): 3.98MM **Privately Held**
Web: www.didionvessel.com
SIC: **3499** 8711 Fire- or burglary-resistive products; Engineering services

(G-1124)
HB FULLER COMPANY
400 N Buckeye St (44811-1210)
PHONE.............................833 672-1482
EMP: 6
SALES (corp-wide): 3.57B **Publicly Held**
Web: www.hbfuller.com
SIC: **2891** Adhesives and sealants
PA: H.B. Fuller Company
1200 Willow Lake Blvd
Saint Paul MN 55110
651 236-5900

(G-1125)
INTERNATIONAL METAL HOSE CO
520 Goodrich Rd (44811-1160)
PHONE.............................419 483-7690
◆ **EMP:** 75 **EST:** 1956
SALES (est): 8.9MM **Privately Held**
Web: www.metalhose.com
SIC: **3599** Flexible metal hose, tubing, and bellows

(G-1126)
MITSUBISHI CHEMICAL AMER INC
Also Called: McPp
350 N Buckeye St (44811-1208)
PHONE.............................419 483-2931
Lee Wilson, *Brnch Mgr*
EMP: 95
Web: www.mitsubishi3d.com
SIC: **5511** 2891 Automobiles, new and used; Adhesives
HQ: Mitsubishi Chemical America, Inc.
9115 Hrris Crners Pkwy St
Charlotte NC 28269
980 580-2839

(G-1127)
MITSUBISHI CHEMICAL AMER INC
Also Called: McPp-Detroit
350 N Buckeye St (44811-1208)
PHONE.............................586 755-1660
Keith Thomas, *Manager*
EMP: 188
Web: www.mitsubishi3d.com
SIC: **2821** 2822 Plastics materials and resins ; Synthetic rubber
HQ: Mitsubishi Chemical America, Inc.
9115 Hrris Crners Pkwy St
Charlotte NC 28269
980 580-2839

(G-1128)
QUALITY WELDING INC
104 Ronald Ln (44811)
P.O. Box 273 (44811-0273)
PHONE.............................419 483-6067
Charles Tinnel, *Pr*
EMP: 25 **EST:** 1976
SQ FT: 2,800
SALES (est): 1.18MM **Privately Held**
Web: www.qwi-inc.com
SIC: **7692** Welding repair

(G-1129)
R AND S TECHNOLOGIES INC
2474 State Route 4 (44811-9742)
PHONE.............................419 483-3691
Paul Ritz, *Pr*
Gary Shingledecker, *VP*
EMP: 11 **EST:** 1985
SQ FT: 2,400
SALES (est): 2.37MM **Privately Held**
Web: www.r-s-t-inc.com
SIC: **3089** 3599 Molding primary plastics; Machine and other job shop work

(G-1130)
SCS GEARBOX INC
739 W Main St (44811-9312)
PHONE.............................419 483-7278
Craig Sage, *Pr*
EMP: 11 **EST:** 1979
SQ FT: 10,000
SALES (est): 790.92K **Privately Held**
Web: www.scsgearbox.com
SIC: **3714** Gears, motor vehicle

(G-1131)
SENECA RAILROAD & MINING CO
Also Called: Seneca
1075 W Main St (44811-9012)
PHONE.............................419 483-7764
Raymond Wasson, *Pr*
Pat Mira, *Sec*
EMP: 6 **EST:** 1981
SQ FT: 16,300
SALES (est): 573.76K **Privately Held**
Web: www.senecarail.com
SIC: **3312** Rail joints or fastenings

(G-1132)
SOLAE LLC
Also Called: Solae Central Soya
300 Great Lakes Pkwy (44811)
P.O. Box 369 (44811-0369)
PHONE.............................419 483-0400
Dale Perman, *Mgr*
EMP: 79
SALES (corp-wide): 11.48B **Publicly Held**
SIC: **2075** Soybean oil, cake or meal
HQ: Solae, Llc
4300 Ducan Ave
Saint Louis MO 63110
314 659-3000

(G-1133)
SOLAE LLC
605 Goodrich Rd (44811-1142)
PHONE.............................419 483-5340
Dale Hoffman, *Mgr*
EMP: 10 **EST:** 2013
SALES (est): 3.12MM
SALES (corp-wide): 11.48B **Publicly Held**
SIC: **2099** Food preparations, nec
PA: International Flavors & Fragrances Inc.
521 W 57th St
New York NY 10019
212 765-5500

(G-1134)
SPIRALCOOL COMPANY
186 Sheffield St Ste 188 (44811-1528)
P.O. Box 128 (44811-0128)
PHONE.............................419 483-2510
Thomas Artino, *Pr*
Richard A Hopkins, *Pr*
EMP: 9
SQ FT: 5,000
SALES (est): 999.73K **Privately Held**
Web: www.bestbackingpad.com
SIC: **3069** Hard rubber and molded rubber products

(G-1135)
THOMAS STEEL INC
305 Elm St (44811-1564)
PHONE.............................419 483-7540
Jake Thomas, *CEO*
Steve Roth, *
Carl Koselke, *
Lynn E Thomas, *
Chuck Gerber, *
EMP: 38 **EST:** 1959
SQ FT: 50,000
SALES (est): 4MM **Privately Held**
Web: www.tsifab.com
SIC: **3441** Building components, structural steel

(G-1136)
TOWER ATMTIVE OPRTONS USA I LL
630 Southwest St (44811-9314)
PHONE.............................419 483-1500
Mike Jenkins, *Brnch Mgr*
EMP: 192
SALES (corp-wide): 4.41B **Privately Held**
Web: www.autokiniton.com
SIC: **3714** Motor vehicle parts and accessories
HQ: Tower Automotive Operations Usa I, Llc
17757 Woodland Dr
New Boston MI 48164

Bellville
Richland County

(G-1137)
D H BOWMAN & SONS INC
1201 Mill Rd (44813-1282)

PHONE......................419 886-2711
John Ellis, *Pr*
EMP: 7 **EST:** 1946
SQ FT: 1,200
SALES (est): 800K **Privately Held**
SIC: 1771 1794 1442 Blacktop (asphalt) work
; Excavation work; Sand mining

(G-1138)
GATTON PACKAGING INC
99 East St (44813-1003)
PHONE......................419 886-2577
John R Gatton, *Pr*
Larry Gatton, *Sec*
EMP: 6 **EST:** 1987
SQ FT: 10,000
SALES (est): 140.6K **Privately Held**
SIC: 2653 Boxes, corrugated: made from
    purchased materials

(G-1139)
JACKSON WELLS SERVICES
1201 Mill Rd (44813-1282)
PHONE......................419 886-2017
Cory Jackson, *Owner*
EMP: 10 **EST:** 2011
SALES (est): 1.4MM **Privately Held**
Web: www.jacksonwellservices.com
SIC: 1381 Service well drilling

(G-1140)
NATURAL OPTONS ARMATHERAPY
LLC
Also Called: Holistic Botanicals
610 State Route 97 W (44813-8813)
PHONE......................419 886-3736
George Cox, *Prin*
EMP: 10 **EST:** 2010
SALES (est): 465.48K **Privately Held**
Web:
www.bestaromatherapyproducts.com
SIC: 2833 Medicinals and botanicals

(G-1141)
NORTH CENTRAL INSULATION INC
(PA)
7539 State Route 13 (44813-8943)
P.O. Box 368 (44813-0368)
PHONE......................419 886-2030
TOLL FREE: 800
D Brent Dudgeon, *Pr*
Andrew Dungeon, *VP*
Linda Dudgeon, *Sec*
John Dudgeon, *Sls Mgr*
▲ **EMP:** 18 **EST:** 1980
SQ FT: 10,000
SALES (est): 11.22MM
SALES (corp-wide): 11.22MM **Privately**
Held
Web: www.nci-ins.com
SIC: 1741 1742 3231 Foundation building;
    Insulation, buildings; Products of purchased
    glass

(G-1142)
PROTEUS ELECTRONICS INC
161 Spayde Rd (44813-9011)
P.O. Box 725 (44813-0725)
PHONE......................419 886-2296
Thomas Clabaugh, *Pr*
Mark Molnar, *VP*
EMP: 8 **EST:** 1980
SQ FT: 3,500
SALES (est): 3.22MM **Privately Held**
Web: www.proteuselectronics.com
SIC: 3629 Electronic generation equipment

(G-1143)
TIMOTHY WHATMAN
6617 Stoffer Rd (44813-9362)
PHONE......................419 883-2443

Tim Whatman, *Brnch Mgr*
EMP: 23
Web: www.whatmanhardwoods.com
SIC: 2426 Flooring, hardwood
PA: Timothy Whatman
    847 Wagner Rd
    Bellville OH 44813

Beloit
Mahoning County

(G-1144)
BENDER ENGINEERING COMPANY
17934 Mill St (44609-9027)
P.O. Box 238 (44609-0238)
PHONE......................330 938-2355
Dennis Patterson, *Pr*
Lois Patterson, *VP*
EMP: 7 **EST:** 1983
SQ FT: 2,000
SALES (est): 96.14K **Privately Held**
SIC: 8711 3545 Engineering services;
    Machine tool accessories

(G-1145)
MAHONING VALLEY MFG INC
17796 Rte 62 (44609)
P.O. Box 247 (44619-0247)
PHONE......................330 537-4492
Tony Sampedro, *CEO*
Susan Sampedro, *VP*
EMP: 20 **EST:** 1973
SQ FT: 35,000
SALES (est): 2.06MM **Privately Held**
Web: www.mvmi.com
SIC: 3944 3469 Strollers, baby (vehicle);
    Stamping metal for the trade

Belpre
Washington County

(G-1146)
EDI HOLDING COMPANY LLC (PA)
100 Ayers Blvd (45714-9303)
PHONE......................740 401-4000
Richard Wynn, *Pr*
EMP: 6 **EST:** 2010
SALES (est): 4.76MM
SALES (corp-wide): 4.76MM **Privately**
Held
Web: www.cimarron.com
SIC: 3533 5084 Oil and gas field machinery;
    Oil refining machinery, equipment, and
    supplies

(G-1147)
ELECTRNIC DSIGN FOR INDUST INC
Also Called: E D I
100 Ayers Blvd (45714-9303)
PHONE......................740 401-4000
Richard Wynn, *Pr*
Nancy Wynn, *VP*
Jay Pottmeyer, *VP*
Sam Wynn, *Sec*
EMP: 21 **EST:** 1981
SQ FT: 2,700
SALES (est): 4.76MM
SALES (corp-wide): 4.76MM **Privately**
Held
Web: www.cimarron.com
SIC: 3533 5084 Oil and gas field machinery;
    Oil refining machinery, equipment, and
    supplies
PA: Edi Holding Company, Llc
    100 Ayers Blvd
    Belpre OH 45714
    740 401-4000

(G-1148)
KRATON CORPORATION
2419 State Route 618 (45714-2086)
PHONE......................740 423-7571
EMP: 33
Web: www.kraton.com
SIC: 2821 Plastics materials and resins
PA: Kraton Corporation
    9950 Wdloch Frest Dr Ste
    The Woodlands TX 77380

(G-1149)
KRATON EMPLYEES RECREATION
CLB
2419 State Route 618 (45714-2086)
P.O. Box 235 (45714-0235)
PHONE......................740 423-7571
Nanette Pettit, *Prin*
EMP: 9 **EST:** 2011
SALES (est): 212.09K **Privately Held**
Web: www.kraton.com
SIC: 2822 Synthetic rubber

(G-1150)
KRATON POLYMERS US LLC
Also Called: Kraton Polymers
2419 State Route 618 (45714-2086)
P.O. Box 235 (45714-0235)
PHONE......................740 423-7571
Bob Rose, *Brnch Mgr*
EMP: 400
Web: www.kraton.com
SIC: 2822 5169 2821 Synthetic rubber;
    Synthetic resins, rubber, and plastic
    materials; Plastics materials and resins
HQ: Kraton Polymers U.S. Llc
    9950 Woodloch Forest Dr
    Spring TX 77380
    281 504-4700

(G-1151)
ORION ENGINEERED CARBONS LLC
11135 State Route 7 (45714-9496)
PHONE......................740 423-9571
Donnie Loubiere, *Manager*
EMP: 54
SALES (corp-wide): 2.67MM **Privately**
Held
Web: www.orioncarbons.com
SIC: 2869 Industrial organic chemicals, nec
HQ: Orion Engineered Carbons Llc
    1700 City Plz Dr Ste 300
    Spring TX 77389
    832 445-3300

(G-1152)
OVP INC
Also Called: Ohio Dalley Press
305 Washington Blvd (45714-2458)
PHONE......................740 423-5171
John E Baker, *Pr*
EMP: 8 **EST:** 1967
SQ FT: 4,000
SALES (est): 494.76K **Privately Held**
SIC: 2752 Commercial printing, lithographic

(G-1153)
PIONEER CITY CASTING COMPANY
904 Campus Dr (45714-2342)
P.O. Box 425 (45714-0425)
PHONE......................740 423-7533
Don W Simmons, *Pr*
EMP: 30 **EST:** 1946
SQ FT: 55,000
SALES (est): 2.28MM **Privately Held**
Web: www.pioneercitycasting.com
SIC: 3321 3322 Gray iron castings, nec;
    Malleable iron foundries

(G-1154)
SKYLINE STEEL LLC
Also Called: Casteel
12355 State Route 7 (45714-9473)
PHONE......................740 423-8544
Ed Martin, *Brnch Mgr*
EMP: 8
SALES (corp-wide): 30.73B **Publicly Held**
Web: www.nucorskyline.com
SIC: 3444 Pile shells, sheet metal
HQ: Skyline Steel, Llc
    300 Tchnlogy Ctr Way Ste
    Rock Hill SC 29730
    803 620-8516

(G-1155)
WAL-BON OF OHIO INC (PA)
Also Called: Napoli's Pizza
210 Main St (45714-1612)
P.O. Box 508 (45714-0508)
PHONE......................740 423-6351
Wayne D Waldeck, *Ch Bd*
William D Waldeck, *Pr*
Charles A Bonnist, *Prin*
Doris C Celli, *Prin*
Guy J Celli Senior, *Prin*
EMP: 15 **EST:** 1966
SQ FT: 6,000
SALES (est): 29.21MM
SALES (corp-wide): 29.21MM **Privately**
Held
Web: www.napolis.com
SIC: 2051 5812 Bakery: wholesale or
    wholesale/retail combined; Pizzeria,
    independent

(G-1156)
WAL-BON OF OHIO INC
Also Called: Mc Happy's Bake Shoppe
708 Main St (45714-1622)
P.O. Box 508 (45714-0508)
PHONE......................740 423-8178
William Waldeck, *Mgr*
EMP: 41
SQ FT: 8,000
SALES (corp-wide): 29.21MM **Privately**
Held
Web: www.mchappys.com
SIC: 5461 2051 2099 Doughnuts;
    Doughnuts, except frozen; Food
    preparations, nec
PA: Wal-Bon Of Ohio, Inc.
    210 Main St
    Belpre OH 45714
    740 423-6351

Berea
Cuyahoga County

(G-1157)
A & F MACHINE PRODUCTS CO
454 Geiger St (44017-1392)
PHONE......................440 826-0959
Fred J Helwig Senior, *Pr*
Fred J Helwig Junior, *VP*
EMP: 25 **EST:** 1960
SQ FT: 12,000
SALES (est): 9.05MM **Privately Held**
Web: www.helwigpumps.com
SIC: 3561 Industrial pumps and parts

(G-1158)
ALLOY ENGINEERING COMPANY
(PA)
844 Thacker St (44017-1698)
PHONE......................440 243-6800
Lou Petonovich, *Pr*
Jeffrey Hood, *
▼ **EMP:** 65 **EST:** 1943

▲ = Import ▼ = Export
◆ = Import/Export

SQ FT: 45,000
SALES (est): 19.38MM
SALES (corp-wide): 19.38MM **Privately Held**
Web: www.alloyengineering.com
SIC: 3443 Plate work for the metalworking trade

(G-1159)
AUDION AUTOMATION LTD
Clamco
775 Berea Industrial Pkwy (44017-2948)
PHONE...........................216 267-1911
Mark E Goldman, *Brnch Mgr*
EMP: 25
SALES (corp-wide): 9.82MM **Privately Held**
Web: www.pacmachinery.com
SIC: 3565 Packaging machinery
PA: Audion Automation, Ltd.
775 Berea Industrial Pkwy
Berea OH 44017
216 267-1911

(G-1160)
AUDION AUTOMATION LTD (PA)
775 Berea Industrial Pkwy (44017-2948)
PHONE...........................216 267-1911
Mark Goldman, *CEO*
▲ **EMP:** 10 **EST:** 2001
SQ FT: 64,000
SALES (est): 9.82MM
SALES (corp-wide): 9.82MM **Privately Held**
Web: www.pacmachinery.com
SIC: 3565 Packing and wrapping machinery

(G-1161)
BEREA PRINTING COMPANY
95 Pelret Industrial Pkwy (44017-2940)
P.O. Box 38251 (44138-0251)
PHONE...........................440 243-1080
James Dettmer, *Pr*
Linda Dettmer, *Sec*
EMP: 9 **EST:** 1967
SALES (est): 1.07MM **Privately Held**
Web: www.bereaprinting.com
SIC: 2752 2759 Offset printing; Letterpress printing

(G-1162)
CLEVELAND METAL STAMPING CO
1231 W Bagley Rd Ste 1 (44017-2911)
PHONE...........................440 234-0010
Frank Ghinga, *VP*
Florian Ghinga, *Manager*
EMP: 15 **EST:** 1974
SQ FT: 23,000
SALES (est): 2.2MM **Privately Held**
Web: www.cmstamping.com
SIC: 3469 Stamping metal for the trade

(G-1163)
COLORMATRIX CORPORATION (HQ)
680 N Rocky River Dr (44017-1628)
PHONE...........................216 622-0100
◆ **EMP:** 120 **EST:** 1978
SALES (est): 9.85MM **Publicly Held**
Web: www.avient.com
SIC: 2865 2816 Dyes and pigments; Inorganic pigments
PA: Avient Corporation
33587 Walker Rd
Avon Lake OH 44012

(G-1164)
COLORMATRIX GROUP INC
680 N Rocky River Dr (44017-1628)
PHONE...........................216 622-0100
Stephen Newlin, *Pr*
EMP: 161 **EST:** 2006

SALES (est): 4.38MM **Publicly Held**
Web: www.colormatrixgroup.com
SIC: 2865 2816 Dyes and pigments; Inorganic pigments
PA: Avient Corporation
33587 Walker Rd
Avon Lake OH 44012

(G-1165)
COLORMATRIX HOLDINGS INC (HQ)
680 N Rocky River Dr (44017-1628)
PHONE...........................440 930-3162
Gerry Corrigan, *Prin*
EMP: 16 **EST:** 2006
SALES (est): 3.36MM **Publicly Held**
SIC: 2865 2816 Dyes and pigments; Inorganic pigments
PA: Avient Corporation
33587 Walker Rd
Avon Lake OH 44012

(G-1166)
DEARBORN INC
678 Front St (44017-1607)
PHONE...........................440 234-1353
Kenneth Dearborn, *Pr*
EMP: 50 **EST:** 1944
SQ FT: 30,000
SALES (est): 4.77MM **Privately Held**
Web: www.dearborninc.com
SIC: 3599 Machine shop, jobbing and repair

(G-1167)
DENTAL PURE WATER INC
336 Daisy Ave Ste 102b (44017-1729)
PHONE...........................440 234-0890
Frank Falat, *Prin*
EMP: 10 **EST:** 2001
SALES (est): 389.21K **Privately Held**
Web: www.dentalpurewaterinc.com
SIC: 5499 3843 Water: distilled mineral or spring; Dental chairs

(G-1168)
EFG HOLDINGS LLC
777 W Bagley Rd (44017-2901)
PHONE...........................440 325-4337
EMP: 613
SALES (corp-wide): 70MM **Privately Held**
Web: www.mwcomponents.com
SIC: 3965 Fasteners
PA: Efg Holdings, Llc
288 Holbrook Dr
Wheeling IL 60090
812 689-8990

(G-1169)
EMPIRE PLOW COMPANY INC (DH)
343 W Bagley Rd Ste 214 (44017-1357)
P.O. Box 39 (50220-0039)
PHONE...........................216 641-2290
David Pitt, *Pr*
EMP: 25 **EST:** 1840
SALES (est): 20.52MM
SALES (corp-wide): 838.71K **Privately Held**
Web: www.mckaytillage.com
SIC: 3523 3423 Farm machinery and equipment; Hand and edge tools, nec
HQ: Ralph Mckay Industries Inc
130 Hodsman Rd
Regina SK S4N 5
306 721-9292

(G-1170)
ES THERMAL INC
Also Called: Brown Fired Heater Div
388 Cranston Dr (44017-2205)
PHONE...........................440 323-3291
David Hoecke, *Pr*
John Somodi, *

Keith J Phillips, *
EMP: 25 **EST:** 1974
SALES (est): 2.41MM **Privately Held**
Web: www.es-thermal.com
SIC: 3433 Oil burners, domestic or industrial

(G-1171)
ESTABROOK ASSEMBLY SVCS INC
Also Called: Easi
700 W Bagley Rd (44017-2900)
P.O. Box 804 (44017-0804)
PHONE...........................440 243-3350
Jeffrey W Tarr, *Pr*
Rich Zsigray, *VP*
▼ **EMP:** 15 **EST:** 1991
SQ FT: 14,000
SALES (est): 3.64MM **Privately Held**
Web: www.easiassembly.com
SIC: 3822 Energy cutoff controls, residential or commercial types

(G-1172)
FASTENER INDUSTRIES INC
Also Called: Ohio Nut & Bolt Company Div
33 Lou Groza Blvd (44017-1237)
PHONE...........................440 891-2031
Tim Morgan, *Mgr*
EMP: 50
SALES (corp-wide): 46.16MM **Privately Held**
Web: www.fastenerind.com
SIC: 3452 5084 Bolts, nuts, rivets, and washers; Lift trucks and parts
PA: Fastener Industries, Inc.
1 Berea Commons Ste 209
Berea OH 44017
440 243-0034

(G-1173)
FASTENER INDUSTRIES INC (PA)
Also Called: Buckeye Fasteners Company
1 Berea Cmns Ste 209 (44017-2577)
PHONE...........................440 243-0034
◆ **EMP:** 7 **EST:** 1905
SALES (est): 46.16MM
SALES (corp-wide): 46.16MM **Privately Held**
Web: www.fastenerind.com
SIC: 3452 5084 Bolts, nuts, rivets, and washers; Lift trucks and parts

(G-1174)
FLAMING RIVER INDUSTRIES INC
800 Poertner Dr (44017-2936)
PHONE...........................440 826-4488
Jeanette Ladina, *Pr*
Ralph A Deluca, *Treas*
▲ **EMP:** 18 **EST:** 1987
SQ FT: 25,000
SALES (est): 4.03MM **Privately Held**
Web: www.flamingriver.com
SIC: 3714 Motor vehicle engines and parts

(G-1175)
HORIZON METALS INC
8059 Lewis Rd Ste 102 (44017-2943)
P.O. Box 38310 (44138-0310)
PHONE...........................440 235-3338
Paul Froehlich, *Pr*
James Batcha, *VP*
▲ **EMP:** 20 **EST:** 1997
SQ FT: 38,000
SALES (est): 3.53MM **Privately Held**
Web: www.horizonmetals.net
SIC: 3441 Fabricated structural metal

(G-1176)
HUNT IMAGING LLC (PA)
210 Sheldon Rd (44017-1234)
PHONE...........................440 826-0433
Jeff Johnson, *Prin*

William M Schmitt, *Managing Member*
John J Margherio, *Managing Member*
Peter Calabrese, *Prin*
◆ **EMP:** 31 **EST:** 1930
SQ FT: 2,040
SALES (est): 7.29MM **Privately Held**
Web: www.huntimaging.com
SIC: 2869 2899 Industrial organic chemicals, nec; Chemical preparations, nec

(G-1177)
JACO MANUFACTURING COMPANY
90 Karl St (44017-1320)
P.O. Box 619 (44017-0619)
PHONE...........................440 234-4000
Annmarie Brian, *Mgr*
EMP: 20
SQ FT: 12,000
SALES (corp-wide): 22.24MM **Privately Held**
Web: www.jacomfg.com
SIC: 3089 3559 Injection molded finished plastics products, nec; Plastics working machinery
PA: Jaco Manufacturing Company
468 Geiger St
Berea OH 44017
440 234-4000

(G-1178)
JACO MANUFACTURING COMPANY (PA)
468 Geiger St (44017-1319)
P.O. Box 619 (44017-0619)
PHONE...........................440 234-4000
Stephen C Campbell, *Ch*
Thomas Campell, *
Susan Sexton, *SYS*
EMP: 100 **EST:** 1949
SQ FT: 70,000
SALES (est): 22.24MM
SALES (corp-wide): 22.24MM **Privately Held**
Web: www.jacomfg.com
SIC: 3089 Injection molding of plastics

(G-1179)
JOYCE MANUFACTURING CO
Also Called: Joyce Windows
1125 Berea Industrial Pkwy (44017-2928)
PHONE...........................440 239-9100
Russell Schmidt, *Pr*
Gary Winkler, *
John Caputo, *
EMP: 70 **EST:** 1955
SQ FT: 100,000
SALES (est): 8.51MM **Privately Held**
Web: www.joycemfg.com
SIC: 3448 3446 3444 Prefabricated metal buildings; Architectural metalwork; Awnings, sheet metal

(G-1180)
MASTER PRINTING GROUP INC
Also Called: Master Printing & Mailing
95 Pelret Industrial Pkwy (44017-2940)
PHONE...........................216 351-2246
Jeremy Dobos, *Pr*
EMP: 13 **EST:** 1928
SALES (est): 2.91MM **Privately Held**
Web: www.masterprintinggroup.com
SIC: 2752 7331 Commercial printing, lithographic; Mailing service

(G-1181)
MEDINA SUPPLY COMPANY
Also Called: Schwab Industries
661 Front St (44017-1606)
PHONE...........................440 234-1321
Jerry Lance, *Mgr*
EMP: 7

SQ FT: 19,749
SALES (corp-wide): 34.95B **Privately Held**
Web: www.madeinmedinacounty.com
SIC: 3273 Ready-mixed concrete
HQ: Medina Supply Company
230 E Smith Rd
Medina OH 44256
330 723-3681

(G-1182)
MGM CONSTRUCTION INC
Also Called: MGM Roofing
1480 W Bagley Rd Ste 1 (44017-2951)
PHONE..........................440 234-7660
Michael Lyon, *Pr*
EMP: 7 **EST:** 2000
SALES (est): 1.02MM **Privately Held**
SIC: 1389 1542 1761 1799 Construction,
repair, and dismantling services;
Commercial and office building contractors;
Roofing contractor; Athletic and recreation
facilities construction

(G-1183)
NORTH COAST MEDICAL EQP INC
96 Lincoln Ave (44017-1662)
PHONE..........................440 243-6189
Edward Gibbs, *CEO*
EMP: 10 **EST:** 1982
SQ FT: 2,694
SALES (est): 829.17K **Privately Held**
SIC: 3844 X-ray apparatus and tubes

(G-1184)
NOSHOK INC (PA)
1010 W Bagley Rd (44017-2906)
PHONE..........................440 243-0888
Jeff N Scott, *Pr*
Christian F L, *Coll Vice President*
Jeffrey S Mendrala, *
▲ **EMP:** 33 **EST:** 1980
SQ FT: 50,000
SALES (est): 1.56MM
SALES (corp-wide): 1.56MM **Privately
Held**
Web: www.noshok.com
SIC: 3823 Process control instruments

(G-1185)
POLYONE CORPORATION
Also Called: POLYONE CORPORATION
680 N Rocky River Dr (44017-1628)
PHONE..........................216 622-0100
EMP: 6
Web: www.avient.com
SIC: 2821 Plastics materials and resins
PA: Avient Corporation
33587 Walker Rd
Avon Lake OH 44012

(G-1186)
QRP INC
1000 W Bagley Rd Ste 101 (44017-2906)
PHONE..........................910 371-0700
Dave Werner, *Pr*
Jordan Law, *
Gabriel Yuen, *
EMP: 85 **EST:** 1986
SQ FT: 63,000
SALES (est): 8.13MM
SALES (corp-wide): 15.37B **Publicly Held**
SIC: 3452 Bolts, metal
HQ: Consolidated Aerospace
Manufacturing, Llc
1425 S Acacia Ave
Fullerton CA 92831
714 989-2797

(G-1187)
RADS LLC
Also Called: Radcliffe Steel
135 Blaze Industrial Pkwy (44017-2930)
P.O. Box 13862 (44334-3862)
PHONE..........................330 671-0464
EMP: 11 **EST:** 1992
SQ FT: 16,000
SALES (est): 2.47MM **Privately Held**
Web: www.dcradcliffe.com
SIC: 3441 Fabricated structural metal

(G-1188)
**STANDBY SCREW MACHINE PDTS
CO**
1122 W Bagley Rd (44017-2908)
PHONE..........................440 243-8200
Frederick W Marcell, *Ch Bd*
Sal Caroniti, *
Patt Hanna, *
E J Miller, *
J Albert Lowell, *
◆ **EMP:** 375 **EST:** 1939
SALES (est): 16.08MM **Privately Held**
Web: www.standbyscrew.com
SIC: 3599 Machine shop, jobbing and repair

(G-1189)
SUN ART DECALS INC
83 Dorland Ave (44017-2801)
PHONE..........................440 234-9045
John J Soppelsa, *Pr*
James A Soppelsa, *VP*
Nikki Soppelsa, *Sec*
EMP: 7 **EST:** 1975
SALES (est): 265.89K **Privately Held**
Web: www.sunartdecals.com
SIC: 2752 Decals, lithographed

(G-1190)
TALENT TOOL & DIE INC
777 Berea Industrial Pkwy (44017-2948)
PHONE..........................440 239-8777
Tam Pham, *Ch Bd*
Thanh Pham, *
Kha Vu, *
▲ **EMP:** 40 **EST:** 1981
SQ FT: 80,000
SALES (est): 9.95MM **Privately Held**
Web: www.talent-tool.com
SIC: 3469 3544 Metal stampings, nec;
Special dies, tools, jigs, and fixtures

(G-1191)
**TIMCO RUBBER PRODUCTS INC
(PA)**
125 Blaze Industrial Pkwy (44017-2930)
PHONE..........................216 267-6242
John Kuzmick, *CEO*
Joe Hoffman, *
Randy Dahlke, *
EMP: 27 **EST:** 1956
SQ FT: 4,500
SALES (est): 3.37MM
SALES (corp-wide): 3.37MM **Privately
Held**
Web: www.timcorubber.com
SIC: 3069 Bags, rubber or rubberized fabric

(G-1192)
**TMG PERFORMANCE PRODUCTS
LLC**
Also Called: Volant Performance
140 Blaze Industrial Pkwy (44017-2930)
PHONE..........................440 891-0999
▲ **EMP:** 60 **EST:** 1988
SALES (est): 10.27MM
SALES (corp-wide): 195.05MM **Privately
Held**
Web: www.tmgperformance.com

SIC: 3714 Exhaust systems and parts, motor
vehicle
PA: Race Winning Brands, Inc.
7201 Industrial Park Blvd
Mentor OH 44060
440 951-6600

(G-1193)
VOSS INDUSTRIES LLC
1000 W Bagley Rd (44017-2906)
PHONE..........................216 771-7655
James Callan, *Pr*
EMP: 99
SALES (corp-wide): 15.37B **Publicly Held**
Web: www.vossindustries.com
SIC: 3429 Hardware, nec
HQ: Voss Industries, Llc
2168 W 25th St
Cleveland OH 44113
216 771-7655

(G-1194)
VRC INC
Also Called: Vrc Manufacturers
696 W Bagley Rd (44017-1350)
PHONE..........................440 243-6666
Christopher W Lovell, *CEO*
EMP: 54 **EST:** 1967
SQ FT: 42,000
SALES (est): 3.71MM **Privately Held**
Web: www.vrcmfg.com
SIC: 3599 Machine shop, jobbing and repair

Bergholz
Jefferson County

(G-1195)
**DENOON LUMBER COMPANY LLC
(PA)**
571 County Road 52 (43908-7961)
PHONE..........................740 768-2220
EMP: 96 **EST:** 1963
SALES (est): 4.93MM
SALES (corp-wide): 4.93MM **Privately
Held**
Web: www.denoon.com
SIC: 2421 2449 2431 2426 Lumber: rough,
sawed, or planed; Wood containers, nec;
Millwork; Hardwood dimension and flooring
mills

(G-1196)
ROSEBUD MINING COMPANY
Also Called: Bergholz 7
9076 County Road 53 (43908-7948)
PHONE..........................740 768-2275
William Denoon, *Brnch Mgr*
EMP: 83
SALES (corp-wide): 134.46MM **Privately
Held**
Web: www.rosebudmining.com
SIC: 1222 1221 Bituminous coal-
underground mining; Bituminous coal and
lignite-surface mining
PA: Rosebud Mining Company
301 Market St
Kittanning PA 16201
724 545-6222

(G-1197)
WITTS SERVICES LLC
Also Called: Welding and Fabrication
553 County Road 59 (43908-7932)
PHONE..........................740 543-8526
David Raveaux, *CEO*
David Raveaux, *Prin*
EMP: 6 **EST:** 2020
SALES (est): 1.25MM **Privately Held**

SIC: 1799 7692 Welding on site; Welding
repair

Berlin
Holmes County

(G-1198)
HOLMES LIMESTONE CO (PA)
4255 State Rte 39 (44610)
P.O. Box 295 (44610-0295)
PHONE..........................330 893-2721
Merle Mullet, *Pr*
Wade Mullet, *Sec*
William Hummel, *Treas*
EMP: 7 **EST:** 1949
SQ FT: 10,000
SALES (est): 1.86MM
SALES (corp-wide): 1.86MM **Privately
Held**
Web: www.holmeslimestone.com
SIC: 1221 Strip mining, bituminous

(G-1199)
ROBIN INDUSTRIES INC
5200 County Rd 120 (44610)
P.O. Box 330 (44610-0330)
PHONE..........................330 893-3501
David Theiss, *Brnch Mgr*
EMP: 35
SALES (corp-wide): 74.78MM **Privately
Held**
Web: www.robin-industries.com
SIC: 3061 3069 1481 Mechanical rubber
goods; Molded rubber products; Mine
development, nonmetallic minerals
PA: Robin Industries, Inc.
8562 Port Jackson Ave Nw
North Canton OH 44720
216 631-7000

(G-1200)
TGS INTERNATIONAL INC
Also Called: CAM Books
4464 Oh-39 (44610)
P.O. Box 355 (44610-0355)
PHONE..........................330 893-4828
David N Troyer, *Pr*
Roman Mullet, *Prin*
Philip Troyer, *Prin*
James Mullet, *Prin*
Nolan Byler, *Prin*
EMP: 18 **EST:** 1987
SALES (est): 3.4MM
SALES (corp-wide): 147.97MM **Privately
Held**
Web: www.cambooks.org
SIC: 2731 Books, publishing only
PA: Christian Aid Ministries
4464 State Rte 39 E
Millersburg OH 44654
330 893-2428

Berlin Center
Mahoning County

(G-1201)
MASTROPIETRO WINERY INC
14558 Ellsworth Rd (44401-9742)
PHONE..........................330 547-2151
Daniel Mastropietro, *Pr*
Marianne Mastropietro, *VP*
EMP: 8 **EST:** 2004
SQ FT: 1,512
SALES (est): 295.45K **Privately Held**
Web: www.mastropietrowinery.com
SIC: 2084 Wines

(G-1202)
PARKER-HANNIFIN CORPORATION
Also Called: Parker Hannifin
14010 Ellsworth Rd (44401-9749)
PHONE..................................330 261-1618
EMP: 16
SALES (corp-wide): 19.93B **Publicly Held**
Web: www.parker.com
SIC: 3594 Fluid power pumps and motors
PA: Parker-Hannifin Corporation
6035 Parkland Blvd
Cleveland OH 44124
216 896-3000

Berlin Heights
Erie County

(G-1203)
AUTOGATE INC
7306 Driver Rd (44814-9661)
P.O. Box 50 (44814-0050)
PHONE..................................419 588-2796
TOLL FREE: 800
William Rodwancy, *Pr*
Donald Rodwancy, *
Diane Mongiardo, *
EMP: 34 **EST:** 1985
SQ FT: 28,750
SALES (est): 8.63MM **Privately Held**
Web: www.autogate.com
SIC: 3446 Gates, ornamental metal

(G-1204)
ELITE INDUSTRIAL CONTROLS INC
7308 Driver Rd (44814-9661)
PHONE..................................567 234-1057
EMP: 24 **EST:** 2018
SALES (est): 6.61MM **Privately Held**
Web: www.eliteindustrialcontrols.com
SIC: 3625 Relays and industrial controls

(G-1205)
KERNELLS AUTMTC MACHINING INC
10511 State Rte 61 N (44814)
P.O. Box 41 (44814-0041)
PHONE..................................419 588-2164
Claude Kernell, *Pr*
Vicky Seck, *
Jeff Kernell, *
▲ **EMP:** 50 **EST:** 1969
SQ FT: 20,500
SALES (est): 1.81MM **Privately Held**
Web: www.kernellsautomatic.com
SIC: 3451 Screw machine products

(G-1206)
WELD TECH LLC
12316 Berlin Rd (44814-9504)
PHONE..................................419 357-3214
Walt Wlodarsky, *Admn*
EMP: 6 **EST:** 2010
SALES (est): 1.51MM **Privately Held**
Web: www.weldtech-metalfab.com
SIC: 3444 Sheet metalwork

Bettsville
Seneca County

(G-1207)
CARMEUSE LIME INC
Also Called: Carmeuse Natural Chemicals
1967 W County Rd 42 (44815)
P.O. Box 708 (44815-0708)
PHONE..................................419 986-5200
Thomas A Buck, *CEO*
EMP: 56
SALES (corp-wide): 2.67MM **Privately Held**

Web: www.carmeuse.com
SIC: 1422 Crushed and broken limestone
HQ: Carmeuse Lime, Inc.
11 Stanwix St Fl 21
Pittsburgh PA 15222
412 995-5500

Beverly
Washington County

(G-1208)
SCHILLING TRUSS INC
230 Stony Run Rd (45715-5051)
P.O. Box 187 (45715-0187)
PHONE..................................740 984-2396
Charles L Schilling, *Pr*
Jeff Schilling, *Pr*
Charles L Schilling, *VP*
Lori Meek, *Sec*
EMP: 10 **EST:** 1986
SALES (est): 2.01MM **Privately Held**
Web: www.schillingtruss.com
SIC: 2439 Trusses, wooden roof

(G-1209)
SKINNER FIRESTONE INC
Also Called: Firestone
232 5th St (45715-1165)
P.O. Box 428 (45715-0428)
PHONE..................................740 984-4247
Vernon Skinner, *Pr*
William Leroy Skinner, *Prin*
EMP: 7 **EST:** 1961
SQ FT: 6,600
SALES (est): 1.17MM **Privately Held**
Web: www.skinnerfirestone.com
SIC: 5531 7534 Automotive tires; Tire recapping

(G-1210)
UNLIMITED ENERGY SERVICES LLC
19371 State Route 60 (45715-5055)
P.O. Box 474 (26378-0474)
PHONE..................................304 517-7097
Michael Goodwin, *Pr*
EMP: 10 **EST:** 2018
SALES (est): 2.29MM
SALES (corp-wide): 96.85MM **Privately Held**
SIC: 4953 1382 Refuse systems; Oil and gas exploration services
PA: American Environmental Partners, Inc.
645 Hamilton St
Allentown PA 18101
610 217-3275

(G-1211)
WATERFORD TANK FABRICATION LTD
203 State Route 83 (45715-8938)
P.O. Box 392 (45744-0392)
PHONE..................................740 984-4100
Matt Brook, *Pr*
Matt Brook, *Pr*
Larry Lang, *
▲ **EMP:** 80 **EST:** 2006
SQ FT: 80,000
SALES (est): 10.13MM **Privately Held**
Web: www.waterfordtanks.com
SIC: 3399 3441 Iron ore recovery from open hearth slag; Building components, structural steel

Bidwell
Gallia County

(G-1212)
BOB EVANS FARMS INC
Also Called: Bob Evans
791 Farmview Rd (45614-9230)
P.O. Box 198 (45674-0198)
PHONE..................................740 245-5305
Rain Mckinniss, *Mgr*
EMP: 1685
Web: www.bobevansgrocery.com
SIC: 2011 Sausages, from meat slaughtered on site
HQ: Bob Evans Farms, Inc.
8200 Walton Pkwy
New Albany OH 43054
614 492-7700

(G-1213)
OHIO VALLEY TRACKWORK INC
39 Fairview Rd (45614-1100)
P.O. Box 153 (45674-0153)
PHONE..................................740 446-0181
Mike Little, *Pr*
Bret Little, *VP*
Adam Little, *Dir*
EMP: 8 **EST:** 2001
SALES (est): 996.21K **Privately Held**
Web: www.ohiovalleytrackwork.com
SIC: 3743 Railroad equipment

(G-1214)
RUTLAND TOWNSHIP
33325 Jessie Creek Rd (45614-9600)
P.O. Box 203 (45775-0203)
PHONE..................................740 742-2805
Opal Dyer, *Ofcr*
EMP: 6 **EST:** 2011
SALES (est): 193.19K **Privately Held**
SIC: 2951 Asphalt paving mixtures and blocks

(G-1215)
SOUTHERN CABINETRY INC
41 International Blvd (45614-8002)
PHONE..................................740 245-5992
Don Strieter, *Pr*
EMP: 35 **EST:** 1994
SALES (est): 2.14MM **Privately Held**
SIC: 3083 Plastics finished products, laminated

Big Prairie
Holmes County

(G-1216)
DOMETIC SANITATION CORPORATION
Also Called: Dometic Sanitation
13128 State Route 226 (44611-9522)
P.O. Box 38 (44611-0038)
PHONE..................................330 439-5550
Doug Whyte, *Pr*
▲ **EMP:** 22 **EST:** 1998
SALES (est): 9.82MM
SALES (corp-wide): 2.26B **Privately Held**
Web: www.dometicsanitation.com
SIC: 3089 Plastics containers, except foam
HQ: Dometic Corporation
5600 N River Rd Ste 250
Rosemont IL 60018

(G-1217)
PRIDE OF THE HILLS MANUFACTURING INC
8275 State Route 514 (44611-9692)

PHONE..................................330 567-3108
EMP: 100
Web: www.lastarrowmfg.com
SIC: 3533 Oil and gas field machinery

Blacklick
Franklin County

(G-1218)
ABRANDA LLC
Also Called: Cycle Cat
7175 Havens Rd (43004-9549)
PHONE..................................614 577-8080
EMP: 10 **EST:** 1998
SQ FT: 12,000
SALES (est): 140.74K **Privately Held**
SIC: 5571 3711 Motorcycle parts and accessories; Mobile lounges (motor vehicle), assembly of

(G-1219)
ACTION GROUP INC
411 Reynoldsburg New Albany Rd
(43004-9796)
PHONE..................................614 868-8868
Nancy Denutte, *Pr*
EMP: 45 **EST:** 1983
SQ FT: 155,000
SALES (est): 4.95MM **Privately Held**
Web: www.actiongroupinc.com
SIC: 3441 Fabricated structural metal

(G-1220)
BESA LIGHTING CO INC
6695 Taylor Rd (43004-9614)
PHONE..................................614 475-7046
Bernd Hoffbauer, *Pr*
◆ **EMP:** 47 **EST:** 1993
SQ FT: 48,500
SALES (est): 4.99MM **Privately Held**
Web: www.besalighting.com
SIC: 3646 3645 Commercial lighting fixtures; Residential lighting fixtures

(G-1221)
BLACKLICK MACHINE COMPANY
265 North St (43004-9139)
P.O. Box 105 (43004-0105)
PHONE..................................614 866-9300
John Boggs, *Pr*
Morgan Brooks, *Rgnl Mgr*
EMP: 7 **EST:** 1061
SQ FT: 7,200
SALES (est): 641.53K **Privately Held**
Web: www.machinedesignohio.com
SIC: 3599 Machine shop, jobbing and repair

(G-1222)
CEDAR CRAFT PRODUCTS INC
776 Reynoldsburg New Albany Rd
(43004-0145)
P.O. Box 9 (43004-0009)
PHONE..................................614 759-1600
Rick Van Walsen, *Pr*
Magdlen Maggie Van Walsen, *Sec*
EMP: 7 **EST:** 1986
SQ FT: 4,800
SALES (est): 1.18MM **Privately Held**
Web: www.cedar-craft.com
SIC: 2441 Boxes, wood

(G-1223)
HP LIQUIDATING INC
725 Reynoldsburg New Albany Rd
(43004-9638)
P.O. Box 350 (43004-0350)
PHONE..................................614 861-1791
EMP: 90 **EST:** 1971
SQ FT: 72,000

G E O G R A P H I C

SALES (est): 14.16MM **Privately Held**
Web: www.hubplastics.com
SIC: 3089 Plastics containers, except foam

(G-1224)
MARINE JET POWER INC
6740 Commerce Court Dr (43004-9200)
PHONE....................................614 759-9000
Kevin Kirby, *Pr*
▲ EMP: 6 EST: 1981
SQ FT: 7,000
SALES (est): 1MM
SALES (corp-wide): 78.18MM **Privately Held**
Web: www.marinejetpower.com
SIC: 3483 Jet propulsion projectiles
HQ: Marine Jet Power Ab
　　Hanselisgatan 6
　　Uppsala 754 5
　　101651000

(G-1225)
MCGRAW-HILL EDUCATION INC
860 Taylor Station Rd (43004-9540)
PHONE....................................760 931-1290
EMP: 6
Web: www.mheducation.com
SIC: 2731 Book publishing
HQ: Mcgraw-Hill Education, Inc.
　　1325 Ave Of The Americas
　　New York NY 10019
　　646 766-2000

(G-1226)
MCGRAW-HILL GLOBAL EDUCATN LLC
860 Taylor Station Rd (43004-9540)
P.O. Box 182605 (43218-2605)
PHONE....................................614 755-4151
EMP: 500
Web: www.mheducation.com
SIC: 2731 Book publishing
HQ: Mcgraw-Hill Global Education, Llc
　　2 Penn Plz Fl 20
　　New York NY 10121
　　646 766-2000

(G-1227)
MURPHY DOG LLC
225 Business Center Dr (43004-9452)
PHONE....................................614 755-4278
◆ EMP: 45 EST: 2006
SQ FT: 27,000
SALES (est): 10.93MM **Privately Held**
Web: www.artbrands.com
SIC: 2759 Screen printing

(G-1228)
REYNOLDS INDUSTRIES GROUP LLC
97 Hallowell Dr (43004-6054)
P.O. Box 563 (43004-0563)
PHONE....................................614 363-9149
David Reynolds, *Pr*
EMP: 45 EST: 2010
SALES (est): 301.12K **Privately Held**
SIC: 2731 Book publishing

(G-1229)
RICHARDSON WOODWORKING
3834 Mann Rd (43004-9741)
PHONE....................................614 893-8850
Craig Richardson, *Pr*
EMP: 6 EST: 2000
SALES (est): 157.96K **Privately Held**
SIC: 2431 Interior and ornamental woodwork
　　and trim

(G-1230)
TRADES RESTORE LLC
405 N Brice Rd (43004-9453)
PHONE....................................440 614-0480
Denise A Dolly, *Prin*
EMP: 11 EST: 2013
SALES (est): 400.6K **Privately Held**
Web: www.rightrestoration.com
SIC: 3069 Plumbers' rubber goods

(G-1231)
WIRELESS RETAIL LLC
Also Called: Cricket
6750 Commerce Court Dr (43004-9200)
PHONE....................................614 657-5182
Matt Starkin, *Managing Member*
EMP: 10 EST: 2018
SALES (est): 665.45K **Privately Held**
SIC: 3663 Mobile communication equipment

Bladensburg
Knox County

(G-1232)
DERRICK PETROLEUM INC
Market Street (43005)
P.O. Box 145 (43005-0145)
PHONE....................................740 668-5711
Duane Dugan, *Pr*
Duane Dugan, *Pr*
Vickie Dugan, *Sec*
EMP: 6 EST: 1977
SQ FT: 500
SALES (est): 990K **Privately Held**
SIC: 1311 Crude petroleum production

Blanchester
Clinton County

(G-1233)
BIC PRECISION MACHINE CO INC
3004 Cherry St (45107-7915)
P.O. Box 188 (45107-0188)
PHONE....................................937 783-1406
Sarah Burns, *CEO*
EMP: 42 EST: 1997
SQ FT: 4,000
SALES (est): 6.52MM **Privately Held**
Web: www.bicprecisionmachine.com
SIC: 3599 Machine shop, jobbing and repair

(G-1234)
CCPI INC (PA)
Also Called: Consolidated Ceramic Products
838 Cherry St (45107-1316)
PHONE....................................937 783-2476
◆ EMP: 50 EST: 1957
SALES (est): 22.69MM
SALES (corp-wide): 22.69MM **Privately Held**
Web: www.ccpi-inc.com
SIC: 3297 3479 Castable refractories,
　　nonclay; Enameling, including porcelain, of
　　metal products

(G-1235)
CURLESS PRINTING COMPANY
202 E Main St Unit 1 (45107-1247)
P.O. Box 97 (45107-0097)
PHONE....................................937 783-2403
Donald S Hadley, *Pr*
Parker M Beebe, *
EMP: 24 EST: 1953
SQ FT: 23,500
SALES (est): 2.26MM **Privately Held**
Web: www.curlessprinting.com
SIC: 2752 Offset printing

(G-1236)
HITACHI ASTEMO AMERICAS INC
960 Cherry St (45107-7883)
PHONE....................................937 783-4961
EMP: 245
Web: www.hitachi-automotive.us
SIC: 3694 Engine electrical equipment
HQ: Hitachi Astemo Americas, Inc.
　　955 Warwick Rd
　　Harrodsburg KY 40330
　　859 734-9451

(G-1237)
R & R TOOL INC
1449a Middleboro Rd (45107-8765)
PHONE....................................937 783-8665
Bonnie Reed, *Pr*
Dan Reed, *
Daniel Reed, *
▲ EMP: 46 EST: 1985
SQ FT: 30,000
SALES (est): 9.62MM **Privately Held**
Web: www.rrtoolinc.com
SIC: 3429 Hardware, nec

(G-1238)
RUTHMAN PUMP AND ENGINEERING
Fulflo Specialties Co
459 E Fancy St (45107-1462)
PHONE....................................937 783-2411
David Locaputo, *Mgr*
EMP: 8
SALES (corp-wide): 29.79MM **Privately Held**
Web: www.ruthmancompanies.com
SIC: 3494 5085 3491 Valves and pipe
　　fittings, nec; Valves and fittings; Industrial
　　valves
PA: Ruthman Pump And Engineering, Inc
　　7236 Tylers Corner Dr
　　West Chester OH 45069
　　513 559-1901

Bloomingburg
Fayette County

(G-1239)
BLOOMNGBURG SPRING WIRE FORM I
83 Main St (43106-9008)
P.O. Box 158 (43106-0158)
PHONE....................................740 437-7614
James Van Horn, *Pr*
Tim Van Horn, *VP*
▲ EMP: 20 EST: 1946
SQ FT: 27,000
SALES (est): 2.39MM **Privately Held**
Web: www.bloomingburgspring.com
SIC: 3495 3496 Wire springs; Miscellaneous
　　fabricated wire products

Bloomville
Seneca County

(G-1240)
HEIDELBERG MTLS MDWEST AGG INC
4575 S County Road 49 (44818-8400)
P.O. Box 128 (44818-0128)
PHONE....................................419 983-2211
Dan Lepp, *Mgr*
EMP: 8
SALES (corp-wide): 22.37B **Privately Held**
SIC: 2951 1422 Asphalt paving mixtures and
　　blocks; Limestones, ground
HQ: Heidelberg Materials Midwest Agg, Inc.
　　300 E John Crptr Fwy Ste
　　Irving TX

Blue Ash
Hamilton County

(G-1241)
ABSTRACT DISPLAYS INC
6465 Creek Rd (45242-4113)
PHONE....................................513 985-9700
Carla Eng, *Pr*
Michael Eng, *VP*
EMP: 15 EST: 2001
SALES (est): 7.65MM **Privately Held**
Web: www.abstractdisplays.com
SIC: 5046 7389 3577 7336 Display
　　equipment, except refrigerated; Exhibit
　　construction by industrial contractors;
　　Graphic displays, except graphic terminals;
　　Graphic arts and related design

(G-1242)
ADDUP INC
5101 Creek Rd (45242-3931)
PHONE....................................513 745-4510
Ken Wright, *CEO*
Clement Mailet, *CFO*
Rodney Teach, *Sec*
EMP: 20 EST: 2017
SQ FT: 10,000
SALES (est): 14.68MM
SALES (corp-wide): 1.92MM **Privately Held**
Web: www.addupsolutions.com
SIC: 3499 5084 Friction material, made from
　　powdered metal; Welding machinery and
　　equipment
HQ: Fives
　　3 Rue Drouot
　　Paris IDF 75009
　　145237575

(G-1243)
ADVANTAGE PRODUCTS CORPORATION (PA)
11559 Grooms Rd (45242-1409)
PHONE....................................513 489-2283
Robert Weber, *Pr*
EMP: 9 EST: 1990
SALES (est): 1.23MM **Privately Held**
Web: www.treds.com
SIC: 3021 Protective footwear, rubber or
　　plastic

(G-1244)
AERPIO THERAPEUTICS LLC
9987 Carver Rd Ste 420 (45242-5563)
PHONE....................................513 985-1920
Joseph H Gardner, *CEO*
Kevin Peters, *CSO*
Steve Pakola, *CMO*
EMP: 21 EST: 2011
SALES (est): 1.9MM
SALES (corp-wide): 25.98MM **Publicly Held**
SIC: 2834 Pharmaceutical preparations
PA: Whitehawk Therapeutics
　　17383 Snset Blvd Ste A250
　　Pacific Palisades CA 90272
　　424 744-8055

(G-1245)
ALIMENTO VENTURES INC
10001 Alliance Rd (45242-4750)
PHONE....................................855 510-2866
Kevin R Feazell, *Pr*
EMP: 17 EST: 2013
SALES (est): 1.85MM **Privately Held**
Web: www.alimentoventures.com
SIC: 2099 Seasonings and spices

▲ = Import ▼ = Export
◆ = Import/Export

(G-1246)
APSX LLC
11121 Kenwood Rd (45242-1817)
PHONE....................513 716-5992
Cevik Burak, *Prin*
EMP: 10 **EST:** 2006
SALES (est): 1.43MM **Privately Held**
Web: www.apsx.com
SIC: 3541 3089 Milling machines; Injection molding of plastics

(G-1247)
BAXTERS NORTH AMERICA INC
Also Called: Right Away Division
4700 Creek Rd (45242-2808)
PHONE....................513 552-7463
Matt Femia, *Contrlr*
EMP: 28
SALES (corp-wide): 477.56MM **Privately Held**
Web: www.baxtersna.com
SIC: 2032 Canned specialties
HQ: Baxters North America, Inc.
4700 Creek Rd
Cincinnati OH 45242
513 552-7485

(G-1248)
BAXTERS NORTH AMERICA INC
10825 Kenwood Rd (45242-2808)
PHONE....................513 552-7400
John Geisler, *Brnch Mgr*
EMP: 106
SALES (corp-wide): 477.56MM **Privately Held**
Web: www.baxtersna.com
SIC: 2032 Canned specialties
HQ: Baxters North America, Inc.
4700 Creek Rd
Cincinnati OH 45242
513 552-7485

(G-1249)
BAXTERS NORTH AMERICA INC
Also Called: Wornick Foods
4602 Ilmenau Way (45242-7563)
PHONE....................513 552-7728
Diana Frazier, *Mgr*
EMP: 38
SALES (corp-wide): 477.56MM **Privately Held**
Web: www.baxtersna.com
SIC: 2032 Baby foods, including meats: packaged in cans, jars, etc.
HQ: Baxters North America, Inc.
4700 Creek Rd
Cincinnati OH 45242
513 552-7485

(G-1250)
BEEBE WORLDWIDE GRAPHICS SIGN
Also Called: Worldwide Graphics and Sign
9933 Alliance Rd Ste 2 (45242-5662)
PHONE....................513 241-2726
Christian Beebe, *Pr*
EMP: 6 **EST:** 2006
SQ FT: 6,000
SALES (est): 402.29K **Privately Held**
Web: www.worldwidegraphics.com
SIC: 3993 Signs, not made in custom sign painting shops

(G-1251)
BERMAN INDUSTRIES INC
10999 Reed Hartman Hwy Ste 204 (45242-8331)
PHONE....................513 874-7477
Dolph Berman, *Pr*
Nancy C Berman, *Sec*
▲ **EMP:** 10 **EST:** 1987

SQ FT: 53,000
SALES (est): 957.97K **Privately Held**
Web: www.bermanindustries.com
SIC: 3089 Tableware, plastics

(G-1252)
BEVERAGES HOLDINGS LLC
10300 Alliance Rd Ste 500 (45242-4767)
PHONE....................513 483-3300
EMP: 860
SIC: 2086 2037 Fruit drinks (less than 100% juice): packaged in cans, etc.; Fruit juice concentrates, frozen

(G-1253)
BINDUSA
6819 Ashfield Dr (45242-4108)
PHONE....................513 247-3000
EMP: 11
SALES (est): 1.48MM **Privately Held**
Web: www.bindusa.com
SIC: 2789 Bookbinding and related work

(G-1254)
BLUE ASH TOOL & DIE CO INC
4245 Creek Rd (45241-2999)
PHONE....................513 793-4530
Ronald Siderits, *Pr*
Otto Siderits, *Stockholder*
Anna Siderits, *VP*
Caroline Siderits, *VP*
Michael Siderits, *Stockholder*
EMP: 15 **EST:** 1965
SQ FT: 20,000
SALES (est): 2.33MM **Privately Held**
Web: www.batd.com
SIC: 3545 3544 Gauge blocks; Special dies, tools, jigs, and fixtures

(G-1255)
BRAMKAMP PRINTING COMPANY INC
9933 Alliance Rd Ste 2 (45242-5662)
PHONE....................513 241-1865
Kevin Murray, *VP*
Larry Kuhlman, *
EMP: 8 **EST:** 1921
SQ FT: 200,000
SALES (est): 543.46K **Privately Held**
Web: www.graphicvillage.com
SIC: 2759 2752 Letterpress printing; Offset printing

(G-1256)
BROWN PUBLISHING INC LLC
4229 Saint Andrews Pl (45236-1057)
PHONE....................513 794-5040
EMP: 7 **EST:** 2010
SALES (est): 439.17K **Privately Held**
SIC: 2711 Newspapers: publishing only, not printed on site

(G-1257)
C M M S - RE LLC
Also Called: Forward Technologies
6130 Interstate Cir (45242-1425)
PHONE....................513 489-5111
Bradley Meyers, *Pr*
Brian Collins, *VP*
Scott Mayson, *VP*
Andrew Schultz, *VP*
EMP: 15 **EST:** 2014
SQ FT: 6,500
SALES (est): 4.67MM **Privately Held**
SIC: 3365 3541 Aluminum foundries; Machine tools, metal cutting: exotic (explosive, etc.)

(G-1258)
CANDLE-LITE COMPANY LLC (HQ)
Also Called: Candle-Lite
10521 Millington Ct Ste B (45242-4022)
PHONE....................937 780-2563
Lori Gonzalez, *CEO*
Ryan E Skeldon, *
EMP: 60 **EST:** 2014
SQ FT: 900,000
SALES (est): 64.01MM
SALES (corp-wide): 260.78MM **Privately Held**
Web: www.candle-lite.com
SIC: 3999 Candles
PA: Luminex Home Decor & Fragrance Holding Corporation
10521 Millington Ct
Cincinnati OH 45242
513 563-1113

(G-1259)
CECO ENVIRONMENTAL CORP
6245 Creek Rd (45242-4104)
PHONE....................513 458-2606
T Kroeger, *Brnch Mgr*
EMP: 10
Web: www.cecoenviro.com
SIC: 3564 Purification and dust collection equipment
PA: Ceco Environmental Corp.
5080 Spectrum Dr Ste 800e
Addison TX 75001

(G-1260)
CEQUENCE SECURITY INC
10805 Indeco Dr Ste B (45241-2965)
PHONE....................650 437-6338
EMP: 19
SALES (corp-wide): 4.09MM **Privately Held**
SIC: 7372 Prepackaged software
PA: Cequence Security, Inc.
5201 Great Amer Pkwy Ste
Santa Clara CA
650 437-6338

(G-1261)
CERKL INCORPORATED
Also Called: Cerkl
11126 Kenwood Rd (45242-1897)
P.O. Box 42458 (45242-0458)
PHONE....................513 813-8425
Tarek Kamil, *CEO*
EMP: 100 **EST:** 2014
SALES (est): 2.14MM **Privately Held**
Web: www.cerkl.com
SIC: 2741 7371 7372 Internet publishing and broadcasting; Software programming applications; Prepackaged software

(G-1262)
CINCINNATI FAMILY MAGAZINE
10945 Reed Hartman Hwy Ste 221 (45242-2853)
PHONE....................513 842-0077
Jeffrey Pyle, *Prin*
EMP: 7 **EST:** 2007
SALES (est): 110.12K **Privately Held**
Web: www.cincinnatifamilymagazine.com
SIC: 2721 Magazines: publishing only, not printed on site

(G-1263)
CINCINNATI THERMAL SPRAY INC
5901 Creek Rd (45242-4011)
PHONE....................513 793-1037
Scott Paschke, *Brnch Mgr*
EMP: 50
Web: www.cts-inc.net

SIC: 3479 Coating of metals and formed products
PA: Cincinnati Thermal Spray, Inc.
10904 Deerfield Rd
Cincinnati OH 45242

(G-1264)
COVAP INC
10829 Millington Ct Ste 1 (45242-4023)
P.O. Box 42510 (45242-0510)
PHONE....................513 793-1855
Arnold Stoller, *Pr*
Stephanie Stoller, *VP*
EMP: 18 **EST:** 1934
SQ FT: 9,000
SALES (est): 2.36MM **Privately Held**
Web: www.covap.com
SIC: 5112 7331 2752 Stationery and office supplies; Mailing service; Commercial printing, lithographic

(G-1265)
CREST GRAPHICS INC
9933 Alliance Rd Ste 1 (45242-5662)
PHONE....................513 271-2200
Robert Sparks, *Pr*
Mike Hickle, *VP*
Andy Bregger, *VP*
EMP: 16 **EST:** 1999
SQ FT: 22,000
SALES (est): 1.65MM **Privately Held**
Web: www.crestgraphics.com
SIC: 2752 Offset printing

(G-1266)
CUMMINS - ALLISON CORP
Also Called: Cummins
11256 Cornell Park Dr (45242-1821)
PHONE....................513 469-2924
Jack Prather, *Mgr*
EMP: 7
SALES (corp-wide): 1.49B **Publicly Held**
Web: www.cranepi.com
SIC: 5046 3519 Commercial equipment, nec ; Internal combustion engines, nec
HQ: Cummins-Allison Corp.
852 Feehanville Dr
Mount Prospect IL 60056
800 786-5528

(G-1267)
DORAN MFG LLC
4362 Glendale Milford Rd (45242-3706)
PHONE....................866 816-7233
Dave Robinson, *CFO*
EMP: 75 **EST:** 2003
SQ FT: 10,000
SALES (est): 1.95MM **Privately Held**
Web: www.doranmfg.com
SIC: 5013 3714 Motor vehicle supplies and new parts; Sanders, motor vehicle safety
PA: Evolving Enterprises, Inc.
6306 Beach Dr Sw
Seattle WA 98136

(G-1268)
DSK IMAGING LLC
Also Called: Allegra Marketing Print Mail
6839 Ashfield Dr (45242-4108)
PHONE....................513 554-1797
Steve Kapuscinski, *Prin*
EMP: 10 **EST:** 2005
SQ FT: 4,000
SALES (est): 901.13K **Privately Held**
Web: www.allegramarketingprint.com
SIC: 2752 Offset printing

(G-1269)
EAJ SERVICES LLC
Also Called: Nextstep Networking
4350 Glendale Milford Rd Ste 170 (45242-3700)

PHONE..................................513 792-3400
Andrew Johnson, *VP*
EMP: 18 **EST:** 1986
SQ FT: 5,500
SALES (est): 4.39MM **Privately Held**
Web: www.nextstepnetworking.com
SIC: 7373 7378 3571 Computer integrated systems design; Computer maintenance and repair; Electronic computers

(G-1270)
EASTERN SHEET METAL INC (DH)
8959 Blue Ash Rd (45242-7800)
PHONE..................................513 793-3440
William K Stout Senior, *Ch Bd*
William K Stout Junior, *Pr*
Robert Fedders, *Sec*
Margaret Geiger, *Treas*
▲ **EMP:** 61 **EST:** 1978
SQ FT: 80,000
SALES (est): 13.22MM **Privately Held**
Web: www.easternsheetmetal.com
SIC: 3444 Ducts, sheet metal
HQ: Johnson Controls, Inc.
    5757 N Green Bay Ave
    Milwaukee WI 53209
    866 496-1999

(G-1271)
ELITAIRE LLC
4280 Glendale Milford Rd (45242-3704)
PHONE..................................513 475-3803
Matt Beecroft, *
EMP: 75 **EST:** 2020
SALES (est): 6.03MM **Privately Held**
Web: www.elitaire.com
SIC: 3585 Refrigeration and heating equipment

(G-1272)
ETHICON INC
Also Called: Ethicon Endo - Surgery
10123 Alliance Rd (45242-4707)
PHONE..................................513 786-7000
Frank J Ryan, *Mgr*
EMP: 225
SALES (corp-wide): 88.82B **Publicly Held**
SIC: 3842 Surgical appliances and supplies
HQ: Ethicon Inc.
    1000 Route 202
    Raritan NJ 08869
    800 384-4266

(G-1273)
EVERYTHINGS IMAGE INC
9933 Alliance Rd Ste 2 (45242-5662)
PHONE..................................513 469-6727
Kirk Morris, *Pr*
Daniel Mcbride, *VP*
EMP: 6 **EST:** 2002
SQ FT: 5,500
SALES (est): 483.42K **Privately Held**
Web: www.everythingsimage.com
SIC: 2759 Promotional printing

(G-1274)
F+W MEDIA INC
Also Called: Novel Writing Workshop
9912 Carver Rd Ste 100 (45242-5541)
P.O. Box 78000 (48278-0001)
PHONE..................................513 531-2690
▲ **EMP:** 650
Web: www.goldenpeakmedia.com
SIC: 2721 2731 4813 Magazines: publishing only, not printed on site; Books, publishing only; Online service providers

(G-1275)
FOOD PLANT ENGINEERING LLC
10816 Millington Ct Ste 110 (45242-4026)
PHONE..................................513 618-3165

EMP: 14 **EST:** 2015
SALES (est): 1.16MM **Privately Held**
Web: www.foodplantengineering.com
SIC: 2011 5149 5451 Meat packing plants; Bakery products; Cheese

(G-1276)
GATE WEST COAST VENTURES LLC
Also Called: Tsjmedia
4901 Hunt Rd Ste 200 (45242-6990)
PHONE..................................513 891-1000
Josh Guttman, *Genl Mgr*
Brian Wiles, *Mgr*
EMP: 11 **EST:** 2005
SALES (est): 642.07K **Privately Held**
SIC: 2711 Newspapers, publishing and printing

(G-1277)
GLENROCK COMPANY
10852 Millington Ct (45242-4017)
PHONE..................................513 489-6710
Joe Amrein, *Prin*
EMP: 7
SALES (corp-wide): 1.5MM **Privately Held**
Web: www.glenrockcompany.com
SIC: 2891 Adhesives and sealants
PA: Glenrock Company
    200 W Wrightwood Ave
    Elmhurst IL 60126
    630 530-9600

(G-1278)
GRAPHIC VILLAGE LLC
4440 Creek Rd (45242-2802)
PHONE..................................513 241-1865
EMP: 171 **EST:** 2012
SALES (est): 17.16MM **Privately Held**
Web: www.graphicvillage.com
SIC: 2752 Offset printing

(G-1279)
GRIFFIN INDUSTRIES LLC
11315 Reed Hartman Hwy (45241-2429)
PHONE..................................513 549-0041
EMP: 11
SALES (corp-wide): 6.79B **Publicly Held**
Web: www.griffinind.com
SIC: 5159 2077 Furs, raw; Animal and marine fats and oils
HQ: Griffin Industries Llc
    4221 Alexandria Pike
    Cold Spring KY 41076
    859 781-2010

(G-1280)
H & G EQUIPMENT INC (PA)
10837 Millington Ct (45242-4019)
PHONE..................................513 761-2060
Eric Kuehne, *Pr*
Dave Meiners, *VP*
EMP: 11 **EST:** 1978
SQ FT: 4,400
SALES (est): 4.25MM
SALES (corp-wide): 4.25MM **Privately Held**
Web: www.hgequipment.us
SIC: 3565 Packaging machinery

(G-1281)
H MACK CHARLES & ASSOCIATES INC
Also Called: Ch Mack
10101 Alliance Rd Ste 10 (45242-4715)
PHONE..................................513 791-4456
EMP: 22
Web: www.chmack.com
SIC: 7371 7372 Computer software development; Prepackaged software

(G-1282)
HB FULLER COMPANY
Also Called: Adhesves Sealants Coatings Div
4450 Malsbary Rd (45242-5695)
PHONE..................................513 719-3600
Todd Trushenski, *Mgr*
EMP: 53
SQ FT: 23,000
SALES (corp-wide): 3.57B **Publicly Held**
Web: www.hbfuller.com
SIC: 2891 Adhesives
PA: H.B. Fuller Company
    1200 Willow Lake Blvd
    Saint Paul MN 55110
    651 236-5900

(G-1283)
HB FULLER COMPANY
4440 Malsbary Rd (45242-5623)
PHONE..................................513 719-3600
Todd Trushenski, *Brnch Mgr*
EMP: 11
SALES (corp-wide): 3.57B **Publicly Held**
Web: www.hbfuller.com
SIC: 2891 Adhesives
PA: H.B. Fuller Company
    1200 Willow Lake Blvd
    Saint Paul MN 55110
    651 236-5900

(G-1284)
HELIUM SEO
11311 Cornell Park Dr (45242-1889)
PHONE..................................513 563-3065
EMP: 36 **EST:** 2018
SALES (est): 2.48MM **Privately Held**
Web: www.helium-seo.com
SIC: 2813 Helium

(G-1285)
HERITAGE HILL LLC
11563 Grooms Rd (45242-1409)
PHONE..................................513 237-0240
EMP: 6 **EST:** 2019
SALES (est): 842.63K **Privately Held**
Web: www.hhcoop.org
SIC: 2211 Apparel and outerwear fabrics, cotton

(G-1286)
ILLINOIS TOOL WORKS INC
Also Called: ITW Evercoat
6600 Cornell Rd (45242-2033)
PHONE..................................513 489-7600
Steven Levine, *Genl Mgr*
EMP: 130
SALES (corp-wide): 16.11B **Publicly Held**
Web: www.itw.com
SIC: 2821 3714 2891 Polyesters; Motor vehicle parts and accessories; Adhesives and sealants
PA: Illinois Tool Works Inc.
    155 Harlem Ave
    Glenview IL 60025
    847 724-7500

(G-1287)
ILSCO LLC (DH)
Also Called: Utilco Div
4701 Creek Rd Ste 110 (45242-8330)
PHONE..................................513 533-6200
▲ **EMP:** 250 **EST:** 1894
SALES (est): 40.8MM **Privately Held**
Web: www.ilsco.com
SIC: 3643 3369 3451 3678 Electric connectors; Nonferrous foundries, nec; Screw machine products; Electronic connectors
HQ: Ecm Industries, Llc
    16250 W Woods Edge Rd
    New Berlin WI 53151
    800 624-4320

(G-1288)
INFINIT NUTRITION LLC
11240 Cornell Park Dr Ste 110 (45242-1800)
PHONE..................................513 791-3500
Michael Folan, *Managing Member*
▲ **EMP:** 10 **EST:** 2004
SALES (est): 791.09K **Privately Held**
Web: www.infinitnutrition.us
SIC: 2023 Dietary supplements, dairy and non-dairy based

(G-1289)
JENZABAR INC
10260 Alliance Rd (45242-4741)
PHONE..................................513 563-4542
EMP: 28
SALES (corp-wide): 42.98MM **Privately Held**
Web: www.jenzabar.com
SIC: 7372 Educational computer software
PA: Jenzabar, Inc.
    111 Hntington Ave Ste 530
    Boston MA 02199
    617 492-9099

(G-1290)
JOHNSON & JOHNSON
4545 Creek Rd (45242-2803)
PHONE..................................513 786-7000
EMP: 29
SALES (corp-wide): 88.82B **Publicly Held**
SIC: 2834 2676 3842 3841 Pharmaceutical preparations; Sanitary paper products; Surgical appliances and supplies; Surgical and medical instruments
PA: Johnson & Johnson
    1 Johnson And Johnson Plz
    New Brunswick NJ 08933
    732 524-0400

(G-1291)
JPS TECHNOLOGIES INC (PA)
11110 Deerfield Rd (45242-2022)
PHONE..................................513 984-6400
Robert J Brandner, *Pr*
Nancy K Meyer, *VP*
EMP: 10 **EST:** 1970
SQ FT: 7,500
SALES (est): 9.77MM
SALES (corp-wide): 9.77MM **Privately Held**
Web: www.jpstechnologies.com
SIC: 5084 3089 Industrial machinery and equipment; Plastics processing

(G-1292)
JPS TECHNOLOGIES INC
11118 Deerfield Rd (45242-2022)
PHONE..................................513 984-6400
Nancy Meyers, *Mgr*
EMP: 12
SALES (corp-wide): 9.77MM **Privately Held**
Web: www.jpstechnologies.com
SIC: 5084 3089 Industrial machinery and equipment; Plastics processing
PA: Jps Technologies, Inc.
    11110 Deerfield Rd
    Blue Ash OH 45242
    513 984-6400

(G-1293)
KARDOL QUALITY PRODUCTS LLC (PA)
9933 Alliance Rd Ste 2 (45242-5662)
PHONE..................................513 933-8206
Eric Kahn, *CEO*
Mike Darding, *CFO*
Mark Bedwell, *Pr*
◆ **EMP:** 6 **EST:** 1984

2025 Harris Ohio
Industrial Directory

▲ = Import ▼ = Export
◆ = Import/Export

SQ FT: 5,000
SALES (est): 9.27MM
SALES (corp-wide): 9.27MM **Privately Held**
Web: www.kardol.com
SIC: 2672 2841 2842 2821 Paper; coated and laminated, nec; Soap and other detergents; Polishes and sanitation goods; Plastics materials and resins

(G-1294)
KOLINAHR SYSTEMS INC
6840 Ashfield Dr (45242-4108)
PHONE......................513 745-9401
Gary Jenkins, *Pr*
EMP: 15 **EST:** 1993
SALES (est): 2.27MM **Privately Held**
Web: www.kolinahrsystems.com
SIC: 3535 5084 3565 Conveyors and conveying equipment; Industrial machinery and equipment; Packaging machinery

(G-1295)
LANDRUM BROWN WRLDWIDE SVCS LL
Also Called: Landrum & Brown
4445 Lake Forest Dr Ste 700 (45242-3739)
PHONE......................513 530-5333
Dennis Peters, *Prin*
EMP: 8 **EST:** 2000
SALES (est): 507.92K **Privately Held**
Web: www.landrumbrown.com
SIC: 3812 Aircraft/aerospace flight instruments and guidance systems

(G-1296)
LARMAX INC
Also Called: Kwik Kopy Printing
10945 Reed Hartman Hwy Ste 210 (45242-2828)
PHONE......................513 984-0783
Larry Richardson, *Pr*
Maxine Richardson, *VP*
EMP: 6 **EST:** 1980
SQ FT: 1,500
SALES (est): 264.17K **Privately Held**
Web: www.kwikkopyblueash.com
SIC: 2752 Offset printing

(G-1297)
LEGRAND AV INC
Polacoat Divison
11500 Williamson Rd (45241-2271)
PHONE......................574 267-8101
Bob St Martin, *Mgr*
EMP: 25
SQ FT: 41,700
Web: www.legrandav.com
SIC: 3861 3643 Motion picture apparatus and equipment; Current-carrying wiring services
HQ: Legrand Av Inc.
6436 City W Pkwy
Eden Prairie MN 55344
866 977-3901

(G-1298)
LMG HOLDINGS INC (PA)
Also Called: Scram Systems
4290 Glendale Milford Rd (45242-3704)
PHONE......................905 829-3541
Marc Jourlait, *Ch*
Kyle Macemore, *CFO*
Concetta Rand, *CRO*
EMP: 21 **EST:** 2010
SALES (est): 98.79MM
SALES (corp-wide): 98.79MM **Privately Held**
Web: www.lifesafer.com
SIC: 3829 Measuring and controlling devices, nec

(G-1299)
LSI INDUSTRIES INC
LSI Midwest Lighting
10000 Alliance Rd (45242-4706)
PHONE......................913 281-1100
Dennis Oberling, *Mgr*
EMP: 200
SALES (corp-wide): 469.64MM **Publicly Held**
Web: www.lsicorp.com
SIC: 3646 5063 Commercial lighting fixtures; Lighting fixtures
PA: Lsi Industries Inc.
10000 Alliance Rd
Cincinnati OH 45242
513 793-3200

(G-1300)
LSI LIGHTRON INC
10000 Alliance Rd (45242-4706)
PHONE......................845 562-5500
Gene Littman, *CEO*
Barry White, *
▲ **EMP:** 1000 **EST:** 1946
SALES (est): 6.19MM
SALES (corp-wide): 469.64MM **Publicly Held**
Web: www.lsicorp.com
SIC: 3646 5063 Commercial lighting fixtures; Electrical apparatus and equipment
PA: Lsi Industries Inc.
10000 Alliance Rd
Cincinnati OH 45242
513 793-3200

(G-1301)
MAPVISION INC
5601 Creek Rd Ste C (45242-4038)
PHONE......................513 400-1038
Joakim Siirilae, *Pr*
EMP: 9 **EST:** 2017
SALES (est): 5MM **Privately Held**
SIC: 3829 Measuring and controlling devices, nec

(G-1302)
MAT BASICS INCORPORATED
4546 Cornell Rd (45241-2425)
PHONE......................513 793-0313
Suzie L Johnson, *Prin*
EMP: 6 **EST:** 2011
SALES (est): 245.67K **Privately Held**
Web: www.matbasics.com
SIC: 2273 Carpets and rugs

(G-1303)
MATDAN CORPORATION
10855 Millington Ct (45242-4019)
PHONE......................513 794-0500
David Arand, *Pr*
▲ **EMP:** 35 **EST:** 1992
SQ FT: 10,000
SALES (est): 3.72MM **Privately Held**
Web: www.matdanfasteners.com
SIC: 3452 3429 Bolts, metal; Hardware, nec

(G-1304)
MAVERICK CORPORATION
11285 Grooms Rd (45242-1428)
PHONE......................513 469-9919
Robert Gray, *Pr*
Eric Collins, *Ch*
EMP: 14 **EST:** 1993
SQ FT: 2,300
SALES (est): 2.49MM **Privately Held**
Web: www.maverickcorp.com
SIC: 3089 3299 Thermoformed finished plastics products, nec; Ceramic fiber

(G-1305)
MAVERICK MOLDING CO
11359 Grooms Rd (45242-1405)
PHONE......................513 387-6100
Jack Rubino, *Ex VP*
Laurel Mesing, *Prin*
Brad Love, *Prin*
▲ **EMP:** 17 **EST:** 2005
SALES (est): 4.83MM **Privately Held**
Web: www.maverickmolding.com
SIC: 3728 Aircraft parts and equipment, nec

(G-1306)
MBAS PRINTING INC
11401 Deerfield Rd (45242-2106)
PHONE......................513 489-3000
Richard P Vollet, *Pr*
EMP: 8 **EST:** 2009
SALES (est): 111.81K **Privately Held**
SIC: 2752 Offset printing

(G-1307)
MEGADYNE MEDICAL PRODUCTS INC
4545 Creek Rd (45242-2803)
PHONE......................801 576-9669
Paul Borgmeier, *Admn*
Robert Farnsworth, *
Andrew K Ekdahl, *
Veera Rastogi, *
Michael Facer, *
▼ **EMP:** 140 **EST:** 1985
SALES (est): 8.98MM
SALES (corp-wide): 88.82B **Publicly Held**
SIC: 3841 Surgical instruments and apparatus
HQ: Ethicon Endo-Surgery, Inc.
4545 Creek Rd
Cincinnati OH 45242
513 337-7000

(G-1308)
META MANUFACTURING CORPORATION
8901 Blue Ash Rd Ste 1 (45242-7809)
PHONE......................513 793-6382
David Mc Swain, *Pr*
EMP: 50 **EST:** 1988
SQ FT: 54,000
SALES (est): 6.7MM **Privately Held**
Web: www.metamfg.com
SIC: 3599 7692 Machine shop, jobbing and repair; Welding repair

(G-1309)
METAL IMPROVEMENT COMPANY LLC
11131 Luschek Dr (45241-2434)
PHONE......................513 489-6484
Dan Richardson, *Mgr*
EMP: 74
SQ FT: 15,031
SALES (corp-wide): 3.12B **Publicly Held**
Web: www.imrtest.com
SIC: 3398 Shot peening (treating steel to reduce fatigue)
HQ: Metal Improvement Company, Llc
80 Route 4 E Ste 310
Paramus NJ 07652
201 843-7800

(G-1310)
METALEX MANUFACTURING INC (PA)
5750 Cornell Rd (45242-2083)
PHONE......................513 489-0507
Kevin Kummerle, *CEO*
Werner Kummerle, *
Sue Kummerle, *
◆ **EMP:** 112 **EST:** 1972

SQ FT: 120,000
SALES (est): 23.72MM
SALES (corp-wide): 23.72MM **Privately Held**
Web: www.metalexmfg.com
SIC: 3599 3511 3544 3769 Custom machinery; Turbines and turbine generator sets; Special dies, tools, jigs, and fixtures; Space vehicle equipment, nec

(G-1311)
MILLENNIUM PRINTING LLC
Also Called: Millprint
11401 Deerfield Rd (45242-2106)
PHONE......................513 489-3000
EMP: 6 **EST:** 2003
SALES (est): 320.86K **Privately Held**
Web: www.perfectionprintmedia.com
SIC: 2752 Offset printing

(G-1312)
MULTI-CRAFT LITHO INC
4440 Creek Rd (45242-2802)
PHONE......................859 581-2754
EMP: 48
SIC: 2791 2789 2759 2732 Typesetting; Bookbinding and related work; Commercial printing, nec; Book printing

(G-1313)
NEW PUBLISHING HOLDINGS LLC
10151 Carver Rd Ste 200 (45242-4760)
PHONE......................513 531-2690
Gregory J Osberg, *CEO*
David Nussbaum, *
EMP: 651 **EST:** 2005
SALES (est): 1.22MM **Privately Held**
SIC: 2731 2721 Books, publishing only; Magazines: publishing only, not printed on site

(G-1314)
NUTONE INC
9825 Kenwood Rd Ste 301 (45242-6252)
P.O. Box 270140 (53027-7140)
PHONE......................888 336-3948
EMP: 625
Web: www.broan-nutone.com
SIC: 3634 Electric housewares and fans

(G-1315)
ORGANIZED LIGHTNING LLC
Also Called: Shelter Studios
5601 Belleview Ave (45242-7427)
PHONE......................407 965-2730
Jonathan Weiner, *Managing Member*
EMP: 6 **EST:** 2013
SQ FT: 3,500
SALES (est): 124.29K **Privately Held**
SIC: 2741 Internet publishing and broadcasting

(G-1316)
OSBORNE COINAGE COMPANY LLC (PA)
Also Called: Doran Manufacturing Co.
4362 Glendale Milford Rd (45242-3706)
PHONE......................877 480-0456
Thomas E Stegman, *Pr*
Todd R Stegman, *
Jeffrey J Stegman, *
▲ **EMP:** 70 **EST:** 1835
SALES (est): 6.56MM
SALES (corp-wide): 6.56MM **Privately Held**
Web: www.osbornecoin.com
SIC: 3644 3613 5999 Terminal boards; Panelboards and distribution boards, electric; Coins and stamps

(G-1317)
PACIFIC PISTON RING CO INC
11379 Grooms Rd (45242-1405)
PHONE...................................513 387-6100
Dirkson Charles, *Pr*
Glenn Dalessandro, *
EMP: 50 **EST:** 1959
SALES (est): 14MM **Privately Held**
SIC: 3728 Aircraft body assemblies and parts

(G-1318)
PATHEON PHARMACEUTICALS INC
4750 Lake Forest Dr (45242-3852)
PHONE...................................513 948-9111
EMP: 1873
SALES (corp-wide): 42.86B **Publicly Held**
SIC: 2834 Pharmaceutical preparations
HQ: Patheon Pharmaceuticals Inc.
3900 Paramount Pkwy
Morrisville NC 27560
919 226-3200

(G-1319)
PLASTIC MOLDINGS COMPANY LLC (PA)
Also Called: P M C
9825 Kenwood Rd Ste 302 (45242-6252)
PHONE...................................513 921-5040
Thomas R Gerdes, *
Lisa Jennings, *
▲ **EMP:** 75 **EST:** 1929
SQ FT: 63,500
SALES (est): 24.78MM
SALES (corp-wide): 24.78MM **Privately Held**
Web: www.pmcsmartsolutions.com
SIC: 3089 Injection molding of plastics

(G-1320)
PMC SMART SOLUTIONS LLC
9825 Kenwood Rd Ste 300 (45242-6252)
PHONE...................................513 921-5040
Lisa Jennings, *Pr*
EMP: 93 **EST:** 2013
SALES (est): 5.84MM **Privately Held**
Web: www.pmcsmartsolutions.com
SIC: 3089 Injection molding of plastics

(G-1321)
PMP INDUSTRIES INC
4460 Lake Forest Dr Ste 228 (45242-3755)
PHONE...................................513 563-3028
Alessandro Borsetti, *Pr*
EMP: 6 **EST:** 2007
SALES (est): 5.48MM **Privately Held**
Web: www.pmp-industries.com
SIC: 3612 Transformers, except electric
HQ: Pmp Pro Mec Spa
Via Dell'industria 2
Coseano UD 33030
043 286-3611

(G-1322)
POSITECH CORP
11310 Williamson Rd (45241-2233)
PHONE...................................513 942-7411
Jeff Hauck, *Pr*
▲ **EMP:** 13 **EST:** 1996
SQ FT: 12,400
SALES (est): 2.65MM **Privately Held**
Web: www.positechcorp.net
SIC: 3599 Machine shop, jobbing and repair

(G-1323)
PRECISION ANLYTICAL INSTRS INC
Also Called: P A I
10857 Millington Ct (45242-4019)
PHONE...................................513 984-1600
EMP: 6
SQ FT: 2,100

SALES (est): 966.3K **Privately Held**
Web: www.toolsforanalysis.com
SIC: 3826 Analytical instruments

(G-1324)
PRESTIGE ENTERPRISE INTL INC
11343 Grooms Rd (45242-1405)
PHONE...................................513 469-6044
Charles Gabbour, *Pr*
Jeff Gabbour, *
◆ **EMP:** 51 **EST:** 1977
SQ FT: 10,000
SALES (est): 2.69MM **Privately Held**
Web: www.prestigefloor.com
SIC: 2426 Flooring, hardwood

(G-1325)
PROCTER & GAMBLE COMPANY
Also Called: Procter & Gamble
11530 Reed Hartman Hwy (45241-2422)
PHONE...................................513 626-2500
Gale Britton, *Mgr*
EMP: 38
SALES (corp-wide): 84.04B **Publicly Held**
Web: us.pg.com
SIC: 2844 Deodorants, personal
PA: The Procter & Gamble Company
1 Procter & Gamble Plz
Cincinnati OH 45202
513 983-1100

(G-1326)
RA CONSULTANTS LLC
10856 Kenwood Rd (45242-2812)
PHONE...................................513 469-6600
Marijo Flamm, *
EMP: 30 **EST:** 2004
SALES (est): 5.26MM **Privately Held**
Web: www.raconsultantsllc.com
SIC: 8711 3679 Civil engineering;
Commutators, electronic

(G-1327)
ROSS GROUP INC
4555 Lake Forest Dr Ste 650 (45242-3785)
PHONE...................................937 427-3069
Steve Woody, *Brnch Mgr*
EMP: 6
Web: www.rossgroupinc.com
SIC: 7372 Business oriented computer
software
PA: The Ross Group Inc
3400 Chapel Hill Rd
Douglasville GA

(G-1328)
RSW DISTRIBUTORS LLC
Also Called: Culinary Standards
4700 Ashwood Dr Ste 200 (45241-2424)
PHONE...................................502 587-8877
Mark A Littman, *
EMP: 10 **EST:** 2008
SQ FT: 27,111
SALES (est): 1.16MM **Privately Held**
SIC: 2038 Frozen specialties, nec

(G-1329)
SAMUEL L PETERS LLC
10001 Alliance Rd Ste 1 (45242-4751)
PHONE...................................513 745-1500
Samuel L Peters, *Prin*
EMP: 7 **EST:** 2016
SALES (est): 593.98K **Privately Held**
SIC: 2711 Commercial printing and
newspaper publishing combined

(G-1330)
SAMUELS PRODUCTS INC
9851 Redhill Dr (45242-5694)
PHONE...................................513 891-4456

Millard Samuels, *Pr*
Thomas J Samuels, *
William Fitzpatric, *
EMP: 30 **EST:** 1903
SQ FT: 61,000
SALES (est): 4.99MM **Privately Held**
Web: www.samuelsproducts.com
SIC: 2759 5122 Flexographic printing;
Druggists' sundries, nec

(G-1331)
SCHAEFFERS INVESTMENT RESEARCH INC
Also Called: Option Advisor, The
5151 Pfeiffer Rd Ste 450 (45242-4865)
PHONE...................................513 589-3800
EMP: 65 **EST:** 1981
SALES (est): 4.62MM **Privately Held**
Web: www.schaeffersresearch.com
SIC: 2741 6282 2721 Newsletter publishing;
Investment advice; Periodicals

(G-1332)
ST MEDIA GROUP INTL INC
Also Called: St Media Group International
11262 Cornell Park Dr (45242-1828)
PHONE...................................513 421-2050
Jerry Swormstedt, *Ch*
Tedd Swormstedt, *
Murray Kasmenn, *
Wade Swormstedt, *
Brian Soos, *
▲ **EMP:** 65 **EST:** 1906
SQ FT: 30,000
SALES (est): 1.6MM **Privately Held**
Web: www.stmediagroupintl.com
SIC: 2721 2731 2791 Magazines: publishing
only, not printed on site; Book publishing;
Typesetting

(G-1333)
STACK CONSTRUCTION TECH INC (PA)
9999 Carver Rd (45242-5584)
PHONE...................................513 445-5122
Phil Ogilby, *CEO*
Ray Dezenzo, *
EMP: 15 **EST:** 2007
SALES (est): 9.18MM
SALES (corp-wide): 9.18MM **Privately Held**
Web: www.stackct.com
SIC: 7372 Business oriented computer
software

(G-1334)
STANDARD BARIATRICS INC
4300 Glendale Milford Rd (45242-3706)
PHONE...................................513 620-7751
Jonathan Thompson, *Pr*
Matt Sokany, *CEO*
Adam Dunki-jacobs, *COO*
Kurt Azarbarzin, *Ch Bd*
EMP: 27 **EST:** 2016
SALES (est): 4.99MM **Privately Held**
Web: www.standardbariatrics.com
SIC: 3841 Surgical and medical instruments

(G-1335)
STOLLE PROPERTIES INC
6954 Cornell Rd Ste 100 (45242-3001)
P.O. Box 815 (45036-0815)
PHONE...................................513 932-8664
William Faulkner, *Pr*
EMP: 580 **EST:** 1999
SQ FT: 1,876
SALES (est): 971.97K
SALES (corp-wide): 24.82MM **Privately Held**
SIC: 3469 Metal stampings, nec
PA: The Ralph J Stolle Company

6990 Cornell Rd
Blue Ash OH 45242
513 489-7184

(G-1336)
SUPERALLOY MFG SOLUTIONS CORP
11495 Deerfield Rd (45242-2106)
PHONE...................................513 605-8380
EMP: 10 **EST:** 1986
SALES (est): 813.2K **Privately Held**
Web: www.superalloymfg.com
SIC: 3599 Machine shop, jobbing and repair

(G-1337)
SUPERALLOY MFG SOLUTIONS CORP
11230 Deerfield Rd (45242-2024)
PHONE...................................513 489-9800
John Wilbur, *CEO*
Robert Segal, *
Leonard Levie, *
▲ **EMP:** 200 **EST:** 1945
SQ FT: 175,000
SALES (est): 50MM **Privately Held**
Web: www.superalloymfg.com
SIC: 3724 Aircraft engines and engine parts

(G-1338)
SURGRX INC
4545 Creek Rd (45242-2803)
PHONE...................................650 482-2400
David Clapper, *Pr*
Edward Unkard, *CFO*
EMP: 14 **EST:** 2000
SQ FT: 20,000
SALES (est): 4.78MM
SALES (corp-wide): 88.82B **Publicly Held**
SIC: 3841 Surgical and medical instruments
HQ: Ethicon Endo-Surgery, Inc.
4545 Creek Rd
Cincinnati OH 45242
513 337-7000

(G-1339)
SUTTER LLC
Also Called: BBC Technology Solutions
11105 Deerfield Rd (45242-2021)
PHONE...................................513 891-2261
Michael Sutter, *Managing Member*
EMP: 10 **EST:** 2006
SALES (est): 505.53K **Privately Held**
Web: www.enlivenedtech.com
SIC: 8748 3577 7373 Business consulting,
nec; Computer peripheral equipment, nec;
Value-added resellers, computer systems

(G-1340)
TAPPAN CHAIRS LLC
Also Called: Shaker Workshops
9115 Blue Ash Rd (45242-6821)
PHONE...................................800 840-9121
EMP: 8 **EST:** 2013
SALES (est): 234.26K **Privately Held**
Web: www.tappanchairs.com
SIC: 2511 Wood household furniture

(G-1341)
TECHNOSOFT INC
11180 Reed Hartman Hwy Ste 200
(45242-1824)
PHONE...................................513 985-9877
Adel Chemaly, *Pr*
EMP: 10 **EST:** 1992
SALES (est): 1.31MM **Privately Held**
Web: www.technosoft.com
SIC: 7372 7371 Prepackaged software;
Custom computer programming services

(G-1342)

THE FECHHEIMER BROTHERS CO (HQ)
4545 Malsbary Rd (45242-5624)
PHONE.....................513 793-5400
Dan Dudley, *CEO*
Fred Heldman, *
◆ EMP: 200 EST: 1842
SQ FT: 108,000
SALES (est): 122.99MM
SALES (corp-wide): 424.23B **Publicly Held**
Web: www.flyingcross.com
SIC: 2311 2337 2339 5699 Men's and boys' uniforms; Women's and misses' suits and coats; Women's and misses' outerwear, nec ; Uniforms
PA: Berkshire Hathaway Inc.
3555 Farnam St Ste 1440
Omaha NE 68131
402 346-1400

(G-1343)

THERMO FISHER SCIENTIFIC INC
4750 Lake Forest Dr Ste 114 (45242-3852)
PHONE.....................513 948-6290
EMP: 10
SALES (corp-wide): 42.86B **Publicly Held**
Web: www.thermofisher.com
SIC: 3826 3845 3823 3629 Analytical instruments; Electromedical equipment; Process control instruments; Electronic generation equipment
PA: Thermo Fisher Scientific Inc.
168 3rd Ave
Waltham MA 02451
781 622-1000

(G-1344)

TORAX MEDICAL INC
4545 Creek Rd (45242-2803)
PHONE.....................651 361-8900
Tod Berg, *
Chas Mckhann, *CCO*
EMP: 18 EST: 2002
SALES (est): 5.61MM
SALES (corp-wide): 88.82B **Publicly Held**
SIC: 3845 Electromedical apparatus
HQ: Ethicon Inc.
1000 Route 202
Raritan NJ 08869
800 384-4266

(G-1345)

UNITED AIR SPECIALISTS INC
Also Called: UAS
4440 Creek Rd (45242-2802)
PHONE.....................513 891-0400
TOLL FREE: 800
◆ EMP: 250
Web: www.uasinc.com
SIC: 3563 3564 Spraying and dusting equipment; Air cleaning systems

(G-1346)

VALENTINE RESEARCH INC
10280 Alliance Rd (45242-4710)
PHONE.....................513 984-8900
Michael Valentine, *Pr*
Stephen Scholl, *
Margaret Valentine, *
EMP: 21 EST: 1983
SQ FT: 11,000
SALES (est): 3.52MM **Privately Held**
Web: www.valentine1.com
SIC: 3812 Radar systems and equipment

(G-1347)

VORTEC AND PAXTON PRODUCTS
10125 Carver Rd (45242-4719)
PHONE.....................513 891-7474

David Spears, *CEO*
William Ooh, *Genl Mgr*
EMP: 14 EST: 1957
SQ FT: 25,000
SALES (est): 924.61K **Privately Held**
Web: www.paxtonproducts.com
SIC: 3564 Blowers and fans

(G-1348)

VORTEC CORPORATION
Also Called: Vortec-An Illinois TI Works Co
10125 Carver Rd (45242-4798)
PHONE.....................513 891-7485
Lois Lannigan, *Pr*
EMP: 22 EST: 1992
SALES (est): 3.17MM
SALES (corp-wide): 16.11B **Publicly Held**
Web: www.vortec.com
SIC: 3585 3499 3699 3498 Refrigeration and heating equipment; Nozzles, spray: aerosol, paint, or insecticide; Electrical equipment and supplies, nec; Fabricated pipe and fittings
PA: Illinois Tool Works Inc.
155 Harlem Ave
Glenview IL 60025
847 724-7500

(G-1349)

WHATIFSPORTSCOM INC
10200 Alliance Rd Ste 301 (45242-4716)
PHONE.....................513 333-0313
Tarek Kamil, *Pr*
EMP: 7 EST: 2000
SALES (est): 305.81K **Privately Held**
Web: www.whatifsports.com
SIC: 7372 Home entertainment computer software

(G-1350)

WHITEHOUSE BROS INC
4393 Creek Rd (45241-2923)
P.O. Box 2981 (45201-2981)
PHONE.....................513 621-2259
Joseph G Vogelsang, *Pr*
Gary Domsher, *Mgr*
▲ EMP: 9 EST: 1906
SQ FT: 1,200
SALES (est): 256.91K **Privately Held**
Web: www.whitehousebrothers.com
SIC: 3911 Jewelry, precious metal

(G-1351)

WITTROCK WDWKG & MFG CO INC
4201 Malsbary Rd (45242-5509)
PHONE.....................513 891-5800
David Wittrock, *Pr*
Joseph Wittrock, *
Christopher Wittrock, *
▲ EMP: 70 EST: 1963
SQ FT: 11,000
SALES (est): 9.44MM **Privately Held**
Web: www.wittrockinc.com
SIC: 2431 Millwork

(G-1352)

WOLF MACHINE COMPANY (PA)
5570 Creek Rd (45242-4004)
PHONE.....................513 791-5194
Scott E Andre, *Pr*
EMP: 35 EST: 1888
SQ FT: 50,000
SALES (est): 17.69MM
SALES (corp-wide): 17.69MM **Privately Held**
Web: www.wolfmachine.com
SIC: 5084 3552 3556 3546 Machine tools and accessories; Textile machinery; Food products machinery; Power-driven handtools

(G-1353)

WOODLAWN RUBBER CO
11268 Williamson Rd (45241-2281)
PHONE.....................513 489-1718
Kirk Heithaus, *Pr*
Donald Heithaus, *Treas*
EMP: 18 EST: 1964
SQ FT: 21,000
SALES (est): 2.47MM **Privately Held**
Web: www.woodlawnrubber.com
SIC: 3069 3061 Molded rubber products; Mechanical rubber goods

(G-1354)

WORNICK HOLDING COMPANY INC
4700 Creek Rd (45242-2808)
PHONE.....................513 794-9800
Jon P Geisler, *Pr*
Dustin Mcdulin, *CFO*
Michael Hyche, *
John Kowalchik, *
EMP: 22 EST: 2008
SALES (est): 864.92K
SALES (corp-wide): 41.04MM **Privately Held**
Web: www.baxtersna.com
SIC: 2032 Canned specialties
HQ: Polen Capital Credit, Llc
1075 Main St Ste 320
Waltham MA 02451

(G-1355)

XOMOX CORPORATION
Also Called: Crane Xomox
4477 Malsbary Rd (45242-5622)
PHONE.....................513 745-6000
William Hayes, *Brnch Mgr*
EMP: 6
SALES (corp-wide): 2.13B **Publicly Held**
Web: www.cranecpe.com
SIC: 3491 Process control regulator valves
HQ: Xomox Corporation
4526 Res Frest Dr Ste 400
The Woodlands TX 77381
936 271-6500

Bluffton
Allen County

(G-1356)

A TO Z PORTION CTRL MEATS INC
201 N Main St (45817-1283)
PHONE.....................419 358-2926
Lee Ann Kagy, *Pr*
Sean Kagy, *
Leslie Barnes, *
EMP: 34 EST: 1945
SQ FT: 20,000
SALES (est): 4.87MM **Privately Held**
Web: www.atozmeats.com
SIC: 5142 2013 Meat, frozen: packaged; Sausages and other prepared meats

(G-1357)

BLUFFTON NEWS PUBG & PRTG CO (PA)
Also Called: Bluffton News, The
101 S Main St (45817-1249)
P.O. Box 105 (45856-0105)
PHONE.....................419 358-8010
Thomas M Edwards, *Pr*
Marilyn Edwards, *VP*
EMP: 12 EST: 1875
SQ FT: 4,500
SALES (est): 114.86K
SALES (corp-wide): 114.86K **Privately Held**
Web: www.blufftonnews.com

SIC: 2711 2721 Job printing and newspaper publishing combined; Magazines: publishing and printing

(G-1358)

BLUFFTON STONE CO
310 Quarry Dr (45817)
P.O. Box 26 (45817-0026)
PHONE.....................419 358-6941
Brent Gerken, *Pr*
Mike Gerken, *Sec*
EMP: 18 EST: 1930
SQ FT: 1,800
SALES (est): 5.05MM **Privately Held**
Web: www.bluffton.edu
SIC: 1422 3274 2951 Crushed and broken limestone; Lime; Asphalt paving mixtures and blocks

(G-1359)

CARPE DIEM INDUSTRIES LLC
Also Called: Diamond Machine and Mfg
505 E Jefferson St (45817-1349)
PHONE.....................419 358-0129
Ryan Smith, *Mgr*
EMP: 55
SQ FT: 271,000
SALES (corp-wide): 9.25MM **Privately Held**
Web: www.colonialsurfacesolutions.com
SIC: 3471 3398 3479 1799 Cleaning and descaling metal products; Metal heat treating; Painting of metal products; Coating of metal structures at construction site
PA: Carpe Diem Industries, Llc
4599 Campbell Rd
Columbus Grove OH 45830
419 659-5639

(G-1360)

DIAMOND MFG BLUFFTON LTD
505 E Jefferson St (45817-1349)
PHONE.....................419 358-0129
Tom Langhals, *
EMP: 65 EST: 2010
SQ FT: 120,000
SALES (est): 8.54MM **Privately Held**
Web: www.diamondmb.com
SIC: 3441 Fabricated structural metal

(G-1361)

GROB SYSTEMS INC
Also Called: Machine Tool Division
1070 Navajo Dr (45817-9666)
PHONE.....................419 358-9015
Michael Hutecker, *CEO*
David Kuenzli, *Sec*
◆ EMP: 590 EST: 1981
SQ FT: 262,000
SALES (est): 42.35MM
SALES (corp-wide): 355.83K **Privately Held**
Web: www.grobgroup.com
SIC: 3535 7699 Robotic conveyors; Industrial equipment services
PA: Grob-Werke Burkhart Grob E.K.
Industriestr. 4
Mindelheim BY 87719
82619960

(G-1362)

MASTERPIECE SIGNS GRAPHICS INC
902 N Main St (45817-9710)
P.O. Box 124 (45817-0124)
PHONE.....................419 358-0077
Tim Boutwell, *Owner*
EMP: 10 EST: 2016
SALES (est): 1.66MM **Privately Held**
Web: www.masterpiecesign.com

SIC: 3993 Signs and advertising specialties

(G-1363)
RICHLAND TOWNSHIP BD TRUSTEES
8435 Dixie Hwy (45817-9543)
PHONE..............................419 358-4897
Rod Goldsberry, *Pr*
Gary Lugibihl, *Prin*
Donald Brauen, *Prin*
Neil Reichenbach, *Prin*
EMP: 15 EST: 2019
SALES (est): 976.88K Privately Held
SIC: 3531 Road construction and
　　maintenance machinery

(G-1364)
RILEY CREEK HOLDINGS INC
8950 Dixie Hwy (45817-8566)
P.O. Box 161 (45817-0161)
PHONE..............................419 358-6946
David P Akin, *Pr*
Michael J Akin, *VP Opers*
James D Akin, *Stockholder*
Carlin Porter, *Sec*
EMP: 24 EST: 1963
SQ FT: 3,000
SALES (est): 4.14MM Privately Held
Web: www.blufftonprecast.com
SIC: 3272 Septic tanks, concrete

(G-1365)
SUMIRIKO OHIO INC (DH)
320 Snider Rd (45817-9573)
PHONE..............................419 358-2121
Takeo Endoh, *Pr*
M Fujiwara, *
Yuichi Ariga, *
◆ **EMP: 81 EST: 1988**
SQ FT: 240,000
SALES (est): 162.06MM Privately Held
Web: us.sumiriko.com
SIC: 3052 3069 3829 3714 Automobile
　　hose, rubber; Molded rubber products;
　　Measuring and controlling devices, nec;
　　Motor vehicle parts and accessories
HQ: Sumitomo Riko America, Inc.
　　41441 11 Mile Rd
　　Novi MI 48375
　　248 946-4915

(G-1366)
TOWER ATMTIVE OPRTONS USA I LL
Also Called: Tower Automotive
18717 County Road 15 (45817-9693)
PHONE..............................419 358-8966
Mike Jenkins, *Mgr*
EMP: 283
SALES (corp-wide): 4.41B Privately Held
Web: www.autokiniton.com
SIC: 3465 Automotive stampings
HQ: Tower Automotive Operations Usa I, Llc
　　17757 Woodland Dr
　　New Boston MI 48164

(G-1367)
TRIPLETT BLUFFTON CORPORATION
Also Called: Lfe Instruments
1 Triplett Dr (45817-1055)
P.O. Box 13 (45817-0013)
PHONE..............................419 358-8750
Warren J Hess, *Pr*
Kyle Apkarian, *CFO*
▲ **EMP: 9 EST: 1932**
SQ FT: 150,000
SALES (est): 921.9K Privately Held
Web: www.triplett.com
SIC: 3825 3824 Test equipment for
　　electronic and electrical circuits; Fluid
　　meters and counting devices

Boardman
Mahoning County

(G-1368)
BOARDMAN NEWS
8302 Southern Blvd Ste 2 (44512-3390)
PHONE..............................330 758-6397
Jack Darnell, *Owner*
EMP: 8 EST: 1947
SQ FT: 3,500
SALES (est): 67.63K Privately Held
Web: www.boardmannews.net
SIC: 2711 Newspapers, publishing and
　　printing

(G-1369)
CARTERS INC
389 Boardman Poland Rd (44512-4904)
PHONE..............................330 758-0390
EMP: 9
SALES (corp-wide): 2.84B Publicly Held
Web: www.carters.com
SIC: 5641 5137 5136 2389 Children's wear;
　　Women's and children's outerwear; Men's
　　and boys' hats, scarves, and gloves; Men's
　　miscellaneous accessories
PA: Carter's, Inc.
　　3438 Pchtree Rd Ne Ste 18
　　Atlanta GA 30326
　　678 791-1000

(G-1370)
EMPYRACOM INC (PA)
7510 Market St Ste 8 (44512-6021)
PHONE..............................330 744-5570
Shanthi Subramanyam, *Pr*
Viswanath Subramanya, *VP*
EMP: 16 EST: 1994
SQ FT: 2,500
SALES (est): 2.8MM
SALES (corp-wide): 2.8MM Privately Held
Web: www.empyra.com
SIC: 7379 7372 7371 Computer related
　　consulting services; Prepackaged software;
　　Computer software systems analysis and
　　design, custom

(G-1371)
EXCALIBUR BARBER LLC
7401 Market St (44512-5621)
PHONE..............................330 729-9006
Kelan Bilal, *Pr*
EMP: 10 EST: 2010
SALES (est): 106.31K Privately Held
Web: www.excaliburbarber.com
SIC: 7241 3999 5087 Barber shops; Barber
　　and beauty shop equipment; Beauty salon
　　and barber shop equipment and supplies

(G-1372)
GORANT CHOCOLATIER LLC (PA)
Also Called: Gorant's Yum Yum Tree
8301 Market St (44512-6257)
P.O. Box 1014 (44406-5014)
PHONE..............................330 726-8821
Joseph M Miller, *Managing Member*
Gary Weiss, *Pr*
EMP: 120 EST: 1946
SQ FT: 60,000
SALES (est): 3.22MM
SALES (corp-wide): 3.22MM Privately Held
Web: www.gorant.com
SIC: 5441 5947 5145 3999 Candy; Greeting
　　cards; Candy; Candles

(G-1373)
GREENHART RSTORATION MLLWK LLC

6001 Southern Blvd Ste 105 (44512-2900)
PHONE..............................330 502-6050
John Angelilli, *Prin*
EMP: 9 EST: 2017
SALES (est): 180.05K Privately Held
Web: www.greenheartcompanies.com
SIC: 2431 Millwork

(G-1374)
HERCULES LED LLC
5411 Market St (44512-2615)
PHONE..............................844 437-2533
James Rosan, *Managing Member*
EMP: 35 EST: 2014
SALES (est): 3.99MM Privately Held
Web: www.herculesled.com
SIC: 3646 7349 Ceiling systems, luminous;
　　Building component cleaning service

(G-1375)
PITA WRAP LLC
4721 Market St (44512-1526)
PHONE..............................330 886-8091
Marlene A Bassil, *Pr*
EMP: 7 EST: 2012
SQ FT: 3,700
SALES (est): 487.97K Privately Held
Web: www.sauceeino.com
SIC: 2099 Food preparations, nec

(G-1376)
SDS NATIONAL LLC
Also Called: SDS Logistics Services
143 Boardman Canfield Rd Pmb 333
(44512-4804)
PHONE..............................330 759-8066
Andrew Weiss, *Managing Member*
EMP: 6 EST: 2001
SALES (est): 2.79MM Privately Held
Web: www.sdslogistics.com
SIC: 3559 4731 Recycling machinery;
　　Freight transportation arrangement

(G-1377)
STRUGGLE GRIND SUCCESS LLC
6414 Market St (44512-3434)
PHONE..............................330 834-6738
EMP: 6 EST: 2019
SALES (est): 120.88K Privately Held
SIC: 7389 2211 Apparel designers,
　　commercial; Apparel and outerwear fabrics,
　　cotton

(G-1378)
TREEMEN INDUSTRIES INC
Also Called: Tii Treeman Industries
691 Mcclurg Rd (44513)
P.O. Box 3777 (44513-3777)
PHONE..............................330 965-3777
George Ogletree, *Pr*
Daniel Solmen, *
Violet Ogletree, *
EMP: 40 EST: 1998
SQ FT: 35,900
SALES (est): 8.93MM Privately Held
Web: www.treemen.com
SIC: 3479 3089 3646 3647 Aluminum
　　coating of metal products; Injection molding
　　of plastics; Commercial lighting fixtures;
　　Vehicular lighting equipment

(G-1379)
ZIDIAN MANAGEMENT LLC (PA)
574 Mcclurg Rd (44512-6405)
PHONE..............................330 743-6050
Tom Zidian, *Pr*
Michelle Gross, *
EMP: 25 EST: 2000
SALES (est): 91.82MM
SALES (corp-wide): 91.82MM Privately Held

Web: www.summergardenfood.com
SIC: 2099 Food preparations, nec

(G-1380)
ZIDIAN MANUFACTURING LLC
Also Called: Summer Garden Food Mfg
500 Mcclurg Rd (44512-6405)
PHONE..............................330 965-8455
Tom Zidian, *CEO*
▲ **EMP: 54 EST: 2000**
SALES (est): 14.09MM
SALES (corp-wide): 402.06MM Privately Held
Web: www.summergardenfood.com
SIC: 2099 Sauce, gravy, dressing, and dip
　　mixes
HQ: Lassonde Industries Inc.
　　755 Rue Principale
　　Rougemont QC J0L 1
　　450 469-4926

Bolivar
Tuscarawas County

(G-1381)
AMERICAN HIGHWAY PRODUCTS LLC
11723 Strasburg Bolivar Rd Nw
(44612-8554)
P.O. Box 640 (44612-0640)
PHONE..............................330 874-3270
Scott Fier, *Pr*
Eric Fier, *VP*
EMP: 10 EST: 1978
SQ FT: 10,400
SALES (est): 2.47MM Privately Held
Web: www.ahp1.com
SIC: 3531 Road construction and
　　maintenance machinery

(G-1382)
ELEET CRYOGENICS INC (PA)
11132 Industrial Pkwy Nw (44612-8993)
PHONE..............................330 874-4009
Garry Sears, *Pr*
Tenia Sears, *
▲ **EMP: 33 EST: 1997**
SQ FT: 47,000
SALES (est): 9.87MM Privately Held
Web: www.eleetcryogenics.com
SIC: 3443 7353 2761 5088 Cryogenic tanks,
　　for liquids and gases; Oil field equipment,
　　rental or leasing; Manifold business forms;
　　Tanks and tank components

(G-1383)
GEMINI FIBER CORPORATION
11145 Industrial Pkwy Nw (44612-8993)
P.O. Box 487 (44612-0487)
PHONE..............................330 874-4131
Stanley F Lakota, *Pr*
▲ **EMP: 12 EST: 1993**
SQ FT: 15,000
SALES (est): 4.49MM Privately Held
Web: www.geminifiber.com
SIC: 2679 Paper products, converted, nec

(G-1384)
HOLDSWORTH INDUSTRIAL FABG LLC
10407 Welton Rd Ne (44612-8833)
P.O. Box 643 (44697-0643)
PHONE..............................330 874-3945
Randy Holdsworth, *Owner*
EMP: 6 EST: 1980
SQ FT: 5,000
SALES (est): 486.63K Privately Held
SIC: 1799 7692 Welding on site; Welding
　　repair

(G-1385)
MYERS MACHINING INC
11789 Strasburg Bolivar Rd Nw
(44612-8555)
P.O. Box 645 (44612-0645)
PHONE..................................330 874-3005
David Myers, *Pr*
Brenda Myers, *VP*
EMP: 6 **EST:** 1981
SQ FT: 16,000
SALES (est): 1.51MM **Privately Held**
SIC: 3599 Machine shop, jobbing and repair

(G-1386)
NILODOR INC
10966 Industrial Pkwy Nw (44612-8991)
P.O. Box 660 (44612-0660)
PHONE..................................800 443-4321
Les Mitson, *Pr*
Kurt Peterson, *
Jeff Wilkof, *
◆ **EMP:** 43 **EST:** 1956
SQ FT: 43,000
SALES (est): 9.69MM
SALES (corp-wide): 523.82MM **Privately
Held**
Web: www.hospecobrands.com
SIC: 2842 Deodorants, nonpersonal
PA: The Tranzonic Companies
26301 Crtiss Wrght Pkwy S
Cleveland OH 44143
216 535-4300

(G-1387)
OSTER SAND AND GRAVEL INC
3467 Dover Zoar Rd Ne (44612-8922)
PHONE..................................330 874-3322
Dan Morrisset, *Mgr*
EMP: 6
SALES (corp-wide): 3.25MM **Privately
Held**
Web:
www.ostersandandgravelnorthcantonoh.com
SIC: 1442 Construction sand and gravel
PA: Oster Sand And Gravel, Inc.
5947 Whipple Ave Nw
Canton OH 44720
330 494-5472

(G-1388)
PREMERE ENTERPRISES INC
10882 Fort Laurens Rd Nw (44612-8942)
PHONE..................................330 874-3000
Garry D Martin, *Pr*
Richard D Dodez, *Prin*
EMP: 6 **EST:** 1996
SALES (est): 910.58K **Privately Held**
Web: www.premereinc.com
SIC: 3544 Special dies, tools, jigs, and
fixtures

(G-1389)
PREMIERE MOLD AND MACHINE CO
10882 Fort Laurens Rd Nw (44612-8942)
PHONE..................................330 874-3000
Robert L Martin, *Ch Bd*
Garry Martin, *Pr*
Richard Dodez, *Sec*
EMP: 6 **EST:** 1972
SQ FT: 33,000
SALES (est): 656.95K **Privately Held**
Web: www.premereinc.com
SIC: 3089 Injection molding of plastics

(G-1390)
**PROGRSSIVE MOLDING BOLIVAR
INC**
10882 Fort Laurens Rd Nw (44612-8942)
PHONE..................................330 874-3000
James C Dukat, *Prin*
Garry Martin, *

Robert L Martin, *
Richard D Dodez, *
Sandra K Scott, *
EMP: 6 **EST:** 1976
SQ FT: 33,000
SALES (est): 685.58K **Privately Held**
Web: www.premereinc.com
SIC: 3544 3089 Dies, plastics forming;
Thermoformed finished plastics products,
nec

(G-1391)
RHC INC
Also Called: Ragon House Collection
10841 Fisher Rd Nw (44612-8487)
PHONE..................................330 874-3750
Mary Ragon, *Pr*
Joshua Ragon, *VP Opers*
Kerrie Thomas, *Sec*
▲ **EMP:** 22 **EST:** 2004
SALES (est): 2.23MM **Privately Held**
Web: www.ragonhouse.com
SIC: 3999 5023 5999 Christmas tree
ornaments, except electrical and glass;
Decorating supplies; Christmas lights and
decorations

(G-1392)
SUBURBAN PLASTICS CO (PA)
509 Water St Sw (44612-8986)
PHONE..................................847 741-4900
Stuart Buzz Baxter, *Pr*
Jeremy Baxter, *
Cheri A Baxter, *
◆ **EMP:** 325 **EST:** 1946
SALES (est): 4.54MM
SALES (corp-wide): 4.54MM **Privately
Held**
Web: www.suburbanplastics.com
SIC: 3089 Injection molding of plastics

(G-1393)
**TORQUE 2020 CMA ACQISITION LLC
(PA)**
Also Called: Cablecraft Motion Controls
10896 Industrial Pkwy Nw (44612-8990)
P.O. Box 409 (44612)
PHONE..................................330 874-2900
Daniel Pappano, *Pr*
Kimberly Mcbride, *CFO*
▲ **EMP:** 200 **EST:** 1974
SQ FT: 61,000
SALES (est): 100.09MM
SALES (corp-wide): 100.09MM **Privately
Held**
Web: www.cablecraft.com
SIC: 3315 3568 3714 Cable, steel: insulated
or armored; Ball joints, except aircraft and
auto; Ball joints, motor vehicle

(G-1394)
US TECHNOLOGY MEDIA INC
509 Water St Sw (44612-8986)
P.O. Box 526 (44612-0526)
PHONE..................................330 874-3094
EMP: 10 **EST:** 2015
SALES (est): 1MM **Privately Held**
SIC: 3291 Abrasive products

(G-1395)
USA LABEL EXPRESS INC
11206 Industrial Pkwy Nw (44612-8994)
P.O. Box 518 (44612-0518)
PHONE..................................330 874-1001
Chris Helwig, *Pr*
EMP: 25 **EST:** 1971
SQ FT: 25,000
SALES (est): 2.49MM **Privately Held**
Web: www.usalabelexpress.com
SIC: 2759 Labels and seals: printing, nsk

Botkins
Shelby County

(G-1396)
BOOMERANG RUBBER INC
105 Dinsmore St (45306-9632)
P.O. Box 538 (45306)
PHONE..................................937 693-4611
Mark Sultman, *Pr*
EMP: 22 **EST:** 2009
SALES (est): 4.53MM **Privately Held**
Web: www.boomerangrubber.com
SIC: 3069 Reclaimed rubber and specialty
rubber compounds

(G-1397)
BROWN INDUSTRIAL INC
311 W South St (45306-8019)
P.O. Box 74 (45306-0074)
PHONE..................................937 693-3838
Christopher D Brown, *Pr*
Ruth C Brown, *
Craig D Brown, *
EMP: 45 **EST:** 1937
SQ FT: 32,000
SALES (est): 9.14MM **Privately Held**
Web: www.brownindustrial.com
SIC: 3713 5012 5084 7692 Truck bodies
(motor vehicles); Truck bodies; Industrial
machinery and equipment; Automotive
welding

(G-1398)
RIDLEY USA INC
Also Called: Hubbard Feeds
104 Oak St (45306-8031)
P.O. Box 1105 (42241-1105)
PHONE..................................800 837-8222
Roger Allen, *Mgr*
EMP: 10
SALES (corp-wide): 1.49B **Privately Held**
Web: www.hubbardfeeds.com
SIC: 2048 5191 Livestock feeds; Animal
feeds
HQ: Ridley Usa Inc.
111 W Cherry St Ste 500
Mankato MN 56001
507 388-9400

Bowerston
Harrison County

(G-1399)
BOWERSTON SHALE COMPANY (PA)
515 Main St (44695-9512)
P.O. Box 199 (44695-0199)
PHONE..................................740 269-2921
Mark Willard, *Pr*
Edward C Milliken, *
Beth Hillyer, *
EMP: 30 **EST:** 1929
SQ FT: 100,000
SALES (est): 23.2MM
SALES (corp-wide): 23.2MM **Privately
Held**
Web: www.bowerstonshale.com
SIC: 3255 3251 2951 Clay refractories; Brick
clay: common face, glazed, vitrified, or
hollow; Asphalt paving mixtures and blocks

(G-1400)
NOLAN COMPANY
300 Boyce Dr (44695-9760)
PHONE..................................740 269-1512
Dan Chew, *Mgr*
EMP: 7
SALES (corp-wide): 47.2MM **Privately
Held**

Web: www.nolancompany.com
SIC: 3743 3532 Railroad equipment; Mining
machinery
HQ: The Nolan Company
1016 9th St Sw
Canton OH 44707

(G-1401)
NOVO MANUFACTURING LLC (DH)
Also Called: L J Smith Stair System
35280 Scio Bowerston Rd (44695-9731)
PHONE..................................740 269-2221
Rob Brown, *CEO*
Jordan Stephens, *
Jeff Leys, *
Jeff Broene, *
Faiz Karmally, *
▲ **EMP:** 49 **EST:** 1991
SQ FT: 180,000
SALES (est): 61.7MM
SALES (corp-wide): 2.58B **Privately Held**
Web: www.ljsmith.com
SIC: 2431 Staircases, stairs and railings
HQ: Novo Building Products Holdings, Llc
8181 Logistic Dr
Zeeland MI 49464
800 253-9000

Bowersville
Greene County

(G-1402)
PREMIER GRAIN LLC
5827 E Xenia St (45307)
PHONE..................................937 584-6552
John Heinz, *VP*
EMP: 9
SALES (corp-wide): 764.62K **Privately
Held**
Web: www.premiergrainllc.com
SIC: 2048 Prepared feeds, nec
PA: Premier Grain, Llc
1 Solutions Ave
Sabina OH 45169
937 584-6552

Bowling Green
Wood County

(G-1403)
A-GAS US HOLDINGS INC (DH)
Also Called: A-Gas Americas
1100 Haskins Rd (43402-9363)
PHONE..................................419 867-8990
Monte Roach, *Pr*
Patricia Burns, *VP*
Jason Zilles, *CFO*
EMP: 14 **EST:** 2012
SALES (est): 158.73MM **Privately Held**
Web: www.agas.com
SIC: 5099 2869 4953 3399 Fire extinguishers
; Freon; Chemical detoxification;
Reclaiming ferrous metals from clay
HQ: A-Gas International Limited
Banyard Road
Bristol BS20
127 537-6600

(G-1404)
**AARDVARK SCREEN PRTG & EMB
LLC**
123 S Main St (43402-2910)
P.O. Box 128 (43402-0128)
PHONE..................................419 354-6686
TOLL FREE: 888
EMP: 10 **EST:** 2016
SQ FT: 3,000
SALES (est): 379.2K **Privately Held**

(PA)=Parent Co (HQ)=Headquarters
✪ = New Business established in last 2 years

Web: www.aardvarkspe.com
SIC: **2759** 7311 Screen printing; Advertising agencies

(G-1405)
ABSORBENT PRODUCTS COMPANY INC
455 W Woodland Cir (43402-8834)
PHONE..........................419 352-5353
Paul Rankin, *Pr*
◆ **EMP: 35 EST:** 1989
SALES (est): 1.79MM
SALES (corp-wide): 45.62MM **Privately Held**
SIC: **2676** Diapers, paper (disposable): made from purchased paper
PA: Principle Business Enterprises, Inc.
20189 Pine Lk Rd
Bowling Green OH 43402
419 352-1551

(G-1406)
AEROPACT MANUFACTURING LLC
Also Called: Martin Machine
435 W Woodland Cir (43402-8834)
PHONE..........................419 373-1711
Rajkumar Nagarajan, *Pr*
EMP: 11 EST: 2019
SALES (est): 5.86MM **Privately Held**
Web: www.aeropact.com
SIC: **3324** Aerospace investment castings, ferrous

(G-1407)
BARNES INTERNATIONAL LLC
Also Called: Henry Filters
555 Van Camp Rd (43402-9011)
PHONE..........................419 352-7501
Steve Volmer, *Brnch Mgr*
EMP: 28
SALES (corp-wide): 92.18MM **Privately Held**
Web: www.barnesintl.com
SIC: **3677** Electronic coils and transformers
HQ: Barnes International, Llc
814 Chestnut St
Rockford IL 61102
815 964-8661

(G-1408)
BASIC COATINGS LLC
400 Van Camp Rd (43402-9062)
PHONE..........................419 241-2156
EMP: 10 EST: 2005
SALES (est): 1.25MM
SALES (corp-wide): 90.43MM **Privately Held**
Web: www.basiccoatings.com
SIC: **2851** Paints and allied products
PA: Betco Corporation
400 Van Camp Rd
Bowling Green OH 43402
419 241-2156

(G-1409)
BETCO CORPORATION LTD (HQ)
400 Van Camp Rd (43402-9062)
PHONE..........................419 241-2156
Paul C Betz, *CEO*
Tony Lyons, *VP*
James Betz, *Sec*
◆ **EMP: 200 EST:** 1994
SALES (est): 6.69MM
SALES (corp-wide): 90.43MM **Privately Held**
Web: www.betco.com
SIC: **2842** Polishes and sanitation goods
PA: Betco Corporation
400 Van Camp Rd
Bowling Green OH 43402
419 241-2156

(G-1410)
BIO-SYSTEMS CORPORATION
Also Called: BSC Environmental
400 Van Camp Rd (43402-9062)
PHONE..........................608 365-9550
Malcolm Peacock, *Pr*
Marilyn Peacock, *
Lisa Peacock, *
EMP: 7 EST: 1986
SALES (est): 505.25K **Privately Held**
Web: www.envirozyme.com
SIC: **2819** Industrial inorganic chemicals, nec

(G-1411)
BIOFIT ENGINEERED PRODUCTS LIMITED PARTNERSHIP (PA)
15500 Bio Fit Way (43402-9290)
P.O. Box 109 (43566-0109)
PHONE..........................419 823-1089
▲ **EMP: 45 EST:** 1992
SALES (est): 9.29MM **Privately Held**
Web: www.biofit.com
SIC: **3444** 2531 2599 2522 Sheet metalwork ; Public building and related furniture; Stools, factory; Chairs, office: padded or plain: except wood

(G-1412)
CENTAUR TOOL & DIE INC
2019 Wood Bridge Blvd (43402-8913)
PHONE..........................419 352-7704
Paul E Faykosh, *Pr*
Jack Faykosh, *VP*
Jeff Faykosh, *VP*
EMP: 12 EST: 1973
SQ FT: 16,400
SALES (est): 2.4MM **Privately Held**
Web: www.centaurtool.com
SIC: **3544** Die sets for metal stamping (presses)

(G-1413)
CENTURY MARKETING CORPORATION
1145 Fairview Ave (43402-1204)
PHONE..........................419 354-2591
EMP: 149
SALES (corp-wide): 48.89MM **Privately Held**
Web: www.centurylabel.com
SIC: **2759** Labels and seals: printing, nsk
HQ: Century Marketing Corporation
12836 S Dixie Hwy
Bowling Green OH 43402
419 354-2591

(G-1414)
CLARK FIXTURE TECHNOLOGIES INC
410 N Dunbridge Rd (43402-8963)
PHONE..........................419 354-1541
EMP: 36 EST: 1980
SALES (est): 7.01MM **Privately Held**
Web: www.clarkfixtures.com
SIC: **3829** 3544 Measuring and controlling devices, nec; Special dies, tools, jigs, and fixtures

(G-1415)
CMC GROUP INC (PA)
12836 S Dixie Hwy (43402-9697)
PHONE..........................419 354-2591
Jeffrey Gayer, *
Jeff Palmer, *
Bob Copple, *
Tammy Corral, *
▲ **EMP: 67 EST:** 1999
SQ FT: 2,268
SALES (est): 48.89MM
SALES (corp-wide): 48.89MM **Privately Held**

Web: www.cmcgp.com
SIC: **2759** 7389 Labels and seals: printing, nsk; Telemarketing services

(G-1416)
COOPER-STANDARD AUTOMOTIVE INC
Also Called: Cooper
1175 N Main St (43402-1310)
P.O. Box 1108 (43402-1108)
PHONE..........................419 352-3533
Robert Huey, *Brnch Mgr*
EMP: 90
SALES (corp-wide): 2.73B **Publicly Held**
Web: www.cooperstandard.com
SIC: **3052** Automobile hose, rubber
HQ: Cooper-Standard Automotive Inc.
40300 Traditions Dr
Northville MI 48168
248 596-5900

(G-1417)
DOW JONES & COMPANY INC
Also Called: Dow Jones
1100 Brim Rd (43402-9351)
PHONE..........................419 352-4696
Nick Barbosa, *Brnch Mgr*
EMP: 39
SALES (corp-wide): 10.09B **Publicly Held**
Web: www.dowjones.com
SIC: **2711** Newspapers, publishing and printing
HQ: Dow Jones & Company, Inc.
1211 Ave Of The Americas
New York NY 10036
800 369-5663

(G-1418)
DOWA THT AMERICA INC
2130 S Woodland Cir (43402-8832)
PHONE..........................419 354-4144
Masanari Konomi, *Pr*
Sandy Hill, *
▲ **EMP: 35 EST:** 1997
SALES (est): 7.45MM **Privately Held**
Web: www.dowa-tht.com
SIC: **3398** Metal heat treating
HQ: Dowa Thermotech Co., Ltd.
19-1, Ukishimacho, Mizuho-Ku
Nagoya AIC 467-0

(G-1419)
ENVIROZYME LLC
Also Called: Envirozyme
400 Van Camp Rd (43402-9062)
PHONE..........................800 232-2847
EMP: 19 EST: 2010
SALES (est): 5.21MM **Privately Held**
Web: www.envirozyme.com
SIC: **2836** Bacteriological media

(G-1420)
GELOK INTERNATIONAL CORP
20189 Pine Lake Rd (43402-4091)
P.O. Box 69 (43414-0069)
PHONE..........................419 352-1482
Charles Stocking, *Pr*
Micheal Kirby, *CFO*
Carol Stocking, *Sec*
▲ **EMP: 6 EST:** 1983
SQ FT: 20,000
SALES (est): 1.35MM **Privately Held**
Web: www.gelok.com
SIC: **3842** Surgical appliances and supplies

(G-1421)
GKN DRIVELINE BOWL GREEN INC (DH)
2223 Wood Bridge Blvd (43402-8873)
PHONE..........................419 373-7700

Kevin Cumming, *CEO*
▲ **EMP: 30 EST:** 1998
SALES (est): 16.06MM
SALES (corp-wide): 6.06B **Privately Held**
Web: www.bowlinggreen-oh.com
SIC: **3999** Barber and beauty shop equipment
HQ: Gkn America Corp.
1180 Pchtree St Ne Ste 24
Atlanta GA 30309
630 972-9300

(G-1422)
GKN DRIVELINE NORTH AMER INC
Also Called: GKN Driveline Bowling Green
2223 Wood Bridge Blvd (43402-8873)
PHONE..........................419 354-3955
Hideo Miyagi, *Brnch Mgr*
EMP: 91
SALES (corp-wide): 6.06B **Privately Held**
SIC: **3714** Motor vehicle parts and accessories
HQ: Gkn Driveline North America, Inc.
2200 N Opdyke Rd
Auburn Hills MI 48326
248 296-7000

(G-1423)
KEL-MAR INC
436 N Enterprise St (43402)
P.O. Box 424 (43402-0424)
PHONE..........................419 806-4600
Burr Sterling, *Pr*
EMP: 25 EST: 1981
SALES (est): 186.49K **Privately Held**
SIC: **3471** Finishing, metals or formed products

(G-1424)
LBZB RESTAURANTS INC
132 E Wooster St (43402-2919)
PHONE..........................567 413-4700
Zachariah Baroudi, *CEO*
EMP: 12 EST: 2018
SALES (est): 472.97K **Privately Held**
SIC: **2035** 5812 2099 Dressings, salad: raw and cooked (except dry mixes); Fast-food restaurant, chain; Dressings, salad: dry mixes

(G-1425)
LIFEFORMATIONS INC
Also Called: Lifeformations
2029 Wood Bridge Blvd (43402-8913)
PHONE..........................419 352-2101
Rodney Hailigmann, *Pr*
EMP: 50 EST: 1991
SQ FT: 8,000
SALES (est): 3.65MM **Privately Held**
Web: www.lfstudios.com
SIC: **3559** Robots, molding and forming plastics

(G-1426)
LUBRIZOL GLOBAL MANAGEMENT
Also Called: LUBRIZOL GLOBAL MANAGEMENT, INC
1142 N Main St (43402-1309)
PHONE..........................419 352-5565
Dennis Callan, *Prin*
EMP: 46
SALES (corp-wide): 424.23B **Publicly Held**
Web: www.lubrizol.com
SIC: **2899** Chemical preparations, nec
HQ: Lubrizol Global Management, Inc.
9911 Brecksville Rd
Cleveland OH 44141
216 447-5000

▲ = Import ▼ = Export
◆ = Import/Export

(G-1427)
MACK INDUSTRIES
507 Derby Ave (43402-3973)
PHONE..............................419 353-7081
Betsie Mack, *Pr*
EMP: 19 **EST:** 1910
SALES (est): 4.41MM
SALES (corp-wide): 86.93MM **Privately Held**
Web: www.mackconcrete.com
SIC: 3272 5211 1711 Burial vaults, concrete or precast terrazzo; Masonry materials and supplies; Septic system construction
PA: Mack Industries, Inc.
1321 Indus Pkwy N Ste 500
Brunswick OH 44212
330 460-7005

(G-1428)
MARATHON SPECIAL PRODUCTS CORP
427 Van Camp Rd (43402-9020)
P.O. Box 468 (43402-0468)
PHONE..............................419 352-8441
Bret Banks, *VP*
EMP: 175 **EST:** 1956
SQ FT: 68,000
SALES (est): 4.7MM
SALES (corp-wide): 6.03B **Publicly Held**
Web: www.marathonsp.com
SIC: 3613 3643 Fuses and fuse equipment; Current-carrying wiring services
HQ: Regal Beloit America, Inc.
111 W Michigan St
Milwaukee WI 53203
608 364-8800

(G-1429)
MESTEK INC
American Warming & Vent Div
219 S Church St # 200 (43402-2816)
PHONE..............................419 288-2703
Paul Quinlan, *Mgr*
EMP: 61
SALES (corp-wide): 689.94MM **Privately Held**
Web: www.mestek.com
SIC: 3822 3444 3442 Air flow controllers, air conditioning and refrigeration; Sheet metalwork; Metal doors, sash, and trim
PA: Mestek, Inc.
260 N Elm St
Westfield MA 01085
413 568-9571

(G-1430)
NOVAVISION LLC (PA)
Also Called: Sealock
524 E Woodland Cir (43402-8966)
PHONE..............................419 354-1427
Steve Wirrig, *CEO*
Albert Caperna, *
Mike Messmer, *
Bill Schoenherr, *
▲ **EMP:** 58 **EST:** 1994
SQ FT: 39,000
SALES (est): 13.7MM **Privately Held**
Web: www.novavisioninc.com
SIC: 2672 Adhesive papers, labels, or tapes: from purchased material

(G-1431)
NRG INDUSTRIAL LIGHTING MFG CO
7458 Linwood Rd (43402-9545)
P.O. Box 12 (43402-0012)
PHONE..............................419 354-8207
Kenneth Stinehart, *Pr*
EMP: 8 **EST:** 2005
SALES (est): 690K **Privately Held**
SIC: 3646 Commercial lighting fixtures

(G-1432)
PALM PLASTICS LTD
843 Miller Dr (43402-8601)
PHONE..............................561 776-6700
EMP: 7 **EST:** 2017
SALES (est): 86.67K **Privately Held**
SIC: 3843 Dental equipment and supplies

(G-1433)
PALMER BROS TRANSIT MIX CON (PA)
Also Called: Fostoria Concrete
12205 E Gypsy Lane Rd (43402-9516)
PHONE..............................419 352-4681
Randolph G Schmeltz, *Pr*
Jesse Schmeltz, *VP*
EMP: 15 **EST:** 1974
SQ FT: 2,000
SALES (est): 5.86MM
SALES (corp-wide): 5.86MM **Privately Held**
SIC: 3273 Ready-mixed concrete

(G-1434)
PHOENIX TECHNOLOGIES INTL LLC (HQ)
Also Called: Pti
1098 Fairview Ave (43402-1233)
PHONE..............................419 353-7738
Thomas E Brady, *Managing Member*
Elizabeth C Brady, *
▲ **EMP:** 50 **EST:** 1992
SQ FT: 100,000
SALES (est): 15.72MM **Privately Held**
Web: www.phoenixtechnologies.net
SIC: 3085 5169 Plastics bottles; Synthetic resins, rubber, and plastic materials
PA: Far Eastern New Century Corporation
36f, No. 207, Dunhua S. Rd., Sec. 2
Taipei City TAP 10605

(G-1435)
PINNACLE INDUSTRIAL ENTPS INC
Also Called: Pinnacle Plastic Products
513 Napoleon Rd (43402-4822)
P.O. Box 286 (43402-0286)
PHONE..............................419 352-8688
Kevin J Tearney, *Pr*
Gary Gratop, *
Mike Hagen, *
▲ **EMP:** 125 **EST:** 1995
SQ FT: 90,000
SALES (est): 9.24MM **Privately Held**
Web: www.pinnacleplasticproducts.com
SIC: 3089 Injection molding of plastics

(G-1436)
PIONEER PACKING CO
510 Napoleon Rd (43402-4821)
P.O. Box 171 (43402-0171)
PHONE..............................419 352-5283
Brian Contris, *Pr*
EMP: 70 **EST:** 1945
SQ FT: 30,000
SALES (est): 6.92MM **Privately Held**
Web: www.pioneerpacking.com
SIC: 2011 Meat packing plants

(G-1437)
PRINCIPLE BUSINESS ENTPS INC (PA)
Also Called: Tranquility
20189 Pine Lake Rd (43402-4091)
P.O. Box 129 (43414-0129)
PHONE..............................419 352-1551
Andrew Stocking, *Pr*
Carol Stocking, *Vice Chairman*
Charles A Stocking, *
Michael Kirby, *
Chuck Tull, *

▲ **EMP:** 200 **EST:** 1961
SQ FT: 105,000
SALES (est): 45.62MM
SALES (corp-wide): 45.62MM **Privately Held**
Web:
www.principlebusinessenterprises.com
SIC: 2676 3142 Diapers, paper (disposable): made from purchased paper; House slippers

(G-1438)
RECLAMATION TECHNOLOGIES INC
Also Called: Remtec International
1100 Haskins Rd (43402-9363)
PHONE..............................800 372-1301
◆ **EMP:** 38
SIC: 2869 Freon

(G-1439)
REGAL BELOIT AMERICA INC
Marathon Special Products
427 Van Camp Rd (43402-9020)
P.O. Box 468 (43402-0468)
PHONE..............................419 352-8441
Larry Minnich, *Genl Mgr*
EMP: 200
SALES (corp-wide): 6.03B **Publicly Held**
Web: www.marathonsp.com
SIC: 3613 3644 Fuse mountings, electric power; Noncurrent-carrying wiring devices
HQ: Regal Beloit America, Inc.
111 W Michigan St
Milwaukee WI 53203
608 364-8800

(G-1440)
SOUTHEASTERN CONTAINER INC
307 Industrial Pkwy (43402-1347)
PHONE..............................419 352-6300
John Johnson, *Brnch Mgr*
EMP: 55
SALES (corp-wide): 80.49MM **Privately Held**
Web: www.secontainer.com
SIC: 3085 3089 Plastics bottles; Plastics containers, except foam
PA: Southeastern Container, Inc.
1250 Sand Hill Rd
Enka NC 28728
828 350-7200

(G-1441)
TBT HAULING LLC
500 Lehman Ave Ste 103 (43402-3068)
PHONE..............................904 635-7631
EMP: 6 **EST:** 2021
SALES (est): 1.75MM **Privately Held**
SIC: 3537 Trucks: freight, baggage, etc.: industrial, except mining

(G-1442)
TH PLASTICS INC
843 Miller Dr (43402-8601)
PHONE..............................419 352-2770
Patrick Haas, *Owner*
EMP: 78
SALES (corp-wide): 49.59MM **Privately Held**
Web: www.thplastics.com
SIC: 3089 Injection molding of plastics
PA: Th Plastics, Inc.
106 E Main St
Mendon MI 49072
269 496-8495

(G-1443)
TOLEDO MOLDING & DIE LLC
515 E Gypsy Lane Rd (43402-8739)
PHONE..............................419 354-6050
Tom Pasche, *Mgr*

EMP: 127
SALES (corp-wide): 7.28B **Privately Held**
Web: www.tmdinc.com
SIC: 3089 Injection molding of plastics
HQ: Toledo Molding & Die, Llc
1429 Coining Dr
Toledo OH 43612

(G-1444)
TRENCHLESS RSRCES GLOBL HLDNGS
Also Called: Vylon Pipe
420 Industrial Pkwy (43402-1326)
PHONE..............................419 419-6498
George Foos, *CEO*
Matthew Holl, *Prin*
EMP: 11 **EST:** 2018
SALES (est): 4.16MM **Privately Held**
Web: www.vylonpipe.com
SIC: 3312 Pipes and tubes

(G-1445)
VEHTEK SYSTEMS INC
2125 Wood Bridge Blvd (43402-9164)
PHONE..............................419 373-8741
Christian Holzer, *Prin*
◆ **EMP:** 700 **EST:** 2004
SALES (est): 40.08MM
SALES (corp-wide): 42.84B **Privately Held**
SIC: 3465 Body parts, automobile: stamped metal
PA: Magna International Inc
337 Magna Dr
Aurora ON L4G 7
905 726-2462

(G-1446)
VITAL & FHR NORTH AMERICA LLC
1201 Brim Rd (43402-9393)
PHONE..............................650 405-9975
Feng Xiong, *Managing Member*
EMP: 35 **EST:** 2022
SALES (est): 9.12MM **Privately Held**
SIC: 3399 Primary metal products

(G-1447)
WILLIAMS INDUSTRIAL SVC INC
Also Called: Williams Industrial
2120 Wood Bridge Blvd (43402-9164)
PHONE..............................419 353-2120
Jason Williams, *Pr*
Nancy Williams, *Treas*
Barry E Savage, *Prin*
Mary E Geremski, *Prin*
Mary Helen Nowak, *Prin*
EMP: 22 **EST:** 1971
SQ FT: 56,000
SALES (est): 5.56MM **Privately Held**
Web: www.wisfurnaces.com
SIC: 3567 Heating units and devices, industrial: electric

(G-1448)
WOOD COUNTY OHIO
Also Called: Laser Cartridge Express
991 S Main St (43402-4708)
PHONE..............................419 353-1227
Gaile Brooker, *Mgr*
EMP: 8
SALES (corp-wide): 158.18MM **Privately Held**
Web: www.lasercartridgeexpress.com
SIC: 3955 Print cartridges for laser and other computer printers
PA: County Of Wood
1 Courthouse Sq
Bowling Green OH 43402
419 354-9100

(G-1449)
XORB CORPORATION
455 W Woodland Cir (43402-8834)
PHONE..............................419 354-6021
Ralph Temple, *Pr*
Paul Dunlavey, *Sec*
EMP: 7 **EST:** 1992
SQ FT: 10,000
SALES (est): 3.3MM **Privately Held**
Web: www.xorbcorp.com
SIC: 3826 Analytical instruments

(G-1450)
ZERES INC
2018 Clearwater Cir (43402-8778)
P.O. Box 487 (43402-0487)
PHONE..............................419 354-5555
EMP: 26 **EST:** 1984
SALES (est): 462.48K **Privately Held**
Web: www.zeresinc.com
SIC: 2893 Printing ink

Bradford
Miami County

(G-1451)
C F POEPPELMAN INC (PA)
Also Called: Pepcon Concrete
4755 N State Route 721 (45308-9425)
PHONE..............................937 448-2191
James Poeppelman, *Pr*
Fred Poeppelman, *VP*
EMP: 20 **EST:** 1950
SQ FT: 1,500
SALES (est): 5.78MM
SALES (corp-wide): 5.78MM **Privately Held**
Web: www.poeppelmanmaterials.com
SIC: 3273 1442 Ready-mixed concrete;
　　Construction sand and gravel

(G-1452)
PRODUCTION PAINT FINISHERS INC
Also Called: P P F
140 Center St (45308-1202)
P.O. Box 127 (45308-0127)
PHONE..............................937 448-2627
Kenneth L Robertson, *Prin*
Lawrence F Francis, *
Allen J Francis, *
Russell Francis, *
Barbara Francis, *
EMP: 80 **EST:** 1970
SQ FT: 67,000
SALES (est): 4.97MM **Privately Held**
Web: www.productionpaint.com
SIC: 3479 Coating of metals and formed
　　products

(G-1453)
TWENTY ONE BARRELS LTD
9717 Horatio Harris Creek Rd
(45308-9686)
PHONE..............................937 467-4498
Danielle Pierce, *CEO*
EMP: 8 **EST:** 2020
SALES (est): 1.05MM **Privately Held**
Web: www.21barrels.com
SIC: 2084 Wines

Bradner
Wood County

(G-1454)
MESTEK INC
America Wariming & Ventraling
120 Plin St (43406-7735)
P.O. Box 677 (43406-0677)
PHONE..............................419 288-2703
Todd Whightman, *Brnch Mgr*
EMP: 11
SALES (corp-wide): 689.94MM **Privately Held**
Web: www.mestek.com
SIC: 3822 3564 3444 3442 Hardware for
　environmental regulators; Blowers and fans
　; Sheet metalwork; Metal doors, sash, and
　trim
PA: Mestek, Inc.
　　260 N Elm St
　　Westfield MA 01085
　　413 568-9571

Brecksville
Cuyahoga County

(G-1455)
AB RESOURCES LLC
6802 W Snowville Rd Ste E (44141-3296)
PHONE..............................440 922-1098
EMP: 25 **EST:** 2005
SQ FT: 7,500
SALES (est): 859.97K **Privately Held**
Web: www.abresourcesllc.com
SIC: 1382 Oil and gas exploration services

(G-1456)
AGRANA FRUIT US INC (DH)
6850 Southpointe Pkwy (44141-3260)
PHONE..............................440 546-1199
◆ **EMP:** 50 **EST:** 1977
SALES (est): 236.54MM
SALES (corp-wide): 2.67MM **Privately Held**
Web: us.agrana.com
SIC: 2087 Flavoring extracts and syrups, nec
HQ: Agrana Fruit Austria Gmbh
　　MuhlwaldstraBe 1
　　Gleisdorf 8200
　　311222260

(G-1457)
APPLIED MEDICAL TECHNOLOGY INC (PA)
Also Called: Amt
8006 Katherine Blvd (44141-4202)
PHONE..............................440 717-4000
George J Picha, *Pr*
Robert J Crump, *
EMP: 11 **EST:** 1979
SQ FT: 14,000
SALES (est): 10.46MM
SALES (corp-wide): 10.46MM **Privately Held**
Web: www.appliedmedical.net
SIC: 3841 3083 8731 Surgical and medical
　instruments; Laminated plastics plate and
　sheet; Medical research, commercial

(G-1458)
BARNES GROUP INC
Also Called: Hyson Products
10367 Brecksville Rd (44141-3335)
PHONE..............................440 526-5900
Mike Gaudiani, *Brnch Mgr*
EMP: 8
SQ FT: 53,593
SALES (corp-wide): 2.6B **Privately Held**
Web: www.hysonproducts.com
SIC: 3469 3495 Metal stampings, nec; Wire
　springs
HQ: Barnes Group Inc.
　　123 Main St
　　Bristol CT 06010
　　860 583-7070

(G-1459)
BENJAMIN MEDIA INC
10050 Brecksville Rd (44141-3219)
P.O. Box 190 (44264-0190)
PHONE..............................330 467-7588
Bernard P Krzys, *Pr*
▲ **EMP:** 28 **EST:** 1992
SQ FT: 2,744
SALES (est): 5.01MM **Privately Held**
Web: www.benjaminmedia.com
SIC: 2721 Trade journals: publishing and
　printing

(G-1460)
BLACK BOX CORPORATION
6650 W Snowville Rd Ste R (44141-4301)
PHONE..............................800 676-8850
Randy Reffert, *Brnch Mgr*
EMP: 10
Web: www.blackbox.com
SIC: 3577 Computer peripheral equipment,
　nec
HQ: Black Box Corporation
　　2701 N Dllas Pkwy Ste 510
　　Plano TX 75093
　　724 746-5500

(G-1461)
CURTISS-WRIGHT FLOW CTRL CORP
Also Called: Sprague Products
10195 Brecksville Rd (44141-3205)
PHONE..............................440 838-7690
EMP: 30
SQ FT: 77,847
SALES (corp-wide): 3.12B **Publicly Held**
Web: www.curtisswright.com
SIC: 3491 Industrial valves
HQ: Curtiss-Wright Flow Control
　　Corporation
　　1966 Broadhollow Rd Ste E
　　Farmingdale NY 11735
　　631 293-3800

(G-1462)
DEMATIC CORP
6930 Treeline Dr (44141-3367)
PHONE..............................440 526-2770
John Baysore, *Pr*
EMP: 95
SALES (corp-wide): 12.16B **Privately Held**
Web: www.dematic.com
SIC: 3535 Conveyors and conveying
　equipment
HQ: Dematic Corp.
　　756 W Peachtree St Nw
　　Atlanta GA 30308

(G-1463)
DIRECT DISPOSABLES LLC
10605 Snowville Rd (44141-3446)
P.O. Box 470451 (44147-0451)
PHONE..............................440 717-3335
EMP: 7 **EST:** 2000
SALES (est): 485.26K **Privately Held**
Web: www.directdisposables.com
SIC: 2389 Disposable garments and
　accessories

(G-1464)
EAGLESTONE PRODUCTS LLC
8057 Amber Ln (44141-1915)
PHONE..............................440 463-8715
Stephen C Hudak, *Managing Member*
EMP: 9 **EST:** 2002
SALES (est): 492.08K **Privately Held**
Web: www.eaglestoneproducts.com
SIC: 3993 Signs and advertising specialties

(G-1465)
EXACT CUTTING SERVICE INC
Also Called: Experimental Machine
6892 W Snowville Rd Ste 108
(44141-3249)
P.O. Box 470535 (44147-0535)
PHONE..............................440 546-1319
Jerry Narduzzi, *Pr*
▲ **EMP:** 8 **EST:** 1974
SQ FT: 20,000
SALES (est): 338.24K **Privately Held**
Web: www.exactcut.com
SIC: 7389 3599 Metal cutting services;
　Machine shop, jobbing and repair

(G-1466)
FULTON MANUFACTURING INDS LLC
6600 W Snowville Rd # 6500 (44141-3257)
EMP: 34 **EST:** 2004
SQ FT: 55,000
SALES (est): 1.8MM **Privately Held**
SIC: 3469 Metal stampings, nec

(G-1467)
GENERATIONS COFFEE COMPANY LLC (HQ)
60100 West Snowell (44141)
PHONE..............................440 546-0901
Michael Caruso, *Genl Mgr*
EMP: 11 **EST:** 2006
SALES (corp-wide): 290.57K
SALES (corp-wide): 78.56B **Publicly Held**
SIC: 2095 5149 5499 Roasted coffee;
　Groceries and related products, nec; Coffee
PA: Coffee Holding Co., Inc.
　　3475 Victory Blvd
　　Staten Island NY 10314
　　718 832-0800

(G-1468)
GLOBAL LIGHTING TECH INC
55 Andrews Cir Ste 1 (44141-3269)
PHONE..............................440 922-4584
Jeffery Parker, *Pr*
Michael Mayer, *General Vice President**
▲ **EMP:** 24 **EST:** 2000
SQ FT: 16,500
SALES (est): 9.96MM **Privately Held**
Web: www.glthome.com
SIC: 3648 3993 Lighting equipment, nec;
　Signs and advertising specialties
PA: Global Lighting Technologies Inc.
　　C/O: Maples & Calder Limited
　　George Town GR CAYMAN

(G-1469)
GOODRICH CORPORATION
9921 Brecksville Rd (44141-3201)
PHONE..............................440 262-1400
S Lau, *Brnch Mgr*
EMP: 8
SALES (corp-wide): 80.74B **Publicly Held**
Web: www.collinsaerospace.com
SIC: 3728 Aircraft parts and equipment, nec
HQ: Goodrich Corporation
　　2730 W Tyvola Rd
　　Charlotte NC 28217
　　704 423-7000

(G-1470)
HOMBRE CAPITAL INC
5945 W Snowville Rd (44141-3266)
PHONE..............................440 838-5335
Jim Urbanski, *Pr*
EMP: 10 **EST:** 1991
SQ FT: 24,000
SALES (est): 3.4MM **Privately Held**
Web: info.triadtechnologies.com

SIC: 3492 5074 Hose and tube fittings and assemblies, hydraulic/pneumatic; Plumbing and heating valves

(G-1471)
INDEPENDENCE CEMENT LLC
9240 Noble Park Dr (44141-3258)
P.O. Box 311009 (44131-8109)
PHONE...................................216 264-1212
Domenic Gangale, *Managing Member*
EMP: 25 **EST:** 2017
SALES (est): 3.51MM **Privately Held**
Web: www.independencecement.com
SIC: 3241 Natural cement

(G-1472)
INDUSTRIAL MFG CO LLC (HQ)
8223 Brecksville Rd Ste 100 (44141-1361)
PHONE...................................440 838-4700
◆ **EMP:** 10 **EST:** 1979
SQ FT: 4,700
SALES (est): 458.33MM
SALES (corp-wide): 459.42MM **Privately Held**
Web: www.mfgco.com
SIC: 2542 3728 3566 Lockers (not refrigerated): except wood; Aircraft body and wing assemblies and parts; Speed changers, drives, and gears
PA: Summa Holdings, Inc.
8223 Brcksvlle Rd Ste 100
Cleveland OH 44141
440 838-4700

(G-1473)
INTEGRATED CHEM CONCEPTS INC
Also Called: ICC
6650 W Snowville Rd Ste F (44141-4301)
PHONE...................................440 838-5666
Richard H Fagher, *Pr*
Christine Lease, *Sec*
EMP: 9 **EST:** 1989
SQ FT: 9,300
SALES (est): 481.25K **Privately Held**
Web: www.electrostaticdissipationcleveland.com
SIC: 2821 Plastics materials and resins

(G-1474)
JOHNSON CONTROLS INC
Also Called: Johnson Controls
6650 W Snowville Rd (44141-4301)
PHONE...................................216 587-0100
Todd Van Denbosche, *Prin*
EMP: 53
Web: www.johnsoncontrols.com
SIC: 2531 Seats, automobile
HQ: Johnson Controls, Inc.
5757 N Green Bay Ave
Milwaukee WI 53209
866 496-1999

(G-1475)
KNIGHT ERGONOMICS INC
Also Called: Gemini Products
6650 W Snowville Rd Ste G (44141-4301)
PHONE...................................440 746-0044
Robert Haller, *Pr*
Nicholas Pyros, *VP*
EMP: 10 **EST:** 1992
SALES (est): 824.54K **Privately Held**
Web: www.knightergo.com
SIC: 3423 Hand and edge tools, nec

(G-1476)
LUBRIZOL ADVANCED MTLS INC (HQ)
9911 Brecksville Rd (44141-3201)
PHONE...................................216 447-5000
Arnau Pano, *Pr*
Rebecca Liebert, *CEO*

EMP: 16 **EST:** 2000
SALES (est): 23.45MM
SALES (corp-wide): 424.23B **Publicly Held**
Web: www.lubrizol.com
SIC: 2899 Chemical preparations, nec
PA: Berkshire Hathaway Inc.
3555 Farnam St Ste 1440
Omaha NE 68131
402 346-1400

(G-1477)
NATURES OWN SOURCE LLC
7033 Mill Rd (44141-1813)
PHONE...................................440 838-5135
EMP: 8 **EST:** 2013
SALES (est): 415.57K **Privately Held**
Web: www.naturesownsource.com
SIC: 2899 Desalter kits, sea water

(G-1478)
NAUTICUS INC
8080 Snowville Rd (44141-3413)
PHONE...................................440 746-1290
John Agro, *Pr*
John Deagro, *Pr*
▲ **EMP:** 6 **EST:** 1998
SALES (est): 452.88K **Privately Held**
Web: www.nauticusinc.com
SIC: 3732 Motorized boat, building and repairing

(G-1479)
PRECISION INTERNATIONAL LLC
7000 S Edgerton Rd Ste 106 (44141-3199)
P.O. Box 513 (44210-0513)
PHONE...................................330 793-0900
Anthony P Crisalli, *Pr*
Kurt Walcutt, *CFO*
EMP: 20 **EST:** 2016
SALES (est): 5.06MM **Privately Held**
Web: www.precisioninc.net
SIC: 3441 Fabricated structural metal

(G-1480)
RBR ENTERPRISES LLC
Also Called: Hudson Workwear
6910 Miller Rd (44141-3227)
PHONE...................................866 437-9327
Heidi Sweeney, *Managing Member*
EMP: 11 **EST:** 2000
SALES (est): 460.2K **Privately Held**
Web: www.hudsonworkwear.com
SIC: 5136 5137 5699 3143 Apparel belts, men's and boys'; Apparel belts, women's and children's; Uniforms and work clothing; Work shoes, men's

(G-1481)
SYSTEM SEALS INC
Also Called: System Seals, Inc.
6600 W Snowville Rd (44141-3257)
PHONE...................................216 220-1800
EMP: 28
SALES (corp-wide): 779.39K **Privately Held**
Web: www.systemseals.com
SIC: 3953 5084 Embossing seals and hand stamps; Hydraulic systems equipment and supplies
HQ: System Seals, Llc
9505 Midwest Ave
Cleveland OH 44125

(G-1482)
TELEHEALTH CARE SOLUTIONS LLC
2551 Sweetwater Dr (44141-4102)
PHONE...................................440 823-6023
James Cireddu, *Prin*
EMP: 7 **EST:** 2014

SALES (est): 370K **Privately Held**
SIC: 7372 Publisher's computer software

(G-1483)
TEST-FUCHS CORPORATION
10325 Brecksville Rd (44141-3335)
PHONE...................................440 708-3505
Peter Barnhart, *CEO*
EMP: 8 **EST:** 2017
SQ FT: 168
SALES (est): 4.11MM **Privately Held**
Web: www.test-fuchs.com
SIC: 3826 3829 3728 Analytical instruments; Measuring and controlling devices, nec; Military aircraft equipment and armament

(G-1484)
TRACKER MANAGEMENT SYSTEMS
10091 Brecksville Rd (44141-3396)
PHONE...................................800 445-2438
James Weaver, *Pr*
Terri Weaver, *VP*
EMP: 7 **EST:** 1984
SALES (est): 351.45K **Privately Held**
Web: www.traxero.com
SIC: 7372 Business oriented computer software

(G-1485)
WICKED PREMIUMS LLC
8748 Brecksville Rd Ste 224 (44141-1986)
PHONE...................................216 364-0322
Ken Chelko, *Prin*
EMP: 6 **EST:** 2013
SALES (est): 73.66K **Privately Held**
Web: www.wickedpremiums.com
SIC: 2752 Commercial printing, lithographic

Bremen
Fairfield County

(G-1486)
INLINE UNDGRD HRZNTAL DRCTNAL
Also Called: Inline Underground Hdd
5440 Marietta Rd Sw (43107-9503)
PHONE...................................740 808-0316
Steven Thompson, *Prin*
EMP: 8 **EST:** 2020
SALES (est): 527.86K **Privately Held**
Web: www.inlinehdd.com
SIC: 1389 Construction, repair, and dismantling services

(G-1487)
STUART BURIAL VAULT CO INC
527 Ford St (43107-1111)
P.O. Box 146 (43107-0146)
PHONE...................................740 569-4158
John A Boone, *Pr*
Mary Lyle Boone, *VP*
EMP: 11 **EST:** 1919
SQ FT: 16,500
SALES (est): 1.09MM **Privately Held**
Web: www.stuartburialvaults.com
SIC: 3272 Burial vaults, concrete or precast terrazzo

(G-1488)
WESTERMAN INC (PA)
245 N Broad St (43107-1003)
P.O. Box 125 (43107-0125)
PHONE...................................800 338-8265
John Moorefield, *Ch*
Jacob Garrett, *
Nick Chrzanowski, *
Dave Cline, *
Brian Kariker, *
◆ **EMP:** 185 **EST:** 1957
SQ FT: 150,000

SALES (est): 87.41MM
SALES (corp-wide): 87.41MM **Privately Held**
Web: www.westermaninc.com
SIC: 3825 1389 Electrical energy measuring equipment; Oil field services, nec

(G-1489)
WORTHINGTON CYLINDER CORP
245 N Broad St (43107-1003)
P.O. Box 125 (43107-0125)
PHONE...................................740 569-4143
EMP: 178
SALES (corp-wide): 1.25B **Publicly Held**
Web: www.worthingtonenterprises.com
SIC: 3443 Cylinders, pressure: metal plate
HQ: Worthington Cylinder Corporation
200 W Old Wilson Bridge Rd
Worthington OH 43085
614 840-3210

Brewster
Stark County

(G-1490)
BREWSTER CHEESE COMPANY (PA)
Also Called: Brewster Cheese
800 Wabash Ave S (44613-1464)
PHONE...................................330 767-3492
Katsy Flarida, *CEO*
Fritz Leeman, *
Thomas Murphy, *
Emil Alecusan, *
▼ **EMP:** 200 **EST:** 1964
SQ FT: 78,914
SALES (est): 96.78MM
SALES (corp-wide): 96.78MM **Privately Held**
Web: www.brewstercheese.com
SIC: 2022 Natural cheese

(G-1491)
BREWSTER SUGARCREEK TWP HISTO
Also Called: BREWSTER HISTORICAL SOCIETY
45 Wabash Ave S (44613-1210)
PHONE...................................330 767-0045
Robert Lucking, *Owner*
EMP: 10 **EST:** 1976
SQ FT: 3,196
SALES (est): 131.7K **Privately Held**
Web: www.brewster-sugarcreektwp-hist.org
SIC: 3732 8412 Boat kits, not models; Museum

(G-1492)
MICRO MACHINE LTD
275 7th St Sw (44613-1457)
PHONE...................................330 438-7078
Ronald Pollock, *Pt*
Harold Byer, *Pt*
EMP: 7 **EST:** 2001
SALES (est): 466.12K **Privately Held**
SIC: 3599 Machine shop, jobbing and repair

(G-1493)
SHEARERS FOODS LLC
Also Called: Shearer's Snacks
692 Wabash Ave N (44613-1020)
PHONE...................................330 767-3426
Angie Hostetler, *Brnch Mgr*
EMP: 7
SALES (corp-wide): 14.54B **Privately Held**
Web: www.shearers.com
SIC: 2096 Potato chips and similar snacks
HQ: Shearer's Foods, Llc
100 Lincoln Way E

Massillon OH 44646
800 428-6843

Bridgeport
Belmont County

(G-1494)
JERRY HAROLDS DOORS UNLIMITED
Also Called: Doors Unlimited
415 Hall St (43912-1343)
PHONE.............................740 635-4949
Jerry Brocht, *Pr*
Harold Games, *VP*
EMP: 7 **EST:** 1987
SQ FT: 1,600
SALES (est): 497.86K **Privately Held**
Web: www.doorsunlimited.net
SIC: 5031 3446 5211 Doors, nec;
Architectural metalwork; Garage doors,
sale and installation

(G-1495)
RECON
54382 National Rd (43912-9804)
PHONE.............................740 609-3050
Ray Hieronymus, *Pr*
EMP: 10 **EST:** 2017
SALES (est): 9.91MM **Privately Held**
Web: www.reconoilfieldservices.com
SIC: 1389 Oil field services, nec

(G-1496)
SKYLINER
225 Main St (43912-1345)
PHONE.............................740 738-0874
Donald Rhodes, *Owner*
Robyn Rhodes, *Prin*
Witney Stewski, *Prin*
EMP: 8 **EST:** 2015
SALES (est): 144.3K **Privately Held**
SIC: 7299 2051 Party planning service;
Bakery: wholesale or wholesale/retail
combined

Brilliant
Jefferson County

(G-1497)
STEEL VALLEY TANK & WELDING
24 County Road 7e (43913-1079)
P.O. Box 8 (43913-0008)
PHONE.............................740 598-4994
Gary Kessler, *Owner*
EMP: 10 **EST:** 1987
SALES (est): 2.31MM **Privately Held**
SIC: 3443 Industrial vessels, tanks, and
containers

Bristolville
Trumbull County

(G-1498)
M B K INC
Also Called: King Bros Feed & Supply
1306 State Route 88 (44402-8743)
P.O. Box 240 (44402-0240)
PHONE.............................330 889-3451
Marlene King, *Pr*
Rex King, *
EMP: 14 **EST:** 1956
SQ FT: 4,200
SALES (est): 1.92MM **Privately Held**
SIC: 3273 5211 5261 5191 Ready-mixed
concrete; Lumber and other building
materials; Fertilizer; Feed

Broadview Heights
Cuyahoga County

(G-1499)
BENJAMIN P FORBES COMPANY
Also Called: Forbes Chocolate
800 Ken Mar Industrial Pkwy (44147-2922)
PHONE.............................440 838-4400
Keith Geringer, *Pr*
▲ **EMP:** 13 **EST:** 1913
SQ FT: 16,687
SALES (est): 6.54MM **Privately Held**
Web: www.forbeschocolate.com
SIC: 2066 Powdered cocoa

(G-1500)
CHICAGO PNEUMATIC TOOL CO LLC
9100 Market Pl Rear (44147-2861)
PHONE.............................704 883-3500
EMP: 19
Web: www.cp.com
SIC: 3546 Power-driven handtools
HQ: Chicago Pneumatic Tool Company Llc
1815 Clubhouse Dr
Rock Hill SC 29730
803 817-7100

(G-1501)
CLINICL OTCMS MNGMNT SYST LLC
Also Called: Coms Interactive
9200 S Hills Blvd Ste 200 (44147-3520)
PHONE.............................330 650-9900
Edward J Tromczynski, *CEO*
Terry Sullivan, *CMO*
Bill Stuart, *CFO*
EMP: 59 **EST:** 2009
SQ FT: 1,400
SALES (est): 2.45MM
SALES (corp-wide): 77.37MM **Privately
Held**
SIC: 7372 Business oriented computer
software
HQ: Pointclickcare Technologies Inc
5570 Explorer Dr
Mississauga ON L4W 0
905 858-8885

(G-1502)
EVERON LLC
9200 Market Pl (44147-2863)
PHONE.............................440 397-4428
EMP: 27
SALES (corp-wide): 1.5B **Privately Held**
Web: www.everonsolutions.com
SIC: 3699 Security devices
HQ: Everon, Llc
1501 W Yamato Rd
Boca Raton FL 33431
844 538-3766

(G-1503)
KEBAN INDUSTRIES INC
Also Called: Stefan Restoration
1263 Royalwood Rd (44147-1728)
PHONE.............................216 446-0159
Ken Stefan, *Prin*
EMP: 7 **EST:** 1997
SALES (est): 719.06K **Privately Held**
SIC: 3599 Custom machinery

(G-1504)
KONECRANES INC
Also Called: Crane Pro Services
331 Treeworth Blvd (44147-2985)
PHONE.............................440 461-8400
Denise Collins, *Admn*
EMP: 10
Web: www.konecranes.com

SIC: 3536 7389 Hoists, cranes, and
monorails; Crane and aerial lift service
HQ: Konecranes, Inc.
4401 Gateway Blvd
Springfield OH 45502

(G-1505)
MOREL LANDSCAPING LLC
9396 Broadview Rd (44147-2306)
P.O. Box 41420 (44141-0420)
PHONE.............................216 551-4395
EMP: 11 **EST:** 2012
SQ FT: 9,000
SALES (est): 2.74MM **Privately Held**
Web: www.morellandscaping.com
SIC: 1771 0783 3645 0781 Patio
construction, concrete; Planting services,
ornamental bush; Garden, patio, walkway
and yard lighting fixtures: electric;
Landscape services

(G-1506)
NATIONAL POLISHING SYSTEMS INC
Also Called: NPS
9299 Market Pl (44147-2866)
PHONE.............................330 659-6547
Robert Tetmayer, *Pr*
EMP: 28 **EST:** 2007
SALES (est): 4.75MM **Privately Held**
Web: www.nationalpolishing.com
SIC: 3471 Cleaning, polishing, and finishing

(G-1507)
NELSON LABS FAIRFIELD INC
9100 S Hills Blvd (44147-3518)
PHONE.............................973 227-6882
Daniel L Prince, *Pr*
EMP: 50 **EST:** 1970
SALES (est): 2.48MM
SALES (corp-wide): 1.1B **Publicly Held**
Web: www.nelsonlabs.com
SIC: 3841 8734 Diagnostic apparatus,
medical; Testing laboratories
PA: Sotera Health Company
9100 S Hills Blvd Ste 300
Broadview Heights OH 44147
440 262-1410

(G-1508)
NRKA CORP
Also Called: Fastsigns
1100 W Royalton Rd Ste A (44147-3947)
PHONE.............................440 817-0700
Bob Bottomley, *Prin*
EMP: 6 **EST:** 2017
SALES (est): 265.71K **Privately Held**
Web: www.fastsigns.com
SIC: 3993 Signs and advertising specialties

(G-1509)
OHIO MACHINERY CO (PA)
Also Called: Caterpillar Authorized Dealer
3993 E Royalton Rd (44147-2898)
PHONE.............................440 526-6200
Ken Taylor, *Pr*
Paul Liesem, *
Kelly Love, *
Eric W Emch, *
David J Blocksom, *
◆ **EMP:** 160 **EST:** 1946
SQ FT: 92,000
SALES (est): 185.86MM
SALES (corp-wide): 185.86MM **Privately
Held**
Web: www.ohiocat.com
SIC: 7513 6159 7699 5082 Truck rental,
without drivers; Machinery and equipment
finance leasing; Aircraft and heavy
equipment repair services; General
construction machinery and equipment

(G-1510)
UFO BIKES LLC
9930 Hidden Hollow Trl (44147-4504)
PHONE.............................724 986-1417
Timothy Betts, *Managing Member*
EMP: 6 **EST:** 2018
SALES (est): 1.1MM **Privately Held**
SIC: 3751 Motorcycles, bicycles and parts

Brook Park
Cuyahoga County

(G-1511)
CERAMIC HOLDINGS INC (DH)
Also Called: Cetek
20600 Sheldon Rd (44142-1312)
PHONE.............................216 362-3900
Derek Scott, *Pr*
Kathlene Stevens, *
◆ **EMP:** 120 **EST:** 1981
SALES (est): 23.7MM **Privately Held**
Web: www.fosbel.com
SIC: 7629 7692 Electrical repair shops;
Welding repair
HQ: Fosbel Holding, Inc.
20600 Sheldon Rd
Cleveland OH 44142

(G-1512)
DIVERSIFIED MCH COMPONENTS LLC
6346 Eastland Rd (44142-1302)
PHONE.............................440 942-5701
Gregory J O'brien, *Managing Member*
EMP: 18 **EST:** 2005
SALES (est): 3.76MM **Privately Held**
Web: www.dmcparts.net
SIC: 3599 Machine shop, jobbing and repair

(G-1513)
H&M MTAL STAMPING ASSEMBLY INC
5325 W 140th St (44142-1759)
PHONE.............................216 898-9030
Kathryn Mabin, *Pr*
EMP: 11 **EST:** 2008
SALES (est): 3.96MM **Privately Held**
Web: www.hm-metalstamping.com
SIC: 3469 Stamping metal for the trade

Brookfield
Trumbull County

(G-1514)
ENREVO PYRO LLC
6874 Strimbu Dr (44403-9526)
PHONE.............................203 517-5002
Philip Smith, *CEO*
EMP: 6 **EST:** 2012
SQ FT: 15,000
SALES (est): 636.42K **Privately Held**
SIC: 1311 2911 Coal pyrolysis; Fractionation
products of crude petroleum, hydrocarbons,
nec

(G-1515)
INDUSTRIAL TANK & CONTAINMENT
411 State Route 7 Se Ste 3 (44403-9555)
P.O. Box 267 (44403-0267)
PHONE.............................330 448-4876
Raymond Graff, *Pr*
EMP: 10 **EST:** 2001
SQ FT: 10,000
SALES (est): 810.56K **Privately Held**
Web: www.apitankrepair.com
SIC: 3443 Fabricated plate work (boiler shop)

▲ = Import ▼ = Export
◆ = Import/Export

(G-1516)
IPSCO TUBULARS INC
Also Called: IPSCO TUBULARS, INC.
6880 Parkway Dr (44403-9797)
PHONE...............................330 448-6772
EMP: 61
Web: www.tenaris.com
SIC: 3498 Fabricated pipe and fittings
HQ: Ipsco Tubulars Inc.
 2200 West Loop S Ste 800
 Houston TX 77027

(G-1517)
PANELMATIC BLDG SOLUTIONS INC
6882 Parkway Dr (44403-9797)
PHONE...............................330 619-5235
Richard Leach, *Prin*
Sean Fightmaster, *
Dan Vodhanel, *
EMP: 30 **EST:** 2019
SALES (est): 23.14MM
SALES (corp-wide): 56.9MM **Privately Held**
Web: www.panelmatic.com
SIC: 3613 Control panels, electric
PA: Panelmatic, Inc.
 6806 Willowbrook Park
 Houston TX 77066
 888 757-1957

(G-1518)
SILCOR OILFIELD SERVICES INC
6874 Strimbu Dr (44403-9526)
PHONE...............................330 448-8500
Terri D Presco, *Prin*
EMP: 8 **EST:** 1992
SALES (est): 1.36MM **Privately Held**
SIC: 1382 Oil and gas exploration services

Brooklyn
Cuyahoga County

(G-1519)
AREWAY ACQUISITION INC
8525 Clinton Rd (44144-1014)
PHONE...............................216 651-9022
John S Hadgis, *Pr*
John Hadgis, *
EMP: 99 **EST:** 2010
SQ FT: 100,000
SALES (est): 4.22MM **Privately Held**
SIC: 3471 Polishing, metals or formed products

(G-1520)
AREWAY LLC
8525 Clinton Rd (44144-1014)
PHONE...............................216 651-9022
▲ **EMP:** 99 **EST:** 1967
SALES (est): 5.06MM **Privately Held**
SIC: 3714 3541 Motor vehicle engines and parts; Buffing and polishing machines

(G-1521)
ENESPRO PPE ✪
10601 Memphis Ave (44144-2053)
PHONE...............................800 553-0672
EMP: 14 **EST:** 2023
SALES (est): 893.85K **Privately Held**
Web: www.enesproppe.com
SIC: 3699 Electrical equipment and supplies, nec

(G-1522)
HMI INDUSTRIES INC (PA)
Also Called: Health-Mor
1 American Rd Ste 1250 (44144-2355)
PHONE...............................440 846-7800
Daniel Duggan, *CEO*

Timothy Duggan, *VP*
Sorin Fulea, *Treas*
Ken Skoczen, *VP*
◆ **EMP:** 50 **EST:** 1928
SQ FT: 73,000
SALES (est): 9.54MM
SALES (corp-wide): 9.54MM **Privately Held**
Web: www.filterqueen.com
SIC: 3634 Air purifiers, portable

(G-1523)
MMI TEXTILES INC (PA)
Also Called: Ndw Textiles
1 American Rd Ste 950 (44144-2356)
PHONE...............................440 899-8050
Amy Hammond, *CEO*
Nick Rivera, *Pr*
Kathleen Stevens, *CFO*
▲ **EMP:** 7 **EST:** 2000
SQ FT: 5,000
SALES (est): 9.67MM **Privately Held**
Web: www.mmitextiles.com
SIC: 2211 2221 2262 5131 Duck, cotton; Manmade and synthetic broadwoven fabrics ; Chemical coating or treating of manmade broadwoven fabrics; Broadwoven fabrics

(G-1524)
MPC PLATING INC
9921 Clinton Rd (44144-1035)
PHONE...............................216 881-7220
EMP: 7 **EST:** 2022
SALES (est): 453.27K **Privately Held**
Web: www.mpcplating.com
SIC: 3471 Electroplating of metals or formed products

(G-1525)
RHINOSYSTEMS INC
Also Called: Navage
1 American Rd Ste 1100 (44144-2357)
PHONE...............................216 351-6262
EMP: 10 **EST:** 2007
SQ FT: 9,000
SALES (est): 965.08K **Privately Held**
Web: www.navage.com
SIC: 3841 Inhalation therapy equipment

(G-1526)
YOURWAY COATINGS LLC
8617 Clinton Rd (44144-1016)
PHONE...............................216 651-9022
John S Hadgis, *Managing Member*
EMP: 17 **EST:** 2018
SALES (est): 713.44K **Privately Held**
SIC: 3471 Finishing, metals or formed products

Brooklyn Heights
Cuyahoga County

(G-1527)
APPLIED MATERIALS FINSHG LTD
1040 Valley Belt Rd (44131-1433)
PHONE...............................330 336-5645
Faith Ortiz, *Prin*
EMP: 25 **EST:** 2012
SALES (est): 1.3MM **Privately Held**
SIC: 3341 Secondary nonferrous metals

(G-1528)
APPLIED METALS TECH LTD
1040 Valley Belt Rd (44131-1433)
PHONE...............................216 741-3236
Lisa Virost, *Pr*
EMP: 47 **EST:** 2001
SQ FT: 30,000
SALES (est): 6.34MM **Privately Held**

Web: www.amtcleveland.com
SIC: 3471 Finishing, metals or formed products

(G-1529)
BRILLIANT ELECTRIC SIGN CO LTD
4811 Van Epps Rd (44131-1082)
PHONE...............................216 741-3800
James R Groh, *Managing Member*
EMP: 55 **EST:** 1929
SQ FT: 55,000
SALES (est): 5.13MM **Privately Held**
Web: www.brilliantsign.com
SIC: 3993 1799 Electric signs; Sign installation and maintenance

(G-1530)
CI DISPOSITION CO
1000 Valley Belt Rd (44131-1433)
PHONE...............................216 587-5200
Gary Tarnowski, *VP*
EMP: 12 **EST:** 1952
SQ FT: 56,000
SALES (est): 2.55MM **Privately Held**
SIC: 3699 5085 Linear accelerators; Industrial supplies

(G-1531)
GRAFTECH INTERNATIONAL LTD (PA)
Also Called: GRAFTECH INTERNATIONAL
982 Keynote Cir Ste 6 (44131-1873)
PHONE...............................216 676-2000
Timothy K Flanagan, *Pr*
Henry R Keizer, *Ch Bd*
Jeremy S Halford, *Ex VP*
Gina K Gunning, *CLO*
Inigo Perez Ortiz, *Sr VP*
EMP: 91 **EST:** 1886
SALES (est): 538.78MM **Publicly Held**
Web: graftech2022cr.q4web.com
SIC: 3624 Carbon and graphite products

(G-1532)
GRAFTECH INTL HOLDINGS INC (HQ)
Also Called: UCAR Carbon
982 Keynote Cir Ste 6 (44131-1873)
PHONE...............................216 676-2000
David Rintaul, *CEO*
◆ **EMP:** 197 **EST:** 1988
SQ FT: 10,000
SALES (est): 35.13MM **Publicly Held**
Web: graftech2022cr.q4web.com
SIC: 3624 Electrodes, thermal and electrolytic uses: carbon, graphite
PA: Graftech International Ltd.
 982 Keynote Cir
 Brooklyn Heights OH 44131

(G-1533)
J & L BODY INC
4848 Van Epps Rd (44131-1016)
PHONE...............................216 661-2323
Mike Litteria, *Pr*
Rosemary Nelson, *Sec*
Robert Daley, *VP*
EMP: 10 **EST:** 1963
SQ FT: 16,000
SALES (est): 785.03K **Privately Held**
Web: www.jlbody.com
SIC: 3715 7549 7539 Truck trailers; Trailer maintenance; Trailer repair

(G-1534)
KWEEN AND CO
994 Valley Belt Rd (44131-1446)
PHONE...............................440 724-4342
Alexandra Bonar, *CEO*
Alexandra Kathryn Bonar, *CEO*

EMP: 15 **EST:** 2019
SALES (est): 528.49K **Privately Held**
Web: www.oat.haus
SIC: 2045 2043 Bread and bread type roll mixes: from purchased flour; Cereal breakfast foods

(G-1535)
MIDWEST PRECISION
1000 Valley Belt Rd (44131-1433)
PHONE...............................216 658-0058
EMP: 7 **EST:** 2014
SALES (est): 73.41K **Privately Held**
Web: www.midwestllc.com
SIC: 3599 Machine shop, jobbing and repair

(G-1536)
NORTH SHORE STRAPPING COMPANY (PA)
1400 Valley Belt Rd (44131-1441)
PHONE...............................216 661-5200
Bridget A Leneghan, *Pr*
Kevin Leneghan, *
David M Leneghan, *
▲ **EMP:** 50 **EST:** 1982
SQ FT: 225,000
SALES (est): 1.99MM
SALES (corp-wide): 1.99MM **Privately Held**
Web: www.northshorestrapping.com
SIC: 3081 3499 3312 2992 Unsupported plastics film and sheet; Strapping, metal; Wire products, steel or iron; Lubricating oils and greases

(G-1537)
R&D MARKETING GROUP INC
Also Called: Proforma Signature Solutions
4597 Van Epps Rd (44131-1009)
PHONE...............................216 398-9100
Dave Mader, *Pr*
Tony Zayas, *Dir*
EMP: 8 **EST:** 2011
SALES (est): 406.39K **Privately Held**
Web: www.proforma-solutions.com
SIC: 6794 2759 2752 Franchises, selling or licensing; Commercial printing, nec; Commercial printing, lithographic

(G-1538)
REL ENTERPRISES INC (DH)
Also Called: Diversified Air Systems
4760 Van Epps Rd (44131-1014)
PHONE...............................216 741-1700
Bob Lisi, *Pr*
Vincent Lisi, *Sec*
EMP: 20 **EST:** 1995
SQ FT: 20,000
SALES (est): 449.9K **Privately Held**
Web: www.diversifiedair.com
SIC: 5084 5075 7694 Compressors, except air conditioning; Compressors, air conditioning; Armature rewinding shops
HQ: Motion & Control Enterprises Llc
 100 Williams Dr
 Zelienople PA 16063
 724 452-6000

(G-1539)
RS INDUSTRIES INC
1455 E Schaaf Rd (44131-1321)
PHONE...............................216 351-8200
Nicholas J Russo Senior, *Pr*
Nick Russo Junior, *CFO*
EMP: 9 **EST:** 1987
SALES (est): 2.24MM **Privately Held**
Web: www.rsind.com
SIC: 5046 3556 Commercial cooking and food service equipment; Food products machinery

---

(G-1540)
SIMS-LOHMAN INC
1500 Valley Belt Rd (44131-1450)
PHONE.................................440 799-8285
EMP: 61
SALES (corp-wide): 96.65MM **Privately Held**
Web: www.sims-lohman.com
SIC: 3281 Cut stone and stone products
PA: Sims-Lohman, Inc.
6325 Este Ave
Cincinnati OH 45232
513 651-3510

(G-1541)
TREK DIAGNOSTICS INC
982 Keynote Cir (44131-1872)
PHONE.................................440 808-0000
EMP: 10 EST: 2017
SALES (est): 2.64MM **Privately Held**
SIC: 3826 Analytical instruments

(G-1542)
TRIONETICS INC
4924 Schaaf Ln (44131-1008)
PHONE.................................216 812-3570
Colleen Maitino, *CEO*
Phillip Maitino, *Pr*
Matthew Maitino, *Sec*
Jared Maitino, *Treas*
Sheryl Maitino, *Prin*
EMP: 14 EST: 1989
SQ FT: 2,100
SALES (est): 4.46MM **Privately Held**
Web: www.trionetics.com
SIC: 3589 Water treatment equipment,
industrial

Brookpark
Cuyahoga County

(G-1543)
AMERICAN SOLVING INC
6519 Eastland Rd Ste 5 (44142-1347)
PHONE.................................440 234-7373
Orley Aten, *Pr*
Julia Aten, *Treas*
▲ EMP: 6 EST: 1991
SQ FT: 5,000
SALES (est): 500.02K **Privately Held**
Web: www.solvinginc.com
SIC: 3535 5084 Pneumatic tube conveyor
systems; Materials handling machinery

(G-1544)
**AMPEX METAL PRODUCTS
COMPANY (PA)**
5581 W 164th St (44142-1513)
PHONE.................................216 267-9242
Andrew S Pastor, *Pr*
Robert Pastor, *Product Vice President**
EMP: 55 EST: 1960
SQ FT: 24,000
SALES (est): 4.96MM
SALES (corp-wide): 4.96MM **Privately
Held**
Web: www.ampexmetal.com
SIC: 3469 3544 3452 3429 Stamping metal
for the trade; Special dies, tools, jigs, and
fixtures; Bolts, nuts, rivets, and washers;
Hardware, nec

(G-1545)
CRITERION TOOL & DIE INC
Also Called: Criterion Instrument
5349 W 161st St (44142-1609)
PHONE.................................216 267-1733
Tanya Disalvo, *Pr*
Dennis M Ondercin, *

Theodore D Ward, *
EMP: 40 EST: 1953
SQ FT: 20,000
SALES (est): 3.89MM **Privately Held**
Web: www.criteriontool.com
SIC: 3599 3544 3541 Machine shop, jobbing
and repair; Special dies, tools, jigs, and
fixtures; Machine tools, metal cutting type

(G-1546)
CUSTOM FLOATERS LLC
6519 Eastland Rd Ste 101 (44142-1347)
PHONE.................................216 536-8979
EMP: 6 EST: 2017
SALES (est): 2.41MM **Privately Held**
Web: www.customfloaters.com
SIC: 3714 Motor vehicle parts and
accessories

(G-1547)
**CUYAHOGA MACHINE COMPANY
LLC**
5250 W 137th St (44142-1828)
PHONE.................................216 267-3560
Irene Bogdan, *Managing Member*
Nona Betz, *Sec*
EMP: 19 EST: 2013
SALES (est): 1.26MM **Privately Held**
Web: www.cuyahogamachine.com
SIC: 7699 3599 Industrial machinery and
equipment repair; Machine shop, jobbing
and repair

(G-1548)
DD FOUNDRY INC (PA)
15583 Brookpark Rd (44142-1618)
PHONE.................................216 362-4100
David Dolata, *CEO*
Jerry Kovatch, *
Mary Miller, *Stockholder**
Sandra Catlett, *
David Zanto, *
▲ EMP: 12 EST: 1946
SQ FT: 80,000
SALES (est): 7.03MM
SALES (corp-wide): 7.03MM **Privately
Held**
SIC: 3364 3324 3369 3365 Nonferrous die-
castings except aluminum; Commercial
investment castings, ferrous; Nonferrous
foundries, nec; Aluminum foundries

(G-1549)
E L MUSTEE & SONS INC (PA)
5431 W 164th St (44142-1586)
PHONE.................................216 267-3100
Kevin Mustee, *Pr*
◆ EMP: 98 EST: 1932
SQ FT: 140,000
SALES (est): 8.61MM
SALES (corp-wide): 8.61MM **Privately
Held**
Web: www.mustee.com
SIC: 3088 Tubs (bath, shower, and laundry),
plastics

(G-1550)
FORD MOTOR COMPANY
Also Called: Ford
17601 Brookpark Rd (44142-1518)
P.O. Box 9900 (44142)
PHONE.................................216 676-7918
Timothy M Duperron, *Brnch Mgr*
EMP: 101
SQ FT: 2,320,000
SALES (corp-wide): 184.99B **Publicly
Held**
Web: www.ford.com
SIC: 3714 3321 Motor vehicle parts and
accessories; Gray and ductile iron foundries
PA: Ford Motor Company

1 American Rd
Dearborn MI 48126
313 322-3000

(G-1551)
GREENKOTE USA INC
6435 Eastland Rd (44142-1305)
PHONE.................................440 243-2865
Mark Gore, *Dir*
James Thomson, *Sec*
▲ EMP: 8 EST: 2008
SALES (est): 1.34MM **Privately Held**
Web: www.greenkote.com
SIC: 3479 Coating of metals and formed
products

(G-1552)
HONEYWELL INTERNATIONAL INC
Also Called: Honeywell
2100 Apollo Dr (44142-4103)
PHONE.................................216 459-6048
Dan Stankey, *CFO*
EMP: 18
SALES (corp-wide): 38.5B **Publicly Held**
Web: www.honeywell.com
SIC: 3724 Turbines, aircraft type
PA: Honeywell International Inc.
855 S Mint St
Charlotte NC 28202
704 627-6200

(G-1553)
IVOSTUD LLC
6430 Eastland Rd Ste C (44142-1340)
PHONE.................................440 925-4227
Mike Quinn, *CEO*
EMP: 7 EST: 2018
SALES (est): 5.08MM
SALES (corp-wide): 408.18K **Privately
Held**
Web: www.ivostud.com
SIC: 3452 3548 Bolts, nuts, rivets, and
washers; Electric welding equipment
HQ: Avistud Gmbh
Schutzenstr. 6-8
Breckerfeld
233 887-0990

(G-1554)
K-M-S INDUSTRIES INC
Also Called: K.M.S.
6519 Eastland Rd Ste 1 (44142-1347)
PHONE.................................440 243-6680
Gerald Korman, *Pr*
Richard Malone Junior, *VP*
Diane Malone, *Treas*
EMP: 6 EST: 1980
SQ FT: 25,000
SALES (est): 918.76K **Privately Held**
Web: www.kmsindustries.com
SIC: 3599 5531 7692 Machine shop, jobbing
and repair; Automotive parts; Welding repair

(G-1555)
LAKE ERIE GRAPHICS INC
5372 W 130th St (44142-1801)
PHONE.................................216 575-1333
James K Dietz, *Pr*
EMP: 30 EST: 1990
SQ FT: 25,000
SALES (est): 5.15MM **Privately Held**
Web: www.lakeeriegraphics.com
SIC: 3993 Signs and advertising specialties

(G-1556)
**NORTH COAST SEAL
INCORPORATED**
Also Called: Ncs
5163 W 137th St (44142-1809)
PHONE.................................216 898-5000
Thomas Sasura, *Pr*

Edward D Montgomery, *Pr*
▲ EMP: 10 EST: 1985
SQ FT: 14,000
SALES (est): 3.14MM **Privately Held**
Web: www.northcoastseal.com
SIC: 5085 3069 3053 3089 Gaskets and
seals; Sponge rubber and sponge rubber
products; Gaskets; packing and sealing
devices; Extruded finished plastics
products, nec

(G-1557)
RELIACHECK MANUFACTURING INC
Also Called: Ecil Met TEC
6550 Eastland Rd (44142-1307)
P.O. Box 303 (44012-0303)
PHONE.................................440 933-6162
Luis Antonio Srerie, *Pr*
David Updegraff, *
▲ EMP: 26 EST: 2002
SALES (est): 4.82MM
SALES (corp-wide): 2.41B **Privately Held**
SIC: 3317 Seamless pipes and tubes
PA: Vesuvius Plc
165 Fleet Street
London EC4A
207 822-0000

(G-1558)
ROLL-IN SAW INC
15851 Commerce Park Dr (44142-2020)
PHONE.................................216 459-9001
Donald Borman, *Pr*
Marcus Borman, *VP*
▼ EMP: 10 EST: 1940
SQ FT: 15,000
SALES (est): 2.38MM **Privately Held**
Web: www.rollinsaw.com
SIC: 3541 Sawing and cutoff machines
(metalworking machinery)

(G-1559)
THERMAL SOLUTIONS MFG INC
15600 Commerce Park Dr (44142-2015)
PHONE.................................800 776-4225
EMP: 8 EST: 2013
SALES (est): 1.72MM **Privately Held**
Web: www.thermalsolutionsmfg.com
SIC: 3714 Radiators and radiator shells and
cores, motor vehicle

(G-1560)
WELDERS SUPPLY INC
5575 Engle Rd (44142-1533)
PHONE.................................216 267-4470
EMP: 45
SALES (corp-wide): 6.29MM **Privately
Held**
SIC: 7692 5999 5984 Welding repair;
Welding supplies; Propane gas, bottled
HQ: Welders Supply Inc
2020 Train Ave
Cleveland OH 44113
216 241-1696

Brookville
Montgomery County

(G-1561)
ADMARK PRINTING INC
310 Sycamore St (45309-1731)
PHONE.................................937 833-5111
Patrick J Bruchs, *Pr*
EMP: 6 EST: 1980
SQ FT: 15,000
SALES (est): 194.26K **Privately Held**
SIC: 2752 Offset printing

(G-1562)
ANTIQUE AUTO SHEET METAL INC
718 Albert Rd (45309-9202)
PHONE...............................937 833-4422
Raymond Gollahon, *Pr*
Donna Gollahon, *
EMP: 10 **EST:** 1972
SQ FT: 21,000
SALES (est): 2.01MM **Privately Held**
Web: www.brookvilleroadster.com
SIC: 3711 3444 3465 Motor vehicles and car
bodies; Sheet metalwork; Body parts,
automobile: stamped metal

(G-1563)
BROOKVILLE ROADSTER INC
718 Albert Rd (45309-9202)
PHONE...............................937 833-4605
Ray Gollahon, *Pr*
EMP: 9 **EST:** 1986
SALES (est): 914.23K **Privately Held**
Web: www.brookvilleroadster.com
SIC: 3711 5013 Automobile assembly,
including specialty automobiles; Automotive
supplies and parts

(G-1564)
CYCLE ELECTRIC INC
8734 Dayton Greenville Pike (45309-9232)
P.O. Box 81 (45322-0081)
PHONE...............................937 884-7300
Karl Fahringer, *Pr*
Roxanne Fahringer, *VP*
EMP: 10 **EST:** 1982
SQ FT: 8,000
SALES (est): 953.64K **Privately Held**
Web: www.cycleelectricinc.com
SIC: 3694 Generators, automotive and
aircraft

(G-1565)
D M TOOL & PLASTICS INC
11150 Baltimore Phillipsburg Rd
(45309-8687)
PHONE...............................937 962-4140
Pat Meyer, *Mgr*
EMP: 11
SALES (corp-wide): 9.47MM **Privately Held**
SIC: 3089 3599 Injection molding of plastics;
Machine shop, jobbing and repair
PA: D M Tool & Plastics, Inc.
4140 Us Route 40 E
Lewisburg OH 45338
937 962-4140

(G-1566)
DIGISOFT SYSTEMS CORPORATION
4520 Clayton Rd (45309-9332)
PHONE...............................937 833-5016
Gary E Brazier, *Pr*
Betty L Brazier, *VP*
Christopher F Cowan, *Sec*
EMP: 7 **EST:** 1986
SQ FT: 600
SALES (est): 325.06K **Privately Held**
SIC: 7372 Business oriented computer
software

(G-1567)
**FIBRE GLAST DVLPMENTS CORP
LLC**
385 Carr Dr (45309-1921)
PHONE...............................937 833-5200
Mark Knight, *Managing Member*
EMP: 15 **EST:** 2021
SALES (est): 3.05MM **Privately Held**
Web: www.fibreglast.com
SIC: 2821 Plastics materials and resins

(G-1568)
FLOW DRY TECHNOLOGY INC (HQ)
379 Albert Rd (45309-9247)
P.O. Box 190 (45309-0190)
PHONE...............................937 833-2161
Douglas Leconey, *Pr*
▲ **EMP:** 111 **EST:** 1946
SQ FT: 65,000
SALES (est): 20.55MM
SALES (corp-wide): 1.05B **Privately Held**
Web: www.flowdry.com
SIC: 3053 2834 Gasket materials; Druggists'
preparations (pharmaceuticals)
PA: Filtration Group Corporation
1 Tower Ln
Oakbrook Terrace IL 60181
630 968-1730

(G-1569)
FTD INVESTMENTS LLC
379 Albert Rd (45309-9247)
PHONE...............................937 833-2161
Doug Le, *Prin*
EMP: 880 **EST:** 2006
SQ FT: 65,000
SALES (est): 1.72MM **Privately Held**
Web: www.flowdry.com
SIC: 3714 2834 Air conditioner parts, motor
vehicle; Druggists' preparations
(pharmaceuticals)
PA: Blackstreet Capital Management, Llc
7250 Woodmont Ave Ste 210
Bethesda MD 20814

(G-1570)
GREEN TOKAI CO LTD (DH)
Also Called: GTC
55 Robert Wright Dr (45309-1931)
PHONE...............................937 833-5444
Daniel Bowers, *Pr*
◆ **EMP:** 525 **EST:** 1987
SQ FT: 246,000
SALES (est): 48.26MM **Privately Held**
Web: www.greentokai.com
SIC: 3714 3069 Motor vehicle body
components and frame; Rubber automotive
products
HQ: Tokai Kogyo Co.,Ltd.
4-1, Naganecho
Obu AIC 474-0

(G-1571)
IMAGE PAVEMENT MAINTENANCE
425 Carr Dr (45309-1935)
P.O. Box 157 (45309-0157)
PHONE...............................937 833-9200
Michael Gartrell, *Pr*
EMP: 6 **EST:** 1992
SALES (est): 1.08MM **Privately Held**
Web: www.imagepavement.com
SIC: 1611 2951 1799 1771 Surfacing and
paving; Asphalt paving mixtures and blocks
; Parking lot maintenance; Driveway
contractor

(G-1572)
KUHNS MOLD & TOOL CO INC
Also Called: K & B Molded Products
9360 National Rd (45309-9675)
PHONE...............................937 833-2178
EMP: 75 **EST:** 1964
SALES (est): 9.47MM **Privately Held**
Web: www.kandbmoldedproducts.com
SIC: 3089 3544 Injection molded finished
plastics products, nec; Industrial molds

(G-1573)
MCGREGOR & ASSOCIATES INC
Also Called: McGregor Surmount
365 Carr Dr (45309-1921)
PHONE...............................937 629-4346
Larry Mcgregor, *Pr*
Beverly Mcgregor, *Sec*
Don Wurst, *
▲ **EMP:** 120 **EST:** 1971
SQ FT: 16,000
SALES (est): 15.97MM **Privately Held**
Web: www.mcgregor-surmount.com
SIC: 3672 Printed circuit boards

(G-1574)
NORGREN LLC
Also Called: IMI Precision
325 Carr Dr (45309-1929)
PHONE...............................937 833-4033
Michael Vinski, *Brnch Mgr*
EMP: 147
SALES (corp-wide): 2.8B **Privately Held**
Web: www.norgren.com
SIC: 3625 Actuators, industrial
HQ: Norgren Llc
7979 E Tufts Ave Ste 1150
Denver CO 80237
303 794-5000

(G-1575)
R & J TOOL INC
10550 Upper Lewisburg Salem Rd
(45309-8804)
P.O. Box 118 (45309-0118)
PHONE...............................937 833-3200
Richard Rohrer, *Pr*
Marilyn K Rohrer, *VP*
EMP: 10 **EST:** 1974
SQ FT: 5,000
SALES (est): 901.25K **Privately Held**
Web: www.rjtoolinc.com
SIC: 3599 Machine shop, jobbing and repair

(G-1576)
SOELTER CORPORATION
385 Carr Dr (45309-1921)
PHONE...............................800 838-8984
Marilyn Soelter, *Pr*
▼ **EMP:** 17 **EST:** 1955
SALES (est): 6.33MM **Privately Held**
Web: www.fibreglast.com
SIC: 2821 Plastics materials and resins

Brunswick
Medina County

(G-1577)
696 LEDGEROCK CIR
2950 Westway Dr (44212-5665)
PHONE...............................330 289-0996
Allen Higgins, *Prin*
EMP: 6 **EST:** 2010
SALES (est): 584.98K **Privately Held**
SIC: 3571 Minicomputers

(G-1578)
A G INDUSTRIES INC
2963 Interstate Pkwy (44212-4327)
PHONE...............................330 220-0050
Albert Gawel, *Pr*
EMP: 10 **EST:** 1991
SQ FT: 4,000
SALES (est): 922.81K **Privately Held**
Web: www.agind.co
SIC: 3544 Special dies, tools, jigs, and
fixtures

(G-1579)
ALTERNATIVE SURFACE GRINDING
Also Called: Ring Masters
1093 Industrial Pkwy N (44212-4319)
PHONE...............................330 273-3443
Kent Shutey, *Pr*
EMP: 6 **EST:** 2010
SALES (est): 1.4MM **Privately Held**
Web: www.alternativesurfacegrind.com
SIC: 3599 Machine shop, jobbing and repair

(G-1580)
AMERICAN CUBE MOLD INC
Also Called: Acm
1636 W 130th St (44212-2322)
PHONE...............................330 558-0044
Frank J Kichurchak, *Pr*
EMP: 6 **EST:** 1986
SQ FT: 3,800
SALES (est): 2.33MM **Privately Held**
Web: www.americancubemold.com
SIC: 3544 3829 Industrial molds; Testing
equipment: abrasion, shearing strength, etc.

(G-1581)
BEST PROCESS SOLUTIONS INC
1071 Industrial Pkwy N (44212-4319)
PHONE...............................330 220-1440
Mike Desalvo, *Pr*
EMP: 30 **EST:** 2012
SALES (est): 7.52MM **Privately Held**
Web: www.bpsvibes.com
SIC: 3441 Fabricated structural metal

(G-1582)
**CHEMICAL METHODS
INCORPORATED**
2853 Westway Dr # A (44212-5657)
PHONE...............................216 476-8400
Daniel E Richards, *Pr*
EMP: 30 **EST:** 1971
SALES (est): 2.41MM **Privately Held**
Web: www.chemicalmethods.com
SIC: 2842 3471 2992 2899 Cleaning or
polishing preparations, nec; Plating and
polishing; Lubricating oils and greases;
Chemical preparations, nec

(G-1583)
COLONY MACHINE & TOOL INC
1300 Industrial Pkwy N (44212-2346)
P.O. Box 126 (44212-0126)
PHONE...............................330 225-3410
Roger Reich, *Pr*
Mark Borcoman, *VP*
EMP: 8 **EST:** 1967
SQ FT: 20,000
SALES (est): 841.5K **Privately Held**
Web: www.colonymachine.com
SIC: 3751 Motorcycle accessories

(G-1584)
**COLUMBIA CHEMICAL
CORPORATION**
1000 Western Dr (44212-4330)
PHONE...............................330 225-3200
Brett Larick, *Pr*
D J Hudak, *Prin*
William E Rosenberg, *Prin*
Herbert H Geduld, *Prin*
◆ **EMP:** 22 **EST:** 1975
SALES (est): 4.63MM **Privately Held**
Web: www.columbiachemical.com
SIC: 2819 Zinc chloride

(G-1585)
COMPONENT MFG & DESIGN INC
3121 Interstate Pkwy (44212-4329)
P.O. Box 845 (44212-0845)
PHONE...............................330 225-8080
Edward C Crist, *Pr*
EMP: 6 **EST:** 1976
SQ FT: 12,000
SALES (est): 1.76MM **Privately Held**
Web: www.cmd-tip.com
SIC: 3599 Machine shop, jobbing and repair

GEOGRAPHIC

(G-1586)
CONTROLLED ACCESS INC
Also Called: Sentronic
1535 Industrial Pkwy (44212-2359)
P.O. Box 430 (44233)
PHONE................................330 273-6185
Michelle Sherba, *Pr*
Mike Sherba, *Stockholder*
Sylvia Hayes, *Treas*
▲ **EMP: 16 EST:** 1984
SALES (est): 2.28MM **Privately Held**
Web: www.controlledaccess.com
SIC: 3829 Turnstiles, equipped with counting
mechanisms

(G-1587)
D C SYSTEMS INC
1251 Industrial Pkwy N (44212-2341)
PHONE................................330 273-3030
Thomas E Schira, *Pr*
Katherine Schira, *Sec*
EMP: 10 EST: 1967
SQ FT: 22,600
SALES (est): 994.83K **Privately Held**
Web: www.associatedequip.com
SIC: 5063 3692 7699 3629 Batteries; Dry
cell batteries, single or multiple cell; Battery
service and repair; Battery chargers,
rectifying or nonrotating

(G-1588)
DESTINY MANUFACTURING INC
2974 Interstate Pkwy (44212-4323)
PHONE................................330 273-9000
Josef Schuessler, *Pr*
Reinhold Rock, *
Michael Schuessler, *
Bernard Karthan, *
◆ **EMP: 24 EST:** 1998
SQ FT: 100,000
SALES (est): 4.98MM **Privately Held**
Web: www.destinymfg.com
SIC: 3469 3399 Appliance parts, porcelain
enameled; Metal powders, pastes, and
flakes

(G-1589)
DIE-MENSION CORPORATION
3020 Nationwide Pkwy (44212-2360)
PHONE................................330 273-5872
Karen Thompson, *Pr*
Rick Thompson, *VP*
▼ **EMP: 12 EST:** 1985
SQ FT: 14,250
SALES (est): 854.45K **Privately Held**
Web: www.diemension.com
SIC: 3544 3469 Special dies and tools;
Metal stampings, nec

(G-1590)
FORMATECH INC
3024 Interstate Pkwy (44212-4324)
PHONE................................330 273-2800
Craig F Wahl, *Pr*
Carol Wahl, *Sec*
▲ **EMP: 20 EST:** 1985
SALES (est): 6.74MM **Privately Held**
Web: www.formatechexhibits.com
SIC: 2542 2541 Counters or counter display
cases, except wood; Counters or counter
display cases, wood

(G-1591)
FPC HOLDINGS INC
Also Called: Cnc Machine Shop
2867 Nationwide Pkwy (44212-2363)
PHONE................................216 362-7888
Christopher Fredericks, *CEO*
David Tenny, *
Joe Tako, *
Diane Bokar, *

EMP: 36 EST: 2000
SALES (est): 8.28MM **Privately Held**
Web: www.firstarcnc.com
SIC: 3599 Machine shop, jobbing and repair

(G-1592)
FREMAR INDUSTRIES INC
2808 Westway Dr (44212-5656)
PHONE................................330 220-3700
Marcus Bauman, *CEO*
Donald Brandt, *
▼ **EMP: 22 EST:** 1982
SQ FT: 26,000
SALES (est): 2.4MM **Privately Held**
Web: www.fre-mar.com
SIC: 3544 Special dies and tools

(G-1593)
GALLEY PRINTING INC
Also Called: Galley Printing Company
2892 Westway Dr (44212-5656)
PHONE................................330 220-5577
Richard Stitch, *CEO*
Barbara Stitch, *
EMP: 25 EST: 1959
SALES (est): 4.35MM **Privately Held**
Web: www.galleyprinting.com
SIC: 2752 Offset printing

(G-1594)
GEM INSTRUMENT COMPANY INC
2832 Nationwide Pkwy (44212-2362)
P.O. Box 830 (44212-0830)
PHONE................................330 273-6117
Spiras Arfaras, *Pr*
Joan Arfaras, *VP*
EMP: 6 EST: 1937
SQ FT: 10,000
SALES (est): 940.58K **Privately Held**
Web: www.gem-instrument.com
SIC: 3823 3829 Digital displays of process
variables; Measuring and controlling
devices, nec

(G-1595)
GLOBAL SPECIALTIES INC
2950 Westway Dr Ste 110 (44212-5666)
PHONE................................800 338-0814
Clyde Kanz, *Prin*
EMP: 6 EST: 2004
SALES (est): 464.04K **Privately Held**
SIC: 3965 Fasteners

(G-1596)
GRIND-ALL CORPORATION
1113 Industrial Pkwy N (44212-2371)
PHONE................................330 220-1600
Henry Matousek Senior, *Pr*
Mary Matousek, *
EMP: 25 EST: 1974
SALES (est): 2.88MM **Privately Held**
Web: www.grindall.com
SIC: 3541 Grinding machines, metalworking

(G-1597)
ID IMAGES INC
1120 W 130th St (44212-2317)
PHONE................................330 220-7300
EMP: 21
SALES (est): 5.37MM **Privately Held**
Web: www.idimages.com
SIC: 3577 Bar code (magnetic ink) printers

(G-1598)
ID IMAGES LLC (PA)
1120 W 130th St (44212-2317)
PHONE................................330 220-7300
Jeff Fielkow, *CEO*
Rick Dodson, *
▲ **EMP: 65 EST:** 1995

SQ FT: 24,200
SALES (est): 39.4MM **Privately Held**
Web: www.idimages.com
SIC: 2672 Chemically treated papers, made
from purchased materials

(G-1599)
INTERNATIONAL MACHINING INC
2885 Nationwide Pkwy (44212-4314)
PHONE................................330 225-1963
John Strobel, *Pr*
Bruce Sherman, *
EMP: 40 EST: 1981
SQ FT: 26,000
SALES (est): 6.59MM **Privately Held**
Web: www.imimachining.com
SIC: 3599 Machine shop, jobbing and repair

(G-1600)
JET DI INC
1736 W 130th St Ste 200 (44212-6338)
PHONE................................330 607-7913
David Dempsey, *Pr*
EMP: 7 EST: 2013
SALES (est): 1.1MM **Privately Held**
Web: www.jet-di.com
SIC: 3544 8711 Special dies, tools, jigs, and
fixtures; Machine tool design

(G-1601)
L & R RACING INC
Also Called: Drr USA
1261 Industrial Pkwy N Ste 1a
(44212-4310)
P.O. Box 875 (44212-0875)
PHONE................................330 220-3102
Louis Allan, *CEO*
◆ **EMP: 20 EST:** 2000
SALES (est): 2.37MM **Privately Held**
Web: www.drrusa.com
SIC: 5012 5013 3799 Motorcycles;
Motorcycle parts; Recreational vehicles

(G-1602)
MURPHY TRACTOR & EQP CO INC
Also Called: John Deere Authorized Dealer
1550 Industrial Pkwy (44212-2349)
PHONE................................330 220-4999
Bob Cumberledge, *Svc Mgr*
EMP: 8
Web: www.murphytractor.com
SIC: 3531 5082 Construction machinery;
Construction and mining machinery
HQ: Murphy Tractor & Equipment Co., Inc.
5375 N Deere Rd
Park City KS 67219
855 246-9124

(G-1603)
NUFACTURING INC
2845 Center Rd (44212-2331)
PHONE................................330 814-5259
Jordan Adair, *Pr*
Jordan Adair, *Managing Member*
EMP: 24 EST: 2022
SALES (est): 936.84K **Privately Held**
Web: www.nufacturing.com
SIC: 2833 Vitamins, natural or synthetic:
bulk, uncompounded

(G-1604)
OPTICS INCORPORATED
2936 Westway Dr (44212-5658)
PHONE................................800 362-1337
Dale Springer Senior, *Pr*
Cheryl Springer, *Sec*
EMP: 22 EST: 1960
SQ FT: 10,000
SALES (est): 2.59MM **Privately Held**
Web: www.opticsinc.com

SIC: 3827 Optical instruments and lenses

(G-1605)
PHILPOTT RUBBER LLC (HQ)
Also Called: Philpott Rubber Company
1010 Industrial Pkwy N (44212-4318)
PHONE................................330 225-3344
David Ferrell, *CEO*
Mike Baach, *
Russell E Schabel, *
Gregory C Stafford, *
Jeffrey Rog, *
▲ **EMP: 28 EST:** 1889
SQ FT: 30,000
SALES (est): 7.25MM
SALES (corp-wide): 28.02MM **Privately
Held**
Web: www.philpottsolutions.com
SIC: 3069 Medical sundries, rubber
PA: Philpott Solutions Group Inc.
1010 Industrial Pkwy N
Brunswick OH 44212
330 225-3344

(G-1606)
POMACON INC
2996 Interstate Pkwy (44212-4323)
PHONE................................330 273-1576
Rodger Post, *Pr*
EMP: 15 EST: 1985
SQ FT: 14,000
SALES (est): 5.31MM **Privately Held**
Web: www.pomacon.com
SIC: 3535 5084 5999 Conveyors and
conveying equipment; Conveyor systems;
Alcoholic beverage making equipment and
supplies

(G-1607)
PRAGMATIC MFG LLC
2774 Nationwide Pkwy Unit 18
(44212-2357)
PHONE................................330 222-6051
EMP: 8 EST: 2019
SALES (est): 2.13MM **Privately Held**
Web: www.pragmaticmanufacturing.com
SIC: 3999 Manufacturing industries, nec

(G-1608)
PRISM POWDER COATINGS LTD
2890 Carquest Dr (44212-4352)
PHONE................................330 225-5626
Alex Asour, *Pr*
Livio Agnoletto, *
▲ **EMP: 35 EST:** 1990
SQ FT: 4,000
SALES (est): 4.5MM **Privately Held**
Web: www.prismpowder.com
SIC: 3479 Coating of metals and formed
products

(G-1609)
PROKLEAN SERVICES LLC (PA)
3041 Nationwide Pkwy (44212-2361)
P.O. Box 729 (44212-0729)
PHONE................................330 273-0122
EMP: 24 EST: 2016
SALES (est): 2.35MM
SALES (corp-wide): 2.35MM **Privately
Held**
Web: www.prokleanservices.com
SIC: 2899 Chemical preparations, nec

(G-1610)
QUAD FLUID DYNAMICS INC
2826 Westway Dr (44212-5656)
P.O. Box 429 (44212-0429)
PHONE................................330 220-3005
Kenneth H Oleksiak, *Pr*
Barbara Oleksiak, *VP*
David E Williams, *VP*

▲ = Import ▼ = Export
◆ = Import/Export

EMP: 10 EST: 1978
SQ FT: 10,000
SALES (est): 1.66MM **Privately Held**
Web: www.quadfluiddynamics.com
SIC: 5085 3594 7699 Valves and fittings;
  Fluid power pumps and motors; Hydraulic
  equipment repair

(G-1611)
REALEFLOW LLC
150 Pearl Rd (44212-1116)
PHONE...............................855 545-2095
EMP: 7 EST: 2007
SALES (est): 2.51MM **Privately Held**
Web: www.realeflow.com
SIC: 7372 Business oriented computer
  software

(G-1612)
ROCKSTEDT TOOL & DIE INC
2974 Interstate Pkwy (44212-4323)
PHONE...............................330 273-9000
Josef Schuessler, Pr
EMP: 6 EST: 1965
SQ FT: 100,000
SALES (est): 880.77K **Privately Held**
Web: www.rockstedtwireedm.com
SIC: 3544 Special dies and tools

(G-1613)
RONLEN INDUSTRIES INC
2809 Nationwide Pkwy (44212-2363)
PHONE...............................330 273-6468
Leonard Lutch, Pr
Ron Bryant, *
Greg Lutch, *
EMP: 26 EST: 1978
SQ FT: 25,000
SALES (est): 7.27MM **Privately Held**
Web: www.ronlen.com
SIC: 3469 3544 Stamping metal for the trade
  ; Special dies and tools

(G-1614)
SCHERBA INDUSTRIES INC
Also Called: Inflatable Images
2880 Interstate Pkwy (44212-4322)
PHONE...............................330 273-3200
Robert J Scherba, Pr
David M Scherba, *
▲ EMP: 100 EST: 1982
SQ FT: 63,000
SALES (est): 5.01MM **Privately Held**
Web: www.inflatableimages.com
SIC: 3081 3069 2394 Vinyl film and sheet;
  Balloons, advertising and toy: rubber;
  Canvas and related products

(G-1615)
SENECA LABEL INC
1120 W 130th St (44212-2317)
PHONE...............................440 237-1600
Michael Hoopingarner, Pr
John Hoopingarner, *
EMP: 35 EST: 1968
SALES (est): 4.79MM **Privately Held**
Web: www.senecalabel.com
SIC: 2759 Labels and seals: printing, nsk

(G-1616)
STANDOUT STICKERS INC
2991 Interstate Pkwy (44212-4327)
PHONE...............................877 449-7703
Jeffrey Nemecek, CEO
EMP: 6 EST: 2010
SALES (est): 923.02K **Privately Held**
Web: www.standoutstickers.com
SIC: 2759 Screen printing

(G-1617)
TECHNICAL TOOL & GAUGE INC
2914 Westway Dr (44212-5658)
PHONE...............................330 273-1778
Jeff Butcher, Owner
EMP: 11 EST: 1989
SALES (est): 1.55MM **Privately Held**
SIC: 3544 Special dies and tools

(G-1618)
TIGER CAT FURNITURE
294 Marks Rd (44212-1042)
PHONE...............................330 220-7232
Audrey F Bledsoe, Owner
EMP: 8 EST: 1999
SALES (est): 349.71K **Privately Held**
Web: www.tigercatsfurniture.com
SIC: 3999 Novelties, bric-a-brac, and hobby
  kits

(G-1619)
**TINNERMAN PALNUT ENGINEERED
PR**
1060 W 130th St (44212-2316)
PHONE...............................330 220-5100
Jim Finley, Prin
◆ EMP: 14 EST: 2011
SALES (est): 2.72MM **Privately Held**
SIC: 3452 Screws, metal

(G-1620)
TURF CARE SUPPLY LLC (PA)
Also Called: Allied Nutrients
50 Pearl Rd Ste 200 (44212-5703)
PHONE...............................877 220-1014
Mark Mangan, Pr
Michael Randall, *
▼ EMP: 64 EST: 1974
SQ FT: 5,000
SALES (est): 115.19MM **Privately Held**
Web: www.turfcaresupply.com
SIC: 2873 Nitrogenous fertilizers

(G-1621)
**UNITED MEDICAL SUPPLY
COMPANY**
2948 Nationwide Pkwy (44212-2364)
P.O. Box 862 (44212-0862)
PHONE...............................866 678-8633
Ted Walsh, CEO
Anthony Fidram, Pr
EMP: 18 EST: 2016
SALES (est): 7.64MM **Privately Held**
Web: www.unitedmedsupply.com
SIC: 3841 5047 Surgical and medical
  instruments; Hospital equipment and
  supplies, nec

(G-1622)
**VERSATILE AUTOMATION TECH
CORP**
2853 Westway Dr (44212-5657)
PHONE...............................330 220-2600
James Byrne, Pr
EMP: 6 EST: 2018
SALES (est): 248K **Privately Held**
SIC: 3569 5084 Robots, assembly line:
  industrial and commercial; Robots, industrial

(G-1623)
WALEST INCORPORATED
Also Called: Kol-Cap Manufacturing Co
306 Aynesly Way (44212-4610)
PHONE...............................216 362-8110
Mike Gorbulja, Pr
EMP: 8 EST: 1958
SALES (est): 932.21K **Privately Held**
SIC: 3544 3599 Special dies and tools;
  Machine shop, jobbing and repair

(G-1624)
WIFI-PLUS INC
2950 Westway Dr Ste 101 (44212-5666)
PHONE...............................330 273-3665
Allen Higgins Mg, Pt
Dennis Broderick, Pt
Jack Nilsson, Pt
EMP: 6 EST: 2003
SQ FT: 6,000
SALES (est): 267.98K **Privately Held**
Web: www.wifi-plus.com
SIC: 5063 3679 Antennas, receiving,
  satellite dishes; Antennas, receiving

Bryan
Williams County

(G-1625)
AIRMATE CO INC
16280 County Road D (43506-9552)
PHONE...............................419 636-3184
Carol Schreder Czech, Pr
Carol Schreder, *
Neil Oberlin, *
▲ EMP: 57 EST: 1946
SQ FT: 24,000
SALES (est): 5.16MM **Privately Held**
Web: www.airmateplasticfabrication.com
SIC: 3823 7311 Process control instruments;
  Advertising consultant

(G-1626)
**ALLIED MOULDED PRODUCTS INC
(PA)**
222 N Union St (43506-1450)
PHONE...............................419 636-4217
Aaron T Herman, Pr
◆ EMP: 234 EST: 1958
SQ FT: 110,000
SALES (est): 62MM
SALES (corp-wide): 62MM **Privately Held**
Web: www.alliedmoulded.com
SIC: 3089 3699 Injection molded finished
  plastics products, nec; Electrical equipment
  and supplies, nec

(G-1627)
ALTENLOH BRINCK & CO INC
2105 County Road 12c (43506-8301)
PHONE...............................419 636-6715
Brian Roth, Pr
D Kip Winzeler, *
▲ EMP: 135 EST: 1981
SQ FT: 200,000
SALES (est): 7.34MM
SALES (corp-wide): 341.65MM **Privately
Held**
Web: www.spax.us
SIC: 3452 Pins
HQ: Altenloh, Brinck & Co. Us, Inc.
  2105 Williams Co Rd 12c
  Bryan OH 43506

(G-1628)
**ALTENLOH BRINCK & CO US INC
(DH)**
Also Called: Trufast
2105 County Road 12c (43506-8301)
PHONE...............................419 636-6715
Brian Roth, Pr
Kip Winzeler, *
▲ EMP: 18 EST: 2005
SALES (est): 49.18MM
SALES (corp-wide): 341.65MM **Privately
Held**
Web: www.spax.us
SIC: 3452 Screws, metal

HQ: Abc Finanzierungs- Und Beteiligungs
  Gmbh
  Kolner Str. 71-77
  Ennepetal NW
  23337990

(G-1629)
ANDERSON & VREELAND INC
Also Called: Anderson Vreeland Midwest
15348 Us Highway 127 Ew (43506-9191)
P.O. Box 527 (43506-0527)
PHONE...............................419 636-5002
EMP: 80
SQ FT: 3,000
SALES (corp-wide): 41.02MM **Privately
Held**
Web: www.andersonvreeland.com
SIC: 5084 3555 3542 2796 Printing trades
  machinery, equipment, and supplies;
  Printing trades machinery; Machine tools,
  metal forming type; Platemaking services
PA: Anderson & Vreeland, Inc.
  8 Evans St
  Fairfield NJ 07004
  973 227-2270

(G-1630)
ARROW TRU-LINE INC
720 E Perry St (43506-2223)
P.O. Box 704 (43506-0704)
PHONE...............................419 636-7013
Curtis Anderson, Ch Bd
EMP: 8
SALES (corp-wide): 46.8MM **Privately
Held**
Web: www.arrowtruline.com
SIC: 3429 3469 3449 Builders' hardware;
  Metal stampings, nec; Miscellaneous
  metalwork
PA: Arrow Tru-Line, Inc.
  2211 S Defiance St
  Archbold OH 43502
  419 446-2785

(G-1631)
**BARD MANUFACTURING COMPANY
INC (PA)**
1914 Randolph Dr (43506-2253)
P.O. Box 607 (43506-0607)
PHONE...............................419 636-1194
Pam Bard Steel, Pr
Bill Steel, *
▼ EMP: 51 EST: 2006
SALES (est): 12.5MM **Privately Held**
Web: www.bardhvac.com
SIC: 3585 Air conditioning equipment,
  complete

(G-1632)
BRICKER PLATING INC
612 E Edgerton St (43506-1408)
PHONE...............................419 636-1990
Tim Bricker, Pr
EMP: 6 EST: 1950
SQ FT: 4,800
SALES (est): 328.98K **Privately Held**
SIC: 3471 Electroplating of metals or formed
  products

(G-1633)
BRYAN PACKAGING INC
620 E Perry St (43506-2221)
PHONE...............................419 636-2600
Leo Deiger, Pr
EMP: 12 EST: 1998
SALES (est): 4.67MM
SALES (corp-wide): 25.21MM **Privately
Held**
SIC: 5199 2653 Packaging materials; Boxes,
  corrugated: made from purchased materials
PA: Pro-Pak Industries, Inc.

1125 Ford St
Maumee OH 43537
419 729-0751

(G-1634)
BRYAN PUBLISHING COMPANY (PA)
Also Called: County Line
211 W High St Ste A (43506-1604)
PHONE.....................................419 636-1111
Christopher Cullis, *Pr*
Tom Voight, *
Elizabeth Cullis, *
EMP: 80 **EST:** 1863
SALES (est): 4.8MM
SALES (corp-wide): 4.8MM **Privately Held**
Web: www.bryantimes.com
SIC: 2711 Newspapers, publishing and
printing

(G-1635)
C E ELECTRONICS INC
2107 Industrial Dr (43506-8773)
PHONE.....................................419 636-6705
Garry L Courtney, *Pr*
EMP: 85 **EST:** 1980
SALES (est): 8.36MM **Privately Held**
Web: www.ceelectronics.com
SIC: 3679 3672 Electronic circuits; Printed
circuit boards

(G-1636)
CLARIOS LLC
Also Called: Johnson Controls
918 S Union St (43506-2246)
PHONE.....................................419 636-4211
Kevin Cagala, *Mgr*
EMP: 48
SALES (corp-wide): 69.83B **Privately Held**
Web: www.clarios.com
SIC: 2531 Seats, automobile
HQ: Clarios, Llc
5757 N Green Bay Ave Flor
Glendale WI 53209

(G-1637)
DAAVLIN DISTRIBUTING CO
Also Called: Daavlin
205 W Bement St (43506-1264)
P.O. Box 626 (43506-0626)
PHONE.....................................419 636-6304
David W Swanson, *Pr*
Tracey Mckelvey, *VP*
Traci Hartman, *
Sandrine Woolace, *
▼ **EMP:** 48 **EST:** 1981
SQ FT: 24,000
SALES (est): 8.87MM **Privately Held**
Web: www.daavlin.com
SIC: 3841 Diagnostic apparatus, medical

(G-1638)
DIGIMANUFACTURING TECH LLC
207 Brown Dr (43506-8954)
PHONE.....................................419 212-6414
Chad Walls, *Prin*
EMP: 6 **EST:** 2018
SALES (est): 81.32K **Privately Held**
Web: www.digimanufacturing.com
SIC: 3999 Manufacturing industries, nec

(G-1639)
**DURACOAT POWDER FINISHING
INC (PA)**
1012 E Wilson St (43506-9358)
P.O. Box 715 (43517-0715)
PHONE.....................................419 636-3111
Frank Monosmith, *Pr*
Dock Pigmon, *CFO*
EMP: 13 **EST:** 1992
SQ FT: 45,000
SALES (est): 465.62K **Privately Held**

Web: www.duracoatpowderfinishing.com
SIC: 3479 Coating of metals and formed
products

(G-1640)
ENVASES MEDIA INC
1 Toy St (43506-1853)
P.O. Box 524 (43506-0524)
PHONE.....................................419 636-5461
Thomas P Dillon, *Pr*
▲ **EMP:** 21 **EST:** 2007
SALES (est): 4.76MM **Privately Held**
Web: www.envases.mx
SIC: 3411 3221 Food and beverage
containers; Bottles for packing, bottling, and
canning: glass
HQ: Envases Europe A/S
Hedenstedvej 14
Losning 8723
63124200

(G-1641)
FLUID EQUIPMENT CORPORATION
7671 County Rd 7 G (43506-9118)
P.O. Box 689 (43506-0689)
PHONE.....................................419 636-0777
Edward T Ward, *Pr*
EMP: 7 **EST:** 1989
SALES (est): 308.25K **Privately Held**
Web: www.fluidequipmentcorp.com
SIC: 8748 8711 3823 Systems engineering
consultant, ex. computer or professional;
Consulting engineer; Fluidic devices,
circuits, and systems for process control

(G-1642)
FLUID HANDLING DYNAMICS LTD
815 Navarre Ave (43506-1528)
PHONE.....................................419 633-0560
Nick Kozumplik Junior, *Prin*
EMP: 10 **EST:** 2019
SALES (est): 491.63K **Privately Held**
SIC: 3652 Prerecorded records and tapes

(G-1643)
GENDRON INC
520 W Mulberry St Ste 100 (43506-1159)
PHONE.....................................419 636-0848
EMP: 22
Web: www.gendroninc.com
SIC: 3842 Surgical appliances and supplies

(G-1644)
ILLINOIS TOOL WORKS INC
Also Called: ITW Powertrain Components
730 E South St (43506-2433)
PHONE.....................................419 633-3236
Martin Collins, *Brnch Mgr*
EMP: 100
SALES (corp-wide): 16.11B **Publicly Held**
Web: www.itw.com
SIC: 3089 Injection molding of plastics
PA: Illinois Tool Works Inc.
155 Harlem Ave
Glenview IL 60025
847 724-7500

(G-1645)
ILLINOIS TOOL WORKS INC
Also Called: ITW Filtration Products
730 E South St (43506-2433)
PHONE.....................................262 248-8277
Bob Hamilton, *Genl Mgr*
EMP: 22
SALES (corp-wide): 16.11B **Publicly Held**
Web: www.itw.com
SIC: 3677 3714 3564 Filtration devices,
electronic; Motor vehicle parts and
accessories; Blowers and fans
PA: Illinois Tool Works Inc.
155 Harlem Ave

Glenview IL 60025
847 724-7500

(G-1646)
ILLINOIS TOOL WORKS INC
ITW Tomco
730 E South St (43506-2433)
PHONE.....................................419 636-3161
Tom Mack, *VP*
EMP: 9
SQ FT: 75,000
SALES (corp-wide): 16.11B **Publicly Held**
Web: www.itw.com
SIC: 3089 Injection molding of plastics
PA: Illinois Tool Works Inc.
155 Harlem Ave
Glenview IL 60025
847 724-7500

(G-1647)
KENLEY ENTERPRISES LLC
418 N Lynn St (43506-1218)
P.O. Box 7036 (43506-7036)
PHONE.....................................419 630-0921
EMP: 9 **EST:** 2004
SALES (est): 1.09MM **Privately Held**
Web: www.kenleyenterprises.com
SIC: 3549 3498 3714 Wiredrawing and
fabricating machinery and equipment, ex.
die; Tube fabricating (contract bending and
shaping); Motor vehicle parts and
accessories

(G-1648)
LCKBM COMPANY (HQ)
1030 E Wilson St (43506-9358)
P.O. Box 766 (43506-0766)
PHONE.....................................419 636-4555
Laura Juarez, *Pr*
Craig Francisco, *
Mindy Hess, *
Steve Smith, *
Mari Ivan, *
▲ **EMP:** 100 **EST:** 1950
SQ FT: 90,000
SALES (est): 18.03MM **Privately Held**
Web: www.lesmith.com
SIC: 2431 5072 2541 Interior and
ornamental woodwork and trim; Builders'
hardware, nec; Wood partitions and fixtures
PA: Cutting Edge Countertops, Inc.
1300 Flagship Dr
Perrysburg OH 43551

(G-1649)
**LEADER ENGNRNG-FABRICATION
INC**
County Rd D-50 (43506)
PHONE.....................................419 636-1731
John Hill, *Mgr*
EMP: 6
SALES (corp-wide): 8.29MM **Privately
Held**
Web: www.axisengineering.com
SIC: 3599 Machine shop, jobbing and repair
PA: Leader Engineering-Fabrication, Inc.
695 Independence Dr
Napoleon OH 43545
419 592-0008

(G-1650)
**MANUFACTURED HOUSING ENTPS
INC**
Also Called: Mansion Homes
9302 Us Highway 6 (43506-9516)
PHONE.....................................419 636-4511
Mary Jane Fitzcharles, *CEO*
Nathan Kimpel, *
Janet Rice, *
EMP: 17 **EST:** 1966
SQ FT: 250,000

SALES (est): 4.45MM **Privately Held**
Web: www.mheinc.com
SIC: 2451 1521 Mobile homes, except
recreational; Single-family housing
construction

(G-1651)
MINTEQ INTERNATIONAL INC
719 E High St (43506-1824)
PHONE.....................................419 636-4561
Tim Connors, *Mgr*
EMP: 12
Web: www.mineralstech.com
SIC: 3297 High temperature mortar, nonclay
HQ: Minteq International Inc.
35 Highland Ave
Bethlehem PA 18017

(G-1652)
NASG SEATING BRYAN LLC
633 Commerce Dr (43506-9197)
PHONE.....................................419 633-0662
David Vondeylen, *Managing Member*
▲ **EMP:** 92 **EST:** 2001
SQ FT: 80,000
SALES (est): 8.64MM **Privately Held**
Web: www.nasg.net
SIC: 3469 Stamping metal for the trade

(G-1653)
NOSTRUM LABORATORIES INC
705 E Mulberry St Unit A (43506-1734)
PHONE.....................................419 636-1168
EMP: 46
SQ FT: 91,100
Web: www.nostrumlabs.com
SIC: 2834 Syrups, pharmaceutical
PA: Nostrum Laboratories Inc.
1800 N Topping Ave
Kansas City MO 64120

(G-1654)
OBIC LLC
525 Winzeler Dr # 1 (43506-8303)
PHONE.....................................419 633-3147
EMP: 10 **EST:** 2018
SALES (est): 3.69MM **Privately Held**
Web: www.obicproducts.com
SIC: 3589 Water filters and softeners,
household type

(G-1655)
OHIO ART COMPANY (PA)
1 Toy St (43506-1853)
P.O. Box 111 (43506-0111)
PHONE.....................................419 636-3141
William C Killgallon, *Ch Bd*
Martin L Killgallon Ii, *Pr*
Martin L Killgallon Iii, *Sr VP*
Larry Killgallon, *
▲ **EMP:** 77 **EST:** 1908
SQ FT: 661,000
SALES (est): 9.93MM
SALES (corp-wide): 9.93MM **Privately
Held**
Web: www.ohioart.com
SIC: 2752 5945 Commercial printing,
lithographic; Toys and games

(G-1656)
OTTOKEE GROUP INC
17768 County Road H 50 (43506-9429)
PHONE.....................................419 636-1932
Keith Krovath, *Mgr*
EMP: 6
SALES (corp-wide): 126.56K **Privately
Held**
SIC: 2875 Fertilizers, mixing only
PA: Ottokee Group, Inc.
21450 County Rd J
Archbold OH 43502

▲ = Import ▼ = Export
◆ = Import/Export

419 445-0446

(G-1657)
PAHL READY MIX CONCRETE INC (PA)
Also Called: Pahl Ready Mix Concrete
14586 Us Highway 127 Ew (43506-9754)
PHONE..............................419 636-4238
TOLL FREE: 800
Thomas G Weber, *Pr*
Judy Weber, *VP*
EMP: 17 EST: 1968
SQ FT: 500
SALES (est): 4.87MM
SALES (corp-wide): 4.87MM **Privately Held**
Web: www.pahlreadymix.com
SIC: 3273 Ready-mixed concrete

(G-1658)
PRECISE METAL FORM INC
810 Commerce Dr (43506-8861)
P.O. Box 764 (43506-0764)
PHONE..............................419 636-5221
James Bloir, *Pr*
Linda Bloir, *Sec*
EMP: 10 EST: 1969
SALES (est): 1.76MM **Privately Held**
SIC: 3441 Fabricated structural metal

(G-1659)
S & H AUTOMATION & EQP CO INC
815 Commerce Dr (43506-8862)
P.O. Box 662 (43506-0662)
PHONE..............................419 636-0020
Johnathan Stewart, *Managing Member*
Jimmy Stewart, *Pr*
EMP: 12 EST: 1993
SALES (est): 1.57MM **Privately Held**
Web: www.autobenders.com
SIC: 3599 Machine shop, jobbing and repair

(G-1660)
SPANGLER CANDY COMPANY (PA)
400 N Portland St (43506-1257)
P.O. Box 71 (43506-0071)
PHONE..............................419 636-4221
▲ EMP: 175 EST: 1906
SALES (est): 45.8MM
SALES (corp-wide): 45.8MM **Privately Held**
Web: www.spanglercandy.com
SIC: 2064 Candy and other confectionery products

(G-1661)
TGM LLC
401 N Union St (43506-1455)
PHONE..............................419 636-8567
Ed Berhoff, *Managing Member*
EMP: 15 EST: 2011
SQ FT: 17,000
SALES (est): 300K **Privately Held**
Web: www.tgminc.com
SIC: 3599 Machine shop, jobbing and repair

(G-1662)
TITAN TIRE CORPORATION
Also Called: Titan Tire Corporation Bryan
927 S Union St (43506-2252)
PHONE..............................419 633-4221
Tom Jagielski, *Mgr*
EMP: 400
SQ FT: 750,000
SALES (corp-wide): 1.85B **Publicly Held**
Web: www.titan-intl.com
SIC: 3011 Tires and inner tubes
HQ: Titan Tire Corporation
2345 E Market St
Des Moines IA 50317

(G-1663)
TITAN TIRE CORPORATION BRYAN
927 S Union St (43506-2252)
PHONE..............................419 633-4224
Paul Reitz, *Pr*
EMP: 36 EST: 2006
SALES (est): 3.18MM
SALES (corp-wide): 1.85B **Publicly Held**
Web: www.titan-intl.com
SIC: 3011 Tires and inner tubes
PA: Titan International, Inc.
1525 Kautz Rd Ste 600
West Chicago IL 60185
630 377-0486

(G-1664)
TRANE TECHNOLOGIES COMPANY LLC
Ingersoll-Rand
1 Aro Ctr (43506)
PHONE..............................419 636-4242
EMP: 10
Web: www.tranetechnologies.com
SIC: 3561 Pumps and pumping equipment
HQ: Trane Technologies Company Llc
800-E Beaty St
Davidson NC 28036
704 655-4000

(G-1665)
TRANE TECHNOLOGIES COMPANY LLC
Also Called: Ingersoll-Rand
209 N Main St (43506-1319)
P.O. Box 151 (43506-0151)
PHONE..............................419 633-6800
Larry White, *Mgr*
EMP: 43
Web: www.tranetechnologies.com
SIC: 3546 4225 3823 3594 Power-driven handtools; General warehousing and storage; Process control instruments; Fluid power pumps and motors
HQ: Trane Technologies Company Llc
800-E Beaty St
Davidson NC 28036
704 655-4000

(G-1666)
WEBER SAND & GRAVEL INC
14586 Us Highway 127 Ew (43506-9754)
PHONE..............................419 636-7920
Tom Weber, *Pr*
EMP: 8 EST: 1968
SALES (est): 531.44K **Privately Held**
SIC: 1442 Gravel mining

(G-1667)
WESTAR PLASTICS LLC
Also Called: Westar Plastics
4271 County Road 15d (43506-9442)
PHONE..............................419 636-1333
Steve Goltare, *Managing Member*
EMP: 7 EST: 1996
SQ FT: 12,000
SALES (est): 1.09MM **Privately Held**
Web: www.westarplastics.com
SIC: 3089 Injection molding of plastics

(G-1668)
YANFENG INTL AUTO TECH US I LL
918 S Union St (43506-2246)
PHONE..............................419 633-1873
EMP: 51
Web: www.yanfeng.com
SIC: 3089 3465 3479 3714 Injection molding of plastics; Automotive stampings; Painting, coating, and hot dipping; Motor vehicle parts and accessories

HQ: Yanfeng International Automotive Technology Us I Llc
41935 W 12 Mile Rd
Novi MI 48377
248 319-7333

(G-1669)
YANFENG INTL AUTO TECH US I LL
715 E South St (43506)
PHONE..............................616 834-9422
Joseph Magdy, *Brnch Mgr*
EMP: 100
Web: www.yanfeng.com
SIC: 3714 Motor vehicle parts and accessories
HQ: Yanfeng International Automotive Technology Us I Llc
41935 W 12 Mile Rd
Novi MI 48377
248 319-7333

(G-1670)
YANFENG INTL AUTO TECH US II L
918 S Union St (43506-2246)
PHONE..............................419 636-4211
Kevin Cagala, *Mgr*
EMP: 7
SIC: 3089 Injection molding of plastics
HQ: Yanfeng International Automotive Technology Us Ii Llc
41935 W 12 Mile Rd
Novi MI 48377
248 319-7333

Bucyrus
Crawford County

(G-1671)
ADVANCED FIBER LLC
100 Crossroads Blvd (44820-1361)
PHONE..............................419 562-1337
Doug Leuthold, *Pr*
EMP: 20 EST: 2018
SALES (est): 2.25MM
SALES (corp-wide): 2.94B **Publicly Held**
Web: www.advanced-fiber.com
SIC: 2821 2951 2823 Cellulose derivative materials; Asphalt paving mixtures and blocks; Cellulosic manmade fibers
PA: Installed Building Products, Inc.
495 S High St Ste 50
Columbus OH 43215
614 221-3399

(G-1672)
BUCYRUS BLADES INC (DH)
260 E Beal Ave (44820-3492)
PHONE..............................419 562-6015
Alvin Collins, *Ch*
Jon Owens, *
Kevin Thomas, *
Eric Blackburn, *
◆ EMP: 154 EST: 1951
SQ FT: 130,000
SALES (est): 60MM
SALES (corp-wide): 3.18B **Privately Held**
Web: www.escocorp.com
SIC: 3531 Blades for graders, scrapers, dozers, and snow plows
HQ: Esco Group Llc
1631 Nw Thurman St
Portland OR 97209
503 228-2141

(G-1673)
BUCYRUS GRAPHICS INC
Also Called: Quality Printing Co
214 W Liberty St (44820-2639)
P.O. Box 454 (44820-0454)

PHONE..............................419 562-2906
W Gary Mc Kee, *Pr*
Judy Mc Kee, *Sec*
EMP: 10 EST: 1968
SQ FT: 5,000
SALES (est): 281.3K **Privately Held**
Web: www.1officesolution.com
SIC: 2752 Offset printing

(G-1674)
BUCYRUS PRECISION TECH INC
Also Called: B P T
200 Crossroads Blvd (44820-1363)
P.O. Box 2748 (44906-0748)
PHONE..............................419 563-9950
Keiji Nishio, *Pr*
Terry Pence, *
▲ EMP: 189 EST: 1995
SQ FT: 107,000
SALES (est): 9.7MM **Privately Held**
Web: www.bucyrusprecisiontech.com
SIC: 3714 3568 5531 Motor vehicle engines and parts; Power transmission equipment, nec; Automotive accessories
PA: Kaneta Kogyo Co.,Ltd.
3-18-5, Takaokahigashi, Chuo-Ku
Hamamatsu SZO 433-8

(G-1675)
CHECKMATE MARINE INC
3691 State Route 4 (44820-9466)
P.O. Box 351 (44820-0351)
PHONE..............................419 562-3881
Doug Smith, *Pr*
EMP: 7 EST: 2006
SALES (est): 433.96K **Privately Held**
SIC: 3732 Boatbuilding and repairing

(G-1676)
COOPERS MILL INC
1414 N Sandusky Ave (44820-1330)
P.O. Box 149 (44820-0149)
PHONE..............................419 562-4215
Jason Mcmullan, *Pr*
Justin Mcmullan, *VP*
EMP: 8 EST: 1969
SQ FT: 17,300
SALES (est): 830.88K **Privately Held**
Web: www.crossroadscandles.com
SIC: 2033 5431 5149 Jams, jellies, and preserves, packaged in cans, jars, etc.; Fruit stands or markets; Pickles, preserves, jellies, and jams

(G-1677)
D PICKING & CO
119 S Walnut St (44820-2325)
PHONE..............................419 562-6891
Helen Picking Neff, *Owner*
EMP: 6 EST: 1874
SQ FT: 5,000
SALES (est): 450.08K **Privately Held**
Web: www.bucyruscopperkettle.com
SIC: 3364 3931 3366 3321 Copper and copper alloy die-castings; Musical instruments; Copper foundries; Gray and ductile iron foundries

(G-1678)
DIAMOND WIPES INTL INC
1375 Isaac Beal Rd (44820-9604)
PHONE..............................419 562-3575
Diane Belcher, *Prin*
EMP: 8
SALES (corp-wide): 51.1MM **Privately Held**
Web: www.diamondwipes.com
SIC: 3441 Fabricated structural metal
PA: Diamond Wipes International, Inc.
4651 Schaefer Ave
Chino CA 91710

909 230-9888

(G-1679)
EAGLE CRUSHER CO INC
521 E Southern Ave (44820-3258)
P.O. Box 537 (44833-0537)
PHONE..............................419 562-1183
Susan Cobey, *Brnch Mgr*
EMP: 95
SQ FT: 200,000
SALES (corp-wide): 13.19MM **Privately Held**
Web: www.eaglecrusher.com
SIC: 3531 Construction machinery
PA: Eagle Crusher Co Inc
    525 S Market St
    Galion OH 44833
    419 468-2288

(G-1680)
EAST SIDE FUEL PLUS OPERATIONS
1505 N Sandusky Ave (44820-1333)
PHONE..............................419 563-0777
Bridgette J Liedorff, *Prin*
EMP: 6 EST: 2011
SALES (est): 168.31K **Privately Held**
SIC: 2869 Fuels

(G-1681)
GANYMEDE TECHNOLOGIES CORP
Also Called: J3 Point-Of-Sale
1685 Marion Rd (44820-3116)
P.O. Box 1138 (44820-1138)
PHONE..............................419 562-5522
George Fred Fischer, *Pr*
EMP: 6 EST: 2005
SALES (est): 905.55K **Privately Held**
Web: www.j3pos.biz
SIC: 7371 3578 Computer software
    development; Calculators and adding
    machines

(G-1682)
GENERAL ELECTRIC COMPANY
Also Called: GE
1250 S Walnut St (44820-3266)
PHONE..............................419 563-1200
Peter Gabriel, *Brnch Mgr*
EMP: 32
SALES (corp-wide): 38.7B **Publicly Held**
Web: geaerospace.com
SIC: 3641 Lamps, fluorescent, electric
PA: General Electric Company
    1 Aviation Way
    Cincinnati OH 45215
    617 443-3000

(G-1683)
IMASEN BUCYRUS TECHNOLOGY INC
Also Called: I B-Tech
260 Crossroads Blvd (44820-1363)
PHONE..............................419 563-9590
Katsumi Ito, *Pr*
Joe Downing, *
Koichi Fukui, *
◆ **EMP:** 220 EST: 1997
SALES (est): 49.08MM **Privately Held**
Web: www.bucyrusohio.com
SIC: 3714 Motor vehicle parts and
    accessories
PA: Imasen Electric Industrial Co., Ltd.
    1, Kakibata
    Inuyama AIC 484-0

(G-1684)
NATIONAL LIME AND STONE CO
4580 Bethel Rd (44820-9754)
P.O. Box 69 (44820-0069)
PHONE..............................419 562-0771
Eric Johnson, *Prin*

EMP: 27
SALES (corp-wide): 86.85MM **Privately Held**
Web: www.natlime.com
SIC: 1411 3281 1422 Limestone, dimension-
    quarrying; Cut stone and stone products;
    Crushed and broken limestone
PA: The National Lime And Stone
    Company
    551 Lake Cascade Pkwy
    Findlay OH 45840
    419 422-4341

(G-1685)
OAK VIEW ENTERPRISES INC
100 Crossroads Blvd (44820-1361)
PHONE..............................513 860-4446
Doug Leuthold, *Pr*
Jeff Miller, *Prin*
Phil Taylor, *Prin*
Sandi Leuthold, *Prin*
EMP: 20 EST: 1988
SQ FT: 51,500
SALES (est): 7.76MM **Privately Held**
Web: www.advanced-fiber.com
SIC: 2821 5084 Cellulose derivative
    materials; Paper manufacturing machinery

(G-1686)
QUALITOR SUBSIDIARY H INC
1232 Whetstone St (44820-3539)
PHONE..............................419 562-7987
Andrew Ason, *Pr*
Ralph Reins, *
EMP: 40 EST: 1984
SALES (est): 2.31MM
SALES (corp-wide): 7.28B **Privately Held**
SIC: 3714 3451 3429 5013 Motor vehicle
    brake systems and parts; Screw machine
    products; Hardware, nec; Automotive
    supplies and parts
HQ: Transportation Aftermarket Enterprise
    Inc
    1840 Mccullough St
    Lima OH

(G-1687)
R L RUSH TOOL & PATTERN INC
Also Called: Rush, R L Tool & Pattern
1620 Whetstone St (44820-3557)
P.O. Box 763 (44820-0763)
PHONE..............................419 562-9849
Roger Rush, *Pr*
Phyllis Rush, *Sec*
EMP: 7 EST: 1974
SQ FT: 7,000
SALES (est): 1.01MM **Privately Held**
Web: www.rushtool.com
SIC: 3543 3469 Industrial patterns;
    Stamping metal for the trade

(G-1688)
RANDYS TIRE & AUTO REPAIR INC
1000 N Sandusky Ave (44820-1457)
P.O. Box 551 (44820)
PHONE..............................419 562-2926
Randall Scheffler, *Pr*
Louri Shepard, *VP*
EMP: 9 EST: 1963
SQ FT: 8,000
SALES (est): 852.5K **Privately Held**
Web: www.randystire.com
SIC: 5531 7538 7534 7539 Automotive tires;
    General automotive repair shops; Tire
    retreading and repair shops; Automotive
    repair shops, nec

(G-1689)
REGO MANUFACTURING CO INC
1870 E Mansfield St (44820-2018)
P.O. Box 838 (44820-0838)

PHONE..............................419 562-0466
Raymond L Kincaid, *Ch Bd*
Timothy Stenson, *
Ken Kincaid, *
Claudia Kincaid, *
EMP: 63 EST: 1973
SQ FT: 15,000
SALES (est): 1.31MM **Privately Held**
Web: www.regoonline.com
SIC: 3911 Jewelry apparel

(G-1690)
RYDER-HEIL BRONZE INC
126 E Irving St (44820-1409)
P.O. Box 647 (44820-0647)
PHONE..............................419 562-2841
Herbert D Kleine, *Pr*
EMP: 35 EST: 1910
SQ FT: 39,750
SALES (est): 4.47MM **Privately Held**
Web: www.ryderheil.com
SIC: 3366 Copper foundries

(G-1691)
VAL CASTING INC
108 E Rensselaer St (44820-2320)
P.O. Box 374 (44820-0374)
PHONE..............................419 562-2499
Val Fawley, *Pr*
Michael Romanoff, *
EMP: 6 EST: 1983
SQ FT: 4,500
SALES (est): 725.43K **Privately Held**
Web: www.valjewelry.com
SIC: 3911 Jewelry, precious metal

(G-1692)
VASIL CO INC
Also Called: Vasil Fashions
119 E Mary St (44820-1828)
PHONE..............................419 562-2901
Nicholas G Vasil, *Treas*
Nicholas G Vasil, *Pr*
Margaret Ann Vasil, *VP*
EMP: 8 EST: 1958
SQ FT: 12,000
SALES (est): 297.35K **Privately Held**
Web: www.thevasilcompany.com
SIC: 2396 2395 Screen printing on fabric
    articles; Art goods for embroidering,
    stamped: purchased materials

(G-1693)
VELVET ICE CREAM COMPANY
Also Called: Bucyrus Ice Company
1233 Whetstone St (44820-3540)
PHONE..............................419 562-2009
TOLL FREE: 800
Jack Rogers, *Mgr*
EMP: 30
SALES (corp-wide): 21.87MM **Privately Held**
Web: www.velveticecream.com
SIC: 5143 2097 Ice cream and ices;
    Manufactured ice
PA: Velvet Ice Cream Company
    11324 Mount Vernon Rd
    Utica OH 43080
    740 892-3921

(G-1694)
W E LOTT COMPANY
1432 Isaac Beal Rd (44820-9604)
P.O. Box 628 (44820-0628)
PHONE..............................419 563-9400
Richard Olt, *Pr*
W E Lott, *Sec*
▲ **EMP:** 11 EST: 1958
SQ FT: 20,000
SALES (est): 3.23MM **Privately Held**
Web: www.welott.com

SIC: 3462 3321 3322 3324 Iron and steel
    forgings; Gray and ductile iron foundries;
    Malleable iron foundries; Steel investment
    foundries

(G-1695)
W M DAUCH CONCRETE INC
900 Nevada Rd (44820-1744)
PHONE..............................419 562-6917
William Dauch, *Pr*
EMP: 7 EST: 1968
SALES (est): 108.96K **Privately Held**
Web: www.dauchconcrete.com
SIC: 3273 1771 Ready-mixed concrete;
    Concrete work

(G-1696)
WILLIAM DAUCH CONCRETE COMPANY
900 Nevada Wynford Rd (44820-9440)
PHONE..............................419 562-6917
Tim Corrigan, *Mgr*
EMP: 10
SALES (corp-wide): 9.78MM **Privately Held**
Web: www.dauchconcrete.com
SIC: 3273 Ready-mixed concrete
PA: William Dauch Concrete Company Inc
    84 Cleveland Rd
    Norwalk OH 44857
    419 668-4458

Burghill
Trumbull County

(G-1697)
DESIGNER DOORS INC
4810 State Route 7 (44404-9701)
PHONE..............................330 772-6391
Ron Seidle Junior, *Pr*
Robert Seidle, *
◆ **EMP:** 9 EST: 1972
SQ FT: 23,500
SALES (est): 233.45K **Privately Held**
Web: www.cambek.com
SIC: 2431 Doors, wood

Burkettsville
Mercer County

(G-1698)
WERLING AND SONS INC
Also Called: Burkettsville Stockyard
100 Plum St (45310-5017)
P.O. Box 148 (45310-0148)
PHONE..............................937 338-3281
Edward J Werling, *Pr*
James R Werling, *Sec*
EMP: 10 EST: 1886
SALES (est): 212.63K **Privately Held**
Web: www.werlingandsons.com
SIC: 5154 2011 Livestock; Meat packing
    plants

Burton
Geauga County

(G-1699)
HEXPOL COMPOUNDING LLC
Also Called: Burton Rubber Processing
14330 Kinsman Rd (44021-9648)
PHONE..............................440 834-4644
John Gorrell, *Mgr*
EMP: 200
SALES (corp-wide): 6.47MM **Privately Held**

▲ = Import ▼ = Export
◆ = Import/Export

Web: www.burtonchamberofcommerce.org
SIC: 3087 2865 5162 2899 Custom compound purchased resins; Dyes and pigments; Resins; Chemical preparations, nec
HQ: Hexpol Compounding Llc
14330 Kinsman Rd
Burton OH 44021
440 834-4644

(G-1700)
HEXPOL COMPOUNDING LLC (DH)
Also Called: Hexpol Polymers
14330 Kinsman Rd (44021-9648)
P.O. Box 415000 (37241-5000)
PHONE..............................440 834-4644
Gary Moore, *Pr*
Tracy Garrison, *
Ernie Ulmer, *
▲ **EMP:** 50 **EST:** 2004
SALES (est): 491.43MM
SALES (corp-wide): 6.47MM **Privately Held**
Web: www.hexpol.com
SIC: 3087 2821 Custom compound purchased resins; Thermoplastic materials
HQ: Hexpol Holding Inc.
14330 Kinsman Rd
Burton OH 44021
440 834-4644

(G-1701)
HEXPOL HOLDING INC (HQ)
14330 Kinsman Rd (44021-9648)
PHONE..............................440 834-4644
Georg Brunstam, *Pr*
EMP: 10 **EST:** 2012
SALES (est): 782.08MM
SALES (corp-wide): 6.47MM **Privately Held**
Web: www.hexpol.com
SIC: 3087 6719 2821 Custom compound purchased resins; Investment holding companies, except banks; Plastics materials and resins
PA: Hexpol Ab
Skeppsbron 3
Malmo 211 2
40254660

(G-1702)
KEN EMERICK MACHINE PRODUCTS
14504 Main Market Rd (44021-9615)
PHONE..............................440 834-1601
Ken Emerick, *Pr*
Pam Emerick, *VP*
EMP: 8 **EST:** 1965
SQ FT: 12,500
SALES (est): 943.59K **Privately Held**
Web: www.emerickmachine.com
SIC: 3451 Screw machine products

(G-1703)
OHIO BOX & CRATE INC
Also Called: Ohio Box and Crate Co
16751 Tavern Rd (44021-9605)
PHONE..............................440 526-3133
Sarmite S Grava, *Pr*
EMP: 7 **EST:** 1975
SQ FT: 15,000
SALES (est): 474.15K **Privately Held**
SIC: 2441 2448 Boxes, wood; Skids, wood and wood with metal

(G-1704)
STEPHEN M TRUDICK
Also Called: Hardwood Lumber Co
13813 Station Road (44021)
P.O. Box 15 (44021-0015)
PHONE..............................440 834-1891
Stephen M Trudick, *Owner*

▲ **EMP:** 41 **EST:** 1958
SQ FT: 80,000
SALES (est): 4.99MM **Privately Held**
Web: www.hardwood-lumber.com
SIC: 3991 2426 5031 3442 Brooms and brushes; Dimension, hardwood; Lumber: rough, dressed, and finished; Metal doors, sash, and trim

(G-1705)
TROY CHEMICAL INDUSTRIES INC (PA)
Also Called: Troy Chemical
17040 Rapids Rd (44021-9754)
P.O. Box 430 (44021-0430)
PHONE..............................440 834-4408
Lee Imhof, *Pr*
Richard B Keyse, *VP*
Joyce Pope, *Sec*
▲ **EMP:** 19 **EST:** 1971
SQ FT: 25,000
SALES (est): 4.53MM
SALES (corp-wide): 4.53MM **Privately Held**
Web: www.troychemical.com
SIC: 2842 Polishes and sanitation goods

(G-1706)
TROY MANUFACTURING CO
Also Called: Troy
17090 Rapids Rd (44021-9754)
P.O. Box 448 (44021-0448)
PHONE..............................440 834-8262
David Cseplo, *Pr*
Charles Fath, *
Wynne Bogert, *
Richard Taylor, *
EMP: 22 **EST:** 1952
SQ FT: 40,000
SALES (est): 4.76MM **Privately Held**
Web: www.troy-mfg.com
SIC: 3599 Machine shop, jobbing and repair

(G-1707)
TROY PRECISION CARBIDE DIE INC
Also Called: Troy Precision Carbide
17720 Claridon Troy Rd (44021-9658)
PHONE..............................440 834-4477
James Dewalt, *Pr*
Kelly Amon, *VP*
Jeff Amon, *Sec*
EMP: 6 **EST:** 1952
SQ FT: 10,000
SALES (est): 901.14K **Privately Held**
Web: www.troyprecisioncarbidedie.com
SIC: 3544 Special dies and tools

Byesville
Guernsey County

(G-1708)
DAVID R HILL INC
132 S 2nd St (43723-1304)
P.O. Box 247 (43723-0247)
PHONE..............................740 685-5168
David R Hill, *CEO*
EMP: 6 **EST:** 1982
SALES (est): 802.5K **Privately Held**
SIC: 1382 Geological exploration; oil and gas field

(G-1709)
DETROIT DESL RMNFCTRNG-AST INC
60703 Country Club Rd (43723-9730)
PHONE..............................740 439-7701
Roger S Penske, *Ch Bd*
James Morrow, *
Mike Chuich, *General Vice President*

◆ **EMP:** 500 **EST:** 1989
SQ FT: 128,000
SALES (est): 17.56MM
SALES (corp-wide): 57.19B **Privately Held**
Web: northamerica.daimlertruck.com
SIC: 3519 Diesel engine rebuilding
HQ: Detroit Diesel Remanufacturing Llc
100 Lodestone Way
Tooele UT 84074

(G-1710)
DETROIT DIESL SPECIALTY TL INC
60703 Country Club Rd (43723-9730)
PHONE..............................740 435-4452
Wayne Prouty, *Pr*
▲ **EMP:** 38 **EST:** 2001
SALES (est): 6.66MM
SALES (corp-wide): 57.19B **Privately Held**
SIC: 3599 Electrical discharge machining (EDM)
HQ: Detroit Diesel Corporation
13400 W Outer Dr
Detroit MI 48239
313 592-5000

(G-1711)
FAMOUS INDUSTRIES INC
Also Called: L B Manufacturing
356 Main St (43723-1123)
PHONE..............................740 685-2592
Bob Badnell, *Mgr*
EMP: 13
SALES (corp-wide): 3.97B **Privately Held**
Web: www.johnsoncontrols.com
SIC: 3469 3585 3564 3498 Stamping metal for the trade; Refrigeration and heating equipment; Blowers and fans; Fabricated pipe and fittings
HQ: Famous Industries, Inc.
2620 Ridgewood Rd Ste 200
Akron OH 44313
330 535-1811

(G-1712)
FAMOUS REALTY CLEVELAND INC
Also Called: Famous Supply
354 Main St (43723-1123)
PHONE..............................740 685-2533
Eric St Claire, *Mgr*
EMP: 10
SALES (corp-wide): 664.34K **Privately Held**
SIC: 3585 5074 Heating and air conditioning combination units; Plumbing fittings and supplies
PA: Famous Realty Of Cleveland, Inc.
109 N Union St
Akron OH 44304
330 762-9621

(G-1713)
GUERNSEY INDUSTRIES
60772 Southgate Rd (43723-9731)
PHONE..............................740 439-4452
Ken Harper, *Ex Dir*
EMP: 110 **EST:** 1977
SALES (est): 1.01MM **Privately Held**
Web: www.guernseyindustries.com
SIC: 8331 2511 2448 Sheltered workshop; Wood household furniture; Wood pallets and skids

(G-1714)
ISLAND ASEPTICS LLC
100 Hope Ave (43723-9460)
P.O. Box 280 (43723-0280)
PHONE..............................740 685-2548
▲ **EMP:** 150
SIC: 2656 Food containers (liquid tight), including milk cartons

(G-1715)
KERRY INC
Also Called: Kerry Ingredients
100 Hope Ave (43723-9460)
PHONE..............................760 685-2548
EMP: 45
Web: www.kerry.com
SIC: 2656 5149 Food containers (liquid tight), including milk cartons; Condiments
HQ: Kerry Inc.
3400 Millington Rd
Beloit WI 53511
608 363-1200

(G-1716)
TIMCO INC
57051 Marietta Rd (43723-9709)
PHONE..............................740 685-2594
Tim Brown, *Pr*
EMP: 6 **EST:** 1982
SQ FT: 2,000
SALES (est): 923.17K **Privately Held**
Web: www.timcoinc.net
SIC: 1381 3533 Drilling oil and gas wells; Oil and gas field machinery

(G-1717)
VELOCITY CONCEPT DEV GROUP LLC
8824 Clay Pike (43723-9712)
PHONE..............................740 685-2637
Eric Fehrman, *Brnch Mgr*
EMP: 8
SALES (corp-wide): 4.25MM **Privately Held**
Web: www.velocityfast.com
SIC: 3544 Industrial molds
PA: Velocity Concept Development Group, Llc
4393 Digital Way
Mason OH 45040
513 204-2100

(G-1718)
W P BROWN ENTERPRISES INC
57051 Marietta Rd (43723-9709)
PHONE..............................740 685-2594
William P Brown, *Pr*
EMP: 6 **EST:** 1978
SALES (est): 438.68K **Privately Held**
Web: www.brownrentalsinc.com
SIC: 1311 Crude petroleum production

Cadiz
Harrison County

(G-1719)
MARKWEST ENERGY PARTNERS LP
Also Called: Mark West Energy
78405 Cadiz New Athens Rd (43907-9665)
PHONE..............................740 942-0463
Mark West, *Brnch Mgr*
EMP: 11
Web: www.markwest.com
SIC: 1321 Natural gas liquids
HQ: Markwest Energy Partners, L.P.
1515 Arphoe St Twr 1 Ste
Denver CO 80202
303 925-9200

(G-1720)
STANLEY BITTINGER
Also Called: Bittinger Carbide
81331 Hines Rd (43907-9535)
PHONE..............................740 942-4302
Stanley Bittinger, *Owner*
Sheila Bittinger, *Off Mgr*
EMP: 7 **EST:** 1981
SQ FT: 1,800

SALES (est): 505.69K **Privately Held**
Web: www.bittingercarbide.com
SIC: **3546** 5084 3545 Power-driven
  handtools; Industrial machinery and
  equipment; Machine tool accessories

Cairo
Allen County

(G-1721)
CHEMTRADE REFINERY SVCS INC
7680 Ottawa Rd (45820)
PHONE.................................419 641-4151
Tim Handiford, *Brnch Mgr*
EMP: 10
SALES (corp-wide): 1.34B **Privately Held**
Web: www.chemtradelogistics.com
SIC: **2819** Industrial inorganic chemicals, nec
HQ: Chemtrade Refinery Services Inc.
  440 N 9th St
  Lawrence KS 66044
  785 843-2290

Caldwell
Noble County

(G-1722)
ANTERO RESOURCES
CORPORATION
44510 Marietta Rd (43724-9209)
PHONE.................................303 357-7310
Austin Beeler, *Mgr*
EMP: 34
Web: www.anteroresources.com
SIC: **1382** Oil and gas exploration services
PA: Antero Resources Corporation
  1615 Wynkoop St
  Denver CO 80202

(G-1723)
BEAR WELDING SERVICES LLC
18210 Myrtle Ake Rd (43724-9136)
PHONE.................................740 630-7538
Jeremy Leonard, *Managing Member*
EMP: 10 EST: 2014
SALES (est): 231.89K **Privately Held**
SIC: **7692** Welding repair

(G-1724)
CALDWELL LUMBER & SUPPLY CO
Also Called: Do It Best
17990 Woodsfield Rd (43724-9435)
PHONE.................................740 732-2306
Edward Crock, *Pr*
Brandon Crock, *
EMP: 11 EST: 1948
SQ FT: 25,000
SALES (est): 1.44MM **Privately Held**
Web: caldwell.doitbest.com
SIC: **5251** 3273 Hardware stores; Ready-
  mixed concrete

(G-1725)
MAGNUM MAGNETICS
CORPORATION
17289 Industrial Hwy (43724-9779)
PHONE.................................740 516-6237
EMP: 39
Web: www.magnummagnetics.com
SIC: **2893** Printing ink
PA: Magnum Magnetics Corporation
  801 Masonic Park Rd
  Marietta OH 45750

(G-1726)
MAGNUM TAPES FILMS
17289 Industrial Hwy (43724-9779)

PHONE.................................877 460-8402
EMP: 9 EST: 2018
SALES (est): 447.42K **Privately Held**
Web: www.magnumtapes.com
SIC: **2672** 3069 3081 Adhesive papers,
  labels, or tapes: from purchased material;
  Film, rubber; Polyethylene film

(G-1727)
R C MOORE LUMBER CO
820 Miller St (43724-1044)
P.O. Box 139 (43724-0139)
PHONE.................................740 732-4950
Chad Moore, *Pr*
EMP: 12
SALES (corp-wide): 386.26K **Privately
Held**
Web: www.rcmooredoors.com
SIC: **2431** 5211 Doors, combination screen-
  storm, wood; Lumber products
PA: R. C. Moore Lumber Co.
  46000 County Road 56
  Caldwell OH
  740 732-2326

(G-1728)
SHARON STONE INC
44895 Sharon Stone Rd (43724-9534)
P.O. Box 100 (45727-0100)
PHONE.................................740 732-7100
John Mccort, *Pr*
Carl Baker Junior, *VP*
Robert Cunningham, *Sec*
EMP: 6 EST: 1985
SQ FT: 980
SALES (est): 695.64K **Privately Held**
SIC: **1422** Limestones, ground

(G-1729)
SOUTHEAST PUBLICATIONS INC
Also Called: Journal Leader
309 Main St (43724-1321)
P.O. Box 315 (43724-0315)
PHONE.................................740 732-2341
David Evans, *Pr*
Jack Cartener, *Dir*
Ann Velgari, *Dir*
EMP: 10 EST: 1941
SQ FT: 3,360
SALES (est): 290.09K **Privately Held**
Web: www.journal-leader.com
SIC: **2711** 2752 Commercial printing and
  newspaper publishing combined;
  Commercial printing, lithographic

(G-1730)
TRINITY WATER SOLUTIONS LLC
17226 Industrial Hwy (43724-9779)
P.O. Box 4074 (45750-7074)
PHONE.................................740 318-0585
EMP: 25 EST: 2021
SALES (est): 3.13MM **Privately Held**
Web: www.trinityenergysolutionsllc.com
SIC: **3589** Water treatment equipment,
  industrial

Caledonia
Marion County

(G-1731)
GLEN-GERY CORPORATION
Also Called: Glen-Gery Caledonia Plant
5692 Rinker Rd (43314-9791)
P.O. Box 207 (43325-0207)
PHONE.................................419 845-3321
Ken Hagberg, *Mgr*
EMP: 94
Web: www.glengery.com

SIC: **3251** 5211 3255 Brick clay: common
  face, glazed, vitrified, or hollow; Brick; Clay
  refractories
HQ: Glen-Gery Corporation
  1166 Spring St
  Reading PA 19610
  610 374-4011

(G-1732)
INSTA-GRO MANUFACTURING INC
8217 Linn Hipsher Rd (43314-9736)
PHONE.................................419 845-3046
Allan Farrow, *Pr*
EMP: 6 EST: 1978
SALES (est): 491.09K **Privately Held**
Web: www.instagro.com
SIC: **2875** 5261 Fertilizers, mixing only;
  Fertilizer

(G-1733)
PILLSBURY COMPANY LLC
Also Called: Pillsbury
4136 Martel Rd (43314-9634)
PHONE.................................419 845-3751
Craig Olinger, *Brnch Mgr*
EMP: 74
SALES (corp-wide): 19.86B **Publicly Held**
Web: www.pillsbury.com
SIC: **2041** 2033 Flour and other grain mill
  products; Canned fruits and specialties
HQ: The Pillsbury Company Llc
  1 General Mills Blvd
  Minneapolis MN 55426

Cambridge
Guernsey County

(G-1734)
ACI SERVICES INC (HQ)
Also Called: Gas Products
125 Steubenville Ave (43725-2212)
PHONE.................................740 435-0240
Chad Brahler, *Pr*
Joe Reiheld, *
Dwayne A Hickman, *OF ERCM
PRODUCTS AND SERVICES*
Brett Kyle, *
Les Wymer, *
EMP: 40 EST: 1960
SQ FT: 25,000
SALES (est): 13.46MM
SALES (corp-wide): 317.01MM **Privately
Held**
Web: www.aciservices.com
SIC: **3563** Air and gas compressors
  including vacuum pumps
PA: Cooper Machinery Services Llc
  16250 Port Nw Dr
  Houston TX 77041
  713 354-1900

(G-1735)
AMG ALUMINUM NORTH AMERICA
LLC (HQ)
Also Called: AMG Aluminum
60790 Southgate Rd (43725-9414)
PHONE.................................659 348-3620
Tom Centa, *Managing Member*
◆ EMP: 15 EST: 1986
SALES (est): 16.98MM
SALES (corp-wide): 937.12MM **Privately
Held**
Web: www.amg-al.com
SIC: **3355** 3354 3365 3339 Aluminum rod
  and bar; Aluminum extruded products;
  Aluminum foundries; Primary nonferrous
  metals, nec
PA: Amg Critical Materials N.V.
  Strawinskylaan 1343
  Amsterdam NH 1077

207147140

(G-1736)
APPALACHIAN WELL SURVEYS INC
10291 Ohio Ave (43725-3201)
P.O. Box 1058 (43725-6058)
PHONE.................................740 255-7652
Jonathan W Hudson, *Pr*
Mary Ann Hudson, *VP*
EMP: 8 EST: 1987
SALES (est): 1.03MM **Privately Held**
Web:
www.appalachianwellsurveysinc.com
SIC: **1389** Oil field services, nec

(G-1737)
BLUE RACER MIDSTREAM LLC
11388 E Pike Rd Unit B (43725-9669)
PHONE.................................740 630-7556
EMP: 16 EST: 2013
SALES (est): 2.31MM **Privately Held**
Web: www.blueracermidstream.com
SIC: **1382** Oil and gas exploration services

(G-1738)
CAMBRIDGE PACKAGING INC
Also Called: Cambridge Box & Gift Shop
60794 Southgate Rd (43725-9414)
PHONE.................................740 432-3351
Larry Knellinger, *Pr*
Margaret F Knellinger, *
Bill Knellinger, *
Rick Knellinger, *
EMP: 31 EST: 1982
SQ FT: 26,000
SALES (est): 11.04MM **Privately Held**
Web: www.cambridgepackaging.com
SIC: **2653** 5199 Boxes, corrugated: made
  from purchased materials; Packaging
  materials

(G-1739)
COLGATE-PALMOLIVE COMPANY
Also Called: Colgate-Palmolive
8800 Guernsey Industrial Blvd
(43725-8913)
PHONE.................................212 310-2000
Rick Spann, *Mgr*
EMP: 250
SALES (corp-wide): 20.1B **Publicly Held**
Web: www.colgatepalmolive.com
SIC: **2844** Perfumes, cosmetics and other
  toilet preparations
PA: Colgate-Palmolive Company
  300 Park Ave
  New York NY 10022
  212 310-2000

(G-1740)
CRESCENT SERVICES LLC
11137 E Pike Rd (43725-8949)
PHONE.................................405 603-1200
Susan Leonard, *Prin*
EMP: 6 EST: 2012
SALES (est): 179.1K **Privately Held**
SIC: **1389** Oil field services, nec

(G-1741)
DETROIT DESL RMNUFACTURING
LLC
8475 Reitler Rd (43725-8660)
PHONE.................................740 439-7701
Cheryl Meyer, *Brnch Mgr*
EMP: 121
SALES (corp-wide): 57.19B **Privately Held**
SIC: **3519** Diesel engine rebuilding
HQ: Detroit Diesel Remanufacturing Llc
  100 Lodestone Way
  Tooele UT 84074

▲ = Import ▼ = Export
◆ = Import/Export

(G-1742)
EMERSON PROFESSIONAL TOOLS LLC
9877 Brick Church Rd (43725-9420)
PHONE..............................740 432-8782
EMP: 26 **EST:** 2019
SALES (est): 12.93MM
SALES (corp-wide): 17.49B **Publicly Held**
SIC: 3823 Process control instruments
PA: Emerson Electric Co.
8027 Forsyth Boulevard
Saint Louis MO 63105
888 889-9170

(G-1743)
ENCORE INDUSTRIES INC (DH)
Also Called: Encore Plastics
725 Water St (43725-1241)
PHONE..............................419 626-8000
Timothy J Rathbun, *CEO*
Craig Rathbun, *
▲ **EMP:** 41 **EST:** 2000
SQ FT: 250,000
SALES (est): 45.52MM
SALES (corp-wide): 816.52K **Privately Held**
SIC: 3089 Thermoformed finished plastics products, nec
HQ: Plastiques Ipl Inc
1155 Boul Rene-Levesque O Bureau 4100
Montreal QC H3B 3
418 789-2880

(G-1744)
GEORGETOWN VINEYARDS INC
Also Called: Georgetown Vineyards
62920 Georgetown Rd (43725-9749)
PHONE..............................740 435-3222
John Nicolozakes, *Pr*
Kay Nicolozakes, *VP*
Emma Mcvicker, *Sec*
Sam Nicolozakes, *Treas*
EMP: 25 **EST:** 2004
SQ FT: 600
SALES (est): 1.28MM **Privately Held**
Web: www.georgetowntavern.com
SIC: 2084 5812 2082 Wine cellars, bonded: engaged in blending wines; Pizza restaurants; Near beer

(G-1745)
J E NICOLOZAKES CO
62920 Georgetown Rd (43725-9749)
PHONE..............................740 310-1606
John Nicolozakes, *Prin*
EMP: 6 **EST:** 1992
SALES (est): 95.06K **Privately Held**
SIC: 2084 Wines

(G-1746)
KENNEDYS BAKERY INC
1025 Wheeling Ave (43725-2441)
P.O. Box 396 (43725-0396)
PHONE..............................740 432-2301
T Noralee Kennedy, *Pr*
Bob Kennedy, *VP*
EMP: 8 **EST:** 1925
SQ FT: 8,000
SALES (est): 505.65K **Privately Held**
Web: www.kennedysbakery.com
SIC: 5461 2052 2051 Doughnuts; Cookies and crackers; Bread, cake, and related products

(G-1747)
KINGSLY COMPRESSION INC
Also Called: Kingsly Compression
3956 Glenn Hwy (43725-8575)
PHONE..............................740 439-0772
Jeffrey B Sable, *Brnch Mgr*

EMP: 8
Web: www.kingslycompression.com
SIC: 3563 5084 Air and gas compressors; Processing and packaging equipment
PA: Kingsly Compression, Inc.
3750 S Noah Dr
Saxonburg PA 16056

(G-1748)
MATTMARK PARTNERS INC
Also Called: Mattmark Drilling Company
61234 Southgate Rd (43725-8945)
PHONE..............................740 439-3109
Gerald J Benson, *Pr*
Georgia Benson, *VP*
EMP: 14 **EST:** 1985
SQ FT: 5,400
SALES (est): 671.97K **Privately Held**
SIC: 1381 Drilling oil and gas wells

(G-1749)
METAL COATERS
Also Called: Centria Coil Coating Services
530 N 2nd St (43725-1214)
PHONE..............................740 432-7351
Charlie Hamilton, *Mgr*
EMP: 100
SALES (corp-wide): 30.73B **Publicly Held**
Web: www.bluescopecoatedproducts.com
SIC: 3444 Sheet metalwork
HQ: Centria, Inc.
1550 Corpls Hts Rd # 500
Moon Township PA 15108
412 299-8000

(G-1750)
MO-TRIM INC
240 Steubenville Ave (43725-2215)
P.O. Box 850 (43725-0850)
PHONE..............................740 439-2725
Jack O Cartner, *Pr*
EMP: 7 **EST:** 1962
SQ FT: 10,000
SALES (est): 1.02MM **Privately Held**
Web: www.motrim.net
SIC: 3524 Lawn and garden tractors and equipment

(G-1751)
MOSSER GLASS INC
9279 Cadiz Rd (43725-9564)
PHONE..............................740 439-1827
Timmy J Mosser, *Pr*
Thomas R Mosser, *
Timmy J Mosser, *VP*
Mindy Hartly, *
▲ **EMP:** 30 **EST:** 1961
SALES (est): 2.91MM **Privately Held**
Web: www.mosserglass.com
SIC: 3229 5199 5719 Novelty glassware; Glassware, novelty; Glassware

(G-1752)
OHIO BRIDGE CORPORATION
Also Called: U.S. Bridge
201 Wheeling Ave (43725-2256)
P.O. Box 757 (43725-0757)
PHONE..............................740 432-6334
Daniel Rogovin, *CEO*
Richard Rogovin, *
▼ **EMP:** 140 **EST:** 1952
SQ FT: 250,000
SALES (est): 23.78MM **Privately Held**
Web: www.usbridge.com
SIC: 1622 3449 Bridge construction; Bars, concrete reinforcing: fabricated steel

(G-1753)
PACKAGING MATERIALS INC
62805 Bennett Ave (43725-9490)
P.O. Box 731 (43725-0731)
PHONE..............................740 432-6337
Marc Radasky, *Pr*
▼ **EMP:** 38 **EST:** 1970
SQ FT: 48,000
SALES (est): 4.5MM
SALES (corp-wide): 9.06MM **Privately Held**
Web: www.packagingmaterialsinc.com
SIC: 3081 2759 2673 Unsupported plastics film and sheet; Commercial printing, nec; Bags: plastic, laminated, and coated
PA: Columbia Burlap And Bag Company, Inc.
1475 Walnut St
Kansas City MO 64106
816 421-4121

(G-1754)
PANHANDLE OLFLD SVC CMPNIES IN
62787 Philips Rd (43725-8684)
PHONE..............................330 340-9525
EMP: 20
Web: www.posci.net
SIC: 1389 Oil field services, nec
PA: Panhandle Oilfield Service Companies, Inc.
14000 Qail Sprng Pkwy Ste
Oklahoma City OK 73134

(G-1755)
PLASTIC COMPOUNDERS INC
1125 Utica Dr (43725-2578)
P.O. Box 664 (43725-0664)
PHONE..............................740 432-7371
Dick Eubanks, *Pr*
Scott Eubanks, *
EMP: 40 **EST:** 1965
SQ FT: 50,000
SALES (est): 9.53MM **Privately Held**
Web: www.plasticcompounders.net
SIC: 2821 Plastics materials and resins

(G-1756)
QUANEX IG SYSTEMS INC
Also Called: Quanex Custom Mixing
804 Byesville Rd (43725-9327)
PHONE..............................740 435-0444
Jim Nixon, *Brnch Mgr*
EMP: 74
Web: www.quanex.com
SIC: 2891 Rubber cement
HQ: Quanex Ig Systems, Inc.
388 S Main St Ste 700
Akron OH 44311

(G-1757)
QUANEX IG SYSTEMS INC
Also Called: Quanex Building Products
800 Cochran Ave (43725-9317)
PHONE..............................740 439-2338
Michael Hovan, *Brnch Mgr*
EMP: 28
Web: www.quanex.com
SIC: 3061 3053 Mechanical rubber goods; Gaskets; packing and sealing devices
HQ: Quanex Ig Systems, Inc.
388 S Main St Ste 700
Akron OH 44311

(G-1758)
RIDGE TOOL COMPANY
Also Called: North American Dist Ctr
9877 Brick Church Rd (43725-9420)
PHONE..............................740 432-8782
Brian Shanahann, *Mgr*
EMP: 81

SALES (corp-wide): 17.49B **Publicly Held**
Web: www.ridgid.com
SIC: 3541 Machine tools, metal cutting type
HQ: Ridge Tool Company
400 Clark St
Elyria OH 44035
440 323-5581

(G-1759)
SMITH CONCRETE
61539 Southgate Rd (43725-9456)
PHONE..............................740 439-7714
EMP: 15 **EST:** 2019
SALES (est): 329.74K **Privately Held**
Web: www.shellyco.com
SIC: 3273 Ready-mixed concrete

(G-1760)
SNIDER TIRE INC
Also Called: Snider General Tire
9501 Sunrise Rd (43725-9116)
PHONE..............................740 439-2741
Jerry Vandyne, *Mgr*
EMP: 18
SALES (corp-wide): 501.16MM **Privately Held**
Web: www.sniderfleet.com
SIC: 5531 7534 Automotive tires; Tire retreading and repair shops
PA: Snider Tire, Inc.
1081 Red Ventures Dr
Fort Mill SC 29707
800 528-2840

(G-1761)
SPORTSMANS HAVEN INC
14695 E Pike Rd (43725-9166)
P.O. Box 403 (43773-0403)
PHONE..............................740 432-7243
Brent Umberger, *Pr*
EMP: 6 **EST:** 1961
SQ FT: 600
SALES (est): 146.93K **Privately Held**
SIC: 2426 7699 5941 Gun stocks, wood; Gunsmith shop; Firearms

(G-1762)
SUPERIOR HARDWOODS OHIO INC
Also Called: Superior Hardwoods Cambridge
9911 Ohio Ave (43725-9307)
P.O. Box 1358 (43725-6358)
PHONE..............................740 439-2727
Fred Lander, *Mgr*
EMP: 20
SALES (corp-wide): 8.88MM **Privately Held**
Web: www.superiorhardwoodsofohio.com
SIC: 2421 2426 Sawmills and planing mills, general; Hardwood dimension and flooring mills
PA: Superior Hardwoods Of Ohio, Inc.
134 Wellston Indus Pk Rd
Wellston OH 45692
740 384-5677

(G-1763)
TAYLOR QUICK PRINT
Also Called: Quick Print
1008 Woodlawn Ave # A (43725-2951)
PHONE..............................740 439-2208
Brenda Taylor, *Prin*
EMP: 6 **EST:** 2007
SALES (est): 103.35K **Privately Held**
SIC: 2752 Offset printing

(G-1764)
TELLING INDUSTRIES LLC
2105 Larrick Rd (43725-3064)
PHONE..............................740 435-8900
Steve Linch, *Mgr*

EMP: 37
SALES (corp-wide): 24.7MM **Privately Held**
Web: www.tellingindustries.com
SIC: 3316 Bars, steel, cold finished, from purchased hot-rolled
PA: Telling Industries, Llc
4420 Sherwin Rd Ste 4
Willoughby OH 44094
440 974-3370

(G-1765)
VARIETY GLASS INC
201 Foster Ave (43725-1219)
PHONE..............................740 432-3643
Thomas R Mosser, *Pr*
Timothy J Mosser, *VP*
EMP: 10 **EST:** 1959
SQ FT: 16,000
SALES (est): 989.99K **Privately Held**
Web: www.mosserglass.com
SIC: 3229 Scientific glassware

(G-1766)
ZEKELMAN INDUSTRIES INC
Also Called: Wheatland Tube Company
9208 Jeffrey Dr (43725-9417)
PHONE..............................740 432-2146
Ned Feeney, *Pr*
EMP: 186
SQ FT: 58,000
Web: www.zekelman.com
SIC: 3317 3498 5074 3644 Pipes, seamless steel; Fabricated pipe and fittings; Plumbing fittings and supplies; Noncurrent-carrying wiring devices
PA: Zekelman Industries, Inc.
227 W Monroe St Ste 2600
Chicago IL 60606

Camden
Preble County

(G-1767)
CAMDEN READY MIX CO (PA)
478 Camden College Corner Rd (45311-9520)
P.O. Box 5 (45381-0005)
PHONE..............................937 456-4539
John D Wysong, *Pr*
Carroll Wysong, *VP*
EMP: 6 **EST:** 1947
SALES (est): 458.44K
SALES (corp-wide): 458.44K **Privately Held**
Web: www.preblecountystorage.com
SIC: 3273 Ready-mixed concrete

(G-1768)
PRECISION WOOD PRODUCTS INC (PA)
2456 Aukerman Creek Rd (45311-9706)
P.O. Box 10 (45311-0010)
PHONE..............................937 787-3523
Anthony Metzger, *Pr*
Lloyd W Kinzie, *Pr*
Glen D Knaus, *VP*
H Ronald Knaus, *VP*
Barbara Knaus, *Sec*
EMP: 10 **EST:** 1977
SQ FT: 32,000
SALES (est): 3.23MM
SALES (corp-wide): 3.23MM **Privately Held**
Web: www.precisionwoodproducts.com
SIC: 2431 Doors, wood

(G-1769)
WYSONG GRAVEL CO INC
120 Camden College Corner Rd (45311-9520)
P.O. Box 5 (45381-0005)
PHONE..............................937 452-1523
Tom Caden, *Genl Mgr*
EMP: 7
SQ FT: 3,452
SALES (corp-wide): 2.59MM **Privately Held**
Web: www.preblecountystorage.com
SIC: 1442 Gravel mining
PA: Wysong Gravel Co Inc
2332 State Route 503 N
West Alexandria OH 45381
937 456-4539

Campbell
Mahoning County

(G-1770)
SEACOR PAINTING CORPORATION
98 Creed Cir (44405-1277)
P.O. Box 588 (44405-0588)
PHONE..............................330 755-6361
Nicholas Frangos, *Pr*
EMP: 8 **EST:** 1997
SALES (est): 429.02K **Privately Held**
Web: www.seacorpainting.com
SIC: 3479 Painting of metal products

(G-1771)
STEEL CITY CONTRACTORS LLC
419 Blossom Ave (44405-1432)
PHONE..............................330 519-8873
EMP: 10 **EST:** 2021
SALES (est): 1.15MM **Privately Held**
SIC: 3441 Fabricated structural metal

Canal Fulton
Stark County

(G-1772)
ASTRO-TEC MFG INC
550 Elm Ridge Ave (44614-9369)
P.O. Box 608 (44614-0608)
PHONE..............................330 854-2209
Stephanie Hopper, *Pr*
◆ **EMP:** 22 **EST:** 1963
SQ FT: 15,328
SALES (est): 2.95MM **Privately Held**
Web: www.astro-tec.com
SIC: 3441 Fabricated structural metal

(G-1773)
BIRDS EYE FOODS INC
611 Elm Ridge Ave (44614-8476)
PHONE..............................330 854-0818
Bill Gaster, *Brnch Mgr*
EMP: 77
SALES (corp-wide): 45.76MM **Privately Held**
SIC: 2096 3523 Potato chips and similar snacks; Peanut combines, diggers, packers, and threshers
PA: Birds Eye Foods, Inc.
121 Woodcrest Rd
Cherry Hill NJ 08003

(G-1774)
C MASSOUH PRINTING CO INC
Also Called: C Massouh Printing
590 Elm Ridge Ave (44614-9369)
PHONE..............................330 408-7330
Carl Massouh, *Pr*
Chris Massouh, *VP*
EMP: 10 **EST:** 1989

SALES (est): 986.65K **Privately Held**
Web: www.cmassouhprinting.com
SIC: 2752 Offset printing

(G-1775)
COMMUNICATION EXHIBITS INC
1119 Milan St N (44614-9737)
PHONE..............................330 854-4040
EMP: 60 **EST:** 1977
SALES (est): 8.96MM **Privately Held**
Web: www.ceilink.com
SIC: 3993 2542 Signs and advertising specialties; Partitions and fixtures, except wood

(G-1776)
JONMAR GEAR AND MACHINE INC
13786 Warwick Dr Nw (44614-9738)
PHONE..............................330 854-6500
Larry Murgatroyd, *Pr*
Brent A Murgatroyd, *VP*
EMP: 6 **EST:** 2000
SQ FT: 18,000
SALES (est): 1.68MM **Privately Held**
Web: www.jonmargear.com
SIC: 3566 7699 Gears, power transmission, except auto; Industrial machinery and equipment repair

(G-1777)
LINDSAY PRECAST LLC (PA)
6845 Erie Ave Nw (44614-8509)
PHONE..............................800 837-7788
TOLL FREE: 800
Roland Lindsay Senior, *Pr*
Timothy Gesaman, *VP*
Linda Lindsay, *VP*
▼ **EMP:** 49 **EST:** 1968
SALES (est): 35.62MM
SALES (corp-wide): 35.62MM **Privately Held**
Web: www.lindsayprecast.com
SIC: 3272 3699 Septic tanks, concrete; Security devices

(G-1778)
MIDWEST KNIFE GRINDING INC
492 Elm Ridge Ave Ste 4 (44614-9369)
PHONE..............................330 854-1030
James M Richmond Ii, *Pr*
EMP: 10 **EST:** 1986
SQ FT: 12,000
SALES (est): 1.01MM **Privately Held**
Web: www.midwestknife.com
SIC: 7699 3541 3423 Knife, saw and tool sharpening and repair; Machine tools, metal cutting type; Hand and edge tools, nec

(G-1779)
SUMMIT ENGINEERED PRODUCTS INC
516 Elm Ridge Ave (44614-9369)
PHONE..............................330 854-5388
Dick Lutz, *Pr*
EMP: 10 **EST:** 2006
SALES (est): 949.51K **Privately Held**
SIC: 3315 Steel wire and related products

(G-1780)
TEK GROUP INTERNATIONAL
Also Called: Tek Manufacturing
567 Elm Ridge Ave (44614-9369)
PHONE..............................330 706-0000
Chris Willison, *Pr*
Cliff Willison, *
EMP: 35 **EST:** 2003
SQ FT: 12,000
SALES (est): 5.4MM **Privately Held**
Web: www.tekusa.com

SIC: 3599 Machine shop, jobbing and repair

(G-1781)
USA PRECAST CONCRETE LIMITED
801 Elm Ridge Ave (44614-9396)
P.O. Box 613 (44614-0613)
PHONE..............................330 854-9600
Jeffrey Augustine, *VP*
Timothy Gesaman, *
Krista Gesaman, *
Jeff Augustine, *
Wendy Potashnik, *
EMP: 50 **EST:** 2016
SALES (est): 5.03MM **Privately Held**
Web: www.usaprecast.com
SIC: 3241 Cement, hydraulic

Canal Winchester
Franklin County

(G-1782)
A K ATHLETIC EQUIPMENT INC
8015 Howe Industrial Pkwy (43110-7890)
PHONE..............................614 920-3069
Angela Katz, *Pr*
EMP: 34 **EST:** 1993
SQ FT: 32,000
SALES (est): 7.5MM **Privately Held**
Web: www.akathletics.com
SIC: 3496 5091 Mats and matting; Gymnasium equipment

(G-1783)
AEROSPORT MODELING DESIGN LLC
Also Called: Aerosport Additive
8090 Howe Industrial Pkwy (43110-7889)
PHONE..............................614 834-5227
Jeff Combs, *Pr*
Laurel Combs, *Sec*
EMP: 10 **EST:** 1989
SQ FT: 10,000
SALES (est): 2.12MM **Privately Held**
Web: www.aerosportadditive.com
SIC: 7389 7699 2821 Hand tool designers; Industrial equipment services; Plasticizer/ additive based plastic materials

(G-1784)
ATWOOD ROPE MANUFACTURING INC
121 N Trine St (43110-1154)
PHONE..............................614 920-0534
Curtis Atwood, *Pr*
Curtis Atwood, *Owner*
▲ **EMP:** 40 **EST:** 2000
SALES (est): 1.86MM **Privately Held**
Web: www.atwoodrope.com
SIC: 5091 5085 2298 Boat accessories and parts; Rope, cord, and thread; Ropes and fiber cables

(G-1785)
BABBERT REAL ESTATE INV CO LTD (PA)
7415 Diley Rd (43110-8813)
P.O. Box 203 (43110-0203)
PHONE..............................614 837-8444
Ervin C Babbert, *CEO*
Chuck Babbert, *
Ronald Babbert, *
Bonnie Babbert, *
EMP: 100 **EST:** 1998
SQ FT: 20,000
SALES (est): 1.34MM
SALES (corp-wide): 1.34MM **Privately Held**
Web: www.ecbabbert.com

SIC: 3272 Liquid catch basins, tanks, and covers: concrete

(G-1786)
BREWDOG BREWING COMPANY LLC (PA)
Also Called: Brewdog
96 Gender Rd (43110-7539)
PHONE..............................614 908-3051
Martin Macdonald, *Genl Mgr*
EMP: 18 EST: 2016
SALES (est): 9.83MM
SALES (corp-wide): 9.83MM **Privately Held**
Web: www.brewdog.com
SIC: 2082 5813 Beer (alcoholic beverage); Bars and lounges

(G-1787)
BRIDGESTONE RET OPERATIONS LLC
Also Called: Firestone
6574 Winchester Blvd (43110-2056)
PHONE..............................614 834-3672
EMP: 7
Web: www.bridgestoneamericas.com
SIC: 5531 7534 Automotive tires; Tire retreading and repair shops
HQ: Bridgestone Retail Operations, Llc
200 4th Ave S Ste 100
Nashville TN 37201
615 937-1000

(G-1788)
CAPSA SOLUTIONS LLC
8170 Dove Pkwy (43110-9674)
PHONE..............................800 437-6633
David Burns, *CEO*
EMP: 90
SALES (corp-wide): 96.35MM **Privately Held**
Web: www.capsahealthcare.com
SIC: 3572 Computer storage devices
PA: Capsa Solutions Llc
8170 Dove Pkwy
Canal Winchester OH 43110
800 437-6633

(G-1789)
E C BABBERT INC
7415 Diley Rd (43110-8813)
P.O. Box 203 (43110-0203)
PHONE..............................614 837-8444
Ervin C Babbert, *CEO*
Charles Babbert, *
Rick Gibbs Cntllr, *Prin*
EMP: 72 EST: 2009
SALES (est): 8.63MM **Privately Held**
Web: www.ecbabbert.com
SIC: 3272 Liquid catch basins, tanks, and covers: concrete

(G-1790)
FIFTH AVENUE LUMBER CO
Lumbercraft
5200 Winchester Pike (43110-9723)
PHONE..............................614 833-6655
Chris Kealey, *Mgr*
EMP: 27
SALES (corp-wide): 27.16MM **Privately Held**
Web: www.straitandlamp.com
SIC: 2431 2439 2452 2435 Millwork; Trusses, wooden roof; Prefabricated wood buildings; Hardwood veneer and plywood
HQ: Fifth Avenue Lumber Co (Inc)
479 E 5th Ave
Columbus OH 43201
614 294-0068

(G-1791)
HFI LLC (PA)
59 Gender Rd (43110-9733)
PHONE..............................614 491-0700
Brian Grady, *CEO*
Tony Konarzewski, *
◆ EMP: 350 EST: 1969
SQ FT: 140,000
SALES (est): 277MM
SALES (corp-wide): 277MM **Privately Held**
Web: www.hfi-inc.com
SIC: 2396 2821 3714 3429 Automotive trimmings, fabric; Polyurethane resins; Motor vehicle parts and accessories; Hardware, nec

(G-1792)
KELLOGG CABINETS INC
Also Called: Kci Works
7711 Diley Rd (43110-9616)
PHONE..............................614 833-9596
Judy A Kellogg, *CEO*
Douglas E Kellogg, *VP*
Judy Kellogg, *CEO*
◆ EMP: 9 EST: 1975
SQ FT: 28,850
SALES (est): 1.82MM **Privately Held**
Web: www.kciworks.com
SIC: 2541 2542 2434 Cabinets, except refrigerated: show, display, etc.: wood; Partitions and fixtures, except wood; Wood kitchen cabinets

(G-1793)
MANIFOLD & PHALOR INC
Also Called: US Die & Mold
10385 Busey Rd Nw (43110-8883)
PHONE..............................614 920-1200
Thomas J Creek, *Pr*
▼ EMP: 45 EST: 1946
SQ FT: 28,800
SALES (est): 5.15MM **Privately Held**
Web: www.manifoldphalor.com
SIC: 3441 3599 3559 Fabricated structural metal; Machine shop, jobbing and repair; Glass making machinery: blowing, molding, forming, etc.

(G-1794)
NIFCO AMERICA CORPORATION (HQ)
8015 Dove Pkwy (43110-9697)
PHONE..............................614 920-6800
Masaharu Shibao, *CEO*
Toshiyuki Yamamoto, *CSO**
Tom Day, *
John Kosik, *
▲ EMP: 312 EST: 1996
SQ FT: 50,000
SALES (est): 223.73MM **Privately Held**
Web: www.nifcousa.com
SIC: 3089 Automotive parts, plastic
PA: Nifco Inc.
5-3, Hikarinooka
Yokosuka KNG 239-0

(G-1795)
NIFCO AMERICA CORPORATION
Also Called: Canal Winchester Facility
7877 Robinett Way (43110-8165)
PHONE..............................614 836-3808
Tom Day, *Genl Mgr*
EMP: 55
Web: www.nifcousa.com
SIC: 3089 Automotive parts, plastic
HQ: Nifco America Corporation
8015 Dove Pkwy
Canal Winchester OH 43110
614 920-6800

(G-1796)
NORDIC LIGHT AMERICA INC
6320 Winchester Blvd (43110-6536)
PHONE..............................614 981-9497
Kenneth Johansson, *Pr*
▲ EMP: 10 EST: 2011
SALES (est): 7.79MM
SALES (corp-wide): 603.72MM **Privately Held**
Web: www.itab.com
SIC: 7389 3646 Interior design services; Ceiling systems, luminous
HQ: Nordic Light Ab
Svedjevagen 12
SkellefteA 931 3
910733790

(G-1797)
OLAN PLASTICS INC
6550 Olan Dr (43110-9685)
PHONE..............................614 834-6526
Olan Long, *CEO*
James Long, *
Marcella Long, *
EMP: 40 EST: 1980
SQ FT: 30,000
SALES (est): 2.91MM **Privately Held**
Web: www.olanplastics.shop
SIC: 3089 Plastics containers, except foam

(G-1798)
TARMAN MACHINE COMPANY INC
8215 Dove Pkwy (43110-7717)
P.O. Box 192 (43147-0192)
PHONE..............................614 834-4010
Randy Tarman, *Pr*
EMP: 17 EST: 1966
SQ FT: 13,000
SALES (est): 3.29MM **Privately Held**
Web: www.tarmanmachine.com
SIC: 3599 Machine shop, jobbing and repair

(G-1799)
TS TRIM INDUSTRIES INC (DH)
6380 Canal St (43110-9640)
PHONE..............................614 837-4114
▲ EMP: 400 EST: 1986
SALES (est): 40.26MM **Privately Held**
Web: www.tstech.com
SIC: 5013 3465 3714 3083 Automotive supplies and parts; Moldings or trim, automobile: stamped metal; Motor vehicle parts and accessories; Laminated plastics plate and sheet
HQ: Ts Tech Americas, Inc.
8458 E Broad St
Reynoldsburg OH 43068
614 575-4100

(G-1800)
WORLD HARVEST CHURCH INC (PA)
Also Called: Breakthrough Media Ministries
4595 Gender Rd (43110-9149)
P.O. Box 428 (43110-0428)
PHONE..............................614 837-1990
Pastor Rodney Parsley, *Prin*
EMP: 200 EST: 1976
SQ FT: 200,000
SALES (est): 7.56MM
SALES (corp-wide): 7.56MM **Privately Held**
Web: www.whc.life
SIC: 7812 2731 Video tape production; Books, publishing and printing

Canfield
Mahoning County

(G-1801)
ADVETECH INC (PA)
Also Called: Perfection In Carbide
445 W Main St (44406-1436)
PHONE..............................330 533-2227
David Scott Owens, *CEO*
David Smith, *
EMP: 30 EST: 1917
SQ FT: 30,000
SALES (est): 858.54K
SALES (corp-wide): 858.54K **Privately Held**
Web: www.advetech.com
SIC: 3421 3599 3423 3541 Knife blades and blanks; Machine shop, jobbing and repair; Knives, agricultural or industrial; Machine tools, metal cutting type

(G-1802)
ADVETECH INC
451 W Main St (44406-1425)
P.O. Box 163216 (43216-3216)
PHONE..............................330 533-2227
Dave Smith, *Mgr*
EMP: 34
SALES (corp-wide): 858.54K **Privately Held**
Web: www.advetech.com
SIC: 3423 Knives, agricultural or industrial
PA: Advetech, Inc.
445 W Main St
Canfield OH 44406
330 533-2227

(G-1803)
ALSTART ENTERPRISES LLC
Also Called: USA Rolls
451 W Main St (44406-1425)
P.O. Box 1076 (44406-5076)
PHONE..............................330 533-3222
Kevin M Sheldon, *Pr*
EMP: 18 EST: 2009
SQ FT: 55,000
SALES (est): 2.73MM **Privately Held**
Web: www.usarolls.com
SIC: 3559 Plastics working machinery

(G-1804)
BAIRD BROTHERS SAWMILL INC
7060 Crory Rd (44406-9720)
PHONE..............................330 533-3122
TOLL FREE: 800
Paul Baird, *Pr*
Helen Perrine, *
EMP: 115 EST: 1960
SQ FT: 350,000
SALES (est): 16.89MM **Privately Held**
Web: www.bairdbrothers.com
SIC: 2431 Doors and door parts and trim, wood

(G-1805)
BETTS COMPANY
Also Called: Betts Hd
430 W Main St (44406-1434)
PHONE..............................330 533-0111
EMP: 24
SALES (corp-wide): 39.88MM **Privately Held**
SIC: 3495 Wire springs
PA: Betts Company
2843 S Maple Ave
Fresno CA 93725
559 498-3304

(G-1806)
CANFIELD COATING LLC
460 W Main St (44406-1434)
PHONE...........................330 533-3311
EMP: 24 EST: 2013
SALES (est): 3.39MM
SALES (corp-wide): 107.19MM **Privately Held**
Web: www.materialsciencescorp.com
SIC: 3479 5051 Galvanizing of iron, steel, or end-formed products; Metals service centers and offices
PA: Material Sciences Corporation
6855 Commerce Blvd
Canton MI 48187
734 207-4444

(G-1807)
CANFIELD METAL COATING CORP
460 W Main St (44406-1434)
PHONE...........................330 702-3876
Ronald W Jandrokovic, *Pr*
George S Bokros, *
Paul Pirko, *
EMP: 52 EST: 2001
SALES (est): 2.33MM
SALES (corp-wide): 2.03B **Publicly Held**
Web: www.materialsciencescorp.com
SIC: 3479 5051 Galvanizing of iron, steel, or end-formed products; Metals service centers and offices
HQ: Handy & Harman Ltd.
590 Madison Ave Fl 32
New York NY 10022

(G-1808)
DLAC INDUSTRIES INC
3755 Sugarbush Dr (44406-9107)
PHONE...........................330 519-4789
D L Cicoretti, *Prin*
EMP: 6 EST: 2011
SALES (est): 74K **Privately Held**
SIC: 3999 Manufacturing industries, nec

(G-1809)
EVERFLOW EASTERN PARTNERS LP (PA)
585 W Main St (44406-9733)
P.O. Box 629 (44406-0629)
PHONE...........................330 533-2692
Brian A Staebler, *Pr*
Michael W Rathburn, *CAO*
EMP: 7 EST: 1990
SQ FT: 6,400
SALES (est): 4.96MM **Privately Held**
SIC: 1382 1311 Oil and gas exploration services; Crude petroleum and natural gas

(G-1810)
HORSESHOE EXPRESS INC
8045 Camden Way (44406-8165)
PHONE...........................330 692-1209
Margaret Garwood, *Prin*
EMP: 6 EST: 2012
SALES (est): 517.75K **Privately Held**
SIC: 3462 Horseshoes

(G-1811)
IES SYSTEMS INC
464 Lisbon St (44406-1423)
P.O. Box 89 (44406-0089)
PHONE...........................330 533-6683
Mark Brucoli, *Pr*
Rob Mcandrew, *Ex VP*
David Wigal, *
Bill Yobi, *
Kelly Weiss, *
EMP: 45 EST: 2000
SQ FT: 27,000
SALES (est): 4.23MM **Privately Held**
Web: www.ies-us.com

SIC: 7389 3821 Design, commercial and industrial; Laboratory apparatus and furniture

(G-1812)
LHY POWERTRAIN CORPORATION (DH)
Also Called: Linde Hydraulics Corporation
5089 W Western Reserve Rd (44406-9564)
PHONE...........................330 533-6801
Doctor Ferdinand Megerlin, *Ch Bd*
Frank Cobb, *
Lewis P Kasper, *
John Kumler, *
▲ EMP: 38 EST: 1970
SQ FT: 80,000
SALES (est): 11.43MM **Publicly Held**
Web: www.lhy.com
SIC: 3594 3566 3714 3621 Pumps, hydraulic power transfer; Gears, power transmission, except auto; Motor vehicle parts and accessories; Motors and generators
HQ: Lhy Powertrain Gmbh & Co. Kg
Wailandtstr. 13
Aschaffenburg BY 63741
602115000

(G-1813)
MATERIAL SCIENCES CORPORATION
460 W Main St (44406-1434)
PHONE...........................330 702-3882
EMP: 105
SALES (corp-wide): 107.19MM **Privately Held**
Web: www.materialsciencescorp.com
SIC: 3479 Painting of metal products
PA: Material Sciences Corporation
6855 Commerce Blvd
Canton MI 48187
734 207-4444

(G-1814)
R J MANRAY INC
Also Called: Simply Bags
7320 Akron Canfield Rd Ste B (44406-9750)
PHONE...........................330 559-6716
Joanne Shirilla, *Pr*
Robert Shirilla, *Mktg Dir*
EMP: 8 EST: 1982
SALES (est): 77.28K **Privately Held**
Web: www.simply-bags.com
SIC: 5947 7389 2393 2211 Gift shop; Advertising, promotional, and trade show services; Duffle bags, canvas: made from purchased materials; Blankets and blanketings, cotton

(G-1815)
RUST BELT BRONCOS LLC
6145 State Route 446 (44406-9428)
PHONE...........................330 533-0048
Nathan Miller, *Managing Member*
EMP: 20 EST: 2014
SALES (est): 1.01MM **Privately Held**
Web: www.rustbeltbroncos.com
SIC: 3052 5531 Transmission belting, rubber; Automotive parts

(G-1816)
STAR EXTRUDED SHAPES LLC
7055 Herbert Rd (44406-8660)
P.O. Box 553 (44406-0553)
PHONE...........................330 533-9863
EMP: 300 EST: 1983
SALES (est): 14.11MM
SALES (corp-wide): 35.16MM **Privately Held**
Web: www.starext.com

SIC: 3354 Aluminum extruded products
PA: Astro Shapes Llc
65 Main St
Struthers OH 44471
330 755-1414

(G-1817)
STAR FAB LLC (HQ)
7055 Herbert Rd (44406-8660)
P.O. Box 553 (44406-0553)
PHONE...........................330 533-9863
Kenneth George, *Pr*
Gary Griswold, *
▲ EMP: 120 EST: 2001
SQ FT: 100,000
SALES (est): 5.1MM
SALES (corp-wide): 35.16MM **Privately Held**
Web: www.starext.com
SIC: 3354 3479 Aluminum extruded products; Painting of metal products
PA: Astro Shapes Llc
65 Main St
Struthers OH 44471
330 755-1414

(G-1818)
UNITED EXTRUSION DIES INC
5171 W Western Reserve Rd (44406-8112)
P.O. Box 117 (44406-0117)
PHONE...........................330 533-2915
John Fritz, *Pr*
James Rektor, *VP*
Sharon Crawford, *Sec*
EMP: 10 EST: 1984
SQ FT: 8,000
SALES (est): 582.33K **Privately Held**
Web: www.extrusionsupplies.com
SIC: 3544 Special dies and tools

Canton
Stark County

(G-1819)
3D PARTNERS LLC
1817 20th St Ne (44714-2123)
PHONE...........................330 323-6453
EMP: 8 EST: 2019
SALES (est): 1.18MM **Privately Held**
SIC: 3441 Fabricated structural metal

(G-1820)
ABC TECHNOLOGIES DLHB INC
2310 Leo Ave Sw (44706)
PHONE...........................330 479-7595
Tom Huskey, *Brnch Mgr*
EMP: 44
SALES (corp-wide): 26.11B **Publicly Held**
Web: www.dlhbowles.com
SIC: 3089 Injection molding of plastics
HQ: Abc Technologies Dlhb, Inc
2422 Leo Ave Sw
Canton OH 44706
330 478-2503

(G-1821)
ABC TECHNOLOGIES DLHB INC (DH)
Also Called: Genex Mold
2422 Leo Ave Sw (44706-2344)
PHONE...........................330 478-2503
Daniel Konrad, *Pr*
◆ EMP: 450 EST: 1977
SQ FT: 107,000
SALES (est): 100.08MM
SALES (corp-wide): 26.11B **Publicly Held**
Web: www.dlhbowles.com
SIC: 3714 Motor vehicle parts and accessories

HQ: Abc Technologies Inc
2 Norelco Dr
North York ON M9L 2
416 246-1782

(G-1822)
ACCU-RITE TOOL & DIE CO CORP
7295 Sunset Strip Ave Nw (44720-7038)
P.O. Box 2651 (44720-0651)
PHONE...........................330 497-9959
John Snyder, *Pr*
Susan Snyder, *Sec*
Tom Snyder, *VP*
EMP: 6 EST: 1979
SQ FT: 5,000
SALES (est): 1.21MM **Privately Held**
Web: www.accuritetool.com
SIC: 3544 Special dies and tools

(G-1823)
ADELMANS TRUCK PARTS CORP (PA)
Also Called: Adelman's Truck Sales
2000 Waynesburg Dr Se (44707-2194)
PHONE...........................330 456-0206
Carl Adelman, *Pr*
Larry Adelman, *
◆ EMP: 30 EST: 1921
SQ FT: 120,000
SALES (est): 16.85MM
SALES (corp-wide): 16.85MM **Privately Held**
Web: www.adelmans.com
SIC: 5013 3714 Truck parts and accessories; Power transmission equipment, motor vehicle

(G-1824)
AIRFASCO INC
2655 Harrison Ave Sw (44706-3047)
PHONE...........................330 430-6190
Dennis Dent, *CEO*
Jeff Parker, *
Marlene Veobides, *
Tim West, *OF CORP Quality**
EMP: 42 EST: 1984
SQ FT: 25,000
SALES (est): 4.17MM **Privately Held**
Web: www.airfasco.com
SIC: 3452 Bolts, metal

(G-1825)
AIRFASCO INDS FSTNER GROUP LLC
2655 Harrison Ave Sw (44706-3047)
PHONE...........................330 430-6190
EMP: 40 EST: 2009
SALES (est): 1.32MM **Privately Held**
Web: www.airfasco.com
SIC: 3452 Bolts, nuts, rivets, and washers

(G-1826)
AIRGAS USA LLC
2505 Shepler Ave Sw (44706)
PHONE...........................330 454-1330
Rod St John, *Brnch Mgr*
EMP: 26
SALES (corp-wide): 114.13MM **Privately Held**
Web: www.airgas.com
SIC: 2813 Oxygen, compressed or liquefied
HQ: Airgas Usa, Llc
259 N Rdnor Chster Rd Ste
Radnor PA 19087
216 642-6600

(G-1827)
AK FABRICATION INC
1500 Allen Ave Se (44707-3768)
PHONE...........................330 458-1037

▲ = Import ▼ = Export
◆ = Import/Export

Chris Kulenics, *Pr*
EMP: 12 **EST:** 1999
SQ FT: 10,000
SALES (est): 973.91K **Privately Held**
SIC: 1751 3548 Carpentry work; Welding
apparatus

(G-1828)
ALL POWER BATTERY INC
1387 Clarendon Ave Sw Ste 6
(44710-2190)
PHONE..............................330 453-5236
William Ferris, *Pr*
EMP: 6 **EST:** 1986
SQ FT: 4,000
SALES (est): 133.13K **Privately Held**
Web: www.allpowerbattery.com
SIC: 7699 5013 3691 Battery service and
repair; Automotive batteries; Lead acid
batteries (storage batteries)

(G-1829)
AMBAFLEX INC
1530 Raff Rd Sw (44710-2322)
PHONE..............................330 478-1858
David Spencer, *Genl Mgr*
◆ **EMP:** 22 **EST:** 2010
SALES (est): 7.94MM **Privately Held**
Web: www.ambaflex.com
SIC: 3535 Conveyors and conveying
equipment

(G-1830)
AMERICAN ALUMINUM EXTRUSIONS
Also Called: A A E
4416 Louisville St Ne (44705-4848)
PHONE..............................330 458-0300
Samuel Popa, *Pr*
Ken Hendricks, *Managing Member**
Barb Kepner, *
Diane Hendricks, *Managing Member**
▲ **EMP:** 105 **EST:** 2001
SQ FT: 240,000
SALES (est): 10.96MM **Privately Held**
Web: www.americanaluminum.com
SIC: 3354 Aluminum extruded products

(G-1831)
ARCHER CORPORATION
Also Called: Archer Sign
1917 Henry Ave Sw (44706-2941)
PHONE..............................330 455-9995
Jerry Archer, *CEO*
Michael Minor, *
EMP: 40 **EST:** 1965
SQ FT: 70,000
SALES (est): 7.44MM **Privately Held**
Web: www.archersign.com
SIC: 1799 3993 Sign installation and
maintenance; Signs and advertising
specialties

(G-1832)
ARCONIC
1935 Warner Rd Se (44707-2273)
PHONE..............................330 471-1844
EMP: 12 **EST:** 2019
SALES (est): 272.36K **Privately Held**
Web: www.arconic.com
SIC: 2816 Inorganic pigments

(G-1833)
ASSOCTED VSUAL CMMNCATIONS INC
Also Called: A V C
7000 Firestone Ave Ne (44721-2594)
PHONE..............................330 452-4449
Raymond Gonzalez, *Pr*
Paul Anthony, *
EMP: 25 **EST:** 1983
SALES (est): 1.51MM **Privately Held**

Web: www.avcprint.com
SIC: 2759 Screen printing

(G-1834)
AZZ INC
1723 Cleveland Ave Sw (44707-3646)
PHONE..............................330 456-3241
Tim Myers, *Mgr*
EMP: 58
SALES (corp-wide): 1.58B **Publicly Held**
Web: www.azz.com
SIC: 3699 Electrical equipment and supplies,
nec
PA: Azz Inc.
3100 W 7th St Ste 500
Fort Worth TX 76107
817 810-0095

(G-1835)
BADBOY BLASTERS INCORPORATED
1720 Wallace Ave Ne (44705-4056)
PHONE..............................330 454-2699
Andrea Bandi Cain, *Pr*
Mark Cain, *VP*
▲ **EMP:** 10 **EST:** 2006
SQ FT: 13,000
SALES (est): 1.02MM **Privately Held**
Web: www.badboyblasters.com
SIC: 3471 Sand blasting of metal parts

(G-1836)
BALL CORPORATION
2121 Warner Rd Se (44707-2273)
PHONE..............................234 360-2141
EMP: 11
SALES (corp-wide): 11.79B **Publicly Held**
Web: www.ball.com
SIC: 2631 Paperboard mills
PA: Ball Corporation
9200 W 108th Cir
Westminster CO 80021
303 469-3131

(G-1837)
BARNHART PRINTING CORP
Also Called: Barnhart Publishing
1107 Melchoir Pl Sw (44707-4220)
PHONE..............................330 456-2279
Brent A Barnhart, *Ch*
John F Waechter, *Pr*
EMP: 8 **EST:** 1930
SQ FT: 10,000
SALES (est): 443.78K **Privately Held**
SIC: 2752 2759 2789 Offset printing;
Letterpress printing; Bookbinding and
related work

(G-1838)
BDI INC
Also Called: Bdi
417 Applegrove St Nw (44720-1617)
PHONE..............................330 498-4980
Tom Carlouzzi, *Brnch Mgr*
EMP: 145
SALES (corp-wide): 1.51B **Privately Held**
Web: www.bdiexpress.com
SIC: 3568 Power transmission equipment,
nec
HQ: Bdi, Inc.
8000 Hub Pkwy
Cleveland OH 44125
216 642-9100

(G-1839)
BETTER LIVING CONCEPTS INC
Also Called: Compu-Print
7233 Freedom Ave Nw (44720-7123)
P.O. Box 2340 (44720-0340)
PHONE..............................330 494-2213
Jeff Davies, *Pr*

EMP: 6 **EST:** 1984
SQ FT: 5,400
SALES (est): 187.02K **Privately Held**
Web: www.gbscorp.com
SIC: 2759 Imprinting

(G-1840)
BIG KAHUNA GRAPHICS LLC
Also Called: Big Kahuna Graphics
1255 Prospect Ave Sw (44706-1627)
PHONE..............................330 455-2625
EMP: 9 **EST:** 1987
SALES (est): 1.04MM **Privately Held**
Web: www.bigkahunagraphics.com
SIC: 2396 2395 2759 Stamping fabric articles
; Pleating and stitching; Screen printing

(G-1841)
BOLER COMPANY
Hendrickson Trailer Commercial
2070 Industrial Pl Se (44707-2641)
PHONE..............................330 445-6728
Perry Bahr, *Brnch Mgr*
EMP: 250
SALES (corp-wide): 758.84MM **Privately Held**
Web: www.hendrickson-intl.com
SIC: 3714 Motor vehicle parts and
accessories
PA: The Boler Company
2021 Parkside Dr
Schaumburg IL 60173
630 773-9111

(G-1842)
BOLONS CUSTOM KITCHENS INC
6287 Promler St Nw (44720-7609)
PHONE..............................330 499-0092
Guy Bolon, *CEO*
Terry Bolon, *Pr*
EMP: 6 **EST:** 1976
SQ FT: 1,500
SALES (est): 551.56K **Privately Held**
Web: www.bolonskitchens.com
SIC: 5722 2599 Kitchens, complete (sinks,
cabinets, etc.); Cabinets, factory

(G-1843)
BOWDIL COMPANY
2030 Industrial Pl Se (44707-2641)
PHONE..............................800 356-8663
Brite Morrow, *Pr*
J Britton Morrow, *Sec*
EMP: 17 **EST:** 1923
SQ FT: 50,000
SALES (est): 3.53MM **Privately Held**
Web: www.bowdil.com
SIC: 3532 3599 3398 Mining machinery;
Custom machinery; Metal heat treating

(G-1844)
BRENDEL PRODUCING COMPANY
8215 Arlington Ave Nw (44720-5111)
PHONE..............................330 854-4151
Frank Brendel Junior, *Pr*
Kay Morgan, *Mgr*
EMP: 8 **EST:** 1928
SQ FT: 1,200
SALES (est): 475.41K **Privately Held**
Web: www.doylepc.com
SIC: 1381 1311 Directional drilling oil and
gas wells; Crude petroleum and natural gas

(G-1845)
BRIDGESTONE RET OPERATIONS LLC
Also Called: Firestone
3032 Atlantic Blvd Ne (44705-3929)
PHONE..............................330 454-9478
David Rapp, *Mgr*
EMP: 8

SQ FT: 2,340
Web: www.bridgestoneamericas.com
SIC: 5531 7534 Automotive tires; Rebuilding
and retreading tires
HQ: Bridgestone Retail Operations, Llc
200 4th Ave S Ste 100
Nashville TN 37201
615 937-1000

(G-1846)
BRIGHTWAVE ENTERPRISES INC
545 Market Ave N Ste 100 (44702-1545)
PHONE..............................812 331-2391
Ceo Principal, *CEO*
EMP: 10
SALES (est): 1.21MM **Privately Held**
SIC: 7372 Application computer software

(G-1847)
BUCKEYE PAPER CO INC
5233 Southway St Sw Ste 523
(44706-1943)
P.O. Box 711 (44648-0711)
PHONE..............................330 477-5925
Edward N Bast Senior, *Pr*
Edward Bast Junior, *VP*
▼ **EMP:** 32 **EST:** 1981
SQ FT: 54,000
SALES (est): 1.87MM **Privately Held**
Web: www.buckeyepaper.com
SIC: 2679 5113 Paper products, converted,
nec; Industrial and personal service paper

(G-1848)
BUCKEYE TERMINALS
807 Hartford Ave Se (44707-3376)
PHONE..............................330 453-4170
EMP: 6 **EST:** 2018
SALES (est): 997.25K **Privately Held**
Web: www.buckeye.com
SIC: 2999 Petroleum and coal products, nec

(G-1849)
BUGH INC
8933 Cleveland Ave Nw (44720-4565)
PHONE..............................330 305-0978
Roger Bugh, *Pr*
Barbara Bugh, *VP*
EMP: 8 **EST:** 2002
SQ FT: 3,600
SALES (est): 997.63K **Privately Held**
Web: www.bughinc.com
SIC: 5211 3089 Fencing; Fences, gates, and
accessories: plastics

(G-1850)
CAGE GEAR & MACHINE LLC
1776 Gateway Blvd Se (44707-3503)
PHONE..............................330 452-1532
EMP: 23 **EST:** 2000
SQ FT: 22,900
SALES (est): 8.06MM **Privately Held**
Web: www.cagegear.com
SIC: 3599 3566 Machine shop, jobbing and
repair; Gears, power transmission, except
auto

(G-1851)
CAMMEL SAW COMPANY
4898 Hills And Dales Rd Nw (44708-1495)
PHONE..............................330 477-3764
Dennis Cammel, *Pr*
EMP: 14 **EST:** 1968
SQ FT: 10,000
SALES (est): 827.53K **Privately Held**
Web: www.cammelsaw.com
SIC: 7699 5072 5251 3425 Knife, saw and
tool sharpening and repair; Saw blades;
Tools; Saws, hand: metalworking or
woodworking

(G-1852)
CANTON ASPHALT CO
5947 Whipple Ave Nw (44720-7692)
PHONE..................................330 499-6888
Marlene Oster, *Pr*
Brian Oster, *Rep*
EMP: 6
SQ FT: 3,000
SALES (est): 917.13K **Privately Held**
Web:
www.ostersandandgravelnorthcantonoh.com
SIC: 1442 Construction sand and gravel

(G-1853)
CANTON BANDAG CO
922 Benskin Ave Sw (44710-1438)
PHONE..................................330 454-3025
TOLL FREE: 800
Dave Richards Junior, *CEO*
EMP: 7 EST: 1962
SALES (est): 840.06K **Privately Held**
Web: www.cantonbandag.com
SIC: 5531 7534 Automotive tires; Tire
retreading and repair shops

(G-1854)
CANTON DROP FORGE INC
Also Called: Canton Drop Forge
4575 Southway St Sw (44706-1995)
PHONE..................................330 477-4511
Brad Ahbe, *Pr*
◆ EMP: 259 EST: 1903
SQ FT: 245,000
SALES (est): 51.35MM
SALES (corp-wide): 1.66B **Publicly Held**
Web: www.cantondropforge.com
SIC: 3462 3463 3356 3312 Iron and steel
forgings; Nonferrous forgings; Nonferrous
rolling and drawing, nec; Blast furnaces and
steel mills
PA: Park-Ohio Holdings Corp.
6065 Parkland Blvd
Cleveland OH 44124
440 947-2000

(G-1855)
CANTON GALVANIZING LLC
1821 Moore Ave Se (44707-2233)
PHONE..................................330 685-9060
Anthony Codispoti, *Managing Member*
EMP: 27 EST: 2015
SALES (est): 4.61MM **Privately Held**
SIC: 3479 Etching and engraving

(G-1856)
CANTON GEAR MFG DESIGNING INC
1600 Tuscarawas St E (44707-3199)
PHONE..................................330 455-2771
Matthew Weida, *Pr*
Barbara Bettis, *VP*
EMP: 10 EST: 1960
SALES (est): 2.51MM **Privately Held**
Web: www.cagegear.com
SIC: 3566 Gears, power transmission,
except auto

(G-1857)
CANTON OH RUBBER SPECLTY PRODS
Also Called: Cors Products
1387 Clarendon Ave Sw Bldg 13
(44710-2190)
P.O. Box 20188 (44701-0188)
PHONE..................................330 454-3847
EMP: 8 EST: 2008
SQ FT: 15,000
SALES (est): 953.23K **Privately Held**
Web: www.corsproducts.com

SIC: 3061 2869 3069 2822 Appliance rubber
goods (mechanical); Silicones; Weather
strip, sponge rubber; Ethylene-propylene
rubbers, EPDM polymers

(G-1858)
CANTON OIL WELL SERVICE INC
7793 Pittsburg Ave Nw (44720-6947)
PHONE..................................330 494-1221
Robert J Hutcheson, *Prin*
Thomas R Hutcheson, *CEO*
James Paumier, *VP*
Kevin W Hutcheson, *Pr*
EMP: 16 EST: 1962
SQ FT: 7,500
SALES (est): 4.06MM **Privately Held**
SIC: 1382 Oil and gas exploration services

(G-1859)
CANTON PLATING CO INC
903 9th St Ne (44704-1400)
PHONE..................................330 452-7808
Mark Kast, *Pr*
Denise Kast, *Sec*
EMP: 6 EST: 1955
SQ FT: 3,480
SALES (est): 463.31K **Privately Held**
SIC: 3471 Electroplating of metals or formed
products

(G-1860)
CANTON STERILIZED WIPING CLOTH
Also Called: Sentry Products
1401 Waynesburg Dr Se (44707-2115)
P.O. Box 7227 (44705-0227)
PHONE..................................330 455-5179
Robert Shapiro, *Pr*
Ronald Shapiro, *VP*
EMP: 8 EST: 1924
SQ FT: 42,000
SALES (est): 805.99K **Privately Held**
Web: www.sentryproducts.com
SIC: 2211 5199 5113 Scrub cloths; Chamois
leather; Napkins, paper

(G-1861)
CARMEL PUBLISHING INC
4501 Hills And Dales Rd Nw (44708-1572)
PHONE..................................330 478-9200
Ernie Blood, *Pr*
Melody Blood, *
Karen Hought, *
EMP: 8 EST: 1989
SALES (est): 480.13K **Privately Held**
SIC: 2721 2731 Magazines: publishing and
printing; Book publishing

(G-1862)
CENTRAL ALLIED ENTERPRISES INC (PA)
1243 Raff Rd Sw (44710-1455)
P.O. Box 80449 (44708-0449)
PHONE..................................330 477-6751
EMP: 50 EST: 1929
SALES (est): 21.96MM
SALES (corp-wide): 21.96MM **Privately Held**
Web: www.shellyco.com
SIC: 1611 2951 1442 Highway and street
construction; Asphalt and asphaltic paving
mixtures (not from refineries); Construction
sand and gravel

(G-1863)
CHECKPOINT SYSTEMS INC
Alpha Security
1510 4th St Se (44707-3206)
PHONE..................................330 456-7776
Tim Williams, *Brnch Mgr*

EMP: 198
SALES (corp-wide): 4.84B **Privately Held**
Web: www.checkpointsystems.com
SIC: 3699 Security control equipment and
systems
HQ: Checkpoint Systems, Inc.
101 Wolf Dr
West Deptford NJ 08086
800 257-5540

(G-1864)
CHEMSPEC LTD (DH)
Also Called: Chemspec Polymer Additives
4450 Belden Village St Nw Ste 507
(44718-2564)
PHONE..................................330 896-0355
David Moreland, *Pr*
Chris Wagner, *COO*
Aaron Shaffer, *CFO*
◆ EMP: 20 EST: 2003
SQ FT: 1,500
SALES (est): 38.67MM
SALES (corp-wide): 166.77K **Privately Held**
Web: www.safic-alcan.com
SIC: 2891 2952 3011 Adhesives and
sealants; Mastic roofing composition;
Automobile tires, pneumatic
HQ: Safic Alcan
Tour Pacific
Puteaux IDF 92800
146926464

(G-1865)
CINTAS CORPORATION NO 2
Also Called: Cintas
3865 Highland Park Nw (44720-4537)
P.O. Box 3010 (44720-8010)
PHONE..................................330 966-7800
TOLL FREE: 800
Allen Kocsis, *Mgr*
EMP: 81
SQ FT: 17,084
SALES (corp-wide): 9.6B **Publicly Held**
Web: www.cintas.com
SIC: 5084 2326 2337 Safety equipment;
Work uniforms; Uniforms, except athletic:
women's, misses', and juniors'
HQ: Cintas Corporation No. 2
6800 Cintas Blvd
Mason OH 45040

(G-1866)
CITY OF CANTON
Also Called: Traffic Engineering Department
2436 30th St Ne (44705-2568)
PHONE..................................330 489-3370
Dan Moeglin, *Admn*
EMP: 38
Web: www.cantonohio.gov
SIC: 3669 9111 Traffic signals, electric;
Mayors' office
PA: City Of Canton
218 Cleveland Ave Sw
Canton OH 44702
330 438-4300

(G-1867)
CLARK OPTIMIZATION LLC
1222 Easton St Ne (44721-2455)
PHONE..................................330 417-2164
Steve Clark, *Pr*
Douglas B Crawford, *Financial Chief*
EMP: 20 EST: 2011
SALES (est): 146.24K **Privately Held**
Web: www.clarkoptimization.com
SIC: 2741 Internet publishing and
broadcasting

(G-1868)
CLARK SUBSTATIONS LLC
Also Called: Clark Substations
2240 Allen Ave Se (44707-3612)
PHONE..................................330 452-5200
EMP: 6 EST: 1950
SALES (est): 907.43K **Privately Held**
Web: www.vsschuler.com
SIC: 3612 3699 3625 Distribution
transformers, electric; Electrical equipment
and supplies, nec; Relays and industrial
controls

(G-1869)
COLLINS & AIKMAN AUTO MATS LLC
1212 7th St Nw (44711)
PHONE..................................330 456-4543
EMP: 30 EST: 2007
SALES (est): 1.05MM **Privately Held**
SIC: 2221 Automotive fabrics, manmade fiber

(G-1870)
COMBI PACKAGING SYSTEMS LLC
6299 Dressler Rd Nw (44720-7607)
P.O. Box 9326 (44711)
PHONE..................................330 456-9333
John F Fisher, *CEO*
Barbara A Karch, *
◆ EMP: 70 EST: 1979
SQ FT: 119,000
SALES (est): 23MM **Privately Held**
Web: www.combi.com
SIC: 3565 Packaging machinery

(G-1871)
COPLEY OHIO NEWSPAPERS INC (HQ)
Also Called: Repository
500 Market Ave S (44702-2112)
PHONE..................................585 598-0030
Garrett J Cummings Attorney, *Prin*
Kevin Kampman, *
Darryl Hudson, *
James Porter, *
EMP: 47 EST: 2000
SALES (est): 84.58MM
SALES (corp-wide): 2.51B **Publicly Held**
Web: www.cantonrep.com
SIC: 2711 Commercial printing and
newspaper publishing combined
PA: Gannett Co., Inc.
175 Sully's Trl Ste 203
Pittsford NY 14534
703 854-6000

(G-1872)
CORDIER GROUP HOLDINGS INC
4575 Southway St Sw (44706-1933)
PHONE..................................330 477-4511
James J O'sullivan Junior, *Ch*
EMP: 301 EST: 1985
SALES (est): 1.95MM **Privately Held**
Web: www.cantondropforge.com
SIC: 3462 Iron and steel forgings

(G-1873)
CRAMERS INC
4944 Southway St Sw (44706-1990)
PHONE..................................330 477-4571
E Robert Schellhase, *Prin*
Don Hoover, *
Lynn Herdlick, *
Dana Cramer, *
R C Cramer, *
EMP: 25 EST: 1946
SQ FT: 15,000
SALES (est): 5.94MM **Privately Held**
Web: www.cramersinc.com

SIC: **3444** 3446 3443 3441 Sheet metal specialties, not stamped; Architectural metalwork; Fabricated plate work (boiler shop); Fabricated structural metal

(G-1874)

CUSTOM TRUCK ONE SOURCE LP
3522 Middlebranch Ave Ne (44705-5012)
PHONE...............................330 409-7291
Paul Sackett, *Acctg Mgr*
EMP: 93
SALES (corp-wide): 1.8B **Publicly Held**
Web: www.customtruck.com
SIC: **3713** Utility truck bodies
HQ: Custom Truck One Source, L.P.
   7701 Independence Ave
   Kansas City MO 64125
   855 931-1852

(G-1875)

CUSTOM WELD & MACHINE CORP
1500 Henry Ave Sw (44706-2852)
PHONE...............................330 452-3935
Tom Greening, *CEO*
Tim Savage, *VP*
EMP: 6 EST: 1957
SQ FT: 31,500
SALES (est): 312.73K **Privately Held**
SIC: **7692** Welding repair

(G-1876)

D & L ENERGY INC
3930 Fulton Dr Nw Ste 200 (44718-3040)
PHONE...............................330 270-1201
Ben W Lupo, *CEO*
Susan A Faith, *Pr*
EMP: 8 EST: 1986
SQ FT: 13,637
SALES (est): 2.4MM **Privately Held**
SIC: **1311** Natural gas production

(G-1877)

DARTING AROUND LLC
3058 Cromer Ave Nw (44709-2908)
PHONE...............................330 639-3990
Jeff Bowman, *Prin*
EMP: 6 EST: 2007
SALES (est): 720.47K **Privately Held**
Web: www.dartingaround.com
SIC: **3949** Darts and table sports equipment and supplies

(G-1878)

DE VORE ENGRAVING CO
1017 Tuscarawas St E (44707-3154)
PHONE...............................330 454-6820
Alan J De Vore, *Pr*
Chris De Vore, *VP*
EMP: 6 EST: 1963
SQ FT: 400
SALES (est): 652.34K **Privately Held**
Web: www.devoreengraving.com
SIC: **3479** Painting, coating, and hot dipping

(G-1879)

DECISION SYSTEMS INC
Also Called: Midland Engineering
2935 Woodcliff Dr Nw (44718-3331)
PHONE...............................330 456-7600
Peter E Voss, *Pr*
E R Frederick, *Ex VP*
Kay Wieschaus, *Treas*
EMP: 13 EST: 1978
SQ FT: 5,000
SALES (est): 4.28MM **Privately Held**
SIC: **3559** 8711 3535 Separation equipment, magnetic; Engineering services; Conveyors and conveying equipment

(G-1880)

DELTA PLATING INC
Also Called: Olymco
2125 Harrison Ave Sw (44706-3005)
PHONE...............................330 452-2300
Gregory Kalikas, *Pr*
Alex Sklavenitis, *
Stephanie Kalikas, *
EMP: 43 EST: 1986
SQ FT: 46,000
SALES (est): 2.77MM **Privately Held**
Web: www.olymco.com
SIC: **3471** Electroplating of metals or formed products

(G-1881)

DIANO CONSTRUCTION AND SUP CO
Also Called: Diano Supply Co
1000 Warner Rd Se (44707-3398)
PHONE...............................330 456-7229
Anthony Diano Junior, *Pr*
Darlene Guynup, *VP*
EMP: 10 EST: 1929
SQ FT: 1,500
SALES (est): 1.01MM **Privately Held**
Web: www.dianosupplyco.com
SIC: **3273** Ready-mixed concrete

(G-1882)

DIEBOLD NIXDORF INCORPORATED
818 Mulberry Rd Se (44707-3201)
PHONE...............................330 490-4000
Diane Pellegrene, *Brnch Mgr*
EMP: 59
SALES (corp-wide): 3.75B **Publicly Held**
Web: www.dieboldnixdorf.com
SIC: **3578** Automatic teller machines (ATM)
PA: Diebold Nixdorf, Incorporated
   350 Orchard Ave Ne
   North Canton OH 44720
   330 490-4000

(G-1883)

DIOGUARDIS ITALIAN FOODS INC
3116 Market Ave N (44714-1430)
PHONE...............................330 492-3777
Jeff Labowitz, *Pr*
EMP: 15 EST: 2010
SALES (est): 683.84K **Privately Held**
Web: www.dioguardis.com
SIC: **2038** 5411 Spaghetti and meatballs, frozen; Grocery stores, independent

(G-1884)

EDW C LEVY CO
3715 Whipple Ave Sw (44706-3535)
PHONE...............................330 484-6328
Jack Sines, *Mgr*
EMP: 8
SQ FT: 5,200
SALES (corp-wide): 486.96MM **Privately Held**
Web: www.edwclevy.com
SIC: **5093** 3295 Scrap and waste materials; Minerals, ground or treated
PA: Edw. C. Levy Co.
   9300 Dix Ave
   Dearborn MI 48120
   313 429-2200

(G-1885)

ELECTRA TARP INC
2900 Perry Dr Sw (44706-2268)
PHONE...............................330 477-7168
TOLL FREE: 800
Susan Paul, *Pr*
Betsy Paul, *Pr*
EMP: 19 EST: 1974
SQ FT: 20,000
SALES (est): 2.46MM **Privately Held**

Web: www.electratarp.com
SIC: **2394** 5091 2591 2391 Canvas and related products; Sporting and recreation goods; Shade, curtain, and drapery hardware; Cottage sets (curtains), made from purchased materials

(G-1886)

EMAXX NORTHEAST OHIO LLC
Also Called: Akron Canton Waste Oil
1701 Sherrick Rd Se (44707-2201)
PHONE...............................844 645-6299
EMP: 6 EST: 2018
SALES (est): 1.17MM **Privately Held**
SIC: **2992** Lubricating oils and greases

(G-1887)

EMBROIDME
3611 Cleveland Ave S (44707-1447)
PHONE...............................330 484-8484
Scott Leuenberger, *Mgr*
EMP: 6 EST: 2010
SALES (est): 194.62K **Privately Held**
Web: www.fullypromoted.com
SIC: **2395** Embroidery and art needlework

(G-1888)

ESMET INC
1406 5th St Sw (44702-2062)
P.O. Box 9238 (44711-9238)
PHONE...............................330 452-9132
◆ EMP: 34 EST: 1937
SALES (est): 9.83MM **Privately Held**
Web: www.esmet.com
SIC: **3429** 2542 Keys, locks, and related hardware; Racks, merchandise display or storage: except wood
PA: Tuscany Inc
   1406 5th St Sw
   Canton OH

(G-1889)

EVANS INDUSTRIES INC
606 Walnut Ave Ne (44702-1029)
PHONE...............................330 453-1122
Sue Ann Evans, *Pr*
Bevan Evans, *Sec*
EMP: 10 EST: 1977
SQ FT: 15,000
SALES (est): 4.37MM **Privately Held**
Web: www.evansind.net
SIC: **3089** Injection molding of plastics

(G-1890)

EVERHARD PRODUCTS INC (PA)
Also Called: Everhard
1016 9th St Sw (44707-4100)
PHONE...............................330 453-7786
G R Lucas, *Ch Bd*
James L Anderson, *
Scott Anderson, *
Rick Lucas, *
J D Anderson, *
◆ EMP: 119 EST: 1960
SQ FT: 154,000
SALES (est): 24.57MM
SALES (corp-wide): 24.57MM **Privately Held**
Web: www.everhard.com
SIC: **3423** Hand and edge tools, nec

(G-1891)

FOLTZ MACHINE LLC
2030 Allen Ave Se (44707-3691)
PHONE...............................330 453-9235
David Dicola, *Pr*
Lee Dicola, *Pr*
Linda R Polsinelli, *
EMP: 30 EST: 1970
SQ FT: 37,500
SALES (est): 4.68MM **Privately Held**

Web: www.foltzmachine.com
SIC: **3599** Machine shop, jobbing and repair

(G-1892)

FORMCO INC
5175 Stoneham Rd (44720-1540)
PHONE...............................330 966-2111
Richard Bourne, *Pr*
Carol Bourne, *Sec*
Christopher Bourne, *Treas*
EMP: 7 EST: 1976
SQ FT: 9,000
SALES (est): 687.98K **Privately Held**
Web: www.moldeddevices.com
SIC: **3089** Injection molding of plastics

(G-1893)

FOUNDATION SYSTEMS ANCHORS INC (PA)
Also Called: F S A
2300 Allen Ave Se (44707-3673)
PHONE...............................330 454-1700
Anthony Codispoti, *Pr*
Dennis Dinarda, *VP*
Karen Hawk, *Sec*
▲ EMP: 15 EST: 1985
SQ FT: 2,500
SALES (est): 4.58MM
SALES (corp-wide): 4.58MM **Privately Held**
Web: www.fsabolt.com
SIC: **3449** Fabricated bar joists and concrete reinforcing bars

(G-1894)

FRESH MARK INC
1600 Harmont Ave Ne (44705-3398)
PHONE...............................330 455-5253
EMP: 873
SALES (corp-wide): 1.38B **Privately Held**
Web: www.freshmark.com
SIC: **2011** 2013 Meat packing plants; Sausages and other prepared meats
PA: Fresh Mark, Inc.
   1888 Southway St Sw
   Massillon OH 44646
   330 832-7491

(G-1895)

FRITO-LAY NORTH AMERICA INC
Also Called: Frito-Lay
4030 16th St Sw (44710-2354)
PHONE...............................330 477-7009
Mike Kulbacki, *Brnch Mgr*
EMP: 71
SQ FT: 36,400
SALES (corp-wide): 91.47B **Publicly Held**
Web: www.fritolay.com
SIC: **2096** 2099 Potato chips and other potato-based snacks; Food preparations, nec
HQ: Frito-Lay North America, Inc.
   7701 Legacy Dr
   Plano TX 75024

(G-1896)

GALT ALLOYS ENTERPRISE
1550 Marietta Ave Se (44707-2568)
PHONE...............................330 309-8194
Phil Pennington, *Pr*
EMP: 11 EST: 2010
SALES (est): 973.1K **Privately Held**
Web: www.galtalloys.com
SIC: **1081** Metal mining exploration and development services

(G-1897)

GALT ALLOYS INC MAIN OFC
122 Central Plz N (44702-1448)
PHONE...............................330 453-4678
Stephen R Giangiordano, *Prin*

EMP: 6 EST: 2010
SALES (est): 165.94K **Privately Held**
SIC: 3339 Primary nonferrous metals, nec

(G-1898)
GASPAR INC
Also Called: Gaspar
1545 Whipple Ave Sw (44710-1373)
PHONE..............................330 477-2222
Gary W Gaspar, *Pr*
Judy Gaspar, *
EMP: 55 EST: 1967
SQ FT: 36,000
SALES (est): 10.31MM **Privately Held**
Web: www.gasparinc.com
SIC: 3443 7692 3444 Tanks, standard or
custom fabricated: metal plate; Welding
repair; Sheet metalwork

(G-1899)
GENERAL ELECTRIC COMPANY
Also Called: GE
5555 Massillon Rd Bldg D (44720-1339)
PHONE..............................330 458-3200
June Mutter, *Mgr*
EMP: 13
SALES (corp-wide): 38.7B **Publicly Held**
Web: www.ge.com
SIC: 3646 Commercial lighting fixtures
PA: General Electric Company
1 Aviation Way
Cincinnati OH 45215
617 443-3000

(G-1900)
**GERDAU MCSTEEL ATMSPHERE
ANNLI**
Also Called: Advanced Bar Technology
1501 Raff Rd Sw (44710-2356)
PHONE..............................330 478-0314
Saminathan Ramaswamy, *Prin*
EMP: 28
SQ FT: 31,316
SIC: 7389 3398 Metal cutting services; Metal
heat treating
HQ: Gerdau Macsteel Atmosphere
Annealing
209 W Mt Hope Ave Ste 1
Lansing MI 48910
517 782-0415

(G-1901)
GLASSES GUY LLC
5151 Tuscarawas St W (44708-5015)
PHONE..............................970 624-9019
Frank Soto, *CEO*
EMP: 20 EST: 2019
SALES (est): 1.14MM **Privately Held**
SIC: 3851 Eyeglasses, lenses and frames

(G-1902)
GMELECTRIC INC
4606 Southway St Sw (44706-1935)
PHONE..............................330 477-3392
George H Mountcastle, *Prin*
EMP: 6 EST: 2008
SALES (est): 669.81K **Privately Held**
Web: www.gmelectric.biz
SIC: 3694 5013 3679 Engine electrical
equipment; Automotive supplies and parts;
Harness assemblies, for electronic use:
wire or cable

(G-1903)
GONZOIL INC
5260 Fulton Dr Nw (44718-1806)
PHONE..............................330 497-5888
Douglas W Gonzalez, *Pr*
Frank W Gonzalez, *Sec*
EMP: 9 EST: 1988
SQ FT: 1,000

SALES (est): 824.63K **Privately Held**
Web: www.gonzoilinc.com
SIC: 1382 Oil and gas exploration services

(G-1904)
**GOODYEAR TIRE & RUBBER
COMPANY**
Also Called: Goodyear
6850 Frank Ave Nw (44720-7010)
PHONE..............................330 966-1274
Lenny Mullen, *Mgr*
EMP: 6
SALES (corp-wide): 18.88B **Publicly Held**
Web: www.goodyear.com
SIC: 5531 7534 Automotive tires; Tire repair
shop
PA: The Goodyear Tire & Rubber Company
200 Innovation Way
Akron OH 44316
330 796-2121

(G-1905)
GREGORY INDUSTRIES INC (PA)
4100 13th St Sw (44710-1464)
PHONE..............................330 477-4800
T Stephen Gregory, *Prin*
T Stephen Gregory, *CEO*
Joseph Weaver, *
◆ EMP: 80 EST: 1957
SQ FT: 145,000
SALES (est): 24.44MM
SALES (corp-wide): 24.44MM **Privately
Held**
Web: www.gregorycorp.com
SIC: 3441 Fabricated structural metal

(G-1906)
GREGORY ROLL FORM INC
4100 13th St Sw (44710-1464)
P.O. Box 80508 (44708-0508)
PHONE..............................330 477-4800
T Stephen Gregory, *CEO*
T Raymond Gregory, *
Joseph Weaver, *
EMP: 55 EST: 1978
SQ FT: 160,000
SALES (est): 1.48MM
SALES (corp-wide): 24.44MM **Privately
Held**
Web: www.gregorycorp.com
SIC: 3312 Galvanized pipes, plates, sheets,
etc.: iron and steel
PA: Gregory Industries, Inc.
4100 13th St Sw
Canton OH 44710
330 477-4800

(G-1907)
HAINES PUBLISHING INC
8050 Freedom Ave Nw (44720-6912)
P.O. Box 900820 (84090-0820)
PHONE..............................330 494-9111
William Haines Junior, *Pr*
EMP: 13 EST: 1991
SQ FT: 20,000
SALES (est): 218.03K **Privately Held**
Web: www.haines.com
SIC: 2741 Directories, nec: publishing and
printing

(G-1908)
HANNON COMPANY (PA)
Also Called: Charles Rewinding Div
1605 Waynesburg Dr Se (44707-2137)
PHONE..............................330 456-4728
Christopher Meister, *Pr*
Mike Mcallister, *Superintnt*
Gary Gonzalez, *
Gary Griswold, *
Ann Paris, *
EMP: 75 EST: 1926

SQ FT: 65,000
SALES (est): 23.88MM
SALES (corp-wide): 23.88MM **Privately
Held**
Web: www.hannonelectric.com
SIC: 3621 3825 5084 3699 Motors, electric;
Test equipment for electronic and electrical
circuits; Industrial machinery and equipment
; Electrical equipment and supplies, nec

(G-1909)
HARRISON PAINT COMPANY (PA)
Also Called: Harrison Paint
1329 Harrison Ave Sw (44706-1596)
PHONE..............................330 455-5120
Patrick Lauber, *Pr*
◆ EMP: 27 EST: 1911
SQ FT: 173,000
SALES (est): 6.88MM
SALES (corp-wide): 6.88MM **Privately
Held**
Web: www.harrisonpaint.com
SIC: 2851 Paints and allied products

(G-1910)
HEINEMANN SAW COMPANY
2017 Navarre Rd Sw (44706-5499)
PHONE..............................330 456-4721
Thomas Dickey, *Pr*
Arthur Poorman, *
▲ EMP: 45 EST: 1917
SQ FT: 20,000
SALES (est): 4.76MM **Privately Held**
Web: www.heinemannsaw.com
SIC: 3425 3421 Saw blades and handsaws;
Knives: butchers', hunting, pocket, etc.

(G-1911)
HENDRICKSON USA LLC
Also Called: Hendrckson Trlr Coml Vhcl Syst
2070 Industrial Pl Se (44707-2641)
PHONE..............................330 456-7288
Perry Bahr, *Genl Mgr*
EMP: 150
SALES (corp-wide): 758.84MM **Privately
Held**
Web: www.hendrickson-intl.com
SIC: 3714 Motor vehicle parts and
accessories
HQ: Hendrickson Usa, L.L.C.
840 S Frontage Rd
Woodridge IL 60517

(G-1912)
HOLMES LUMBER & BLDG CTR INC
1532 Perry Dr Sw (44710-1039)
PHONE..............................330 479-8314
EMP: 46
SALES (corp-wide): 9.13MM **Privately
Held**
Web: www.holmeslumber.com
SIC: 5031 5211 2439 2434 Lumber,
plywood, and millwork; Lumber and other
building materials; Structural wood
members, nec; Wood kitchen cabinets
PA: Holmes Lumber & Building Center, Inc.
6139 Hc 39
Millersburg OH 44654
330 674-9060

(G-1913)
HUNTER HYDRAULICS INC
Also Called: Hhi
2512 Columbus Rd Ne (44705-3707)
P.O. Box 7117 (44705-0117)
PHONE..............................330 455-3983
Larry R Hunter, *Pr*
Judith Kay Hunter, *VP*
EMP: 6 EST: 1968
SQ FT: 10,000
SALES (est): 1.61MM

SALES (corp-wide): 2.97MM **Privately
Held**
SIC: 3542 7699 Presses: hydraulic and
pneumatic, mechanical and manual;
Hydraulic equipment repair
PA: The H H I Company Inc
2512 Columbus Rd Ne
Canton OH 44705
330 455-3983

(G-1914)
HYDRODEC INC (PA)
2021 Steinway Blvd Se (44707-2644)
PHONE..............................330 454-8202
Mark Mcnamara, *CEO*
EMP: 9 EST: 2006
SALES (est): 9.98MM **Privately Held**
Web: www.hydrodec.com
SIC: 2911 Oils, partly refined: sold for
rerunning

(G-1915)
**HYDRODEC OF NORTH AMERICA
LLC**
2021 Steinway Blvd Se (44707-2644)
PHONE..............................330 454-8202
Ian Smale, *CEO*
Colin Moynihan, *Ch*
Chris Ellis, *CFO*
▼ EMP: 29 EST: 2007
SQ FT: 15,000
SALES (est): 9.98MM **Privately Held**
Web: www.hydrodec.com
SIC: 2911 Oils, partly refined: sold for
rerunning
PA: Hydrodec Inc.
2021 Steinway Blvd Se
Canton OH 44707

(G-1916)
**IMPERIAL CONVEYING SYSTEMS
LLC**
4155 Martindale Rd Ne (44705-2727)
PHONE..............................330 491-3200
Brian Rostedt, *Managing Member*
EMP: 14 EST: 2020
SALES (est): 5.45MM **Privately Held**
Web:
www.imperialconveyingsystems.com
SIC: 3535 Robotic conveyors

(G-1917)
**INDUSTRIAL FABRICATION AND
MCH**
3216 Kuemerle Ct Ne (44705-5076)
PHONE..............................330 454-7644
Jim Stout, *Pt*
Ray Meyers, *Pt*
EMP: 8 EST: 1992
SQ FT: 11,000
SALES (est): 210.17K **Privately Held**
SIC: 3443 Fabricated plate work (boiler shop)

(G-1918)
INTERIOR GRAPHIC SYSTEMS LLC
4550 Aultman Rd (44720-1525)
PHONE..............................330 244-0100
Jim Weisburn, *Managing Member*
EMP: 8 EST: 1980
SQ FT: 10,000
SALES (est): 407.49K **Privately Held**
Web: www.igssignage.com
SIC: 3993 Signs, not made in custom sign
painting shops

(G-1919)
INVUE SECURITY PRODUCTS INC
1510 4th St Se (44707-3206)
PHONE..............................330 456-7776
Farrokh Abadi, *Pr*

▼ **EMP:** 21 **EST:** 2003
SALES (est): 1.93MM
SALES (corp-wide): 4.84B **Privately Held**
Web: www.invue.com
SIC: 3699 Security devices
HQ: Checkpoint Systems, Inc.
101 Wolf Dr
West Deptford NJ 08086
800 257-5540

(G-1920)
JACODAR FSA LLC
2300 Allen Ave Se (44707-3673)
PHONE..............................330 454-1832
Vincent Codispoti, *Prin*
EMP: 21 **EST:** 2013
SALES (est): 3.55MM
SALES (corp-wide): 4.58MM **Privately Held**
Web: www.jacodar.com
SIC: 3452 Bolts, metal
PA: Foundation Systems And Anchors, Inc.
2300 Allen Ave S E
Canton OH 44707
330 454-1700

(G-1921)
JANSON INDUSTRIES
1200 Garfield Ave Sw (44706-1639)
P.O. Box 6090 (44706-0090)
PHONE..............................330 455-7029
Richard Janson, *Pt*
Eric H Janson, *Mng Pt*
EMP: 100 **EST:** 1927
SQ FT: 120,000
SALES (est): 14.9MM **Privately Held**
Web: www.jansonindustries.com
SIC: 1799 2391 3999 Rigging and scaffolding
; Curtains and draperies; Stage hardware
and equipment, except lighting

(G-1922)
JMW WELDING AND MFG INC
512 45th St Sw (44706-4432)
PHONE..............................330 484-2428
John Slutz, *Pr*
Michael Slutz, *
Neal Slutz, *
EMP: 30 **EST:** 1983
SQ FT: 12,000
SALES (est): 2.71MM **Privately Held**
Web: www.jmwcompanies.net
SIC: 3443 7692 Industrial vessels, tanks,
and containers; Welding repair

(G-1923)
JUNKER INC
1601 Perry Dr Sw (44706-1919)
P.O. Box 80423 (44708-0423)
PHONE..............................630 231-3770
Jason Drury, *CEO*
EMP: 9 **EST:** 1985
SALES (est): 2.16MM
SALES (corp-wide): 217.73K **Privately Held**
Web: www.otto-junker.com
SIC: 3549 Metalworking machinery, nec
HQ: Otto Junker Gesellschaft Mit
Beschrankter Haftung
Jagerhausstr. 22
Simmerath NW 52152
24736010

(G-1924)
**KEBCO PRCISION FABRICATORS
INC**
2006 Allen Ave Se (44707-3608)
P.O. Box 20057 (44701)
PHONE..............................330 456-0808
Eric Keblesh, *Admn*
Eric James Keblesh, *Prin*

Michael Todd Cogan, *Prin*
EMP: 12 **EST:** 2008
SALES (est): 2.09MM **Privately Held**
Web: www.kebcofab.com
SIC: 3441 Fabricated structural metal

(G-1925)
KLENK INDUSTRIES INC
Also Called: Klenk
1016 9th St Sw (44707-4108)
PHONE..............................330 453-7857
James Andreson, *Pr*
EMP: 6 **EST:** 1934
SQ FT: 5,000
SALES (est): 224.1K **Privately Held**
Web: www.everhard.com
SIC: 3421 Shears, hand

(G-1926)
KLINGSTEDT BROTHERS COMPANY
425 Schroyer Ave Sw (44702-2012)
P.O. Box 6088 (44706-0088)
PHONE..............................330 456-8319
James R Cassler, *Pr*
Janet Cassler, *Sec*
EMP: 10 **EST:** 1912
SQ FT: 15,000
SALES (est): 1.03MM **Privately Held**
Web: www.klingstedtbrothers.com
SIC: 2752 2754 Offset printing; Rotary
photogravure printing

(G-1927)
KMS 2000 INC (PA)
Also Called: P P I Graphics
315 12th St Nw (44703-1806)
P.O. Box 21220 (44701-1220)
PHONE..............................330 454-9444
Kevin Smith, *Pr*
EMP: 14 **EST:** 1932
SALES (est): 5.16MM
SALES (corp-wide): 5.16MM **Privately Held**
Web: www.ppigraphics.com
SIC: 2752 2759 Offset printing; Letterpress
printing

(G-1928)
KNOTTY PALLET LLC
4801 Munson St Nw (44718-3614)
P.O. Box 263 (44432-0263)
PHONE..............................330 451-9838
Yvette Marie B Grubb, *CEO*
Yvette Marie B Grubb, *Managing Member*
EMP: 6 **EST:** 2018
SALES (est): 1.66MM **Privately Held**
Web: knotty-pallet.com
SIC: 2448 Pallets, wood

(G-1929)
KOHLER COATING INC
Also Called: KOHLER COATING
1205 5th St Sw (44707-4625)
PHONE..............................330 499-1407
Herb Kohler, *Pr*
▲ **EMP:** 29 **EST:** 2001
SALES (est): 6.44MM **Privately Held**
Web: www.kohlercoating.com
SIC: 3554 Paper industries machinery

(G-1930)
LANE FIELD MATERIALS INC
530 Walnut Ave Ne (44702-1273)
PHONE..............................330 526-8082
Jason D Terrell, *Prin*
Krystal Fisher, *Prin*
EMP: 7 **EST:** 2020
SALES (est): 2.14MM **Privately Held**
SIC: 3537 Industrial trucks and tractors

(G-1931)
**LAZARS ART GLLERY CRTIVE
FRMNG**
2940 Woodlawn Ave Nw (44708)
PHONE..............................330 477-8351
TOLL FREE: 800
Lazer Tarzan, *Pr*
Elizabeth Tarzan, *VP*
EMP: 8 **EST:** 1969
SALES (est): 78.76K **Privately Held**
Web: www.lazarsartgallery.com
SIC: 2499 5999 Picture and mirror frames,
wood; Art dealers

(G-1932)
LEGALCRAFT INC
302 Hallum St Sw (44720-4217)
P.O. Box 8500 (44711-8500)
PHONE..............................330 494-1261
Robert Beck, *Pr*
EMP: 7 **EST:** 1933
SQ FT: 2,000
SALES (est): 725.5K **Privately Held**
SIC: 2752 Offset printing

(G-1933)
LUSTROUS METAL COATINGS INC
1541 Raff Rd Sw (44710-2321)
PHONE..............................330 478-4653
Michael Paxos, *Pr*
EMP: 40 **EST:** 1980
SQ FT: 34,000
SALES (est): 4.48MM **Privately Held**
Web: www.lustrousmetal.com
SIC: 3471 Electroplating of metals or formed
products

(G-1934)
M A C MACHINE
1111 Faircrest St Se (44707-1229)
PHONE..............................410 944-6171
Allen Craig, *Owner*
EMP: 6 **EST:** 1980
SQ FT: 5,400
SALES (est): 241.73K **Privately Held**
SIC: 3599 Machine shop, jobbing and repair

(G-1935)
M K MORSE COMPANY (PA)
1101 11th St Se (44707-3400)
P.O. Box 8677 (44711-8677)
PHONE..............................330 453-8187
Nancy Sonner, *CEO*
Sally Dale, *
James Batchelder, *
Thomas Herrick Junior, *CFO*
George Briercheck, *
◆ **EMP:** 447 **EST:** 1963
SQ FT: 375,000
SALES (est): 44.92MM
SALES (corp-wide): 44.92MM **Privately
Held**
Web: www.mkmorse.com
SIC: 3425 Saw blades, for hand or power
saws

(G-1936)
M T SYSTEMS INC
400 Schroyer Ave Sw (44702-2013)
P.O. Box 2086 (61834-2086)
PHONE..............................330 453-4646
Mark E Church, *Pr*
EMP: 8 **EST:** 1985
SQ FT: 12,500
SALES (est): 3.89MM **Privately Held**
Web: www.mt-systems.com
SIC: 7373 3823 3561 Computer integrated
systems design; Process control
instruments; Pumps and pumping
equipment

(G-1937)
M TECHNOLOGIES INC
Also Called: Northern Mobile Electric
1818 Hopple Ave Sw (44706-1909)
PHONE..............................330 477-9009
Rodney Mccauley, *Mng Pt*
Diane Broderick, *Pt*
EMP: 12 **EST:** 1981
SQ FT: 6,000
SALES (est): 2.3MM **Privately Held**
Web: www.northernmobile.com
SIC: 3625 5531 Starter, electric motor;
Automotive parts

(G-1938)
**MARY ANN DONUT SHOPPE INC
(PA)**
Also Called: Mary Ann Donuts
5032 Yukon St Nw (44708-5018)
PHONE..............................330 478-1655
Patrick J Welden, *Pr*
Dorothy Schweitzer, *VP*
EMP: 8 **EST:** 1947
SALES (est): 2.5MM
SALES (corp-wide): 2.5MM **Privately Held**
Web: www.maryanndonuts.com
SIC: 5461 2051 Doughnuts; Doughnuts,
except frozen

(G-1939)
MATALCO (US) INC (HQ)
4420 Louisville St Ne (44705-4848)
PHONE..............................330 452-4760
Gina Mason, *Pr*
▲ **EMP:** 20 **EST:** 2010
SALES (est): 21.47MM
SALES (corp-wide): 10.75MM **Privately
Held**
Web: www.matalco.com
SIC: 3363 Aluminum die-castings
PA: Matalco Inc
850 Intermodal Dr
Brampton ON L6T 0
905 790-2511

(G-1940)
MATRIX MANAGEMENT SOLUTIONS
5200 Stoneham Rd (44720-1584)
PHONE..............................330 470-3700
Mark Terpylak, *Pr*
EMP: 7 **EST:** 2007
SALES (est): 2.94MM **Privately Held**
Web: www.nextgen.com
SIC: 7372 7373 Prepackaged software;
Computer integrated systems design
HQ: Nextgen Healthcare, Inc.
1551 Emnception Hwy Ste 20
Fredericksburg VA 22401
949 255-2600

(G-1941)
MC CONCEPTS LLC
2459 55th St Ne (44721-3425)
PHONE..............................330 933-6402
EMP: 7 **EST:** 2008
SALES (est): 461.8K **Privately Held**
SIC: 2095 Roasted coffee

(G-1942)
MCCANN COLOR INC
Also Called: Team Remington Cadillac
8562 Port Jackson Ave Nw (44720-5467)
PHONE..............................330 498-4840
EMP: 24
SIC: 2816 2851 Color pigments; Paints and
allied products

(G-1943)
MCCANN PLASTICS LLC
Also Called: McCann

GEOGRAPHIC

5600 Mayfair Rd (44720-1539)
PHONE................................330 499-1515
Nicole Windemuth, *
EMP: 85 **EST:** 1989
SQ FT: 157,800
SALES (est): 16.5MM
SALES (corp-wide): 6.47MM **Privately Held**
SIC: 3087 Custom compound purchased resins
PA: Hexpol Ab
   Skeppsbron 3
   Malmo 211 2
   40254660

(G-1944)
METALLUS INC (PA)
1835 Dueber Ave Sw (44706-2728)
PHONE................................330 471-7000
Michael S Williams, *Pr*
Ronald A Rice, *Non-Executive Chairman of the Board*
Kristopher R Westbrooks, *Ex VP*
Kristine C Syrvalin, *Chief Human Resources Officer*
Kevin A Raketich, *CCO*
◆ **EMP:** 1245 **EST:** 1899
SALES (est): 1.08B
SALES (corp-wide): 1.08B **Publicly Held**
Web: www.metallus.com
SIC: 3312 Blast furnaces and steel mills

(G-1945)
METALLUS INC
2311 Shepler Church Ave Sw (44706-3073)
PHONE................................216 825-2533
EMP: 9
SALES (corp-wide): 1.08B **Publicly Held**
Web: www.metallus.com
SIC: 3312 Blast furnaces and steel mills
PA: Metallus Inc.
   1835 Dueber Ave Sw
   Canton OH 44706
   330 471-7000

(G-1946)
METALLUS INC
4748 Navarre Rd Sw (44706-2339)
PHONE................................800 967-1218
EMP: 17
SALES (corp-wide): 1.08B **Publicly Held**
Web: www.metallus.com
SIC: 3312 Blast furnaces and steel mills
PA: Metallus Inc.
   1835 Dueber Ave Sw
   Canton OH 44706
   330 471-7000

(G-1947)
METALLUS INC
Also Called: Harrison Plant
1835 Dueber Ave Sw (44706-2728)
PHONE................................330 471-7000
EMP: 50
SALES (corp-wide): 1.08B **Publicly Held**
Web: www.metallus.com
SIC: 3312 Blast furnaces and steel mills
PA: Metallus Inc.
   1835 Dueber Ave Sw
   Canton OH 44706
   330 471-7000

(G-1948)
METALLUS INC
Also Called: Timkensteel Fircrest Stl Plant
4511 Faircrest St Sw (44706-3513)
PHONE................................330 471-7000
Ron Balyint, *Prin*
EMP: 36
SALES (corp-wide): 1.08B **Publicly Held**
Web: www.metallus.com

SIC: 3317 Steel pipe and tubes
PA: Metallus Inc.
   1835 Dueber Ave Sw
   Canton OH 44706
   330 471-7000

(G-1949)
MIDLANDS MILLROOM SUPPLY INC
1911 36th St Ne (44705-5023)
P.O. Box 7007 (44705-0007)
PHONE................................330 453-9100
Fred Clark, *Pr*
◆ **EMP:** 28 **EST:** 1991
SQ FT: 17,000
SALES (est): 5.37MM **Privately Held**
Web: www.midlands-technologies.com
SIC: 5084 3061 Materials handling machinery; Mechanical rubber goods

(G-1950)
MILK HNEY CNDY SODA SHOPPE LLC
3400 Cleveland Ave Nw Ste 1 (44709-2784)
PHONE................................330 492-5884
Dwayne Cornell, *Pt*
EMP: 6 **EST:** 1954
SQ FT: 2,500
SALES (est): 482.89K **Privately Held**
Web: www.milkandhoneychocolates.com
SIC: 5451 5812 2066 2064 Ice cream (packaged); Restaurant, lunch counter; Chocolate and cocoa products; Candy and other confectionery products

(G-1951)
MONIQUE BATH AND BODY LTD
6545 Market Ave N (44721-2430)
PHONE................................513 440-7370
Monique Blue, *Managing Member*
EMP: 8 **EST:** 2020
SALES (est): 381.04K **Privately Held**
Web: www.purebymonique.com
SIC: 2844 Shampoos, rinses, conditioners: hair

(G-1952)
MPLX TERMINALS LLC
Also Called: Marathon Canton Refinery
2408 Gambrinus Ave Sw (44706-2365)
PHONE................................330 479-5539
Mike Armbrester, *Brnch Mgr*
EMP: 14
SIC: 5172 2951 Gasoline; Asphalt paving mixtures and blocks
HQ: Mplx Terminals Llc
   200 E Hardin St
   Findlay OH 45840
   419 421-2414

(G-1953)
MULTI GALVANIZING LLC
825 Navarre Rd Sw (44707-4058)
PHONE................................330 453-1441
Charles E Decker Ii, *Managing Member*
EMP: 6 **EST:** 2003
SQ FT: 30,000
SALES (est): 1.06MM **Privately Held**
Web: www.multigalvanizing.com
SIC: 3547 Galvanizing lines (rolling mill equipment)

(G-1954)
MURPHY TRACTOR & EQP CO INC
Also Called: John Deere Authorized Dealer
1509 Raff Rd Sw (44710-2321)
PHONE................................330 477-9304
Chris Mears, *Brnch Mgr*
EMP: 8
Web: www.murphytractor.com

SIC: 3531 5082 Construction machinery; Construction and mining machinery
HQ: Murphy Tractor & Equipment Co., Inc.
   5375 N Deere Rd
   Park City KS 67219
   855 246-9124

(G-1955)
MYERS CONTROLLED POWER LLC
133 Taft Ave Ne (44720-2527)
PHONE................................909 923-1800
James Fink, *Brnch Mgr*
EMP: 103
SALES (corp-wide): 172.09MM **Privately Held**
Web: www.myerspower.com
SIC: 3629 Inverters, nonrotating: electrical
HQ: Myers Controlled Power, Llc
   219 E Maple Ste 100-200 E
   North Canton OH 44720
   330 834-3200

(G-1956)
NEW BLTMORE ICE CREAM PDTS INC
2932 Clearview Ave Nw (44718-3428)
PHONE................................330 904-6687
Tana Gerwin, *Pr*
EMP: 31 **EST:** 2009
SALES (est): 471.64K **Privately Held**
SIC: 2024 Ice cream and frozen deserts

(G-1957)
NEWCO INDUSTRIES
4057 Glenmoor Rd Nw (44718-2253)
PHONE................................717 566-9560
Patricia Newell, *Owner*
EMP: 10 **EST:** 2000
SALES (est): 396.1K **Privately Held**
SIC: 3569 Assembly machines, non-metalworking

(G-1958)
NOLAN COMPANY (HQ)
1016 9th St Sw (44707-4108)
PHONE................................330 453-7922
Dan Epstein, *CEO*
EMP: 13 **EST:** 1909
SQ FT: 52,000
SALES (est): 12.08MM
SALES (corp-wide): 47.2MM **Privately Held**
Web: www.nolancompany.com
SIC: 3743 3532 Railroad equipment; Mining machinery
PA: Resource Pro Llc
   60 E 42nd St Ste 1500
   New York NY 10165
   888 577-7552

(G-1959)
NORCIA BAKERY
624 Belden Ave Ne (44704-2229)
PHONE................................330 454-1077
Donald C Horne, *Pr*
Jim Butler, *
EMP: 9 **EST:** 1920
SQ FT: 3,200
SALES (est): 862.51K **Privately Held**
Web: www.norciabakery.com
SIC: 2051 5461 5149 2052 Bakery: wholesale or wholesale/retail combined; Bread; Groceries and related products, nec; Cookies and crackers

(G-1960)
NORRIS NORTH MANUFACTURING
1500 Henry Ave Sw (44706-2852)
PHONE................................330 691-0449
Tyler Palumbo, *Prin*
EMP: 12 **EST:** 2014

SALES (est): 4.19MM **Privately Held**
SIC: 3999 Manufacturing industries, nec

(G-1961)
NORTHEASTERN PLASTICS INC
112 Navarre Rd Sw (44707-3950)
PHONE................................330 453-5925
Allen Richards, *Pr*
EMP: 6 **EST:** 1993
SQ FT: 4,800
SALES (est): 483.17K **Privately Held**
Web: www.northeasternplastics.com
SIC: 2759 2396 Screen printing; Automotive and apparel trimmings

(G-1962)
OBS INC
Also Called: Obs Specialty Vehicles
1324 Tuscarawas St W (44702-2036)
PHONE................................330 453-3725
Robert Ferne, *Pr*
▲ **EMP:** 13 **EST:** 1998
SQ FT: 28,000
SALES (est): 1.3MM **Privately Held**
Web: www.mycompanies.com
SIC: 3711 7532 Mobile lounges (motor vehicle), assembly of; Body shop, automotive

(G-1963)
OGC INDUSTRIES INC
934 Wells Ave Nw (44703-3500)
PHONE................................330 456-1500
Orlando Chiarucci, *Pr*
EMP: 10 **EST:** 1984
SQ FT: 80,000
SALES (est): 492.91K **Privately Held**
Web: www.ogcind.com
SIC: 4731 3679 Brokers, shipping; Harness assemblies, for electronic use: wire or cable

(G-1964)
OHIO AUTO SUPPLY COMPANY
Also Called: Professional Detailing Pdts
1128 Tuscarawas St W (44702-2086)
PHONE................................330 454-5105
Michael Dickson, *Pr*
Stanley R Rubin, *
EMP: 7 **EST:** 1933
SQ FT: 15,000
SALES (est): 2.23MM **Privately Held**
Web: www.professionaldetailingproducts.com
SIC: 5013 2842 5531 3714 Automotive supplies and parts; Cleaning or polishing preparations, nec; Automotive parts; Motor vehicle parts and accessories

(G-1965)
OHIO EMBROIDERY LLC
1321 Davis St Sw (44706-4503)
PHONE................................330 479-0029
Sarah Kennedy, *Prin*
EMP: 6 **EST:** 2014
SALES (est): 145.03K **Privately Held**
Web: www.ohioembroidery.com
SIC: 2395 Embroidery and art needlework

(G-1966)
OHIO GRATINGS INC (PA)
5299 Southway St Sw (44706-1992)
PHONE................................800 321-9800
John Bartley, *Pr*
David Bartley, *
Ronald Lenney, *
Jeff Davis, *
Juanita Finley, *
◆ **EMP:** 300 **EST:** 1970
SQ FT: 150,000
SALES (est): 40.22MM
SALES (corp-wide): 40.22MM **Privately Held**

▲ = Import ▼ = Export
◆ = Import/Export

Web: www.ohiogratings.com
SIC: 3446 3444 3441 3312 Gratings, open steel flooring; Sheet metalwork; Fabricated structural metal; Blast furnaces and steel mills

(G-1967)
OHIO PAPER TUBE CO
3422 Navarre Rd Sw (44706-1856)
PHONE.............................330 478-5171
William Natale Junior, *Pr*
Dennis Natale, *
Timothy Natale, *
EMP: 26 **EST:** 1968
SQ FT: 46,000
SALES (est): 7.91MM **Privately Held**
Web: www.ohiopapertube.com
SIC: 2655 5113 Tubes, fiber or paper: made from purchased material; Paper tubes and cores

(G-1968)
OHIO PRECISION INC
1239 Market Ave S (44707-3968)
PHONE.............................330 453-9710
Susan Stabler, *Pr*
David Boord, *VP*
EMP: 8 **EST:** 1995
SALES (est): 846.23K **Privately Held**
SIC: 3599 Machine shop, jobbing and repair

(G-1969)
OMWP COMPANY
3620 Progress St Ne (44705-4438)
P.O. Box 7069 (44705-0069)
PHONE.............................330 453-8438
EMP: 35 **EST:** 1954
SALES (est): 239.78K **Privately Held**
SIC: 3545 Machine tool accessories

(G-1970)
OSTER SAND AND GRAVEL INC (PA)
5947 Whipple Ave Nw (44720-7692)
PHONE.............................330 494-5472
Marlene Oster, *Pr*
Valerie Newman, *Treas*
Scott Oster, *VP*
EMP: 7 **EST:** 1967
SQ FT: 3,000
SALES (est): 3.25MM
SALES (corp-wide): 3.25MM **Privately Held**
Web:
www.ostersandandgravelnorthcantonoh.com
SIC: 1442 Gravel mining

(G-1971)
PARAGRAPHICS INC
2011 29th St Nw (44709-3218)
PHONE.............................330 493-1074
James S Bosworth, *Pr*
Peter A Bosworth, *
Andrew Bosworth, *
▲ **EMP:** 30 **EST:** 1975
SQ FT: 18,000
SALES (est): 4.27MM **Privately Held**
Web: www.para-inc.com
SIC: 2752 Offset printing

(G-1972)
PATRIOT SOFTWARE LLC
4883 Dressler Rd Nw Ste 301
(44718-3665)
PHONE.............................877 968-7147
Michael J Kappel, *Pr*
Todd Schmitt, *
EMP: 100 **EST:** 2002
SQ FT: 1,120
SALES (est): 13.67MM **Privately Held**
Web: www.patriotsoftware.com

SIC: 7372 Business oriented computer software

(G-1973)
PATRIOT SPECIAL METALS INC
2201 Harrison Ave Sw (44706-3076)
P.O. Box 1562 (14092-8562)
PHONE.............................330 580-9600
Frank Carchidi, *CEO*
Paul Olah, *
Ron Brattin, *Managing Member*
EMP: 70 **EST:** 1994
SALES (est): 4.18MM
SALES (corp-wide): 51.08MM **Privately Held**
Web: www.republicspecialmetals.com
SIC: 3356 Nonferrous rolling and drawing, nec
PA: Patriot Forge Co.
280 Henry St
Brantford ON N3S 7
519 758-8100

(G-1974)
PAXOS PLATING INC
4631 Navarre Rd Sw (44706-2336)
PHONE.............................330 479-0022
Mike Paxos, *Pr*
EMP: 25 **EST:** 1996
SQ FT: 35,000
SALES (est): 2.53MM **Privately Held**
Web: www.paxosplating.com
SIC: 3471 Electroplating of metals or formed products

(G-1975)
PHASE II ENTERPRISES INC
Also Called: Marino Maintenance Co
2154 Bolivar Rd Sw (44706-3055)
PHONE.............................330 484-2113
Richard Marino, *Pr*
EMP: 8 **EST:** 1989
SQ FT: 5,200
SALES (est): 1.02MM **Privately Held**
Web: www.cobraroloff.com
SIC: 7349 3446 Building maintenance services, nec; Stairs, fire escapes, balconies, railings, and ladders

(G-1976)
PINNACLE PRESS INC
2960 Harrisburg Rd Ne (44705-2562)
PHONE.............................330 453-7060
Robert Kettlewell, *Pr*
Shelly Poyser, *Treas*
EMP: 6 **EST:** 1976
SQ FT: 9,700
SALES (est): 579.49K **Privately Held**
Web: www.pinnaclepressinc.com
SIC: 2752 Offset printing

(G-1977)
PJS FABRICATING INC
Also Called: Pj's
1511 Linwood Ave Sw (44710-2313)
PHONE.............................330 478-1120
Francis C Bell, *Pr*
Harry Spurrier, *
Kathleen Hohler, *
EMP: 30 **EST:** 1977
SQ FT: 33,000
SALES (est): 5.03MM **Privately Held**
Web: www.pjsfab.com
SIC: 3441 Fabricated structural metal

(G-1978)
POLYTECH AMERICA LLC
3021 Saratoga Ave Sw (44706-2275)
PHONE.............................904 728-7458
Yabuta Naomi, *CEO*
EMP: 6 **EST:** 2016

SALES (est): 5.1MM **Privately Held**
Web: www.polytech-america.com
SIC: 3353 Coils, sheet aluminum

(G-1979)
PRECISION COMPONENT INDS LLC ✪
5325 Southway St Sw (44706-1943)
PHONE.............................330 477-6287
Karen Bartley, *Managing Member*
EMP: 25 **EST:** 2023
SALES (est): 2.93MM **Privately Held**
Web: www.precision-component.com
SIC: 3599 Machine shop, jobbing and repair

(G-1980)
PRECISION POWDER COATING INC
1530 Raff Rd Sw (44710-2322)
PHONE.............................330 478-0741
Chris Paxos, *Pr*
Myron Cybyk, *CFO*
Carl Talsma, *VP*
Dave Manns, *VP*
John Bertrand, *VP*
EMP: 10 **EST:** 1995
SQ FT: 100,000
SALES (est): 409.82K **Privately Held**
SIC: 3398 3471 Metal heat treating; Finishing, metals or formed products

(G-1981)
PRIDE 821 LLC
401 Cherry Ave Ne (44702-1154)
PHONE.............................330 754-6320
EMP: 8 **EST:** 2020
SALES (est): 396.99K **Privately Held**
SIC: 2599 Bar, restaurant and cafeteria furniture

(G-1982)
PRIME ENGINEERED PLASTICS CORP
1505 Howington Cir Se (44707-2214)
PHONE.............................330 452-5110
Patrick M Nolan, *Pr*
EMP: 15 **EST:** 1996
SQ FT: 14,400
SALES (est): 2.15MM **Privately Held**
Web: www.prime-plastics.com
SIC: 3089 Injection molding of plastics

(G-1983)
PRINT SHOP OF CANTON INC
6536 Promler St Nw (44720-7630)
PHONE.............................330 497-3212
Jeff Grametbauer, *Pr*
Joyce Grametbauer, *Sec*
EMP: 11 **EST:** 1972
SQ FT: 2,600
SALES (est): 1MM **Privately Held**
Web: www.printshopinc.com
SIC: 2752 Offset printing

(G-1984)
PRO-DECAL INC
3638 Cleveland Ave S (44707-1448)
PHONE.............................330 484-0089
Shane Branning, *Pr*
Robin Branning, *Sec*
Kim Schott, *VP*
EMP: 6 **EST:** 1996
SQ FT: 800
SALES (est): 650K **Privately Held**
Web: www.pro-decal.com
SIC: 2752 3993 Decals, lithographed; Signs and advertising specialties

(G-1985)
PROFILE PLASTICS INC
1226 Prospect Ave Sw (44706-1628)

PHONE.............................330 452-7000
Bryan Knowles, *Prin*
Sandra Knowles, *Sec*
EMP: 21 **EST:** 1993
SQ FT: 16,000
SALES (est): 4.72MM **Privately Held**
Web: www.profileplastics.com
SIC: 3089 Extruded finished plastics products, nec

(G-1986)
QUASS SHEET METAL INC
5018 Yukon St Nw (44708-5018)
PHONE.............................330 477-4841
John Angerer, *Pr*
Joyce Angerer, *VP*
EMP: 9 **EST:** 1936
SQ FT: 9,500
SALES (est): 957.34K **Privately Held**
Web: www.metalfabricationquass.com
SIC: 3444 Sheet metalwork

(G-1987)
QUICKDRAFT INC
1525 Perry Dr Sw (44710-1098)
PHONE.............................330 477-4574
Matthew C Litler, *Pr*
Matthew C Litzler, *Pr*
William J Urban, *Treas*
EMP: 45 **EST:** 1953
SQ FT: 45,000
SALES (est): 8.4MM
SALES (corp-wide): 25.05MM **Privately Held**
Web: www.quickdraft.com
SIC: 3535 3564 Conveyors and conveying equipment; Blowers and fans
PA: C.A. Litzler Holding Company
4800 W 160th St
Cleveland OH 44135
216 267-8020

(G-1988)
R G SMITH COMPANY (PA)
Also Called: Rgs
1249 Dueber Ave Sw (44706-1635)
P.O. Box P.O. Box 9067 (44711-9067)
PHONE.............................330 456-3415
EMP: 95 **EST:** 1909
SALES (est): 21.47MM
SALES (corp-wide): 21.47MM **Privately Held**
Web: www.rgscontractors.com
SIC: 3444 1761 1611 3106 Ducts, sheet metal; Roofing contractor; Industrial buildings and warehouses; Miscellaneous fabricated wire products

(G-1989)
R H LITTLE CO
4434 Southway St Sw (44706-1894)
PHONE.............................330 477-3455
David Little, *Pr*
Robert Brady, *VP*
Genevieve Little, *Sec*
EMP: 8 **EST:** 1940
SQ FT: 22,000
SALES (est): 476.89K **Privately Held**
Web: www.jbardmcleaninc.com
SIC: 3743 Railroad equipment

(G-1990)
R W SIDLEY INCORPORATED
7545 Pittsburg Ave Nw (44720-6943)
PHONE.............................330 499-5616
R W Sidley, *Pr*
EMP: 21
SALES (corp-wide): 43.09MM **Privately Held**
Web: www.rwsidley.com

SIC: 3273 Ready-mixed concrete
PA: R. W. Sidley Incorporated
436 Casement Ave
Painesville OH 44077
440 352-9343

(G-1991)
RANDALL RICHARD & MOORE LLC
Also Called: Cutter Equipment Company
3710 Progress St Ne (44705-4438)
PHONE..............................330 455-8873
EMP: 28 EST: 1998
SALES (est): 3.22MM Privately Held
Web: www.cutteronline.com
SIC: 3523 Turf and grounds equipment

(G-1992)
RELADYNE RELIABILITY SVCS INC
(HQ)
3713 Progress St Ne (44705-4437)
PHONE..............................888 478-6996
Larry Stoddard, CEO
▲ EMP: 27 EST: 2011
SALES (est): 23.89MM Privately Held
SIC: 3569 Lubrication machinery, automatic
PA: Reladyne Inc.
8280 Mntgomery Rd Ste 101
Cincinnati OH 45236

(G-1993)
RELIABLE READY MIX CO
1606 Allen Ave Se (44706)
P.O. Box 6359 (44706-0359)
PHONE..............................330 453-8266
James Lombardi, CEO
EMP: 42 EST: 2003
SALES (est): 5.67MM Privately Held
Web: www.reliablereadymix.com
SIC: 3273 Ready-mixed concrete

(G-1994)
REPUBLIC STEEL
Also Called: Canton Hot Rolled Plant
2633 8th St Ne (44704-2311)
PHONE..............................330 438-5533
John Ridgeway, Mgr
EMP: 10
Web: www.republicsteel.com
SIC: 3312 Blast furnaces and steel mills
HQ: Republic Steel
2633 8th St
Canton OH 44704
330 438-5435

(G-1995)
REPUBLIC STEEL (DH)
2633 8th St Ne (44704-2311)
PHONE..............................330 438-5435
Jaime Vigil, Pr
Noel J Huettich, *
Ted Thielens, *
John A Willoughby, *
Joseph A Kaczka, *
◆ EMP: 34 EST: 1993
SQ FT: 800,000
SALES (est): 162.57MM Privately Held
Web: www.republicsteel.com
SIC: 3312 Bars, iron: made in steel mills
HQ: Grupo Simec, S.A.B. De C.V.
Av. Lazaro Cardenas No. 601 Edif. A
Guadalajara JAL 44470

(G-1996)
REPUBLIC STORAGE SYSTEMS LLC
1038 Belden Ave Ne (44705-1454)
PHONE..............................330 438-5800
EMP: 400
SIC: 2542 3441 Lockers (not refrigerated):
except wood; Fabricated structural metal

(G-1997)
RMI TITANIUM COMPANY LLC
Also Called: Galt Alloys
208 15th St Sw (44707-4009)
PHONE..............................330 471-1844
Bruce Whatzel, Mgr
EMP: 355
SALES (corp-wide): 7.43B Publicly Held
Web: www.galtalloys.com
SIC: 3312 3341 Blast furnace and related
products; Secondary nonferrous metals
HQ: Rmi Titanium Company, Llc
1000 Warren Ave
Niles OH 44446
330 652-9952

(G-1998)
RMI TITANIUM COMPANY LLC
Also Called: Rti Alloys
1550 Marietta Ave Se (44707-2568)
PHONE..............................330 453-2118
George Hilana, Mgr
EMP: 326
SALES (corp-wide): 7.43B Publicly Held
SIC: 3312 3341 Tool and die steel and alloys
; Secondary nonferrous metals
HQ: Rmi Titanium Company, Llc
1000 Warren Ave
Niles OH 44446
330 652-9952

(G-1999)
RMI TITANIUM COMPANY LLC
Also Called: Rti Alloys Tpd
1935 Warner Rd Se (44707-2273)
PHONE..............................330 455-4010
Cheryl Lyons, Prin
EMP: 326
SALES (corp-wide): 7.43B Publicly Held
Web: www.howmet.com
SIC: 3499 Friction material, made from
powdered metal
HQ: Rmi Titanium Company, Llc
1000 Warren Ave
Niles OH 44446
330 652-9952

(G-2000)
ROBERT SMART INC
Also Called: Superior Machine Co
1100 High Ave Sw (44707-4116)
PHONE..............................330 454-8881
Robert Scott Smart, Pr
EMP: 8 EST: 1939
SALES (est): 2.1MM Privately Held
SIC: 3599 Machine shop, jobbing and repair

(G-2001)
SELF MADE HOLDINGS LLC
5325 Southway St Sw (44706-1943)
PHONE..............................330 477-1052
Patricia Gerak, CEO
Anthony J Gerak, *
EMP: 30 EST: 1957
SQ FT: 56,000
SALES (est): 823.7K Privately Held
Web: www.precision-component.com
SIC: 3599 3544 3545 Machine shop, jobbing
and repair; Special dies and tools; Shear
knives

(G-2002)
SEQUA CAN MACHINERY INC
Also Called: C I P
4150 Belden Village St Nw Ste 504
(44718-2595)
PHONE..............................330 493-0444
James Mcclung, Pr
Manuel Rubalcava, *
EMP: 24 EST: 1993
SQ FT: 2,000

SALES (est): 1.6MM
SALES (corp-wide): 1.58B Publicly Held
Web: www.stollemachinery.com
SIC: 3599 5084 Custom machinery;
Industrial machinery and equipment
PA: Azz Inc.
3100 W 7th St Ste 500
Fort Worth TX 76107
817 810-0095

(G-2003)
SHAHEEN ORIENTAL RUG CO INC
(PA)
Also Called: Abbey Carpet
4120 Whipple Ave Nw (44718-2970)
PHONE..............................330 493-9000
Nicholas H Shaheen Junior, Pr
Dawn Shaheen, VP
EMP: 10 EST: 1901
SQ FT: 12,800
SALES (est): 915.2K
SALES (corp-wide): 915.2K Privately Held
Web: www.shaheenrugs.com
SIC: 5713 7217 2295 Carpets; Carpet and
furniture cleaning on location; Tape,
varnished: plastic, and other coated (except
magnetic)

(G-2004)
SHANAFELT MANUFACTURING CO
(PA)
2633 Winfield Way Ne (44705-2069)
P.O. Box 7040 (44705-0040)
PHONE..............................330 455-0315
Leo Kovachic, Pr
Jon Lindseth, *
Joseph Sullivan, *
EMP: 35 EST: 1893
SQ FT: 50,000
SALES (est): 2.79MM
SALES (corp-wide): 2.79MM Privately
Held
Web: www.shanafelt.com
SIC: 3537 3451 Containers (metal), air cargo
; Screw machine products

(G-2005)
SHEETMETAL CRAFTERS INC
325 5th St Se (44702-1314)
P.O. Box 20648 (44701-0648)
PHONE..............................330 452-6700
David Grabowsky, Pr
EMP: 15 EST: 1989
SQ FT: 600
SALES (est): 2.21MM Privately Held
Web: www.sheetmetalcrafters.com
SIC: 3444 Sheet metalwork

(G-2006)
SJV INVESTMENT INC
Also Called: U.S. Casting Company
722 Mulberry Rd Se (44707-3255)
PHONE..............................330 452-9711
EMP: 20 EST: 1983
SALES (est): 3.86MM Privately Held
Web: www.uscastingco.com
SIC: 3325 Alloy steel castings, except
investment

(G-2007)
SLIMANS PRINTERY INC
Also Called: SPI Mailing
624 5th St Nw (44703-2625)
PHONE..............................330 454-9141
Samuel Sliman Junior, Pr
Judy Sliman Humphries, VP
EMP: 14 EST: 1947
SQ FT: 9,000
SALES (est): 3.88MM Privately Held
Web: www.slimansprintery.com

SIC: 2752 2759 Offset printing; Letterpress
printing

(G-2008)
SOLMET TECHNOLOGIES INC
2716 Shepler Church Ave Sw (44706-4114)
PHONE..............................330 915-4160
Joseph R Halter Junior, Pr
E Scott Jackson, *
Lee Dicola, *
Matthew Halter, *
EMP: 50 EST: 1985
SALES (est): 8.54MM Privately Held
Web: www.solmet.net
SIC: 3462 Iron and steel forgings

(G-2009)
SPARTA EMBROIDERY INC
3611 Cleveland Ave S (44707-1447)
PHONE..............................330 484-8484
Ed Hampshire, Pr
EMP: 9 EST: 2011
SALES (est): 1.1MM Privately Held
SIC: 2395 Embroidery products, except
Schiffli machine

(G-2010)
SPECIAL PACK INC
5555 Massillon Rd (44720-1339)
PHONE..............................330 458-3204
Greg Brumbaugh, Genl Mgr
◆ EMP: 40 EST: 1997
SALES (est): 1.54MM Privately Held
SIC: 2621 Packaging paper

(G-2011)
SPERLING RAILWAY SERVICES INC
4313 Southway St Sw (44706-1809)
PHONE..............................330 479-2004
Fred Sperling, Pr
Nancy Sperling, Sec
EMP: 10 EST: 1996
SQ FT: 17,000
SALES (est): 2.32MM Privately Held
Web: www.sperlingrailway.com
SIC: 3743 Railroad equipment

(G-2012)
STANDARD PRINTING CO OF
CANTON
Also Called: Standard Printing Company
1115 Cherry Ave Ne (44704-1325)
P.O. Box 9276 (44711-9276)
PHONE..............................330 453-8247
EMP: 70 EST: 1923
SALES (est): 10.3MM Privately Held
Web: www.spcoc.com
SIC: 2752 2791 2789 Offset printing;
Typesetting; Bookbinding and related work

(G-2013)
STARK CNTY FDRTION CNSRVTION
C
6323 Richville Dr Sw (44706-3131)
PHONE..............................330 268-1652
Michael W Rutledge, Prin
Jim Adkins, *
Kathy Griffin, *
Debbie Bonk, *
Bob Hess, *
EMP: 25 EST: 2018
SALES (est): 472.55K Privately Held
Web: www.the-review.com
SIC: 2711 Newspapers, publishing and
printing

(G-2014)
STARK MATERIALS INC
Also Called: Northstar Asphalt
7345 Sunset Strip Ave Nw (44720-7040)

P.O. Box 2646 (44720-0646)
PHONE..........................330 497-1648
Howard Wenger, *Pr*
EMP: 13 **EST:** 1985
SQ FT: 1,404
SALES (est): 1.07MM **Privately Held**
Web: www.northstarasphalt.com
SIC: 2911 2951 Asphalt or asphaltic
materials, made in refineries; Asphalt
paving mixtures and blocks

(G-2015)
STARK TRUSS COMPANY INC
Also Called: Stark Forest Products
4933 Southway St Sw (44706-1979)
PHONE..........................330 478-2100
Rob Blyer, *Brnch Mgr*
EMP: 97
SALES (corp-wide): 90.76MM **Privately
Held**
Web: www.starktruss.com
SIC: 2439 2511 Trusses, wooden roof; Wood
household furniture
PA: Stark Truss Company, Inc.
109 Miles Ave Sw
Canton OH 44710
330 478-2100

(G-2016)
STARK TRUSS COMPANY INC
Stark Forest Products
1601 Perry Dr Sw (44706-1919)
P.O. Box 80469 (44708-0469)
PHONE..........................330 478-6063
Tim Harold, *Brnch Mgr*
EMP: 7
SALES (corp-wide): 90.76MM **Privately
Held**
Web: www.starkforest.com
SIC: 2439 Trusses, wooden roof
PA: Stark Truss Company, Inc.
109 Miles Ave Sw
Canton OH 44710
330 478-2100

(G-2017)
STARK TRUSS COMPANY INC (PA)
Also Called: S T C
109 Miles Ave Sw (44710-1261)
P.O. Box 80469 (44708-0469)
PHONE..........................330 478-2100
Abner Yoder, *CEO*
Stephen Yoder, *Pr*
Javan Yoder, *Ex VP*
Todd Pallotta, *VP*
Wendy Spillman, *Sec*
EMP: 18 **EST:** 1968
SQ FT: 4,300
SALES (est): 90.76MM
SALES (corp-wide): 90.76MM **Privately
Held**
Web: www.starktruss.com
SIC: 5031 2439 Lumber, plywood, and
millwork; Trusses, wooden roof

(G-2018)
**STOLLE MACHINERY COMPANY
LLC**
Also Called: Canton Tool
1007 High Ave Sw (44707-4131)
PHONE..........................330 244-0555
Mike Felpovich, *Mgr*
EMP: 50
SALES (corp-wide): 492.99MM **Privately
Held**
Web: www.stollemachinery.com
SIC: 3411 Tin cans
PA: Stolle Machinery Company, Llc
6949 S Potomac St
Centennial CO 80112
303 708-9044

(G-2019)
STUDIO ARTS AND GLASS INC
7495 Strauss Ave Nw (44720-7103)
PHONE..........................330 494-9779
TOLL FREE: 800
Robert Joliet, *Pr*
Wendy Warren, *VP*
EMP: 10 **EST:** 1983
SQ FT: 7,000
SALES (est): 1.26MM **Privately Held**
Web: www.studioartsandglass.com
SIC: 3231 8299 Stained glass: made from
purchased glass; Arts and crafts schools

(G-2020)
SUN STATE PLASTICS INC
4045 Kevin St Nw (44720-6981)
PHONE..........................330 494-5220
Rick Dewees, *Pr*
EMP: 40 **EST:** 1949
SQ FT: 37,000
SALES (est): 3.7MM **Privately Held**
Web: www.sunstateplastics.com
SIC: 3089 Injection molding of plastics

(G-2021)
SUPERIOR DAIRY INC
Also Called: Creative Edge Group
4719 Navarre Rd Sw (44706-2300)
PHONE..........................330 477-4515
EMP: 220 **EST:** 1922
SALES (est): 35.29MM **Privately Held**
Web: www.mimilk.com
SIC: 2026 2024 Fluid milk; Ice cream and
frozen deserts

(G-2022)
TECHNIBUS INC
1501 Raff Rd Sw Ste 6 (44710-2356)
PHONE..........................330 479-4202
Mike Rice, *Pr*
Jacob Isaacson, *
▲ **EMP:** 100 **EST:** 2006
SQ FT: 150,000
SALES (est): 50MM **Publicly Held**
Web: www.technibus.com
SIC: 3444 Ducts, sheet metal
HQ: Ies Infrastructure Solutions, Llc
800 Nave Rd Se
Massillon OH 44646
330 830-3500

(G-2023)
TEK GEAR & MACHINE INC
1220 Camden Ave Sw (44706-1618)
PHONE..........................330 455-3331
Kevin Aronhalt, *Pr*
Thomas Mertz, *VP*
Emil Bueno, *Treas*
EMP: 8 **EST:** 1990
SQ FT: 6,000
SALES (est): 3.07MM **Privately Held**
Web: www.tekgearinc.com
SIC: 3599 Machine shop, jobbing and repair

(G-2024)
**THE BELDEN BRICK COMPANY LLC
(HQ)**
700 Tuscarawas St W Uppr (44702-2063)
P.O. Box 20910 (44701-0910)
PHONE..........................330 456-0031
◆ **EMP:** 34 **EST:** 1885
SALES (est): 94.32MM
SALES (corp-wide): 113.08MM **Privately
Held**
Web: www.beldenbrick.com
SIC: 3251 Structural brick and blocks
PA: Belden Holding & Acquisition
Company, Inc.
700 W Tuscarawas St
Canton OH 44702

330 456-0031

(G-2025)
TIMKENSTEEL MATERIAL SVCS LLC
1835 Dueber Ave Sw (44706-2728)
P.O. Box 90246 (77290-0246)
PHONE..........................281 449-0319
Tim Timken, *Prin*
Barbara Moore, *
Shawn Seanor, *
Phillip R Cox, *Prin*
Randall Edwards, *Prin*
▼ **EMP:** 120 **EST:** 1972
SALES (est): 5.28MM
SALES (corp-wide): 1.08B **Publicly Held**
Web: www.metallus.com
SIC: 3599 Machine shop, jobbing and repair
PA: Metallus Inc.
1835 Dueber Ave Sw
Canton OH 44706
330 471-7000

(G-2026)
TRAIL SPRAYER & SERVICE LLC
2830 Cleveland Ave Nw (44709-3204)
PHONE..........................330 720-2966
Jeremy Davidson, *Managing Member*
EMP: 13 **EST:** 2015
SALES (est): 6.35MM
SALES (corp-wide): 6.35MM **Privately
Held**
Web: www.trailsprayer.com
SIC: 3563 Spraying and dusting equipment
PA: Sprayworks Equipment Group, Llc
2830 Cleveland Ave Nw
Canton OH 44709
330 587-4141

(G-2027)
**TRANSFORMER ASSOCIATES
LIMITED**
831 Market Ave N (44702-1175)
PHONE..........................330 430-0750
Rodney Herndon, *Pr*
Tonya Cihon, *Mgr*
EMP: 6 **EST:** 2004
SALES (est): 1.49MM **Privately Held**
Web: www.transformerassociates.com
SIC: 3612 Voltage regulating transformers,
electric power

(G-2028)
TRI-K ENTERPRISES INC
935 Mckinley Ave Sw (44707-4163)
PHONE..........................330 832-7380
Robert S Black, *Pr*
Kerry Black, *VP*
Kevin Black, *VP*
Joan Black, *Sec*
EMP: 6 **EST:** 1977
SALES (est): 1.96MM **Privately Held**
SIC: 3451 3542 Screw machine products;
Presses: hydraulic and pneumatic,
mechanical and manual

(G-2029)
TRUCKCORP LLC
Also Called: American Road Machinery Co
3026 Saratoga Ave Sw (44706-2236)
PHONE..........................234 666-5702
Nick Ballas, *Pr*
EMP: 63 **EST:** 2020
SALES (est): 2.04MM **Privately Held**
Web: www.truckcorpllc.com
SIC: 3537 Trucks: freight, baggage, etc.:
industrial, except mining

(G-2030)
UHRDEN INC
Also Called: Tubar Eureka Industrial Group
700 Tuscarawas St W (44702-2048)

P.O. Box 705 (44681-0705)
PHONE..........................330 456-0031
Kenneth L Cook, *Ch Bd*
Hemmy Acharya, *
▲ **EMP:** 46 **EST:** 1952
SQ FT: 82,000
SALES (est): 6.47MM **Privately Held**
Web: www.tubareureka.com
SIC: 3535 3561 3537 3536 Conveyors and
conveying equipment; Pumps and pumping
equipment; Industrial trucks and tractors;
Hoists, cranes, and monorails

(G-2031)
UNI CORP
Also Called: Unitec
1300 Market Ave N (44714-2606)
PHONE..........................800 782-3296
Richard C Gattuso, *Pr*
Margherita Gattuso, *Sec*
▲ **EMP:** 20 **EST:** 1989
SQ FT: 20,000
SALES (est): 653.66K **Privately Held**
Web: www.unitecproducts.com
SIC: 3161 3651 Cases, carrying, nec;
Speaker monitors

(G-2032)
UNION METAL CORPORATION
1432 Maple Ave Ne (44705-1700)
PHONE..........................330 456-7653
◆ **EMP:** 390
Web: www.unionmetal.com
SIC: 3648 Public lighting fixtures

(G-2033)
UNION METAL INDUSTRIES CORP
1432 Maple Ave Ne (44705-1700)
PHONE..........................330 456-7653
Ryan Macvoy, *CEO*
Zach Macvoy, *CEO*
EMP: 46 **EST:** 2018
SALES (est): 8.66MM **Privately Held**
Web: www.unionmetal.com
SIC: 3669 Traffic signals, electric

(G-2034)
UNITED ENGINEERING & FNDRY CO
1400 Grace Ave Ne (44705-2035)
PHONE..........................330 456-2761
Ronald A Martin, *Pr*
Edward Bauer, *COO*
EMP: 6 **EST:** 1986
SQ FT: 5,000
SALES (est): 209.48K **Privately Held**
Web: www.whemco.com
SIC: 3325 Rolling mill rolls, cast steel

(G-2035)
**UNITED GRINDING AND MACHINE
CO**
2315 Ellis Ave Ne (44705-4696)
PHONE..........................330 453-7402
Allan J Pfabe, *Pr*
Dennis Pfabe, *
Karen Essig, *
▲ **EMP:** 22 **EST:** 1967
SQ FT: 65,000
SALES (est): 4.84MM **Privately Held**
Web: www.unitedgrinding.com
SIC: 3599 Machine shop, jobbing and repair

(G-2036)
UNITED ROLLS INC (DH)
Also Called: Whemco
1400 Grace Ave Ne (44705-2035)
◆ **EMP:** 83 **EST:** 2010
SQ FT: 225,000
SALES (est): 53.56MM
SALES (corp-wide): 645.61MM **Privately
Held**

Web: www.whemco.com
SIC: **3547** 3613 Rolling mill machinery; Control panels, electric
HQ: Whemco Inc.
    5 Hot Metal St Ste 300
    Pittsburgh PA 15203
    412 390-2700

(G-2037)
UNITED SURFACE FINISHING INC
2202 Gilbert Ave Ne (44705-4634)
PHONE.....................................330 453-2786
Robert R Horger, *Pr*
Beth Horger, *VP*
EMP: 19 EST: 1954
SQ FT: 18,000
SALES (est): 2.59MM **Privately Held**
Web: www.unitedsurfacefinishing.com
SIC: **3471** Electroplating of metals or formed products

(G-2038)
UNIVERSAL METALS CUTTING INC
2656 Harrison Ave Sw (44706-3085)
PHONE.....................................330 580-5192
Joseph Halter Junior, *Pr*
Lee J Dicola, *Sec*
EMP: 7 EST: 1996
SQ FT: 8,140
SALES (est): 412.5K **Privately Held**
SIC: **3312** Tubes, steel and iron

(G-2039)
US TECHNOLOGY CORPORATION
4200 Munson St Nw (44718-2981)
PHONE.....................................330 455-1181
Raymond F Williams, *Pr*
Robert B Putnam, *
◆ EMP: 42 EST: 1985
SQ FT: 2,000
SALES (est): 2.29MM **Privately Held**
Web: www.ustechnology.com
SIC: **3291** 3728 Abrasive products; Aircraft parts and equipment, nec

(G-2040)
USA QUICKPRINT INC (PA)
Also Called: Quick Print
409 3rd St Sw (44702-1910)
PHONE.....................................330 455-5119
Gerald Hohler, *Pr*
Jocelyn Hohler, *VP*
EMP: 15 EST: 1979
SQ FT: 2,000
SALES (est): 2.7MM
SALES (corp-wide): 2.7MM **Privately Held**
Web: www.usaqp.com
SIC: **2752** Offset printing

(G-2041)
V & S SCHULER ENGINEERING INC (DH)
2240 Allen Ave Se (44707-3612)
PHONE.....................................330 452-5200
Brian Miller, *Pr*
Paul Balster Ctrl, *Prin*
EMP: 33 EST: 1939
SQ FT: 40,000
SALES (est): 21.76MM
SALES (corp-wide): 1.08B **Privately Held**
Web: www.vsschuler.com
SIC: **3441** 3444 Fabricated structural metal; Sheet metalwork
HQ: Voigt & Schweitzer Llc
    987 Buckeye Park Rd
    Columbus OH 43207
    614 449-8281

(G-2042)
VERSALIFT EAST INC
Also Called: VERSALIFT EAST, INC.
4884 Corporate St Sw (44706-1907)
PHONE.....................................610 866-1400
Keith W Joseph, *Brnch Mgr*
EMP: 191
SALES (corp-wide): 266.43MM **Privately Held**
Web: east.versalift.com
SIC: **3534** Elevators and moving stairways
HQ: Versalift East, L.L.C.
    7601 Imperial Dr
    Waco TX 76712

(G-2043)
W W CROSS INDUSTRIES INC
2510 Allen Ave Se (44707-3614)
PHONE.....................................330 588-8400
Thomas Trudeau, *Pr*
Phillip Lattavo, *VP*
Christine Trudeau, *Treas*
EMP: 10 EST: 2002
SALES (est): 2.32MM **Privately Held**
Web: www.wwcross.com
SIC: **3965** Fasteners

(G-2044)
WACKER CHEMICAL CORPORATION
Also Called: Silmix Division
2215 International Pkwy (44720-1372)
PHONE.....................................330 899-0847
Jake Miller, *Off Mgr*
EMP: 115
SALES (corp-wide): 6.96B **Privately Held**
Web: www.wacker.com
SIC: **2869** Silicones
HQ: Wacker Chemical Corporation
    3301 Sutton Rd
    Adrian MI 49221
    517 264-8500

(G-2045)
WALLACE FORGE COMPANY
3700 Georgetown Rd Ne (44704-2697)
PHONE.....................................330 488-1203
Dean Wallace, *Pr*
Sheila A Ghezzi, *
William A Peterson, *
▲ EMP: 65 EST: 1966
SQ FT: 55,000
SALES (est): 8.68MM **Privately Held**
Web: www.wallaceforge.com
SIC: **3462** 3321 3463 3452 Iron and steel forgings; Gray and ductile iron foundries; Nonferrous forgings; Bolts, nuts, rivets, and washers

(G-2046)
WERNET INC
Also Called: Commercial Press
606 Cherry Ave Ne (44702-1046)
PHONE.....................................330 452-2200
Greg Wernet, *Pr*
Susan Wernet, *Sec*
EMP: 6 EST: 1926
SQ FT: 8,800
SALES (est): 59.6K **Privately Held**
SIC: **2752** Offset printing

(G-2047)
WESTERN BRANCH DIESEL LLC
Also Called: John Deere Authorized Dealer
1616 Metric Ave Sw (44706-3087)
PHONE.....................................330 454-8800
Mike Mcelwain, *Brnch Mgr*
EMP: 17
SQ FT: 22,400
SALES (corp-wide): 107.64MM **Privately Held**
Web: www.westernbranchdiesel.com

SIC: **5084** 5531 5063 3714 Engines and parts, diesel; Truck equipment and parts; Generators; Motor vehicle parts and accessories
HQ: Western Branch Diesel, Llc
    3504 Shipwright St
    Portsmouth VA 23703
    757 673-7000

(G-2048)
WHITACRE ENGINEERING COMPANY (PA)
4645 Rebar Ave Ne (44705-4473)
P.O. Box 8444 (44711-8444)
PHONE.....................................330 455-8505
▲ EMP: 37 EST: 1920
SALES (est): 9.82MM
SALES (corp-wide): 9.82MM **Privately Held**
Web: www.whitacrerebar.com
SIC: **3441** Fabricated structural metal

(G-2049)
WYOMING CASING SERVICE INC
1414 Raff Rd Sw (44710-2320)
PHONE.....................................330 479-8785
EMP: 83
SALES (corp-wide): 8.26MM **Privately Held**
Web: www.wyomingcasing.com
SIC: **1389** Oil field services, nec
PA: Wyoming Casing Service, Inc.
    198 40th St E
    Dickinson ND 58601
    701 225-8521

(G-2050)
XCEL MOLD AND MACHINE INC
7661 Freedom Ave Nw (44720-6987)
PHONE.....................................330 499-8450
Bruce Cain, *Pr*
Bob Johnson, *VP*
EMP: 14 EST: 1956
SQ FT: 25,000
SALES (est): 1.63MM **Privately Held**
SIC: **3544** Industrial molds

(G-2051)
ZEIGER INDUSTRIES INC
4704 Wiseland Ave Se (44707-1054)
PHONE.....................................330 484-4413
Donald Zeiger, *Pr*
Sandi Zeiger, *VP*
EMP: 22 EST: 1981
SQ FT: 2,500
SALES (est): 2.4MM **Privately Held**
Web: www.zeigerindustries.com
SIC: **3599** Machine shop, jobbing and repair

(G-2052)
ZIEGLER TIRE AND SUPPLY CO
Also Called: Affordable Tire
4300 Tuscarawas St W (44708-5427)
PHONE.....................................330 477-3463
Rick Hall, *Brnch Mgr*
EMP: 9
SALES (corp-wide): 93.71MM **Privately Held**
Web: www.zieglertire.com
SIC: **5531** 7534 Automotive tires; Tire retreading and repair shops
PA: The Ziegler Tire And Supply Company
    4150 Millennium Blvd Se
    Massillon OH 44646
    330 834-3332

Cardington
Morrow County

(G-2053)
CARDINGTON YUTAKA TECH INC (DH)
575 W Main St (43315-9796)
PHONE.....................................419 864-8777
Masato Hattori, *Pr*
Fred Razavi, *
▲ EMP: 750 EST: 1995
SQ FT: 300,000
SALES (est): 94.19MM **Privately Held**
Web: www.yutakatech.com
SIC: **3714** Exhaust systems and parts, motor vehicle
HQ: Yutaka Giken Co.,Ltd.
    508-1, Yutakacho, Chuo-Ku
    Hamamatsu SZO 431-3

(G-2054)
HOFFMAN MEAT PROCESSING
157 S 4th St (43315-9726)
PHONE.....................................419 864-3994
Mike Hoffman, *Owner*
EMP: 7 EST: 1969
SALES (est): 506.5K **Privately Held**
SIC: **2013** 5421 Sausages and other prepared meats; Meat markets, including freezer provisioners

(G-2055)
MARENGO FABRICATED STEEL LTD (PA)
Also Called: Lincoln Center Manufacturing
2896 State Route 61 (43315-9427)
P.O. Box 8 (43321)
PHONE.....................................800 919-2652
Rick Howell, *Pt*
Robert C Howell, *Pt*
EMP: 17 EST: 1996
SQ FT: 60,000
SALES (est): 4.69MM **Privately Held**
Web: www.lcmohio.com
SIC: **3713** 5084 7692 Dump truck bodies; Food product manufacturing machinery; Welding repair

Carey
Wyandot County

(G-2056)
BOSSERMAN AVIATION EQUIPMENT INC
2327 State Highway 568 (43316-9583)
PHONE.....................................419 722-2879
◆ EMP: 50
Web: www.bossermanaviationequip.com
SIC: **3728** Fuel tanks, aircraft

(G-2057)
CAREY PRECAST CONCRETE COMPANY
3420 Township Highway 98 (43316-9763)
P.O. Box 129 (43316-0129)
PHONE.....................................419 396-7142
TOLL FREE: 800
Kathryn Beck, *Pr*
Dean Beck, *Sec*
EMP: 6 EST: 1985
SQ FT: 2,000
SALES (est): 857.39K **Privately Held**
Web: www.careyprecast.com
SIC: **3272** Concrete products, precast, nec

▲ = Import ▼ = Export
◆ = Import/Export

(G-2058)
HANON SYSTEMS USA LLC
581 Arrowhead Dr (43316-7503)
PHONE.....................313 920-0583
Thomas Charnesky, *Manager*
EMP: 140
Web: www.hanonsystems.com
SIC: 3714 3585 3699 Air conditioner parts,
motor vehicle; Compressors for
refrigeration and air conditioning equipment
; Heat emission operating apparatus
HQ: Hanon Systems Usa, Llc
39600 Lewis Dr
Novi MI 48377
248 907-8000

(G-2059)
MINERAL PROCESSING COMPANY
1855 County Highway 99 (43316-9722)
PHONE.....................419 396-3501
Daniel Allen, *Pr*
John Uliveto, *VP*
Harry Allen, *Sec*
Victoria C Allen, *Treas*
EMP: 6 **EST:** 1988
SQ FT: 15,000
SALES (est): 682.21K
SALES (corp-wide): 11.26B **Publicly Held**
SIC: 3275 3274 Gypsum products; Lime
PA: The Andersons Inc
1947 Briarfield Blvd
Maumee OH 43537
419 893-5050

(G-2060)
NATIONAL LIME AND STONE CO
370 N Patterson St (43316-1057)
P.O. Box 8 (43316-0008)
PHONE.....................419 396-7671
Ryan Phillips, *Brnch Mgr*
EMP: 37
SALES (corp-wide): 86.85MM **Privately Held**
Web: www.natlime.com
SIC: 1422 3291 3281 3274 Lime rock,
ground; Abrasive products; Cut stone and
stone products; Lime
PA: The National Lime And Stone
Company
551 Lake Cascade Pkwy
Findlay OH 45840
419 422-4341

(G-2061)
OHIO POWER SYSTEMS LLC
Also Called: Ops Wireless
807 E Findlay St (43316-1331)
PHONE.....................419 396-4041
Michael R Brooks, *Managing Member*
Dustin Brooks, *Contrlr*
EMP: 14 **EST:** 2004
SQ FT: 10,500
SALES (est): 2.95MM **Privately Held**
Web: www.opscontrols.com
SIC: 3679 Video triggers, except remote
control TV devices

(G-2062)
PROGRESSOR TIMES
1198 E Findlay St (43316-9760)
P.O. Box 37 (43316-0037)
PHONE.....................419 396-7567
Stephen Zender, *Owner*
EMP: 6 **EST:** 1873
SALES (est): 116.5K **Privately Held**
Web: www.theprogressortimes.com
SIC: 7313 2711 Newspaper advertising
representative; Newspapers

(G-2063)
TEIJIN AUTOMOTIVE TECH INC
Also Called: CSP Carey
2915 County Highway 96 (43316-1155)
PHONE.....................419 396-1980
Mike Bishop, *Brnch Mgr*
EMP: 253
Web: www.teijinautomotive.com
SIC: 3089 3714 Injection molding of plastics;
Motor vehicle parts and accessories
HQ: Teijin Automotive Technologies, Inc.
255 Rex Blvd
Auburn Hills MI 48326
248 237-7800

(G-2064)
WYANDOT DOLOMITE INC
Also Called: Stoneco
1794 County Highway 99 (43316-9722)
P.O. Box 99 (43316-0099)
PHONE.....................419 396-7641
Dennis Overacker, *Prin*
EMP: 25 **EST:** 1949
SQ FT: 3,500
SALES (est): 1.87MM **Privately Held**
SIC: 1411 1611 2951 3272 Limestone,
dimension-quarrying; Surfacing and paving;
Asphalt and asphaltic paving mixtures (not
from refineries); Concrete products, nec

Carlisle
Warren County

(G-2065)
CONVERTERS/PREPRESS INC
301 Industry Dr (45005-6330)
PHONE.....................937 743-0935
Mike Zimmer, *Brnch Mgr*
EMP: 17
SALES (corp-wide): 2.2MM **Privately Held**
Web: www.cpinc.net
SIC: 2796 7336 Engraving platemaking
services; Commercial art and graphic
design
PA: Converters/Prepress, Inc.
1070 Tower Ln
Bensenville IL 60106
630 860-9400

(G-2066)
INDUSTRIAL ELECTRONIC SERVICE
Also Called: De Digital
325 Industry Dr (45005-6309)
PHONE.....................937 746-9750
Jim Staffan, *Prin*
Pete Staffan, *Prin*
EMP: 11 **EST:** 1965
SQ FT: 3,700
SALES (est): 1MM **Privately Held**
Web: www.ledscoreboard.com
SIC: 3993 3579 7622 1731 Scoreboards,
electric; Time clocks and time recording
devices; Intercommunication equipment
repair; Electronic controls installation

(G-2067)
KITTYHAWK MOLDING COMPANY INC
10 Eagle Ct (45005-6321)
PHONE.....................937 746-3663
Wilbur V Wisecup Junior, *CEO*
Dave Holmes, *
Anita Holmes, *
Sue Little, *
EMP: 29 **EST:** 1989
SQ FT: 20,500
SALES (est): 4.99MM **Privately Held**
Web: www.kittyhawkmolding.com

SIC: 3089 Injection molding of plastics

(G-2068)
MAR-FLEX SYSTEMS LLC
Also Called: Mar-Flex Wtrproofing Bldg Pdts
500 Business Pkwy (45005-6337)
PHONE.....................513 422-7285
◆ **EMP:** 20 **EST:** 1987
SALES (est): 8.72MM **Privately Held**
Web: www.mar-flex.com
SIC: 2899 Waterproofing compounds

(G-2069)
NARROW WAY CUSTOM TECH INC
100 Industry Dr (45005-6304)
PHONE.....................937 743-1611
Timothy Williams, *Pr*
EMP: 29 **EST:** 1998
SQ FT: 5,600
SALES (est): 4.54MM **Privately Held**
Web: www.narrowway100.com
SIC: 3599 7629 Custom machinery;
Electrical repair shops

(G-2070)
PATRIOT MFG GROUP INC
512 Linden Ave (45005-3345)
PHONE.....................937 746-2117
Phillip Hubbell, *Pr*
EMP: 54 **EST:** 2005
SALES (est): 4.74MM **Privately Held**
Web: www.patriot-mg.com
SIC: 3599 Machine shop, jobbing and repair

(G-2071)
QIBCO BUFFING PADS INC (PA)
Also Called: American Buffing
301 Industry Dr Ste B (45005-6330)
PHONE.....................937 743-0805
Jeff Phipps, *VP*
▲ **EMP:** 6 **EST:** 1996
SALES (est): 194.64K **Privately Held**
Web: www.americanbuffing.com
SIC: 3291 Abrasive buffs, bricks, cloth,
paper, stones, etc.

(G-2072)
REFRESCO US INC
Also Called: Refresco North America
300 Industry Dr (45005-6308)
PHONE.....................937 790-1400
EMP: 110
Web: www.refresco.com
SIC: 2033 Fruit juices: packaged in cans,
jars, etc.
HQ: Refresco Us, Inc.
6655 S Lewis Ave
Tulsa OK 74136

Carroll
Fairfield County

(G-2073)
ARTISAN EQUIPMENT INC
5770 Winchester Rd (43112-9204)
P.O. Box 500 (43112-0500)
PHONE.....................740 756-9135
Stuart Brengman, *Pr*
Keith C Brengman, *VP*
Marsha Brengman, *Sec*
EMP: 10 **EST:** 1975
SQ FT: 12,700
SALES (est): 1.71MM **Privately Held**
Web: www.artisanequipment.com
SIC: 3599 3469 3544 Custom machinery;
Machine parts, stamped or pressed metal;
Special dies, tools, jigs, and fixtures

(G-2074)
CW MACHINE WORX LTD
4805 Scooby Ln (43112-9446)
PHONE.....................740 654-5304
Shannon Heston, *Managing Member*
EMP: 12 **EST:** 2009
SQ FT: 15,000
SALES (est): 3.12MM **Privately Held**
Web: www.companywrench.com
SIC: 3531 Construction machinery

(G-2075)
F C BRENGMAN AND ASSOC LLC
86 High St (43112-9793)
P.O. Box 470 (43112-0470)
PHONE.....................740 756-4308
Bill Mason, *Owner*
Bill Mason, *Managing Member*
Robert Mason, *
EMP: 28 **EST:** 1949
SQ FT: 12,000
SALES (est): 5.79MM **Privately Held**
Web: www.fcbrengman.com
SIC: 3469 Stamping metal for the trade

(G-2076)
FAIRFIELD MACHINED PDTS INC
6215 Columbus Lancaster Rd Nw
(43112-9202)
P.O. Box 410 (43112-0410)
PHONE.....................740 756-4409
David Riggenbach, *Pr*
Frederick Marshall, *VP*
Ronnie Wyne, *Sec*
EMP: 7 **EST:** 2002
SALES (est): 874.63K **Privately Held**
Web:
www.fairfieldmachinedproducts.com
SIC: 3451 Screw machine products

(G-2077)
RELIABLE MANUFACTURING LLC
5594 Winchester Rd (43112-9202)
PHONE.....................740 756-9373
Jesse Whittington, *Managing Member*
EMP: 23 **EST:** 2021
SALES (est): 10MM **Privately Held**
Web: www.reliablemfggas.com
SIC: 3824 Fluid meters and counting devices

(G-2078)
RELIABLE MFG CO LLC
4411 Carroll Southern Rd (43112-9794)
PHONE.....................740 756-9373
EMP: 6 **EST:** 2002
SQ FT: 8,500
SALES (est): 1.05MM **Privately Held**
SIC: 2813 Industrial gases

Carrollton
Carroll County

(G-2079)
AERO PALLETS INC
348 Raley Ave Se (44615-1443)
P.O. Box 311 (44663-0311)
PHONE.....................330 260-7107
Paul Collier, *Pr*
EMP: 30 **EST:** 2015
SALES (est): 1.78MM **Privately Held**
SIC: 2448 Wood pallets and skids

(G-2080)
CARROLL HILLS INDUSTRIES
540 High St Nw (44615-1116)
P.O. Box 567 (44615)
PHONE.....................330 627-5524
Matt Champbell, *Superintnt*
EMP: 8 **EST:** 1980

SQ FT: 4,640
SALES (est): 527.16K **Privately Held**
Web: www.carrollcbdd.org
SIC: 8331 3999 Sheltered workshop; Barber
and beauty shop equipment

(G-2081)
CARROLLTON PUBLISHING COMPANY
Also Called: Free Press Standard
43 E Main St (44615-1221)
P.O. Box 37 (44615-0037)
PHONE..............................330 627-5591
William Peterson, *Genl Mgr*
Maynard Buck, *Sec*
EMP: 6 EST: 1965
SQ FT: 4,800
SALES (est): 215.58K **Privately Held**
Web: www.freepressstandard.com
SIC: 2711 Commercial printing and
newspaper publishing combined

(G-2082)
ERNST ENTERPRISES INC
Also Called: Valley Concrete
4710 Soldiers Home Rd (44615)
P.O. Box 638 (44615-0638)
PHONE..............................937 866-9441
John Mcafee, *Genl Mgr*
EMP: 13
SALES (corp-wide): 240.08MM **Privately Held**
Web: www.ernstconcrete.com
SIC: 3273 Ready-mixed concrete
PA: Ernst Enterprises, Inc.
993 Falls Creek Dr
Vandalia OH 45377
937 233-5555

(G-2083)
FUSION CERAMICS INC (PA)
160 Scio Rd Se (44615-9502)
P.O. Box 127 (44615-0127)
PHONE..............................330 627-5821
Richard Hannon Junior, *Pr*
Dave Schneider, *
Joyce J Hannon, *
◆ EMP: 25 EST: 1971
SQ FT: 20,000
SALES (est): 9.78MM
SALES (corp-wide): 9.78MM **Privately Held**
Web: www.fusionceramics.com
SIC: 2899 Chemical preparations, nec

(G-2084)
HALL ACQUISITION LLC
1209 N Lisbon St (44615-9404)
P.O. Box 24 (44615-0024)
PHONE..............................330 627-2119
Donald Hall, *Pr*
EMP: 6 EST: 1965
SQ FT: 11,800
SALES (est): 965.53K **Privately Held**
SIC: 3599 Machine shop, jobbing and repair

(G-2085)
HERITAGE PLASTICS LIQUIDATION INC
Also Called: Heritage Plastics
861 N Lisbon St (44615-9401)
PHONE..............................330 627-8002
▼ EMP: 70
Web: www.atkore.com
SIC: 3084 Plastics pipe

(G-2086)
J P INDUSTRIAL PRODUCTS INC
755 N Lisbon St (44615-9401)
PHONE..............................330 627-1377

EMP: 10
SALES (corp-wide): 14.93MM **Privately Held**
Web: www.jpindustrial.com
SIC: 2821 Plastics materials and resins
PA: J. P. Industrial Products, Inc.
11988 State Route 45
Lisbon OH 44432
330 424-1110

(G-2087)
JOMAC LTD
Also Called: Jones Propane Supply
182 Scio Rd Se (44615-8521)
P.O. Box 337 (44615-0337)
PHONE..............................330 627-7727
Richard Jones, *Pr*
Lori Jones, *
EMP: 38 EST: 1983
SALES (est): 6.72MM **Privately Held**
Web: www.jomacltd.com
SIC: 3441 5984 Fabricated structural metal;
Propane gas, bottled

(G-2088)
RCE HEAT EXCHANGERS LLC
3165 Folsam Rd Nw (44615-8201)
PHONE..............................330 627-0300
Mike Earl, *Mng Pt*
Robert Strobel, *VP*
EMP: 20 EST: 2005
SALES (est): 883.4K **Privately Held**
Web: www.rceheatexchangers.com
SIC: 3443 Heat exchangers, condensers,
and components

(G-2089)
REINALT-THOMAS CORPORATION
5125 Canton Rd Nw (44615-9015)
PHONE..............................330 863-1936
Gene Dunn, *Brnch Mgr*
EMP: 6
SALES (corp-wide): 3.69B **Privately Held**
SIC: 3089 Automotive parts, plastic
PA: The Reinalt-Thomas Corporation
20225 N Scottsdale Rd
Scottsdale AZ 85255
480 606-6000

(G-2090)
SEVEN RANGES MFG CORP
330 Industrial Dr Sw (44615-8569)
P.O. Box 206 (44615-0206)
PHONE..............................330 627-7155
Fred D Tarr Senior, *Pr*
David Richard Tarr, *
EMP: 26 EST: 1982
SQ FT: 29,000
SALES (est): 2.16MM **Privately Held**
Web: www.sevenranges.com
SIC: 3469 Stamping metal for the trade

(G-2091)
TWIN CITIES CONCRETE CO
1031 Kensington Rd Ne (44615-9403)
P.O. Box 400 (44622-0400)
PHONE..............................330 627-2158
Louis Cline, *Mgr*
EMP: 483
SALES (corp-wide): 34.95B **Privately Held**
SIC: 3273 Ready-mixed concrete
HQ: Twin Cities Concrete Co.
141 S Tuscarawas Ave
Dover OH 44622
330 343-4491

Casstown
Miami County

(G-2092)
STEEL AVIATION AIRCRAFT SALES
4433 E State Route 55 (45312-9579)
PHONE..............................937 332-7587
Jaime Steel, *Prin*
EMP: 7 EST: 2004
SALES (est): 340.87K **Privately Held**
Web: www.steelaviation.com
SIC: 3721 Airplanes, fixed or rotary wing

Castalia
Erie County

(G-2093)
ABJ EQUIPFIX LLC
Also Called: Abj
202 Lucas St W (44824-9254)
PHONE..............................419 684-5236
Alan D Strause, *CEO*
EMP: 20 EST: 2001
SQ FT: 7,000
SALES (est): 2.1MM **Privately Held**
Web: www.abjequipment.com
SIC: 7699 3556 Industrial machinery and
equipment repair; Food products machinery

(G-2094)
CASTALIA TRENCHING & RDYMX LLC
4814 State Route 269 S (44824-9359)
PHONE..............................419 684-5502
Joe Verb, *Prin*
Denise Verb, *Prin*
EMP: 16 EST: 2013
SALES (est): 1.46MM **Privately Held**
Web: www.ctrmohio.com
SIC: 3273 Ready-mixed concrete

(G-2095)
CASTALIA TRENCHING & READY MIX
4814 State Route 269 S (44824-9359)
PHONE..............................419 684-5502
TOLL FREE: 800
Francis Winkel, *Pr*
James Winkel, *Sec*
Larry Winkel, *VP*
John Winkel, *VP*
EMP: 10 EST: 1954
SQ FT: 8,000
SALES (est): 304.51K **Privately Held**
Web: www.ctrmohio.com
SIC: 3273 1794 Ready-mixed concrete;
Excavation work

(G-2096)
WALLSEYE CONCRETE CORP
8802 Portland Rd (44824-9259)
PHONE..............................419 483-2738
TOLL FREE: 800
Marvin Brenzo, *Mgr*
EMP: 10
Web: www.westviewconcrete.com
SIC: 3241 5032 Portland cement; Brick,
stone, and related material
PA: Wallseye Concrete Corp.
26000 Sprague Rd
Cleveland OH 44138

Casstown
Miami County

(G-2097)
APPLIED SCIENCES INC
141 W Xenia Ave (45314-9529)
P.O. Box 579 (45314-0579)
PHONE..............................937 766-2020
Max Lake, *Pr*
Inga Lake, *
EMP: 35 EST: 1984
SQ FT: 6,600
SALES (est): 1.81MM **Privately Held**
Web: www.apsci.com
SIC: 8731 3624 Commercial research
laboratory; Carbon and graphite products

Celina
Mercer County

(G-2098)
BUCKEYE VALLEY PIZZA HUT LTD
Also Called: Pizza Hut
1152 E Market St (45822-1934)
PHONE..............................419 586-5900
EMP: 34
SALES (corp-wide): 2.43MM **Privately Held**
Web: www.pizzahut.com
SIC: 5812 2099 Pizzeria, chain; Food
preparations, nec
PA: Buckeye Valley Pizza Hut, Ltd.
65 S Main St
Springboro OH 45066
937 748-3338

(G-2099)
CELINA ALUM PRECISION TECH INC
Also Called: Capt
7059 Staeger Rd (45822-9395)
PHONE..............................419 586-2278
Takenori Yamaguchi, *Pr*
Jay James, *
▲ EMP: 500 EST: 1994
SQ FT: 160,000
SALES (est): 40.97MM **Privately Held**
Web: www.capt-celina.com
SIC: 3592 Pistons and piston rings
HQ: Honda Foundry Co., Ltd.
1620, Matoba
Kawagoe STM 350-1

(G-2100)
CELINA PERCISION MACHINE
1201 Havemann Rd (45822-1391)
PHONE..............................419 586-9222
EMP: 10 EST: 2019
SALES (est): 490.69K **Privately Held**
Web: www.machine-pro.com
SIC: 3599 Machine shop, jobbing and repair

(G-2101)
CELINA TENT INC (PA)
5373 State Route 29 (45822-9210)
PHONE..............................419 586-3610
Jeff Grieshop, *Pr*
Janice Grieshop, *
◆ EMP: 91 EST: 1996
SQ FT: 27,000
SALES (est): 1.91MM **Privately Held**
Web: www.celina.com
SIC: 2394 Tents: made from purchased
materials

(G-2102)
CROWN EQUIPMENT CORPORATION
Also Called: Crown Lift Trucks
410 Grand Lake Rd (45822-1869)

PHONE..............................419 586-1100
Chuck Post, *Brnch Mgr*
EMP: 42
SALES (corp-wide): 7.12B **Privately Held**
Web: www.crown.com
SIC: 3537 Lift trucks, industrial: fork, platform, straddle, etc.
PA: Crown Equipment Corporation
44 S Washington St
New Bremen OH 45869
419 629-2311

(G-2103)
DOLL INC
Also Called: Doll Printing
1901 Havemann Rd (45822)
P.O. Box 412 (45822-0412)
PHONE..............................419 586-7880
Robert A Doll, *Pr*
Phyllis Doll, *Sec*
EMP: 8 **EST:** 1928
SQ FT: 6,200
SALES (est): 437.09K **Privately Held**
Web: www.dollprinting.com
SIC: 2752 Offset printing

(G-2104)
EIGHTH FLOOR PROMOTIONS LLC
Also Called: Awardcraft
1 Visions Pkwy (45822-7500)
P.O. Box 42501 (45042-0501)
PHONE..............................419 586-6433
Dave Willis, *Pr*
Les Dorfman, *
▲ **EMP:** 190 **EST:** 1977
SQ FT: 83,000
SALES (est): 5.45MM **Privately Held**
Web: www.8thfloorpromotions.com
SIC: 3993 Signs and advertising specialties

(G-2105)
ERGO DESKTOP LLC
457 Grand Lake Rd (45822-1839)
PHONE..............................567 890-3746
Kathy Sharkey, *Managing Member*
Derrick Walls, *Managing Member*
▲ **EMP:** 23 **EST:** 2009
SQ FT: 2,500
SALES (est): 869.62K **Privately Held**
Web: www.ergodesktop.com
SIC: 2522 7389 Office furniture, except wood ; Business Activities at Non-Commercial Site

(G-2106)
FALLEN OAK CANDLES INC
917 Lilac St (45822-1326)
PHONE..............................419 204-8162
Brian Brim, *Pr*
EMP: 7 **EST:** 2009
SALES (est): 275.65K **Privately Held**
SIC: 3999 Candles

(G-2107)
GRYPMAT INC
6886 Nancy Ave (45822-9268)
PHONE..............................419 953-7607
Tom Burden, *CEO*
EMP: 7 **EST:** 2017
SALES (est): 484.92K **Privately Held**
Web: www.grypmat.com
SIC: 3069 Trays, rubber

(G-2108)
HAULETTE MANUFACTURING INC
8271 Us Route 127 (45822-9416)
PHONE..............................419 586-1717
Fred Kremer, *CEO*
Steven Braun, *
EMP: 53 **EST:** 1958
SQ FT: 50,000

SALES (est): 4.15MM **Privately Held**
Web: www.haulette.com
SIC: 3599 3715 Machine shop, jobbing and repair; Trailer bodies

(G-2109)
HEITKAMP & KREMER PRINTING INC
Also Called: Messenger Press
6184 State Route 274 (45822-9505)
PHONE..............................419 925-4121
Alan Kremer, *Pr*
Randy Heitkamp, *VP*
Jenny Schwenzer, *Sec*
EMP: 9 **EST:** 1992
SALES (est): 460.97K **Privately Held**
Web: www.messenger-press.com
SIC: 2752 Offset printing

(G-2110)
INNOVTIVE MCHNING SLUTIONS LLC
6190 Franklin St (45822-9628)
PHONE..............................419 925-2060
EMP: 11 **EST:** 2018
SALES (est): 5.92MM **Privately Held**
SIC: 3541 8711 Machine tools, metal cutting type; Engineering services

(G-2111)
JAVANATION
108 S Main St (45822-2228)
PHONE..............................419 584-1705
Vance Nation, *Owner*
EMP: 10 **EST:** 2009
SALES (est): 253.47K **Privately Held**
Web: www.hexxen.com
SIC: 3269 Pottery products, nec

(G-2112)
JES FOODS/CELINA INC
1800 Industrial Dr (45822-1376)
PHONE..............................419 586-7446
Elaine Freed, *Pr*
William Freed, *VP*
EMP: 13 **EST:** 1995
SQ FT: 24,000
SALES (est): 1.19MM **Privately Held**
Web: www.jesfoods.com
SIC: 2033 2035 2032 Canned fruits and specialties; Pickles, sauces, and salad dressings; Canned specialties
PA: J.E.S. Foods, Inc.
865 W Liberty St Ste 200
Medina OH 44256

(G-2113)
MACHINE-PRO TECHNOLOGIES INC
1321 W Market St (45822-9285)
PHONE..............................419 584-0086
Tim Klosterman, *Pr*
▲ **EMP:** 57 **EST:** 1994
SQ FT: 24,000
SALES (est): 4.63MM **Privately Held**
Web: www.machine-pro.com
SIC: 3599 Machine shop, jobbing and repair

(G-2114)
PAX MACHINE WORKS INC
5139 Monroe Rd (45822-9033)
P.O. Box 338 (45822-0338)
PHONE..............................419 586-2337
Francis J Pax, *Pr*
Michael Pax, *
Deborah Guingrich, *
▼ **EMP:** 65 **EST:** 1948
SQ FT: 451,000
SALES (est): 7.65MM **Privately Held**
Web: www.paxmachine.com
SIC: 3469 Stamping metal for the trade

(G-2115)
PAX PRODUCTS INC
5097 Monroe Rd (45822-9033)
P.O. Box 257 (45822-0257)
PHONE..............................419 586-2337
Francis J Pax, *Pr*
Steven Pax, *VP*
Michael Pax, *Treas*
Deborah Guingrich, *Sec*
EMP: 11 **EST:** 1980
SQ FT: 36,500
SALES (est): 4.58MM **Privately Held**
Web: www.paxproducts.com
SIC: 3569 Lubricating equipment

(G-2116)
PHI WERKES LLC
1201 Havemann Rd (45822-1391)
PHONE..............................419 586-9222
EMP: 8 **EST:** 2003
SQ FT: 13,800
SALES (est): 304.46K **Privately Held**
SIC: 3599 Machine shop, jobbing and repair

(G-2117)
REYNOLDS AND REYNOLDS COMPANY
Reynolds & Reynolds
824 Murlin Ave (45822-2459)
P.O. Box 999 (45822-0999)
PHONE..............................419 584-7000
Ray Grassman, *Brnch Mgr*
EMP: 10
SALES (corp-wide): 1.54B **Privately Held**
Web: www.reyrey.com
SIC: 2761 2759 2752 Manifold business forms; Commercial printing, nec; Commercial printing, lithographic
HQ: The Reynolds And Reynolds Company
1 Reynolds Way
Kettering OH 45430
937 485-2000

(G-2118)
S & K PRODUCTS COMPANY
Also Called: Plant 1
4540 St Rt 127 (45822)
P.O. Box 166 (45828-0166)
PHONE..............................419 268-2244
EMP: 45 **EST:** 1949
SALES (est): 6.82MM **Privately Held**
Web: www.skproductsco.com
SIC: 3469 3429 Metal stampings, nec; Hardware, nec

(G-2119)
SCHUCK MTAL FBRCTION DSIGN INC
8319 Us 127 N (45822)
P.O. Box 354 (45822-0354)
PHONE..............................419 586-1054
Daniel Schuck, *Pr*
EMP: 15 **EST:** 1985
SQ FT: 15,000
SALES (est): 597.32K **Privately Held**
Web: www.schuckcushionhitches.com
SIC: 3441 Fabricated structural metal

(G-2120)
SOCIETY OF THE PRECIOUS BLOOD
Also Called: Messenger Press
2860 Us Route 127 (45822-9533)
PHONE..............................419 925-4516
Father James Seibert, *Brnch Mgr*
EMP: 40
SALES (corp-wide): 899.52K **Privately Held**
Web: www.messenger-press.com

SIC: 2732 8661 8211 Pamphlets: printing only, not published on site; Brethren Church ; Private elementary and secondary schools
PA: The Society Of The Precious Blood
431 E 2nd St
Dayton OH 45402
937 228-9263

(G-2121)
STANDARD PRINTING CO INC
Also Called: Daily Standard The
123 E Market St (45822-1730)
P.O. Box 140 (45822-0140)
PHONE..............................419 586-2371
Frank Snyder, *Pr*
EMP: 9 **EST:** 1851
SQ FT: 20,000
SALES (est): 429.29K **Privately Held**
Web: www.dailystandard.com
SIC: 2711 Commercial printing and newspaper publishing combined

(G-2122)
STEALTH ARMS LLC
4939 Kittle Rd (45822-9191)
PHONE..............................419 925-7005
EMP: 8 **EST:** 2013
SALES (est): 1.29MM **Privately Held**
Web: www.stealtharms.net
SIC: 3484 Guns (firearms) or gun parts, 30 mm. and below

(G-2123)
TECH SOLUTIONS LLC
Also Called: Instantorder
658 N Main St (45822-1463)
PHONE..............................419 852-7190
EMP: 8 **EST:** 2011
SALES (est): 129.51K **Privately Held**
Web: www.instantorder.io
SIC: 7371 5961 7372 Computer software development and applications; Food, mail order; Application computer software

(G-2124)
THEES MACHINE & TOOL COMPANY
2007 State Route 703 (45822-2525)
PHONE..............................419 586-4766
John E Thees, *Pr*
Carolann Thees, *VP*
EMP: 6 **EST:** 1973
SQ FT: 7,000
SALES (est): 474.74K **Privately Held**
SIC: 3599 Machine shop, jobbing and repair

(G-2125)
THIEMAN TAILGATES INC
600 E Wayne St (45822-1566)
PHONE..............................419 586-7727
Thomas A Thieman, *Pr*
Sandra Thieman, *Sec*
Todd Thieman, *VP*
EMP: 90 **EST:** 1987
SQ FT: 130,000
SALES (est): 11.08MM **Privately Held**
Web: www.thiemantailgates.com
SIC: 3561 Industrial pumps and parts

(G-2126)
VAN TILBURG FARMS INC
Also Called: Vantilburg Farms
8398 Celina Mendon Rd (45822-9339)
PHONE..............................419 586-3077
James Van Tilburg, *Pr*
Brenda Vantilburg, *Sec*
EMP: 12 **EST:** 1942
SQ FT: 2,000
SALES (est): 6.73MM **Privately Held**
Web: www.vantilburgfarms.com
SIC: 5153 2875 Grains; Compost

(G-2127)
VERSA-PAK LTD
500 Staeger Rd (45822-9373)
P.O. Box 69 (45822-0069)
PHONE..............................419 586-5466
Jeffrey C Bruns, *Rep*
Kenneth Gerlach, *
Mark A Bruns, *
EMP: 45 **EST:** 2000
SQ FT: 23,000
SALES (est): 3.47MM **Privately Held**
Web: www.versa-pak.com
SIC: 5199 2671 Packaging materials; Plastic film, coated or laminated for packaging

Centerburg
Knox County

(G-2128)
TRADYE MACHINE & TOOL INC
3116a Wilson Rd (43011-9467)
PHONE..............................740 625-7550
Tracy Payne, *Pr*
Diana Payne, *Mgr*
EMP: 7 **EST:** 1994
SQ FT: 12,000
SALES (est): 1.14MM **Privately Held**
Web: www.tradye.com
SIC: 3544 3599 Special dies and tools; Machine shop, jobbing and repair

Centerville
Montgomery County

(G-2129)
ASSOCIATES TIRE AND SVC INC
Also Called: Grismer Tire
1099 S Main St (45458-3840)
PHONE..............................937 436-4692
Andrew Stewart, *Brnch Mgr*
EMP: 10
SALES (corp-wide): 2.02MM **Privately Held**
Web: www.grismertire.com
SIC: 5014 5531 7534 Automobile tires and tubes; Automotive tires; Tire repair shop
PA: Associates Tire And Service Inc.
3411 Office Park Dr
Dayton OH
937 643-2526

(G-2130)
B & P COMPANY INC
301 Miamisburg Centerville Rd
(45459-4705)
P.O. Box 41184 (45441-0184)
PHONE..............................937 298-0265
Margaret Wright, *Pr*
EMP: 9 **EST:** 1996
SQ FT: 13,000
SALES (est): 5.58MM **Privately Held**
Web: www.frownies.com
SIC: 2844 Cosmetic preparations

(G-2131)
DIMCOGRAY CORPORATION (PA)
Also Called: Dimco-Gray Company
900 Dimco Way (45458-2709)
PHONE..............................937 433-7600
TOLL FREE: 800
Michael Sieron, *CEO*
Terry Tate, *
▲ **EMP:** 90 **EST:** 1924
SQ FT: 48,000
SALES (est): 3.81MM
SALES (corp-wide): 3.81MM **Privately Held**
Web: www.dimcogray.com

SIC: 3089 3873 3965 3625 Injection molding of plastics; Watches, clocks, watchcases, and parts; Fasteners; Relays and industrial controls

(G-2132)
GRISMER TIRE COMPANY (PA)
1099 S Main St (45458-3840)
P.O. Box 337 (45401-0337)
PHONE..............................937 643-2526
Charles L Marshall Ii, *Pr*
John L Marshall, *
Robert Hupp, *
▲ **EMP:** 28 **EST:** 1932
SQ FT: 40,000
SALES (est): 18.33MM
SALES (corp-wide): 18.33MM **Privately Held**
Web: www.grismertire.com
SIC: 5531 7538 5014 7534 Automotive tires; General automotive repair shops; Automobile tires and tubes; Rebuilding and retreading tires

Chagrin Falls
Cuyahoga County

(G-2133)
1-2-3 GLUTEN FREE INC
125 Orange Tree Dr (44022-1560)
PHONE..............................216 378-9233
Kim Ullner, *Prin*
EMP: 6 **EST:** 2007
SALES (est): 319.3K **Privately Held**
Web: www.123glutenfree.com
SIC: 2041 Flour mixes

(G-2134)
11 92 HOLDINGS LLC
8 E Washington St Ste 200 (44022-3057)
PHONE..............................216 920-7790
Mike Owens, *Prin*
EMP: 10 **EST:** 2014
SALES (est): 1.22MM **Privately Held**
SIC: 2591 Blinds vertical
HQ: Vertical Knowledge Llc
4 E Washington St
Chagrin Falls OH 44022
216 920-7790

(G-2135)
ADVERTISING JOE LLC MEAN
33 River St Ste 7 (44022-3020)
PHONE..............................440 247-8200
Todd Berk, *Pr*
EMP: 7 **EST:** 2012
SALES (est): 521.79K **Privately Held**
Web: www.meanjoeadvertising.com
SIC: 7311 2759 Advertising agencies; Commercial printing, nec

(G-2136)
C4 POLYMERS INC (PA)
Also Called: C4 Group, The
33 River St (44022-3020)
PHONE..............................440 543-3866
Eric Smith, *Pr*
▼ **EMP:** 9 **EST:** 1996
SALES (est): 4.38MM **Privately Held**
Web: www.c4poly.com
SIC: 2821 Plastics materials and resins

(G-2137)
CABINETWORKS GROUP MICH LLC
25 N Franklin St (44022-3009)
PHONE..............................440 247-3091
EMP: 37
SALES (corp-wide): 486.01MM **Privately Held**

Web: www.cabinetworksgroup.com
SIC: 2434 Wood kitchen cabinets
PA: Cabinetworks Group Michigan, Llc
20000 Victor Pkwy
Livonia MI 48152
734 205-4600

(G-2138)
CATERPILLAR INDUSTRIAL INC
45 E Washington St Ste 203 (44022-3040)
PHONE..............................440 247-8484
EMP: 7 **EST:** 1965
SALES (est): 654.89K
SALES (corp-wide): 64.81B **Publicly Held**
Web: www.ohiocat.com
SIC: 3531 Construction machinery
PA: Caterpillar Inc.
5205 N Ocnnor Blvd Ste 10
Irving TX 75039
972 891-7700

(G-2139)
CHAGRIN VALLEY PUBLISHING CO
Also Called: Chagrin Valley Times
525 Washington St (44022-4455)
P.O. Box 150 (44022-0150)
PHONE..............................440 247-5335
Harold Douthit, *Pr*
EMP: 17 **EST:** 1971
SQ FT: 4,000
SALES (est): 988.44K **Privately Held**
Web: www.chagrinvalleytoday.com
SIC: 2711 Newspapers, publishing and printing

(G-2140)
E TECHNOLOGIES INC
300 Industrial Pkwy Ste A (44022-4420)
PHONE..............................440 247-7000
John Englhardt, *Pr*
Suellen Englehardt, *VP*
EMP: 6 **EST:** 1998
SQ FT: 2,500
SALES (est): 4.33MM **Privately Held**
Web: www.etechnologies.com
SIC: 3612 Transformers, except electric

(G-2141)
E-Z GRADER COMPANY
300 Industrial Pkwy Ste A (44022-4420)
PHONE..............................440 247-7511
Jill Richards, *Pr*
Bruce Richards, *VP*
EMP: 8 **EST:** 1952
SALES (est): 167.71K **Privately Held**
Web: www.ezgrader.com
SIC: 5961 2679 Educational supplies and equipment, mail order; Paperboard products, converted, nec

(G-2142)
EDMAR CHEMICAL COMPANY
539 Washington St (44022-4407)
P.O. Box 598 (44022-0598)
PHONE..............................440 247-9560
Jack Binder, *Pr*
Dan Berick, *Sec*
Jack Ahem, *Treas*
EMP: 9 **EST:** 1940
SALES (est): 946.62K **Privately Held**
Web: www.edmarchem.com
SIC: 2841 2842 Soap: granulated, liquid, cake, flaked, or chip; Fabric softeners

(G-2143)
EL OSTENDORF INC
Also Called: Shuler Pewter
3425 Roundwood Rd (44022-6634)
PHONE..............................440 247-7631
Ed L Ostendorf, *Pr*
EMP: 7 **EST:** 1956

SQ FT: 12,000
SALES (est): 340.58K **Privately Held**
SIC: 6531 3645 Real estate agent, commercial; Residential lighting fixtures

(G-2144)
FMX 2018 INC
Also Called: Sedona Office
547 Washington St Ste 11 (44022-4436)
PHONE..............................440 247-5602
Michael Marks, *Pr*
EMP: 15 **EST:** 1996
SALES (est): 1.67MM **Privately Held**
Web: www.boldgroup.com
SIC: 7372 Business oriented computer software

(G-2145)
GLX POWER SYSTEMS INC
46 Chagrin Plz Ste 201 (44022-2731)
PHONE..............................440 338-6526
Kent Kristensen, *Pr*
EMP: 9 **EST:** 2018
SALES (est): 333.62K **Privately Held**
SIC: 3692 3691 Primary batteries, dry and wet; Storage batteries

(G-2146)
INTEGRATED DEVELOPMENT & MFG (PA)
Also Called: Environmental Growth Chambers
510 Washington St (44022-4448)
PHONE..............................440 247-5100
Adrian Rule, *Pr*
Adrian Rule Iv, *VP*
Raymond F Pletcher, *Treas*
EMP: 16 **EST:** 1952
SQ FT: 28,000
SALES (est): 9.94MM
SALES (corp-wide): 9.94MM **Privately Held**
Web:
integrated-development-manufacturing.sbcontract.com
SIC: 3822 1711 Environmental controls; Refrigeration contractor

(G-2147)
KATIMEX USA INC
15241 Hemlock Point Rd (44022-3832)
P.O. Box 4000 (44065-0299)
PHONE..............................440 338-3500
Mary Ann Ondrus, *Pr*
Tom Ondrus, *VP*
EMP: 9 **EST:** 1984
SALES (est): 89.88K **Privately Held**
SIC: 2298 Cable, fiber

(G-2148)
MEYER COMPANY (PA)
Also Called: Tomlinson Industries
7180 Sugar Bush Ln (44022-2666)
PHONE..............................216 587-3400
H F Meyer, *Pr*
Donald Calkins, *
Michael E Figas, *
H F Meyer Iii, *VP*
Heidi Figas, *
◆ **EMP:** 170 **EST:** 1897
SALES (est): 4.83MM
SALES (corp-wide): 4.83MM **Privately Held**
Web: www.meyerinc.com
SIC: 3556 Food products machinery

(G-2149)
MILLENNIUM ADHESIVE PDTS LLC
178 E Washington St Ste 1 (44022-2978)
PHONE..............................440 708-1212
Ronald Janoski, *Pr*
Mark Rundo, *VP Sls*

EMP: 10 **EST:** 1997
SQ FT: 7,000
SALES (est): 2.2MM
SALES (corp-wide): 3.57B **Publicly Held**
SIC: 2891 Adhesives and sealants
PA: H.B. Fuller Company
1200 Willow Lake Blvd
Saint Paul MN 55110
651 236-5900

(G-2150)
RSP INDUSTRIES INC
415 Hazelwood Dr (44022-3926)
PHONE..............................440 823-4502
EMP: 8 **EST:** 2016
SALES (est): 2.32MM **Privately Held**
Web: www.sapproductsllc.com
SIC: 2493 Wall tile, fiberboard

(G-2151)
SHOOK MANUFACTURED PDTS INC
3801 Wiltshire Rd (44022-1151)
PHONE..............................440 247-9130
Thomas John, *Mgr*
EMP: 8
SALES (corp-wide): 976.14K **Privately Held**
Web: www.shookmfg.com
SIC: 3545 Chucks: drill, lathe, or magnetic (machine tool accessories)
PA: Shook Manufactured Products, Inc.
1017 Kenmore Blvd
Akron OH 44314
330 848-9780

Chagrin Falls
Geauga County

(G-2152)
AB TIRE & REPAIR
9685 Washington St (44023-2757)
PHONE..............................440 543-2929
Edward Klempay, *Owner*
EMP: 7 **EST:** 2007
SALES (est): 254.73K **Privately Held**
Web: www.radiatorinfo.com
SIC: 5531 7538 7534 7539 Automotive tires; General automotive repair shops; Tire retreading and repair shops; Automotive repair shops, nec

(G-2153)
ABANAKI CORPORATION (PA)
Also Called: Aerodyne
17387 Munn Rd (44023-5400)
PHONE..............................440 543-7400
Mark Thomas Hobson, *Pr*
▲ **EMP:** 14 **EST:** 1968
SQ FT: 7,700
SALES (est): 5.34MM
SALES (corp-wide): 5.34MM **Privately Held**
Web: www.abanaki.com
SIC: 3569 Filters

(G-2154)
ACTIVE CHEMICAL SYSTEMS INC
16755 Park Circle Dr (44023-4562)
PHONE..............................440 543-7755
Bruno Thut, *CEO*
Kristine Thut, *Pr*
EMP: 17 **EST:** 1974
SQ FT: 16,000
SALES (est): 660.67K **Privately Held**
Web: www.activechemicalsystems.com
SIC: 3443 3624 Heat exchangers, condensers, and components; Carbon and graphite products

(G-2155)
ARCHITCTRAL MLLWK CBINETRY INC
16715 W Park Circle Dr (44023-4549)
PHONE..............................440 708-0086
Gary Spaeth, *Pr*
EMP: 8 **EST:** 2002
SALES (est): 231.21K **Privately Held**
SIC: 5031 5211 3442 1751 Molding, all materials; Cabinets, kitchen; Molding, trim, and stripping; Cabinet and finish carpentry

(G-2156)
BUMMIN BEAVER BREWERY LLC
11610 Washington St (44023-9214)
PHONE..............................440 543-9900
David Rutana, *Managing Member*
EMP: 7 **EST:** 2019
SALES (est): 126.67K **Privately Held**
Web: www.bumminbeaver.com
SIC: 2082 Beer (alcoholic beverage)

(G-2157)
CRAFTED SURFACE AND STONE LLC
16625 Wren Rd (44023-4517)
PHONE..............................440 658-3799
Allen Gleine, *Managing Member*
EMP: 25 **EST:** 2018
SALES (est): 1.87MM **Privately Held**
Web: www.craftedss.com
SIC: 1799 2541 Counter top installation; Counter and sink tops

(G-2158)
DESIGNED IMAGES INC
10121 Stafford Rd Ste C (44023-5128)
PHONE..............................440 708-2526
Thomas Hoenigman, *Pr*
Renee Hoenigman, *VP*
EMP: 7 **EST:** 2001
SALES (est): 211.58K **Privately Held**
Web: www.designedimages.net
SIC: 3083 Plastics finished products, laminated

(G-2159)
DYNAMIC DESIGN & SYSTEMS INC
7639 Washington St (44023-4403)
PHONE..............................440 708-1010
Richard E Doerr, *Pr*
Marilyn N Doerr, *VP*
◆ **EMP:** 8 **EST:** 1992
SQ FT: 3,000
SALES (est): 386.57K **Privately Held**
Web: www.dynamicdes.com
SIC: 2759 2752 Screen printing; Decals, lithographed

(G-2160)
ESPI ENTERPRISES INC (PA)
Also Called: Essential Sealing Products
10145 Queens Way (44023-5407)
P.O. Box 23699 (44023)
PHONE..............................440 543-8108
Joshua Botnick, *CEO*
Joshua Botnick, *Pr*
Bruce Pyle, *VP*
Pat Stipp, *Treas*
EMP: 8 **EST:** 1981
SQ FT: 30,000
SALES (est): 1.7MM
SALES (corp-wide): 1.7MM **Privately Held**
Web: www.espsealing.com
SIC: 3053 Gaskets, all materials

(G-2161)
ETNA PRODUCTS INCORPORATED
Also Called: Master Draw Lubricants
16824 Park Circle Dr (44023-4516)

P.O. Box 23609 (44023-0609)
PHONE..............................440 543-9845
Catharine Tripp Golden, *CEO*
Mike Washington, *
◆ **EMP:** 30 **EST:** 1943
SQ FT: 35,000
SALES (est): 5.4MM **Privately Held**
Web: www.etna.com
SIC: 2992 2821 2899 Oils and greases, blending and compounding; Polyethylene resins; Chemical preparations, nec

(G-2162)
GEAUGA GROUP LLC
11024 Wingate Dr (44023-6181)
PHONE..............................440 543-8797
Henry Milnark, *Pr*
James Mecsko, *VP*
Janet Mecsko, *Treas*
EMP: 9 **EST:** 2010
SALES (est): 86.86K **Privately Held**
Web: geauga.oh.gov
SIC: 2326 2339 7213 Aprons, work, except rubberized and plastic: men's; Aprons, except rubber or plastic: women's, misses', juniors'; Apron supply

(G-2163)
GLOBAL METAL SERVICES LTD
8401 Chagrin Rd Ste 14a (44023-4702)
P.O. Box 297 (44021)
PHONE..............................440 591-1264
Chi Cheung, *Managing Member*
▲ **EMP:** 6 **EST:** 2012
SALES (est): 937.41K **Privately Held**
Web: www.gmsamerica.com
SIC: 3312 Plate, steel

(G-2164)
HB FULLER COMPANY
17340 Munn Rd (44023-5476)
PHONE..............................440 708-1212
Ron Janoski, *Brnch Mgr*
EMP: 10
SALES (corp-wide): 3.57B **Publicly Held**
Web: www.hbfuller.com
SIC: 2891 Adhesives
PA: H.B. Fuller Company
1200 Willow Lake Blvd
Saint Paul MN 55110
651 236-5900

(G-2165)
HIGH TEMPERATURE SYSTEMS INC
16755 Park Circle Dr (44023-4562)
PHONE..............................440 543-8271
Bruno Thut, *CEO*
Bruno Thut, *Ch Bd*
Kristine Thut, *Pr*
▲ **EMP:** 11 **EST:** 1971
SQ FT: 16,000
SALES (est): 1.86MM **Privately Held**
Web: www.hitemp.com
SIC: 3559 Smelting and refining machinery and equipment

(G-2166)
IBI BRAKE PRODUCTS INC
Also Called: Brake Products
16751 Hilltop Park Pl (44023-4500)
P.O. Box 23547 (44023-0547)
PHONE..............................440 543-7962
John Hooper, *Pr*
EMP: 6 **EST:** 1985
SQ FT: 9,000
SALES (est): 927.7K **Privately Held**
Web: www.brakeproducts.com

SIC: 3499 5084 7389 3536 Wheels: wheelbarrow, stroller, etc.: disc, stamped metal; Industrial machinery and equipment; Crane and aerial lift service; Hoists, cranes, and monorails

(G-2167)
INTEGRATED DEVELOPMENT & MFG
8401 Washington St (44023-4511)
PHONE..............................440 543-2423
Adrian O Rule Iii, *Mgr*
EMP: 19
SALES (corp-wide): 9.94MM **Privately Held**
Web:
integrated-development-manufacturing.sbcontract.com
SIC: 3822 Environmental controls
PA: Integrated Development & Mfg
510 Washington St
Chagrin Falls OH 44022
440 247-5100

(G-2168)
L HABERNY CO INC
10115 Queens Way (44023-5407)
PHONE..............................440 543-5999
Dale Haberny, *Pr*
EMP: 12 **EST:** 1983
SQ FT: 7,000
SALES (est): 1.63MM **Privately Held**
Web: www.lhaberny.com
SIC: 3567 1796 Industrial furnaces and ovens; Pollution control equipment installation

(G-2169)
LASER AUTOMATION INC
16771 Hilltop Park Pl (44023-4500)
PHONE..............................440 543-9291
John Herkes, *Pr*
Carol Scerba, *Sec*
EMP: 7 **EST:** 1977
SQ FT: 12,000
SALES (est): 1.29MM **Privately Held**
Web: www.laserautomationinc.com
SIC: 3699 5049 3535 Laser welding, drilling, and cutting equipment; Scientific and engineering equipment and supplies; Conveyors and conveying equipment

(G-2170)
MAR-BAL INC (PA)
10095 Queens Way (44023-5406)
PHONE..............................440 543-7526
Scott Balogh, *Pr*
Steven Balogh, *
Carolyn E Balogh, *
Kevin Casey, *
Jim Wojtila, *
◆ **EMP:** 93 **EST:** 1970
SALES (est): 46.61MM
SALES (corp-wide): 46.61MM **Privately Held**
Web: www.mar-bal.com
SIC: 3089 2821 3081 Molding primary plastics; Polyesters; Unsupported plastics film and sheet

(G-2171)
NATIONAL POLYMER INC
10200 Gottschalk Pkwy (44023-5470)
P.O. Box 343 (44065-0343)
PHONE..............................440 708-1245
Adrian De Krom, *Pr*
Daniel Bess, *Dir*
EMP: 11 **EST:** 2004
SQ FT: 6,000
SALES (est): 2.25MM **Privately Held**
Web: www.nationalpolymer.com

SIC: 8734 5169 2891 Testing laboratories; Adhesives and sealants; Adhesives, plastic

(G-2172)
NATURES WAY BIRD PRODUCTS LLC
9054 Washington St (44023-2744)
PHONE..................................440 554-6166
Keith Moone, *CEO*
EMP: 20 EST: 2011
SALES (est): 20MM **Privately Held**
Web: www.natureswaybirds.com
SIC: 2048 7389 Bird food, prepared; Business services, nec

(G-2173)
NELSON ALUMINUM FOUNDRY INC
17093 Munn Rd (44023-5412)
PHONE..................................440 543-1941
Russell Nelson, *Pr*
EMP: 6 EST: 1951
SALES (est): 519.25K **Privately Held**
SIC: 3365 3369 Machinery castings, aluminum; Nonferrous foundries, nec

(G-2174)
ODYSSEY SPIRITS INC
Also Called: Odyssey Printwear
7409 Pettibone Rd (44023-4940)
PHONE..................................330 562-1523
Mark Hoehn, *Pr*
Laura Hoehn, *VP*
EMP: 12 EST: 1974
SALES (est): 633.01K **Privately Held**
Web: www.odysseyprintwear.com
SIC: 2759 5651 5699 5947 Screen printing; Family clothing stores; T-shirts, custom printed; Gift shop

(G-2175)
P & T MILLWORK INC
10090 Queens Way (44023-5403)
PHONE..................................440 543-2151
Joe Tesauro, *CEO*
Randall Pistone, *VP*
David Koci, *Sec*
EMP: 10 EST: 1987
SQ FT: 21,500
SALES (est): 638.09K **Privately Held**
Web: www.ptmillwork.com
SIC: 2499 5211 2431 Decorative wood and woodwork; Door and window products; Millwork

(G-2176)
PANELTECH LLC
17525 Haskins Rd (44023-5729)
PHONE..................................440 516-1300
EMP: 9 EST: 2012
SALES (est): 3.45MM **Privately Held**
Web: www.paneltech.com
SIC: 3825 Test equipment for electronic and electric measurement

(G-2177)
PERSISTENCE OF VISION INC
Also Called: Pov Print Communications
16715 W Park Circle Dr (44023-4549)
PHONE..................................440 591-5443
Chris Yuhasz, *Pr*
EMP: 9 EST: 1993
SQ FT: 3,000
SALES (est): 954.56K **Privately Held**
Web: www.povprintingservices.com
SIC: 2752 Offset printing

(G-2178)
PHOENIX ASSOCIATES
16760 W Park Circle Dr (44023-4550)
PHONE..................................440 543-9701

EMP: 25 EST: 1972
SQ FT: 12,000
SALES (est): 2.49MM **Privately Held**
Web: www.phoenixassociates.com
SIC: 3053 Gaskets, all materials

(G-2179)
QUBE CORPORATION
16744 W Park Circle Dr (44023-4550)
PHONE..................................440 543-2393
William C Mc Coy, *Pr*
Steve L Clark, *VP*
EMP: 11 EST: 1992
SQ FT: 13,000
SALES (est): 4.55MM **Privately Held**
Web: www.qubeinc.com
SIC: 3089 Injection molding of plastics

(G-2180)
RESERVE ENERGY EXPLORATION CO
10155 Gottschalk Pkwy Ste 1 (44023-5465)
P.O. Box 23278 (44023-0278)
PHONE..................................440 543-0770
Joseph Haas, *Pr*
EMP: 8 EST: 2001
SALES (est): 943.22K **Privately Held**
Web: www.reserve-energy.com
SIC: 1382 Oil and gas exploration services

(G-2181)
ROYAL ADHESIVES & SEALANTS LLC
17340 Munn Rd (44023-5476)
PHONE..................................440 708-1212
Ron Janoski, *Pr*
EMP: 12
SALES (corp-wide): 3.57B **Publicly Held**
Web: www.hbfuller.com
SIC: 2891 Sealants
HQ: Royal Adhesives And Sealants Llc
　　2001 W Washington St
　　South Bend IN 46628
　　574 246-5000

(G-2182)
SAPPHIRE CREEK WNERY GRDNS LLC
16965 Park Circle Dr (44023-6502)
PHONE..................................440 543-7777
EMP: 10 EST: 2018
SALES (est): 1.29MM **Privately Held**
Web: www.sapphire-creek.com
SIC: 2084 Wines

(G-2183)
SPECTRE INDUSTRIES LLC
10185 Gottschalk Pkwy Ste 1 (44023-5461)
P.O. Box 39562 (44139-0562)
PHONE..................................440 665-2600
EMP: 6 EST: 2018
SALES (est): 328.87K **Privately Held**
Web: www.spectreind.com
SIC: 3999 Manufacturing industries, nec

(G-2184)
STOCK EQUIPMENT COMPANY INC
Also Called: Stock
16490 Chillicothe Rd (44023-4398)
PHONE..................................440 543-6000
◆ EMP: 240
SIC: 3535 Conveyors and conveying equipment

(G-2185)
STOUTHEART CORPORATION
7205 Chagrin Rd Ste 4 (44023-1127)
P.O. Box 39219 (44139-0219)
PHONE..................................800 556-6470
David Martinelli, *Pr*

EMP: 37 EST: 2002
SQ FT: 500
SALES (est): 347.13K **Privately Held**
SIC: 3351 Strip, copper and copper alloy

(G-2186)
TANGENT COMPANY LLC
10175 Queens Way Ste 1 (44023-5435)
P.O. Box 23008 (44023-0008)
PHONE..................................440 543-2775
James Bolton, *Managing Member*
EMP: 9 EST: 2008
SALES (est): 589.5K **Privately Held**
Web: www.tangentcompany.com
SIC: 3999 8711 8734 8733 Grinding and pulverizing of materials, nec; Engineering services; Testing laboratories; Noncommercial research organizations

(G-2187)
TARKETT INC
16910 Munn Rd (44023-5411)
PHONE..................................440 543-8916
Bruce Ziegler, *Dir*
EMP: 41
Web: www.tarkettna.com
SIC: 3069 Flooring, rubber: tile or sheet
HQ: Tarkett, Inc.
　　30000 Aurora Rd
　　Solon OH 44139
　　800 899-8916

(G-2188)
TARKETT USA INC
16910 Munn Rd (44023-5411)
PHONE..................................440 543-8916
Jeff Fenwick, *Pr*
EMP: 297
Web: www.tarkett-group.com
SIC: 3253 Ceramic wall and floor tile
HQ: Tarkett Usa Inc.
　　30000 Aurora Rd
　　Solon OH 44139
　　877 827-5388

(G-2189)
UTILITY RELAY CO LTD
Also Called: Urc
10100 Queens Way (44023-5404)
PHONE..................................440 708-1000
Helmut Weiher, *Managing Member*
EMP: 42 EST: 1994
SQ FT: 15,000
SALES (est): 7.53MM **Privately Held**
Web: www.utilityrelay.com
SIC: 3625 Industrial electrical relays and switches

(G-2190)
VENTCO INC
66 Windward Way (44023-6706)
PHONE..................................440 834-8888
Joseph Ventimiglia, *Pr*
Frank Ventimiglia, *VP*
▼ EMP: 10 EST: 1983
SQ FT: 15,500
SALES (est): 189.87K **Privately Held**
SIC: 2842 2992 Cleaning or polishing preparations, nec; Lubricating oils and greases

(G-2191)
WHIP GUIDE CO
Also Called: Gizmo
16829 Park Circle Dr (44023-4515)
PHONE..................................440 543-5151
Morton C Mc Clennan, *Pt*
Walter C Mc Clennan, *Pt*
EMP: 10 EST: 1946
SQ FT: 10,000
SALES (est): 163.49K **Privately Held**

Web: www.hypertool.com
SIC: 3545 3366 Drilling machine attachments and accessories; Copper foundries

(G-2192)
WIHOLI INC
17050 Munn Rd (44023-5413)
PHONE..................................440 543-8233
George C Wick Junior, *Pr*
George F Howson Junior, *VP*
Craig Liechty, *CFO*
EMP: 15 EST: 1945
SQ FT: 31,000
SALES (est): 2.13MM **Privately Held**
Web: www.speedselector.com
SIC: 3568 Power transmission equipment, nec

(G-2193)
XACT SPEC INDUSTRIES LLC
Aerospace Operations
16959 Munn Rd (44023-5410)
PHONE..................................440 543-8157
Peter Barnhart, *Mng Pt*
EMP: 9
Web: www.xactspec.com
SIC: 3599 Machine shop, jobbing and repair
PA: Xact Spec Industries Llc
　　16959 Munn Rd
　　Chagrin Falls OH 44023

(G-2194)
XACT SPEC INDUSTRIES LLC (PA)
16959 Munn Rd (44023-5410)
PHONE..................................440 543-8157
Peter Barnhart, *Managing Member*
EMP: 33 EST: 2008
SQ FT: 32,000
SALES (est): 3.07MM **Privately Held**
Web: www.xactspec.com
SIC: 3599 Machine shop, jobbing and repair

(G-2195)
ZOOK ENTERPRISES LLC (PA)
16809 Park Circle Dr (44023-4515)
P.O. Box 419 (44022-0419)
PHONE..................................440 543-1010
Gregory D Clark, *CEO*
▲ EMP: 20 EST: 1971
SQ FT: 8,400
SALES (est): 8.01MM
SALES (corp-wide): 8.01MM **Privately Held**
Web: www.zookdisk.com
SIC: 3559 Petroleum refinery equipment

Chardon
Geauga County

(G-2196)
9/10 CASTINGS INC
313 Greenway Dr (44024-1481)
PHONE..................................216 406-8907
EMP: 6 EST: 2011
SALES (est): 183.15K **Privately Held**
Web: www.910castings.com
SIC: 3272 Concrete products, nec

(G-2197)
CHARDON CUSTOM POLYMERS LLC
373 Washington St (44024-1129)
PHONE..................................440 285-2161
Marian Devoe, *Pr*
EMP: 16 EST: 2010
SALES (est): 5.48MM **Privately Held**
Web: www.chardoncp.com

SIC: 3061 3069 Mechanical rubber goods; Molded rubber products

(G-2198)
CHARDON METAL PRODUCTS CO
206 5th Ave (44024-1007)
PHONE...............................440 285-2147
Anderson Allyn Junior, *Ch Bd*
Duke Allyn, *
Aric Allyn, *
Anderson Allyn Iii, *CFO*
EMP: 32 EST: 1945
SQ FT: 31,000
SALES (est): 4.68MM **Privately Held**
Web: www.chardonmetal.com
SIC: 3498 3451 3599 Tube fabricating (contract bending and shaping); Screw machine products; Machine shop, jobbing and repair

(G-2199)
CHARDON SQUARE AUTO & BODY INC (PA)
Also Called: Chardon Tire and Brake
525 Water St (44024-1146)
PHONE...............................440 286-7600
John Colello, *Pr*
EMP: 10 EST: 1991
SQ FT: 7,800
SALES (est): 1.2MM **Privately Held**
Web: www.csautoandtire.com
SIC: 7532 7534 7539 Body shop, automotive ; Tire retreading and repair shops; Brake services

(G-2200)
CHARDON TOOL & SUPPLY CO INC
115 Parker Ct (44024-1112)
P.O. Box 291 (44024-0291)
PHONE...............................440 286-6440
Weldon Bennett, *Pr*
EMP: 40 EST: 1986
SQ FT: 4,800
SALES (est): 2.43MM **Privately Held**
Web: www.chardontool.com
SIC: 3545 5085 Diamond cutting tools for turning, boring, burnishing, etc.; Diamonds, industrial: natural, crude

(G-2201)
CITY OF CHARDON
Also Called: Water & Sewer
201 N Hambden St (44024-1175)
PHONE...............................440 286-2657
David Lelki, *Mgr*
EMP: 27
Web: www.chardon.cc
SIC: 3589 Sewage and water treatment equipment
PA: City Of Chardon
111 Water St 2nd Fl
Chardon OH 44024
440 286-2600

(G-2202)
DAVE KRISSINGER
12335 Old State Rd (44024-9560)
PHONE...............................440 669-9957
Dave Krissinger, *Prin*
EMP: 6 EST: 2010
SALES (est): 85.88K **Privately Held**
Web: www.garlicdave.com
SIC: 2035 Spreads, garlic

(G-2203)
DE NORA TECH INC
DE NORA TECH, INC.
464 Center St (44024-1068)
PHONE...............................440 285-0100
Dennis L Baxendale, *Brnch Mgr*
EMP: 161

SALES (corp-wide): 930.89MM **Privately Held**
Web: business.painesvilleohchamber.org
SIC: 3643 3823 Current-carrying wiring services; Electrolytic conductivity instruments, industrial process
HQ: De Nora Tech, Llc
7590 Discovery Ln
Painesville OH 44077
440 710-5334

(G-2204)
EGC OPERATING COMPANY LLC (PA)
Also Called: Egc Enterprises
140 Parker Ct (44024-1112)
PHONE...............................440 285-5835
Hugh Slater, *CEO*
John Popovich, *VP*
Paul Clark, *COO*
Lisa Sutton, *Contrlr*
EMP: 66 EST: 2014
SALES (est): 10.55MM
SALES (corp-wide): 10.55MM **Privately Held**
Web: www.egcgraphite.com
SIC: 2891 3053 Sealants; Gaskets; packing and sealing devices

(G-2205)
EUCLID JALOUSIES INC
11668 Fowlers Mill Rd (44024-9314)
PHONE...............................440 953-1112
Timothy Huquila, *Pr*
Bob Dunmire, *VP*
EMP: 7 EST: 1954
SALES (est): 489.32K **Privately Held**
Web: www.euclidjalousies.com
SIC: 3442 5211 Screen and storm doors and windows; Windows, storm: wood or metal

(G-2206)
GEAUGA COATINGS LLC
15120 Sisson Rd (44024-8507)
PHONE...............................440 221-7286
Brian Milks, *Prin*
EMP: 7 EST: 2011
SALES (est): 2.49MM **Privately Held**
Web: www.geaugacoatings.com
SIC: 3312 Chemicals and other products derived from coking

(G-2207)
HI-TECH EXTRUSIONS LTD
12621 Chardon Windsor Rd (44024-8969)
PHONE...............................440 286-4000
Donald J Michalek, *Genl Pt*
Matt Michalek, *Pt*
Julius Wilson, *Pt*
EMP: 30 EST: 1997
SQ FT: 25,000
SALES (est): 7.95MM **Privately Held**
Web: www.hitechextrusions.com
SIC: 3089 Injection molding of plastics

(G-2208)
HUTTER RACING ENGINES LTD
12550 Gar Hwy (44024-8232)
PHONE...............................440 285-2175
Ronald Hutter, *Pt*
Thalia Hutter, *Pt*
Trevor Hutter, *Pt*
EMP: 10 EST: 1970
SQ FT: 6,000
SALES (est): 793.39K **Privately Held**
Web: www.hutterperformance.com
SIC: 3599 7538 Machine shop, jobbing and repair; General automotive repair shops

(G-2209)
KEOUGH AND ASSOCIATES LLC
Also Called: Kevin Is Always Mixing
106 Cherry Ave (44024-1158)
PHONE...............................440 682-0514
EMP: 6 EST: 2014
SALES (est): 649.56K **Privately Held**
SIC: 2053 Cakes, bakery: frozen

(G-2210)
KEY MANEUVERS INC (PA)
Also Called: K.M.I. Printing
10639 Grant St Ste C (44024-1282)
P.O. Box 51 (44024-0051)
PHONE...............................440 285-0774
Randy Bennett, *Pr*
EMP: 7 EST: 1988
SQ FT: 3,000
SALES (est): 566.91K **Privately Held**
Web: www.kmiprinting.com
SIC: 2752 Offset printing

(G-2211)
KONA BLACKBIRD INC
Also Called: Black Lab Custom Products
11730 Ravenna Rd (44024-7005)
PHONE...............................440 285-3189
▲ EMP: 29
SIC: 2899 3241 3251 2842 Fluxes: brazing, soldering, galvanizing, and welding; Masonry cement; Flooring brick, clay; Cleaning or polishing preparations, nec

(G-2212)
KTS CSTM LGS/XCLSVELY YOU INC
602 South St Ste C-2 (44024-1459)
PHONE...............................440 285-9803
Kevin R Temple, *Pr*
Melissa Temple, *VP*
EMP: 7 EST: 2002
SQ FT: 2,800
SALES (est): 139.8K **Privately Held**
Web: www.ktscustomlogos.com
SIC: 2395 7389 Embroidery and art needlework; Advertising, promotional, and trade show services

(G-2213)
KTS CUSTOM LOGOS
602 South St Ste C-2 (44024-1459)
PHONE...............................440 285-9803
Kevin Temple, *Pr*
Melissa Temple, *VP*
Ken Temple, *Prin*
EMP: 7 EST: 1998
SALES (est): 198.37K **Privately Held**
Web: www.ktscustomlogos.com
SIC: 2395 Embroidery and art needlework

(G-2214)
MAPLEDALE FARM INC
Also Called: Mapledale Landscaping
12613 Woodin Rd (44024-9177)
PHONE...............................440 286-3389
David P Johnson, *Pr*
Arthur L Johnson Senior, *VP*
Judy Johnson, *Sec*
EMP: 10 EST: 1982
SALES (est): 1.05MM **Privately Held**
Web: www.mapledalelandscaping.com
SIC: 0782 4959 2087 5251 Landscape contractors; Snowplowing; Beverage bases, concentrates, syrups, powders and mixes; Snowblowers

(G-2215)
NOF METAL COATINGS N AMER INC (HQ)
275 Industrial Pkwy (44024-1052)
PHONE...............................440 285-2231

Shin Masuda, *Pr*
Norman Gertz, *
▲ EMP: 50 EST: 1984
SQ FT: 20,000
SALES (est): 17.72MM **Privately Held**
Web: www.nofmetalcoatings.com
SIC: 2899 Chemical preparations, nec
PA: Nof Corporation
4-20-3, Ebisu
Shibuya-Ku TKY 150-0

(G-2216)
NORTH AMERICAN CAST STONE INC
11546 Claridon Troy Rd (44024-8437)
PHONE...............................440 286-1999
Richard T Rickelman, *Prin*
EMP: 6 EST: 2002
SALES (est): 187.54K **Privately Held**
Web: www.northamericancaststone.com
SIC: 3272 Concrete products, precast, nec

(G-2217)
OHIO ORDNANCE WORKS INC
310 Park Dr (44024-1057)
P.O. Box 687 (44024-0687)
PHONE...............................440 285-3481
Robert I Landies, *Pr*
Robert E Conroy Junior, *VP*
◆ EMP: 40 EST: 1992
SALES (est): 8.48MM **Privately Held**
Web: www.oowinc.com
SIC: 3484 Guns (firearms) or gun parts, 30 mm. and below

(G-2218)
ORWELL PRINTING
10639 Grant St Ste C (44024-1282)
P.O. Box 51 (44024-0051)
PHONE...............................440 285-2233
Randy Bennett, *Pr*
EMP: 8 EST: 1948
SQ FT: 1,900
SALES (est): 184.14K **Privately Held**
Web: www.orwellprinting.com
SIC: 2752 Offset printing
PA: Key Maneuvers, Inc.
10639 Grant St Ste C
Chardon OH 44024

(G-2219)
QUANTUM ENERGY LLC (PA)
10405 Locust Grove Dr (44024-8861)
PHONE...............................440 285-7381
EMP: 15 EST: 1996
SALES (est): 452.73K
SALES (corp-wide): 452.73K **Privately Held**
SIC: 1382 Oil and gas exploration services

(G-2220)
RHEIN CHEMIE CORPORATION
145 Parker Ct (44024-1112)
PHONE...............................440 279-2367
◆ EMP: 250
Web: www.lanxess.com
SIC: 3069 5169 Reclaimed rubber and specialty rubber compounds; Industrial chemicals

(G-2221)
RICHARDS MAPLE PRODUCTS INC
545 Water St (44024-1142)
PHONE...............................440 286-4160
TOLL FREE: 800
Debra Richards, *Pr*
Colin Rennie, *VP*
Annette Polson, *Sec*
EMP: 6 EST: 1910
SALES (est): 976.18K **Privately Held**
Web: www.richardsmapleproducts.com

SIC: 2064 5149 Candy and other confectionery products; Syrups, except for fountain use

(G-2222)
SHIFFLER EQUIPMENT SALES INC (PA)
745 South St (44024-2800)
P.O. Box 232 (44024-0232)
PHONE...................................440 285-9175
John Shiffler, *CEO*
Gloria S Shiffler, *
Mark C Lewis, *
▲ **EMP:** 42 **EST:** 1971
SQ FT: 30,000
SALES (est): 28.92MM
SALES (corp-wide): 28.92MM **Privately Held**
Web: www.shifflerequip.com
SIC: 2531 School furniture

(G-2223)
SOLON MANUFACTURING COMPANY
425 Center St (44024-1054)
PHONE...................................440 286-7149
David J Carpenter, *Ch*
J Timothy Dunn, *
George Davet, *
Perry Blossom, *
Jim Young, *
▲ **EMP:** 38 **EST:** 1949
SQ FT: 30,000
SALES (est): 9.39MM **Privately Held**
Web: www.solonmfg.com
SIC: 3823 3493 3643 3495 Pressure measurement instruments, industrial; Cold formed springs; Current-carrying wiring services; Wire springs

(G-2224)
SPALDING
12860 Mayfield Rd (44024-8963)
PHONE...................................440 286-5717
Richard Spalding, *Prin*
EMP: 10 **EST:** 2010
SALES (est): 237.96K **Privately Held**
Web: www.spalding.com
SIC: 2253 Jerseys, knit

(G-2225)
THE Q-P MANUFACTURING CO INC
215 5th Ave (44024-1001)
PHONE...................................440 946-2120
EMP: 15 **EST:** 2006
SQ FT: 74,000
SALES (est): 5.31MM **Privately Held**
Web: www.qpmfg.com
SIC: 3599 Machine shop, jobbing and repair

(G-2226)
WECALL INC
510 Center St (44024-1004)
P.O. Box 39 (44076-0039)
PHONE...................................440 437-8202
Paul David Doherty, *Pr*
Bernard Doherty, *VP*
EMP: 9 **EST:** 1969
SALES (est): 2.82MM **Privately Held**
Web: www.wecallinc.com
SIC: 3429 3452 Metal fasteners; Bolts, nuts, rivets, and washers

Charm
Holmes County

(G-2227)
RABER LUMBER CO
4112 State Rte 557 (44617)
P.O. Box 26 (44617-0026)

PHONE...................................330 893-2797
Edward Raber, *Pt*
EMP: 7 **EST:** 1965
SQ FT: 1,000
SALES (est): 499.4K **Privately Held**
SIC: 2421 2448 Sawmills and planing mills, general; Pallets, wood

Chesapeake
Lawrence County

(G-2228)
AQUA OHIO INC
Also Called: Union Rome Sewer System
32 Private Drive 11100 (45619-6500)
P.O. Box 430 (45619-0430)
PHONE...................................740 867-8700
EMP: 10
SALES (corp-wide): 2.09B **Publicly Held**
Web: www.lawcomunicourt.com
SIC: 3589 Sewage and water treatment equipment
HQ: Aqua Ohio, Inc.
      6650 South Ave
      Youngstown OH 44512
      330 726-8151

(G-2229)
G BIG INC (PA)
Also Called: Pickett Concrete
441 Rockwood Ave (45619-1120)
PHONE...................................740 867-5758
John W Galloway, *Pr*
Todd A Galloway, *VP*
James W Galloway, *VP*
EMP: 20 **EST:** 1960
SQ FT: 2,000
SALES (est): 6.2MM
SALES (corp-wide): 6.2MM **Privately Held**
Web: www.pickettconcrete.com
SIC: 3273 1771 Ready-mixed concrete; Concrete work

(G-2230)
PRECISION COMPONENT & MCH INC
17 Rosslyn Rd (45619)
P.O. Box 580 (45619-0580)
PHONE...................................740 867-6366
Steve Chatteron, *Pr*
Stephanie Black, *
EMP: 38 **EST:** 1996
SQ FT: 24,000
SALES (est): 7.45MM **Privately Held**
Web: www.pcmohio.com
SIC: 3599 Machine shop, jobbing and repair

Cheshire
Gallia County

(G-2231)
ENVIRI CORPORATION
5486 State Route 7 N (45620-9522)
P.O. Box 371 (45620-0371)
PHONE...................................740 367-7322
James D Taylor, *Mgr*
EMP: 9
SQ FT: 300
SALES (corp-wide): 2.34B **Publicly Held**
Web: www.enviri.com
SIC: 3295 Slag, crushed or ground
PA: Enviri Corporation
      100-120 N 18th St # 17
      Philadelphia PA 19103
      267 857-8715

Chesterland
Geauga County

(G-2232)
AEROTECH ENTERPRISE
8511 Mulberry Rd (44026-1437)
P.O. Box 596 (44026-0596)
PHONE...................................440 729-2616
Mike Matic, *Pr*
Andrea Matic, *Sec*
EMP: 15 **EST:** 1973
SQ FT: 6,000
SALES (est): 2.87MM **Privately Held**
Web: www.aerotechcnc.com
SIC: 3599 Machine shop, jobbing and repair

(G-2233)
DARRAH ELECTRIC COMPANY (PA)
8834 Mayfield Rd Ste A (44026-2696)
PHONE...................................216 631-0912
David J Darrah, *Pr*
Robert J Darrah, *Ch Bd*
John A Darrah, *VP*
Neal A Darrah, *Sec*
EMP: 19 **EST:** 1960
SALES (est): 4.69MM
SALES (corp-wide): 4.69MM **Privately Held**
Web: www.darrahelectric.com
SIC: 3679 3612 3674 Rectifiers, electronic; Power and distribution transformers; Semiconductors and related devices

(G-2234)
INNOVEST ENERGY GROUP LLC
8834 Mayfield Rd Ste A (44026-2696)
P.O. Box 179 (44045-0179)
PHONE...................................440 644-1027
Mike Yukich, *Prin*
EMP: 7 **EST:** 2019
SALES (est): 1.45MM **Privately Held**
Web: www.innovestenergygroup.com
SIC: 3643 Lightning protection equipment

(G-2235)
MEISTERMATIC INC
12446 Bentbrook Dr (44026-2459)
PHONE...................................216 481-7773
Edward Kurnava, *Pr*
Terry Kurnava, *
EMP: 8 **EST:** 1963
SQ FT: 70,000
SALES (est): 1.5MM **Privately Held**
SIC: 3451 Screw machine products

(G-2236)
METZENBAUM SHELTERED INDS INC
Also Called: MSI
8090 Cedar Rd (44026-3465)
P.O. Box 538 (44065)
PHONE...................................440 729-1919
Robert Voss, *Prgrm Mgr*
Robert Preston, *
Diane Buehner, *Head Secretary**
EMP: 49 **EST:** 1969
SQ FT: 12,000
SALES (est): 1.68MM **Privately Held**
Web: www.geaugadd.org
SIC: 8331 7389 3672 Sheltered workshop; Packaging and labeling services; Printed circuit boards

(G-2237)
NITROJECTION
8430 Mayfield Rd (44026-2580)
PHONE...................................440 729-2711
Ana Leben, *Prin*
EMP: 6 **EST:** 2011

SALES (est): 2.34MM **Privately Held**
Web: www.nitrojection.com
SIC: 3089 Injection molding of plastics

(G-2238)
ORGANON INC
7407 Cedar Rd (44026-3464)
PHONE...................................440 729-2290
EMP: 11 **EST:** 2009
SALES (est): 233.73K **Privately Held**
Web: www.organon.com
SIC: 2834 Pharmaceutical preparations

(G-2239)
PNEUMATIC SPECIALTIES INC
Also Called: PSI
11677 Chillicothe Rd Unit 1 (44026-1905)
PHONE...................................440 729-4400
Lisa Labanc, *CEO*
Lisa Labanc, *Pr*
EMP: 6 **EST:** 1987
SALES (est): 2.53MM **Privately Held**
Web: www.psiproductspecialists.com
SIC: 2841 2842 5999 7218 Soap and other detergents; Degreasing solvent; Safety supplies and equipment; Safety glove supply

Chickasaw
Mercer County

(G-2240)
CHICKASAW MACHINE & TL CO INC
3050 Chickasaw Rd (45826-4523)
P.O. Box 35 (45826-0035)
PHONE...................................419 925-4325
Norbert B Tangeman, *Pr*
Ted Homan, *VP*
Dave Tangeman, *VP*
▼ **EMP:** 11 **EST:** 1960
SQ FT: 18,000
SALES (est): 2.59MM **Privately Held**
Web: www.chickasawmachine.com
SIC: 3599 Machine shop, jobbing and repair

Chillicothe
Ross County

(G-2241)
ADVANTAGE TENT FITTINGS INC
11661 Pleasant Valley Rd (45601-8315)
PHONE...................................740 773-3015
Benjamin Hall, *Pr*
Robert Hall, *Ch Bd*
▼ **EMP:** 15 **EST:** 1991
SQ FT: 14,000
SALES (est): 2.09MM **Privately Held**
Web: www.advantagetent.com
SIC: 2431 5091 2394 Millwork; Sporting and recreation goods; Canvas and related products

(G-2242)
ALL SIGNS OF CHILLICOTHE INC
Also Called: All Signs
12035 Pleasant Valley Rd (45601-9785)
PHONE...................................740 773-5016
Kris Oliver, *VP*
EMP: 9 **EST:** 1989
SALES (est): 993.17K **Privately Held**
Web: www.allsignsofohio.com
SIC: 3993 1799 Electric signs; Sign installation and maintenance

(G-2243)
AUTOMATOR MARKING SYSTEMS INC

▲ = Import ▼ = Export
◆ = Import/Export

475 Douglas Ave (45601-3663)
PHONE................................740 983-0157
Gregory Mcdaniel, *Pr*
EMP: 10 **EST:** 2017
SALES (est): 1.46MM **Privately Held**
Web: www.automator.com
SIC: 3599 Machine and other job shop work

(G-2244)
BBB MUSIC LLC
643 Central Ctr (45601-2249)
P.O. Box 903 (45601-0903)
PHONE................................740 772-2262
EMP: 8 **EST:** 2009
SALES (est): 316.26K **Privately Held**
Web: www.bbbmusiccenter.com
SIC: 3931 5736 Musical instruments;
Musical instrument stores

(G-2245)
BELL LOGISTICS CO
27311 Old Route 35 (45601-8110)
P.O. Box 91 (45601-0091)
PHONE................................740 702-9830
Jon Bell, *Pr*
Deana Bell, *
EMP: 30 **EST:** 2007
SQ FT: 25,000
SALES (est): 4.53MM **Privately Held**
Web: www.jbexpress.com
SIC: 3715 Truck trailers

(G-2246)
BROCK RAD WLDG FABRICATION INC
Also Called: Brocks RAD Wldg Fabrication I
370 Douglas Ave (45601-3662)
PHONE................................740 773-2540
David J Brock, *Pr*
Nancy Brock, *Sec*
EMP: 8 **EST:** 1945
SQ FT: 12,000
SALES (est): 156.93K **Privately Held**
SIC: 7539 7692 Radiator repair shop,
automotive; Automotive welding

(G-2247)
CHILLICOTHE PACKAGING CORP
Also Called: Churmac Industries
4168 State Route 159 (45601-8695)
P.O. Box 466 (45601-0466)
PHONE................................740 773-5800
Michael Mccarty, *Pr*
EMP: 40 **EST:** 1978
SQ FT: 60,000
SALES (est): 4.5MM **Privately Held**
SIC: 2653 Boxes, corrugated: made from
purchased materials

(G-2248)
CHURMAC INDUSTRIES INC
Also Called: Chillicothe Packing
4168 State Route 159 (45601-8695)
P.O. Box 205 (45601-0205)
PHONE................................740 773-5800
Michael Mccarty, *Pr*
EMP: 7 **EST:** 1983
SQ FT: 60,000
SALES (est): 864.73K **Privately Held**
SIC: 2631 Paperboard mills

(G-2249)
CRISPIE CREME CHILLICOTHE INC
Also Called: Grandpa Jack's
47 N Bridge St (45601-2615)
PHONE................................740 774-3770
Richard Renison, *Pr*
James M Renison, *
EMP: 6 **EST:** 1929
SQ FT: 2,500
SALES (est): 429.68K **Privately Held**

Web: www.chillicotheohio.com
SIC: 2051 5461 Doughnuts, except frozen;
Doughnuts

(G-2250)
DOUGLAS INDUSTRIES LLC
379 Douglas Ave (45601-3663)
P.O. Box 6188 (45601-6188)
PHONE................................740 775-2400
Larry Eyre, *
EMP: 24 **EST:** 2004
SALES (est): 3.06MM **Privately Held**
Web: www.douglas-industries.com
SIC: 3599 Machine shop, jobbing and repair

(G-2251)
FIFTY WEST BREWING COMPANY LLC
1 N Paint St (45601-3116)
PHONE................................740 775-2337
EMP: 25
SALES (corp-wide): 4.15MM **Privately Held**
Web: www.fiftywestbrew.com
SIC: 2082 Beer (alcoholic beverage)
PA: Fifty West Brewing Company, Llc
7668 Wooster Pike
Cincinnati OH 45227
513 834-8789

(G-2252)
G & J PEPSI-COLA BOTTLERS INC
Also Called: Pepsico
400 E 7th St (45601-3455)
PHONE................................740 774-2148
Henry Thrapp, *Brnch Mgr*
EMP: 22
SALES (corp-wide): 404.54MM **Privately Held**
Web: www.pepsico.com
SIC: 2086 Carbonated soft drinks, bottled
and canned
PA: G & J Pepsi-Cola Bottlers Inc
9435 Wrstone Blvd Ste 39
Cincinnati OH 45249
513 785-6060

(G-2253)
GLATFELTER CORPORATION
Also Called: Glatfelter Corporation
353 S Paint St (45601-3814)
P.O. Box 2500 (45601-0997)
PHONE................................740 772-3893
EMP: 9
SALES (corp-wide): 1.39B **Publicly Held**
Web: www.glatfelter.com
SIC: 2621 Book paper
PA: Magnera Corporation
9335 Hrris Crners Pkwy St
Charlotte NC 28269
866 744-7380

(G-2254)
GLATFELTER CORPORATION
Also Called: Glatfelter Corporation
311 Caldwell St (45601-3332)
PHONE................................740 775-6119
Dawn Limle, *Brnch Mgr*
EMP: 11
SALES (corp-wide): 1.39B **Publicly Held**
Web: www.glatfelter.com
SIC: 2621 Book paper
PA: Magnera Corporation
9335 Hrris Crners Pkwy St
Charlotte NC 28269
866 744-7380

(G-2255)
GLATFELTER CORPORATION
Also Called: Chillicothe Facility
232 E 8th St (45601-3364)

P.O. Box 2500 (45601-0997)
PHONE................................740 772-3111
John R Blind, *VP*
EMP: 100
SALES (corp-wide): 1.39B **Publicly Held**
Web: www.glatfelter.com
SIC: 2621 Book paper
PA: Magnera Corporation
9335 Hrris Crners Pkwy St
Charlotte NC 28269
866 744-7380

(G-2256)
HERR FOODS INCORPORATED
476 E 7th St (45601-3455)
PHONE................................740 773-8282
Scott Carmenan, *Mgr*
EMP: 53
SQ FT: 1,000
SALES (corp-wide): 392.21MM **Privately Held**
Web: www.herrs.com
SIC: 2096 Potato chips and other potato-
based snacks
PA: Herr Foods Incorporated
20 Herr Dr
Nottingham PA 19362
610 932-9330

(G-2257)
HERR FOODS INCORPORATED
104 S Mcarthur St (45601-3600)
PHONE................................800 344-3777
EMP: 16
SALES (corp-wide): 392.21MM **Privately Held**
Web: www.herrs.com
SIC: 2096 Potato chips and other potato-
based snacks
PA: Herr Foods Incorporated
20 Herr Dr
Nottingham PA 19362
610 932-9330

(G-2258)
HITE PARTS EXCHANGE INC
933 E Main St (45601-2843)
PHONE................................614 272-5115
Thomas A Blake, *Pr*
Dona Blake, *
EMP: 8 **EST:** 1937
SALES (est): 489.48K **Privately Held**
Web: www.hiteparts.com
SIC: 5013 3714 3626 3601 Automotive
supplies and parts; Motor vehicle engines
and parts; Relays and industrial controls;
Fluid power pumps and motors

(G-2259)
INDUSTRIAL RLBLITY SPCLSTS INC (PA)
Also Called: Irr
370 Douglas Ave (45601-3662)
PHONE................................800 800-6345
Robert A Rivenbark Senior, *Prin*
EMP: 6 **EST:** 2018
SALES (est): 871.67K
SALES (corp-wide): 871.67K **Privately Held**
SIC: 3542 Arbor presses

(G-2260)
INFOSIGHT CORPORATION
20700 Us Highway 23 (45601-9016)
P.O. Box 5000 (45601-7000)
PHONE................................740 642-3600
John A Robertson, *CEO*
G D Hudelson, *
Barbara Robertson, *
Rob Underhill, *
▲ **EMP:** 65 **EST:** 1993

SQ FT: 30,000
SALES (est): 15.53MM **Privately Held**
Web: www.infosight.com
SIC: 3953 Figures (marking devices), metal

(G-2261)
INGLE-BARR INC (PA)
Also Called: Ibi
20 Plyleys Ln (45601-2005)
P.O. Box 874 (45601-0874)
PHONE................................740 702-6117
Jeffrey Poole, *Pr*
Rod Poole, *
EMP: 100 **EST:** 1967
SQ FT: 6,500
SALES (est): 8.96MM
SALES (corp-wide): 8.96MM **Privately Held**
Web: www.4ibi.com
SIC: 1521 1541 1542 2541 General
remodeling, single-family houses;
Renovation, remodeling and repairs:
industrial buildings; Commercial and office
building, new construction; Bar fixtures,
wood

(G-2262)
LOMA SYSTEMS
151 Discovery Dr (45601-3946)
PHONE................................740 274-9047
EMP: 21 **EST:** 2018
SALES (est): 793.24K **Privately Held**
Web: www.loma.com
SIC: 3577 Computer peripheral equipment,
nec

(G-2263)
M & M FABRICATION INC
18828 Us Highway 50 (45601-9268)
PHONE................................740 779-3071
Gary Timmons, *Pr*
Ardath I Wise Incorp, *Prin*
Jessie B Wise Incorp, *Prin*
Joseph S Wise Incorp, *Prin*
EMP: 10 **EST:** 2001
SALES (est): 983.62K **Privately Held**
Web: www.mmfabrication.com
SIC: 3441 Building components, structural
steel

(G-2264)
MCNEAL ENTERPRISES LLC
807 E 2nd St (45601-2750)
PHONE................................740 703-7108
EMP: 8 **EST:** 2015
SALES (est): 1.23MM **Privately Held**
SIC: 3089 Injection molding of plastics

(G-2265)
MCRD ENTERPRISES LLC
Also Called: Art Tech
337 E Main St (45601-3415)
PHONE................................740 775-2377
EMP: 10 **EST:** 2007
SALES (est): 161.8K **Privately Held**
SIC: 3993 Signs, not made in custom sign
painting shops

(G-2266)
MIDWEST MOTOPLEX LLC
98 Consumer Center Dr (45601-2667)
PHONE................................740 772-5300
EMP: 7 **EST:** 2011
SQ FT: 13,000
SALES (est): 503.55K **Privately Held**
SIC: 3799 5012 All terrain vehicles (ATV);
Motorcycles

(G-2267)
NATIONAL INDUS CONCEPTS INC
Also Called: Nic Global
170 N Park Dr (45601-7823)
PHONE..................................615 989-9101
EMP: 10
SALES (corp-wide): 75.33MM **Privately Held**
Web: www.nicglobalms.com
SIC: 3444 Sheet metal specialties, not stamped
PA: National Industrial Concepts, Inc.
23518 63rd Ave Se
Woodinville WA 98072
425 489-4300

(G-2268)
ON THE MANTLE LLC
Also Called: W.britain Model Figures
20 E Water St (45601-2534)
PHONE..................................740 702-1803
Edward Kunzelman, *Managing Member*
EMP: 6 **EST:** 2020
SALES (est): 271.06K **Privately Held**
SIC: 3999 Miniatures

(G-2269)
PACCAR INC
Paccar
65 Kenworth Dr (45601-8829)
P.O. Box 2345 (45601-0998)
PHONE..................................740 774-5111
Doug Littick, *Brnch Mgr*
EMP: 90
SALES (corp-wide): 33.66B **Publicly Held**
Web: www.paccar.com
SIC: 3711 3715 3713 Truck and tractor truck assembly; Truck trailers; Truck and bus bodies
PA: Paccar Inc
777 106th Ave Ne
Bellevue WA 98004
425 468-7400

(G-2270)
PELLETIER BROTHERS MFG INC
4000 Sulphur Lick Rd (45601-8972)
PHONE..................................740 774-4704
Chris Pelletier, *Pr*
Mark Pelletier, *VP*
EMP: 16 **EST:** 1992
SQ FT: 7,000
SALES (est): 911.28K **Privately Held**
Web: www.pellbro.com
SIC: 3479 Coating of metals and formed products

(G-2271)
PITTSBURGH PAINTS CO
Also Called: Porter Paints
848 Southern Ave (45601-9123)
PHONE..................................740 774-7600
EMP: 29
SALES (corp-wide): 388.64MM **Privately Held**
Web: www.ppgpaints.com
SIC: 2851 Paints and allied products
PA: The Pittsburgh Paints Co
400 Bertha Lamme Dr
Cranberry Township PA 16066
724 742-5200

(G-2272)
PIXELLE SPCIALTY SOLUTIONS LLC
232 E 8th St (45601-3364)
PHONE..................................740 772-3111
EMP: 1009
SALES (corp-wide): 760.06MM **Privately Held**
Web: www.pixelle.com

SIC: 2621 Specialty or chemically treated papers
PA: Pixelle Specialty Solutions Llc
228 S Main St
Spring Grove PA 17362
717 225-4711

(G-2273)
PPG INDUSTRIES INC
Also Called: PPG Chillicothe
7012 Chillicoth (45601)
PHONE..................................740 774-8734
Amanda Moore, *Acctnt*
EMP: 17
SALES (corp-wide): 18.25B **Publicly Held**
Web: www.ppg.com
SIC: 2851 Paints and allied products
PA: Ppg Industries, Inc.
1 Ppg Pl
Pittsburgh PA 15272
412 434-3131

(G-2274)
PPG INDUSTRIES INC
Also Called: PPG Regional Support Center
848 Southern Ave (45601-9123)
PHONE..................................740 774-7600
Melissa Wills, *Brnch Mgr*
EMP: 37
SALES (corp-wide): 18.25B **Publicly Held**
Web: www.ppg.com
SIC: 2851 Paints and allied products
PA: Ppg Industries, Inc.
1 Ppg Pl
Pittsburgh PA 15272
412 434-3131

(G-2275)
PPG INDUSTRIES INC
Also Called: PPG Aerospace
848 Southern Ave (45601-9123)
P.O. Box 7011 (45601)
PHONE..................................740 774-7600
EMP: 15
SALES (corp-wide): 18.25B **Publicly Held**
Web: www.ppg.com
SIC: 2851 Paints and allied products
PA: Ppg Industries, Inc.
1 Ppg Pl
Pittsburgh PA 15272
412 434-3131

(G-2276)
PRINTEX INCORPORATED (PA)
Also Called: Printex-Same Day Printing
185 E Main St (45601-2507)
P.O. Box 1626 (45601-5626)
PHONE..................................740 773-0088
TOLL FREE: 800
Jeffrey G Marshall, *Pr*
Gene T Marshall, *VP*
EMP: 10 **EST:** 1975
SQ FT: 3,000
SALES (est): 1.21MM
SALES (corp-wide): 1.21MM **Privately Held**
Web: www.visitprintex.com
SIC: 2759 2752 Letterpress printing; Offset printing

(G-2277)
R L S CORPORATION
Also Called: R L S Recycling
990 Eastern Ave (45601-3658)
P.O. Box 327 (45601-0327)
PHONE..................................740 773-1440
Charles Stevens, *Pr*
EMP: 6 **EST:** 1923
SQ FT: 14,000
SALES (est): 200.61K **Privately Held**

SIC: 5093 3341 Ferrous metal scrap and waste; Secondary nonferrous metals

(G-2278)
R L WALLER CONSTRUCTION INC
645 Alum Cliff Rd (45601-8533)
PHONE..................................740 772-6185
R I Waller, *Pr*
EMP: 7 **EST:** 2002
SALES (est): 883.13K **Privately Held**
SIC: 1521 3441 General remodeling, single-family houses; Building components, structural steel

(G-2279)
RIFFLE MACHINE WORKS INC (PA)
Also Called: Riffle & Sons
5746 State Route 159 (45601-8956)
PHONE..................................740 775-2838
Bob Riffle, *Pr*
Mike Riffle, *VP*
Tim Riffle, *VP*
Mark Riffle, *VP*
EMP: 8 **EST:** 1980
SQ FT: 3,500
SALES (est): 5.39MM **Privately Held**
SIC: 3599 Machine shop, jobbing and repair

(G-2280)
ROSS-CO REDI-MIX CO INC (PA)
6430 State Route 159 (45601-8956)
PHONE..................................740 775-4466
Todd Wrightsel, *Pr*
Connie Wrightsel, *Sec*
Thomas Overly, *Prin*
EMP: 15 **EST:** 1962
SALES (est): 1.69MM
SALES (corp-wide): 1.69MM **Privately Held**
SIC: 3273 Ready-mixed concrete

(G-2281)
SHELLY MATERIALS INC
1177 Hopetown Rd (45601-8224)
PHONE..................................740 775-4567
Rusty Scott, *Mgr*
EMP: 27
SALES (corp-wide): 34.95B **Privately Held**
Web: www.shellyco.com
SIC: 3273 Ready-mixed concrete
HQ: Shelly Materials, Inc.
80 Park Dr
Thornville OH 43076
740 246-6315

(G-2282)
STAT INDUSTRIES INC (PA)
Also Called: Stat Index Tab
137 Stone Rd (45601-9709)
PHONE..................................740 779-6561
Robert Kellough, *CEO*
Susanna Kellough, *CFO*
Chris Kellough, *Prin*
EMP: 7 **EST:** 1991
SQ FT: 6,000
SALES (est): 871.31K **Privately Held**
Web: www.statindex.com
SIC: 2675 Index cards, die-cut: made from purchased materials

(G-2283)
STAT INDUSTRIES INC
Also Called: Stat Index Tab Company
137 Stone Rd (45601-9709)
PHONE..................................740 779-6561
Robert Kellough, *Pr*
EMP: 6
Web: www.statindex.com
SIC: 2675 Index cards, die-cut: made from purchased materials
PA: Stat Industries, Inc.

137 Stone Rd
Chillicothe OH 45601

(G-2284)
THE KITCHEN COLLECTION LLC
Also Called: Le Gourmet Chef
71 E Water St (45601-2535)
PHONE..................................740 773-9150
▲ **EMP:** 1495
SIC: 3634 5719 Toasters, electric: household ; Kitchenware

(G-2285)
TRIM SYSTEMS OPERATING CORP
75 Chamber Dr (45601-7612)
PHONE..................................740 772-5998
Eric Conley, *Brnch Mgr*
EMP: 373
SALES (corp-wide): 723.36MM **Publicly Held**
Web: www.cvgrp.com
SIC: 2396 Automotive and apparel trimmings
HQ: Trim Systems Operating Corp.
7800 Walton Pkwy
New Albany OH 43054
614 289-5360

(G-2286)
TYKMA INC
Also Called: Tykma Electrox
370 Gateway Dr (45601-3976)
P.O. Box 917 (45601-0917)
PHONE..................................740 779-9918
Paul R Dupee, *Pr*
Terry Allison, *
Karen Cyrus, *
Gregory Cox, *
EMP: 53 **EST:** 1970
SQ FT: 50,000
SALES (est): 8.83MM
SALES (corp-wide): 31.96MM **Privately Held**
Web: www.permanentmarking.com
SIC: 3541 3555 Machine tools, metal cutting type; Engraving machinery and equipment, except plates
PA: The 600 Group Limited
42 Berkeley Square
London W1J 5

(G-2287)
VITATOE INDUSTRIES INC (PA)
100 Chamber Dr (45601-7612)
P.O. Box 224 (45601-0224)
PHONE..................................740 773-2425
EMP: 68 **EST:** 1981
SALES (est): 7.96MM
SALES (corp-wide): 7.96MM **Privately Held**
Web: www.vitatoe.com
SIC: 3713 Truck and bus bodies

(G-2288)
YSK CORPORATION
1 Colomet Rd (45601-8819)
PHONE..................................740 774-7315
Kenzaburo Matsuo, *Pr*
H Naiki, *
Reiichi Hohda, *
▲ **EMP:** 279 **EST:** 1988
SQ FT: 200,000
SALES (est): 24.66MM **Privately Held**
SIC: 3469 Machine parts, stamped or pressed metal
HQ: Yanagawa Seiki Co., Ltd.
1012, Wadacho
Kameyama MIE 519-0

Cincinnati
Clermont County

(G-2289)
5ME LLC
4270 Ivy Pointe Blvd Ste 100 (45245-0004)
P.O. Box 541085 (45254-1085)
PHONE.................................513 719-1600
William A Horwarth, *Pr*
Jeffery Price, *
Chris Chapman, *
EMP: 45 **EST:** 2013
SALES (est): 2.28MM
SALES (corp-wide): 2.5MM **Privately Held**
Web: www.5me.com
SIC: 3544 8742 Special dies, tools, jigs, and fixtures; Business management consultant
PA: 5me Holdings Llc
4270 Ivy Pointe Blvd # 240
Cincinnati OH 45245
859 534-4872

(G-2290)
A & P TECHNOLOGY INC
4622 E Tech Dr (45245-1000)
PHONE.................................513 688-3200
Andrew Head, *Brnch Mgr*
EMP: 50
Web: www.braider.com
SIC: 2241 Narrow fabric mills
PA: A & P Technology, Inc.
4595 E Tech Dr
Cincinnati OH 45245

(G-2291)
A & P TECHNOLOGY INC
4578 E Tech Dr (45245-1054)
PHONE.................................513 688-3200
Andrew Head, *Brnch Mgr*
EMP: 50
Web: www.braider.com
SIC: 2241 Narrow fabric mills
PA: A & P Technology, Inc.
4595 E Tech Dr
Cincinnati OH 45245

(G-2292)
A & P TECHNOLOGY INC
4624 E Tech Dr (45245)
PHONE.................................513 688-3200
Rhonda Slominski, *Brnch Mgr*
EMP: 50
SQ FT: 1,880
Web: www.braider.com
SIC: 2241 Narrow fabric mills
PA: A & P Technology, Inc.
4595 E Tech Dr
Cincinnati OH 45245

(G-2293)
A & P TECHNOLOGY INC
4599 E Tech Dr (45245-1055)
PHONE.................................513 688-3200
Keith Cnarr, *Mgr*
EMP: 50
Web: www.braider.com
SIC: 2241 Webbing, braids and belting
PA: A & P Technology, Inc.
4595 E Tech Dr
Cincinnati OH 45245

(G-2294)
A & P TECHNOLOGY INC (PA)
4595 E Tech Dr (45245-1055)
PHONE.................................513 688-3200
Andrew A Head, *Pr*
Luke Domet, *CFO*
◆ **EMP:** 20 **EST:** 1994
SQ FT: 75,000

SALES (est): 24.57MM **Privately Held**
Web: www.braider.com
SIC: 2241 Webbing, braids and belting

(G-2295)
ADGO INCORPORATED
3988 Mcmann Rd (45245-2308)
PHONE.................................513 752-6880
Robert C Reynolds, *Pr*
Rick Elliott, *
Mike Cliett, *
Kelly Throckmorton, *
EMP: 23 **EST:** 1957
SQ FT: 30,000
SALES (est): 4.45MM **Privately Held**
Web: www.adgoinc.com
SIC: 3613 Control panels, electric

(G-2296)
ALUFAB INC
Also Called: Alufab
1018 Seabrook Way (45245-1963)
PHONE.................................513 528-7281
Doug Nimmo, *Pr*
Fred Mileham, *VP*
▲ **EMP:** 6 **EST:** 2005
SQ FT: 4,000
SALES (est): 2.16MM **Privately Held**
Web: www.alufabinc.com
SIC: 3354 Aluminum extruded products

(G-2297)
BEACHS TREES SLCTIVE HRVSTG LL
Also Called: Beachs Trees
915 Wilma Cir (45245-2220)
PHONE.................................513 289-5976
Brian Beach, *Prin*
EMP: 6 **EST:** 2013
SQ FT: 2,500
SALES (est): 596.46K **Privately Held**
Web: www.beachstrees.com
SIC: 2411 Logging camps and contractors

(G-2298)
CINCINNATI EYE INST - ESTGATE
601 Ivy Gtwy Ste 301 (45245-1899)
PHONE.................................513 984-5133
EMP: 6 **EST:** 1945
SALES (est): 75.74K **Privately Held**
Web: www.cincinnatieye.com
SIC: 8049 3827 Offices of health practitioner ; Optical instruments and lenses

(G-2299)
CLIPPER PRODUCTS INC
Also Called: Clipper Products
675 Cincinnati Batavia Pike (45245-1028)
PHONE.................................513 688-7300
David J Durham, *Pr*
Gerold J Zobrist, *Ch Bd*
▲ **EMP:** 6 **EST:** 1971
SQ FT: 16,000
SALES (est): 282.72K **Privately Held**
Web: www.clippercorp.com
SIC: 3161 Cases, carrying, nec

(G-2300)
CURTISS-WRIGHT FLOW CTRL CORP
Also Called: Qualtech NP
4600 E Tech Dr (45245-1000)
PHONE.................................513 528-7900
Marion Mitchell, *Brnch Mgr*
EMP: 82
SALES (corp-wide): 3.12B **Publicly Held**
Web: www.curtisswright.com
SIC: 3443 8734 Fabricated plate work (boiler shop); Testing laboratories

HQ: Curtiss-Wright Flow Control Corporation
1966 Broadhollow Rd Ste E
Farmingdale NY 11735
631 293-3800

(G-2301)
DRS LEONARDO INC
4043 Mcmann Rd (45245-1960)
PHONE.................................513 943-1111
Rich Reynolds, *Brnch Mgr*
EMP: 26
SALES (corp-wide): 16.62B **Publicly Held**
Web: www.leonardodrs.com
SIC: 3812 Search and navigation equipment
HQ: Leonardo Drs, Inc.
2345 Crystal Dr Ste 1000
Arlington VA 22202
703 416-8000

(G-2302)
ELITE BIOMEDICAL SOLUTIONS LLC
756 Cincinnati Batavia Pike Ste C (45245-1277)
PHONE.................................513 207-0602
Jeff Smith, *Managing Member*
Alex Heileman, *COO*
EMP: 13 **EST:** 2012
SALES (est): 7.05MM **Privately Held**
Web: www.elitebiomedicalsolutions.com
SIC: 3841 7699 7389 Surgical and medical instruments; Medical equipment repair, non-electric; Business services, nec

(G-2303)
FUNTOWN PLAYGROUNDS INC
839 Cypresspoint Ct (45245-3352)
PHONE.................................513 871-8585
Orville Wright, *Pr*
Marty Kremer, *VP*
EMP: 6 **EST:** 1979
SALES (est): 420.44K **Privately Held**
Web: www.thinklocalsouthernindiana.com
SIC: 3949 Playground equipment

(G-2304)
GENERAL DATA COMPANY INC (PA)
4354 Ferguson Dr (45245-1667)
P.O. Box 541165 (45254-1165)
PHONE.................................513 752-7978
Peter Wenzel, *Pr*
Jim Burns, *
Erin Johnson, *
Michele Marsh, *
◆ **EMP:** 280 **EST:** 1980
SQ FT: 175,000
SALES (est): 36.8MM
SALES (corp-wide): 36.8MM **Privately Held**
Web: www.general-data.com
SIC: 2679 5046 5084 2759 Labels, paper: made from purchased material; Commercial equipment, nec; Printing trades machinery, equipment, and supplies; Commercial printing, nec

(G-2305)
HAWKS & ASSOCIATES INC
Also Called: Hawks Tag
1029 Seabrook Way (45245-1964)
P.O. Box 541207 (45254-1207)
PHONE.................................513 752-4311
James M Hawks, *Pr*
EMP: 28 **EST:** 1973
SQ FT: 15,000
SALES (est): 3.05MM **Privately Held**
Web: www.hawkstag.com
SIC: 2759 2752 Flexographic printing; Commercial printing, lithographic

(G-2306)
HDT EXPEDITIONARY SYSTEMS INC
1032 Seabrook Way (45245-1963)
PHONE.................................513 943-1111
EMP: 14
Web: www.hdtglobal.com
SIC: 3429 Hardware, nec
HQ: Hdt Expeditionary Systems, Inc.
30500 Aurora Rd Ste 100
Solon OH 44139
216 438-6111

(G-2307)
HUNTER DEFENSE TECH INC
1032 Seabrook Way (45245-1963)
PHONE.................................513 943-7880
Angela Cowan, *Brnch Mgr*
EMP: 24
Web: www.hdtglobal.com
SIC: 3812 Search and navigation equipment
PA: Hunter Defense Technologies, Inc.
30500 Aurora Rd Ste 100
Solon OH 44139

(G-2308)
J BEST INC
Also Called: Fastsigns
4476 Glen Este Withamsville Rd (45245-1356)
PHONE.................................513 943-7000
EMP: 6 **EST:** 2020
SALES (est): 619.52K **Privately Held**
Web: www.fastsigns.com
SIC: 3993 Signs and advertising specialties

(G-2309)
L3 TECHNOLOGIES INC
Electro Fab Division
3975 Mcmann Rd (45245-2307)
PHONE.................................513 943-2000
Charls King, *Genl Mgr*
EMP: 40
SALES (corp-wide): 21.32B **Publicly Held**
Web: www.l3harris.com
SIC: 3672 Printed circuit boards
HQ: L3 Technologies, Inc.
600 3rd Ave Fl 34
New York NY 10016
321 727-9100

(G-2310)
L3HARRIS ELECTRODYNAMICS INC
3975 Mcmann Rd (45245-2307)
PHONE.................................847 259-0740
Donald A Spetter, *Pr*
Stephen Post, *
Steven M Post, *
EMP: 195 **EST:** 1981
SQ FT: 46,000
SALES (est): 22.75MM
SALES (corp-wide): 21.32B **Publicly Held**
Web: www.l3harris.com
SIC: 3577 3812 3824 3823 Data conversion equipment, media-to-media: computer; Flight recorders; Controls, revolution and timing instruments; Process control instruments
HQ: L3 Technologies, Inc.
600 3rd Ave Fl 34
New York NY 10016
321 727-9100

(G-2311)
L3HARRIS FZING ORD SYSTEMS INC
3975 Mcmann Rd (45245-2307)
PHONE.................................513 943-2000
Michael T Strianese, *CEO*
Eric Ellis, *Pr*
Curtis Brunson, *Ex VP*
Ralph G D'ambrosio, *CFO*
Steven M Post, *Sr VP*

EMP: 575 **EST:** 1967
SQ FT: 236,000
SALES (est): 90.91MM
SALES (corp-wide): 21.32B **Publicly Held**
Web: www.l3harris.com
SIC: 3483 Arming and fusing devices for missiles
HQ: L3 Technologies, Inc.
    600 3rd Ave Fl 34
    New York NY 10016
    321 727-9100

(G-2312)
LINTECH ELECTRONICS LLC
4435 Aicholtz Rd Ste 500 (45245-1692)
P.O. Box 54436 (45254-0436)
PHONE..............................513 528-6190
EMP: 22 **EST:** 1994
SALES (est): 3.15MM **Privately Held**
Web: www.lintech-electronics.com
SIC: 8711 3679 Electrical or electronic engineering; Electronic circuits

(G-2313)
MCDONALDS
812 Eastgate North Dr (45245-1588)
PHONE..............................513 752-2008
EMP: 11 **EST:** 2019
SALES (est): 57.19K **Privately Held**
Web: www.mcdonalds.com
SIC: 5813 5812 5499 2038 Drinking places; Eating places; Miscellaneous food stores; Frozen specialties, nec

(G-2314)
PRO AUDIO
671 Cincinnati Batavia Pike (45245-1002)
PHONE..............................513 752-7500
Frank Marino, *Owner*
EMP: 6 **EST:** 2002
SALES (est): 248.94K **Privately Held**
Web: www.proaudio.com
SIC: 3651 Audio electronic systems

(G-2315)
QUEEN CITY FORGING COMPANY
Also Called: Qcforge.com
1019 Seabrook Way (45245-1964)
PHONE..............................513 321-2003
Howard R Mayer, *Ch Bd*
John Mayer, *VP*
Ron Secen, *VP*
George C Allen, *Prin*
▲ **EMP:** 16 **EST:** 1881
SQ FT: 36,000
SALES (est): 4.69MM **Privately Held**
Web: www.qcforge.com
SIC: 3462 Iron and steel forgings

(G-2316)
TAKE IT FOR GRANITE LLC
3898 Mcmann Rd (45245-2347)
PHONE..............................513 735-0555
Dustin Wallace, *Managing Member*
Amy Jo Wallace, *Managing Member*
▲ **EMP:** 15 **EST:** 2002
SQ FT: 12,000
SALES (est): 820.25K **Privately Held**
Web: www.takeitforgranitecincy.com
SIC: 3281 Cut stone and stone products

(G-2317)
UNITED TOOL SUPPLY INC
Also Called: K M I
851 Ohio Pike Ste 101 (45245-2293)
PHONE..............................513 752-6000
Russell F Young, *Pr*
EMP: 6 **EST:** 1973
SQ FT: 8,000
SALES (est): 2.43MM **Privately Held**
Web: www.united-tool.com

SIC: 5085 3823 Industrial supplies; Process control instruments

(G-2318)
XCITE SYSTEMS CORPORATION
675 Cincinnati Batavia Pike (45245-1028)
PHONE..............................513 965-0300
Terry A Dunlap, *Pr*
Gerald J Zobrist, *Ch*
EMP: 6 **EST:** 1997
SQ FT: 2,000
SALES (est): 692.56K **Privately Held**
Web: www.xcitesystems.com
SIC: 3829 8711 Stress, strain, and flaw detecting/measuring equipment; Engineering services

---

Cincinnati
Hamilton County

(G-2319)
1 A LIFESAFER INC (PA)
Also Called: Ignition Interlock
3630 Park 42 Dr Ste 140c (45241-2131)
PHONE..............................513 651-9560
Chris Linchwaite, *CEO*
Richard Freund, *
Craig Armstrong, *
Glenn Kermes, *
EMP: 21 **EST:** 1992
SALES (est): 9.39MM **Privately Held**
Web: www.lifesafer.com
SIC: 3829 Measuring and controlling devices, nec

(G-2320)
400 SW 7TH STREET PARTNERS LTD
Also Called: Ohio Construction News
3825 Edwards Rd Ste 800 (45209-1289)
PHONE..............................440 826-4700
Tim Blaicher, *Brnch Mgr*
EMP: 39
Web: www.constructionjournal.com
SIC: 2721 Periodicals
PA: 400 Sw 7th Street Partners, Ltd.
    3825 Edwards Rd Ste 800
    Cincinnati OH 45209

(G-2321)
400 SW 7TH STREET PARTNERS LTD (PA)
Also Called: Construction Journal
3825 Edwards Rd Ste 800 (45209-1289)
PHONE..............................772 781-2144
Richard J Goldman, *Pr*
EMP: 41 **EST:** 1996
SALES (est): 7.67MM **Privately Held**
Web: www.constructionjournal.com
SIC: 2721 Trade journals: publishing only, not printed on site

(G-2322)
7OCTOPUS7 INC
8790 Governors Hill Dr Ste 102 (45249-1374)
PHONE..............................513 677-5044
B J Becker, *Pr*
John Gallagher, *VP*
EMP: 10 **EST:** 1984
SQ FT: 3,000
SALES (est): 965.36K **Privately Held**
Web: www.beckergallagher.com
SIC: 2741 Miscellaneous publishing

(G-2323)
A & B DEBURRING COMPANY
Also Called: A & B
525 Carr St (45203-1815)
PHONE..............................513 723-0444

TOLL FREE: 800
Robert Wegman, *Pr*
EMP: 14 **EST:** 1946
SQ FT: 25,000
SALES (est): 5.55MM **Privately Held**
Web: www.abdeburr.com
SIC: 5084 3471 Metal refining machinery and equipment; Polishing, metals or formed products

(G-2324)
A AND V GRINDING INC
Also Called: Midwest Centerless Grinding
1115 Straight St 17 (45214-1735)
PHONE..............................937 444-4141
Albert Benedetti, *Pr*
Vera Benedetti, *VP*
EMP: 6 **EST:** 1982
SQ FT: 12,500
SALES (est): 497.19K **Privately Held**
Web: www.mpgrinding.com
SIC: 3599 Machine shop, jobbing and repair

(G-2325)
A GOOD MOBILE DETAILING LLC
2464 8 Mile Rd (45244-2614)
PHONE..............................513 316-3802
Todd Knight, *Managing Member*
EMP: 6 **EST:** 2022
SALES (est): 441.61K **Privately Held**
Web: www.agoodmobiledetailing.com
SIC: 3714 7389 Cleaners, air, motor vehicle; Business Activities at Non-Commercial Site

(G-2326)
A Z PRINTING INC (PA)
Also Called: A-Z Discount Printing
10122 Reading Rd (45241-3110)
PHONE..............................513 733-3900
Bruce Hassel, *Pr*
EMP: 6 **EST:** 1978
SQ FT: 4,000
SALES (est): 377.51K
SALES (corp-wide): 377.51K **Privately Held**
Web: www.printing-cincinnati.com
SIC: 2752 Offset printing

(G-2327)
A&E SIGNS AND LIGHTING LLC
1030 Straight St (45214-1734)
PHONE..............................513 541-0024
Elvera Maier, *Prin*
EMP: 15
SALES (est): 292.74K **Privately Held**
SIC: 3993 Signs and advertising specialties

(G-2328)
AA HAND SANITIZER
2230 Park Ave Ste 202 (45206-2782)
PHONE..............................513 506-7575
Alex Ebner, *Mgr*
Alex Ebner, *Pt*
David Bade, *COO*
EMP: 9 **EST:** 2020
SALES (est): 118.27K **Privately Held**
Web: saferhands.zachzeltman.com
SIC: 2844 Cosmetic preparations

(G-2329)
AAA GALVANIZING - JOLIET INC
Also Called: Azz Galvanizing - Cincinnati
4454 Steel Pl (45209-1135)
PHONE..............................513 871-5700
Lori Wilp, *Manager*
EMP: 12
SALES (corp-wide): 1.58B **Publicly Held**
SIC: 3479 Hot dip coating of metals or formed products
HQ: Aaa Galvanizing - Joliet, Inc.
    625 Mills Rd

Joliet IL 60433

(G-2330)
AB BONDED LOCKSMITHS INC
Also Called: Tri County Locksmith
4344 Montgomery Rd (45212-3104)
PHONE..............................513 531-7334
Russell Mcgurrin, *Pr*
Russell Mcgurrin, *CEO*
Cindy Mcgurrin, *CFO*
EMP: 7 **EST:** 1933
SQ FT: 5,000
SALES (est): 398.1K **Privately Held**
Web: www.ablocks.com
SIC: 7699 3429 Locksmith shop; Hardware, nec

(G-2331)
ABC SIGNS INC
2336 Iowa Ave (45206-2313)
PHONE..............................513 407-4367
Cliff Meyer, *Pr*
Thomas Meyer, *VP*
EMP: 10 **EST:** 1979
SQ FT: 30,500
SALES (est): 844.41K **Privately Held**
Web: www.abcsign.com
SIC: 3993 2394 1799 7359 Electric signs; Awnings, fabric: made from purchased materials; Sign installation and maintenance ; Sign rental

(G-2332)
ABEL FBRCTION PRCSION PDTS INC
Also Called: Abel Fabrication & Precision
3474 Beekman St (45223-2425)
PHONE..............................513 681-5000
Deborah Smith, *Pr*
EMP: 10 **EST:** 2001
SQ FT: 14,000
SALES (est): 912.92K **Privately Held**
Web: www.abelfab.com
SIC: 3451 Screw machine products

(G-2333)
ABEL MANUFACTURING COMPANY
3474 Beekman St (45223-2425)
PHONE..............................513 681-5000
Carl Abel Junior, *Pr*
Michael Nagel, *VP*
Ardath Abel, *Sec*
Katherine Nagel, *Treas*
Mark Abel, *VP*
EMP: 15 **EST:** 1966
SQ FT: 14,000
SALES (est): 3.29MM **Privately Held**
Web: www.abelusa.com
SIC: 3451 Screw machine products

(G-2334)
ABLE TOOL CORPORATION
617 N Wayne Ave (45215-2250)
PHONE..............................513 733-8989
Daniel R Hayes, *Pr*
Daniel R Hayes, *Pr*
Sara Hayes, *
Janice M Hayes, *
EMP: 30 **EST:** 1984
SQ FT: 22,400
SALES (est): 6.68MM **Privately Held**
Web: www.abletool.com
SIC: 3599 3565 3545 Machine shop, jobbing and repair; Packing and wrapping machinery; Machine tool accessories

(G-2335)
ABRASIVE PRODUCTS
1028 Rosetree Ln (45230-4041)
PHONE..............................513 502-9150
Brent Cassil, *Prin*
EMP: 8 **EST:** 2016

SALES (est): 67.51K Privately Held
Web: www.surfaceprep.com
SIC: 3291 Abrasive products

(G-2336)
ACCRETECH SBS INC (PA)
8790 Governors Hill Dr (45249-1307)
PHONE..............................513 373-4844
Shigeru Umenaka, Pr
▲ EMP: 7 EST: 2009
SALES (est): 1.19MM
SALES (corp-wide): 1.19MM Privately
Held
Web: toseiengineering.accretech.com
SIC: 5045 3545 Computers, peripherals, and
software; Balancing machines (machine
tool accessories)

(G-2337)
ACCURATE GEAR MFG CO INC
16 E 73rd St (45216-2038)
PHONE..............................513 761-3220
Dennis M Pauly, Pr
David Schachere, VP
EMP: 9 EST: 1974
SQ FT: 10,500
SALES (est): 987.06K Privately Held
Web: www.accurategearmfg.com
SIC: 3462 Iron and steel forgings

(G-2338)
ADVANCED GROUND SYSTEMS
Also Called: Agse Tooling
1650 Magnolia Dr (45215-1976)
PHONE..............................513 402-7226
Roy Stone, Mgr
EMP: 18
SALES (corp-wide): 24.58MM Privately
Held
Web: www.agsecorp.com
SIC: 3724 Aircraft engines and engine parts
HQ: Advanced Ground Systems
Engineering Llc
10805 Painter Ave
Santa Fe Springs CA 90670
562 906-9300

(G-2339)
ADVENTUROUS CHILD INC
4781 Duck Creek Rd (45227-1419)
PHONE..............................513 531-7700
Clark Kugler, Pr
EMP: 7 EST: 1986
SQ FT: 4,000
SALES (est): 331.36K Privately Held
Web: www.adventurouschild.com
SIC: 3949 Playground equipment

(G-2340)
AFFINITY DISP EXPOSITIONS INC
Also Called: Adex International
1375 Spring Park Walk (45215-0046)
PHONE..............................513 771-2339
Tim Murphy, Pr
EMP: 12
SALES (corp-wide): 19.2MM Privately
Held
Web: www.adex-intl.com
SIC: 3993 Signs and advertising specialties
PA: Affinity Displays & Expositions, Inc.
1301 Glendale Milford Rd
Cincinnati OH 45215
513 771-2339

(G-2341)
AFFINITY DISP EXPOSITIONS INC (PA)
Also Called: Adex International
1301 Glendale Milford Rd (45215-1210)
PHONE..............................513 771-2339
Timothy Murphy, Pr

Walt Pottschmidt, Ex VP
Mike Pierdiluca, VP
Joe Rickard, CFO
▲ EMP: 100 EST: 1978
SQ FT: 250,000
SALES (est): 19.2MM
SALES (corp-wide): 19.2MM Privately
Held
Web: www.adex-intl.com
SIC: 3993 Displays and cutouts, window and
lobby

(G-2342)
AFFINITY DISP EXPOSITIONS INC
Also Called: Adex International
1375 Glendale Milford Rd (45215-1210)
PHONE..............................513 771-2339
EMP: 11
SALES (corp-wide): 19.2MM Privately
Held
Web: www.adex-intl.com
SIC: 3993 Displays and cutouts, window and
lobby
PA: Affinity Displays & Expositions, Inc.
1301 Glendale Milford Rd
Cincinnati OH 45215
513 771-2339

(G-2343)
AGNONE-KELLY ENTERPRISES INC
Also Called: Thermalgraphics
11658 Baen Rd (45242-1600)
P.O. Box 428543 (45242-8543)
PHONE..............................800 634-6503
Kevin Kelly, Pr
Elizabeth Kelly, VP
EMP: 6 EST: 1987
SQ FT: 20,000
SALES (est): 96.76K Privately Held
SIC: 2759 Commercial printing, nec

(G-2344)
AHALOGY
1140 Main St # 3 (45202-7236)
PHONE..............................314 974-5599
Michael Wohlschlaeger, CEO
EMP: 28 EST: 2014
SALES (est): 915.89K Privately Held
Web: www.quotient.com
SIC: 2741 Internet publishing and
broadcasting

(G-2345)
AIRECON MANUFACTURING CORP
5271 Brotherton Rd (45227-2103)
PHONE..............................513 561-5522
Joseph E Gutierrez, Pr
Timothy Kidd, *
David W Miller, *
▲ EMP: 50 EST: 1979
SQ FT: 30,000
SALES (est): 9.92MM Privately Held
Web: www.airecon.com
SIC: 3564 Air purification equipment

(G-2346)
AIRTX INTERNATIONAL LTD
6320 Wiehe Rd (45237-4214)
PHONE..............................513 631-0660
Michael Rawlings, Pt
Michael Rawlings, Pr
EMP: 10 EST: 1993
SQ FT: 7,500
SALES (est): 914.87K Privately Held
Web: www.airtx.com
SIC: 3563 Air and gas compressors

(G-2347)
ALL AROUND PRIMO LOGISTICS LLC
6027 Magnolia Woods Way (45247-2608)

PHONE..............................513 725-7888
EMP: 6 EST: 2021
SALES (est): 2.14MM Privately Held
SIC: 3537 Trucks: freight, baggage, etc.:
industrial, except mining

(G-2348)
ALL CRAFT MANUFACTURING CO
Also Called: Talisman Racing
6500 Glenway Ave Side 2 (45211-4451)
P.O. Box 58651 (45258-0651)
PHONE..............................513 661-3383
Robert W Farrell, Pr
Paula Farrell, VP
EMP: 15 EST: 1987
SQ FT: 3,200
SALES (est): 4.5MM Privately Held
Web: www.allcraftmfg.com
SIC: 3599 Machine shop, jobbing and repair

(G-2349)
ALLERGAN SALES LLC
Also Called: Allergan
5000 Brotherton Rd (45209-1105)
PHONE..............................513 271-6800
Doug Yelton, Brnch Mgr
EMP: 190
SALES (corp-wide): 56.33B Publicly Held
Web: www.abbvie.com
SIC: 2834 Pharmaceutical preparations
HQ: Allergan Sales, Llc
2525 Dupont Dr
Irvine CA 92612

(G-2350)
ALLERGAN SALES LLC
3941 Brotherton Rd (45209)
PHONE..............................513 271-6800
Greg Yurchak, Brnch Mgr
EMP: 13
SALES (corp-wide): 56.33B Publicly Held
Web: www.abbvie.com
SIC: 2834 Pharmaceutical preparations
HQ: Allergan Sales, Llc
2525 Dupont Dr
Irvine CA 92612

(G-2351)
ALLGEIER & SON INC (PA)
6386 Bridgetown Rd (45248-2933)
PHONE..............................513 574-3735
Michael Allgeier, Owner
Margaret A Steigerwald, Treas
EMP: 18 EST: 1964
SQ FT: 800
SALES (est): 1.41MM
SALES (corp-wide): 1.41MM Privately
Held
Web: www.allgeierandson.com
SIC: 1794 1422 1795 Excavation and
grading, building construction; Crushed and
broken limestone; Wrecking and demolition
work

(G-2352)
ALLU INC
Also Called: Franklin's Printing
432 Bishopsbridge Dr (45255-3900)
PHONE..............................513 624-9333
Dean Hicks, Pr
Fern Hicks, Sec
EMP: 7 EST: 1990
SQ FT: 2,800
SALES (est): 177.57K Privately Held
Web: www.allu.net
SIC: 2752 Commercial printing, lithographic

(G-2353)
ALUCHEM INC (PA)
1 Landy Ln Ste 1 (45215-3489)
PHONE..............................513 733-8519

Ronald P Zapletal, Pr
Ronald L Bell, *
Edward L Butera, *
William A Kist, *
◆ EMP: 47 EST: 1978
SQ FT: 200,000
SALES (est): 24.04MM
SALES (corp-wide): 24.04MM Privately
Held
Web: www.aluchem.com
SIC: 2819 Industrial inorganic chemicals, nec

(G-2354)
ALUMINUM EXTRUDED SHAPES INC
Also Called: AES
10549 Reading Rd (45241-2524)
PHONE..............................513 563-2205
Robert E Hoeweler, Pr
Alan Hoeweler, Prin
Reuven Katz, Prin
EMP: 115 EST: 1946
SQ FT: 130,000
SALES (est): 4.09MM Privately Held
Web: www.alum-ext.com
SIC: 3354 3471 3444 Aluminum extruded
products; Plating and polishing; Sheet
metalwork

(G-2355)
AMANTEA NONWOVENS LLC
6715 Steger Dr (45237-3097)
PHONE..............................513 842-6600
Gianni Boscolo, *
Tom Grabo, *
▲ EMP: 6 EST: 2004
SQ FT: 77,000
SALES (est): 230.78K Privately Held
SIC: 2297 Nonwoven fabrics

(G-2356)
AMERICAN BOTTLING COMPANY
125 E Court St Ste 820 (45202-1201)
PHONE..............................513 381-4891
EMP: 70
Web: www.keurigdrpepper.com
SIC: 2086 Soft drinks: packaged in cans,
bottles, etc.
HQ: The American Bottling Company
6425 Hall Of Fame Ln
Frisco TX 75034

(G-2357)
AMERICAN BOTTLING COMPANY
Also Called: 7 Up/ Royal Crown
5151 Fischer Ave (45217-1157)
PHONE..............................513 242-5151
Mark Wendling, Mgr
EMP: 78
Web: www.keurigdrpepper.com
SIC: 2086 Soft drinks: packaged in cans,
bottles, etc.
HQ: The American Bottling Company
6425 Hall Of Fame Ln
Frisco TX 75034

(G-2358)
AMERICAN CITY BUS JOURNALS INC
Also Called: Cincinnati Business Courier
120 E 4th St Ste 230 (45202-4099)
PHONE..............................513 337-9450
Douglas Bolton, Brnch Mgr
EMP: 72
SALES (corp-wide): 2.88B Privately Held
Web: www.acbj.com
SIC: 2711 2741 Newspapers: publishing
only, not printed on site; Miscellaneous
publishing
HQ: American City Business Journals, Inc.
120 W Morehead St Ste 400
Charlotte NC 28202
704 973-1000

(G-2359)

AMERICAN GILD OF ENGLISH HNDBE

201 E 5th St (45202-4152)
PHONE...........................937 438-0085
Jennifer Cauhorn, *Ex Dir*
EMP: 9 **EST:** 1986
SQ FT: 2,253
SALES (est): 683.86K **Privately Held**
Web: www.handbellmusicians.org
SIC: 8699 7929 2741 7041 Personal interest organization; Entertainers and entertainment groups; Music, sheet; publishing only, not printed on site; Membership-basis organization hotels

(G-2360)

AMERICAN ISRAELITE COMPANY INC

Also Called: American Israelite Newspaper
18 W 9th St Ste 2 (45202-2037)
PHONE...........................513 621-3145
Ted Deustch, *Pr*
EMP: 8 **EST:** 1854
SQ FT: 1,000
SALES (est): 166K **Privately Held**
Web: www.americanisraelite.com
SIC: 2711 Newspapers, publishing and printing

(G-2361)

AMERICAN LEGAL PUBLISHING CORP

525 Vine St Ste 300 (45202-3121)
PHONE...........................513 421-4248
Stephen G Wolf, *Pr*
Cynthia Poweleit, *
EMP: 40 **EST:** 1978
SALES (est): 2.1MM **Privately Held**
Web: www.amlegal.com
SIC: 2731 2741 Books, publishing only; Miscellaneous publishing

(G-2362)

AMERICAN QUICKSILVER COMPANY

646 Rushton Rd (45226-1124)
PHONE...........................513 871-4517
Barney Pogue, *Pr*
Mara Pogue, *Sec*
▲ **EMP:** 9 **EST:** 1993
SALES (est): 440.82K **Privately Held**
Web: www.americanquicksilverco.com
SIC: 3421 Knife blades and blanks

(G-2363)

AMERICRAFT MFG CO INC

7937 School Rd (45249-1533)
PHONE...........................513 489-1047
Erin Giblin, *Pr*
EMP: 11 **EST:** 1979
SQ FT: 55,000
SALES (est): 5.3MM **Privately Held**
Web: www.americraftmfg.com
SIC: 3564 Blowers and fans

(G-2364)

AMERIDIAN SPECIALTY SERVICES

11520 Rockfield Ct (45241-1919)
P.O. Box 62808 (45262-0808)
PHONE...........................513 769-0150
Betty Owens, *Pr*
EMP: 50 **EST:** 1999
SQ FT: 32,000
SALES (est): 1.09MM **Privately Held**
Web: www.ameridiancommercial.com
SIC: 8741 1761 3441 Construction management; Architectural sheet metal work; Fabricated structural metal

(G-2365)

AMPAC HOLDINGS LLC (HQ)

Also Called: Proampac
12025 Tricon Rd (45246-1719)
PHONE...........................513 671-1777
Greg Tucker, *Managing Member*
Jon Dill, *
Tom Geyer, *
Eric Bradford, *
◆ **EMP:** 700 **EST:** 2001
SQ FT: 220,000
SALES (est): 429.03MM
SALES (corp-wide): 1.58B **Privately Held**
Web: www.proampac.com
SIC: 2673 2677 3081 2674 Plastic bags: made from purchased materials; Envelopes; Unsupported plastics film and sheet; Shopping bags: made from purchased materials
PA: Proampac Holdings Inc.
　　12025 Tricon Rd
　　Cincinnati OH 45246
　　513 671-1777

(G-2366)

AMPAC PACKAGING LLC (HQ)

Also Called: Ampac
12025 Tricon Rd (45246-1719)
PHONE...........................513 671-1777
John Baumann, *CEO*
◆ **EMP:** 112 **EST:** 2006
SALES (est): 412.5MM
SALES (corp-wide): 1.58B **Privately Held**
Web: www.proampac.com
SIC: 3086 5084 Packaging and shipping materials, foamed plastics; Processing and packaging equipment
PA: Proampac Holdings Inc.
　　12025 Tricon Rd
　　Cincinnati OH 45246
　　513 671-1777

(G-2367)

AMPAC PLASTICS LLC

Also Called: Ampac
12025 Tricon Rd (45246-1792)
PHONE...........................513 671-1777
Greg Tucker, *CEO*
Eric Bradford, *
Bob Wheeler, *
▲ **EMP:** 300 **EST:** 1965
SQ FT: 210,000
SALES (est): 14.69MM
SALES (corp-wide): 1.58B **Privately Held**
Web: www.proampac.com
SIC: 2621 2671 Packaging paper; Paper, coated or laminated for packaging
HQ: Ampac Holdings, Llc
　　12025 Tricon Rd
　　Cincinnati OH 45246
　　513 671-1777

(G-2368)

AMPACET CORPORATION

4705 Duke Dr # 400 (45249)
PHONE...........................513 247-5400
Vicky Willsey, *Mgr*
EMP: 13
SALES (corp-wide): 410.74MM **Privately Held**
Web: www.ampacet.com
SIC: 3089 5162 Coloring and finishing of plastics products; Plastics materials and basic shapes
PA: Ampacet Corporation
　　660 White Plins Rd Ste 36
　　Tarrytown NY 10591
　　914 631-6600

(G-2369)

ANCHOR FLANGE COMPANY (PA)

Also Called: Anchor Fluid Power
5553 Murray Ave (45227-2707)
PHONE...........................513 527-3512
▲ **EMP:** 79 **EST:** 1983
SALES (est): 17.98MM
SALES (corp-wide): 17.98MM **Privately Held**
Web: www.anchorfluidpower.com
SIC: 3462 5085 3594 3494 Flange, valve, and pipe fitting forgings, ferrous; Industrial supplies; Fluid power pumps and motors; Valves and pipe fittings, nec

(G-2370)

ANDYS MDTERRANEAN FD PDTS LLC

906 Nassau St (45206-2508)
PHONE...........................513 281-9791
▲ **EMP:** 6 **EST:** 2008
SQ FT: 9,000
SALES (est): 236.9K **Privately Held**
Web: www.andyskabob.com
SIC: 2099 Food preparations, nec

(G-2371)

ANTHONY FLOTTEMESCH & SON INC

8201 Camargo Rd Ste 1 (45243-1469)
PHONE...........................513 561-1212
James Flottemesch, *Pr*
James Flottimish Junior, *VP*
EMP: 10 **EST:** 1942
SQ FT: 13,000
SALES (est): 664.99K **Privately Held**
Web: www.aflottemesch.com
SIC: 2511 2434 2431 Wood household furniture; Wood kitchen cabinets; Millwork

(G-2372)

ANZA INC

3265 Colerain Ave Ste 2 (45225-3301)
PHONE...........................513 542-7337
John Busse, *Pr*
David Burbink, *VP*
▲ **EMP:** 8 **EST:** 1985
SQ FT: 6,000
SALES (est): 508.74K **Privately Held**
Web: www.anzadesign.com
SIC: 3999 Models, general, except toy

(G-2373)

APEX CABINETRY INC

Also Called: Apex Cabinetry
4536 W Mitchell Ave (45232-1912)
PHONE...........................513 832-7905
Denise Martin, *Pr*
Dave Smith, *VP*
EMP: 20 **EST:** 1997
SALES (est): 2.06MM **Privately Held**
Web: www.apexcabinetry.com
SIC: 2434 Wood kitchen cabinets

(G-2374)

ARCHER COUNTER DESIGN INC

4433 Verne Ave (45209-1223)
PHONE...........................513 396-7526
Robert Lewis, *Pr*
Tony Williams, *VP*
▲ **EMP:** 9 **EST:** 1983
SQ FT: 15,000
SALES (est): 499.78K **Privately Held**
SIC: 2541 Table or counter tops, plastic laminated

(G-2375)

ARKU INC (HQ)

7251 E Kemper Rd (45249-1030)
PHONE...........................513 985-0500
Nicholas Miller, *Pr*
Franck Hirschmann, *
▲ **EMP:** 15 **EST:** 2004
SALES (est): 4.38MM
SALES (corp-wide): 65.95MM **Privately Held**
Web: www.arku.com
SIC: 3549 3444 Wiredrawing and fabricating machinery and equipment, ex. die; Sheet metalwork
PA: Arku Maschinenbau Gmbh
　　Siemensstr. 11
　　Baden-Baden BW 76532
　　722150090

(G-2376)

ARMSTRONG STATIONERY CO CORP

10235 Spartan Dr Ste G (45215-1243)
PHONE...........................513 891-0667
David Hertlein, *Pr*
EMP: 7 **EST:** 1903
SQ FT: 5,000
SALES (est): 172.09K **Privately Held**
Web: www.armstrongstationery.com
SIC: 2752 Offset printing

(G-2377)

ARSCO CUSTOM METALS LLC

Also Called: Arsco Manufacturing Company
3330 E Kemper Rd (45241-1538)
PHONE...........................513 385-0555
Gregory Hemmert, *Managing Member*
EMP: 69 **EST:** 1926
SQ FT: 3,000
SALES (est): 8.72MM **Privately Held**
Web: www.arscometals.com
SIC: 3444 Sheet metalwork

(G-2378)

ART GUILD BINDERS INC

Also Called: Happy Booker
1068 Meta Dr (45237-5008)
PHONE...........................513 242-3000
TOLL FREE: 800
Timothy Hugenberg, *Pr*
Gregory M Hugenberg, *
Donald F Cooper, *
▲ **EMP:** 23 **EST:** 1948
SQ FT: 28,000
SALES (est): 3.03MM **Privately Held**
Web: www.artguildbinders.com
SIC: 2782 2675 2789 Looseleaf binders and devices; Die-cut paper and board; Bookbinding and repairing: trade, edition, library, etc.

(G-2379)

ART WOODWORKING & MFG CO

4238 Dane Ave (45223-1856)
PHONE...........................513 681-2986
Ralph R Dickman, *Pr*
EMP: 30 **EST:** 1922
SQ FT: 23,000
SALES (est): 4.91MM **Privately Held**
Web: www.artwoodmfg.net
SIC: 2431 Millwork

(G-2380)

ASPEC INC

5810 Carothers St (45227-2350)
PHONE...........................513 561-9922
Kerry L Bollmer, *Pr*
EMP: 9 **EST:** 1978
SQ FT: 11,000
SALES (est): 943.78K **Privately Held**
Web: www.aspecplastics.com
SIC: 3089 3544 Injection molding of plastics; Forms (molds), for foundry and plastics working machinery

(G-2381)
ASSOCIATED PREMIUM CORPORATION
1870 Summit Rd (45237-2804)
PHONE..................513 679-4444
◆ **EMP:** 40 **EST:** 1975
SALES (est): 2.06MM **Privately Held**
Web: www.apcpromos.com
SIC: 5199 5064 3993 3911 Advertising specialties; Electrical appliances, television and radio; Signs and advertising specialties ; Jewelry, precious metal

(G-2382)
ASTERION LLC
3630 E Kemper Rd (45241-2011)
P.O. Box 68809 (46268-0809)
PHONE..................317 875-0051
Blair R Vandivier, *Pr*
Roger Sowinski, *Sr VP*
◆ **EMP:** 23 **EST:** 2010
SALES (est): 10MM **Privately Held**
Web: www.asterionstc.com
SIC: 2899 Plating compounds

(G-2383)
ASTRO MET INC (PA)
9974 Springfield Pike (45215-1425)
PHONE..................513 772-1242
Donald Graham, *Pr*
EMP: 18 **EST:** 1961
SQ FT: 39,000
SALES (est): 2.54MM
SALES (corp-wide): 2.54MM **Privately Held**
Web: www.astromet.com
SIC: 3299 Ceramic fiber

(G-2384)
AT&T ENTERPRISES LLC
Also Called: AT&T
7875 Montgomery Rd Ofc (45236-4305)
PHONE..................513 792-9300
Vicky Valento, *Brnch Mgr*
EMP: 9
SALES (corp-wide): 122.34B **Publicly Held**
Web: www.att.com
SIC: 4813 3661 3357 3571 Local and long distance telephone communications; Telephone and telegraph apparatus; Communication wire; Electronic computers
HQ: At&T Enterprises, Llc
208 S Akard St
Dallas TX 75202
800 403-3302

(G-2385)
ATLANTIC SIGN COMPANY INC
2328 Florence Ave (45206-2431)
PHONE..................513 383-1504
William Yusko, *Pr*
Cj Mcdonald, *VP*
Aleisa Yusko, *
EMP: 27 **EST:** 2003
SQ FT: 15,000
SALES (est): 2.58MM **Privately Held**
Web: www.atlanticsigncompany.com
SIC: 3993 Signs and advertising specialties

(G-2386)
ATLAS VAC MACHINE CO LLC
Also Called: Atlas Vac
9150 Reading Rd (45215-3343)
P.O. Box 42633 (45242-0633)
PHONE..................513 407-3513
John Abraham, *Managing Member*
▼ **EMP:** 6 **EST:** 2008
SQ FT: 8,800
SALES (est): 4.52MM **Privately Held**
Web: www.atlasvac.com

SIC: 3565 Packaging machinery

(G-2387)
ATR DISTRIBUTING COMPANY (PA)
Also Called: Atr Automation
11857 Kemper Springs Dr (45240-1641)
P.O. Box 85 (45002-0085)
PHONE..................513 353-1800
EMP: 8 **EST:** 1981
SALES (est): 12.09MM
SALES (corp-wide): 12.09MM **Privately Held**
Web: www.atrautomation.com
SIC: 7371 7372 Computer software systems analysis and design, custom; Business oriented computer software

(G-2388)
ATR DISTRIBUTING COMPANY
Wonderware Cincinnati
11857 Kemper Springs Dr (45240-1641)
PHONE..................513 353-1800
Joe Murray, *Brnch Mgr*
EMP: 19
SALES (corp-wide): 12.09MM **Privately Held**
Web: www.atrautomation.com
SIC: 7372 Prepackaged software
PA: Atr Distributing Company
11857 Kemper Springs Dr
Cincinnati OH 45240
513 353-1800

(G-2389)
ATRIUM CENTERS INC
1400 Mallard Cove Dr (45246-3941)
PHONE..................513 830-5014
Jason Reese, *Brnch Mgr*
EMP: 18
SALES (corp-wide): 34.18MM **Privately Held**
Web: www.atriumlivingcenters.com
SIC: 3442 Metal doors, sash, and trim
PA: Atrium Centers, Inc.
2550 Corp Exchange Dr # 200
Columbus OH 43231
614 416-0600

(G-2390)
AUBREY ROSE APPAREL LLC
3862 Race Rd (45211-4346)
PHONE..................513 728-2681
EMP: 6 **EST:** 2009
SALES (est): 158.11K **Privately Held**
Web: www.aubreyrose.org
SIC: 7389 2395 Advertising, promotional, and trade show services; Embroidery and art needlework

(G-2391)
AUTOMTED CMPNENT SPCALISTS LLC
7740 Reinhold Dr (45237-2806)
PHONE..................513 335-4285
Andy Hillard, *Managing Member*
EMP: 25 **EST:** 2020
SALES (est): 1.07MM **Privately Held**
Web:
www.automatedcomponentspecialists.com
SIC: 2298 8711 7389 3442 Ropes and fiber cables; Engineering services; Field warehousing; Molding, trim, and stripping

(G-2392)
AVARI AERO LLC
Also Called: Avari Aerospace
7711 Affinity Pl (45231-3567)
PHONE..................513 828-0860
EMP: 8
SALES (est): 539.58K **Privately Held**
Web: www.avariaero.com

SIC: 3721 Aircraft

(G-2393)
AVERY DENNISON CORPORATION
11101 Mosteller Rd Ste 2 (45241-1882)
PHONE..................513 682-7500
Dennis Cain, *Brnch Mgr*
EMP: 50
SALES (corp-wide): 8.76B **Publicly Held**
Web: www.averydennison.com
SIC: 2672 Adhesive backed films, foams and foils
PA: Avery Dennison Corporation
8080 Norton Pkwy
Mentor OH 44060
440 534-6000

(G-2394)
B & J BAKING COMPANY
4056 Colerain Ave (45223-2561)
PHONE..................513 541-2386
Steve Toleski, *Pr*
Tatsa Toleski, *Sec*
EMP: 10 **EST:** 1924
SQ FT: 10,000
SALES (est): 842.56K **Privately Held**
SIC: 2051 Buns, bread type: fresh or frozen

(G-2395)
B & R FABRICATORS & MAINT INC
4524 W Mitchell Ave (45232-1912)
P.O. Box 17211 (45217-0211)
PHONE..................513 641-2222
Randy Allen, *Pr*
Bruce Allen, *VP*
EMP: 12 **EST:** 1993
SQ FT: 5,000
SALES (est): 508.17K **Privately Held**
SIC: 7692 Welding repair

(G-2396)
B R PRINTERS INC
Also Called: BR Ohio
3962 Virginia Ave (45227-3412)
PHONE..................513 271-6035
Adam Damaestri, *Pr*
EMP: 80
Web: www.brprinters.com
SIC: 2752 Offset printing
PA: B R Printers, Inc.
665 Lenfest Rd
San Jose CA 95133

(G-2397)
B&G FOODS INC
5204 Spring Grove Ave (45217-1031)
PHONE..................513 482-8226
EMP: 86
SALES (corp-wide): 1.93B **Publicly Held**
Web: www.bgfoods.com
SIC: 2013 2032 2033 2035 Canned meats (except baby food), from purchased meat; Beans and bean sprouts, canned, jarred, etc.; Canned fruits and specialties; Pickles, sauces, and salad dressings
PA: B&G Foods, Inc.
4 Gatehall Dr
Parsippany NJ 07054
973 401-6500

(G-2398)
BAERLOCHER PRODUCTION USA LLC
5890 Highland Ridge Dr (45232-1440)
PHONE..................513 482-6300
David Kuebel, *
▲ **EMP:** 50 **EST:** 1999
SQ FT: 50,000
SALES (est): 47.46MM
SALES (corp-wide): 525.26MM **Privately Held**

Web: www.baerlocherusa.com
SIC: 2819 Nonmetallic compounds
HQ: Baerlocher Gmbh
Freisinger Str. 1
UnterschleiBheim BY 85716
89143730

(G-2399)
BANBURY INVESTMENTS INC
Also Called: AlphaGraphics
9160 Union Cemetery Rd (45249-2006)
PHONE..................513 677-4500
Doug Banbury, *Pr*
Malisa Banbury, *Treas*
EMP: 8 **EST:** 1991
SQ FT: 4,800
SALES (est): 100.35K **Privately Held**
Web: www.alphagraphics.com
SIC: 2752 Commercial printing, lithographic

(G-2400)
BARR LABORATORIES INC
Also Called: BARR LABORATORIES, INC.
5040 Duramed Rd (45213-2520)
PHONE..................513 731-9900
S Goldstein, *Prin*
EMP: 973
Web: www.tevausa.com
SIC: 2834 Pharmaceutical preparations
HQ: Barr Laboratories Llc
400 Interpace Pkwy Bldg A
Parsippany NJ 07054
215 591-3000

(G-2401)
BASF CORP
3131 Spring Grove Ave (45225-1862)
PHONE..................513 681-9100
EMP: 8 **EST:** 2018
SALES (est): 683.96K **Privately Held**
Web: www.basf.com
SIC: 2869 Industrial organic chemicals, nec

(G-2402)
BASF CORPORATION
4900 Este Ave (45232-1491)
PHONE..................513 482-3000
Tasso Rigopoulos, *Mgr*
EMP: 145
SALES (corp-wide): 69.01B **Privately Held**
Web: www.basf.com
SIC: 2869 Industrial organic chemicals, nec
HQ: Basf Corporation
100 Park Ave
Florham Park NJ 07932
800 962-7831

(G-2403)
BAXTER BURIAL VAULT SVC INC
Also Called: Baxter-Wilbert Burial Vault
909 E Ross Ave (45217-1159)
PHONE..................513 641-1010
R Douglas Baxter, *Pr*
EMP: 14 **EST:** 1924
SALES (est): 1.33MM **Privately Held**
Web: www.baxterburialvault.com
SIC: 5087 3272 Concrete burial vaults and boxes; Concrete products, nec

(G-2404)
BAXTERS NORTH AMERICA INC (DH)
Also Called: Wornick Foods
4700 Creek Rd (45242-2808)
P.O. Box 42634 (45242)
PHONE..................513 552-7485
John Kowalchik, *CEO*
Jack Fields, *
Doug Herald, *
Randy Newbold, *
Dustin Mcdulin, *CFO*

▼ **EMP: 26 EST:** 2003
SQ FT: 600,000
SALES (est): 489.6MM
SALES (corp-wide): 477.56MM **Privately Held**
Web: www.baxtersna.com
SIC: 2032 Baby foods, including meats: packaged in cans, jars, etc.
HQ: Baxters Food Group Limited
Fochabers IV32
134 382-0393

(G-2405)
BECKMAN MACHINE LLC
4684 Paddock Rd (45229-1002)
P.O. Box 37655 (45222-0655)
PHONE.............................513 242-2700
Mary Kathryn Lynch, *Pr*
Charles Beckman, *VP*
EMP: 20 EST: 1989
SALES (est): 1.97MM **Privately Held**
Web: www.beckmanmachine.com
SIC: 3599 Machine shop, jobbing and repair

(G-2406)
BERGHAUSEN CORPORATION
4524 Este Ave (45232-1763)
P.O. Box 43400 (45243-0400)
PHONE.............................513 591-4491
Fritz Berghausen, *Pr*
August Ritt, *Prin*
◆ **EMP: 20 EST:** 1863
SQ FT: 38,000
SALES (est): 916.73K **Privately Held**
Web: www.berghausen.com
SIC: 2843 2087 2865 Emulsifiers, except food and pharmaceutical; Extracts, flavoring ; Food dyes or colors, synthetic

(G-2407)
BERNARD LABORATORIES INC
1738 Townsend St (45223-2710)
PHONE.............................513 681-7373
Boyd J Piper Junior, *Pr*
▲ **EMP: 22 EST:** 1980
SQ FT: 30,000
SALES (est): 3.09MM **Privately Held**
Web: www.bernardlab.com
SIC: 7389 2899 Packaging and labeling services; Chemical preparations, nec

(G-2408)
BERRY COMPANY
312 Plum St Ste 600 (45202-4809)
PHONE.............................513 768-7800
Pete Luongo, *Pr*
EMP: 6 EST: 1910
SALES (est): 105.36K **Privately Held**
Web: www.thryv.com
SIC: 2741 Directories, telephone: publishing and printing

(G-2409)
BEST GRAPHICS & PRINTING INC
11836 Stone Mill Rd (45251-4128)
PHONE.............................513 535-3529
Jeffrey Best, *Prin*
EMP: 6 EST: 2012
SALES (est): 132.63K **Privately Held**
SIC: 2752 Commercial printing, lithographic

(G-2410)
BIOWISH TECHNOLOGIES INC
Also Called: Biowish
2724 Erie Ave Ste B (45208-2125)
PHONE.............................312 572-6700
Bill Diederich, *CEO*
Richard Carpenter, *Prin*
Rod Vautier, *VP*
Bill Diederich, *VP*
John Schroeder, *VP*

▲ **EMP: 9 EST:** 2009
SALES (est): 9.82MM **Privately Held**
Web: www.biowishtechnologies.com
SIC: 2869 Enzymes

(G-2411)
BIOWISH TECHNOLOGIES INC
2717 Erie Ave (45208-2103)
PHONE.............................312 572-6700
EMP: 44 EST: 2009
SALES (est): 2.25MM **Privately Held**
Web: www.biowishtechnologies.com
SIC: 2869 Industrial organic chemicals, nec

(G-2412)
BLACK SQUIRREL HOLDINGS INC
Also Called: Frame Usa, Inc.
225 Northland Blvd (45246-3603)
PHONE.............................513 577-7107
Greg Clark, *CEO*
Daniel P Regenold, *Ch Bd*
Dana Gore, *Pr*
◆ **EMP: 20 EST:** 1990
SQ FT: 7,000
SALES (est): 3.94MM
SALES (corp-wide): 4.96MM **Privately Held**
Web: www.frameusa.com
SIC: 2499 5999 3499 Picture frame molding, finished; Picture frames, ready made; Picture frames, metal
PA: Posterservice, Incorporated
225 Northland Blvd
Cincinnati OH 45246
513 577-7100

(G-2413)
BLU BIRD LLC
Also Called: Stone Center
4820 Stafford St (45227-2539)
PHONE.............................513 271-5646
Steve Piehl, *Mgr*
EMP: 11
SQ FT: 7,500
SALES (corp-wide): 3.41MM **Privately Held**
Web: www.stonecenters.com
SIC: 3281 Cut stone and stone products
PA: Blu Bird Llc
1736 Mckinley Ave
Columbus OH 43222
614 276-3585

(G-2414)
BLUE CHIP TOOL INC
11511 Goldcoast Dr (45249-1620)
PHONE.............................513 489-3561
William Riehle, *Pr*
John Kilgore, *VP Mfg*
Eileen Riehle, *Sec*
EMP: 11 EST: 1983
SQ FT: 5,000
SALES (est): 3.18MM **Privately Held**
Web: www.bluechiptool.com
SIC: 3599 Machine shop, jobbing and repair

(G-2415)
BODOR VENTS INC
Also Called: Vents US
400 Murray Rd (45217-1013)
PHONE.............................513 348-3853
Zoltan Bodor, *Managing Member*
EMP: 7 EST: 2005
SALES (est): 992.03K **Privately Held**
Web: www.vents-us.com
SIC: 3585 Refrigeration and heating equipment

(G-2416)
BODYCOTE THERMAL PROC INC
710 Burns St (45204-1904)
PHONE.............................513 921-2300
Kevin Mccurdy, *Brnch Mgr*
EMP: 46
SALES (corp-wide): 959.76MM **Privately Held**
Web: www.bodycote.com
SIC: 3398 Metal heat treating
HQ: Bodycote Thermal Processing, Inc.
12750 Merit Dr Ste 1400
Dallas TX 75251
214 904-2420

(G-2417)
BONSAL AMERICAN INC
5155 Fischer Ave (45217-1157)
PHONE.............................513 398-7300
Marshal Lewis, *Mgr*
EMP: 26
SQ FT: 8,100
SALES (corp-wide): 34.95B **Privately Held**
SIC: 1442 Construction sand and gravel
HQ: Bonsal American, Inc.
625 Griffith Rd Ste 100
Charlotte NC 28217
704 525-1621

(G-2418)
BOSE CORPORATION
Also Called: Bose Showcase Store
7875 Montgomery Rd Spc 2422 (45236-4608)
PHONE.............................513 891-4384
Donna Davis, *Owner*
EMP: 6
SALES (corp-wide): 3.6B **Privately Held**
Web: www.bose.com
SIC: 5731 3651 High fidelity stereo equipment; Household audio equipment
PA: Bose Corporation
100 The Mountain Rd
Framingham MA 01701
508 879-7330

(G-2419)
BOSTON BEER COMPANY
1625 Central Pkwy (45214-2423)
PHONE.............................267 240-4429
Jeremy Roza, *Prin*
▲ **EMP: 29 EST:** 2010
SALES (est): 8.39MM **Privately Held**
Web: www.samueladams.com
SIC: 3585 Beer dispensing equipment

(G-2420)
BRACKISH MEDIA LLC
2662 Mckinley Ave (45211-7206)
PHONE.............................513 394-2871
Terrell Hill, *CEO*
EMP: 11 EST: 2014
SALES (est): 706.75K **Privately Held**
SIC: 4899 3577 7313 Communication services, nec; Data conversion equipment, media-to-media: computer; Radio, television, publisher representatives

(G-2421)
BRENTWOOD PRINTING & STY
8630 Winton Rd (45231-4817)
PHONE.............................513 522-2679
Scott Finke, *Owner*
EMP: 8 EST: 1979
SQ FT: 1,250
SALES (est): 290K **Privately Held**
Web: www.brentwood-printing.com
SIC: 2752 Offset printing

(G-2422)
BREWER COMPANY
7300 Main St (45244-3015)
PHONE.............................513 576-6300
Laura Graber, *Plng Mgr*
EMP: 7
SALES (corp-wide): 12.34MM **Privately Held**
Web: www.thebrewerco.com
SIC: 2952 2891 Coating compounds, tar; Adhesives and sealants
PA: The Brewer Company
25 Whitney Dr Ste 104
Milford OH 45150
800 394-0017

(G-2423)
BREWPRO INC
Also Called: Brewer Products Co
9483 Reading Rd (45215-3550)
P.O. Box 62065 (45262-0065)
PHONE.............................513 577-7200
David Brewer, *Pr*
EMP: 6 EST: 1987
SALES (est): 461.42K **Privately Held**
Web: www.brewerproducts.com
SIC: 5082 3531 7353 5169 Road construction equipment; Airport construction machinery; Heavy construction equipment rental; Adhesives and sealants

(G-2424)
BRIDGESTONE RET OPERATIONS LLC
Also Called: Firestone
7800 Montgomery Rd Unit 18 (45236-4388)
PHONE.............................513 793-4550
Derek Lester, *Mgr*
EMP: 8
SQ FT: 6,000
Web: www.bridgestoneamericas.com
SIC: 5531 7534 Automotive tires; Tire retreading and repair shops
HQ: Bridgestone Retail Operations, Llc
200 4th Ave S Ste 100
Nashville TN 37201
615 937-1000

(G-2425)
BRIDGESTONE RET OPERATIONS LLC
Also Called: Firestone
9107 Fields Ertel Rd (45249-8209)
PHONE.............................513 677-5200
John May, *Mgr*
EMP: 6
SQ FT: 6,600
Web: www.bridgestoneamericas.com
SIC: 5531 7534 Automotive tires; Tire retreading and repair shops
HQ: Bridgestone Retail Operations, Llc
200 4th Ave S Ste 100
Nashville TN 37201
615 937-1000

(G-2426)
BRIDGESTONE RET OPERATIONS LLC
Also Called: Michel Tires Plus 227565
272 W Mitchell Ave (45232-1908)
PHONE.............................513 681-7682
Ryan Murray, *Mgr*
EMP: 8
Web: www.bebridgestone.com
SIC: 7534 5531 Tire retreading and repair shops; Automotive tires
HQ: Bridgestone Retail Operations, Llc
200 4th Ave S Ste 100
Nashville TN 37201
615 937-1000

▲ = Import ▼ = Export
◆ = Import/Export

(G-2427)
BROADWAY PRINTING LLC
530 Reading Rd (45202-1407)
PHONE..............................513 621-3429
EMP: 6 EST: 2000
SALES (est): 79.42K Privately Held
SIC: 2759 Commercial printing, nec

(G-2428)
BROCAR PRODUCTS INC
4335 River Rd (45204-1041)
P.O. Box 42295 (45242-0295)
PHONE..............................513 922-2888
John Helmsderfer, Pr
EMP: 21 EST: 1992
SQ FT: 16,000
SALES (est): 1.35MM Privately Held
Web: www.ceobrocar.com
SIC: 2531 Chairs, table and arm

(G-2429)
BRODWILL LLC
3900 Rose Hill Ave Ste C (45229-1454)
PHONE..............................513 258-2716
Rick Williams, Pr
EMP: 8 EST: 2005
SALES (est): 240.73K Privately Held
Web: www.brodwill.com
SIC: 2599 Hospital furniture, except beds

(G-2430)
BROOKWOOD GROUP INC
Also Called: Schauer Battery Chargers
3210 Wasson Rd (45209-2382)
PHONE..............................513 791-3030
Jonathan Chaiken, CEO
▲ EMP: 10 EST: 2009
SQ FT: 10,000
SALES (est): 1.07MM Privately Held
Web: www.battery-chargers.com
SIC: 3629 Battery chargers, rectifying or
   nonrotating

(G-2431)
BSN SPORTS
11480 Enterprise Park Dr (45241-1500)
PHONE..............................513 821-7575
EMP: 6 EST: 2019
SALES (est): 147.08K Privately Held
Web: www.bsnsports.com
SIC: 2759 Commercial printing, nec

(G-2432)
**BUCKLEY MANUFACTURING
COMPANY**
148 Caldwell Dr (45216-1522)
P.O. Box 62117 (45262)
PHONE..............................513 821-4444
Michael G Strotman, Pr
Mary Reardon, Sec
Thomas M Strotman, Treas
Kathleen Strotman, Asst Tr
C M Pulskamp, Prin
EMP: 18 EST: 1947
SALES (est): 4.55MM Privately Held
SIC: 3469 3714 Stamping metal for the trade
   ; Gas tanks, motor vehicle

(G-2433)
BUILDING CTRL INTEGRATORS LLC
300 E Business Way Ste 200 (45241-2389)
PHONE..............................513 247-6154
Dave Milar, Brnch Mgr
EMP: 6
SALES (corp-wide): 8.5MM Privately Held
Web: www.bcicontrols.com
SIC: 3822 Temperature controls, automatic
PA: Building Control Integrators, Llc
   383 N Liberty St
   Powell OH 43065

614 334-3300

(G-2434)
BUSKEN BAKERY INC (PA)
2675 Madison Rd (45208-1389)
PHONE..............................513 871-2114
D Page Busken, Pr
Brian Busken, *
EMP: 90 EST: 1928
SQ FT: 21,000
SALES (est): 29.48MM
SALES (corp-wide): 29.48MM Privately
Held
Web: www.busken.com
SIC: 2045 5461 5149 Blended flour: from
   purchased flour; Bread; Bakery products

(G-2435)
C & W CUSTOM WDWKG CO INC
11949 Tramway Dr (45241-1666)
PHONE..............................513 891-6340
Dave Williams, Prin
Steven Cornett, Prin
EMP: 9 EST: 2000
SQ FT: 3,000
SALES (est): 557.96K Privately Held
Web:
www.candwcustomwoodworking.com
SIC: 2431 Millwork

(G-2436)
CAMARGO PHRM SVCS LLC (DH)
1 E 4th St Ste 1400 (45202-3708)
PHONE..............................513 561-3329
Daniel S Duffy, CEO
Ray Dawkins, CMO
Jim Beach, COO
Carter Gaither, CFO
Reeves Mcgee, CCO
EMP: 11 EST: 2003
SALES (est): 8.12MM
SALES (corp-wide): 21.62MM Privately
Held
Web: www.premierconsulting.com
SIC: 2834 Proprietary drug products
HQ: Premier Research International Llc
   3800 Parmnt Pkwy Ste 400
   Morrisville NC 27560

(G-2437)
CAPTIVE-AIRE SYSTEMS INC
Also Called: Cincinnati Fdsrvice A Slutions
1329 E Kemper Rd Ste 4210 (45246-5100)
PHONE..............................513 860-5555
EMP: 9
SALES (corp-wide): 485.13MM Privately
Held
Web: www.captiveaire.com
SIC: 3444 Restaurant sheet metalwork
PA: Captive-Aire Systems, Inc.
   4641 Pragon Pk Rd Ste 104
   Raleigh NC 27616
   919 882-2410

(G-2438)
CARAUSTAR INDUSTRIES INC
Also Called: Cincinnati Paperboard
5500 Wooster Pike (45226-2227)
PHONE..............................513 871-7112
Allen Hall, Manager
EMP: 45
SALES (corp-wide): 5.45B Publicly Held
Web: www.greif.com
SIC: 2631 Paperboard mills
HQ: Caraustar Industries, Inc.
   5000 Astell Pwdr Sprng Rd
   Austell GA 30106
   770 948-3101

(G-2439)
CARLISLE AND FINCH COMPANY
4562 W Mitchell Ave (45232-1759)
PHONE..............................513 681-6080
Kurtis Finch, CEO
Brent R Finch, *
Garth Finch, *
EMP: 30 EST: 1897
SQ FT: 45,000
SALES (est): 4.48MM Privately Held
Web: www.carlislefinch.com
SIC: 3648 3471 3641 Searchlights; Plating
   and polishing; Electric lamps

(G-2440)
CARUSO FOODS LLC ✪
3465 Hauck Rd (45241-1601)
PHONE..............................513 860-9200
James S Caruso, CEO
Jeff Burt, Pr
Steven J Caruso, Ex VP
David Brown, CFO
EMP: 59 EST: 2023
SALES (est): 4.48MM
SALES (corp-wide): 43MM Privately Held
SIC: 2099 Sandwiches, assembled and
   packaged: for wholesale market
PA: Caruso, Inc.
   3465 Hauck Rd
   Cincinnati OH 45241
   513 860-9200

(G-2441)
CASCO MFG SOLUTIONS INC
3107 Spring Grove Ave (45225-1821)
PHONE..............................513 681-0003
Thomas Mangold, Ch
Melissa Mangold, *
Terri Mangold, *
▲ EMP: 60 EST: 1959
SQ FT: 72,000
SALES (est): 9.93MM Privately Held
Web: www.cascomfg.com
SIC: 2515 7641 3841 2522 Mattresses,
   containing felt, foam rubber, urethane, etc.;
   Upholstery work; Surgical and medical
   instruments; Office furniture, except wood

(G-2442)
CAST-FAB TECHNOLOGIES INC (PA)
3040 Forrer St (45209-1016)
PHONE..............................513 758-1000
EMP: 241 EST: 1940
SALES (est): 9.05MM
SALES (corp-wide): 9.05MM Privately
Held
Web: www.cast-fab.com
SIC: 3499 3321 3441 3322 Machine bases,
   metal; Gray iron castings, nec; Fabricated
   structural metal; Malleable iron foundries

(G-2443)
CATALOG MERCHANDISER INC
Also Called: Portico Merchandising
10525 Chester Rd Ste A (45215-1254)
P.O. Box 196 (52052-0196)
▲ EMP: 11 EST: 1997
SALES (est): 390.69K Privately Held
SIC: 3993 Signs, not made in custom sign
   painting shops

(G-2444)
CBP CO INC
6545 Wiehe Rd (45237-4217)
PHONE..............................513 860-9053
James Yockey, Pr
EMP: 13 EST: 1990
SALES (est): 2.32MM
SALES (corp-wide): 4MM Privately Held
Web: www.cpprinters.com
SIC: 2752 Offset printing

PA: Sjs Packaging Group, Inc.
   6545 Wiehe Rd
   Cincinnati OH 45237
   513 841-1351

(G-2445)
CBST ACQUISITION LLC
Also Called: Dynus Technologies
6900 Steger Dr (45237-3096)
PHONE..............................513 361-9600
EMP: 90 EST: 1983
SQ FT: 80,000
SALES (est): 377.34K Privately Held
SIC: 5065 7629 3357 7622 Telephone
   equipment; Telecommunication equipment
   repair (except telephones); Fiber optic
   cable (insulated); Radio and television
   repair

(G-2446)
CECO ENVIRONMENTAL CORP
Effox-Flextor
9759 Inter Ocean Dr (45246-1027)
PHONE..............................513 874-8915
Jack Neiser, Mgr
EMP: 52
Web: www.cecoenviro.com
SIC: 3443 3441 Fabricated plate work (boiler
   shop); Fabricated structural metal
PA: Ceco Environmental Corp.
   5080 Spectrum Dr Ste 800e
   Addison TX 75001

(G-2447)
CECO FILTERS INC
4625 Red Bank Rd Ste 200 (45227-1552)
PHONE..............................513 458-2600
Mary Buckius, Pr
EMP: 9 EST: 2015
SALES (est): 682.49K Publicly Held
Web: www.cecoenviro.com
SIC: 3564 Filters, air: furnaces, air
   conditioning equipment, etc.
PA: Ceco Environmental Corp.
   5080 Spectrum Dr Ste 800e
   Addison TX 75001

(G-2448)
**CECO GROUP GLOBAL HOLDINGS
LLC (HQ)**
4625 Red Bank Rd Ste 200 (45227-1552)
PHONE..............................513 458-2600
EMP: 13 EST: 2013
SALES (est): 3.87MM Publicly Held
SIC: 3564 Purification and dust collection
   equipment
PA: Ceco Environmental Corp.
   5080 Spectrum Dr Ste 800e
   Addison TX 75001

(G-2449)
CENTRAL FABRICATORS INC
408 Poplar St (45214-2481)
PHONE..............................513 621-1240
David J Angner, Pr
Daniel Meade, *
Micheal Lewis, *
EMP: 26 EST: 1945
SQ FT: 65,000
SALES (est): 3.86MM Privately Held
Web: www.centralfabricators.com
SIC: 3443 Tanks, standard or custom
   fabricated: metal plate

(G-2450)
CENTRAL INVESTMENT LLC (PA)
7265 Kenwood Rd Ste 240 (45236-4411)
PHONE..............................513 563-4700
Keven Shell, Pr
Carl Myers, VP
Manny Zapata, VP

William P Martin, *Sec*
EMP: 16 EST: 2004
SALES (est): 41.54MM **Privately Held**
Web: www.pepsico.com
SIC: 2086 Carbonated soft drinks, bottled
and canned

(G-2451)
CENTRAL READY MIX LLC (PA)
6310 E Kemper Rd Ste 125 (45241-2370)
P.O. Box 70 (45050-0070)
PHONE..............................513 402-5001
TOLL FREE: 888
EMP: 30 EST: 1934
SQ FT: 8,000
SALES (est): 3.38MM
SALES (corp-wide): 3.38MM **Privately
Held**
Web: www.centralrm.com
SIC: 3273 1442 Ready-mixed concrete;
Sand mining

(G-2452)
CENTRAL READY-MIX OF OHIO LLC
6310 E Kemper Rd Ste 125 (45241-2370)
PHONE..............................614 252-3452
EMP: 8 EST: 2000
SALES (est): 896.89K **Privately Held**
SIC: 3273 Ready-mixed concrete

(G-2453)
CENTRAL USA WIRELESS LLC
11210 Montgomery Rd (45249-2311)
PHONE..............................513 469-1500
EMP: 8 EST: 2013
SALES (est): 827.43K **Privately Held**
Web: www.centralusawireless.com
SIC: 7622 3663 Antenna repair and
installation; Antennas, transmitting and
communications

(G-2454)
CFGSC LLC
Also Called: Madisono's Gelato
5927 Belmont Ave (45224-2365)
PHONE..............................513 772-5920
Bryan Madison, *Managing Member*
EMP: 6 EST: 2010
SALES (est): 151.53K **Privately Held**
Web: www.madisonogelato.com
SIC: 2024 Ice cream and ice milk

(G-2455)
CFM INTERNATIONAL INC
111 Merchant St (45246-3730)
PHONE..............................513 563-4180
EMP: 11
SALES (corp-wide): 8.65MM **Privately
Held**
Web: www.cfmaeroengines.com
SIC: 3724 Aircraft engines and engine parts
PA: Cfm International, Inc.
6440 Aviation Way
West Chester OH 45069
513 552-2787

(G-2456)
CFM INTERNATIONAL INC
1 Neumann Way (45215-1900)
PHONE..............................513 563-4180
Pierre Fabre, *Brnch Mgr*
EMP: 11
SALES (corp-wide): 8.65MM **Privately
Held**
Web: www.cfmaeroengines.com
SIC: 3724 Aircraft engines and engine parts
PA: Cfm International, Inc.
6440 Aviation Way
West Chester OH 45069
513 552-2787

(G-2457)
**CH TRANSITION COMPANY LLC
(DH)**
Also Called: Campbell Group
225 Pictoria Dr Ste 210 (45246-1616)
PHONE..............................800 543-6400
Terry Atwater, *Pr*
Dave Kohlmayer, *
◆ **EMP: 112 EST:** 1987
SQ FT: 3,000
SALES (est): 24.57MM
SALES (corp-wide): 424.23B **Publicly
Held**
SIC: 3563 3546 3548 Air and gas
compressors including vacuum pumps;
Power-driven handtools; Welding apparatus
HQ: The Marmon Group Llc
181 W Madison St Ste 3900
Chicago IL 60602

(G-2458)
CHAMPION OPCO LLC (DH)
Also Called: Champion Window
12121 Champion Way (45241-6419)
PHONE..............................513 327-7338
Jim Mishler, *CEO*
Donald R Jones, *
Joe Faisant, *
▲ **EMP: 300 EST:** 2007
SQ FT: 500,000
SALES (est): 496.44MM **Privately Held**
Web: www.championwindow.com
SIC: 3089 1761 3442 Window frames and
sash, plastics; Siding contractor; Storm
doors or windows, metal
HQ: Great Day Improvements, Llc
700 E Highland Rd
Macedonia OH 44056

(G-2459)
CHC FABRICATING CORP (PA)
10270 Wayne Ave (45215-1127)
PHONE..............................513 821-7757
EMP: 58 EST: 1961
SALES (est): 2.6MM
SALES (corp-wide): 2.6MM **Privately Held**
Web: www.chcfab.com
SIC: 1791 3446 3441 Structural steel
erection; Stairs, staircases, stair treads:
prefabricated metal; Fabricated structural
metal

(G-2460)
CHC MANUFACTURING INC (PA)
10270 Wayne Ave (45215-1127)
PHONE..............................513 821-7757
Patrick Mclaughlin, *CEO*
Mark Lambert, *Pr*
Robert J Christen, *VP*
EMP: 21 EST: 2007
SALES (est): 7.33MM
SALES (corp-wide): 7.33MM **Privately
Held**
Web: www.chcfab.com
SIC: 3446 3441 Stairs, staircases, stair
treads: prefabricated metal; Fabricated
structural metal

(G-2461)
CHESTER LABS INC
900 Section Rd Ste A (45237)
PHONE..............................513 458-3871
Robert King, *Prin*
EMP: 25 EST: 1946
SALES (est): 1.58MM **Privately Held**
SIC: 2834 Pharmaceutical preparations

(G-2462)
CHOICE BRANDS ADHESIVES LTD
Also Called: Choice Adhesives
666 Redna Ter Ste 500 (45215-1166)

PHONE..............................800 330-5566
Robert Johnson, *CEO*
EMP: 25 EST: 2010
SALES (est): 2.78MM
SALES (corp-wide): 639.69MM **Privately
Held**
Web: www.choicebrandsadhesives.com
SIC: 2891 Adhesives
PA: Innovative Chemical Products Group,
Llc
150 Dascomb Rd
Andover MA 01810
978 623-9980

(G-2463)
**CHRIS ERHART FOUNDRY & MCH
CO**
Also Called: Erhart Foundry
1240 Mehring Way (45203-1836)
PHONE..............................513 421-6550
Daniel J Erhart, *Pr*
EMP: 10 EST: 1854
SQ FT: 40,000
SALES (est): 1.83MM **Privately Held**
Web: www.erhart.com
SIC: 3321 Gray iron castings, nec

(G-2464)
CIMX LLC
Also Called: Cimx Software
2368 Victory Pkwy Ste 120 (45206-2810)
PHONE..............................513 248-7700
Anthony Cuilwik, *Prin*
Anthony Cuilwik, *Managing Member*
Kristin Cuilwik, *OF Business Operations**
Comfort Wendel, *
EMP: 30 EST: 1996
SALES (est): 4.22MM **Privately Held**
Web: www.cimx.com
SIC: 7372 7371 Prepackaged software;
Custom computer programming services

(G-2465)
CINCINNATI - VULCAN COMPANY
5353 Spring Grove Ave (45217-1026)
PHONE..............................513 242-5300
Garry C Ferraris, *Pr*
EMP: 87 EST: 1912
SQ FT: 6,000
SALES (est): 977.59K
SALES (corp-wide): 5.67MM **Privately
Held**
SIC: 5983 2992 5171 2899 Fuel oil dealers;
Oils and greases, blending and
compounding; Petroleum bulk stations;
Chemical preparations, nec
HQ: Great River Re, Inc.
5353 Spring Grove Ave
Cincinnati OH 45217
513 471-8770

(G-2466)
CINCINNATI A FLTER SLS SVC INC
Also Called: Cafco Filter
4815 Para Dr (45237-5009)
PHONE..............................513 242-3400
TOLL FREE: 800
Edward W Flick, *CEO*
Mark Flick, *Pr*
EMP: 21 EST: 1945
SQ FT: 12,500
SALES (est): 10.61MM **Privately Held**
Web: www.cafcoservices.com
SIC: 5075 7349 3564 Air filters; Building
component cleaning service; Filters, air:
furnaces, air conditioning equipment, etc.

(G-2467)
CINCINNATI ADVG PDTS LLC
Also Called: Wear Magic
12150 Northwest Blvd (45246-1231)

PHONE..............................513 346-7310
Jesse King, *
EMP: 250 EST: 1983
SQ FT: 40,000
SALES (est): 2.36MM
SALES (corp-wide): 229.65MM **Privately
Held**
Web: www.wearmagic.com
SIC: 2262 Screen printing: manmade fiber
and silk broadwoven fabrics
PA: Hit Promotional Products, Inc.
10810 72nd St
Largo FL 33777
727 541-5561

(G-2468)
CINCINNATI AIR CONDITIONING CO
Also Called: Honeywell Authorized Dealer
2080 Northwest Dr (45231-1700)
PHONE..............................513 721-5622
Mark Radtke, *Pr*
Michael Geiger, *
EMP: 55 EST: 1939
SQ FT: 30,000
SALES (est): 15.51MM **Privately Held**
Web: www.cincinnatiair.com
SIC: 1711 3822 Warm air heating and air
conditioning contractor; Environmental
controls

(G-2469)
CINCINNATI ASSN FOR THE BLIND
Also Called: CINCINNATI ASSOCIATION
FOR THE
2045 Gilbert Ave (45202-1490)
PHONE..............................513 221-8558
TOLL FREE: 888
John Mitchell, *CEO*
Ginny Backscheider, *SERVICES**
Jennifer Dubois, *
Amy Scrivner, *OF Development
COMMUNITY Relations**
Bill Neyer, *OF Business Development**
▲ **EMP: 125 EST:** 1910
SQ FT: 88,000
SALES (est): 11.43MM **Privately Held**
Web: www.cincyblind.org
SIC: 8331 8322 2891 7371 Sheltered
workshop; Association for the handicapped;
Adhesives and sealants; Computer
software development

(G-2470)
CINCINNATI BEVERAGE COMPANY
242 W Mcmicken Ave (45214-2314)
PHONE..............................513 904-8910
Jay Woffington, *CEO*
Stacey Schultz, *Prin*
EMP: 20 EST: 2020
SALES (est): 4.44MM **Privately Held**
Web: www.mmamckinney.com
SIC: 2082 Beer (alcoholic beverage)

(G-2471)
**CINCINNATI BIOREFINING CORP
(HQ)**
470 Este Ave (45232)
PHONE..............................513 482-8800
EMP: 10 EST: 2009
SALES (est): 18.97MM **Publicly Held**
SIC: 2079 Edible fats and oils
PA: Marathon Petroleum Corporation
539 S Main St
Findlay OH 45840

(G-2472)
CINCINNATI CONVERTORS INC
1730 Cleneay Ave (45212-3506)
PHONE..............................513 731-6600
Kristin Goltra, *Pr*
EMP: 8 EST: 1973

SQ FT: 15,000
SALES (est): 535.47K **Privately Held**
Web: www.cincinnaticonvertors.com
SIC: 2752 Commercial printing, lithographic

(G-2473)
CINCINNATI CTRL DYNAMICS INC
4924 Para Dr (45237-5012)
PHONE.................................513 242-7300
Jeffrey Bao, *Pr*
Jeffrey Bad, *Dir*
Kweesun Ng, *Dir*
EMP: 8 **EST:** 1976
SQ FT: 20,000
SALES (est): 2.38MM **Privately Held**
Web: www.airflowmachines.com
SIC: 3625 3829 7373 Control equipment,
electric; Measuring and controlling devices,
nec; Systems software development
services

(G-2474)
CINCINNATI ENQUIRER
312 Elm St Fl 18 (45202-2721)
PHONE.................................513 721-2700
Mike Ballman, *Prin*
EMP: 132 **EST:** 2008
SALES (est): 4.07MM **Privately Held**
Web: www.cincinnati.com
SIC: 2711 Newspapers, publishing and
printing

(G-2475)
CINCINNATI GASKET PKG MFG INC
Also Called: Cincinnati Gasket & Indus GL
40 Illinois Ave (45215-5512)
PHONE.................................513 761-3458
Lawrence Uhlenbrock, *Pr*
Pete Knecht, *
Frank Duttenhofer, *
Henry D Hopf, *
◆ **EMP:** 45 **EST:** 1907
SQ FT: 75,000
SALES (est): 3.6MM **Privately Held**
Web: www.cgindustrialglass.com
SIC: 3229 3053 Glassware, industrial;
Gaskets, all materials

(G-2476)
CINCINNATI GEARING SYSTEMS INC
(PA)
5757 Mariemont Ave (45227-4216)
PHONE.................................513 527-8600
Kenneth Kiehl, *Pr*
Walter L Rye, *
EMP: 75 **EST:** 1941
SQ FT: 100,000
SALES (est): 22.68MM
SALES (corp-wide): 22.68MM **Privately
Held**
Web:
www.cincinnatigearingsystems.com
SIC: 3398 3471 Metal heat treating; Plating
and polishing

(G-2477)
CINCINNATI GEARING SYSTEMS INC
301 Milford Pkwy (45227)
PHONE.................................513 527-8634
Kenneth Kiehl, *VP*
EMP: 41
SALES (corp-wide): 22.68MM **Privately
Held**
Web:
www.cincinnatigearingsystems.com
SIC: 3462 Gears, forged steel
PA: Cincinnati Gearing Systems
Incorporated
5757 Mariemont Ave
Cincinnati OH 45227
513 527-8600

(G-2478)
CINCINNATI GILBERT MCH TL LLC
3366 Beekman St (45223-2424)
PHONE.................................513 541-4815
▲ **EMP:** 8 **EST:** 1995
SQ FT: 50,000
SALES (est): 2.03MM **Privately Held**
Web: www.cincinnatigilbert.com
SIC: 3541 Drilling machine tools (metal
cutting)

(G-2479)
CINCINNATI LASER CUTTING LLC
Also Called: Cincinnati Metal Fabricating
891 Redna Ter (45215-1110)
PHONE.................................513 779-7200
Eric Hill, *Pr*
EMP: 40 **EST:** 1999
SQ FT: 45,000
SALES (est): 9.08MM **Privately Held**
Web: www.cincymetalfab.com
SIC: 3441 Fabricated structural metal

(G-2480)
CINCINNATI MARLINS INC
616 W North Bend Rd (45224-1424)
PHONE.................................513 761-3320
Brian Bridgeford, *Pr*
EMP: 8 **EST:** 1961
SQ FT: 500
SALES (est): 935.34K **Privately Held**
Web: www.cincy-marlins.com
SIC: 7997 2086 Country club, membership;
Soft drinks: packaged in cans, bottles, etc.

(G-2481)
CINCINNATI MEDIA LLC
Also Called: Cincinnati Magazine
1818 Race St Ste 301 (45202-7740)
PHONE.................................513 562-2755
Stefan Wanczyk, *CEO*
John Balardo, *Pr*
EMP: 8 **EST:** 2017
SALES (est): 290.69K **Privately Held**
Web: www.cincinnatimedia.com
SIC: 2721 Magazines: publishing and printing

(G-2482)
CINCINNATI MINE MACHINERY CO
(PA)
2950 Jonrose Ave (45239-5319)
PHONE.................................513 522-7777
Robert J Stenger, *Pr*
William D Stenger, *
Jane Wegman, *
Ron Paolello, *
▲ **EMP:** 30 **EST:** 1924
SQ FT: 75,000
SALES (est): 9.41MM
SALES (corp-wide): 9.41MM **Privately
Held**
Web: www.cinmine.com
SIC: 3541 3535 Machine tools, metal cutting
type; Conveyors and conveying equipment

(G-2483)
CINCINNATI PATTERN COMPANY INC
2405 Spring Grove Ave (45214-1727)
PHONE.................................513 241-9872
Michael J Ballard, *Pr*
EMP: 8 **EST:** 1972
SQ FT: 8,000
SALES (est): 1.71MM **Privately Held**
Web: www.cinpat.com
SIC: 3543 Foundry patternmaking

(G-2484)
CINCINNATI RENEWABLE FUELS
LLC
4700 Este Ave (45232-1415)

PHONE.................................513 482-8800
Jeffrie Defraties, *
Rajive Khosla, *
◆ **EMP:** 75 **EST:** 2002
SALES (est): 18.97MM **Publicly Held**
Web: www.twinriverstechnologies.com
SIC: 2079 Edible fats and oils
HQ: Cincinnati Biorefining Corp
470 Este Ave
Cincinnati OH 45232

(G-2485)
CINCINNATI SITE SOLUTIONS LLC
36 E 7th St Ste 1650 (45202-4452)
PHONE.................................513 373-5001
Stephen R Ramsey Esq, *Admn*
EMP: 6 **EST:** 2017
SALES (est): 67.98K **Privately Held**
Web: www.cincinnati.com
SIC: 2711 Newspapers, publishing and
printing

(G-2486)
CINCINNATI STAIR & HANDRAIL
1220 Hill Smith Dr Ste C (45215-1250)
PHONE.................................513 722-3947
Dustin Kreiger, *Owner*
EMP: 11 **EST:** 1975
SALES (est): 451.6K **Privately Held**
Web: www.cincinnatistair.com
SIC: 2431 Millwork

(G-2487)
CINCINNATI STL TREATING CO LLC
5701 Mariemont Ave (45227-4299)
PHONE.................................513 271-3173
Robert W Rye, *Pr*
Walter L Rye, *Ch Bd*
Michael Reichling, *VP*
EMP: 40 **EST:** 2013
SALES (est): 5.39MM **Privately Held**
Web: www.steeltreating.com
SIC: 3398 Metal heat treating

(G-2488)
CINCINNATI THERMAL SPRAY INC
(PA)
Also Called: CTS
10904 Deerfield Rd (45242-4110)
PHONE.................................513 793-0670
▲ **EMP:** 10 **EST:** 1987
SALES (est): 26.54MM **Privately Held**
Web: www.cts-inc.net
SIC: 3479 Coating of metals and formed
products

(G-2489)
CINCINNATI WINDOW SHADE INC
(PA)
Also Called: Cincinnati Window Decor
3004 Harris Ave (45212-2404)
PHONE.................................513 631-7200
James G Frederick, *Pr*
Janet Frederick, *Treas*
James M Frederick, *Sec*
EMP: 16 **EST:** 1934
SQ FT: 15,000
SALES (est): 6.37MM
SALES (corp-wide): 6.37MM **Privately
Held**
Web: www.blindsplusandmore.com
SIC: 5023 5719 2591 Window furnishings;
Window shades, nec; Window shades

(G-2490)
CINCY GLASS INC
3249 Fredonia Ave (45229-3309)
P.O. Box 141476 (45250-1476)
PHONE.................................513 241-0455
Michael T Brown, *Pr*

EMP: 8 **EST:** 1994
SALES (est): 969.3K **Privately Held**
Web: www.cincyglassig.com
SIC: 3441 Fabricated structural metal

(G-2491)
CINDUS CORPORATION
Also Called: Ptp of Mississippi
515 Station Ave (45215-6899)
PHONE.................................513 948-9951
▲ **EMP:** 100 **EST:** 1923
SALES (est): 22.52MM **Privately Held**
Web: www.cindus.com
SIC: 2679 Crepe paper or crepe paper
products: purchased material

(G-2492)
CINEX INC
2641 Cummins St (45225-2099)
PHONE.................................513 921-2825
Gary R Smith, *Pr*
Judith A Smith, *
EMP: 7 **EST:** 1966
SQ FT: 35,000
SALES (est): 968.62K **Privately Held**
Web: www.cinex.com.ve
SIC: 3599 Machine shop, jobbing and repair

(G-2493)
CINFAB LLC
Also Called: Cinfab
5240 Lester Rd (45213-2522)
PHONE.................................513 396-6100
EMP: 140 **EST:** 1982
SQ FT: 36,500
SALES (est): 1.72MM **Privately Held**
Web: www.cinfab.com
SIC: 3444 Sheet metalwork

(G-2494)
CINTAS CORPORATION
Also Called: Cintas Uniforms AP Fcilty Svcs
5570 Ridge Ave (45213-2516)
PHONE.................................513 631-5750
Marie Seng, *Brnch Mgr*
EMP: 100
SALES (corp-wide): 9.6B **Publicly Held**
Web: www.cintas.com
SIC: 2326 2337 7218 5084 Work uniforms;
Uniforms, except athletic: women's,
misses', and juniors'; Industrial uniform
supply; Safety equipment
PA: Cintas Corporation
6800 Cintas Blvd
Mason OH 45040
513 459-1200

(G-2495)
CINTAS SALES CORPORATION (HQ)
Also Called: Cintas
6800 Cintas Blvd (45262)
PHONE.................................513 459-1200
Richard T Farmer, *Ch Bd*
Robert J Kohlhepp, *
Scott Farmer, *
Bill Gale, *
EMP: 450 **EST:** 1987
SALES (est): 6.88MM
SALES (corp-wide): 9.6B **Publicly Held**
Web: www.cintas.com
SIC: 7218 2326 5136 5137 Industrial uniform
supply; Work uniforms; Uniforms, men's
and boys'; Uniforms, women's and
children's
PA: Cintas Corporation
6800 Cintas Blvd
Mason OH 45040
513 459-1200

(G-2496)
CITYWIDE MATERIALS INC
Also Called: Citywide Ready Mix
5263 Wooster Pike (45226-2228)
PHONE.................................513 533-1111
Jerry Powell Junior, *Ch Bd*
Mark Cassiere, *Pr*
EMP: 20 **EST:** 1992
SQ FT: 560
SALES (est): 2.4MM **Privately Held**
Web: www.citywidematerials.com
SIC: 3273 Ready-mixed concrete

(G-2497)
CLARKE POWER SERVICES INC
Also Called: Clarke Fire Protection Product
3133 E Kemper Rd (45241-1516)
PHONE.................................513 771-2200
Dane Petrie, *Mgr*
EMP: 24
SALES (corp-wide): 225.9MM **Privately Held**
Web: www.clarkepowerservices.com
SIC: 3463 Pump, compressor, turbine, and engine forgings, except auto
PA: Clarke Power Services, Inc.
　3133 E Kemper Rd
　Cincinnati OH 45241
　513 771-2200

(G-2498)
CLEARVIEW CONSTRUCTION LLC
Also Called: Clearview Roof and Remodelling
4520 Bridgetown Rd # 1 (45211-4440)
PHONE.................................513 206-6415
Antionette Sibert, *Admn*
EMP: 9 **EST:** 2013
SALES (est): 327.2K **Privately Held**
Web: www.clearviewconstructionllc-oh.com
SIC: 1521 1761 3069 Single-family housing construction; Roofing and gutter work; Roofing, membrane rubber

(G-2499)
CLIPSONS METAL WORKING INC
Also Called: Clipson S Metalworking
127 Novner Dr (45215-1300)
PHONE.................................513 772-6393
Stuart Clipson, *Pr*
Patricia Clipson, *VP*
EMP: 7 **EST:** 1982
SQ FT: 7,500
SALES (est): 962.44K **Privately Held**
SIC: 3599 7692 3441 Machine shop, jobbing and repair; Welding repair; Fabricated structural metal

(G-2500)
CLOVERNOOK CTR FOR BLIND VSLLY (PA)
7000 Hamilton Ave (45231-5240)
PHONE.................................513 522-3860
Robin Usalis, *Pr*
Christopher Faust, *
Douglas Jacques, *
Betsy Baugh, *
Jacqueline L Conner, *
EMP: 125 **EST:** 1958
SQ FT: 40,000
SALES (est): 9.05MM
SALES (corp-wide): 9.05MM **Privately Held**
Web: www.clovernook.org
SIC: 2656 8322 7389 Paper cups, plates, dishes, and utensils; Rehabilitation services ; Fund raising organizations

(G-2501)
CLUB 513 LLC
201 E 5th St 19th Fl (45202-4152)
PHONE.................................800 530-2574
Aaron R Chiles, *Managing Member*
EMP: 6 **EST:** 2004
SQ FT: 3,500
SALES (est): 182.96K **Privately Held**
Web: www.club513llc.com
SIC: 7929 2759 5099 Entertainment group; Letterpress and screen printing; Novelties, durable

(G-2502)
CMT IMPORTS INC (PA)
2930 Glendale Milford Rd Ste 330 (45241-3398)
PHONE.................................513 615-1851
Wendell Hunsucker, *Pr*
Emily Triantos, *VP Sls*
Brent Atrick, *VP Opers*
▲ **EMP:** 6 **EST:** 2001
SQ FT: 2,300
SALES (est): 9.58MM
SALES (corp-wide): 9.58MM **Privately Held**
Web: www.cmtimports.com
SIC: 5051 3363 3321 3324 Castings, rough: iron or steel; Aluminum die-castings; Ductile iron castings; Commercial investment castings, ferrous

(G-2503)
COCA-COLA CONSOLIDATED INC
Also Called: Coca-Cola
5100 Duck Creek Rd (45227-1450)
PHONE.................................513 527-6600
John Whitaker, *Mgr*
EMP: 1571
SALES (corp-wide): 6.9B **Publicly Held**
Web: www.cokeconsolidated.com
SIC: 2086 Bottled and canned soft drinks
PA: Coca-Cola Consolidated, Inc.
　4100 Coca-Cola Plz
　Charlotte NC 28211
　980 392-8298

(G-2504)
COMBINED CONTAINERBOARD INC
7741 School Rd (45249-1513)
PHONE.................................513 530-5700
Phil Wenger, *Genl Mgr*
EMP: 52 **EST:** 1987
SQ FT: 162,000
SALES (est): 13.73MM
SALES (corp-wide): 5.45B **Publicly Held**
SIC: 2653 Sheets, corrugated: made from purchased materials
HQ: Greif Packaging Llc
　5800 Cane Run Rd
　Louisville KY 40258

(G-2505)
COMMUNICATIONS AID INC
Also Called: University Hring Aid Assctions
222 Piedmont Ave Ste 5200 (45219-4222)
PHONE.................................513 475-8453
Stephanie Lockhart, *Pr*
Myles Pensak, *Dir*
EMP: 10 **EST:** 1978
SALES (est): 84.88K **Privately Held**
SIC: 5999 3842 Communication equipment; Hearing aids

(G-2506)
COMPLETE CYLINDER SERVICE INC
1240 Glendale Milford Rd (45215-1269)
PHONE.................................513 772-1500
David Kleier, *Prin*
EMP: 8 **EST:** 2012
SALES (est): 485.98K **Privately Held**
Web: complete-cylinder-service.business.site
SIC: 3272 Cylinder pipe, prestressed or pretensioned concrete

(G-2507)
COMPLETE MECHANICAL SVCS LLC
Also Called: Cincinnati Mechanical Svcs LLC
11399 Grooms Rd (45242-1405)
PHONE.................................513 489-3080
Bruce Ducker, *
Daniel G Dulle, *
Robert Sambrookes, *
Wyane Miller, *
EMP: 97 **EST:** 2000
SQ FT: 20,000
SALES (est): 28.93MM **Privately Held**
Web: www.completemech.com
SIC: 1711 3443 Mechanical contractor; Tank towers, metal plate

(G-2508)
COMPUTER PRODUCTS CORPORATION (PA)
3950 Virginia Ave (45227-3412)
PHONE.................................513 221-0600
Kurtis Lindemann, *Owner*
Tom Volpenhein, *
Jim Volpenhein, *
Carla Brose, *
▲ **EMP:** 29 **EST:** 1962
SQ FT: 40,000
SALES (est): 25.05MM
SALES (corp-wide): 25.05MM **Privately Held**
Web: www.cpc-i.com
SIC: 5734 7372 7379 Computer peripheral equipment; Business oriented computer software; Online services technology consultants

(G-2509)
CONCENTRIX CVG LLC (DH)
201 E 4th St (45202-4248)
PHONE.................................972 454-8000
James A Milton, *Managing Member*
David W Branderburg, *
Michael J Willner, *
Craig E Holmes, *
Dean C Howell, *
EMP: 97 **EST:** 2011
SALES (est): 22.47MM
SALES (corp-wide): 9.62B **Publicly Held**
SIC: 3661 PBX equipment, manual or automatic
HQ: Concentrix Cvg Corporation
　201 E 4th St
　Cincinnati OH 45202
　800 747-0583

(G-2510)
CONSOLDTED ANLYTCAL SYSTEMS IN
Also Called: Cas
2629 Spring Grove Ave (45214-1731)
PHONE.................................513 542-1200
Seth Cloran, *Pr*
Jim Tish, *VP*
John Tish, *Sec*
EMP: 14 **EST:** 2012
SALES (est): 4.59MM **Privately Held**
Web: www.cas-en.com
SIC: 8711 2452 3448 3823 Consulting engineer; Prefabricated buildings, wood; Prefabricated metal buildings and components; Chromatographs, industrial process type

(G-2511)
CONSOLIDATED METAL PDTS INC (PA)
1028 Depot St (45204-2073)
PHONE.................................513 251-2624
John Bernloehr, *Pr*
Hugh M Gallagher Junior, *Pr*
John J Kropp, *
EMP: 77 **EST:** 1945
SQ FT: 150,000
SALES (est): 9.84MM
SALES (corp-wide): 9.84MM **Privately Held**
Web: www.cmpubolt.com
SIC: 3452 3316 3356 Bolts, metal; Cold finishing of steel shapes; Nonferrous rolling and drawing, nec

(G-2512)
CONTACT CONTROL INTERFACES LLC
231 W 12th St Ste 201c (45202-8001)
PHONE.................................609 333-3264
Thomas Buchanan, *Prin*
EMP: 9 **EST:** 2016
SALES (est): 7.45MM **Privately Held**
Web: www.contact.ci
SIC: 3577 Computer peripheral equipment, nec

(G-2513)
CONTINENTAL MINERAL PROCESSING CORPORATION
11817 Mosteller Rd (45241-1524)
P.O. Box 62005 (45262-0005)
PHONE.................................513 771-7190
◆ **EMP:** 20 **EST:** 1948
SALES (est): 4.31MM **Privately Held**
Web: www.continentalmineral.com
SIC: 3295 Minerals, ground or treated

(G-2514)
CONTROL CRAFT LLC
1123 Hickorywood Ct (45233-4845)
PHONE.................................513 674-0056
EMP: 10 **EST:** 2000
SALES (est): 823.23K **Privately Held**
Web: www.controlcraftllc.com
SIC: 3613 Control panels, electric

(G-2515)
CONTROLS AND SHEET METAL INC (PA)
1051 Sargent St (45203-1858)
PHONE.................................513 721-3610
Rick Schaible, *Pr*
Danny D Bishop, *Prin*
Anthony S Knuckles, *Prin*
EMP: 21 **EST:** 1983
SQ FT: 40,000
SALES (est): 9.33MM
SALES (corp-wide): 9.33MM **Privately Held**
SIC: 5075 3444 Warm air heating and air conditioning; Ducts, sheet metal

(G-2516)
COOPERSURGICAL INC
P.O. Box 712280 (45271-2280)
PHONE.................................203 601-5200
EMP: 6
SALES (corp-wide): 3.9B **Publicly Held**
Web: www.coopersurgical.com
SIC: 5047 3842 3841 3845 Medical equipment and supplies; Gynecological supplies and appliances; Surgical and medical instruments; Electromedical equipment
HQ: Coopersurgical, Inc.
　75 Corporate Dr

▲ = Import ▼ = Export
◆ = Import/Export

Trumbull CT 06611

(G-2517)
CORE OPTIX INC
821 Melbourne St (45229-3311)
PHONE.....................855 267-3678
Joseph Kreidler, *Pr*
Joseph Kriedler, *Pr*
John Thomson, *VP*
◆ **EMP:** 10 **EST:** 2011
SQ FT: 8,000
SALES (est): 516.9K **Privately Held**
Web: www.coreoptix.com
SIC: 2298 3357 3351 Cable, fiber; Fiber optic cable (insulated); Wire, copper and copper alloy

(G-2518)
CORPORATE DCMENT SOLUTIONS INC (PA)
11120 Ashburn Rd (45240-3813)
PHONE.....................513 595-8200
Mary C Percy, *Pr*
Harold B Percy Junior, *VP*
EMP: 9 **EST:** 1992
SQ FT: 15,000
SALES (est): 2.66MM **Privately Held**
Web: www.cdsprint.com
SIC: 7334 2752 2759 Photocopying and duplicating services; Offset and photolithographic printing; Commercial printing, nec

(G-2519)
CORRUGATED CHEMICALS INC
Also Called: Corrugated Chemicals
3865 Virginia Ave (45227-3409)
PHONE.....................513 561-7773
Tod Sistrunk, *Mgr*
EMP: 6
SQ FT: 23,940
SALES (corp-wide): 5.1MM **Privately Held**
Web: www.corrugatedchemicals.com
SIC: 2869 5169 Industrial organic chemicals, nec; Chemicals and allied products, nec
PA: Corrugated Chemicals, Inc.
5410 Homberg Dr Ste 20
Knoxville TN 37919
865 588-2471

(G-2520)
COVIDIEN HOLDING INC
Also Called: Covidien
2111 E Galbraith Rd (45237-1624)
PHONE.....................513 948-7219
EMP: 182
Web: www.medtronic.com
SIC: 3841 Surgical and medical instruments
HQ: Covidien Holding Inc.
710 Medtronic Pkwy
Minneapolis MN 55432

(G-2521)
CPG - OHIO LLC (HQ)
470 Northland Blvd (45240-3211)
PHONE.....................513 825-4800
Chaim Kaufman, *
EMP: 51 **EST:** 2016
SALES (est): 7.78MM
SALES (corp-wide): 57.46MM **Privately Held**
Web: www.conpackgroup.com
SIC: 2671 2673 Plastic film, coated or laminated for packaging; Plastic bags: made from purchased materials
PA: Consolidated Packaging Group, Inc.
30 Bergen Tpke
Ridgefield Park NJ 07660
201 440-4240

(G-2522)
CRACO EMBROIDERY INC
37 Techview Dr (45215-1980)
PHONE.....................513 563-6999
Bob Crable, *Pr*
Rick Crable, *VP*
EMP: 9 **EST:** 1991
SQ FT: 1,200
SALES (est): 97.02K **Privately Held**
SIC: 2395 Emblems, embroidered

(G-2523)
CRANIAL TECHNOLOGIES INC
4030 Smith Rd Ste 105 (45209-0008)
PHONE.....................844 447-5894
Tammy Jones, *Brnch Mgr*
EMP: 6
Web: www.cranialtech.com
SIC: 3842 Braces, orthopedic
PA: Cranial Technologies, Inc.
1405 W Auto Dr Ste 201
Tempe AZ 85284

(G-2524)
CREE LOGISTICS LLC
Also Called: UPS Store 7395
7439 Wooster Pike (45227-3895)
PHONE.....................513 978-1112
James W Cree, *Mgr*
EMP: 6 **EST:** 2021
SALES (est): 300K **Privately Held**
SIC: 3861 Printing frames, photographic

(G-2525)
CREST CRAFT CO
4460 Lake Forest Dr Ste 232 (45242-3755)
PHONE.....................513 271-4858
Bradley Olsen, *Pr*
EMP: 10 **EST:** 1946
SQ FT: 44,000
SALES (est): 994.32K **Privately Held**
Web: www.crestcraft.com
SIC: 3499 Novelties and giftware, including trophies

(G-2526)
CROHM LLC
1640 Lionel Ave (45214-1571)
PHONE.....................513 921-9400
Michael C Crowe, *Admn*
Michael C Crowe, *Prin*
John C Crowe, *Prin*
EMP: 8 **EST:** 2019
SALES (est): 507.29K **Privately Held**
Web: www.crohm.com
SIC: 8742 3629 Business management consultant; Blasting machines, electrical

(G-2527)
CROWN EQUIPMENT CORPORATION
Also Called: Crown Lift Trucks
10685 Medallion Dr (45241-4827)
PHONE.....................513 874-2600
Dave Kelly, *Mgr*
EMP: 85
SALES (corp-wide): 7.12B **Privately Held**
Web: www.crown.com
SIC: 3537 Lift trucks, industrial: fork, platform, straddle, etc.
PA: Crown Equipment Corporation
44 S Washington St
New Bremen OH 45869
419 629-2311

(G-2528)
CSP GROUP INC
7141 E Kemper Rd (45249-1028)
PHONE.....................513 984-9500
EMP: 20
Web: www.lumisigns.com

SIC: 3993 Signs and advertising specialties

(G-2529)
CTEK TOOL & MACHINE COMPANY
11310 Southland Rd (45240-3201)
PHONE.....................513 742-0423
Phyllis Couch, *Pr*
James Couch, *VP*
EMP: 6 **EST:** 1993
SQ FT: 6,500
SALES (est): 1.41MM **Privately Held**
Web: www.ctektool.com
SIC: 3599 Machine shop, jobbing and repair

(G-2530)
CTL-AEROSPACE INC (PA)
Also Called: OEM
5616 Spellmire Dr (45246-4898)
PHONE.....................513 874-7900
James T Irwin, *Pr*
Robert W Buechner, *
Vicki Osborne, *
John Irwin, *
John Macleod, *
EMP: 205 **EST:** 1946
SQ FT: 100,000
SALES (est): 47.06MM
SALES (corp-wide): 47.06MM **Privately Held**
Web: www.ctlaerospace.com
SIC: 3728 Aircraft assemblies, subassemblies, and parts, nec

(G-2531)
CUSTOM MATERIAL HDLG EQP LLC
7868 Gapstow Brg (45231-6058)
PHONE.....................513 235-5336
EMP: 6 **EST:** 2006
SALES (est): 410.87K **Privately Held**
SIC: 2411 Logging camps and contractors

(G-2532)
CUSTOM QUALITY PRODUCTS INC
1645 Blue Rock St (45223-7500)
EMP: 23 **EST:** 1982
SALES (est): 2.2MM **Privately Held**
Web: www.cqpinc.com
SIC: 3442 Metal doors, sash, and trim

(G-2533)
CUSTOM TOOLING COMPANY
603 Wayne Park Dr (45215-2848)
PHONE.....................513 733-5790
Thomas Brune, *Pr*
Charles Brune, *VP*
EMP: 10 **EST:** 1963
SQ FT: 5,000
SALES (est): 1.62MM **Privately Held**
Web: www.custom-tooling.com
SIC: 3599 Machine shop, jobbing and repair

(G-2534)
D & J MANUFACTURING JEWELER
7793 Colerain Ave Ste B (45239-4503)
PHONE.....................513 541-5200
Joachim V Daskevics, *Prin*
Joachim Daskevics, *Owner*
Pam Daskevics, *Mgr*
EMP: 7 **EST:** 1985
SQ FT: 2,000
SALES (est): 104.33K **Privately Held**
SIC: 5944 3911 Jewelry, precious stones and precious metals; Jewelry, precious metal

(G-2535)
D & M SAW & TOOL INC
Also Called: Eccles Saw & Tool
2974 P G Graves Ln (45241-3155)
PHONE.....................513 871-5433

Michael Hugenberg, *Pr*
EMP: 9 **EST:** 1954
SQ FT: 6,000
SALES (est): 255.97K **Privately Held**
Web: www.ecclessaw.com
SIC: 7699 5251 3423 Knife, saw and tool sharpening and repair; Chainsaws; Cutting dies, except metal cutting

(G-2536)
D C MORRISON COMPANY INC
11959 Tramway Dr (45241-1666)
P.O. Box 12586 (41012-0586)
PHONE.....................859 581-7511
Henry E Reder, *Pr*
Roger E Reder, *
Bernice Reder, *
Greg Reder, *
EMP: 30 **EST:** 1963
SALES (est): 2.33MM **Privately Held**
Web: www.dcmorrison.com
SIC: 3545 3542 Machine tool attachments and accessories; Machine tools, metal forming type

(G-2537)
D F ELECTRONICS INC
200 Novner Dr (45215-6002)
PHONE.....................513 772-7792
Donald Fine, *Pr*
Ann Fine, *
EMP: 75 **EST:** 1975
SQ FT: 27,000
SALES (est): 3.89MM **Privately Held**
Web: www.dfelectronics.com
SIC: 3674 Solid state electronic devices, nec

(G-2538)
D+H USA CORPORATION
Also Called: DH
312 Plum St Ste 500 (45202-4810)
PHONE.....................513 381-9400
EMP: 173
SALES (corp-wide): 1.24B **Privately Held**
SIC: 7372 Application computer software
HQ: D+H Usa Corporation
1320 Sw Broadway Ste 100
Portland OR 97204
407 804-6600

(G-2539)
DADCO INC
Also Called: Rpp Containers
10111 Evendale Commons Dr
(45241-2689)
PHONE.....................513 489-2244
Scott Denoma, *Pr*
Jim West, *VP*
EMP: 17 **EST:** 1998
SALES (est): 11.76MM **Privately Held**
Web: www.rppcontainers.com
SIC: 5085 3089 Bins and containers, storage; Plastics containers, except foam

(G-2540)
DALE KESTLER
Also Called: Apollo GL Mirror Win Screen Co
3475 Cardiff Ave (45209-1317)
PHONE.....................513 871-9000
Dale Kestler, *Pr*
EMP: 8 **EST:** 1991
SQ FT: 1,500
SALES (est): 637.84K **Privately Held**
Web: www.apolloglassmirror.com
SIC: 5231 5719 5211 3442 Glass; Mirrors; Door and window products; Screens, window, metal

(G-2541)

DARLING INGREDIENTS INC
Also Called: Cincinnati Transfer Station
3105 Spring Grove Ave (45225-1821)
PHONE......................972 717-0300
Tim Fontaine, *Mgr*
EMP: 9
SALES (corp-wide): 6.79B **Publicly Held**
Web: www.darlingii.com
SIC: 2077 Animal and marine fats and oils
PA: Darling Ingredients Inc.
5601 N Macarthur Blvd
Irving TX 75038
972 717-0300

(G-2542)

DATA PROCESSING SCIENCES CORPORATION
Also Called: Dpsciences
2 Camargo Cyn (45243-2945)
PHONE......................513 791-7100
▼ **EMP:** 65
SIC: 4813 5045 3669 3577 Telephone communication, except radio; Computers, peripherals, and software; Intercommunication systems, electric; Computer peripheral equipment, nec

(G-2543)

DEBRA-KUEMPEL INC (HQ)
Also Called: De Bra - Kuempel
3976 Southern Ave (45227-3562)
P.O. Box 701620 (45227)
PHONE......................513 271-6500
Fred B De Bra, *Ch Bd*
Joe D Clark, *
Morris H Reed, *
Debbie Biggs, *
Bill Flaugher, *
EMP: 73 **EST:** 1944
SQ FT: 20,079
SALES (est): 46.84MM
SALES (corp-wide): 14.57B **Publicly Held**
Web: www.dkemcor.com
SIC: 3446 1711 3443 3441 Architectural metalwork; Mechanical contractor; Fabricated plate work (boiler shop); Fabricated structural metal
PA: Emcor Group, Inc.
301 Merritt 7
Norwalk CT 06851
203 849-7800

(G-2544)

DEGUSSA INCORPORATED
620 Shepherd Dr (45215-2104)
PHONE......................513 733-5111
Probyn Forbes, *Prin*
▲ **EMP:** 6 **EST:** 2008
SALES (est): 241.82K **Privately Held**
SIC: 2816 Inorganic pigments

(G-2545)

DELTA POWER SUPPLY INC
10330 Chester Rd (45215-1225)
PHONE......................513 771-3835
Rodney G Thiemann, *CEO*
Rodney Thiemann, *CEO*
Denny Beasley, *Sr VP*
▲ **EMP:** 11 **EST:** 1995
SQ FT: 7,500
SALES (est): 946.76K **Privately Held**
SIC: 3648 Lighting equipment, nec

(G-2546)

DERRICK COMPANY INC
4560 Kellogg Ave (45226-2499)
PHONE......................513 321-8122
Gary Schmid, *CEO*
Jason Schmid, *
Kathie Schmid, *

EMP: 25 **EST:** 1923
SQ FT: 170,000
SALES (est): 5.46MM **Privately Held**
Web: www.derrickcompany.com
SIC: 3398 3471 Metal heat treating; Sand blasting of metal parts

(G-2547)

DESIGN MASTERS INC
800 Redna Ter (45215-1111)
PHONE......................513 772-7175
Terry Masters, *Pr*
EMP: 6 **EST:** 1994
SALES (est): 452.25K **Privately Held**
Web: www.dmisigns.com
SIC: 3993 7532 7319 Signs, not made in custom sign painting shops; Truck painting and lettering; Display advertising service

(G-2548)

DEVICOR MED PDTS HOLDINGS INC
300 E Business Way Fl 5 (45241-2384)
PHONE......................513 864-9000
Thomas D Daulton, *CEO*
David Nuty, *
Jonathan Salkin, *
EMP: 550 **EST:** 2010
SALES (est): 48.56MM **Privately Held**
Web: www.mammotome.com
SIC: 3841 Surgical and medical instruments

(G-2549)

DIGITAL FACTORY TECH INC
Also Called: Digital Factory
407 Race St (45202-3757)
PHONE......................513 560-4074
Lawrence Griffith, *CEO*
Allan Tsao, *
EMP: 33 **EST:** 2016
SALES (est): 436.19K **Privately Held**
Web: www.dgtl-factory.com
SIC: 3993 Signs and advertising specialties

(G-2550)

DIMENSION MACHINE COMPANY INC
6614 Lebanon St (45216-1931)
PHONE......................513 242-9996
Donald P Barth, *Pr*
EMP: 8 **EST:** 1994
SQ FT: 12,000
SALES (est): 956.68K **Privately Held**
Web: www.dimensionmachinecompany.com
SIC: 3599 Machine shop, jobbing and repair

(G-2551)

DITSCH USA LLC
1100 E Kemper Rd (45246-3321)
PHONE......................513 782-8888
Thorsten Schroeder, *Brnch Mgr*
EMP: 42
SIC: 2052 Cookies and crackers
HQ: Ditsch Usa, Llc
311 Northland Blvd
Cincinnati OH 45246
513 782-8888

(G-2552)

DITSCH USA LLC (DH)
311 Northland Blvd (45246-3690)
PHONE......................513 782-8888
Gary Gottenbusch, *CEO*
Brian Tooley, *CFO*
EMP: 8 **EST:** 2014
SQ FT: 100,000
SALES (est): 3.38MM **Privately Held**
Web: www.ditsch.com
SIC: 2052 5149 Pretzels; Bakery products
HQ: Valora Holding Ag
Hofackerstrasse 40
Muttenz BL 4132

(G-2553)

DIVERSEYLEVER INC
3630 E Kemper Rd (45241-2011)
PHONE......................513 554-4200
Richard Koch, *Pr*
EMP: 8 **EST:** 2017
SALES (est): 343.2K **Privately Held**
Web: www.duboischemicals.com
SIC: 2819 Industrial inorganic chemicals, nec

(G-2554)

DIVERSIFIED OPHTHALMICS INC
Also Called: Diversified SE Division
250 Mccullough St (45226-2145)
PHONE......................803 783-3454
Sara Baldwin, *Mgr*
EMP: 47
SIC: 5048 3851 5049 Contact lenses; Contact lenses; Optical goods
HQ: Diversified Ophthalmics, Inc.
250 Mccullough St
Cincinnati OH
800 852-8089

(G-2555)

DIVERSIPAK INC
838 Reedy St (45202-2216)
PHONE......................513 321-7884
Dan Kunkemoeller, *CEO*
Jennifer Kunkemoeller, *
Greg Lamping, *
Douglas Hearn, *
Jake Linz, *
EMP: 50 **EST:** 1998
SQ FT: 15,000
SALES (est): 2.48MM **Privately Held**
Web: www.diversipak.com
SIC: 2671 Paper, coated or laminated for packaging

(G-2556)

DIVISION OVERHEAD DOOR INC (PA)
Also Called: Cincinnati Prof Door Sls Div
861 Dellway St (45229-3305)
P.O. Box 12588 (41012-0588)
PHONE......................513 872-0888
Robert H Mc Kibben Junior, *Pr*
Pat Higgins, *VP*
Jim Morrison, *Sec*
EMP: 19 **EST:** 1942
SQ FT: 12,000
SALES (est): 2.96MM
SALES (corp-wide): 2.96MM **Privately Held**
Web: www.divisionoverheaddoor.com
SIC: 3442 2431 7699 1751 Garage doors, overhead: metal; Garage doors, overhead, wood; Garage door repair; Garage door, installation or erection

(G-2557)

DOMINION LIQUID TECH LLC
Also Called: D L T
3965 Virginia Ave (45227-3411)
PHONE......................513 272-2824
Charles Cain, *Managing Member*
EMP: 41 **EST:** 2003
SQ FT: 54,000
SALES (est): 12.45MM **Privately Held**
Web: www.dltdelivers.com
SIC: 2087 2033 Syrups, drink; Barbecue sauce: packaged in cans, jars, etc.

(G-2558)

DOMTAR CORP
9435 Waterstone Blvd Ste 360
(45249-8227)
PHONE......................803 802-7500
EMP: 8 **EST:** 2018
SALES (est): 243.3K **Privately Held**
Web: www.domtar.com

SIC: 2621 Paper mills

(G-2559)

DOSMATIC USA INC
3798 Round Bottom Rd (45244-2413)
PHONE......................972 245-9765
Jeff Rowe, *Pr*
Steve Vogel, *
▲ **EMP:** 30 **EST:** 1990
SQ FT: 25,000
SALES (est): 258.67K **Privately Held**
Web: www.hydrosystemsco.com
SIC: 3569 Liquid automation machinery and equipment

(G-2560)

DOVER WIPES COMPANY
1 Procter And Gamble Plz (45202-3315)
PHONE......................513 983-1100
EMP: 14 **EST:** 1999
SALES (est): 25.88MM
SALES (corp-wide): 84.04B **Publicly Held**
SIC: 2844 Deodorants, personal
PA: The Procter & Gamble Company
1 Procter & Gamble Plz
Cincinnati OH 45202
513 983-1100

(G-2561)

DOWNHOME INC
Also Called: Down Decor Ohio Feather
1910 South St (45204-2034)
PHONE......................513 921-3373
EMP: 33
Web: www.downdecor.com
SIC: 2392 Pillows, bed: made from purchased materials
PA: Downhome, Inc.
1 Kovach Dr
Cincinnati OH 45215

(G-2562)

DOWNHOME INC (PA)
Also Called: Down Decor
1 Kovach Dr (45215-1000)
PHONE......................513 921-3373
Daniel Guigui, *Pr*
▲ **EMP:** 44 **EST:** 1994
SALES (est): 8.14MM **Privately Held**
Web: www.downdecor.com
SIC: 2392 Pillows, bed: made from purchased materials

(G-2563)

DSS INSTALLATIONS LTD
Also Called: Dss/Drect Tv/Rfs/Ms/rmediation
6721 Montgomery Rd Ste 1 (45236-3890)
P.O. Box 36520 (45236-0520)
PHONE......................513 761-7000
Allen Sheff, *Pt*
Allen Sheff, *Managing Member*
EMP: 8 **EST:** 1990
SALES (est): 429.31K **Privately Held**
Web: www.dssinstallations.com
SIC: 5731 1731 7622 3825 Antennas, satellite dish; Cable television installation; Antenna repair and installation; Radio frequency measuring equipment

(G-2564)

DSWDWK LLC
Also Called: Taft's Ale House
4831 Spring Grove Ave (45232-1938)
PHONE......................513 853-5021
EMP: 6 **EST:** 2013
SALES (est): 6.75MM **Privately Held**
Web: www.taftsbeer.com
SIC: 2082 Malt beverages

▲ = Import ▼ = Export
◆ = Import/Export

(G-2565)
DURO BAG MANUFACTURING COMPANY (PA)
Also Called: Duro Standard Products Company
441 Vine St Ste 200 (45202-2836)
PHONE...............................800 879-3876
Charles Shor, *Pr*
Gerry Otto, *
◆ **EMP:** 100 **EST:** 1953
SQ FT: 30,000
SALES (est): 6.3MM
SALES (corp-wide): 6.3MM **Privately Held**
Web: www.novolex.com
SIC: 2674 Paper bags: made from purchased materials

(G-2566)
DWD2 INC
10200 Wayne Ave (45215-1127)
P.O. Box 15627 (45215-0627)
PHONE...............................513 563-0070
David Draginoff, *CEO*
Sandra Draginoff, *Sec*
Jack Taylor Contl, *Prin*
Mike Trovillo, *VP*
EMP: 17 **EST:** 1972
SQ FT: 11,500
SALES (est): 5.41MM **Privately Held**
Web: www.pridetool.com
SIC: 3599 Machine shop, jobbing and repair

(G-2567)
DYNAMIC INDUSTRIES INC
3611 Woodburn Ave (45207-1019)
PHONE...............................513 861-6767
Phillip J Mitchell, *Pr*
Henry W Ochs, *
EMP: 33 **EST:** 1985
SQ FT: 150,000
SALES (est): 6.79MM **Privately Held**
Web: www.dynamicindustries.com
SIC: 3599 Machine shop, jobbing and repair

(G-2568)
E & J GALLO WINERY
125 E Court St (45202-1212)
PHONE...............................513 381-4050
Holly Mcclelland, *Mgr*
EMP: 38
SALES (corp-wide): 2.11B **Privately Held**
Web: www.gallo.com
SIC: 2084 Wines
PA: E. & J. Gallo Winery
600 Yosemite Blvd
Modesto CA 95354
877 687-9463

(G-2569)
E C SHAW COMPANY OF OHIO
1242 Mehring Way (45203-1836)
PHONE...............................513 721-6334
Joseph Grome, *Pr*
Robert Grome, *OF Purchasing*
Kenneth Grome, *
EMP: 30 **EST:** 1912
SQ FT: 12,000
SALES (est): 5.69MM **Privately Held**
Web: www.ecshaw.com
SIC: 3555 3953 3469 2821 Printing plates; Marking devices; Metal stampings, nec; Plastics materials and resins

(G-2570)
E I CERAMICS LLC
2600 Commerce Blvd (45241-1552)
PHONE...............................513 772-7001
Graham J Roberts, *Managing Member*
▲ **EMP:** 60 **EST:** 2002
SALES (est): 11.8MM **Privately Held**

SIC: 3297 Graphite refractories: carbon bond or ceramic bond
HQ: Ifgl Refractories Limited
3, Netaji Subash Road,
Kolkata WB 70000

(G-2571)
E P S SPECIALISTS LTD INC
7875 School Rd (45249-1531)
PHONE...............................513 489-3676
Ed L Wilkson, *Pr*
Lee Wilkinson, *VP*
EMP: 6 **EST:** 1989
SALES (est): 170.46K **Privately Held**
Web: www.lamlite.com
SIC: 2821 Plastics materials and resins

(G-2572)
EAGLE CREEK INC
Also Called: EAGLE CREEK, INC.
9799 Prechtel Rd (45252-2117)
PHONE...............................513 385-4442
EMP: 83
SALES (corp-wide): 980.45K **Privately Held**
Web: www.eaglecreek.com
SIC: 3161 Traveling bags
PA: Eagle Creek Ip, Llc
2620 S Cop Frntge Rd Uni
Steamboat Springs CO 80487
760 431-6400

(G-2573)
EAGLEBURGMANN INDUSTRIES LP
3478 Hauck Rd Ste A (45241-4604)
PHONE...............................513 563-7325
Matt Vaupel, *Mgr*
EMP: 10
SALES (corp-wide): 12.96B **Privately Held**
Web: www.eagleburgmann.us
SIC: 3053 Gaskets; packing and sealing devices
HQ: Eagleburgmann Industries Lp
10035 Brookriver Dr
Houston TX 77040
713 939-9515

(G-2574)
EARL D ARNOLD PRINTING COMPANY
Also Called: Arnold Printing Co
630 Lunken Park Dr (45226-1800)
PHONE...............................513 533-6900
Earl D Arnold Senior, *Pr*
Timothy A Arnold, *
EMP: 35 **EST:** 1910
SQ FT: 30,000
SALES (est): 5.17MM **Privately Held**
Web: www.arnoldprinting.com
SIC: 2752 2759 2796 2791 Offset printing; Letterpress printing; Platemaking services; Typesetting

(G-2575)
EASTGATE CUSTOM GRAPHICS LTD
Also Called: Loveland Graphics
4459 Mount Carmel Tobasco Rd (45244-2225)
PHONE...............................513 528-7922
Donald R Hall, *Pt*
EMP: 7 **EST:** 1994
SQ FT: 42,000
SALES (est): 480.43K **Privately Held**
Web: www.ecgraphix.com
SIC: 7336 5999 2395 Silk screen design; Banners; Embroidery and art needlework

(G-2576)
EASY WAY LEISURE COMPANY LLC (PA)

Also Called: Easy Way Products
8950 Rossash Rd (45236-1210)
PHONE...............................513 731-5640
Jon Randman, *Pr*
Scott Szymkowicz, *
Steve Coppel, *
Pamela Ruvle, *
◆ **EMP:** 40 **EST:** 1947
SQ FT: 100,000
SALES (est): 16.11MM
SALES (corp-wide): 16.11MM **Privately Held**
Web: www.easywayproducts.com
SIC: 2392 Cushions and pillows

(G-2577)
EBEL-BINDER PRINTING CO INC
Also Called: Ebel Tape & Label
1630 Dalton Ave # 1 (45214-2020)
PHONE...............................513 471-1067
Thomas Heidemann, *Pr*
Marian Dulle, *VP*
James Dulle, *Treas*
EMP: 7 **EST:** 1937
SQ FT: 3,000
SALES (est): 398.75K **Privately Held**
SIC: 2759 Flexographic printing

(G-2578)
ECM INDUSTRIES LLC
Also Called: Ecm Industries, Llc
3898 Duck Creek Rd (45227)
PHONE...............................513 533-6242
EMP: 14
Web: www.ilsco.com
SIC: 3643 3369 3451 3678 Current-carrying wiring services; Nonferrous foundries, nec; Screw machine products; Electronic connectors
HQ: Ilsco, Llc
4701 Creek Rd Ste 110
Blue Ash OH 45242
513 533-6200

(G-2579)
ECU CORPORATION (PA)
11500 Goldcoast Dr (45249-1621)
PHONE...............................513 898-9294
Mike Fox, *Pr*
Hank Worsley, *VP*
◆ **EMP:** 19 **EST:** 2006
SQ FT: 25,000
SALES (est): 4.65MM **Privately Held**
Web: www.ecucorp.com
SIC: 3585 Air conditioning units, complete: domestic or industrial

(G-2580)
ELECTRIC SERVICE CO INC
5331 Hetzell St (45227-1513)
PHONE...............................513 271-6387
Helen Snyder, *Pr*
EMP: 34 **EST:** 1912
SQ FT: 35,000
SALES (est): 2.43MM **Privately Held**
Web: www.elscotransformers.com
SIC: 7629 3677 3621 Electronic equipment repair; Transformers power supply, electronic type; Phase or rotary converters (electrical equipment)

(G-2581)
ELECTRONAUTS LLC
621 Wilmer Ave (45226-1859)
PHONE...............................859 261-3600
Douglas E Gilb, *Managing Member*
◆ **EMP:** 18 **EST:** 1979
SQ FT: 55,000
SALES (est): 5.4MM **Privately Held**
Web: www.electronauts.com

SIC: 3679 Electronic circuits

(G-2582)
ELEEO BRANDS LLC
Also Called: Boogie Wipes
2150 Winchell Ave (45214-1853)
PHONE...............................513 572-8100
Richard Palmer, *CEO*
▲ **EMP:** 6 **EST:** 2020
SALES (est): 11.52MM **Privately Held**
Web: www.boogiewipes.com
SIC: 2676 Sanitary paper products

(G-2583)
EMERSON ELECTRIC CO
Also Called: Emerson
6000 Fernview Ave (45212-1312)
PHONE...............................513 731-2020
Brent Schroeder, *Mgr*
EMP: 200
SALES (corp-wide): 17.49B **Publicly Held**
Web: www.emerson.com
SIC: 3823 Process control instruments
PA: Emerson Electric Co.
8027 Forsyth Boulevard
Saint Louis MO 63105
888 889-9170

(G-2584)
EMERY OLEOCHEMICALS LLC (HQ)
Also Called: Emery
4900 Este Ave (45232-1491)
PHONE...............................513 762-2500
Robert J Squires, *Managing Member*
◆ **EMP:** 32 **EST:** 2005
SQ FT: 4,032
SALES (est): 122.99MM **Privately Held**
Web: www.emeryoleo.com
SIC: 2899 Acids
PA: Edenor Oleochemicals (M) Sdn. Bhd.
Lot 1 Jalan Perak
Telok Panglima Garang 42500

(G-2585)
EMPIRICAL MANUFACTURING CO INC
7616 Reinhold Dr (45237-3312)
PHONE...............................513 948-1616
Gloria Tarver, *Pr*
Gloria Jenkins, *Pr*
EMP: 18 **EST:** 1986
SQ FT: 8,200
SALES (est): 432.01K **Privately Held**
Web: www.empirical-co.com
SIC: 2311 Men's and boys' uniforms

(G-2586)
ENCLOSURE SUPPLIERS LLC
Also Called: Champion
12119 Champion Way (45241-6419)
PHONE...............................513 782-3900
▲ **EMP:** 30 **EST:** 1990
SQ FT: 160,000
SALES (est): 8.83MM **Privately Held**
Web: www.esi-blinds.com
SIC: 3448 5031 3231 Prefabricated metal buildings; Lumber, plywood, and millwork; Products of purchased glass
HQ: Champion Opco, Llc
12121 Champion Wy
Cincinnati OH 45241
513 327-7338

(G-2587)
ENCOMPASS WOODWORKING LLC
1303 Monmouth St (45225-1349)
PHONE...............................513 569-2841
Adam Schwoeppe, *Managing Member*
EMP: 9 **EST:** 2014
SALES (est): 975.69K **Privately Held**
Web: www.encompasswoodworking.com

SIC: 2431 Millwork

(G-2588)
ENDURANCE INDUSTRIES LLC
5055 Madison Rd (45227-1431)
PHONE..................................513 285-8503
EMP: 11 EST: 2018
SALES (est): 3.46MM Privately Held
Web: www.endurance.industries
SIC: 3999 Manufacturing industries, nec

(G-2589)
ENERFAB INC
ENERFAB, INC.
11861 Mosteller Rd (45241-1524)
PHONE..................................513 771-2300
Steve Zoller, Genl Mgr
EMP: 6
SQ FT: 250,000
SALES (corp-wide): 483.98MM Privately
Held
Web: www.enerfab.com
SIC: 3559 Pharmaceutical machinery
PA: Enerfab, Llc
4430 Chickering Ave
Cincinnati OH 45232
513 641-0500

(G-2590)
ENERFAB LLC (PA)
4430 Chickering Ave (45232-1931)
PHONE..................................513 641-0500
Wendell R Bell, CEO
Dave Herche, *
Jeffrey P Hock, *
Daniel J Sillies, *
Mark Schoettmer, *
◆ EMP: 330 EST: 1912
SQ FT: 180,000
SALES (est): 483.98MM
SALES (corp-wide): 483.98MM Privately
Held
Web: www.enerfab.com
SIC: 3443 1629 1541 1711 Tanks, standard
or custom fabricated: metal plate; Power
plant construction; Industrial buildings and
warehouses; Mechanical contractor

(G-2591)
ENQUIRER PRINTING CO INC
7188 Main St (45244-3019)
PHONE..................................513 241-1956
John G Anderson, Pr
Michael W Anderson, VP
Steve Anderson, Treas
EMP: 10 EST: 1894
SQ FT: 19,000
SALES (est): 979.4K Privately Held
SIC: 2752 Offset printing

(G-2592)
ENTERPRISE MACHINE INC
Also Called: Boye & Emmes Machine
3640 Llewellyn Ave (45223-2336)
PHONE..................................513 681-4409
Scott Hammer, Pr
Steve Wernke, Pr
Timothy Orr, VP
EMP: 8 EST: 1961
SQ FT: 10,000
SALES (est): 1.01MM Privately Held
Web: www.enterprisemachineinc.com
SIC: 3363 3599 3451 3498 Aluminum die-
castings; Amusement park equipment;
Screw machine products; Fabricated pipe
and fittings

(G-2593)
ENVOI DESIGN INC
1332 Main St Frnt (45202-7849)
PHONE..................................513 651-4229

Denise Calmus, Pr
Steve Weinstein, VP
EMP: 7 EST: 1988
SQ FT: 1,200
SALES (est): 211.37K Privately Held
Web: www.envoidesign.com
SIC: 2752 7336 Commercial printing,
lithographic; Graphic arts and related design

(G-2594)
EP BOLLINGER LLC
Also Called: Myrlen
2664 Saint Georges Ct (45233-4290)
PHONE..................................513 941-1101
Ed P Bollinger, Managing Member
EMP: 501 EST: 2015
SQ FT: 22,000
SALES (est): 3.26MM Privately Held
Web: www.controlconceptsusa.com
SIC: 2821 Plastics materials and resins

(G-2595)
EPS SPECIALTIES LTD INC
7875 School Rd # 77 (45249-1531)
PHONE..................................513 489-3676
Edgar L Wilkinson, Pr
Lee Wilkinson, VP
▲ EMP: 12 EST: 1983
SALES (est): 2.04MM Privately Held
Web: www.lamlite.com
SIC: 3086 Packaging and shipping
materials, foamed plastics

(G-2596)
**EQM TECHNOLOGIES & ENERGY
INC (PA)**
1800 Carillion Blvd (45240-2788)
PHONE..................................513 825-7500
Jon Colin, CEO
Jack S Greber, Sr VP
Robert Galvin, CFO
EMP: 33 EST: 2008
SQ FT: 1,000
SALES (est): 8.86MM Privately Held
Web: www.eqm.com
SIC: 2869 Industrial organic chemicals, nec

(G-2597)
EQUIPPING MINISTRIES INTL INC
3908 Plainville Rd # 200 (45227-3202)
PHONE..................................513 742-1100
David Ping, Interim Director
EMP: 8 EST: 1972
SALES (est): 155.82K Privately Held
Web: www.equippingministries.org
SIC: 8299 2731 Religious school;
Pamphlets: publishing and printing

(G-2598)
EQUISTAR CHEMICALS LP
11530 Northlake Dr (45249-1642)
PHONE..................................513 530-4000
Peter Hanik, Brnch Mgr
EMP: 68
Web: www.lyondellbasell.com
SIC: 2869 Industrial organic chemicals, nec
HQ: Equistar Chemicals, Lp
1221 Mckinney St Ste 300
Houston TX 77010

(G-2599)
ESSENTIAL ELEMENTS USA LLC
4775 Paddock Rd (45229-1003)
P.O. Box 29075 (45229-0075)
PHONE..................................513 482-5700
Todd Wisener, Genl Mgr
EMP: 25
SALES (corp-wide): 3.9MM Privately Held
Web: www.solvay.com

SIC: 2819 2899 Catalysts, chemical;
Chemical preparations, nec
PA: Essential Elements Usa, Llc
100 Overlook Ctr Fl 2
Princeton NJ 08540
609 375-2003

(G-2600)
ETHICON ENDO-SURGERY INC (HQ)
4545 Creek Rd (45242-2803)
PHONE..................................513 337-7000
Andrew K Ekdahl, Pr
▲ EMP: 1440 EST: 1992
SQ FT: 31,330
SALES (est): 489.67MM
SALES (corp-wide): 88.82B Publicly Held
SIC: 3841 5047 Surgical instruments and
apparatus; Medical equipment and supplies
PA: Johnson & Johnson
1 Johnson And Johnson Plz
New Brunswick NJ 08933
732 524-0400

(G-2601)
EUROSTAMPA NORTH AMERICA INC
1440 Seymour Ave (45237-3006)
PHONE..................................513 821-2275
Gianmario Cillario, CEO
▲ EMP: 217 EST: 2007
SALES (est): 90.73MM Privately Held
Web: www.eurostampa.com
SIC: 2752 Offset printing
HQ: Industria Grafica Eurostampa Spa
Viale Rimembranza 20
Bene Vagienna CN 12041
017 265-1811

(G-2602)
EVERON LLC
2300 Wall St Ste H (45212-2794)
PHONE..................................513 258-2409
EMP: 75
SALES (corp-wide): 1.5B Privately Held
Web: www.everonsolutions.com
SIC: 3699 Security control equipment and
systems
HQ: Everon, Llc
1501 W Yamato Rd
Boca Raton FL 33431
844 538-3766

(G-2603)
EVERS ENTERPRISES INC
Aurand Manufacturing & Eqp Co
1210 Ellis St (45223-1843)
PHONE..................................513 541-7200
Ray Evers, Pr
EMP: 6
SALES (corp-wide): 2.88MM Privately
Held
Web: www.aurand.net
SIC: 3589 Commercial cleaning equipment
PA: Evers Enterprises Inc
4849 Blue Rock Rd
Cincinnati OH

(G-2604)
EVERS WELDING CO INC
4849 Blue Rock Rd (45247-5504)
P.O. Box 53426 (45253-0426)
PHONE..................................513 385-7352
Edward G Evers, Pr
Jacqueline Evers, *
EMP: 8 EST: 1957
SQ FT: 3,000
SALES (est): 527.61K Privately Held
Web: www.everssteel.com
SIC: 1791 3441 Structural steel erection;
Fabricated structural metal

(G-2605)
EVOLUTION CRTIVE SOLUTIONS INC
7107 Shona Dr (45237-3808)
PHONE..................................513 681-4450
Cathy Lindemann, Pr
EMP: 45 EST: 1994
SQ FT: 22,000
SALES (est): 4.46MM Privately Held
Web: www.evo-creative.com
SIC: 2752 Color lithography

(G-2606)
EVONIK CORPORATION
Also Called: Coatings & Colorants
620 Shepherd Dr (45215-2104)
PHONE..................................513 554-8969
Joseph Won, Manager
EMP: 36
SALES (corp-wide): 16.03B Privately Held
Web: corporate.evonik.com
SIC: 2819 Industrial inorganic chemicals, nec
HQ: Evonik Corporation
2 Turner Pl
Piscataway NJ 08854
732 981-5060

(G-2607)
EVP INTERNATIONAL LLC
Also Called: Mn8-Foxfire
2701 Short Vine St # 200 (45219-2018)
PHONE..................................513 761-7614
EMP: 6 EST: 2010
SALES (est): 3.6MM Privately Held
Web: www.mn8foxfire.com
SIC: 3646 Commercial lighting fixtures

(G-2608)
EXAIR LLC
11510 Goldcoast Dr (45249-1621)
P.O. Box 00766 (45264)
PHONE..................................513 671-3322
Kirk Edwards, Pr
Brian Peters, *
Jackie Sweeney, *
Bob West, *
EMP: 50 EST: 1983
SQ FT: 42,000
SALES (est): 10.18MM Privately Held
Web: www.exair.com
SIC: 3499 Nozzles, spray: aerosol, paint, or
insecticide

(G-2609)
**EXPRESS GRPHICS PRTG DSIGN
INC**
9695 Hamilton Ave (45231-2351)
PHONE..................................513 728-3344
Craig Keller, Owner
EMP: 8 EST: 1998
SQ FT: 2,400
SALES (est): 447.11K Privately Held
Web: www.xgraph1.com
SIC: 2752 Offset printing

(G-2610)
FABRIC FORMS INC
1320 Bates Ave (45225-1310)
PHONE..................................513 281-6300
Michael Goldfarb, Pr
EMP: 7 EST: 1991
SQ FT: 4,000
SALES (est): 465.25K Privately Held
Web: www.fabricformsawnings.com
SIC: 2394 Awnings, fabric: made from
purchased materials

(G-2611)
**FAMILY MOTOR COACH ASSN INC
(PA)**
8291 Clough Pike (45244-2796)

▲ = Import ▼ = Export
◆ = Import/Export

PHONE..........................513 474-3622
Lana Makin, *CEO*
EMP: 46 **EST:** 1963
SQ FT: 22,000
SALES (est): 4.08MM
SALES (corp-wide): 4.08MM **Privately Held**
Web: www.fmca.com
SIC: 8641 2721 Social associations; Magazines: publishing and printing

(G-2612)
FAMILY MOTOR COACHING INC
Also Called: Family Motor Coaching
8291 Clough Pike (45244-2756)
PHONE..........................513 474-3622
Don Moore, *Pr*
Don Eversmann, *
EMP: 57 **EST:** 1963
SQ FT: 20,000
SALES (est): 2.1MM
SALES (corp-wide): 4.08MM **Privately Held**
Web: www.fmca.com
SIC: 2721 Magazines: publishing only, not printed on site
PA: Family Motor Coach Association, Inc.
8291 Clough Pike
Cincinnati OH 45244
513 474-3622

(G-2613)
FAWN CONFECTIONERY INC (PA)
4271 Harrison Ave (45211-3340)
PHONE..........................513 574-9612
Kathy Guenther, *CEO*
Jane Guenther, *Treas*
Jackie Copenhaver, *Sec*
EMP: 15 **EST:** 1946
SALES (est): 806.43K
SALES (corp-wide): 806.43K **Privately Held**
Web: www.fawncandy.com
SIC: 5441 2064 2066 Candy; Candy and other confectionery products; Chocolate and cocoa products

(G-2614)
FAXON MACHINING LLC
11101 Adwood Dr (45240-3235)
PHONE..........................513 851-4644
Robert Faxon, *CEO*
Barry A Faxon, *
David K Faxon, *
D K Faxon Ii, *Prin*
B W Faxon, *
▲ **EMP:** 145 **EST:** 1978
SQ FT: 155,000
SALES (est): 14.48MM **Privately Held**
Web: www.faxon-machining.com
SIC: 3599 3483 Machine shop, jobbing and repair; Ammunition, except.for small arms, nec

(G-2615)
FBF LIMITED
Also Called: Queen City Steel Treating Co
2980 Spring Grove Ave (45225-2146)
PHONE..........................513 541-6300
Judith T Houchens, *Pr*
Michael E Fourney, *
William L Fourney, *
EMP: 35 **EST:** 1922
SALES (est): 1.69MM **Privately Held**
Web: www.qcst.com
SIC: 3398 Brazing (hardening) of metal

(G-2616)
FEDERAL EQUIPMENT COMPANY (DH)
5298 River Rd (45233-1688)

PHONE..........................513 621-5260
George Whittier, *CEO*
Doug Ridenour, *
Robert Starr, *
Jay Mcfadyen, *CCO*
Jared Barefield, *CAO*
▲ **EMP:** 70 **EST:** 1982
SALES (est): 45.42MM
SALES (corp-wide): 1.27B **Privately Held**
Web: www.fairbanksmorsedefense.com
SIC: 3699 3728 3534 3535 Electrical equipment and supplies, nec; Aircraft parts and equipment, nec; Elevators and moving stairways; Conveyors and conveying equipment
HQ: Fairbanks Morse, Llc
701 White Ave
Beloit WI 53511
800 356-6955

(G-2617)
FEINTOOL CINCINNATI INC (DH)
11280 Cornell Park Dr (45242-1888)
PHONE..........................513 247-0110
Christoph Trachsler, *CEO*
Ralph Hardt, *
Karl Frydryk, *
Paul Frauchiger, *
Rolf Haag, *
▲ **EMP:** 240 **EST:** 1978
SALES (est): 33.32MM **Privately Held**
Web: www.feintool.com
SIC: 3465 Automotive stampings
HQ: Feintool U.S. Operations, Inc.
11280 Cornell Park Dr
Cincinnati OH 45242
513 247-0110

(G-2618)
FEINTOOL US OPERATIONS INC (DH)
11280 Cornell Park Dr (45242-1888)
PHONE..........................513 247-0110
Richard Surico, *CEO*
Ralph E Hardt, *
Christoph Trachsler, *
▲ **EMP:** 250 **EST:** 1978
SALES (est): 96.5MM **Privately Held**
Web: www.feintool.com
SIC: 3469 3465 Metal stampings, nec; Automotive stampings
HQ: Feintool International Holding Ag
Industriering 8
Lyss BE 3260

(G-2619)
FELD PRINTING CO
6806 Main St (45244-3435)
P.O. Box 44188 (45244)
PHONE..........................513 271-6806
Robert A Feld Senior, *Pr*
Robert A Feld Junior, *VP*
David A Feld, *VP*
Marilyn Feld Mitchell, *Sec*
EMP: 7 **EST:** 1943
SQ FT: 5,000
SALES (est): 164.59K **Privately Held**
Web: www.feldprinting.com
SIC: 2752 Offset printing

(G-2620)
FIEDELDEY STL FABRICATORS INC
8487 E Miami River Rd (45247-2208)
PHONE..........................513 353-3300
Bernard A Fiedeldey Junior, *Pr*
EMP: 20 **EST:** 1974
SQ FT: 20,000
SALES (est): 3.37MM **Privately Held**
Web: www.fiedeldeysteel.com
SIC: 3441 Fabricated structural metal

(G-2621)
FIELD APPARATUS SERVICE & TSTG
Also Called: F A S T
4040 Rev Dr (45232-1914)
PHONE..........................513 353-9399
Kathy Jones, *Pr*
EMP: 7 **EST:** 1995
SALES (est): 91.85K **Privately Held**
SIC: 8711 3825 Electrical or electronic engineering; Test equipment for electronic and electric measurement

(G-2622)
FIELD AVIATION INC (PA)
8044 Montgomery Rd Ste 530 (45236-2924)
PHONE..........................513 792-2282
John Mactaggart, *CEO*
EMP: 23 **EST:** 2010
SALES (est): 20.91MM **Privately Held**
Web: www.fieldav.com
SIC: 3728 Aircraft parts and equipment, nec

(G-2623)
FIFTH THIRD PROC SOLUTIONS INC
38 Fountain Square Plz (45202-3102)
PHONE..........................800 972-3030
EMP: 36 **EST:** 2011
SALES (est): 9.26MM **Privately Held**
SIC: 7372 Prepackaged software

(G-2624)
FINN GRAPHICS INC
220 Stille Dr (45233-1647)
PHONE..........................513 941-6161
Dan Finn, *Pr*
Robert Finn, *
Jack Roch, *
EMP: 40 **EST:** 1958
SQ FT: 30,000
SALES (est): 2.42MM **Privately Held**
Web: www.finn-line.com
SIC: 2752 3993 2395 Offset printing; Advertising novelties; Pleating and stitching

(G-2625)
FLAVOR PRODUCERS LLC
2429 E Kemper Rd (45241-1811)
PHONE..........................513 771-0777
EMP: 32
SALES (corp-wide): 57.58MM **Privately Held**
Web: www.flavorproducers.com
SIC: 2087 Concentrates, flavoring (except drink)
PA: Flavor Producers, Llc
8521 Fllbrook Ave Ste 380
West Hills CA 91304
661 257-3400

(G-2626)
FLAVOR SYSTEMS INTL INC (HQ)
5404 Duff Dr (45246-1323)
PHONE..........................513 870-4900
William W Wasz, *Pr*
John Disebastian, *VP*
William Baker, *VP*
▲ **EMP:** 21 **EST:** 1994
SQ FT: 50,000
SALES (est): 2.66MM
SALES (corp-wide): 11.48B **Publicly Held**
Web: www.flavorsystems.com
SIC: 2087 Flavoring extracts and syrups, nec
PA: International Flavors & Fragrances Inc.
521 W 57th St
New York NY 10019
212 765-5500

(G-2627)
FLEXOMATION LLC
11701 Chesterdale Rd (45246-3405)
P.O. Box 40537 (45240-0537)
PHONE..........................513 825-0555
EMP: 6 **EST:** 2004
SALES (est): 1.24MM **Privately Held**
Web: www.flexomation.com
SIC: 3549 Assembly machines, including robotic

(G-2628)
FLINT CPS INKS NORTH AMER LLC
410 Glendale Milford Rd (45215-1103)
PHONE..........................513 619-2089
Mike Ledford, *Brnch Mgr*
EMP: 24
SALES (corp-wide): 1.91B **Privately Held**
Web: www.flintgrp.com
SIC: 2865 2893 Color pigments, organic; Printing ink
HQ: Flint Cps Inks North America Llc
17177 N Lrel Pk Dr Ste 30
Livonia MI 48152
734 781-4600

(G-2629)
FLOW TECHNOLOGY INC
4444 Cooper Rd (45242-0259)
PHONE..........................513 745-6000
Bill Hayes, *Pr*
Bill Hays, *Pr*
EMP: 7 **EST:** 1978
SALES (est): 885.99K
SALES (corp-wide): 2.13B **Publicly Held**
Web: www.ftimeters.com
SIC: 3491 Valves, automatic control
HQ: Xomox Corporation
4526 Res Frest Dr Ste 400
The Woodlands TX 77381
936 271-6500

(G-2630)
FLUFF BOUTIQUE
6539 Harrison Ave (45247-7822)
PHONE..........................513 227-6614
Laura White, *Owner*
EMP: 6 **EST:** 2013
SQ FT: 2,000
SALES (est): 189.68K **Privately Held**
SIC: 7363 5621 5137 5963 Help supply services; Women's clothing stores; Women's and children's clothing; Clothing sales, house-to-house

(G-2631)
FLYPAPER STUDIO INC
311 Elm St Ste 200 (45202-2743)
PHONE..........................602 801-2208
Patrick Sullivan, *CEO*
Don Perison, *
Pat Stoner, *
Greg Head, *
Sunil Padiyar, *
EMP: 6 **EST:** 2003
SQ FT: 16,778
SALES (est): 778.18K **Privately Held**
SIC: 7372 Educational computer software

(G-2632)
FOODIES VEGAN LTD
Also Called: Five Star Foodies
4524 Este Ave (45232-1763)
PHONE..........................513 487-3037
Valerie Williams, *CEO*
Christian Stroud, *CFO*
EMP: 12 **EST:** 2007
SALES (est): 1.2MM **Privately Held**
Web: www.foodiesvegan.com
SIC: 5142 2099 Packaged frozen goods; Tofu, except frozen desserts

(G-2633)
FORCAM INC
3825 Edwards Rd Ste 103 (45209-1262)
PHONE..................................513 878-2780
Franz Gruber, *CEO*
EMP: 15 **EST:** 2012
SALES (est): 866.11K **Privately Held**
Web: www.forcam.com
SIC: 7371 7372 Computer software
　development and applications; Application
　computer software

(G-2634)
FOREST CONVERTING CO INC
4701 Forest Ave (45212-3399)
P.O. Box 12238 (45212)
PHONE..................................513 631-4190
R Douglas Lojinger, *Pr*
EMP: 6 **EST:** 1949
SQ FT: 22,000
SALES (est): 182.39K **Privately Held**
Web: www.forestconverting.com
SIC: 2675 Paper die-cutting

(G-2635)
FORMICA CORPORATION (DH)
10155 Reading Rd (45241-4805)
PHONE..................................513 786-3400
Frank Riddick, *Pr*
Michael Fischer V, *President SFCE America*
Catherine Vernon, *VP*
Mitchell P Quint, *Pr*
R Gerard Bollman, *VP*
◆ **EMP:** 20 **EST:** 1913
SQ FT: 14,000
SALES (est): 292.94MM
SALES (corp-wide): 355.83K **Privately
Held**
Web: www.formica.com
SIC: 2541 2679 Counter and sink tops;
　Paperboard products, converted, nec
HQ: Broadview Holding B.V.
　Willemsplein 2
　's-Hertogenbosch NB 5211

(G-2636)
FORWARD MOVEMENT
Also Called: Forward Day By Day
412 Sycamore St (45202-6202)
PHONE..................................513 721-6659
Scott Gunn, *Ex Dir*
▲ **EMP:** 21 **EST:** 1935
SALES (est): 1.9MM **Privately Held**
Web: www.forwardmovement.org
SIC: 2759 Publication printing

(G-2637)
FOSTER TRANSFORMER COMPANY
3820 Colerain Ave (45223-2586)
PHONE..................................513 681-2420
◆ **EMP:** 25 **EST:** 1937
SALES (est): 2.14MM
SALES (corp-wide): 3.86MM **Privately
Held**
Web: www.foster-transformer.com
SIC: 3677 3612 Electronic transformers;
　Transformers, except electric
PA: Harrison Corporation
　3820 Colerain Ave
　Cincinnati OH 45223
　513 681-2420

(G-2638)
FRANK L HARTER & SON INC
3778 Frondorf Ave (45211-4421)
PHONE..................................513 574-1330
Michael Harter, *Pr*
Barb Harter, *Sec*
EMP: 6 **EST:** 1928
SQ FT: 800
SALES (est): 358.8K **Privately Held**

SIC: 5143 5144 5148 2099 Butter; Eggs;
　Fresh fruits and vegetables; Salads, fresh
　or refrigerated

(G-2639)
FRANKLIN COVEY CO
7875 Montgomery Rd Spc 1202
(45236-4344)
PHONE..................................513 680-0975
Jason Mast, *Mgr*
EMP: 8
SALES (corp-wide): 287.23MM **Publicly
Held**
Web: www.franklincovey.com
SIC: 2741 Miscellaneous publishing
PA: Franklin Covey Co.
　2200 W Parkway Blvd
　Salt Lake City UT 84119
　801 817-1776

(G-2640)
FRANKS ELECTRIC INC
Also Called: Franks Electric Motor Repair
2640 Colerain Ave (45214-1712)
PHONE..................................513 313-5883
Brian Knue, *Pr*
Diana Grady, *VP*
EMP: 8 **EST:** 1944
SQ FT: 10,000
SALES (est): 237.42K **Privately Held**
Web: www.frankselectric.org
SIC: 1731 7694 5999 General electrical
　contractor; Electric motor repair; Motors,
　electric

(G-2641)
FREDERICK STEEL COMPANY LLC
Also Called: Bfs Supply
630 Glendale Milford Rd (45215-1105)
PHONE..................................513 821-6400
Burke Byer, *Prin*
Timothy Nagy, *Sec*
Jay Binder, *Prin*
Jeff Ginter, *Prin*
Jonas Allen, *Prin*
EMP: 60 **EST:** 2013
SALES (est): 10.48MM
SALES (corp-wide): 41.34MM **Privately
Held**
Web: www.fredericksteel.com
SIC: 1791 3441 Structural steel erection;
　Building components, structural steel
PA: Benjamin Steel Company, Inc.
　777 Benjamin Dr
　Springfield OH 45502
　937 322-8600

(G-2642)
FROST ENGINEERING INC
3408 Beekman St (45223-2425)
PHONE..................................513 541-6330
Charles E Frost, *Pr*
EMP: 42 **EST:** 1995
SQ FT: 15,000
SALES (est): 2.1MM **Privately Held**
Web: www.frostengineering.com
SIC: 3556 8711 Smokers, food processing
　equipment; Engineering services

(G-2643)
FRUTAROM USA INC (HQ)
Also Called: Frutarom
5404 Duff Dr (45246-1323)
PHONE..................................513 870-4900
Ori Yehudai, *Pr*
Luis Gayo, *
Alon Granot, *
Michael J Gill, *
Kevin Woten, *
◆ **EMP:** 120 **EST:** 1933
SQ FT: 360,000

SALES (est): 32.67MM
SALES (corp-wide): 11.48B **Publicly Held**
SIC: 2099 2833 2087 Spices, including
　grinding; Botanical products, medicinal:
　ground, graded, or milled; Extracts, flavoring
PA: International Flavors & Fragrances Inc.
　521 W 57th St
　New York NY 10019
　212 765-5500

(G-2644)
**G & J PEPSI-COLA BOTTLERS INC
(PA)**
Also Called: Pepsi-Cola
9435 Waterstone Blvd Ste 390
(45249-8227)
PHONE..................................513 785-6060
Timothy S Trant, *CEO*
Daniel D Sweeney, *COO*
Tim Hardid, *COO*
Stanley Kaplan, *Ch*
Thomas D Heekin, *V Ch Bd*
EMP: 10 **EST:** 1968
SQ FT: 8,052
SALES (est): 404.54MM
SALES (corp-wide): 404.54MM **Privately
Held**
Web: www.gjpepsi.com
SIC: 2086 Carbonated soft drinks, bottled
　and canned

(G-2645)
G A AVRIL COMPANY (PA)
Also Called: BRASS & BRONZE INGOT
DIVISION
2108 Eagle Ct (45237-4754)
P.O. Box 32066 (45232-0066)
PHONE..................................513 641-0566
Thomas B Avril, *Pr*
John G Avril, *VP*
EMP: 10 **EST:** 1946
SQ FT: 47,000
SALES (est): 37.58K
SALES (corp-wide): 37.58K **Privately Held**
Web: www.gaavril.com
SIC: 3341 3356 Brass smelting and refining
　(secondary); Nonferrous rolling and
　drawing, nec

(G-2646)
G A AVRIL COMPANY
White Metal Products Division
2108 Eagle Ct (45237-4754)
P.O. Box 12050 (45212-0050)
PHONE..................................513 731-5133
Philip V Schneider, *Mgr*
EMP: 10
SQ FT: 66,782
SALES (corp-wide): 37.58K **Privately Held**
Web: www.gaavril.com
SIC: 3356 Lead and lead alloy bars, pipe,
　plates, shapes, etc.
PA: The G A Avril Company
　2108 Eagle Ct
　Cincinnati OH 45237
　513 641-0566

(G-2647)
G L PIERCE INC
Also Called: Cincinnati GL Blck Dyton GL Bl
12100 Mosteller Rd Ste 500 (45241-6404)
PHONE..................................513 772-7202
Gregory Pierce, *Pr*
Gregory L Pierce, *Pr*
EMP: 7 **EST:** 2018
SALES (est): 942.08K **Privately Held**
Web: www.daytonglassblock.com
SIC: 3229 1741 Blocks and bricks, glass;
　Concrete block masonry laying

(G-2648)
**GANNETT STLLITE INFO NTWRK
LLC**
6223 Lakewood Dr (45201)
PHONE..................................513 768-8451
Harry M Whipple, *Brnch Mgr*
EMP: 18
SALES (corp-wide): 2.51B **Publicly Held**
Web: www.gannett.com
SIC: 2711 Newspapers, publishing and
　printing
HQ: Gannett Satellite Information Network,
　Llc
　1675 Broadway Fl 23
　New York NY 10019
　703 854-6000

(G-2649)
**GARDEN STREET IRON & METAL
INC (PA)**
2885 Spring Grove Ave (45225-2222)
PHONE..................................513 721-4660
Earl J Weber Junior, *Pr*
Margaret Weber, *
▲ **EMP:** 39 **EST:** 1959
SQ FT: 43,000
SALES (est): 4.67MM
SALES (corp-wide): 4.67MM **Privately
Held**
Web: www.gardenst.com
SIC: 4953 3341 3312 Recycling, waste
　materials; Secondary nonferrous metals;
　Blast furnaces and steel mills

(G-2650)
GARDNER BUSINESS MEDIA INC
6925 Valley Ln (45244-3029)
PHONE..................................513 527-8800
Margaret Kline, *Mgr*
EMP: 10
SQ FT: 17,600
SALES (corp-wide): 34.92MM **Privately
Held**
Web: www.gardnerweb.com
SIC: 2721 2731 Trade journals: publishing
　only, not printed on site; Books, publishing
　and printing
PA: Gardner Business Media, Inc.
　6915 Valley Ave
　Cincinnati OH 45244
　513 527-8800

(G-2651)
**GARDNER BUSINESS MEDIA INC
(PA)**
6915 Valley Ln (45244-3029)
PHONE..................................513 527-8800
EMP: 120 **EST:** 1928
SALES (est): 34.92MM
SALES (corp-wide): 34.92MM **Privately
Held**
Web: www.gardnerweb.com
SIC: 2721 2731 2741 Trade journals:
　publishing only, not printed on site; Books,
　publishing only; Miscellaneous publishing

(G-2652)
**GARYS CHESECAKES FINE
DESSERTS**
1875 Jonte St (45214-1310)
PHONE..................................513 574-1700
Gary Haas, *Owner*
EMP: 8 **EST:** 2003
SALES (est): 224.49K **Privately Held**
Web: www.garyscheesecakes.com
SIC: 2051 Bread, cake, and related products

(G-2653)
GCI DIGITAL IMAGING INC
5031 Winton Rd (45232-1506)

▲ = Import ▼ = Export
◆ = Import/Export

PHONE..............................513 521-7446
Tom Bedacht, *Pr*
▲ **EMP:** 14 **EST:** 1992
SQ FT: 10,000
SALES (est): 6.05MM **Privately Held**
Web: www.gci-digital.com
SIC: 2752 Offset printing

(G-2654)
GE AVIATION SYSTEMS LLC
Also Called: GE Aviation
10270 Saint Rita Ln (45215-1215)
PHONE..............................513 470-2889
EMP: 40
SALES (corp-wide): 38.7B **Publicly Held**
Web: www.geaerospace.com
SIC: 3812 Aircraft control systems, electronic
HQ: Ge Aviation Systems Llc
1 Neumann Way
Cincinnati OH 45215
937 898-9600

(G-2655)
GE AVIATION SYSTEMS LLC (HQ)
Also Called: GE Aviation
1 Neumann Way (45215-1915)
PHONE..............................937 898-9600
R F Ehr, *Pr*
J B Hines, *Pr*
Peter Page, *Ex VP*
Jeff Immelt, *Ch*
▲ **EMP:** 8 **EST:** 1987
SALES (est): 2.46B
SALES (corp-wide): 38.7B **Publicly Held**
Web: www.geaerospace.com
SIC: 3812 Aircraft control systems, electronic
PA: General Electric Company
1 Aviation Way
Cincinnati OH 45215
617 443-3000

(G-2656)
GE ENGINE SERVICES LLC
Also Called: GE
201 W Crescentville Rd (45246-1713)
PHONE..............................513 977-1500
John Ousley, *Brnch Mgr*
EMP: 300
SALES (corp-wide): 38.7B **Publicly Held**
Web: www.geaerospace.com
SIC: 3728 Aircraft parts and equipment, nec
HQ: Ge Engine Services, Llc
1 Neumann Way
Cincinnati OH 45215
513 243-2000

(G-2657)
GE HEALTHCARE INC
346 Gest St (45203-1822)
PHONE..............................513 241-5955
Mark Nybo, *Mgr*
EMP: 15
SALES (corp-wide): 19.67B **Publicly Held**
Web: www.cytivalifesciences.com
SIC: 2835 Diagnostic substances
HQ: Ge Healthcare Inc.
3350 N Ridge Ave
Arlington Heights IL 60004
732 457-8667

(G-2658)
GE MILITARY SYSTEMS
1 Neumann Way (45215-1915)
PHONE..............................513 243-2000
Russ Sparks, *Of Mil Strat*
EMP: 8 **EST:** 1996
SALES (est): 2.6MM
SALES (corp-wide): 38.7B **Publicly Held**
Web: www.geaerospace.com
SIC: 3728 Aircraft parts and equipment, nec
PA: General Electric Company

1 Aviation Way
Cincinnati OH 45215
617 443-3000

(G-2659)
GENERAL CHAIN & MFG CORP
3274 Beekman St (45223-2490)
PHONE..............................513 541-6005
Eric Schaumloffel, *Pr*
EMP: 40 **EST:** 1919
SALES (est): 3.83MM **Privately Held**
Web: www.generalchain.com
SIC: 3496 Miscellaneous fabricated wire products

(G-2660)
GENERAL ELECTRIC COMPANY
Also Called: GE
445 S Cooper Ave (45215-4565)
PHONE..............................513 948-4170
Carol Mase, *Mgr*
EMP: 8
SALES (corp-wide): 38.7B **Publicly Held**
Web: geaerospace.com
SIC: 3724 Aircraft engines and engine parts
PA: General Electric Company
1 Aviation Way
Cincinnati OH 45215
617 443-3000

(G-2661)
GENERAL ELECTRIC COMPANY
GE Aviation
1 Neumann Way (45215-1988)
PHONE..............................513 956-9051
EMP: 41
SALES (corp-wide): 38.7B **Publicly Held**
Web: geaerospace.com
SIC: 3812 Search and navigation equipment
PA: General Electric Company
1 Aviation Way
Cincinnati OH 45215
617 443-3000

(G-2662)
GENERAL ELECTRIC COMPANY
Also Called: GE
201 W Crescentville Rd (45246-1733)
PHONE..............................513 977-1500
Bill Fitzgerald, *Mgr*
EMP: 23
SALES (corp-wide): 38.7B **Publicly Held**
Web: geaerospace.com
SIC: 7629 3769 3728 3537 Aircraft electrical equipment repair; Space vehicle equipment, nec; Aircraft parts and equipment, nec; Industrial trucks and tractors
PA: General Electric Company
1 Aviation Way
Cincinnati OH 45215
617 443-3000

(G-2663)
GENERAL MILLS INC
General Mills
11301 Mosteller Rd (45241-1827)
PHONE..............................513 771-8200
Jerry Kelley, *Brnch Mgr*
EMP: 92
SALES (corp-wide): 19.86B **Publicly Held**
Web: www.generalmills.com
SIC: 2043 2099 Cereal breakfast foods; Food preparations, nec
PA: General Mills, Inc.
1 General Mills Blvd
Minneapolis MN 55426
763 764-7600

(G-2664)
GENERAL NANO LLC
Also Called: Veelo Technologies
10340 Julian Dr (45215-1131)
PHONE..............................513 309-5947
EMP: 14 **EST:** 2007
SALES (est): 3.74MM **Privately Held**
Web: www.veelotech.com
SIC: 3399 Metal powders, pastes, and flakes

(G-2665)
GENERAL PLASTICS NORTH CORP
5220 Vine St (45217-1028)
PHONE..............................800 542-2466
Zetta Bouligaraki, *Pr*
EMP: 108 **EST:** 1950
SQ FT: 150,000
SALES (est): 900.5K
SALES (corp-wide): 1.71B **Privately Held**
Web: www.generalplasticscorp.com
SIC: 3479 Coating of metals and formed products
HQ: Pmc, Inc.
12243 Branford St
Sun Valley CA 91352
818 896-1101

(G-2666)
GENERAL TOOL COMPANY (PA)
101 Landy Ln (45215-3495)
PHONE..............................513 733-5500
William J Kramer Junior, *CEO*
William J Kramer Iii, *CFO*
John Cozad, *
Elliot Adams, *
Paul Kramer, *
▲ **EMP:** 235 **EST:** 1947
SQ FT: 150,000
SALES (est): 39.89MM
SALES (corp-wide): 39.89MM **Privately Held**
Web: www.gentool.com
SIC: 3599 3443 3444 3544 Machine shop, jobbing and repair; Fabricated plate work (boiler shop); Sheet metalwork; Special dies and tools

(G-2667)
GENPACT LLC
100 Tri County Pkwy Ste 200 (45246-3244)
PHONE..............................513 763-7660
EMP: 43
Web: www.genpact.com
SIC: 8711 3812 Mechanical engineering; Electronic field detection apparatus (aeronautical)
HQ: Genpact Llc
521 5th Ave
New York NY 10175
442 072-2752

(G-2668)
GENTHERM MEDICAL LLC (HQ)
12011 Mosteller Rd (45241-1528)
PHONE..............................513 772-8810
EMP: 236 **EST:** 1940
SALES (est): 44.91MM **Publicly Held**
Web: www.gentherm.com
SIC: 3823 3841 Controllers, for process variables, all types; Surgical and medical instruments
PA: Gentherm Incorporated
28875 Cabot Dr
Novi MI 48377

(G-2669)
GERALD L HERRMANN COMPANY INC
Also Called: Master Print Center
3325 Harrison Ave (45211-5618)
P.O. Box 11560 (45211-0560)

PHONE..............................513 661-1818
TOLL FREE: 800
Gerald Herrmann, *Pr*
Suzanne Herrmann, *Sec*
EMP: 11 **EST:** 1961
SQ FT: 7,500
SALES (est): 2.12MM **Privately Held**
Web: www.addresserbasedsystems.com
SIC: 7331 2752 Addressing service; Photo-offset printing

(G-2670)
GILLETTE COMPANY LLC
Also Called: Gillette
1 Procter And Gamble Plz (45202-3315)
P.O. Box 5319 (45201-5319)
PHONE..............................513 983-1100
David S Taylor, *Ch Bd*
EMP: 54 **EST:** 2016
SALES (est): 21.87MM
SALES (corp-wide): 84.04B **Publicly Held**
Web: www.gillette.com
SIC: 3421 Razor blades and razors
PA: The Procter & Gamble Company
1 Procter & Gamble Plz
Cincinnati OH 45202
513 983-1100

(G-2671)
GIRINDUS AMERICA INC
Also Called: Avecia
10608 Deercreek Ln (45249-3506)
PHONE..............................513 679-3000
EMP: 30
SIC: 2834 Pharmaceutical preparations

(G-2672)
GIVAUDAN FLAVORS CORPORATION
100 E 69th St (45216-2008)
PHONE..............................513 948-3428
EMP: 24
Web: www.givaudan.com
SIC: 2869 Flavors or flavoring materials, synthetic
HQ: Givaudan Flavors Corporation
1199 Edison Dr 1-2
Cincinnati OH 45216

(G-2673)
GIVAUDAN FLAVORS CORPORATION (DH)
Also Called: Givaudan
1199 Edison Dr 1-2 (45216-2265)
P.O. Box 17038 (45216)
PHONE..............................513 948-8000
◆ **EMP:** 199 **EST:** 1988
SALES (est): 543.21MM **Privately Held**
SIC: 2869 2087 Flavors or flavoring materials, synthetic; Flavoring extracts and syrups, nec
HQ: Givaudan Flavors And Fragrances, Inc.
1199 Edison Dr
Cincinnati OH 45216

(G-2674)
GIVAUDAN FLAVORS CORPORATION
110 E 70th St (45216-2011)
PHONE..............................513 948-8000
Felix Mayr Harting, *Brnch Mgr*
EMP: 8
SIC: 2087 Flavoring extracts and syrups, nec
HQ: Givaudan Flavors Corporation
1199 Edison Dr 1-2
Cincinnati OH 45216

(G-2675)
GIVAUDAN FRAGRANCES CORP
100 E 69th St (45216-2008)
PHONE..............................513 948-3428
Gary Schmidt, *Mgr*
EMP: 63

SIC: 2869 2087 Flavors or flavoring materials, synthetic; Flavoring extracts and syrups, nec
HQ: Givaudan Fragrances Corporation
1199 Edison Dr Ste 1-2
Cincinnati OH 45216
513 948-8000

(G-2676)
GIVAUDAN FRAGRANCES CORP (DH)
1199 Edison Dr Ste 1-2 (45216-2265)
P.O. Box 17038 (45216)
PHONE...............................513 948-8000
Gilles Andrier, CEO
◆ EMP: 386 EST: 2000
SQ FT: 78,000
SALES (est): 259.15MM Privately Held
SIC: 2869 Perfume materials, synthetic
HQ: Givaudan Flavors And Fragrances, Inc.
1199 Edison Dr
Cincinnati OH 45216

(G-2677)
GLOBAL SRCING SUPPORT SVCS LLC
260 E University Ave (45219-2356)
PHONE...............................800 645-2986
▲ EMP: 6 EST: 2005
SALES (est): 809.98K Privately Held
SIC: 3599 Custom machinery

(G-2678)
GM PALLET LLC
Also Called: G.M. Pallet Co.
121 Citycentre Dr (45216-1657)
P.O. Box 16116 (45216-0116)
PHONE...............................859 408-1781
EMP: 7 EST: 2017
SALES (est): 918.62K Privately Held
Web: www.gmpalletsco.com
SIC: 2448 Pallets, wood

(G-2679)
GMP WELDING & FABRICATION INC
11175 Adwood Dr (45240-3235)
PHONE...............................513 825-7861
Leonard J Mee, Pr
Tyler Mee, VP
Linda Conrad, Sec
EMP: 6 EST: 1979
SALES (est): 1.03MM Privately Held
Web: www.gmpwelding.com
SIC: 7692 Welding repair

(G-2680)
GOLD MEDAL PRODUCTS CO (PA)
Also Called: Gold Medal-Carolina
10700 Medallion Dr (45241-4807)
PHONE...............................513 769-7676
◆ EMP: 300 EST: 1931
SALES (est): 48.47MM
SALES (corp-wide): 48.47MM Privately Held
Web: www.gmpopcorn.com
SIC: 3556 3589 5145 3581 Food products machinery; Cooking equipment, commercial ; Confectionery; Automatic vending machines

(G-2681)
GOLD STAR CHILI INC (PA)
Also Called: Gold Star Chili
650 Lunken Park Dr (45226-1800)
PHONE...............................513 231-4541
Roger David, Pr
Suhaila B David, Stockholder*
Fahid S Daoud, Stockholder*
Frank S Daoud, Stockholder*
Basheer S David, Stockholder*

EMP: 33 EST: 1965
SQ FT: 5,000
SALES (est): 22.38MM
SALES (corp-wide): 22.38MM Privately Held
Web: www.goldstarchili.com
SIC: 5812 2099 6794 5499 Chili stand; Food preparations, nec; Franchises, selling or licensing; Spices and herbs

(G-2682)
GOLD STAR CHILI INC
Also Called: Gold Star Chili
5420 Ridge Ave (45213-2514)
PHONE...............................513 631-1990
Rusa Abusway, Owner
EMP: 53
SALES (corp-wide): 22.38MM Privately Held
Web: www.goldstarchili.com
SIC: 5812 2099 Chili stand; Food preparations, nec
PA: Gold Star Chili, Inc.
650 Lunkenpark Dr
Cincinnati OH 45226
513 231-4541

(G-2683)
GOMEZ SALSA LLC
8575 Coolwood Ct (45236-1301)
PHONE...............................513 314-1978
Andrew Gomez, Prin
EMP: 11 EST: 2012
SALES (est): 1.05MM Privately Held
Web: www.gomezsalsa.com
SIC: 2099 Dips, except cheese and sour cream based

(G-2684)
GOSUN INC
5151 Fischer Ave (45217-1157)
PHONE...............................888 868-6154
Patrick Sherwin, CEO
EMP: 10 EST: 2016
SALES (est): 5.87MM Privately Held
Web: www.gosun.co
SIC: 3631 Barbecues, grills, and braziers (outdoor cooking)

(G-2685)
GOVERNMENT ACQUISITIONS INC
2060 Reading Rd Fl 4 (45202-1400)
PHONE...............................513 721-8700
Roger Brown, CEO
Roger Brown, Owner
Stan Jones, *
Bobby Brown, *
EMP: 35 EST: 1989
SQ FT: 20,000
SALES (est): 41.69MM Privately Held
Web: www.gov-acq.com
SIC: 7378 3577 5045 Computer maintenance and repair; Computer peripheral equipment, nec; Computer software

(G-2686)
GOYAL ENTERPRISES INC
Also Called: Bharat Trading
4836 Business Center Way (45246-1318)
P.O. Box 1728 (45071-1728)
PHONE...............................513 874-9303
Arun Goyal, Genl Mgr
Kavita Goyal, Pr
EMP: 10 EST: 1991
SQ FT: 4,500
SALES (est): 543.67K Privately Held
Web: www.geminijewelers.com
SIC: 5094 5944 3911 Jewelry; Jewelry, precious stones and precious metals; Bracelets, precious metal

(G-2687)
GRAETERS ICE CREAM COMPANY (PA)
1175 Regina Graeter Way (45216-1998)
PHONE...............................513 721-3323
Richard Graeter Ii, Pr
Tom Kunzelman, *
EMP: 60 EST: 1870
SQ FT: 25,000
SALES (est): 26.74MM
SALES (corp-wide): 26.74MM Privately Held
Web: www.graeters.com
SIC: 2024 2051 2064 2066 Ice cream, packaged: molded, on sticks, etc.; Bread, cake, and related products; Candy and other confectionery products; Chocolate and cocoa products

(G-2688)
GREAT RIVER RE INC (HQ)
Also Called: Coolant Control, Inc.
5353 Spring Grove Ave (45217-1026)
PHONE...............................513 471-8770
Greg Battle, CEO
Garry C Ferraris, Pr
Jorge Costa, Ofcr
Larry Schirmann, CFO
▲ EMP: 33 EST: 1975
SQ FT: 30,000
SALES (est): 5.67MM
SALES (corp-wide): 5.67MM Privately Held
Web: www.coolantcontrol.com
SIC: 2899 2819 Chemical preparations, nec; Industrial inorganic chemicals, nec
PA: Kodiak, Llc
1800 Murray Ave
Pittsburgh PA 15217
724 812-6595

(G-2689)
GREATER CINCINNATI BOWL ASSN
611 Mercury Dr (45215)
P.O. Box 54290 (45254-0290)
PHONE...............................513 761-7387
Willie Dean, Pr
Tom Taylor, VP
Joe Mcfarland, VP
EMP: 22 EST: 1895
SQ FT: 1,700
SALES (est): 779.22K Privately Held
Web: www.pincincinnati.org
SIC: 8699 2721 7933 Bowling club; Periodicals; Bowling centers

(G-2690)
GREENDALE HOME FASHIONS LLC
5500 Muddy Creek Rd (45238-2030)
PHONE...............................859 916-5475
▲ EMP: 80 EST: 1954
SALES (est): 5.26MM Privately Held
Web: www.greendalehomefashions.com
SIC: 3842 2392 Life preservers, except cork and inflatable; Cushions and pillows

(G-2691)
GREG G WRIGHT & SONS LLC
10200 Springfield Pike (45215-1116)
PHONE...............................513 721-3310
Tracey A Chriske, Prin
EMP: 30 EST: 1860
SQ FT: 34,000
SALES (est): 693.66K Privately Held
Web: www.gregwrightandsons.com
SIC: 3953 3993 Textile marking stamps, hand: rubber or metal; Name plates: except engraved, etched, etc.: metal

(G-2692)
GRIFFIN FISHER CO INC
1126 William Howard Taft Rd (45206-2031)
PHONE...............................513 961-2110
Whitney Fisher, CEO
Branden Fisher, Pr
EMP: 9 EST: 1909
SQ FT: 3,800
SALES (est): 436.94K Privately Held
Web: www.fishergriffinco.com
SIC: 2394 2396 2399 Convertible tops, canvas or boat: from purchased materials; Automotive trimmings, fabric; Seat covers, automobile

(G-2693)
GRIPPO FOODS INC (PA)
6750 Colerain Ave (45239-5542)
PHONE...............................513 923-1900
Teri Nicole Baker, Pr
James Pagel, *
Linda Foster, *
Nancy Schreiber, *
Dorothy Saylor, *
EMP: 79 EST: 1919
SQ FT: 27,000
SALES (est): 21.21MM
SALES (corp-wide): 21.21MM Privately Held
Web: www.grippos.com
SIC: 2096 Potato chips and similar snacks

(G-2694)
GRIPPO POTATO CHIP CO INC
6750 Colerain Ave (45239-5542)
PHONE...............................513 923-1900
Ralph W Pagel Ii, Pr
James Pagel, *
Linda Foster, *
Dorothy Saylor, *
EMP: 10 EST: 1919
SQ FT: 27,000
SALES (est): 1.4MM Privately Held
Web: www.grippos.com
SIC: 2096 2099 Potato chips and other potato-based snacks; Food preparations, nec

(G-2695)
GT INDUSTRIAL SUPPLY INC
Also Called: Gt Industrial Supply
7775 E Kemper Rd (45249-1611)
PHONE...............................513 771-7000
Michael Griffie Junior, Pr
Stephen Tino, VP
EMP: 10 EST: 2009
SALES (est): 6MM Privately Held
Web: www.gtindustrialsupply.com
SIC: 2671 5063 5087 5199 Paper; coated and laminated packaging; Lighting fixtures; Janitors' supplies; Packaging materials

(G-2696)
GTLP HOLDINGS LLC (PA)
Also Called: Premier Southern Ticket
7911 School Rd (45249-1533)
PHONE...............................513 489-6700
Phillip R Sorensen, Pr
Kirk Schulz, VP
EMP: 28 EST: 2009
SQ FT: 35,000
SALES (est): 2.23MM Privately Held
Web: www.premiersouthern.com
SIC: 2752 Tag, ticket, and schedule printing: lithographic

(G-2697)
GUS HOLTHAUS SIGNS INC
Also Called: Holthaus Lackner Signs
817 Ridgeway Ave (45229-3222)
P.O. Box 29373 (45229-0373)

PHONE.............................513 861-0060
Kevin Holthaus, *Pr*
Scott Holthaus, *
Kerry Holthaus, *
EMP: 40 **EST:** 1929
SQ FT: 38,600
SALES (est): 6.9MM **Privately Held**
Web: www.hlsigns.com
SIC: 3993 1799 Electric signs; Sign installation and maintenance

(G-2698)
H HAFNER & SONS INC
5445 Wooster Pike (45226-2226)
P.O. Box 30435 (45230)
PHONE.............................513 321-1895
Justin Cooper, *Pr*
Linda Hafner, *
Andrew O Haefner, *
Maryellen Maltry, *
Paul J Hengge, *
EMP: 42 **EST:** 1923
SQ FT: 5,500
SALES (est): 7.17MM **Privately Held**
Web: www.hafners.com
SIC: 5191 2499 4212 4953 Soil, potting and planting; Mulch, wood and bark; Dump truck haulage; Recycling, waste materials

(G-2699)
H LEE PHILIPPI CO
3660 Hyde Park Ave (45208-1497)
P.O. Box 9845 (45209-0845)
PHONE.............................513 321-5330
Hiram Lee Philippi, *Pr*
Richard W Scott, *VP*
EMP: 15 **EST:** 1964
SQ FT: 20,000
SALES (est): 988.44K **Privately Held**
SIC: 2679 Paperboard products, converted, nec

(G-2700)
H NAGEL & SON CO
Also Called: Brighton Mills
2641 Spring Grove Ave (45214-1731)
PHONE.............................513 665-4550
Brian Mitchell, *Genl Mgr*
EMP: 10
SALES (corp-wide): 7.35MM **Privately Held**
Web: www.brightonmills.com
SIC: 2041 Flour: blended, prepared, or self-rising
PA: H. Nagel & Son Co.
707 Harrison Brkvl Rd Uni
West Harrison IN 47060
513 665-4550

(G-2701)
H&G LEGACY CO (PA)
Also Called: Hill and Griffith Co
1085 Summer St (45204-2037)
PHONE.............................513 921-1075
Mike Lawry, *CEO*
Ryan Canfield, *Pr*
EMP: 14 **EST:** 1896
SALES (est): 8.69MM
SALES (corp-wide): 8.69MM **Privately Held**
Web: www.hillandgriffith.com
SIC: 2899 2869 3565 3542 Chemical preparations, nec; Industrial organic chemicals, nec; Packaging machinery; Machine tools, metal forming type

(G-2702)
HADRONICS INC
4570 Steel Pl (45209-1189)
PHONE.............................513 321-9350
Michael G Green, *Pr*

Kenneth J Green, *
Jeffrey Mccarty, *S&M/VP*
Pat Mcdonough, *Pr*
EMP: 56 **EST:** 1970
SALES (est): 5.39MM **Privately Held**
Web: www.hadronics.com
SIC: 3471 3479 3555 3366 Electroplating of metals or formed products; Etching and engraving; Printing trades machinery; Copper foundries

(G-2703)
HANCHETT PAPER COMPANY
Also Called: Shorr Packaging
12121 Best Pl (45241-6402)
PHONE.............................513 782-4440
Mark Trainer, *Prin*
EMP: 63
SALES (corp-wide): 245.19MM **Privately Held**
Web: www.shorr.com
SIC: 2621 Paper mills
PA: Hanchett Paper Company
4000 Ferry Rd
Aurora IL 60502
888 885-0055

(G-2704)
HANDSHAKERS CONSTRUCTION LLC
213 Assisiknoll Ct (45238-5974)
PHONE.............................513 370-1371
Steven Allen Calendine, *Managing Member*
EMP: 10 **EST:** 2020
SALES (est): 329.31K **Privately Held**
Web: www.handshakersconstructions.com
SIC: 1799 1521 7299 1389 Kitchen and bathroom remodeling; Single-family home remodeling, additions, and repairs; Handyman service; Construction, repair, and dismantling services

(G-2705)
HARBISON WALKER INTL MNRL INC
1085 Summer St (45204-2037)
PHONE.............................513 251-1010
Mark Pine, *Mgr*
EMP: 6
Web:
www.imerys-performance-minerals.com
SIC: 3295 Minerals, ground or treated
HQ: Harbison Walker International Minerals Inc.
2000 Park Ln Ste 400
Pittsburgh PA 15275
412 375-6600

(G-2706)
HARLAN GRAPHIC ARTS SVCS INC
4752 River Rd (45233-1633)
P.O. Box 643806 (45264-3806)
PHONE.............................513 251-5700
Larry Ehrman, *Pr*
Jeff Ehrman, *VP*
Kim Springer, *CFO*
EMP: 22 **EST:** 1980
SQ FT: 40,000
SALES (est): 5.26MM **Privately Held**
Web: www.harlangraphics.com
SIC: 2791 Typesetting

(G-2707)
HARRAY LLC
266 W Mitchell Ave (45232-1908)
PHONE.............................888 568-8371
EMP: 6 **EST:** 2005
SALES (est): 964.5K **Privately Held**
Web: www.archlouvers.com
SIC: 3444 Sheet metalwork

(G-2708)
HARRISON CORPORATION (PA)
3820 Colerain Ave (45223-2571)
PHONE.............................513 681-2420
EMP: 9 **EST:** 1974
SALES (est): 3.86MM
SALES (corp-wide): 3.86MM **Privately Held**
SIC: 3677 3612 3674 Electronic transformers ; Transformers, except electric; Light emitting diodes

(G-2709)
HARTCO INC
1280 Glendale Milford Rd (45215-1209)
P.O. Box 6129 (45206-0129)
PHONE.............................513 771-4430
EMP: 20 **EST:** 1981
SALES (est): 6.37MM **Privately Held**
Web: www.hartcoservice.com
SIC: 2295 Resin or plastic coated fabrics

(G-2710)
HARVEY BROTHERS INC (PA)
3492 Spring Grove Ave (45223-2495)
PHONE.............................513 541-2622
Stephen Kyle, *Pr*
EMP: 8 **EST:** 1920
SQ FT: 5,600
SALES (est): 2.29MM
SALES (corp-wide): 2.29MM **Privately Held**
Web: www.harveybrothersinc.com
SIC: 3441 Fabricated structural metal

(G-2711)
HASON USA CORP
1080 Nimitzview Dr Ste 402 (45230-4332)
PHONE.............................513 248-0287
Dennis Blain, *Prin*
EMP: 9 **EST:** 2014
SALES (est): 1.14MM **Privately Held**
SIC: 3443 Tanks, standard or custom fabricated: metal plate

(G-2712)
HATHAWAY STAMP CO
Also Called: Hathaway Stamp
304 E 8th St (45202-2231)
PHONE.............................513 621-1052
Peter Ruttenberg, *Pr*
Robert C Ruwe, *VP*
EMP: 15 **EST:** 1902
SALES (est): 1.26MM
SALES (corp-wide): 9.65MM **Privately Held**
Web: www.hathawaystamps.com
SIC: 3953 3089 5999 5943 Embossing seals and hand stamps; Engraving of plastics; Rubber stamps; Office forms and supplies
PA: Volk Corporation
47808 Galleon Dr
Plymouth MI 48170
248 477-6700

(G-2713)
HATHAWAY STAMP IDNTFCTION CNCN
Also Called: Hathaway Stamp Identification
304 E 8th St (45202-2231)
PHONE.............................513 621-1052
EMP: 7 **EST:** 2012
SALES (est): 1.34MM
SALES (corp-wide): 9.65MM **Privately Held**
Web: www.hathawaystamps.com
SIC: 3953 3479 Marking devices; Name plates: engraved, etched, etc.
PA: Volk Corporation
47808 Galleon Dr
Plymouth MI 48170

248 477-6700

(G-2714)
HCC/SEALTRON (DH)
9705 Reading Rd (45215-3515)
PHONE.............................513 733-8400
Wes Hausman, *Prin*
EMP: 184 **EST:** 1986
SQ FT: 38,000
SALES (est): 7.94MM
SALES (corp-wide): 6.94B **Publicly Held**
SIC: 3678 Electronic connectors
HQ: Hcc Industries Leasing, Inc.
4232 Temple City Blvd
Rosemead CA 91770
626 443-8933

(G-2715)
HELMART COMPANY INC
Also Called: Countertops Helmart
4960 Hillside Ave (45233-1621)
PHONE.............................513 941-3095
Jeff Wittwer, *Pr*
Marlene Wittwer, *Treas*
Mark Wittwer, *Prin*
EMP: 7 **EST:** 1979
SQ FT: 6,000
SALES (est): 999.03K **Privately Held**
Web:
www.helmartgranitecountertops.com
SIC: 5032 1411 2541 Marble building stone; Granite dimension stone; Table or counter tops, plastic laminated

(G-2716)
HEN OF WOODS LLC
Also Called: Wholesale
2116 Colerain Ave (45214-1838)
P.O. Box 867 (45201-0867)
PHONE.............................513 954-8871
Nick Marckwald, *CEO*
Jason Dranschak, *CFO*
EMP: 7 **EST:** 2012
SQ FT: 9,000
SALES (est): 1.45MM **Privately Held**
Web: www.henofthewoods.com
SIC: 5145 2099 2087 5961 Snack foods; Seasonings and spices; Beverage bases, concentrates, syrups, powders and mixes; Catalog and mail-order houses

(G-2717)
HENKEL US OPERATIONS CORP
9435 Waterstone Blvd (45249-8226)
PHONE.............................513 830-0260
Daniel Henkel, *Brnch Mgr*
EMP: 28
SALES (corp-wide): 22.83B **Privately Held**
Web: www.henkel.com
SIC: 2891 Adhesives
HQ: Henkel Us Operations Corporation
1 Henkel Way
Rocky Hill CT 06067
860 571-5100

(G-2718)
HENTY USA LLC
7260 Edington Dr (45249-1063)
PHONE.............................513 984-5590
Tyler Scott, *Prin*
Tylor Scott, *CEO*
▲ **EMP:** 10 **EST:** 2013
SALES (est): 212.01K **Privately Held**
Web: www.henty-usa.com
SIC: 2392 Bags, garment storage: except paper or plastic film

(G-2719)
HERMETIC SEAL TECHNOLOGY INC
Also Called: Hst
2150 Schappelle Ln (45240-4602)

PHONE..................................513 851-4899
John Wendeln, *Pr*
EMP: 10 **EST:** 1994
SALES (est): 1.11MM **Privately Held**
Web: www.glass-to-metal.com
SIC: 3643 Connectors and terminals for electrical devices

(G-2720)
HESKAMP PRINTING CO INC
5514 Fair Ln (45227-3402)
PHONE..................................513 871-6770
J David Heskamp, *Pr*
Jane Heskamp, *Sec*
EMP: 6 **EST:** 1922
SQ FT: 7,500
SALES (est): 252.12K **Privately Held**
SIC: 2752 2759 Offset printing; Letterpress printing

(G-2721)
HICKMAN WILLIAMS & COMPANY (PA)
250 E 5th St Ste 300 (45202-4198)
P.O. Box 538 (45201)
PHONE..................................513 621-1946
Robert E Davis, *Pr*
Robert J Gray, *VP*
Terry L Meadors, *VP*
Steven W Stark, *VP*
Stuart M Shroyer, *VP*
◆ **EMP:** 11 **EST:** 1890
SQ FT: 5,000
SALES (est): 36.57MM
SALES (corp-wide): 36.57MM **Privately Held**
Web: www.hicwilco.com
SIC: 5051 5052 5169 5085 Steel; Coal and other minerals and ores; Chemicals and allied products, nec; Abrasives

(G-2722)
HILLTOP BASIC RESOURCES INC
Also Called: Hilltop Cmpnies St Brnard Rdym
900 Kieley Pl (45217-1153)
PHONE..................................513 242-8400
Cody Steele, *Brnch Mgr*
EMP: 8
SALES (corp-wide): 49.96MM **Privately Held**
Web: www.hilltopcompanies.com
SIC: 3273 Ready-mixed concrete
PA: Hilltop Basic Resources, Inc.
50 E Rvrcnter Blvd Ste 10
Covington KY 41011
513 651-5000

(G-2723)
HILLTOP BASIC RESOURCES INC
Also Called: Hilltop Concrete
511 W Water St (45202-3400)
PHONE..................................513 621-1500
Mike Marchioni, *Mgr*
EMP: 103
SQ FT: 1,758
SALES (corp-wide): 49.96MM **Privately Held**
Web: www.hilltopcompanies.com
SIC: 3273 3272 1442 Ready-mixed concrete ; Concrete products, nec; Construction sand and gravel
PA: Hilltop Basic Resources, Inc.
50 E Rvrcnter Blvd Ste 10
Covington KY 41011
513 651-5000

(G-2724)
HILLTOP BIG BEND QUARRY LLC
1 W 4th St Ste 1100 (45202-3610)
PHONE..................................513 651-5000
John F Steele Junior, *Prin*

EMP: 11 **EST:** 2005
SALES (est): 699.97K **Privately Held**
Web: www.hilltopcompanies.com
SIC: 3273 Ready-mixed concrete

(G-2725)
HLSIGNS
817 Ridgeway Ave (45229-3222)
PHONE..................................513 703-6363
Kevin Holthaus, *Pr*
EMP: 6 **EST:** 2013
SALES (est): 119.97K **Privately Held**
Web: www.hlsigns.com
SIC: 3993 Signs and advertising specialties

(G-2726)
HOLLAENDER MANUFACTURING CO
10285 Wayne Ave (45215-1199)
P.O. Box 156399 (45215-6399)
PHONE..................................513 772-8800
Robert P Hollaender Ii, *CEO*
Marc E Cetrulo, *
John Reifschneider, *
Ron Crebo, *
▼ **EMP:** 51 **EST:** 1943
SQ FT: 33,000
SALES (est): 8.88MM **Privately Held**
Web: www.hollaender.com
SIC: 3498 Fabricated pipe and fittings

(G-2727)
HOLLAND ASSOCTS LLC DBA ARCHOU
Also Called: Archoustics Mid-America
316 W 4th St Ste 201 (45202-2675)
PHONE..................................513 891-0006
EMP: 10 **EST:** 2007
SALES (est): 1.01MM **Privately Held**
Web: www.rhcontract.com
SIC: 5065 3699 1742 Sound equipment, electronic; Electric sound equipment; Acoustical and insulation work

(G-2728)
HOMAN METALS LLC
1253 Knowlton St (45223-1844)
PHONE..................................513 721-5010
EMP: 8 **EST:** 1940
SQ FT: 60,000
SALES (est): 422.35K **Privately Held**
Web: www.homanmetals.com
SIC: 5093 3334 4953 3355 Ferrous metal scrap and waste; Aluminum ingots and slabs; Recycling, waste materials; Aluminum ingot

(G-2729)
HOME CITY ICE COMPANY
11920 Kemper Springs Dr (45240-1642)
PHONE..................................513 851-4040
Jason Dugas, *Brnch Mgr*
EMP: 9
SQ FT: 14,040
SALES (corp-wide): 100.42MM **Privately Held**
Web: www.homecityice.com
SIC: 2097 Ice cubes
PA: The Home City Ice Company
6045 Bridgetown Rd Ste 1
Cincinnati OH 45248
513 574-1800

(G-2730)
HONEYBAKED HAM COMPANY (PA)
11935 Mason Montgomery Rd Ste 200 (45249-3702)
PHONE..................................513 583-9700
Craig Kurz, *CEO*
George J Kurz, *
George S Kurz, *
Keith Kurz, *

EMP: 25 **EST:** 1957
SQ FT: 12,000
SALES (est): 9.92MM
SALES (corp-wide): 9.92MM **Privately Held**
Web: www.honeybaked.com
SIC: 5421 2099 2024 2013 Meat markets, including freezer provisioners; Food preparations, nec; Ice cream and frozen deserts; Sausages and other prepared meats

(G-2731)
HORMEL FOODS CORP SVCS LLC
Also Called: Hormel
4055 Executive Park Dr Ste 300 (45241-4020)
PHONE..................................513 563-0211
Jim Tupy, *Mgr*
EMP: 17
SALES (corp-wide): 11.92B **Publicly Held**
Web: www.hormelfoods.com
SIC: 2011 Meat packing plants
HQ: Hormel Foods Corporate Services, Llc
1 Hormel Pl
Austin MN 55912

(G-2732)
HORNELL BREWING CO INC
Also Called: Arizona Beverages
635 W 7th St (45203-1513)
PHONE..................................516 812-0384
Francie Patton, *VP*
EMP: 6
SALES (corp-wide): 99.65MM **Privately Held**
SIC: 2086 Bottled and canned soft drinks
PA: Hornell Brewing Co., Inc.
60 Crossways Park Dr W # 400
Woodbury NY 11797
516 812-0300

(G-2733)
HORRORHOUND LTD
1706 Republic St (45202-6421)
P.O. Box 710 (45150-0710)
PHONE..................................513 239-7263
Jeremy Sheldon, *Pt*
EMP: 13 **EST:** 2005
SALES (est): 970.13K **Privately Held**
Web: www.horrorhound.com
SIC: 2731 Book publishing

(G-2734)
HRH DOOR CORP
2136 Stapleton Ct (45240-2780)
PHONE..................................513 674-9300
EMP: 31
SALES (corp-wide): 616.75MM **Privately Held**
SIC: 3442 2431 Garage doors, overhead: metal; Garage doors, overhead, wood
PA: Hrh Door Corp.
1 Door Dr
Mount Hope OH 44660
850 208-3400

(G-2735)
HUNKAR TECHNOLOGIES INC (PA)
2368 Victory Pkwy Ste 210 (45206-2810)
PHONE..................................513 272-1010
Eric R Thiemann, *Pr*
C Kevin Whaley, *
Jeannine Martin, *
James K Rice, *Corporate Secretary*
EMP: 140 **EST:** 1962
SQ FT: 47,000
SALES (est): 24.81MM
SALES (corp-wide): 24.81MM **Privately Held**
Web: www.hunkar.com

SIC: 3565 3823 3577 3441 Labeling machines, industrial; Controllers, for process variables, all types; Bar code (magnetic ink) printers; Fabricated structural metal

(G-2736)
HYDE PARK LUMBER COMPANY
Also Called: Do It Best
3360 Red Bank Rd (45227-4107)
P.O. Box 8085 (45208-0085)
PHONE..................................513 271-1500
Mills C Judy Junior, *Pr*
Vicki Clephane, *
EMP: 35 **EST:** 1902
SQ FT: 80,000
SALES (est): 7.32MM
SALES (corp-wide): 7.32MM **Privately Held**
Web: www.hydeparklumber.com
SIC: 5251 2431 Hardware stores; Millwork
PA: The Judy Mills Company Inc
3360 Red Bank Rd
Cincinnati OH 45227
513 271-4241

(G-2737)
HYDRATECH ENGINEERED PDTS LLC
10448 Chester Rd (45215-1202)
PHONE..................................513 827-9169
Peter Blais, *Managing Member*
EMP: 10 **EST:** 2009
SALES (est): 2.31MM **Privately Held**
Web: www.hydratechllc.com
SIC: 2891 Sealing compounds for pipe threads or joints

(G-2738)
I T VERDIN CO (PA)
Also Called: Verdin Company
444 Reading Rd (45202-1465)
PHONE..................................513 241-4010
F B Wersel, *CEO*
Robert R Verdin Junior, *CEO*
James R Verdin, *
David E Verdin, *
F B Wersel, *Prin*
◆ **EMP:** 30 **EST:** 1842
SQ FT: 13,000
SALES (est): 18.87MM
SALES (corp-wide): 18.87MM **Privately Held**
Web: www.verdin.com
SIC: 3931 3699 3873 Carillon bells; Bells, electric; Clocks, except timeclocks

(G-2739)
IGEL TECHNOLOGY AMERICA LLC
2106 Florence Ave (45206-2427)
PHONE..................................954 739-9990
Jim Volpenhein, *CEO*
EMP: 14 **EST:** 2009
SALES (est): 886.96K **Privately Held**
Web: www.igel.com
SIC: 7372 Prepackaged software

(G-2740)
IMI REAL ESTATE LLC
2792 Glendale Milford Rd (45241-3127)
PHONE..................................513 769-3666
Jay Snider, *Brnch Mgr*
EMP: 6
SALES (corp-wide): 440.22MM **Privately Held**
Web: www.irvmat.com
SIC: 3273 Ready-mixed concrete
PA: Imi Real Estate, Llc
8032 N State Rd 9
Greenfield IN 46140
317 326-3101

▲ = Import ▼ = Export
◆ = Import/Export

(G-2741)
IMPERIAL ADHESIVES
6315 Wiehe Rd (45237-4213)
PHONE..............................513 351-1300
Pete Smith, *VP*
EMP: 7 **EST:** 2008
SALES (est): 360.62K **Privately Held**
SIC: 2891 Adhesives

(G-2742)
IMPERIAL POOLS INC
12090 Best Pl (45241-1569)
PHONE..............................513 771-1506
Mike Grant, *Brnch Mgr*
EMP: 20
SALES (corp-wide): 38.91MM **Privately Held**
Web: www.imperialpoolsb2b.com
SIC: 3949 Swimming pools, except plastic
PA: Imperial Pools, Inc.
     33 Wade Rd
     Latham NY 12110
     518 786-1200

(G-2743)
INDRA HOLDINGS CORP (PA)
Also Called: Totes Isotoner
9655 International Blvd (45246-4861)
PHONE..............................513 682-8200
Daniel S Rajczak, *Pr*
Ronald P Spogli, *Prin*
EMP: 219 **EST:** 2014
SALES (est): 3.04MM
SALES (corp-wide): 3.04MM **Privately Held**
SIC: 5632 2396 5699 2389 Apparel accessories; Apparel and other linings, except millinery; Customized clothing and apparel; Men's miscellaneous accessories

(G-2744)
INDUSTRIAL COATING TECH INC
Also Called: Ict Sales
1011 Sunset Ave (45205-1503)
PHONE..............................513 376-9945
Michael Hernandez, *Prin*
EMP: 6 **EST:** 2017
SALES (est): 90.18K **Privately Held**
SIC: 3479 Metal coating and allied services

(G-2745)
INDUSTRIAL THERMAL SYSTEMS INC
3914 Virginia Ave (45227-3412)
PHONE..............................513 561-2100
Robert Jackson, *Pr*
Susan Jackson, *Treas*
◆ **EMP:** 15 **EST:** 1982
SQ FT: 34,000
SALES (est): 2.63MM **Privately Held**
Web: www.industrialthermal.com
SIC: 3559 3613 Kilns; Control panels, electric

(G-2746)
INNOVATIVE WOODWORKING INC
1901 Ross Ave (45212-2019)
PHONE..............................513 531-1940
Robert Rodenfels, *Pr*
Robert W Rodenfels Ii, *Pr*
Janet A Rodenfels, *VP*
EMP: 9 **EST:** 1984
SQ FT: 13,000
SALES (est): 929.23K **Privately Held**
SIC: 2522 2521 Office bookcases, wallcases and partitions, except wood; Wood office filing cabinets and bookcases

(G-2747)
INSTRMNTATION CTRL SYSTEMS INC

Also Called: Ics Electrical Services
11355 Sebring Dr (45240-2796)
PHONE..............................513 662-2600
John Guenther, *Pr*
▲ **EMP:** 43 **EST:** 1997
SQ FT: 15,500
SALES (est): 10.58MM **Privately Held**
Web: www.icselectricalservices.com
SIC: 1731 7629 3613 General electrical contractor; Electrical measuring instrument repair and calibration; Control panels, electric

(G-2748)
INTER AMERICAN PRODUCTS INC (HQ)
Also Called: Kenlake Foods
1240 State Ave (45204-1728)
PHONE..............................800 645-2233
David B Dillon, *Ch*
Rodney Mcmullen, *Pr*
Bill Lucia, *Genl Mgr*
David Hipenbecker, *Dir*
EMP: 54 **EST:** 1989
SALES (est): 3.11MM
SALES (corp-wide): 147.12B **Publicly Held**
Web: www.interamericanproducts.com
SIC: 2095 2099 2033 2079 Roasted coffee; Spices, including grinding; Jellies, edible, including imitation: in cans, jars, etc.; Salad oils, except corn: vegetable refined
PA: The Kroger Co
     1014 Vine St
     Cincinnati OH 45202
     513 762-4000

(G-2749)
INTERCONTINENTAL CHEMICAL CORP (PA)
4660 Spring Grove Ave (45232-1995)
PHONE..............................513 541-7100
Cameron W Cord, *Pr*
Paul Shaver, *
EMP: 25 **EST:** 1964
SQ FT: 54,000
SALES (est): 3.09MM
SALES (corp-wide): 3.09MM **Privately Held**
Web: www.icc-chemicals.com
SIC: 2899 Chemical preparations, nec

(G-2750)
INTERLUBE CORPORATION
Also Called: Lube & Chem Products
4646 Baker St (45212-2594)
PHONE..............................513 531-1777
Elmer Cleave, *Pr*
Elmer B Cleves, *Pr*
EMP: 10 **EST:** 1969
SQ FT: 4,464
SALES (est): 8.56MM **Privately Held**
Web: www.interlubecorp.com
SIC: 2992 Lubricating oils and greases

(G-2751)
INTERNATIONAL BRAND SERVICES
Also Called: Graeter's Ice Cream
3397 Erie Ave Apt 215 (45208-1638)
PHONE..............................513 376-8209
Kellie Manning, *Genl Mgr*
EMP: 6 **EST:** 2003
SALES (est): 108.8K **Privately Held**
Web: www.graeters.com
SIC: 2024 5812 Ice cream and ice milk; Ice cream stands or dairy bars

(G-2752)
INTERNATIONAL MOTORS LLC
Also Called: Navistar
11775 Highway Dr (45241-2005)

PHONE..............................513 733-8500
David Mannin, *Brnch Mgr*
EMP: 6
SALES (corp-wide): 343.33B **Privately Held**
Web: www.internationaltrucks.com
SIC: 3711 Truck and tractor truck assembly
HQ: International Motors, Llc
     2701 International Dr
     Lisle IL 60532
     331 332-5000

(G-2753)
IOWA QUALITY MEATS LTD
805 E Kemper Rd (45246-2515)
PHONE..............................515 225-6868
Pat Watkins, *Genl Mgr*
EMP: 160 **EST:** 1980
SQ FT: 24,000
SALES (est): 1.89MM **Publicly Held**
SIC: 2013 Prepared pork products, from purchased pork
HQ: Smithfield Packaged Meats Corp.
     805 E Kemper Rd
     Cincinnati OH 45246
     513 782-3800

(G-2754)
IREPORTSOURCE
7864 Camargo Rd (45243-2652)
PHONE..............................888 294-9578
Nancy Koors, *Prin*
EMP: 13 **EST:** 2017
SALES (est): 2.5MM **Privately Held**
Web: www.ireportsource.com
SIC: 7372 Prepackaged software

(G-2755)
J & P INVESTMENTS INC
Also Called: Advance Printing Company
6006 Squirrelwood Ct (45247-5972)
P.O. Box 37633 (45222)
PHONE..............................513 821-2299
Paul Erdman, *Pr*
Thomas Schamer, *VP*
EMP: 13 **EST:** 1980
SALES (est): 494.25K **Privately Held**
Web: www.advanceprinting.com
SIC: 2752 Offset printing

(G-2756)
JACOBS MECHANICAL CO
Also Called: Jacobs
4500 W Mitchell Ave (45232-1912)
PHONE..............................513 681-6800
John E Mc Donald, *Pr*
EMP: 125 **EST:** 1922
SQ FT: 20,000
SALES (est): 5.49MM **Privately Held**
Web: www.jacobsmech.com
SIC: 1711 3444 Ventilation and duct work contractor; Sheet metalwork

(G-2757)
JAKE SWEENEY MAZDA TRI-COUNTY
135 Northland Blvd (45246-3121)
PHONE..............................513 782-1150
EMP: 6 **EST:** 2020
SALES (est): 266.05K **Privately Held**
Web: www.jakesweeneymazda.com
SIC: 5599 3714 Automotive dealers, nec; Motor vehicle parts and accessories

(G-2758)
JAKMAR INCORPORATED
3280 Hageman Ave (45241-1907)
PHONE..............................513 631-4303
William Thaman, *Pr*
EMP: 6 **EST:** 2001
SALES (est): 446.61K **Privately Held**

SIC: 3061 Mechanical rubber goods

(G-2759)
JAMES C FREE INC
Also Called: James Free Jewellers
9555 Main St Ste 1 (45242-7670)
PHONE..............................513 793-0133
Zackery Karaman, *VP*
EMP: 6
SALES (corp-wide): 2.02MM **Privately Held**
Web: www.jamesfree.com
SIC: 3911 5944 Jewelry, precious metal; Jewelry, precious stones and precious metals
PA: James C. Free, Inc.
     3100 Far Hills Ave
     Dayton OH 45429
     937 298-0171

(G-2760)
JAMES C ROBINSON
Also Called: J C Robinson Products
442 Chestnut St Apt 1 (45203-1454)
PHONE..............................513 969-7482
James C Robinson, *Owner*
EMP: 9 **EST:** 1981
SALES (est): 118.16K **Privately Held**
SIC: 5149 7231 2842 Dried or canned foods; Beauty shops; Automobile polish

(G-2761)
JAMES L DECKEBACH LLC
4575 Eastern Ave (45226-1805)
PHONE..............................513 321-3733
James Deckebach, *Owner*
EMP: 6 **EST:** 2016
SALES (est): 401.42K **Privately Held**
SIC: 2511 Wood household furniture

(G-2762)
JATIGA INC (PA)
Also Called: Hanser Music Group
5823 Ravens Ridge Ln (45247-5862)
PHONE..............................859 817-7100
John Hanser Iii, *Pr*
Gary Hanser, *
Timothy Hanser, *
David Rasfeld, *
▲ **EMP:** 80 **EST:** 1924
SALES (est): 1.63MM
SALES (corp-wide): 1.63MM **Privately Held**
SIC: 3931 5099 Musical instruments; Musical instruments

(G-2763)
JBNOVEMBER LLC
3950 Virginia Ave (45227-3412)
PHONE..............................513 272-7000
EMP: 30
SIC: 2752 Offset printing

(G-2764)
JEN-COAT INC (DH)
Also Called: Prolamina
12025 Tricon Rd (45246-1719)
P.O. Box 274 (01086)
PHONE..............................513 671-1777
Gregory Tucker, *CEO*
Eric Bradford, *CFO*
◆ **EMP:** 230 **EST:** 1972
SQ FT: 375,000
SALES (est): 48.75MM
SALES (corp-wide): 1.58B **Privately Held**
Web: www.proampac.com
SIC: 3554 Die cutting and stamping machinery; paper converting
HQ: Prolamina Corporation
     132 N Elm St
     Westfield MA 01086

(G-2765)
JERRY TOOLS INC
6200 Vine St (45216-2199)
PHONE...................................513 242-3211
David Inboldt, *Pr*
David Imholt, *Pr*
Don Daniels, *VP*
Debra Imholt, *VP*
EMP: 16 **EST:** 1965
SQ FT: 15,625
SALES (est): 2.12MM **Privately Held**
Web: www.jerrytools.com
SIC: 3545 3452 Chucks: drill, lathe, or magnetic (machine tool accessories); Nuts, metal

(G-2766)
JFDB LTD
Also Called: Hvac Mech Cntrcto Plbg Ppfttin
10036 Springfield Pike (45215-1452)
PHONE...................................513 870-0601
Jonathan Feldkamp, *Pr*
Joel Feldkamp, *
EMP: 150 **EST:** 2006
SQ FT: 18,000
SALES (est): 21.84MM **Privately Held**
Web: www.jfeldkampdesignbuild.com
SIC: 1711 3499 Mechanical contractor; Aerosol valves, metal

(G-2767)
JOHN FRIEDA PROF HAIR CARE INC (DH)
2535 Spring Grove Ave (45214-1729)
P.O. Box 145444 (45250)
PHONE...................................800 521-3189
William J Gentner, *Pr*
Joseph B Workman, *
EMP: 40 **EST:** 1990
SALES (est): 490.3K **Privately Held**
Web: www.mykaoshop.com
SIC: 2844 Hair preparations, including shampoos
HQ: Kao Usa Inc.
　　2535 Spring Grove Ave
　　Cincinnati OH 45214
　　513 421-1400

(G-2768)
JOHN R JURGENSEN CO (PA)
11641 Mosteller Rd (45241-1520)
PHONE...................................513 771-0820
▲ **EMP:** 440 **EST:** 1930
SALES (est): 225.16MM
SALES (corp-wide): 225.16MM **Privately Held**
Web: www.jrjnet.com
SIC: 1611 1442 General contractor, highway and street construction; Sand mining

(G-2769)
JOHN STEHLIN & SONS CO
Also Called: Stehlin, John & Sons Meats
10134 Colerain Ave (45251-4902)
PHONE...................................513 385-6164
John Stehlin, *Pr*
Ronald Stehlin, *VP*
Richard Stehlin, *Sec*
Dennis Stehlin, *VP*
EMP: 6 **EST:** 1913
SQ FT: 3,600
SALES (est): 515.31K **Privately Held**
Web: www.stehlinsmeatmarket.com
SIC: 5421 2013 2011 Meat markets, including freezer provisioners; Sausages and other prepared meats; Beef products, from beef slaughtered on site

(G-2770)
JOHNSON & JOHNSON SERVICES LLC
273 Mccormick Pl (45219-2811)
PHONE...................................513 289-4514
Danny Johnson, *Mgr*
EMP: 10 **EST:** 2021
SALES (est): 100K **Privately Held**
Web: www.jnj.com
SIC: 3524 Lawnmowers, residential: hand or power

(G-2771)
JOHNSON CONTROLS INC
Also Called: Johnson Controls
7863 Palace Dr (45249-1635)
PHONE...................................513 489-0950
Brian Ballitch, *Brnch Mgr*
EMP: 52
Web: www.johnsoncontrols.com
SIC: 2531 Seats, automobile
HQ: Johnson Controls, Inc.
　　5757 N Green Bay Ave
　　Milwaukee WI 53209
　　866 496-1999

(G-2772)
JOHNSON CONTROLS INC
Also Called: Johnson Controls
11648 Springfield Pike (45246-3019)
PHONE...................................513 671-6338
Lawrence W Gundler, *Pr*
EMP: 16
Web: www.johnsoncontrols.com
SIC: 2531 7382 Seats, automobile; Security systems services
HQ: Johnson Controls, Inc.
　　5757 N Green Bay Ave
　　Milwaukee WI 53209
　　866 496-1999

(G-2773)
JOS BERNING PRINTING CO
1850 Dalton Ave (45214-2056)
PHONE...................................513 721-0781
Michael Berning, *Pr*
EMP: 11 **EST:** 1883
SQ FT: 11,800
SALES (est): 435.3K **Privately Held**
Web: www.josberningprinting.com
SIC: 2752 Offset printing

(G-2774)
JRM 2 COMPANY
Also Called: Cushman Foundry Div
425 Shepherd Ave (45215-3114)
P.O. Box 15527 (45215-0527)
PHONE...................................513 554-1700
▲ **EMP:** 100
SIC: 3365 3325 3369 3341 Aluminum and aluminum-based alloy castings; Alloy steel castings, except investment; Nonferrous foundries, nec; Secondary nonferrous metals

(G-2775)
JUDY MILLS COMPANY INC (PA)
3360 Red Bank Rd (45227-4107)
PHONE...................................513 271-4241
Mike Judy, *Pr*
EMP: 36 **EST:** 1922
SALES (est): 7.32MM
SALES (corp-wide): 7.32MM **Privately Held**
Web: www.doitbest.com
SIC: 5251 5211 2431 Hardware stores; Lumber and other building materials; Millwork

(G-2776)
K F T INC
726 Mehring Way (45203-1809)
PHONE...................................513 241-5910
Ronald Eubanks, *Pr*
Richard Eubanks, *Stockholder*
EMP: 60 **EST:** 1941
SQ FT: 45,000
SALES (est): 2.15MM **Privately Held**
Web: www.tkf.com
SIC: 1796 3535 Millwright; Overhead conveyor systems

(G-2777)
KAFFENBARGER TRUCK EQP CO
3260 E Kemper Rd (45241-1519)
PHONE...................................513 772-6800
Rodney Swigert, *Mgr*
EMP: 25
SQ FT: 18,280
SALES (corp-wide): 22.65MM **Privately Held**
Web: www.knapheide.com
SIC: 7538 5531 3713 3532 Truck engine repair, except industrial; Truck equipment and parts; Truck bodies and parts; Mining machinery
PA: Kaffenbarger Truck Equipment Co Inc
　　10991 Ballentine Pike
　　New Carlisle OH 45344
　　937 845-3804

(G-2778)
KAHNY PRINTING INC
4766 River Rd (45233-1633)
PHONE...................................513 251-2911
John S Kahny, *Pr*
Linda Knierim, *
EMP: 25 **EST:** 1956
SQ FT: 14,000
SALES (est): 4.78MM **Privately Held**
Web: www.kahny.com
SIC: 2752 Offset printing

(G-2779)
KAISER FOODS INC (PA)
500 York St (45214-2490)
PHONE...................................513 621-2053
David Kaiser, *Ch*
Donald J Kaiser, *VP*
Kim Speed, *VP*
Kimberly Speed, *COO*
▲ **EMP:** 20 **EST:** 1920
SQ FT: 50,000
SALES (est): 21.06MM
SALES (corp-wide): 21.06MM **Privately Held**
Web: www.kaiserpickles.com
SIC: 5149 2035 Pickles, preserves, jellies, and jams; Cucumbers, pickles and pickle salting

(G-2780)
KAISER PICKLES LLC (HQ)
500 York St (45214-2416)
PHONE...................................513 621-2053
David Kaiser, *CEO*
Kim Speed, *
EMP: 6 **EST:** 2003
SALES (est): 21.06MM
SALES (corp-wide): 21.06MM **Privately Held**
Web: www.kaiserpickles.com
SIC: 2035 Pickled fruits and vegetables
PA: Kaiser Foods, Inc.
　　500 York St
　　Cincinnati OH 45214
　　513 621-2053

(G-2781)
KAISER PICKLES LLC
422 York St (45214-2414)
PHONE...................................513 621-2053
EMP: 16
SALES (corp-wide): 21.06MM **Privately Held**
Web: www.kaiserpickles.com
SIC: 2035 Pickled fruits and vegetables
HQ: Kaiser Pickles, Llc
　　500 York St
　　Cincinnati OH 45214
　　513 621-2053

(G-2782)
KAO USA INC (HQ)
2535 Spring Grove Ave (45214-1729)
P.O. Box 145444 (45250-5444)
PHONE...................................513 421-1400
Karen B Frank, *Ch Bd*
John Nosek, *
◆ **EMP:** 400 **EST:** 1971
SQ FT: 489,000
SALES (est): 457.85MM **Privately Held**
Web: www.kao.com
SIC: 2844 2841 Cosmetic preparations; Soap: granulated, liquid, cake, flaked, or chip
PA: Kao Corporation
　　1-14-10, Nihombashikayabacho
　　Chuo-Ku TKY 103-0

(G-2783)
KAO USA INC
312 Plum St (45202-2697)
PHONE...................................513 629-5210
Bill Gentner, *Pr*
EMP: 15
Web: www.kaoprint.com
SIC: 2844 Cosmetic preparations
HQ: Kao Usa Inc.
　　2535 Spring Grove Ave
　　Cincinnati OH 45214
　　513 421-1400

(G-2784)
KARRIKIN SPIRITS COMPANY LLC
3717 Jonlen Dr (45227-4103)
PHONE...................................513 561-5000
EMP: 16 **EST:** 2017
SALES (est): 1.96MM **Privately Held**
Web: www.karrikinspirits.com
SIC: 2085 5812 Distilled and blended liquors ; Eating places

(G-2785)
KATCH KITCHEN LLC
4172 Hamilton Ave (45223-2247)
PHONE...................................513 537-8056
EMP: 20 **EST:** 2020
SALES (est): 540K **Privately Held**
SIC: 2499 Food handling and processing products, wood

(G-2786)
KAWS INC
Also Called: RB Tool & Mfg. Co.
2680 Civic Center Dr (45231-1312)
PHONE...................................513 521-8292
Kathy Schaeper, *CEO*
Al Schaeper, *
EMP: 25 **EST:** 1995
SQ FT: 20,000
SALES (est): 4.59MM **Privately Held**
Web: www.rbtoolandmfg.com
SIC: 3599 Machine shop, jobbing and repair

(G-2787)
KDM SIGNS INC (PA)
Also Called: Kdm Screen Printing

10450 Medallion Dr (45241-3199)
PHONE.............................513 769-1932
Robert J Kissel, *Pr*
Kathy Mcqueen, *Sec*
▲ EMP: 230 EST: 1984
SQ FT: 150,000
SALES (est): 49.21MM
SALES (corp-wide): 49.21MM **Privately Held**
Web: www.kdmpop.com
SIC: 3993 2759 Signs and advertising specialties; Screen printing

(G-2788)
KDM SIGNS INC
2996 Exon Ave (45241-2521)
PHONE.............................513 554-1393
EMP: 20
SALES (corp-wide): 49.21MM **Privately Held**
Web: www.kdmpop.com
SIC: 2759 Commercial printing, nec
PA: Kdm Signs, Inc.
    10450 N Medallion Dr
    Cincinnati OH 45241
    513 769-1932

(G-2789)
KDM SIGNS INC
Kdm Retail
3000 Exon Ave (45241-2550)
PHONE.............................513 769-3900
Lee Diss, *Brnch Mgr*
EMP: 20
SALES (corp-wide): 49.21MM **Privately Held**
Web: www.kdmpop.com
SIC: 2541 Display fixtures, wood
PA: Kdm Signs, Inc.
    10450 N Medallion Dr
    Cincinnati OH 45241
    513 769-1932

(G-2790)
KEEBLER COMPANY
Also Called: Keebler
1 Trade St (45227-4509)
PHONE.............................513 271-3500
Sam Bristle, *Mgr*
EMP: 186
SALES (corp-wide): 12.75B **Publicly Held**
Web: www.keebler.com
SIC: 2052 Cookies
HQ: Keebler Company
    1 Kellogg Sq
    Battle Creek MI 49017
    269 961-2000

(G-2791)
KEMPF SURGICAL APPLIANCES INC
10567 Montgomery Rd (45242-4416)
PHONE.............................513 984-5758
Steven Kempf, *Pr*
Susan Kempf, *Treas*
EMP: 9 EST: 1963
SALES (est): 661.48K **Privately Held**
Web: www.kempfsurgical.com
SIC: 5999 5047 7352 3842 Hospital equipment and supplies; Hospital equipment and supplies, nec; Medical equipment rental; Surgical appliances and supplies

(G-2792)
KENDALL/HUNT PUBLISHING CO
Also Called: Rcl Benziger
8805 Governors Hill Dr Ste 400
(45249-3314)
PHONE.............................877 275-4725
Peter Ashpostio, *Brnch Mgr*
EMP: 109

SALES (corp-wide): 39.18MM **Privately Held**
Web: www.rclbenziger.com
SIC: 2731 Books, publishing and printing
PA: Kendall/Hunt Publishing Company
    4050 Westmark Dr
    Dubuque IA 52002
    563 589-1000

(G-2793)
KENNEDY INK COMPANY INC (PA)
5230 Wooster Pike (45226-2229)
PHONE.............................513 871-2515
Jim Scott, *Pr*
James H Scott, *Prin*
Ralph W Wagner, *Prin*
Donald M Kennedy, *Prin*
EMP: 10 EST: 1956
SQ FT: 8,000
SALES (est): 3.95MM
SALES (corp-wide): 3.95MM **Privately Held**
Web: www.perfectdomain.com
SIC: 2893 Printing ink

(G-2794)
KENVUE BRANDS LLC
8044 Montgomery Rd Ste 510
(45236-2924)
PHONE.............................513 985-1540
Sue Strunk, *Brnch Mgr*
EMP: 18
SALES (corp-wide): 15.46B **Publicly Held**
Web: www.kenvue.com
SIC: 2834 Pharmaceutical preparations
HQ: Kenvue Brands Llc
    1 Kenvue Way
    Summit NJ 07901
    908 874-1000

(G-2795)
KING BAG AND MANUFACTURING CO (PA)
1500 Spring Lawn Ave (45223-1699)
PHONE.............................513 541-5440
Connie M Kirsch, *Pr*
Ronald Kirsch Senior, *VP*
Ronald Kirsch Junior, *VP*
◆ EMP: 25 EST: 1985
SQ FT: 18,000
SALES (est): 4.31MM
SALES (corp-wide): 4.31MM **Privately Held**
Web: www.kingbag.com
SIC: 2393 2221 Textile bags; Polyethylene broadwoven fabrics

(G-2796)
KINSELLA MANUFACTURING CO INC
7880 Camargo Rd (45243-2652)
PHONE.............................513 561-5285
George P Kinsella, *Pr*
John Kinsella, *Sec*
Kevin Kinsella, *VP*
EMP: 10 EST: 1961
SQ FT: 10,000
SALES (est): 469.79K **Privately Held**
Web: www.kinsellakitchens.com
SIC: 5211 2541 2434 Cabinets, kitchen; Counters or counter display cases, wood; Wood kitchen cabinets

(G-2797)
KIRK & BLUM MANUFACTURING CO (DH)
4625 Red Bank Rd Ste 200 (45227-1552)
PHONE.............................513 458-2600
◆ EMP: 200 EST: 1907
SQ FT: 250,000
SALES (est): 43.18MM **Publicly Held**
Web: www.cecoenviro.com

SIC: 1761 3444 3443 Sheet metal work, nec; Sheet metal specialties, not stamped; Fabricated plate work (boiler shop)
HQ: Ceco Group, Inc.
    4625 Red Bank Rd Ste 200
    Cincinnati OH 45227
    513 458-2600

(G-2798)
KIRWAN INDUSTRIES INC
8390 Ridge Rd (45236-1338)
PHONE.............................513 333-0766
Ronan Kirwan, *Pr*
EMP: 8 EST: 1994
SALES (est): 207.09K **Privately Held**
Web: www.kirwanindustries.com
SIC: 3441 Building components, structural steel

(G-2799)
KITCHENS BY RUTENSCHROER INC (PA)
Also Called: Kbr
950 Laidlaw Ave (45237-5004)
PHONE.............................513 251-8333
Steven Rutenschroer, *Pr*
Missy Rutenschroer, *VP*
G Robert Hines, *Prin*
Kathy Frisby, *Prin*
Steven D Rutenschroer, *Prin*
▲ EMP: 9 EST: 1978
SQ FT: 8,000
SALES (est): 4.29MM
SALES (corp-wide): 4.29MM **Privately Held**
Web: www.kbrmfg.com
SIC: 5722 2519 2541 2511 Kitchens, complete (sinks, cabinets, etc.); Household furniture, except wood or metal: upholstered; Wood partitions and fixtures; Wood household furniture

(G-2800)
KLOSTERMAN BAKING CO LLC
1000 E Ross Ave (45217-1191)
PHONE.............................513 242-5667
Larry Moore, *Mgr*
EMP: 133
SALES (corp-wide): 93.13MM **Privately Held**
Web: www.klostermanbakery.com
SIC: 5149 2051 Bakery products; Bread, cake, and related products
PA: Klosterman Baking Co., Llc
    2100 Litton Ln
    Hebron KY 41048
    513 242-1004

(G-2801)
KN8DESIGNS LLC
4016 Allston St (45209-1743)
PHONE.............................859 380-5926
Nathan Ward, *Prin*
EMP: 6 EST: 2009
SALES (est): 508.65K **Privately Held**
Web: www.kn8designs.com
SIC: 2621 Printing paper

(G-2802)
KNOBLE GLASS & METAL INC (PA)
Also Called: K G M
8650 Green Rd (45255-5016)
PHONE.............................513 753-1246
David Knoble, *Pr*
EMP: 9 EST: 1999
SALES (est): 896.42K
SALES (corp-wide): 896.42K **Privately Held**
Web: www.knobelglassandmetal.com
SIC: 3229 3354 Glass fibers, textile; Aluminum extruded products

(G-2803)
KNOWLTON MANUFACTURING CO INC
2524 Leslie Ave (45212-4299)
PHONE.............................513 631-7353
Kenneth Jenkins, *Pr*
John Fricker, *VP*
Allan Marcuse, *CFO*
Karen Fanroy, *Dir*
EMP: 15 EST: 2009
SQ FT: 44,000
SALES (est): 4.25MM **Privately Held**
Web: www.knowltonmfg.com
SIC: 3469 3544 Stamping metal for the trade ; Special dies and tools

(G-2804)
KOHL & MADDEN INC
5000 Spring Grove Ave (45232-1926)
PHONE.............................513 326-6900
Rudi Lenz, *Prin*
EMP: 6 EST: 2008
SALES (est): 146.87K **Privately Held**
Web: www.sunchemical.com
SIC: 2893 Printing ink

(G-2805)
KOOP DIAMOND CUTTERS INC
214 E 8th St Fl 4 (45202-2173)
PHONE.............................513 621-2838
Clarence E Koop, *Pr*
Richard J Louis, *Sec*
EMP: 10 EST: 1965
SQ FT: 4,300
SALES (est): 573.97K **Privately Held**
Web: www.koopdiamondcutters.com
SIC: 3911 7631 3915 Jewelry, precious metal ; Jewelry repair services; Jewel cutting, drilling, polishing, recutting, or setting

(G-2806)
KOST USA INC (DH)
Also Called: Kgi Holdings
1000 Tennessee Ave (45229-1008)
PHONE.............................513 583-7070
EMP: 23 EST: 1985
SALES (est): 22.62MM
SALES (corp-wide): 86.97MM **Privately Held**
Web: www.kostusa.com
SIC: 2899 2992 Antifreeze compounds; Lubricating oils
HQ: Recochem Inc.
    6250 N River Rd # 6000
    Rosemont IL 60018
    888 269-0750

(G-2807)
KREHBIEL HOLDINGS INC
3962 Virginia Ave (45227-3412)
PHONE.............................513 271-6035
Tim Ruppert, *CEO*
▼ EMP: 93 EST: 1871
SQ FT: 170,000
SALES (est): 6.87MM **Privately Held**
Web: www.cjkusa.com
SIC: 2752 Offset printing

(G-2808)
KUHLS HOT SPORTSPOT
6701 Beechmont Ave (45230-2905)
PHONE.............................513 474-2282
Robert Kuhl, *Owner*
EMP: 10 EST: 1987
SALES (est): 461.66K **Privately Held**
Web: www.cincysportsshop.com
SIC: 2395 Embroidery products, except Schiffli machine

(G-2809)
KYOCERA SENCO INDUS TLS INC (HQ)
8450 Broadwell Rd (45244-1612)
PHONE..................................513 388-2000
Cliff Mentrup, *CEO*
▲ **EMP:** 70 **EST:** 1948
SALES (est): 48.68MM **Privately Held**
Web: www.senco.com
SIC: 3546 7389 Power-driven handtools;
Business services, nec
PA: Kyocera Corporation
6, Takedatobadonocho, Fushimi-Ku
Kyoto KYO 612-8

(G-2810)
LA MFG INC
Also Called: Brewer Products
9483 Reading Rd (45215-3550)
P.O. Box 62065 (45262-0065)
PHONE..................................513 577-7200
David Brewer, *Pr*
EMP: 6 **EST:** 1989
SALES (est): 493.29K **Privately Held**
Web: www.brewerproducts.com
SIC: 3569 5199 5082 General industrial
machinery, nec; Nondurable goods, nec;
Construction and mining machinery

(G-2811)
LANGDON INC
9865 Wayne Ave (45215-1403)
P.O. Box 15308 (45215-0308)
PHONE..................................513 733-5955
David Sandman, *Pr*
Michael Sandman, *
▲ **EMP:** 40 **EST:** 1966
SQ FT: 42,000
SALES (est): 5.17MM **Privately Held**
Web: www.langdonsheetmetal.com
SIC: 3444 1711 3564 3446 Ducts, sheet
metal; Warm air heating and air
conditioning contractor; Blowers and fans;
Architectural metalwork

(G-2812)
LATE FOR SKY PRODUCTION CO
1292 Glendale Milford Rd (45215-1209)
PHONE..................................513 531-4400
Robyn L Wilson, *Prin*
William C Schulte Junior, *VP*
Mark Hunter, *
Chris Niehaus, *
▲ **EMP:** 48 **EST:** 1985
SQ FT: 60,000
SALES (est): 5.11MM **Privately Held**
Web: www.lateforthesky.com
SIC: 3944 Board games, children's and
adults'

(G-2813)
LAUNCH SCOUT LLC
Also Called: Gaslight
5910 Hamilton Ave (45224-3027)
PHONE..................................513 449-6940
Peter Kananen, *CEO*
Doug Alcorn, *COO*
EMP: 17 **EST:** 2017
SALES (est): 4.85MM **Privately Held**
Web: www.launchscout.com
SIC: 7372 Prepackaged software

(G-2814)
LAURENEE LTD
Also Called: Deerfield Digital
3509 Harrison Ave (45211-5544)
PHONE..................................513 662-2225
Timothy R Roedersheimer, *Managing
Member*
EMP: 8 **EST:** 1975
SQ FT: 8,500

SALES (est): 928.37K **Privately Held**
Web: www.deerfielddigital.com
SIC: 2752 2791 Offset printing; Typesetting

(G-2815)
LEADEC CORP (HQ)
Also Called: Leadec Services
9395 Kenwood Rd Ste 200 (45242-6819)
PHONE..................................513 731-3590
William Bell, *CEO*
Donald G Morsch, *
▲ **EMP:** 34 **EST:** 1984
SQ FT: 18,000
SALES (est): 341.34MM
SALES (corp-wide): 1.69B **Privately Held**
Web: www.leadec-services.com
SIC: 7349 8741 3714 Building cleaning
service; Management services; Motor
vehicle parts and accessories
PA: Leadec Holding Bv & Co. Kg
Meitnerstr. 11
Stuttgart BW 70563
71178410

(G-2816)
LEARN21 A FLXBLE LRNG CLLBRTIV
11802 Conrey Rd (45249-1074)
PHONE..................................513 402-2121
William Fritz, *Ex Dir*
EMP: 15 **EST:** 2008
SALES (est): 1.19MM **Privately Held**
Web: www.learn21.org
SIC: 8351 7372 Child day care services;
Educational computer software

(G-2817)
LEE CORPORATION
Also Called: Lee Printers
12055 Mosteller Rd (45241-1589)
PHONE..................................513 771-3602
Thomas Krieg, *Pr*
Carol Krieg, *Sec*
Ronald Krieg, *Treas*
Lee Krieg, *VP*
EMP: 7 **EST:** 1905
SQ FT: 35,000
SALES (est): 248.19K **Privately Held**
Web: www.leeprinters.com
SIC: 2752 2759 2791 2789 Offset printing;
Letterpress printing; Typesetting;
Bookbinding and related work

(G-2818)
LEICA BIOSYSTEMS - TAS
300 E Business Way Fl 5 (45241-2384)
PHONE..................................513 864-9671
EMP: 41 **EST:** 2018
SALES (est): 7.97MM **Privately Held**
SIC: 3841 Surgical and medical instruments

(G-2819)
LEONHARDT PLATING COMPANY
5753 Este Ave (45232-1499)
PHONE..................................513 242-1410
Kerry Leonhardt, *Pr*
Daniel Leonhardt, *Stockholder*
EMP: 8 **EST:** 1950
SQ FT: 20,500
SALES (est): 991.64K **Privately Held**
Web: www.leonhardtplating.com
SIC: 3471 2899 2851 2842 Electroplating of
metals or formed products; Chemical
preparations, nec; Paints and allied
products; Polishes and sanitation goods

(G-2820)
LIB THERAPEUTICS INC
5375 Medpace Way (45227-1543)
PHONE..................................859 240-7764
David Cory, *CEO*

Dennis Thompson, *CFO*
EMP: 10 **EST:** 2017
SALES (est): 2.35MM **Privately Held**
Web: www.libtherapeutics.com
SIC: 2834 Pharmaceutical preparations

(G-2821)
LIFE IS SWEET LLC (PA)
6926 Main St (45244-3009)
PHONE..................................330 342-0172
EMP: 13 **EST:** 2018
SALES (est): 15.37MM
SALES (corp-wide): 15.37MM **Privately
Held**
Web: www.lisbrands.com
SIC: 2064 Candy and other confectionery
products

(G-2822)
LIGHT VISION
1776 Mentor Ave (45212-3554)
PHONE..................................513 351-9444
EMP: 6 **EST:** 1996
SQ FT: 3,000
SALES (est): 341.71K **Privately Held**
SIC: 2064 Candy and other confectionery
products

(G-2823)
LINDE GAS & EQUIPMENT INC
Also Called: Praxair
8376 Reading Rd (45237-1407)
PHONE..................................513 821-2192
Joe R Smith, *Mgr*
EMP: 8
Web: www.lindeus.com
SIC: 2813 5084 5999 Carbon dioxide;
Welding machinery and equipment;
Welding supplies
HQ: Linde Gas & Equipment Inc.
10 Riverview Dr
Danbury CT 06810
844 445-4633

(G-2824)
LISTERMANN MFG CO INC
Also Called: Listermann Brewery Supply
4120 Forest Ave (45212-3340)
PHONE..................................513 731-1130
Daniel Listermann, *Pr*
Sue Listermann, *VP*
EMP: 8 **EST:** 1991
SALES (est): 3.69MM **Privately Held**
Web: www.listermannbrewing.com
SIC: 3556 Brewers' and maltsters' machinery

(G-2825)
LIVE OFF LOYALTY INC
12019 Hitchcock Dr (45240-1816)
PHONE..................................513 413-2401
Derrick Ferguson, *CEO*
EMP: 7 **EST:** 2015
SALES (est): 226.54K **Privately Held**
SIC: 2782 Record albums

(G-2826)
LONG-LOK LLC (PA)
10630 Chester Rd (45215-1249)
PHONE..................................336 343-7319
Bryan Perkins, *Managing Member*
EMP: 30 **EST:** 2019
SALES (est): 9.6MM
SALES (corp-wide): 9.6MM **Privately Held**
Web: www.longlok.com
SIC: 3728 R and D by manuf., aircraft parts
and auxiliary equipment

(G-2827)
**LONG-LOK FASTENERS
CORPORATION**

10630 Chester Rd (45215-1249)
PHONE..................................513 772-1880
Aaron Dollenmeyer, *Mgr*
EMP: 35
SQ FT: 33,000
SALES (corp-wide): 7.76MM **Privately
Held**
Web: www.longlok.com
SIC: 3452 Bolts, nuts, rivets, and washers
HQ: Long-Lok Fasteners Corporation
14755 Preston Rd Ste 520
Dallas TX 75254
888 656-9450

(G-2828)
LOROCO INDUSTRIES INC
Also Called: Royal Pad Products
10600 Evendale Dr (45241-2518)
PHONE..................................513 891-9544
James Lallathin, *Pr*
Lee Rozin, *
Jim Myers, *
▼ **EMP:** 75 **EST:** 1898
SALES (est): 1.91MM **Privately Held**
Web: www.lorocoindustries.com
SIC: 2675 2671 3479 3544 Paperboard die-
cutting; Paper; coated and laminated
packaging; Painting, coating, and hot
dipping; Dies, steel rule

(G-2829)
LOSANTIVILLE WINERY LLC
38 W Mcmicken Ave (45202-7718)
PHONE..................................513 918-3015
EMP: 6 **EST:** 2014
SALES (est): 237.14K **Privately Held**
Web: www.skeletonroot.com
SIC: 2084 Wines

(G-2830)
LSI INDUSTRIES INC (PA)
Also Called: LSI Industries
10000 Alliance Rd (45242-4738)
P.O. Box 42728 (45242-0728)
PHONE..................................513 793-3200
James A Clark, *Pr*
Wilfred T O'gara, *Ch Bd*
James E Galeese, *Ex VP*
Thomas A Caneris, *Sr VP*
EMP: 234 **EST:** 1976
SQ FT: 243,000
SALES (est): 469.64MM
SALES (corp-wide): 469.64MM **Publicly
Held**
Web: www.lsicorp.com
SIC: 3648 3993 3663 Lighting equipment,
nec; Electric signs; Light communications
equipment

(G-2831)
**LUMINEX HM DCOR FRGRNCE
HLDG C (PA)**
Also Called: Luminex HD&f Company
10521 Millington Ct (45242-4022)
PHONE..................................513 563-1113
Calvin Johnston, *CEO*
EMP: 687 **EST:** 2016
SALES (est): 260.78MM
SALES (corp-wide): 260.78MM **Privately
Held**
Web: www.candle-lite.com
SIC: 5023 2844 Decorative home furnishings
and supplies; Perfumes, cosmetics and
other toilet preparations

(G-2832)
LUXFER MAGTECH INC (HQ)
Also Called: Heatermeals
2940 Highland Ave Ste 210 (45212-2402)
PHONE..................................513 772-3066
Brian Purves, *CEO*

▲ = Import ▼ = Export
◆ = Import/Export

Marc Lamensdorf, *
Deborah Simsen, *
Deepak Madan, *
EMP: 10 **EST:** 2014
SALES (est): 11.43MM
SALES (corp-wide): 405MM **Privately Held**
Web: www.heatermeals.com
SIC: 2899 5149 Desalter kits, sea water; Groceries and related products, nec
PA: Luxfer Holdings Plc
Ancorage Gateway
Salford LANCS M50 3
161 300-0611

(G-2833)
LYONDELL CHEMICAL COMPANY
11530 Northlake Dr (45249-1642)
PHONE...........................513 530-4000
Norma Maraschin, *Mgr*
EMP: 232
Web: www.lyondellbasell.com
SIC: 2869 2822 8731 Olefins; Polyethylene, chlorosulfonated, hypalon; Commercial physical research
HQ: Lyondell Chemical Company
1221 Mckinney St Ste 300
Houston TX 77010
713 309-7200

(G-2834)
M R I EDUCATION FOUNDATION
5400 Kennedy Ave (45213-2664)
PHONE...........................513 281-3400
EMP: 24 **EST:** 1988
SQ FT: 5,600
SALES (est): 368.34K **Privately Held**
Web: www.proscan.com
SIC: 8249 2741 Medical training services; Miscellaneous publishing

(G-2835)
M ROSENTHAL COMPANY
3125 Exon Ave (45241-2547)
PHONE...........................513 563-0081
Edward L Etter Iii, *Mng Pt*
EMP: 19 **EST:** 1888
SQ FT: 30,000
SALES (est): 1.35MM **Privately Held**
Web: www.mrosenthal.com
SIC: 2759 2752 Letterpress printing; Offset and photolithographic printing

(G-2030)
MACHINE DEVELOPMENT CORP
Also Called: Marine Development
7707 Affinity Pl (45240)
PHONE...........................513 825-5885
Gary Fay, *Pr*
EMP: 8 **EST:** 1979
SQ FT: 7,800
SALES (est): 248.6K **Privately Held**
Web: cnc-machinists.cmac.ws
SIC: 3599 Machine shop, jobbing and repair

(G-2837)
MACHINE DRIVE COMPANY
2513 Crescentville Rd (45241-1575)
PHONE...........................513 793-7077
EMP: 52
SIC: 5063 3625 Electrical apparatus and equipment; Control equipment, electric

(G-2838)
MACKE BROTHERS INC
10355 Spartan Dr (45215-1220)
PHONE...........................513 771-7500
Joseph D Macke Senior, *Pr*
Joseph D Macke Junior, *VP*
Bill Macke, *
Nick Macke, *

EMP: 7 **EST:** 1908
SQ FT: 43,000
SALES (est): 462.26K **Privately Held**
Web: www.mackebrothers.com
SIC: 2789 7331 Pamphlets, binding; Mailing service

(G-2839)
MADISON PROPERTY HOLDINGS INC
5055 Madison Rd (45227-1431)
PHONE...........................800 215-3210
EMP: 25 **EST:** 1940
SALES (est): 8.04MM **Privately Held**
Web: www.kett-tool.com
SIC: 3546 3542 3421 Power-driven handtools; Machine tools, metal forming type; Cutlery

(G-2840)
MAGNA MACHINE CO (PA)
11180 Southland Rd (45240-3202)
PHONE...........................513 851-6900
Scott Kramer, *CEO*
Scott Kramer, *Pr*
William Kramer Junior, *Sec*
James Parker, *
Greg Bodenburg, *
▼ **EMP:** 101 **EST:** 1953
SQ FT: 80,000
SALES (est): 21.65MM
SALES (corp-wide): 21.65MM **Privately Held**
Web: www.magna-machine.com
SIC: 3556 3554 3599 Bakery machinery; Paper industries machinery; Machine shop, jobbing and repair

(G-2841)
MAGNA THREE LLC
2668 Cyclorama Dr (45211-8315)
PHONE...........................513 389-0776
John Dorey, *Prin*
EMP: 8 **EST:** 2016
SALES (est): 103.91K **Privately Held**
SIC: 3829 Measuring and controlling devices, nec

(G-2842)
MAIN AWNING & TENT INC
415 W Seymour Ave (45216-1842)
PHONE...........................513 621-6947
Hyman Goldfarb, *Pr*
Leslie Goldfarb, *Pr*
Robert Goldfarb, *VP*
◆ **EMP:** 9 **EST:** 1933
SALES (est): 520.54K **Privately Held**
Web: www.awningscincinnati.com
SIC: 2394 Awnings, fabric: made from purchased materials

(G-2843)
MANE INC
10261 Chester Rd (45215-1581)
PHONE...........................513 248-9876
EMP: 74
Web: www.mane.com
SIC: 2087 Flavoring extracts and syrups, nec
HQ: Mane, Inc.
2501 Henkle Dr
Lebanon OH 45036
513 248-9876

(G-2844)
MANUFACTURING COMPANY LLC
3468 Cornell Pl (45220-1502)
PHONE...........................414 708-7583
Michael Fleisch, *Prin*
EMP: 10 **EST:** 2012
SALES (est): 182.95K **Privately Held**

SIC: 3999 Manufacturing industries, nec

(G-2845)
MARCH FIRST MANUFACTURING LLC (PA)
Also Called: March First Brewing
7885 E Kemper Rd (45249-1622)
PHONE...........................513 266-3076
Mark Stuhlreyer, *Pr*
EMP: 8 **EST:** 2016
SALES (est): 2.63MM
SALES (corp-wide): 2.63MM **Privately Held**
Web: www.marchfirstbrewing.com
SIC: 2085 Distilled and blended liquors

(G-2846)
MARINERS LANDING INC
Also Called: Mariner's Landing Marina
7405 Forbes Rd (45233-1014)
PHONE...........................513 941-3625
Pamela Tonne, *Pr*
EMP: 8 **EST:** 1990
SQ FT: 6,992
SALES (est): 174.53K **Privately Held**
Web: www.mariners-landing.com
SIC: 4493 5551 3732 Boat yards, storage and incidental repair; Boat dealers; Boatbuilding and repairing

(G-2847)
MARKLEY ENTERPRISES LLC
Also Called: Die Craft Division
1705 Magnolia Dr (45215-1979)
PHONE...........................513 771-1290
▲ **EMP:** 22 **EST:** 1970
SQ FT: 32,000
SALES (est): 7.23MM **Privately Held**
Web: www.diecraftmachine.com
SIC: 3449 8711 3599 Miscellaneous metalwork; Mechanical engineering; Machine shop, jobbing and repair

(G-2848)
MARKUS JEWELERS LLC
Also Called: Marcus Jewelers
2022 8 Mile Rd (45244-2607)
PHONE...........................513 474-4950
Mark Ogier, *Owner*
EMP: 7 **EST:** 1990
SQ FT: 1,100
SALES (est): 166.46K **Privately Held**
SIC: 3911 5944 Jewelry, precious metal; Jewelry stores

(G-2849)
MASTER COMMUNICATIONS INC
Also Called: Asia For Kids
2692 Madison Rd Ste N1-307 (45208-1321)
P.O. Box 9096 (45209-0096)
PHONE...........................208 821-3473
Selina Yoon, *Pr*
Frederick Chen, *VP*
▲ **EMP:** 9 **EST:** 1994
SALES (est): 452.61K **Privately Held**
Web: www.master-comm.com
SIC: 7812 2731 Video tape production; Book publishing

(G-2850)
MATLOCK ELECTRIC CO INC
2780 Highland Ave (45212-2494)
PHONE...........................513 731-9600
TOLL FREE: 800
Thomas J Geoppinger, *Ch*
Joseph P Geoppinger, *Pr*
▼ **EMP:** 36 **EST:** 1920
SQ FT: 25,000
SALES (est): 8.3MM **Privately Held**
Web: www.matlockelectric.com

SIC: 7694 5063 3699 3612 Electric motor repair; Motors, electric; Electrical equipment and supplies, nec; Transformers, except electric

(G-2851)
MCRON FINANCE CORP
3010 Disney St (45209-5028)
PHONE...........................513 487-5000
EMP: 136
SALES (est): 2.1MM **Publicly Held**
SIC: 3544 Forms (molds), for foundry and plastics working machinery
HQ: Milacron Holdings Corp.
4165 Half Acre Rd
Batavia OH 45103
513 487-5000

(G-2852)
MCSWAIN MANUFACTURING LLC
Also Called: Midstate Machine
189 Container Pl (45246-1708)
PHONE...........................513 619-1222
Michael Meshay, *Pr*
◆ **EMP:** 180 **EST:** 1942
SQ FT: 70,000
SALES (est): 24.13MM **Privately Held**
Web: www.midstateusa.com
SIC: 3599 Machine shop, jobbing and repair

(G-2853)
MECHANICAL FINISHERS INC LLC
Also Called: Mfi
6350 Este Ave (45232-1450)
PHONE...........................513 641-5419
Nico Cottone, *CEO*
EMP: 30 **EST:** 2015
SALES (est): 2.51MM **Privately Held**
Web: www.mechfin.com
SIC: 3471 Electroplating of metals or formed products

(G-2854)
MECHANICAL FINISHING INC
6350 Este Ave (45232-1450)
PHONE...........................513 641-5419
Jerry Stenger, *Pr*
EMP: 6 **EST:** 1992
SQ FT: 40,000
SALES (est): 598.44K **Privately Held**
Web: www.mechfin.com
SIC: 3471 Finishing, metals or formed products

(G-2855)
MEDER SPECIAL-TEES LTD
618 Delhi Ave (45204-1222)
PHONE...........................513 921-3800
Jerome A Meder, *Owner*
EMP: 8 **EST:** 1984
SQ FT: 3,000
SALES (est): 334.95K **Privately Held**
Web: www.medertees.com
SIC: 2759 Screen printing

(G-2856)
MEDPACE CORE LABORATORIES LLC
5375 Medpace Way (45227-1543)
PHONE...........................513 579-9911
EMP: 10 **EST:** 2017
SALES (est): 2.1MM
SALES (corp-wide): 2.11B **Publicly Held**
Web: www.medpace.com
SIC: 2834 Pharmaceutical preparations
PA: Medpace Holdings, Inc.
5375 Medpace Way
Cincinnati OH 45227
513 579-9911

(G-2857)
MEDPACE HOLDINGS INC (PA)
Also Called: Medpace
5375 Medpace Way (45227-1543)
PHONE...........................513 579-9911
August J Troendle, *Ch Bd*
Jesse J Geiger, *LABORATORY Operations*
Susan E Burwig, *Ofcr*
Stephen P Ewald, *Corporate Secretary*
EMP: 246 EST: 1992
SQ FT: 600,000
SALES (est): 2.11B
SALES (corp-wide): 2.11B **Publicly Held**
Web: www.medpace.com
SIC: 2834 8731 Pharmaceutical preparations
; Commercial physical research

(G-2858)
MEGGITT (ERLANGER) LLC
Also Called: Edac Composites
10293 Burlington Rd (45231-1901)
PHONE...........................513 851-5550
Steve Hartke, *Brnch Mgr*
EMP: 70
SALES (corp-wide): 19.93B **Publicly Held**
Web: www.parkwayproducts.com
SIC: 3089 3544 2851 2822 Molding primary
plastics; Special dies, tools, jigs, and
fixtures; Paints and allied products;
Synthetic rubber
HQ: Meggitt (Erlanger), Llc
1400 Jamike Ave
Erlanger KY 41018
859 525-8040

(G-2859)
MEGGITT POLYMERS &
COMPOSITES
10293 Burlington Rd (45231-1901)
PHONE...........................513 851-5550
EMP: 10 EST: 2016
SALES (est): 4.17MM **Privately Held**
Web: www.meggitt.com
SIC: 3728 Aircraft parts and equipment, nec

(G-2860)
MEIERJOHAN-WENGLER INC
10340 Julian Dr (45215-1131)
PHONE...........................513 771-6074
Steve Jones, *Pr*
▲ EMP: 25 EST: 1941
SQ FT: 34,000
SALES (est): 2.31MM
SALES (corp-wide): 1.8B **Publicly Held**
SIC: 3366 Bronze foundry, nec
HQ: Aurora Casket Company, Llc
10944 Marsh Rd
Aurora IN 47001
800 457-1111

(G-2861)
MEIERS WINE CELLARS INC
Also Called: John C Meier Grape Juice Co
6955 Plainfield Rd (45236-3793)
PHONE...........................513 891-2900
Paul Lux, *Pr*
Barbara Boyd Ctrl, *Prin*
◆ EMP: 30 EST: 1895
SQ FT: 20,000
SALES (est): 9.95MM
SALES (corp-wide): 283.23MM **Privately
Held**
Web: www.drinkmeiers.com
SIC: 2033 2084 2086 Fruit juices: fresh;
Wines; Bottled and canned soft drinks
PA: Vintage Wine Estates, Inc. (Nv)
937 Tahoe Blvd Ste 210
Incline Village NV 89451
707 346-3640

(G-2862)
MELVIN STONE CO LLC
11641 Mosteller Rd Ste 2 (45241-1520)
PHONE...........................513 771-0820
Susan B Salyer, *Prin*
EMP: 18 EST: 2006
SALES (est): 1.56MM **Privately Held**
Web: www.jrjnet.com
SIC: 3281 Cut stone and stone products

(G-2863)
MENARD INC
2789 Cunningham Rd (45241-1390)
PHONE...........................513 250-4566
EMP: 12
SALES (corp-wide): 1.7B **Privately Held**
Web: www.menards.com
SIC: 2431 Millwork
PA: Menard, Inc.
5101 Menard Dr
Eau Claire WI 54703
715 876-2000

(G-2864)
MERIDIAN BIOSCIENCE INC (PA)
Also Called: Meridian Bioscience
3471 River Hills Dr (45244-3023)
PHONE...........................513 271-3700
Jack Kenny, *CEO*
Andrew S Kitzmiller, *
Tony Serafini-Iamanna, *Ex VP*
Lourdes G Weltzien, *Ex VP*
Julie Smith, *CAO*
EMP: 188 EST: 1976
SALES (est): 333.02MM
SALES (corp-wide): 333.02MM **Privately
Held**
Web: www.meridianbioscience.com
SIC: 2835 2834 Diagnostic substances;
Pharmaceutical preparations

(G-2865)
MERIDIAN LIFE SCIENCE INC (HQ)
Also Called: Viral Antigens
3471 River Hills Dr (45244-3023)
PHONE...........................513 271-3700
Rick Eberly, *Pr*
EMP: 19 EST: 1982
SQ FT: 34,000
SALES (est): 9.8MM
SALES (corp-wide): 333.02MM **Privately
Held**
Web: www.meridianbioscience.com
SIC: 2835 Veterinary diagnostic substances
PA: Meridian Bioscience, Inc.
3471 River Hills Dr
Cincinnati OH 45244
513 271-3700

(G-2866)
MESA INDUSTRIES INC (PA)
Also Called: Airplaco Equipment Company
4027 Eastern Ave (45226-1747)
PHONE...........................513 321-2950
Terry S Segerberg, *CEO*
Kent Sexton, *
James R Sexton, *
◆ EMP: 32 EST: 1966
SQ FT: 100,000
SALES (est): 9.91MM
SALES (corp-wide): 9.91MM **Privately
Held**
Web: www.gunitesupply.com
SIC: 3531 5085 5082 Bituminous, cement
and concrete related products and equip.;
Hose, belting, and packing; Construction
and mining machinery

(G-2867)
MESA INDUSTRIES INC
4141 Airport Rd (45226-1643)
PHONE...........................513 999-9781
EMP: 15
SALES (corp-wide): 9.91MM **Privately
Held**
Web: www.mesa-intl.com
SIC: 3531 Bituminous, cement and concrete
related products and equip.
PA: Mesa Industries, Inc.
4027 Eastern Ave
Cincinnati OH 45226
513 321-2950

(G-2868)
MET-PRO TECHNOLOGIES LLC (HQ)
4625 Red Bank Rd (45277)
PHONE...........................513 458-2600
Dennis Sadlowski, *Pr*
EMP: 15 EST: 2013
SALES (est): 2.32MM **Publicly Held**
Web: www.cecoenviro.com
SIC: 3564 Air purification equipment
PA: Ceco Environmental Corp.
5080 Spectrum Dr Ste 800e
Addison TX 75001

(G-2869)
METAL PANEL SYSTEMS LLC
Also Called: Metal Panel Systems
11401 Rockfield Ct (45241-1916)
PHONE...........................513 554-6120
Mike O'brien, *CEO*
EMP: 20 EST: 2019
SALES (est): 5.06MM **Privately Held**
SIC: 3444 Metal roofing and roof drainage
equipment

(G-2870)
METALPHOTO OF CINCINNATI INC
1080 Skillman Dr (45215-1137)
PHONE...........................513 772-8281
Herbert Wainer, *Prin*
Patrick Hollis, *
EMP: 26 EST: 1959
SQ FT: 21,000
SALES (est): 4.83MM
SALES (corp-wide): 27.81MM **Privately
Held**
Web: www.mpofcinci.com
SIC: 3993 Name plates: except engraved,
etched, etc.: metal
PA: Horizons Incorporated
18531 S Miles Rd
Cleveland OH 44128
216 475-0555

(G-2871)
**METCUT RESEARCH ASSOCIATES
INC (PA)**
Also Called: Metcut Research, Inc.
3980 Rosslyn Dr (45209-1110)
PHONE...........................513 271-5100
John P Kahles, *Pr*
John H Clippinger, *
William P Koster, *
John H More, *
Robert T Keeler, *
EMP: 85 EST: 1948
SQ FT: 25,000
SALES (est): 24.93MM
SALES (corp-wide): 24.93MM **Privately
Held**
Web: www.metcut.com
SIC: 8734 3599 Metallurgical testing
laboratory; Machine and other job shop
work

(G-2872)
METRO CONTAINERS INC
4927 Beech St (45212-2315)
PHONE...........................513 351-6800
EMP: 77
SIC: 2653 Boxes, corrugated: made from
purchased materials

(G-2873)
METZGER MACHINE CO
2165 Spring Grove Ave (45214-1790)
PHONE...........................513 241-3360
David L Brown, *Pr*
Virginia Brown, *Sec*
EMP: 10 EST: 1876
SQ FT: 10,000
SALES (est): 1.08MM **Privately Held**
Web: www.metzgermachine.com
SIC: 3599 5085 Machine shop, jobbing and
repair; Industrial supplies

(G-2874)
MEYER TOOL INC (PA)
3055 Colerain Ave (45225-1827)
PHONE...........................513 681-7362
Arlyn Easton, *Pr*
Larry Allen, *
Jerry Flyr, *General Vice President*
Christine Steele, *
◆ EMP: 650 EST: 1951
SQ FT: 365,000
SALES (est): 344.81MM
SALES (corp-wide): 344.81MM **Privately
Held**
Web: www.meyertool.com
SIC: 3724 3599 Aircraft engines and engine
parts; Machine shop, jobbing and repair

(G-2875)
MICHELMAN INC (PA)
Also Called: Michelman
9080 Shell Rd (45236-1232)
P.O. Box 538702 (45253-8702)
PHONE...........................513 793-7766
◆ EMP: 160 EST: 1949
SALES (est): 83.67MM
SALES (corp-wide): 83.67MM **Privately
Held**
Web: www.michelman.com
SIC: 2869 Industrial organic chemicals, nec

(G-2876)
MICRO METAL FINISHING LLC
3448 Spring Grove Ave (45225-1328)
PHONE...........................513 541-3095
John A Rose, *Pr*
Karen Lafkas, *
EMP: 61 EST: 1995
SQ FT: 100,000
SALES (est): 2.29MM **Privately Held**
Web: www.micrometalfinishing.com
SIC: 3471 Finishing, metals or formed
products

(G-2877)
MICROPYRETICS HEATERS INTL INC
Also Called: Mhi
750 Redna Ter (45215-1109)
PHONE...........................513 772-0404
Anu Vissa, *COO*
▲ EMP: 11 EST: 1991
SALES (est): 2.61MM **Privately Held**
Web: www.mhi-inc.com
SIC: 3567 Industrial furnaces and ovens

(G-2878)
MIDSTATE MACHINE OHIO FACILITY
189 Container Pl (45246-1708)
PHONE...........................513 619-1222
EMP: 6 EST: 2016

▲ = Import ▼ = Export
◆ = Import/Export

SALES (est): 329.57K **Privately Held**
Web: www.midstateusa.com
SIC: **3599** Machine shop, jobbing and repair

(G-2879)
MIDWEST FILTRATION LLC
9775 International Blvd (45246-4855)
PHONE....................................513 874-6510
Steven Vollmer, *Managing Member*
Frank Strittmatter, *
▲ EMP: 79 EST: 1985
SQ FT: 110,000
SALES (est): 35.83MM **Privately Held**
Web: www.midwestfiltration.com
SIC: **3569** 2653 Filters, general line:
  industrial; Corrugated and solid fiber boxes

(G-2880)
MILACRON LLC (DH)
10200 Alliance Rd Ste 200 (45242-4716)
PHONE....................................513 487-5000
Tom Goeke, *CEO*
Hugh Odonnell, *
Bruce Chalmers, *
Ron Krisanda, *
John Gallagher, *
◆ EMP: 35 EST: 2009
SALES (est): 1.22B **Publicly Held**
Web: www.milacron.com
SIC: **3549** 2899 Metalworking machinery, nec
  ; Correction fluid
HQ: Milacron Intermediate Holdings Inc.
  3010 Disney St
  Cincinnati OH 45209
  513 536-2000

(G-2881)
MILLSTONE COFFEE INC (HQ)
1 Procter And Gamble Plz (45202-3315)
PHONE....................................513 983-1100
R Kerry Clark, *Pr*
Clayton C Daley Junior, *VP Fin*
S P Donovan Junior, *VP*
Doctor Walker, *VP*
H J Kangis, *
▲ EMP: 80 EST: 1981
SALES (est): 14.79MM
SALES (corp-wide): 8.18B **Publicly Held**
SIC: **2095** Coffee roasting (except by
  wholesale grocers)
PA: The J M Smucker Company
  1 Strawberry Ln
  Orrville OH 44667
  330 682 3000

(G-2882)
MINUTEMAN PRESS INC
Also Called: Minuteman Press
9904 Colerain Ave (45251-1431)
PHONE....................................513 741-9056
Portia Ash, *Prin*
EMP: 6 EST: 2010
SALES (est): 228.74K **Privately Held**
Web: www.mmpcolerain.com
SIC: **2752** Commercial printing, lithographic

(G-2883)
MMP PRINTING INC
Also Called: Minuteman Press
10570 Chester Rd (45215-1263)
PHONE....................................513 381-0990
Melody Tuttle, *Pr*
William Tuttle, *VP*
EMP: 17 EST: 1995
SQ FT: 30,000
SALES (est): 850.13K **Privately Held**
Web: www.mmpcincy.com
SIC: **2752** 2791 2789 2759 Commercial
  printing, lithographic; Typesetting;
  Bookbinding and related work; Commercial
  printing, nec

(G-2884)
MODEL PATTERN & FOUNDRY CO
3242 Spring Grove Ave (45225-1373)
PHONE....................................513 542-2322
Shirley Kipp, *Pr*
Kenneth Kipp, *
David Kipp, *
EMP: 6 EST: 1943
SQ FT: 16,500
SALES (est): 1.22MM **Privately Held**
Web: www.mpfoundry.com
SIC: **3363** 3364 3366 3365 Aluminum die-
  castings; Brass and bronze die-castings;
  Copper foundries; Aluminum foundries

(G-2885)
**MODERN ICE EQUIPMENT & SUP CO
(PA)**
Also Called: Modern Tour
5709 Harrison Ave (45248-1601)
PHONE....................................513 367-2101
Gary E Jerow, *Pr*
John Murphy, *VP*
◆ EMP: 20 EST: 1990
SQ FT: 12,000
SALES (est): 24.34MM **Privately Held**
Web: www.modernice.com
SIC: **5078** 3444 Refrigeration equipment and
  supplies; Sheet metalwork

(G-2886)
MONTI INCORPORATED (PA)
4510 Reading Rd (45229-1230)
PHONE....................................513 761-7775
Gavin J Narburgh, *CEO*
Gavin J Narburgh, *Pr*
Beverly Narburgh, *
John Narburgh, *
Brian Tibbs, *
▲ EMP: 72 EST: 1971
SQ FT: 137,000
SALES (est): 30.82MM
SALES (corp-wide): 30.82MM **Privately
Held**
Web: www.monti-inc.com
SIC: **3599** 3644 3674 Machine shop, jobbing
  and repair; Insulators and insulation
  materials, electrical; Semiconductors and
  related devices

(G-2887)
MORGAN4140 LLC
Also Called: Sixteen Brcks Artsan Bakehouse
4760 Paddock Rd Ste B (45229-1048)
PHONE....................................513 873-1426
Ryan Morgan, *Managing Member*
EMP: 10 EST: 2012
SALES (est): 1.03MM **Privately Held**
Web: www.sixteenbricks.com
SIC: **2051** Bread, cake, and related products

(G-2888)
MORRIS TECHNOLOGIES INC
11988 Tramway Dr (45241-1664)
PHONE....................................513 733-1611
Gregory M Morris, *CEO*
William G Noack, *Pr*
Wendell H Morris, *Treas*
EMP: 20 EST: 1994
SQ FT: 25,000
SALES (est): 2.32MM **Privately Held**
SIC: **8711** 3999 3313 3841 Mechanical
  engineering; Models, except toy; Alloys,
  additive, except copper: not made in blast
  furnaces; Surgical and medical instruments

(G-2889)
**MORROW GRAVEL COMPANY INC
(PA)**
11641 Mosteller Rd (45241-1520)

PHONE....................................513 771-0820
James P Jurgensen, *Pr*
Tim St Clair, *VP*
EMP: 20 EST: 1958
SQ FT: 15,000
SALES (est): 21.28MM
SALES (corp-wide): 21.28MM **Privately
Held**
Web: www.jrjnet.com
SIC: **1442** 1771 2951 Construction sand
  mining; Blacktop (asphalt) work; Asphalt
  and asphaltic paving mixtures (not from
  refineries)

(G-2890)
MORTON SALT INC
Also Called: Morton Salt
5336 River Rd (45233-1686)
PHONE....................................513 941-1578
Jim Benton, *Brnch Mgr*
EMP: 9
SALES (corp-wide): 3.82B **Privately Held**
Web: www.mortonsalt.com
SIC: **2899** Salt
HQ: Morton Salt, Inc.
  444 W Lake St Ste 3000
  Chicago IL 60606

(G-2891)
MR LABEL INC
5018 Gray Rd (45232-1514)
PHONE....................................513 681-2088
Patrick H Meehan Junior, *Pr*
Timothy F Meehan, *
Brigid Hoffman, *
▼ EMP: 25 EST: 1976
SQ FT: 19,200
SALES (est): 4.47MM **Privately Held**
Web: www.mrlabelco.com
SIC: **2759** 2672 Flexographic printing;
  Paper; coated and laminated, nec

(G-2892)
MWGH LLC
Also Called: Metalworking Group, The
9070 Pippin Rd (45251-3174)
PHONE....................................513 521-4114
Doug J Watts, *Managing Member*
EMP: 135 EST: 2019
SALES (est): 42.2MM
SALES (corp-wide): 42.2MM **Privately
Held**
SIC: **3444** Sheet metalwork
PA: Mwg Holdings, Inc.
  9070 Pippin Rd
  Cincinnati OH 45251
  513 521-4119

(G-2893)
NATIONAL ACCESS DESIGN LLC
Also Called: N A D
1871 Summit Rd (45237-2803)
PHONE....................................513 351-3400
Cheryl White, *Pr*
EMP: 13 EST: 2011
SALES (est): 3.39MM **Privately Held**
Web: www.nationalaccessdesign.com
SIC: **3442** 3089 Metal doors, sash, and trim;
  Doors, folding: plastics or plastics coated
  fabric

(G-2894)
**NATIONAL MACHINE TOOL
COMPANY**
2013 E Galbraith Rd (45215-5633)
PHONE....................................513 541-6682
Harold J Rembold, *Pr*
Chris K Rembold, *VP*
EMP: 9 EST: 1903
SQ FT: 5,998
SALES (est): 998.66K **Privately Held**

Web: www.keyseaters.com
SIC: **3541** Machine tools, metal cutting:
  exotic (explosive, etc.)

(G-2895)
NATIONAL SCOREBOARDS LLC
Also Called: N S B
8044 Montgomery Rd Ste 700
  (45236-2926)
PHONE....................................513 791-5244
Nick Mckenzie, *Managing Member*
Aaron Todd, *Managing Member*
EMP: 7 EST: 2003
SQ FT: 1,000
SALES (est): 394.83K **Privately Held**
SIC: **3993** Scoreboards, electric

(G-2896)
NAVISTONE INC
231 W 12th St Ste 200w (45202-8001)
PHONE....................................844 677-3667
Larry Kavanagh, *CEO*
Allen Abbott, *COO*
Efrain Torres, *CFO*
Lori Paikin, *CRO*
EMP: 53 EST: 2016
SALES (est): 2.38MM **Privately Held**
Web: www.navistone.com
SIC: **7371** 7372 Computer software
  development; Application computer software

(G-2897)
**NEHEMIAH MANUFACTURING CO
LLC**
1907 South St (45204-2033)
PHONE....................................513 351-5700
Daniel Meyer, *CEO*
Richard T Palmer, *Pr*
Mike Pachko, *COO*
▲ EMP: 100 EST: 2009
SQ FT: 33,706
SALES (est): 24.26MM **Privately Held**
Web: www.nehemiahmfg.com
SIC: **2844** 5122 Perfumes, cosmetics and
  other toilet preparations; Toiletries

(G-2898)
NEPTUNE EQUIPMENT COMPANY
11082 Southland Rd (45240-3713)
PHONE....................................513 851-8008
Robert W Becker, *Pr*
Mary Ellen Shouse, *Sec*
EMP: 17 EST: 1934
SQ FT: 4,000
SALES (est): 5.27MM **Privately Held**
Web: www.necowater.com
SIC: **3825** 1623 Meters: electric, pocket,
  portable, panelboard, etc.; Aqueduct
  construction

(G-2899)
**NETHERLAND RUBBER COMPANY
(PA)**
2931 Exon Ave (45241-2593)
P.O. Box 62165 (45262-0165)
PHONE....................................513 733-0883
Timothy Clarke, *Pr*
Robert Pater, *VP*
Sue Clarke, *Treas*
EMP: 17 EST: 1931
SQ FT: 69,000
SALES (est): 9.87MM
SALES (corp-wide): 9.87MM **Privately
Held**
Web: www.netherlandrubber.com
SIC: **5085** 3053 3492 5099 Rubber goods,
  mechanical; Gaskets, all materials; Hose
  and tube fittings and assemblies, hydraulic/
  pneumatic; Safety equipment and supplies

(G-2900)
NEW DAIRY CINCINNATI LLC
415 John St (45215-5481)
PHONE................................214 258-1200
Gregg Engles, *CEO*
EMP: 70 EST: 2020
SALES (est): 381.23K
SALES (corp-wide): 403.14MM **Privately Held**
SIC: 2021 Creamery butter
PA: New Dairy Opco, Llc
12400 Coit Rd Ste 200
Dallas TX 75251
214 258-1200

(G-2901)
NEW DIRY CINCINNATI TRNSPT LLC
415 John St (45215-5481)
PHONE................................214 258-1200
Gregg Engles, *CEO*
EMP: 56 EST: 2020
SALES (est): 236.29K
SALES (corp-wide): 403.14MM **Privately Held**
SIC: 2023 Dry, condensed and evaporated dairy products
PA: New Dairy Opco, Llc
12400 Coit Rd Ste 200
Dallas TX 75251
214 258-1200

(G-2902)
NEW LIFE CHAPEL
10195 Giverny Blvd (45241-3276)
P.O. Box 62047 (45262-0047)
PHONE................................513 298-2980
Pastor Lonnie Snell, *Prin*
EMP: 10 EST: 2009
SALES (est): 336.69K **Privately Held**
Web: www.newlifechapel.net
SIC: 8661 7372 Non-denominational church; Application computer software

(G-2903)
NEW PME INC
Also Called: Plant Maintenance Engineering
518 W Crescentville Rd (45246-1222)
PHONE................................513 671-1717
Charles Walter, *Pr*
EMP: 14 EST: 1980
SALES (est): 1.64MM **Privately Held**
Web: www.pmebabbittbearings.com
SIC: 3599 Machine shop, jobbing and repair

(G-2904)
NEW VULCO MFG & SALES CO LLC
Also Called: Vulcan Oil Company
5353 Spring Grove Ave (45217-1026)
PHONE................................513 242-2672
Larry Schirmann, *
EMP: 60 EST: 2005
SALES (est): 3.3MM **Privately Held**
Web: www.vulcanoil.com
SIC: 5983 2992 5171 2899 Fuel oil dealers; Oils and greases, blending and compounding; Petroleum bulk stations; Chemical preparations, nec

(G-2905)
NEWMAN BROTHERS INC
5609 Center Hill Ave (45216-2305)
P.O. Box 43460 (45243-0460)
EMP: 6 EST: 1882
SQ FT: 65,000
SALES (est): 704.56K **Privately Held**
Web: www.newmanbrothers.com
SIC: 3446 Ornamental metalwork

(G-2906)
NEXTGEN FIBER OPTICS LLC (PA)
720 E Pete Rose Way Ste 410 (45202-3579)
PHONE................................513 549-4691
EMP: 7 EST: 2002
SALES (est): 808.65K
SALES (corp-wide): 808.65K **Privately Held**
SIC: 3229 Fiber optics strands

(G-2907)
NEXTMED SYSTEMS INC (PA)
16 Triangle Park Dr (45246-3411)
PHONE................................216 674-0511
David Shute, *CEO*
James Bennett, *
EMP: 44 EST: 1999
SQ FT: 3,000
SALES (est): 894.12K
SALES (corp-wide): 894.12K **Privately Held**
SIC: 7372 Business oriented computer software

(G-2908)
NEYRA INTERSTATE INC (PA)
10700 Evendale Dr (45241-2536)
PHONE................................513 733-1000
EMP: 25 EST: 1975
SALES (est): 21.26MM
SALES (corp-wide): 21.26MM **Privately Held**
Web: www.neyra.com
SIC: 2952 2891 2865 Coating compounds, tar; Adhesives and sealants; Cyclic crudes and intermediates

(G-2909)
NILPETER USA INC
Also Called: Next
11550 Goldcoast Dr (45249-1640)
PHONE................................513 489-4400
Lenny Degirolmo, *Prin*
Timothy Taggart, *
Eric Vandenburg, *
◆ EMP: 110 EST: 1987
SQ FT: 35,000
SALES (est): 23.22MM
SALES (corp-wide): 104.11K **Privately Held**
Web: www.nilpeter.com
SIC: 3555 3554 3565 2759 Printing trades machinery; Die cutting and stamping machinery, paper converting; Packaging machinery; Commercial printing, nec
PA: Nilpeter-Fonden
Elmedalsvej 20-22
Slagelse
58528311

(G-2910)
NINE GIANT BREWING LLC
6095 Montgomery Rd (45213-1617)
PHONE................................510 220-5104
Brandon Hughes, *Owner*
EMP: 9 EST: 2016
SALES (est): 859.6K **Privately Held**
Web: www.ninegiant.com
SIC: 2082 Malt beverages

(G-2911)
NKH-SAFETY INC
1375 Kemper Meadow Dr Ste 12 (45240-1650)
PHONE................................513 771-3839
William Neal, *Pr*
EMP: 10 EST: 1990
SQ FT: 4,000
SALES (est): 877.41K **Privately Held**
Web: www.nkhsafety.com

SIC: 3845 8748 Electromedical equipment; Safety training service

(G-2912)
NNODUM PHARMACEUTICALS CORP
483 Northland Blvd (45240-3210)
P.O. Box 19725 (45219-0725)
PHONE................................513 861-2329
Nnodum Iheme, *Pr*
Peggy Iheme, *VP*
EMP: 12 EST: 1995
SQ FT: 16,000
SALES (est): 924.84K **Privately Held**
Web: www.zikspain.com
SIC: 2834 Pharmaceutical preparations

(G-2913)
NOBLE DENIM WORKSHOP
2929 Spring Grove Ave (45225-2157)
PHONE................................513 560-5640
EMP: 6 EST: 2013
SALES (est): 136.7K **Privately Held**
Web: www.nobledenim.com
SIC: 2211 Denims

(G-2914)
NOLTE PRECISE MANUFACTURING INC
6850 Colerain Ave (45239-5544)
PHONE................................513 923-3100
EMP: 54 EST: 1916
SALES (est): 9.11MM **Privately Held**
Web: www.nolteprecise.com
SIC: 3451 Screw machine products

(G-2915)
NORTON OUTDOOR ADVERTISING
5280 Kennedy Ave (45213-2620)
PHONE................................513 631-4864
Thomas Norton, *CEO*
Thomas Norton, *Pr*
Daniel Norton, *
Michael Norton, *
EMP: 24 EST: 1949
SQ FT: 7,500
SALES (est): 2.24MM **Privately Held**
Web: www.norton-outdoor.com
SIC: 7312 3993 Poster advertising, outdoor; Signs and advertising specialties

(G-2916)
NU-TECH POLYMERS CO INC
3220 E Sharon Rd (45241-1945)
PHONE................................513 942-6003
R Douglas Pendery, *Pr*
EMP: 8 EST: 1985
SALES (est): 2.96MM **Privately Held**
Web: www.nu-techpolymers.com
SIC: 2821 Plastics materials and resins

(G-2917)
NUCOR CORPORATION
P.O. Box 5810 (45201-5810)
PHONE................................407 855-2990
EMP: 27
SALES (corp-wide): 30.73B **Publicly Held**
Web: www.nucor.com
SIC: 3312 Blast furnaces and steel mills
PA: Nucor Corporation
1915 Rexford Rd
Charlotte NC 28211
704 366-7000

(G-2918)
NUCOR CORPORATION
Also Called: Nucor Load Center
300 Pike St Fl 4 (45202-4241)
PHONE................................901 275-3826
Susie Eaddy, *Brnch Mgr*

EMP: 15
SALES (corp-wide): 30.73B **Publicly Held**
Web: www.nucor.com
SIC: 3312 Blast furnaces and steel mills
PA: Nucor Corporation
1915 Rexford Rd
Charlotte NC 28211
704 366-7000

(G-2919)
NUCOR LOGISTICS LLC
300 Pike St (45202-4222)
PHONE................................901 275-3826
EMP: 14
SALES (est): 3.99MM **Privately Held**
Web: www.nucor.com
SIC: 3312 Blast furnaces and steel mills

(G-2920)
OAK HILLS CARTON CO
6310 Este Ave (45232-1450)
PHONE................................513 948-4200
Kenneth Kabel, *Pr*
EMP: 25 EST: 1951
SQ FT: 40,000
SALES (est): 5.4MM **Privately Held**
Web: www.oakhillscarton.com
SIC: 2679 2657 Paperboard products, converted, nec; Folding paperboard boxes

(G-2921)
OHIO CBD GUY LLC
7875 Montgomery Rd (45236-4344)
PHONE................................513 417-9806
Jason Friedman, *Owner*
EMP: 6 EST: 2018
SALES (est): 715.35K **Privately Held**
Web: www.ohiocbdguy.com
SIC: 3999

(G-2922)
OHIO FEATHER COMPANY INC
1910 South St (45204-2034)
PHONE................................513 921-3373
Gabriel Guigui, *Pr*
Daniel Guigui, *VP*
▲ EMP: 6 EST: 1986
SALES (est): 709.5K **Privately Held**
Web: www.downdecor.com
SIC: 3999 Feathers and feather products

(G-2923)
OHIO FLAME HARDENING COMPANY (PA)
3944 Miami Rd Apt 106 (45227-3736)
PHONE................................513 336-6160
Robert Bokon, *Pr*
EMP: 24 EST: 1975
SALES (est): 856.27K
SALES (corp-wide): 856.27K **Privately Held**
SIC: 3398 Brazing (hardening) of metal

(G-2924)
OHIO HYDRAULICS INC
2510 E Sharon Rd (45241-1891)
PHONE................................513 771-2590
Kathleen Hilliard, *Pr*
John Davis, *
Robert Farwick, *
Tamera Fair, *
EMP: 25 EST: 1971
SQ FT: 13,500
SALES (est): 3.88MM **Privately Held**
Web: www.ohiohydraulics.com
SIC: 3492 3599 5084 7699 Hose and tube fittings and assemblies, hydraulic/pneumatic; Flexible metal hose, tubing, and bellows; Hydraulic systems equipment and supplies; Tank repair and cleaning services

(G-2925)
OHIO PULP MILLS INC
2100 Losantiville Ave Ste 3 (45237-7100)
PHONE.............................513 631-7400
Steve Baker, *Mgr*
EMP: 25
SQ FT: 19,000
SALES (corp-wide): 4.85MM **Privately Held**
Web: www.doncosolutions.com
SIC: 2621 Paper mills
PA: Ohio Pulp Mills Inc
737 N Mich Ave Ste 1450
Chicago IL 60611
312 337-7822

(G-2926)
OHIO TILE & MARBLE CO
3809 Spring Grove Ave (45223-2693)
PHONE.............................513 541-4211
Sean Dowers, *Pr*
Ruth Dowers, *VP*
Clyde Dowers, *Stockholder*
▲ EMP: 23 EST: 1937
SQ FT: 21,500
SALES (est): 2.1MM **Privately Held**
Web: www.ohiotile.com
SIC: 5032 5211 3281 3253 Tile, clay or other
ceramic, excluding refractory; Tile, ceramic;
Marble, building: cut and shaped; Ceramic
wall and floor tile

(G-2927)
OHIO WOODWORKING CO INC
5035 Beech St (45212-2399)
PHONE.............................513 631-0870
Thomas R Frank Junior, *Pr*
Peggy Frank, *Sec*
EMP: 8 EST: 1931
SQ FT: 17,000
SALES (est): 922.99K **Privately Held**
Web:
www.ohiowoodworkingcompany.com
SIC: 2541 2431 Display fixtures, wood;
Millwork

(G-2928)
OKL CAN LINE INC
11235 Sebring Dr (45240-2714)
◆ EMP: 47 EST: 1983
SQ FT: 50,000
SALES (est): 7.37MM
SALES (corp-wide): 8.07MM **Privately
Held**
Web: www.oklcan.com
SIC: 3565 7699 Bottling and canning
machinery; Industrial machinery and
equipment repair
PA: Allcan Global Services, Inc
11235 Sebring Dr
Cincinnati OH 45240
513 825-1655

(G-2929)
OMI SURGICAL PRODUCTS
4900 Charlemar Dr (45227-1550)
PHONE.............................513 561-2241
Teck Awa, *Engr*
EMP: 8 EST: 2013
SALES (est): 2.56MM **Privately Held**
SIC: 3841 Surgical and medical instruments

(G-2930)
OMYA INC (DH)
Also Called: Callahan AMS Machine
Company
9987 Carver Rd Ste 300 (45242-5563)
PHONE.............................513 387-4600
◆ EMP: 150 EST: 1894
SALES (est): 193.19MM **Privately Held**
Web: www.omya.com

SIC: 2819 Calcium compounds and salts,
inorganic, nec
HQ: Omya Industries Inc.
4605 Duke Dr
Mason OH 45040
513 387-4600

(G-2931)
ONE CLOUD SERVICES LLC
Also Called: Zimcom Internet Solutions
1080 Nimitzview Dr Ste 400 (45230-4314)
PHONE.............................513 231-9500
Anne Zimmerman, *Pr*
Steve Searles, *VP*
EMP: 6 EST: 2016
SALES (est): 1.14MM **Privately Held**
Web: www.zimcom.net
SIC: 7372 Business oriented computer
software
PA: Liberty Noc, Llc
4815 Delemere Ave
Royal Oak MI 48073

(G-2932)
ONE THREE ENERGY INC
Also Called: Edgeenergy
1311 Vine St (45202-7118)
PHONE.............................513 996-6973
Greg York, *CEO*
Ben Morris, *VP*
Jon Holland, *CFO*
EMP: 10 EST: 2020
SALES (est): 4.77MM **Privately Held**
Web: www.edgeenergyev.com
SIC: 3621 Storage battery chargers, motor
and engine generator type

(G-2933)
ONETOUCHPOINT EAST CORP
Also Called: Touch Print Solution
1441 Western Ave (45214-2041)
PHONE.............................513 421-1600
Christopher A Illman, *CEO*
William Pearson, *
Larry Halenkamp, *
EMP: 87 EST: 1969
SQ FT: 102,000
SALES (est): 8.23MM
SALES (corp-wide): 412.03MM **Privately
Held**
Web: www.1touchpoint.com
SIC: 2789 2752 2759 2791 Bookbinding and
related work; Commercial printing,
lithographic; Commercial printing, nec;
Typesetting
HQ: Onetouchpoint Corp.
1225 Walnut Ridge
Hartland WI 53029

(G-2934)
ONLINE ENGINEERING CORP
6732 High Meadows Dr (45230-3805)
PHONE.............................513 561-8878
Richard Hittinger, *Pr*
Jane Hittinger, *Stockholder*
▼ EMP: 6 EST: 2005
SALES (est): 494.97K **Privately Held**
Web: www.onlineengineeringcorp.com
SIC: 3914 Stainless steel ware

(G-2935)
ONX HOLDINGS LLC (DH)
Also Called: Onx Enterprise Solutions
221 E 4th St (45202-4124)
PHONE.............................866 587-2287
EMP: 49 EST: 2006
SALES (est): 9.65MM
SALES (corp-wide): 3.15B **Privately Held**
Web: www.altafiber.com

SIC: 7379 7372 Computer related consulting
services; Business oriented computer
software
HQ: Cincinnati Bell Inc.
221 E 4th St
Cincinnati OH 45202
513 397-9900

(G-2936)
**OPTUM INFUSION SVCS 550 LLC
(DH)**
Also Called: Diplomat Spclty Infusion Group
7167 E Kemper Rd (45249-1028)
PHONE.............................866 442-4679
EMP: 63 EST: 2004
SALES (est): 31.89MM
SALES (corp-wide): 400.28B **Publicly
Held**
Web: www.biorxhemophilia.com
SIC: 5122 8748 2834 5047 Pharmaceuticals;
Business consulting, nec; Pharmaceutical
preparations; Medical and hospital
equipment
HQ: Optum, Inc.
11000 Optum Cir
Eden Prairie MN 55344
952 936-1300

(G-2937)
ORFLEX INC
470 Northland Blvd (45240-3211)
EMP: 270
SIC: 2671 Paper; coated and laminated
packaging

(G-2938)
ORGANIZED LIVING
12115 Ellington Ct (45249-1000)
PHONE.............................513 277-3700
EMP: 7 EST: 2019
SALES (est): 1.17MM **Privately Held**
Web: www.organizedliving.com
SIC: 3499 Fabricated metal products, nec

(G-2939)
ORGANIZED LIVING INC (PA)
Also Called: Organized Living
3100 E Kemper Rd (45241-1517)
PHONE.............................513 489-9300
John D Kokenge, *CEO*
Patrick Taylor, *
Steve Mccamley, *VP Mktg*
Robert J Lamping, *
Kevin Ball, *
◆ EMP: 40 EST: 1919
SQ FT: 16,000
SALES (est): 15.06MM
SALES (corp-wide): 15.06MM **Privately
Held**
Web: www.organizedliving.com
SIC: 3083 3411 2542 1799 Laminated
plastics plate and sheet; Metal cans;
Partitions and fixtures, except wood; Home/
office interiors finishing, furnishing and
remodeling

(G-2940)
PA TECHNOLOGIES LLC
10176 Evendale Commons Dr
(45241-2688)
PHONE.............................513 800-3541
Gene Harbstreit, *Pr*
EMP: 12 EST: 2018
SALES (est): 7.1MM **Privately Held**
Web: www.p-a-technologies.com
SIC: 8711 3613 Engineering services;
Control panels, electric

(G-2941)
PANEL-FAB INC
10520 Taconic Ter (45215-1125)
PHONE.............................513 771-1462
Robert A Harrison, *Pr*
Stephen T Williford, *
Nancy J Shurlow, *
EMP: 90 EST: 1979
SQ FT: 25,000
SALES (est): 23.49MM **Privately Held**
Web: www.panel-fab.com
SIC: 3613 Control panels, electric

(G-2942)
PARKER MEGGITT ✪
10293 Burlington Rd (45231-1901)
PHONE.............................513 851-5550
EMP: 15 EST: 2023
SALES (est): 992.18K **Privately Held**
SIC: 3728 Aircraft parts and equipment, nec

(G-2943)
PATHEON PHARMACEUTICALS INC
2110 E Galbraith Rd (45237-1625)
PHONE.............................513 948-9111
Teresa C Turnbow, *Mgr*
EMP: 1873
SALES (corp-wide): 42.86B **Publicly Held**
Web: www.patheon.com
SIC: 2834 Pharmaceutical preparations
HQ: Patheon Pharmaceuticals Inc.
3900 Paramount Pkwy
Morrisville NC 27560
919 226-3200

(G-2944)
PATIO ENCLOSURES (PA)
11949 Tramway Dr (45241-1666)
PHONE.............................513 733-4646
Ronald J Molnar, *Pr*
Donna Molnar, *Sec*
EMP: 19 EST: 1973
SQ FT: 10,000
SALES (est): 438.16K
SALES (corp-wide): 438.16K **Privately
Held**
Web: www.patioenclosures.com
SIC: 5039 2452 1521 Prefabricated
structures; Prefabricated wood buildings;
Patio and deck construction and repair

(G-2945)
PATRICK J BURKE & CO
Also Called: Burke & Company
901 Adams Crossing Fl 1 (45202-1693)
PHONE.............................513 455-8200
Patrick Burke, *Owner*
EMP: 35 EST: 1984
SALES (est): 2.03MM **Privately Held**
Web: www.burkecpa.com
SIC: 8721 7372 Certified public accountant;
Prepackaged software

(G-2946)
PATRIOT SIGNAGE INC
5725 Dragon Way (45227-4519)
PHONE.............................859 655-9009
Kevin L Keefe, *Pr*
Mike Maier, *Prin*
EMP: 9 EST: 1991
SALES (est): 924.09K **Privately Held**
Web: www.patriotsigns.com
SIC: 3993 Signs, not made in custom sign
painting shops

(G-2947)
PAUL WILKE & SON INC
1965 Grand Ave (45214-1505)
PHONE.............................513 921-3163
Charles S Wilke, *Pr*

G
E
O
G
R
A
P
H
I
C

EMP: 14 **EST:** 1920
SQ FT: 22,000
SALES (est): 2.31MM **Privately Held**
Web: www.paulwilkeandson.com
SIC: 3444 3599 7692 Sheet metal specialties, not stamped; Machine shop, jobbing and repair; Welding repair

(G-2948)
PAVESTONE LLC
8479 Broadwell Rd (45244-1693)
PHONE..............................513 474-3783
Dave Lemmon, *Mgr*
EMP: 70
SQ FT: 54,837
Web: www.pavestone.com
SIC: 3272 3281 Paving materials, prefabricated concrete; Cut stone and stone products
HQ: Pavestone, Llc
   5 Concourse Pkwy Ste 1900
   Atlanta GA 30328
   404 926-3167

(G-2949)
PAYCOR HCM INC (HQ)
Also Called: Paycor
4811 Montgomery Rd (45212-2163)
PHONE..............................800 381-0053
Raul Villar Junior, *CEO*
Adam Ante, *CFO*
Alice Geene, *CLO*
Ryan Bergstrom, *CPO*
Charles Mueller, *CRO*
EMP: 14 **EST:** 1990
SQ FT: 135,577
SALES (est): 654.95MM
SALES (corp-wide): 654.95MM **Privately Held**
Web: www.paycor.com
SIC: 7372 8742 Prepackaged software; Human resource consulting services
PA: Pride Aggregator, Lp
   601 Lexington Ave Fl 53
   New York NY 10022
   212 753-6300

(G-2950)
PE USA LLC
Also Called: P.E. Labellers
89 Partnership Way (45241-1580)
P.O. Box 62067 (45262-0067)
PHONE..............................513 771-7374
▲ **EMP:** 16 **EST:** 1961
SALES (est): 6.01MM **Privately Held**
Web: www.pelabellers.com
SIC: 5084 3565 3469 Packaging machinery and equipment; Packaging machinery; Machine parts, stamped or pressed metal

(G-2951)
PEASE ENTERPRISES INC
Also Called: Brisker Products
1402 Riverside Dr (45202-1754)
PHONE..............................513 871-8907
David Pease, *Pr*
▲ **EMP:** 15 **EST:** 1999
SALES (est): 872.87K **Privately Held**
Web: www.brisker.com
SIC: 8748 5039 2431 5211 Testing services; Prefabricated structures; Doors and door parts and trim, wood; Doors, wood or metal, except storm

(G-2952)
PEERLESS PRINTING COMPANY
2250 Gilbert Ave Ste 1 (45206-2531)
PHONE..............................513 721-4657
Ken Schrand, *Pr*
Paul Dimario, *Prin*
Jay Heidemann, *Prin*

Steve Lyons, *Prin*
Ryan Schrand, *Prin*
EMP: 15 **EST:** 1900
SQ FT: 4,400
SALES (est): 1.72MM **Privately Held**
Web: www.peerlessprinting.com
SIC: 2752 Offset printing

(G-2953)
PERFECT PROBATE
2036 8 Mile Rd (45244-2607)
PHONE..............................513 791-4100
Shawn Wood, *Owner*
EMP: 6 **EST:** 1994
SALES (est): 277.82K **Privately Held**
Web: www.perfectprobate.com
SIC: 7372 8111 Prepackaged software; Legal services

(G-2954)
PERFORMANCE ELECTRONICS LTD
11529 Goldcoast Dr (45249-1620)
PHONE..............................513 777-5233
Brian Lewis, *Mng Pt*
EMP: 8 **EST:** 1999
SALES (est): 1.73MM **Privately Held**
Web: www.pe-ltd.com
SIC: 3679 Electronic circuits

(G-2955)
PERFORMANCE PLASTICS LTD
Also Called: Performance Plastics
4435 Brownway Ave (45209-1264)
PHONE..............................513 321-8404
EMP: 75 **EST:** 1982
SQ FT: 20,000
SALES (est): 20.9MM
SALES (corp-wide): 295.68MM **Privately Held**
Web: www.performanceplastics.com
SIC: 3089 Injection molding of plastics
PA: Pexco Llc
   3440 Preston Ridge Rd
   Alpharetta GA 30005
   678 990-1523

(G-2956)
PETE GAIETTO & ASSOCIATES INC
1900 Section Rd (45237-3308)
PHONE..............................513 771-0903
Jordan Gaietto, *CEO*
▲ **EMP:** 75 **EST:** 2005
SQ FT: 3,880
SALES (est): 8.61MM **Privately Held**
Web: www.petergaietto.com
SIC: 2542 Office and store showcases and display fixtures

(G-2957)
PETER CREMER N AMER ENRGY INC
Also Called: Peter Cremer North America
3131 River Rd (45204-1211)
PHONE..............................513 557-3943
EMP: 30 **EST:** 2009
SALES (est): 11.92MM **Privately Held**
Web: www.petercremerna.com
SIC: 2843 Surface active agents

(G-2958)
PETER CREMER NORTH AMERICA LP (DH)
Also Called: Pcna
3131 River Rd (45204-1211)
PHONE..............................513 471-7200
Ian Van Handel, *CEO*
◆ **EMP:** 60 **EST:** 1998
SALES (est): 115.36MM
SALES (corp-wide): 188.69K **Privately Held**
Web: www.petercremerna.com

SIC: 2899 Oils and essential oils
HQ: Peter Cremer Gmbh
   GlockengieBerwall 3
   Hamburg HH 20095
   40320110

(G-2959)
PETNET SOLUTIONS INC
2139 Auburn Ave (45219-2906)
PHONE..............................865 218-2000
Barry Scott, *CEO*
EMP: 6
SALES (corp-wide): 84.78B **Privately Held**
Web: www.siemens.com
SIC: 2835 Radioactive diagnostic substances
HQ: Petnet Solutions, Inc.
   810 Innovation Dr
   Knoxville TN 37932
   865 218-2000

(G-2960)
PFPC ENTERPRISES INC
5750 Hillside Ave (45233-1508)
PHONE..............................513 941-6200
Peter F Coffaro, *Ch Bd*
James Coffaro, *
Stephen Stout, *
Jerry Jung, *Prin*
EMP: 6 **EST:** 1963
SQ FT: 52,000
SALES (est): 234.36K **Privately Held**
SIC: 5023 5084 3594 3535 Floor coverings; Industrial machinery and equipment; Fluid power pumps and motors; Conveyors and conveying equipment

(G-2961)
PHOENIX GRAPHIX INC
817 W Court St (45203-1308)
PHONE..............................513 751-4433
Rich Hartman, *Pr*
Jo Ann Hartman, *VP*
EMP: 7 **EST:** 2003
SQ FT: 6,000
SALES (est): 88.48K **Privately Held**
SIC: 2752 5111 Offset printing; Printing paper

(G-2962)
PICKENS WINDOW SERVICE INC
7824 Hamilton Ave (45231-3106)
PHONE..............................513 931-4432
Brian Pickens, *Pr*
Kendall Pickens, *Sec*
EMP: 6 **EST:** 1952
SQ FT: 10,000
SALES (est): 395.59K **Privately Held**
Web: www.pickenswindowparts.com
SIC: 5211 7699 2431 Windows, storm: wood or metal; Door and window repair; Window screens, wood frame

(G-2963)
PINNACLE ROLLER CO
2147 Spring Grove Ave (45214-1721)
PHONE..............................513 369-4830
Mike Brown, *Prin*
EMP: 10 **EST:** 2004
SALES (est): 973.7K **Privately Held**
Web: www.pinnacleroller.com
SIC: 3069 Rubber rolls and roll coverings

(G-2964)
PIQUA MATERIALS INC (PA)
11641 Mosteller Rd Ste 1 (45241-1520)
PHONE..............................513 771-0820
James Jurgensen, *Pr*
Tim Saintclair, *Sec*
James Jurgenson Ii, *VP*
EMP: 21 **EST:** 1989
SALES (est): 8.6MM **Privately Held**
Web: www.jrjnet.com

SIC: 1422 Limestones, ground

(G-2965)
PITTSBURGH PAINTS CO
Porter Paints
4600 Reading Rd (45229-1232)
PHONE..............................513 242-3050
Beny Cado, *Mgr*
EMP: 10
SQ FT: 1,600
SALES (corp-wide): 388.64MM **Privately Held**
Web: www.ppgpaints.com
SIC: 2851 Paints and allied products
PA: The Pittsburgh Paints Co
   400 Bertha Lamme Dr
   Cranberry Township PA 16066
   724 742-5200

(G-2966)
PITTSBURGH PAINTS CO
Glidden Professional Paint Ctr
2960 Exon Ave (45241-2521)
PHONE..............................513 563-0220
Dave Gerding, *Brnch Mgr*
EMP: 10
SALES (corp-wide): 388.64MM **Privately Held**
Web: www.ppgpaints.com
SIC: 2851 Paints and allied products
PA: The Pittsburgh Paints Co
   400 Bertha Lamme Dr
   Cranberry Township PA 16066
   724 742-5200

(G-2967)
PKI INC
Also Called: Powder Kote Industries
4500 Reading Rd (45229-1230)
PHONE..............................513 832-8749
Jeff Cox, *Pr*
EMP: 10 **EST:** 1973
SQ FT: 10,000
SALES (est): 941.56K **Privately Held**
Web: www.powdercoatinc.com
SIC: 3479 3471 Coating of metals and formed products; Sand blasting of metal parts

(G-2968)
PLANK AND HIDE CO
2721 E Sharon Rd (45241-1944)
PHONE..............................888 462-6852
Erik Mueller, *CEO*
EMP: 20 **EST:** 2014
SALES (est): 4.62MM **Privately Held**
Web: www.plankandhide.com
SIC: 2426 Carvings, furniture: wood

(G-2969)
PLASTICRAFT USA LLC
3101 Exon Ave (45241-2547)
PHONE..............................513 761-2999
EMP: 6 **EST:** 1996
SQ FT: 2,800
SALES (est): 431.86K **Privately Held**
SIC: 3229 3089 Industrial-use glassware; Molding primary plastics

(G-2970)
PLASTIGRAPHICS INC
722 Redna Ter (45215-1109)
PHONE..............................513 771-8848
Robert Heinold, *Pr*
Sandy Miller, *Sec*
EMP: 12 **EST:** 1971
SQ FT: 6,500
SALES (est): 1.08MM **Privately Held**
Web: www.plastigraphics.com

SIC: **3993** 3861 Signs, not made in custom sign painting shops; Graphic arts plates, sensitized

(G-2971)
PMC SPECIALTIES GROUP INC (DH)
Also Called: Pmcsg
501 Murray Rd (45217-1014)
PHONE..............................513 242-3300
Zoe Bouligaraki, *CEO*
◆ **EMP:** 21 **EST:** 1984
SQ FT: 7,500
SALES (est): 12.36MM
SALES (corp-wide): 1.71B **Privately Held**
Web: www.pmcsg.com
SIC: **2819** 2816 Industrial inorganic chemicals, nec; Inorganic pigments
HQ: Pmc, Inc.
    12243 Branford St
    Sun Valley CA 91352
    818 896-1101

(G-2972)
PMC SPECIALTIES GROUP INC
5220 Vine St (45217-1028)
PHONE..............................513 242-3300
EMP: 18
SALES (corp-wide): 1.71B **Privately Held**
Web: www.pmcsg.com
SIC: **2819** 2816 Industrial inorganic chemicals, nec; Inorganic pigments
HQ: Pmc Specialties Group, Inc.
    501 Murray Rd
    Cincinnati OH 45217

(G-2973)
PME OF OHIO INC (PA)
Also Called: PME- Babbit Bearings
518 W Crescentville Rd (45246-1222)
PHONE..............................513 671-1717
Charles Walter, *Pr*
EMP: 20 **EST:** 1980
SQ FT: 20,000
SALES (est): 8.47MM
SALES (corp-wide): 8.47MM **Privately Held**
Web: www.pmebabbittbearings.com
SIC: **3599** Machine shop, jobbing and repair

(G-2974)
PORTER PRECISION PRODUCTS CO (PA)
Also Called: Porter
2734 Banning Rd (45239-5504)
PHONE..............................513 385-1569
John Cipriani Junior, *Pr*
Mary M Cipriani, *
Dale Warlaumont, *
EMP: 79 **EST:** 1947
SQ FT: 33,200
SALES (est): 7.69MM
SALES (corp-wide): 7.69MM **Privately Held**
Web: www.porterpunch.com
SIC: **3544** Special dies and tools

(G-2975)
PORTER-GUERTIN CO INC
2150 Colerain Ave (45214-1873)
P.O. Box 14177 (45250-0177)
PHONE..............................513 241-7663
James F Gentil, *Pr*
Kathleen Gentil, *Sec*
EMP: 6 **EST:** 1953
SQ FT: 12,000
SALES (est): 780.76K **Privately Held**
Web: www.porterguertinco.com
SIC: **3471** Electroplating of metals or formed products

(G-2976)
POSITROL INC
Also Called: Positrol Workholding
3890 Virginia Ave (45227-3410)
PHONE..............................513 272-0500
David C Weber, *Pr*
Jonathan T Weber, *
EMP: 30 **EST:** 1947
SQ FT: 11,000
SALES (est): 3.83MM **Privately Held**
Web: www.positrol.com
SIC: **3545** Machine tool attachments and accessories

(G-2977)
POSTERSERVICE INCORPORATED (PA)
225 Northland Blvd (45246-3603)
PHONE..............................513 577-7100
Daniel P Regenold, *Ch*
Dana W Gore, *Pr*
Rebecca Regenold, *Sec*
▲ **EMP:** 6 **EST:** 1983
SQ FT: 30,000
SALES (est): 4.96MM
SALES (corp-wide): 4.96MM **Privately Held**
Web: www.artandcanvas.com
SIC: **5199** 2741 Posters; Posters: publishing and printing

(G-2978)
PRECISION SWISS LLC
9580 Wayne Ave (45215-2252)
PHONE..............................513 716-7000
Ron Hinks, *Owner*
Tatyana Hinks, *CFO*
EMP: 9 **EST:** 2011
SQ FT: 17,000
SALES (est): 1.37MM **Privately Held**
SIC: **3843** Dental equipment and supplies

(G-2979)
PREMIER INDUSTRIES INC
5721 Dragon Way Ste 113 (45227-4518)
PHONE..............................513 271-2550
J Paul Taylor, *Pr*
Suzanne Gerwin, *
EMP: 39 **EST:** 1935
SQ FT: 45,000
SALES (est): 534.95K
SALES (corp-wide): 720.21K **Privately Held**
SIC: **2656** 3556 Plates, paper: made from purchased material; Food products machinery
PA: Taylor Company
    5721 Dragon Way Ste 117
    Cincinnati OH 45227
    513 271-2550

(G-2980)
PREMIER SOUTHERN TICKET CO INC
7911 School Rd (45249-1596)
PHONE..............................513 489-6700
Kirk Schulz, *Pr*
Jim Raike, *
◆ **EMP:** 38 **EST:** 1883
SQ FT: 38,000
SALES (est): 408.44K **Privately Held**
Web: www.premiersouthern.com
SIC: **2759** Tickets: printing, nsk
PA: Gtlp Holdings, Llc
    7911 School Rd
    Cincinnati OH 45249

(G-2981)
PRIDE CAST METALS INC
2737 Colerain Ave (45225-2263)
PHONE..............................513 541-1295
Thomas Hamm, *Pr*
Kenneth Bechtol, *
▲ **EMP:** 100 **EST:** 1983
SQ FT: 150,000
SALES (est): 1.92MM **Privately Held**
Web: www.pridecastmetals.com
SIC: **3365** 3366 3599 Aluminum and aluminum-based alloy castings; Castings (except die), nec, bronze; Machine shop, jobbing and repair

(G-2982)
PRIMO SERVICES LLC
1937 Clarion Ave (45207-1242)
PHONE..............................513 725-7888
Shanel Gentry, *CEO*
EMP: 15 **EST:** 2014
SALES (est): 4.39MM **Privately Held**
Web: www.primoservicesllc.com
SIC: **1389** 7349 Construction, repair, and dismantling services; Janitorial service, contract basis

(G-2983)
PRINTERY INC
Also Called: Pink Pages
4460 Bridgetown Rd (45211-4411)
P.O. Box 20206 (45220-0206)
PHONE..............................513 574-1099
Donald B Flick, *Pr*
EMP: 6 **EST:** 1970
SQ FT: 1,500
SALES (est): 63.65K **Privately Held**
SIC: **2741** 2791 Directories, telephone: publishing only, not printed on site; Photocomposition, for the printing trade

(G-2984)
PRO MACH INC
89 Partnership Way (45241-1580)
PHONE..............................513 771-7374
EMP: 36 **EST:** 2019
SALES (est): 8.26MM **Privately Held**
SIC: **3535** Conveyors and conveying equipment
HQ: Pro Mach, Inc.
    50 E Rvrcnter Blvd Ste 18
    Covington KY 41011
    513 831-8778

(G-2985)
PROAMPAC LLC
Also Called: Proampac
12025 Tricon Rd (45246-1719)
PHONE..............................513 671-1777
Greg Tucker, *CEO*
Eric Bradford, *
EMP: 2400 **EST:** 2015
SALES (est): 18.05MM **Privately Held**
SIC: **2671** Paper, coated or laminated for packaging

(G-2986)
PROCESSALL INC
Also Called: Mixmill
4600 N Mason Montgomery Road (45215)
PHONE..............................513 771-2266
Albert J Shohet, *Pr*
EMP: 10 **EST:** 1983
SQ FT: 9,500
SALES (est): 504.47K **Privately Held**
Web: www.processall.com
SIC: **3559** 3556 Chemical machinery and equipment; Food products machinery

(G-2987)
PROCTER & GAMBLE COMPANY
Also Called: Procter & Gamble
6210 Center Hill Ave (45224-1708)
PHONE..............................513 983-1100
Matt Wagner, *Pr*
EMP: 47
SALES (corp-wide): 84.04B **Publicly Held**
Web: us.pg.com
SIC: **2844** 2676 3421 2842 Deodorants, personal; Towels, napkins, and tissue paper products; Razor blades and razors; Specialty cleaning
PA: The Procter & Gamble Company
    1 Procter & Gamble Plz
    Cincinnati OH 45202
    513 983-1100

(G-2988)
PROCTER & GAMBLE COMPANY
Also Called: Procter & Gamble
5280 Vine St (45217-1028)
PHONE..............................513 266-4375
Ed Allie, *Mgr*
EMP: 26
SALES (corp-wide): 84.04B **Publicly Held**
Web: us.pg.com
SIC: **2844** 2676 3421 2842 Deodorants, personal; Towels, napkins, and tissue paper products; Razor blades and razors; Specialty cleaning
PA: The Procter & Gamble Company
    1 Procter & Gamble Plz
    Cincinnati OH 45202
    513 983-1100

(G-2989)
PROCTER & GAMBLE COMPANY
Also Called: Procter & Gamble
654 Wilmer Ave Hngr 4 (45226-1860)
PHONE..............................513 871-7557
David Tobertge, *Mgr*
EMP: 11
SALES (corp-wide): 84.04B **Publicly Held**
Web: us.pg.com
SIC: **2844** 2676 3421 2842 Deodorants, personal; Towels, napkins, and tissue paper products; Razor blades and razors; Specialty cleaning
PA: The Procter & Gamble Company
    1 Procter & Gamble Plz
    Cincinnati OH 45202
    513 983-1100

(G-2990)
PROCTER & GAMBLE COMPANY
Also Called: Procter & Gamble
5299 Spring Grove Ave (45217-1025)
PHONE..............................513 983-1100
John E Pepper, *Ch Bd*
EMP: 65
SALES (corp-wide): 84.04B **Publicly Held**
Web: us.pg.com
SIC: **2844** Deodorants, personal
PA: The Procter & Gamble Company
    1 Procter & Gamble Plz
    Cincinnati OH 45202
    513 983-1100

(G-2991)
PROCTER & GAMBLE COMPANY
Also Called: Procter & Gamble
4460 Kings Run Rd. (45232)
PHONE..............................513 482-6789
Joe Kelly, *Opers Mgr*
EMP: 10
SALES (corp-wide): 84.04B **Publicly Held**
Web: us.pg.com
SIC: **2844** 2676 3421 2842 Deodorants, personal; Towels, napkins, and tissue paper products; Razor blades and razors; Specialty cleaning
PA: The Procter & Gamble Company
    1 Procter & Gamble Plz
    Cincinnati OH 45202
    513 983-1100

(G-2992)
PROCTER & GAMBLE COMPANY
Also Called: Procter & Gamble
6300 Center Hill Ave Fl 2 (45224-1795)
PHONE...............................513 634-5069
D L Miller, *Mgr*
EMP: 50
SALES (corp-wide): 84.04B **Publicly Held**
Web: us.pg.com
SIC: 2844 Deodorants, personal
PA: The Procter & Gamble Company
    1 Procter & Gamble Plz
    Cincinnati OH 45202
    513 983-1100

(G-2993)
PROCTER & GAMBLE COMPANY
Also Called: Procter & Gamble
1 Plaza (45246)
PHONE...............................513 983-3000
EMP: 205
SALES (corp-wide): 84.04B **Publicly Held**
Web: us.pg.com
SIC: 2844 2676 3421 2842 Deodorants,
    personal; Towels, napkins, and tissue paper
    products; Razor blades and razors;
    Specialty cleaning
PA: The Procter & Gamble Company
    1 Procter & Gamble Plz
    Cincinnati OH 45202
    513 983-1100

(G-2994)
PROCTER & GAMBLE COMPANY
Also Called: Procter & Gamble
5348 Vine St (45217-1030)
PHONE...............................513 627-7115
Joe Barbro, *Brnch Mgr*
EMP: 53
SALES (corp-wide): 84.04B **Publicly Held**
Web: us.pg.com
SIC: 2844 2676 3421 2842 Deodorants,
    personal; Towels, napkins, and tissue paper
    products; Razor blades and razors;
    Specialty cleaning
PA: The Procter & Gamble Company
    1 Procter & Gamble Plz
    Cincinnati OH 45202
    513 983-1100

(G-2995)
PROCTER & GAMBLE COMPANY
Also Called: Procter & Gamble
1340 Clay St (45202-7608)
PHONE...............................513 658-9853
David Kuehler, *Brnch Mgr*
EMP: 9
SALES (corp-wide): 84.04B **Publicly Held**
Web: us.pg.com
SIC: 2844 Deodorants, personal
PA: The Procter & Gamble Company
    1 Procter & Gamble Plz
    Cincinnati OH 45202
    513 983-1100

(G-2996)
PROCTER & GAMBLE COMPANY
Also Called: Procter & Gamble
2 Procter And Gamble Plz (45202-3315)
PHONE...............................513 983-1100
Sharon Shea, *Brnch Mgr*
EMP: 500
SALES (corp-wide): 84.04B **Publicly Held**
Web: us.pg.com
SIC: 2844 Deodorants, personal
PA: The Procter & Gamble Company
    1 Procter & Gamble Plz
    Cincinnati OH 45202
    513 983-1100

(G-2997)
PROCTER & GAMBLE COMPANY
Also Called: Procter & Gamble
6280 Center Hill Ave (45224-1708)
PHONE...............................513 945-0340
EMP: 50
SALES (corp-wide): 84.04B **Publicly Held**
Web: us.pg.com
SIC: 2844 2676 3421 2842 Deodorants,
    personal; Towels, napkins, and tissue paper
    products; Razor blades and razors;
    Specialty cleaning
PA: The Procter & Gamble Company
    1 Procter & Gamble Plz
    Cincinnati OH 45202
    513 983-1100

(G-2998)
PROCTER & GAMBLE COMPANY
Procter & Gamble
5289 Vine St (45217-1027)
PHONE...............................513 242-5752
Tia Maurer, *Brnch Mgr*
EMP: 48
SALES (corp-wide): 84.04B **Publicly Held**
Web: us.pg.com
SIC: 2844 Deodorants, personal
PA: The Procter & Gamble Company
    1 Procter & Gamble Plz
    Cincinnati OH 45202
    513 983-1100

(G-2999)
PROCTER & GAMBLE COMPANY
(PA)
Also Called: P&G
1 Procter And Gamble Plz (45202-3393)
P.O. Box 599 (45201)
PHONE...............................513 983-1100
Jon R Moeller, *Ch Bd*
Shailesh Jejurikar, *COO*
Andre Schulten, *CFO*
M Tracey Grabowski, *Chief Human
    Resources Officer*
Susan Street Whaley, *CLO*
◆ EMP: 2997 EST: 1837
SALES (est): 84.04B
SALES (corp-wide): 84.04B **Publicly Held**
Web: us.pg.com
SIC: 2844 2842 2676 3634 Hair
    preparations, including shampoos;
    Specialty cleaning; Towels, napkins, and
    tissue paper products; Razors, electric

(G-3000)
**PROCTER & GAMBLE FAR EAST
INC (HQ)**
1 Procter And Gamble Plz (45202-3393)
PHONE...............................513 983-1100
C Daley, *Prin*
A G Lafley, *Pr*
RI Antoine, *VP*
F Benvegnu, *VP*
Rg Pease, *VP*
EMP: 110 EST: 1837
SQ FT: 1,600,000
SALES (est): 4.07MM
SALES (corp-wide): 84.04B **Publicly Held**
SIC: 2842 2844 2676 Laundry cleaning
    preparations; Toilet preparations; Napkins,
    sanitary: made from purchased paper
PA: The Procter & Gamble Company
    1 Procter & Gamble Plz
    Cincinnati OH 45202
    513 983-1100

(G-3001)
**PROCTER & GAMBLE HAIR CARE
LLC**
1 Procter And Gamble Plz (45202-3393)
PHONE...............................513 983-4502

David S Taylor, *Ch Bd*
EMP: 32 EST: 2001
SALES (est): 59.45MM
SALES (corp-wide): 84.04B **Publicly Held**
SIC: 2844 Shampoos, rinses, conditioners:
    hair
PA: The Procter & Gamble Company
    1 Procter & Gamble Plz
    Cincinnati OH 45202
    513 983-1100

(G-3002)
PROCTER & GAMBLE MFG CO (HQ)
Also Called: Procter & Gamble
1 Procter And Gamble Plz (45202-3393)
P.O. Box 599 (45201-0599)
PHONE...............................513 983-1100
Jon R Moeller, *Ch Bd*
John Jensen, *VP*
C Daley Junior, *Prin*
John Goodwin, *VP*
Chris Walther, *Sec*
◆ EMP: 15 EST: 1910
SQ FT: 1,600,000
SALES (est): 1.27B
SALES (corp-wide): 84.04B **Publicly Held**
Web: us.pg.com
SIC: 2841 2079 2099 2844 Soap:
    granulated, liquid, cake, flaked, or chip;
    Shortening and other solid edible fats;
    Peanut butter; Toilet preparations
PA: The Procter & Gamble Company
    1 Procter & Gamble Plz
    Cincinnati OH 45202
    513 983-1100

(G-3003)
**PROCTER & GAMBLE PAPER PDTS
CO (HQ)**
Also Called: Procter & Gamble
1 Procter And Gamble Plz (45202-3315)
P.O. Box 599 (45201)
PHONE...............................513 983-1100
David S Taylor, *Pr*
Doctor Walker, *VP*
E G Nelson, *VP Fin*
C C Daley, *VP*
T L Overbey, *Sec*
◆ EMP: 15 EST: 1893
SQ FT: 1,600,000
SALES (est): 1.96B
SALES (corp-wide): 84.04B **Publicly Held**
Web: us.pg.com
SIC: 2676 Towels, napkins, and tissue paper
    products
PA: The Procter & Gamble Company
    1 Procter & Gamble Plz
    Cincinnati OH 45202
    513 983-1100

(G-3004)
**PROCTER & GAMBLE PAPER PDTS
CO**
Also Called: Procter & Gamble
301 E 6th St (45202-3339)
PHONE...............................513 983-2222
EMP: 25
SALES (corp-wide): 84.04B **Publicly Held**
Web: us.pg.com
SIC: 2676 Towels, paper: made from
    purchased paper
HQ: The Procter & Gamble Paper Products
    Company
    1 Procter And Gamble Plz
    Cincinnati OH 45202
    513 983-1100

(G-3005)
PROFESSIONAL AWARD SERVICE
Also Called: ID Plastech Engraving
3901 N Bend Rd (45211-4814)

PHONE...............................513 389-3600
Ronald Jeremiah, *Pr*
EMP: 8 EST: 1982
SQ FT: 3,818
SALES (est): 310.1K **Privately Held**
Web: www.awardsanddesign.com
SIC: 3914 7389 Silverware and plated ware;
    Engraving service

(G-3006)
PROFILES IN DESIGN INC
860 Dellway St (45229-3306)
PHONE...............................513 751-2212
Joe Pfaltzgraff, *Pr*
Gary Stacy, *VP*
Sarah Albert, *Sec*
EMP: 10 EST: 1996
SQ FT: 20,000
SALES (est): 907.92K **Privately Held**
Web: www.profilesindesign.com
SIC: 2434 Vanities, bathroom: wood

(G-3007)
PROFT & GAMBLE
6280 Center Hill Ave (45224-1708)
PHONE...............................513 945-0340
Debbie Schurgast, *Prin*
▲ EMP: 7 EST: 2005
SALES (est): 505.68K **Privately Held**
SIC: 2844 Shampoos, rinses, conditioners:
    hair

(G-3008)
**PROMINENCE ENERGY
CORPORATION**
1325 Spring St (45202-7420)
PHONE...............................513 818-8329
Howard M Plevyak Junior, *Prin*
EMP: 6 EST: 2016
SALES (est): 2.26MM **Privately Held**
Web: www.prominenceenergy.com.au
SIC: 1382 Oil and gas exploration services

(G-3009)
PROSPIANT INC (HQ)
5513 Vine St (45217-1022)
PHONE...............................513 242-0310
Mark Dunson, *Pr*
EMP: 53 EST: 1999
SALES (est): 20.1MM
SALES (corp-wide): 1.31B **Publicly Held**
Web: www.prospiant.com
SIC: 3448 Greenhouses, prefabricated metal
PA: Gibraltar Industries, Inc.
    3556 Lake Shore Rd
    Buffalo NY 14219
    716 826-6500

(G-3010)
**PROTECTIVE PACKG SOLUTIONS
LLC**
10345 S Medallion Dr (45241-4825)
PHONE...............................513 769-5777
Thomas Mcnamara, *CEO*
Dave Rettig, *
EMP: 30 EST: 2011
SALES (est): 4.02MM **Privately Held**
Web: www.ppspkg.com
SIC: 2653 5199 Boxes, corrugated: made
    from purchased materials; Packaging
    materials

(G-3011)
PROTEIN TECHNOLOGIES LTD
4015 Executive Park Dr (45241-4017)
PHONE...............................513 769-0840
F Harrison Green, *Prin*
EMP: 7 EST: 2010
SALES (est): 248.75K **Privately Held**

SIC: **2836** Biological products, except diagnostic

(G-3012)
PURETI GROUP LLC
10931 Reed Hartman Hwy Ste C (45242-2862)
PHONE...........................513 708-3631
Brian R Haas, *Prin*
EMP: 6 EST: 2013
SALES (est): 983.48K **Privately Held**
Web: www.pureti.com
SIC: **2819** Chemicals, high purity: refined from technical grade

(G-3013)
QC SOFTWARE LLC
50 E Business Way (45241-2397)
PHONE...........................513 469-1424
Kevin Tedford, *CEO*
EMP: 50 EST: 1996
SQ FT: 2,900
SALES (corp-wide): 44.25MM **Privately Held**
Web: www.kpisolutions.com
SIC: **7371 7372** Computer software development; Prepackaged software
PA: Kuecker Pulse Integration, L.P.
801 W Markey Rd
Belton MO 64012
844 574-1010

(G-3014)
QCA INC
2832 Spring Grove Ave (45225-2220)
PHONE...........................513 681-8400
James Bosken, *Pr*
Andrea Winterhalter, *VP*
EMP: 23 EST: 1950
SQ FT: 35,000
SALES (est): 202.49K **Privately Held**
Web: www.go-qca.com
SIC: **3652** Master records or tapes, preparation of

(G-3015)
QUALITY CONTROLS INC
3411 Church St (45244-3409)
PHONE...........................513 272-3900
Thomas M Pulskamp, *Pr*
Annette Pulskamp, *Sec*
EMP: 11 EST: 1994
3Q FT: 15,000
SALES (est): 4.09MM **Privately Held**
Web: www.qcipanels.com
SIC: **3625 3829** Motor control accessories, including overload relays; Measuring and controlling devices, nec

(G-3016)
QUALITY MECHANICALS INC
1225 Streng St (45223-2642)
PHONE...........................513 559-0998
Richard Doll, *Pr*
Denise Albright, *
EMP: 35 EST: 1985
SQ FT: 4,000
SALES (est): 7.17MM **Privately Held**
Web: www.qualitymechanicals.com
SIC: **3498** Fabricated pipe and fittings

(G-3017)
QUALITY MFG COMPANY INC
4323 Spring Grove Ave (45223-1834)
PHONE...........................513 921-4500
Edward J Bemerer, *Pr*
Richard Lipps, *VP*
Paul A Kapper, *Sec*
EMP: 8 EST: 1975
SQ FT: 16,000

SALES (est): 3.19MM **Privately Held**
Web: www.qmfgco.com
SIC: **3599** Machine shop, jobbing and repair

(G-3018)
QUANTA INTERNATIONAL LLC
1 Landy Ln (45215-3405)
PHONE...........................513 354-3639
Augusto Quinones, *Pr*
EMP: 11 EST: 2011
SALES (est): 728.7K **Privately Held**
SIC: **2819** Industrial inorganic chemicals, nec

(G-3019)
QUEBECOR WORLD JOHNSON HARDIN
3600 Red Bank Rd (45227-4142)
PHONE...........................614 326-0299
Chuck Miotke, *Pr*
James H Bossart, *
Jeffery R Herman, *
EMP: 8 EST: 1902
SQ FT: 200,000
SALES (est): 207.16K **Privately Held**
SIC: **2759 2752 2732** Magazines: printing, nsk; Offset printing; Books, printing only

(G-3020)
QUEEN CITY AWNING & TENT CO
Also Called: Queen City Awning
7225 E Kemper Rd (45249-1030)
PHONE...........................513 530-9660
Peter Weingartner, *Pr*
Robert P Weingartner Senior, *Ch*
James Weingartner, *
EMP: 35 EST: 1877
SQ FT: 27,000
SALES (est): 4.45MM **Privately Held**
Web: www.queencityawning.com
SIC: **2394 5712** Awnings, fabric: made from purchased materials; Outdoor and garden furniture

(G-3021)
QUEEN CITY CARPETS LLC
6539 Harrison Ave 304 (45247-7822)
PHONE...........................513 823-8238
Terry Hensley, *VP*
EMP: 10 EST: 2012
SALES (est): 157.96K **Privately Held**
SIC: **2393** Cushions, except spring and carpet: purchased materials

(G-3022)
QUEEN CITY OFFICE MACHINE
3984 Trevor Ave (45211-3407)
PHONE...........................513 251-7200
Ronald Swing, *Prin*
EMP: 10 EST: 1971
SQ FT: 6,000
SALES (est): 965.63K **Privately Held**
Web: www.queencityoffice.com
SIC: **5112 7629 2759** Office supplies, nec; Business machine repair, electric; Laser printing

(G-3023)
QUEEN CITY PALLETS INC
Also Called: Qcp Pallet Services
7744 Reinhold Dr (45237-2806)
PHONE...........................513 821-6700
Mike Unthank, *CEO*
Garry Unthank, *
EMP: 40 EST: 2006
SQ FT: 30,000
SALES (est): 4.54MM **Privately Held**
Web: www.qcpallets.com
SIC: **2448** Pallets, wood

(G-3024)
QUEEN CITY REPROGRAPHICS
2863 E Sharon Rd (45241-1923)
PHONE...........................513 326-2300
EMP: 105 EST: 1963
SALES (est): 5.76MM
SALES (corp-wide): 281.2MM **Privately Held**
SIC: **5049 7334 7335 2752** Drafting supplies ; Blueprinting service; Commercial photography; Lithographing on metal
PA: Arc Document Solutions, Inc.
12657 Alcsta Blvd Ste 200
San Ramon CA 94583
925 949-5100

(G-3025)
QUEEN CITY SAUSAGE & PROV INC
Also Called: Queen City Sausage
1136 Straight St (45214-1736)
PHONE...........................513 541-5581
Elmer J Hensler, *Pr*
EMP: 43 EST: 1965
SQ FT: 17,000
SALES (est): 4.74MM **Privately Held**
Web: www.queencitysausage.com
SIC: **5421 2013** Meat markets, including freezer provisioners; Sausages and related products, from purchased meat

(G-3026)
QUEEN CITY SPIRIT LLC
Also Called: Queen City Mascots and Logos
8211 Blue Ash Rd (45236-1987)
PHONE...........................513 533-2662
Deanna Regruth, *Owner*
EMP: 10 EST: 2011
SALES (est): 737.21K **Privately Held**
SIC: **2395 2759 7389** Embroidery and art needlework; Screen printing; Engraving service

(G-3027)
R A HELLER COMPANY
10530 Chester Rd (45215-1262)
PHONE...........................513 771-6100
Steve Heller, *Pr*
Laura Heller, *Sec*
EMP: 11 EST: 1946
SQ FT: 20,000
SALES (est): 1.11MM **Privately Held**
Web: www.raheller.com
SIC: **3471 3599 3545** Chromium plating of metals or formed products; Machine shop, jobbing and repair; Cutting tools for machine tools

(G-3028)
R E SMITH INC
10330 Chester Rd (45215-1225)
PHONE...........................513 771-0645
Kenneth J Koncelik, *Pr*
EMP: 10 EST: 2000
SQ FT: 2,000
SALES (est): 816.64K **Privately Held**
Web: www.rs485andrs232.com
SIC: **3621** Frequency converters (electric generators)

(G-3029)
R VANDEWALLE INC
Also Called: Van Engineering Co
4030 Delhi Ave (45204-1276)
PHONE...........................513 921-2657
Robert Vandewalle, *Pr*
Richard Vandewalle, *VP*
EMP: 8 EST: 1942
SQ FT: 7,000
SALES (est): 665.73K **Privately Held**
SIC: **3599** Machine shop, jobbing and repair

(G-3030)
RAD TECHNOLOGIES INCORPORATED
Also Called: Precision Temp
3428 Hauck Rd Ste G (45241-4603)
P.O. Box 498004 (45249)
PHONE...........................513 641-0523
Robert Muhlhauser, *CEO*
Gerry Wolters, *Prin*
Fred Rothzeid, *CFO*
▲ **EMP: 12 EST:** 2010
SALES (est): 2.13MM **Privately Held**
Web: www.precisiontemp.com
SIC: **3639** Hot water heaters, household

(G-3031)
RAILROAD TOOLS & SOLUTIONS INC ✪
4729 Red Bank Rd (45227-1527)
PHONE...........................513 533-7070
Wayne Cash, *Pr*
Michael Mccammon, *Sec*
EMP: 9 EST: 2023
SALES (est): 1.12MM **Privately Held**
SIC: **3531** Railway track equipment

(G-3032)
RANDY GRAY
Also Called: Brat Printing
4142 Airport Rd Unit 1 (45226-1627)
PHONE...........................513 533-3200
Randy Gray, *Owner*
EMP: 6 EST: 1993
SQ FT: 9,000
SALES (est): 942.32K **Privately Held**
Web: www.bratprinting.com
SIC: **3552 2395 2396** Textile machinery; Emblems, embroidered; Automotive and apparel trimmings

(G-3033)
RCL PUBLISHING GROUP LLC
8805 Governors Hill Dr Ste 400 (45249-3314)
PHONE...........................972 390-6400
Rcl Benziger, *Prin*
▼ **EMP: 6 EST:** 2011
SALES (est): 220.43K **Privately Held**
SIC: **2741** Miscellaneous publishing

(G-3034)
READING ROCK INCORPORATED (PA)
4600 Devitt Dr (45246-1130)
P.O. Box 46387 (45246-0387)
PHONE...........................513 874-2345
Gordon Rich, *Pr*
Mark Swortwood, *
▲ **EMP: 97 EST:** 1946
SQ FT: 64,000
SALES (est): 20.55MM
SALES (corp-wide): 20.55MM **Privately Held**
Web: www.readingrock.com
SIC: **3271 2951** Blocks, concrete or cinder: standard; Asphalt paving mixtures and blocks

(G-3035)
RECORD HERALD PUBLISHING CO (DH)
Also Called: Record Herald
5050 Kingsley Dr (45227-1115)
P.O. Box 271 (17268-0271)
PHONE...........................717 762-2151
Denise Igram, *Genl Mgr*
Denise Igram, *Mgr*
EMP: 50 EST: 1847
SALES (est): 1.57MM
SALES (corp-wide): 2.51B **Publicly Held**

Web: www.therecordherald.com
SIC: 2711 2752 Commercial printing and newspaper publishing combined; Commercial printing, lithographic
HQ: Gatehouse Media, Llc
175 Sllys Trl Fl 3 Corp C
Pittsford NY 14534
585 598-0030

(G-3036)
RECTO MOLDED PRODUCTS INC
4425 Appleton St (45209-1290)
PHONE.................................513 871-5544
Per Flem, *Pr*
EMP: 65 **EST:** 1913
SQ FT: 65,000
SALES (est): 8.5MM **Privately Held**
Web: www.rectomolded.com
SIC: 3089 3083 Injection molding of plastics; Laminated plastics plate and sheet

(G-3037)
RELIABLE CASTINGS CORPORATION (PA)
3530 Spring Grove Ave (45223-2742)
PHONE.................................513 541-2627
EMP: 100 **EST:** 1922
SALES (est): 15.32MM
SALES (corp-wide): 15.32MM **Privately Held**
Web: www.reliablecastings.com
SIC: 3365 3543 Aluminum and aluminum-based alloy castings; Industrial patterns

(G-3038)
RENEE GRACE LLC
Also Called: Renee Grace Bridal
11176 Main St (45241-2672)
PHONE.................................513 399-5616
Teresa Eklund, *Prin*
EMP: 8 **EST:** 2018
SALES (est): 205.86K **Privately Held**
Web: www.reneegrace.com
SIC: 2335 Bridal and formal gowns

(G-3039)
RESIDEO LLC
Also Called: ADI Global Distribution
5601 Creek Rd Ste A (45242-4038)
PHONE.................................513 772-1851
Erin Fletcher, *Brnch Mgr*
EMP: 10
SALES (corp-wide): 6.76B **Publicly Held**
Web: www.adiglobaldistribution.us
SIC: 5063 3669 3822 Alarm systems, nec; Emergency alarms; Environmental controls
HQ: Resideo Llc
275 Bradhollow Rd Ste 400
Melville NY 11747
631 692-1000

(G-3040)
RHGS COMPANY
1150 W 8th St Ste 111 (45203-1245)
PHONE.................................513 721-6299
Gregg Sample, *Pr*
Ronald E Heithaus, *Prin*
EMP: 6 **EST:** 2004
SQ FT: 8,000
SALES (est): 395.7K **Privately Held**
Web: www.thetormaxxcompany.com
SIC: 3545 Machine tool accessories

(G-3041)
RHI US LTD (DH)
3956 Virginia Ave (45227-3412)
PHONE.................................513 527-6160
Phil Poulin, *Pr*
Hans Joerg Junger, *VP*
Friedrich Schweighofer, *VP*
Erica Soller, *Sec*

◆ **EMP:** 9 **EST:** 2010
SALES (est): 13.78MM **Privately Held**
Web: www.interstop-usa.com
SIC: 3823 Refractometers, industrial process type
HQ: Dutch Us Holding B.V.
Hofplein 19
Rotterdam ZH 3032
263635763

(G-3042)
RHINEGEIST HOLDING COMPANY INC
1910 Elm St (45202-7751)
PHONE.................................513 381-1367
Robert Bonder, *Prin*
EMP: 6 **EST:** 2021
SALES (est): 170.95K **Privately Held**
Web: www.rhinegeist.com
SIC: 2082 Malt beverages

(G-3043)
RIBS KING INC
9406 Main St (45242-7616)
PHONE.................................513 791-1942
Evan Andrews, *VP*
Thomas Gregory, *Pr*
Dean Gregory, *VP*
Victoria Siegel, *VP*
EMP: 9 **EST:** 1990
SQ FT: 21,000
SALES (est): 253.12K **Privately Held**
Web: www.montgomeryinnribsking.com
SIC: 2035 Seasonings and sauces, except tomato and dry

(G-3044)
RICHARDS INDUSTRIALS INC (PA)
Also Called: Richards Industrials
3170 Wasson Rd (45209-2360)
PHONE.................................513 533-5600
Jordan Bast, *Pr*
John Speridakos, *
Bill Metz, *
Jim Gray, *
▲ **EMP:** 75 **EST:** 1961
SQ FT: 150,000
SALES (est): 11.77MM
SALES (corp-wide): 11.77MM **Privately Held**
Web: www.richardsind.com
SIC: 3491 3494 3823 Industrial valves; Pipe fittings; Process control instruments

(G-3045)
RIDGE ENGINEERING INC
Also Called: Delhi Welding Co
1700 Blue Rock St (45223-2505)
PHONE.................................513 681-5500
Rob Shean, *Genl Mgr*
EMP: 9 **EST:** 1984
SQ FT: 14,000
SALES (est): 223.34K **Privately Held**
Web: www.ridgeeng.com
SIC: 7692 Welding repair

(G-3046)
RINA SYSTEMS LLC
8180 Corporate Park Dr Ste 140 (45242-3309)
PHONE.................................513 469-7462
Leo G Samasqui, *Pr*
EMP: 6 **EST:** 1995
SALES (est): 842.09K **Privately Held**
Web: www.rinasystems.com
SIC: 7372 Prepackaged software

(G-3047)
RIVER CITY BODY COMPANY
2660 Commerce Blvd (45241-1552)
PHONE.................................513 772-9317

John Mc Henry, *Pr*
EMP: 11 **EST:** 1989
SQ FT: 10,000
SALES (est): 2.24MM **Privately Held**
Web: www.rivercitybody.com
SIC: 3537 5531 Trucks, tractors, loaders, carriers, and similar equipment; Truck equipment and parts

(G-3048)
RIVERSIDE CNSTR SVCS INC
218 W Mcmicken Ave (45214-2314)
PHONE.................................513 723-0900
Robert S Krejci, *Pr*
Timothy L Pierce, *
EMP: 32 **EST:** 1993
SQ FT: 21,000
SALES (est): 5.39MM **Privately Held**
Web: www.riversidearchitectural.com
SIC: 2431 1751 2434 Millwork; Carpentry work; Wood kitchen cabinets

(G-3049)
RM ADVISORY GROUP INC
5300 Vine St (45217-1030)
PHONE.................................513 242-2100
Robert Moskowitz, *Pr*
Ira Moskowitz, *
EMP: 35 **EST:** 1901
SQ FT: 70,000
SALES (est): 864.77K **Privately Held**
SIC: 5093 3341 Ferrous metal scrap and waste; Secondary nonferrous metals

(G-3050)
RMT ACQUISITION INC
Also Called: Young & Bertke Air Systems Co.
3111 Spring Grove Ave (45225-1821)
PHONE.................................513 241-5566
Roger Young, *Pr*
Tim Rohrer, *
Michael Munafo, *
Phillip C Young, *Stockholder*
EMP: 28 **EST:** 1920
SQ FT: 51,000
SALES (est): 5.29MM
SALES (corp-wide): 54.5MM **Privately Held**
Web: www.youngbertke.com
SIC: 1761 3441 3564 3444 Sheet metal work, nec; Fabricated structural metal; Blowers and fans; Sheet metalwork
PA: Anguil Environmental Systems, Inc.
8855 N 55th St
Milwaukee WI 53223
414 365-6400

(G-3051)
ROBBINS SPORTS SURFACES LLC (PA)
Also Called: Robbins Sports Surfaces
4777 Eastern Ave (45226-2339)
PHONE.................................513 871-8988
Dave Fulton, *CEO*
Matt Femia, *
Mike Niese, *
John Williams, *
Beth Smith, *
◆ **EMP:** 35 **EST:** 1970
SQ FT: 3,000
SALES (est): 8.4MM
SALES (corp-wide): 8.4MM **Privately Held**
Web: www.robbinsfloor.com
SIC: 2426 Flooring, hardwood

(G-3052)
ROLCON INC
510 Station Ave (45215-5439)
PHONE.................................513 821-7259
Don Mileham, *Admn*
EMP: 10

Web: www.rolconrollers.com
SIC: 3535 3561 Conveyors and conveying equipment; Cylinders, pump
PA: Rolcon, Inc
134 Carthage Ave
Cincinnati OH 45215

(G-3053)
ROTEX GLOBAL LLC
Also Called: Gundlach
1230 Knowlton St (45223-1800)
P.O. Box 630317 (45263-0317)
PHONE.................................513 541-1236
William J Herkamp, *Pr*
Robert W Dieckman, *
Gary Armstrong, *
Mark J Moore, *
Richard B Paulsen, *
◆ **EMP:** 165 **EST:** 1844
SQ FT: 150,000
SALES (est): 24.88MM **Publicly Held**
Web: www.rotex.com
SIC: 3569 3826 Sifting and screening machines; Particle size analyzers
PA: Hillenbrand, Inc.
1 Batesville Blvd
Batesville IN 47006

(G-3054)
ROUGH BROTHERS MFG INC
5513 Vine St (45217-1049)
PHONE.................................513 242-0310
Richard Reilly, *Pr*
David Roberts, *
◆ **EMP:** 90 **EST:** 1992
SQ FT: 100,000
SALES (est): 44.68MM
SALES (corp-wide): 1.31B **Publicly Held**
Web: www.prospiant.com
SIC: 1542 3448 Greenhouse construction; Greenhouses, prefabricated metal
HQ: Rough Brothers Holding Co., Inc
3556 Lk Shore Rd Ste 100
Buffalo NY 14219
716 826-6500

(G-3055)
RPI COLOR SERVICE INC
Also Called: RPI Graphic Data Solutions
1950 Radcliff Dr (45204-1823)
PHONE.................................513 471-4040
Patricia A Raker, *Pr*
Karen E Rellar, *Communication Secretary*
Denise L Rellar, *
William E Rellar, *
EMP: 70 **EST:** 1980
SQ FT: 65,000
SALES (est): 7.06MM **Privately Held**
Web: www.rpigraphic.com
SIC: 2752 Offset printing

(G-3056)
RUDD EQUIPMENT COMPANY INC
11807 Enterprise Dr (45241-1511)
PHONE.................................513 321-7833
Mike Rudd, *Pr*
EMP: 40
Web: www.ruddequipment.com
SIC: 3462 7699 Construction or mining equipment forgings, ferrous; Industrial machinery and equipment repair
HQ: Rudd Equipment Company, Inc.
4344 Poplar Level Rd
Louisville KY 40213
502 456-4050

(G-3057)
RUMPKE TRANSPORTATION CO LLC
Also Called: Rumpke Container Service
553 Vine St (45202-3105)
PHONE.................................513 242-4600

Jeff Rumpke, *Mgr*
EMP: 263
Web: www.rumpke.com
SIC: 4953 3341 3231 2611 Recycling, waste materials; Secondary nonferrous metals; Products of purchased glass; Pulp mills
HQ: Rumpke Transportation Company, Llc
10795 Hughes Rd
Cincinnati OH 45251
513 851-0122

(G-3058)
RUMPKE TRANSPORTATION CO LLC (HQ)
10795 Hughes Rd (45251-4598)
PHONE..............................513 851-0122
William J Rumpke, *Pr*
Phil Wehrman, *CFO*
EMP: 10 **EST:** 1999
SQ FT: 10,000
SALES (est): 19.56MM **Privately Held**
Web: www.rumpke.com
SIC: 3561 5084 7537 4953 Pumps and pumping equipment; Hydraulic systems equipment and supplies; Automotiv e transmission repair shops; Refuse systems
PA: Rumpke Consolidated Companies, Inc.
3990 Generation Drive
Cincinnati OH 45251

(G-3059)
S J ROTH ENTERPRISES INC
900 Kieley Pl (45217-1153)
PHONE..............................513 543-1140
Steven Roth, *Pr*
Frank J Roth, *
EMP: 70 **EST:** 1980
SQ FT: 1,200
SALES (est): 2.14MM **Privately Held**
SIC: 3273 Ready-mixed concrete

(G-3060)
SAKRETE INC
5155 Fischer Ave (45217-1157)
PHONE..............................513 242-3644
John G Avril, *Ch Bd*
J Craig Avril, *
EMP: 35 **EST:** 1936
SQ FT: 35,000
SALES (est): 575.1K **Privately Held**
SIC: 3273 6794 Ready-mixed concrete; Patent buying, licensing, leasing

(G-3001)
SAMHAIN PUBLISHING LTD (LLC)
11821 Mason Montgomery Rd # 2
(45249-3705)
PHONE..............................513 453-4688
EMP: 9
SALES (est): 932.68K **Privately Held**
SIC: 2741 Miscellaneous publishing

(G-3062)
SAMUEL ADAMS BREWERY COMPANY LTD
1625 Central Pkwy (45214-2423)
PHONE..............................513 412-3200
◆ **EMP:** 100
Web: www.samadamscincy.com
SIC: 2082 Beer (alcoholic beverage)

(G-3063)
SANGER HOLDINGS LLC
501 Chestnut St (45203-1420)
PHONE..............................513 784-9046
Donna Eby, *Pt*
Lisa Sanger, *Pt*
EMP: 16 **EST:** 1988
SQ FT: 6,300
SALES (est): 2.44MM **Privately Held**

Web: www.sangereby.com
SIC: 7336 7372 Graphic arts and related design; Application computer software

(G-3064)
SATURDAY KNIGHT LTD (PA)
Also Called: Skl Home
4330 Winton Rd (45232-1827)
PHONE..............................513 641-1400
Kristen Vransky, *Pr*
Frank Kling, *
◆ **EMP:** 99 **EST:** 1976
SQ FT: 450,000
SALES (est): 3.75MM
SALES (corp-wide): 3.75MM **Privately Held**
Web: www.sklhome.com
SIC: 2392 Towels, fabric and nonwoven: made from purchased materials

(G-3065)
SAUERWEIN WELDING
605 Wayne Park Dr (45215-2848)
P.O. Box 15033 (45215-0033)
PHONE..............................513 563-2979
Donald Sauerwein, *Pr*
EMP: 7 **EST:** 1964
SQ FT: 5,000
SALES (est): 258.37K **Privately Held**
Web: www.sauerweinwelding.com
SIC: 7692 Welding repair

(G-3066)
SB TRANS LLC
300 E Business Way Ste 200 (45241-2389)
PHONE..............................407 477-2545
EMP: 10 **EST:** 2018
SALES (est): 1.02MM **Privately Held**
SIC: 3537 Trucks: freight, baggage, etc.: industrial, except mining

(G-3067)
SCHAAF CO INC
2440 Spring Grove Ave (45214-1755)
PHONE..............................513 241-7044
TOLL FREE: 800
Walter A Smith, *Pr*
Chuck Smith, *VP*
Barb Meeks, *Sec*
EMP: 9 **EST:** 1928
SQ FT: 6,500
SALES (est): 499.17K **Privately Held**
Web: www.schaafcincy.com
SIC: 2394 Awnings, fabric: made from purchased materials

(G-3068)
SCHURMAN FINE PAPERS
Also Called: Papyrus
7875 Montgomery Rd Spc 81 (45236-4391)
PHONE..............................513 791-5554
Margo Pollak, *Brnch Mgr*
EMP: 25
SALES (corp-wide): 38.97MM **Privately Held**
Web: www.srgretail.com
SIC: 2771 Greeting cards
PA: Schurman Fine Papers
300 Oak Bluff Ln
Goodlettsville TN 37072
707 425-8006

(G-3069)
SCIATH AIM FORGE INC ✪
11560 Goldcoast Dr (45249-1640)
PHONE..............................574 933-3479
Chad Barden, *CEO*
EMP: 7 **EST:** 2024
SALES (est): 1.23MM **Privately Held**
SIC: 3531 Construction machinery

(G-3070)
SCOTT MODELS INC
607 Redna Ter Ste 400 (45215-1183)
PHONE..............................513 771-8005
Thomas Scott, *Pr*
EMP: 15 **EST:** 1974
SQ FT: 10,000
SALES (est): 419.32K **Privately Held**
Web: www.scottmodels.com
SIC: 3999 Models, except toy

(G-3071)
SCS CONSTRUCTION SERVICES INC
2130 Western Ave (45214-1744)
PHONE..............................513 929-0260
Jerry Back, *Pr*
Larry Back, *
EMP: 20 **EST:** 2000
SQ FT: 8,000
SALES (est): 5.33MM **Privately Held**
Web: www.scscincinnati.com
SIC: 1542 3231 1761 3449 Commercial and office building, new construction; Doors, glass: made from purchased glass; Skylight installation; Curtain walls for buildings, steel

(G-3072)
SDI INDUSTRIES
8561 New England Ct (45236-2093)
PHONE..............................513 561-4032
Edward Boll, *Prin*
EMP: 6 **EST:** 2010
SALES (est): 178.85K **Privately Held**
Web: www.sdi.systems
SIC: 3999 Manufacturing industries, nec

(G-3073)
SEALTRON INC
9705 Reading Rd (45215-3515)
PHONE..............................513 733-8400
Andy Goldfarb, *Pr*
Christopher Bateman, *
EMP: 144 **EST:** 1971
SQ FT: 38,000
SALES (est): 7.72MM
SALES (corp-wide): 6.94B **Publicly Held**
SIC: 3823 Process control instruments
PA: Ametek, Inc.
1100 Cassatt Rd
Berwyn PA 19312
610 647-2121

(G-3074)
SECURITY FENCE GROUP INC (PA)
4260 Dane Ave (45223-1855)
PHONE..............................513 681-3700
Christine Frankenstein, *CEO*
Christine Frankenstein, *Pr*
George Frankenstein, *
Angela Case, *
EMP: 37 **EST:** 1960
SQ FT: 140,000
SALES (est): 18.5MM **Privately Held**
Web: www.sfence.com
SIC: 1611 1799 5039 1731 Guardrail construction, highways; Fence construction; Wire fence, gates, and accessories; General electrical contractor

(G-3075)
SEEMLESS PRINTING LLC
717 Linn St (45203-1703)
PHONE..............................513 871-2366
Alicia Wilhelmy, *Pt*
EMP: 6 **EST:** 2002
SALES (est): 872.66K **Privately Held**
Web: www.seemlessprinting.com
SIC: 2752 Offset printing

(G-3076)
SEILKOP INDUSTRIES INC
Also Called: Hitech Shapes & Designs
7211 Market Pl (45216-2020)
PHONE..............................513 679-5680
Ken Seilkop, *Owner*
EMP: 11
SALES (corp-wide): 19.44MM **Privately Held**
Web: www.seilkopindustries.com
SIC: 3543 3369 3365 3363 Foundry patternmaking; Nonferrous foundries, nec; Aluminum foundries; Aluminum die-castings
PA: Seilkop Industries, Inc.
425 W N Bend Rd
Cincinnati OH 45216
513 761-1035

(G-3077)
SEILKOP INDUSTRIES INC (PA)
Also Called: Epcor Foundries
425 W North Bend Rd (45216-1731)
PHONE..............................513 761-1035
Dave Seilkop, *Pr*
Ken Seilkop, *
Robin Vogel, *
EMP: 50 **EST:** 1946
SQ FT: 35,000
SALES (est): 19.44MM
SALES (corp-wide): 19.44MM **Privately Held**
Web: www.seilkopindustries.com
SIC: 3363 3544 3553 3469 Aluminum die-castings; Special dies and tools; Pattern makers' machinery, woodworking; Patterns on metal

(G-3078)
SELBY SERVICE/ROXY PRESS INC
2020 Elm St (45202-4911)
PHONE..............................513 241-3445
Clarence Stricker, *Ch Bd*
Robert Stricker, *Pr*
Loretta Stricker, *Treas*
Jeanne Meinzen, *Sec*
Bob Furnish, *VP*
EMP: 6 **EST:** 1938
SALES (est): 176.89K **Privately Held**
SIC: 2752 7331 2759 Offset printing; Addressographing service; Letterpress printing

(G-3079)
SENIOR IMPACT PUBLICATIONS LLC
5980 Kugler Mill Rd (45236-2075)
PHONE..............................513 791-8800
Robert Jutze, *Pr*
EMP: 10 **EST:** 1997
SALES (est): 90.78K **Privately Held**
Web: www.seniorimpact.com
SIC: 2741 Miscellaneous publishing

(G-3080)
SENNECA HOLDINGS INC (HQ)
Also Called: Door Engineering and Mfg
10021 Commerce Park Dr (45246-1333)
PHONE..............................800 543-4455
Robert G Isaman, *CEO*
Jeffrey Stark, *
Michael Rubiera, *CCO**
Karl Adrian, *
Pat Mcmullen, *CFO*
EMP: 33 **EST:** 2010
SALES (est): 129.54MM
SALES (corp-wide): 1.01B **Privately Held**
Web: www.senneca.com
SIC: 3442 Metal doors, sash, and trim
PA: Kohlberg & Co., L.L.C.
111 Radio Cir
Mount Kisco NY 10549
914 241-7430

(G-3081)
SENSE DIAGNOSTICS INC
1776 Mentor Ave Ste 426 (45212-3583)
PHONE..............................513 702-0376
Geoff Klass, *CEO*
Dan Kincaid, *COO*
Matt Flaherty, *CCO*
Ope Adeoye, *CMO*
EMP: 9 **EST:** 2013
SALES (est): 1.62MM **Privately Held**
Web: www.senseneuro.com
SIC: 3841 Diagnostic apparatus, medical

(G-3082)
SENSORY ROBOTICS INC
9711 Winton Hills Ln (45215-2059)
PHONE..............................513 545-9501
Chris Edwards, *CEO*
EMP: 7 **EST:** 2020
SALES (est): 157.3K **Privately Held**
Web: www.sensoryrobotics.com
SIC: 3569 Robots, assembly line: industrial
and commercial

(G-3083)
SERVATII INC
3774 Paxton Ave (45209-2306)
PHONE..............................513 271-5040
Becky Free, *Mgr*
EMP: 9
SALES (corp-wide): 14.87MM **Privately
Held**
Web: www.servatii.com
SIC: 2051 Bread, cake, and related products
PA: Servatii, Inc.
3888 Virginia Ave
Cincinnati OH 45227
513 271-5040

(G-3084)
SESH COMMUNICATIONS
Also Called: N J E M A Magazine
3440 Burnet Ave Ste 130 (45229-2857)
PHONE..............................513 851-1693
Eric Kearney, *Pr*
Wilton Blake, *VP*
Jan-michele Kearney, *VP*
Ronda Gooden, *VP*
EMP: 15 **EST:** 1998
SALES (est): 863.37K **Privately Held**
Web: www.thecincinnatiherald.com
SIC: 2711 2721 Newspapers, publishing and
printing; Periodicals

(G-3085)
SETCO INDUSTRIES INC
5880 Hillside Ave (45233-1524)
PHONE..............................513 941-5110
Jeff Clark, *CEO*
EMP: 60 **EST:** 2017
SALES (est): 4.98MM **Privately Held**
Web: www.setco.com
SIC: 3545 Machine tool accessories

(G-3086)
SHAMROCK MATERIALS INC
11641 Mosteller Rd (45241-1520)
PHONE..............................513 988-0647
James P Jurgensen, *Pr*
James King, *VP*
EMP: 10 **EST:** 1979
SQ FT: 800
SALES (est): 206.75K **Privately Held**
Web: www.shamrockmaterials.com
SIC: 3273 Ready-mixed concrete

(G-3087)
SHAWNEE SYSTEMS INC
4221 Brandonmore Dr (45255-3656)
P.O. Box 1446 (30009-1446)

PHONE..............................513 561-9932
▲ **EMP:** 57
Web: www.shawneesystems.com
SIC: 2761 2752 Manifold business forms;
Commercial printing, lithographic

(G-3088)
SIEBTECHNIK TEMA INC
7806 Redsky Dr (45249-1632)
PHONE..............................513 489-7811
Michael Mullins, *Pr*
J Neal Gardner, *
▲ **EMP:** 26 **EST:** 1977
SQ FT: 15,000
SALES (est): 20.16MM
SALES (corp-wide): 510.34MM **Privately
Held**
Web: www.siebtechnik-tema.com
SIC: 3599 3589 3532 3569 Custom
machinery; Commercial cooking and
foodwarming equipment; Mineral
beneficiation equipment; Centrifuges,
industrial
HQ: Siebtechnik Gmbh
Platanenallee 46
Mulheim An Der Ruhr NW 45478
208580100

(G-3089)
SIGMATEK SYSTEMS LLC (HQ)
Also Called: Sigma T E K
1445 Kemper Meadow Dr (45240-1637)
PHONE..............................513 674-0005
Ben Terreblanche, *CEO*
EMP: 65 **EST:** 1993
SQ FT: 23,000
SALES (est): 24.4MM
SALES (corp-wide): 12.03B **Privately Held**
Web: www.sigmanest.com
SIC: 7372 Prepackaged software
PA: Sandvik Ab
Spangvagen 10
Sandviken 811 3
26260000

(G-3090)
SIGNALYSIS INC
539 Glenrose Ln (45244-1509)
PHONE..............................513 528-6164
Robert Neil Coleman, *Pr*
Kyle Coleman, *VP*
Phil Wilkin, *Stockholder*
EMP: 12 **EST:** 1987
SALES (est): 4.06MM **Privately Held**
Web: www.signalysis.com
SIC: 8711 7371 3695 7389 Consulting
engineer; Computer software development
and applications; Computer software tape
and disks: blank, rigid, and floppy; Business
Activities at Non-Commercial Site

(G-3091)
SIMPLEVMS LLC
7373 Beechmont Ave Ste 130
(45230-4100)
PHONE..............................888 255-8918
Jason Oswald, *Pr*
EMP: 19 **EST:** 2011
SALES (est): 8.95MM **Privately Held**
Web: www.simplevms.com
SIC: 7372 7371 8742 8748 Business
oriented computer software; Computer
software development and applications;
Human resource consulting services;
Business consulting, nec
PA: Avionte, Llc
4300 Marketpointe Dr
Minneapolis MN 55435

(G-3092)
SIMPLY UNIQUE SNACKS LLC
4420 Haight Ave (45223-1705)
PHONE..............................513 223-7736
Steve Hofford, *Pr*
EMP: 6 **EST:** 2014
SALES (est): 330K
SALES (corp-wide): 1.1MM **Privately Held**
Web: www.simplyuniquesnacks.com
SIC: 2013 2037 2068 7389 Snack sticks,
including jerky: from purchased meat; Fruit
juices, frozen; Salted and roasted nuts and
seeds; Business services, nec
PA: United Snacks Of America Llc
42 Phipps Ln
Plainview NY 11803
516 319-9448

(G-3093)
SIMS-LOHMAN INC (PA)
Also Called: Sims-Lohman Fine Kitchens
Gran
6325 Este Ave (45232-1458)
PHONE..............................513 651-3510
Steve Steinman, *CEO*
John Beiersdorfer, *
▲ **EMP:** 50 **EST:** 1974
SQ FT: 153,000
SALES (est): 96.65MM
SALES (corp-wide): 96.65MM **Privately
Held**
Web: www.sims-lohman.com
SIC: 2435 5031 Hardwood veneer and
plywood; Kitchen cabinets

(G-3094)
SK TEXTILE INC
Also Called: Sk
1 Knollcrest Dr (45237-1608)
PHONE..............................800 888-9112
Kim Morris Heiman, *Pr*
▲ **EMP:** 105 **EST:** 1986
SALES (est): 2.68MM **Privately Held**
Web: www.standardtextile.com
SIC: 2391 2211 Curtains and draperies;
Bedspreads, cotton

(G-3095)
SKY WIRELESS AND SMOKE SP LLC
100 S Cooper Ave (45215-4560)
PHONE..............................513 488-5992
Mahmoud Alili, *Pr*
EMP: 21 **EST:** 2010
SALES (est): 254.39K **Privately Held**
SIC: 5999 2752 Miscellaneous retail stores,
nec; Advertising posters, lithographed

(G-3096)
SMITH ELECTRO CHEMICAL CO
5936 Carthage Ct (45212-1103)
PHONE..............................513 351-7227
Donald W Kifer, *Pr*
Robert Kifer, *
EMP: 9 **EST:** 1948
SQ FT: 25,000
SALES (est): 947.28K **Privately Held**
Web: www.smithelectrochemical.com
SIC: 3471 Electroplating of metals or formed
products

(G-3097)
**SMITHFIELD PACKAGED MEATS
CORP (DH)**
805 E Kemper Rd (45246-2515)
P.O. Box 405020 (45240-5020)
PHONE..............................513 782-3800
Joseph B Sebring, *Pr*
Mike Corbett, *
Mark Dorsey, *
◆ **EMP:** 125 **EST:** 1957
SQ FT: 10,000

SALES (est): 598.83MM **Publicly Held**
SIC: 2011 Pork products, from pork
slaughtered on site
HQ: Smithfield Foods, Inc.
200 Commerce St
Smithfield VA 23430
757 365-3000

(G-3098)
SO-LOW ENVIRONMENTAL EQP CO
10310 Spartan Dr (45215-1279)
PHONE..............................513 772-9410
Walter Schum, *Pr*
James Schum, *
Jean Schum, *
EMP: 48 **EST:** 1959
SQ FT: 66,000
SALES (est): 9.32MM **Privately Held**
Web: www.so-low.com
SIC: 3821 3585 Laboratory apparatus and
furniture; Refrigeration equipment, complete

(G-3099)
SOLID SURFACE CONCEPTS INC
7660 Production Dr (45237-3209)
P.O. Box 43335 (45243-0335)
PHONE..............................513 948-8677
Rob Butler, *Pr*
Kenneth Granger, *
Bill Butler, *
Steve Butler, *
EMP: 24 **EST:** 1989
SQ FT: 6,956
SALES (est): 165.44K **Privately Held**
Web: www.solidsurfaceconcepts.com
SIC: 2431 3281 2541 1411 Millwork; Cut
stone and stone products; Wood partitions
and fixtures; Dimension stone

(G-3100)
SOLO PRODUCTS INC
838 Reedy St (45202-2216)
PHONE..............................513 321-7884
Steve Kunkemoeller, *CEO*
Doug Hearn, *CFO*
EMP: 12 **EST:** 1987
SALES (est): 1.21MM **Privately Held**
Web:
www.soloproductsandcontainers.com
SIC: 5085 3086 Rubber goods, mechanical;
Carpet and rug cushions, foamed plastics

(G-3101)
**SOUTHERN GRAPHIC SYSTEMS
LLC**
9435 Waterstone Blvd Ste 300
(45249-8226)
PHONE..............................513 648-4641
Kerri Randolph, *Brnch Mgr*
EMP: 21
SALES (corp-wide): 998.42MM **Privately
Held**
Web: www.sgsco.com
SIC: 2796 Platemaking services
HQ: Southern Graphic Systems, Llc
626 W Main St Ste 400
Louisville KY 40202
502 637-5443

(G-3102)
SOUTHERN OHIO PRINTING
2230 Gilbert Ave (45206-2531)
PHONE..............................513 241-5150
Robert Van Lear, *Owner*
EMP: 7 **EST:** 1998
SALES (est): 170.59K **Privately Held**
SIC: 2752 Offset printing

▲ = Import ▼ = Export
◆ = Import/Export

(G-3103)
SPECIALTY LITHOGRAPHING CO
1035 W 7th St (45203-1285)
PHONE.................................513 621-0222
Elmer A Babey, *CEO*
Mark Babey, *Pr*
James Babey, *VP*
Carol Evans, *Sec*
EMP: 17 **EST:** 1947
SQ FT: 20,000
SALES (est): 1.69MM **Privately Held**
Web: www.specialtylitho.com
SIC: 2752 Offset printing

(G-3104)
SPECTEX LLC
6156 Wesselman Rd (45248-1204)
PHONE.................................603 330-3334
Kelley Mckenzie, *Admn*
EMP: 17 **EST:** 2001
SALES (est): 2.1MM **Privately Held**
Web: www.sur-seal.com
SIC: 3554 Die cutting and stamping
machinery, paper converting

(G-3105)
SPEEDPRO IMAGING
2888 E Kemper Rd (45241-1820)
PHONE.................................513 771-4776
Dave Sperry, *Prin*
EMP: 7 **EST:** 2006
SALES (est): 752.92K **Privately Held**
Web: www.speedpro.com
SIC: 3993 Signs and advertising specialties

(G-3106)
SPORTSCO IMPRINTING
8277 Wicklow Ave (45236-1613)
PHONE.................................513 641-5111
Joe Eigel, *Pt*
Eric Kattus, *Pt*
EMP: 8 **EST:** 1993
SQ FT: 1,800
SALES (est): 384.17K **Privately Held**
SIC: 2262 2395 Screen printing: manmade
fiber and silk broadwoven fabrics;
Emblems, embroidered

(G-3107)
**SPRING GROVE MANUFACTURING
INC**
Also Called: Cinncinati Bindery
2838 Spring Grove Ave (45225-2268)
PHONE.................................513 542-6900
Jeff Best, *Pr*
EMP: 6 **EST:** 1989
SALES (est): 338.56K **Privately Held**
Web: www.cincybindery.com
SIC: 2789 Binding only: books, pamphlets,
magazines, etc.

(G-3108)
SPRINGDOT INC (PA)
Also Called: Springdot
2611 Colerain Ave (45214-1711)
PHONE.................................513 542-4000
Josh Deutsch, *Pr*
Jeff Deutsch, *
John Brenner, *
Thomas Deutsch, *Stockholder**
EMP: 60 **EST:** 1904
SQ FT: 70,000
SALES (est): 9.93MM
SALES (corp-wide): 9.93MM **Privately
Held**
Web: www.springdot.com
SIC: 2752 4899 2759 2675 Offset printing;
Data communication services; Commercial
printing, nec; Die-cut paper and board

(G-3109)
SQUEAKY CLEAN CINCINNATI INC
Also Called: Squeaky Clean Off & Coml Clg
1500 Goodman Ave (45224-1005)
P.O. Box 31055 (45231-0055)
PHONE.................................513 729-2712
Larry Vaughan, *Pr*
EMP: 10 **EST:** 1986
SALES (est): 182.36K **Privately Held**
Web: floor-cleaning-services.cmac.ws
SIC: 3589 Commercial cleaning equipment

(G-3110)
STAINLESS CRAFTS INC
6660 Russell Heights Dr (45248-1015)
PHONE.................................513 353-4578
Michael Woodrey, *Pr*
Linda Woodrey, *VP*
EMP: 6 **EST:** 1982
SQ FT: 5,500
SALES (est): 76.66K **Privately Held**
SIC: 2599 1796 Restaurant furniture, wood
or metal; Installing building equipment

(G-3111)
STANDARD PUBLISHING LLC
8805 Governors Hill Dr Ste 400
(45249-3314)
PHONE.................................513 931-4050
▲ **EMP:** 200 **EST:** 2004
SALES (est): 1.13MM **Privately Held**
Web: www.standardpub.com
SIC: 2721 Magazines: publishing only, not
printed on site
PA: Cfm Religion Publishing Group Llc
8805 Governors Hill Dr # 40
Cincinnati OH 45249

(G-3112)
STANDARD TEXTILE CO INC (PA)
Also Called: Pridecraft Enterprises
1 Knollcrest Dr (45237-1608)
P.O. Box 371805 (45222-1805)
PHONE.................................513 761-9255
Gary Heiman, *CEO*
Alex Heiman, *
Edward Frankel, *CAO**
Norman Frankel, *SALES**
Chris Bopp, *CIO**
◆ **EMP:** 300 **EST:** 1940
SQ FT: 150,000
SALES (est): 393.56MM
SALES (corp-wide): 393.56MM **Privately
Held**
Web: www.standardtextile.com
SIC: 2299 7389 5023 Linen fabrics; Textile
designers; Linens and towels

(G-3113)
STARKS PLASTICS LLC
11236 Sebring Dr (45240-2715)
PHONE.................................513 541-4591
Larry Clark, *Managing Member*
EMP: 10 **EST:** 1993
SQ FT: 1,400
SALES (est): 1.5MM **Privately Held**
Web: www.starksplastics.com
SIC: 3089 5046 Plastics processing; Store
fixtures

(G-3114)
STARR SERVICES INC
3625 Spring Grove Ave (45223-2458)
PHONE.................................513 241-7708
Robert Meade, *Pr*
EMP: 7 **EST:** 1975
SQ FT: 5,000
SALES (est): 459.82K **Privately Held**
Web: www.starrprinting.net
SIC: 2752 2759 Offset printing; Letterpress
printing

(G-3115)
STEEL IT LLC
250 Mccullough St (45226-2145)
PHONE.................................513 253-3111
Craig Freeman, *Managing Member**
EMP: 34 **EST:** 2015
SALES (est): 6.31MM **Privately Held**
SIC: 3441 Fabricated structural metal

(G-3116)
STEEL QUEST INC
8180 Corporate Park Dr Ste 250
(45242-3319)
PHONE.................................513 772-5030
Matthew S Kuhnell, *Pr*
EMP: 9 **EST:** 1993
SQ FT: 3,500
SALES (est): 6.26MM **Privately Held**
Web: www.steelquest.com
SIC: 3441 Fabricated structural metal

(G-3117)
STEGEMEYER MACHINE INC
212 Mccullough St (45226-2120)
PHONE.................................513 321-5651
Richard Stegemeyer, *Pr*
Deanna Stegemeyer, *Sec*
EMP: 7 **EST:** 1907
SQ FT: 4,500
SALES (est): 506.04K **Privately Held**
SIC: 3599 Machine shop, jobbing and repair

(G-3118)
STELLAR SYSTEMS INC
1944 Harrison Ave (45214-1176)
PHONE.................................513 921-8748
William L Spetz, *Pr*
EMP: 7 **EST:** 1980
SQ FT: 8,000
SALES (est): 129.89K **Privately Held**
Web: www.stellarsystems.com
SIC: 7371 3577 Computer software
development; Computer peripheral
equipment, nec

(G-3119)
STEVENSON COLOR INC
Also Called: SGS Cincinnati
535 Wilmer Ave (45226-1828)
PHONE.................................513 321-7500
Thomas Stevenson, *Pr*
EMP: 190 **EST:** 1926
SQ FT: 116,800
SALES (est): 11.43MM
SALES (corp-wide): 998.42MM **Privately
Held**
Web: www.sgsco.com
SIC: 2796 2752 Color separations, for
printing; Commercial printing, lithographic
HQ: Southern Graphic Systems, Llc
626 W Main St Ste 400
Louisville KY 40202
502 637-5443

(G-3120)
**STONE STATEMENTS
INCORPORATED**
7451 Fields Ertel Rd (45241-0003)
PHONE.................................513 489-7866
Douglas R Beyersdoerfer, *Pr*
▲ **EMP:** 8 **EST:** 2004
SALES (est): 1.87MM **Privately Held**
Web: www.stonestatements.com
SIC: 1411 1799 Granite dimension stone;
Counter top installation

(G-3121)
STOROPACK INC (DH)
Also Called: Foam Pac Materials Company
4758 Devitt Dr (45246-1106)

PHONE.................................513 874-0314
Hans Reichenecker, *Ch Bd*
Daniel Wachter, *
Gregg Battaglia, *
Joe Lagrasta, *
Lester Whisnant, *
▲ **EMP:** 50 **EST:** 1978
SQ FT: 35,000
SALES (est): 152.02MM
SALES (corp-wide): 655.85MM **Privately
Held**
Web: www.storopack.us
SIC: 5199 3086 2671 Packaging materials;
Packaging and shipping materials, foamed
plastics; Paper; coated and laminated
packaging
HQ: Storopack Hans Reichenecker Gmbh
Untere Rietstr. 30
Metzingen BW 72555
71231640

(G-3122)
SUGAR CREEK PACKING CO (PA)
Also Called: Sugar Creek
4320 Indeco Ct (45241-2925)
PHONE.................................513 551-5280
John Richardson, *Ch Bd*
Michael Richardson, *
Daniel Hammer, *
Jennifer Richardson-hutcheson, *CRO*
Tom Bollinger, *
◆ **EMP:** 299 **EST:** 1966
SQ FT: 80,000
SALES (est): 700MM
SALES (corp-wide): 700MM **Privately
Held**
Web: www.sugarcreek.com
SIC: 2013 Bacon, side and sliced: from
purchased meat

(G-3123)
SUN CHEMICAL CORPORATION
General Printing Ink Division
12049 Centron Pl (45246-1789)
PHONE.................................513 671-0407
Pat Myers, *Brnch Mgr*
EMP: 52
SQ FT: 11,000
Web: www.sunchemical.com
SIC: 2893 2899 Printing ink; Ink or writing
fluids
HQ: Sun Chemical Corporation
35 Waterview Blvd
Parsippany NJ 07054
973 404-6000

(G-3124)
SUN CHEMICAL CORPORATION
Also Called: Sun Chemical US Rycoline
5020 Spring Grove Ave (45232-1988)
P.O. Box 16097 (45216-0097)
PHONE.................................513 681-5950
EMP: 27
Web: www.sunchemical.com
SIC: 2893 Printing ink
HQ: Sun Chemical Corporation
35 Waterview Blvd
Parsippany NJ 07054
973 404-6000

(G-3125)
SUN CHEMICAL CORPORATION
Kohl & Madden Printing Ink Div
5020 Spring Grove Ave (45232-1988)
P.O. Box 32040 (45232)
PHONE.................................513 681-5950
Lou Schulte, *Mgr*
EMP: 39
Web: www.sunchemical.com
SIC: 2893 Printing ink
HQ: Sun Chemical Corporation

35 Waterview Blvd
Parsippany NJ 07054
973 404-6000

(G-3126)
SUN CHEMICAL CORPORATION
5000 Spring Grove Ave (45232-1926)
PHONE..............................513 830-8667
Milt Barnes, *Brnch Mgr*
EMP: 46
Web: www.sunchemical.com
SIC: 2893 2865 Printing ink; Dyes and
pigments
HQ: Sun Chemical Corporation
35 Waterview Blvd
Parsippany NJ 07054
973 404-6000

(G-3127)
SUN CHEMICAL CORPORATION
Also Called: Pigments Division
4526 Chickering Ave (45232-1935)
PHONE..............................513 681-5950
Brian Leen, *Brnch Mgr*
EMP: 210
SQ FT: 91,671
Web: www.sunchemical.com
SIC: 2816 2865 Inorganic pigments; Cyclic
crudes and intermediates
HQ: Sun Chemical Corporation
35 Waterview Blvd
Parsippany NJ 07054
973 404-6000

(G-3128)
SUPER SYSTEMS INC (PA)
7205 Edington Dr (45249-1064)
PHONE..............................513 772-0060
Stephen Thompson, *Pr*
Scott Johnstone, *
Jim Oakes, *
EMP: 32 **EST:** 1993
SQ FT: 5,000
SALES (est): 9.69MM **Privately Held**
Web: www.supersystems.com
SIC: 3829 5084 Measuring and controlling
devices, nec; Industrial machinery and
equipment

(G-3129)
**SUPERIOR PROPERTY
RESTORATION**
Also Called: Remodeling
2144 Schappelle Ln (45240-4602)
PHONE..............................513 509-6849
Roy Payne, *Pr*
EMP: 12 **EST:** 2000
SALES (est): 799.78K **Privately Held**
Web:
www.superiorpropertyrestoration.com
SIC: 1389 1521 Construction, repair, and
dismantling services; Single-family home
remodeling, additions, and repairs

(G-3130)
SUR-SEAL LLC (PA)
6156 Wesselman Rd (45248-1204)
PHONE..............................513 574-8500
Pete Futia, *CEO*
◆ **EMP:** 135 **EST:** 1965
SQ FT: 67,000
SALES (est): 82.97MM
SALES (corp-wide): 82.97MM **Privately
Held**
Web: www.sur-seal.com
SIC: 3053 3069 Gaskets, all materials;
Molded rubber products

(G-3131)
**SURFACE ENHANCEMENT TECH
LLC**
3929 Virginia Ave (45227-3411)
PHONE..............................513 561-1520
EMP: 17 **EST:** 2000
SQ FT: 28,000
SALES (est): 2.01MM **Privately Held**
Web: www.lambdatechs.com
SIC: 3398 Brazing (hardening) of metal

(G-3132)
**SURGICAL APPLIANCE INDS INC
(PA)**
3960 Rosslyn Dr (45209-1195)
PHONE..............................513 271-4594
L Thomas Applegate, *CEO*
▲ **EMP:** 200 **EST:** 1893
SQ FT: 225,000
SALES (est): 21.4MM
SALES (corp-wide): 21.4MM **Privately
Held**
Web: www.saibrands.com
SIC: 3842 Surgical appliances and supplies

(G-3133)
SWEETS AND MEATS LLC
Also Called: Sweets & Meats Bbq
2249 Beechmont Ave (45230-5318)
PHONE..............................513 888-4227
Kristen Bailey, *CEO*
EMP: 12 **EST:** 2014
SALES (est): 1.04MM **Privately Held**
Web: www.sweetsandmeatsbbq.com
SIC: 5812 2599 Restaurant, family:
independent; Food wagons, restaurant

(G-3134)
SYCAMORE TIRE & AUTO REPAIR
9372 Kenwood Rd (45242-6810)
PHONE..............................513 793-0726
Bruce Mc Goron, *Pr*
Martha Mc Goron, *Sec*
Jeff Gordon, *VP*
EMP: 8 **EST:** 1951
SQ FT: 8,000
SALES (est): 112.86K **Privately Held**
SIC: 5531 7538 7534 7539 Automotive tires;
General automotive repair shops; Tire
retreading and repair shops; Automotive
repair shops, nec

(G-3135)
T-SHIRT CO
413 Northland Blvd (45240-3210)
PHONE..............................513 821-7100
EMP: 9 **EST:** 2017
SALES (est): 118.5K **Privately Held**
Web: www.cincytshirts.com
SIC: 2759 Screen printing

(G-3136)
TAMARRON TECHNOLOGY INC
8044 Montgomery Rd (45236-2919)
PHONE..............................800 277-3207
John Gill, *VP*
EMP: 10 **EST:** 2007
SQ FT: 4,000
SALES (est): 342.3K **Privately Held**
Web: www.tamarrontechnology.biz
SIC: 3272 5032 Building materials, except
block or brick: concrete; Concrete building
products

(G-3137)
TAMBRANDS SALES CORP (HQ)
Also Called: Tampax
1 Procter And Gamble Plz (45202-3315)
PHONE..............................513 983-1100
Wolfgang C Berndt, *Pr*

Erik G Nelson, *VP Fin*
▲ **EMP:** 130 **EST:** 1936
SQ FT: 100,000
SALES (est): 20.91MM
SALES (corp-wide): 84.04B **Publicly Held**
Web: www.tampax.com
SIC: 2676 Tampons, sanitary: made from
purchased paper
PA: The Procter & Gamble Company
1 Procter & Gamble Plz
Cincinnati OH 45202
513 983-1100

(G-3138)
TARGET HOLDINGS INC
Also Called: Target World
2300 E Kemper Rd Unit 5 (45241-6505)
PHONE..............................513 474-4409
Joseph Blanco, *Pr*
Mark W Reis, *
EMP: 25 **EST:** 1999
SQ FT: 13,560
SALES (est): 609.18K **Privately Held**
Web: www.targetworld.info
SIC: 5941 7997 3499 Firearms; Gun and
hunting clubs; Safes and vaults, metal

(G-3139)
TAYLOR & MOORE CO
807 Wachendorf St (45215-4743)
PHONE..............................513 733-5530
George R Taylor Prestreas, *Prin*
George R Taylor, *Pr*
EMP: 10 **EST:** 1991
SQ FT: 11,898
SALES (est): 816.49K **Privately Held**
SIC: 3585 Air conditioning units, complete:
domestic or industrial

(G-3140)
TEAMCENTRAL INC
7875 Montgomery Rd (45236-4344)
PHONE..............................513 382-1497
Marc Johnson, *CEO*
EMP: 7 **EST:** 2021
SALES (est): 1.1MM **Privately Held**
SIC: 7372 Prepackaged software

(G-3141)
TECHNO ADHESIVES CO
12113 Mosteller Rd (45241-1591)
PHONE..............................513 771-1584
EMP: 6 **EST:** 1965
SALES (est): 994.21K **Privately Held**
Web: www.technoadhesives.com
SIC: 2891 Adhesives

(G-3142)
TEKWORX LLC
3094 Madison Rd (45209-1723)
PHONE..............................513 533-4777
Larry Tillack, *Research & Development*
EMP: 15 **EST:** 2002
SALES (est): 3.73MM **Privately Held**
Web: www.tekworx.us
SIC: 8748 8711 1731 3625 Systems analysis
and engineering consulting services;
Energy conservation engineering; Energy
management controls; Electric controls and
control accessories, industrial

(G-3143)
TESTLINK USA INC
11445 Century Cir W (45246-3303)
PHONE..............................513 272-1081
Greg Hughes, *CEO*
Nick Beer, *Ch*
Simon Yeomans, *Pr*
EMP: 22 **EST:** 2013
SALES (est): 2.44MM **Privately Held**
Web: www.testlink.co.uk

SIC: 3578 Automatic teller machines (ATM)

(G-3144)
TEVA PHARMACEUTICALS USA INC
5040 Duramed Rd (45213-2520)
PHONE..............................513 731-9900
EMP: 131
Web: www.tevausa.com
SIC: 2834 Pharmaceutical preparations
HQ: Teva Pharmaceuticals Usa, Inc.
400 Interpace Pkwy Bldg A
Parsippany NJ 07054
215 591-3000

(G-3145)
TEVA WOMENS HEALTH LLC (DH)
5040 Duramed Rd (45213-2520)
PHONE..............................513 731-9900
Bruce L Downey, *Prin*
Lawrence A Glassman, *
Timothy J Holt, *
EMP: 250 **EST:** 1982
SQ FT: 28,200
SALES (est): 24.84MM **Privately Held**
Web: www.duramed.com
SIC: 5122 2834 7389 Patent medicines;
Pharmaceutical preparations; Packaging
and labeling services
HQ: Teva Pharmaceuticals Usa, Inc.
400 Interpace Pkwy Bldg A
Parsippany NJ 07054
215 591-3000

(G-3146)
TH MAGNESIUM INC
9435 Waterstone Blvd Ste 290
(45249-8226)
PHONE..............................513 285-7568
Stephen Norris, *Pr*
Oliver Haun, *VP Sls*
EMP: 6 **EST:** 2015
SALES (est): 677.13K **Privately Held**
SIC: 3356 Magnesium

(G-3147)
THE F L EMMERT CO INC
Also Called: Emmert Grains
2007 Dunlap St (45214-2309)
PHONE..............................513 721-5808
EMP: 18 **EST:** 1881
SALES (est): 2.49MM **Privately Held**
Web: www.emmert.com
SIC: 2048 Prepared feeds, nec

(G-3148)
**THE KORDENBROCK TOOL AND DIE
CO**
10250 Wayne Ave (45215-2299)
PHONE..............................513 326-4390
EMP: 12 **EST:** 1953
SALES (est): 3.08MM **Privately Held**
Web: www.kordenbrocktoolanddie.com
SIC: 3544 3469 3599 Special dies and tools;
Stamping metal for the trade; Electrical
discharge machining (EDM)

(G-3149)
**THE PHOTO-TYPE ENGRAVING
COMPANY (PA)**
Also Called: Olberding Brand Family
2141 Gilbert Ave (45206-3021)
PHONE..............................513 281-0999
EMP: 60 **EST:** 1919
SALES (est): 25.66MM
SALES (corp-wide): 25.66MM **Privately
Held**
Web: www.phototype.com

▲ = Import ▼ = Export
◆ = Import/Export

SIC: 2754 7336 7335 2796 Commercial printing, gravure; Commercial art and graphic design; Commercial photography; Platemaking services

(G-3150)
THE SHEFFER CORPORATION (HQ)
6990 Cornell Rd (45242-3025)
PHONE..................513 489-9770
▲ EMP: 85 EST: 1956
SALES (est): 23.85MM
SALES (corp-wide): 24.82MM Privately Held
Web: www.sheffercorp.com
SIC: 3593 3492 3494 Fluid power cylinders, hydraulic or pneumatic; Control valves, fluid power: hydraulic and pneumatic; Valves and pipe fittings, nec
PA: The Ralph J Stolle Company
6990 Cornell Rd
Cincinnati OH 45242
513 489-7184

(G-3151)
THE SHEPHERD COLOR COMPANY (PA)
4539 Dues Dr (45246-1098)
P.O. Box 465627 (45246)
PHONE..................513 874-0714
◆ EMP: 175 EST: 1920
SALES (est): 95.5MM
SALES (corp-wide): 95.5MM Privately Held
Web: www.shepherdcolor.com
SIC: 2816 Metallic and mineral pigments, nec

(G-3152)
THERMO FISHER SCIENTIFIC INC
2110 E Galbraith Rd (45237-1625)
PHONE..................800 955-6288
EMP: 8
SALES (corp-wide): 42.86B Publicly Held
Web: www.patheon.com
SIC: 3826 Analytical instruments
PA: Thermo Fisher Scientific Inc.
168 3rd Ave
Waltham MA 02451
781 622-1000

(G-3153)
THINKWARE INCORPORATED
4055 Executive Park Dr Ste 240 (45241-2019)
PHONE..................513 598-3300
Kevin Eickmann, Pr
EMP: 28 EST: 1993
SALES (est): 1.45MM Privately Held
Web: www.thinkwareinc2.com
SIC: 7371 7374 7372 Computer software development; Data processing and preparation; Prepackaged software

(G-3154)
THIS IS L INC
1100 Sycamore St Ste 300 (45202-1376)
PHONE..................415 630-5172
Talia Frenkel, CEO
EMP: 7 EST: 2011
SALES (est): 404.65K
SALES (corp-wide): 84.04B Publicly Held
Web: www.thisisl.com
SIC: 2676 Tampons, sanitary: made from purchased paper
PA: The Procter & Gamble Company
1 Procter & Gamble Plz
Cincinnati OH 45202
513 983-1100

(G-3155)
THOMAS PRODUCTS CO INC (PA)
3625 Spring Grove Ave (45223-2458)
PHONE..................513 756-9009
Joseph Thomas, CEO
Paul Cecil Green, Pr
EMP: 25 EST: 1959
SQ FT: 25,000
SALES (est): 2.39MM
SALES (corp-wide): 2.39MM Privately Held
SIC: 2759 3842 2761 2672 Flexographic printing; Surgical appliances and supplies; Manifold business forms; Paper; coated and laminated, nec

(G-3156)
TI MARIE CANDLE COMPANY LLC
311 Elm St Ste 270 (45202-2781)
PHONE..................513 746-7798
Kimberly Jenkins, CEO
EMP: 12 EST: 2020
SALES (est): 469.31K Privately Held
Web: www.timariecandleco.com
SIC: 3999 7389 Candles; Business services, nec

(G-3157)
TKF CONVEYOR SYSTEMS LLC
5298 River Rd (45233-1643)
PHONE..................513 621-5260
EMP: 110 EST: 2011
SALES (est): 3.77MM Privately Held
Web: www.tkf.com
SIC: 3535 Conveyors and conveying equipment

(G-3158)
TL KRIEG OFFSET LLC
10600 Chester Rd (45215-1206)
PHONE..................513 542-1522
Thomas Schaefer, Pr
Terry L Krieg, *
EMP: 33 EST: 1975
SQ FT: 30,000
SALES (est): 4.95MM Privately Held
Web: www.kriegoffset.com
SIC: 2752 2789 Offset printing; Bookbinding and related work

(G-3159)
TOTES ISOTONER CORPORATION (PA)
Also Called: Isotoner
9655 International Blvd (45246-4861)
PHONE..................513 682-8200
Daniel Rajczak, Pr
Chris Lutz, CFO
John O Spiegel, Sec
▲ EMP: 96 EST: 1924
SQ FT: 450,000
SALES (est): 49.56MM
SALES (corp-wide): 49.56MM Privately Held
Web: www.totes.com
SIC: 2385 5699 Waterproof outerwear; Umbrellas

(G-3160)
TOTES ISOTONER HOLDINGS LLC (PA)
9655 International Blvd (45246-4861)
PHONE..................513 682-8200
Daniel S Rajczak, CEO
Daniel S Rajczak, Pr
Donna Deye, CFO
Joshua Beckenstein, VP
▲ EMP: 200 EST: 1994
SALES (est): 4.79MM
SALES (corp-wide): 4.79MM Privately Held

Web: www.totes.com
SIC: 2381 3151 2211 3021 Gloves, woven or knit: made from purchased materials; Leather gloves and mittens; Umbrella cloth, cotton; Rubber and plastics footwear

(G-3161)
TPF INC
313 S Wayne Ave (45215-4522)
P.O. Box 15171 (45215-0171)
PHONE..................513 761-9968
Charles Stiens, Pr
Robert Stiens, Ch
Kenneth Stiens, VP
Charlotte Stiens, Sec
EMP: 8 EST: 1969
SQ FT: 2,400
SALES (est): 2.4MM Privately Held
Web: www.tpftherm.com
SIC: 3823 7699 Thermometers, filled system: industrial process type; Industrial machinery and equipment repair

(G-3162)
TRANE TECHNOLOGIES COMPANY LLC
Also Called: Ingersoll-Rand
10300 Springfield Pike (45215-1118)
PHONE..................513 459-4580
Brandon Gibbons, Mgr
EMP: 22
SQ FT: 10,000
Web: www.trane.com
SIC: 3561 Pumps and pumping equipment
HQ: Trane Technologies Company Llc
800-E Beaty St
Davidson NC 28036
704 655-4000

(G-3163)
TRANE US INC
Also Called: Trane
10300 Springfield Pike (45215-1118)
PHONE..................513 771-8884
Al Fullerton, Mgr
EMP: 132
Web: www.trane.com
SIC: 3585 Refrigeration and heating equipment
HQ: Trane U.S. Inc.
800-E Beaty St
Davidson NC 28036
704 655-4000

(G-3164)
TRANS ASH INC
Also Called: Gibbco
360 S Wayne Ave (45215-4523)
PHONE..................859 341-1528
Brian Keplinger, Mgr
EMP: 10
SALES (corp-wide): 776.44MM Privately Held
Web: www.transash.com
SIC: 3295 Slag, crushed or ground
HQ: Trans Ash, Inc.
617 Shepherd Dr
Cincinnati OH 45215
513 733-4770

(G-3165)
TRANS-ACC INC (PA)
11167 Deerfield Rd (45242-2021)
PHONE..................513 793-6410
John Weinkam, Pr
Mary Weinkam, *
EMP: 24 EST: 1967
SQ FT: 27,000
SALES (est): 2.4MM
SALES (corp-wide): 2.4MM Privately Held
Web: www.trans-acc.com

SIC: 3471 3479 Finishing, metals or formed products; Coating of metals and formed products

(G-3166)
TRANSDUCERS DIRECT LLC
Also Called: Transducers Direct
12115 Ellington Ct (45249-1000)
PHONE..................513 247-0601
◆ EMP: 16 EST: 1999
SALES (est): 6.59MM Privately Held
Web: www.transducersdirect.com
SIC: 3543 5084 Industrial patterns; Industrial machine parts

(G-3167)
TREVED EXTERIORS
10235 Spartan Dr Ste T (45215-1243)
PHONE..................513 771-3888
Eddie Oblinger, Prin
EMP: 7 EST: 2006
SALES (est): 132.72K Privately Held
Web: www.trevedexteriors.com
SIC: 2851 Paint removers

(G-3168)
TRI-STATE WIRE ROPE SUPPLY INC (HQ)
5246 Wooster Pike (45226-2229)
PHONE..................513 871-8656
Mel Fireovid, Pr
Patricia Fireovid, Sec
▲ EMP: 9 EST: 1989
SQ FT: 6,500
SALES (est): 10.13MM
SALES (corp-wide): 19.56MM Privately Held
Web: www.fulcrumlifting.com
SIC: 5051 3496 Rope, wire (not insulated); Slings, lifting: made from purchased wire
PA: Fulcrum Lifting, Llc
5246 Wooster Pike
Cincinnati OH 45226
513 871-8656

(G-3169)
TRISTATE STEEL CONTRACTORS LLC
2508 Civic Center Dr Ste A (45231-1363)
PHONE..................513 648-9000
EMP: 8 EST: 2004
SALES (est): 1.29MM Privately Held
Web: www.tscsteel.com
SIC: 3441 Fabricated structural metal

(G-3170)
TROYKE MANUFACTURING COMPANY
11294 Orchard St (45241-1996)
PHONE..................513 769-4242
Bernard R Froehlich, Pr
Eric N Froehlich, VP
EMP: 12 EST: 1952
SQ FT: 40,000
SALES (est): 2.42MM Privately Held
Web: www.troyke.com
SIC: 3545 Machine tool accessories

(G-3171)
TRU-TEX INTERNATIONAL CORP
11050 Southland Rd (45240-3713)
P.O. Box 40107 (45240)
PHONE..................513 825-8844
Christopher Henn, Pr
Ruth Henn, CEO
Sandy Whitaker, Off Mgr
EMP: 9 EST: 1966
SQ FT: 8,000
SALES (est): 885.11K Privately Held
Web: www.trutexint.com

SIC: 3544 Dies and die holders for metal cutting, forming, die casting

(G-3172)
TRUCK CAB MANUFACTURERS INC (PA)
2420 Anderson Ferry Rd (45238-3345)
P.O. Box 58400 (45258-8400)
PHONE..............................513 922-1300
▲ EMP: 35 EST: 1948
SALES (est): 1.68MM
SALES (corp-wide): 1.68MM **Privately Held**
Web: www.truckcab.com
SIC: 3713 3441 Truck cabs, for motor vehicles; Fabricated structural metal

(G-3173)
TRUE DINERO RECORDS & TECH LLC
2611 Kemper Ln Uppr Level1 (45206-1220)
PHONE..............................513 428-4610
Aaron Savage, *Pr*
Tracy Savage, *Prin*
David Thompson, *Prin*
EMP: 8 EST: 2012
SALES (est): 108.45K **Privately Held**
Web: truedinerorecords.yolasite.com
SIC: 5735 7336 2759 2752 Records; Commercial art and graphic design; Laser printing; Offset printing

(G-3174)
TRULOU HOLDINGS INC
5311 Robert Ave Ste A (45248-7200)
PHONE..............................513 347-0100
Michael L Dinkelacker, *Pr*
James C Dinkelacker, *VP*
EMP: 22 EST: 1995
SQ FT: 12,000
SALES (est): 5.13MM **Privately Held**
Web: www.tristatetoolgrinding.com
SIC: 3599 Machine shop, jobbing and repair

(G-3175)
TSS ACQUISITION COMPANY
1201 Hill Smith Dr (45215-1228)
PHONE..............................513 772-7000
Bob Queen, *Brnch Mgr*
EMP: 6
SALES (corp-wide): 97.71MM **Privately Held**
Web: www.miqpartners.com
SIC: 3599 Machine shop, jobbing and repair
HQ: Tss Acquisition Company
8800 Global Way
West Chester OH

(G-3176)
TULKOFF FOOD PRODUCTS OHIO LLC
3015 E Kemper Rd (45241-1514)
PHONE..............................410 864-0523
Dawn Wade, *Managing Member*
EMP: 6 EST: 2020
SALES (est): 2.43MM **Privately Held**
Web: www.tulkoff.com
SIC: 2035 Dressings, salad: raw and cooked (except dry mixes)

(G-3177)
TVONE NCSA
Also Called: Tvone Ncsa - N Centl & S Amer
621 Wilmer Ave (45226-1859)
PHONE..............................859 282-7303
EMP: 7 EST: 2017
SALES (est): 1.31MM **Privately Held**
Web: www.tvone.com
SIC: 3651 Electronic kits for home assembly: radio, TV, phonograph

(G-3178)
UNCLE JAYS CAKES LLC
2516 Clifton Ave (45219-1004)
PHONE..............................513 882-3433
EMP: 6 EST: 2021
SALES (est): 221.85K **Privately Held**
SIC: 2051 Cakes, bakery: except frozen

(G-3179)
UNDERGROUND SPORTS SHOP INC
1233 Findlay St Ste Frnt (45214-2049)
PHONE..............................513 751-1662
Sean Mason, *Pr*
Jim Hebert, *Sec*
Andy Wolterman, *VP*
▲ EMP: 10 EST: 1992
SQ FT: 12,000
SALES (est): 1.22MM **Privately Held**
Web: www.undergroundsportsshop.com
SIC: 2759 7389 5199 Screen printing; Embroidery advertising; Advertising specialties

(G-3180)
UNITED - MAIER SIGNS INC
1030 Straight St (45214-1734)
PHONE..............................513 681-6600
Antony E Maier, *Pr*
Elvera Maier, *
EMP: 54 EST: 1964
SQ FT: 18,000
SALES (est): 4.68MM **Privately Held**
Web: www.united-maier.com
SIC: 3993 1799 Electric signs; Sign installation and maintenance

(G-3181)
UNITED DAIRY FARMERS INC (PA)
Also Called: U D F
3955 Montgomery Rd (45212-3798)
PHONE..............................513 396-8700
Brad Lindner, *Pr*
Marilyn Mitchell, *
EMP: 200 EST: 1940
SALES (est): 446.66MM
SALES (corp-wide): 446.66MM **Privately Held**
Web: www.udfinc.com
SIC: 5411 5143 2026 2024 Convenience stores, chain; Ice cream and ices; Milk processing (pasteurizing, homogenizing, bottling); Ice cream and ice milk

(G-3182)
UNITED ENVELOPE LLC
4890 Spring Grove Ave (45232-1933)
PHONE..............................513 542-4700
Stuart Grover, *Brnch Mgr*
EMP: 280
SALES (corp-wide): 45.76MM **Privately Held**
SIC: 2677 Envelopes
HQ: United Envelope, Llc
65 Railroad Ave
Ridgefield NJ 07657

(G-3183)
UNITED GROUP SERVICES INC (PA)
9740 Near Dr (45246-1013)
PHONE..............................800 633-9690
Mark Mosley, *Stockholder*
Daniel Freese, *
Kevin Sell, *
Don Mattingly, *
EMP: 200 EST: 1982
SQ FT: 45,500
SALES (est): 22.58MM
SALES (corp-wide): 22.58MM **Privately Held**
Web: www.united-gs.com

SIC: 3498 1711 Fabricated pipe and fittings; Process piping contractor

(G-3184)
UNITED PRECISION SERVICES INC
Also Called: Union America
11183 Southland Rd (45240-3206)
PHONE..............................513 851-6900
Paul Kramer, *Pr*
▲ EMP: 9 EST: 2001
SQ FT: 10,000
SALES (est): 963.96K **Privately Held**
Web: www.unitedprecisionservices.com
SIC: 3599 Machine shop, jobbing and repair

(G-3185)
UNITED STATES DRILL HEAD CO
5298 River Rd (45233-1688)
PHONE..............................513 941-0300
J H Nymberg Junior, *Pr*
Joseph E Bashor, *
EMP: 10 EST: 1915
SQ FT: 47,772
SALES (est): 2.4MM **Privately Held**
Web: www.usdrillhead.com
SIC: 3545 3363 3543 Cutting tools for machine tools; Aluminum die-castings; Industrial patterns

(G-3186)
UNIVERSAL PACKG SYSTEMS INC
Also Called: Paklab
470 Northland Blvd (45240-3211)
PHONE..............................513 674-9400
Jeff Topits, *Brnch Mgr*
EMP: 158
SALES (corp-wide): 379.38MM **Privately Held**
Web: www.paklab.com
SIC: 2844 7389 3565 2671 Cosmetic preparations; Packaging and labeling services; Bottling machinery: filling, capping, labeling; Plastic film, coated or laminated for packaging
PA: Universal Packaging Systems, Inc.
14570 Monte Vista Ave
Chino CA 91710
909 517-2442

(G-3187)
UPRISING FOOD INC
4200 Plainville Rd (45227-3247)
PHONE..............................513 313-1087
William Schumacher, *CEO*
Kristen Schumacher, *Chief Brand Officer*
Mark Frommeyer, *Banker*
Sara Frommeyer, *Banker*
EMP: 6 EST: 2019
SALES (est): 985.16K **Privately Held**
Web: www.uprisingfood.com
SIC: 2051 Bread, cake, and related products

(G-3188)
UPSHIFT WORK LLC
Also Called: Upshift
2300 Montana Ave Ste 301 (45211-3890)
PHONE..............................513 813-5695
Steve Anevski, *CEO*
EMP: 34 EST: 2016
SALES (est): 3.28MM **Privately Held**
Web: www.upshift.work
SIC: 7372 7363 Application computer software; Temporary help service

(G-3189)
US INDUSTRIAL LUBRICANTS INC
Also Called: Oil Kraft Div
3330 Beekman St (45223-2424)
PHONE..............................513 541-2225
Donald L Mattcheck, *Pr*
David E Ziegler, *VP*

Adam Freeman, *VP*
Jenny Anderson, *Sec*
EMP: 20 EST: 1976
SQ FT: 45,000
SALES (est): 559.86K **Privately Held**
Web: www.duboischemicals.com
SIC: 2842 2992 2841 Specialty cleaning; Oils and greases, blending and compounding; Soap and other detergents

(G-3190)
VALCO CINCINNATI INC (PA)
Also Called: Valco Melton
411 Circle Freeway Dr (45246-1284)
P.O. Box 465619 (45246-5619)
PHONE..............................513 874-6550
Richard Santefort, *Pr*
Gregory T Amend, *
▲ EMP: 180 EST: 1952
SQ FT: 43,000
SALES (est): 23.19MM
SALES (corp-wide): 23.19MM **Privately Held**
Web: www.valco-cp.com
SIC: 3586 2891 3561 Measuring and dispensing pumps; Adhesives and sealants ; Industrial pumps and parts

(G-3191)
VALLEY ASPHALT CORPORATION (HQ)
Also Called: Asphalt
11641 Mosteller Rd (45241-1520)
PHONE..............................513 771-0820
EMP: 20 EST: 1934
SALES (est): 26.83MM
SALES (corp-wide): 225.16MM **Privately Held**
Web: www.jrjnet.com
SIC: 1611 2951 General contractor, highway and street construction; Asphalt and asphaltic paving mixtures (not from refineries)
PA: John R. Jurgensen Co.
11641 Mosteller Rd
Cincinnati OH 45241
513 771-0820

(G-3192)
VALLEY METAL WORKS INC
698 W Columbia Ave (45215-3184)
PHONE..............................513 554-1022
James Steinbeck, *Pr*
Kevin Graham, *
James Stiebeck, *
Fred Horst, *
EMP: 25 EST: 1934
SQ FT: 19,000
SALES (est): 5.57MM **Privately Held**
Web: www.valleymetalworks.com
SIC: 3444 Sheet metal specialties, not stamped

(G-3193)
VAN-GRINER LLC
1009 Delta Ave (45208-3103)
PHONE..............................419 733-7951
EMP: 6 EST: 2010
SALES (est): 106.96K **Privately Held**
Web: www.van-griner.com
SIC: 2741 Miscellaneous publishing

(G-3194)
VANTAGE ORTHOPEDICS INC
41 Techview Dr (45215-1980)
PHONE..............................513 563-1690
Craig Robinson, *Pr*
▲ EMP: 19 EST: 1991
SQ FT: 6,800
SALES (est): 1.43MM **Privately Held**
Web: www.vantageortho.com

▲ = Import ▼ = Export
◆ = Import/Export

SIC: 3842 Braces, orthopedic

(G-3195)
VARLAND METAL SERVICE INC
Also Called: Varland Plating Company
3231 Fredonia Ave (45229-3394)
PHONE.................................513 861-0555
EMP: 48 EST: 1946
SALES (est): 6.13MM Privately Held
Web: www.varland.com
SIC: 3471 Electroplating of metals or formed
products

(G-3196)
VENCO MANUFACTURING INC
Also Called: Collins & Venco Venturo
12110 Best Pl (45241-1569)
PHONE.................................513 772-8448
Larry R Collins, Pr
Ronald A Collins, VP
Mike Strittholt, Treas
Barbara Duke, Sec
▲ EMP: 13 EST: 1979
SQ FT: 35,000
SALES (est): 5.47MM
SALES (corp-wide): 23.07MM Privately
Held
Web: www.venturo.com
SIC: 3714 Motor vehicle parts and
accessories
PA: Venco Venturo Industries Llc
12110 Best Pl
Cincinnati OH 45241
513 772-8448

(G-3197)
**VENCO VENTURO INDUSTRIES LLC
(PA)**
Also Called: Venco/Venturo Div
12110 Best Pl (45241-1569)
PHONE.................................513 772-8448
Brett Collins, Pr
Mike Strittholt, *
Dave Foster, *
▲ EMP: 41 EST: 1952
SQ FT: 100,000
SALES (est): 23.07MM
SALES (corp-wide): 23.07MM Privately
Held
Web: www.venturo.com
SIC: 3713 5012 3714 5084 Truck bodies
(motor vehicles); Truck bodies; Motor
vehicle parts and accessories; Cranes,
industrial

(G-3198)
VENTILATION SYSTEMS JSC
Also Called: Vents - US
400 Murray Rd (45217-1013)
PHONE.................................513 348-3853
Zoltan Bodor, Mgr
EMP: 19
Web: www.vents-us.com
SIC: 3634 Fans, exhaust and ventilating,
electric: household
HQ: Ventilation Systems Llc
1 Vul.Kotsiubynskoho Mykhaila
Kyiv 01030

(G-3199)
VENTURO MANUFACTURING INC
12110 Best Pl (45241-1569)
PHONE.................................513 772-8448
Ronald A Collins, VP
Larry Collins, Pr
Mike Strittholt, Treas
Barbara Duke, Sec
EMP: 12 EST: 1952
SQ FT: 5,000
SALES (est): 5.75MM
SALES (corp-wide): 23.07MM Privately
Held

Web: www.venturo.com
SIC: 3537 5084 Cranes, industrial truck;
Industrial machinery and equipment
PA: Venco Venturo Industries Llc
12110 Best Pl
Cincinnati OH 45241
513 772-8448

(G-3200)
VENUE LIFESTYLE & EVENT GUIDE
11959 Tramway Dr (45241-1666)
PHONE.................................513 405-6822
Kim Wanamaker, Pr
Steve Wanamaker, VP
EMP: 7 EST: 2010
SALES (est): 132.96K Privately Held
SIC: 2721 Magazines: publishing and printing

(G-3201)
VEOLIA WTS SYSTEMS USA INC
Also Called: General Ionics
11799 Enterprise Dr (45241-1510)
PHONE.................................513 794-1010
Dan Goins, Mgr
EMP: 8
Web: www.suezwatertechnologies.com
SIC: 3589 Water treatment equipment,
industrial
HQ: Veolia Wts Systems Usa, Inc.
3600 Horizon Blvd Ste 100
Trevose PA 19053
866 439-2837

(G-3202)
VERTIFLO PUMP COMPANY
7807 Redsky Dr (45249-1636)
PHONE.................................513 530-0888
Mark Werner, Pr
EMP: 17 EST: 1979
SQ FT: 18,000
SALES (est): 4.86MM Privately Held
Web: www.vertiflopump.com
SIC: 3594 3561 Fluid power pumps; Pumps
and pumping equipment

(G-3203)
VESI INCORPORATED
Also Called: Vesi
7289 Kirkridge Dr (45233-4232)
PHONE.................................513 563-6002
Greg Visconti, CEO
Dale Davidson, *
Susan Litster, *
▲ EMP: 45 EST: 1992
SALES (est): 1.45MM Privately Held
Web: www.clublevelbrands.com
SIC: 2329 2339 Men's and boys' sportswear
and athletic clothing; Sportswear, women's

(G-3204)
VICAS MANUFACTURING CO INC
8407 Monroe Ave (45236-1909)
P.O. Box 36310 (45236-0310)
PHONE.................................513 791-7741
Virginia Willoughby, Pr
Pon May, *
EMP: 47 EST: 1972
SQ FT: 25,600
SALES (est): 4.78MM Privately Held
Web: www.vi-cas.com
SIC: 3089 3599 Injection molding of plastics;
Machine shop, jobbing and repair

(G-3205)
VILLAGE CABINET SHOP INC
Also Called: Reynolds Cabinetry & Millwork
1820 Loisview Ln (45255-2617)
PHONE.................................704 966-0801
Derrick A Reynolds, Brnch Mgr
EMP: 6

SIC: 2541 Cabinets, except refrigerated:
show, display, etc.: wood
PA: The Village Cabinet Shop Inc
17746 93rd Pl N
Osseo MN 55311

(G-3206)
VINOKLET WINERY INC
11069 Colerain Rd (45252-1425)
PHONE.................................513 385-9309
Kreso Mikulic, CEO
EMP: 21 EST: 2004
SALES (est): 609.93K Privately Held
Web: www.vinokletwines.com
SIC: 2084 Wines

(G-3207)
VOLK CORPORATION
Also Called: Hathaway
635 Main St Ste 1 (45202-2524)
PHONE.................................513 621-1052
Larry Schultz, Brnch Mgr
EMP: 8
SALES (corp-wide): 9.65MM Privately
Held
Web: www.volkcorp.com
SIC: 3953 Marking devices
PA: Volk Corporation
47808 Galleon Dr
Plymouth MI 48170
248 477-6700

(G-3208)
VULCAN INTERNATIONAL CORP
30 Garfield Pl Ste 1000 (45202-4308)
PHONE.................................513 621-2850
Benjamin Gattler, Brnch Mgr
EMP: 9
SALES (corp-wide): 2.49MM Privately
Held
Web: www.oddballstocks.com
SIC: 3069 Medical and laboratory rubber
sundries and related products
PA: Vulcan International Corporation
300 Delaware Ave Ste 1704
Wilmington DE 19801
302 428-3181

(G-3209)
VURVEY LABS INC
1008 Race St Ste 4 (45202-1091)
PHONE.................................513 379-3595
EMP: 13 EST: 2022
SALES (est): 1.14MM Privately Held
Web: www.vurvey.com
SIC: 7372 Application computer software

(G-3210)
VYA INC
Also Called: Docustar
1325 Glendale Milford Rd (45215-1210)
P.O. Box 634015 (45263-4015)
PHONE.................................513 772-5400
Jay Brokamp, Pr
Terry Brokamp, *
EMP: 41 EST: 1991
SQ FT: 56,000
SALES (est): 8.67MM Privately Held
Web: www.vyasystems.com
SIC: 2759 2675 2752 Commercial printing,
nec; Die-cut paper and board; Commercial
printing, lithographic

(G-3211)
WALL COLMONOY CORPORATION
Aerobraze Division
940 Redna Ter (45215-1113)
PHONE.................................513 842-4200
Ken Coldfelter, Brnch Mgr
EMP: 69
SALES (corp-wide): 98.07MM Privately
Held

Web: www.wallcolmonoy.com
SIC: 3812 Search and navigation equipment
HQ: Wall Colmonoy Corporation
101 W Girard Ave
Madison Heights MI 48071
248 585-6400

(G-3212)
WAYGATE TECHNOLOGIES USA LP
1 Neumann Way (45215-1900)
PHONE.................................866 243-2638
David Calhoun, Brnch Mgr
EMP: 89
SALES (corp-wide): 27.83B Publicly Held
Web:
www.waygateinspectionacademy.com
SIC: 3829 3844 Ultrasonic testing equipment
; Radiographic X-ray apparatus and tubes
HQ: Waygate Technologies Usa, Lp
721 Visions Dr
Skaneateles NY 13152
315 554-2000

(G-3213)
WCM HOLDINGS INC
11500 Canal Rd (45241-1862)
PHONE.................................513 705-2100
David Herche, CEO
Tim Fogarty, *
Melvyn Fisher, *
▲ EMP: 120 EST: 1978
SALES (est): 1.45MM Privately Held
SIC: 5099 2381 3842 Safety equipment and
supplies; Gloves, work: woven or knit,
made from purchased materials; Clothing,
fire resistant and protective

(G-3214)
WELAGE CORPORATION
7712 Reinhold Dr (45237-2810)
P.O. Box 37665 (45222-0665)
PHONE.................................513 681-2300
David Welage, Pr
Brad Ruter, VP
EMP: 15 EST: 1937
SQ FT: 15,000
SALES (est): 2.69MM Privately Held
Web: www.welagecorp.com
SIC: 3441 3469 3544 Fabricated structural
metal; Metal stampings, nec; Special dies,
tools, jigs, and fixtures

(G-3215)
WELCH FOODS INC A COOPERATIVE
Also Called: Welch Foods
720 E Pete Rose Way (45202-3579)
PHONE.................................513 632-5610
EMP: 60
SALES (corp-wide): 766.83MM Privately
Held
Web: www.welchs.com
SIC: 2033 Canned fruits and specialties
HQ: Welch Foods Inc., A Cooperative
575 Virginia
Concord MA 01742
978 371-1000

(G-3216)
WELCH HOLDINGS INC
8953 E Miami River Rd (45247-2232)
PHONE.................................513 353-3220
James R Welch, Pr
Ronnie L Welch, *
EMP: 24 EST: 1955
SQ FT: 3,400
SALES (est): 1.33MM Privately Held
Web: www.welchsand.com
SIC: 1442 Common sand mining

GEOGRAPHIC

(G-3217)
WELCH SAND & GRAVEL INC
8953 E Miami River Rd (45247-2232)
P.O. Box 531700 (45253-1700)
PHONE....................................513 353-3220
Chris Stalker, Prin
EMP: 11 **EST:** 2008
SALES (est): 2.5MM **Privately Held**
Web: www.welchsand.com
SIC: 1442 Construction sand and gravel

(G-3218)
WELDCO INC
2121 Spring Grove Ave (45214-1721)
PHONE....................................513 744-9353
EMP: 33
SIC: 5084 3264 Welding machinery and
equipment; Porcelain electrical supplies

(G-3219)
**WELLMAN CONTAINER
CORPORATION**
412 S Cooper Ave (45215-4555)
PHONE....................................513 860-3040
Barbara J Wellman, Pr
Ronald J Wellman, *
EMP: 25 **EST:** 1981
SQ FT: 60,000
SALES (est): 1.05MM **Privately Held**
SIC: 2653 2631 3993 2448 Boxes,
corrugated: made from purchased materials
; Container, packaging, and boxboard;
Displays and cutouts, window and lobby;
Pallets, wood

(G-3220)
WEST CHESTER HOLDINGS LLC
Also Called: West Chester Protective Gear
11500 Canal Rd (45241-1862)
PHONE....................................513 705-2100
Tim Fogarty, CEO
Jim Wilson, *
▲ **EMP:** 134 **EST:** 1995
SQ FT: 200,000
SALES (est): 45.5MM
SALES (corp-wide): 2.61B **Privately Held**
Web: www.westchesterclothing.com
SIC: 3842 5136 5099 5137 Clothing, fire
resistant and protective; Men's and boy's
clothing; Safety equipment and supplies;
Women's and children's clothing
HQ: Protective Industrial Products, Inc.
25 British American Blvd
Latham NY 12110
518 861-0133

(G-3221)
**WESTERN & SOUTHERN LF INSUR
CO (DH)**
Also Called: WESTERN & SOUTHERN
400 Broadway St Stop G (45202-3341)
P.O. Box 1119 (45201-1119)
PHONE....................................513 629-1800
John F Barrett, Pr
James Vance, *
Danald J Wuebbling, Sec
EMP: 982 **EST:** 1888
SQ FT: 600,000
SALES (est): 60.14MM **Privately Held**
Web: www.westernsouthern.com
SIC: 6211 6311 2511 Investment firm,
general brokerage; Life insurance; Play
pens, children's: wood
HQ: Western & Southern Financial Group,
Inc.
400 Broadway
Cincinnati OH 45202
877 367-9734

(G-3222)
WHEATLEY ELECTRIC SERVICE CO
2046 Ross Ave (45212-2040)
PHONE....................................513 531-4951
Dorothy Elsbrock, Pr
Jim Elsbrock, VP
EMP: 7 **EST:** 1934
SQ FT: 5,000
SALES (est): 171.5K **Privately Held**
Web: www.electricmotortech.com
SIC: 7694 5999 5063 Electric motor repair;
Motors, electric; Motors, electric

(G-3223)
WHITE CASTLE SYSTEM INC
White Castle
3126 Exon Ave (45241-2548)
PHONE....................................513 563-2290
Jarrett Cook, Mgr
EMP: 68
SALES (corp-wide): 187.89MM **Privately
Held**
Web: www.whitecastle.com
SIC: 5812 2099 Fast-food restaurant, chain;
Sandwiches, assembled and packaged: for
wholesale market
PA: White Castle System, Inc.
555 Edgar Waldo Way
Columbus OH 43215
614 228-5781

(G-3224)
WILLIAM POWELL COMPANY (PA)
Also Called: Powell Valve
3261 Spring Grove Ave (45225-1329)
PHONE....................................513 852-2000
David R Cowart, Pr
Jeff Thompson, *
Brandy Cowart, *
◆ **EMP:** 70 **EST:** 1846
SALES (est): 22.28MM
SALES (corp-wide): 22.28MM **Privately
Held**
Web: www.powellvalves.com
SIC: 3494 3491 Valves and pipe fittings, nec;
Pressure valves and regulators, industrial

(G-3225)
WILLIS MUSIC COMPANY
11700 Princeton Pike Unit E209
(45246-2535)
PHONE....................................513 671-3288
Robert Mooney, Mgr
EMP: 10
SALES (corp-wide): 4.6MM **Privately Held**
Web: www.willismusic.com
SIC: 2741 5736 Music, sheet: publishing and
printing; Musical instrument stores
PA: Willis Music Company
7567 Mall Rd
Florence KY 41042
859 283-2050

(G-3226)
WIN PLASTIC EXTRUSIONS LLC
Also Called: TMI
11502 Century Blvd (45246-3305)
PHONE....................................330 929-1999
Patrick Mcmullen, CFO
EMP: 7 **EST:** 2007
SALES (est): 486.08K **Privately Held**
SIC: 2821 Polyvinyl chloride resins, PVC

(G-3227)
WINE CELLAR INNOVATIONS LLC
Also Called: Honeywell Authorized Dealer
4575 Eastern Ave (45226-1805)
P.O. Box 8879 (45208)
PHONE....................................513 321-3733
▼ **EMP:** 157 **EST:** 1978
SQ FT: 350,000

SALES (est): 9.72MM **Privately Held**
Web: www.winecellarinnovations.com
SIC: 2511 2541 Wood household furniture;
Wood partitions and fixtures

(G-3228)
WJF ENTERPRISES LLC
Also Called: Specialty Wood Products
1347 Custer Ave (45208-2556)
PHONE....................................513 871-7320
EMP: 6 **EST:** 1999
SQ FT: 32,000
SALES (est): 283.58K **Privately Held**
SIC: 2448 Wood pallets and skids

(G-3229)
WM LANG & SONS COMPANY
3280 Beekman St (45223-2423)
PHONE....................................513 541-3304
Robert Schutte, Pr
Howard Schutte Junior, Asst VP
Joseph Schutte, Corporate Secretary
Jeffrey Tuttle, VP
EMP: 18 **EST:** 1892
SQ FT: 16,800
SALES (est): 2.73MM **Privately Held**
Web: www.langironworks.com
SIC: 3441 Building components, structural
steel

(G-3230)
WOOD GRAPHICS INC (PA)
Also Called: United Engraving
8075 Reading Rd Ste 301 (45237-1416)
PHONE....................................513 771-6300
Mark Richler, Pr
Gaylord H Fill, *
◆ **EMP:** 30 **EST:** 1972
SQ FT: 21,500
SALES (est): 434.61K
SALES (corp-wide): 434.61K **Privately
Held**
SIC: 3555 7699 2796 Printing trades
machinery; Industrial machinery and
equipment repair; Platemaking services

(G-3231)
WORKS IN PROGRESS INC (PA)
3825 Edwards Rd Ste 800 (45209-1289)
PHONE....................................802 658-3797
Larry Cain, Pr
Cara Cain V, Pr
EMP: 14 **EST:** 1993
SALES (est): 252.59K **Privately Held**
Web: projects.constructconnect.com
SIC: 2741 Miscellaneous publishing

(G-3232)
WRIGHT BROTHERS INC (PA)
7825 Cooper Rd (45242-7605)
PHONE....................................513 731-2222
Charles Wright, Pr
Denetria Wright, Sec
EMP: 15 **EST:** 1977
SALES (est): 7.52MM
SALES (corp-wide): 7.52MM **Privately
Held**
Web: www.wrightbros.com
SIC: 2813 3446 5084 Industrial gases;
Architectural metalwork; Welding
machinery and equipment

(G-3233)
**WRIGHT BROTHERS GLOBAL GAS
LLC**
7825 Cooper Rd (45242-7605)
PHONE....................................513 731-2222
Ashley Werthaiser, Pr
Neal O Willmann, Prin
Cyndi Blalock, COO
EMP: 12 **EST:** 2004

SALES (est): 4.13MM **Privately Held**
Web: www.globalgassupply.com
SIC: 2813 Industrial gases

(G-3234)
WT ACQUISITION COMPANY LTD
Also Called: Waltek & Company
2130 Waycross Rd (45240-2719)
PHONE....................................513 577-7980
EMP: 30
SIC: 3449 3211 Curtain wall, metal;
Construction glass

(G-3235)
WULCO INC (PA)
Also Called: Jet Machine & Manufacturing
6899 Steger Dr Ste A (45237-3059)
PHONE....................................513 679-2600
Richard G Wulfeck, Pr
Gary Wulfeck, *
Ken Wulfeck, *
▲ **EMP:** 100 **EST:** 1970
SQ FT: 100,000
SALES (est): 153.68MM **Privately Held**
Web: www.wulco.com
SIC: 5085 3599 Industrial supplies; Machine
shop, jobbing and repair

(G-3236)
WULCO INC
Also Called: Jet Machine
6900 Steger Dr (45237-3096)
PHONE....................................513 679-2600
Adam Wulfeck, VP
EMP: 99
SQ FT: 80,000
Web: www.jet-machine.com
SIC: 3599 Machine shop, jobbing and repair
PA: Wulco, Inc.
6899 Steger Dr Ste A
Cincinnati OH 45237

(G-3237)
XOMOX CORPORATION
Also Called: Crane Chempharma & Energy
4444 Cooper Rd (45242-5686)
PHONE....................................936 271-6500
EMP: 20
SALES (corp-wide): 2.13B **Publicly Held**
Web: www.cranecpe.com
SIC: 3491 3593 3494 Boiler gauge cocks;
Fluid power actuators, hydraulic or
pneumatic; Plumbing and heating valves
HQ: Xomox Corporation
4526 Res Frest Dr Ste 400
The Woodlands TX 77381
936 271-6500

(G-3238)
XOMOX PFT CORP
4444 Cooper Rd (45242-5686)
PHONE....................................936 271-6500
William Hayes, Pr
William Metz, *
Dale Friemoth, *
EMP: 418 **EST:** 2021
SALES (est): 21.19MM
SALES (corp-wide): 2.13B **Publicly Held**
SIC: 3491 3593 3494 Process control
regulator valves; Fluid power cylinders and
actuators; Valves and pipe fittings, nec
PA: Crane Company
100 1st Stmford Pl Ste 40
Stamford CT 06902
203 363-7300

(G-3239)
XS SMITH INC (PA)
5513 Vine St Ste 1 (45217-1022)
PHONE....................................252 940-5060
Richard W Smith Junior, Pr

▲ = Import ▼ = Export
◆ = Import/Export

Scott Thompson, *Ex VP*
Cheryl Difiore, *Treas*
EMP: 20 **EST:** 1946
SQ FT: 40,000
SALES (est): 201.65K
SALES (corp-wide): 201.65K **Privately Held**
Web: www.structures-unlimited.com
SIC: 5191 3448 3231 Greenhouse equipment and supplies; Greenhouses, prefabricated metal; Products of purchased glass

(G-3240)
XTEK INC (PA)
11451 Reading Rd (45241-2283)
PHONE...............................513 733-7800
Roger Miller, *Pr*
Frank Petrek, *
James J Raible, *
Albert Schreiver Iv, *VP Fin*
◆ **EMP:** 336 **EST:** 1909
SQ FT: 363,440
SALES (est): 83.6MM
SALES (corp-wide): 83.6MM **Privately Held**
Web: www.xtek.com
SIC: 3568 3547 3398 3312 Power transmission equipment, nec; Rolling mill machinery; Metal heat treating; Wheels, locomotive and car: iron and steel

(G-3241)
ZEDA INC
11560 Goldcoast Dr (45249-1640)
PHONE...............................513 966-4633
Greg Morris, *CEO*
Greg Morris, *Prin*
Steve Rengers, *Prin*
EMP: 10 **EST:** 2019
SALES (est): 4.44MM **Privately Held**
Web: www.z8a.com
SIC: 3499 Fabricated metal products, nec

(G-3242)
ZIPSCENE LLC
Also Called: Zipscene
615 Main St Fl 5 (45202-2538)
PHONE...............................513 201-5174
Rick Lamy, *
EMP: 62 **EST:** 2010
SQ FT: 2,000
SALES (est): 4.73MM **Privately Held**
Web: www.zipscene.com
SIC: 7372 Business oriented computer software

(G-3243)
ZTS INC
5628 Wooster Pike (45227-4121)
PHONE...............................513 271-2557
Dave Zimmerman, *Pr*
Marge Zimmerman, *Sec*
Phil Zimmerman, *Prin*
▲ **EMP:** 10 **EST:** 1970
SQ FT: 8,000
SALES (est): 1.02MM **Privately Held**
Web: www.ztsinc.com
SIC: 3825 Battery testers, electrical

(G-3244)
ZWANENBERG FOOD GROUP (USA) INC (DH)
3640 Muddy Creek Rd (45238-2044)
PHONE...............................513 682-6000
◆ **EMP:** 15 **EST:** 1990
SALES (est): 127.85MM
SALES (corp-wide): 647.54MM **Privately Held**
Web: www.zwanfoods.com

SIC: 5141 2013 Groceries, general line; Canned meats (except baby food), from purchased meat
HQ: Zwanenberg Food Group B.V.
Twentepoort Oost 5
Almelo OV
546547000

(G-3245)
ZYGO INC
Also Called: Cincy Deli & Carryout
2832 Jefferson Ave (45219-1920)
PHONE...............................513 281-0888
Jim Powers, *CEO*
EMP: 8 **EST:** 1970
SQ FT: 1,500
SALES (est): 250.01K **Privately Held**
Web: www.zygo.com
SIC: 5411 2097 Delicatessen stores; Ice cubes

Circleville
Pickaway County

(G-3246)
ALL - DO WELD & FAB LLC
28155 River Dr (43113-9726)
PHONE...............................740 477-2133
Sheng Stack, *Opers Mgr*
EMP: 6 **EST:** 2005
SALES (est): 411.93K **Privately Held**
SIC: 7692 Welding repair

(G-3247)
AMERICAN WOOD FIBERS INC
Also Called: AMERICAN WOOD FIBERS, INC.
2500 Owens Rd (43113-8963)
PHONE...............................740 420-3233
Mark Roth, *Mgr*
EMP: 32
SALES (corp-wide): 44.7MM **Privately Held**
Web: www.awf.com
SIC: 2499 Mulch or sawdust products, wood
PA: American Wood Fibers, Inc
9740 Ptxent Wods Dr Ste 5
Columbia MD 21046
800 624-9663

(G-3248)
BEAZER EAST INC
200 E Corwin St (43113-1906)
P.O. Box 268 (43113-0268)
PHONE...............................740 474-3169
Leonard Mcferren, *Mgr*
EMP: 16
SALES (corp-wide): 22.37B **Privately Held**
SIC: 3273 3271 Ready-mixed concrete; Blocks, concrete or cinder: standard
HQ: Beazer East, Inc.
600 River Ave Ste 200
Pittsburgh PA 15212
412 428-9407

(G-3249)
CARBON ENTERPRISES INC (PA)
Also Called: C E I
28205 Scippo Creek Rd (43113-8835)
PHONE...............................740 420-6472
Ryan Carter, *Pr*
Richard Ciminello, *Pr*
Ryan Carter, *VP*
Louis Ciminello, *Sec*
Brad Verne, *Prin*
◆ **EMP:** 7 **EST:** 1998
SQ FT: 20,500
SALES (est): 7.93MM
SALES (corp-wide): 7.93MM **Privately Held**

Web: www.ceifiltration.com
SIC: 5085 4731 1231 Filters, industrial; Freight forwarding; Anthracite preparation and screening

(G-3250)
CENTRAL COCA-COLA BTLG CO INC
Also Called: Coca-Cola
387 Walnut St (43113-2225)
PHONE...............................740 474-2180
EMP: 28
SALES (corp-wide): 45.75B **Publicly Held**
Web: www.coca-cola.com
SIC: 2086 8741 Bottled and canned soft drinks; Management services
HQ: Central Coca-Cola Bottling Company, Inc.
555 Taxter Rd Ste 550
Elmsford NY 10523
914 789-1100

(G-3251)
CIRCLEVILLE OIL CO
Also Called: Subway
224 Lancaster Pike (43113-1507)
P.O. Box 123 (43113-0123)
PHONE...............................740 477-3341
Lori Whited, *Mgr*
EMP: 8
SALES (corp-wide): 3.35MM **Privately Held**
Web: www.subway.com
SIC: 1389 7539 5812 Construction, repair, and dismantling services; Brake services; Sandwiches and submarines shop
PA: Circleville Oil Co (Inc)
315 Town St
Circleville OH 43113
740 474-7544

(G-3252)
CLINE MACHINE AND AUTOMTN INC
Also Called: Suburban Metal Products
1050 Tarlton Rd (43113-9132)
PHONE...............................740 474-4237
Joey R Cline, *Pr*
EMP: 22 **EST:** 2010
SALES (est): 3.13MM **Privately Held**
SIC: 3549 Metalworking machinery, nec

(G-3253)
DAN PATRICK ENTERPRISES INC
8564 Zane Trail Rd (43113-9745)
PHONE...............................740 477-1006
Daniel E Patrick, *Pr*
Christine Patrick, *Sec*
EMP: 6 **EST:** 1985
SQ FT: 3,500
SALES (est): 508.18K **Privately Held**
Web: www.samson4x4.com
SIC: 3713 5013 7538 Truck bodies and parts ; Truck parts and accessories; General truck repair

(G-3254)
DUPONT SPECIALTY PDTS USA LLC
Also Called: Dupont Vespel Parts and Shapes
800 Dupont Rd (43113)
PHONE...............................740 474-0635
Wayne Macdonald, *Mgr*
EMP: 75
SALES (corp-wide): 12.39B **Publicly Held**
Web: www.dupont.com
SIC: 2821 Plastics materials and resins
HQ: Dupont Specialty Products Usa, Llc
974 Centre Rd
Wilmington DE 19805
302 295-5783

(G-3255)
DUPONT SPECIALTY PDTS USA LLC
Also Called: Dupont
Rt 23 S Dupont Rd (43113)
P.O. Box 89 (43113-0089)
PHONE...............................740 474-0220
Tony Eichstadt, *Mgr*
EMP: 50
SALES (corp-wide): 12.39B **Publicly Held**
Web: www.dupont.com
SIC: 2821 3861 3081 Polyesters; Photographic equipment and supplies; Unsupported plastics film and sheet
HQ: Dupont Specialty Products Usa, Llc
974 Centre Rd
Wilmington DE 19805
302 295-5783

(G-3256)
EASTERN TRUCK & TRAILER LLC
177 Neville St (43113-9129)
PHONE...............................866 240-4422
EMP: 21 **EST:** 2000
SALES (est): 2.27MM **Privately Held**
Web: www.easterntruck.com
SIC: 3715 Truck trailers

(G-3257)
ERNIE GREEN INDUSTRIES INC
Also Called: Earnie Green Industries
30627 Orr Rd (43113-9731)
PHONE...............................740 420-5252
Mark Sells, *Brnch Mgr*
EMP: 47
SALES (corp-wide): 86.16MM **Privately Held**
Web: www.epcmfg.com
SIC: 3714 Motor vehicle parts and accessories
PA: Ernie Green Industries, Inc.
1785 Big Hill Rd
Dayton OH 45439
614 219-1423

(G-3258)
FLORIDA PRODUCTION ENGRG INC
Also Called: Eg Industries
30627 Orr Rd (43113-9731)
PHONE...............................740 420-5252
Chuck Reisinger, *Mgr*
EMP: 160
SALES (corp-wide): 86.16MM **Privately Held**
SIC: 3089 Injection molding of plastics
HQ: Florida Production Engineering, Inc.
2 E Tower Cir
Ormond Beach FL 32174
386 677-2566

(G-3259)
FPE INC
30627 Orr Rd (43113-9731)
PHONE...............................740 420-5252
EMP: 200
SIC: 3089 Automotive parts, plastic

(G-3260)
GEORGIA-PACIFIC LLC
Also Called: Georgia-Pacific
2850 Owens Rd (43113-9079)
P.O. Box 379 (43113-0379)
PHONE...............................740 477-3347
Terry Gaffney, *Mgr*
EMP: 130
SALES (corp-wide): 64.44B **Privately Held**
Web: www.gp.com
SIC: 2653 3412 2675 2671 Boxes, corrugated: made from purchased materials ; Metal barrels, drums, and pails; Die-cut paper and board; Paper; coated and laminated packaging

---

HQ: Georgia-Pacific Llc
133 Peachtree St Ne
Atlanta GA 30303
404 652-4000

(G-3261)
OHIOHEALTH IMAGING SERVICES
1434 Circleville Plaza Dr (43113-2269)
PHONE................................740 420-7925
EMP: 12 EST: 2019
SALES (est): 1.01MM Privately Held
Web: www.ohiohealth.com
SIC: 3841 Surgical and medical instruments

(G-3262)
PPG INDUSTRIES INC
559 Pittsburgh Rd (43113-9436)
P.O. Box 457 (43113-0457)
PHONE................................740 474-3161
Dave Moss, *Brnch Mgr*
EMP: 64
SALES (corp-wide): 18.25B Publicly Held
Web: www.ppg.com
SIC: 2851 Paints and allied products
PA: Ppg Industries, Inc.
1 Ppg Pl
Pittsburgh PA 15272
412 434-3131

(G-3263)
SUBURBAN METAL PRODUCTS INC
1050 Tarlton Rd (43113-9132)
PHONE................................740 474-4237
Linda Kempton, *Sec*
EMP: 18 EST: 1987
SQ FT: 12,000
SALES (est): 2.33MM Privately Held
Web: www.cline-machine.com
SIC: 3599 3441 7692 3544 Machine shop,
jobbing and repair; Fabricated structural
metal; Welding repair; Special dies, tools,
jigs, and fixtures

(G-3264)
TANGENT AIR INC
127 Edison Ave (43113-2117)
PHONE................................740 474-1114
John Morehead, *Pr*
Jerry Jones, *
EMP: 38 EST: 1993
SQ FT: 17,000
SALES (est): 1.52MM Privately Held
Web: www.tangentairinc.com
SIC: 3321 3444 Cast iron pipe and fittings;
Sheet metalwork

(G-3265)
TECHNICOLOR USA INC
Also Called: Circleville Glass Operations
24200 Us Highway 23 S (43113-7566)
PHONE................................614 474-8821
Chet Kucinski, *Mgr*
EMP: 1065
SQ FT: 325,000
Web: www.technicolor.com
SIC: 3651 3231 Household audio and video
equipment; Products of purchased glass
HQ: Technicolor Usa, Inc.
6040 Sunset Blvd
Hollywood CA 90028
317 587-4287

(G-3266)
TELESIS TECHNOLOGIES INC (DH)
Also Called: Telesis Marking Systems
28181 River Dr (43113-9726)
PHONE................................740 477-5000
Steve Sheng, *Pr*
Warren R Knipple, *
▲ **EMP: 135 EST: 1971**
SQ FT: 39,900

SALES (est): 27.6MM Privately Held
Web: www.telesis.com
SIC: 3953 Canceling stamps, hand: rubber
or metal
HQ: Hitachi Industrial Equipment Systems
Co., Ltd.
1-5-1, Sotokanda
Chiyoda-Ku TKY 101-0

(G-3267)
TOOLTEX INC
17287 Florence Chapel Pike (43113-9556)
PHONE................................614 539-3222
Paul Spurgeon, *Pr*
EMP: 15 EST: 1987
SALES (est): 2.43MM Privately Held
Web: www.tooltex.com
SIC: 5084 3559 Industrial machinery and
equipment; Plastics working machinery

(G-3268)
TRIMOLD LLC
200 Pittsburgh Rd (43113-9288)
PHONE................................740 474-7591
Yoshimasa Okada, *Managing Member*
Yoshimasa Okada, *Managing Member*
Katsuya Kanda, *
EMP: 360 EST: 2005
SALES (est): 18.17MM Privately Held
Web: www.tstech.com
SIC: 3089 Injection molding of plastics
HQ: Ts Trim Industries Inc.
6380 Canal St
Canal Winchester OH 43110
614 837-4114

(G-3269)
TS TECH CO LTD
200 Pittsburgh Rd (43113-9288)
PHONE................................740 420-5617
EMP: 6 EST: 2018
SALES (est): 2.72MM Privately Held
Web: www.tstech.com
SIC: 3089 Plastics products, nec

Clarington
Monroe County

(G-3270)
AMERICAN HVY PLATE SLTIONS LLC
42722 State Route 7 Ste 12 (43915-9583)
PHONE................................740 331-4620
Roxana Stoicea, *Managing Member*
Roxana Stoicea, *CFO*
EMP: 148 EST: 2017
SALES (est): 12.62MM Privately Held
Web: www.ahplates.com
SIC: 3312 Sheet or strip, steel, cold-rolled:
own hot-rolled

Clayton
Montgomery County

(G-3271)
ANCHOR FABRICATORS INC
386 Talmadge Rd (45315-9621)
P.O. Box 99 (45315-0099)
PHONE................................937 836-5117
Tom Saldoff, *Pr*
Marshall Ruchman, *
Randee Saldoff, *Stockholder*
EMP: 43 EST: 1949
SQ FT: 60,000
SALES (est): 7.97MM Privately Held
Web: www.anchorfab.com
SIC: 3471 3599 3469 Buffing for the trade;
Machine shop, jobbing and repair; Metal
stampings, nec

(G-3272)
BLACKTHORN LLC
6113 Brookville Salem Rd (45315-9701)
PHONE................................937 836-9296
Greg Benedict, *Managing Member*
Sharon Yoakum, *VP*
Sharon Buehler, *Sec*
EMP: 10 EST: 1985
SQ FT: 20,000
SALES (est): 1.12MM Privately Held
Web: www.blackthorn-inc.com
SIC: 3053 2899 3089 3296 Gaskets, all
materials; Concrete curing and hardening
compounds; Plastics hardware and building
products; Fiberglass insulation

(G-3273)
**HOFACKER PRCSION MACHINING
LLC**
7560 Jacks Ln (45315-8779)
PHONE................................937 832-7712
EMP: 18 EST: 1997
SQ FT: 2,500
SALES (est): 4.32MM Privately Held
Web: www.hofackerprecision.com
SIC: 3599 3544 Machine shop, jobbing and
repair; Special dies and tools

(G-3274)
KITTO KATSU INC
7445 Lockwood St (45315)
PHONE................................818 256-6997
Hiran Jayasinghe, *Pr*
EMP: 7 EST: 2017
SALES (est): 238.18K Privately Held
SIC: 3999 8742 Manufacturing industries,
nec; Marketing consulting services

(G-3275)
SLUTERBECK TOOL & DIE CO INC
Also Called: Sluterbeck Tool Co
7540 Jacks Ln (45315-8779)
P.O. Box 87 (45315-0087)
PHONE................................937 836-5736
Ronald Sluterbeck, *Pr*
Anne Goss, *Sec*
Steve Sluterbeck, *VP*
Greg Sluterbeck, *VP*
EMP: 10 EST: 1953
SQ FT: 6,000
SALES (est): 1MM Privately Held
SIC: 3544 Special dies and tools

Cleveland
Cuyahoga County

(G-3276)
2 RETRIEVERS LLC
Also Called: Elugen Pharmaceuticals
2515 Jay Ave (44113-3091)
PHONE................................216 200-9040
Kevin Lenahan, *CEO*
EMP: 8 EST: 2019
SALES (est): 331.01K Privately Held
Web: www.2retrievers.com
SIC: 2834 Pharmaceutical preparations

(G-3277)
4WALLSCOM LLC
4700 Lakeside Ave E Unit 173a
(44114-3863)
PHONE................................216 432-1400
Gale Flanagan, *General Member*
EMP: 10 EST: 2004
SALES (est): 2.04MM Privately Held
Web: www.4walls.com
SIC: 2679 Wallpaper

(G-3278)
A & W TABLE PAD CO
Also Called: Pioneer Table Pad
6520 Carnegie Ave (44103-4697)
PHONE................................800 541-0271
TOLL FREE: 800
Tamara Christman, *Pr*
EMP: 10 EST: 1915
SQ FT: 12,000
SALES (est): 413.54K Privately Held
Web: www.pioneertablepads.com
SIC: 2392 Table mats, plastic and textile

(G-3279)
A AABACO PLASTICS INC
Also Called: United Plastic Film
9520 Midwest Ave (44125-2463)
PHONE................................216 663-9494
Daniel R Lee, *Pr*
Jonathan Lee, *VP*
David Lee, *Sec*
A R Mays, *Prin*
Elliott M Kaufman, *Prin*
EMP: 10 EST: 1968
SQ FT: 25,000
SALES (est): 2.12MM Privately Held
Web: www.aabacoplastics.com
SIC: 3089 Blister or bubble formed
packaging, plastics

(G-3280)
A F KRAINZ CO
1364 E 47th St (44103-1220)
PHONE................................216 431-4341
Andrew F Krainz Junior, *Owner*
EMP: 8 EST: 1974
SALES (est): 444.31K Privately Held
SIC: 2752 Offset printing

(G-3281)
A G INDUSTRIES INC
1 American Rd (44144-2354)
PHONE................................216 252-7300
Jeff White, *Pr*
EMP: 9 EST: 1960
SQ FT: 30,000
SALES (est): 4.65MM
SALES (corp-wide): 14.54B Privately Held
SIC: 2541 Display fixtures, wood
HQ: American Greetings Corporation
1 American Blvd
Cleveland OH 44145
216 252-7300

(G-3282)
A H MARTY CO LTD
6900 Union Ave (44105-1383)
PHONE................................216 641-8950
Diane Champion, *Pr*
Tom Champion, *VP*
EMP: 12 EST: 1910
SQ FT: 15,000
SALES (est): 3.21MM Privately Held
Web: www.ahmarty.com
SIC: 3443 Weldments

(G-3283)
A JACKS MANUFACTURING CO
1441 Chardon Rd (44117-1510)
PHONE................................216 531-1010
Charlie Crout, *Pr*
▲ **EMP: 21 EST: 2003**
SALES (est): 4.77MM
SALES (corp-wide): 1.66B Publicly Held
SIC: 3567 Industrial furnaces and ovens
HQ: Park-Ohio Industries, Inc.
6065 Parkland Blvd
Cleveland OH 44124
440 947-2000

(G-3284)
AAA STAMPING INC
4001 Pearl Rd Uppr (44109-3198)
PHONE..............................216 749-4494
Stan Gawor, *Pr*
EMP: 22 **EST:** 1985
SQ FT: 25,000
SALES (est): 3.83MM **Privately Held**
Web: www.aaastampinginc.com
SIC: 3469 Stamping metal for the trade

(G-3285)
AAJAJ HAIR COMPANY LLC
3905 W 18th St (44109-3074)
PHONE..............................216 309-0816
EMP: 10 **EST:** 2019
SALES (est): 129.37K **Privately Held**
SIC: 3999 Hair and hair-based products

(G-3286)
ABEL METAL PROCESSING INC
2105 E 77th St (44103-4990)
PHONE..............................216 881-4156
Eugene Schoenmeyer, *Pr*
Joan Kern, *VP*
EMP: 11 **EST:** 1975
SQ FT: 8,000
SALES (est): 1.17MM **Privately Held**
Web: www.abelmetal.com
SIC: 3471 Electroplating of metals or formed products

(G-3287)
ABEONA THERAPEUTICS INC (PA)
Also Called: Abeona
6555 Carnegie Ave Fl 4 (44103-4637)
PHONE..............................646 813-4701
Vishwas Seshadri, *Pr*
Michael Amoroso, *Ch Bd*
Joseph Vazzano, *CFO*
EMP: 59 **EST:** 1974
SQ FT: 45,705
Web: www.abeonatherapeutics.com
SIC: 2834 Pharmaceutical preparations

(G-3288)
ABI INC
Also Called: ABI
5350 Transportation Blvd Ste 18b (44125-5307)
P.O. Box 389 (44286-0389)
PHONE..............................800 847-8950
Lloyd Ray Parr, *Pr*
Thomas L Feher, *Sec*
EMP: 10 **EST:** 1991
SALES (est): 992.41K **Privately Held**
Web: www.ultraclear.com
SIC: 2836 Biological products, except diagnostic

(G-3289)
ACADEMY GRAPHIC COMM INC
1000 Brookpark Rd (44109-5824)
PHONE..............................216 661-2550
James M Champion, *Pr*
Elaine Champion, *
EMP: 10 **EST:** 1966
SQ FT: 1,400
SALES (est): 1.35MM **Privately Held**
Web: www.visitagc.com
SIC: 2752 7336 Offset printing; Graphic arts and related design

(G-3290)
ACME LIFTING PRODUCTS INC
Also Called: Universal Cargo
6892 W Snowville Rd Ste 2 (44141-3288)
PHONE..............................440 838-4430
Laura Davis, *Pr*
Arnold Davis, *VP*
EMP: 8 **EST:** 1986
SQ FT: 6,000
SALES (est): 880K **Privately Held**
SIC: 3536 Hoisting slings

(G-3291)
ACME SPRLLY WOUND PPR PDTS INC
Also Called: Acme Paper Tube
4810 W 139th St (44135-5036)
P.O. Box 35320 (44135-0320)
PHONE..............................216 267-2950
Dan Kobrak, *CEO*
Donald H Kobak Junior, *CEO*
EMP: 17 **EST:** 1953
SQ FT: 36,000
SALES (est): 5.6MM **Privately Held**
Web: www.acmespiral.com
SIC: 2655 Tubes, fiber or paper: made from purchased material

(G-3292)
ACOR ORTHOPAEDIC INC
Also Called: Cleveland Prosthetic Center
18700 S Miles Rd (44128-4242)
PHONE..............................440 532-0117
EMP: 14
SALES (corp-wide): 8.41MM **Privately Held**
Web: www.acor.com
SIC: 3842 Orthopedic appliances
PA: Acor Orthopaedic, Llc
18530 S Miles Rd
Cleveland OH 44128
216 662-4500

(G-3293)
ACOR ORTHOPAEDIC LLC (PA)
18530 S Miles Rd (44128-4200)
PHONE..............................216 662-4500
Joseph Merolla, *Managing Member*
Greg Alaimo, *
Jeff Alaimo, *
▲ **EMP:** 34 **EST:** 1965
SQ FT: 35,000
SALES (est): 8.41MM
SALES (corp-wide): 8.41MM **Privately Held**
Web: www.acor.com
SIC: 3144 3143 3842 3086 Women's footwear, except athletic; Men's footwear, except athletic; Prosthetic appliances; Plastics foam products

(G-3294)
AD PISTON RING LLC
Also Called: Ad Piston Ring
3145 Superior Ave E (44114-4342)
PHONE..............................216 781-5200
Craig Duber, *Managing Member*
Bob Lee, *Managing Member*
Craig Duber, *Genl Mgr*
EMP: 10 **EST:** 1921
SQ FT: 12,000
SALES (est): 2.74MM **Privately Held**
Web: www.adpistonring.com
SIC: 3592 Pistons and piston rings

(G-3295)
ADALET/SCOTT FETZER COMPANY
Also Called: Meriam Instrument
10920 Madison Ave (44102-2526)
PHONE..............................440 892-3074
Dave Thomas, *Prin*
EMP: 50 **EST:** 1987
SALES (est): 5.55MM **Privately Held**
Web: www.meriam.com
SIC: 3823 Process control instruments

(G-3296)
ADCHEM ADHESIVES INC
4111 E Royalton Rd (44147-2931)
PHONE..............................440 526-1976
Claude Dandurande, *Pr*
Brett Joint, *Mgr*
▲ **EMP:** 10 **EST:** 1996
SQ FT: 15,000
SALES (est): 96.91K **Privately Held**
SIC: 2891 Adhesives

(G-3297)
ADCRAFT DECALS INCORPORATED
7708 Commerce Park Oval (44131-2394)
PHONE..............................216 524-2934
Robert W Talion, *Pr*
Ciliox Rendina, *
EMP: 27 **EST:** 1961
SQ FT: 21,200
SALES (est): 4.9MM **Privately Held**
Web: www.adcraftdecals.com
SIC: 2759 3993 2752 2672 Screen printing; Signs and advertising specialties; Commercial printing, lithographic; Paper; coated and laminated, nec

(G-3298)
ADDED EDGE ASSEMBLY INC
26800 Fargo Ave Ste A (44146-1341)
PHONE..............................216 464-4305
Kurt Kodrich, *Pr*
Janet Kodrich, *Sec*
EMP: 9 **EST:** 1991
SQ FT: 3,000
SALES (est): 643.9K **Privately Held**
Web: www.addedge.com
SIC: 3549 Assembly machines, including robotic

(G-3299)
ADMIRAL PRODUCTS COMPANY INC
4101 W 150th St (44135-1303)
PHONE..............................216 671-0600
Vincent C Hvizda, *CEO*
Paul Hvizda, *
Margaret Schroeder Hvizda, *
EMP: 37 **EST:** 1948
SQ FT: 39,000
SALES (est): 4.2MM **Privately Held**
Web: www.admiralproducts.com
SIC: 2752 2759 2754 2672 Offset printing; Flexographic printing; Labels: gravure printing; Paper; coated and laminated, nec

(G-3300)
ADMJ HOLDINGS LLC
Also Called: Advance Door Co.
5260 Commerce Pkwy W (44130-1271)
PHONE..............................216 588-0038
Jerry Oflanagan, *Prin*
Mary Oflanagan, *
EMP: 35 **EST:** 2019
SALES (est): 4.19MM **Privately Held**
Web: www.advance-door.com
SIC: 2381 Fabric dress and work gloves

(G-3301)
ADVANCE INDUSTRIES GROUP LLC
3636 W 58th St (44102-5641)
PHONE..............................216 741-1800
EMP: 20 **EST:** 2006
SQ FT: 35,000
SALES (est): 4.53MM **Privately Held**
Web: www.advancewireforming.com
SIC: 3441 3315 Fabricated structural metal; Wire and fabricated wire products

(G-3302)
ADVANCE MANUFACTURING CORP
6800 Madison Ave (44102-4099)
PHONE..............................216 333-1684
Herman Bredenbeck, *Pr*
Jon Bredenbeck, *
Kenneth Bailey, *
Doug Carlson, *
EMP: 48 **EST:** 1936
SQ FT: 64,000
SALES (est): 7.03MM **Privately Held**
Web: www.advancemanuf.com
SIC: 3599 3549 Machine shop, jobbing and repair; Metalworking machinery, nec

(G-3303)
ADVANCE METAL PRODUCTS INC
3636 W 58th St (44102-5641)
PHONE..............................216 741-1800
James Williams, *Pr*
EMP: 6 **EST:** 1996
SQ FT: 30,000
SALES (est): 492.02K **Privately Held**
Web: www.advancewireforming.com
SIC: 3441 Fabricated structural metal

(G-3304)
ADVANCE WIRE FORMING INC
3636 W 58th St (44102-5641)
PHONE..............................216 432-3250
Jeff Stein, *Pr*
James Williams, *VP*
EMP: 10 **EST:** 2000
SQ FT: 30,000
SALES (est): 1.53MM **Privately Held**
Web: www.advancewireforming.com
SIC: 3496 Miscellaneous fabricated wire products

(G-3305)
ADVANCED FLUIDS INC
18127 Roseland Rd (44112-1001)
PHONE..............................216 692-3050
Emil T Rosul, *Pr*
EMP: 7 **EST:** 1996
SQ FT: 12,800
SALES (est): 1.04MM **Privately Held**
Web: www.advancedfluidsinc.com
SIC: 2992 Lubricating oils

(G-3306)
ADVANCED KIFFER SYSTEMS INC
4905 Rocky River Dr (44135-3245)
PHONE..............................216 267-8181
Dale C Phillip, *Pr*
Lars Eriksson, *VP*
Susan Phillip, *Sec*
EMP: 24 **EST:** 1988
SQ FT: 85,000
SALES (est): 4.58MM
SALES (corp-wide): 9.17MM **Privately Held**
Web: www.akscutting.com
SIC: 3825 Test equipment for electronic and electric measurement
PA: Kiffer Industries, Inc.
4905 Rocky River Dr
Cleveland OH 44135
216 267-1818

(G-3307)
ADVANCED PAPER TUBE INC
1951 W 90th St (44102-2742)
PHONE..............................216 281-5691
Leon Lasky, *Pr*
Dorothy Lasky, *VP*
EMP: 6 **EST:** 1982
SQ FT: 27,000
SALES (est): 1.3MM **Privately Held**
Web: www.advancedpapertube.com

SIC: **2655** Tubes, fiber or paper: made from purchased material

(G-3308)
ADVANCED SURFACE TECHNOLOGY
12211 Sobieski Ave (44135-4857)
PHONE.................................216 476-8600
Joseph Lardner, *Pr*
James Mason, *VP*
EMP: 7 EST: 2000
SALES (est): 497.42K **Privately Held**
Web: www.advancedsurfaceinc.com
SIC: **3471** Electroplating of metals or formed products

(G-3309)
AERO-INSTRUMENTS CO LLC
Also Called: Aero Instruments
4223 Monticello Blvd (44121-2814)
P.O. Box 932066 (44193-0007)
PHONE.................................216 671-3133
EMP: 50
Web: www.aeroinstruments.com
SIC: **3812** Search and navigation equipment

(G-3310)
AEROLL ENGINEERING CORP
18511 Euclid Ave Rear (44112-1018)
PHONE.................................216 481-2266
Carl E Weaver Iii, *Pr*
Sherri Weaver, *Sec*
EMP: 7 EST: 1942
SQ FT: 8,000
SALES (est): 489.88K **Privately Held**
Web: www.wickertengineering.com
SIC: **3545** Thread cutting dies

(G-3311)
AEROSCENA LLC
Also Called: Ascents
10000 Cedar Ave (44106-2119)
PHONE.................................800 671-1890
Mark Kohoot, *CEO*
EMP: 7 EST: 2010
SALES (est): 435.61K **Privately Held**
Web: www.aeroscena.com
SIC: **2844** Perfumes, natural or synthetic

(G-3312)
AETNA PLATING CO
6511 Morgan Ave (44127-1947)
PHONE.................................216 341-9111
Peter Sobey, *Pr*
Joel Newman, *Sec*
EMP: 15 EST: 1934
SQ FT: 55,000
SALES (est): 1.95MM **Privately Held**
Web: www.aetnaplating.com
SIC: **3471** Electroplating of metals or formed products

(G-3313)
AFFYMETRIX INC
26111 Miles Rd (44128-5933)
P.O. Box 68 (92018-0068)
PHONE.................................800 321-9322
EMP: 78
SALES (corp-wide): 42.86B **Publicly Held**
Web: www.thermofisher.com
SIC: **3826** Analytical instruments
HQ: Affymetrix, Inc.
3450 Central Expy
Santa Clara CA 95051

(G-3314)
AGMET LLC
5533 Dunham Rd (44137-3679)
PHONE.................................216 663-8200
Dave Crose, *Brnch Mgr*
EMP: 10

SALES (corp-wide): 42.96MM **Privately Held**
Web: www.agmet1.com
SIC: **5093** 3341 Ferrous metal scrap and waste; Secondary nonferrous metals
PA: Agmet Llc
7800 Medusa Rd
Cleveland OH 44146
440 439-7400

(G-3315)
AIN INDUSTRIES INC
13901 Aspinwall Ave (44110-2210)
P.O. Box 464 (44011-0464)
PHONE.................................440 781-0950
Bill Kavila, *Pr*
Steve Misch, *VP*
Ted Black, *Sec*
EMP: 6 EST: 1986
SQ FT: 6,500
SALES (est): 228.08K **Privately Held**
SIC: **2841** 5169 5087 Soap and other detergents; Chemicals and allied products, nec; Service establishment equipment

(G-3316)
AIR-RITE INC
Also Called: Air Rite Service Supply
1290 W 117th St (44107-3096)
PHONE.................................216 228-8200
TOLL FREE: 800
David Harris, *Pr*
Marilyn Harris, *
▼ EMP: 24 EST: 1951
SQ FT: 28,000
SALES (est): 4.94MM **Privately Held**
Web: www.airrite-supply.com
SIC: **7623** 7699 5075 3564 Air conditioning repair; Boiler and heating repair services; Warm air heating equipment and supplies; Blowers and fans

(G-3317)
AIRCRAFT & AUTO FITTINGS CO
17120 Saint Clair Ave (44110-2531)
PHONE.................................216 486-0047
Martin Sexton, *Pr*
John Markulin, *Sec*
EMP: 8 EST: 1960
SQ FT: 4,800
SALES (est): 725.67K **Privately Held**
SIC: **3599** Machine shop, jobbing and repair

(G-3318)
ALABAMA SLING CENTER INC
21000 Aerospace Pkwy (44142-1000)
PHONE.................................440 239-7000
Tony Mazzela, *Prin*
EMP: 11 EST: 2013
SALES (est): 1.15MM **Privately Held**
SIC: **3496** Miscellaneous fabricated wire products

(G-3319)
ALBION MACHINE & TOOL CO INC
13200 Enterprise Ave (44135-5104)
PHONE.................................216 267-9627
Michael Gierscher, *Pr*
Regina Gierscher, *VP*
EMP: 6 EST: 1987
SQ FT: 9,000
SALES (est): 680.39K **Privately Held**
SIC: **3599** Machine shop, jobbing and repair

(G-3320)
ALCAN CORPORATION (HQ)
6060 Parkland Blvd (44124-4225)
◆ EMP: 22 EST: 2003
SQ FT: 11,000
SALES (est): 38.22MM
SALES (corp-wide): 53.66B **Privately Held**

SIC: **3351** 3355 3496 3357 Wire, copper and copper alloy; Wire, aluminum: made in rolling mills; Miscellaneous fabricated wire products; Nonferrous wiredrawing and insulating
PA: Rio Tinto Plc
6 St. James's Square
London SW1Y
207 781-2000

(G-3321)
ALCON INDUSTRIES INC
7990 Baker Ave (44102-1900)
PHONE.................................216 961-1100
Richard J Chalet, *Ch Bd*
Richard J Chalet, *Ch Bd*
▲ EMP: 100 EST: 1977
SQ FT: 130,000
SALES (est): 14.31MM **Privately Held**
Web: www.alconindustries.com
SIC: **3325** 3441 3369 Alloy steel castings, except investment; Fabricated structural metal; Nonferrous foundries, nec

(G-3322)
ALFRED MACHINE CO (HQ)
29500 Solon Rd (44139-3449)
PHONE.................................440 248-4600
Art Anton, *CEO*
EMP: 85 EST: 1964
SQ FT: 100,000
SALES (est): 3.84MM
SALES (corp-wide): 881.02MM **Privately Held**
SIC: **3599** Machine shop, jobbing and repair
PA: Swagelok Company
29500 Solon Rd
Solon OH 44139
440 248-4600

(G-3323)
ALKID CORPORATION
6035 Parkland Blvd (44124-4186)
PHONE.................................216 896-3000
Jon P Marten, *CEO*
EMP: 46 EST: 1953
SALES (est): 1.59MM
SALES (corp-wide): 19.93B **Publicly Held**
SIC: **3594** Fluid power pumps
PA: Parker-Hannifin Corporation
6035 Parkland Blvd
Cleveland OH 44124
216 896-3000

(G-3324)
ALL METAL FABRICATORS INC
15400 Commerce Park Dr (44142-2011)
PHONE.................................216 267-0033
William Yankovich, *Pr*
Mike Yankovich, *VP*
Carol Yankovich, *Sec*
EMP: 15 EST: 1978
SQ FT: 14,000
SALES (est): 1.74MM **Privately Held**
Web: www.all-metalfab.com
SIC: **3444** Sheet metal specialties, not stamped

(G-3325)
ALL OHIO COMPANIES INC
2735 Scranton Rd (44113-5181)
PHONE.................................216 420-9274
Paul Colletti, *Prin*
EMP: 6 EST: 2013
SQ FT: 5,088
SALES (est): 1.58MM **Privately Held**
Web: www.allohiopressurewash.com
SIC: **3446** 1721 1799 Gates, ornamental metal; Exterior residential painting contractor; Exterior cleaning, including sandblasting

(G-3326)
ALL OHIO THREADED ROD CO INC
5349 Saint Clair Ave (44103-1311)
PHONE.................................216 426-1800
James Wolford, *CEO*
Rick Fien, *
James Wolford, *VP*
▲ EMP: 28 EST: 1981
SQ FT: 40,000
SALES (est): 6.7MM **Privately Held**
Web: www.allohiorod.com
SIC: **3312** 5085 3316 Bar, rod, and wire products; Industrial supplies; Cold finishing of steel shapes

(G-3327)
ALL STREETS AUTO LLC
15317 Chatfield Ave (44111-4301)
PHONE.................................330 714-7717
Dalton Lindesmith, *Managing Member*
EMP: 12 EST: 2022
SALES (est): 1.61MM **Privately Held**
SIC: **2396** Automotive and apparel trimmings

(G-3328)
ALL TRADES CONTRACTORS LLC
9920 Olivet Ave (44108-3546)
PHONE.................................440 850-5693
EMP: 8 EST: 2020
SALES (est): 270.27K **Privately Held**
SIC: **1389** Construction, repair, and dismantling services

(G-3329)
ALL-TYPE WELDING & FABRICATION
7690 Bond St (44139-5351)
PHONE.................................440 439-3990
Mike Distaulo, *Pr*
Dennis Whitaker, *
EMP: 40 EST: 1974
SQ FT: 34,000
SALES (est): 7.64MM **Privately Held**
Web: www.atwf-inc.com
SIC: **3599** 7692 1761 Machine and other job shop work; Welding repair; Sheet metal work, nec

(G-3330)
ALLEGION ACCESS TECH LLC
Stanley Assembly Technologies
5335 Avion Park Dr (44143-1916)
P.O. Box 50400 (46250-0400)
PHONE.................................440 461-5500
John E Turpin, *Brnch Mgr*
EMP: 32
SQ FT: 40,000
Web: www.stanleyaccess.com
SIC: **3423** 3546 Hand and edge tools, nec; Power-driven handtools
HQ: Allegion Access Technologies Llc
65 Scott Swamp Rd
Farmington CT 06032

(G-3331)
ALLIED TOOL & DIE INC
16146 Puritas Ave (44135-2691)
PHONE.................................216 941-6196
Fred Montag, *Pr*
Walter Montag, *Stockholder*
EMP: 19 EST: 1946
SALES (est): 3.39MM **Privately Held**
Web: www.alliedtool-die.com
SIC: **3469** 3544 Stamping metal for the trade ; Special dies and tools

(G-3332)
ALPHA PACKAGING HOLDINGS INC
Also Called: Progressive Plastics
14801 Emery Ave (44135-1476)
PHONE.................................216 252-5595

A J Busa, *Mgr*
EMP: 275
SALES (corp-wide): 491.41MM **Privately Held**
Web: www.pretiumpkg.com
SIC: 3089 3085 Molding primary plastics; Plastics bottles
HQ: Alpha Packaging Holdings, Inc.
1555 Page Industrial Blvd
Saint Louis MO 63132

(G-3333)
ALPHA TOOL & MOLD INC
83 Alpha Park (44143-2265)
PHONE.............................440 473-2343
Robert Pischel, *Pr*
Al Pischel, *Sec*
Alfred Pischel, *Prin*
Helen Pischel, *Prin*
William M Fumich, *Prin*
▲ **EMP:** 12 **EST:** 1976
SQ FT: 8,500
SALES (est): 2.57MM **Privately Held**
Web: www.alphatoolandmold.com
SIC: 3544 Special dies and tools

(G-3334)
ALPHA ZETA HOLDINGS INC (PA)
2981 Independence Rd (44115-3615)
PHONE.............................216 271-1601
Joseph T Turgeon, *CEO*
James B Krimmel, *Pr*
EMP: 6 **EST:** 2003
SALES (est): 24.62MM
SALES (corp-wide): 24.62MM **Privately Held**
SIC: 2819 2869 6799 Industrial inorganic chemicals, nec; Industrial organic chemicals, nec; Investors, nec

(G-3335)
ALTHAR LLC
5432 Broadway Ave (44127-1509)
PHONE.............................216 408-9860
EMP: 10 **EST:** 2021
SALES (est): 215.86K **Privately Held**
Web: www.atssounds.com
SIC: 3651 Speaker systems

(G-3336)
ALUMINUM BEARING CO OF AMERICA
Also Called: Albeco
4775 W 139th St (44135-5033)
PHONE.............................216 267-8560
Jane Beyer, *Pr*
EMP: 9 **EST:** 1956
SQ FT: 3,000
SALES (est): 915.45K **Privately Held**
Web: www.albeco.com
SIC: 5051 3429 Aluminum bars, rods, ingots, sheets, pipes, plates, etc.; Hardware, nec

(G-3337)
AMAC ENTERPRISES INC
5925 W 130th St (44130-1076)
PHONE.............................216 362-1880
Dean Caimples, *Mgr*
EMP: 13
SQ FT: 160,000
SALES (corp-wide): 5.32MM **Privately Held**
Web: www.amacent.com
SIC: 3471 Anodizing (plating) of metals or formed products
PA: Amac Enterprises, Inc.
5909 W 130th St
Parma OH 44130
216 362-1880

(G-3338)
AMANI VINES LLC
3100 E 45th St Ste 512 (44127-1095)
PHONE.............................440 335-5432
EMP: 10 **EST:** 2021
SALES (est): 103K **Privately Held**
SIC: 2084 Wines

(G-3339)
AMECO USA MET FBRCTION SLTONS
4600 W 160th St (44135-2630)
PHONE.............................440 899-9400
EMP: 13 **EST:** 2010
SALES (est): 6.24MM **Privately Held**
Web: www.ameco-usa.com
SIC: 3441 Fabricated structural metal
PA: American Manufacturing And Engineering Company
4600 W 160th Street
Cleveland OH 44135

(G-3340)
AMERICAN ALLOY CORPORATION
9501 Allen Dr (44125-4603)
PHONE.............................216 642-9638
▲ **EMP:** 37
SIC: 3531 Construction machinery

(G-3341)
AMERICAN BRASS MFG CO
5000 Superior Ave (44103-1299)
PHONE.............................216 431-6565
Robert Mc Conville Junior, *Ch*
▲ **EMP:** 8 **EST:** 1894
SQ FT: 40,000
SALES (est): 948.19K **Privately Held**
Web: www.rvfaucets.com
SIC: 3432 Plumbers' brass goods: drain cocks, faucets, spigots, etc.

(G-3342)
AMERICAN BRONZE CORPORATION
2941 Broadway Ave (44115-3692)
PHONE.............................216 341-7800
Gerald Goldstein, *Pr*
Joshua Goldstein, *
EMP: 25 **EST:** 1924
SQ FT: 50,000
SALES (est): 10MM **Privately Held**
Web: www.americanbronzecorp.com
SIC: 3366 Copper foundries

(G-3343)
AMERICAN FRICTION TECH LLC
9300 Midwest Ave (44125-2418)
PHONE.............................216 823-0861
Gregory C Soukup, *Managing Member*
Horst Becker, *
Andrew C Freeman, *
▲ **EMP:** 65 **EST:** 1996
SQ FT: 54,000
SALES (est): 9.93MM **Privately Held**
Web: www.americanfriction.net
SIC: 3339 Primary nonferrous metals, nec

(G-3344)
AMERICAN GREETINGS CORPORATION (HQ)
Also Called: American Greetings
1 American Blvd (44145-8151)
PHONE.............................216 252-7300
Joe Arcuri, *CEO*
Aaron Siegel, *VP*
Chad Anderson, *Ex Dir*
Gregory M Steinberg, *CFO*
◆ **EMP:** 1700 **EST:** 1906
SQ FT: 1,194,414
SALES (est): 689.67MM
SALES (corp-wide): 14.54B **Privately Held**

Web: www.americangreetings.com
SIC: 2771 2679 2656 2678 Greeting cards; Gift wrap, paper: made from purchased material; Cups, paper: made from purchased material; Stationery: made from purchased materials
PA: Clayton, Dubilier & Rice, Inc.
375 Park Ave Fl 18
New York NY 10152
212 407-5200

(G-3345)
AMERICAN IR MET CLEVELAND LLC
1240 Marquette St (44114-3920)
PHONE.............................216 266-0509
◆ **EMP:** 20 **EST:** 1983
SQ FT: 70,000
SALES (est): 4.79MM
SALES (corp-wide): 407.17MM **Privately Held**
Web: www.aim-recycling.com
SIC: 5051 3441 Steel; Fabricated structural metal
HQ: American Iron & Metal (U.S.A.), Inc.
25 Kenney Dr
Cranston RI 02920
401 463-5605

(G-3346)
AMERICAN METAL TREATING CO
1043 E 62nd St (44103-1094)
PHONE.............................216 431-4492
Richard Roenn, *Pr*
Carol Roenn, *Sec*
▲ **EMP:** 22 **EST:** 1926
SQ FT: 15,830
SALES (est): 2.77MM **Privately Held**
Web: www.americanmetaltreating.com
SIC: 3398 Brazing (hardening) of metal

(G-3347)
AMERICAN PRECISION SPINDLES
Also Called: SKF Machine Tools Service
670 Alpha Dr (44143-2123)
PHONE.............................267 436-6000
EMP: 8 **EST:** 1997
SQ FT: 10,000
SALES (est): 2.25MM
SALES (corp-wide): 740.17MM **Privately Held**
Web: www.precisionspindleinc.com
SIC: 3552 Spindles, textile
HQ: Skf Usa Inc.
801 Lakeview Dr Ste 120
Blue Bell PA 19422
267 436-6000

(G-3348)
AMERICAN TANK & FABRICATING CO (PA)
Also Called: A T & F Co
12314 Elmwood Ave (44111-5906)
PHONE.............................216 252-1500
Terry Ripich, *Ch Bd*
Michael Ripich, *
Kenneth Ripich, *
Brian Spitz, *
Michael Puleo, *HEAVY FABRICATING*
▲ **EMP:** 100 **EST:** 1940
SQ FT: 300,000
SALES (est): 57.84MM
SALES (corp-wide): 57.84MM **Privately Held**
Web: www.atfco.com
SIC: 5051 3443 Metals service centers and offices; Weldments

(G-3349)
AMERICLEAN 2 LLC
2061 Gehring Ave (44113-4120)
PHONE.............................216 781-3720

Randy Zimmerman, *Brnch Mgr*
EMP: 15
SALES (corp-wide): 8.2MM **Privately Held**
Web: www.ejthomascompany.com
SIC: 3714 Cleaners, air, motor vehicle
PA: Americlean 2 Llc
5101 Forrest Dr Ste C
New Albany OH 43054
614 294-3373

(G-3350)
AMIR FOODS INC
761 Beta Dr Ste A (44143-2329)
PHONE.............................440 646-9388
Butch Rassi, *Pr*
Sam Rassi, *VP*
Tony Rassi, *Sec*
EMP: 7 **EST:** 1993
SQ FT: 7,100
SALES (est): 475.2K **Privately Held**
Web: www.amirfoods.com
SIC: 2099 Food preparations, nec

(G-3351)
AMROS INDUSTRIES INC
14701 Industrial Pkwy (44135-4547)
PHONE.............................216 433-0010
Gregory Shteyngarts, *Pr*
EMP: 15 **EST:** 1986
SQ FT: 65,000
SALES (est): 961.56K **Privately Held**
Web: www.clamshellusa.com
SIC: 7389 2821 Packaging and labeling services; Thermoplastic materials

(G-3352)
ANALIZA INC (PA)
3615 Superior Ave E Ste 4407b (44114-4139)
PHONE.............................216 432-9050
Amon Chait, *Pr*
EMP: 9 **EST:** 1996
SQ FT: 5,000
SALES (est): 4.89MM **Privately Held**
Web: www.analiza.com
SIC: 2834 Pharmaceutical preparations

(G-3353)
ANCHOR INDUSTRIES INCORPORATED
30775 Solon Industrial Pkwy (44139-4338)
PHONE.............................440 473-1414
Doug Kaufman, *Pr*
▲ **EMP:** 47 **EST:** 1999
SALES (est): 5.08MM **Privately Held**
Web: www.anchor-online.com
SIC: 3462 Automotive forgings, ferrous: crankshaft, engine, axle, etc.

(G-3354)
ANCHOR METAL PROCESSING INC
12200 Brookpark Rd (44130-1146)
PHONE.............................216 362-6463
Fred Pfaff, *Brnch Mgr*
EMP: 15
Web: www.anchor-mfg.com
SIC: 3599 1761 3444 Machine shop, jobbing and repair; Sheet metal work, nec; Sheet metalwork
PA: Anchor Metal Processing, Inc.
11830 Brookpark Rd
Cleveland OH 44130

(G-3355)
ANCHOR METAL PROCESSING INC (PA)
11830 Brookpark Rd (44130-1103)
PHONE.............................216 362-1850
Edward Pfaff, *Ch Bd*
Frederick Pfaff, *

Jeff Pfaff, *
Robert Pfaff, *
EMP: 30 **EST:** 1992
SQ FT: 46,000
SALES (est): 7.01MM **Privately Held**
Web: www.anchor-mfg.com
SIC: 3599 1761 3444 Machine shop, jobbing and repair; Sheet metal work, nec; Sheet metalwork

(G-3356)
ANCHOR TOOL & DIE CO
Also Called: Anchor Manufacturing Group
12200 Brookpark Rd (44130-1146)
PHONE..................................216 362-1850
Edward Pfaff, *Ch*
Frederick A Pfaff, *
Jeff Pfaff, *
Jim Walker, *
Robert Pfaff, *
▲ **EMP:** 275 **EST:** 1970
SQ FT: 350,000
SALES (est): 24.16MM **Privately Held**
Web: www.anchor-mfg.com
SIC: 3465 3544 3469 Automotive stampings; Special dies, tools, jigs, and fixtures; Metal stampings, nec

(G-3357)
ANDEEN-HAGERLING INC
31200 Bainbridge Rd Ste 2 (44139-2298)
PHONE..................................440 349-0370
Carl W Hagerling, *Pr*
Carl G Andeen, *VP*
EMP: 14 **EST:** 1982
SQ FT: 7,600
SALES (est): 713.63K **Privately Held**
Web: www.andeen-hagerling.com
SIC: 3825 Bridges: Kelvin, Wheatstone, vacuum tube, megohm, etc.

(G-3358)
ANDERSON DOOR CO
18090 Miles Rd (44128-3435)
PHONE..................................216 475-5700
James B Anderson Junior, *Pr*
James B Anderson Iii, *VP*
Virginia Anderson, *
EMP: 11 **EST:** 1920
SQ FT: 30,000
SALES (est): 1.92MM **Privately Held**
Web: www.andersondoor.com
SIC: 2431 3442 Garage doors, overhead, wood; Garage doors, overhead: metal

(G-3359)
ANDERSOUND PA SERVICE
15911 Harvard Ave (44128-2049)
PHONE..................................216 401-4631
Clarence Anderson Junior, *Owner*
EMP: 6 **EST:** 1975
SALES (est): 229.2K **Privately Held**
SIC: 3651 Audio electronic systems

(G-3360)
ANGEL PRTG & REPRODUCTION CO
1400 W 57th St (44102-3044)
PHONE..................................216 631-5225
Frank Petkovsek, *Pr*
Mary Louise Petkovsek, *VP*
EMP: 10 **EST:** 1965
SQ FT: 16,000
SALES (est): 1.3MM **Privately Held**
Web: www.angelprinting.com
SIC: 2752 Offset printing

(G-3361)
APEX ADVANCED TECHNOLOGIES LLC
4857 W 130th St A (44135-5137)
PHONE..................................216 898-1595

Dennis Hammond, *Managing Member*
▲ **EMP:** 6 **EST:** 2000
SQ FT: 12,000
SALES (est): 545.09K **Privately Held**
Web: www.apexadvancedtechnologies.com
SIC: 2899 Corrosion preventive lubricant

(G-3362)
APPROVED PLUMBING CO
Also Called: Approved Plbg & Sewer Clg Co
770 Ken Mar Industrial Pkwy (44147-2920)
PHONE..................................216 663-5063
Dennis Schlekie, *Pr*
EMP: 10 **EST:** 1940
SALES (est): 1.99MM **Privately Held**
Web: www.approvedplumbing.com
SIC: 1711 2434 Plumbing contractors; Wood kitchen cabinets

(G-3363)
ARC DRILLING INC (PA)
9551 Corporate Cir (44125-4261)
PHONE..................................216 525-0920
Jason Busse, *CEO*
Lee Trem, *Pr*
Kevin Trem, *VP*
Will Houghtaling, *CFO*
Will Houghtaling, *CFO*
EMP: 25 **EST:** 1947
SQ FT: 5,000
SALES (est): 5.15MM
SALES (corp-wide): 5.15MM **Privately Held**
Web: www.arcdrilling.com
SIC: 3599 Machine shop, jobbing and repair

(G-3364)
ARCHITECTURAL FIBERGLASS INC
8300 Bessemer Ave (44127-1839)
PHONE..................................216 641-8300
Michael Dobronos, *Pr*
Tanya Dobronos, *
▲ **EMP:** 30 **EST:** 1990
SQ FT: 20,000
SALES (est): 5.35MM **Privately Held**
Web: www.fiberglassafi.com
SIC: 2221 Glass and fiberglass broadwoven fabrics

(G-3365)
ARISDYNE SYSTEMS INC
17830 Englewood Dr Ste 11 (44130-3485)
PHONE..................................216 458-1991
Peter Reimers, *CEO*
Frederick W Clarke, *Ex VP*
Peter Reimers, *Pr*
Cheryl Petrencsik, *CFO*
Scott Incorvia, *COO*
EMP: 15 **EST:** 2006
SALES (est): 4.71MM **Privately Held**
Web: www.arisdyne.com
SIC: 3612 Saturable reactors

(G-3366)
ARMOUR SPRAY SYSTEMS INC
210 Hayes Dr Ste I (44131-1056)
PHONE..................................216 398-3838
Michael J Mihna Junior, *Pr*
Michael J Mihna Iii, *VP*
▲ **EMP:** 10 **EST:** 1976
SQ FT: 5,000
SALES (est): 3.99MM **Privately Held**
Web: www.armourspray.com
SIC: 5084 3563 Pumps and pumping equipment, nec; Spraying outfits: metals, paints, and chemicals (compressor)

(G-3367)
ARROW INTERNATIONAL INC (PA)
9900 Clinton Rd (44144-1097)
PHONE..................................216 961-3500
John E Gallagher, *CEO*
◆ **EMP:** 85 **EST:** 1965
SALES (est): 9.23MM
SALES (corp-wide): 9.23MM **Privately Held**
Web: www.arrowinternational.com
SIC: 3944 Board games, puzzles, and models, except electronic

(G-3368)
ART GALVANIZING WORKS INC
3935 Valley Rd (44109-3092)
PHONE..................................216 749-0020
James Klein, *Pr*
Adrienne Klein, *VP*
EMP: 9 **EST:** 1935
SQ FT: 9,775
SALES (est): 1.56MM **Privately Held**
Web: www.artgalvanizing.com
SIC: 3479 Coating of metals and formed products

(G-3369)
ARTISAN ALES LLC
17448 Lorain Ave (44111-4028)
PHONE..................................216 544-8703
Richard Skains, *Pr*
EMP: 9 **EST:** 2016
SALES (est): 381.8K **Privately Held**
SIC: 5813 2082 Drinking places; Beer (alcoholic beverage)

(G-3370)
ARTISAN CONSTRUCTORS LLC
Also Called: Artisan Renovations
600 Superior Ave E (44114-2614)
PHONE..................................216 800-7641
James Abrams, *Managing Member*
James Abrams, *Prin*
EMP: 25 **EST:** 2008
SALES (est): 1.52MM **Privately Held**
SIC: 1522 7299 1521 1389 Residential construction, nec; Home improvement and renovation contractor agency; Single-family home remodeling, additions, and repairs; Construction, repair, and dismantling services

(G-3371)
ARTISAN TOOL & DIE CORP
4911 Grant Ave (44125-1027)
PHONE..................................216 883-2769
James Berkes, *Pr*
David Dross, *
▼ **EMP:** 10 **EST:** 1968
SQ FT: 65,000
SALES (est): 888.59K **Privately Held**
Web: www.alacriant.com
SIC: 3469 3544 Metal stampings, nec; Special dies and tools

(G-3372)
ARTISTIC METAL SPINNING INC
Also Called: Zoia
4700 Lorain Ave (44102-3443)
PHONE..................................216 961-3336
Lorraine Hangauer, *Pr*
Donald E Hangauer, *Sec*
Ronald W Hangauer, *VP*
EMP: 6 **EST:** 1930
SQ FT: 12,000
SALES (est): 919.04K **Privately Held**
Web: www.artisticmetalspinning.com
SIC: 3469 Stamping metal for the trade

(G-3373)
ARZEL TECHNOLOGY INC
Also Called: Arzel Zoning Technology
4801 Commerce Pkwy (44128-5905)
PHONE..................................216 831-6068
Lenny Roth, *Sr VP*
Adam Bush, *
▼ **EMP:** 29 **EST:** 1983
SQ FT: 40,000
SALES (est): 2.44MM **Privately Held**
Web: www.arzelzoning.com
SIC: 3823 Process control instruments

(G-3374)
ASCO POWER TECHNOLOGIES LP
6255 Halle Dr (44125-4615)
PHONE..................................216 573-7600
Bob Daniels, *Genl Mgr*
EMP: 104
SALES (corp-wide): 1.09K **Privately Held**
Web: www.ascopower.com
SIC: 3613 3625 Switchgear and switchboard apparatus; Resistors and resistor units
HQ: Asco Power Technologies, L.P.
160 Park Ave
Florham Park NJ 07932

(G-3375)
ASCON TECNOLOGIC N AMER LLC
Also Called: Ascon Tecnologic
1111 Brookpark Rd (44109-5825)
PHONE..................................216 485-8350
Steven Craig, *Genl Mgr*
EMP: 6 **EST:** 2012
SALES (est): 627.94K **Privately Held**
Web: www.ascontecnologic.com
SIC: 3823 Process control instruments

(G-3376)
ASG
15700 S Waterloo Rd (44110-3814)
PHONE..................................216 486-6163
Bryon Schafer, *Mgr*
EMP: 10 **EST:** 2014
SALES (est): 1.27MM **Privately Held**
Web: www.asg-jergens.com
SIC: 3423 Hand and edge tools, nec

(G-3377)
ASG DIVISION JERGENS INC
15700 S Waterloo Rd Jergens Way (44110-3814)
PHONE..................................888 486-6163
EMP: 24 **EST:** 2015
SALES (est): 4.05MM **Privately Held**
Web: www.asg-jergens.com
SIC: 3423 3629 1731 Screw drivers, pliers, chisels, etc. (hand tools); Battery chargers, rectifying or nonrotating; Electric power systems contractors

(G-3378)
ASHLAND CHEMCO INC
Also Called: Ask Chemicals
2191 W 110th St (44102-3593)
PHONE..................................216 961-4690
EMP: 14
SALES (corp-wide): 2.11B **Publicly Held**
SIC: 2899 Chemical preparations, nec
HQ: Ashland Chemco Inc.
1979 Atlas St
Columbus OH 43228
859 815-3333

(G-3379)
ASHTA FORGE & MACHINE INC
3001 W 121st St (44111-1638)
PHONE..................................216 252-7000
Wayne Phelps, *Pr*
Karen Mason, *Sec*

EMP: 19 EST: 1992
SALES (est): 220.52K Privately Held
Web: www.bulaforge.com
SIC: 3599 Machine shop, jobbing and repair

(G-3380)
ASPRA INDUSTRIAL LLC
1311 Brookpark Rd (44109-5829)
PHONE...................................216 459-9200
EMP: 11 EST: 2021
SALES (est): 1.28MM Privately Held
Web: www.aspraind.com
SIC: 3541 Milling machines

(G-3381)
ASSEMBLY SPECIALTY PDTS INC
14700 Brookpark Rd (44135-5166)
PHONE...................................216 676-5600
Erno Nagy, Pr
Attila Nagy, VP
EMP: 22 EST: 1971
SQ FT: 33,500
SALES (est): 7.22MM Privately Held
Web: www.assemblyspecialty.com
SIC: 3496 Cable, uninsulated wire: made
from purchased wire

(G-3382)
AT HOLDINGS CORPORATION
23555 Euclid Ave (44117-1732)
PHONE...................................216 692-6000
Michael S Lipscomb, Ch Bd
Frances S St Clair, *
David Scaife, *
EMP: 736 EST: 1990
SQ FT: 1,800,000
SALES (est): 5.53MM Privately Held
SIC: 3724 3728 6512 Pumps, aircraft engine
; Aircraft parts and equipment, nec;
Commercial and industrial building
operation
HQ: Eaton Corporation
1000 Eaton Blvd
Cleveland OH 44122
440 523-5000

(G-3383)
AT&F ADVANCED METALS LLC (PA)
12314 Elmwood Ave (44111-5906)
PHONE...................................330 684-1122
▲ EMP: 23 EST: 2002
SQ FT: 15,000
SALES (est): 5.04MM
SALES (corp-wide): 5.04MM Privately
Held
Web: www.atfco.com
SIC: 3446 3443 Railings, prefabricated metal
; Process vessels, industrial: metal plate

(G-3384)
ATHENS FOODS INC
13600 Snow Rd (44142-2546)
PHONE...................................216 676-8500
Eric Moscahlaidis, Ch Bd
Robert Tansing, *
William Buckingham, Marketing*
Jeff Swint, *
Sandy Sanders, *
EMP: 180 EST: 1958
SQ FT: 114,000
SALES (est): 17.63MM Privately Held
Web: www.athensfoods.com
SIC: 2038 2045 Frozen specialties, nec;
Prepared flour mixes and doughs

(G-3385)
ATOTECH USA LLC
1000 Harvard Ave (44109-3048)
PHONE...................................216 398-0550
Steve Bellavita, Brnch Mgr
EMP: 11

SALES (corp-wide): 3.59B Publicly Held
Web: www.atotech.com
SIC: 2899 4225 Chemical supplies for
foundries; General warehousing and
storage
HQ: Atotech Usa, Llc
1750 Overview Dr
Rock Hill SC 29730

(G-3386)
AUSTIN POWDER COMPANY (DH)
25800 Science Park Dr Ste 300
(44122-7386)
PHONE...................................216 464-2400
William Jack Davis, Ch Bd
David M Gleason, *
Jason F Rawlings, *
Michael A Gleason, *
▲ EMP: 70 EST: 1833
SQ FT: 25,000
SALES (est): 270.59MM
SALES (corp-wide): 749.73MM Privately
Held
Web: www.austinpowder.com
SIC: 2892 Explosives
HQ: Austin Powder Holdings Company
25800 Scnce Pk Dr Ste 300
Cleveland OH 44122

(G-3387)
**AUSTIN POWDER HOLDINGS
COMPANY (HQ)**
25800 Science Park Dr Ste 300
(44122-7386)
PHONE...................................216 464-2400
William Jack Davis, Ch Bd
David M Gleason, *
Michael Gleason, *
◆ EMP: 60 EST: 1837
SQ FT: 25,000
SALES (est): 749.73MM
SALES (corp-wide): 749.73MM Privately
Held
Web: www.austinpowder.com
SIC: 2892 Explosives
PA: Davis Mining & Manufacturing, Inc.
5957 Windswept Blvd
Wise VA 24293
276 395-3354

(G-3388)
AUTO BOLT COMPANY
Also Called: Auto Bolt and Nut Company, The
4740 Manufacturing Ave (44135-2040)
PHONE...................................216 881-3913
Robert Kocian, Pr
EMP: 60 EST: 2005
SQ FT: 64,100
SALES (est): 9.81MM Privately Held
Web: www.autobolt.net
SIC: 3452 Bolts, metal

(G-3389)
AUTO-TAP INC
3317 W 140th St (44111-2428)
PHONE...................................216 671-1043
Jim Sullivan, Pr
Mike Peteras, Stockholder
Frank Suarez, Stockholder
EMP: 9 EST: 1972
SQ FT: 18,000
SALES (est): 1.09MM Privately Held
Web: www.auto-tap.net
SIC: 3559 Degreasing machines, automotive
and industrial

(G-3390)
AUTOMATIC STAMP PRODUCTS INC
6700 Thornapple Dr (44143-2317)
PHONE...................................216 781-7933
Raymond L Haserodt, VP

EMP: 7 EST: 1946
SALES (est): 1.63MM Privately Held
Web: www.automaticstamp.com
SIC: 3469 Stamping metal for the trade

(G-3391)
AVERY DENNISON CORPORATION
15939 Industrial Pkwy (44135-3321)
PHONE...................................216 267-8700
EMP: 7
SALES (corp-wide): 8.76B Publicly Held
Web: www.averydennison.com
SIC: 2672 Adhesive papers, labels, or tapes:
from purchased material
PA: Avery Dennison Corporation
8080 Norton Pkwy
Mentor OH 44060
440 534-6000

(G-3392)
AVILES CONSTRUCTION CO INC
7011 Clark Ave (44102-5316)
PHONE...................................216 939-1084
Jose Aviles, Pr
Elisa E Velez, Sec
Maria Aviles, Treas
Alex Aviles, VP
Jose E Aviles, Pr
EMP: 6 EST: 1983
SALES (est): 818.3K Privately Held
Web: www.avilesenergysolutions.com
SIC: 2821 Cellulose acetate (plastics)

(G-3393)
AVTRON AEROSPACE INC
7900 E Pleasant Valley Rd (44131-5529)
PHONE...................................216 750-5152
John Pesec, Pr
Joseph Flower, *
EMP: 117 EST: 1953
SQ FT: 65,000
SALES (est): 24.8MM Privately Held
Web: www.testek.com
SIC: 3351 3728 Bars and bar shapes,
copper and copper alloy; Aircraft parts and
equipment, nec

(G-3394)
AVTRON HOLDINGS LLC
7900 E Pleasant Valley Rd (44131-5529)
PHONE...................................216 642-1230
James Ettamarna, *
Theodore A Laufik, *
Peter Taft, *
Karen Tuleta, *
EMP: 40 EST: 2007
SQ FT: 47,707
SALES (est): 1.28MM Privately Held
Web: www.testek.com
SIC: 3625 3825 Electric controls and control
accessories, industrial; Instruments to
measure electricity

(G-3395)
AVTRON LOADBANK INC
6255 Halle Dr (44125-4615)
P.O. Box 4100 (63136-8506)
PHONE...................................216 573-7600
EMP: 109
SIC: 3613 3625 Switchgear and switchboard
apparatus; Resistors and resistor units

(G-3396)
AW FABER-CASTELL USA INC
Also Called: Creativity For Kids
9000 Rio Nero Dr (44125)
PHONE...................................216 643-4660
Scott Flynn, CEO
Don Fischer, *
Phyllis Brody, *
▲ EMP: 79 EST: 1996

SALES (est): 46.1MM
SALES (corp-wide): 671.09MM Privately
Held
Web: www.fabercastell.com
SIC: 5092 5112 3944 Arts and crafts
equipment and supplies; Stationery and
office supplies; Games, toys, and children's
vehicles
HQ: Faber-Castell Ag
Nurnberger Str. 2
Stein BY 90547
91199650

(G-3397)
AWNING FABRI CATERS INC
10237 Lorain Ave (44111-5435)
P.O. Box 182 (44012-0182)
PHONE...................................216 476-4888
TOLL FREE: 800
Todd Krupa, Pr
EMP: 7 EST: 1987
SALES (est): 421.87K Privately Held
Web:
awning-and-canopy-dealers.cmac.ws
SIC: 2394 Awnings, fabric: made from
purchased materials

(G-3398)
B & P SPRING PROD CO INC
19520 Nottingham Rd (44110-2730)
PHONE...................................216 486-4260
Ken Godnavec, Pr
Lorraine Ray, Sec
EMP: 10 EST: 1952
SQ FT: 13,000
SALES (est): 982.84K Privately Held
Web: www.bpspring.com
SIC: 3495 Precision springs

(G-3399)
B & R MACHINE CO
2216 W 65th St (44102-5302)
PHONE...................................216 961-7370
William E Graham, Pr
Teala Graham, Sec
EMP: 18 EST: 1958
SQ FT: 12,000
SALES (est): 4.83MM Privately Held
Web: www.brmachineco.com
SIC: 3545 3599 Machine tool accessories;
Machine shop, jobbing and repair

(G-3400)
B&A ISON STEEL INC
Also Called: Buckeye Metals Industries
3238 E 82nd St (44104-4338)
P.O. Box 31528 (44131-0528)
PHONE...................................216 663-4300
Bruce Ison, Pr
EMP: 10 EST: 1997
SQ FT: 45,000
SALES (est): 4.92MM
SALES (corp-wide): 21.6MM Privately
Held
Web: www.buckeye-metals.com
SIC: 3469 5051 Metal stampings, nec; Steel
PA: Paragon Steel Enterprises, Llc
4211 County Road 61
Butler IN 46721
260 868-1100

(G-3401)
B-R-O-T INCORPORATED
4730 Briar Rd (44135-2595)
PHONE...................................216 267-5335
Kenneth Ott, Pr
Patricia Ott, *
Robert Ott, *
▲ EMP: 25 EST: 1946
SQ FT: 22,000
SALES (est): 6.54MM Privately Held

Web: www.brot-inc.com
SIC: **3444** 2542 Sheet metalwork; Partitions
and fixtures, except wood

(G-3402)
B2D SOLUTIONS INC
Also Called: Ballastshop
3558 Lee Rd (44120-5123)
PHONE..............................855 484-1145
John Mahoney, *Pr*
EMP: 7 **EST:** 2000
SALES (est): 1.14MM **Privately Held**
Web: www.ballastshop.com
SIC: **5063** 3648 Lighting fixtures; Decorative
area lighting fixtures

(G-3403)
BAR 25 LLC (PA)
Also Called: Market Garden Brewery
1939 W 25th St (44113-3474)
PHONE..............................216 621-4000
EMP: 6 **EST:** 2004
SQ FT: 35,000
SALES (est): 3.17MM
SALES (corp-wide): 3.17MM **Privately
Held**
Web: www.marketgardenbrewery.com
SIC: **5813** 2082 Beer garden (drinking
places); Beer (alcoholic beverage)

(G-3404)
BAR 25 LLC
Also Called: Market Garden Brewery
1849 W 24th St (44113-3513)
PHONE..............................216 373-3700
EMP: 45
SALES (corp-wide): 3.17MM **Privately
Held**
SIC: **2082** Beer (alcoholic beverage)
PA: Bar 25, Llc
1939 W 25th St
Cleveland OH 44113
216 621-4000

(G-3405)
BARBS GRAFFITI INC (PA)
Also Called: Graffiti Co
3111 Carnegie Ave (44115-2632)
PHONE..............................216 881-5550
Abe Miller, *Pr*
Barbara Miller, *
▲ **EMP:** 38 **EST:** 1984
SQ FT: 18,000
SALES (est): 1.63MM
SALES (corp-wide): 1.63MM **Privately
Held**
Web: www.graffiticaps.com
SIC: **2353** 2395 5136 5137 Baseball caps;
Pleating and stitching; Sportswear, men's
and boys'; Sportswear, women's and
children's

(G-3406)
BARKER PRODUCTS COMPANY
1028 E 134th St (44110-2248)
P.O. Box 10845 (44110-0845)
▲ **EMP:** 30 **EST:** 1945
SALES (est): 515.69K **Privately Held**
Web: www.barkerplating.com
SIC: **3471** Electroplating of metals or formed
products

(G-3407)
BARTH INDUSTRIES CO LLC (PA)
Also Called: Landis Machine Division
12650 Brookpark Rd (44130-1154)
PHONE..............................216 267-1950
Richard Legan, *Pr*
Russ Lauer, *
▲ **EMP:** 27 **EST:** 2006
SQ FT: 120,700

SALES (est): 6MM
SALES (corp-wide): 6MM **Privately Held**
Web: www.barthindustries.com
SIC: **3541** 3542 3535 3699 Machine tools,
metal cutting type; Machine tools, metal
forming type; Conveyors and conveying
equipment; Electrical equipment and
supplies, nec

(G-3408)
BASF CATALYSTS LLC
Also Called: BASF
23800 Mercantile Rd (44122-5908)
P.O. Box 22126 (44122-0126)
PHONE..............................216 360-5005
John Ferek, *Brnch Mgr*
EMP: 830
SALES (corp-wide): 69.01B **Privately Held**
Web: catalysts.basf.com
SIC: **2819** 8731 Catalysts, chemical;
Commercial physical research
HQ: Basf Catalysts Llc
33 Wood Ave
Iselin NJ 08830
732 205-5000

(G-3409)
BASIC CASES INC
19561 Miles Rd (44128-4111)
PHONE..............................216 662-3900
Kenneth Wieder, *Pr*
Ruth Wieder, *VP*
EMP: 8 **EST:** 1980
SQ FT: 22,000
SALES (est): 304.98K **Privately Held**
Web: www.basiccases.com
SIC: **2511** 2521 Wood household furniture;
Wood office furniture

(G-3410)
BD LAPLACE LLC (PA)
Also Called: Bayou Steel Group
28026 Gates Mills Blvd (44124-4730)
PHONE..............................985 652-4900
Robert Simon, *CEO*
Alton Davis, *
◆ **EMP:** 410 **EST:** 1979
SALES (est): 3.06MM
SALES (corp-wide): 3.06MM **Privately
Held**
Web: www.stjohnig.com
SIC: **3312** Structural and rail mill products

(G-3411)
BEA-ECC APPARELS INC
1287 W 76th St (44102-2050)
PHONE..............................216 650-6336
Siba Beavogui, *Prin*
EMP: 8 **EST:** 2002
SALES (est): 195.71K **Privately Held**
SIC: **2311** Men's and boy's suits and coats

(G-3412)
BEACON METAL FABRICATORS INC
5425 Hamilton Ave Ste D (44114-3983)
PHONE..............................216 391-7444
Kenneth Grobolsek, *Pr*
Robert Groboissek, *VP*
EMP: 6 **EST:** 1987
SQ FT: 11,000
SALES (est): 1.01MM **Privately Held**
Web: www.beaconmetalfab.com
SIC: **3599** 3444 3446 Machine and other job
shop work; Bins, prefabricated sheet metal;
Railings, prefabricated metal

(G-3413)
BECKETT-GREENHILL LLC
Also Called: Colony Hardware
1800 E 30th St (44114-4410)
PHONE..............................216 861-5730

EMP: 15 **EST:** 2007
SQ FT: 40,000
SALES (est): 2.6MM **Privately Held**
Web: www.colonyhardware.com
SIC: **3965** Fasteners

(G-3414)
BELLAS JEWELS LLC
975 Parkwood Dr Apt 10ste1 (44108-3052)
PHONE..............................216 551-9593
Tyreka Williams, *Managing Member*
EMP: 8 **EST:** 2021
SALES (est): 136.59K **Privately Held**
SIC: **3961** Jewelry apparel, non-precious
metals

(G-3415)
BERGSTROM COMPANY LTD PARTNR
Also Called: Weldon Pump
640 Golden Oak Pkwy (44146-6504)
PHONE..............................440 232-2282
Tony Coletto, *CEO*
Blane Mckelvey, *Genl Pt*
Walter T Bergstrom, *Pt*
Jon Bergstrom, *Pt*
Barbara Bergstrom, *Pt*
EMP: 18 **EST:** 1918
SQ FT: 13,600
SALES (est): 3.33MM **Privately Held**
Web: www.weldonpumps.com
SIC: **3714** 3594 3586 3561 Fuel pumps,
motor vehicle; Fluid power pumps and
motors; Measuring and dispensing pumps;
Pumps and pumping equipment

(G-3416)
BERKSHIRE ROAD HOLDINGS INC
3344 E 80th St (44127-1851)
PHONE..............................216 883-4200
James Lamantia, *Pr*
Jay E Irvin, *Ex VP*
EMP: 18 **EST:** 1958
SQ FT: 60,000
SALES (est): 2.46MM **Privately Held**
Web: www.genstlcorp.com
SIC: **5051** 3398 3441 Steel; Metal heat
treating; Fabricated structural metal

(G-3417)
BEVERAGE MCH & FABRICATORS INC
13301 Lakewood Heights Blvd
(44107-6219)
PHONE..............................216 252-5100
John D Geiger, *Pr*
Nancy Geiger, *Sec*
EMP: 15 **EST:** 1932
SQ FT: 15,000
SALES (est): 697.81K **Privately Held**
Web: www.bevmachine.com
SIC: **3599** Machine shop, jobbing and repair

(G-3418)
BIG GUS ONION RINGS INC
4500 Turney Rd (44105-6716)
PHONE..............................216 883-9045
Peter George, *Pr*
Thomas George, *VP*
Angela George, *Sec*
EMP: 9 **EST:** 1968
SQ FT: 5,000
SALES (est): 916.89K **Privately Held**
Web: www.biggusonionrings.com
SIC: **2037** 5148 2099 Vegetables, quick
frozen & cold pack, excl. potato products;
Fruits, fresh; Food preparations, nec

(G-3419)
BIZALL INC
Also Called: Promote-U-Graphics
1935 W 96th St Ste H (44102-2600)
PHONE..............................216 939-9580
Brent White, *Pr*
Tyrone White, *VP*
EMP: 7 **EST:** 1992
SQ FT: 15,000
SALES (est): 138.14K **Privately Held**
SIC: **5734** 2759 Printers and plotters:
computers; Commercial printing, nec

(G-3420)
BLACK & DECKER CORPORATION
Also Called: Black & Decker
12100 Snow Rd Ste 1 (44130-9319)
PHONE..............................440 842-9100
Mark Konecek, *Brnch Mgr*
EMP: 7
SALES (corp-wide): 15.37B **Publicly Held**
Web: www.blackanddecker.com
SIC: **3546** Power-driven handtools
HQ: The Black & Decker Corporation
701 E Joppa Rd
Towson MD 21286
410 716-3900

(G-3421)
BLAINS FOLDING SERVICE INC
4103 Detroit Ave (44113-2721)
PHONE..............................216 631-4700
Edward Blain, *Pr*
Carol Blain, *Sec*
EMP: 7 **EST:** 1967
SALES (est): 505.33K **Privately Held**
SIC: **2789** Binding only: books, pamphlets,
magazines, etc.

(G-3422)
BLASTER HOLDINGS LLC (PA)
Also Called: Gunk
8500 Sweet Valley Dr (44125-4214)
PHONE..............................216 901-5800
Randy Pindor, *Pr*
EMP: 45 **EST:** 2020
SALES (est): 14.97MM
SALES (corp-wide): 14.97MM **Privately
Held**
Web: www.blasterholdings.com
SIC: **2911** 2819 2842 Fuel additives;
Catalysts, chemical; Automobile polish

(G-3423)
BLASTER LLC (PA)
8500 Sweet Valley Dr (44125-4214)
PHONE..............................216 901-5800
Randy Pindor, *Pr*
EMP: 39 **EST:** 1959
SQ FT: 20,000
SALES (est): 32.62MM
SALES (corp-wide): 32.62MM **Privately
Held**
Web: www.blasterproducts.com
SIC: **2911** 2819 2842 2992 Fuel additives;
Catalysts, chemical; Automobile polish;
Lubricating oils and greases

(G-3424)
BOARD OF PARK COMMISSIONERS
4101 Fulton Pkwy (44144-1923)
PHONE..............................216 635-3200
Dan T Moore, *Prin*
EMP: 7 **EST:** 2005
SALES (est): 678.61K **Privately Held**
Web: www.clevelandmetroparks.com
SIC: **3949** Shafts, golf club

▲ = Import ▼ = Export
◆ = Import/Export

(G-3425)
BODYCOTE THERMAL PROC INC
5475 Avion Park Dr (44143-1918)
PHONE..............................440 473-2020
Ron Perkins, *Brnch Mgr*
EMP: 42
SALES (corp-wide): 959.76MM **Privately Held**
Web: www.bodycote.com
SIC: 3398 Metal heat treating
HQ: Bodycote Thermal Processing, Inc.
12750 Merit Dr Ste 1400
Dallas TX 75251
214 904-2420

(G-3426)
BOMEN MARKING PRODUCTS INC
12905 York Delta Dr Ste A (44133-3551)
PHONE..............................440 582-0053
Joseph Mendyka, *Pr*
EMP: 9 EST: 1987
SQ FT: 3,800
SALES (est): 363.47K **Privately Held**
Web: www.bomenmarking.com
SIC: 2796 3599 Steel line engraving, for the printing trade; Custom machinery

(G-3427)
BONFOEY CO
1710 Euclid Ave (44115-2134)
PHONE..............................216 621-0178
Richard G Moore, *Pr*
Mina V Moore, *Sec*
Olga Merela, *Treas*
EMP: 15 EST: 1893
SQ FT: 9,300
SALES (est): 2.42MM **Privately Held**
Web: www.bonfoey.com
SIC: 2499 5719 8999 Picture and mirror frames, wood; Pictures, wall; Art restoration

(G-3428)
BORDEN DAIRY CO CINCINNATI LLC (DH)
Also Called: H. Meyer Dairy
3068 W 106th St (44111-1801)
PHONE..............................513 948-8811
EMP: 27 EST: 1976
SALES (est): 4.9MM **Privately Held**
Web: www.bordendairy.com
SIC: 2026 2086 5143 5144 Milk processing (pasteurizing, homogenizing, bottling); Bottled and canned soft drinks; Dairy products, except dried or canned; Poultry and poultry products
HQ: National Dairy, Llc
8750 N Central Expy # 400
Dallas TX 75231
214 459-1100

(G-3429)
BORMAN ENTERPRISES INC
Also Called: Cleveland Indus Training Ctr
1311 Brookpark Rd (44109-5829)
PHONE..............................216 459-9292
Donald Borman, *Pr*
Marybeth Borman, *Sec*
Joseph Scheall, *VP*
EMP: 10 EST: 1975
SQ FT: 13,000
SALES (est): 842.86K **Privately Held**
Web: www.aspratechcenter.com
SIC: 3599 8222 Machine shop, jobbing and repair; Technical institute

(G-3430)
BOXIT CORPORATION
3000 Quigley Rd B (44113-4591)
PHONE..............................216 416-9475
Mark Cassese, *Prin*
EMP: 40

(G-3431)
BOXIT CORPORATION (HQ)
5555 Walworth Ave (44102-4430)
PHONE..............................216 631-6900
Joel Zaas, *Pr*
Carole Holowecky, *
Donald Zaas, *
Mark Cassese, *
EMP: 12 EST: 1971
SQ FT: 100,000
SALES (est): 8.63MM
SALES (corp-wide): 23.79MM **Privately Held**
Web: www.boxit.com
SIC: 2652 2657 Setup paperboard boxes; Folding paperboard boxes
PA: The Apex Paper Box Company
5601 Walworth Ave
Cleveland OH 44102
216 631-4000

(G-3432)
BRAKE PARTS HOLDINGS INC (DH)
127 Public Sq Ste 5110 (44114-1313)
PHONE..............................216 589-0198
EMP: 500 EST: 2020
SALES (est): 413.59MM
SALES (corp-wide): 7.28B **Privately Held**
SIC: 6719 3544 3089 Investment holding companies, except banks; Special dies, tools, jigs, and fixtures; Injection molded finished plastics products, nec
HQ: First Brands Group, Llc
127 Public Sq Ste 5300
Cleveland OH 44114
888 565-9632

(G-3433)
BRAKE PARTS INC CHINA LLC (DH)
127 Public Sq Ste 5110 (44114-1313)
PHONE..............................216 589-0198
EMP: 6
SALES (est): 20.25MM
SALES (corp-wide): 7.28B **Privately Held**
SIC: 3714 Motor vehicle brake systems and parts
HQ: Bpi Holdings International, Inc.
4400 Prime Pkwy
Mchenry IL 60050
815 363-9000

(G-3434)
BRANTLEY PARTNERS IV LP
3550 Lander Rd Ste 160 (44124-5727)
PHONE..............................216 464-8400
Robert Pinkas, *Ch*
Michael J Finn, *Pr*
Tab A Keplinger, *VP*
EMP: 8 EST: 2000
SALES (est): 232.83K **Privately Held**
Web: www.brantleypartners.com
SIC: 6799 5141 2066 2099 Investors, nec; Groceries, general line; Chocolate and cocoa products; Food preparations, nec

(G-3435)
BREINING MECH SYSTEMS INC (PA)
883 Addison Rd (44103-1607)
PHONE..............................216 391-2400
John Sickle Junior, *Pr*
EMP: 8 EST: 1947
SALES (est): 734.2K
SALES (corp-wide): 734.2K **Privately Held**
Web: www.breiningmechanicalsystems.com
SIC: 3444 Sheet metalwork

(G-3436)
BRIDGESTONE RET OPERATIONS LLC
Also Called: Firestone
6874 Pearl Rd (44130-3615)
PHONE..............................440 842-3200
Sunil Rebello, *Mgr*
EMP: 8
Web: www.bridgestoneamericas.com
SIC: 5531 7534 Automotive tires; Tire repair shop
HQ: Bridgestone Retail Operations, Llc
200 4th Ave S Ste 100
Nashville TN 37201
615 937-1000

(G-3437)
BRIDGESTONE RET OPERATIONS LLC
Also Called: Firestone
5117 Wilson Mills Rd (44143-3005)
PHONE..............................440 461-4747
Zach Grashik, *Mgr*
EMP: 6
Web: www.firestonecompleteautocare.com
SIC: 5531 7534 Automotive tires; Rebuilding and retreading tires
HQ: Bridgestone Retail Operations, Llc
200 4th Ave S Ste 100
Nashville TN 37201
615 937-1000

(G-3438)
BRIDGESTONE RET OPERATIONS LLC
Also Called: Firestone
12420 Cedar Rd (44106-3129)
PHONE..............................216 229-2550
Adam Coyle, *Mgr*
EMP: 8
SQ FT: 8,366
Web: www.firestonecompleteautocare.com
SIC: 5531 7534 Automotive tires; Rebuilding and retreading tires
HQ: Bridgestone Retail Operations, Llc
200 4th Ave S Ste 100
Nashville TN 37201
615 937-1000

(G-3439)
BRIDGESTONE RET OPERATIONS LLC
Also Called: Firestone
700 Richmond Rd (44143-2918)
PHONE..............................216 382-8970
Stephen Park, *Mgr*
EMP: 7
SQ FT: 10,010
Web: www.firestonecompleteautocare.com
SIC: 5531 7534 Automotive tires; Rebuilding and retreading tires
HQ: Bridgestone Retail Operations, Llc
200 4th Ave S Ste 100
Nashville TN 37201
615 937-1000

(G-3440)
BRITTANY STAMPING LLC
50 Public Sq Ste 4000 (44113-2243)
PHONE..............................216 267-0850
Frederick W Clarke, *CEO*
Charles P Bolton, *
Forrest D Hayes, *Vice Chairman**
Jerome R Gratry, *
Janet M Tilton, *
EMP: 1300 EST: 1978
SQ FT: 8,000
SALES (est): 1.35MM **Privately Held**
SIC: 3469 3321 3089 3269 Metal stampings, nec; Gray iron castings, nec; Thermoformed finished plastics products, nec; Stoneware pottery products

(G-3441)
BROCO PRODUCTS INC
8510 Bessemer Ave (44127-1843)
PHONE..............................216 531-0880
Barry Brown, *Pr*
Joyce Brown, *VP*
EMP: 9 EST: 1968
SALES (est): 2.28MM **Privately Held**
Web: www.brocoproducts.com
SIC: 3559 2899 Metal finishing equipment for plating, etc.; Metal treating compounds

(G-3442)
BROOKLYN MACHINE & MFG CO INC
5180 Grant Ave (44125-1065)
PHONE..............................216 341-1846
Walter Spann, *Pr*
Frederick Spann, *Sec*
EMP: 7 EST: 1923
SQ FT: 8,500
SALES (est): 2.22MM **Privately Held**
Web: www.brooklynmachinemfg.com
SIC: 3599 Machine shop, jobbing and repair

(G-3443)
BROST FOUNDRY COMPANY (PA)
2934 E 55th St (44127-1207)
PHONE..............................216 641-1131
Tom Peretti, *Pr*
EMP: 28 EST: 1910
SQ FT: 45,000
SALES (est): 3.88MM
SALES (corp-wide): 3.88MM **Privately Held**
Web: www.brostfoundry.com
SIC: 3366 3365 3369 3325 Castings (except die), nec, bronze; Aluminum and aluminum-based alloy castings; Nonferrous foundries, nec; Steel foundries, nec

(G-3444)
BROTHERS PRINTING CO INC
2000 Euclid Ave (44115-2276)
PHONE..............................216 621-6050
Dotty Kaufman, *CEO*
Jay Kaufman, *Pr*
David Kaufman, *Treas*
EMP: 9 EST: 1925
SQ FT: 36,000
SALES (est): 917.98K **Privately Held**
Web: www.brosprintcle.com
SIC: 2752 2759 Offset printing; Letterpress printing

(G-3445)
BRUENING GLASS WORKS INC
Also Called: Konys, Mark Glass Design
20157 Lake Rd (44116-1514)
PHONE..............................440 333-4768
Marc Konys, *Pr*
Chris Konys, *VP*
EMP: 6 EST: 1945
SQ FT: 1,500
SALES (est): 447.47K **Privately Held**
Web: www.brueningglass.com
SIC: 3231 5719 5712 Mirrored glass; Mirrors ; Furniture stores

(G-3446)
BRUSHES INC
5400 Smith Rd (44142-2025)
PHONE..............................216 267-8084
Mary Drews, *Pr*

EMP: 8 **EST:** 1958
SQ FT: 9,600
SALES (est): 499.12K **Privately Held**
Web: www.malinco.com
SIC: 3991 Brushes, household or industrial

(G-3447)
BRUSHES INC
Also Called: Malin Company
5400 Smith Rd (44142-2025)
PHONE...............................216 267-8084
▲ **EMP:** 18
SALES (est): 4.14MM **Privately Held**
Web: www.malinco.com
SIC: 3496 Miscellaneous fabricated wire products

(G-3448)
BUCKINGHAM SRC INC
Also Called: SRC Worldwide
3425 Service Rd (44111-2421)
PHONE...............................216 941-6115
◆ **EMP:** 10
SIC: 2899 Fluxes: brazing, soldering, galvanizing, and welding

(G-3449)
BUD MAY INC
Also Called: Maynard Company, The
16850 Hummel Rd (44142-2131)
PHONE...............................216 676-8850
John Maynard, *Pr*
Tom Maynard, *VP*
Joan Santoro, *Mgr*
EMP: 10 **EST:** 1974
SQ FT: 18,000
SALES (est): 505.67K **Privately Held**
SIC: 3541 Grinding, polishing, buffing, lapping, and honing machines

(G-3450)
BUFFEX METAL FINISHING INC
1935 W 96th St Ste L (44102-2600)
PHONE...............................216 631-2202
Orlando Joe R Quintana, *Pr*
Louis Quintana, *VP*
EMP: 6 **EST:** 1987
SQ FT: 10,000
SALES (est): 727.33K **Privately Held**
Web: www.buffex.net
SIC: 3471 Electroplating of metals or formed products

(G-3451)
BULA FORGE & MACHINE INC (PA)
Also Called: Bula Defense Systems
3001 W 121st St (44111-1638)
PHONE...............................216 252-7600
Wayne Phelps, *Pr*
Karen Mason, *VP*
EMP: 17 **EST:** 1973
SALES (est): 4.92MM
SALES (corp-wide): 4.92MM **Privately Held**
Web: www.bulaforge.com
SIC: 3462 Iron and steel forgings

(G-3452)
BULA FORGE MACHINE
12117 Berea Rd Ste 1 (44111-1600)
PHONE...............................216 252-7600
EMP: 8 **EST:** 2020
SALES (est): 7.45MM **Privately Held**
Web: www.bulaforge.com
SIC: 3599 Machine shop, jobbing and repair

(G-3453)
BUSCHMAN CORPORATION
4100 Payne Ave Ste 1 (44103-2340)
PHONE...............................216 431-6633

Tom Buschman, *CEO*
Ross Defelice, *Pr*
▲ **EMP:** 19 **EST:** 1977
SQ FT: 90,000
SALES (est): 3.72MM **Privately Held**
Web: www.buschman.com
SIC: 3312 2679 2295 Rods, iron and steel: made in steel mills; Paper products, converted, nec; Tape, varnished: plastic, and other coated (except magnetic)

(G-3454)
BUSH INC
15901 Industrial Pkwy (44135-3321)
PHONE...............................216 362-6700
H Russell Bush, *Pr*
EMP: 6 **EST:** 1999
SALES (est): 348.17K **Privately Held**
SIC: 2752 Offset printing

(G-3455)
BWXT NCLEAR OPRTIONS GROUP INC
24703 Euclid Ave (44117-1714)
PHONE...............................216 912-3000
Mary Salomone, *Brnch Mgr*
EMP: 1842
Web: www.bwxt.com
SIC: 3443 Fabricated plate work (boiler shop)
HQ: Bwxt Nuclear Operations Group, Inc.
2016 Mount Athos Rd
Lynchburg VA 24504

(G-3456)
BYG INDUSTRIES INC
Also Called: Guerin-Zimmerman Co
8003 Clinton Rd (44144-1004)
PHONE...............................216 961-5436
James R Brasty, *Pr*
John Brasty Senior, *VP*
EMP: 6 **EST:** 1934
SQ FT: 10,000
SALES (est): 974.12K **Privately Held**
Web: www.stressandpainclinic.com
SIC: 3444 3599 Sheet metalwork; Machine shop, jobbing and repair

(G-3457)
C A LITZLER CO INC
4800 W 160th St (44135-2689)
PHONE...............................216 267-8020
Matthew C Litzler, *Pr*
J H Rogers, *
P S Sprague, *
William J Urban, *
Julia Mayer, *
▲ **EMP:** 42 **EST:** 1953
SQ FT: 32,000
SALES (est): 1.56MM
SALES (corp-wide): 25.05MM **Privately Held**
Web: www.calitzler.com
SIC: 3567 3535 3552 3549 Industrial furnaces and ovens; Conveyors and conveying equipment; Textile machinery; Metalworking machinery, nec
PA: C.A. Litzler Holding Company
4800 W 160th St
Cleveland OH 44135
216 267-8020

(G-3458)
CA LITZLER HOLDING COMPANY (PA)
4800 W 160th St (44135-2634)
PHONE...............................216 267-8020
Matthew C Litzler, *CEO*
William J Urban, *
Juila L Mayer, *
▲ **EMP:** 59 **EST:** 1999
SALES (est): 25.05MM

SALES (corp-wide): 25.05MM **Privately Held**
Web: www.calitzler.com
SIC: 3567 Industrial furnaces and ovens

(G-3459)
CAILIN DEVELOPMENT LLC
896 E 70th St (44103-1706)
PHONE...............................216 408-6261
Louis Finucane, *Managing Member*
EMP: 10 **EST:** 1996
SALES (est): 930.61K **Privately Held**
Web: www.cailindev.com
SIC: 3523 3532 3965 3462 Farm machinery and equipment; Mining machinery; Straight pins: steel or brass; Iron and steel forgings

(G-3460)
CAKE HOUSE CLEVELAND LLC
1536 Saint Clair Ave Ne Ste 65 (44114-2004)
PHONE...............................216 870-4659
EMP: 10 **EST:** 2019
SALES (est): 929.32K **Privately Held**
SIC: 2051 Cakes, bakery: except frozen

(G-3461)
CAM-LEM INC
1768 E 25th St (44114-4418)
PHONE...............................216 391-7750
Brian Mathewson, *CEO*
Terrell Pin, *COO*
EMP: 9 **EST:** 1993
SQ FT: 1,100
SALES (est): 466.87K **Privately Held**
Web: www.camlem.com
SIC: 3559 3544 3264 Robots, molding and forming plastics; Special dies, tools, jigs, and fixtures; Porcelain electrical supplies

(G-3462)
CANARY HEALTH TECHNOLOGIES INC
5005 Rockside Rd Ste 600 (44131-6827)
PHONE...............................617 784-4021
Raj Reddy, *Pr*
EMP: 10 **EST:** 2018
SALES (est): 10MM **Privately Held**
SIC: 3845 Ultrasonic scanning devices, medical

(G-3463)
CANSTO COATINGS LTD
9320 Woodland Ave (44104-2410)
P.O. Box 241303 (44124-8303)
PHONE...............................216 231-6115
Sam P Cannata, *Mng Pt*
EMP: 10 **EST:** 2010
SALES (est): 317.38K **Privately Held**
Web: www.cansto.com
SIC: 2851 Paints and allied products

(G-3464)
CANSTO PAINT AND VARNISH CO
9320 Woodland Ave (44104-2489)
EMP: 7 **EST:** 1932
SQ FT: 18,000
SALES (est): 370.49K **Privately Held**
SIC: 2851 Paints and paint additives

(G-3465)
CANVAS SPECIALTY MFG CO
4045 Saint Clair Ave (44103-1117)
PHONE...............................216 881-0647
Carl E Heilman, *Pr*
EMP: 7 **EST:** 1930
SQ FT: 8,500
SALES (est): 443.93K **Privately Held**
Web: www.canvasspecialty.com

SIC: 2394 7699 Awnings, fabric: made from purchased materials; Nautical repair services

(G-3466)
CAPCO AUTOMOTIVE PRODUCTS CORP
1111 Superior Ave Eaton Ctr (44114-2522)
PHONE...............................216 523-5000
Francisco E Bertolaccina, *Ch Bd*
Cal E Cheesbrough, *Sec*
Jose Roberto Morato, *VP*
EMP: 2300 **EST:** 1959
SQ FT: 226,270
SALES (est): 76.6MM **Privately Held**
SIC: 3714 Transmissions, motor vehicle
HQ: Eaton Corporation
1000 Eaton Blvd
Cleveland OH 44122
440 523-5000

(G-3467)
CAPITAL TOOL COMPANY
1110 Brookpark Rd (44109-5871)
PHONE...............................216 661-5750
Richard Crane, *Pr*
EMP: 45 **EST:** 1962
SQ FT: 20,000
SALES (est): 1.49MM **Privately Held**
Web: www.capitaltoolco.com
SIC: 3544 3545 3443 Special dies and tools; Machine tool accessories; Fabricated plate work (boiler shop)

(G-3468)
CARAUSTAR INDUSTRIES INC
Also Called: Cleveland Digital Imaging Svcs
7960 Lorain Ave (44102-4256)
PHONE...............................216 939-3001
Petrelli Tony, *VP*
EMP: 19
SALES (corp-wide): 5.45B **Publicly Held**
Web: www.greif.com
SIC: 2631 Paperboard mills
HQ: Caraustar Industries, Inc.
5000 Astell Pwdr Sprng Rd
Austell GA 30106
770 948-3101

(G-3469)
CARAVAN PACKAGING INC (PA)
6427 Eastland Rd (44142-1305)
PHONE...............................440 243-4100
Fred Hitti, *Pr*
Chris Pisanelli, *VP*
Sue Hitti, *Treas*
▲ **EMP:** 9 **EST:** 1962
SQ FT: 40,000
SALES (est): 2.22MM
SALES (corp-wide): 2.22MM **Privately Held**
Web: www.caravanpackaging.com
SIC: 4783 2441 6512 Packing goods for shipping; Nailed wood boxes and shook; Commercial and industrial building operation

(G-3470)
CARGILL INCORPORATED
Also Called: Cargill
2400 Ships Channel (44113-2673)
P.O. Box 6920 (44101-1920)
PHONE...............................216 651-7200
Bob Soupko, *Brnch Mgr*
EMP: 205
SALES (corp-wide): 159.59B **Privately Held**
Web: www.cargill.com
SIC: 2048 2899 Prepared feeds, nec; Chemical preparations, nec
PA: Cargill, Incorporated

▲ = Import ▼ = Export
◆ = Import/Export

15407 Mcginty Rd W
Wayzata MN 55391
800 227-4455

(G-3471)
CARR BROS BLDRS SUP & COAL CO
7177 Northfield Rd (44146-5403)
PHONE......................440 232-3700
Floyd E Carr Junior, *Pr*
Duane Carr, *
Michael Carr, *
Amy Rickleman, *
EMP: 35 EST: 1892
SQ FT: 3,000
SALES (est): 336.5K **Privately Held**
Web: www.carrbros.net
SIC: 3273 Ready-mixed concrete

(G-3472)
CARRERA HOLDINGS INC
101 W Prospect Ave (44115-1093)
PHONE......................216 687-1311
James B Mooney, *Prin*
EMP: 6 EST: 1999
SALES (est): 1.56MM **Privately Held**
SIC: 2329 2339 Knickers, dress (separate):
men's and boys'; Aprons, except rubber or
plastic: women's, misses', juniors'
HQ: Carrera Spa
Via Sant'irene 1
Caldiero VR 37042
045 232-0506

(G-3473)
CARTER CARBURETOR LLC ✪
127 Public Sq Ste 5300 (44114-1219)
PHONE......................216 314-2711
Shekhar Kumar, *
EMP: 1600 EST: 2023
SALES (est): 130MM
SALES (corp-wide): 7.28B **Privately Held**
SIC: 3621 Motors and generators
HQ: Carter Carburetor Holdings, Llc
127 Public Sq Ste 5300
Cleveland OH 44114
216 906-2744

(G-3474)
CASE OHIO BURIAL CO (PA)
1720 Columbus Rd (44113-2410)
P.O. Box 26020 (44126-0020)
PHONE......................440 779-1992
Grace Caffo, *Pr*
Ronald Caffo, *VP*
Wanda Armburger, *Sec*
EMP: 13 EST: 1944
SQ FT: 70,000
SALES (est): 983.14K
SALES (corp-wide): 983.14K **Privately Held**
SIC: 3995 5087 Burial caskets; Caskets

(G-3475)
CAST SPECIALTIES INC
26711 Miles Rd (44128-5927)
PHONE......................216 292-7393
Martin Dragich, *Pr*
Benjamin G Ammons, *
Michael Paskevich, *
Elaine Zelch, *
EMP: 38 EST: 1960
SQ FT: 40,000
SALES (est): 7.13MM **Privately Held**
Web: www.castspecialties.com
SIC: 3364 3363 Zinc and zinc-base alloy die-
castings; Aluminum die-castings

(G-3476)
CASTALLOY INC
7990 Baker Ave (44102-1903)
PHONE......................216 961-7990

Richard J Chalet, *Prin*
Michael Wood, *
Thomas Waldin, *
▲ **EMP: 55 EST:** 1977
SQ FT: 40,000
SALES (est): 2.71MM **Privately Held**
Web: www.alconindustries.com
SIC: 3324 Steel investment foundries

(G-3477)
CASTELLI MARBLE LLC (PA)
3958 Superior Ave E (44114-4130)
PHONE......................216 361-1222
Luigi Castelli, *CEO*
Luigi Castelli, *Managing Member*
Gina Vicio, *Sec*
▲ **EMP: 7 EST:** 1987
SQ FT: 10,000
SALES (est): 2.24MM
SALES (corp-wide): 2.24MM **Privately
Held**
Web: www.castellimarbleinc.com
SIC: 5032 3281 Marble building stone; Cut
stone and stone products

(G-3478)
CB GRAPHICS LLC
5725 Brookpark Rd (44129-1207)
PHONE......................216 749-5577
EMP: 9 EST: 1982
SQ FT: 2,000
SALES (est): 339.45K **Privately Held**
Web: www.cbg-printing.com
SIC: 2752 Offset printing

(G-3479)
**CBTS TECHNOLOGY SOLUTIONS
LLC**
5910 Landerbrook Dr Ste 250
(44124-6508)
PHONE......................440 569-2300
Theodore H Torbeck, *CEO*
EMP: 270
SALES (corp-wide): 255.4K **Privately Held**
Web: www.cbts.com
SIC: 7379 7372 Computer related consulting
services; Business oriented computer
software
HQ: Cbts Technology Solutions Llc
25 Merchant St
Cincinnati OH 45246

(G-3480)
CCL LABEL INC
CCL Design
15939 Industrial Pkwy (44135-3321)
PHONE......................216 676-2703
Chief Anderson, *Mgr*
EMP: 42
SALES (corp-wide): 4.84B **Privately Held**
Web: www.cclind.com
SIC: 2672 3081 3497 2678 Adhesive
papers, labels, or tapes: from purchased
material; Unsupported plastics film and
sheet; Metal foil and leaf; Stationery
products
HQ: Ccl Label, Inc.
161 Worcester Rd Ste 603
Framingham MA 01701
508 872-4511

(G-3481)
CDI INDUSTRIES INC
Also Called: Coaxial Dynamics
6800 Lake Abrams Dr (44130-3455)
PHONE......................440 243-1100
Joseph D Kluha, *Pr*
EMP: 24 EST: 1969
SQ FT: 16,000
SALES (est): 2.62MM **Privately Held**
Web: www.coaxial.com

SIC: 3663 3825 3613 Receivers, radio
communications; Instruments to measure
electricity; Switchgear and switchboard
apparatus

(G-3482)
CEN-TROL MACHINE CO
7601 Commerce Park Oval (44131-2303)
PHONE......................216 524-1932
Henry J Kuska, *Prin*
Theresa Kuska, *VP*
Allen Straka, *Sec*
EMP: 6 EST: 1964
SQ FT: 11,000
SALES (est): 475.19K **Privately Held**
SIC: 3599 Machine shop, jobbing and repair

(G-3483)
CENTERLESS GRINDING SVC INC
Also Called: C G S
19500 S Miles Rd (44128-4251)
P.O. Box 535 (44202-0535)
PHONE......................216 251-4100
Jim Daso, *Pr*
Terry Daso, *Treas*
EMP: 8 EST: 1959
SQ FT: 3,632
SALES (est): 242.66K **Privately Held**
Web: www.profilegrinding.com
SIC: 3999 3599 Grinding and pulverizing of
materials, nec; Machine shop, jobbing and
repair

(G-3484)
CHALFANT SEW FABRICATORS INC
Also Called: Chalfant Loading Dock Eqp
11525 Madison Ave (44102-2392)
PHONE......................216 521-7922
Jeff Chalfant, *Pr*
Stephanie Chalfant, *
◆ **EMP: 30 EST:** 1940
SQ FT: 50,000
SALES (est): 4.8MM **Privately Held**
Web: www.chalfantusa.com
SIC: 3069 2394 Sponge rubber and sponge
rubber products; Canvas and related
products

(G-3485)
CHARIZMA CORP
Also Called: National Screen Production
1400 E 30th St Ste 201 (44114-4050)
P.O. Box 33520 (44133-0520)
PHONE......................216 621-2220
Marcy Szabados, *Pr*
EMP: 7 EST: 1980
SQ FT: 5,000
SALES (est): 209.05K **Privately Held**
Web: www.nsp-screenprinting.com
SIC: 2396 5199 Screen printing on fabric
articles; Advertising specialties

(G-3486)
CHARLES C LEWIS COMPANY
1 W Interstate St Ste 200 (44146-4256)
PHONE......................440 439-3150
Steve Mccoy, *Mgr*
EMP: 10
SALES (corp-wide): 8.81MM **Privately
Held**
Web: www.charleslewis.com
SIC: 3312 Blast furnaces and steel mills
PA: The Charles C Lewis Company
209 Page Blvd
Springfield MA 01104
413 733-2121

(G-3487)
CHART ASIA INC
1 Infinity Corporate Centre Dr (44125-5369)
PHONE......................440 753-1490

Samuel F Thomas, *Pr*
EMP: 39 EST: 1995
SALES (est): 2.37MM **Publicly Held**
Web: www.chartindustries.com
SIC: 3443 Heat exchangers, plate type
HQ: Chart Inc.
5615 S 129th E Ave
Tulsa OK 74134

(G-3488)
CHART INDUSTRIES INC
5885 Landerbrook Dr Ste 150
(44124-4045)
PHONE......................440 753-1490
Samuel F Thomas, *Pr*
Arthur S Holmes, *
EMP: 181 EST: 1992
SALES (est): 5.34MM **Publicly Held**
Web: www.chartindustries.com
SIC: 3443 Heat exchangers, plate type
HQ: Chart Inc.
5615 S 129th E Ave
Tulsa OK 74134

(G-3489)
CHART INTERNATIONAL INC (HQ)
1 Infinity Corporate Centre Dr (44125-5369)
PHONE......................440 753-1490
Samuel F Thomas, *Pr*
EMP: 67 EST: 1998
SALES (est): 19.9MM **Publicly Held**
Web: www.chartindustries.com
SIC: 3443 3317 3559 3569 Heat
exchangers, plate type; Steel pipe and
tubes; Cryogenic machinery, industrial;
Separators for steam, gas, vapor, or air
(machinery)
PA: Chart Industries, Inc.
2200 Arprt Indus Dr Ste 1
Ball Ground GA 30107

(G-3490)
CHARTER MANUFACTURING CO INC
Charter Steel Division
4300 E 49th St (44125-1004)
PHONE......................216 883-3800
Kevin Burg, *Brnch Mgr*
EMP: 71
SALES (corp-wide): 570.48MM **Privately
Held**
Web: www.chartersteel.com
SIC: 3312 Rods, iron and steel: made in
steel mills
PA: Charter Manufacturing Company, Inc.
12121 Corporate Pkwy
Mequon WI 53092
262 243-4700

(G-3491)
CHECK POINT SOFTWARE TECH INC
6100 Oak Tree Blvd Ste 200 (44131-6914)
PHONE......................440 748-0900
EMP: 45
SALES (corp-wide): 999.82MM **Privately
Held**
Web: www.checkpoint.com
SIC: 7372 Prepackaged software
HQ: Check Point Software Technologies,
Inc.
100 Oracle Pkwy
Redwood City CA 94065

(G-3492)
CHEMICAL SOLVENTS INC (PA)
3751 Jennings Rd (44109-2889)
PHONE......................216 741-9310
Edward Pavlish, *Ch Bd*
E H Pavlish, *
Gerald J Schill, *
Patricia Pavlish, *
Thos A Mason, *

▲ **EMP:** 45 **EST:** 1970
SQ FT: 30,000
SALES (est): 55.44MM
SALES (corp-wide): 55.44MM **Privately Held**
Web: www.chemicalsolvents.com
SIC: 5169 7349 3471 2992 Detergents and soaps, except specialty cleaning; Chemical cleaning services; Cleaning and descaling metal products; Oils and greases, blending and compounding

(G-3493)
CHEMTRADE LOGISTICS INC
2545 W 3rd St (44113-2512)
PHONE.................................216 566-8070
EMP: 10 **EST:** 2019
SALES (est): 1.46MM **Privately Held**
Web: www.chemtradelogistics.com
SIC: 2819 Industrial inorganic chemicals, nec

(G-3494)
CHI CORPORATION (PA)
Also Called: CHI Storage Solutions Corp
5265 Naiman Pkwy Ste H (44139-1013)
PHONE.................................440 498-2300
John R Thome Senior, *Ch*
John Thome Junior, *Pr*
EMP: 9 **EST:** 1994
SALES (est): 4.6MM **Privately Held**
Web: www.chicorporation.com
SIC: 7373 3572 Systems software development services; Computer tape drives and components

(G-3495)
CHILCOTE COMPANY
Also Called: Oliver Inc.
4600 Tiedeman Rd (44144-2332)
PHONE.................................216 781-6000
Mark Mcelhinny, *Pr*
Matthew Moir, *
Daniel Malloy, *
◆ **EMP:** 140 **EST:** 1906
SALES (est): 23.48MM
SALES (corp-wide): 196.73MM **Privately Held**
Web: www.oliverinc.com
SIC: 2675 2652 2657 Die-cut paper and board; Setup paperboard boxes; Folding paperboard boxes
PA: Oliver Printing And Packaging, Inc.
10 Gilpin Ave
Hauppauge NY 11788
631 234-1400

(G-3496)
CHOCOLATE PIG INC (PA)
Also Called: Fantasy Candies
5338 Mayfield Rd (44124-2479)
PHONE.................................440 461-4511
Joel Fink, *Pr*
EMP: 6 **EST:** 1990
SQ FT: 3,500
SALES (est): 590.39K **Privately Held**
Web: www.fantasycandies.com
SIC: 2064 5441 2066 Candy and other confectionery products; Candy, nut, and confectionery stores; Chocolate and cocoa products

(G-3497)
CHROMATIC INC
839 E 63rd St (44103-1018)
PHONE.................................216 881-2228
Dennis L Paul, *Pr*
EMP: 10 **EST:** 1984
SQ FT: 12,000
SALES (est): 965.73K **Privately Held**
Web: www.chromaticplating.com

SIC: 3471 Electroplating of metals or formed products

(G-3498)
CHROMIUM CORPORATION
8701 Union Ave (44105-1611)
PHONE.................................216 271-4910
Richard Young, *Mgr*
EMP: 50
SALES (corp-wide): 6.35B **Privately Held**
SIC: 3443 3471 Fabricated plate work (boiler shop); Plating and polishing
HQ: Chromium Corporation
14911 Quorum Dr Ste 600
Dallas TX 75254
972 851-0500

(G-3499)
CITY OF CLEVELAND
Also Called: Printing & Reproduction Div
1735 Lakeside Ave E (44114-1118)
PHONE.................................216 664-3013
Michael Hewett, *Commsnr*
EMP: 21
SALES (corp-wide): 1.12B **Privately Held**
Web: www.clevelandohio.gov
SIC: 2752 9199 Commercial printing, lithographic; General government administration
PA: City Of Cleveland
601 Lakeside Ave E Rm 227
Cleveland OH 44114
216 664-2000

(G-3500)
CITY OF CLEVELAND
Also Called: Parking Facilities
500 Lakeside Ave E (44114-1019)
PHONE.................................216 664-2711
Paul Bender, *Dir*
EMP: 36 **EST:** 2009
SALES (est): 4.73MM
SALES (corp-wide): 1.12B **Privately Held**
Web: www.clevelandohio.gov
SIC: 3559 Parking facility equipment and supplies
PA: City Of Cleveland
601 Lakeside Ave E Rm 227
Cleveland OH 44114
216 664-2000

(G-3501)
CITY PLATING AND POLISHING LLC
Also Called: City Plating
4821 W 130th St (44135-5137)
PHONE.................................216 267-8158
Randy Solganik, *Managing Member*
EMP: 7 **EST:** 2001
SQ FT: 20,000
SALES (est): 1.27MM **Privately Held**
Web: www.cityplate.com
SIC: 3471 Electroplating of metals or formed products

(G-3502)
CLARKE-BOXIT CORPORATION
5601 Walworth Ave (44102-4432)
PHONE.................................716 487-1950
Donald Zaas, *CEO*
Joel Zaas, *Pr*
Mark Cassese, *VP*
Carole Halowecky, *CFO*
EMP: 20 **EST:** 1992
SALES (est): 2.36MM
SALES (corp-wide): 23.79MM **Privately Held**
SIC: 2652 Setup paperboard boxes
PA: The Apex Paper Box Company
5601 Walworth Ave
Cleveland OH 44102
216 631-4000

(G-3503)
CLEANLIFE ENERGY LLC
Also Called: Unibat
7620 Hub Pkwy (44125-5736)
PHONE.................................800 316-2532
Justin Miller, *CEO*
Jonathan Koslo, *VP*
▲ **EMP:** 15 **EST:** 2011
SALES (est): 4.19MM **Privately Held**
Web: www.cleanlifeled.com
SIC: 3356 3679 5063 Battery metal; Liquid crystal displays (LCD); Lighting fixtures

(G-3504)
CLEARVUE INSULATING GLASS CO
14735 Lorain Ave Ste 1 (44111-3175)
PHONE.................................216 651-1140
Jeffrey Fogel, *Pr*
EMP: 6 **EST:** 1970
SALES (est): 1.1MM **Privately Held**
Web: www.clearvueig.com
SIC: 3211 5039 Insulating glass, sealed units ; Exterior flat glass: plate or window

(G-3505)
CLECORR INC
Also Called: Clecorr Packaging
10610 Berea Rd Rear (44102-2595)
PHONE.................................216 961-5500
Kevin L Smith, *Pr*
Christopher Dye, *
EMP: 29 **EST:** 1987
SQ FT: 67,000
SALES (est): 7.8MM **Privately Held**
Web: www.clecorrpackaging.com
SIC: 2653 Boxes, corrugated: made from purchased materials

(G-3506)
CLEVELAND AEC WEST LLC
14000 Keystone Pkwy (44135-5170)
PHONE.................................216 362-6000
Deepmala Agarwal, *Prin*
EMP: 6 **EST:** 2015
SALES (est): 165.78K **Privately Held**
SIC: 2835 Veterinary diagnostic substances

(G-3507)
CLEVELAND BLACK OXIDE INC
11400 Brookpark Rd (44130-1131)
PHONE.................................216 861-4431
Bob Mcelwee, *Pr*
Kim Elliott, *VP*
EMP: 12 **EST:** 2013
SALES (est): 1.94MM **Privately Held**
Web: www.clevelandblackoxide.com
SIC: 3471 Electroplating of metals or formed products

(G-3508)
CLEVELAND CANVAS GOODS MFG CO
1960 E 57th St (44103-3804)
PHONE.................................216 361-4567
William Morton Iii, *Pr*
William J Morton Iii, *Pr*
Tyler Martinez, *
EMP: 26 **EST:** 1922
SQ FT: 29,500
SALES (est): 3MM **Privately Held**
Web: www.clevelandcanvas.com
SIC: 2394 2393 2326 2296 Canvas and related products; Textile bags; Men's and boy's work clothing; Tire cord and fabrics

(G-3509)
CLEVELAND CIRCUITS CORP
Also Called: Instrumatics
15516 Industrial Pkwy (44135-3314)
PHONE.................................216 267-9020

Sumir Amin, *Pr*
Jay Amin, *VP*
EMP: 25 **EST:** 1994
SQ FT: 18,500
SALES (est): 5.35MM **Privately Held**
SIC: 3672 Printed circuit boards

(G-3510)
CLEVELAND CONTROLS INC
1111 Brookpark Rd (44109-5825)
PHONE.................................216 398-0330
Steve Craig, *Pr*
EMP: 10 **EST:** 1942
SQ FT: 10,000
SALES (est): 2.19MM **Privately Held**
Web: www.clevelandcontrols.com
SIC: 3823 Combustion control instruments

(G-3511)
CLEVELAND GEAR COMPANY INC (DH)
3249 E 80th St (44104-4395)
P.O. Box 70100-T (44190-0001)
PHONE.................................216 641-9000
Dana Lynch, *Pr*
Robert Wightman, *Contrlr*
Russell Warner, *VP Mfg*
John M Atkinson, *VP Sls*
▲ **EMP:** 83 **EST:** 1912
SALES (est): 23.82MM
SALES (corp-wide): 459.42MM **Privately Held**
Web: www.clevelandgear.com
SIC: 3566 3569 Speed changers, drives, and gears; Lubricating equipment
HQ: Industrial Manufacturing Company Llc
8223 Brcksvlle Rd Ste 100
Brecksville OH 44141
440 838-4700

(G-3512)
CLEVELAND GRANITE & MARBLE LLC
4121 Carnegie Ave (44103-4336)
PHONE.................................216 291-7637
Kimberly K Lisboa, *Managing Member*
▲ **EMP:** 33 **EST:** 2000
SQ FT: 50,000
SALES (est): 849.38K **Privately Held**
Web: www.clevelandgranite.com
SIC: 3291 1799 Abrasive metal and steel products; Home/office interiors finishing, furnishing and remodeling

(G-3513)
CLEVELAND IGNITION CO INC
600 Golden Oak Pkwy (44146-6504)
PHONE.................................440 439-3688
Walt Lemonovith, *Pr*
Charles O'toole, *Prin*
▲ **EMP:** 9 **EST:** 1917
SQ FT: 8,000
SALES (est): 2.23MM **Privately Held**
Web: www.clevelandignition.com
SIC: 3714 Motor vehicle parts and accessories

(G-3514)
CLEVELAND JEWISH PUBL CO
Also Called: Cleveland Jewish News
23880 Commerce Park Ste 1 (44122-5830)
PHONE.................................216 454-8300
Rob Certner, *CEO*
Cynthia Dettelbach, *
EMP: 38 **EST:** 1964
SQ FT: 9,000
SALES (est): 3.08MM **Privately Held**
Web: www.clevelandjewishnews.com
SIC: 2711 Newspapers, publishing and printing

▲ = Import ▼ = Export
◆ = Import/Export

(G-3515)
CLEVELAND MEDICAL DEVICES INC
Also Called: Clevemed
4415 Euclid Ave Ste 400 (44103-3757)
PHONE...................................216 619-5928
Robert N Schmidt, *Ch*
Hani Kayyali, *Pr*
Bryan Kolkowski, *VP*
EMP: 20 **EST:** 1991
SQ FT: 9,000
SALES (est): 4.05MM **Privately Held**
Web: www.clevemed.com
SIC: 3845 3842 Electromedical apparatus;
Surgical appliances and supplies

(G-3516)
CLEVELAND MENU PRINTING INC
1441 E 17th St (44114-2012)
PHONE...................................216 241-5256
Tom Ramella, *Pr*
Jerry Ramella, *
Gerry Ramella, *
Daniel Payne, *
George Maxwell, *
▼ **EMP:** 25 **EST:** 1930
SQ FT: 15,000
SALES (est): 5.37MM **Privately Held**
Web: www.clevelandmenu.com
SIC: 2759 Menus: printing, nsk

(G-3517)
CLEVELAND METAL PROCESSING INC (PA)
20303 1st Ave (44130-2433)
PHONE...................................440 243-3404
Juan Chahda, *Pr*
Liliana Chahda, *
EMP: 114 **EST:** 1947
SQ FT: 119,000
SALES (est): 773.55K
SALES (corp-wide): 773.55K **Privately Held**
Web: www.clevelandmetroparks.com
SIC: 3465 3544 Automotive stampings;
Special dies and tools

(G-3518)
CLEVELAND PLATING LLC
1028 E 134th St (44110-2248)
PHONE...................................216 249-0300
Elva Wade, *Managing Member*
EMP: 7 **EST:** 2015
SALES (est): 1.38MM **Privately Held**
Web: www.clevelandplating.com
SIC: 3471 Plating of metals or formed products

(G-3519)
CLEVELAND PRESS
452 Bishop Rd (44143-1957)
PHONE...................................440 442-5101
Lynne Bolivar-wolford, *Prin*
EMP: 6 **EST:** 2010
SALES (est): 76.67K **Privately Held**
Web: www.clevelandmemory.org
SIC: 2741 Miscellaneous publishing

(G-3520)
CLEVELAND PRESS
30628 Detroit Rd (44145-5844)
PHONE...................................440 289-3227
EMP: 6 **EST:** 2014
SALES (est): 90.05K **Privately Held**
Web: www.clevelandpress.com
SIC: 2741 Miscellaneous publishing

(G-3521)
CLEVELAND PRINTWEAR INC
13300 Madison Ave (44107-4894)
PHONE...................................216 521-5500

Michael Cannon, *Pr*
Karen Cannon, *Sec*
EMP: 9 **EST:** 1983
SQ FT: 8,000
SALES (est): 2.04MM **Privately Held**
Web: www.clevelandprintwear.com
SIC: 2759 Screen printing

(G-3522)
CLEVELAND RANGE LLC (DH)
Also Called: Manitwoc Ovens Advnced
Cooking
760 Beta Dr Ste G (44143-2334)
PHONE...................................216 481-4900
Robert Pritt, *Managing Member*
John Stevenson, *
▲ **EMP:** 209 **EST:** 1922
SALES (est): 25.92MM
SALES (corp-wide): 4.67B **Privately Held**
Web: www.clevelandrange.com
SIC: 3589 3556 3634 Commercial cooking
and foodwarming equipment; Food
products machinery; Electric housewares
and fans
HQ: Welbilt, Inc.
2227 Welbilt Blvd
New Port Richey FL 34655
727 375-7010

(G-3523)
CLEVELAND REBABBITTING SVC INC
15593 Brookpark Rd (44142-1618)
PHONE...................................216 433-0123
Kenneth Roller, *Pr*
Bradford Roller, *VP*
EMP: 9
SQ FT: 15,000
SALES (est): 938.13K **Privately Held**
Web: www.rebabbit.com
SIC: 3568 Bearings, bushings, and blocks

(G-3524)
CLEVELAND ROLL FORMING CO
3170 W 32nd St (44109-1529)
PHONE...................................216 281-0202
William P Ekey, *Pr*
Edward L Ekey, *VP*
EMP: 7 **EST:** 1947
SQ FT: 11,700
SALES (est): 920.5K **Privately Held**
Web: www.clevelandrollforming.com
SIC: 3544 Special dies and tools

(G-3525)
CLEVELAND SPECIALTY PDTS INC
2130 W 110th St (44102-3510)
PHONE...................................216 281-8300
Manuel P Glynias, *Pr*
EMP: 22 **EST:** 2009
SALES (est): 5.87MM **Privately Held**
Web: www.clevelandlumber.com
SIC: 3089 Extruded finished plastics products, nec

(G-3526)
CLEVELAND STEEL TOOL COMPANY
474 E 105th St (44108-1378)
PHONE...................................216 681-7400
Mark Dawson, *Pr*
Wayne Haas, *
◆ **EMP:** 26 **EST:** 1908
SQ FT: 25,000
SALES (est): 3.82MM **Privately Held**
Web: www.clevelandsteeltool.com
SIC: 3544 Punches, forming and stamping

(G-3527)
CLEVELAND SUPPLYONE INC (DH)
Also Called: Supplyone Retail
26801b Fargo Ave (44146-1338)

PHONE...................................216 514-7000
◆ **EMP:** 50 **EST:** 1914
SALES (est): 23.65MM
SALES (corp-wide): 841.65MM **Privately Held**
Web: www.supplyone.com
SIC: 5113 5162 5085 2653 Industrial and
personal service paper; Plastics film; Glass
bottles; Corrugated and solid fiber boxes
HQ: Supplyone, Inc.
11 Campus Blvd Ste 150
Newtown Square PA 19073
484 582-5005

(G-3528)
CLEVELAND TOOL AND MACHINE INC
4717 Hinckley Industrial Pkwy
(44109-6004)
PHONE...................................216 267-6010
Victor Bota, *Pr*
Maria Bota, *VP*
Douglas Neece, *VP*
◆ **EMP:** 15 **EST:** 1996
SALES (est): 2.84MM **Privately Held**
Web: www.clevtool.com
SIC: 3599 Machine shop, jobbing and repair

(G-3529)
CLEVELAND VIBRATOR COMPANY
4544 Hinckley Industrial Pkwy
(44109-6010)
PHONE...................................800 221-3298
Jeffrey Chokel, *Ch Bd*
EMP: 6 **EST:** 2016
SALES (est): 643.73K **Privately Held**
Web: www.vibestrength.com
SIC: 3532 Mining machinery

(G-3530)
CLEVELAND WIND COMPANY LLC
4176 Hinsdale Rd (44121-2704)
PHONE...................................216 269-7667
Robert Parins, *Prin*
EMP: 6 **EST:** 2010
SALES (est): 104.19K **Privately Held**
SIC: 3621 Windmills, electric generating

(G-3531)
CLEVELAND WIRE CLOTH MFG LLC
3573 E 78th St (44105-1517)
PHONE...................................216 341-1832
Nicholas A Reif, *Managing Member*
EMP: 26 **EST:** 2022
SALES (est): 9.46MM
SALES (corp-wide): 9.46MM **Privately Held**
Web: www.wirecloth.com
SIC: 3496 Hardware cloth, woven wire
PA: Freshwater Capital Llc
1375 E 9th St Fl 29
Cleveland OH

(G-3532)
CLEVELAND-CLIFFS INC (PA)
Also Called: Cliffs
200 Public Sq Ste 3300 (44114-2315)
PHONE...................................216 694-5700
Lourenco Goncalves, *Pr*
Lourenco Goncalves, *Ch Bd*
Clifford Smith, *Ex VP*
Celso Goncalves, *Ex VP*
James D Graham, *Legal*
◆ **EMP:** 175 **EST:** 1847
SALES (est): 19.18B
SALES (corp-wide): 19.18B **Publicly Held**
Web: www.clevelandcliffs.com
SIC: 3312 Blast furnaces and steel mills

(G-3533)
CLEVELAND-CLIFFS STEEL CORP (DH)
Also Called: Cleveland-Cliffs
200 Public Sq Ste 3300 (44114-2315)
PHONE...................................216 694-5700
Lourenco Goncalves, *Pr*
◆ **EMP:** 88 **EST:** 1989
SQ FT: 136,000
SALES (est): 1.9B
SALES (corp-wide): 19.18B **Publicly Held**
Web: www.clevelandcliffs.com
SIC: 3312 Sheet or strip, steel, hot-rolled
HQ: Cleveland-Cliffs Steel Holding
Corporation
200 Public Sq Ste 3300
Cleveland OH 44114

(G-3534)
CLEVELANDCOM
4800 Tiedeman Rd (44144-2336)
PHONE...................................216 862-7159
EMP: 8 **EST:** 2013
SALES (est): 619.47K **Privately Held**
Web: www.cleveland.com
SIC: 2711 Newspapers

(G-3535)
CLEVELND-CLFFS CLVLAND WRKS LL (HQ)
3060 Eggers Ave (44105-1012)
PHONE...................................216 429-6000
Dan Boone, *Pr*
▲ **EMP:** 230 **EST:** 2002
SQ FT: 40,000
SALES (est): 462.89MM
SALES (corp-wide): 19.18B **Publicly Held**
Web: www.clevelandcliffs.com
SIC: 3312 Blast furnaces and steel mills
PA: Cleveland-Cliffs Inc.
200 Public Sq Ste 3300
Cleveland OH 44114
216 694-5700

(G-3536)
CLEVELND-CLFFS CLVLAND WRKS LL
3100 E 4th St (44127)
PHONE...................................216 429-6000
Sylvia Gerkin, *Brnch Mgr*
EMP: 30
SALES (corp-wide): 19.18B **Publicly Held**
Web: www.clevelandcliffs.com
SIC: 3312 Blast furnaces and steel mills
HQ: Cleveland Cleveland-Cliffs Works Llc
3060 Eggers Ave
Cleveland OH 44105
216 429-6000

(G-3537)
CLEVELND-CLIFFS STL HOLDG CORP (DH)
200 Public Sq Ste 3300 (44114-2315)
PHONE...................................216 694-5700
C Lourenco Goncalves, *Ch Bd*
C Lourenco Goncalves, *Ch Bd*
Terry G Fedor, *
R Christopher Cebula, *CAO*
Celso L Goncalves Junior, *VP*
◆ **EMP:** 300 **EST:** 1993
SALES (est): 5.35B
SALES (corp-wide): 19.18B **Publicly Held**
Web: www.cleveland-cliffs.com
SIC: 3312 Sheet or strip, steel, hot-rolled
HQ: Cliffs Steel Inc.
200 Public Sq Ste 3300
Cleveland OH 44114
216 694-5700

(G-3538)
CLIFFS & ASSOCIATES LTD
1100 Superior Ave E Ste 1500
(44114-2530)
PHONE..................216 694-5700
W R Calfee, *Pr*
Rainald Von Bitter, *VP*
EMP: 6 **EST:** 1996
SQ FT: 65,000
SALES (est): 563.25K **Privately Held**
Web: www.clevelandcliffs.com
SIC: 1011 Iron ores

(G-3539)
CLIFFS MINING COMPANY
200 Public Sq Ste 3300 (44114-2315)
PHONE..................216 694-5700
Lourenco Goncalves, *Ch Bd*
Celso Goncalves, *Ex VP*
Clifford Smith, *Ex VP*
EMP: 19 **EST:** 1883
SQ FT: 40,000
SALES (est): 7.14MM
SALES (corp-wide): 19.18B **Publicly Held**
Web: www.clevelandcliffs.com
SIC: 1011 Iron ores
PA: Cleveland-Cliffs Inc.
    200 Public Sq Ste 3300
    Cleveland OH 44114
    216 694-5700

(G-3540)
CLIFFS STEEL INC (HQ)
200 Public Sq Ste 3300 (44114-2315)
PHONE..................216 694-5700
Cliford T Smith, *Pr*
Celso L Goncalves Junior, *Ex VP*
James D Graham, *Ex VP*
Kimberly A Floriani, *Sr VP*
Denise M Caruso,, *VP*
EMP: 29 **EST:** 2021
SALES (est): 6.38B
SALES (corp-wide): 19.18B **Publicly Held**
Web: www.clevelandcliffs.com
SIC: 3312 Blast furnaces and steel mills
PA: Cleveland-Cliffs Inc.
    200 Public Sq Ste 3300
    Cleveland OH 44114
    216 694-5700

(G-3541)
CLIMATE PROS LLC
5309 Hamilton Ave (44114-3909)
PHONE..................216 881-5200
Todd Ernest, *CEO*
EMP: 85
Web: www.climatepros.com
SIC: 1711 5078 2541 2434 Refrigeration
    contractor; Commercial refrigeration
    equipment; Cabinets, except refrigerated:
    show, display, etc.: wood; Wood kitchen
    cabinets
PA: Climate Pros, Llc
    2190 Gladstone Ct Ste E
    Glendale Heights IL 60139

(G-3542)
CO-PAC SERVICES INC
3113 W 110th St (44111-2753)
PHONE..................216 688-1780
Craig Jaworski, *Pr*
Mike Marfeka, *VP*
Phil Puhala, *Sec*
▲ **EMP:** 15 **EST:** 1994
SQ FT: 65,000
SALES (est): 2.46MM **Privately Held**
Web: www.copac.com
SIC: 3993 Displays and cutouts, window and
    lobby

(G-3543)
COCHEM INC
Also Called: Clark Oil & Chemical Division
7555 Bessemer Ave (44127-1821)
PHONE..................216 341-8914
Tom Mesterhazy, *Pr*
Patrick J Amer, *
EMP: 29 **EST:** 1912
SQ FT: 18,000
SALES (est): 23.8MM **Privately Held**
Web: www.clarkoilandchemical.com
SIC: 2992 Lubricating oils and greases
PA: Mco, Inc.
    7555 Bessemer Ave
    Cleveland OH 44127

(G-3544)
CODONICS INC (PA)
17991 Englewood Dr Ste B (44130-3493)
PHONE..................800 444-1198
Peter Botten, *CEO*
◆ **EMP:** 208 **EST:** 1982
SALES (est): 24.98MM
SALES (corp-wide): 24.98MM **Privately
Held**
Web: www.codonics.com
SIC: 3841 Surgical and medical instruments

(G-3545)
**COLLINWOOD SHALE BRICK SUP
CO (PA)**
16219 Saranac Rd (44110-2435)
PHONE..................216 587-2700
Dorothy Strohm, *Ch Bd*
Scott Terhune, *Pr*
Cynthia S Terhune, *Treas*
EMP: 50 **EST:** 1921
SQ FT: 10,000
SALES (est): 2.37MM
SALES (corp-wide): 2.37MM **Privately
Held**
SIC: 3273 5032 Ready-mixed concrete;
    Brick, stone, and related material

(G-3546)
**COLOR BAR PRINTING CENTERS
INC**
4576 Renaissance Pkwy (44128-5702)
P.O. Box 1922 (44234-1922)
PHONE..................216 595-3939
Roger Perlmuter, *Pr*
Mary Ann Perlmuter, *VP*
EMP: 6 **EST:** 1992
SQ FT: 16,248
SALES (est): 209.87K **Privately Held**
Web: www.colorbar.net
SIC: 2752 Offset printing

(G-3547)
COLUMBIA INDUSTRIAL PDTS INC
4100 Payne Ave (44103-2346)
PHONE..................216 431-6633
Ross Defelice, *Pr*
EMP: 15 **EST:** 2001
SQ FT: 80,000
SALES (est): 536.99K **Privately Held**
Web: www.buschman.com
SIC: 3561 Industrial pumps and parts

(G-3548)
COM-CORP INDUSTRIES INC
7601 Bittern Ave (44103-1060)
PHONE..................216 431-6266
Thomas Stanciu, *CEO*
William Beckwith, *
Kimberly Watroba, *
John Strazzanti, *Stockholder**
◆ **EMP:** 100 **EST:** 1980
SQ FT: 150,000
SALES (est): 8.67MM **Privately Held**

Web: www.ccioh.com
SIC: 3469 Stamping metal for the trade

(G-3549)
COMBER HOLDINGS INC
3304 W 67th Pl (44102-5243)
PHONE..................216 961-8600
Dean Comber, *Pr*
EMP: 40 **EST:** 1984
SQ FT: 30,000
SALES (est): 3.18MM **Privately Held**
Web: www.shakervalleyfoods.com
SIC: 5141 2011 Food brokers; Meat packing
    plants

(G-3550)
COMCORP INC (HQ)
Also Called: Sun Newspaper Div
1801 Superior Ave E (44114-2135)
PHONE..................718 981-1234
John Urbancich, *Pr*
Douglas J Lightner, *
EMP: 175 **EST:** 1969
SQ FT: 22,500
SALES (est): 16.33K
SALES (corp-wide): 2.88B **Privately Held**
SIC: 2711 Newspapers: publishing only, not
    printed on site
PA: Advance Publications, Inc.
    1 World Trade Ctr Fl 43
    New York NY 10007
    718 981-1234

(G-3551)
COMEX NORTH AMERICA INC (HQ)
Also Called: Comex Group
101 W Prospect Ave Ste 1020
(44115-1093)
PHONE..................303 307-2100
Leon Cohen, *Pr*
Christopher Connor, *
◆ **EMP:** 90 **EST:** 2000
SQ FT: 2,900
SALES (est): 896.73K
SALES (corp-wide): 23.1B **Publicly Held**
SIC: 2851 8742 5198 5231 Paints and paint
    additives; Corporation organizing consultant
    ; Paints; Paint
PA: The Sherwin-Williams Company
    101 W Prospect Ave
    Cleveland OH 44115
    216 566-2000

(G-3552)
**COMMERCIAL ELECTRIC PDTS
CORP (PA)**
1821 E 40th St (44103-3503)
PHONE..................216 241-2886
Roger Meyer, *Pr*
Kenneth Culp, *
EMP: 44 **EST:** 1927
SQ FT: 32,000
SALES (est): 17.02MM
SALES (corp-wide): 17.02MM **Privately
Held**
Web: www.commercialelectric.com
SIC: 5085 3661 3824 7699 Power
    transmission equipment and apparatus;
    Telephones and telephone apparatus;
    Mechanical and electromechanical
    counters and devices; Industrial equipment
    services

(G-3553)
COMMERCIAL STEEL TREATING CO
1394 E 39th St (44114-4163)
PHONE..................216 431-8204
Jeff Seitz, *Pr*
Lisa Seitz, *Sec*
Donna Seitz, *Sec*
EMP: 10 **EST:** 1941

SQ FT: 36,000
SALES (est): 942.54K **Privately Held**
Web: www.commercialsteeltreating.com
SIC: 3398 3471 Metal heat treating; Plating
    and polishing

(G-3554)
**COMMUNITY CARE NETWORK INC
(PA)**
4614 Prospect Ave Ste 240 (44103-4365)
PHONE..................216 671-0977
David Lundeen, *Pr*
Christopher Cassidy, *CFO*
EMP: 49 **EST:** 2005
SALES (est): 2.18MM
SALES (corp-wide): 2.18MM **Privately
Held**
Web: www.ccnms.org
SIC: 3825 Network analyzers

(G-3555)
**COMPLIANT HEALTHCARE TECH
LLC (PA)**
Also Called: C H T
7123 Pearl Rd Ste 305 (44130-4944)
PHONE..................216 255-9607
Jason Di Marco, *Managing Member*
Scot Wederquist, *
EMP: 25 **EST:** 2006
SQ FT: 8,200
SALES (est): 4.13MM **Privately Held**
Web: www.chthealthcare.com
SIC: 7389 3826 Gas system conversion;
    Gas testing apparatus

(G-3556)
COMPONENT SYSTEMS INC
Also Called: A-Wall
5350 Tradex Pkwy (44102-5887)
PHONE..................216 252-9292
Tim Nelson, *Pr*
Thomas A Nelson, *VP*
Gineen Nelson, *Sec*
EMP: 20 **EST:** 1978
SALES (est): 3.41MM **Privately Held**
Web: www.a-wall.com
SIC: 2542 Partitions and fixtures, except
    wood

(G-3557)
COMPUTER WORKSHOP INC
6100 Rockside Woods Blvd N Ste 235
(44131-2366)
PHONE..................216 901-0106
David Williams, *Mgr*
EMP: 6
SALES (corp-wide): 2.37MM **Privately
Held**
Web: www.tcworkshop.com
SIC: 8243 7371 2741 Software training,
    computer; Custom computer programming
    services; Miscellaneous publishing
PA: The Computer Workshop Inc
    5200 Upper Metro Pl # 140
    Dublin OH 43017
    614 798-9505

(G-3558)
CONDOR TOOL & DIE INC
Also Called: Anchor Die Technologies
4541 Industrial Pkwy (44135-4598)
PHONE..................216 671-6000
Edward Pfaff, *Ch Bd*
Frederick Pfaff, *
Robert Pfaff, *
Jeff Pfaff, *
EMP: 35 **EST:** 1982
SQ FT: 25,000
SALES (est): 2.47MM **Privately Held**
SIC: 3544 Special dies and tools

(G-3559)
CONSOLDATED GRAPHICS GROUP INC
Also Called: Consolidated Solutions
1614 E 40th St (44103-2319)
PHONE...............................216 881-9191
Kenneth A Lanci, *Ch Bd*
Terry Hartman, *
Oliver Moeritz, *
Matthew Reville, *
▲ EMP: 170 EST: 1984
SQ FT: 75,000
SALES (est): 20.67MM **Privately Held**
Web: www.csinc.com
SIC: 2752 2759 7331 2791 Offset printing;
Commercial printing, nec; Direct mail
advertising services; Typesetting

(G-3560)
CONSOLDTED PRECISION PDTS CORP (PA)
Also Called: Cpp
1621 Euclid Ave Ste 1850 (44115-2126)
PHONE...............................216 453-4800
James Stewart, *CEO*
Steve Clodfelter, *
Ali Ghavami, *
Debbie Comstock, *
Mel Crosier, *
▲ EMP: 250 EST: 1991
SQ FT: 10,000
SALES (est): 1.9B
SALES (corp-wide): 1.9B **Privately Held**
Web: www.cppcorp.com
SIC: 5088 3812 3721 Aircraft engines and
engine parts; Aircraft/aerospace flight
instruments and guidance systems;
Research and development on aircraft by
the manufacturer

(G-3561)
CONSOLIDATED COATINGS CORP
3735 Green Rd (44122-5705)
PHONE...............................216 514-7596
J K Milliken, *Genl Mgr*
Thomas C Sullivan, *
Paul A Granzier, *
EMP: 973 EST: 1904
SQ FT: 4,000
SALES (est): 2.21MM
SALES (corp-wide): 7.34B **Publicly Held**
SIC: 5169 2891 2851 2842 Adhesives and
sealants; Adhesives and sealants; Paints
and allied products; Polishes and sanitation
goods
HQ: Republic Powdered Metals, Inc.
2628 Pearl Rd
Medina OH 44256
330 225-3192

(G-3562)
CONSOLIDATED FOUNDRIES INC (HQ)
Also Called: C P P
1621 Euclid Ave Ste 1850 (44115-2126)
PHONE...............................909 595-2252
James Stewart, *CEO*
▲ EMP: 98 EST: 1991
SALES (est): 24.77MM
SALES (corp-wide): 1.9B **Privately Held**
Web: www.cppcorp.com
SIC: 3324 Aerospace investment castings,
ferrous
PA: Consolidated Precision Products Corp.
1621 Euclid Ave Ste 1850
Cleveland OH 44115
216 453-4800

(G-3563)
CONTINENTAL METAL PROC CO (PA)
18711 Cleveland Ave (44110)
P.O. Box 18130 (44118-0130)
PHONE...............................216 268-0000
Joseph Freund, *Pr*
Rubin Freund, *VP*
Mike Freund, *VP*
EMP: 19 EST: 1957
SQ FT: 328,000
SALES (est): 514.86K
SALES (corp-wide): 514.86K **Privately Held**
SIC: 3341 Aluminum smelting and refining
(secondary)

(G-3564)
CONTINENTAL METAL PROC CO
14919 Saranac Rd (44110-2344)
PHONE...............................216 268-0000
Michael Freund, *VP*
EMP: 22
SQ FT: 320,000
SALES (corp-wide): 514.86K **Privately Held**
SIC: 3341 Aluminum smelting and refining
(secondary)
PA: Continental Metal Processing Co (Inc)
18711 Cleveland Ave
Cleveland OH 44110
216 268-0000

(G-3565)
CONTROL LINE EQUIPMENT INC
14750 Industrial Pkwy (44135-4548)
PHONE...............................216 433-7766
Mike Rotella, *CEO*
Robert May, *VP*
▲ EMP: 12 EST: 1979
SQ FT: 12,000
SALES (est): 3.49MM **Privately Held**
Web: www.control-line.com
SIC: 5084 3593 Hydraulic systems
equipment and supplies; Fluid power
cylinders and actuators

(G-3566)
COOPER WIRING DEVICES INC
1000 Eaton Blvd (44122-6058)
PHONE...............................440 523-5000
EMP: 65
SIC: 3643 Plugs, electric
HQ: Cooper Wiring Devices, Inc.
203 Cooper Cir
Peachtree City GA 30269
770 631-2100

(G-3567)
COPY KING INC
3333 Chester Ave (44114-4600)
PHONE...............................216 861-3377
Margaret Walsh, *Pr*
John Schneeberger, *VP*
EMP: 19 EST: 1990
SQ FT: 15,000
SALES (est): 2.25MM **Privately Held**
Web: www.copy-king.com
SIC: 2752 Offset printing

(G-3568)
CORNER ALLEY LLC (PA)
402 Euclid Ave (44114-2215)
P.O. Box 14100 (44114-0100)
PHONE...............................216 298-4070
Michael Grasso, *Genl Mgr*
EMP: 34 EST: 2010
SALES (est): 2.48MM
SALES (corp-wide): 2.48MM **Privately Held**
Web: www.thecorneralley.com

SIC: 3949 Bowling alleys and accessories

(G-3569)
COSMO PLASTICS COMPANY (HQ)
Also Called: Cosmo
30201 Aurora Rd (44139-2745)
PHONE...............................440 498-7500
▲ EMP: 150 EST: 1968
SALES (est): 37.71K
SALES (corp-wide): 33.37K **Privately Held**
Web: www.cosmocorp.com
SIC: 3082 3089 Unsupported plastics profile
shapes; Plastics hardware and building
products
PA: Marbeach Corp.
30201 Aurora Rd
Cleveland OH
440 498-7500

(G-3570)
COUNTRY PARLOUR ICE CREAM CO
12905 York Delta Dr Ste C (44133-3551)
PHONE...............................440 237-4040
Jeri Hovanec, *Prin*
Craig Hovanec, *Sec*
EMP: 8 EST: 1988
SALES (est): 872.14K **Privately Held**
Web: www.countryparlouricecream.com
SIC: 2024 2099 5143 Ice cream, bulk; Food
preparations, nec; Dairy products, except
dried or canned

(G-3571)
COVENTRY STEEL SERVICES INC
4200 E 71st St Ste 1 (44105-5721)
P.O. Box 25077 (44125-0077)
PHONE...............................216 883-4477
Brian Migchelbrink, *Pr*
Joseph Hustosky, *VP*
Jeff Migchelbrink, *Sec*
EMP: 7 EST: 1985
SQ FT: 35,000
SALES (est): 843.99K **Privately Held**
Web: www.coventrysteel.com
SIC: 3441 5051 Fabricated structural metal;
Steel

(G-3572)
CPC HOLDING INC
2926 Chester Ave (44114-4414)
PHONE...............................216 383-3932
Miriam Strebeck, *Ch Bd*
Emerson O Mcarthur Iii, *Pr*
EMP: 30 EST: 1916
SALES (est): 6.45MM **Privately Held**
Web: www.continentalprod.com
SIC: 2851 Paints and paint additives

(G-3573)
CPI GROUP LIMITED
Also Called: Puremonics
13858 Tinkers Creek Rd (44125-5661)
P.O. Box 25411 (44125-0411)
PHONE...............................216 525-0046
EMP: 11 EST: 2005
SQ FT: 2,000
SALES (est): 1.3MM **Privately Held**
Web: www.cpigroupltd.com
SIC: 3675 8711 Electronic capacitors;
Electrical or electronic engineering

(G-3574)
CPP GROUP HOLDINGS LLC (PA)
1621 Euclid Ave Ste 1850 (44115-2126)
PHONE...............................216 453-4800
James V Stewart, *CEO*
Timothy Trombetta I, *
Rick Legenza, *
EMP: 50 EST: 2019
SALES (est): 690.77MM
SALES (corp-wide): 690.77MM **Privately Held**

Web: www.cppcorp.com
SIC: 6719 3089 Investment holding
companies, except banks; Automotive
parts, plastic

(G-3575)
CRAIN COMMUNICATIONS INC
Also Called: Crain's Cleveland Business
700 W Saint Clair Ave Ste 310
(44113-1230)
PHONE...............................216 522-1383
Elizabeth Mcintyre, *Mgr*
EMP: 29
SALES (corp-wide): 249.16MM **Privately Held**
Web: www.crain.com
SIC: 2721 2711 Magazines: publishing only,
not printed on site; Newspapers
PA: Crain Communications, Inc.
1155 Gratiot Ave
Detroit MI 48207
313 446-6000

(G-3576)
CRAWFORD UNITED CORPORATION (PA)
Also Called: Crawford United
10514 Dupont Ave Ste 200 (44108-1348)
PHONE...............................216 243-2614
Brian E Powers, *Pr*
Edward F Crawford, *Ch Bd*
Jeffrey J Salay, *CFO*
EMP: 50 EST: 1910
SQ FT: 37,000
SALES (est): 150.2MM
SALES (corp-wide): 150.2MM **Publicly Held**
Web: www.crawfordunited.com
SIC: 3823 3829 Industrial process
measurement equipment; Measuring and
controlling devices, nec

(G-3577)
CROWNE GROUP LLC (PA)
127 Public Sq Ste 5110 (44114-1313)
PHONE...............................216 589-0198
Robert Henderson, *Managing Member*
EMP: 14 EST: 2013
SALES (est): 54.77MM
SALES (corp-wide): 54.77MM **Privately Held**
SIC: 3559 8711 Degreasing machines,
automotive and industrial; Industrial
engineers

(G-3578)
CTS NATIONAL CORPORATION
101 W Prospect Ave Ste 1020
(44115-1093)
PHONE...............................216 566-2000
EMP: 23 EST: 2019
SALES (est): 24.87MM
SALES (corp-wide): 23.1B **Publicly Held**
SIC: 2851 Paints and allied products
PA: The Sherwin-Williams Company
101 W Prospect Ave
Cleveland OH 44115
216 566-2000

(G-3579)
CUMMINS - ALLISON CORP
Also Called: Cummins
6777 Engle Rd Ste H (44130-7941)
PHONE...............................440 824-5050
David Profera, *Brnch Mgr*
EMP: 8
SALES (corp-wide): 1.49B **Publicly Held**
Web: www.cranepi.com

SIC: 5046 5087 5044 3519 Commercial equipment, nec; Shredders, industrial and commercial; Check writing, signing, and endorsing machines; Internal combustion engines, nec
HQ: Cummins-Allison Corp.
852 Feehanville Dr
Mount Prospect IL 60056
800 786-5528

(G-3580)
CURRENT LIGHTING SOLUTIONS LLC
Also Called: GE Current
1099 Ivanhoe Rd (44110-3232)
PHONE..............................216 266-4416
Manish Bhandari, *Brnch Mgr*
EMP: 285
SALES (corp-wide): 179.66MM **Privately Held**
Web: www.led.com
SIC: 3646 Commercial lighting fixtures
PA: Current Lighting Solutions, Llc
6085 Parkland Blvd
Cleveland OH 44124
216 462-4700

(G-3581)
CURRENT LIGHTING SOLUTIONS LLC (PA)
Also Called: GE Current, A Daintree Company
6085 Parkland Blvd (44124-4184)
PHONE..............................216 462-4700
Steve Harris, *CEO*
◆ **EMP:** 50 **EST:** 1998
SALES (est): 179.66MM
SALES (corp-wide): 179.66MM **Privately Held**
Web: www.led.com
SIC: 3646 3641 2819 Commercial lighting fixtures; Electric lamps; Industrial inorganic chemicals, nec

(G-3582)
CURTIS INDUSTIRES
1301 E 9th St Ste 700 (44114-1800)
PHONE..............................216 430-5759
Curtis Wilson, *Prin*
EMP: 13 **EST:** 2010
SALES (est): 1.29MM **Privately Held**
SIC: 3531 Construction machinery

(G-3583)
CURTISS-WRIGHT FLOW CTRL CORP
Nova Machine Div
18001 Sheldon Rd (44130-2465)
PHONE..............................216 267-3200
David Linton, *CEO*
EMP: 60
SALES (corp-wide): 3.12B **Publicly Held**
Web: www.curtisswright.com
SIC: 3452 3429 3369 3356 Bolts, metal; Hardware, nec; Nonferrous foundries, nec; Nonferrous rolling and drawing, nec
HQ: Curtiss-Wright Flow Control Corporation
1966 Broadhollow Rd Ste E
Farmingdale NY 11735
631 293-3800

(G-3584)
CUSTOM CLTCH JINT HYDRLICS INC (PA)
3417 Saint Clair Ave Ne (44114-4186)
PHONE..............................216 431-1630
David Ballantyne, *CEO*
Donald Meintel, *Pr*
Patricia Beason, *Treas*
Scott Ballantyne, *Sec*

Elmer T Elbrecht, *Prin*
EMP: 11 **EST:** 1960
SQ FT: 52,000
SALES (est): 2.39MM
SALES (corp-wide): 2.39MM **Privately Held**
Web: www.customclutch.com
SIC: 3714 3594 3561 3492 Motor vehicle transmissions, drive assemblies, and parts; Fluid power pumps; Cylinders, pump; Hose and tube couplings, hydraulic/pneumatic

(G-3585)
CUSTOM CONNECTOR CORPORATION
1821 E 40th St (44103-3503)
PHONE..............................216 241-1679
Roger Meyer, *Pr*
Robert Meyer, *Pr*
Larry Weider, *VP*
▲ **EMP:** 20 **EST:** 1969
SQ FT: 15,000
SALES (est): 3.67MM
SALES (corp-wide): 17.02MM **Privately Held**
Web: www.customconnector.com
SIC: 3678 Electronic connectors
PA: Commercial Electric Products Corporation
1821 E 40th St
Cleveland OH 44103
216 241-2886

(G-3586)
CUSTOM PAPER TUBES INC
6030 Carey Dr (44125-4260)
P.O. Box 35140 (44135-0140)
PHONE..............................216 362-2964
EMP: 25 **EST:** 1962
SALES (est): 3.1MM **Privately Held**
Web: www.custompapertubes.com
SIC: 2655 Tubes, for chemical or electrical uses: paper or fiber

(G-3587)
CUSTOM RUBBER CORPORATION
1274 E 55th St (44103-1029)
PHONE..............................216 391-2928
William Braun, *Pr*
◆ **EMP:** 75 **EST:** 1956
SQ FT: 70,000
SALES (est): 9.72MM **Privately Held**
Web: www.customrubbercorp.com
SIC: 3069 Molded rubber products

(G-3588)
CUTTERCROIX LLC
7251 Engle Rd Ste 350 (44130-3419)
PHONE..............................330 289-6185
EMP: 27 **EST:** 2016
SALES (est): 1.09MM **Privately Held**
Web: www.cuttercroix.com
SIC: 3652 Prerecorded records and tapes

(G-3589)
CUTTING EDGE TECHNOLOGIES INC
Also Called: Telos Systems
1241 Superior Ave E (44114-3204)
PHONE..............................216 574-4759
Steve Church, *CEO*
Frank J Foti, *
Anthony Foti, *
EMP: 6 **EST:** 1988
SALES (est): 890.96K **Privately Held**
SIC: 3679 3661 Electronic circuits; Telephone and telegraph apparatus

(G-3590)
CUTTING SYSTEMS INC
15593 Brookpark Rd (44142-1618)
PHONE..............................216 928-0500

Kris Asadorian, *Pr*
George Asadorian, *Pr*
Kevan Asadorian, *VP*
Sergey Edilyan, *VP*
▲ **EMP:** 16 **EST:** 1996
SQ FT: 44,500
SALES (est): 4.16MM **Privately Held**
Web: www.cuttingsystems.com
SIC: 3541 Plasma process metal cutting machines

(G-3591)
CUYAHOGA FENCE LLC
3100 E 45th St Ste 504 (44127-1095)
P.O. Box 43547 (44143-0547)
PHONE..............................216 830-2200
Rita Samorezov, *Prin*
EMP: 15 **EST:** 2008
SALES (est): 1.3MM **Privately Held**
SIC: 1799 3446 Fence construction; Grillwork, ornamental metal

(G-3592)
CUYAHOGA REBUILDERS INC
5111 Brookpark Rd (44134-1047)
PHONE..............................216 635-0659
Randolph Treudler, *Pr*
EMP: 6 **EST:** 1967
SQ FT: 2,500
SALES (est): 407.83K **Privately Held**
SIC: 3694 Alternators, automotive

(G-3593)
CW LIQUIDATION INC
1801 E 9th St Ste 1100 (44114-3103)
EMP: 100
SIC: 3441 Fabricated structural metal

(G-3594)
CWD LLC (DH)
Also Called: Centric Parts
127 Public Sq Ste 5110 (44114-1313)
PHONE..............................310 218-1082
Marc Weinsweig, *Managing Member*
Henry Hippert, *
Jayme Farina, *
Jason Soika, *
Gary Nix, *
◆ **EMP:** 37 **EST:** 2000
SQ FT: 80,000
SALES (est): 24.46MM
SALES (corp-wide): 7.28B **Privately Held**
Web: www.centricparts.com
SIC: 3714 Motor vehicle parts and accessories
HQ: Cwd Intermediate Holdings Ii, Llc
127 Public Sq Ste 5110
Cleveland OH

(G-3595)
CYBERUTILITY LLC
1599 Maywood Rd (44121-4101)
PHONE..............................216 291-8723
John Scott Minor, *Managing Member*
EMP: 8 **EST:** 1999
SALES (est): 148.94K **Privately Held**
SIC: 2911 Petroleum refining

(G-3596)
D JACOB INDUSTRIES LLC
13995 Enterprise Ave (44135-5117)
PHONE..............................440 292-7277
Daniel Ganim, *Prin*
EMP: 9 **EST:** 2017
SALES (est): 2.4MM **Privately Held**
SIC: 3999 Manufacturing industries, nec

(G-3597)
DAKOTA SOFTWARE CORPORATION (PA)

1375 Euclid Ave Ste 500 (44115-1808)
PHONE..............................216 765-7100
Reginald C Shiverick, *Pr*
EMP: 61 **EST:** 1988
SALES (est): 7.48MM
SALES (corp-wide): 7.48MM **Privately Held**
Web: www.dakotasoft.com
SIC: 7372 Prepackaged software

(G-3598)
DAL-LITTLE FABRICATING INC
Also Called: Megna Plastics
11707 Putnam Ave (44105-5416)
P.O. Box 44067 (44144-0067)
PHONE..............................216 883-3323
Betty J Massielle, *Pr*
Joe Massielle, *Pr*
EMP: 8 **EST:** 1991
SQ FT: 13,000
SALES (est): 517.99K **Privately Held**
Web: www.dallittle.com
SIC: 3229 3441 Glass fiber products; Fabricated structural metal

(G-3599)
DARLING INGREDIENTS INC
1002 Peltnine Ave (44109)
PHONE..............................216 651-9300
Lorie Shorvath, *Mgr*
EMP: 7
SQ FT: 28,122
SALES (corp-wide): 6.79B **Publicly Held**
Web: www.darlingii.com
SIC: 2077 5191 Animal and marine fats and oils; Farm supplies
PA: Darling Ingredients Inc.
5601 N Macarthur Blvd
Irving TX 75038
972 717-0300

(G-3600)
DARLING INGREDIENTS INC
1002 Belt Line Ave (44109-2848)
PHONE..............................216 351-3440
Howard Murray, *Mgr*
EMP: 7
SALES (corp-wide): 6.79B **Publicly Held**
Web: www.darlingii.com
SIC: 2077 Animal and marine fats and oils
PA: Darling Ingredients Inc.
5601 N Macarthur Blvd
Irving TX 75038
972 717-0300

(G-3601)
DAWN ENTERPRISES INC (PA)
Also Called: Sportwing
9155 Sweet Valley Dr (44125-4223)
PHONE..............................216 642-5506
Robert Kovach, *Pr*
Lawrence De Laat, *General Vice President*
Lori M Kovach, *
▲ **EMP:** 40 **EST:** 1973
SQ FT: 69,900
SALES (est): 4.2MM
SALES (corp-wide): 4.2MM **Privately Held**
Web: www.sportwing.com
SIC: 3089 5521 Injection molding of plastics; Used car dealers

(G-3602)
DAY-GLO COLOR CORP (DH)
4515 Saint Clair Ave (44103-1268)
PHONE..............................216 391-7070
Alice J Walker, *Prin*
Arthur A Sayre, *
John D Steele, *
Phil Rozick, *Research*
▲ **EMP:** 140 **EST:** 1931
SQ FT: 36,000

▲ = Import ▼ = Export
◆ = Import/Export

SALES (est): 49.02MM
SALES (corp-wide): 7.34B **Publicly Held**
Web: www.dayglo.com
SIC: **2816** 2851 Inorganic pigments;
Lacquers, varnishes, enamels, and other
coatings
HQ: Republic Powdered Metals, Inc.
2628 Pearl Rd
Medina OH 44256
330 225-3192

(G-3603)
DAY-GLO COLOR CORP
4518 Hamilton Ave (44114-3854)
PHONE..............................216 391-7070
Steven Jackson, *Brnch Mgr*
EMP: 15
SALES (corp-wide): 7.34B **Publicly Held**
Web: www.dayglo.com
SIC: **2816** 2851 Inorganic pigments;
Lacquers, varnishes, enamels, and other
coatings
HQ: Day-Glo Color Corp.
4515 St Clair Ave
Cleveland OH 44103
216 391-7070

(G-3604)
DB REDIHEAT INC
Also Called: National Bios Fabric Company
4516 Saint Clair Ave (44103-1204)
PHONE..............................216 361-0530
David Breen, *Pr*
◆ EMP: 20 EST: 2009
SQ FT: 28,000
SALES (est): 1.98MM **Privately Held**
Web: www.rediheat.com
SIC: **5131** 2241 7389 Textile converters;
Bindings, textile; Sewing contractor

(G-3605)
DCD TECHNOLOGIES INC
17920 S Waterloo Rd (44119-3222)
PHONE..............................216 481-0056
Dave Hodgson, *Pr*
EMP: 11 EST: 1974
SQ FT: 18,000
SALES (est): 1.19MM **Privately Held**
Web: www.dcdtech.com
SIC: **3544** Dies and die holders for metal
cutting, forming, die casting

(G-3606)
DCM MANUFACTURING INC (HQ)
4540 W 160th St (44135-2628)
PHONE..............................216 265-8006
Theodore Berger, *Ch*
Theodore Berger Junior, *Pr*
Kevin J Berger, *
Marilyn J Berger, *
◆ EMP: 50 EST: 1994
SQ FT: 68,000
SALES (est): 8.72MM
SALES (corp-wide): 43.22MM **Privately
Held**
Web: www.dcm-mfg.com
SIC: **3621** 3433 3714 Motors, electric;
Heating equipment, except electric; Motor
vehicle parts and accessories
PA: Dreison International, Inc.
4540 W 160th St
Cleveland OH 44135
216 362-0755

(G-3607)
DCW ACQUISITION INC
Also Called: Regol-G Industries
10646 Leuer Ave (44108-1352)
P.O. Box 608957 (44108-0957)
PHONE..............................216 451-0666
Dan Waite, *Pr*

EMP: 7 EST: 1986
SQ FT: 20,000
SALES (est): 460.73K **Privately Held**
Web: www.regol-g.com
SIC: **7389** 2394 2393 2392 Sewing
contractor; Canvas and related products;
Textile bags; Household furnishings, nec

(G-3608)
DEFENSE CO INC
600 Superior Ave E (44114-2614)
PHONE..............................413 998-1637
Kent Rosenthal, *Pr*
EMP: 7 EST: 1976
SALES (est): 1.07MM **Privately Held**
SIC: **3769** Guided missile and space vehicle
parts and aux. equip., R&D

(G-3609)
DEPENDABLE STAMPING COMPANY
1160 E 222nd St (44117-1176)
PHONE..............................216 486-5522
Jeffrey N Beres, *Pr*
Michael Beres, *General Vice President**
Roy Beres, *
EMP: 25 EST: 1981
SQ FT: 20,000
SALES (est): 8.29MM **Privately Held**
Web: www.dependablestamping.com
SIC: **3469** Stamping metal for the trade

(G-3610)
DESMOND ENGRAVING CO INC
3264 W 105th St (44111-2865)
PHONE..............................216 265-8338
William Bozak, *Pr*
Brett J May, *VP*
EMP: 7 EST: 1968
SALES (est): 426.06K **Privately Held**
Web: www.truemarkengraving.com
SIC: **3953** Date stamps, hand: rubber or
metal

(G-3611)
DETREX CORPORATION (DH)
Also Called: Research Technologies Intl
1000 Belt Line Ave (44109-2848)
PHONE..............................216 749-2605
Thomas E Mark, *Pr*
Robert M Currie, *VP*
◆ EMP: 10 EST: 1920
SQ FT: 5,000
SALES (est): 90.62MM **Privately Held**
Web: www.detrexchemicals.com
SIC: **2819** 3589 Inorganic acids except nitric
and phosphoric; Commercial cleaning
equipment
HQ: Italmatch Chemicals Spa
Via Magazzini Del Cotone 17
Genova GE 16128

(G-3612)
DI IORIO SHEET METAL INC
5002 Clark Ave (44102-4552)
P.O. Box 602210 (44102-0210)
PHONE..............................216 961-3703
Anthony Di Iorio, *Pr*
Anna Di Iorio, *Sec*
EMP: 12 EST: 1963
SQ FT: 34,000
SALES (est): 1.85MM **Privately Held**
SIC: **3444** Sheet metalwork

(G-3613)
DIAMOND MACHINERY LLC
Also Called: Diamond Machinery Company
19525 Hilliard Blvd Unit 16729
(44116-4750)
PHONE..............................216 312-1235
William T Danicki, *Pr*
EMP: 8 EST: 2019

SALES (est): 350.02K **Privately Held**
Web: www.diamondmachineryco.com
SIC: **3553** 7699 Woodworking machinery;
Industrial machinery and equipment repair

(G-3614)
DIASOME PHARMACEUTICALS INC
10000 Cedar Ave Ste 6 (44106-2119)
PHONE..............................216 444-7110
Robert Geho, *CEO*
Todd Hobbs, *CMO*
Peter Tollman, *Ch Bd*
EMP: 10 EST: 2008
SALES (est): 2.21MM **Privately Held**
Web: www.diasome.com
SIC: **2834** Pharmaceutical preparations

(G-3615)
DIE-CUT PRODUCTS CO
Also Called: D C
1801 E 30th St (44114-4471)
PHONE..............................216 771-6994
Ari Comet, *Pr*
Steve A Comet, *Pr*
Arlene R Comet, *VP*
EMP: 10 EST: 1944
SQ FT: 10,600
SALES (est): 3.33MM **Privately Held**
Web: www.diecut.com
SIC: **3069** 3452 3053 3499 Washers, rubber;
Washers; Gaskets; packing and sealing
devices; Shims, metal

(G-3616)
DIRECTCONNECTGROUP LTD
Also Called: D C G
5501 Cass Ave (44102-2121)
PHONE..............................216 281-2866
Robert A Durham, *Pt*
Scott L Durham, *Pt*
James E Pinkin, *Pt*
Steven J Pinkin, *Pt*
Terry Storms, *Pt*
EMP: 7 EST: 2003
SALES (est): 528.02K **Privately Held**
Web: www.dcgone.com
SIC: **2752** 7331 Offset printing; Mailing
service

(G-3617)
DISCOUNT FLORAL SUPPLY INC
Also Called: Ribbon Warehouse
1734 Ivanhoe Rd (44112-1674)
EMP: 6 EST: 1985
SQ FT: 9,000
SALES (est): 74.93K **Privately Held**
SIC: **2396** Ribbons and bows, cut and sewed

(G-3618)
DISH ONE UP SATELLITE INC
3634 Euclid Ave Ste 100 (44115-2535)
PHONE..............................216 482-3875
Firas Essa, *Pr*
EMP: 99 EST: 2001
SALES (est): 4.93MM **Privately Held**
Web: www.dish1up.com
SIC: **3679** 5731 Antennas, satellite:
household use; Antennas, satellite dish

(G-3619)
DISTILLATA COMPANY (PA)
1608 E 24th St (44114-4212)
P.O. Box 93845 (44101-5845)
PHONE..............................216 771-2900
TOLL FREE: 800
William E Schroeder, *Pr*
Herbert Buckman, *
J C Little, *
R M Egan, *
Dalphne Axline, *
EMP: 70 EST: 1897

SQ FT: 100,000
SALES (est): 9.76MM
SALES (corp-wide): 9.76MM **Privately
Held**
Web: www.distillata.com
SIC: **2899** 5149 Distilled water; Mineral or
spring water bottling

(G-3620)
DISTRIBUTOR GRAPHICS INC
6909 Engle Rd Ste 13 (44130-3484)
PHONE..............................440 260-0024
Richard Doerr, *Pr*
James F Gottschalk, *VP*
Robert Wilson, *Treas*
EMP: 8 EST: 1985
SQ FT: 8,500
SALES (est): 313.93K **Privately Held**
Web: www.magicmkt.com
SIC: **2752** Offset printing

(G-3621)
DIVERSIFIED MOLD CASTINGS LLC
Also Called: Diversified Mold & Castings Co
19800 Miles Rd (44128-4118)
PHONE..............................216 663-1814
Vince Costello, *Prin*
EMP: 37 EST: 2008
SALES (est): 4.46MM **Privately Held**
Web: www.diversifiedmolds.com
SIC: **3544** Special dies and tools

(G-3622)
DOAN/PYRAMID SOLUTIONS LLC
5069 Corbin Dr (44128-5413)
PHONE..............................216 587-9510
EMP: 22 EST: 2004
SALES (est): 2.36MM **Privately Held**
SIC: **3822** Environmental controls

(G-3623)
DOLLARS N CENT INC
1057 S Belvoir Blvd (44121-2944)
PHONE..............................971 381-0406
Roderick Byers, *CEO*
EMP: 11 EST: 2005
SALES (est): 545.41K **Privately Held**
SIC: **1389** Construction, repair, and
dismantling services

(G-3624)
DOMINION ENTERPRISES
26301 Curtiss Wright Pkwy (44143-4413)
PHONE..............................216 472-1870
Michelle Dubblestyne, *Prin*
EMP: 18
Web: www.dominionenterprises.com
SIC: **2721** Periodicals
HQ: Dominion Enterprises
150 Granby St Ste 150 # 150
Norfolk VA 23510

(G-3625)
DOMINO FOODS INC
Also Called: Domino Sugar
2075 E 65th St (44103-4630)
PHONE..............................216 432-3222
Jeffrey Bender, *Brnch Mgr*
EMP: 164
SALES (corp-wide): 2.16B **Privately Held**
Web: www.dominosugar.com
SIC: **2099** 7389 Sugar; Packaging and
labeling services
HQ: Domino Foods Inc.
99 Wood Ave S Ste 901
Iselin NJ 08830
732 590-1173

(G-3626)
DONNELLEY FINANCIAL LLC
1300 E 9th St Ste 1200 (44114-1513)
PHONE....................................216 621-8384
Andrew Komer, *Mgr*
EMP: 6
SALES (corp-wide): 781.9MM **Publicly Held**
Web: www.dfinsolutions.com
SIC: 2752 Offset printing
HQ: Donnelley Financial, Llc
35 W Wacker Dr
Chicago IL 60601
844 866-4337

(G-3627)
DORN COLOR LLC
11555 Berea Rd (44102-3522)
PHONE....................................216 634-2252
▲ EMP: 118 EST: 1929
SALES (est): 20.73MM
SALES (corp-wide): 25.28MM **Privately Held**
Web: www.dorncolor.com
SIC: 2752 Cards, lithographed
PA: Signum Llc
32000 Aurora Rd Ste C
Solon OH 44139
440 248-2233

(G-3628)
DOVE DIE AND STAMPING COMPANY
15665 Brookpark Rd (44142-1619)
PHONE....................................216 267-3720
Gerald Wagner, *Pr*
Norma Wagner, *
EMP: 30 EST: 1952
SQ FT: 42,000
SALES (est): 5.69MM **Privately Held**
Web: www.dovedie.com
SIC: 3469 3544 Stamping metal for the trade
; Special dies and tools

(G-3629)
DRABIK MANUFACTURING INC
15601 Commerce Park Dr (44142-2016)
PHONE....................................216 267-1616
James Drabik, *Pr*
EMP: 17 EST: 1962
SQ FT: 13,000
SALES (est): 2.27MM **Privately Held**
Web: www.drabikinc.com
SIC: 3599 7692 Machine shop, jobbing and repair; Welding repair

(G-3630)
DRAPERY STITCH - CLEVELAND INC
Also Called: Drapery Stitch
12890 Berea Rd (44111-1624)
PHONE....................................216 252-3857
George Beckmann, *Pr*
Wayne Monar, *VP*
EMP: 7 EST: 1978
SQ FT: 7,200
SALES (est): 671.62K **Privately Held**
Web: www.draperystitch.com
SIC: 2211 2221 Draperies and drapery fabrics, cotton; Draperies and drapery fabrics, manmade fiber and silk

(G-3631)
DREAMZONE MEDIA LLC
850 Euclid Ave Ste 819 (44114-3315)
PHONE....................................216 532-3301
EMP: 10 EST: 2017
SALES (est): 319.66K **Privately Held**
Web: www.dreamzonemedia.com
SIC: 3577 Data conversion equipment, media-to-media: computer

(G-3632)
DREISON INTERNATIONAL INC (PA)
4540 W 160th St (44135-2628)
PHONE....................................216 362-0755
John Berger Junior, *Pr*
Theodore Berger Junior, *Pr*
Theodore J Berger Senior, *Ch Bd*
Marilyn J Berger, *
Whitney Slaght, *
◆ EMP: 190 EST: 1986
SQ FT: 210,000
SALES (est): 43.22MM
SALES (corp-wide): 43.22MM **Privately Held**
Web: www.dreison.com
SIC: 3643 3621 3561 3564 Current-carrying wiring services; Motors, electric; Pumps and pumping equipment; Purification and dust collection equipment

(G-3633)
DRINK MODERN TECHNOLOGIES LLC
4125 Lorain Ave 2nd Fl (44113-3718)
PHONE....................................216 577-1536
Mike Dougherty, *Managing Member*
EMP: 8 EST: 2022
SALES (est): 4.06MM **Privately Held**
SIC: 3556 Beverage machinery

(G-3634)
DUBLIN PLASTICS INC
9202 Reno Ave (44105-2125)
PHONE....................................216 641-5904
Donald R Newman, *Pr*
James Newman, *Sec*
EMP: 8 EST: 1983
SALES (est): 659.33K **Privately Held**
SIC: 3089 Injection molding of plastics

(G-3635)
DUCK-T PRINTING LLC
Also Called: Duck-T Printing
1544 E 86th St (44106-3748)
PHONE....................................216 312-0838
Lashun Duckworth, *Prin*
EMP: 10 EST: 2014
SALES (est): 207.32K **Privately Held**
Web: www.kennyskarsllc.com
SIC: 2752 Commercial printing, lithographic

(G-3636)
DUCT FABRICATORS INC
Also Called: Fab3 Group
883 Addison Rd (44103-1607)
PHONE....................................216 391-2400
John Sickle, *Prin*
Steven Haydu, *Prin*
EMP: 8 EST: 2011
SALES (est): 1.52MM **Privately Held**
Web: www.tinshops.com
SIC: 3444 Sheet metalwork

(G-3637)
DUCTS INC
883 Addison Rd (44103-1607)
PHONE....................................216 391-2400
Charlotte Sickle, *Ch*
Patricia Sickle Mc Elroy, *
John E Sickle Junior, *Pr*
James Sickle, *
EMP: 6 EST: 1962
SQ FT: 30,000
SALES (est): 352.16K **Privately Held**
SIC: 1761 3444 Sheet metal work, nec; Sheet metalwork

(G-3638)
DUPONT SPECIALTY PDTS USA LLC
Also Called: Dupont Vespel Parts and Shapes
6200 Hillcrest Dr (44125-4624)
PHONE....................................216 901-3600
Anthony Adetayo, *Brnch Mgr*
EMP: 118
SALES (corp-wide): 12.39B **Publicly Held**
Web: www.dupont.com
SIC: 3366 3568 Bushings and bearings; Power transmission equipment, nec
HQ: Dupont Specialty Products Usa, Llc
974 Centre Rd
Wilmington DE 19805
302 295-5783

(G-3639)
DURABLE PLATING CO
4404 Saint Clair Ave (44103-1188)
PHONE....................................216 391-2132
Joe Akers, *Pr*
Tim Akers, *VP*
Shirley Akers, *Sec*
EMP: 7 EST: 1935
SQ FT: 6,500
SALES (est): 1MM **Privately Held**
Web: www.renzettilaw.com
SIC: 3471 Electroplating of metals or formed products

(G-3640)
DURAY PLATING COMPANY INC
13701 Triskett Rd (44111-1520)
PHONE....................................216 941-5540
Christine Roth, *Pr*
Kenneth R Roth, *Pr*
EMP: 20 EST: 1963
SQ FT: 6,000
SALES (est): 2.03MM **Privately Held**
Web: www.durayplatingco.com
SIC: 3471 Electroplating of metals or formed products

(G-3641)
DVUV LLC
4641 Hinckley Industrial Pkwy (44109-6002)
PHONE....................................216 741-5511
▼ EMP: 16 EST: 2005
SQ FT: 20,000
SALES (est): 4.38MM **Privately Held**
Web: www.dvuv.com
SIC: 2521 Wood office furniture

(G-3642)
DYNAMIC TOOL & MOLD INC
12126 York Rd Unit N (44133-3688)
PHONE....................................440 237-8665
Dale English, *Pr*
John Getchell, *VP*
EMP: 7 EST: 1996
SQ FT: 3,500
SALES (est): 708.72K **Privately Held**
Web: www.dynamictoolandmold.com
SIC: 3544 Special dies and tools

(G-3643)
E & K PRODUCTS CO INC
3520 Cesko Ave (44109-1487)
PHONE....................................216 631-2510
Lee Klimek, *Pr*
Lee Klimek, *Ch Bd*
David Klimek, *VP*
Joyce Klimek, *Sec*
EMP: 8 EST: 1966
SQ FT: 25,000
SALES (est): 687.84K **Privately Held**
Web: www.ekproducts.com
SIC: 3599 3444 Machine shop, jobbing and repair; Sheet metalwork

(G-3644)
E D M FASTAR INC
13410 Enterprise Ave (44135-5162)
PHONE....................................216 676-0100
Frank Star, *Pr*
EMP: 7 EST: 1999
SQ FT: 3,000
SALES (est): 681.79K **Privately Held**
Web: www.fastaredm.com
SIC: 3544 Special dies and tools

(G-3645)
E POMPILI SONS INC
Also Called: Pompili Precast Concrete
12307 Broadway Ave (44125-1847)
PHONE....................................216 581-8080
William Pompili, *Pr*
EMP: 8 EST: 1953
SQ FT: 14,500
SALES (est): 460.87K **Privately Held**
Web: www.pompiliprecastconcrete.com
SIC: 3272 Concrete products, precast, nec

(G-3646)
E-Z ELECTRIC MOTOR SVC CORP
8510 Bessemer Ave (44127-1843)
P.O. Box 22531 (44122-0531)
PHONE....................................216 581-8820
Demetrius Ledgyard, *Pr*
EMP: 8 EST: 1965
SQ FT: 15,000
SALES (est): 857.18K **Privately Held**
Web: www.ezelectricmotor.com
SIC: 7694 Electric motor repair

(G-3647)
EAGLE FAMILY FOODS GROUP LLC (PA)
1975 E 61st St (44103-3810)
PHONE....................................330 382-3725
Paul Smucker Wagstaff, *CEO*
Paul Smucker Wagstaff, *Managing Member*
Larry Herman, *
Jeff Boyle, *CAO*
Dan Gentile, *
EMP: 25 EST: 2015
SALES (est): 101.8MM
SALES (corp-wide): 101.8MM **Privately Held**
Web: www.eaglefoods.com
SIC: 2023 Condensed milk

(G-3648)
EAST WEST COPOLYMER LLC (PA)
Also Called: East West Copolymer
28026 Gates Mills Blvd (44124-4730)
PHONE....................................225 267-3400
Gregory Nelson, *Pr*
Celso Goncalves, *Sr VP*
Patrick Bowers, *VP*
Bobby Rikhoff, *VP*
◆ EMP: 54 EST: 2005
SALES (est): 5.23MM **Privately Held**
SIC: 2822 Synthetic rubber

(G-3649)
EAST WOODWORKING COMPANY
2044 Random Rd (44106-2392)
P.O. Box 221185 (44122-0995)
PHONE....................................216 791-5950
Zigmund T Hersh, *Pr*
Albert Hersh, *VP*
Coby Hersh, *Mgr*
Ken Hersh, *Mgr*
EMP: 8 EST: 1956
SQ FT: 12,400
SALES (est): 449.67K **Privately Held**

SIC: 1751 2521 2522 3261 Cabinet building and installation; Cabinets, office: wood; Office cabinets and filing drawers, except wood; Vitreous plumbing fixtures

(G-3650)
EATON AEROQUIP LLC (HQ)
Also Called: Eaton Global Hose
1000 Eaton Blvd (44122-6058)
PHONE...............................440 523-5000
Alexander M Cutler, *CEO*
E R Franklin, *
◆ EMP: 220 EST: 1940
SQ FT: 21,000
SALES (est): 92.92MM **Privately Held**
SIC: 3052 3492 3429 3069 Rubber hose; Hose and tube fittings and assemblies, hydraulic/pneumatic; Clamps and couplings, hose; Molded rubber products
PA: Eaton Corporation Public Limited Company
30 Pembroke Road
Dublin

(G-3651)
EATON CORPORATION
Also Called: NA Financial Service Center
6055 Rockside Woods Blvd N
(44131-2301)
P.O. Box 818035 (44181-8035)
PHONE...............................440 826-1115
EMP: 217
Web: www.dix-eaton.com
SIC: 3625 Relays and industrial controls
HQ: Eaton Corporation
1000 Eaton Blvd
Cleveland OH 44122
440 523-5000

(G-3652)
EATON CORPORATION (HQ)
Also Called: Eaton
1000 Eaton Blvd (44122-6058)
PHONE...............................440 523-5000
Craig Arnold, *Ch*
Mark Mcguire, *Ex VP*
Thomas Moran, *Sr VP*
David Foster, *Senior Vice President Corporate Development*
Katrina R Redmond Scp, *CIO*
◆ EMP: 450 EST: 1916
SALES (est): 1.95B **Privately Held**
Web: eaton.eightfold.ai
SIC: 3625 3714 3594 3559 Motor controls and accessories; Motor vehicle engines and parts; Pumps, hydraulic power transfer; Semiconductor manufacturing machinery
PA: Eaton Corporation Public Limited Company
30 Pembroke Road
Dublin

(G-3653)
EATON CORPORATION
Airflex Div
9919 Clinton Rd (44144-1077)
PHONE...............................216 281-2211
James W Fisher, *Brnch Mgr*
EMP: 200
Web: www.dix-eaton.com
SIC: 3714 3625 3542 3568 Air brakes, motor vehicle; Electromagnetic clutches or brakes ; Brakes, metal forming; Clutches, except vehicular
HQ: Eaton Corporation
1000 Eaton Blvd
Cleveland OH 44122
440 523-5000

(G-3654)
EATON ELECTRIC HOLDINGS LLC (HQ)
1000 Eaton Blvd (44122-6058)
PHONE...............................440 523-5000
Kirk Hachigian, *Pr*
Bruce M Taten, *
David Barta, *
Tyler Johnson, *
▲ EMP: 406 EST: 1996
SALES (est): 2.02B **Privately Held**
Web: www.eaton.com
SIC: 3612 3613 3644 3536 Transformers, except electric; Panel and distribution boards and other related apparatus; Noncurrent-carrying wiring devices; Hoists, cranes, and monorails
PA: Eaton Corporation Public Limited Company
30 Pembroke Road
Dublin

(G-3655)
EATON ELECTRICAL
23555 Euclid Ave (44117-1703)
P.O. Box 818021 (44181-8021)
PHONE...............................787 257-4470
EMP: 17 EST: 2017
SALES (est): 6.05MM **Privately Held**
SIC: 3625 Motor controls and accessories

(G-3656)
EATON INDUSTRIAL CORPORATION (HQ)
23555 Euclid Ave (44117-1732)
PHONE...............................216 523-4205
Craig Arnold, *CEO*
Paul R Keen, *
John S Glover, *
Earl R Franklin, *
EMP: 433 EST: 1990
SQ FT: 1,800,000
SALES (est): 24.34MM **Privately Held**
SIC: 3724 3728 Pumps, aircraft engine; Aircraft parts and equipment, nec
PA: Eaton Corporation Public Limited Company
30 Pembroke Road
Dublin

(G-3657)
EATON INDUSTRIAL CORPORATION
Also Called: Argo Tech Fluid Elec Dist Div
1000 Eaton Blvd (44122-6058)
PHONE...............................216 692-5456
Heath Monesmith, *Brnch Mgr*
EMP: 101
SIC: 7699 3728 Pumps and pumping equipment repair; Aircraft parts and equipment, nec
HQ: Eaton Industrial Corporation
23555 Euclid Ave
Cleveland OH 44117
216 523-4205

(G-3658)
EG ENTERPRISE SERVICES INC
5000 Euclid Ave Ste 100 (44103-3752)
P.O. Box 18029 (44118-0029)
PHONE...............................216 431-3300
Evon Gocan, *Pr*
Karla Shim, *VP*
EMP: 6 EST: 1993
SQ FT: 10,000
SALES (est): 105.88K **Privately Held**
SIC: 2752 7331 7334 Offset printing; Mailing service; Photocopying and duplicating services

(G-3659)
ELCO CORPORATION (DH)
Also Called: Elco
1000 Belt Line Ave (44109-2800)
PHONE...............................800 321-0467
Dave Millin, *CEO*
Bob Lunoe, *
◆ EMP: 33 EST: 1974
SQ FT: 72,000
SALES (est): 4.83MM **Privately Held**
Web:
www.lubeperformanceadditives.com
SIC: 2869 Industrial organic chemicals, nec
HQ: Detrex Corporation
1000 Belt Line Ave
Cleveland OH 44109
216 749-2605

(G-3660)
ELECTRIC CORD SETS INC (PA)
Also Called: Happy Trails Rv
4700 Manufacturing Ave (44135-2640)
PHONE...............................216 261-1000
Thomas Benbow, *Ch Bd*
Cathy Gilmour, *Treas*
Edward Benbow, *VP Opers*
Tammy Liloie, *VP*
◆ EMP: 6 EST: 1947
SQ FT: 3,500
SALES (est): 4.51MM
SALES (corp-wide): 4.51MM **Privately Held**
Web: www.ecspremier.com
SIC: 3643 Current-carrying wiring services

(G-3661)
ELECTROLIZING CORP OF OHIO (PA)
1325 E 152nd St (44112-2075)
P.O. Box 12007 (44112-0007)
PHONE...............................800 451-8655
Lawrence E Noble, *Pr*
Scott Noble, *Ex VP*
Todd Noble, *VP*
EMP: 20 EST: 1948
SQ FT: 20,000
SALES (est): 5.22MM
SALES (corp-wide): 5.22MM **Privately Held**
Web: www.ecofohio.com
SIC: 3471 Electroplating of metals or formed products

(G-3662)
ELECTROLIZING CORPORATION OHIO
Also Called: ELECTROLIZING CORPORATION OF OHIO
1655 Collamer Ave (44110-3201)
PHONE...............................216 451-8653
Daral Cook, *Mgr*
EMP: 10
SQ FT: 12,342
SALES (corp-wide): 5.22MM **Privately Held**
Web: www.ecofohio.com
SIC: 3471 Electroplating of metals or formed products
PA: The Electrolizing Corporation Of Ohio
1325 E 152nd St
Cleveland OH 44112
800 451-8655

(G-3663)
ELMET TECHNOLOGIES INC
21801 Tungsten Rd (44117-1117)
PHONE...............................216 692-3990
Larry Mchugh, *CEO*
John Durham, *Sr VP*
Pete Calfo, *Sr VP*
Joel Hoffman, *Sr VP*
EMP: 11 EST: 1995

SQ FT: 150,000
SALES (est): 1.23MM **Privately Held**
Web: www.hcstarcksolutions.com
SIC: 3339 Primary nonferrous metals, nec

(G-3664)
ELYRIA SPRING SPCLTY HOLDG INC (PA)
14577 Lorain Ave (44111-3156)
PHONE...............................440 323-5502
Eric G Turk, *CEO*
EMP: 7 EST: 2016
SALES (est): 2.74MM
SALES (corp-wide): 2.74MM **Privately Held**
Web: www.elyriaspring.com
SIC: 3469 5085 3495 Stamping metal for the trade; Springs; Wire springs

(G-3665)
EM ES BE COMPANY LLC
Also Called: M.S. Barkin Company
18210 Saint Clair Ave (44110-2610)
PHONE...............................216 761-9500
EMP: 8 EST: 1966
SQ FT: 2,500
SALES (est): 290.74K **Privately Held**
Web: www.msbarkinco.com
SIC: 3911 5944 Jewelry, precious metal; Jewelry, precious stones and precious metals

(G-3666)
EM4 LLC
Also Called: G&H Baltimore
676 Alpha Dr (44143-2123)
PHONE...............................410 987-5600
Mark Webster, *Brnch Mgr*
EMP: 25
SALES (corp-wide): 9.86MM **Privately Held**
Web: www.gandh.com
SIC: 3661 Fiber optics communications equipment
PA: Em4, Llc
7 Oak Park Dr
Bedford MA 01730
781 275-7501

(G-3667)
EM4 LLC
676 Alpha Dr (44143-2123)
PHONE...............................608 240-4800
Brian Engstrom, *Brnch Mgr*
EMP: 25
SALES (corp-wide): 9.86MM **Privately Held**
Web: www.gandh.com
SIC: 3674 Semiconductors and related devices
PA: Em4, Llc
7 Oak Park Dr
Bedford MA 01730
781 275-7501

(G-3668)
EMERSON INDUSTRIAL AUTOMATION
7800 Hub Pkwy (44125-5711)
PHONE...............................216 901-2400
EMP: 9 EST: 2015
SALES (est): 2.98MM **Privately Held**
Web: www.emerson.com
SIC: 3823 Process control instruments

(G-3669)
EMX INDUSTRIES LLC (HQ)
Also Called: Emx Industries, Inc.
5660 Transportation Blvd (44125-5363)
PHONE...............................216 518-9888

GEOGRAPHIC

Joseph Williams, *Pr*
▲ **EMP: 16 EST:** 1992
SALES (est): 9.85MM
SALES (corp-wide): 15.34MM **Privately Held**
Web: www.emxinc.com
SIC: 3699 Security control equipment and systems
PA: Watervale Equity Partners Fund I G.P., Llc
29525 Chagrin Blvd
Beachwood OH 44122
216 926-7219

(G-3670)
ENAMELAC COMPANY
18103 Roseland Rd (44112-1001)
P.O. Box 5058 (44085-0258)
PHONE..................................216 481-8878
John M Kanuch Junior, *Pr*
EMP: 10 **EST:** 1950
SQ FT: 10,000
SALES (est): 227.81K **Privately Held**
Web: www.enamelac.com
SIC: 3479 Enameling, including porcelain, of metal products

(G-3671)
ENERCO GROUP INC (PA)
Also Called: Mr Heater
4560 W 160th St (44135-2628)
P.O. Box P.O. Box 6660 (44101-1660)
PHONE..................................216 916-3000
Franco Pozzi, *CEO*
Jeff Bush, *
Mark Przypyfz, *
Allen Haire, *
▲ **EMP:** 101 **EST:** 1957
SQ FT: 120,875
SALES (est): 47.02MM
SALES (corp-wide): 47.02MM **Privately Held**
Web: www.enerco.com
SIC: 3433 Gas infrared heating units

(G-3672)
ENERCO TECHNICAL PRODUCTS INC
Also Called: Mr. Heater
4560 W 160th St (44135-2628)
P.O. Box 6660 (44101-1660)
PHONE..................................216 916-3000
Allen L Haire, *CEO*
John D Duross, *
Francis Verchick, *
▲ **EMP:** 58 **EST:** 1986
SQ FT: 48,000
SALES (est): 1.79MM
SALES (corp-wide): 47.02MM **Privately Held**
Web: www.heatstarbyenerco.com
SIC: 3433 Gas infrared heating units
PA: Enerco Group, Inc.
4560 W 160th St
Cleveland OH 44135
216 916-3000

(G-3673)
ENERSYS
12690 Elmwood Ave (44111-5912)
PHONE..................................216 252-4242
Walter Sauerteig, *Genl Mgr*
EMP: 168
SALES (corp-wide): 3.58B **Publicly Held**
Web: www.enersys.com
SIC: 3691 Lead acid batteries (storage batteries)
PA: Enersys
2366 Bernville Rd
Reading PA 19605
610 208-1991

(G-3674)
ENESPRO LLC
15825 Industrial Pkwy (44135-3319)
PHONE..................................630 332-2801
Chuck Grossman, *CEO*
Michael Enright, *Pr*
EMP: 8 **EST:** 2017
SALES (est): 2.91MM
SALES (corp-wide): 472.43MM **Privately Held**
Web: www.enesproppe.com
SIC: 3842 Gloves, safety
HQ: National Safety Apparel, Llc
15825 Industrial Pkwy
Cleveland OH 44135

(G-3675)
ENPROTECH INDUSTRIAL TECH LLC (DH)
Also Called: Enprotech Mechanical Services
4259 E 49th St (44125-1001)
PHONE..................................216 883-3220
Chris Pascarella, *CEO*
▲ **EMP:** 23 **EST:** 1950
SQ FT: 96,000
SALES (est): 32.23MM **Privately Held**
Web: www.enprotech.com
SIC: 3547 3365 3599 8711 Rolling mill machinery; Machinery castings, aluminum; Custom machinery; Engineering services
HQ: Industrious Group Inc.
4259 E 49th St
Cleveland OH 44125
216 206-0080

(G-3676)
ENSIGN PRODUCT COMPANY INC
3528 E 76th St (44105-1510)
P.O. Box 27167 (44127-0167)
PHONE..................................216 341-5911
Birney R Walker Iii, *Pr*
Christopher Walker, *VP*
Charles Snyder, *Sec*
EMP: 6 **EST:** 1920
SQ FT: 9,000
SALES (est): 310.78K **Privately Held**
SIC: 2992 2899 Lubricating oils; Chemical preparations, nec

(G-3677)
ENTERPRISE TOOL & DIE COMPANY
4940 Schaaf Ln (44131-1008)
PHONE..................................216 351-1300
Robert C Schweikert, *Pr*
Richard W Schweikert, *VP*
Todd Schweikert, *Sec*
EMP: 10 **EST:** 1954
SQ FT: 10,000
SALES (est): 974.84K **Privately Held**
SIC: 3544 Dies and die holders for metal cutting, forming, die casting

(G-3678)
ENVIRI CORPORATION
Sherwood Divisions of Harsco
7900 Hub Pkwy (44125-5713)
PHONE..................................216 961-1570
Tom Hensley, *Mgr*
EMP: 7
SALES (corp-wide): 2.34B **Publicly Held**
Web: www.enviri.com
SIC: 3443 Industrial vessels, tanks, and containers
PA: Enviri Corporation
100-120 N 18th St # 17
Philadelphia PA 19103
267 857-8715

(G-3679)
ENVIROFAB INC
7914 Lake Ave (44102-1933)
P.O. Box 602750 (44102-0750)
PHONE..................................216 651-1767
Thomas J Rusnak, *Pr*
Richard Rusnak, *VP*
EMP: 6 **EST:** 1974
SQ FT: 42,000
SALES (est): 729.19K **Privately Held**
Web: www.envirofab.net
SIC: 3564 Dust or fume collecting equipment, industrial

(G-3680)
EOS TECHNOLOGY INC
8525 Clinton Rd (44144-1014)
PHONE..................................216 281-2999
John Hadgis, *Pr*
Gregory Hadgis, *VP*
EMP: 7 **EST:** 1996
SALES (est): 581.96K **Privately Held**
SIC: 3599 Machine shop, jobbing and repair

(G-3681)
EPSILON MANAGEMENT CORPORATION
Also Called: Areway
8525 Clinton Rd (44144-1014)
PHONE..................................216 634-2500
◆ **EMP:** 200
Web: www.epsilonmgmt.com
SIC: 2851 3471 Paints and allied products; Polishing, metals or formed products

(G-3682)
EQUIPMENT MFRS INTL INC
Also Called: E M I
16151 Puritas Ave (44135-2617)
P.O. Box 94725 (44101)
PHONE..................................216 651-6700
Jerry Senk, *Prin*
R T Mackin, *
Joe Mcfarland, *Prin*
Bill Vondriska, *Prin*
Dave Bowman, *Prin*
▲ **EMP:** 30 **EST:** 1982
SQ FT: 65,000
SALES (est): 7.51MM **Privately Held**
Web: www.emi-inc.com
SIC: 3559 5084 Foundry machinery and equipment; Industrial machinery and equipment

(G-3683)
ERICO PRODUCTS INC
Also Called: Erico
34600 Solon Rd (44139-2695)
PHONE..................................440 248-0100
▲ **EMP:** 428
SIC: 3644 3441 3629 3643 Noncurrent-carrying wiring devices; Fabricated structural metal; Electronic generation equipment; Rail bonds, electric: for propulsion and signal circuits

(G-3684)
ERIE STREET THEA SVCS INC
1621 E 41st St (44103-2305)
PHONE..................................216 426-0050
Angie Davis, *Pr*
EMP: 8 **EST:** 1993
SALES (est): 129.87K **Privately Held**
Web: www.eriestreet.net
SIC: 5049 3999 Theatrical equipment and supplies; Theatrical scenery

(G-3685)
ERIEVIEW METAL TREATING CO
Also Called: Apex Metals

4465 Johnston Pkwy (44128-2998)
PHONE..................................216 663-1780
Alex Kappos, *Pr*
Dennis Kappos, *
George Kappos Junior, *Sec*
EMP: 100 **EST:** 1961
SQ FT: 70,000
SALES (est): 8.96MM **Privately Held**
Web: www.erieviewmetal.com
SIC: 3471 Electroplating of metals or formed products

(G-3686)
ESSI ACOUSTICAL PRODUCTS
11750 Berea Rd Ste 1 (44111-1603)
P.O. Box 643 (44107-0943)
PHONE..................................216 251-7888
Mark Essi, *Pr*
EMP: 10 **EST:** 1984
SQ FT: 6,000
SALES (est): 1.07MM **Privately Held**
Web: www.essiacoustical.com
SIC: 3296 Acoustical board and tile, mineral wool

(G-3687)
ESTERLINE TECHNOLOGIES CORP (HQ)
Also Called: Esterline
1350 Euclid Ave Ste 1600 (44114)
PHONE..................................216 706-2960
Curtis C Reusser, *Pr*
Stephen M Nolan, *Ex VP*
Paul P Benson, *Chief Human Resources Officer*
Donald E Walther, *Ex VP*
▼ **EMP:** 35 **EST:** 1967
SALES (est): 1.54B
SALES (corp-wide): 7.94B **Publicly Held**
Web: www.transdigm.com
SIC: 3728 3812 3429 Aircraft assemblies, subassemblies, and parts, nec; Aircraft control instruments; Aircraft hardware
PA: Transdigm Group Incorporated
1350 Euclid Ave Ste 1600
Cleveland OH 44115
216 706-2960

(G-3688)
EUCLID CHEMICAL COMPANY (DH)
19215 Redwood Rd (44110-2735)
PHONE..................................800 321-7628
Thomas Gairing, *Pr*
◆ **EMP:** 20 **EST:** 1910
SALES (est): 111.09MM
SALES (corp-wide): 7.34B **Publicly Held**
Web: www.euclidchemical.com
SIC: 2899 4213 3272 Chemical preparations, nec; Trucking, except local; Concrete products, nec
HQ: Tremco Cpg Inc.
3735 Green Rd
Beachwood OH 44122
216 292-5000

(G-3689)
EUCLID COFFEE CO INC
17230 S Waterloo Rd (44110-3811)
PHONE..................................216 481-3330
James M Repak, *Pr*
M J Repak, *CEO*
EMP: 8 **EST:** 1935
SQ FT: 10,000
SALES (est): 388.38K **Privately Held**
Web: www.euclidcoffee.com
SIC: 2095 Coffee roasting (except by wholesale grocers)

(G-3690)
EUCLID MEDIA GROUP LLC (PA)
Also Called: Do 210
737 Bolivar Rd (44115-1259)
P.O. Box 1028 (44096-1028)
PHONE................................216 241-7550
Daniel N Zelman, *Managing Member*
EMP: 10 **EST:** 1998
SALES (est): 5.05MM
SALES (corp-wide): 5.05MM **Privately Held**
Web: www.chavagroup.com
SIC: 2711 Newspapers, publishing and printing

(G-3691)
EUREKA SCREW MACHINE PDTS CO
Also Called: Eureka Screw Machine Co
3960 E 91st St (44105-3964)
PHONE................................216 883-1715
William Rubick, *Pr*
Irene Rubick, *Treas*
EMP: 6 **EST:** 1950
SQ FT: 5,136
SALES (est): 533.03K **Privately Held**
Web: www.eurekamachine.com
SIC: 3451 Screw machine products

(G-3692)
EVEN CUT ABRASIVE COMPANY
850 E 72nd St (44103-1007)
PHONE................................216 881-9595
Art Ellison, *Pr*
EMP: 17 **EST:** 1932
SALES (est): 778.41K **Privately Held**
Web: www.evencut.com
SIC: 3291 Abrasive products

(G-3693)
EVEREADY PRINTING INC
Also Called: Weprintquick.com
20700 Miles Pkwy (44128-5506)
PHONE................................216 587-2389
Roger Wolfson, *Prin*
Roger Wolfson, *Pr*
Scott Wolfson, *VP*
EMP: 20 **EST:** 1905
SALES (est): 2.45MM **Privately Held**
Web: www.evereadyprint.com
SIC: 2752 Offset printing

(G-3694)
EVEREADY PRODUCTS CORPORATION
1101 Belt Line Ave (44109-2849)
PHONE................................216 661-2755
Samuel Vandivort, *Ch Bd*
Daniel Harrington, *Pr*
EMP: 14 **EST:** 1951
SQ FT: 36,000
SALES (est): 6.28MM **Privately Held**
Web: www.evereadyproducts.com
SIC: 2813 Aerosols

(G-3695)
EVERYTHING IN AMERICA
Also Called: Eia
4141 Stilmore Rd (44121-3129)
PHONE................................347 871-6872
Patrick Hadley, *VP*
Renee Hawkins, *Asst VP*
EMP: 8 **EST:** 2013
SALES (est): 82.33K **Privately Held**
SIC: 5211 2452 7389 Modular homes; Modular homes, prefabricated, wood; Business services, nec

(G-3696)
EXACT-TOOL & DIE INC
5425 W 140th St (44142-1704)

PHONE................................216 676-9140
Frank K Chesek, *CEO*
John J Melnik, *
Mark S Klepper, *
Robert Matis, *
Ron Gunter, *
EMP: 35 **EST:** 1977
SQ FT: 60,000
SALES (est): 6.27MM **Privately Held**
Web: www.exact-tool.com
SIC: 3465 3469 3544 3694 Automotive stampings; Metal stampings, nec; Special dies, tools, jigs, and fixtures; Engine electrical equipment

(G-3697)
EXCELLENT TOOL & DIE INC
10921 Briggs Rd (44111-5333)
PHONE................................216 671-9222
John Kinsch, *Pr*
John Kinsch, *Pr*
Edith Burnside, *VP*
EMP: 6 **EST:** 1983
SQ FT: 4,800
SALES (est): 1.92MM **Privately Held**
Web: www.excellent-tool.com
SIC: 3599 Machine shop, jobbing and repair

(G-3698)
EXPLORYS INC
1111 Superior Ave E (44114-2522)
PHONE................................216 767-4700
Stephen Mchale, *CEO*
Charles Lougheed, *
Aaron Cornell, *
Thomas Chickerella, *
EMP: 24 **EST:** 2009
SALES (est): 13.59MM
SALES (corp-wide): 62.75B **Publicly Held**
Web: www.ibm.com
SIC: 7372 Application computer software
PA: International Business Machines Corporation
1 New Orchard Rd
Armonk NY 10504
914 499-1900

(G-3699)
EXPO PACKAGING INC
Also Called: Expo Machinery
4832 Ridge Rd (44144-3329)
PHONE................................216 267-9700
Patricia Kaszas, *Pr*
Lorena J Kaszas, *Conl Mgr*
Tim Kaszas Senior, *VP*
Jim Kaszas Junior, *VP*
EMP: 6 **EST:** 1982
SALES (est): 100.81K **Privately Held**
SIC: 7389 3565 Packaging and labeling services; Packaging machinery

(G-3700)
EXPRESS GROUND SERVICES INC
Also Called: Eminent Transport
1241 E 172nd St (44119-3128)
PHONE................................216 870-9374
Rashid Sharif, *Pr*
EMP: 6 **EST:** 2021
SALES (est): 892.91K **Privately Held**
SIC: 3537 7389 Trucks: freight, baggage, etc.: industrial, except mining; Business Activities at Non-Commercial Site

(G-3701)
EZ BRITE BRANDS INC
806 Sharon Dr Ste C (44145-7701)
P.O. Box 40025 (44140-0025)
PHONE................................440 871-7817
Edmond Aghajanian, *Pr*
Marcia Meermans, *Ofcr*
EMP: 11 **EST:** 1989

SQ FT: 11,000
SALES (est): 1.1MM **Privately Held**
SIC: 2842 Dusting cloths, chemically treated

(G-3702)
FABRICATING MACHINE TOOLS LTD
12360 Plaza Dr (44130-1043)
PHONE................................440 666-9187
TOLL FREE: 800
EMP: 6 **EST:** 1997
SQ FT: 6,000
SALES (est): 1.29MM **Privately Held**
SIC: 3599 Machine shop, jobbing and repair

(G-3703)
FALCON INNOVATIONS INC
3316 W 118th St (44111-1723)
PHONE................................216 252-0676
Robert A Jewell Junior, *Pr*
EMP: 6 **EST:** 1964
SQ FT: 6,400
SALES (est): 505.45K **Privately Held**
Web: www.falconinnovations.com
SIC: 3599 Machine shop, jobbing and repair

(G-3704)
FALLON PHARAOHS
3911 Grosvenor Rd (44118-2315)
PHONE................................216 990-2746
Lavelle Moore, *Pr*
EMP: 7 **EST:** 2019
SALES (est): 250K **Privately Held**
SIC: 2329 Men's and boy's clothing, nec

(G-3705)
FALLS STAMPING & WELDING CO
Also Called: Plant Two
1720 Fall St (44113-2416)
PHONE................................216 771-9635
John Hall, *Frmn Supr*
EMP: 13
SALES (corp-wide): 11.15MM **Privately Held**
Web: www.falls-stamping.com
SIC: 3465 Automotive stampings
PA: Falls Stamping & Welding Company
2900 Vincent St
Cuyahoga Falls OH 44221
330 928-1191

(G-3706)
FARASEY STEEL FABRICATORS INC
4000 Iron Ct (44115-3582)
PHONE................................216 641-1853
Don J Henderson, *Pr*
Don J Henderson, *Pr*
Robert L Henderson, *VP*
George R Henderson, *VP*
EMP: 15 **EST:** 1859
SQ FT: 14,000
SALES (est): 1.72MM **Privately Held**
Web: www.faraseysteelfabricators.com
SIC: 3441 Fabricated structural metal

(G-3707)
FBC CHEMICAL CORPORATION
7301 Bessemer Ave (44127-1817)
PHONE................................216 341-2000
EMP: 21
SALES (corp-wide): 43.14MM **Privately Held**
Web: www.fbcchem.com
SIC: 3312 Chemicals and other products derived from coking
PA: Fbc Chemical Corporation
634 Route 228
Mars PA 16046
724 625-3116

(G-3708)
FCI INC
4801 W 160th St (44135-2633)
PHONE................................216 251-5200
Kenneth Edgar, *Pr*
Irene Edgar, *
EMP: 80 **EST:** 1958
SALES (est): 6.33MM **Privately Held**
Web: www.jbtc.com
SIC: 3089 Injection molding of plastics

(G-3709)
FDI ENTERPRISES
17700 Saint Clair Ave (44110-2621)
PHONE................................440 269-8282
EMP: 6 **EST:** 2016
SALES (est): 3.4MM **Privately Held**
Web: www.tripolymer.com
SIC: 3089 Plastics products, nec

(G-3710)
FEDERAL HOSE MANUFACTURING LLC
10514 Dupont Ave (44108-1348)
PHONE................................800 346-4673
EMP: 25 **EST:** 2021
SALES (est): 1.37MM **Privately Held**
Web: www.federalhose.com
SIC: 3599 Hose, flexible metallic

(G-3711)
FEDPRO INC (HQ)
Also Called: Gasoila Thred-Taper
4520 Richmond Rd (44128-5757)
PHONE................................216 464-6440
Jon Outcalt Junior, *CEO*
Jon Outcalt Senior, *Ch*
Jon Outcalt Junior, *Pr*
▲ **EMP:** 28 **EST:** 1915
SQ FT: 4,000
SALES (est): 33.03MM
SALES (corp-wide): 33.03MM **Privately Held**
Web: www.fpcintl.com
SIC: 2891 Sealing compounds, synthetic rubber or plastic
PA: Fpc International, Inc.
4520 Richmond Rd
Cleveland OH 44128
216 464-6440

(G-3712)
FENCE ONE INC
Also Called: Great Lake Fence
11111 Broadway Ave (44125-1659)
PHONE................................216 441-2600
Michael Ely, *Pr*
EMP: 14 **EST:** 1951
SQ FT: 12,000
SALES (est): 2.46MM **Privately Held**
Web: www.greatlakesfence.com
SIC: 1521 1799 3496 General remodeling, single-family houses; Fence construction; Miscellaneous fabricated wire products

(G-3713)
FERRALLOY INC
28001 Ranney Pkwy (44145-1159)
PHONE................................440 250-1900
William Habansky Junior, *Pr*
Sherri Habansky, *Sec*
▲ **EMP:** 8 **EST:** 1978
SQ FT: 15,000
SALES (est): 4.1MM **Privately Held**
Web: www.ferralloy.com
SIC: 5051 3599 Castings, rough: iron or steel; Machine shop, jobbing and repair

(G-3714)
FERROTHERM CORPORATION
4758 Warner Rd (44125-1117)
PHONE.............................216 883-9350
Haakon Egeland, *CEO*
Haakon Egeland, *Ch Bd*
Emery Ceo, *Pr*
Alf Egeland, *
Thor Egeland, *
▲ EMP: 105 EST: 1939
SQ FT: 90,000
SALES (est): 22.76MM **Privately Held**
Web: www.ferrotherm.com
SIC: 3462 3724 3812 3694 Turbine engine forgings, ferrous; Aircraft engines and engine parts; Search and navigation equipment; Engine electrical equipment

(G-3715)
FIBERCORE LLC
15625 Saranac Rd (44110-2427)
PHONE.............................216 249-2100
Brian Wood, *Pr*
▲ EMP: 14 EST: 2004
SALES (est): 922.56K **Privately Held**
Web: www.fibercorellc.com
SIC: 3999 3053 Pet supplies; Packing materials

(G-3716)
FIELDS PROCESS TECHNOLOGY INC
1849 W 24th St (44113-3513)
P.O. Box 91806 (44101-3806)
PHONE.............................216 781-4787
Joseph Fields, *Owner*
EMP: 6 EST: 2001
SALES (est): 340.73K **Privately Held**
SIC: 3089 Plastics containers, except foam

(G-3717)
FINELLI ORNAMENTAL IRON CO
Also Called: Finelli Architectural Iron Co
30815 Solon Rd (44139-3485)
PHONE.............................440 248-0050
Frank Finelli, *Pr*
Angelo Finelli, *VP*
James Korosec, *VP*
EMP: 22 EST: 1962
SQ FT: 15,000
SALES (est): 2.26MM **Privately Held**
Web: www.finelliironworks.com
SIC: 3446 1751 Ornamental metalwork; Carpentry work

(G-3718)
FIRST BRANDS GROUP LLC (DH)
127 Public Sq Ste 5300 (44114-1219)
PHONE.............................888 565-9632
Patrick James, *Managing Member*
EMP: 21 EST: 2013
SALES (est): 6.49B
SALES (corp-wide): 7.28B **Privately Held**
Web: www.framfilters.ca
SIC: 3714 Windshield wiper systems, motor vehicle
HQ: First Brands Group Intermediate, Llc
127 Public Sq Ste 5110
Cleveland OH 44114
216 589-0198

(G-3719)
FIRST BRNDS GROUP HOLDINGS LLC (PA)
127 Public Sq Ste 5300 (44114-1219)
PHONE.............................216 589-0198
Patrick James, *CEO*
EMP: 33 EST: 2020
SALES (est): 7.28B
SALES (corp-wide): 7.28B **Privately Held**

SIC: 3069 Tubing, rubber

(G-3720)
FIRST BRNDS GROUP INTRMDATE LL (HQ)
Also Called: Luber-Finer
127 Public Sq Ste 5110 (44114-1313)
PHONE.............................216 589-0198
Patrick James, *Managing Member*
EMP: 13 EST: 2018
SALES (est): 6.49B
SALES (corp-wide): 7.28B **Privately Held**
SIC: 3069 Tubing, rubber
PA: First Brands Group Holdings, Llc
127 Public Sq Ste 5300
Cleveland OH 44114
216 589-0198

(G-3721)
FIVES N AMERCN COMBUSTN INC (DH)
4455 E 71st St (44105-5601)
PHONE.............................216 271-6000
Luigi Russo, *Ch Bd*
Erik Paulhardt, *Pr*
Kathy E Ruekberg, *VP*
Philippe Guerreau, *Sec*
◆ EMP: 244 EST: 1917
SQ FT: 400,000
SALES (est): 49.88MM
SALES (corp-wide): 1.92MM **Privately Held**
Web: www.fivesgroup.com
SIC: 3433 Heating equipment, except electric
HQ: Fives Inc.
46912 Liberty Dr
Wixom MI 48393
248 477-0800

(G-3722)
FLAGSHIP TRADING CORPORATION
Also Called: Manufacturers Wholesale Lumber
734 Alpha Dr Ste J (44143-2135)
EMP: 35 EST: 1983
SALES (est): 4.96MM **Privately Held**
SIC: 2491 5031 Structural lumber and timber, treated wood; Lumber, plywood, and millwork

(G-3723)
FLASH INDUSTRIAL TECH LTD
30 Industry Dr (44146-4414)
PHONE.............................440 786-8979
Lawrence P Zajac, *Prin*
Mary Elizabeth Zajac, *Prin*
▲ EMP: 9 EST: 1995
SQ FT: 18,000
SALES (est): 2.08MM **Privately Held**
Web: www.flashindustrial.com
SIC: 3599 Machine shop, jobbing and repair

(G-3724)
FLEXNOVA INC (PA)
6100 Oak Tree Blvd Ste 200 (44131-2544)
PHONE.............................216 288-6961
Steve Rossi, *Pr*
EMP: 11 EST: 2003
SQ FT: 1,000
SALES (est): 1.93MM
SALES (corp-wide): 1.93MM **Privately Held**
Web: www.flexnova.com
SIC: 7372 Prepackaged software

(G-3725)
FLEXRACK BY QCELLS LLC (PA)
Also Called: NSM
23000 Harvard Rd Ste B (44122-7234)
P.O. Box 270666 (06127)

PHONE.............................216 998-5988
◆ EMP: 145 EST: 1986
SALES (est): 9.12MM
SALES (corp-wide): 9.12MM **Privately Held**
Web: www.extrusions.com
SIC: 3354 Aluminum rod and bar

(G-3726)
FLIGHT BRIGHT LTD
23100 Miles Rd (44128-5441)
P.O. Box 391718 (44139-8718)
PHONE.............................216 663-6677
Allen Warner, *Pr*
EMP: 15 EST: 2004
SALES (est): 276.01K **Privately Held**
Web: www.flitebrite.com
SIC: 3471 Cleaning, polishing, and finishing

(G-3727)
FLOWCRETE NORTH AMERICA INC
19218 Redwood Rd (44110-2736)
PHONE.............................936 539-6700
Mark Greaves, *Pr*
Edward W Moore, *
▲ EMP: 24 EST: 2004
SALES (est): 1.05MM
SALES (corp-wide): 7.34B **Publicly Held**
Web: www.flowcrete.in
SIC: 3996 Tile, floor: supported plastic
HQ: Flowcrete Group Limited
Computershare Governance Serv.
Bristol

(G-3728)
FLUID SYSTEM SERVICE INC
13825 Triskett Rd (44111-1523)
P.O. Box 771414 (44107-0057)
PHONE.............................216 651-2450
John C Balliett, *Pr*
D Thomas George, *Sec*
EMP: 8 EST: 1981
SALES (est): 2.33MM **Privately Held**
Web: www.fluidsystemsohio.com
SIC: 3511 7699 Hydraulic turbines; Hydraulic equipment repair

(G-3729)
FLUKE ELECTRONICS CORPORATION
28775 Aurora Rd (44139-1837)
PHONE.............................800 850-4608
EMP: 9 EST: 2004
SALES (est): 2.88MM
SALES (corp-wide): 6.23B **Publicly Held**
Web: www.fluke.com
SIC: 3825 Instruments to measure electricity
PA: Fortive Corporation
6920 Seaway Blvd
Everett WA 98203
425 446-5000

(G-3730)
FOAM SEAL INC
5109 Hamilton Ave (44114-3907)
PHONE.............................216 881-8111
Sarah Nash, *Ch Bd*
Ronald Moeller, *
EMP: 120 EST: 1977
SQ FT: 250,000
SALES (est): 22.68K **Privately Held**
Web: www.novagard.com
SIC: 2891 2911 Adhesives and sealants; Greases, lubricating
PA: Novagard Solutions, Inc.
5109 Hamilton Ave
Cleveland OH 44114

(G-3731)
FOAM-TEX SOLUTIONS CORP
13981 W Parkway Rd (44135-4511)
PHONE.............................216 889-2702
Donald Abshire, *CEO*
Alan Abshire, *VP Prd*
▲ EMP: 6 EST: 1999
SQ FT: 6,700
SALES (est): 243.15K **Privately Held**
Web: www.foam-tex.com
SIC: 2841 Soap and other detergents

(G-3732)
FOLLOW PRINT CLUB ON FACEBOOK
11150 East Blvd (44106-1711)
PHONE.............................216 707-2579
EMP: 7 EST: 2011
SALES (est): 257.38K **Privately Held**
Web: www.printclubcleveland.org
SIC: 2752 Commercial printing, lithographic

(G-3733)
FOOD DESIGNS INC
Also Called: Ohio City Pasta
5299 Crayton Ave (44104-2829)
PHONE.............................216 651-9221
Gary W Thomas, *Pr*
EMP: 10 EST: 1991
SALES (est): 2.4MM **Privately Held**
Web: www.ohiocitypasta.com
SIC: 2099 2032 Pasta, uncooked: packaged with other ingredients; Ravioli: packaged in cans, jars, etc.

(G-3734)
FOOTE PRINTING COMPANY INC
Also Called: Audit Forms
2800 E 55th St (44104-2862)
PHONE.............................216 431-1757
Michael Duhr, *Pr*
Karl-heinz Duhr, *Pr*
Steven Duhr, *VP*
Steven Duhhr, *CEO*
EMP: 10 EST: 1907
SQ FT: 16,000
SALES (est): 2.18MM **Privately Held**
Web: www.footeprinting.com
SIC: 2752 2759 Offset printing; Letterpress printing

(G-3735)
FOREST CITY COMPANIES INC
Also Called: Forest City Packaging
3607 W 56th St (44102-5739)
PHONE.............................216 586-5279
Anthony Galang, *Pr*
Dawn Galang, *
EMP: 23 EST: 2003
SQ FT: 42,000
SALES (est): 6.93MM **Privately Held**
Web: www.forestcityco.com
SIC: 4783 2441 2394 Packing goods for shipping; Boxes, wood; Canvas and related products

(G-3736)
FORGE PRODUCTS CORPORATION
Also Called: Forged Products
9503 Woodland Ave (44104-2487)
PHONE.............................216 231-2600
Charles E Thayer Ii, *Pr*
EMP: 26 EST: 1962
SQ FT: 31,600
SALES (est): 4.4MM **Privately Held**
Web: www.forgeproducts.com
SIC: 3312 3463 3462 Forgings, iron and steel ; Nonferrous forgings; Iron and steel forgings

(G-3737)
FORMTEK INC (DH)
Also Called: Formtek International
4899 Commerce Pkwy (44128-5905)
PHONE..................................216 292-4460
Joe Mayer, *Pr*
▲ **EMP:** 60 **EST:** 1984
SQ FT: 56,000
SALES (est): 25.38MM
SALES (corp-wide): 689.94MM **Privately Held**
Web: www.formtekgroup.com
SIC: 3547 3549 3535 Pipe and tube mills; Coiling machinery; Conveyors and conveying equipment
HQ: Formtek Inc
711 Ogden Ave
Lisle IL 60532
630 285-1500

(G-3738)
FORMTEK METAL FORMING INC
Yoder Manufacturing Division
4899 Commerce Pkwy (44128-5905)
PHONE..................................216 292-4460
Glenn Ertel, *Brnch Mgr*
EMP: 95
SALES (corp-wide): 689.94MM **Privately Held**
Web: www.formtekgroup.com
SIC: 3547 Rolling mill machinery
HQ: Formtek, Inc.
4899 Commerce Pkwy
Cleveland OH 44128
216 292-4460

(G-3739)
FOUNDRY ARTISTS INC
Also Called: Studio Foundry
4404 Perkins Ave (44103-3544)
PHONE..................................216 391-9030
Mark Olitsky, *Pr*
Craig Horstman, *Treas*
John Ranally, *Sec*
Lisa Kenion, *VP*
EMP: 7 **EST:** 1988
SQ FT: 3,000
SALES (est): 880.32K **Privately Held**
Web: www.studiofoundry.net
SIC: 3366 Bronze foundry, nec

(G-3740)
FPT CLEVELAND LLC (DH)
Also Called: Ferrous Processing and Trading
8550 Aetna Rd (44105-1607)
PHONE..................................216 441-3800
Andrew M Luntz, *
▲ **EMP:** 105 **EST:** 1999
SALES (est): 40MM
SALES (corp-wide): 19.18B **Publicly Held**
Web: www.fptscrap.com
SIC: 4953 5051 5093 3341 Recycling, waste materials; Iron and steel (ferrous) products; Ferrous metal scrap and waste; Secondary nonferrous metals
HQ: Ferrous Processing And Trading Company
1333 Brewery Park Blvd
Detroit MI 48207
313 567-9710

(G-3741)
FRAM GROUP
127 Public Sq Ste 5110 (44114-1313)
PHONE..................................479 271-7934
Ike Peterson, *Owner*
EMP: 9 **EST:** 2012
SALES (est): 4MM **Privately Held**
SIC: 3714 Motor vehicle parts and accessories

(G-3742)
FRANCK AND FRIC INCORPORATED
7919 Old Rockside Rd (44131-2300)
P.O. Box 31148 (44131-0148)
PHONE..................................216 524-4451
Donald R Skala Senior, *Pr*
David R Skala, *VP*
Donald C Skala Junior, *VP*
Stacey Carson, *Asst VP*
EMP: 51 **EST:** 1934
SQ FT: 20,000
SALES (est): 4.42MM **Privately Held**
Web: franck-fric-inc.business.site
SIC: 1711 1761 3441 3444 Ventilation and duct work contractor; Sheet metal work, nec ; Fabricated structural metal; Sheet metalwork

(G-3743)
FREEWAY CORPORATION (PA)
9301 Allen Dr (44125-4688)
PHONE..................................216 524-9700
◆ **EMP:** 110 **EST:** 1944
SALES (est): 22.2MM
SALES (corp-wide): 22.2MM **Privately Held**
Web: www.freewaycorp.com
SIC: 3469 Metal stampings, nec

(G-3744)
FUNNY TIMES INC
2176 Lee Rd (44118-2908)
P.O. Box 18530 (44118-0530)
PHONE..................................216 371-8600
Raymond Lesser, *Pr*
Susan Wolpert, *Sec*
EMP: 6 **EST:** 1985
SALES (est): 482.99K **Privately Held**
Web: www.funnytimes.com
SIC: 2711 Newspapers, publishing and printing

(G-3745)
FURNITURE CONCEPTS INC
4925 Galaxy Pkwy Ste G (44128-5961)
PHONE..................................216 292-9100
Karyl Walker, *Pr*
Karyl Walker, *CEO*
EMP: 12 **EST:** 1991
SQ FT: 1,700
SALES (est): 846.28K **Privately Held**
Web: www.furnitureconcepts.com
SIC: 7641 2599 2426 Furniture repair and maintenance; Factory furniture and fixtures; Furniture squares, hardwood

(G-3746)
FX DIGITAL MEDIA INC (PA)
1600 E 23rd St (44114-4208)
PHONE..................................216 241-4040
John Gadd, *CEO*
Columbus Woodruff, *Pr*
Nikki Woodruff, *Stockholder*
EMP: 18 **EST:** 1997
SQ FT: 15,000
SALES (est): 1.77MM **Privately Held**
SIC: 7336 2754 Commercial art and graphic design; Color printing: gravure

(G-3747)
FX DIGITAL MEDIA INC
Also Called: Hot Cards.com
2400 Superior Ave E Ste 100 (44114-4236)
PHONE..................................216 241-4040
Columbus Woodruff, *Brnch Mgr*
EMP: 7
SIC: 2752 Offset printing
PA: Fx Digital Media, Inc.
1600 E 23rs St
Cleveland OH 44114

(G-3748)
G & S METAL PRODUCTS CO INC (PA)
3330 E 79th St (44127-1831)
P.O. Box 78510 (44105-8510)
PHONE..................................216 441-0700
◆ **EMP:** 165 **EST:** 1949
SALES (est): 19.15MM
SALES (corp-wide): 19.15MM **Privately Held**
Web: www.gsmetal.com
SIC: 3411 5023 5072 3556 Pans, tinned; Kitchenware; Hardware; Food products machinery

(G-3749)
G AND J AUTOMATIC SYSTEMS INC
Also Called: G & J Packaging
14701 Industrial Pkwy (44135-4547)
PHONE..................................216 741-6070
Gregory Shteyngarts, *Pr*
EMP: 30 **EST:** 1985
SQ FT: 23,000
SALES (est): 123.5K **Privately Held**
SIC: 7389 3565 Packaging and labeling services; Packaging machinery

(G-3750)
G T METAL FABRICATORS INC
Also Called: Acromet Metal Fabricators
12126 York Rd Unit E (44133-3688)
PHONE..................................440 237-8745
Gary Callahan, *Pr*
Judy Callahan, *VP*
EMP: 12 **EST:** 1966
SQ FT: 9,000
SALES (est): 993.98K **Privately Held**
Web: www.acromet.com
SIC: 3444 Sheet metal specialties, not stamped

(G-3751)
G W COBB CO
3914 Broadway Ave 16 (44115-3694)
PHONE..................................216 341-0100
George W Cobb Junior, *Pr*
EMP: 12 **EST:** 1940
SQ FT: 15,000
SALES (est): 999.26K **Privately Held**
Web: www.gwcobb.com
SIC: 3411 5084 Food containers, metal; Industrial machinery and equipment

(G-3752)
G2 MATERIALS LLC
17325 Euclid Ave Ste 3038 (44112-1255)
PHONE..................................216 293-4211
Timothy Gascoigne, *Managing Member*
EMP: 6 **EST:** 2021
SALES (est): 1.5MM **Privately Held**
Web: www.g2materials.com
SIC: 3444 Machine guards, sheet metal

(G-3753)
GALAXY BALLOONS INCORPORATED
11750 Berea Rd Ste 3 (44111-1603)
P.O. Box 698 (44107-0998)
PHONE..................................216 476-3360
Terry Brizz, *Pr*
▲ **EMP:** 130 **EST:** 1990
SQ FT: 50,000
SALES (est): 9.91MM **Privately Held**
Web: www.galaxyballoon.com
SIC: 2752 7336 5092 5199 Offset printing; Silk screen design; Balloons, novelty; Advertising specialties

(G-3754)
GARFIELD ALLOYS INC (PA)
4878 Chaincraft Rd (44125-1807)
PHONE..................................216 587-4843
Chuck Slovich, *Pr*
Mike Slovich Junior, *Sec*
◆ **EMP:** 12 **EST:** 1950
SQ FT: 60,000
SALES (est): 3.01MM
SALES (corp-wide): 3.01MM **Privately Held**
SIC: 3369 Magnesium and magnes.-base alloy castings, exc. die-casting

(G-3755)
GARICK LLC (HQ)
Also Called: Ogg Garick
8400 Sweet Valley Dr Ste 408 (44125-4244)
PHONE..................................216 581-0100
Gary P Trinetti, *Managing Member*
EMP: 20 **EST:** 1980
SALES (est): 44.9MM
SALES (corp-wide): 22.06B **Publicly Held**
Web: www.garick.com
SIC: 2875 0711 2499 5091 Potting soil, mixed; Soil preparation services; Mulch or sawdust products, wood; Athletic goods
PA: Waste Management, Inc.
800 Capitol St Ste 3000
Houston TX 77002
713 512-6200

(G-3756)
GARLAND COMMERCIAL INDUSTRIES LLC
1333 E 179th St (44110-4500)
PHONE..................................800 338-2204
◆ **EMP:** 6 **EST:** 1973
SALES (est): 1.46MM
SALES (corp-wide): 4.67B **Privately Held**
Web: www.garland-group.com
SIC: 3556 3589 3631 3567 Ovens, bakery; Cooking equipment, commercial; Household cooking equipment; Industrial furnaces and ovens
HQ: Welbilt, Inc.
2227 Welbilt Blvd
New Port Richey FL 34655
727 375-7010

(G-3757)
GARLAND INDUSTRIES INC (PA)
3800 E 91st St (44105-2197)
PHONE..................................216 641-7500
David Sokol, *Pr*
Melvin Chrostowski, *VP Mktg*
G Richard Olivier, *Admn Execs*
William Oley, *VP Sls*
Joe Orlando, *Sls Mgr*
EMP: 8 **EST:** 1895
SQ FT: 150,000
SALES (est): 706.22MM
SALES (corp-wide): 706.22MM **Privately Held**
Web: www.garlandco.com
SIC: 2952 6512 8712 Roofing materials; Commercial and industrial building operation; Architectural services

(G-3758)
GARLAND/DBS INC
3800 E 91st St (44105-2103)
PHONE..................................216 641-7500
Dave Sokol, *Pr*
Richard Debacco, *VP*
Melvin Chrostowski, *VP Mktg*
Chuck Ripepi, *CFO*
EMP: 250 **EST:** 2009
SALES (est): 13.45MM
SALES (corp-wide): 706.22MM **Privately Held**

Web: www.dbsgarland.com
SIC: 2952 6512 8712 Roofing materials; Commercial and industrial building operation; Architectural services
HQ: The Garland Company Inc
3800 E 91st St
Cleveland OH 44105
216 641-7500

(G-3759)
GE LIGHTING INC
Also Called: GE
1975 Noble Rd (44112-1719)
Rural Route 1975 Noble Rd (44112)
PHONE..............................216 266-2121
Bill Lacey, *CEO*
Ken Friesen, *
EMP: 80 EST: 1996
SALES (est): 20.9MM
SALES (corp-wide): 399.47MM **Privately Held**
Web: www.gelighting.com
SIC: 3646 Commercial lighting fixtures
PA: Savant Systems, Inc.
45 Perseverance Way
Hyannis MA 02601
508 683-2500

(G-3760)
GEAR COMPANY OF AMERICA INC
14300 Lorain Ave (44111-2297)
PHONE..............................216 671-5400
Edward Morel, *Pr*
EMP: 60 EST: 1946
SQ FT: 96,000
SALES (est): 7.2MM **Privately Held**
Web: www.gearcoa.com
SIC: 3462 3714 3566 Gears, forged steel; Gears, motor vehicle; Gears, power transmission, except auto

(G-3761)
GEBAUER COMPANY
4444 E 153rd St (44128-2955)
PHONE..............................216 581-3030
John Giltinan, *CEO*
Margaret Giltinan, *
David O'halloran, *Pr*
Ted Kulak, *
▲ EMP: 34 EST: 1957
SQ FT: 16,000
SALES (est): 12.49MM **Privately Held**
Web: www.gebauer.com
SIC: 2834 Pharmaceutical preparations

(G-3762)
GENERAL AWNING COMPANY INC
1350 E Granger Rd (44131-1206)
P.O. Box 275 (44402-0275)
PHONE..............................216 749-0110
Paul Gall, *Pr*
EMP: 6 EST: 1950
SQ FT: 10,000
SALES (est): 686.19K **Privately Held**
SIC: 3444 1751 1761 Awnings, sheet metal; Window and door (prefabricated) installation ; Siding contractor

(G-3763)
GENERAL ELECTRIC COMPANY
Also Called: GE
1099 Ivanhoe Rd (44110-3293)
PHONE..............................216 268-3846
James C Wiester, *Brnch Mgr*
EMP: 7
SALES (corp-wide): 38.7B **Publicly Held**
Web: geaerospace.com
SIC: 2819 2899 2851 Industrial inorganic chemicals, nec; Chemical preparations, nec ; Paints and allied products
PA: General Electric Company

1 Aviation Way
Cincinnati OH 45215
617 443-3000

(G-3764)
GENERAL ELECTRIC COMPANY
Also Called: GE
1814 E 45th St (44103-2321)
PHONE..............................216 391-8741
Mike Kridle, *Mgr*
EMP: 11
SALES (corp-wide): 38.7B **Publicly Held**
Web: geaerospace.com
SIC: 3641 Lamps, incandescent filament, electric
PA: General Electric Company
1 Aviation Way
Cincinnati OH 45215
617 443-3000

(G-3765)
GENERAL ELECTRIC COMPANY
Also Called: GE
18683 S Miles Rd (44128-4297)
PHONE..............................216 663-2110
Steve Hilgendorf, *Mgr*
EMP: 11
SQ FT: 53,462
SALES (corp-wide): 38.7B **Publicly Held**
Web: geaerospace.com
SIC: 3844 Radiographic X-ray apparatus and tubes
PA: General Electric Company
1 Aviation Way
Cincinnati OH 45215
617 443-3000

(G-3766)
GENERAL ELECTRIC COMPANY
Also Called: GE
4477 E 49th St (44125-1097)
PHONE..............................216 883-1000
Donald Mysliwiec, *Mgr*
EMP: 27
SQ FT: 12,000
SALES (corp-wide): 38.7B **Publicly Held**
Web: geaerospace.com
SIC: 7629 3621 3613 3612 Electrical repair shops; Motors and generators; Switchgear and switchboard apparatus; Transformers, except electric
PA: General Electric Company
1 Aviation Way
Cincinnati OH 45215
617 443-3000

(G-3767)
GENERAL MOTORS LLC
General Motors
5400 Chevrolet Blvd (44130-1451)
PHONE..............................216 265-5000
Al Maclauhlin, *Mgr*
EMP: 2028
Web: www.gm.com
SIC: 5511 3465 3714 2531 Automobiles, new and used; Body parts, automobile: stamped metal; Motor vehicle parts and accessories; Public building and related furniture
HQ: General Motors Llc
300 Rnaissance Ctr Ste L1
Detroit MI 48243

(G-3768)
GENERAL SHEAVE COMPANY INC
1335 Main Ave (44113-2389)
PHONE..............................216 781-8120
Antun Bunjevac, *Pr*
EMP: 9 EST: 1951
SQ FT: 7,500
SALES (est): 724.96K **Privately Held**

Web: www.generalsheave.com
SIC: 3599 Machine shop, jobbing and repair

(G-3769)
GENIE REPROS INC
2211 Hamilton Ave (44114-1154)
PHONE..............................216 696-6677
Barry Bishop, *Pr*
EMP: 6 EST: 1968
SQ FT: 7,900
SALES (est): 228.31K **Privately Held**
Web: www.reprosinc.com
SIC: 2752 Lithographing on metal

(G-3770)
GENT MACHINE COMPANY
12315 Kirby Ave (44108-1616)
PHONE..............................216 481-2334
Richard W Gent Junior, *Pr*
Diane Gent, *
Richard W Gent Iv, *VP*
EMP: 50 EST: 1927
SALES (est): 9.64MM **Privately Held**
Web: www.gentmachine.com
SIC: 3451 Screw machine products

(G-3771)
GEON COMPANY
6100 Oak Tree Blvd (44131-2544)
PHONE..............................216 447-6000
Thomas A Waltermire, *Pr*
Thomas A Waltermire, *Ch Bd*
Donald P Knechtges Senior, *Vice President Business*
Gregory L Rutman, *
W David Wilson, *
EMP: 3200 EST: 1993
SQ FT: 387,877
SALES (est): 9.91MM **Privately Held**
Web: www.geon.com
SIC: 2821 2869 2812 Polyvinyl chloride resins, PVC; Ethylene; Chlorine, compressed or liquefied

(G-3772)
GEROW EQUIPMENT COMPANY INC
706 E 163rd St (44110-2453)
PHONE..............................216 383-8800
Robert L Gerow, *CEO*
EMP: 7 EST: 1943
SQ FT: 1,500
SALES (est): 2.17MM **Privately Held**
Web: gerow-equipment-co.business.site
SIC: 3561 5084 Industrial pumps and parts; Heat exchange equipment, industrial

(G-3773)
GES AGM
12300 Snow Rd (44130-1001)
PHONE..............................216 658-6528
EMP: 26 EST: 2017
SALES (est): 6MM **Privately Held**
Web: www.ges-agm.com
SIC: 3624 Fibers, carbon and graphite

(G-3774)
GEW INC
11941 Abbey Rd Ste X (44133-2663)
PHONE..............................440 237-4439
Brian Wenger, *Pr*
▲ EMP: 9 EST: 1999
SALES (est): 3.64MM **Privately Held**
Web: www.gewuv.com
SIC: 3555 Printing trades machinery

(G-3775)
GIE MEDIA INC (PA)
5811 Canal Rd (44125-3430)
PHONE..............................800 456-0707
Richard J W Foster, *CEO*

Chris Foster, *
Dan Moreland, *
EMP: 35 EST: 1980
SQ FT: 6,500
SALES (est): 9.25MM
SALES (corp-wide): 9.25MM **Privately Held**
Web: www.giemedia.com
SIC: 2721 2731 Magazines: publishing only, not printed on site; Books, publishing only

(G-3776)
GLASS BLOCK HEADQUARTERS INC
15501 Munn Rd (44111-2002)
PHONE..............................216 941-5470
Sophia Fernandez, *Pr*
Elias Fernandez, *VP*
EMP: 6 EST: 2004
SALES (est): 954.94K **Privately Held**
Web: www.glassblockhq.com
SIC: 3229 Blocks and bricks, glass

(G-3777)
GLF INTERNATIONAL INC (PA)
3690 Orange Pl Ste 495 (44122-4465)
PHONE..............................216 621-6901
James Mcclurg, *Pr*
Gary Mcclurg, *Pr*
EMP: 10 EST: 1993
SQ FT: 20,000
SALES (est): 1.8MM **Privately Held**
SIC: 1479 Fluorspar mining

(G-3778)
GLOBE PIPE HANGER PRODUCTS INC
14601 Industrial Pkwy (44135-4545)
PHONE..............................216 362-6300
E Scot Kennedy, *Ch Bd*
Dan Collins, *Marketing*
Dale Zeleznik, *VP Fin*
Gary Horvath, *COO*
◆ EMP: 20 EST: 1978
SQ FT: 30,000
SALES (est): 5.41MM **Privately Held**
Web: www.globepipehanger.com
SIC: 3569 Firefighting and related equipment

(G-3779)
GOLDEN DRAPERY SUPPLY INC
Also Called: Golden Window Fashions
2500 Brookpark Rd Unit 3 (44134-1450)
PHONE..............................216 351-3283
Bernard Golden Junior, *Pr*
EMP: 28 EST: 1983
SQ FT: 25,000
SALES (est): 122.83K **Privately Held**
SIC: 5023 2591 Window furnishings; Window blinds

(G-3780)
GRABO INTERIORS INC
3605 Perkins Ave (44114-4632)
PHONE..............................216 391-6677
Joseph Grabo, *Pr*
Paul Grabo, *VP*
EMP: 6 EST: 1979
SQ FT: 4,400
SALES (est): 499.42K **Privately Held**
Web: www.grabointeriors.com
SIC: 2511 Wood household furniture

(G-3781)
GRAFTECH GLOBAL ENTPS INC
12900 Snow Rd (44130-1012)
PHONE..............................216 676-2000
Joel Hawthorne, *Pr*
EMP: 6 EST: 2016
SALES (est): 1.96MM **Publicly Held**

Web: graftech2022cr.q4web.com
SIC: 3629 Electrical industrial apparatus, nec
PA: Graftech International Ltd.
982 Keynote Cir
Brooklyn Heights OH 44131

(G-3782)
GRAFTECH INTL TRDG INC
12900 Snow Rd (44130-1012)
PHONE...............................216 676-2000
EMP: 24
SALES (est): 5.43MM Privately Held
Web: graftech2022cr.q4web.com
SIC: 3624 Carbon and graphite products

(G-3783)
GRAND ARCHT ETRNL EYE 314 LLC
Also Called: Grand Architect
10413 Nelson Ave (44105-4250)
PHONE...............................800 377-8147
EMP: 10 EST: 2021
SALES (est): 250K Privately Held
SIC: 1389 3531 0783 1731 Construction,
repair, and dismantling services;
Construction machinery attachments;
Removal services, bush and tree; Electrical
work

(G-3784)
GRAND HARBOR YACHT SALES & SVC
Also Called: Sneller Machine Tool Division
706 Alpha Dr (44143-2125)
PHONE...............................440 442-2919
John Bennington, Pr
EMP: 6 EST: 1973
SQ FT: 7,000
SALES (est): 486.24K Privately Held
Web: www.snellermachine.com
SIC: 3599 5084 3537 3531 Machine shop,
jobbing and repair; Industrial machinery
and equipment; Industrial trucks and
tractors; Construction machinery

(G-3785)
GRAPHIC ART SYSTEMS INC
Also Called: Grafix
5800 Pennsylvania Ave (44137-4331)
PHONE...............................216 581-9050
Jordan Katz, Pr
Hayley Ann Prendergast, *
◆ EMP: 27 EST: 1963
SQ FT: 45,000
SALES (est): 9.24MM Privately Held
Web: www.grafixarts.com
SIC: 3089 Injection molding of plastics

(G-3786)
GRAPHIC IMAGINATIONS
2160 Superior Ave E (44114-2102)
PHONE...............................216 781-4880
David Hein, BD
EMP: 6 EST: 2017
SALES (est): 218.06K Privately Held
SIC: 2782 Blankbooks and looseleaf binders

(G-3787)
GRAY & COMPANY PUBLISHERS
1588 E 40th St Ste 1b (44103-2386)
PHONE...............................216 431-2665
David Gray, Pr
EMP: 6 EST: 1991
SALES (est): 234.87K Privately Held
Web: www.grayco.com
SIC: 2741 Miscellaneous publishing

(G-3788)
GREAT LAKES BREWING CO
1947 W 28th St (44113-3422)
PHONE...............................216 771-4404

Robert Centa, Admn
EMP: 40
SALES (corp-wide): 24.22MM Privately
Held
Web: www.greatlakesbrewing.com
SIC: 2082 Malt beverages
PA: The Great Lakes Brewing Co
2516 Market Ave
Cleveland OH 44113
216 771-4404

(G-3789)
GREAT LAKES BREWING CO (PA)
2516 Market Ave (44113-3434)
PHONE...............................216 771-4404
Patrick F Conway, Pr
Daniel J Conway, Sec
Steven Pauwels, COO
◆ EMP: 105 EST: 1988
SQ FT: 20,000
SALES (est): 24.22MM
SALES (corp-wide): 24.22MM Privately
Held
Web: www.greatlakesbrewing.com
SIC: 2082 5813 5812 Beer (alcoholic
beverage); Bar (drinking places); American
restaurant

(G-3790)
GREAT LAKES ETCHING FINSHG CO
7010 Krick Rd (44146-4445)
PHONE...............................440 439-3624
Ronald Pool, Owner
Ronald Pool Senior, Pr
Ronald Pool Iii, VP
Joanne Marold, VP
EMP: 7 EST: 1962
SALES (est): 1.2MM Privately Held
SIC: 3479 Etching on metals

(G-3791)
GREAT LAKES GRAPHICS INC
3354 Superior Ave E (44114-4123)
PHONE...............................216 391-0077
Anthony R Lux, Pr
EMP: 9 EST: 1983
SQ FT: 15,000
SALES (est): 1.56MM Privately Held
SIC: 3555 7336 Plates, offset; Graphic arts
and related design

(G-3792)
GREAT LAKES GROUP
Also Called: Great Lakes Towing
4500 Division Ave (44102-2228)
PHONE...............................216 621-4854
Sheldon Guren, Ch Bd
Ronald Rasmus, *
George Sogar, *
EMP: 120 EST: 1978
SQ FT: 6,000
SALES (est): 1.92MM Privately Held
Web: www.thegreatlakesgroup.com
SIC: 3731 4492 Shipbuilding and repairing;
Marine towing services

(G-3793)
**GREAT LAKES PUBLISHING
COMPANY (PA)**
Also Called: Cleveland Magazine
1422 Euclid Ave Ste 730 (44115-2001)
PHONE...............................216 771-2833
Lute Harmon Senior, Ch Bd
Lute Harmon Junior, Pr
Christopher Valantasis, *
Nicole Stoner, *
Geli Valli, *
EMP: 75 EST: 1972
SQ FT: 19,000
SALES (est): 9.01MM
SALES (corp-wide): 9.01MM Privately
Held

Web: www.glpublishing.com
SIC: 2721 7374 Magazines: publishing only,
not printed on site; Computer graphics
service

(G-3794)
**GREAT LKES NROTECHNOLOGIES
INC**
6100 Rockside Woods Blvd N Ste 415
(44131-2366)
PHONE...............................855 456-3876
Robert N Schmidt, Ch Bd
Joseph P Giuffrida, Pr
Brian M Kolkowski, Ex VP
EMP: 20 EST: 2010
SALES (est): 3.55MM Privately Held
Web: www.glneurotech.com
SIC: 3845 Electromedical apparatus

(G-3795)
GREATER CLEVE PIPE FTTING FUND
6305 Halle Dr (44125-4617)
PHONE...............................216 524-8334
Niel Ginley, Pr
EMP: 10 EST: 2002
SALES (est): 1.83MM Privately Held
Web: www.pipefitters120.org
SIC: 3494 Pipe fittings

(G-3796)
GROUP INDUSTRIES INC (PA)
Also Called: Drum Parts
7580 Garfield Blvd (44125-1216)
P.O. Box 25409 (44125-0409)
PHONE...............................216 271-0702
Martin Tiernan, Ch Bd
Lane A Zamin, *
Dale Zeleznik, *
Curtis Crowder, *
◆ EMP: 32 EST: 1968
SQ FT: 24,000
SALES (est): 7.26MM
SALES (corp-wide): 7.26MM Privately
Held
Web: www.drumpartsinc.com
SIC: 3429 3592 3452 Hardware, nec;
Carburetors, pistons, piston rings and
valves; Bolts, nuts, rivets, and washers

(G-3797)
**GROVER MUSICAL PRODUCTS INC
(PA)**
Also Called: Grover Trophy Musical Products
9287 Midwest Ave (44125-2415)
PHONE...............................216 391-1188
Richard I Berger, Pr
Dann Skutt, *
Daniel Greene, *
▲ EMP: 22 EST: 1923
SQ FT: 60,000
SALES (est): 1.26MM
SALES (corp-wide): 1.26MM Privately
Held
Web: www.grotro.com
SIC: 3931 Musical instruments

(G-3798)
GSH INDUSTRIES INC
15242 Foltz Pkwy (44149-4733)
PHONE...............................440 238-3009
EMP: 30 EST: 1986
SALES (est): 11.13MM Privately Held
Web: www.gshindustries.com
SIC: 2821 Plastics materials and resins

(G-3799)
GSI OF OHIO LLC
Also Called: Sidari's Italian Foods
3820 Lakeside Ave E (44114-3848)
PHONE...............................216 431-3344

▲ EMP: 18
SIC: 2099 Pasta, rice, and potato, packaged
combination products

(G-3800)
**GUARANTEED FNSHG UNLIMITED
INC**
3200 W 121st St (44111-1720)
PHONE...............................216 252-8200
William Kozak, CEO
Joseph Janke, *
▲ EMP: 35 EST: 1983
SQ FT: 50,000
SALES (est): 2.49MM Privately Held
Web: www.gfuinc.com
SIC: 3471 Electroplating of metals or formed
products

(G-3801)
GUSTAVE JULIAN JEWELERS INC
7432 State Rd (44134-5858)
PHONE...............................440 888-1100
Jim Julian, Pr
Jayne Julian, Sec
Edward Julian, VP
EMP: 7 EST: 1948
SQ FT: 2,400
SALES (est): 327.92K Privately Held
Web: www.julianjeweler.com
SIC: 5944 7631 3911 Silverware; Jewelry
repair services; Jewelry, precious metal

(G-3802)
GWJ LIQUIDATION INC
Also Called: Perfection Fine Products
16153 Libby Rd (44137-1219)
PHONE...............................216 475-5770
Jack M Goldberg, Pr
William Overton, VP
EMP: 18 EST: 1951
SQ FT: 30,000
SALES (est): 1.8MM Privately Held
Web: www.greatwesternjuice.com
SIC: 2033 2087 Fruit juices: fresh; Cocktail
mixes, nonalcoholic

(G-3803)
GZJB HOLDINGS INC
24000 Lakeland Blvd (44132-2618)
PHONE...............................216 731-0500
John F Zagar, Pr
David Arnold, *
◆ EMP: 25 EST: 1941
SQ FT: 50,000
SALES (est): 8.48MM Privately Held
Web: www.zagar.com
SIC: 3546 3541 Power-driven handtools;
Machine tools, metal cutting type

(G-3804)
H & H TRUCK PARTS LLC
5500s Cloverleaf Pkwy (44125-4802)
PHONE...............................216 642-4540
EMP: 30 EST: 2004
SQ FT: 12,000
SALES (est): 4.41MM Privately Held
Web: www.hhtruckparts.com
SIC: 3713 5531 Truck bodies and parts;
Truck equipment and parts

(G-3805)
H P MANUFACTURING CO
3740 Prospect Ave E (44115-2706)
PHONE...............................216 361-6500
EMP: 6 EST: 2015
SALES (est): 1.41MM Privately Held
Web: www.hpmanufacturing.com
SIC: 3089 Injection molding of plastics

(G-3806)
HAFCO-CASE INC
12212 Sprecher Ave (44135-5122)
PHONE..............................216 267-4644
Phyllis Tarnawsky, *Pr*
Bohdan Tarnawsky, *General Vice President*
Natalie Tarnawsky, *Sec*
EMP: 8 **EST:** 1951
SQ FT: 8,000
SALES (est): 934.78K **Privately Held**
SIC: 3599 Machine shop, jobbing and repair

(G-3807)
HAHN MANUFACTURING COMPANY
5332 Hamilton Ave (44114-3984)
PHONE..............................216 391-9300
Robert E Hahn, *Pr*
Laura L Hahn, *
Greg Hahn, *
EMP: 28 **EST:** 1916
SQ FT: 17,000
SALES (est): 4.83MM **Privately Held**
Web: www.hahnmfg.com
SIC: 3549 3599 Metalworking machinery, nec
; Machine shop, jobbing and repair

(G-3808)
HALO METAL PREP INC
5712 Brookpark Rd Unit C (44129-1208)
PHONE..............................216 741-0506
Dean M Mella, *Prin*
EMP: 6 **EST:** 2019
SALES (est): 2.6MM **Privately Held**
Web: www.halometalprep.com
SIC: 3599 Machine shop, jobbing and repair

(G-3809)
HALVORSEN COMPANY
7500 Grand Division Ave Ste 1
(44125-1282)
P.O. Box 25625 (44125-0625)
PHONE..............................216 341-7500
Ross C Frick, *Pr*
Francis J Talty, *
John F Ray Junior, *Prin*
William Patrick Clyne, *
◆ **EMP:** 32 **EST:** 1954
SQ FT: 68,000
SALES (est): 3.5MM **Privately Held**
Web: www.halvorsenusa.com
SIC: 3441 3444 3443 Fabricated structural
metal; Sheet metalwork; Fabricated plate
work (boiler shop)

(G-3810)
HANLON INDUSTRIES INC
Also Called: Fiberglass Engineering Co
1280 E 286th St (44132-2195)
PHONE..............................216 261-7056
Bernard M Hanlon, *Pr*
EMP: 10 **EST:** 1959
SALES (est): 968.02K **Privately Held**
Web: www.fiberglasshanlon.com
SIC: 3089 Injection molding of plastics

(G-3811)
HARTLINE PRODUCTS COINC
15035 Woodworth Rd Ste 3 (44110-3345)
PHONE..............................216 851-7189
Becky Hart, *Manager*
EMP: 9
SALES (corp-wide): 2.6MM **Privately Held**
Web: www.hartlineproducts.com
SIC: 2891 3241 Cement, except linoleum
and tile; Cement, hydraulic
PA: Hartline Products Co.Inc.
4568 Mayfield Rd Ste 202
Cleveland OH 44121
216 291-2303

(G-3812)
HARVARD COIL PROCESSING INC
5400 Harvard Ave (44105-4828)
PHONE..............................216 883-6366
Eileen Jacobs, *Pr*
EMP: 13 **EST:** 1996
SQ FT: 2,000
SALES (est): 2.05MM **Privately Held**
Web: www.harvardcoilprocessing.com
SIC: 3312 Blast furnaces and steel mills

(G-3813)
HCC HOLDINGS INC
4700 W 160th St (44135-2632)
PHONE..............................800 203-1155
EMP: 6 **EST:** 2011
SALES (est): 1.05MM
SALES (corp-wide): 304.6MM **Privately
Held**
SIC: 3444 Metal roofing and roof drainage
equipment
PA: Oatey Co.
20600 Emerald Pkwy
Cleveland OH 44135
800 203-1155

(G-3814)
HEALTH AID OF OHIO INC (PA)
6940 Engle Rd Ste A (44130-3435)
P.O. Box 35107 (44135-0107)
PHONE..............................216 252-3900
Carol Gilligan, *Pr*
Cortney B Mcdowell, *VP*
Kristin O'neil, *Mgr*
David Tatka, *
Sheila Harrison, *
EMP: 50 **EST:** 1983
SALES (est): 18.94MM
SALES (corp-wide): 18.94MM **Privately
Held**
Web: www.healthaidofohio.com
SIC: 5999 7352 3821 Medical apparatus and
supplies; Medical equipment rental;
Incubators, laboratory

(G-3815)
HEALTH NUTS MEDIA LLC
4225 W 229th St (44126-1834)
PHONE..............................818 802-5222
EMP: 6 **EST:** 2012
SALES (est): 234.83K **Privately Held**
SIC: 7371 5999 7389 7372 Computer
software writing services; Educational aids
and electronic training materials; Business
services, nec; Educational computer
software

(G-3816)
HEAT SEAL LLC
Also Called: Ampak
4922 E 49th St Ste 100 (44125-1002)
PHONE..............................216 341-2022
Bryan Rakovec, *Prin*
R J Skalsky, *
James Sovacool, *
Thomas Dougherty, *
Bryan Rakovec, *Prin*
◆ **EMP:** 110 **EST:** 1956
SQ FT: 80,000
SALES (est): 21.9MM **Privately Held**
Web: www.heatsealco.com
SIC: 2542 3565 Fixtures, store: except wood
; Wrapping machines

(G-3817)
HEDALLOY DIE CORPORATION
3266 E 49th St (44127-1092)
PHONE..............................216 341-3768
John Susa, *Pr*
Joseph Susa, *Genl Mgr*
John Susa Junior, *VP*

EMP: 6 **EST:** 1991
SQ FT: 10,000
SALES (est): 815.32K **Privately Held**
SIC: 3544 Dies, steel rule

(G-3818)
HEILIND ELECTRONICS INC
Also Called: Maverick Electronics
5300 Avion Park Dr (44143-1917)
PHONE..............................440 473-9600
Rick Nemeth, *Mgr*
EMP: 20
SALES (corp-wide): 475.94MM **Privately
Held**
Web: www.heilind-electronic.uk
SIC: 5065 3315 Electronic parts; Cable,
steel: insulated or armored
PA: Heiland Electronics, Inc.
58 Jonspin Rd
Wilmington MA 01887
978 657-4870

(G-3819)
HELLAN STRAINER COMPANY
3249 E 80th St (44104-4341)
PHONE..............................216 206-4200
Philip Haynes, *Pr*
▲ **EMP:** 9 **EST:** 2000
SALES (est): 6.32MM
SALES (corp-wide): 459.42MM **Privately
Held**
Web: www.hellanstrainer.com
SIC: 3569 Filters and strainers, pipeline
HQ: Industrial Manufacturing Company Llc
8223 Brcksvlle Rd Ste 100
Brecksville OH 44141
440 838-4700

(G-3820)
HELLER MACHINE PRODUCTS INC
1971 W 90th St (44102-2742)
PHONE..............................216 281-2951
Jeff Evin, *Pr*
Mary Heller, *VP*
David Heller, *VP*
Eda Heller, *Dir*
Joyce Evin, *Dir*
EMP: 8 **EST:** 1953
SQ FT: 10,000
SALES (est): 758.83K **Privately Held**
SIC: 3451 3812 3728 3429 Screw machine
products; Search and navigation equipment
; Aircraft parts and equipment, nec;
Hardware, nec

(G-3821)
HENKEL US OPERATIONS CORP
Cleveland Manufacturing Fcilty
18731 Cranwood Pkwy (44128-4037)
PHONE..............................216 475-3600
Doug Karns, *Mgr*
EMP: 250
SALES (corp-wide): 22.83B **Privately Held**
Web: www.henkel-northamerica.com
SIC: 2891 2851 2842 Adhesives; Paints and
allied products; Polishes and sanitation
goods
HQ: Henkel Us Operations Corporation
1 Henkel Way
Rocky Hill CT 06067
860 571-5100

(G-3822)
HENNINGS QUALITY SERVICE INC
3115 Berea Rd (44111-1505)
PHONE..............................216 941-9120
Herbert Morrow, *Pr*
James Brinker, *VP*
EMP: 17 **EST:** 1981
SQ FT: 20,000
SALES (est): 1.67MM **Privately Held**

Web: www.hqs1.com
SIC: 7694 Electric motor repair

(G-3823)
HENRY & WRIGHT CORPORATION
1387 E 168th St (44110-2522)
PHONE..............................216 851-3750
Austin W Moore, *Pr*
Jonathan Moore, *VP*
EMP: 13 **EST:** 1997
SALES (est): 899.88K **Privately Held**
Web: www.henrywright.com
SIC: 3542 3829 3823 Presses: hydraulic and
pneumatic, mechanical and manual;
Measuring and controlling devices, nec;
Process control instruments

(G-3824)
HENRY TOOLS INC
498 S Belvoir Blvd (44121-2351)
PHONE..............................216 291-1011
Clara Henry, *Ch Bd*
Richard Henry Senior, *Pr*
David Henry, *VP*
▲ **EMP:** 9 **EST:** 1973
SALES (est): 984.64K **Privately Held**
Web: www.henrytools.com
SIC: 3724 Aircraft engines and engine parts

(G-3825)
HEPHAESTUS TECHNOLOGIES LLC
Also Called: Gray Tech International
3811 W 150th St (44111-5806)
PHONE..............................216 252-0430
Helun Chahda, *CEO*
Helun Bachour Chahda, *
Eric Attel, *
Mario Chahda, *
EMP: 24 **EST:** 1987
SQ FT: 20,000
SALES (est): 4.57MM **Privately Held**
Web: www.graytechintl.com
SIC: 3599 Machine shop, jobbing and repair

(G-3826)
HERD MANUFACTURING INC
Also Called: Herd
9227 Clinton Rd (44144-1088)
PHONE..............................216 651-4221
Erich J Rock, *Pr*
Rita Laurenci, *Sec*
Erick M Rock Shdr, *Prin*
EMP: 40 **EST:** 1972
SQ FT: 25,000
SALES (est): 2.36MM **Privately Held**
Web: www.herdmfg.com
SIC: 3469 3544 3599 Stamping metal for the
trade; Special dies and tools; Custom
machinery

(G-3827)
HERMAN MANUFACTURING LLC
Also Called: Walsh Manufacturing
13825 Triskett Rd (44111-1523)
PHONE..............................216 251-6400
Martin Herman, *Managing Member*
EMP: 16 **EST:** 1963
SQ FT: 25,000
SALES (est): 5MM **Privately Held**
Web: www.walshmfg.com
SIC: 3564 3441 Dust or fume collecting
equipment, industrial; Fabricated structural
metal

(G-3828)
HEROLD SALADS INC
17512 Miles Ave (44128-3404)
PHONE..............................216 991-7500
Cathy L Herold, *Pr*
EMP: 13 **EST:** 1935
SQ FT: 20,000

▲ = Import ▼ = Export
◆ = Import/Export

SALES (est): 852.7K **Privately Held**
Web: www.heroldssalads.com
SIC: 2099 Salads, fresh or refrigerated

(G-3829)
HEXAGON INDUSTRIES INC
1135 Ivanhoe Rd (44110-3249)
PHONE..............................216 249-0200
Stephen R Jackson, *Pr*
Peter M Jackson, *
▲ EMP: 50 EST: 1979
SQ FT: 270,000
SALES (est): 5.23MM **Privately Held**
Web: www.hexagonindustries.com
SIC: 3452 Screws, metal

(G-3830)
HICKOK WAEKON LLC
10514 Dupont Ave (44108-1348)
PHONE..............................216 541-8060
EMP: 55 EST: 2018
SALES (est): 5.11MM **Privately Held**
Web: www.hickokwaekon.com
SIC: 3841 Diagnostic apparatus, medical

(G-3831)
HITTI ENTERPRISES INC
6427 Eastland Rd (44142-1305)
PHONE..............................440 243-4100
Fred Hitti, *Pr*
EMP: 10 EST: 1989
SQ FT: 40,000
SALES (est): 467.09K **Privately Held**
SIC: 3086 6531 Packaging and shipping
materials, foamed plastics; Real estate
agents and managers

(G-3832)
**HKM DRECT MKT CMMNICATIONS
INC (PA)**
Also Called: H K M
5501 Cass Ave (44102-2121)
PHONE..............................800 860-4456
Rob Durham, *Pr*
Scott Durham, *
EMP: 140 EST: 1922
SQ FT: 86,000
SALES (est): 26.5MM
SALES (corp-wide): 26.5MM **Privately
Held**
Web: www.hkmdirectmarket.com
SIC: 2752 7375 2791 2759 Commercial
printing, lithographic; Information retrieval
services, Typesetting, Commercial printing,
nec

(G-3833)
HOLCIM (US) INC
2500 Elm St (44113-1114)
PHONE..............................216 781-9330
Thomas Peck, *Brnch Mgr*
EMP: 7
Web: www.holcim.us
SIC: 3241 Cement, hydraulic
HQ: Holcim (Us) Inc.
8700 W Bryn Mawr Ste
Chicago IL 60631

(G-3834)
HOLLY ROBAKOWSKI
641 E 185th St (44119-1764)
PHONE..............................440 854-9317
Holly Robakowski, *Owner*
EMP: 6
SALES (est): 271.05K **Privately Held**
SIC: 1389 7389 Construction, repair, and
dismantling services; Business services,
nec

(G-3835)
HOLMES MADE FOODS LLC
21315 Fairmount Blvd (44118-4805)
PHONE..............................216 618-5043
Bruce Holmes, *Prin*
EMP: 6 EST: 2011
SALES (est): 444.08K **Privately Held**
Web: www.holmesmouthwatering.com
SIC: 2099 Food preparations, nec

(G-3836)
HOME STOR & OFF SOLUTIONS INC
Also Called: Closet Factory, The
5305 Commerce Pkwy W (44130-1274)
PHONE..............................216 362-4660
Kathy Pietrick, *Pr*
Robert J Pietrick Junior, *VP*
EMP: 26 EST: 1994
SQ FT: 5,000
SALES (est): 3.67MM **Privately Held**
Web: www.closetfactory.com
SIC: 5211 5712 2541 Closets, interiors and
accessories; Furniture stores; Wood
partitions and fixtures

(G-3837)
**HORIZON GLOBAL CORPORATION
(DH)**
127 Public Sq Ste 5300 (44114-1219)
PHONE..............................734 656-3000
Patrick James, *Pr*
Stephen Graham, *CFO*
EMP: 37 EST: 2015
SALES (est): 782.12MM
SALES (corp-wide): 7.28B **Privately Held**
Web: www.horizonglobal.com
SIC: 3714 3711 5531 Trailer hitches, motor
vehicle; Wreckers (tow truck), assembly of;
Auto and truck equipment and parts
HQ: Phnx Acquisition Corp
127 Public Sq Ste 5110
Cleveland OH

(G-3838)
HORIZONS INCORPORATED (PA)
Also Called: Panam Imaging Systems
18531 S Miles Rd (44128-4237)
PHONE..............................216 475-0555
Herbert A Wainer, *Pr*
Robert Miller, *
Micheal Rish, *
◆ EMP: 115 EST: 1967
SQ FT: 51,000
SALES (est): 27.81MM
SALES (corp-wide): 27.81MM **Privately
Held**
Web: www.horizons-inc.com
SIC: 3861 Plates, photographic (sensitized)

(G-3839)
HORSBURGH & SCOTT CO (PA)
5114 Hamilton Ave (44114-3985)
PHONE..............................216 431-3900
Lloyd G Trotter, *Ch Bd*
Randy Burdick, *
Damian Thomas, *
Monty Yort, *
David Ottesen, *
◆ EMP: 158 EST: 2007
SQ FT: 240,000
SALES (est): 40.69MM
SALES (corp-wide): 40.69MM **Privately
Held**
Web: www.horsburgh-scott.com
SIC: 3566 Gears, power transmission,
except auto

(G-3840)
HOSE MASTER LLC (PA)
1233 E 222nd St (44117-1121)
PHONE..............................216 481-2020

◆ EMP: 275 EST: 1982
SALES (est): 71.25MM
SALES (corp-wide): 71.25MM **Privately
Held**
Web: www.hosemaster.com
SIC: 3599 Hose, flexible metallic

(G-3841)
**HP MANUFACTURING COMPANY
INC (PA)**
Also Called: House of Plastics
3705 Carnegie Ave (44115-2750)
PHONE..............................216 361-6500
John R Melchiorre, *Pr*
EMP: 62 EST: 1948
SQ FT: 110,000
SALES (corp-wide): 7.9MM **Privately Held**
Web: www.hpmanufacturing.com
SIC: 3089 5162 3993 3082 Injection molding
of plastics; Plastics sheets and rods; Signs
and advertising specialties; Unsupported
plastics profile shapes

(G-3842)
HUBBELL MACHINE TOOLING INC
7507 Exchange St (44125-3305)
PHONE..............................216 524-1797
Claude Petek, *CEO*
EMP: 15 EST: 1943
SQ FT: 16,000
SALES (est): 3.64MM **Privately Held**
Web: www.hubbellmachine.com
SIC: 3599 Machine shop, jobbing and repair

(G-3843)
HUDSON SUPPLY COMPANY INC
4500 Lee Rd Ste 120 (44128-2959)
PHONE..............................216 518-3000
Richard Kopittke, *Pr*
▲ EMP: 6 EST: 2005
SALES (est): 972.36K **Privately Held**
Web: www.hudsonsupply.com
SIC: 3545 Machine tool accessories

(G-3844)
HUMONGOUS HOLDINGS LLC
Also Called: Humongous Fan
23103 Miles Rd (44128-5475)
PHONE..............................216 663-8830
James Meskill, *Pr*
EMP: 10 EST: 2010
SALES (est): 4.14MM **Privately Held**
Web: www.humongousfan.com
SIC: 3564 Ventilating fans: industrial or
commercial

(G-3845)
HUSQVARNA US HOLDING INC (HQ)
Also Called: Husqvarna Construction Pdts
20445 Emerald Pkwy Ste 205
(44135-6009)
P.O. Box 35920 (44135-0920)
PHONE..............................216 898-1800
George Weigand, *Sr VP*
Ronald Zajaczkowski, *
Marie-louise Wingard, *Treas*
Richard Pietch, *
▲ EMP: 70 EST: 2001
SQ FT: 18,000
SALES (est): 13.19MM
SALES (corp-wide): 2.23B **Privately Held**
SIC: 3582 Dryers, laundry: commercial,
including coin-operated
PA: Husqvarna Ab
Drottninggatan 2
Huskvarna 561 3
36146500

(G-3846)
HY-GRADE CORPORATION (PA)
3993 E 93rd St (44105-4052)
PHONE..............................216 341-7711
Michael Pemberton, *Pr*
EMP: 35 EST: 1951
SQ FT: 25,000
SALES (est): 1.86MM
SALES (corp-wide): 1.86MM **Privately
Held**
Web: www.uniquepavingmaterials.com
SIC: 5032 2952 2951 Asphalt mixture;
Asphalt felts and coatings; Asphalt paving
mixtures and blocks

(G-3847)
HYSTER-YALE INC (PA)
Also Called: HYSTER
5875 Landerbrook Dr Ste 300
(44124-4069)
PHONE..............................440 449-9600
Rajiv K Prasad, *Pr*
Alfred M Rankin Junior, *Ex Ch Bd*
Scott A Minder, *Sr VP*
Suzanne S Taylor, *Sr VP*
Dena R Mckee, *CAO*
EMP: 120 EST: 1989
SALES (est): 4.31B **Publicly Held**
Web: www.hyster-yalecareers.com
SIC: 3537 Forklift trucks

(G-3848)
I JALCITE INC
25 W Prospect Ave (44115-1066)
PHONE..............................216 622-5000
William H Bricker, *Pr*
George T Henning, *VP*
Glenn J Moran, *VP*
John C Skurek, *VP*
Richard J Hipple, *Dir*
EMP: 11 EST: 2000
SALES (est): 205.87K **Privately Held**
SIC: 3312 Blast furnaces and steel mills

(G-3849)
IM GREENBERG INC
Also Called: IMG
5470 Mayfield Rd (44124-2924)
PHONE..............................440 461-4464
Steven Greenberg, *Pr*
EMP: 6 EST: 1968
SQ FT: 5,500
SALES (est): 565.19K **Privately Held**
Web: www.imgjewelers.com
SIC: 3911 7631 Jewelry, precious metal;
Diamond setter

(G-3850)
IMAGE CONCEPTS INC
Also Called: AlphaGraphics Valley View
8200 Sweet Valley Dr 107
(44125-4240)
PHONE..............................216 524-9000
Patrick Delahunty, *VP*
Karey Zorv, *Pr*
EMP: 10 EST: 1998
SQ FT: 8,000
SALES (est): 984.63K **Privately Held**
Web: www.imageconceptsprint.com
SIC: 2752 Offset printing

(G-3851)
IMALUX CORPORATION
11000 Cedar Ave Ste 250 (44106-3056)
PHONE..............................216 502-0755
Michael Burke, *Pr*
Bill R Sanford, *Ch*
Thomas F Barnish, *VP*
Paul G Amazeen, *Ex VP*
Nancy J Tresser, *CMO*
EMP: 10 EST: 1996

SQ FT: 1,000
SALES (est): 1.36MM **Privately Held**
Web: www.imalux.com
SIC: 3845 Electromedical apparatus

(G-3852)
IMET CORPORATION
13400 Glenside Rd (44110-3528)
P.O. Box 10753 (44110-0753)
PHONE..............................440 799-3135
Mehmet Gencer, *CEO*
Paul Zakriski, *Pr*
Carol Mills, *Treas*
EMP: 7 EST: 1997
SQ FT: 700
SALES (est): 737.89K **Privately Held**
Web: www.imet.net
SIC: 3589 Water treatment equipment,
industrial

(G-3853)
IMPACT ARMOR TECHNOLOGIES LLC
17000 Saint Clair Ave Ste 106
(44110-2535)
PHONE..............................216 706-2024
EMP: 10 EST: 2009
SALES (est): 485.79K **Privately Held**
SIC: 3297 Nonclay refractories

(G-3854)
IMPERIAL METAL SOLUTIONS LLC
2284 Scranton Rd (44113-4310)
PHONE..............................216 781-4094
EMP: 18 EST: 2001
SQ FT: 23,000
SALES (est): 2.46MM **Privately Held**
Web: www.imspowder.net
SIC: 3479 Coating of metals and formed
products

(G-3855)
IMPERIAL METAL SPINNING CO
7600 Exchange St (44125-3308)
PHONE..............................216 524-5020
Christopher Bindel, *Pr*
Timothy Bindel, *VP*
EMP: 8 EST: 1954
SQ FT: 7,000
SALES (est): 423.02K **Privately Held**
Web: www.imperialmetalspinning.com
SIC: 3469 Stamping metal for the trade

(G-3856)
IMPRINT LLC
3654 W 104th St (44111-3817)
PHONE..............................216 233-0066
Julia Garmon, *Prin*
EMP: 7 EST: 2014
SALES (est): 117.04K **Privately Held**
Web: www.customimprint.com
SIC: 2752 Commercial printing, lithographic

(G-3857)
INDEPENDENT STAMPING INC
12025 Zelis Rd (44135-4699)
PHONE..............................216 251-3500
William Nester, *Pr*
EMP: 10 EST: 1965
SQ FT: 11,000
SALES (est): 4.24MM **Privately Held**
Web: www.indstamping.com
SIC: 3469 3544 Stamping metal for the trade
; Special dies and tools

(G-3858)
INFINITE ENERGY MFG LLC
4517 Industrial Pkwy (44135-4541)
PHONE..............................440 759-5920
Gilbert Sherman, *Pr*

EMP: 10
SALES (est): 1.49MM **Privately Held**
SIC: 3499 Fabricated metal products, nec

(G-3859)
INFORMA MEDIA INC
Also Called: INFORMA MEDIA, INC.
1300 E 9th St (44114-1501)
PHONE..............................216 696-7000
Bill Fallon, *Dir*
EMP: 650
SALES (corp-wide): 4.5B **Privately Held**
Web: www.informa.com
SIC: 2721 Magazines: publishing only, not
printed on site
HQ: Informa Media Llc
605 3rd Ave # 22
New York NY 10158
212 204-4200

(G-3860)
INK TECHNOLOGY CORPORATION
18320 Lanken Ave (44119-3216)
PHONE..............................216 486-6720
Ian Walker, *Pr*
David Ringler, *
Ernest Walker, *
Ethel R Haff, *
Robert Jenson, *
◆ EMP: 26 EST: 1980
SQ FT: 20,000
SALES (est): 1.86MM **Privately Held**
Web: www.inktechnology.com
SIC: 2893 Printing ink

(G-3861)
INNOPLAST INC (PA)
5718 Transportation Blvd (44125-5343)
P.O. Box 23681 (44023-0681)
PHONE..............................440 543-8660
Craig Mcconnell, *CEO*
Gary Bowling, *Pr*
Lisa Mcconnell, *VP*
Steve Budinsky, *Genl Mgr*
◆ EMP: 14 EST: 2006
SALES (est): 12.64MM **Privately Held**
Web: www.innoplast.com
SIC: 2822 3559 Ethylene-propylene rubbers,
EPDM polymers; Parking facility equipment
and supplies

(G-3862)
INNOVATIONS IN PLASTIC INC
1643 Eddy Rd (44112-4207)
PHONE..............................216 541-6060
Charles Hazle, *Pr*
Mary Ann Hazle, *Sec*
EMP: 7 EST: 1972
SQ FT: 13,000
SALES (est): 888K **Privately Held**
Web: www.innovationsinplastic.com
SIC: 3089 Injection molding of plastics

(G-3863)
INTEGRATED POWER SERVICES LLC
Also Called: Monarch
5325 W 130th St (44130-1034)
PHONE..............................216 433-7808
Bridgette Gullatta, *Pr*
EMP: 100
Web: www.ips.us
SIC: 7694 Electric motor repair
PA: Integrated Power Services Llc
250 Exctive Ctr Dr Ste 20
Greenville SC 29615

(G-3864)
INTERIOR PRODUCTS CO INC
3615 Superior Ave E Ste 3104f
(44114-4138)

PHONE..............................216 641-1919
Joseph J Frisse, *Pr*
EMP: 9 EST: 1971
SQ FT: 14,000
SALES (est): 3.1MM **Privately Held**
Web: www.reclaimedcleveland.com
SIC: 2521 Cabinets, office: wood

(G-3865)
INTERSTATE DIESEL SERVICE INC (PA)
Also Called: American Diesel
5300 Lakeside Ave E (44114-3916)
PHONE..............................216 881-0015
Alfred J Buescher, *CEO*
Ann Buescher, *
Brad Buescher, *
◆ EMP: 125 EST: 1947
SQ FT: 70,000
SALES (est): 8.48MM
SALES (corp-wide): 8.48MM **Privately Held**
Web: www.interstate-mcbee.com
SIC: 5013 3714 Automotive engines and
engine parts; Fuel systems and parts,
motor vehicle

(G-3866)
INTERSTATE TOOL CORPORATION
4538 W 130th St (44135-3574)
PHONE..............................216 671-1077
Warren Thompson, *Pr*
EMP: 20 EST: 1962
SQ FT: 22,000
SALES (est): 1.79MM **Privately Held**
Web: www.itctoolcorp.com
SIC: 5084 3545 3541 Machine tools and
accessories; Cutting tools for machine tools
; Machine tools, metal cutting type

(G-3867)
INX INTERNATIONAL INK CO
18001 Englewood Dr Unit P (44130-3422)
PHONE..............................440 239-1766
Kyle Hurrle, *Mgr*
EMP: 16
Web: www.inxinternational.com
SIC: 2893 Printing ink
HQ: Inx International Ink Co.
150 N Mrtngale Rd Ste 700
Schaumburg IL 60173
630 382-1800

(G-3868)
ION VACUUM IVAC TECH CORP
Also Called: Ion Vacuum Technologies
18678 Cranwood Pkwy (44128-4036)
PHONE..............................216 662-5158
Bela Fischer, *Pr*
George Fischer, *Sec*
EMP: 12 EST: 1987
SQ FT: 4,000
SALES (est): 909.17K **Privately Held**
Web: www.ivactech.com
SIC: 3479 8731 Coating of metals and
formed products; Commercial physical
research

(G-3869)
IONBOND LLC
24700 Highpoint Rd (44122-6005)
PHONE..............................216 831-0880
Heidi Froelich, *Brnch Mgr*
EMP: 11
Web: www.ionbond.com
SIC: 3479 Coating of metals and formed
products
HQ: Ionbond, Llc
1823 E Whitcomb
Madison Heights MI 48071

(G-3870)
IROCK CRUSHERS LLC
Also Called: Irock Crushers
5531 Canal Rd (44125-4874)
PHONE..............................866 240-0201
Nancy Frognowski, *Managing Member*
Kenneth E Taylor, *
John Reynolds, *
Taylor Kenneth, *
Taylor Martha, *
▲ EMP: 25 EST: 2001
SALES (est): 7.71MM **Privately Held**
Web: www.irockcrushers.com
SIC: 3532 Rock crushing machinery,
stationary

(G-3871)
IRONUNITS LLC
Also Called: Metallics
200 Public Sq Ste 3300 (44114-2315)
PHONE..............................216 694-5303
Lourenco Goncalves, *CEO*
EMP: 25 EST: 2000
SALES (est): 26.27MM
SALES (corp-wide): 19.18B **Publicly Held**
SIC: 1011 Iron ore beneficiating
PA: Cleveland-Cliffs Inc.
200 Public Sq Ste 3300
Cleveland OH 44114
216 694-5700

(G-3872)
IRWIN ENGRAVING & PRINTING CO
5318 Saint Clair Ave Ste 1 (44103-1355)
PHONE..............................216 391-7300
TOLL FREE: 800
Milan L Nass, *Pr*
Milan L Nass, *CEO*
Martha Ness, *Sec*
EMP: 9 EST: 1922
SQ FT: 16,000
SALES (est): 375.72K **Privately Held**
Web: www.irwinengraving.com
SIC: 2759 2752 Engraving, nec; Offset
printing

(G-3873)
ITALMATCH SC LLC
1000 Belt Line Ave (44109-2848)
PHONE..............................216 749-2605
Belinda Rosario, *CFO*
EMP: 17 EST: 2017
SALES (est): 2.17MM **Privately Held**
Web: www.italmatch.com
SIC: 2899 Chemical preparations, nec

(G-3874)
ITL CORP (HQ)
Also Called: Industrial Timber & Lumber Co
23925 Commerce Park (44122-5821)
PHONE..............................216 831-3140
Larry Evans, *Pr*
◆ EMP: 30 EST: 1957
SQ FT: 10,000
SALES (est): 5.16MM **Privately Held**
Web: www.itlcorp.com
SIC: 2421 2426 Kiln drying of lumber;
Hardwood dimension and flooring mills
PA: Northwest Hardwoods, Inc.
2600 Network Blvd Ste 600
Frisco TX 75034

(G-3875)
ITT TORQUE SYSTEMS INC
Also Called: C M C
7550 Hub Pkwy (44125-5705)
PHONE..............................216 524-8800
▲ EMP: 230

▲ = Import ▼ = Export
◆ = Import/Export

SIC: 3625 3823 3566 Controls for adjustable speed drives; Process control instruments; Speed changers, drives, and gears

(G-3876)
J & C INDUSTRIES INC
4808 W 130th St (44135-5138)
PHONE..............................216 362-8867
Bruce Jasen, *Pr*
EMP: 6 EST: 1973
SQ FT: 16,000
SALES (est): 1.05MM Privately Held
Web: www.jcindinc.com
SIC: 3599 Machine shop, jobbing and repair

(G-3877)
J B STAMPING INC
7413 Associate Ave (44144-1190)
PHONE..............................216 631-0013
James Bailey, *Pr*
Stacy Zadar, *
EMP: 43 EST: 1973
SQ FT: 35,000
SALES (est): 5.08MM Privately Held
Web: www.jbstamping.com
SIC: 3469 Stamping metal for the trade

(G-3878)
J R M CHEMICAL INC
4881 Neo Pkwy (44128-3101)
PHONE..............................216 475-8488
Dave Czehut, *VP*
Scott Wiesler, *VP*
▲ **EMP: 11 EST: 1988**
SQ FT: 12,000
SALES (est): 4.21MM Privately Held
Web: www.soilmoist.com
SIC: 2819 Industrial inorganic chemicals, nec

(G-3879)
J SCHRADER COMPANY
4603 Fenwick Ave (44102-4597)
PHONE..............................216 961-2890
Len Gagnon, *Pr*
EMP: 6 EST: 1922
SQ FT: 34,000
SALES (est): 1.14MM Privately Held
Web: www.jschraderco.com
SIC: 3469 3645 3646 Spinning metal for the trade; Table lamps; Commercial lighting fixtures

(G-3880)
J W HARWOOD CO (PA)
18001 Roseland Rd (44112-1109)
PHONE..............................216 531-6230
Walter B Harwood, *Pr*
Madeleine Harwood, *VP*
Marilyn Harwood, *Sec*
EMP: 12 EST: 1934
SQ FT: 12,000
SALES (est): 3.98MM
SALES (corp-wide): 3.98MM Privately Held
SIC: 3544 Special dies and tools

(G-3881)
JAKPRINTS INC
3133 Chester Ave (44114-4616)
PHONE..............................877 246-3132
Jacob Edwards, *Pr*
Dameon Guess, *
EMP: 127 EST: 1994
SQ FT: 32,000
SALES (est): 24.48MM Privately Held
Web: www.jakprints.com
SIC: 2752 Offset printing

(G-3882)
JAMESTOWN CONT CLEVELAND INC
4500 Renaissance Pkwy (44128-5702)
PHONE..............................216 831-3700
Glen Jenowsky, *Ch Bd*
Bruce Janowsky, *
Dick Weimer, *
EMP: 350 EST: 1961
SQ FT: 100,000
SALES (est): 9.88MM
SALES (corp-wide): 163.21MM Privately Held
Web: www.jamestowncontainer.com
SIC: 2653 Boxes, corrugated: made from purchased materials
PA: Jamestown Container Corp
14 Deming Dr
Falconer NY 14733
716 665-4623

(G-3883)
JASMINE DISTRIBUTING LTD
12117 Berea Rd (44111-1600)
PHONE..............................216 251-9420
Fady Chamoun, *Owner*
▲ **EMP: 20 EST: 1986**
SALES (est): 2.53MM Privately Held
Web: www.jasminebakery.com
SIC: 2051 Breads, rolls, and buns

(G-3884)
JBAR A/C INC
Also Called: Jbar
15501 Chatfield Ave (44111-4311)
PHONE..............................216 447-4294
Kevin R Keogh, *CEO*
Michael Pease, *Pr*
Kim Pease, *Sec*
▲ **EMP: 12 EST: 2001**
SQ FT: 21,000
SALES (est): 3MM Privately Held
Web: www.jbar-ac.com
SIC: 3714 3585 Heaters, motor vehicle; Air conditioning, motor vehicle

(G-3885)
JERGENS INC (PA)
Also Called: Tooling Components Division
15700 S Waterloo Rd (44110-3898)
PHONE..............................216 486-5540
Jack H Schron Junior, *Pr*
Sue Evans, *
Kurt Schron, *
▲ **EMP: 195 EST: 1942**
SQ FT: 104,000
SALES (est): 93.96MM
SALES (corp-wide): 93.96MM Privately Held
Web: www.jergensinc.com
SIC: 3443 3452 5084 3545 Fabricated plate work (boiler shop); Bolts, nuts, rivets, and washers; Machine tools and accessories; Drill bushings (drilling jig)

(G-3886)
JET DOCK SYSTEMS INC
9601 Corporate Cir (44125-4261)
PHONE..............................216 750-2264
David Faber, *Pr*
W Allen Eva Iii Esq, *VP*
▼ **EMP: 30 EST: 1993**
SQ FT: 30,000
SALES (est): 7.93MM Privately Held
Web: www.jetdock.com
SIC: 3448 Docks, prefabricated metal

(G-3887)
JET INC
750 Alpha Dr (44143-2146)
PHONE..............................440 461-2000
◆ **EMP: 40 EST: 1959**

SALES (est): 8.48MM Privately Held
Web: www.jetincorp.com
SIC: 3589 Sewage treatment equipment

(G-3888)
JIS DISTRIBUTION LLC (HQ)
15700 S Waterloo Rd (44110-3814)
PHONE..............................216 706-6552
Matt Schron, *Managing Member*
EMP: 13 EST: 2020
SALES (est): 4.24MM
SALES (corp-wide): 93.96MM Privately Held
Web: www.jergensinc.com
SIC: 5084 3443 Machine tools and accessories; Fabricated plate work (boiler shop)
PA: Jergens, Inc.
15700 S Waterloo Rd
Cleveland OH 44110
216 486-5540

(G-3889)
JOHN KRUSINSKI
Also Called: Krusinski's Meat Market
6300 Heisley Ave (44105-1226)
PHONE..............................216 441-0100
John Krusinski, *Owner*
EMP: 10 EST: 1952
SQ FT: 10,000
SALES (est): 495.49K Privately Held
SIC: 5147 5421 2099 2013 Meats, fresh; Meat markets, including freezer provisioners; Food preparations, nec; Sausages and other prepared meats

(G-3890)
JOHN P ELLIS CLINIC PODIATRY
730 Som Center Rd Ste 350 (44143-2362)
PHONE..............................440 460-0444
John P Ellis, *Owner*
EMP: 6 EST: 2015
SALES (est): 890.84K Privately Held
SIC: 2835 8071 0783 Diagnostic substances ; Ultrasound laboratory; Surgery services, ornamental bush

(G-3891)
JORDON AUTO SERVICE & TIRE INC
5201 Carnegie Ave (44103-4357)
PHONE..............................216 214-6528
Jordan Kaminsky, *Owner*
EMP: 7 EST: 2011
SALES (est): 796.63K Privately Held
SIC: 2653 7539 Pallets, corrugated: made from purchased materials; Automotive repair shops, nec

(G-3892)
JOSEPH T SNYDER INDUSTRIES INC
9210 Loren Ave (44105-2133)
PHONE..............................216 883-6900
Gregory Snyder, *Pr*
Robert Snyder, *VP*
EMP: 9 EST: 1969
SQ FT: 12,000
SALES (est): 987.79K Privately Held
Web: www.jtsnyder.com
SIC: 7389 2671 2653 Packaging and labeling services; Paper; coated and laminated packaging; Corrugated and solid fiber boxes

(G-3893)
JOSLYN HI-VOLTAGE COMPANY LLC
4000 E 116th St (44105-4310)
PHONE..............................216 271-6600
Jim Domo, *Pr*
▲ **EMP: 11 EST: 1947**
SQ FT: 100,000

SALES (est): 4.42MM Privately Held
SIC: 3613 Switchgear and switchboard apparatus
HQ: Abb Installation Products Inc.
860 Rdg Lake Blvd
Memphis TN 38120
901 252-5000

(G-3894)
JOSLYN SUNBANK COMPANY LLC (DH)
1000 Eaton Blvd (44122-6058)
PHONE..............................805 238-2840
Mike Ritter, *Dir Opers*
Kirsten Park, *VP*
EMP: 14 EST: 1997
SQ FT: 80,000
SALES (est): 21.45MM Privately Held
Web:
joslyn-sunbank-company-llc-in-paso-robles-ca.cityfos.com
SIC: 3678 3643 5065 Electronic connectors; Connectors and terminals for electrical devices; Connectors, electronic
HQ: Eaton Corporation
1000 Eaton Blvd
Cleveland OH 44122
440 523-5000

(G-3895)
JOY GLOBAL UNDERGROUND MIN LLC
6160 Cochran Rd (44139-3306)
PHONE..............................440 248-7970
Mark Sanders, *Brnch Mgr*
EMP: 21
SIC: 3535 Bucket type conveyor systems
HQ: Joy Global Underground Mining Llc
40 Pennwood Pl Ste 100
Warrendale PA 15086
724 779-4500

(G-3896)
JP CABINETS LLC
20910 Miles Pkwy (44128-5510)
PHONE..............................440 232-9780
EMP: 6 EST: 2002
SALES (est): 483.07K Privately Held
Web: www.jpcabinets.com
SIC: 2434 Wood kitchen cabinets

(G-3897)
JSJ SB HOLDINGS INC
4653 Spring Rd (44131-1021)
PHONE..............................216 398-7774
Andy Balog, *Rgnl Mgr*
EMP: 6
SQ FT: 13,800
SALES (corp-wide): 497.25MM Privately Held
Web: www.sparksbelting.com
SIC: 3535 Conveyors and conveying equipment
HQ: Jsj Sb Holdings, Inc.
5005 Kraft Ave Se
Grand Rapids MI 49512

(G-3898)
JT PREMIER PRINTING CORP
Also Called: Premier Printing
18780 Cranwood Pkwy (44128-4038)
PHONE..............................216 831-8785
James Trombo, *Pr*
EMP: 6 EST: 1999
SALES (est): 413.94K Privately Held
Web: www.premierprintingcorp.com
SIC: 2752 Offset printing

(G-3899)

JUST NATURAL PROVISION COMPANY

4800 Crayton Ave (44104-2822)

PHONE..................................216 431-7922

Dennis Parker, *Pr*

EMP: 6 **EST:** 2001

SALES (est): 2MM **Privately Held**

SIC: 2015 5144 Poultry slaughtering and processing; Poultry and poultry products

(G-3900)

K & G MACHINE COMPANY

26981 Tungsten Rd (44132-2992)

PHONE..................................216 732-7115

Monte Curtis, *Pr*

EMP: 11 **EST:** 1953

SQ FT: 24,000

SALES (est): 1.61MM **Privately Held**

Web: www.kandgmachine.com

SIC: 3599 3743 Machine shop, jobbing and repair; Railroad equipment

(G-3901)

K S MACHINE INC

3215 Superior Ave E (44114-4344)

PHONE..................................216 687-0459

Thomas Wallace, *Pr*

EMP: 7 **EST:** 1931

SALES (est): 679.84K **Privately Held**

Web: www.ksmachineinc.com

SIC: 3599 Machine shop, jobbing and repair

(G-3902)

K&M AVIATION LLC

Also Called: Nextant Aerospace Holdings LLC

355 Richmond Rd (44143-4405)

PHONE..................................216 261-9000

Kenneth C Ricci, *CEO*

Jim Miller, *

Sean Mcgeough, *Pr*

Mark O' Donell, *

Michael A Rossi, *

EMP: 75 **EST:** 2007

SQ FT: 3,000

SALES (est): 24.2MM

SALES (corp-wide): 160.16MM **Privately Held**

Web: www.nextantaerospace.com

SIC: 3721 Aircraft

HQ: Flight Options International, Inc.

355 Richmond Rd

Richmond Heights OH 44143

216 261-3500

(G-3903)

K-B PLATING INC

3685 E 78th St (44105-2048)

PHONE..................................216 341-1115

David Kopea, *Pr*

Thomas Thome, *VP*

Gordon Loux, *Sec*

Doris Kopea, *Treas*

EMP: 10 **EST:** 1961

SQ FT: 21,000

SALES (est): 926.5K **Privately Held**

Web: www.kbplating.com

SIC: 3471 Electroplating of metals or formed products

(G-3904)

KABAB-G INC

6676 Rochelle Blvd (44130-3977)

PHONE..................................216 476-3335

Ghazi Slailati, *Prin*

EMP: 6 **EST:** 2010

SALES (est): 217.91K **Privately Held**

SIC: 3421 Table and food cutlery, including butchers'

(G-3905)

KALIBURN INC

22801 Saint Clair Ave (44117-2524)

PHONE..................................843 695-4073

George Blankenship, *Prin*

EMP: 11 **EST:** 2013

SALES (est): 14.25MM

SALES (corp-wide): 4.01B **Publicly Held**

Web: www.lincolnelectriccutting.com

SIC: 3548 Welding and cutting apparatus and accessories, nec

PA: Lincoln Electric Holdings, Inc.

22801 St Clair Ave

Cleveland OH 44117

216 481-8100

(G-3906)

KARYALL-TELDAY INC

8221 Clinton Rd (44144-1008)

PHONE..................................216 281-4063

James Mindek, *Pr*

EMP: 6 **EST:** 1947

SQ FT: 43,000

SALES (est): 520.29K **Privately Held**

Web: www.karyalltelday.com

SIC: 2851 3499 Paints and paint additives; Boxes for packing and shipping, metal

(G-3907)

KASE EQUIPMENT CORPORATION

7400 Hub Pkwy (44125-5735)

PHONE..................................216 642-9040

Edward Hawkins, *Ch Bd*

Partick Hawkins, *

Dave Hodgson, *

◆ **EMP:** 100 **EST:** 1962

SQ FT: 68,360

SALES (est): 4.51MM **Privately Held**

Web: www.kaseequip.com

SIC: 3555 Printing trades machinery

(G-3908)

KAUFMAN CONTAINER COMPANY (PA)

1000 Keystone Pkwy Ste 100 (44135-5119)

P.O. Box 35902 (44135-0902)

PHONE..................................216 898-2000

Roger Seid, *Ch*

Ken Slater, *

Karen D Melton, *

Charles Borowiak, *

Anita Seid, *

◆ **EMP:** 118 **EST:** 1910

SQ FT: 180,000

SALES (est): 38.96MM

SALES (corp-wide): 38.96MM **Privately Held**

Web: www.kaufmancontainer.com

SIC: 5085 2759 Commercial containers; Screen printing

(G-3909)

KAWNEER COMPANY INC

4536 Industrial Pkwy (44135-4593)

PHONE..................................216 252-3203

Janice Gibson, *Genl Mgr*

EMP: 157

SALES (corp-wide): 4.39B **Privately Held**

Web: www.kawneer.us

SIC: 3442 Metal doors

HQ: Kawneer Company, Inc.

555 Guthridge Ct

Norcross GA 30092

770 449-5555

(G-3910)

KEENE BUILDING PRODUCTS CO (PA)

2926 Chester Ave (44114-4414)

P.O. Box 241353 (44124)

PHONE..................................440 605-1020

James Keene, *Pr*

▲ **EMP:** 39 **EST:** 2002

SALES (est): 29.15MM

SALES (corp-wide): 29.15MM **Privately Held**

Web: www.keenebuilding.com

SIC: 2677 3625 Envelopes; Noise control equipment

(G-3911)

KEENER PRINTING INC

Also Called: Keener

401 E 200th St (44119-1594)

PHONE..................................216 531-7595

Duane Pecjak, *Pr*

EMP: 6 **EST:** 1976

SQ FT: 3,600

SALES (est): 674.61K **Privately Held**

Web: www.keenerprinting.com

SIC: 2752 2791 Offset printing; Typesetting

(G-3912)

KELLY PLATING CO

10316 Madison Ave (44102-3594)

PHONE..................................216 961-1080

Donald J Kelly, *Pr*

James Kelly, *

Lauralee Paukert, *

EMP: 9 **EST:** 1932

SQ FT: 20,000

SALES (est): 2.47MM **Privately Held**

Web: www.kellyplating.com

SIC: 3471 Electroplating of metals or formed products

(G-3913)

KENCO PRODUCTS CO INC

3204 Sackett Ave (44109-2016)

PHONE..................................216 351-7610

John Kennedy, *Pr*

EMP: 9 **EST:** 1953

SQ FT: 32,000

SALES (est): 271.59K **Privately Held**

SIC: 3317 Steel pipe and tubes

(G-3914)

KEREK INDUSTRIES LTD LBLTY CO

750 Beta Dr Ste A (44143-2333)

EMP: 13 **EST:** 1986

SQ FT: 22,000

SALES (est): 2.53MM **Privately Held**

Web: www.kerekindustries.com

SIC: 3599 Machine shop, jobbing and repair

(G-3915)

KERN INC

755 Alpha Dr (44143-2124)

PHONE..................................440 930-7315

Thomas Brock, *Pr*

EMP: 144

SALES (corp-wide): 19.62MM **Privately Held**

Web: www.kerninc.com

SIC: 3579 3577 Envelope stuffing, sealing, and addressing machines; Computer peripheral equipment, nec

HQ: Kern, Inc.

3940 Gantz Rd Ste A

Grove City OH 43123

614 317-2600

(G-3916)

KEYSTONE BOLT & NUT COMPANY

Also Called: Keystone Threaded Products

7600 Hub Pkwy (44125-5707)

P.O. Box 31059 (44131-0059)

PHONE..................................216 524-9626

James W Krejci, *Pr*

Betsy Mitchell, *

▲ **EMP:** 60 **EST:** 1919

SQ FT: 30,000

SALES (est): 9.32MM **Privately Held**

Web: www.keystonethreaded.com

SIC: 3452 Bolts, metal

(G-3917)

KG63 LLC

Also Called: Multiple Products Company

15501 Chatfield Ave (44111-4311)

PHONE..................................216 941-7766

William F Anderson, *Pr*

Joseph T Anderson, *VP*

Joel Newman, *Sec*

◆ **EMP:** 11 **EST:** 1945

SQ FT: 22,000

SALES (est): 1.33MM **Privately Held**

Web: www.multipleproducts.com

SIC: 3469 3861 Stamping metal for the trade ; Photographic equipment and supplies

(G-3918)

KIEFER TOOL & MOLD INC

3855 W 150th St (44111-5806)

PHONE..................................216 251-0076

John Kiefer Junior, *Pr*

Jim Kiefer, *VP*

Thomas Kiefer, *Sec*

EMP: 15 **EST:** 1966

SQ FT: 12,000

SALES (est): 2.96MM **Privately Held**

Web: www.kiefertool.com

SIC: 3599 Machine shop, jobbing and repair

(G-3919)

KIFFER INDUSTRIES INC (PA)

4905 Rocky River Dr (44135-3245)

PHONE..................................216 267-1818

EMP: 36 **EST:** 1912

SALES (est): 9.17MM

SALES (corp-wide): 9.17MM **Privately Held**

Web: www.kiffer.com

SIC: 3544 3599 3545 Special dies and tools; Custom machinery; Machine tool accessories

(G-3920)

KILROY COMPANY (PA)

Also Called: Trust Technologies

17325 Euclid Ave Ste 2042 (44112-1250)

PHONE..................................440 951-8700

Brett Jaffe, *Pr*

William S Kilroy Ii, *Ch Bd*

Paul Cardinale, *

Mark Plush, *

Frank Lamanna, *

EMP: 75 **EST:** 1967

SALES (est): 4.93MM

SALES (corp-wide): 4.93MM **Privately Held**

SIC: 3544 3549 3545 3541 Jigs and fixtures; Metalworking machinery, nec; Machine tool accessories; Machine tools, metal cutting type

(G-3921)

KING MEDIA ENTERPRISES INC

Also Called: Call & Post

11800 Shaker Blvd (44120-1919)

P.O. Box 22872 (44122-0872)

PHONE..................................216 588-6700

Don King, *Pr*

Constance Harper, *Ex Dir*

EMP: 13 **EST:** 1998

SALES (est): 1.02MM **Privately Held**

Web: www.callandpost.com

SIC: 2711 Commercial printing and newspaper publishing combined

▲ = Import ▼ = Export
◆ = Import/Export

(G-3922)
KINKOS INC
Also Called: Kinko's
4832 Ridge Rd (44144-3329)
PHONE.............................216 661-9950
Jim Wood, *Prin*
EMP: 9 **EST:** 2010
SALES (est): 134.38K **Privately Held**
SIC: 2752 Commercial printing, lithographic

(G-3923)
KINZUA ENVIRONMENTAL INC
1176 E 38th St Ste 1 (44114-3898)
PHONE.............................216 881-4040
Bradley R Waxman, *Pr*
EMP: 20 **EST:** 1974
SQ FT: 20,000
SALES (est): 5.94MM **Privately Held**
Web: www.kinzuachemical.com
SIC: 2842 Specialty cleaning

(G-3924)
KIP-CRAFT INCORPORATED (PA)
Also Called: Schoolbelles
4747 W 160th St (44135-2631)
PHONE.............................216 898-5500
Bruce J Carroll, *Pr*
Elaine Stephens, *
Mary Carroll, *
EMP: 60 **EST:** 1958
SALES (est): 4.29MM
SALES (corp-wide): 4.29MM **Privately
Held**
Web: www.schoolbelles.com
SIC: 5699 2339 2326 Uniforms; Women's
and misses' outerwear, nec; Men's and
boy's work clothing

(G-3925)
KIRKWOOD HOLDING INC (PA)
1239 Rockside Rd (44134-2772)
PHONE.............................216 267-6200
L Thomas Koechley, *CEO*
Paul Hensen, *VP Opers*
Donna Ross, *VP*
Frederick Assini, *Sec*
EMP: 7 **EST:** 2004
SQ FT: 3,500
SALES (est): 27.27MM **Privately Held**
Web: www.toledocommutator.com
SIC: 3621 Commutators, electric motor

(G-3926)
KNUTSEN MACHINE PRODUCTS INC
15020 Miles Ave (44128-2370)
PHONE.............................216 751-6500
Lee Downey, *Pr*
William Downey, *VP*
Paul E Landis, *Stockholder*
EMP: 6 **EST:** 1946
SQ FT: 20,000
SALES (est): 158.07K **Privately Held**
SIC: 3599 Machine shop, jobbing and repair

(G-3927)
KOWALSKI HEAT TREATING CO
3611 Detroit Ave (44113-2790)
PHONE.............................216 631-4411
Robert Kowalski, *Pr*
Carole Kowalski, *VP*
Stephen Kowalski, *VP*
Nancy Vermilye, *Sec*
EMP: 13 **EST:** 1975
SQ FT: 11,000
SALES (est): 3.62MM **Privately Held**
Web: www.khtheat.com
SIC: 3398 Metal heat treating

(G-3928)
KRAFTS EXOTIKA LLC
3553 Bosworth Rd (44111-6028)
PHONE.............................216 563-1178
Harry Larweh, *Prin*
EMP: 6 **EST:** 2016
SALES (est): 94.78K **Privately Held**
SIC: 2022 Natural cheese

(G-3929)
KROY LLC
Also Called: Buckeye Business Products
3830 Kelley Ave (44114-4534)
PHONE.............................800 837-4323
Stephen Kalette, *Managing Member*
Robert Kanner, *
▲ **EMP:** 177 **EST:** 1997
SQ FT: 110,000
SALES (est): 80.95MM
SALES (corp-wide): 85.24MM **Privately
Held**
Web: www.buckeyebusiness.com
SIC: 2671 3955 2761 Paper; coated and
laminated packaging; Carbon paper and
inked ribbons; Manifold business forms
PA: Pubco Corporation
3830 Kelley Ave
Cleveland OH 44114
216 881-5300

(G-3930)
KRUMOR INC
7655 Hub Pkwy Ste 206 (44125-5739)
PHONE.............................216 328-9802
Robert Mikals, *Pr*
Herbert H Sher, *VP*
EMP: 10 **EST:** 1972
SALES (est): 2.34MM **Privately Held**
Web: www.krumor.com
SIC: 3829 Temperature sensors, except
industrial process and aircraft

(G-3931)
KTRI HOLDINGS INC (DH)
127 Public Sq Ste 5110 (44114-1313)
PHONE.............................216 400-9308
Patrick James, *Pr*
Stephen Graham, *CFO*
EMP: 400 **EST:** 2007
SALES (est): 743.54MM
SALES (corp-wide): 7.28B **Privately Held**
Web: www.ktriholdings.com
SIC: 3714 Motor vehicle parts and
accessories
HQ: First Brands Group, Llc
127 Public Sq Ste 5300
Cleveland OH 44114
888 565-9632

(G-3932)
L BROWN LOANS & INVESTMENTS
1879 Colonnade Rd (44112-1567)
PHONE.............................216 308-1820
Lamone Brown, *Pr*
EMP: 6 **EST:** 2011
SALES (est): 506.25K **Privately Held**
SIC: 6519 1389 Real property lessors, nec;
Construction, repair, and dismantling
services

(G-3933)
L T V STEEL COMPANY INC
200 Public Sq (44114-2316)
P.O. Box 6778 (44101-1778)
PHONE.............................216 622-5000
J Peter Kelly, *COO*
Richard Hipple, *Pr*
A Cole Tremain, *PUBLIC AFFAIRS*
John C Skurek, *VP*
Glen J Moran, *Sr VP*
EMP: 13500 **EST:** 1899

SQ FT: 315,000
SALES (est): 3.11MM **Privately Held**
SIC: 3312 Sheet or strip, steel, hot-rolled

(G-3934)
LACHINA CREATIVE INC
3791 Green Rd (44122-5705)
PHONE.............................216 292-7959
Jeff Lachina, *Pr*
EMP: 36 **EST:** 1978
SALES (est): 1.76MM **Privately Held**
Web: www.lachina.com
SIC: 2731 Book publishing

(G-3935)
LAIRD TECHNOLOGIES INC
4707 Detroit Ave (44102-2216)
PHONE.............................216 939-2300
Martin Rapp, *Pr*
EMP: 75
SALES (corp-wide): 12.39B **Publicly Held**
Web: www.lairdtech.com
SIC: 2891 Adhesives and sealants
HQ: Laird Technologies, Inc.
16401 Swngley Rdge Rd Ste
Chesterfield MO 63017
636 898-6000

(G-3936)
LAKE BUILDING PRODUCTS INC
1361 Chardon Rd Ste 4 (44117-1557)
PHONE.............................216 486-1500
John Pogacnik, *Pr*
EMP: 24 **EST:** 1977
SQ FT: 34,000
SALES (est): 2.43MM **Privately Held**
Web: www.lbpsteel.com
SIC: 3441 1791 5051 Building components,
structural steel; Structural steel erection;
Metals service centers and offices

(G-3937)
LALAC ONE LLC
18451 Euclid Ave (44112-1016)
PHONE.............................216 432-4422
EMP: 31 **EST:** 2003
SQ FT: 30,000
SALES (est): 2.32MM **Privately Held**
Web: www.lefcoworthington.com
SIC: 4783 2441 4226 Packing and crating;
Boxes, wood; Special warehousing and
storage, nec

(G-3938)
LAM PRO INC
4701 Crayton Ave Ste A (44104-2819)
PHONE.............................216 426-0661
Kerry Stewart, *Pr*
Debbie Dragar, *Sec*
EMP: 13 **EST:** 1992
SQ FT: 33,000
SALES (est): 1.8MM **Privately Held**
Web: www.lampro.com
SIC: 3089 2789 2675 2672 Laminating of
plastics; Bookbinding and related work; Die-
cut paper and board; Paper; coated and
laminated, nec

(G-3939)
**LANGENAU MANUFACTURING
COMPANY**
7306 Madison Ave (44102-4094)
PHONE.............................216 651-3400
W C Strangward, *Pr*
EMP: 11 **EST:** 1884
SQ FT: 40,000
SALES (est): 1.09MM **Privately Held**
Web: www.langenau.com

SIC: 3432 3465 3469 3544 Plastic plumbing
fixture fittings, assembly; Automotive
stampings; Metal stampings, nec; Special
dies, tools, jigs, and fixtures

(G-3940)
LANIER & ASSOCIATES INC
Also Called: Cleveland Black Pages
1814 E 40th St Ste 1c (44103-3500)
PHONE.............................216 391-7735
Bob Lanier, *Pr*
Linda Lanier, *VP*
EMP: 6 **EST:** 1991
SALES (est): 122.76K **Privately Held**
SIC: 2741 Directories, telephone: publishing
only, not printed on site

(G-3941)
LANLY COMPANY
26201 Tungsten Rd (44132-2997)
PHONE.............................216 731-1115
Joe Vitale, *Pr*
Dennis W Hill, *
David Fowle, *
EMP: 44 **EST:** 1938
SQ FT: 68,000
SALES (est): 9.33MM **Privately Held**
Web: www.lanly.com
SIC: 3567 Heating units and devices,
industrial: electric

(G-3942)
LARMCO WINDOWS INC (PA)
8400 Sweet Valley Dr Ste 404
(44125-4243)
PHONE.............................216 502-2832
William Simon, *Ch Bd*
Joe Talmon, *Pr*
EMP: 30 **EST:** 1959
SALES (est): 2.17MM
SALES (corp-wide): 2.17MM **Privately
Held**
Web: www.larmco.com
SIC: 3089 Windows, plastics

(G-3943)
LAS AMERICAS INC
5722 Mayfield Rd (44124-2918)
PHONE.............................440 459-2030
Jefferson Evangelista, *Prin*
EMP: 6 **EST:** 2014
SALES (est): 62.38K **Privately Held**
SIC: 2099 Food preparations, nec

(G-3944)
LASER PRINTING SOLUTIONS INC
Also Called: L P S I
6040 Hillcrest Dr (44125-4620)
PHONE.............................216 351-4444
Mike Piaser, *Pr*
Bob Lasser, *Ch Bd*
EMP: 7 **EST:** 1994
SQ FT: 5,000
SALES (est): 501.88K **Privately Held**
Web: www.laserprintingsolutions.com
SIC: 2759 Laser printing

(G-3945)
LAU HOLDINGS LLC (HQ)
16900 S Waterloo Rd (44110-3808)
PHONE.............................216 486-4000
Megan Fellinger, *Pr*
EMP: 79 **EST:** 2017
SQ FT: 50,000
SALES (est): 48MM
SALES (corp-wide): 184.04MM **Privately
Held**
Web: www.lauparts.com
SIC: 3564 Ventilating fans: industrial or
commercial
PA: Morrison Products, Inc.

GEOGRAPHIC

16900 S Waterloo Rd
Cleveland OH 44110
216 486-4000

(G-3946)
LAWRENCE INDUSTRIES INC (PA)
4500 Lee Rd Ste 120 (44128-2959)
PHONE...........................216 518-7000
Lawrence A Kopittke Senior, *Pr*
Richard L Kopittke, *
Arthur Kopittke, *
◆ **EMP:** 50 **EST:** 1969
SQ FT: 160,000
SALES (est): 3.36MM
SALES (corp-wide): 3.36MM **Privately Held**
Web: www.lawrenceindustriesinc.com
SIC: 3599 3541 7699 5084 Machine shop, jobbing and repair; Sawing and cutoff machines (metalworking machinery); Tool repair services; Metalworking tools, nec (such as drills, taps, dies, files)

(G-3947)
LAWRENCE INDUSTRIES INC
Also Called: Arte Limited
4500 Lee Rd Ste 120 (44128-2959)
PHONE...........................216 518-1400
Robert Kopittke, *Brnch Mgr*
EMP: 101
SALES (corp-wide): 3.36MM **Privately Held**
Web: www.lawrenceindustriesinc.com
SIC: 3599 3541 Machine shop, jobbing and repair; Sawing and cutoff machines (metalworking machinery)
PA: Lawrence Industries, Inc.
4500 Lee Rd Ste 120
Cleveland OH 44128
216 518-7000

(G-3948)
LAWSON TWING AUTO WRECKING LLC
14114 Miles Ave (44128-2329)
PHONE...........................216 883-9050
Edward Maurice Lawson, *Owner*
EMP: 10 **EST:** 2009
SALES (est): 312.63K **Privately Held**
SIC: 5093 3711 Junk and scrap; Wreckers (tow truck), assembly of

(G-3949)
LEGAL NEWS PUBLISHING CO
Also Called: Daily Legal News
2935 Prospect Ave E (44115-2607)
PHONE...........................216 696-3322
Lucien B Karlovec Junior, *Pr*
Jeffrey Karlovec, *
Charles E Bergstresser, *
EMP: 28 **EST:** 1885
SQ FT: 14,238
SALES (est): 2.47MM **Privately Held**
Web: www.dln.com
SIC: 2791 2711 2752 2789 Typesetting; Newspapers, publishing and printing; Offset printing; Bookbinding and related work

(G-3950)
LEIMKUEHLER INC (PA)
4625 Detroit Ave (44102-2295)
PHONE...........................440 899-7842
Robert Leimkuehler, *Pr*
EMP: 21 **EST:** 1948
SQ FT: 10,000
SALES (est): 2.74MM
SALES (corp-wide): 2.74MM **Privately Held**
Web: www.leimkuehlerinc.com

(G-3951)
LENNOX INDUSTRIES INC
Also Called: Lennox
4562 Hinckley Industrial Pkwy Unit 8 (44109-6025)
PHONE...........................216 739-1909
John Kelley, *Mgr*
EMP: 9
SALES (corp-wide): 5.34B **Publicly Held**
Web: www.lennoxpros.com
SIC: 3585 Refrigeration and heating equipment
HQ: Lennox Industries Inc.
2100 Lake Park Blvd
Richardson TX 75080
972 497-5000

(G-3952)
LEWART PLASTICS LLC
3562 W 69th St (44102-5420)
PHONE...........................216 281-2333
EMP: 10 **EST:** 2018
SALES (est): 2.85MM **Privately Held**
Web: www.lewartplastics.com
SIC: 3089 Injection molding of plastics

(G-3953)
LEXTECH INDUSTRIES LTD
6800 Union Ave (44105-1326)
PHONE...........................216 883-7900
David N Bortz, *Pr*
EMP: 6 **EST:** 1998
SQ FT: 143,000
SALES (est): 2.18MM **Privately Held**
Web: www.lextechindustries.com
SIC: 3469 3568 3462 Stamping metal for the trade; Power transmission equipment, nec; Iron and steel forgings

(G-3954)
LICENSE AD PLATE COMPANY
13110 Enterprise Ave Side B (44135-5174)
PHONE...........................216 265-4200
Richard Russell, *Pr*
Loretta Patten, *Sec*
EMP: 10 **EST:** 1946
SQ FT: 6,000
SALES (est): 450.88K **Privately Held**
SIC: 3993 2759 Advertising novelties; Screen printing

(G-3955)
LINCOLN ELECTRIC COMPANY (HQ)
22801 Saint Clair Ave (44117-1199)
PHONE...........................216 481-8100
Christopher L Mapes, *Ch Bd*
Frederick G Stueber, *
Anthony Battle, *
Geoffrey P Allman, *
◆ **EMP:** 3200 **EST:** 1895
SQ FT: 2,658,410
SALES (est): 446.08MM
SALES (corp-wide): 4.01B **Publicly Held**
Web: www.lincolnelectric.com
SIC: 3548 Arc welding generators, a.c. and d.c.
PA: Lincoln Electric Holdings, Inc.
22801 St Clair Ave
Cleveland OH 44117
216 481-8100

(G-3956)
LINCOLN ELECTRIC HOLDINGS INC (PA)
Also Called: LINCOLN ELECTRIC
22801 Saint Clair Ave (44117-1199)
PHONE...........................216 481-8100

Christopher L Mapes, *Ch Bd*
Steven B Hedlund, *Pr*
Christopher L Mapes, *Ex Ch Bd*
Gabriel Bruno, *Ex VP*
Jennifer I Ansberry, *Ex VP*
EMP: 485 **EST:** 1895
SQ FT: 3,017,090
SALES (est): 4.01B
SALES (corp-wide): 4.01B **Publicly Held**
Web: ir.lincolnelectric.com
SIC: 3548 Welding and cutting apparatus and accessories, nec

(G-3957)
LINCOLN FOODSERVICE PRODUCTS LLC
Also Called: Lincoln Foodservice Products
1333 E 179th St (44110-2501)
PHONE...........................260 459-8200
▲ **EMP:** 340
SIC: 3556 Ovens, bakery

(G-3958)
LINDE INC
Praxair
14788 York Rd (44133-4508)
PHONE...........................440 237-8690
Brian Pasquerlo, *Superintnt*
EMP: 12
Web: www.lindeus.com
SIC: 2813 Industrial gases
HQ: Linde Inc.
10 Riverview Dr
Danbury CT 06810
203 837-2000

(G-3959)
LINEAR ACOUSTIC INC
1241 Superior Ave E (44114-3204)
PHONE...........................717 735-3611
EMP: 6 **EST:** 2018
SALES (est): 1.54MM **Privately Held**
Web: www.telosalliance.com
SIC: 3663 Radio and t.v. communications equipment

(G-3960)
LINEAR TECHNOLOGY LLC
7550 Lucerne Dr Ste 106 (44130-6503)
PHONE...........................440 239-0817
Todd Sloan, *Mgr*
EMP: 7
SALES (corp-wide): 9.43B **Publicly Held**
Web: www.analog.com
SIC: 3674 Semiconductors and related devices
HQ: Linear Technology Llc
1630 Mccarthy Blvd
Milpitas CA 95035
408 432-1900

(G-3961)
LINESTREAM TECHNOLOGIES INC
1468 W 9th St Ste 435 (44113-1316)
PHONE...........................216 862-7874
James G Dawson, *Prin*
Dave Neundorfer, *CEO*
EMP: 7 **EST:** 2008
SALES (est): 943.55K **Privately Held**
Web: www.linestream.com
SIC: 7372 Business oriented computer software

(G-3962)
LINSALATA CPITL PRTNERS FUND I
5900 Landerbrook Dr Ste 280 (44124-4020)
PHONE...........................440 684-1400
Frank Linsalata, *Pt*
EMP: 9 **EST:** 1985
SALES (est): 1.01MM **Privately Held**

Web: www.linsalatacapital.com
SIC: 6282 6799 3499 2676 Investment advisory service; Venture capital companies; Safes and vaults, metal; Sanitary paper products

(G-3963)
LIQUID IMAGE CORP AMERICA
3700 Prospect Ave E (44115-2706)
PHONE...........................216 458-9800
Lea Wiertel, *Pr*
Michael Wiertel, *VP*
EMP: 7 **EST:** 1997
SQ FT: 2,500
SALES (est): 1.28MM **Privately Held**
Web: www.liquid-image.com
SIC: 3663 Digital encoders

(G-3964)
LITURGICAL PUBLICATIONS INC
Also Called: LPI
4560 E 71st St (44105-5604)
PHONE...........................216 325-6825
Lou Anthes, *Mgr*
EMP: 68
SALES (corp-wide): 47.85MM **Privately Held**
Web: www.4lpi.com
SIC: 2731 2789 2752 2721 Pamphlets: publishing and printing; Bookbinding and related work; Commercial printing, lithographic; Periodicals
PA: Liturgical Publications, Inc.
2875 S James Dr
New Berlin WI 53151
262 785-1188

(G-3965)
LKD AEROSPACE HOLDINGS INC (PA)
25101 Chagrin Blvd Ste 350 (44122-5643)
PHONE...........................216 262-8481
Mark Chamberlain, *CEO*
Steven H Rosen, *Pr*
Jonathan Crandall, *VP*
EMP: 11 **EST:** 2016
SALES (est): 37.48MM
SALES (corp-wide): 37.48MM **Privately Held**
SIC: 3728 Aircraft parts and equipment, nec

(G-3966)
LOGAN CLUTCH CORPORATION
Also Called: Lc
28855 Ranney Pkwy (44145-1173)
PHONE...........................440 808-4258
William A Logan, *Pr*
Madelon Logan, *
Elyse Logan, *
▲ **EMP:** 30 **EST:** 1975
SQ FT: 33,000
SALES (est): 9.8MM **Privately Held**
Web: www.loganclutch.com
SIC: 3568 5085 Clutches, except vehicular; Industrial supplies

(G-3967)
LOTUS PIPES & ROCKDRILLS USA
1700 E 12th St (44114)
PHONE...........................516 209-6995
EMP: 10 **EST:** 2017
SALES (est): 487.75K **Privately Held**
Web: www.lotuspipesandrockdrills.com
SIC: 3089 Plastics processing

(G-3968)
LOUS SAUSAGE LTD
Also Called: Lou's Sausage
14723 Miles Ave (44128-2397)
PHONE...........................216 752-5060
EMP: 6 **EST:** 1958

(G-3951)

SIC: **5999** 3842 Orthopedic and prosthesis applications; Surgical appliances and supplies

SQ FT: 7,500
SALES (est): 1.37MM Privately Held
Web: www.loussausage.com
SIC: 2013 Sausages, from purchased meat

(G-3969)
LUBRIQUIP INC
Also Called: Other Styles - See Operation
18901 Cranwood Pkwy (44128-4041)
P.O. Box 1441 (55440-1441)
PHONE..................................216 581-2000
EMP: 300
SIC: 3714 Lubrication systems and parts,
motor vehicle

(G-3970)
LUBRIZOL GLOBAL MANAGEMENT INC (DH)
Also Called: Lubrizol
9911 Brecksville Rd (44141-3201)
PHONE..................................216 447-5000
Rebecca Liebert, CEO
Rick Tolin, Pr
Brian A Valentine, VP
John J King, VP
Leslie M Reynolds, Sec
◆ EMP: 10 EST: 1870
SQ FT: 380,000
SALES (est): 689.17MM
SALES (corp-wide): 424.23B Publicly Held
Web: www.lubrizol.com
SIC: 2899 2891 3088 2834 Chemical
preparations, nec; Adhesives and sealants;
Plastics plumbing fixtures; Pharmaceutical
preparations
HQ: The Lubrizol Corporation
29400 Lakeland Blvd
Wickliffe OH 44092
440 943-4200

(G-3971)
LUCKY THIRTEEN INC
Also Called: Lucky Thirteen Laser
7413 Associate Ave (44144-1104)
PHONE..................................216 631-0013
James Bailey, Pr
Francis J Dempsey, Prin
James P Bailey, Prin
Thomas G Scheiman, Prin
EMP: 8 EST: 2009
SALES (est): 1.33MM Privately Held
Web: www.jbstamping.com
SIC: 3600 Laser welding, drilling, and cutting
equipment

(G-3972)
LUXCO INC
Also Called: Paramount Distillers
3116 Berea Rd (44111-1501)
PHONE..................................216 671-6300
Paul A Lux, Brnch Mgr
EMP: 6
SALES (corp-wide): 703.63MM Publicly
Held
Web: www.luxco.com
SIC: 2085 Bourbon whiskey
HQ: Luxco, Inc.
540 Mryvlle Cntre Dr Ste
Saint Louis MO 63141
314 772-2626

(G-3973)
M & M DIES INC
3502 Beyerle Rd (44105-1016)
PHONE..................................216 883-6628
Donald Dostie, Pr
EMP: 7 EST: 1968
SQ FT: 2,940
SALES (est): 242.86K Privately Held
Web: www.mmdci.com

SIC: 3364 3544 Nonferrous die-castings
except aluminum; Special dies and tools

(G-3974)
M ARGUESO & CO INC
Also Called: Paramelt
12651 Elmwood Ave (44111-5911)
PHONE..................................216 252-4122
Rob Deck, Genl Mgr
EMP: 134
SALES (corp-wide): 879.5MM Privately
Held
Web: www.paramelt.com
SIC: 2891 Adhesives and sealants
HQ: M. Argueso & Co., Inc.
1300 E Mount Garfield Rd
Norton Shores MI 49441
231 759-7304

(G-3975)
M B SAXON CO INC
Also Called: Saxon Jewelers
47 Alpha Park (44143-2219)
PHONE..................................440 229-5006
Michael B Saxon, Pr
EMP: 6 EST: 1979
SQ FT: 3,200
SALES (est): 1MM Privately Held
Web: www.saxonjewelers.com
SIC: 3911 5944 5094 Jewelry, precious metal
; Jewelry, precious stones and precious
metals; Jewelry

(G-3976)
M-BOSS INC
4510 E 71st St (44105-5637)
PHONE..................................216 441-6080
William Perk, Pr
EMP: 20 EST: 1999
SQ FT: 6,000
SALES (est): 1.38MM Privately Held
Web: www.mbossinc.com
SIC: 3646 Ceiling systems, luminous

(G-3977)
M3 TECHNOLOGIES INC
13910 Enterprise Ave (44135-5118)
PHONE..................................216 898-9936
Roger May, Pr
Danny May, Sec
Barry May, Treas
EMP: 10 EST: 2001
SALES (est): 1.82MM Privately Held
Web: www.m3techfab.com
SIC: 3444 Sheet metal specialties, not
stamped

(G-3978)
MACE PERSONAL DEF & SEC INC (HQ)
4400 Carnegie Ave (44103-4342)
PHONE..................................440 424-5321
Carl Smith, CFO
◆ EMP: 30 EST: 2002
SQ FT: 30,000
SALES (est): 258.66K
SALES (corp-wide): 22.34MM Publicly
Held
Web: www.mace.com
SIC: 3999 5065 Self-defense sprays;
Security control equipment and systems
PA: Mace Security International, Inc.
4400 Carnegie Ave
Cleveland OH 44103
440 424-5325

(G-3979)
MACE SECURITY INTL INC (PA)
Also Called: Mace
4400 Carnegie Ave (44103-4342)
PHONE..................................440 424-5325

Sanjay Singh, Ch Bd
Carl R Smith, *
Eric Crawford, *
Paul Hughes, *
Mark Barrus, *
◆ EMP: 42 EST: 1993
SQ FT: 5,000
SALES (est): 22.34MM
SALES (corp-wide): 22.34MM Publicly
Held
Web: www.mace.com
SIC: 3699 3999 Security devices; Self-
defense sprays

(G-3980)
MAGNESIUM REFINING TECHNOLOGIES INC
29695 Pettibone Rd (44139-5462)
PHONE..................................419 483-9199
▲ EMP: 90
SIC: 3339 Magnesium refining (primary)

(G-3981)
MAGNUM COMPUTERS INC
868 Montford Rd (44121-2012)
PHONE..................................216 781-1757
Dan Hanson, Pr
EMP: 10 EST: 1970
SQ FT: 3,000
SALES (est): 323.68K Privately Held
Web: www.magnuminc.com
SIC: 5045 1731 8748 7378 Computers,
peripherals, and software; General
electrical contractor; Business consulting,
nec; Computer maintenance and repair

(G-3982)
MALIN CO
5400 Smith Rd (44142-2081)
PHONE..................................216 267-9080
Leonard Defino, Pr
Frank Defino, VP
Mary Defino, Sec
◆ EMP: 27 EST: 1894
SQ FT: 56,000
SALES (est): 15.65MM Privately Held
Web: www.malinco.com
SIC: 3496 3469 Miscellaneous fabricated
wire products; Metal stampings, nec
PA: A.J.D. Holding Co.
2181 Enterprise Pkwy
Twinsburg OH 44087

(G-3983)
MALLEYS CANDIES LLC (PA)
Also Called: Malley's Chocolates
13400 Brookpark Rd (44135-5145)
PHONE..................................216 362-8700
Mike Malley, Prin
William Malley, *
▲ EMP: 62 EST: 1935
SQ FT: 60,000
SALES (est): 25.28MM
SALES (corp-wide): 25.28MM Privately
Held
Web: www.malleys.com
SIC: 5441 5451 2064 2068 Candy; Ice
cream (packaged); Candy bars, including
chocolate covered bars; Nuts: dried,
dehydrated, salted or roasted

(G-3984)
MAMECO INTERNATIONAL INC
4475 E 175th St (44128-3599)
PHONE..................................216 752-4400
Jeff Korach, Prin
EMP: 10 EST: 1913
SQ FT: 77,000
SALES (est): 2.95MM
SALES (corp-wide): 7.34B Publicly Held

SIC: 2891 2851 3069 Sealants; Paints and
allied products; Floor coverings, rubber
PA: Rpm International Inc.
2628 Pearl Rd
Medina OH 44258
330 273-5090

(G-3985)
MANUFACTURERS SERVICE INC
11440 Brookpark Rd (44130-1131)
PHONE..................................216 267-3771
Carl C Jordan, Pr
Edward Jordan, *
David C Jordan, *
EMP: 25 EST: 1949
SQ FT: 40,000
SALES (est): 2.63MM Privately Held
Web: www.mobilewindshieldpro.com
SIC: 3469 3544 Metal stampings, nec;
Special dies and tools

(G-3986)
MARADYNE CORPORATION (HQ)
4540 W 160th St (44135-2628)
PHONE..................................216 362-0755
▲ EMP: 58 EST: 1981
SALES (est): 12.55MM
SALES (corp-wide): 43.22MM Privately
Held
Web: www.maradyne.com
SIC: 3714 Motor vehicle electrical equipment
PA: Dreison International, Inc.
4540 W 160th St
Cleveland OH 44135
216 362-0755

(G-3987)
MARCUS UPPE INC
Also Called: Clicks Document Management
815 Superior Ave E Ste 714 (44114-2706)
PHONE..................................216 263-4000
Mark Sukie, Brnch Mgr
EMP: 27
SIC: 2759 Commercial printing, nec
PA: Marcus Uppe Inc.
320 Fort Duquesne Blvd # 300
Pittsburgh PA 15222

(G-3988)
MARICH MACHINE AND TOOL CO
3815 Lakeside Ave E (44114-3843)
PHONE..................................216 391-5502
Andrew Marich, Pr
EMP: 9 EST: 1981
SQ FT: 10,000
SALES (est): 853.92K Privately Held
Web: www.marichmachine.com
SIC: 3599 Machine shop, jobbing and repair

(G-3989)
MARKING DEVICES INC
3110 Payne Ave (44114-4504)
PHONE..................................216 861-4498
Theodore Cutts, Pr
EMP: 8 EST: 1936
SALES (est): 957.75K
SALES (corp-wide): 3.96MM Privately
Held
SIC: 3953 Embossing seals and hand
stamps
PA: Royal Acme Corporation
3110 Payne Ave
Cleveland OH 44114
216 241-1477

(G-3990)
MARLIN MANUFACTURING CORP (PA)
12800 Corporate Dr (44130-9311)
PHONE..................................216 676-1340
John Tymkewicz, Prin

John H Breisch, *
Wallace B Heiser, *
Andy Gehrisch, *
◆ **EMP:** 64 **EST:** 1952
SQ FT: 42,000
SALES (est): 8.35MM
SALES (corp-wide): 8.35MM **Privately
Held**
Web: www.marlinmfg.com
SIC: 3823 Pyrometers, industrial process
type

(G-3991)
MARLOW-2000 INC
Also Called: Martin Industrial Truck
13811 Enterprise Ave (44135-5115)
PHONE..........................216 362-8500
Danny E Martin, *Pr*
Sandra Martin, *Treas*
EMP: 13 **EST:** 1997
SQ FT: 22,000
SALES (est): 2.42MM **Privately Held**
Web: www.clevelandforklift.com
SIC: 5531 3537 7513 Truck equipment and
parts; Forklift trucks; Truck rental and
leasing, no drivers

(G-3992)
MARTIN PULTRUSION GROUP INC
20801 Miles Rd Ste B (44128-4530)
PHONE..........................440 439-9130
Jeff Martin, *Pr*
▼ **EMP:** 6 **EST:** 1993
SQ FT: 7,360
SALES (est): 990.01K **Privately Held**
Web: www.martinpultrusion.com
SIC: 3544 Special dies, tools, jigs, and
fixtures

(G-3993)
MARTIN SHEET METAL INC
Also Called: Martin Cab Div
7108 Madison Ave (44102-4093)
PHONE..........................216 377-8200
Pauline Martin, *Ch Bd*
Robert P Martin Senior, *VP*
George F Voinovich, *
Frank Bendyck, *
EMP: 24 **EST:** 1920
SQ FT: 100,000
SALES (est): 4.21MM **Privately Held**
Web: www.martincab.com
SIC: 3537 3713 Cabs, for industrial trucks
and tractors; Truck and bus bodies

(G-3994)
MARTINDALE ELECTRIC COMPANY
1375 Hird Ave (44107-3008)
P.O. Box 72419 (44192)
PHONE..........................216 521-8567
Jim Satterthwaite, *Pr*
Jeffrey Snyder, *
F Z Marty, *
EMP: 48 **EST:** 1913
SQ FT: 33,000
SALES (est): 3.31MM **Privately Held**
Web: www.martindaleco.com
SIC: 3425 3541 Saw blades and handsaws;
Machine tools, metal cutting type

(G-3995)
MARZANO INC
Also Called: Nunzios Cabinet Shop
4147 Pearl Rd (44109-3332)
PHONE..........................216 459-2051
Nunzio Marzano, *Pr*
Carlena Marzano, *Sec*
EMP: 8 **EST:** 1977
SQ FT: 10,000
SALES (est): 751.26K **Privately Held**
Web: www.nunzioscabinets.com

SIC: 2434 Wood kitchen cabinets

(G-3996)
MASTER CRAFT PRODUCTS INC
10621 Briggs Rd (44111-5329)
PHONE..........................216 281-5910
Jim Szente Junior, *Pr*
Cyndi Szente, *Treas*
EMP: 12 **EST:** 2002
SQ FT: 4,400
SALES (est): 946.86K **Privately Held**
Web: www.mastercraftdies.com
SIC: 3544 Special dies and tools

(G-3997)
MASTER MFG CO INC
Also Called: Master Caster Company
9200 Inman Ave (44105-2110)
PHONE..........................216 641-0500
Iris Rubinfield, *Pr*
Penny Heinzmann, *
Pamela Vestal, *
◆ **EMP:** 34 **EST:** 1951
SQ FT: 10,000
SALES (est): 2.29MM **Privately Held**
Web: www.mastermfgco.com
SIC: 3429 2599 2392 3069 Furniture,
builders' and other household hardware;
Factory furniture and fixtures; Household
furnishings, nec; Hard rubber and molded
rubber products

(G-3998)
MASTER PRODUCTS COMPANY
6400 Park Ave (44105-4991)
PHONE..........................216 341-1740
R Jeffrey Walters, *Pr*
Greg Walters, *
David Mitskavich, *
Lisa Sparenga, *
EMP: 57 **EST:** 1919
SQ FT: 70,000
SALES (est): 9.71MM **Privately Held**
Web: www.masterproducts.com
SIC: 3452 3469 3568 Washers, metal;
Stamping metal for the trade; Power
transmission equipment, nec

(G-3999)
MAX - PRO TOOLS INC
8999 W Pleasant Valley Rd (44130-7644)
PHONE..........................800 456-0931
Steven Kurr, *Pr*
EMP: 10 **EST:** 2004
SALES (est): 174.54K **Privately Held**
SIC: 3541 Machine tools, metal cutting type

(G-4000)
MAXIM INTEGRATED PRODUCTS LLC
9000 Yale Ave (44108-2140)
PHONE..........................216 375-1057
EMP: 50 **EST:** 2019
SALES (est): 250K **Privately Held**
SIC: 3299 Architectural sculptures: gypsum,
clay, papier mache, etc.

(G-4001)
MAY TOOL & DIE CO
9981 York Theta Dr Ste 1 (44133-3582)
PHONE..........................440 237-8012
Gus May, *Engg Mgr*
EMP: 7 **EST:** 1980
SALES (est): 785.19K **Privately Held**
SIC: 3444 Sheet metalwork

(G-4002)
MAYFAIR GRANITE CO INC
Also Called: Mayfair Memorial
4202 Mayfield Rd (44121-3008)

PHONE..........................216 382-8150
Michael J Johns Senior, *Pr*
Monica Johns, *VP*
Nicolette L Johns, *Sec*
Michael N Johns, *VP*
EMP: 7 **EST:** 1937
SALES (est): 458.18K **Privately Held**
Web: www.jcmemorials.com
SIC: 5999 5032 3993 Monuments, finished
to custom order; Granite building stone;
Signs and advertising specialties

(G-4003)
MAYFRAN INTERNATIONAL INC (HQ)
6650 Beta Dr (44143-2352)
PHONE..........................440 461-4100
Naoshige Sakai, *Pr*
Steve Carlson, *
▲ **EMP:** 247 **EST:** 1983
SQ FT: 154,000
SALES (est): 37.68MM **Privately Held**
Web: www.mayfran.com
SIC: 3535 Belt conveyor systems, general
industrial use
PA: Tsubakimoto Chain Co.
3-3-3, Nakanoshima, Kita-Ku
Osaka OSK 530-0

(G-4004)
MAZZELLA JHH COMPANY INC
Also Called: J Henry Holland
21000 Aerospace Pkwy (44142-1000)
PHONE..........................440 239-7000
EMP: 56 **EST:** 2012
SALES (est): 2.35MM **Privately Held**
Web: www.mazzellacompanies.com
SIC: 3496 Miscellaneous fabricated wire
products

(G-4005)
MAZZELLA LIFTING TECH INC (HQ)
Also Called: Rouster Lfting Rgging A Mzzlla
21000 Aerospace Pkwy (44142-1072)
PHONE..........................440 239-7000
Anthony Mazzella, *CEO*
James J Mazzella, *
▲ **EMP:** 80 **EST:** 1959
SQ FT: 50,000
SALES (est): 34.93MM **Privately Held**
Web: www.mazzellacompanies.com
SIC: 3496 Miscellaneous fabricated wire
products
PA: Mazzella Holding Company, Inc.
21000 Aerospace Pkwy
Cleveland OH 44142

(G-4006)
MB DYNAMICS INC
25865 Richmond Rd (44146-1431)
PHONE..........................216 292-5850
Richard Mccormick, *CEO*
▼ **EMP:** 29 **EST:** 1984
SQ FT: 25,000
SALES (est): 4.32MM **Privately Held**
Web: www.mbdynamics.com
SIC: 3829 Testing equipment: abrasion,
shearing strength, etc.

(G-4007)
MC MACHINE LLC
9000 Brookpark Rd (44129-6832)
PHONE..........................216 398-3666
▲ **EMP:** 25
SIC: 7539 7692 3444 3443 Machine shop,
automotive; Welding repair; Sheet
metalwork; Fabricated plate work (boiler
shop)

(G-4008)
MCDONALD STEEL PLATE INC
Also Called: General Steel Corporation
3344 E 80th St (44127-1851)
PHONE..........................216 883-4200
James Grasso, *Pr*
EMP: 13 **EST:** 2022
SALES (est): 2.35MM
SALES (corp-wide): 4.98MM **Privately
Held**
Web: www.genstlcorp.com
SIC: 5051 3398 3441 Steel; Metal heat
treating; Fabricated structural metal
PA: Mcdonald Steel Corporation
100 Ohio Ave
Mc Donald OH 44437
330 530-9118

(G-4009)
MCGEAN-ROHCO INC (PA)
Also Called: McGean
2910 Harvard Ave (44105-3010)
PHONE..........................216 441-4900
◆ **EMP:** 75 **EST:** 1929
SALES (est): 41.26MM
SALES (corp-wide): 41.26MM **Privately
Held**
Web: www.mcgean.com
SIC: 2899 2819 3471 Chemical
preparations, nec; Industrial inorganic
chemicals, nec; Plating and polishing

(G-4010)
MCHAEL D GORONOK STRING INSTRS
10823 Magnolia Dr (44106-1807)
PHONE..........................216 421-4227
Michael D Goronok, *Owner*
EMP: 9 **EST:** 1992
SQ FT: 8,000
SALES (est): 149.01K **Privately Held**
SIC: 3931 5099 String instruments and parts
; Musical instruments

(G-4011)
MCKECHNIE AROSPC HOLDINGS INC
1301 E 9th St Ste 3000 (44114-1871)
PHONE..........................216 706-2960
Tariq M Jesrai, *CEO*
Dirkson Charles, *Ex VP*
Glenn D'alessandro, *VP*
Michael Manella, *VP*
EMP: 7 **EST:** 2007
SALES (est): 7.86MM
SALES (corp-wide): 7.94B **Publicly Held**
SIC: 3728 Aircraft parts and equipment, nec
HQ: Transdigm, Inc.
1350 Euclid Ave
Cleveland OH 44115

(G-4012)
MCM IND CO INC (PA)
Also Called: McM Industries
22901 Millcreek Blvd Ste 250 (44122-5729)
P.O. Box 284 (44065-0284)
PHONE..........................216 292-4506
Gloria Reljanovic, *CEO*
Michael Reljanovic, *Pr*
◆ **EMP:** 12 **EST:** 1981
SQ FT: 1,000
SALES (est): 4.96MM **Privately Held**
Web: www.mcmindustries.com
SIC: 3496 Miscellaneous fabricated wire
products

(G-4013)
MCM IND CO INC
7800 Finney Ave (44105-5125)
PHONE..........................216 641-6300

Mike Zlojutro, *Brnch Mgr*
EMP: 16
SQ FT: 51,055
Web: www.mcmindustries.com
SIC: 3496 Miscellaneous fabricated wire products
PA: Mcm Ind. Co., Inc.
22901 Millcreek Blvd Ste 2
Cleveland OH 44122

(G-4014)
MCO INC (PA)
7555 Bessemer Ave (44127-1821)
PHONE..................................216 341-8914
Tom Mesterhazy, *Pr*
EMP: 6 **EST:** 1989
SQ FT: 18,000
SALES (est): 23.8MM **Privately Held**
SIC: 2992 Lubricating oils and greases

(G-4015)
MEASUREMENT COMPUTING CORP (DH)
Also Called: Iotech
25971 Cannon Rd (44146-1833)
PHONE..................................440 439-4091
Mark Marini, *Pr*
EMP: 32 **EST:** 1982
SQ FT: 30,000
SALES (est): 5.78MM
SALES (corp-wide): 17.49B **Publicly Held**
Web: www.digilent.com
SIC: 3823 Computer interface equipment, for industrial process control
HQ: National Instruments Corporation
11500 N Mopac Expy
Austin TX 78759
512 683-0100

(G-4016)
MEDIVIEW XR INC
10000 Cedar Ave (44106-2119)
PHONE..................................419 270-2774
John Black, *CEO*
EMP: 13 **EST:** 2019
SALES (est): 9.95MM **Privately Held**
Web: www.mediview.com
SIC: 3841 Medical instruments and equipment, blood and bone work

(G-4017)
MEDTRONIC INC
Also Called: Medtronic
5005 Rockside Rd Ste 1160 (44131-6801)
PHONE..................................216 642-1977
Larry Saunders, *Brnch Mgr*
EMP: 14
Web: www.medtronic.com
SIC: 3841 Surgical and medical instruments
HQ: Medtronic, Inc.
710 Medtronic Pkwy
Minneapolis MN 55432
763 514-4000

(G-4018)
MEGA TECHWAY INC (PA)
760 Beta Dr Ste F (44143-2334)
PHONE..................................440 605-0700
Richard Sadler, *Pr*
Karl Weinfurtner, *
EMP: 87 **EST:** 2004
SQ FT: 3,500
SALES (est): 19.56MM
SALES (corp-wide): 19.56MM **Privately Held**
Web: www.megatechway.com
SIC: 3679 Harness assemblies, for electronic use: wire or cable

(G-4019)
MELIN TOOL COMPANY INC
5565 Venture Dr Ste C (44130-9302)
PHONE..................................216 362-4200
Mike Wochna, *Pr*
Mildred Rathberger, *
John Stickney, *
EMP: 70 **EST:** 1938
SQ FT: 25,000
SALES (est): 10.02MM
SALES (corp-wide): 12.03B **Privately Held**
Web: www.melintool.com
SIC: 3545 3541 Cutting tools for machine tools; Machine tools, metal cutting type
HQ: Walter Ag
Derendinger Str. 53
Tubingen BW 72072
70717010

(G-4020)
MEMPHIS SMOKEHOUSE INC
Also Called: Tobacco Company
8463 Memphis Ave (44144-2126)
PHONE..................................216 351-5321
Dwight Hughes, *Pr*
Jim Seward, *Pr*
EMP: 7 **EST:** 1995
SQ FT: 1,200
SALES (est): 263.11K **Privately Held**
SIC: 2111 Cigarettes

(G-4021)
MERIT BRASS CO (PA)
Also Called: Merit Brass
1 Merit Dr (44143-1457)
P.O. Box 43127 (44143-0127)
PHONE..................................216 261-9800
▲ **EMP:** 236 **EST:** 1961
SALES (est): 44.19MM
SALES (corp-wide): 44.19MM **Privately Held**
Web: www.meritbrass.com
SIC: 3432 5051 5074 Plumbing fixture fittings and trim; Metals service centers and offices; Plumbing fittings and supplies

(G-4022)
MESSER LLC
6300 Halle Dr (44125-4618)
PHONE..................................216 533-7256
EMP: 34
SALES (corp-wide): 2.29B **Privately Held**
Web: www.messeramericas.com
SIC: 2813 Oxygen, compressed or liquefied
HQ: Messer Llc
200 Smrset Corp Blvd Ste
Bridgewater NJ 08807
800 755-9277

(G-4023)
METAL FABRICATING CORPORATION
10408 Berea Rd (44102-2506)
PHONE..................................216 631-8121
Bernard Golias Senior, *Ch*
Judy Kalski, *
Joseph Golias, *
Robert Golias, *
EMP: 87 **EST:** 1932
SQ FT: 150,000
SALES (est): 6.17MM **Privately Held**
Web: www.metalfabricatingcorp.com
SIC: 2542 3444 3469 3443 Cabinets: show, display, or storage: except wood; Bins, prefabricated sheet metal; Stamping metal for the trade; Fabricated plate work (boiler shop)

(G-4024)
MEYER PRODUCTS LLC
18513 Euclid Ave (44112-1084)
PHONE..................................216 486-1313
Louis Berkman, *Managing Member*
EMP: 48 **EST:** 2004
SALES (est): 8.28MM **Privately Held**
Web: www.meyerproducts.com
SIC: 3531 Construction machinery
HQ: Aebi Schmidt Holding Ag
Schulstrasse 4
Frauenfeld TG 8500

(G-4025)
MFH PARTNERS INC (PA)
6650 Beta Dr (44143-2352)
P.O. Box 43038 (44143-0045)
PHONE..................................440 461-4100
J D Sullivan, *Ch Bd*
Carron Redena, *
EMP: 279 **EST:** 2004
SQ FT: 4,000
SALES (est): 4.33MM
SALES (corp-wide): 4.33MM **Privately Held**
SIC: 5084 3535 3568 2296 Industrial machinery and equipment; Belt conveyor systems, general industrial use; Power transmission equipment, nec; Tire cord and fabrics

(G-4026)
MIC-RAY METAL PRODUCTS INC
9016 Manor Ave (44104-4524)
PHONE..................................216 791-2206
Michael Konicky Junior, *Pr*
Raymond Konicky, *Treas*
EMP: 10 **EST:** 1947
SQ FT: 5,000
SALES (est): 838.26K **Privately Held**
SIC: 3469 Metal stampings, nec

(G-4027)
MICELI DAIRY PRODUCTS CO (PA)
2721 E 90th St (44104-3396)
PHONE..................................216 791-6222
Joseph D Miceli, *CEO*
John J Miceli Junior, *Ex VP*
Joseph Lograsso, *
Charles Surace, *
Carol Lograsso, *
▲ **EMP:** 90 **EST:** 1946
SQ FT: 25,000
SALES (est): 50.14MM
SALES (corp-wide): 50.14MM **Privately Held**
Web: www.miceli-dairy.com
SIC: 2022 0241 Natural cheese; Milk production

(G-4028)
MICROPURE FILTRATION INC
Also Called: Wfs Filter Co
837 E 79th St (44103-1807)
PHONE..................................952 472-2323
Trey Senney, *CEO*
Robert Pollmann, *Pr*
Marcy Pollmann, *Sec*
◆ **EMP:** 9 **EST:** 1980
SQ FT: 10,000
SALES (est): 2.09MM **Privately Held**
Web: www.micropure.com
SIC: 3677 Filtration devices, electronic

(G-4029)
MICROSHEEN CORPORATION
1100 E 222nd St Ste 1 (44117-1127)
PHONE..................................216 481-5610
Lisa Habe, *Owner*
Mark Scanlon, *Genl Mgr*
Dan Roe, *Supervisor*

EMP: 10 **EST:** 1960
SQ FT: 30,000
SALES (est): 1.09MM
SALES (corp-wide): 24.2MM **Privately Held**
Web: www.microsheencorporation.com
SIC: 3471 Electroplating of metals or formed products
PA: Interlake Industries, Inc.
4732 E 355th St
Willoughby OH 44094
440 942-0800

(G-4030)
MICROSOFT CORPORATION
Also Called: Microsoft
6050 Oak Tree Blvd Ste 300 (44131-6929)
PHONE..................................216 986-1440
Chris Caster, *Mgr*
EMP: 7
SALES (corp-wide): 245.12B **Publicly Held**
Web: www.microsoft.com
SIC: 7372 Application computer software
PA: Microsoft Corporation
1 Microsoft Way
Redmond WA 98052
425 882-8080

(G-4031)
MID AMERICAN VENTURES INC
Also Called: Cookie Cupboard
7600 Wall St Ste 205 (44125-3358)
PHONE..................................216 524-0974
Richard A Pignatiello, *Pr*
Ellen Pignatiello, *VP*
EMP: 10 **EST:** 1983
SALES (est): 2.37MM **Privately Held**
Web: www.cookiecupboard.com
SIC: 2045 2099 Doughs, frozen or refrigerated: from purchased flour; Food preparations, nec

(G-4032)
MID-AMERICA CHEMICAL CORP
4701 Spring Rd (44131-1025)
PHONE..................................216 749-0100
Frank J Martinek Junior, *Pr*
Julienne C Martinek, *VP*
Doris Hallaman, *Sec*
Debra Matrinek, *VP*
EMP: 9 **EST:** 1978
SQ FT: 19,000
SALES (est): 1.26MM **Privately Held**
Web: www.midamericachem.com
SIC: 2851 2869 Paints and allied products; Solvents, organic

(G-4033)
MID-AMERICA STEEL CORP
Also Called: Mid-America Stainless
20900 Saint Clair Ave Rear (44117-1130)
PHONE..................................800 282-3466
EMP: 50
Web: www.masteel.com
SIC: 5051 3469 3316 3312 Steel; Metal stampings, nec; Cold finishing of steel shapes; Blast furnaces and steel mills

(G-4034)
MID-CONTINENT MINERALS CORP (PA)
20600 Chagrin Blvd Ste 850 (44122-5341)
PHONE..................................216 283-5700
Thomas G Gibbs, *Pr*
Harold Geiss, *Treas*
Mike Bakonyi, *CFO*
◆ **EMP:** 10 **EST:** 1975
SALES (est): 31.31MM
SALES (corp-wide): 31.31MM **Privately Held**

Web: www.midcontinentcoke.com
SIC: 3296 Insulation: rock wool, slag, and
silica minerals

(G-4035)
MIDWEST BOX COMPANY
9801 Walford Ave Ste C (44102-4788)
PHONE.....................................216 281-9021
Susan Hecht Remer, *CEO*
EMP: 20 EST: 1964
SQ FT: 150,000
SALES (est): 9.96MM **Privately Held**
Web: www.jamestowncontainer.com
SIC: 2653 Boxes, corrugated: made from
purchased materials

(G-4036)
MIDWEST CURTAINWALLS INC
5171 Grant Ave (44125-1031)
PHONE.................................216 641-7900
Donald F Kelly Junior, *Pr*
EMP: 80 EST: 1986
SQ FT: 55,000
SALES (est): 2.67MM
SALES (corp-wide): 4.47MM **Privately
Held**
Web: www.midwestcurtainwalls.com
SIC: 3449 3442 1751 Curtain wall, metal;
Window and door frames; Window and
door (prefabricated) installation
PA: Innovest Global, Inc.
8834 Mayfield Rd
Chesterland OH 44026
216 815-1122

(G-4037)
MIDWEST MACHINE SERVICE INC
4700 Train Ave Ste 1 (44102-4591)
PHONE.................................216 631-8151
Kevin Klapcic, *Pr*
EMP: 15 EST: 1976
SQ FT: 6,000
SALES (est): 1.47MM **Privately Held**
Web: www.midwestmachineservice.com
SIC: 3599 Machine shop, jobbing and repair

(G-4038)
**MIDWEST RLWY PRSRVTION SOC
INC**
2800 W 3rd St (44113-2516)
PHONE.................................216 781-3629
Steven Korpos, *Ex Dir*
EMP: 7 EST: 1955
SALES (est): 200.28K **Privately Held**
Web: www.midwestrailway.org
SIC: 7699 3743 Antique repair and
restoration, except furniture, autos;
Railroad equipment

(G-4039)
MILAN TOOL CORP
8989 Brookpark Rd (44129-6819)
P.O. Box 29336 (44129-0336)
PHONE.................................216 661-1078
Mark Milan, *Pr*
▲ EMP: 30 EST: 1946
SQ FT: 20,000
SALES (est): 5.06MM **Privately Held**
Web: www.milantool.com
SIC: 3728 3541 Aircraft body assemblies
and parts; Grinding machines, metalworking

(G-4040)
MILES MIDPRINT INC
1215 W 10th St Ste B (44113-1291)
PHONE.................................216 860-4770
Nicholas Martin, *CEO*
EMP: 11 EST: 2018
SALES (est): 488.53K **Privately Held**

SIC: 7372 5045 7371 Business oriented
computer software; Computer software;
Computer software development and
applications

(G-4041)
MILLCRAFT PURCHASING CORP
6800 Grant Ave (44105-5628)
PHONE.................................216 441-5505
Carol Braunschweig, *Prin*
EMP: 6 EST: 1998
SALES (est): 2.94MM **Privately Held**
Web: www.millcraft.com
SIC: 2631 Container, packaging, and
boxboard
HQ: The Millcraft Paper Company
9010 Rio Nero Dr
Independence OH 44131
216 441-5500

(G-4042)
MILLWOOD INC
Also Called: Cleveland Cstm Pallet & Crate
4201 Lakeside Ave E (44114-3814)
PHONE.................................216 881-1414
EMP: 24
Web: www.millwoodinc.com
SIC: 2448 Pallets, wood
PA: Millwood, Inc.
3708 International Blvd
Vienna OH 44473

(G-4043)
MODERN INDUSTRIES INC
6610 Metta Ave (44103-1618)
PHONE.................................216 432-2855
Gregory Senn, *Pr*
Steve Seredick, *Ch Bd*
EMP: 7 EST: 1966
SQ FT: 22,000
SALES (est): 366.44K **Privately Held**
Web: www.modernind.com
SIC: 3599 Machine shop, jobbing and repair

(G-4044)
MONACO PLATING INC
3555 E 91st St (44105-1601)
PHONE.................................216 206-2360
Louis C Monaco, *Pr*
EMP: 11 EST: 2008
SALES (est): 200.01K **Privately Held**
SIC: 3471 Plating of metals or formed
products

(G-4045)
MONARCH STEEL COMPANY INC
Also Called: Monarch
4650 Johnston Pkwy (44128-3219)
PHONE.................................216 587-8000
Josh Kaufman, *CEO*
Robert L Meyer, *
Steve Lefkowitz, *
▲ EMP: 40 EST: 1934
SQ FT: 118,000
SALES (est): 19.87MM **Privately Held**
Web: www.monarchsteel.com
SIC: 5051 5049 3353 Steel; Precision tools;
Coils, sheet aluminum
PA: American Consolidated Industries, Inc.
4650 Johnston Pkwy
Cleveland OH 44128

(G-4046)
MONROE TOOL AND MFG CO
3900 E 93rd St (44105-4094)
PHONE.................................216 883-7360
Herbert C Brosnan Junior, *Pr*
Herbert Brosnan Iii, *VP*
Anne Brosnan, *Treas*
EMP: 11 EST: 1940
SQ FT: 7,200

SALES (est): 2.82MM **Privately Held**
Web: www.monroetoolmfg.com
SIC: 3599 Machine shop, jobbing and repair

(G-4047)
MORRISON PRODUCTS INC (PA)
16900 S Waterloo Rd (44110-3895)
PHONE.................................216 486-4000
▼ EMP: 131 EST: 1923
SALES (est): 184.04MM
SALES (corp-wide): 184.04MM **Privately
Held**
Web: www.morrisonproducts.com
SIC: 3443 Heat exchangers, condensers,
and components

(G-4048)
MORTON SALT INC
2100 W 3rd St (44113-2505)
PHONE.................................216 664-0728
EMP: 23
SALES (corp-wide): 3.82B **Privately Held**
Web: www.mortonsalt.com
SIC: 2899 Salt
HQ: Morton Salt, Inc.
444 W Lake St Ste 3000
Chicago IL 60606

(G-4049)
MPC PLASTICS INC
1859 E 63rd St (44103-3832)
PHONE.................................216 881-7220
Albert Walcutt, *Pr*
EMP: 7 EST: 1984
SQ FT: 26,000
SALES (est): 988.25K **Privately Held**
Web: www.mpcplating.com
SIC: 3471 Electroplating of metals or formed
products

(G-4050)
MPC PLATING LLC
9921 Clinton Rd (44144-1035)
PHONE.................................216 881-7220
Albert N Walcutt, *Pr*
Rose Ann Walcutt, *
▲ EMP: 100 EST: 1980
SALES (est): 11.27MM **Privately Held**
Web: www.mpcplating.com
SIC: 3471 Electroplating of metals or formed
products

(G-4051)
MR HEATER INC
Also Called: Heatstar
4560 W 160th St (44135-2628)
P.O. Box 44101 (44144-0101)
PHONE.................................216 916-3000
Allen L Haire, *Ch Bd*
John D Duross, *Vice Chairman*
Jeff Mack, *Pr*
Kevin Mcdonough, *VP Fin*
▲ EMP: 41 EST: 1986
SQ FT: 100,000
SALES (est): 628.82K
SALES (corp-wide): 47.02MM **Privately
Held**
Web: www.heatstarbyenerco.com
SIC: 3433 Gas infrared heating units
PA: Enerco Group, Inc.
4560 W 160th St
Cleveland OH 44135
216 916-3000

(G-4052)
MRPICKER
595 Miner Rd (44143-2131)
PHONE.................................440 354-6497
Robert Blankenship, *CFO*
EMP: 9 EST: 2017
SALES (est): 334.18K **Privately Held**

SIC: 3845 Electromedical equipment

(G-4053)
MURRAY FABRICS INC (PA)
837 E 79th St (44103-1807)
PHONE.................................216 881-4041
Walter Senney, *Pr*
Joyce Senney, *Sec*
EMP: 10 EST: 1954
SALES (est): 403.09K
SALES (corp-wide): 403.09K **Privately
Held**
Web: www.murrayfabrics.com
SIC: 2258 Net and netting products

(G-4054)
MURRAY MACHINE AND TOOL INC
17801 Sheldon Rd Side (44130-7992)
PHONE.................................216 267-1126
Frank P Ondercik Junior, *Pr*
EMP: 7 EST: 1927
SQ FT: 8,500
SALES (est): 499.12K **Privately Held**
SIC: 3599 3451 Machine shop, jobbing and
repair; Screw machine products

(G-4055)
MYERS PRECISION GRINDING INC
19500 S Miles Rd (44128-4251)
P.O. Box 535 (44202)
PHONE.................................216 587-3737
Joseph Tenebria, *Pr*
Gail Myers Tenebria, *Sec*
Ben Tenebria, *Treas*
EMP: 10 EST: 1973
SQ FT: 15,600
SALES (est): 2.02MM **Privately Held**
Web: www.myersprecision.com
SIC: 3599 Machine shop, jobbing and repair

(G-4056)
NACCO INDUSTRIES INC (PA)
22901 Millcreek Blvd Ste 600 (44122-5724)
PHONE.................................440 229-5151
J C Butler Junior, *Pr*
Alfred M Rankin Junior, *Non-Executive
Chairman of the Board*
Elizabeth I Loveman, *CTRL*
John D Neumann, *Sr VP*
Thomas A Maxwell, *FIN PLANNING
ANALYSIS*
EMP: 39 EST: 1913
SALES (est): 237.71MM
SALES (corp-wide): 237.71MM **Publicly
Held**
Web: www.nacco.com
SIC: 1221 Surface mining, lignite, nec

(G-4057)
**NAGELE MANUFACTURING
COMPANY**
5201 W 164th St (44142-1507)
PHONE.................................216 433-1100
Fred Nagele, *CEO*
Ronald Nagele, *
Gary Single, *
Tom Cachat, *
EMP: 45 EST: 1956
SQ FT: 80,000
SALES (est): 1.88MM **Privately Held**
Web: www.nagelemfg.com
SIC: 2541 2431 1751 2511 Cabinets, except
refrigerated: show, display, etc.: wood;
Millwork; Cabinet building and installation;
Wood household furniture

(G-4058)
NATIONAL BIAS FABRIC CO
4516 Saint Clair Ave (44103-1288)
PHONE.................................216 361-0530
James R Engelbert, *Pr*

▲ = Import ▼ = Export
◆ = Import/Export

James R Engelbert, *Pr*
Keith Engelbert, *
Carol Ann Engelbert, *
EMP: 6 EST: 1902
SQ FT: 33,000
SALES (est): 411.76K **Privately Held**
Web: www.nationalbias.com
SIC: 2396 2631 2394 Bindings, bias: made
from purchased materials; Paperboard mills
; Canvas and related products

(G-4059)
NATIONAL ELECTRO-COATINGS INC
Also Called: National Office Services
15655 Brookpark Rd (44142-1619)
PHONE..........................216 898-0080
Robert W Schneider, *Ch*
Gregory R Schneider, *
Richard Corl, *
▲ **EMP:** 90 EST: 1967
SQ FT: 175,000
SALES (est): 16.89MM **Privately Held**
Web: www.natoffice.com
SIC: 2522 7641 1799 5021 Office furniture,
except wood; Office furniture repair and
maintenance; Office furniture installation;
Office and public building furniture

(G-4060)
NATIONAL FOODS PACKAGING INC
8200 Madison Ave (44102-2727)
PHONE..........................216 622-2740
John Pallas, *Pr*
▲ **EMP:** 30 EST: 2001
SQ FT: 57,261
SALES (est): 8.12MM **Privately Held**
Web: www.nationalfoodsonline.com
SIC: 2099 2035 2045 5149 Seasonings and
spices; Pickles, sauces, and salad
dressings; Bread and bread type roll mixes:
from purchased flour; Breakfast cereals

(G-4061)
NATIONAL PLATING CORPORATION
6701 Hubbard Ave Ste 1 (44127-1479)
PHONE..........................216 341-6707
Mark Palik, *Pr*
Sherrie Jezerinac, *
EMP: 48 EST: 1946
SQ FT: 100,000
SALES (est): 3.69MM **Privately Held**
Web: www.nationalplatingcorp.com
SIC: 3471 Electroplating of metals or formed
products

(G-4062)
NATIONAL SAFETY APPAREL LLC
(HQ)
15825 Industrial Pkwy (44135-3319)
PHONE..........................800 553-0672
◆ **EMP:** 60 EST: 1991
SALES (est): 23.13MM
SALES (corp-wide): 472.43MM **Privately
Held**
Web: www.thinknsa.com
SIC: 3842 Gloves, safety
PA: Blue Point Capital Partners Llc
127 Public Sq Ste 5100
Cleveland OH 44114
216 535-4700

(G-4063)
NBW INC
4556 Industrial Pkwy (44135-4542)
PHONE..........................216 377-1700
Burgess J Holt, *Ch*
Thomas Graves, *
Todd Holt, *
Buck L Holt, *
EMP: 48 EST: 1935
SQ FT: 25,000

SALES (est): 9.69MM **Privately Held**
Web: www.nbwinc.com
SIC: 1711 1796 7699 3443 Boiler setting
contractor; Installing building equipment;
Boiler and heating repair services;
Fabricated plate work (boiler shop)

(G-4064)
NDI MEDICAL LLC (PA)
22901 Millcreek Blvd Ste 110 (44122-5724)
PHONE..........................216 378-9106
Geoff Thrope, *CEO*
◆ **EMP:** 22 EST: 2002
SALES (est): 1.92MM
SALES (corp-wide): 1.92MM **Privately
Held**
Web: www.ndimedical.com
SIC: 3845 Electromedical equipment

(G-4065)
NEON
15201 Euclid Ave (44112-2803)
PHONE..........................216 541-5600
EMP: 6 EST: 2010
SALES (est): 711.38K **Privately Held**
Web: www.neonhealth.org
SIC: 2813 Neon

(G-4066)
NEON HEALTH SERVICES INC
4800 Payne Ave (44103-2443)
PHONE..........................216 231-7700
Willie Austin, *Prin*
EMP: 22 EST: 2010
SALES (est): 7.22MM **Privately Held**
Web: www.neonhealth.org
SIC: 2813 Neon

(G-4067)
NERVIVE INC
Also Called: Nervive
5900 Landerbrook Dr Ste 350
(44124-4085)
PHONE..........................847 274-1790
Mark K Borsody, *Prin*
Dagmar Nikles, *Prin*
EMP: 10 EST: 2010
SALES (est): 775.96K **Privately Held**
Web: www.nervive.com
SIC: 3841 Medical instruments and
equipment, blood and bone work

(G-4068)
NESCO INC (PA)
Also Called: Nesco Resource
6140 Parkland Blvd Ste 110 (44124-6106)
PHONE..........................440 461-6000
Robert Tomsich, *Pr*
Frank Rzicznek, *VP*
◆ **EMP:** 20 EST: 1988
SQ FT: 55,000
SALES (est): 450.24MM
SALES (corp-wide): 450.24MM **Privately
Held**
Web: www.nescoresource.com
SIC: 3535 3541 3544 8711 Conveyors and
conveying equipment; Machine tools, metal
cutting type; Special dies, tools, jigs, and
fixtures; Engineering services

(G-4069)
NESTAWAY LLC
9100 Bank St Ste 1 (44125-3432)
PHONE..........................216 587-1500
▲ **EMP:** 100
SIC: 1799 2392 Home/office interiors
finishing, furnishing and remodeling;
Household furnishings, nec

(G-4070)
NESTLE USA INC
Also Called: Nestle Food Service Factory
2621 W 25th St (44113-4708)
PHONE..........................216 861-8350
Ingolf Nitsch, *Brnch Mgr*
EMP: 100
Web: www.nestleusa.com
SIC: 5499 2023 Health foods; Dry,
condensed and evaporated dairy products
HQ: Nestle Usa, Inc.
1812 N Moore St
Arlington VA 22209
800 225-2270

(G-4071)
NEUROLOGIX TECHNOLOGIES INC
10000 Cedar Ave Ste 3-160 (44106-2119)
PHONE..........................512 914-7941
Frank Carruba, *CEO*
EMP: 10 EST: 2015
SALES (est): 326.9K **Privately Held**
Web: www.neurologixtech.com
SIC: 3841 8742 7389 Diagnostic apparatus,
medical; Management information systems
consultant; Business services, nec

(G-4072)
NEURONOFF INC
11000 Cedar Ave Ste 290 (44106-3052)
PHONE..........................216 505-1818
Shaher Ahmad, *Prin*
EMP: 24 EST: 2020
SALES (est): 915.59K **Privately Held**
Web: www.neuronoff.com
SIC: 2833 Medicinals and botanicals

(G-4073)
NEW DAIRY OHIO LLC
3068 W 106th St (44111-1801)
PHONE..........................214 258-1200
Gregg Engles, *CEO*
EMP: 84 EST: 2020
SALES (est): 2.54MM
SALES (corp-wide): 403.14MM **Privately
Held**
SIC: 2021 Creamery butter
PA: New Dairy Opco, Llc
12400 Coit Rd Ste 200
Dallas TX 75251
214 258-1200

(G-4074)
NEW DAIRY OHIO TRANSPORT LLC
3068 W 106th St (44111-1801)
PHONE..........................214 258-1200
Gregg Engles, *CEO*
EMP: 56 EST: 2020
SALES (est): 273.18K
SALES (corp-wide): 403.14MM **Privately
Held**
SIC: 2023 Condensed, concentrated, and
evaporated milk products
PA: New Dairy Opco, Llc
12400 Coit Rd Ste 200
Dallas TX 75251
214 258-1200

(G-4075)
NEXTANT AEROSPACE LLC
Also Called: Nextant Aerospace
18601 Cleveland Pkwy Dr (44135-3231)
PHONE..........................216 898-4800
Jacqueline Disanto, *Admn*
EMP: 30 EST: 2012
SALES (est): 4.64MM **Privately Held**
Web: www.nextantaerospace.com
SIC: 3721 Aircraft

(G-4076)
NIDEC MOTOR CORPORATION
Also Called: Nidec Industrial Solutions
243 Tuxedo Ave (44131-1107)
PHONE..........................216 642-1230
Anna Marie Kennedy, *Mgr*
EMP: 150
Web: www.nidec-conversion.com
SIC: 3823 Process control instruments
HQ: Nidec Motor Corporation
8050 W Florissant Ave
Saint Louis MO 63136

(G-4077)
NIDEC MOTOR CORPORATION
Also Called: Nidec Industrial Solutions
7555 E Pleasant Valley Rd (44131-5562)
PHONE..........................216 642-1230
EMP: 30
Web: acim.nidec.com
SIC: 3823 3829 Process control instruments;
Aircraft and motor vehicle measurement
equipment
HQ: Nidec Motor Corporation
8050 W Florissant Ave
Saint Louis MO 63136

(G-4078)
NIPPON PAINT (USA) INC
11110 Berea Rd Ste 1 (44102-2540)
PHONE..........................216 651-5900
EMP: 202
SIC: 2851 Paints and paint additives
HQ: Nippon Paint (Usa) Inc.
2701 E 170th St
Lansing IL 60438

(G-4079)
NOBLE BEAST BREWING LLC
1864 W 45th St (44102-3406)
PHONE..........................570 809-6405
Shaun Yasaki, *Prin*
EMP: 6 EST: 2015
SALES (est): 1.2MM **Privately Held**
Web: www.noblebeastbeer.com
SIC: 2082 Malt beverages

(G-4080)
NOOK INDUSTRIES LLC (DH)
4950 E 49th St (44125-1016)
PHONE..........................216 271-7900
Scott Benigni, *Managing Member*
Bradly Lodge, *
Todd Patriacca, *
Glenn E Deegan, *
▲ **EMP:** 204 EST: 2021
SQ FT: 110,000
SALES (est): 46MM
SALES (corp-wide): 6.03B **Publicly Held**
Web: www.nookindustries.com
SIC: 3451 Screw machine products
HQ: Altra Industrial Motion Corp.
300 Granite St Ste 201
Braintree MA 02184
781 917-0600

(G-4081)
NORMAN NOBLE INC
Also Called: N N I
5507 Avion Park Dr (44143-1921)
PHONE..........................216 761-5387
Kevin Noble, *Prin*
EMP: 85
SALES (corp-wide): 42.44MM **Privately
Held**
Web: www.nnoble.com
SIC: 3599 Machine shop, jobbing and repair
PA: Norman Noble, Inc.
5507 Avion Park Dr
Highland Heights OH 44143
216 761-5387

(G-4082)

NORTH COAST COMPOSITES INC
4605 Spring Rd (44131-1021)
PHONE..............................216 398-8550
Richard L Petrovich, *Pr*
▲ EMP: 12 EST: 2003
SALES (est): 23.24MM
SALES (corp-wide): 189.21MM **Privately Held**
Web: www.nctm.com
SIC: 2655 Cans, composite: foil-fiber and other: from purchased fiber
PA: Applied Composites Holdings, Llc
25692 Atlantic Ocean Dr
Lake Forest CA 92630
949 716-3511

(G-4083)

NORTH COAST CONTAINER LLC (HQ)
Also Called: Ncc
8806 Crane Ave (44105-1622)
PHONE..............................216 441-6214
EMP: 30 EST: 1930
SQ FT: 120,000
SALES (est): 22.77MM
SALES (corp-wide): 32.94MM **Privately Held**
Web: www.northcoastcontainer.com
SIC: 3412 Drums, shipping: metal
PA: General Steel Drum, Llc
4500 South Blvd
Charlotte NC 28209
704 525-7160

(G-4084)

NORTH COAST EXOTICS INC
3159 W 68th St (44102-5305)
PHONE..............................216 651-5512
Earl Gibbs Junior, *Pr*
EMP: 6 EST: 1984
SQ FT: 15,000
SALES (est): 238.6K **Privately Held**
Web:
north-coast-exotics-inc.business.site
SIC: 7699 3714 Miscellaneous automotive repair services; Motor vehicle parts and accessories

(G-4085)

NORTH COAST INSTRUMENTS INC
14615 Lorain Ave (44111-3166)
PHONE..............................216 251-2353
James Irwin, *Pr*
James Irwin, *Pr*
Charlotte G Irwin, *Sec*
Julia W Irwin, *Treas*
EMP: 9 EST: 2003
SQ FT: 20,000
SALES (est): 1.61MM
SALES (corp-wide): 1.61MM **Privately Held**
SIC: 3593 Fluid power cylinders and actuators
PA: Ohio Pipe & Supply Company Incorporated
14615 Lorain Ave
Cleveland OH
216 251-2345

(G-4086)

NORTH COAST LITHO INC
4701 Manufacturing Ave (44135-2639)
PHONE..............................216 881-1952
Keith P Jaworski, *Pr*
EMP: 20 EST: 1993
SQ FT: 12,000
SALES (est): 4.26MM **Privately Held**
Web: www.northcoastlitho.com
SIC: 2752 Offset printing

(G-4087)

NORTH COAST MEDIA LLC
Also Called: NCM
1360 E 9th St Ste 1070 (44114-1754)
PHONE..............................216 706-3700
Kevin Stoltman, *Pr*
Kevin Stoltman, *Pr*
Steve Galperin, *
EMP: 75 EST: 2011
SALES (est): 3.67MM **Privately Held**
Web: www.northcoastmedia.net
SIC: 2731 Book publishing

(G-4088)

NORTH COAST MINORITY MEDIA LLC
Also Called: North Coast Publications
1360 E 9th St (44114-1737)
PHONE..............................216 407-4327
EMP: 9 EST: 2012
SALES (est): 436.49K **Privately Held**
Web: www.northcoastmedia.net
SIC: 2721 Magazines: publishing and printing

(G-4089)

NORTH COAST TIRE CO INC
7810 Old Rockside Rd (44131-2314)
P.O. Box 31273 (44131-0273)
PHONE..............................216 447-1690
Victor J Appenzeller, *Pr*
Julie A Appenzeller, *VP*
EMP: 8 EST: 1983
SQ FT: 8,500
SALES (est): 468.37K **Privately Held**
Web: www.northcoasttire.com
SIC: 7534 5014 Tire repair shop; Truck tires and tubes

(G-4090)

NORTH STAR BUILDING PDTS LLC
1281 E 38th St (44114-3844)
P.O. Box 22352 (44122-0352)
PHONE..............................216 431-1000
David Gordon, *Prin*
EMP: 6 EST: 2012
SALES (est): 630.42K **Privately Held**
Web: www.northstarbp.com
SIC: 5211 2434 Lumber and other building materials; Wood kitchen cabinets

(G-4091)

NORTHAST OHIO NGHBRHOOD HLTH S
Also Called: Southeast Health Center
13301 Miles Ave (44105-5521)
PHONE..............................216 751-3100
EMP: 31
SALES (corp-wide): 28.01MM **Privately Held**
Web: www.neonhealth.org
SIC: 2813 Neon
PA: Northeast Ohio Neighborhood Health Services, Inc.
4800 Payne Ave
Cleveland OH 44103
216 231-7700

(G-4092)

NORTHEAST BLUEPRINT AND SUP CO
1230 E 286th St (44132-2138)
PHONE..............................216 261-7500
Timothy Yurick, *Pr*
James Yurick, *Pr*
EMP: 7 EST: 1962
SQ FT: 7,000
SALES (est): 986.01K **Privately Held**
Web: www.northeastblueprint.com
SIC: 7334 2752 Blueprinting service; Commercial printing, lithographic

(G-4093)

NORTHERN CHEM BLNDING CORP INC
360 Literary Rd (44113-4560)
PHONE..............................216 781-7799
John Zemaitis, *Pr*
▲ EMP: 9 EST: 1983
SQ FT: 35,000
SALES (est): 2.64MM **Privately Held**
Web: ncbcohio.lookchem.com
SIC: 2899 Metal treating compounds

(G-4094)

NORTHERN OHIO PRINTING INC
4721 Hinckley Industrial Pkwy (44109-6004)
PHONE..............................216 398-0000
Gary Chmielewski, *Pr*
EMP: 30 EST: 1994
SQ FT: 5,000
SALES (est): 6.41MM **Privately Held**
Web: nohioprint.secureprintorder.com
SIC: 2752 Offset printing

(G-4095)

NORTHERN STAMPING CO
5900 Harvard Ave (44105-4850)
PHONE..............................216 883-8888
EMP: 10
SALES (corp-wide): 471.87MM **Privately Held**
Web: www.northernstamping.com
SIC: 3465 3469 Automotive stampings; Metal stampings, nec
HQ: Northern Stamping Co.
6600 Chapek Pkwy
Cleveland OH 44125
216 883-8888

(G-4096)

NORTHERN STAMPING CO (HQ)
Also Called: Northern Stamping
6600 Chapek Pkwy (44125-1049)
PHONE..............................216 883-8888
Matthew Friedman, *Pr*
Scott Sheffield, *
Ian Hessel, *
◆ EMP: 215 EST: 1989
SQ FT: 118,000
SALES (est): 88.38MM
SALES (corp-wide): 471.87MM **Privately Held**
Web: www.northernstamping.com
SIC: 3465 3469 Automotive stampings; Metal stampings, nec
PA: Bear Diversified, Inc.
4580 E 71st St
Cleveland OH 44125
216 883-8888

(G-4097)

NORTHERN STAMPING CO
Also Called: Northern Stamping Plant 2
7750 Hub Pkwy (44125-5709)
PHONE..............................216 642-8081
Scott Sheffield, *Pdt Mgr*
EMP: 12
SALES (corp-wide): 471.87MM **Privately Held**
Web: www.northernstamping.com
SIC: 3465 3714 Automotive stampings; Motor vehicle parts and accessories
HQ: Northern Stamping Co.
6600 Chapek Pkwy
Cleveland OH 44125
216 883-8888

(G-4098)

NORTHSHORE MOLD INC
2861 E Royalton Rd (44147-2827)
PHONE..............................440 838-8212

Joseph E Pajestka Junior, *Pr*
Vivian Pajestka, *VP*
EMP: 7 EST: 1985
SQ FT: 6,000
SALES (est): 477.56K **Privately Held**
Web: www.northshoremold.com
SIC: 3599 3089 Machine and other job shop work; Injection molding of plastics

(G-4099)

NORTHWIND INDUSTRIES INC
11324 Brookpark Rd (44130-1129)
PHONE..............................216 433-0666
Garry Patla, *Pr*
Christine Klukan, *VP*
EMP: 8 EST: 1985
SALES (est): 943.1K **Privately Held**
SIC: 3599 7692 3469 3444 Machine shop, jobbing and repair; Welding repair; Metal stampings, nec; Sheet metalwork

(G-4100)

NOVA STRUCTURAL STEEL INC
Also Called: Structural Steel Fabrication
900 E 69th St (44103-1736)
PHONE..............................216 938-7476
Michael Ciofani, *CEO*
Mariella Kaufman, *CEO*
Michael Ciofani, *Pr*
EMP: 20 EST: 2013
SALES (est): 3.8MM **Privately Held**
Web: www.novastructuralsteel.com
SIC: 3312 1531 3441 Structural shapes and pilings, steel; Building components, structural steel

(G-4101)

NOVAGARD SOLUTIONS INC (PA)
Also Called: Foam Seal
5109 Hamilton Ave (44114-3907)
PHONE..............................216 881-8111
Sarah Nash, *Ch Bd*
Ron Moeller, *
EMP: 71 EST: 2002
SQ FT: 250,000
SALES (est): 22.68MM **Privately Held**
Web: www.novagard.com
SIC: 5169 2822 2869 3567 Adhesives and sealants; Silicone rubbers; Silicones; Incinerators, thermal, fume & catalytic

(G-4102)

NOVAK J F MANUFACTURING CO LLC
Also Called: Cleveland Church Supply
2701 Meyer Ave (44109-1532)
PHONE..............................216 741-5112
Sharon Campbell, *Mgr*
EMP: 6 EST: 1932
SQ FT: 7,000
SALES (est): 166.05K **Privately Held**
Web:
www.policesupplystorecleveland.com
SIC: 2395 5049 Emblems, embroidered; Religious supplies

(G-4103)

NOVOLYTE TECHNOLOGIES INC
Also Called: Novolyte Performance
8001 E Pleasant Valley Rd (44131-5526)
PHONE..............................216 867-1040
▲ EMP: 305
Web: www.novolyte.com
SIC: 2621 Specialty or chemically treated papers

(G-4104)

NPA COATINGS INC
Also Called: Npa Coatings
11110 Berea Rd Ste 1 (44102-2540)
PHONE..............................216 651-5900

▲ **EMP:** 180
Web: www.npacoatings.com
SIC: 2851 Paints and allied products

(G-4105)
NU-DI PRODUCTS CO INC
Also Called: Nu-Di
12730 Triskett Rd (44111-2529)
PHONE.....................216 251-9070
Kenneth Bihn, *Pr*
Tim Bihn, *
EMP: 85 **EST:** 1969
SQ FT: 38,000
SALES (est): 5.76MM **Privately Held**
Web: www.nu-di.com
SIC: 3825 5013 Engine electrical test
  equipment; Testing equipment, electrical:
  automotive

(G-4106)
**OASIS CONSUMER HEALTHCARE
LLC**
Also Called: Ochc
425 Literary Rd Apt 100 (44113-4506)
PHONE.....................216 394-0544
EMP: 6 **EST:** 2008
SALES (est): 409.87K **Privately Held**
Web: www.oasisbeautyrx.com
SIC: 2844 Mouthwashes

(G-4107)
OATEY CO (PA)
20600 Emerald Pkwy (44135-6022)
P.O. Box 35906 (44135-0906)
PHONE.....................800 203-1155
▲ **EMP:** 300 **EST:** 1916
SALES (est): 304.6MM
SALES (corp-wide): 304.6MM **Privately
Held**
Web: www.oatey.com
SIC: 3444 Metal roofing and roof drainage
  equipment

(G-4108)
**OATEY SUPPLY CHAIN SVCS INC
(HQ)**
Also Called: Oatey
20600 Emerald Pkwy (44135-6022)
PHONE.....................216 267-7100
John H Mcmillan, *Ch*
Neal Restivo, *
◆ **EMP:** 200 **EST:** 2001
SQ FT: 165,000
SALES (est): 2.5MM
SALES (corp-wide): 304.6MM **Privately
Held**
Web: www.oatey.com
SIC: 3444 5074 Metal roofing and roof
  drainage equipment; Plumbing and
  hydronic heating supplies
PA: Oatey Co.
  20600 Emerald Pkwy
  Cleveland OH 44135
  800 203-1155

(G-4109)
**OGLEBAY NORTON MAR SVCS CO
LLC**
1001 Lakeside Ave E 15th Fl (44114-1158)
PHONE.....................216 861-3300
Michael D Lundin, *Pr*
EMP: 1500 **EST:** 1999
SALES (est): 2.34MM **Privately Held**
SIC: 1422 Crushed and broken limestone

(G-4110)
OHIO ALUMINUM INDUSTRIES INC
4840 Warner Rd (44125-1193)
PHONE.....................216 641-8865
Kurt Blemaster, *CEO*

James E Herkner, *
Willem Der Velde, *
▲ **EMP:** 163 **EST:** 1970
SQ FT: 78,000
SALES (est): 23.58MM **Privately Held**
Web: www.ohioaluminum.com
SIC: 3363 Aluminum die-castings

(G-4111)
**OHIO AWNING & MANUFACTURING
CO**
5777 Grant Ave (44105-5605)
PHONE.....................216 861-2400
TOLL FREE: 800
Andrew Morse, *Pr*
Anne L Morse, *
▲ **EMP:** 30 **EST:** 1864
SQ FT: 80,000
SALES (est): 3.48MM **Privately Held**
Web: www.ohioawning.com
SIC: 2394 3993 Awnings, fabric: made from
  purchased materials; Electric signs

(G-4112)
OHIO BEVERAGE SYSTEMS INC
9200 Midwest Ave (44125-2416)
PHONE.....................216 475-3900
James Rickon, *Pr*
EMP: 15 **EST:** 1983
SQ FT: 28,000
SALES (est): 4.24MM **Privately Held**
Web: www.ohiobev.net
SIC: 2086 Fruit drinks (less than 100%
  juice): packaged in cans, etc.

(G-4113)
OHIO BLOW PIPE COMPANY (PA)
Also Called: Ohio Blow Pipe
446 E 131st St (44108-1684)
PHONE.....................216 681-7379
Edward Fakeris, *Pr*
William Roberts, *
Lisa Kern, *
EMP: 33 **EST:** 1967
SQ FT: 45,000
SALES (est): 9.44MM
SALES (corp-wide): 9.44MM **Privately
Held**
Web: www.innoveyance.com
SIC: 8711 3564 3444 Engineering services;
  Blowers and fans; Sheet metalwork

(G-4114)
**OHIO ENVELOPE MANUFACTURING
CO**
5161 W 164th St (44142-1592)
PHONE.....................216 267-2920
David Rick Gould III, *Pr*
David Rick Gould Iii, *Pr*
Carol J Gould, *
EMP: 35 **EST:** 1936
SQ FT: 35,000
SALES (est): 4.21MM **Privately Held**
Web: www.ohioenvelope.com
SIC: 2759 2754 2677 Envelopes: printing,
  nsk; Envelopes: gravure printing; Envelopes

(G-4115)
OHIO IRISH AMERICAN NEWS
14615 Triskett Rd (44111-3123)
PHONE.....................216 647-1144
EMP: 8 **EST:** 2014
SALES (est): 226.28K **Privately Held**
Web: www.iirish.us
SIC: 2711 Newspapers, publishing and
  printing

(G-4116)
OHIO MILLS CORPORATION (PA)
Also Called: Ohio Mill Supply

1719 E 39th St (44114-4530)
PHONE.....................216 431-3979
Ronald Katz, *Pr*
EMP: 8 **EST:** 1983
SQ FT: 15,000
SALES (est): 497.36K
SALES (corp-wide): 497.36K **Privately
Held**
Web: www.sodonate.com
SIC: 5651 2842 Unisex clothing stores;
  Dusting cloths, chemically treated

(G-4117)
OKM LLC
Also Called: Ohio Knitting Mills
4701 Perkins Ave (44103-3525)
PHONE.....................216 272-6375
Steven Tatar, *Pr*
EMP: 7 **EST:** 2006
SQ FT: 4,000
SALES (est): 74.18K **Privately Held**
Web: www.ohioknittingmills.com
SIC: 2253 Knit outerwear mills

(G-4118)
OLDKOR INC
10410 Berea Rd (44102-2506)
PHONE.....................216 631-7800
Gordon Barr, *Pr*
EMP: 20 **EST:** 1972
SQ FT: 23,000
SALES (est): 1.63MM **Privately Held**
Web: www.newkor.com
SIC: 2655 Tubes, for chemical or electrical
  uses: paper or fiber

(G-4119)
OLYMPIC FOREST PRODUCTS CO
2280 W 11th St (44113-3662)
PHONE.....................216 421-2775
Daniel Andrews, *Pr*
Howard A Steindler, *
EMP: 25 **EST:** 1980
SALES (est): 4.59MM **Privately Held**
Web: www.olyforest.com
SIC: 2448 Pallets, wood

(G-4120)
OM GROUP INC
127 Public Sq Ste 3900 (44114-1291)
PHONE.....................216 781-0083
EMP: 11 **EST:** 2019
SALES (est): 1.93MM **Privately Held**
web: www.omgroupinc.us
SIC: 2819 Industrial inorganic chemicals, nec

(G-4121)
OMNI TECHNICAL PRODUCTS INC
Also Called: Wire Lab Company
15300 Industrial Pkwy (44135-3310)
PHONE.....................216 433-1970
Robert J Fulop, *Pr*
Robert L Fulop, *VP*
EMP: 11 **EST:** 1980
SQ FT: 20,000
SALES (est): 1.97MM **Privately Held**
Web: www.wirelab.com
SIC: 3599 Machine shop, jobbing and repair

(G-4122)
ORACLE CORPORATION
1300 E 9th St Ste 1600 (44114-1573)
PHONE.....................216 706-1500
EMP: 13 **EST:** 2019
SALES (est): 842.85K **Privately Held**
Web: www.oracle.com
SIC: 7372 Prepackaged software

(G-4123)
ORBYTEL PRINT AND PACKG INC
Also Called: Orbytel
4901 Johnston Pkwy (44128-3201)
PHONE.....................216 267-8734
Albert Uvlin, *Pr*
Cynthia Uvlin, *Sec*
Mark Uvlin, *COO*
Clarence D Finke, *Prin*
James R Bingham, *Prin*
EMP: 8 **EST:** 1964
SQ FT: 12,300
SALES (est): 9.88MM **Privately Held**
Web: www.orbytel.com
SIC: 2679 5085 Tags and labels, paper;
  Industrial supplies

(G-4124)
ORLANDO BAKING COMPANY (PA)
Also Called: Orlando
7777 Grand Ave (44104-3099)
PHONE.....................216 361-1872
TOLL FREE: 800
Chester Orlando, *Pr*
Joseph Orlando, *
Christine Brindle, *
Edna Rosenblum, *
Glenn W Eckert, *
▲ **EMP:** 230 **EST:** 1872
SQ FT: 80,000
SALES (est): 49.39MM
SALES (corp-wide): 49.39MM **Privately
Held**
Web: www.orlandobaking.com
SIC: 2051 Bread, all types (white, wheat,
  rye, etc); fresh or frozen

(G-4125)
OSBORNE INC
26481 Cannon Rd (44146-1843)
PHONE.....................440 232-1440
Patrick Donnelly, *Genl Mgr*
EMP: 10
SQ FT: 6,000
SALES (corp-wide): 14.18MM **Privately
Held**
Web: www.osbornecompaniesinc.com
SIC: 3273 Ready-mixed concrete
PA: Osborne, Inc.
  7954 Reynolds Rd
  Mentor OH 44060
  440 942-7000

(G-4126)
OSTEOSYMBIONICS LLC
1768 E 25th St Ste 316 (44114-4418)
P.O. Box 128 (44202-0128)
PHONE.....................216 881-8500
Cynthia Brogan, *Managing Member*
EMP: 10 **EST:** 2006
SALES (est): 574.88K **Privately Held**
Web: www.osteosymbionics.com
SIC: 3842 Implants, surgical

(G-4127)
OTIS ELEVATOR COMPANY
9800 Rockside Rd Ste 1200 (44125-6270)
PHONE.....................216 573-2333
Gordy Sell, *Mgr*
EMP: 44
SALES (corp-wide): 14.26B **Publicly Held**
Web: www.otis.com
SIC: 5084 1796 3534 Elevators; Elevator
  installation and conversion; Elevators and
  equipment
HQ: Otis Elevator Company
  1 Carrier Pl
  Farmington CT 06032
  860 674-3000

(G-4128)
OTTO KONIGSLOW MFG CO
13300 Coit Rd (44110-2285)
PHONE..............................216 851-7900
J P Lawson, *Pr*
Cofer Mcintosh, *CEO*
EMP: 15 EST: 1876
SQ FT: 72,500
SALES (est): 2.79MM **Privately Held**
Web: www.ottokonigslowmfg.com
SIC: 3724 3548 Aircraft engines and engine
　　parts; Welding and cutting apparatus and
　　accessories, nec

(G-4129)
P & P MACHINE TOOL INC
26189 Broadway Ave (44146-6512)
PHONE..............................440 232-7404
Wayne Pelcarsky, *Pr*
Thomas Pelcarsky, *VP*
EMP: 6 EST: 1980
SQ FT: 4,000
SALES (est): 481.12K **Privately Held**
SIC: 3599 Machine shop, jobbing and repair

(G-4130)
P S C INC
21761 Tungsten Rd (44117-1116)
PHONE..............................216 531-3375
Matthew C Litzler, *Pr*
William J Urban, *COO*
▲ **EMP: 8 EST:** 1970
SQ FT: 12,000
SALES (est): 4.43MM
SALES (corp-wide): 25.05MM **Privately
Held**
Web: www.pscrfheat.com
SIC: 3567 1731 Dielectric heating equipment
　; General electrical contractor
PA: C.A. Litzler Holding Company
　　4800 W 160th St
　　Cleveland OH 44135
　　216 267-8020

(G-4131)
PACK LINE CORP
22900 Miles Rd (44128-5445)
PHONE..............................212 564-0664
Michael Beilinson, *Prin*
▲ **EMP: 6 EST:** 2003
SALES (est): 1.97MM **Privately Held**
SIC: 3565 Packaging machinery
PA: Packline Ltd
　　59 Prof. Shor
　　Holon 58811

(G-4132)
PALISIN & ASSOCIATES INC (PA)
Also Called: Sup-R-Die
10003 Memphis Ave (44144-2031)
PHONE..............................216 252-3930
David L Palisin, *Pr*
Marilyn J Palisin, *VP*
EMP: 22 EST: 1956
SQ FT: 11,000
SALES (est): 4.99MM
SALES (corp-wide): 4.99MM **Privately
Held**
Web: www.suprdie.com
SIC: 3544 Special dies and tools

(G-4133)
PARAMELT ARGUESO KINDT INC
Also Called: Paramelt
12651 Elmwood Ave (44111-5911)
PHONE..............................216 252-4122
David P Kindt, *Pr*
▲ **EMP: 7 EST:** 2010
SALES (est): 2.49MM **Privately Held**
Web: www.paramelt.com
SIC: 2891 Adhesives

(G-4134)
PARAMOUNT DISTILLERS INC
Also Called: Lonz Winery
3116 Berea Rd (44111-1596)
PHONE..............................216 671-6300
▲ **EMP:** 337
SIC: 2084 2085 5182 5812 Wines; Distilled
　　and blended liquors; Wine; Eating places

(G-4135)
**PARK PLACE TECHNOLOGIES LLC
(PA)**
747 Alpha Dr (44143-2124)
EMP: 161 EST: 1991
SQ FT: 41,000
SALES (est): 367.44MM **Privately Held**
Web: www.parkplacetechnologies.com
SIC: 7379 3571 7378 3572 Computer
　　related consulting services; Electronic
　　computers; Computer peripheral equipment
　　repair and maintenance; Computer storage
　　devices

(G-4136)
PARK-OHIO HOLDINGS CORP (PA)
6065 Parkland Blvd Ste 1 (44124-6145)
PHONE..............................440 947-2000
Matthew Crawford, *Ch*
Patrick Fogarty, *VP*
Robert Vilsack, *CLO CAO*
◆ **EMP: 18 EST:** 1998
SALES (est): 1.66B
SALES (corp-wide): 1.66B **Publicly Held**
Web: www.pkoh.com
SIC: 3069 3567 3363 3524 Molded rubber
　　products; Induction heating equipment;
　　Aluminum die-castings; Lawn and garden
　　tractors and equipment

(G-4137)
PARK-OHIO INDUSTRIES INC (HQ)
Also Called: Park-Ohio
6065 Parkland Blvd Ste 1 (44124-6145)
PHONE..............................440 947-2000
Matthew V Crawford, *Pr*
Patrick W Fogarty, *CAO*
EMP: 129 EST: 1984
SQ FT: 60,450
SALES (est): 1.66B
SALES (corp-wide): 1.66B **Publicly Held**
Web: www.pkoh.com
SIC: 3462 3069 3567 3363 Iron and steel
　　forgings; Molded rubber products; Induction
　　heating equipment; Aluminum die-castings
PA: Park-Ohio Holdings Corp.
　　6065 Parkland Blvd
　　Cleveland OH 44124
　　440 947-2000

(G-4138)
PARK-OHIO PRODUCTS INC
7000 Denison Ave (44102-5247)
PHONE..............................216 961-7200
Craig Cowan, *Pr*
Robert Vilsack, *
Richard Paul Elliott, *
Anthony Hall, *
Robert Poeppleman, *Tax Vice President**
▲ **EMP: 100 EST:** 1995
SQ FT: 40,000
SALES (est): 11.55MM
SALES (corp-wide): 1.66B **Publicly Held**
Web: www.pkoh.com
SIC: 3069 Molded rubber products
HQ: Park-Ohio Industries, Inc.
　　6065 Parkland Blvd
　　Cleveland OH 44124
　　440 947-2000

(G-4139)
PARKER AEROSPACE
19600 Five Points Rd (44135-3109)
PHONE..............................216 225-2721
Cody Risker, *Mgr*
EMP: 6 EST: 2018
SALES (est): 1.27MM **Privately Held**
SIC: 3812 Search and navigation equipment

(G-4140)
PARKER HANNIFIN PARTNER B LLC
6035 Parkland Blvd (44124-4186)
PHONE..............................216 896-3000
EMP: 7 EST: 2012
SALES (est): 5.62MM
SALES (corp-wide): 19.93B **Publicly Held**
SIC: 3594 Fluid power pumps and motors
PA: Parker-Hannifin Corporation
　　6035 Parkland Blvd
　　Cleveland OH 44124
　　216 896-3000

(G-4141)
PARKER ROYALTY PARTNERSHIP
6035 Parkland Blvd (44124-4186)
PHONE..............................216 896-3000
EMP: 9 EST: 2008
SALES (est): 9.08MM
SALES (corp-wide): 19.93B **Publicly Held**
SIC: 3594 Fluid power pumps and motors
PA: Parker-Hannifin Corporation
　　6035 Parkland Blvd
　　Cleveland OH 44124
　　216 896-3000

(G-4142)
**PARKER RST-PROOF CLEVELAND
INC**
1688 Arabella Rd (44112-1489)
PHONE..............................216 481-6680
Frederick A Fruscella, *Ch Bd*
Sharon Bodine, *
EMP: 37 EST: 1935
SQ FT: 75,000
SALES (est): 7.97MM **Privately Held**
Web: www.parkerhq.com
SIC: 3479 3471 Rust proofing (hot dipping)
　　of metals and formed products; Plating and
　　polishing

(G-4143)
**PARKER-HANNIFIN CORPORATION
(PA)**
Also Called: Parker
6035 Parkland Blvd (44124-4186)
PHONE..............................216 896-3000
Jennifer A Parmentier, *Ch Bd*
Andrew D Ross, *Pr*
Todd M Leombruno, *Ex VP*
Joseph R Leonti, *VP*
Angela R Ives, *Care Vice President*
▲ **EMP: 4558 EST:** 1917
SALES (est): 19.93B
SALES (corp-wide): 19.93B **Publicly Held**
Web: www.parker.com
SIC: 3593 3492 3594 Fluid power cylinders
　　and actuators; Control valves, fluid power:
　　hydraulic and pneumatic; Fluid power
　　pumps

(G-4144)
PARKER-HANNIFIN CORPORATION
Also Called: Flight Operations
19600 Five Points Rd (44135-3109)
PHONE..............................216 433-1795
Allen Maurer, *Dir*
EMP: 15
SALES (corp-wide): 19.93B **Publicly Held**
Web: www.parker.com

SIC: 5084 3822 Hydraulic systems
　　equipment and supplies; Environmental
　　controls
PA: Parker-Hannifin Corporation
　　6035 Parkland Blvd
　　Cleveland OH 44124
　　216 896-3000

(G-4145)
PARKING & TRAFFIC CONTROL SEC
Also Called: Ptc Industries
13651 Newton Rd (44130-2735)
PHONE..............................440 243-7565
Donald Shorts, *CEO*
Lee Shorts, *Pr*
EMP: 15 EST: 1979
SQ FT: 20,000
SALES (est): 1.69MM **Privately Held**
Web: www.obardoorandgate.com
SIC: 3824 1799 8711 Parking meters;
　　Parking facility equipment and maintenance
　; Designing: ship, boat, machine, and
　　product

(G-4146)
PARKOHIO WORLDWIDE LLC (HQ)
6065 Parkland Blvd Ste 1 (44124-6145)
PHONE..............................440 947-2000
Matthew Crawford, *Ch*
EMP: 48 EST: 2018
SALES (est): 4.5MM
SALES (corp-wide): 1.66B **Publicly Held**
Web: www.pkoh.com
SIC: 3069 Molded rubber products
PA: Park-Ohio Holdings Corp.
　　6065 Parkland Blvd
　　Cleveland OH 44124
　　440 947-2000

(G-4147)
PARMA HEIGHTS LICENSE BUREAU
6339 Olde York Rd (44130-3059)
PHONE..............................440 888-0388
Dan Hughes, *Owner*
EMP: 7 EST: 1999
SALES (est): 581.57K **Privately Held**
Web: bmv.ohio.gov
SIC: 3469 Automobile license tags, stamped
　　metal

(G-4148)
PCC AIRFOILS LLC
Also Called: Sherwood Refractores
1781 Octavia Rd (44112-1410)
PHONE..............................216 692-7900
Thomas Lenard, *Genl Mgr*
EMP: 313
SALES (corp-wide): 424.23B **Publicly
Held**
Web: www.pccairfoils.com
SIC: 3369 3812 3677 3543 Castings, except
　　die-castings, precision; Search and
　　navigation equipment; Electronic coils and
　　transformers; Foundry cores
HQ: Pcc Airfoils, Llc
　　3401 Entp Pkwy Ste 200
　　Beachwood OH 44122
　　216 831-3590

(G-4149)
PEERLESS METAL PRODUCTS INC
6017 Superior Ave (44103-1447)
PHONE..............................216 431-6905
Thomas Banyas, *Pr*
Judy Szabo, *Treas*
EMP: 7 EST: 1996
SQ FT: 32,000
SALES (est): 937.22K **Privately Held**
Web: www.peerlessmetalproducts.com
SIC: 3469 Stamping metal for the trade

(G-4150)
PEMCO INC
5663 Brecksville Rd (44131-1593)
PHONE..............................216 524-2990
William J Koteles, *Pr*
William John Koteles, *Pr*
Ivan Kovacs, *
Kathleen Koteles, *
EMP: 43 EST: 1942
SQ FT: 25,000
SALES (est): 4.98MM **Privately Held**
Web: www.pemcomedical.com
SIC: 3841 3599 3845 3545 Surgical and
medical instruments; Machine shop,
jobbing and repair; Electromedical
equipment; Machine tool accessories

(G-4151)
PEMRO CORPORATION
Also Called: Pemro Distribution
125 Alpha Park (44143-2224)
PHONE..............................800 440-5441
Jon C Raney, *Pr*
Shari Raney, *Sec*
Gregory J Dziak, *Prin*
Todd Chaston, *Sls Mgr*
Matt Raney, *Genl Mgr*
EMP: 10 EST: 2001
SQ FT: 3,500
SALES (est): 6.71MM **Privately Held**
Web: www.pemro.com
SIC: 5065 2899 5045 Electronic parts;
Fluxes: brazing, soldering, galvanizing, and
welding; Anti-static equipment and devices

(G-4152)
PERITEC BIOSCIENCES LTD
Also Called: Peritec Biosciences
3291 Bremerton Rd (44124-5346)
PHONE..............................216 445-3756
Nancy Rubin, *CFO*
Naga Mallika Sattiraju, *Mgr*
EMP: 8 EST: 2005
SALES (est): 480.86K **Privately Held**
Web: www.peritecbio.com
SIC: 3841 Surgical and medical instruments

(G-4153)
PERSONNEL SELECTION SERVICES
31517 Walker Rd (44140-1415)
PHONE..............................440 835-3255
Paul Michalko, *Pr*
EMP: 10 EST: 1990
SALES (est): 260.84K **Privately Held**
SIC: 1389 8071 Testing, measuring,
surveying, and analysis services; Testing
laboratories

(G-4154)
PETFIBER LLC
Also Called: Fiberworx
17000 Saint Clair Ave Ste 105
(44110-2535)
PHONE..............................216 767-4535
Daniel T Moore, *Managing Member*
EMP: 12 EST: 2013
SALES (est): 1.25MM **Privately Held**
Web: www.fiberwx.com
SIC: 2295 Resin or plastic coated fabrics

(G-4155)
PETNET SOLUTIONS CLEVELAND LLC
2035 E 86th St Rm Jb122 (44106-2963)
PHONE..............................865 218-2000
Michele Abbott, *Contrlr*
EMP: 12 EST: 2007
SALES (est): 838.83K
SALES (corp-wide): 84.78B **Privately Held**

SIC: 2834 2835 Pharmaceutical preparations
; Radioactive diagnostic substances
HQ: Petnet Solutions, Inc.
810 Innovation Dr
Knoxville TN 37932
865 218-2000

(G-4156)
PETRO GEAR CORPORATION (PA)
3901 Hamilton Ave (44114-3831)
PHONE..............................216 431-2820
EMP: 10 EST: 1917
SQ FT: 40,000
SALES (est): 4.87MM
SALES (corp-wide): 4.87MM **Privately Held**
Web: www.stahlgear.com
SIC: 3566 Gears, power transmission,
except auto

(G-4157)
PG SQUARE LLC
6035 Parkland Blvd (44124-4186)
PHONE..............................216 896-3000
EMP: 10 EST: 2008
SALES (est): 2.91MM
SALES (corp-wide): 19.93B **Publicly Held**
SIC: 3823 Process control instruments
PA: Parker-Hannifin Corporation
6035 Parkland Blvd
Cleveland OH 44124
216 896-3000

(G-4158)
PHIL VEDDA & SONS INC
Also Called: Vedda Printing
12000 Berea Rd (44111-1608)
PHONE..............................216 671-2222
Phillip Vedda, *Pr*
James Vedda, *VP*
Grace Vedda, *Sec*
EMP: 8 EST: 1956
SQ FT: 20,000
SALES (est): 2.97MM **Privately Held**
Web: www.veddaprinting.com
SIC: 2752 Offset printing

(G-4159)
PHILIPS MED SYSTEMS CLVLAND IN (HQ)
Also Called: Philips Healthcare
595 Miner Rd (44143-2131)
PHONE..............................440 483-3000
David A Dripchak, *CEO*
Jerry C Cirino, *Ex VP*
William J Cull Senior, *VP*
Robert Blankenship, *CFO*
◆ **EMP: 500 EST:** 1970
SQ FT: 495,000
SALES (est): 450.77MM
SALES (corp-wide): 18.51B **Privately Held**
Web: www.emergin.com
SIC: 3844 5047 5137 3842 X-ray apparatus
and tubes; X-ray film and supplies; Hospital
gowns, women's and children's; Surgical
appliances and supplies
PA: Koninklijke Philips N.V.
High Tech Campus 52
Eindhoven NB 5656
402791111

(G-4160)
PHILLIPS ELECTRIC CO
Also Called: Phillips Electric
4126 Saint Clair Ave (44103-1120)
PHONE..............................216 361-0014
Jennifer Marriott, *CEO*
Jennifer Marriott, *Pr*
EMP: 16 EST: 1946
SQ FT: 40,000
SALES (est): 4.87MM **Privately Held**

Web: www.redmondwaltz.com
SIC: 7694 5063 Electric motor repair;
Motors, electric

(G-4161)
PHUNKENSHIP - PLATFORM BEER CO
3137 Sackett Ave (44109-2013)
PHONE..............................216 417-7743
EMP: 10 EST: 2019
SALES (est): 87.42K **Privately Held**
SIC: 2082 Beer (alcoholic beverage)

(G-4162)
PIEDMONT WATER SERVICES LLC
21400 Lorain Rd (44126-2125)
P.O. Box 1369 (58702-1369)
PHONE..............................216 554-4747
David Niederst, *Managing Member*
EMP: 6 EST: 2014
SALES (est): 527.1K **Privately Held**
SIC: 2834 Chlorination tablets and kits
(water purification)

(G-4163)
PIERCE-WRIGHT PRECISION INC
13606 Enterprise Ave (44135-5112)
PHONE..............................216 362-2870
David B Pierce, *Pr*
EMP: 7 EST: 1978
SQ FT: 10,000
SALES (est): 526.73K **Privately Held**
Web: www.conceptdesigns.com
SIC: 3599 Machine shop, jobbing and repair

(G-4164)
PIERRES ICE CREAM COMPANY INC
6200 Euclid Ave (44103-3724)
PHONE..............................216 432-1144
Doug Smith, *CEO*
Matthew J Anderson, *CFO*
EMP: 80 EST: 2022
SALES (est): 10.77MM **Privately Held**
Web: www.pierres.com
SIC: 2024 Ice cream and frozen deserts

(G-4165)
PILE DYNAMICS INC
Also Called: Pdi
30725 Aurora Rd (44139-2735)
PHONE..............................216 831-6131
Garland Likins, *Pr*
George Piscsalko, *
Doctor Frank Rausche, *Sec*
Adrian Rausche, *
Mohamad Hussein, *Stockholder*
▲ **EMP: 35 EST:** 1972
SQ FT: 12,000
SALES (est): 9.53MM **Privately Held**
Web: www.pile.com
SIC: 3825 Test equipment for electronic and
electrical circuits

(G-4166)
PIONEER CLDDING GLZING SYSTEMS
2550 Brookpark Rd (44134-1407)
PHONE..............................216 816-4242
Michael Robinson, *Brnch Mgr*
EMP: 35
SALES (corp-wide): 50.53MM **Privately Held**
Web: www.pioneerglazing.com
SIC: 1793 1741 3448 Glass and glazing work
; Masonry and other stonework;
Prefabricated metal components
PA: Pioneer Cladding And Glazing Systems
4074 Bethany Rd
Mason OH 45040
513 583-5925

(G-4167)
PIONEER MANUFACTURING INC (PA)
Also Called: Pioneer Athletics
4529 Industrial Pkwy (44135-4505)
PHONE..............................216 671-5500
▲ **EMP: 99 EST:** 1906
SALES (est): 26.54MM
SALES (corp-wide): 26.54MM **Privately Held**
Web: www.pioneerathletics.com
SIC: 2952 5087 2842 2841 Asphalt felts and
coatings; Cleaning and maintenance
equipment and supplies; Polishes and
sanitation goods; Soap and other detergents

(G-4168)
PJ BUSH ASSOCIATES INC
Also Called: Bush Integrated
15901 Industrial Pkwy (44135-3321)
PHONE..............................216 362-6700
Kathleen Bush, *CEO*
Patrick J Bush, *Prin*
EMP: 18 EST: 1985
SQ FT: 40,000
SALES (est): 2.37MM **Privately Held**
Web: www.bushprinting.com
SIC: 2759 Business forms: printing, nsk

(G-4169)
PLASMAN AB LP
Also Called: Plasman Cleveland Mfg
3000 W 121st St (44111-1639)
PHONE..............................216 252-2995
David Wiskel, *Pt*
Hal Leitch, *Pt*
EMP: 112 EST: 1992
SQ FT: 58,000
SALES (est): 8.68MM
SALES (corp-wide): 2.37B **Privately Held**
Web: www.plasman.com
SIC: 3471 Electroplating of metals or formed
products
HQ: Plasman Us Holdco Llc
1301 W Long Lk Rd Ste 255
Troy MI 48098
248 205-7004

(G-4170)
PLASTER PROCESS CASTINGS CO
Also Called: Diversified Mold and Castings
19800 Miles Rd (44128-4118)
PHONE..............................216 663-1814
Vince Costello, *Pr*
EMP: 30 EST: 1939
SQ FT: 7,500
SALES (est): 3.09MM **Privately Held**
Web: www.diversifiedmolds.com
SIC: 3363 3364 Aluminum die-castings; Zinc
and zinc-base alloy die-castings

(G-4171)
PLASTIC WORKS INC
Also Called: The Plastic Works Inc
19851 Ingersoll Dr (44116-1817)
P.O. Box 369 (44839-0369)
PHONE..............................440 331-5575
Eric Kvame, *Mgr*
EMP: 12
SALES (corp-wide): 1.2MM **Privately Held**
SIC: 3086 2671 Packaging and shipping
materials, foamed plastics; Paper; coated
and laminated packaging
PA: The Plastic Works Inc
10502 Mudbrook Rd
Huron OH 44839
419 433-6576

(G-4172)
PLASTICS FAMILY HOLDINGS INC
Also Called: Total Plastics International
17851 Englewood Dr Ste A (44130-3489)

PHONE.................................440 891-1140
TOLL FREE: 877
Chris Terrell, *Brnch Mgr*
EMP: 6
Web: www.totalplastics.com
SIC: 3089 5162 Injection molding of plastics;
  Plastics sheets and rods
HQ: Plastics Family Holdings, Inc.
  5800 Cmpus Cir Dr E Ste 1
  Irving TX 75063
  469 299-7000

(G-4173)
PLATFORM BEERS LLC
Also Called: Platform Beer
4125 Lorain Ave (44113-3718)
PHONE.................................440 539-3245
Paul Benner, *Managing Member*
EMP: 12 EST: 2013
SQ FT: 5,000
SALES (est): 4.63MM
SALES (corp-wide): 1.7B Privately Held
Web: www.platformbeer.co
SIC: 2082 Near beer
HQ: Anheuser-Busch, Llc
  1 Busch Pl
  Saint Louis MO 63118
  800 342-5283

(G-4174)
PLUS MARK LLC
1 American Rd (44144-2354)
PHONE.................................216 252-6770
Kurt Schoen, *Pr*
Dick Gygi, *VP*
Stephen J Smith, *Treas*
Chris Haffke, *Sec*
Jim Kaiser, *Asst Tr*
◆ EMP: 100 EST: 1977
SQ FT: 1,600,000
SALES (est): 24.69MM
SALES (corp-wide): 14.54B Privately Held
SIC: 2621 2396 2771 Wrapping paper;
  Automotive and apparel trimmings;
  Greeting cards
HQ: American Greetings Corporation
  1 American Blvd
  Cleveland OH 44145
  216 252-7300

(G-4175)
POLY PRODUCTS INC
837 E 79th St (44103-1807)
PHONE.................................216 391-7659
Walter Senney, *Pr*
Joyce Senney, *VP*
EMP: 6 EST: 1983
SQ FT: 12,000
SALES (est): 606.51K Privately Held
Web: www.poly-products.com
SIC: 3559 3568 Refinery, chemical
  processing, and similar machinery;
  Bearings, bushings, and blocks

(G-4176)
PORATH BUSINESS SERVICES INC
Also Called: Porath Printing
21000 Miles Pkwy (44128-5515)
PHONE.................................216 626-0060
Gerald A Engelhart, *Pr*
EMP: 17 EST: 1951
SQ FT: 5,000
SALES (est): 2.07MM Privately Held
Web: www.porathprintsource.com
SIC: 2752 7331 Offset printing; Mailing
  service

(G-4177)
POSTLE INDUSTRIES INC (PA)
Also Called: Cermet Technologies
5500 W 164th St (44142-1512)

PHONE.................................216 265-9000
John G Postle, *Pr*
Chris J Postle, *
▲ EMP: 24 EST: 1968
SQ FT: 15,000
SALES (est): 5.58MM
SALES (corp-wide): 5.58MM Privately
Held
Web: www.hardbandingsolutions.com
SIC: 3548 2851 Welding and cutting
  apparatus and accessories, nec; Epoxy
  coatings

(G-4178)
POTTERS INDUSTRIES LLC
Potters Industries
2380 W 3rd St (44113-2509)
PHONE.................................216 621-0840
Bob Hooper, *Mgr*
EMP: 53
SALES (corp-wide): 406.19MM Privately
Held
Web: www.pottersindustries.com
SIC: 3231 Reflector glass beads, for
  highway signs or reflectors
HQ: Potters Industries, Llc
  3222 Phnxvlle Pike Ste 10
  Malvern PA 19355
  484 895-3200

(G-4179)
PPG INDUSTRIES INC
14800 Emery Ave (44135-1477)
PHONE.................................216 671-7793
Dian Lind, *Brnch Mgr*
EMP: 9
SALES (corp-wide): 18.25B Publicly Held
Web: www.ppg.com
SIC: 2851 Paints and allied products
PA: Ppg Industries, Inc.
  1 Ppg Pl
  Pittsburgh PA 15272
  412 434-3131

(G-4180)
PPG INDUSTRIES OHIO INC (HQ)
Also Called: PPG Oak Creek
3800 W 143rd St (44111-4901)
PHONE.................................216 671-0050
Charles E Bunch, *CEO*
Bill Silvestri, *
J Rich Alexander, *
Dennis N Taljan, *
◆ EMP: 602 EST: 1999
SQ FT: 439,551
SALES (est): 493.21MM
SALES (corp-wide): 18.25B Publicly Held
Web: www.ppg.com
SIC: 2851 Paints and paint additives
PA: Ppg Industries, Inc.
  1 Ppg Pl
  Pittsburgh PA 15272
  412 434-3131

(G-4181)
PPG INDUSTRIES OHIO INC
Also Called: PPG Deco USA
P.O. Box 94995 (44101-4995)
PHONE.................................412 434-3888
EMP: 245
SALES (corp-wide): 18.25B Publicly Held
Web: www.ppg.com
SIC: 2851 Paints and paint additives
HQ: Ppg Industries Ohio, Inc.
  3800 West 143rd St
  Cleveland OH 44111
  216 671-0050

(G-4182)
PRECISE TOOL & MFG CORP
5755 Canal Rd (44125-3429)

PHONE.................................216 524-1500
Ronald Volandt, *Pr*
EMP: 10 EST: 1950
SQ FT: 5,200
SALES (est): 1.05MM Privately Held
SIC: 3545 Cutting tools for machine tools

(G-4183)
PRECISION COATINGS INC
Also Called: Precison Coating Technology
3289 E 80th St (44104-4341)
PHONE.................................216 441-0805
Dale Palik, *Pr*
Lucille Palik, *Sec*
Mike Palik, *VP*
EMP: 9 EST: 1981
SQ FT: 22,000
SALES (est): 1.99MM Privately Held
Web: www.precisioncoatingscorp.com
SIC: 3479 Coating of metals and formed
  products

(G-4184)
PRECISION ENGINEERED PLAS INC
7000 Denison Ave (44102-5247)
PHONE.................................216 334-1105
Leonard Annaloro, *Pr*
EMP: 20 EST: 1997
SALES (est): 2.05MM
SALES (corp-wide): 1.66B Publicly Held
SIC: 3089 Automotive parts, plastic
HQ: Park-Ohio Industries, Inc.
  6065 Parkland Blvd
  Cleveland OH 44124
  440 947-2000

(G-4185)
PRECISION METAL PRODUCTS INC
Also Called: Metal Stamping
5745 Canal Rd (44125-3402)
PHONE.................................216 447-1900
George Jacin, *Pr*
George A Jacin, *
Aaron Jason, *
Amber Jacon, *
EMP: 30 EST: 1961
SQ FT: 16,000
SALES (est): 5.08MM Privately Held
Web: www.pmpstamping.com
SIC: 3469 3549 Stamping metal for the trade
  ; Assembly machines, including robotic

(G-4186)
PRECISION METAL PRODUCTS INC
9005 Bank St (44125-3425)
PHONE.................................216 447-1900
EMP: 10 EST: 2020
SALES (est): 2.85MM Privately Held
Web: www.pmpstamping.com
SIC: 3469 Stamping metal for the trade

(G-4187)
PRECISION WELDING
CORPORATION
7900 Exchange St (44125-3334)
P.O. Box 25548 (44125-0548)
PHONE.................................216 524-6110
Dennis Nader, *Pr*
Randy Nader, *
EMP: 32 EST: 1946
SQ FT: 26,000
SALES (est): 3.52MM Privately Held
Web: www.precisionweldingcorp.net
SIC: 7692 3444 3441 Welding repair; Sheet
  metalwork; Fabricated structural metal

(G-4188)
PREDICOR LLC
2728 Euclid Ave Ste 300 (44115-2428)
PHONE.................................419 460-1831
Timothy Walker, *Managing Member*

Timothy Walker, *Prin*
Dhruv Seshadri, *Prin*
Evan Davies, *Prin*
EMP: 6 EST: 2019
SALES (est): 391.78K Privately Held
SIC: 3571 Electronic computers

(G-4189)
PREMIER CONTAINER INC (PA)
Also Called: Premier Container
4500 Crayton Ave (44104-2816)
PHONE.................................800 230-7132
Mike Hanzak, *Pr*
EMP: 23 EST: 2012
SALES (est): 4.51MM
SALES (corp-wide): 4.51MM Privately
Held
Web: www.premier-container.com
SIC: 3537 Containers (metal), air cargo

(G-4190)
PREMIER MANUFACTURING CORP
(HQ)
3003 Priscilla Ave (44134-4230)
PHONE.................................216 941-9700
Paul Kara, *Pr*
Steve Koss, *
Donald C Dawson, *
◆ EMP: 118 EST: 1962
SALES (est): 10.34MM
SALES (corp-wide): 482.27MM Privately
Held
Web: www.sswtechnologies.com
SIC: 3496 3296 Miscellaneous fabricated
  wire products; Mineral wool
PA: Ssw Advanced Technologies, Llc
  435 N Whttngton Pkwy Ste
  Louisville KY 40222
  800 942-0286

(G-4191)
PREMIER PRINTING CORPORATION
18780 Cranwood Pkwy (44128-4038)
PHONE.................................216 478-9720
James Trombo, *Pr*
Jeffrey Trombo, *VP*
EMP: 10 EST: 2000
SQ FT: 10,000
SALES (est): 896.15K Privately Held
Web: www.premierprintingcorp.com
SIC: 2752 Offset printing

(G-4192)
PRESQUE ISLE ORTHTICS
PRSTHTIC
Also Called: Presque Isle Medical Tech
14055 Cedar Rd Ste 107 (44118-3333)
PHONE.................................216 371-0660
Solomon Heifetz, *Managing Member*
EMP: 8 EST: 2013
SALES (est): 659.09K Privately Held
Web: www.presqueislemedical.com
SIC: 8011 5999 3842 Primary care medical
  clinic; Orthopedic and prosthesis
  applications; Prosthetic appliances

(G-4193)
PRESRITE CORPORATION (PA)
3665 E 78th St (44105-2048)
PHONE.................................216 441-5990
Donald J Diemer, *Ch Bd*
George Longhour, *
William Berglund, *
Keith Vanderburg, *
Chris Carman, *
EMP: 300 EST: 1969
SQ FT: 180,000
SALES (est): 47.58MM
SALES (corp-wide): 47.58MM Privately
Held
Web: www.presrite.com

▲ = Import ▼ = Export
◆ = Import/Export

SIC: 3462 Automotive and internal combustion engine forgings

(G-4194)
PRESSCO TECHNOLOGY INC (PA)
Also Called: Pressco
29200 Aurora Rd (44139-1847)
PHONE..............................440 498-2600
Don W Cochran, *Pr*
Thomas P O'brien, *SLS*
Ed Morgan, *
William C Holmes, *
James R Bridgeland Junior, *Prin*
▲ EMP: 90 EST: 1990
SQ FT: 60,000
SALES (est): 16.64MM
SALES (corp-wide): 16.64MM **Privately Held**
Web: www.pressco.com
SIC: 3829 3825 Physical property testing equipment; Instruments to measure electricity

(G-4195)
PRIME INSTRUMENTS INC
9805 Walford Ave (44102-4734)
PHONE..............................216 651-0400
Robert Krupa, *Pr*
Alexander Krupa, *
Anthony Krupa, *Pdt Mgr*
▲ EMP: 75 EST: 1970
SQ FT: 37,000
SALES (est): 7.81MM **Privately Held**
Web: www.primeinstruments.com
SIC: 3823 Process control instruments

(G-4196)
PRINCE & IZANT LLC (PA)
12999 Plaza Dr (44130-1093)
P.O. Box 931247 (44193)
PHONE..............................216 362-7000
▲ EMP: 22 EST: 1927
SALES (est): 18.99MM
SALES (corp-wide): 18.99MM **Privately Held**
Web: www.princeizant.com
SIC: 3915 7692 3911 Jewelry soldering for the trade; Brazing; Jewel settings and mountings, precious metal

(G-4197)
PRO PRESS INC
3135 Berea Rd Ste 1 (44111-1513)
PHONE..............................216 631-8200
Steve Forster, *Pr*
Steve Forster, *Pt*
Teresa Tarantino, *Pt*
James Branagan, *Pt*
EMP: 10 EST: 1995
SQ FT: 3,000
SALES (est): 463.31K **Privately Held**
Web: www.propressinc.com
SIC: 2741 7311 Telephone and other directory publishing; Advertising agencies

(G-4198)
PRODUCTS CHEMICAL COMPANY LLC
4005 Clark Ave (44109-1128)
PHONE..............................216 218-1155
James Purcell, *CEO*
EMP: 15 EST: 2019
SALES (est): 807.54K **Privately Held**
Web: www.prod-chem.com
SIC: 2842 Polishes and sanitation goods

(G-4199)
PROFILE GRINDING INC
4593 Spring Rd (44131-1023)
PHONE..............................216 351-0600
Karen Homer, *Pr*

EMP: 19 EST: 1945
SQ FT: 20,000
SALES (est): 2.92MM **Privately Held**
Web: www.profilegrinding.com
SIC: 3451 3599 Screw machine products; Machine shop, jobbing and repair

(G-4200)
PROGRESS RAIL SERVICES CORP
Also Called: Cleveland Track Material
6600 Bessemer Ave (44127-1804)
PHONE..............................216 641-4000
EMP: 260
SALES (corp-wide): 64.81B **Publicly Held**
Web: www.progressrailstore.com
SIC: 3743 Railroad equipment
HQ: Progress Rail Services Corporation
1600 Progress Dr
Albertville AL 35950
800 476-8769

(G-4201)
PROJITECH INC
Also Called: Onstation
2310 Superior Ave E Ste 200 (44114-4245)
PHONE..............................216 999-6228
Patrick Russo, *CEO*
Jake Bailosky, *
EMP: 24 EST: 2013
SALES (est): 1.87MM **Privately Held**
Web: www.onstationapp.com
SIC: 7372 Application computer software

(G-4202)
PROTECH POWDER COATINGS INC
11110 Berea Rd (44102-2539)
PHONE..............................216 244-2761
EMP: 9
SALES (corp-wide): 202.63K **Privately Held**
Web: www.theprotechgroup.com
SIC: 3479 Coating of metals and formed products
HQ: Protech Powder Coatings, Inc.
21 Audrey Pl
Fairfield NJ 07004

(G-4203)
PROTOTYPE FABRICATORS CO
10911 Briggs Rd (44111-5300)
PHONE..............................216 252-0080
Richard Poddubny, *Pr*
EMP: 10 EST: 1971
SQ FT: 7,200
SALES (est): 2.77MM **Privately Held**
SIC: 3441 Fabricated structural metal

(G-4204)
PS SUPERIOR INC
Also Called: P S Awards
9257 Midwest Ave (44125-2415)
PHONE..............................216 587-1000
Elizabeth Sudyk, *Pr*
Joanne Sudyk, *Sec*
EMP: 8 EST: 1958
SQ FT: 10,000
SALES (est): 1.83MM **Privately Held**
Web: www.psawards.com
SIC: 3499 7389 5199 Trophies, metal, except silver; Lettering service; Advertising specialties

(G-4205)
PUBCO CORPORATION (PA)
3830 Kelley Ave (44114-4534)
PHONE..............................216 881-5300
William Dillingham, *Pr*
Stephen R Kalette, *
Maria Szubski, *
◆ EMP: 85 EST: 1996
SQ FT: 312,000

SALES (est): 85.24MM
SALES (corp-wide): 85.24MM **Privately Held**
Web: www.buckeyebusiness.com
SIC: 3531 3955 6512 Construction machinery; Carbon paper and inked ribbons ; Nonresidential building operators

(G-4206)
PUCEL ENTERPRISES INC
1440 E 36th St (44114-4117)
PHONE..............................216 881-4604
Robert A Mlakar, *Pr*
Kathleen M Mlakar-cook, *VP*
Ann Marie Mlakar-leissa, *VP*
Anthony F Mlakar, *
Rita T Mlakar, *
EMP: 55 EST: 1949
SQ FT: 105,000
SALES (est): 8.1MM **Privately Held**
Web: www.pucelenterprises.com
SIC: 3499 3441 3537 3443 Furniture parts, metal; Fabricated structural metal; Industrial trucks and tractors; Fabricated plate work (boiler shop)

(G-4207)
PUCEL ENTERPRISES INC
1401 E 34th St (44114-4136)
PHONE..............................800 336-4986
EMP: 6
SALES (est): 72K **Privately Held**
Web: www.pucelenterprises.com
SIC: 3499 Furniture parts, metal

(G-4208)
PULSAR ECOPRODUCTS LLC
Also Called: Pulsar Products
3615 Superior Ave E Ste 4402a (44114-4139)
PHONE..............................216 861-8800
Eric Ludwig, *Managing Member*
▲ EMP: 13 EST: 1998
SQ FT: 7,500
SALES (est): 4.36MM **Privately Held**
Web: www.pulsarproducts.com
SIC: 5112 3861 3952 5947 Stationery and office supplies; Photographic equipment and supplies; Lead pencils and art goods; Gift, novelty, and souvenir shop

(G-4209)
PYRAMID PLASTICS INC
9202 Reno Ave (44105-2187)
PHONE..............................216 641-5904
Donald Newman, *Ch Bd*
Mike Dezort, *
James E Newman, *
EMP: 8 EST: 1931
SQ FT: 10,000
SALES (est): 1.19MM **Privately Held**
SIC: 3089 Injection molding of plastics

(G-4210)
QCSM LLC
Also Called: Columbia Industries
9335 Mccracken Blvd (44125-2311)
PHONE..............................216 650-8731
EMP: 6 EST: 2013
SALES (est): 219.74K **Privately Held**
Web: www.columbiaind.com
SIC: 3451 8711 3599 3593 Screw machine products; Mechanical engineering; Machine and other job shop work; Fluid power cylinders, hydraulic or pneumatic

(G-4211)
QUALITOR INC (DH)
127 Public Sq Ste 5300 (44114-1219)
PHONE..............................248 204-8600
Gary Cohen, *CEO*

Scott Gibaratz, *CFO*
▲ EMP: 6 EST: 1999
SQ FT: 2,500
SALES (est): 48.95MM
SALES (corp-wide): 7.28B **Privately Held**
SIC: 3714 5013 Motor vehicle engines and parts; Motor vehicle supplies and new parts
HQ: Qualitor Acquisition Inc
127 Public Sq Ste 5110
Cleveland OH

(G-4212)
QUALITY BORATE CO LLC
3690 Orange Pl Ste 495 (44122-4465)
PHONE..............................216 896-1949
▲ EMP: 10 EST: 2000
SQ FT: 3,500
SALES (est): 374.68K **Privately Held**
Web: www.qualityborate.com
SIC: 5169 2879 Chemicals and allied products, nec; Agricultural chemicals, nec

(G-4213)
QUALITY CUTTER GRINDING CO
15501 Commerce Park Dr (44142-2014)
PHONE..............................216 362-6444
Carl Scafuro, *Pr*
Debbie Ebert, *Sec*
EMP: 13 EST: 1978
SQ FT: 13,500
SALES (est): 1.23MM **Privately Held**
Web: www.qualitycuttergrinding.com
SIC: 3545 7699 Cutting tools for machine tools; Knife, saw and tool sharpening and repair

(G-4214)
QUALITY INDUSTRIES INC
3716 Clark Ave (44109-1142)
PHONE..............................216 961-5566
Jerry Kaplan, *Pr*
Jim Kaplan, *VP*
EMP: 6 EST: 1945
SQ FT: 12,000
SALES (est): 489.01K **Privately Held**
Web: www.qualityindustries.com
SIC: 3599 Machine shop, jobbing and repair

(G-4215)
QUALITY PLATING CO
1443 E 40th St (44103-1182)
P.O. Box 603247 (44103-0247)
PHONE..............................216 361-0151
Daniel Miller, *Pr*
▲ EMP: 9 EST: 1944
SQ FT: 11,895
SALES (est): 981.14K **Privately Held**
Web: www.qualityplatinginc.com
SIC: 3471 8711 Chromium plating of metals or formed products; Engineering services

(G-4216)
QUALITY SOLUTIONS INC
Also Called: QUALITY SOLUTIONS INC
P.O. Box 40147 (44140-0147)
PHONE..............................440 933-9946
Francis P Toolan Junior, *Brnch Mgr*
EMP: 27
Web: www.qualitysolutions.com
SIC: 2741 8742 8732 Business service newsletters: publishing and printing; Management consulting services; Market analysis or research
HQ: Quality Solutions, Inc.
44 Merrimac St Ste 22
Newburyport MA 01950

(G-4217)
QUALITY STAMPING PRODUCTS CO (PA)
5322 Bragg Rd (44127-1283)

PHONE..............................216 441-2700
Alan Nayman, *Pr*
Kenneth Nayman, *VP*
Dorothy Nayman, *Sec*
Nan Nayman, *VP*
EMP: 16 **EST:** 1951
SQ FT: 20,000
SALES (est): 2.2MM
SALES (corp-wide): 2.2MM **Privately Held**
SIC: 3469 Stamping metal for the trade

(G-4218)
QUES INDUSTRIES INC
5420 W 140th St (44142-1703)
PHONE..............................216 267-8989
Quentin Meng, *Pr*
▲ **EMP:** 16 **EST:** 1983
SQ FT: 50,000
SALES (est): 1.16MM **Privately Held**
Web: www.quesinc.com
SIC: 2899 Water treating compounds

(G-4219)
R & T ESTATE LLC
Also Called: Gray Area Bistro Ultra Lounge
17001 Euclid Ave (44112-1431)
PHONE..............................216 862-0822
Willis Tabron, *Managing Member*
EMP: 15 **EST:** 2018
SQ FT: 2,600
SALES (est): 256.54K **Privately Held**
SIC: 5812 2084 Cafe; Wines

(G-4220)
R E MAY INC
1401 E 24th St (44114-2124)
PHONE..............................216 771-6332
Betty D Pangrace, *Pr*
John E Pangrace, *VP*
EMP: 6 **EST:** 1973
SQ FT: 5,000
SALES (est): 715.05K **Privately Held**
Web: www.brandingsuite.com
SIC: 2796 Lithographic plates, positives or
negatives

(G-4221)
R H INDUSTRIES INC
3155 W 33rd St (44109-1524)
P.O. Box 609040 (44109-0040)
PHONE..............................216 281-5210
Tina Haddad, *Pr*
EMP: 21 **EST:** 1972
SQ FT: 10,000
SALES (est): 4.05MM **Privately Held**
Web: www.rhindustries.com
SIC: 3429 3599 3511 Motor vehicle hardware
; Machine shop, jobbing and repair;
Turbines and turbine generator sets

(G-4222)
RAM SENSORS INC
875 Canterbury Rd (44145-1488)
PHONE..............................440 835-3540
Ron Miller, *Pr*
Caroline J Miller, *
EMP: 25 **EST:** 1981
SQ FT: 16,000
SALES (est): 3.22MM **Privately Held**
Web: www.ramsensors.com
SIC: 3823 3315 Temperature instruments:
industrial process type; Wire, steel:
insulated or armored

(G-4223)
RANDYS PICKLES LLC
2203 Superior Ave E (44114-4222)
PHONE..............................440 864-6611
Andrew Rainey, *CEO*
EMP: 7
SQ FT: 3,000

SALES (corp-wide): 49.93K **Privately Held**
Web: www.randysartisanal.com
SIC: 2035 Pickles, sauces, and salad
dressings
PA: Randys Pickles Llc
615 Eastern Heights Blvd
Elyria OH 44035
440 935-2785

(G-4224)
RANGE IMPACT INC (PA)
200 Park Ave Ste 400 (44122-4297)
PHONE..............................216 304-6556
Michael Cavanaugh, *CEO*
Edward Feighan, *Ch Bd*
Patricia Missal, *CFO*
EMP: 7 **EST:** 2007
SALES (est): 9.01MM
SALES (corp-wide): 9.01MM **Publicly
Held**
Web: www.malachiteinnovations.com
SIC: 2833 8731 Medicinals and botanicals;
Commercial physical research

(G-4225)
RAY FOGG CONSTRUCTION INC
981 Keynote Cir Ste 15 (44131-1842)
PHONE..............................216 351-7976
Raymon B Fogg Senior, *Pr*
Richard Neiden, *VP*
Michael J Merle, *Ex VP*
Virginia Fogg, *Sec*
Raymon B Fogg Junior, *Ex VP*
EMP: 8 **EST:** 1980
SQ FT: 5,760
SALES (est): 604.26K **Privately Held**
Web: www.fogg.com
SIC: 2821 Plastics materials and resins

(G-4226)
RAYS SAUSAGE INC
3146 E 123rd St (44120-3179)
PHONE..............................216 921-8782
Renee Cash, *Pr*
Raymond Cash, *VP*
Leslie Lester, *CFO*
EMP: 8 **EST:** 1952
SQ FT: 660
SALES (est): 492.49K **Privately Held**
Web: www.rayssausage.com
SIC: 2013 Sausages, from purchased meat

(G-4227)
REBIZ LLC
1925 Saint Clair Ave Ne (44114-2028)
PHONE..............................844 467-3249
Jumaid Hasan, *Managing Member*
EMP: 50 **EST:** 2014
SALES (est): 5.08MM **Privately Held**
Web: www.rebiz.com
SIC: 7372 7374 Business oriented computer
software; Optical scanning data service

(G-4228)
RED SEAL ELECTRIC COMPANY
3835 W 150th St (44111-5891)
PHONE..............................216 941-3900
Samuel Stryffeler, *Pr*
Daniel T Stryffeler, *
Judy Stryffeler, *
Jeff Stryffeler, *
▲ **EMP:** 38 **EST:** 1946
SQ FT: 28,000
SALES (est): 5.95MM **Privately Held**
Web: www.redseal.com
SIC: 3644 Insulators and insulation
materials, electrical

(G-4229)
RED TIE GROUP INC (PA)
Also Called: Braden-Sutphin Ink Company
4521 Industrial Pkwy (44135-4541)
▲ **EMP:** 36 **EST:** 1913
SALES (est): 9.34MM
SALES (corp-wide): 9.34MM **Privately
Held**
Web: www.bsink.com
SIC: 2893 Printing ink

(G-4230)
REDLAND QUARRIES NY INC
560 Harrison Street (44113)
PHONE..............................216 566-0545
EMP: 27
SALES (corp-wide): 20.63MM **Privately
Held**
SIC: 3241 Cement, hydraulic
PA: Redland Quarries Ny Inc.
6211 N Ann Arbor Rd
Dundee MI

(G-4231)
REFOCUS HOLDINGS INC
2310 Superior Ave E Ste 210 (44114-4244)
PHONE..............................216 751-8384
Greg Shick, *Pr*
EMP: 42 **EST:** 2004
SALES (est): 1.56MM **Privately Held**
Web: www.lightspec.com
SIC: 3674 Light emitting diodes

(G-4232)
RELIABLE PATTERN WORKS INC
590 Golden Oak Pkwy (44146-6502)
PHONE..............................440 232-8820
Stephanie Kapcio, *Pr*
Stephanie Kacio, *Sec*
EMP: 7 **EST:** 1913
SQ FT: 7,500
SALES (est): 978.45K **Privately Held**
Web: www.reliablepattern.com
SIC: 3543 Industrial patterns

(G-4233)
RENEGADE BRANDS LLC
3201 Enterprise Pkwy Ste 490
(44122-7330)
PHONE..............................216 342-4347
Cathy Horton, *CEO*
EMP: 7 **EST:** 2012
SQ FT: 5,000
SALES (est): 424.11K **Privately Held**
Web: www.renegadebrands.com
SIC: 2841 Soap: granulated, liquid, cake,
flaked, or chip

(G-4234)
REPKO MACHINE INC
5081 W 164th St (44142-1599)
PHONE..............................216 267-1144
John Palmer Iii, *Pr*
Valentyna Palmer, *Sec*
EMP: 9 **EST:** 1951
SQ FT: 16,000
SALES (est): 867.76K **Privately Held**
Web: www.repko.com
SIC: 3599 Machine shop, jobbing and repair

(G-4235)
REPRO ACQUISITION COMPANY LLC
Also Called: Reprocenter, The
25001 Rockwell Dr (44117-1239)
PHONE..............................216 738-3800
▲ **EMP:** 7 **EST:** 1999
SQ FT: 32,000
SALES (est): 785.38K **Privately Held**
Web: www.reprocenter.com

SIC: 2752 7375 2789 Offset printing;
Information retrieval services; Bookbinding
and related work

(G-4236)
RESEARCH ORGANICS LLC
Also Called: Safc Cleveland
4353 E 49th St (44125-1083)
PHONE..............................216 883-8025
Rob Sternfeld, *Pr*
Fred Sternfeld, *
▲ **EMP:** 75 **EST:** 1966
SQ FT: 100,000
SALES (est): 24.9MM
SALES (corp-wide): 22.37B **Privately Held**
Web: resorg.lookchem.com
SIC: 2899 2869 Chemical preparations, nec;
Industrial organic chemicals, nec
HQ: Sigma-Aldrich Corporation
3050 Spruce St
Saint Louis MO 63103
314 771-5765

(G-4237)
RESILIENCE FUND III LP (PA)
25101 Chagrin Blvd Ste 350 (44122-5687)
PHONE..............................216 292-0200
David Glickman, *Pt*
Ki Mixon, *Pt*
William Tobin, *Pt*
EMP: 16 **EST:** 2010
SALES (est): 85.81MM
SALES (corp-wide): 85.81MM **Privately
Held**
Web: www.resiliencecapital.com
SIC: 6799 3567 Investors, nec; Industrial
furnaces and ovens

(G-4238)
REVOLUTION MACHINE WORKS INC
5613 Cloverleaf Pkwy (44125-4816)
P.O. Box 1063 (44021-1063)
PHONE..............................706 505-6525
Kris Fugate, *Pr*
EMP: 8 **EST:** 2018
SALES (est): 4.16MM **Privately Held**
Web: www.revolutionmw.net
SIC: 3599 Machine shop, jobbing and repair

(G-4239)
RFW HOLDINGS INC
Also Called: R F W
1200 Smith Ct (44116-1520)
PHONE..............................440 331-8300
Richard Wilber, *Pr*
EMP: 8 **EST:** 1984
SALES (est): 490.4K **Privately Held**
Web: www.sobstad.com
SIC: 2394 Sails: made from purchased
materials

(G-4240)
RICHARD STEEL COMPANY INC
11110 Avon Ave (44105-4223)
P.O. Box 31516 (44131-0516)
PHONE..............................216 520-6390
Richard Jereb, *Pr*
EMP: 9 **EST:** 1981
SQ FT: 5,000
SALES (est): 266.9K **Privately Held**
SIC: 3441 Fabricated structural metal

(G-4241)
RICKING HOLDING CO
5800 Grant Ave (44105-5608)
PHONE..............................513 825-3551
Carl Ricking Junior, *Pr*
Joyce Ricking, *
Julie Ricking, *
Carla Droll, *
Preston M Simpson, *

▲ = Import ▼ = Export
◆ = Import/Export

EMP: 14 EST: 1974
SALES (est): 1.26MM **Privately Held**
Web: www.joshen.com
SIC: 5141 2656 5113 Groceries, general line
; Cups, paper: made from purchased
material; Bags, paper and disposable plastic

(G-4242)
RITIME INCORPORATED
6363 York Rd Ste 104 (44130-3031)
PHONE..................330 273-3443
William E Avis, *Pr*
EMP: 6 EST: 1966
SQ FT: 10,000
SALES (est): 124.64K **Privately Held**
SIC: 3599 3542 Machine shop, jobbing and
repair; Machine tools, metal forming type

(G-4243)
RIVERSIDE DRIVES INC
Also Called: Riverside Drives
4509 W 160th St (44135-2627)
P.O. Box 35166 (44135)
PHONE..................216 362-1211
Bernard Dillemuth, *Pr*
David Dillemuth, *
Kathleen Dillemuth, *
▼ **EMP: 28 EST:** 1985
SQ FT: 7,500
SALES (est): 2.5MM **Privately Held**
Web: www.riversidedrives.com
SIC: 5063 3699 Power transmission
equipment, electric; Electrical equipment
and supplies, nec

(G-4244)
RIVERSIDE MFG ACQUISITION LLC
5344 Bragg Rd (44127-1274)
PHONE..................585 458-2090
Mike Hill, *Pr*
Gerard Shafer, *
EMP: 7 EST: 1973
SQ FT: 120,000
SALES (est): 406.13K **Privately Held**
SIC: 2789 Binding only: books, pamphlets,
magazines, etc.

(G-4245)
ROBERTS DEMAND NO 3 CORP
Also Called: Electro-Plating & Fabricating
4008 E 89th St (44105-3919)
P.O. Box 605635 (44105-0635)
PHONE..................216 641-0660
Les Demand, *Pr*
William Demand, *VP*
Don Paukert, *Stockholder*
EMP: 9 EST: 1939
SQ FT: 13,500
SALES (est): 554.36K **Privately Held**
SIC: 3471 Cleaning and descaling metal
products

(G-4246)
ROCK AWAY CAPITAL INC
Also Called: Rockport Ready Mix
3092 Rockefeller Ave (44115-3612)
PHONE..................216 432-9465
Ann Nock, *Pr*
EMP: 25 EST: 1993
SALES (est): 4.48MM **Privately Held**
Web: www.rockportreadymix.com
SIC: 3273 Ready-mixed concrete

(G-4247)
ROCKWELL AUTOMATION INC
6680 Beta Dr (44143-2352)
PHONE..................440 646-7900
Michael Bless, *Brnch Mgr*
EMP: 10
Web: www.rockwellautomation.com

SIC: 3625 Relays and industrial controls
PA: Rockwell Automation, Inc.
1201 S 2nd St
Milwaukee WI 53204

(G-4248)
ROECHLING INDUS CLEVELAND LP (DH)
Also Called: Rochling Glastic Composites
4321 Glenridge Rd (44121-2805)
PHONE..................216 486-0100
Jim Azzarello, *Pt*
◆ **EMP: 200 EST:** 1988
SQ FT: 127,000
SALES (est): 122.03MM
SALES (corp-wide): 2.96B **Privately Held**
Web: www.roechling.com
SIC: 3089 2821 3083 3644 Thermoformed
finished plastics products, nec; Molding
compounds, plastics; Laminated plastics
sheets; Noncurrent-carrying wiring devices
HQ: Rochling Industrial Se & Co. Kg
Rochlingstr. 1
Haren (Ems) NI 49733
59347010

(G-4249)
ROL- FAB INC
4949 Johnston Pkwy (44128-3201)
PHONE..................216 662-2500
Robert Hansen, *Pr*
▼ **EMP: 32 EST:** 1969
SQ FT: 70,000
SALES (est): 6.27MM **Privately Held**
Web: www.rol-fab.com
SIC: 3441 Building components, structural
steel

(G-4250)
ROSE METAL INDUSTRIES LLC (PA)
1536 E 43rd St (44103-2310)
PHONE..................216 881-3355
Robert B Rose, *Managing Member*
EMP: 11 EST: 1904
SQ FT: 10,000
SALES (est): 6.25MM
SALES (corp-wide): 6.25MM **Privately Held**
Web: www.rosemetalindustries.com
SIC: 3441 7692 3462 3443 Fabricated
structural metal; Welding repair; Iron and
steel forgings; Ladles, metal plate

(G-4251)
ROSE METAL INDUSTRIES LLC
1155 Marquette St (44114-3919)
PHONE..................216 426-8615
Robert Rose, *Pr*
EMP: 24
SALES (corp-wide): 6.25MM **Privately Held**
Web: www.rosemetalindustries.com
SIC: 3441 Fabricated structural metal
PA: Rose Metal Industries, Llc
1536 E 43rd St
Cleveland OH 44103
216 881-3355

(G-4252)
ROSE PROPERTIES INC
Also Called: Rose Metal Industries
1536 E 43rd St (44103-2310)
PHONE..................216 881-6000
Robert Rose, *Pr*
EMP: 8 EST: 1952
SQ FT: 10,000
SALES (est): 1.43MM **Privately Held**
Web: www.roseironworks.com
SIC: 3441 Fabricated structural metal

(G-4253)
ROSENFELD JEWELRY INC
5668 Mayfield Rd (44124-2916)
PHONE..................440 446-0099
Henry Rosenfeld, *Pr*
Ruth Rosenfeld, *VP*
Arthur Rosenfeld, *Sec*
EMP: 8 EST: 1967
SQ FT: 1,350
SALES (est): 570.44K **Privately Held**
Web: www.rosenfeldjewelry.com
SIC: 3911 5944 Jewelry, precious metal;
Jewelry stores

(G-4254)
ROSSBOROUGH AUTOMOTIVE CORP
3425 Service Rd (44111-2421)
PHONE..................216 941-6115
Chet Scholtz, *Prin*
EMP: 11 EST: 2006
SALES (est): 177.1K **Privately Held**
Web: www.src-worldwide.com
SIC: 2899 Fluxes: brazing, soldering,
galvanizing, and welding

(G-4255)
ROSSBOROUGH SUPPLY CO
3425 Service Rd (44111-2421)
PHONE..................216 941-6115
EMP: 8 EST: 2017
SALES (est): 753.38K **Privately Held**
Web: www.src-worldwide.com
SIC: 3369 Machinery castings, exc. die,
nonferrous, exc. alum. copper

(G-4256)
ROYAL ACME CORPORATION (PA)
Also Called: Adsetting Service
3110 Payne Ave (44114-4504)
PHONE..................216 241-1477
Theodore D Cutts, *Pr*
▲ **EMP: 22 EST:** 1932
SALES (est): 3.96MM
SALES (corp-wide): 3.96MM **Privately Held**
Web: www.artgonewild.com
SIC: 3953 2791 3993 3053 Embossing seals
and hand stamps; Typesetting; Signs and
advertising specialties; Gaskets; packing
and sealing devices

(G-4257)
ROYAL APPLIANCE INTL CO
7005 Cochran Rd (44139-4303)
PHONE..................440 996-2000
Chris Gurieri, *Pr*
Andy Klaus, *CFO*
Pat Sullivan, *CEO*
EMP: 10 EST: 1953
SALES (est): 8.71MM **Privately Held**
Web: www.dirtdevil.com
SIC: 3635 Household vacuum cleaners
HQ: Royal Appliance Mfg. Co.
8405 Ibm Dr
Charlotte NC 28262
888 321-1134

(G-4258)
ROYAL CABINET DESIGN CO INC
15800 Commerce Park Dr (44142-2019)
PHONE..................216 267-5330
Joseph Estephan, *Pr*
Elie Estephan, *VP*
Georgette Estephan, *Sec*
EMP: 12 EST: 1982
SALES (est): 4.73MM **Privately Held**
Web: www.royalcabinetdesign.com
SIC: 2434 Wood kitchen cabinets

(G-4259)
ROYAL POWDER CORPORATION
4800 Briar Rd (44135-5040)
PHONE..................216 898-0074
Kirit Patel, *Pr*
EMP: 6 EST: 2003
SQ FT: 1,300
SALES (est): 960.97K **Privately Held**
Web: www.royalpowder.com
SIC: 3399 Metal powders, pastes, and flakes

(G-4260)
ROYS MUELLER BOX CO
5140 Richmond Rd (44146-1331)
PHONE..................216 464-1191
Sue Horky, *Owner*
Paul Horky, *VP*
EMP: 7 EST: 1922
SQ FT: 1,900
SALES (est): 419.21K **Privately Held**
SIC: 2657 Folding paperboard boxes

(G-4261)
RP HOSKINS INC
3033 W 44th St (44113-4817)
PHONE..................216 631-1000
Christopher S Hoskins, *Pr*
Richard P Hoskins, *
Flo Roll, *Finance**
EMP: 8 EST: 1978
SQ FT: 10,000
SALES (est): 856.65K **Privately Held**
Web: www.trucocoatings.com
SIC: 2899 2952 Waterproofing compounds;
Roofing felts, cements, or coatings, nec

(G-4262)
RSB SPINE LLC
2530 Superior Ave E Ste 703 (44114-4200)
P.O. Box 250 (44070-0250)
PHONE..................216 241-2804
John Redmond, *Managing Member*
EMP: 6 EST: 2001
SALES (est): 2.22MM **Privately Held**
Web: www.rsbspine.com
SIC: 3841 Surgical instruments and
apparatus

(G-4263)
RTI REMMELE ENGINEERING INC
5801 Postal Rd (44181-2184)
P.O. Box 81292 (44181-0292)
PHONE..................651 635-4179
EMP: 101
SALES (corp-wide): 7.43B **Publicly Held**
Web: www.howmet.com
SIC: 3569 Gas generators
HQ: Rti Remmele Engineering, Inc.
10 Old Highway 8 Sw
Saint Paul MN 55112
651 635-4100

(G-4264)
RUDYS STRUDEL SHOP
Also Called: Rudy's Strudel & Bakery
5580 Ridge Rd (44129-2396)
PHONE..................440 886-4430
Eugenia Polatajko, *Owner*
EMP: 6 EST: 1948
SQ FT: 7,900
SALES (est): 358.05K **Privately Held**
Web: www.rudysstrudel.com
SIC: 2051 2052 Bakery: wholesale or
wholesale/retail combined; Cookies and
crackers

(G-4265)
RUSH FIXTURE & MILLWORK CO
1978 W 3rd St (44113-2525)
PHONE..................216 241-9100

Roger Solomon, *Pr*
EMP: 15 **EST:** 1999
SALES (est): 232.93K **Privately Held**
SIC: 2431 Millwork

(G-4266)
S & H INDUSTRIES INC
Also Called: Keysco Tools
5200 Richmond Rd (44146-1387)
PHONE..............................216 831-0550
John Turk, *Pr*
Steven Perney, *
Edward Clancy, *
▲ **EMP:** 24 **EST:** 1952
SQ FT: 23,000
SALES (est): 916.7K
SALES (corp-wide): 2.41MM **Privately Held**
Web: www.shindustries.com
SIC: 3423 Mechanics' hand tools
PA: S & H Industries Inc
5200 Richmond Rd
Bedford OH 44146
216 831-0550

(G-4267)
S A LANGMACK COMPANY
Also Called: Niagara Custombilt Mfg
13400 Glenside Rd (44110-3528)
PHONE..............................216 541-0500
Chris Langmack, *Pr*
John C Langmack, *Prin*
Clark B Langmack, *VP*
Virginia Langmack, *Sec*
EMP: 9 **EST:** 1934
SQ FT: 25,000
SALES (est): 989.61K **Privately Held**
SIC: 3565 3569 Bottle washing and sterilizing machines; Filters, general line: industrial

(G-4268)
S R P M INC
30300 Bruce Industrial Pkwy Ste B (44139-3921)
PHONE..............................440 248-8440
Mark Steinmeyer, *Pr*
Craig Steinmeyer, *
EMP: 30 **EST:** 1953
SQ FT: 15,000
SALES (est): 5.42MM **Privately Held**
Web: www.srpm.com
SIC: 3599 Machine shop, jobbing and repair

(G-4269)
SAINT CTHERINES METALWORKS INC
1985 W 68th St (44102-3906)
PHONE..............................216 409-0576
Van Peplin, *Pr*
EMP: 9 **EST:** 2001
SQ FT: 20,000
SALES (est): 278K **Privately Held**
Web: www.scmetalworks.com
SIC: 2842 8661 Metal polish; Religious organizations

(G-4270)
SAINT-GOBAIN HYCOMP LLC
17960 Englewood Dr (44130-3438)
PHONE..............................440 234-2002
EMP: 120 **EST:** 1992
SQ FT: 48,600
SALES (est): 6MM
SALES (corp-wide): 402.18MM **Privately Held**
Web: www.omniseal-solutions.com
SIC: 3089 Injection molding of plastics
HQ: Saint Gobain Performance Plastics
France
34 Rue Du Moulin Des Aulnaies

Charny Oree De Puisaye BFC 89120
386637878

(G-4271)
SAMSCO CORP
837 E 79th St (44103-1807)
PHONE..............................216 400-8207
Walter F Senney, *Pr*
Jason Verderber, *CFO*
EMP: 10 **EST:** 2005
SQ FT: 100,000
SALES (est): 2.49MM **Privately Held**
Web: www.samsco.com
SIC: 5084 3589 Pollution control equipment, water (environmental); Water treatment equipment, industrial

(G-4272)
SAMSEL ROPE & MARINE SUPPLY CO (PA)
Also Called: Samsel Supply Company
1285 Old River Rd Uppr (44113-1279)
PHONE..............................216 241-0333
Kathleen A Petrick, *Pr*
F Michael Samsel, *
Wentworth J Marshall, *
Scott Balser, *
Grace F Wilcox, *
▲ **EMP:** 32 **EST:** 1958
SQ FT: 100,000
SALES (est): 6.1MM
SALES (corp-wide): 6.1MM **Privately Held**
Web: www.samselsupply.com
SIC: 2394 5051 4959 5085 Canvas and related products; Rope, wire (not insulated); Environmental cleanup services; Industrial supplies

(G-4273)
SANDVIK ROCK PROC SLTONS N AME
1214 Marquette St (44114-3920)
PHONE..............................216 431-2600
Leo Matthews, *Mgr*
EMP: 10
SALES (corp-wide): 12.03B **Privately Held**
Web: www.rammer.com
SIC: 3531 Construction machinery
HQ: Sandvik Rock Processing Solutions North America, Llc
3900 Kelley Ave
Cleveland OH 44114
216 431-2600

(G-4274)
SANDVIK ROCK PROC SLTONS N AME (HQ)
3900 Kelley Ave (44114-4536)
PHONE..............................216 431-2600
Phil Paranic, *Pr*
Kathy Toth, *CFO*
◆ **EMP:** 47 **EST:** 1942
SQ FT: 110,000
SALES (est): 22.78MM
SALES (corp-wide): 12.03B **Privately Held**
Web: www.rammer.com
SIC: 3531 Bituminous batching plants
PA: Sandvik Ab
Spangvagen 10
Sandviken 811 3
26260000

(G-4275)
SCHOOL UNIFORMS AND MORE INC
13721 Lorain Ave (44111-3439)
PHONE..............................216 365-1957
Nadia Habeeb, *Prin*
EMP: 7 **EST:** 2008
SALES (est): 190K **Privately Held**
Web: www.affuniforms.com
SIC: 2326 Work uniforms

(G-4276)
SCHUMANN ENTERPRISES INC
Also Called: E.C. Kitzel & Sons
12340 Plaza Dr (44130-1043)
PHONE..............................216 267-6850
Thomas Schumann, *Pr*
Meredith Schumann, *Corporate Secretary**
EMP: 30 **EST:** 1927
SALES (est): 4.98MM **Privately Held**
Web: www.kitzel.com
SIC: 3545 3291 Diamond cutting tools for turning, boring, burnishing, etc.; Abrasive wheels and grindstones, not artificial

(G-4277)
SCHWEIZER DIPPLE INC
7227 Division St (44146-5405)
PHONE..............................440 786-8090
Michael J Kelley, *Pr*
Lynn E Ulrich, *
Peter A Mcgrogan, *VP*
Roy Page, *
Dennis J Clark, *
EMP: 55 **EST:** 1932
SQ FT: 27,000
SALES (est): 21.1MM
SALES (corp-wide): 40.37MM **Privately Held**
Web: www.schweizer-dipple.com
SIC: 1711 3496 3444 3443 Mechanical contractor; Miscellaneous fabricated wire products; Sheet metalwork; Fabricated plate work (boiler shop)
PA: Kelley Steel Erectors, Inc.
7220 Division St
Cleveland OH 44146
440 232-1573

(G-4278)
SCOTT FETZER COMPANY
Adalet
4801 W 150th St (44135-3301)
PHONE..............................216 267-9000
Fred Lemke, *Brnch Mgr*
EMP: 150
SALES (corp-wide): 226 **Privately Held**
Web: www.scottfetzer.com
SIC: 5063 3469 3357 3613 Wire and cable; Metal stampings, nec; Nonferrous wiredrawing and insulating; Control panels, electric
PA: The Scott Fetzer Company
28800 Clemens Rd
Westlake OH 44145
440 892-3000

(G-4279)
SCOTT FETZER COMPANY
Cwp Technologies
3881 W 150th St (44111-5806)
PHONE..............................216 252-1190
Ryan Pereira, *Genl Mgr*
EMP: 45
SQ FT: 15,280
SALES (corp-wide): 226 **Privately Held**
Web: www.cwptechnologies.com
SIC: 3635 Household vacuum cleaners
PA: The Scott Fetzer Company
28800 Clemens Rd
Westlake OH 44145
440 892-3000

(G-4280)
SCOTTCARE CORPORATION (HQ)
Also Called: Scottcare Crdvscular Solutions
4791 W 150th St (44135-3301)
PHONE..............................216 362-0550
Deepak Malhotra, *Pr*
EMP: 30 **EST:** 1990
SALES (est): 2.6MM
SALES (corp-wide): 226 **Privately Held**

Web: www.scottcare.com
SIC: 3841 Surgical instruments and apparatus
PA: The Scott Fetzer Company
28800 Clemens Rd
Westlake OH 44145
440 892-3000

(G-4281)
SCOVIL HANNA LLC
Also Called: Arrowhead Industries
4545 Johnston Pkwy (44128-2954)
PHONE..............................216 581-1500
▲ **EMP:** 40 **EST:** 1974
SALES (est): 11.67MM
SALES (corp-wide): 2.67MM **Privately Held**
Web: www.bfc-profile.com
SIC: 3315 Wire and fabricated wire products
HQ: Bfcc U.S. Inc.
742 J A Cochran By Pass
Chester SC 29706

(G-4282)
SDG INC
10000 Cedar Ave (44106-2119)
P.O. Box 91023 (44101-3023)
PHONE..............................440 893-0771
W Blair Geho, *Pr*
Robert Geho, *VP*
Hans C Geho, *Sec*
EMP: 13 **EST:** 1981
SQ FT: 12,000
SALES (est): 369.37K **Privately Held**
Web: www.sdgpharma.com
SIC: 8733 2869 Noncommercial research organizations; Industrial organic chemicals, nec

(G-4283)
SDO SPORTS LTD
10250 Brecksville Rd (44141-3342)
PHONE..............................440 546-9998
Rick Greenberg, *Prin*
EMP: 7 **EST:** 1995
SQ FT: 3,000
SALES (est): 72.75K **Privately Held**
SIC: 2752 Commercial printing, lithographic

(G-4284)
SECURASTOCK LLC
11470 Euclid Ave (44106-3934)
PHONE..............................844 732-8727
Apryle Davis, *Ex Dir*
Bill Warren, *COO*
EMP: 24 **EST:** 2013
SALES (est): 4.23MM **Privately Held**
Web: www.securastock.com
SIC: 3581 Automatic vending machines

(G-4285)
SEEMRAY LLC
261 Alpha Park (44143-2225)
PHONE..............................440 536-8705
Bogdan Glushko, *CEO*
EMP: 23 **EST:** 2017
SALES (est): 309.43K **Privately Held**
Web: www.seemray.com
SIC: 2431 1751 5211 Windows and window parts and trim, wood; Window and door installation and erection; Door and window products

(G-4286)
SERVICE STATION EQUIPMENT CO (PA)
Also Called: Sseco Solutions
1294 E 55th St (44103-1029)
PHONE..............................216 431-6100
TOLL FREE: 800
David Chrien, *Pr*

Diana Chrien, *VP*
EMP: 9 **EST:** 1960
SQ FT: 45,000
SALES (est): 4.86MM
SALES (corp-wide): 4.86MM **Privately Held**
Web: www.ssecosolutions.com
SIC: 5087 3559 Carwash equipment and supplies; Petroleum refinery equipment

(G-4287)
SHALIX INC
10910 Briggs Rd (44111-5332)
PHONE.....................216 941-3546
David Schultheis, *Pr*
EMP: 10 **EST:** 1996
SALES (est): 446.77K **Privately Held**
SIC: 3544 Special dies and tools

(G-4288)
SHARP TOOL SERVICE INC
4735 W 150th St Unit H (44135-3352)
PHONE.....................330 273-4144
Richard Schirripa, *CEO*
Jeff Schirripa, *
Laura Schirripa, *
Rick Schirripa, *Stockholder*
Joe Schirripa, *Stockholder*
EMP: 25 **EST:** 1985
SQ FT: 22,000
SALES (est): 2.38MM **Privately Held**
Web: www.sharptool-service.com
SIC: 3545 Cutting tools for machine tools

(G-4289)
SHEAR SERVICE INC
Also Called: Shear Service, The
3175 E 81st St (44104-4386)
PHONE.....................216 341-2700
Kim Curtis, *Pr*
EMP: 8 **EST:** 1972
SALES (est): 495.64K **Privately Held**
SIC: 7389 3312 Metal slitting and shearing; Blast furnaces and steel mills

(G-4290)
SHEFFIELD BRONZE PAINT CORP
17814 S Waterloo Rd (44119-3295)
P.O. Box 19206 (44119-0206)
PHONE.....................216 481-8330
Mel Hart, *Pr*
EMP: 20 **EST:** 1925
SQ FT: 100,000
SALES (est): 2.44MM **Privately Held**
Web: www.sheffieldbronze.com
SIC: 2851 Paints and paint additives

(G-4291)
SHELLY COMPANY
4431 W 130th St (44135-3011)
PHONE.....................216 688-0684
Gary Eaton, *Brnch Mgr*
EMP: 6
SALES (corp-wide): 34.95B **Privately Held**
Web: www.shellyco.com
SIC: 1422 Crushed and broken limestone
HQ: Shelly Company
80 Park Dr
Thornville OH 43076
740 246-6315

(G-4292)
SHERIDAN WOODWORKS INC
17801 S Miles Rd (44128-4249)
PHONE.....................216 663-9333
Edward Sheridan, *Pr*
EMP: 8 **EST:** 1985
SQ FT: 16,000
SALES (est): 2.5MM **Privately Held**
Web: www.sheridanwoodworks.com

SIC: 2431 1751 Millwork; Cabinet building and installation

(G-4293)
SHERWIN-WILLIAMS COMPANY (PA)
Also Called: Sherwin-Williams
101 W Prospect Ave Ste 1020 (44115-1027)
PHONE.....................216 566-2000
Heidi G Petz, *Ch Bd*
Allen J Mistysyn, *Sr VP*
Mary L Garceau, *CLO*
J Paul Lang, *CAO*
Marlena K Boyce, *Sr VP*
EMP: 1200 **EST:** 1866
SALES (est): 23.1B
SALES (corp-wide): 23.1B **Publicly Held**
Web: www.sherwin-williams.com
SIC: 2851 5231 Paints and allied products; Paint and painting supplies

(G-4294)
SHERWIN-WILLIAMS MFG CO
101 W Prospect Ave Ste 1020 (44115-1027)
PHONE.....................216 566-2000
Allen J Mistysyn, *VP*
Mary L Garceau, *VP*
Jeffrey J Miklich, *Asst VP*
Stephen J Perisutti, *Asst VP*
Lawrence J Boron, *Asst VP*
EMP: 10 **EST:** 2017
SALES (est): 21.52MM
SALES (corp-wide): 23.1B **Publicly Held**
Web: www.sherwin-williams.com
SIC: 2851 5198 Paints and allied products; Paint or varnish thinner
PA: The Sherwin-Williams Company
101 W Prospect Ave
Cleveland OH 44115
216 566-2000

(G-4295)
SHERWN-WLLAMS AUTO FNSHES CORP (HQ)
4440 Warrensville Center Rd (44128-2837)
PHONE.....................216 332-8330
Christopher Connor, *CEO*
Thomas Havlitzel, *
◆ **EMP:** 30 **EST:** 1995
SALES (est): 10.39MM
SALES (corp-wide): 23.1B **Publicly Held**
Web: industrial.sherwin-williams.com
SIC: 5231 2851 Paint; Paints and allied products
PA: The Sherwin-Williams Company
101 W Prospect Ave
Cleveland OH 44115
216 566-2000

(G-4296)
SHERWOOD VALVE LLC
7900 Hub Pkwy (44125-5713)
PHONE.....................216 264-5023
Richard Gravagna, *Brnch Mgr*
EMP: 35
Web: www.sherwoodvalve.com
SIC: 3491 Industrial valves
HQ: Sherwood Valve Llc
100 Business Center Dr # 400
Pittsburgh PA 15205

(G-4297)
SHORELINE MACHINE PRODUCTS CO (PA)
19301 Saint Clair Ave (44117-1087)
PHONE.....................216 481-8033
Robert Arth, *Pr*
Larry Arth, *VP*
John J Ewers, *Prin*
Joseph Frank Tekavic, *Prin*

Richard Kaufman, *Prin*
EMP: 11 **EST:** 1967
SQ FT: 15,000
SALES (est): 952.24K
SALES (corp-wide): 952.24K **Privately Held**
Web: www.shorelineproducts.com
SIC: 3599 Machine shop, jobbing and repair

(G-4298)
SIFCO APPLIED SRFC CNCEPTS LLC (PA)
Also Called: Sifco ASC
5708 E Schaaf Rd (44131-1308)
PHONE.....................216 524-0099
Charles Allen, *Managing Member*
Norman Hay, *
EMP: 34 **EST:** 2012
SQ FT: 18,000
SALES (est): 10.03MM
SALES (corp-wide): 10.03MM **Privately Held**
Web: www.sifcoasc.com
SIC: 3471 Plating of metals or formed products

(G-4299)
SIFCO INDUSTRIES INC (PA)
Also Called: Sifco
970 E 64th St (44103-1694)
PHONE.....................216 881-8600
George Scherff, *CEO*
Alayne L Reitman, *Ch Bd*
Jennifer Wilson Skuhrovec, *CFO*
◆ **EMP:** 78 **EST:** 1916
SQ FT: 280,000
SALES (est): 79.63MM
SALES (corp-wide): 79.63MM **Publicly Held**
Web: www.sifco.com
SIC: 3724 3462 3471 Aircraft engines and engine parts; Aircraft forgings, ferrous; Anodizing (plating) of metals or formed products

(G-4300)
SIGMA-ALDRICH CORPORATION
Research Organics
4353 E 49th St (44125-1003)
P.O. Box 14508 (63178-4508)
PHONE.....................216 206-5424
EMP: 67
SALES (corp-wide): 22.37B **Privately Held**
Web: www.sigmaaldrich.com
SIC: 2899 5169 Chemical preparations, nec; Chemicals and allied products, nec
HQ: Sigma-Aldrich Corporation
3050 Spruce St
Saint Louis MO 63103
314 771-5765

(G-4301)
SIGNATURE SIGN CO INC
1776 E 43rd St (44103-2314)
PHONE.....................216 426-1234
Bruce Farkas, *Pr*
EMP: 6 **EST:** 1987
SQ FT: 10,000
SALES (est): 462.1K **Privately Held**
Web: www.signaturesigncompany.com
SIC: 1799 2499 Sign installation and maintenance; Signboards, wood

(G-4302)
SINGLETON CORPORATION
3280 W 67th Pl (44102-5241)
PHONE.....................216 651-7800
Raymund Singleton, *Pr*
Eric Singleton, *VP*
Carol Singleton, *Sec*
Laura Singleton, *Treas*

▼ **EMP:** 17 **EST:** 1947
SQ FT: 30,000
SALES (est): 4.67MM **Privately Held**
Web: www.singletoncorp.com
SIC: 3559 5169 Anodizing equipment; Anti-corrosion products

(G-4303)
SKF USA INC
Also Called: SKF Machine Tool Services
670 Alpha Dr (44143-2123)
PHONE.....................800 589-5563
David Rodgers, *Brnch Mgr*
EMP: 29
SQ FT: 4,000
SALES (corp-wide): 740.17MM **Privately Held**
Web: www.skf.com
SIC: 3053 Gaskets; packing and sealing devices
HQ: Skf Usa Inc.
801 Lakeview Dr Ste 120
Blue Bell PA 19422
267 436-6000

(G-4304)
SKYBRYTE COMPANY INC
3125 Perkins Ave (44114-4627)
PHONE.....................216 771-1590
Cecil Stanley, *Pr*
Terry Wise, *VP*
EMP: 7 **EST:** 1915
SQ FT: 7,500
SALES (est): 907.67K **Privately Held**
Web: www.skybryte.com
SIC: 2842 Rust removers

(G-4305)
SMART BUSINESS NETWORK INC (PA)
Also Called: Smart Business Magazine
835 Sharon Dr Ste 200 (44145-7703)
PHONE.....................440 250-7000
Fred Koury, *CEO*
EMP: 25 **EST:** 1988
SQ FT: 10,000
SALES (est): 9.06MM **Privately Held**
Web: www.sbnonline.com
SIC: 2711 Newspapers: publishing only, not printed on site

(G-4306)
SMART SONIC CORPORATION
Also Called: Smart Snic Stencil Clg Systems
837 E 79th St (44103-1807)
PHONE.....................818 610-7900
William C Schreiber, *Pr*
EMP: 8 **EST:** 1993
SQ FT: 4,400
SALES (est): 2.73MM **Privately Held**
Web: www.smartsonic.com
SIC: 3699 2842 3589 Cleaning equipment, ultrasonic, except medical and dental; Polishes and sanitation goods; Sewage and water treatment equipment

(G-4307)
SMARTSODA HOLDINGS INC (PA)
6095 Parkland Blvd (44124-6139)
PHONE.....................888 998-9668
Lior Shafir, *CEO*
Julia Solooki, *Ch*
Solomon Sol Mayer, *Ofcr*
EMP: 7 **EST:** 2019
SALES (est): 8.57MM
SALES (corp-wide): 8.57MM **Privately Held**
Web: www.smartsoda.com
SIC: 2099 5963 Syrups; Beverage services, direct sales

(G-4308)

SNAP RITE MANUFACTURING INC
14300 Darley Ave (44110-2172)
PHONE..............................910 897-4080
Bill Gray, *Brnch Mgr*
EMP: 35
SALES (corp-wide): 5.21MM **Privately Held**
Web: www.snaprite.com
SIC: 3585 Air conditioning equipment, complete
PA: Snap Rite Manufacturing, Inc.
232 N Ida St
Coats NC 27521
910 897-4080

(G-4309)

SNOW DRAGON LLC
1441 Chardon Rd (44117-1510)
PHONE..............................440 295-0238
John Allin, *Managing Member*
EMP: 12 **EST:** 2005
SALES (est): 3.39MM
SALES (corp-wide): 1.66B **Publicly Held**
Web: www.snowdragonmelters.com
SIC: 3531 Snow plow attachments
HQ: Park-Ohio Industries, Inc.
6065 Parkland Blvd
Cleveland OH 44124
440 947-2000

(G-4310)

SNYDER INTL BREWING GROUP LLC (PA)
Also Called: Sibg
1940 E 6th St Ste 200 (44114-2202)
PHONE..............................216 619-7424
Dave Snyder, *Pt*
Christopher Livingston, *
EMP: 25 **EST:** 1998
SALES (est): 2.51MM
SALES (corp-wide): 2.51MM **Privately Held**
SIC: 2082 Beer (alcoholic beverage)

(G-4311)

SOBEL CORRUGATED CONTAINERS INC
Also Called: Miles Folding Box Co Div
1111 Superior Ave E Ste 1111 (44114-2522)
PHONE..............................216 475-2100
EMP: 200
Web: www.sobelcorr.com
SIC: 2653 Boxes, corrugated: made from purchased materials

(G-4312)

SOLARFLO CORPORATION
22901 Aurora Rd (44146-1701)
PHONE..............................440 439-1680
W H Thompson, *Ch Bd*
John P Streisel, *Pr*
EMP: 17 **EST:** 1918
SQ FT: 35,000
SALES (est): 1.04MM **Privately Held**
Web: www.solarflo.com
SIC: 3433 Gas burners, domestic

(G-4313)

SOLON GLASS CENTER INC
Also Called: Solon Glass Ctr
33001 Station St (44139-2935)
PHONE..............................440 248-5018
Roy Kucia, *Pr*
EMP: 10 **EST:** 1962
SALES (est): 996.65K **Privately Held**
Web: www.solonglass.com
SIC: 1793 3231 Glass and glazing work; Products of purchased glass

(G-4314)

SONOGAGE INC
26650 Renaissance Pkwy Ste 3 (44128-5776)
PHONE..............................216 464-1119
Alex Dybbs, *Pr*
EMP: 10 **EST:** 1985
SALES (est): 481.08K **Privately Held**
Web: www.sonogage.com
SIC: 3841 Diagnostic apparatus, medical

(G-4315)

SOUNDWICH INC
17000 Saint Clair Ave (44110-2535)
PHONE..............................216 249-4900
EMP: 20
SALES (corp-wide): 24.66MM **Privately Held**
Web: www.soundwich.com
SIC: 3714 Motor vehicle engines and parts
PA: Soundwich, Inc.
881 Wayside Rd
Cleveland OH 44110
216 486-2666

(G-4316)

SOUNDWICH INC (PA)
881 Wayside Rd (44110-2961)
PHONE..............................216 486-2666
Perry Peck, *CEO*
Kevin Cleary, *
Steve Tomoba, *
Jeff Kristofeld, *
J Patrick Morris, *
EMP: 80 **EST:** 1988
SQ FT: 46,974
SALES (est): 24.66MM
SALES (corp-wide): 24.66MM **Privately Held**
Web: www.soundwich.com
SIC: 3714 Motor vehicle engines and parts

(G-4317)

SOUTH SHORE FINISHERS INC
1720 Willey Ave (44113-4367)
PHONE..............................216 664-1792
Fran Dickson, *Pr*
Dom Dickson, *VP*
EMP: 6 **EST:** 1983
SQ FT: 25,000
SALES (est): 113.48K **Privately Held**
Web: www.southshorefinishers.com
SIC: 3471 Plating of metals or formed products

(G-4318)

SP MOUNT PRINTING COMPANY
1306 E 55th St (44103-1302)
PHONE..............................216 881-3316
Scott C Mc Gill, *Pr*
Gerald Mc Gill Senior, *Treas*
Gerald Mcgill Junior, *VP*
EMP: 21 **EST:** 1867
SQ FT: 45,000
SALES (est): 1.9MM **Privately Held**
Web: www.spmount.com
SIC: 2752 Offset printing

(G-4319)

SPECIALTY HARDWARE INC
2200 Kerwin Rd Apt 710 (44118-3954)
PHONE..............................216 291-1160
Lisa Hayzlett, *Pr*
James Hayzlett, *VP*
◆ **EMP:** 8 **EST:** 1996
SALES (est): 344.75K **Privately Held**
SIC: 3429 3999 5072 Luggage hardware; Handles, handbag and luggage; Hardware

(G-4320)

SPRINGCO METAL COATINGS INC
12500 Elmwood Ave (44111-5910)
PHONE..............................216 941-0020
Paul W Springer, *Pr*
David Starn, *VP*
Jason Conn, *VP*
EMP: 250 **EST:** 1977
SQ FT: 140,000
SALES (est): 11.81MM **Privately Held**
Web: www.springcometalcoating.com
SIC: 3479 3471 Painting of metal products; Plating and polishing

(G-4321)

SRC & COMPANY
3214 Prospect Ave E (44115-2614)
PHONE..............................216 417-7477
EMP: 10 **EST:** 2018
SALES (est): 206.5K **Privately Held**
Web: www.astrategicmove.com
SIC: 2752 Commercial printing, lithographic

(G-4322)

SRC WORLDWIDE INC (HQ)
3425 Service Rd (44111-2421)
PHONE..............................216 941-6115
Marc Pignataro, *CEO*
Cary Nordan, *Pr*
Brian Kucia, *CFO*
Jonathan Ward, *Sec*
▲ **EMP:** 15 **EST:** 2014
SQ FT: 70,000
SALES (est): 8.25MM **Publicly Held**
Web: www.src-worldwide.com
SIC: 2899 Fluxes: brazing, soldering, galvanizing, and welding
PA: Barings Bdc, Inc.
300 S Tryon St Ste 2500
Charlotte NC 28202

(G-4323)

STAHL GEAR & MACHINE CO
3901 Hamilton Ave (44114-3831)
PHONE..............................216 431-2820
Herman Bronstein, *Pr*
Joel Bronstein, *
Mike Kramer, *
EMP: 8 **EST:** 1917
SQ FT: 40,000
SALES (est): 1.03MM **Privately Held**
Web: www.stahlgear.com
SIC: 3566 3561 3462 Gears, power transmission, except auto; Pumps and pumping equipment; Iron and steel forgings

(G-4324)

STAINLESS AUTOMATION
1978 W 74th St (44102-2987)
PHONE..............................216 961-4550
Lois Martin, *Owner*
EMP: 7 **EST:** 1984
SQ FT: 3,000
SALES (est): 493.45K **Privately Held**
Web: www.stainlessautomation.com
SIC: 3549 3559 Metalworking machinery, nec ; Vibratory parts handling equipment

(G-4325)

STAMCO INDUSTRIES INC
26650 Lakeland Blvd (44132-2644)
PHONE..............................216 731-9333
William Sopko, *Pr*
◆ **EMP:** 38 **EST:** 1983
SQ FT: 130,000
SALES (est): 9.98MM **Privately Held**
Web: www.stamcoind.com
SIC: 3465 Automotive stampings

(G-4326)

STANDARD MACHINE INC
1952 W 93rd St (44102-2790)
PHONE..............................216 631-4440
Jim Dopoulos, *Pr*
Eli Manos, *
Linda S Kratky, *
Marion R Herrington, *
EMP: 32 **EST:** 1969
SQ FT: 31,000
SALES (est): 4.16MM **Privately Held**
Web: www.standardmachineinc.com
SIC: 3599 Machine shop, jobbing and repair

(G-4327)

STANLEY INDUSTRIES INC
19120 Cranwood Pkwy (44128-4088)
PHONE..............................216 475-4000
Jay Cusick, *Pr*
▼ **EMP:** 11 **EST:** 1946
SQ FT: 20,000
SALES (est): 1.05MM **Privately Held**
Web: www.stanley-industries.com
SIC: 3599 5084 Machine shop, jobbing and repair; Metal refining machinery and equipment

(G-4328)

STAR CALENDAR & PRINTING INC
4354 Pearl Rd (44109-4269)
PHONE..............................216 741-3223
Robert Cortelezzi, *Pr*
EMP: 6 **EST:** 1946
SQ FT: 4,000
SALES (est): 530.55K **Privately Held**
Web: www.starcalendarprinting.com
SIC: 2752 5199 2759 Offset printing; Advertising specialties; Letterpress printing

(G-4329)

STATE INDUSTRIAL PRODUCTS CORP (PA)
Also Called: State Chemical Manufacturing
5915 Landerbrook Dr Ste 300 (44124-4034)
PHONE..............................877 747-6986
Harold Uhrman, *Pr*
Robert M San Julian, *
William Barnett, *
Brian Limbert, *
Dan Prugar, *
◆ **EMP:** 300 **EST:** 1911
SQ FT: 240,000
SALES (est): 86.95MM
SALES (corp-wide): 86.95MM **Privately Held**
Web: www.stateindustrial.com
SIC: 2841 5072 2842 2992 Soap: granulated, liquid, cake, flaked, or chip; Bolts, nuts, and screws; Polishes and sanitation goods; Lubricating oils and greases

(G-4330)

STEELTEC PRODUCTS LLC
13000 Saint Clair Ave (44108-2033)
PHONE..............................216 681-1114
John Bargar, *Managing Member*
EMP: 10 **EST:** 2002
SQ FT: 100,000
SALES (est): 2.15MM **Privately Held**
Web: www.steeltecproducts.com
SIC: 3441 Fabricated structural metal

(G-4331)

STEIN LLC
2032 Campbell Rd (44105-1059)
P.O. Box 470548 (44147-0548)
PHONE..............................216 883-7444
Dave Bilek, *Brnch Mgr*
EMP: 75

▲ = Import ▼ = Export
◆ = Import/Export

Web: www.steininc.com
SIC: 3399 3549 Iron ore recovery from open hearth slag; Metalworking machinery, nec
HQ: Stein, Llc
3 Summit Park Dr Ste 425
Independence OH 44131
440 526-9301

(G-4332)
STIBER FABRICATING INC
Also Called: Mailposts By Mike
1678 Leonard St (44113-2436)
P.O. Box 347175 (44134-7175)
PHONE..................................216 771-7210
Michael Stiber, *Pr*
Genmarie Stiber, *VP*
EMP: 13 EST: 1987
SQ FT: 10,000
SALES (est): 643.04K Privately Held
SIC: 2542 5211 Counters or counter display cases, except wood; Lumber and other building materials

(G-4333)
STRETCHTAPE INC
3100 Hamilton Ave (44114-3701)
PHONE..................................216 486-9400
Alex F Mc Donald, *CEO*
Harry Mc Donald, *
Vonna Mc Donald, *
▲ EMP: 40 EST: 1984
SQ FT: 55,000
SALES (est): 21.18MM
SALES (corp-wide): 23.65MM **Privately Held**
Web: www.stretchtape.com
SIC: 2672 2671 3861 Adhesive papers, labels, or tapes: from purchased material; Paper; coated and laminated packaging; Sensitized film, cloth, and paper
PA: Adherex Group
3100 Hamilton Ave
Cleveland OH

(G-4334)
STRICKER REFINISHING INC
2060 Hamilton Ave (44114-1115)
PHONE..................................216 696-2906
Tom Stricker, *Pr*
Greg Stricker, *Sec*
EMP: 7 EST: 1984
SQ FT: 4,000
SALES (est): 920.23K Privately Held
Web: www.srcplating.com
SIC: 3471 Electroplating of metals or formed products

(G-4335)
STRICTLY STITCHERY INC
Also Called: In Sttches Ctr For Ltrgcal Art
13801 Shaker Blvd Apt 4a (44120-5628)
PHONE..................................440 543-7128
Brenda Grauer, *Pr*
EMP: 10 EST: 1984
SQ FT: 800
SALES (est): 409.47K Privately Held
SIC: 3269 5999 Art and ornamental ware, pottery; Religious goods

(G-4336)
STRIPMATIC PRODUCTS INC
5301 Grant Ave Ste 200 (44125-1053)
PHONE..................................216 241-7143
William J Adler Junior, *Pr*
Elizabeth R Adler, *
▲ EMP: 29 EST: 1946
SQ FT: 42,000
SALES (est): 4.12MM Privately Held
Web: www.stripmatic.com

SIC: 3469 3465 3568 3498 Stamping metal for the trade; Automotive stampings; Power transmission equipment, nec; Fabricated pipe and fittings

(G-4337)
STRONG BINDERY INC
13015 Larchmere Blvd (44120-1147)
PHONE..................................216 231-0001
Ellen Strong, *Pr*
EMP: 9 EST: 1985
SALES (est): 175.2K Privately Held
Web: www.strongbindery.com
SIC: 2789 Binding only: books, pamphlets, magazines, etc.

(G-4338)
STUART-DEAN CO INC
2615 Saint Clair Ave Ne (44114-4014)
PHONE..................................412 765-2752
Aaron Wolk, *Mgr*
EMP: 8
SALES (corp-wide): 65.45MM **Privately Held**
Web: www.stuartdean.com
SIC: 1799 1743 3471 Ornamental metal work ; Terrazzo, tile, marble and mosaic work; Plating and polishing
PA: Stuart-Dean Co. Inc.
43-50 10th St
Long Island City NY 11101
800 322-3180

(G-4339)
STUDGIONSGROUP LLC
10413 Way Ave (44105-2766)
PHONE..................................216 804-1561
EMP: 20 EST: 2020
SALES (est): 367.75K Privately Held
SIC: 2051 5999 Bakery: wholesale or wholesale/retail combined; Cosmetics

(G-4340)
SUBURBAN PRESS INCORPORATED
3818 Lorain Ave (44113-3785)
PHONE..................................216 961-0766
William C Mueller, *Pr*
Paul R Mueller, *VP*
Ellen Mueller, *Sec*
Richard M Mueller, *VP*
EMP: 16 EST: 1955
SALES (est): 2.7MM Privately Held
Web: www.suburbanpressinc.com
SIC: 2752 2791 2789 2759 Offset printing; Typesetting; Bookbinding and related work; Commercial printing, nec

(G-4341)
SUMMERS ACQUISITION CORP (DH)
Also Called: Summers Rubber Company
12555 Berea Rd (44111-1619)
PHONE..................................216 941-7700
Mike Summers, *Pr*
William M Summers, *
Gene Mayo, *
Gwendolyn M Summers, *
Eugene Mayo, *
▲ EMP: 26 EST: 1949
SQ FT: 63,000
SALES (est): 17.4MM
SALES (corp-wide): 4.71B Privately Held
Web: www.summersrubber.com
SIC: 5085 3429 Rubber goods, mechanical; Hardware, nec
HQ: Hampton Rubber Company
1669 W Pembroke Ave
Hampton VA 23661
757 722-9818

(G-4342)
SUN POLISHING CORP
13800 Progress Pkwy Ste E (44133-4354)
PHONE..................................440 237-5525
Frank Schumacher, *Pr*
EMP: 8 EST: 1978
SQ FT: 3,160
SALES (est): 416.54K Privately Held
Web: www.sunpolishcorp.com
SIC: 3471 Polishing, metals or formed products

(G-4343)
SUPERIOR FLUX & MFG CO
6615 Parkland Blvd (44139-4345)
PHONE..................................440 349-3000
Yehuda Baskin, *Pr*
Barbara Baskin, *VP Opers*
John Dunn, *Sec*
◆ EMP: 13 EST: 1932
SQ FT: 16,500
SALES (est): 5.89MM Privately Held
Web: www.superiorflux.com
SIC: 2899 Fluxes: brazing, soldering, galvanizing, and welding

(G-4344)
SUPERIOR HOLDING LLC (DH)
3786 Ridge Rd (44144-1127)
PHONE..................................216 651-9400
Thomas Farrel, *Pr*
EMP: 7 EST: 2009
SALES (est): 12MM
SALES (corp-wide): 7.75B **Publicly Held**
Web: www.superiorprod.com
SIC: 3494 5085 3492 Valves and pipe fittings, nec; Industrial supplies; Fluid power valves and hose fittings
HQ: Engineered Controls International, Llc
100 Rego Dr
Elon NC 27244

(G-4345)
SUPERIOR PRECISION PDTS INC
968 E 69th Pl (44103-1760)
PHONE..................................216 881-3696
Zeljko Tokic, *Pr*
EMP: 6 EST: 1976
SQ FT: 16,000
SALES (est): 500.64K Privately Held
SIC: 3599 Machine shop, jobbing and repair

(G-4346)
SUPERIOR PRINTING INK CO INC
7655 Hub Pkwy Ste 205 (44125-5739)
PHONE..................................216 328-1720
Scott Allen, *Mgr*
EMP: 7
SALES (corp-wide): 23.66MM **Privately Held**
Web: www.superiorink.com
SIC: 2851 2893 Varnishes, nec; Gravure ink
PA: Superior Printing Ink Co Inc
10 York Ave
West Caldwell NJ 07006
201 478-5600

(G-4347)
SUPERIOR PRODUCTS LLC
3786 Ridge Rd (44144-1127)
PHONE..................................216 651-9400
Donald L Mottinger, *Pr*
Tim Giesse, *
Tim Austin, *
Gregory K Gens, *
EMP: 65 EST: 2009
SQ FT: 75,000
SALES (est): 12MM
SALES (corp-wide): 7.75B **Publicly Held**
Web: www.superiorprod.com

SIC: 3494 5085 3492 Valves and pipe fittings, nec; Industrial fittings; Fluid power valves and hose fittings
HQ: Superior Holding, Llc
3786 Ridge Rd
Cleveland OH 44144
216 651-9400

(G-4348)
SUPERIOR TOOL CORPORATION
Also Called: Superior Tool Company
100 Hayes Dr Ste C (44131-1057)
PHONE..................................216 398-8600
◆ EMP: 50
Web: www.superiortool.com
SIC: 3423 Plumbers' hand tools

(G-4349)
SUPERIOR WELD AND FABG CO INC
15002 Woodworth Rd (44110-3310)
PHONE..................................216 249-5122
Howard Holmes, *Pr*
Joanne Holmes, *Mgr*
EMP: 6 EST: 1994
SQ FT: 7,000
SALES (est): 774.06K Privately Held
Web: www.superiorweldfab.com
SIC: 3442 7692 Metal doors, sash, and trim; Welding repair

(G-4350)
SUPERTRAPP INDUSTRIES INC
Also Called: Supertrapp
4540 W 160th St (44135-2628)
PHONE..................................216 265-8400
Kevin Berger, *Pr*
Theodore Berger, *
Whitney Slaght Iii, *Sec*
James M Smith, *
▲ EMP: 83 EST: 1988
SQ FT: 210,000
SALES (est): 11.47MM
SALES (corp-wide): 43.22MM **Privately Held**
Web: www.supertrapp.com
SIC: 3714 Mufflers (exhaust), motor vehicle
PA: Dreison International, Inc.
4540 W 160th St
Cleveland OH 44135
216 362-0755

(G-4351)
SUPPLY TECHNOLOGIES LLC (HQ)
Also Called: I L S
6065 Parkland Blvd Ste 1 (44124-6145)
P.O. Box 248199 (44124)
PHONE..................................440 947-2100
Brian Norris, *Managing Member*
◆ EMP: 150 EST: 1998
SQ FT: 7,000
SALES (est): 7.4MM
SALES (corp-wide): 1.66B **Publicly Held**
Web: supplytechnologies.com
SIC: 5085 3452 3469 Fasteners, industrial: nuts, bolts, screws, etc.; Bolts, nuts, rivets, and washers; Stamping metal for the trade
PA: Park-Ohio Holdings Corp.
6065 Parkland Blvd
Cleveland OH 44124
440 947-2000

(G-4352)
SURE-FOOT INDUSTRIES CORP
Also Called: Skid Guard
20260 1st Ave (44130-2430)
P.O. Box 707 (44017-0707)
PHONE..................................440 234-4446
Clarence Haas, *Pr*
Raymond Buckley, *
Shirley Haas, *
▲ EMP: 32 EST: 1979

SQ FT: 65,000
SALES (est): 5.66MM **Privately Held**
Web: www.surefootcorp.com
SIC: 3291 Abrasive products

(G-4353)
SWAGELOK COMPANY
358 Bishop Rd (44143-1446)
PHONE..............................440 461-7714
Robin Lavigne, *Mgr*
EMP: 52
SALES (corp-wide): 881.02MM **Privately Held**
Web: www.aldvalve.com
SIC: 3599 Machine shop, jobbing and repair
PA: Swagelok Company
    29500 Solon Rd
    Solon OH 44139
    440 248-4600

(G-4354)
SWAGELOK COMPANY
318 Bishop Rd (44143-1446)
PHONE..............................440 473-1050
William Cosgrove, *Mgr*
EMP: 56
SALES (corp-wide): 881.02MM **Privately Held**
Web: www.aldvalve.com
SIC: 3494 Pipe fittings
PA: Swagelok Company
    29500 Solon Rd
    Solon OH 44139
    440 248-4600

(G-4355)
SWAGELOK COMPANY
Also Called: Flight Operations
328 Bishop Rd (44143-1446)
PHONE..............................440 442-6611
Bob Parmelee, *Mgr*
EMP: 10
SALES (corp-wide): 881.02MM **Privately Held**
Web: www.aldvalve.com
SIC: 4581 3494 Hangar operation; Valves and pipe fittings, nec
PA: Swagelok Company
    29500 Solon Rd
    Solon OH 44139
    440 248-4600

(G-4356)
SWIGER COIL SYSTEMS LTD
4677 Manufacturing Ave (44135-2673)
PHONE..............................216 362-7500
Michael Aladjem, *Managing Member*
▲ EMP: 190 EST: 2010
SALES (est): 22.53MM **Privately Held**
Web: www.swigercoil.com
SIC: 3621 3677 Electric motor and generator parts; Electronic coils and transformers

(G-4357)
SWIMMER PRINTING INC
Also Called: AlphaGraphics
1215 Superior Ave E Ste 110 (44114-3249)
PHONE..............................216 623-1005
Judith Swimmer, *Pr*
Brad Swimmer, *VP*
EMP: 8 EST: 1990
SALES (est): 965.54K **Privately Held**
Web: www.alphagraphics.com
SIC: 2752 Offset printing

(G-4358)
SWITCHBACK GROUP INC (HQ)
Also Called: Mpac Switchback
5638 Transportation Blvd (44125-5363)
PHONE..............................216 290-6040
David Shepherd, *Pr*

EMP: 25 EST: 2004
SALES (est): 22.1MM
SALES (corp-wide): 142.34MM **Privately Held**
Web: www.switchbackgroup.com
SIC: 3565 Packaging machinery
PA: Mpac Group Plc
    Station Estate
    Tadcaster LS24
    247 642-1100

(G-4359)
SYSTEM SEALS LLC (HQ)
9505 Midwest Ave (44125-2421)
PHONE..............................440 735-0200
Arnold V Engelbrechten, *Pr*
▲ EMP: 22 EST: 1995
SQ FT: 10,000
SALES (est): 23.96MM
SALES (corp-wide): 779.39K **Privately Held**
Web: www.systemseals.com
SIC: 3953 5084 Embossing seals and hand stamps; Hydraulic systems equipment and supplies
PA: System Seals Europe Ltd
    Carlton House
    Rushden NORTHANTS NN10
    132 783-0954

(G-4360)
T & B FOUNDRY COMPANY
2469 E 71st St (44104-1967)
PHONE..............................216 391-4200
Edward Pruc, *Pr*
Ted Pruc, *
EMP: 8 EST: 1992
SQ FT: 275,000
SALES (est): 799.55K **Privately Held**
SIC: 3321 3369 3322 Gray iron castings, nec; Nonferrous foundries, nec; Malleable iron foundries

(G-4361)
T A BACON CO
Also Called: Tabco
235 E 131st St (44108-1605)
P.O. Box 21150 (44121-0150)
PHONE..............................216 595-1310
Timothy Bacon, *Pr*
▲ EMP: 7 EST: 1975
SQ FT: 45,000
SALES (est): 2.45MM **Privately Held**
Web: www.tabcoparts.com
SIC: 3465 5013 Automotive stampings; Automotive stampings

(G-4362)
T D DYNAMICS INC
Also Called: Morgan Litho
4101 Commerce Ave (44103-3507)
PHONE..............................216 881-0800
Dale Fellows, *Pr*
Thomas M Baginski, *VP*
EMP: 10 EST: 1961
SQ FT: 19,800
SALES (est): 388.35K **Privately Held**
Web: www.morganlitho.com
SIC: 2752 Offset printing

(G-4363)
TALAN PRODUCTS INC
18800 Cochran Ave (44110-2700)
PHONE..............................216 458-0170
Steve Peplin, *CEO*
Peter Accorti, *
Adam Snyder, *
▲ EMP: 60 EST: 1986
SQ FT: 100,000
SALES (est): 1.38MM **Privately Held**
Web: www.talanproducts.com

SIC: 3469 Stamping metal for the trade

(G-4364)
TATHAM SCHULZ INCORPORATED
Also Called: Cleveland Black Oxide
11400 Brookpark Rd (44130-1131)
PHONE..............................216 861-4431
David Tatham, *Pr*
Ken Schulz, *
Richard Tatham, *
EMP: 35 EST: 1981
SALES (est): 2.32MM **Privately Held**
Web: tatham.openfos.com
SIC: 3471 Electroplating of metals or formed products

(G-4365)
TBC RETAIL GROUP INC
Also Called: Ntb
5370 W 130th St (44142-1801)
PHONE..............................216 267-8040
Jim Zeuli, *Mgr*
EMP: 30
SALES (corp-wide): 2.41B **Privately Held**
Web: jobs.tbccorp.com
SIC: 7534 5531 Tire retreading and repair shops; Automotive tires
HQ: Tbc Retail Group, Inc.
    4280 Prof Ctr Dr Ste 400
    Palm Beach Gardens FL 33410
    561 383-3000

(G-4366)
TEAM PLASTICS INC
3901 W 150th St (44111-5810)
PHONE..............................216 251-8270
Ed Busch, *Pr*
Robert Timko, *VP*
William Madar, *Treas*
EMP: 10 EST: 1994
SQ FT: 14,000
SALES (est): 2.21MM **Privately Held**
Web: teamplasticscom.homestead.com
SIC: 3089 Injection molding of plastics

(G-4367)
TEAM WENDY LLC
17000 Saint Clair Ave Bldg 1 (44110-2535)
PHONE..............................216 738-2518
Dan T Moore Iii, *Ch*
Thomas J Prodouz, *Pr*
▲ EMP: 60 EST: 1997
SQ FT: 60,000
SALES (est): 10.38MM **Privately Held**
Web: www.teamwendy.com
SIC: 3086 Padding, foamed plastics

(G-4368)
TECH INDUSTRIES INC
1313 Washington Ave (44113-2332)
PHONE..............................216 861-7337
Bruno Aldons, *Pr*
James Weiskittel, *VP*
Arnold Lowe, *VP*
EMP: 10 EST: 1953
SQ FT: 10,000
SALES (est): 1.29MM **Privately Held**
Web: www.tech-ind.com
SIC: 3544 Special dies and tools

(G-4369)
TECH READY MIX INC
5000 Crayton Ave (44104-2826)
P.O. Box 5270 (44101-0270)
PHONE..............................216 361-5000
Janice Knight, *Prin*
Mark F Perkins, *
EMP: 45 EST: 2008
SALES (est): 5.79MM **Privately Held**
Web: www.techreadymix.com

SIC: 3273 Ready-mixed concrete

(G-4370)
TECHNICAL MACHINE PRODUCTS INC
5500 Walworth Ave (44102-4431)
P.O. Box 920 (45356-0920)
▲ EMP: 10 EST: 1978
SALES (est): 2.79MM
SALES (corp-wide): 20.79MM **Privately Held**
Web: www.frenchoil.com
SIC: 3559 3542 Rubber working machinery, including tires; Pressing machines
PA: The French Oil Mill Machinery Company
    1035 W Greene St
    Piqua OH 45356
    937 773-3420

(G-4371)
TECHNLOGY INSTALL PARTNERS LLC
Also Called: Security Designs
13701 Enterprise Ave (44135-5113)
PHONE..............................888 586-7040
Erica Temple, *Pr*
Ryan Temple, *
EMP: 40 EST: 2014
SALES (est): 4.67MM **Privately Held**
Web: www.technologyinstallpartners.com
SIC: 3699 Security control equipment and systems

(G-4372)
TEMPCRAFT CORPORATION
3960 S Marginal Rd (44114-3835)
PHONE..............................216 391-3885
John Plant, *Ch Bd*
EMP: 70 EST: 1960
SQ FT: 100,000
SALES (est): 2.77MM
SALES (corp-wide): 7.43B **Publicly Held**
SIC: 3544 3543 Industrial molds; Industrial patterns
HQ: Howmet Corporation
    3850 White Lake Dr
    Whitehall MI 49461
    231 894-5686

(G-4373)
TEMPEST INC
12750 Berea Rd (44111-1622)
PHONE..............................216 883-6500
Charles Ruebensaal, *Pr*
◆ EMP: 25 EST: 2000
SQ FT: 65,000
SALES (est): 2.07MM **Privately Held**
Web: www.tempest-eng.com
SIC: 3585 Refrigeration and heating equipment
PA: Great Lakes Management, Inc.
    2700 E 40th St Ste 1
    Cleveland OH 44115

(G-4374)
TENDON MANUFACTURING INC
20805 Aurora Rd (44146-1005)
PHONE..............................216 663-3200
Gregory F Tench, *Pr*
Michael J Gordon, *
EMP: 46 EST: 1988
SQ FT: 36,000
SALES (est): 5.25MM **Privately Held**
Web: www.tendon.com
SIC: 3599 3479 1761 7692 Machine shop, jobbing and repair; Painting of metal products; Sheet metal work, nec; Welding repair

(G-4375)
TERNION INC (PA)
Also Called: Skyline Trisource Exhibits
12400 Plaza Dr (44130-1057)
PHONE..............................216 642-6180
Kristie Damalas, *Pr*
Wendy Ressing-seitz, *Pr*
Kristie Jones-damalas, *Sec*
◆ **EMP:** 23 **EST:** 1989
SQ FT: 23,000
SALES (est): 4.35MM
SALES (corp-wide): 4.35MM **Privately
Held**
SIC: 5046 3993 2542 Display equipment,
except refrigerated; Signs and advertising
specialties; Partitions and fixtures, except
wood

(G-4376)
THA PRESIDENTIAL SUITE LLC
3863 E 112th St (44105-4258)
PHONE..............................216 338-7287
Lionel Langford, *Pr*
EMP: 7 **EST:** 2019
SALES (est): 144.68K **Privately Held**
SIC: 5999 2253 8742 Miscellaneous retail
stores, nec; Lounge, bed, and leisurewear;
Business management consultant

(G-4377)
**THE APEX PAPER BOX COMPANY
(PA)**
Also Called: Sweet Packaing
5601 Walworth Ave (44102-4432)
PHONE..............................216 631-4000
▼ **EMP:** 9 **EST:** 1932
SALES (est): 23.79MM
SALES (corp-wide): 23.79MM **Privately
Held**
Web: www.boxit.com
SIC: 2652 2657 Setup paperboard boxes;
Folding paperboard boxes

(G-4378)
**THE BASIC ALUMINUM CASTINGS
CO**
1325 E 168th St (44110-2522)
PHONE..............................216 481-5606
EMP: 85 **EST:** 1946
SALES (est): 4.23MM **Privately Held**
Web: www.basicaluminum.com
SIC: 3363 3542 Aluminum die-castings; Die
casting machines

(G-4379)
THE BLONDER COMPANY
Also Called: Blonder Home Accents
3950 Prospect Ave E (44115-2710)
PHONE..............................216 431-3560
◆ **EMP:** 245
Web: www.blonderhome.com
SIC: 5198 2679 5719 Wallcoverings;
Wallpaper: made from purchased paper;
Housewares, nec

(G-4380)
THE CLEVELAND-CLIFFS IRON CO
1100 Superior Ave E Ste 1500
(44114-2530)
PHONE..............................216 694-5700
J A Carrabba, *CEO*
D S Gallagher, *
W R Calfee, *
Laurie Brlas, *
EMP: 176 **EST:** 1847
SQ FT: 40,000
SALES (est): 9.89MM
SALES (corp-wide): 19.18B **Publicly Held**
Web: www.clevelandcliffs.com
SIC: 1011 Iron ore mining

PA: Cleveland-Cliffs Inc.
200 Public Sq Ste 3300
Cleveland OH 44114
216 694-5700

(G-4381)
THE FISCHER & JIROUCH COMPANY
9105 Sapphire Ct (44130-7686)
PHONE..............................216 361-3840
Robert Mattei, *Pr*
Salvatore Grandinetti, *Sec*
Carloina Cretoni, *Stockholder*
EMP: 8 **EST:** 1902
SALES (est): 922.22K **Privately Held**
Web: www.fischerandjirouch.com
SIC: 3299 Architectural sculptures: gypsum,
clay, papier mache, etc.

(G-4382)
THE GARLAND COMPANY INC (HQ)
3800 E 91st St (44105-2197)
PHONE..............................216 641-7500
EMP: 100 **EST:** 1988
SALES (est): 288.45MM
SALES (corp-wide): 706.22MM **Privately
Held**
Web: www.garlandco.com
SIC: 2952 2851 Roofing materials; Epoxy
coatings
PA: Garland Industries, Inc.
3800 E 91st St
Cleveland OH 44105
216 641-7500

(G-4383)
**THE GREAT LAKES TOWING
COMPANY (PA)**
Also Called: Great Lakes Shipyard
4500 Division Ave (44102-2228)
PHONE..............................216 621-4854
EMP: 73 **EST:** 1899
SALES (est): 21.99MM
SALES (corp-wide): 21.99MM **Privately
Held**
Web: www.thegreatlakesgroup.com
SIC: 4492 3731 Tugboat service;
Shipbuilding and repairing

(G-4384)
THE HATTENBACH COMPANY
Also Called: Hattenbach
5309 Hamilton Ave (44114-3909)
PHONE..............................216 881-5200
EMP: 85
Web: www.hattenbach.com
SIC: 1711 5078 2541 2434 Refrigeration
contractor; Commercial refrigeration
equipment; Cabinets, except refrigerated:
show, display, etc.: wood; Wood kitchen
cabinets

(G-4385)
THE HOLTKAMP ORGAN CO
2909 Meyer Ave (44109-1536)
P.O. Box 609396 (44109-0396)
PHONE..............................216 741-5180
F Christian Holtkamp, *Pr*
Thomas Lucchesi, *Sec*
EMP: 12 **EST:** 1855
SQ FT: 15,700
SALES (est): 884.99K **Privately Held**
Web: www.holtkamporgan.com
SIC: 3931 Pipes, organ

(G-4386)
**THE IDEAL BUILDERS SUPPLY &
FUEL CO INC (PA)**
4720 Brookpark Rd (44134-1014)
PHONE..............................216 741-1600
EMP: 12 **EST:** 1906

SALES (est): 485.18K
SALES (corp-wide): 485.18K **Privately
Held**
Web: www.idealbuilders.com
SIC: 3271 5032 5211 Concrete block and
brick; Brick, except refractory; Brick

(G-4387)
THE KINDT-COLLINS COMPANY LLC
12651 Elmwood Ave (44111-5994)
PHONE..............................216 252-4122
◆ **EMP:** 72
Web: www.kindt-collins.com
SIC: 5085 2999 3363 3364 Industrial
supplies; Waxes, petroleum: not produced
in petroleum refineries; Aluminum die-
castings; Brass and bronze die-castings

(G-4388)
**THE NATIONAL TELEPHONE
SUPPLY COMPANY**
5100 Superior Ave (44103-1284)
PHONE..............................216 361-0221
▼ **EMP:** 50 **EST:** 1910
SALES (est): 4.76MM **Privately Held**
Web: www.nicopress.com
SIC: 3643 Connectors and terminals for
electrical devices

(G-4389)
THEB INC
Also Called: A Quick Copy Center
3700 Kelley Ave (44114-4533)
PHONE..............................216 391-4800
Rhonda Garcia, *Pr*
Tom Garcia, *Sec*
EMP: 7 **EST:** 1962
SQ FT: 4,000
SALES (est): 180.18K **Privately Held**
SIC: 2752 Offset printing

(G-4390)
THERMAGON INC
Also Called: Laird Technologies
4707 Detroit Ave (44102-2216)
PHONE..............................216 939-2300
▲ **EMP:** 75
Web: www.thermagon.com
SIC: 2891 Adhesives and sealants

(G-4391)
**THERMO SYSTEMS TECHNOLOGY
INC**
2000 Auburn Dr Ste 200 (44122-4328)
PHONE..............................216 292-8250
Henry A Becker, *Pr*
EMP: 6 **EST:** 1990
SALES (est): 808.14K **Privately Held**
Web: www.thermosys.com
SIC: 3567 3433 Heating units and devices,
industrial: electric; Heating equipment,
except electric

(G-4392)
THERMOPRENE INC
5718 Transportation Blvd (44125-5343)
P.O. Box 23681 (44023-0681)
PHONE..............................440 543-8660
Richard K Raymond, *Pr*
Craig Mcconnell, *VP*
▲ **EMP:** 10 **EST:** 1997
SALES (est): 2.48MM **Privately Held**
Web: www.thermoprene.com
SIC: 3089 Injection molding of plastics

(G-4393)
**THOMPSON ALUMINUM CASTING
CO**
Also Called: Thompson Castings
5161 Canal Rd (44125-1143)

PHONE..............................216 206-2781
Dave Oberg, *Prin*
▲ **EMP:** 45 **EST:** 1948
SQ FT: 60,000
SALES (est): 4.35MM **Privately Held**
Web: www.thompsoncasting.com
SIC: 3364 3369 3363 3365 Magnesium and
magnesium-base alloy die-castings;
Magnesium and magnes.-base alloy
castings, exc. die-casting; Aluminum die-
castings; Aluminum foundries

(G-4394)
**THOSE CHRCTERS FROM CLVLAND
LL**
Also Called: T C F C
1 American Rd (44144-2354)
PHONE..............................216 252-7300
Ed Fructembaum, *Ch*
Thomas Schneider, *VP*
William Meyer, *VP*
Howard Weinshenker, *VP*
Dale A Cable, *Treas*
EMP: 7 **EST:** 1984
SQ FT: 5,000
SALES (est): 590.33K **Privately Held**
SIC: 8999 2771 Art related services;
Greeting cards

(G-4395)
TILDEN MINING COMPANY LC (HQ)
200 Public Sq Ste 3300 (44114-2315)
PHONE..............................216 694-5700
Lourenco Goncalves, *Pr*
Terry Fedor, *Ex VP*
Timothy K Flanagan, *CFO*
James Graham, *CLO*
EMP: 580 **EST:** 1995
SALES (est): 369.3MM
SALES (corp-wide): 19.18B **Publicly Held**
SIC: 1011 Iron ore mining
PA: Cleveland-Cliffs Inc.
200 Public Sq Ste 3300
Cleveland OH 44114
216 694-5700

(G-4396)
TLS CORP (PA)
Also Called: Telos Alliance, The
1241 Superior Ave E (44114-3204)
PHONE..............................216 574-4759
Frank Foti, *CEO*
Timothy Carroll, *
◆ **EMP:** 55 **EST:** 1980
SQ FT: 10,500
SALES (est): 14.52MM
SALES (corp-wide): 14.52MM **Privately
Held**
Web: www.telosalliance.com
SIC: 3663 3679 3823 3661 Radio and t.v.
communications equipment; Electronic
circuits; Process control instruments;
Telephone and telegraph apparatus

(G-4397)
TMS INTERNATIONAL LLC
4300 E 49th St (44125-1004)
PHONE..............................216 441-9702
Keith Kelley, *Prin*
EMP: 22
Web: www.tmsinternational.com
SIC: 3312 Blast furnaces and steel mills
HQ: Tms International, Llc
2835 East Carson Street
Pittsburgh PA 15203
412 678-6141

(G-4398)
TODD INDUSTRIES INC
7300 Northfield Rd Ste 1 (44146-6106)
PHONE..............................440 439-2900

Gerald Boehnlein Senior, *Pr*
Gerald Boehnlein Junior, *VP*
Judith A Boehnlein, *
EMP: 45 **EST:** 1972
SQ FT: 45,000
SALES (est): 951.75K **Privately Held**
Web: www.allmachining.com
SIC: 3549 3599 Metalworking machinery, nec
; Machine shop, jobbing and repair

(G-4399)
TOMLINSON INDUSTRIES LLC
4350 Renaissance Pkwy (44128-5793)
PHONE..............................216 587-3400
Michael E Figas, *Pr*
▲ **EMP:** 170 **EST:** 1989
SALES (est): 2.69MM **Privately Held**
Web: www.tomlinsonind.com
SIC: 3556 Food products machinery

(G-4400)
TOOLBOLD CORPORATION (PA)
5330 Commerce Pkwy W (44130-1273)
PHONE..............................216 676-9840
Harry Eisengrein, *CEO*
Barbara Blech, *Pr*
EMP: 20 **EST:** 1976
SQ FT: 14,000
SALES (est): 5.01MM
SALES (corp-wide): 5.01MM **Privately Held**
Web: www.toolbold.com
SIC: 3599 Machine shop, jobbing and repair

(G-4401)
TOOLBOLD CORPORATION
Leadfree Faucets Division
5330 Commerce Pkwy W (44130-1273)
PHONE..............................440 543-1660
Harry Eisengrein, *Brnch Mgr*
EMP: 10
SALES (corp-wide): 5.01MM **Privately Held**
Web: www.toolbold.com
SIC: 3432 Faucets and spigots, metal and plastic
PA: Toolbold Corporation
5330 Commerce Pkwy W
Cleveland OH 44130
216 676-9840

(G-4402)
TOP KNOTCH PRODUCTS INC
819 Colonel Dr (44109-3768)
PHONE..............................419 543-2266
Lance E Larson, *Pr*
EMP: 8 **EST:** 1990
SQ FT: 5,000
SALES (est): 687.24K **Privately Held**
Web: www.topknotchproducts.com
SIC: 3496 Miscellaneous fabricated wire products

(G-4403)
TOP TOOL & DIE INC
15500 Brookpark Rd (44135-3334)
PHONE..............................216 267-5878
Anton Schiro, *Pr*
Irma Schiro, *Treas*
Bob Schiro, *VP*
EMP: 6 **EST:** 1979
SQ FT: 12,000
SALES (est): 608.53K **Privately Held**
Web: www.toptoolanddie.com
SIC: 3544 Special dies and tools

(G-4404)
TOPPS PRODUCTS INC
3201 E 66th St (44127-1403)
P.O. Box 1632 (39046-1632)
PHONE..............................913 685-2500

John Fry, *Ch*
Arlan Koppel, *Pr*
William B Schmidt, *Sec*
▼ **EMP:** 18 **EST:** 1994
SQ FT: 8,500
SALES (est): 2.48MM **Privately Held**
Web: www.toppsproducts.com
SIC: 3069 Roofing, membrane rubber

(G-4405)
TORRMETAL LLC
12125 Bennington Ave (44135-3729)
PHONE..............................216 671-1616
EMP: 32 **EST:** 2021
SALES (est): 3.66MM **Privately Held**
Web: www.torrmetal.com
SIC: 3469 3544 Stamping metal for the trade
; Special dies, tools, jigs, and fixtures

(G-4406)
TORRMETAL CORPORATION
12125 Bennington Ave (44135-3729)
PHONE..............................216 671-1616
Patrick Sheehan, *Pr*
Lisa M Habe, *Mng Pt*
EMP: 21 **EST:** 1992
SQ FT: 25,000
SALES (est): 4.98MM
SALES (corp-wide): 24.2MM **Privately Held**
Web: www.torrmetal.com
SIC: 3469 3544 Stamping metal for the trade
; Special dies, tools, jigs, and fixtures
PA: Interlake Industries, Inc.
4732 E 355th St
Willoughby OH 44094
440 942-0800

(G-4407)
TORTILLERIA LA BAMBA LLC
12119 Bennington Ave (44135-3729)
PHONE..............................216 515-1600
▼ **EMP:** 6 **EST:** 2012
SALES (est): 876.15K **Privately Held**
Web: www.labambagroup.com
SIC: 2099 Tortillas, fresh or refrigerated

(G-4408)
TOTAL TOUCH LLC
250 W Huron Rd Ste 400 (44113-1411)
PHONE..............................800 726-2117
EMP: 15 **EST:** 2018
SALES (est): 1.14MM
SALES (corp-wide): 27.42MM **Privately Held**
Web: www.totaltouchpos.com
SIC: 3578 Point-of-sale devices
PA: Electronic Merchant Systems, Llc
250 W Huron Rd Ste 300
Cleveland OH 44113
216 524-0900

(G-4409)
TRACER SPECIALTIES INC
1842 Columbus Rd (44113-2412)
PHONE..............................216 696-2363
Tejinder Singh, *Pr*
EMP: 8 **EST:** 1969
SQ FT: 7,500
SALES (est): 727.65K **Privately Held**
SIC: 3599 Machine shop, jobbing and repair

(G-4410)
TRANE INC
Also Called: Trane Cleveland
9555 Rockside Rd Ste 350 (44125-6283)
PHONE..............................440 946-7823
EMP: 30
Web: www.trane.com
SIC: 3585 Refrigeration and heating equipment

HQ: Trane Inc.
1 Centennial Ave Ste 101
Piscataway NJ 08854
732 652-7100

(G-4411)
TRANSDIGM INC
Also Called: Aerocontrolex
4223 Monticello Blvd (44121-2814)
PHONE..............................216 291-6025
Cathy Leak, *Prin*
EMP: 21
SALES (corp-wide): 7.94B **Publicly Held**
Web: www.aerocontrolex.com
SIC: 3561 3492 3563 3625 Pumps and pumping equipment; Fluid power valves and hose fittings; Air and gas compressors; Relays and industrial controls
HQ: Transdigm, Inc.
1350 Euclid Ave
Cleveland OH 44115

(G-4412)
TRANSDIGM INC (HQ)
1350 Euclid Ave Ste 1601 (44115-1825)
PHONE..............................216 706-2960
W Nicholas Howley, *Ch Bd*
Kevin Stein, *Pr*
Robert S Henderson, *Vice Chairman*
Jorge L Valladares Iii, *COO*
Michael Lisman, *CFO*
EMP: 8 **EST:** 1993
SALES (est): 624.86MM
SALES (corp-wide): 7.94B **Publicly Held**
Web: www.aerocontrolex.com
SIC: 3812 Defense systems and equipment
PA: Transdigm Group Incorporated
1350 Euclid Ave Ste 1600
Cleveland OH 44115
216 706-2960

(G-4413)
TRANSDIGM GROUP INCORPORATED (PA)
Also Called: Transdigm
1350 Euclid Ave Ste 1601 (44115-1825)
PHONE..............................216 706-2960
Kevin Stein, *Pr*
W Nicholas Howley, *Ch Bd*
Sarah Wynne, *CFO*
EMP: 257 **EST:** 1993
SQ FT: 26,000
SALES (est): 7.94B
SALES (corp-wide): 7.94B **Publicly Held**
Web: www.transdigm.com
SIC: 3728 5088 Aircraft parts and equipment, nec; Aircraft equipment and supplies, nec

(G-4414)
TRANZONIC COMPANIES
26301 Curtiss Wright Pkwy Ste 200 (44143-1454)
PHONE..............................440 446-0643
Ken F Vuylsteke, *Pr*
EMP: 233
SALES (corp-wide): 523.82MM **Privately Held**
Web: www.tranzonic.com
SIC: 2211 2326 2842 2273 Scrub cloths; Work garments, except raincoats: waterproof; Sanitation preparations, disinfectants and deodorants; Mats and matting
PA: The Tranzonic Companies
26301 Crtiss Wrght Pkwy S
Cleveland OH 44143
216 535-4300

(G-4415)
TREC INDUSTRIES INC
4713 Spring Rd (44131-1025)
PHONE..............................216 741-4114
James M Trecokas, *Pr*
Laurel Trecokas, *Sec*
EMP: 14 **EST:** 1979
SQ FT: 10,000
SALES (est): 2.21MM **Privately Held**
Web: www.trecindustries.com
SIC: 3599 Machine shop, jobbing and repair

(G-4416)
TREMONT ELECTRIC INCORPORATED
Also Called: Delaware Company
2112 W 7th St (44113-3622)
PHONE..............................888 214-3137
Aaron Lemieux, *Prin*
Charles Ames, *Pr*
Aaron Lemiuex, *CEO*
Jill Lemiuex, *VP*
Benjamin Brooks, *Dir*
EMP: 9 **EST:** 2007
SALES (est): 527.83K **Privately Held**
Web: www.greennpower.com
SIC: 3621 Motors and generators

(G-4417)
TRI COUNTY CONCRETE INC
Also Called: Tri County Ready Mixed Con Co
10155 Royalton Rd (44133-4426)
P.O. Box 665 (44087-0665)
PHONE..............................330 425-4464
Tony Farinacci, *Pr*
EMP: 11
SQ FT: 23,282
SALES (corp-wide): 3.06MM **Privately Held**
Web: www.tricountyconcretecompany.com
SIC: 3273 Ready-mixed concrete
PA: Tri County Concrete Inc
9423 Darrow Rd
Twinsburg OH 44087
330 425-4464

(G-4418)
TRI-CRAFT INC
17941 Englewood Dr (44130-3488)
PHONE..............................440 826-1050
Kathleen Byrnes, *Pr*
Monica Hargis, *VP*
EMP: 34 **EST:** 1967
SQ FT: 30,000
SALES (est): 4.07MM **Privately Held**
Web: www.tc-tm.com
SIC: 3089 3544 3469 Injection molded finished plastics products, nec; Special dies, tools, jigs, and fixtures; Metal stampings, nec

(G-4419)
TRIAD CAPITAL GROUP LLC
4641 Spring Rd (44131-1021)
PHONE..............................440 236-6677
EMP: 6
SALES (corp-wide): 1.08MM **Privately Held**
Web: evenmix.com
SIC: 3441 Fabricated structural metal
PA: Triad Capital Group, Llc
4641 Spring Rd
Independence OH 44131
440 236-6677

(G-4420)
TRIANGLE MACHINE PRODUCTS CO
6055 Hillcrest Dr (44125-4687)
PHONE..............................216 524-5872
Robb Scherler, *Pr*

Raymond Scherler, *
Roy Scherler, *
Michael Rosegger, *
Randy Scherler, *
EMP: 35 **EST:** 1950
SQ FT: 42,000
SALES (est): 2.8MM
SALES (corp-wide): 22.2MM **Privately Held**
Web: www.freewaycorp.com
SIC: 3451 Screw machine products
PA: Freeway Corporation
9301 Allen Dr
Cleveland OH 44125
216 524-9700

(G-4421)
TRIBCO INCORPORATED
18901 Cranwood Pkwy (44128-4041)
P.O. Box 202148 (44120-8119)
PHONE..........................216 486-2000
David N Bortz, Pr
EMP: 40 **EST:** 1980
SALES (est): 4.3MM **Privately Held**
Web: www.tribco.com
SIC: 3499 Friction material, made from powdered metal

(G-4422)
TRIBOTECH COMPOSITES INC
7800 Exchange St (44125-3332)
PHONE..........................216 901-1300
Arnold Von, Pr
◆ **EMP:** 9 **EST:** 2012
SALES (est): 5.2MM
SALES (corp-wide): 779.39K **Privately Held**
Web: www.tribotechcomposites.com
SIC: 2821 Plastics materials and resins
HQ: System Seals, Llc
9505 Midwest Ave
Cleveland OH 44125

(G-4423)
TRICO HOLDING CORPORATION (DH)
127 Public Sq Ste 5110 (44114-1313)
PHONE..........................216 589-0198
EMP: 6 **EST:** 1986
SALES (est): 39.65MM
SALES (corp-wide): 7.28B **Privately Held**
Web: www.tricocorp.com
SIC: 3714 Motor vehicle parts and accessories
HQ: Trico Products Corporation
127 Public Sq
Cleveland OH 44114
800 388-7428

(G-4424)
TRICO MACHINE PRODUCTS CORP
5081 Corbin Dr (44128-5413)
PHONE..........................216 662-4194
Julius Szorady Junior, Pr
James Szorady, VP
Mark Szorady, Treas
EMP: 10 **EST:** 1953
SQ FT: 8,000
SALES (est): 902.24K **Privately Held**
Web: www.tricomachine.com
SIC: 3599 Machine and other job shop work

(G-4425)
TRICO PRODUCTS CORPORATION (DH)
Also Called: Trico
127 Public Sq (44114-1217)
PHONE..........................800 388-7428
Patrick James, Pr
◆ **EMP:** 150 **EST:** 1920
SALES (est): 161.69MM

SALES (corp-wide): 7.28B **Privately Held**
Web: www.tricoproducts.com
SIC: 8734 3082 3069 8731 Testing laboratories; Tubes, unsupported plastics; Tubing, rubber; Commercial physical research
HQ: Ktri Holdings, Inc.
127 Public Sq Ste 5110
Cleveland OH 44114
216 400-9308

(G-4426)
TRIM TOOL & MACHINE INC
3431 Service Rd (44111)
PHONE..........................216 889-1916
Dane Willis, Pr
EMP: 20 **EST:** 1998
SALES (est): 2.43MM **Privately Held**
Web: www.trimtoolmachine.com
SIC: 3544 Special dies and tools

(G-4427)
TRINEL INC
5251 W 137th St (44142-1800)
PHONE..........................216 265-9190
Jimmy M Martella, Pr
Thomas A Martella, Asst VP
Rose Martella, Sec
EMP: 8 **EST:** 1986
SQ FT: 22,000
SALES (est): 1.19MM **Privately Held**
Web: www.trinelinc.com
SIC: 3599 Grinding castings for the trade

(G-4428)
TRIPLE A BUILDERS INC
540 E 105th St (44108-4301)
PHONE..........................216 249-0327
Cynthia Mumford, Pr
EMP: 7 **EST:** 2000
SQ FT: 1,800
SALES (est): 482.97K **Privately Held**
SIC: 0782 1751 1752 1761 Lawn and garden services; Carpentry work; Floor laying and floor work, nec; Roofing, siding, and sheetmetal work

(G-4429)
TRITON DURO WERKS INC
12200 Sprecher Ave (44135-5122)
PHONE..........................216 267-1117
Victor De Leon, CEO
EMP: 19 **EST:** 1967
3Q FT: 12,000
SALES (est): 4.61MM **Privately Held**
Web: www.ziptool.com
SIC: 3465 3469 Automotive stampings; Metal stampings, nec

(G-4430)
TRU FORM METAL PRODUCTS INC
12305 Grimsby Ave (44135-4843)
PHONE..........................216 252-3700
Ron Seith, Pr
EMP: 8 **EST:** 2001
SALES (est): 923.85K **Privately Held**
Web: www.truform-metal.com
SIC: 3444 Sheet metalwork

(G-4431)
TRUCK FAX INC
17700 S Woodland Rd (44120-1767)
PHONE..........................216 921-8866
Brian Luntz, Pr
Melissa Beesley, Ex Sec
◆ **EMP:** 8 **EST:** 1996
SALES (est): 247.63K **Privately Held**
SIC: 3399 7371 3999 Iron, powdered; Computer software development; Atomizers, toiletry

(G-4432)
TUGZ INTERNATIONAL LLC
4500 Division Ave (44102-2228)
PHONE..........................216 621-4854
George Sogor, Pr
EMP: 15 **EST:** 1994
SALES (est): 363.21K **Privately Held**
Web: www.thegreatlakesgroup.com
SIC: 3732 7389 Boatbuilding and repairing; Design, commercial and industrial

(G-4433)
TURBINE ENG CMPNENTS TECH CORP
Also Called: Whitcraft Cleveland
23555 Euclid Ave (44117-1703)
PHONE..........................216 692-5200
Doug Folsom, Mgr
EMP: 318
SALES (corp-wide): 48.64MM **Privately Held**
SIC: 3724 3728 3463 Airfoils, aircraft engine; Aircraft parts and equipment, nec; Nonferrous forgings
PA: Turbine Engine Components Technologies Corporation
1211 Old Albany Rd
Thomasville GA 31792
229 228-2600

(G-4434)
TW MANUFACTURING CO
Also Called: Production Pattern Company
6065 Parkland Blvd (44124-6119)
PHONE..........................440 439-3243
David Drunelle, Manager
EMP: 7 **EST:** 2008
SALES (est): 1.56MM
SALES (corp-wide): 1.66B **Publicly Held**
Web: www.prodpatt.com
SIC: 3543 3544 Foundry cores; Industrial molds
HQ: Park-Ohio Industries, Inc.
6065 Parkland Blvd
Cleveland OH 44124
440 947-2000

(G-4435)
TYCO FIRE PRODUCTS LP
Also Called: Tyco Fire Protection Products
5565 Venture Dr Ste A (44130-9302)
PHONE..........................216 265-0505
Keith Bredenkamp, Brnch Mgr
EMP: /
Web: www.tyco-fire.com
SIC: 3569 Sprinkler systems, fire: automatic
HQ: Tyco Fire Products Lp
1467 Elmwood Ave
Cranston RI 02910
215 362-0700

(G-4436)
TYLOK INTERNATIONAL INC
1061 E 260th St (44132-2877)
PHONE..........................216 261-7310
Carole Hahl, Pr
Sandy Carroll, *
▲ **EMP:** 55 **EST:** 1955
SQ FT: 72,000
SALES (est): 9.95MM **Privately Held**
Web: www.tylok.com
SIC: 3494 3492 3491 Valves and pipe fittings, nec; Hose and tube fittings and assemblies, hydraulic/pneumatic; Pressure valves and regulators, industrial

(G-4437)
TYMEX PLASTICS INC
5300 Harvard Ave (44105-4826)
PHONE..........................216 429-8950
Michael Turkovich, Pr

EMP: 45 **EST:** 2001
SQ FT: 160,000
SALES (est): 10.23MM **Privately Held**
Web: www.tymexplastics.com
SIC: 3087 Custom compound purchased resins

(G-4438)
U S ALLOY DIE CORP
4007 Brookpark Rd (44134-1131)
PHONE..........................216 749-9700
Anthony Corrao Senior, Pr
Dyann Corrao, VP
Rachelle Corrao, VP
Anthony Carrao Junior, VP
EMP: 11 **EST:** 1955
SQ FT: 12,000
SALES (est): 1.04MM **Privately Held**
Web: www.usalloydie.com
SIC: 3544 3599 3541 Special dies and tools; Electrical discharge machining (EDM); Machine tools, metal cutting type

(G-4439)
UCI CONTROLS INC (PA)
Also Called: Cleveland Controls
1111 Brookpark Rd (44109-5825)
PHONE..........................216 398-0330
Matthew Churchill, Pr
Jim Ransbury, CFO
EMP: 34 **EST:** 2022
SALES (est): 34.34MM
SALES (corp-wide): 34.34MM **Privately Held**
Web: www.clevelandcontrols.com
SIC: 3613 Power switching equipment

(G-4440)
UNION CARBIDE CORPORATION
11709 Madison Ave (44107-5230)
P.O. Box 1153 (44055-0153)
PHONE..........................216 529-3784
Al Miller, Prin
EMP: 13
SALES (corp-wide): 42.96B **Publicly Held**
Web: www.unioncarbide.com
SIC: 2869 Industrial organic chemicals, nec
HQ: Union Carbide Corporation
7501 State Hwy 185 N
Seadrift TX 77983
361 553-2997

(G-4441)
UNISON UCI INC
Also Called: Hays Cleveland
1111 Brookpark Rd (44109-5825)
▲ **EMP:** 7
Web: www.clevelandcontrols.com
SIC: 3823 Combustion control instruments

(G-4442)
UNITED FINSHG & DIE CUTNG INC
3875 King Ave (44114-3727)
PHONE..........................216 881-0239
Laurie Jacbec, Pr
Aaron Jacbec, Admn Execs
EMP: 6 **EST:** 2004
SALES (est): 868.24K **Privately Held**
Web: www.unitedfdc.com
SIC: 3544 Special dies and tools

(G-4443)
UNITED IGNITION WIRE CORP
15620 Industrial Pkwy (44135-3316)
PHONE..........................216 898-1112
Richard L Maxwell, Pr
Marie Maxwell, Sec
▲ **EMP:** 8 **EST:** 1988
SQ FT: 20,000
SALES (est): 840.7K **Privately Held**
Web: www.unitedmotorproducts.com

SIC: 3694 5521 Ignition apparatus, internal combustion engines; Used car dealers

(G-4444)
UNITED READY MIX INC
7820 Carnegie Ave (44103-4904)
PHONE..........................216 696-1600
Harvey J Newsom, *Pr*
Alvin Robinson, *Sr VP*
EMP: 6 **EST:** 1972
SQ FT: 4,000
SALES (est): 197.01K **Privately Held**
SIC: 3273 Ready-mixed concrete

(G-4445)
UNIVERSAL GRINDING CORPORATION
1234 W 78th St (44102-1914)
PHONE..........................216 631-9410
Donald R Toth, *Pr*
Nancy Toth, *
Kevin Decaire, *
▼ **EMP:** 49 **EST:** 1940
SQ FT: 86,000
SALES (est): 5.54MM **Privately Held**
Web: www.universalgrinding.com
SIC: 3599 Machine shop, jobbing and repair

(G-4446)
UNIVERSAL MANUFACTURING
9900 Clinton Rd (44144-1034)
PHONE..........................816 396-0101
EMP: 7 **EST:** 2016
SALES (est): 292.66K **Privately Held**
SIC: 3999 Manufacturing industries, nec

(G-4447)
UNIVERSAL OIL INC
265 Jefferson Ave (44113-2594)
PHONE..........................216 771-4300
TOLL FREE: 800
John J Purcell, *Pr*
EMP: 30 **EST:** 1875
SQ FT: 25,000
SALES (est): 29.58MM **Privately Held**
Web: www.universaloil.com
SIC: 5171 2992 Petroleum bulk stations; Lubricating oils

(G-4448)
UNIVERSAL STEEL COMPANY
6600 Grant Ave (44105-5692)
PHONE..........................216 883-4972
David P Miller, *Ch*
Richard W Williams, *Pr*
Stephen F Ruscher, *VP*
▲ **EMP:** 100 **EST:** 1925
SQ FT: 200,000
SALES (est): 2.74MM
SALES (corp-wide): 42.22MM **Privately Held**
Web: www.univsteel.com
SIC: 3444 5051 Sheet metalwork; Steel
PA: Columbia National Group, Inc.
6600 Grant Ave
Cleveland OH 44105
216 883-4972

(G-4449)
UPRIGHT STEEL LLC
9110 George Ave (44105-1630)
PHONE..........................216 923-0852
EMP: 20 **EST:** 2010
SALES (est): 2.29MM **Privately Held**
Web: www.uprightsteelfab.com
SIC: 3441 3446 1791 Fabricated structural metal; Stairs, fire escapes, balconies, railings, and ladders; Concrete reinforcement, placing of

(G-4450)
URETHANE POLYMERS INTL (HQ)
Also Called: U P I
3800 E 91st St (44105-2103)
PHONE..........................216 430-3655
Kevin Mcnulty, *CEO*
Charles Ripepi, *CFO*
EMP: 10 **EST:** 1989
SQ FT: 72,000
SALES (est): 23.26MM
SALES (corp-wide): 23.26MM **Privately Held**
Web: www.urethanepolymers.com
SIC: 2899 2851 2821 Waterproofing compounds; Paints and allied products; Plastics materials and resins
PA: O S L, Inc
1308 E Wakeham Ave
Santa Ana CA 92705
714 505-4923

(G-4451)
US COTTON LLC
15501 Industrial Pkwy (44135-3313)
PHONE..........................216 676-6400
John Levinsky, *Mgr*
EMP: 94
SALES (corp-wide): 1.44B **Privately Held**
Web: www.uscotton.us
SIC: 2844 2241 Perfumes, cosmetics and other toilet preparations; Cotton narrow fabrics
HQ: U.S. Cotton, Llc
531 Cotton Blossom Cir
Gastonia NC 28054
216 676-6400

(G-4452)
US WELLNESS LLC
1200 E 55th St Ste A (44103-1080)
PHONE..........................216 772-3364
Nikola Matic, *CEO*
Marko Matic, *Pr*
EMP: 7 **EST:** 2014
SQ FT: 2,000
SALES (est): 145.31K **Privately Held**
Web: www.us-wellness.com
SIC: 2099 5149 Tea blending; Tea bagging

(G-4453)
USA HEAT TREATING INC
4500 Lee Rd Ste B (44128-2959)
PHONE..........................216 587-4700
Norman R Fisher Junior, *Pr*
Forest Delaine, *
EMP: 26 **EST:** 1992
SQ FT: 50,000
SALES (est): 3.55MM **Privately Held**
Web: www.usaheattreating.com
SIC: 3398 Metal heat treating

(G-4454)
USB CORPORATION
26111 Miles Rd (44128-5933)
P.O. Box 68 (92018-0068)
PHONE..........................216 765-5000
Michael Lachman, *Pr*
Fred Leffler, *Marketing**
Frank Maenpa, *Quality Vice President**
Kathy Fortney, *
EMP: 10 **EST:** 1998
SQ FT: 60,000
SALES (est): 3.04MM
SALES (corp-wide): 42.86B **Publicly Held**
Web: usbcorporation.lookchem.com
SIC: 2833 2834 2835 Medicinals and botanicals; Pharmaceutical preparations; Radioactive diagnostic substances
HQ: Affymetrix, Inc.
3450 Central Expy
Santa Clara CA 95051

(G-4455)
UTILITY WIRE PRODUCTS INC
3302 E 87th St (44127-1849)
PHONE..........................216 441-2180
Ronald F Anzells, *Pr*
Donald J Anzells, *Treas*
Marcia Anzells, *Sec*
EMP: 8 **EST:** 1953
SQ FT: 48,000
SALES (est): 515.25K **Privately Held**
Web: www.utilitywire.com
SIC: 3496 Woven wire products, nec

(G-4456)
VACONO AMERICA LLC
1163 E 40th St Ste 301 (44114-3869)
PHONE..........................216 938-7428
▲ **EMP:** 29 **EST:** 2011
SALES (est): 582.34K **Privately Held**
Web: www.vacono.com
SIC: 3479 Aluminum coating of metal products

(G-4457)
VARBROS LLC (PA)
16025 Brookpark Rd (44142-1623)
PHONE..........................216 267-5200
Rick Vargo, *
Dave Gido, *
Ernest R Vargo Junior, *Treas*
Joseph G Corsaro, *
▼ **EMP:** 90 **EST:** 1951
SQ FT: 113,000
SALES (est): 22.16MM
SALES (corp-wide): 22.16MM **Privately Held**
Web: www.varbroscorp.com
SIC: 3469 3714 Stamping metal for the trade ; Motor vehicle parts and accessories

(G-4458)
VARMLAND INC
Also Called: All Cstom Fabricators Erectors
1200 Brookpark Rd (44109-5828)
PHONE..........................216 741-1510
Erik V Schneider, *Pr*
Karl M Schneider, *VP*
Deborah Schneider, *Sec*
EMP: 12 **EST:** 1943
SQ FT: 20,000
SALES (est): 1.4MM **Privately Held**
SIC: 3444 Sheet metal specialties, not stamped

(G-4459)
VE GLOBAL VENDING INC
Also Called: Vegv
8700 Brookpark Rd (44129-6810)
PHONE..........................216 785-2611
Aviel Dafna, *Pr*
Nate Stansell, *COO*
▲ **EMP:** 7 **EST:** 2003
SALES (est): 613.78K **Privately Held**
Web: www.vesolutions.co
SIC: 3581 Automatic vending machines

(G-4460)
VECTOR MECHANICAL LLC
10917 Dale Ave (44111-4846)
PHONE..........................216 337-4042
Ildiko Sarai, *Managing Member*
EMP: 8 **EST:** 2017
SALES (est): 442.8K **Privately Held**
SIC: 1711 1799 3564 Mechanical contractor; Dock equipment installation, industrial; Ventilating fans: industrial or commercial

(G-4461)
VERTIV GROUP CORPORATION
5900 Landerbrook Dr Ste 300
(44124-4020)

PHONE..........................440 460-3600
Steven M Barto, *Brnch Mgr*
EMP: 6
SALES (corp-wide): 8.01B **Publicly Held**
Web: www.vertiv.com
SIC: 3661 1731 Telephone and telegraph apparatus; Communications specialization
HQ: Vertiv Group Corporation
505 N Cleveland Ave
Westerville OH 43082
614 888-0246

(G-4462)
VETERANS STEEL INC
900 E 69th St (44103-1736)
PHONE..........................216 938-7476
Karen Black, *Pr*
EMP: 13 **EST:** 2014
SALES (est): 779.51K **Privately Held**
SIC: 3449 Bars, concrete reinforcing: fabricated steel

(G-4463)
VGS INC
2239 E 55th St (44103-4451)
PHONE..........................216 431-7800
Robert Comben Junior, *Pr*
Donald E Carlton, *
Mick Latkovich, *
James Huduk, *
EMP: 200 **EST:** 1998
SQ FT: 36,000
SALES (est): 4.1MM **Privately Held**
Web: www.vgsjob.org
SIC: 8331 2326 2311 Job training and related services; Work uniforms; Military uniforms, men's and youths': purchased materials

(G-4464)
VGU INDUSTRIES INC
Also Called: Vinyl Graphics
4747 Manufacturing Ave (44135-2639)
PHONE..........................216 676-9093
Brian Stransky, *Pr*
▲ **EMP:** 35 **EST:** 1973
SQ FT: 40,000
SALES (est): 2.36MM **Privately Held**
Web: www.mosoundmusic.com
SIC: 3993 2759 2396 Signs, not made in custom sign painting shops; Screen printing ; Automotive and apparel trimmings

(G-4465)
VIBRANTZ CORPORATION
4150 E 56th St (44105-4890)
P.O. Box 519 (15301-0519)
PHONE..........................724 207-2152
David Klimas, *Mgr*
EMP: 41
SALES (corp-wide): 1.88B **Privately Held**
Web: www.vibrantz.com
SIC: 2816 Color pigments
HQ: Vibrantz Corporation
6060 Prkland Blvd Ste 250
Mayfield Heights OH 44124
216 875-5600

(G-4466)
VIBRANTZ CORPORATION
6060 Parkland Blvd Ste 250 (44124-4225)
PHONE..........................442 224-6100
Mike Steele, *Mgr*
EMP: 10
SALES (corp-wide): 1.88B **Privately Held**
Web: www.vibrantz.com
SIC: 2819 Industrial inorganic chemicals, nec
HQ: Vibrantz Corporation
6060 Prkland Blvd Ste 250
Mayfield Heights OH 44124
216 875-5600

▲ = Import ▼ = Export
◆ = Import/Export

(G-4467)
VIBRANTZ CORPORATION
Also Called: Porcelain Enamels
6060 Parkland Blvd (44124-4225)
PHONE...........................216 875-5600
Robert Szabo, *Mgr*
EMP: 23
SALES (corp-wide): 1.88B Privately Held
Web: www.vibrantz.com
SIC: 2899 Chemical preparations, nec
HQ: Vibrantz Corporation
6060 Prkland Blvd Ste 250
Mayfield Heights OH 44124
216 875-5600

(G-4468)
VIBRANTZ CORPORATION
Ferro Crmic Glaze Prcln Enl Di
4150 E 56th St (44105-4890)
P.O. Box 6550 (44101-1550)
PHONE...........................216 875-6213
John V Belcastro, *Prin*
EMP: 250
SALES (corp-wide): 1.88B Privately Held
Web: www.vibrantz.com
SIC: 2899 2851 3264 2893 Frit; Lacquers,
varnishes, enamels, and other coatings;
Porcelain electrical supplies; Printing ink
HQ: Vibrantz Corporation
6060 Prkland Blvd Ste 250
Mayfield Heights OH 44124
216 875-5600

(G-4469)
VIBRANTZ CORPORATION
6060 Parkland Blvd (44124-4225)
PHONE...........................732 287-4925
Thomas Loschiazo, *Brnch Mgr*
EMP: 73
SALES (corp-wide): 1.88B Privately Held
Web: www.vibrantz.com
SIC: 2865 2851 2816 Color lakes or toners;
Lacquers, varnishes, enamels, and other
coatings; Inorganic pigments
HQ: Vibrantz Corporation
6060 Prkland Blvd Ste 250
Mayfield Heights OH 44124
216 875-5600

(G-4470)
VICS TURNING COINC
16911 Saint Clair Ave (44110-2536)
PHONE...........................216 531-5016
John Lamovec, *Pr*
Ann Maher, *Sec*
EMP: 6 EST: 1972
SQ FT: 16,500
SALES (est): 450.37K Privately Held
Web: www.vicsturning.com
SIC: 3599 Machine shop, jobbing and repair

(G-4471)
VICTOR BODIE TIRE CO
1750 E 55th St (44103-3118)
PHONE...........................216 431-1700
Marc L Blum, *CEO*
EMP: 6 EST: 1948
SQ FT: 12,000
SALES (est): 450K Privately Held
SIC: 7534 5531 5014 Tire recapping;
Automotive tires; Tires and tubes

(G-4472)
**VICTORY WHITE METAL COMPANY
(PA)**
6100 Roland Ave (44127-1353)
P.O. Box 605187 (44105-0187)
PHONE...........................216 271-1400
Alex J Stanwick, *Pr*
Jennifer Sturman, *
▲ EMP: 60 EST: 1920

SQ FT: 60,000
SALES (est): 10.66MM
SALES (corp-wide): 10.66MM Privately
Held
Web: www.victorywhitemetal.com
SIC: 5085 3356 Valves and fittings; Solder:
wire, bar, acid core, and rosin core

(G-4473)
VICTORY WHITE METAL COMPANY
Also Called: Vwm Republic Metals
7930 Jones Rd (44105-3908)
P.O. Box 605217 (44105-0217)
PHONE...........................216 641-2575
Lynn Carlson, *Mgr*
EMP: 12
SALES (corp-wide): 10.66MM Privately
Held
Web: www.victorywhitemetal.com
SIC: 5051 3356 Lead; Lead and zinc
PA: The Victory White Metal Company
6100 Roland Ave
Cleveland OH 44127
216 271-1400

(G-4474)
VICTORY WHITE METAL COMPANY
3027 E 55th St (44127-1275)
P.O. Box 605187 (44105-0187)
PHONE...........................216 271-1400
Tim Hess, *Mgr*
EMP: 19
SQ FT: 50,000
SALES (corp-wide): 10.66MM Privately
Held
Web: www.victorywhitemetal.com
SIC: 3341 4941 4225 Lead smelting and
refining (secondary); Water supply; General
warehousing and storage
PA: The Victory White Metal Company
6100 Roland Ave
Cleveland OH 44127
216 271-1400

(G-4475)
VINYLMNG LLC
8001 Krueger Ave (44105)
PHONE...........................440 261-5799
Stephen Donnelly, *Managing Member*
EMP: 20 EST: 2019
SALES (est): 5.56MM Privately Held
SIC: 2821 Plastics materials and resins

(G-1176)
VISI-TRAK WORLDWIDE LLC (PA)
8400 Sweet Valley Dr Ste 406
(44125-4244)
PHONE...........................216 524-2363
Jack Vann, *Pr*
EMP: 13 EST: 2000
SQ FT: 8,050
SALES (est): 2.33MM
SALES (corp-wide): 2.33MM Privately
Held
Web: www.visi-trak.com
SIC: 3823 Process control instruments

(G-4477)
VITEX CORPORATION
2960 Broadway Ave (44115-3606)
PHONE...........................216 883-0920
Robert Vitek Senior, *Pr*
Robert Vitek Junior, *VP*
Marie Vitek, *Sec*
EMP: 15 EST: 1970
SQ FT: 60,000
SALES (est): 3MM Privately Held
Web: www.vitexcorporation.com
SIC: 2842 Cleaning or polishing
preparations, nec

(G-4478)
VOCATIONAL SERVICES INC
2239 E 55th St (44103-4451)
PHONE...........................216 431-8085
Robert Comben, *Pr*
Donald E Carlson, *
EMP: 10 EST: 1980
SQ FT: 17,541
SALES (est): 1.19MM Privately Held
Web: www.vsiserve.org
SIC: 2391 2511 8331 Curtains and draperies
; Wood household furniture; Job training
and related services

(G-4479)
VOICE PRODUCTS INC
23715 Mercantile Rd Ste A200
(44122-5926)
PHONE...........................216 360-0433
Michael Kaufman, *Pr*
EMP: 10 EST: 1992
SALES (est): 710K Privately Held
Web: www.vproducts.com
SIC: 3669 Smoke detectors

(G-4480)
VOLPE MILLWORK INC
4500 Lee Rd (44128-2963)
PHONE...........................216 581-0200
John Volpe, *Pr*
Salvatore Volpe, *Sec*
William Roy Laubscher, *Stockholder*
Mary Ellen Volpe, *Stockholder*
EMP: 7 EST: 1988
SQ FT: 9,000
SALES (est): 717.98K Privately Held
Web: www.volpemillworkinc.com
SIC: 1521 2431 General remodeling, single-
family houses; Millwork

(G-4481)
VON ROLL USA INC
Also Called: Von Roll Isola
4853 W 130th St (44135-5137)
PHONE...........................216 433-7474
Larry Schwener, *Brnch Mgr*
EMP: 72
SALES (corp-wide): 4.44B Privately Held
Web: www.vonroll.com
SIC: 3644 Insulators and insulation
materials, electrical
HQ: Von Roll Usa, Inc.
200 Von Roll Dr
Schenectady NY 12306
518 344-7100

(G-4482)
VOSS INDUSTRIES LLC (DH)
2168 W 25th St (44113-4172)
PHONE...........................216 771-7655
Daniel W Sedor Senior, *Pr*
Mark Schodowski, *
Nicola Antonelli, *
John F Fritskey, *
◆ EMP: 104 EST: 1957
SQ FT: 240,000
SALES (est): 49.01MM
SALES (corp-wide): 15.37B Publicly Held
Web: www.vossindustries.com
SIC: 3429 3469 3369 3499 Clamps and
couplings, hose; Machine parts, stamped or
pressed metal; Aerospace castings,
nonferrous: except aluminum; Strapping,
metal
HQ: Consolidated Aerospace
Manufacturing, Llc
1425 S Acacia Ave
Fullerton CA 92831
714 989-2797

(G-4483)
**VOYALE MINORITY ENTERPRISE
LLC**
5855 Grant Ave (44105-5607)
PHONE...........................216 271-3661
EMP: 20 EST: 2004
SQ FT: 116,000
SALES (est): 1.71MM Privately Held
Web: www.vmellc.com
SIC: 3499 Metal household articles

(G-4484)
VWM-REPUBLIC INC
Also Called: Republic Metals
7930 Jones Rd (44105-3908)
P.O. Box 605217 (44105-0217)
PHONE...........................216 641-2575
Lynn Carlson, *Mgr*
EMP: 9 EST: 1924
SALES (est): 3.17MM Privately Held
Web: www.republicmetals.com
SIC: 2816 Lead pigments: white lead, lead
oxides, lead sulfate

(G-4485)
WABTEC CORPORATION
4677 Manufacturing Ave (44135-2637)
PHONE...........................216 362-7500
EMP: 10
Web: www.wabteccorp.com
SIC: 3621 3677 Electric motor and generator
parts; Electronic coils and transformers
HQ: Wabtec Corporation
30 Isabella St
Pittsburgh PA 15212

(G-4486)
**WABUSH MNES CLFFS MIN MNGING
A**
200 Public Sq Ste 3300 (44114-2315)
PHONE...........................216 694-5700
John Tuomi, *Managing Member*
Terrance Taridei, *CFO*
EMP: 15 EST: 1957
SALES (est): 3.09MM
SALES (corp-wide): 19.18B Publicly Held
SIC: 1011 Iron ore mining
PA: Cleveland-Cliffs Inc.
200 Public Sq Ste 3300
Cleveland OH 44114
216 694-5700

(G-4487)
**WACO SCAFFOLDING &
EQUIPMENT INC**
4545 Spring Rd (44131-1023)
P.O. Box 318028 (44131-8028)
PHONE...........................216 749-8900
EMP: 550
SIC: 7359 3446 5082 1799 Equipment rental
and leasing, nec; Scaffolds, mobile or
stationary: metal; Scaffolding; Scaffolding

(G-4488)
WADE DYNAMICS INC
1411 E 39th St (44114-4120)
PHONE...........................216 431-8484
Dennis Wade, *Pr*
Denise Wade, *Treas*
Peter Wade, *VP*
EMP: 9 EST: 1963
SQ FT: 6,000
SALES (est): 896.31K Privately Held
Web: www.wadedynamics.com
SIC: 3599 Machine shop, jobbing and repair

(G-4489)
WALLSEYE CONCRETE CORP (PA)
Also Called: Avon
26000 Sprague Rd (44138-2743)

P.O. Box 38159 (44138-0159)
PHONE..............................440 235-1800
Sandra Hill, *Sec*
Brock Walls, *VP*
EMP: 11 **EST:** 1992
SQ FT: 3,400
SALES (est): 874.59K **Privately Held**
Web: www.westviewconcrete.com
SIC: 3241 Portland cement

(G-4490)
WARREN CASTINGS INC
2934 E 55th St (44127-1207)
PHONE..............................216 883-2520
Willie Warren, *Pr*
EMP: 7 **EST:** 1983
SALES (est): 609.97K **Privately Held**
SIC: 3369 Castings, except die-castings, precision

(G-4491)
WARWICK PRODUCTS COMPANY
5350 Tradex Pkwy (44102-5887)
PHONE..............................216 334-1200
Matthew Beverstock, *Pr*
Mike Beverstock, *
John Beverstock, *
Kathryn Koz, *
▼ **EMP:** 30 **EST:** 1949
SQ FT: 17,000
SALES (est): 9.91MM **Privately Held**
Web: www.warwickproducts.com
SIC: 3089 Cases, plastics

(G-4492)
WATERLOO INDUSTRIES INC
12487 Plaza Dr (44130-1056)
P.O. Box 30382 (44130-0382)
PHONE..............................800 833-8851
EMP: 7 **EST:** 2013
SALES (est): 202.57K **Privately Held**
SIC: 3999 Manufacturing industries, nec

(G-4493)
WATERLOX COATINGS CORPORATION
9808 Meech Ave (44105-4191)
PHONE..............................216 641-4877
John Wilson Hawkins, *Pr*
Kellie Hawkins Schaffner, *VP*
▼ **EMP:** 13 **EST:** 1910
SQ FT: 40,000
SALES (est): 2.88MM **Privately Held**
Web: www.waterlox.com
SIC: 2851 Paints: oil or alkyd vehicle or water thinned

(G-4494)
WATTERS MANUFACTURING CO INC
1931 W 47th St (44102-3413)
PHONE..............................216 281-8600
Charles D Watters, *Pr*
EMP: 6 **EST:** 1959
SQ FT: 2,500
SALES (est): 469.52K **Privately Held**
SIC: 3451 Screw machine products

(G-4495)
WDI GROUP INC
Also Called: Solid Surfaces Plus
4031 W 150th St (44135-1301)
PHONE..............................216 251-5509
EMP: 78 **EST:** 1979
SALES (est): 4.66MM **Privately Held**
Web: www.rocksolid-surfaces.com
SIC: 2541 Table or counter tops, plastic laminated

(G-4496)
WEDGEWORKS MCH TL BORING INC
3169 E 80th St (44104-4343)
PHONE..............................216 441-1200
Bradford Braude, *Pr*
Sherry Braude, *Sec*
EMP: 6 **EST:** 1990
SQ FT: 20,000
SALES (est): 1.33MM **Privately Held**
SIC: 3599 Machine shop, jobbing and repair

(G-4497)
WEIDMANN ELECTRICAL TECH INC
Also Called: Weidmann
1300 E 9th St (44114-1501)
P.O. Box 903 (05819-0903)
PHONE..............................937 508-2112
Ulrich W Suter, *Ch*
Franziska A Tschudi Sauber, *CEO*
Oliver Kopp, *CFO*
Daniel J Tschudi, *Prin*
▲ **EMP:** 8 **EST:** 1877
SALES (est): 1.69MM **Privately Held**
Web: www.weidmann-group.com
SIC: 1731 3826 Electrical work; Analytical instruments

(G-4498)
WEISKOPF INDUSTRIES CORP
54 Alpha Park (44143-2208)
P.O. Box 24390 (44124-0390)
PHONE..............................440 442-4400
Edward A Weiskopf, *Pr*
Geoffrey Weiskopf, *
Pam Keidel, *
EMP: 6 **EST:** 1981
SALES (est): 1.19MM **Privately Held**
Web: www.wicwipers.com
SIC: 2211 Tracing cloth, cotton

(G-4499)
WELDED RING PRODUCTS CO (PA)
2180 W 114th St (44102-3582)
PHONE..............................216 961-3800
James C Janosek, *Pr*
Gary Horvath, *
▲ **EMP:** 80 **EST:** 1960
SQ FT: 250,000
SALES (est): 11.63MM
SALES (corp-wide): 11.63MM **Privately Held**
Web: www.weldedring.com
SIC: 3724 Aircraft engines and engine parts

(G-4500)
WELDERS SUPPLY INC (HQ)
Also Called: Lake Erie Iron and Metal
2020 Train Ave (44113-4205)
PHONE..............................216 241-1696
Richard Osborne, *Pr*
Martin Hathy, *VP*
EMP: 12 **EST:** 1946
SQ FT: 8,000
SALES (est): 1.4MM
SALES (corp-wide): 6.29MM **Privately Held**
SIC: 2813 5084 5999 Oxygen, compressed or liquefied; Welding machinery and equipment; Welding supplies
PA: Osair, Inc.
7001 Center St
Mentor OH 44060
440 974-6500

(G-4501)
WERNER G SMITH INC
1730 Train Ave (44113-4289)
PHONE..............................216 861-3676
▼ **EMP:** 12 **EST:** 1950
SALES (est): 3.47MM **Privately Held**
Web: www.wernergsmith.com

SIC: 5088 2869 2077 Marine supplies; Amines, acids, salts, esters; Animal and marine fats and oils

(G-4502)
WEST-CAMP PRESS INC
1538 E 41st St (44103-2337)
PHONE..............................216 426-2660
EMP: 53
SALES (corp-wide): 24.84MM **Privately Held**
Web: www.westcamppress.com
SIC: 2261 Screen printing of cotton broadwoven fabrics
PA: West-Camp Press, Inc.
39 Collegeview Rd
Westerville OH 43081
614 882-2378

(G-4503)
WHITEROCK PIGMENTS INC
1768 E 25th St (44114-4418)
PHONE..............................216 391-7765
Robert L Meyer, *CEO*
Thomas M Forman, *Ch*
EMP: 10 **EST:** 2013
SALES (est): 1.19MM **Privately Held**
SIC: 2816 Titanium dioxide, anatase or rutile (pigments)

(G-4504)
WHITNEY STAINED GL STUDIO INC
5939 Broadway Ave (44127-1718)
PHONE..............................216 348-1616
Peter Billington, *Pr*
Glenn Billington, *VP*
EMP: 9 **EST:** 1994
SQ FT: 12,000
SALES (est): 234.93K **Privately Held**
Web: www.whitneystainedglass.com
SIC: 8999 3231 Stained glass art; Stained glass: made from purchased glass

(G-4505)
WILD FIRE SYSTEMS
535 Ransome Rd (44143-1993)
PHONE..............................440 442-8999
James Berilla, *Owner*
EMP: 6 **EST:** 1975
SALES (est): 483.38K **Privately Held**
Web: www.cleveland19.com
SIC: 3823 7379 Computer interface equipment, for industrial process control; Computer related consulting services

(G-4506)
WILLIAM EXLINE INC
12301 Bennington Ave (44135-3796)
PHONE..............................216 941-0800
William B Exline, *Pr*
August Tischer, *VP Fin*
Michael P Exline, *VP*
EMP: 8 **EST:** 1929
SQ FT: 35,000
SALES (est): 860.67K **Privately Held**
Web: www.williamexline.com
SIC: 2782 Passbooks: bank, etc.

(G-4507)
WILLIAMS STEEL RULE DIE CO
1633 E 40th St (44103-2304)
P.O. Box 43518 (44143-0518)
PHONE..............................216 431-3232
Jeff Jazbec, *Pr*
EMP: 6 **EST:** 1961
SQ FT: 52,000
SALES (est): 470.95K **Privately Held**
Web: www.valve3.com

SIC: 3544 3953 2675 3993 Paper cutting dies; Embossing seals, corporate and official; Paper die-cutting; Signs and advertising specialties

(G-4508)
WINDSOR TOOL INC
10714 Bellaire Rd (44111-5324)
PHONE..............................216 671-1900
Marc Ravas, *Pr*
EMP: 10 **EST:** 1946
SQ FT: 5,000
SALES (est): 819.84K **Privately Held**
SIC: 3544 Special dies and tools

(G-4509)
WIRE PRODUCTS COMPANY INC
Also Called: WIRE PRODUCTS COMPANY, INC.
14700 Industrial Pkwy (44135-4548)
PHONE..............................216 267-0777
Dale Zeleznik, *Mgr*
EMP: 10
SQ FT: 56,625
SALES (corp-wide): 5.69MM **Privately Held**
Web: www.wire-products.com
SIC: 3495 3315 3469 Mechanical springs, precision; Hangers (garment); wire; Metal stampings, nec
PA: Wire Products Company, Llc
14601 Industrial Pkwy
Cleveland OH 44135
216 267-0777

(G-4510)
WIRE PRODUCTS COMPANY LLC (PA)
14601 Industrial Pkwy (44135-4595)
PHONE..............................216 267-0777
E Scot Kennedy, *Pr*
Winston Breeden Junior, *Ex VP*
Dale Zeleznik, *
Gail Breeden, *Stockholder*
Dan Collins, *
EMP: 100 **EST:** 1951
SQ FT: 43,000
SALES (est): 5.69MM
SALES (corp-wide): 5.69MM **Privately Held**
Web: www.wire-products.com
SIC: 3496 Miscellaneous fabricated wire products

(G-4511)
WLS STAMPING CO (PA)
Also Called: Wls Stamping & Fabricating
3292 E 80th St (44104-4392)
PHONE..............................216 271-5100
Robert Guy, *Dir*
Daniel C Cronin, *
Craig Kotnik, *
Susan Nash, *
▲ **EMP:** 74 **EST:** 1944
SQ FT: 30,000
SALES (est): 10.51MM
SALES (corp-wide): 10.51MM **Privately Held**
Web: www.wlsstamping.com
SIC: 3469 3544 Stamping metal for the trade ; Special dies and tools

(G-4512)
WM PLOTZ MACHINE AND FORGE CO
Also Called: Peerless Pump Clveland Svc Ctr
2514 Center St (44113-1111)
PHONE..............................216 861-0441
James W Plotz, *Pr*
Thomas D Plotz, *Sec*
EMP: 17 **EST:** 1888

SQ FT: 21,000
SALES (est): 1.33MM Privately Held
Web: www.plotzmachine.com
SIC: 3599 7699 Machine shop, jobbing and
repair; Pumps and pumping equipment
repair

(G-4513)
WODIN INC
5441 Perkins Rd (44146-1891)
PHONE...............................440 439-4222
R Grant Murphy, Pr
EMP: 35 EST: 1967
SQ FT: 30,000
SALES (est): 1.37MM Privately Held
Web: www.wodin.com
SIC: 3462 3463 3599 3965 Machinery
forgings, ferrous; Nonferrous forgings;
Machine shop, jobbing and repair;
Fasteners

(G-4514)
WOOD-SEBRING CORPORATION
13800 Enterprise Ave (44135-5116)
PHONE...............................216 267-3191
Joseph Kronander, Pr
Joseph Kronander, Pr
Mary Kronander, Sec
EMP: 7 EST: 1944
SQ FT: 10,000
SALES (est): 495.02K Privately Held
SIC: 3451 Screw machine products

(G-4515)
**WOODHILL PLATING WORKS
COMPANY**
9114 Reno Ave (44105-2123)
P.O. Box 605304 (44105-0304)
PHONE...............................216 883-1344
John W Sparano Senior, Pr
James Sparano, *
John W Sparano Junior, VP
Jeff Sparano, *
Jerry Sparano, *
EMP: 25 EST: 1932
SQ FT: 25,000
SALES (est): 2.58MM Privately Held
Web: www.woodhillplating.com
SIC: 3471 Electroplating of metals or formed
products

(G-4516)
WOODSTOCK PRODUCTS INC
2914 Broadway Ave (44115-3606)
PHONE...............................216 641-3811
Terry Dunay, Pr
Clara Dunay, Sec
EMP: 6 EST: 1958
SQ FT: 5,000
SALES (est): 932.13K Privately Held
Web: www.woodstockproductsinc.com
SIC: 2048 Feed concentrates

(G-4517)
**WORTHINGTON MID-RISE CNSTR
INC (HQ)**
Also Called: Worthington Industries
3100 E 45th St Ste 400 (44127-1095)
PHONE...............................216 472-1511
Marybeth Bosko, Pr
Michael Whitticar, *
EMP: 40 EST: 2002
SQ FT: 14,000
SALES (est): 15.92MM
SALES (corp-wide): 1.25B Publicly Held
Web: www.worthingtonenterprises.com
SIC: 3446 Purlins, light gauge steel
PA: Worthington Enterprises, Inc.
200 W Old Wlson Bridge Rd
Worthington OH 43085
614 438-3210

(G-4518)
WRKCO INC
16645 Granite Rd (44137-4301)
PHONE...............................216 663-3344
EMP: 32
SIC: 2631 Paperboard mills
HQ: Wrkco Inc.
1000 Abrnthy Rd Ne Ste 12
Atlanta GA 30328
770 448-2193

(G-4519)
WYMAN-GORDON COMPANY
Also Called: Wyman Gordon
3097 E 61st St (44127-1312)
PHONE...............................216 341-0085
Tim Herron, Brnch Mgr
EMP: 48
SALES (corp-wide): 424.23B Publicly
Held
Web: www.pccforgedproducts.com
SIC: 3462 Iron and steel forgings
HQ: Wyman-Gordon Company
244 Worcester St
North Grafton MA 01536
508 839-8252

(G-4520)
XAPC CO
Also Called: Avalon
15583 Brookpark Rd (44142-1618)
PHONE...............................216 362-4100
Doug Ciabotti, CEO
Lindsey Krauth, Prs Mgr
Tom Ward, VP Sls
▲ EMP: 238 EST: 1982
SQ FT: 36,000
SALES (est): 8.69MM Privately Held
SIC: 3324 Steel investment foundries

(G-4521)
YOUR CARPENTER INC
2403 Saint Clair Ave Ne (44114-4020)
P.O. Box 14519 (44114-0519)
PHONE...............................216 621-2166
Matt Howells, Prin
EMP: 8 EST: 2006
SALES (est): 739.38K Privately Held
SIC: 3423 Carpenters' hand tools, except
saws: levels, chisels, etc.

(G-4522)
ZACLON LLC
2981 Independence Rd (44115-3699)
PHONE...............................216 271-1601
◆ EMP: 25 EST: 2003
SALES (est): 24.62MM
SALES (corp-wide): 24.62MM Privately
Held
Web: www.zaclon.com
SIC: 2819 Industrial inorganic chemicals, nec
PA: Alpha Zeta Holdings, Inc.
2981 Independence Rd
Cleveland OH 44115
216 271-1601

(G-4523)
ZEN INDUSTRIES INC
Also Called: American Mine Door
6200 Harvard Ave (44105-4861)
PHONE...............................216 432-3240
Kim Zenisek, Pr
Ed Ebner, *
EMP: 35 EST: 1906
SQ FT: 70,000
SALES (est): 4.27MM Privately Held
Web: www.minedoor.com
SIC: 3532 Mining machinery

(G-4524)
ZF ACTIVE SAFETY & ELEC US LLC
8333 Rockside Rd (44125-6134)
PHONE...............................216 750-2400
Richard Rowan, Mgr
EMP: 84
SALES (corp-wide): 144.19K Privately
Held
Web: www.exactcarepharmacy.com
SIC: 3714 Motor vehicle parts and
accessories
HQ: Zf Active Safety & Electronics Us Llc
15811 Centennial Dr
Northville MI 48168
765 429-1936

(G-4525)
ZIPPITYCOM PRINT LLC
1600 E 23rd St (44114-4208)
PHONE...............................216 438-0001
J P Dell'aquila, Managing Member
Dennis Dimitrov, COO
EMP: 12 EST: 2017
SALES (est): 1.38MM Privately Held
Web: www.zippityprint.com
SIC: 2752 Offset printing

(G-4526)
ZIRCOA INC (PA)
31501 Solon Rd (44139-3526)
PHONE...............................440 248-0500
John Kaniuk, Pr
▲ EMP: 130 EST: 1956
SQ FT: 120,000
SALES (est): 13.47MM
SALES (corp-wide): 13.47MM Privately
Held
Web: www.zircoa.com
SIC: 3339 3297 2851 Zirconium metal,
sponge and granules; Nonclay refractories;
Paints and allied products

Cleveland Heights
Cuyahoga County

(G-4527)
**AUGUSTE MOONE ENTERPRISES
LTD**
3355 Tullamore Rd (44118-2938)
PHONE...............................216 333-9248
Augustin Jackson, CEO
EMP: 25 EST: 2010
SALES (est): 192.51K Privately Held
SIC: 8299 2731 5942 8999 Educational
services; Books, publishing only; Children's
books; Writing for publication

(G-4528)
**DATA COOLING TECHNOLOGIES
LLC**
3092 Euclid Heights Blvd (44118-2026)
PHONE...............................330 954-3800
Gregory Gyllstrom, CEO
William M Weber, *
EMP: 42 EST: 2005
SQ FT: 100,000
SALES (est): 2.57MM Privately Held
SIC: 3433 Heating equipment, except electric

(G-4529)
MADE MEN CIRCLE LLC
2883 Mayfield Rd Apt 2 (44118-1698)
PHONE...............................216 501-0414
EMP: 6 EST: 2020
SALES (est): 60K Privately Held
SIC: 3161 Clothing and apparel carrying
cases

(G-4530)
MOMMA JS BLAZING KITCHEN LLC
2281 S Overlook Rd (44106-3141)
PHONE...............................216 551-8791
EMP: 8
SALES (est): 111.58K Privately Held
SIC: 2099 7389 Food preparations, nec;
Business services, nec

(G-4531)
TALUS RENEWABLES INC (PA)
3762 Bainbridge Rd (44118-2244)
PHONE...............................650 248-5374
Hiro Iwanaga, CEO
EMP: 17 EST: 2021
SALES (est): 1.83MM
SALES (corp-wide): 1.83MM Privately
Held
SIC: 4911 2873
; Anhydrous ammonia

Cleves
Hamilton County

(G-4532)
BRUEWER WOODWORK MFG CO
10000 Cilley Rd (45002-9735)
PHONE...............................513 353-3505
Ralph H Bruewer, Pr
August Bruewer, *
Gary A Bruewer, *
Richard M Ruffing, *
▲ EMP: 55 EST: 1973
SQ FT: 155,000
SALES (est): 3.33MM Privately Held
Web: mail.bruewerwoodwork.com
SIC: 3083 2541 2435 2434 Plastics finished
products, laminated; Office fixtures, wood;
Hardwood veneer and plywood; Wood
kitchen cabinets

(G-4533)
CONVEYOR SOLUTIONS LLC
6705 Dry Fork Rd (45002-9732)
PHONE...............................513 367-4845
EMP: 10 EST: 2001
SQ FT: 6,200
SALES (est): 5.18MM Privately Held
Web: www.conveyorsolutionsllc.com
SIC: 3535 Belt conveyor systems, general
industrial use

(G-4534)
CORNHOLE WORLDWIDE LLC
5337 Hamilton Cleves Rd (45002-7502)
PHONE...............................513 324-2777
Adam Brinkman, Managing Member
EMP: 6 EST: 2010
SALES (est): 1.07MM Privately Held
Web: www.cornholeworldwide.com
SIC: 3944 Games, toys, and children's
vehicles

(G-4535)
**EPOXY SYSTEMS BLSTG CATING
INC**
5640 Morgan Rd (45002-8720)
PHONE...............................513 924-1800
Ray Litmer, Pr
Barbara Ferneding, Prin
EMP: 15 EST: 2007
SALES (est): 2MM Privately Held
Web:
www.epoxy-systems-blast-powder-paint.com
SIC: 2851 Epoxy coatings

(G-4536)
ERNST ENTERPRISES INC
Also Called: Ernst Concrete
7340 Dry Fork Rd (45002-9431)
PHONE.....................................513 367-1939
Dick England, *Mgr*
EMP: 8
SALES (corp-wide): 240.08MM **Privately Held**
Web: www.ernstconcrete.com
SIC: 3273 Ready-mixed concrete
PA: Ernst Enterprises, Inc.
    993 Falls Creek Dr
    Vandalia OH 45377
    937 233-5555

(G-4537)
FDI CABINETRY LLC
Also Called: Fdi
5555 Dry Fork Rd (45002-9733)
P.O. Box 832 (45041-0832)
PHONE.....................................513 353-4500
Diane Hart, *Managing Member*
EMP: 9 **EST:** 2011
SQ FT: 12,000
SALES (est): 1.97MM **Privately Held**
Web: www.fdicabinetry.com
SIC: 2434 3993 1799 3083 Wood kitchen cabinets; Signs and advertising specialties; Home/office interiors finishing, furnishing and remodeling; Plastics finished products, laminated

(G-4538)
HANSON AGGREGATES EAST
7000 Dry Fork Rd (45002-9732)
PHONE.....................................513 353-1100
Tom Rodurbush, *Prin*
EMP: 6 **EST:** 2004
SALES (est): 472.32K **Privately Held**
SIC: 1442 Construction sand and gravel

(G-4539)
HEALTHWARES MANUFACTURING
5838b Hamilton Cleves Rd (45002-9529)
PHONE.....................................513 353-3691
Greg Overman, *Pr*
Joe Overman, *VP*
EMP: 12 **EST:** 1996
SALES (est): 1.19MM **Privately Held**
Web: www.healthwares.com
SIC: 3842 Wheelchairs

(G-4540)
JAMES BUNNELL INC
7000 Dry Fork Rd (45002-9732)
PHONE.....................................513 353-1100
Jack Ernest, *Pr*
Vicki Earnst, *Sec*
EMP: 10 **EST:** 1955
SQ FT: 1,160
SALES (est): 792.78K **Privately Held**
SIC: 1442 Construction sand and gravel

(G-4541)
JOHNSON PRCISION MACHINING INC
5919 Hamilton Cleves Rd (45002-9051)
PHONE.....................................513 353-4252
Mary C Hubbard, *Pr*
Ellis Hubbard, *VP*
EMP: 8 **EST:** 1983
SQ FT: 7,500
SALES (est): 651.69K **Privately Held**
SIC: 3599 Machine shop, jobbing and repair

(G-4542)
KINNEMYERS CORNERSTONE CAB INC
Also Called: Kinnemeyers Cornerstone Cab Co

6000 Hamilton Cleves Rd (45002-9530)
PHONE.....................................513 353-3030
Ken Kinnemeyer, *Pr*
EMP: 6 **EST:** 2004
SALES (est): 222.06K **Privately Held**
Web: www.cornerstonecabinets.com
SIC: 2599 2434 Cabinets, factory; Wood kitchen cabinets

(G-4543)
L & L ORNAMENTAL IRON CO
Also Called: L & L Railings
6024 Hamilton Cleves Rd (45002-9530)
PHONE.....................................513 353-1930
Randy Seiler, *Pr*
Dean Seiler, *VP*
EMP: 11 **EST:** 1959
SQ FT: 8,000
SALES (est): 6.06MM **Privately Held**
Web: www.llrailings.com
SIC: 2431 3446 3354 Railings, stair: wood; Ornamental metalwork; Aluminum extruded products

(G-4544)
METAL MAINTENANCE INC
Also Called: Architectural Metal Maint
322 N Finley St (45002-1005)
P.O. Box 41 (45001-0041)
PHONE.....................................513 661-3300
Steve Campbell, *Pr*
EMP: 10 **EST:** 1997
SALES (est): 243.25K **Privately Held**
Web: www.metalmaintenance.com
SIC: 3446 Architectural metalwork

(G-4545)
MODERN SHEET METAL WORKS INC
6037 Hamilton Cleves Rd (45002-9530)
P.O. Box 53187 (45253-0187)
PHONE.....................................513 353-3666
Dorothy Johnson, *Pr*
Cynthia Freppon, *
Pamela Rosenacher, *
William Freppon, *
Jennifer Sucher, *
EMP: 25 **EST:** 1936
SQ FT: 16,000
SALES (est): 4.39MM **Privately Held**
Web: www.modernsheetmetal.com
SIC: 3444 Sheet metalwork

(G-4546)
POHL MACHINING INC (PA)
Also Called: Miami Machine
4901 Hamilton Cleves Rd (45002-9753)
P.O. Box 10 (45002-0010)
PHONE.....................................513 353-2929
Shawna Vanderpohl, *Pr*
Irvin Vanderpohl, *
EMP: 26 **EST:** 2013
SALES (est): 9.58MM
SALES (corp-wide): 9.58MM **Privately Held**
Web: www.miamimachine.com
SIC: 3599 Machine shop, jobbing and repair

(G-4547)
POWERCLEAN EQUIPMENT COMPANY
5945 Dry Fork Rd (45002-9794)
PHONE.....................................513 202-0001
Tom Ossege, *Pr*
Gary Ossege, *VP*
EMP: 16 **EST:** 2005
SALES (est): 2.46MM **Privately Held**
Web: www.powercleanequipment.com

SIC: 7359 3635 5084 Equipment rental and leasing, nec; Household vacuum cleaners; Cleaning equipment, high pressure, sand or steam

(G-4548)
SPURLINO MATERIALS LLC
6600 Dry Fork Rd (45002-9392)
PHONE.....................................513 202-1111
Allan Roelle, *Mgr*
EMP: 9
SALES (corp-wide): 1.56MM **Privately Held**
Web: www.spurlino.net
SIC: 3273 Ready-mixed concrete
PA: Spurlino Materials, Llc
    4000 Oxford State Rd
    Middletown OH 45044
    513 705-0111

(G-4549)
STOCK MFG & DESIGN CO INC (PA)
Also Called: Q M P
10040 Cilley Rd (45002-9735)
P.O. Box 68 (45002-0068)
PHONE.....................................513 353-3600
William H Reyering, *Pr*
Dennis K Stock, *
Anthony Stock, *
EMP: 15 **EST:** 1974
SQ FT: 80,000
SALES (est): 20.91MM
SALES (corp-wide): 20.91MM **Privately Held**
Web: www.stockmfg.com
SIC: 3441 Fabricated structural metal

(G-4550)
TAKK INDUSTRIES INC
5838a Hamilton Cleves Rd (45002-9529)
PHONE.....................................513 353-4306
Joseph Overman, *Pr*
Gregory Overman, *Ex VP*
▲ **EMP:** 16 **EST:** 1944
SALES (est): 2.28MM **Privately Held**
Web: www.takk.com
SIC: 3629 3469 Static elimination equipment, industrial; Metal stampings, nec

(G-4551)
TISCH ENVIRONMENTAL INC (PA)
145 S Miami Ave (45002-1250)
PHONE.....................................513 467-9000
Wilbur John Tisch, *Pr*
James Paul Tisch, *VP*
▲ **EMP:** 22 **EST:** 1998
SQ FT: 12,000
SALES (est): 10MM
SALES (corp-wide): 10MM **Privately Held**
Web: www.tisch-env.com
SIC: 3564 Blowers and fans

(G-4552)
W & W CUSTOM FABRICATION INC
4801 Hamilton Cleves Rd (45002-9752)
P.O. Box 288 (45002-0288)
PHONE.....................................513 353-4617
Steve Webb, *Pr*
Mike Hutchison, *Genl Mgr*
EMP: 6 **EST:** 1994
SALES (est): 3.79MM **Privately Held**
Web: www.wwcustomfab.com
SIC: 3441 Fabricated structural metal

Clinton
Summit County

(G-4553)
CLARK WOOD SPECIALTIES INC
9235 Shadybrook St Nw (44216-9546)
PHONE.....................................330 499-8711
Paul Clark, *Pr*
Kimberly Ann Clark, *VP*
EMP: 8 **EST:** 1980
SQ FT: 12,500
SALES (est): 332.68K **Privately Held**
Web: www.clarkwoodspecialties.com
SIC: 2431 5031 Moldings, wood: unfinished and prefinished; Kitchen cabinets

(G-4554)
J & M FABRICATIONS LLC
3000 S 1st St (44216-9110)
PHONE.....................................330 860-4346
EMP: 6 **EST:** 2017
SALES (est): 2.56MM **Privately Held**
SIC: 3441 Fabricated structural metal

Cloverdale
Putnam County

(G-4555)
JONASHTONS LLC
12485 State Route 634 (45827-9723)
PHONE.....................................419 488-2363
Susan Knippen, *Owner*
EMP: 7 **EST:** 1994
SALES (est): 488.19K **Privately Held**
SIC: 3599 Machine shop, jobbing and repair

Clyde
Sandusky County

(G-4556)
ALLIANCE-MCALPIN NY LLC
401 Elm St (43410-2148)
PHONE.....................................585 426-5310
EMP: 296 **EST:** 2008
SALES (est): 5.88MM
SALES (corp-wide): 33.16MM **Privately Held**
Web: www.allianceppc.com
SIC: 3089 Injection molded finished plastics products, nec
HQ: Revere Plastics Systems, Llc
    39555 Orchard Hill Pl
    Novi MI 48375

(G-4557)
CLYDE TOOL & DIE INC
Also Called: Clyde Foam
524 S Church St (43410-2100)
PHONE.....................................419 547-9574
Bruce G Schrader, *Pr*
EMP: 18 **EST:** 1942
SQ FT: 30,000
SALES (est): 2.32MM **Privately Held**
Web: www.clydetool.com
SIC: 3544 2821 Special dies and tools; Molding compounds, plastics

(G-4558)
EVERGREEN RECYCLING LLC (DH)
Also Called: Evergreen Midwest
202 Watertower Dr (43410-2154)
PHONE.....................................419 547-1400
Greg Johnson, *Managing Member*
EMP: 22 **EST:** 1998
SALES (est): 5.32MM **Privately Held**
Web: www.evergreentogether.com

▲ = Import ▼ = Export
◆ = Import/Export

SIC: 2821 Polystyrene resins
HQ: Polychem, Llc
6277 Heisley Rd
Mentor OH 44060
440 357-1500

(G-4559)
J TEK TOOL & MOLD INC
304 Elm St (43410-2124)
PHONE..............................419 547-9476
John Cattano, *Pr*
EMP: 10 **EST:** 1989
SQ FT: 10,000
SALES (est): 830.57K **Privately Held**
Web: www.jtektool.com
SIC: 3544 Special dies and tools

(G-4560)
MIDWEST COMPOST INC
7250 State Route 101 E (43410-8519)
PHONE..............................419 547-7979
Eugene F Windau, *Pr*
Joseph Tauch, *VP*
John Steager, *Sec*
EMP: 11 **EST:** 1988
SQ FT: 2,432
SALES (est): 2.94MM **Privately Held**
SIC: 2875 Compost

(G-4561)
POLYCHEM LLC
Also Called: Evergreen Plastics
202 Watertower Dr (43410-2154)
PHONE..............................419 547-1400
Mark Jeckering, *Genl Mgr*
EMP: 75
Web: www.polychem.com
SIC: 3052 4953 Plastic belting; Recycling, waste materials
HQ: Polychem, Llc
6277 Heisley Rd
Mentor OH 44060
440 357-1500

(G-4562)
REVERE PLAS SYSTEMS GROUP LLC (HQ)
401 Elm St (43410-2148)
PHONE..............................419 547-6918
EMP: 450 **EST:** 2005
SALES (est): 18.84MM **Privately Held**
Web: www.surflo.com
SIC: 3089 Injection molding of plastics
PA: Old Rev, Llc
16855 Suthpark Dr Ste 100
Westfield IN 46074

(G-4563)
REVERE PLASTICS SYSTEMS LLC
401 Elm St (43410-2148)
PHONE..............................573 785-0871
Danny Neff, *Mgr*
EMP: 236
SALES (corp-wide): 33.16MM **Privately Held**
Web: www.revereplasticssystems.com
SIC: 3089 Injection molding of plastics
HQ: Revere Plastics Systems, Llc
39555 Orchard Hill Pl
Novi MI 48375

(G-4564)
SANDCO INDUSTRIES
567 Premier Dr (43410-2157)
PHONE..............................419 547-3273
Donald Nalley, *Dir*
EMP: 35 **EST:** 1964
SALES (est): 2.06MM **Privately Held**
Web: www.sandcoind.com

SIC: 8331 3639 Sheltered workshop; Major kitchen appliances, except refrigerators and stoves

(G-4565)
WHIRLPOOL CORPORATION
Also Called: Whirlpool
119 Birdseye St (43410-1397)
PHONE..............................419 547-7711
Casey Drabik, *VP*
EMP: 159
SQ FT: 1,500,000
SALES (corp-wide): 16.61B **Publicly Held**
Web: www.whirlpoolcorp.com
SIC: 3632 3639 3582 3633 Freezers, home and farm; Dishwashing machines, household; Commercial laundry equipment; Washing machines, household: including coin-operated
PA: Whirlpool Corporation
2000 N M-63
Benton Harbor MI 49022
269 923-5000

(G-4566)
WHIRLPOOL CORPORATION
Also Called: Whirlpool
1081 W Mcpherson Hwy (43410-1001)
PHONE..............................419 547-2610
Tom Borro, *Mgr*
EMP: 9
SALES (corp-wide): 16.61B **Publicly Held**
Web: www.whirlpoolcorp.com
SIC: 3633 Household laundry equipment
PA: Whirlpool Corporation
2000 N M-63
Benton Harbor MI 49022
269 923-5000

Coldwater
Mercer County

(G-4567)
ALUMETAL MANUFACTURING COMPANY
4555 Sr 127 (45828)
P.O. Box 166 (45828-0166)
PHONE..............................419 268-2311
Lavern W Gross, *Pr*
Oliver Giere, *Sec*
EMP: 21 **EST:** 1950
SQ FT: 25,000
SALES (est): 319.45K **Privately Held**
Web: www.alumetalmfg.com
SIC: 3444 Awnings, sheet metal

(G-4568)
BASIC GRAIN PRODUCTS INC
Also Called: Tastemorr Snacks
300 E Vine St 310 (45828-1399)
PHONE..............................419 678-2304
Carol Knapke, *Pr*
Amy Day, *
Ralph F Keister, *
Brent Aleong, *
EMP: 100 **EST:** 1994
SQ FT: 100,000
SALES (est): 10.79MM **Privately Held**
SIC: 2052 2099 2096 Rice cakes; Food preparations, nec; Potato chips and similar snacks

(G-4569)
CAMELOT MANUFACTURING INC
210 Butler St (45828-1103)
P.O. Box 44 (45828-0044)
PHONE..............................419 678-2603
Charles A Froning, *Pr*
EMP: 9 **EST:** 1981

SQ FT: 14,000
SALES (est): 785.99K **Privately Held**
SIC: 3441 7692 3469 Fabricated structural metal; Welding repair; Metal stampings, nec

(G-4570)
CASAD COMPANY INC
Also Called: Totally Promotional
450 S 2nd St (45828-1803)
PHONE..............................419 586-9457
Thomas R Casad, *Pr*
▲ **EMP:** 15 **EST:** 1992
SQ FT: 7,000
SALES (est): 3.59MM **Privately Held**
Web: www.totallypromotional.com
SIC: 2759 3993 Screen printing; Signs and advertising specialties

(G-4571)
COLDWATER MACHINE COMPANY LLC
911 N 2nd St (45828-8736)
PHONE..............................419 678-4877
EMP: 113 **EST:** 1956
SALES (est): 6.5MM
SALES (corp-wide): 4.01B **Publicly Held**
Web: www.coldwatermachine.com
SIC: 3545 3544 Machine tool accessories; Special dies and tools
PA: Lincoln Electric Holdings, Inc.
22801 St Clair Ave
Cleveland OH 44117
216 481-8100

(G-4572)
DERUIJTER INTL USA INC
Also Called: Dri Rubber
120 Harvest Dr (45828-8733)
P.O. Box 90 (45828-0090)
PHONE..............................419 678-3909
Roger Deruijter, *Pr*
Michael Lindsay, *VP*
Hans Van Kleef, *CFO*
◆ **EMP:** 10 **EST:** 1995
SQ FT: 35,000
SALES (est): 6.58MM **Privately Held**
Web: www.deruijterusa.com
SIC: 3069 Plumbers' rubber goods
HQ: De Ruijter International B.V.
Prof. Minckelersweg 1
Waalwijk NB 5144
416674000

(G-4573)
EXCEL MACHINE & TOOL INC
212 Butler St (45828-1103)
PHONE..............................419 678-3318
Timothy Moorman, *Pr*
Dale Kahlig, *VP*
EMP: 10 **EST:** 1991
SALES (est): 960.04K **Privately Held**
Web: www.tubebenders.com
SIC: 3599 Machine shop, jobbing and repair

(G-4574)
FORM MANUFACTURING LLC
149 Harvest Dr (45828-8748)
PHONE..............................419 678-1400
Kevin Myer, *Engr*
EMP: 10 **EST:** 2015
SALES (est): 158.19K **Privately Held**
Web: www.4mmfg.com
SIC: 2295 Plastic coated yarns or fabrics

(G-4575)
FORTY NINE DEGREES LLC
149 Harvest Dr (45828-8748)
PHONE..............................419 678-0100
EMP: 11 **EST:** 2003
SALES (est): 2.72MM **Privately Held**
Web: www.fortyninedegrees.com

SIC: 3993 Signs and advertising specialties

(G-4576)
HARDIN CREEK MACHINE & TL INC
200 Hardin St (45828-9794)
PHONE..............................419 678-4913
Joseph Wenning, *Pr*
Randy Schmitz, *VP*
EMP: 10 **EST:** 1984
SQ FT: 6,000
SALES (est): 1.25MM **Privately Held**
SIC: 3544 3599 Special dies and tools; Machine and other job shop work

(G-4577)
HEALTH CARE PRODUCTS INC
410 Nisco St (45828-8750)
P.O. Box 116 (45828-0116)
PHONE..............................419 678-9620
Michael Bruns, *Pr*
▲ **EMP:** 38 **EST:** 2005
SQ FT: 50,000
SALES (est): 8.58MM **Privately Held**
Web: www.hcp3.com
SIC: 2676 Napkins, sanitary: made from purchased paper

(G-4578)
HOME BAKERY
109 W Main St (45828-1702)
PHONE..............................419 678-3018
Carl Brunson, *Owner*
Bruce A Fox, *Owner*
EMP: 10 **EST:** 1885
SQ FT: 3,000
SALES (est): 220.91K **Privately Held**
SIC: 2051 Bakery: wholesale or wholesale/ retail combined

(G-4579)
K VENTURES INC
Also Called: EMB Designs
211 E Main St (45828-1720)
P.O. Box 112 (45828-0112)
PHONE..............................419 678-2308
Michelle Ebbing, *Pr*
Mike Knapschaefer, *Sec*
EMP: 10 **EST:** 2003
SQ FT: 24,000
SALES (est): 418.16K **Privately Held**
Web: www.designsemb.com
SIC: 5099 5137 5699 2395 Signs, except electric; Women's and children's sportswear and swimsuits; Uniforms; Embroidery and art needlework

(G-4580)
LEFELD WELDING & STL SUPS INC (PA)
Also Called: Lefeld Supplies Rental
600 N 2nd St (45828-9777)
PHONE..............................419 678-2397
Stanley E Lefeld, *CEO*
Gary Lefeld, *
▲ **EMP:** 43 **EST:** 1953
SQ FT: 10,400
SALES: 8.95MM
SALES (corp-wide): 8.95MM **Privately Held**
Web: www.lefeld.com
SIC: 5084 7353 1799 3441 Welding machinery and equipment; Heavy construction equipment rental; Welding on site; Fabricated structural metal

(G-4581)
LINCOLN ELECTRIC AUTOMTN INC
911 N 2nd St (45828-8736)
PHONE..............................419 678-4877
John Campbell, *Brnch Mgr*
EMP: 115

SALES (corp-wide): 4.01B **Publicly Held**
Web: www.coldwatermachine.com
SIC: 3545 3443 Machine tool accessories;
　Special dies and tools
HQ: Lincoln Electric Automation, Inc.
　407 S Main St
　Fort Loramie OH 45845
　937 295-2120

(G-4582)
MERCER COLOR CORPORATION
425 Hardin St (45828-8742)
P.O. Box 113 (45828-0113)
PHONE...............................419 678-8273
Mark A Baumer, *Pr*
Patrick J Berger, *VP*
EMP: 9 **EST:** 1981
SQ FT: 12,000
SALES (est): 747.69K **Privately Held**
Web: www.mercercolor.com
SIC: 2752 Offset printing

(G-4583)
RANDALL BEARINGS INC
821 Weis St (45828-9612)
PHONE...............................419 678-2486
Jeff Hager, *Brnch Mgr*
EMP: 12
Web: www.randallbearings.com
SIC: 3568 3624 3366 Bearings, bushings,
　and blocks; Carbon and graphite products;
　Copper foundries
HQ: Randall Bearings, Inc.
　240 Jay Begg Pkwy
　Lima OH 45804
　419 223-1075

(G-4584)
SIGNATURE PARTNERS INC
Also Called: Signature 4 Image
149 Harvest Dr (45828-8748)
PHONE...............................419 678-1400
Bradley Meyer, *Pr*
Paul Meikemp, *
▲ **EMP:** 65 **EST:** 1992
SALES (est): 9.05MM **Privately Held**
Web: www.signature4.com
SIC: 3479 Name plates: engraved, etched,
　etc.

(G-4585)
TAYLOR COMMUNICATIONS INC
Also Called: Standard Register
515 W Sycamore St (45828-1663)
P.O. Box 109 (45828-0109)
PHONE...............................419 678-6000
Barry Paynter, *Brnch Mgr*
EMP: 32
SALES (corp-wide): 3.81B **Privately Held**
Web: www.taylor.com
SIC: 2759 Commercial printing, nec
HQ: Taylor Communications, Inc.
　1725 Roe Crest Dr
　North Mankato MN 56003
　866 541-0937

(G-4586)
VAL-CO PAX INC (DH)
Also Called: Val Products
　210 E Main St (45828-1751)
　P.O. Box 117 (45828-0117)
PHONE...............................717 354-4586
Frederick Steudler, *CEO*
Steve Hough, *
William Kramer, *
▲ **EMP:** 67 **EST:** 1935
SQ FT: 130,000
SALES (est): 8.18MM
SALES (corp-wide): 30.96MM **Privately
Held**
Web: www.val-co.com

SIC: 3523 3443 Hog feeding, handling, and
　watering equipment; Fabricated plate work
　(boiler shop)
HQ: Val Products, Inc.
　2599 Old Phladelphia Pike
　Bird In Hand PA 17505
　717 392-3978

Collins
Huron County

(G-4587)
FACILITY SERVICE PROS LLC
3206 Townsend Angling Rd (44826-9723)
PHONE...............................419 577-6123
Misty Bainbridge, *CEO*
Michael Bainbridge, *Managing Member*
Misty Bainbridge, *Managing Member*
EMP: 6 **EST:** 2016
SALES (est): 446.85K **Privately Held**
Web: www.fs-pros.com
SIC: 1542 8744 1389 Commercial and office
　buildings, renovation and repair; Facilities
　support services; Construction, repair, and
　dismantling services

Columbia Station
Lorain County

(G-4588)
AQUATIC TECHNOLOGY
26966 Royalton Rd (44028-9758)
PHONE...............................440 236-8330
Greg Smith, *Owner*
◆ **EMP:** 10 **EST:** 1991
SQ FT: 4,300
SALES (est): 109.35K **Privately Held**
Web: www.aquatictech.com
SIC: 5999 5199 3999 Aquarium supplies;
　Pets and pet supplies; Pet supplies

(G-4589)
ATOM BLASTING AND FINSHG INC
24933 Sprague Rd (44028-9671)
PHONE...............................440 235-4765
Richard Ferry, *Pr*
Karen Widener, *VP*
▲ **EMP:** 6 **EST:** 1970
SALES (est): 587.41K **Privately Held**
SIC: 3471 Finishing, metals or formed
　products

(G-4590)
CAL SALES EMBROIDERY
13975 Station Rd (44028-9401)
PHONE...............................440 236-3820
Edward L Pete Houston, *Owner*
EMP: 6 **EST:** 1986
SQ FT: 1,800
SALES (est): 137.64K **Privately Held**
Web: www.calsalesembroidery.com
SIC: 2395 2396 5199 Embroidery products,
　except Schiffli machine; Screen printing on
　fabric articles; Advertising specialties

(G-4591)
COLUMBIA STAMPING INC
Also Called: Total Automation
13676 Station Rd (44028-9538)
PHONE...............................440 236-6677
James D Galvin, *Pr*
Ken Dillinger, *Sec*
EMP: 9 **EST:** 1990
SQ FT: 37,000
SALES (est): 615.25K **Privately Held**
Web: www.specialmetalstamping.com
SIC: 3544 3542 Die sets for metal stamping
　(presses); Die casting machines

(G-4592)
CONTROL ELECTRIC CO
12130 Eaton Commerce Pkwy
　(44028-9208)
PHONE...............................216 671-8010
Mike Vogt, *Pr*
EMP: 23 **EST:** 1963
SQ FT: 6,800
SALES (est): 4.81MM **Privately Held**
Web: www.controlelectric.com
SIC: 3625 8711 2542 Industrial electrical
　relays and switches; Engineering services;
　Partitions and fixtures, except wood

(G-4593)
DIMENSION INDUSTRIES INC
27335 Royalton Rd (44028-9159)
P.O. Box 1130 (44028-1130)
PHONE...............................440 236-3265
William Biljes, *Pr*
EMP: 6 **EST:** 1986
SQ FT: 7,200
SALES (est): 1.2MM **Privately Held**
Web: www.dimensionindustries.com
SIC: 3599 Machine and other job shop work

(G-4594)
MODERN MOLD CORPORATION
27684 Royalton Rd (44028-9073)
PHONE...............................440 236-9600
David Bowes, *Pr*
EMP: 7 **EST:** 1984
SALES (est): 1.95MM **Privately Held**
Web: www.tonerplastics.com
SIC: 3089 Injection molding of plastics

(G-4595)
OBHC INC
Also Called: Original Beverage Holder Co
33549 E Royalton Rd Unit 9 (44028-9306)
PHONE...............................440 236-5112
Tim Jenkins, *Pr*
EMP: 7 **EST:** 2007
SQ FT: 6,000
SALES (est): 954.48K **Privately Held**
Web: www.obhcinc.com
SIC: 3585 3993 5149 Soda fountain and
　beverage dispensing equipment and parts;
　Scoreboards, electric; Wine makers'
　equipment and supplies

(G-4596)
PERRONS PRINTING COMPANY INC
Also Called: Image Graphics
27500 Royalton Rd Ste D (44028-9713)
P.O. Box 669 (44028-0669)
PHONE...............................440 236-8870
Edward Perron Senior, *Pr*
Linda Perron, *Pr*
George D Maurer Senior, *Prin*
EMP: 6 **EST:** 1982
SQ FT: 10,000
SALES (est): 486.91K **Privately Held**
Web: www.printdirectforless.com
SIC: 2752 7336 Offset printing; Graphic arts
　and related design

(G-4597)
PIER TOOL & DIE INC
27369 Royalton Rd (44028-9159)
P.O. Box 452 (44028-0452)
PHONE...............................440 236-3188
Mario J Pierzchala, *Pr*
Karen Pierzchala, *VP*
Randy Pierzchala, *Manager*
EMP: 15 **EST:** 1985
SQ FT: 15,000
SALES (est): 2.27MM **Privately Held**
Web: www.piertool.com
SIC: 3544 Special dies and tools

(G-4598)
PRINT DIRECT FOR LESS 2 INC
27500 Royalton Rd (44028-9713)
P.O. Box 669 (44028-0669)
PHONE...............................440 236-8870
Edward M Perron Junior, *Pr*
Linda Perron, *Pr*
Edward M Perron Junior, *VP*
Nellie Akalp, *Prin*
▼ **EMP:** 15 **EST:** 2004
SALES (est): 2.44MM **Privately Held**
Web: www.printdirectforless.com
SIC: 2752 Offset printing

(G-4599)
ROLLER SOURCE INC
34100 E Royalton Rd (44028-9759)
PHONE...............................440 748-4033
Steve Leuschel, *Pr*
George Novak, *VP*
EMP: 10 **EST:** 1985
SALES (est): 1.55MM **Privately Held**
Web: www.therollersource.com
SIC: 3069 Medical and laboratory rubber
　sundries and related products

(G-4600)
ROYALTON INDUSTRIES INC
12450 Eaton Commerce Pkwy Ste 1
　(44028-9213)
PHONE...............................440 748-9900
William A Baltes Senior, *Ch Bd*
William A Baltes Junior, *Treas*
EMP: 10 **EST:** 1979
SQ FT: 10,000
SALES (est): 1.87MM **Privately Held**
SIC: 3599 Custom machinery

(G-4601)
RURAL-URBAN RECORD INC
24487 Squire Rd (44028-9672)
P.O. Box 966 (44028-0966)
PHONE...............................440 236-8982
Leonard Boise, *Pr*
EMP: 6 **EST:** 1956
SQ FT: 1,966
SALES (est): 181.54K **Privately Held**
Web: www.rural-urbanrecord.com
SIC: 2711 Newspapers, publishing and
　printing

(G-4602)
**SEAWAY BOLT AND SPECIALS
COMPANY**
Also Called: Seaway
11561 Station Rd (44028-9503)
P.O. Box 908 (44028-0908)
PHONE...............................440 236-5015
EMP: 84 **EST:** 1957
SALES (est): 5.37MM **Privately Held**
Web: www.seawaybolt.com
SIC: 3499 3399 Drain plugs, magnetic; Metal
　fasteners

(G-4603)
SUPERIOR ENERGY SYSTEMS LLC
13660 Station Rd (44028-9538)
PHONE...............................440 236-6009
Donald Fernald, *CEO*
Derek Rimko, *VP*
William J Young, *VP*
Mike Walters, *VP*
Philip J Lombardo, *Prin*
▼ **EMP:** 17 **EST:** 2002
SQ FT: 14,000
SALES (est): 8.68MM **Privately Held**
Web: www.superiornrg.com
SIC: 3714 Propane conversion equipment,
　motor vehicle

Columbiana
Columbiana County

(G-4604)
A PLUS POWDER COATERS INC
1384 Kauffman Ave (44408-9750)
PHONE.................................330 482-4389
Robert Bertelsen, *CEO*
EMP: 44 **EST:** 1996
SQ FT: 20,250
SALES (est): 4.39MM **Privately Held**
Web: www.apluspowder.com
SIC: 3479 Coating of metals and formed
products

(G-4605)
ALLOY MACHINING AND FABG INC
1028 Lower Elkton Rd (44408-8427)
P.O. Box 49 (44408-0049)
PHONE.................................330 482-5543
Ed Keating, *Pr*
EMP: 7 **EST:** 2005
SALES (est): 990.29K **Privately Held**
SIC: 3599 Machine shop, jobbing and repair

(G-4606)
BOARDMAN STEEL INC
156 Nulf Dr (44408-9720)
PHONE.................................330 758-0951
Dave Deibel, *Pr*
EMP: 55 **EST:** 1963
SQ FT: 49,000
SALES (est): 4.57MM **Privately Held**
Web: www.boardmansteel.com
SIC: 3441 Building components, structural
steel

(G-4607)
BUCKEYE COMPONENTS LLC
1340 State Route 14 (44408-9648)
PHONE.................................330 482-5163
EMP: 30 **EST:** 1993
SQ FT: 8,000
SALES (est): 2.5MM **Privately Held**
SIC: 5031 2439 Lumber, plywood, and
millwork; Trusses, wooden roof

(G-4608)
CENTURY CONTAINER LLC
32 W Railroad St (44408-1203)
PHONE.................................330 457-2367
Don R Di, *CEO*
EMP: 25
Web: www.centurycontainercorporation.com
SIC: 3089 Plastics containers, except foam
HQ: Century Container, Llc
5331 State Rte 7
New Waterford OH 44445
330 457-2367

(G-4609)
COBBLERS CORNER LLC
1115 Village Plz (44408-8480)
PHONE.................................330 482-4005
EMP: 7 **EST:** 1975
SQ FT: 8,000
SALES (est): 436.1K **Privately Held**
Web: www.cobblerscorner1.com
SIC: 5661 3021 7251 Men's boots; Rubber
and plastics footwear; Footwear, custom
made

(G-4610)
COL-PUMP COMPANY INC
131 E Railroad St (44408-1318)
PHONE.................................330 482-1029
Thomas Bowker, *Pr*
Paul Rance, *
EMP: 60 **EST:** 1882

SQ FT: 100,000
SALES (est): 4.61MM **Privately Held**
Web: www.col-pump.net
SIC: 3321 Gray iron castings, nec

(G-4611)
**COLUMBIANA BOILER COMPANY
LLC**
Also Called: Cbc Global
200 W Railroad St (44408-1281)
PHONE.................................330 482-3373
Michael J Sherwin, *CEO*
Thomas F Dougherty, *
Alan G Eckert, *
Gerianne Klepfer, *
Charles R Moore, *
◆ **EMP:** 45 **EST:** 1894
SQ FT: 50,000
SALES (est): 8.44MM
SALES (corp-wide): 8.44MM **Privately
Held**
Web: www.cbco.com
SIC: 1791 3443 Storage tanks, metal:
erection; Process vessels, industrial: metal
plate
PA: Columbiana Holding Co Inc
200 W Railroad St
Columbiana OH 44408
330 482-3373

(G-4612)
COLUMBIANA FOUNDRY COMPANY
501 Lisbon St (44408-1267)
P.O. Box 98 (44408-0098)
PHONE.................................330 482-3336
EMP: 130 **EST:** 1933
SALES (est): 5.43MM **Privately Held**
Web: www.columbianafoundry.com
SIC: 3321 3325 3369 3312 Gray iron
castings, nec; Steel foundries, nec;
Nonferrous foundries, nec; Blast furnaces
and steel mills

(G-4613)
**COMPCO COLUMBIANA COMPANY
(HQ)**
Also Called: Compco Industries
400 W Railroad St (44408-1213)
PHONE.................................330 482-0200
Gregory Smith, *Ch Bd*
Clarence Smith Senior, *Ch Bd*
Joel Sofranko, *CFO*
EMP: 63 **EST:** 1998
SALES (est): 18.55MM
SALES (corp-wide): 27.79MM **Privately
Held**
Web: www.compco.com
SIC: 3469 3443 Metal stampings, nec;
Tanks, standard or custom fabricated: metal
plate
PA: S-P Company, Inc.
400 W Railroad St Ste 1
Columbiana OH 44408
330 782-5651

(G-4614)
COMPCO YOUNGSTOWN COMPANY
Also Called: Compco Industries
400 W Railroad St (44408-1213)
PHONE.................................330 482-6488
Gregory Smith, *Ch Bd*
Clarence R Smith Junior, *Ch Bd*
James B Greene, *CCO*
EMP: 88 **EST:** 1952
SQ FT: 200,000
SALES (est): 9.21MM
SALES (corp-wide): 27.79MM **Privately
Held**
Web: www.compco.com

(G-4615)
E-1 (2012) HOLDINGS INC
Also Called: Envelope 1
41969 State Route 344 (44408-9421)
PHONE.................................330 482-3900
▲ **EMP:** 180
SIC: 2677 Envelopes

(G-4616)
ENVELOPE 1 INC (PA)
41969 State Route 344 (44408-9421)
PHONE.................................330 482-3900
Tarry Pidgeon, *CEO*
Cody Stokes, *
▲ **EMP:** 97 **EST:** 2012
SALES (est): 41.98MM
SALES (corp-wide): 41.98MM **Privately
Held**
Web: www.envelope1.com
SIC: 2677 Envelopes

(G-4617)
FEDERAL IRON WORKS COMPANY
42082 State Route 344 (44408-9421)
P.O. Box 150 (44408-0150)
PHONE.................................330 482-5910
Edward M Sferra, *Pr*
Edward M Sferra Junior, *Pr*
Marcella A Sferra, *VP*
EMP: 8 **EST:** 1920
SALES (est): 2.25MM **Privately Held**
Web: www.cycomsolutions.com
SIC: 3446 1761 Architectural metalwork;
Architectural sheet metal work

(G-4618)
HORST PACKING INC
3535 Renkenberger Rd (44408-9763)
PHONE.................................330 482-2997
David Horst, *Pr*
Debra Horst, *Sec*
EMP: 6 **EST:** 1981
SQ FT: 1,500
SALES (est): 470.16K **Privately Held**
Web: horst-packing-inc.hub.biz
SIC: 2011 Meat packing plants

(G-4619)
HUMTOWN PATTERN COMPANY
Also Called: Humtown Products
44708 Columbiana Waterford Rd
(44408-9605)
P.O. Box 367 (44408-0367)
PHONE.................................330 482-5555
Mark Lamoncha, *Pr*
Criss La Moncha, *
Brandon Lamoncha, *
Terrie Marshall, *
Sheri Lamoncha, *
EMP: 67 **EST:** 1959
SQ FT: 55,000
SALES (est): 9.22MM **Privately Held**
Web: www.humtown.com
SIC: 2759 3543 Commercial printing, nec;
Foundry cores

(G-4620)
J & H MANUFACTURING LLC
Also Called: J & H Mfg
1652 Columbiana Lisbon Rd (44408-9443)
P.O. Box 12 (44408-0012)
PHONE.................................330 482-2636
John Kephart, *Managing Member*

▲ **EMP:** 6 **EST:** 2003
SQ FT: 41,000
SALES (est): 1.51MM **Privately Held**
Web: www.jhmfgllc.com
SIC: 3462 Iron and steel forgings

(G-4621)
J&J PRECISION FABRICATORS LTD
Also Called: J&J Precision Fabrication
1341 Heck Rd (44408-9599)
PHONE.................................330 482-4964
Timothy D Mckinzie, *Managing Member*
EMP: 11 **EST:** 2001
SQ FT: 11,500
SALES (est): 1.09MM **Privately Held**
SIC: 7692 3599 Welding repair; Crankshafts
and camshafts, machining

(G-4622)
MILLER CASTINGS INC
1634 Lower Elkton Rd (44408-9404)
P.O. Box 440 (44408-0440)
PHONE.................................330 482-2923
Mike Miller, *Pr*
EMP: 22 **EST:** 1993
SALES (est): 1.44MM **Privately Held**
SIC: 3365 Aluminum foundries

(G-4623)
NEWELL - PSN LLC (PA)
235 E State Route 14 Ste 104
(44408-8494)
P.O. Box 48 (44408-0048)
PHONE.................................304 387-2700
Rick Stanley, *Pr*
▲ **EMP:** 6 **EST:** 2005
SALES (est): 1.33MM **Privately Held**
Web: www.newellporcelain.com
SIC: 3264 Insulators, electrical: porcelain

(G-4624)
OAKS WELDING INC
201 Prospect St (44408)
P.O. Box 23 (44408-0023)
PHONE.................................330 482-4216
Jack Guy, *Pr*
Jeff Guy, *Pr*
Maribell Guy, *Sec*
Geri Rubicky, *Treas*
EMP: 8 **EST:** 1927
SQ FT: 11,025
SALES (est): 1.03MM **Privately Held**
Web: www.oakswelding.com
SIC: 3599 7692 7629 Machine shop, jobbing
and repair; Welding repair; Electrical repair
shops

(G-4625)
QFM STAMPING INC
400 W Railroad St Ste 1 (44408-1294)
PHONE.................................330 337-3311
EMP: 7 **EST:** 2016
SALES (est): 1.87MM **Privately Held**
SIC: 3469 Stamping metal for the trade

(G-4626)
RANCE INDUSTRIES INC
1361 Heck Rd (44408-9599)
P.O. Box 325 (44408-0325)
PHONE.................................330 482-1745
John Rance, *Pr*
Karen Rance, *Treas*
EMP: 15 **EST:** 1997
SQ FT: 20,000
SALES (est): 2.86MM **Privately Held**
Web: www.ranceindustries.com
SIC: 3441 Fabricated structural metal

(G-4627)
S-P COMPANY INC (PA)
400 W Railroad St Ste 1 (44408-1294)
PHONE..................................330 782-5651
Gregory Smith, *CEO*
Clarence R Smith Junior, *Ch Bd*
Douglas Hagy, *
Richard Kamperman, *
EMP: 90 **EST:** 1946
SQ FT: 44,000
SALES (est): 27.79MM
SALES (corp-wide): 27.79MM **Privately Held**
Web: www.spplus.com
SIC: 3469 3443 3498 6512 Metal stampings, nec; Tanks, standard or custom fabricated: metal plate; Tube fabricating (contract bending and shaping); Commercial and industrial building operation

(G-4628)
SITLER PRINTER INC
707 E Park Ave (44408-1447)
PHONE..................................330 482-4463
Christine R Davis, *Pr*
Christine R Davis, *Pr*
Lee Davis, *VP*
EMP: 8 **EST:** 1909
SQ FT: 2,000
SALES (est): 413.74K **Privately Held**
Web: www.sitlertheprinter.com
SIC: 2752 2759 Offset printing; Letterpress printing

(G-4629)
SPECIALTY CERAMICS INC
41995 State Route 344 (44408-9421)
PHONE..................................330 482-0800
Richard Ludwig, *Pr*
Richard F Wilk, *
EMP: 100 **EST:** 1990
SQ FT: 47,000
SALES (est): 3.76MM **Privately Held**
Web: scilogs.spektrum.de
SIC: 3433 3255 Logs, gas fireplace; Clay refractories
PA: Unifrax Holding Llc
    600 Riverwalk Pkwy
    Tonawanda NY 14150

(G-4630)
STAR FAB INC
Also Called: STAR FAB, INC.
400 W Railroad St Ste 8 (44408-1294)
P.O. Box 553 (44406-0553)
PHONE..................................330 482-1601
John Zepernick, *Brnch Mgr*
EMP: 40
SALES (corp-wide): 35.16MM **Privately Held**
Web: www.starext.com
SIC: 3354 3711 Aluminum extruded products; Automobile assembly, including specialty automobiles
HQ: Star Fab, Llc
    7055 Herbert Rd
    Canfield OH 44406
    330 533-9863

(G-4631)
VARI-WALL TUBE SPECIALISTS INC
1350 Wardingsley Ave (44408-9727)
P.O. Box 340 (44408-0340)
PHONE..................................330 482-0000
Randall Alexoff, *Pr*
Peter Alexoff, *
Thomas Lodge, *
▲ **EMP:** 100 **EST:** 1985
SQ FT: 60,000
SALES (est): 3.73MM **Privately Held**
Web: www.vari-wall.com

SIC: 3354 3751 3714 Shapes, extruded aluminum, nec; Motorcycles, bicycles and parts; Motor vehicle parts and accessories

(G-4632)
VINEYARDS AT PINE LAKE INC
14101 Market St (44408-9788)
PHONE..................................330 549-0195
Eric Glista, *Prin*
Catherine A Glista, *
EMP: 25 **EST:** 2015
SALES (est): 652.07K **Privately Held**
Web: www.thevineyardsatpinelake.com
SIC: 2084 Wines

(G-4633)
VIVO BROTHERS LLC
1387 Columbiana Lisbon Rd (44408-9485)
PHONE..................................330 629-8686
Vince Vivo, *Prin*
EMP: 10 **EST:** 2000
SALES (est): 2.58MM **Privately Held**
Web: www.vivobrothers.com
SIC: 2599 Cabinets, factory

(G-4634)
VPL LLC
14101 Market St (44408-9788)
PHONE..................................330 549-0195
EMP: 10 **EST:** 2017
SALES (est): 363.94K **Privately Held**
SIC: 2084 Wines

(G-4635)
ZARBANA ALUM EXTRUSIONS LLC
41738 Esterly Dr (44408-9448)
P.O. Box 46 (44408-0046)
PHONE..................................330 482-5092
Billy Joe Miller, *Administration Finance*
EMP: 37 **EST:** 2005
SALES (est): 11.5MM
SALES (corp-wide): 436.99K **Privately Held**
Web: www.zarbana.com
SIC: 3354 Aluminum extruded products
HQ: Roccafranca Spa
    Via Rudiana 4
    Roccafranca BS 25030

(G-4636)
ZARBANA INDUSTRIES INC
41738 Esterly Dr (44408-9448)
P.O. Box 46 (44408-0046)
PHONE..................................330 482-5092
EMP: 37
Web: www.zarbana.com
SIC: 3354 Aluminum extruded products

(G-4637)
ZORICH INDUSTRIES INC
1400 Wardingsley Ave (44408-9727)
PHONE..................................330 482-9803
Frank Phillips, *Prin*
EMP: 7 **EST:** 2004
SALES (est): 938.3K **Privately Held**
Web: www.zorichind.com
SIC: 3999 Atomizers, toiletry

Columbus
Delaware County

(G-4638)
3GTMS LLC (PA)
8760 Orion Pl Ste 300 (43240-2109)
PHONE..................................877 722-3538
Paul Brady, *CEO*
EMP: 36 **EST:** 2010
SALES (est): 8.37MM
SALES (corp-wide): 8.37MM **Privately Held**

Web: www.3gtms.com
SIC: 7372 Prepackaged software

(G-4639)
CABINET SHOP
9075 Antares Ave (43240-2012)
PHONE..................................614 885-9676
Hans Jurawitz, *Owner*
EMP: 9 **EST:** 2007
SALES (est): 1.65MM **Privately Held**
Web: www.thecabshop.com
SIC: 2434 Wood kitchen cabinets

(G-4640)
EXACT EQUIPMENT CORPORATION (HQ)
1900 Polaris Pkwy (43240-4035)
PHONE..................................215 295-2000
Robert C Enichan, *Pr*
EMP: 10 **EST:** 1986
SQ FT: 9,000
SALES (est): 3.32MM
SALES (corp-wide): 3.87B **Publicly Held**
SIC: 3565 3596 3824 Packaging machinery; Industrial scales; Fluid meters and counting devices
PA: Mettler-Toledo International Inc.
    1900 Polaris Pkwy
    Columbus OH 43240
    614 438-4511

(G-4641)
HEADLEE ENTERPRISES LTD
Also Called: AlphaGraphics
9015 Antares Ave (43240-2012)
PHONE..................................614 785-1476
Chad Headlee, *Pt*
Murray Headlee, *Pt*
EMP: 8 **EST:** 2001
SQ FT: 4,200
SALES (est): 953.1K **Privately Held**
Web: www.alphagraphics.com
SIC: 2752 Commercial printing, lithographic

(G-4642)
MCGRAW-HILL SCHL EDCATN HLDNGS
8787 Orion Pl (43240-4027)
PHONE..................................614 430-4000
Chris Wiggens, *Prin*
EMP: 750
Web: www.mheducation.com
SIC: 2731 Book publishing
HQ: Mcgraw-Hill School Education Holdings, Llc
    2 Penn Plz Fl 20
    New York NY 10121
    646 766-2000

(G-4643)
METTLER-TOLEDO INTL INC (PA)
Also Called: METTLER-TOLEDO
1900 Polaris Pkwy (43240-4035)
PHONE..................................614 438-4511
Patrick Kaltenbach, *Pr*
Roland Diggelmann, *Ch Bd*
Shawn P Vadala, *CFO*
◆ **EMP:** 3182 **EST:** 1991
SALES (est): 3.87B
SALES (corp-wide): 3.87B **Publicly Held**
Web: www.mt.com
SIC: 3826 3596 3821 3823 Analytical instruments; Industrial scales; Laboratory measuring apparatus; Process control instruments

(G-4644)
METTLER-TOLEDO LLC (HQ)
1900 Polaris Pkwy (43240-4055)
PHONE..................................614 438-4511

◆ **EMP:** 1000 **EST:** 1901
SALES (est): 2B
SALES (corp-wide): 3.87B **Publicly Held**
Web: www.mt.com
SIC: 3596 5049 7699 3821 Industrial scales; Analytical instruments; Professional instrument repair services; Pipettes, hemocytometer
PA: Mettler-Toledo International Inc.
    1900 Polaris Pkwy
    Columbus OH 43240
    614 438-4511

(G-4645)
METTLR-TLEDO GLOBL HLDNGS LLC (HQ)
1900 Polaris Pkwy (43240-4035)
PHONE..................................614 438-4511
Mary T Finnegan, *Treas*
EMP: 48 **EST:** 2010
SALES (est): 2.76MM
SALES (corp-wide): 3.87B **Publicly Held**
SIC: 3451 3826 Screw machine products; Analytical instruments
PA: Mettler-Toledo International Inc.
    1900 Polaris Pkwy
    Columbus OH 43240
    614 438-4511

(G-4646)
MICROSOFT CORPORATION
Also Called: Microsoft
8800 Lyra Dr Ste 400 (43240-2100)
PHONE..................................614 719-5900
Marrida Davis, *Genl Mgr*
EMP: 7
SALES (corp-wide): 245.12B **Publicly Held**
Web: www.microsoft.com
SIC: 7372 Application computer software
PA: Microsoft Corporation
    1 Microsoft Way
    Redmond WA 98052
    425 882-8080

(G-4647)
RAININ INSTRUMENT LLC
1900 Polaris Pkwy (43240-4035)
PHONE..................................510 564-1600
Ruben Rosso, *Prin*
EMP: 8 **EST:** 2008
SALES (est): 5.61MM **Privately Held**
Web: www.mt.com
SIC: 3596 Scales and balances, except laboratory

(G-4648)
READY MEDIA LLC
1491 Polaris Pkwy Ste 81 (43240-2041)
PHONE..................................614 441-8178
Gail Dudley Eic, *Prin*
Dominiq Dudley Crtv Edtr, *Prin*
EMP: 8 **EST:** 2018
SALES (est): 87.14K **Privately Held**
Web: www.readypublication.com
SIC: 2741 Miscellaneous publishing

(G-4649)
RENEWAL BY ANDERSEN LLC
400 Lazelle Rd Ste 1 (43240-2077)
PHONE..................................614 781-9600
Jake Zahnow, *Prin*
EMP: 7
SALES (corp-wide): 1.78B **Privately Held**
Web: www.renewalbyandersen.com
SIC: 3442 2431 Screens, window, metal; Millwork
HQ: Renewal By Andersen Llc
    9900 Jamaica Ave S
    Cottage Grove MN 55016
    855 871-7377

▲ = Import ▼ = Export
◆ = Import/Export

(G-4650)
VEEAM GOVERNMENT SOLUTIONS LLC
8800 Lyra Dr Ste 350 (43240-2151)
PHONE..........................614 339-8200
William Largent, *Prin*
Ming Miranda, *
EMP: 25 EST: 2018
SALES (est): 5.48MM **Privately Held**
SIC: 7372 Prepackaged software

(G-4651)
VIAVI SOLUTIONS INC
8740 Orion Pl Ste 100 (43240-4063)
PHONE..........................316 522-4981
EMP: 12
SALES (corp-wide): 1B **Publicly Held**
Web: www.viavisolutions.com
SIC: 3826 3674 Analytical instruments;
Optical isolators
PA: Viavi Solutions Inc.
1445 S Spctrum Blvd Ste 1
Chandler AZ 85286
408 404-3600

Columbus
Franklin County

(G-4652)
1ONE STOP PRINTING INC
1509 Blatt Blvd Ste 8303 (43230-6925)
P.O. Box 30101 (43230-0101)
PHONE..........................614 216-1438
Deon Pollard, *Pr*
EMP: 10 EST: 2019
SALES (est): 168.83K **Privately Held**
Web: www.1onestopinc.com
SIC: 2752 Commercial printing, lithographic

(G-4653)
4MATIC VALVE AUTOMTN OHIO LLC
4993 Cleveland Ave (43231-4734)
PHONE..........................614 806-1221
EMP: 10 EST: 2021
SALES (est): 732.36K **Privately Held**
SIC: 3491 Industrial valves

(G-4654)
614 MEDIA GROUP LLC
Also Called: 614 Magazine
458 E Main St (43215-5344)
PHONE..........................014 400-4400
EMP: 18 EST: 2008
SALES (est): 2.27MM **Privately Held**
Web: www.614mediagroup.com
SIC: 2721 Magazines: publishing and printing

(G-4655)
889 GLOBAL SOLUTIONS LTD
1943 W 5th Ave (43212-1902)
PHONE..........................614 235-8889
Judy Huang, *CEO*
Judy Huang, *Managing Member*
John Lewis, *Managing Member*
◆ EMP: 10 EST: 2000
SALES (est): 2.45MM **Privately Held**
Web: www.889globalsolutions.com
SIC: 7389 5047 8742 3365 Advertising,
promotional, and trade show services;
Medical equipment and supplies;
Manufacturing management consultant;
Machinery castings, aluminum

(G-4656)
A L D PRECAST CORP (PA)
400 Frank Rd (43207-2423)
PHONE..........................614 449-3366
William E Anderson, *Prin*
EMP: 8 EST: 2007

SALES (est): 4.9MM **Privately Held**
Web: www.aldprecast.com
SIC: 3272 Concrete products, precast, nec

(G-4657)
A-DISPLAY SERVICE CORP
Also Called: Signature Store Fixtures
541 Dana Ave (43223-5202)
PHONE..........................614 469-1230
Anthony Grilli, *Pr*
Nancy Grilli, *Sec*
Mario Grilli, *CEO*
EMP: 10 EST: 1978
SQ FT: 8,500
SALES (est): 825.12K **Privately Held**
Web: www.signaturemillshop.com
SIC: 2434 Wood kitchen cabinets

(G-4658)
AAT USA LLC (PA)
Also Called: Able Applied Technologies
1850 Denune Ave (43211-1718)
P.O. Box 12515 (43212-0515)
PHONE..........................614 388-8866
Michael Mcnamara, *Managing Member*
EMP: 7 EST: 1989
SQ FT: 150,000
SALES (est): 4.71MM
SALES (corp-wide): 4.71MM **Privately Held**
Web: www.ableat.com
SIC: 3648 3699 Lighting equipment, nec;
Electrical equipment and supplies, nec

(G-4659)
ABBOTT
923 Dennison Ave (43201-3400)
PHONE..........................608 931-1057
Stephanie Ferguson, *Prin*
EMP: 7 EST: 2015
SALES (est): 261.72K **Privately Held**
SIC: 2834 Pharmaceutical preparations

(G-4660)
ABBOTT LABORATORIES
Also Called: Abbott Nutrition
585 Cleveland Ave (43215-1755)
P.O. Box 16546 (43216)
PHONE..........................614 624-3191
Eric Christensen, *Mgr*
EMP: 550
SQ FT: 378,500
SALES (corp-wide): 41.95B **Publicly Held**
Web: www.abbottnutrition.com
SIC: 2834 2087 2086 2032 Pharmaceutical
preparations; Flavoring extracts and
syrups, nec; Bottled and canned soft drinks;
Canned specialties
PA: Abbott Laboratories
100 Abbott Park Rd
Abbott Park IL 60064
224 667-6100

(G-4661)
ABBOTT LABORATORIES
350 N 5th St (43215-2103)
PHONE..........................614 624-3192
EMP: 13
SALES (corp-wide): 41.95B **Publicly Held**
Web: www.abbottstore.com
SIC: 2834 Pharmaceutical preparations
PA: Abbott Laboratories
100 Abbott Park Rd
Abbott Park IL 60064
224 667-6100

(G-4662)
ABBOTT LABORATORIES
Also Called: Tobal Products
2900 Easton Square Pl (43219-6225)
PHONE..........................847 937-6100

Steven K Williams, *Brnch Mgr*
EMP: 92
SALES (corp-wide): 41.95B **Publicly Held**
Web: www.similacstore.com
SIC: 2834 3841 2879 4226 Pharmaceutical
preparations; Surgical and medical
instruments; Insecticides, agricultural or
household; Special warehousing and
storage, nec
PA: Abbott Laboratories
100 Abbott Park Rd
Abbott Park IL 60064
224 667-6100

(G-4663)
ABBOTT LABORATORIES
625 Cleveland Ave (43215-1754)
P.O. Box 16718 (43216-6718)
PHONE..........................800 551-5838
EMP: 227
SALES (corp-wide): 41.95B **Publicly Held**
Web: www.abbott.com
SIC: 2834 Pharmaceutical preparations
PA: Abbott Laboratories
100 Abbott Park Rd
Abbott Park IL 60064
224 667-6100

(G-4664)
ABBOTT LABORATORIES
Abbott Nutrition
3300 Stelzer Rd (43219-3034)
PHONE..........................614 624-7677
Don Paton, *Brnch Mgr*
EMP: 3000
SALES (corp-wide): 41.95B **Publicly Held**
Web: www.abbottnutrition.com
SIC: 2834 Druggists' preparations
(pharmaceuticals)
PA: Abbott Laboratories
100 Abbott Park Rd
Abbott Park IL 60064
224 667-6100

(G-4665)
ABITEC CORPORATION (HQ)
501 W 1st Ave (43215-1101)
PHONE..........................614 429-6464
Jeff Walton, *CEO*
Susan Taylor, *CFO*
◆ EMP: 20 EST: 1994
SQ FT: 12,000
SALES (est): 98.1MM
SALES (corp-wide): 26.94B **Privately Held**
Web: www.abiteccorp.com
SIC: 2844 2834 2869 2045 Perfumes,
cosmetics and other toilet preparations;
Pharmaceutical preparations; Industrial
organic chemicals, nec; Prepared flour
mixes and doughs
PA: Wittington Investments Limited
10 Grosvenor Street
London W1K 4
207 399-6565

(G-4666)
ABLE PALLET MFG & REPR
1271 Harmon Ave (43223-3306)
P.O. Box 23083 (43223-0083)
PHONE..........................614 444-2115
Charles O'hara, *Pr*
EMP: 7 EST: 1984
SQ FT: 5,089
SALES (est): 293.77K **Privately Held**
SIC: 7699 2448 Pallet repair; Wood pallets
and skids

(G-4667)
ACCENT DRAPERY CO INC
Also Called: Accent Drapery Supply Co
1180 Goodale Blvd (43212-3793)

PHONE..........................614 488-0741
Patrick Casbarro, *Pr*
Brian Whiteside, *
EMP: 27 EST: 1967
SQ FT: 19,500
SALES (est): 3.16MM **Privately Held**
Web: www.accentdraperies.com
SIC: 5714 5023 2391 Draperies; Draperies;
Curtains and draperies

(G-4668)
ACCLAIMD INC
1275 Kinnear Rd (43212-1180)
PHONE..........................614 219-9519
David Lyons, *Pr*
EMP: 6 EST: 2012
SALES (est): 801.63K
SALES (corp-wide): 102.92K **Privately Held**
Web: domains.squadhelp.com
SIC: 7372 Application computer software
PA: Eboss Online Recruitment Solutions
(Eboss) Limited
Unit 13
Poole
207 183-0675

(G-4669)
ACCULON ENERGY INC
1275 Kinnear Rd (43212-1180)
PHONE..........................614 259-7792
Andrew Thomas, *Pr*
EMP: 20 EST: 2022
SALES (est): 3.75MM **Privately Held**
Web: www.acculonenergy.com
SIC: 3691 Storage batteries

(G-4670)
ACCUSCAN INSTRUMENTS INC
Also Called: Omni Tech Electronics
5098 Trabue Rd (43228-9391)
PHONE..........................614 878-6644
R H Mandalaywala, *Pr*
R H, *Pr*
EMP: 10 EST: 1996
SQ FT: 10,000
SALES (est): 744.8K **Privately Held**
Web: www.omnitech-usa.com
SIC: 3821 Laboratory apparatus, except
heating and measuring

(G-4671)
ACME HOME IMPROVEMENT CO INC
2909 E 4th Ave (43219-2827)
P.O. Box 13063 (43213-0063)
PHONE..........................614 252-2129
Judith Hinckley, *Pr*
James Linthwaite, *VP*
Vicki Romanoff, *Sec*
EMP: 10 EST: 1958
SQ FT: 7,800
SALES (est): 253.84K **Privately Held**
SIC: 1521 3441 1761 1751 General
remodeling, single-family houses;
Fabricated structural metal; Roofing, siding,
and sheetmetal work; Carpentry work

(G-4672)
ACTION EXPRESS INC
Also Called: Acex
100 E Campus View Blvd Ste 250
(43235-4682)
PHONE..........................929 351-3620
Levan Lomidze, *Pr*
EMP: 7 EST: 2018
SALES (est): 1.01MM **Privately Held**
SIC: 2741 Miscellaneous publishing

(G-4673)
ACTUAL INDUSTRIES LLC
655 N James Rd (43219-1837)
PHONE..............................614 379-2739
Fredrick Lee, *Prin*
EMP: 7 EST: 2012
SALES (est): 197.5K **Privately Held**
Web: www.actualindustries.com
SIC: 3999 Manufacturing industries, nec

(G-4674)
ADSR ENT LLC
1888 Noe Bixby Rd (43232-2675)
PHONE..............................773 280-2129
EMP: 10
SALES (est): 873.04K **Privately Held**
SIC: 3537 7389 Trucks: freight, baggage,
etc.: industrial, except mining; Business
Activities at Non-Commercial Site

(G-4675)
ADVANCE SIGN GROUP LLC
5150 Walcutt Ct (43228-9641)
P.O. Box 698 (43216-0698)
PHONE..............................614 429-2111
James L Wasserstrom, *Managing Member*
Roger Wallace, *
EMP: 41 EST: 2001
SALES (est): 9.4MM **Privately Held**
Web: www.advancesigngroup.com
SIC: 3993 Electric signs

(G-4676)
ADVANCED FUEL SYSTEMS INC
841 Alton Ave (43219-3710)
PHONE..............................614 252-8422
Timothy L Thickstun, *Pr*
Steve Thickstun, *VP*
Joanne Thickstun, *Sec*
▼ **EMP: 8 EST:** 1998
SQ FT: 8,500
SALES (est): 4.02MM **Privately Held**
Web: www.advfuel.com
SIC: 3561 3728 Pumps and pumping
equipment; Aircraft parts and equipment,
nec

(G-4677)
ADVANTAGE PRINT SOLUTIONS LLC
79 Acton Rd (43214-3301)
PHONE..............................614 519-2392
Debbie Smith, *Prin*
EMP: 6 EST: 2009
SALES (est): 443.28K **Privately Held**
Web: www.advantageprintsolutions.com
SIC: 2752 Offset printing

(G-4678)
AEROSPACE LUBRICANTS LLC
1600 Georgesville Rd (43228-3616)
PHONE..............................614 878-3600
Steven Gates, *Pr*
▲ **EMP: 15 EST:** 1973
SQ FT: 25,000
SALES (est): 4.49MM
SALES (corp-wide): 240.81MM **Privately
Held**
Web: www.aerospacelubricants.com
SIC: 5172 2992 Lubricating oils and greases
; Lubricating oils
PA: Amsoil Inc.
925 Tower Ave
Superior WI 54880
715 392-7101

(G-4679)
AGRI COMMUNICATORS INC
Also Called: Ohio's Country Journal
280 N High St Fl 6 (43215-2594)
PHONE..............................614 273-0465

Bart Johnson, *Pr*
Marilyn Johnson, *Sec*
EMP: 7 EST: 1972
SALES (est): 246.05K **Privately Held**
Web: www.ocj.com
SIC: 7313 2721 Radio, television, publisher
representatives; Periodicals, publishing only

(G-4680)
AGRIUM ADVANCED TECH US INC
701 Kaderly Dr (43228-1031)
PHONE..............................614 276-5103
Karl Creighton, *Brnch Mgr*
EMP: 7
SALES (corp-wide): 29.06B **Privately Held**
Web: www.nutrien.com
SIC: 2873 Nitrogenous fertilizers
HQ: Agrium Advanced Technologies (U.S.)
Inc.
2915 Rcky Mtn Ave Ste 400
Loveland CO 80538

(G-4681)
AHMF INC (PA)
Also Called: Original Mattress Factory
2245 Wilson Rd (43228-9594)
PHONE..............................614 921-1223
Ronald E Trzcinski, *Ch Bd*
Jeffrey C Merill, *VP*
Lawrence S Carlson, *VP*
Perry Doermann, *Sec*
Tony Dempsey, *VP*
EMP: 20 EST: 1992
SQ FT: 22,000
SALES (est): 5.86MM **Privately Held**
SIC: 2515 5712 5021 Mattresses and
foundations; Bedding and bedsprings;
Mattresses

(G-4682)
AKRON BRASS COMPANY
Also Called: Weldon Technologies
3656 Paragon Dr (43228-9750)
PHONE..............................614 529-7230
Sean Tillinghast, *Prin*
EMP: 23
SALES (corp-wide): 3.27B **Publicly Held**
Web: www.akronbrass.com
SIC: 3647 3699 3648 Vehicular lighting
equipment; Electrical equipment and
supplies, nec; Lighting equipment, nec
HQ: Akron Brass Company
343 Venture Blvd
Wooster OH 44691

(G-4683)
AKZO NOBEL COATINGS INC
1313 Windsor Ave Ste 1313 (43211-2851)
PHONE..............................614 294-3361
Paul Hoelzer, *Genl Mgr*
EMP: 127
SALES (corp-wide): 11.6B **Privately Held**
SIC: 2851 Paints and allied products
HQ: Akzo Nobel Coatings Inc.
535 Marriott Dr Ste 500
Nashville TN 37214
440 297-5100

(G-4684)
**ALL PRO OVRHD DOOR SYSTEMS
LLC**
1985 Oakland Park Ave (43224-3636)
P.O. Box 361478 (43236-1478)
PHONE..............................614 444-3667
EMP: 8 EST: 2007
SALES (est): 2.56MM **Privately Held**
Web: www.allprodoors.com
SIC: 3442 2431 Metal doors, sash, and trim;
Door frames, wood

(G-4685)
ALL STAR SIGN COMPANY
112 S Glenwood Ave (43222-1406)
P.O. Box 23071 (43223-0071)
PHONE..............................614 461-9052
James E Waller, *Pr*
Howard Berridge, *VP*
EMP: 6 EST: 1985
SQ FT: 7,600
SALES (est): 396.91K **Privately Held**
Web: www.allstarohio.com
SIC: 3993 Electric signs

(G-4686)
ALLFAB INC
2273 Williams Rd (43207-5121)
PHONE..............................614 491-4944
Lise S Roth, *Pr*
Russell W Roth, *VP*
EMP: 15 EST: 1985
SQ FT: 15,000
SALES (est): 2.46MM **Privately Held**
Web: www.allfabinc.com
SIC: 3444 Sheet metalwork

(G-4687)
ALLIED FABRICATING & WLDG CO
5699 Chantry Dr (43232-4731)
PHONE..............................614 868-8680
Douglas Martin, *Pr*
Tim Cundiff, *
EMP: 34 EST: 1971
SQ FT: 30,000
SALES (est): 5.16MM **Privately Held**
Web: www.afaw.net
SIC: 3444 7692 3535 3441 Sheet metal
specialties, not stamped; Welding repair;
Conveyors and conveying equipment;
Fabricated structural metal

(G-4688)
**ALLIED MINERAL PRODUCTS LLC
(PA)**
2700 Scioto Pkwy (43221-4660)
PHONE..............................614 876-0244
Paul Jamieson, *Pr*
Anthony S Disaia, *
John S Halsted Junior, *VP*
Paul D Jamieson, *
Douglas K Doza, *
◆ **EMP: 290 EST:** 1961
SQ FT: 450,000
SALES (est): 91.72MM
SALES (corp-wide): 91.72MM **Privately
Held**
Web: www.alliedmineral.com
SIC: 3297 Brick refractories

(G-4689)
ALLIED SIGN CO
818 Marion Rd (43207-2553)
P.O. Box 7760 (43207-0760)
PHONE..............................614 443-9656
Richard L Frost, *Pr*
EMP: 7 EST: 1955
SQ FT: 8,000
SALES (est): 609.81K **Privately Held**
Web: www.alliedsignco.com
SIC: 3993 Signs and advertising specialties

(G-4690)
ALRO STEEL CORPORATION
555 Hilliard Rome Rd (43228-9265)
PHONE..............................614 878-7271
Steve White, *Mgr*
EMP: 22
SALES (corp-wide): 3.04B **Privately Held**
Web: www.alro.com

SIC: 5051 5085 5162 3444 Steel; Industrial
supplies; Plastics materials, nec; Sheet
metalwork
PA: Alro Steel Corporation
3100 E High St
Jackson MI 49203
517 787-5500

(G-4691)
AMATECH INC
1633 Woodland Ave (43219-1135)
PHONE..............................614 252-2506
Rick Bittner, *Brnch Mgr*
EMP: 25
Web: www.amatechinc.com
SIC: 3086 7336 2671 Plastics foam products
; Package design; Plastic film, coated or
laminated for packaging
PA: Amatech, Inc.
1460 Grimm Dr
Erie PA 16501

(G-4692)
AMERICAN BOTTLING COMPANY
Also Called: Dr. Pepper 7 Up Columbus
960 Stelzer Rd (43219-3740)
PHONE..............................614 237-4201
Dan Grassbaugh, *Brnch Mgr*
EMP: 75
Web: www.keurigdrpepper.com
SIC: 2086 Soft drinks: packaged in cans,
bottles, etc.
HQ: The American Bottling Company
6425 Hall Of Fame Ln
Frisco TX 75034

(G-4693)
AMERICAN BOTTLING COMPANY
Also Called: 7 Up / R C/Canada Dry Btlg Co
950 Stelzer Rd (43219-3740)
PHONE..............................614 237-4201
Mike Stall, *Brnch Mgr*
EMP: 114
Web: www.keurigdrpepper.com
SIC: 2086 5149 Soft drinks: packaged in
cans, bottles, etc.; Groceries and related
products, nec
HQ: The American Bottling Company
6425 Hall Of Fame Ln
Frisco TX 75034

(G-4694)
AMERICAN COLORSCANS INC
Also Called: ACS Commercial Graphics
5178 Sinclair Rd (43229-5437)
PHONE..............................614 895-0233
EMP: 22
SIC: 2752 Color lithography

(G-4695)
**AMERICAN COMMUNITY
NEWSPAPERS**
5255 Sinclair Rd (43229-5042)
PHONE..............................614 888-4567
Leanne Brandell, *Prin*
EMP: 7 EST: 2009
SALES (est): 109.38K **Privately Held**
SIC: 2711 Newspapers, publishing and
printing

(G-4696)
**AMERICAN CORRUGATED
PRODUCTS INC**
4700 Alkire Rd (43228-3495)
PHONE..............................614 870-2000
EMP: 220

▲ = Import ▼ = Export
◆ = Import/Export

SIC: 2653 3086 2671 2657 Boxes, corrugated: made from purchased materials ; Plastics foam products; Paper; coated and laminated packaging; Folding paperboard boxes

(G-4697)
AMERICAN IMPRSSIONS SPORTSWEAR
Also Called: American Imprssions Sportswear
5523 Mercer St (43235-7596)
PHONE..............................614 848-6677
Robert Midkiff, *Pr*
EMP: 9 **EST:** 1992
SALES (est): 1MM **Privately Held**
SIC: 2396 2759 Screen printing on fabric articles; Promotional printing

(G-4698)
AMERICAN ISOSTATIC PRESSES INC
Also Called: A I P
1205 S Columbus Airport Rd (43207-4304)
PHONE..............................614 497-3148
Rajendra Persaud, *Pr*
Cliff Orcutt, *VP*
Lisa Persaud, *Sec*
Carol Sprang, *Prin*
▲ **EMP:** 16 **EST:** 1992
SQ FT: 14,000
SALES (est): 6.06MM **Privately Held**
Web: www.aiphip.com
SIC: 3821 Furnaces, laboratory

(G-4699)
AMERICAN LED-GIBLE INC
Also Called: Led-Andon
4734 Funston Ct (43232-6122)
PHONE..............................614 851-1100
Charles R Morrison, *Pr*
Robin L Morrison, *CFO*
▲ **EMP:** 10 **EST:** 1976
SALES (est): 1.07MM **Privately Held**
Web: www.ledgible.com
SIC: 3993 Electric signs

(G-4700)
AMERICAN ORTHOPEDICS INC (PA)
1151 W 5th Ave (43212-2529)
PHONE..............................614 291-6454
Richard F Nitsch, *Pr*
Ronald Kidd, *Pr*
Loretta Kidd, *Sec*
Zachary Ruhl, *VP*
Barbara Berndt, *Mgr*
EMP: 19 **EST:** 1970
SQ FT: 7,000
SALES (est): 2.7MM
SALES (corp-wide): 2.7MM **Privately Held**
Web: www.amerortho.com
SIC: 3842 Prosthetic appliances

(G-4701)
AMERICAN REGENT INC
960 Crupper Ave (43229-1109)
PHONE..............................614 436-2222
Joseph Kenneth Keller, *CEO*
EMP: 100
Web: www.americanregent.com
SIC: 2834 Pharmaceutical preparations
HQ: American Regent, Inc.
5 Ramsey Rd
Shirley NY 11967
631 924-4000

(G-4702)
AMERICAN SCIENTIFIC LLC
6420 Fiesta Dr (43235-5208)
PHONE..............................614 764-9002
Sanjay Sadana, *Managing Member*
▲ **EMP:** 7 **EST:** 1999
SALES (est): 1.03MM **Privately Held**

Web: www.american-scientific.com
SIC: 3826 Analytical instruments

(G-4703)
AMERISOURCE HEALTH SVCS LLC
Also Called: American Health Packaging
2550 John Glenn Ave Ste A (43217-1188)
PHONE..............................614 492-8177
Steve Collis, *Pr*
Richard Greenhall, *
▲ **EMP:** 89 **EST:** 1996
SQ FT: 153,000
SALES (est): 49.88MM
SALES (corp-wide): 293.96B **Publicly Held**
Web:
www.americanhealthpackaging.com
SIC: 2064 4783 Cough drops, except pharmaceutical preparations; Packing goods for shipping
HQ: Amerisourcebergen Drug Corporation
1 W 1st Ave
Conshohocken PA 19428
610 727-7000

(G-4704)
AMERITECH PUBLISHING INC
Also Called: SBC
2550 Corporate Exchange Dr Ste 310 (43231-7659)
PHONE..............................614 895-6123
David Lobdell, *Mgr*
EMP: 1328
SALES (corp-wide): 122.34B **Publicly Held**
SIC: 2741 Directories, telephone: publishing only, not printed on site
HQ: Ameritech Publishing, Inc.
23500 Northwestern Hwy
Southfield MI

(G-4705)
AMETEK INC
Also Called: Ametek Aerospace & Defense
875 Dearborn Dr (43085-1586)
PHONE..............................302 636-5401
EMP: 7
SALES (corp-wide): 6.94B **Publicly Held**
Web: www.ametek.com
SIC: 3621 Motors and generators
PA: Ametek, Inc.
1100 Cassatt Rd
Berwyn PA 19312
610 647-2121

(G-4706)
AMPSCO DIVISION
2301 Fairwood Ave (43207-2768)
PHONE..............................614 444-2181
Dennis J Leukart, *Pr*
Matthew Leukart, *VP*
EMP: 170 **EST:** 1960
SQ FT: 250,000
SALES (est): 736.88K
SALES (corp-wide): 18.78MM **Privately Held**
Web: www.superior-dietool.com
SIC: 3599 Machine shop, jobbing and repair
PA: Superior Production Llc
2301 Fairwood Ave
Columbus OH 43207
614 444-2181

(G-4707)
AMT MACHINE SYSTEMS LIMITED
1760 Zollinger Rd Ste 2 (43221-2843)
PHONE..............................740 965-2693
Dennis R Pugh, *Pt*
Howard Ubert, *Pt*
Gregory Knight, *Pt*
Eric Ribble, *Pt*

EMP: 10 **EST:** 1996
SQ FT: 2,000
SALES (est): 1.14MM **Privately Held**
SIC: 3451 Screw machine products

(G-4708)
AMTEKCO INDUSTRIES LLC (HQ)
Also Called: Amtekco
2300 Lockbourne Rd (43207-2167)
PHONE..............................614 228-6590
Earl B Sisson, *Pr*
John Mccormick, *Pr*
Bruce Wasserstrom, *
Hugh E Kirkwood Junior, *Pr*
Ollie Rossman, *
EMP: 100 **EST:** 1962
SALES (est): 4.62MM
SALES (corp-wide): 378.09MM **Privately Held**
Web: www.amtekco.com
SIC: 3469 2541 Kitchen fixtures and equipment: metal, except cast aluminum; Cabinets, except refrigerated: show, display, etc.: wood
PA: The Wasserstrom Company
4500 E Broad St
Columbus OH 43213
614 228-6525

(G-4709)
AMTEKCO INDUSTRIES INC
Also Called: AMTEKCO INDUSTRIES INC
33 W Hinman Ave (43207-1809)
PHONE..............................614 228-6525
Ron Bower, *Pr*
EMP: 50
SALES (corp-wide): 378.09MM **Privately Held**
Web: www.amtekco.com
SIC: 2541 3469 Wood partitions and fixtures; Metal stampings, nec
HQ: Amtekco Industries, Llc
2300 Lockbourne Rd
Columbus OH 43207
614 228-6590

(G-4710)
ANADEM INC
3620 N High St Ste 201 (43214-3643)
PHONE..............................614 262-2539
Will Kuhlmann, *CEO*
Mike Cheadle, *VP*
EMP: 7 **EST:** 1977
SALES (est): 204.16K **Privately Held**
Web: www.anadem.com
SIC: 2741 Miscellaneous publishing

(G-4711)
ANCHOR HOCKING LLC (HQ)
Also Called: Anchor Hocking Company, The
1600 Dublin Rd Ste 200 (43215-2872)
PHONE..............................740 687-2500
Mark Eichhorn, *Pr*
Mark Hedstrom, *
Joe Sundberg, *
Bert Filice, *
◆ **EMP:** 1200 **EST:** 1905
SALES (est): 479.42MM
SALES (corp-wide): 509.79MM **Privately Held**
Web: www.anchorhocking.com
SIC: 3089 3229 3411 3221 Cups, plastics, except foam; Tableware, glass or glass ceramic; Metal cans; Glass containers
PA: Anchor Hocking Holdings, Inc.
1600 Dublin Rd Ste 200
Columbus OH 43215
740 687-2500

(G-4712)
ANCHOR HOCKING CORPORATION
1600 Dublin Rd (43215-2095)
PHONE..............................614 633-4247
EMP: 8 **EST:** 1928
SALES (est): 1.27MM **Privately Held**
Web: www.anchorhocking.com
SIC: 3229 Pressed and blown glass, nec

(G-4713)
ANCHOR HOCKING HOLDINGS INC (PA)
1600 Dublin Rd Ste 200 (43215-2872)
PHONE..............................740 687-2500
Mark Eichhorn, *Pr*
Bert Filice, *CSO*
Mike Hanson, *
Jamie Keller, *
EMP: 567 **EST:** 2011
SALES (est): 509.79MM
SALES (corp-wide): 509.79MM **Privately Held**
Web: www.theoneidagroup.com
SIC: 3089 3469 Plastics kitchenware, tableware, and houseware; Kitchen fixtures and equipment, porcelain enameled

(G-4714)
ANCHOR PATTERN COMPANY
748 Frebis Ave (43206-3709)
PHONE..............................614 443-2221
Wilbur S Smith Iii, *Pr*
Barbara L Smith, *Sec*
EMP: 6 **EST:** 1967
SQ FT: 4,000
SALES (est): 1.08MM **Privately Held**
Web: www.anchorpattern.com
SIC: 3543 Industrial patterns

(G-4715)
ANDELYN BIOSCIENCES INC (HQ)
1180 Arthur E Adams Dr (43221-3542)
PHONE..............................844 228-2366
Adam Lauber, *Admn*
Michael Osborne, *VP*
Wade Macedone, *COO*
EMP: 20 **EST:** 1998
SALES (est): 23.59MM
SALES (corp-wide): 3.67B **Privately Held**
Web: www.andelynbio.com
SIC: 2834 Pharmaceutical preparations
PA: Nationwide Children's Hospital
700 Children's Dr
Columbus OH 43205
614 722-2000

(G-4716)
ANDERSON CONCRETE CORP
Also Called: Buckeye Ready Mix
400 Frank Rd (43207-2456)
P.O. Box Po Box 398 (43216-0398)
PHONE..............................614 443-0123
Douglas Anderson, *Pr*
Richard D Anderson, *
William Feltz, *Product Vice President*
John Mynes, *
William S Dunn, *
EMP: 150 **EST:** 1921
SALES (est): 22.88MM **Privately Held**
Web: www.andersonconcrete.com
SIC: 3273 Ready-mixed concrete

(G-4717)
ANDERSON GLASS CO INC
2816 Morse Rd (43231-6094)
PHONE..............................614 476-4877
Bradley Anderson, *Pr*
Helena Anderson, *
EMP: 8 **EST:** 1949
SQ FT: 32,000
SALES (est): 616.77K **Privately Held**

Web: www.andersoncompanies.com
SIC: 5039 3231 3229 Exterior flat glass;
plate or window; Products of purchased
glass; Pressed and blown glass, nec

(G-4718)
ANHEUSER-BUSCH LLC
Also Called: Anheuser-Busch
700 Schrock Rd (43229-1159)
PHONE..............................614 847-6213
Kevin Lee, *Mgr*
EMP: 500
SALES (corp-wide): 1.7B Privately Held
Web: www.budweisertours.com
SIC: 2082 Beer (alcoholic beverage)
HQ: Anheuser-Busch, Llc
1 Busch Pl
Saint Louis MO 63118
800 342-5283

(G-4719)
ANTHONY-THOMAS CANDY
COMPANY (PA)
Also Called: Anthony-Thomas Candy
Shoppes
1777 Arlingate Ln (43228-4114)
P.O. Box 21865 (43221-0865)
PHONE..............................614 274-8405
Joseph Zanetos, *Pr*
Candi Trifelos, *
Nick Trifelos, *
▲ EMP: 125 EST: 1952
SQ FT: 152,000
SALES (est): 25.61MM
SALES (corp-wide): 25.61MM Privately
Held
Web: www.anthony-thomas.com
SIC: 2064 5441 2068 2066 Candy and other
confectionery products; Candy, nut, and
confectionery stores; Salted and roasted
nuts and seeds; Chocolate and cocoa
products

(G-4720)
APERA INSTRUMENTS LLC
6656 Busch Blvd (43229-1125)
PHONE..............................614 285-3080
Qingxiang Wu, *Admn*
EMP: 11 EST: 2016
SALES (est): 4.76MM Privately Held
Web: www.aperainst.com
SIC: 3826 Analytical instruments

(G-4721)
APPIAN MANUFACTURING CORP
2025 Camaro Ave (43207-1716)
PHONE..............................614 445-2230
Fran A Vendetta, *Pr*
▲ EMP: 30 EST: 1990
SQ FT: 40,000
SALES (est): 4.44MM Privately Held
Web: www.appianmfg.com
SIC: 3441 3498 Fabricated structural metal;
Fabricated pipe and fittings
PA: Necco K.K.
1-7-44, Namiki
Kawaguchi STM 332-0

(G-4722)
APPLICATION LINK INCORPORATED
4449 Easton Way Fl 2 (43219-7005)
PHONE..............................614 934-1735
Michael Reed, *Pr*
EMP: 6 EST: 1979
SQ FT: 2,000
SALES (est): 1.21MM Privately Held
Web: www.genesisearth.com
SIC: 7372 5045 7371 Business oriented
computer software; Computers,
peripherals, and software; Custom
computer programming services

(G-4723)
AQUA SCIENCE INC
1877 E 17th Ave (43219-1006)
PHONE..............................614 252-5000
Dan L Smucker, *Pr*
Darrell L Miller Junior, *VP*
EMP: 34 EST: 1983
SQ FT: 28,000
SALES (est): 9MM Privately Held
Web: www.aquascience.com
SIC: 2899 Water treating compounds

(G-4724)
ARBENZ INC
Also Called: Edwards Steel
1777 Mckinley Ave (43222-1050)
PHONE..............................614 274-6800
EMP: 15 EST: 1932
SALES (est): 3.75MM Privately Held
Web: www.edwardssteel.com
SIC: 3441 3444 Fabricated structural metal;
Sheet metalwork

(G-4725)
ARIEZHAIR COLLECTION LLC
1747 Olentangy River Rd (43212-1453)
PHONE..............................614 964-5748
Alexis Whitfield, *Managing Member*
EMP: 10
SALES (est): 283.15K Privately Held
SIC: 3999 Hair and hair-based products

(G-4726)
ARMOR
2218 Bristol Rd (43221-1204)
PHONE..............................614 459-1414
EMP: 8 EST: 2016
SALES (est): 93.02K Privately Held
Web: www.highcomarmor.com
SIC: 3555 Printing trades machinery

(G-4727)
ASHLAND CHEMCO INC
Also Called: Ashland Distribution
1979 Atlas St (43228-9645)
P.O. Box 2219 (43216-2219)
PHONE..............................614 790-3333
Ted Harris, *Distribution Vice President*
EMP: 150
SALES (corp-wide): 2.11B Publicly Held
Web: www.ashland.com
SIC: 2899 5169 Chemical preparations, nec;
Chemicals and allied products, nec
HQ: Ashland Chemco Inc.
1979 Atlas St
Columbus OH 43228
859 815-3333

(G-4728)
ASHLAND SPCALTY INGREDIENTS
GP
1979 Atlas St (43228-9645)
PHONE..............................614 529-3311
EMP: 132
SALES (corp-wide): 2.11B Publicly Held
Web: www.ashland.com
SIC: 2899 Chemical preparations, nec
HQ: Ashland Specialty Ingredients G.P.
8145 Blazer Dr
Wilmington DE 19808
302 594-5000

(G-4729)
ASIST TRANSLATION SERVICES
Also Called: Asist Translation Services
4891 Sawmill Rd Ste 200 (43235-7266)
PHONE..............................614 451-6744
Elena Tsinman, *Pr*
EMP: 12 EST: 1983
SQ FT: 8,000
SALES (est): 2.41MM Privately Held
Web: www.asisttranslations.com
SIC: 7389 2791 Translation services;
Typesetting

(G-4730)
ASSEMBLY MACHINING WIRE PDTS
Also Called: A M W
2375 Refugee Park (43207-2173)
PHONE..............................614 443-1110
Gregory Allan Donovan, *Pr*
EMP: 7 EST: 1974
SQ FT: 10,000
SALES (est): 382.94K Privately Held
SIC: 3599 Machine shop, jobbing and repair

(G-4731)
ATCHLEY SIGNS & GRAPHICS LLC
Also Called: 360 Wrapz
1616 Transamerica Ct (43228-9332)
PHONE..............................614 421-7446
Derek Atchley, *Prin*
Christine Atchley, *Prin*
EMP: 13 EST: 2006
SALES (est): 992.14K Privately Held
Web: www.atchleysigns.com
SIC: 3993 7389 Signs, not made in custom
sign painting shops; Printed circuitry
graphic layout

(G-4732)
ATLAS INDUSTRIAL CONTRS LLC
(HQ)
Also Called: Atlas Industrial Contractors
5275 Sinclair Rd (43229-5042)
PHONE..............................614 841-4500
George Ghanem, *Pr*
Timothy Seils, *
EMP: 300 EST: 1923
SQ FT: 20,000
SALES (est): 50.1MM Privately Held
Web: www.atlascos.com
SIC: 1731 3498 1796 Electrical work;
Fabricated pipe and fittings; Machine
moving and rigging
PA: Gmg Holdings, Llc
5275 Sinclair Rd
Columbus OH 43229

(G-4733)
ATM NERDS LLC
175 S 3rd St Ste 200 (43215-5194)
PHONE..............................614 983-3056
EMP: 10 EST: 2021
SALES (est): 750K Privately Held
SIC: 3578 Automatic teller machines (ATM)

(G-4734)
AULD CORPORATION
1569 Westbelt Dr (43228-3839)
P.O. Box 218373 (43221)
PHONE..............................614 454-1010
Dan Auld, *CEO*
EMP: 9 EST: 2014
SALES (est): 961.24K Privately Held
SIC: 3446 2752 Architectural metalwork;
Commercial printing, lithographic

(G-4735)
AUTOBODY SUPPLY COMPANY INC
212 N Grant Ave (43215-2691)
PHONE..............................614 228-4328
EMP: 68
SIC: 3563 5013 5198 Air and gas
compressors including vacuum pumps;
Automotive supplies; Paints, varnishes, and
supplies

(G-4736)
AVATION MEDICAL INC
1375 Perry St (43201-3177)
PHONE..............................614 591-4201
Jason Whiting, *CEO*
Kevin Wasserstein, *Ch*
Chris Hobbs, *CFO*
EMP: 10 EST: 2016
SQ FT: 2,500
SALES (est): 5.58MM Privately Held
Web: www.avation.com
SIC: 3845 Electromedical equipment

(G-4737)
AWC TRANSITION CORPORATION
6540 Huntley Rd (43229-1087)
PHONE..............................614 846-2918
Kelly Davirro, *Pr*
▲ EMP: 14 EST: 1957
SQ FT: 5,000
SALES (est): 1.38MM Privately Held
Web: www.americanwhistle.com
SIC: 3949 Sporting and athletic goods, nec

(G-4738)
B & A HOLISTIC FD & HERBS LLC
Also Called: Holistic Foods Herbs and Books
4550 Heaton Rd Ste B7 (43229-6611)
PHONE..............................614 747-2200
Sonya Robinson, *Managing Member*
EMP: 10 EST: 2011
SALES (est): 200K Privately Held
SIC: 2833 Drugs and herbs: grading,
grinding, and milling

(G-4739)
B & G TOOL COMPANY
4832 Kenny Rd (43220-2793)
PHONE..............................614 451-2538
Michael Plahuta, *Pr*
Daniel Plahuta, *VP*
EMP: 7 EST: 1965
SQ FT: 8,800
SALES (est): 2.16MM Privately Held
Web: www.b-gtool.com
SIC: 3599 3312 Machine shop, jobbing and
repair; Tool and die steel

(G-4740)
B B BRADLEY COMPANY INC
2699 Scioto Pkwy (43221-4658)
PHONE..............................614 777-5600
Bruce Beaty, *Pr*
EMP: 7
SALES (corp-wide): 5.06MM Privately
Held
Web: www.bbbradley.com
SIC: 3086 5199 Packaging and shipping
materials, foamed plastics; Packaging
materials
PA: The B B Bradley Company Inc
7755 Crile Rd
Concord Township OH 44077
440 354-2005

(G-4741)
BAKELITE CHEMICALS LLC
1975 Watkins Rd (43207-3443)
PHONE..............................404 652-4000
Rick Urschel, *Pr*
EMP: 88
SALES (corp-wide): 1.34B Privately Held
Web: www.bakelite.com
SIC: 2821 Melamine resins, melamine-
formaldehyde
HQ: Bakelite Chemicals Llc
1040 Crown Pnte Pkwy Ste
Atlanta GA 30338

(G-4742)
BALL CORPORATION
Also Called: Ball Metal Food Container
2690 Charter St (43228-4600)
PHONE....................................614 771-9112
Gordan Freeman, *Brnch Mgr*
EMP: 65
SALES (corp-wide): 11.79B **Publicly Held**
Web: www.ball.com
SIC: 3411 Metal cans
PA: Ball Corporation
9200 W 108th Cir
Westminster CO 80021
303 469-3131

(G-4743)
BANNER METALS GROUP INC
1308 Holly Ave (43212-3115)
PHONE....................................614 291-3105
Bronson Jones, *CEO*
John E O'brien Iii, *CEO*
C Bronson Jones, *General Vice President**
F M Jaeger, *
James H Kennedy, *
EMP: 40 EST: 1921
SQ FT: 70,000
SALES (est): 10.71MM **Privately Held**
Web: www.bannermetalsgroup.com
SIC: 3469 3544 Stamping metal for the trade
; Special dies and tools

(G-4744)
BARR ENGINEERING
INCORPORATED (PA)
Also Called: National Engrg Archtctral Svcs
2800 Corporate Exchange Dr Ste 240
(43231-7628)
PHONE....................................614 714-0299
Jawdat Siddiqi, *Pr*
Enoch Chipukaizer, *
EMP: 35 EST: 1992
SQ FT: 1,500
SALES (est): 4.92MM **Privately Held**
Web: www.neasinc.com
SIC: 8711 8713 8734 1799 Civil engineering;
Surveying services; Testing laboratories;
Core drilling and cutting

(G-4745)
BASF CORPORATION
Also Called: Midwest Distribution Center
9565 Logistics Ct (43217-0001)
PHONE....................................614 662-5682
Larry Baker, *Brnch Mgr*
EMP: 70
SALES (corp-wide): 69.01B **Privately Held**
Web: www.basf.com
SIC: 2869 2819 2899 2843 Industrial organic
chemicals, nec; Industrial inorganic
chemicals, nec; Antifreeze compounds;
Surface active agents
HQ: Basf Corporation
100 Park Ave
Florham Park NJ 07932
800 962-7831

(G-4746)
BEAM TECHNOLOGIES INC
80 E Rich St Ste 400 (43215-5286)
PHONE....................................800 648-1179
Alex Frommeyer, *CEO*
Alexander Curry, *
Daniel Dykes, *
EMP: 330 EST: 2012
SALES (est): 42.82MM **Privately Held**
Web: www.beambenefits.com
SIC: 3841 6411 Surgical and medical
instruments; Insurance agents, brokers,
and service

(G-4747)
BECKMAN XMO
376 Morrison Rd Ste D (43213-1447)
PHONE....................................614 864-2232
Tracy Beckman, *Prin*
EMP: 6 EST: 2010
SALES (est): 663.03K **Privately Held**
Web: www.beckmanxmo.com
SIC: 2752 Offset printing

(G-4748)
BEEHEX INC
1130 Gahanna Pkwy (43230-6615)
PHONE....................................512 633-5304
Benjamin Felnter, *COO*
EMP: 7 EST: 2016
SALES (est): 643.87K **Privately Held**
Web: www.beehex.com
SIC: 3555 Printing trades machinery

(G-4749)
BEEHEX LLC
1130 Gahanna Pkwy (43230-6615)
PHONE....................................512 633-5304
EMP: 11 EST: 2015
SALES (est): 1.17MM **Privately Held**
Web: www.beehex.com
SIC: 2099 Baking powder and soda, yeast,
and other leavening agents

(G-4750)
BELEM GROUP LLC
6012 E Main St (43213-3355)
PHONE....................................614 604-6870
Shad Bucher, *Pr*
EMP: 6 EST: 2019
SALES (est): 411.85K **Privately Held**
SIC: 2711 Commercial printing and
newspaper publishing combined

(G-4751)
BENCHMARK ARCHTECTURAL
SYSTEMS
Also Called: Kingspan Benchmark
720 Marion Rd (43207-2553)
PHONE....................................614 444-0110
Russel Shiels, *Pr*
Ilhan Eser, *
▲ EMP: 40 EST: 1997
SQ FT: 96,000
SALES (est): 9.4MM **Privately Held**
SIC: 3448 Prefabricated metal buildings and
components
HQ: Kingspan Insulated Panels Inc.
726 Summerhill Dr
Deland FL 32724
386 626-6789

(G-4752)
BERTEC CORPORATION
2500 Citygate Dr (43219-3677)
P.O. Box 360358 (43236-0358)
PHONE....................................614 543-8099
Necip Berme, *Pr*
EMP: 47 EST: 1987
SQ FT: 26,790
SALES (est): 9.65MM **Privately Held**
Web: www.bertec.com
SIC: 8711 3829 Consulting engineer;
Measuring and controlling devices, nec

(G-4753)
BEXLEY FABRICS INC
2476 E Main St (43209-2441)
P.O. Box 124 (43119-0124)
PHONE....................................614 231-7272
Edward E Goldin, *Owner*
EMP: 8 EST: 1939
SALES (est): 84.01K **Privately Held**

SIC: 2295 Sleeving, textile: saturated

(G-4754)
BIO-BLOOD COMPONENTS INC
1393 N High St (43201-2459)
PHONE....................................614 294-3183
Jane Hancock, *Mgr*
EMP: 86
SALES (corp-wide): 2.06MM **Privately Held**
SIC: 8099 2836 Blood bank; Biological
products, except diagnostic
PA: Bio-Blood Components, Inc.
5700 Pleasant View Rd
Memphis TN 38134
901 384-6250

(G-4755)
BIOBENT HOLDINGS LLC
Also Called: Biobent Polymers
1275 Kinnear Rd Ste 239 (43212-1180)
PHONE....................................513 658-5560
Keith Masavage, *CEO*
Michele Cole, *Prin*
EMP: 6 EST: 2012
SALES (est): 238.72K **Privately Held**
SIC: 2821 Plastics materials and resins

(G-4756)
BISON BUILDERS LLC
Also Called: Cabinet Guys, The
6999 Huntley Rd Ste M (43229-1031)
PHONE....................................614 636-0365
EMP: 18
SALES (est): 1.68MM **Privately Held**
SIC: 1522 2434 5031 Hotel/motel and multi-
family home renovation and remodeling;
Vanities, bathroom: wood; Kitchen cabinets

(G-4757)
BIZZY BEE PRINTING INC
Also Called: Innovative Computer Forms
1500 W 3rd Ave Ste 106 (43212-2887)
PHONE....................................614 771-1222
Chris Schmelzer, *Pr*
Rosemary Schmelzer, *Sec*
Rick Schmelzer, *Treas*
EMP: 6 EST: 1987
SALES (est): 165.8K **Privately Held**
Web: www.biggprint.com
SIC: 2752 Offset printing

(G-4758)
BJ EQUIPMENT LTD
Also Called: Rent-A-John
4522 Lockbourne Rd (43207-4231)
P.O. Box 753 (43216-0753)
PHONE....................................614 497-1188
William Reynolds Senior, *Pr*
William Reynolds Junior, *VP*
Bonnie Jean Reynolds, *Sec*
EMP: 14 EST: 1956
SALES (est): 2.41MM **Privately Held**
Web: www.potty4u.com
SIC: 7359 3444 3443 3431 Portable toilet
rental; Sheet metalwork; Fabricated plate
work (boiler shop); Metal sanitary ware

(G-4759)
BJOND INC
1463 Briarmeadow Dr (43235-1612)
PHONE....................................614 537-7246
Kenneth Leachman, *CEO*
EMP: 8 EST: 2013
SALES (est): 568.42K **Privately Held**
Web: www.researchgermany.com
SIC: 7372 7389 Business oriented computer
software; Business services, nec

(G-4760)
BLACK & DECKER (US) INC
1948 Schrock Rd (43229-1563)
PHONE....................................614 895-3112
Dave Burica, *Mgr*
EMP: 7
SALES (corp-wide): 15.37B **Publicly Held**
Web: www.dewalt.com
SIC: 3546 Power-driven handtools
HQ: Black & Decker (U.S.) Inc.
1000 Stanley Dr
New Britain CT 06053
860 225-5111

(G-4761)
BLACK GOLD CAPITAL LLC
2121 Bethel Rd Ste A (43220-1804)
PHONE....................................614 348-7460
Ernie Malas, *Managing Member*
Darshan Vyas, *Managing Member*
EMP: 20 EST: 2019
SALES (est): 4MM **Privately Held**
SIC: 3533 5013 Oil and gas field machinery;
Pumps, oil and gas

(G-4762)
BLACKBURNS FABRICATION INC
2467 Jackson Pike (43223-3846)
PHONE....................................614 875-0784
Mark A Blackburn, *Pr*
Edsel L Blackburn Senior, *VP*
Carolyn Blackburn, *
Kim Green, *
EMP: 30 EST: 1995
SQ FT: 50,000
SALES (est): 5.08MM **Privately Held**
Web:
www.blackburnsfabricationcolumbus.com
SIC: 3441 5051 Fabricated structural metal;
Structural shapes, iron or steel

(G-4763)
BLACKSTAR INTERNATIONAL INC
361 Indian Mound Rd (43213-2629)
PHONE....................................917 510-5482
Robert Black, *Pr*
EMP: 7
SALES (est): 1.14MM **Privately Held**
SIC: 3999 Manufacturing industries, nec

(G-4764)
BLACKWOOD SHEET METAL INC
844 Kerr St (43215-1499)
PHONE....................................614 291-3115
Diana Blackwood Newby, *Pr*
Charles Newby, *VP*
EMP: 8 EST: 1908
SQ FT: 10,000
SALES (est): 246.69K **Privately Held**
SIC: 7692 3443 Welding repair; Fabricated
plate work (boiler shop)

(G-4765)
BLOCKAMERICA CORPORATION
Also Called: Glass Block Warehouse, The
750 Kaderly Dr (43228-1032)
PHONE....................................614 274-0700
John Heisler, *Pr*
Carol Heisler, *VP*
John Heisler Ii, *VP*
EMP: 6 EST: 1987
SQ FT: 2,500
SALES (est): 475.5K **Privately Held**
Web: www.theglassblockwarehouse.com
SIC: 3229 5031 5231 Blocks and bricks,
glass; Windows; Glass

(G-4766)
BLU BIRD LLC (PA)
Also Called: Stone Center

GEOGRAPHIC

1736 Mckinley Ave (43222-1051)
PHONE.................................614 276-3585
EMP: 9 **EST:** 2020
SALES (est): 3.41MM
SALES (corp-wide): 3.41MM **Privately Held**
Web: www.stonecenters.com
SIC: 3281 Cut stone and stone products

(G-4767)
BLUE CHIP MANUFACTURING & SALES INC
3155 Lamb Ave (43219-2344)
PHONE.................................614 475-3853
EMP: 36
SIC: 3441 Fabricated structural metal

(G-4768)
BOB SUMEREL TIRE CO INC
2807 International St (43228-4616)
PHONE.................................614 527-9700
Timothy Hooker, *Mgr*
EMP: 11
SALES (corp-wide): 35.8MM **Privately Held**
Web: www.bobsumereltire.com
SIC: 5014 5015 7534 Tires and tubes; Batteries, used: automotive; Tire retreading and repair shops
PA: Bob Sumerel Tire Co., Inc.
1257 Cox Ave
Erlanger KY 41018
859 283-2700

(G-4769)
BOSC & BRIE
7625 N High St (43235-1499)
PHONE.................................614 985-2215
EMP: 12 **EST:** 2017
SALES (est): 252.66K **Privately Held**
Web: www.boscandbrie.com
SIC: 2034 Dried and dehydrated fruits, vegetables and soup mixes

(G-4770)
BOSTIK INC
802 Harmon Ave (43223-2410)
PHONE.................................614 232-8510
Al Lombardi, *Brnch Mgr*
EMP: 35
SALES (corp-wide): 134.78MM **Privately Held**
Web: www.bostik.com
SIC: 2891 Adhesives and sealants
HQ: Bostik, Inc.
11320 W Wtertown Plank Rd
Wauwatosa WI 53226
414 774-2250

(G-4771)
BOWDEN FENCE CO LLC
1560 Harmon Ave (43223-3312)
PHONE.................................614 272-8923
Terry Bowden, *Managing Member*
EMP: 9 **EST:** 1982
SALES (est): 719.36K **Privately Held**
Web: www.bowdenfence.com
SIC: 3446 1799 Acoustical suspension systems, metal; Fence construction

(G-4772)
BOWMANMULTIMEDIA LLC
470 W Broad St (43215-2759)
PHONE.................................419 405-8648
EMP: 10
SALES (est): 413.11K **Privately Held**
SIC: 2741 Miscellaneous publishing

(G-4773)
BRATTIEGIRLZ LLC
175 S 3rd St Ste 200 (43215-5194)
PHONE.................................513 607-4757
Giovonni Myers, *CEO*
EMP: 8 **EST:** 2020
SALES (est): 2.64MM **Privately Held**
SIC: 3537 Trucks, tractors, loaders, carriers, and similar equipment

(G-4774)
BREWPUB RESTAURANT CORPORATION
Also Called: Barley's Brewing Company
467 N High St (43215-2007)
PHONE.................................614 228-2537
Tiffany Jezerinac, *Pr*
EMP: 19 **EST:** 1992
SALES (est): 938.92K **Privately Held**
Web: www.smokehousebrewing.com
SIC: 5812 2082 American restaurant; Malt beverages

(G-4775)
BRIDGE COMPONENTS INCORPORATED
3476 Millikin Ct (43228-9765)
P.O. Box 1228 (43017-6228)
PHONE.................................614 873-0777
Neil Spears, *Pr*
EMP: 7 **EST:** 2001
SALES (est): 467.46K **Privately Held**
Web: www.bridgecomponentsind.com
SIC: 2824 3449 Elastomeric fibers; Bars, concrete reinforcing: fabricated steel

(G-4776)
BRIDGE COMPONENTS INDS INC
3476 Millikin Ct (43228-9765)
PHONE.................................614 873-0777
Tyler Spears, *Pr*
EMP: 10 **EST:** 2011
SALES (est): 1.96MM **Privately Held**
Web: www.bridgecomponentsind.com
SIC: 3312 Railroad crossings, steel or iron

(G-4777)
BRIDGESTONE RET OPERATIONS LLC
Also Called: Firestone
4015 E Broad St (43213-1130)
PHONE.................................614 864-3350
Brian Roper, *Mgr*
EMP: 10
Web: www.firestonecompleteautocare.com
SIC: 5531 7534 Automotive tires; Rebuilding and retreading tires
HQ: Bridgestone Retail Operations, Llc
200 4th Ave S Ste 100
Nashville TN 37201
615 937-1000

(G-4778)
BRIDGESTONE RET OPERATIONS LLC
Also Called: Firestone
35 Great Southern Blvd (43207-4001)
PHONE.................................614 491-8062
Tom Dummar, *Mgr*
EMP: 10
Web: www.firestonecompleteautocare.com
SIC: 5531 7534 7539 Automotive tires; Rebuilding and retreading tires; Brake services
HQ: Bridgestone Retail Operations, Llc
200 4th Ave S Ste 100
Nashville TN 37201
615 937-1000

(G-4779)
BRIDGESTONE RET OPERATIONS LLC
Also Called: Firestone
180 N 3rd St (43215-2920)
PHONE.................................614 224-4221
Joe Struewing, *Mgr*
EMP: 9
SQ FT: 5,550
Web: www.bridgestoneamericas.com
SIC: 5531 7534 Automotive tires; Rebuilding and retreading tires
HQ: Bridgestone Retail Operations, Llc
200 4th Ave S Ste 100
Nashville TN 37201
615 937-1000

(G-4780)
BRILISTA FOODS COMPANY INC (PA)
Also Called: Krema Nut Co
1000 Goodale Blvd (43212-3827)
PHONE.................................614 299-4132
Michael Giunta, *Pr*
Peggy Giunta, *VP*
Brian Giunta, *VP*
David Block, *VP*
EMP: 8 **EST:** 1991
SQ FT: 8,500
SALES (est): 2.43MM **Privately Held**
Web: www.krema.com
SIC: 2038 Snacks, incl. onion rings, cheese sticks, etc.

(G-4781)
BRISKHEAT CORPORATION (DH)
4800 Hilton Corporate Dr (43232-4150)
PHONE.................................614 294-3376
Domenic Federico, *CEO*
▲ **EMP:** 159 **EST:** 1949
SQ FT: 40,000
SALES (est): 31.21MM
SALES (corp-wide): 4.57MM **Privately Held**
Web: www.briskheat.com
SIC: 3585 Refrigeration and heating equipment
HQ: Backer Ehp Inc.
4700 John Bragg Hwy
Murfreesboro TN 37127

(G-4782)
BROCADE CMMNCTIONS SYSTEMS LLC
4200 Regent St Ste 200 (43219-6229)
PHONE.................................614 232-8015
EMP: 6
SALES (corp-wide): 51.57B **Publicly Held**
Web: www.broadcom.com
SIC: 3674 Semiconductors and related devices
HQ: Brocade Communications Systems Llc
3421 Hillview Ave
Palo Alto CA 94304

(G-4783)
BUCKEYE BOXES INC (PA)
601 N Hague Ave (43204-1498)
PHONE.................................614 274-8484
Craig Hoyt, *Pr*
Judd Hauenstein, *
Ken Churchill, *
▲ **EMP:** 60 **EST:** 1966
SQ FT: 100,000
SALES (est): 3.2MM
SALES (corp-wide): 3.2MM **Privately Held**
Web: www.buckeyeboxes.com

SIC: 2653 3993 2675 2631 Boxes, corrugated: made from purchased materials; Signs and advertising specialties; Die-cut paper and board; Paperboard mills

(G-4784)
BUCKEYE BUSINESS FORMS INC
Also Called: Proforma Buckeye
1695 Northam Rd (43221-3358)
PHONE.................................614 882-1890
Ann Kaylor Patton, *Pr*
James Patton, *Sec*
EMP: 6 **EST:** 1966
SALES (est): 223.74K **Privately Held**
Web: proformabuckeye.proforma.com
SIC: 7311 2752 7331 Advertising agencies; Offset printing; Mailing service

(G-4785)
BUCKEYE METAL WORKS INC
3240 Petzinger Rd (43232-3912)
PHONE.................................614 239-8000
Matthew Daniel, *Pr*
Walt Daniel, *VP*
EMP: 8 **EST:** 1994
SQ FT: 15,000
SALES (est): 2.35MM **Privately Held**
Web: www.buckeyemetal.com
SIC: 3444 Sheet metal specialties, not stamped

(G-4786)
BUCKEYE STAMPING COMPANY
Also Called: Buckeye Shapeform
555 Marion Rd (43207-2501)
PHONE.................................877 728-0776
Jon Hettinger, *Ch Bd*
C A Morningstar, *
Ken Tumblison, *
Larry Doza, *
EMP: 60 **EST:** 1902
SQ FT: 80,000
SALES (est): 9.64MM **Privately Held**
Web: www.buckeyeshapeform.com
SIC: 3469 3443 3089 3449 Electronic enclosures, stamped or pressed metal; Containers, shipping (bombs, etc.): metal plate; Plastics hardware and building products; Miscellaneous metalwork

(G-4787)
BUCKS FOR PUPS CONFECTIONS LLC
Also Called: Buckeye Lady, The
4493 N High St (43214-2637)
PHONE.................................614 359-4672
Alicia Hindman, *Managing Member*
EMP: 10 **EST:** 2020
SALES (est): 69.18K **Privately Held**
SIC: 2064 5812 Candy bars, including chocolate covered bars; Eating places

(G-4788)
BURTON METAL FINISHING INC
Also Called: Burton Mtal Fnshg Inc Pwdr Cti
1711 Woodland Ave (43219-1137)
PHONE.................................614 252-9523
Daniel Burton, *Pr*
Scott Burton, *
Victoria Burton, *
EMP: 25 **EST:** 1987
SQ FT: 5,000
SALES (est): 6.66MM **Privately Held**
Web: www.burtonmetal.com
SIC: 3471 Electroplating of metals or formed products

(G-4789)
BUSINESS IDNTFCTION SYSTEMS IN
Also Called: Sign-A-Rama
6185 Huntley Rd Ste M (43229-1094)

▲ = Import ▼ = Export
◆ = Import/Export

PHONE..................614 841-1255
Stephen M Thompson, *Pr*
EMP: 6 **EST:** 1993
SQ FT: 5,200
SALES (est): 497.81K **Privately Held**
Web: www.signarama.com
SIC: 3993 5999 Signs and advertising
specialties; Banners, flags, decals, and
posters

(G-4790)
BYBE INC
107 S High St (43215-3408)
PHONE..................614 706-3050
EMP: 10 **EST:** 2017
SALES (est): 1.21MM **Privately Held**
Web: www.bybe.com
SIC: 7372 Application computer software

(G-4791)
CALGON CARBON CORPORATION
835 N Cassady Ave (43219-2203)
PHONE..................614 258-9501
Maria D'amico, *Brnch Mgr*
EMP: 10
Web: www.calgoncarbon.com
SIC: 2819 Charcoal (carbon), activated
HQ: Calgon Carbon Corporation
3000 Gsk Dr
Moon Township PA 15108
412 787-6700

(G-4792)
CALLAHAN CUTTING TOOLS INC
Also Called: Blade Manufacturing Co, The
915 Distribution Dr Ste A (43228-1009)
PHONE..................614 294-1649
Marc A Callahan, *Pr*
◆ **EMP:** 7 **EST:** 2004
SQ FT: 10,000
SALES (est): 880.89K **Privately Held**
SIC: 3541 3425 Machine tools, metal cutting
type; Saw blades and handsaws

(G-4793)
CANDLE LAB
1251 Grandview Ave (43212-3457)
PHONE..................614 488-2009
Steve Weaver, *Pr*
EMP: 7 **EST:** 2008
SALES (est): 130.25K **Privately Held**
Web: www.thecandlelab.com
SIC: 3999 Candles

(G-4794)
CAP & ASSOCIATES INC
Also Called: Cap Fixtures
445 Mccormick Blvd (43213-1526)
PHONE..................614 863-3363
Jason Prosnik, *
Joseph Chaulk, *
◆ **EMP:** 170 **EST:** 1981
SQ FT: 110,000
SALES (est): 2.46MM **Privately Held**
Web: www.capfixtures.com
SIC: 2541 2542 Store fixtures, wood;
Fixtures, store: except wood

(G-4795)
CAPEHART ENTERPRISES LLC
Also Called: Minuteman Press
1724 Northwest Blvd Ste B (43212-2272)
PHONE..................614 769-7746
Gerald C Capehart, *Managing Member*
EMP: 15 **EST:** 1998
SQ FT: 1,500
SALES (est): 320.4K **Privately Held**
Web: www.minuteman.com
SIC: 2752 5199 8742 Commercial printing,
lithographic; Advertising specialties;
Marketing consulting services

(G-4796)
CAPITAL CITY AWNING CO INC
577 N 4th St (43215-2183)
PHONE..................614 221-5404
TOLL FREE: 800
Timothy Kellogg, *Pr*
Michael Mc Connell, *
Eugene E Mc Connell Junior, *Stockholder*
EMP: 50 **EST:** 1944
SQ FT: 25,600
SALES (est): 4.15MM **Privately Held**
Web: www.capitalcityawning.com
SIC: 2394 2393 Awnings, fabric: made from
purchased materials; Canvas bags

(G-4797)
CAPITAL PRSTHTIC ORTHTIC CTR I
(PA)
4678 Larwell Dr (43220-3621)
PHONE..................614 451-0446
Lisa Crawford, *CEO*
Patricia W Kozersky, *Sec*
EMP: 12 **EST:** 1982
SQ FT: 3,200
SALES (est): 6.35MM
SALES (corp-wide): 6.35MM **Privately
Held**
Web: www.capitalprosthetics.net
SIC: 3842 Limbs, artificial

(G-4798)
CAPITAL RESIN CORPORATION
324 Dering Ave (43207-2956)
PHONE..................614 445-7177
Judithe Wensinger, *CEO*
▲ **EMP:** 76 **EST:** 1976
SQ FT: 6,000
SALES (est): 11.79MM **Privately Held**
Web: www.capitalresin.com
SIC: 2819 2821 Inorganic acids except nitric
and phosphoric; Acrylic resins

(G-4799)
CAPITOL CITICOM INC
Also Called: Citicom
2225 Citygate Dr Ste A (43219-3651)
P.O. Box 361563 (43236)
PHONE..................614 472-2679
Kevin Oakes, *Pr*
Gail E Oakes, *VP*
Michael Oakes, *VP*
EMP: 20 **EST:** 1985
SQ FT: 11,500
SALES (est): 4.85MM **Privately Held**
Web: www.citicomprint.com
SIC: 7372 7389 7334 2752 Publisher's
computer software; Printers' services:
folding, collating, etc.; Photocopying and
duplicating services; Offset and
photolithographic printing

(G-4800)
CAPITOL SQUARE PRINTING INC
59 E Gay St (43215-3103)
PHONE..................614 221-2850
Marilyn S Smith, *Pr*
Craig Poland, *VP*
EMP: 7 **EST:** 1975
SQ FT: 4,500
SALES (est): 410.71K **Privately Held**
Web: www.capitolsquareprinting.com
SIC: 2752 Offset printing

(G-4801)
CARDINAL BUILDERS INC
4409 E Main St (43213-3061)
PHONE..................614 237-1000
Tim Coady, *Pr*
Tim Kane, *Stockholder*
EMP: 6 **EST:** 1965
SQ FT: 22,000

SALES (est): 686.66K **Privately Held**
SIC: 3541 1521 1522 1761 Machine tool
replacement & repair parts, metal cutting
types; General remodeling, single-family
houses; Hotel/motel and multi-family home
renovation and remodeling; Siding
contractor

(G-4802)
CATHOLIC DIOCESE OF COLUMBUS
Also Called: Catholic Times
197 E Gay St Ste 4 (43215-3229)
PHONE..................614 224-5195
Teresa Ianaggi, *Mgr*
EMP: 9
SALES (corp-wide): 12.29MM **Privately
Held**
Web: www.catholictimescolumbus.org
SIC: 2711 Newspapers
PA: Catholic Diocese Of Columbus
198 E Broad St
Columbus OH 43215
614 224-2251

(G-4803)
CENTRAL OIL ASPHALT CORP (PA)
8 E Long St Ste 400 (43215-2914)
PHONE..................614 224-8111
F L Shafer, *Pr*
EMP: 7 **EST:** 1934
SQ FT: 4,600
SALES (est): 573.76K
SALES (corp-wide): 573.76K **Privately
Held**
SIC: 2951 Asphalt and asphaltic paving
mixtures (not from refineries)

(G-4804)
CGMW INCORPORATED
Also Called: Interface Logic Systems
1020 Taylor Station Rd Ste F (43230-6675)
P.O. Box 30772 (43230-0772)
PHONE..................614 236-8388
James Gottliebson, *Pr*
EMP: 8 **EST:** 1986
SALES (est): 164.65K **Privately Held**
Web: www.interfacelogic.com
SIC: 5046 3596 Commercial equipment, nec
; Industrial scales

(G-4805)
CHAMPION STRAPPING PDTS INC
1819 Walcutt Rd Ste 13 (43228-9149)
PHONE..................614 527-1454
Andrew Sandberg, *Prin*
EMP: 6 **EST:** 2010
SALES (est): 2.15MM **Privately Held**
SIC: 3499 Strapping, metal

(G-4806)
CHEAP DUMPSTERS LLC
5042 Astoria Ave (43207-4924)
PHONE..................614 285-5865
Vanessa Nakanishi, *Prin*
EMP: 6 **EST:** 2012
SALES (est): 133.14K **Privately Held**
SIC: 3443 Dumpsters, garbage

(G-4807)
CHEP (USA) INC
2130 New World Dr (43207-3433)
PHONE..................614 497-9448
Matt Mallory, *Mgr*
EMP: 15
Web: www.chep.com
SIC: 2448 Pallets, wood
HQ: Chep (U.S.A.) Inc.
5897 Windward Pkwy
Alpharetta GA 30005
770 668-8100

(G-4808)
CHOICE MARKETING
5130 Transamerica Dr (43228-9269)
PHONE..................614 638-8404
Cullan Laing, *Prin*
EMP: 15 **EST:** 2018
SALES (est): 118.54K **Privately Held**
Web:
www.choice-marketing-partners.com
SIC: 2711 Newspapers

(G-4809)
CLARK GRAVE VAULT COMPANY
(PA)
Also Called: C.T.L. Steel Division
375 E 5th Ave (43201-2819)
P.O. Box 8250 (43201-0250)
PHONE..................614 294-3761
David Beck, *Pr*
Mark Beck, *
David A Beck Ii, *VP*
Douglas A Beck, *Marketing*
Nancy M Beck, *
EMP: 140 **EST:** 1898
SQ FT: 300,000
SALES (est): 23.5MM
SALES (corp-wide): 23.5MM **Privately
Held**
Web: www.clarkvault.com
SIC: 3316 3272 Strip, steel, flat bright, cold-
rolled: purchased hot-rolled; Precast
terrazzo or concrete products

(G-4810)
CLASSIC STONE COMPANY INC
4090 Janitrol Rd (43228-1396)
PHONE..................614 833-3946
R G Reitter, *Pr*
Steven Waits, *VP*
EMP: 10 **EST:** 1998
SQ FT: 20,000
SALES (est): 312.44K **Privately Held**
SIC: 3281 Cut stone and stone products

(G-4811)
CLEVELAND PLANT AND FLOWER
CO
2370 Marilyn Park Ln (43219-1792)
P.O. Box 30837 (43230-0837)
PHONE..................614 478-9900
Brian Davis, *Mgr*
EMP: 8
SQ FT: 3,000
SALES (corp-wide): 22.39MM **Privately
Held**
Web: www.cpfco.com
SIC: 5193 5992 3999 Flowers, fresh;
Flowers, fresh; Candles
PA: The Cleveland Plant And Flower
Company
12920 Corporate Dr
Cleveland OH 44130
216 898-3500

(G-4812)
CLEVELAND-CLIFFS COLUMBUS
LLC
4300 Alum Creek Dr (43207-4519)
PHONE..................614 492-8287
Heather Paarlberg, *Brnch Mgr*
EMP: 25
SALES (corp-wide): 19.18B **Publicly Held**
Web: www.clevelandcliffs.com
SIC: 3312 Galvanized pipes, plates, sheets,
etc.: iron and steel
HQ: Cleveland-Cliffs Columbus Llc
4020 Knross Lkes Pkwy Ste
Richfield OH 44286
614 492-6800

(G-4813)
CLOCKINGME LLC
3280 Morse Rd Ste 211 (43231-6175)
PHONE..............................614 400-9727
EMP: 10
SALES (est): 180.56K Privately Held
SIC: 3695 Computer software tape and
　disks: blank, rigid, and floppy

(G-4814)
CMD MEDTECH LLC
3585 Interchange Rd (43204-1400)
PHONE..............................614 364-4243
EMP: 15 EST: 2016
SALES (est): 2.91MM Privately Held
Web: www.cmdmedtech.com
SIC: 3841 Surgical and medical instruments

(G-4815)
COCA-COLA COMPANY
Also Called: Coca-Cola
2455 Watkins Rd (43207-3488)
P.O. Box 2589 (43216-2589)
PHONE..............................614 491-6305
Willi Pete, Mgr
EMP: 47
SALES (corp-wide): 45.75B Publicly Held
Web: www.coca-colacompany.com
SIC: 2086 Bottled and canned soft drinks
PA: The Coca-Cola Company
　1 Coca Cola Plz Nw
　Atlanta GA 30313
　404 676-2121

(G-4816)
COLORTECH GRAPHICS &
PRINTING (PA)
4000 Business Park Dr (43204-5023)
PHONE..............................614 766-2400
C Wayne Booker, Pr
EMP: 19 EST: 1985
SQ FT: 1,600
SALES (est): 873.83K
SALES (corp-wide): 873.83K Privately
Held
Web: www.colortechdesign.com
SIC: 7334 2791 Photocopying and
　duplicating services; Typesetting

(G-4817)
COLUMBUS APPAREL STUDIO LLC
Also Called: Columbus Apparel Studio
757 Garden Rd Ste 110 (43214-2294)
PHONE..............................614 706-7292
Denise Falter, CEO
EMP: 10 EST: 2018
SALES (est): 441.9K Privately Held
Web: www.columbusapparelstudio.com
SIC: 2331 2339 2321 2329 Women's and
　misses' blouses and shirts; Women's and
　misses' athletic clothing and sportswear;
　Men's and boys' dress shirts; Men's and
　boy's clothing, nec

(G-4818)
COLUMBUS ART MEMORIAL INC
606 W Broad St (43215-2712)
PHONE..............................614 221-9333
Mel Lee, Mgr
EMP: 8
SQ FT: 5,000
SALES (corp-wide): 801.88K Privately
Held
Web: www.columbusartmemorial.com
SIC: 3272 Monuments, concrete
PA: Art Columbus Memorial Inc
　766 Greenlawn Ave
　Columbus OH 43223
　614 443-5778

(G-4819)
COLUMBUS CANVAS PRODUCTS
INC
Also Called: Columbus Canvas Products
577 N 4th St (43215-2101)
PHONE..............................614 375-1397
Janet M Kellogg, Pr
Michael Mcconnell, VP
Timothy Kellogg, VP
EMP: 10 EST: 1958
SQ FT: 10,000
SALES (est): 1.72MM Privately Held
Web:
www.columbuscanvasproducts.com
SIC: 2394 2393 3949 2392 Canvas and
　related products; Cushions, except spring
　and carpet: purchased materials; Sporting
　and athletic goods, nec; Household
　furnishings, nec

(G-4820)
COLUMBUS CONTROLS INC
3573 Johnny Appleseed Ct (43231-4985)
PHONE..............................614 882-9029
EMP: 30 EST: 1981
SALES (est): 4.64MM Privately Held
Web: www.columbuscontrols.com
SIC: 3822 3613 Environmental controls;
　Control panels, electric

(G-4821)
COLUMBUS CUSTOM TEES
6419 Nicholas Dr (43235-5204)
PHONE..............................614 573-5556
EMP: 11 EST: 2018
SALES (est): 247.8K Privately Held
Web: www.columbuscustomtees.com
SIC: 2759 Screen printing

(G-4822)
COLUMBUS DESIGN & MFG LLC
3303 E 11th Ave (43219-5716)
PHONE..............................414 534-3273
Patrick Montag, Prin
EMP: 9 EST: 2013
SALES (est): 1.1MM Privately Held
Web: www.cdmohio.com
SIC: 3541 7389 Machine tools, metal cutting
　type; Design services

(G-4823)
COLUMBUS HEATING & VENT CO
182 N Yale Ave (43222-1127)
PHONE..............................614 274-1177
Charles R Gulley, Pr
Greogy Yoak, *
Mikel Plythe, *
Michael Blythe, *
EMP: 135 EST: 1874
SALES (est): 2.37MM Privately Held
Web: www.columbusheat.com
SIC: 1711 3585 Warm air heating and air
　conditioning contractor; Furnaces, warm
　air: electric

(G-4824)
COLUMBUS INCONTACT
555 S Front St (43215-5668)
PHONE..............................801 245-8369
EMP: 9 EST: 2017
SALES (est): 2.1MM Privately Held
Web: www.nice.com
SIC: 7372 Prepackaged software

(G-4825)
COLUMBUS INSTRUMENTS LLC
950 N Hague Ave (43204-2121)
PHONE..............................614 276-0861
EMP: 25 EST: 2020
SALES (est): 5.6MM Privately Held

Web: www.colinst.com
SIC: 3826 Analytical instruments

(G-4826)
COLUMBUS INSTRUMENTS INTL
CORP
Also Called: Columbus Instruments
950 N Hague Ave (43204-2121)
PHONE..............................614 276-0593
Jan A Czekajewski, Pr
Laura Damas, *
◆ EMP: 48 EST: 1970
SQ FT: 19,460
SALES (est): 2.99MM Privately Held
Web: www.colinst.com
SIC: 3826 Analytical instruments

(G-4827)
COLUMBUS INTERNATIONAL CORP
(PA)
200 E Campus View Blvd Ste 200
(43235-4678)
PHONE..............................614 323-1086
Rajeev Kumar, Pr
EMP: 8 EST: 2001
SQ FT: 2,000
SALES (est): 1.17MM
SALES (corp-wide): 1.17MM Privately
Held
Web: www.columbuscorp.com
SIC: 7372 Business oriented computer
　software

(G-4828)
COLUMBUS KOMBUCHA COMPANY
LLC
930 Freeway Dr N (43229-5424)
PHONE..............................614 262-0000
EMP: 8 EST: 2011
SQ FT: 5,000
SALES (est): 243.39K Privately Held
SIC: 2082 Malt beverages

(G-4829)
COLUMBUS MACHINE WORKS INC
2491 Fairwood Ave (43207-2709)
PHONE..............................614 409-0244
Michael Stacey, Pr
Diana Stacey, Sec
EMP: 11 EST: 1997
SQ FT: 3,729
SALES (est): 2.73MM Privately Held
Web: www.columbusmachine.com
SIC: 3599 Machine shop, jobbing and repair

(G-4830)
COLUMBUS MESSENGER
COMPANY (PA)
Also Called: Madison Messenger
3500 Sullivant Ave (43204-1887)
PHONE..............................614 272-5422
Phillip Daubel, Owner
EMP: 25 EST: 1972
SQ FT: 4,000
SALES (est): 2.38MM
SALES (corp-wide): 2.38MM Privately
Held
Web: www.columbusmessenger.com
SIC: 2711 Newspapers, publishing and
　printing

(G-4831)
COLUMBUS PIPE AND EQUIPMENT
CO
Also Called: Steel Warehouse Division
763 E Markison Ave (43207-1393)
P.O. Box 07843 (43207-0843)
PHONE..............................614 444-7871
TOLL FREE: 800
Bruce Jay Silberstein, Pr

Jonathan Silberstein, VP
Mike Denoewer, CFO
Helen Silberstein, Sec
Roberta Silberstein, Stockholder
EMP: 15 EST: 1932
SQ FT: 50,000
SALES (est): 4.3MM Privately Held
Web:
plumbing-equipment-dealers.cmac.ws
SIC: 5082 7692 5074 Construction and
　mining machinery; Welding repair;
　Plumbing fittings and supplies

(G-4832)
COLUMBUS ROOF TRUSSES INC
(PA)
2525 Fisher Rd (43204-3588)
P.O. Box 578 (47970)
PHONE..............................614 272-6464
TOLL FREE: 800
Tony Iacovetta, Pr
Eugene R Iacovetta, *
Rose A Pritchard, *
EMP: 30 EST: 1959
SQ FT: 51,000
SALES (est): 4.98MM
SALES (corp-wide): 4.98MM Privately
Held
Web: www.columbusrooftruss.com
SIC: 2439 Trusses, wooden roof

(G-4833)
COLUMBUS SIGN COMPANY
1515 E 5th Ave (43219-2483)
PHONE..............................614 252-3133
Michael Hoy, Pr
Michael S Hoy, *
EMP: 33 EST: 1911
SQ FT: 15,000
SALES (est): 2.57MM Privately Held
Web: www.columbussign.com
SIC: 3993 Neon signs

(G-4834)
COLUMBUS STEEL CASTINGS CO
Also Called: Columbus Castings
2211 Parsons Ave (43207-2448)
PHONE..............................614 444-2121
▲ EMP: 750
SIC: 3325 Steel foundries, nec

(G-4835)
COLUMBUS STEELMASTERS INC
660 Concrea Rd (43219-1822)
PHONE..............................614 231-2141
Brenda Neale, CEO
Steven Neale, Pr
EMP: 12 EST: 1971
SQ FT: 17,000
SALES (est): 950.81K Privately Held
SIC: 3444 Sheet metal specialties, not
　stamped

(G-4836)
COLUMBUS V&S GALVANIZING LLC
987 Buckeye Park Rd (43207-2596)
PHONE..............................614 449-8281
Werner Niehaus, Pr
Brian Miller, Managing Member*
EMP: 90 EST: 2001
SALES (est): 9.18MM Privately Held
Web: www.hotdipgalvanizing.com
SIC: 3479 Galvanizing of iron, steel, or end-
　formed products

(G-4837)
COLUMBUS WATER SECTION
PERMIT
910 Dublin Rd (43215-1169)
PHONE..............................614 645-8039
EMP: 6 EST: 2019

SALES (est): 360.5K **Privately Held**
Web: new.columbus.gov
SIC: 3542 Machine tools, metal forming type

(G-4838)
COLUMBUS-SPORTS PUBLICATIONS
Also Called: Buckeye Sports Bulletin
1200 Chambers Rd (43212-1703)
P.O. Box 12453 (43212-0453)
PHONE..................................614 486-2202
Frank L Moskowitz, *Pr*
EMP: 7 EST: 1981
SALES (est): 235.55K **Privately Held**
Web: www.buckeyesports.com
SIC: 2711 Newspapers, publishing and
printing

(G-4839)
COMPUTER ALLIED TECHNOLOGY CO
3385 Somerford Rd (43221-1438)
PHONE..................................614 457-2292
Mark Taylor, *Pr*
Pat Taylor, *Sec*
EMP: 7 EST: 1986
SALES (est): 205.19K **Privately Held**
SIC: 7371 3569 Computer software
development; Robots, assembly line:
industrial and commercial

(G-4840)
CONCEPT 9 INC
1604 Clara St (43211-2664)
PHONE..................................614 294-3743
Kenneth J Nienkirchen, *Ch Bd*
Karl Nienkirchen, *Pr*
Kris Nienkirchen, *VP*
EMP: 6 EST: 1981
SQ FT: 5,000
SALES (est): 178.72K **Privately Held**
SIC: 2759 Screen printing

(G-4841)
CONNECT HOUSING BLOCKS LLC
3251 Westerville Rd (43224-3751)
PHONE..................................614 503-4344
Brad Dehays, *Managing Member*
EMP: 25 EST: 2020
SALES (est): 4.83MM **Privately Held**
Web: www.connecthousingblocks.com
SIC: 3448 Prefabricated metal buildings and
components

(G-4842)
CONNS POTATO CHIP CO INC
1271 Alum Creek Dr (43209-2721)
PHONE..................................614 252-2150
Nick Miller, *Mgr*
EMP: 45
SQ FT: 1,050
SALES (corp-wide): 9.37MM **Privately Held**
Web: www.connspotatochips.com
SIC: 2096 Potato chips and similar snacks
PA: Conn's Potato Chip Co., Inc.
1805 Kemper Ct
Zanesville OH 43701
740 452-4615

(G-4843)
CONQUEST MAPS LLC (PA)
5696 Westbourne Ave (43213-1487)
PHONE..................................614 654-1627
Ross Worden, *CEO*
Ross Worden, *Pr*
EMP: 6 EST: 2012
SALES (est): 2.66MM
SALES (corp-wide): 2.66MM **Privately Held**
Web: www.conquestmaps.com

SIC: 5023 8699 3861 Decorative home
furnishings and supplies; Travel club;
Printing frames, photographic

(G-4844)
CONTRACT LUMBER INC
200 Schofield Dr (43213-3803)
PHONE..................................614 751-1109
EMP: 15
SALES (corp-wide): 101.14MM **Privately Held**
Web: www.contractlumber.com
SIC: 7349 5211 5031 2421 Building
maintenance services, nec; Lumber and
other building materials; Lumber: rough,
dressed, and finished; Lumber: rough,
sawed, or planed
PA: Contract Lumber, Inc.
3245 Hazelton-Etna Rd
Pataskala OH 43062
740 964-3147

(G-4845)
CONTROL-X INC
3546 Rosburg Dr (43228-7089)
PHONE..................................614 777-9729
Zsigmond Kovacs, *Pr*
EMP: 7 EST: 1990
SALES (est): 490.92K **Privately Held**
SIC: 3844 X-ray apparatus and tubes

(G-4846)
CONVAULT OF OHIO INC
841 Alton Ave (43219-3710)
P.O. Box 89 (43068-0089)
PHONE..................................614 252-8422
Tim Thickstun, *Pr*
Steven Thickstun, *Sec*
Joanne Thickstun, *VP*
EMP: 9 EST: 1990
SALES (est): 359.77K **Privately Held**
Web: www.mastohio.com
SIC: 3443 Fuel tanks (oil, gas, etc.), metal
plate

(G-4847)
COOKIE BOUQUETS INC
Also Called: Cookie Bouquet
6665 Huntley Rd Ste F (43229-1045)
PHONE..................................614 888-2171
Christian Mccoy, *Pr*
EMP: 7 EST: 1984
SQ FT: 4,500
SALES (est): 409.14K **Privately Held**
Web: www.cookiebouquets.com
SIC: 5461 5947 2052 Cookies; Gift baskets;
Cookies and crackers

(G-4848)
COOPER LIGHTING LLC
Also Called: Cooper Lighting Solutions
P.O. Box 182368 (43218-2368)
PHONE..................................800 334-6871
EMP: 6 EST: 2012
SALES (est): 1.14MM **Privately Held**
SIC: 3648 Lighting equipment, nec

(G-4849)
COPIER RESOURCES INC
Also Called: Cri Digital
4800 Evanswood Dr (43229-6207)
P.O. Box 14824 (43214-0824)
PHONE..................................614 268-1100
Scott Di Francesco, *Pr*
EMP: 6 EST: 1991
SQ FT: 4,000
SALES (est): 896.33K **Privately Held**
Web: www.cridigital.net

SIC: 7629 7359 5734 3575 Electrical repair
shops; Office machine rental, except
computers; Computer and software stores;
Cathode ray tube (CRT), computer terminal

(G-4850)
CORE MOLDING TECHNOLOGIES INC (PA)
800 Manor Park Dr (43228-9762)
PHONE..................................614 870-5000
David L Duvall, *Pr*
Thomas R Cellitti, *Non-Executive Chairman
of the Board**
Eric L Palomaki, *COO*
John P Zimmer, *Ex VP*
▲ EMP: 518 EST: 1988
SALES (est): 302.38MM **Publicly Held**
Web: www.coremt.com
SIC: 3089 Injection molding of plastics

(G-4851)
CORPORATE ELEVATOR LLC
35 E Gay St Ste 218 (43215-8128)
P.O. Box 538 (43054-0538)
PHONE..................................614 288-1847
Ivan Isreal, *Prin*
EMP: 7 EST: 2014
SALES (est): 267.9K **Privately Held**
Web: www.corporate-elevator.net
SIC: 8243 7372 7371 Repair training,
computer; Application computer software;
Custom computer programming services

(G-4852)
COSTUME SPECIALISTS INC
1801 Lone Eagle St (43228-3647)
PHONE..................................614 464-2115
Wendy C Goldstein, *Pr*
EMP: 36 EST: 1979
SALES (est): 9.35MM **Privately Held**
Web: www.costumespecialists.com
SIC: 2389 7299 Theatrical costumes;
Costume rental

(G-4853)
COTT SYSTEMS INC
2800 Corporate Exchange Dr Ste 300
(43231-1678)
PHONE..................................614 847-4405
Deborah A Ball, *CEO*
Jodie Bare, ***
Karen L Bailey, ***
Drew Shepppared, ***
Mike Sosh, ***
EMP: 95 EST: 1888
SQ FT: 20,000
SALES (est): 16.43MM **Privately Held**
Web: www.cottsystems.com
SIC: 7373 7371 2789 Computer integrated
systems design; Computer software
development and applications; Beveling of
cards

(G-4854)
COW INDUSTRIES INC (PA)
Also Called: Central Ohio Welding
1875 Progress Ave (43207-1781)
PHONE..................................614 443-6537
John Burns, *Pr*
Michael Netto, ***
Gary Carter, ***
Christina Bradford, ***
EMP: 40 EST: 1911
SQ FT: 80,000
SALES (est): 9.44MM
SALES (corp-wide): 9.44MM **Privately Held**
Web: www.cowind.com
SIC: 3499 3444 Machine bases, metal;
Sheet metalwork

(G-4855)
COX INTERIOR INC
Also Called: Cox's Interior Supply
2220 Citygate Dr (43219-3565)
PHONE..................................614 473-9169
Mick Householder, *Mgr*
EMP: 8
SALES (corp-wide): 44.6MM **Privately Held**
Web: www.coxinterior.com
SIC: 2431 Millwork
HQ: Cox Interior, Inc.
1751 Old Columbia Rd
Campbellsville KY 42718
270 789-3129

(G-4856)
COZMYK ENTERPRISES INC
3757 Courtright Ct (43227-2250)
PHONE..................................614 231-1370
Alan L Cozmyk, *Pr*
Christopher J Minnillo, *Prin*
EMP: 15 EST: 1986
SQ FT: 20,000
SALES (est): 2.28MM **Privately Held**
Web: www.cozmykenterprises.com
SIC: 3446 Ornamental metalwork

(G-4857)
CPMM SERVICES GROUP INC
3785 Indianola Ave (43214-3754)
PHONE..................................614 447-0165
Dan Dimitroff, *Pr*
EMP: 8 EST: 1984
SQ FT: 12,500
SALES (est): 786.97K **Privately Held**
Web: www.cpmmservicesinc.com
SIC: 7331 2752 7374 Mailing list compilers;
Offset printing; Data processing service

(G-4858)
CRANE BLENDING CENTER
2141 Fairwood Ave (43207-1753)
P.O. Box 1058 (43216-1058)
PHONE..................................614 542-1199
Phil Stobart, *Pr*
EMP: 40 EST: 2000
SALES (est): 2.66MM **Privately Held**
SIC: 2821 Polyvinyl chloride resins, PVC

(G-4859)
CRAWFORD PRODUCTS INC
3637 Corporate Dr (43231-7997)
PHONE..................................614 890-1822
William A Crawford, *CEO*
Kevin P Crawford, *Pr*
Scott Stauch, *VP*
▲ EMP: 21 EST: 1970
SQ FT: 12,500
SALES (est): 4.22MM **Privately Held**
Web: www.crawfordproducts.com
SIC: 5085 3452 Fasteners, industrial: nuts,
bolts, screws, etc.; Bolts, nuts, rivets, and
washers

(G-4860)
CRIMSON CUP INC (PA)
Also Called: Crimson Cup Coffee Roasters
700 Alum Creek Dr Ste 400 (43205-1640)
PHONE..................................614 252-3335
TOLL FREE: 888
Greg Ubert, *Pr*
Howard Ubert, *Sec*
EMP: 11 EST: 1991
SQ FT: 6,000
SALES (est): 8.57MM **Privately Held**
Web: www.crimsoncup.com
SIC: 5499 2095 Coffee; Coffee roasting
(except by wholesale grocers)

(G-4861)
CRMD LLC
1190 N High St (43201-2411)
PHONE..................................440 225-7179
EMP: 8 EST: 2017
SALES (est): 1.17MM **Privately Held**
Web: www.getcrmd.com
SIC: 2024 Ice cream and frozen deserts

(G-4862)
CSG SOFTWARE
700 Taylor Ave (43219-2527)
PHONE..................................614 986-2600
Rick Lueckel, *Prin*
EMP: 9 EST: 2007
SALES (est): 537.29K **Privately Held**
SIC: 7372 7699 Prepackaged software;
Cleaning services

(G-4863)
CUSTOM RETAIL GROUP LLC
Also Called: Crg Worldwide
6311 Busch Blvd (43229-1802)
PHONE..................................614 409-9720
Colin Leveque, *Managing Member*
EMP: 9 EST: 2013
SQ FT: 25,000
SALES (est): 820.2K **Privately Held**
Web: www.crgworldwide.com
SIC: 3993 Displays, paint process

(G-4864)
CUSTOM SIGN CENTER
400 N Wilson Rd (43204-1208)
PHONE..................................614 279-6035
EMP: 10 EST: 2018
SALES (est): 432.17K **Privately Held**
Web: www.customsigncenter.com
SIC: 3993 Signs and advertising specialties

(G-4865)
CUSTOM SIGN CENTER INC
3200 Valleyview Dr (43204-2080)
PHONE..................................614 279-6700
Tim W Sheehy, *Pr*
Judy Ramsburg, *
EMP: 50 EST: 1969
SQ FT: 40,000
SALES (est): 3.99MM **Privately Held**
Web: www.customsigncenter.com
SIC: 3993 Electric signs

(G-4866)
CUSTOMWORKS INC
330 Lenappe Dr (43214-3118)
PHONE..................................614 262-1002
Jon Fotis, *Pr*
EMP: 9 EST: 1946
SQ FT: 14,500
SALES (est): 161.09K **Privately Held**
Web: www.customworksinc.com
SIC: 2541 Table or counter tops, plastic
laminated

(G-4867)
DABAR INDUSTRIES LLC
7630 Copper Glen St (43235-1637)
PHONE..................................614 873-3949
Cliff Baseler, *Pr*
EMP: 15 EST: 2015
SALES (est): 965.92K **Privately Held**
SIC: 3443 Tanks, standard or custom
fabricated: metal plate

(G-4868)
DAILY FANTASY CIRCUIT INC
5 E Long St Ste 603 (43215-2931)
PHONE..................................614 989-8689
Justin Fox, *Prin*
EMP: 6 EST: 2016

SALES (est): 62.99K **Privately Held**
SIC: 2711 Newspapers, publishing and
printing

(G-4869)
DAILY REPORTER
580 S High St Ste 316 (43215-5659)
PHONE..................................614 224-4835
Ed Frederickson, *Pr*
Dan Shillingburg, *
EMP: 29 EST: 1896
SQ FT: 5,500
SALES (est): 1.04MM
SALES (corp-wide): 3.92MM **Privately
Held**
Web: www.thedailyreporteronline.com
SIC: 2711 Newspapers, publishing and
printing
PA: Calcomco, Inc.
5544 S Red Pine Cir
Kalamazoo MI 49009
313 885-9228

(G-4870)
DANITE HOLDINGS LTD
Also Called: Danite Sign Co
1640 Harmon Ave (43223-3321)
PHONE..................................614 444-3333
Tim Mccord, *Pr*
Shelley Mccord, *Sec*
Calvin Lutz, *Stockholder**
C William Klausman, *
EMP: 50 EST: 1954
SQ FT: 33,500
SALES (est): 9.83MM **Privately Held**
Web: www.danitesign.com
SIC: 3993 1799 Electric signs; Sign
installation and maintenance

(G-4871)
DAYTON ROGERS OF OHIO INC
2309 Mcgaw Rd (43207-4806)
PHONE..................................614 491-1477
EMP: 60 EST: 1973
SALES (est): 2.61MM
SALES (corp-wide): 43.79MM **Privately
Held**
Web: www.daytonrogers.com
SIC: 3469 Stamping metal for the trade
PA: Dayton Rogers Manufacturing Co.
8401 W 35 W Service Dr
Minneapolis MN 55449
763 717-6450

(G-4872)
**DAZPAK FLEXIBLE PACKAGING
CORP (PA)**
2901 E 4th Ave (43219-2896)
PHONE..................................614 252-2121
James Rooney, *CEO*
Mike Mc Coy, *CFO*
▲ EMP: 152 EST: 1964
SQ FT: 50,000
SALES (est): 3.02MM
SALES (corp-wide): 3.02MM **Privately
Held**
Web: www.dazpak.com
SIC: 2673 5113 Plastic bags: made from
purchased materials; Bags, paper and
disposable plastic

(G-4873)
DC REPROGRAPHICS CO
Also Called: AlphaGraphics
1254 Courtland Ave (43201-2829)
PHONE..................................614 297-1200
Daniel R Cannell, *Pr*
EMP: 15 EST: 2012
SALES (est): 1.19MM **Privately Held**
Web: www.alphagraphics.com

SIC: 2752 Commercial printing, lithographic

(G-4874)
DEE PRINTING INC
4999 Transamerica Dr (43228-9381)
P.O. Box 85 (43026-0085)
PHONE..................................614 777-8700
Dorothy J Murnane, *Pr*
EMP: 14 EST: 1974
SQ FT: 4,000
SALES (est): 2MM **Privately Held**
Web: www.deeprinting.com
SIC: 2759 7311 Letterpress printing;
Advertising agencies

(G-4875)
DEFABCO INC
3765 E Livingston Ave (43227-2258)
PHONE..................................614 231-2700
EMP: 60 EST: 1972
SALES (est): 9.72MM **Privately Held**
Web: www.defabco.com
SIC: 1761 3443 3535 3444 Sheet metal
work, nec; Pipe, standpipe, and culverts;
Conveyors and conveying equipment;
Sheet metalwork

(G-4876)
DELILLE OXYGEN COMPANY (PA)
772 Marion Rd (43207-2595)
P.O. Box 7809 (43207-0809)
PHONE..................................614 444-1177
Richard F Carlile, *Prin*
Joseph R Smith, *
Tom Smith, *
Jim Smith, *
EMP: 40 EST: 1964
SQ FT: 20,000
SALES (est): 25.83MM
SALES (corp-wide): 25.83MM **Privately
Held**
Web: www.delille.com
SIC: 2813 5085 Acetylene; Welding supplies

(G-4877)
DELPHIA CONSULTING LLC
1550 Old Henderson Rd (43220-3626)
PHONE..................................614 421-2000
Brian Delphia, *Pr*
Brian Delphia, *CEO*
Alexander Main, *
EMP: 40 EST: 1999
SALES (est): 8.63MM **Privately Held**
Web: www.delphiaconsulting.com
SIC: 8742 7372 Human resource consulting
services; Business oriented computer
software

(G-4878)
DEPUY SYNTHES INC
374 W Spring St (43215-2321)
PHONE..................................614 472-8008
EMP: 6
SALES (corp-wide): 88.82B **Publicly Held**
Web: www.jnjmedicaldevices.com
SIC: 3842 Surgical appliances and supplies
HQ: Depuy Synthes, Inc.
700 Orthopaedic Dr
Warsaw IN 46582

(G-4879)
DEWITT GROUP INC
Also Called: Capital Office Supply
777 Dearborn Park Ln Ste E (43085-5716)
PHONE..................................614 847-5919
Bill Dewitt, *Ch Bd*
Jory Dewitt, *Sec*
EMP: 10 EST: 1982
SQ FT: 9,000
SALES (est): 2.37MM **Privately Held**
Web: www.friendsoffice.com

SIC: 5112 2752 Office supplies, nec; Offset
printing

(G-4880)
DIAMOND INNOVATIONS INC (PA)
Also Called: Hyperion
6325 Huntley Rd (43229-1007)
P.O. Box 568 (43085-0568)
PHONE..................................614 438-2000
Ron Voigt, *CEO*
◆ EMP: 406 EST: 1955
SALES (est): 44.95MM
SALES (corp-wide): 44.95MM **Privately
Held**
Web: www.hyperionmt.com
SIC: 3291 Abrasive products

(G-4881)
DIRCKSEN AND ASSOCIATES INC
743 S Front St (43206-1905)
P.O. Box 13662 (43213-0662)
PHONE..................................614 238-0413
Daniel W Dircksen, *Pr*
EMP: 6 EST: 1983
SALES (est): 852.07K **Privately Held**
Web: www.dircksenassociates.com
SIC: 3728 5088 Military aircraft equipment
and armament; Transportation equipment
and supplies

(G-4882)
DISCOVER PUBLICATIONS
6425 Busch Blvd (43229-1862)
PHONE..................................877 872-3080
Leo Zupam, *Prin*
EMP: 9 EST: 2009
SALES (est): 466.8K **Privately Held**
Web: www.discoverpubs.com
SIC: 2741 Miscellaneous publishing

(G-4883)
DISPATCH PRINTING COMPANY (PA)
62 E Broad St (43215-3503)
PHONE..................................614 220-5833
Michael J Fiorile, *CEO*
Joseph Y Gallo, *
John F Wolfe, *Golf Chairman of the Board**
Charles D Simeral, *
Joseph J Gill, *
EMP: 600 EST: 1871
SQ FT: 200,000
SALES (est): 48.78MM
SALES (corp-wide): 48.78MM **Privately
Held**
Web: www.dispatch.com
SIC: 2711 Newspapers, publishing and
printing

(G-4884)
DISPATCH PRINTING COMPANY
Also Called: Columbus Dispatch
34 S 3rd St (43215-3081)
PHONE..................................614 461-5000
EMP: 13
SALES (corp-wide): 48.78MM **Privately
Held**
Web: www.dispatch.com
SIC: 2711 Newspapers, publishing and
printing
PA: The Dispatch Printing Company
62 E Broad St.
Columbus OH 43215
614 220-5833

(G-4885)
DISTINCTIVE SURFACES LLC
4600 Bridgeway Ave (43219-1893)
PHONE..................................614 431-0898
Jonathan Ruper, *Managing Member*
EMP: 18 EST: 2013
SALES (est): 4.94MM **Privately Held**

Web: www.distinctivekitchen.com
SIC: 2434 Wood kitchen cabinets

(G-4886)
DISTRICT BREWING COMPANY INC
Also Called: Columbus Brewing Company
2555 Harrison Rd (43204-3511)
PHONE..............................614 224-3626
Eric Bean, *Pr*
Susie Edwards, *
Ben Pridgeon, *
▲ EMP: 48 EST: 1988
SQ FT: 6,000
SALES (est): 5.7MM **Privately Held**
Web: www.columbusbrewing.com
SIC: 5813 2082 Bars and lounges; Beer
(alcoholic beverage)

(G-4887)
DLZ OHIO INC (HQ)
6121 Huntley Rd (43229-1003)
PHONE..............................614 888-0040
Vikram Raj Rajadhyaksha, *Ch*
A James Siebert, *
David Cutlip, *
Allan C Strange, *
P V Rajadhyaksha, *
EMP: 200 EST: 1950
SQ FT: 45,000
SALES (est): 9.37MM **Privately Held**
Web: www.dlz.com
SIC: 8711 1382 8712 8713 Consulting
engineer; Geophysical exploration, oil and
gas field; Architectural services; Surveying
services
PA: Dlz Corporation
6121 Huntley Rd
Columbus OH 43229

(G-4888)
DM PALLET SERVICE INC
2019 Rathmell Rd (43207-5012)
PHONE..............................614 491-0881
Dexter Mounts Ii, *Pr*
Dexter Mounts Senior, *Sec*
EMP: 8 EST: 1985
SQ FT: 800
SALES (est): 885.5K **Privately Held**
Web: www.dmpallet.com
SIC: 2448 Pallets, wood

(G-4889)
DNO INC
3650 E 5th Ave (43219-1805)
PHONE..............................614 231-3601
Anthony Dinovo, *Pr*
Carol Dinovo, *
EMP: 80 EST: 1989
SQ FT: 10,000
SALES (est): 11.2MM **Privately Held**
Web: www.dnoinc.com
SIC: 2099 5148 Salads, fresh or refrigerated;
Fruits, fresh

(G-4890)
DRIVELINE 1 INC
1369 Frank Rd (43223-3729)
P.O. Box 40 (43123-0040)
PHONE..............................614 279-7734
Bruce Hickman, *Pr*
EMP: 9 EST: 1993
SQ FT: 7,500
SALES (est): 1.3MM **Privately Held**
Web: www.driveline1.com
SIC: 3714 Motor vehicle parts and
accessories

(G-4891)
DURE FOODS US LLC
6967 Alum Creek Dr (43217-1244)
PHONE..............................614 409-9030

EMP: 15 EST: 2004
SQ FT: 50,000
SALES (est): 1.05MM
SALES (corp-wide): 13.48MM **Privately
Held**
Web: www.durefoods.com
SIC: 2099 Food preparations, nec
PA: Dure Foods Limited
120 Roy Blvd
Brantford ON N3R 7
519 753-5504

(G-4892)
DWR GRAPHICS INC
Also Called: Advance Digital
850 Science Blvd (43230-6609)
PHONE..............................614 863-6966
David W Ramsey, *CEO*
Brian Nordmoe, *
EMP: 25 EST: 1985
SQ FT: 10,000
SALES (est): 477.62K **Privately Held**
SIC: 2262 Screen printing: manmade fiber
and silk broadwoven fabrics

(G-4893)
E BEE PRINTING INC
70 S 4th St (43215-4315)
PHONE..............................614 224-0416
Debbi Bussman, *Prin*
EMP: 7 EST: 2009
SALES (est): 223.89K **Privately Held**
SIC: 2752 Offset printing

(G-4894)
E RETAILING ASSOCIATES LLC
Also Called: Customized Girl
2282 Westbrooke Dr (43228-9416)
PHONE..............................614 300-5785
Taj Schaffnit, *Managing Member*
Kurt J Schmalz, *
EMP: 64 EST: 2004
SALES (est): 3.77MM **Privately Held**
Web: www.eretailing.com
SIC: 8748 5961 2253 Business consulting,
nec; Electronic shopping; T-shirts and tops,
knit

(G-4895)
EARTHLEY WELLNESS
320 Outerbelt St Ste J (43213-1537)
PHONE..............................614 625-1064
Benjamin Tietje, *CEO*
EMP: 34 EST: 2016
SALES (est): 1.48MM **Privately Held**
Web: www.earthley.com
SIC: 2833 Medicinals and botanicals

(G-4896)
ECLIPSE 3D/PI LLC
825 Taylor Rd (43230-6235)
PHONE..............................614 626-8536
Jeff Burt, *CEO*
Sandra Burt, *
Scott Wolfe, *
EMP: 45 EST: 1994
SALES (est): 2.38MM **Privately Held**
Web: www.eclipsecreative.com
SIC: 7335 2621 Photographic studio,
commercial; Printing paper

(G-4897)
EDEN CRYOGENICS LLC
7630 Copper Glen St (43235-1637)
PHONE..............................614 873-3949
Steve L Hensley, *Pr*
▲ EMP: 45 EST: 2006
SALES (est): 2.44MM **Privately Held**
Web: www.edencryogenics.com
SIC: 3559 Cryogenic machinery, industrial

(G-4898)
EDGE EXPONENTIAL LLC
1140 Gahanna Pkwy (43230-6615)
PHONE..............................614 226-4421
Jim Droty, *Pr*
Craig Ryan Turner, *Dir*
EMP: 10 EST: 2020
SALES (est): 1.24MM **Privately Held**
Web: www.edgeinnovationhub.com
SIC: 3556 Food products machinery

(G-4899)
EICKHOLT GLASS INC
401 W Town St Fl 2 (43215-4034)
P.O. Box 21142 (43221)
PHONE..............................614 638-4903
Robert Eickholt, *Pr*
EMP: 15 EST: 1980
SQ FT: 12,000
SALES (est): 1.13MM **Privately Held**
Web: www.eickholtglassstudio.com
SIC: 3229 Pressed and blown glass, nec

(G-4900)
ELMERS PRODUCTS INC
180 E Broad St Fl 4 (43215-3763)
PHONE..............................614 225-4000
Michael Endres, *Brnch Mgr*
EMP: 130
SALES (corp-wide): 7.58B **Publicly Held**
Web: www.elmers.com
SIC: 2891 Adhesives and sealants
HQ: Elmer's Products, Inc.
6655 Pachtree Dunwoody Rd
Atlanta GA 30328

(G-4901)
**ENDLESS HOME IMPROVEMENTS
LLC**
3897 Fergus Rd (43207-4253)
PHONE..............................614 599-1799
EMP: 6
SALES (est): 408.84K **Privately Held**
SIC: 1389 7389 Construction, repair, and
dismantling services; Business Activities at
Non-Commercial Site

(G-4902)
ENGINEERED MARBLE INC
4064 Fisher Rd (43228-1020)
PHONE..............................614 308-0041
Jeff Schmidt, *Pr*
Jeff Klein, *VP*
EMP: 6 EST: 1994
SQ FT: 6,100
SALES (est): 237.55K **Privately Held**
Web: www.engineeredmarbleinc.com
SIC: 3281 Marble, building: cut and shaped

(G-4903)
ENGINEERED PROFILES LLC
2141 Fairwood Ave (43207-1753)
PHONE..............................614 754-3700
Mike Davis, *Pr*
Brian Davis, *
Adam Wachter, *
EMP: 328 EST: 1999
SQ FT: 300,000
SALES (est): 49.14MM **Privately Held**
Web: www.engineeredprofiles.com
SIC: 3089 Injection molding of plastics
HQ: The Crane Group Companies Limited
330 W Spring St Ste 200
Columbus OH 43215
614 754-3000

(G-4904)
ENTROCHEM INC
1245 Kinnear Rd (43212-1155)
PHONE..............................614 946-7602

Jim Mcguire, *Pr*
EMP: 10 EST: 1999
SALES (est): 970.79K **Privately Held**
Web: www.entrotech.com
SIC: 2891 Adhesives

(G-4905)
ENTROTECH INC
1245 Kinnear Rd (43212-1155)
PHONE..............................614 946-7602
James E Mcguire Junior, *Pr*
Dave Bragg, *VP*
Jim Koch, *VP*
Elizabeth Maag, *Prin*
▲ EMP: 18 EST: 1999
SQ FT: 6,000
SALES (est): 9.46MM **Privately Held**
Web: www.entrotech.com
SIC: 3081 Plastics film and sheet

(G-4906)
EP FERRIS & ASSOCIATES INC
2130 Quarry Trails Dr # 2 (43228-8981)
PHONE..............................614 299-2999
Edward P Ferris, *Ch Bd*
Matthew Ferris, *Dir*
EMP: 40 EST: 1987
SALES (est): 4.16MM **Privately Held**
Web: www.epferris.com
SIC: 8742 8711 1389 Management
consulting services; Construction and civil
engineering; Testing, measuring, surveying,
and analysis services

(G-4907)
ERNST ENTERPRISES INC
4252 Truro Station Service Rd
(43232-4171)
PHONE..............................614 308-0063
EMP: 13
SALES (corp-wide): 240.08MM **Privately
Held**
Web: www.ernstconcrete.com
SIC: 3273 Ready-mixed concrete
PA: Ernst Enterprises, Inc.
993 Falls Creek Dr
Vandalia OH 45377
937 233-5555

(G-4908)
ERNST ENTERPRISES INC
569 N Wilson Rd (43204-1459)
PHONE..............................614 308-0063
EMP: 13
SALES (corp-wide): 240.08MM **Privately
Held**
Web: www.ernstconcrete.com
SIC: 3273 Ready-mixed concrete
PA: Ernst Enterprises, Inc.
993 Falls Creek Dr
Vandalia OH 45377
937 233-5555

(G-4909)
ERNST ENTERPRISES INC
711 Stimmel Rd (43223-2905)
PHONE..............................614 443-9456
John C Ernst Junior, *Brnch Mgr*
EMP: 32
SALES (corp-wide): 240.08MM **Privately
Held**
Web: www.ernstconcrete.com
SIC: 5211 3273 Cement; Ready-mixed
concrete
PA: Ernst Enterprises, Inc.
993 Falls Creek Dr
Vandalia OH 45377
937 233-5555

(G-4910)
ESTR PUBLICATIONS
7464 Mapleleaf Ct (43235-4216)
PHONE......................................614 940-9996
Kevin Anderson, *Prin*
EMP: 6 **EST:** 2013
SALES (est): 96.63K **Privately Held**
Web: www.estr.net
SIC: 2741 Miscellaneous publishing

(G-4911)
ETHERIUM LIGHTING LLC
6969 Alum Creek Dr Ste 4 (43217-1244)
PHONE......................................614 388-9893
Steve Smitson, *CEO*
EMP: 7 **EST:** 2017
SALES (est): 2.5MM **Privately Held**
Web: www.etheriumled.com
SIC: 3646 Commercial lighting fixtures

(G-4912)
EVANS ADHESIVE CORPORATION
(HQ)
925 Old Henderson Rd (43220-3779)
PHONE......................................614 451-2665
C Russell Thompson, *Pr*
EMP: 27 **EST:** 1900
SALES (est): 24MM
SALES (corp-wide): 97.52MM **Privately
Held**
Web: www.evansadhesive.com
SIC: 2891 5085 Adhesives; Abrasives and
adhesives
PA: Meridian Adhesives Group Llc
15720 Brxham Hl Ave Ste 5
Charlotte NC

(G-4913)
EVANS ADHESIVE CORPORATION
LTD
925 Old Henderson Rd (43220-3779)
PHONE......................................614 451-2665
◆ **EMP:** 39
SIC: 2891 2821 Adhesives; Plastics
materials and resins

(G-4914)
EVANS CREATIVE GROUP LLC
Also Called: Columbus Underground
11 E Gay St (43215-3125)
PHONE......................................614 657-9439
EMP: 9 **EST:** 2008
SQ FT: 2,600
SALES (est): 494.2K **Privately Held**
Web: www.columbusunderground.com
SIC: 2741 Internet publishing and
broadcasting

(G-4915)
EXPRESS PHARMACY & DME LLC
2750 S Hamilton Rd Ste 19 (43232-5188)
PHONE......................................210 981-9690
Daniel Winston Amoh Junior, *Managing
Member*
EMP: 6 **EST:** 2019
SALES (est): 210.37K **Privately Held**
Web:
www.expresspharmacyanddme.com
SIC: 5912 3069 Drug stores and proprietary
stores; Medical and laboratory rubber
sundries and related products

(G-4916)
EXTERIOR PORTFOLIO LLC
1441 Universal Rd (43207-1730)
P.O. Box 1058 (43216-1058)
PHONE......................................614 754-3400
EMP: 250
SIC: 3089 Siding, plastics

(G-4917)
EYE SURGERY CENTER OHIO INC
(PA)
Also Called: Arena Eye Surgeons
262 Neil Ave Ste 320 (43215-4624)
PHONE......................................614 228-3937
TOLL FREE: 800
Peter Utrata, *Prin*
EMP: 25 **EST:** 1984
SQ FT: 2,200
SALES (est): 5.53MM
SALES (corp-wide): 5.53MM **Privately
Held**
Web: www.arenaeyesurgeons.com
SIC: 3841 8011 Eye examining instruments
and apparatus; Offices and clinics of
medical doctors

(G-4918)
FABX LLC
1819 Walcutt Rd Ste 100 (43228-9149)
PHONE......................................614 565-5835
Todd Wurstner, *Managing Member*
EMP: 10 **EST:** 2020
SALES (est): 2.43MM **Privately Held**
SIC: 3441 Building components, structural
steel

(G-4919)
FACILITIES MANAGEMENT EX LLC
800 Yard St Ste 115 (43212-3866)
PHONE......................................614 519-2186
Jeffery Wilkins, *CEO*
Brian Gregory, *
Jeffery Wilkins Ceojeffery Wilkins, *CEO*
EMP: 56 **EST:** 2014
SQ FT: 3,200
SALES (est): 4.31MM **Privately Held**
Web: www.gofmx.com
SIC: 7372 Application computer software

(G-4920)
FBG BOTTLING GROUP LLC
Also Called: Frostop
818 S Yearling Rd (43213-3056)
P.O. Box 9841 (43209-0841)
PHONE......................................614 580-7063
Mike Gutter, *Pr*
EMP: 7 **EST:** 2012
SALES (est): 727.06K **Privately Held**
Web: www.frostop.com
SIC: 2086 Bottled and canned soft drinks

(G-4921)
FCBDD
2879 Johnstown Rd (43219-1719)
PHONE......................................614 475-6440
EMP: 17 **EST:** 2014
SALES (est): 1.69MM **Privately Held**
Web: www.fcbdd.org
SIC: 3999

(G-4922)
FCX PERFORMANCE INC (HQ)
Also Called: Jh Instruments
3000 E 14th Ave (43219-2355)
PHONE......................................614 253-1996
Thomas Cox, *Ch*
Russell S Frazee, *
Chris Hill, *
Theron Neese, *
Brian Miller, *
▲ **EMP:** 40 **EST:** 1999
SQ FT: 44,000
SALES (est): 544.13MM
SALES (corp-wide): 4.48B **Publicly Held**
Web: www.fcxperformance.com
SIC: 5084 5085 3494 Instruments and
control equipment; Industrial supplies;
Valves and pipe fittings, nec
PA: Applied Industrial Technologies, Inc.

1 Applied Plz
Cleveland OH 44115
216 426-4000

(G-4923)
FERGUSON FIRE FABRICATION INC
1640 Clara St (43211-2628)
PHONE......................................614 299-2070
Dan Tober, *Brnch Mgr*
EMP: 47
SALES (est): 29.73B **Privately Held**
Web: www.ferguson.com
SIC: 5074 3999 Plumbing fittings and
supplies; Atomizers, toiletry
HQ: Ferguson Fire & Fabrication, Inc.
2750 S Towne Ave
Pomona CA 91766
909 517-3085

(G-4924)
FINE LINE GRAPHICS CORP
Also Called: Fine Line Graphics
2364 Featherwood Dr (43228-8236)
P.O. Box 163370 (43216-3370)
PHONE......................................614 486-0276
James Basch, *Pr*
Mark Carro, *
Gregory Davis, *
▲ **EMP:** 170 **EST:** 1979
SALES (est): 4.99MM **Privately Held**
Web: www.finelinegraphics.com
SIC: 2752 7331 Offset printing; Mailing
service

(G-4925)
FIREHOUSE FOODS
917 E Whittier St (43206-1584)
PHONE......................................614 592-8115
EMP: 6
SALES (est): 425.67K **Privately Held**
SIC: 2099 Food preparations, nec

(G-4926)
FISHEL COMPANY
Johnson Brothers Construction
1600 Walcutt Rd (43228-9394)
PHONE......................................614 850-4400
Ed Evans, *Mgr*
EMP: 167
SALES (corp-wide): 758.15MM **Privately
Held**
Web: www.teamfishel.com
SIC: 1623 8711 1731 3612 Telephone and
communication line construction;
Engineering services; Electrical work;
Transformers, except electric
PA: The Fishel Company
1366 Dublin Rd
Columbus OH 43215
614 274-8100

(G-4927)
FLAG LADY INC
Also Called: Flag Lady's Flag Store, The
4567 N High St (43214-2042)
PHONE......................................614 263-1776
Mary Leavitt, *Pr*
Lori Leavitt Watson, *VP*
EMP: 9 **EST:** 1979
SQ FT: 5,000
SALES (est): 503.55K **Privately Held**
Web: www.flagladyusa.com
SIC: 5999 2399 Flags; Flags, fabric

(G-4928)
FLEXSYS AMERICA LP
1658 Williams Rd (43207-5109)
PHONE......................................618 482-6371
EMP: 15
SALES (corp-wide): 142.37MM **Privately
Held**

SIC: 3069 Reclaimed rubber and specialty
rubber compounds
HQ: Flexsys America L.P.
260 Springside Dr
Akron OH 44333

(G-4929)
FLIGHTSAFETY INTERNATIONAL
INC (HQ)
3100 Easton Square Pl Ste 100
(43219-6290)
PHONE......................................614 324-3500
Barbara Telek, *Pr*
Patricia Arundell Lampe, *
Brian Moore, *
Tina Rourk, *CIO**
Stephen Phillips, *OK Vice President**
▲ **EMP:** 110 **EST:** 1951
SQ FT: 36,000
SALES (est): 403.58MM
SALES (corp-wide): 424.23B **Publicly
Held**
Web: www.flightsafety.com
SIC: 8249 3699 Aviation school; Flight
simulators (training aids), electronic
PA: Berkshire Hathaway Inc.
3555 Farnam St Ste 1440
Omaha NE 68131
402 346-1400

(G-4930)
FLOYD BELL INC (PA)
720 Dearborn Park Ln (43085-5703)
PHONE......................................614 294-4000
▲ **EMP:** 69 **EST:** 1971
SALES (est): 7.39MM
SALES (corp-wide): 7.39MM **Privately
Held**
Web: www.floydbell.com
SIC: 3669 5065 3661 3651 Emergency
alarms; Telephone equipment; Telephone
and telegraph apparatus; Household audio
and video equipment

(G-4931)
FORIS EXTRAORDINARY MEATS
LLC
1145 Chesapeake Ave Ste E (43212-2286)
PHONE......................................614 670-5726
James Forbes, *Managing Member*
EMP: 10 **EST:** 2014
SALES (est): 600K **Privately Held**
Web: www.forismeats.com
SIC: 5421 2011 5147 2013 Meat markets,
including freezer provisioners; Meat
packing plants; Meats and meat products;
Bacon, side and sliced: from purchased
meat

(G-4932)
FORMWARE INC
3441 Winchester Pike (43232-5566)
PHONE......................................614 231-9387
Christopher R Kessler, *Pr*
Margaret Kessler, *Sec*
EMP: 12 **EST:** 1983
SALES (est): 979.4K **Privately Held**
Web: www.weaverautorepair.com
SIC: 2434 Wood kitchen cabinets

(G-4933)
FORTERRA PIPE & PRECAST LLC
1500 Haul Rd (43207-1888)
PHONE......................................614 445-3830
Wayne Greene, *Pr*
EMP: 11 **EST:** 2016
SALES (est): 3.38MM **Privately Held**
Web: www.rinkerpipe.com
SIC: 3272 Concrete products, nec

▲ = Import ▼ = Export
◆ = Import/Export

(G-4934)
FORTIN WELDING & MFG INC
Also Called: Fortin Ironworks
944 W 5th Ave (43212-2657)
PHONE..............................614 291-4342
Joe Vangundy, *Pr*
Dan Fortin, *
Fred Fortin, *
John Fortin, *
Robert Fortin, *
EMP: 39 **EST:** 1946
SQ FT: 60,000
SALES (est): 4.12MM **Privately Held**
Web: www.fortinironworks.com
SIC: 3449 3446 Miscellaneous metalwork;
Ornamental metalwork

(G-4935)
FORTIS PARENT INC (HQ) ✪
Also Called: Alta Performance Materials
955 Yard St (43212-3915)
PHONE..............................614 790-9299
Andrew Miller, *CEO*
EMP: 60 **EST:** 2024
SALES (est): 110.36MM
SALES (corp-wide): 4.41B **Privately Held**
SIC: 2821 Plastics materials and resins
PA: Kps Capital Partners, Lp
1 Vanderbilt Ave Fl 52
New York NY 10017
212 338-5100

(G-4936)
FORTNER UPHOLSTERING INC
2050 S High St (43207-2425)
PHONE..............................614 475-8282
David F Fortner Junior, *Pr*
Diana Orum, *Sec*
Glen Mcallister, *Pr*
David F Fortner Junior, *Prin*
Wanda L Fortner, *Prin*
▲ **EMP:** 16 **EST:** 1967
SQ FT: 7,000
SALES (est): 1.98MM **Privately Held**
Web: www.fortnerupholstering.com
SIC: 5712 2512 7641 3429 Furniture stores;
Upholstered household furniture;
Reupholstery and furniture repair;
Furniture, builders' and other household
hardware

(G-4937)
FRANKLIN ART GLASS STUDIOS
222 E Sycamore St (43206-2198)
PHONE..............................614 221-2972
Gary L Helf, *Ch Bd*
Andrea Reid, *
▲ **EMP:** 20 **EST:** 1900
SQ FT: 55,000
SALES (est): 3.91MM **Privately Held**
Web: www.franklinartglass.com
SIC: 3231 5231 5945 Stained glass: made
from purchased glass; Glass, leaded or
stained; Hobby, toy, and game shops

(G-4938)
FRANKLIN INTERNATIONAL INC (PA)
Also Called: Constrction Adhsves Slants Div
2020 Bruck St (43207-2382)
PHONE..............................614 443-0241
◆ **EMP:** 378 **EST:** 1935
SALES (est): 92.31MM
SALES (corp-wide): 92.31MM **Privately
Held**
Web: www.franklininternational.com
SIC: 2891 2821 Adhesives; Plastics
materials and resins

(G-4939)
FRED D PFENING COMPANY (PA)
1075 W 5th Ave (43212-2691)
PHONE..............................614 294-5361
Fred D Pfening Junior, *CEO*
Fred D Pfening Iii, *Pr*
Ed Brackman, *VP*
Timothy D Pfening, *Sec*
William F Kearns, *VP*
EMP: 41 **EST:** 1919
SQ FT: 55,000
SALES (est): 11.58MM
SALES (corp-wide): 11.58MM **Privately
Held**
Web: pfening.openfos.com
SIC: 3535 3585 3556 Pneumatic tube
conveyor systems; Air conditioning units,
complete: domestic or industrial; Mixers,
commercial, food

(G-4940)
FRED D PFENING COMPANY
Also Called: Plant 2
1075 W 5th Ave (43212-2691)
PHONE..............................614 294-5361
John Legg, *Brnch Mgr*
EMP: 7
SALES (corp-wide): 11.58MM **Privately
Held**
Web: www.pfening.com
SIC: 3556 Bakery machinery
PA: The Fred D Pfening Company
1075 W 5th Ave
Columbus OH 43212
614 294-5361

(G-4941)
FUTURE POLYTECH INC (PA)
2215 Citygate Dr Ste D (43219-3589)
PHONE..............................614 942-1209
Tony Durieux, *Pr*
EMP: 22 **EST:** 2011
SALES (est): 1.31MM
SALES (corp-wide): 1.31MM **Privately
Held**
Web: www.futurepolytech.com
SIC: 2671 Plastic film, coated or laminated
for packaging

(G-4942)
G & J PEPSI-COLA BOTTLERS INC
Also Called: Pepsico
870 N 22nd St (43219-2427)
PHONE..............................866 647-2734
EMP: 31
SALES (corp-wide): 404.54MM **Privately
Held**
Web: www.gjpepsi.com
SIC: 2086 Carbonated soft drinks, bottled
and canned
PA: G & J Pepsi-Cola Bottlers Inc
9435 Wtrstone Blvd Ste 39
Cincinnati OH 45249
513 785-6060

(G-4943)
G & J PEPSI-COLA BOTTLERS INC
Also Called: Pepsico
1241 Gibbard Ave (43219-2438)
PHONE..............................614 253-8771
Thomas Pendrey, *Brnch Mgr*
EMP: 550
SQ FT: 200,000
SALES (corp-wide): 404.54MM **Privately
Held**
Web: www.gjpepsi.com
SIC: 2086 Carbonated soft drinks, bottled
and canned
PA: G & J Pepsi-Cola Bottlers Inc
9435 Wtrstone Blvd Ste 39
Cincinnati OH 45249

513 785-6060

(G-4944)
GALACTIC PRINTING LLC
3923 E Main St (43213-2948)
EMP: 8 **EST:** 2006
SQ FT: 10,000
SALES (est): 116.42K **Privately Held**
SIC: 2759 Commercial printing, nec

(G-4945)
GARDNER INC (PA)
3641 Interchange Rd (43204-1499)
PHONE..............................614 456-4000
John F Finn, *Ch*
James P Finn, *
Michael L Finn, *
John T Finn, *
◆ **EMP:** 222 **EST:** 1975
SQ FT: 204,000
SALES (est): 49.05MM
SALES (corp-wide): 49.05MM **Privately
Held**
Web: www.gardnerinc.com
SIC: 3524 Lawn and garden equipment

(G-4946)
GAWA TRADERS LLC
250 West St (43215-7513)
PHONE..............................614 697-1440
EMP: 30 **EST:** 2020
SALES (est): 821.61K **Privately Held**
Web: www.gawatraders.com
SIC: 2051 Bakery: wholesale or wholesale/
retail combined

(G-4947)
GEN DIGITAL INC
Also Called: Symantec
2720 Airport Dr Ste 100 (43219-2219)
PHONE..............................614 418-1700
Michael Sederer, *Brnch Mgr*
EMP: 6
SALES (corp-wide): 3.81B **Publicly Held**
Web: www.nortonlifelock.com
SIC: 3674 Semiconductors and related
devices
PA: Gen Digital Inc.
60 E Rio Slado Pkwy Ste 1
Tempe AZ 85281
650 527-8000

(G-4948)
GENERAL THEMING CONTRS LLC
Also Called: GTC Artist With Machines
3750 Courtright Ct (43227-2253)
P.O. Box 27173 (43227-0173)
PHONE..............................614 252-6342
Richard D Rogovin, *Prin*
Kim Schanzenbach, *
Rich Witherspoon, *
▲ **EMP:** 105 **EST:** 1999
SQ FT: 60,000
SALES (est): 1.71MM **Privately Held**
Web: www.artistswithmachines.com
SIC: 7389 7336 2759 2396 Sign painting
and lettering shop; Commercial art and
graphic design; Commercial printing, nec;
Automotive and apparel trimmings

(G-4949)
GENERALS BOOKS
Also Called: The General's Books
522 Norton Rd (43228-2617)
P.O. Box 28685 (43228-0685)
PHONE..............................614 870-1861
David Roth, *Pr*
Robin Patricia Roth, *Pr*
EMP: 8 **EST:** 1983
SQ FT: 1,980
SALES (est): 418.06K **Privately Held**

Web: www.bluegraymagazine.com
SIC: 2721 Magazines: publishing only, not
printed on site

(G-4950)
GENPAK LLC
845 Kaderly Dr (43228-1033)
PHONE..............................614 276-5156
Scott Wilson, *Mgr*
EMP: 50
Web: www.genpak.com
SIC: 3089 Plastics containers, except foam
HQ: Genpak Llc
10601 Westlake Dr
Charlotte NC 28273
800 626-6695

(G-4951)
GEORGIA-PACIFIC LLC
Also Called: Georgia-Pacific
1975 Watkins Rd (43207-3443)
PHONE..............................614 491-9100
Kurt Miller, *Mgr*
EMP: 40
SALES (corp-wide): 64.44B **Privately Held**
Web: www.gp.com
SIC: 2621 Paper mills
HQ: Georgia-Pacific Llc
133 Peachtree St Ne
Atlanta GA 30303
404 652-4000

(G-4952)
**GFL ENVIRONMENTAL SVCS USA
INC**
Also Called: Heartland Petroleum
4001 E 5th Ave (43219-1812)
PHONE..............................614 441-4001
Sayed Atiyeah, *Manager*
EMP: 45
SALES (corp-wide): 5.6B **Privately Held**
SIC: 2911 5172 Mineral oils, natural; Fuel oil
HQ: Gfl Environmental Services Usa, Inc.
18927 Hckry Creek Dr Ste
Mokena IL 60448
866 579-6900

(G-4953)
GFS CHEMICALS INC
800 Kaderly Dr (43228-1034)
PHONE..............................614 351-5347
John Pringle, *Mgr*
EMP: 27
SALES (corp-wide): 25.94MM **Privately
Held**
Web: www.gfschemicals.com
SIC: 2819 Industrial inorganic chemicals, nec
PA: Gfs Chemicals, Inc.
155 Hidden Ravines Dr
Powell OH 43065
740 881-5501

(G-4954)
GFS CHEMICALS INC
851 Mckinley Ave (43222-1148)
P.O. Box 245 (43065-0245)
PHONE..............................614 224-5345
Robert Pierro, *Brnch Mgr*
EMP: 60
SALES (corp-wide): 25.94MM **Privately
Held**
Web: www.gfschemicals.com
SIC: 2819 2899 2869 Chemicals, reagent
grade: refined from technical grade;
Chemical preparations, nec; Industrial
organic chemicals, nec
PA: Gfs Chemicals, Inc.
155 Hidden Ravines Dr
Powell OH 43065
740 881-5501

(G-4955)
GLAXOSMITHKLINE LLC
741 Chaffin Rdg (43214-2905)
PHONE..............................937 623-2680
EMP: 6
SALES (corp-wide): 39.77B Privately Held
Web: us.gsk.com
SIC: 2834 Pharmaceutical preparations
HQ: Glaxosmithkline Llc
　　2929 Walnut St Ste 1700
　　Philadelphia PA 19112
　　888 825-5249

(G-4956)
GLAXOSMITHKLINE LLC
359 Garden Rd (43214-2133)
PHONE..............................614 570-5970
EMP: 6
SALES (corp-wide): 39.77B Privately Held
Web: us.gsk.com
SIC: 2834 Pharmaceutical preparations
HQ: Glaxosmithkline Llc
　　2929 Walnut St Ste 1700
　　Philadelphia PA 19112
　　888 825-5249

(G-4957)
GLISTER INC
Also Called: Kingswood Company, The
830 Harmon Ave (43223-2410)
PHONE..............................614 252-6400
Kristie Nicolosi, *Pr*
EMP: 49 EST: 2005
SALES (est): 4.9MM Privately Held
Web: www.thekingswoodcompany.com
SIC: 2842 Polishes and sanitation goods

(G-4958)
GLOBAL RETAIL PARTNERS LLC
Also Called: Mid-America Store Fixtures
2195 Broehm Rd (43207-5206)
PHONE..............................614 409-9850
Richleigh Lemon, *
EMP: 32 EST: 2011
SALES (est): 5.52MM Privately Held
Web: www.midasf.com
SIC: 6153 2541 Factoring services; Wood
　　partitions and fixtures

(G-4959)
GLOBAL TRUCKING LLC
3723 Ellerdale Dr (43230-4086)
PHONE..............................614 598-6264
Ayan Hassan Abdinizak, *Admn*
Ayan Abdirizak, *Managing Member*
EMP: 10 EST: 2016
SALES (est): 1.47MM Privately Held
SIC: 3537 Trucks, tractors, loaders, carriers,
　　and similar equipment

(G-4960)
**GOLDEN ANGLE ARCHTCTRAL
GROUP**
Also Called: General Contractor
4207 E Broad St Ste C (43213-1200)
PHONE..............................614 531-7932
Jermaine Wilson, *CEO*
EMP: 8 EST: 2014
SALES (est): 250.76K Privately Held
SIC: 1761 8712 1751 1521 Roofing, siding,
　　and sheetmetal work; Architectural services
　　; Window and door installation and erection;
　　Patio and deck construction and repair

(G-4961)
GOLDEN DYNAMIC INC
676 Brook Holw Ste 104 (43230-6276)
PHONE..............................614 575-1222
Judy Sheu, *Pr*
▲ EMP: 7 EST: 1993

SALES (est): 841.56K Privately Held
Web: www.goldendynamic.com
SIC: 3291 Abrasive grains

(G-4962)
GONGWER NEWS SERVICE INC (PA)
Also Called: Ohio Report
175 S 3rd St (43215-5188)
PHONE..............................614 221-1992
Alan A Miller, *Pr*
Scott Miller, *Asst VP*
EMP: 11 EST: 1906
SALES (est): 1.6MM
SALES (corp-wide): 1.6MM Privately Held
Web: www.gongwer-oh.com
SIC: 2721 8111 Magazines: publishing only,
　　not printed on site; Legal services

(G-4963)
GRAFFITI FOODS LIMITED
333 Outerbelt St (43213-1529)
PHONE..............................614 759-1921
EMP: 13 EST: 2004
SQ FT: 7,600
SALES (est): 3.28MM
SALES (corp-wide): 48.97MM Privately
Held
Web: www.graffitifoods.com
SIC: 2099 Food preparations, nec
PA: New Horizons Baking Company, Llc
　　211 Woodlawn Ave
　　Norwalk OH 44857
　　419 668-8226

(G-4964)
GRAHAM ELECTRIC
2855 Banwick Rd (43232-3821)
PHONE..............................614 231-8500
EMP: 9 EST: 2015
SALES (est): 2.15MM Privately Held
Web: www.graham-electric.com
SIC: 3699 1731 Electrical equipment and
　　supplies, nec; Electrical work

(G-4965)
GRAMKE ENTERPRISES LTD
3021 E 4th Ave Ste B (43219-2888)
PHONE..............................614 252-8711
▲ EMP: 7 EST: 2001
SALES (est): 514.26K Privately Held
SIC: 3479 Painting, coating, and hot dipping

(G-4966)
GREEN ROOM BREWING LLC
Also Called: Seventh Son Brewing
1101 N 4th St (43201-3683)
PHONE..............................614 421-2337
EMP: 7 EST: 2010
SALES (est): 629.55K Privately Held
SIC: 5813 2082 Bars and lounges; Near beer

(G-4967)
HAKE HEAD LLC
Also Called: Maramor Chocolates
1855 E 17th Ave (43219-1006)
PHONE..............................614 291-2244
Michael Ryan, *Managing Member*
▲ EMP: 7 EST: 2002
SQ FT: 30,000
SALES (est): 455.77K Privately Held
Web: www.maramor.com
SIC: 2064 Candy and other confectionery
　　products

(G-4968)
HAMAN ENTERPRISES INC
Also Called: Haman Midwest
75 W Southington Ave (43085-3852)
PHONE..............................614 888-7574
Tod Haman, *Pr*

▲ EMP: 19 EST: 1984
SALES (est): 2.33MM Privately Held
Web: www.hamanmidwest.com
SIC: 2752 2759 Offset printing; Calendars:
　　printing, nsk

(G-4969)
HAMILTON TANKS LLC
2200 Refugee Rd (43207-2898)
PHONE..............................614 445-8446
TOLL FREE: 800
EMP: 17 EST: 1915
SQ FT: 30,000
SALES (est): 7.58MM
SALES (corp-wide): 30.29MM Privately
Held
Web: www.hamiltontanks.com
SIC: 3443 Tanks, lined: metal plate
PA: Meeker Equipment Co., Inc.
　　4381 Front Mountain Rd
　　Belleville PA 17004
　　717 667-6000

(G-4970)
**HARPER ENGRAVING & PRINTING
CO (PA)**
2626 Fisher Rd (43204-3561)
P.O. Box 426 (43216-0426)
PHONE..............................614 276-0700
Donald Mueller, *Pr*
EMP: 73 EST: 1891
SQ FT: 40,000
SALES (est): 4.21MM
SALES (corp-wide): 4.21MM Privately
Held
Web: www.harperengraving.com
SIC: 2759 2752 Commercial printing, nec;
　　Offset printing

(G-4971)
HARRIS PAPER CRAFTS INC
266 E 5th Ave (43201-2818)
PHONE..............................614 299-2141
Richard Potts, *Pr*
EMP: 10 EST: 1983
SALES (est): 486.62K Privately Held
Web: www.harrispapercrafts.com
SIC: 2679 2796 2789 2675 Paper products,
　　converted, nec; Platemaking services;
　　Bookbinding and related work; Die-cut
　　paper and board

(G-4972)
HARROP INDUSTRIES INC
3470 E 5th Ave (43219-1797)
PHONE..............................614 231-3621
◆ EMP: 49 EST: 1919
SALES (est): 11MM Privately Held
Web: www.harropusa.com
SIC: 3567 Ceramic kilns and furnaces

(G-4973)
HAZELBAKER INDUSTRIES LTD
Also Called: Wellnitz
1661 Old Henderson Rd (43220-3617)
EMP: 7 EST: 1994
SQ FT: 2,500
SALES (est): 1.53MM Privately Held
Web: www.wellnitz.com
SIC: 3271 5211 3272 Blocks, concrete or
　　cinder: standard; Masonry materials and
　　supplies; Concrete products, nec

(G-4974)
HEARTLAND GROUP HOLDINGS LLC
4001 E 5th Ave (43219-1812)
PHONE..............................614 441-4001
EMP: 90
SIC: 3559 Refinery, chemical processing,
　　and similar machinery

(G-4975)
HELENA AGRI-ENTERPRISES LLC
800 Distribution Dr (43228-1004)
PHONE..............................614 275-4200
Helena Cwu, *Brnch Mgr*
EMP: 9
Web: www.helenaagri.com
SIC: 5191 2819 Chemicals, agricultural;
　　Chemicals, high purity: refined from
　　technical grade
HQ: Helena Agri-Enterprises, Llc
　　225 Schlling Blvd Ste 300
　　Collierville TN 38017
　　901 761-0050

(G-4976)
HEXION INC (PA)
Also Called: Hexion
180 E Broad St (43215-3707)
P.O. Box 1310 (43216)
PHONE..............................888 443-9466
Michael Lefenfeld, *Pr*
Mark Bidstrup, *Ex VP*
Douglas A Johns, *Ex VP*
Matthew A Sokol, *Ex VP*
EMP: 241 EST: 1899
SALES (est): 1.26B
SALES (corp-wide): 1.26B Privately Held
Web: www.hexion.com
SIC: 8711 2821 5169 4911 Chemical
　　engineering; Epoxy resins; Chemicals,
　　industrial and heavy

(G-4977)
HEXION LLC (HQ)
180 E Broad St Fl 26 (43215-3707)
PHONE..............................614 225-4000
William H Carter, *
George Knight, *
Mary N Jorgensen, *
◆ EMP: 100 EST: 2004
SQ FT: 200,000
SALES (est): 43.78MM Privately Held
Web: www.hexion.com
SIC: 2821 2899 Thermosetting materials;
　　Chemical preparations, nec
PA: Hexion Topco, Llc
　　180 E Broad St
　　Columbus OH 43215

(G-4978)
HEXION TOPCO LLC (PA)
180 E Broad St (43215-3707)
PHONE..............................614 225-4000
Craig A Rogerson, *Ch Bd*
Dale N Plante, *Pr*
George F Knight, *Ex VP*
Judith A Sonnett, *Ex VP*
▼ EMP: 68 EST: 2010
SALES (est): 439.43MM Privately Held
Web: www.hexion.com
SIC: 2821 2869 6719 Thermosetting
　　materials; Silicones; Investment holding
　　companies, except banks

(G-4979)
HEXION US FINANCE CORP
180 E Broad St (43215-3707)
PHONE..............................614 225-4000
Bill Klosterman, *Dir*
▼ EMP: 18 EST: 2009
SALES (est): 10.05MM
SALES (corp-wide): 1.26B Privately Held
Web: www.hexion.com
SIC: 2821 Plastics materials and resins
PA: Hexion Inc.
　　180 E Broad St
　　Columbus OH 43215
　　888 443-9466

▲ = Import ▼ = Export
◆ = Import/Export

(G-4980)

HI LITE PLASTIC PRODUCTS
Also Called: Capital Toe Grinding
3760 E 5th Ave (43219-1807)
PHONE.................................614 235-9050
Offie Bartley, *Owner*
EMP: 6 **EST:** 1977
SALES (est): 459.01K **Privately Held**
Web: www.hiliteplastics.com
SIC: 3089 Kitchenware, plastics

(G-4981)

HIGHCOM GLOBAL SECURITY INC (HQ)
Also Called: Blastwrap
2901 E 4th Ave Unit J (43219-2896)
PHONE.................................727 592-9400
Francis Michaud, *Ch Bd*
Francis Michaud, *Interim Chairman of the Board*
Michael L Bundy, *COO*
EMP: 7 **EST:** 1999
SQ FT: 32,155
SALES (est): 30.29MM
SALES (corp-wide): 1.5MM **Publicly Held**
Web: www.blastgardtech.com
SIC: 3699 Fire control or bombing
equipment, electronic
PA: 2538093 Ontario Inc
4400-181 Bay St
Toronto ON M5J 2

(G-4982)

HIGHLIGHTS CONSUMER SVCS INC
1800 Watermark Dr (43216)
P.O. Box 269 (43216)
PHONE.................................570 253-1164
Kent Johnson, *CEO*
Lece Lohr, *Pr*
EMP: 15 **EST:** 2011
SALES (est): 7.87MM
SALES (corp-wide): 72.35MM **Privately Held**
Web: shop.highlights.com
SIC: 2731 Books, publishing only
PA: Highlights For Children, Inc.
1800 Watermark Dr
Columbus OH 43215
614 486-0631

(G-4983)

HIGHLIGHTS FOR CHILDREN INC (PA)
Also Called: Highlights For Children Publr
1800 Watermark Dr (43215-1035)
P.O. Box 269 (43216-0269)
PHONE.................................614 486-0631
▲ **EMP:** 250 **EST:** 1946
SALES (est): 72.35MM
SALES (corp-wide): 72.35MM **Privately Held**
Web: shop.highlights.com
SIC: 2721 Magazines: publishing and printing

(G-4984)

HIKMA LABS INC
Also Called: Roxane Laboratories
1900 Arlingate Ln (43228-3175)
PHONE.................................614 276-4000
Chris Boneham, *Brnch Mgr*
EMP: 8
SALES (corp-wide): 3.13B **Privately Held**
Web: www.hikma-specialty.com
SIC: 2834 Pharmaceutical preparations
HQ: Hikma Labs Inc.
1809 Wilson Rd
Columbus OH 43216

(G-4985)

HIKMA LABS INC (DH)
1809 Wilson Rd (43216)
P.O. Box 16532 (43216-6532)
PHONE.................................614 276-4000
Michael Raya, *CEO*
Brian Hoffmann, *
Mohammed Obeidat, *
George J Muench Iii, *Treas*
David Berger, *
▲ **EMP:** 116 **EST:** 2005
SALES (est): 51.97MM
SALES (corp-wide): 3.13B **Privately Held**
Web: www.hikma.com
SIC: 2834 Druggists' preparations
(pharmaceuticals)
HQ: West-Ward Holdings Limited
1 New Burlington Place
London W1S 2
207 399-2760

(G-4986)

HIKMA PHARMACEUTICALS USA INC
Also Called: Non-Injectable Manufacturing
1809 Wilson Rd (43228-9579)
PHONE.................................614 276-4000
EMP: 39
SALES (corp-wide): 3.13B **Privately Held**
Web: www.hikma.com
SIC: 2834 Pharmaceutical preparations
HQ: Hikma Pharmaceuticals Usa Inc.
200 Connell Dr 4th Fl
Berkeley Heights NJ 07922
908 673-1030

(G-4987)

HIKMA SPECIALTY USA INC
1900 Arlingate Ln (43228-3175)
PHONE.................................856 489-2110
Frank Savastano, *Pr*
George J Muench Iii, *Treas*
David Berger, *Sec*
Rebecca Jewell, *Sec*
EMP: 10 **EST:** 2013
SALES (est): 2.4MM
SALES (corp-wide): 3.13B **Privately Held**
Web: www.hikma.com
SIC: 2834 Pharmaceutical preparations
HQ: Eurohealth (U.S.A.), Inc
200 Connell Dr Fl 4
Berkeley Heights NJ 07922

(G-4988)

HILL SIGN COMPANY INC
4555 Groves Rd Ste 1 (43232-4135)
PHONE.................................614 367-9227
Gene Johnson, *Pr*
EMP: 7 **EST:** 1970
SQ FT: 9,432
SALES (est): 205.03K **Privately Held**
SIC: 3993 2759 5131 Signs and advertising
specialties; Screen printing; Flags and
banners

(G-4989)

HJ SYSTEMS INC
230 N Central Ave (43222-1001)
PHONE.................................614 351-9777
James E Stang, *Pr*
EMP: 10 **EST:** 1993
SQ FT: 20,000
SALES (est): 1.1MM **Privately Held**
Web: www.hjsystemsinc.com
SIC: 2431 Millwork

(G-4990)

HONEYWELL INTERNATIONAL INC
Also Called: Honeywell
2080 Arlingate Ln (43228-4112)
PHONE.................................302 327-8920
Brad Forry, *Brnch Mgr*

EMP: 22
SALES (corp-wide): 38.5B **Publicly Held**
Web: www.honeywell.com
SIC: 3829 3674 Pressure transducers;
Semiconductors and related devices
PA: Honeywell International Inc.
855 S Mint St
Charlotte NC 28202
704 627-6200

(G-4991)

HONEYWELL LEBOW PRODUCTS
Also Called: Honeywell Senfopec
2080 Arlingate Ln (43228-4112)
PHONE.................................614 850-5000
Phil Geraffo, *Pr*
▲ **EMP:** 200 **EST:** 2000
SALES (est): 2.73MM
SALES (corp-wide): 38.5B **Publicly Held**
SIC: 3724 Aircraft engines and engine parts
PA: Honeywell International Inc.
855 S Mint St
Charlotte NC 28202
704 627-6200

(G-4992)

HOSTER GRAPHICS COMPANY INC
Also Called: Advance Graphics
2580 Westbelt Dr (43228-3827)
PHONE.................................614 299-9770
Frank Hoster, *Pr*
EMP: 13 **EST:** 1929
SALES (est): 2.1MM **Privately Held**
Web: www.advancecolumbus.com
SIC: 2752 7334 Offset printing;
Photocopying and duplicating services

(G-4993)

HOWARD INDUSTRIES INC
1840 Progress Ave (43207-1707)
PHONE.................................614 444-9900
EMP: 15 **EST:** 1964
SALES (est): 2.15MM **Privately Held**
Web: www.howardchem.com
SIC: 7389 2843 5051 3087 Packaging and
labeling services; Emulsifiers, except food
and pharmaceutical; Miscellaneous
nonferrous products; Custom compound
purchased resins

(G-4994)

HYPE SOCKS LLC
204 S Front St Apt 400 (43215-4753)
PHONE.................................855 497-3769
Josh M Wintermantel, *Managing Member*
EMP: 15 **EST:** 2015
SALES (est): 3.95MM **Privately Held**
Web: www.hypesocks.com
SIC: 2252 Socks

(G-4995)

HYPER TECH RESEARCH INC
539 Industrial Mile Rd (43228-2412)
PHONE.................................614 481-8050
Michael Tomsic, *Pr*
Lawrence Walley, *CFO*
Sarah Tomsic, *Stockholder*
Sherrie Cantu, *Stockholder*
David Doll, *Prin*
EMP: 16 **EST:** 2001
SQ FT: 50,000
SALES (est): 2.49MM **Privately Held**
Web: www.hypertechresearch.com
SIC: 3674 Semiconductors and related
devices

(G-4996)

I H SCHLEZINGER INC
Also Called: Schlezinger Metals
1041 Joyce Ave (43219-2448)
P.O. Box 83624 (43203-0624)

PHONE.................................614 252-1188
Kenneth Cohen, *Pr*
John Miller, *
Jack Joseph, *
Donald Zulanch, *
Neil Cohen, *
EMP: 42 **EST:** 1915
SQ FT: 9,000
SALES (est): 4.51MM **Privately Held**
Web: www.ihsrecycling.com
SIC: 3341 5093 Secondary nonferrous
metals; Ferrous metal scrap and waste

(G-4997)

IABF INC
Also Called: Industrial Aluminum Foundry
1890 Mckinley Ave (43222-1004)
PHONE.................................614 279-4498
Andrew B Kientz, *Pr*
EMP: 8 **EST:** 1966
SQ FT: 7,500
SALES (est): 986.7K **Privately Held**
Web: www.iabfinc.com
SIC: 3365 3369 Aluminum and aluminum-
based alloy castings; Nonferrous foundries,
nec

(G-4998)

ICC SAFETY SERVICE INC
1070 Leona Ave (43201-3039)
PHONE.................................614 261-4557
Tiffany Adair, *Pr*
Christopher Duger, *VP*
EMP: 6 **EST:** 2004
SQ FT: 3,900
SALES (est): 863.37K **Privately Held**
Web: www.iccsafetysurfaces.com
SIC: 3271 Blocks, concrete: insulating

(G-4999)

IDENTIFICATION SYSTEMS INC
Also Called: Identity Systems
1324 Stimmel Rd (43223-2917)
PHONE.................................614 448-1741
▲ **EMP:** 50 **EST:** 1987
SALES (est): 4.47MM **Privately Held**
Web: www.identitysystemsinc.com
SIC: 3089 Identification cards, plastics

(G-5000)

IKE SMART CITY
250 N Hartford Ave (43222-1100)
PHONE.................................614 294-4898
Pete Scantland, *CEO*
EMP: 20 **EST:** 2017
SALES (est): 923.52K **Privately Held**
Web: www.ikesmartcity.com
SIC: 3993 7312 Signs and advertising
specialties; Outdoor advertising services

(G-5001)

IMH LLC
160 Easton Town Ctr (43219-6074)
PHONE.................................513 800-9830
EMP: 10
SIC: 2844 Perfumes and colognes
PA: I.M.H. Llc
7020 Huntley Rd Ste C
Columbus OH 43229

(G-5002)

IMH LLC (PA)
7020 Huntley Rd Ste C (43229-1050)
PHONE.................................614 436-0991
EMP: 8 **EST:** 2011
SALES (est): 2MM **Privately Held**
SIC: 2844 Perfumes and colognes

(G-5003)

IMPACT PRINTING AND DESIGN LLC
4670 Groves Rd (43232-4164)
PHONE.............................833 522-6200
EMP: 12 EST: 2008
SALES (est): 171.96K **Privately Held**
Web: www.impactprintanddesign.com
SIC: 7389 3953 5699 2759 Design services;
Screens, textile printing; T-shirts, custom
printed; Poster and decal printing and
engraving

(G-5004)

INDUSTRIAL PATTERN & MFG CO
899 N 20th St (43219-2420)
PHONE.............................614 252-0934
Thomas C Birkefeld, *Pr*
Charles J Birkefeld, *VP*
Jay Hrun, *VP Engg*
EMP: 11 EST: 1947
SQ FT: 5,000
SALES (est): 1.55MM **Privately Held**
Web: www.industrialpattern.com
SIC: 3543 Industrial patterns

(G-5005)

INHANCE TECHNOLOGIES LLC
6575 Huntley Rd Ste D (43229-1039)
PHONE.............................614 846-6400
Tom Gardener, *Mgr*
EMP: 35
SQ FT: 7,500
SALES (corp-wide): 225.67MM **Privately
Held**
Web: www.inhancetechnologies.com
SIC: 3089 Injection molding of plastics
HQ: Inhance Technologies Llc
22008 N Berwick Dr
Houston TX 77095
800 929-1743

(G-5006)

INLAND PRODUCTS INC (PA)
599 Frank Rd (43223-3813)
P.O. Box 2228 (43216-2228)
PHONE.............................614 443-3425
Gary H Baas, *Pr*
EMP: 21 EST: 1867
SQ FT: 40,000
SALES (est): 2.56MM
SALES (corp-wide): 2.56MM **Privately
Held**
SIC: 2077 5159 Grease rendering, inedible;
Hides

(G-5007)

INNOVATIVE GRAPHICS LTD
2580 Westbelt Dr (43228-3827)
PHONE.............................877 406-3636
Michael Foley, *Pr*
EMP: 13 EST: 2018
SALES (est): 1.48MM **Privately Held**
SIC: 2752 Commercial printing, lithographic

(G-5008)

INSKEEP BROTHERS INC
Also Called: Inskeep Brothers Printers
3193 E Dublin Granville Rd (43231-4035)
PHONE.............................614 898-6620
Jeff Inskeep, *Pr*
Paula Inskeep, *VP*
EMP: 6 EST: 1888
SQ FT: 11,000
SALES (est): 729.71K **Privately Held**
Web: www.inskeepbrothers.com
SIC: 2752 Offset printing

(G-5009)

INSTALLED BUILDING PDTS LLC
Swan Freedom
1320 Mckinley Ave Ste A (43222-1115)
PHONE.............................614 308-9900
Mark Lomax, *Brnch Mgr*
EMP: 319
SALES (corp-wide): 2.94B **Publicly Held**
Web: www.swanfreedom.com
SIC: 2511 2514 3231 3442 Whatnot shelves:
wood; Medicine cabinets and vanities: metal
; Mirrored glass; Shutters, door or window:
metal
HQ: Installed Building Products Llc
495 S High St Ste 150
Columbus OH 43215
614 221-3399

(G-5010)

**INSTANTWHIP CONNECTICUT INC
(PA)**
2200 Cardigan Ave (43215-1092)
PHONE.............................614 488-2536
Douglas A Smith, *Pr*
Clifton J Smith, *Ch Bd*
Robert Pavlick, *General Vice President*
G Frederick Smith, *Sec*
Thomas G Michaelides, *Treas*
EMP: 18 EST: 1946
SQ FT: 10,300
SALES (est): 2.47MM
SALES (corp-wide): 2.47MM **Privately
Held**
Web: www.instantwhip.com
SIC: 2026 5143 Whipped topping, except
frozen or dry mix; Dairy products, except
dried or canned

(G-5011)

INSTANTWHIP FOODS INC (PA)
2200 Cardigan Ave (43215-1092)
PHONE.............................614 488-2536
Douglas A Smith, *Pr*
Thomas G Michaelides, *VP*
EMP: 18 EST: 1934
SQ FT: 10,300
SALES (est): 47.63MM
SALES (corp-wide): 47.63MM **Privately
Held**
Web: www.instantwhip.com
SIC: 6794 8741 2026 5143 Franchises,
selling or licensing; Administrative
management; Fluid milk; Dairy products,
except dried or canned

(G-5012)

**INSTANTWHIP PRODUCTS CO PA
(HQ)**
Also Called: Instantwhip of Pennsylvania
2200 Cardigan Ave (43215-1092)
PHONE.............................614 488-2536
Douglas A Smith, *Pr*
EMP: 18 EST: 1940
SQ FT: 20,300
SALES (est): 2.26MM
SALES (corp-wide): 47.63MM **Privately
Held**
Web: www.instantwhip.com
SIC: 2026 5143 Whipped topping, except
frozen or dry mix; Dairy products, except
dried or canned
PA: Instantwhip Foods, Inc.
2200 Cardigan Ave
Columbus OH 43215
614 488-2536

(G-5013)

INSTANTWHIP-BUFFALO INC (HQ)
2200 Cardigan Ave (43215-1092)
PHONE.............................614 488-2536
Douglas A Smith, *Pr*

Thomas G Michaelides, *Treas*
G Frederick Smith, *Sec*
John Beck, *VP*
EMP: 10 EST: 1939
SQ FT: 10,300
SALES (est): 6.27MM
SALES (corp-wide): 47.63MM **Privately
Held**
Web: www.instantwhip.com
SIC: 2026 5143 Whipped topping, except
frozen or dry mix; Dairy products, except
dried or canned
PA: Instantwhip Foods, Inc.
2200 Cardigan Ave
Columbus OH 43215
614 488-2536

(G-5014)

INSTANTWHIP-CHICAGO INC (PA)
2200 Cardigan Ave (43215-1092)
PHONE.............................614 488-2536
Douglas A Smith, *Pr*
Clifton J Smith, *
G Frederick Smith, *
Thomas G Michaelides, *
Jim Ring, *
EMP: 36 EST: 1946
SQ FT: 10,300
SALES (est): 2.87MM
SALES (corp-wide): 2.87MM **Privately
Held**
Web: www.instantwhip.com
SIC: 2026 Cream, whipped

(G-5015)

INSTANTWHIP-SYRACUSE INC (PA)
2200 Cardigan Ave (43215-1092)
PHONE.............................614 488-2536
Douglas A Smith, *Pr*
Raymond Winslow, *General Vice President*
Thomas G Michaelides, *Treas*
G Frederick Smith, *Sec*
Clifton J Smith, *Ch Bd*
EMP: 17 EST: 1940
SQ FT: 10,300
SALES (est): 353.49K
SALES (corp-wide): 353.49K **Privately
Held**
SIC: 2026 Whipped topping, except frozen
or dry mix

(G-5016)

INSULPRO INC
4650 Indianola Ave (43214-1884)
PHONE.............................614 262-3768
Greg Freed, *Pr*
EMP: 10 EST: 1989
SALES (est): 912.19K **Privately Held**
SIC: 3494 Line strainers, for use in piping
systems

(G-5017)

INTELLINETICS INC (PA)
2190 Dividend Dr (43228-3806)
PHONE.............................614 388-8908
James F Desocio, *Pr*
Michael N Taglich, *Interim Chairman of the
Board*
Matthew L Chretien, *CSO*
Joseph D Spain, *CFO*
EMP: 97 EST: 1996
SQ FT: 6,000
SALES (est): 18.02MM
SALES (corp-wide): 18.02MM **Publicly
Held**
Web: www.intellinetics.com
SIC: 7372 Prepackaged software

(G-5018)

INTERBAKE FOODS LLC (HQ)
Also Called: Norse Dairy Systems

1740 Joyce Ave (43219-1026)
PHONE.............................614 294-4931
Raymond Baxter, *Pr*
Paul M Desjardins, *
◆ EMP: 55 EST: 1972
SALES (est): 486.26MM **Privately Held**
Web: www.interbake.com
SIC: 2052 2051 Cookies; Bread, cake, and
related products
PA: Hearthside Food Solutions, Llc
3333 Finley Rd Ste 800
Downers Grove IL 60515

(G-5019)

**INTERNATIONAL CONFECTIONS
COMPANY LLC**
Also Called: Maxfield Candy Company
1855 E 17th Ave (43219-1006)
PHONE.............................800 288-8002
▼ EMP: 200
SIC: 2064 Chocolate candy, except solid
chocolate

(G-5020)

INTERNTNAL PDTS SRCING GROUP I
Also Called: Ipsg
2701 Charter St Ste A (43228-4639)
PHONE.............................614 334-1500
EMP: 266
SALES (corp-wide): 824.57MM **Privately
Held**
SIC: 3571 Electronic computers
HQ: International Products Sourcing Group,
Inc.
4119 Leap Rd
Hilliard OH 43026

(G-5021)

**INTERNTNAL TCHNCAL CATINGS
INC**
Also Called: Itc Manufacturing
845 E Markison Ave (43207-1388)
PHONE.............................800 567-6592
Judith Fernandez, *Brnch Mgr*
EMP: 187
Web: www.itcmfg.com
SIC: 3496 Shelving, made from purchased
wire
PA: International Technical Coatings, Inc.
110 S 41st Ave
Phoenix AZ 85009

(G-5022)

INTERSTATE TRUCKWAY INC
5440 Renner Rd (43228-8941)
PHONE.............................614 771-1220
Willy Walraven, *Brnch Mgr*
EMP: 15
Web: www.interstatetrailer.com
SIC: 3799 5012 Trailers and trailer
equipment; Automobiles and other motor
vehicles
PA: Interstate Truckway Inc
1755 Dreman Ave
Cincinnati OH 45223

(G-5023)

INVIRSA INC
1275 Kinnear Rd Ste 217 (43212-0017)
PHONE.............................614 344-1765
Robert Shalwitz, *CEO*
EMP: 7 EST: 2016
SALES (est): 518.57K **Privately Held**
Web: www.invirsa.com
SIC: 2834 Pharmaceutical preparations

(G-5024)

IPA LTD
Also Called: Zed Digital
199 Mckenna Creek Dr (43230-6127)

PHONE.................................614 523-3974
Sumithra Jagannath, *Pr*
EMP: 13 **EST:** 2014
SQ FT: 1,500
SALES (est): 193.17K **Privately Held**
SIC: 7371 7373 2741 7374 Computer software development; Computer integrated systems design; Internet publishing and broadcasting; Computer graphics service

(G-5025)
IRONFAB LLC
1771 Progress Ave (43207-1749)
PHONE.................................614 443-3900
EMP: 13 **EST:** 2003
SALES (est): 2.36MM **Privately Held**
Web: www.ironfabllc.com
SIC: 3441 Fabricated structural metal

(G-5026)
ISP CHEMICALS LLC
1979 Atlas St (43228-9645)
PHONE.................................614 876-3637
Doctor Paul Taylor, *Dir*
EMP: 70
SALES (corp-wide): 2.11B **Publicly Held**
SIC: 2834 Pharmaceutical preparations
HQ: Isp Chemicals Llc
     455 N Main St
     Calvert City KY 42029
     270 395-4165

(G-5027)
J S C PUBLISHING
958 King Ave (43212-2655)
PHONE.................................614 424-6911
Joe Paxton, *Owner*
EMP: 6 **EST:** 2000
SALES (est): 228.05K **Privately Held**
SIC: 2731 Pamphlets: publishing and printing

(G-5028)
J SOLUTIONS LLC
216 E Hinman Ave (43207-1182)
PHONE.................................614 732-4857
Jennifer Williams, *Prin*
EMP: 7 **EST:** 2012
SALES (est): 79.66K **Privately Held**
Web: www.jsolutions.us
SIC: 2752 Commercial printing, lithographic

(G-5029)
JACOBI CARBONS INC
432 Mccormick Blvd (43215)
PHONE.................................215 546-3900
Bill Eubanks, *Pr*
◆ **EMP:** 79 **EST:** 2001
SALES (est): 4.48MM **Privately Held**
Web: www.jacobi.net
SIC: 2895 Carbon black
HQ: Jacobi Carbons Ab
     Scheelegatan 8
     Kalmar 392 3
     480417550

(G-5030)
JAIN AMERICA FOODS INC (HQ)
Also Called: Jain Americas
1819 Walcutt Rd Ste I (43228-9149)
PHONE.................................614 850-9400
Anil Jain, *CEO*
Nerinder Gupta, *COO*
John Donovan, *CFO*
◆ **EMP:** 7 **EST:** 1998
SQ FT: 30,000
SALES (est): 26.91MM **Privately Held**
Web: www.jainamericas.com
SIC: 3086 2821 3081 Plastics foam products ; Molding compounds, plastics; Polyvinyl film and sheet

PA: Jain Irrigation Systems Limited
     Jain Plastic Park, N.H. No. 6,
     Jalgaon MH 42500

(G-5031)
JAMES K GREEN ENTERPRISES INC
Also Called: Columbus Gasket & Supply
1875 Lone Eagle St (43228-3647)
PHONE.................................614 878-6041
James K Green, *Pr*
▲ **EMP:** 9 **EST:** 1976
SQ FT: 14,000
SALES (est): 891.04K **Privately Held**
Web: www.columbusgasket.com
SIC: 3053 3069 Gaskets, all materials; Molded rubber products

(G-5032)
JAPO INC
3902 Indianola Ave (43214-3156)
P.O. Box 630 (43216-0630)
PHONE.................................614 263-2850
▼ **EMP:** 47
Web: www.lcpinc.com
SIC: 5085 3089 Industrial supplies; Injection molding of plastics

(G-5033)
JAX WAX INC
3145 E 17th Ave (43219-2329)
PHONE.................................614 476-6769
Jack Minor, *Pr*
EMP: 10 **EST:** 1993
SQ FT: 5,600
SALES (est): 2.32MM **Privately Held**
Web: www.jaxwax.com
SIC: 2842 Automobile polish

(G-5034)
JBS INDUSTRIES LTD
1001 Atlantic Ave Apt 783 (43229-1777)
PHONE.................................513 314-5599
EMP: 6 **EST:** 2005
SALES (est): 88.7K **Privately Held**
Web: www.jbsindustries.com
SIC: 3999 Manufacturing industries, nec

(G-5035)
JE GROTE COMPANY INC (PA)
Also Called: Grote
1160 Gahanna Pkwy (43230-6615)
PHONE.................................614 868-8414
James E Grote, *Ch Bd*
Bob Grote, *
◆ **EMP:** 100 **EST:** 1969
SQ FT: 73,500
SALES (est): 49.98MM
SALES (corp-wide): 49.98MM **Privately Held**
Web: www.grotecompany.com
SIC: 3589 3556 Cooking equipment, commercial; Food products machinery

(G-5036)
JENIS SPLENDID ICE CREAMS LLC (PA)
401 N Front St Ste 300 (43215-2263)
PHONE.................................614 488-3224
Charles Bauer, *Managing Member*
EMP: 23 **EST:** 2003
SALES (est): 19.98MM
SALES (corp-wide): 19.98MM **Privately Held**
Web: www.jenis.com
SIC: 5451 2024 Ice cream (packaged); Custard, frozen

(G-5037)
JENTGEN STEEL SERVICES LLC
611 E Weber Rd Ste 201 (43211-1097)

PHONE.................................614 268-6340
EMP: 12 **EST:** 2011
SALES (est): 1.25MM **Privately Held**
SIC: 3448 Trusses and framing, prefabricated metal

(G-5038)
JET CONTAINER COMPANY
1033 Brentnell Ave Ste 100 (43219-2186)
PHONE.................................614 444-2133
Stephen J Schmitt, *Pr*
Richard Prohl, *Managing Member*
Mike Schmitt, *
EMP: 57 **EST:** 1977
SQ FT: 175,000
SALES (est): 12.75MM **Privately Held**
Web: www.jetcontainer.com
SIC: 2653 Boxes, corrugated: made from purchased materials

(G-5039)
JETCOAT LLC
Also Called: Jetcoat
472 Brehl Ave (43223-1973)
P.O. Box 23054 (43223-0054)
PHONE.................................800 394-0047
David L Thorson, *Managing Member*
EMP: 20 **EST:** 2007
SQ FT: 5,000
SALES (est): 12.62MM **Privately Held**
Web: www.jetcoatinc.com
SIC: 2891 Sealants
PA: Thorworks Industries, Inc.
     2520 Campbell St
     Sandusky OH 44870

(G-5040)
JLS FUNERAL HOME
2322 Randy Ct (43232-8470)
PHONE.................................614 625-1220
Jimmie Spurlock, *Prin*
EMP: 10
SALES (est): 180.06K **Privately Held**
SIC: 2396 5087 7389 Veils and veiling: bridal, funeral, etc.; Cemetery and funeral director's equipment and supplies; Business Activities at Non-Commercial Site

(G-5041)
JMAC INC (PA)
200 W Nationwide Blvd Unit 1 (43215-2561)
PHONE.................................614 436-2418
John P Mcconnell, *Ch Bd*
Michael A Priest, *Pr*
George N Corey, *Prin*
▲ **EMP:** 28 **EST:** 1980
SQ FT: 6,000
SALES (est): 46.13MM
SALES (corp-wide): 46.13MM **Privately Held**
SIC: 3325 5198 7999 5511 Steel foundries, nec; Paints; Ice skating rink operation; Automobiles, new and used

(G-5042)
JOHNSONS REAL ICE CREAM LLC
Also Called: Wilcoxon, James H Jr
2728 E Main St (43209-2534)
PHONE.................................614 231-0014
James H Wilcoxon Junior, *Pr*
EMP: 53 **EST:** 1950
SQ FT: 4,600
SALES (est): 2.75MM **Privately Held**
Web: www.johnsonsrealicecream.com
SIC: 5812 5143 2024 Ice cream stands or dairy bars; Dairy products, except dried or canned; Ice cream and frozen deserts

(G-5043)
JUDITH LEIBER LLC (PA)
4300 E 5th Ave (43219-1816)
PHONE.................................614 449-4217
EMP: 20 **EST:** 2000
SALES (est): 1.55MM
SALES (corp-wide): 1.55MM **Privately Held**
SIC: 3171 Women's handbags and purses

(G-5044)
KAMPS PALLETS
2132 Refugee Rd (43207-2841)
PHONE.................................616 818-4323
EMP: 6 **EST:** 2018
SALES (est): 381.46K **Privately Held**
Web: www.kampspallets.com
SIC: 2448 Pallets, wood

(G-5045)
KANTNER INGREDIENTS INC
Also Called: AME Nutrition Ingredients
975 Worthington Woods Loop Rd (43085-5743)
PHONE.................................614 766-3638
Douglas E Kantner, *Pr*
◆ **EMP:** 7 **EST:** 2004
SALES (est): 858.76K **Privately Held**
Web: www.kantnergroup.com
SIC: 2099 Food preparations, nec

(G-5046)
KARN MEATS INC
Also Called: Central Market Specialty Meats
922 Taylor Ave (43219-2558)
PHONE.................................614 252-3712
Richard Karn, *Pr*
EMP: 50 **EST:** 1971
SQ FT: 50,000
SALES (est): 9.97MM **Privately Held**
Web: www.karnmeats.com
SIC: 2011 2013 Meat packing plants; Sausages and other prepared meats

(G-5047)
KEFFS INC
2117 S High St (43207-2428)
P.O. Box 1310 (43017-6310)
PHONE.................................614 443-0586
K R Gay, *Pr*
Kenneth Robert Gay, *Pr*
Elizabeth Sue Gay, *VP*
EMP: 7 **EST:** 1962
SQ FT: 35,000
SALES (est): 852.5K **Privately Held**
Web: www.accredocbs.com
SIC: 3496 Shelving, made from purchased wire

(G-5048)
KENAN ADVANTAGE GROUP INC
Also Called: Advantage Truck Trailers
500 Manor Park Dr (43228-9396)
PHONE.................................614 878-4050
Dan Peckinpaugh, *Mgr*
EMP: 9
SALES (corp-wide): 1.55B **Privately Held**
Web: www.thekag.com
SIC: 3715 Truck trailers
PA: The Kenan Advantage Group Inc
     4366 Mt Pleasant St Nw
     North Canton OH 44720
     800 969-5419

(G-5049)
KENDALL HOLDINGS LTD (PA)
Also Called: Phpk Technologies
2111 Builders Pl (43204-4886)
PHONE.................................614 486-4750
Richard Coleman, *Pt*

GEOGRAPHIC

▲ **EMP:** 49 **EST:** 2004
SQ FT: 60,000
SALES (est): 10.1MM
SALES (corp-wide): 10.1MM **Privately Held**
Web: www.phpk.com
SIC: 3443 Fabricated plate work (boiler shop)

(G-5050)
KENWEL PRINTERS INC
4272 Indianola Ave (43214-2891)
PHONE..........................614 261-1011
David G Starner, *Pr*
Mike Fisher, *
EMP: 36 **EST:** 1969
SQ FT: 15,000
SALES (est): 6.25MM **Privately Held**
Web: www.kenwelprinters.com
SIC: 2752 2789 2759 Offset printing;
Bookbinding and related work; Commercial
printing, nec

(G-5051)
KEURIG DR PEPPER INC
950 Stelzer Rd (43219-3740)
PHONE..........................614 237-4201
David Gerics, *Brnch Mgr*
EMP: 51
Web: www.keurigdrpepper.com
SIC: 2086 Soft drinks: packaged in cans,
bottles, etc.
PA: Keurig Dr Pepper Inc.
53 South Ave
Burlington MA 01803

(G-5052)
KEVIN NOESNER
2672 Eastcleft Dr (43221-1708)
PHONE..........................614 451-5459
Kevin Noesner, *Prin*
EMP: 7 **EST:** 2017
SALES (est): 240.84K **Privately Held**
SIC: 2752 Commercial printing, lithographic

(G-5053)
KEY FINISHES LLC
727 Harrison Dr (43204-3507)
PHONE..........................614 351-8393
James H Mccurdy, *CFO*
▲ **EMP:** 9 **EST:** 2010
SALES (est): 1.47MM **Privately Held**
Web: www.keyfinishes.com
SIC: 3399 Powder, metal

(G-5054)
KIRK EXCAVATING &
CONSTRUCTION
1399 Stimmel Rd (43223-2949)
P.O. Box 8 (43123-0008)
PHONE..........................614 444-4008
Charles Kirk, *Pr*
Tamara Pleskach, *VP*
EMP: 20 **EST:** 2001
SALES (est): 4.8MM **Privately Held**
Web: www.kirkexcavating.com
SIC: 1381 Directional drilling oil and gas
wells

(G-5055)
KOKOSING MATERIALS INC
4755 S High St (43207-4028)
P.O. Box 334 (43019-0334)
PHONE..........................614 491-1199
Bill Burgett, *Pr*
Bob Bailey, *
EMP: 8 **EST:** 1996
SALES (est): 363.68K **Privately Held**
Web: www.kokosing.biz
SIC: 2951 Asphalt and asphaltic paving
mixtures (not from refineries)

(G-5056)
KRIGBAUM INC
Also Called: Signs By Tomorrow
373 Vista Dr (43230-5902)
PHONE..........................614 478-6472
Richard Krigbaum, *Pr*
Marilyn Krigbaum, *VP*
EMP: 20 **EST:** 2001
SALES (est): 412.74K **Privately Held**
Web: www.signsbytomorrow.com
SIC: 3993 Signs and advertising specialties

(G-5057)
KRISPY KREME DOUGHNUT CORP
Also Called: Krispy Kreme 322
3690 W Dublin Granville Rd (43235-7987)
PHONE..........................614 798-0812
James Lewis, *Mgr*
EMP: 23
SQ FT: 2,158
SALES (corp-wide): 1.69B **Publicly Held**
Web: www.krispykreme.com
SIC: 5461 2051 Doughnuts; Pastries, e.g.
danish: except frozen
HQ: Krispy Kreme Doughnut Corp
2116 Hawkins St Ste 102
Charlotte NC 28203
980 270-7117

(G-5058)
KRISPY KREME DOUGHNUT CORP
Also Called: Krispy Kreme
2557 Westbelt Dr (43228-3826)
PHONE..........................614 876-0058
Ron Snyder, *Mgr*
EMP: 70
SALES (corp-wide): 1.69B **Publicly Held**
Web: www.krispykreme.com
SIC: 5461 2051 Doughnuts; Pastries, e.g.
danish: except frozen
HQ: Krispy Kreme Doughnut Corp
2116 Hawkins St Ste 102
Charlotte NC 28203
980 270-7117

(G-5059)
KYRON TOOL & MACHINE CO INC
2900 Banwick Rd (43232-3838)
PHONE..........................614 231-6000
Charles P Haueisen, *Pr*
Randal Hauesein, *VP*
Rosemary Hauesein, *Treas*
EMP: 10 **EST:** 1949
SQ FT: 50,000
SALES (est): 2.49MM **Privately Held**
Web: www.kyrontool.com
SIC: 3599 Machine shop, jobbing and repair

(G-5060)
LA MARQUISE INC
Also Called: La Chatelaine
1550 W Lane Ave (43221-3921)
PHONE..........................614 488-1911
Stan Wielezynsky, *Prin*
EMP: 60 **EST:** 1990
SALES (est): 2.36MM **Privately Held**
Web: www.lachatelainebakery.com
SIC: 5461 5812 2052 2051 Retail bakeries;
French restaurant; Cookies and crackers;
Bread, cake, and related products

(G-5061)
LAMBERT SHEET METAL INC
Also Called: Lsmi
1625 W Mound St (43223-1809)
PHONE..........................614 237-0384
Carl Lambert, *Pr*
Betty Lambert, *VP*
EMP: 15 **EST:** 1969
SALES (est): 2.31MM **Privately Held**
Web: www.lambertsheetmetal.com

SIC: 3444 Sheet metal specialties, not
stamped

(G-5062)
LANCASTER COMMERCIAL PDTS
LLC
2353 Westbrooke Dr (43228-9557)
PHONE..........................844 324-1444
◆ **EMP:** 34 **EST:** 2013
SALES (est): 4.82MM **Privately Held**
Web: www.lcpinc.com
SIC: 5085 3089 Industrial supplies; Injection
molding of plastics

(G-5063)
LANDON VAULT COMPANY
1477 Frebis Ave (43206-3763)
PHONE..........................614 443-5505
Martin Pehrson, *Pr*
Autumn Epperson, *Sec*
EMP: 11 **EST:** 1920
SQ FT: 3,600
SALES (est): 2.17MM **Privately Held**
SIC: 3272 Burial vaults, concrete or precast
terrazzo

(G-5064)
LANG STONE COMPANY INC (PA)
4099 E 5th Ave (43219-1812)
P.O. Box 360747 (43236-0747)
PHONE..........................614 235-4099
TOLL FREE: 800
E Dean Coffman, *Pr*
Joann Coffman, *
▲ **EMP:** 39 **EST:** 1856
SQ FT: 10,000
SALES (est): 10.12MM
SALES (corp-wide): 10.12MM **Privately
Held**
Web: www.langstone.com
SIC: 5032 5211 3281 3272 Granite building
stone; Lumber and other building materials;
Cut stone and stone products; Concrete
products, nec

(G-5065)
LAPHAM-HICKEY STEEL CORP
Lapham-Hickey
753 Marion Rd (43207-2554)
PHONE..........................614 443-4881
Eric Sattler, *Mgr*
EMP: 54
SQ FT: 110,000
SALES (corp-wide): 235.89MM **Privately
Held**
Web: www.lapham-hickey.com
SIC: 5051 3443 3441 3398 Steel; Fabricated
plate work (boiler shop); Fabricated
structural metal; Metal heat treating
PA: Lapham-Hickey Steel Corp.
5500 W 73rd St
Bedford Park IL 60638
708 496-6111

(G-5066)
LH MARSHALL COMPANY
1601 Woodland Ave (43219-1135)
PHONE..........................614 294-6433
Dorothy B Roberts, *Pr*
Cynthia R Padilla, *Sec*
Janet Forgue, *Treas*
Courtney Roberts, *VP*
▲ **EMP:** 18 **EST:** 1927
SALES (est): 2.22MM **Privately Held**
Web: www.lhmarshall.com
SIC: 3829 Measuring and controlling
devices, nec

(G-5067)
LIFE SUPPORT DEVELOPMENT LTD
777 Dearborn Park Ln Ste R (43085-5716)
PHONE..........................614 221-1765
EMP: 8 **EST:** 2010
SALES (est): 464.9K **Privately Held**
Web: www.lifesupport.com
SIC: 2086 Fruit drinks (less than 100%
juice): packaged in cans, etc.

(G-5068)
LIFELINE MOBILE INC
2050 Mcgaw Rd (43207-4800)
PHONE..........................614 497-8300
▼ **EMP:** 65 **EST:** 1991
SALES (est): 9.75MM **Privately Held**
Web: www.lifelinemobile.com
SIC: 3713 Specialty motor vehicle bodies

(G-5069)
LIFETIME PRODUCTS INC
4364 Sullivant Ave (43228-2819)
PHONE..........................614 272-1255
Chris Roberts, *Mgr*
EMP: 8
SALES (corp-wide): 291.23MM **Privately
Held**
Web: www.lifetime.com
SIC: 3949 Sporting and athletic goods, nec
PA: Lifetime Products Inc.
Freeport Ctr Bldg D11
Clearfield UT 84016
801 776-1532

(G-5070)
LINCOLN ELECTRIC AUTOMTN INC
1700 Jetway Blvd (43219-1675)
PHONE..........................614 471-5926
John Campbell, *Brnch Mgr*
EMP: 45
SALES (corp-wide): 4.01B **Publicly Held**
Web: www.rimrockcorp.com
SIC: 3563 3569 3443 3541 Spraying outfits:
metals, paints, and chemicals (compressor)
; Robots, assembly line: industrial and
commercial; Ladles, metal plate; Machine
tools, metal cutting type
HQ: Lincoln Electric Automation, Inc.
407 S Main St
Fort Loramie OH 45845
937 295-2120

(G-5071)
LINDE GAS & EQUIPMENT INC
Praxair
450 Greenlawn Ave (43223-2611)
PHONE..........................614 443-7687
Pratt Thompson, *Mgr*
EMP: 27
Web: www.lindedirect.com
SIC: 2813 Industrial gases
HQ: Linde Gas & Equipment Inc.
10 Riverview Dr
Danbury CT 06810
844 445-4633

(G-5072)
LOAD32 LLC
265 N Oakley Ave (43204-3762)
PHONE..........................614 984-6648
Durrell Burgess, *Managing Member*
EMP: 10 **EST:** 2020
SALES (est): 489.82K **Privately Held**
SIC: 3537 Trucks: freight, baggage, etc.:
industrial, except mining

(G-5073)
LOFT VIOLIN SHOP
4604 N High St (43214-2002)
PHONE..........................614 267-7221

▲ = Import ▼ = Export
◆ = Import/Export

David Schlub, *Owner*
Richard C Schlub, *Pt*
EMP: 9 **EST:** 1976
SALES (est): 480.02K **Privately Held**
Web: www.theloftviolinshop.com
SIC: 7699 5736 3931 7359 Musical instrument repair services; Musical instrument stores; Musical instruments; Musical instrument rental services

(G-5074)
LONOLIFE INC
432 W 2nd Ave (43201-3314)
PHONE..............................614 296-2250
EMP: 6 **EST:** 2015
SALES (est): 980.63K **Privately Held**
Web: www.lonolife.com
SIC: 2032 Soups and broths, canned, jarred, etc.

(G-5075)
LOTUS LOVE LLC
Also Called: Custom Dsign Chakra Reiki Jwly
1091 Fountain Ln Apt B (43213-4157)
P.O. Box 47 (43109-0047)
PHONE..............................614 964-8477
EMP: 25 **EST:** 2018
SALES (est): 253.57K **Privately Held**
SIC: 3911 Jewelry apparel

(G-5076)
LOUIS INSTANTWHIP-ST INC
2200 Cardigan Ave (43215-1092)
PHONE..............................614 488-2536
Douglas A Smith, *Pr*
G Frederick Smith, *Sec*
Thomas G Michaelides, *VP*
EMP: 18 **EST:** 1971
SQ FT: 10,300
SALES (est): 1.04MM **Privately Held**
Web: www.instantwhip.com
SIC: 2026 5143 Whipped topping, except frozen or dry mix; Dairy products, except dried or canned

(G-5077)
LVD ACQUISITION LLC (HQ)
Also Called: Oasis International
222 E Campus View Blvd (43235-4634)
PHONE..............................614 861-1350
Jeff Chiarugi, *Pr*
Michael Leibold, *
◆ **EMP:** 69 **EST:** 1910
SQ FT: 15,000
SALES (est): 361.88K
SALES (corp-wide): 652.75MM **Privately Held**
Web: www.oasiscoolers.com
SIC: 3585 3431 5078 Coolers, milk and water: electric; Drinking fountains, metal; Drinking water coolers, mechanical
PA: Culligan International Company
9399 W Hggins Rd Ste 1100
Rosemont IL 60018
847 430-2800

(G-5078)
MAC LEAN J S CO
5454 Alkire Rd (43228-3606)
PHONE..............................614 878-5454
J Bruce Lean Mac, *Pr*
M Richard Lean Mac, *Genl Mgr*
Richard Gomez, *
Mike Hunter, *
EMP: 6 **EST:** 1888
SQ FT: 86,000
SALES (est): 390.12K **Privately Held**
SIC: 2541 2542 2435 2434 Store fixtures, wood; Partitions and fixtures, except wood; Hardwood veneer and plywood; Wood kitchen cabinets

(G-5079)
MAK MAGIC INC
3900 Fisher Rd Ste G (43228-1054)
P.O. Box 28688 (43228-0688)
PHONE..............................614 591-3551
Mary Ann King, *Pr*
▲ **EMP:** 8 **EST:** 1973
SALES (est): 524.42K **Privately Held**
Web: www.makmagic.com
SIC: 3944 3999 Games, toys, and children's vehicles; Magic equipment, supplies, and props

(G-5080)
MARATHON AT SAWMILL
Also Called: Sawmill Marathon
7200 Sawmill Rd (43235-5964)
PHONE..............................614 734-0836
Donald Spangler, *Owner*
EMP: 10 **EST:** 1983
SALES (est): 229.75K **Privately Held**
SIC: 2421 Sawmills and planing mills, general

(G-5081)
MARFO COMPANY (PA)
Also Called: Trading Corp of America
799 N Hague Ave (43204-1424)
PHONE..............................614 276-3352
Bill Giovanello, *CEO*
Alan Johnson, *
EMP: 97 **EST:** 1977
SQ FT: 41,000
SALES (est): 4.71MM
SALES (corp-wide): 4.71MM **Privately Held**
Web: www.marsala.com
SIC: 5094 3911 Jewelry; Jewelry apparel

(G-5082)
MARK W THRUMAN
85 Mcnaughten Rd (43213-2174)
PHONE..............................614 754-5500
Mark W Thruman, *Prin*
EMP: 6 **EST:** 2010
SALES (est): 761.69K **Privately Held**
Web: www.ohiogastro.com
SIC: 3841 Gastroscopes, except electromedical

(G-5083)
MARS PETCARE US INC
Also Called: Masterfoods USA
5115 Fisher Rd (43228-9146)
P.O. Box 28146 (43228-0146)
PHONE..............................614 878-7242
Goodwyn Morgan, *Brnch Mgr*
EMP: 25
SQ FT: 175,000
SALES (corp-wide): 42.84B **Privately Held**
Web: www.marspetcare.com
SIC: 2047 Dog food
HQ: Mars Petcare Us, Inc.
1676 Intl Dr 10th Fl
Mclean VA 22102
615 807-4626

(G-5084)
MARSHALLTOWN PACKAGING INC
601 N Hague Ave (43204-1422)
PHONE..............................641 753-5272
Gary Bolar, *Pr*
▲ **EMP:** 9 **EST:** 1993
SQ FT: 54,000
SALES (est): 2.5MM
SALES (corp-wide): 3.2MM **Privately Held**
SIC: 2653 Boxes, corrugated: made from purchased materials
PA: Buckeye Boxes, Inc.
601 N Hague Ave
Columbus OH 43204

614 274-8484

(G-5085)
MARTINA METAL LLC
1575 Shawnee Ave (43211-2643)
PHONE..............................614 291-9700
EMP: 20
Web: www.smcco.org
SIC: 1761 3444 3441 3364 Sheet metal work, nec; Sheet metalwork; Fabricated structural metal; Nonferrous die-castings except aluminum

(G-5086)
MATERIALS SCIENCE INTL INC
1660 Georgesville Rd (43228-3613)
PHONE..............................614 870-0400
Neil Crabbe, *Pr*
William F Bailey, *
▲ **EMP:** 30 **EST:** 1987
SQ FT: 12,500
SALES (est): 4.29MM **Privately Held**
Web: www.msitarget.com
SIC: 3599 Machine shop, jobbing and repair

(G-5087)
MATTHEW WARREN INC
Also Called: Capital Spring
2000 Jetway Blvd (43219-1673)
PHONE..............................614 418-0250
William Hunsucker, *Prin*
EMP: 47
SALES (corp-wide): 400.43MM **Privately Held**
Web: www.mwcomponents.com
SIC: 3493 3495 Steel springs, except wire; Wire springs
PA: Matthew Warren, Inc.
3426 Tringdon Way Ste 400
Charlotte NC 28277

(G-5088)
MB RENOVATIONS & DESIGNS LLC
4449 Easton Way Ste 200 (43219-7005)
PHONE..............................614 772-6139
Marcus Bryant, *Prin*
Meagan Sparks, *Prin*
EMP: 9 **EST:** 2017
SALES (est): 706.27K **Privately Held**
SIC: 1389 Construction, repair, and dismantling services

(G-5089)
MCGILL AIRCLEAN LLC
Also Called: McGill Airclean
1777 Refugee Rd (43207-2119)
PHONE..............................614 829-1200
Paul R Hess, *Managing Member*
Jerry Childress, *
◆ **EMP:** 70 **EST:** 2004
SQ FT: 15,000
SALES (est): 14.73MM
SALES (corp-wide): 67.2MM **Privately Held**
Web: www.mcgillairclean.com
SIC: 3564 1796 Precipitators, electrostatic; Pollution control equipment installation
HQ: United Mcgill Corporation
1 Mission Park
Groveport OH 43125
614 829-1200

(G-5090)
MCGILL AIRFLOW LLC
2400 Fairwood Ave (43207-2708)
PHONE..............................614 829-1200
Ed Kromer, *Mgr*
EMP: 64
SALES (corp-wide): 67.2MM **Privately Held**
Web: www.mcgillairflow.com

SIC: 3444 Ducts, sheet metal
HQ: Mcgill Airflow Llc
1 Mission Park
Groveport OH 43125
614 829-1200

(G-5091)
MCGLENNON METAL PRODUCTS INC
940 N 20th St (43219-2423)
P.O. Box 188 (45315-0188)
PHONE..............................614 252-7114
Thomas Saldoff, *Pr*
EMP: 15 **EST:** 1988
SQ FT: 22,000
SALES (est): 2.19MM **Privately Held**
Web: www.mcglennonmetal.com
SIC: 3469 Stamping metal for the trade

(G-5092)
MCL INC
Also Called: McL Whitehall
5240 E Main St (43213-2501)
PHONE..............................614 861-6259
Jim Bell, *Mgr*
EMP: 24
SALES (corp-wide): 39.05MM **Privately Held**
Web: www.mclhomemade.com
SIC: 2051 Bakery: wholesale or wholesale/ retail combined
PA: Mcl, Inc.
2730 E 62nd St
Indianapolis IN 46220
317 257-5425

(G-5093)
MCNEIL GROUP INC
Also Called: Pinnacle Metal Products
1701 Woodland Ave (43219-1137)
PHONE..............................614 298-0300
Susan Mcneil, *Pr*
Michael Mcneil, *VP*
EMP: 32 **EST:** 1992
SQ FT: 41,000
SALES (est): 7.41MM **Privately Held**
Web: www.pinnmetalstairs.com
SIC: 3499 Furniture parts, metal

(G-5094)
MCNEIL HOLDINGS LLC
1701 Woodland Ave (43219-1137)
PHONE..............................614 298-0300
EMP: 6 **EST:** 1998
SALES (est): 743.15K **Privately Held**
Web: www.pinnmetalstairs.com
SIC: 3441 Fabricated structural metal

(G-5095)
MEDRANO USA INC (PA)
Also Called: Medrano USA
4311 Janitrol Rd Ste 500 (43228-1390)
PHONE..............................614 272-5856
Gerardo Fernandez, *CEO*
Luis Fernandez, *CFO*
Gerardo Santiago, *Sec*
EMP: 30 **EST:** 2016
SQ FT: 700
SALES (est): 11.78MM
SALES (corp-wide): 11.78MM **Privately Held**
Web: www.grupomedrano.com
SIC: 3537 Platforms, stands, tables, pallets, and similar equipment

(G-5096)
METTLER-TOLEDO LLC
Toledo Scales & Systems
6600 Huntley Rd (43229-1048)
PHONE..............................614 841-7300
Al Herold, *Mgr*

GEOGRAPHIC

EMP: 170
SQ FT: 71,000
SALES (corp-wide): 3.87B **Publicly Held**
Web: www.mt.com
SIC: 3596 Industrial scales
HQ: Mettler-Toledo, Llc
　　1900 Polaris Pkwy Fl 6
　　Columbus OH 43240
　　614 438-4511

(G-5097)
MGF SOURCING US LLC (HQ)
Also Called: MGF Sourcing
4200 Regent St Ste 205　(43219-6229)
PHONE.............................614 904-3300
Michael Yee, *CEO*
James Schwartz, *
Jennie Wilson, *
▲ **EMP:** 60 **EST:** 2011
SQ FT: 16,000
SALES (est): 54.71MM **Publicly Held**
Web: www.mgfsourcing.com
SIC: 2211 Twills, drills, denims and other
　　ribbed fabrics; cotton
PA: Sycamore Partners Management, L.P.
　　9 W 57th St Ste 3100
　　New York NY 10019

(G-5098)
MID-OHIO ELECTRIC CO
1170 Mckinley Ave　(43222-1113)
PHONE.............................614 274-8000
Cynthia Langhirt, *Pr*
Bruce A Langhirt, *
Vince Langhirt, *
EMP: 26 **EST:** 1955
SQ FT: 13,800
SALES (est): 2.04MM **Privately Held**
Web: www.mid-ohioelectric.com
SIC: 7694 5063 7629 8711　Electric motor
　　repair; Motors, electric; Circuit board repair;
　　Electrical or electronic engineering

(G-5099)
MID-STATE SALES INC (PA)
Also Called: Mid-State Sales
1101 Gahanna Pkwy　(43230-6600)
PHONE.............................614 864-1811
▲ **EMP:** 56 **EST:** 1969
SALES (est): 10.43MM
SALES (corp-wide): 10.43MM **Privately
Held**
Web: www.midstate-sales.com
SIC: 5084 3494 3492　Hydraulic systems
　　equipment and supplies; Pipe fittings; Hose
　　and tube fittings and assemblies, hydraulic/
　　pneumatic

(G-5100)
MIDWEST MOTOR SUPPLY CO (PA)
Also Called: Kimball Midwest
4800 Roberts Rd　(43228-9791)
P.O. Box 2470　(43216-2470)
PHONE.............................800 233-1294
Patrick J Mccurdy Junior, *CEO*
Patrick J Mccurdy Junior, *Pr*
Ed Mccurdy, *VP*
David Mccurdy, *VP*
Charles Mccurdy, *VP*
▲ **EMP:** 200 **EST:** 1955
SQ FT: 85,000
SALES (est): 85.6MM
SALES (corp-wide): 85.6MM **Privately
Held**
Web: www.kimballmidwest.com
SIC: 3965 3399 8742　Fasteners; Metal
　　fasteners; Materials mgmt. (purchasing,
　　handling, inventory) consultant

(G-5101)
MIDWEST STRAPPING PRODUCTS
1819 Walcutt Rd Ste 13　(43228-9149)
PHONE.............................614 527-1454
Nancy Blaski, *Pr*
David Starr, *VP*
EMP: 9 **EST:** 2000
SALES (est): 960K **Privately Held**
SIC: 3499 Strapping, metal

(G-5102)
MILATHAN WHOLESALERS
423 N Front St 237　(43215-2228)
PHONE.............................614 697-1458
EMP: 30 **EST:** 2020
SALES (est): 480.69K **Privately Held**
Web: www.milathan.com
SIC: 3613 Distribution boards, electric

(G-5103)
MILLWORK ELEMENTS LLC
6663 Huntley Rd Ste A　(43229-1033)
PHONE.............................614 905-8163
EMP: 6 **EST:** 2017
SALES (est): 897.99K **Privately Held**
Web: www.millworkelements.com
SIC: 2431 Millwork

(G-5104)
MINIMALLY INVASIVE DEVICES INC
Also Called: Mid
1275 Kinnear Rd　(43212-1180)
PHONE.............................614 484-5036
Wayne Poll, *CEO*
Caroline Crisafulli, *VP Opers*
Kenneth Jones, *CFO*
EMP: 8 **EST:** 2007
SALES (est): 1.04MM **Privately Held**
Web: www.floshield.com
SIC: 3841 Surgical and medical instruments

(G-5105)
MMF INC
Rainbow Custom Powder Coaters
1977 Mcallister Ave　(43205-1614)
PHONE.............................614 252-2522
Brian Mills, *Mgr*
EMP: 9
SALES (corp-wide): 2.32MM **Privately
Held**
Web: www.millsmetal.net
SIC: 3471 Plating of metals or formed
　　products
PA: Mmf Incorporated
　　1977 Mcallister Ave
　　Columbus OH 43205
　　614 252-0078

(G-5106)
MMF INCORPORATED (PA)
Also Called: Mills Metal Finishing
1977 Mcallister Ave　(43205-1614)
PHONE.............................614 252-0078
Brian L Mills, *Pr*
Cheryl Camp, *VP*
Foster Mills, *Dir*
Steven Mills, *Stockholder*
EMP: 11 **EST:** 1974
SQ FT: 9,400
SALES (est): 2.32MM
SALES (corp-wide): 2.32MM **Privately
Held**
Web: www.millsmetaloh.com
SIC: 3479 Coating of metals and formed
　　products

(G-5107)
MOBILE SOLUTIONS LLC
149 N Hamilton Rd　(43213-1308)
PHONE.............................614 286-3944

EMP: 10 **EST:** 2012
SQ FT: 2,500
SALES (est): 468.04K **Privately Held**
Web: www.mobilesolutions-usa.com
SIC: 3711 Cars, electric, assembly of

(G-5108)
MODE INDUSTRIES INC
3000 E Main St Ste 134　(43209-3717)
PHONE.............................614 504-8008
EMP: 8 **EST:** 2019
SALES (est): 186.41K **Privately Held**
SIC: 3999 Manufacturing industries, nec

(G-5109)
**MOMENTIVE PERFORMANCE MTLS
INC**
180 E Broad St　(43215-3707)
PHONE.............................614 986-2495
Steve Delarge, *Opers Mgr*
EMP: 1500
Web: www.momentive.com
SIC: 2869 Silicones
HQ: Momentive Performance Materials Inc.
　　2750 Balltown Rd
　　Niskayuna NY 12309

(G-5110)
MONKS COPY SHOP INC
47 E Gay St　(43215-3103)
PHONE.............................614 461-6438
Edward M Smith, *Pr*
EMP: 18 **EST:** 1980
SQ FT: 15,718
SALES (est): 2.16MM **Privately Held**
Web: www.monkscopyshop.com
SIC: 7334 2752　Photocopying and
　　duplicating services; Commercial printing,
　　lithographic

(G-5111)
MORI SHUJI
Also Called: Geodyne One
3755 Mountview Rd　(43220-4801)
PHONE.............................614 459-1296
Shuji Mori, *Owner*
EMP: 7 **EST:** 1992
SALES (est): 399.75K **Privately Held**
SIC: 1382 Oil and gas exploration services

(G-5112)
MORRISON SIGN COMPANY INC
2757 Scioto Pkwy　(43221-4658)
PHONE.............................614 276-1181
David Morrison, *Pr*
Helen Morrison, *
EMP: 27 **EST:** 1979
SQ FT: 18,000
SALES (est): 4.24MM **Privately Held**
Web: www.morrisonsigns.com
SIC: 3993 2759　Signs, not made in custom
　　sign painting shops; Screen printing

(G-5113)
**MOTHERSON YCHIYO AUTO TECH
PDT (HQ)**
Also Called: Yachiyo Manufacturing America
2285 Walcutt Rd　(43228-9575)
PHONE.............................614 876-3220
Toshihiko Ogawa, *Pr*
Poshio Yanada, *CEO*
▲ **EMP:** 83 **EST:** 1997
SALES (est): 43.2MM **Privately Held**
Web: www.yachiyo-of-america.com
SIC: 3465 3089 3714　Automotive stampings;
　　Novelties, plastics; Acceleration equipment,
　　motor vehicle
PA: Samvardhana Motherson International
　　Limited
　　Corporate Tower, 11th Floor,

Noida UP 20130

(G-5114)
MOVE EZ INC
Also Called: Moveeasy
855 Grandview Ave Ste 140　(43215-1189)
PHONE.............................844 466-8339
Venkatesh Ganapathy, *CEO*
EMP: 57 **EST:** 2014
SALES (est): 1.52MM
SALES (corp-wide): 794.2MM **Publicly
Held**
Web: www.moveeasy.com
SIC: 7372 6411 4212　Application computer
　　software; Insurance agents, brokers, and
　　service; Moving services
PA: Appfolio, Inc.
　　70 Castilian Dr
　　Santa Barbara CA 93117
　　805 364-6093

(G-5115)
MRS INDUSTRIAL INC
Also Called: M R S
2583 Harrison Rd　(43204-3511)
PHONE.............................614 308-1070
Scott J Cosgrove, *Pr*
Scott Cosgrove, *
Kenneth Michael Cosgrove, *
Ronald L Belford, *
▲ **EMP:** 24 **EST:** 1997
SQ FT: 60,000
SALES (est): 5.3MM **Privately Held**
Web: www.mrsindustrial.com
SIC: 3444 Sheet metalwork

(G-5116)
MURPHY TRACTOR & EQP CO INC
Also Called: John Deere Authorized Dealer
2121 Walcutt Rd　(43228-9575)
PHONE.............................614 876-1141
Mike Slinger, *Rgnl Mgr*
EMP: 8
Web: www.murphytractor.com
SIC: 3531 5082　Construction machinery;
　　Construction and mining machinery
HQ: Murphy Tractor & Equipment Co., Inc.
　　5375 N Deere Rd
　　Park City KS 67219
　　855 246-9124

(G-5117)
MVP PHARMACY
1931 Parsons Ave　(43207-2364)
PHONE.............................614 449-8000
EMP: 7 **EST:** 2013
SALES (est): 363.76K **Privately Held**
SIC: 2834 Pharmaceutical preparations

(G-5118)
N WASSERSTROM & SONS INC (HQ)
Also Called: Wasserstrom Marketing Division
2300 Lockbourne Rd　(43207-6111)
PHONE.............................614 228-5550
William Wasserstrom, *Pr*
John H Mc Cormick, *Sr VP*
Reid Wasserstrom, *Sec*
◆ **EMP:** 250 **EST:** 1933
SQ FT: 175,000
SALES (est): 37.15MM
SALES (corp-wide): 378.09MM **Privately
Held**
Web: www.wasserstrom.com
SIC: 3556 5046 3444　Food products
　　machinery; Restaurant equipment and
　　supplies, nec; Sheet metalwork
PA: The Wasserstrom Company
　　4500 E Broad St
　　Columbus OH 43213
　　614 228-6525

(G-5119)
N WASSERSTROM & SONS INC
Also Called: Select Seating
862 E Jenkins Ave (43207-1317)
PHONE..................................614 737-5410
Greg Pell, *Mgr*
EMP: 14
SALES (corp-wide): 378.09MM **Privately Held**
Web: www.wasserstrom.com
SIC: 2511 2531 Wood household furniture; Public building and related furniture
HQ: N. Wasserstrom & Sons, Inc.
2300 Lockbourne Rd
Columbus OH 43207
614 228-5550

(G-5120)
NATIONAL ELECTRIC COIL INC (PA)
Also Called: N E C Columbus
800 King Ave (43212-2644)
P.O. Box 370 (43216-0370)
PHONE..................................614 488-1151
Robert Barton, *CEO*
◆ EMP: 300 EST: 1994
SQ FT: 500,000
SALES (est): 76.95MM **Privately Held**
Web: www.national-electric-coil.com
SIC: 7694 Electric motor repair

(G-5121)
NATIONAL FRT VGTABLE TECH CORP
Also Called: Fresh Vegetable Technology
250 Civic Center Dr (43215-5086)
PHONE..................................740 400-4055
Daniel Cashman, *CEO*
Mitch Adams, *
Keith Stoll, *
Richard Cashman, *Stockholder*
EMP: 10 EST: 1986
SQ FT: 150,000
SALES (est): 578.35K **Privately Held**
SIC: 2037 Fruits, quick frozen and cold pack (frozen)

(G-5122)
NATIONAL SKILLED TRADES NETWRK
5950 Sharon Woods Blvd (43229-2645)
PHONE..................................614 230-2852
Howard Williams, *Ex Dir*
EMP: 10 EST: 2009
SALES (est): 216.77K **Privately Held**
Web: www.nstnetwork.org
SIC: 3423 Carpenters' hand tools, except saws: levels, chisels, etc.

(G-5123)
NELSON COMPANY
2160 Refugee Rd (43207-2841)
PHONE..................................614 444-1164
EMP: 6
SALES (corp-wide): 29.09MM **Privately Held**
Web: www.nelsoncompany.com
SIC: 2448 Pallets, wood
PA: The Nelson Company
4517 N Point Blvd
Baltimore MD 21219
410 477-3000

(G-5124)
NETWORK PRINTING & GRAPHICS
443 Crestview Rd (43202-2244)
PHONE..................................614 230-2084
Cathy Ann Dawson, *Pr*
EMP: 10 EST: 1989
SQ FT: 7,500
SALES (est): 258.17K **Privately Held**

SIC: 2752 7331 2791 2789 Offset printing; Direct mail advertising services; Typesetting ; Bookbinding and related work

(G-5125)
NEW AQUA LLC
Also Called: NEW AQUA LLC
3707 Interchange Rd (43204-1435)
PHONE..................................614 265-9000
EMP: 11
SALES (corp-wide): 35.47MM **Privately Held**
Web: www.aquasystems.com
SIC: 3589 Water filters and softeners, household type
HQ: New Aqua, Llc
7785 E Us Hwy 36
Avon IN 46123
317 272-3000

(G-5126)
NEW HORIZONS FD SOLUTIONS LLC (PA)
2300 Citygate Dr (43219-3664)
PHONE..................................614 861-3639
Trina Bediako, *CEO*
EMP: 29 EST: 2021
SALES (est): 7.91MM
SALES (corp-wide): 7.91MM **Privately Held**
Web: www.coalescencellc.com
SIC: 2099 Baking powder and soda, yeast, and other leavening agents

(G-5127)
NEWALL ELECTRONICS INC
1803 Obrien Rd (43228-3866)
PHONE..................................614 771-0213
Martha Sullivan, *Pr*
Paul Vasington, *CFO*
▲ EMP: 14 EST: 1989
SQ FT: 7,000
SALES (est): 2.22MM
SALES (corp-wide): 4.05B **Privately Held**
Web: www.newall.com
SIC: 3829 Measuring and controlling devices, nec
HQ: Custom Sensors & Technologies, Inc.
1461 Lawrence Dr
Thousand Oaks CA 91320
805 716-0322

(G-5128)
NORSE DAIRY SYSTEMS INC
1700 E 17th Ave (43219-1005)
P.O. Box 1869 (43216-1869)
PHONE..................................614 294-4931
Ralph Denisco, *Pr*
Randy Harvey, *
EMP: 201 EST: 1995
SQ FT: 850
SALES (corp-wide): 43.77B **Privately Held**
SIC: 6719 3565 3556 2671 Investment holding companies, except banks; Packaging machinery; Food products machinery; Paper; coated and laminated packaging
PA: George Weston Limited
22 St. Clair Ave E
Toronto ON M4T 2
416 922-2500

(G-5129)
NORSE DAIRY SYSTEMS LP
1740 Joyce Ave (43219-1026)
P.O. Box 1869 (43216-1869)
PHONE..................................614 294-4931
Scott Fullbright, *Pt*
◆ EMP: 340 EST: 1995
SALES (est): 9.25MM **Privately Held**
Web: www.norse.com

SIC: 3556 2052 2656 Ice cream manufacturing machinery; Cones, ice cream ; Ice cream containers: made from purchased material
HQ: Interbake Foods Llc
1740 Joyce Ave
Columbus OH 43219
614 294-4931

(G-5130)
NORTHEAST CABINET CO LLC
6063 Taylor Rd (43230-3211)
PHONE..................................614 759-0800
James P Yankle, *Prin*
EMP: 8 EST: 2006
SALES (est): 920.98K **Privately Held**
Web: www.jyanklecompany.com
SIC: 2434 Wood kitchen cabinets

(G-5131)
NORTHWOOD ENERGY CORPORATION
941 Chatham Ln Ste 100 (43221-2471)
PHONE..................................614 457-1024
Ralph W Talmage, *Pr*
Dave Haid, *VP*
Frederick H Kennedy, *Prin*
Joan S Talmage, *Prin*
EMP: 13 EST: 1983
SQ FT: 5,000
SALES (est): 2.64MM **Privately Held**
Web: www.northwoodenergy.com
SIC: 1382 Oil and gas exploration services

(G-5132)
NUCON INTERNATIONAL INC (PA)
7000 Huntley Rd (43229-1022)
P.O. Box 29151 (43229-0151)
PHONE..................................614 846-5710
J Louis Kovach, *Pr*
Joseph C Enneking, *VP*
Paul E Kovach, *Sec*
▲ EMP: 11 EST: 1972
SQ FT: 22,000
SALES (est): 15.34MM
SALES (corp-wide): 15.34MM **Privately Held**
Web: www.nucon-int.com
SIC: 5199 8711 8734 3829 Charcoal; Pollution control engineering; Pollution testing; Nuclear radiation and testing apparatus

(G-5133)
NUTS ARE GOOD INC (PA)
Also Called: Buffalo Peanuts
Busch Blvd (43229)
PHONE..................................586 619-2400
Daniel B Levy, *Pr*
EMP: 12 EST: 1989
SQ FT: 10,000
SALES (est): 718.51K **Privately Held**
Web: www.freshroastedalmondco.com
SIC: 2068 5145 Salted and roasted nuts and seeds; Nuts, salted or roasted

(G-5134)
NUVO PACKAGING LLC ✪
845 Kaderly Dr (43228-1033)
PHONE..................................216 400-9676
Ira Naroofiam, *Managing Member*
EMP: 50 EST: 2023
SALES (est): 5.07MM **Privately Held**
SIC: 2656 Sanitary food containers

(G-5135)
O E MEYER CO
5677 Chantry Dr (43232-4731)
PHONE..................................614 428-5656
EMP: 21
Web: www.oemeyer.com

SIC: 3548 Welding apparatus
PA: O. E. Meyer Co.
3303 Tiffin Ave Rte 101
Sandusky OH 44870

(G-5136)
O J C PUBLISHING CO INC
Also Called: Senior Times
2862 Johnstown Rd (43219-1793)
P.O. Box 30965 (43230-0965)
PHONE..................................614 337-2055
Stephen N Pinsky, *Pr*
EMP: 7 EST: 1989
SQ FT: 1,200
SALES (est): 164.97K **Privately Held**
Web: www.ohiojewishchronicle.com
SIC: 2711 Newspapers

(G-5137)
OBERFIELDS LLC
1165 Alum Creek Dr (43209-2719)
PHONE..................................614 252-0955
Chris Buttke, *Mgr*
EMP: 19
SALES (corp-wide): 21.04MM **Privately Held**
Web: www.oberfields.com
SIC: 3272 3271 2531 Concrete products, nec ; Concrete block and brick; Public building and related furniture
HQ: Oberfield's, Llc
528 London Rd
Delaware OH 43015
740 369-7644

(G-5138)
OCTSYS SECURITY CORP
Also Called: O S C
341 S 3rd St Ste 100-42 (43215-5463)
P.O. Box 1071 (43216-1071)
PHONE..................................614 470-4510
Vincent King, *CEO*
EMP: 9 EST: 2013
SALES (est): 408.84K **Privately Held**
SIC: 3089 3999 Identification cards, plastics; Stereographs, photographic

(G-5139)
OHIO COFFEE COLLABORATIVE LTD
Also Called: One Line Coffee
745 N High St (43215-1425)
PHONE..................................614 564-9852
Ralph Miller, *Brnch Mgr*
EMP: 15
SALES (corp-wide): 2.57MM **Privately Held**
Web: www.onelinecoffee.com
SIC: 5812 5149 5499 2095 Coffee shop; Coffee, green or roasted; Coffee; Roasted coffee
PA: Ohio Coffee Collaborative Ltd
2084 Taylor Ln
Newark OH 43055
614 289-2939

(G-5140)
OHIO DEPARTMENT TRANSPORTATION
1606 W Broad St (43223-1202)
PHONE..................................614 351-2898
EMP: 20
SIC: 3669 9621 Transportation signaling devices; Regulation, administration of transportation, State government
HQ: Ohio Department Of Transportation
1980 W Broad St
Columbus OH 43223

(G-5141)
OHIO DESIGNER CRAFTSMEN ENTPS (HQ)
Also Called: Columbus Winter Fair
1665 W 5th Ave (43212-2315)
PHONE..............................614 486-7119
Sharon Kokot, *Dir*
EMP: 12 EST: 1963
SQ FT: 2,000
SALES (est): 899.93K Privately Held
Web: www.ohiocraft.org
SIC: 5947 8741 2721 Artcraft and carvings;
Management services; Periodicals,
publishing only
PA: Ohio Designer-Craftsmen
1665 W 5th Ave
Columbus OH 43212

(G-5142)
OHIO DISTINCTIVE ENTERPRISES
Also Called: Ohio Distinctive Software
6500 Fiesta Dr (43235-5201)
PHONE..............................614 459-0453
Stanford Apseloff, *Pr*
Glen Apseloff, *VP*
Timothy M Clark, *Sec*
EMP: 9 EST: 1986
SQ FT: 12,000
SALES (est): 1.52MM Privately Held
Web:
ohiodistinctivebucket.s3-website.us-
east-2.amazonaws.com
SIC: 7372 Prepackaged software

(G-5143)
OHIO ELECTRIC MOTOR SERVICE CENTER INC
1854 S High St (43207-2373)
PHONE..............................614 444-1451
EMP: 12
SIC: 7694 5063 Electric motor repair;
Motors, electric

(G-5144)
OHIO ELECTRIC MOTOR SVC LLC (PA)
1909 E Livingston Ave (43209-2733)
P.O. Box 425 (43216)
PHONE..............................614 444-1451
EMP: 11 EST: 2011
SALES (est): 1.93MM
SALES (corp-wide): 1.93MM Privately
Held
Web:
www.ohioelectricmotorservicecenter.com
SIC: 7694 Electric motor repair

(G-5145)
OHIO FOAM CORPORATION
1513 Alum Creek Dr (43209-2712)
PHONE..............................614 252-4877
Phil Johnson, *Brnch Mgr*
EMP: 8
SALES (corp-wide): 8.08MM Privately
Held
Web: www.ohiofoam.com
SIC: 3069 3086 Foam rubber; Plastics foam
products
PA: Ohio Foam Corporation
820 Plymouth St
Bucyrus OH 44820
419 563-0399

(G-5146)
OHIO LABEL INC
5005 Transamerica Dr (43228-9381)
P.O. Box 179 (43026)
PHONE..............................614 777-0180
Stacy Graham, *CEO*
EMP: 10 EST: 1990

SQ FT: 12,000
SALES (est): 984.16K Privately Held
Web: www.ohiolabel.com
SIC: 2759 Labels and seals: printing, nsk

(G-5147)
OHIO MODEL PRODUCTS LLC
Also Called: Buddy RC
4180 Fisher Rd (43228-1024)
PHONE..............................614 808-4488
EMP: 10 EST: 2022
SALES (est): 489.21K Privately Held
Web: www.ohiomodelplanes.com
SIC: 3944 Airplane models, toy and hobby

(G-5148)
OHIO NEWS NETWORK
Also Called: Ohio News Network
770 Twin Rivers Dr (43215-1127)
PHONE..............................614 460-3700
Tom Greidorn, *Genl Mgr*
EMP: 7 EST: 1996
SALES (est): 235.68K Privately Held
Web: www.onnradio.com
SIC: 7383 2711 4841 News syndicates;
Newspapers; Cable and other pay
television services

(G-5149)
OHIO NEWSPAPER SERVICES INC
Also Called: Adohio
1335 Dublin Rd Ste 216b (43215-1000)
PHONE..............................614 486-6677
Frank Deaner, *Ex Dir*
EMP: 8 EST: 1933
SALES (est): 181.18K
SALES (corp-wide): 249.12K Privately
Held
Web: www.adohio.net
SIC: 7313 2711 Newspaper advertising
representative; Newspapers, publishing
and printing
PA: Ohio News Media Association
1335 Dublin Rd Ste 216b
Columbus OH 43215
614 486-6677

(G-5150)
OHIO NEWSPAPERS FOUNDATION
1335 Dublin Rd Ste 216b (43215-1000)
PHONE..............................614 486-6677
Al Sahafa, *Prin*
EMP: 7 EST: 2010
SALES (est): 261.06K Privately Held
SIC: 2711 Newspapers, publishing and
printing

(G-5151)
OHIO PACKING COMPANY
1306 Harmon Ave (43223-3365)
P.O. Box 30961 (43230-0961)
PHONE..............................614 445-0627
Walter Wilke Junior, *Pr*
Carla Jones, *
Edward Wilke Junior, *Sec*
James Wilke, *
EMP: 190 EST: 1907
SQ FT: 70,000
SALES (est): 9.19MM Privately Held
Web: www.ohiopacking.com
SIC: 2011 Pork products, from pork
slaughtered on site

(G-5152)
OHIO RIGHTS GROUP
1021 E Broad St (43205-1357)
PHONE..............................614 300-0529
Chad Callender, *Prin*
EMP: 9 EST: 2015
SALES (est): 205.94K Privately Held
Web: www.ohiorightsgroup.info

SIC: 2711 Newspapers, publishing and
printing

(G-5153)
OHIO STATE PLASTICS
1917 Joyce Ave (43219-1029)
PHONE..............................614 299-5618
Dwayne Margin, *Mgr*
EMP: 19 EST: 1998
SALES (est): 3.29MM
SALES (corp-wide): 17.51B Publicly Held
SIC: 2656 Food containers (liquid tight),
including milk cartons
HQ: Altium Packaging Llc
2500 Windy Ridge Pkwy Se # 1400
Atlanta GA 30339
678 742-4600

(G-5154)
OHIO STEEL INDUSTRIES INC (PA)
2575 Ferris Rd (43224-2597)
PHONE..............................614 471-4800
◆ EMP: 75 EST: 1958
SALES (est): 16.31MM
SALES (corp-wide): 16.31MM Privately
Held
Web: www.osiplastics.com
SIC: 3441 Fabricated structural metal

(G-5155)
OHIO TRAILER SUPPLY INC
Also Called: Ots
2966 Westerville Rd (43224-4563)
PHONE..............................614 471-9121
Jet Chrysler, *Pr*
EMP: 7 EST: 1980
SQ FT: 8,000
SALES (est): 453.63K Privately Held
Web: www.ohiotrailer.com
SIC: 7692 5013 Welding repair; Trailer parts
and accessories

(G-5156)
OHIO WIRE FORM & SPRING CO
2270 S High St (43207-2432)
PHONE..............................614 444-3676
P E Van Horn Junior, *Ch*
Stephen A Van Horn, *Pr*
Samuel E Van Horn, *VP*
EMP: 19 EST: 1947
SQ FT: 43,800
SALES (est): 3.18MM Privately Held
Web: www.ohiowireform.com
SIC: 3496 3495 Miscellaneous fabricated
wire products; Wire springs

(G-5157)
OHLINGER DEV & EDITORIAL CO
Also Called: Ohlinger Studios
28 W Henderson Rd (43214-2628)
PHONE..............................614 261-5360
Monica Ohlinger, *Pr*
EMP: 52 EST: 2019
SALES (est): 814.51K Privately Held
Web: www.ohlingerstudios.com
SIC: 2741 Miscellaneous publishing

(G-5158)
OHLINGER PUBLISHING SVCS INC
Also Called: Ohlinger Studios
28 W Henderson Rd (43214-2628)
PHONE..............................614 261-5360
Monica Ohlinger, *Pr*
EMP: 30 EST: 2001
SALES (est): 391.81K Privately Held
Web: www.ohlingerstudios.com
SIC: 2741 Miscellaneous publishing

(G-5159)
OLD TRAIL PRINTING COMPANY
Also Called: Old Trail Printing Co
100 Fornoff Rd (43207-2475)
PHONE..............................614 443-4852
Mary Held, *Pr*
Michael Held, *Stockholder Principal**
Dave Held, *Stockholder Principal**
Susan Horn, *Stockholder Principal**
Jeff Lampert, *
EMP: 125 EST: 1924
SQ FT: 55,000
SALES (est): 9.94MM Privately Held
Web: www.oldtrailprinting.com
SIC: 2752 2791 2789 2759 Offset printing;
Typesetting; Bookbinding and related work;
Commercial printing, nec

(G-5160)
OMETEK LLC
790 Cross Pointe Rd (43230-6685)
PHONE..............................614 861-6729
EMP: 90 EST: 1977
SALES (est): 9.43MM Privately Held
Web: www.ometek.com
SIC: 3599 Machine shop, jobbing and repair

(G-5161)
OPC POLYMERS LLC
Also Called: OPC Polymers
1920 Leonard Ave (43219-2514)
P.O. Box 369004 (43236-9004)
PHONE..............................614 253-8511
EMP: 94 EST: 1919
SALES (est): 1.6MM Privately Held
Web: www.yenkin-majestic.com
SIC: 2851 2821 2869 Paints and paint
additives; Plastics materials and resins;
Plasticizers, organic: cyclic and acyclic

(G-5162)
ORANGE BARREL MEDIA LLC
250 N Hartford Ave (43222-1100)
PHONE..............................614 294-4898
Pete Scantland, *CEO*
Adam Borchers, *
EMP: 75 EST: 2004
SALES (est): 12.72MM Privately Held
Web: www.obm.com
SIC: 3993 7312 Signs and advertising
specialties; Outdoor advertising services

(G-5163)
ORBIS RPM LLC
592 Claycraft Rd (43230-5319)
PHONE..............................419 307-8511
Chad Goodwin, *Brnch Mgr*
EMP: 8
SALES (corp-wide): 1.94B Privately Held
Web: www.orbiscorporation.com
SIC: 3081 Unsupported plastics film and
sheet
HQ: Orbis Rpm, Llc
1055 Corporate Center Dr
Oconomowoc WI 53066
262 560-5000

(G-5164)
OSI GLOBAL SOURCING LLC
2575 Ferris Rd (43224-2540)
PHONE..............................614 471-4800
Tom Martini, *Pr*
▲ EMP: 6 EST: 2008
SALES (est): 147.29K Privately Held
Web: www.ohiosteel.com
SIC: 2821 Plastics materials and resins

(G-5165)
OTC INDUSTRIAL TECHNOLOGIES (PA)

▲ = Import ▼ = Export
◆ = Import/Export

1900 Jetway Blvd (43219-1681)
PHONE...............................800 837-6827
Bill Canady, *CEO*
EMP: 11 EST: 2021
SALES (est): 34.71MM
SALES (corp-wide): 34.71MM **Privately Held**
Web: www.otcindustrial.com
SIC: 3531 Construction machinery

(G-5166)
OWENS CORNING
Also Called: 1-800-Usa-home.com
2050 Integrity Dr S (43209-2728)
PHONE...............................614 754-4098
Stephen Brooks, *Mgr*
EMP: 8
Web: www.owenscorning.com
SIC: 3296 Fiberglass insulation
PA: Owens Corning
1 Owens Corning Pkwy
Toledo OH 43659

(G-5167)
P-AMERICAS LLC
Also Called: Pepsico
1241 Gibbard Ave (43219-2438)
PHONE...............................614 253-8771
Dale Watkins, *CFO*
EMP: 25
SALES (corp-wide): 91.47B **Publicly Held**
Web: www.pepsico.com
SIC: 2086 Carbonated soft drinks, bottled
and canned
HQ: P-Americas Llc
1 Pepsi Way
Somers NY 10589
336 896-5740

(G-5168)
PACTIV LLC
2120 Westbelt Dr (43228-3820)
P.O. Box 28147 (43228-0147)
PHONE...............................614 771-5400
Joe Deal, *Opers Mgr*
EMP: 101
SALES (corp-wide): 26.11B **Publicly Held**
Web: www.pactivevergreen.com
SIC: 2631 7389 Paperboard mills;
Packaging and labeling services
HQ: Pactiv Llc
1900 W Field Ct
Lake Forest IL 60045
847 482-2000

(G-5169)
PAKRA LLC
449 E Mound St (43215-5514)
PHONE...............................614 477-6965
Rini Das, *Managing Member*
EMP: 10 EST: 2007
SQ FT: 900
SALES (est): 379.38K **Privately Held**
Web: www.pakragames.com
SIC: 7372 8331 8249 8742 Business
oriented computer software; Job training
and related services; Business training
services; Management consulting services

(G-5170)
PANACEA PRODUCTS
CORPORATION
1825 Joyce Ave (43219-1027)
PHONE...............................614 429-6320
Frank Panancea, *Brnch Mgr*
EMP: 24
SALES (corp-wide): 49.68MM **Privately Held**
Web: www.panaceaproducts.com

SIC: 3496 3423 2542 Miscellaneous
fabricated wire products; Hand and edge
tools, nec; Partitions and fixtures, except
wood
PA: Panacea Products Corporation
2711 International St
Columbus OH 43228
614 850-7000

(G-5171)
PANACEA PRODUCTS
CORPORATION (PA)
Also Called: J-Mak Industries
2711 International St (43228-4604)
PHONE...............................614 850-7000
Frank A Paniccia, *Pr*
Gregg Paniccia, *
Jim Fancelli, *
Fred Pagura, *
Louis Calderone, *
◆ EMP: 40 EST: 1967
SALES (est): 49.68MM
SALES (corp-wide): 49.68MM **Privately Held**
Web: www.panaceaproducts.com
SIC: 5051 2542 3496 Metals service centers
and offices; Partitions and fixtures, except
wood; Miscellaneous fabricated wire
products

(G-5172)
PANTRYBAG INC
769 Sullivant Ave (43222-1678)
PHONE...............................614 812-8073
Chiahanam C Ani, *CEO*
Chiahanam C Ani, *Pr*
EMP: 10 EST: 2019
SALES (est): 96.8K **Privately Held**
SIC: 2674 Shipping and shopping bags or
sacks

(G-5173)
PAPEL COUTURE
Also Called: PC
6522 Singletree Dr (43229-1119)
PHONE...............................614 848-5700
Vadim Daskal, *Owner*
Scott Vogel, *Genl Mgr*
EMP: 6 EST: 2011
SQ FT: 600
SALES (est): 304.37K
SALES (corp-wide): 1.5MM **Privately Held**
Web: www.papelcouture.com
SIC: 2760 Invitation and stationery printing
and engraving
PA: Daskal Enterprise, Llc
6522 Singletree Dr
Columbus OH 43229
614 848-5700

(G-5174)
PARKER-HANNIFIN CORPORATION
Also Called: Tube Fittings Division
3885 Gateway Blvd (43228-9723)
PHONE...............................614 279-7070
William Bowman, *Brnch Mgr*
EMP: 120
SALES (corp-wide): 19.93B **Publicly Held**
Web: www.parker.com
SIC: 3494 5074 Pipe fittings; Plumbing
fittings and supplies
PA: Parker-Hannifin Corporation
6035 Parkland Blvd
Cleveland OH 44124
216 896-3000

(G-5175)
PART 2 SCREEN PRTG DESIGN INC
935 King Ave (43212-2656)
PHONE...............................614 294-4429
Cliff Ryan, *Pr*

EMP: 6 EST: 1996
SQ FT: 5,000
SALES (est): 410K **Privately Held**
SIC: 2759 2395 Screen printing; Embroidery
products, except Schiffli machine

(G-5176)
PATH ROBOTICS INC
3950 Business Park Dr (43204-5008)
PHONE...............................330 808-2788
Andrew Lonsberry, *CEO*
EMP: 120 EST: 2018
SALES (est): 29.39MM **Privately Held**
Web: www.path-robotics.com
SIC: 3599 Custom machinery

(G-5177)
PATIO PRINTING INC
Also Called: Patio Print & Promotions
6663 Huntley Rd Ste S (43229-1040)
PHONE...............................614 785-9553
Dieter Thellman, *Pr*
Dieter Thellmann, *Pr*
Margit Thellmann, *VP*
EMP: 7 EST: 1983
SQ FT: 1,400
SALES (est): 450.2K **Privately Held**
Web: www.patioprintinginc.com
SIC: 2752 2759 Offset printing; Screen
printing

(G-5178)
PAUL PETERSON COMPANY (PA)
950 Dublin Rd (43215-1169)
P.O. Box 1510 (43216-1510)
PHONE...............................614 486-4375
Paul Peterson Junior, *Ch Bd*
Parr Peterson, *CEO*
Aaron Peterson, *Pr*
Colette Peterson, *Sec*
EMP: 13 EST: 1932
SQ FT: 2,000
SALES (est): 6.33MM
SALES (corp-wide): 6.33MM **Privately Held**
Web: www.ppco.net
SIC: 1611 1799 3669 5084 Guardrail
construction, highways; Waterproofing;
Traffic signals, electric; Safety equipment

(G-5179)
PAUL PETERSON SAFETY DIV INC
950 Dublin Rd (43215-1169)
P.O. Box 1510 (43216-1510)
PHONE...............................614 486-4375
Paul Peterson Junior, *Pr*
Parr Peterson, *
Gary Boylan, *
Colette Peterson, *
EMP: 34 EST: 1975
SQ FT: 3,800
SALES (est): 1.46MM
SALES (corp-wide): 6.33MM **Privately Held**
SIC: 3993 7359 5999 Signs, not made in
custom sign painting shops; Work zone
traffic equipment (flags, cones, barrels, etc.)
; Safety supplies and equipment
PA: The Paul Peterson Company
950 Dublin Rd
Columbus OH 43215
614 486-4375

(G-5180)
PEARSON EDUCATION INC
4350 Equity Dr (43228-4801)
PHONE...............................614 876-0371
Sheila Hickle, *Brnch Mgr*
EMP: 6
SALES (corp-wide): 4.5B **Privately Held**
Web: www.pearson.com

SIC: 2721 Periodicals
HQ: Pearson Education, Inc.
221 River St
Hoboken NJ 07030
201 236-7000

(G-5181)
PEARSON EDUCATION INC
800 N High St (43215-1430)
PHONE...............................614 841-3700
Bruce Johnson, *Mgr*
EMP: 49
SALES (corp-wide): 4.5B **Privately Held**
Web: www.pearson.com
SIC: 2721 Periodicals
HQ: Pearson Education, Inc.
221 River St
Hoboken NJ 07030
201 236-7000

(G-5182)
PEEBLES - HERZOG INC
50 Hayden Ave (43222-1019)
PHONE...............................614 279-2211
Michael B Herzog, *Pr*
Michael Lauffer, *VP*
Molly Herzog, *Sec*
EMP: 7 EST: 1975
SQ FT: 6,500
SALES (est): 489.17K **Privately Held**
Web: www.peeblesherzog.com
SIC: 3931 7699 Pipes, organ; Organ tuning
and repair

(G-5183)
PENNANT INC
Also Called: Pennant Manufacturing
401 N Front St Ste 350 (43215-2249)
PHONE...............................937 584-5411
Mike Gaby, *CEO*
Jim Tighe, *CFO*
Mike Ryan, *VP*
Kathy Rupp, *Dir Opers*
EMP: 15 EST: 1998
SALES (est): 1.32MM **Privately Held**
Web: www.pennant-us.com
SIC: 3496 Clips and fasteners, made from
purchased wire

(G-5184)
PENNY FAB LLC
Also Called: Penny Fab
1055 Gibbard Ave (43201-3052)
PHONE...............................740 967-3669
Charles Evans, *Pr*
Charles Ray Evans, *Owner*
EMP: 12 EST: 1990
SQ FT: 50,000
SALES (est): 2.59MM **Privately Held**
Web: www.pennyfab.com
SIC: 3441 3499 Fabricated structural metal
for ships; Fire- or burglary-resistive products

(G-5185)
PEPSI-COLA METRO BTLG CO INC
Also Called: Pepsico
2553 N High St (43202-2555)
PHONE...............................614 261-8193
Al Vogt, *Mgr*
EMP: 16
SALES (corp-wide): 91.47B **Publicly Held**
Web: www.pepsico.com
SIC: 2086 Carbonated soft drinks, bottled
and canned
HQ: Pepsi-Cola Metropolitan Bottling
Company, Inc.
700 Anderson Hill Rd
Purchase NY 10577
914 767-6000

(G-5186)
PERCUVISION LLC
2030 Dividend Dr (43228-3847)
PHONE.............................614 891-4800
Errol Singh Md Facs, *CEO*
Earl Singh J.d., *COO*
Rick Karr Mba, *VP Opers*
David Busick Mba M S Me, *Marketing Communication Director*
EMP: 9 EST: 2007
SQ FT: 7,500
SALES (est): 981.8K **Privately Held**
Web: www.percuvision.com
SIC: 3841 Surgical and medical instruments

(G-5187)
PERFORMANCE RESEARCH INC
Also Called: PRI Marine
3328 Westerville Rd (43224-3700)
PHONE.............................614 475-8300
Robert M Proffit, *Pr*
EMP: 7 EST: 1953
SQ FT: 10,000
SALES (est): 880.04K **Privately Held**
SIC: 3519 Marine engines

(G-5188)
PERFORMANCE RESULTS PLUS INC
Also Called: Prp
1700 Joyce Ave (43219-1026)
P.O. Box 2817 (43086)
PHONE.............................614 297-9877
Michael L Adkins, *Pr*
Monty W Walker, *Prin*
EMP: 12 EST: 2020
SQ FT: 5,200
SALES (est): 3.03MM **Privately Held**
Web: www.prph2o.com
SIC: 3829 Gauging instruments, thickness ultrasonic

(G-5189)
PERSONALITEEZ LLC
144 1/2 Brunson Ave (43203-1758)
PHONE.............................614 354-9108
EMP: 10 EST: 2020
SALES (est): 106.46K **Privately Held**
Web: www.personaliteez.com
SIC: 2396 7389 Printing and embossing on plastics fabric articles; Business services, nec

(G-5190)
PHARMAFORCE INC
960 Crupper Ave (43229-1109)
EMP: 250
SIC: 2834 Adrenal pharmaceutical preparations

(G-5191)
PHILADELPHIA INSTANTWHIP INC
2200 Cardigan Ave (43215-1092)
PHONE.............................614 488-2536
Douglas A Smith, *Pr*
G Frederick Smith, *Sec*
Thomas G Michaelides, *Treas*
Tom Willard, *Genl Mgr*
EMP: 14 EST: 1954
SALES (est): 689.53K
SALES (corp-wide): 47.63MM **Privately Held**
Web: www.instantwhip.com
SIC: 2026 5143 Whipped topping, except frozen or dry mix; Dairy products, except dried or canned
PA: Instantwhip Foods, Inc.
　　2200 Cardigan Ave
　　Columbus OH 43215
　　614 488-2536

(G-5192)
PITT PLASTICS INC (DH)
3980 Groves Rd Ste A (43232-4172)
PHONE.............................614 868-8660
Terry Callow, *Parent*
EMP: 65 EST: 1972
SQ FT: 120,000
SALES (est): 23MM **Privately Held**
Web: www.pittplastics.com
SIC: 2821 2673 Polyethylene resins; Bags: plastic, laminated, and coated
HQ: Pitt Plastics, Inc.
　　1400 Atkinson Ave
　　Pittsburg KS 66762
　　620 231-4030

(G-5193)
PJS WHOLESALE INC
2551 Westbelt Dr (43228-3826)
PHONE.............................614 402-9363
Azmi Azzam Alhamouri, *Prin*
Mahmoud T Almahmoud, *Prin*
▲ EMP: 6 EST: 2009
SALES (est): 109.74K **Privately Held**
SIC: 2253 T-shirts and tops, knit

(G-5194)
PLASKOLITE LLC (PA)
400 W Nationwide Blvd Ste 400 (43215-2394)
PHONE.............................614 294-3281
Michael Gilbert, *Pr*
Peter Lynch, *
John Szlag, *Chief Commercial Officer**
Roger Hamilton, *
◆ EMP: 238 EST: 2015
SQ FT: 508,000
SALES (est): 542.25MM
SALES (corp-wide): 542.25MM **Privately Held**
Web: www.plaskolite.com
SIC: 2821 Plastics materials and resins

(G-5195)
PLASKOLITE LLC
Also Called: Retail Display Group
400 W Nationwide Blvd Ste 400 (43215-2394)
P.O. Box 1497 (43216-1497)
PHONE.............................614 294-3281
James R Dunn, *Brnch Mgr*
EMP: 63
SALES (corp-wide): 542.25MM **Privately Held**
Web: www.plaskolite.com
SIC: 2821 3083 Acrylic resins; Laminated plastics plate and sheet
PA: Plaskolite, Llc
　　400 W Ntnwide Blvd Ste 40
　　Columbus OH 43215
　　614 294-3281

(G-5196)
PLASTICS FAMILY HOLDINGS INC
Also Called: Laird Plastics
2220 International St (43228-4630)
PHONE.............................614 272-0777
Chet Thompson, *Brnch Mgr*
EMP: 10
Web: www.lairdplastics.com
SIC: 5162 3089 Plastics materials, nec; Windows, plastics
HQ: Plastics Family Holdings, Inc.
　　5800 Cmpus Cir Dr E Ste 1
　　Irving TX 75063
　　469 299-7000

(G-5197)
PLCC2 LLC
Also Called: PLC Connections
673 N Wilson Rd (43204-1461)

PHONE.............................614 279-1796
Tadashi Miyashita, *Managing Member*
◆ EMP: 8 EST: 2014
SQ FT: 7,000
SALES (est): 1.71MM **Privately Held**
Web: www.plcconnections.com
SIC: 3678 8711 Electronic connectors; Engineering services

(G-5198)
POPS PRINTED APPAREL LLC
1758 N High St Unit 2 (43201-4422)
PHONE.............................614 372-5651
Austin Pence, *Managing Member*
EMP: 6 EST: 2014
SQ FT: 2,000
SALES (est): 513.08K **Privately Held**
Web: www.printedbypops.com
SIC: 2759 Screen printing

(G-5199)
PORCELAIN STEEL BUILDINGS COMPANY
Also Called: Psb Company
555 W Goodale St (43215-1104)
P.O. Box 1089 (43216-1089)
PHONE.............................614 228-5781
▲ EMP: 80
SIC: 3479 3444 Coating of metals and formed products; Restaurant sheet metalwork

(G-5200)
POWER DISTRIBUTORS LLC (PA)
Also Called: Central Power Systems
3700 Paragon Dr (43228-9750)
PHONE.............................614 876-3533
Matthew Finn, *Pr*
▲ EMP: 83 EST: 2012
SALES (est): 48.45MM
SALES (corp-wide): 48.45MM **Privately Held**
Web: www.powerdistributors.com
SIC: 5084 3524 Engines and parts, air-cooled; Lawn and garden equipment

(G-5201)
PPAFCO INC
1096 Ridge St (43215-1154)
PHONE.............................614 488-7259
Laura Bowman, *Pr*
EMP: 10 EST: 1978
SQ FT: 15,000
SALES (est): 1.81MM **Privately Held**
Web: www.ppafco.com
SIC: 3089 3069 5074 Fittings for pipe, plastics; Nipples, rubber; Pipes and fittings, plastic

(G-5202)
PRECISION DUCT FABRICATION LLC
182 N Yale Ave (43222-1127)
PHONE.............................614 580-9385
EMP: 10 EST: 2020
SALES (est): 1.07MM **Privately Held**
Web: www.precisionductandfab.com
SIC: 3444 Ducts, sheet metal

(G-5203)
PREISSER INC
Also Called: PIP Printing
3560 Millikin Ct Ste A (43228-9765)
P.O. Box 827 (43017-6827)
PHONE.............................614 345-0199
Gail Preisser, *Pr*
Thomas Preisser, *Sec*
EMP: 6 EST: 1974
SALES (est): 229.17K **Privately Held**
Web: www.pip.com

SIC: 2752 2791 Offset printing; Typesetting

(G-5204)
PRESSURE CONNECTIONS CORP
610 Claycraft Rd (43230-5328)
PHONE.............................614 863-6930
◆ EMP: 56 EST: 1981
SALES (est): 8.61MM **Privately Held**
Web: www.pressureconnections.com
SIC: 3498 5085 3494 3492 Tube fabricating (contract bending and shaping); Industrial supplies; Valves and pipe fittings, nec; Fluid power valves and hose fittings

(G-5205)
PRIME EQUIPMENT GROUP LLC
Also Called: Diversfied Mch Pdts Gnsvlle GA
2001 Courtright Rd (43232-4216)
PHONE.............................614 253-8590
Joseph Gasbarro, *Pr*
David Kreim, *CFO*
Nick Gasbarro, *
◆ EMP: 100 EST: 1986
SALES (est): 36.64MM **Publicly Held**
Web: www.jbtc.com
SIC: 3556 Poultry processing machinery
PA: Jbt Marel Corporation
　　70 W Madison St Ste 4400
　　Chicago IL 60602

(G-5206)
PRINT SYNDICATE INC
2282 Westbrooke Dr (43228-9416)
PHONE.............................617 290-9550
James Keller, *COO*
EMP: 19 EST: 2014
SALES (est): 508.13K **Privately Held**
Web: www.printsyndicate.com
SIC: 2752 Commercial printing, lithographic

(G-5207)
PRINTED IMAGE
Also Called: The Printed Image
41 S Grant Ave (43215-3979)
PHONE.............................614 221-1412
Cathleen Siech, *Pr*
Vicki Hamer, *VP*
EMP: 10 EST: 1998
SALES (est): 392.05K **Privately Held**
Web: www.printedimage.com
SIC: 2752 2791 2789 Offset printing; Typesetting; Bookbinding and related work

(G-5208)
PRO TIRE INC
61 N Brice Rd (43213-1580)
PHONE.............................614 864-8662
Thomas Geiger, *Pr*
Thomas Geiger Senior, *Sec*
EMP: 10 EST: 1997
SQ FT: 40,000
SALES (est): 250.41K **Privately Held**
Web: www.tirepros.com
SIC: 7534 5014 Tire retreading and repair shops; Automobile tires and tubes

(G-5209)
PROFILE IMAGING COLUMBUS LLC
Also Called: Profile Discovery
815 Grandview Ave Ste 650 (43215-1893)
PHONE.............................614 301-3444
Andrew Keck, *Prin*
Larry Kotterman, *Pr*
EMP: 12 EST: 2005
SALES (est): 1.7MM **Privately Held**
Web: www.profilediscovery.com
SIC: 7372 Prepackaged software

(G-5210)
PROFORM GROUP INC
1715 Georgesville Rd (43228-3619)
PHONE...............................614 332-9654
Joe Vannata, *Brnch Mgr*
EMP: 15
SALES (corp-wide): 3MM **Privately Held**
Web: www.proformtrailers.com
SIC: 3713 Truck bodies (motor vehicles)
PA: Proform Group, Inc.
76138 Highway 69
Wagoner OK 74467
918 682-8666

(G-5211)
PROGRESS RAIL SERVICES CORP
2351 Westbelt Dr (43228-3823)
PHONE...............................614 850-1730
David Heatter, *Brnch Mgr*
EMP: 18
SALES (corp-wide): 64.81B **Publicly Held**
Web: www.progressrailstore.com
SIC: 3743 Railroad equipment
HQ: Progress Rail Services Corporation
1600 Progress Dr
Albertville AL 35950
800 476-8769

(G-5212)
PROVIDENCE REES INC
2111 Builders Pl (43204-4886)
P.O. Box 12535 (43212-0535)
PHONE...............................614 833-6231
Leo Steger, *Sec*
Billy Parsley, *
Lee Nichols, *
EMP: 6 **EST:** 1982
SQ FT: 36,000
SALES (est): 477.99K **Privately Held**
SIC: 3496 8711 Wire winding; Engineering services

(G-5213)
PUBLISHING GROUP LTD
781 Northwest Blvd Ste 202 (43212-3874)
PHONE...............................614 572-1240
Chuck Steie, *CEO*
Dave Prosser, *Pr*
Kathy Gillis, *VP Opers*
Chuck Stein, *CEO*
EMP: 10 **EST:** 1990
SALES (est): 962.88K **Privately Held**
Web: www.cityscenecolumbus.com
SIC: 2721 7389 2741 5199 Magazines: publishing and printing; Trade show arrangement; Art copy: publishing and printing; Advertising specialties

(G-5214)
PURPLE ORCHID BOUTIQUE LLC
1535 Cunard Rd (43227-3279)
PHONE...............................614 554-7686
EMP: 7 **EST:** 2020
SALES (est): 60K **Privately Held**
SIC: 2335 Women's, junior's, and misses' dresses

(G-5215)
PYRAMID INDUSTRIES LLC
327 Briarwood Dr (43213-2055)
PHONE...............................614 783-1543
Eric Joyner, *Prin*
EMP: 10 **EST:** 2017
SALES (est): 120.89K **Privately Held**
SIC: 3999 Manufacturing industries, nec

(G-5216)
Q T COLUMBUS LLC
1330 Stimmel Rd (43223-2917)
PHONE...............................800 758-2410
EMP: 6 **EST:** 2005
SALES (est): 231.05K **Privately Held**
SIC: 7532 5531 3713 Body shop, trucks; Automotive tires; Utility truck bodies
PA: Q.T. Equipment Company
151 W Dartmore Ave
Akron OH 44301

(G-5217)
QAF TECHNOLOGIES INC
1212 E Dublin Granville Rd Ste 105 (43229-3302)
PHONE...............................440 941-4348
Athar Ashraf, *Pr*
Aila Ashraf, *
EMP: 25 **EST:** 2012
SALES (est): 1.98MM **Privately Held**
Web: www.qaftech.com
SIC: 3621 Power generators

(G-5218)
QUALITY BAKERY COMPANY INC
Also Called: Mountain Top Frozen Pies Div
50 N Glenwood Ave (43222-1206)
P.O. Box 453 (43216-0453)
PHONE...............................614 224-1424
Jeff Waller, *Mgr*
EMP: 135
SQ FT: 32,836
SALES (corp-wide): 1.87B **Publicly Held**
SIC: 2051 Bread, cake, and related products
HQ: The Quality Bakery Company Inc
380 Polaris Pkwy Ste 400
Westerville OH 43082
614 846-2232

(G-5219)
QUANTUM SOLUTIONS GROUP
1555 Bethel Rd (43220-2003)
PHONE...............................614 442-0664
EMP: 6 **EST:** 2019
SALES (est): 289.93K **Privately Held**
Web: www.quantum-health.com
SIC: 3572 Computer storage devices

(G-5220)
QUIKRETE COMPANIES LLC
6225 Huntley Rd (43229-1005)
PHONE...............................614 885-4406
Robert Miller, *Brnch Mgr*
EMP: 51
SQ FT: 10,000
Web: www.quikrete.com
SIC: 3272 3241 2899 Dry mixture concrete; Cement, hydraulic; Chemical preparations, nec
HQ: The Quikrete Companies Llc
5 Concourse Pkwy Ste 1900
Atlanta GA 30328
404 634-9100

(G-5221)
R & J BARDON INC
4676 Larwell Dr (43220-3621)
PHONE...............................614 457-5500
Chris Swearingen, *Pr*
Leslie Swearingen, *VP*
EMP: 9 **EST:** 1979
SQ FT: 3,000
SALES (est): 358.74K **Privately Held**
Web: www.rjbardon.com
SIC: 2752 Offset printing

(G-5222)
R & S MONITIONS INC
181 Rosslyn Ave (43214-1474)
PHONE...............................614 846-0597
Ron Herman, *Pr*
Sherry Herman, *VP*
EMP: 6 **EST:** 1986
SALES (est): 169.06K **Privately Held**
SIC: 3482 5941 Small arms ammunition; Firearms

(G-5223)
RAMSEY STAIRS & WDWKG LLC
4134 Little Pine Dr (43230-1166)
PHONE...............................614 694-2101
Robert Ramsey, *Pr*
EMP: 6 **EST:** 2020
SALES (est): 176.15K **Privately Held**
Web: www.ramseystairs.com
SIC: 2431 Millwork

(G-5224)
RAPID MR INTERNATIONAL LLC
1500 Lake Shore Dr Ste 310 (43204-3936)
PHONE...............................614 486-6300
EMP: 7 **EST:** 2006
SALES (est): 1.76MM **Privately Held**
Web: www.rapidmri.com
SIC: 3677 Electronic coils and transformers

(G-5225)
RAYMAR HOLDINGS CORPORATION
3700 Lockbourne Rd (43207-5133)
PHONE...............................614 497-3033
Charles Marcum, *Pr*
Mike Marcum, *
EMP: 50 **EST:** 1972
SQ FT: 29,000
SALES (est): 22.1MM **Privately Held**
Web: www.cardinalcontainer.com
SIC: 2653 Boxes, corrugated: made from purchased materials
HQ: Stronghaven, Incorporated
2727 Paces Ferry Rd Se
Atlanta GA 30336
678 235-2713

(G-5226)
RED BARAKUDA LLC
4439 Shoupmill Dr (43230-1489)
PHONE...............................614 596-5432
EMP: 7 **EST:** 2009
SALES (est): 244.83K **Privately Held**
SIC: 3949 7389 Flies, fishing: artificial; Business services, nec

(G-5227)
RESILIENT HOLDINGS INC
Also Called: Magnum Press
6155 Huntley Rd Ste F (43229-1096)
PHONE...............................614 847-5600
David G Umbreit, *Prin*
Douglas J Conley, *Prin*
EMP: 10 **EST:** 1988
SALES (est): 490.61K **Privately Held**
Web: www.magnum-press.com
SIC: 2752 Offset printing

(G-5228)
RESPIRONICS NOVAMETRIX LLC
9570 Logistics Ct (43217-7500)
PHONE...............................800 345-6443
EMP: 1919
SALES (corp-wide): 18.51B **Privately Held**
SIC: 3841 3845 Surgical and medical instruments; Electromedical equipment
HQ: Respironics Novametrix, Llc
3000 Minuteman Rd
Andover MA 01810
724 882-4120

(G-5229)
RICKLY HYDROLOGICAL CO
1700 Joyce Ave (43219-1026)
P.O. Box 2817 (43086-2817)
PHONE...............................614 297-9877
Michael Rickly, *Owner*
EMP: 24 **EST:** 1925

SALES (est): 2.31MM **Privately Held**
Web: www.prph2o.com
SIC: 3823 Industrial process measurement equipment

(G-5230)
RIMROCK CORPORATION
1700 Jetway Blvd (43219-1675)
PHONE...............................614 471-5926
▲ **EMP:** 50
Web: www.rimrockcorp.com
SIC: 3563 3569 3443 3541 Spraying outfits: metals, paints, and chemicals (compressor); Robots, assembly line: industrial and commercial; Ladles, metal plate; Machine tools, metal cutting type

(G-5231)
RIMROCK HOLDINGS CORPORATION
1700 Jetway Blvd (43219-1675)
PHONE...............................614 471-5926
Tom Dejong, *Pr*
Tom Dejong, *Pr*
EMP: 150 **EST:** 1999
SALES (est): 17.48MM
SALES (corp-wide): 4.01B **Publicly Held**
Web: www.rimrockcorp.com
SIC: 3563 3569 3443 3541 Spraying outfits: metals, paints, and chemicals (compressor); Robots, assembly line: industrial and commercial; Ladles, metal plate; Machine tools, metal cutting type
PA: Lincoln Electric Holdings, Inc.
22801 St Clair Ave
Cleveland OH 44117
216 481-8100

(G-5232)
RNM HOLDINGS INC
2350 Refugee Park (43207-2173)
PHONE...............................614 444-5556
Matt Milton, *Pr*
EMP: 15
Web: www.crane1.com
SIC: 7353 5084 3536 Cranes and aerial lift equipment, rental or leasing; Cranes, industrial; Cranes, overhead traveling
PA: Rnm Holdings, Inc.
550 Conover Dr
Franklin OH 45005

(G-5233)
ROACH STUDIOS LLC
Also Called: Ctc / Roach Studios
441 E Hudson St (43202-2704)
PHONE...............................614 725-1405
EMP: 10 **EST:** 2011
SALES (est): 1.57MM **Privately Held**
Web: www.roach-studios.com
SIC: 2396 2211 Screen printing on fabric articles; Apparel and outerwear fabrics, cotton

(G-5234)
ROADSAFE TRAFFIC SYSTEMS INC
1350 Stimmel Rd (43223-2917)
PHONE...............................614 274-9782
Steve Fisher, *Mgr*
EMP: 6
Web: www.roadsafetraffic.com
SIC: 3531 Construction machinery
PA: Roadsafe Traffic Systems, Inc.
8750 W Bryn Mawr Ave Ste
Chicago IL 60631

(G-5235)
ROSATIS WINDOW CO LLC
Also Called: Rosati Windows
4200 Roberts Rd (43228-9663)
PHONE...............................614 777-4806

G
E
O
G
R
A
P
H
I
C

EMP: 70 **EST:** 2000
SALES (est): 7.57MM **Privately Held**
Web: www.rosatiwindows.com
SIC: 3442 5211 Window and door frames; Windows, storm: wood or metal

(G-5236)
ROY RETRAC INCORPORATED
Also Called: Phyllis Ann's
100 E Campus View Blvd Ste 250
(43235-4682)
PHONE..............................740 564-5552
Katherine Carter, *CEO*
EMP: 6 **EST:** 2020
SALES (est): 700K **Privately Held**
SIC: 2099 Food preparations, nec

(G-5237)
RR DONNELLEY & SONS COMPANY
Also Called: Bowne of Columbus
41 S High St Ste 3750 (43215-6161)
PHONE..............................614 221-8385
FAX: 614 221-8427
EMP: 8
SALES (corp-wide): 6.9B **Publicly Held**
SIC: 2791 Typesetting
PA: R. R. Donnelley & Sons Company
35 W Wacker Dr Ste 3650
Chicago IL 60606
312 326-8000

(G-5238)
RUSSELL GROUP UNITED LLC
Also Called: Trg United
1250 Arthur E Adams Dr Ste 205
(43221-3560)
P.O. Box 1087 (43054-1087)
PHONE..............................614 353-6853
George Nelson, *CEO*
EMP: 10 **EST:** 2013
SALES (est): 1.73MM **Privately Held**
Web: www.trgunited.com
SIC: 3679 8712 8742 8748 Harness assemblies, for electronic use: wire or cable ; Architectural engineering; Management consulting services; Business consulting, nec

(G-5239)
RV MOBILE POWER LLC (PA)
Also Called: Rvmp
830 Kinnear Rd (43212-1442)
PHONE..............................855 427-7978
James Conroy Ii, *CEO*
EMP: 23 **EST:** 2018
SQ FT: 39,413
SALES (est): 21.8MM
SALES (corp-wide): 21.8MM **Privately Held**
Web: www.rvmp.co
SIC: 5063 3621 3674 3639 Generators; Generators and sets, electric; Solar cells; Hot water heaters, household

(G-5240)
S BECKMAN PRINT GRPHIC SLTONS
Also Called: Beckman Xmo
376 Morrison Rd Ste D (43213-1447)
PHONE..............................614 864-2232
Tracy Beckman, *Pr*
EMP: 6 **EST:** 1979
SQ FT: 4,100
SALES (est): 451.54K **Privately Held**
SIC: 2752 Offset printing

(G-5241)
S&S SIGN SERVICE
485 Ternstedt Ln (43228-2128)
PHONE..............................614 279-9722
Robert Sherry, *CEO*
EMP: 6 **EST:** 2005

SALES (est): 384.6K **Privately Held**
SIC: 3993 Signs and advertising specialties

(G-5242)
SAFECOR HEALTH LLC (PA)
Also Called: R S C
4060 Business Park Dr Ste B (43204-5047)
PHONE..............................800 447-1006
Mark Saxon, *CEO*
Gary Binkoski, *CFO*
Steve Fischbach, *Ex VP*
Ryan O'dell, *Prin*
EMP: 52 **EST:** 2008
SALES (est): 32.74MM **Privately Held**
Web: www.safecorhealth.com
SIC: 2834 Pharmaceutical preparations

(G-5243)
SAFECOR HEALTH LLC
4000 Business Park Dr (43204-5023)
PHONE..............................614 351-6117
EMP: 9
Web: www.safecorhealth.com
SIC: 7389 2834 Packaging and labeling services; Pharmaceutical preparations
PA: Safecor Health, Llc
4060 Business Pk Dr Ste B
Columbus OH 43204

(G-5244)
SAFELITE GROUP INC (DH)
Also Called: Safelite Autoglass
7400 Safelite Way (43235-5086)
P.O. Box 182827 (43218-2827)
PHONE..............................614 210-9000
Renee Cacchillo, *Pr*
Douglas Herron, *
Tim Spencer, *
Dino Lano, *
Natalie Crede, *
◆ **EMP:** 1000 **EST:** 1947
SALES (est): 1.38B
SALES (corp-wide): 452.95K **Privately Held**
Web: www.safelite.com
SIC: 7536 3231 6411 Automotive glass replacement shops; Windshields, glass: made from purchased glass; Insurance claim processing, except medical
HQ: Belron Group Sca
Boulevard Prince Henri 9b
Luxembourg 1724
27478860

(G-5245)
SALEM MANUFACTURING & SLS INC
171 N Hamilton Rd (43213-1300)
PHONE..............................614 572-4242
W Thomas Goble, *Pr*
EMP: 6 **EST:** 1978
SQ FT: 5,000
SALES (est): 703.47K **Privately Held**
SIC: 3599 Machine shop, jobbing and repair

(G-5246)
SAMMY S AUTO DETAIL
3514 Cleveland Ave (43224-2908)
PHONE..............................614 263-2728
Sam Cavin, *CEO*
EMP: 10 **EST:** 2003
SALES (est): 531.44K **Privately Held**
Web: www.sammysautospa.com
SIC: 3589 7538 Car washing machinery; General automotive repair shops

(G-5247)
SAMSON
772 N High St Ste 101 (43215-1457)
PHONE..............................614 504-8038
Nicholas Dwane Starns, *Prin*
EMP: 6 **EST:** 2015

SALES (est): 1.34MM **Privately Held**
Web: www.samsonmensemporium.com
SIC: 2326 Men's and boy's work clothing

(G-5248)
SANDVIK INC
Also Called: Sandvik Hyperion
6325 Huntley Rd (43229-1007)
PHONE..............................614 438-6579
EMP: 211
SALES (corp-wide): 12.03B **Privately Held**
Web: www.home.sandvik
SIC: 3316 Strip, steel, cold-rolled, nec: from purchased hot-rolled,
HQ: Sandvik, Inc.
1483 Dogwood Way
Mebane NC 27302
919 563-5008

(G-5249)
SAREPTA THERAPEUTICS INC
4201 Easton Cmns (43219-6510)
PHONE..............................380 324-3973
EMP: 99
SALES (corp-wide): 1.9B **Publicly Held**
Web: www.sarepta.com
SIC: 2834 Pharmaceutical preparations
PA: Sarepta Therapeutics, Inc.
215 1st St Ste 415
Cambridge MA 02142
617 274-4000

(G-5250)
SAVKO PLASTIC PIPE & FITTINGS
Also Called: Bath & Brass Emporium The
683 E Lincoln Ave (43229-5021)
PHONE..............................614 885-8420
Chuck Savko, *Pr*
Andrew C Puskas, *Pr*
Lindo Spinosi, *VP*
EMP: 13 **EST:** 1967
SQ FT: 9,000
SALES (est): 3.01MM **Privately Held**
Web: www.savko.com
SIC: 3084 5719 5074 Plastics pipe; Bath accessories; Plumbing and hydronic heating supplies

(G-5251)
SAWMILL ROAD MANAGEMENT CO LLC (PA)
370 S 5th St (43215-5433)
PHONE..............................937 342-9071
Judy Ross, *Managing Member*
EMP: 30 **EST:** 1996
SALES (est): 1.94MM
SALES (corp-wide): 1.94MM **Privately Held**
Web: www.sawmillroadmgt.com
SIC: 6531 2421 Buying agent, real estate; Sawmills and planing mills, general

(G-5252)
SCAREFACTORY INC
350 Mccormick Blvd # C (43213-1550)
PHONE..............................614 565-3590
David Fachman, *Pr*
EMP: 15 **EST:** 1993
SQ FT: 38,000
SALES (est): 1.66MM **Privately Held**
Web: www.scarefactory.com
SIC: 3999 Theatrical scenery

(G-5253)
SCHODORF TRUCK BODY & EQP CO
885 Harmon Ave (43223-2411)
P.O. Box 23322 (43223-0322)
PHONE..............................614 228-6793
Joe Schodorf, *Pr*
Paul F Schodorf, *
EMP: 18 **EST:** 1882

SQ FT: 52,000
SALES (est): 3.4MM **Privately Held**
Web: www.schodorftruck.com
SIC: 5012 3713 3211 Truck bodies; Truck bodies (motor vehicles); Flat glass

(G-5254)
SCHOOL PRIDE LIMITED
3511 Johnny Appleseed Ct (43231-4985)
PHONE..............................614 568-0697
Daren Brown, *Pr*
Janet Brown, *
EMP: 19 **EST:** 2000
SALES (est): 1.89MM **Privately Held**
Web: www.schoolpride.com
SIC: 2399 Banners, pennants, and flags

(G-5255)
SCI ENGINEERED MATERIALS INC
Also Called: SCI
2839 Charter St (43228-4607)
PHONE..............................614 486-0261
Jeremiah R Young, *Pr*
Laura F Shunk, *Ch Bd*
Gerald S Blaskie, *CAO*
EMP: 23 **EST:** 1987
SQ FT: 32,000
SALES (est): 22.87MM **Privately Held**
Web: www.sciengineeredmaterials.com
SIC: 3674 Semiconductors and related devices

(G-5256)
SCIOTO FLEET SERVICES LLC
659 Marion Rd (43207-2552)
PHONE..............................614 749-2318
Michael Afaghi, *Managing Member*
EMP: 6 **EST:** 2021
SALES (est): 28.25K **Privately Held**
SIC: 2899 Fluxes: brazing, soldering, galvanizing, and welding

(G-5257)
SCORECARDS UNLIMITED LLC
Also Called: Golf Dsgn Screcards Unlimited
1820 W Dublin Granville Rd (43085-3461)
PHONE..............................614 885-0796
Paul Filing, *Managing Member*
EMP: 8 **EST:** 1976
SALES (est): 427.45K **Privately Held**
Web: www.scorecardsunlimited.net
SIC: 2752 Offset printing

(G-5258)
SCRIPTEL CORPORATION
2222 Dividend Dr (43228-3808)
PHONE..............................877 848-6824
John Powers, *CEO*
Kristal Scott, *Mgr*
▲ **EMP:** 17 **EST:** 2001
SALES (est): 7.62MM **Privately Held**
Web: www.scriptel.com
SIC: 3577 Computer peripheral equipment, nec
PA: Sutisoft, Inc.
333 Camarillo Ter Ste 2
Sunnyvale CA 94085

(G-5259)
SEEKIRK INC
2420 Scioto Harper Dr (43204-3480)
PHONE..............................614 278-9200
Douglas Seeley, *CEO*
Pamela Seeley, *Treas*
EMP: 14 **EST:** 1982
SQ FT: 11,000
SALES (est): 856.78K **Privately Held**
Web: www.seekirk.com
SIC: 3823 Annunciators, relay and solid state types

(G-5260)
SELECTEON CORPORATION
2041 Arlingate Ln (43228-4113)
PHONE..................................614 710-1132
Thomas J Ward, *Pr*
EMP: 26 EST: 2004
SQ FT: 20,000
SALES (est): 5.65MM Privately Held
Web: www.selecteon.com
SIC: 3599 Machine shop, jobbing and repair

(G-5261)
SENTEK CORPORATION
1300 Memory Ln N (43209-2736)
PHONE..................................614 586-1123
Niklas Almstedt, *Pr*
Ann Almstedt, *VP*
EMP: 7 EST: 1999
SQ FT: 9,000
SALES (est): 2.6MM Privately Held
Web: www.sentekcorp.com
SIC: 3547 8748 Ferrous and nonferrous mill
    equipment, auxiliary; Systems analysis and
    engineering consulting services

(G-5262)
**SERMONIX PHARMACEUTICALS
INC**
250 E Broad St Ste 250 (43215-3778)
PHONE..................................614 864-4919
Miriam Portman, *CEO*
David Portman, *CEO*
Miriam Portman, *COO*
EMP: 10 EST: 2019
SALES (est): 1.76MM Privately Held
Web: www.sermonixpharma.com
SIC: 2834 Pills, pharmaceutical

(G-5263)
SHOEMAKER ELECTRIC COMPANY
Also Called: Shoemaker Industrial Solutions
831 Bonham Ave (43211-2999)
PHONE..................................614 294-5626
Fred N Kletrovets, *Pr*
Betty Kletrovets, *
Teri Richardson, *
▲ EMP: 29 EST: 1935
SQ FT: 16,000
SALES (est): 4.53MM Privately Held
Web: www.shoemakerindustrial.com
SIC: 7694 5063 Electric motor repair;
    Motors, electric

(G-5264)
SHOUT OUT LOUD PRINTS
809 Phillipi Rd (43228-1041)
PHONE..................................614 432-8990
EMP: 8 EST: 2010
SALES (est): 209.74K Privately Held
Web: www.shoutoutloudprints.com
SIC: 2752 Commercial printing, lithographic

(G-5265)
SIGNAL INTERACTIVE
401 W Town St # B (43215-4034)
PHONE..................................614 360-3938
EMP: 14 EST: 2017
SALES (est): 245.99K Privately Held
Web: www.signal-interactive.com
SIC: 7372 Application computer software

(G-5266)
SIGNATURE CABINETRY INC
1285 Alum Creek Dr (43209-2721)
PHONE..................................614 252-2227
Jack E Mc Vey, *Pr*
EMP: 15 EST: 1993
SALES (est): 5.08MM Privately Held
Web: www.signaturecabinetryinc.com

SIC: 2434 Wood kitchen cabinets

(G-5267)
SIGNATURE FLEXIBLE PACKG LLC
2901 E 4th Ave (43219-2896)
PHONE..................................614 252-2121
Adrian Backer, *Brnch Mgr*
EMP: 16
SALES (corp-wide): 25MM Privately Held
Web: www.dazpak.com
SIC: 2891 2673 Adhesives and sealants;
    Bags: plastic, laminated, and coated
PA: Signature Flexible Packaging, Llc
    19310 San Jose Ave
    City Of Industry CA 91748
    909 598-7844

(G-5268)
SIGNCOM INCORPORATED
527 W Rich St (43215-4903)
PHONE..................................614 228-9999
Jim Hartley, *Pr*
EMP: 12 EST: 1982
SALES (est): 2.5MM Privately Held
Web: www.signcominc.com
SIC: 3993 Neon signs

(G-5269)
SIGNME LLC
Also Called: Binkley, Geoffrey
39 E Gay St (43215-3103)
PHONE..................................614 221-7803
Geoffrey M Binkley, *Prin*
EMP: 7 EST: 2006
SALES (est): 160K Privately Held
SIC: 2399 Fabricated textile products, nec

(G-5270)
SIMPLE TIMES LLC
750 Cross Pointe Rd Ste M (43230-6692)
P.O. Box 639 (43004-0639)
PHONE..................................614 504-3551
EMP: 9 EST: 2018
SALES (est): 2.08MM Privately Held
Web: www.simpletimesmixers.com
SIC: 2085 Cordials and premixed alcoholic
    cocktails

(G-5271)
**SIMPSON STRONG-TIE COMPANY
INC**
2600 International St (43228-4617)
PHONE   614 876-8060
Dave Williams, *Brnch Mgr*
EMP: 253
SALES (corp-wide): 2.23B Publicly Held
Web: www.strongtie.com
SIC: 5082 3643 3452 Construction and
    mining machinery; Current-carrying wiring
    services; Bolts, nuts, rivets, and washers
HQ: Simpson Strong-Tie Company Inc.
    5956 W Las Positos Blvd
    Pleasanton CA 94588
    925 560-9000

(G-5272)
SIRAJ RECOVERY LLC
4088 Seigman Ave (43213-2324)
PHONE..................................614 893-3507
EMP: 6
SALES (est): 226.5K Privately Held
SIC: 3799 7389 Towing bars and systems;
    Business Activities at Non-Commercial Site

(G-5273)
SIRIUS STEEL SERVICES INC
1985 Henderson Rd Ste 2211
(43220-2401)
PHONE..................................937 797-3975
Sam Wilson, *Pr*

EMP: 10 EST: 2020
SALES (est): 385.88K Privately Held
Web: www.siriussteelservices.com
SIC: 3441 Building components, structural
    steel

(G-5274)
SOLIDSTATE CONTROLS LLC (HQ)
Also Called: Ametek Solidstate Controls
875 Dearborn Dr (43085-1596)
PHONE..................................614 846-7500
▲ EMP: 160 EST: 1962
SALES (est): 23.74MM
SALES (corp-wide): 6.94B Publicly Held
Web: www.solidstatecontrolsinc.com
SIC: 3629 Power conversion units, a.c. to
    d.c.: static-electric
PA: Ametek, Inc.
    1100 Cassatt Rd
    Berwyn PA 19312
    610 647-2121

(G-5275)
**SOLSTICE SLEEP PRODUCTS INC
(PA)**
Also Called: Bel-Air Mattress Company
3720 W Broad St (43228-1443)
PHONE..................................614 279-8850
Dennis Straily, *Pr*
◆ EMP: 30 EST: 2009
SALES (est): 25.65MM
SALES (corp-wide): 25.65MM Privately
    Held
Web: www.jamisonbedding.com
SIC: 2515 Mattresses and bedsprings

(G-5276)
SONOCO PRODUCTS COMPANY
444 Mccormick Blvd (43213-1525)
PHONE..................................614 759-8470
Greg Ickes, *Prin*
EMP: 24
SALES (corp-wide): 5.31B Publicly Held
Web: www.sonoco.com
SIC: 2631 2671 2653 2655 Paperboard mills
    ; Paper; coated and laminated packaging;
    Corrugated and solid fiber boxes; Fiber
    cans, drums, and similar products
PA: Sonoco Products Company
    1 N 2nd St
    Hartsville SC 29550
    843 383-7000

(G-5277)
SOONDOOK LLC
6344 Nicholas Dr (43235-5206)
PHONE..................................614 389-5757
EMP: 20 EST: 2018
SALES (est): 975.16K Privately Held
Web: www.soondook.net
SIC: 2752 Commercial printing, lithographic

(G-5278)
SPECIAL DESIGN PRODUCTS INC
520 Industrial Mile Rd (43228-2413)
P.O. Box 28126 (43228)
PHONE..................................614 272-6700
Nancy Evanichko, *CEO*
Nancy Evanichko, *Pr*
Stan Evanichko, *
Suzette King, *Stockholder*
EMP: 32 EST: 1990
SALES (est): 6.33MM Privately Held
Web: www.sdpfab.com
SIC: 3086 Packaging and shipping
    materials, foamed plastics

(G-5279)
SPECIALTY NAMEPLATE CORP
4670 Groves Rd (43232-4164)
PHONE..................................614 444-6876

Frank Schreck, *Genl Mgr*
Denise Crawford, *Sec*
EMP: 14 EST: 1960
SQ FT: 7,600
SALES (est): 932.88K Privately Held
Web: www.specialty-printing.com
SIC: 2759 Screen printing

(G-5280)
SPECIALTY PRINTING AND PROC
4670 Groves Rd (43232-4164)
PHONE..................................614 322-9035
Frank Schreck, *Owner*
EMP: 17 EST: 2000
SALES (est): 2.04MM Privately Held
Web: www.specialty-printing.com
SIC: 2759 Screen printing

(G-5281)
SPECIALTY SVCS CABINETRY INC
1253 Essex Ave (43201-2927)
PHONE..................................614 421-1599
Michael Melton, *Pr*
Joann Melton, *Sec*
EMP: 8 EST: 1985
SALES (est): 557.27K Privately Held
Web: www.specialty-services.net
SIC: 2521 2511 Cabinets, office: wood;
    Wood household furniture

(G-5282)
SPECIALTY TECHNOLOGY & RES
Also Called: Star
1150 Milepost Dr (43228-9388)
PHONE..................................614 870-0744
Girish Dubey, *Pr*
▼ EMP: 6 EST: 1986
SQ FT: 4,500
SALES (est): 1.69MM Privately Held
Web: www.starseal.com
SIC: 2951 8731 Paving mixtures;
    Commercial physical research

(G-5283)
SPECTRUM NEWS OHIO
580 N 4th St Ste 350 (43215-2159)
PHONE..................................614 384-2640
EMP: 14 EST: 2019
SALES (est): 228.06K Privately Held
Web: www.ohiotavernnews.com
SIC: 2711 Newspapers, publishing and
    printing

(G-5284)
SPIRIT AVIONICS LTD (PA)
Also Called: Spirit Aeronautics
465 Waterbury Ct Ste C (43230-5312)
PHONE..................................614 237-4271
Tony Bailey, *Pr*
EMP: 15 EST: 2000
SALES (est): 3.72MM Privately Held
Web: www.spiritaeronautics.com
SIC: 7629 4581 2396 3629 Aircraft electrical
    equipment repair; Aircraft servicing and
    repairing; Automotive trimmings, fabric;
    Electronic generation equipment

(G-5285)
SPLENDID LLC
1415 E Dublin Granville Rd Ste 219
(43229-3356)
P.O. Box 141528 (43214-6528)
PHONE..................................614 396-6481
Shurki Mire, *Managing Member*
Moe Lee, *Prin*
EMP: 14 EST: 2017
SALES (est): 4.59MM Privately Held
SIC: 3531 Crane carriers

(G-5286)

SPRING WORKS INCORPORATED
3201 Alberta St (43204-2029)
PHONE..............................614 351-9345
Edgar Weil, *CEO*
EMP: 20 EST: 1981
SQ FT: 27,000
SALES (est): 777.2K **Privately Held**
Web: www.thespringworks.com
SIC: 3495 Mechanical springs, precision

(G-5287)

SRICO INC
2724 Sawbury Blvd (43235-4579)
PHONE..............................614 799-0664
Sri Sriram, *Pr*
Sri Sriram, *Pr*
Judith C Sriram, *VP*
EMP: 8 EST: 1990
SQ FT: 3,600
SALES (est): 981.42K **Privately Held**
Web: www.srico.com
SIC: 3229 8731 Fiber optics strands;
Electronic research

(G-5288)

STAQ PHARMA OF OHIO LLC
255 Phillipi Rd (43228-1307)
PHONE..............................833 397-0106
Joseph Bagan, *Managing Member*
EMP: 13 EST: 2021
SALES (est): 1.38MM **Privately Held**
Web: www.ohiolifesciences.org
SIC: 2834 Pharmaceutical preparations

(G-5289)

STAR JET LLC
4130 E 5th Ave (43219-1802)
PHONE..............................614 338-4379
EMP: 7 EST: 2005
SALES (est): 872.94K **Privately Held**
SIC: 3721 Aircraft

(G-5290)

STAUFS COFFEE ROASTERS LIMITED
705 Hadley Dr (43228-1029)
PHONE..............................614 486-4479
EMP: 8
SALES (est): 561.37K **Privately Held**
Web: www.staufs.com
SIC: 2095 Coffee roasting (except by
wholesale grocers)

(G-5291)

STEER & GEAR INC
Also Called: Steer & Geer
1000 Barnett Rd (43227-1188)
PHONE..............................614 231-4064
Gerald Ries, *Pr*
Susan Ries, *
EMP: 6 EST: 1979
SALES (est): 1.04MM **Privately Held**
Web: www.steerandgear.com
SIC: 3714 Power steering equipment, motor
vehicle

(G-5292)

STERLING PROCESS EQUIPMENT & SERVICES INC (PA)
333 Mccormick Blvd (43213-1526)
PHONE..............................614 868-5151
EMP: 24 EST: 1983
SALES (est): 6.44MM
SALES (corp-wide): 6.44MM **Privately Held**
Web: www.sterlingpe.com
SIC: 3556 1623 Food products machinery;
Pipeline construction, nsk

(G-5293)

STEWARD EDGE BUS SOLUTIONS
23 N Westgate Ave (43204-1344)
PHONE..............................614 826-5305
Linda Steward, *Pr*
EMP: 10 EST: 2016
SALES (est): 123.78K **Privately Held**
SIC: 8741 7371 8721 7372 Business
management; Computer software systems
analysis and design, custom; Billing and
bookkeeping service; Operating systems
computer software

(G-5294)

STOCKER & SITLER OIL COMPANY (HQ)
4770 Indianola Ave (43214-1862)
PHONE..............................614 888-9588
Judson K Byrd, *Pr*
EMP: 7 EST: 1962
SALES (est): 2.84MM
SALES (corp-wide): 7.98MM **Privately Held**
SIC: 1311 1389 Crude petroleum and natural
gas production; Pumping of oil and gas
wells
PA: Cgas Inc
110 E Wilson Bridge Rd # 250
Worthington OH 43085
614 975-4697

(G-5295)

STYLE-LINE INCORPORATED (PA)
Also Called: Chelsea House Fabrics
901 W 3rd Ave Ste A (43212-3108)
P.O. Box 2706 (43216-2706)
PHONE..............................614 291-0600
Laura R Prophater, *Pr*
William H Prophater, *
EMP: 35 EST: 1969
SQ FT: 54,000
SALES (est): 2.35MM
SALES (corp-wide): 2.35MM **Privately Held**
Web: www.lookhuman.com
SIC: 5023 5131 2391 1799 Venetian blinds;
Drapery material, woven; Curtains, window:
made from purchased materials; Drapery
track installation

(G-5296)

SUBURBAN STL SUP CO LTD PARTNR
Also Called: Suburban Steel of Indiana
1900 Deffenbaugh Ct (43230-8604)
PHONE..............................317 783-6555
Mark Debellis, *Pr*
EMP: 8
SALES (corp-wide): 10.37MM **Privately Held**
Web: www.suburbansteelsupply.com
SIC: 3441 Fabricated structural metal
PA: Suburban Steel Supply Co. Limited
Partnership
1900 Deffenbaugh Ct
Gahanna OH 43230
614 737-5501

(G-5297)

SUNRISE FOODS INC
Also Called: Sunrise Foods
2097 Corvair Blvd (43207-1701)
PHONE..............................614 276-2880
Mark Pi Junior, *Pr*
Mark Pi Senior Stk Hld, *Prin*
Men Ma Stk Hld, *Prin*
EMP: 48 EST: 1997
SQ FT: 38,000
SALES (est): 5.12MM **Privately Held**
Web: www.sunrisefoodsohio.com

SIC: 2038 2013 2035 2099 Ethnic foods,
nec, frozen; Frozen meats, from purchased
meat; Pickles, sauces, and salad dressings;
Food preparations, nec

(G-5298)

SUPERIOR METAL WORX LLC
1239 Alum Creek Dr (43209-2721)
PHONE..............................614 879-9400
EMP: 15 EST: 2013
SALES (est): 3.88MM **Privately Held**
Web: www.superiormetalworx.com
SIC: 3441 Fabricated structural metal

(G-5299)

SUPERIOR PRODUCTION LLC (PA)
Also Called: Superior Die Tool & Machine Co
2301 Fairwood Ave (43207-2768)
PHONE..............................614 444-2181
▲ **EMP: 200 EST:** 1914
SALES (est): 18.78MM
SALES (corp-wide): 18.78MM **Privately Held**
Web: www.superior-dietool.com
SIC: 3714 3544 3469 5531 Bumpers and
bumperettes, motor vehicle; Special dies
and tools; Metal stampings, nec;
Automotive accessories

(G-5300)

SUPERIOR WELDING CO
906 S Nelson Rd (43205-3098)
PHONE..............................614 252-8539
Steve Shipley, *Pr*
Sandra R Shipley, *VP*
EMP: 7 EST: 1947
SQ FT: 22,000
SALES (est): 1.01MM **Privately Held**
Web: www.superior-welding.com
SIC: 3599 Machine shop, jobbing and repair

(G-5301)

SUPPLY TECHNOLOGIES LLC
590 Claycraft Rd (43230-5319)
PHONE..............................614 759-9939
Thomas Gisczinski, *Mgr*
EMP: 25
SALES (corp-wide): 1.66B **Publicly Held**
Web: supplytechnologies.com
SIC: 3452 Bolts, nuts, rivets, and washers
HQ: Supply Technologies Llc
6065 Parkland Blvd
Cleveland OH 44124
440 947-2100

(G-5302)

SUSTAINMENT ACTIONS LLC
20 S 3rd St Ste 210 (43215-4206)
PHONE..............................330 805-3468
Bradford Klusmann, *Prin*
EMP: 11 EST: 2021
SALES (est): 235.24K **Privately Held**
SIC: 3199 Leather goods, nec

(G-5303)

SWAPIL INC
2740 Airport Dr Ste 310 (43219-2295)
P.O. Box 4087 (60174-9081)
▼ **EMP: 55 EST:** 1986
SALES (est): 3.05MM
SALES (corp-wide): 1.15B **Privately Held**
SIC: 3089 Stock shapes, plastics
PA: New Enterprise Stone & Lime Co., Inc.
3912 Brumbaugh Rd
New Enterprise PA 16664
814 766-2211

(G-5304)

SYSCOM ADVANCED MATERIALS INC

1305 Kinnear Rd (43212-1574)
PHONE..............................614 487-3626
Jar Wha Lee, *CEO*
Jar-wha Lee, *Pr*
Iqbal Haider, *Treas*
EMP: 21 EST: 2005
SALES (est): 2.81MM **Privately Held**
Web: www.metalcladfibers.com
SIC: 3357 Fiber optic cable (insulated)

(G-5305)

T E Q HI INC
1525 Alum Creek Dr (43209-2712)
PHONE..............................877 448-3701
Satyen Prabhu, *Pr*
Fatyen Prabhu, *
EMP: 35 EST: 1988
SQ FT: 17,000
SALES (est): 498.2K
SALES (corp-wide): 645.5MM **Privately
Held**
SIC: 3567 Industrial furnaces and ovens
HQ: Inductotherm Corp.
10 Indel Ave
Rancocas NJ 08073
609 267-9000

(G-5306)

TAIKISHA USA INC
1939 Refugee Rd (43207-1743)
PHONE..............................614 444-5602
Mark Swedni, *Brnch Mgr*
EMP: 65
Web: www.tksindustrial.com
SIC: 3559 Metal finishing equipment for
plating, etc.
HQ: Taikisha Usa, Inc
901 Tower Dr Ste 300
Troy MI 48098
248 786-5000

(G-5307)

TALLY HO SLIPCOVERS
2019 Andover Rd (43212-1006)
PHONE..............................614 448-6170
Marian Tanner, *Prin*
EMP: 6 EST: 2012
SALES (est): 112.45K **Privately Held**
SIC: 2392 Slip covers: made of fabric,
plastic, etc.

(G-5308)

TARAHILL INC
Also Called: Pet Goods Mfg
3985 Groves Rd (43232-4138)
PHONE..............................706 864-0808
Floyd E Seal, *Pr*
◆ **EMP: 7 EST:** 1972
SALES (est): 162.42K **Privately Held**
SIC: 3199 Dog furnishings: collars, leashes,
muzzles, etc.: leather

(G-5309)

TARIGMA CORPORATION
Also Called: Ooteksofpak
6161 Busch Blvd Ste 110 (43229-2553)
PHONE..............................614 436-3734
J Declan Smith, *Pr*
Keith Sarbaugh, *Treas*
Winthrop Worcester, *Sec*
EMP: 10 EST: 1995
SQ FT: 1,000
SALES (est): 1.03MM **Privately Held**
Web: www.tarigma.com
SIC: 7372 Prepackaged software

(G-5310)

TARRIER FOODS CORP
Also Called: Tarrier
2700 International St (43228-4640)
PHONE..............................614 876-8594

Timothy A Tarrier, *Pr*
Ann Tarrier, *
Julia A Grooms, *
EMP: 42 **EST:** 1978
SQ FT: 54,000
SALES (est): 2.4MM **Privately Held**
Web: www.tarrierfoods.com
SIC: 5149 5145 2099 Dried or canned foods; Nuts, salted or roasted; Food preparations, nec

(G-5311)
TARRIER STEEL COMPANY INC
1379 S 22nd St (43206-3083)
P.O. Box 7885 (43207)
PHONE..............................614 444-4000
Todd Tarrier, *Pr*
EMP: 41 **EST:** 1920
SQ FT: 36,000
SALES (est): 9.83MM **Privately Held**
Web: www.tarrier.com
SIC: 3441 3446 Fabricated structural metal; Ornamental metalwork

(G-5312)
TAYLOR COMMUNICATIONS INC
3950 Business Park Dr (43204-5008)
PHONE..............................614 351-6868
EMP: 13
SALES (corp-wide): 3.81B **Privately Held**
Web: www.taylor.com
SIC: 2752 4225 Commercial printing, lithographic; General warehousing and storage
HQ: Taylor Communications, Inc.
       1725 Roe Crest Dr
       North Mankato MN 56003
       866 541-0937

(G-5313)
TDS CUSTOM CABINETS LLC
1819 Walcutt Rd Ste 9 (43228-9149)
P.O. Box 56 (43026)
PHONE..............................614 850-7590
Dustin Sauer, *Pr*
Terry Sauer, *Managing Member*
EMP: 6 **EST:** 2006
SQ FT: 36,000
SALES (est): 4.11MM **Privately Held**
Web: www.tdsmanufacturingllc.com
SIC: 2434 Wood kitchen cabinets

(G-5314)
TEAM INC
Tsi Manufacturing
3005 Silver Dr (43224-3945)
PHONE..............................614 263-1808
Sam Dematteo, *VP*
EMP: 12
SALES (corp-wide): 852.27MM **Publicly Held**
Web: www.teaminc.com
SIC: 3398 Metal heat treating
HQ: Team, Inc.
       5095 Paris St
       Denver CO 80239

(G-5315)
TECH4IMAGING LLC
1910 Crown Park Ct Ste B (43235-2404)
PHONE..............................614 214-2655
Qussai Marashdeh, *CEO*
EMP: 12 **EST:** 2007
SALES (est): 2.47MM **Privately Held**
Web: www.tech4imaging.com
SIC: 7371 8711 3826 5049 Computer software development; Consulting engineer ; Laser scientific and engineering instruments; Scientific and engineering equipment and supplies

(G-5316)
TECHNICAL ARTISTRY INC
Also Called: Tech Art Productions
1340b Emig Rd (43207)
P.O. Box 1239 (43026-6239)
PHONE..............................614 299-7777
Tim Mclaughlin, *Pr*
Tim Mclaughlin, *CEO*
EMP: 6 **EST:** 2003
SALES (est): 973.79K **Privately Held**
Web: www.techartproductions.com
SIC: 5063 7929 5099 7359 Lighting fixtures; Entertainment service; Video and audio equipment; Sound and lighting equipment rental

(G-5317)
TERRASMART LLC
1000 Buckeye Park Rd (43207-2509)
PHONE..............................239 362-0211
EMP: 20
SALES (corp-wide): 1.31B **Publicly Held**
Web: www.terrasmart.com
SIC: 3441 3317 1711 Fabricated structural metal; Boiler tubes (wrought); Solar energy contractor
HQ: Terrasmart Llc
       14590 Global Pkwy
       Fort Myers FL 33913

(G-5318)
THE COLUMBUS SHOW CASE COMPANY
Also Called: CSC Worldwide
4401 Equity Dr (43228-3856)
P.O. Box 21205 (43221-0205)
▲ **EMP:** 170
SIC: 2541 3585 2522 Showcases, except refrigerated: wood; Counters and counter display cases, refrigerated; Panel systems and partitions, office: except wood

(G-5319)
THE CRANE GROUP COMPANIES LIMITED (HQ)
330 W Spring St Ste 200 (43215-2389)
P.O. Box 1047 (43216)
PHONE..............................614 754-3000
EMP: 28 **EST:** 1947
SALES (est): 69.38MM **Privately Held**
Web: www.cranegroup.com
SIC: 3089 Extruded finished plastics products, nec
PA: Crane Group Co.
       330 W Spring St
       Columbus OH 43215

(G-5320)
THE HARTMAN CORP
Also Called: Hartman Trophies
3216 Morse Rd (43231-6132)
PHONE..............................614 475-5035
Larry Hartman, *Pr*
Linda Hartman, *Sec*
Gary Hartman, *VP*
EMP: 6 **EST:** 1968
SQ FT: 6,500
SALES (est): 330.81K **Privately Held**
Web: www.hartmancorporation.com
SIC: 5999 5941 5947 3993 Trophies and plaques; Bowling equipment and supplies; Trading cards: baseball or other sports, entertainment, etc.; Signs and advertising specialties

(G-5321)
THE OLEN CORPORATION (PA)
4755 S High St (43207-4080)
PHONE..............................614 491-1515
TOLL FREE: 800

EMP: 62 **EST:** 1951
SALES (est): 32.6MM
SALES (corp-wide): 32.6MM **Privately Held**
Web: www.kokosing.biz
SIC: 1442 Construction sand and gravel

(G-5322)
THERMAL SOLUTIONS INC
3005 Silver Dr (43224-3945)
PHONE..............................614 263-1808
EMP: 23
Web: www.thermalsolutionsinc.com
SIC: 3398 Metal heat treating
HQ: Thermal Solutions, Inc.
       9329 County Rd 107
       Proctorville OH 45669
       740 886-2861

(G-5323)
THURNS BAKERY & DELI
541 S 3rd St (43215-5721)
PHONE..............................614 221-9246
Marilyn Plank, *Pr*
Dan Plank, *
Chris Plank, *
Bill Plank, *
EMP: 7 **EST:** 1972
SQ FT: 2,100
SALES (est): 396.24K **Privately Held**
SIC: 5461 5149 2051 Retail bakeries; Bakery products; Bread, cake, and related products

(G-5324)
TIBA LLC (DH)
Also Called: Signature Control Systems
2228 Citygate Dr (43219-3565)
PHONE..............................614 328-2040
Jon Dawsher, *Managing Member*
EMP: 30 **EST:** 1987
SALES (est): 10.22MM
SALES (corp-wide): 366.96K **Privately Held**
Web: www.tibaparking.com
SIC: 3559 Parking facility equipment and supplies
HQ: Faac Spa
       Via Monaldo Calari 10
       Zola Predosa BO 40069

(G-5325)
TOTAL TENNIS INC
Also Called: TTI Sports Equipment
1733 Cardiff Rd (43221-3806)
PHONE..............................614 488-5004
James Lathrop, *Pr*
Sally Ann Lathrop, *VP*
EMP: 10 **EST:** 1979
SALES (est): 683.75K **Privately Held**
Web: www.totaltennisinc.com
SIC: 3949 5091 Tennis equipment and supplies; Sporting and recreation goods

(G-5326)
TRANE US INC
Trane
2300 Citygate Dr Ste 100 (43219-3664)
PHONE..............................614 473-3131
Al Fullerton, *Dist Mgr*
EMP: 150
Web: www.trane.com
SIC: 3585 Refrigeration and heating equipment
HQ: Trane U.S. Inc.
       800-E Beaty St
       Davidson NC 28036
       704 655-4000

(G-5327)
TRANE US INC
Also Called: Trane National Account Service
2300 Citygate Dr Ste 250 (43219-3664)
PHONE..............................614 473-8701
EMP: 6
Web: www.trane.com
SIC: 3585 Refrigeration and heating equipment
HQ: Trane U.S. Inc.
       800-E Beaty St
       Davidson NC 28036
       704 655-4000

(G-5328)
TRANSMET CORPORATION
4290 Perimeter Dr (43228-1036)
PHONE..............................614 276-5522
Douglas Shull, *Pr*
▼ **EMP:** 8 **EST:** 1979
SQ FT: 17,000
SALES (est): 1.71MM **Privately Held**
Web: www.transmet.com
SIC: 3399 Flakes, metal

(G-5329)
TRAXLER PRINTING
310 W Pacemont Rd Apt A (43202-1071)
PHONE..............................614 593-1270
Zachary Traxler, *CEO*
EMP: 8 **EST:** 2016
SALES (est): 204.72K **Privately Held**
Web: www.traxlerprinting.com
SIC: 2752 Offset printing

(G-5330)
TREWBRIC III INC
1701 Moler Rd (43207-1684)
P.O. Box 07847 (43207)
PHONE..............................614 444-2184
Ted Coons, *Ch*
Ted Coons, *CEO*
Don Mcnutt, *Pr*
Lynn Coons, *
◆ **EMP:** 34 **EST:** 1948
SQ FT: 37,000
SALES (est): 5MM **Privately Held**
Web: www.afinitas.com
SIC: 1771 5084 3446 Concrete work; Cement making machinery; Architectural metalwork

(G-5331)
TRI-STATE SUPPLY CO INC
3840 Fisher Rd (43228-1016)
PHONE..............................614 272-6767
Jim Bruce, *Prin*
EMP: 10 **EST:** 1950
SQ FT: 10,000
SALES (est): 113.31K **Privately Held**
SIC: 2493 5046 2531 Bulletin boards, wood; Partitions; Blackboards, wood

(G-5332)
TRI-W GROUP INC
Also Called: Military Spec Packaging
835 Goodale Blvd (43212-3824)
PHONE..............................614 228-5000
▲ **EMP:** 1241
SIC: 3694 7538 7537 Distributors, motor vehicle engine; Diesel engine repair: automotive; Automotiv e transmission repair shops

(G-5333)
TROY FILTERS LTD
1680 Westbelt Dr (43228-3812)
P.O. Box 21295 (43221-0295)
PHONE..............................614 777-8222
Cory Elliott, *Managing Member*

EMP: 20 EST: 1993
SQ FT: 16,000
SALES (est): 2.16MM **Privately Held**
Web: www.troyfiltersusa.com
SIC: 3564 Filters, air: furnaces, air
conditioning equipment, etc.

(G-5334)
TRUTECH CABINETRY LLC
2121 S James Rd (43232-3829)
PHONE...............................614 338-0680
Nick Willis, *Owner*
EMP: 8 EST: 2007
SALES (est): 1.96MM **Privately Held**
Web: www.trutechcabinetry.com
SIC: 2434 Wood kitchen cabinets

(G-5335)
TURN-KEY TUNNELING INC
1247 Stimmel Rd (43223-2915)
PHONE...............................614 275-4832
Christine Froehrlich, *Pr*
Deborah Tingler, *
Brian Froehrlich, *
Michael J Fusco, *
EMP: 35 EST: 2005
SALES (est): 4.68MM **Privately Held**
Web: www.turn-keytunneling.com
SIC: 3531 Tunneling machinery

(G-5336)
U S HAIR INC
3727 E Broad St (43213-1127)
PHONE...............................614 235-5190
Tom Jeon, *Pr*
EMP: 6 EST: 2001
SALES (est): 483.45K **Privately Held**
Web: www.ushairbeauty.com
SIC: 3999 Hair and hair-based products

(G-5337)
UNITED SECURITY SEALS INC (PA)
Also Called: United Seal Company
2000 Fairwood Ave (43207-1607)
P.O. Box 7852 (43207-0852)
PHONE...............................614 443-7633
Herbert Cook, *Pr*
Daniel P Sander, *
▲ EMP: 30 EST: 1900
SQ FT: 20,000
SALES (est): 2.54MM
SALES (corp-wide): 2.54MM **Privately
Held**
Web: www.unitedsecurityseals.com
SIC: 3312 3089 Bar, rod, and wire products;
Plastics processing

(G-5338)
UNIVERSAL FABG CNSTR SVCS INC
Also Called: UNI-Facs
1241 Mckinley Ave (43222-1114)
PHONE...............................614 274-1128
Steve Finkel, *Pr*
Robert Watts, *
▲ EMP: 14 EST: 1987
SQ FT: 120,000
SALES (est): 1.99MM **Privately Held**
SIC: 1541 3441 3599 1799 Renovation,
remodeling and repairs: industrial buildings;
Building components, structural steel;
Catapults; Sandblasting of building exteriors

(G-5339)
UNIVERSAL PALLETS INC
611 Marion Rd (43207-2552)
PHONE...............................614 444-1095
Mike Afaghi, *Brnch Mgr*
EMP: 27
SALES (corp-wide): 1.82MM **Privately
Held**
Web: www.48forty.com

SIC: 5031 2448 Pallets, wood; Cargo
containers, wood
PA: Universal Pallets Inc.
659 Marion Rd
Columbus OH 43207
614 444-1095

(G-5340)
UPPER ARLINGTON CREW INC
5257 Sinclair Rd (43229-5042)
P.O. Box 211086 (43221)
PHONE...............................614 485-0089
Betty Callender, *Prin*
EMP: 6 EST: 2010
SALES (est): 406.78K **Privately Held**
Web: www.uacrew.org
SIC: 2711 Newspapers, publishing and
printing

(G-5341)
URBN TIMBER LLC
29 Kingston Ave (43207-2437)
PHONE...............................614 981-3043
Tyler Sirak, *Managing Member*
Treg Sherman, *Managing Member*
Tyler Hillyard, *Managing Member*
EMP: 6 EST: 2016
SALES (est): 530.17K **Privately Held**
Web: www.urbntimber.com
SIC: 2491 2426 5712 5021 Structural lumber
and timber, treated wood; Carvings,
furniture: wood; Custom made furniture,
except cabinets; Furniture

(G-5342)
USTEK INCORPORATED
4663 Executive Dr Ste 3 (43220-3627)
PHONE...............................614 538-8000
Robert M Simon, *Pr*
Wendy Simon, *Sec*
▲ EMP: 10 EST: 1986
SQ FT: 650
SALES (est): 1.63MM **Privately Held**
Web: www.ustek.com
SIC: 3674 Semiconductors and related
devices

(G-5343)
V & C ENTERPRISES CO
Also Called: Printed Image, The
41 S Grant Ave (43215-3979)
PHONE...............................614 221-1412
Cathleen Siech, *Prin*
Vicki Hamer, *Prin*
EMP: 7 EST: 1991
SALES (est): 786.13K **Privately Held**
SIC: 2752 Offset printing

(G-5344)
VALLEY VITAMINS II INC
4449 Easton Way Fl 2 (43219-7005)
PHONE...............................330 533-0051
Adam Crouch, *CEO*
EMP: 10 EST: 2008
SALES (est): 184.25K **Privately Held**
SIC: 2833 Medicinals and botanicals

(G-5345)
VECTRA INC
Also Called: Vectra Visual
3950 Business Park Dr (43204-5021)
PHONE...............................614 351-6868
◆ EMP: 200
Web: www.taylor.com
SIC: 2752 4225 Commercial printing,
lithographic; General warehousing and
storage

(G-5346)
VERIFONE INC
Also Called: 2checkout
855 Grandview Ave Ste 110 (43215-1102)
PHONE...............................800 837-4366
EMP: 114
SALES (corp-wide): 695.17MM **Privately
Held**
Web: www.2checkout.com
SIC: 3578 Point-of-sale devices
HQ: Verifone, Inc.
2744 N University Dr
Coral Springs FL 33065
800 837-4366

(G-5347)
VERITIV
2344 Limestone Way (43228-9197)
P.O. Box 183028 (43218-3028)
PHONE...............................614 323-3335
EMP: 15 EST: 2019
SALES (est): 1.65MM **Privately Held**
SIC: 2621 Paper mills

(G-5348)
VERTIV JV HOLDINGS LLC
1050 Dearborn Dr (43085-1544)
PHONE...............................614 888-0246
Eva M Kalawski, *Sec*
EMP: 6488 EST: 2016
SALES (est): 4.9MM **Privately Held**
SIC: 3679 3585 6719 Power supplies, all
types: static; Air conditioning units,
complete: domestic or industrial;
Investment holding companies, except
banks

(G-5349)
VIGILANTE LOVE LLC
191 Broad Meadows Blvd (43214-1001)
PHONE...............................380 258-5983
Keveante Smoot, *Managing Member*
EMP: 12
SALES (est): 1.49MM **Privately Held**
SIC: 1389 Construction, repair, and
dismantling services

(G-5350)
VIRGINIA AIR DISTRIBUTORS INC
2821 Silver Dr (43211-1052)
PHONE...............................614 262-1129
Ken Baker, *CEO*
EMP: 8
SALES (corp-wide): 104.5MM **Privately
Held**
Web: www.virginiaair.com
SIC: 3585 Parts for heating, cooling, and
refrigerating equipment
PA: Virginia Air Distributors Inc
2501 Waterford Lake Dr
Midlothian VA 23112
804 608-3600

(G-5351)
**VISTA INDUSTRIAL PACKAGING LLC
(PA)**
Also Called: Vista Packaging & Logistics
4700 Fisher Rd (43228-9752)
PHONE...............................800 454-6117
▲ EMP: 45 EST: 1985
SQ FT: 350,000
SALES (est): 19.5MM
SALES (corp-wide): 19.5MM **Privately
Held**
Web: www.vistaindustrialpackaging.com
SIC: 4783 7389 4226 2679 Packing and
crating; Inspection and testing services;
Special warehousing and storage, nec;
Pressed fiber and molded pulp products,
except food products

(G-5352)
VOIGT & SCHWEITZER LLC (HQ)
987 Buckeye Park Rd (43207-2596)
PHONE...............................614 449-8281
Werner Niehaus, *Pr*
Brian Miller, *Sr VP*
▲ EMP: 12 EST: 1968
SQ FT: 55,000
SALES (est): 56.22MM
SALES (corp-wide): 1.08B **Privately Held**
Web: www.hotdipgalvanizing.com
SIC: 3479 Galvanizing of iron, steel, or end-
formed products
PA: Hill & Smith Plc
Westhaven House
Solihull W MIDLANDS B90 4
121 704-7430

(G-5353)
WALKER NATIONAL INC
2195 Wright Brothers Ave (43217-1157)
PHONE...............................614 492-1614
Richard Longo, *Pr*
Deborah Krikorian, *
◆ EMP: 30 EST: 1988
SALES (est): 2.37MM
SALES (corp-wide): 34.45MM **Privately
Held**
SIC: 3499 7699 Magnets, permanent:
metallic; Industrial equipment services
PA: Industrial Magnetics, Inc.
1385 M 75 S
Boyne City MI 49712
231 582-3100

(G-5354)
WALOR NORTH AMERICA INC
2230 S 3rd St (43207-2402)
PHONE...............................614 445-6060
Arun Thandapani, *CEO*
Felix Schmieder, *
Mark Hoosier, *
Robert Hartwell, *
Charles Bentz, *
◆ EMP: 322 EST: 1988
SQ FT: 155,000
SALES (est): 49.47MM
SALES (corp-wide): 5.1B **Privately Held**
Web: www.hirschvogel.com
SIC: 3714 Motor vehicle parts and
accessories
HQ: Walor International
92 Rue Saint Melaine
Laval PDL 53000

(G-5355)
WARD ENGINEERING INC
2041 Arlingate Ln (43228-4113)
PHONE...............................614 442-8063
EMP: 7 EST: 2019
SALES (est): 1.75MM **Privately Held**
SIC: 3841 Surgical and medical instruments

(G-5356)
WASSERSTROM COMPANY (PA)
Also Called: National Smallwares
4500 E Broad St (43213-1360)
PHONE...............................614 228-6525
Rodney Wasserstrom, *Pr*
Reid Wasserstrom, *
Dennis Blank, *
Alan Wasserstrom, *
David A Tumen, *
◆ EMP: 395 EST: 1902
SQ FT: 250,000
SALES (est): 378.09MM
SALES (corp-wide): 378.09MM **Privately
Held**
Web: www.wasserstrom.com

▲ = Import ▼ = Export
◆ = Import/Export

SIC: **5087** 3566 5021 5046 Restaurant supplies; Speed changers, drives, and gears; Office furniture, nec; Commercial cooking and food service equipment

(G-5357)
WATERSHED DISTILLERY LLC
1145 Chesapeake Ave Ste D (43212-2284)
PHONE..................................614 357-1936
Dave Rigo, *Pt*
Greg Lehman, *Pt*
EMP: 50 **EST:** 2010
SQ FT: 4,700
SALES (est): 8.61MM **Privately Held**
Web: www.watersheddistillery.com
SIC: **5182** 2085 Wine; Distilled and blended liquors

(G-5358)
WATKINS PRINTING COMPANY
1401 E 17th Ave (43211-2849)
P.O. Box 11618 (43211)
PHONE..................................614 297-8270
Tamara Watkins Green, *Sec*
Eric Watkins, *
David Watkins, *
EMP: 45 **EST:** 1949
SQ FT: 35,000
SALES (est): 4.7MM **Privately Held**
Web: www.watkinsprinting.com
SIC: **2752** 2791 2789 Offset printing; Typesetting; Bookbinding and related work

(G-5359)
WELCH PACKAGING GROUP INC
Also Called: Welch Packaging Columbus
4700 Alkire Rd (43228-3495)
PHONE..................................614 870-2000
Tayler Darling, *Mgr*
EMP: 110
SALES (corp-wide): 457.79MM **Privately Held**
Web: www.welchpkg.com
SIC: **2621** 7389 Wrapping and packaging papers; Packaging and labeling services
PA: Welch Packaging Group, Inc.
1020 Herman St
Elkhart IN 46516
574 295-2460

(G-5360)
WELDING CONSULTANTS INC
889 N 22nd St (43219-2426)
PHONE..................................614 258-7018
William A Svekric Senior, *Pr*
William Svekric Junior, *VP*
EMP: 6 **EST:** 1981
SQ FT: 4,800
SALES (est): 394.81K **Privately Held**
Web:
welding-consultants-llc.myshopify.com
SIC: **8742** 8734 8711 7692 Management consulting services; Testing laboratories; Engineering services; Welding repair

(G-5361)
WELDING CONSULTANTS LLC
889 N 22nd St (43219-2426)
PHONE..................................614 258-7018
Richard Holdren, *Pr*
EMP: 7 **EST:** 2016
SALES (est): 243.39K **Privately Held**
Web:
welding-consultants-llc.myshopify.com
SIC: **7692** Welding repair

(G-5362)
WEST-CAMP PRESS INC
Also Called: American Colorscans
5178 Sinclair Rd (43229-5437)
PHONE..................................614 895-0233

EMP: 22
SALES (corp-wide): 24.84MM **Privately Held**
Web: www.westcamppress.com
SIC: **2752** Color lithography
PA: West-Camp Press, Inc.
39 Collegeview Rd
Westerville OH 43081
614 882-2378

(G-5363)
WEST-WARD COLUMBUS INC
Also Called: Hikma Pharmaceuticals
1809 Wilson Rd (43228-9579)
P.O. Box 16532 (43216-6532)
PHONE..................................614 276-4000
◆ **EMP:** 1100 **EST:** 1890
SALES (est): 24.7MM
SALES (corp-wide): 3.13B **Privately Held**
SIC: **2834** Druggists' preparations (pharmaceuticals)
HQ: West-Ward Holdings Limited
1 New Burlington Place
London W1S 2
207 399-2760

(G-5364)
WESTLAKE CORPORATION
Also Called: Westlake Epoxy
180 E Broad St (43215-3707)
PHONE..................................614 986-2497
EMP: 78
Web: www.westlake.com
SIC: **2821** Epoxy resins
PA: Westlake Corporation
2801 Post Oak Blvd Ste 60
Houston TX 77056

(G-5365)
WESTLAKE RYAL BLDG PDTS USA IN (DH)
Also Called: Royal Building Products
1441 Universal Rd (43207-1730)
PHONE..................................800 366-8472
Scott Szwejbka, *Pr*
Mark J Orcutt, *Ex VP*
Chris Bitsakakis, *VP*
Guy Prentice, *VP*
Simon Bates, *Genl Mgr*
EMP: 25 **EST:** 1997
SALES (est): 8.85MM **Publicly Held**
Web: www.royalbuildingproducts.com
SIC: **5932** 2952 2431 1761 Building materials, secondhand; Siding materials; Windows and window parts and trim, wood; Roofing, siding, and sheetmetal work
HQ: Westlake Petrochemicals Llc
2801 Post Oak Blvd
Houston TX 77056

(G-5366)
WHEEL GROUP HOLDINGS LLC
Also Called: Wheel One
2901 E 4th Ave Ste 3 (43219-2896)
PHONE..................................614 253-6247
Joseph Nantle, *Off Mgr*
EMP: 6
SALES (corp-wide): 74.55MM **Privately Held**
Web: www.thewheelgroup.com
SIC: **3714** 3452 Wheel rims, motor vehicle; Nuts, metal
PA: Wheel Group Holdings, Llc
1050 N Vineyard Ave
Ontario CA 91764
888 399-8885

(G-5367)
WHITE CASTLE SYSTEM INC (PA)
Also Called: White Castle
555 Edgar Waldo Way (43215-1158)

P.O. Box 1498 (43216-1498)
PHONE..................................614 228-5781
Edgar W Ingram Iii, *Ch Bd*
Russell J Meyer, *
Nicholas Zuk, *
Elizabeth Ingram, *
Andrew Prakel, *Corporate Controller**
◆ **EMP:** 275 **EST:** 1921
SQ FT: 143,000
SALES (est): 187.89MM
SALES (corp-wide): 187.89MM **Privately Held**
Web: www.whitecastle.com
SIC: **5812** 5142 2051 2013 Fast-food restaurant, chain; Meat, frozen: packaged; Bread, cake, and related products; Sausages and other prepared meats

(G-5368)
WILD OHIO BREWING COMPANY
2025 S High St (43207-2426)
PHONE..................................614 262-0000
Russell Pinto, *Prin*
EMP: 8 **EST:** 2017
SALES (est): 2.19MM **Privately Held**
Web: www.wildohiobrewing.com
SIC: **5181** 2082 Beer and ale; Ale (alcoholic beverage)

(G-5369)
WILSONART LLC
2500 International St (43228-4601)
PHONE..................................614 876-1515
Buddy Mohler, *Mgr*
EMP: 34
SALES (corp-wide): 982.77MM **Privately Held**
Web: www.wilsonart.com
SIC: **2821** 2541 Plastics materials and resins ; Table or counter tops, plastic laminated
HQ: Wilsonart Llc
2501 Wilsonart Dr
Temple TX 76504
254 207-7000

(G-5370)
WOLF COMPOSITE SOLUTIONS
3991 Fondorf Dr (43228-1025)
PHONE..................................614 219-6990
Alex Wolford, *Pr*
Bethany Wolford, *Off Mgr*
▼ **EMP:** 17 **EST:** 1999
SQ FT: 53,000
SALES (est): 2.21MM **Privately Held**
Web: www.wolfcomposites.com
SIC: **3624** Fibers, carbon and graphite

(G-5371)
WOLF METALS INC
1625 W Mound St (43223-1809)
PHONE..................................614 461-6361
James Wolf, *Pr*
Donna Wolf, *VP*
Karen Gould, *Sec*
EMP: 6 **EST:** 1974
SQ FT: 10,000
SALES (est): 2.19MM **Privately Held**
Web: www.wolfmetals.com
SIC: **3444** Sheet metal specialties, not stamped

(G-5372)
WORLD WIDE RECYCLERS INC
3755 S High St (43207-4011)
PHONE..................................614 554-3296
Jeffery May Senior, *Pr*
EMP: 9 **EST:** 2006
SALES (est): 240.99K **Privately Held**
SIC: **2611** 5064 Pulp mills, mechanical and recycling processing; Electric household appliances, nec

(G-5373)
WORTHINGTON CYLINDER CORP
1085 Dearborn Dr (43085-1542)
PHONE..................................614 438-7900
EMP: 196
SALES (corp-wide): 1.25B **Publicly Held**
Web: www.worthingtonenterprises.com
SIC: **3443** 3593 Cylinders, pressure: metal plate; Fluid power cylinders, hydraulic or pneumatic
HQ: Worthington Cylinder Corporation
200 W Old Wlson Bridge Rd
Worthington OH 43085
614 840-3210

(G-5374)
WORTHINGTON STEEL INC (PA) ✪
Also Called: WORTHINGTON STEEL
100 W Old Wilson Bridge Rd (43085-2255)
PHONE..................................614 840-3462
Geoffrey G Gilmore, *Pr*
John B Blystone, *Ex Ch Bd*
Jeff R Klingler, *Ex VP*
Timothy A Adams, *VP*
Joseph Y Heuer, *VP*
EMP: 278 **EST:** 2023
SALES (est): 3.43B
SALES (corp-wide): 3.43B **Publicly Held**
Web: www.worthingtonsteel.com
SIC: **3316** Cold-rolled strip or wire

(G-5375)
WORTHNGTON STELPAC SYSTEMS LLC (HQ)
1205 Dearborn Dr (43085-4769)
PHONE..................................614 438-3205
Mark Russell, *CEO*
EMP: 250 **EST:** 1999
SALES (est): 20.69MM
SALES (corp-wide): 1.25B **Publicly Held**
Web: www.worthingtonenterprises.com
SIC: **3325** 5051 Steel foundries, nec; Metals service centers and offices
PA: Worthington Enterprises, Inc.
200 W Old Wlson Bridge Rd
Worthington OH 43085
614 438-3210

(G-5376)
WYANDOTTE WINERY LLC
4640 Wyandotte Dr (43230-1258)
PHONE..................................614 357-7522
Robin Coolidge, *Prin*
Alena Miller, *Prin*
EMP: 10 **EST:** 1977
SALES (est): 1.15MM **Privately Held**
Web: www.wyandottewinery.com
SIC: **2084** Wines

(G-5377)
Y O H INC
Also Called: Pengywn
2550 W 5th Ave (43204-3815)
PHONE..................................614 488-2861
Jim Kime, *Pr*
Sheila Kime, *Sec*
EMP: 20 **EST:** 1986
SQ FT: 20,000
SALES (est): 4.47MM **Privately Held**
Web: www.pengwyn.com
SIC: **3531** 3594 Snow plow attachments; Fluid power pumps and motors

(G-5378)
Z M O COMPANY (PA)
Also Called: Z M O Oil
2140 Eakin Rd (43223-6258)
P.O. Box 8587 (44906-8587)
PHONE..................................614 875-0230
Philip Schaffner, *Pr*
Don Schaffner, *VP*

Marie Schaffner, *Sec*
Valerie Schaffner, *Treas*
EMP: 6 **EST:** 1965
SALES (est): 234.21K
SALES (corp-wide): 234.21K **Privately Held**
Web: www.zmocompany.com
SIC: 2834 Liniments

(G-5379)
ZANE PETROLEUM INC
Also Called: Hopewell Oil and Gas
575 S 3rd St (43215-5755)
PHONE...............................740 454-8779
Jerry S Henderson, *Pr*
EMP: 10 **EST:** 1982
SALES (est): 1.05MM **Privately Held**
SIC: 1382 Oil and gas exploration services

(G-5380)
ZANER-BLOSER INC (HQ)
Also Called: Superkids Reading Program
1800 Watermark Dr (43215-1048)
P.O. Box 16764 (43216-6764)
PHONE...............................614 486-0221
Lisa Carmona, *Pr*
▲ **EMP:** 149 **EST:** 1972
SALES (est): 37.78MM
SALES (corp-wide): 72.35MM **Privately Held**
Web: www.zaner-bloser.com
SIC: 5192 5049 8249 2731 Books; School supplies; Correspondence school; Book publishing
PA: Highlights For Children, Inc.
1800 Watermark Dr
Columbus OH 43215
614 486-0631

(G-5381)
ZENNI USA INC
Also Called: Zenni USA LLC
4531 Industrial Center Dr (43207-4589)
PHONE...............................614 439-9850
EMP: 100 **EST:** 2020
SALES (est): 6.01MM
SALES (corp-wide): 104.56MM **Privately Held**
SIC: 3851 5995 Eyeglasses, lenses and frames; Optical goods stores
PA: Zenni Optical, Inc.
448 Ignacio Blvd Ste 332
Novato CA 94949
800 211-2105

Columbus Grove
Putnam County

(G-5382)
CARPE DIEM INDUSTRIES LLC (PA)
Also Called: Colonial Surface Solutions
4599 Campbell Rd (45830-9403)
PHONE...............................419 659-5639
Patricia Langhals, *Pr*
Darren Langhals, *
EMP: 55 **EST:** 1989
SQ FT: 750
SALES (est): 9.25MM
SALES (corp-wide): 9.25MM **Privately Held**
Web: www.colonialsurfacesolutions.com
SIC: 3479 3471 3398 1799 Painting of metal products; Cleaning and descaling metal products; Metal heat treating; Coating of metal structures at construction site

(G-5383)
GROVE ENGINEERED PRODUCTS
201 E Cross St (45830-1302)

PHONE...............................419 659-5939
Larry Clymer, *Pr*
▲ **EMP:** 6 **EST:** 2002
SALES (est): 1.91MM **Privately Held**
Web:
www.groveengineeredproducts.com
SIC: 2241 3011 Spindle banding; Tire and inner tube materials and related products

(G-5384)
PRODUCTION PRODUCTS INC
200 Sugar Grove Ln (45830-9627)
PHONE...............................734 241-7242
Sam Modica, *Pr*
Grace Viers, *VP*
◆ **EMP:** 76 **EST:** 2004
SQ FT: 20,000
SALES (est): 21.61MM **Privately Held**
Web: www.midwayproducts.com
SIC: 3469 3548 Metal stampings, nec; Electric welding equipment
PA: Midway Products Group, Inc.
One Lyman E Hoyt Dr
Monroe MI 48161

Concord Township
Lake County

(G-5385)
AVERY DENNISON CORPORATION
7600 Auburn Rd Bldg 18 (44077-9608)
PHONE...............................440 358-4691
Martina Mcissac, *Mgr*
EMP: 328
SALES (corp-wide): 8.76B **Publicly Held**
Web: www.averydennison.com
SIC: 2672 2679 Adhesive papers, labels, or tapes: from purchased material; Building, insulating, and packaging paper
PA: Avery Dennison Corporation
8080 Norton Pkwy
Mentor OH 44060
440 534-6000

(G-5386)
B B BRADLEY COMPANY INC (PA)
7755 Crile Rd (44077-9702)
PHONE...............................440 354-2005
Bruce Beaty, *Pr*
EMP: 40 **EST:** 1977
SALES (est): 5.06MM
SALES (corp-wide): 5.06MM **Privately Held**
Web: www.bbbradley.com
SIC: 3086 Packaging and shipping materials, foamed plastics

(G-5387)
BELLCO FEEDERS LLC
7757 Auburn Rd Ste 23 (44077-9604)
PHONE...............................440 728-5590
EMP: 10
SALES (est): 1.69MM **Privately Held**
SIC: 3569 Assembly machines, non-metalworking

(G-5388)
CEMCO CONSTRUCTION CORPORATION
10176 Page Dr (44060-6816)
PHONE...............................440 567-7708
Gianmichele Bruno, *Pr*
EMP: 6 **EST:** 2004
SALES (est): 174.96K **Privately Held**
Web: www.cem-co.com
SIC: 3273 Ready-mixed concrete

(G-5389)
DE NORA HOLDINGS US INC
7590 Discovery Ln (44077-9190)
PHONE...............................440 710-5300
Paolo Dellacha, *Pr*
Angelo Ferrari, *
Silvia Bertini, *
EMP: 370 **EST:** 2015
SALES (est): 5.03MM
SALES (corp-wide): 930.89MM **Privately Held**
SIC: 3589 Water purification equipment, household type
HQ: De Nora Holding (Uk) Limited
C/O Pirola Pennuto Zei & Associati Ltd
London EC4N

(G-5390)
ELTECH SYSTEMS CORPORATION (PA)
7590 Discovery Ln (44077-9190)
PHONE...............................440 285-0380
Dennis L Baxendale, *Prin*
EMP: 6 **EST:** 2018
SALES (est): 215.32K
SALES (corp-wide): 215.32K **Privately Held**
SIC: 2812 Alkalies and chlorine

(G-5391)
GENESIS PLASTIC TECH LLC
7540 W Pond Ct (44077-8962)
PHONE...............................440 542-0722
EMP: 80 **EST:** 2006
SALES (est): 9.63MM **Privately Held**
Web: www.genesisplastic.com
SIC: 3089 Injection molding of plastics

(G-5392)
ISK AMERICAS INCORPORATED (HQ)
7474 Auburn Rd (44077-9703)
PHONE...............................440 357-4600
Fujio Tamara, *Ch Bd*
F O Hicks, *
Marvin Hosokawa, *
R C Andrews, *
EMP: 16 **EST:** 1997
SQ FT: 4,400
SALES (est): 35.79MM **Privately Held**
Web: www.iskbc.com
SIC: 2816 2491 Titanium dioxide, anatase or rutile (pigments); Wood preserving
PA: Ishihara Sangyo Kaisha,Ltd.
1-3-15, Edobori, Nishi-Ku
Osaka OSK 550-0

(G-5393)
PRESSURE TECHNOLOGY OHIO INC
7996 Auburn Rd (44077-9701)
P.O. Box 357336 (32635-7336)
PHONE...............................215 628-1975
David Bowles, *Pr*
EMP: 20 **EST:** 2002
SALES (est): 2.27MM **Privately Held**
Web: www.pressuretechnology.com
SIC: 3398 Metal heat treating

(G-5394)
RANPAK HOLDINGS CORP (PA)
7990 Auburn Rd (44077-9701)
PHONE...............................440 354-4445
Omar M Asali, *Ch Bd*
Bill Drew, *Ex VP*
EMP: 52 **EST:** 1972
SALES (est): 368.9MM
SALES (corp-wide): 368.9MM **Publicly Held**
Web: www.ranpak.com

SIC: 2657 Paperboard backs for blister or skin packages

(G-5395)
ROBERTSON MANUFACTURING CO
10150 Colton Ave (44077-2195)
PHONE...............................216 531-8222
John S Green, *Pr*
Shannon Catalano, *Dir*
Sandra Essick, *Treas*
EMP: 10 **EST:** 1948
SALES (est): 2.3MM **Privately Held**
Web: www.robertsongears.com
SIC: 3568 3566 Sprockets (power transmission equipment); Gears, power transmission, except auto

(G-5396)
VAL-CON INC
7201 Hermitage Rd (44077-9718)
PHONE...............................440 357-1898
Richard Vertocnik, *Pr*
Jonell Vertocnik, *VP*
EMP: 7 **EST:** 1982
SALES (est): 167.54K **Privately Held**
SIC: 3825 Energy measuring equipment, electrical

(G-5397)
WATER STAR INC
7590 Discovery Ln (44077-9190)
P.O. Box 710 (44080-0710)
PHONE...............................440 996-0800
Dan Longhenry, *Pr*
Andrew Niksa, *VP*
▲ **EMP:** 14 **EST:** 2002
SALES (est): 752.65K
SALES (corp-wide): 1.29B **Publicly Held**
Web: americas.denora.com
SIC: 3356 3479 Titanium; Coating of metals and formed products
PA: Tennant Company
10400 Clean St
Eden Prairie MN 55344
763 540-1200

(G-5398)
ZSI MANUFACTURING INC
Also Called: American Belleville
8059 Crile Rd (44077-9180)
PHONE...............................440 266-0701
Steve Fowler, *CEO*
Christopher P Blossom, *CFO*
EMP: 11 **EST:** 2016
SQ FT: 21,500
SALES (est): 3.83MM **Privately Held**
Web: www.americanbelleville.com
SIC: 3493 Steel springs, except wire

Conneaut
Ashtabula County

(G-5399)
CASCADE OHIO INC
Also Called: C W Ohio
1209 Maple Ave (44030-2120)
PHONE...............................440 593-5800
Nicholas N Noirot, *Pr*
Gary C Trapp, *
▲ **EMP:** 282 **EST:** 1991
SQ FT: 250,000
SALES (est): 3.29MM **Privately Held**
Web: www.cwohio.com
SIC: 2431 3442 Windows and window parts and trim, wood; Metal doors, sash, and trim

(G-5400)
EXOMET INC
1100 Maple Ave (44030-2119)

PHONE..............................440 593-1161
Roger Stanbridge, *Prin*
EMP: 19 **EST:** 2008
SALES (est): 853.86K
SALES (corp-wide): 2.41B **Privately Held**
SIC: 5084 3559 Industrial machinery and
  equipment; Foundry machinery and
  equipment
HQ: Foseco, Inc.
  20200 Sheldon Rd
  Cleveland OH 44142
  440 826-4548

(G-5401)
GENERAL ALUMINUM MFG LLC
1370 Chamberlain Blvd (44030-1100)
P.O. Box 28 (44030-0028)
PHONE..............................440 593-6225
EMP: 300
Web: www.generalaluminum.com
SIC: 3365 3369 Aluminum and aluminum-
  based alloy castings; Nonferrous foundries,
  nec
HQ: General Aluminum Mfg. Llc
  5159 S Prospect St
  Ravenna OH 44266
  330 297-1225

(G-5402)
HARBOR INDUSTRIAL CORP
859 W Jackson St (44030-2255)
PHONE..............................440 599-8366
Michael D Legeza, *Pr*
Dale Hoskins, *Sec*
EMP: 18 **EST:** 1985
SQ FT: 92,000
SALES (est): 2.01MM **Privately Held**
Web: www.harborindustrialcorp.com
SIC: 3089 Plastics hardware and building
  products

(G-5403)
HEAVENLY CREAMERY INC
264 Sandusky St (44030-2568)
PHONE..............................440 593-6080
Joseph Ericksen, *Pr*
Christine Ericksen, *Sec*
John Ericksen, *Treas*
EMP: 6 **EST:** 2015
SALES (est): 200.14K **Privately Held**
Web: www.heavenlycreamery.com
SIC: 2021 3556 Creamery butter; Ice cream
  manufacturing machinery

(G-5404)
HMT INC
360 Commerce St (44030-2200)
P.O. Box 88 (44030-0088)
PHONE..............................440 599-7005
Darrell Maukonen, *Pr*
EMP: 8 **EST:** 1987
SQ FT: 5,000
SALES (est): 241.14K **Privately Held**
SIC: 3398 Metal heat treating

(G-5405)
INDEPENDENT CAN COMPANY
1049 Chamberlain Blvd (44030-1168)
PHONE..............................440 593-5300
Nancy Kalinowski, *Brnch Mgr*
EMP: 14
SALES (corp-wide): 39.47MM **Privately
Held**
Web: www.independentcan.com
SIC: 3411 Tin cans
PA: Independent Can Company
  1300 Brass Mill Rd
  Belcamp MD 21017
  410 272-0090

(G-5406)
KELLYS WLDG & FABRICATION LTD
285 N Amboy Rd (44030-3098)
PHONE..............................440 593-6040
Herbert Kelly Junior, *Pr*
EMP: 8 **EST:** 1991
SALES (est): 458.06K **Privately Held**
SIC: 7692 3441 1799 1542 Welding repair;
  Fabricated structural metal; Welding on site
  ; Nonresidential construction, nec

(G-5407)
**LEATHER RESOURCE OF AMERICA
INC**
Also Called: Cortina Leathers
494 E Main Rd (44030-8666)
PHONE..............................440 262-5761
▲ **EMP:** 49 **EST:** 2005
SALES (est): 1.53MM **Privately Held**
Web: www.cortinaleathers.com
SIC: 3111 3199 Finishing of leather; Boxes,
  leather

(G-5408)
LIGHTNING MOLD & MACHINE INC
Also Called: Lightning Mold & Machine
509 W Main Rd (44030-2975)
PHONE..............................440 593-6460
Ronald R Newhart, *Pr*
Loretta Newhart, *Sec*
Erik Newhart, *VP*
EMP: 10 **EST:** 1992
SQ FT: 2,700
SALES (est): 368.63K **Privately Held**
SIC: 3544 3599 Industrial molds; Custom
  machinery

(G-5409)
**LUKJAN METAL PDTS HOLDG CO
INC**
645 Industry Rd (44030-3045)
P.O. Box 357 (44030-0357)
PHONE..............................440 599-8127
EMP: 6 **EST:** 2017
SALES (est): 1.21MM **Privately Held**
Web: www.lukjan.com
SIC: 3444 Sheet metalwork

(G-5410)
**LUKJAN METAL PRODUCTS INC
(PA)**
645 Industry Rd (44030-3045)
P.O. Box P.O. Box 357 (44030)
PHONE..............................440 599-8127
Daniel Korda, *Pr*
Elena Kelly, *
EMP: 140 **EST:** 1964
SQ FT: 100,000
SALES (est): 23.47MM
SALES (corp-wide): 23.47MM **Privately
Held**
Web: www.lukjan.com
SIC: 3312 3444 Blast furnaces and steel mills
  ; Ducts, sheet metal

(G-5411)
**LYONDLLBSELL ADVNCED
PLYMERS I**
Also Called: A Schulman
3365 E Center St (44030-3333)
PHONE..............................440 224-7291
EMP: 78
Web: www.lyondellbasell.com
SIC: 2869 Industrial organic chemicals, nec
HQ: Lyondellbasell Advanced Polymers Inc.
  1221 Mckinney St Ste 300
  Houston TX 77010
  713 309-7200

(G-5412)
MODERN ENGINEERING INC
527 W Adams St (44030-2272)
PHONE..............................440 593-5414
David Mc Laughin, *Owner*
EMP: 6 **EST:** 1985
SALES (est): 494.92K **Privately Held**
SIC: 3469 3599 Machine parts, stamped or
  pressed metal; Machine shop, jobbing and
  repair

(G-5413)
OVERHEAD DOOR CORPORATION
Also Called: Wayne - Dalton Plastics
1001 Chamberlain Blvd (44030-1168)
PHONE..............................440 593-5226
EMP: 11
Web: www.overheaddoor.com
SIC: 1751 3089 3083 Garage door,
  installation or erection; Extruded finished
  plastics products, nec; Laminated plastics
  plate and sheet
HQ: Overhead Door Corporation
  2501 S State Hwy 121 Ste
  Lewisville TX 75067
  469 549-7100

(G-5414)
**PREMIX-HADLOCK COMPOSITES
LLC (DH)**
3365 E Center St (44030-3333)
PHONE..............................440 335-4301
Terry Morgan, *Pr*
▲ **EMP:** 26 **EST:** 2008
SQ FT: 110,000
SALES (est): 23.09MM
SALES (corp-wide): 49.93MM **Privately
Held**
Web: www.premix-hadlock.com
SIC: 3089 Injection molding of plastics
HQ: Hpc Holdings, Llc
  3637 Ridgewood Rd
  Fairlawn OH 44333

(G-5415)
S AND S TOOL INC
576 Blair St (44030-1463)
P.O. Box 127 (44030-0127)
PHONE..............................440 593-4000
Paul Sedmak, *Pr*
Joe Sedmak, *VP*
EMP: 8 **EST:** 1983
SQ FT: 5,000
SALES (est): 866.39K **Privately Held**
Web: www.sstool1inc.com
SIC: 3599 Machine shop, jobbing and repair

(G-5416)
SECONDARY MACHINING SVCS INC
539 Center Rd (44030-2308)
P.O. Box 296 (44030-0296)
PHONE..............................440 593-3040
Art Distelrath Junior, *Pr*
Madelon L Distelrath, *Treas*
Amy Distelrath, *VP*
EMP: 7 **EST:** 1985
SALES (est): 183.81K **Privately Held**
SIC: 3599 Machine shop, jobbing and repair

(G-5417)
TEIJIN AUTOMOTIVE TECH INC
333 Gore Rd (44030-2909)
PHONE..............................440 945-4800
Dave Murtha, *Brnch Mgr*
EMP: 197
Web: www.teijinautomotive.com
SIC: 3089 Injection molding of plastics
HQ: Teijin Automotive Technologies, Inc.
  255 Rex Blvd
  Auburn Hills MI 48326
  248 237-7800

(G-5418)
THE GAZETTE PRINTING CO INC
Also Called: Gazette Publishing
218 Washington St (44030-2605)
P.O. Box 212 (44030-0212)
PHONE..............................440 593-6030
John Lampson, *Prin*
EMP: 9
SALES (corp-wide): 7.8MM **Privately Held**
Web: www.gazettenews.com
SIC: 2752 2711 Offset printing; Newspapers
PA: The Gazette Printing Co Inc
  46 W Jefferson St
  Jefferson OH 44047
  440 576-9125

(G-5419)
VESUVIUS U S A CORPORATION
Also Called: Foseco Metallurgical
1100 Maple Ave (44030-2119)
PHONE..............................440 593-1161
Jeremy Wilkinson, *Mgr*
EMP: 6
SALES (corp-wide): 2.41B **Privately Held**
SIC: 2899 Chemical preparations, nec
HQ: Vesuvius U S A Corporation
  1404 Newton Dr
  Champaign IL 61822
  217 351-5000

Conover
Miami County

(G-5420)
CONOVER LUMBER COMPANY INC
Also Called: Staely Custom Crating
7960 N Alcony Conover Rd (45317-3503)
P.O. Box 464 (45317-0464)
PHONE..............................937 368-3010
John D Staley, *Pr*
EMP: 14 **EST:** 2000
SQ FT: 3,584
SALES (est): 918.18K **Privately Held**
Web: www.conoverlumber.net
SIC: 5211 2421 Lumber products; Flooring
  (dressed lumber), softwood

(G-5421)
MAGNUM MOLDING INC
7435 N Bollinger Rd (45317-9738)
P.O. Box 459 (45317-0459)
PHONE..............................937 368-3040
Greg Gross, *Pr*
EMP: 9 **EST:** 1989
SQ FT: 7,000
SALES (est): 968.25K **Privately Held**
Web: www.magnummolding.com
SIC: 3089 3544 Injection molding of plastics;
  Industrial molds

Continental
Putnam County

(G-5422)
HELENA AGRI-ENTERPRISES LLC
200 N Main St (45831-9172)
PHONE..............................419 596-3806
Wayne Nossfinger, *Brnch Mgr*
EMP: 6
Web: www.helenaagri.com
SIC: 2819 5191 Chemicals, high purity:
  refined from technical grade; Fertilizers and
  agricultural chemicals
HQ: Helena Agri-Enterprises, Llc
  225 Schlling Blvd Ste 300
  Collierville TN 38017
  901 761-0050

(G-5423)
SOCAR OF OHIO INC (PA)
21739 Road E16 (45831-9003)
PHONE......................419 596-3100
Ken Charles, *
Cary Andrews, *
Donald G Smith, *
John Morris, *
EMP: 89 EST: 1971
SQ FT: 90,000
SALES (est): 832.6K
SALES (corp-wide): 832.6K Privately Held
SIC: 3441 2439 Joists, open web steel: long-span series; Structural wood members, nec

(G-5424)
VERHOFF MACHINE & WELDING INC
7300 Road 18 (45831-8826)
PHONE......................419 596-3202
Edward Verhoff, *Pr*
Joseph Verhoff, *
Leonard J Verhoff, *
EMP: 120 EST: 1955
SQ FT: 150,000
SALES (est): 21.66MM Privately Held
Web: www.verhoff.com
SIC: 3599 3469 3444 3443 Machine shop, jobbing and repair; Metal stampings, nec; Sheet metalwork; Fabricated plate work (boiler shop)

Convoy
Van Wert County

(G-5425)
SHELLY MATERIALS INC
2364 Richey Rd (45832-9643)
PHONE......................419 622-2101
Gary Ferguson, *CEO*
EMP: 18
SALES (corp-wide): 34.95B Privately Held
Web: www.shellyco.com
SIC: 2951 Asphalt paving mixtures and blocks
HQ: Shelly Materials, Inc.
80 Park Dr
Thornville OH 43076
740 246-6315

Coolville
Athens County

(G-5426)
MIDDLETON LLYD DOLLS INC (PA)
Also Called: Middlton Lloyd Doll Fctry Outl
23689 Mountain Bell Rd (45723-9463)
PHONE......................740 989-2082
Janice Middleton, *Pr*
Lloyd Middleton, *Pr*
Janice Middleton, *VP*
EMP: 7 EST: 1990
SQ FT: 8,000
SALES (est): 626.32K Privately Held
SIC: 3942 5945 5092 Dolls, except stuffed toy animals; Hobby, toy, and game shops; Dolls

Copley
Summit County

(G-5427)
ACE BOILER & WELDING CO INC
118 Brookrun Dr (44321-1373)
PHONE......................330 745-4443
Robert Kille, *Pr*
Cynthia Kille, *Stockholder*

EMP: 8 EST: 1962
SALES (est): 583.71K Privately Held
Web: www.aceboilerandwelding.com
SIC: 3599 3441 Machine shop, jobbing and repair; Fabricated structural metal

(G-5428)
AKRON DISPERSIONS INC
3291 Sawmill Rd (44321-1637)
P.O. Box 4195 (44321-0195)
PHONE......................330 666-0045
Michael Giustino, *CEO*
James Finn, *
Diane Hunsicker, *
▲ **EMP: 25 EST: 1958**
SQ FT: 56,000
SALES (est): 9.94MM Privately Held
Web: www.akrondispersions.com
SIC: 2819 2899 Industrial inorganic chemicals, nec; Chemical preparations, nec

(G-5429)
ALL FIRED UP PNT YOUR OWN POT
30 Rothrock Loop (44321-1331)
PHONE......................330 865-5858
Janelle Wertz, *Owner*
EMP: 6 EST: 2002
SALES (est): 194.51K Privately Held
Web: www.allfiredupakron.com
SIC: 3269 5719 Art and ornamental ware, pottery; Pottery

(G-5430)
BKT USA INC
Also Called: Bkt
202 Montrose West Ave Ste 240
(44321-2903)
PHONE......................330 836-1090
▲ **EMP: 15 EST: 2009**
SALES (est): 2.39MM Privately Held
Web: www.bkt-tires.com
SIC: 5531 3011 Automotive tires; Tires and inner tubes
PA: Balkrishna Industries Limited
Bkt House, C/15, Trade World, Kamala Mills Compound,
Mumbai MH 40001

(G-5431)
BLOCH PRINTING COMPANY
3569 Copley Rd (44321-1646)
PHONE......................330 576-6760
David Bloch, *Pr*
Maria Bloch, *VP*
EMP: 6 EST: 1977
SALES (est): 336.41K Privately Held
Web: www.blochprinting.com
SIC: 5112 2752 Business forms; Commercial printing, lithographic

(G-5432)
CARAUSTAR INDUSTRIES INC
Also Called: Caraustar
202 Montrose West Ave Ste 315
(44321-2904)
PHONE......................330 665-7700
EMP: 22
SALES (corp-wide): 5.45B Publicly Held
Web: www.caraustar.com
SIC: 2679 2655 3275 3089 Paperboard products, converted, nec; Tubes, fiber or paper: made from purchased material; Gypsum products; Injection molded finished plastics products, nec
HQ: Caraustar Industries, Inc.
5000 Astell Pwdr Sprng Rd
Austell GA 30106
770 948-3101

(G-5433)
COPLEY FIRE & RESCUE ASSN
Also Called: Copley Township Fire Dept
1540 S Cleveland Massillon Rd
(44321-1908)
PHONE......................330 666-6464
Chief Joseph Ezzi, *Prin*
Joseph Ezzi, *Prin*
EMP: 10 EST: 1977
SALES (est): 308.78K Privately Held
Web: www.copley.oh.us
SIC: 3711 Fire department vehicles (motor vehicles), assembly of

(G-5434)
MEECH STTIC ELMINATORS USA INC
1298 Centerview Cir (44321-1632)
PHONE......................330 564-2000
Matt Fyffe, *Genl Mgr*
▲ **EMP: 15 EST: 1995**
SALES (est): 4.01MM Privately Held
Web: www.meech.com
SIC: 3823 Industrial process measurement equipment

(G-5435)
MILLER EXPRESS INC
828 Dogwood Ter (44321-1406)
PHONE......................330 714-6751
Douglas Miller, *Prin*
EMP: 6 EST: 2008
SALES (est): 256.39K Privately Held
SIC: 2741 Miscellaneous publishing

(G-5436)
POWER MEDIA INC
152 Hunt Club Dr Apt 3c (44321-2722)
PHONE......................330 475-0500
Jon Erisey, *Pr*
EMP: 8 EST: 1997
SALES (est): 487.41K Privately Held
Web: www.gopowermedia.com
SIC: 3993 3999 Advertising novelties; Advertising display products

(G-5437)
PRCC HOLDINGS INC
Also Called: Preferred Compounding
175 Montrose West Ave Ste 200
(44321-3122)
PHONE......................330 798-4790
Kenneth Bloom, *Pr*
Kenneth Bloom, *CEO*
David Kantor, *CFO*
EMP: 238 EST: 2010
SQ FT: 5,000
SALES (est): 205MM Privately Held
SIC: 3069 Custom compounding of rubber materials

(G-5438)
PRIMAL LIFE ORGANICS LLC
405 Rothrock Rd Ste 105 (44321-3146)
PHONE......................800 260-4946
Trina Felber, *CEO*
EMP: 20 EST: 2012
SALES (est): 3.98MM Privately Held
Web: www.primallifeorganics.com
SIC: 2844 5999 Perfumes, cosmetics and other toilet preparations; Cosmetics

(G-5439)
PVS CHEMICAL SOLUTIONS INC
3149 Copley Rd (44321-2127)
P.O. Box 4143 (44321-0143)
PHONE......................330 666-0888
Bob Vorhees, *Mgr*
EMP: 10
SQ FT: 27,596
SALES (corp-wide): 483.42MM Privately Held

Web: www.pvschemicals.com
SIC: 2819 5169 Sulfur chloride; Chemicals and allied products, nec
HQ: Pvs Chemical Solutions, Inc.
10900 Harper Ave
Detroit MI 48213

Corning
Perry County

(G-5440)
ALTIER BROTHERS INC
155 Walnut St (43730)
P.O. Box 430 (43730-0430)
PHONE......................740 347-4329
Louis Altier, *Pr*
EMP: 6 EST: 1950
SQ FT: 5,000
SALES (est): 927.58K Privately Held
Web: altier-bros-inc.business.site
SIC: 1389 Oil field services, nec

(G-5441)
JT PLUS WELL SERVICE LLC
140 E Main St (43730-9550)
PHONE......................740 347-0070
Patrick W Altier, *Prin*
EMP: 10 EST: 2001
SALES (est): 1.16MM Privately Held
SIC: 1389 Oil field services, nec

Cortland
Trumbull County

(G-5442)
BORTNICK TRACTOR SALES INC
6192 Warren Rd (44410-9736)
PHONE......................330 924-2555
Dana W Harju, *Prin*
EMP: 20 EST: 2013
SALES (est): 1.94MM Privately Held
Web: www.bortnicktractorsales.com
SIC: 5261 3541 5083 Lawn and garden equipment; Saws and sawing machines; Agricultural machinery and equipment

(G-5443)
CONTROL TRANSFORMER INC
Also Called: Geneva Rubber Company
3701 Warren Meadville Rd (44410-9423)
PHONE......................330 637-6015
William J Martin, *Pr*
▲ **EMP: 45 EST: 2002**
SQ FT: 30,000
SALES (est): 10.32MM
SALES (corp-wide): 1.66B Publicly Held
Web: www.control-transformer.com
SIC: 3612 Power transformers, electric
HQ: Ajax Tocco Magnethermic Corporation
1745 Overland Avenue Ne
Warren OH 44483
800 547-1527

(G-5444)
EXTREME CASTER SERVICES INC
3333 Niles Cortland Rd Ne (44410-1786)
PHONE......................330 637-9030
John C Grundy, *Prin*
EMP: 6 EST: 2008
SALES (est): 506.31K Privately Held
SIC: 3562 Casters

(G-5445)
HOWLAND PRINTING INC
Also Called: Proforma
3117 Niles Cortland Rd Ne (44410-1737)
PHONE......................330 637-8255
Norma Harned, *Pr*

EMP: 7 **EST:** 1994
SQ FT: 1,500
SALES (est): 178.97K **Privately Held**
Web: www.proforma.com
SIC: 2752 Offset printing

(G-5446)
LAWBRE CO
Also Called: Architechual Etc
3311 Warren Meadville Rd (44410-8808)
PHONE..................................330 637-3363
Christopher Riekert, *Pr*
EMP: 6 **EST:** 1974
SQ FT: 5,000
SALES (est): 111.9K **Privately Held**
Web: www.lawbre.com
SIC: 3944 Dollhouses and furniture

Coshocton
Coshocton County

(G-5447)
ANNIN & CO INC
Annin Flagmakers
700 S 3rd St (43812-2062)
PHONE..................................740 622-4447
Vane Scott Iii, *Mgr*
EMP: 167
SQ FT: 15,000
SALES (corp-wide): 52.62MM **Privately Held**
Web: www.annin.com
SIC: 2399 5999 3446 3429 Flags, fabric;
  Banners, flags, decals, and posters;
  Architectural metalwork; Hardware, nec
PA: Annin & Co., Inc.
  430 Mountain Ave
  New Providence NJ 07974
  973 228-9400

(G-5448)
ANSELL HEALTHCARE PRODUCTS LLC
Also Called: Ansell Edmont Div
925 Chestnut St (43812-1302)
PHONE..................................740 622-4369
Kendall Cranston, *Mgr*
EMP: 240
Web: www.ansell.com
SIC: 3842 2822 2259 Gloves, safety;
  Synthetic rubber; Gloves, knit, except dress
  and semidress gloves
HQ: Ansell Healthcare Products Llc
  111 Wood Ave S Ste 210
  Iselin NJ 08830
  732 345-5400

(G-5449)
ANSELL HEALTHCARE PRODUCTS LLC
925 Chestnut St (43812-1302)
PHONE..................................740 622-4311
Allan Roman, *Mgr*
EMP: 26
Web: www.ansell.com
SIC: 3842 3069 Gloves, safety; Rubber
  coated fabrics and clothing
HQ: Ansell Healthcare Products Llc
  111 Wood Ave S Ste 210
  Iselin NJ 08830
  732 345-5400

(G-5450)
ARMCO INC
17400 State Route 16 (43812-9268)
PHONE..................................740 829-3000
Edward F Smith, *Prin*
EMP: 6 **EST:** 2010
SALES (est): 197.57K **Privately Held**

SIC: 3315 Steel wire and related products

(G-5451)
BAIRD CONCRETE PRODUCTS INC
15 Locust St (43812-1136)
P.O. Box 1028 (43812-5028)
PHONE..................................740 623-8600
John Baird, *Pr*
Margie Baird, *VP*
Cynthia Albertson, *Sec*
Tom Albertson, *VP*
EMP: 10 **EST:** 1989
SQ FT: 13,700
SALES (est): 1.08MM **Privately Held**
Web: www.bairdconcrete.biz
SIC: 3273 Ready-mixed concrete

(G-5452)
BRYDET DEVELOPMENT CORPORATION
16867 State Route 83 (43812-9460)
P.O. Box 199 (43811-0199)
PHONE..................................740 623-0455
Paul E Bryant, *Pr*
Ron Deeter, *
▼ **EMP:** 6 **EST:** 1987
SQ FT: 4,500
SALES (est): 497.72K **Privately Held**
Web: www.brydet.com
SIC: 3532 Auger mining equipment

(G-5453)
BUCKEYE FABRIC FINISHERS INC
Also Called: Buckeye Fabric Finishing Co
1260 E Main St (43812-1700)
PHONE..................................740 622-3251
▲ **EMP:** 18 **EST:** 1988
SALES (est): 2.37MM **Privately Held**
Web: www.be-fabric.com
SIC: 2295 2899 2851 Waterproofing fabrics,
  except rubberizing; Chemical preparations,
  nec; Paints and allied products

(G-5454)
EXCELLO FABRIC FINISHERS INC
802 S 2nd St (43812-1916)
P.O. Box 848 (43812)
PHONE..................................740 622-7444
Kevin Lee, *Pr*
Charles Milligan, *Prin*
Edward L Lee, *Ch Bd*
William J Stenner, *VP*
Eugene Weir, *Prin*
EMP: 6 **EST:** 1966
SQ FT: 1,000
SALES (est): 977.59K **Privately Held**
Web: www.be-fabric.com
SIC: 2295 Waterproofing fabrics, except
  rubberizing

(G-5455)
FRANCISCO JAUME
Also Called: Coshocton Orthopedic Center
311 S 15th St Ste 206 (43812-1875)
P.O. Box 490 (43812-0490)
PHONE..................................740 622-1200
Francisco Jaume, *Owner*
EMP: 6 **EST:** 1997
SALES (est): 275.4K **Privately Held**
SIC: 3842 8011 Surgical appliances and
  supplies; Offices and clinics of medical
  doctors

(G-5456)
GENERAL ELECTRIC COMPANY
Also Called: GE
1350 S 2nd St (43812-1980)
PHONE..................................740 623-5379
Bob Callahan, *Mgr*
EMP: 6
SALES (corp-wide): 38.7B **Publicly Held**

Web: geaerospace.com
SIC: 3083 Plastics finished products,
  laminated
PA: General Electric Company
  1 Aviation Way
  Cincinnati OH 45215
  617 443-3000

(G-5457)
ITM MARKETING INC
Also Called: Intellitarget Marketing Svcs
331 Main St (43812-1510)
PHONE..................................740 295-3575
Lawrence W Farrell, *Pr*
Bruce Collen, *
EMP: 124 **EST:** 1996
SALES (est): 2.13MM **Privately Held**
Web: www.itmmarketing.com
SIC: 8742 7374 2741 7322 Marketing
  consulting services; Data processing and
  preparation; Telephone and other directory
  publishing; Adjustment and collection
  services

(G-5458)
KRAFT HEINZ FOODS COMPANY
Also Called: Heinz
1660 S 2nd St (43812-1977)
PHONE..................................740 622-0523
Carol Villa, *Mgr*
EMP: 109
SQ FT: 120,000
SALES (corp-wide): 25.85B **Publicly Held**
Web: www.kraftheinzcompany.com
SIC: 2013 Sausages and other prepared
  meats
HQ: Kraft Heinz Foods Company
  1 Ppg Pl Ste 3400
  Pittsburgh PA 15222
  412 456-5700

(G-5459)
MCWANE INC
Clow Water Systems Company
2266 S 6th St (43812-8906)
P.O. Box 6001 (43812-6001)
PHONE..................................740 622-6651
Jeff Otterstedt, *Mgr*
EMP: 400
SALES (corp-wide): 970.37MM **Privately Held**
Web: www.mcwane.com
SIC: 3321 5085 5051 3444 Cast iron pipe
  and fittings; Industrial supplies; Pipe and
  tubing, steel; Sheet metalwork
PA: Mcwane, Inc.
  2900 Hwy 280 S Ste 300
  Birmingham AL 35223
  205 414-3100

(G-5460)
MFC DRILLING INC
Also Called: Medina Fuel
46281 Us Highway 36 (43812-8707)
P.O. Box 715 (43812-0715)
PHONE..................................740 622-5600
James S Aslanides, *Pr*
Jackie Wilkins, *Admn*
Randy Matheny, *VP*
EMP: 10 **EST:** 1988
SQ FT: 2,200
SALES (est): 970.79K **Privately Held**
SIC: 1382 Oil and gas exploration services

(G-5461)
MFM BUILDING PRODUCTS CORP
425 Brewer Ln (43812-8965)
PHONE..................................740 622-2645
EMP: 25
SALES (corp-wide): 17.49MM **Privately Held**

Web: www.mfmbp.com
SIC: 2952 Asphalt felts and coatings
PA: Mfm Building Products Corp
  525 Orange St
  Coshocton OH 43812
  740 622-2645

(G-5462)
MFM BUILDING PRODUCTS CORP (PA)
525 Orange St (43812-2178)
P.O. Box 340 (43812-0340)
PHONE..................................740 622-2645
◆ **EMP:** 43 **EST:** 1952
SALES (est): 17.49MM
SALES (corp-wide): 17.49MM **Privately Held**
Web: www.mfmbp.com
SIC: 2952 Roof cement: asphalt, fibrous, or
  plastic

(G-5463)
MUSKINGUM GRINDING AND MCH CO
2155 Otsego Ave (43812-9401)
P.O. Box 396 (43812-0396)
PHONE..................................740 622-4741
Jeff Mulett, *Pr*
Janel Richards, *Sec*
EMP: 15 **EST:** 1945
SQ FT: 14,000
SALES (est): 1.33MM **Privately Held**
SIC: 3599 Machine shop, jobbing and repair

(G-5464)
NGO DEVELOPMENT CORPORATION
Also Called: Energy Corportive
504 N 3rd St (43812-1113)
P.O. Box 662 (43812-0662)
PHONE..................................740 622-9560
Scott Kees, *Mgr*
EMP: 7
SALES (corp-wide): 13.4MM **Privately Held**
Web: www.myenergycoop.com
SIC: 1382 4923 5984 Oil and gas
  exploration services; Gas transmission and
  distribution; Propane gas, bottled
HQ: Ngo Development Corporation
  1500 Granville Rd
  Newark OH 43055
  740 344-3790

(G-5465)
NOVELTY ADVERTISING CO INC
Also Called: Kenyon Co
1148 Walnut St (43812-1769)
PHONE..................................740 622-3113
Gregory Coffman, *Pr*
James Mcconnel, *VP*
◆ **EMP:** 50 **EST:** 1895
SQ FT: 100,000
SALES (est): 1.63MM **Privately Held**
Web: www.noveltyadv.com
SIC: 2752 5199 Calendars, lithographed;
  Advertising specialties

(G-5466)
OFCO INC
Also Called: Ohio Fabricators
111 N 14th St (43812-1710)
P.O. Box 218 (43812-0218)
PHONE..................................740 622-5922
Michael Shaw, *CEO*
Harold R Shaw, *
▲ **EMP:** 65 **EST:** 1945
SQ FT: 50,000
SALES (est): 9.22MM **Privately Held**
Web: www.ohfab.com
SIC: 3496 Wire cloth and woven wire
  products

(G-5467)
OHIO FABRICATORS COMPANY
1321 Elm St (43812-2216)
PHONE..............................740 622-5922
Marcia Bush, *CEO*
EMP: 10 **EST:** 2008
SALES (est): 1.86MM **Privately Held**
Web: www.ohfab.com
SIC: 3441 Fabricated structural metal

(G-5468)
OXFORD MINING COMPANY INC (DH)
544 Chestnut St (43812-1209)
P.O. Box 1027 (43812-5027)
PHONE..............................740 622-6302
Charles C Ungurean, *Pr*
Thomas T Ungurean, *Sec*
Jeffrey M Gutman, *Sr VP*
Gregory J Honish, *Sr VP*
Daniel M Maher, *Sr VP*
EMP: 6 **EST:** 1985
SQ FT: 3,200
SALES (est): 9.37MM
SALES (corp-wide): 449.53MM **Privately Held**
SIC: 1221 Bituminous coal and lignite-surface mining
HQ: Westmoreland Resource Partners, Lp
9540 S Maroon Cir Ste 300
Englewood CO 80112

(G-5469)
OXFORD MINING COMPANY LLC (DH)
544 Chestnut St (43812-1209)
PHONE..............................740 622-6302
EMP: 12 **EST:** 1985
SALES (est): 2.62MM
SALES (corp-wide): 449.53MM **Privately Held**
SIC: 1221 Bituminous coal and lignite-surface mining
HQ: Westmoreland Resource Partners, Lp
9540 S Maroon Cir Ste 300
Englewood CO 80112

(G-5470)
OXFORD MINING COMPANY - KY LLC
544 Chestnut St (43812-1209)
PHONE..............................740 622-6302
EMP: 32 **EST:** 2010
SALES (est): 1.09MM
SALES (corp-wide): 449.53MM **Privately Held**
SIC: 1221 Strip mining, bituminous
HQ: Oxford Mining Company, Llc
544 Chestnut St
Coshocton OH 43812

(G-5471)
SANCAST INC
535 Clow Ln (43812-9782)
PHONE..............................740 622-8660
Don Hutchins, *Prin*
Don Popernik, *
John Fox, *
Nancy Foster, *
Julie Starcher, *
EMP: 50 **EST:** 1975
SQ FT: 56,000
SALES (est): 7.87MM **Publicly Held**
SIC: 3321 3322 Ductile iron castings; Malleable iron foundries
HQ: Wabtec Componenfs Llc
30 Isabella St
Pittsburgh PA 15212
412 825-1000

(G-5472)
SHAWNE SPRINGS WINERY
20093 County Road 6 (43812-9149)
PHONE..............................740 623-0744
Randy Hall, *Prin*
EMP: 7 **EST:** 2007
SALES (est): 161.01K **Privately Held**
Web: www.shawneespringswinery.com
SIC: 2084 Wines

(G-5473)
SPRINT PRINT INC
Also Called: Market Media Creations
520 Main St (43812-1612)
PHONE..............................740 622-4429
Jeff Eikenberry, *Pr*
EMP: 9 **EST:** 1999
SQ FT: 6,000
SALES (est): 362.48K **Privately Held**
SIC: 2752 7319 Offset printing; Poster advertising service, except outdoor

(G-5474)
THOMAS J WEAVER INC (PA)
Also Called: Coshocton Pallet & Door Co
1501 Kenilworth Ave (43812-2430)
P.O. Box 412 (43812-0412)
PHONE..............................740 622-2040
Thomas J Weaver, *Pr*
EMP: 12 **EST:** 1963
SALES (est): 684.5K
SALES (corp-wide): 684.5K **Privately Held**
SIC: 1542 1541 1521 2448 Commercial and office building, new construction; Industrial buildings, new construction, nec; New construction, single-family houses; Pallets, wood

(G-5475)
WESTMORELAND RESOURCES GP LLC
544 Chestnut St (43812-1209)
PHONE..............................740 622-6302
Martin Purvis, *CEO*
EMP: 48 **EST:** 2007
SALES (est): 3.27MM
SALES (corp-wide): 449.53MM **Privately Held**
SIC: 1221 Bituminous coal and lignite-surface mining
PA: Westmoreland Mining Llc
10375 Pk Mdows Dr Ste 400
Lone Tree CO 80124
303 922-6463

(G-5476)
WILEY COMPANIES (PA)
Also Called: Organic Technologies
545 Walnut St (43812-1656)
P.O. Box 1665 (43812)
PHONE..............................740 622-0755
▲ **EMP:** 130 **EST:** 1981
SALES (est): 22.04MM
SALES (corp-wide): 22.04MM **Privately Held**
Web: www.wileyco.com
SIC: 2087 8731 2869 Concentrates, flavoring (except drink); Commercial physical research; Industrial organic chemicals, nec

(G-5477)
WILEY COMPANIES
Also Called: Organic Technologies
1245 S 6th St (43812-2809)
PHONE..............................740 622-0755
David Wiley, *Pr*
EMP: 200
SALES (corp-wide): 22.04MM **Privately Held**
Web: www.wileyco.com

SIC: 2869 Industrial organic chemicals, nec
PA: Wiley Companies
545 Walnut St
Coshocton OH 43812
740 622-0755

(G-5478)
WILEYS FINEST LLC (PA)
545 Walnut St (43812-1656)
P.O. Box 1665 (43812-6665)
PHONE..............................740 622-1072
Sam Wiley, *Managing Member*
Shane Griffiths, *Prin*
EMP: 191 **EST:** 2013
SALES (est): 7.71MM
SALES (corp-wide): 7.71MM **Privately Held**
Web: www.wileysfinest.com
SIC: 2077 2079 2023 5499 Animal fats, oils, and meals; Edible fats and oils; Dietary supplements, dairy and non-dairy based; Health foods

---

Coventry Township
Summit County

(G-5479)
AKRON DESIGN & COSTUME LLC
888 Tippecanoe Dr (44319-2140)
PHONE..............................330 644-0425
Debbie Meridith, *Owner*
EMP: 8 **EST:** 1981
SALES (est): 190.23K **Privately Held**
Web: www.akrondesign.com
SIC: 2389 7299 Costumes; Costume rental

(G-5480)
ALSCOMMUNITY ✿
665 Cove Blvd (44319-1041)
PHONE..............................215 478-5095
Jeff Oppenheimer, *Pr*
EMP: 13 **EST:** 2024
SALES (est): 698.39K **Privately Held**
SIC: 2741 8399 Internet publishing and broadcasting; Health and welfare council

(G-5481)
CHEMEQUIP SALES INC
Also Called: R & R Engine & Machine
1004 Swartz Rd (44319-1340)
PHONE..............................330 724-8300
Jeanie Menke, *Pr*
EMP: 30 **EST:** 1968
SQ FT: 2,500
SALES (est): 4.81MM **Privately Held**
Web: www.rrengine.com
SIC: 3519 3621 Diesel engine rebuilding; Motors and generators

(G-5482)
FRIESS WELDING INC
Also Called: Summit Trailer Sales & Svcs
3342 S Main St (44319-3099)
PHONE..............................330 644-8160
Jeff Friess, *Pr*
Russell C Friess, *CEO*
Betty Friess, *Sec*
EMP: 6 **EST:** 1968
SQ FT: 7,000
SALES (est): 510.56K **Privately Held**
Web: www.friessandsummit.com
SIC: 7692 7539 5511 Welding repair; Radiator repair shop, automotive; Trucks, tractors, and trailers: new and used

(G-5483)
GARDNER PIE COMPANY
191 Logan Pkwy (44319-1188)
PHONE..............................330 245-2030

EMP: 140 **EST:** 1944
SALES (est): 39.11MM **Privately Held**
Web: www.gardnerpie.com
SIC: 2053 2051 Pies, bakery; frozen; Bread, cake, and related products

(G-5484)
KEN-DAL CORPORATION
644 Killian Rd (44319-2599)
PHONE..............................330 644-7118
William Keasling, *Pr*
Alan Place, *VP*
▲ **EMP:** 10 **EST:** 1962
SQ FT: 12,000
SALES (est): 1.28MM **Privately Held**
Web: admiral.kendal.org
SIC: 3599 Machine shop, jobbing and repair

(G-5485)
KUHLMAN CORPORATION
Also Called: B&G Contractors Supply
999 Swartz Rd (44319-1335)
PHONE..............................330 724-9900
Jeff Johnston, *Brnch Mgr*
EMP: 21
SALES (corp-wide): 42.49MM **Privately Held**
Web: www.gerkencompanies.com
SIC: 3273 Ready-mixed concrete
PA: Kuhlman Corporation
1845 Indian Wood Cir
Maumee OH 43537
419 897-6000

(G-5486)
L & S HOME IMPROVEMENT
549 Saunders Ave (44319-2270)
PHONE..............................330 906-3199
Lezjon Mantz, *Owner*
EMP: 6 **EST:** 2019
SALES (est): 200K **Privately Held**
SIC: 1389 Construction, repair, and dismantling services

(G-5487)
PACKAGING CORPORATION AMERICA
Also Called: PCA/Akron 312
708 Killian Rd (44319-2559)
PHONE..............................330 644-9542
Ralph Snyder, *Mgr*
EMP: 44
SALES (corp-wide): 7.73B **Publicly Held**
Web: www.packagingcorp.com
SIC: 2653 Boxes, corrugated: made from purchased materials
PA: Packaging Corporation Of America
1 N Field Ct
Lake Forest IL 60045
847 482-3000

Covington
Miami County

(G-5488)
ARENS CORPORATION (PA)
395 S High St (45318-1121)
P.O. Box 69 (45318-0069)
PHONE..............................937 473-2028
Gary Godfrey Senior, *Pr*
Ginger Godfrey, *VP*
Gary Godfrey, *Sec*
EMP: 17 **EST:** 1954
SQ FT: 2,000
SALES (est): 643.59K
SALES (corp-wide): 643.59K **Privately Held**
Web: www.arenspub.com

▲ = Import ▼ = Export
◆ = Import/Export

SIC: **2711** 2721 2752 Newspapers:
publishing only, not printed on site;
Magazines: publishing only, not printed on
site; Offset printing

(G-5489)
ARENS CORPORATION
Also Called: Arens Publications & Printing
22 N High St (45318-1306)
PHONE....................................937 473-2028
Connie Didier, *Mgr*
EMP: 6
SALES (corp-wide): 643.59K **Privately
Held**
Web: www.arenspub.com
SIC: **2711** 2721 2752 Newspapers:
publishing only, not printed on site;
Magazines: publishing only, not printed on
site; Offset printing
PA: The Arens Corporation
395 S High St
Covington OH 45318
937 473-2028

(G-5490)
B K PLASTICS INC
1400 Mote Dr (45318-1217)
P.O. Box 250 (45318-0250)
PHONE....................................937 473-2087
Robert Robbins, *Pr*
Karen Robbins, *Treas*
EMP: 6 **EST:** 1983
SQ FT: 12,000
SALES (est): 272.09K **Privately Held**
Web: www.bkpi.net
SIC: **2673** Plastic bags: made from
purchased materials

(G-5491)
CONCEPT MACHINE & TOOL INC
2065 Industrial Ct (45318-1265)
P.O. Box 9 (45318-0009)
PHONE....................................937 473-3334
EMP: 22 **EST:** 1993
SALES (est): 3.68MM **Privately Held**
Web: www.conceptmach.com
SIC: **3599** Machine shop, jobbing and repair

(G-5492)
**D&D CLSSIC AUTO RSTORATION
INC**
Also Called: D&D Classic Restoration
2300 Mote Dr (45318-1200)
PHONE....................................937 473-2229
Dale Sotsing, *Pr*
Rodger James, *VP*
Mark Kennison, *Sec*
EMP: 9 **EST:** 1985
SQ FT: 8,000
SALES (est): 636.14K **Privately Held**
Web: www.cristinapowerhouse.com
SIC: **7389** 3711 5521 7532 Automobile
recovery service; Motor vehicles and car
bodies; Automobiles, used cars only; Tops
(canvas or plastic), installation or repair:
automotive

(G-5493)
GENERAL FILMS INC
645 S High St (45318-1182)
PHONE....................................888 436-3456
Roy J Weikert, *Ch*
Tim Weikert, *Pr*
Marilyn Dennings, *Sec*
Tom Granata, *VP*
EMP: 80 **EST:** 1938
SQ FT: 55,000
SALES (est): 9.92MM **Privately Held**
Web: www.generalfilms.com
SIC: **3081** 2673 Polyethylene film; Plastic
and pliofilm bags

(G-5494)
HITACHI AUTOMATION OHIO INC
Also Called: Kec America
2000 Industrial Ct (45318-1266)
PHONE....................................937 753-1148
Hiroshi Ichiki, *Pr*
EMP: 10 **EST:** 2011
SALES (est): 5.95MM **Privately Held**
Web: www.kec-corp.jp
SIC: **3569** Robots, assembly line: industrial
and commercial
PA: Hitachi, Ltd.
1-6-6, Marunouchi
Chiyoda-Ku TKY 100-0

(G-5495)
J&I DUCT FAB LLC
7502 W State Route 41 (45318-9746)
P.O. Box 190 (45318-0190)
PHONE....................................937 473-2121
EMP: 12 **EST:** 2013
SALES (est): 1.1MM **Privately Held**
Web: www.jiduct.com
SIC: **3585** Heating and air conditioning
combination units

(G-5496)
NEW TECH PLASTICS LLC
1300 Mote Dr (45318-1218)
P.O. Box 99 (45318-0099)
PHONE....................................937 473-3011
EMP: 87 **EST:** 1980
SALES (est): 1.42MM **Privately Held**
Web: www.newtechplastics.com
SIC: **3081** Polyethylene film

(G-5497)
PBM COVINGTON LLC
400 Hazel St (45318-1724)
PHONE....................................937 473-2050
Scott F Jamison, *Managing Member*
EMP: 9 **EST:** 2008
SALES (est): 1MM **Privately Held**
SIC: **2834** Vitamin, nutrient, and hematinic
preparations for human use

(G-5498)
PERRIGO
400 Hazel St (45318-1724)
PHONE....................................937 473-2050
EMP: 22 **EST:** 2013
SALES (est): 3.42MM **Privately Held**
Web: www.perrigo.com
SIC: **2834** Pharmaceutical preparations

(G-5499)
**ROSEBUDS RANCH AND GARDEN
LLC**
Also Called: Rosebud's Real Food
473 E Troy Pike (45318-1196)
PHONE....................................937 214-1801
EMP: 10 **EST:** 2016
SALES (est): 775.62K **Privately Held**
Web: www.rosebudsrealfood.com
SIC: **2099** 2033 2095 Seasonings and spices
; Canned fruits and specialties; Roasted
coffee

(G-5500)
TUSCARORA WOOD MIDWEST LLC
6506 W Us Route 36 (45318-9661)
PHONE....................................937 603-8882
Rodney Long, *Prin*
EMP: 6 **EST:** 2007
SALES (est): 433.93K **Privately Held**
Web: www.tuscarorawoodmidwest.com
SIC: **2431** Millwork

Crestline
Crawford County

(G-5501)
DRIVEN EXCAVATING LLC
121 S Washington Ave (44827-1931)
P.O. Box 320 (44827-0320)
PHONE....................................567 224-1421
Darrin Feichtner, *Managing Member*
Jason Stober, *
EMP: 25 **EST:** 2019
SALES (est): 5.91MM **Privately Held**
Web: www.drivenexcavating.com
SIC: **3531** Plows: construction, excavating,
and grading

(G-5502)
FOWLER PRODUCTS INC
810 Colby Rd (44827-1799)
PHONE....................................419 683-4057
Mark Fowler, *Pr*
Phyllis Fowler, *Ch*
Robert Stauffer, *Stockholder*
Jean E Cole, *Stockholder*
Marcia A Dishon, *Stockholder*
▲ **EMP:** 6 **EST:** 1976
SQ FT: 52,000
SALES (est): 859.15K **Privately Held**
Web: www.fowler-inc.com
SIC: **3089** 3829 3084 3083 Extruded
finished plastics products, nec; Measuring
and controlling devices, nec; Plastics pipe;
Laminated plastics plate and sheet

(G-5503)
INTERSTATE SIGN PRODUCTS INC
432 E Main St (44827-1118)
P.O. Box 187 (44827-0187)
PHONE....................................419 683-1962
Robin Wittmer, *Pr*
EMP: 6 **EST:** 1985
SQ FT: 4,000
SALES (est): 971.4K **Privately Held**
Web: www.interstate911.com
SIC: **5085** 3993 Signmaker equipment and
supplies; Letters for signs, metal

(G-5504)
NIESE FARMS
7506 Cole Rd (44827-9742)
PHONE....................................419 347-1204
Patrick Niese, *Pt*
EMP: 7 **EST:** 1965
SQ FT: 2,150
SALES (est): 249.73K **Privately Held**
SIC: **2043** Oatmeal: prepared as cereal
breakfast food

Creston
Wayne County

(G-5505)
ATLANTIC VEAL & LAMB LLC
2416 E West Salem Rd (44217-9650)
PHONE....................................330 435-6400
Phillip Peerless, *Managing Member*
EMP: 9 **EST:** 2008
SALES (est): 2.13MM
SALES (corp-wide): 4.4MM **Privately Held**
SIC: **2011** Veal, from meat slaughtered on
site
PA: Atlantic Veal And Lamb, Inc.
275 Morgan Ave
Brooklyn NY 11211
718 599-6400

(G-5506)
FRANK CSAPO
Also Called: Frank Csapo Oil & Gas Producer
157 Myers St (44217-9704)
PHONE....................................330 435-4458
Frank Csapo, *Owner*
EMP: 6 **EST:** 1970
SALES (est): 499.24K **Privately Held**
SIC: **1381** Drilling oil and gas wells

(G-5507)
MELLOTT BRONZE INC
4634 E Sterling Rd (44217-9241)
PHONE....................................330 435-6304
Ron Mellott, *Pr*
Ed Mellott, *VP*
Linda Mellott, *Sec*
EMP: 13 **EST:** 1985
SQ FT: 11,800
SALES (est): 2.32MM **Privately Held**
Web: www.mellottbronze.com
SIC: **3599** Machine shop, jobbing and repair

Crooksville
Perry County

(G-5508)
BEAUMONT BROS STONEWARE INC
Also Called: Beaumont Brothers Pottery
410 Keystone St (43731-1034)
PHONE....................................740 982-0055
Roger Beaumont, *Pr*
Margie Beaumont, *
EMP: 24 **EST:** 1989
SQ FT: 14,000
SALES (est): 219.68K **Privately Held**
SIC: **3269** Stoneware pottery products

(G-5509)
CHRISTY CATALYTICS LLC
713 Keystone St (43731-1039)
PHONE....................................740 982-1302
EMP: 7
Web: www.christycatalytics.com
SIC: **2819** Catalysts, chemical
HQ: Christy Catalytics, Llc
4641 Mcree Ave
Saint Louis MO 63110

(G-5510)
I CERCO INC
416 Maple Ave (43731-1305)
P.O. Box 151 (43731-0151)
PHONE....................................740 982-2050
Mick Pease, *Brnch Mgr*
EMP: 220
SALES (corp-wide): 24.08MM **Privately
Held**
Web: www.cercocorp.com
SIC: **3255** 3567 3297 Clay refractories;
Industrial furnaces and ovens; Nonclay
refractories
PA: I Cerco Inc
453 W Mcconkey St
Shreve OH 44676
330 567-2145

(G-5511)
PCC AIRFOILS LLC
101 China St (43731-1111)
P.O. Box 206 (43731-0206)
PHONE....................................740 982-6025
Ryan Thrush, *Brnch Mgr*
EMP: 269
SALES (corp-wide): 424.23B **Publicly
Held**
Web: www.pccairfoils.com

SIC: **3369** 3728 Castings, except die-castings, precision; Aircraft parts and equipment, nec
HQ: Pcc Airfoils, Llc
　　3401 Entp Pkwy Ste 200
　　Beachwood OH 44122
　　216 831-3590

(G-5512)
PETRO WARE INC
Also Called: Swingle Drilling
713 Keystone St (43731-1039)
P.O. Box 220 (43731-0220)
PHONE..............................740 982-1302
Mark B Swingle, *Pr*
James R Swingle, *
EMP: 6 **EST:** 1985
SQ FT: 2,000
SALES (est): 1.04MM **Privately Held**
Web: www.christycatalytics.com
SIC: **3569** 3264 Filters, general line: industrial; Porcelain electrical supplies

(G-5513)
TEMPLE OIL AND GAS LLC
Also Called: Speed-O-Print
6626 Ceramic Rd Ne (43731-9419)
P.O. Box 70 (43731-0070)
PHONE..............................740 452-7878
Robert Swingle, *Pr*
EMP: 8 **EST:** 1969
SQ FT: 8,000
SALES (est): 1.99MM **Privately Held**
SIC: **1381** 1311 Directional drilling oil and gas wells; Natural gas production

Croton
Licking County

(G-5514)
MULLER PIPE ORGAN CO
Also Called: Muller Pipe Organ Company
122 N High St (43013-9007)
P.O. Box 353 (43013-0353)
PHONE..............................740 893-1700
John W Muller, *Pr*
Mary J Muller, *Sec*
EMP: 10 **EST:** 1986
SQ FT: 8,650
SALES (est): 615K **Privately Held**
Web: www.mullerpipeorgan.com
SIC: **3931** Musical instruments

(G-5515)
OHIO FRESH EGGS LLC (PA)
11212 Croton Rd (43013-9725)
PHONE..............................740 893-7200
Gary Bethel, *Managing Member*
▲ **EMP:** 6 **EST:** 1984
SQ FT: 5,000
SALES (est): 12.19MM
SALES (corp-wide): 12.19MM **Privately Held**
SIC: **5144** 2015 Eggs; Egg processing

Cumberland
Guernsey County

(G-5516)
CUMBERLAND LIMESTONE LLC
53681 Spencer Rd (43732-9709)
PHONE..............................740 638-3942
Cris Sidwell, *Managing Member*
EMP: 21 **EST:** 2010
SALES (est): 6.23MM **Privately Held**
Web: www.cumberlandlimestone.com
SIC: **1422** Crushed and broken limestone

Curtice
Ottawa County

(G-5517)
OTTAWA PRODUCTS CO
1602 N Curtice Rd Ste A (43412-9507)
PHONE..............................419 836-5115
Jeffery Hepner, *Pr*
Bruce Miller, *Dir*
George F Wasmer, *Ch*
EMP: 20 **EST:** 1997
SQ FT: 19,000
SALES (est): 2.25MM **Privately Held**
Web: www.ottawaproducts.com
SIC: **3429** 3469 Clamps, metal; Spinning metal for the trade

(G-5518)
TAT MACHINE & TOOL LTD
1313 S Cousino Rd (43412-9100)
P.O. Box 184 (43412-0184)
PHONE..............................419 836-7706
Thomas A Truman, *Pt*
Joan C Truman, *Pt*
EMP: 8 **EST:** 1983
SQ FT: 7,500
SALES (est): 876.49K **Privately Held**
SIC: **3599** Machine shop, jobbing and repair

Cuyahoga Falls
Summit County

(G-5519)
4R ENTERPRISES INCORPORATED
Also Called: Radioshack
700 Portage Trl (44221-3057)
PHONE..............................330 923-9799
M Grimes, *Pr*
Norman B Rice, *Techl Dir*
Marsha Grimes, *Pr*
EMP: 6 **EST:** 1985
SQ FT: 2,000
SALES (est): 432.95K **Privately Held**
Web: www.4r-inc.com
SIC: **5731** 3826 3821 7389 Radio, television, and electronic stores; Surface area analyzers; Laboratory measuring apparatus ; Industrial and commercial equipment inspection service

(G-5520)
ADVANCED HOLDING DESIGNS INC
Also Called: Ahd
3332 Cavalier Trl (44224-4906)
PHONE..............................330 928-4456
Mark Smrekar, *Pr*
Anne Daugherty, *Mgr*
EMP: 6 **EST:** 1988
SQ FT: 12,000
SALES (est): 708.11K **Privately Held**
Web: www.ahd-flex-e-on.com
SIC: **3545** Collets (machine tool accessories)

(G-5521)
ALTEC INDUSTRIES INC
307 Munroe Falls Ave (44221-2827)
PHONE..............................205 408-2341
Tim Smith, *Brnch Mgr*
EMP: 10
SALES (corp-wide): 1.21B **Privately Held**
Web: www.altec.com
SIC: **3531** 3536 3713 Derricks, except oil and gas field; Cranes, overhead traveling; Truck bodies (motor vehicles)
HQ: Altec Industries, Inc.
　　210 Inverness Center Drv
　　Birmingham AL 35242
　　205 991-7733

(G-5522)
AMERICAN DE ROSA LAMPARTS LLC (HQ)
Also Called: Luminance
370 Falls Commerce Pkwy (44224-1062)
◆ **EMP:** 85 **EST:** 1951
SALES (est): 18.95MM
SALES (corp-wide): 19.21MM **Privately Held**
Web: luminance.us.com
SIC: **5063** 3364 3229 Lighting fixtures; Brass and bronze die-castings; Bulbs for electric lights
PA: Luminance Acquisition, Llc
　　25101 Chagrin Blvd # 350
　　Cleveland OH

(G-5523)
AMERICHEM INC (PA)
2000 Americhem Way (44221-3303)
PHONE..............................330 929-4213
Matthew Hellstern, *CEO*
Tom Gannon, *
John Volcheck, *
◆ **EMP:** 100 **EST:** 1941
SQ FT: 83,000
SALES (est): 188.64MM
SALES (corp-wide): 188.64MM **Privately Held**
Web: www.americhem.com
SIC: **2851** 2865 2816 2819 Paints and allied products; Color pigments, organic; Inorganic pigments; Industrial inorganic chemicals, nec

(G-5524)
AMERICHEM INC
Also Called: Americhem
155 E Steels Corners Rd (44224-4919)
PHONE..............................330 926-3185
Rod Manfull, *Mgr*
EMP: 50
SQ FT: 78,214
SALES (corp-wide): 188.64MM **Privately Held**
Web: www.americhem.com
SIC: **2865** 2816 Color pigments, organic; Inorganic pigments
PA: Americhem, Inc.
　　2000 Americhem Way
　　Cuyahoga Falls OH 44221
　　330 929-4213

(G-5525)
AMH HOLDINGS II INC
3773 State Rd (44223-2603)
PHONE..............................330 929-1811
Thomas N Chieffe, *CEO*
EMP: 500 **EST:** 2002
SALES (est): 2.28MM **Privately Held**
Web: www.alside.com
SIC: **3355** Coils, wire aluminum: made in rolling mills

(G-5526)
APPLIED VISION CORPORATION (PA)
2020 Vision Ln (44223-4706)
PHONE..............................330 926-2222
Amir Novini, *CEO*
Manijeh Novini, *CFO*
EMP: 60 **EST:** 1997
SQ FT: 80,000
SALES (est): 20.26MM
SALES (corp-wide): 20.26MM **Privately Held**
Web: www.antaresvisiongroup.com
SIC: **3577** Magnetic ink and optical scanning devices

(G-5527)
ASCOT VALLEY FOODS LTD
205 Ascot Pkwy (44223-3701)
PHONE..............................330 376-9411
Robert J Zab, *Prin*
EMP: 50 **EST:** 2017
SALES (est): 2.32MM **Privately Held**
Web: www.ascotvalleyfoods.com
SIC: **2099** Food preparations, nec

(G-5528)
ASSOCIATED MATERIALS LLC (PA)
Also Called: Alside Supply Center
3773 State Rd (44223-2603)
P.O. Box 2010 (44310)
PHONE..............................330 929-1811
James Drexinger, *CEO*
Erik D Ragatz, *
Brian C Strauss, *
Scott F Stephens, *
William L Topper, *
▲ **EMP:** 230 **EST:** 1947
SQ FT: 63,000
SALES (est): 1.18B
SALES (corp-wide): 1.18B **Privately Held**
Web: www.associatedmaterials.com
SIC: **3089** 5033 5031 3442 Plastics hardware and building products; Roofing and siding materials; Windows; Metal doors, sash, and trim

(G-5529)
ASSOCIATED MATERIALS GROUP INC (PA)
3773 State Rd (44223-2603)
PHONE..............................330 929-1811
Brian C Strauss, *Pr*
EMP: 55 **EST:** 2010
SALES (est): 83.76MM **Privately Held**
Web: www.associatedmaterials.com
SIC: **3089** 5033 5031 3442 Plastics hardware and building products; Roofing and siding materials; Windows; Metal doors, sash, and trim

(G-5530)
ASSOCIATED MTLS HOLDINGS LLC
3773 State Rd (44223-2603)
P.O. Box 2010 (44309-2010)
PHONE..............................330 929-1811
Ira D Kleinman, *Ch Bd*
EMP: 2000 **EST:** 1947
SALES (est): 4.77MM **Privately Held**
Web: www.associatedmaterials.com
SIC: **5033** 5031 5063 3442 Roofing and siding materials; Windows; Wire and cable; Metal doors, sash, and trim
PA: Associated Materials Group, Inc.
　　3773 State Rd
　　Cuyahoga Falls OH 44223

(G-5531)
ATA TOOLS INC
7 Ascot Pkwy (44223-3326)
PHONE..............................330 928-7744
Hector Diaz-stringel, *Pr*
EMP: 107 **EST:** 2012
SALES (est): 9.68MM **Privately Held**
Web: www.atagroup.com
SIC: **3545** Machine tool accessories

(G-5532)
BARRY-WEHMILLER COMPANIES INC
4485 Allen Rd (44224-1033)
PHONE..............................330 923-0491
Jim Foley, *Brnch Mgr*
EMP: 14
Web: www.bwpackaging.com

▲ = Import ▼ = Export
◆ = Import/Export

SIC: 3565 Packaging machinery
HQ: Barry-Wehmiller Companies, Inc.
8020 Forsyth Blvd
Saint Louis MO 63105
314 862-8000

(G-5533)
BOURBON PLASTICS INC
111 Stow Ave Ste 100 (44221-2560)
P.O. Box 23 (46504-0023)
PHONE..............................574 342-0893
EMP: 35
SIC: 3644 3089 Insulators and insulation
materials, electrical; Injection molded
finished plastics products, nec

(G-5534)
CIRCLE PRIME MANUFACTURING INC
2114 Front St (44221-3220)
P.O. Box 112 (44221)
PHONE..............................330 923-0019
James Mothersbaugh, *Pr*
Robert Mothersbaugh, *
EMP: 27 **EST:** 1989
SQ FT: 50,000
SALES (est): 8.55MM **Privately Held**
Web: www.circleprime.com
SIC: 3672 8731 3663 3812 Printed circuit
boards; Commercial physical research;
Radio broadcasting and communications
equipment; Antennas, radar or
communications

(G-5535)
CORTAPE INC
60 Marc Dr (44223-2628)
PHONE..............................330 929-6700
Matthew Mc Clellan, *Pr*
Erik W Akins, *Ch Bd*
◆ **EMP:** 17 **EST:** 1976
SQ FT: 25,000
SALES (est): 7.55MM **Privately Held**
Web: www.cortape.com
SIC: 2672 Tape, pressure sensitive: made
from purchased materials

(G-5536)
CRAIN COMMUNICATIONS INC
Also Called: Rubber & Plastics News
2291 Riverfront Pkwy Ste 1000
(44221-2580)
PHONE..............................330 836-9180
Robert S Simmons, *VP*
EMP: 47
SALES (corp-wide): 249.16MM **Privately Held**
Web: www.tirebusiness.com
SIC: 2711 2721 7389 Newspapers:
publishing only, not printed on site;
Periodicals; Advertising, promotional, and
trade show services
PA: Crain Communications, Inc.
1155 Gratiot Ave
Detroit MI 48207
313 446-6000

(G-5537)
DBCR INC
Also Called: G.S. Steel Company
3400 Cavalier Trl (44224-4908)
PHONE..............................330 920-1900
Donald E Potoczek, *Pr*
Beth Potoczek, *Treas*
EMP: 20 **EST:** 2005
SALES (est): 6.89MM **Privately Held**
Web: www.gssteel.com
SIC: 3541 7389 7692 Plasma process metal
cutting machines; Metal cutting services;
Welding repair

(G-5538)
DENTRONIX INC
235 Ascot Pkwy (44223-3701)
PHONE..............................330 916-7300
Jerry Sullivan, *Pr*
Joseph Fasano, *
EMP: 53 **EST:** 1976
SQ FT: 16,000
SALES (est): 2.57MM **Privately Held**
Web: www.diatechusa.com
SIC: 3843 5047 3842 3841 Orthodontic
appliances; Dental equipment and supplies;
Surgical appliances and supplies; Surgical
and medical instruments
HQ: Coltene/Whaledent Inc.
235 Ascot Pkwy
Cuyahoga Falls OH 44223

(G-5539)
EWART-OHLSON MACHINE COMPANY
1435 Main St (44221-4926)
P.O. Box 359 (44222-0359)
PHONE..............................330 928-2171
David L Ewart, *Ch*
Brian L Ewart, *
Earl Norrod, *
Margaret Ewart, *
David Achauer, *
▲ **EMP:** 28 **EST:** 1942
SQ FT: 39,000
SALES (est): 5.41MM **Privately Held**
Web: www.ewart-ohlson.com
SIC: 3599 Machine shop, jobbing and repair

(G-5540)
FACTS INC
2737 Front St (44221-1904)
PHONE..............................330 928-2332
Albert H Curry, *Pr*
Thomas W Fisher Iii, *VP*
EMP: 20 **EST:** 1992
SQ FT: 10,000
SALES (est): 4.95MM **Privately Held**
Web: www.facts-inc.com
SIC: 7371 3823 Computer software systems
analysis and design, custom; Industrial
process control instruments

(G-5541)
FALLS STAMPING & WELDING CO (PA)
2900 Vincent St (44221-1954)
PHONE..............................330 928-1191
Rick Boettner, *Ch*
David Cesar, *
Jason Taft, *
EMP: 125 **EST:** 1919
SQ FT: 95,000
SALES (est): 11.15MM
SALES (corp-wide): 11.15MM **Privately Held**
Web: www.falls-stamping.com
SIC: 3465 3469 3544 3711 Automotive
stampings; Stamping metal for the trade;
Special dies, tools, jigs, and fixtures;
Chassis, motor vehicle

(G-5542)
FLEX-E-ON INC
3332 Cavalier Trl (44224-4906)
PHONE..............................330 928-4496
Mark Smrekar, *Pr*
EMP: 10 **EST:** 1965
SQ FT: 12,000
SALES (est): 856.35K **Privately Held**
Web: www.ahd-flex-e-on.com
SIC: 3545 Chucks: drill, lathe, or magnetic
(machine tool accessories)

(G-5543)
FOX TOOL CO INC
1471 Main St (44221-4926)
PHONE..............................330 928-3402
Nathan Fox, *Pr*
EMP: 8 **EST:** 1973
SQ FT: 5,120
SALES (est): 471.09K **Privately Held**
Web: www.foxtoolcompany.com
SIC: 7699 3545 Knife, saw and tool
sharpening and repair; Cutting tools for
machine tools

(G-5544)
GENTEK BUILDING PRODUCTS INC (HQ)
Also Called: Revere Building Products
3773 State Rd (44223-2603)
PHONE..............................800 548-4542
Thomas Chieffe, *CEO*
Michael Caporale, *Pr*
D Keith Lavanway, *VP*
▲ **EMP:** 18 **EST:** 1994
SQ FT: 8,000
SALES (est): 26.64MM
SALES (corp-wide): 1.18B **Privately Held**
Web: www.alside.com
SIC: 3444 3089 Siding, sheet metal; Siding,
plastics
PA: Associated Materials, Llc
3773 State Rd
Cuyahoga Falls OH 44223
330 929-1811

(G-5545)
GOJO INDUSTRIES INC
Also Called: Production
3783 State Rd (44223-2698)
P.O. Box 991 (44309-0991)
PHONE..............................330 255-6000
Joseph Kanfer, *Brnch Mgr*
EMP: 18
SALES (corp-wide): 802.21MM **Privately Held**
Web: www.gojo.com
SIC: 2842 Polishes and sanitation goods
PA: Gojo Industries, Inc.
1 Gojo Plz Ste 500
Akron OH 44311
330 255-6000

(G-5546)
GOJO INDUSTRIES INC
3783 State Rd (44223-2698)
PHONE..............................330 255-6527
Jeffrey Vengrow, *Brnch Mgr*
▼ **EMP:** 12
SALES (corp-wide): 802.21MM **Privately Held**
Web: www.gojo.com
SIC: 2842 Polishes and sanitation goods
PA: Gojo Industries, Inc.
1 Gojo Plz Ste 500
Akron OH 44311
330 255-6000

(G-5547)
HARBOR CASTINGS INC (PA)
2508 Bailey Rd (44221-2585)
PHONE..............................330 499-7178
C Richard Lynham, *CEO*
EMP: 45 **EST:** 1992
SQ FT: 13,000
SALES (est): 15.26MM
SALES (corp-wide): 15.26MM **Privately Held**
Web:
www.harborinvestmentcastings.com
SIC: 3324 3369 3325 Steel investment
foundries; Nonferrous foundries, nec; Steel
foundries, nec

(G-5548)
HARWOOD ENTP HOLDINGS INC
1365 Orlen Ave (44221-2957)
PHONE..............................330 923-3256
Richard Harwood, *Pr*
John H Eblen, *VP*
Lundy Mills, *Sec*
Donald R Harwood, *Stockholder*
EMP: 12 **EST:** 1952
SQ FT: 22,000
SALES (est): 2.2MM **Privately Held**
Web: www.harwoodrubber.com
SIC: 3479 3061 Coating of metals with
plastic or resins; Mechanical rubber goods

(G-5549)
INNOVATED HEALTH LLC
2241 Front St 1st Fl (44221-2501)
P.O. Box 963 (44223-0963)
PHONE..............................330 858-0651
Fred Guerra, *Managing Member*
EMP: 9 **EST:** 2014
SQ FT: 2,000
SALES (est): 384.24K **Privately Held**
SIC: 2023 Dietary supplements, dairy and
non-dairy based

(G-5550)
INTER-ION INC
157 Ascot Pkwy (44223-3747)
PHONE..............................330 928-9655
Adam Antonas, *Pr*
Panos Panayiotou, *
EMP: 25 **EST:** 1988
SQ FT: 25,000
SALES (est): 2.35MM **Privately Held**
Web: www.inter-ion.com
SIC: 3479 Coating of metals and formed
products

(G-5551)
JAY-EM AEROSPACE CORPORATION
75 Marc Dr (44223-2627)
PHONE..............................330 923-0333
Michael E Bell Senior, *CEO*
EMP: 25 **EST:** 1992
SQ FT: 34,000
SALES (est): 6.02MM **Privately Held**
SIC: 3728 3599 Wheels, aircraft; Machine
shop, jobbing and repair

(G-5552)
JJ&PL SERVICES-CONSULTING LLC
1474 Main St (44221-4927)
PHONE..............................330 923-5783
Hans R Leitner, *CEO*
EMP: 38 **EST:** 2010
SALES (est): 4.74MM **Privately Held**
Web: www.mach3machining.com
SIC: 3441 7699 Building components,
structural steel; Industrial machinery and
equipment repair

(G-5553)
JULIUS ZORN INC
Also Called: Juzo USA
3690 Zorn Dr (44223-3580)
P.O. Box 1088 (44223-1088)
PHONE..............................330 923-4999
Anne Rose Zorn, *Pr*
Petra Zorn, *
Uwe Schettler, *
▲ **EMP:** 75 **EST:** 1980
SQ FT: 30,000
SALES (est): 24.48MM
SALES (corp-wide): 135.9MM **Privately Held**
Web: www.juzo.ca
SIC: 5047 3842 Medical equipment and
supplies; Hosiery, support
PA: Julius Zorn Gmbh

Juliusplatz 1
Aichach BY 86551
82519010

(G-5554)
KEUCHEL & ASSOCIATES INC
Also Called: Spunfab
175 Muffin Ln (44223-3359)
P.O. Box 3435 (44223-3435)
PHONE...............................330 945-9455
Ken Keuchel, *Pr*
Herb Keuchel, *Stockholder**
Herbert W Keuchel, *
Richard W Staehle, *
◆ **EMP:** 50 **EST:** 1979
SQ FT: 40,000
SALES (est): 4.64MM **Privately Held**
Web: www.spunfab.com
SIC: 2241 8711 Narrow fabric mills;
   Consulting engineer

(G-5555)
KOLPIN OUTDOORS CORPORATION
Also Called: Premier O.E.M.
3479 State Rd (44223-2553)
PHONE...............................330 328-0772
James Nagy, *Pr*
▲ **EMP:** 23 **EST:** 2015
SALES (est): 2.53MM **Privately Held**
Web: www.kolpin.com
SIC: 3799 All terrain vehicles (ATV)

(G-5556)
KYOCERA HARDCOATING TECH LTD
220 Marc Dr (44223-2651)
PHONE...............................330 686-2136
EMP: 9 **EST:** 1995
SALES (est): 2.31MM **Privately Held**
Web: www.kyocera-hardcoating.com
SIC: 3479 Coating of metals and formed
   products

(G-5557)
**KYOCERA SGS PRECISION TLS INC
(PA)**
Also Called: Kyocera Precision Tools
150 Marc Dr (44223-2630)
P.O. Box 187 (44262)
PHONE...............................330 688-6667
Thomas Haag, *Pr*
Jeff Burton, *Prin*
Aaron Holb, *
▲ **EMP:** 50 **EST:** 1961
SALES (est): 36.3MM
SALES (corp-wide): 36.3MM **Privately
Held**
Web: www.kyocera-sgstool.com
SIC: 3545 5084 Cutting tools for machine
   tools; Industrial machinery and equipment

(G-5558)
KYOCERA SGS PRECISION TLS INC
238 Marc Dr (44223-2651)
PHONE...............................330 922-1953
Richard G Tichon, *Brnch Mgr*
EMP: 86
SALES (corp-wide): 36.3MM **Privately
Held**
Web: www.kyocera-sgstool.com
SIC: 3545 Cutting tools for machine tools
PA: Kyocera Sgs Precision Tools, Inc.
   150 Marc Dr
   Cuyahoga Falls OH 44223
   330 688-6667

(G-5559)
LINDEN-TWO INC
137 Ascot Pkwy (44223-3355)
PHONE...............................330 928-4064
Peter Tilgner, *Pr*
Ken Erwin, *

Bob Hughey, *
EMP: 42 **EST:** 1985
SQ FT: 26,000
SALES (est): 5.62MM **Privately Held**
Web: www.lindenindustries.com
SIC: 3559 5084 Plastics working machinery;
   Industrial machinery and equipment

(G-5560)
MAIN STREET GOURMET LLC
Also Called: Main Street Cambritt Cookies
170 Muffin Ln (44223-3358)
PHONE...............................330 929-0000
David Choe, *
Alex Schneider, *
Steven Marks, *
Harvey Nelson, *
EMP: 108 **EST:** 1987
SQ FT: 60,000
SALES (est): 19.64MM **Privately Held**
Web: www.mainstreetgourmet.com
SIC: 2053 2099 2052 2051 Frozen bakery
   products, except bread; Food preparations,
   nec; Cookies and crackers; Bread, cake,
   and related products

(G-5561)
MOORE MC MILLEN HOLDINGS (PA)
1850 Front St (44221-3912)
PHONE...............................330 745-3075
Robert S Mc Millen, *Pr*
EMP: 35 **EST:** 1994
SQ FT: 19,141
SALES (est): 13.07MM **Privately Held**
SIC: 3398 Metal heat treating

(G-5562)
NANOTRONICS IMAGING INC (PA)
Also Called: Nanotronics
2251 Front St Ste 110 (44221-2577)
P.O. Box 306 (44222-0306)
PHONE...............................330 926-9809
Matthew Putman, *CEO*
Matthew Putnam, *CEO*
John Putman, *Pr*
EMP: 6 **EST:** 2007
SQ FT: 2,000
SALES (est): 24.23MM
SALES (corp-wide): 24.23MM **Privately
Held**
Web: www.nanotronics.co
SIC: 3826 3825 Analytical instruments;
   Semiconductor test equipment

(G-5563)
NSK INDUSTRIES INC (PA)
150 Ascot Pkwy (44223-3354)
P.O. Box 1089 (44223-0089)
PHONE...............................330 923-4112
◆ **EMP:** 67 **EST:** 1980
SALES (est): 14.81MM
SALES (corp-wide): 14.81MM **Privately
Held**
Web: www.nskind.com
SIC: 5085 3479 3451 Fasteners, industrial:
   nuts, bolts, screws, etc.; Coating of metals
   and formed products; Screw machine
   products

(G-5564)
**PNEUMATIC SCALE CORPORATION
(DH)**
Also Called: Pneumatic Scale Angelus
10 Ascot Pkwy (44223-3325)
PHONE...............................330 923-0491
Timothy J Sullivan, *CEO*
William J Morgan, *Pr*
David M Gianini, *VP*
Robert H Chapman, *Ch*
Gregory L Coonrod Mr, *Dir*
◆ **EMP:** 225 **EST:** 1895

SQ FT: 102,000
SALES (est): 86.08MM **Privately Held**
Web: www.psangelus.com
SIC: 3535 3569 3565 Conveyors and
   conveying equipment; Centrifuges, industrial
   ; Bottling machinery: filling, capping, labeling
HQ: Barry-Wehmiller Companies, Inc.
   8020 Forsyth Blvd
   Saint Louis MO 63105
   314 862-8000

(G-5565)
POLYMERICS INC (PA)
2828 2nd St (44221-1953)
PHONE...............................330 928-2210
C Robert Samples, *Ch Bd*
Joe Arhar, *
▲ **EMP:** 50 **EST:** 1974
SQ FT: 24,000
SALES (est): 1.27MM
SALES (corp-wide): 1.27MM **Privately
Held**
Web: www.polymericsinc.com
SIC: 3069 2819 2891 2865 Custom
   compounding of rubber materials; Industrial
   inorganic chemicals, nec; Adhesives and
   sealants; Cyclic crudes and intermediates

(G-5566)
PROSPECT MOLD & DIE COMPANY
Also Called: Prospect Mold
1100 Main St (44221-4922)
PHONE...............................330 929-3311
Brandon Wenzlik, *CEO*
Bruce W Wright, *
Walter Nagel, *
▲ **EMP:** 120 **EST:** 1945
SQ FT: 100,000
SALES (est): 24.01MM **Privately Held**
Web: www.prospectgroup.com
SIC: 5084 3544 Industrial machinery and
   equipment; Forms (molds), for foundry and
   plastics working machinery

(G-5567)
PROTO CIRCUIT INC
7 Ascot Pkwy (44223-3326)
PHONE...............................330 572-3400
EMP: 7 **EST:** 2019
SALES (est): 1.03MM **Privately Held**
SIC: 3672 Printed circuit boards

(G-5568)
RECYCLING EQP SOLUTIONS CORP
276 Remington Rd Ste C (44224-4900)
PHONE...............................330 920-1500
Gary Gaither, *Pr*
Mary Gaither, *VP*
▼ **EMP:** 8 **EST:** 2001
SALES (est): 880.13K **Privately Held**
Web: www.therescorp.com
SIC: 3542 Mechanical (pneumatic or
   hydraulic) metal forming machines

(G-5569)
REUTHER MOLD & MFG CO INC
Also Called: Reuther Mold & Manufacturing
1225 Munroe Falls Ave (44221-3598)
PHONE...............................330 923-5266
Karl A Reuther Ii, *Pr*
Jessica Rhodes, *
EMP: 60 **EST:** 1950
SQ FT: 61,000
SALES (est): 9.41MM **Privately Held**
Web: www.reuthermold.com
SIC: 3544 3599 Industrial molds; Machine
   shop, jobbing and repair

(G-5570)
RMS EQUIPMENT LLC
Also Called: RMS Equipment Company
1 Vision Ln (44223-4710)
PHONE...............................330 564-1360
Armand Massary, *Pr*
▲ **EMP:** 1527 **EST:** 1917
SQ FT: 50,000
SALES (est): 2.24MM **Privately Held**
Web: www.steelastic.com
SIC: 3559 Rubber working machinery,
   including tires
HQ: Pettibone L.L.C.
   27501 Bella Vista Pkwy
   Warrenville IL 60555
   630 353-5000

(G-5571)
SARAHS VINEYARD INC
1204 W Steels Corners Rd (44223-3115)
PHONE...............................330 929-8057
Micheal Lytz, *Pr*
EMP: 8 **EST:** 2007
SALES (est): 1.4MM **Privately Held**
Web: www.sarahsvineyardwinery.com
SIC: 2084 Wines

(G-5572)
SILICONE SOLUTIONS INC
338 Remington Rd (44224-4916)
PHONE...............................330 920-3125
David M Brassard, *Pr*
Lorraine R Brassard, *Treas*
EMP: 10 **EST:** 1996
SQ FT: 10,000
SALES (est): 7.57MM **Privately Held**
Web: www.siliconesolutions.com
SIC: 2869 2891 Silicones; Adhesives and
   sealants

(G-5573)
**SPECTRUM PLASTICS
CORPORATION**
99 E Ascot Ln (44223-3788)
PHONE...............................330 926-9766
Mohammad Malik, *Pr*
▲ **EMP:** 9 **EST:** 1988
SQ FT: 25,000
SALES (est): 2.32MM **Privately Held**
Web: www.splastics.com
SIC: 3089 Injection molding of plastics

(G-5574)
STEELASTIC COMPANY LLC
1 Vision Ln (44223-4710)
PHONE...............................330 633-0505
Jim Vogel, *Pr*
Brian Fetzer, *Managing Member**
▲ **EMP:** 46 **EST:** 1970
SQ FT: 34,500
SALES (est): 21.11MM **Privately Held**
Web: www.steelastic.com
SIC: 3559 Automotive related machinery
HQ: Pettibone L.L.C.
   27501 Bella Vista Pkwy
   Warrenville IL 60555
   630 353-5000

(G-5575)
SUMMIT MILLWORK LLC
1619 Main St (44221-4047)
PHONE...............................330 920-4000
EMP: 8 **EST:** 2003
SQ FT: 30,000
SALES (est): 2.6MM **Privately Held**
Web: www.summitmillwork.com
SIC: 2431 Millwork

▲ = Import ▼ = Export
◆ = Import/Export

(G-5576)
TECHNICOTE INC
70 Marc Dr (44223-2628)
PHONE..........................330 928-1476
Dave Bolanz, *Mgr*
EMP: 40
SALES (corp-wide): 49.86MM **Privately Held**
Web: www.technicote.com
SIC: 2891 Adhesives
PA: Technicote, Inc.
222 Mound Ave
Miamisburg OH 45342
800 358-4448

(G-5577)
TRM MANUFACTURING INC (PA)
Also Called: Gem Attachments
607 Munroe Falls Ave (44221-3437)
PHONE..........................330 769-2600
Yong-chang Tang, *CEO*
EMP: 13 EST: 2011
SALES (est): 10.74MM
SALES (corp-wide): 10.74MM **Privately Held**
Web: www.trmmfg.com
SIC: 3462 Iron and steel forgings

(G-5578)
TRM MANUFACTURING INC
601 Munroe Falls Ave (44221-3437)
PHONE..........................330 769-2600
EMP: 15
SALES (corp-wide): 10.74MM **Privately Held**
Web: www.trmmfg.com
SIC: 3462 Iron and steel forgings
PA: Trm Manufacturing, Inc.
607 Munroe Falls Ave
Cuyahoga Falls OH 44221
330 769-2600

(G-5579)
TRU-BORE MACHINE CO INC
1220 Orlen Ave (44221-2956)
PHONE..........................330 928-6215
Michele Crandall, *Pr*
EMP: 6 EST: 1966
SQ FT: 10,000
SALES (est): 377.39K **Privately Held**
SIC: 3599 Custom machinery

(G-5580)
ULTRA TECH MACHINERY INC
297 Ascot Pkwy (44223-3701)
PHONE..........................330 929-5544
Don Hagarty, *Pr*
Robert Hagarty, *
Jim Hagarty, *
▲ EMP: 30 EST: 1986
SQ FT: 11,000
SALES (est): 8.44MM **Privately Held**
Web: www.utmachinery.com
SIC: 3599 7389 Machine shop, jobbing and repair; Design, commercial and industrial

(G-5581)
WEAVER PROPACK - MARC DRIVE
129 Marc Dr (44223-2629)
PHONE..........................330 379-3660
EMP: 6 EST: 2016
SALES (est): 70.58K **Privately Held**
Web: www.weaverindustries.org
SIC: 3999 Manufacturing industries, nec

(G-5582)
WIN CD INC
Also Called: Win Plex
3333 Win St (44223-3790)
PHONE..........................330 929-1999

David K Pulk, *Pr*
EMP: 16 EST: 1995
SQ FT: 42,000
SALES (est): 549.67K **Privately Held**
Web: www.chasedoors.com
SIC: 2821 Plastics materials and resins

Dalton
Wayne County

(G-5583)
DENDRATEC LTD
1417 Zuercher Rd (44618-9776)
PHONE..........................330 473-4878
Clarence Jennings, *Prin*
EMP: 6 EST: 2008
SALES (est): 452.33K **Privately Held**
Web: www.dendratec.com
SIC: 2431 Millwork

(G-5584)
EGR PRODUCTS COMPANY INC (PA)
55 Eckard Rd (44618-9664)
PHONE..........................330 833-6554
Jeffery Daley, *Pr*
Jerome T Daley, *Pr*
Mary Ann Daley, *VP*
EMP: 16 EST: 1975
SQ FT: 30,000
SALES (est): 392.29K
SALES (corp-wide): 392.29K **Privately Held**
SIC: 3694 3714 Generators, automotive and aircraft; Motor vehicle parts and accessories

(G-5585)
FLEXTUR CORP
16875 Jericho Rd (44618-9657)
PHONE..........................877 435-3988
Daniel Wengerd, *Pr*
Leon Wengerd, *
◆ EMP: 55 EST: 1986
SALES (est): 953.58K **Privately Held**
Web: www.flextur.com
SIC: 3315 3441 Steel wire and related products; Fabricated structural metal

(G-5586)
J HORST MANUFACTURING CO
Also Called: 2cravealloys
279 E Main St (44618-9601)
PHONE..........................330 828-2216
Roland Horst, *Pr*
Richard Horst, *
Mary Steiner, *
Don E Flath, *
EMP: 53 EST: 1963
SQ FT: 78,000
SALES (est): 8.77MM **Privately Held**
Web: www.jhorst.com
SIC: 3599 3441 3549 3547 Machine shop, jobbing and repair; Fabricated structural metal; Metalworking machinery, nec; Rolling mill machinery

(G-5587)
LAKE REGION OIL INC
26 N Cochran St (44618-9808)
P.O. Box 1478 (44648-1478)
PHONE..........................330 828-8420
Robert Dervin Ii, *Pr*
EMP: 6 EST: 1979
SQ FT: 2,500
SALES (est): 786.67K **Privately Held**
Web: www.lakeregionoilinc.com
SIC: 1382 Oil and gas exploration services

(G-5588)
MARS HORSECARE US INC
Also Called: Mars Horsecare
330 E Schultz St (44618-9072)
P.O. Box 505 (44618-0505)
PHONE..........................330 828-2251
EMP: 45 EST: 1943
SALES (est): 9.23MM
SALES (corp-wide): 42.84B **Privately Held**
Web: www.buckeyenutrition.com
SIC: 2048 Alfalfa or alfalfa meal, prepared as animal feed
PA: Mars, Incorporated
6885 Elm St
Mclean VA 22101
703 821-4900

(G-5589)
MASSILLON MATERIALS INC (PA)
26 N Cochran St (44618-9808)
P.O. Box 499 (44618-0499)
PHONE..........................330 837-4767
Howard J Wenger, *Pr*
EMP: 16 EST: 1985
SQ FT: 6,000
SALES (est): 2.9MM **Privately Held**
Web: www.massillon-materials.com
SIC: 1442 Sand mining

(G-5590)
OVERHEAD DOOR CORPORATION
14512 Lincoln Way E (44618-9014)
PHONE..........................330 828-2291
EMP: 6
Web: www.overheaddoor.com
SIC: 3442 2431 Garage doors, overhead: metal; Doors, wood
HQ: Overhead Door Corporation
2501 S State Hwy 121 Ste
Lewisville TX 75067
469 549-7100

(G-5591)
P GRAHAM DUNN INC
630 Henry St (44618-9280)
P.O. Box 263 (44667)
PHONE..........................330 828-2105
Patrick Helmuth, *CEO*
Joe Knutson, *
Robert Shetler, *
▲ EMP: 300 EST: 1976
SQ FT: 100,000
SALES (est): 24.74MM
SALES (corp-wide): 47.33MM **Privately Held**
Web: www.pgrahamdunn.com
SIC: 2499 Laundry products, wood
PA: Cbc Group, Inc.
5226 S 31st Pl
Phoenix AZ 85040
602 441-1401

(G-5592)
PETER GRAHAM DUNN INC
1417 Zuercher Rd (44618-9776)
PHONE..........................330 816-0035
Peter G Dunn, *Pr*
Leanna Dunn, *
◆ EMP: 6 EST: 1987
SQ FT: 36,000
SALES (est): 901.19K **Privately Held**
Web: www.pgrahamdunn.com
SIC: 3499 5199 Novelties and giftware, including trophies; Advertising specialties

(G-5593)
ROBURA LLC (PA)
Also Called: Lehman's
4779 Kidron Rd (44618-9287)
P.O. Box P.O. Box 270 (44636-0270)
PHONE..........................800 438-5346

◆ EMP: 94 EST: 1954
SALES (est): 21.4MM
SALES (corp-wide): 21.4MM **Privately Held**
Web: www.lehmans.com
SIC: 3639 Major kitchen appliances, except refrigerators and stoves

(G-5594)
S LEHMAN CENTRAL WAREHOUSE
289 Kurzen Rd N (44618-9009)
PHONE..........................330 828-8828
EMP: 6 EST: 2014
SALES (est): 253.87K **Privately Held**
Web: www.crownplacebrands.com
SIC: 5251 3429 Hardware stores; Hardware, nec

(G-5595)
SPRINGHILL DIMENSIONS
4530 Mount Eaton Rd S (44618-9128)
PHONE..........................330 359-5972
Levi Beachy, *Owner*
EMP: 14 EST: 1996
SQ FT: 6,000
SALES (est): 1.02MM **Privately Held**
Web: www.springhilldimensions.com
SIC: 3553 Furniture makers machinery, woodworking

(G-5596)
WORLD CLASS CARRIAGES LLC
5090 Mount Eaton Rd S (44618-9643)
PHONE..........................330 857-7811
EMP: 8 EST: 2020
SALES (est): 524.77K **Privately Held**
Web: www.worldclasscarriages.com
SIC: 3799 Carriages, horse drawn

(G-5597)
ZIMMERMAN STEEL & SUP CO LLC
18543 Davis Rd (44618-9697)
PHONE..........................330 828-1010
EMP: 10 EST: 1995
SQ FT: 11,700
SALES (est): 3.31MM **Privately Held**
Web: www.zimmersteel.com
SIC: 3441 Fabricated structural metal

Danville
Knox County

(G-5598)
COUNTRY LANE CUSTOM BUILDINGS
Also Called: Countryside Construction
21318 Pealer Mill Rd (43014-9640)
PHONE..........................740 485-8481
Andrew C Nisley, *Owner*
EMP: 9 EST: 2017
SALES (est): 1.64MM **Privately Held**
SIC: 3999 7389 Miniatures; Business services, nec

(G-5599)
GDN WELDING LLC
26697 Danville Amity Rd (43014-9769)
PHONE..........................740 398-6109
Grant Nyhart, *Pr*
EMP: 30 EST: 2014
SALES (est): 1.04MM **Privately Held**
Web: www.gdnwelding.com
SIC: 7692 1389 1799 3469 Welding repair; Oil and gas field services, nec; Welding on site; Machine parts, stamped or pressed metal

(G-5600)
VALLEY VIEW PALLETS LLC
Also Called: Valley View Pallets Partners
22414 Hostetler Rd (43014-9638)
PHONE....................................740 599-0010
Ephraim Yoder, *Managing Member*
EMP: 9 **EST:** 1996
SALES (est): 820.08K **Privately Held**
SIC: 2448 7389 Pallets, wood; Business
Activities at Non-Commercial Site

(G-5601)
YOUNGS LOCKER SERVICE INC
Also Called: Youngs Locker Serv & Meat Proc
16201 Nashville Rd (43014-9738)
P.O. Box Y (43014-0625)
PHONE....................................740 599-6833
Lawrence Payne, *Pr*
EMP: 10 **EST:** 1945
SQ FT: 10,000
SALES (est): 430.69K **Privately Held**
Web: www.youngscountrymarket.com
SIC: 2011 4222 2013 Meat packing plants;
Warehousing, cold storage or refrigerated;
Sausages and other prepared meats

Dayton
Greene County

(G-5602)
AES BEAVER VALLEY LLC
1065 Woodman Dr (45432-1423)
▲ **EMP:** 62 **EST:** 1983
SALES (est): 2.53MM
SALES (corp-wide): 12.28B **Publicly Held**
Web: www.aes.com
SIC: 3612 Power transformers, electric
PA: The Aes Corporation
4300 Wilson Blvd
Arlington VA 22203
703 522-1315

(G-5603)
AMCO PRODUCTS INC
500 N Smithville Rd (45431-1069)
PHONE....................................937 433-7982
Joseph M Raby, *CEO*
Ronald J Raby, *Pr*
Karla Simmons, *VP*
EMP: 10 **EST:** 1966
SQ FT: 58,600
SALES (est): 983.16K **Privately Held**
Web: www.amco-products.com
SIC: 3451 Screw machine products

(G-5604)
CAPITAL PRECISION MACHINE & TL
1865 Radio Rd (45431-1034)
PHONE....................................937 258-1176
Paul Powers Senior, *Owner*
Cliff Smith, *Prin*
EMP: 8 **EST:** 1978
SQ FT: 10,000
SALES (est): 717.56K **Privately Held**
Web: www.cpmtool.com
SIC: 3544 Special dies and tools

(G-5605)
CASSADY WOODWORKS INC
446 N Smithville Rd (45431-1080)
PHONE....................................937 256-7948
Tom Joch, *Pr*
EMP: 13 **EST:** 1958
SQ FT: 12,000
SALES (est): 3.84MM **Privately Held**
Web: www.cassadywoodworks.com
SIC: 2431 2441 2541 Millwork; Nailed wood
boxes and shook; Display fixtures, wood

(G-5606)
CPM TOOL CO LLC
1865 Radio Rd (45431-1034)
PHONE....................................937 258-1176
EMP: 7 **EST:** 2020
SALES (est): 600K **Privately Held**
Web: www.cpmtool.com
SIC: 3312 Tool and die steel and alloys

(G-5607)
D & B INDUSTRIES INC
5031 Linden Ave Ste B (45432-1893)
PHONE....................................937 253-8658
Brent Gillott, *Pr*
EMP: 7 **EST:** 1973
SQ FT: 5,000
SALES (est): 528.59K **Privately Held**
Web: www.d-bindustries.com
SIC: 3599 Machine shop, jobbing and repair

(G-5608)
DAYTON INDUSTRIAL DRUM INC
1880 Radio Rd (45431-1035)
P.O. Box 172 (45371-0172)
PHONE....................................937 253-8933
David Hussong, *Pr*
Kylene Hussong, *
Ruth M Hussong, *
EMP: 25 **EST:** 1955
SQ FT: 25,000
SALES (est): 598.71K **Privately Held**
Web: www.daytonindustrialdrum.com
SIC: 7699 5085 5113 2673 Industrial
equipment services; Drums, new or
reconditioned; Industrial and personal
service paper; Bags: plastic, laminated, and
coated

(G-5609)
DEFENSE RESEARCH ASSOC INC
3915 Germany Ln Ste 102 (45431-1688)
PHONE....................................937 431-1644
Leroy E Anderson, *CEO*
Ray Trimmer, *
Jeanette Anderson, *
Rebecca Trimmer, *
EMP: 25 **EST:** 1973
SQ FT: 15,000
SALES (est): 3.8MM **Privately Held**
Web: www.dra-engineering.com
SIC: 8731 8748 3724 Commercial physical
research; Systems analysis and
engineering consulting services; Research
and development on aircraft engines and
parts

(G-5610)
DLA DOCUMENT SERVICES
4165 Communications Blvd Ste 2
(45433-5601)
PHONE....................................937 257-6014
Leonard Xavier, *Dir*
EMP: 12
Web: www.dla.mil
SIC: 2752 9711 Commercial printing,
lithographic; National security
HQ: Dla Document Services
5450 Carlisle Pike Bldg 9
Mechanicsburg PA 17050
717 605-2362

(G-5611)
DOXIE INC
Also Called: Signs Now Dayton
3197 Beaver Vu Dr (45434-6366)
PHONE....................................937 427-3431
James Jackson, *Pr*
Carol Jackson, *VP*
EMP: 7 **EST:** 2016
SALES (est): 1.47MM **Privately Held**
Web: www.signsnow.com

SIC: 3993 Signs and advertising specialties

(G-5612)
GREEN MACHINE TOOL INC
1865 Radio Rd (45431-1034)
PHONE....................................937 253-0771
Eugene Green, *Pr*
Mary Ann Green, *VP*
EMP: 8 **EST:** 1979
SQ FT: 12,000
SALES (est): 804.7K **Privately Held**
Web: www.greenmachinetool.com
SIC: 3599 3544 Machine shop, jobbing and
repair; Forms (molds), for foundry and
plastics working machinery

(G-5613)
GREENE COUNTY
Also Called: Green County Wtr Sup & Trtmnt
1122 Beaver Valley Rd (45434-7014)
PHONE....................................937 429-0127
EMP: 8
SIC: 3589 4941 Sewage and water
treatment equipment; Water supply
PA: Greene County
35 Greene St
Xenia OH 45385
937 562-5006

(G-5614)
INNOVATIVE MECH SYSTEMS LLC
Also Called: American Metal Fabricators
3100 Plainfield Rd Ste A (45432-3725)
PHONE....................................937 813-8713
EMP: 9 **EST:** 1986
SQ FT: 37,000
SALES (est): 2.93MM **Privately Held**
SIC: 3444 Sheet metalwork

(G-5615)
KETCO INC
1348 Research Park Dr (45432-2818)
PHONE....................................937 426-9331
Richard D Harding, *Pr*
Steven Gerbic, *VP*
EMP: 20 **EST:** 1973
SQ FT: 15,000
SALES (est): 2.11MM **Privately Held**
Web: www.ketco.com
SIC: 3543 Industrial patterns

(G-5616)
L3 TECHNOLOGIES INC
Also Called: Raytheon
47 Alf/ Raytheon Arospace Bld 201 Area C
5 (45433)
PHONE....................................937 257-8501
Dave Riegel, *Prin*
EMP: 6
SALES (corp-wide): 21.32B **Publicly Held**
Web: www.l3harris.com
SIC: 3663 Telemetering equipment,
electronic
HQ: L3 Technologies, Inc.
600 3rd Ave Fl 34
New York NY 10016
321 727-9100

(G-5617)
LAU HOLDINGS LLC
4509 Springfield St (45431-1042)
PHONE....................................937 476-6500
Daniel Hake, *Brnch Mgr*
EMP: 46
SALES (corp-wide): 184.04MM **Privately
Held**
Web: www.lauparts.com
SIC: 3564 Ventilating fans: industrial or
commercial
HQ: Lau Holdings, Llc
16900 S Waterloo Rd

Cleveland OH 44110
216 486-4000

(G-5618)
LAU INDUSTRIES INC
Also Called: Supreme Fan/Industrial Air
4509 Springfield St (45431-1042)
PHONE....................................937 476-6500
Damian Macaluso, *Pr*
Christopher Wampler, *
Dan Disser, *
▼ **EMP:** 1865 **EST:** 1929
SQ FT: 50,000
SALES (est): 17.13MM **Privately Held**
SIC: 3564 Ventilating fans: industrial or
commercial
HQ: Johnson Controls, Inc.
5757 N Green Bay Ave
Milwaukee WI 53209
866 496-1999

(G-5619)
MANTYCH METALWORKING INC
3175 Plainfield Rd (45432-3712)
PHONE....................................937 258-1373
Kathleen Mantych, *CEO*
Colleen Mantych, *Pr*
Cristy Mantych, *VP*
EMP: 15 **EST:** 1971
SQ FT: 24,000
SALES (est): 3.19MM **Privately Held**
Web: www.mantych.net
SIC: 3599 3444 Machine shop, jobbing and
repair; Sheet metalwork

(G-5620)
MIAMI VALLEY LIGHTING LLC
1065 Woodman Dr (45432-1423)
PHONE....................................937 224-6000
Joyce Reives, *Managing Member*
EMP: 7 **EST:** 2001
SQ FT: 1,500
SALES (est): 88.12K
SALES (corp-wide): 12.28B **Publicly Held**
Web: www.lightingsimplified.com
SIC: 3648 Street lighting fixtures
HQ: Dpl Llc
1065 Woodman Dr
Dayton OH 45432
937 259-7215

(G-5621)
MIAMI VLY MFG & ASSEMBLY INC
1889 Radio Rd (45431-1034)
PHONE....................................937 254-6665
Joseph S Rosenkranz, *Pr*
EMP: 12 **EST:** 1993
SQ FT: 5,000
SALES (est): 1MM **Privately Held**
Web: www.mvmainc.com
SIC: 3599 Machine shop, jobbing and repair

(G-5622)
REGIONAL SHEETMETAL MFG L
4401 Springfield St (45431-1040)
PHONE....................................937 425-6972
Allen Cruze, *Prin*
EMP: 8 **EST:** 2006
SALES (est): 885.93K **Privately Held**
Web: www.regionalsheetmetal.net
SIC: 3444 Sheet metalwork

(G-5623)
SELECT SIGNS
1755 Spaulding Rd (45432-3727)
PHONE....................................937 262-7095
Jon Cowell, *Prin*
EMP: 22 **EST:** 2007
SALES (est): 2.44MM **Privately Held**
Web: www.selectsigns.com

▲ = Import ▼ = Export
◆ = Import/Export

SIC: 3993 Signs and advertising specialties

(G-5624)
TOASTMASTERS INTERNATIONAL
1854 Redleaf Ct (45432-4103)
PHONE.................................937 429-2680
Dan Reeves, *Treas*
EMP: 10
SALES (corp-wide): 27.95MM **Privately Held**
Web: www.toastmasters.org
SIC: 8299 2721 Educational service, nondegree granting: continuing educ.; Magazines: publishing only, not printed on site
PA: Toastmasters International
9127 S Jamaica St # 400
Englewood CO 80112
949 858-8255

(G-5625)
UNISON INDUSTRIES LLC
2455 Dayton Xenia Rd (45434-7148)
PHONE.................................904 667-9904
Belinda Kidwell, *Mgr*
EMP: 400
SALES (corp-wide): 38.7B **Publicly Held**
Web: www.unisonindustries.com
SIC: 3728 4581 3714 3498 Aircraft parts and equipment, nec; Aircraft servicing and repairing; Motor vehicle parts and accessories; Fabricated pipe and fittings
HQ: Unison Industries, Llc
7575 Baymeadows Way
Jacksonville FL 32256
904 739-4000

(G-5626)
YOUNGS PUBLISHING INC
4130 Linden Ave Ste 150 (45432-3088)
PHONE.................................937 259-6575
Ronald K Young Senior, *Pr*
Ronald K Young Junior, *VP*
EMP: 6 EST: 1988
SALES (est): 522.86K **Privately Held**
Web: www.reforsale.org
SIC: 2721 Magazines: publishing and printing

Dayton
Montgomery County

(G-5627)
4 OVER LLC
7801 Technology Blvd (45424-1574)
PHONE.................................937 610-0629
Frank Johnston, *VP*
EMP: 40
SALES (corp-wide): 172.36MM **Privately Held**
Web: www.4over.com
SIC: 2759 Commercial printing, nec
HQ: 4 Over, Llc
1225 Loa Angeles St
Glendale CA 91204
818 246-1170

(G-5628)
5 AXIS GRINDING INC
86 Westpark Rd (45459-4813)
PHONE.................................937 312-9797
Scott Ameduri, *Pr*
Barbara Ameduri, *Sec*
EMP: 7 EST: 2005
SALES (est): 3.84MM **Privately Held**
Web: www.5axisgrinding.com
SIC: 3541 Machine tools, metal cutting type

(G-5629)
A & B IRON & METAL CO INC
329 Washington St (45402-2541)
P.O. Box 123 (45301)
PHONE.................................937 228-1561
Greg Thoma, *Pr*
Joseph Caperna, *Pr*
Rosalia Caperna, *VP*
EMP: 12 EST: 1949
SQ FT: 500
SALES (est): 888.64K **Privately Held**
Web: www.abironmetal.com
SIC: 5093 4953 3341 3231 Metal scrap and waste materials; Refuse systems; Secondary nonferrous metals; Products of purchased glass

(G-5630)
ACCRO-CAST CORPORATION
4147 Gardendale Ave (45427)
PHONE.................................937 228-0497
Fred Luther, *Pr*
EMP: 6 EST: 1964
SQ FT: 5,000
SALES (est): 1.11MM **Privately Held**
Web: www.accrocast.com
SIC: 3363 Aluminum die-castings

(G-5631)
ACCU-GRIND & MFG CO INC
272 Leo St (45404-1006)
P.O. Box 117 (45337-0117)
PHONE.................................937 224-3303
Jeff Heisey, *Pr*
EMP: 43 EST: 1988
SQ FT: 39,500
SALES (est): 3.11MM **Privately Held**
Web: www.accugrind.net
SIC: 3599 Machine shop, jobbing and repair

(G-5632)
ACCUTECH PLASTIC MOLDING INC
5015 Kitridge Rd (45424-4433)
P.O. Box 24272 (45424-0272)
PHONE.................................937 233-0017
William Stoddard Junior, *Pr*
EMP: 7 EST: 1977
SQ FT: 6,000
SALES (est): 977.99K **Privately Held**
SIC: 3089 Injection molding of plastics

(G-5633)
ACTION RUBBER CO INC
601 Fame Rd (45449-2355)
PHONE.................................937 866-5975
Ron Mc Croson, *Pr*
EMP: 10 EST: 1984
SQ FT: 12,500
SALES (est): 651.71K **Privately Held**
Web: www.actionrubber.com
SIC: 3069 Molded rubber products

(G-5634)
AD INDUSTRIES INC
6450 Poe Ave Ste 109 (45414-2646)
PHONE.................................303 744-1911
◆ EMP: 7776
SIC: 3634 3564 3535 3714 Fans, exhaust and ventilating, electric: household; Ventilating fans: industrial or commercial; Conveyors and conveying equipment; Motor vehicle parts and accessories

(G-5635)
ADCURA MFG
1314 Farr Dr (45404-2736)
PHONE.................................937 222-3800
Russel Phie, *Owner*
EMP: 6 EST: 2005
SALES (est): 876.44K **Privately Held**

Web: www.adcuramfg.com
SIC: 3496 Miscellaneous fabricated wire products

(G-5636)
ADEPT MANUFACTURING CORP
1710 E 1st St (45403-1128)
PHONE.................................937 222-7110
Mike Mueller, *Pr*
Sandy Mueller, *Treas*
EMP: 10 EST: 1992
SALES (est): 861.39K **Privately Held**
SIC: 3544 Special dies and tools

(G-5637)
AERO JET WASH LLC
450 Gargrave Rd (45449-2462)
PHONE.................................866 381-7955
Shawn Tadayon, *Managing Member*
Mike Vahedy, *Managing Member*
EMP: 10 EST: 2006
SALES (est): 1.31MM **Privately Held**
Web: www.aerojetwash.com
SIC: 3724 4581 Aircraft engines and engine parts; Aircraft cleaning and janitorial service

(G-5638)
AEROSEAL LLC
Also Called: Aerobarrier
1851 S Metro Pkwy (45459-2523)
PHONE.................................937 428-9300
Amit Gupta, *Brnch Mgr*
EMP: 30
SALES (corp-wide): 14MM **Privately Held**
Web: www.aeroseal.com
SIC: 8748 3679 Energy conservation consultant; Hermetic seals, for electronic equipment
PA: Aeroseal Llc
225 Byers Rd # 1
Miamisburg OH 45342
937 428-9300

(G-5639)
AFC STAMPING & PRODUCTION INC
4900 Webster St (45414-4831)
PHONE.................................937 275-8700
EMP: 115 EST: 1971
SALES (est): 8.86MM
SALES (corp-wide): 43.81MM **Privately Held**
Web: www.afcstamping.com
SIC: 3469 Metal stampings, nec
PA: Fc Industries, Inc.
4900 Webster St
Dayton OH 45414
937 275-8700

(G-5640)
AFC TOOL CO INC
4900 Webster St (45414-4831)
PHONE.................................937 275-8700
EMP: 30 EST: 1972
SALES (est): 6.21MM
SALES (corp-wide): 43.81MM **Privately Held**
Web: www.afctool.com
SIC: 3544 Special dies and tools
PA: Fc Industries, Inc.
4900 Webster St
Dayton OH 45414
937 275-8700

(G-5641)
AFS TECHNOLOGY LLC
6649 Deer Bluff Dr (45424-7029)
PHONE.................................937 545-0627
John Tiernan, *Pr*
EMP: 13 EST: 2005
SALES (est): 4.42MM **Privately Held**
Web: www.afstechnologyusa.com

SIC: 3523 Elevators, farm

(G-5642)
AGILE MANUFACTURING TECH LLC
220 N Jersey St (45403-1220)
PHONE.................................937 258-3338
EMP: 10 EST: 2019
SALES (est): 4.86MM **Privately Held**
SIC: 3999 Manufacturing industries, nec

(G-5643)
AIDA-AMERICA CORPORATION
7600 Center Point 70 Blvd (45424-6365)
PHONE.................................937 237-2382
EMP: 15
SIC: 3542 Machine tools, metal forming type
HQ: Aida-America Corporation
7660 Center Point 70 Blvd
Dayton OH 45424

(G-5644)
AIDA-AMERICA CORPORATION (HQ)
7660 Center Point 70 Blvd (45424-6365)
PHONE.................................937 237-2382
◆ EMP: 65 EST: 1995
SALES (est): 23.82MM **Privately Held**
Web: www.aida-global.com
SIC: 3542 Presses: forming, stamping, punching, sizing (machine tools)
PA: Aida Engineering, Ltd.
2-10, Oyamacho, Midori-Ku
Sagamihara KNG 252-0

(G-5645)
ALLEY CAT DESIGNS INC
919 Senate Dr (45459-4017)
PHONE.................................937 291-8803
Ron Dallessandris, *Pr*
Joyce Dallessandris, *VP*
Mariana Neal, *VP*
Patty Dallessandris, *Sec*
EMP: 8 EST: 1996
SQ FT: 2,800
SALES (est): 1.91MM **Privately Held**
Web: www.alleycatworldwide.com
SIC: 3552 2395 Printing machinery, textile; Embroidery products, except Schiffli machine

(G-5646)
ALLIED MOTION AT DAYTON
2275 Stanley Ave (45404-1226)
PHONE.................................937 228-3171
EMP: 25 EST: 2018
SALES (est): 8.21MM **Privately Held**
SIC: 3621 Motors, electric

(G-5647)
ALLIED SILK SCREEN INC
2740 Thunderhawk Ct (45414-3464)
PHONE.................................937 223-4921
Dennis Brzozowski, *Pr*
David Brzozowski, *VP*
EMP: 7 EST: 1970
SQ FT: 10,000
SALES (est): 127.03K **Privately Held**
Web: www.alliedsilkscreen.com
SIC: 2759 Screen printing

(G-5648)
ALRO STEEL CORPORATION
821 Springfield St (45403-1252)
PHONE.................................937 253-6121
TOLL FREE: 800
Tim Elliott, *Mgr*
EMP: 40
SQ FT: 120,000
SALES (corp-wide): 3.04B **Privately Held**
Web: www.alro.com

SIC: 5051 3441 3317 3316 Steel; Fabricated structural metal; Steel pipe and tubes; Cold finishing of steel shapes
PA: Alro Steel Corporation
3100 E High St
Jackson MI 49203
517 787-5500

(G-5649)
AMERICAN AERO COMPONENTS LLC
2601 W Stroop Rd Ste 62 (45439-2030)
PHONE..................937 367-5068
Ajitesh Kakade, *Managing Member*
EMP: 7 EST: 2015
SQ FT: 50,000
SALES (est): 1.27MM Privately Held
SIC: 3451 3599 3728 3724 Screw machine products; Machine and other job shop work; Aircraft parts and equipment, nec; Aircraft engines and engine parts

(G-5650)
AMERICAN BOTTLING COMPANY
7 Up Bottling Co of Dayton
3131 Transportation Rd (45404-2372)
PHONE..................937 236-0333
Michael Eichner, *Mgr*
EMP: 110
SQ FT: 100,000
Web: www.keurigdrpepper.com
SIC: 2086 Soft drinks: packaged in cans, bottles, etc.
HQ: The American Bottling Company
6425 Hall Of Fame Ln
Frisco TX 75034

(G-5651)
AMERICAN CITY BUS JOURNALS INC
Also Called: Dayton Business Journal
40 N Main St Ste 810 (45423-1053)
PHONE..................937 528-4400
Neil Arthur, *Mgr*
EMP: 104
SALES (corp-wide): 2.88B Privately Held
Web: www.acbj.com
SIC: 2711 7313 Newspapers: publishing only, not printed on site; Newspaper advertising representative
HQ: American City Business Journals, Inc.
120 W Morehead St Ste 400
Charlotte NC 28202
704 973-1000

(G-5652)
AMERICAN CONCRETE PRODUCTS INC
Also Called: American Brick & Block
1433 S Euclid Ave (45417-3839)
PHONE..................937 224-1433
Lee Snyder, *Pr*
Lee E Snyder, *Treas*
EMP: 7 EST: 1987
SQ FT: 10,000
SALES (est): 232.14K Privately Held
Web: www.snyderonline.com
SIC: 3271 5211 Blocks, concrete or cinder: standard; Brick

(G-5653)
AMERICAN INDUS MAINTENENCE
605 Springfield St (45403-1248)
PHONE..................937 254-3400
Marvin Price, *Pr*
Cari Price, *VP*
EMP: 8 EST: 1991
SQ FT: 19,000
SALES (est): 495.37K Privately Held
Web: www.aimsandblasting.com

SIC: 5231 3471 Paint and painting supplies; Sand blasting of metal parts

(G-5654)
AMERICAN POWER LLC
Also Called: Apowermedia
1819 Troy St (45404-2400)
PHONE..................937 235-0418
Adil Baguirov, *CEO*
Adil Baguirov, *Managing Member*
EMP: 12 EST: 2013
SALES (est): 652.81K Privately Held
Web: www.americanpowertransport.com
SIC: 5047 3842 5088 7379 Medical equipment and supplies; Surgical appliances and supplies; Transportation equipment and supplies; Computer related consulting services

(G-5655)
AMERICAN RESCUE TECHNOLOGY INC
2780 Culver Ave (45429-3724)
PHONE..................937 293-6240
Richard S Michalo, *Pr*
◆ EMP: 10 EST: 1993
SQ FT: 11,000
SALES (est): 5.2MM Privately Held
Web: www.art4rescue.com
SIC: 5084 3569 Safety equipment; Firefighting and related equipment

(G-5656)
AMERICAN WAY EXTERIORS LLC
900 E Franklin St (45459-5620)
PHONE..................937 221-8860
Stephen Moad, *Pr*
EMP: 7 EST: 2014
SALES (est): 1.51MM Privately Held
Web: www.americanwayexteriors.com
SIC: 3292 1761 1799 Roofing, asbestos felt roll; Roofing, siding, and sheetmetal work; Asbestos removal and encapsulation

(G-5657)
AMERIWATER LLC
3345 Stop 8 Rd (45414-3425)
PHONE..................937 461-8833
Greg Reny, *Pr*
James Baker, *
▲ EMP: 47 EST: 1992
SQ FT: 48,000
SALES (est): 14.48MM Privately Held
Web: www.ameriwater.com
SIC: 3589 Water treatment equipment, industrial

(G-5658)
ANALYTICA USA INC (PA)
711 E Monument Ave Ste 309 (45402-1320)
PHONE..................513 348-2333
Vikram Seshadri, *CEO*
EMP: 9 EST: 2006
SALES (est): 1.69MM
SALES (corp-wide): 1.69MM Privately Held
Web: www.analytica.net
SIC: 7371 3825 Software programming applications; Radio apparatus analyzers, nec

(G-5659)
ANNARINO FOODS LTD
2787 Armstrong Ln (45414-4225)
PHONE..................937 274-3663
Jonathan Annarino, *Pr*
Anthony Annarino, *Pt*
Leonard M Annarino, *Pt*
EMP: 20 EST: 1990
SQ FT: 6,000

SALES (est): 4.95MM Privately Held
Web: www.annarinofoods.com
SIC: 2035 2033 2099 Dressings, salad: raw and cooked (except dry mixes); Barbecue sauce: packaged in cans, jars, etc.; Sauce, gravy, dressing, and dip mixes

(G-5660)
AOG INC
Also Called: Agents of Gaming
7672 Mcewen Rd (45459-3908)
P.O. Box 31571 (45437-0571)
PHONE..................937 436-2412
Bruce Graw, *Pr*
Robert Glass, *VP*
Kelly Lofgren, *Treas*
EMP: 7 EST: 1997
SQ FT: 6,000
SALES (est): 104.53K Privately Held
Web: www.agentsofgaming.com
SIC: 3944 Games, toys, and children's vehicles

(G-5661)
APEX TOOL GROUP LLC
762 W Stewart St (45417-3971)
PHONE..................937 222-7871
EMP: 128
SALES (corp-wide): 2.81B Privately Held
Web: www.apextoolgroup.com
SIC: 3546 Power-driven handtools
HQ: Apex Tool Group, Llc
910 Ridgebrook Rd Ste 200
Sparks Glencoe MD 21152

(G-5662)
APS-MATERIALS INC (PA)
Also Called: A P S
4011 Riverside Dr (45405-2364)
P.O. Box 1106 (45401-1106)
PHONE..................937 278-6547
Michael C Wilson, *Pr*
Joseph T Cheng, *
▲ EMP: 65 EST: 1975
SQ FT: 50,000
SALES (est): 23.4MM
SALES (corp-wide): 23.4MM Privately Held
Web: www.apsmaterials.com
SIC: 3479 2899 2851 Coating of metals and formed products; Chemical preparations, nec; Paints and allied products

(G-5663)
APS-MATERIALS INC
314 Leo St (45404-1078)
PHONE..................937 278-6547
EMP: 9
SALES (corp-wide): 23.4MM Privately Held
Web: www.apsmaterials.com
SIC: 3479 Coating of metals and formed products
PA: Aps-Materials, Inc.
4011 Riverside Dr
Dayton OH 45405
937 278-6547

(G-5664)
AQUA PRECISION LLC
165 Janney Rd (45404-1225)
PHONE..................937 912-9582
Michael Witt, *Prin*
EMP: 8 EST: 2016
SALES (est): 2.06MM Privately Held
Web: www.aquaprecision.net
SIC: 3599 Machine shop, jobbing and repair

(G-5665)
ARTISAN GRINDING SERVICE INC
1300 Stanley Ave (45404-1092)
P.O. Box 131 (45404-0131)
PHONE..................937 667-7383
Carolyn M Buechly, *Pr*
Jeryl L Yantis, *Sec*
Teresa Landers, *Asst VP*
EMP: 11 EST: 1977
SQ FT: 14,000
SALES (est): 970.04K Privately Held
Web: www.artisangrinding.com
SIC: 3599 Machine shop, jobbing and repair

(G-5666)
ASIDACO LLC (PA)
Also Called: Alterntive Sltons Innvtion Dev
400 Linden Ave Ste 95 (45403-2574)
PHONE..................800 204-1544
Andrea T Bashaw, *Managing Member*
EMP: 9 EST: 2008
SALES (est): 1.2MM
SALES (corp-wide): 1.2MM Privately Held
Web: www.asidaco.com
SIC: 1731 1711 4911 3694 Electric power systems contractors; Solar energy contractor; Battery charging alternators and generators

(G-5667)
AUGUST INCORPORATED
2122 Pelwood Dr (45459-5139)
PHONE..................937 434-2520
Lee Fister Junior, *Pr*
Lee Fister Junior, *Pr*
Judith W Fister, *VP*
David Idle, *VP*
EMP: 20 EST: 1975
SQ FT: 20,000
SALES (est): 725.61K Privately Held
Web: www.augustinc.com
SIC: 2521 Wood office furniture

(G-5668)
AUTO-VALVE INC
1707 Guenther Rd (45417-9398)
PHONE..................937 854-3037
Raymond C Clark, *Pr*
Beth Seall, *
EMP: 50 EST: 1948
SQ FT: 17,800
SALES (est): 9.89MM Privately Held
Web: www.autovalve.com
SIC: 3728 Aircraft parts and equipment, nec

(G-5669)
AUTOMATION SYSTEMS DESIGN INC
Also Called: A S D
3540 Vance Rd (45439-7939)
PHONE..................937 387-0351
Sunny Kullar, *Prin*
Sukhi Kullar, *CFO*
EMP: 20 EST: 2000
SALES (est): 4.97MM Privately Held
Web: www.asddayton.com
SIC: 3535 Robotic conveyors

(G-5670)
AUTOMATION TECHNOLOGY INC
1900 Troy St (45404-2194)
PHONE..................937 233-6084
Robert Storar, *CEO*
N Chris Storar, *
Jeff Storar, *
EMP: 25 EST: 1982
SQ FT: 20,000
SALES (est): 4.44MM Privately Held
Web: www.atidayton.com

SIC: 3625 3825 3829 3823 Actuators, industrial; Test equipment for electronic and electrical circuits; Measuring and controlling devices, nec; Process control instruments

(G-5671)
AZTECA SYSTEMS INC
5475 Kellenburger Rd (45424-1013)
PHONE..................................801 523-2751
Brian Haslam, *Pr*
Brent Haslam, *
Peter S Hristou, *
EMP: 97 EST: 1986
SALES (est): 2.14MM **Privately Held**
Web: assetlifecycle.trimble.com
SIC: 7372 Prepackaged software

(G-5672)
B S F INC (PA)
8895 N Dixie Dr (45414-1803)
P.O. Box 459 (45377-0459)
PHONE..................................937 890-6121
Kathryn Keel, *Pr*
Mike Coale, *VP*
Chris Bright, *Prin*
Eric Metzger, *Prin*
Jackie Frank, *Prin*
EMP: 10 EST: 1974
SQ FT: 2,000
SALES (est): 2.47MM
SALES (corp-wide): 2.47MM **Privately Held**
Web: www.bsfinc.net
SIC: 3498 3568 Couplings, pipe: fabricated from purchased pipe; Couplings, shaft: rigid, flexible, universal joint, etc.

(G-5673)
BACKGROUND MUSIC & SOUND INC
8529 N Dixie Dr Ste 325 (45414-2497)
PHONE..................................937 898-9871
Sal Chirico Senior, *Pr*
EMP: 8 EST: 1980
SQ FT: 2,900
SALES (est): 120.73K **Privately Held**
SIC: 5065 1731 3651 Sound equipment, electronic; Sound equipment specialization; Sound reproducing equipment

(G-5674)
BARSPLICE PRODUCTS INC
4900 Webster St (45414-4831)
PHONE..................................937 275-8700
▼ **EMP: 48 EST:** 1988
SALES (est): 7.87MM
SALES (corp-wide): 43.81MM **Privately Held**
Web: www.barsplice.com
SIC: 3449 Bars, concrete reinforcing: fabricated steel
PA: Fc Industries, Inc.
4900 Webster St
Dayton OH 45414
937 275-8700

(G-5675)
BEIJING WEST INDUSTRIES
3100 Research Blvd Ste 10 (45420-4032)
PHONE..................................937 455-5281
EMP: 7 EST: 2010
SALES (est): 2.87MM **Privately Held**
Web: www.bwigroup.com
SIC: 3714 Motor vehicle parts and accessories

(G-5676)
BELTON FOODS LLC
Also Called: Belton Foods
2701 Thunderhawk Ct (45414-3445)
P.O. Box 13605 (45413-0605)
PHONE..................................937 890-7768

David V Sipos, *Pr*
Cindy Gillespie, *
Ted Dorow, *
Barbara Berer, *
Eleanor Sipos, *Stockholder**
EMP: 36 EST: 1949
SQ FT: 24,800
SALES (est): 9.54MM **Privately Held**
Web: www.beltonfoods.com
SIC: 2087 2086 2035 Concentrates, drink; Bottled and canned soft drinks; Pickles, sauces, and salad dressings

(G-5677)
BETA INDUSTRIES INC (PA)
2860 Culver Ave (45429-3794)
PHONE..................................937 299-7385
William B Walcott, *Pr*
Kenneth Walcott, *Dev*
Phyllis Walcott, *Sec*
EMP: 12 EST: 1968
SQ FT: 12,600
SALES (est): 4.76MM
SALES (corp-wide): 4.76MM **Privately Held**
Web: www.betaindustries.net
SIC: 3599 3699 Machine shop, jobbing and repair; Electrical equipment and supplies, nec

(G-5678)
BLAIRS CNC TURNING INC
Also Called: Blair's Cnc
245 Leo St (45404-1005)
P.O. Box 2840 (45401-2840)
PHONE..................................937 461-1100
James Trochelman, *Pr*
Marina Trochelman, *VP*
EMP: 7 EST: 1986
SQ FT: 13,100
SALES (est): 855.34K **Privately Held**
SIC: 3599 Machine shop, jobbing and repair

(G-5679)
BLANG ACQUISITION LLC
Also Called: Kap Signs
7464 Webster St (45414-5816)
PHONE..................................937 223-2155
John D Blang, *Managing Member*
EMP: 9 EST: 1969
SQ FT: 12,000
SALES (est): 756.3K **Privately Held**
Web: www.kapsigns.com
SIC: 2400 5000 5100 3003 Signboards, wood; Banners; Decals; Signs and advertising specialties

(G-5680)
BLUE CREEK ENTERPRISES INC
Also Called: Tabtronics
2153 Winners Cir (45404-1150)
PHONE..................................937 222-9969
EMP: 10
SALES (corp-wide): 37.64MM **Privately Held**
Web: www.miracllc.com
SIC: 3672 Printed circuit boards
PA: Blue Creek Enterprises, Inc.
316 N Main St
Lynchburg OH 45142

(G-5681)
BOB SUMEREL TIRE CO INC
7711 Center Point 70 Blvd (45424-6368)
PHONE..................................937 235-0062
Dennis Lavoie, *Mgr*
EMP: 8
SALES (corp-wide): 35.8MM **Privately Held**
Web: www.bobsumereltire.com

SIC: 5531 7534 Automotive tires; Tire retreading and repair shops
PA: Bob Sumerel Tire Co., Inc.
1257 Cox Ave
Erlanger KY 41018
859 283-2700

(G-5682)
BOOKFACTORY LLC
2302 S Edwin C Moses Blvd (45417-4662)
PHONE..................................937 226-7100
Andrew Gilmore, *
▼ **EMP: 30 EST:** 2002
SQ FT: 20,000
SALES (est): 4.85MM **Privately Held**
Web: www.bookfactory.com
SIC: 5942 2678 2731 2789 Book stores; Memorandum books, notebooks, and looseleaf filler paper; Book publishing; Bookbinding and related work

(G-5683)
BRANCH & BONE ARTISAN ALES LLC
905 Wayne Ave (45410-1247)
PHONE..................................937 723-7608
John Joyce, *Managing Member*
EMP: 14 EST: 2016
SALES (est): 1.41MM **Privately Held**
Web: www.branchandboneales.com
SIC: 2082 Beer (alcoholic beverage)

(G-5684)
BRIDGITS BATH LLC
1226 Pursell Ave (45420-1974)
PHONE..................................937 259-1960
EMP: 7 EST: 2008
SALES (est): 248.57K **Privately Held**
Web: www.bridgitsbath.com
SIC: 3261 7389 Soap dishes, vitreous china; Business services, nec

(G-5685)
BRINKMAN TOOL & DIE INC
325 Kiser St (45404-1621)
PHONE..................................937 222-1161
John R Brinkman, *Pr*
John C Brinkman, *VP*
Charlene Brinkman, *Sec*
▲ **EMP: 25 EST:** 1913
SQ FT: 24,000
SALES (est): 970.8K **Privately Held**
Web: www.brinkmantool.com
SIC: 3544 Special dies and tools

(G-5686)
BROADWAY SAND AND GRAVEL LLC
130 W 2nd St Ste 2000 (45402-1502)
PHONE..................................937 853-5555
Michael Marshall, *Prin*
EMP: 6 EST: 2016
SALES (est): 69.55K **Privately Held**
SIC: 1442 Construction sand and gravel

(G-5687)
BUCKEYE OIL EQUIPMENT CO
20 Innovation Ct (45414-3968)
PHONE..................................937 387-0671
Tim Stovell, *Prin*
EMP: 10 EST: 1977
SALES (est): 246.55K **Privately Held**
Web: www.jfpetrogroup.com
SIC: 3533 Oil and gas drilling rigs and equipment

(G-5688)
BUDDE PRECISION MACHINING CORP
2608 Nordic Rd (45414-3424)
PHONE..................................937 278-1962

Michael Budde, *Pr*
EMP: 15 EST: 2018
SALES (est): 3.56MM **Privately Held**
Web: www.buddeprecision.com
SIC: 3599 Machine shop, jobbing and repair

(G-5689)
BUDDE SHEET METAL WORKS INC (PA)
305 Leo St (45404-1083)
PHONE..................................937 224-0868
Candice Budde, *Pr*
Thomas Budde, *
Stephen L Budde, *
William R Budde Junior, *Sec*
EMP: 25 EST: 1922
SQ FT: 20,000
SALES (est): 9.15MM
SALES (corp-wide): 9.15MM **Privately Held**
Web: www.buddesheetmetal.com
SIC: 1761 3444 1711 Sheet metal work, nec; Sheet metalwork; Plumbing, heating, air-conditioning

(G-5690)
C & M RUBBER CO INC
414 Littell Ave (45419-3608)
P.O. Box 185 (45401-0185)
PHONE..................................937 299-2782
James Mccloskey, *Pr*
Eric Weber, *VP*
EMP: 10 EST: 1964
SQ FT: 10,000
SALES (est): 963.29K **Privately Held**
Web: www.cmrubber.com
SIC: 3061 Mechanical rubber goods

(G-5691)
C B MFG & SLS CO INC
American Cutting Edge
4475 Infirmary Rd (45449)
PHONE..................................937 866-5986
Charles Biehn, *Mgr*
EMP: 19
SALES (corp-wide): 25.37MM **Privately Held**
Web: www.americancuttingedge.com
SIC: 3423 Hand and edge tools, nec
PA: C. B. Manufacturing And Sales Company, Inc.
4455 Infirmary Rd
Miamisburg OH 45342
937 866-5986

(G-5692)
C-LINK ENTERPRISES LLC
Also Called: Southern Ohio Kitchens
1825 Webster St (45404-1147)
PHONE..................................937 222-2829
EMP: 10 EST: 1968
SQ FT: 25,000
SALES (est): 195.5K **Privately Held**
SIC: 1521 2514 5722 General remodeling, single-family houses; Kitchen cabinets: metal; Kitchens, complete (sinks, cabinets, etc.)

(G-5693)
CARGILL INCORPORATED
Also Called: Cargill
3201 Needmore Rd (45414-4321)
PHONE..................................937 236-1971
Sheila Willhoite, *Brnch Mgr*
EMP: 49
SALES (corp-wide): 159.59B **Privately Held**
Web: www.cargill.com
SIC: 2046 2087 2041 Corn starch; Flavoring extracts and syrups, nec; Flour and other grain mill products

PA: Cargill, Incorporated
15407 Mcginty Rd W
Wayzata MN 55391
800 227-4455

(G-5694)
CARSON-SAEKS INC (PA)
Also Called: Karen Carson Creations
2601 Timber Ln (45414-4733)
P.O. Box 13297 (45413-0297)
PHONE..............................937 278-5311
William Smith, *Ch Bd*
Terrence Mollaun, *
Jeff Smith, *
◆ **EMP: 35 EST:** 1985
SQ FT: 20,000
SALES (est): 1.62MM
SALES (corp-wide): 1.62MM **Privately Held**
Web: www.karencarson.com
SIC: 2869 Perfume materials, synthetic

(G-5695)
CASSANOS INC (PA)
Also Called: Cassano's Pizza & Subs
1700 E Stroop Rd (45429-5095)
PHONE..............................937 294-8400
Vic Cassano Junior, *Ch Bd*
EMP: 45 EST: 1949
SQ FT: 37,500
SALES (est): 20.38MM
SALES (corp-wide): 20.38MM **Privately Held**
Web: www.cassanos.com
SIC: 5812 5149 6794 2045 Pizzeria, chain; Baking supplies; Franchises, selling or licensing; Pizza doughs, prepared: from purchased flour

(G-5696)
CASSIS PACKAGING CO
1235 Mccook Ave (45404-2812)
PHONE..............................937 223-8868
TOLL FREE: 800
Sheila Cassis, *Pr*
Cassandra Cassis, *VP*
EMP: 13 EST: 1957
SQ FT: 26,000
SALES (est): 354.87K **Privately Held**
Web: www.cassispackaging.com
SIC: 2449 4783 Rectangular boxes and crates, wood; Crating goods for shipping

(G-5697)
CERTIFIED HEAT TREATING INC (PA)
4475 Infirmary Rd (45449)
P.O. Box 354 (45449)
PHONE..............................937 866-0245
Joseph Biehn, *Pr*
EMP: 7 EST: 1970
SQ FT: 20,000
SALES (est): 882.75K
SALES (corp-wide): 882.75K **Privately Held**
Web: www.heattreating.com
SIC: 3398 Metal heat treating

(G-5698)
CHAOS ENTERTAINMENT
Also Called: CD / Dvd Distribution
7570 Mount Whitney St (45424-6944)
PHONE..............................937 520-5260
EMP: 8 EST: 2008
SALES (est): 456.88K **Privately Held**
SIC: 3561 Pumps and pumping equipment

(G-5699)
CHEMCORE INC (PA)
20 Madison St (45402-2106)
P.O. Box 802 (45401-0802)

PHONE..............................937 228-6118
Mike Klaus, *CEO*
Reiff Lorenz, *Pr*
Geoffrey Lorenz, *VP*
EMP: 10 EST: 2000
SALES (est): 725.17K
SALES (corp-wide): 725.17K **Privately Held**
SIC: 5169 2869 Chemical additives; Industrial organic chemicals, nec

(G-5700)
CHEMINEER INC
Also Called: Kenics
5870 Poe Ave (45414-3442)
P.O. Box 1123 (45401-1123)
PHONE..............................937 454-3200
◆ **EMP:** 160
Web: www.nov.com
SIC: 3559 3556 3554 3531 Chemical machinery and equipment; Food products machinery; Paper industries machinery; Construction machinery

(G-5701)
CHEMSTATION INTERNATIONAL INC (PA)
Also Called: Chemstation
3400 Encrete Ln (45439-1946)
PHONE..............................937 294-8265
EMP: 45 EST: 1982
SALES (est): 56.36MM
SALES (corp-wide): 56.36MM **Privately Held**
Web: www.chemstation.com
SIC: 6794 2842 2899 2841 Franchises, selling or licensing; Cleaning or polishing preparations, nec; Chemical preparations, nec; Soap and other detergents

(G-5702)
CHROMALLOY CORPORATION
7425 Webster St (45414-5817)
PHONE..............................937 890-3775
Pete Stodd, *Pr*
EMP: 11
SALES (corp-wide): 502.01MM **Privately Held**
Web: www.chromalloy.com
SIC: 3569 Assembly machines, non-metalworking
PA: Chromalloy Corporation
3999 Rca Blvd
Palm Beach Gardens FL 33410
561 935-3571

(G-5703)
CLINTS PRINTING INC
Also Called: Clint's Prntng
1176 Little Sugar Creek Rd (45440-3941)
PHONE..............................937 426-2771
Clinton Whittaker, *CEO*
Lucille Whittaker, *Pr*
Lawrence Bernard, *VP*
EMP: 6 EST: 1952
SALES (est): 64.22K **Privately Held**
Web: www.clintsprinting.com
SIC: 2791 2789 2752 Typesetting; Bookbinding and related work; Offset printing

(G-5704)
COCA-COLA CONSOLIDATED INC
Also Called: Coca-Cola
1000 Coca Cola Blvd (45424-6375)
PHONE..............................937 878-5000
Bob Tiootson, *Mgr*
EMP: 573
SALES (corp-wide): 6.9B **Publicly Held**
Web: www.cokeconsolidated.com

SIC: 2086 Bottled and canned soft drinks
PA: Coca-Cola Consolidated, Inc.
4100 Coca-Cola Plz
Charlotte NC 28211
980 392-8298

(G-5705)
COLBY WOODWORKING INC
1912 Lucille Dr (45404-1109)
PHONE..............................937 224-7676
Steven Colby, *Pr*
EMP: 20 EST: 1985
SALES (est): 1.16MM **Privately Held**
SIC: 2434 Wood kitchen cabinets

(G-5706)
COMBINED TECH GROUP INC
6061 Milo Rd (45414-3417)
PHONE..............................937 274-4866
Chad Kuhns, *Managing Member*
Kurtis Vanburen, *
Tina Vanburen, *
EMP: 28 EST: 1998
SQ FT: 50,000
SALES (est): 7.46MM **Privately Held**
Web: www.comtechgrp.com
SIC: 5084 3549 Industrial machinery and equipment; Assembly machines, including robotic

(G-5707)
COMMERCIAL MTAL FBRICATORS INC
150 Commerce Park Dr (45404-1273)
PHONE..............................937 233-4911
Patrick Dakin, *Pr*
James D Utrecht, *
Molly Dakin, *
EMP: 40 EST: 1954
SALES (est): 4.5MM **Privately Held**
Web:
www.commercialmetalfabricators.com
SIC: 3441 3444 3443 Fabricated structural metal; Sheet metalwork; Fabricated plate work (boiler shop)

(G-5708)
COMPONENT SOLUTIONS GROUP INC (HQ)
7755 Paragon Rd Ste 104 (45459-4052)
PHONE..............................937 434-8100
Ernie Riling, *Pr*
Sam Pfabe, *CFO*
EMP: 12 EST: 1998
SQ FT: 3,500
SALES (est): 40.3MM **Privately Held**
Web:
www.componentsolutionsgroup.com
SIC: 5031 3452 Pallets, wood; Bolts, nuts, rivets, and washers
PA: Bufab Ab (Publ)
Stenfalksvagen 1
VArnamo 331 4

(G-5709)
COMPOSITE TECHNOLOGIES CO LLC
401 N Keowee St (45404-1602)
PHONE..............................937 228-2880
Mike Dematto, *Managing Member*
Jay Binder, *Managing Member*
EMP: 80 EST: 1998
SQ FT: 100,000
SALES (est): 5.36MM
SALES (corp-wide): 22.45MM **Privately Held**
Web: www.ctcplastics.com
SIC: 3089 Plastics containers, except foam
PA: Soin International, Llc
1129 Mmsburg Cntrvlle Rd
Dayton OH 45449

937 427-7646

(G-5710)
CONTECH BRIDGE SOLUTIONS LLC
Also Called: Bridgetek
7941 New Carlisle Pike (45424-1507)
PHONE..............................937 878-2170
Jim Feltner, *Mgr*
EMP: 10
Web: www.conteches.com
SIC: 3272 Concrete products, nec
HQ: Contech Bridge Solutions Llc
9025 Cntrpinte Dr Ste 400
West Chester OH 45069

(G-5711)
COUCH BUSINESS DEVELOPMENT INC
Also Called: Fordyce Custom Finishing
32 Bates St (45402-1326)
PHONE..............................937 253-1099
David Couch, *Pr*
EMP: 8 EST: 2010
SQ FT: 49,250
SALES (est): 444.22K **Privately Held**
Web: www.artifexfinishing.com
SIC: 2541 2491 1751 Display fixtures, wood; Millwork, treated wood; Store fixture installation

(G-5712)
COX PUBLISHING HQ
1611 S Main St (45409-2547)
PHONE..............................937 225-2000
Michael Joseph, *Prin*
EMP: 9 EST: 2007
SALES (est): 247.99K **Privately Held**
SIC: 2741 Miscellaneous publishing

(G-5713)
CREATIVE FOAM DAYTON MOLD
3337 N Dixie Dr (45414-5645)
PHONE..............................937 279-9987
EMP: 14 EST: 2013
SALES (est): 3.73MM **Privately Held**
Web: www.creativefoam.com
SIC: 3086 Plastics foam products

(G-5714)
CREATIVE IMPRESSIONS INC
4611 Gateway Cir (45440-1713)
PHONE..............................937 435-5296
Dennis C Carter, *Pr*
Linda S Carter, *VP*
EMP: 10 EST: 1975
SQ FT: 7,500
SALES (est): 896.2K **Privately Held**
Web: www.creativeimpressions.biz
SIC: 2752 Offset printing

(G-5715)
CROWN CORK & SEAL USA INC
5005 Springboro Pike (45439-2974)
PHONE..............................937 299-2027
Robert Mason, *Mgr*
EMP: 102
SQ FT: 50,000
SALES (corp-wide): 11.8B **Publicly Held**
Web: www.crowncork.com
SIC: 3411 Metal cans
HQ: Crown Cork & Seal Usa, Inc.
770 Township Line Rd
Yardley PA 19067
215 698-5100

(G-5716)
CTC PLASTICS (HQ)
401 N Keowee St (45404-1602)
PHONE..............................937 228-9184
Vishal Soin, *CEO*

Mike Dematto, *COO*
William R Senften, *CFO*
EMP: 22 **EST:** 2012
SALES (est): 7.81MM
SALES (corp-wide): 22.45MM **Privately Held**
Web: www.ctcplastics.com
SIC: 3089 Injection molding of plastics
PA: Soin International, Llc
1129 Mmsburg Cntrvlle Rd
Dayton OH 45449
937 427-7646

(G-5717)
CUSTOM BLIND CORPORATION
Also Called: Castle Blinds and Draperies
2895 Culver Ave (45429-3725)
PHONE..................................937 643-2907
FAX: 937 643-1119
EMP: 12
SQ FT: 6,000
SALES (est): 1.29MM **Privately Held**
SIC: 2591 5023 1521 Drapery hardware and window blinds and shades; Vertical blinds; Single-family home remodeling, additions, and repairs

(G-5718)
CUSTOM METAL SHEARING INC
80 Commerce Park Dr (45404-1212)
PHONE..................................937 233-6950
Robert Colby, *Pr*
Marlene Kitty Colby, *VP*
Richard Colby, *VP*
EMP: 13 **EST:** 1992
SQ FT: 20,000
SALES (est): 2.16MM **Privately Held**
Web: www.custommetalshearing.com
SIC: 3444 7389 2819 Sheet metalwork; Metal slitting and shearing; Aluminum oxide

(G-5719)
CUSTOM NICKEL LLC
45 N Clinton St (45402-1346)
PHONE..................................937 222-1995
EMP: 6 **EST:** 1980
SALES (est): 976.51K **Privately Held**
Web: www.custom-nickel.com
SIC: 3471 Plating of metals or formed products

(G-5720)
DAYTON ARMOR LLC
2300 W Dorothy Ln Ste 107 (45439-1001)
PHONE..................................937 723-8675
EMP: 7 **EST:** 2010
SALES (est): 1.09MM **Privately Held**
Web: www.daytonarmor.com
SIC: 3999 Barber and beauty shop equipment

(G-5721)
DAYTON BAG & BURLAP CO
448 Huffman Ave (45403-2506)
PHONE..................................937 253-1722
Dave Barcus, *Pr*
EMP: 10
SALES (corp-wide): 3.15MM **Privately Held**
Web: www.daybag.com
SIC: 4225 2299 General warehousing and storage; Burlap, jute
PA: The Dayton Bag & Burlap Co
322 Davis Ave
Dayton OH 45403
937 258-8000

(G-5722)
DAYTON BINDERY SERVICE INC
3757 Inpark Dr (45414-4417)
PHONE..................................937 235-3111

FAX: 937 235-5070
EMP: 20
SALES (est): 2.15MM **Privately Held**
SIC: 2789 Bookbinding and related work

(G-5723)
DAYTON CITY PAPER GROUP LLC
Also Called: Impact Weekly
126 N Main St Ste 240 (45402-1766)
P.O. Box 10065 (45402-7065)
PHONE..................................937 222-8855
Mehdi Adineh, *Managing Member*
EMP: 10 **EST:** 1993
SALES (est): 183.21K **Privately Held**
SIC: 2711 Newspapers, publishing and printing

(G-5724)
DAYTON CLUTCH & JOINT INC (PA)
2005 Troy St 1 (45404-2936)
P.O. Box 163 (45404-0163)
PHONE..................................937 236-9770
Keith Knight, *Pr*
Nancy Knight, *Sec*
EMP: 16 **EST:** 1956
SQ FT: 16,000
SALES (est): 2.31MM
SALES (corp-wide): 2.31MM **Privately Held**
Web: www.daytonclutch.com
SIC: 3714 Motor vehicle parts and accessories

(G-5725)
DAYTON COATING TECH LLC
1926 E Siebenthaler Ave (45414-5334)
PHONE..................................937 278-2060
EMP: 6 **EST:** 1999
SQ FT: 15,000
SALES (est): 1.05MM **Privately Held**
Web: www.toolgrindcoat.com
SIC: 3479 Coating of metals and formed products

(G-5726)
DAYTON FORGING HEAT TREATING
215 N Findlay St (45403-1200)
PHONE..................................937 253-4126
Eric Wilson, *Pr*
Martha Todd Wilson, *
EMP: 65 **EST:** 1919
SQ FT: 100,000
SALES (est): 9.71MM **Privately Held**
Web: www.daytonforging.com
SIC: 3398 3462 Metal heat treating; Machinery forgings, ferrous

(G-5727)
DAYTON GEAR AND TOOL CO
500 Fame Rd (45449-2387)
PHONE..................................937 866-4327
Thomas R Baird, *Pr*
EMP: 20 **EST:** 1946
SQ FT: 3,000
SALES (est): 5.26MM **Privately Held**
Web: www.daytongear.com
SIC: 3566 Gears, power transmission, except auto

(G-5728)
DAYTON HAWKER CORPORATION
2844 Culver Ave (45429-3726)
PHONE..................................937 293-8147
William Darrow, *Pr*
▲ **EMP:** 10 **EST:** 1918
SQ FT: 12,000
SALES (est): 807.99K **Privately Held**
Web: www.hawkermfg.com
SIC: 3553 3841 3915 Lathes, wood turning: including accessories; Forceps, surgical; Pin stems

(G-5729)
DAYTON LEGAL BLANK INC
Also Called: Signature Printing
875 Congress Park Dr (45459-4047)
P.O. Box 750788 (45475-0788)
PHONE..................................937 435-4405
EMP: 6 **EST:** 1873
SALES (est): 487.14K **Privately Held**
SIC: 2791 2759 2752 2789 Typesetting; Commercial printing, nec; Commercial printing, lithographic; Bookbinding and related work

(G-5730)
DAYTON MACHINE TOOL COMPANY
Also Called: M D Tool
1314 Webster St (45404-1565)
PHONE..................................937 222-6444
EMP: 8 **EST:** 1950
SALES (est): 815.95K **Privately Held**
Web: www.firsttoolcorp.com
SIC: 3541 3549 7699 Machine tools, metal cutting type; Metalworking machinery, nec; Industrial machinery and equipment repair

(G-5731)
DAYTON MAILING SERVICES INC
100 S Keowee St (45402-2241)
P.O. Box 2436 (45401-2436)
PHONE..................................937 222-5056
Christine Soward, *Pr*
EMP: 30 **EST:** 1984
SQ FT: 100,000
SALES (est): 3.74MM **Privately Held**
Web: www.dmsink.us
SIC: 7331 2759 Mailing service; Commercial printing, nec

(G-5732)
DAYTON MOLDED URETHANES LLC
Also Called: D M U
3337 N Dixie Dr (45414-5645)
PHONE..................................937 279-9987
William Palmer, *Pr*
EMP: 9 **EST:** 2001
SQ FT: 50,000
SALES (est): 3.98MM
SALES (corp-wide): 198.24MM **Privately Held**
SIC: 3089 Injection molding of plastics
PA: Creative Foam Corporation
300 N Alloy Dr
Fenton MI 48430
810 629-4149

(G-5733)
DAYTON MOLDED URETHANES LLC
6400 Sand Lake Rd (45414-2635)
PHONE..................................937 279-1910
EMP: 36 **EST:** 2013
SALES (est): 1.11MM
SALES (corp-wide): 198.24MM **Privately Held**
SIC: 3061 Mechanical rubber goods
PA: Creative Foam Corporation
300 N Alloy Dr
Fenton MI 48430
810 629-4149

(G-5734)
DAYTON ONE LLC
212 Heid Ave (45404-1220)
PHONE..................................937 265-0227
EMP: 6 **EST:** 2016
SALES (est): 2.99MM **Privately Held**
Web: www.daytonone.com
SIC: 3599 Machine shop, jobbing and repair

(G-5735)
DAYTON PATTERN INC
5591 Wadsworth Rd (45414-3446)
P.O. Box 13779 (45413-0779)
PHONE..................................937 277-0761
Erik Zimmer, *Pr*
Janice Zimmer, *Sec*
EMP: 6 **EST:** 1965
SQ FT: 7,000
SALES (est): 227.84K **Privately Held**
Web: www.daytonpattern.com
SIC: 3543 Industrial patterns

(G-5736)
DAYTON POLYMERIC PRODUCTS INC
3337 N Dixie Dr (45414-5645)
PHONE..................................937 279-9987
EMP: 60 **EST:** 2001
SALES (est): 2.29MM **Privately Held**
SIC: 3086 Packaging and shipping materials, foamed plastics

(G-5737)
DAYTON PROGRESS CORPORATION (DH)
500 Progress Rd (45449-2351)
P.O. Box 39 (45449)
PHONE..................................937 859-5111
David Turpin, *Pr*
Randy Wissinger, *VP Fin*
Sawato Hayashi, *Prin*
▲ **EMP:** 525 **EST:** 1946
SALES (est): 47.7MM **Privately Held**
Web: www.daytonprogress.com
SIC: 3544 3545 3495 3493 Punches, forming and stamping; Machine tool accessories; Wire springs; Steel springs, except wire
HQ: Dayton Lamina Corporation
500 Progress Rd
Dayton OH 45449
937 859-5111

(G-5738)
DAYTON PROGRESS INTL CORP
500 Progress Rd (45449-2326)
PHONE..................................937 859-5111
Alan Shaffer, *Pr*
David Turpin, *VP*
Randy S Wissinger, *VP Fin*
Bill Mills, *VP*
EMP: 7 **EST:** 1969
SALES (est): 1.78MM **Privately Held**
Web: www.daytonlamina.com
SIC: 3544 Special dies and tools
HQ: Dayton Progress Corporation
500 Progress Rd
Dayton OH 45449
937 859-5111

(G-5739)
DAYTON STENCIL WORKS COMPANY
Also Called: Datono Products
113 E 2nd St (45402-1753)
P.O. Box 126 (45401-0126)
PHONE..................................937 223-3233
TOLL FREE: 800
Edward Jauch, *Pr*
Larry Horwath, *VP*
David Jauch, *Sec*
John Jauch, *Treas*
EMP: 19 **EST:** 1859
SQ FT: 18,000
SALES (est): 2.48MM **Privately Held**
Web: www.datono.com
SIC: 3949 3953 3544 5085 Golf equipment; Marking devices; Special dies, tools, jigs, and fixtures; Industrial supplies

GEOGRAPHIC

(G-5740)
DAYTON WHEEL CONCEPTS INC
Also Called: Dayton Wire Wheel
115 Compark Rd (45459-4803)
PHONE.....................937 438-0100
Charles Schroeder, *Prin*
▲ **EMP:** 30 **EST:** 1953
SQ FT: 150,000
SALES (est): 4.51MM **Privately Held**
Web: www.daytonwirewheels.com
SIC: 3714 Wheels, motor vehicle

(G-5741)
DAYTON WIRE PRODUCTS INC
7 Dayton Wire Pkwy (45404-1282)
PHONE.....................937 236-8000
David Leiser, *Pr*
Brian Schissler, *
EMP: 40 **EST:** 1965
SQ FT: 62,500
SALES (est): 2.48MM **Privately Held**
Web: www.ncttech.com
SIC: 3496 3993 Miscellaneous fabricated
wire products; Signs and advertising
specialties

(G-5742)
DAYTON-PHOENIX GROUP INC (PA)
1619 Kuntz Rd (45404-1240)
PHONE.....................937 496-3900
Gale Kooken, *Pr*
Roger Fleming, *
John Murphy, *
◆ **EMP:** 104 **EST:** 1992
SALES (est): 114.96MM **Privately Held**
Web: www.dayton-phoenix.com
SIC: 3621 3743 Motors and generators;
Railroad equipment

(G-5743)
DB UNLIMITED LLC
Also Called: Db Products USA
61 Marco Ln (45458-3818)
PHONE.....................937 401-2602
John Sackett, *Genl Mgr*
EMP: 8 **EST:** 2013
SALES (est): 259.81K **Privately Held**
Web: www.dbunlimitedco.com
SIC: 3651 5065 Audio electronic systems;
Sound equipment, electronic

(G-5744)
DCM SOUNDEX INC
Also Called: Soundex Communications Group
1901 E 5th St (45403-2347)
P.O. Box 1942 (45401-1942)
PHONE.....................937 522-0371
Sam Nicolosi, *Pr*
EMP: 15 **EST:** 1974
SALES (est): 538.86K **Privately Held**
SIC: 3678 3679 Electronic connectors;
Transducers, electrical

(G-5745)
DELMA CORP
Also Called: Dayton Manufacturing Company
3327 Elkton Ave (45403-1357)
PHONE.....................937 253-2142
Robert J Davis, *Pr*
Lisa Davis, *
Ronald Connelly, *
Lisa D Houseman, *
Mary W Davis, *
EMP: 65 **EST:** 1991
SQ FT: 52,000
SALES (est): 2.15MM **Privately Held**
Web: www.daytonmanufacturing.com
SIC: 3444 Metal housings, enclosures,
casings, and other containers

(G-5746)
DESIGN PATTERN WORKS INC
2312 E 3rd St (45403-2015)
PHONE.....................937 252-0797
George Weckler, *Pr*
James Weckler, *VP*
EMP: 8 **EST:** 1977
SALES (est): 484.7K **Privately Held**
SIC: 3543 Industrial patterns

(G-5747)
DGL WOODWORKING INC
5931 Wolf Creek Pike (45426-2439)
PHONE.....................937 837-7091
FAX: 937 854-7568
EMP: 10
SQ FT: 10,000
SALES (est): 820K **Privately Held**
Web: www.dglwoodworking.com
SIC: 2522 2434 1751 Cabinets, office:
except wood; Wood kitchen cabinets;
Cabinet and finish carpentry

(G-5748)
DIK JAXON PRODUCTS CO INC
Also Called: Jaxon's
6195 Webster St (45414-3447)
PHONE.....................937 890-7350
Barry Jackson, *Pr*
EMP: 10 **EST:** 1896
SQ FT: 5,400
SALES (est): 389.7K **Privately Held**
Web: www.jaxonmush.com
SIC: 2041 Flour and other grain mill products

(G-5749)
DIMCO GRAY
8200 S Suburban Dr (45458-2709)
PHONE.....................937 291-4720
Terry Tate, *Contrlr*
EMP: 9 **EST:** 2018
SALES (est): 2.45MM **Privately Held**
SIC: 3089 Injection molding of plastics

(G-5750)
DOUBLE D D MTLS INSTLLTION INC
Also Called: Double D D Mtls Instllation In
7733 N Main St (45415-2551)
PHONE.....................937 898-2534
George Dahling, *Pr*
EMP: 8 **EST:** 1996
SQ FT: 2,000
SALES (est): 276.79K **Privately Held**
SIC: 5211 5031 1799 3699 Fencing;
Fencing, wood; Fence construction; Door
opening and closing devices, electrical

(G-5751)
**DRAGOON TECHNOLOGIES INC
(PA)**
Also Called: Dragoonitcn
900 Senate Dr (45459-4017)
PHONE.....................937 439-9223
Kathy Appenzeller, *CEO*
EMP: 6 **EST:** 1993
SQ FT: 51,000
SALES (est): 931.44K
SALES (corp-wide): 931.44K **Privately
Held**
Web: www.dragoonitcn.com
SIC: 3812 Radar systems and equipment

(G-5752)
DRONE EXPRESS INC (PA)
123 Webster St (45402-1391)
PHONE.....................513 577-5152
EMP: 18 **EST:** 2022
SALES (est): 4.82MM
SALES (corp-wide): 4.82MM **Privately
Held**

Web: www.droneexpress.com
SIC: 3728 Target drones

(G-5753)
DRT HOLDINGS LLC (PA)
618 Greenmount Blvd (45419-3271)
PHONE.....................937 298-7391
Robert S Cohen, *CEO*
Greg Martin, *
Joseph Zehenny, *
EMP: 60 **EST:** 2008
SALES (est): 177.41MM **Privately Held**
Web: www.drtholdingsllc.com
SIC: 6719 3599 3728 Investment holding
companies, except banks; Machine shop,
jobbing and repair; Aircraft parts and
equipment, nec

(G-5754)
DRT MFG CO LLC (HQ)
Also Called: Drt
4201 Little York Rd (45414-2507)
PHONE.....................937 297-6670
Gregory S Martin, *VP Opers*
Stephen Barnes, *
◆ **EMP:** 63 **EST:** 1949
SALES (est): 26.38MM **Privately Held**
Web: mp.drtholdingsllc.com
SIC: 3544 3545 Special dies and tools;
Machine tool accessories
PA: Drt Holdings, Llc
618 Greenmount Blvd
Dayton OH 45419

(G-5755)
DRT MFG CO LLC
618 Greenmount Blvd (45419-3271)
PHONE.....................937 298-7391
EMP: 150 **EST:** 2019
SALES (est): 1.52MM **Privately Held**
Web: www.drtholdingsllc.com
SIC: 3599 Machine shop, jobbing and repair

(G-5756)
**DUPONT ELECTRONIC POLYMERS
LP**
1515 Nicholas Rd (45417-6712)
PHONE.....................937 268-3411
Ellen Kullman, *Ch Bd*
Craig F Binetti, *Pr*
David G Bills, *Sr VP*
James C Borel, *Ex VP*
Benito Cachinero-snchez, *Sr VP*
EMP: 65 **EST:** 2001
SALES (est): 21.49MM
SALES (corp-wide): 16.91B **Publicly Held**
Web: www.dupont.com
SIC: 2819 Industrial inorganic chemicals, nec
HQ: Eidp, Inc.
9330 Zionsville Rd
Indianapolis IN 46268
833 267-8382

(G-5757)
DYSINGER INCORPORATED (PA)
4316 Webster St (45414-4936)
PHONE.....................937 297-7761
EMP: 44 **EST:** 1973
SALES (est): 1.3MM
SALES (corp-wide): 1.3MM **Privately Held**
Web: www.dysinger.com
SIC: 3545 3544 3496 Cutting tools for
machine tools; Special dies, tools, jigs, and
fixtures; Miscellaneous fabricated wire
products

(G-5758)
EASTMAN KODAK COMPANY
Also Called: Kodak
3000 Research Blvd (45420-4003)
PHONE.....................937 259-3000

Patty A Cord, *Brnch Mgr*
EMP: 20
SALES (corp-wide): 1.04B **Publicly Held**
Web: www.kodak.com
SIC: 3355 3577 5043 Aluminum rolling and
drawing, nec; Computer peripheral
equipment, nec; Projection apparatus,
motion picture and slide
PA: Eastman Kodak Company
343 State St
Rochester NY 14650
800 356-3259

(G-5759)
ECO-GROUPE INC (PA)
6161 Ventnor Ave (45414-2651)
PHONE.....................937 898-2603
William Gaiser, *CEO*
Karin Gaiser, *Pr*
Kelly Ferguson, *VP*
EMP: 16 **EST:** 2011
SALES (est): 3.47MM
SALES (corp-wide): 3.47MM **Privately
Held**
SIC: 3085 Plastics bottles

(G-5760)
EDFA LLC
Also Called: Martin-Palmer Tool
90 Vermont Ave (45404-1521)
PHONE.....................937 222-1415
Flem Messer, *Prin*
April Messer, *Prin*
EMP: 7 **EST:** 2019
SALES (est): 2.17MM **Privately Held**
Web: www.martinpalmertool.com
SIC: 3544 Special dies and tools

(G-5761)
ELECTRO POLISH COMPANY
332 Vermont Ave (45404-1597)
PHONE.....................937 222-3611
Kent Kumbroch, *Pr*
Stuart Price, *
EMP: 24 **EST:** 1949
SQ FT: 8,000
SALES (est): 2.47MM **Privately Held**
Web: www.electro-polish.com
SIC: 3471 Electroplating of metals or formed
products

(G-5762)
ELECTRO-LINE INC
118 S Terry St (45403-2312)
P.O. Box 1688 (45401-1688)
PHONE.....................937 461-5683
Bruce Jump, *Pr*
Bruce Jump, *Pr*
Jeffrey J Bucher, *VP*
Jeff Bucher, *VP*
EMP: 15 **EST:** 1958
SQ FT: 15,000
SALES (est): 2.49MM **Privately Held**
Web: www.rpaelect.com
SIC: 3679 5065 Electronic circuits;
Electronic parts and equipment, nec

(G-5763)
**ELLIOTT TOOL TECHNOLOGIES LTD
(PA)**
Also Called: Elliott
1760 Tuttle Ave (45403-3428)
PHONE.....................937 253-6133
EMP: 66 **EST:** 1892
SQ FT: 37,000
SALES (est): 11.87MM **Privately Held**
Web: www.elliott-tool.com
SIC: 7359 3542 5072 3541 Equipment rental
and leasing, nec; Machine tools, metal
forming type; Hand tools; Machine tools,
metal cutting type

▲ = Import ▼ = Export
◆ = Import/Export

(G-5764)
EMERSON HELIX
40 W Stewart St (45409-2667)
PHONE...................................937 710-5771
EMP: 17 **EST:** 2018
SALES (est): 1.4MM **Privately Held**
Web: www.emerson.com
SIC: 3823 Process control instruments

(G-5765)
ENCON INC
Also Called: Encon
6161 Ventnor Ave (45414-2651)
P.O. Box 13418 (45413-0418)
PHONE...................................937 898-2603
◆ **EMP:** 140
Web: www.anyon.info
SIC: 3085 3089 Plastics bottles; Plastics
containers, except foam

(G-5766)
EPIX TUBE CO INC (PA)
5800 Wolf Creek Pike (45426-2438)
PHONE...................................937 529-4858
Paul Kasperski, *Pr*
Angela Salazar, *CFO*
EMP: 10 **EST:** 2009
SALES (est): 9.72MM
SALES (corp-wide): 9.72MM **Privately
Held**
Web: www.epixtube.com
SIC: 2599 5531 Factory furniture and fixtures
; Automotive accessories

(G-5767)
**ERNST METAL TECHNOLOGIES LLC
(DH)**
2920 Kreitzer Rd (45439-1644)
PHONE...................................937 434-3133
James Burt, *Managing Member*
▲ **EMP:** 44 **EST:** 2005
SALES (est): 22.13MM
SALES (corp-wide): 130.82MM **Privately
Held**
Web: www.ernst.de
SIC: 3469 3312 Stamping metal for the trade
; Tool and die steel and alloys
HQ: Ernst Umformtechnik Gmbh
Am Wiesenbach 1
Oberkirch BW 77704
78054060

(G-5768)
ESTEE 2 INC
612 Linden Ave (45403-2513)
PHONE...................................937 224-7853
Dan Rinehart, *Pr*
Werner Triftshouser, *Stockholder*
Gerhard Triftshouser, *Stockholder*
EMP: 9 **EST:** 1945
SQ FT: 28,000
SALES (est): 2.46MM **Privately Held**
Web: www.esteemold.com
SIC: 3544 Special dies and tools

(G-5769)
**ESTHER PRICE CANDIES
CORPORATION (PA)**
Also Called: Esther Price Candies & Gifts
1709 Wayne Ave (45410-1711)
PHONE...................................937 253-2121
EMP: 25 **EST:** 1926
SALES (est): 8.17MM
SALES (corp-wide): 8.17MM **Privately
Held**
Web: www.estherprice.com
SIC: 2064 5441 5145 Candy and other
confectionery products; Candy, nut, and
confectionery stores; Confectionery

(G-5770)
EUGENE STEWART
Also Called: Spectrum Printing & Design
5671 Webster St (45414-3518)
PHONE...................................937 898-1117
Eugene Stewart, *Owner*
EMP: 8 **EST:** 1991
SQ FT: 6,000
SALES (est): 279.33K **Privately Held**
SIC: 2791 7336 2789 2752 Typesetting; Art
design services; Bookbinding and related
work; Commercial printing, lithographic

(G-5771)
EVANS BAKERY INC
700 Troy St (45404-1851)
P.O. Box 64 (45404-0064)
PHONE...................................937 228-4151
Edward William Evans, *Pr*
Rose Mary Evans, *VP*
EMP: 8 **EST:** 1952
SQ FT: 1,600
SALES (est): 211.29K **Privately Held**
Web: www.evansbakery.com
SIC: 2051 5461 Bakery: wholesale or
wholesale/retail combined; Doughnuts

(G-5772)
EVER SECURE SEC SYSTEMS INC
Also Called: Ess
5523 Salem Ave Ste 134 (45426-1451)
PHONE...................................937 369-8294
Victor Nwufoh, *Pr*
Victor Nwufoh, *Pr*
Robert Todd, *Ex VP*
EMP: 16 **EST:** 1998
SQ FT: 1,500
SALES (est): 209.11K **Privately Held**
SIC: 8711 3699 Civil engineering; Security
devices

(G-5773)
FALCON TOOL & MACHINE INC
2795 Lance Dr (45409-1519)
PHONE...................................937 534-9999
Don Voehringer, *Pr*
John Noble, *Treas*
Mark Metter, *Sec*
EMP: 7 **EST:** 1994
SQ FT: 7,000
SALES (est): 801.52K **Privately Held**
Web: www.falcon-tool.com
SIC: 3541 3599 Machine tools, metal cutting
type; Machine shop, jobbing and repair

(G-5774)
FC INDUSTRIES INC (PA)
4900 Webster St (45414-4831)
PHONE...................................937 275-8700
EMP: 46 **EST:** 1988
SALES (est): 43.81MM
SALES (corp-wide): 43.81MM **Privately
Held**
Web: www.fcindinc.com
SIC: 3544 3469 3449 Special dies and tools;
Metal stampings, nec; Miscellaneous
metalwork

(G-5775)
**FERNANDES ENTERPRISES LLC
(PA)**
Also Called: Fourjay Industries
2801 Ontario Ave (45414-5136)
PHONE...................................937 890-6444
Vernon Fernandes, *Pr*
▲ **EMP:** 18 **EST:** 1956
SQ FT: 9,600
SALES (est): 4.35MM
SALES (corp-wide): 4.35MM **Privately
Held**
Web: www.fourjay.com

SIC: 3699 Electric sound equipment

(G-5776)
FIDELITY ORTHOPEDIC INC
8514 N Main St (45415-1325)
PHONE...................................937 228-0682
TOLL FREE: 800
Hillmo Hodzic, *Pr*
Adam Murka, *Dir*
Mark Murka, *Dir*
EMP: 6 **EST:** 1929
SQ FT: 4,000
SALES (est): 1.31MM **Privately Held**
Web: www.fidelityorthopedic.com
SIC: 3842 Limbs, artificial

(G-5777)
FIRST TOOL CORP (PA)
612 Linden Ave (45403-2589)
PHONE...................................937 254-6197
Robert J Davis, *Pr*
Lisa Davis, *
Ron Connelly, *
Pauline Miller, *
Seymour D Ramby, *
EMP: 40 **EST:** 1966
SQ FT: 60,000
SALES (est): 9.65MM
SALES (corp-wide): 9.65MM **Privately
Held**
Web: www.firsttoolcorp.com
SIC: 3542 3544 Machine tools, metal
forming type; Jigs and fixtures

(G-5778)
FISCHER ENGINEERING CO LLC
8220 Expansion Way (45424-6382)
PHONE...................................937 754-1750
Ben Finney, *Prin*
EMP: 7 **EST:** 1976
SQ FT: 14,400
SALES (est): 3.71MM **Privately Held**
Web: www.fischerengr.com
SIC: 3829 5999 8734 Tensile strength
testing equipment; Welding supplies;
Testing laboratories

(G-5779)
FLEET GRAPHICS INC
1701 Thomas Paine Pkwy (45459-2540)
PHONE...................................937 252-2552
Scott Waggoner, *Pr*
Val R Waggoner, *VP*
Richard Brice, *Sec*
EMP: 9 **EST:** 1954
SQ FT: 6,000
SALES (est): 2.18MM **Privately Held**
Web: www.fltgfx.com
SIC: 3571 2752 Computers, digital, analog
or hybrid; Commercial printing, lithographic

(G-5780)
FLOWSERVE CORPORATION
Flowserve
2200 E Monument Ave (45402-1362)
PHONE...................................937 226-4000
John Carano, *Brnch Mgr*
EMP: 51
SALES (corp-wide): 4.56B **Publicly Held**
Web: www.flowserve.com
SIC: 3561 Industrial pumps and parts
PA: Flowserve Corporation
5215 N Ocnnor Blvd Ste 70
Irving TX 75039
972 443-6500

(G-5781)
FMH ENTERPRISES LLC ✪
Also Called: Westendorf Printing
4220 Interpoint Blvd (45424-8717)
PHONE...................................937 478-2739

Frank Hiti, *Managing Member*
EMP: 15 **EST:** 2023
SALES (est): 1.56MM **Privately Held**
SIC: 2752 Commercial printing, lithographic

(G-5782)
FORGELINE MOTORSPORTS LLC
Also Called: Forgeline Motorsports
3522 Kettering Blvd (45439-2000)
PHONE...................................800 886-0093
David Schardt, *Managing Member*
EMP: 25 **EST:** 1994
SQ FT: 5,600
SALES (est): 5.2MM **Privately Held**
Web: www.forgeline.com
SIC: 3714 Wheels, motor vehicle

(G-5783)
FOUR AMBITION LLC
2821 Kenmore Ave (45420-2231)
PHONE...................................937 239-4479
Shannon Thomas, *Prin*
EMP: 6 **EST:** 2007
SALES (est): 258.58K **Privately Held**
Web: www.fourambition.com
SIC: 2759 Screen printing

(G-5784)
FRANKLIN IRON & METAL CORP
1939 E 1st St (45403-1131)
PHONE...................................937 253-8184
Jack Edelman, *Pr*
Debra Edelman, *
▲ **EMP:** 105 **EST:** 1961
SQ FT: 60,000
SALES (est): 7.32MM **Privately Held**
Web: www.franklin-iron.com
SIC: 5093 3341 3312 Ferrous metal scrap
and waste; Secondary nonferrous metals;
Blast furnaces and steel mills

(G-5785)
FRIENDS SERVICE CO INC
4604 Salem Ave (45416-1712)
PHONE...................................800 427-1704
Kenneth J Schroeder, *Brnch Mgr*
EMP: 15
Web: www.friendsoffice.com
SIC: 5112 5021 5087 2752 Stationery and
office supplies; Furniture; Service
establishment equipment; Commercial
printing, lithographic
PA: Friends Service Co., Inc.
2300 Bright Rd
Findlay OH 45840

(G-5786)
FRIES MACHINE & TOOL INC
5729 Webster St (45414-3520)
PHONE...................................937 898-6432
Arland Fries, *CEO*
Tony E Fries, *Pr*
Lisa A Fries, *Sec*
EMP: 7 **EST:** 1999
SQ FT: 4,000
SALES (est): 900.68K **Privately Held**
Web: www.friesmachineandtool.com
SIC: 3599 Machine shop, jobbing and repair

(G-5787)
FUKUVI USA INC
7631 Progress Ct (45424-6378)
PHONE...................................937 236-7288
S Yagi, *Pr*
K Takagi, *Marketing*
▲ **EMP:** 65 **EST:** 1996
SQ FT: 84,000
SALES (est): 21.67MM **Privately Held**
Web: www.fukuvi-usa.com
SIC: 3089 Injection molding of plastics
PA: Fukuvi Chemical Industry Co.,Ltd.

33-66, Sanjuhasshacho
Fukui FKI 918-8

(G-5788)
FURNITURE BY OTMAR INC (PA)
301 Miamisburg Centerville Rd
(45459-4705)
PHONE.....................937 435-2039
Josef Otmar Iv, *Pr*
Alberto Otmar, *VP*
▲ EMP: 12 EST: 1960
SQ FT: 10,000
SALES (est): 986.26K
SALES (corp-wide): 986.26K **Privately Held**
Web: www.furniturebyotmar.com
SIC: 2511 5712 Wood household furniture;
Furniture stores

(G-5789)
GALAPAGOS INC (PA)
3345 Old Salem Rd (45415-1232)
PHONE.....................937 890-3068
Onno Van De Stolpe, *CEO*
EMP: 19 EST: 2003
SALES (est): 2.5MM **Privately Held**
Web: www.glpg.com
SIC: 2833 2899 Medicinals and botanicals;
Chemical preparations, nec

(G-5790)
GDC INDUSTRIES LLC
170 Gracewood Dr (45458-2505)
PHONE.....................937 367-7229
Louis Luedtke, *CEO*
EMP: 6 EST: 2015
SALES (est): 496.44K **Privately Held**
SIC: 3339 Tin-base alloys (primary)

(G-5791)
GE AVIATION SYSTEMS LLC
Also Called: Tech Development
6800 Poe Ave (45414-2530)
PHONE.....................937 898-9600
EMP: 82
SALES (corp-wide): 38.7B **Publicly Held**
Web: www.geaerospace.com
SIC: 3812 Aircraft control systems, electronic
HQ: Ge Aviation Systems Llc
1 Neumann Way
Cincinnati OH 45215
937 898-9600

(G-5792)
GEM CITY ENGINEERING CO (DH)
Also Called: Libra Industries
401 Leo St (45404-1009)
PHONE.....................937 223-5544
Jim Kircher, *CEO*
Luis Montiel, *
EMP: 120 EST: 1936
SQ FT: 250,000
SALES (est): 23.33MM
SALES (corp-wide): 144.38MM **Privately Held**
Web: www.libraindustries.com
SIC: 3679 3544 3569 3549 Antennas,
receiving; Special dies and tools; Assembly
machines, non-metalworking; Metalworking
machinery, nec
HQ: Libra Industries, Llc
7770 Division Dr
Mentor OH 44060
440 974-7770

(G-5793)
GEM CITY METAL TECH LLC
Also Called: Gem City
1825 E 1st St (45403-1129)
PHONE.....................937 252-8998
Dennis Nystrom, *Managing Member*

Don Nystron, *Managing Member**
Norb Overla, *
Dennis Mc Wright, *
EMP: 49 EST: 1990
SQ FT: 53,000
SALES (est): 7.53MM **Privately Held**
Web: www.gcmetalspinning.com
SIC: 3356 3446 3444 3469 Nonferrous
rolling and drawing, nec; Architectural
metalwork; Sheet metalwork; Spinning
metal for the trade

(G-5794)
GENERAL DYNMICS MSSION SYSTEMS
Also Called: Electronics & Communications
1900 Founders Dr Ste 106 (45420-4030)
PHONE.....................937 723-2001
Jay Ebersohl, *Brnch Mgr*
EMP: 6
SALES (corp-wide): 47.72B **Publicly Held**
Web: www.gdmissionsystems.com
SIC: 3571 Electronic computers
HQ: General Dynamics Mission Systems,
Inc.
12450 Fair Lakes Cir
Fairfax VA 22033
877 449-0600

(G-5795)
GINKO VOTING SYSTEMS LLC
Also Called: Ginko Systems
600 Progress Rd (45449-2300)
PHONE.....................937 291-4060
Franklin Dunkin, *CEO*
Lawrence Whitehead, *VP*
EMP: 21 EST: 2004
SQ FT: 12,000
SALES (est): 6.14MM **Privately Held**
Web: www.ginkosystemsllc.com
SIC: 3578 3695 Automatic teller machines
(ATM); Computer software tape and disks:
blank, rigid, and floppy

(G-5796)
GLEASON METROLOGY SYSTEMS CORP (HQ)
Also Called: Gleason M & M Precision
300 Progress Rd (45449-2322)
PHONE.....................937 384-8901
Terry Turner, *Ex VP*
Douglas Beerck, *
◆ EMP: 49 EST: 1951
SQ FT: 68,000
SALES (est): 8.71MM
SALES (corp-wide): 469.63MM **Privately Held**
Web: www.gleason.com
SIC: 3829 3823 3769 3621 Measuring and
controlling devices, nec; Process control
instruments; Space vehicle equipment, nec;
Motors and generators
PA: Gleason Corporation
1000 University Ave
Rochester NY 14607
585 473-1000

(G-5797)
GLEN D LALA
Also Called: Innovative Creations
2610 Willowburn Ave (45417-9434)
P.O. Box 328 (45066-0328)
PHONE.....................937 274-7770
Glen D Lala, *Owner*
EMP: 6 EST: 1986
SQ FT: 12,000
SALES (est): 109.58K **Privately Held**
SIC: 2759 7699 Screen printing; Printing
trades machinery and equipment repair

(G-5798)
GLOBE MOTORS INC (HQ)
Also Called: Globe Motors
2275 Stanley Ave (45404-1226)
PHONE.....................334 983-3542
Steven Mchenry, *CEO*
William Gillespie, *CFO*
▲ EMP: 150 EST: 1945
SALES (est): 25.6MM
SALES (corp-wide): 529.97MM **Publicly Held**
Web: www.alliedmotion.com
SIC: 3621 Motors, electric
PA: Allient Inc.
495 Commerce Dr Ste 3
Amherst NY 14228
716 242-8634

(G-5799)
GLOBE PRODUCTS INC (PA)
5051 Kitridge Rd (45424-4433)
P.O. Box 77 (45404-0077)
PHONE.....................937 233-0233
Scott Kroencke, *Pr*
James E Kroencke, *CEO*
W Patrick Winton, *Stockholder*
▲ EMP: 19 EST: 1919
SQ FT: 100,000
SALES (est): 2.36MM
SALES (corp-wide): 2.36MM **Privately Held**
Web: www.globe-usa.com
SIC: 3599 Machine shop, jobbing and repair

(G-5800)
GLT INC (PA)
Also Called: Johnson Contrls Authorized Dlr
3341 Successful Way (45414-4317)
PHONE.....................937 237-0055
Kevin Knight, *Pr*
Chris Knight, *VP*
◆ EMP: 12 EST: 1987
SQ FT: 75,000
SALES (est): 5.6MM
SALES (corp-wide): 5.6MM **Privately Held**
Web: www.gltonline.com
SIC: 3541 5075 Machine tools, metal cutting
type; Warm air heating and air conditioning

(G-5801)
GMD INDUSTRIES LLC
Also Called: Production Screw Machine
1414 E 2nd St (45403-1023)
PHONE.....................937 252-3643
Michael Mcquinn, *Ex Dir*
David Musgrave, *
▼ EMP: 25 EST: 2000
SQ FT: 35,000
SALES (est): 9.77MM **Privately Held**
Web: www.psmco.com
SIC: 3599 Machine shop, jobbing and repair

(G-5802)
GRB HOLDINGS INC
131 Janney Rd (45404-1225)
P.O. Box 173 (45404-0173)
PHONE.....................937 236-3250
David Gitridge, *Pr*
David Gutridge, *
EMP: 8 EST: 1913
SQ FT: 50,000
SALES (est): 300.21K **Privately Held**
SIC: 3295 3471 Minerals, ground or treated;
Plating and polishing

(G-5803)
GREEN LEAF PRINTING AND DESIGN
1001 E 2nd St Ste 2485 (45402-1498)
PHONE.....................937 222-3634
Larry Blevins, *Prin*

EMP: 6 EST: 2009
SALES (est): 1.02MM **Privately Held**
Web: www.greenleafprinting.com
SIC: 2759 Screen printing

(G-5804)
GREEN TOKAI CO LTD
3700 Inpark Dr (45414-4418)
PHONE.....................937 237-1630
Charlie Sapp, *Brnch Mgr*
EMP: 144
Web: www.greentokai.com
SIC: 3714 Motor vehicle parts and
accessories
HQ: Green Tokai Co., Ltd.
55 Robert Wright Dr
Brookville OH 45309
937 833-5444

(G-5805)
GREGORY STONE CO INC
1860 N Gettysburg Ave (45417-9585)
PHONE.....................937 275-7455
Thomas L Call, *Pr*
Jackie K Call, *VP*
EMP: 9 EST: 1936
SQ FT: 7,000
SALES (est): 303.17K **Privately Held**
Web: www.gregorystonecompany.com
SIC: 5211 1411 Masonry materials and
supplies; Limestone, dimension-quarrying

(G-5806)
H GERSTNER & SONS INC
Also Called: Gerstner International
20 Gerstner Way (45402-8408)
PHONE.....................937 228-1662
John Campbell, *Pr*
Nancy Campbell, *Sec*
▲ EMP: 20 EST: 1906
SQ FT: 30,000
SALES (est): 2.5MM **Privately Held**
Web: www.gerstnerusa.com
SIC: 2441 Tool chests, wood

(G-5807)
HAM SIGNS LLC DBA FASTSIGNS
6020 N Dixie Dr (45414-4018)
PHONE.....................937 890-6770
EMP: 12 EST: 1995
SALES (est): 513.78K **Privately Held**
SIC: 3993 7532 Signs and advertising
specialties; Truck painting and lettering

(G-5808)
HEC INVESTMENTS INC
4800 Wadsworth Rd (45414-4224)
PHONE.....................937 278-9123
▲ EMP: 144 EST: 1975
SALES (est): 2.81MM **Privately Held**
Web: www.superiorabrasives.com
SIC: 3291 Abrasive products

(G-5809)
HESS ADVANCED SOLUTIONS LLC
7415 Chambersburg Rd (45424-3921)
P.O. Box 17669 (45417-0669)
PHONE.....................937 829-4794
Frederick Edmonds, *CEO*
EMP: 8 EST: 2016
SQ FT: 15,000
SALES (est): 1.11MM **Privately Held**
SIC: 3699 1731 8711 1711 Electrical
equipment and supplies, nec; Electrical
work; Heating and ventilation engineering;
Heating and air conditioning contractors

(G-5810)
HINKLE FINE FOODS INC
4800 Wadsworth Rd (45414-4224)

▲ = Import ▼ = Export
◆ = Import/Export

PHONE...............................937 836-3665
Benny S Hinkle, *Pr*
Marlene M Hinkle, *Sec*
Craig Frost, *Pt*
Micheal Beller, *Pt*
EMP: 10 **EST:** 1975
SQ FT: 8,200
SALES (est): 3.71MM **Privately Held**
Web: www.hinklefinefoods.com
SIC: 2035 Seasonings and sauces, except tomato and dry

(G-5811)
HOCKER TOOL AND DIE INC
5161 Webster St (45414-4227)
PHONE...............................937 274-3443
Ronald S Hocker, *Pr*
William K Hocker, *VP*
EMP: 26 **EST:** 1972
SQ FT: 12,000
SALES (est): 9.08MM **Privately Held**
Web: www.hockertoolanddie.com
SIC: 3544 Special dies and tools

(G-5812)
HOME CITY ICE COMPANY
1020 Gateway Dr (45404-2281)
PHONE...............................937 461-6028
Joel Heck, *Mgr*
EMP: 7
SALES (corp-wide): 100.42MM **Privately Held**
Web: www.homecityice.com
SIC: 2097 5999 Manufactured ice; Ice
PA: The Home City Ice Company
6045 Bridgetown Rd Ste 1
Cincinnati OH 45248
513 574-1800

(G-5813)
HOUSE OF 10000 PICTURE FRAMES
2210 Wilmington Pike (45420-1433)
PHONE...............................937 254-5541
William Heath, *Owner*
EMP: 9 **EST:** 1971
SQ FT: 4,000
SALES (est): 155.78K **Privately Held**
Web:
www.houseof10kpictureframes.com
SIC: 5999 5719 2499 Picture frames, ready made; Pictures, wall; Picture frame molding, finished

(G 5814)
HOWMEDICA OSTEONICS CORP
474 Windsor Park Dr (45459-4111)
PHONE...............................937 291-3900
Patrick Barnes, *Brnch Mgr*
EMP: 59
SALES (corp-wide): 22.59B **Publicly Held**
Web: www.patientwebsitecontent.com
SIC: 3841 Surgical and medical instruments
HQ: Howmedica Osteonics Corp.
325 Corporate Dr
Mahwah NJ 07430
201 831-5000

(G-5815)
HR MACHINE LLC
1300 Stanley Ave (45404-1016)
P.O. Box 213 (45301-0213)
PHONE...............................937 222-7644
Jennifer Hudson, *Mgr*
Larry Hudson, *VP*
EMP: 8 **EST:** 2010
SALES (est): 1.89MM **Privately Held**
Web: www.hrmachine.net
SIC: 3441 3914 Fabricated structural metal; Trophies, stainless steel

(G-5816)
HTEC SYSTEMS INC
561 Congress Park Dr (45459-4036)
PHONE...............................937 438-3010
Phillip Hayden, *Ch*
Peter A Flaherty, *Pr*
Christopher Hayden, *Sec*
▼ **EMP:** 10 **EST:** 2005
SQ FT: 4,000
SALES (est): 173.69K **Privately Held**
Web: www.htecsystems.com
SIC: 8711 7389 1629 3599 Consulting engineer; Design services; Industrial plant construction; Custom machinery

(G-5817)
HYLAND MACHINE COMPANY
Also Called: Hyland Screw Machine Products
1900 Kuntz Rd (45404-1251)
P.O. Box 133 (45404-0133)
PHONE...............................937 233-8600
Forest Hyland, *Pr*
Dan Hyland, *
▲ **EMP:** 27 **EST:** 1928
SQ FT: 42,000
SALES (est): 4.56MM **Privately Held**
Web: www.hylandmach.com
SIC: 3451 Screw machine products

(G-5818)
IDX DAYTON LLC
Also Called: Universal Forest Products
2875 Needmore Rd (45414-4301)
PHONE...............................937 401-3460
Isaac Bokros, *Asst Mgr*
▲ **EMP:** 123 **EST:** 2012
SALES (est): 27.41MM
SALES (corp-wide): 6.65B **Publicly Held**
Web: www.idxcorporation.com
SIC: 2542 2541 Partitions and fixtures, except wood; Store and office display cases and fixtures
PA: Ufp Industries, Inc.
2801 E Beltline Ave Ne
Grand Rapids MI 49525
616 364-6161

(G-5819)
IGNYTE ASSURANCE PLATFORM
714 E Monument Ave (45402-1382)
PHONE...............................833 446-9831
Narinder Aulakh, *Prin*
EMP: 20 **EST:** 2018
SALES (est): 1.21MM **Privately Held**
Web: www.ignyteplatform.com
SIC: 7372 Prepackaged software

(G-5820)
INDEPENDENT AWNING & CANVAS CO
791 Ashton Cir Apt 102 (45429-3497)
PHONE...............................937 223-9661
Fred Utzinger Iii, *Pr*
Shirley Utzinger, *Sec*
EMP: 7 **EST:** 1990
SALES (est): 247.97K **Privately Held**
Web: www.independentawning.com
SIC: 2394 Awnings, fabric: made from purchased materials

(G-5821)
INDOOR ENVMTL SPECIALISTS INC
Also Called: Environmental Doctor
438 Windsor Park Dr (45459-4111)
PHONE...............................937 433-5202
Brenden Gitzinger, *Pr*
Margie Gitzinger, *VP*
EMP: 22 **EST:** 2006
SQ FT: 3,000
SALES (est): 2.01MM **Privately Held**
Web: www.envirodoc.com

SIC: 7349 5999 1799 3564 Air duct cleaning; Air purification equipment; Waterproofing; Air purification equipment

(G-5822)
INNOVATIVE VEND SOLUTIONS LLC
740 Royal Ridge Dr (45449-2334)
PHONE...............................866 931-9413
Patrick Mcdonald, *Prin*
EMP: 10 **EST:** 2008
SALES (est): 2.94MM **Privately Held**
Web:
www.innovativevendingsolutions.com
SIC: 3581 Automatic vending machines

(G-5823)
INSTANTWHIP-DAYTON INC (PA)
Also Called: Tiller Foods
5820 Executive Blvd (45424-1451)
PHONE...............................937 235-5930
Donald Tiller Junior, *Pr*
Donald Tiller Junior, *Pr*
William B Tiller, *VP*
David Yost, *Sec*
▲ **EMP:** 9 **EST:** 1936
SQ FT: 15,000
SALES (est): 658.32K
SALES (corp-wide): 658.32K **Privately Held**
SIC: 2026 2023 5143 Half and half; Cream substitutes; Dairy products, except dried or canned

(G-5824)
INSTANTWHIP-DAYTON INC
Also Called: Tiller Foods
967 Senate Dr (45459-4017)
PHONE...............................937 435-4371
David Yost, *Genl Mgr*
EMP: 6
SALES (corp-wide): 658.32K **Privately Held**
SIC: 2026 2023 Half and half; Cream substitutes
PA: Instantwhip-Dayton, Inc.
5820 Executive Blvd
Dayton OH 45424
937 235-5930

(G-5825)
INTEGRITY MANUFACTURING CORP
3723 Inpark Dr (45414-4417)
P.O. Box 312 (45404)
PHONE...............................937 233-6792
Richard L Halderman, *Pr*
Gretchen Halderman, *VP*
EMP: 10 **EST:** 1977
SQ FT: 11,950
SALES (est): 557.43K **Privately Held**
Web: www.integrity-mfg.com
SIC: 3451 3599 Screw machine products; Machine shop, jobbing and repair

(G-5826)
JAMES C FREE INC (PA)
Also Called: James Free Jewelers
3100 Far Hills Ave (45429-2512)
PHONE...............................937 298-0171
Michael S Karaman, *Pr*
▲ **EMP:** 20 **EST:** 1940
SQ FT: 6,000
SALES (est): 2.02MM
SALES (corp-wide): 2.02MM **Privately Held**
Web: www.jamesfree.com
SIC: 3911 5944 Jewelry, precious metal; Jewelry, precious stones and precious metals

(G-5827)
JASON POFFENBERGER
122 Willowwood Dr (45405-3027)
PHONE...............................937 369-1358
Jason Poffenberger, *Prin*
EMP: 6
SALES (est): 1.44MM **Privately Held**
SIC: 1389 7389 Construction, repair, and dismantling services; Business Activities at Non-Commercial Site

(G-5828)
JEFF BONHAM ELECTRIC INC
3647 Wright Way Rd (45424-5165)
PHONE...............................937 233-7662
Jeff Bonham, *Pr*
Bryan Farlow, *VP*
EMP: 22 **EST:** 1959
SQ FT: 1,500
SALES (est): 5.38MM **Privately Held**
Web: www.jeffbonhamelectric.com
SIC: 1731 3613 General electrical contractor ; Panel and distribution boards and other related apparatus

(G-5829)
JET PRODUCTS INCORPORATED
535 E Dixie Dr (45449-1828)
PHONE...............................937 866-7969
Wayne Busdiecker, *Pr*
Lawrence Larsen, *VP*
▲ **EMP:** 9 **EST:** 1974
SQ FT: 7,500
SALES (est): 739.95K **Privately Held**
Web: www.sajetproducts.com
SIC: 3537 Lift trucks, industrial: fork, platform, straddle, etc.

(G-5830)
JOYCE/DAYTON CORP
P.O. Box 1630 (45401-1630)
PHONE...............................937 294-6261
Michael Harris, *Pr*
EMP: 23
SALES (corp-wide): 4.79B **Publicly Held**
Web: www.joycedayton.com
SIC: 3569 Filters
HQ: Joyce/Dayton Corp.
3300 S Dixie Dr Ste 101
Dayton OH 45439
937 294-6261

(G-5831)
JOYCE/DAYTON CORP (HQ)
3300 S Dixie Dr Ste 101 (45439-2318)
P.O. Box 635789 (45263-5789)
PHONE...............................937 294-6261
Michael Harris, *Pr*
▲ **EMP:** 30 **EST:** 1893
SQ FT: 20,000
SALES (est): 22.14MM
SALES (corp-wide): 4.79B **Publicly Held**
Web: www.joycedayton.com
SIC: 3569 Jacks, hydraulic
PA: Graham Holdings Company
1300 17th St N Ste 1700 F
Arlington VA 22209
703 345-6300

(G-5832)
JTL ENTERPRISES LLC (PA)
5700 Webster St (45414-3521)
P.O. Box 13027 (45413-0027)
PHONE...............................937 890-8189
EMP: 20 **EST:** 2001
SALES (est): 27.92MM
SALES (corp-wide): 27.92MM **Privately Held**
SIC: 5531 7534 Automotive tires; Tire recapping

(G-5833)
JUDO STEEL COMPANY INC
Also Called: Judo Steel
1526 Nicholas Rd (45417-6713)
P.O. Box 751586 (45475-1586)
EMP: 10 **EST:** 1994
SQ FT: 6,000
SALES (est): 543.64K **Privately Held**
SIC: 3441 Building components, structural
steel

(G-5834)
JULIE MAYNARD INC
Also Called: Consolidated Vehicle Converter
4991 Hempstead Station Dr (45429-5159)
PHONE.................................937 443-0408
Julie Maynard, *Pr*
Tim Prugh, *Sec*
▲ **EMP:** 10 **EST:** 1996
SQ FT: 20,000
SALES (est): 4.43MM **Privately Held**
SIC: 3714 3566 Motor vehicle parts and
accessories; Speed changers, drives, and
gears

(G-5835)
JUST BUSINESS INC
Also Called: Onstage Publications
1612 Prosser Ave Ste 100 (45409-2041)
PHONE.................................866 577-3303
Norman L Orlowski, *Pr*
Kyle Orlowski, *VP Sls*
Garett Orlowski, *VP Opers*
EMP: 14 **EST:** 2001
SQ FT: 2,000
SALES (est): 2.25MM **Privately Held**
Web: www.audienceaccess.co
SIC: 8742 2731 7311 Marketing consulting
services; Book publishing; Advertising
consultant

(G-5836)
JUSTICE
2700 Miamisburg Centerville Rd Ste 260
(45459-3752)
PHONE.................................937 435-6928
EMP: 6 **EST:** 2019
SALES (est): 376.5K **Privately Held**
Web: www.justice.gov
SIC: 2361 Girl's and children's dresses,
blouses

(G-5837)
K & B ACQUISITIONS INC
Also Called: Mehaffie Pie Company
3013 Linden Ave (45410-3028)
PHONE.................................937 253-1163
Greg Hay, *Pr*
Jim Columbus, *VP*
Barb Columbus, *Treas*
Bruce Kouse, *VP*
EMP: 10 **EST:** 1930
SQ FT: 9,000
SALES (est): 278.68K **Privately Held**
SIC: 2051 5461 Pies, bakery: except frozen;
Pies

(G-5838)
KELLEY COMMUNICATION DEV
Also Called: Kelley Bible Books
2312 Candlewood Dr (45419-2825)
P.O. Box 292113 (45429-0113)
PHONE.................................937 298-6132
Robert Kelley, *Owner*
EMP: 7 **EST:** 1979
SALES (est): 235.69K **Privately Held**
Web: www.kcdev.com
SIC: 2731 Books, publishing only

(G-5839)
**KOLHFAB CSTM PLSTIC
FBRICATION**
2025 Webster St (45404-1143)
PHONE.................................937 237-2098
Bernie Kohlbarg, *CEO*
EMP: 6 **EST:** 2011
SALES (est): 507.46K **Privately Held**
SIC: 3089 Injection molding of plastics

(G-5840)
L3 TECHNOLOGIES INC
3155 Research Blvd Ste 101 (45420-4015)
PHONE.................................937 223-3285
Walker Larimer, *Brnch Mgr*
EMP: 7
SALES (corp-wide): 21.32B **Publicly Held**
Web: www.l3harris.com
SIC: 3812 Navigational systems and
instruments
HQ: L3 Technologies, Inc.
600 3rd Ave Fl 34
New York NY 10016
321 727-9100

(G-5841)
LAHM-TROSPER INC
Also Called: Lahm Tool
1030 Springfield St (45403-1350)
P.O. Box 336 (45401-0336)
PHONE.................................937 252-8791
James Trosper, *Pr*
EMP: 10 **EST:** 1997
SQ FT: 10,000
SALES (est): 1.01MM **Privately Held**
Web: www.lahmtool.com
SIC: 3541 3544 Machine tools, metal cutting
type; Special dies, tools, jigs, and fixtures

(G-5842)
LAWRENCE TECHNOLOGIES INC
2571 Timber Ln (45414-4731)
PHONE.................................937 274-7771
Lawrence J Richards, *Pr*
Linda Heider, *VP*
▲ **EMP:** 8 **EST:** 1987
SQ FT: 5,000
SALES (est): 996.41K **Privately Held**
Web: www.lawrencetechnologies.com
SIC: 3714 3728 3569 8711 Motor vehicle
parts and accessories; Aircraft parts and
equipment, nec; Filters; Professional
engineer

(G-5843)
LEGRAND NORTH AMERICA LLC
Also Called: C2g
6500 Poe Ave (45414-2527)
PHONE.................................937 224-0639
EMP: 420
Web: www.legrand.us
SIC: 1731 5063 5045 3643 Communications
specialization; Cable conduit; Computer
peripheral equipment; Current-carrying
wiring services
HQ: Legrand North America, Llc
60 Woodlawn St
West Hartford CT 06110
860 233-6251

(G-5844)
LENZ INC
Also Called: Lenz Company
3301 Klepinger Rd (45406-1823)
P.O. Box 1044 (45401-1044)
PHONE.................................937 277-9364
Robert Wagner, *Pr*
▲ **EMP:** 50 **EST:** 1955
SQ FT: 15,000
SALES (est): 4.48MM **Privately Held**
Web: www.lenzinc.com

SIC: 6531 3089 Real estate brokers and
agents; Fittings for pipe, plastics

(G-5845)
LEWARK METAL SPINNING INC
2746 Keenan Ave (45414-4912)
PHONE.................................937 275-3303
Larry W Lewark, *Pr*
Pete Hagenbuch, *
EMP: 50 **EST:** 1993
SQ FT: 35,000
SALES (est): 9.05MM **Privately Held**
Web: www.lewarkmetalspinning.com
SIC: 3499 3469 Friction material, made from
powdered metal; Spinning metal for the
trade

(G-5846)
**LIFE SCIENCES - VANDALIA LLC
(HQ)**
4201 Little York Rd (45414-2507)
PHONE.................................937 387-0880
Simon Newman, *CEO*
EMP: 138 **EST:** 2005
SALES (est): 5.96MM
SALES (corp-wide): 6.94B **Publicly Held**
Web: mp.drtholdingsllc.com
SIC: 3841 Surgical and medical instruments
PA: Ametek, Inc.
1100 Cassatt Rd
Berwyn PA 19312
610 647-2121

(G-5847)
LION APPAREL INC (DH)
7200 Poe Ave Ste 400 (45414-2798)
PHONE.................................937 898-1949
Steve Schwartz, *CEO*
Andrew Schwartz, *Legal**
Theodore Schwartz, *
Mark Berliant, *
Mark Jahnke, *
◆ **EMP:** 150 **EST:** 1930
SQ FT: 37,000
SALES (est): 92.05MM
SALES (corp-wide): 18.69MM **Privately
Held**
Web: www.lionprotects.com
SIC: 2311 Firemen's uniforms: made from
purchased materials
HQ: Lion Group, Inc.
7200 Poe Ave Ste 400
Dayton OH 45414
800 421-2926

(G-5848)
LION APPAREL INC
Bodyguard
6450 Poe Ave Ste 300 (45414-2600)
P.O. Box 13576 (45413-0576)
PHONE.................................937 898-1949
Richard Lapedes, *Pr*
EMP: 100
SALES (corp-wide): 18.69MM **Privately
Held**
Web: www.lionprotects.com
SIC: 2311 Firemen's uniforms: made from
purchased materials
HQ: Lion Apparel, Inc.
7200 Poe Ave Ste 400
Dayton OH 45414
937 898-1949

(G-5849)
LION FIRST RESPONDER PPE INC
7200 Poe Ave Ste 400 (45414-2798)
PHONE.................................937 898-1949
Steve Schwartz, *CEO*
David Cook, *
EMP: 57 **EST:** 2015
SALES (est): 6.66MM

SALES (corp-wide): 18.69MM **Privately
Held**
SIC: 2311 3842 5047 Firemen's uniforms:
made from purchased materials; Clothing,
fire resistant and protective; Medical
equipment and supplies
HQ: Lion Safety Resources Group, Inc.
7200 Poe Ave Ste 400
Dayton OH 45414
937 898-1949

(G-5850)
LION GROUP INC (HQ)
7200 Poe Ave Ste 400 (45414-2798)
PHONE.................................800 421-2926
Steve Schwartz, *CEO*
Andrew Schwartz, *
James Disanto, *
Richard Musick, *
EMP: 90 **EST:** 2014
SQ FT: 3,700
SALES (est): 327.39MM
SALES (corp-wide): 18.69MM **Privately
Held**
Web: www.lionprotects.com
SIC: 6719 2311 5047 Investment holding
companies, except banks; Firemen's
uniforms: made from purchased materials;
Medical equipment and supplies
PA: Lion Protects B.V.
Rheastraat 14
Tilburg NB 5047
135076800

(G-5851)
LITEFLEX DISC LLC
3251 Mccall St (45417-1907)
P.O. Box 69 (45322)
PHONE.................................937 836-7025
John Prikkel Iii, *Pr*
Daniel Chien, *
Ray Blatz, *
▲ **EMP:** 55 **EST:** 2001
SALES (est): 2.32MM **Privately Held**
Web: www.liteflex.com
SIC: 3493 Leaf springs: automobile,
locomotive, etc.

(G-5852)
LITHO-PRINT LTD
848 E Monument Ave (45402-1312)
PHONE.................................937 222-4351
Darrell Templeton, *Pt*
Sandra Templeton, *Pt*
Leanore Obelewicz, *Pt*
Paul Obolwicz, *Pt*
EMP: 16 **EST:** 1951
SQ FT: 15,500
SALES (est): 2.21MM **Privately Held**
Web: www.lithoprintco.com
SIC: 2752 Offset printing

(G-5853)
LOCK 27 BREWING LLC
Also Called: Dayton Brewery & Pub
1024 Quail Run Dr (45458-9619)
PHONE.................................937 433-2739
Steve Barnhart, *Prin*
EMP: 14 **EST:** 2013
SALES (est): 2.43MM **Privately Held**
Web: www.lock27brewing.com
SIC: 5813 2082 Beer garden (drinking
places); Beer (alcoholic beverage)

(G-5854)
LORD CORPORATION
Mechanical Products Division
4644 Wadsworth Rd (45414-4220)
PHONE.................................937 278-9431
Janet Eastep, *Mgr*
EMP: 150

SQ FT: 30,000
SALES (corp-wide): 19.93B **Publicly Held**
Web: www.lord.com
SIC: 3545 3769 Machine tool accessories;
 Space vehicle equipment, nec
HQ: Lord Corporation
 111 Lord Dr
 Cary NC 27511
 919 468-5979

(G-5855)
LORENZ CORPORATION (PA)
Also Called: Show What You Know
501 E 3rd St (45402-2280)
P.O. Box 802 (45401-0802)
PHONE...............................937 228-6118
Reiff Lorenz, *Pr*
Reiff Lorenz, *Ch Bd*
Geoffrey R Lorenz, *
John Schimtz, *
Kris Kropff, *
▲ EMP: 60 EST: 1890
SQ FT: 55,000
SALES (est): 2.3MM
SALES (corp-wide): 2.3MM **Privately Held**
Web: www.lorenz.com
SIC: 2759 5049 2721 2741 Music, sheet:
 printing, nsk; School supplies; Periodicals,
 publishing only; Music, sheet: publishing
 only, not printed on site

(G-5856)
M & J TOOLING LTD
Also Called: M & J Tooling
420 Davis Ave (45403-2912)
PHONE...............................937 951-3527
Matthew Hemmerich, *Pt*
EMP: 10 EST: 2006
SALES (est): 906.36K **Privately Held**
Web: www.mjtoolingllc.com
SIC: 3545 Machine tool accessories

(G-5857)
M & R ELECTRIC MOTOR SVC INC
Also Called: M & R Electric Motor
1516 E 5th St (45403-2397)
PHONE...............................937 701-0475
Ronald Mader, *VP*
Ronald Mader, *VP*
Anthony Mader, *
Craig Mader, *
Le Romer, *Pr*
EMP: 28 EST: 1949
SQ FT: 8,000
SALES (est): 11.02MM **Privately Held**
Web: www.mrelectricsales.com
SIC: 5063 7694 Motors, electric; Electric
 motor repair

(G-5858)
M T M MOLDED PRODUCTS COMPANY
3370 Obco Ct (45414-3513)
P.O. Box 13117 (45413-0117)
PHONE...............................937 890-7461
Steven Minneman, *Pr*
Steve Minneman, *
Allen Minneman, *
◆ EMP: 65 EST: 1966
SQ FT: 92,000
SALES (est): 4.9MM **Privately Held**
Web: www.mtmcase-gard.com
SIC: 3089 Cases, plastics

(G-5859)
M21 INDUSTRIES LLC
Also Called: Module 21 Bldg Company
721 Springfield St (45403-1250)
P.O. Box 4044 (45401-4044)
PHONE...............................937 781-1377
Jeffrey Levine, *Managing Member*

Wolfgang Dalichau, *Managing Member*
David Allen, *VP*
Don Carter, *VP*
Rusty Brown, *VP*
EMP: 7 EST: 1975
SQ FT: 230,000
SALES (est): 971.38K **Privately Held**
Web: www.m21industries.com
SIC: 2541 2431 Office fixtures, wood;
 Windows, wood

(G-5860)
MACHINE PRODUCTS COMPANY
5660 Webster St (45414-3596)
P.O. Box 618 (45068)
PHONE...............................937 890-6600
Robert C Appenzeller, *Pr*
Rebecca A Cain, *
EMP: 16 EST: 1956
SQ FT: 40,000
SALES (est): 2.51MM **Privately Held**
Web: www.mpcdayton.com
SIC: 3599 3825 3694 Machine shop, jobbing
 and repair; Instruments to measure
 electricity; Engine electrical equipment

(G-5861)
MAGNUM TOOL CORP
1407 Stanley Ave (45404-1110)
PHONE...............................937 228-0900
Christopher S Grooms, *Pr*
Gregory S Grooms, *Sec*
◆ EMP: 10 EST: 1972
SQ FT: 6,000
SALES (est): 911.87K **Privately Held**
Web: www.magnumtoolcorp.com
SIC: 3544 Special dies and tools

(G-5862)
MAHLE BEHR DAYTON LLC
1600 Webster St (45404-1144)
PHONE...............................937 369-2000
EMP: 2000
SALES (corp-wide): 504.65K **Privately Held**
SIC: 3443 3585 Heat exchangers,
 condensers, and components; Refrigeration
 and heating equipment
HQ: Mahle Behr Dayton L.L.C.
 1600 Webster St
 Dayton OH 45404
 937 369-2900

(G-5863)
MAHLE BEHR DAYTON LLC (DH)
1600 Webster St (45404-1144)
PHONE...............................937 369-2900
Ing Heinz K Junker, *Ch Bd*
Willm Uhlenbecker, *
Wolf Hennig Scheider, *
Bruce Moorehouse, *
Milan Belans, *
◆ EMP: 93 EST: 2002
SALES (est): 63.22MM
SALES (corp-wide): 3.75MM **Privately Held**
SIC: 3714 Motor vehicle parts and
 accessories
HQ: Mahle Behr Gmbh & Co. Kg
 Mauserstr. 3
 Stuttgart BW
 7115010

(G-5864)
MAHLE BEHR DAYTON LLC
1720 Webster St (45404-1128)
PHONE...............................937 369-2900
Rob Baker, *Brnch Mgr*
EMP: 856
SALES (corp-wide): 3.75MM **Privately Held**

SIC: 3714 Air conditioner parts, motor vehicle
HQ: Mahle Behr Dayton L.L.C.
 1600 Webster St
 Dayton OH 45404
 937 369-2900

(G-5865)
MAHLE INDUSTRIES INCORPORATED
Also Called: Delphi-T - Vandalia Ptc
1600 Webster St (45404-1144)
PHONE...............................937 890-2739
EMP: 30
SALES (corp-wide): 504.65K **Privately Held**
SIC: 3714 Motor vehicle parts and
 accessories
HQ: Mahle Industries, Incorporated
 23030 Mahle Dr
 Farmington Hills MI 48335
 248 305-8200

(G-5866)
MANCOR OHIO INC (HQ)
1008 Leonhard St (45404-1666)
PHONE...............................937 228-6141
Art Church, *Ch Bd*
Dale Harper, *
EMP: 50 EST: 2006
SALES (est): 47.42MM
SALES (corp-wide): 156.64MM **Privately Held**
Web: www.mancor.com
SIC: 3713 Truck bodies and parts
PA: Mancor Canada Inc
 2485 Speers Rd
 Oakville ON L6L 2
 905 827-3737

(G-5867)
MANCOR OHIO INC
600 Kiser St (45404-1644)
PHONE...............................937 228-6141
George Mcnight, *Genl Mgr*
EMP: 170
SALES (corp-wide): 156.64MM **Privately Held**
Web: www.mancor.com
SIC: 3713 Truck bodies and parts
HQ: Mancor Ohio Inc.
 1008 Leonhard St
 Dayton OH 45404

(G-5868)
MAR-VEL TOOL CO
858 Hall Ave (45404-1142)
PHONE...............................937 223-2137
John G Glaser, *Pr*
Brett R Glaser, *VP*
EMP: 10 EST: 1984
SQ FT: 23,000
SALES (est): 743.88K **Privately Held**
Web: www.mar-veltool.com
SIC: 3544 Special dies and tools

(G-5869)
MATRIX RESEARCH INC
3844 Research Blvd (45430-2104)
PHONE...............................937 427-8433
Robert Hawley, *Pr*
Robert W Hawley, *
James Lutz, *
William Pierson, *
EMP: 80 EST: 2005
SQ FT: 4,000
SALES (est): 8.63MM **Privately Held**
Web: www.matrixresearch.com
SIC: 3829 8711 Measuring and controlling
 devices, nec; Engineering services

(G-5870)
MATTHEW BRUN ENTERPRISES INC
Also Called: Champion Equipment
3600 Valley St (45424-5142)
P.O. Box 27 (45404-0027)
PHONE...............................937 604-0057
Matthew Brun, *Pr*
Matthew Brun, *CEO*
EMP: 43 EST: 2008
SALES (est): 9.98MM **Privately Held**
Web: www.gotochampion.com
SIC: 2611 5191 Pulp manufactured from
 waste or recycled paper; Garden supplies

(G-5871)
MCINTOSH SAFE CORP
603 Leo St (45404-1507)
PHONE...............................937 222-7008
John Mcintosh, *Pr*
EMP: 10 EST: 1996
SALES (est): 796.17K **Privately Held**
Web: www.mcintoshsafe.com
SIC: 3499 5044 Safes and vaults, metal;
 Vaults and safes

(G-5872)
MEASUREMENT SPECIALTIES INC
2670 Indian Ripple Rd (45440-3605)
PHONE...............................937 427-1231
Brian Ream, *Brnch Mgr*
EMP: 157
SALES (corp-wide): 400.61MM **Privately Held**
Web: www.te.com
SIC: 3674 3676 Diodes, solid state
 (germanium, silicon, etc.); Thermistors,
 except temperature sensors
PA: Measurement Specialties, Inc.
 1000 Lucas Way
 Hampton VA 23666
 757 766-1500

(G-5873)
MEDICAL DEVICE BUS SVCS INC
2747 Armstrong Ln (45414-4225)
PHONE...............................937 274-5850
David Smith, *Brnch Mgr*
EMP: 28
SALES (corp-wide): 88.82B **Publicly Held**
Web: www.selectmcohio.com
SIC: 3842 Orthopedic appliances
HQ: Medical Device Business Services, Inc.
 700 Orthopaedic Dr
 Warsaw IN 46582

(G-5874)
METALBRITE POLISHING LLC
2445 Neff Rd Unit 4 (45414-5067)
PHONE...............................937 278-9739
Michael Barr, *Owner*
EMP: 11 EST: 1998
SALES (est): 506.94K **Privately Held**
Web: www.metal-britepolishing.com
SIC: 3471 Plating of metals or formed
 products

(G-5875)
METOKOTE CORPORATION
8040 Center Point 70 Blvd (45424-6373)
PHONE...............................937 233-1565
EMP: 8
SALES (corp-wide): 18.25B **Publicly Held**
Web: www.ppgcoatingsservices.com
SIC: 3479 Coating of metals and formed
 products
HQ: Metokote Corporation
 1340 Neubrecht Rd
 Lima OH 45801
 419 996-7800

(G-5876)
MEYERS PRINTING & DESIGN INC
254 Leo St (45404-1006)
PHONE..................................937 461-6000
Gregory Meyers, *Pr*
EMP: 10 **EST:** 1999
SALES (est): 439.15K **Privately Held**
Web: www.mpdink.com
SIC: 2752 Offset printing

(G-5877)
MIAMI CONTROL SYSTEMS INC
4433 Interpoint Blvd (45424-5708)
P.O. Box 96 (45383-0096)
PHONE..................................937 233-8146
Andy Minniear, *Pr*
EMP: 9 **EST:** 1994
SALES (est): 908.68K **Privately Held**
Web: www.miamicontrol.com
SIC: 3625 Electric controls and control
accessories, industrial

(G-5878)
MIAMI VALLEY MEALS INC
428 S Edwin C Moses Blvd (45402-8418)
PHONE..................................937 938-7141
Amanda Delotelle, *Prin*
EMP: 13 **EST:** 2020
SALES (est): 885.87K **Privately Held**
Web: www.miamivalleymeals.org
SIC: 2099 Food preparations, nec

(G-5879)
MIAMI VLY PACKG SOLUTIONS INC
1752 Stanley Ave (45404-1117)
P.O. Box 296 (45404-0296)
PHONE..................................937 224-1800
James Williams, *Pr*
Kenneth Phegley, *VP*
Donald Chmiel, *VP Sls*
▲ **EMP:** 19 **EST:** 2009
SQ FT: 6,000
SALES (est): 7.3MM **Privately Held**
Web: www.mvpsohio.com
SIC: 2653 Boxes, corrugated: made from
purchased materials

(G-5880)
MICHELE CALDWELL
Also Called: MRC & Associates
3421 Olive Rd (45426-2655)
PHONE..................................937 505-7744
F Michele Caldwell, *Owner*
Michele Caldwell, *Owner*
EMP: 6 **EST:** 1993
SALES (est): 225.69K **Privately Held**
SIC: 8742 7389 7372 7291 Management
consulting services; Business oriented
computer software; Tax return preparation
services

(G-5881)
MICROSUN LAMPS LLC
7890 Center Point 70 Blvd (45424-6369)
PHONE..................................888 328-8701
Bob Conner, *CEO*
▲ **EMP:** 8 **EST:** 2014
SALES (est): 476.56K **Privately Held**
Web: www.microsunlamps.com
SIC: 5719 3645 Lighting, lamps, and
accessories; Desk lamps

(G-5882)
MIDWEST SECURITY SERVICES
4050 Benfield Dr (45429-4651)
PHONE..................................937 853-9000
Terry Rogers, *Pr*
Jeremy Filia, *Ex VP*
EMP: 20 **EST:** 2012
SALES (est): 1.98MM **Privately Held**

Web: www.mwsecurityservices.com
SIC: 3699 Security control equipment and
systems

(G-5883)
MIDWEST TOOL & ENGINEERING CO
112 Webster St (45402-1363)
P.O. Box 481 (45409-0481)
EMP: 9 **EST:** 1920
SQ FT: 27,750
SALES (est): 506.55K **Privately Held**
Web: www.themidwesttool.com
SIC: 3544 3594 3545 Special dies and tools;
Fluid power pumps and motors; Machine
tool accessories

(G-5884)
MIKE-SELLS POTATO CHIP CO
Also Called: Mikesells Snack Fd Co Dist Ctr
1610 Stanley Ave (45404-1115)
PHONE..................................937 228-9400
Lucas Mapp, *Prin*
EMP: 92 **EST:** 1947
SALES (est): 2.31MM **Privately Held**
Web: www.mikesells.com
SIC: 2096 Potato chips and similar snacks

(G-5885)
MIKE-SELLS POTATO CHIP CO (HQ)
333 Leo St (45404-1007)
P.O. Box 13749 (45413-0749)
PHONE..................................937 228-9400
D W Mikesell, *
Martha J Mikesell, *
EMP: 30 **EST:** 1910
SQ FT: 95,000
SALES (est): 34.32MM
SALES (corp-wide): 34.32MM **Privately
Held**
Web: www.mikesells.com
SIC: 2096 5145 Potato chips and other
potato-based snacks; Snack foods
PA: Mike-Sell's West Virginia, Inc.
333 Leo St
Dayton OH 45404
937 228-9400

(G-5886)
**MIKE-SELLS WEST VIRGINIA INC
(PA)**
333 Leo St (45404-1080)
P.O. Box 115 (45404-0115)
PHONE..................................937 228-9400
EMP: 75 **EST:** 1910
SALES (est): 34.32MM
SALES (corp-wide): 34.32MM **Privately
Held**
SIC: 2096 5145 Potato chips and other
potato-based snacks; Pretzels

(G-5887)
MILLAT INDUSTRIES CORP
7611 Center Point 70 Blvd (45424-6366)
PHONE..................................937 535-1500
Yogi Singhal, *Prin*
EMP: 13
SALES (corp-wide): 35MM **Privately Held**
Web: www.millatindustries.com
SIC: 3714 Motor vehicle parts and
accessories
PA: Millat Industries, Corp.
4901 Croftshire Dr
Dayton OH 45440
937 434-6666

(G-5888)
MILLAT INDUSTRIES CORP (PA)
4901 Croftshire Dr (45440-1709)
P.O. Box 931188 (44193-1449)
PHONE..................................937 434-6666
Gregory Millat, *Pr*

Robert Millat, *
▲ **EMP:** 100 **EST:** 1969
SQ FT: 99,000
SALES (est): 35MM
SALES (corp-wide): 35MM **Privately Held**
Web: www.millatindustries.com
SIC: 3769 3599 3714 Space vehicle
equipment, nec; Machine shop, jobbing and
repair; Motor vehicle parts and accessories

(G-5889)
MINCO TOOL AND MOLD INC (PA)
Also Called: Minco Group, The
5690 Webster St (45414-3519)
P.O. Box 13545 (45413-0545)
PHONE..................................937 890-7905
EMP: 64 **EST:** 1956
SALES (est): 9.39MM
SALES (corp-wide): 9.39MM **Privately
Held**
Web: www.mincogroup.com
SIC: 3544 Forms (molds), for foundry and
plastics working machinery

(G-5890)
MKGS CORP
1712 Springfield St Ste 2 (45403-1447)
PHONE..................................937 254-8181
Raymond P Horan, *Pr*
EMP: 7 **EST:** 1994
SQ FT: 25,000
SALES (est): 1.47MM **Privately Held**
Web: www.intlam.com
SIC: 3083 Plastics finished products,
laminated

(G-5891)
MODERN MACHINE DEVELOPMENT
400 Linden Ave Ste 3 (45403-2558)
PHONE..................................937 253-4576
Bruce Vicory, *Pr*
David Wolfe, *VP*
Iva Nelson, *Sec*
EMP: 10 **EST:** 1968
SQ FT: 70,000
SALES (est): 486.03K **Privately Held**
SIC: 3599 5084 7692 Custom machinery;
Welding machinery and equipment;
Welding repair

(G-5892)
MONAGHAN & ASSOCIATES INC
Also Called: Monaghan Tooling Group
30 N Clinton St (45402-1327)
P.O. Box 1012 (45401-1012)
PHONE..................................937 253-7706
Scott Monaghan, *Pr*
EMP: 13 **EST:** 1986
SALES (est): 2.4MM **Privately Held**
Web: www.monaghantooling.com
SIC: 3545 5084 3541 Cutting tools for
machine tools; Industrial machinery and
equipment; Machine tools, metal cutting
type

(G-5893)
MORBERN USA
3265 Dryden Rd (45439-1461)
PHONE..................................937 298-2176
Erica Rines, *Brnch Mgr*
EMP: 15
SALES (corp-wide): 94.6MM **Privately
Held**
Web: www.morbern.com
SIC: 2821 5162 Vinyl resins, nec; Plastics
materials and basic shapes
PA: Morbern Inc
80 Boundary Rd
Cornwall ON
613 932-8811

(G-5894)
MORNING PRIDE MFG LLC (HQ)
Also Called: Honeywell First Responder Pdts
1 Innovation Ct (45414-3967)
PHONE..................................937 264-2662
William L Grilliot, *Managing Member*
▲ **EMP:** 521 **EST:** 1998
SQ FT: 56,000
SALES (est): 47.38MM
SALES (corp-wide): 38.5B **Publicly Held**
Web: 91512-us.all.biz
SIC: 3842 2326 Respirators; Men's and
boy's work clothing
PA: Honeywell International Inc.
855 S Mint St
Charlotte NC 28202
704 627-6200

(G-5895)
MORNING PRIDE MFG LLC
4978 Riverton Dr (45414-3964)
PHONE..................................937 264-1726
Patrick Walls, *Supervisor*
EMP: 521
SALES (corp-wide): 38.5B **Publicly Held**
SIC: 3842 Respirators
HQ: Morning Pride Mfg Llc
1 Innovation Ct
Dayton OH 45414
937 264-2662

(G-5896)
**MOUND MANUFACTURING CENTER
INC**
33 Commerce Park Dr (45404-1211)
PHONE..................................937 236-8387
Albert J Hodapp Iii, *Pr*
Steve Priser, *VP*
EMP: 12 **EST:** 1994
SQ FT: 9,000
SALES (est): 2.37MM **Privately Held**
Web: www.moundmanufacturing.com
SIC: 8711 3599 Machine tool design;
Machine shop, jobbing and repair

(G-5897)
MRS ELECTRONIC INC
6680 Poe Ave Ste 100 (45414-2855)
PHONE..................................937 660-6767
Franz Hoffmann, *CEO*
Guenther Doergeloh, *COO*
EMP: 12 **EST:** 2015
SALES (est): 2.51MM **Privately Held**
Web: www.mrs-electronics.com
SIC: 3714 Motor vehicle electrical equipment

(G-5898)
MULLINS RUBBER PRODUCTS INC
2949 Valley Pike (45404-2693)
P.O. Box 24830 (45424-0830)
PHONE..................................937 233-4211
William D Mullins, *Prin*
Dennis Mullins, *
William R Mullins Junior, *VP*
EMP: 52 **EST:** 1939
SQ FT: 75,000
SALES (est): 2.19MM **Privately Held**
Web: www.mullinsrubber.com
SIC: 3069 Molded rubber products

(G-5899)
MVGG INC
Also Called: Focke Rubber Products Div
1222 E 3rd St (45402-2255)
PHONE..................................937 228-0781
TOLL FREE: 800
Robin Cunningham, *Pr*
Jim Focke, *
EMP: 25 **EST:** 1948
SQ FT: 29,000
SALES (est): 702.57K **Privately Held**

Web: www.miamivalleygasket.com
SIC: 3053 Gaskets, all materials

(G-5900)
MW METALS GROUP LLC
461 Homestead Ave (45417-3921)
P.O. Box 546 (45401-0546)
PHONE...............................937 222-5992
Joel Frydman, *CEO*
Farley Frydman, *Pr*
EMP: 65 EST: 1955
SQ FT: 150,000
SALES (est): 4.62MM **Privately Held**
Web: www.mwmetals.com
SIC: 3341 5093 Secondary nonferrous
metals; Scrap and waste materials

(G-5901)
NATIONAL OILWELL VARCO LP
Also Called: Chemineer
5870 Poe Ave (45414-3442)
P.O. Box 1123 (45401)
PHONE...............................937 454-4660
Joel Staff, *Pt*
EMP: 192
SALES (corp-wide): 8.87B **Publicly Held**
Web: www.nov.com
SIC: 3556 3554 Food products machinery;
Paper industries machinery
HQ: National Oilwell Varco, L.P.
10353 Richmond Ave
Houston TX 77042
713 375-3700

(G-5902)
NATIONAL PALLET & MULCH LLC
3550 Intercity Dr (45424-5124)
PHONE...............................937 237-1643
EMP: 10 EST: 2005
SALES (est): 385.58K **Privately Held**
SIC: 2448 Pallets, wood

(G-5903)
NCR TECHNOLOGY CENTER
1560 S Patterson Blvd (45409-2108)
PHONE...............................937 445-1936
EMP: 6 EST: 2014
SALES (est): 827.06K **Privately Held**
Web: www.ncr.com
SIC: 3578 7379 7374 7371 Point-of-sale
devices; Computer related maintenance
services; Data processing and preparation;
Software programming applications

(G-5904)
ND PAPER INC
7777 Washington Village Dr Ste 210
(45459-3995)
PHONE...............................937 528-3822
EMP: 245
Web: us.ndpaper.com
SIC: 2611 Pulp manufactured from waste or
recycled paper
HQ: Nd Paper Inc.
2001 Spring Rd Ste 500
Oak Brook IL 60523
513 200-0908

(G-5905)
NDC TECHNOLOGIES INC
Also Called: Nordson MCS
8001 Technology Blvd (45424-1568)
PHONE...............................937 233-9935
Bromley Beadle, *Pr*
EMP: 115
SALES (corp-wide): 2.69B **Publicly Held**
Web: www.ndc.com
SIC: 3826 Analytical instruments
HQ: Ndc Technologies, Inc.
8001 Technology Blvd
Dayton OH 45424
937 233-9935

(G-5906)
NDC TECHNOLOGIES INC (HQ)
Also Called: NDC Technologies
8001 Technology Blvd (45424-1568)
PHONE...............................937 233-9935
Marti Nyman, *Pr*
▲ EMP: 105 EST: 1987
SQ FT: 45,000
SALES (est): 21.17MM
SALES (corp-wide): 2.69B **Publicly Held**
Web: www.ndc.com
SIC: 3829 Measuring and controlling
devices, nec
PA: Nordson Corporation
28601 Clemens Rd
Westlake OH 44145
440 892-1580

(G-5907)
NIOBIUM MICROSYSTEMS INC
444 E 2nd St (45402-1724)
PHONE...............................937 203-8117
Rob Wiltbank, *CEO*
EMP: 6
SALES (corp-wide): 6.08MM **Privately
Held**
Web: www.niobiummicrosystems.com
SIC: 3674 Semiconductors and related
devices
PA: Niobium Microsystems, Inc.
421 Sw 6th Ave Ste 300
Portland OR 97204
503 626-6616

(G-5908)
NOBLE TOOL CORP
1535 Stanley Ave (45404-1112)
PHONE...............................937 461-4040
Thomas Biegel, *Pr*
Nick Rosenkranz, *
EMP: 31 EST: 1980
SQ FT: 7,500
SALES (est): 4.54MM **Privately Held**
Web: www.nobletool.com
SIC: 3544 Special dies and tools

(G-5909)
NON-FERROUS CASTING COMPANY
736 Albany St (45417-3486)
P.O. Box 364 (45409-0364)
PHONE...............................937 228-1162
James D Claffey, *Prin*
James D Claffey Junior Prinic, *Prin*
EMP: 0 EST: 1954
SQ FT: 12,000
SALES (est): 572.78K **Privately Held**
Web: www.nonferrouscasting.com
SIC: 3366 3365 Brass foundry, nec; Masts,
cast aluminum

(G-5910)
**NORTHROP GRMMN SPCE & MSSN
SYS**
1900 Founders Dr Ste 202 (45420-1182)
PHONE...............................937 259-4956
EMP: 60
SIC: 7372 7374 Prepackaged software; Data
processing and preparation
HQ: Northrop Grumman Space & Mission
Systems Corp.
6379 San Ignacio Ave
San Jose CA 95119
703 280-2900

(G-5911)
NORTHWESTERN TOOLS INC
4800 Hempstead Station Dr (45429-3900)
PHONE...............................937 298-9994
EMP: 16 EST: 1942
SALES (est): 1.98MM **Privately Held**
Web: www.northwesterntools.com

SIC: 3544 Jigs and fixtures

(G-5912)
NORWOOD MEDICAL LLC (DH)
Also Called: Norwood Medical
2122 Winners Cir (45404-1148)
P.O. Box 3806 (45401)
PHONE...............................937 228-4101
Kenneth Hemmelgarn Senior, *Pr*
Kenneth J Hemmelgarn Senior, *Pr*
Kenneth J Hemmelgarn Junior, *VP Fin*
Brian Hemmelgarn, *
EMP: 75 EST: 1926
SQ FT: 65,000
SALES (est): 98.48MM
SALES (corp-wide): 2.67MM **Privately
Held**
Web: www.norwoodmedical.com
SIC: 3841 3845 Surgical and medical
instruments; Electromedical apparatus
HQ: Heraeus Holding Gesellschaft Mit
Beschrankter Haftung
Heraeusstr. 12-14
Hanau HE 63450
6181350

(G-5913)
NORWOOD MEDICAL LLC
2101 Winners Cir (45404-1176)
P.O. Box 3806 (45401-3806)
PHONE...............................937 228-4101
Ken Hammelgarn, *Mgr*
EMP: 1061
SALES (corp-wide): 2.67MM **Privately
Held**
Web: www.norwoodmedical.com
SIC: 3469 Metal stampings, nec
HQ: Norwood Medical Llc
2122 Winners Cir
Dayton OH 45404
937 228-4101

(G-5914)
NORWOOD TOOL COMPANY
Also Called: NORWOOD TOOL COMPANY
2055 Winners Cir (45404-1182)
PHONE...............................937 228-4101
EMP: 7
SALES (corp-wide): 2.67MM **Privately
Held**
Web: www.norwoodmedical.com
SIC: 3469 Metal stampings, nec
HQ: Norwood Medical Llc
2122 Winners Cir
Dayton OH 45404
937 228-4101

(G-5915)
NOV INC
Also Called: Chemineer
5870 Poe Ave (45414-3442)
PHONE...............................937 454-3200
Daniel Margolien, *Genl Mgr*
EMP: 88
SALES (corp-wide): 8.87B **Publicly Held**
Web: www.nov.com
SIC: 3569 3531 Liquid automation
machinery and equipment; Construction
machinery
PA: Nov Inc.
10353 Richmond Ave
Houston TX 77042
346 223-3000

(G-5916)
**NOV PROCESS & FLOW TECH US
INC**
5870 Poe Ave (45414-3442)
PHONE...............................937 454-3300
EMP: 12
SALES (corp-wide): 8.87B **Publicly Held**

Web: www.petrostartools.com
SIC: 3823 Industrial flow and liquid
measuring instruments
HQ: Nov Process & Flow Technologies Us,
Inc.
10353 Richmond Ave
Houston TX 77042
346 223-3000

(G-5917)
NTECH INDUSTRIES INC
5475 Kellenburger Rd (45424-1013)
PHONE...............................707 467-3747
John Mayfield, *CEO*
EMP: 6 EST: 2001
SQ FT: 1,600
SALES (est): 1.01MM
SALES (corp-wide): 3.68B **Publicly Held**
SIC: 3523 Farm machinery and equipment
PA: Trimble Inc.
10368 Westmoor Dr
Westminster CO 80021
720 887-6100

(G-5918)
NU STREAM FILTRATION INC
1257 Stanley Ave (45404-1013)
PHONE...............................937 949-3174
James Baker, *Pr*
EMP: 10 EST: 2017
SQ FT: 20,000
SALES (est): 4.41MM **Privately Held**
Web: www.nustreamfiltration.com
SIC: 3677 Filtration devices, electronic

(G-5919)
OAKLEY INC
1421 Springfield St Unit 2 (45403-1435)
P.O. Box 8302 (45040-5302)
PHONE...............................949 672-6560
Sheila Oakley, *Brnch Mgr*
EMP: 11
SALES (corp-wide): 7.66MM **Privately
Held**
Web: www.oakley.com
SIC: 3851 Ophthalmic goods
HQ: Oakley, Inc.
1 Icon
Foothill Ranch CA 92610
949 951-0991

(G-5920)
OBERFIELDS LLC
10075 Sheehan Rd (45458-4301)
PHONE...............................937 885-3711
Bruce Loris, *Pr*
EMP: 7
SALES (corp-wide): 21.04MM **Privately
Held**
Web: www.oberfields.com
SIC: 3272 Concrete products, precast, nec
HQ: Oberfield's, Llc
528 London Rd
Delaware OH 43015
740 369-7644

(G-5921)
**OERLIKON FRCTION SYSTEMS US
IN**
Also Called: Plant 5
240 Detrick St (45404-1699)
PHONE...............................937 233-9191
Joe Caffano, *Brnch Mgr*
EMP: 34
Web: www.oerlikon.com
SIC: 3465 Automotive stampings
HQ: Oerlikon Friction Systems (Us) Inc.
240 Detrick St
Dayton OH 45404
937 449-4000

GEOGRAPHIC

(G-5922)
OERLIKON FRICTION SYSTEMS
14 Heid Ave (45404-1216)
P.O. Box 745 (45401-0745)
PHONE..................937 449-4000
EMP: 34
Web: www.oerlikon.com
SIC: 3714 Acceleration equipment, motor vehicle
HQ: Oerlikon Friction Systems (Us) Inc.
　240 Detrick St
　Dayton OH 45404
　937 449-4000

(G-5923)
OERLIKON FRICTION SYSTEMS (HQ)
240 Detrick St (45404-1699)
P.O. Box 745 (45401-0745)
PHONE..................937 449-4000
Eric A Schueler, Pr
John Parker, *
Mark Szporka, *
◆ EMP: 54 EST: 2002
SQ FT: 115,000
SALES (est): 3.45MM Privately Held
Web: www.oerlikon.com
SIC: 3714 Transmission housings or parts, motor vehicle
PA: Oc Oerlikon Corporation Ag, Pfaffikon
　Churerstrasse 120
　PfAffikon SZ 8808

(G-5924)
OHIO METAL FABRICATING INC
6057 Milo Rd (45414-3417)
PHONE..................937 233-2400
Gary Brandeberry, Pr
Leta Brandeberry, Prin
EMP: 17 EST: 2007
SQ FT: 18,000
SALES (est): 2.13MM Privately Held
Web: www.ohiometalfab.com
SIC: 3599 Machine shop, jobbing and repair

(G-5925)
OHIO METAL PRODUCTS COMPANY
35 Bates St (45402-1395)
PHONE..................937 228-6101
John D Moore, Pr
Janet A Simpson, *
▲ EMP: 13 EST: 1909
SQ FT: 32,000
SALES (est): 2.71MM Privately Held
Web: www.ohio-metal.com
SIC: 3451 3471 Screw machine products; Plating and polishing

(G-5926)
OHIO NEWSPAPERS INC (DH)
Also Called: Cox Media Group
1611 S Main St (45409-2547)
PHONE..................937 225-2000
Julia Wallace, VP
Charles D Shook, *
Edward L Shank, *
Sylvia J Planck, *
EMP: 550 EST: 1898
SQ FT: 150,000
SALES (est): 21.17MM
SALES (corp-wide): 961.55MM Privately Held
Web: www.cmglocalsolutions.com
SIC: 2711 Commercial printing and newspaper publishing combined
HQ: Cox Newspapers, Inc.
　6205 Pchtree Dnwody Rd N
　Atlanta GA 30328

(G-5927)
OMNIPRESENCE CLEANING LLC
302 W Fairview Ave (45405-3304)
P.O. Box 20042 (45420-0042)
PHONE..................937 250-4749
Sabrina Monegan, Ex Dir
EMP: 17 EST: 2009
SALES (est): 260.9K Privately Held
SIC: 7349 1389 8322 2741 Building maintenance services, nec; Construction, repair, and dismantling services; Senior citizens' center or association; Business service newsletters: publishing and printing

(G-5928)
OP DAWG LOGISTICS LLC
1700 Shroyer Rd Apt 4 (45419-3216)
PHONE..................937 844-3135
EMP: 20
SALES (est): 1.37MM Privately Held
SIC: 3537 7389 Trucks: freight, baggage, etc.: industrial, except mining; Business Activities at Non-Commercial Site

(G-5929)
OPEN ADDITIVE LLC
2750 Indian Ripple Rd (45440-3638)
PHONE..................937 306-6140
EMP: 11 EST: 2019
SALES (est): 4.06MM Privately Held
Web: www.arctos-us.com
SIC: 3552 8731 Textile machinery; Commercial physical research

(G-5930)
OREGON VLG PRINT SHOPPE INC
Also Called: Oregon Printing
29 N June St (45403-1015)
P.O. Box 750334 (45475)
PHONE..................937 222-9418
Judd Plattenburg, Pr
EMP: 14 EST: 1974
SQ FT: 5,300
SALES (est): 1.01MM Privately Held
Web: www.oregonprinting.com
SIC: 2752 Offset printing

(G-5931)
OUTLOOK TOOL INC
360 Fame Rd (45449-2313)
PHONE..................937 235-6330
Eric Staeuble, Pr
Ted Nevels, Sec
EMP: 6 EST: 1997
SQ FT: 3,200
SALES (est): 506.68K Privately Held
Web: www.outlooktool.com
SIC: 3599 Machine shop, jobbing and repair

(G-5932)
OVASE MANUFACTURING LLC
Also Called: Global Tool
1990 Berwyck Ave (45414-5556)
P.O. Box 3 (45066-0003)
PHONE..................937 275-0617
EMP: 8 EST: 2005
SALES (est): 1.02MM Privately Held
SIC: 3599 Machine shop, jobbing and repair

(G-5933)
P J TOOL COMPANY INC
1115 Springfield St (45403-1420)
PHONE..................937 254-2817
Paul Hedrick, Pr
Jim Fedor, Sec
EMP: 6 EST: 1987
SQ FT: 2,600
SALES (est): 582.55K Privately Held

SIC: 3599 3544 Machine shop, jobbing and repair; Special dies, tools, jigs, and fixtures

(G-5934)
PAVE TECHNOLOGY CO
2751 Thunderhawk Ct (45414-3451)
PHONE..................937 890-1100
Walter D Wood, Ch Bd
Brad Boomershine, *
EMP: 45 EST: 1980
SQ FT: 20,000
SALES (est): 9.4MM Privately Held
Web: www.pavetechnologyco.com
SIC: 3643 3089 Current-carrying wiring services; Injection molding of plastics

(G-5935)
PENTAGEAR PRODUCTS LLC
6161 Webster St (45414-3435)
PHONE..................937 660-8182
EMP: 7 EST: 2005
SALES (est): 1.31MM Privately Held
Web: www.pentagear.com
SIC: 3566 7389 Speed changers, drives, and gears; Business services, nec

(G-5936)
PEPSI-COLA METRO BTLG CO INC
Also Called: Pepsi-Cola
526 Milburn Ave (45404-1678)
PHONE..................937 461-4664
Tim Trant, Genl Mgr
EMP: 61
SQ FT: 115,000
SALES (corp-wide): 91.47B Publicly Held
Web: www.pepsico.com
SIC: 2086 5149 Soft drinks: packaged in cans, bottles, etc.; Groceries and related products, nec
HQ: Pepsi-Cola Metropolitan Bottling Company, Inc.
　700 Anderson Hill Rd
　Purchase NY 10577
　914 767-6000

(G-5937)
PERMA EDGE INDUSTRIES LLC
8579 N Dixie Dr (45414-2463)
PHONE..................937 623-7819
EMP: 6 EST: 2016
SALES (est): 2.32MM Privately Held
Web: www.permapaveredging.com
SIC: 3999 Manufacturing industries, nec

(G-5938)
PERMA-FIX OF DAYTON INC
300 Cherokee Dr (45417-8113)
PHONE..................937 268-6501
Brad Malatesta, Pr
Richard Kelecy, VP
EMP: 13 EST: 1941
SQ FT: 25,000
SALES (est): 2.52MM Publicly Held
Web: www.perma-fix.com
SIC: 4953 2992 Recycling, waste materials; Lubricating oils and greases
PA: Perma-Fix Environmental Services, Inc.
　8302 Dunwoody Pl Ste 250
　Atlanta GA 30350

(G-5939)
PHOENIX METAL WORKS INC
Also Called: Phoenix Metal Fabricators
2528 Ashcraft Rd (45414-3402)
PHONE..................937 274-5555
Carl Abshire, Pr
EMP: 9 EST: 1989
SQ FT: 10,000
SALES (est): 2.37MM Privately Held
Web: www.phoenixdayton.com

SIC: 3441 Fabricated structural metal

(G-5940)
PIETRA NATURALE INC
2425 Stanley Ave (45404-2728)
PHONE..................937 438-8882
Michael Carnevale Junior, Pr
Robert Carnevale, *
Michael Ricky Carnevale, Treas
EMP: 12 EST: 1990
SALES (est): 1.05MM Privately Held
Web: www.pietranaturaleinc.com
SIC: 1799 3281 Counter top installation; Marble, building: cut and shaped

(G-5941)
PLATING TECHNOLOGY INC
1525 W River Rd (45417-6740)
PHONE..................937 268-6882
Jody Pollack Blazar, Prin
▲ EMP: 70 EST: 1953
SQ FT: 190,000
SALES (est): 9.89MM Privately Held
Web: www.platingtech.com
SIC: 3471 3469 Electroplating of metals or formed products; Machine parts, stamped or pressed metal

(G-5942)
PLUMB BUILDERS INC
2367 S Dixie Dr (45409-1858)
PHONE..................937 293-1111
Larry Freed, Pr
EMP: 10 EST: 1991
SALES (est): 77.85K Privately Held
SIC: 1521 5999 3999 Single-family housing construction; Technical aids for the handicapped; Wheelchair lifts

(G-5943)
PRATT INDUSTRIES INC
98 Quality Ln (45449-2141)
PHONE..................513 262-6253
EMP: 17
Web: www.prattindustries.com
SIC: 2653 Boxes, corrugated: made from purchased materials
PA: Pratt Industries, Inc.
　4004 Smmit Blvd Ne Ste 10
　Atlanta GA 30319

(G-5944)
PRECISION ARCFT COMPONENTS INC
2787 Armstrong Ln (45414-4225)
PHONE..................937 278-0265
Emsy Little Junior, CEO
Jonathan Hurlow, Sec
EMP: 9 EST: 1985
SQ FT: 17,500
SALES (est): 986.12K Privately Held
SIC: 3599 Machine shop, jobbing and repair

(G-5945)
PRECISION FINISHING SYSTEMS
6101 Webster St (45414-3435)
PHONE..................937 415-5794
Barbara Lipuma, Pt
EMP: 45 EST: 2012
SALES (est): 4MM Privately Held
Web: www.pfs-finishing.com
SIC: 3471 Cleaning, polishing, and finishing

(G-5946)
PRECISION GAGE & TOOL COMPANY
375 Gargrave Rd (45449-2465)
PHONE..................937 866-9666
Vicki Waltz, Pr
Leslie Heaton, VP

▲ = Import ▼ = Export
◆ = Import/Export

EMP: 20 EST: 1929
SQ FT: 16,000
SALES (est): 3.16MM Privately Held
Web: www.pgtgage.com
SIC: 3545 7699 Gauges (machine tool accessories); Caliper, gauge, and other machinists' instrument repair

(G-5947)
PRECISION MACHINING SERVICES
Also Called: Universal Tool Co
365 Leo St (45404-1007)
PHONE..................................937 222-4608
Eric Kleinschmidt, Pr
Mike Farmer, *
EMP: 7 EST: 1936
SQ FT: 45,000
SALES (est): 1.7MM Privately Held
Web: www.thomasnet.com
SIC: 3599 Machine shop, jobbing and repair

(G-5948)
PRECISION MANUFACTURING CO INC
2149 Valley Pike (45404-2542)
PHONE..................................937 236-2170
Faye Ledwick, CEO
EMP: 70 EST: 1967
SQ FT: 30,000
SALES (est): 4.13MM Privately Held
Web: www.precmfgco.com
SIC: 3679 Electronic circuits

(G-5949)
PRECISION MFG & ASSEMBLY LLC
2240 Richard St (45403-2551)
PHONE..................................937 252-3507
William Bill Duckro, Managing Member
EMP: 65 EST: 2002
SALES (est): 703.78K Privately Held
SIC: 3089 Automotive parts, plastic

(G-5950)
PRECISION MTAL FABRICATION INC (PA)
191 Heid Ave (45404-1217)
PHONE..................................937 235-9261
Jim Hackenberger, Pr
John Limberg, *
EMP: 57 EST: 1984
SQ FT: 30,000
SALES (est): 3.61MM
SALES (corp-wide): 3.61MM Privately Held
Web: www.premetfab.com
SIC: 7692 3444 Welding repair; Sheet metalwork

(G-5951)
PRECISION PRESSED POWDERED MET
295 S Alex Rd (45449-1910)
PHONE..................................937 433-6802
Stephen G England, Ch
David Warner, Pr
EMP: 10 EST: 1983
SALES (est): 2.45MM Privately Held
Web:
www.precisionpressedpowderedmetals.com
SIC: 3399 Powder, metal

(G-5952)
PREMIER AEROSPACE GROUP LLC
Also Called: Jbk Manufacturing & Dev Co
2127 Troy St (45404-2162)
PHONE..................................937 233-8300
Steve Olson, Managing Member
EMP: 35 EST: 2021
SALES (est): 8.32MM Privately Held
Web: www.jbkmfg.com

(G-5953)
PRIDE INVESTMENTS LLC
Also Called: American Heat Treating
1346 Morris Ave (45417-3829)
PHONE..................................937 461-1121
Lawrence Gray, Owner
EMP: 15 EST: 2004
SQ FT: 32,000
SALES (est): 2.23MM Privately Held
Web: www.ahtdayton.com
SIC: 3398 Metal heat treating

(G-5954)
PRIMARY PDTS INGRDNTS AMRCAS L
Also Called: Tate & Lyle
5584 Webster St (45414-3517)
PHONE..................................937 235-4074
EMP: 10
SALES (corp-wide): 1.16B Privately Held
Web: www.tateandlyle.com
SIC: 2046 Wet corn milling
HQ: Primary Products Ingredients Americas Llc
20 N Mrtingale Rd Ste 350
Schaumburg IL 60173
217 423-4411

(G-5955)
PRIMARY PDTS INGRDNTS AMRCAS L
5600 Brentlinger Dr (45414-3512)
PHONE..................................937 236-5906
Dana Johnson, Brnch Mgr
EMP: 100
SALES (corp-wide): 1.16B Privately Held
Web: www.primient.com
SIC: 2899 2819 2087 Chemical preparations, nec; Industrial inorganic chemicals, nec; Flavoring extracts and syrups, nec
HQ: Primary Products Ingredients Americas Llc
20 N Mrtingale Rd Ste 350
Schaumburg IL 60173
217 423-4411

(G-5956)
PRIME PRINTING INC (PA)
8929 Kingsridge Dr (45458-1621)
P.O. Box 751591 (45475-1591)
PHONE..................................937 438-3707
Gary Smith, Pr
Dan Cornelius, *
Tim Cox, *
EMP: 33 EST: 1991
SQ FT: 12,000
SALES (est): 455.69K Privately Held
SIC: 2752 2796 2791 2789 Offset printing; Platemaking services; Typesetting; Bookbinding and related work

(G-5957)
PRINTING DIMENSIONS INC
500 N Irwin St (45403-1335)
PHONE..................................937 256-0044
Michael E Feeley, Pr
Michael D Hornick, VP
John A Feeley, Sec
EMP: 12 EST: 1982
SALES (est): 1MM Privately Held
SIC: 2752 2759 Offset printing; Commercial printing, nec

(G-5958)
PRINTPOINT INC
150 S Patterson Blvd (45402-2421)
PHONE..................................937 223-9041

Mike Munch, Pr
EMP: 7 EST: 1976
SQ FT: 13,000
SALES (est): 379.08K Privately Held
Web: www.printpointprinting.com
SIC: 2752 Offset printing

(G-5959)
PRO LINE COLLISION AND PNT LLC (PA)
Also Called: Proline Finishing
1 Armor Pl (45417-3443)
PHONE..................................937 223-7611
EMP: 8 EST: 2005
SQ FT: 44,000
SALES (est): 3.3MM Privately Held
Web: www.prolinefinishing.com
SIC: 3471 Finishing, metals or formed products

(G-5960)
PRODIGY PRINT INC
Also Called: Prodigy Print Ink
884 Valley St (45404-2066)
▲ EMP: 10 EST: 1982
SALES (est): 309.43K Privately Held
SIC: 2759 2789 Screen printing; Bookbinding and related work

(G-5961)
PRODUCTION CONTROL UNITS INC
2280 W Dorothy Ln (45439-1892)
PHONE..................................937 299-5594
Thomas Hoge, Pr
Fred Bayer, *
▼ EMP: 100 EST: 1946
SQ FT: 58,000
SALES (est): 20.34MM Privately Held
Web: www.pcuinc.com
SIC: 3829 3823 Measuring and controlling devices, nec; Industrial process control instruments

(G-5962)
PRODUCTION DESIGN SERVICES INC (PA)
Also Called: Pdsi Technical Services
313 Mound St (45402-8370)
PHONE..................................937 866-3377
John H Schultz, Pr
John H Schultz, Pr
Jeffrey R Schultz, *
James A Schultz, *
EMP: 76 EST: 1978
SQ FT: 48,000
SALES (est): 6.6MM
SALES (corp-wide): 6.6MM Privately Held
Web: www.pdsitech.com
SIC: 3559 3559 Custom machinery; Sewing machines and hat and zipper making machinery

(G-5963)
PRODUCTION TUBE CUTTING INC
1100 S Smithville Rd (45403-3423)
PHONE..................................937 254-6138
◆ EMP: 43 EST: 1959
SALES (est): 8.84MM Privately Held
Web: www.productiontubecutting.com
SIC: 3498 3559 3351 3083 Tube fabricating (contract bending and shaping); Refinery, chemical processing, and similar machinery; Copper rolling and drawing; Laminated plastics plate and sheet

(G-5964)
PROFICIENT INFO TECH INC
Also Called: Pi-Tech
301 W 1st St (45402-3033)
PHONE..................................937 470-1300

Tina Bustillo, Pr
EMP: 8 EST: 1994
SALES (est): 314.46K Privately Held
Web: www.pi-tech-inc.com
SIC: 7371 7372 7379 8742 Custom computer programming services; Application computer software; Computer related maintenance services; Marketing consulting services

(G-5965)
PROFILE DIGITAL PRINTING LLC
5449 Marina Dr (45449-1833)
PHONE..................................937 866-4241
Terry Harmeyer, Genl Mgr
June Helmers, *
Tom Helmers, *
EMP: 25 EST: 2002
SALES (est): 720.08K Privately Held
Web: www.profiledpi.com
SIC: 7334 2759 2752 Blueprinting service; Commercial printing, nec; Commercial printing, lithographic

(G-5966)
PROFOUND LOGIC SOFTWARE INC (PA)
396 Congress Park Dr (45459-4149)
P.O. Box 12559 (92658)
PHONE..................................937 439-7925
Alex Roytman, CEO
Alex Roytman, Pr
EMP: 27 EST: 2000
SALES (est): 6.38MM Privately Held
Web: www.profoundlogic.com
SIC: 7372 7379 7371 Prepackaged software ; Computer related consulting services; Software programming applications

(G-5967)
PROGRESSIVE PRINTERS INC
6700 Homestretch Rd (45414-2516)
PHONE..................................937 222-1267
Dennis Livesay, Pr
Sharon L Staggs, *
Sheena Simmons, *
Dennis Livesay, CEO
Phil Bondi, Genl Mgr
EMP: 55 EST: 2004
SQ FT: 26,000
SALES (est): 1.82MM Privately Held
Web: www.progressiveprinters.com
SIC: 2752 2759 Offset printing; Commercial printing, nec

(G-5968)
PROJECTS UNLIMITED INC (PA)
6300 Sand Lake Rd (45414-2649)
PHONE..................................937 918-2200
EMP: 170 EST: 1954
SALES (est): 23.79MM
SALES (corp-wide): 23.79MM Privately Held
Web: www.pui.com
SIC: 3672 3679 3643 3625 Printed circuit boards; Harness assemblies, for electronic use: wire or cable; Current-carrying wiring services; Relays and industrial controls

(G-5969)
PUTNAM PLASTICS INC
Also Called: Farm Products Division
255 S Alex Rd (45449-1910)
PHONE..................................937 866-6261
Gary Spacht, Mgr
EMP: 8
SALES (corp-wide): 5.42MM Privately Held
Web: www.putnamplasticsinc.com

SIC: 5199 5113 3081 Packaging materials; Industrial and personal service paper; Polyethylene film
PA: Putnam Plastics Inc
30 W Stardust Rd
Cloverdale IN 46120
765 795-6102

(G-5970)
QUARTER CENTURY DESIGN LLC
2555 S Dixie Dr Ste 232 (45409-1518)
PHONE..............................937 434-5127
EMP: 6 EST: 2006
SALES (est): 1.42MM Privately Held
Web: www.quartercenturydesign.com
SIC: 3672 Printed circuit boards

(G-5971)
R D BAKER ENTERPRISES INC
Also Called: Alpha Water Conditioning Co
765 Liberty Ln (45449-2134)
PHONE..............................937 461-5225
Bill Miller, *Brnch Mgr*
EMP: 6
SALES (corp-wide): 3.1MM Privately Held
Web: www.daytonsoftwater.com
SIC: 3589 8734 5074 Water purification equipment, household type; Water testing laboratory; Water softeners
PA: R. D. Baker Enterprises, Inc.
765 Liberty Ln
Dayton OH 45449
937 461-5225

(G-5972)
RAM PRECISION INDUSTRIES INC
Also Called: R A M Precision Tool
11125 Yankee St Ste A (45458-3698)
PHONE..............................937 885-7700
Rick Mount, *CEO*
▲ EMP: 75 EST: 1974
SQ FT: 55,000
SALES (est): 8.87MM Privately Held
Web: www.ramprecision.com
SIC: 3599 Machine shop, jobbing and repair

(G-5973)
RAM TOOL INC
1944 Neva Dr (45414-5525)
PHONE..............................937 277-0717
Robert Coblentz, *Pr*
Forrest Lemaster, *Pr*
EMP: 7 EST: 1973
SQ FT: 4,000
SALES (est): 899.37K Privately Held
Web: www.ramtoolohio.com
SIC: 3544 Special dies and tools

(G-5974)
RAMBASEK REALTY INC
Also Called: Crystal Water Company
827 S Patterson Blvd (45402-2622)
PHONE..............................937 228-1189
Tom Rambasek, *Pr*
Nancy F Rambasek, *VP*
EMP: 19 EST: 1919
SQ FT: 16,000
SALES (est): 2.28MM Privately Held
SIC: 5149 5963 2899 7359 Water, distilled; Bottled water delivery; Distilled water; Equipment rental and leasing, nec

(G-5975)
RANDD ASSOC PRTG & PROMOTIONS
330 Progress Rd (45449-2322)
PHONE..............................937 294-1874
Rick Dobson, *Pr*
Rick Dobson, *Pr*
Pam Dobson, *Sec*
EMP: 7 EST: 1980

SQ FT: 3,200
SALES (est): 2.17MM Privately Held
Web: www.randdassociates.com
SIC: 2752 5199 Offset printing; Advertising specialties

(G-5976)
RCF KITCHENS INDIANA LLC
Also Called: Really Cool Foods
87 Shelford Way (45440-3657)
PHONE..............................765 478-6600
Don Gillun, *Managing Member*
EMP: 6 EST: 2007
SQ FT: 1,500
SALES (est): 839.94K Privately Held
SIC: 2015 Chicken, processed: fresh

(G-5977)
RCT INDUSTRIES INC
Also Called: Adcura Mfg
1314 Farr Dr (45404-2736)
PHONE..............................937 602-1100
Russell Thie, *Pr*
EMP: 10 EST: 2000
SQ FT: 4,000
SALES (est): 1.05MM Privately Held
Web: www.adcuramfg.com
SIC: 3679 Electronic circuits

(G-5978)
READY TECHNOLOGY INC (HQ)
Also Called: Standard Die Supply
333 Progress Rd (45449-2490)
PHONE..............................937 866-7200
Michael Danly, *Pr*
▲ EMP: 14 EST: 1981
SQ FT: 10,000
SALES (est): 5.01MM Privately Held
Web: www.readytechnology.com
SIC: 5084 3544 3542 Metalworking tools, nec (such as drills, taps, dies, files); Special dies, tools, jigs, and fixtures; Bending machines
PA: Danly Corporation
3121 Commodore Plz Ph 5
Miami FL 33133

(G-5979)
RELY-ON MANUFACTURING INC
955 Springfield St (45403-1347)
PHONE..............................937 254-0118
Marsha Mosher, *Pr*
Peter T Mosher, *VP*
EMP: 6 EST: 1983
SALES (est): 2.06MM Privately Held
SIC: 3451 Screw machine products

(G-5980)
RESONANT SCIENCES LLC
3975 Research Blvd (45430-2107)
PHONE..............................937 431-8180
J Micah North, *Pr*
EMP: 49 EST: 2014
SALES (est): 13.92MM Privately Held
Web: www.resonantsciences.com
SIC: 3825 8711 Radio frequency measuring equipment; Aviation and/or aeronautical engineering

(G-5981)
RESPONSE METAL FABRICATORS
521 Kiser St (45404-1641)
PHONE..............................937 222-9000
Janice Morton, *Pr*
T R Morton, *VP*
EMP: 11 EST: 1998
SQ FT: 3,000
SALES (est): 627.26K Privately Held
Web:
www.commercialmetalfabricators.com

SIC: 3441 Fabricated structural metal

(G-5982)
REX AMERICAN RESOURCES CORP (PA)
Also Called: Rex
7720 Paragon Rd (45459-4050)
PHONE..............................937 276-3931
Zafar Rizvi, *Pr*
Stuart A Rose, *
Edward M Kress, *
Douglas L Bruggeman, *VP Fin*
EMP: 102 EST: 1980
SQ FT: 7,500
SALES (est): 642.49MM
SALES (corp-wide): 642.49MM Publicly Held
Web: www.rexamerican.com
SIC: 2869 Fuels

(G-5983)
REYNOLDS MACHINERY INC
760 Liberty Ln (45449-2135)
PHONE..............................937 847-8121
Scott D Mays, *Pr*
Jeffrey J Jaske, *CFO*
Steve Mays, *VP*
Carl Mays, *Prin*
EMP: 14 EST: 1976
SQ FT: 12,500
SALES (est): 2.35MM Privately Held
Web: www.reynoldsmachinery.com
SIC: 3599 Machine shop, jobbing and repair

(G-5984)
RIXAN ASSOCIATES INC
7560 Paragon Rd (45459-5317)
PHONE..............................937 438-3005
Stephen Harris, *Pr*
Aaron Rick Harris, *Ch*
Beatrice Harris, *Sec*
EMP: 20 EST: 1959
SQ FT: 14,000
SALES (est): 4.31MM Privately Held
Web: www.rixan.com
SIC: 5084 3569 5065 Robots, industrial; Robots, assembly line: industrial and commercial; Electronic parts

(G-5985)
RMT CORPORATION
2552 Titus Ave (45414-4217)
PHONE..............................937 274-2121
Brent Shreiner, *Pr*
EMP: 10 EST: 1986
SQ FT: 1,267
SALES (est): 856.36K Privately Held
Web: www.rmt-corp.com
SIC: 3544 Special dies and tools

(G-5986)
ROBBINS & MYERS INC
5870 Poe Ave Ste A (45414-3442)
P.O. Box 1123 (45401-1123)
PHONE..............................937 454-3200
Kevin Brown, *Brnch Mgr*
EMP: 6
SALES (corp-wide): 8.87B Publicly Held
Web: www.robn.com
SIC: 3533 Oil and gas field machinery
HQ: Robbins & Myers, Inc.
10586 Hwy 75 N
Willis TX 77378
936 890-1064

(G-5987)
ROBS WELDING TECHNOLOGIES LTD
Also Called: Rob's Welding Technologies
2920 Production Ct (45414-3537)

PHONE..............................937 890-4963
Dean Shoup, *Pt*
Rob Shoup, *Pt*
EMP: 9 EST: 1987
SQ FT: 10,000
SALES (est): 494.97K Privately Held
Web: www.robsweldingtech.com
SIC: 3312 3441 1799 Tool and die steel; Fabricated structural metal; Welding on site

(G-5988)
RONALD T DODGE CO
Also Called: Dodge Company
55 Westpark Rd (45459-4812)
PHONE..............................937 439-4497
Ronald J Versic, *Pr*
Ronald J Versic, *Pr*
Linda J Versic, *VP*
EMP: 10 EST: 1979
SQ FT: 8,000
SALES (est): 4.81MM Privately Held
Web: www.rtdodge.com
SIC: 2869 8731 High purity grade chemicals, organic; Commercial research laboratory

(G-5989)
RUBBER-TECH INC
5208 Wadsworth Rd (45414-3592)
PHONE..............................937 274-1114
Forest Back, *Pr*
L Irene Back, *Sec*
EMP: 14 EST: 1953
SQ FT: 10,000
SALES (est): 849.26K Privately Held
Web: www.rubber-tech.com
SIC: 3069 3061 Molded rubber products; Mechanical rubber goods

(G-5990)
RYANWORKS INC
Also Called: Woodcraft
175 E Alex Bell Rd Ste 264 (45459-2701)
PHONE..............................937 438-1282
Alan Ryan, *Pr*
EMP: 35 EST: 1998
SALES (est): 4.92MM Privately Held
SIC: 5084 2499 Woodworking machinery; Decorative wood and woodwork

(G-5991)
S F MOCK & ASSOCIATES LLC
105 Westpark Rd (45459-4814)
PHONE..............................937 438-0196
EMP: 10 EST: 2016
SALES (est): 125.99K Privately Held
Web: www.safeguardmpg.com
SIC: 2761 5611 2759 Manifold business forms; Men's and boys' clothing stores; Business forms: printing, nsk

(G-5992)
SAFE-GRAIN INC
Also Called: Safe Grain Max Tronix
10522 Success Ln (45458-3561)
PHONE..............................513 398-2500
Greg Stevens, *Dir*
EMP: 8
SALES (corp-wide): 2.6MM Privately Held
Web: www.safegrain.com
SIC: 3523 Farm machinery and equipment
PA: Safe-Grain, Inc.
417 Wards Corner Rd Ste B
Loveland OH 45140
513 398-2500

(G-5993)
SAMPLE MACHINING INC
Also Called: Bitec
220 N Jersey St (45403-1220)
PHONE..............................937 258-3338
Beverly Bleicher, *Pr*

▲ = Import ▼ = Export
◆ = Import/Export

Kevin Bleicher, *
EMP: 45 **EST:** 1985
SQ FT: 19,000
SALES (est): 9.71MM **Privately Held**
Web: www.bitecsmi.com
SIC: 3599 8734 Custom machinery; Testing laboratories

(G-5994)
SANTOS INDUSTRIAL LTD (PA)
Also Called: Bimac
3034 Dryden Rd (45439-1620)
PHONE..................937 299-7333
Roberto Santos, *Pr*
▲ **EMP:** 41 **EST:** 1958
SQ FT: 33,280
SALES (est): 4.57MM
SALES (corp-wide): 4.57MM **Privately Held**
Web: www.bimac.com
SIC: 3366 Copper foundries

(G-5995)
SCARLETT KITTY LLC
Also Called: Scarlett Ktty Bath Made Pretty
2786 Wilmington Pike (45419-2141)
PHONE..................678 438-3796
Joy Coleman, *CEO*
EMP: 10 **EST:** 2014
SQ FT: 3,000
SALES (est): 142.67K **Privately Held**
SIC: 2844 Depilatories (cosmetic)

(G-5996)
SCENIC SOLUTIONS LTD LBLTY CO
355 Gargrave Rd (45449-2465)
PHONE..................937 866-5062
Dan Mclaughlin, *Managing Member*
▲ **EMP:** 12 **EST:** 2000
SQ FT: 26,000
SALES (est): 1.89MM **Privately Held**
Web: www.scenicsolutions.com
SIC: 7922 2541 Scenery design, theatrical; Display fixtures, wood

(G-5997)
SCHUERHOLZ INC
3540 Marshall Rd (45429-4916)
PHONE..................937 294-5218
Charles Schuerholz, *Pr*
EMP: 7 **EST:** 1961
SQ FT: 4,500
SALES (est): 665.5K **Privately Held**
Web: www.schuerholzprinting.com
SIC: 2752 7336 Offset printing; Graphic arts and related design

(G-5998)
SCIENCE/ELECTRONICS INC
Also Called: Earth and Atmospheric Sciences
521 Kiser St (45404-1641)
PHONE..................937 224-4444
Ted Morton, *CEO*
Janice Morton, *CFO*
EMP: 6 **EST:** 1978
SQ FT: 90,000
SALES (est): 175.56K **Privately Held**
Web: www.se-one.com
SIC: 5049 3829 Scientific instruments; Measuring and controlling devices, nec

(G-5999)
SCOTTS COMPANY LLC
20 Innovation Ct (45414-3968)
PHONE..................937 454-2782
Kevin Laughlin, *Mgr*
EMP: 15
SALES (corp-wide): 3.55B **Publicly Held**
Web: www.scotts.com
SIC: 2873 Fertilizers: natural (organic), except compost

HQ: The Scotts Company Llc
14111 Co Hwy 105
Marysville OH 43040
937 644-0011

(G-6000)
SCREEN WORKS INC (PA)
3970 Image Dr (45414-2524)
PHONE..................937 264-9111
Jeff Cottrell, *Prin*
Jeff Cottrell, *Prin*
Ron Witters, *Prin*
EMP: 48 **EST:** 1987
SQ FT: 42,000
SALES (est): 1.58MM
SALES (corp-wide): 1.58MM **Privately Held**
Web: www.screenworksinc.com
SIC: 7336 5199 7389 3993 Silk screen design; Advertising specialties; Embroidery advertising; Signs and advertising specialties

(G-6001)
SELECT INDUSTRIES CORPORATION
60 Heid Ave (45404-1216)
P.O. Box P.O. Box 887 (45401-0887)
PHONE..................937 233-9191
Kelly Wogoman, *Ch*
Robert Whited, *Prin*
Mark Wogoman, *Pr*
◆ **EMP:** 200 **EST:** 1999
SQ FT: 250,000
SALES (est): 43.91MM **Privately Held**
Web: www.select.org
SIC: 3544 Special dies and tools
PA: Select International Corp.
60 Heid Avenue
Dayton OH 45404

(G-6002)
SHAWN FLEMING IND TRCKG LLC
4982 Aquilla Dr (45415-3401)
PHONE..................937 707-8539
Shawn Fleming, *Managing Member*
EMP: 7 **EST:** 2015
SALES (est): 513.26K **Privately Held**
SIC: 4212 3537 4213 Local trucking, without storage; Trucks, tractors, loaders, carriers, and similar equipment; Trucking, except local

(G-6003)
SHILOH INDUSTRIES INC
5988 Executive Blvd Ste B (45424-1453)
PHONE..................937 236-5100
John Dixon, *Pr*
David W Dixon, *VP*
EMP: 18 **EST:** 1974
SQ FT: 18,000
SALES (est): 4.82MM **Privately Held**
SIC: 3679 3089 Electronic circuits; Injection molding of plastics

(G-6004)
SHORE TO SHORE INC (DH)
8170 Washington Village Dr (45458-1848)
PHONE..................937 866-1908
Howard Kurdin, *Pr*
John Lau, *
Chuck Rowland, *
◆ **EMP:** 100 **EST:** 1991
SQ FT: 30,000
SALES (est): 4.58MM
SALES (corp-wide): 4.84B **Privately Held**
SIC: 2679 2241 Labels, paper: made from purchased material; Labels, woven
HQ: Checkpoint Systems, Inc.
101 Wolf Dr
West Deptford NJ 08086
800 257-5540

(G-6005)
SHOUSHA TRUCKING LLC
3695 Barbarosa Dr (45416-1935)
PHONE..................937 270-4471
Kedir Enday, *Owner*
EMP: 10 **EST:** 2022
SALES (est): 3.49MM **Privately Held**
SIC: 3537 7389 Trucks, tractors, loaders, carriers, and similar equipment; Business Activities at Non-Commercial Site

(G-6006)
SIGN CONNECTION INC
90 Compark Rd Ste B (45459-4967)
PHONE..................937 435-4070
Jane Fiehrer, *Pr*
EMP: 11 **EST:** 1997
SALES (est): 1.26MM **Privately Held**
Web: www.signconnectioninc.com
SIC: 3993 Signs, not made in custom sign painting shops

(G-6007)
SIGN TECHNOLOGIES LLC
Also Called: Signetics
2001 Kuntz Rd (45404-1221)
PHONE..................937 439-3970
Shari Brown, *Finance*
EMP: 6 **EST:** 1960
SQ FT: 6,000
SALES (est): 491.67K **Privately Held**
Web: www.signetics1.com
SIC: 3993 Signs and advertising specialties

(G-6008)
SIGNWIRE WORLDWIDE INC
Also Called: Signwire.com
2781 Thunderhawk Ct (45414-3445)
PHONE..................937 428-6189
Jeffrey L Becht, *Pr*
EMP: 6 **EST:** 2008
SQ FT: 10,000
SALES (est): 280.63K **Privately Held**
SIC: 3993 Signs and advertising specialties

(G-6009)
SIMON ELLIS SUPERABRASIVES INC
501 Progress Rd (45449-2325)
P.O. Box 510 (28666-0510)
PHONE..................937 226-0683
David Rawson, *Pr*
Beverly Greene, *Sec*
Thomas Greene, *VP*
EMP: 9 **EST:** 1992
SQ FT: 5,000
SALES (est): 430.1K **Privately Held**
Web: www.simonellis.com
SIC: 3423 Hand and edge tools, nec

(G-6010)
SINEL COMPANY INC
4811 Pamela Sue Dr (45429-5349)
PHONE..................937 433-4772
Mitchell S Siler, *Pr*
EMP: 10 **EST:** 1934
SQ FT: 5,000
SALES (est): 489.63K **Privately Held**
Web: www.excelvent.com
SIC: 3543 Foundry cores

(G-6011)
SNYDER CONCRETE PRODUCTS INC
Also Called: Snyder Brick and Block
1433 S Euclid Ave (45417-3839)
PHONE..................937 224-1433
Chip Lytel, *Mgr*
EMP: 9
SALES (corp-wide): 24.02MM **Privately Held**

Web: www.snyderonline.com
SIC: 5032 3271 Brick, except refractory; Blocks, concrete or cinder: standard
PA: Snyder Concrete Products, Inc.
2301 W Dorothy Ln
Moraine OH 45439
937 885-5176

(G-6012)
SOFTWARE SOLUTIONS INC (PA)
8534 Yankee St Ste 2b (45458-1889)
PHONE..................513 932-6667
John Rettig, *Pr*
EMP: 23 **EST:** 1978
SALES (est): 7.78MM
SALES (corp-wide): 7.78MM **Privately Held**
Web: www.mysoftwaresolutions.com
SIC: 5045 7372 7373 Computer software; Application computer software; Computer integrated systems design

(G-6013)
SOUTHWSTERN OHIO INSTRCTNAL TE
Also Called: S O I T A
1205 E 5th St (45402-2221)
PHONE..................937 746-6333
David Gibson, *Dir*
Dave Mc Williams, *Sec*
Larry Pogue, *Ex Dir*
EMP: 10 **EST:** 1968
SQ FT: 2,000
SALES (est): 440.08K **Privately Held**
Web: www.soita.org
SIC: 7372 Educational computer software

(G-6014)
SPAOS INC (PA)
Also Called: Quality Office Products
6012 N Dixie Dr (45414-4018)
P.O. Box 13661 (45413-0661)
PHONE..................937 890-0783
Jack Roberts, *Pr*
Bonnie Roberts, *Sec*
EMP: 6 **EST:** 1980
SALES (est): 187.82K
SALES (corp-wide): 187.82K **Privately Held**
Web: www.superiorprintingpromo.com
SIC: 2752 Offset printing

(G-6015)
SPECIALTY MACHINES INC
5370 Salem Ave (45426-1626)
PHONE..................937 837-8852
Donna Suess, *Pr*
Richard Suess, *VP*
William C Hoyer, *CEO*
EMP: 20 **EST:** 1947
SQ FT: 15,000
SALES (est): 4.16MM **Privately Held**
Web: www.specialtymachinesinc.com
SIC: 3599 Machine shop, jobbing and repair

(G-6016)
SPECTRACAM LTD
1112 East Race Dr (45404)
PHONE..................937 223-3805
Joseph Wendling, *Managing Member*
EMP: 7 **EST:** 1998
SQ FT: 6,300
SALES (est): 3.74MM **Privately Held**
Web: www.spectracam.com
SIC: 3544 3543 Special dies, tools, jigs, and fixtures; Industrial patterns

(G-6017)
SPECTRON INC
132 S Terry St (45403-2340)
P.O. Box 3518 (45401-3518)

PHONE..................937 461-5590
Betty Burnett, *Pr*
Jeff Bucher, *Pr*
EMP: 6 **EST:** 1966
SQ FT: 4,000
SALES (est): 426.14K **Privately Held**
Web: www.spectronus.com
SIC: 3679 Electronic circuits

(G-6018)
SPIEGLER BRAKE SYSTEMS USA LLC
Also Called: Spiegler Brake Systems USA
1699 Thomas Paine Pkwy (45459-2538)
PHONE..................937 291-1735
Matthias Schaub, *Managing Member*
▲ **EMP:** 6 **EST:** 1999
SQ FT: 3,500
SALES (est): 1.09MM **Privately Held**
Web: www.spieglerusa.com
SIC: 3751 5571 Motorcycles, bicycles and parts; Motorcycle parts and accessories

(G-6019)
SRC LIQUIDATION LLC (PA)
111 W 1st St (45402-1154)
P.O. Box 1167 (45401)
PHONE..................937 221-1000
Landen Williams, *Pr*
F David Clarke Iii, *Ch Bd*
Diana Tullio, *CIO*
Benjamin T Cutting, *CFO*
James M Vaughn, *Treas*
◆ **EMP:** 600 **EST:** 1912
SALES (est): 447.06MM
SALES (corp-wide): 447.06MM **Privately Held**
Web: www.taylor.com
SIC: 2761 2672 2677 2759 Manifold business forms; Labels (unprinted), gummed: made from purchased materials; Envelopes; Promotional printing

(G-6020)
STACO ENERGY PRODUCTS CO
301 Gaddis Blvd (45403-1314)
PHONE..................937 253-1191
EMP: 28
SALES (corp-wide): 51.25MM **Privately Held**
Web: www.stacoenergy.com
SIC: 3677 3612 Baluns; Instrument transformers (except portable)
HQ: Staco Energy Products Co.
2425 Technical Dr
Miamisburg OH 45342
937 253-1191

(G-6021)
STAFFORD GAGE & TOOL INC
4606 Webster St (45414-4826)
P.O. Box 433 (45377-0433)
PHONE..................937 277-9944
Jeff Stafford, *Pr*
Judy Stafford, *Pr*
Jean Stafford, *VP*
Teresa Stafford, *VP*
EMP: 9 **EST:** 1947
SQ FT: 10,500
SALES (est): 2.03MM **Privately Held**
Web: www.staffordgt.com
SIC: 3599 Machine shop, jobbing and repair

(G-6022)
STANCO PRECISION MFG INC
Also Called: Ss Industries
1 Walbrook Ave (45405-2341)
PHONE..................937 274-1785
Stephen P Stanoikovich, *Pr*
Rhonda Stanoikovich, *Mgr*
▲ **EMP:** 9 **EST:** 1988

SQ FT: 8,000
SALES (est): 765.32K **Privately Held**
Web: www.stancoprecision.com
SIC: 3599 3544 Machine shop, jobbing and repair; Special dies and tools

(G-6023)
STANDARD REGISTER TECHNOLOGIES
600 Albany St (45417-3405)
PHONE..................937 443-1000
Joseph P Morgan Junior, *CEO*
EMP: 26
SALES (est): 479.13K **Privately Held**
Web: www.taylor.com
SIC: 2759 Commercial printing, nec

(G-6024)
STARWIN INDUSTRIES LLC
3387 Woodman Dr (45429-4100)
PHONE..................937 293-8568
Matthew Eberhardt, *CEO*
Rick Little, *
EMP: 50 **EST:** 1973
SQ FT: 30,000
SALES (est): 8.68MM
SALES (corp-wide): 38.58MM **Privately Held**
Web: www.starwin-ind.com
SIC: 7372 3728 3663 3599 Prepackaged software; Aircraft parts and equipment, nec; Radio and t.v. communications equipment; Machine and other job shop work
PA: Eti Mission Controls, Llc
3387 Woodman Dr
Dayton OH 45429
937 832-4200

(G-6025)
STAUB LASER CUTTING INC
Also Called: Staub Manufacturing Solutions
2501 Thunderhawk Ct (45414-3466)
PHONE..................937 890-4486
Steve Staub, *Pr*
Sandy Keplinger, *
EMP: 40 **EST:** 1997
SQ FT: 15,000
SALES (est): 8.94MM **Privately Held**
Web: www.staubmfg.com
SIC: 3599 Machine shop, jobbing and repair

(G-6026)
STECK MANUFACTURING CO LLC
1200 Leo St (45404-1650)
PHONE..................937 222-0062
Greg Carlson, *Pr*
▲ **EMP:** 13 **EST:** 1945
SALES (est): 13.51MM
SALES (corp-wide): 71.7MM **Privately Held**
Web: www.steckmfg.com
SIC: 3714 3599 Motor vehicle parts and accessories; Machine shop, jobbing and repair
PA: Cnl Strategic Capital, Llc
450 S Orange Ave Ste 1400
Orlando FL 32801
407 650-1000

(G-6027)
STOLLE MACHINERY COMPANY LLC
Also Called: Ultra Punch
7425 Webster St (45414-5817)
PHONE..................937 497-5400
Keith Gilmore, *Mgr*
EMP: 113
SALES (corp-wide): 492.99MM **Privately Held**
Web: www.stollemachinery.com

SIC: 3544 3496 Punches, forming and stamping; Miscellaneous fabricated wire products
PA: Stolle Machinery Company, Llc
6949 S Potomac St
Centennial CO 80112
303 708-9044

(G-6028)
STRYVER MFG INC
15 N Broadway St (45426-3555)
PHONE..................937 854-3048
Bruce J Flora, *Pr*
Thomas E Flora, *
Lucille Flora, *
EMP: 30 **EST:** 1994
SQ FT: 30,000
SALES (est): 4.32MM **Privately Held**
Web: www.stryver.com
SIC: 3599 3548 Machine shop, jobbing and repair; Welding apparatus

(G-6029)
SUGAR CREEK PACKING CO
1241 N Gettysburg Ave (45417-9513)
PHONE..................937 268-6601
Steve Shutte, *Mgr*
EMP: 6
SQ FT: 20,000
SALES (corp-wide): 700MM **Privately Held**
Web: www.sugarcreek.com
SIC: 2013 2011 Bacon, side and sliced: from purchased meat; Meat packing plants
PA: Sugar Creek Packing Co.
4320 Indeco Ct
Cincinnati OH 45241
513 551-5280

(G-6030)
SUPERIOR MACHINING INC
2946 Lindale Ave (45414-5521)
PHONE..................937 236-9619
Thomas Gilhooly, *CEO*
James Lewis, *
EMP: 32 **EST:** 2001
SQ FT: 16,764
SALES (est): 592.2K **Privately Held**
SIC: 3541 Milling machines

(G-6031)
SUPPLIER INSPECTION SVCS INC (PA)
2941 S Gettysburg Ave (45439-7912)
PHONE..................877 263-7097
Paul A Bowell, *Pr*
EMP: 11 **EST:** 1986
SQ FT: 50,000
SALES (est): 4.67MM
SALES (corp-wide): 4.67MM **Privately Held**
Web: www.sis-inspection.net
SIC: 3545 7389 Machine tool accessories; Inspection and testing services

(G-6032)
SUPPLY TECHNOLOGIES LLC
4704 Wadsworth Rd (45414-4222)
PHONE..................937 898-5795
EMP: 8
SALES (corp-wide): 1.66B **Publicly Held**
Web: supplytechnologies.com
SIC: 5085 3452 3469 Fasteners, industrial: nuts, bolts, screws, etc.; Bolts, nuts, rivets, and washers; Stamping metal for the trade
HQ: Supply Technologies Llc
6065 Parkland Blvd
Cleveland OH 44124
440 947-2100

(G-6033)
SURE TOOL & MANUFACTURING CO
429 Winston Ave (45403-1400)
PHONE..................937 253-9111
Jerrald Kuriger, *Pr*
Ruth Kuriger, *Sec*
Russell B Kuriger, *VP*
EMP: 23 **EST:** 1969
SQ FT: 14,000
SALES (est): 3.67MM **Privately Held**
Web: www.suretool.net
SIC: 3544 Special dies and tools

(G-6034)
SWIHART INDUSTRIES INC
5111 Webster St (45414-4227)
PHONE..................937 277-4796
EMP: 30 **EST:** 1978
SALES (est): 2.72MM **Privately Held**
Web: www.swihartindustries.com
SIC: 3599 Machine shop, jobbing and repair

(G-6035)
SYSTEMAX MANUFACTURING INC
6450 Poe Ave Ste 200 (45414-2655)
PHONE..................937 368-2300
Curt Rush, *Sec*
▲ **EMP:** 8 **EST:** 1980
SQ FT: 185,000
SALES (est): 748.31K **Publicly Held**
SIC: 5961 7373 3577 3571 Computers and peripheral equipment, mail order; Systems integration services; Computer peripheral equipment, nec; Electronic computers
PA: Global Industrial Company
11 Harbor Park Dr
Port Washington NY 11050

(G-6036)
T & L CUSTOM SCREENING INC
3464 Successful Way (45414-4320)
PHONE..................937 237-3121
Louise Edwards, *Pr*
Tonya Snapp, *Sec*
EMP: 7 **EST:** 1996
SQ FT: 6,500
SALES (est): 426.57K **Privately Held**
Web: www.tlcustomtees.com
SIC: 2759 5199 2395 2396 Screen printing; Advertising specialties; Embroidery products, except Schiffli machine; Automotive and apparel trimmings

(G-6037)
T & R WELDING SYSTEMS INC
1 Janney Rd (45404-1263)
PHONE..................937 228-7517
Mike Bozzo, *Pr*
▼ **EMP:** 15 **EST:** 1969
SQ FT: 15,000
SALES (est): 2.07MM **Privately Held**
Web: www.trwelding.com
SIC: 3496 7692 Miscellaneous fabricated wire products; Welding repair

(G-6038)
TARGETED CMPUND MONITORING LLC
2790 Indian Ripple Rd Ste A (45440-3639)
PHONE..................937 825-0842
Willie Steinecker, *CEO*
EMP: 6 **EST:** 2016
SALES (est): 848.48K **Privately Held**
Web: www.tcmglobalinc.com
SIC: 3826 Automatic chemical analyzers

(G-6039)
TAYLOR COMMUNICATIONS INC
600 Albany St (45417-3405)
PHONE..................937 221-1000

▲ = Import ▼ = Export
◆ = Import/Export

Jim Miller, *Mgr*
EMP: 24
SALES (corp-wide): 3.81B **Privately Held**
Web: www.taylor.com
SIC: 2761 2759 2752 8744 Manifold business forms; Commercial printing, nec; Commercial printing, lithographic; Facilities support services
HQ: Taylor Communications, Inc.
  1725 Roe Crest Dr
  North Mankato MN 56003
  866 541-0937

(G-6040)
TAYLOR COMMUNICATIONS INC
7755 Paragon Rd Ste 101 (45459-4052)
PHONE..............................732 356-0081
Brian Clark, *Mgr*
EMP: 13
SALES (corp-wide): 3.81B **Privately Held**
Web: shoptaylorpromo.espwebsite.com
SIC: 2761 Manifold business forms
HQ: Taylor Communications, Inc.
  1725 Roe Crest Dr
  North Mankato MN 56003
  866 541-0937

(G-6041)
TDI CO
6800 Poe Ave (45414-2530)
P.O. Box 13557 (45413-0557)
PHONE..............................937 898-9600
EMP: 7 **EST:** 2019
SALES (est): 2.83MM **Privately Held**
Web: www.tdi-airstarter.com
SIC: 3714 Motor vehicle parts and accessories

(G-6042)
TECHMETALS INC (PA)
345 Springfield St (45403-1240)
P.O. Box 1266 (45401-1266)
PHONE..............................937 253-5311
EMP: 93 **EST:** 1968
SALES (est): 13.81MM
SALES (corp-wide): 13.81MM **Privately Held**
Web: www.techmetals.com
SIC: 3471 Plating of metals or formed products

(G-6043)
TEKNOL INC (PA)
Also Called: Rubber Seal Products
5751 Webster St (45414-3520)
P.O. Box 13387 (45413-0387)
PHONE..............................937 264-0190
Kent Von Behren, *Pr*
R Von Behren, *Stockholder**
▲ **EMP:** 57 **EST:** 1976
SQ FT: 60,000
SALES (est): 11.69MM
SALES (corp-wide): 11.69MM **Privately Held**
Web: www.medallionrefinish.com
SIC: 2899 2891 5198 2851 Chemical preparations, nec; Sealants; Paints, varnishes, and supplies; Paints and allied products

(G-6044)
TERRA SURFACES LLC
6350 Frederick Pike (45414-2972)
PHONE..............................937 836-1900
▲ **EMP:** 8 **EST:** 2004
SQ FT: 20,000
SALES (est): 389.17K **Privately Held**
SIC: 3281 Stone, quarrying and processing of own stone products

(G-6045)
TESSEC LLC
5621 Webster St (45414-3518)
PHONE..............................937 576-0010
David Evans, *Pr*
EMP: 70 **EST:** 2007
SALES (est): 3.01MM **Privately Held**
Web: www.tessec.com
SIC: 3721 3599 3365 3724 Motorized aircraft ; Machine shop, jobbing and repair; Aerospace castings, aluminum; Aircraft engines and engine parts

(G-6046)
TESSEC MANUFACTURING SVCS LLC
Also Called: Tessec
5621 Webster St (45414-3518)
PHONE..............................937 985-3552
David Evans, *Pr*
EMP: 21 **EST:** 2010
SALES (est): 3.27MM **Privately Held**
Web: www.tessec.com
SIC: 3452 3544 3721 3761 Bolts, nuts, rivets, and washers; Special dies, tools, jigs, and fixtures; Aircraft; Guided missiles and space vehicles

(G-6047)
TESSEC TECHNOLOGY SERVICES LLC
5621 Webster St (45414-3518)
PHONE..............................513 240-5601
David Evans, *Prin*
EMP: 38 **EST:** 2013
SALES (est): 2.84MM **Privately Held**
SIC: 3728 Aircraft parts and equipment, nec

(G-6048)
THE F A REQUARTH COMPANY
Also Called: Requarth Lumber Co.
447 E Monument Ave (45402-1226)
P.O. Box 38 (45401-0038)
PHONE..............................937 224-1141
EMP: 30 **EST:** 1860
SALES (est): 4.78MM **Privately Held**
Web: www.requarth.com
SIC: 2431 2491 5211 2421 Millwork; Wood preserving; Lumber and other building materials; Sawmills and planing mills, general

(G-6049)
THE MEAD CORPORATION
4751 Hempstead Station Dr (45429-5165)
PHONE..............................937 495-6323
▲ **EMP:** 500
SIC: 2621 2631 2653 2656 Printing paper; Corrugating medium; Boxes, corrugated: made from purchased materials; Sanitary food containers

(G-6050)
THE VULCAN TOOL COMPANY
730 Lorain Ave (45410-2400)
PHONE..............................937 253-6194
▲ **EMP:** 7
Web: www.vulcantoolcompany.com
SIC: 3544 3542 3541 3643 Special dies and tools; Machine tools, metal forming type; Machine tools, metal cutting type; Current-carrying wiring services

(G-6051)
THOMAS CABINET SHOP INC
321 Gargrave Rd (45449-2465)
PHONE..............................937 847-8239
Jon Thomas, *Pr*
Don Thomas, *VP Opers*
Cherie Thomas, *Sec*

EMP: 10 **EST:** 1961
SQ FT: 11,800
SALES (est): 1.53MM **Privately Held**
SIC: 1542 1751 2541 2434 Commercial and office buildings, renovation and repair; Cabinet building and installation; Wood partitions and fixtures; Wood kitchen cabinets

(G-6052)
THREE BOND INTERNATIONAL INC
101 Daruma Pkwy (45439-7908)
PHONE..............................937 610-3000
EMP: 33
Web: www.threebond.com
SIC: 2891 Adhesives
HQ: Three Bond International, Inc.
  6184 Schumacher Park Dr
  West Chester OH 45069
  513 779-7300

(G-6053)
THRIFT TOOL INC
5916 Milo Rd (45414-3416)
PHONE..............................937 275-3600
Walter Jones, *Pr*
Jeff Jones, *VP*
EMP: 6 **EST:** 1990
SQ FT: 8,000
SALES (est): 484.2K **Privately Held**
Web: www.thrifttool.com
SIC: 3312 Tool and die steel and alloys

(G-6054)
THT PRESSES INC
Also Called: Tht Presses
7475 Webster St (45414-5817)
PHONE..............................937 898-2012
Mike Thieman, *Pr*
▲ **EMP:** 25 **EST:** 1977
SQ FT: 51,000
SALES (est): 4.83MM **Privately Held**
Web: www.thtpresses.com
SIC: 3542 Die casting machines

(G-6055)
TIPP MACHINE & TOOL INC
4201 Little York Rd (45414-2507)
PHONE..............................937 890-8428
EMP: 124
SIC: 3544 3599 7389 Special dies and tools; Machine shop, jobbing and repair; Grinding, precision: commercial or industrial

(G-6056)
TOGA-PAK INC
2208 Sandridge Dr (45439-1814)
P.O. Box Rr&Box363 (45409)
PHONE..............................937 294-7311
EMP: 40 **EST:** 1981
SALES (est): 3.33MM **Privately Held**
Web: www.ipack.com
SIC: 3081 5084 5199 Unsupported plastics film and sheet; Packaging machinery and equipment; Packaging materials

(G-6057)
TONEY TOOL MANUFACTURING INC
Also Called: Toney Tool
3488 Stop 8 Rd (45414-3428)
PHONE..............................937 890-8535
EMP: 9 **EST:** 1982
SALES (est): 2.36MM **Privately Held**
Web: www.toneytool.com
SIC: 3559 3544 7692 Automotive related machinery; Special dies and tools; Welding repair

(G-6058)
TOOLCRAFT PRODUCTS INC
1265 Mccook Ave (45404-2800)
P.O. Box 482 (45401-0482)
PHONE..............................937 223-8271
Mark W Klug, *Pr*
Thomas W Thompson, *
Henry Wagner Junior, *Treas*
Hugh E Wall Iii, *Sec*
Cherilynn M O'malley, *CFO*
EMP: 23 **EST:** 1939
SQ FT: 56,000
SALES (est): 2.88MM **Privately Held**
Web: www.toolcraftproducts.com
SIC: 3544 Die sets for metal stamping (presses)

(G-6059)
TOOLRITE MANUFACTURING INC
2608 Nordic Rd (45414-3424)
PHONE..............................937 278-1962
David Tangeman, *Pr*
Cindy Loy, *Mgr*
Tim Ryan, *VP*
EMP: 12 **EST:** 1996
SALES (est): 994.32K **Privately Held**
SIC: 3544 Special dies and tools

(G-6060)
TREADWAY MANUFACTURING LLC
8800 Frederick Pike (45414-1235)
PHONE..............................937 266-3423
Kenny Treadway, *CEO*
EMP: 8 **EST:** 2005
SALES (est): 888.75K **Privately Held**
Web: www.treadwaymfg.com
SIC: 3599 Machine shop, jobbing and repair

(G-6061)
TRI-STATE PAPER INC
9000 Kenrick Rd (45458-5300)
P.O. Box 447 (45068-0447)
PHONE..............................937 885-3365
EMP: 13 **EST:** 1979
SALES (est): 2.42MM **Privately Held**
SIC: 5199 2653 Packaging materials; Boxes, corrugated: made from purchased materials

(G-6062)
TRIANGLE PRECISION INDS INC
1650 Delco Park Dr (45420-1392)
PHONE..............................937 299-6776
Gerald D Schriml, *Pr*
Paul S Holzinger, *
EMP: 57 **EST:** 1982
SQ FT: 23,400
SALES (est): 3.92MM **Privately Held**
Web: www.triangleprecision.com
SIC: 3599 7692 3446 3444 Machine shop, jobbing and repair; Welding repair; Architectural metalwork; Sheet metalwork

(G-6063)
TRIFECTA TOOL AND ENGRG LLC
4648 Gateway Cir (45440-1714)
PHONE..............................937 291-0933
Bret West, *Managing Member*
▲ **EMP:** 9 **EST:** 2004
SQ FT: 15,000
SALES (est): 3.09MM **Privately Held**
SIC: 3089 Automotive parts, plastic

(G-6064)
TRIMBLE INC
Trimble Engineering
5475 Kellenburger Rd (45424-1013)
PHONE..............................937 233-8921
Chris Shephard, *Brnch Mgr*
EMP: 11
SALES (corp-wide): 3.68B **Publicly Held**

GEOGRAPHIC

Web: www.trimble.com
SIC: **3812** Navigational systems and instruments
PA: Trimble Inc.
10368 Westmoor Dr
Westminster CO 80021
720 887-6100

(G-6065)
TROY ENGNRED CMPNNTS ASSMBLIES
Also Called: Teca
4900 Webster St (45414-4831)
PHONE..............................937 335-8070
Marvin Sauner, *Pr*
Jack Spencer, *VP*
Tony Vukufich, *AR Vice President*
Larry Ishmael, *Sec*
EMP: 8 EST: 2005
SALES (est): 879.56K **Privately Held**
Web: www.tecaassembly.com
SIC: **3011** Tire and inner tube materials and related products

(G-6066)
TRUSSCORE USA INC
6161 Ventnor Ave (45414-2651)
P.O. Box 695 (45377-0695)
PHONE..............................888 418-4679
Steve Bosman, *Dir*
David Caputo, *
Joel Koops, *
EMP: 45 EST: 2017
SALES (est): 30MM **Privately Held**
Web: www.trusscore.com
SIC: **3089** Plastics hardware and building products

(G-6067)
TUF-TUG INC
3434 Encrete Ln (45439-1946)
PHONE..............................937 299-1213
Joseph F Deuer Junior, *Pr*
Louise Deuer, *Treas*
▲ EMP: 18 EST: 1987
SQ FT: 27,000
SALES (est): 3.69MM **Privately Held**
Web: www.tuf-tug.com
SIC: **3544** 7539 Special dies, tools, jigs, and fixtures; Machine shop, automotive

(G-6068)
U S CHROME CORPORATION OHIO
Also Called: Production Plant
107 Westboro St (45417-4055)
PHONE..............................877 872-7716
Greg Santo, *Brnch Mgr*
EMP: 12
SQ FT: 8,000
SALES (corp-wide): 38.62MM **Privately Held**
Web: www.uschrome.com
SIC: **3471** Electroplating of metals or formed products
HQ: U.S. Chrome Corporation Of Ohio
175 Garfield Ave
Stratford CT
937 224-0548

(G-6069)
UNIVERSAL TOOL TECHNOLOGY LLC
3488 Stop 8 Rd (45414-3428)
P.O. Box 31249 (45437-0249)
PHONE..............................937 222-4608
Michael Farmer, *Managing Member*
EMP: 6 EST: 2001
SQ FT: 45,000
SALES (est): 938.76K **Privately Held**
Web: www.universal-systems.net

SIC: **3544** 3599 Special dies and tools; Machine shop, jobbing and repair

(G-6070)
US AEROTEAM INC
2601 W Stroop Rd Ste 60 (45439-2030)
PHONE..............................937 458-0344
Suhas Kakde, *Pr*
Jeff Maag, *
EMP: 48 EST: 2005
SALES (est): 3.16MM **Privately Held**
Web: www.usaeroteam.com
SIC: **3728** Aircraft parts and equipment, nec

(G-6071)
VENTURE MFG CO
Also Called: Venture
3636 Dayton Park Dr (45414-4492)
PHONE..............................937 233-8792
▲ EMP: 25 EST: 1971
SALES (est): 7.56MM **Privately Held**
Web: www.venturemfgco.com
SIC: **3625** Actuators, industrial

(G-6072)
VITALS MATTER LLC
1398 Nature Ct (45440-4324)
PHONE..............................937 848-8871
EMP: 6
SALES (est): 513.4K **Privately Held**
Web: www.vitalsmatter.com
SIC: **7372** 7389 Application computer software; Business Activities at Non-Commercial Site

(G-6073)
VYRAL LLC
2078 E Dorothy Ln (45420-1112)
PHONE..............................937 993-7765
EMP: 12 EST: 2020
SALES (est): 3.86MM **Privately Held**
Web: www.vyralteq.com
SIC: **3577** Computer peripheral equipment, nec

(G-6074)
WALTER NORTH
900 Pimlico Dr Apt 2a (45459-8265)
PHONE..............................937 204-6050
Walter North, *Owner*
EMP: 11 EST: 2017
SALES (est): 498.93K **Privately Held**
SIC: **3571** 7389 Electronic computers; Business services, nec

(G-6075)
WASCA LLC
750 Rosedale Dr (45402-5758)
PHONE..............................937 723-9031
EMP: 50
SIC: **3089** Plastics and fiberglass tanks

(G-6076)
WATSON HARAN & COMPANY INC
Also Called: Manoranjan Shaffer & Heidkamp
1500 Yankee Park Pl (45458-1878)
PHONE..............................937 436-1414
Angie Shaffer, *Mgr*
EMP: 6
Web: www.haranwatson.com
SIC: **8721** 2759 Certified public accountant; Financial note and certificate printing and engraving
PA: Watson Haran & Company Inc
445 Hutchinson Ave # 695
Columbus OH 43235

(G-6077)
WELDMENTS INC
167 Heid Ave (45404-1217)

P.O. Box 320 (45404-0320)
PHONE..............................937 235-9261
James Hackenberger, *Pr*
John Limberg, *Sec*
Chuck Kraft, *VP*
EMP: 12 EST: 1985
SQ FT: 10,000
SALES (est): 939.44K
SALES (corp-wide): 3.61MM **Privately Held**
Web: www.weldments.com
SIC: **7692** 1799 Welding repair; Welding on site
PA: Precision Metal Fabrication, Inc.
191 Heid Ave
Dayton OH 45404
937 235-9261

(G-6078)
WESTBROOK MFG INC
Also Called: Westbrook Manufacturing
600 N Irwin St (45403-1388)
PHONE..............................937 254-2004
▲ EMP: 270
Web: www.westbrookohio.com
SIC: **3599** 3679 3714 3613 Machine and other job shop work; Harness assemblies, for electronic use: wire or cable; Motor vehicle parts and accessories; Switchgear and switchboard apparatus

(G-6079)
WESTROCK MWV LLC
Consumer & Office Products Div
10 W 2nd St (45402-1791)
PHONE..............................937 495-6323
Patricia B Robinson, *Mgr*
EMP: 56
Web: www.westrock.com
SIC: **2678** Stationery products
HQ: Westrock Mwv, Llc
3500 45th St Sw
Lanett AL 36863
804 444-1000

(G-6080)
WESTWOOD FBRCTION SHTMETAL INC
1752 Stanley Ave (45404-1117)
PHONE..............................937 837-0494
Larry Highlander, *Pr*
EMP: 27 EST: 1995
SQ FT: 25,000
SALES (est): 4.64MM **Privately Held**
Web: www.westwoodfabrication.com
SIC: **3441** Fabricated structural metal

(G-6081)
WFSR HOLDINGS LLC
220 E Monument Ave (45402-1287)
PHONE..............................877 735-4966
Tim Tatman, *Pr*
Tom Koenig, *VP*
▲ EMP: 1032 EST: 2010
SALES (est): 891.89K
SALES (corp-wide): 447.06MM **Privately Held**
SIC: **2752** 2754 2759 2761 Commercial printing, lithographic; Commercial printing, gravure; Commercial printing, nec; Manifold business forms
PA: Src Liquidation Llc
111 W First St
Dayton OH 45402
937 221-1000

(G-6082)
WINKLER CO INC
Also Called: Oakwood Register, The
435 Patterson Rd (45419-4344)
P.O. Box 572 (45409-0572)

PHONE..............................937 294-2662
Dolores Winkler, *Pr*
Lance A Winkler, *VP*
Dana M Winkler, *Sec*
EMP: 6 EST: 1960
SQ FT: 2,700
SALES (est): 241.37K **Privately Held**
Web: www.oakwoodregister.com
SIC: **2711** 2791 Newspapers: publishing only, not printed on site; Typesetting

(G-6083)
WINSTON HEAT TREATING INC
711 E 2nd St (45402-1319)
P.O. Box 1551 (45401-1551)
PHONE..............................937 226-0110
TOLL FREE: 800
John L Reger, *Pr*
EMP: 33 EST: 1967
SQ FT: 26,000
SALES (est): 4.67MM **Privately Held**
Web: www.winstonht.com
SIC: **3398** Metal heat treating

(G-6084)
WISCO PRODUCTS INCORPORATED
109 Commercial St (45402-2297)
PHONE..............................937 228-2101
Mark Paxson, *Pr*
EMP: 30 EST: 1935
SQ FT: 23,000
SALES (est): 4.39MM **Privately Held**
Web: www.wiscoproducts.com
SIC: **3469** 3089 Metal stampings, nec; Caps, plastics

(G-6085)
WOODBURN PRESS LTD
405 Littell Ave (45419-3609)
P.O. Box 329 (45409-0329)
PHONE..............................937 293-9245
EMP: 6 EST: 1996
SQ FT: 10,000
SALES (est): 446.66K **Privately Held**
Web: www.woodburnpress.com
SIC: **2731** 2741 Book publishing; Posters: publishing and printing

(G-6086)
WORKER AUTOMATION INC
953 Belfast Dr (45440-3851)
PHONE..............................937 473-2111
Joe Hickey, *Pr*
Margrett Hickey, *Sec*
EMP: 8 EST: 1997
SQ FT: 14,000
SALES (est): 1.02MM **Privately Held**
SIC: **3548** 5084 7373 Welding apparatus; Robots, industrial; Computer integrated systems design

(G-6087)
WORKFLOWONE LLC
220 E Monument Ave (45402-1287)
P.O. Box 1167 (45401-1167)
PHONE..............................877 735-4966
◆ EMP: 2000
SIC: **2754** 2791 4225 4731 Forms, business: gravure printing; Typesetting; General warehousing and storage; Freight transportation arrangement

(G-6088)
WORLDWIDE BRANDS DIRECT LLC
Also Called: Custom Reptile Habitats
2609 Nordic Rd (45414-3423)
P.O. Box 27 (45377)
PHONE..............................937 991-0999
Paul Barclay, *CEO*
EMP: 10 EST: 2018
SALES (est): 1.02MM **Privately Held**

▲ = Import ▼ = Export
◆ = Import/Export

Web: www.customreptilehabitats.com
SIC: 3999 5999 Pet supplies; Miscellaneous retail stores, nec

(G-6089)
YODER INDUSTRIES INC (PA)
2520 Needmore Rd (45414-4204)
PHONE....................937 278-5769
Charles W Slicer, *Ch*
Ron Zeverka, *
Pam Stewart, *
Charles W Slicer, *Prin*
J B Yoder, *
EMP: 110 **EST:** 1956
SQ FT: 32,000
SALES (est): 4.51MM
SALES (corp-wide): 4.51MM **Privately Held**
Web: www.yoderindustries.com
SIC: 3363 3369 3471 3365 Aluminum die-castings; Nonferrous foundries, nec; Plating and polishing; Aluminum foundries

(G-6090)
ZIMMER ENTERPRISES INC (PA)
Also Called: Kettering Monogramming
911 Senate Dr (45459-4017)
PHONE....................937 428-1057
Jeffrey Zimmer, *Pr*
Patricia M Zimmer, *
▲ **EMP:** 24 **EST:** 1982
SALES (est): 2.43MM
SALES (corp-wide): 2.43MM **Privately Held**
Web: www.pbj-sport.com
SIC: 5137 2395 Women's and children's clothing; Embroidery products, except Schiffli machine

De Graff
Logan County

(G-6091)
ALAN BORTREE
Also Called: HI Standard Machine Co
8176 State Route 508 (43318-9624)
PHONE....................937 585-6962
Alan Bortree, *Owner*
EMP: 6 **EST:** 1967
SQ FT: 5,500
SALES (est): 1.33MM **Privately Held**
Web: www.hi-standardmachine.com
SIC: 3535 Conveyors and conveying equipment

(G-6092)
NATES NECTAR LLC
Also Called: Nate's Nectar
4684 Township Road 53 (43318-9669)
PHONE....................937 935-3289
EMP: 7 **EST:** 2017
SALES (est): 681.39K **Privately Held**
Web: www.natesnectarandmore.com
SIC: 2099 Honey, strained and bottled

Deerfield
Portage County

(G-6093)
FOUNDERS SERVICE & MFG INC (PA)
Also Called: Founder's Service Co
879 State Route 14 (44411-9777)
P.O. Box 56 (44449-0056)
PHONE....................330 584-7759
Doug Stanley, *Pr*
Thad Stanley, *Sec*
EMP: 6 **EST:** 1984

SQ FT: 8,000
SALES (est): 6.62MM
SALES (corp-wide): 6.62MM **Privately Held**
SIC: 3543 3544 Foundry cores; Forms (molds), for foundry and plastics working machinery

Defiance
Defiance County

(G-6094)
ADVANTAGE POWDER COATING INC (PA)
2090 E 2nd St Ste 102 (43512-8654)
PHONE....................419 782-2363
Joellen Hornish, *Pr*
Sam Hornish, *
EMP: 70 **EST:** 1992
SQ FT: 51,000
SALES (est): 919.79K **Privately Held**
Web: www.hornishgroup.com
SIC: 3479 Coating of metals and formed products

(G-6095)
AL-FE HEAT TREATING LLC
Aalberts Surface Technologies
2066 E 2nd St (43512-8654)
PHONE....................419 782-7200
Ernie Lackner, *Brnch Mgr*
EMP: 19
SALES (corp-wide): 41.55MM **Privately Held**
Web: www.aalberts-ht.us
HQ: Al-Fe Heat Treating, Llc
209 W Mount Hope Ave
Lansing MI 48910
517 485-5090

(G-6096)
APACHE ACQUISITIONS LLC
1008 Jackson Ave (43512-2797)
PHONE....................419 782-8003
Eric Westrick, *Prin*
EMP: 6 **EST:** 2008
SALES (est): 621.57K **Privately Held**
SIC: 1311 Crude petroleum production

(G-6097)
APACKAGING GROUP OHIO INC
25925 Commerce Dr (43512-1708)
PHONE....................419 785-8600
Helga Arminak, *CEO*
EMP: 10 **EST:** 2022
SALES (est): 4.49MM
SALES (corp-wide): 4.49MM **Privately Held**
Web: www.apackaginggroup.com
SIC: 3565 Packaging machinery
PA: Apackaging Group Llc
1350 Mountain View Cir
Azusa CA 91702
626 385-5858

(G-6098)
ARPS DAIRY INC
136 Fox Run Dr (43512-1394)
P.O. Box 803 (43512-0803)
PHONE....................419 782-9116
Stephen L Boomer, *Pr*
EMP: 18 **EST:** 1936
SALES (est): 5.16MM **Privately Held**
Web: www.arpsdairy.com
SIC: 5143 2026 Dairy products, except dried or canned; Fluid milk

(G-6099)
B & B MOLDED PRODUCTS INC
1250 Ottawa Ave (43512-3004)
P.O. Box 213 (43545)
PHONE....................419 592-8700
Donald V Gillett, *Pr*
▲ **EMP:** 40 **EST:** 1993
SQ FT: 55,000
SALES (est): 8.22MM **Privately Held**
Web: www.bbmolded.com
SIC: 3089 Injection molded finished plastics products, nec

(G-6100)
BAKER-SHINDLER CONTRACTING CO (PA)
Also Called: Baker-Shindler Builders Sup Co
525 Cleveland Ave (43512-3546)
P.O. Box 488 (43512-0488)
PHONE....................419 782-5080
TOLL FREE: 800
Douglas Shindler, *Pr*
EMP: 20 **EST:** 1921
SQ FT: 8,500
SALES (est): 4.64MM
SALES (corp-wide): 4.64MM **Privately Held**
Web: www.baker-shindler.com
SIC: 1542 1541 3273 Specialized public building contractors; Industrial buildings, new construction, nec; Ready-mixed concrete

(G-6101)
CBS BORING AND MCH CO INC
2064 E 2nd St (43512-8654)
PHONE....................419 784-9500
Dave Hodell, *Mgr*
EMP: 15
SALES (corp-wide): 24.88MM **Privately Held**
Web: www.cbsboring.com
SIC: 3599 Machine shop, jobbing and repair
PA: C.B.S. Boring And Machine Company, Inc.
33750 Riviera
Fraser MI 48026
586 294-7540

(G-6102)
CENTER CONCRETE INC
24187 Jewell Rd (43512-9135)
PHONE....................419 782-2495
Don Pahl, *Brnch Mgr*
EMP: 9
Web: www.centerconcreteinc.com
SIC: 3273 Ready-mixed concrete
PA: Center Concrete, Inc.
8790 Us Rt 6
Edgerton OH 43517

(G-6103)
CLEMENS MOBILE WELDING LLC
25239 Commerce Dr (43512-1790)
PHONE....................419 782-4220
Scott Clemens, *Managing Member*
Sherri Hammersmith, *
EMP: 25 **EST:** 1989
SALES (est): 1.54MM **Privately Held**
Web: www.clemensmobilewelding.com
SIC: 7692 Welding repair

(G-6104)
DECKED LLC
25401 Elliott Rd (43512-9003)
PHONE....................208 806-0251
Bryan Perry, *Brnch Mgr*
EMP: 10
SALES (corp-wide): 34.7MM **Privately Held**
Web: www.decked.com

SIC: 3542 Machine tools, metal forming type
PA: Decked, L.L.C.
110 Lindsay Cir
Ketchum ID 83340
208 806-0251

(G-6105)
DEFIANCE METAL PRODUCTS CO (HQ)
21 Seneca St (43512-2274)
PHONE....................419 784-5332
Stephen Mance, *CEO*
Sam Strausbaugh, *
Joellen Frederick, *
Don Johnson, *
Rick Creedmore, *
▲ **EMP:** 475 **EST:** 1939
SQ FT: 165,000
SALES (est): 68.44MM
SALES (corp-wide): 581.6MM **Publicly Held**
Web: www.mecinc.com
SIC: 3443 3544 Fabricated plate work (boiler shop); Special dies and tools
PA: Mayville Engineering Co Inc
135 S 84th St Ste 300
Milwaukee WI 53214
414 381-2860

(G-6106)
DEFIANCE PUBLISHING CO LTD
Also Called: Defiance Crescent News, The
624 W 2nd St (43512-2161)
P.O. Box 249 (43512-0249)
PHONE....................419 784-5441
Mark Adams, *Pr*
EMP: 476 **EST:** 1888
SQ FT: 9,000
SALES (est): 1.51MM
SALES (corp-wide): 38.43MM **Privately Held**
Web: www.crescent-news.com
SIC: 2711 Commercial printing and newspaper publishing combined
PA: Dix 1898, Inc.
212 E Liberty St
Wooster OH
330 264-3511

(G-6107)
GENERAL MOTORS LLC
Also Called: General Motors
26427 State Route 281 (43512-6781)
PHONE....................419 792-7010
Thomas Galither, *Mgr*
EMP: 505
Web: www.gm.com
SIC: 3321 3322 3365 3369 Gray iron castings, nec; Malleable iron foundries; Aluminum and aluminum-based alloy castings; Nonferrous foundries, nec
HQ: General Motors Llc
300 Rnaissance Ctr Ste L1
Detroit MI 48243

(G-6108)
GODFREY & WING INC
2066 E 2nd St (43512-8654)
PHONE....................419 980-4616
John Horvath, *Brnch Mgr*
EMP: 10
SALES (corp-wide): 10.26MM **Privately Held**
Web: www.godfreywing.com
SIC: 3823 Absorption analyzers: infrared, x-ray, etc.: industrial
PA: Godfrey & Wing Inc.
220 Campus Dr
Aurora OH 44202
330 562-1440

(G-6109)
GT TECHNOLOGIES INC
Also Called: Defiance Operations
1125 Precision Way (43512-1919)
PHONE..............................419 782-8955
Joe Molnar, *Manager*
EMP: 50
SALES (corp-wide): 283.29MM **Privately Held**
Web: www.gttechnologies.com
SIC: 3714 3562 3599 3398 Motor vehicle engines and parts; Ball and roller bearings; Machine shop, jobbing and repair; Metal heat treating
PA: Gt Technologies, Inc.
5859 E Executive Dr
Westland MI 48185
734 467-8371

(G-6110)
HILLTOP PRINTING
1815 Baltimore St (43512-1913)
PHONE..............................419 782-9898
Verle L Harner, *Owner*
EMP: 6 **EST:** 1970
SQ FT: 5,000
SALES (est): 138.7K **Privately Held**
Web: www.hilltopprinting.ca
SIC: 2752 Offset printing

(G-6111)
HUBBARD COMPANY
612 Clinton St (43512-2637)
P.O. Box 100 (43512-0100)
PHONE..............................419 784-4455
E Keith Hubbard, *Ch Bd*
Thomas K Hubbard, *
Stephen F Hubbard, *
Jean A Hubbard, *
EMP: 44 **EST:** 1906
SQ FT: 20,000
SALES (est): 2.24MM **Privately Held**
Web: www.friendsoffice.com
SIC: 5943 5192 2752 2732 Office forms and supplies; Books; Offset printing; Book printing

(G-6112)
INNOVATIVE FOOD PROCESSORS INC
136 Fox Run Dr (43512-1394)
PHONE..............................507 334-2730
EMP: 6 **EST:** 2019
SALES (est): 737.47K **Privately Held**
SIC: 2899 Chemical preparations, nec

(G-6113)
JOHNS MANVILLE CORPORATION
1410 Columbus Ave (43512-3181)
P.O. Box 7188 (43512-7188)
PHONE..............................419 782-0180
Randy Engel, *Genl Mgr*
EMP: 60
SALES (corp-wide): 424.23B **Publicly Held**
Web: www.jm.com
SIC: 3296 Mineral wool
HQ: Johns Manville Corporation
717 17th St
Denver CO 80202
303 978-2000

(G-6114)
JOHNS MANVILLE CORPORATION
925 Carpenter Rd (43512-1765)
PHONE..............................419 784-7000
Roger Snow, *Mgr*
EMP: 90
SALES (corp-wide): 424.23B **Publicly Held**
Web: www.jm.com

SIC: 3296 Fiberglass insulation
HQ: Johns Manville Corporation
717 17th St
Denver CO 80202
303 978-2000

(G-6115)
JOHNS MANVILLE CORPORATION
3rd And Perry (43512)
P.O. Box 158 (43512-0158)
PHONE..............................419 784-7000
Jerry Henry, *Pr*
EMP: 25
SALES (corp-wide): 424.23B **Publicly Held**
Web: www.jm.com
SIC: 3296 Fiberglass insulation
HQ: Johns Manville Corporation
717 17th St
Denver CO 80202
303 978-2000

(G-6116)
JOHNS MANVILLE CORPORATION
408 Perry St (43512-2122)
PHONE..............................419 878-8111
Craig Mckibben, *Mgr*
EMP: 37
SALES (corp-wide): 424.23B **Publicly Held**
Web: www.jm.com
SIC: 3296 Fiberglass insulation
HQ: Johns Manville Corporation
717 17th St
Denver CO 80202
303 978-2000

(G-6117)
KOESTER MACHINED PRODUCTS CO
136 Fox Run Dr (43512-1394)
PHONE..............................419 782-0291
William C Koester, *Dir*
Jeanette Spiller, *Sec*
Michael Koester, *Pr*
EMP: 6 **EST:** 1990
SQ FT: 21,000
SALES (est): 157.85K **Privately Held**
SIC: 3599 Machine shop, jobbing and repair

(G-6118)
M W SOLUTIONS LLC
1802 Baltimore St Ste B (43512-2081)
PHONE..............................419 782-1611
Matthew Winzeler, *Managing Member*
EMP: 10 **EST:** 2010
SALES (est): 2.15MM **Privately Held**
Web: www.mwsolutionsllc.com
SIC: 3089 3694 3559 Automotive parts, plastic; Alternators, automotive; Automotive related machinery

(G-6119)
MARC V CONCEPTS INC
Also Called: Figley Stamping Company
401 Agnes St (43512-3072)
PHONE..............................419 782-6505
Christopher Slee, *Pr*
Rick Behnfeldt, *VP*
▼ **EMP:** 10 **EST:** 1993
SQ FT: 23,000
SALES (est): 1.31MM **Privately Held**
Web: www.figleystamping.com
SIC: 3469 Stamping metal for the trade

(G-6120)
MARTIN DIESEL INC
27809 County Road 424 (43512-8147)
P.O. Box 1000 (43512-1000)
PHONE..............................419 782-9911
James M Martin Junior, *Pr*

Cliff Martin, *VP*
EMP: 21 **EST:** 1977
SQ FT: 17,500
SALES (est): 2.4MM **Privately Held**
Web: www.martindiesel.com
SIC: 3621 5013 5531 5084 Generators and sets, electric; Automotive supplies and parts ; Truck equipment and parts; Engines and parts, diesel

(G-6121)
MEEKS PASTRY SHOP
315 Clinton St (43512-2113)
PHONE..............................419 782-4871
William Meek, *Owner*
EMP: 6 **EST:** 1925
SQ FT: 2,500
SALES (est): 256.76K **Privately Held**
SIC: 2051 5461 Bread, cake, and related products; Pastries

(G-6122)
NOSTALGIC IMAGES INC
26012 Nostalgic Rd (43512-7108)
PHONE..............................419 784-1728
William Westrick, *Pr*
Lynda Sue Westrick, *
Clay W Balyeat, *
▲ **EMP:** 24 **EST:** 1997
SQ FT: 60,000
SALES (est): 2.01MM **Privately Held**
Web: www.nostalgicimages.com
SIC: 3499 Picture frames, metal

(G-6123)
SENSORYFFCTS POWDR SYSTEMS INC
136 Fox Run Dr (43512-1394)
PHONE..............................419 783-5518
Charles A Nicolais, *CEO*
◆ **EMP:** 70 **EST:** 1870
SQ FT: 160,000
SALES (est): 14.46MM
SALES (corp-wide): 953.68MM **Publicly Held**
Web: www.balchem.com
SIC: 2099 Food preparations, nec
HQ: Sensoryeffects, Inc.
13723 Rverport Dr Ste 201
Maryland Heights MO 63043

(G-6124)
STANDRIDGE COLOR CORPORATION
1122 Integrity Dr (43512-1948)
PHONE..............................770 464-3362
EMP: 12
SALES (corp-wide): 345MM **Privately Held**
Web: www.standridgecolor.com
SIC: 2865 Cyclic crudes and intermediates
PA: Standridge Color Corporation
1196 E Hightower Trl
Social Circle GA 30025
770 464-3362

(G-6125)
SUPERIOR BAR PRODUCTS INC
1710 Spruce St (43512-2457)
PHONE..............................419 784-2590
Mark Crandall, *Pr*
Deb Wittenmyer, *Treas*
EMP: 6 **EST:** 1988
SQ FT: 7,000
SALES (est): 461.14K **Privately Held**
Web: www.superiorbarproducts.com
SIC: 3451 Screw machine products

(G-6126)
TRESSLERS PLUMBING LLC
9170 State Route 15 (43512-8642)
P.O. Box 433 (43512-0433)
PHONE..............................419 784-2142
EMP: 7 **EST:** 1987
SALES (est): 942.59K **Privately Held**
SIC: 1481 Pumping or draining, nonmetallic mineral mines

(G-6127)
WERLOR INC
Also Called: Werlor Waste Control
1420 Ralston Ave (43512-1380)
PHONE..............................419 784-4285
Casey Wertz, *Pr*
Gerald Wertz, *
Mark Hageman, *
Tom Taylor, *
Casey Wertz, *VP*
EMP: 16 **EST:** 1969
SQ FT: 8,000
SALES (est): 2.37MM **Privately Held**
Web: www.werlor.com
SIC: 2875 4212 4953 Compost; Garbage collection and transport, no disposal; Recycling, waste materials

---

Delaware
Delaware County

(G-6128)
ACI INDUSTRIES LTD (PA)
970 Pittsburgh Dr Frnt (43015-3872)
PHONE..............................740 368-4160
Ralph Paglieri, *Pt*
Scott H Fischer, *
Helen Harper, *
◆ **EMP:** 49 **EST:** 1984
SQ FT: 225,000
SALES (est): 10MM
SALES (corp-wide): 10MM **Privately Held**
Web: www.aci-industries.com
SIC: 3341 5093 3339 Secondary nonferrous metals; Scrap and waste materials; Primary nonferrous metals, nec

(G-6129)
ACI INDUSTRIES CONVERTING LTD (HQ)
Also Called: J and J Sales
970 Pittsburgh Dr (43015-3872)
PHONE..............................740 368-4160
Mike Paglieri, *Genl Pt*
◆ **EMP:** 17 **EST:** 1990
SQ FT: 232,000
SALES (est): 4.25MM
SALES (corp-wide): 10MM **Privately Held**
Web: www.aci-industries.com
SIC: 2676 5113 Towels, napkins, and tissue paper products; Towels, paper
PA: Aci Industries, Ltd.
970 Pittsburgh Dr
Delaware OH 43015
740 368-4160

(G-6130)
AMERICAN APEX CORPORATION
105 Innovation Ct Ste I (43015-4351)
PHONE..............................614 652-2000
Charles Torson, *Pr*
Charles R Torson, *Pr*
Sherry H Torson, *Sec*
▲ **EMP:** 10 **EST:** 1991
SQ FT: 16,000
SALES (est): 2.25MM **Privately Held**
Web: www.americanapex.com

SIC: 3484 3489 3795 8748 Small arms; Ordnance and accessories, nec; Tanks and tank components; Safety training service

(G-6131)
ASSOCIATED HYGIENIC PDTS LLC
2332 Us Highway 42 S (43015-9502)
PHONE..................................770 497-9800
EMP: 560
SALES (corp-wide): 34.36MM Privately Held
Web: www.attindas.com
SIC: 2621 Paper mills
PA: Associated Hygienic Products Llc
1029 Old Creek Rd
Greenville NC 27834
800 428-8363

(G-6132)
ATKINS CUSTOM FRAMING LTD
3116 Troy Rd (43015-8799)
PHONE..................................740 816-1501
Mark A Atkins, *Prin*
EMP: 8 EST: 2015
SALES (est): 1.19MM Privately Held
Web: www.atkinscustomframing.com
SIC: 2499 Picture frame molding, finished

(G-6133)
ATTENDS HEALTHCARE PDTS INC
Also Called: Attindas Hygiene Partners
2332 Us Highway 42 S (43015-9502)
PHONE..................................740 368-7880
EMP: 8
SALES (corp-wide): 90.15MM Privately Held
Web: www.attends.com
SIC: 2676 Sanitary paper products
PA: Attends Healthcare Products Inc.
8020 Arco Corp Dr Ste 200
Raleigh NC 27617
800 428-8363

(G-6134)
BLACK WING SHOOTING CENTER LLC
3722 Marysville Rd (43015-9527)
PHONE..................................740 363-7555
Rex Gore, *Pr*
EMP: 9 EST: 2002
SALES (est): 2.36MM Privately Held
Web: www.blackwingsc.com
SIC: 7999 3949 Shooting range operation; Bases, baseball

(G-6135)
BUNS OF DELAWARE INC
Also Called: Buns Restaurant & Bakery
14 W Winter St (43015-1919)
PHONE..................................740 363-2867
Vasili Konstantinidis, *Pr*
EMP: 13 EST: 1864
SQ FT: 11,184
SALES (est): 162.74K Privately Held
Web: www.bunsrestaurant.com
SIC: 5812 5461 7299 2051 Eating places; Retail bakeries; Banquet hall facilities; Bread, cake, and related products

(G-6136)
CEDEE CEDAR INC (PA)
Also Called: Cedar Woodworking
3903 Us Highway 42 S (43015-9517)
PHONE..................................740 363-3148
Carl Reynolds, *CEO*
Kris Bargram, *Mgr*
EMP: 10 EST: 1985
SALES (est): 161.85K
SALES (corp-wide): 161.85K Privately Held

SIC: 2434 Wood kitchen cabinets

(G-6137)
CHARTER NEX FILMS - DELAWARE OH INC
Also Called: Charter Nex Films
1188 S Houk Rd (43015-3857)
PHONE..................................740 369-2770
EMP: 45
Web: cng-development.flywheelsites.com
SIC: 3081 2673 Unsupported plastics film and sheet; Plastic and pliofilm bags

(G-6138)
CHARTER NEXT GENERATION INC
1188 S Houk Rd (43015-3857)
PHONE..................................740 369-2770
EMP: 128
SALES (corp-wide): 1.5B Privately Held
Web: cng-development.flywheelsites.com
SIC: 2671 Plastic film, coated or laminated for packaging
PA: Charter Next Generation, Inc.
300 N La Slle Dr Ste 1575
Chicago IL 60654
608 868-5757

(G-6139)
CHROMA COLOR CORPORATION
100 Colomet Dr (43015-3846)
P.O. Box 690 (43015-0690)
PHONE..................................740 363-6622
Jeff Smik, *Brnch Mgr*
EMP: 55
SALES (corp-wide): 78.23MM Privately Held
Web: www.carolinacolor.com
SIC: 2821 Plastics materials and resins
PA: Chroma Color Corporation
3900 W Dayton St
Mc Henry IL 60050
877 385-8777

(G-6140)
CONCRETE ONE CONSTRUCTION LLC ✪
755 Us Highway 23 N Ste E (43015-6004)
PHONE..................................740 595-9680
Gerald Rowe Junior, *Managing Member*
EMP: 15 EST: 2023
SALES (est): 3.63MM Privately Held
SIC: 1389 1771 Construction, repair, and dismantling services; Concrete work

(G-6141)
DELAWARE CITY VINEYARD
32 Troy Rd (43015-4503)
PHONE..................................740 362-6383
Robb Morgan, *Prin*
EMP: 10 EST: 2009
SALES (est): 231.11K Privately Held
Web: www.delawarecityvineyard.org
SIC: 2084 Wines

(G-6142)
DELAWARE DATA PRODUCTS INC
Also Called: Ddp Mailing & Printing
439 Dunlap St (43015-4140)
PHONE..................................740 369-5449
Larry Garrett, *CEO*
Joe Garrett, *Pr*
EMP: 7 EST: 1986
SQ FT: 4,000
SALES (est): 266.08K Privately Held
SIC: 7389 2752 7374 Mailing and messenger services; Commercial printing, lithographic; Data processing service

(G-6143)
DELAWARE GAZETTE COMPANY
Also Called: Mid Ohio Net
40 N Sandusky St Ste 202 (43015-1973)
PHONE..................................740 363-1161
Roy Brown, *Pr*
Walter D Thomson Ii, *Pr*
Thomas T Thomson, *
Henry C Thomson, *
EMP: 11 EST: 1818
SQ FT: 20,000
SALES (est): 248.06K Privately Held
Web: www.delgazette.com
SIC: 2711 Commercial printing and newspaper publishing combined

(G-6144)
DIVERSE MFG SOLUTIONS LLC
970 Pittsburgh Dr Ste 22 (43015-3872)
PHONE..................................740 363-3600
EMP: 10 EST: 2010
SALES (est): 2.19MM Privately Held
Web: www.dms-site.com
SIC: 3542 Sheet metalworking machines

(G-6145)
EMERSON CORP
975 Pittsburgh Dr (43015-2858)
PHONE..................................614 841-5498
EMP: 7 EST: 2019
SALES (est): 1.66MM Privately Held
Web: www.emerson.com
SIC: 3823 Process control instruments

(G-6146)
ENGINEERED CONDUCTIVE MTL LLC
132 Johnson Dr (43015-8699)
PHONE..................................740 362-4444
Chuck Feeny, *Prin*
EMP: 8 EST: 2004
SALES (est): 122.96K Privately Held
SIC: 2891 Adhesives and sealants

(G-6147)
FEDERAL HEATH SIGN COMPANY LLC
1020 Pittsburgh Dr Ste A (43015-3878)
PHONE..................................740 369-0999
Ken Hermes, *Manager*
EMP: 57
Web: www.federalheath.com
SIC: 3993 Electric signs
HQ: Federal Heath Sign Company, Llc
1845 Prcnct Line Rd Ste 1
Hurst TX 76054

(G-6148)
FOUR NATURES KEEPERS INC
4651 Marysville Rd (43015-9528)
PHONE..................................740 363-8007
Willis J Whittaker, *Pr*
Nancy Pintavalli, *Sec*
EMP: 10 EST: 1997
SALES (est): 88.8K Privately Held
Web: www.natureskeepers.com
SIC: 2048 Bird food, prepared

(G-6149)
GREIF INC (PA)
Also Called: Greif
425 Winter Rd (43015-8903)
P.O. Box 8014 (43015)
PHONE..................................740 549-6000
Ole Rosgaard, *Pr*
Bruce Edwards, *
Lawrence A Hilsheimer, *Ex VP*
Gary R Martz, *Ex VP*
Bala V Sathyanarayanan, *Chief Human Resources Officer*

◆ EMP: 50 EST: 1926
SALES (est): 5.45B
SALES (est): 5.45B Publicly Held
Web: www.greif.com
SIC: 2449 2655 3412 3089 Shipping cases and drums, wood: wirebound and plywood; Fiber cans, drums, and similar products; Drums, shipping: metal; Plastics containers, except foam

(G-6150)
GREIF INC
Also Called: Grief Brothers
366 Greif Pkwy (43015-8260)
PHONE..................................740 657-6500
Kathy King, *Mgr*
EMP: 46
SALES (corp-wide): 5.45B Publicly Held
Web: www.greif.com
SIC: 2449 2655 3412 2653 Shipping cases and drums, wood: wirebound and plywood; Drums, fiber: made from purchased material; Drums, shipping: metal; Boxes, corrugated: made from purchased materials
PA: Greif, Inc.
425 Winter Rd
Delaware OH 43015
740 549-6000

(G-6151)
GREIF INC
Also Called: Independent Container
366 Greif Pkwy (43015-8260)
PHONE..................................740 657-6500
Max Marley, *Genl Mgr*
EMP: 6
SQ FT: 113,400
SALES (corp-wide): 5.45B Publicly Held
Web: www.greif.com
SIC: 2655 Fiber cans, drums, and similar products
PA: Greif, Inc.
425 Winter Rd
Delaware OH 43015
740 549-6000

(G-6152)
GREIF PACKAGING LLC (HQ)
Also Called: Corrchoice
366 Greif Pkwy (43015-8260)
PHONE..................................740 549-6000
Brian Dum, *CEO*
▲ EMP: 30 EST: 1983
SALES (est): 404.30MM
SALES (corp-wide): 5.45B Publicly Held
Web: www.greif.com
SIC: 3086 Packaging and shipping materials, foamed plastics
PA: Greif, Inc.
425 Winter Rd
Delaware OH 43015
740 549-6000

(G-6153)
GREIF USA LLC (DH)
366 Greif Pkwy (43015-8260)
PHONE..................................740 549-6000
EMP: 96 EST: 2005
SALES (est): 99.94MM
SALES (corp-wide): 5.45B Publicly Held
Web: www.greif.com
SIC: 2655 Fiber cans, drums, and similar products
HQ: Greif Packaging Llc
366 Greif Pkwy
Delaware OH 43015

(G-6154)
HALLIDAY TECHNOLOGIES INC
105 Innovation Ct Ste F (43015-4351)
PHONE..................................614 504-4150

Don Halliday, *CEO*
Don Halliday, *Pr*
Patricia Halliday, *VP*
EMP: 7 **EST:** 1994
SQ FT: 400
SALES (est): 3.03MM **Privately Held**
Web: www.hallidaytech.com
SIC: 3829 8711 Measuring and controlling devices, nec; Consulting engineer

(G-6155)
HARRIS INSTRUMENT CORPORATION
155 Johnson Dr (43015-8500)
P.O. Box 982 (43015)
PHONE..............................740 369-3580
Cathy Harris, *Pr*
David E Harris, *Stockholder*
Gary E Saum, *Stockholder*
John Harris, *Pr*
EMP: 9 **EST:** 1979
SQ FT: 10,000
SALES (est): 790.03K **Privately Held**
Web: www.harris-instrument.com
SIC: 3829 3823 3625 Measuring and controlling devices, nec; Process control instruments; Relays and industrial controls

(G-6156)
HENKEL US OPERATIONS CORP
Also Called: Henkel Surface Technologies
421 London Rd (43015-2493)
P.O. Box 363 (43015-0363)
PHONE..............................740 363-1351
Tony Neal, *Brnch Mgr*
EMP: 223
SQ FT: 1,634
SALES (corp-wide): 22.83B **Privately Held**
Web: www.henkel.com
SIC: 2841 2842 Detergents, synthetic organic or inorganic alkaline; Polishes and sanitation goods
HQ: Henkel Us Operations Corporation
　1 Henkel Way
　Rocky Hill CT 06067
　860 571-5100

(G-6157)
HOME CITY ICE COMPANY
150 Johnson Dr (43015-8699)
PHONE..............................419 562-4953
TOLL FREE: 800
Bryan Stuckman, *Mgr*
EMP: 10
SALES (corp-wide): 100.42MM **Privately Held**
Web: www.homecityice.com
SIC: 2024 2097 Ice cream and frozen deserts ; Manufactured ice
PA: The Home City Ice Company
　6045 Bridgetown Rd Ste 1
　Cincinnati OH 45248
　513 574-1800

(G-6158)
INTERNATIONAL PAPER COMPANY
International Paper
875 Pittsburgh Dr (43015-2860)
P.O. Box 8005 (43015-8005)
PHONE..............................740 369-7691
David Harbaugh, *Mgr*
EMP: 172
SALES (corp-wide): 18.62B **Publicly Held**
Web: www.internationalpaper.com
SIC: 2653 Boxes, corrugated: made from purchased materials
PA: International Paper Company
　6400 Poplar Ave
　Memphis TN 38197
　901 419-7000

(G-6159)
KHEMPCO BLDG SUP CO LTD PARTNR (PA)
Also Called: Arlington-Blaine Lumber Co
130 Johnson Dr (43015-8699)
PHONE..............................740 549-0465
James D Klingbeil Junior, *Genl Pt*
Richard Robinson, *Pt*
Donny Bowman, *Pt*
EMP: 100 **EST:** 1963
SALES (est): 2.04MM
SALES (corp-wide): 2.04MM **Privately Held**
Web: www.khempco.com
SIC: 5031 5211 2439 2431 Lumber: rough, dressed, and finished; Lumber and other building materials; Trusses, except roof: laminated lumber; Doors, wood

(G-6160)
LIBERTY CASTING COMPANY LLC (PA)
550 Liberty Rd (43015-8670)
PHONE..............................740 363-1941
William B Shearer, *Managing Member*
Jerry Harmeyer, *
Tom James, *
Troy Fischer, *
Viera Maruli, *
▲ **EMP:** 70 **EST:** 2003
SQ FT: 400,000
SALES (est): 24.41MM
SALES (corp-wide): 24.41MM **Privately Held**
Web: www.libertycasting.com
SIC: 3321 Gray iron castings, nec

(G-6161)
LUVATA OHIO INC (HQ)
Also Called: Luvata
1376 Pittsburgh Dr (43015-3814)
PHONE..............................740 363-1981
Jussi Helavirta, *Ch Bd*
Jyrki Vesaluona, *CEO*
Dirk Greywitt, *VP*
Carla Grispino, *Treas*
Robert Fleming, *Sec*
◆ **EMP:** 85 **EST:** 1946
SQ FT: 60,000
SALES (est): 27MM **Privately Held**
Web: www.luvata.com
SIC: 3548 Welding and cutting apparatus and accessories, nec
PA: Mitsubishi Materials Corporation
　3-2-3, Marunouchi
　Chiyoda-Ku TKY 100-0

(G-6162)
NAGASE CHEMTEX AMERICA LLC
100 Innovation Ct (43015-7532)
PHONE..............................740 362-4444
Somari De Wet Cntrl, *Prin*
▲ **EMP:** 49 **EST:** 1992
SQ FT: 20,000
SALES (est): 12.39MM **Privately Held**
Web: www.emsadhesives.com
SIC: 2891 Adhesives
HQ: Nagase Holdings America Corporation
　546 5th Ave Fl 19
　New York NY 10036
　212 703-1340

(G-6163)
NATIONAL LIME AND STONE CO
Also Called: National Lime Stone Clmbus Reg
2406 S Section Line Rd (43015-9518)
P.O. Box 537 (43015-0537)
PHONE..............................740 548-4206
Carolyn Coder, *Off Mgr*
EMP: 27
SALES (corp-wide): 86.85MM **Privately Held**

Web: www.natlime.com
SIC: 1422 Crushed and broken limestone
PA: The National Lime And Stone Company
　551 Lake Cascade Pkwy
　Findlay OH 45840
　419 422-4341

(G-6164)
NATIONAL METAL SHAPES INC
425 S Sandusky St Ste 1 (43015-3604)
PHONE..............................740 363-9559
John Vogel, *Pr*
▲ **EMP:** 25 **EST:** 1971
SQ FT: 85,000
SALES (est): 4.38MM **Privately Held**
Web: www.nationalmetalshapes.com
SIC: 3354 Aluminum extruded products

(G-6165)
OBERFIELDS LLC (HQ)
528 London Rd (43015-2850)
P.O. Box 362 (43015-0362)
PHONE..............................740 369-7644
Bruce Loris, *Pr*
EMP: 70 **EST:** 1961
SQ FT: 52,000
SALES (est): 21.04MM
SALES (corp-wide): 21.04MM **Privately Held**
Web: www.oberfields.com
SIC: 3272 Concrete products, precast, nec
PA: Oberfields Holdings Llc
　528 London Rd
　Delaware OH 43015
　740 369-7644

(G-6166)
PPG INDUSTRIES INC
Also Called: P P G Refinishing Group
760 Pittsburgh Dr (43015-3811)
PHONE..............................740 363-9610
Mike Tiehurst, *Mgr*
EMP: 6
SALES (corp-wide): 18.25B **Publicly Held**
Web: www.ppg.com
SIC: 2851 Paints and allied products
PA: Ppg Industries, Inc.
　1 Ppg Pl
　Pittsburgh PA 15272
　412 434-3131

(G-6167)
PPG INDUSTRIES OHIO INC
760 Pittsburgh Dr (43015-3811)
PHONE..............................740 363-9610
James Boyd, *Brnch Mgr*
EMP: 214
SALES (corp-wide): 18.25B **Publicly Held**
Web: www.ppg.com
SIC: 2851 Paints and allied products
HQ: Ppg Industries Ohio, Inc.
　3800 West 143rd St
　Cleveland OH 44111
　216 671-0050

(G-6168)
PRICE FARMS ORGANICS LTD
4838 Warrensburg Rd (43015-8589)
PHONE..............................740 369-1000
Tom Price, *Managing Member*
EMP: 13 **EST:** 1998
SQ FT: 1,000
SALES (est): 488.68K **Privately Held**
Web: www.pricefarms.org
SIC: 2875 Compost

(G-6169)
RJW TRUCKING COMPANY LTD
Also Called: Henderson Trucking
124 Henderson Ct (43015-8479)

PHONE..............................740 363-5343
Jack Henderson, *Managing Member*
EMP: 20 **EST:** 2000
SALES (est): 2.99MM **Privately Held**
Web: www.hendersontruckingohio.com
SIC: 1442 4212 Construction sand and gravel; Local trucking, without storage

(G-6170)
SAM DONG AMERICA INC
801 Pittsburgh Dr (43015-2860)
PHONE..............................740 363-1985
Ee Joo Lee, *Pr*
EMP: 14 **EST:** 2016
SALES (est): 2.55MM **Privately Held**
Web: www.samdongamerica.com
SIC: 3357 Magnet wire, nonferrous

(G-6171)
SAM DONG OHIO INC
801 Pittsburgh Dr (43015-2860)
PHONE..............................740 363-1985
Ee Joo Lee, *Pr*
▲ **EMP:** 75 **EST:** 2009
SALES (est): 26.29MM **Privately Held**
Web: www.samdongamerica.com
SIC: 3331 Primary copper
PA: Sam Dong Co.,Ltd.
　816-41 Samyang-Ro, Daeso-Myeon
　Eumseong 27673

(G-6172)
SANDRA WEDDINGTON
Also Called: Blend of Seven Winery
1400 Stratford Rd (43015-2922)
PHONE..............................740 417-4286
Sandra Weddington, *Owner*
EMP: 15 **EST:** 2011
SALES (est): 967.71K **Privately Held**
Web: www.blendofsevenwinery.com
SIC: 2084 5182 5921 Wines; Wine; Wine

(G-6173)
SKY CLIMBER FABRICATING LLC
1600 Pittsburgh Dr (43015-3884)
PHONE..............................740 990-9430
EMP: 7 **EST:** 2016
SQ FT: 84,000
SALES (est): 2.98MM **Privately Held**
Web: www.skyclimber.com
SIC: 3449 7692 Bars, concrete reinforcing: fabricated steel; Welding repair

(G-6174)
SKY CLIMBER WIND SOLUTIONS LLC
1800 Pittsburgh Dr (43015-3870)
PHONE..............................740 203-3900
EMP: 24 **EST:** 2007
SALES (est): 1.1MM **Privately Held**
Web: www.skyclimber-re.com
SIC: 3446 Scaffolds, mobile or stationary: metal

(G-6175)
STOVER INTERNATIONAL LLC
222 Stover Dr (43015-8601)
PHONE..............................740 363-5251
Dan Bloom, *Managing Member*
EMP: 25 **EST:** 2007
SALES (est): 2.4MM **Privately Held**
SIC: 3441 3549 3542 Fabricated structural metal; Assembly machines, including robotic ; Machine tools, metal forming type

(G-6176)
TJ CLARK INTERNATIONAL LLC
320 London Rd Ste 608 (43015-6407)
PHONE..............................614 388-8869
Eric Jenkusky, *CEO*

▲ = Import ▼ = Export
◆ = Import/Export

Eric Jenkusky, *Pr*
EMP: 15 **EST:** 2015
SQ FT: 2,200
SALES (est): 3.37MM **Privately Held**
Web: www.tjclarkintl.com
SIC: 3561 3441 Pumps and pumping
equipment; Fabricated structural metal

(G-6177)
VERTIV CORPORATION
Vertiv
975 Pittsburgh Dr (43015-2858)
P.O. Box 29186 (43229-0186)
PHONE.............................614 841-6078
Chris Crawrford, *Engr*
EMP: 111
SQ FT: 200,000
SALES (corp-wide): 8.01B **Publicly Held**
Web: www.vertiv.com
SIC: 3585 Air conditioning units, complete:
domestic or industrial
HQ: Vertiv Corporation
505 N Cleveland Ave
Westerville OH 43082
614 888-0246

(G-6178)
VITAMIN SHOPPE FLORIDA LLC
(DH)
Also Called: Nutri-Force Nutrition
109 Innovation Ct Ste J (43015-7759)
◆ **EMP:** 11 **EST:** 2001
SQ FT: 120,000
SALES (est): 3.71MM
SALES (corp-wide): 4.4B **Privately Held**
SIC: 2833 Vitamins, natural or synthetic:
bulk, uncompounded
HQ: Vitamin Shoppe Industries Llc
109 Innovation Ct Ste J
Delaware OH 43015

(G-6179)
VITAMIN SHOPPE INDUSTRIES LLC
(DH)
Also Called: Vitamin Shoppe, The
109 Innovation Ct Ste J (43015-7759)
EMP: 540 **EST:** 1977
SQ FT: 230,000
SALES (est): 437.24MM
SALES (corp-wide): 4.4B **Privately Held**
Web: www.vitaminshoppe.com
SIC: 5499 5961 2833 Vitamin food stores;
Pharmaceuticals, mail order; Vitamins,
natural or synthetic: bulk, uncompounded
HQ: Valor Acquisition, Llc
1716 Corp Landing Pkwy
Virginia Beach VA 23454

(G-6180)
WANNER METAL WORX INC
525 London Rd (43015-2849)
P.O. Box 1004 (43015-7104)
PHONE.............................740 369-4034
Craig Wanner, *Pr*
Richard Wanner Junior, *VP*
Rick Wanner, *
EMP: 50 **EST:** 1989
SQ FT: 250,000
SALES (est): 4.53MM **Privately Held**
Web: www.wannermetalworx.com
SIC: 3441 Fabricated structural metal

(G-6181)
WHITESIDE MANUFACTURING CO
309 Hayes St (43015-2189)
P.O. Box 322 (43015-0322)
PHONE.............................740 363-1179
Kirt Whiteside, *CEO*
Robert Whiteside, *
Terry Whiteside, *
▲ **EMP:** 40 **EST:** 1954

SQ FT: 75,000
SALES (est): 4.45MM **Privately Held**
Web: www.whitesidemfg.com
SIC: 3537 3429 Platforms, stands, tables,
pallets, and similar equipment; Hardware,
nec

Dellroy
Carroll County

(G-6182)
RNP INC
Also Called: Robert's Men's Shop
8014 Linden Dr Sw (44620-9747)
EMP: 7 **EST:** 1989
SALES (est): 680K **Privately Held**
SIC: 5661 5611 5699 2395 Men's shoes;
Clothing accessories: men's and boys';
Formal wear; Embroidery products, except
Schiffli machine

Delphos
Allen County

(G-6183)
A & J WOODWORKING INC
808 Ohio St (45833-1824)
PHONE.............................419 695-5655
Arnold Mohler, *Pr*
Jeff Mohler, *VP*
Jill Mohler, *Sec*
EMP: 8 **EST:** 1985
SALES (est): 862.9K **Privately Held**
Web: www.ajwoodworking.com
SIC: 1751 2541 2434 2431 Cabinet building
and installation; Wood partitions and fixtures
; Wood kitchen cabinets; Millwork

(G-6184)
DELPHOS HERALD INC (PA)
Also Called: Eagle Print
405 N Main St (45833-1598)
PHONE.............................419 695-0015
Murray Cohen, *Ch Bd*
Ray Geary, *Asst Tr*
EMP: 83 **EST:** 1962
SQ FT: 14,000
SALES (est): 8.87MM
SALES (corp-wide): 8.87MM **Privately**
Held
Web: www.dolphooherald.com
SIC: 2711 2752 Newspapers, publishing and
printing; Offset printing

(G-6185)
DELPHOS RUBBER COMPANY
1450 N Main St (45833-1150)
PHONE.............................419 692-3000
EMP: 20
SIC: 3069 Floor coverings, rubber
HQ: Delphos Rubber Company
715 Fountain Ave
Lancaster PA 17601
717 295-3400

(G-6186)
DELPHOS TENT AND AWNING INC
1454 N Main St (45833-1150)
PHONE.............................419 692-5776
TOLL FREE: 800
Andrew Wurst, *Pr*
Shellie Wurst, *VP*
Charlie Gerdeman, *Dir*
EMP: 9 **EST:** 1920
SQ FT: 5,000
SALES (est): 778.4K **Privately Held**
Web: www.delphostentawning.com

SIC: 2394 Canvas and related products

(G-6187)
HYDROFRESH LTD
Also Called: Hydrofresh Hpp
1571 Gressel Dr (45833-9187)
PHONE.............................567 765-1010
Don Klausing, *Pr*
Mike Billig, *VP*
EMP: 7 **EST:** 2017
SQ FT: 36,616
SALES (est): 2.12MM
SALES (corp-wide): 30.4MM **Privately**
Held
SIC: 2099 Food preparations, nec
HQ: Universal Pure, Llc
1601 Pioneer Blvd
Lincoln NE 68502
402 474-9500

(G-6188)
KNIPPEN CHRYSLER DDGE JEEP
INC
Also Called: Knippen Chrysler Dodge Jeep
800 W 5th St (45833-9212)
PHONE.............................419 695-4976
Ronald Knippen, *Pr*
John Klausing, *
Ronald Baumgarte, *
▲ **EMP:** 15 **EST:** 1981
SQ FT: 13,500
SALES (est): 972.19K **Privately Held**
Web:
www.knippenchryslerdodgejeep.com
SIC: 5511 5521 3714 7513 Automobiles,
new and used; Used car dealers; Motor
vehicle parts and accessories; Truck rental
and leasing, no drivers

(G-6189)
KRENDL MACHINE COMPANY
1201 Spencerville Rd (45833-2381)
PHONE.............................419 692-3060
Joe Krendl, *Pr*
Jeffrey Krendl, *Plant Operator*
Joseph Krendl, *Vice President Business*
Lee Krendl, *
▼ **EMP:** 70 **EST:** 1958
SQ FT: 55,000
SALES (est): 8.21MM **Privately Held**
Web: www.krendlmachine.com
SIC: 3599 3432 3827 Machine shop, jobbing
and repair; Plumbing fixture fittings and trim
; Optical instruments and lenses

(G-6190)
LAKEVIEW FARMS LLC (PA)
1600 Gressel Dr (45833-9153)
P.O. Box 98 (45833-0098)
PHONE.............................419 695-9925
Tom Davis, *CEO*
John Kopilchack, *VP*
Martin Garlock, *Treas*
EMP: 140 **EST:** 2011
SQ FT: 36,250
SALES (est): 1.12B
SALES (corp-wide): 1.12B **Privately Held**
Web: www.lakeviewfarms.com
SIC: 2099 2026 2022 Dips, except cheese
and sour cream based; Cream, sour;
Cheese; natural and processed

(G-6191)
ORVAL KENT FOOD COMPANY LLC
1600 Gressel Dr (45833-9153)
P.O. Box 369 (45833-0369)
PHONE.............................419 695-5015
EMP: 29
SIC: 2099 Ready-to-eat meals, salads, and
sandwiches

(G-6192)
RUBBER GRINDING INC
1430 N Main St (45833-1150)
P.O. Box 466 (45833-0466)
PHONE.............................419 692-3000
Ted Horstman, *Pr*
Rick Horstman, *VP*
◆ **EMP:** 100 **EST:** 1992
SQ FT: 50,000
SALES (est): 5.59MM
SALES (corp-wide): 5B **Publicly Held**
Web: www.midwestelastomers.com
SIC: 3069 5941 Mats or matting, rubber, nec
; Exercise equipment
HQ: Ultimate Rb, Inc.
1430 N Main St
Delphos OH 45833
419 692-3000

(G-6193)
TOLEDO MOLDING & DIE LLC
Also Called: Delphos Plant 2
24086 State Route 697 (45833-9203)
P.O. Box 393 (45833-0393)
PHONE.............................419 692-6022
Keith Riegle, *Mgr*
EMP: 189
SALES (corp-wide): 7.28B **Privately Held**
Web: www.tmdinc.com
SIC: 5031 3714 Molding, all materials; Motor
vehicle parts and accessories
HQ: Toledo Molding & Die, Llc
1429 Coining Dr
Toledo OH 43612

(G-6194)
TOLEDO MOLDING & DIE LLC
900 Gressel Dr (45833-9154)
P.O. Box 393 (45833-0393)
PHONE.............................419 692-6022
Jack Ruhe, *Mgr*
EMP: 161
SALES (corp-wide): 7.28B **Privately Held**
Web: www.tmdinc.com
SIC: 3089 3714 Injection molding of plastics;
Motor vehicle parts and accessories
HQ: Toledo Molding & Die, Llc
1429 Coining Dr
Toledo OH 43612

(G-6195)
ULTIMATE RB INC (DH)
1430 N Main St (45833-1150)
PHONE.............................419 692-3000
Marvin Wool, *Pr*
EMP: 12 **EST:** 2014
SALES (est): 6.7MM
SALES (corp-wide): 5B **Publicly Held**
Web: www.ultimaterb.com
SIC: 3069 Mats or matting, rubber, nec
HQ: Accella Performance Materials Inc.
2500 Adie Rd
Maryland Heights MO
314 432-3200

(G-6196)
ULTIMATE SYSTEMS LTD
1430 N Main St (45833-1150)
P.O. Box 465 (45833-0465)
PHONE.............................419 692-3005
◆ **EMP:** 50
Web: www.ultimatesystemsltd.com
SIC: 3069 Door mats, rubber

(G-6197)
US METALCRAFT INC
101 S Franklin St (45833-1936)
P.O. Box 308 (45833-0308)
PHONE.............................419 692-4962
Joel Birkmeier, *Pr*
Steve Birkmeier, *VP*

◆ **EMP:** 16 **EST:** 1959
SQ FT: 20,000
SALES (est): 4.09MM **Privately Held**
Web: www.usmetalcraft.com
SIC: 3365 Aluminum and aluminum-based alloy castings

(G-6198)
VAN WERT MACHINE INC
Also Called: Progressive Tool Division
210 E Cleveland St (45833-1941)
P.O. Box 40 (45833-0040)
PHONE..............................419 692-6836
Jesse F Hitchcock, *Pr*
Donald E Bechtol, *VP*
Gloria Bechtol, *Sec*
EMP: 6 **EST:** 1961
SQ FT: 18,600
SALES (est): 717.25K **Privately Held**
Web: www.progressive-tool.com
SIC: 3544 Special dies and tools

(G-6199)
VANAMATIC COMPANY
701 Ambrose Dr (45833-9179)
PHONE..............................419 692-6085
Jeffrey S Wiltsie, *Pr*
Perry J Wiltsie, *VP*
Patricia M Morris, *Sec*
EMP: 85 **EST:** 1954
SQ FT: 75,000
SALES (est): 8.47MM **Privately Held**
Web: www.vanamatic.com
SIC: 3451 Screw machine products

(G-6200)
WOOD CREATIONS
12805 State Rd (45833-9073)
PHONE..............................419 692-2624
Mark Wurst, *Owner*
EMP: 6 **EST:** 1996
SQ FT: 7,200
SALES (est): 323.58K **Privately Held**
Web: www.woodcreationscabinets.com
SIC: 2431 Millwork

Delta
Fulton County

(G-6201)
AREA 419 FIREARMS LLC
Also Called: Area 419
4750 County Road 5 (43515-9262)
PHONE..............................419 830-8353
EMP: 13 **EST:** 2013
SALES (est): 920.96K **Privately Held**
Web: www.area419.com
SIC: 5941 3489 Firearms; Artillery or artillery parts, over 30 mm.

(G-6202)
BEAVERSON MACHINE INC
11600 County Road 10 2 (43515-9748)
PHONE..............................419 923-8064
Ralph Beaverson, *Pr*
James Beaverson, *VP*
EMP: 6 **EST:** 1984
SQ FT: 3,000
SALES (est): 487.17K **Privately Held**
Web: www.beaversonmachine.com
SIC: 3599 Machine shop, jobbing and repair

(G-6203)
DELTA TOOL & DIE STL BLOCK INC
Also Called: Delta Tool & Die
5226 County Road 6 (43515-9648)
PHONE..............................419 822-5939
EMP: 28 **EST:** 1999
SQ FT: 27,500

SALES (est): 2.31MM **Privately Held**
Web: www.deltastamping.com
SIC: 3544 3469 Jigs and fixtures; Metal stampings, nec

(G-6204)
DESIGNER WINDOW TREATMENTS INC
302 Superior St (43515-1335)
P.O. Box 146 (43515-0146)
PHONE..............................419 822-4967
Leslie Zalecki, *Pr*
EMP: 8 **EST:** 1989
SALES (est): 303.06K **Privately Held**
SIC: 2591 Window blinds

(G-6205)
EDW C LEVY CO
Also Called: Fullton Mill Services
6565 County Road 9 (43515-9449)
P.O. Box 86 (43515-0086)
PHONE..............................419 822-8286
Paul Ruffner, *Mgr*
EMP: 8
SALES (corp-wide): 486.96MM **Privately Held**
Web: www.edwclevy.com
SIC: 4212 3295 Dump truck haulage; Minerals, ground or treated
PA: Edw. C. Levy Co.
9300 Dix Ave
Dearborn MI 48120
313 429-2200

(G-6206)
FULTON COUNTY PROCESSING LTD
7800 State Route 109 (43515-9335)
P.O. Box 67 (43515-0067)
PHONE..............................419 822-9266
James J Vanpoppel, *Managing Member*
▲ **EMP:** 125 **EST:** 2001
SALES (est): 24.45MM
SALES (corp-wide): 230.06MM **Privately Held**
Web: www.fcpltd.com
SIC: 3312 Stainless steel
HQ: Heidtman Steel Products, Inc.
2401 Front St
Toledo OH 43605
419 691-4646

(G-6207)
GB MANUFACTURING COMPANY (PA)
Also Called: Gb
1120 E Main St (43515)
P.O. Box 8 (43515-0008)
PHONE..............................419 822-5323
Nelson U Reyes, *Pr*
Annette Y Petree, *
Michael Pechette, *
Mark Ries, *
▲ **EMP:** 53 **EST:** 2005
SQ FT: 50,000
SALES (est): 69.43MM
SALES (corp-wide): 69.43MM **Privately Held**
Web: www.gbmfg.com
SIC: 3469 Machine parts, stamped or pressed metal

(G-6208)
GLENN HUNTER & ASSOCIATES INC
1222 County Road 6 (43515-9644)
PHONE..............................419 533-0925
Dean Daenens, *Prin*
James Clark, *
Glenn Hunter, *
Suzanne Hunter, *
▼ **EMP:** 75 **EST:** 1993
SQ FT: 2,500

SALES (est): 1.47MM **Privately Held**
Web:
www.glennhunterandassociates.com
SIC: 3559 Recycling machinery

(G-6209)
INDUSTRIAL REPAIR AND MFG
265 Rogers Rd (43515-9478)
PHONE..............................419 822-0314
EMP: 12
Web: www.irmworldwide.com
SIC: 7363 3443 Help supply services; Fabricated plate work (boiler shop)
PA: Industrial Repair And Manufacturing Inc
1140 East Main St
Delta OH 43515

(G-6210)
INDUSTRIAL REPAIR AND MFG (PA)
1140 E Main St (43515-9406)
PHONE..............................419 822-4232
TOLL FREE: 877
William H Toedter, *Pr*
Peggy J Toedter, *
▲ **EMP:** 42 **EST:** 1995
SQ FT: 48,000
SALES (est): 2.27MM **Privately Held**
Web: www.irmworldwide.com
SIC: 7699 7363 3443 Industrial machinery and equipment repair; Truck driver services ; Containers, shipping (bombs, etc.): metal plate

(G-6211)
MESSER LLC
6744 County Road 10 (43515-9453)
PHONE..............................419 822-3909
Mike Murphy, *Mgr*
EMP: 7
SALES (corp-wide): 2.29B **Privately Held**
Web: www.messeramericas.com
SIC: 2813 Industrial gases
HQ: Messer Llc
200 Smrset Corp Blvd Ste
Bridgewater NJ 08807
800 755-9277

(G-6212)
MID AMERICAN PUBLISHING
Also Called: Mid-American Publishing
7227 County Road D (43515-9623)
P.O. Box 329 (43515-0329)
PHONE..............................419 822-5662
Nancy J Cole, *Owner*
EMP: 6 **EST:** 1971
SALES (est): 226.93K **Privately Held**
SIC: 2721 2741 2711 Magazines: publishing only, not printed on site; Telephone and other directory publishing; Newspapers

(G-6213)
NATION TOOL & DIE LTD
5226 County Road 6 (43515-9648)
PHONE..............................419 822-5939
Jerami Nation, *Pr*
Lynette Nation, *CFO*
EMP: 20 **EST:** 2022
SALES (est): 1.24MM **Privately Held**
SIC: 3544 3469 Jigs and fixtures; Metal stampings, nec

(G-6214)
TWIN POINT INC (PA)
Also Called: Workman Electronics
11955 County Road 10-2 (43515-9748)
PHONE..............................419 923-7525
Jerry Twining, *CEO*
▲ **EMP:** 7 **EST:** 1977
SALES (est): 1.54MM
SALES (corp-wide): 1.54MM **Privately Held**

SIC: 3679 Electronic circuits

(G-6215)
WORKMAN ELECTRONIC PDTS INC
Also Called: Electrical Insulation Company
11955 County Road 10-2 (43515-9748)
PHONE..............................419 923-7525
Jerry Twining, *Pr*
Judy Eyer, *Ch Bd*
James Twining, *Sr VP*
Thomas A Yoder, *Prin*
▲ **EMP:** 6 **EST:** 1936
SQ FT: 24,400
SALES (est): 1.54MM
SALES (corp-wide): 1.54MM **Privately Held**
Web: www.workmanelectronics.com
SIC: 3679 Electronic circuits
PA: Twin Point Inc
11955 County Road 10 2
Delta OH 43515
419 923-7525

Dennison
Tuscarawas County

(G-6216)
BLOOMS PRINTING INC
Also Called: Blooming Services
4792 N 4th Street Ext Se (44621-8929)
PHONE..............................740 922-1765
Richard Bloom, *Pr*
Kay Bloom, *Sec*
EMP: 7 **EST:** 1990
SALES (est): 447.68K **Privately Held**
Web: www.bloomsprinting.com
SIC: 2752 Offset printing

(G-6217)
CLAPP & HANEY BRAZED TL CO INC
901 Race St (44621-1509)
P.O. Box 105 (44621-0105)
PHONE..............................740 922-3515
Richard Liggett, *Pt*
Tom Benner, *Pt*
EMP: 9 **EST:** 1935
SALES (est): 2.49MM **Privately Held**
Web:
www.clappandhaneybrazedtool.com
SIC: 3545 3599 Cutting tools for machine tools; Machine shop, jobbing and repair

(G-6218)
SERVICES ACQUISITION CO LLC
Also Called: Tank Services
4412 Pleasant Valley Rd Se (44621-9038)
P.O. Box 71 (44621-0071)
PHONE..............................330 479-9267
James Milano, *CEO*
EMP: 9 **EST:** 2014
SALES (est): 1.48MM **Privately Held**
Web: www.tankservices.com
SIC: 3731 Tankers, building and repairing

(G-6219)
UTICA EAST OHIO MIDSTREAM LLC
8349 Azalea Rd Sw (44621-9100)
PHONE..............................740 431-4168
EMP: 233 **EST:** 2012
SALES (est): 1.37MM
SALES (corp-wide): 10.5B **Publicly Held**
SIC: 1382 Oil and gas exploration services
HQ: Utica Gas Services, L.L.C.
525 Central Park Dr # 1005
Oklahoma City OK 73105
877 413-1023

(G-6220)
VALLEY MINING INC
4412 Pleasant Valley Rd Se (44621-9038)
P.O. Box 152 (44683-0152)
PHONE.............................740 922-3942
EMP: 130
SIC: 1221 1629 Auger mining, bituminous;
Land preparation construction

Derwent
Guernsey County

(G-6221)
BI-CON SERVICES INC
Also Called: BSI Group, The
10901 Clay Pike Rd (43733-9900)
P.O. Box 10 (43733)
PHONE.............................740 685-2542
EMP: 400 **EST:** 1971
SALES (est): 171.41MM **Privately Held**
Web: www.bi-conservices.com
SIC: 1623 3498 3443 Water, sewer, and
utility lines; Fabricated pipe and fittings;
Fabricated plate work (boiler shop)

Deshler
Henry County

(G-6222)
GRAMINEX LLC
2300 County Road C (43516-9756)
PHONE.............................419 278-1023
Justin Ritter, *Manager*
EMP: 15
SALES (corp-wide): 9.1MM **Privately Held**
Web: www.graminex.com
SIC: 2834 2833 Extracts of botanicals:
powdered, pilular, solid, or fluid; Medicinals
and botanicals
PA: Graminex, L.L.C.
95 Midland Rd
Saginaw MI 48638
989 797-5502

Dexter City
Noble County

(G-6223)
AMES COMPANIES INC
21460 Ames Ln (45727-9702)
P.O. Box 644 (13849-0644)
PHONE.............................740 783-2535
Jim Basham, *Brnch Mgr*
EMP: 27
SALES (corp-wide): 2.62B **Publicly Held**
Web: www.homebyames.com
SIC: 3423 Garden and farm tools, including
shovels
HQ: The Ames Companies Inc
13485 Veterans Way
Orlando FL 32827

(G-6224)
B&N COAL INC
38455 Marietta Rd (45727-6500)
P.O. Box 100 (45727-0100)
PHONE.............................740 783-3575
Carl Baker, *Pr*
Roger Osborne, *
Bob Cunningham, *
EMP: 33 **EST:** 1962
SQ FT: 21,000
SALES (est): 3.99MM **Privately Held**
SIC: 1221 8711 Strip mining, bituminous;
Engineering services

(G-6225)
WARREN DRILLING CO INC
Also Called: Warren Trucking
305 Smithson St (45727-9749)
P.O. Box 103 (45727-0103)
PHONE.............................740 783-2775
Dan R Warren, *Pr*
Randy C Warren, *
Emily Warren, *
Lewis D Warren, *
Paul H Warren, *
EMP: 110 **EST:** 1939
SALES (est): 9.89MM **Privately Held**
Web: www.warrendrilling.biz
SIC: 1381 Directional drilling oil and gas
wells

Diamond
Portage County

(G-6226)
CEMEX MATERIALS LLC
4200 Universal Dr (44412-9700)
PHONE.............................330 654-2501
Chris Rowland, *Mgr*
EMP: 113
SIC: 3273 Ready-mixed concrete
HQ: Cemex Materials Llc
1720 Cntrpark Dr E Ste 10
West Palm Beach FL 33401
561 833-5555

Donnelsville
Clark County

(G-6227)
BEACH MANUFACTURING CO
118 N Hampton Rd (45319-5011)
P.O. Box 129 (45319-0129)
PHONE.............................937 882-6372
Ted Beach, *Pr*
Carrie M Ridenaur, *
Louis Beach, *
EMP: 120 **EST:** 1943
SQ FT: 20,000
SALES (est): 8.97MM **Privately Held**
Web: www.beachmfgco.com
SIC: 3714 3231 Motor vehicle parts and
accessories; Mirrors, truck and automobile:
made from purchased glass

Dover
Tuscarawas County

(G-6228)
**ALLIED MACHINE & ENGRG CORP
(PA)**
120 Deeds Dr (44622-9652)
P.O. Box 36 (44622-0036)
PHONE.............................330 343-4283
Bill Stokey, *CEO*
Michael A Stokey, *
Steve Stokey, *
Gary Kropf, *
Dave Triplett, *
▲ **EMP:** 219 **EST:** 1933
SALES (est): 32.56MM
SALES (corp-wide): 32.56MM **Privately
Held**
Web: www.alliedmachine.com
SIC: 3545 Machine tool attachments and
accessories

(G-6229)
BAERLOCHER USA LLC (DH)
Also Called: Baerlocher

3676 Davis Rd Nw (44622-9771)
PHONE.............................330 364-6000
Ray Buehler, *CEO*
David Keubel, *CFO*
▲ **EMP:** 10 **EST:** 1990
SQ FT: 10,000
SALES (est): 21.44MM
SALES (corp-wide): 525.26MM **Privately
Held**
Web: www.baerlocher-usa.com
SIC: 2819 Nonmetallic compounds
HQ: Baerlocher Gmbh
Freisinger Str. 1
UnterschleiBheim BY 85716
89143730

(G-6230)
BFC INC (PA)
Also Called: Farmer Smiths Market
1213 E 3rd St (44622-1227)
PHONE.............................330 364-6645
William Barkett, *CEO*
James Barkett, *
Thomas Barkett, *
Ronald Barkett, *
EMP: 36 **EST:** 1924
SQ FT: 20,000
SALES (est): 1.22MM
SALES (corp-wide): 1.22MM **Privately
Held**
Web: www.barkettfruit.com
SIC: 5148 5143 5144 2099 Vegetables;
Dairy products, except dried or canned;
Eggs; Salads, fresh or refrigerated

(G-6231)
BOB SUMEREL TIRE CO INC
Also Called: Bandag
204 Deeds Dr (44622-9652)
PHONE.............................330 602-1733
EMP: 7
SALES (corp-wide): 35.8MM **Privately
Held**
Web: www.bandag.com
SIC: 7534 Tire retreading and repair shops
PA: Bob Sumerel Tire Co., Inc.
1257 Cox Ave
Erlanger KY 41018
859 283-2700

(G-6232)
BREITENBACH WINE CELLARS INC
Also Called: Breitenbach Bed & Breakfast
5934 Old Route 39 Nw (44622-7787)
PHONE.............................330 343-3603
Cynthia Bixler, *Pr*
EMP: 8 **EST:** 1980
SALES (est): 908.79K **Privately Held**
Web: www.breitenbachwine.com
SIC: 2084 5812 7011 Wines; Eating places;
Bed and breakfast inn

(G-6233)
CHO BEDFORD INC (PA)
2997 Progress St (44622-9639)
PHONE.............................330 343-8896
Jeff Headlee, *Mgr*
Jeff Headlee, *Managing Member*
EMP: 60 **EST:** 1950
SALES (est): 9.77MM
SALES (corp-wide): 9.77MM **Privately
Held**
Web: www.commercialfluidpower.com
SIC: 3492 Fluid power valves and hose
fittings

(G-6234)
CHO BEDFORD INC
Commercial Fluid Power
2997 Progress St (44622-9639)
PHONE.............................330 343-8896

Melvin White, *Brnch Mgr*
EMP: 25
SALES (corp-wide): 9.77MM **Privately
Held**
Web: www.commercialfluidpower.com
SIC: 3593 Fluid power cylinders, hydraulic or
pneumatic
PA: Cho Bedford, Inc.
2997 Progress St
Dover OH 44622
330 343-8896

(G-6235)
COMMERCIAL HONING LLC (DH)
Also Called: Commercial Fluid Power
2997 Progress St (44622-9639)
PHONE.............................330 343-8896
Jeff Headley, *Managing Member*
▲ **EMP:** 60 **EST:** 1946
SQ FT: 15,000
SALES (est): 11.13MM
SALES (corp-wide): 296.11MM **Privately
Held**
Web: www.commercialfluidpower.com
SIC: 3599 3471 3317 Machine shop, jobbing
and repair; Plating and polishing; Steel pipe
and tubes
HQ: National Tube Supply Company
925 Central Ave
University Park IL 60484

(G-6236)
DIRECT ACTION CO INC
Also Called: Dac
6668 Old Route 39 Nw (44622-7794)
P.O. Box 2205 (44622-1000)
PHONE.............................330 364-3219
Randy Jacobs, *Pr*
James Rhodes, *VP*
EMP: 15 **EST:** 1997
SALES (est): 5.53MM **Privately Held**
Web: www.feeddac.com
SIC: 5122 2048 Vitamins and minerals; Feed
supplements

(G-6237)
DOVER CABINET INDUSTRIES INC
1568 State Route 39 Nw (44622-7346)
PHONE.............................330 343-9074
John A Perkowski, *Pr*
Lori Ann Perkowski, *VP*
EMP: 16 **EST:** 1982
SQ FT: 16,000
SALES (est): 2.10MM **Privately Held**
Web: www.dovercabinet.com
SIC: 2434 Wood kitchen cabinets

(G-6238)
**DOVER CHEMICAL CORPORATION
(HQ)**
3676 Davis Rd Nw (44622-9771)
PHONE.............................330 343-7711
Jack Teat Junior, *Pr*
Chuck Fletcher, *
Darren Schwede, *
Don Stevenson, *
Tom Freeman, *
◆ **EMP:** 170 **EST:** 1975
SQ FT: 260,000
SALES (est): 202.07MM
SALES (corp-wide): 2.03B **Privately Held**
Web: www.doverchem.com
SIC: 2819 2869 2899 5169 Industrial
inorganic chemicals, nec; Industrial organic
chemicals, nec; Chemical preparations, nec
; Chemicals and allied products, nec
PA: Icc Industries Inc.
725 5th Ave
New York NY 10022
212 521-1700

(G-6239)

DOVER FABRICATION AND BURN INC (HQ)
2996 Progress St (44622-9639)
PHONE..............................330 339-1057
Robert Sensel, *Pr*
EMP: 7 **EST:** 2012
SALES (est): 293.11K
SALES (corp-wide): 12.58MM **Privately Held**
Web: www.doverhydraulics.com
SIC: 1799 7692 7353 Welding on site; Welding repair; Oil well drilling equipment, rental or leasing
PA: Dover Hydraulics, Inc.
　　2996 Progress St
　　Dover OH 44622
　　330 364-1617

(G-6240)

DOVER HIGH PRFMCE PLAS INC
Also Called: Dhpp
140 Williams Dr Nw (44622-7662)
PHONE..............................330 343-3477
Mary L Schwab, *Pr*
George Maksim, *
EMP: 36 **EST:** 1990
SQ FT: 60,000
SALES (est): 7.73MM **Privately Held**
Web: www.dhpp.net
SIC: 3089 Injection molding of plastics

(G-6241)

DOVER MACHINE CO
2208 State Route 516 Nw (44622-7081)
PHONE..............................330 343-4123
Wayne Amistadi, *Pr*
EMP: 6 **EST:** 1955
SQ FT: 10,000
SALES (est): 300.6K **Privately Held**
Web: www.candbmachine.com
SIC: 3599 7692 3544 Machine shop, jobbing and repair; Welding repair; Special dies, tools, jigs, and fixtures

(G-6242)

DOVER TANK AND PLATE COMPANY
5725 Crown Rd Nw (44622-9649)
P.O. Box 70 (44622-0070)
PHONE..............................330 343-4443
David Lawless, *Pr*
Earl Lawless, *
Joseph Lawless, *
Luke Lawless, *
EMP: 45 **EST:** 1922
SQ FT: 40,000
SALES (est): 4.8MM **Privately Held**
Web: www.dovertank.com
SIC: 3441 3446 3444 3443 Fabricated structural metal; Architectural metalwork; Sheet metalwork; Fabricated plate work (boiler shop)

(G-6243)

DYNAMIC HYDRAULIC SVCS CO LLC
205 Deeds Dr (44622-9652)
PHONE..............................330 447-8967
Shawn Endlich, *Mgr*
EMP: 32 **EST:** 2012
SQ FT: 30,000
SALES (est): 4MM **Privately Held**
Web: www.dynamichsc.com
SIC: 3593 7699 3594 3053 Fluid power cylinders and actuators; Hydraulic equipment repair; Fluid power pumps and motors; Gaskets; packing and sealing devices

(G-6244)

E WARTHER & SONS INC
Also Called: Warther Cutlery
924 N Tuscarawas Ave (44622-2752)
PHONE..............................330 343-7513
Steve Cunningham, *Pr*
Joan Warther, *Sec*
EMP: 15 **EST:** 1946
SQ FT: 14,000
SALES (est): 702.93K **Privately Held**
Web: www.warthercutlery.com
SIC: 3421 5947 Table cutlery, except with handles of metal; Gift shop

(G-6245)

FARSIGHT MANAGEMENT INC
6790 Middle Run Rd Nw (44622-7648)
PHONE..............................330 602-8338
Robert A Bennett, *Pr*
EMP: 10 **EST:** 2000
SALES (est): 959.03K **Privately Held**
Web: www.usefarsight.com
SIC: 1446 Molding sand mining

(G-6246)

HANNON COMPANY
Charles Rewinding Division
801 Commercial Pkwy (44622-3152)
P.O. Box 398 (44622-0398)
PHONE..............................330 343-7758
Timothy Welch, *Brnch Mgr*
EMP: 15
SQ FT: 12,200
SALES (corp-wide): 23.88MM **Privately Held**
Web: www.hanco.com
SIC: 7629 5063 7699 7694 Electrical repair shops; Motors, electric; Welding equipment repair; Electric motor repair
PA: The Hannon Company
　　1605 Waynesburg Rd Se
　　Canton OH 44707
　　330 456-4728

(G-6247)

HVAC INC
Also Called: Dover Phila Heating & Cooling
133 W 3rd St (44622-2933)
PHONE..............................330 343-5511
Dana Moser, *Genl Mgr*
David Kinsey, *Pr*
James Moser, *Sec*
EMP: 15 **EST:** 1981
SQ FT: 10,000
SALES (est): 1.34MM **Privately Held**
Web: www.doverphilahvac.com
SIC: 1711 3444 Warm air heating and air conditioning contractor; Sheet metalwork

(G-6248)

INCA PRESSWOOD-PALLETS LTD (PA)
3005 Progress St (44622-9640)
P.O. Box 248 (44622-0248)
PHONE..............................330 343-3361
Wolfgang Ketzer, *Ltd Pt*
Hans Inselkammer, *Ltd Pt*
▲ **EMP:** 35 **EST:** 1979
SQ FT: 45,000
SALES (est): 15.61MM
SALES (corp-wide): 15.61MM **Privately Held**
Web: www.litco.com
SIC: 2448 Pallets, wood

(G-6249)

J & J TOOL & DIE INC
203 W 4th St (44622-2994)
PHONE..............................330 343-4721
Scott Sherer, *Pr*
Carol Belt, *Sec*

EMP: 7 **EST:** 1966
SQ FT: 5,000
SALES (est): 365.96K **Privately Held**
Web: www.jjtooldie.com
SIC: 3544 Special dies and tools

(G-6250)

KIMBLE COMPANY (PA)
Also Called: Kimble Clay & Limestone
3596 State Route 39 Nw (44622-7232)
PHONE..............................330 343-1226
EMP: 160 **EST:** 1952
SALES (est): 39.13MM
SALES (corp-wide): 39.13MM **Privately Held**
Web: www.kimblecompanies.com
SIC: 1221 Bituminous coal and lignite-surface mining

(G-6251)

KRUZ INC
Also Called: Ravens Sales & Service
6332 Columbia Rd Nw (44622-7676)
PHONE..............................330 878-5595
Rufus Hall, *Mgr*
EMP: 30
SALES (corp-wide): 9.7MM **Privately Held**
Web: www.kruzinc.com
SIC: 3713 Dump truck bodies
PA: Kruz Inc.
　　1201 W Culver Rd
　　Knox IN 46534
　　574 772-6673

(G-6252)

MARLITE INC (DH)
1 Marlite Dr (44622-2361)
PHONE..............................330 343-6621
Daryl Rosser, *Pr*
Greg Triplett, *
Kimberly Mcbride, *CFO*
Mark Jutte, *
Greg Leary, *
◆ **EMP:** 150 **EST:** 2004
SQ FT: 450,000
SALES (est): 32.83MM **Privately Held**
Web: www.marlite.com
SIC: 2542 Partitions and fixtures, except wood
HQ: Nudo Products, Inc.
　　1500 Taylor Ave
　　Springfield IL 62703
　　217 528-5636

(G-6253)

METEOR SEALING SYSTEMS LLC
Also Called: Meteor Automotive
400 S Tuscarawas Ave (44622-2342)
PHONE..............................330 343-9595
Joerg Busse, *
▲ **EMP:** 155 **EST:** 1998
SALES (est): 44.93MM
SALES (corp-wide): 355.83K **Privately Held**
Web: www.meteor-sealingsystems.com
SIC: 3069 Tubing, rubber
HQ: Meteor Creative, Inc.
　　1414 Commerce Park Dr
　　Tipp City OH 45371
　　800 273-1535

(G-6254)

MINTEQ INTERNATIONAL INC
5864 Crown Street Ext Nw (44622)
PHONE..............................330 343-8821
Ron Nanni, *Brnch Mgr*
EMP: 31
SQ FT: 150,000
Web: www.mineralstech.com

SIC: 3297 3255 3251 Brick refractories; Clay refractories; Brick and structural clay tile
HQ: Minteq International Inc.
　　35 Highland Ave
　　Bethlehem PA 18017

(G-6255)

NEXT SALES LLC
3258 Dogwood Ln Nw (44622-6822)
PHONE..............................330 704-4126
Michael R Ludwig, *Prin*
EMP: 17 **EST:** 2012
SALES (est): 267.62K **Privately Held**
Web: www.nextind.com
SIC: 3275 Acoustical plaster, gypsum

(G-6256)

NORRIS MANUFACTURING LLC
317 E Broadway St (44622-1914)
PHONE..............................330 602-5005
EMP: 17 **EST:** 2002
SQ FT: 55,000
SALES (est): 440.13K **Privately Held**
Web: www.cnorrismanufacturing.com
SIC: 3531 Construction machinery

(G-6257)

OERLIKON BLZERS CATING USA INC
120 Deeds Dr (44622-9652)
PHONE..............................330 343-9892
EMP: 7
Web: www.oerlikon.com
SIC: 3479 Coating of metals and formed products
HQ: Oerlikon Balzers Coating Usa Inc.
　　1700 E Golf Rd Ste 200
　　Schaumburg IL 60173
　　847 619-5541

(G-6258)

PERFORMANCE TANK SALES INC
424 W 3rd St (44622-3169)
PHONE..............................330 602-8800
Douglas Stiffler, *Prin*
EMP: 6 **EST:** 1998
SALES (est): 420.73K **Privately Held**
SIC: 3795 3799 Tanks and tank components ; Trailers and trailer equipment

(G-6259)

REAM AND HAAGER LABORATORY INC
179 W Broadway St (44622-1916)
P.O. Box 706 (44622-0706)
PHONE..............................330 343-3711
Tim Levengood, *Pr*
EMP: 13 **EST:** 1960
SQ FT: 4,300
SALES (est): 1.4MM **Privately Held**
Web: www.rhlab.us
SIC: 8748 8734 0711 1389 Business consulting, nec; Water testing laboratory; Soil testing services; Pipe testing, oil field service

(G-6260)

SCHINDLERS BROAD RUN CHSHUSE I
Also Called: Broad Run Cheese House
6011 Old Route 39 Nw (44622-7788)
PHONE..............................330 343-4108
Chad Schindler, *Pr*
Nancy Schindler, *Treas*
EMP: 10 **EST:** 1933
SQ FT: 16,600
SALES (est): 878.95K **Privately Held**
Web: www.broadruncheese.com
SIC: 2022 5451 5947 Natural cheese; Cheese; Gift shop

▲ = Import ▼ = Export
◆ = Import/Export

(G-6261)
SCHWAB INDUSTRIES INC (HQ)
2301 Progress St (44622-9641)
P.O. Box 400 (44622-0400)
PHONE..............................330 364-4411
Jerry A Schwab, *Pr*
David A Schwab, *VP*
Mary Lynn Hites, *Treas*
Donna Schwab, *Sec*
EMP: 15 **EST:** 1950
SQ FT: 2,500
SALES (est): 9.88MM
SALES (corp-wide): 34.95B **Privately Held**
SIC: 3273 5031 5032 Ready-mixed concrete
; Lumber, plywood, and millwork; Concrete
and cinder block
PA: Crh Public Limited Company
Stonemason S Way
Rathfarnham
14041000

(G-6262)
SMITH CONCRETE CO (PA)
Also Called: Division of Selling Materials
2301 Progress St (44622-9641)
P.O. Box 356 (45750-0356)
PHONE..............................740 373-7441
Mike Murphy, *Genl Mgr*
EMP: 50 **EST:** 1922
SQ FT: 2,000
SALES (est): 5.77MM
SALES (corp-wide): 5.77MM **Privately
Held**
Web: www.shellyco.com
SIC: 3272 3273 1442 Dry mixture concrete;
Ready-mixed concrete; Construction sand
and gravel

(G-6263)
SNYDER MANUFACTURING INC
3001 Progress St (44622-9640)
P.O. Box 188 (44622-0188)
PHONE..............................330 343-4456
Dennis Snyder, *Pr*
Goerge Mokodean, *
▲ **EMP:** 60 **EST:** 1985
SQ FT: 50,000
SALES (est): 9.89MM **Privately Held**
Web: www.snyderman.com
SIC: 3083 Laminated plastics plate and sheet

(G-6264)
SUGARCREEK LIME SERVICE
Also Called: M D Trucking
2068 Gordon Rd Nw (44622-7741)
PHONE..............................330 364-4460
Matthew Beachy, *Owner*
EMP: 8 **EST:** 1979
SALES (est): 465.81K **Privately Held**
SIC: 3274 Lime

(G-6265)
TCB AUTOMATION LLC
601 W 15th St (44622-9763)
PHONE..............................330 556-6444
Joseph Dalessandro, *Managing Member*
EMP: 13 **EST:** 2013
SALES (est): 2MM **Privately Held**
Web: www.tcbautomation.com
SIC: 1731 3613 General electrical contractor
; Control panels, electric

(G-6266)
TWIN CITIES CONCRETE CO (DH)
141 S Tuscarawas Ave (44622-1951)
PHONE..............................330 343-4491
Jerry Schwab, *Pr*
David Schwab, *VP*
Jerry Gwinn, *Genl Mgr*
Donna Schwab, *Sec*
Mary Lynn Schwab, *Treas*

EMP: 17 **EST:** 1949
SQ FT: 1,500
SALES (est): 1.15MM
SALES (corp-wide): 34.95B **Privately Held**
SIC: 3273 5072 Ready-mixed concrete;
Builders' hardware, nec
HQ: Schwab Industries, Inc.
2301 Progress St
Dover OH 44622
330 364-4411

(G-6267)
ZIEGLER TIRE AND SUPPLY CO
Also Called: Ziegler Oil Co
411 Commercial Pkwy (44622-3125)
PHONE..............................330 343-7739
Tom West, *Mgr*
EMP: 36
SQ FT: 100,000
SALES (corp-wide): 93.71MM **Privately
Held**
Web: www.zieglertire.com
SIC: 5531 7534 Automotive tires; Rebuilding
and retreading tires
PA: The Ziegler Tire And Supply Company
4150 Millennium Blvd Se
Massillon OH 44646
330 834-3332

(G-6268)
ZIMMER SURGICAL INC
Also Called: Zimmer Orthopaedic Surgical
200 W Ohio Ave (44622-9642)
PHONE..............................800 321-5533
Kenneth R Coonce, *VP*
James T Crines, *
▲ **EMP:** 300 **EST:** 2002
SALES (est): 95.44MM
SALES (corp-wide): 7.68B **Publicly Held**
Web: www.zimmerbiomet.com
SIC: 3842 Orthopedic appliances
PA: Zimmer Biomet Holdings, Inc.
345 E Main St
Warsaw IN 46580
574 373-3333

Doylestown
Wayne County

(G-6269)
ADAPT OIL
Also Called: Marathon Oil
188 N Portage St (44230-1370)
PHONE..............................330 658-1482
Clark Mowen, *Prin*
EMP: 6 **EST:** 2003
SALES (est): 527.54K **Privately Held**
Web: www.marathonoil.com
SIC: 1389 Oil and gas field services, nec

(G-6270)
THE GALEHOUSE COMPANIES INC
Also Called: Galehouse Lumber
12667 Portage St (44230-9735)
P.O. Box 267 (44230-0267)
PHONE..............................330 658-2023
EMP: 30 **EST:** 1968
SALES (est): 6.96MM **Privately Held**
Web: www.galehouse.com
SIC: 5031 5211 1531 1521 Lumber: rough,
dressed, and finished; Millwork and lumber;
Condominium developers; New
construction, single-family houses

Dublin
Franklin County

(G-6271)
A GRADE NOTES INC (PA)
6385 Shier Rings Rd Ste 1 (43016-1261)
P.O. Box 4175 (43016-0617)
PHONE..............................614 299-9999
Gary V Stoep, *CEO*
Gary Vander Stoep, *CEO*
Kathy Gatton Eshelman, *Pr*
David Kiess, *VP*
Rita Wood, *Sec*
EMP: 8 **EST:** 1987
SQ FT: 1,000
SALES (est): 481.79K
SALES (corp-wide): 481.79K **Privately
Held**
Web: www.gradeanotes.com
SIC: 2752 7334 Offset printing;
Photocopying and duplicating services

(G-6272)
**ACCURATE MANUFACTURING
COMPANY**
5765 Richgrove Ln (43016-2233)
P.O. Box 28666 (43228-0666)
PHONE..............................614 878-6510
Tom Lindblom, *CEO*
Angela Merrill, *VP*
EMP: 10 **EST:** 1943
SALES (est): 3.14MM **Privately Held**
Web:
www.accuratemanufacturingco.com
SIC: 3542 3599 3548 Presses: hydraulic and
pneumatic, mechanical and manual;
Machine shop, jobbing and repair; Welding
apparatus

(G-6273)
**ADVANCED PRGRM RESOURCES
INC (PA)**
Also Called: Touchmark
2715 Tuller Pkwy (43017-2310)
PHONE..............................614 761-9994
Danial Chacho, *CEO*
Larry Dado, *
Douglas Heagren, *
Jennifer Heagren, *
EMP: 47 **EST:** 1989
SQ FT: 5,100
SALES (est): 631.8K **Privately Held**
SIC: 7379 7373 8742 7372 Computer
related consulting services; Systems
integration services; Management
consulting services; Application computer
software

(G-6274)
ALKON CORPORATION
6750 Crosby Ct (43016-7644)
PHONE..............................614 799-6650
Mark Marino, *Brnch Mgr*
EMP: 11
SALES (corp-wide): 28.32MM **Privately
Held**
Web: www.alkoncorp.com
SIC: 3491 3082 5084 5085 Industrial valves;
Unsupported plastics profile shapes;
Industrial machinery and equipment;
Industrial supplies
PA: Alkon Corporation
728 Graham Dr
Fremont OH 43420
419 355-9111

(G-6275)
ANDELYN BIOSCIENCES INC
Also Called: Andelyn Development Center

5185 Blazer Pkwy (43017-3308)
PHONE..............................614 332-0554
EMP: 189
SALES (corp-wide): 3.67B **Privately Held**
Web: www.andelynbio.com
SIC: 2834 Pharmaceutical preparations
HQ: Andelyn Biosciences, Inc.
1180 Arthur E Adams Dr
Columbus OH 43221
844 228-2366

(G-6276)
APPALACHIAN FUELS LLC (PA)
6375 Riverside Dr Ste 200 (43017-5045)
PHONE..............................606 928-0460
EMP: 247 **EST:** 2001
SALES (est): 1.05MM
SALES (corp-wide): 1.05MM **Privately
Held**
SIC: 1241 Coal mining services

(G-6277)
ASK CHEMICALS LLC
495 Metro Pl S (43017-5331)
PHONE..............................800 848-7485
Frank Goede, *CEO*
Stefan Sommer, *
Scott Hoertz, *
◆ **EMP:** 305 **EST:** 2010
SQ FT: 3,200
SALES (est): 95.3MM **Privately Held**
Web: www.ask-chemicals.com
SIC: 2899 Chemical preparations, nec
HQ: Ask Chemicals Gmbh
Reisholzstr. 16-18
Hilden NW 40721
211711030

(G-6278)
AUTO DES SYS INC
4242 Tuller Rd Ste B1 (43017-5108)
PHONE..............................614 488-8838
David Kropp, *Pr*
Chris Yessios, *Pr*
David Kropp, *VP*
EMP: 10 **EST:** 1989
SQ FT: 2,000
SALES (est): 2.42MM **Privately Held**
Web: www.autodessys.com
SIC: 7371 7372 Computer software
development; Prepackaged software

(G-6279)
AUTOMATION AND CTRL TECH INC
Also Called: Act
6141 Avery Rd (43016-8761)
P.O. Box 3667 (43016-0338)
PHONE..............................614 495-1120
Charles Totel, *Pr*
Michael Iaquinta, *
Dave Pond, *
EMP: 26 **EST:** 1998
SQ FT: 21,000
SALES (est): 885.91K **Privately Held**
Web: www.advanzgauge.com
SIC: 3829 3823 Measuring and controlling
devices, nec; Process control instruments

(G-6280)
AVIDYNE
5980 Wilcox Pl Ste I (43016-6809)
PHONE..............................800 284-3963
Paul A Ryan, *Prin*
EMP: 6 **EST:** 2010
SALES (est): 665.46K **Privately Held**
Web: www.avidyne.com
SIC: 3724 Aircraft engines and engine parts

(G-6281)
BIOSORTIA PHARMACEUTICALS INC
4266 Tuller Rd (43017-5007)
PHONE...........................614 636-4850
Ross O Youngs, *Pr*
Haiyin He, *
Guy T Carter, *
Michele H Cole, *
EMP: 16 **EST:** 2009
SALES (est): 2.52MM **Privately Held**
Web: www.algaevs.com
SIC: 2834 Pharmaceutical preparations

(G-6282)
BLACK BOX CORPORATION
5400 Frantz Rd Ste 240 (43016-6102)
PHONE...........................800 837-7777
Chris Tjotjos, *Brnch Mgr*
EMP: 8
Web: www.blackbox.com
SIC: 3577 Computer peripheral equipment,
nec
HQ: Black Box Corporation
2701 N Dllas Pkwy Ste 510
Plano TX 75093
724 746-5500

(G-6283)
BOY-RAD INC
Also Called: Goodyear
7742 Sawmill Rd (43016-8522)
PHONE...........................614 766-1228
Lance Boyer, *Pr*
EMP: 7 **EST:** 1989
SALES (est): 1.14MM **Privately Held**
Web: www.boyradtire.com
SIC: 5531 7534 Automotive tires; Tire
retreading and repair shops

(G-6284)
CAKE LLC
6724 Perimeter Loop Rd Unit 254
(43017-3202)
PHONE...........................614 592-7681
Lesley Blake, *Asst Sec*
EMP: 7 **EST:** 2013
SALES (est): 441.34K **Privately Held**
SIC: 7372 Home entertainment computer
software

(G-6285)
CARDINAL HEALTH INC
7200 Cardinal Pl W (43017-1094)
PHONE...........................614 553-3830
EMP: 27
SALES (corp-wide): 226.83B **Publicly
Held**
Web: www.cardinalhealth.com
SIC: 5122 5047 8741 3842 Pharmaceuticals;
Surgical equipment and supplies;
Management services; Surgical appliances
and supplies
PA: Cardinal Health, Inc.
7000 Cardinal Pl
Dublin OH 43017
614 757-5000

(G-6286)
CARDINAL HEALTH INC (PA)
Also Called: Cardinalhealth
7000 Cardinal Pl (43017-1091)
PHONE...........................614 757-5000
Jason M Hollar, *CEO*
Gregory B Kenny, *Non-Executive Chairman
of the Board*
Aaron E Alt, *
Ola M Snow, *Chief Human Resource
Officer*
Jessica L Mayer, *CLO CCO*
◆ **EMP:** 2800 **EST:** 1979
SALES (est): 226.83B

SALES (corp-wide): 226.83B **Publicly
Held**
Web: www.cardinalhealth.com
SIC: 5122 5047 8741 3842 Pharmaceuticals;
Surgical equipment and supplies;
Management services; Surgical appliances
and supplies

(G-6287)
CARDINAL HEALTH 110 LLC
Also Called: Parmed Pharmaceuticals
7000 Cardinal Pl (43017-1091)
PHONE...........................800 727-6331
Robert Walter, *Pr*
EMP: 28 **EST:** 1988
SALES (est): 4.68MM
SALES (corp-wide): 226.83B **Publicly
Held**
Web: ir.cardinalhealth.com
SIC: 5047 2834 Instruments, surgical and
medical; Proprietary drug products
PA: Cardinal Health, Inc.
7000 Cardinal Pl
Dublin OH 43017
614 757-5000

(G-6288)
CARDINAL HEALTH 414 LLC (HQ)
7000 Cardinal Pl (43017-1091)
PHONE...........................614 757-5000
Jason Hollar, *CEO*
Aaron Alt, *
▲ **EMP:** 155 **EST:** 1985
SQ FT: 60,967
SALES (est): 483.45MM
SALES (corp-wide): 226.83B **Publicly
Held**
SIC: 2834 2835 8052 Proprietary drug
products; Radioactive diagnostic
substances; Home for the mentally
retarded, with health care
PA: Cardinal Health, Inc.
7000 Cardinal Pl
Dublin OH 43017
614 757-5000

(G-6289)
COFFMAN MEDIA LLC
5995 Wilcox Pl Ste A (43016-9267)
PHONE...........................614 956-7015
Jason Ault, *COO*
EMP: 12 **EST:** 2010
SALES (est): 2.86MM **Privately Held**
Web: www.coffmanmedia.com
SIC: 3571 Computers, digital, analog or
hybrid

(G-6290)
COMMAND ALKON INCORPORATED
6750 Crosby Ct (43016-7644)
PHONE...........................614 799-0600
Randy Willaman, *Brnch Mgr*
EMP: 38
SALES (corp-wide): 55.1MM **Privately
Held**
Web: www.commandalkon.com
SIC: 3823 7371 3625 Industrial process
measurement equipment; Custom
computer programming services; Relays
and industrial controls
PA: Command Alkon Incorporated
1800 Intl Pk Dr Ste 400
Birmingham AL 35243
205 879-3282

(G-6291)
COMPUTER WORKSHOP INC (PA)
5200 Upper Metro Pl Ste 140 (43017-5322)
PHONE...........................614 798-9505
Thelma Tippie, *Pr*
Terri Williams, *COO*

EMP: 20 **EST:** 1988
SALES (est): 2.37MM
SALES (corp-wide): 2.37MM **Privately
Held**
Web: www.tcworkshop.com
SIC: 8243 7371 2741 Operator training,
computer; Custom computer programming
services; Miscellaneous publishing

(G-6292)
**CRIMSON GATE CONSULTING CO
(PA)**
6457 Reflections Dr S200 (43017-2352)
PHONE...........................614 805-0897
Brent Dyke, *CEO*
Glenn Foote, *Dir Opers*
Brian Rogers, *Proj Mgr*
EMP: 9 **EST:** 2010
SQ FT: 300
SALES (est): 152.44K
SALES (corp-wide): 152.44K **Privately
Held**
SIC: 8742 7372 Business management
consultant; Business oriented computer
software

(G-6293)
DIOCESAN PUBLICATIONS INC (PA)
6161 Wilcox Rd (43016-1264)
PHONE...........................614 718-9500
Robert Zielke, *Pr*
Donald Zielke, *
EMP: 35 **EST:** 1972
SALES (est): 5.89MM
SALES (corp-wide): 5.89MM **Privately
Held**
Web: www.diocesan.com
SIC: 2759 2741 Letterpress printing;
Miscellaneous publishing

(G-6294)
DUBLIN MILLWORK CO INC
7575 Fishel Dr S (43016-8821)
PHONE...........................614 889-7776
Wilbur C Strait, *Ch Bd*
Scott Evisol, *Genl Mgr*
EMP: 15 **EST:** 1981
SQ FT: 100,000
SALES (est): 2.48MM
SALES (corp-wide): 27.16MM **Privately
Held**
Web: www.straitandlamp.com
SIC: 5031 2431 Trim, sheet metal; Millwork
PA: The Strait & Lamp Lumber Company
Incorporated
269 National Rd Se
Hebron OH 43025
740 928-4501

(G-6295)
DUPONT WEALTH SOLUTIONS LLC
655 Metro Pl S Ste 600 (43017-3394)
PHONE...........................614 384-5246
EMP: 10 **EST:** 2017
SALES (est): 3.1MM **Privately Held**
Web: www.advocatewealthsolutions.com
SIC: 2879 Agricultural chemicals, nec

(G-6296)
ECI MACOLA/MAX LLC (DH)
5455 Rings Rd Ste 100 (43017-7519)
PHONE...........................978 539-6186
Alex Braverman, *
James A Workman, *
Lisa Wise, *
EMP: 170 **EST:** 1971
SQ FT: 30,000
SALES (est): 3.78MM **Privately Held**
Web: www.ecisolutions.com

SIC: 7371 7372 5045 2759 Computer
software development; Prepackaged
software; Computer software; Letterpress
printing
HQ: Exact Holding B.V.
Molengraaffsingel 33
Delft ZH 2629
157115000

(G-6297)
GCONSENT LLC
Also Called: Gconsent Logistics
5412 Talladega Dr (43016-7857)
PHONE...........................614 886-2416
Unyime Akpan, *CEO*
EMP: 12 **EST:** 2018
SALES (est): 3.18MM **Privately Held**
Web: www.gconsent.com
SIC: 3537 Trucks, tractors, loaders, carriers,
and similar equipment

(G-6298)
GLOBAL COAL SALES GROUP LLC
6641 Dublin Center Dr (43017-5077)
P.O. Box 340290 (43234)
PHONE...........................614 221-0101
Steven Read, *Pr*
Wayne M Boich, *Managing Member*
▼ **EMP:** 9 **EST:** 2008
SALES (est): 4.85MM
SALES (corp-wide): 4.85MM **Privately
Held**
Web: www.globalcoalsales.com
SIC: 1241 Coal mining services
PA: Global Mining Holding Company, Llc
41 S High St Ste 3750
Columbus OH 43215
614 221-0101

(G-6299)
GUILD ASSOCIATES INC
Also Called: Guild Biosciences
4412 Tuller Rd (43017-5033)
PHONE...........................843 573-0095
Nick Dinovo, *Mgr*
EMP: 7
SALES (corp-wide): 24.49MM **Privately
Held**
Web: www.guildbiosciences.com
SIC: 8731 3559 Chemical laboratory, except
testing; Chemical machinery and equipment
PA: Guild Associates, Inc.
5750 Shier Rings Rd
Dublin OH 43016
614 798-8215

(G-6300)
GUILD ASSOCIATES INC (PA)
5750 Shier Rings Rd (43016-1234)
PHONE...........................614 798-8215
Henry Berns, *CEO*
Dominic Dinovo, *
Dolores Dinovo, *
▲ **EMP:** 65 **EST:** 1981
SQ FT: 53,000
SALES (est): 24.49MM
SALES (corp-wide): 24.49MM **Privately
Held**
Web: www.guildassociates.com
SIC: 3559 8731 Chemical machinery and
equipment; Chemical laboratory, except
testing

(G-6301)
HARTCO PRINTING COMPANY (PA)
Also Called: Hartco Products, The
4106 Delancy Park Dr (43016-7246)
PHONE...........................614 761-1292
Carlton W Hartley, *Pr*
Louann Hartley, *VP*
EMP: 8 **EST:** 1955

▲ = Import ▼ = Export
◆ = Import/Export

SQ FT: 9,900
SALES (est): 790.15K
SALES (corp-wide): 790.15K **Privately Held**
SIC: 2752 Offset printing

(G-6302)
HBD INDUSTRIES INC (PA)
565 Metro Pl S Ste 250 (43017-7312)
PHONE................................614 526-7000
◆ **EMP:** 25 **EST:** 1987
SALES (est): 241.4MM
SALES (corp-wide): 241.4MM **Privately Held**
Web: www.hbdindustries.com
SIC: 3052 3621 3566 3812 Rubber hose; Motors and generators; Speed changers (power transmission equipment), except auto; Magnetic field detection apparatus

(G-6303)
HIDAKA USA INC
5761 Shier Rings Rd (43016-1233)
PHONE................................614 889-8611
Yoshihiro Hidaka, *Pr*
Mikihiro Hidaka, *
▲ **EMP:** 40 **EST:** 1989
SQ FT: 90,000
SALES (est): 4.02MM **Privately Held**
Web: www.hidakausainc.com
SIC: 3444 3469 Sheet metalwork; Machine parts, stamped or pressed metal
HQ: Hidaka Seiki Co., Ltd.
3-28-5, Nishirokugo
Ota-Ku TKY 144-0

(G-6304)
HOMETOWN TICKETING INC
4305 W Dublin Granville Rd (43017-2041)
PHONE................................866 488-4849
Nate Nale, *CEO*
Wesley Haines, *
EMP: 191 **EST:** 2015
SALES (est): 12.89MM **Privately Held**
Web: www.easypeasyticketing.com
SIC: 7372 Application computer software

(G-6305)
ICU MEDICAL INC
5200 Upper Metro Pl Ste 200 (43017-5379)
PHONE................................614 210-7300
EMP: 60
SALES (corp-wide): 2.38B **Publicly Held**
SIC: 3841 5047 Diagnostic apparatus, medical; Electro-medical equipment
PA: Icu Medical, Inc.
951 Calle Amanecer
San Clemente CA 92673
949 366-2183

(G-6306)
IMPERIAL STUCCO LLC
P.O. Box 1579 (43017-6579)
PHONE................................614 787-5888
Jeffrey S Parenteau, *Prin*
EMP: 6 **EST:** 2010
SALES (est): 229.15K **Privately Held**
SIC: 3299 Stucco

(G-6307)
INEOS JOLIET LLC
5220 Blazer Pkwy (43017-3494)
PHONE................................815 314-4317
Rebecca Gray, *Mgr*
EMP: 11
SALES (corp-wide): 1.38MM **Privately Held**
Web: www.ineos.com
SIC: 2821 Plastics materials and resins
HQ: Ineos Joliet, Llc
23425 Amoco Rd

Channahon IL 60410
815 467-3200

(G-6308)
INEOS NEAL LLC
5220 Blazer Pkwy (43017-3494)
PHONE................................610 790-3333
Ralston Skinner, *Pr*
EMP: 46 **EST:** 2019
SALES (est): 9.77MM
SALES (corp-wide): 2.11B **Publicly Held**
SIC: 2851 2821 2911 Paints and allied products; Plastics materials and resins; Heavy distillates
HQ: Ashland Chemco Inc.
1979 Atlas St
Columbus OH 43228
859 815-3333

(G-6309)
INEOS SOLVENTS SALES US CORP
5220 Blazer Pkwy (43017-3494)
PHONE................................614 790-3333
Ralston Skinner, *Pr*
EMP: 400 **EST:** 2019
SALES (est): 4.83MM
SALES (corp-wide): 2.11B **Publicly Held**
SIC: 2851 2821 Paints and allied products; Plastics materials and resins
HQ: Ashland Chemco Inc.
1979 Atlas St
Columbus OH 43228
859 815-3333

(G-6310)
INSIGHTS SCCESS MEDIA TECH LI C
555 Metro Pl N Ste 100 (43017-1389)
PHONE................................614 602-1754
Manish Bansal, *Managing Member*
EMP: 24 **EST:** 2016
SALES (est): 314.8K **Privately Held**
Web: www.insightssuccess.com
SIC: 2721 Magazines: publishing and printing

(G-6311)
INTERSTATE GAS SUPPLY LLC (PA)
Also Called: Interstate Gas Supply
6100 Emerald Pkwy (43016-3248)
P.O. Box 9060 (43017)
PHONE................................877 995-4447
Scott White, *Pr*
Doug Austin, *
Jim Baich, *
Tami Wilson Chu, *Prin*
EMP: 241 **EST:** 1989
SQ FT: 100,000
SALES (est): 91.18MM **Privately Held**
Web: www.igs.com
SIC: 1311 Natural gas production

(G-6312)
INVENTUS POWER (OHIO) INC (DH)
Also Called: Iccnexergy
5115 Parkcenter Ave Ste 275 (43017-7544)
PHONE................................614 351-2191
Patrick Trippel, *Pr*
▲ **EMP:** 10 **EST:** 1961
SQ FT: 46,000
SALES (est): 9.98MM
SALES (corp-wide): 389.64MM **Privately Held**
SIC: 3692 Primary batteries, dry and wet
HQ: Inventus Power, Inc.
1200 Internationale Pkwy
Woodridge IL 60517

(G-6313)
JASSTEK INC
555 Metro Pl N Ste 100 (43017-1389)
PHONE................................614 808-3600
Sulakshana Singh, *Pr*

EMP: 11 **EST:** 2004
SQ FT: 1,200
SALES (est): 499.08K **Privately Held**
Web: www.jasstek.com
SIC: 7371 7372 7379 8748 Custom computer programming services; Business oriented computer software; Online services technology consultants; Systems engineering consultant, ex. computer or professional

(G-6314)
KASAI NORTH AMERICA INC
655 Metro Pl S Ste 560 (43017-3382)
PHONE................................614 356-1494
Yoichi Yamaguchi, *Brnch Mgr*
EMP: 35
Web: www.kasai-na.com
SIC: 3089 3714 3429 Injection molded finished plastics products, nec; Motor vehicle parts and accessories; Hardware, nec
HQ: Kasai North America, Inc.
1225 Garrison Dr
Murfreesboro TN 37129
615 546-6040

(G-6315)
KENTROX INC (HQ)
5800 Innovation Dr (43016-3271)
PHONE................................614 798-2000
Richard S Cremona, *CEO*
Jeffrey S Estuesta, *
Charlie Vogt, *
Michael P Keegan, *
Eric Langille, *
▲ **EMP:** 100 **EST:** 2004
SALES (est): 1.55MM **Publicly Held**
Web: www.westell.com
SIC: 3661 Telephone central office equipment, dial or manual
PA: Westell Technologies, Inc.
750 N Commons Dr
Aurora IL 60504

(G-6316)
KINETICS NOISE CONTROL INC (PA)
Also Called: Hammond Kinetics
6300 Irelan Pl (43017)
P.O. Box 655 (43017-0655)
PHONE................................614 889-0480
◆ **EMP:** 135 **EST:** 1958
SALES (est): 38.42MM
SALES (corp-wide): 38.42MM **Privately Held**
Web: www.kineticsnoise.com
SIC: 3829 3625 3446 5084 Vibration meters, analyzers, and calibrators; Noise control equipment; Acoustical suspension systems, metal; Industrial machinery and equipment

(G-6317)
LANCASTER COLONY CORPORATION
Also Called: Lancaster Colony Design Group
280 Cramer Creek Ct (43017-2584)
PHONE................................614 792-9774
EMP: 13
SALES (corp-wide): 1.22B **Publicly Held**
SIC: 2035 Dressings, salad: raw and cooked (except dry mixes)
PA: Lancaster Colony Corporation
380 Polaris Pkwy Ste 400
Westerville OH 43082
614 224-7141

(G-6318)
LSP TECHNOLOGIES INC
6161 Shamrock Ct (43016-1275)
PHONE................................614 718-3000
Jeff L Dulaney, *Pr*

Mark O'loughlin, *VP*
David Lahrman, *VP*
Beth Mitchell, *Ex Sec*
EMP: 22 **EST:** 1994
SQ FT: 18,000
SALES (est): 9.73MM **Privately Held**
Web: www.lsptechnologies.com
SIC: 3724 Aircraft engines and engine parts

(G-6319)
MATRIX MEATS INC
5164 Blazer Pkwy (43017-1339)
PHONE................................614 602-1846
Eric Jenkusky, *CEO*
EMP: 11 **EST:** 2019
SALES (est): 539.69K **Privately Held**
Web: www.derbyshiredistillery.com
SIC: 2824 Protein fibers

(G-6320)
MIRUS ADAPTED TECH LLC
Also Called: Adapted Tech
288 Cramer Creek Ct (43017-2584)
PHONE................................614 402-4585
Stephan Mertik, *Managing Member*
EMP: 20 **EST:** 2015
SALES (est): 1.88MM **Privately Held**
Web: www.adapted.tech
SIC: 1731 7372 Electrical work; Home entertainment computer software

(G-6321)
MODULAR ASSMBLY INNVATIONS LLC (PA)
600 Stonehenge Pkwy Ste 100 (43017-6027)
PHONE................................614 389-4860
Billy R Vickers, *Pr*
EMP: 24 **EST:** 2010
SALES (est): 30.75MM
SALES (corp-wide): 30.75MM **Privately Held**
Web: www.modularai.com
SIC: 3559 Automotive related machinery

(G-6322)
NANOFIBER SOLUTIONS LLC
5164 Blazer Pkwy (43017-1339)
PHONE................................614 319-3075
Ross Kayuha, *Pr*
John Lannutti, *CSO*
EMP: 12 **EST:** 2009
SQ FT: 20,000
SALES (est): 7.14MM **Privately Held**
Web: www.nanofibersolutions.com
SIC: 2835 2834 2821 Diagnostic substances ; Liniments; Plasticizer/additive based plastic materials

(G-6323)
NATIONAL GLASS SVC GROUP LLC
Also Called: National Glass Service Group
5500 Frantz Rd Ste 120 (43017-3545)
PHONE................................614 652-3699
Haytham Elzayn, *CEO*
EMP: 10 **EST:** 2008
SALES (est): 294.67K **Privately Held**
Web: www.nationalglassservicegroup.com
SIC: 2671 Paper; coated and laminated packaging

(G-6324)
NAVIDEA BIOPHARMACEUTICALS INC (PA)
Also Called: Navidea
4995 Bradenton Ave Ste 240 (43017-3552)
PHONE................................614 793-7500
Michael S Rosol, *CMO*
Alexander L Cappello, *Ch Bd*
John K Scott Junior, *V Ch Bd*

Michel Mikhail, *CRO*
Erika L Eves, *VP Fin*
EMP: 7 **EST:** 1983
SQ FT: 5,000
SALES (est): 65.65K
SALES (corp-wide): 65.65K **Publicly Held**
Web: www.navidea.com
SIC: 2834 2835 Pharmaceutical preparations
; Diagnostic substances

(G-6325)
NORTH AMERICAN ASSEMBLIES LLC
600 Stonehenge Pkwy (43017-6026)
PHONE..............................843 420-5354
EMP: 27 **EST:** 2004
SALES (est): 1.82MM **Privately Held**
Web: www.modularai.com
SIC: 3011 Tires and inner tubes

(G-6326)
OHIO REFINING COMPANY LLC
5550 Blazer Pkwy Ste 200 (43017-3478)
PHONE..............................614 210-2300
Scott Howard, *Managing Member*
Daniel Syphard, *Sec*
EMP: 560 **EST:** 2008
SALES (est): 4B **Privately Held**
SIC: 2911 Petroleum refining

(G-6327)
ORACLE AMERICA INC
4378 Tuller Rd (43017-5030)
PHONE..............................650 506-7000
EMP: 6
SALES (corp-wide): 52.96B **Publicly Held**
Web: www.oracle.com
SIC: 3571 Minicomputers
HQ: Oracle America, Inc.
    500 Oracle Pkwy
    Redwood Shores CA 94065
    650 506-7000

(G-6328)
PARALLEL TECHNOLOGIES INC
4868 Blazer Pkwy (43017-3302)
PHONE..............................614 798-9700
Joseph Redman, *Pr*
Martin B Jacobs, *
EMP: 80 **EST:** 1984
SQ FT: 8,500
SALES (est): 34.75MM
SALES (corp-wide): 23.49MM **Privately Held**
Web: www.paralleltech.com
SIC: 1623 7372 Telephone and
communication line construction; Business
oriented computer software
PA: R C I Communications Inc
    4868 Blazer Pkwy
    Dublin OH 43017
    614 798-9700

(G-6329)
PEEBLES CREATIVE GROUP INC
4260 Tuller Rd Ste 200 (43017-5026)
PHONE..............................614 487-2011
Doug Peebles, *Prin*
Doug Peebles, *Prin*
EMP: 9 **EST:** 1997
SQ FT: 3,500
SALES (est): 927.55K **Privately Held**
Web: www.peeblescreativegroup.com
SIC: 2741 2759 Miscellaneous publishing;
Commercial printing, nec

(G-6330)
PEERLESS-WINSMITH INC
Peerless Winsmith
5200 Upper Metro Pl Ste 110 (43017-5377)
PHONE..............................330 399-3651

Paul Petrich, *Mgr*
EMP: 328
SALES (corp-wide): 241.4MM **Privately Held**
SIC: 3621 Motors and generators
HQ: Peerless-Winsmith, Inc.
    5200 Upper Metro Pl Ste 11
    Dublin OH 43017
    614 526-7000

(G-6331)
PENTAGON PROTECTION USA LLC
5500 Frantz Rd Ste 120 (43017-3545)
PHONE..............................614 734-7240
Sam Elzein, *Pr*
EMP: 10 **EST:** 2005
SALES (est): 393.51K **Privately Held**
Web: www.pentagonprotectionus.com
SIC: 1793 3699 Glass and glazing work;
Security control equipment and systems

(G-6332)
PM POWER PRODUCTS LLC
4393 Tuller Rd Ste A (43017-5106)
PHONE..............................614 652-6509
EMP: 7 **EST:** 2017
SALES (est): 689.75K **Privately Held**
Web: www.pmpowerproducts.com
SIC: 3669 Communications equipment, nec

(G-6333)
POWER ACQUISITION LLC
5025 Bradenton Ave Ste 130 (43017-3506)
PHONE..............................614 228-5000
John B Simmons, *CEO*
J Michael Kirksey, *CFO*
EMP: 993 **EST:** 2016
SALES (est): 5.96MM
SALES (corp-wide): 411.88MM **Privately Held**
SIC: 3694 7538 7537 Distributors, motor
vehicle engine; Diesel engine repair:
automotive; Automotiv e transmission
repair shops
PA: Oep Capital Advisors, L.P.
    510 Madison Ave Fl 19
    New York NY 10022
    212 277-1500

(G-6334)
PRECISION METAL PRODUCTS INC
5200 Upper Metro Pl (43017-5377)
PHONE..............................614 526-7000
Thomas Pozda, *CEO*
EMP: 108 **EST:** 2007
SALES (est): 6.62MM
SALES (corp-wide): 241.4MM **Privately Held**
Web: www.hbdindustries.com
SIC: 3444 Sheet metalwork
PA: Hbd Industries, Inc.
    565 Metro Pl S Ste 250
    Dublin OH 43017
    614 526-7000

(G-6335)
PRO ONCALL TECHNOLOGIES LLC
Also Called: Digital & Analog Design
4374 Tuller Rd Ste B (43017-5030)
PHONE..............................614 761-1400
David Myers, *Mgr*
EMP: 11
SALES (corp-wide): 24.76MM **Privately Held**
Web: www.prooncall.com
SIC: 5065 3661 Telephone equipment;
Telephone and telegraph apparatus
PA: Pro Oncall Technologies, Llc
    6902 E Kemper Road
    Cincinnati OH 45249
    513 489-7660

(G-6336)
PROFESSIONAL PLASTICS CORP
4863 Rays Cir (43016-6069)
PHONE..............................614 336-2498
Mark Casey, *VP Sls*
EMP: 7 **EST:** 2012
SALES (est): 821.41K **Privately Held**
SIC: 3089 Injection molding of plastics

(G-6337)
QUEST SOFTWARE INC
Aeilita Div
6500 Emerald Pkwy Ste 400 (43016-6234)
PHONE..............................614 336-9223
Ratmir Timashev, *Mgr*
EMP: 61
SALES (corp-wide): 647.68MM **Privately Held**
Web: www.quest.com
SIC: 7372 Prepackaged software
PA: Quest Software Inc.
    20 Enterprise Ste 100
    Aliso Viejo CA 92656
    949 754-8000

(G-6338)
QUESTLINE INC
5500 Frantz Rd Ste 156 (43017-3548)
PHONE..............................614 255-3166
David Reim, *CEO*
Robert L Hines, *
EMP: 36 **EST:** 2011
SQ FT: 8,000
SALES (est): 4.13MM **Privately Held**
Web: www.questline.com
SIC: 2741 Business service newsletters:
publishing and printing

(G-6339)
RENASCENT PRTCTION SLTIONS LLC
Also Called: Allegiance Select
5500 Frantz Rd Ste 100 (43017-3545)
PHONE..............................678 910-0412
Loreto Grimaldi, *CEO*
Brian Leslie, *
EMP: 70 **EST:** 2018
SALES (est): 7.76MM **Privately Held**
Web: www.renascentps.com
SIC: 1061 8741 Nickel ore mining;
Administrative management

(G-6340)
ROBERT W JOHNSON INC (PA)
Also Called: Diamond Cellar, The
6280 Sawmill Rd (43017-1470)
PHONE..............................614 336-4545
R Andrew Johnson, *CEO*
Ron Croft, *
EMP: 70 **EST:** 1946
SQ FT: 23,000
SALES (est): 8.31MM
SALES (corp-wide): 8.31MM **Privately Held**
Web: www.diamondcellar.com
SIC: 5944 3911 Jewelry, precious stones
and precious metals; Jewelry, precious
metal

(G-6341)
RUSCILLI REAL ESTATE SERVICES
5100 Parkcenter Ave Ste 100 (43017-7563)
PHONE..............................614 923-6400
Timothy Kelton, *Pr*
Timothy D Kelton, *Pr*
David C Wade, *Treas*
EMP: 10 **EST:** 1978
SQ FT: 1,000
SALES (est): 404.77K **Privately Held**
Web: www.ruscillire.com

SIC: 6531 1389 Real estate agent, residential
; Roustabout service

(G-6342)
SAINT-GOBAIN PRFMCE PLAS CORP
Also Called: Medex
6250 Shier Rings Rd (43016-1270)
PHONE..............................614 889-2220
Ralph Dickman, *Brnch Mgr*
EMP: 110
SALES (corp-wide): 402.18MM **Privately Held**
Web: plastics.saint-gobain.com
SIC: 2821 Plastics materials and resins
HQ: Saint-Gobain Performance Plastics
    Corporation
    20 Moores Rd
    Malvern PA 19355
    440 836-6900

(G-6343)
SALIENT SYSTEMS INC
4393 Tuller Rd Ste K (43017-5106)
PHONE..............................614 792-5800
Robert Bower, *CEO*
EMP: 24 **EST:** 1984
SQ FT: 16,000
SALES (est): 4.58MM
SALES (corp-wide): 543.74MM **Publicly Held**
Web: www.salientsys.com
SIC: 3674 8742 Microprocessors; Business
management consultant
HQ: L. B. Foster Rail Technologies, Inc.
    415 Holiday Dr Ste 1
    Pittsburgh PA 15220
    412 928-3400

(G-6344)
SERTEK LLC
6399 Shier Rings Rd (43016-3213)
PHONE..............................614 504-5828
EMP: 100 **EST:** 2009
SALES (est): 4.73MM **Privately Held**
Web: www.franke.com
SIC: 3312 Blast furnaces and steel mills
HQ: Franke Coffee Systems Americas Llc
    800 Aviation Pkwy
    Smyrna TN 37167
    615 287-8200

(G-6345)
SMITHS MEDICAL ASD INC
5200 Upper Metro Pl Ste 200 (43017-5379)
P.O. Box 8106 (43016-2106)
PHONE..............................800 796-8701
Eller Erock, *Mgr*
EMP: 23
SALES (corp-wide): 2.38B **Publicly Held**
SIC: 3841 Surgical and medical instruments
HQ: Smiths Medical Asd, Inc.
    6000 Nathan Ln N
    Plymouth MN 55442
    763 383-3000

(G-6346)
SMITHS MEDICAL ASD INC
6250 Shier Rings Rd (43016-1270)
PHONE..............................614 889-2220
Heather Wise, *Mgr*
EMP: 242
SALES (corp-wide): 2.38B **Publicly Held**
SIC: 3841 IV transfusion apparatus
HQ: Smiths Medical Asd, Inc.
    6000 Nathan Ln N
    Plymouth MN 55442
    763 383-3000

▲ = Import ▼ = Export
◆ = Import/Export

(G-6347)
SMITHS MEDICAL NORTH AMERICA
5200 Upper Metro Pl Ste 200 (43017-5377)
PHONE..............................614 210-7300
Srini Seshadri, *Pr*
Rob White, *VP*
EMP: 8 **EST:** 2019
SALES (est): 1.99MM **Privately Held**
SIC: 3841 5047 Surgical and medical
instruments; Medical and hospital
equipment

(G-6348)
SOLEO HEALTH INC
6190 Shamrock Ct Ste 100 (43016-1279)
PHONE..............................844 467-8200
EMP: 38
Web: www.soleohealth.com
SIC: 2834 5912 Druggists' preparations
(pharmaceuticals); Drug stores and
proprietary stores
HQ: Soleo Health Inc.
950 Calcon Hook Rd Ste 19
Sharon Hill PA 19079
888 244-2340

(G-6349)
**STANLEY INDUSTRIAL & AUTO LLC
(HQ)**
Also Called: Mac Tools
5195 Blazer Pkwy (43017-3308)
PHONE..............................614 755-7000
Phillip Cox, *Pr*
James Ritter, *
Craig Douglas, *
Bruce Beatt, *
▲ **EMP:** 72 **EST:** 2013
SALES (est): 345.09MM
SALES (corp-wide): 15.37B **Publicly Held**
Web: www.mactools.com
SIC: 3546 5251 3423 3452 Power-driven
handtools; Tools; Hand and edge tools, nec
; Bolts, nuts, rivets, and washers
PA: Stanley Black & Decker, Inc.
1000 Stanley Dr
New Britain CT 06053
860 225-5111

(G-6350)
STANLEY STEEMER INTL INC (PA)
Also Called: Stanley Steemer Carpet Cleaner
5800 Innovation Dr (43016-3271)
P.O. Box 8004 (43016-2004)
PHONE..............................614 764-2007
Wesley C Bates, *CEO*
Justin Bates, *
Eric Smith, *
Philip P Ryser, *
Mark Bunner C.p.a., *VP*
▲ **EMP:** 250 **EST:** 1947
SQ FT: 55,000
SALES (est): 263.72MM
SALES (corp-wide): 263.72MM **Privately
Held**
Web: www.stanleysteemer.com
SIC: 7217 3635 6794 5713 Carpet and
furniture cleaning on location; Household
vacuum cleaners; Franchises, selling or
licensing; Carpets

(G-6351)
STERLING COMMERCE LLC
4600 Lakehurst Ct (43016-2248)
PHONE..............................614 798-2192
EMP: 2500
SIC: 7372 Business oriented computer
software

(G-6352)
STRYKER ORTHOPEDIC
4420 Tuller Rd (43017-5033)
PHONE..............................614 766-2990
John Tripp, *Prin*
EMP: 8 **EST:** 2007
SALES (est): 1.69MM **Privately Held**
SIC: 3841 Surgical and medical instruments

(G-6353)
SUTPHEN CORPORATION (PA)
Also Called: Sutphen
6450 Eiterman Rd (43016-8711)
P.O. Box 158 (43002-0158)
PHONE..............................800 726-7030
Drew Sutphen, *Pr*
Thomas C Sutphen, *
Julie S Phelps, *
Robert M Sutphen, *Stockholder**
Greg Mallon, *
▼ **EMP:** 180 **EST:** 1962
SQ FT: 90,000
SALES (est): 173.19MM
SALES (corp-wide): 173.19MM **Privately
Held**
Web: www.sutphen.com
SIC: 3711 5087 Fire department vehicles
(motor vehicles), assembly of; Firefighting
equipment

(G-6354)
TECH-SONIC INC (PA)
4330 Tuller Rd (43017-5008)
PHONE..............................614 792-3117
Byoung Ou, *Pr*
Hyun Ou, *Treas*
EMP: 8 **EST:** 2005
SALES (est): 2.18MM **Privately Held**
Web: www.tech-sonic.us
SIC: 3548 3699 Electric welding equipment;
Generators, ultrasonic

(G-6355)
TERRADYN CORPORATION
6457 Reflections Dr Ste 200 (43017-2352)
PHONE..............................614 805-0897
Robert Shane Jones, *CFO*
EMP: 15 **EST:** 2019
SALES (est): 1.11MM **Privately Held**
SIC: 1241 Coal mining services

(G-6356)
TOUCH BIONICS INC (DH)
6640 Riverside Dr (43017-9531)
PHONE..............................800 233-6263
Ian Stevens, *CEO*
Melissa Peloquin, *Sec*
Jill Mcgregor, *CFO*
EMP: 7 **EST:** 2007
SQ FT: 6,200
SALES (est): 2.18MM
SALES (corp-wide): 787.61MM **Privately
Held**
SIC: 3842 Prosthetic appliances
HQ: Ossur Europe B.V.
De Schakel 70
Eindhoven NB
499462840

(G-6357)
TRU COMFORT MATTRESS
8994 Mediterra Pl (43016-6098)
PHONE..............................614 595-8600
Samuel Wang, *Admn*
EMP: 6 **EST:** 2012
SALES (est): 123.33K **Privately Held**
SIC: 2515 Mattresses and foundations

(G-6358)
UNITED TRADE PRINTERS LLC
94 N High St Ste 290 (43017-1110)
PHONE..............................614 326-4829
▼ **EMP:** 20
SQ FT: 6,000
SALES (est): 5MM **Privately Held**
SIC: 2752 Commercial printing, lithographic

(G-6359)
UNIVAR SOLUTIONS USA LLC
6000 Parkwood Pl (43016-1213)
PHONE..............................800 531-7106
Dale Leachman, *Brnch Mgr*
EMP: 17
SALES (corp-wide): 11.48B **Privately Held**
Web: www.univarsolutions.com
SIC: 5169 5162 2821 Industrial chemicals;
Plastics materials and basic shapes;
Plastics materials and resins
HQ: Univar Solutions Usa Llc
3075 Hghland Pkwy Ste 200
Downers Grove IL 60515
331 777-6000

(G-6360)
VICTORY POSTCARDS INC
Also Called: Victory Postcards & Souvenirs
6129 Balmoral Dr (43017-8528)
PHONE..............................614 764-8975
Scott Armstrong, *Pr*
Kimberly Armstrong, *VP*
EMP: 6 **EST:** 1989
SALES (est): 527.15K **Privately Held**
Web: www.victorypostcards.com
SIC: 2759 5099 Post cards, picture: printing,
nsk; Souvenirs

(G-6361)
WONDER-SHIRTS INC
7695 Crawley Dr (43017-8820)
PHONE..............................917 679-2336
Matthew Mohr, *Pr*
EMP: 6 **EST:** 2002
SALES (est): 151.02K **Privately Held**
Web: www.wonder-shirts.com
SIC: 2253 2211 T-shirts and tops, knit;
Apparel and outerwear fabrics, cotton

(G-6362)
WW WILLIAMS COMPANY LLC (PA)
400 Metro Pl N Ste 201 (43017-3577)
PHONE..............................614 228-5000
John Simmons, *CEO*
Andy Gasser, *
EMP: 60 **EST:** 1912
SALES (est): 292.86MM
SALES (corp-wide): 292.86MM **Privately
Held**
Web: www.wwwilliams.com
SIC: 3694 7538 7537 Distributors, motor
vehicle engine; Diesel engine repair:
automotive; Automotiv e transmission
repair shops

(G-6363)
ZILLA
6728 Liggett Rd Ste 110 (43016-8306)
PHONE..............................614 763-5311
EMP: 8 **EST:** 2018
SALES (est): 1.07MM **Privately Held**
Web: www.zillaexhibits.com
SIC: 3993 Signs and advertising specialties

Dundee
Tuscarawas County

(G-6364)
ALPINE DAIRY LLC
1658 Township Road 660 (44624-9601)
P.O. Box 209 (44690-0209)
PHONE..............................330 359-6291
Jon Solivan, *Managing Member*
EMP: 46 **EST:** 2012
SALES (est): 5.28MM **Privately Held**
SIC: 2022 Processed cheese

(G-6365)
**GALION-GODWIN TRUCK BDY CO
LLC**
Also Called: Galion Dump Bodies
7415 Township Road 666 (44624-9272)
PHONE..............................330 359-5495
▲ **EMP:** 11 **EST:** 2003
SALES (est): 2.66MM **Privately Held**
Web: www.galiongodwin.com
SIC: 3713 3711 5531 3441 Truck bodies
(motor vehicles); Motor vehicles and car
bodies; Truck equipment and parts;
Fabricated structural metal

(G-6366)
KANN CUSTOM WELDING LLC
2425 Township Road 414 (44624-9239)
PHONE..............................330 231-2719
Norman Nisley, *Pt*
EMP: 6 **EST:** 2021
SALES (est): 553.51K **Privately Held**
SIC: 7692 Welding repair

(G-6367)
L AND J WOODWORKING
9035 Senff Rd (44624-9414)
PHONE..............................330 359-3216
Ray Yoder Junior, *Owner*
EMP: 14 **EST:** 2003
SALES (est): 939.34K **Privately Held**
SIC: 2431 Millwork

(G-6368)
MILLWOOD INC
Also Called: Millwood Pallet Co
18279 Dover Rd (44624-9425)
PHONE..............................330 359-5220
Jim Caughey, *Mgr*
EMP: 63
Web: www.millwoodinc.com
SIC: 2448 Pallets, wood
PA: Millwood, Inc.
3708 International Blvd
Vienna OH 44473

(G-6369)
MILLWOOD WHOLESALE INC
7969 Township Road 662 (44624-9602)
PHONE..............................330 359-6109
David Miller, *Pr*
EMP: 10 **EST:** 2005
SALES (est): 353.51K **Privately Held**
Web: www.millwoodqualityfurniture.com
SIC: 1751 2431 2511 5021 Carpentry work;
Millwork; Kitchen and dining room furniture;
Chairs

(G-6370)
TROYERS TRAIL BOLOGNA INC
6552 State Route 515 (44624-9226)
PHONE..............................330 893-2414
Dale Troyer, *Pr*
Greg Troyer, *VP*
Kenneth Troyer, *Sec*
Darrin Troyer, *VP*
Kevin Troyer, *VP*

GEOGRAPHIC

EMP: 6 **EST:** 1925
SQ FT: 1,050
SALES (est): 1.57MM **Privately Held**
Web: www.troyerstrail.com
SIC: 2011 5411 Cured meats, from meat slaughtered on site; Grocery stores, independent

(G-6371)
TWIN OAKS BARNS LLC
3337 Us Route 62 (44624-9270)
PHONE................................330 893-3126
Melvin Miller, *Owner*
EMP: 10 **EST:** 1973
SALES (est): 986.5K **Privately Held**
Web: www.twinoaksbarnsllc.com
SIC: 2452 3999 Prefabricated buildings, wood; Lawn ornaments

(G-6372)
WENGERD WOOD INC
1760 County Road 200 (44624-9694)
PHONE................................330 359-4300
Wayne Wengerd, *Pr*
Dean Wengerd, *Sec*
Weyne Wengerd, *Pr*
EMP: 17 **EST:** 1998
SALES (est): 699.69K **Privately Held**
Web: www.wengerdwood.com
SIC: 2431 Millwork

(G-6373)
YODER SHARPENING LTD
14280 Durstine Rd (44624-9446)
PHONE................................330 359-0767
David Yoder, *Owner*
David Yoder, *Pt*
EMP: 10 **EST:** 1987
SQ FT: 4,176
SALES (est): 463.29K **Privately Held**
Web: yodersharpeningltd.business.site
SIC: 7699 3545 Knife, saw and tool sharpening and repair; Cutting tools for machine tools

(G-6374)
YUTZY WOODWORKING LTD
2441 Us Route 62 (44624-9233)
PHONE................................330 359-6166
Dennis Yutzy, *Owner*
▲ **EMP:** 22 **EST:** 1999
SALES (est): 2.28MM **Privately Held**
Web: www.urbancollectionsohiousa.com
SIC: 2431 Millwork

Dunkirk
Hardin County

(G-6375)
NORTH COAST CUSTOM MOLDING INC
211 W Geneva St (45836-1008)
PHONE................................419 905-6447
Jim Braeunig, *Pr*
Jane Miller, *VP*
Chad Erick Miller, *VP*
EMP: 15 **EST:** 1988
SQ FT: 9,700
SALES (est): 399.96K **Privately Held**
Web: www.nccmolding.com
SIC: 3089 Molding primary plastics

East Canton
Stark County

(G-6376)
ABC TECHNOLOGIES DLHB INC
336 Wood St S (44730-1348)
P.O. Box 6030 (44706-0030)
PHONE................................330 488-0716
Debbie Seaburn, *Brnch Mgr*
EMP: 49
SALES (corp-wide): 26.11B **Publicly Held**
Web: www.dlhbowles.com
SIC: 3089 3082 Injection molding of plastics; Tubes, unsupported plastics
HQ: Abc Technologies Dlhb, Inc
　　2422 Leo Ave Sw
　　Canton OH 44706
　　330 478-2503

(G-6377)
BARBCO INC
Also Called: Barbco
315 Pekin Dr Se (44730-9462)
P.O. Box 30189 (44730-0189)
PHONE................................330 488-9400
Anthony R Barbera, *Prin*
Tony Barbera, *
David Barbera, *
John F Boggins, *
Richard C Kettler, *
▲ **EMP:** 46 **EST:** 1989
SQ FT: 15,000
SALES (est): 7.99MM **Privately Held**
Web: www.barbco.com
SIC: 3531 3541 Tunneling machinery; Drilling and boring machines

(G-6378)
KNIGHT MATERIAL TECH LLC (PA)
5385 Orchardview Dr Se (44730-9568)
P.O. Box 30070 (44730-0070)
PHONE................................330 488-1651
Kevin Brooks, *Pr*
◆ **EMP:** 41 **EST:** 2001
SALES (est): 19.58MM
SALES (corp-wide): 19.58MM **Privately Held**
Web: www.knightmaterials.com
SIC: 2911 5172 5169 4922 Petroleum refining; Petroleum products, nec; Chemicals and allied products, nec; Natural gas transmission

(G-6379)
RECON SYSTEMS LLC
330 Wood St S (44730-1348)
P.O. Box 30100 (44730-0100)
PHONE................................330 488-0368
Brandon Ballos, *Managing Member*
EMP: 6 **EST:** 2004
SALES (est): 4.57MM **Privately Held**
Web: www.reconsystems.com
SIC: 3565 Packaging machinery

(G-6380)
RESCO PRODUCTS INC
6878 Osnaburg St Se (44730-9529)
P.O. Box 30169 (44730-0169)
PHONE................................330 488-1226
Kurt Bletzacker, *Mgr*
EMP: 9
SQ FT: 1,500
Web: www.rescoproducts.com
SIC: 3255 Clay refractories
HQ: Resco Products, Inc.
　　1 Robinson Plz Ste 300
　　Pittsburgh PA 15205
　　412 494-4491

(G-6381)
WORTHIGNTON PRODUCTS INC
1520 Wood Ave Se (44730-9591)
PHONE................................330 452-7400
Paul Meeks, *Pr*
Jeffrey S Sanger, *VP*
▲ **EMP:** 6 **EST:** 2003
SALES (est): 228.47K **Privately Held**
Web: www.tuffboom.com
SIC: 3443 3429 3089 Buoys, metal; Marine hardware; Buoys and floats, plastics

East Cleveland
Cuyahoga County

(G-6382)
SAVANT TECHNOLOGIES LLC (HQ)
Also Called: GE Lighting, A Savant Company
1975 Noble Rd (44112-1719)
PHONE................................800 435-4448
Kathy Sterio, *Managing Member*
Royal Simmons, *
EMP: 19 **EST:** 2018
SALES (est): 10.82MM
SALES (corp-wide): 399.47MM **Privately Held**
Web: www.gelighting.com
SIC: 3641 Electric lamps
PA: Savant Systems, Inc.
　　45 Perseverance Way
　　Hyannis MA 02601
　　508 683-2500

East Liberty
Logan County

(G-6383)
C & F FABRICATIONS INC
3100 State St (43319-9453)
P.O. Box 258 (43319-0258)
PHONE................................937 666-3234
William D Mercer, *CEO*
Betty J Mercer, *Pr*
Karen Lyon, *Contrlr*
W Douglas Mercer, *Treas*
EMP: 6 **EST:** 1959
SQ FT: 26,000
SALES (est): 1.25MM **Privately Held**
Web: www.cffabcorp.com
SIC: 3496 Miscellaneous fabricated wire products

(G-6384)
CHEMTREAT
11000 State Route 347 (43319-9470)
PHONE................................937 644-2525
Jack Juchcinski, *Pr*
EMP: 7 **EST:** 2017
SALES (est): 918.42K **Privately Held**
Web: www.chemtreat.com
SIC: 3589 Water treatment equipment, industrial

(G-6385)
GREAT LAKES ASSEMBLIES LLC
11590 Township Road 298 (43319-9487)
PHONE................................937 645-3900
Billy R Vickers, *Pr*
EMP: 70 **EST:** 2004
SQ FT: 90,000
SALES (est): 9.49MM
SALES (corp-wide): 30.75MM **Privately Held**
Web: www.modularai.com
SIC: 3711 Automobile assembly, including specialty automobiles
PA: Modular Assembly Innovations Llc
　　600 Stnhnge Pkwy Ste 100a

Dublin OH 43017
614 389-4860

(G-6386)
HARDING MACHINE ACQUISITION CO
Also Called: Global Precision Parts
13060 State Route 287 (43319-9439)
P.O. Box 752 (45891-0752)
PHONE................................937 666-3031
Todd Kriegel, *Pr*
Dave Kriegel, *
Susan Mosier, *
EMP: 75 **EST:** 2006
SALES (est): 4.74MM **Privately Held**
Web: www.globalprecisionpartsinc.com
SIC: 3599 Machine shop, jobbing and repair

East Liverpool
Columbiana County

(G-6387)
C A JOSEPH CO (PA)
13712 Old Fredericktown Rd (43920-9531)
PHONE................................330 385-6869
Charles Chuck Joseph, *Pr*
Mike Joseph, *VP*
Chris Joseph, *VP*
▲ **EMP:** 8 **EST:** 1974
SQ FT: 200,000
SALES (est): 3.09MM
SALES (corp-wide): 3.09MM **Privately Held**
Web: www.cajoseph.com
SIC: 3089 3599 Plastics processing; Machine shop, jobbing and repair

(G-6388)
CAMPBELL SIGNS & APPAREL LLC
47366 Y And O Rd (43920-8747)
PHONE................................330 386-4768
Jodi H Campbell, *CFO*
EMP: 8 **EST:** 1989
SQ FT: 9,600
SALES (est): 921.9K **Privately Held**
Web: www.campbellsa.com
SIC: 3993 2759 2395 Signs, not made in custom sign painting shops; Screen printing ; Embroidery and art needlework

(G-6389)
CF INDUSTRIES INC
425 River Rd (43920-3451)
PHONE................................330 385-5424
Joe Palyan, *Brnch Mgr*
EMP: 128
Web: www.cfindustries.com
SIC: 2873 Anhydrous ammonia
HQ: Cf Industries, Inc.
　　2375 Waterview Dr
　　Northbrook IL 60062
　　847 405-2400

(G-6390)
COMMERCIAL DECAL OHIO INC
46686 Y And O Rd (43920-9710)
P.O. Box 2747 (43920-0747)
PHONE................................330 385-7178
David Dunn, *Pr*
EMP: 6 **EST:** 1939
SQ FT: 11,000
SALES (est): 589.2K **Privately Held**
SIC: 2759 Decals: printing, nsk

(G-6391)
DECARIA BROTHERS INC
104 E 5th St (43920-3031)
PHONE................................330 385-0825
Erin Mccart, *Prin*

EMP: 6
SALES (corp-wide): 1.41MM **Privately Held**
Web: www.portersrx.com
SIC: 2836 Vaccines and other immunizing products
PA: Decaria Brothers, Inc.
4201 Sunset Blvd
Steubenville OH 43952
740 264-1669

(G-6392)
DELTA MANUFACTURING INC
Also Called: Twister Displays
49207 Calcutta Smithferry Rd (43920-9570)
P.O. Box 2704 (43920-0704)
PHONE..................................330 386-1270
Harry Smith, *Pr*
Jeff Smith, *VP*
EMP: 15 **EST:** 1972
SQ FT: 800,000
SALES (est): 2.22MM **Privately Held**
SIC: 3599 Amusement park equipment

(G-6393)
KENTAK PRODUCTS COMPANY
1308 Railroad St (43920-3430)
PHONE..................................330 386-3700
Doug Gomoll, *Pr*
EMP: 60
SALES (corp-wide): 5.1MM **Privately Held**
Web: www.kentak.com
SIC: 3082 3052 Tubes, unsupported plastics ; Plastic hose
PA: Kentak Products Company
1230 Railroad St Ste 1
East Liverpool OH 43920
330 382-2000

(G-6394)
KENTAK PRODUCTS COMPANY (PA)
1230 Railroad St Ste 1 (43920-3406)
PHONE..................................330 382-2000
Douglas A Gomoll, *Pr*
Otto H Gomoll Junior, *Ch Bd*
William Mays, *
▲ **EMP:** 45 **EST:** 1969
SQ FT: 50,000
SALES (est): 5.1MM
SALES (corp-wide): 5.1MM **Privately Held**
Web: www.kentak.com
SIC: 3082 3052 Tubes, unsupported plastics ; Plastic hose

(G-6395)
MASON COLOR WORKS INC
250 E 2nd St (43920-3110)
P.O. Box 76 (43920-5076)
PHONE..................................330 385-4400
▲ **EMP:** 16 **EST:** 1902
SALES (est): 2.15MM **Privately Held**
Web: www.masoncolor.com
SIC: 2816 Inorganic pigments

(G-6396)
SH BELL COMPANY
Also Called: S.H. BELL COMPANY
2217 Michigan Ave (43920-3637)
PHONE..................................412 963-9910
Rusty Davis, *Mgr*
EMP: 33
Web: www.shbellco.com
SIC: 3479 4226 4225 Aluminum coating of metal products; Special warehousing and storage, nec; General warehousing and storage
HQ: S.H. Bell Company, Llc
644 Alpha Dr
Pittsburgh PA 15238
412 963-9910

(G-6397)
SMITH & THOMPSON ENTPS LLC
Also Called: Smith and Thompson Enterprise
46368 Y And O Rd (43920-3869)
PHONE..................................330 386-9345
Diana Smith, *Managing Member*
Frank C Smith, *Owner*
EMP: 17 **EST:** 1972
SALES (est): 429.2K **Privately Held**
SIC: 0783 4959 0782 2951 Planting, pruning, and trimming services; Snowplowing; Lawn and garden services; Asphalt paving mixtures and blocks

(G-6398)
THE CHINA HALL COMPANY
Also Called: Hall Closet
1 Anna St (43920-3675)
P.O. Box 989 (43920-5989)
PHONE..................................330 385-2900
◆ **EMP:** 120 **EST:** 1903
SALES (est): 2.2MM
SALES (corp-wide): 47.97MM **Privately Held**
Web: www.hallchina.com
SIC: 3262 China cookware
PA: The Fiesta Tableware Company
672 Fiesta Dr
Newell WV 26050
304 387-1300

(G-6399)
W C BUNTING CO INC
Also Called: Advertising Specialty Co
1425 Globe St (43920-2110)
PHONE..................................330 385-2050
D Terrence O'hara, *Pr*
Tim O'hara, *VP*
EMP: 6 **EST:** 1880
SQ FT: 23,200
SALES (est): 311.99K **Privately Held**
Web: www.eastliverpoolchina.com
SIC: 3269 3993 Decalcomania work on china and glass; Advertising novelties

---

East Palestine
Columbiana County

(G-6400)
CARDINAL WELDING INC
895 E Taggart St (44413-2465)
P.O. Box 405 (44413-0405)
PHONE..................................330 426-2404
Daniel Shofstahl, *Pr*
EMP: 6 **EST:** 1999
SQ FT: 25,000
SALES (est): 556.69K **Privately Held**
Web: www.cardinalwelding.com
SIC: 7692 3411 Welding repair; Metal cans

(G-6401)
CERAMSOURCE INC
Also Called: Intersource USA
193 N James St (44413-2062)
P.O. Box 6026 (08816)
PHONE..................................732 257-5002
Yong Gong Wang, *Prin*
▲ **EMP:** 16 **EST:** 2011
SALES (est): 2.42MM **Privately Held**
Web: www.ceramsource.com
SIC: 3299 Ceramic fiber

(G-6402)
E R ADVANCED CERAMICS INC
Also Called: US Group
600 E Clark St (44413-2430)
P.O. Box 270 (44413-0270)
PHONE..................................330 426-9433
John Hayday, *Pr*

David A Early, *
Michael Dematteo, *
◆ **EMP:** 34 **EST:** 1990
SQ FT: 68,274
SALES (est): 4.21MM **Privately Held**
Web: www.usstoneware.com
SIC: 3531 3269 3547 3821 Construction machinery; Grinding media, pottery; Rolling mill machinery; Particle size reduction apparatus, laboratory

(G-6403)
EAST PALESTINE CHINA DCTG LLC
870 W Main St (44413-1328)
P.O. Box 109 (44413-0109)
PHONE..................................330 426-9600
▲ **EMP:** 10 **EST:** 2006
SALES (est): 672.21K **Privately Held**
Web: www.eastpalestinechamber.com
SIC: 3231 Decorated glassware: chipped, engraved, etched, etc.

(G-6404)
LIQUID LUGGERS LLC
183 Edgeworth Ave (44413-1554)
PHONE..................................330 426-2538
Lynn Neely, *Prin*
EMP: 50 **EST:** 2011
SALES (est): 4.79MM **Privately Held**
Web: www.liquidluggers.com
SIC: 3443 Tanks for tank trucks, metal plate

(G-6405)
RBS MANUFACTURING INC
145 E Martin St (44413-2337)
P.O. Box 430 (44413-0430)
PHONE..................................330 426-9486
Dennis Garrett, *Prin*
George P Garrett, *
Rosemarie Garrett, *
EMP: 26 **EST:** 1977
SALES (est): 2.42MM **Privately Held**
Web: www.medartglobal.com
SIC: 3999 Dock equipment and supplies, industrial

(G-6406)
ROBERT MAYO INDUSTRIES
Also Called: Mayo, R A Industries
157 E Martin St (44413-2315)
PHONE..................................330 426-2587
Robert A Mayo, *Owner*
EMP: 6 **EST:** 1963
SQ FT: 1,500
SALES (est): 489.23K **Privately Held**
Web: www.mayoindustries.com
SIC: 2512 7641 Upholstered household furniture; Reupholstery and furniture repair

(G-6407)
STROHECKER INCORPORATED
213 N Pleasant Dr (44413-2497)
PHONE..................................330 426-9496
Richard Strohecker, *Pr*
Tony J Moran, *
◆ **EMP:** 40 **EST:** 1947
SQ FT: 4,000
SALES (est): 4.48MM **Privately Held**
Web: www.strohecker.com
SIC: 3567 3443 Industrial furnaces and ovens; Metal parts

(G-6408)
TEST MARK INDUSTRIES INC
995 N Market St (44413-1109)
PHONE..................................330 426-2200
William F Tyger, *Pr*
Martin R Napolitano, *Sec*
William Quinlan, *Dir*
▼ **EMP:** 12 **EST:** 1991
SQ FT: 8,500

SALES (est): 3.67MM **Privately Held**
Web: www.testmark.net
SIC: 5049 3829 Laboratory equipment, except medical or dental; Physical property testing equipment

(G-6409)
TUBETECH INC (PA)
Also Called: Tubetech North America
900 E Taggart St (44413-2424)
P.O. Box 470 (44413-0470)
PHONE..................................330 426-9476
Steve Oliphant, *CEO*
Stephen D Oliphant, *
Jon Roscow, *
Richard Downey, *
EMP: 25 **EST:** 1988
SQ FT: 80,000
SALES (est): 996.27K
SALES (corp-wide): 996.27K **Privately Held**
SIC: 3317 3471 Tubes, wrought: welded or lock joint; Plating of metals or formed products

(G-6410)
UNITY TUBE INC
1862 State Route 165 (44413-9737)
P.O. Box 425 (44413-0425)
PHONE..................................330 426-4282
Robert Howe, *Pr*
EMP: 18 **EST:** 2003
SALES (est): 3.33MM **Privately Held**
Web: www.unitytube.com
SIC: 3498 Tube fabricating (contract bending and shaping)

East Sparta
Stark County

(G-6411)
CLARK SON ACTN LIQUIDATION INC
Also Called: Clark & Son
10233 Sandyville Ave Se (44626-9333)
PHONE..................................330 866-9330
Clark J Barkheimer, *Pr*
▲ **EMP:** 8 **EST:** 2003
SALES (est): 8.12MM **Privately Held**
Web: www.clarkandsoninc.com
SIC: 2434 Wood kitchen cabinets

(G-6412)
LAND SPECIALTIES LLC
2293 Ullet St Sw (44626-9485)
PHONE..................................330 663-6974
Tyler Cookson, *Prin*
EMP: 6 **EST:** 2019
SALES (est): 73.52K **Privately Held**
SIC: 3599 Machine shop, jobbing and repair

(G-6413)
WILLIAM NICCUM
Also Called: L.A.m Wldg & Met Fabrication
11882 Sandyville Ave Se (44626-9340)
PHONE..................................330 415-0154
William Niccum, *Owner*
EMP: 6 **EST:** 2014
SALES (est): 993.66K **Privately Held**
SIC: 3441 Fabricated structural metal

Eastlake
Lake County

(G-6414)
2-M MANUFACTURING COMPANY INC
34560 Lakeland Blvd (44095-5221)

PHONE.................440 269-1270
Mirko Cukelj, *Pr*
Katherine Cukelj, *
EMP: 25 EST: 1969
SALES (est): 4.03MM **Privately Held**
SIC: 3599 Machine shop, jobbing and repair

(G-6415)
AGILE SIGN & LTG MAINT INC
35280 Lakeland Blvd (44095-5359)
PHONE.................440 918-1311
Tim Ruff, *Pr*
EMP: 20 EST: 2007
SQ FT: 10,000
SALES (est): 4.54MM **Privately Held**
Web: www.agilesignohio.com
SIC: 3993 Signs and advertising specialties

(G-6416)
AGR CONSULTING INC
35400 Lakeland Blvd (44095-5304)
PHONE.................440 974-4030
Rob Murnyack, *Pr*
EMP: 11 EST: 1994
SALES (est): 844.53K **Privately Held**
Web: www.absoluteepg.com
SIC: 3599 Machine shop, jobbing and repair

(G-6417)
ASTRO MANUFACTURING &
DESIGN INC (PA)
Also Called: Astro Manufacturing & Design
34459 Curtis Blvd (44095-4011)
PHONE.................888 215-1746
▲ EMP: 175 EST: 1977
SALES (est): 24.29MM
SALES (corp-wide): 24.29MM **Privately**
Held
Web: www.astromfg.com
SIC: 3569 3599 3089 3444 Assembly
machines, non-metalworking; Machine
shop, jobbing and repair; Molding primary
plastics; Sheet metalwork

(G-6418)
ASTRO MODEL DEVELOPMENT
CORP
34459 Curtis Blvd (44095-4011)
PHONE.................440 946-8855
Ken Anderson, *Mgr*
EMP: 6 EST: 2018
SALES (est): 2.35MM **Privately Held**
Web: www.astromfg.com
SIC: 3089 Injection molding of plastics

(G-6419)
ATS MACHINE & TOOL CO
37033 Lake Shore Blvd (44095-1103)
PHONE.................440 255-1120
Robert E Dutko, *Pr*
Denise Dutko, *VP*
EMP: 12 EST: 1981
SALES (est): 851.02K **Privately Held**
Web: www.atsmachine.com
SIC: 3599 Machine shop, jobbing and repair

(G-6420)
BOND DISTRIBUTING LLC
Also Called: One Time
35585 Curtis Blvd Unit D (44095-4104)
PHONE.................440 461-7920
Scott Fishel, *Managing Member*
EMP: 6 EST: 2000
SALES (est): 504.57K **Privately Held**
Web: www.onetimewood.com
SIC: 2899 Chemical preparations, nec

(G-6421)
CONSOLDTED PRECISION PDTS
CORP

Also Called: Cpp Cleveland
34000 Lakeland Blvd (44095-5215)
PHONE.................440 953-0053
Carol Robinson, *Brnch Mgr*
EMP: 228
SALES (corp-wide): 1.9B **Privately Held**
Web: www.cppcorp.com
SIC: 3369 Castings, except die-castings,
precision
PA: Consolidated Precision Products Corp.
1621 Euclid Ave Ste 1850
Cleveland OH 44115
216 453-4800

(G-6422)
CPP-CLEVELAND INC
Also Called: Cpp-Eastlake
34000 Lakeland Blvd (44095-5215)
PHONE.................440 953-0053
James Stewart, *CEO*
EMP: 200
SALES (corp-wide): 1.9B **Privately Held**
Web: www.cppcorp.com
SIC: 3369 Lead castings, except die-castings
HQ: Cpp-Cleveland, Inc.
26855 Bluestone Blvd
Euclid OH 44132
216 453-4800

(G-6423)
DIE CO INC
1889 E 337th St (44095-5231)
P.O. Box 5248 (44095-0248)
PHONE.................440 942-8856
Donald G Hawk, *Pr*
Michael T Hawk, *
Donna Corrigan, *
▲ EMP: 48 EST: 1963
SQ FT: 35,000
SALES (est): 4.86MM
SALES (corp-wide): 46.16MM **Privately**
Held
Web: www.diecoinc.com
SIC: 3469 3496 3471 3429 Stamping metal
for the trade; Miscellaneous fabricated wire
products; Plating and polishing; Hardware,
nec
PA: Fastener Industries, Inc.
1 Berea Commons Ste 209
Berea OH 44017
440 243-0034

(G-6424)
EAGLEHEAD MANUFACTURING CO
35280 Lakeland Blvd Ste K (44095-5359)
PHONE.................440 951-0400
Jeffery Cotman, *CEO*
Teresa Cotman, *VP*
EMP: 18 EST: 1996
SALES (est): 986.21K **Privately Held**
Web: www.eaglehead.com
SIC: 3599 Machine shop, jobbing and repair

(G-6425)
ENPAC LLC
34355 Melinz Pkwy (44095-4033)
PHONE.................440 975-0070
Timothy Reed, *Pt*
Timothy D Reed, *CFO*
▼ EMP: 80 EST: 2001
SQ FT: 66,500
SALES (est): 5.53MM **Privately Held**
Web: www.enpac.com
SIC: 3089 Plastics containers, except foam

(G-6426)
ENPRESS LLC
34899 Curtis Blvd (44095-4015)
PHONE.................440 510-0108
Douglas Honer, *Managing Member*
Timothy Reid, *Managing Member*

▼ EMP: 40 EST: 2002
SALES (est): 9.13MM **Privately Held**
Web: www.enpress.com
SIC: 3089 Injection molding of plastics

(G-6427)
ESCO TURBINE TECH CLEVELAND
34000 Lakeland Blvd (44095-5215)
PHONE.................440 953-0053
EMP: 14 EST: 2015
SALES (est): 2.04MM **Privately Held**
Web: www.cppcorp.com
SIC: 3535 Conveyors and conveying
equipment

(G-6428)
ESCO TURBINE TECHNOLOGIES -
CLEVELAND INC
Also Called: Consolidated Precision Pdts
34000 Lakeland Blvd (44095-5215)
P.O. Box 10123 (97296-0123)
PHONE.................440 953-0053
EMP: 170
Web: www.cppcorp.com
SIC: 3369 Castings, except die-castings,
precision

(G-6429)
EUCLID PRECISION GRINDING CO
35400 Lakeland Blvd (44095-5304)
PHONE.................440 946-8888
Eric Barbe, *Pr*
EMP: 6 EST: 1945
SQ FT: 9,600
SALES (est): 849.27K **Privately Held**
SIC: 3599 Machine shop, jobbing and repair

(G-6430)
H & R METAL FINISHING INC
1052 E 347th St (44095-2635)
PHONE.................440 942-6656
Rosemarie Cruz, *Pr*
Rose Espendez, *Sec*
EMP: 6 EST: 1984
SALES (est): 495.4K **Privately Held**
Web: www.hrmetal.com
SIC: 3471 Electroplating of metals or formed
products

(G-6431)
HEETER PRINTING COMPANY INC
33212 Lakeland Blvd (44095-5205)
PHONE.................440 946-0606
Blake Laduc, *Mgr*
EMP: 50
SALES (corp-wide): 37.12MM **Privately**
Held
Web: www.heeter.com
SIC: 2752 Offset printing
PA: Heeter Printing Company, Inc.
441 Technology Drive
Canonsburg PA 15317
724 746-8900

(G-6432)
HI CARB CORP
1857 E 337th St # A (44095-5231)
PHONE.................216 486-5000
John R Sonnie, *Pr*
EMP: 8 EST: 1955
SALES (est): 851.53K **Privately Held**
SIC: 3545 Tools and accessories for
machine tools

(G-6433)
HIGH QUALITY TOOLS INC (PA)
Also Called: High Quality Tools
34940 Lakeland Blvd (44095-5226)
PHONE.................440 975-9684
Mirko Cukelj, *Pr*

▲ EMP: 12 EST: 1983
SQ FT: 3,000
SALES (est): 4.43MM
SALES (corp-wide): 4.43MM **Privately**
Held
Web: www.hqtinc.com
SIC: 5085 3545 Industrial tools; Tools and
accessories for machine tools

(G-6434)
KRENGEL EQUIPMENT LLC
Also Called: Krengel Manufacturing
34580 Lakeland Blvd (44095-5221)
PHONE.................440 946-3570
EMP: 140 EST: 2013
SALES (est): 8.94MM **Privately Held**
Web: www.krengelmfg.com
SIC: 3363 3544 Aluminum die-castings; Dies
and die holders for metal cutting, forming,
die casting

(G-6435)
MICONVI PROPERTIES INC
Also Called: Bevcorp Properties
37200 Research Dr (44095-1869)
PHONE.................440 954-3500
Michael Connelly, *Pr*
Vicki Connelly, *
◆ EMP: 6 EST: 1991
SALES (est): 450.6K **Privately Held**
Web: www.bevcorp.com
SIC: 3565 Bottling machinery: filling,
capping, labeling

(G-6436)
MIDWEST PRECISION HOLDINGS
INC (HQ)
34700 Lakeland Blvd (44095-5223)
PHONE.................440 497-4086
Wayne Foley, *Pr*
EMP: 13 EST: 1953
SALES (est): 11.01MM
SALES (corp-wide): 47.95MM **Privately**
Held
Web: www.midwestllc.com
SIC: 3812 Acceleration indicators and
systems components, aerospace
PA: Tribus Aerospace Llc
10 S Wacker Dr Ste 3300
Chicago IL 60606
312 876-7267

(G-6437)
MIDWEST PRECISION LLC
34700 Lakeland Blvd (44095-5223)
PHONE.................440 951-2333
E Wayne Foley, *Managing Member*
William Marlowe, *
EMP: 52 EST: 2010
SQ FT: 38,000
SALES (est): 11.01MM
SALES (corp-wide): 47.95MM **Privately**
Held
Web: www.midwestllc.com
SIC: 3451 Screw machine products
HQ: Midwest Precision Holdings Inc.
34700 Lakeland Blvd
Eastlake OH 44095
440 497-4086

(G-6438)
MOLD MASTERS INTL LLC
34000 Melinz Pkwy (44095-4054)
PHONE.................440 953-0220
Jim Allen, *CEO*
George Goodrich, *
Robert Soltis, *
Vic Sirotek, *
Ron Kern, *
EMP: 170 EST: 1961
SQ FT: 54,000

SALES (est): 5.2MM **Privately Held**
Web: www.pccairfoils.com
SIC: 3324 2842 Steel investment foundries; Polishes and sanitation goods

(G-6439)
NATIONAL BULLET CO
34971 Glen Dr (44095-2622)
PHONE..............................800 317-9506
Ken M Bayko, *Pr*
Nick Sasso, *CEO*
EMP: 9 **EST:** 1976
SQ FT: 2,000
SALES (est): 332.93K **Privately Held**
Web: www.nationalbullet.com
SIC: 3482 5941 Small arms ammunition; Sporting goods and bicycle shops

(G-6440)
PCC AIRFOILS LLC
34300 Melinz Pkwy (44095-4026)
PHONE..............................440 585-8247
EMP: 279
SALES (corp-wide): 424.23B **Publicly Held**
Web: www.pccairfoils.com
SIC: 3369 Castings, except die-castings, precision
HQ: Pcc Airfoils, Llc
      3401 Entp Pkwy Ste 200
      Beachwood OH 44122
      216 831-3590

(G-6441)
POLYMER & STEEL TECH INC
34899 Curtis Blvd (44095-4015)
PHONE..............................440 510-0108
Douglas Horner, *Pr*
▼ **EMP:** 50 **EST:** 1988
SQ FT: 66,000
SALES (est): 1.14MM **Privately Held**
Web: polymer-steel-technologies-inc.sbcontract.com
SIC: 3089 Plastics containers, except foam

(G-6442)
RVTRONIX CORPORATION
34099 Melinz Pkwy Unit E (44095-4001)
PHONE..............................440 359-7200
Paul Spivak, *CEO*
EMP: 28 **EST:** 1998
SALES (est): 5.74MM
SALES (corp-wide): 6.0MM **Privately Held**
Web: www.intellitronix.com
SIC: 3647 Automotive lighting fixtures, nec
PA: Evergreen Cooperative Corporation
      4205 St Clair Ave
      Cleveland OH 44103
      216 268-5399

(G-6443)
STAINLESS SPECIALTIES INC
33240 Lakeland Blvd (44095-5205)
PHONE..............................440 942-4242
Dennis O'brien, *Pr*
Joan Podmore, *
EMP: 25 **EST:** 1993
SQ FT: 26,000
SALES (est): 2.71MM **Privately Held**
Web: www.hoodmart.com
SIC: 3441 3312 Fabricated structural metal; Blast furnaces and steel mills

(G-6444)
SUBURBAN MANUFACTURING CO
1924 E 337th St (44095-5229)
PHONE..............................440 953-2024
Richard E Grice, *Pr*
EMP: 60 **EST:** 1979
SQ FT: 31,000

SALES (est): 2.41MM **Privately Held**
Web: www.submfg.com
SIC: 3599 3546 3469 3561 Machine shop, jobbing and repair; Power-driven handtools; Metal stampings, nec; Pumps and pumping equipment

(G-6445)
T & D FABRICATING INC
Also Called: T & D Fabricating
1489 E 363rd St (44095-4137)
PHONE..............................440 951-5646
Dallas Adkins, *Pr*
Helen Adkins, *Sec*
Todd Adkins, *VP*
EMP: 20 **EST:** 1996
SALES (est): 2.88MM **Privately Held**
Web: www.tdfabricating.com
SIC: 3469 3498 3354 3351 Metal stampings, nec; Fabricated pipe and fittings; Aluminum extruded products; Copper rolling and drawing

(G-6446)
TYMOCA PARTNERS LLC
Also Called: Federal Gear
33220 Lakeland Blvd (44095-5205)
PHONE..............................440 946-4327
EMP: 10 **EST:** 2007
SALES (est): 2.91MM **Privately Held**
Web: www.fg-machine.com
SIC: 3462 Iron and steel forgings

(G-6447)
UNITED MACHINE AND TOOL INC
1956 E 337th St (44095-5229)
PHONE..............................440 946-7677
Martha Klatt, *CEO*
Harry Klatt, *Pr*
EMP: 8 **EST:** 1965
SQ FT: 10,000
SALES (est): 704.52K **Privately Held**
Web: www.unitedmachandtool.com
SIC: 3599 Machine shop, jobbing and repair

Eaton
Preble County

(G-6448)
AUKERMAN J F STEEL RULE DIE
5582 Ozias Rd (45320-9716)
P.O. Box 374 (45320-0374)
PHONE..............................937 456-4498
John F Aukerman Junior, *Pr*
EMP: 7 **EST:** 1975
SALES (est): 275.29K **Privately Held**
SIC: 3544 Dies, steel rule

(G-6449)
BRUBAKER METALCRAFTS INC
209 N Franklin St (45320-1819)
P.O. Box 353 (45320-0353)
PHONE..............................937 456-5834
Paul Brubaker, *Pr*
Wilma Brubaker, *Sec*
EMP: 7 **EST:** 1973
SQ FT: 3,000
SALES (est): 468.98K **Privately Held**
Web: www.brubakermetalcrafts.com
SIC: 3229 Lantern globes

(G-6450)
BULLEN ULTRASONICS INC
Also Called: Bullen
1301 Miller Williams Rd (45320-8507)
PHONE..............................937 456-7133
Mary A Bullen, *Pr*
Mary A Moreland, *
▲ **EMP:** 65 **EST:** 1969

SQ FT: 4,748
SALES (est): 8.29MM **Privately Held**
Web: www.bullentech.com
SIC: 3599 Machine shop, jobbing and repair

(G-6451)
CAMDEN CONCRETE PRODUCTS LLC
Also Called: Shawnee Molds
4952 State Route 732 W (45320-9574)
PHONE..............................937 456-1229
▼ **EMP:** 6 **EST:** 1983
SALES (est): 447.88K **Privately Held**
Web: www.shawneemolds.com
SIC: 3544 Industrial molds

(G-6452)
CORNERSTONE MANUFACTURING INC
861 Us Route 35 (45320-8638)
P.O. Box 682 (45320-0682)
PHONE..............................937 456-5930
Ronnie J Kutter, *Pr*
Trisha Kutter, *VP*
EMP: 9 **EST:** 1980
SQ FT: 4,000
SALES (est): 758.03K **Privately Held**
Web: www.cornerstone-manufacturing.com
SIC: 3544 Special dies and tools

(G-6453)
ELECTRO-CAP INTERNATIONAL INC
1011 W Lexington Rd (45320-9290)
P.O. Box 87 (45320-0087)
PHONE..............................937 456-6099
W Nelson Hardin, *Pr*
Janet L Hardin, *Sec*
EMP: 18 **EST:** 1988
SQ FT: 10,000
SALES (est): 1.63MM **Privately Held**
Web: www.electro-cap.com
SIC: 3089 5047 Caps, plastics; Hospital equipment and furniture

(G-6454)
HENNY PENNY CORPORATION (PA)
1219 U S 35 W (45320)
P.O. Box 60 (45320-0060)
PHONE..............................937 456-8400
Steve Cobb, *Ch*
Rob Connelly, *
◆ **EMP:** 508 **EST:** 1986
SQ FT: 400,000
SALES (est): 128.51MM
SALES (corp-wide): 128.51MM **Privately Held**
Web: www.hennypenny.com
SIC: 3589 Cooking equipment, commercial

(G-6455)
I DREAM OF CAKES
995 Camden Rd (45320-9511)
PHONE..............................937 533-6024
Julie Rosfeld, *Prin*
EMP: 6 **EST:** 2006
SALES (est): 158.3K **Privately Held**
Web: www.idreamofcakes.net
SIC: 5461 2041 Cakes; Flour and other grain mill products

(G-6456)
INTERNATIONAL PAPER COMPANY
Also Called: International Paper
900 Us Route 35 (45320-8647)
PHONE..............................937 456-4131
John Winters, *Brnch Mgr*
EMP: 92
SALES (corp-wide): 18.62B **Publicly Held**
Web: www.internationalpaper.com
SIC: 2621 Paper mills

PA: International Paper Company
      6400 Poplar Ave
      Memphis TN 38197
      901 419-7000

(G-6457)
KRAMER POWER EQUIPMENT CO
2388 State Route 726 N (45320-9217)
PHONE..............................937 456-2232
Joseph Kramer, *Pr*
C Jason Kramer, *VP*
EMP: 6 **EST:** 1975
SQ FT: 20,000
SALES (est): 653.62K **Privately Held**
Web: www.kramerusa.com
SIC: 3599 3444 3441 7692 Machine shop, jobbing and repair; Sheet metalwork; Fabricated structural metal; Welding repair

(G-6458)
LAM RESEARCH CORPORATION
Also Called: Lam Research
960 S Franklin St (45320-9421)
PHONE..............................937 472-3311
Mike Snell, *Genl Mgr*
EMP: 11
SALES (corp-wide): 14.91B **Publicly Held**
Web: www.lamresearch.com
SIC: 3674 Semiconductors and related devices
PA: Lam Research Corporation
      4650 Cushing Pkwy
      Fremont CA 94538
      510 572-0200

(G-6459)
LEE PLASTIC COMPANY LLC
1100 Us Route 35 (45320-8620)
P.O. Box 271 (45320-0271)
PHONE..............................937 456-5720
EMP: 8 **EST:** 1990
SQ FT: 8,000
SALES (est): 476.48K **Privately Held**
Web: www.lee-plastic.com
SIC: 3089 Injection molding of plastics

(G-6460)
NEATON AUTO PRODUCTS MFG INC (HQ)
975 S Franklin St (45320-9400)
PHONE..............................937 456-7103
Naoki Horikawa, *Pr*
David Gulling, *
Kazuhiro Watanabe, *
▲ **EMP:** 25 **EST:** 1984
SQ FT: 500,000
SALES (est): 45.53MM **Privately Held**
Web: www.neaton.com
SIC: 3714 Motor vehicle engines and parts
PA: Nihon Plast Co.,Ltd.
      3507-15, Yamamiya
      Fujinomiya SZO 418-0

(G-6461)
OLDE SCHLHUSE VNYRD WINERY LLC
152 State Route 726 N (45320-9203)
P.O. Box 230 (45321-0230)
PHONE..............................937 472-9463
Mark Zdobinski, *Managing Member*
EMP: 15 **EST:** 2015
SALES (est): 394.96K **Privately Held**
Web: www.oshwinery.com
SIC: 2084 Wines

(G-6462)
PARKER-HANNIFIN CORPORATION
Tube Fittings Division
725 N Beech St (45320-1499)
PHONE..............................937 456-5571

GEOGRAPHIC

William Bowman, *Brnch Mgr*
EMP: 237
SALES (corp-wide): 19.93B **Publicly Held**
Web: www.parker.com
SIC: 3494 5074 3498 3492 Pipe fittings;
Plumbing fittings and supplies; Tube
fabricating (contract bending and shaping);
Fluid power valves and hose fittings
PA: Parker-Hannifin Corporation
6035 Parkland Blvd
Cleveland OH 44124
216 896-3000

(G-6463)
SILFEX INC (HQ)
950 S Franklin St (45320-9421)
PHONE.............................937 472-3311
Kit Armstrong, *Prin*
▲ **EMP:** 49 **EST:** 2006
SALES (est): 48.15MM
SALES (corp-wide): 14.91B **Publicly Held**
Web: www.silfex.com
SIC: 3674 Semiconductors and related
devices
PA: Lam Research Corporation
4650 Cushing Pkwy
Fremont CA 94538
510 572-0200

Edgerton
Williams County

(G-6464)
BUILDING CONCEPTS INC (PA)
Also Called: Cardinal Truss & Components
444 N Michigan Ave (43517-9811)
P.O. Box 579 (43517-0579)
PHONE.............................419 298-2371
TOLL FREE: 800
William H Lutterbein, *Pr*
Dennis Imbrock, *VP*
Donald C Landel, *VP*
EMP: 16 **EST:** 1924
SQ FT: 14,000
SALES (est): 941.95K
SALES (corp-wide): 941.95K **Privately Held**
Web: www.lutterbein.com
SIC: 5211 1521 2439 Lumber and other
building materials; Single-family housing
construction; Trusses, wooden roof

(G-6465)
CENTER CONCRETE INC (PA)
8790 Us Highway 6 (43517-9712)
P.O. Box 340 (43517-0340)
PHONE.............................800 453-4224
Don Pahl, *Pr*
Gary Weber, *Sec*
EMP: 10 **EST:** 1990
SQ FT: 800
SALES (est): 2.22MM **Privately Held**
Web: www.centerconcreteinc.com
SIC: 3273 Ready-mixed concrete

(G-6466)
EDGERTON FORGE INC (HQ)
257 E Morrison St (43517-9302)
PHONE.............................419 298-2333
Richard Horton, *CEO*
Skip Dietrick, *
Mark A Cluadio, *
Gordon Miller, *
EMP: 61 **EST:** 1972
SQ FT: 70,000
SALES (est): 10.15MM
SALES (corp-wide): 474.53MM **Privately Held**
Web: www.edgertonforge.com

SIC: 3462 3714 3423 Iron and steel forgings;
Motor vehicle parts and accessories; Hand
and edge tools, nec
PA: Avis Industrial Corporation
1909 S Main St
Upland IN 46989
765 998-8100

(G-6467)
MATSU OHIO INC
228 E Morrison St (43517-9389)
PHONE.............................419 298-2394
Dave Rutila, *Pr*
Art Artuso, *
Galliano Tiberini, *
Becky Algeo, *
◆ **EMP:** 122 **EST:** 2009
SQ FT: 220,000
SALES (est): 44.09MM
SALES (corp-wide): 97.29MM **Privately Held**
Web: www.matcor-matsu.com
SIC: 3465 Body parts, automobile: stamped
metal
PA: Matsu Manufacturing Inc
7657 Bramalea Rd
Brampton ON L6T 5
905 291-5000

(G-6468)
OREN ELLIOT PRODUCTS LLC
128 W Vine St (43517-8606)
PHONE.............................419 298-0015
Steven Elloitt, *CEO*
EMP: 50 **EST:** 2021
SALES (est): 5.38MM **Privately Held**
Web: www.orenelliottproducts.com
SIC: 3675 Electronic capacitors

(G-6469)
SOEMHEJEE INC
128 W Vine St (43517-8606)
P.O. Box 638 (43517-0638)
PHONE.............................419 298-2306
June Elliott, *Pr*
Oren Elliott, *
EMP: 45 **EST:** 1925
SQ FT: 24,000
SALES (est): 9.57MM **Privately Held**
Web: www.orenelliottproducts.com
SIC: 3675 3451 3469 Electronic capacitors;
Screw machine products; Metal stampings,
nec

(G-6470)
STAFFORD GRAVEL INC
4225 Co Rd 79 (43517)
P.O. Box 340 (43517-0340)
PHONE.............................419 298-2440
Gerry Weber, *Prin*
EMP: 6 **EST:** 2008
SALES (est): 1.71MM **Privately Held**
Web: www.staffordgravel.com
SIC: 1442 Construction sand and gravel

(G-6471)
STARK TRUSS COMPANY INC
400 Component Dr (43517)
P.O. Box 535 (43517-0535)
PHONE.............................419 298-3777
Duane Miller, *Brnch Mgr*
EMP: 46
SQ FT: 45,000
SALES (corp-wide): 90.76MM **Privately Held**
Web: www.starktruss.com
SIC: 2439 2511 2411 Trusses, wooden roof;
Wood household furniture; Logging
PA: Stark Truss Company, Inc.
109 Miles Ave Sw
Canton OH 44710

330 478-2100

Edon
Williams County

(G-6472)
AGRIDRY LLC
3460 Us Highway 20 (43518-9733)
P.O. Box 336 (43518-0336)
PHONE.............................419 459-4399
Eli P Troyer, *Managing Member*
EMP: 7 **EST:** 2005
SALES (est): 1.03MM **Privately Held**
Web: www.agridrylink.com
SIC: 3567 1541 Driers and redriers,
industrial process; Grain elevator
construction

(G-6473)
DIMENSION HARDWOOD VENEERS INC
509 Woodville St (43518)
P.O. Box 59 (43518-0059)
PHONE.............................419 272-2245
Paul Horstman, *Pr*
▲ **EMP:** 50 **EST:** 1977
SQ FT: 56,000
SALES (est): 8.55MM **Privately Held**
Web: www.dimensionhardwoods.com
SIC: 2435 Hardwood veneer and plywood

(G-6474)
L & L MACHINE INC
2919 County Road 2I (43518-9771)
PHONE.............................419 272-5000
Laurie Lehman, *CEO*
Michael Lehman, *Pr*
EMP: 11 **EST:** 2002
SQ FT: 40,000
SALES (est): 966.38K **Privately Held**
Web: www.landlmachine.com
SIC: 3599 Machine shop, jobbing and repair

(G-6475)
LINAMAR STRCTURES USA MICH INC
Also Called: Mobex Global
507 W Indiana St (43518-9644)
P.O. Box 77 (46701)
PHONE.............................260 636-7030
EMP: 94
SALES (corp-wide): 7.54B **Privately Held**
Web: www.mobexglobal.com
SIC: 3714 Motor vehicle engines and parts
HQ: Linamar Structures Usa (Michigan) Inc.
32233 W 8 Mile Rd
Livonia MI 48152
248 477-6240

(G-6476)
LINAMAR STRCTURES USA MICH INC
Also Called: Mobex Global
201 Leanne St (43518)
PHONE.............................567 249-0838
EMP: 200
SALES (corp-wide): 7.54B **Privately Held**
Web: www.mobexglobal.com
SIC: 3714 Motor vehicle engines and parts
HQ: Linamar Structures Usa (Michigan) Inc.
32233 W 8 Mile Rd
Livonia MI 48152
248 477-6240

(G-6477)
NORTHWEST MOLDED PLASTICS
14372 County Road 4 (43518-9765)
PHONE.............................419 459-4414
Richard L Lemmon, *Owner*

EMP: 9 **EST:** 1976
SQ FT: 25,000
SALES (est): 495.29K **Privately Held**
Web: www.cubscoutwheelsandtires.com
SIC: 3089 Injection molding of plastics

(G-6478)
PLAS-TEC CORP
601 W Indiana St (43518-9645)
PHONE.............................419 272-2731
Kenneth Sharlow, *Genl Mgr*
Dennis Cox, *
EMP: 60 **EST:** 1970
SQ FT: 85,000
SALES (est): 5.34MM **Privately Held**
Web: www.plasteccorp.com
SIC: 3089 Injection molding of plastics

(G-6479)
PTC ENTERPRISES INC
3047 County Road K (43518-9551)
PHONE.............................419 272-2524
Bill Patton, *Pr*
David C Newcomer, *
▲ **EMP:** 50 **EST:** 1993
SALES (est): 4.96MM **Privately Held**
Web: www.ptc-enterprises.com
SIC: 3089 Injection molding of plastics

Eldorado
Preble County

(G-6480)
MIAMI VALLEY PLASTICS INC
310 S Main St (45321-9731)
PHONE.............................937 273-3200
George W Halderman, *CEO*
▲ **EMP:** 35 **EST:** 1967
SQ FT: 2,569
SALES (est): 2.45MM **Privately Held**
Web: www.miamivalleyplastics.com
SIC: 3089 Injection molding of plastics

Elida
Allen County

(G-6481)
A & D WOOD PRODUCTS INC (PA)
4220 Sherrick Rd (45807-9783)
PHONE.............................419 331-8859
Joseph Peters, *Pr*
EMP: 9 **EST:** 1991
SALES (est): 897.11K **Privately Held**
SIC: 2448 Pallets, wood

(G-6482)
AIRCRAFT DYNAMICS CORPORATION
Also Called: Aircraft Dynamics
418 E Kiracofe Ave (45807-1030)
P.O. Box 3038 (45807-0038)
PHONE.............................419 331-0371
Jack D Jones, *Pr*
Doug Thackery, *VP*
Steve Jones, *Ex VP*
Alice White, *Sec*
▲ **EMP:** 18 **EST:** 1935
SQ FT: 12,000
SALES (est): 3.22MM **Privately Held**
Web: www.aircraftdynamics.com
SIC: 7359 3546 Equipment rental and
leasing, nec; Power-driven handtools

(G-6483)
LIMA MILLWORK INC
4251 East Rd (45807-1534)
PHONE.............................419 331-3303

Mark Niemeyer, *Pr*
Thelma Neimeyer, *VP*
EMP: 8
SQ FT: 16,000
SALES (est): 881.68K **Privately Held**
Web: www.limamillwork.com
SIC: 2431 2511 2434 3281 Millwork; Wood household furniture; Wood kitchen cabinets ; Cut stone and stone products

(G-6484)
ORICK STAMPING INC
614 E Kiracofe Ave (45807-1034)
PHONE..........................419 331-0600
Paul Orick, *CEO*
Greg Orick, *
Monica Orick, *
EMP: 80 **EST:** 1969
SQ FT: 100,000
SALES (est): 12.98MM **Privately Held**
Web: www.orickstamping.com
SIC: 3469 3544 Stamping metal for the trade ; Special dies, tools, jigs, and fixtures

(G-6485)
PETERS FAMILY ENTERPRISES INC
5959 Allentown Rd (45807-9413)
P.O. Box 3133 (45807-0133)
PHONE..........................419 339-0555
Dave Peters, *Pr*
EMP: 8 **EST:** 2003
SALES (est): 448.19K **Privately Held**
SIC: 2499 Decorative wood and woodwork

(G-6486)
PRECISION TOOL GRINDING INC
216 S Greenlawn Ave Ste 5a (45807-1380)
PHONE..........................419 339-9959
Gary Schneer, *Pr*
EMP: 8 **EST:** 1988
SQ FT: 6,200
SALES (est): 748.47K **Privately Held**
Web: www.precisiontoolgrinding.com
SIC: 3599 Machine shop, jobbing and repair

(G-6487)
RANGE KLEEN MFG INC
4240 East Rd (45807-1533)
P.O. Box 696 (45802-0696)
PHONE..........................419 331-8000
Patrick O'connor, *Pr*
▲ **EMP:** 403 **EST:** 1971
SQ FT: 50,000
SALES (est): 10.54MM **Privately Held**
Web: www.rangekleen.com
SIC: 3365 3469 Cooking/kitchen utensils, cast aluminum; Metal stampings, nec

Elmore
Ottawa County

(G-6488)
CALVIN J MAGSIG
Also Called: Elmore Mfg Co
343 Clinton St (43416-7703)
P.O. Box 32 (43416-0032)
PHONE..........................419 862-3311
Calvin J Magsig, *Owner*
EMP: 7 **EST:** 1945
SQ FT: 15,000
SALES (est): 614.59K **Privately Held**
SIC: 3599 3494 Machine shop, jobbing and repair; Valves and pipe fittings, nec

(G-6489)
MACHINING TECHNOLOGIES INC (PA)
Also Called: M T
468 Maple St (43416-9423)

P.O. Box 287 (43416-0287)
PHONE..........................419 862-3110
William M Van Dorn, *CEO*
Thomas C Van Dorn, *
▲ **EMP:** 41 **EST:** 1985
SQ FT: 32,000
SALES (est): 8.99MM
SALES (corp-wide): 8.99MM **Privately Held**
Web: www.machiningtech.com
SIC: 3082 3545 Unsupported plastics profile shapes; Precision tools, machinists'

(G-6490)
MARTIN INDUSTRIES INC
473 Maple St (43416-9402)
P.O. Box 569 (43416-0569)
PHONE..........................419 862-2694
Tim Gerkensmeyer, *Pr*
EMP: 6 **EST:** 1985
SQ FT: 10,000
SALES (est): 1.15MM **Privately Held**
SIC: 3069 3061 Hard rubber and molded rubber products; Mechanical rubber goods

(G-6491)
MATERION BRUSH INC
14710 W Portage River South Rd (43416-9500)
PHONE..........................419 862-2745
Art Tupper, *Brnch Mgr*
EMP: 700
SQ FT: 100,000
Web: www.materion.com
SIC: 3339 3369 3341 Beryllium metal; Nonferrous foundries, nec; Secondary nonferrous metals
HQ: Materion Brush Inc.
6070 Parkland Blvd
Mayfield Heights OH 44124
216 486-4200

Elyria
Lorain County

(G-6492)
AEROWAVE INC
361 Windward Dr (44035-1633)
PHONE..........................440 731-8464
Bob Avon, *CEO*
EMP: 7 **EST:** 2012
SALES (est): 490.46K **Privately Held**
SIC: 3548 Welding apparatus

(G-6493)
ALCO MANUFACTURING CORP LLC (PA)
10584 Middle Ave (44035-7812)
PHONE..........................440 458-5165
Matt Dietrich, *CEO*
EMP: 22 **EST:** 2006
SALES (est): 24.84MM **Privately Held**
Web: www.alco.com
SIC: 3451 Screw machine products

(G-6494)
ALEXIS CONCRETE ENTERPRISE INC
672 Sugar Ln (44035-6310)
PHONE..........................440 366-0031
Edward Machovia, *Pr*
EMP: 7 **EST:** 2000
SALES (est): 963.21K **Privately Held**
Web: www.alexisconcrete.com
SIC: 3273 Ready-mixed concrete

(G-6495)
AMERICAN FLUID POWER INC
144 Reaser Ct (44035-6285)
PHONE..........................877 223-8742
Robert Weltman, *COO*
EMP: 7 **EST:** 2012
SALES (est): 2.23MM **Privately Held**
Web: www.amerfluidpower.com
SIC: 3542 Bending machines

(G-6496)
AMERICAN TURF RECYCLING LLC
860 Taylor St (44035-6232)
PHONE..........................440 323-0306
Daniel Macphee, *Pr*
EMP: 8 **EST:** 2014
SQ FT: 15,000
SALES (est): 590.06K **Privately Held**
SIC: 2821 Cellulose acetate (plastics)

(G-6497)
APPLIED ENGNEERED SURFACES INC
535 Ternes Ln Rear (44035-6280)
PHONE..........................440 366-0440
Lauren Yoakam, *Pr*
EMP: 19 **EST:** 1999
SALES (est): 4.78MM **Privately Held**
Web: www.uhpsurfaces.com
SIC: 3441 Building components, structural steel

(G-6498)
ARNCO CORPORATION
860 Garden St (44035-4877)
PHONE..........................800 847-7661
Arlene P Tengel, *Prin*
William E Smith, *
◆ **EMP:** 16 **EST:** 1985
SALES (est): 5.3MM
SALES (corp-wide): 2.61B **Privately Held**
Web: www.duraline.com
SIC: 3661 3829 3644 3429 Telephones and telephone apparatus; Measuring and controlling devices, nec; Noncurrent-carrying wiring devices; Hardware, nec
PA: Audax Group, L.P.
101 Huntington Ave
Boston MA 02199
617 859-1500

(G-6499)
AVIENT CORPORATION
1404 Lowell St (44035-4867)
PHONE..........................440 930-1000
EMP: 12
SIC: 2821 Plastics materials and resins
PA: Avient Corporation
33587 Walker Rd
Avon Lake OH 44012

(G-6500)
B&B DISTRIBUTORS LLC
Also Called: Builders Straight Edge
811 Taylor St (44035-6231)
PHONE..........................440 324-1293
George Hovanitz, *Managing Member*
EMP: 10 **EST:** 2004
SALES (est): 935.33K **Privately Held**
Web: www.bandbdistributors.com
SIC: 3353 Aluminum sheet, plate, and foil

(G-6501)
BAKEMARK USA LLC
6325 Gateway Blvd S (44035-5447)
PHONE..........................440 323-5100
EMP: 12
SALES (corp-wide): 194.2MM **Privately Held**
Web: www.yourbakemark.com

SIC: 2045 Flours and flour mixes, from purchased flour
PA: Bakemark Usa Llc
7351 Crider Ave
Pico Rivera CA 90660
562 949-1054

(G-6502)
BASF CATALYSTS LLC
120 Pine St (44035-5228)
P.O. Box 4017 (44036-2017)
PHONE..........................440 322-3741
Randolph C Turk, *Brnch Mgr*
EMP: 830
SALES (corp-wide): 69.01B **Privately Held**
Web: catalysts.basf.com
SIC: 2819 Catalysts, chemical
HQ: Basf Catalysts Llc
33 Wood Ave
Iselin NJ 08830
732 205-5000

(G-6503)
BASF CORPORATION
120 Pine St (44035-5228)
PHONE..........................440 329-2525
EMP: 58
SALES (corp-wide): 69.01B **Privately Held**
Web: www.basf.com
SIC: 2869 Industrial organic chemicals, nec
HQ: Basf Corporation
100 Park Ave
Florham Park NJ 07932
800 962-7831

(G-6504)
BRIDGESTONE RET OPERATIONS LLC
Also Called: Firestone
1951 Midway Mall (44035-2480)
PHONE..........................440 324-3327
Ricargo Vega, *Mgr*
EMP: 8
Web: www.bridgestoneamericas.com
SIC: 5531 7534 Automotive tires; Rebuilding and retreading tires
HQ: Bridgestone Retail Operations, Llc
200 4th Ave S Ste 100
Nashville TN 37201
615 937-1000

(G-6505)
BRIDGESTONE RET OPERATIONS LLC
Also Called: Firestone
520 Abbe Rd S (44035-6302)
PHONE..........................440 365-8308
Richard Cerro, *Mgr*
EMP: 7
Web: www.bridgestoneamericas.com
SIC: 5531 7534 Automotive tires; Rebuilding and retreading tires
HQ: Bridgestone Retail Operations, Llc
200 4th Ave S Ste 100
Nashville TN 37201
615 937-1000

(G-6506)
BUCKEYE STATE WLDG & FABG INC (PA)
131 Buckeye St (44035-5216)
P.O. Box 837 (44036-0837)
PHONE..........................440 322-0319
Kenneth E Reddinger, *Pr*
Patrick J Reddinger, *VP*
Christopher R Reddinger, *Sec*
EMP: 13 **EST:** 1957
SQ FT: 12,000
SALES (est): 2.74MM
SALES (corp-wide): 2.74MM **Privately Held**

Web: www.buckeyeweldfab.com
SIC: 3599 Machine shop, jobbing and repair

(G-6507)
BUCKEYE STATE WLDG & FABG INC
175 Woodford Ave (44035-5436)
P.O. Box 837 (44036-0837)
PHONE....................................440 322-0344
Chris Reddinger, *Owner*
EMP: 8
SALES (corp-wide): 2.74MM **Privately Held**
Web: www.buckeyeweldfab.com
SIC: 7692 Welding repair
PA: Buckeye State Welding & Fabricating, Inc.
131 Buckeye St
Elyria OH 44035
440 322-0319

(G-6508)
CABLETEK WIRING PRODUCTS INC
1150 Taylor St (44035-6281)
PHONE....................................800 562-9378
Stan Leonowigh, *Pr*
EMP: 25 EST: 1998
SALES (est): 1.75MM **Privately Held**
Web: www.cable-tek.com
SIC: 3444 Metal housings, enclosures, casings, and other containers

(G-6509)
CASCADE PATTERN COMPANY INC
519 Ternes Ln (44035-6286)
PHONE....................................440 323-4300
Charles A Petek, *CEO*
Rick Petek, *
Nick Petek, *
EMP: 20 EST: 1972
SALES (est): 6.09MM **Privately Held**
Web: www.cascadepattern.com
SIC: 3543 Industrial patterns

(G-6510)
CASTEK INC
527 Ternes Ln (44035-6286)
PHONE....................................440 365-2333
Daniel C Petek, *Pr*
EMP: 40 EST: 1921
SALES (est): 5.47MM **Privately Held**
Web: www.castekusa.com
SIC: 3365 Aluminum and aluminum-based alloy castings

(G-6511)
CENTRAL COCA-COLA BTLG CO INC
Also Called: Coca-Cola
1410 Lake Ave (44035-3124)
PHONE....................................440 324-3335
Scott Dickerhoff, *Mgr*
EMP: 46
SALES (corp-wide): 45.75B **Publicly Held**
Web: www.coca-cola.com
SIC: 2086 Bottled and canned soft drinks
HQ: Central Coca-Cola Bottling Company, Inc.
555 Taxter Rd Ste 550
Elmsford NY 10523
914 789-1100

(G-6512)
CHAPIN CUSTOMER MOLDING INC
635 Oberlin Elyria Rd (44035-7727)
PHONE....................................440 458-6550
EMP: 9 EST: 2019
SALES (est): 4.53MM **Privately Held**
Web: www.chapincustommolding.com
SIC: 3089 Injection molding of plastics

(G-6513)
CITY ELYRIA COMMUNICATION
851 Garden St (44035-4874)
PHONE....................................440 322-3329
EMP: 6
SALES (est): 369.14K **Privately Held**
SIC: 3669 Traffic signals, electric

(G-6514)
CONSUN FOOD INDUSTRIES INC
Also Called: Sunshine Farms Dairy
123 Gateway Blvd N (44035-4923)
PHONE....................................440 322-6301
Dennis Walter, *Pr*
EMP: 20
SALES (corp-wide): 2.2MM **Privately Held**
Web: www.myconvenient.com
SIC: 2026 Fluid milk
PA: Consun Food Industries, Inc.
123 Gateway Blvd N
Elyria OH 44035
440 322-6301

(G-6515)
COOLBREEZE TECHNOLOGIES LLC
Also Called: Janna Access
827 Walnut St (44035-3352)
PHONE....................................440 748-1911
Reggie Hetsler, *Managing Member*
EMP: 7 EST: 2020
SALES (est): 140.29K **Privately Held**
SIC: 2431 Doors and door parts and trim, wood

(G-6516)
DIAMOND PRODUCTS LIMITED
1201 Taylor St (44035-6247)
PHONE....................................440 323-4616
EMP: 6
SALES (corp-wide): 3.33B **Privately Held**
SIC: 3545 Machine tool accessories
HQ: Diamond Products, Limited
333 Prospect St
Elyria OH 44035
440 323-4616

(G-6517)
DIAMOND PRODUCTS LIMITED
1111 Taylor St (44035-6245)
PHONE....................................440 323-4616
EMP: 6
SALES (corp-wide): 3.33B **Privately Held**
Web: www.diamondproducts.com
SIC: 3545 Machine tool accessories
HQ: Diamond Products, Limited
333 Prospect St
Elyria OH 44035
440 323-4616

(G-6518)
DIAMOND PRODUCTS LIMITED (DH)
333 Prospect St (44035-6154)
P.O. Box 1080 (44036-1080)
PHONE....................................440 323-4616
◆ EMP: 300 EST: 1945
SALES (est): 44.67MM
SALES (corp-wide): 3.33B **Privately Held**
Web: www.diamondproducts.com
SIC: 3545 Machine tool accessories
HQ: Tyrolit Limited
Eldon Close
Northampton NORTHANTS NN6 7
178 882-3738

(G-6519)
DIAMONDS PRODUCTS LLC
1250 E Broad St (44035-6311)
PHONE....................................440 323-4616
▲ EMP: 7 EST: 2003
SALES (est): 326.06K **Privately Held**

Web: www.diamondproducts.com
SIC: 3545 Diamond cutting tools for turning, boring, burnishing, etc.

(G-6520)
DIY HOLSTER LLC
Also Called: Diy Holster
781 Finwood Ct (44035-1616)
PHONE....................................419 921-2168
C Patrick, *Managing Member*
EMP: 8 EST: 2013
SALES (est): 483K **Privately Held**
Web: www.diyholster.com
SIC: 3199 5072 5961 Holsters, leather; Hardware; Tools and hardware, mail order

(G-6521)
DURA-LINE SERVICES LLC
860 Garden St (44035-4826)
PHONE....................................440 322-1000
Steven Sminth, *Brnch Mgr*
EMP: 64
Web: www.duraline.com
SIC: 3084 Plastics pipe
HQ: Dura-Line Services Llc
11400 Parkside Dr Ste 300
Knoxville TN 37934
865 218-3460

(G-6522)
DURA-LINE SERVICES LLC
669 Sugar Ln (44035-6309)
PHONE....................................440 322-1000
Anette Fargo, *Plant Administrator*
EMP: 21
Web: www.duraline.com
SIC: 3084 Plastics pipe
HQ: Dura-Line Services Llc
11400 Parkside Dr Ste 300
Knoxville TN 37934
865 218-3460

(G-6523)
DYNATECH SYSTEMS INC
161 Reaser Ct (44035-6285)
P.O. Box 1589 (44036-1589)
PHONE....................................440 365-1774
Sue A Everett, *Pr*
EMP: 10 EST: 1984
SQ FT: 5,000
SALES (est): 1.28MM **Privately Held**
Web: www.dynatech.com
SIC: 3425 5085 Saw blades and handsaws; Industrial supplies

(G-6524)
E C S CORP
Also Called: Elyria Concrete Step Company
8015 Murray Ridge Rd (44035-2071)
PHONE....................................440 323-1707
Betty Goad, *Pr*
Everett G Goad, *Pr*
Thomas R Goad, *VP*
Leanne Odel, *Sec*
Thomas Goad, *VP*
EMP: 6 EST: 1957
SQ FT: 9,300
SALES (est): 890.59K **Privately Held**
Web: www.elyriaconcretestep.com
SIC: 3446 3272 3271 Grillwork, ornamental metal; Steps, prefabricated concrete; Paving blocks, concrete

(G-6525)
E M SERVICE INC
600 Lowell St (44035-4841)
PHONE....................................440 323-3260
TOLL FREE: 800
EMP: 14 EST: 1918
SALES (est): 2.41MM **Privately Held**
Web: www.emserviceinc.com

SIC: 5999 7694 Motors, electric; Electric motor repair

(G-6526)
E P P INC
Also Called: Elyria Plastic Products
710 Taylor St (44035-6230)
PHONE....................................440 322-8577
James Reichlin, *Pr*
Jim Kastler, *VP*
R Stephen Laux, *Prin*
▲ EMP: 75 EST: 1988
SQ FT: 6,000
SALES (est): 9.83MM **Privately Held**
Web: www.elyriapp.com
SIC: 3089 Injection molding of plastics

(G-6527)
ELITE PROPERTY GROUP LLC
Also Called: 1st Choice Contractor
1036 N Pasadena Ave (44035-2966)
PHONE....................................216 356-7469
EMP: 12 EST: 2017
SALES (est): 130.79K **Privately Held**
SIC: 8742 8741 6531 1389 Construction project management consultant; Construction management; Real estate managers; Construction, repair, and dismantling services

(G-6528)
ELYRIA CONCRETE INC
400 Lowell St (44035-4837)
PHONE....................................440 322-2750
John Walls, *Pr*
Dave Walls, *VP*
Chad Walls, *VP*
EMP: 12 EST: 2004
SALES (est): 891.42K **Privately Held**
Web: www.eci-concrete.com
SIC: 3273 Ready-mixed concrete

(G-6529)
ELYRIA FOUNDRY COMPANY LLC (PA)
120 Filbert St (44035-5357)
PHONE....................................440 322-4657
EMP: 112 EST: 1905
SALES (est): 49.84MM
SALES (corp-wide): 49.84MM **Privately Held**
Web: www.elyriafoundry.com
SIC: 3321 3369 3325 2821 Gray iron castings, nec; Nonferrous foundries, nec; Steel foundries, nec; Plastics materials and resins

(G-6530)
ELYRIA MANUFACTURING CORP (PA)
Also Called: EMC Precision Machining
145 Northrup St (44035-6163)
P.O. Box 479 (44036-0479)
PHONE....................................440 365-4171
Bradley R Ohlemacher, *
Willim Ohlemacher, *
Bob Graney, *
▲ EMP: 50 EST: 1925
SQ FT: 86,000
SALES (est): 10.77MM
SALES (corp-wide): 10.77MM **Privately Held**
Web: www.emcprecision.com
SIC: 3451 Screw machine products

(G-6531)
ELYRIA METAL SPINNING FABG CO
Also Called: Metal Manufacturing
7511 W River Rd S (44035-6972)
P.O. Box 992 (44036-0992)

PHONE..............................440 323-8068
Donald Didomenico, *Pr*
EMP: 8 **EST:** 1962
SQ FT: 18,000
SALES (est): 1.87MM **Privately Held**
Web: www.elyriametalspinning.com
SIC: 3469 3599 Spinning metal for the trade; Machine shop, jobbing and repair

(G-6532)
ELYRIA PATTERN CO INC
6785 W River Rd S (44035-7052)
PHONE..............................440 323-1526
James A Schroeder, *Pr*
James W Schroeder, *VP*
EMP: 7 **EST:** 1947
SALES (est): 696.35K **Privately Held**
Web: www.lorainmodern.com
SIC: 3543 Industrial patterns

(G-6533)
ELYRIA PLATING CORPORATION
118 Olive St (44035-4000)
PHONE..............................440 365-8300
Kevin J Flanigan, *CEO*
E F Gookins, *
EMP: 40 **EST:** 1937
SQ FT: 35,000
SALES (est): 2.38MM **Privately Held**
Web: www.elyriaplating.com
SIC: 3471 Electroplating of metals or formed products

(G-6534)
EMC PRECISION MACHINING II LLC
(PA)
145 Northrup St (44035-6147)
P.O. Box 479 (44036-0479)
PHONE..............................440 365-4171
EMP: 16 **EST:** 2010
SALES (est): 7.19MM
SALES (corp-wide): 7.19MM **Privately Held**
Web: www.emcprecision.com
SIC: 3599 Machine shop, jobbing and repair

(G-6535)
ENVELOPE MART OF OHIO INC
1540 Lowell St (44035-4869)
PHONE..............................440 365-8177
Robert T Thompson, *Pr*
EMP: 11 **EST:** 2008
SALES (est): 906.56K **Privately Held**
Web: www.emprintgroup.com
SIC: 5112 2677 Envelopes; Envelopes

(G-6536)
FELLER TOOL CO
6285 Lake Ave (44035-1021)
PHONE..............................440 324-6277
Doug Feller, *Pr*
Deborah Feller, *VP*
EMP: 10 **EST:** 1959
SALES (est): 931.53K **Privately Held**
SIC: 3544 3599 Special dies and tools; Machine shop, jobbing and repair

(G-6537)
FLORIDA INVACARE HOLDINGS LLC
1 Invacare Way (44035-4190)
P.O. Box 4028 (44036-2028)
PHONE..............................800 333-6900
EMP: 11 **EST:** 2005
SALES (est): 3.38MM
SALES (corp-wide): 741.73MM **Privately Held**
Web: global.invacare.com
SIC: 3842 Surgical appliances and supplies
PA: Invacare Corporation
1 Invacare Way
Elyria OH 44035

440 329-6000

(G-6538)
GASFLUX COMPANY
32 Hawthorne St (44035-4008)
P.O. Box 1170 (44036-1170)
PHONE..............................440 365-1941
Robert C Farquhar, *Pr*
William K Farquhar, *Ch Bd*
Richard Hoffman, *VP*
Mary Ann Farquhar, *Treas*
◆ **EMP:** 8 **EST:** 1938
SQ FT: 20,000
SALES (est): 4.58MM **Privately Held**
Web: www.gasflux.com
SIC: 2899 Fluxes: brazing, soldering, galvanizing, and welding

(G-6539)
GATEWAY INDUSTRIAL PDTS INC
160 Freedom Ct (44035-2245)
P.O. Box 95 (44036-0095)
PHONE..............................440 324-4112
Peter Delaporte, *Pr*
Gayle Delaporte, *Genl Mgr*
▼ **EMP:** 25 **EST:** 1979
SQ FT: 25,000
SALES (est): 4.65MM **Privately Held**
Web: www.gatewayindustrial.com
SIC: 3089 2431 Window screening, plastics; Doors and door parts and trim, wood

(G-6540)
GEON PERFORMANCE SOLUTIONS LLC
835 Leo Bullocks Pkwy (44035-4895)
PHONE..............................440 987-4553
EMP: 53
Web: www.geon.com
SIC: 2821 Plastics materials and resins
HQ: Geon Performance Solutions, Llc
25777 Detroit Rd Ste 202
Westlake OH 44145
800 438-4366

(G-6541)
GREBER MACHINE TOOL INC
Also Called: Custom Powdr Coating By Greber
313 Clark St (44035-6105)
PHONE..............................440 322-3685
Ken Greber, *Pr*
Tammy Greber, *Treas*
EMP: 7 **EST:** 2004
SQ FT: 600
SALES (est): 982.53K **Privately Held**
Web: www.greberracing.com
SIC: 3479 7692 Coating of metals and formed products; Welding repair

(G-6542)
HONEYWELL INTERNATIONAL INC
Also Called: Honeywell
P.O. Box 419 (44036-0419)
PHONE..............................440 329-9000
EMP: 41
SALES (corp-wide): 38.5B **Publicly Held**
Web: www.honeywell.com
SIC: 3724 Aircraft engines and engine parts
PA: Honeywell International Inc.
855 S Mint St
Charlotte NC 28202
704 627-6200

(G-6543)
HYDRO-AIRE INC
Also Called: Lear Romec
241 Abbe Rd S (44035-6239)
P.O. Box 4014 (44036-2014)
PHONE..............................440 323-3211
Tazewell Rowe, *Treas*

EMP: 236
SALES (corp-wide): 2.13B **Publicly Held**
Web: www.craneae.com
SIC: 3728 Aircraft parts and equipment, nec
HQ: Hydro-Aire, Inc.
3000 Winona Ave
Burbank CA 91504

(G-6544)
HYDRO-AIRE AEROSPACE CORP (HQ)
249 Abbe Rd S (44035-6239)
PHONE..............................440 323-3211
Jay Higgs, *Pr*
EMP: 200 **EST:** 2011
SALES (est): 8.48MM
SALES (corp-wide): 2.13B **Publicly Held**
SIC: 3728 3369 Aircraft parts and equipment, nec; Aerospace castings, nonferrous: except aluminum
PA: Crane Company
100 1st Stmford Pl Ste 40
Stamford CT 06902
203 363-7300

(G-6545)
INTERTEK LLC
6805 W River Rd S (44035-7054)
PHONE..............................440 323-3325
Dave W Dennis, *Pr*
EMP: 10 **EST:** 1969
SQ FT: 24,000
SALES (est): 1.88MM **Privately Held**
Web: www.intertekllc.com
SIC: 3599 Machine shop, jobbing and repair

(G-6546)
INVACARE CANADIAN HOLDINGS INC
1 Invacare Way (44035-4190)
PHONE..............................440 329-6000
EMP: 6 **EST:** 2003
SALES (est): 1.12MM
SALES (corp-wide): 741.73MM **Privately Held**
Web: global.invacare.com
SIC: 3842 Surgical appliances and supplies
PA: Invacare Corporation
1 Invacare Way
Elyria OH 44035
440 329-6000

(G-6547)
INVACARE CANADIAN HOLDINGS LLC
1 Invacare Way (44035-4190)
PHONE..............................440 329-6000
EMP: 6 **EST:** 2009
SALES (est): 1.11MM
SALES (corp-wide): 741.73MM **Privately Held**
Web: global.invacare.com
SIC: 3842 Surgical appliances and supplies
PA: Invacare Corporation
1 Invacare Way
Elyria OH 44035
440 329-6000

(G-6548)
INVACARE CONTINUING CARE INC
1 Invacare Way (44035-4190)
PHONE..............................800 668-2337
Matthew Monaghan, *Pr*
EMP: 6 **EST:** 2015
SALES (est): 576.16K **Privately Held**
Web: global.invacare.com
SIC: 3842 Surgical appliances and supplies

(G-6549)
INVACARE CORPORATION (PA)
Also Called: Invacare America
1 Invacare Way (44035-4196)
P.O. Box 4028 (44036-2028)
PHONE..............................440 329-6000
Geoffrey P Purtill, *Pr*
Anthony C Laplaca, *Sr VP*
Rick A Cassiday, *Sr VP*
Kai Zhu, *Sr VP*
◆ **EMP:** 662 **EST:** 1971
SALES (est): 741.73MM
SALES (corp-wide): 741.73MM **Privately Held**
Web: global.invacare.com
SIC: 3842 2514 2813 Surgical appliances and supplies; Beds, including folding and cabinet, household: metal; Industrial gases

(G-6550)
INVACARE CORPORATION
1200 Taylor St (44035-6248)
PHONE..............................440 329-6000
John Dmytriw, *Brnch Mgr*
EMP: 14
SQ FT: 13,000
SALES (corp-wide): 741.73MM **Privately Held**
Web: global.invacare.com
SIC: 3842 Wheelchairs
PA: Invacare Corporation
1 Invacare Way
Elyria OH 44035
440 329-6000

(G-6551)
INVACARE CORPORATION
1320 Taylor St (44035-6250)
PHONE..............................800 333-6900
EMP: 8
SALES (corp-wide): 741.73MM **Privately Held**
Web: global.invacare.com
SIC: 2514 2813 3842 Beds, including folding and cabinet, household: metal; Industrial gases; Wheelchairs
PA: Invacare Corporation
1 Invacare Way
Elyria OH 44035
440 329-6000

(G-6552)
INVACARE HCS LLC
Also Called: Bargmann Management, L.L.C.
1 Invacare Way (44035-4190)
PHONE..............................330 634-9925
Lisa Bargmann, *Managing Member*
EMP: 10 **EST:** 2005
SALES (est): 2.85MM
SALES (corp-wide): 741.73MM **Privately Held**
Web: global.invacare.com
SIC: 3842 Surgical appliances and supplies
PA: Invacare Corporation
1 Invacare Way
Elyria OH 44035
440 329-6000

(G-6553)
INVACARE HOLDINGS LLC
1 Invacare Way (44035-4190)
PHONE..............................440 329-6000
EMP: 8 **EST:** 2001
SALES (est): 1.25MM
SALES (corp-wide): 741.73MM **Privately Held**
Web: global.invacare.com
SIC: 3842 Surgical appliances and supplies
PA: Invacare Corporation
1 Invacare Way

Elyria OH 44035
440 329-6000

(G-6554)
**INVACARE HOLDINGS
CORPORATION**
1 Invacare Way (44036)
PHONE..................440 329-6000
Gerald Blouch, *CEO*
A Malachi Mixon Iii, *Ch Bd*
Joseph B Richey Ii, *Pr*
Anthony C Laplaca, *
Kai Zhu, *
▲ **EMP:** 310 **EST:** 1984
SALES (est): 3.63MM
SALES (corp-wide): 741.73MM **Privately
Held**
Web: global.invacare.com
SIC: 2514 3841 3842 Beds, including folding
and cabinet, household; metal; Inhalation
therapy equipment; Wheelchairs
HQ: Invacare International Corporation
1 Invacare Way
Elyria OH 44035

(G-6555)
J&M PRECISION DIE CASTING LLC
Also Called: J & M Precision Die Cast Inc
1329 Taylor St (44035-6249)
PHONE..................440 365-7388
Michael Prokop, *Pr*
EMP: 19 **EST:** 2015
SQ FT: 8,000
SALES (est): 5.97MM
SALES (corp-wide): 6.43MM **Privately
Held**
Web: www.jmdiecasting.com
SIC: 3599 Machine shop, jobbing and repair
PA: Rhenium Alloys, Inc.
38683 Taylor Pkwy
North Ridgeville OH 44035
440 365-7388

(G-6556)
JET FUEL STRATEGIES LLC
44050 Russia Rd (44035-6800)
PHONE..................440 323-4220
Josi U Ren, *Prin*
EMP: 8 **EST:** 2014
SALES (est): 2.16MM **Privately Held**
Web: www.jetsfbo.com
SIC: 2911 Jet fuels

(G-6557)
LANXESS CORPORATION
Also Called: Ingredient Technology Division
110 Liberty Ct (44035-2237)
PHONE..................440 324-6060
Ronald Nicolson, *Mgr*
EMP: 6
SQ FT: 10,000
SALES (corp-wide): 6.73B **Privately Held**
Web: www.lanxess.com
SIC: 2869 Industrial organic chemicals, nec
HQ: Lanxess Corporation
111 Ridc Park W Dr
Pittsburgh PA 15275
412 809-1000

(G-6558)
LEAR MFG CO INC
147 Freedom Ct (44035-2245)
PHONE..................440 324-1111
Bonnie Lear, *Pr*
EMP: 10 **EST:** 2014
SALES (est): 2.03MM **Privately Held**
Web: www.learmfg.com
SIC: 3452 Nuts, metal

(G-6559)
LORAIN MODERN PATTERN INC
159 Woodbury St (44035-4011)
PHONE..................440 365-6780
Todd R Roth, *Pr*
Sheila I Kelly-roth, *VP*
EMP: 10
SQ FT: 5,500
SALES (est): 1.1MM **Privately Held**
Web: www.lorainmodern.com
SIC: 3543 Industrial patterns

(G-6560)
LTI POWER SYSTEMS INC
10800 Middle Ave Hngr B (44035-7893)
PHONE..................440 327-5050
Robert J Morog, *CEO*
Mary Morog, *Sec*
▲ **EMP:** 20 **EST:** 1995
SQ FT: 35,000
SALES (est): 4.98MM **Privately Held**
Web: www.ltipowersystems.com
SIC: 3612 Specialty transformers

(G-6561)
MASTER BOLT LLC
811 Taylor St (44035-6231)
PHONE..................440 323-5529
EMP: 35 **EST:** 2020
SALES (est): 5.57MM **Privately Held**
Web: www.masterbolt.com
SIC: 3965 Fasteners

(G-6562)
METAL BUILDING INTR PDTS CO
750 Adams St (44035)
PHONE..................440 322-6500
EMP: 16
SALES (corp-wide): 5.72MM **Privately
Held**
Web: www.mbiproducts.com
SIC: 3296 Fiberglass insulation
PA: Metal Building Interior Products Co Inc
801 Bond St
Elyria OH
440 322-6500

(G-6563)
METRO DESIGN INC
10740 Middle Ave (44035-7816)
P.O. Box 248 (44036-0248)
PHONE..................440 458-4200
Jeffery Kraps, *Pr*
EMP: 17 **EST:** 1982
SQ FT: 10,000
SALES (est): 2.25MM **Privately Held**
Web: www.metrodesigninc.com
SIC: 3599 7699 3844 Custom machinery; X-
ray equipment repair; X-ray apparatus and
tubes

(G-6564)
METRO DESIGN INC
7515 W Ridge Rd (44035-1959)
P.O. Box 248 (44036-0248)
PHONE..................440 324-4700
William Grieve, *Manager*
EMP: 6 **EST:** 2018
SALES (est): 554.7K **Privately Held**
Web: www.metrodesigninc.com
SIC: 3599 Machine shop, jobbing and repair

(G-6565)
ML ERECTORS LLC
827 Walnut St (44035-3352)
PHONE..................440 328-3227
Matthew J Loftin, *Managing Member*
EMP: 7 **EST:** 2003
SQ FT: 26,000
SALES (est): 451.45K **Privately Held**

Web: www.mlerectors.com
SIC: 2759 Publication printing

(G-6566)
MULTILINK INC
Also Called: Multifab
580 Ternes Ln (44035-6252)
PHONE..................440 366-6966
Steven Kaplan, *Pr*
Kathy Kaplan, *
Steve Cannon, *
◆ **EMP:** 140 **EST:** 1983
SQ FT: 110,000
SALES (est): 23.74MM **Privately Held**
Web: www.gomultilink.com
SIC: 5063 3829 Wire and cable; Cable
testing machines

(G-6567)
NATIONAL MOLDED PRODUCTS INC
131 Samuel St (44035-3129)
PHONE..................440 365-3400
Robert E Brown, *Pr*
Brian Brown, *
Charlene Brown, *
EMP: 30 **EST:** 1985
SALES (est): 2.37MM **Privately Held**
Web: www.platformos.com
SIC: 3089 Injection molding of plastics

(G-6568)
NELSON STUD WELDING INC (HQ)
7900 W Ridge Rd (44035-1952)
P.O. Box 4019 (44036-2019)
PHONE..................440 329-0400
Ken Caratelli, *Pr*
Debbie Hunnel, *
David Bubar, *
◆ **EMP:** 81 **EST:** 2000
SALES (est): 96MM
SALES (corp-wide): 15.37B **Publicly Held**
Web:
www.stanleyengineeredfastening.com
SIC: 3452 3548 Bolts, nuts, rivets, and
washers; Welding apparatus
PA: Stanley Black & Decker, Inc.
1000 Stanley Dr
New Britain CT 06053
860 225-5111

(G-6569)
NICE BODY AUTOMOTIVE LLC
Also Called: Nice Body Automotive
818 Cleveland St (44035-4108)
PHONE..................440 752-5568
Dezmon Lawrence, *CEO*
EMP: 7 **EST:** 2020
SALES (est): 222.28K **Privately Held**
SIC: 7539 7699 7538 3011 Automotive air
conditioning repair; Miscellaneous
automotive repair services; General
automotive repair shops; Automobile tires,
pneumatic

(G-6570)
**NORTH AMERCN KIT SOLUTIONS
INC (PA)**
172 Reaser Ct (44035-6285)
PHONE..................800 854-3267
Steve Bersticker, *VP*
EMP: 19 **EST:** 2016
SALES (est): 4.17MM
SALES (corp-wide): 4.17MM **Privately
Held**
Web: www.naksinc.com
SIC: 2511 Kitchen and dining room furniture

(G-6571)
NORTH COAST RIVET INC
700 Sugar Ln (44035-6312)
P.O. Box 1441 (44036-1441)

PHONE..................440 366-6829
Wesley L Shirley, *CEO*
Kathy Shirley, *Sec*
EMP: 10 **EST:** 1985
SQ FT: 6,000
SALES (est): 466.54K **Privately Held**
Web: www.valleyfastener.com
SIC: 3452 Rivets, metal

(G-6572)
OHIO DISPLAYS INC
Also Called: Odi
825 Leona St (44035-2300)
PHONE..................216 961-5600
Thomas R Mc Kay, *Ch Bd*
Judy Miller, *VP*
EMP: 15 **EST:** 1918
SQ FT: 70,000
SALES (est): 2.35MM **Privately Held**
Web: www.ohiodisplays.com
SIC: 3993 2542 Displays, paint process;
Partitions and fixtures, except wood

(G-6573)
**OHIO METALLURGICAL SERVICE
INC**
Also Called: Ohiomet
1033 Clark St (44035-6257)
P.O. Box 1228 (44036-1228)
PHONE..................440 365-4104
Donald S Gaydosh, *Pr*
John Gaydosh, *
Glenn E Shoemaker, *
R E Baird, *
William D Latiano, *
EMP: 69 **EST:** 1947
SQ FT: 50,000
SALES (est): 5.08MM **Privately Held**
Web: www.ohiomet.com
SIC: 3398 Metal heat treating

(G-6574)
OHIO SCREW PRODUCTS INC
818 Lowell St (44035-4876)
P.O. Box 4027 (44036-2027)
PHONE..................440 322-6341
Daniel Imbrogno, *Pr*
Dan Imbrogno, *
Edward N Imbrogno, *
Elmer Brown, *
Joseph Sullivan, *
EMP: 75 **EST:** 1945
SQ FT: 65,000
SALES (est): 930.3K **Privately Held**
Web: www.ohioscrew.com
SIC: 3541 3451 Screw machines, automatic;
Screw machine products

(G-6575)
P-AMERICAS LLC
Also Called: Pepsico
925 Lorain Blvd (44035-2819)
PHONE..................440 323-5524
Mike Schonberg, *Brnch Mgr*
EMP: 13
SALES (corp-wide): 91.47B **Publicly Held**
Web: www.pepsico.com
SIC: 2086 Carbonated soft drinks, bottled
and canned
HQ: P-Americas Llc
1 Pepsi Way
Somers NY 10589
336 896-5740

(G-6576)
PARKER-HANNIFIN CORPORATION
Fluid Systems Division
711 Taylor St (44035-6229)
P.O. Box 4032 (44036-4032)
PHONE..................440 284-6277
Eric Mitchell, *Mgr*

EMP: 200
SALES (corp-wide): 19.93B **Publicly Held**
Web: www.parker.com
SIC: 3728 3724 Aircraft assemblies, subassemblies, and parts, nec; Aircraft engines and engine parts
PA: Parker-Hannifin Corporation
6035 Parkland Blvd
Cleveland OH 44124
216 896-3000

(G-6577)
PEPSI-COLA METRO BTLG CO INC
Also Called: Pepsi-Cola
925 Lorain Blvd (44035-2819)
PHONE..................................440 323-5524
Mike Schonberg, *Brnch Mgr*
EMP: 14
SALES (corp-wide): 91.47B **Publicly Held**
Web: www.pepsico.com
SIC: 2086 5149 Carbonated soft drinks, bottled and canned; Soft drinks
HQ: Pepsi-Cola Metropolitan Bottling Company, Inc.
700 Anderson Hill Rd
Purchase NY 10577
914 767-6000

(G-6578)
PERFECTION FABRICATORS INC
680 Sugar Ln (44035-6310)
PHONE..................................440 365-5850
James Ennes, *Pr*
David Ennes, *VP*
EMP: 10 **EST:** 1973
SQ FT: 27,000
SALES (est): 1.08MM **Privately Held**
Web: www.perfectionfabricators.com
SIC: 3441 Fabricated structural metal

(G-6579)
PERSONAL PLUMBER SERVICE CORP
Also Called: Value-Rooter
42343 N Ridge Rd (44035-1130)
PHONE..................................440 324-4321
Russell Halstead, *Pr*
Russell A Halstead, *Owner*
Mellisa Halstead, *Treas*
Russel Halstead, *Pr*
EMP: 19 **EST:** 1997
SALES (est): 1.86MM **Privately Held**
SIC: 1711 2842 1794 Plumbing contractors; Drain pipe solvents or cleaners; Excavation work

(G-6580)
PLASTIC ENTERPRISES INC (PA)
41520 Schadden Rd (44035-2227)
PHONE..................................440 324-3240
John Leonowich, *Pr*
William Kaatz, *VP*
▲ **EMP:** 22 **EST:** 1959
SQ FT: 35,000
SALES (est): 6.66MM
SALES (corp-wide): 6.66MM **Privately Held**
Web: www.plastic-enterprises.com
SIC: 3089 3544 Injection molding of plastics; Special dies, tools, jigs, and fixtures

(G-6581)
PLASTIC ENTERPRISES INC
Also Called: Bee Valve
1150 Taylor St (44035-6281)
PHONE..................................440 366-0220
Bill Kaatz, *Mgr*
EMP: 9
SALES (corp-wide): 6.66MM **Privately Held**
Web: www.plastic-enterprises.com

SIC: 3089 Injection molding of plastics
PA: Plastic Enterprises, Inc.
41520 Schadden Rd
Elyria OH 44035
440 324-3240

(G-6582)
PRECISE MODELS INC
195 Canterbury Rd (44035-1720)
PHONE..................................440 365-5701
Paul Schneider, *Pr*
Rita Malanowski, *Sec*
EMP: 8 **EST:** 1960
SQ FT: 10,500
SALES (est): 111.46K **Privately Held**
Web: www.precisemodelsllc.com
SIC: 3999 Miniatures

(G-6583)
QUALITY BLOW MOLDING INC
635 Oberlin Elyria Rd (44035-7727)
PHONE..................................440 458-6550
Ronald E Matcham, *Pr*
Mary Anne Matcham, *Corporate Secretary**
EMP: 90 **EST:** 1994
SQ FT: 30,000
SALES (est): 1.23MM **Privately Held**
Web: www.qualityblowmolding.com
SIC: 3089 Injection molding of plastics

(G-6584)
REAL ALLOY SPECIALTY PDTS LLC
320 Huron St (44035-4829)
PHONE..................................440 322-0072
Erik Leith, *Brnch Mgr*
EMP: 20
SALES (corp-wide): 483.55MM **Publicly Held**
Web: www.realalloy.com
SIC: 3355 Aluminum rolling and drawing, nec
HQ: Real Alloy Specialty Products, Llc
3700 Park E Dr Ste 300
Beachwood OH 44122
844 732-5087

(G-6585)
RECOGNITION ROBOTICS INC (PA)
141 Innovation Dr Pmb 306 (44035-1673)
PHONE..................................440 590-0499
Simon Melikian, *CEO*
Joe Cyrek, *VP*
EMP: 17 **EST:** 2006
SALES (est): 4.58MM
SALES (corp-wide): 4.58MM **Privately Held**
Web: www.recognitionrobotics.com
SIC: 3569 8742 Robots, assembly line: industrial and commercial; Automation and robotics consultant

(G-6586)
RIDGE TOOL COMPANY (HQ)
Also Called: Ridgid
400 Clark St (44035-6100)
P.O. Box 4023 (44036-2023)
PHONE..................................440 323-5581
B J Jones, *Pr*
◆ **EMP:** 800 **EST:** 1966
SQ FT: 600,000
SALES (est): 467.26MM
SALES (corp-wide): 17.49B **Publicly Held**
Web: www.ridgid.com
SIC: 3423 3547 3546 3541 Hand and edge tools, nec; Rolling mill machinery; Power-driven handtools; Pipe cutting and threading machines
PA: Emerson Electric Co.
8027 Forsyth Boulevard
Saint Louis MO 63105
888 889-9170

(G-6587)
RIDGE TOOL COMPANY
321 Sumner St (44035-6125)
PHONE..................................440 329-4737
Ron Farkas, *Mgr*
EMP: 105
SALES (corp-wide): 17.49B **Publicly Held**
Web: www.ridgid.com
SIC: 3541 Machine tools, metal cutting type
HQ: Ridge Tool Company
400 Clark St
Elyria OH 44035
440 323-5581

(G-6588)
RIDGE TOOL MANUFACTURING CO
400 Clark St (44035-6100)
P.O. Box 4023 (44036)
PHONE..................................440 323-5581
Fred Pond, *Pr*
Scott Garfield, *VP Fin*
Ralph Shaw, *CFO*
EMP: 10 **EST:** 1989
SQ FT: 400,000
SALES (est): 2.09MM
SALES (corp-wide): 17.49B **Publicly Held**
Web: www.ridgid.com
SIC: 3541 3423 3547 3546 Machine tools, metal cutting type; Hand and edge tools, nec; Rolling mill machinery; Power-driven handtools
HQ: Ridge Tool Company
400 Clark St
Elyria OH 44035
440 323-5581

(G-6589)
SHALMET CORPORATION
164 Freedom Ct (44035-2245)
PHONE..................................440 236-8840
Hugh O Donnell, *Brnch Mgr*
EMP: 35
SALES (corp-wide): 2.76B **Publicly Held**
Web: www.carpentertechnology.com
SIC: 3471 Polishing, metals or formed products
HQ: Shalmet Corporation
116 Pinedale Indus Rd
Orwigsburg PA 17961
570 366-1414

(G-6590)
SMART MICROSYSTEMS LTD
141 Innovation Dr (44035-1673)
PHONE..................................440 366-4257
Matt Apanius, *Pr*
EMP: 10 **EST:** 2013
SALES (est): 517.35K **Privately Held**
Web: www.smartmicrosystems.us
SIC: 3674 Microcircuits, integrated (semiconductor)

(G-6591)
STANLEY ENGINEERED FASTEN
7900 W Ridge Rd (44035-1952)
PHONE..................................440 657-3537
EMP: 7 **EST:** 2019
SALES (est): 1.6MM **Privately Held**
Web: www.stanleyengineeredfastening.com
SIC: 3965 Fasteners

(G-6592)
STAYS LIGHTING INC
Also Called: Best Fab Co.
936 Taylor St (44035-6234)
PHONE..................................440 328-3254
Joe Jingle, *Pr*
EMP: 8 **EST:** 2005
SQ FT: 9,200
SALES (est): 786.58K **Privately Held**

SIC: 3441 Fabricated structural metal

(G-6593)
STUD WELDING ASSOCIATES
101 Liberty Ct (44035-2238)
PHONE..................................216 392-7808
EMP: 12 **EST:** 2017
SALES (est): 365.07K **Privately Held**
Web: welding-equipment-dealers.cmac.ws
SIC: 7692 Welding repair

(G-6594)
SYMRISE INC
Also Called: Diana Food
110 Liberty Ct (44035-2237)
PHONE..................................440 324-6060
John Cassidy, *Brnch Mgr*
EMP: 117
Web: www.symrise.com
SIC: 2869 Perfume materials, synthetic
HQ: Symrise Inc.
300 N St
Teterboro NJ 07608
201 288-3200

(G-6595)
THE RELIABLE SPRING WIRE FRMS
910 Taylor St (44035-6234)
P.O. Box 58 (44036)
PHONE..................................440 365-7400
Richard Mcbride, *Pr*
Sybil Mcbride, *Sec*
EMP: 41 **EST:** 1937
SALES (est): 2.07MM **Privately Held**
Web: www.reliablespring.com
SIC: 3469 3495 Stamping metal for the trade ; Mechanical springs, precision

(G-6596)
TOOL AND DIE SYSTEMS
38900 Taylor Pkwy (44035-6259)
PHONE..................................440 327-5800
William Flickinger, *VP*
EMP: 6 **EST:** 2020
SALES (est): 2.99MM **Privately Held**
Web: www.tooldiesystems.com
SIC: 3444 Sheet metalwork

(G-6597)
ULTRA MACHINE INC
Also Called: Silver Machine Co
530 Lowell St (44035-4862)
PHONE..................................440 323-7632
Thomas C Guignette, *Pr*
EMP: 7 **EST:** 1977
SQ FT: 2,500
SALES (est): 557.74K **Privately Held**
SIC: 3599 Machine shop, jobbing and repair

(G-6598)
UNITED INITIATORS INC (HQ)
555 Garden St (44035-4870)
PHONE..................................440 323-3112
Ed Hoozemans, *CEO*
William Clements, ***
Johannes Ziegler, ***
◆ **EMP:** 63 **EST:** 2000
SQ FT: 40,000
SALES (est): 103.5MM
SALES (corp-wide): 254.57MM **Privately Held**
Web: www.united-initiators.com
SIC: 2819 2869 Catalysts, chemical; Industrial organic chemicals, nec
PA: United Initiators Gmbh
Dr.-Gustav-Adolph-Str. 3
Pullach I. Isartal BY 82049
897 442-2237

(G-6599)
VAROUH OIL INC
970 Griswold Rd (44035-2321)
PHONE.....................440 482-8686
Ronald Varouh, *Pr*
Ari Varouh, *VP*
Mark Varouh, *Sec*
EMP: 15 **EST:** 1957
SQ FT: 60,000
SALES (est): 4.5MM **Privately Held**
Web: www.varouhoil.com
SIC: 5172 2911 Lubricating oils and greases;
Oils, lubricating

(G-6600)
VECTRON INC
201 Perry Ct (44035-6149)
PHONE.....................440 323-3369
Robert Pustay, *Pr*
EMP: 13 **EST:** 1972
SQ FT: 48,000
SALES (est): 2.41MM **Privately Held**
Web: www.vectron.cc
SIC: 3599 3471 Machine shop, jobbing and
repair; Plating and polishing

(G-6601)
VTD SYSTEMS INC
7600 W River Rd S (44035-6934)
PHONE.....................440 323-4122
Robert Vilagi Junior, *Pr*
EMP: 20 **EST:** 1994
SQ FT: 5,100
SALES (est): 3.5MM **Privately Held**
Web: www.vtdsystems.com
SIC: 3599 Machine shop, jobbing and repair

(G-6602)
WESTVIEW CONCRETE CORP
Also Called: Avon Concrete
40105 Butternut Ridge Rd (44035-7903)
PHONE.....................440 458-5800
TOLL FREE: 800
John Walls, *VP*
EMP: 15
SQ FT: 1,202
SALES (corp-wide): 4.8MM **Privately Held**
Web: www.westviewconcrete.com
SIC: 3273 5211 Ready-mixed concrete;
Masonry materials and supplies
PA: Westview Concrete Corp.
26000 Sprague Rd
Olmsted Falls OH 44138
440 235-1800

(G-6603)
WOOSTER BRUSH COMPANY
870 Infirmary Rd (44035-4899)
PHONE.....................440 322-8081
Rick Dice, *Brnch Mgr*
EMP: 6
SALES (corp-wide): 36.31MM **Privately
Held**
Web: www.woosterbrush.com
SIC: 3991 Paint and varnish brushes
PA: The Wooster Brush Company
604 Madison Ave
Wooster OH 44691
330 264-4440

(G-6604)
ZAYTRAN INC
41535 Schadden Rd (44035-2226)
P.O. Box 1660 (44036-1660)
PHONE.....................440 324-2814
Theodore Zajac Junior, *Pr*
Theodore Zajac Senior, *Ch*
Monica Parker, *
J C Wm Tattersall, *
EMP: 32 **EST:** 1980
SQ FT: 80,000

SALES (est): 2.71MM **Privately Held**
Web: www.zaytran.com
SIC: 3593 3492 Fluid power actuators,
hydraulic or pneumatic; Fluid power valves
and hose fittings

Englewood
Montgomery County

(G-6605)
AIMS-CMI TECHNOLOGY LLC
65 Haas Dr (45322-2842)
PHONE.....................937 832-2000
David A Delph, *Pr*
EMP: 17 **EST:** 2016
SQ FT: 12,000
SALES (est): 784.6K **Privately Held**
Web: www.cmi-technology.com
SIC: 3599 3544 Machine shop, jobbing and
repair; Special dies, tools, jigs, and fixtures

(G-6606)
AIRBASE INDUSTRIES LLC
Also Called: Eaton Compressor & Fabrication
1000 Cass Dr (45315-8844)
PHONE.....................937 540-1140
Matthew Cain, *Managing Member*
◆ **EMP:** 10 **EST:** 2000
SQ FT: 60,000
SALES (est): 1.7MM **Privately Held**
Web: www.emaxcompressor.com
SIC: 3563 Air and gas compressors
including vacuum pumps

(G-6607)
**ANGSTROM FIBER ENGLEWOOD
LLC (PA) ○**
300 Lau Pkwy (45315-8826)
PHONE.....................734 756-1164
Nagesh Palakurthi, *Managing Member*
EMP: 34 **EST:** 2023
SALES (est): 8.94MM
SALES (corp-wide): 8.94MM **Privately
Held**
SIC: 2273 Aircraft and automobile floor
coverings

(G-6608)
C&W SWISS INC
100 Lau Pkwy (45315-8787)
PHONE.....................937 832-2889
Gregory Crabtree, *Pr*
Tammy Crabtree, *VP*
EMP: 18 **EST:** 1998
SALES (est): 2.89MM **Privately Held**
Web: www.cwswiss.com
SIC: 3599 Machine shop, jobbing and repair

(G-6609)
CMI TECHNOLOGY INC
65 Haas Dr (45322-2842)
PHONE.....................937 832-2000
EMP: 17
Web: www.cmi-technology.com
SIC: 3599 3544 Machine shop, jobbing and
repair; Special dies, tools, jigs, and fixtures

(G-6610)
CREATIVE COUNTERTOPS OHIO INC
Also Called: Creative Countertops
477 E Wenger Rd (45322-2831)
PHONE.....................937 540-9450
EMP: 10 **EST:** 2007
SQ FT: 10,000
SALES (est): 466.22K **Privately Held**
Web: www.creative-countertops.com
SIC: 3281 Granite, cut and shaped

(G-6611)
CREATIVE MICROSYSTEMS INC
Also Called: Civica CMI
52 Hillside Ct (45322-2745)
PHONE.....................937 836-4499
Lin Mallott, *CEO*
Arvind Kohli, *
EMP: 80 **EST:** 1979
SQ FT: 14,400
SALES (est): 5.81MM **Privately Held**
Web: www.civica.com
SIC: 7373 7372 Systems integration services
; Prepackaged software

(G-6612)
DISPLAY DYNAMICS INC
1 Display Point Dr (45315-8857)
P.O. Box 27 (45315-0027)
PHONE.....................937 832-2830
Veit Von Parker, *Pr*
EMP: 18 **EST:** 1994
SQ FT: 40,000
SALES (est): 976.05K **Privately Held**
Web: www.disdyn.com
SIC: 7389 2541 7319 1751 Exhibit
construction by industrial contractors; Store
fixtures, wood; Display advertising service;
Cabinet and finish carpentry

(G-6613)
EATON COMPRSR FABRICATION INC
Also Called: Polar Air
1000 Cass Dr (45315-8844)
PHONE.....................937 540-1140
Matt Cain, *Pr*
◆ **EMP:** 58 **EST:** 2006
SQ FT: 50,000
SALES (est): 3.93MM **Privately Held**
Web: www.eatoncompressor.com
SIC: 3563 Air and gas compressors

(G-6614)
HART & COOLEY LLC
1 Lau Pkwy (45315-8754)
PHONE.....................937 832-7800
Bob Mcdonald, *Brnch Mgr*
EMP: 57
Web: www.hartandcooley.com
SIC: 3446 Registers (air), metal
HQ: Hart & Cooley Llc
4460 44th St Se Ste F
Grand Rapids MI 49512
800 433-6341

(G-6615)
IDEAL IMAGE INC
Also Called: Ideal Branding
115 Haas Dr (45322-2845)
PHONE.....................937 832-1660
Dale Paugh, *Pr*
J Belinda Paugh, *
Belinda Paugh, *
▲ **EMP:** 77 **EST:** 1993
SQ FT: 40,000
SALES (est): 8.8MM **Privately Held**
Web: www.idealimageinc.com
SIC: 3999 Barber and beauty shop
equipment

(G-6616)
INTERNATIONAL BELLOWS
2 Ferrari Ct (45315-8988)
PHONE.....................937 294-6261
Thomas Armstrong, *Pr*
Tony Riggs, *VP*
Martin Sherry, *VP*
Tim Gockel, *Treas*
Greg Furlong, *VP*
EMP: 10 **EST:** 1993
SQ FT: 4,800
SALES (est): 998.41K **Privately Held**

Web: www.joycedayton.com
SIC: 3599 Bellows, industrial: metal

(G-6617)
KING KOLD INC
331 N Main St (45322-1333)
PHONE.....................937 836-2731
Douglas Smith, *Pr*
Robert L Smith, *Sec*
EMP: 21 **EST:** 1968
SQ FT: 5,210
SALES (est): 3.42MM **Privately Held**
Web: www.kingkoldinc.com
SIC: 2038 2013 2011 5142 Frozen
specialties, nec; Cooked meats, from
purchased meat; Meat packing plants; Fish,
frozen: packaged

(G-6618)
LIPO TECHNOLOGIES INC
707 Harco Dr (45315-8854)
PHONE.....................937 264-1222
▲ **EMP:** 24
Web: www.lipotechnologies.com
SIC: 2869 Industrial organic chemicals, nec

(G-6619)
NANOLAP TECHNOLOGIES LLC
85 Harrisburg Dr (45322-2835)
PHONE.....................877 658-4949
EMP: 8 **EST:** 2007
SQ FT: 19,000
SALES (est): 208.58K **Privately Held**
Web: www.nanolapabrasives.com
SIC: 3291 Coated abrasive products

(G-6620)
NISSIN PRECISION N AMER INC
375 Union Blvd (45322)
P.O. Box 399 (45322-0399)
PHONE.....................937 836-1910
Todd Shimizu, *Pr*
Cathy Sayer, *
Mike Greer, *
Masatoshi Shimizu, *
Akio Adam Yamamoto, *VP*
▲ **EMP:** 80 **EST:** 1989
SALES (est): 19.4MM **Privately Held**
Web: www.nissinoh.com
SIC: 3663 3444 Television broadcasting and
communications equipment; Sheet
metalwork
PA: Nissin Kogyo Co., Ltd.
1-1-1, Tsukinowa
Otsu SGA 520-2

(G-6621)
POLYCOM INC
35 Rockridge Rd Ste A (45322-2767)
PHONE.....................937 245-1853
David Allen, *Brnch Mgr*
EMP: 7
SALES (corp-wide): 53.56B **Publicly Held**
Web: www.hp.com
SIC: 3571 Personal computers
(microcomputers)
HQ: Polycom, Inc.
6001 America Center Dr
San Jose CA 95002

(G-6622)
**RATLIFF METAL SPINNING
COMPANY**
40 Harrisburg Dr (45322-2834)
PHONE.....................937 836-3900
Michael K Ratliff, *Pr*
James D Ratliff, *VP*
Robin K Ratliff, *Treas*
EMP: 30 **EST:** 1967
SQ FT: 40,000
SALES (est): 7.22MM **Privately Held**

Web: www.ratliffmetal.com
SIC: 3469 Stamping metal for the trade

(G-6623)
SK TECH INC
200 Metro Dr (45315-8700)
PHONE.................................937 836-3535
Nobuyoshi Saigusa, *Pr*
Hidki Kawase, *
Masatoshi Watanabe, *
Hideki Kawase, *
▲ **EMP:** 160 **EST:** 2002
SQ FT: 48,000
SALES (est): 7.28MM **Privately Held**
Web: www.sktechusa.com
SIC: 3694 Engine electrical equipment

(G-6624)
TCS SCHINDLER & CO LLC
Also Called: Yipes Stripes
36 Haas Dr (45322-2808)
PHONE.................................937 836-9473
Todd Schindler, *Managing Member*
EMP: 7 **EST:** 2012
SALES (est): 321.23K **Privately Held**
Web: www.yipesgraphics.com
SIC: 3993 Signs and advertising specialties

(G-6625)
TE-CO MANUFACTURING LLC
100 Quinter Farm Rd (45322-9705)
PHONE.................................937 836-0961
Richard Porter, *Managing Member*
▲ **EMP:** 76 **EST:** 1926
SQ FT: 40,000
SALES (est): 5.07MM **Privately Held**
Web: www.te-co.com
SIC: 3545 3829 3544 3429 Machine tool
attachments and accessories; Measuring
and controlling devices, nec; Special dies,
tools, jigs, and fixtures; Hardware, nec

(G-6626)
TOM SMITH INDUSTRIES INC
Also Called: T S I
500 Smith Dr (45315-8788)
PHONE.................................937 832-1555
Annette H Smith, *CEO*
John A Shay, *
Steven D Good, *
Tarra E Enochs, *
▲ **EMP:** 85 **EST:** 1980
SQ FT: 108,000
SALES (est): 10.92MM **Privately Held**
Web: www.tomsmithindustries.com
SIC: 3544 3089 3714 Industrial molds;
Injection molded finished plastics products,
nec; Motor vehicle parts and accessories

(G-6627)
UNIFIED SCRNING CRSHING - OH I
Also Called: Ohio Wire Cloth
200 Cass Dr (45315-8834)
P.O. Box 280 (45322-0280)
PHONE.................................937 836-3201
Tom Lentsch, *Pr*
Michele Kleason, *Treas*
Devan Donalson, *Prin*
EMP: 6 **EST:** 1961
SQ FT: 10,000
SALES (est): 1.52MM
SALES (corp-wide): 10.8MM **Privately Held**
Web: www.unifiedscreening.com
SIC: 3496 5082 7699 Wire cloth and woven
wire products; Mining machinery and
equipment, except petroleum; Welding
equipment repair
PA: Unified Screening & Crushing - Mn, Inc.
3350 Hwy 149 S
Eagan MN 55121

651 454-8835

(G-6628)
VALUE ADDED PACKAGING INC
44 Lau Pkwy (45315-8777)
PHONE.................................937 832-9595
Jarod D Wenrick, *Pr*
▲ **EMP:** 15 **EST:** 1998
SQ FT: 20,000
SALES (est): 13.12MM **Privately Held**
Web: www.vapmanaged.com
SIC: 2653 Boxes, corrugated: made from
purchased materials

(G-6629)
VANTAGE SPCLTY INGREDIENTS INC
707 Harco Dr (45315-8854)
PHONE.................................937 264-1222
Stephen Doktycz, *CEO*
EMP: 50 **EST:** 2012
SALES (est): 23.98MM
SALES (corp-wide): 599.91MM **Privately Held**
Web: www.lipotechnologies.com
SIC: 2869 Industrial organic chemicals, nec
HQ: Vantage Specialties, Inc
3938 Porett Dr
Gurnee IL 60031
773 376-9000

(G-6630)
WOODBRIDGE ENGLEWOOD INC
Also Called: Hematite
300 Lau Pkwy (45315-8826)
P.O. Box 249 (45315)
PHONE.................................937 540-9889
John C Pavanel, *Pr*
EMP: 24 **EST:** 2014
SALES (est): 18.9MM **Privately Held**
Web: www.englewood.oh.us
SIC: 3089 Automotive parts, plastic

Enon
Clark County

(G-6631)
HARDWOOD STORE INC
350 Enon Rd (45323-1004)
PHONE.................................937 864-2899
John B Clark, *Pr*
John B Clark, *Pr*
Lisa L Clark, *VP*
EMP: 6 **EST:** 1988
SQ FT: 16,000
SALES (est): 719.69K **Privately Held**
Web: www.thehardwoodstore.com
SIC: 2499 5211 Decorative wood and
woodwork; Lumber products

(G-6632)
PROMAC INC
350 Conley Dr (45323-1002)
P.O. Box 158 (45323-0158)
PHONE.................................937 864-1961
Russell Foster, *Pr*
EMP: 8 **EST:** 1971
SQ FT: 22,000
SALES (est): 948.58K **Privately Held**
Web: www.promacinc.net
SIC: 3599 3544 Machine shop, jobbing and
repair; Special dies, tools, jigs, and fixtures

(G-6633)
SEEPEX INC
511 Speedway Dr (45323-1057)
P.O. Box 951454 (44193-0016)
PHONE.................................937 864-7150
Mike Dillon, *Pr*
Ulrich Seeberger, *

◆ **EMP:** 115 **EST:** 1991
SQ FT: 35,000
SALES (est): 24.71MM
SALES (corp-wide): 7.24B **Publicly Held**
Web: www.seepex.com
SIC: 3586 3561 Measuring and dispensing
pumps; Pumps and pumping equipment
HQ: Seepex Gmbh
Scharnholzstr. 344
Bottrop NW 46240
20419960

Etna
Franklin County

(G-6634)
WAIBEL ELECTRIC CO INC
133 Humphries Dr (43068-6801)
PHONE.................................740 964-2956
Carl H Waibel Junior, *Pr*
Sherry Waibel, *Sec*
EMP: 16 **EST:** 1947
SQ FT: 5,200
SALES (est): 833.95K **Privately Held**
Web: www.waibelelectric.com
SIC: 1731 3621 General electrical contractor
; Motors and generators

Etna
Licking County

(G-6635)
JELD-WEN INC
Also Called: Jeld-Wen Millwork Masters
91 Heritage Dr (43062-9805)
PHONE.................................740 964-1431
Scott Farrington, *Brnch Mgr*
EMP: 107
Web: www.jeld-wen.ca
SIC: 2431 Doors, wood
HQ: Jeld-Wen, Inc.
2645 Silver Crescent Dr
Charlotte NC 28273
800 535-3936

(G-6636)
YANKEE CANDLE COMPANY INC
Also Called: Polarpics
175 Heritage Dr (43062-9805)
PHONE.................................413 712-9416
EMP: 6
SALES (corp-wide): 7.58B **Publicly Held**
Web: www.yankeecandle.com
SIC: 3999 Candles
HQ: The Yankee Candle Company Inc
16 Yankee Candle Way
South Deerfield MA 01373
413 665-8306

Euclid
Cuyahoga County

(G-6637)
ABC REFRESHMENTS LLC
19541 Roseland Ave (44117-1374)
PHONE.................................216 692-0697
Thomas Mcginty, *Managing Member*
EMP: 15 **EST:** 2009
SQ FT: 10,000
SALES (est): 201.72K **Privately Held**
Web: www.abcrefreshments.com
SIC: 2096 2024 Potato chips and similar
snacks; Ice cream and frozen deserts

(G-6638)
ADVANCED EQUIPMENT SYSTEMS LLC
22800 Lakeland Blvd (44132-2606)
PHONE.................................216 289-6505
EMP: 8 **EST:** 2012
SQ FT: 65,000
SALES (est): 2.35MM **Privately Held**
Web: www.advancedequipmentsys.com
SIC: 3535 Conveyors and conveying
equipment

(G-6639)
AJAX-CECO
1500 E 219th St (44117-1503)
PHONE.................................440 295-0244
EMP: 6 **EST:** 2017
SALES (est): 1.71MM **Privately Held**
Web: www.ajaxerie.com
SIC: 3599 Machine shop, jobbing and repair

(G-6640)
AMD PLASTICS INC (PA)
27600 Lakeland Blvd (44132-2152)
PHONE.................................216 289-4862
Brian Coll, *Pr*
▲ **EMP:** 18 **EST:** 1984
SQ FT: 50,000
SALES (est): 4.72MM
SALES (corp-wide): 4.72MM **Privately Held**
Web: www.amdplastics.com
SIC: 3089 Thermoformed finished plastics
products, nec

(G-6641)
AMERICAN METAL STAMPING CO LLC
20900 Saint Clair Ave (44117-1040)
PHONE.................................216 531-3100
Diane Rodgers, *CFO*
EMP: 10 **EST:** 2003
SALES (est): 2.5MM **Privately Held**
Web: www.amstamping.com
SIC: 3441 Fabricated structural metal

(G-6642)
AMERICAN PUNCH CO
1655 Century Corners Pkwy (44132-3321)
PHONE.................................216 731-4501
Robert Olson, *Pr*
David G Olson, *Sec*
EMP: 21 **EST:** 1000
SQ FT: 12,000
SALES (est): 6.1MM **Privately Held**
Web: www.americanpunchco.com
SIC: 3599 3544 3421 Machine shop, jobbing
and repair; Special dies, tools, jigs, and
fixtures; Cutlery

(G-6643)
BEAR CABINETRY LLC
23560 Lakeland Blvd (44132-2613)
PHONE.................................216 481-9282
EMP: 6 **EST:** 2006
SALES (est): 489.1K **Privately Held**
Web: www.bear-cabinetry.com
SIC: 2434 Wood kitchen cabinets

(G-6644)
BIC MANUFACTURING INC
Also Called: Brennan Inds Clvland Mfg Group
26420 Century Corners Pkwy (44132-3310)
PHONE.................................216 531-9393
David D Carr, *Pr*
Tom Levicky, *
EMP: 19 **EST:** 1972
SQ FT: 42,000
SALES (est): 2.49MM **Privately Held**

SIC: 3599 Machine shop, jobbing and repair

(G-6645)
BUCKEYE MACHINING INC
25020 Lakeland Blvd (44132-2628)
PHONE...............................216 731-9535
Jerry Mccarthy, *Pr*
Karen Mccarthy, *VP*
EMP: 8 EST: 1983
SQ FT: 7,500
SALES (est): 352.22K Privately Held
SIC: 3366 Bushings and bearings, bronze (nonmachined)

(G-6646)
CPP-CLEVELAND INC (HQ)
Also Called: Cpp-Euclid
26855 Bluestone Blvd (44132-2223)
PHONE...............................216 453-4800
James V Stewart, *CEO*
EMP: 100 EST: 1979
SALES (est): 4.51MM
SALES (corp-wide): 1.9B Privately Held
SIC: 3369 Lead castings, except die-castings
PA: Consolidated Precision Products Corp.
    1621 Euclid Ave Ste 1850
    Cleveland OH 44115
    216 453-4800

(G-6647)
CUYAHOGA MOLDED PLASTICS CO (INC) (PA)
Also Called: Cuyahoga Plastics
1265 Babbitt Rd (44132-2798)
PHONE...............................216 261-2744
EMP: 50 EST: 1960
SALES (est): 5.15MM
SALES (corp-wide): 5.15MM Privately Held
Web: www.cuyahogaplastics.com
SIC: 3089 2821 Molding primary plastics; Plastics materials and resins

(G-6648)
ELMET EUCLID LLC
21801 Tungsten Rd (44117-1117)
PHONE...............................216 692-3990
Jacob Homiller, *Pr*
Paul Leblanc, *
EMP: 95 EST: 2021
SALES (est): 9.42MM
SALES (corp-wide): 77.73MM Privately Held
Web: www.hcstarcksolutions.com
SIC: 3339 Primary nonferrous metals, nec
PA: Elmet Technologies Llc
    1560 Lisbon St
    Lewiston ME 04240
    207 333-6100

(G-6649)
EMMCO INC
19199 Saint Clair Ave (44117-1002)
PHONE...............................216 429-2020
Eugene Mitocky, *Pr*
Loreen Mitocky, *Sec*
EMP: 6 EST: 1988
SALES (est): 2.17MM Privately Held
Web: www.emmcoinc.com
SIC: 3593 Fluid power cylinders, hydraulic or pneumatic

(G-6650)
EUCLID HEAT TREATING CO
Also Called: E H T Company
1408 E 222nd St (44117-1108)
PHONE...............................216 481-8444
TOLL FREE: 800
John Vanas, *Pr*
John H Vanas, *
EMP: 55 EST: 1946

SQ FT: 45,000
SALES (est): 2.85MM Privately Held
Web: www.euclidheattreating.com
SIC: 3398 Metal heat treating

(G-6651)
GLOBAL GLASS BLOCK INC
23570 Lakeland Blvd (44132-2613)
PHONE...............................216 731-2333
Anthony Lacorte, *Pr*
▲ EMP: 8 EST: 1982
SALES (est): 509.25K Privately Held
Web: www.globalglassblock.com
SIC: 3229 5039 Blocks and bricks, glass; Glass construction materials

(G-6652)
GUARDIAN TECHNOLOGIES LLC
Also Called: Germ Guardian
26251 Bluestone Blvd Ste 7 (44132-2826)
PHONE...............................866 603-5900
Richard Farone, *
Ed Vlacich, *
◆ EMP: 36 EST: 2003
SQ FT: 72,000
SALES (est): 4.6MM
SALES (corp-wide): 49.16MM Privately Held
Web: www.lasko.com
SIC: 3564 3585 Air purification equipment; Humidifiers and dehumidifiers
PA: Lasko Group, Inc.
    820 Lincoln Ave
    West Chester PA 19380
    610 692-7400

(G-6653)
HICKMANS CONSTRUCTION CO LLC
21150 Morris Ave (44123-2922)
PHONE...............................866 271-2565
EMP: 10 EST: 2021
SALES (est): 411.21K Privately Held
SIC: 3531 Construction machinery

(G-6654)
INDELCO CUSTOM PRODUCTS INC
25861 Tungsten Rd (44132-2817)
PHONE...............................216 797-7300
Mitchell Opalich, *Pr*
Lorraine Simer, *VP*
EMP: 8 EST: 1964
SQ FT: 21,500
SALES (est): 917.12K Privately Held
Web: www.indelco.com
SIC: 3599 3498 3561 3089 Machine shop, jobbing and repair; Tube fabricating (contract bending and shaping); Pumps and pumping equipment; Fittings for pipe, plastics

(G-6655)
INFINITAIRE INDUSTRIES LLC
Also Called: Infinitaire Industries
24370 Hartland Dr (44123-2210)
PHONE...............................216 600-2051
Alex Shorter, *CEO*
EMP: 6 EST: 2018
SALES (est): 155.13K Privately Held
SIC: 8748 8742 0139 2298 Economic consultant; Financial consultant; Cordage: abaca, sisal, henequen, hemp, jute, or other fiber

(G-6656)
IRONHAWK INDUSTRIAL DIST LLC
Also Called: Ironhawk Industrial
1261 Babbitt Rd Ste B (44132-2754)
PHONE...............................216 502-3700
Patrick Hawkins, *Pr*
EMP: 8 EST: 2010
SALES (est): 2.76MM Privately Held

Web: www.ironhawkindustrial.com
SIC: 8741 3531 Business management; Snow plow attachments

(G-6657)
KERR LAKESIDE INC
26841 Tungsten Rd (44132-2934)
P.O. Box 32220 (44132-0220)
PHONE...............................216 261-2100
▲ EMP: 70 EST: 1948
SALES (est): 10.98MM Privately Held
Web: www.kerrlakeside.com
SIC: 3452 3451 Bolts, nuts, rivets, and washers; Screw machine products

(G-6658)
LALAC - HANLON LLC
1280 E 286th St (44132-2138)
PHONE...............................216 261-7056
Larry E Fulton, *CEO*
Larry E Fulton, *Managing Member*
EMP: 20 EST: 2018
SALES (est): 3.88MM Privately Held
Web: www.hanloncomposites.com
SIC: 3089 Plastics containers, except foam

(G-6659)
MARIE NOBLE WINE COMPANY
1891 Idlehurst Dr (44117-1878)
PHONE...............................216 633-0025
Bertrim Bandy, *CEO*
EMP: 20 EST: 2022
SALES (est): 832.83K Privately Held
SIC: 2084 7389 Wines, brandy, and brandy spirits; Business services, nec

(G-6660)
MART PLUS FUEL
21820 Lake Shore Blvd (44123-1707)
PHONE...............................216 261-0420
Anil Uppal, *Prin*
EMP: 6 EST: 2011
SALES (est): 181.57K Privately Held
Web: www.fuelmart.com
SIC: 2869 Fuels

(G-6661)
MECHANICAL DYNAMICS ANALIS LLC
Also Called: Renewal Parts Maintenance
1250 E 222nd St (44117-1114)
PHONE...............................440 946-0082
John L Vanderhoef, *CEO*
EMP: 21
Web: www.mdaturbines.com
SIC: 7699 3568 3053 Industrial machinery and equipment repair; Power transmission equipment, nec; Gaskets; packing and sealing devices
HQ: Mechanical Dynamics & Analysis Llc
    25 British American Blvd
    Latham NY 12110
    518 399-3616

(G-6662)
MESOCOAT INC
Also Called: Mesocoat Advanced Coating Tech
24112 Rockwell Dr (44117-1252)
PHONE...............................216 453-0866
Stephen Goss, *CEO*
▲ EMP: 18 EST: 2007
SALES (est): 938.3K
SALES (corp-wide): 938.3K Privately Held
Web: www.mesocoat.com
SIC: 3479 1799 5169 7699 Coating of metals and formed products; Corrosion control installation; Anti-corrosion products; Industrial equipment services
PA: Abakan Inc
    2665 S Byshr Dr Ste 450

Miami FL 33133
786 206-5368

(G-6663)
NEWTON MATERION INC
21801 Tungsten Rd (44117-1117)
PHONE...............................216 692-3990
Greg Fuller, *Dir Opers*
EMP: 300
Web: www.hcstarcksolutions.com
SIC: 3356 3313 3339 Tungsten, basic shapes; Molybdenum silicon, not made in blast furnaces; Rhenium refining (primary)
HQ: Newton Materion Inc
    45 Industrial Pl
    Newton MA 02461
    617 630-5800

(G-6664)
NORAMCO INC
1400 E 222nd St (44117-1108)
PHONE...............................216 531-3400
James M Popela, *CEO*
EMP: 58 EST: 1998
SALES (est): 548.41K
SALES (corp-wide): 21.15MM Privately Held
Web: www.noramcobag.com
SIC: 2673 Bags: plastic, laminated, and coated
PA: North American Plastics Chemicals Incorporated
    1400 E 222nd St
    Euclid OH 44117
    216 531-3400

(G-6665)
NORMAN NOBLE INC
931 E 228th St (44123-3201)
PHONE...............................216 851-4007
Lawrence Noble, *Pr*
EMP: 50
SALES (corp-wide): 42.44MM Privately Held
Web: www.nnoble.com
SIC: 3841 Instruments, microsurgical: except electromedical
PA: Norman Noble, Inc.
    5507 Avion Park Dr
    Highland Heights OH 44143
    216 761-5387

(G-6666)
NORTH AMERICAN PLAS CHEM INC (PA)
Also Called: Noramco
1400 E 222nd St (44117-1108)
PHONE...............................216 531-3400
James Popela, *Pr*
EMP: 35 EST: 1974
SQ FT: 25,000
SALES (est): 21.15MM
SALES (corp-wide): 21.15MM Privately Held
Web: www.noramcobag.com
SIC: 2673 2671 Plastic and pliofilm bags; Paper; coated and laminated packaging

(G-6667)
ORTHOTIC & PROSTHETIC SPC INC
20650 Lakeland Blvd (44119-3241)
PHONE...............................216 531-2773
Richard Gaudio, *Pr*
Tom Heckman, *VP*
Jeff Gerl, *Sec*
EMP: 28 EST: 1972
SQ FT: 7,200
SALES (est): 2.36MM Privately Held
SIC: 3842 Orthopedic appliances

(G-6668)
OURNASHONISME ENT LLC
1423 E 263rd St (44132-2917)
PHONE...................................689 276-0367
EMP: 10 **EST:** 2019
SALES (est): 69.11K **Privately Held**
SIC: 7929 8999 3861 7819 Entertainers and
entertainment groups; Artists and artists'
studios; Sound recording and reproducing
equipment, motion picture; Sound effects
and music production, motion picture

(G-6669)
PIONEER SOLUTIONS LLC
1090 E 222nd St (44117-1101)
PHONE...................................216 383-3400
David Juba, *Managing Member*
EMP: 20 **EST:** 2004
SALES (est): 2.69MM **Privately Held**
Web: www.pioneersolutionsllc.com
SIC: 3492 3542 8711 7389 Electrohydraulic
servo valves, metal; Brakes, metal forming;
Consulting engineer; Inspection and testing
services

(G-6670)
POWDERMET INC (PA)
24112 Rockwell Dr (44117-1252)
PHONE...................................216 404-0053
Andrew Sherman, *Pr*
EMP: 49 **EST:** 1996
SQ FT: 7,800
SALES (est): 13.45MM
SALES (corp-wide): 13.45MM **Privately
Held**
Web: www.powdermetinc.com
SIC: 3399 Powder, metal

(G-6671)
POWDERMET POWDER PROD INC
24112 Rockwell Dr Ste D (44117-1252)
PHONE...................................216 404-0053
Andrew Sherman, *CEO*
EMP: 10 **EST:** 2013
SALES (est): 309.9K **Privately Held**
Web: www.powdermetinc.com
SIC: 3821 Crushing and grinding apparatus,
laboratory

(G-6672)
PPG INDUSTRIES OHIO INC
Also Called: Pretreatment & Specialty Pdts
23000 Saint Clair Ave (44117-2503)
PHONE...................................412 434-1542
Jim Driddy, *Prin*
EMP: 66
SALES (corp-wide): 18.25B **Publicly Held**
Web: www.ppg.com
SIC: 2851 Paints and allied products
HQ: Ppg Industries Ohio, Inc.
3800 West 143rd St
Cleveland OH 44111
216 671-0050

(G-6673)
**PRECISION HYDRLIC CNNCTORS
INC**
Also Called: PHC Divison Bic Manufacturing
26420 Century Corners Pkwy (44132-3310)
PHONE...................................440 953-3778
Patrick De Capua, *Pr*
EMP: 15 **EST:** 1988
SQ FT: 12,000
SALES (est): 1.75MM **Privately Held**
SIC: 3599 Machine and other job shop work

(G-6674)
R & A SPORTS INC
Also Called: Adler Team Sports
23780 Lakeland Blvd (44132-2615)

PHONE...................................216 289-2254
John Domo, *Pr*
Richard Domo, *
Ruth Ann Domo, *
EMP: 25 **EST:** 1976
SQ FT: 16,000
SALES (est): 3.9MM **Privately Held**
Web: www.coachesonly.com
SIC: 5091 5136 5137 2396 Sporting and
recreation goods; Sportswear, men's and
boys'; Sportswear, women's and children's;
Screen printing on fabric articles

(G-6675)
RALPHIE GIANNI MFG & CO LTD
250 E 271st St (44132-1606)
PHONE...................................216 507-3873
EMP: 10 **EST:** 2018
SALES (est): 158.79K **Privately Held**
SIC: 2389 Apparel and accessories, nec

(G-6676)
RISHER & CO
27011 Tungsten Rd (44132-2938)
PHONE...................................216 732-8351
William J Risher, *Pr*
EMP: 11 **EST:** 1942
SQ FT: 27,000
SALES (est): 2.89MM **Privately Held**
Web: www.risherandcompany.com
SIC: 3599 Machine shop, jobbing and repair

(G-6677)
S C INDUSTRIES INC
24460 Lakeland Blvd (44132-2622)
P.O. Box 32307 (44132-0307)
PHONE...................................216 732-9000
Earl Lauridsen, *Pr*
▲ **EMP:** 20 **EST:** 1974
SQ FT: 10,000
SALES (est): 2.34MM **Privately Held**
Web: www.scindustriesinc.com
SIC: 3366 7389 Bushings and bearings;
Grinding, precision: commercial or industrial

(G-6678)
SCHWEBEL BAKING COMPANY
Also Called: Mill Brook
345 E 200th St (44119-1157)
PHONE...................................216 481-1880
Ray Paworwlski, *Mgr*
EMP: 12
SALES (corp-wide): 71.65MM **Privately
Held**
Web: www.myschwebels.com
SIC: 2051 Bread, cake, and related products
PA: Schwebel Baking Company
965 E Midlothian Blvd
Youngstown OH 44502
330 783-2860

(G-6679)
TECH-MED INC
Also Called: Shaker Numeric Mfg
1080 E 222nd St (44117-1101)
PHONE...................................216 486-0900
Gary White, *Pr*
Carty White, *Sec*
EMP: 15 **EST:** 1953
SQ FT: 10,000
SALES (est): 4.96MM **Privately Held**
Web: www.shakernumeric.com
SIC: 3469 Machine parts, stamped or
pressed metal

(G-6680)
TOMAHAWK ENTRMT GROUP LLC
26870 Drakefield Ave (44132-2009)
PHONE...................................216 505-0548
Javon Bates, *CEO*
EMP: 10 **EST:** 2011

SALES (est): 852.31K **Privately Held**
SIC: 4832 2731 7389 8742 Radio
broadcasting stations, music format; Book
publishing; Music recording producer;
Marketing consulting services

(G-6681)
TRUST MANUFACTURING LLC (PA)
20080 Saint Clair Ave (44117-1015)
PHONE...................................216 531-8787
EMP: 9 **EST:** 2004
SALES (est): 2.56MM
SALES (corp-wide): 2.56MM **Privately
Held**
Web: www.trustmfg.com
SIC: 3599 Machine shop, jobbing and repair

(G-6682)
US LIGHTING GROUP INC
1148 E 222nd St (44117-1103)
PHONE...................................216 896-7000
Paul Spivak, *CEO*
Susan Tubbs, *CFO*
Taylor Bennington, *VP*
EMP: 40 **EST:** 2013
SALES (est): 3.63MM **Privately Held**
Web: www.uslightinggroup.com
SIC: 3679 Electronic circuits

(G-6683)
VILLAGE PLASTICS CO
Also Called: 3d Systems
23610 Saint Clair Ave (44117-2515)
PHONE...................................330 753-0100
Kevin Gerstenslager, *Prin*
EMP: 8 **EST:** 2004
SALES (est): 1.06MM
SALES (corp-wide): 29.15MM **Privately
Held**
Web: www.villageplastics.com
SIC: 3544 Extrusion dies
PA: Keene Building Products Co.
2926 Chester Ave
Cleveland OH 44114
440 605-1020

Fairborn
Greene County

(G-6684)
ADAPT-A-PAK INC
678 Yellow Springs Fairfield Rd Ste 100
(45324-9762)
PHONE...................................937 845-0386
TOLL FREE: 800
EMP: 49 **EST:** 1987
SALES (est): 2.15MM **Privately Held**
Web: www.adaptapak.com
SIC: 2653 5113 Boxes, corrugated: made
from purchased materials; Shipping supplies

(G-6685)
ALI INDUSTRIES LLC
Also Called: Abrasive Leaders & Innovators
747 E Xenia Dr (45324-8761)
PHONE...................................937 878-3946
Terry Ali, *Pr*
Phillip Ali, *
Christopher Ali, *
Lee Kockentiet, *
◆ **EMP:** 283 **EST:** 1961
SQ FT: 260,360
SALES (est): 19.35MM
SALES (corp-wide): 7.34B **Publicly Held**
Web: www.gatorfinishing.com
SIC: 3291 Abrasive products
HQ: Rust-Oleum Corporation
11 Hawthorn Pkwy
Vernon Hills IL 60061
847 367-7700

(G-6686)
ALL SRVICE PLASTIC MOLDING INC
611 Yellow Springs Fairfield Rd
(45324-9437)
PHONE...................................937 415-3674
Keller Phillip, *Brnch Mgr*
EMP: 114
SALES (corp-wide): 24.44MM **Privately
Held**
Web: www.mincogroup.com
SIC: 3089 Injection molding of plastics
PA: All Service Plastic Molding, Inc.
850 Falls Creek Dr
Vandalia OH 45377
937 890-0322

(G-6687)
APOGEE PLASTICS CORP
8300 Dayton Springfield Rd (45324-1911)
PHONE...................................937 864-1966
Walter S Hoy, *Pr*
EMP: 6 **EST:** 2003
SALES (est): 509.5K **Privately Held**
Web: www.apogeeplastics.com
SIC: 3089 Plastics processing

(G-6688)
CEMEX CEMENT INC
4410 State Route 235 (45324-9773)
PHONE...................................937 873-9858
EMP: 144
SIC: 3273 Ready-mixed concrete
HQ: Cemex Cement, Inc.
10100 Katy Fwy Ste 300
Houston TX 77043
713 650-6200

(G-6689)
CURTISS-WRIGHT DS INC
Also Called: Curtiss-Wrght C5isr Data Slton
2600 Paramount Pl Ste 200 (45324-6816)
PHONE...................................937 252-5601
Ron Taulton, *Brnch Mgr*
EMP: 50
SALES (corp-wide): 3.12B **Publicly Held**
Web: www.curtisswright.com
SIC: 8711 8731 3769 3625 Consulting
engineer; Commercial physical research;
Space vehicle equipment, nec; Relays and
industrial controls
HQ: Curtiss-Wright Ds, Inc.
20130 Lkview Ctr Plz Ste
Ashburn VA 20147

(G-6690)
ERNST ENTERPRISES INC
Also Called: Valley Concrete Division
5325 Medway Rd (45324-9765)
PHONE...................................937 878-9378
John Macfee, *Genl Mgr*
EMP: 13
SALES (corp-wide): 240.08MM **Privately
Held**
Web: www.ernstconcrete.com
SIC: 3273 Ready-mixed concrete
PA: Ernst Enterprises, Inc.
993 Falls Creek Dr
Vandalia OH 45377
937 233-5555

(G-6691)
FAIRBORN CEMENT PLANT
3250 Linebaugh Rd (45324)
PHONE...................................937 879-8466
Bruce Moroz, *Prin*
EMP: 9 **EST:** 2010
SALES (est): 509.12K **Privately Held**
Web: www.fairborncement.com
SIC: 3273 Ready-mixed concrete

(G-6692)
FOX LITE INC
8300 Dayton Springfield Rd (45324-1911)
PHONE..............................937 864-1966
Douglas Hoy, *Pr*
Walter Hoy, *
Mark Hopkins, *
▼ **EMP:** 30 **EST:** 1982
SQ FT: 74,000
SALES (est): 5.21MM **Privately Held**
Web: www.foxlite.com
SIC: 3089 Plastics hardware and building
products

(G-6693)
**GBR PROPERTY MAINTENANCE
LLC**
1260 Spangler Rd Bldg 1 (45324-9504)
PHONE..............................937 879-0200
EMP: 10 **EST:** 2005
SALES (est): 175.54K **Privately Held**
SIC: 2951 Asphalt paving mixtures and
blocks

(G-6694)
GLAWE MANUFACTURING CO INC
Also Called: Glawe Awnings
851 Zapata Dr (45324-5165)
PHONE..............................937 754-0064
L Vernon Schaefer, *Pr*
Katherine Schaefer, *VP*
Thomas R Fridley, *VP*
EMP: 6 **EST:** 1877
SQ FT: 20,500
SALES (est): 852.63K **Privately Held**
Web: www.glaweawning.com
SIC: 2394 7359 Awnings, fabric: made from
purchased materials; Equipment rental and
leasing, nec

(G-6695)
LASERLINC INC
777 Zapata Dr (45324-5160)
PHONE..............................937 318-2440
Dan Dixon, *Pr*
Jeff Kohler, *VP*
Jack Weiss, *VP*
▲ **EMP:** 20 **EST:** 1994
SQ FT: 19,000
SALES (est): 4.9MM **Privately Held**
Web: www.laserlinc.com
SIC: 3826 Analytical instruments

(G-6696)
MIAMI VALLEY PUBLISHING LLC
678 Yellow Springs Fairfield Rd
(45324-9766)
P.O. Box 681 (45324-0681)
PHONE..............................937 879-5678
EMP: 143
Web: www.miamivalleypublishing.com
SIC: 2752 Offset printing

(G-6697)
MORRIS FURNITURE CO INC (PA)
Also Called: Morris Home Furnishing
2377 Commerce Center Blvd Ste A
(45324-6378)
PHONE..............................937 874-7100
▲ **EMP:** 150 **EST:** 1947
SALES (est): 88.44MM
SALES (corp-wide): 88.44MM **Privately
Held**
Web: www.morrisathome.com
SIC: 2512 2511 5719 5712 Living room
furniture: upholstered on wood frames;
Kitchen and dining room furniture;
Beddings and linens; Office furniture

(G-6698)
**RAPISCAN SYSTEMS HIGH ENRGY
IN**
Also Called: Aracor
514 E Dayton Yellow Springs Rd
(45324-6432)
PHONE..............................937 879-4200
Robert Armistead, *Pr*
EMP: 30
SALES (corp-wide): 1.54B **Publicly Held**
Web: www.rapiscansystems.com
SIC: 3845 Electromedical equipment
HQ: Rapiscan Systems High Energy
Inspection Corporation
520 Almanor Ave
Sunnyvale CA 94085
408 733-7780

(G-6699)
STADCO INC
Also Called: Stadco Automatics
632 Yellow Springs Fairfield Rd
(45324-9762)
PHONE..............................937 878-0911
Dennis C Trammell, *Pr*
Kenneth Wilson, *
Jeffrey Lyon, *
EMP: 45 **EST:** 1948
SQ FT: 42,000
SALES (est): 4.57MM **Privately Held**
Web: www.stadcoprecision.com
SIC: 3451 3541 Screw machine products;
Machine tools, metal cutting type

(G-6700)
SURFACE RECOVERY TECH LLC
833 Zapata Dr (45324-5165)
PHONE..............................937 879-5864
Thomas Brooks, *Managing Member*
EMP: 15 **EST:** 2006
SQ FT: 20,000
SALES (est): 1.34MM **Privately Held**
Web: www.surfacerecovery.com
SIC: 3441 Fabricated structural metal

(G-6701)
TANGIBLE SOLUTIONS INC
678 Yellow Springs Fairfield Rd
(45324-9762)
PHONE..............................937 912-4603
Adam Clark, *CEO*
Christopher Collins, *COO*
Linda Terrill, *CFO*
Roger Edwards, *Ch Bd*
EMP: 26 **EST:** 2013
SALES (est): 2.43MM **Privately Held**
Web: www.tangiblesolutions3d.com
SIC: 8748 8711 3544 8299 Systems
engineering consultant, ex. computer or
professional; Engineering services; Special
dies, tools, jigs, and fixtures; Educational
services

(G-6702)
TEE CREATIONS
Also Called: Tca Graphics
701 N Broad St Ste C (45324-5262)
PHONE..............................937 878-2822
Mike Brown, *Owner*
EMP: 9 **EST:** 1962
SQ FT: 5,000
SALES (est): 475.15K **Privately Held**
Web: www.tcagraphics.com
SIC: 2396 5699 Screen printing on fabric
articles; Sports apparel

(G-6703)
WCR INCORPORATED (PA)
Also Called: W C R
2377 Commerce Center Blvd Ste B
(45324-6378)
PHONE..............................937 223-0703
Kim Andreasen, *CEO*
Brad Stevens, *
Greg Pinasco, *
Ralene Stevens, *
◆ **EMP:** 32 **EST:** 1991
SQ FT: 54,000
SALES (est): 43.23MM
SALES (corp-wide): 43.23MM **Privately
Held**
Web: www.wcrhx.com
SIC: 3443 Heat exchangers, condensers,
and components

Fairfield
Butler County

(G-6704)
7 7 PRINT SOLUTIONS LLC
6601 Dixie Hwy Ste C (45014-5495)
PHONE..............................513 600-4597
Benjamin Sasse, *Prin*
EMP: 6 **EST:** 2017
SALES (est): 588.64K **Privately Held**
SIC: 2752 Commercial printing, lithographic

(G-6705)
AAA LAMINATING AND BINDERY INC
Also Called: AAA Laminating & Bindery
7209 Dixie Hwy (45014-5544)
PHONE..............................513 860-2680
Gerald Randall, *Pr*
EMP: 6 **EST:** 2005
SALES (est): 901.23K **Privately Held**
Web: www.aaalaminating.us
SIC: 2789 Bookbinding and related work

(G-6706)
AGFA CORPORATION
6104 Monastery Dr (45014-4460)
PHONE..............................513 829-6292
James Dixon, *Brnch Mgr*
EMP: 35
SALES (corp-wide): 495.38MM **Privately
Held**
Web: www.agfa.com
SIC: 3861 Photographic equipment and
supplies
HQ: Agfa Corporation
580 Gotham Pkwy
Carlstadt NJ 07072
800 540-2432

(G-6707)
AKRO TOOL CO INC
240 Donald Dr (45014-3007)
PHONE..............................513 858-1555
Ken Johnson, *Pr*
Donna Johnson, *Sec*
EMP: 8 **EST:** 1960
SQ FT: 10,000
SALES (est): 386.35K **Privately Held**
Web: www.akrotool.com
SIC: 3599 Machine shop, jobbing and repair

(G-6708)
ALBA MANUFACTURING INC
8950 Seward Rd (45011-9109)
PHONE..............................513 874-0551
Tom Moon, *Pr*
Thomas N Inderhees, *
Mike Kroger, *
EMP: 52 **EST:** 1973
SQ FT: 67,000
SALES (est): 13.03MM **Privately Held**
Web: www.albamfg.com
SIC: 3535 5084 3312 Conveyors and
conveying equipment; Conveyor systems;
Blast furnaces and steel mills

(G-6709)
AMERICAN FAN COMPANY
2933 Symmes Rd (45014-2099)
PHONE..............................513 874-2400
◆ **EMP:** 162
Web: www.fairbanksmorsedefense.com
SIC: 3564 Exhaust fans: industrial or
commercial

(G-6710)
AMERICAN INKS AND COATINGS CO
575 Quality Blvd (45014-2294)
PHONE..............................513 552-7200
George Sickinger, *Pr*
EMP: 6
SALES (corp-wide): 7.06MM **Privately
Held**
Web: www.flintgrp.com
SIC: 2893 Printing ink
PA: American Inks And Coatings Company
3400 N Hutchison St
Pine Bluff AR 71602
870 247-2080

(G-6711)
AMERICAN MANUFACTURING & EQP
Also Called: Cincinnati Retread Systems
4990 Factory Dr (45014-1945)
PHONE..............................513 829-2248
Albert Penter, *Pr*
Carol Penter, *Treas*
Albert Penter Junior, *VP*
EMP: 9 **EST:** 1978
SQ FT: 12,000
SALES (est): 388.03K **Privately Held**
SIC: 3559 3714 3564 Tire retreading
machinery and equipment; Motor vehicle
parts and accessories; Blowers and fans

(G-6712)
BAYER
700 Nilles Rd (45014-3604)
PHONE..............................513 336-6600
Joe Bayer, *Admn*
EMP: 6 **EST:** 2017
SALES (est): 179.55K **Privately Held**
SIC: 2834 Pharmaceutical preparations

(G-6713)
BCS TECHNOLOGIES LTD
1041 Tedia Way (45014-2004)
PHONE..............................513 829-4577
Jeff Bishop, *Pt*
EMP: 10 **EST:** 1995
SQ FT: 8,000
SALES (est): 3.6MM **Privately Held**
Web: www.bcstechnologies.com
SIC: 3613 7373 Control panels, electric;
Computer integrated systems design

(G-6714)
BK TOOL COMPANY INC
300 Security Dr (45014-4243)
PHONE..............................513 870-9622
Robert Reed Junior, *Treas*
EMP: 8 **EST:** 1972
SQ FT: 10,200
SALES (est): 937.2K **Privately Held**
Web: www.bktoolco.com
SIC: 3544 Special dies and tools

(G-6715)
BYRON PRODUCTS INC
3781 Port Union Rd (45014-2207)
PHONE..............................513 870-9111
Mark Byron, *Ch*
Rick Henry, *
▲ **EMP:** 70 **EST:** 1982
SQ FT: 44,000
SALES (est): 5.36MM **Privately Held**

Web: www.byronproducts.com
SIC: 7692 Welding repair

(G-6716)
CALVARY INDUSTRIES INC (PA)
9233 Seward Rd (45014-5407)
PHONE.............................513 874-1113
John P Morelock Junior, *CEO*
Ivan Byers, *
Thomas Rielage, *
▲ **EMP:** 48 **EST:** 1983
SQ FT: 100,000
SALES (est): 425.01K
SALES (corp-wide): 425.01K **Privately Held**
Web: www.calvaryindustries.com
SIC: 2819 5169 Industrial inorganic chemicals, nec; Chemicals and allied products, nec

(G-6717)
CARR TOOL COMPANY
575 Security Dr (45014-4269)
PHONE.............................513 825-2900
Patricia Blum, *CEO*
Alex Blum, *
EMP: 10 **EST:** 1955
SQ FT: 13,000
SALES (est): 2.44MM **Privately Held**
Web: www.carrtool.com
SIC: 3532 Mining machinery

(G-6718)
CEMPLEX GROUP NC LLC
3195 Profit Dr (45014-4234)
PHONE.............................513 671-3300
EMP: 10 **EST:** 2012
SALES (est): 709.68K **Privately Held**
Web: www.cemplexgroup.com
SIC: 2295 Waterproofing fabrics, except rubberizing

(G-6719)
CENT-ROLL PRODUCTS INC
4866 Factory Dr (45014-1915)
PHONE.............................513 829-5201
EMP: 33 **EST:** 1986
SALES (est): 3.61MM **Privately Held**
Web: www.cent-roll.com
SIC: 3069 Roll coverings, rubber

(G-6720)
CINCINNATI BABBITT INC
9217 Seward Rd (45014-5407)
PHONE.............................513 942-5088
Louis M Patterson, *Pr*
Dale A Frye, *Sec*
▲ **EMP:** 10 **EST:** 1990
SQ FT: 20,000
SALES (est): 969.04K **Privately Held**
Web: www.cinbab.com
SIC: 3599 Machine shop, jobbing and repair

(G-6721)
CINCINNATI GRINDING TECHNOLOGIES INC
Also Called: Cg Industries
300 Distribution Cir Ste G (45014-2239)
P.O. Box 47 (45040-0047)
PHONE.............................866 983-1097
EMP: 9
SIC: 3599 Grinding castings for the trade

(G-6722)
CINCINNATI RADIATOR INC
8551a Seward Rd (45011-8652)
PHONE.............................513 874-5555
Rich Sexton, *Pr*
Phyllis Apure, *Sec*
▲ **EMP:** 13 **EST:** 1994

SALES (est): 2.46MM
SALES (corp-wide): 5.19MM **Privately Held**
Web: www.cincyradiator.com
SIC: 7539 3541 3599 Radiator repair shop, automotive; Machine tools, metal cutting type; Machine and other job shop work
PA: Ohio Heat Holdings Llc
945 Mckinney St Ste 572
Houston TX 77002
513 874-5555

(G-6723)
CKS SOLUTION INCORPORATED (PA)
4293 Muhlhauser Rd (45014-5450)
PHONE.............................513 947-1277
Peter Sung, *Pr*
James Braun, *CFO*
▲ **EMP:** 26 **EST:** 2008
SQ FT: 72,000
SALES (est): 5.49MM
SALES (corp-wide): 5.49MM **Privately Held**
Web: www.ckssolution.com
SIC: 3679 3674 Liquid crystal displays (LCD); Light emitting diodes

(G-6724)
COLOR RESOLUTIONS INTERNATIONAL LLC
Also Called: Cri
575 Quality Blvd (45014-2294)
PHONE.............................513 552-7200
EMP: 115
Web: new.colorresolutions.com
SIC: 2899 Ink or writing fluids

(G-6725)
DAMAK 1 LLC
Also Called: Teron Lighting
33 Donald Dr (45014-3025)
PHONE.............................513 858-6004
David Bellos, *CEO*
Micheal Bellos, *Pr*
▲ **EMP:** 45 **EST:** 1980
SQ FT: 51,100
SALES (est): 11.75MM
SALES (corp-wide): 11.75MM **Privately Held**
Web: www.teronlighting.com
SIC: 3646 Fluorescent lighting fixtures, commercial
PA: Tli, Llc
33 Donald Dr Uppr
Fairfield OH 45014
513 858-6004

(G-6726)
DEFFREN MACHINE TOOL SVC INC
Also Called: Akro Tool Company
240 Donald Dr (45014-3007)
PHONE.............................513 858-1555
Richard Deffren, *Pr*
EMP: 10 **EST:** 2003
SALES (est): 1.71MM **Privately Held**
Web: www.akrotool.com
SIC: 3599 Machine shop, jobbing and repair

(G-6727)
DETROIT FLAME HARDENING CO
Also Called: Cincinnati Flame Hardening Co
375 Security Dr (45014-4250)
PHONE.............................513 942-1400
Allen Leach, *Mgr*
EMP: 10
SALES (corp-wide): 4.84MM **Privately Held**
Web: www.detroitflame.com
SIC: 3398 Metal heat treating
PA: Detroit Flame Hardening Company Inc

17644 Mount Elliott St
Detroit MI
313 891-2936

(G-6728)
DIXIE CONTAINER CORPORATION
Also Called: Pca/Fairfielde 329
3840 Port Union Rd (45014-2202)
PHONE.............................513 860-1145
EMP: 60
SIC: 2653 Corrugated and solid fiber boxes

(G-6729)
DIXON BAYCO USA
7280 Union Centre Blvd (45014-2344)
PHONE.............................513 874-8499
Robert Kettinger, *Pr*
▲ **EMP:** 8 **EST:** 2000
SALES (est): 10.27MM
SALES (corp-wide): 439.82MM **Privately Held**
Web: www.dixonvalve.com
SIC: 3823 Liquid level instruments, industrial process type
PA: Dvcc, Llc
1 Dixon Sq
Chestertown MD 21620
410 778-2000

(G-6730)
ECOPAC LLC
Also Called: Distrubutors
258 Donald Dr (45014-3007)
PHONE.............................513 795-6002
Srinivas Bandinani, *Managing Member*
EMP: 20 **EST:** 2022
SALES (est): 1.13MM **Privately Held**
Web: www.ecopackamerica.com
SIC: 2674 Paper bags: made from purchased materials

(G-6731)
EDI CUSTOM INTERIORS INC
Also Called: Exhibit Design International
5648 Lindenwood Ln (45014-3563)
PHONE.............................513 829-3895
William H Snyder, *Pr*
Janice Snyder, *Stockholder*
EMP: 17 **EST:** 1981
SQ FT: 52,000
SALES (est): 262.03K **Privately Held**
SIC: 3999 Advertising display products

(G-6732)
EMPIRE PRINTING INC
9560 Le Saint Dr (45014-2253)
PHONE.............................513 242-3900
Dean Nieporte, *Pr*
EMP: 9 **EST:** 1956
SQ FT: 6,000
SALES (est): 136.96K **Privately Held**
Web: www.empireprintinginc.com
SIC: 2752 2759 Offset printing; Letterpress printing

(G-6733)
ERNST ENTERPRISES INC
107 River Cir Bldg 1 (45014-2333)
PHONE.............................513 829-8683
John Ernst, *Owner*
EMP: 50
SALES (corp-wide): 240.08MM **Privately Held**
Web: www.ernstconcrete.com
SIC: 1771 3273 Concrete work; Ready-mixed concrete
PA: Ernst Enterprises, Inc.
993 Falls Creek Dr
Vandalia OH 45377
937 233-5555

(G-6734)
FAIRFIELD MANUFACTURING INC
8585 Seward Rd (45011-8652)
PHONE.............................513 642-0081
▲ **EMP:** 300
Web: www.takumistamping.com
SIC: 3469 Stamping metal for the trade

(G-6735)
FLOTURN INC (PA)
4236 Thunderbird Ln (45014-5482)
PHONE.............................513 860-8040
Michael North, *Pr*
Don Spillane, *
◆ **EMP:** 120 **EST:** 1962
SQ FT: 75,000
SALES (est): 42.42MM
SALES (corp-wide): 42.42MM **Privately Held**
Web: www.floturn.com
SIC: 3599 Machine shop, jobbing and repair

(G-6736)
FM AF LLC ✪
Also Called: American Fan
2933 Symmes Rd (45014-2001)
PHONE.............................866 771-6266
George Whittier, *CEO*
EMP: 147 **EST:** 2023
SALES (est): 21.6MM
SALES (corp-wide): 1.27B **Privately Held**
SIC: 3564 Blowers and fans
HQ: Fairbanks Morse, Llc
701 White Ave
Beloit WI 53511
800 356-6955

(G-6737)
FORCE CONTROL INDUSTRIES INC
3660 Dixie Hwy (45014-1105)
PHONE.............................513 868-0900
Robert Briede, *Prin*
James C Besl, *
Joseph E Besl, *
Eric Ferry, *
▲ **EMP:** 50 **EST:** 1969
SQ FT: 60,000
SALES (est): 9.43MM **Privately Held**
Web: www.forcecontrol.com
SIC: 3714 3594 3566 3568 Motor vehicle parts and accessories; Fluid power pumps and motors; Speed changers, drives, and gears; Clutches, except vehicular

(G-6738)
G & W PRODUCTS LLC
8675 Seward Rd (45011-9716)
PHONE.............................513 860-4050
Gary Johns, *CEO*
Wayde Hunker, *Pr*
Douglas Henderson, *VP*
Randy Sagraves, *VP*
Michael R Janson, *CFO*
▲ **EMP:** 125 **EST:** 2006
SQ FT: 120,000
SALES (est): 27.94MM **Privately Held**
Web: www.gandwproductsinc.com
SIC: 2541 3441 3469 Cabinets, lockers, and shelving; Fabricated structural metal; Metal stampings, nec

(G-6739)
HI TECH PRINTING CO INC
3741 Port Union Rd (45014-2207)
PHONE.............................513 874-5325
EMP: 36
SIC: 2759 Flexographic printing

(G-6740)
HIPSY LLC
4951 Dixie Hwy (45014-3057)
PHONE...............................513 403-5333
Lerin Buggs, *Brnch Mgr*
EMP: 9
SALES (corp-wide): 475.04K **Privately Held**
Web: www.headbandsforwomen.com
SIC: 2339 Scarves, hoods, headbands, etc.: women's
PA: Hipsy Llc
5321 Cleves Warsaw Pike
Cincinnati OH 45238
513 403-5333

(G-6741)
HONEYMOON PAPER PRODUCTS INC
7100 Dixie Hwy (45014-5543)
PHONE...............................513 755-7200
EMP: 70
Web: www.sctray.com
SIC: 2675 2653 Die-cut paper and board; Corrugated and solid fiber boxes

(G-6742)
HOWDEN NORTH AMERICA INC
Also Called: Howden North America
2933 Symmes Rd (45014-2001)
PHONE...............................513 874-2400
Karl Kimmerling, *Pr*
▲ EMP: 170 EST: 1996
SALES (est): 2.33MM
SALES (corp-wide): 2.74B **Publicly Held**
Web: www.chartindustries.com
SIC: 3564 Blowers and fans
PA: Esab Corporation
909 Rose Ave Fl 8
North Bethesda MD 20852
301 323-9099

(G-6743)
HOWDEN USA COMPANY
Also Called: American Fan
2933 Symmes Rd (45014-2001)
PHONE...............................513 874-2400
Mark Sanders, *Pr*
Mark Paul Lehman, *
▲ EMP: 175 EST: 2013
SALES (est): 41.61MM **Publicly Held**
Web: www.chartindustries.com
SIC: 3564 Blowing fans: industrial or commercial
PA: Chart Industries, Inc.
2200 Arprt Indus Dr Ste 1
Ball Ground GA 30107

(G-6744)
INNOMARK COMMUNICATIONS LLC
375 Northpointe Dr (45014-5474)
PHONE...............................513 285-1040
EMP: 56
SALES (corp-wide): 47.75MM **Privately Held**
Web: www.innomarkcom.com
SIC: 2759 Commercial printing, nec
PA: Innomark Communications Llc
420 Distribution Cir
Fairfield OH 45014
888 466-6627

(G-6745)
IPEX USA LLC
4507 Le Saint Ct (45014-5486)
PHONE...............................513 942-9910
EMP: 9
SALES (corp-wide): 8.01MM **Privately Held**
Web: www.ipexna.com
SIC: 3084 Plastics pipe

HQ: Ipex Usa Llc
10100 Rodney Blvd
Pineville NC 28134

(G-6746)
IVY VENTURES LLC
39 Citadel Dr Apt 2 (45014-8567)
PHONE...............................513 259-3307
Edward Abernathy Senior, *Prin*
EMP: 9 EST: 2008
SALES (est): 89.11K **Privately Held**
Web: www.centaurihs.com
SIC: 7372 Prepackaged software

(G-6747)
IWATA BOLT USA INC (PA)
Also Called: Iwata Bolt
102 Iwata Dr (45014-2298)
PHONE...............................513 942-5050
Shinobu Iwata, *CEO*
Kiyotaka Iwata, *Pr*
▲ EMP: 11 EST: 1971
SQ FT: 35,000
SALES (est): 20.38MM
SALES (corp-wide): 20.38MM **Privately Held**
Web: www.iwatabolt.co.jp
SIC: 5072 3452 Miscellaneous fasteners; Bolts, nuts, rivets, and washers

(G-6748)
JOHNSON-NASH METAL PDTS INC
9265 Seward Rd (45014-5407)
PHONE...............................513 874-7022
Colleen Johnson, *Ch*
Charles Johnson, *Pr*
Craig Johnson, *CEO*
Carol Johnson Dreyer, *Sec*
EMP: 11 EST: 1936
SQ FT: 21,000
SALES (est): 2.22MM **Privately Held**
Web: www.johnsonnash.com
SIC: 3441 Fabricated structural metal

(G-6749)
MACHINTEK CO
3721 Port Union Rd (45014-2200)
PHONE...............................513 551-1000
Roger Hasler, *Pr*
Vaughn Burckard, *Prin*
Andy Holbert, *Prin*
Chris Rubenacker, *Prin*
▲ EMP: 65 EST: 1985
SQ FT: 37,000
SALES (est): 7.94MM **Privately Held**
Web: www.machintek.com
SIC: 3599 Machine shop, jobbing and repair

(G-6750)
MASS-MARKETING INC (PA)
7209 Dixie Hwy (45014-5544)
P.O. Box 40427 (45240)
PHONE...............................513 860-6200
Donald J Mueller, *Pr*
Betsy Engoe, *Mgr*
◆ EMP: 140 EST: 1977
SQ FT: 25,000
SALES (est): 2.1MM
SALES (corp-wide): 2.1MM **Privately Held**
Web: www.massmarketing.com
SIC: 2752 Offset printing

(G-6751)
MASTER-HALCO INC
620 Commerce Center Dr (45011-8664)
PHONE...............................513 869-7600
Paul Smith, *Mgr*
EMP: 16
Web: www.masterhalco.com
SIC: 5051 3315 Steel; Fence gates, posts, and fittings: steel

HQ: Master-Halco, Inc.
3010 Lyndon B Jhnson Fwy
Dallas TX 75234
800 883-8384

(G-6752)
MASTERS PHARMACEUTICAL INC
8695 Seward Rd (45011-9716)
PHONE...............................513 290-2969
Ben Lazel, *Pr*
EMP: 7 EST: 2015
SALES (est): 263.17K **Privately Held**
Web: www.mastersrx.com
SIC: 2834 Pharmaceutical preparations

(G-6753)
MB MANUFACTURING CORP
2904 Symmes Rd (45014-2035)
PHONE...............................513 682-1461
Greg Kelley, *Prin*
EMP: 9 EST: 2003
SALES (est): 1.58MM **Privately Held**
Web: www.mbveneer.com
SIC: 2421 Lumber: rough, sawed, or planed

(G-6754)
MENDENHALL TECHNICAL SERVICES INC
Also Called: M T S I
9175 Seward Rd (45014-5405)
PHONE...............................513 860-1280
◆ EMP: 22 EST: 1980
SALES (est): 8.08MM **Privately Held**
Web: www.mtsigt.com
SIC: 3511 8711 Turbines and turbine generator sets; Engineering services

(G-6755)
MIDWEST SPECIALTY PDTS CO INC
280 Northpointe Dr (45014-5443)
PHONE...............................513 874-7070
Michael Brunst, *Pr*
Thomas Brunst, *VP*
Steven Huesman, *Sec*
▲ EMP: 18 EST: 1965
SQ FT: 52,000
SALES (est): 6.82MM **Privately Held**
Web: www.tubesandcores.com
SIC: 2655 Fiber cans, drums, and similar products

(G-6756)
MT PLEASANT BLACKTOPPING INC
Also Called: Mt.pleasant Blacktopping
3199 Production Dr (45014-4227)
PHONE...............................513 874-3777
William House, *CEO*
Benjamin House, *Pr*
Anna House, *VP*
EMP: 8 EST: 1962
SQ FT: 3,200
SALES (est): 4.61MM **Privately Held**
Web: www.mtpleasantblacktopping.com
SIC: 1623 1771 2951 Sewer line construction; Blacktop (asphalt) work; Asphalt and asphaltic paving mixtures (not from refineries)

(G-6757)
MULHERN BELTING INC
310 Osborne Dr (45014-2247)
PHONE...............................201 337-5700
George Oboer, *Mgr*
EMP: 38
SQ FT: 10,000
SALES (corp-wide): 23.58MM **Privately Held**
Web: www.mulhernbelting.com

SIC: 3021 3535 Rubber and plastics footwear; Conveyors and conveying equipment
PA: Mulhern Belting, Inc.
148 Bauer Dr
Oakland NJ 07436
201 337-5700

(G-6758)
NORTHEND GEAR AND MACHINE INC
475 Security Dr (45014-4251)
PHONE...............................513 860-4334
Dan Rockenfelder, *Pr*
David Shope, *VP*
Duane Ratcliff, *Sec*
EMP: 18 EST: 1988
SQ FT: 18,000
SALES (est): 2.25MM **Privately Held**
Web: www.northendgear.com
SIC: 3599 Machine shop, jobbing and repair

(G-6759)
NORTHERN PRECISION INC
3245 Production Dr (45014-4232)
PHONE...............................513 860-4701
Harold W Jarvis, *Pr*
Dane A Kerby, *Sr VP*
EMP: 15 EST: 1999
SQ FT: 5,000
SALES (est): 2.4MM **Privately Held**
Web: www.npswiss.com
SIC: 3599 Machine shop, jobbing and repair

(G-6760)
OCS INTELLITRAK INC
8660 Seward Rd (45011-9716)
PHONE...............................513 742-5600
Thomas D Robertson, *Pr*
Charles P Tabler, *Pr*
▲ EMP: 12 EST: 1995
SQ FT: 14,500
SALES (est): 9.32MM **Privately Held**
Web: www.intellitrak.com
SIC: 3535 Conveyors and conveying equipment
PA: Lico, Inc.
9230 E 47th St
Kansas City MO 64133

(G-6761)
PACIFIC INDUSTRIES USA INC
8955 Seward Rd (45011-9109)
PHONE...............................513 860-3900
Toru Nishimura, *Pr*
◆ EMP: 25 EST: 1986
SQ FT: 53,000
SALES (est): 7.63MM **Privately Held**
SIC: 3714 Motor vehicle wheels and parts
PA: Pacific Industrial Co.,Ltd.
100, Kyutokucho
Ogaki GIF 503-0

(G-6762)
PACIFIC MANUFACTURING OHIO INC
8955 Seward Rd (45011-9109)
PHONE...............................513 860-3900
Toshiteru Ando, *Pr*
▲ EMP: 450 EST: 1999
SALES (est): 50.79MM **Privately Held**
Web: www.pacific-ind.co.jp
SIC: 3714 3469 Motor vehicle parts and accessories; Metal stampings, nec
PA: Pacific Industrial Co.,Ltd.
100, Kyutokucho
Ogaki GIF 503-0

(G-6763)
PACIFIC MANUFACTURING OHIO INC
8935 Seward Rd (45011-9109)
PHONE...............................513 860-3900
EMP: 9 EST: 2017

▲ = Import ▼ = Export
◆ = Import/Export

SALES (est): 2.65MM **Privately Held**
SIC: **3999** Barber and beauty shop
equipment

(G-6764)
PEASE INDUSTIES INC
7100 Dixie Hwy (45014-5543)
PHONE....................513 870-3600
David H Pease Junior, *Ch Bd*
Leonard W Cavens, *
Neil W Jackman, *National Account Vice
President*
David A Aluise, *MFG*
EMP: 7 EST: 1892
SQ FT: 220,000
SALES (est): 902.17K
SALES (corp-wide): 2.03B **Privately Held**
SIC: **3442** 3089 2431 Metal doors; Doors,
folding; plastics or plastics coated fabric;
Doors, wood
PA: Pella Corporation
102 Main St
Pella IA 50219
641 621-1000

(G-6765)
PERFECTION PRINTING
9560 Le Saint Dr (45014-2253)
PHONE....................513 874-2173
Steve Myers, *Pr*
Scott Myers, *VP*
Joe Myers, *Treas*
EMP: 8 EST: 1984
SQ FT: 10,000
SALES (est): 599.99K **Privately Held**
Web: www.perfectionprinting.com
SIC: **2752** Offset printing

(G-6766)
**PRESTIGE DISPLAY AND
PACKAGING LLC**
420 Distribution Cir (45014-5473)
PHONE....................513 285-1040
▲ EMP: 16
SIC: **2653** Corrugated boxes, partitions,
display items, sheets, and pad

(G-6767)
PRINTER COMPONENTS INC
4236 Thunderbird Ln (45014-5482)
PHONE....................585 924-5190
◆ EMP: 9
SIC: **3861** 5112 3955 5999 Printing
equipment, photographic; Laser printer
supplies; Print cartridges for laser and other
computer printers; Photocopy machines

(G-6768)
PROMOSPARK INC
300 Osborne Dr (45014-2247)
P.O. Box 18-1147 (45018-1147)
PHONE....................513 844-2211
Sarah Johnston, *Pr*
EMP: 12 EST: 2013
SALES (est): 945.01K **Privately Held**
Web: www.promospark.com
SIC: **2396** Apparel and other linings, except
millinery

(G-6769)
QUALITY GOLD INC (PA)
Also Called: Quality Gold
500 Quality Blvd (45014-2292)
P.O. Box 18490 (45018-0490)
PHONE....................513 942-7659
Michael Langhammer, *CEO*
Jason Langhammer, *
◆ EMP: 270 EST: 1979
SQ FT: 110,000
SALES (est): 23.07MM
SALES (corp-wide): 23.07MM **Privately
Held**

Web: www.qgold.com
SIC: **3339** 5944 Gold refining (primary);
Clock and watch stores

(G-6770)
QUEEN CITY TOOL WORKS INC
125 Constitution Dr Ste 2 (45014-2256)
PHONE....................513 874-0111
Martin Oehler, *Pr*
Tim Mayes, *VP*
EMP: 6 EST: 1998
SQ FT: 5,200
SALES (est): 507.07K **Privately Held**
Web: www.queencitytool.com
SIC: **3544** 3599 Special dies and tools;
Machine and other job shop work

(G-6771)
R K METALS LTD
3235 Homeward Way (45014-4237)
PHONE....................513 874-6055
EMP: 30 EST: 1997
SQ FT: 45,000
SALES (est): 4.48MM **Privately Held**
Web: www.rkmetals.net
SIC: **3469** Stamping metal for the trade

(G-6772)
RIVER CITY PHARMA
8695 Seward Rd (45011-9716)
PHONE....................513 870-1680
Danny Smith, *Pr*
Jason Smith, *VP*
EMP: 8 EST: 2012
SALES (est): 224.09K **Privately Held**
Web: www.mastersrx.com
SIC: **2834** 5122 Pharmaceutical preparations
; Pharmaceuticals

(G-6773)
SAF-HOLLAND INC
105 Mercantile Dr (45014-3782)
PHONE....................513 874-7888
EMP: 7
SALES (corp-wide): 1.98B **Privately Held**
Web: www.safholland.com
SIC: **3715** 3568 3537 3452 Truck trailers;
Power transmission equipment, nec;
Industrial trucks and tractors; Bolts, nuts,
rivets, and washers
HQ: Saf-Holland, Inc.
1950 Industrial Blvd
Muskegon MI 49442
231 773-3271

(G-6774)
SCHNEIDER AUTOMATION INC
5855 Union Centre Blvd (45014-2346)
PHONE....................612 426-0709
EMP: 199
SALES (corp-wide): 1.09K **Privately Held**
Web: www.schneider-electric.com
SIC: **3699** Electrical equipment and supplies,
nec
HQ: Schneider Automation Inc.
800 Federal St
Andover MA 01810
978 794-0800

(G-6775)
SHAW INDUSTRIES INC
8580 Seward Rd Ste 400 (45011-8628)
PHONE....................513 942-3692
Jim Brown, *Brnch Mgr*
EMP: 859
SALES (corp-wide): 424.23B **Publicly
Held**
Web: www.shawinc.com
SIC: **2273** Carpets and rugs
HQ: Shaw Industries, Inc.
616 E Walnut Ave

Dalton GA 30722

(G-6776)
SKYLINE CEM HOLDINGS LLC (PA)
Also Called: Skyline Chili
4180 Thunderbird Ln (45014-2235)
PHONE....................513 874-1188
Dick Williams, *Interim Chief Executive
Officer*
▲ EMP: 148 EST: 1949
SQ FT: 42,000
SALES (est): 44.38MM
SALES (corp-wide): 44.38MM **Privately
Held**
Web: www.skylinechili.com
SIC: **5812** 2038 6794 5149 Restaurant,
family: chain; Frozen specialties, nec;
Franchises, selling or licensing; Groceries
and related products, nec

(G-6777)
SOUTHERN CHAMPION TRAY LP
Also Called: Southern Champion Tray, L.P.
7100 Dixie Hwy (45014-5543)
PHONE....................513 755-7200
John Zeiser, *Brnch Mgr*
EMP: 61
Web: www.sctray.com
SIC: **2675** 2653 Die-cut paper and board;
Corrugated and solid fiber boxes
PA: Southern Champion Tray, Llc
220 Compress St
Chattanooga TN 37405

(G-6778)
STANDEX ELECTRONICS INC (HQ)
Also Called: Standex-Meder Electronics
4150 Thunderbird Ln (45014-2235)
PHONE....................513 871-3777
Ramy Shatoot, *CEO*
▲ EMP: 98 EST: 1999
SQ FT: 22,022
SALES (est): 22.6MM
SALES (corp-wide): 720.63MM **Publicly
Held**
Web: www.standexelectronics.com
SIC: **3625** 5065 Motor controls and
accessories; Electronic parts and
equipment, nec
PA: Standex International Corporation
23 Keewaydin Dr
Salem NH 03079
603 893-9701

(G-6779)
STANDEX INTERNATIONAL CORP
Standex Electronics
4150 Thunderbird Ln (45014-2235)
PHONE....................513 533-7171
Jim Suetholz, *Mgr*
EMP: 64
SALES (corp-wide): 720.63MM **Publicly
Held**
Web: www.standex.com
SIC: **3675** 3678 3644 Electronic capacitors;
Electronic connectors; Noncurrent-carrying
wiring devices
PA: Standex International Corporation
23 Keewaydin Dr
Salem NH 03079
603 893-9701

(G-6780)
TAKUMI STAMPING INC
8585 Seward Rd (45011-8652)
PHONE....................513 642-0081
Ken Naruse, *Pr*
EMP: 193 EST: 2016
SALES (est): 9.99MM **Privately Held**
Web: www.takumistamping.com

SIC: **3469** Stamping metal for the trade

(G-6781)
TECH/III INC
Also Called: Printing Plant
2594 Mack Rd (45014-5127)
PHONE....................513 482-7500
James E Oconnor, *Ch*
Carol S Horan, *
EMP: 42 EST: 1970
SALES (est): 5.84MM **Privately Held**
Web: www.printingplant.com
SIC: **2671** 2759 Paper; coated and
laminated packaging; Labels and seals:
printing, nsk

(G-6782)
**THE ELLENBEE-LEGGETT
COMPANY INC**
3765 Port Union Rd (45014-2207)
P.O. Box 8025 (45014)
PHONE....................513 874-3200
EMP: 110
Web: www.performancefoodservice.com
SIC: **5141** 5147 5142 2015 Groceries,
general line; Meats and meat products;
Meat, frozen: packaged; Poultry
slaughtering and processing

(G-6783)
**THE WESTERN STATES MACHINE
COMPANY**
625 Commerce Center Dr (45011-1172)
P.O. Box 327 (45012-0327)
PHONE....................513 863-4758
◆ EMP: 57 EST: 1917
SALES (est): 9.8MM **Privately Held**
Web: www.westernstates.com
SIC: **3569** Centrifuges, industrial

(G-6784)
THE-FISCHER-GROUP
2028- 2052 Bohlke Blvd (45014)
PHONE....................513 285-1281
Vannessa Fisher, *Off Mgr*
EMP: 9 EST: 1997
SALES (est): 902.71K **Privately Held**
Web: www.the-fischer-group.com
SIC: **3915** Lapidary work, contract or other

(G-6785)
TSR MACHINERY SERVICES INC
100 Soourity Dr (16011 1216)
PHONE....................513 874-9697
Todd Routh, *Pr*
Lisa Routh, *
EMP: 10 EST: 1989
SQ FT: 26,000
SALES (est): 981.63K **Privately Held**
Web: www.tsrmachinery.com
SIC: **3599** Machine shop, jobbing and repair

(G-6786)
USALCO FAIRFIELD PLANT LLC
3700 Dixie Hwy (45014-1106)
PHONE....................513 737-7100
EMP: 20 EST: 2009
SALES (est): 2.19MM **Privately Held**
Web: www.usalco.com
SIC: **2899** Water treating compounds

(G-6787)
USALCO MICHIGAN CITY PLANT LLC
Also Called: Usalco
3700 Dixie Hwy (45014-1106)
PHONE....................513 737-7100
Joseph Hickey, *Mgr*
EMP: 10
SALES (corp-wide): 42.96MM **Privately
Held**

GEOGRAPHIC

Web: www.usalco.com
SIC: 2819 Industrial inorganic chemicals, nec
PA: Usalco Michigan City Plant, Llc
2601 Cannery Ave
Baltimore MD 21226
410 918-2230

(G-6788)
VIBRA FINISH CO
8411 Seward Rd (45011-8651)
PHONE..............................513 870-6300
Haskel Hall, *Pr*
EMP: 20
SALES (corp-wide): 5.08MM **Privately Held**
Web: www.vibrafinish.com
SIC: 3291 Abrasive products
PA: Vibra Finish Co.
2220 Shasta Way
Simi Valley CA 93065
805 578-0033

(G-6789)
VISTECH MFG SOLUTIONS LLC
Also Called: Vistech
4274 Thunderbird Ln (45014-5482)
PHONE..............................513 860-1408
Terry Mclaughlin, *Brnch Mgr*
EMP: 11
SALES (corp-wide): 31.21MM **Privately Held**
Web: www.vistechmfg.com
SIC: 3999 Barber and beauty shop equipment
HQ: Vistech Manufacturing Solutions, Llc
1156 Scenic Dr Ste 120
Modesto CA 95350
209 544-9333

(G-6790)
WATCH-US INC
3400 Port Union Rd (45014-4224)
PHONE..............................513 829-8870
Dan Graf, *Pr*
▲ **EMP:** 20 **EST:** 1991
SALES (est): 3.96MM **Privately Held**
Web: www.watchusinc.com
SIC: 3944 Automobile and truck models, toy and hobby

(G-6791)
WATERCO OF THE CENTRAL STATES
Also Called: Culligan
3215 Homeward Way (45014-4237)
PHONE..............................937 294-0375
Jeffery Meyer, *Pr*
Nicole Duckworth, *
Jason Wesley, *
EMP: 25 **EST:** 2011
SALES (est): 2.27MM **Privately Held**
SIC: 3221 Water bottles, glass

(G-6792)
WHOLESALE BAIT CO INC
2619 Bobmeyer Rd (45014-1217)
PHONE..............................513 863-2380
Gregory Fessel, *CEO*
Anthony G Fessel, *Pr*
Benjamin Fessel, *Dir*
EMP: 9 **EST:** 1950
SQ FT: 18,000
SALES (est): 2.03MM **Privately Held**
Web: www.wholesalebait.com
SIC: 5199 3949 Bait, fishing; Sporting and athletic goods, nec

(G-6793)
WORKSTREAM INC (HQ)
Also Called: Hamilton Casework Solutions
3158 Production Dr (45014-4228)

PHONE..............................513 870-4400
Thadius Jaroszewicz, *CEO*
▼ **EMP:** 60 **EST:** 1988
SQ FT: 50,000
SALES (est): 20.65MM **Privately Held**
Web: www.myworkstream.com
SIC: 2521 2522 Panel systems and partitions (free-standing), office: wood; Panel systems and partitions, office: except wood
PA: H S Morgan Limited Partnership
3158 Production Dr
Fairfield OH 45014

(G-6794)
ZEBEC OF NORTH AMERICA INC
210 Donald Dr (45014-3007)
P.O. Box 181570 (45018-1570)
PHONE..............................513 829-5533
Ed Synder, *Pr*
Scott Snyder, *
Chris Snyder, *
◆ **EMP:** 35 **EST:** 1992
SQ FT: 7,000
SALES (est): 7.42MM **Privately Held**
Web: www.zebec.com
SIC: 3949 5091 Sporting and athletic goods, nec; Sporting and recreation goods

Fairfield Township
Butler County

(G-6795)
BUTLER TECH
Also Called: Southwest Ohio Computer Assn
3611 Hamilton Middletown Rd (45011-2241)
PHONE..............................513 867-1028
Mike Crumley, *Superintnt*
EMP: 38
SALES (corp-wide): 78.28K **Privately Held**
Web: www.butlertech.org
SIC: 8211 7372 Public combined elementary and secondary school; Educational computer software
PA: Butler Technology & Career Development Schools
3603 Hmlton Middletown Rd
Hamilton OH 45011
513 868-1911

(G-6796)
INNOVATIVE CONTROL SYSTEMS
5870 Fairham Rd (45011-2035)
PHONE..............................513 894-3712
Steven Saunders, *Pr*
Dave Edester, *VP*
EMP: 6 **EST:** 1992
SALES (est): 247.36K **Privately Held**
Web: www.icscarwashsystems.com
SIC: 3613 Control panels, electric

Fairlawn
Summit County

(G-6797)
BUCKEYE CORRUGATED INC (PA)
Also Called: B C I
822 Kumho Dr Ste 400 (44333-9298)
PHONE..............................330 576-0590
Dale Sommer, *Pr*
Douglas A Bosnik, *Pr*
Mark A Husted, *CFO*
EMP: 9 **EST:** 1999
SQ FT: 11,000
SALES (est): 1.1B
SALES (corp-wide): 1.1B **Privately Held**
Web: www.bcipkg.com

SIC: 2653 Boxes, corrugated: made from purchased materials

(G-6798)
CONTITECH NORTH AMERICA INC (DH)
703 S Cleveland Massillon Rd (44333-3023)
PHONE..............................330 664-7180
Jim Hill, *Pr*
▲ **EMP:** 17 **EST:** 1999
SALES (est): 468.36MM
SALES (corp-wide): 42B **Privately Held**
Web: www.continental-industry.com
SIC: 3061 Mechanical rubber goods
HQ: Contitech Deutschland Gmbh
Continental-Plaza 1
Hannover NI 30175
51193802

(G-6799)
EDUCATIONAL DIRECTION INC
Also Called: Emergency Training Inst Div
150 N Miller Rd Ste 200 (44333-3772)
PHONE..............................330 836-8439
Alexander M Butman, *Pr*
Richard W Vomacka, *VP*
Warren Joblin, *Sec*
▼ **EMP:** 6 **EST:** 1967
SQ FT: 3,000
SALES (est): 59.34K **Privately Held**
SIC: 2741 5999 Technical manual and paper publishing; Audio-visual equipment and supplies

(G-6800)
ELIOKEM INC (DH)
175 Ghent Rd (44333-3330)
PHONE..............................330 734-1100
John F Malloy, *Pr*
Robert Smith, *
Veronique Le Du, *
◆ **EMP:** 85 **EST:** 2001
SQ FT: 100,000
SALES (est): 6.49MM
SALES (corp-wide): 2.52B **Privately Held**
SIC: 2819 Industrial inorganic chemicals, nec
HQ: Synthomer Inc.
25435 Harvard Rd
Beachwood OH 44122
216 682-7000

(G-6801)
FRISBY PRINTING COMPANY
Also Called: Minuteman Press
3571 Brookwall Dr Unit C (44333-9295)
PHONE..............................330 665-4565
Parris Frisby, *Pr*
EMP: 10 **EST:** 2008
SQ FT: 1,600
SALES (est): 1.65MM **Privately Held**
Web: akron.minutemanpress.com
SIC: 2752 Commercial printing, lithographic

(G-6802)
GOT GRAPHIX LLC
3265 W Market St (44333-3337)
PHONE..............................330 703-9047
Meeran Shafeer, *Managing Member*
EMP: 10 **EST:** 2011
SQ FT: 5,500
SALES (est): 148.94K **Privately Held**
SIC: 2759 2395 Screen printing; Embroidery and art needlework

(G-6803)
HGGC CITADEL PLAS HOLDINGS INC
Also Called: Citadel Plastics
3637 Ridgewood Rd (44333-3123)

PHONE..............................330 666-3751
Mike Huff, *CEO*
Kevin Andrews, *OF ENGINEERED COMPOSITES*
Dennis Loughran, *CFO*
EMP: 10 **EST:** 2012
SALES (est): 3.59MM **Privately Held**
SIC: 2821 Plastics materials and resins
HQ: Lyondellbasell Advanced Polymers Inc.
1221 Mckinney St Ste 300
Houston TX 77010
713 309-7200

(G-6804)
HPC HOLDINGS LLC (HQ)
Also Called: Composite Group, The
3637 Ridgewood Rd (44333-3123)
PHONE..............................330 666-3751
Terry Morgan, *CEO*
Tom Meola, *CFO*
EMP: 11 **EST:** 2008
SALES (est): 34.44MM
SALES (corp-wide): 49.93MM **Privately Held**
SIC: 2821 2655 Molding compounds, plastics; Cans, composite: foil-fiber and other: from purchased fiber
PA: Bulk Molding Compounds, Inc.
1600 Powis Ct
West Chicago IL 60185

(G-6805)
INFINITY ENGINEERED PDTS LLC
Also Called: Infinity Engineered Products
3524 Southwestern Blvd (44333-3191)
PHONE..............................234 466-7200
David Brinkman, *CEO*
EMP: 24 **EST:** 2015
SALES (est): 6.08MM **Privately Held**
Web: www.infinityairsprings.com
SIC: 3714 Shock absorbers, motor vehicle

(G-6806)
LEADER PUBLICATIONS INC
Also Called: West Side Leader
3075 Smith Rd Ste 204 (44333-4454)
PHONE..............................330 665-9595
Clark Burns, *Genl Mgr*
EMP: 6 **EST:** 1984
SALES (est): 882.44K **Privately Held**
Web: www.akron.com
SIC: 2711 Newspapers: publishing only, not printed on site

(G-6807)
LITTLERN CORPORATION
1006 Bunker Dr Apt 207 (44333-3079)
PHONE..............................330 848-8847
Ernest L Puskas Junior, *Pr*
EMP: 9 **EST:** 1980
SALES (est): 852.19K **Privately Held**
Web: www.littlern.com
SIC: 2869 2819 4226 Industrial organic chemicals, nec; Industrial inorganic chemicals, nec; Special warehousing and storage, nec

(G-6808)
PROFUSION INDUSTRIES LLC (PA)
822 Kumho Dr Ste 202 (44333-5105)
PHONE..............................800 938-2858
Jack Woodyard, *VP*
Jon Golden, *
William Hatch, *
EMP: 8 **EST:** 2014
SALES (est): 20.85MM
SALES (corp-wide): 20.85MM **Privately Held**
Web: www.profusionindustries.com

▲ = Import ▼ = Export
◆ = Import/Export

SIC: 3081 3089 Unsupported plastics film and sheet; Extruded finished plastics products, nec

(G-6809)
RJF INTERNATIONAL CORPORATION
Also Called: Matting Products Div
3875 Embassy Pkwy (44333-8342)
PHONE..............................330 668-2069
◆ EMP: 850
Web: www.rjfinternational.com
SIC: 3081 3089 3069 Floor or wall covering, unsupported plastics; Battery cases, plastics or plastics combination; Wallcoverings, rubber

(G-6810)
SANCTUARY SOFTWARE STUDIO INC
3090 W Market St Ste 300 (44333-3623)
PHONE..............................330 666-9690
Michael J Terry, Pr
Stacy Simontom, Dir
EMP: 34 EST: 1993
SALES (est): 2.32MM Privately Held
Web: www.sancsoft.com
SIC: 7372 7371 Application computer software; Computer software development

(G-6811)
SENTIENT STUDIOS LTD
2894 Chamberlain Rd Apt 6 (44333-3468)
P.O. Box 13141 (44334-8541)
PHONE..............................330 204-8636
William Genkin, Managing Member
EMP: 41 EST: 2016
SALES (est): 716.58K Privately Held
SIC: 7373 3569 Computer integrated systems design; Robots, assembly line: industrial and commercial

(G-6812)
SIGNET GROUP INC
375 Ghent Rd (44333-4601)
PHONE..............................330 668-5000
Charles E Scharff, Prin
EMP: 24 EST: 2000
SALES (est): 9.64MM Privately Held
Web: www.signetjewelers.com
SIC: 3911 Jewelry, precious metal
PA: Signet Jewelers Limited
C/O Conyers Corporate Services (Bermuda) Limited
Hamilton HM 11

(G-6813)
SIGNET GROUP SERVICES US INC
375 Ghent Rd (44333-4601)
PHONE..............................330 668-5000
EMP: 11 EST: 2021
SALES (est): 11.35MM Privately Held
SIC: 3911 Jewelry, precious metal
PA: Signet Jewelers Limited
C/O Conyers Corporate Services (Bermuda) Limited
Hamilton HM 11

(G-6814)
SSP INDUSTRIAL GROUP INC
3560 W Market St Ste 300 (44333-2687)
PHONE..............................330 665-2900
Richard M Hamlin, Pr
Mark Hamlin Junior, Pr
James Gaul, Sec
James D Van Tiem, Sec
▲ EMP: 9 EST: 1995
SALES (est): 456.3K Privately Held

SIC: 3465 3412 3411 8742 Automotive stampings; Metal barrels, drums, and pails; Food and beverage containers; Management consulting services

(G-6815)
TOTAL EDUCATION SOLUTIONS INC
Also Called: Tes Therapy
3428 W Market St (44333-3339)
PHONE..............................330 668-4041
Tawnia Novak, Dir
EMP: 99 EST: 2008
SALES (est): 434.77K Privately Held
Web: www.tesidea.com
SIC: 3172 Personal leather goods, nec

Fairport Harbor
Lake County

(G-6816)
GEORGE WHALLEY COMPANY
Also Called: Cft Systems
1180 High St Ste 1 (44077-6921)
PHONE..............................216 453-0099
George M Whalley, Pr
Howard M Whalley, VP
EMP: 10 EST: 1937
SQ FT: 25,000
SALES (est): 1.3MM Privately Held
Web: www.cftsystems.com
SIC: 3545 Tool holders

(G-6817)
JM PERFORMANCE PRODUCTS INC
Also Called: J & M Machine
1234 High St (44077-5559)
PHONE..............................440 357-1234
John Stoneback, Pr
Linda Stoneback, VP
EMP: 19 EST: 1965
SQ FT: 19,500
SALES (est): 2.42MM Privately Held
Web: www.jmperformanceproducts.com
SIC: 3545 Milling machine attachments (machine tool accessories)

(G-6818)
LYONDELL CHEMICAL COMPANY
Also Called: Equistar
110 3rd St (44077-5837)
PHONE..............................440 352-9393
Michael Step, Mgr
EMP: 149
Web: www.lyondellbasell.com
SIC: 2821 Plastics materials and resins
HQ: Lyondell Chemical Company
1221 Mckinney St Ste 300
Houston TX 77010
713 309-7200

(G-6819)
MJM INDUSTRIES INC
1200 East St (44077-5571)
PHONE..............................440 350-1230
Eric Wachob, CEO
James E Heighway, Vice Chairman*
Lois Roulston, *
▲ EMP: 110 EST: 1985
SQ FT: 35,500
SALES (est): 12.61MM Privately Held
Web: www.mjmindustries.com
SIC: 3679 Harness assemblies, for electronic use: wire or cable

(G-6820)
QUARTZ SCIENTIFIC INC (PA)
Also Called: Qsi
819 East St (44077-5596)
P.O. Box 1129 (44077-8129)

PHONE..............................360 574-6254
James R Atwell Junior, Pr
EMP: 22 EST: 1963
SQ FT: 44,000
SALES (est): 2.68MM
SALES (corp-wide): 2.68MM Privately Held
Web: www.qsiquartz.com
SIC: 3679 Quartz crystals, for electronic application

(G-6821)
RAMPE MANUFACTURING COMPANY
Also Called: Torque Transmission
1246 High St (44077-5536)
PHONE..............................440 352-8995
John N Rampe, CEO
John W Rampe, Pr
Willam Patrick, Contrlr
EMP: 17 EST: 1947
SQ FT: 40,000
SALES (est): 4.89MM Privately Held
Web: www.torquetrans.com
SIC: 3568 Power transmission equipment, nec

(G-6822)
US WELDING TRAINING LLC
518 5th St (44077-5663)
P.O. Box 1011 (44077-1011)
PHONE..............................440 669-9380
Michael Davison, Prin
EMP: 6 EST: 2012
SALES (est): 126.25K Privately Held
Web: www.usweldingtraining.com
SIC: 7692 Welding repair

Farmersville
Montgomery County

(G-6823)
QUALITY DURABLE INDUS FLOORS
Also Called: Q&D Indrustrial Floors
5005 Farmersville Germantn Pike (45325-9268)
PHONE..............................937 696-2833
Scott Carmack, Pr
Douglas Emrick, VP
Douglas A Emrick, VP
EMP: 14 EST: 2000
SALES (est): 1.13MM Privately Held
Web: www.qdifloors.com
SIC: 2851 7389 Epoxy coatings; Business services, nec

Fayette
Fulton County

(G-6824)
C & K MACHINE CO INC
604 N Park St (43521-9718)
P.O. Box 478 (43521-0478)
PHONE..............................419 237-3203
Ken Cassaubon, Pr
EMP: 7 EST: 1987
SALES (est): 389.05K Privately Held
SIC: 3599 Machine shop, jobbing and repair

(G-6825)
ZF ACTIVE SAFETY US INC
705 N Fayette St (43521-9586)
PHONE..............................419 237-2511
Gary Predki, Genl Mgr
EMP: 16
SALES (corp-wide): 144.19K Privately Held

SIC: 3714 Motor vehicle parts and accessories
HQ: Zf Active Safety Us Inc.
12025 Tech Center Dr
Livonia MI 48150
734 855-2600

Fayetteville
Brown County

(G-6826)
DEUCE MACHINING LLC
3088 Us Highway 50 (45118-9012)
P.O. Box 57 (45118-0057)
PHONE..............................513 875-2291
Tim Boggs, Prin
EMP: 7 EST: 2008
SALES (est): 1.3MM Privately Held
Web: www.deucemachining.com
SIC: 3599 Machine shop, jobbing and repair

(G-6827)
DR PEPPER/SEVEN UP INC
3943 Us Highway 50 (45118-1500)
PHONE..............................513 875-2466
Bill Hamann, Dist Mgr
EMP: 19
Web: www.drpepper.com
SIC: 2086 Soft drinks: packaged in cans, bottles, etc.
HQ: Dr Pepper/Seven Up, Inc.
6425 Hall Of Fame Ln
Frisco TX 75034
800 527-7096

(G-6828)
KILEY MACHINE COMPANY
4196 Anderson State Rd (45118-9777)
PHONE..............................513 875-3223
Dennis E Kiley, Pr
EMP: 8 EST: 1998
SALES (est): 365.46K Privately Held
SIC: 3599 Machine shop, jobbing and repair

Felicity
Clermont County

(G-6829)
FELICITY PLASTICS MACHINERY
892 Neville Penn Schoolhouse Rd (45120-9542)
PHONE..............................513 876-7003
Craig Rigdon, Pr
EMP: 7 EST: 1987
SQ FT: 14,000
SALES (est): 535.01K Privately Held
SIC: 3089 Injection molding of plastics

(G-6830)
L C LIMING & SONS INC
Also Called: L & L Plastics
3200 State Route 756 (45120-9766)
PHONE..............................513 876-2555
James C Liming, Pr
Margaret Laubach, Treas
EMP: 8 EST: 1970
SQ FT: 9,250
SALES (est): 2.12MM Privately Held
SIC: 3089 6515 Injection molding of plastics; Mobile home site operators

Findlay
Hancock County

(G-6831)

ACCENT SIGNAGE SYSTEMS INC
5409 Hamlet Dr (45840-6618)
PHONE.................................612 377-9156
Shereen Rahamim, *CEO*
EMP: 25 EST: 1984
SALES (est): 956.11K Privately Held
Web: www.accentsignage.com
SIC: 3993 Signs and advertising specialties

(G-6832)

ADS
401 Olive St (45840-5358)
P.O. Box 104 (45839)
PHONE.................................419 422-6521
EMP: 8 EST: 2015
SALES (est): 1.2MM Privately Held
Web: www.adspipe.com
SIC: 3084 Plastics pipe

(G-6833)

ADVANCE NOVELTY INCORPORATED
101 Stanford Pkwy (45840-1731)
PHONE.................................419 424-0363
Tom Heimann, *Prin*
EMP: 7 EST: 2007
SALES (est): 323.59K Privately Held
Web: www.advancenovelty2.com
SIC: 5092 3944 Toys, nec; Games, toys, and children's vehicles

(G-6834)

ADVANCED DRAINAGE SYSTEMS INC
12370 Hancock County Rd (45840)
PHONE.................................419 424-8222
EMP: 6
SALES (corp-wide): 2.87B Publicly Held
Web: www.adspipe.com
SIC: 3084 Plastics pipe
PA: Advanced Drainage Systems, Inc.
4640 Trueman Blvd
Hilliard OH 43026
614 658-0050

(G-6835)

ADVANCED DRAINAGE SYSTEMS INC
401 Olive St (45840-5358)
P.O. Box 104 (45839-0104)
PHONE.................................419 424-8324
Bruce Rush, *Brnch Mgr*
EMP: 36
SALES (corp-wide): 2.87B Publicly Held
Web: www.adspipe.com
SIC: 3084 3083 Plastics pipe; Laminated plastics plate and sheet
PA: Advanced Drainage Systems, Inc.
4640 Trueman Blvd
Hilliard OH 43026
614 658-0050

(G-6836)

AMERICAN PLASTICS LLC
Also Called: Centrex Plastics
814 W Lima St (45840-2312)
PHONE.................................419 423-1213
EMP: 240
SALES (corp-wide): 778.2MM Privately Held
Web: www.americanplasticsllc.com
SIC: 2673 3089 Food storage and trash bags (plastic); Plastics processing
HQ: American Plastics Llc
11840 Wstline Indus Dr St

Saint Louis MO 63146
800 325-1051

(G-6837)

ANDEAVOR LOGISTICS LP (DH)
200 E Hardin St (45840-4969)
PHONE.................................419 421-2414
Gregory J Goff, *Pr*
Steven Sterin, *Pr*
Keith Casey, *Ex VP*
Kim K W Rucker, *Ex VP*
Cynthia Cj Warner, *Ex VP*
EMP: 19 EST: 2010
SALES (est): 447.95MM Publicly Held
SIC: 4612 1311 Crude petroleum pipelines; Crude petroleum production
HQ: Mplx Lp
200 E Hardin St
Findlay OH 45840
419 422-2121

(G-6838)

AUSTIN POWDER COMPANY
Also Called: Austin Powder
3518 Township Road 142 (45840-9611)
PHONE.................................419 299-3347
Rita Whelchel, *Mgr*
EMP: 9
SALES (corp-wide): 749.73MM Privately Held
Web: www.austinpowder.com
SIC: 2892 Explosives
HQ: Austin Powder Company
25800 Science Park Dr # 300
Cleveland OH 44122
216 464-2400

(G-6839)

BACK IN BLACK CO
2100 Fostoria Ave (45840-8758)
P.O. Box 842 (45839-0842)
PHONE.................................419 425-5555
Michael Gardner, *Pr*
EMP: 40 EST: 2009
SALES (est): 778.17K Privately Held
SIC: 3537 Industrial trucks and tractors

(G-6840)

BALL CORPORATION
1800 Production Dr (45840-5445)
PHONE.................................419 423-3071
EMP: 29
SALES (corp-wide): 11.79B Publicly Held
Web: www.ball.com
SIC: 3411 Food and beverage containers
PA: Ball Corporation
9200 W 108th Cir
Westminster CO 80021
303 469-3131

(G-6841)

BALL METAL BEVERAGE CONT CORP
Also Called: Ball Metal Beverage Cont Div
12340 Township Rd 99 E (45840)
PHONE.................................419 423-3071
Tom Martin, *Brnch Mgr*
EMP: 204
SALES (corp-wide): 11.79B Publicly Held
Web: www.ball.com
SIC: 3411 Beer cans, metal
HQ: Ball Metal Beverage Container Corp.
9300 W 108th Cir
Westminster CO 80021

(G-6842)

BALLINGER INDUSTRIES INC (PA)
2500 Fostoria Ave (45840-8732)
PHONE.................................419 422-4533
Jon Ballinger, *Pr*
▲ EMP: 42 EST: 1995

SALES (est): 41.12MM
SALES (corp-wide): 41.12MM Privately Held
SIC: 3531 Construction machinery

(G-6843)

BEST ONE TIRE & SVC LIMA INC
10456 W Us Route 224 Unit 1 (45840-1907)
PHONE.................................419 425-3322
Jason Myers, *Brnch Mgr*
EMP: 8
SALES (corp-wide): 4.46MM Privately Held
Web: www.bestonetire.com
SIC: 7534 5531 5014 Tire recapping; Automotive tires; Tires and tubes
PA: Best One Tire & Service Of Lima, Inc.
701 East Hanthorn Road
Lima OH 45804
419 229-2380

(G-6844)

BOSSERMAN AUTOMOTIVE ENGRG LLC
Also Called: Aircraft-Refuelers.com
18919 Olympic Dr (45840-9453)
PHONE.................................419 722-2879
Terry Bosserman, *Pr*
▼ EMP: 6 EST: 2012
SALES (est): 359.89K Privately Held
SIC: 3713 Tank truck bodies

(G-6845)

BREAD KNEADS INC
510 S Blanchard St (45840-5951)
PHONE.................................419 422-3863
Kelley Smith, *Pr*
EMP: 9 EST: 1981
SALES (est): 372.68K Privately Held
Web: www.tarvinart.com
SIC: 5411 5149 2099 2051 Delicatessen stores; Groceries and related products, nec; Food preparations, nec; Bread, cake, and related products

(G-6846)

BRINKMAN TURKEY FARMS INC (PA)
Also Called: Brinkman's Country Corner
16314 State Route 68 (45840-9245)
PHONE.................................419 365-5127
Larry Brinkman, *Pr*
Joe Brinkman, *VP*
EMP: 18 EST: 1950
SQ FT: 6,000
SALES (est): 2.4MM
SALES (corp-wide): 2.4MM Privately Held
Web: www.brinkmanfarms.com
SIC: 5411 2015 2013 0115 Grocery stores, independent; Turkey, processed: canned; Prepared beef products, from purchased beef; Corn

(G-6847)

BROWN COMPANY OF FINDLAY LTD
225 Stanford Pkwy (45840-1733)
P.O. Box 1625 (45839-1625)
PHONE.................................419 425-3002
Melvin J Brown, *Pr*
EMP: 20 EST: 2007
SALES (est): 6.62MM Privately Held
Web: www.tbcfindlay.com
SIC: 3089 7389 Injection molding of plastics; Inspection and testing services

(G-6848)

BUCKMAN LTD
1413 Forest Park (45840-2991)
PHONE.................................419 420-1687

EMP: 7 EST: 2008
SALES (est): 64.78K Privately Held
Web: www.buckman.com
SIC: 2869 Industrial organic chemicals, nec

(G-6849)

C & H ENTERPRISES LTD
2121 Bright Rd (45840-5433)
PHONE.................................510 226-6083
Douglas D Hosey, *Prin*
EMP: 6 EST: 2009
SALES (est): 277.06K Privately Held
Web: www.candhenterprises.com
SIC: 3599 Machine shop, jobbing and repair

(G-6850)

CASCADE CORPORATION
2000 Production Dr (45840-5449)
P.O. Box 841 (45839-0841)
PHONE.................................419 425-3675
Alice Bauer, *Prin*
EMP: 27
Web: www.cascorp.com
SIC: 5084 3569 Materials handling machinery; Assembly machines, non-metalworking
HQ: Cascade Corporation
2201 Ne 201st Ave
Fairview OR 97024
503 669-6300

(G-6851)

CENTREX PLASTICS LLC ✪
814 W Lima St (45840-2312)
PHONE.................................877 504-2768
Terry Reinhart, *Managing Member*
EMP: 50 EST: 2024
SALES (est): 1.51MM Privately Held
SIC: 3089 Injection molding of plastics

(G-6852)

CITY APPAREL INC
116 E Main Cross St (45840-4817)
PHONE.................................419 434-1155
Andrea Kramer, *CEO*
Julie Weber, *Admn*
▲ EMP: 10 EST: 2007
SALES (est): 1.77MM Privately Held
Web: www.cityapparel.net
SIC: 5611 5621 5947 7389 Men's and boys' clothing stores; Women's clothing stores; Gifts and novelties; Embroidery advertising

(G-6853)

CLARK RM INC
400 Crystal Ave (45840-4770)
PHONE.................................419 425-9889
Marshall Clark, *Mgr*
EMP: 14
SIC: 2491 2449 2448 2441 Structural lumber and timber, treated wood; Wood containers, nec; Wood pallets and skids; Nailed wood boxes and shook
PA: Clark Rm Inc
1110 Summerlin Dr
Douglas GA

(G-6854)

CLASSIC SIGN COMPANY LLC
3230 Township Road 232 (45840-9810)
PHONE.................................419 420-0058
Patrick Gaswint, *Pr*
Lisa Gaswint, *Sec*
EMP: 7 EST: 1994
SALES (est): 485.54K Privately Held
Web: www.classicsigncompany.com
SIC: 3993 Signs, not made in custom sign painting shops

▲ = Import ▼ = Export
◆ = Import/Export

(G-6855)
CONTROL INDUSTRIES INC
614 Central Ave (45840-5646)
P.O. Box 889 (43078-0889)
PHONE...........................937 653-7694
James Long, *Pr*
James B Long, *VP*
EMP: 6 **EST:** 1962
SQ FT: 3,200
SALES (est): 400.65K **Privately Held**
Web: www.controlindustriesinc.com
SIC: 3663 Receiver-transmitter units
(transceiver)

(G-6856)
COOPER TIRE & RUBBER CO LLC (HQ)
Also Called: Cooper
701 Lima Ave (45840-2388)
P.O. Box 550 (45840)
PHONE...........................419 423-1321
Bradley E Hughes, *Pr*
Gerald C Bialek, *Interim Vice President**
Paula S Whitesell, *Chief Human Resources Officer**
Stephen Zamansky, *
◆ **EMP:** 1000 **EST:** 1930
SALES (est): 1.78B
SALES (est): 18.88B **Publicly Held**
Web: us.coopertire.com
SIC: 3011 Automobile tires, pneumatic
PA: The Goodyear Tire & Rubber Company
200 Innovation Way
Akron OH 44316
330 796-2121

(G-6857)
COOPER TIRE VHCL TEST CTR INC (DH)
Also Called: Cooper
701 Lima Ave (45840-2315)
PHONE...........................419 423-1321
Brad Hughes, *Pr*
Stephen O Schroeder, *Treas*
James E Kline, *Sec*
▲ **EMP:** 17 **EST:** 1984
SQ FT: 2,500
SALES (est): 2.26MM
SALES (corp-wide): 18.88B **Publicly Held**
SIC: 3011 4225 Automobile tires, pneumatic;
General warehousing and storage
HQ: Cooper Tire & Rubber Company Llc
701 Lima Ave
Findlay OH 45040
419 423-1321

(G-6858)
CUMMINS FILTRATION INC
2150 Industrial Dr (45840-5402)
P.O. Box 708 (45839-0708)
EMP: 250
SIC: 3569 3714 Filters; Motor vehicle parts
and accessories

(G-6859)
DIETSCH BROTHERS INCORPORATED (PA)
400 W Main Cross St (45840-3317)
PHONE...........................419 422-4474
Jeffery Dietsch, *Pr*
Richard Dietsch, *
Thomas Dietsch, *
EMP: 40 **EST:** 1937
SQ FT: 12,000
SALES (est): 5.11MM
SALES (corp-wide): 5.11MM **Privately Held**
Web: www.dietschs.com

SIC: 2066 2024 5441 Chocolate and cocoa
products; Ice cream and frozen deserts;
Confectionery

(G-6860)
DJM PLASTICS LTD
Also Called: DLM Plastics
1530 Harvard Ave (45840-1737)
PHONE...........................419 424-5250
◆ **EMP:** 10 **EST:** 2005
SALES (est): 4.17MM **Privately Held**
Web: www.dlmplastics.com
SIC: 3089 3081 Injection molded finished
plastics products, nec; Unsupported
plastics film and sheet

(G-6861)
DS TECHSTAR INC
Also Called: Techstar
1219 W Main Cross St Ste 204
(45840-0707)
PHONE...........................419 424-0888
D Steve Brown, *Pr*
D D Brown, *Sec*
Warren Brown, *Treas*
▲ **EMP:** 7 **EST:** 1990
SQ FT: 1,000
SALES (est): 1.02MM **Privately Held**
Web: www.techstar-inc.com
SIC: 3441 Bridge sections, prefabricated,
highway

(G-6862)
FABCO INC
2800 Fostoria Ave (45840-8757)
P.O. Box 1545 (45839-1545)
PHONE...........................419 422-4533
▲ **EMP:** 88
Web: www.fabco-inc.com
SIC: 3535 3444 3443 3441 Conveyors and
conveying equipment; Sheet metalwork;
Fabricated plate work (boiler shop);
Fabricated structural metal

(G-6863)
FINDLAY AMRCN PRSTHTIC ORTHTIC
12474 County Road 99 (45840-9736)
PHONE...........................419 424-1622
TOLL FREE: 800
Jeremy Berman, *Pr*
Kenneth Berman Prosthetist, *Prin*
EMP: 6 **EST:** 1996
SALES (est): 1.19MM **Privately Held**
Web: www.findlayprosthetic.com
SIC: 3842 3841 Braces, orthopedic; Medical
instruments and equipment, blood and
bone work

(G-6864)
FINDLAY MACHINE & TOOL LLC
Also Called: Fmt
2000 Industrial Dr (45840-5443)
P.O. Box 1562 (45840)
PHONE...........................419 434-3100
Joe Klein, *Managing Member*
▲ **EMP:** 45 **EST:** 1987
SALES (est): 27.38MM **Privately Held**
Web: www.fmtinc.com
SIC: 3089 Injection molding of plastics

(G-6865)
FINDLAY PALLET INC
300 Bell Ave (45840)
PHONE...........................419 423-0511
Robert Reed, *Pr*
EMP: 9 **EST:** 1979
SALES (est): 1.08MM **Privately Held**
SIC: 2448 Cargo containers, wood and wood
with metal

(G-6866)
FINDLAY PRODUCTS CORPORATION
2045 Industrial Dr (45840-5444)
P.O. Box 1006 (45839-1006)
PHONE...........................419 423-3324
James E Hoyt, *Pr*
Lloyd A Miller, *
◆ **EMP:** 130 **EST:** 1991
SQ FT: 224,000
SALES (est): 22.95MM **Privately Held**
Web: www.midwayproducts.com
SIC: 3465 3469 Automotive stampings;
Metal stampings, nec
PA: Midway Products Group, Inc.
One Lyman E Hoyt Dr
Monroe MI 48161

(G-6867)
FLEETMASTER EXPRESS INC
5250 Distribution Dr (45840-9814)
PHONE...........................866 425-0666
Rob Mahlman, *Brnch Mgr*
EMP: 92
SALES (corp-wide): 49.71MM **Privately Held**
Web: www.fleetmasterexpress.com
SIC: 2741 Miscellaneous publishing
PA: Fleetmaster Express, Incorporated
1814 Hollins Rd Ne Ste A
Roanoke VA 24012
540 344-8834

(G-6868)
FREUDENBERG-NOK GENERAL PARTNR
Also Called: Freudenberg-Nok Findlay
555 Marathon Blvd (45840-1790)
P.O. Box 269 (45839-0269)
PHONE...........................419 427-5221
Roy Sehroeder, *Genl Mgr*
EMP: 170
SALES (corp-wide): 12.96B **Privately Held**
Web: www.freudenberg.com
SIC: 3053 3492 Gaskets, all materials; Fluid
power valves and hose fittings
HQ: Freudenberg-Nok General Partnership
47774 W Anchor Ct
Plymouth MI 48170
734 451-0020

(G-6869)
FRIENDS SERVICE CO INC (PA)
Also Called: Friends Business Source
2300 Bright Rd (45840-5432)
PHONE...........................419 427-1704
Kenneth J Schroeder, *CEO*
Kenneth J Schroeder, *Pr*
Dale Alt, *CIO**
Margaret Schroeder, *
Dennis Mitchell, *
EMP: 48 **EST:** 1991
SQ FT: 65,000
SALES (est): 21.52MM **Privately Held**
Web: www.friendsoffice.com
SIC: 5021 5044 5087 2752 Furniture; Office
equipment; Janitors' supplies;
Photolithographic printing

(G-6870)
GIANT INDUSTRIES INC (DH)
539 S Main St (45840-3229)
PHONE...........................419 421-2121
Jeff A Stevens, *CEO*
Mark J Smith, *
Dennis Calhoun, *
Morgan Gust, *PRES REFINING STRATEGIC Business**
Mark B Cox, *
◆ **EMP:** 78 **EST:** 1961
SQ FT: 60,000
SALES (est): 88.05MM **Publicly Held**

SIC: 2911 5541 5172 Petroleum refining;
Gasoline service stations; Petroleum
products, nec
HQ: Western Refining, Inc.
212 N Clark Dr
El Paso TX 79905

(G-6871)
GILLIG CUSTOM WINERY INC
1720 Northridge Rd (45840-1905)
PHONE...........................419 202-6057
EMP: 7 **EST:** 2015
SALES (est): 560.58K **Privately Held**
Web: www.gilligwinery.com
SIC: 2084 Wines

(G-6872)
GOULD FIRE PROTECTION INC
633 Bristol Dr (45840-6909)
PHONE...........................419 957-2416
Arthur Gould, *Pr*
James Amos, *VP*
EMP: 6 **EST:** 1997
SALES (est): 437.03K **Privately Held**
SIC: 3569 Sprinkler systems, fire: automatic

(G-6873)
GRAHAM PACKG PLASTIC PDTS INC
170 Stanford Pkwy 7 (45840-1732)
PHONE...........................419 421-8037
EMP: 180
SALES (corp-wide): 11.63B **Publicly Held**
SIC: 3085 Plastics bottles
HQ: Graham Packaging Plastic Products
Inc.
1 Seagate Ste 10
Toledo OH 43604
717 849-8500

(G-6874)
GSW MANUFACTURING INC (DH)
1801 Production Dr (45840-5446)
P.O. Box 1045 (45839-1045)
PHONE...........................419 423-7111
Hiro Kojima, *Pr*
Yukinobu Ukai, *
▲ **EMP:** 130 **EST:** 1989
SQ FT: 72,000
SALES (est): 23.07MM **Privately Held**
Web: www.gswiring.com
SIC: 3714 3694 Automotive wiring harness
sets; Engine electrical equipment
HQ: G.S. Wiring Systems, Inc.
1801 Production Dr
Findlay OH 45840
419 427-1238

(G-6875)
GVS FILTRATION INC (DH)
2150 Industrial Dr (45840-5402)
PHONE...........................419 423-9040
Hasnain Merchant, *Pr*
John Byrnes, *
Nick Galambos, *
Gary Rickle, *
Scott Salsburey, *
▲ **EMP:** 400 **EST:** 2011
SQ FT: 100,000
SALES (est): 43.51MM **Privately Held**
Web: www.kussfiltration.com
SIC: 3569 Filters, general line: industrial
HQ: Gvs Spa
Via Roma 50
Zola Predosa BO 40069
051 617-6311

(G-6876)
HAMLET PROTEIN INC
5289 Hamlet Dr (45840)
PHONE...........................567 525-5627
Scott Moore, *Pr*

GEOGRAPHIC

▼ **EMP:** 40 **EST:** 2011
SALES (est): 21.3MM
SALES (corp-wide): 2.67MM **Privately Held**
Web: www.hamletprotein.com
SIC: 2048 Prepared feeds, nec
HQ: Hamlet Protein A/S
    Saturnvej 51
    Horsens 8700
    75631020

(G-6877)
HANCOCK STRUCTURAL STEEL LLC
813 E Bigelow Ave (45840-4256)
P.O. Box 1546 (45839-1546)
PHONE..............................419 424-1217
Charles W Wenner, *CEO*
Charles G Wenner, *Managing Member*
Charles Weston Garrett Wenner, *CEO*
EMP: 22 **EST:** 2007
SQ FT: 15,000
SALES (est): 5.02MM **Privately Held**
Web: www.hancocksteel.com
SIC: 3441 Fabricated structural metal

(G-6878)
HANCOR INC
12370 Jackson Township Rd (45839)
P.O. Box 1047 (45839-1047)
PHONE..............................419 424-8222
Steve Ferell, *Mgr*
EMP: 48
SALES (corp-wide): 2.87B **Publicly Held**
Web: www.adspipe.com
SIC: 3084 Plastics pipe
HQ: Hancor, Inc.
    4640 Trueman Blvd
    Hilliard OH 43026
    614 658-0050

(G-6879)
HANCOR INC
Also Called: Hantech
433 Olive St (45840-5358)
P.O. Box 1047 (45839-1047)
PHONE..............................419 424-8225
Clark Inniger, *Mgr*
EMP: 37
SALES (corp-wide): 2.87B **Publicly Held**
Web: www.adspipe.com
SIC: 3089 3084 2821 Septic tanks, plastics;
   Plastics pipe; Plastics materials and resins
HQ: Hancor, Inc.
    4640 Trueman Blvd
    Hilliard OH 43026
    614 658-0050

(G-6880)
HITACHI ASTEMO AMERICAS INC
1901 Industrial Dr (45840-5442)
PHONE..............................419 425-1259
EMP: 213
Web: www.hitachi-automotive.us
SIC: 3714 Motor vehicle brake systems and
   parts
HQ: Hitachi Astemo Americas, Inc.
    955 Warwick Rd
    Harrodsburg KY 40330
    859 734-9451

(G-6881)
HOLTGREVEN SCALE & ELEC CORP
Also Called: Loadmaster Scale
420 E Lincoln St (45840-4945)
PHONE..............................419 422-4779
Leonard Holtgreven, *Pr*
Mark Holtgreven, *VP*
▲ **EMP:** 11 **EST:** 1958
SQ FT: 20,000
SALES (est): 1.86MM **Privately Held**
Web: www.loadmasterscale.com

SIC: 3596 Industrial scales

(G-6882)
HOUSE OF AWARDS INC
419 N Main St (45840-3378)
PHONE..............................419 422-7877
Jeff Crawford, *Pr*
Karen Crawford, *VP*
EMP: 7 **EST:** 1968
SQ FT: 3,500
SALES (est): 247.69K **Privately Held**
Web:
www.houseofawardsandsports.com
SIC: 3949 5091 Sporting and athletic goods,
   nec; Sporting and recreation goods

(G-6883)
JK-CO LLC
16960 E State Route 12 (45840-9744)
PHONE..............................419 422-5240
Joseph L Kurtz, *Managing Member*
C Leon Thornton, *
▼ **EMP:** 45 **EST:** 2002
SQ FT: 40,000
SALES (est): 9.57MM **Privately Held**
Web: www.jk-co.com
SIC: 3743 4789 Railroad car rebuilding;
   Railroad car repair

(G-6884)
LEGACY FARMERS COOPERATIVE (PA)
6566 County Road 236 (45840-9769)
PHONE..............................419 423-2611
Mark Sunderman, *Pr*
Dave Baer, *Sec*
Gary Herringshaw, *Treas*
Deborah Boger, *Contrlr*
EMP: 15 **EST:** 1989
SQ FT: 10,000
SALES (est): 336.16MM
SALES (corp-wide): 336.16MM **Privately Held**
Web: www.legacyfarmers.com
SIC: 5153 5191 5984 2875 Grains; Farm
   supplies; Liquefied petroleum gas dealers;
   Fertilizers, mixing only

(G-6885)
LFG SPECIALTIES LLC
16406 E Us Route 224 (45840-9772)
PHONE..............................419 424-4999
EMP: 50 **EST:** 1988
SQ FT: 3,000
SALES (est): 4.27MM
SALES (corp-wide): 1.79B **Privately Held**
SIC: 3585 2899 Evaporative condensers,
   heat transfer equipment; Flares
HQ: Cb&I Group Inc.
    4171 Essen Ln
    Baton Rouge LA 70809
    337 685-4725

(G-6886)
MANUFCTRING BUS DEV SLTONS LLC
Also Called: Mbds
1950 Industrial Dr (45840-5441)
P.O. Box 1811 (45839-1811)
PHONE..............................419 294-1313
Brian Robertson, *Pr*
EMP: 60 **EST:** 2003
SQ FT: 50,000
SALES (est): 2.43MM **Privately Held**
Web: www.mbdsna.com
SIC: 3559 Automotive related machinery

(G-6887)
MARATHON INTL PDTS SUP LLC
539 S Main St (45840-3229)
PHONE..............................419 422-2121

EMP: 6 **EST:** 2011
SALES (est): 3.77MM **Publicly Held**
SIC: 2911 Petroleum refining
PA: Marathon Petroleum Corporation
    539 S Main St
    Findlay OH 45840

(G-6888)
MARATHON OIL COMPANY
539 S Main St (45840-3229)
P.O. Box 151 (45839-0151)
PHONE..............................419 422-2121
EMP: 27
SALES (corp-wide): 8.04B **Privately Held**
Web: www.marathonoil.com
SIC: 2911 Petroleum refining
HQ: Marathon Oil Company
    5555 San Flipe St Bsmt B1
    Houston TX 77056
    713 629-6600

(G-6889)
MARATHON PETROLEUM COMPANY LP (HQ)
539 S Main St (45840-3229)
P.O. Box 599500 (78259-9500)
PHONE..............................419 422-2121
Maryann Mannen, *Pr*
Raymond Brooks, *Ex VP*
Suzanne Gagle, *Sr VP*
Fiona Laird, *Chief Human Resource Officer*
C Kristopher Hagedorn, *Sr VP*
◆ **EMP:** 10 **EST:** 1997
SQ FT: 621,000
SALES (est): 3.56B **Publicly Held**
Web: www.marathonpetroleum.com
SIC: 5172 2951 2865 Gasoline; Road
   materials, bituminous (not from refineries);
   Dyes and pigments
PA: Marathon Petroleum Corporation
    539 S Main St
    Findlay OH 45840

(G-6890)
MARATHON PETROLEUM CORPORATION (PA)
Also Called: Marathon Petroleum
539 S Main St (45840-3229)
PHONE..............................419 422-2121
Maryann T Mannen, *CEO*
Michael J Hennigan, *
Fiona C Laird, *Chief Human Resources Officer*
Molly R Benson, *CLO*
John Quaid, *Ex VP*
▲ **EMP:** 887 **EST:** 1887
SALES (est): 140.41B **Publicly Held**
Web: www.marathonpetroleum.com
SIC: 2911 5172 Petroleum refining; Gasoline

(G-6891)
MARBEE INC
Also Called: Marbee Printing & Graphic Art
2703 N Main St Ste 1 (45840-4039)
PHONE..............................419 422-9441
Randy Raymond, *Pr*
Teresa Raymond, *Sec*
EMP: 6 **EST:** 1991
SQ FT: 3,600
SALES (est): 464.44K **Privately Held**
Web: www.marbeeprinting.com
SIC: 2752 2759 Offset printing; Commercial
   printing, nec

(G-6892)
MC BROWN INDUSTRIES INC
10534 Township Road 128 (45840-9315)
PHONE..............................419 963-2800
Lester Brown, *Pr*
Dan Brown, *VP*
Lester John Brown Iii, *Sec*

EMP: 10 **EST:** 1971
SQ FT: 15,000
SALES (est): 293.25K **Privately Held**
SIC: 3441 3599 Fabricated structural metal;
   Machine shop, jobbing and repair

(G-6893)
MIDWAY PRODUCTS GROUP INC
2045 Industrial Dr (45840-5444)
PHONE..............................419 422-7070
Daryl Osburn, *Brnch Mgr*
EMP: 11
Web: www.midwayproducts.com
SIC: 3469 Metal stampings, nec
PA: Midway Products Group, Inc.
    One Lyman E Hoyt Dr
    Monroe MI 48161

(G-6894)
MITEC POWERTRAIN INC
4000 Fostoria Ave (45840-8733)
PHONE..............................567 525-5606
Arnie Jensen, *Ch*
Pavel Gilman, *
Dennis Doren, *
▲ **EMP:** 232 **EST:** 2009
SQ FT: 100,000
SALES (est): 11.21MM
SALES (corp-wide): 230.9MM **Privately Held**
SIC: 3714 Motor vehicle parts and
   accessories
PA: Mtc Ag
    Rennbahn 25
    Eisenach TH 99817

(G-6895)
MOLTEN NORTH AMERICA CORP (DH)
1835 Industrial Dr (45840-5440)
P.O. Box 1451 (45839-1451)
PHONE..............................419 425-2700
Hiddaki Miyamoto, *Pr*
Toshikazu Yamate, *
▲ **EMP:** 189 **EST:** 1990
SQ FT: 100,814
SALES (est): 9.94MM **Privately Held**
Web: www.molten.co.jp
SIC: 3089 Automotive parts, plastic
HQ: Molten Corporation
    4-10-97-21, Kanonshinmachi, Nishi-Ku
    Hiroshima HIR 733-0

(G-6896)
MPLX GP LLC
539 S Main St (45840-3229)
PHONE..............................419 422-2121
Timothy T Griffith, *Sr VP*
Molly R Benson, *CCO*
Thomas Kaczynski, *VP Fin*
John J Quaid, *VP*
C Kristopher Hagedorn, *Ex VP*
EMP: 8 **EST:** 2012
SALES (est): 6.85MM **Publicly Held**
SIC: 2911 Petroleum refining
PA: Marathon Petroleum Corporation
    539 S Main St
    Findlay OH 45840

(G-6897)
NATIONAL LIME AND STONE CO
9860 County Road 313 (45840-9003)
P.O. Box 120 (45839-0120)
PHONE..............................419 423-3400
Denny Swick, *Brnch Mgr*
EMP: 27
SALES (corp-wide): 86.85MM **Privately Held**
Web: www.natlime.com
SIC: 3273 1422 Ready-mixed concrete;
   Crushed and broken limestone

▲ = Import ▼ = Export
◆ = Import/Export

PA: The National Lime And Stone
Company
551 Lake Cascade Pkwy
Findlay OH 45840
419 422-4341

(G-6898)
NICHIDAI AMERICA CORPORATION
Also Called: N A C
15630 E State Route 12 Ste 4
(45840-7771)
PHONE...............................419 423-7511
Yuzuru Mishimura, *Pr*
Kiyoshi Naaadawa, *VP*
EMP: 6 **EST:** 2006
SALES (est): 196.93K **Privately Held**
Web: www.nichidai.jp
SIC: 3312 Tool and die steel

(G-6899)
NICKOLAS PLASTICS LLC
Also Called: Kreate Industries
814 W Lima St (45840-2312)
PHONE...............................419 423-1213
Terrence L Reinhart, *Pr*
◆ **EMP:** 240 **EST:** 2003
SALES (est): 31.33MM **Privately Held**
Web: www.centrexplastics.com
SIC: 3089 Injection molding of plastics

(G-6900)
NORTHWEST INSTALLATIONS INC
1903 Blanchard Ave (45840-6472)
P.O. Box 1563 (45839-1563)
PHONE...............................419 423-5738
Tracy Lopez, *Pr*
EMP: 23 **EST:** 1986
SQ FT: 7,000
SALES (est): 2.79MM **Privately Held**
Web: www.nwiimi.com
SIC: 1796 3444 3443 3441 Machinery
installation; Sheet metalwork; Fabricated
plate work (boiler shop); Fabricated
structural metal

(G-6901)
OHIO ROTATIONAL MOLDING LLC
2330 Heatherwood Dr (45840-7479)
PHONE...............................419 608-5040
EMP: 7 **EST:** 2017
SALES (est): 921.83K **Privately Held**
Web: www.ohiorotationalmolding.com
SIC: 2821 Molding compounds, plastics

(G-6902)
OLDE MAN GRANOLA LLC
7227 W State Route 12 (45840-8802)
PHONE...............................419 819-9576
Kelly Green, *Ex Dir*
Kelly Green, *Mgr*
Rebecca Green, *Mgr*
Mark Plaza, *Mgr*
Fay Plaza, *Dir Opers*
EMP: 10 **EST:** 2013
SALES (est): 334.41K **Privately Held**
Web: www.oldemangranola.com
SIC: 2043 7389 Granola and muesli, except
bars and clusters; Business services, nec

(G-6903)
OLIVER RUBBER CO
701 Lima Ave (45840-2315)
PHONE...............................419 420-6235
Larry Enders, *CEO*
EMP: 10 **EST:** 2019
SALES (est): 829.93K **Privately Held**
Web: www.oliverrubber.com
SIC: 3011 Tires and inner tubes

(G-6904)
OPERATIONAL SUPPORT SVCS LLC
1850 Industrial Dr (45840-5439)
P.O. Box 178 (45839-0178)
PHONE...............................419 425-0889
EMP: 10 **EST:** 2002
SQ FT: 5,000
SALES (est): 1.36MM **Privately Held**
Web: www.operationalss.com
SIC: 2655 Fiber shipping and mailing
containers

(G-6905)
OTTAWA OIL CO INC
Also Called: Findlay Party Mart
1100 Trenton Ave (45840-1920)
PHONE...............................419 425-3301
Karen Roberts, *Mgr*
EMP: 16
SALES (corp-wide): 126.95MM **Privately
Held**
Web: www.ottawaoil.com
SIC: 1389 Pumping of oil and gas wells
HQ: Ottawa Oil Co., Inc.
10305 State Route 224
Ottawa OH
419 523-6441

(G-6906)
P & A INDUSTRIES INC (HQ)
Also Called: Midway Products
600 Crystal Ave (45840-4600)
P.O. Box 737 (48161-0737)
PHONE...............................419 422-7070
▲ **EMP:** 80 **EST:** 1983
SALES (est): 22.17MM **Privately Held**
Web: www.midwayproducts.com
SIC: 3465 Automotive stampings
PA: Midway Products Group, Inc.
One Lyman E Hoyt Dr
Monroe MI 48161

(G-6907)
PARTITIONS PLUS INCORPORATED
Also Called: Partitions Plus, Inc.
12517 County Road 99 (45840-9771)
PHONE...............................419 422-2600
Thomas R Bradford, *Pr*
Douglas J Brink, *
Ben Riblet, *
EMP: 40 **EST:** 2022
SALES (est): 6.56MM
SALES (corp-wide): 49.31MM **Privately
Held**
Web: www.partitions.plus
SIC: 2541 5046 5021 Wood partitions and
fixtures; Partitions; Racks
PA: Bradford Company
13500 Quincy St
Holland MI 49424
616 399-3000

(G-6908)
PIECO INC (PA)
Also Called: Superior Trim
2151 Industrial Dr (45840-5429)
P.O. Box 118 (45839-0118)
PHONE...............................419 422-5335
Michael Gardner, *Pr*
EMP: 50 **EST:** 1997
SQ FT: 50,000
SALES (est): 37.77MM
SALES (corp-wide): 37.77MM **Privately
Held**
Web: www.pieco.com
SIC: 2396 Automotive trimmings, fabric

(G-6909)
PRESSED PAPERBOARD TECH LLC
Also Called: Papertech
115 Bentley Ct (45840-1799)

PHONE...............................419 423-4030
James Morgan, *Managing Member*
Randy Clifton, *
EMP: 160 **EST:** 1999
SALES (est): 23.87MM
SALES (corp-wide): 44.09MM **Privately
Held**
Web: www.papertrays.com
SIC: 2679 Food dishes and utensils, from
pressed and molded pulp
PA: May River Capital, Llc
1 N Wacker Dr Ste 1920
Chicago IL 60606
312 750-1772

(G-6910)
**PROSPIRA AMERICA
CORPORATION (DH)**
2030 Production Dr (45839)
PHONE...............................419 423-9552
Jun Li, *CEO*
Brian Roberts, *Dir Fin*
EMP: 18 **EST:** 2022
SALES (est): 125MM **Privately Held**
Web: www.prospira.us
SIC: 3826 Automatic chemical analyzers
HQ: Prospira Corporation
580, Horikawacho, Saiwai-Ku
Kawasaki KNG 212-0

(G-6911)
PUKKA LLC (DH)
Also Called: Pukka, Inc.
337 S Main St Fl 4 (45840-3373)
P.O. Box 773 (45839-0773)
PHONE...............................419 429-7808
Isaac Fisher, *CEO*
Tate Miller, *
David Pruss, *
Andrea Rogers, *
◆ **EMP:** 37 **EST:** 2003
SALES (est): 9.66MM
SALES (corp-wide): 114.75MM **Privately
Held**
Web: www.pukkainc.com
SIC: 2353 Caps: cloth, straw, and felt
HQ: Paramount Apparel International, Llc
1 Paramount Dr
Bourbon MO 65441
573 732-4411

(G-6912)
RADAR LOVE CO
Also Called: Superior Trim Formed Products
5500 Fostoria Ave (45840-8739)
P.O. Box 578 (45839-0578)
PHONE...............................419 951-4750
Phillip D Gardner, *Pr*
Charles Henry, *Prin*
EMP: 9 **EST:** 1985
SQ FT: 12,000
SALES (est): 1.82MM **Privately Held**
SIC: 3089 3714 3713 Injection molding of
plastics; Motor vehicle parts and
accessories; Truck and bus bodies

(G-6913)
ROKI AMERICA CO LTD
2001 Production Dr (45839)
P.O. Box 1044 (45839-1044)
PHONE...............................419 424-9713
Takaya Shimada, *CEO*
Hiromitsu Shimada Junior, *Ch*
Toshifumi Sasamori, *
Bob Funkhouser, *
◆ **EMP:** 350 **EST:** 1989
SQ FT: 177,000
SALES (est): 46.61MM **Privately Held**
Web: www.roki-us.com
SIC: 3714 Filters: oil, fuel, and air, motor
vehicle

PA: Roki Holdings Co.,Ltd.
2396, Futamatachofutamata, Tenryu-
Ku
Hamamatsu SZO 431-3

(G-6914)
ROWMARK LLC (PA)
Also Called: Johnson Plastic Plus
5409 Hamlet Dr (45840-6618)
P.O. Box 1605 (45839-1605)
PHONE...............................419 425-8974
Eric Hausserman, *CEO*
◆ **EMP:** 100 **EST:** 2006
SQ FT: 65,000
SALES (est): 95.17MM
SALES (corp-wide): 95.17MM **Privately
Held**
Web: www.rowmark.com
SIC: 3089 3083 Extruded finished plastics
products, nec; Laminated plastics plate and
sheet

(G-6915)
SANOH AMERICA INC (HQ)
1849 Industrial Dr (45840-5440)
P.O. Box 1626 (45839-1626)
PHONE...............................419 425-2600
Masahiko Mizukami, *Pr*
Ryuichiro Harada, *
Hirohisa Nakamoto, *
Eric Carroll, *
Jeff Hook, *OK Vice President*
▲ **EMP:** 70 **EST:** 1986
SQ FT: 303,000
SALES (est): 88.44MM **Privately Held**
Web: www.sanoh-america.com
SIC: 3714 Motor vehicle parts and
accessories
PA: Sanoh Industrial Co., Ltd.
758, Konosu
Koga IBR 306-0

(G-6916)
SAUSSER STEEL COMPANY INC
230 Crystal Ave (45840-4796)
PHONE...............................419 422-9632
Joe W Sausser, *Pr*
Larry Cherry, *VP*
Dorothy M Garlow, *Sec*
Donald Hutton, *VP*
▲ **EMP:** 7 **EST:** 1941
SQ FT: 500,000
SALES (est): 2.57MM **Privately Held**
Web: www.saussersteel.com
SIC: 3441 5084 5051 3446 Fabricated
structural metal; Welding machinery and
equipment; Steel; Architectural metalwork

(G-6917)
SHELVES WEST LLC
510 S Main St (45840-3230)
PHONE...............................928 692-1449
EMP: 19
SALES (corp-wide): 778.2MM **Privately
Held**
SIC: 3089 Injection molding of plastics
HQ: Shelves West, Llc
4425 Windrose Ln
Kingman AZ 86401
928 692-1449

(G-6918)
SIMONA PMC LLC
2040 Industrial Dr (45840-5443)
P.O. Box 1123 (45839-1123)
PHONE...............................419 429-0042
Duane Jebbett, *CEO*
EMP: 65 **EST:** 2003
SALES (est): 17.44MM
SALES (corp-wide): 614.67MM **Privately
Held**

Web: www.simona-pmc.com
SIC: 3081 Plastics film and sheet
PA: Simona Ag
Teichweg 16
Kirn RP 55606
6752140

(G-6919)
SKYMARK REFUELERS LLC
1525 Lima Ave (45840-1431)
PHONE.............................419 957-1709
Joe Spoon, *Managing Member*
EMP: 81
SALES (corp-wide): 1.98MM Privately
Held
Web: www.skymarkrefuelers.com
SIC: 3713 Truck and bus bodies
PA: Skymark Refuelers, Llc
4001 E 149th St
Kansas City MO 64147
913 653-8100

(G-6920)
SMITHFIELD DIRECT LLC
4411 Township Road 142 (45840-9607)
PHONE.............................419 422-2233
EMP: 85
Web: carando.sfdbrands.com
SIC: 2011 Meat packing plants
HQ: Smithfield Direct, Llc
4225 Nperville Rd Ste 600
Lisle IL 60532

(G-6921)
SMOKE-RINGS INC
Also Called: Butt Hut
1928 Tiffin Ave (45840-6753)
PHONE.............................419 420-9966
Jean Dove, *Pr*
EMP: 7 EST: 1997
SALES (est): 163.25K Privately Held
Web: www.butthutohio.com
SIC: 2131 5993 Chewing and smoking
tobacco; Tobacco stores and stands

(G-6922)
SQUARE ONE SOLUTIONS LLC
Also Called: Brown Box Company
130 Bentley Ct (45840-1779)
P.O. Box 965 (45839-0965)
PHONE.............................419 425-5445
Stephen Chan, *Pr*
EMP: 22 EST: 2012
SALES (est): 14.14MM Privately Held
Web: www.square1-solutions.com
SIC: 2653 Boxes, corrugated: made from
purchased materials

(G-6923)
STONECO INC (DH)
1700 Fostoria Ave Ste 200 (45840-6218)
P.O. Box 865 (45839-0865)
PHONE.............................419 422-8854
John T Bearss, *Pr*
Don Weber, *VP*
Jack Zouhary, *Sec*
EMP: 33 EST: 1972
SQ FT: 34,000
SALES (est): 21.74MM
SALES (corp-wide): 34.95B Privately Held
Web: www.shellyco.com
SIC: 2951 1411 Asphalt and asphaltic paving
mixtures (not from refineries); Limestone,
dimension-quarrying
HQ: Shelly Company
80 Park Dr
Thornville OH 43076
740 246-6315

(G-6924)
STREAMSIDE MATERIALS LLC
Also Called: Streamside Materials
7440 Township Road 95 (45840-9659)
PHONE.............................419 423-1290
Randall Tucker, *CEO*
Brian Halm, *Dir Opers*
EMP: 6 EST: 2015
SALES (est): 91.12K Privately Held
Web: www.streamside.us
SIC: 8742 1442 Materials mgmt.
(purchasing, handling, inventory) consultant
; Construction sand and gravel

(G-6925)
SUPERIOR PLASTICS INTL INC
1116 Glen Meadow Dr (45840-6256)
PHONE.............................419 424-3113
Robert M Smith, *Pr*
Todd Smith, *VP*
EMP: 7 EST: 1992
SALES (est): 532.9K Privately Held
SIC: 3053 Gaskets and sealing devices

(G-6926)
TH PLASTICS INC
101 Bentley Ct (45840-1799)
PHONE.............................419 425-5825
Elizabeth Mitchell, *Brnch Mgr*
EMP: 77
SALES (corp-wide): 49.59MM Privately
Held
Web: www.thplastics.com
SIC: 3089 Aquarium accessories, plastics
PA: Th Plastics, Inc.
106 E Main St
Mendon MI 49072
269 496-8495

(G-6927)
**THE NATIONAL LIME AND STONE
COMPANY (PA)**
551 Lake Cascade Pkwy (45840-1388)
P.O. Box 120 (45839)
PHONE.............................419 422-4341
EMP: 30 EST: 1903
SALES (est): 86.85MM
SALES (corp-wide): 86.85MM Privately
Held
Web: www.natlime.com
SIC: 1422 1442 3273 1423 Crushed and
broken limestone; Sand mining; Ready-
mixed concrete; Crushed and broken
granite

(G-6928)
VALGROUP LLC
3441 N Main St (45840-4206)
PHONE.............................419 423-6500
Alberto Geronomi, *CEO*
EMP: 49 EST: 2014
SALES (est): 18.86MM
SALES (corp-wide): 47.1MM Privately
Held
Web: www.valgroupco.com
SIC: 3081 Plastics film and sheet
PA: Valgroup North America, Inc.
3441 N Main St
Findlay OH 45840
419 423-6500

(G-6929)
**VALGROUP NORTH AMERICA INC
(PA)**
3441 N Main St (45840-4206)
PHONE.............................419 423-6500
Alberto Geronomi, *CEO*
EMP: 117 EST: 2014
SALES (est): 47.1MM
SALES (corp-wide): 47.1MM Privately
Held

Web: www.valgroupco.com
SIC: 2671 Plastic film, coated or laminated
for packaging

(G-6930)
VENTEK SOLUTIONS LLC
1900 Industrial Dr (45840-5441)
P.O. Box 714 (45840)
PHONE.............................419 420-0029
Rod Williams, *Brnch Mgr*
EMP: 19
SQ FT: 100,000
SALES (corp-wide): 6.44MM Privately
Held
Web: www.sonoco.com
SIC: 3089 3086 2821 Blister or bubble
formed packaging, plastics; Plastics foam
products; Plastics materials and resins
PA: Ventek Solutions Llc
100 Coastal Dr Ste 101
Charleston SC 29492
847 271-5198

(G-6931)
VEONEER BRAKE SYSTEMS LLC
2001 Industrial Dr (45840-5444)
P.O. Box 886 (45839)
PHONE.............................419 425-6725
EMP: 185 EST: 2015
SALES (est): 6.33MM
SALES (corp-wide): 375MM Privately
Held
SIC: 3714 Motor vehicle brake systems and
parts
HQ: Veoneer Us Safety Systems, Llc
26360 American Dr
Southfield MI 48034
248 223-0600

(G-6932)
WABASH NATIONAL CORPORATION
2000 Fostoria Ave (45840-9775)
PHONE.............................419 434-9409
EMP: 17
SALES (corp-wide): 1.95B Publicly Held
Web: www.onewabash.com
SIC: 3715 Truck trailers
PA: Wabash National Corporation
3900 Mccarty Ln
Lafayette IN 47905
765 771-5310

(G-6933)
WERK-BRAU COMPANY (HQ)
Also Called: Werk-Brau
2800 Fostoria Ave (45840-8757)
P.O. Box 1545 (45839)
PHONE.............................419 422-2912
Paul Ballinger, *CEO*
Jon Ballinger, *Pr*
Jim Greulich, *VP*
▲ EMP: 104 EST: 1947
SQ FT: 104,000
SALES (est): 28.54MM
SALES (corp-wide): 41.12MM Privately
Held
Web: www.werk-brau.com
SIC: 3531 3412 Buckets, excavating:
clamshell, concrete, dragline, etc.; Metal
barrels, drums, and pails
PA: Ballinger Industries, Inc.
2500 Fostoria Ave
Findlay OH 45840
419 422-4533

(G-6934)
WERK-BRAU COMPANY
616 N Blanchard St (45840-5706)
PHONE.............................419 422-2912
EMP: 171
SALES (corp-wide): 41.12MM Privately
Held

Web: www.werk-brau.com
SIC: 3531 Buckets, excavating: clamshell,
concrete, dragline, etc.
HQ: Werk-Brau Company
2800 Fostoria Ave
Findlay OH 45840
419 422-2912

(G-6935)
WHIRLPOOL CORPORATION
Whirlpool
4901 N Main St (45840-8847)
PHONE.............................419 423-8123
John Haywood, *Div VP*
EMP: 100
SALES (corp-wide): 16.61B Publicly Held
Web: www.whirlpoolcorp.com
SIC: 3639 3632 Dishwashing machines,
household; Household refrigerators and
freezers
PA: Whirlpool Corporation
2000 N M-63
Benton Harbor MI 49022
269 923-5000

Flushing
Belmont County

(G-6936)
GLENN MICHAEL BRICK
Also Called: Go For Broke Amusement
108 Wood St (43977-9727)
PHONE.............................740 391-5735
Glenn M Brick, *Owner*
EMP: 11 EST: 2007
SALES (est): 2.51MM Privately Held
SIC: 4212 7993 7699 3578 Mail carriers,
contract; Juke box; Automated teller
machine (ATM) repair; Automatic teller
machines (ATM)

(G-6937)
UNIONTOWN STONE
72607 Gun Club Rd (43977)
PHONE.............................740 968-4313
Jeff Sidwell, *Owner*
EMP: 8 EST: 1998
SALES (est): 290.44K Privately Held
Web: www.sidwellmaterials.com
SIC: 1422 Crushed and broken limestone

Forest
Hardin County

(G-6938)
AEROVATION TECH HOLDINGS LLC
11651 Township Rd 81 (45843)
PHONE.............................567 208-5525
EMP: 9 EST: 2011
SALES (est): 86.08K Privately Held
Web: www.aerovation.me
SIC: 8711 3721 Aviation and/or aeronautical
engineering; Research and development on
aircraft by the manufacturer

(G-6939)
**BUCKEYE MCH FABRICATORS INC
(PA)**
610 E Lima St (45843-1182)
PHONE.............................419 273-2521
D Ray Marshall, *Pr*
Nancy Marshall, *Sec*
EMP: 50 EST: 1974
SQ FT: 65,000
SALES (est): 8.55MM
SALES (corp-wide): 8.55MM Privately
Held
Web: www.buckeyemachine.com

SIC: 3599 Machine shop, jobbing and repair

(G-6940)
DUFF QUARRY INC
3798 State Route 53 (45843-9379)
PHONE..................................419 273-2518
James E Duff, *Pr*
EMP: 10
SALES (corp-wide): 5.22MM **Privately Held**
Web: www.duffquarry.com
SIC: 1422 Crushed and broken limestone
PA: Duff Quarry, Inc.
   9042 State Route 117
   Huntsville OH 43324
   937 686-2811

(G-6941)
SHELLY MATERIALS INC
3798 State Route 53 (45843-9379)
PHONE..................................419 273-2510
Norman Cochran, *Brnch Mgr*
EMP: 6
SALES (corp-wide): 34.95B **Privately Held**
Web: www.shellyco.com
SIC: 2951 Asphalt paving mixtures and blocks
HQ: Shelly Materials, Inc.
   80 Park Dr
   Thornville OH 43076
   740 246-6315

(G-6942)
TRIUMPH THERMAL SYSTEMS LLC (HQ)
200 Railroad St (45843-9193)
PHONE..................................419 273-2511
Michael Perhay, *Pr*
EMP: 56 **EST:** 2003
SQ FT: 125,000
SALES (est): 45.9MM **Publicly Held**
Web: www.triumph-thermal.com
SIC: 3728 3443 Aircraft parts and equipment, nec; Heat exchangers, condensers, and components
PA: Triumph Group, Inc.
   555 E Lncster Ave Ste 400
   Radnor PA 19087

(G-6943)
VTS CO LTD
607 E Lima St (45843-1180)
PHONE..................................419 273-4010
Lloyd Swavel, *Pr*
EMP: 7 **EST:** 1996
SALES (est): 711.95K **Privately Held**
SIC: 3089 Extruded finished plastics products, nec

Fort Loramie
Shelby County

(G-6944)
CROWN EQUIPMENT CORPORATION
Also Called: Crown Lift Trucks
300 Tower Dr (45845-8771)
P.O. Box 97 (45869-0097)
PHONE..................................937 295-4062
Sheryl Gray, *Brnch Mgr*
EMP: 56
SALES (corp-wide): 7.12B **Privately Held**
Web: www.fortloramiechamber.com
SIC: 3537 Lift trucks, industrial: fork, platform, straddle, etc.
PA: Crown Equipment Corporation
   44 S Washington St
   New Bremen OH 45869
   419 629-2311

(G-6945)
CUSTOM FOAM PRODUCTS INC (PA)
900 Tower Dr (45845-8712)
P.O. Box 288 (45845-0288)
PHONE..................................937 295-2700
Nick Fullenkamp, *Owner*
Steve Sherman, *VP*
EMP: 19 **EST:** 1998
SQ FT: 48,000
SALES (est): 6.87MM
SALES (corp-wide): 6.87MM **Privately Held**
Web: www.customfoaminc.com
SIC: 3086 Packaging and shipping materials, foamed plastics

(G-6946)
EDWARD D SEGEN & CO LLC
100 Enterprise Dr (45845-9407)
PHONE..................................937 295-3672
EMP: 8 **EST:** 2005
SALES (est): 877.55K **Privately Held**
Web: www.toolingtechgroup.com
SIC: 3599 Machine shop, jobbing and repair

(G-6947)
EDWARDS MACHINE SERVICE INC
8800 State Route 66 (45845-9806)
P.O. Box 33 (45845-0033)
PHONE..................................937 295-2929
Thomas Edwards, *Pr*
Ronald Edwards, *VP*
EMP: 10 **EST:** 1968
SQ FT: 7,500
SALES (est): 842.91K **Privately Held**
Web: www.edwardspressservice.com
SIC: 3599 Machine shop, jobbing and repair

(G-6948)
INDUSTRIAL MACHINING SERVICES
700 Tower Dr (45845-8769)
P.O. Box 228 (45845-0228)
PHONE..................................937 295-2022
John B Puthoff, *Pr*
EMP: 40 **EST:** 1996
SQ FT: 13,500
SALES (est): 5.41MM **Privately Held**
Web: www.ims-spi.com
SIC: 3599 Machine shop, jobbing and repair

(G-6949)
IRON WORKS INC
62 Elm St Ste A (45845-9411)
PHONE..................................937 420-2100
Bill Gelhaus, *Pr*
Dan Gelhaus, *VP*
EMP: 18 **EST:** 2016
SALES (est): 4.09MM **Privately Held**
SIC: 3537 3448 Engine stands and racks, metal; Prefabricated metal components

(G-6950)
LINCOLN ELECTRIC AUTOMTN INC (HQ)
Also Called: Tennessee Rand
407 S Main St (45845-8716)
PHONE..................................937 295-2120
David M Knapke, *Pr*
EMP: 281 **EST:** 1962
SQ FT: 82,000
SALES (est): 137.07MM
SALES (corp-wide): 4.01B **Publicly Held**
Web: www.waynetrail.com
SIC: 3728 3599 7692 3544 Aircraft parts and equipment, nec; Tubing, flexible metallic; Welding repair; Special dies, tools, jigs, and fixtures
PA: Lincoln Electric Holdings, Inc.
   22801 St Clair Ave
   Cleveland OH 44117
   216 481-8100

(G-6951)
MJ BORNHORST ENTERPRISES LLC
400 Enterprise Dr (45845-9413)
P.O. Box 2 (45845-0002)
PHONE..................................937 295-3469
John Bornhorst, *Managing Member*
EMP: 25
SALES (est): 2.8MM **Privately Held**
Web: www.fortloramiechamber.com
SIC: 2752 Commercial printing, lithographic

(G-6952)
PARTNERS IN RECOGNITION INC
405 S Main St (45845-8716)
P.O. Box 27 (45845-0027)
PHONE..................................937 420-2150
Gregory Short, *Pr*
Angela Speelman, *
◆ **EMP:** 28 **EST:** 2001
SQ FT: 10,000
SALES (est): 4.86MM **Privately Held**
Web: www.gopir.com
SIC: 3999 Identification plates

(G-6953)
ROL - TECH INC
Also Called: Marwil
4814 Calvert Dr (45845)
P.O. Box 547 (32790-0547)
PHONE..................................214 905-8050
Roberto Diaz Del Castillo, *Pr*
Zachary Gillett, *VP*
Mark Lang, *Prin*
▲ **EMP:** 8 **EST:** 2002
SALES (est): 944.06K **Privately Held**
SIC: 3545 Machine tool accessories

(G-6954)
SCHMITMEYER INC
Also Called: G W Tool & Die Co
195 Ben St (45845-9350)
P.O. Box 227 (45845-0227)
PHONE..................................937 295-2091
Jarett Schmitmeyer, *Pr*
Nicole Schmitmeyer, *VP*
EMP: 9 **EST:** 1946
SQ FT: 7,200
SALES (est): 896.92K **Privately Held**
Web: www.g-wtool.com
SIC: 3599 3544 Machine shop, jobbing and repair; Special dies and tools

(G-6955)
SELECT-ARC INC (PA)
600 Enterprise Dr (45845-9410)
P.O. Box 259 (45845-0259)
PHONE..................................937 295-5215
Dale Stager, *Pr*
Scott Stager, *VP*
Ottmar Marko, *CFO*
◆ **EMP:** 146 **EST:** 1996
SQ FT: 67,000
SALES (est): 23.65MM **Privately Held**
Web: www.select-arc.com
SIC: 3548 Welding apparatus

(G-6956)
SHARP ENTERPRISES INC
Also Called: A & B Printing
400 Enterprise Dr (45845-9413)
P.O. Box 2 (45845-0002)
PHONE..................................937 295-2965
James R Sharp, *Pr*
EMP: 19 **EST:** 1987
SQ FT: 8,000
SALES (est): 2.33MM **Privately Held**
Web: www.aandbprinting.com
SIC: 2752 Offset printing

(G-6957)
SOUTH SIDE DRIVE THRU
9204 Hilgefort Rd (45845-9717)
PHONE..................................937 295-2927
Ken Barhorst, *Owner*
EMP: 6 **EST:** 1991
SALES (est): 109.05K **Privately Held**
SIC: 2082 Beer (alcoholic beverage)

(G-6958)
STUDIO ELEVEN INC (PA)
301 S Main St (45845-8755)
P.O. Box 315 (45845-0315)
PHONE..................................937 295-2225
Tom Barhorst, *Pr*
Maria Quinter, *Stockholder*
Frances A Barhorst, *Sec*
▲ **EMP:** 19 **EST:** 1992
SALES (est): 1.03MM **Privately Held**
Web: www.studioeleven.net
SIC: 2759 Screen printing

(G-6959)
TOOLING TECH HOLDINGS LLC (HQ)
100 Enterprise Dr (45845-9407)
PHONE..................................937 295-3672
Tony Seger, *CEO*
EMP: 20 **EST:** 2011
SALES (est): 33.02MM **Privately Held**
Web: www.toolingtechgroup.com
SIC: 3089 Thermoformed finished plastics products, nec
PA: Gennx360 Capital Partners, L.P.
   208 W 122nd St
   New York NY 10027

(G-6960)
TOOLING TECHNOLOGY LLC (PA)
Also Called: Tooling Tech Group
100 Enterprise Dr (45845-9407)
P.O. Box 319 (45845-0319)
PHONE..................................937 381-9211
Anthony Seger, *CEO*
Sean Couse, *
Todd Wodzinski, *CCO*
Amy Stegmuller, *Chief Commercial Officer*
Cory Gergar, *
EMP: 80 **EST:** 2006
SQ FT: 42,000
SALES (est): 51MM
SALES (corp-wide): 51MM **Privately Held**
Web: www.toolingtechgroup.com
SIC: 3544 3363 3365 3322 Industrial molds; Aluminum die-castings; Aluminum foundries ; Malleable iron foundries

Fort Recovery
Mercer County

(G-6961)
BUCKEYE DESIGN & ENGR SVC LLC
2600 Wabash Rd (45846-9500)
P.O. Box 168 (45846-0168)
PHONE..................................419 375-4241
James Westgerdes, *Pt*
EMP: 6 **EST:** 2001
SALES (est): 1.37MM **Privately Held**
SIC: 3089 Injection molding of plastics

(G-6962)
FORT RECOVERY EQUIPMENT INC
1201 Industrial Dr (45846-8046)
P.O. Box 646 (45846-0646)
PHONE..................................419 375-1006
Cyril G Le Fevre, *Pr*
Helen Le Fevere, *
Greg Le Fevere, *
◆ **EMP:** 6 **EST:** 1970
SQ FT: 30,000

SALES (est): 1.49MM **Privately Held**
SIC: 5083 3523 Livestock equipment; Barn, silo, poultry, dairy, and livestock machinery

(G-6963)
FORT RECOVERY EQUITY INC (PA)
2351 Wabash Rd (45846-9586)
PHONE.....................419 375-4119
William Glass, *CEO*
Arnie Sumner, *
EMP: 33 EST: 1919
SQ FT: 15,000
SALES (est): 2.44MM
SALES (corp-wide): 2.44MM **Privately Held**
Web: www.fortrecoveryindustries.com
SIC: 2015 5153 Egg processing; Grain elevators

(G-6964)
FORT RECOVERY INDUSTRIES INC (PA)
2440 State Route 49 (45846-9501)
P.O. Box 638 (45846-0638)
PHONE.....................419 375-4121
Wesley M Jetter, *Ch Bd*
Dean Jetter, *
Larry Holmes, *
◆ **EMP: 199 EST:** 1945
SQ FT: 120,000
SALES (est): 18.44MM
SALES (corp-wide): 18.44MM **Privately Held**
Web: www.fortrecoveryindustries.com
SIC: 3432 3363 3429 Plumbing fixture fittings and trim; Aluminum die-castings; Hardware, nec

(G-6965)
FORT RECOVERY INDUSTRIES INC
1200 Industrial Park Dr (45846)
PHONE.....................419 375-3005
Randy Petit, *Mgr*
EMP: 58
SALES (corp-wide): 18.44MM **Privately Held**
Web: www.fortrecoveryindustries.com
SIC: 3432 Plumbing fixture fittings and trim
PA: Fort Recovery Industries, Inc.
2440 State Route 49
Fort Recovery OH 45846
419 375-4121

(G-6966)
HOME IDEA CENTER INC
1100 Commerce St (45846-8003)
P.O. Box 649 (45846-0649)
PHONE.....................419 375-4951
Dan Schoen, *Pr*
Travis Laux, *VP*
EMP: 6 **EST:** 1978
SQ FT: 12,000
SALES (est): 465.38K **Privately Held**
Web: www.ehomeidea.com
SIC: 2599 Cabinets, factory

(G-6967)
J & M MANUFACTURING CO INC
284 Railroad St (45846-8121)
P.O. Box 547 (45846-0547)
PHONE.....................419 375-2376
Michael Grieshop, *Pr*
Jeff Grieshop, *
◆ **EMP: 200 EST:** 1950
SQ FT: 400,000
SALES (est): 14.64MM **Privately Held**
Web: www.jm-inc.com
SIC: 3523 Farm machinery and equipment

(G-6968)
JR MANUFACTURING INC (PA)
900 Industrial Dr W (45846-8043)
P.O. Box 478 (45846-0478)
PHONE.....................419 375-8021
Chad Guggenbiller, *CFO*
Tomo Yamamoto, *
Jeff Roessner, *
Greg Lefevre, *
Cy Lefevre, *Stockholder*
▲ **EMP: 130 EST:** 1992
SQ FT: 48,000
SALES (est): 20.12MM
SALES (corp-wide): 20.12MM **Privately Held**
Web: www.jrmanufacturing.net
SIC: 3315 3441 Steel wire and related products; Fabricated structural metal

(G-6969)
MEL HEITKAMP BUILDERS LTD
635 Secret Judy Rd (45846)
P.O. Box 229 (45846-0229)
PHONE.....................419 375-0405
Joe Heitkamp, *Genl Pt*
Jack Heitkamp, *Pt*
Tony Heitkamp, *Pt*
Doug Heitkamp, *Pt*
EMP: 9 **EST:** 1990
SALES (est): 142.21K **Privately Held**
SIC: 8741 2521 5712 Construction management; Cabinets, office: wood; Customized furniture and cabinets

(G-6970)
ROESSNER HOLDINGS INC
Also Called: Suspension Feeder
482 State Route 119 (45846-9563)
P.O. Box 369 (45883-0369)
PHONE.....................419 356-2123
Jeffrey D Roessner, *Pr*
EMP: 6 **EST:** 2008
SQ FT: 5,000
SALES (est): 326.42K **Privately Held**
Web: www.roessnerenergyproducts.com
SIC: 3555 Printing trades machinery

(G-6971)
STEVE VORE WELDING AND STEEL
Also Called: Vores Steve Welding & Steel
3234 State Route 49 (45846-9507)
P.O. Box 37 (45846-0037)
PHONE.....................419 375-4087
Stephen Vore, *Pr*
EMP: 10 **EST:** 1974
SQ FT: 5,400
SALES (est): 907.03K **Privately Held**
SIC: 3312 7692 1799 3444 Structural shapes and pilings, steel; Welding repair; Welding on site; Sheet metalwork

(G-6972)
SUSPENSION FEEDER CORPORATION
482 State Route 119 (45846-9563)
P.O. Box 369 (45883-0369)
PHONE.....................419 763-1377
Gregory G Baron, *Pr*
Roberta Baron, *Treas*
EMP: 10 **EST:** 1969
SQ FT: 12,000
SALES (est): 981.22K **Privately Held**
Web: www.suspensionfeeder.com
SIC: 3555 Printing trades machinery

(G-6973)
V H COOPER & CO INC (HQ)
Also Called: Cooper Foods
2321 State Route 49 (45846-9501)
P.O. Box 339 (45846-0339)
PHONE.....................419 375-4116

James R Cooper, *Pr*
Gary A Cooper, *
Dianne L Cooper, *
Anada E Cooper, *
Neil Diller, *
EMP: 150 EST: 1975
SQ FT: 4,400
SALES (est): 2.23MM
SALES (corp-wide): 112.29MM **Privately Held**
SIC: 0253 2015 2011 Turkeys and turkey eggs; Chicken slaughtering and processing; Pork products, from pork slaughtered on site
PA: Cooper Hatchery, Inc.
22348 Rd 140
Oakwood OH 45873
419 594-3325

Fostoria
Seneca County

(G-6974)
ALPHA COATINGS INC
622 S Corporate Dr W (44830-9447)
PHONE.....................419 435-5111
Terence White, *Pr*
EMP: 115 **EST:** 1994
SQ FT: 48,000
SALES (est): 17.98MM
SALES (corp-wide): 18.25B **Publicly Held**
Web: powdercoatings.ppg.com
SIC: 3479 2891 Coating of metals and formed products; Adhesives and sealants
HQ: Whitford Worldwide Company, Llc
47 Park Ave
Elverson PA 19520

(G-6975)
ARCHER-DANIELS-MIDLAND COMPANY
Also Called: ADM
608 Findlay St (44830-1850)
P.O. Box 110 (44830-0110)
PHONE.....................419 435-6633
Dale Anderburry, *Mgr*
EMP: 24
SALES (corp-wide): 85.53B **Publicly Held**
Web: www.adm.com
SIC: 2041 2077 2075 Flour and other grain mill products; Animal and marine fats and oils; Soybean oil mills
PA: Archer-Daniels-Midland Company
77 W Wacker Dr Ste 4600
Chicago IL 60601
312 634-8100

(G-6976)
B&D TRUCK PARTS SLS & SVCS LLC
1498 Perrysburg Rd (44830-1351)
PHONE.....................419 701-7041
EMP: 6 **EST:** 2010
SALES (est): 248.24K **Privately Held**
Web: www.banddtruckpartsstore.com
SIC: 8999 3751 Artists and artists' studios; Motorcycle accessories

(G-6977)
CALLIES PERFORMANCE PRODUCTS INC
901 S Union St (44830-2561)
P.O. Box 926 (44830-0926)
PHONE.....................419 435-7448
▲ **EMP:** 60 **EST:** 1989
SALES (est): 9.35MM **Privately Held**
Web: www.callies.com
SIC: 3714 Crankshaft assemblies, motor vehicle

(G-6978)
FABRICATION SHOP INC
1395 Buckley St (44830-9459)
PHONE.....................419 435-7934
Bill Cronauer, *Pr*
Deborah Cronauer, *VP*
EMP: 18 **EST:** 1977
SQ FT: 15,000
SALES (est): 928.63K **Privately Held**
Web: www.fabshop.com
SIC: 7692 3443 3544 Welding repair; Fabricated plate work (boiler shop); Special dies and tools

(G-6979)
FILMTEC FABRICATIONS LLC
1120 Sandusky St (44830-2761)
P.O. Box 9040 (46899-9040)
PHONE.....................419 435-1819
Scott Glaze, *CEO*
EMP: 24 **EST:** 2016
SALES (est): 4.63MM **Privately Held**
Web: www.filmtecfab.com
SIC: 3599 Machine shop, jobbing and repair

(G-6980)
FOSTORIA BSHNGS INSLATORS CORP
602 S Corporate Dr W Ste D (44830-9456)
P.O. Box 1064 (44830-1064)
PHONE.....................419 435-7514
Philip C John, *Pr*
▲ **EMP:** 6 **EST:** 2001
SALES (est): 696.6K **Privately Held**
Web: www.fostoriabushings.com
SIC: 3612 Transformers, except electric

(G-6981)
FOSTORIA BUSHINGS INC
Also Called: FB Ins
602 S Corporate Dr W (44830-9456)
P.O. Box 1064 (44830-1064)
PHONE.....................419 435-7514
Philip C John, *Pr*
Mary G Padanilam, *Prin*
▲ **EMP:** 9 **EST:** 1995
SALES (est): 974.15K **Privately Held**
Web: www.fostoriabushings.com
SIC: 3612 Transformers, except electric

(G-6982)
FOSTORIA MT&F CORP
1401 Sandusky St (44830-2774)
PHONE.....................419 435-7676
Dick Kiser, *Pr*
EMP: 10 **EST:** 2007
SQ FT: 20,400
SALES (est): 4.28MM **Privately Held**
Web: www.machinetoolandfab.com
SIC: 3599 3441 3442 Custom machinery; Fabricated structural metal; Hangar doors, metal

(G-6983)
FRAM GROUP OPERATIONS LLC
Honeywell
1600 N Union St (44830-1958)
P.O. Box 880 (44830-0880)
PHONE.....................419 436-5827
Paul Humphrys, *Dir*
EMP: 25
SALES (corp-wide): 7.28B **Privately Held**
Web: www.fram.com
SIC: 3714 3264 Motor vehicle parts and accessories; Porcelain electrical supplies
HQ: Fram Group Operations Llc
2500 South Adams Rd
Rochester Hills MI 48309

(G-6984)
INLAND TARP & LINER LLC
1600 N Main St (44830-1941)
PHONE................................419 436-6001
Ron Mackenzie, *Brnch Mgr*
EMP: 25
Web: www.inlandtarp.com
SIC: **1389** Oil field services, nec
PA: Inland Tarp & Liner, Llc
   4172 N Frontage Rd E
   Moses Lake WA 98837

(G-6985)
INNOVATION PLASTICS LLC
1150 State St (44830-3007)
PHONE................................513 818-1771
EMP: 20 EST: 2015
SALES (est): 5.13MM **Privately Held**
SIC: **3089** 4953 Casting of plastics;
   Recycling, waste materials

(G-6986)
KUZMA INDUSTRIES LLC
1541 N Township Road 101 (44830-9319)
PHONE................................419 701-7005
Daniel Kuzma, *Pr*
EMP: 9 EST: 2021
SALES (est): 316.73K **Privately Held**
SIC: **3599** Machine shop, jobbing and repair

(G-6987)
**MAMABEES HM GDS LIFESTYLE
LLC**
2186 Mccutchenville Rd (44830-9797)
PHONE................................419 277-2914
EMP: 6 EST: 2021
SALES (est): 50K **Privately Held**
SIC: **2511** Wood household furniture

(G-6988)
MATERIAL PROCESSING & HDLG CO
1150 State St (44830-3007)
PHONE................................419 436-9562
James H Kenyon, *Pr*
EMP: 14 EST: 2019
SALES (est): 2.48MM **Privately Held**
Web: www.mphco.net
SIC: **2821** Plastics materials and resins

(G-6989)
MENNEL MILLING COMPANY
320 Findlay St (44830-1854)
PHONE................................110 436 5130
Donald L Mennel, *Brnch Mgr*
EMP: 60
SALES (corp-wide): 211.12MM **Privately
Held**
Web: www.mennel.com
SIC: **2041** Flour and other grain mill products
PA: The Mennel Milling Company
   319 S Vine St
   Fostoria OH 44830
   419 435-8151

(G-6990)
MENNEL MILLING COMPANY
611 N Corporate Dr W (44830-9445)
PHONE................................419 435-8151
EMP: 12
SALES (corp-wide): 211.12MM **Privately
Held**
Web: www.mennel.com
SIC: **2041** Flour and other grain mill products
PA: The Mennel Milling Company
   319 S Vine St
   Fostoria OH 44830
   419 435-8151

(G-6991)
MENNEL MILLING COMPANY
Also Called: Mennex Processing & Packing
425 S Union St (44830-2342)
PHONE................................419 307-9657
EMP: 10
SALES (corp-wide): 211.12MM **Privately
Held**
Web: www.mennel.com
SIC: **2041** Flour
PA: The Mennel Milling Company
   319 S Vine St
   Fostoria OH 44830
   419 435-8151

(G-6992)
MORGAN ADVANCED MATERIALS
200 N Town St (44830-2835)
PHONE................................419 435-8182
Randy Bishop, *Manager*
▼ EMP: 160 EST: 2013
SALES (est): 24MM
SALES (corp-wide): 1.39B **Privately Held**
Web:
www.morganadvancedmaterials.com
SIC: **3624** Carbon and graphite products
PA: Morgan Advanced Materials Plc
   York House
   Windsor BERKS SL4 1
   175 383-7000

(G-6993)
MORGAN AM&T
200 N Town St (44830-2835)
PHONE................................419 435-8182
EMP: 7 EST: 2019
SALES (est): 2.26MM **Privately Held**
SIC: **3624** Carbon and graphite products

(G-6994)
NIPPON STL INTGRTED CRNKSHAFT
Also Called: Nsi Crankshaft
1815 Sandusky St (44830-2754)
PHONE................................419 435-0411
Makoto Tsuruhara, *Pr*
Leslie P Lipski, *CFO*
Tim Hasegawa, *Ex VP*
EMP: 13 EST: 2007
SQ FT: 225,000
SALES (est): 16.28MM **Privately Held**
Web: www.nsicrankshaft.com
SIC: **3599** 3714 Crankshafts and camshafts,
   machining; Crankshaft assemblies, motor
   vehicle
HQ: Nippon Steel North America, Inc.
   920 Mmrial Cy Way Ste 700
   Houston TX 77024
   212 486-7150

(G-6995)
NORTON MANUFACTURING CO INC
455 W 4th St (44830-1864)
P.O. Box 1127 (44830-1127)
PHONE................................419 435-0411
EMP: 12 EST: 2010
SALES (est): 3.1MM **Privately Held**
Web: www.nsicrankshaft.com
SIC: **3714** Motor vehicle parts and
   accessories

(G-6996)
OK INDUSTRIES INC
2307 W Corporate Dr W (44830-9449)
PHONE................................419 435-2361
James Kenyon, *Pr*
Jim Kenyon, *Pr*
EMP: 27 EST: 1992
SQ FT: 100,000
SALES (est): 936.14K **Privately Held**
Web: www.okindustriesinc.com

SIC: **2821** Plastics materials and resins

(G-6997)
POET BOREFINING - FOSTORIA LLC
Also Called: Poet Brfining- Fostoria 23200
2111 Sandusky St (44830-2790)
PHONE................................419 436-0954
Art Thomas, *Genl Mgr*
Jeff Broin, *
EMP: 40 EST: 2007
SALES (est): 22.95MM **Privately Held**
Web: poetbiorefining-fostoria.aghost.net
SIC: **2869** Ethyl alcohol, ethanol
PA: Poet, Llc
   4615 N Lewis Ave
   Sioux Falls SD 57104

(G-6998)
ROPPE CORPORATION
1602 N Union St (44830-1958)
PHONE................................419 435-8546
Donald P Miller, *Pr*
Judy R Miller, *Community Relations Vice
President*
Bart Rogers, *Sales & Marketing*
Mark J Baker, *Finance Treasurer*
Angela K Briggs, *
◆ EMP: 300 EST: 1986
SALES (est): 135MM
SALES (corp-wide): 245.4MM **Privately
Held**
Web: www.roppe.com
SIC: **3069** Flooring, rubber: tile or sheet
PA: Roppe Holding Company
   1602 N Union St
   Fostoria OH 44830
   419 435-8546

(G-6999)
ROPPE HOLDING COMPANY (PA)
1602 N Union St (44830-1958)
P.O. Box 1158 (44830-1158)
PHONE................................419 435-8546
▲ EMP: 300 EST: 1955
SALES (est): 245.4MM
SALES (corp-wide): 245.4MM **Privately
Held**
Web: www.roppeholdingcompany.com
SIC: **2426** 3069 Hardwood dimension and
   flooring mills; Rubber floorcoverings/mats
   and wallcoverings

(G-7000)
ROPPE HOLDING COMPANY
J Miller and Co
106 N Main St (44830-2223)
PHONE................................419 435-6601
Jessica Sheridan, *Mgr*
EMP: 8
SALES (corp-wide): 245.4MM **Privately
Held**
Web: www.roppeholdingcompany.com
SIC: **3089** 3069 Extruded finished plastics
   products, nec; Rubber floorcoverings/mats
   and wallcoverings
PA: Roppe Holding Company
   1602 N Union St
   Fostoria OH 44830
   419 435-8546

(G-7001)
SENECA MILLWORK INC
300 Court Pl (44830-2453)
P.O. Box 429 (44830-0429)
PHONE................................419 435-6671
Donald Miller, *Pr*
Angela K Gillett, *
Donald Miller, *Prin*
Mark J Baker, *
Judy R Miller, *
▲ EMP: 50 EST: 1873

SQ FT: 120,000
SALES (est): 4.26MM
SALES (corp-wide): 245.4MM **Privately
Held**
Web: www.senecamillwork.com
SIC: **2431** Moldings, wood: unfinished and
   prefinished
PA: Roppe Holding Company
   1602 N Union St
   Fostoria OH 44830
   419 435-8546

(G-7002)
**SENECA WIRE & MANUFACTURING
CO INC (HQ)**
Also Called: Seneca Wires
319 S Vine St (44830-1843)
PHONE................................419 435-9261
EMP: 17 EST: 1905
SALES (est): 2.26MM **Privately Held**
Web: www.senecawire.com
SIC: **3315** Wire products, ferrous/iron: made
   in wiredrawing plants
PA: The Seneca Wire Group Inc
   820 Willipie St
   Wapakoneta OH 45895

(G-7003)
**THE MENNEL MILLING COMPANY
(PA)**
319 S Vine St (44830-1843)
P.O. Box 806 (44830-0806)
PHONE................................419 435-8151
▲ EMP: 24 EST: 1886
SALES (est): 211.12MM
SALES (corp-wide): 211.12MM **Privately
Held**
Web: www.mennel.com
SIC: **2041** 2048 4221 Flour; Prepared feeds,
   nec; Grain elevator, storage only

Frankfort
Ross County

(G-7004)
CONVEYOR METAL WORKS INC
2717 Bush Mill Rd (45628-9791)
PHONE................................740 477-8700
Scott P Kadish, *Pr*
Christy Wolfe, *VP*
EMP: 20 EST: 2000
SQ FT: 30,000
SALES (est): 2.35MM **Privately Held**
Web: www.conveyormetalworks.com
SIC: **3535** Conveyors and conveying
   equipment

(G-7005)
ROCAL INC (PA)
3186 County Road 550 (45628-9503)
PHONE................................740 998-2122
Robert Lightle, *CEO*
▲ EMP: 82 EST: 1962
SQ FT: 200,000
SALES (est): 9.95MM
SALES (corp-wide): 9.95MM **Privately
Held**
Web: www.rocal.com
SIC: **3993** Signs, not made in custom sign
   painting shops

Franklin
Warren County

(G-7006)
**3-D TECHNICAL SERVICES
COMPANY**

Also Called: 3-Dmed
255 Industrial Dr (45005-4429)
PHONE....................937 746-2901
Robert Aumann, *Pr*
EMP: 25 **EST:** 1970
SQ FT: 15,000
SALES (est): 4.87MM **Privately Held**
Web: www.3-dtechnicalservices.com
SIC: 7389 2542 3999 Building scale models;
Partitions and fixtures, except wood;
Models, general, except toy

(G-7007)
A & B FOUNDRY LLC (PA)
835 N Main St (45005-1648)
PHONE....................937 369-3007
EMP: 14 **EST:** 2018
SALES (est): 5.94MM
SALES (corp-wide): 5.94MM **Privately
Held**
Web: www.abfoundry.com
SIC: 3599 Machine shop, jobbing and repair

(G-7008)
A&B FOUNDRY & MACHINING LLC
835 N Main St (45005-1697)
PHONE....................937 746-3634
EMP: 35 **EST:** 1957
SALES (est): 5.09MM **Privately Held**
Web: www.abfoundry.com
SIC: 3599 Machine shop, jobbing and repair

(G-7009)
AAA WASTEWATER SERVICES INC
Also Called: AAA Wastewater
3677 Anthony Ln (45005-4501)
PHONE....................937 746-6361
TOLL FREE: 888
Timothy E Dehart, *Pr*
Eugene Dehart, *VP*
EMP: 11 **EST:** 1954
SQ FT: 800
SALES (est): 2.23MM **Privately Held**
Web: www.calltriplea.com
SIC: 2992 7699 7359 1711 Lubricating oils
and greases; Septic tank cleaning service;
Portable toilet rental; Septic system
construction

(G-7010)
ATLAS ROOFING CORPORATION
Gypsum & Roofing Div
675 Oxford Rd (45005-3678)
PHONE....................937 746-9941
Eric Glowka, *Mgr*
EMP: 170
Web: www.atlasroofing.com
SIC: 3086 2951 2952 Insulation or
cushioning material, foamed plastics;
Asphalt paving mixtures and blocks;
Asphalt felts and coatings
HQ: Atlas Roofing Corporation
802 Hwy 19 N Ste 190
Meridian MS 39307
601 484-8900

(G-7011)
BOND MACHINE COMPANY INC
921 N Main St (45005-1650)
P.O. Box 95 (45005-0095)
PHONE....................937 746-4941
David Bond, *Pr*
Steve Bond, *Sec*
John Bond Junior, *VP*
Tom Bond, *Corporate Secretary*
EMP: 14 **EST:** 1968
SQ FT: 12,000
SALES (est): 2.52MM **Privately Held**
Web: www.bondmachineco.com
SIC: 3599 Machine shop, jobbing and repair

(G-7012)
CHENEY DYNOS INC
1000 Anderson St (45005-2571)
PHONE....................937 746-9991
EMP: 20 **EST:** 2022
SALES (est): 1.34MM **Privately Held**
Web: www.dynosgroup.com
SIC: 2621 Paper mills
HQ: Dynos Gmbh
Mulheimer Str. 26
Troisdorf NW 53840

(G-7013)
CONTAINER GRAPHICS CORP
1 Miller St (45005-4455)
PHONE....................937 746-5666
Steve Woods, *Brnch Mgr*
EMP: 21
SALES (corp-wide): 3.99MM **Privately
Held**
Web: www.containergraphics.com
SIC: 3555 Printing trades machinery
PA: Container Graphics Corp.
114 Ednbrgh S Drv Ste 104
Cary NC 27511
919 481-4200

(G-7014)
COUNTER-ADVICE INC
7002 State Route 123 (45005-2358)
PHONE....................937 291-1600
Brian Donley, *Pr*
EMP: 7 **EST:** 1999
SQ FT: 13,000
SALES (est): 489.56K **Privately Held**
Web: www.counteradvice.com
SIC: 2434 Wood kitchen cabinets

(G-7015)
COX NEWSPAPERS LLC
Also Called: Franklin Chronicle
129 S Main St (45005-2223)
EMP: 6
SALES (corp-wide): 961.55MM **Privately
Held**
Web: www.coxnewspapers.com
SIC: 2711 8611 Newspapers, publishing and
printing; Business associations
HQ: Cox Newspapers, Inc.
6205 Pchtree Dnwody Rd N
Atlanta GA 30328

(G-7016)
COX OHIO PUBLISHING
5000 Commerce Center Dr (45005-7200)
PHONE....................937 743-6700
EMP: 13 **EST:** 2019
SALES (est): 190.86K **Privately Held**
Web: www.daytondailynews.com
SIC: 2731 Book publishing

(G-7017)
DRACOOL-USA INC (PA)
Also Called: Dracool
331 Industrial Dr (45005-4431)
PHONE....................937 743-5899
Javier Avendano, *CEO*
◆ **EMP:** 24 **EST:** 1958
SALES (est): 4.97MM
SALES (corp-wide): 4.97MM **Privately
Held**
Web: www.dracool-usa.com
SIC: 3441 Fabricated structural metal

(G-7018)
**EMSSONS FAURECIA CTRL
SYSTEMS**
Also Called: Franklin Mfg Div
2301 Commerce Center Dr (45005-1896)
PHONE....................937 743-0551

Parker Sykes, *Brnch Mgr*
EMP: 400
SALES (corp-wide): 92.81MM **Privately
Held**
Web: www.faurecia.com
SIC: 3714 3053 Exhaust systems and parts,
motor vehicle; Gaskets; packing and
sealing devices
HQ: Faurecia Emissions Control Systems
Na, Llc
543 Matzinger Rd
Toledo OH 43612
812 341-2000

(G-7019)
F & G TOOL AND DIE CO
130 Industrial Dr (45005-4428)
PHONE....................937 746-3658
Dick Smith, *Brnch Mgr*
EMP: 6
SALES (corp-wide): 8.79MM **Privately
Held**
Web: www.fgtool.com
SIC: 3542 3469 Machine tools, metal
forming type; Metal stampings, nec
PA: F & G Tool And Die Co.
3024 Dryden Rd
Moraine OH 45439
937 294-1405

(G-7020)
FERCO TECH LLC
291 Conover Dr (45005-1944)
P.O. Box 607 (45005-0607)
PHONE....................937 746-6696
Bryan Perkins, *
Jim Clemons, *
EMP: 120 **EST:** 1984
SQ FT: 30,000
SALES (est): 23.01MM
SALES (corp-wide): 218.18MM **Privately
Held**
Web: www.fercoaerospacegroup.com
SIC: 3728 Aircraft parts and equipment, nec
PA: Novaria Group, L.L.C.
6685 Iron Horse Blvd
North Richland Hills TX 76180
214 707-8980

(G-7021)
FINZER ROLLER INC
Also Called: Rotadyne
315 Industrial Dr (45005-4431)
PHONE....................937 746-4069
Pat Lakes, *Sec*
EMP: 10
SALES (corp-wide): 48.01MM **Privately
Held**
Web: www.finzerroller.com
SIC: 3069 Medical and laboratory rubber
sundries and related products
PA: Finzer Roller, Inc.
880 W Thorndale Ave
Itasca IL 60143
847 390-6200

(G-7022)
FRANKLIN CABINET COMPANY INC
2500 Commerce Center Dr (45005-1816)
P.O. Box 68 (45005)
PHONE....................937 743-9606
Mark Duncan, *Pr*
EMP: 29 **EST:** 1991
SQ FT: 50,000
SALES (est): 2.15MM **Privately Held**
Web: www.franklincabinet.com
SIC: 3083 2541 2599 2531 Plastics finished
products, laminated; Cabinets, lockers, and
shelving; Bar, restaurant and cafeteria
furniture; Public building and related
furniture

(G-7023)
GAD-JETS INVESTMENTS INC
Also Called: Associated Technical Sales
323 Industrial Dr (45005-4431)
P.O. Box 13419 (45413-0419)
PHONE....................937 274-2111
Adryana Southerland, *Pr*
EMP: 8 **EST:** 1947
SQ FT: 9,280
SALES (est): 1.01MM **Privately Held**
Web: www.gadjets.com
SIC: 3542 3089 Presses: hydraulic and
pneumatic, mechanical and manual;
Fittings for pipe, plastics

(G-7024)
GENERAL ENGINE PRODUCTS LLC
2000 Watkins Glen Dr (45005-2392)
P.O. Box 488 (45005-0488)
PHONE....................937 704-0160
Charles M Hall, *Pr*
James Armour, *
Daniel J Dell'orto, *
Jeffery Adams, *
▲ **EMP:** 80 **EST:** 2002
SALES (est): 4.62MM
SALES (corp-wide): 4.41B **Privately Held**
Web: www.amgeneral.com
SIC: 3519 Diesel engine rebuilding
HQ: Am General Llc
105 N Niles Ave
South Bend IN 46617
574 237-6222

(G-7025)
GREENPOINT METALS INC
Also Called: GPM
301 Shotwell Dr (45005-4659)
P.O. Box 935 (45005)
PHONE....................937 743-4075
Brian D Williamson, *CEO*
Doug Everhart, *
Travis Hearn, *
Gary Mockabee, *
EMP: 35 **EST:** 2000
SQ FT: 150,000
SALES (est): 13.6MM **Privately Held**
Web: www.greenpointmetals.com
SIC: 3441 Fabricated structural metal

(G-7026)
H & W SCREW PRODUCTS INC
335 Industrial Dr (45005-4431)
PHONE....................937 866-2577
Robert E Wray, *Pr*
Wendy Wray, *Treas*
Richard Carlisle, *Sec*
EMP: 6 **EST:** 1978
SQ FT: 10,000
SALES (est): 902.92K **Privately Held**
Web: www.h-wscrewproducts.com
SIC: 3451 Screw machine products

(G-7027)
HOMECARE MATTRESS INC
303 Conover Dr (45005-1957)
PHONE....................937 746-2556
Debbie Lipps, *Pr*
P Scott Lipps, *VP*
EMP: 13 **EST:** 1991
SQ FT: 6,000
SALES (est): 2.14MM **Privately Held**
Web: www.sleeptitemattress.com
SIC: 3448 2515 5047 5712 Ramps,
prefabricated metal; Mattresses and
foundations; Medical and hospital
equipment; Mattresses

(G-7028)
HUHTAMAKI INC
4000 Commerce Center Dr (45005-1897)
PHONE..................................937 746-9700
EMP: 53
SALES (corp-wide): 4.36B Privately Held
Web: www.huhtamaki.com
SIC: 3565 2656 Labeling machines, industrial
; Ice cream containers: made from
purchased material
HQ: Huhtamaki, Inc.
9201 Packaging Dr
De Soto KS 66018
913 583-3025

(G-7029)
IKO PRODUCTION INC
Also Called: Iko
1200 S Main St (45005-2781)
PHONE..................................937 746-4561
David Foulkes, Brnch Mgr
EMP: 20
SQ FT: 100,000
SALES (corp-wide): 1.26B Privately Held
Web: www.iko.com
SIC: 2952 3083 Roofing felts, cements, or
coatings, nec; Laminated plastics plate and
sheet
HQ: Iko Production, Inc.
6 Denny Rd Ste 200
Wilmington DE 19809

(G-7030)
LEGACY FINISHING INC
415 Oxford Rd (45005-3639)
P.O. Box 249 (45005-0249)
PHONE..................................937 743-7278
Tom Custer, Prin
EMP: 9 EST: 2011
SALES (est): 551.48K Privately Held
Web: www.legacyfinishing.com
SIC: 3479 Coating of metals and formed
products

(G-7031)
**LIQUID MANUFACTURING
SOLUTIONS**
401 Shotwell Dr (45005-4660)
PHONE..................................937 401-0821
Steve Overdeck, CEO
◆ EMP: 36 EST: 2021
SQ FT: 45,000
SALES (est): 2.16MM Privately Held
Web: www.oilvamed.net
SIC: 2079 Olive oil

(G-7032)
MARBLE ARCH PRODUCTS INC
263 Industrial Dr (45005-4429)
PHONE..................................937 746-8388
Keenan Beauchamp, Pr
EMP: 7 EST: 1990
SQ FT: 15,000
SALES (est): 1.67MM Privately Held
Web: www.marblearchproducts.com
SIC: 3088 5211 Bathroom fixtures, plastics;
Bathroom fixtures, equipment and supplies

(G-7033)
MCS MIDWEST LLC (PA)
3876 Hendrickson Rd (45005-9726)
PHONE..................................513 217-0805
EMP: 7 EST: 2008
SALES (est): 4.82MM
SALES (corp-wide): 4.82MM Privately
Held
Web: www.mcsmidwest.com
SIC: 3089 7699 Garbage containers, plastics
; Agricultural equipment repair services

(G-7034)
MIRACLE WELDING INC
Also Called: Miracle Air
141 Industrial Dr Ste 200 (45005-4427)
PHONE..................................937 746-9977
David Miracle, Pr
EMP: 6 EST: 1978
SQ FT: 12,000
SALES (est): 846.04K Privately Held
Web: www.miraclewelding.com
SIC: 3599 3441 Machine shop, jobbing and
repair; Fabricated structural metal

(G-7035)
MODULA INC (DH)
Also Called: Diamond Systems
5000 Commerce Center Dr (45005-7200)
PHONE..................................207 440-5100
Miquel A Fabra, Pr
Umberto Coruzzi, Prod Controller*
Thomas Samsel, *
◆ EMP: 63 EST: 1995
SALES (est): 43.35MM
SALES (corp-wide): 357.54MM Privately
Held
Web: www.modula.us
SIC: 8711 3535 Engineering services;
Conveyors and conveying equipment
HQ: Modula Spa
Via San Lorenzo 41
Casalgrande RE 42013
052 277-4111

(G-7036)
NATION COATING SYSTEMS INC
501 Shotwell Dr (45005-4663)
PHONE..................................937 746-7632
TOLL FREE: 888
Larry F Grimenstein, Pr
Jim Drumm, VP
Lois Grimenstein, Sec
EMP: 15 EST: 1991
SALES (est): 2.3MM Privately Held
Web: www.nationcoating.com
SIC: 3479 Coating of metals and formed
products

(G-7037)
NC WORKS INC
3500 Commerce Center Dr (45005-7202)
PHONE..................................937 514-7781
Simon Chen, Pr
▲ EMP: 19 EST: 2020
SALES (est): 15.34MM Privately Held
Web: www.ncworksinc.com
SIC: 2299 Automotive felts
PA: Fehrer Enterprise Corporation.
1, Miao-Pu Lane, Shau Shin Lee,
Tainan City 74100

(G-7038)
NIKTEC INC
127 Industrial Dr (45005-4427)
PHONE..................................513 282-3747
◆ EMP: 7 EST: 2007
SALES (est): 708.27K Privately Held
Web: www.niktec.com
SIC: 7629 3679 Electrical repair shops;
Electronic circuits

(G-7039)
PFIZER INC
Also Called: Pfizer
160 Industrial Dr (45005-4428)
PHONE..................................937 746-3603
Fred Haller, Mgr
EMP: 18
SALES (corp-wide): 63.63B Publicly Held
Web: www.pfizer.com

SIC: 2833 2844 2099 2834 Antibiotics; Hair
preparations, including shampoos; Cake
fillings, except fruit; Drugs acting on the
cardiovascular system, except diagnostic
PA: Pfizer Inc.
66 Hudson Blvd E
New York NY 10001
212 733-2323

(G-7040)
PHARMACIA HEPAR LLC
160 Industrial Dr (45005-4428)
PHONE..................................937 746-3603
Fred J Haller, Pr
EMP: 8 EST: 1975
SQ FT: 35,000
SALES (est): 4.19MM
SALES (corp-wide): 63.63B Publicly Held
SIC: 2833 2834 Medicinal chemicals;
Pharmaceutical preparations
PA: Pfizer Inc.
66 Hudson Blvd E
New York NY 10001
212 733-2323

(G-7041)
PHE MANUFACTURING INC
Also Called: Phe Manufacturing
331 Industrial Dr (45005-4431)
PHONE..................................937 790-1582
Javier Avendano, CEO
EMP: 6 EST: 2013
SALES (est): 463.06K Privately Held
Web: www.phemfg.com
SIC: 3443 Heat exchangers, condensers,
and components

(G-7042)
PRU INDUSTRIES INC
8401 Claude Thomas Rd Ste 57
(45005-1497)
PHONE..................................937 746-8702
James Riling, Pr
Marcie Marks, VP
Mark See, VP
EMP: 10 EST: 1990
SALES (est): 458.51K Privately Held
SIC: 2448 Wood pallets and skids
HQ: Component Solutions Group, Inc.
7755 Paragon Rd Ste 104
Dayton OH 45459
937 434-8100

(C-7043)
**QUALITY ARCHITECTURAL AND
FABR**
8 Shotwell Dr (45005-4600)
PHONE..................................937 743-2923
Demida Davis, Pr
Theodosa L Davis, VP
EMP: 18 EST: 1997
SQ FT: 15,000
SALES (est): 1.61MM Privately Held
Web: www.qaf.cc
SIC: 3446 Architectural metalwork

(G-7044)
QUEST TECHNOLOGIES INC
Also Called: Quest Lasercut
600 Commerce Center Dr (45005-7205)
PHONE..................................937 743-1200
John Wenning, Pr
Mike Wolters, VP
EMP: 10 EST: 1995
SQ FT: 12,000
SALES (est): 2.47MM Privately Held
Web: www.questlasercut.com
SIC: 3599 3499 7389 Machine shop, jobbing
and repair; Fire- or burglary-resistive
products; Metal cutting services

(G-7045)
RIVERVIEW PACKAGING INC
101 Shotwell Dr (45005-4653)
P.O. Box 155 (45005-0155)
PHONE..................................937 743-9530
Joan K Ferrell, Pr
Randal T Ferrell, *
Robert S Ferrell, *
Marshall D Ruchman, *
EMP: 40 EST: 1987
SQ FT: 75,000
SALES (est): 15.64MM Privately Held
SIC: 2653 Boxes, corrugated: made from
purchased materials

(G-7046)
RNM HOLDINGS INC (PA)
550 Conover Dr (45005-1953)
PHONE..................................937 704-9900
Matt Milton, Pr
▲ EMP: 41 EST: 2007
SQ FT: 13,500
SALES (est): 1.79MM Privately Held
SIC: 3531 Crane carriers

(G-7047)
RTC CONVERTERS INC
300 Shotwell Dr (45005-4662)
PHONE..................................937 743-2300
Bonnie Vogel, Pr
EMP: 12 EST: 1994
SQ FT: 36,000
SALES (est): 509.25K Privately Held
SIC: 3714 3566 Motor vehicle transmissions,
drive assemblies, and parts; Speed
changers, drives, and gears

(G-7048)
SERVING VETERANS MOBILITY INC
303 Conover Dr (45005-1957)
PHONE..................................937 746-4788
Debra Lipps, VP
EMP: 8
SALES (est): 413.71K Privately Held
Web: www.servingveteransmobility.com
SIC: 3999 Wheelchair lifts

(G-7049)
SHUR-FIT DISTRIBUTORS INC
Also Called: Shur-Form Laminates Division
221 N Main St (45005-1629)
PHONE..................................937 746-0567
Paul Gross, Pr
Hershal Nichol, *
Kent Gross, *
EMP: 15 EST: 1958
SQ FT: 58,000
SALES (est): 1.78MM Privately Held
SIC: 2541 Table or counter tops, plastic
laminated

(G-7050)
SRS MANUFACTURING CORP
395 Industrial Dr (45005-4431)
PHONE..................................937 746-3086
Carlos Robinson, Pr
EMP: 11 EST: 1978
SQ FT: 12,000
SALES (est): 1.85MM Privately Held
Web: www.srsmfg.com
SIC: 3599 Machine shop, jobbing and repair

(G-7051)
SUNSTAR ENGRG AMERICAS INC
Also Called: Sunstar Sprockets
700 Watkins Glen Dr (45005-2394)
PHONE..................................937 743-9049
Naoki Achiwa, Prin
EMP: 73
Web: www.sunstar-engineering.com

GEOGRAPHIC

SIC: 3751 Motorcycles, bicycles and parts
HQ: Sunstar Engineering Americas Inc.
85 S Pioneer Blvd
Springboro OH 45066

(G-7052)
TECH-WAY INDUSTRIES INC
301 Industrial Dr (45005-4458)
P.O. Box 517 (45005-0517)
PHONE...............................937 746-1004
Kenneth Parker, *CEO*
Robin Parker, *
Brian Kress, *
EMP: 55 EST: 1964
SQ FT: 90,000
SALES (est): 8.08MM Privately Held
Web: www.tech-wayindustries.com
SIC: 3089 Injection molding of plastics

(G-7053)
TRI STATE PALLET INC (PA)
8401 Claude Thomas Rd (45005-1475)
PHONE...............................937 746-8702
John Sickinger, *Pr*
EMP: 24 EST: 2005
SALES (est): 2.68MM Privately Held
SIC: 2448 Pallets, wood

(G-7054)
VALUED RELATIONSHIPS INC
Also Called: My Alarm
1400 Commerce Center Dr Ste B
(45005-7203)
PHONE...............................800 860-4230
Chris Hendriksen, *CEO*
Andy Schoonover, *
Rich Filler, *
Salli Duncan, *
Dan Vogel, *
EMP: 331 EST: 1989
SQ FT: 10,000
SALES (est): 43.03MM
SALES (corp-wide): 2.79B Publicly Held
Web: www.vricares.com
SIC: 3845 Patient monitoring apparatus, nec
PA: Modivcare Inc.
6900 E Layton Ave Fl 12
Denver CO 80237
303 728-7012

(G-7055)
WALTER F STEPHENS JR INC
415 South Ave (45005-3698)
PHONE...............................937 746-0521
Carla Baker, *VP*
Walter F Stephens Junior, *Pr*
Ruth Ann Stephens, *Ch Bd*
Diane Stephens Maloney, *Sec*
Patty Gleason, *VP*
EMP: 50 EST: 1940
SQ FT: 45,000
SALES (est): 469.2K Privately Held
Web: www.stephenscatalogs.com
SIC: 5999 2389 5122 5023 Police supply
stores; Uniforms and vestments; Toiletries;
Kitchenware

(G-7056)
WALTHER ENGRG & MFG CO INC
Also Called: Walther EMC
3501 Shotwell Dr (45005-4667)
PHONE...............................937 743-8125
Chris Walther, *Pr*
Phil Fensel, *
EMP: 49 EST: 1992
SQ FT: 35,000
SALES (est): 10.85MM Privately Held
Web: www.waltheremc.com
SIC: 3714 Motor vehicle parts and
accessories

(G-7057)
WAYTEK CORPORATION
400 Shotwell Dr (45005-4661)
PHONE...............................937 743-6142
▲ EMP: 42
SIC: 2672 2891 Paper; coated and
laminated, nec; Adhesives and sealants

Franklin Furnace
Scioto County

(G-7058)
G & J PEPSI-COLA BOTTLERS INC
Also Called: Pepsico
4587 Gallia Pike (45629-8777)
P.O. Box 299 (45629-0299)
PHONE...............................740 354-9191
Robert Ross, *Brnch Mgr*
EMP: 350
SALES (corp-wide): 404.54MM Privately
Held
Web: www.pepsico.com
SIC: 2086 5149 Carbonated soft drinks,
bottled and canned; Groceries and related
products, nec
PA: G & J Pepsi-Cola Bottlers Inc
9435 Wtrstone Blvd Ste 39
Cincinnati OH 45249
513 785-6060

Frazeysburg
Muskingum County

(G-7059)
**DK MANFCTURING FRAZEYSBURG
INC (HQ)**
Also Called: DK Manufacturing
119 W 2nd St (43822-9675)
P.O. Box 409 (43822-0409)
PHONE...............................740 828-3291
Allen L Handlan, *Prin*
Brad Williams, *
EMP: 14 EST: 2004
SALES (est): 8.08MM
SALES (corp-wide): 15.67MM Privately
Held
Web: www.dkmanufacturing.com
SIC: 3089 Injection molding of plastics
PA: Dak Enterprises, Inc.
18062 Timber Trails Rd
Marysville OH 43040
740 828-3291

Fredericksburg
Wayne County

(G-7060)
A-1 RESOURCES LTD
8241 Tr 601 (44627)
PHONE...............................330 695-9351
John R Slater, *CEO*
▲ EMP: 10 EST: 2001
SQ FT: 6,700
SALES (est): 1.42MM Privately Held
SIC: 3469 Metal stampings, nec

(G-7061)
CABINET SPECIALTIES INC
10738 Criswell Rd (44627-9719)
PHONE...............................330 695-3463
Ivan Weaver, *Pr*
Robert Weaver, *VP*
EMP: 7 EST: 1988
SQ FT: 15,000
SALES (est): 853.99K Privately Held
Web: www.cabinetspecialties.co

SIC: 2434 Wood kitchen cabinets

(G-7062)
CRISWELL FURNITURE LLC
8139 Criswell Rd (44627-9709)
PHONE...............................330 695-2082
Jonas Mast, *Managing Member*
Eli Mast, *Managing Member*
David Mast, *Managing Member*
EMP: 15 EST: 1997
SALES (est): 818.33K Privately Held
SIC: 2511 Wood household furniture

(G-7063)
DOWEL YODER & MOLDING
4754 Township Road 613 (44627-9661)
PHONE...............................330 231-2962
Mark Miller, *Pt*
Roy Yoder, *Pt*
EMP: 9 EST: 1991
SALES (est): 263.42K Privately Held
SIC: 2431 5211 Moldings and baseboards,
ornamental and trim; Lumber and other
building materials

(G-7064)
HOLMVIEW WELDING LLC
4041 Township Road 606 (44627-9685)
PHONE...............................330 359-5315
Aaron Herscerger, *Managing Member*
EMP: 12 EST: 2014
SALES (est): 734.53K Privately Held
Web: www.novocollc.com
SIC: 7692 Welding repair

(G-7065)
**MRS MLLERS HMMADE NOODLES
LTD**
9140 County Road 192 (44627-9436)
P.O. Box 289 (44627-0289)
PHONE...............................330 694-5814
Leon Miller, *Pt*
Esther Miller, *Pt*
Maria Miller, *Prin*
▲ EMP: 10 EST: 1973
SQ FT: 11,000
SALES (est): 2.83MM Privately Held
Web: www.mmhn.com
SIC: 2099 Food preparations, nec

(G-7066)
NOVOCO LLC ✪
4041 Township Road 606 (44627-9685)
PHONE...............................330 359-5315
David Miller, *Managing Member*
EMP: 24 EST: 2023
SALES (est): 3.25MM Privately Held
Web: www.novocollc.com
SIC: 3443 Fabricated plate work (boiler shop)

(G-7067)
OHIO CUSTOM DOOR LLC
Also Called: Diamond Door Limited
9141 County Road 201 (44627-9402)
PHONE...............................330 695-6301
EMP: 32 EST: 2003
SALES (est): 990.9K Privately Held
Web: www.ohiodoor.co
SIC: 2431 Doors and door parts and trim,
wood

(G-7068)
QUALITY PLASTICS LLC
9620 S Apple Creek Rd (44627-9743)
PHONE...............................330 695-5920
Monroe Yoder, *Treas*
Emmanuel Yoder, *Mgr*
EMP: 18 EST: 2009
SALES (est): 1.74MM
SALES (corp-wide): 9.58MM Privately
Held

SIC: 2821 Plastics materials and resins
PA: Yoders Produce, Inc.
9599 S Apple Creek Rd
Fredericksburg OH 44627
330 695-5900

(G-7069)
QUALITY WOODPRODUCTS LLC
8216 Township Road 568 (44627-9409)
PHONE...............................330 279-2217
Herman Weaver, *Managing Member*
EMP: 6 EST: 2018
SALES (est): 1.6MM Privately Held
SIC: 2431 Moldings, wood: unfinished and
prefinished

(G-7070)
ROBIN INDUSTRIES INC
Also Called: Fredericksburg Facility
300 W Clay St (44627)
P.O. Box 242 (44627-0242)
PHONE...............................330 695-9300
Dave Wingett, *Prin*
EMP: 158
SALES (corp-wide): 74.78MM Privately
Held
Web: www.robin-industries.com
SIC: 3069 3061 Molded rubber products;
Mechanical rubber goods
PA: Robin Industries, Inc.
8562 Port Jackson Ave Nw
North Canton OH 44720
216 631-7000

(G-7071)
**SALT CREEK LUMBER COMPANY
INC**
11657 Salt Creek Rd (44627-9755)
P.O. Box 253 (44627-0253)
PHONE...............................330 695-3500
Norman Boerman, *Pr*
Shirley Boerman, *VP*
EMP: 6 EST: 1981
SQ FT: 8,000
SALES (est): 121.58K Privately Held
SIC: 5031 2421 Lumber: rough, dressed,
and finished; Sawmills and planing mills,
general

(G-7072)
YODER WINDOW & SIDING LTD (PA)
Also Called: Yoder Window and Siding
7846 Harrison Rd (44627-9798)
PHONE...............................330 695-6960
Jonas Yoder, *Pt*
Jonas M Yoder, *Pt*
Derryl R Troyer, *Pt*
EMP: 13 EST: 1992
SQ FT: 6,500
SALES (est): 3.31MM Privately Held
Web: www.yoderswindowandsiding.com
SIC: 2431 1751 1761 Windows, wood;
Window and door (prefabricated) installation
; Gutter and downspout contractor

(G-7073)
YODERS PRODUCE INC (PA)
Also Called: Quality Plastics
9599 S Apple Creek Rd (44627-9743)
PHONE...............................330 695-5900
Monroe Yoder, *Pr*
EMP: 13 EST: 1990
SALES (est): 9.58MM
SALES (corp-wide): 9.58MM Privately
Held
Web: www.yodersproduce.com
SIC: 2821 Molding compounds, plastics

Fredericktown
Knox County

(G-7074)
COMPLETE METAL SERVICES
18581 Divelbiss Rd (43019-9740)
PHONE..................................740 694-0000
Barry Fluty, *Owner*
EMP: 6 **EST:** 2000
SQ FT: 3,600
SALES (est): 201.71K **Privately Held**
Web:
www.peorialandscapingservice.com
SIC: 7692 Welding repair

(G-7075)
COUNTRY MANUFACTURING INC
333 Salem Ave Ext (43019-9186)
P.O. Box 104 (43019-0104)
PHONE..................................740 694-9926
Joe Chattin, *Pr*
Karen Gay Chattin, *Sec*
EMP: 10 **EST:** 1978
SQ FT: 15,000
SALES (est): 2.33MM **Privately Held**
Web: www.countrymfgstore.com
SIC: 3523 Farm machinery and equipment

(G-7076)
DEE-JAYS CSTM BTCHRING PROC
LL
17460 Ankneytown Rd (43019-8015)
PHONE..................................740 694-7492
Mike Jessee, *Managing Member*
Mike Jessee, *Owner*
EMP: 10 **EST:** 1978
SALES (est): 828.23K **Privately Held**
Web:
www.deejayscustombutchering.com
SIC: 2011 5142 5421 Meat packing plants;
Meat, frozen: packaged; Meat markets,
including freezer provisioners

(G-7077)
DIVELBISS CORPORATION
9778 Mount Gilead Rd (43019-9161)
PHONE..................................800 245-2327
Terry L Divelbiss, *Pr*
Alan Divelbiss, *
EMP: 39 **EST:** 1974
SQ FT: 17,000
SALES (est): 9.3MM **Privately Held**
Web: www.divelbiss.com
SIC: 3625 Relays and industrial controls

(G-7078)
EDWARDS SHEET METAL WORKS
INC
Also Called: Edwards Culvert Co
10439 Sparta Rd (43019-9025)
P.O. Box 239 (43019-0239)
PHONE..................................740 694-0010
Richard Well, *Pr*
Catherine Chris Well, *Sec*
EMP: 12 **EST:** 1907
SQ FT: 8,000
SALES (est): 1.34MM **Privately Held**
SIC: 3444 Culverts, sheet metal

(G-7079)
FT PRECISION INC
Also Called: Ftp
9731 Mount Gilead Rd (43019-9167)
PHONE..................................740 694-1500
Tamami Nishimura, *Pr*
▲ **EMP:** 512 **EST:** 1994
SQ FT: 150,000
SALES (est): 86.72MM **Privately Held**
Web: www.ftprecision.com

SIC: 3714 Motor vehicle engines and parts
PA: Tanaka Seimitsu Kogyo Co.,Ltd.
328, Fuchumachishimada
Toyama TYM 939-2

(G-7080)
INDUSTRIAL AND MAR ENG SVC CO
Also Called: Imesco
13843 Armentrout Rd (43019-9717)
P.O. Box 247 (43019-0247)
PHONE..................................740 694-0791
Theresa C Chandler, *CEO*
EMP: 10 **EST:** 1974
SQ FT: 7,200
SALES (est): 472.39K **Privately Held**
Web: www.imescomfg.com
SIC: 3613 3625 3479 3993 Control panels,
electric; Control circuit relays, industrial;
Name plates: engraved, etched, etc.; Signs
and advertising specialties

(G-7081)
KOKOSING MATERIALS INC
11624 Hyatt Rd (43019-9471)
PHONE..................................740 694-5872
John Gallucci Iii, *Prin*
EMP: 12
SALES (corp-wide): 1.17B **Privately Held**
Web: www.kokosing.biz
SIC: 2951 Asphalt and asphaltic paving
mixtures (not from refineries)
HQ: Kokosing Materials, Inc.
17531 Waterford Rd
Fredericktown OH 43019
740 694-9585

(G-7082)
KOKOSING MATERIALS INC (HQ)
17531 Waterford Rd (43019-9159)
P.O. Box 334 (43019-0334)
PHONE..................................740 694-9585
EMP: 10 **EST:** 1980
SALES (est): 22MM
SALES (corp-wide): 1.17B **Privately Held**
Web: www.kokosing.biz
SIC: 2951 Asphalt and asphaltic paving
mixtures (not from refineries)
PA: Kokosing, Inc.
6235 Wstrville Rd Ste 200
Westerville OH 43081
614 212-5700

(G-7083)
OPTION3 PLU3 INCORPORATED
Also Called: Options Plus
143 Tuttle Ave (43019-1029)
PHONE..................................740 694-9811
Camilyn Jo Meleca, *Pr*
Melissa Chattin, *VP*
◆ **EMP:** 10 **EST:** 1976
SQ FT: 25,000
SALES (est): 945.3K **Privately Held**
SIC: 3444 3496 Sheet metalwork;
Miscellaneous fabricated wire products

(G-7084)
SCHAFER DRIVELINE LLC (HQ)
Also Called: Schafer Industries
123 Phoenix Pl (43019-9162)
PHONE..................................740 694-2055
◆ **EMP:** 18 **EST:** 2012
SQ FT: 110,000
SALES (est): 9.08MM
SALES (corp-wide): 24.27MM **Privately**
Held
Web: www.schaferindustries.com
SIC: 3714 Axles, motor vehicle
PA: Schafer Industries, Inc.
4701 Nimtz Pkwy
South Bend IN 46628
574 234-4116

(G-7085)
TD LANDSCAPE INC
16780 Pinkley Rd (43019-9302)
P.O. Box 154 (43019-0154)
PHONE..................................740 694-0244
Teresa Huvler, *Pr*
Scott Huvler, *CEO*
EMP: 15 **EST:** 2016
SALES (est): 2.83MM **Privately Held**
Web: www.tdlandscape.net
SIC: 3523 Grounds mowing equipment

(G-7086)
UMD AUTOMATED SYSTEMS INC
Also Called: U M D
9855 Salem Rd (43019-9301)
P.O. Box 317 (43019-0317)
PHONE..................................740 694-8614
Don Rogers, *Pr*
Laura Rogers, *
EMP: 72 **EST:** 1996
SQ FT: 55,000
SALES (est): 17.67MM **Privately Held**
Web: www.umdautomatedsystems.com
SIC: 3441 Fabricated structural metal

(G-7087)
UMD CONTRACTORS INC
9855 Salem Rd (43019-9301)
P.O. Box 228 (43019-0228)
PHONE..................................740 694-8614
Don Rogers, *Pr*
EMP: 10 **EST:** 2003
SALES (est): 926.2K **Privately Held**
Web: www.umdautomated.com
SIC: 3011 Tires and inner tubes

(G-7088)
WARD/KRAFT FORMS OF OHIO INC
700 Salem Ave Ext (43019-9188)
PHONE..................................740 694-0015
Robert A Horton, *VP*
Robert A Horton, *General Vice President*
Harold E Kraft, *
Fred Mitchelson, *
David Young, *
EMP: 32 **EST:** 1980
SQ FT: 41,400
SALES (est): 476.79K
SALES (corp-wide): 43.4MM **Privately**
Held
SIC: 2759 Commercial printing, nec
HQ: Ward-Kraft, Inc.
2401 Cooper St
Fort Scott KS 66701
800 821-4021

Freeport
Harrison County

(G-7089)
ROSEBUD MINING COMPANY
28490 Birmingham Rd (43973-9754)
PHONE..................................740 658-4217
EMP: 55
SALES (corp-wide): 134.46MM **Privately**
Held
Web: www.rosebudmining.com
SIC: 1241 Coal mining services
PA: Rosebud Mining Company
301 Market St
Kittanning PA 16201
724 545-6222

Fremont
Sandusky County

(G-7090)
ALKON CORPORATION (PA)
728 Graham Dr (43420-4073)
PHONE..................................419 355-9111
Mark Winter, *Pr*
▲ **EMP:** 60 **EST:** 1968
SQ FT: 40,000
SALES (est): 28.32MM
SALES (corp-wide): 28.32MM **Privately**
Held
Web: www.alkoncorp.com
SIC: 3491 3082 5084 5085 Valves, nuclear;
Tubes, unsupported plastics; Industrial
machinery and equipment; Hydraulic and
pneumatic pistons and valves

(G-7091)
ATLAS INDUSTRIES INC
1750 E State St (43420-4056)
PHONE..................................419 355-1000
◆ **EMP:** 1001
Web: www.atlas-industries.com
SIC: 3599 Crankshafts and camshafts,
machining

(G-7092)
AURIA FREMONT LLC
Also Called: Auria Solutions
400 S Stone St (43420-2658)
PHONE..................................419 332-1587
Brian Pour, *CEO*
EMP: 261 **EST:** 2007
SALES (est): 16.85MM
SALES (corp-wide): 19K **Privately Held**
Web: www.auriasolutions.com
SIC: 3714 Motor vehicle parts and
accessories
HQ: Auria Solutions Usa Inc.
26999 Cntl Pk Blvd Ste 30
Southfield MI 48076
248 728-8000

(G-7093)
BAP MANUFACTURING INC
601 N Stone St Ste 1 (43420-1566)
PHONE..................................419 332-5041
W Scott Brown, *Pr*
EMP: 7 **EST:** 1971
SQ FT: 10,000
SALES (est): 1.09MM **Privately Held**
Web: www.bapman.com
SIC: 3545 Cutting tools for machine tools

(G-7094)
BERLEKAMP PLASTICS INC
2587 County Road 99 (43420-9316)
PHONE..................................419 334-4481
Kenneth Berlekamp Junior, *Pr*
Sandra Berlekamp, *Sec*
EMP: 15 **EST:** 1929
SQ FT: 12,000
SALES (est): 2.29MM **Privately Held**
Web: www.berlekamp.com
SIC: 3089 Injection molding of plastics

(G-7095)
BLONDE SWAN
307 W State St (43420-2527)
PHONE..................................419 307-8591
Elizabeth Martin, *Owner*
Alex Poznanski, *Owner*
EMP: 11 **EST:** 2010
SALES (est): 256.42K **Privately Held**
Web: www.blondeswan.com
SIC: 2371 2353 Hats, fur; Hats, caps, and
millinery

(G-7096)
CARBO FORGE INC
150 State Route 523 (43420-9364)
PHONE..............419 334-9788
Jeffrey Woitha, *Pr*
Jeffrey Witham, *
EMP: 44 EST: 1920
SQ FT: 90,000
SALES (est): 9.6MM Privately Held
Web: www.carboforge.com
SIC: 3462 Iron and steel forgings

(G-7097)
CD COMPANY LLC
215 N Stone St (43420-1505)
PHONE..............419 332-2693
EMP: 93 EST: 2011
SALES (est): 8.29MM Privately Held
Web: www.uniloy.com
SIC: 3089 Injection molding of plastics

(G-7098)
CHRISTY MACHINE COMPANY
1110 Napoleon St (43420-2328)
P.O. Box 39 (43420-0039)
PHONE..............419 332-6451
Randy Fielding, *Pr*
EMP: 8 EST: 1953
SALES (est): 2.43MM Privately Held
Web: www.christymachine.com
SIC: 3556 Food products machinery

(G-7099)
**CRESCENT MANUFACTURING
COMPANY (PA)**
Also Called: Crescent Blades
1310 Majestic Dr (43420-9142)
PHONE..............419 332-6484
▲ **EMP: 98 EST: 1898**
SALES (est): 22.43MM
**SALES (corp-wide): 22.43MM Privately
Held**
Web: www.crescentblades.com
SIC: 3421 3425 Cutlery; Saw blades and
handsaws

(G-7100)
**CROWN BATTERY
MANUFACTURING CO (PA)**
Also Called: Crown Battery
1445 Majestic Dr (43420-9190)
P.O. Box 990 (43420-0990)
PHONE..............419 334-7181
Hal Hawk, *Pr*
Tim Hack, *
◆ **EMP: 450 EST: 1926**
SQ FT: 220,000
SALES (est): 80.83MM
**SALES (corp-wide): 80.83MM Privately
Held**
Web: www.crownbattery.com
SIC: 3691 Storage batteries

(G-7101)
**CROWN BATTERY
MANUFACTURING CO**
4750 Oak Harbor Rd (43420-8910)
PHONE..............330 425-3308
Jeff Wharton, *Brnch Mgr*
EMP: 8
**SALES (corp-wide): 80.83MM Privately
Held**
Web: www.crownbattery.com
SIC: 3691 Storage batteries
PA: Crown Battery Manufacturing Company
1445 Majestic Dr
Fremont OH 43420
419 334-7181

(G-7102)
**CUTTING EDGE MANUFACTURING
LLC**
220 Sullivan Rd (43420-9671)
PHONE..............419 355-0921
Joseph Fisher, *Prin*
EMP: 20 EST: 2016
SALES (est): 2.68MM Privately Held
Web: www.cuttingedgemanuf.com
SIC: 3599 Machine shop, jobbing and repair

(G-7103)
DECKER CUSTOM WOOD LLC
Also Called: Decker Custom Wood Working
505 W Mcgormley Rd (43420-8672)
PHONE..............419 332-3464
EMP: 6 EST: 2004
SQ FT: 3,500
SALES (est): 156.87K Privately Held
Web: www.deckerwoodworking.com
SIC: 2431 Millwork

(G-7104)
DENNIS CONSTUCTION SANITATION
Also Called: J D'S Pre Cast
1201 Siler St (43420-3557)
PHONE..............419 332-8026
A James Dennis, *Owner*
EMP: 7 EST: 1973
SALES (est): 163.75K Privately Held
SIC: 1794 1711 3272 Excavation work;
Plumbing contractors; Septic tanks,
concrete

(G-7105)
ENERGY MANUFACTURING LTD
1830 Oak Harbor Rd (43420-1030)
P.O. Box 1127 (44830-1127)
PHONE..............419 355-9304
Richard Norton, *Pr*
EMP: 6 EST: 2011
SQ FT: 40,000
SALES (est): 2.57MM Privately Held
Web: www.energymanufacturing.com
SIC: 3586 Oil pumps, measuring or
dispensing

(G-7106)
ENGLER PRINTING CO
808 W State St (43420-2538)
PHONE..............419 332-2181
Jay Engler, *Owner*
EMP: 9 EST: 1952
SQ FT: 4,000
SALES (est): 247.08K Privately Held
Web: www.englerprinting.com
SIC: 2752 Offset printing

(G-7107)
FIRST CHOICE PACKAGING INC (PA)
Also Called: First Choice Packg Solutions
1501 W State St (43420-1629)
PHONE..............419 333-4100
Paul W Tomick, *Ch*
Frank Wolfinger, *
▲ **EMP: 105 EST: 1985**
SALES (est): 23.18MM
**SALES (corp-wide): 23.18MM Privately
Held**
Web: www.firstchoicepackaging.com
SIC: 3089 7389 Thermoformed finished
plastics products, nec; Packaging and
labeling services

(G-7108)
FREMONT COMPANY (PA)
Also Called: Fremont
802 N Front St (43420-1917)
PHONE..............419 334-8995
Christopher Smith, *CEO*

Richard L Smith, *
Jeff Diehr, *
Christopher Smith, *VP*
Tom Smith, *
▼ **EMP: 55 EST: 1905**
SQ FT: 250,000
SALES (est): 51.18MM
**SALES (corp-wide): 51.18MM Privately
Held**
Web: www.fremontcompany.com
SIC: 2033 Vegetables: packaged in cans,
jars, etc.

(G-7109)
FREMONT CUTTING DIES INC
3179 Us 20 E (43420-9014)
PHONE..............419 334-5153
Gregory Abdoo, *Pr*
EMP: 9 EST: 2000
SQ FT: 1,000
SALES (est): 1.37MM Privately Held
Web: www.fremontcuttingdies.com
SIC: 3544 Die springs

(G-7110)
FREMONT DISCOVER LTD
315 Garrison St (43420-3031)
P.O. Box 172 (43420-0172)
PHONE..............419 332-8696
Thomas Mccrystal, *Prin*
EMP: 6 EST: 2014
SALES (est): 98.97K Privately Held
Web: www.downtownfremontohio.org
SIC: 2711 Newspapers, publishing and
printing

(G-7111)
FREMONT PLASTIC PRODUCTS INC
2101 Cedar St (43420-1015)
PHONE..............419 332-6407
EMP: 250
SIC: 3089 3944 3714 3661 Blow molded
finished plastics products, nec; Games,
toys, and children's vehicles; Motor vehicle
parts and accessories; Telephone and
telegraph apparatus

(G-7112)
FREMONT PRINTING INC
1208 Dickinson St (43420-1647)
PHONE..............480 272-3443
Dennis C Abdoo, *Pr*
EMP: 10 EST: 1950
SQ FT: 10,000
SALES (est): 260.49K Privately Held
SIC: 2752 2679 Commercial printing,
lithographic; Paper products, converted, nec

(G-7113)
**GANNETT STLLITE INFO NTWRK
LLC**
News Messenger, The
1800 E State St Ste B (43420-4083)
P.O. Box 1230 (43420-8230)
PHONE..............419 334-1012
Cindy Bealer, *Admn*
EMP: 44
SQ FT: 2,792
SALES (corp-wide): 2.51B Publicly Held
Web: www.thenews-messenger.com
SIC: 2711 2752 Newspapers, publishing and
printing; Commercial printing, lithographic
HQ: Gannett Satellite Information Network,
Llc
1675 Broadway Fl 23
New York NY 10019
703 854-6000

(G-7114)
GENERAL CUTLERY INC (PA)
1918 N County Road 232 (43420-9595)
PHONE..............419 332-2316
David Reitz, *Pr*
Carleton R Reitz, *VP*
Donna Shoemaker, *Sec*
EMP: 12 EST: 1945
SQ FT: 25,000
SALES (est): 577.28K
**SALES (corp-wide): 577.28K Privately
Held**
SIC: 3421 Cutlery

(G-7115)
GLATFELTER CORPORATION
Glatfelter
2275 Commerce Dr (43420-1045)
PHONE..............419 333-6700
Lloyd Tuskan, *Mgr*
EMP: 8
SALES (corp-wide): 1.39B Publicly Held
Web: www.glatfelter.com
SIC: 2761 2672 Manifold business forms;
Paper; coated and laminated, nec
PA: Magnera Corporation
9335 Hrris Cmers Pkwy St
Charlotte NC 28269
866 744-7380

(G-7116)
**GRAHAM PACKAGING PET TECH
INC**
725 Industrial Dr (43420-8679)
PHONE..............419 334-4197
Rick Van, *Mgr*
EMP: 9
Web: www.grahampackaging.com
SIC: 3085 3089 Plastics bottles; Plastics
containers, except foam
HQ: Graham Packaging Pet Technologies
Inc.
700 Indian Sprng Dr Ste 1
Lancaster PA 17601

(G-7117)
GREEN BAY PACKAGING INC
Fremont Division
2323 Commerce Dr (43420-1052)
PHONE..............419 332-5593
Paul Hasemeyer, *Mgr*
EMP: 129
SALES (corp-wide): 1.87B Privately Held
Web: www.gbpcoated.com
SIC: 2653 3412 Boxes, corrugated: made
from purchased materials; Metal barrels,
drums, and pails
PA: Green Bay Packaging Inc.
1700 N Webster Ave
Green Bay WI 54302
920 433-5111

(G-7118)
JS FABRICATIONS INC
1400 E State St (43420-4061)
PHONE..............419 333-0323
Jack Swint, *Pr*
EMP: 8 EST: 1991
SALES (est): 800.77K Privately Held
Web: www.jsfab1.com
SIC: 3441 1795 1721 Fabricated structural
metal; Demolition, buildings and other
structures; Industrial painting

(G-7119)
K DAVIS INC
Also Called: KDI Med Supply
206 Lynn St (43420-2375)
P.O. Box 162 (43431-0162)
PHONE..............419 307-7051
Londa Davis, *Pr*

▲ = Import ▼ = Export
◆ = Import/Export

Kevin Davis, *Treas*
EMP: 6 **EST:** 1991
SALES (est): 978.85K **Privately Held**
SIC: 3822 3596 Appliance controls,except air-conditioning and refrigeration; Scales and balances, except laboratory

(G-7120)
KRAFT HEINZ FOODS COMPANY
Also Called: Quality Assurance
1200n N 5th St (43420-3935)
PHONE..............................419 332-7357
Bob Jurski, *Brnch Mgr*
EMP: 113
SALES (corp-wide): 25.85B **Publicly Held**
Web: www.kraftheinzcompany.com
SIC: 2099 Food preparations, nec
HQ: Kraft Heinz Foods Company
   1 Ppg Pl Ste 3400
   Pittsburgh PA 15222
   412 456-5700

(G-7121)
LIGHT CRAFT MANUFACTURING INC
Also Called: Light Craft Direct
220 Sullivan Rd (43420-9671)
PHONE..............................419 332-0536
▲ **EMP:** 10 **EST:** 1987
SALES (est): 2.15MM **Privately Held**
Web: www.lightcraftmfg.com
SIC: 3646 Commercial lighting fixtures

(G-7122)
LUDLOW COMPOSITES CORPORATION
Also Called: Crown Mats & Mating
2100 Commerce Dr (43420-1048)
PHONE..............................419 332-5531
Vincent J Dephillips, *Pr*
B Randall Dobbs, *
Joann Northcott, *
Barry Payne, *
Chris Tricozzi, *
◆ **EMP:** 180 **EST:** 1943
SQ FT: 190,000
SALES (est): 24.58MM **Privately Held**
Web: www.crownfoams.com
SIC: 3069 3081 Mats or matting, rubber, nec ; Vinyl film and sheet

(G-7123)
MICHIGAN SUGAR COMPANY
1101 N Front St (43420-1922)
PHONE..............................419 332-9931
Mark Flegenheimer, *Mgr*
EMP: 10
SALES (corp-wide): 189.47MM **Privately Held**
Web: www.michigansugar.com
SIC: 2063 Beet sugar
PA: Michigan Sugar Company
   122 Uptown Dr Ste 300
   Bay City MI 48706
   989 686-0161

(G-7124)
O E MEYER CO
1005 Everett Rd (43420-1432)
PHONE..............................419 332-6931
TOLL FREE: 800
Eric Wharton, *Brnch Mgr*
EMP: 8
Web: www.oemeyer.com
SIC: 3548 Welding and cutting apparatus and accessories, nec
PA: O. E. Meyer Co.
   3303 Tiffin Ave Rte 101
   Sandusky OH 44870

(G-7125)
ORBIS RPM LLC
2100 Cedar St (43420-1008)
PHONE..............................419 355-8310
Jay Neundorfer, *Brnch Mgr*
EMP: 10
SALES (corp-wide): 1.94B **Privately Held**
Web: www.orbiscorporation.com
SIC: 3081 Unsupported plastics film and sheet
HQ: Orbis Rpm, Llc
   1055 Corporate Center Dr
   Oconomowoc WI 53066
   262 560-5000

(G-7126)
PIXELLE SPCIALTY SOLUTIONS LLC
2275 Commerce Dr (43420-1045)
PHONE..............................419 333-6700
EMP: 260
SALES (corp-wide): 760.06MM **Privately Held**
Web: www.pixelle.com
SIC: 2621 Specialty or chemically treated papers
PA: Pixelle Specialty Solutions Llc
   228 S Main St
   Spring Grove PA 17362
   717 225-4711

(G-7127)
PRAIRIE BUILDERS SUPPLY INC
2114 Hayes Ave (43420-2631)
P.O. Box 592 (43420-0592)
PHONE..............................419 332-7546
Richard A Adams, *Pr*
Jeffrey Adams, *Sec*
EMP: 7 **EST:** 1954
SQ FT: 15,000
SALES (est): 94.01K **Privately Held**
SIC: 5211 3271 Concrete and cinder block; Blocks, concrete or cinder: standard

(G-7128)
PROFESSIONAL SUPPLY INC
Also Called: Worthington Energy Innovations
504 Liberty St (43420-1929)
PHONE..............................419 332-7373
Thomas E Kiser, *Pr*
Dave Engeman, *Treas*
EMP: 18 **EST:** 1979
SQ FT: 9,600
SALES (est): 2.88MM **Privately Held**
Web: www.worldenergyinnovations.com
SIC: 3585 1711 Refrigeration and heating equipment; Plumbing, heating, air-conditioning

(G-7129)
ROOTS MEAT MARKET LLC
3721 W State St (43420-9771)
PHONE..............................419 332-0041
EMP: 23 **EST:** 2020
SALES (est): 6.01MM **Privately Held**
Web: www.rootspoultry.com
SIC: 2011 Meat packing plants

(G-7130)
ROOTS POULTRY INC
3721 W State St (43420-9771)
PHONE..............................419 332-0041
Mark Damschroder, *CEO*
Mike Damschroder, *VP*
EMP: 9 **EST:** 1980
SQ FT: 8,000
SALES (est): 2.39MM **Privately Held**
Web: www.rootspoultry.com
SIC: 2015 5144 5499 Chicken, processed: cooked; Poultry and poultry products; Eggs and poultry

(G-7131)
ROWEND INDUSTRIES INC
1035 Napoleon St Ste 101 (43420-2390)
PHONE..............................419 333-8300
Robert Jablonski, *Pr*
EMP: 8 **EST:** 2006
SALES (est): 207.59K **Privately Held**
Web: www.rowend.com
SIC: 3999 Barber and beauty shop equipment

(G-7132)
SEAWIN INC
728 Graham Dr (43420-4073)
PHONE..............................419 355-9111
Prakash Jog, *Pr*
EMP: 54 **EST:** 1991
SALES (est): 1.59MM
SALES (corp-wide): 28.32MM **Privately Held**
SIC: 3491 Industrial valves
PA: Alkon Corporation
   728 Graham Dr
   Fremont OH 43420
   419 355-9111

(G-7133)
STANDARD TECHNOLOGIES LLC
Also Called: Standard Technologies
2641 Hayes Ave (43420-9715)
PHONE..............................419 332-6434
Max Valentine, *Pr*
EMP: 75 **EST:** 1916
SQ FT: 35,000
SALES (est): 9.53MM **Privately Held**
Web: www.standardtechn.com
SIC: 3444 Sheet metalwork

(G-7134)
STYLE CREST ENTERPRISES INC (PA)
2450 Enterprise St (43420-8553)
P.O. Box A (43420-0555)
PHONE..............................419 355-8586
Thomas L Kern, *CEO*
Phillip Burton, *
Henry Valle, *
Bryan T Kern, *Operations*
Tyrone G Frantz, *
EMP: 47 **EST:** 1996
SQ FT: 40,000
SALES (est): 167.61MM
SALES (corp-wide): 167.61MM **Privately Held**
Web: www.stylecrestinc.com
SIC: 3089 5075 Plastics hardware and building products; Warm air heating and air conditioning

(G-7135)
THE FREMONT KRAUT COMPANY
724 N Front St (43420-1915)
PHONE..............................419 332-6481
Russell G Sorg, *Pr*
Orland H Hasselbach, *General Vice President*
Richard L Smith, *
Jan Sorg, *Sec*
EMP: 13 **EST:** 1906
SALES (est): 1.05MM
SALES (corp-wide): 51.18MM **Privately Held**
Web: www.fremontcompany.com
SIC: 2033 Canned fruits and specialties
PA: The Fremont Company
   802 N Front St
   Fremont OH 43420
   419 334-8995

(G-7136)
THE LOUIS G FREEMAN COMPANY LLC (DH)
Also Called: Freeman
911 Graham Dr (43420-4086)
PHONE..............................419 334-9709
▲ **EMP:** 60 **EST:** 1892
SALES (est): 6.83MM **Privately Held**
Web: www.brownmachinegroup.com
SIC: 3544 Special dies and tools
HQ: Brown Machine Group Intermediate Holdings, Inc.
   330 N Ross St
   Beaverton MI 48612
   989 435-7741

(G-7137)
THERMO KING CORPORATION
Also Called: Thermo King Corporation
1750 E State St (43420-4056)
PHONE..............................567 280-9243
EMP: 12
Web: www.thermoking.com
SIC: 3823 Temperature measurement instruments, industrial
HQ: Thermo King Llc
   314 W 90th St
   Bloomington MN 55420
   952 887-2200

(G-7138)
TI INC
2107 Hayes Ave (43420-2630)
PHONE..............................419 332-8484
Clifford A Robinette, *Pr*
EMP: 30 **EST:** 1972
SQ FT: 16,000
SALES (est): 4.29MM **Privately Held**
Web: www.techniform-plastics.com
SIC: 3083 3599 Thermoplastics laminates: rods, tubes, plates, and sheet; Custom machinery

(G-7139)
TRANSPORT BUFF INTL INC
1099 County Road 126 (43420-8617)
PHONE..............................419 332-5110
Robert Dye, *Pr*
Yvonne Martens, *VP*
EMP: 7 **EST:** 1975
SALES (est): 189.31K **Privately Held**
Web: www.transportbuff.com
SIC: 3471 Cleaning, polishing, and finishing

(G-7140)
UNILOY CENTURY LLC
215 N Stone St (43420-1505)
PHONE..............................419 332-2693
Scott Murphy, *Brnch Mgr*
EMP: 65
SALES (corp-wide): 103MM **Privately Held**
Web: www.uniloy.com
SIC: 2821 Molding compounds, plastics
HQ: Uniloy Century, Llc
   5550 S Occidental Rd
   Tecumseh MI 49286
   517 424-8900

(G-7141)
UNIQUE FABRICATIONS INC
2520 Hayes Ave (43420-2639)
PHONE..............................419 355-1700
Karl Skip Honsperger, *Pr*
Anthony Wayne Doble, *VP*
Madeline Doble, *Sec*
Ellen Honsperger, *Treas*
EMP: 17 **EST:** 1988
SQ FT: 12,000
SALES (est): 4.94MM **Privately Held**
Web: www.uniquefabinc.com

SIC: 3441 Building components, structural steel

(G-7142)
VALLEY ELECTRIC COMPANY
432 N Wood St (43420-2561)
PHONE..............................419 332-6405
Cynthia Auxter, *Pr*
Margaret Hoffman, *VP*
EMP: 6 **EST:** 1957
SALES (est): 994.71K **Privately Held**
Web: valley-electric-co.business.site
SIC: 1731 3679 General electrical contractor
; Electronic circuits

(G-7143)
WAHL REFRACTORY SOLUTIONS LLC
Also Called: Wahl
767 S State Route 19 (43420-9260)
PHONE..............................419 334-2658
Timothy M Albertson, *Pr*
◆ **EMP:** 65 **EST:** 2006
SALES (est): 13.52MM **Privately Held**
Web: www.wahlref.com
SIC: 3255 Mortars, clay refractory

(G-7144)
WOODBRIDGE GROUP
Also Called: Woodbridge
827 Graham Dr (43420-4077)
PHONE..............................419 334-3666
Mike Kohout, *Mgr*
EMP: 150
SALES (corp-wide): 10.66B **Publicly Held**
Web: www.woodbridgegroup.com
SIC: 3069 3714 Hard rubber and molded rubber products; Motor vehicle parts and accessories
HQ: The Woodbridge Company Limited
2400-65 Queen St W
Toronto ON M5H 2
416 364-8700

Fresno
Coshocton County

(G-7145)
BORDER LUMBER & LOGGING LTD
31181 County Road 10 (43824-9503)
PHONE..............................330 897-0177
John Hershberger, *Prin*
EMP: 8 **EST:** 2007
SALES (est): 125.68K **Privately Held**
SIC: 2411 Logging camps and contractors

(G-7146)
CF TOOLS LLC
52025 Township Road 509 (43824-9420)
PHONE..............................740 294-0419
Clinton Frye, *Prin*
EMP: 6 **EST:** 2015
SALES (est): 108.47K **Privately Held**
SIC: 3599 Industrial machinery, nec

(G-7147)
PEARL VALLEY CHEESE INC
54760 Township Road 90 (43824-9796)
P.O. Box 68 (43824-0068)
PHONE..............................740 545-6002
W Charles Ellis, *Pr*
John E Stalder, *Pr*
Sally Ellis, *Sec*
EMP: 20 **EST:** 1928
SQ FT: 8,000
SALES (est): 3.82MM **Privately Held**
Web: www.pearlvalleycheese.com
SIC: 2022 Natural cheese

(G-7148)
PENWOOD MFG
30505 Township Road 212 (43824-9537)
PHONE..............................330 359-5600
Paul Nisley, *Owner*
EMP: 6 **EST:** 1999
SALES (est): 340.54K **Privately Held**
Web: www.penwoodbrands.com
SIC: 2511 Wood household furniture

(G-7149)
SUPERFINE MANUFACTURING INC
33715 County Road 10 (43824-9018)
PHONE..............................330 897-9024
Dan Miller, *Prin*
EMP: 10 **EST:** 2000
SALES (est): 475.69K **Privately Held**
Web: www.superfineinc.com
SIC: 3599 Machine shop, jobbing and repair

(G-7150)
TJ OIL & GAS INC
27353 State Route 621 (43824-9747)
PHONE..............................740 623-0190
Rodney Adams, *Pr*
EMP: 7 **EST:** 2011
SALES (est): 369.13K **Privately Held**
SIC: 1389 Construction, repair, and dismantling services

Fulton
Morrow County

(G-7151)
MAE FENCE LLC
109 E Main St (43321-9706)
PHONE..............................614 929-3526
Timothy Surprise, *Managing Member*
EMP: 16 **EST:** 2010
SALES (est): 2.15MM **Privately Held**
Web: www.maefence.com
SIC: 1799 3315 3089 Fence construction; Fence gates, posts, and fittings: steel; Fences, gates, and accessories: plastics

Gahanna
Franklin County

(G-7152)
ADB SAFEGATE AMERICAS LLC
Also Called: ADB
700 Science Blvd (43230-6641)
P.O. Box 30829 (43230-0829)
PHONE..............................614 861-1304
Joe Pokoj, *Managing Member*
Michael Morrow, *
Gary Roser, *
◆ **EMP:** 220 **EST:** 2009
SALES (est): 24.84MM
SALES (corp-wide): 1.1MM **Privately Held**
Web: www.adbsafegate.com
SIC: 3648 3812 Airport lighting fixtures: runway approach, taxi, or ramp; Search and navigation equipment
HQ: Adb Safegate
Leuvensesteenweg 585
Zaventem VBR 1930
27221711

(G-7153)
ADVANCED PLASTIC SYSTEMS INC
990 Gahanna Pkwy (43230-6613)
PHONE..............................614 759-6550
Wolfegang Doerschlag, *Pr*
EMP: 17 **EST:** 1998
SQ FT: 25,000
SALES (est): 2.82MM **Privately Held**
Web: www.advancedplasticsystems.com

SIC: 3089 Injection molding of plastics

(G-7154)
ARCHITCTRAL IDENTIFICATION INC (PA)
1170 Claycraft Rd (43230-6640)
PHONE..............................614 868-8400
William J Cooke, *Pr*
Barbara B Cooke, *Sec*
James W Cooke C O O, *Prin*
Robert C Barnhart Junior, *VP*
EMP: 18 **EST:** 1971
SQ FT: 5,000
SALES (est): 1.74MM
SALES (corp-wide): 1.74MM **Privately Held**
Web: www.archid.net
SIC: 8748 3993 Systems analysis or design; Electric signs

(G-7155)
DEEMSYS INC (PA)
800 Cross Pointe Rd Ste A (43230-6687)
PHONE..............................614 322-9928
Vijiayarani Benjamin, *Ch Bd*
Jacob Benjamin, *
Dexter Benjamin, *
EMP: 52 **EST:** 2002
SQ FT: 5,100
SALES (est): 2.29MM
SALES (corp-wide): 2.29MM **Privately Held**
Web: www.deemsysinc.com
SIC: 8748 2741 7373 8299 Business consulting, nec; Internet publishing and broadcasting; Systems software development services; Educational service, nondegree granting: continuing educ.

(G-7156)
DIVERSITY-VUTEQ LLC
1015 Taylor Rd (43230-6202)
PHONE..............................614 490-5034
EMP: 8 **EST:** 2015
SALES (est): 424.39K **Privately Held**
SIC: 3089 Plastics products, nec

(G-7157)
EXIDE TECHNOLOGIES LLC
861 Taylor Rd Unit G (43230-6275)
PHONE..............................614 863-3866
Mark Patterson, *Mgr*
EMP: 7
SALES (corp-wide): 482.75MM **Privately Held**
Web: www.exide.com
SIC: 5013 3629 Automotive batteries; Battery chargers, rectifying or nonrotating
PA: Exide Technologies, Llc
13000 Drrfeld Pkwy Bldg 20
Milton GA 30004
678 566-9000

(G-7158)
GLOBAL REALMS LLC
81 Mill St Ste 300 (43230-1718)
PHONE..............................614 828-7284
Devin Randolph, *Managing Member*
EMP: 6 **EST:** 2017
SALES (est): 154.21K **Privately Held**
Web: www.globalrealms.com
SIC: 8731 7371 3571 Computer (hardware) development; Computer software development; Electronic computers

(G-7159)
HEAT TREATING INC
675 Cross Pointe Rd (43230-6689)
PHONE..............................614 759-9963
Rod Ingram, *VP*
EMP: 26 **EST:** 2009

SALES (est): 981.3K **Privately Held**
Web: www.heattreatinginc.com
SIC: 3398 Metal heat treating

(G-7160)
HOLLYWOOD IMPRINTS LLC
1000 Morrison Rd Ste D (43230-6669)
PHONE..............................614 501-6040
EMP: 14 **EST:** 2006
SALES (est): 1.29MM **Privately Held**
Web: www.hollywoodimprints.com
SIC: 7336 2396 7319 Silk screen design; Fabric printing and stamping; Poster advertising service, except outdoor

(G-7161)
K PETROLEUM INC (PA)
81 Mill St Ste 205 (43230-1718)
PHONE..............................614 532-5420
Jam Khorrami, *Pr*
EMP: 10 **EST:** 1984
SQ FT: 3,000
SALES (est): 1.74MM
SALES (corp-wide): 1.74MM **Privately Held**
SIC: 1382 Oil and gas exploration services

(G-7162)
KAHIKI FOODS INC
Also Called: Kahiki
1100 Morrison Rd (43230-6645)
PHONE..............................614 322-3180
Alan L Hoover, *Pr*
Tim Tsao, *Marketing**
Frederick A Niebauer, *
▲ **EMP:** 160 **EST:** 1982
SQ FT: 119,000
SALES (est): 55.46MM **Privately Held**
Web: www.kahiki.com
SIC: 2038 Frozen specialties, nec
PA: Cj Corporation
12 Sowol-Ro 2-Gil, Jung-Gu
Seoul 04637

(G-7163)
KONECRANES INC
1110 Claycraft Rd Ste C (43230-6630)
PHONE..............................614 863-0150
Ashley Easter, *Mgr*
EMP: 27
Web: www.konecranes.com
SIC: 3536 Hoists, cranes, and monorails
HQ: Konecranes, Inc.
4401 Gateway Blvd
Springfield OH 45502

(G-7164)
LA BOIT SPECIALTY VEHICLES
700 Cross Pointe Rd (43230-6685)
PHONE..............................614 231-7640
Gil Blais, *Pr*
Anne Blais, *Treas*
Samson Cheng, *
Ryan Depriest, *
EMP: 70 **EST:** 1980
SQ FT: 18,000
SALES (est): 9.76MM **Privately Held**
Web: www.laboit.com
SIC: 3711 3713 Ambulances (motor vehicles), assembly of; Ambulance bodies

(G-7165)
MCNEILUS TRUCK AND MFG INC
1130 Morrison Rd (43230-6646)
P.O. Box 30777 (43230-0777)
PHONE..............................614 868-0760
Paul Ellingen, *Mgr*
EMP: 6
SALES (corp-wide): 10.73B **Publicly Held**
Web: www.mcneilusgarbagetrucks.com

SIC: 3713 5082 Cement mixer bodies; Concrete processing equipment
HQ: Mcneilus Truck And Manufacturing, Inc.
524 East Highway St
Dodge Center MN 55927
507 374-6321

(G-7166)
MIDDLETON PRINTING CO INC
81 Mill St Ste 300 (43230-1718)
PHONE..................................614 294-7277
David H Stewart, *Pr*
Reno Camerucci, *VP*
EMP: 9 EST: 1950
SQ FT: 14,000
SALES (est): 813.83K **Privately Held**
Web: www.middletonprinting.com
SIC: 2752 2791 2759 Offset printing; Typesetting; Commercial printing, nec

(G-7167)
OCSIAL LLC (PA)
950 Taylor Station Rd Ste W (43230-6671)
PHONE..................................415 906-5271
Yuri Koropachinsky, *Pr*
Peter Cuneo, *Ch Bd*
EMP: 10 EST: 2014
SALES (est): 2.44MM
SALES (corp-wide): 2.44MM **Privately Held**
Web: www.ocsial.com
SIC: 3624 Carbon and graphite products

(G-7168)
RIBBON TECHNOLOGY CORPORATION
Also Called: Ribtec
825 Taylor Station Rd (43230-6654)
P.O. Box 30758 (43230-0758)
PHONE..................................614 864-5444
Kevin Jackson, *Pr*
Scott Palmer, *Sec*
◆ EMP: 11 EST: 1971
SQ FT: 40,000
SALES (est): 4.96MM
SALES (corp-wide): 4.55MM **Privately Held**
Web: www.ribtec.com
SIC: 3357 Building wire and cable, nonferrous
HQ: Dynamic-Materials Limited
Brookhill Industrial Estate
Nottingham NOTTS NG16
177 300 0100

(G-7169)
SNOW AVIATION INTL INC
949 Creek Dr (43230)
PHONE..................................614 588-2452
Harry T Snow, *Pr*
Bill Fergusson, *
Donald Smith, *
Richard Heybes, *
EMP: 6 EST: 1987
SQ FT: 28,000
SALES (est): 851.37K **Privately Held**
SIC: 3721 3728 3724 Aircraft; Aircraft assemblies, subassemblies, and parts, nec; Aircraft engines and engine parts

(G-7170)
SUBURBAN STEEL SUPPLY CO LIMITED PARTNERSHIP (PA)
1900 Deffenbaugh Ct (43230-8604)
PHONE..................................614 737-5501
EMP: 65 EST: 1979
SALES (est): 10.37MM
SALES (corp-wide): 10.37MM **Privately Held**
Web: www.suburbansteelsupply.com

SIC: 3312 3498 3441 Sheet or strip, steel, cold-rolled: own hot-rolled; Fabricated pipe and fittings; Fabricated structural metal

(G-7171)
SURPLUS FREIGHT INC (PA)
501 Morrison Rd Ste 100 (43230-3541)
PHONE..................................614 235-7660
David Belford, *CEO*
Alf Karzia, *Pr*
Mike Mess, *Treas*
Douglas A Hanby, *Prin*
EMP: 7 EST: 2000
SALES (est): 10.68MM **Privately Held**
Web: www.surplusfreight.com
SIC: 3537 Trucks: freight, baggage, etc.: industrial, except mining

(G-7172)
VICTORY DIRECT LLC
750 Cross Pointe Rd Ste M (43230-6692)
PHONE..................................614 626-0000
Joe King, *Managing Member*
EMP: 7 EST: 2008
SALES (est): 495.85K **Privately Held**
Web: www.victory-direct.com
SIC: 7331 2752 Mailing service; Business form and card printing, lithographic

Galena
Delaware County

(G-7173)
K-O-K PRODUCTS INC
700 S 3 Bs And K Rd (43021-9725)
PHONE..................................740 548-0526
EMP: 15
Web: www.kokproducts.com
SIC: 2842 5087 Bleaches, household: dry or liquid; Service establishment equipment

(G-7174)
STEVEN A ESNBROWN LK LURE QPRT
4909 Harlem Rd (43021-9302)
PHONE..................................740 965-2200
EMP: 6 EST: 2016
SALES (est): 47.08K **Privately Held**
SIC: 3949 Golf equipment

Galion
Crawford County

(G-7175)
A & G MANUFACTURING CO INC
165 Gelsanliter Rd (44833)
PHONE..................................419 468-7433
Arvin Shifley, *Brnch Mgr*
EMP: 17
SALES (corp-wide): 5.08MM **Privately Held**
Web: www.agmercury.com
SIC: 3599 Machine shop, jobbing and repair
PA: A. & G. Manufacturing Co., Inc.
280 Gelsanliter Rd
Galion OH 44833
419 468-7433

(G-7176)
A & G MANUFACTURING CO INC (PA)
Also Called: A G Mercury
280 Gelsanliter Rd (44833-2234)
P.O. Box 935 (44833-0935)
PHONE..................................419 468-7433
Arvin Shifley, *Pr*
Doug Shifley, *
Glen E Shifley Junior, *Sec*

Glen Shifley Senior, *Prin*
▲ EMP: 40 EST: 1970
SQ FT: 100,000
SALES (est): 5.08MM
SALES (corp-wide): 5.08MM **Privately Held**
Web: www.agmercury.com
SIC: 3599 7692 3446 3444 Machine shop, jobbing and repair; Welding repair; Architectural metalwork; Sheet metalwork

(G-7177)
ALEXANDER WILBERT VAULT CO (PA)
1263 State Hwy 598 (44833)
P.O. Box 177 (44833-0177)
PHONE..................................419 468-3477
C Phillip Longstreth, *Pr*
Sean Longstreth, *VP*
EMP: 9 EST: 1950
SALES (est): 442.85K
SALES (corp-wide): 442.85K **Privately Held**
Web: www.longstrethmemorials.com
SIC: 3272 Burial vaults, concrete or precast terrazzo

(G-7178)
AMERICAN STEEL GRAVE VAULT CO
799 Newberry Dr (44833-1146)
PHONE..................................419 468-6715
Brent Kingseed, *Pr*
Al Kingseed, *VP*
Mary Kingseed, *Sec*
EMP: 10 EST: 1908
SQ FT: 46,300
SALES (est): 149.45K **Privately Held**
Web: www.goibc.com
SIC: 3995 Grave vaults, metal

(G-7179)
BAILLIE LUMBER CO LP
3953 County Road 51 (44833-9630)
PHONE..................................419 462-2000
Russel Jones, *Brnch Mgr*
EMP: 40
SALES (corp-wide): 595.03MM **Privately Held**
Web: www.baillie.com
SIC: 5031 2426 2421 Lumber: rough, dressed, and finished; Hardwood dimension and flooring mills; Sawmills and planing mills, general
PA: Baillie Lumber Co., L.P.
4002 Legion Dr
Hamburg NY 14075
800 950-2850

(G-7180)
BROTHERS BODY AND EQP LLC
352 South St Door 26 (44833-2742)
P.O. Box 926 (44833-0926)
PHONE..................................419 462-1975
▲ EMP: 15 EST: 2006
SQ FT: 30,000
SALES (est): 1.7MM **Privately Held**
Web: www.brothersbande.com
SIC: 3713 Truck bodies and parts

(G-7181)
CASS FRAMES INC
6052 State Route 19 (44833-9771)
P.O. Box 625 (44833-0625)
PHONE..................................419 468-2863
James Cass, *Pr*
Bart Cass, *VP*
Delores Cass, *Sec*
EMP: 9 EST: 1990
SQ FT: 4,200
SALES (est): 731.13K **Privately Held**

SIC: 2499 Picture and mirror frames, wood

(G-7182)
CENTRAL STATE ENTERPRISES INC
1331 Freese Works Pl (Galion Indl Pk) (44833-9368)
PHONE..................................419 468-8191
Donald E Kuenzli Junior, *Pr*
Sandra Kuenzli, *
EMP: 37 EST: 1982
SQ FT: 28,000
SALES (est): 6.22MM **Privately Held**
Web: www.centralstateent.net
SIC: 3599 Machine shop, jobbing and repair

(G-7183)
CMI HOLDING COMPANY CRAWFORD
Also Called: CMI
1310 Freese Works Pl (44833-9368)
PHONE..................................419 468-9122
Kevin Hessey, *Pr*
Joy Hessey, *
Tonya Hoepf Cust Serv Prcng, *Mgr*
Keith Hummel, *
Brad Hessey, *Acting Vice President**
◆ EMP: 70 EST: 2000
SALES (est): 7.11MM
SALES (corp-wide): 175.39MM **Privately Held**
SIC: 3714 Motor vehicle parts and accessories
HQ: Tramec Sloan, L.L.C.
534 E 48th St
Holland MI 49423
800 336-7778

(G-7184)
COVERT MANUFACTURING INC
303 E Parson St (44833-3304)
PHONE..................................419 468-1761
Carl Montgomery, *Brnch Mgr*
EMP: 34
SALES (corp-wide): 20.15MM **Privately Held**
Web: www.covertmfg.com
SIC: 3599 Machine shop, jobbing and repair
PA: Covert Manufacturing, Inc.
328 S East St
Galion OH 44833
419 468-1761

(G-7185)
COVERT MANUFACTURING INC (PA)
Also Called: Covert
328 S East St (44833-2729)
P.O. Box 608 (44833-0608)
PHONE..................................419 468-1761
Donald L Covert Senior, *CEO*
Kym Fox, *
Teri Williams, *
Donna Morrow, *
▲ EMP: 236 EST: 1971
SQ FT: 300,000
SALES (est): 20.15MM
SALES (corp-wide): 20.15MM **Privately Held**
Web: www.covertmfg.com
SIC: 3545 Machine tool accessories

(G-7186)
CRASE COMMUNICATIONS INC
120 Harding Way E Ste 104 (44833-1927)
PHONE..................................419 468-1173
Edward Crase, *Pr*
Linda Crase, *Sec*
EMP: 6 EST: 1986
SALES (est): 423.02K **Privately Held**
Web: www.crasecommunications.com

SIC: **1731** 3661 Telephone and telephone equipment installation; Toll switching equipment, telephone

(G-7187)
EAGLE CRUSHER CO INC (PA)
525 S Market St (44833-2612)
P.O. Box 537 (44833-0537)
PHONE.............................419 468-2288
Susanne Cobey, *CEO*
Michael Tinkey, *
◆ **EMP:** 75 **EST:** 1915
SQ FT: 40,000
SALES (est): 13.19MM
SALES (corp-wide): 13.19MM **Privately Held**
Web: www.eaglecrusher.com
SIC: **3535** 3532 3589 3531 Conveyors and conveying equipment; Crushing, pulverizing, and screening equipment; Sewage and water treatment equipment; Construction machinery

(G-7188)
ECLIPSE
126 N Union St (44833-1736)
PHONE.............................419 564-7482
Teresa Harris, *Prin*
EMP: 6 **EST:** 2016
SALES (est): 1.01MM **Privately Held**
Web: www.eclipsecorp.us
SIC: **7372** Prepackaged software

(G-7189)
ELLIOTT MACHINE WORKS INC
1351 Freese Works Pl (44833-9368)
PHONE.............................419 468-4709
Richard Ekin, *Pr*
Brad Ekin, *
Brent Ekin, *
EMP: 48 **EST:** 1968
SQ FT: 54,000
SALES (est): 9.62MM **Privately Held**
Web: www.elliottmachine.com
SIC: **3713** 3443 3537 Truck bodies (motor vehicles); Tanks for tank trucks, metal plate; Trucks: freight, baggage, etc.: industrial, except mining
PA: Stellar Industries, Inc.
190 State St
Garner IA 50438

(G-7190)
GALION LLC
515 N East St (44833-2142)
P.O. Box 447 (44833-0447)
PHONE.............................419 468-5214
Richard Voorde, *CEO*
Stephen Koch, *Managing Member*
Stan Will, *
Cindy Shepherd, *
EMP: 105 **EST:** 1994
SQ FT: 60,000
SALES (est): 1.82MM **Privately Held**
Web: www.galionllc.com
SIC: **3482** 3444 Small arms ammunition; Sheet metalwork

(G-7191)
GALION CANVAS PRODUCTS (PA)
385 S Market St (44833-2608)
PHONE.............................419 468-5333
TOLL FREE: 800
Steve Siclair, *Owner*
Scott Goldsmith, *Prin*
EMP: 6 **EST:** 1958
SQ FT: 5,000
SALES (est): 244.71K
SALES (corp-wide): 244.71K **Privately Held**

Web:
galioncanvasproducts.wordpress.com
SIC: **7359** 2394 Tent and tarpaulin rental; Canvas and related products

(G-7192)
GEN-RUBBER LLC
352 South St (44833-2742)
P.O. Box 805 (44258-0805)
PHONE.............................440 655-3643
EMP: 6 **EST:** 2008
SALES (est): 736.29K **Privately Held**
Web: www.rubber-master.com
SIC: **3069** Custom compounding of rubber materials

(G-7193)
GLEDHILL ROAD MACHINERY CO
765 Portland Way S (44833-2326)
P.O. Box P.O. Box 567 (44833-0567)
PHONE.............................419 468-4400
Michael D Rarick, *Pr*
Garland Gledhill, *
Sherrie Dill, *
EMP: 50 **EST:** 1930
SQ FT: 57,000
SALES (est): 5.19MM **Privately Held**
Web: www.gledhillonline.com
SIC: **3531** Road construction and maintenance machinery

(G-7194)
GLEN-GERY CORPORATION
3785 Cardington Iberia Rd (44833-9101)
PHONE.............................419 468-4890
Joe Wishan, *Brnch Mgr*
EMP: 24
Web: www.glengery.com
SIC: **3251** Brick and structural clay tile
HQ: Glen-Gery Corporation
1166 Spring St
Reading PA 19610
610 374-4011

(G-7195)
HYDRANAMICS INC
Also Called: Hydranamics Div Carter Mch Co
820 Edward St (44833-2223)
PHONE.............................419 468-3530
Juanita Carter, *Ch*
Andrea Carter, *
EMP: 87 **EST:** 1941
SALES (est): 1.4MM
SALES (corp-wide): 9.8MM **Privately Held**
Web: www.hydranamics.com
SIC: **3593** 3547 Fluid power cylinders, hydraulic or pneumatic; Rolling mill machinery
PA: Carter Machine Company, Inc.
820 Edward St
Galion OH 44833
419 468-3530

(G-7196)
OTTERBACHER TRAILERS LLC
352 South St (44833-2742)
P.O. Box 129 (44827-0129)
PHONE.............................419 462-1975
EMP: 10 **EST:** 2002
SALES (est): 390.68K **Privately Held**
Web: www.brothersbande.com
SIC: **3799** Trailers and trailer equipment

(G-7197)
PRINTS & PAINTS FLR CVG CO INC
Also Called: My Floors By Prints and Paints
888 Bucyrus Rd (44833-1549)
PHONE.............................419 462-5663
Gary Frankhouse Senior, *Pr*
Sandra Frankhouse, *Ex VP*
Gary Frankhose Junior, *Treas*

Steve Frankhouse, *Sec*
EMP: 23 **EST:** 1977
SQ FT: 14,000
SALES (est): 2.66MM **Privately Held**
Web: www.myfloorsohiofa.com
SIC: **5231** 2295 1743 5713 Paint; Laminating of fabrics; Tile installation, ceramic; Carpets

(G-7198)
SCHILLING GRAPHICS INC (PA)
275 Gelsanliter Rd (44833-2235)
P.O. Box 978 (44833-0978)
PHONE.............................419 468-1037
TOLL FREE: 800
Douglas Schilling, *Pr*
EMP: 33 **EST:** 1963
SQ FT: 20,000
SALES (est): 7.03MM
SALES (corp-wide): 7.03MM **Privately Held**
Web: www.schillinginc.com
SIC: **2752** 3552 3555 2759 Decals, lithographed; Silk screens for textile industry ; Printing trades machinery; Commercial printing, nec

(G-7199)
STARKEY MACHINERY INC
254 S Washington St (44833-2616)
P.O. Box 207 (44833-0207)
PHONE.............................419 468-2560
James D Starkey, *Pr*
Don Starkey, *VP*
EMP: 20 **EST:** 1881
SQ FT: 30,000
SALES (est): 2.48MM **Privately Held**
Web: www.starkeymachinery.com
SIC: **3559** 5084 3594 3544 Clay working and tempering machines; Industrial machinery and equipment; Fluid power pumps and motors; Special dies, tools, jigs, and fixtures

(G-7200)
URBAN INDUSTRIES OF OHIO INC
Also Called: Urban Industries
525 King Ave (44833-1850)
P.O. Box 27 (44833-0027)
PHONE.............................419 468-3578
▲ **EMP:** 25 **EST:** 1947
SALES (est): 5.67MM **Privately Held**
Web: www.urbanindustries.com
SIC: **3446** 3354 7389 1531 Architectural metalwork; Aluminum extruded products; Laminating service

(G-7201)
VULCAN PRODUCTS CO INC
208 S Washington St (44833-2616)
P.O. Box 216 (44833-0216)
PHONE.............................419 468-1039
Ralph Chamberlin, *Pr*
EMP: 6 **EST:** 1951
SALES (est): 937.46K **Privately Held**
Web: www.vulcanproducts.net
SIC: **3451** Screw machine products

Gallipolis
Gallia County

(G-7202)
BIG RIVER ELECTRIC INC
Also Called: Big River Electric
299 Upper River Rd (45631-1838)
P.O. Box 244 (45631-0244)
PHONE.............................740 446-4360
Kelly Counts, *Pr*
Geraldine Counts, *VP*
Debra Barcus, *Sec*

EMP: 6 **EST:** 1983
SQ FT: 8,500
SALES (est): 1.04MM **Privately Held**
Web: www.bigriverelec.com
SIC: **5999** 7694 5063 Motors, electric; Electric motor repair; Motors, electric

(G-7203)
ELECTROCRAFT ARKANSAS INC
250 Mccormick Rd (45631-8745)
PHONE.............................501 268-4203
James Elsner, *CEO*
John Arico, *
Logan D Delany Junior, *Ch Bd*
▲ **EMP:** 9 **EST:** 2001
SQ FT: 50,000
SALES (est): 4.28MM **Privately Held**
Web: www.electrocraft.com
SIC: **3621** Electric motor and generator parts
HQ: Electrocraft, Inc.
2 Marin Way Ste3
Stratham NH 03885

(G-7204)
ELECTROCRAFT OHIO INC
250 Mccormick Rd (45631-8745)
PHONE.............................740 441-6200
James Elsner, *Pr*
Mike Karsonovich, *Pr*
John Arico, *VP Fin*
Logan D Delany Junior, *Prin*
▲ **EMP:** 225 **EST:** 2002
SQ FT: 160,000
SALES (est): 46.85MM **Privately Held**
Web: www.electrocraft.com
SIC: **3625** Relays and industrial controls
HQ: Electrocraft, Inc.
2 Marin Way Ste3
Stratham NH 03885

(G-7205)
GKN PLC
Also Called: GKN Sinter Metals
2160 Eastern Ave (45631-1823)
PHONE.............................740 446-9211
Daniel Swannigan, *Brnch Mgr*
EMP: 9
SALES (corp-wide): 4.4B **Privately Held**
Web: www.gknaerospace.com
SIC: **3462** Iron and steel forgings
HQ: Gkn Limited
11th Floor, The Colmore Building
Birmingham W MIDLANDS B4 6A
121 210-9800

(G-7206)
GKN SINTER METALS LLC
Also Called: Precision Forged Products
2160 Eastern Ave (45631-1823)
PHONE.............................740 441-3203
Greg Landis, *Brnch Mgr*
EMP: 139
SALES (corp-wide): 6.06B **Privately Held**
Web: www.gknpm.com
SIC: **3312** 3568 3462 Sinter, iron; Power transmission equipment, nec; Iron and steel forgings
HQ: Gkn Sinter Metals, Llc
1670 Opdyke Ct
Auburn Hills MI 48326
248 883-4500

(G-7207)
KING KUTTER II INC
Also Called: Sfs Truck Sales & Parts
2150 Eastern Ave (45631-1823)
P.O. Box 786 (45631-0786)
PHONE.............................740 446-0351
James Phillip Fraley, *Pr*
Jeff Fraley, *
Deborah Swain, *

▲ **EMP:** 50 **EST:** 1982
SQ FT: 160
SALES (est): 2.12MM **Privately Held**
Web: www.kingkutter2.com
SIC: 5521 3713 Trucks, tractors, and trailers: used; Truck and bus bodies

(G-7208)
RIVERVIEW PRODUCTIONS INC
Also Called: UNIQUE EXPRESSIONS
652 Jackson Pike (45631-1389)
P.O. Box 624 (45692-0624)
PHONE..............................740 441-1150
Thomas Meadows, *Ch*
EMP: 9 **EST:** 1991
SALES (est): 413.05K **Privately Held**
SIC: 5261 2611 Retail nurseries; Pulp mills, mechanical and recycling processing

(G-7209)
THOMAS DO-IT CENTER INC (PA)
Also Called: Thomas Rental
176 Mccormick Rd (45631-8745)
PHONE..............................740 446-2002
Autumn Thomas, *Ex Dir*
Jim Thomas, *Pr*
Marlene Hall, *
Lee Cyrus, *
Jay Hall, *
▲ **EMP:** 45 **EST:** 1988
SALES (est): 11.56MM
SALES (corp-wide): 11.56MM **Privately Held**
Web: www.thomasdoit.com
SIC: 7359 2439 5211 5251 Equipment rental and leasing, nec; Trusses, wooden roof; Lumber products; Hardware stores

Galloway
Franklin County

(G-7210)
PETTITS PALLETS INC
1891 Dauphin Dr (43119-8513)
PHONE..............................614 351-4920
Brenda Pettit, *Pr*
Tim Pettit, *VP*
EMP: 7 **EST:** 1986
SALES (est): 231.33K **Privately Held**
SIC: 2448 Pallets, wood

Gambier
Knox County

(G-7211)
KENYON REVIEW
209 Chase Ave (43022-5024)
PHONE..............................740 427-5208
Abigail Serfass, *Admn*
Meg Galipault, *COO*
David Lynn, *CEO*
EMP: 7 **EST:** 2004
SALES (est): 2.92MM **Privately Held**
Web: www.kenyonreview.org
SIC: 2721 Magazines: publishing and printing

(G-7212)
SMALL SAND & GRAVEL INC
10229 Killduff Rd (43022-9657)
P.O. Box 617 (43022-0617)
PHONE..............................740 427-3130
Michael W Small, *Pr*
William T Small, *
Carol Small, *
EMP: 35 **EST:** 1958
SALES (est): 1.88MM **Privately Held**
Web: www.smallssandandgravel.com

SIC: 3273 Ready-mixed concrete

(G-7213)
SMALLS INC
Also Called: Small's Ready-Mixed Concrete
10229 Killduff Rd (43022-9657)
P.O. Box 503 (43022-0503)
PHONE..............................740 427-3633
Robert Small, *Pr*
Sharon Mills, *Sec*
EMP: 10 **EST:** 1994
SALES (est): 480.51K **Privately Held**
Web: www.smallssandandgravel.com
SIC: 3273 Ready-mixed concrete

(G-7214)
SMALLS ASPHALT PAVING INC
10229 Killduff Rd (43022-9657)
P.O. Box 552 (43022-0552)
PHONE..............................740 427-4096
Robert E Small, *Pr*
Michael Small, *VP*
William T Small, *Treas*
Carol Small, *Sec*
EMP: 6 **EST:** 1978
SALES (est): 423.25K **Privately Held**
Web: www.smallssandandgravel.com
SIC: 1771 2951 1611 Blacktop (asphalt) work ; Asphalt paving mixtures and blocks; Highway and street construction

(G-7215)
YODERS FINE FOODS LLC
Also Called: Yoder's Cider Barn
3361 Martinsburg Rd (43022-9737)
PHONE..............................740 668-4961
Sheldon Yoder, *Managing Member*
▲ **EMP:** 10 **EST:** 1975
SALES (est): 476.86K **Privately Held**
Web: www.yodersfinefoods.com
SIC: 2023 2033 Condensed, concentrated, and evaporated milk products; Jams, including imitation: packaged in cans, jars, etc.

Garfield Heights
Cuyahoga County

(G-7216)
BJS DEMO&HAULING LLC
4937 E 88th St (44125-2013)
P.O. Box 27211 (44127-0211)
PHONE..............................216 904-8909
EMP: 6 **EST:** 2022
SALES (est): 532.48K **Privately Held**
SIC: 3799 7389 Transportation equipment, nec; Business services, nec

Garrettsville
Portage County

(G-7217)
DCA CONSTRUCTION PRODUCTS LLC
10421 Industrial Dr (44231-9764)
PHONE..............................330 527-4308
EMP: 24 **EST:** 2002
SALES (est): 2.26MM **Privately Held**
Web: www.durajoint.com
SIC: 3272 Concrete products, nec

(G-7218)
DISKIN ENTERPRISES LLC
Also Called: Four Seasons Manufacturing
10421 Industrial Dr (44231-9764)
PHONE..............................330 527-4308
Michael E Diskin, *Pr*

Micheal A Diskin, *
EMP: 30 **EST:** 2016
SALES (est): 5.12MM **Privately Held**
Web: www.durajoint.com
SIC: 3089 Injection molding of plastics

(G-7219)
EDGEWELL PER CARE BRANDS LLC
10545 Freedom St (44231-9237)
PHONE..............................330 527-2191
Ronald R Taylor, *Brnch Mgr*
EMP: 10
SQ FT: 50,000
SALES (corp-wide): 2.25B **Publicly Held**
Web: www.edgewell.com
SIC: 3421 Cutlery
HQ: Edgewell Personal Care Brands, Llc
6 Research Dr
Shelton CT 06484
203 944-5500

(G-7220)
HARRISON MCH & PLASTIC CORP (PA)
11614 State Route 88 (44231-9105)
P.O. Box 1826 (44234-1826)
PHONE..............................330 527-5641
Bryson Swanda, *Pr*
EMP: 25 **EST:** 1970
SQ FT: 30,000
SALES (est): 4.94MM
SALES (corp-wide): 4.94MM **Privately Held**
Web: www.harrisonplastic.com
SIC: 3089 3444 3084 Injection molding of plastics; Sheet metalwork; Plastics pipe

(G-7221)
JC ELECTRIC LLC
9717 State Route 88 (44231-9746)
P.O. Box 304 (44231-0304)
PHONE..............................330 760-2915
Jason Carmichael, *Owner*
EMP: 10 **EST:** 2001
SALES (est): 912.05K **Privately Held**
SIC: 1731 3699 1521 General electrical contractor; Door opening and closing devices, electrical; Single-family home remodeling, additions, and repairs

(G-7222)
KECAMM LLC
10404 Industrial Dr (44231-9764)
PHONE..............................330 527-2918
Cheryl A Macek, *CEO*
George Macek, *Pr*
EMP: 7 **EST:** 2003
SQ FT: 10,000
SALES (est): 248.02K **Privately Held**
Web: www.kecam.com
SIC: 3479 5084 Bonderizing of metal or metal products; Paint spray equipment, industrial

(G-7223)
KECOAT LLC
10610 Freedom St (44231-9763)
PHONE..............................330 527-0215
Darrin Macek, *Managing Member*
EMP: 9 **EST:** 2006
SQ FT: 10,000
SALES (est): 1.91MM **Privately Held**
SIC: 3441 Fabricated structural metal

(G-7224)
LHPC INC (PA)
11964 State Route 88 (44231-9115)
P.O. Box P.O. Box 347 (44231-0347)
PHONE..............................330 527-2696
Larry I Hermann, *Pr*
Ruth Hermann, *Treas*

Walter Kaudelka, *CFO*
EMP: 28 **EST:** 1967
SALES (est): 5.51MM
SALES (corp-wide): 5.51MM **Privately Held**
Web: www.hermannpicklecompany.com
SIC: 2035 Pickles, sauces, and salad dressings

(G-7225)
MACHINE TEK SYSTEMS INC
10400 Industrial Dr (44231-9764)
P.O. Box 187 (44231-0187)
PHONE..............................330 527-4450
Tim Paul, *Pr*
EMP: 33 **EST:** 1986
SQ FT: 22,000
SALES (est): 2.64MM **Privately Held**
Web: www.machineteksystemsinc.com
SIC: 3544 3599 3451 Special dies and tools; Machine shop, jobbing and repair; Screw machine products

(G-7226)
MEGA PLASTICS CO
10610 Freedom St (44231-9763)
PHONE..............................330 527-2211
Ronald Porter, *Pr*
Wendi Porter, *VP*
EMP: 20 **EST:** 1998
SQ FT: 25,000
SALES (est): 2.38MM **Privately Held**
Web: www.megaplastics.com
SIC: 3089 Plastics processing

(G-7227)
MODERN RETAIL SOLUTIONS LLC
10421 Industrial Dr (44231-9764)
PHONE..............................330 527-4308
▼ **EMP:** 24 **EST:** 1972
SQ FT: 100,000
SALES (est): 2.11MM **Privately Held**
Web: www.modern-retailsolutions.com
SIC: 2542 Partitions and fixtures, except wood

(G-7228)
THERM-O-LINK INC (PA)
10513 Freedom St (44231-9244)
PHONE..............................330 527-2124
Ronald M Krisher, *Ch Bd*
David Campbell, *
Thomas C B Letson, *
▲ **EMP:** 100 **EST:** 1978
SQ FT: 125,000
SALES (est): 23.71MM
SALES (corp-wide): 23.71MM **Privately Held**
Web: www.tolwire.com
SIC: 3357 3496 Nonferrous wiredrawing and insulating; Miscellaneous fabricated wire products

Gates Mills
Cuyahoga County

(G-7229)
ASSOCIATED PRESS REPAIR INC
7547 Brigham Rd (44040-9782)
PHONE..............................216 881-2288
Anthony Grbavac, *Pr*
Steve Grbavac, *VP*
EMP: 8 **EST:** 1985
SALES (est): 476.55K **Privately Held**
SIC: 3599 Machine shop, jobbing and repair

(G-7230)
LIMINAL ESPORTS LLC
Also Called: Liminal Data

1500 Chagrin River Rd Unit 361
(44040-7414)
PHONE..............................440 423-5856
James Collins, *CEO*
EMP: 8 **EST:** 2019
SALES (est): 294.93K **Privately Held**
SIC: 8732 7372 Research services, except
　laboratory; Educational computer software

Geneva
Ashtabula County

(G-7231)
ADRIA SCIENTIFIC GL WORKS CO
2683 State Route 534 S (44041)
P.O. Box 673 (44041-0673)
PHONE..............................440 474-6691
Milan Krmpotic, *Pr*
Brigitte Krmpotic, *Sec*
EMP: 6 **EST:** 1964
SQ FT: 18,000
SALES (est): 343.11K **Privately Held**
SIC: 3231 Products of purchased glass

(G-7232)
AITKEN PRODUCTS INC
Also Called: Aitken
566 N Eagle St (44041-1099)
P.O. Box 151 (44041-0151)
PHONE..............................440 466-5711
Suzanne Aitken Shannon, *Pr*
Louis J Doria, *Prin*
Thomas A Grabien, *Prin*
EMP: 8 **EST:** 1957
SQ FT: 50,000
SALES (est): 1.58MM **Privately Held**
Web: www.aitkenproducts.com
SIC: 3634 3433 Heating units, electric
　(radiant heat): baseboard or wall; Gas
　infrared heating units

(G-7233)
ARC RUBBER INC
100 Water St (44041-1192)
PHONE..............................440 466-4555
Robert Johnson Junior, *Pr*
Josephine Johnson, *Sec*
Robert Johnson Iii, *VP*
EMP: 10 **EST:** 1965
SQ FT: 20,000
SALES (est): 979.96K **Privately Held**
Web: www.arcrubber.com
SIC: 3069 3061 Molded rubber products;
　Mechanical rubber goods

(G-7234)
BENNETT MACHINE & STAMPING CO
150 D Termination Ave (44041-1173)
PHONE..............................440 415-0401
EMP: 25 **EST:** 1969
SALES (est): 6.2MM **Privately Held**
Web: www.bennettmachine.com
SIC: 3469 Stamping metal for the trade

(G-7235)
DWAYNE BENNETT INDUSTRIES
Also Called: Bennett Displays
6708 N Ridge Rd W (44041-7663)
PHONE..............................440 466-5724
Dwayne Bennett, *Owner*
EMP: 6 **EST:** 1991
SALES (est): 446.09K **Privately Held**
Web: www.bennettind.com
SIC: 2542 3441 Racks, merchandise display
　or storage: except wood; Fabricated
　structural metal

(G-7236)
**ELSTER PERFECTION
CORPORATION (DH)**
Also Called: Honeywell Smart Energy
436 N Eagle St (44041-1157)
PHONE..............................440 428-1171
Barry O'connell, *Pr*
Timothy Stevens, *
◆ **EMP:** 100 **EST:** 1944
SQ FT: 75,000
SALES (est): 24.86MM
SALES (corp-wide): 38.5B **Publicly Held**
Web: automation.honeywell.com
SIC: 3498 3089 3429 3312 Fabricated pipe
　and fittings; Fittings for pipe, plastics;
　Hardware, nec; Blast furnaces and steel
　mills
HQ: Elster American Meter Company, Llc
　855 S Mint St
　Charlotte NC 28202
　402 873-8200

(G-7237)
FERRANTE WINE FARM INC
5585 State Route 307 (44041)
PHONE..............................440 466-8466
Nicholas Ferrante, *Pr*
Nicholas Farrante, *Pr*
Mary Jo Ferrante, *Prin*
Peter Ferrante, *Prin*
Charles Rehor, *Prin*
EMP: 13 **EST:** 1979
SQ FT: 3,023
SALES (est): 1.05MM **Privately Held**
Web: www.ferrantewinery.com
SIC: 0172 2084 5812 Grapes; Wines; Eating
　places

(G-7238)
H & H ENGINEERED MOLDED PDTS
436 N Eagle St (44041-1157)
PHONE..............................440 415-1814
Barry O Connell, *Pr*
Roy Sutterfield, *
Tim Stevens, *
EMP: 125 **EST:** 1971
SQ FT: 26,000
SALES (est): 1.49MM
SALES (corp-wide): 38.5B **Publicly Held**
SIC: 3089 Injection molding of plastics
HQ: Elster Perfection Corporation
　436 N Eagle St
　Geneva OH 44041
　440 428-1171

(G-7239)
HDT EXPEDITIONARY SYSTEMS INC
5455 Route 307 West (44041)
PHONE..............................440 466-6640
James Maurer, *Pr*
EMP: 15
Web: www.hdtglobal.com
SIC: 3585 3564 3433 Air conditioning units,
　complete: domestic or industrial; Filters, air:
　furnaces, air conditioning equipment, etc.;
　Heating equipment, except electric
HQ: Hdt Expeditionary Systems, Inc.
　30500 Aurora Rd Ste 100
　Solon OH 44139
　216 438-6111

(G-7240)
HONEYWELL SMART ENERGY
Also Called: Elster Perfection
436 N Eagle St (44041-1157)
P.O. Box 10 (44057-0010)
PHONE..............................440 415-1606
Tony Pallotta, *Mgr*
EMP: 75
SALES (corp-wide): 38.5B **Publicly Held**
Web: automation.honeywell.com

SIC: 3498 Fabricated pipe and fittings
HQ: Elster Perfection Corporation
　436 N Eagle St
　Geneva OH 44041
　440 428-1171

(G-7241)
**LOUIS ARTHUR STEEL COMPANY
(PA)**
185 Water St (44041-1199)
P.O. Box 229 (44041-0229)
PHONE..............................440 997-5545
J Trombley Kanicki, *Pr*
J Matthew Kanicki, *Asst VP*
Sandra Kanicki, *VP*
James H Kanicki, *Stockholder*
J Barton Kanicki, *Stockholder*
EMP: 8 **EST:** 1949
SQ FT: 80,000
SALES (est): 4.59MM
SALES (corp-wide): 4.59MM **Privately
Held**
Web: www.arthurlouissteel.com
SIC: 3441 5051 3444 3443 Building
　components, structural steel; Steel; Sheet
　metalwork; Fabricated plate work (boiler
　shop)

(G-7242)
LOUIS ARTHUR STEEL COMPANY
Also Called: Arthur Louis Steel Co
200 North Ave E (44041-1166)
PHONE..............................440 997-5545
Andy Housel, *Genl Mgr*
EMP: 50
SALES (corp-wide): 4.59MM **Privately
Held**
Web: www.arthurlouissteel.com
SIC: 3441 Fabricated structural metal
PA: The Louis Arthur Steel Company
　185 Water St
　Geneva OH 44041
　440 997-5545

(G-7243)
**LYONDLLBSELL ADVNCED
PLYMERS I**
Also Called: A Schulman Compression
110 N Eagle St (44041-1107)
PHONE..............................440 224-7544
EMP: 56
Web: www.lyondellbasell.com
SIC: 2821 Plastics materials and resins
HQ: Lyondellbasell Advanced Polymers Inc.
　1221 Mckinney St Ste 300
　Houston TX 77010
　713 309-7200

(G-7244)
OLD FIREHOUSE WINERY INC
Also Called: Old Firehouse Cellars
5499 Lake Rd E (44041-9425)
P.O. Box 310 (44041-0310)
PHONE..............................440 466-9300
Joyce Otto, *Pr*
Dave Otto, *Sec*
Donald Woodward, *Treas*
EMP: 20 **EST:** 1988
SALES (est): 480.15K **Privately Held**
Web: www.oldfirehousewinery.com
SIC: 5921 5182 2084 Wine; Wine; Wines,
　brandy, and brandy spirits

(G-7245)
**PREMIX-HADLOCK COMPOSITES
LLC**
110 N Eagle St (44041-1107)
PHONE..............................440 335-4301
EMP: 81
SALES (corp-wide): 49.93MM **Privately
Held**

SIC: 3089 Injection molding of plastics
HQ: Premix-Hadlock Composites, Llc
　3365 E Center St
　Conneaut OH 44030
　440 335-4301

(G-7246)
TEGAM INC (HQ)
Also Called: Tegam
10 Tegam Way (44041-1144)
PHONE..............................440 466-6100
Andrew Brush, *Genl Mgr*
Adam Fleder, *
EMP: 43 **EST:** 1979
SQ FT: 28,600
SALES (est): 13.43MM
SALES (corp-wide): 1.48B **Publicly Held**
Web: www.tegam.com
SIC: 3829 7629 Measuring and controlling
　devices, nec; Electrical measuring
　instrument repair and calibration
PA: Advanced Energy Industries, Inc.
　1595 Wynkoop St Ste 800
　Denver CO 80202
　800 446-9167

Genoa
Ottawa County

(G-7247)
GRAYMONT DOLIME (OH) INC
21880 State Route 163 (43430-1679)
P.O. Box 158 (43430-0158)
PHONE..............................419 855-8682
Stephane Godin, *Prin*
Mike Brown, *
Kenneth J Lahti, *Prin*
J Graham Weir, *
Kenneth J Lahti, *CFO*
▼ **EMP:** 54 **EST:** 1998
SALES (est): 5.8MM
SALES (corp-wide): 51.97MM **Privately
Held**
Web: www.graymont.com
SIC: 3274 Lime
PA: Graymont, Inc.
　301 S 700 E # 3950
　Salt Lake City UT 84102
　801 262-3942

(G-7248)
JBI CORPORATION
22325 State Route 51 W (43430-1123)
PHONE..............................419 855-3389
John Badger, *Ch Bd*
Joseph Badger, *Pr*
Florence Badger, *Sec*
EMP: 10 **EST:** 1982
SQ FT: 7,500
SALES (est): 978.63K **Privately Held**
Web: www.jbicorp.com
SIC: 8711 3544 8734 Civil engineering; Jigs
　and fixtures; Testing laboratories

(G-7249)
RCR PARTNERSHIP
Also Called: Paul Blausey Farms
424 N Martin Williston Rd (43430-9786)
PHONE..............................419 340-1202
EMP: 6 **EST:** 2013
SALES (est): 986.24K **Privately Held**
SIC: 3443 Farm storage tanks, metal plate

(G-7250)
**RIVERSIDE MCH & AUTOMTN INC
(PA)**
Also Called: Riverside
1240 N Genoa Clay Center Rd
(43430-1206)

PHONE..............................419 855-8308
Gerald Giesler, *CEO*
Jerry Giesler, *
Lester Meyer, *
EMP: 60 **EST:** 1989
SQ FT: 30,000
SALES (est): 4.33MM **Privately Held**
Web: www.riverside-machine.com
SIC: 3599 3549 Machine shop, jobbing and repair; Metalworking machinery, nec

---

Georgetown
Brown County

(G-7251)
BROWN CNTY BD MNTAL RTARDATION
325 W State St Bldg A (45121-1229)
PHONE..............................937 378-4891
Theresa Armstrong, *Prin*
Lena Bradford, *
EMP: 8 **EST:** 1966
SQ FT: 100,000
SALES (est): 93.92K **Privately Held**
Web: www.browncbdd.org
SIC: 8331 3993 2396 Sheltered workshop; Signs and advertising specialties; Automotive and apparel trimmings

---

Germantown
Montgomery County

(G-7252)
POINT SOURCE INC
7996 N Butter St (45327-9484)
PHONE..............................937 855-6020
Steve Mersch, *Pr*
Joyce Mersch, *Sec*
EMP: 12 **EST:** 1992
SQ FT: 3,000
SALES (est): 866.72K **Privately Held**
Web: www.pointsource-inc.com
SIC: 8731 3827 Electronic research; Optical instruments and lenses

(G-7253)
PROJECT ENGINEERING COMPANY
9874 Eby Rd (45327-9776)
PHONE..............................937 743-9114
John L Michael, *Pr*
EMP: 6 **EST:** 2002
SALES (est): 650.18K **Privately Held**
Web: www.projectengineeringcompany.com
SIC: 3544 Special dies and tools

(G-7254)
SMYRNA READY MIX CONCRETE LLC
9151 Township Park Dr (45327-8711)
PHONE..............................937 855-0410
Hank Ernst, *Brnch Mgr*
EMP: 85
SALES (corp-wide): 513.05MM **Privately Held**
Web: www.smyrnareadymix.com
SIC: 5211 5032 3273 Cement; Concrete and cinder building products; Ready-mixed concrete
PA: Smyrna Ready Mix Concrete, Llc
1000 Hollingshead Cir
Murfreesboro TN 37129
615 355-1028

(G-7255)
THE DUPPS COMPANY (PA)
Also Called: Dupps
548 N Cherry St (45327-1185)

P.O. Box 189 (45327)
PHONE..............................937 855-6555
◆ **EMP:** 91 **EST:** 1950
SALES (est): 206.76K
SALES (corp-wide): 206.76K **Privately Held**
Web: www.dupps.com
SIC: 2077 Rendering

(G-7256)
THOMAS D EPPERSON
Also Called: Epco
7440 Weaver Rd (45327-9390)
P.O. Box 19 (45327-0019)
PHONE..............................937 855-3300
Thomas D Epperson, *Owner*
EMP: 7 **EST:** 1981
SQ FT: 2,104
SALES (est): 461.97K **Privately Held**
Web: www.epcostainless.com
SIC: 3751 Motorcycle accessories

(G-7257)
WILSON SIGN CO INC
Also Called: Wilson Electronic Displays
2623 Dayton Germantown Pike (45327-9625)
PHONE..............................937 253-2246
David Wilson, *Pr*
Lattie B Wilson, *Treas*
EMP: 11 **EST:** 1969
SALES (est): 460.44K **Privately Held**
Web: www.wilsonsigncompany.com
SIC: 3993 7629 Electric signs; Electrical equipment repair, high voltage

---

Gibsonburg
Sandusky County

(G-7258)
PROTECH PET LLC
3595 State Route 51 (43431-9746)
PHONE..............................419 552-4617
David Bryan, *Pr*
EMP: 16 **EST:** 2004
SALES (est): 3.51MM **Privately Held**
Web: www.protech-llc.com
SIC: 2821 Plastics materials and resins

(G-7259)
STANDARD WELLNESS COMPANY LLC
105 Commerce Dr (43431-1466)
PHONE..............................330 931-1037
Jared Maloof, *CEO*
Kyle Ciccarello, *
Emily Simmerly, *
EMP: 180 **EST:** 2017
SALES (est): 14.34MM **Privately Held**
Web: www.standardwellness.com
SIC: 2834 7389 Medicines, capsuled or ampuled; Business Activities at Non-Commercial Site

(G-7260)
TRI COUNTY TARP LLC (PA)
13100 Us Highway 23 (43431-9792)
P.O. Box 600 (43406-0600)
PHONE..............................419 288-3350
Gary L Harrison, *Managing Member*
EMP: 24 **EST:** 1977
SQ FT: 82,000
SALES (est): 4.05MM
SALES (corp-wide): 4.05MM **Privately Held**
Web: www.tritarp.com

SIC: 2394 2542 3354 Tarpaulins, fabric: made from purchased materials; Partitions for floor attachment, prefabricated: except wood; Aluminum extruded products

---

Gilboa
Putnam County

(G-7261)
HILLSIDE WINERY
221 Main St (45875-9757)
PHONE..............................419 456-3434
Lou Schaublin, *Prin*
EMP: 7 **EST:** 2008
SALES (est): 254.24K **Privately Held**
Web: www.thehillsidewinery.com
SIC: 2084 Wines

Girard
Trumbull County

(G-7262)
A J CONSTRUCTION CO
870 Shannon Rd (44420-2046)
PHONE..............................330 539-9544
Anthony Guerrieri, *Pr*
EMP: 6 **EST:** 1993
SALES (est): 489.98K **Privately Held**
SIC: 2541 Cabinets, except refrigerated: show, display, etc.: wood

(G-7263)
AIM SERVICES COMPANY
1500 Trumbull Ave (44420-3453)
PHONE..............................800 321-9038
EMP: 30 **EST:** 2017
SALES (est): 5.27MM **Privately Held**
Web: www.aimntls.com
SIC: 1389 Oil and gas field services, nec

(G-7264)
ALTRONIC LLC (DH)
712 Trumbull Ave (44420-3443)
PHONE..............................330 545-9768
Bruce R Beeghly, *Pr*
Joseph Lepley, *VP*
Alexander Steeb, *Prin*
Keith Brooks, *Prin*
David Bell, *Prin*
▲ **EMP:** 150 **EST:** 1955
SQ FT: 80,000
SALES (est): 49.53MM **Privately Held**
Web: www.altronic-llc.com
SIC: 3694 3823 3613 3625 Ignition systems, high frequency; Temperature instruments: industrial process type; Control panels, electric; Relays and industrial controls
HQ: Hoerbiger Holding Ag
Baarerstrasse 18
Zug ZG 6302

(G-7265)
AMEX DIES INC
932 N State St (44420-1796)
PHONE..............................330 545-9766
Ted Dudzik, *Pr*
Sam Bates, *Genl Mgr*
EMP: 17 **EST:** 1961
SQ FT: 6,000
SALES (est): 780K **Privately Held**
Web: www.amexdiesinc.com
SIC: 3544 Extrusion dies

(G-7266)
BARFECTIONS LLC (PA) ✪
1598 Motor Inn Dr (44420-2487)
PHONE..............................330 759-3100
EMP: 15 **EST:** 2023

SALES (est): 10.64MM
SALES (corp-wide): 10.64MM **Privately Held**
SIC: 2064 Candy bars, including chocolate covered bars

(G-7267)
BRAINARD RIVET COMPANY
222 Harry St (44420-1759)
P.O. Box 30 (44420-0030)
PHONE..............................330 545-4931
Clyde Faust, *CEO*
Linda Kerekes, *
EMP: 30 **EST:** 1997
SQ FT: 61,000
SALES (est): 10MM
SALES (corp-wide): 46.16MM **Privately Held**
Web: www.brainardrivet.com
SIC: 3452 Bolts, nuts, rivets, and washers
PA: Fastener Industries, Inc.
1 Berea Commons Ste 209
Berea OH 44017
440 243-0034

(G-7268)
CHECKERED EXPRESS INC
2501 W Liberty St (44420-3112)
PHONE..............................330 530-8169
Csaba Bujdoso, *Pr*
EMP: 15 **EST:** 2005
SALES (est): 1.61MM **Privately Held**
SIC: 2741 Miscellaneous publishing

(G-7269)
CRITICAL CTRL ENRGY SVCS INC
1688 Shannon Rd (44420-1121)
PHONE..............................330 539-4267
Bernie Vogel, *Mgr*
EMP: 12
SALES (corp-wide): 19.99MM **Privately Held**
Web: www.criticalcontrol.com
SIC: 1389 Gas field services, nec
HQ: Critical Control Energy Services, Inc.
8444 Water St
Stonewood WV 26301
304 623-0020

(G-7270)
FIRE FAB CORP
999 Trumbull Ave (44420-3448)
P.O. Box 128 (44410)
PHONE..............................330 759-9834
Ernie Nicholas, *Pr*
Mary Nicholas, *Sec*
Jamie Wilcox, *Acctnt*
EMP: 6 **EST:** 1987
SQ FT: 18,000
SALES (est): 1.02MM **Privately Held**
Web: www.firefoe.com
SIC: 3569 Sprinkler systems, fire: automatic

(G-7271)
FIRE FOE CORP
999 Trumbull Ave (44420-3448)
P.O. Box 128 (44410-0128)
PHONE..............................330 759-9834
Earnest A Nicholas, *Pr*
Mary Nicholas, *
EMP: 35 **EST:** 1978
SQ FT: 18,000
SALES (est): 4.22MM **Privately Held**
Web: www.firefoe.com
SIC: 3569 7699 Sprinkler systems, fire: automatic; Fire control (military) equipment repair

(G-7272)
GIRARD MACHINE COMPANY INC
700 Dot St (44420-1701)
P.O. Box 298 (44420-0298)
PHONE...............................330 545-9731
Carl Malito, *Pr*
Donald Malito, *
Robert Malito, *
EMP: 9 **EST:** 1946
SQ FT: 60,000
SALES (est): 817.63K **Privately Held**
Web: www.morganengineering.com
SIC: 3559 3599 Foundry, smelting, refining,
and similar machinery; Machine shop,
jobbing and repair

(G-7273)
KNIGHT LINE SIGNATURE AP CORP
16 W Liberty St (44420-2840)
PHONE...............................330 545-8108
Patrick K Rubinic, *Pr*
Michael P Rubinic, *VP*
Paul R Rubinic, *Sec*
EMP: 7 **EST:** 1994
SQ FT: 2,000
SALES (est): 502.4K **Privately Held**
Web:
knight-line-signature-apparel-oh-1.hub.biz
SIC: 2759 Screen printing

(G-7274)
LIBERTY IRON & METAL INC
27 Furnace Ln (44420-3214)
P.O. Box 29 (44420-0029)
PHONE...............................724 347-4534
David P Miller, *Ch Bd*
EMP: 30
SALES (corp-wide): 293.57K **Privately
Held**
SIC: 3312 Blast furnaces and steel mills
HQ: Liberty Iron & Metal, Inc.
2144 W Mcdowell Rd
Phoenix AZ 85009

(G-7275)
MARSH TECHNOLOGIES INC
30 W Main St Ste A (44420-2520)
PHONE...............................330 545-0085
Sandra G Marsh, *Pr*
EMP: 12 **EST:** 1985
SQ FT: 10,000
SALES (est): 537.14K **Privately Held**
Web: www.gopwarrencounty.com
SIC: 3544 Special dies, tools, jigs, and
fixtures

(G-7276)
**MORGAN ENGINEERING SYSTEMS
INC**
Also Called: Morgan Mfg Plant No 3
700 Dot St (44420-1701)
PHONE...............................330 545-9731
Mark Fedor, *CEO*
EMP: 32
SQ FT: 120,000
SALES (corp-wide): 24.45MM **Privately
Held**
Web: www.morganengineering.com
SIC: 3559 3599 Foundry, smelting, refining,
and similar machinery; Machine shop,
jobbing and repair
PA: Morgan Engineering Systems, Inc.
1049 S Mahoning Ave
Alliance OH 44601
330 823-6130

(G-7277)
NEW DAWN DISTRIBUTION INC
Also Called: New Dawn Designs
1282 Trumbull Ave Ste E (44420-3475)
PHONE...............................330 759-3500

Linda Barton, *Pr*
Linda Barton, *CEO*
Scott Barton, *VP*
EMP: 6 **EST:** 1998
SQ FT: 8,000
SALES (est): 956.57K **Privately Held**
Web: www.sweetvintagetees.com
SIC: 2759 5441 5699 Screen printing; Candy
; Shirts, custom made

(G-7278)
PETTIT W T & SONS CO INC
1670 Keefer Rd (44420-1434)
PHONE...............................330 539-6100
Francis Poe, *Pr*
Daniel De Genova, *VP*
EMP: 8 **EST:** 1946
SQ FT: 57,000
SALES (est): 889.61K **Privately Held**
Web: www.wtpettit.com
SIC: 3469 7389 Metal stampings, nec; Metal
slitting and shearing

(G-7279)
ROCKY HINGE INC
1660 Harding Ave (44420-1514)
PHONE...............................330 539-6296
Rocky Shamlin, *Owner*
EMP: 6 **EST:** 2006
SQ FT: 3,072
SALES (est): 237.43K **Privately Held**
Web: www.rockyhinge.com
SIC: 5251 3944 Hardware stores; Child
restraint seats, automotive

(G-7280)
SOFT TOUCH WOOD LLC
Also Called: Soft Tuch Furn Repr Rfinishing
1560 S State St (44420-3315)
PHONE...............................330 545-4204
Terry Chudakoff, *Pr*
Bob Leer, *
EMP: 40 **EST:** 2000
SQ FT: 5,000
SALES (est): 2.24MM **Privately Held**
Web: www.softtouchfurniture.com
SIC: 7641 2531 Furniture refinishing; Public
building and related furniture

(G-7281)
VALLOUREC STAR LP
706 S State St (44420-3204)
PHONE...............................330 742-6227
EMP: 144
SALES (corp-wide): 4.93MM **Privately
Held**
Web: www.vallourec.com
SIC: 3317 Steel pipe and tubes
HQ: Vallourec Star, Lp
2669 Mrtin Lther King Jr
Youngstown OH 44510
330 742-6300

(G-7282)
YOUNGSTOWN BURIAL VAULT CO
316 Forsythe Ave (44420-2205)
PHONE...............................330 782-0015
Charles Phillips, *Pr*
EMP: 9 **EST:** 1945
SALES (est): 289.52K **Privately Held**
SIC: 3272 Burial vaults, concrete or precast
terrazzo

Glandorf
Putnam County

(G-7283)
FIELD GYMMY INC
138-143 S Main St (45848)

P.O. Box 121 (45875-0121)
PHONE...............................419 538-6511
Melvin Nienberg, *VP*
Dennis Nienberg, *Pr*
Thomas Russell, *Sec*
EMP: 8 **EST:** 1974
SQ FT: 15,300
SALES (est): 212.43K **Privately Held**
SIC: 3523 3713 3563 3531 Farm machinery
and equipment; Truck and bus bodies; Air
and gas compressors; Construction
machinery

Glenmont
Holmes County

(G-7284)
BRIAR HILL STONE CO INC
12470 State Route 520 (44628-9702)
P.O. Box 398 (44628-0398)
PHONE...............................216 377-5100
Toby Rosen, *Trst*
Bill W Alde, *
Eugene G Rosenthal, *
EMP: 60 **EST:** 1906
SQ FT: 4,000
SALES (est): 429.79K **Privately Held**
Web: www.briarhillstone.com
SIC: 3281 Stone, quarrying and processing
of own stone products

Glenwillow
Cuyahoga County

(G-7285)
**CUSTOM PRODUCTS
CORPORATION (PA)**
7100 Cochran Rd (44139-4306)
PHONE...............................440 528-7100
Timothy Stepanek, *Pr*
John Stepanek, *VP*
William Stepanek Junior, *VP*
▲ **EMP:** 77 **EST:** 1974
SQ FT: 82,000
SALES (est): 11.43MM
SALES (corp-wide): 11.43MM **Privately
Held**
Web: www.customproducts.net
SIC: 7389 5131 5199 2761 Packaging and
labeling services; Labels; Packaging
materials; Manifold business forms

(G-7286)
NOCO COMPANY (PA)
Also Called: Noco
30339 Diamond Pkwy Ste 102
(44139-5473)
PHONE...............................216 464-8131
William Nook Senior, *CEO*
Jonathan Nook, *
◆ **EMP:** 71 **EST:** 1914
SQ FT: 100,000
SALES (est): 24.19MM
SALES (corp-wide): 24.19MM **Privately
Held**
Web: www.no.co
SIC: 2899 5063 5072 3714 Chemical
preparations, nec; Wire and cable; Power
tools and accessories; Booster (jump-start)
cables, automotive

(G-7287)
NORTHSTAR PLASTICS INC
27200 Tinkers Ct (44139-4387)
PHONE...............................216 340-7109
Michael Lerner, *CEO*
EMP: 100 **EST:** 1994
SQ FT: 40,000

SALES (est): 623.05K **Privately Held**
Web: www.plastics-plus.com
SIC: 3089 3421 Injection molding of plastics;
Cutlery

(G-7288)
RIZE HOME LLC (PA)
Also Called: Mantua Bed Frames
31050 Diamond Pkwy (44139-5478)
PHONE...............................800 333-8333
David Jaffe, *CEO*
Edward Weintraub, *
Marc Spector, *
◆ **EMP:** 75 **EST:** 1954
SQ FT: 67,500
SALES (est): 49.2MM
SALES (corp-wide): 49.2MM **Privately
Held**
Web: www.rizehome.com
SIC: 5021 2514 Bedsprings; Frames for box
springs or bedsprings: metal

(G-7289)
STRIDE TOOL LLC
30333 Emerald Valley Pkwy (44139-4394)
P.O. Box 2019 (30096)
PHONE...............................440 247-4600
Ron Ortiz, *CEO*
EMP: 150 **EST:** 2016
SALES (est): 11.75MM
SALES (corp-wide): 529.99MM **Privately
Held**
Web: www.stridetool.com
SIC: 3423 Hand and edge tools, nec
PA: Diversitech Corporation
3039 Prmiere Pkwy Ste 600
Duluth GA 30097
678 542-3600

Glouster
Athens County

(G-7290)
FROG RANCH FOODS LTD
5 S High St (45732-1051)
PHONE...............................740 767-3705
Craig Cornett, *Pr*
Kristi Hewitt, *CFO*
EMP: 10 **EST:** 1994
SQ FT: 10,000
SALES (est): 1.03MM **Privately Held**
Web: www.frogranch.com
SIC: 2099 Food preparations, nec

Gnadenhutten
Tuscarawas County

(G-7291)
MILLWOOD LUMBER INC
Also Called: Millwood Logging
2400 Larson Rd Se (44629-9500)
P.O. Box 871 (44629-0871)
PHONE...............................740 254-4681
Jeffery Miller, *Pr*
EMP: 22 **EST:** 1985
SALES (est): 4.6MM **Privately Held**
Web: www.millwoodlumberinc.com
SIC: 2421 Sawmills and planing mills,
general

(G-7292)
PLYMOUTH FOAM LLC
1 Southern Gateway Dr (44629-5030)
P.O. Box 177 (44629-0177)
PHONE...............................740 254-1188
Chris Coleman, *Mgr*
EMP: 72
Web: www.plymouthfoam.com

▲ = Import ▼ = Export
◆ = Import/Export

SIC: 3069 Medical and laboratory rubber sundries and related products
HQ: Plymouth Foam Llc
1800 Sunset Dr
Plymouth WI 53073
800 669-1176

(G-7293)
STOCKER CONCRETE COMPANY
7574 Us Hwy 36 Se (44629)
P.O. Box 176 (44629-0176)
PHONE..........................740 254-4626
Thomas Stocker, *Pr*
Bryan Stocker, *VP*
Jeffrey Stocker, *Sec*
William Stocker, *Stockholder*
EMP: 15 **EST:** 1933
SQ FT: 15,000
SALES (est): 1.8MM
SALES (corp-wide): 5.21MM **Privately Held**
Web: www.stockerconcrete.com
SIC: 3273 5032 5211 3271 Ready-mixed concrete; Concrete building products; Masonry materials and supplies; Concrete block and brick
PA: Stocker Sand & Gravel Co.
Rr 36
Gnadenhutten OH 44629
740 254-4635

(G-7294)
STOCKER SAND & GRAVEL CO (PA)
Rte 36 (44629)
P.O. Box 176 (44629-0176)
PHONE..........................740 254-4635
Bill Stocker, *Pr*
Jeffrey Stocker, *Pr*
Bryan Stocker, *VP*
Thomas Stocker, *Sec*
EMP: 12 **EST:** 1933
SQ FT: 3,000
SALES (est): 5.21MM
SALES (corp-wide): 5.21MM **Privately Held**
Web: www.stockerconcrete.com
SIC: 1442 3271 Common sand mining; Blocks, concrete or cinder: standard

(G-7295)
TUSCO LIMITED PARTNERSHIP
Also Called: Tusco Display
239 S Chestnut St (44629-5005)
P.O. Box 175 (44629-0175)
PHONE..........................740 254-4343
EMP: 102 **EST:** 1949
SALES (est): 9.96MM **Privately Held**
Web: www.tuscomfg.com
SIC: 3993 2542 2541 Displays and cutouts, window and lobby; Partitions and fixtures, except wood; Wood partitions and fixtures

Goshen
Clermont County

(G-7296)
DANDY PRODUCTS INC (PA)
3314 State Route 131 (45122-8511)
PHONE..........................513 625-3000
Daniel R Reed, *Pr*
Colleen Reed, *VP*
EMP: 6 **EST:** 1989
SQ FT: 15,000
SALES (est): 893.37K **Privately Held**
Web: www.dandyproducts.net
SIC: 3069 Floor coverings, rubber

(G-7297)
LAB QUALITY MACHINING INC
6311 Roudebush Rd (45122-9571)
PHONE..........................513 625-0219
Linda A Brath, *Prin*
James Brath, *Pr*
EMP: 6 **EST:** 1985
SQ FT: 5,200
SALES (est): 604.21K **Privately Held**
Web: www.labqualitymachininginc.com
SIC: 3599 Machine shop, jobbing and repair

(G-7298)
TRIUMPHANT ENTERPRISES INC
7096 Hill Station Rd (45122-9728)
PHONE..........................513 617-1668
Richard G Hughes Senior, *Pr*
Jewell A Hughes, *VP*
EMP: 8 **EST:** 1993
SALES (est): 1.79MM **Privately Held**
SIC: 3537 Trucks: freight, baggage, etc.: industrial, except mining

Grafton
Lorain County

(G-7299)
BANKS MANUFACTURING COMPANY
40259 Banks Rd (44044-9750)
PHONE..........................440 458-8661
Tim Boyd, *Pr*
Sheila Boyd, *VP*
EMP: 10 **EST:** 1948
SQ FT: 10,000
SALES (est): 828.76K **Privately Held**
Web: www.banksmfgco.com
SIC: 1799 1721 3441 Sandblasting of building exteriors; Industrial painting; Fabricated structural metal

(G-7300)
CUSTOMCHROME PLATING INC
Also Called: Custom Chrome Plating
963 Mechanic St (44044-1416)
PHONE..........................440 926-3116
Jon E Wright, *Pr*
EMP: 15 **EST:** 1968
SQ FT: 12,500
SALES (est): 798.09K **Privately Held**
Web: www.customchromeplating.com
SIC: 3471 Electroplating of metals or formed products

(G-7301)
EATON FABRICATING COMPANY INC
1009 Mcalpin Ct (44044-1322)
PHONE..........................440 926-3121
Ray D Roach Junior, *Pr*
Lloyd H Roach Senior, *Prin*
▲ **EMP:** 50 **EST:** 1963
SQ FT: 40,600
SALES (est): 4.67MM **Privately Held**
Web: www.eatonfab.com
SIC: 3599 3444 3443 Machine shop, jobbing and repair; Sheet metalwork; Fabricated plate work (boiler shop)

(G-7302)
GENERAL PLUG AND MFG CO (PA)
455 Main St (44044-1257)
P.O. Box P.O. Box 26 (44044-0026)
PHONE..........................440 926-2411
Kevin J Flanigan, *Pr*
▲ **EMP:** 125 **EST:** 1955
SQ FT: 70,000
SALES (est): 22.33MM
SALES (corp-wide): 22.33MM **Privately Held**
Web: www.generalplug.com

SIC: 3494 3599 3643 Pipe fittings; Machine shop, jobbing and repair; Current-carrying wiring services

(G-7303)
GRAFTON READY MIX CONCRET INC
1155 Elm St (44044-1303)
P.O. Box 823 (44052-0823)
PHONE..........................440 926-2911
Jeffrey Riddell, *Pr*
EMP: 120 **EST:** 1987
SQ FT: 15,000
SALES (est): 828.67K **Privately Held**
SIC: 3273 5032 5211 Ready-mixed concrete; Brick, stone, and related material; Masonry materials and supplies
PA: Consumeracq, Inc.
2509 N Ridge Rd E
Lorain OH 44055

(G-7304)
INSPYRE HEALTH SYSTEMS LLC
1004 Commerce Dr (44044-1273)
PHONE..........................440 412-7916
EMP: 8 **EST:** 2017
SALES (est): 4.68MM **Privately Held**
Web: www.inspyrehs.com
SIC: 3841 Surgical and medical instruments

(G-7305)
VILLAGE OF GRAFTON
Also Called: Fire Department
1013 Chestnut St (44044-1406)
PHONE..........................440 926-2075
Randy Kimbro, *Chief*
EMP: 15
Web: www.villageofgrafton.org
SIC: 3711 Snow plows (motor vehicles), assembly of
PA: Village Of Grafton
960 N Main St
Grafton OH 44044

(G-7306)
WILLIS CNC
1008 Commerce Dr (44044-1275)
PHONE..........................440 926-0434
EMP: 7 **EST:** 2015
SALES (est): 3.92MM **Privately Held**
Web: www.williscnc.com
SIC: 3599 Machine shop, jobbing and repair

Grand Rapids
Wood County

(G-7307)
A+ ENGINEERING FABRICATION INC
17562 Beech St (43522-9728)
P.O. Box 470 (43522-0470)
PHONE..........................419 832-0748
David Arno, *Pr*
Linda Arno, *VP*
EMP: 15 **EST:** 1989
SQ FT: 23,500
SALES (est): 2.58MM **Privately Held**
Web: www.aplusengineering.com
SIC: 3441 3599 8711 Fabricated structural metal; Machine shop, jobbing and repair; Engineering services

(G-7308)
Q S I FABRICATION INC
10333 S River Rd (43522-9350)
PHONE..........................419 832-1680
Tom Zitzelberger, *Pr*
EMP: 7 **EST:** 1998
SQ FT: 400
SALES (est): 728.07K **Privately Held**
Web: www.qsifab.com

SIC: 3441 Fabricated structural metal

(G-7309)
SAYLOR PRODUCTS CORPORATION
17484 Saylor Ln (43522-9792)
PHONE..........................419 832-2125
Douglas Mueller, *CEO*
EMP: 10 **EST:** 1902
SQ FT: 550
SALES (est): 2.51MM **Privately Held**
Web: www.saylorproducts.com
SIC: 3644 Electric conduits and fittings
HQ: Saylor Technical Products, Llc
17484 Saylor Ln
Grand Rapids OH 43522
419 832-2125

Grand River
Lake County

(G-7310)
JED INDUSTRIES INC
320 River St (44045-8214)
P.O. Box 369 (44045-0369)
PHONE..........................440 639-9973
Donald Nye, *Pr*
EMP: 11 **EST:** 1995
SQ FT: 27,000
SALES (est): 2.09MM **Privately Held**
Web: www.jedindustries.com
SIC: 3599 5084 Machine shop, jobbing and repair; Industrial machinery and equipment

(G-7311)
KONGSBERG ACTATION SYSTEMS LLC
Also Called: Kongsberg Automotive
301 Olive St (44045-8221)
P.O. Box 98 (44045-0098)
PHONE..........................440 639-8778
Martin White, *Managing Member*
EMP: 25 **EST:** 2008
SALES (est): 16.78MM **Privately Held**
Web: www.kongsbergautomotive.com
SIC: 3714 Motor vehicle parts and accessories
PA: Kongsberg Automotive Asa
Dyrmyrgata 48
Kongsberg 3611

(G-7312)
SUMITOMO ELC CARBIDE MFG INC (DH)
210 River St (44045-8249)
P.O. Box 188 (44045-0188)
PHONE..........................440 354-0600
Yasuhisa Hashimoto, *Pr*
Takahiro Kimura, *Sec*
EMP: 10 **EST:** 1973
SQ FT: 25,000
SALES (est): 2.5MM **Privately Held**
Web: www.sumicarbide.com
SIC: 3541 3546 3545 3423 Machine tools, metal cutting type; Power-driven handtools; Machine tool accessories; Hand and edge tools, nec
HQ: Sumitomo Electric Carbide Inc
1001 E Business Center Dr
Mount Prospect IL 60056
847 635-0044

Granville
Licking County

(G-7313)
ACUITY BRANDS LIGHTING INC
American Electric Lighting
3825 Columbus Rd Bldg A (43023-8604)

PHONE..................................800 754-0463
EMP: 121
SALES (corp-wide): 3.84B **Publicly Held**
Web: lithonia.acuitybrands.com
SIC: 3646 Commercial lighting fixtures
HQ: Acuity Brands Lighting, Inc.
    1170 Pchtree St Ne Ste 23
    Atlanta GA 30309

(G-7314)
ERATH VENEER CORP VIRGINIA
Also Called: Erath Veneer
2825 Hallie Ln # B (43023-9256)
P.O. Box 507 (24151-0507)
PHONE..................................540 483-5223
Michael G Erath, *Ch*
Michael G Erath, *Pr*
Rbobert C Moore, *Sec*
◆ **EMP:** 7 **EST:** 1952
SALES (est): 1.11MM **Privately Held**
SIC: 2435 Veneer stock, hardwood

(G-7315)
HARVEST COMMISSARY LLC
3825 Columbus Rd Bldg J (43023-8614)
PHONE..................................513 706-1951
EMP: 23
SALES (corp-wide): 1.27MM **Privately Held**
SIC: 2099 2051 Food preparations, nec;
    Bread, cake, and related products
PA: Harvest Commissary Llc
    3579 Raccoon Valley Rd
    Granville OH 43023
    513 706-1951

(G-7316)
HOLOPHANE CORPORATION (HQ)
Also Called: Holophane
3825 Columbus Rd Bldg A (43023-8604)
PHONE..................................866 759-1577
Vernon J Nagel, *CEO*
◆ **EMP:** 116 **EST:** 1989
SALES (est): 21.49MM
SALES (corp-wide): 3.84B **Publicly Held**
Web: holophane.acuitybrands.com
SIC: 3646 3648 Commercial lighting fixtures;
    Outdoor lighting equipment
PA: Acuity Inc.
    1170 Pchtree St Ne Ste 12
    Atlanta GA 30309
    404 853-1400

(G-7317)
MERITOR INC
Also Called: Arvinmrtor Commerical Vhcl Sys
4009 Columbus Rd Unit 111 (43023-8613)
PHONE..................................740 348-3270
Mike Deep, *Mgr*
EMP: 154
SALES (corp-wide): 34.1B **Publicly Held**
Web: www.meritor.com
SIC: 3714 3713 Axles, motor vehicle; Truck
    and bus bodies
HQ: Meritor, Inc.
    2135 W Maple Rd
    Troy MI 48084

(G-7318)
MKFOUR INC
108 Hawks Cove Ct (43023-9031)
PHONE..................................620 629-1120
EMP: 6 **EST:** 2018
SALES (est): 497.97K **Privately Held**
SIC: 2911 Petroleum refining

(G-7319)
NUANCE COMPANY
17 Amanda Dr (43023-9190)
PHONE..................................740 964-0367
Scot Burdette, *Prin*

EMP: 6 **EST:** 2014
SALES (est): 444.86K **Privately Held**
Web: www.nuance.com
SIC: 7372 Prepackaged software

(G-7320)
REED GOWDEY COMPANY
Also Called: Gowdey Reed
101 Glenshire Dr (43023-3400)
PHONE..................................401 723-6114
James H Wilson, *Prin*
▲ **EMP:** 7 **EST:** 1834
SALES (est): 562.89K **Privately Held**
Web: www.gowdeyreed.com
SIC: 3552 Reeds, loom

Gratis
Preble County

(G-7321)
TOLSON PALLET MFG INC
10240 State Rte 122 (45330)
P.O. Box 151 (45330-0151)
PHONE..................................937 787-3511
Keith Tolson, *Pr*
Brent Tolson, *VP*
EMP: 10 **EST:** 1969
SQ FT: 30,000
SALES (est): 328.25K **Privately Held**
SIC: 2448 Pallets, wood

Graysville
Washington County

(G-7322)
WHITACRE ENTERPRISES INC
35651 State Route 537 (45734-7002)
PHONE..................................740 934-2331
Koy Whitacre, *Pr*
EMP: 7 **EST:** 1900
SQ FT: 7,000
SALES (est): 283.38K **Privately Held**
Web: www.whitacrestore.com
SIC: 5411 1382 Convenience stores,
    independent; Oil and gas exploration
    services

Green
Summit County

(G-7323)
MODERN DESIGNS INC
310 Killian Rd (44232)
P.O. Box 247 (44232-0247)
PHONE..................................330 644-1771
Gregg Boyd, *Pr*
EMP: 9 **EST:** 1985
SALES (est): 186.06K **Privately Held**
Web: www.moderndesignsinc.com
SIC: 2434 Wood kitchen cabinets

Greenfield
Highland County

(G-7324)
ADIENT US LLC
1147 N Washington St (45123-9782)
PHONE..................................937 981-2176
Joe Jones, *Prd Mgr*
EMP: 133
SQ FT: 65,000
Web: www.adient.com
SIC: 3714 Motor vehicle parts and
    accessories
HQ: Adient Us Llc

49200 Halyard Dr
Plymouth MI 48170
734 254-5000

(G-7325)
AMERICAN MADE CRRGTED PCKG INC
Also Called: A M C P
1100 N 5th St (45123)
P.O. Box 186 (45123-0186)
PHONE..................................937 981-2111
Arden Fife, *Pr*
Pat Mc Allister, *Sec*
EMP: 7 **EST:** 1987
SQ FT: 21,000
SALES (est): 1.18MM **Privately Held**
SIC: 2653 5113 Boxes, corrugated: made
    from purchased materials; Corrugated and
    solid fiber boxes

(G-7326)
CORVAC COMPOSITES LLC
1025 N Washington St (45123-9780)
PHONE..................................248 807-0969
James Fitzell, *CEO*
EMP: 78
SALES (corp-wide): 126.15MM **Privately Held**
Web: www.corvaccomposites.com
SIC: 3089 Thermoformed finished plastics
    products, nec
HQ: Corvac Composites, Llc
    4450 36th St Se
    Kentwood MI 49512

(G-7327)
GMI COMPANIES INC
Woodware Furniture
512 S Washington St (45123-1645)
PHONE..................................937 981-0244
George L Leasure, *Pr*
EMP: 17
SALES (corp-wide): 41MM **Privately Held**
Web: www.ghent.com
SIC: 2531 2493 2599 2541 Blackboards,
    wood; Bulletin boards, cork; Boards:
    planning, display, notice; Showcases,
    except refrigerated: wood
PA: Gmi Companies, Inc.
    2999 Henkle Dr
    Lebanon OH 45036
    513 932-3445

(G-7328)
GMI COMPANIES INC
Also Called: Waddell A Div GMI Companies
512 S Washington St (45123-1645)
P.O. Box 18 (45123-0018)
PHONE..................................937 981-7724
Tom Septer, *Mgr*
EMP: 18
SALES (corp-wide): 41MM **Privately Held**
Web: www.ghent.com
SIC: 2541 Showcases, except refrigerated:
    wood
PA: Gmi Companies, Inc.
    2999 Henkle Dr
    Lebanon OH 45036
    513 932-3445

(G-7329)
GREENFIELD PRECISION PLAS LLC
175 Industrial Park Dr (45123-9000)
PHONE..................................937 803-0328
Thomas Karns, *VP*
EMP: 10 **EST:** 2018
SALES (est): 2.19MM **Privately Held**
Web:
www.greenfieldprecisionplastics.com
SIC: 3089 Injection molding of plastics

(G-7330)
GREENFIELD RESEARCH INC (PA)
347 Edgewood Ave (45123-1149)
P.O. Box 239 (45123-0239)
PHONE..................................937 981-7763
Michael Penn, *Pr*
Robert Snider, *
▼ **EMP:** 150 **EST:** 1966
SQ FT: 60,000
SALES (est): 22.67MM
SALES (corp-wide): 22.67MM **Privately Held**
Web: www.greenfield-research.com
SIC: 2396 Screen printing on fabric articles

(G-7331)
SKYLINE MATERIAL SALES LLC
Also Called: Alloy Manufacturing
12325 Pommert Rd (45123-9275)
PHONE..................................937 981-5505
EMP: 9 **EST:** 2016
SALES (est): 2.68MM **Privately Held**
Web: www.skylinematerial.com
SIC: 3444 Metal roofing and roof drainage
    equipment

Greentown
Stark County

(G-7332)
CANRON MANUFACTURING INC
3979 State Street N W (44630)
P.O. Box 356 (44630-0356)
PHONE..................................330 497-1131
John Kettering, *Pr*
Heidi Michel, *VP*
EMP: 10 **EST:** 1981
SQ FT: 15,000
SALES (est): 863.31K **Privately Held**
Web: www.canronmfg.com
SIC: 3496 Miscellaneous fabricated wire
    products

Greenville
Darke County

(G-7333)
ALL ABOUT PLASTICS LLC
5339 State Route 571 (45331-9606)
PHONE..................................937 547-0098
EMP: 8 **EST:** 2003
SQ FT: 25,000
SALES (est): 406.28K **Privately Held**
SIC: 3089 Injection molding of plastics

(G-7334)
ANDERSONS MRATHON HOLDINGS LLC
5728 Sebring Warner Rd N (45331-9800)
PHONE..................................937 316-3700
EMP: 40
SALES (corp-wide): 11.26B **Publicly Held**
Web: www.andersonsinc.com
SIC: 2869 Ethyl alcohol, ethanol
HQ: The Andersons Marathon Holdings Llc
    1947 Briarfield Blvd
    Maumee OH 43537
    419 893-5050

(G-7335)
AVIENT CORPORATION
Also Called: Polyone
1050 Landsdowne Ave (45331-8382)
PHONE..................................800 727-4338
John Dimino, *Manager*
EMP: 30
Web: www.avient.com

SIC: 2821 Plastics materials and resins
PA: Avient Corporation
33587 Walker Rd
Avon Lake OH 44012

(G-7336)
BRIDGESTONE RET OPERATIONS LLC
Also Called: Firestone
425 Walnut St (45331-1920)
PHONE..............................937 548-1197
Mark Lacey, *Mgr*
EMP: 6
Web: www.bridgestoneamericas.com
SIC: 5531 7534 Automotive tires; Rebuilding and retreading tires
HQ: Bridgestone Retail Operations, Llc
200 4th Ave S Ste 100
Nashville TN 37201
615 937-1000

(G-7337)
CALMEGO SPECIALIZED PDTS LLC
1569 Martindale Rd (45331-9696)
PHONE..............................937 669-5620
EMP: 10 EST: 2011
SALES (est): 1.7MM Privately Held
Web:
www.calmegospecializedproducts.com
SIC: 3366 Copper foundries

(G-7338)
CLASSIC REPRODUCTIONS
5315 Meeker Rd (45331-9751)
P.O. Box 916 (45331-0916)
PHONE..............................937 548-9839
Thomas Jeffers, *Owner*
EMP: 8 EST: 1984
SQ FT: 48,000
SALES (est): 632.25K Privately Held
SIC: 3714 Motor vehicle body components and frame

(G-7339)
COMMERCIAL PRTG GREENVILLE INC
Also Called: Commercial Printing Co
314 S Broadway St (45331-1905)
PHONE..............................937 548-3835
Jeff Campbell, *Owner*
Joan Brante, *Prin*
Marian Campbell, *Sec*
EMP: 8 EST: 1923
SQ FT: 2,200
SALES (est): 482.71K Privately Held
SIC: 2752 Offset printing

(G-7340)
D A FITZGERALD CO INC
1045 Sater St (45331-1638)
P.O. Box 206 (45331-0206)
PHONE..............................937 548-0511
Don S Fitzgerald, *Pr*
Janice Fitzgerald, *Sec*
Scott Fitzgerald, *Sec*
EMP: 9 EST: 1967
SQ FT: 10,000
SALES (est): 721.48K Privately Held
Web: www.dafitzgerald.com
SIC: 3544 Special dies and tools

(G-7341)
FOUREMANS SAND & GRAVEL INC
2791 Wildcat Rd (45331-9453)
PHONE..............................937 547-1005
Gary B Foureman, *Pr*
Susan Foureman, *Sec*
John Foureman, *VP*
EMP: 6 EST: 1953
SQ FT: 14,000
SALES (est): 425.85K Privately Held

Web: www.fouremansgravel.com
SIC: 1442 1794 Gravel mining; Excavation and grading, building construction

(G-7342)
G S K INC
915 Front St (45331-1606)
P.O. Box 358 (45331-0358)
PHONE..............................937 547-1611
Jack Besecker, *CEO*
Chris Besecker, *Pr*
Patricia Besecker, *Sec*
EMP: 9 EST: 1977
SQ FT: 6,600
SALES (est): 2.21MM Privately Held
SIC: 3089 2631 7389 Molding primary plastics; Paperboard mills; Packaging and labeling services

(G-7343)
JAFE DECORATING INC
1250 Martin St (45331-1870)
PHONE..............................937 547-1888
Randy O'dell, *Pr*
EMP: 120 EST: 1978
SQ FT: 36,000
SALES (est): 9.38MM Privately Held
Web: www.jafedecorating.com
SIC: 3231 Decorated glassware: chipped, engraved, etched, etc.

(G-7344)
JRB INDUSTRIES LLC
3425 State Route 571 (45331-3247)
PHONE..............................567 825-7022
EMP: 25 EST: 2017
SALES (est): 314.83K Privately Held
SIC: 3999 Atomizers, toiletry

(G-7345)
KITCHENAID INC
1700 Kitchen Aid Way (45331-8331)
PHONE..............................937 316-4782
EMP: 11 EST: 2017
SALES (est): 1.58MM Privately Held
SIC: 3633 Household laundry equipment

(G-7346)
KNITTING MACHINERY CO AMER LLC
607 Riffle Ave (45331-1612)
P.O. Box 902 (45331-0902)
PHONE..............................937 548-2338
Chester Rice, *Mgr*
EMP: 10
SALES (corp-wide): 150.2MM Publicly Held
Web: www.knittingmachinerycorp.com
SIC: 3552 Knitting machines
HQ: Knitting Machinery Company Of America Llc
15625 Saranac Rd
Cleveland OH 44110
216 851-9900

(G-7347)
MONSANTO COMPANY
Also Called: Monsanto
1051 Landsdowne Ave (45331-8381)
PHONE..............................937 548-7858
Jim Larkin, *Mgr*
EMP: 10
SALES (corp-wide): 49.29B Privately Held
Web: www.monsanto.com
SIC: 2879 Agricultural chemicals, nec
HQ: Monsanto Technology Llc.
800 North Lindbergh Blvd
Saint Louis MO 63167
314 694-1000

(G-7348)
NEFF MOTIVATION INC (DH)
645 Pine St (45331-1624)
P.O. Box 218 (45331-0218)
PHONE..............................937 548-3194
◆ EMP: 125 EST: 1902
SALES (est): 4.38MM
SALES (corp-wide): 7.58B Publicly Held
Web: www.neffco.com
SIC: 2399 3999 2329 2395 Emblems, badges, and insignia: from purchased materials; Plaques, picture, laminated; Jackets (suede, leatherette, etc.), sport: men's and boys'; Embroidery and art needlework
HQ: Visant Corporation
3601 Minnesota Dr Ste 400
Minneapolis MN 55435
914 595-8200

(G-7349)
PFI USA
5963 Jaysville Saint Johns Rd (45331-9398)
PHONE..............................937 547-0413
Albert Wiebe, *Prin*
EMP: 15 EST: 2014
SALES (est): 5.42MM Privately Held
SIC: 3499 Automobile seat frames, metal

(G-7350)
RAMCO ELECTRIC MOTORS INC
5763 Jaysville Saint Johns Rd (45331-9678)
PHONE..............................937 548-2525
Dave Dunaway, *Pr*
Louis R Dunaway, ***
EMP: 85 EST: 1986
SQ FT: 30,000
SALES (est): 24MM Publicly Held
Web: www.ramcoelectricmotors.com
SIC: 3621 3625 3363 Motors, electric; Relays and industrial controls; Aluminum die-castings
HQ: Arnold Magnetic Technologies Corporation
770 Linden Ave
Rochester NY 14625
585 385-9010

(G-7351)
REBSCO INC
4362 Us Route 36 (45331-9754)
P.O. Box 370 (45331-0370)
PHONE..............................937 548-2246
Tyeis L Baker-baumann, *Pr*
EMP: 15 EST: 1965
SQ FT: 23,000
SALES (est): 1.74MM Privately Held
Web: www.rebsco.com
SIC: 1542 2431 3448 3443 Commercial and office building, new construction; Millwork; Prefabricated metal buildings and components; Tanks, standard or custom fabricated: metal plate

(G-7352)
RUSSELL L GARBER (PA)
Also Called: Garber Farms
4891 Clark Station Rd (45331-9562)
PHONE..............................937 548-6224
Russell L Garber, *Owner*
EMP: 6 EST: 1954
SALES (est): 1.69MM
SALES (corp-wide): 1.69MM Privately Held
SIC: 2448 0161 Pallets, wood; Melon farms

(G-7353)
SPARTECH LLC
1050 Landsdowne Ave (45331-8382)
PHONE..............................937 548-1395
Julie A Mcalindon, *Mgr*
EMP: 235
SALES (corp-wide): 344.31MM Privately Held
Web: www.spartech.com
SIC: 3081 3089 Unsupported plastics film and sheet; Plastics containers, except foam
PA: Spartech Llc
11650 Lkeside Crossing Ct
Saint Louis MO 63146
314 569-7400

(G-7354)
SPECIALIZED CASTINGS LTD
1569 Martindale Rd (45331-9696)
PHONE..............................937 669-5620
▼ EMP: 15 EST: 2003
SQ FT: 50,000
SALES (est): 2.23MM Privately Held
Web: www.spcastings.com
SIC: 3365 Aluminum and aluminum-based alloy castings

(G-7355)
ST HENRY TILE CO INC
Also Called: Wayne Builders Supply
5410 S State Route 49 (45331-1032)
PHONE..............................937 548-1101
Mike Homan, *Mgr*
EMP: 9
SALES (corp-wide): 8.27MM Privately Held
Web: www.sthenrytileco.com
SIC: 3271 5211 3272 Blocks, concrete or cinder: standard; Masonry materials and supplies; Concrete products, precast, nec
PA: The St Henry Tile Co Inc
281 W Washington St
Saint Henry OH 45883
419 678-4841

(G-7356)
STATELINE POWER CORP
Also Called: Southast Diesl Acquisition Sub
650 Pine St (45331-1625)
PHONE..............................937 547-1006
Tom Tracy Iii, *Pr*
EMP: 15 EST: 1978
SQ FT: 45,000
SALES (est): 7.23MM Privately Held
Web: www.statelinepower.com
SIC: 3569 3621 Gas producers, generators, and other gas related equipment; Motors and generators
HQ: Tradewinds Power Corp.
5820 Nw 84th Ave
Doral FL 33166

(G-7357)
TDB ASSOCIATES INC
1014 Front St (45331-1609)
PHONE..............................937 459-5730
Jason Snyder, *CEO*
EMP: 13 EST: 2001
SALES (est): 2.1MM Privately Held
SIC: 3353 8742 Aluminum sheet and strip; Management consulting services

(G-7358)
TREATY CITY INDUSTRIES INC
Also Called: T C I
945 Sater St (45331-1636)
P.O. Box 39 (45331-0039)
PHONE..............................937 548-9000
Mike Jones, *Pr*
Sherri Jones, *Treas*
EMP: 19 EST: 1988

SQ FT: 40,000
SALES (est): 2.41MM **Privately Held**
Web: www.wavebaseball.net
SIC: 3053 3469 Gaskets; packing and
  sealing devices; Metal stampings, nec

(G-7359)
WHIRLPOOL CORPORATION
Whirlpool
1701 Kitchen Aid Way (45331-8331)
PHONE.............................937 548-4126
Eric Joiner, *Brnch Mgr*
EMP: 95
SALES (corp-wide): 16.61B **Publicly Held**
Web: www.whirlpool.com
SIC: 3634 Electric household cooking
  appliances
PA: Whirlpool Corporation
  2000 N M-63
  Benton Harbor MI 49022
  269 923-5000

(G-7360)
WOLF G T AWNING & TENT CO
3352 State Route 571 (45331-3229)
P.O. Box 248 (45331-0248)
PHONE.............................937 548-4161
Susan Miles, *Pr*
Maurie Miles, *VP*
EMP: 10 EST: 1896
SALES (est): 222.79K **Privately Held**
SIC: 7359 2394 Tent and tarpaulin rental;
  Canvas and related products

Greenwich
Huron County

(G-7361)
F SQUARED INC
9 Sunset Dr (44837-1020)
PHONE.............................419 752-7273
William Shipman, *Pr*
Patricia Shipman, *Sec*
EMP: 6 EST: 1981
SALES (est): 437.52K **Privately Held**
SIC: 3825 Electrical power measuring
  equipment

(G-7362)
JOHNSON BROS RUBBER CO INC
Also Called: Johnson Bros Greenwich
41 Center St (44837-1049)
PHONE.............................419 752-4814
Ken Bostic, *Mgr*
EMP: 30
SALES (corp-wide): 9.56MM **Privately
Held**
Web:
www.johnsonbrosrubbercompany.com
SIC: 5199 3743 3634 3545 Foams and
  rubber; Railroad equipment; Electric
  housewares and fans; Machine tool
  accessories
PA: Johnson Bros. Rubber Co.
  42 W Buckeye St
  West Salem OH 44287
  419 853-4122

(G-7363)
LAKEPARK INDUSTRIES INC
Also Called: Midway Products Group
40 Seminary St (44837-1040)
PHONE.............................419 752-4471
James Hoyt, *Pr*
Lloyd A Miller, *
EMP: 150 EST: 1985
SQ FT: 60,000
SALES (est): 21.85MM **Privately Held**
Web: www.midwayproducts.com

SIC: 3469 3465 Stamping metal for the trade
  ; Automotive stampings
PA: Midway Products Group, Inc.
  One Lyman E Hoyt Dr
  Monroe MI 48161

(G-7364)
**RICHLAND LAMINATED COLUMNS
LLC**
8252 State Route 13 (44837-9638)
PHONE.............................419 895-0036
EMP: 10 EST: 2004
SQ FT: 40,000
SALES (est): 3.64MM **Privately Held**
SIC: 2439 Arches, laminated lumber

Grove City
Franklin County

(G-7365)
3359 KINGSTON LLC
1111 London Groveport Rd (43123-9708)
PHONE.............................614 871-8989
James Rauck, *Prin*
EMP: 6 EST: 2007
SALES (est): 317.16K **Privately Held**
SIC: 2273 Carpets and rugs

(G-7366)
ADVANCE APEX INC (PA)
Also Called: Advance Cnc Machining
2375 Harrisburg Pike (43123-1057)
PHONE.............................614 539-3000
Jeremy J Hamilton, *Pr*
▲ EMP: 30 EST: 1987
SQ FT: 40,000
SALES (est): 5.35MM
SALES (corp-wide): 5.35MM **Privately
Held**
Web: www.advancecnc.com
SIC: 3599 Machine shop, jobbing and repair

(G-7367)
ADVANCE INDUSTRIAL MFG INC
1996 Longwood Ave (43123-1218)
P.O. Box 1296 (43123-6296)
PHONE.............................614 871-3333
James Wintzer, *Pr*
James Wintzer, *Pr*
Cynthia T Wintzer, *
Doctor Christopher Wintzer, *Dir*
Gus Wintzer, *
EMP: 49 EST: 1993
SQ FT: 35,000
SALES (est): 4.94MM **Privately Held**
Web: www.advanceind.com
SIC: 3441 3443 3449 Fabricated structural
  metal; Fabricated plate work (boiler shop);
  Miscellaneous metalwork

(G-7368)
AFG INDUSTRIES INC
Also Called: AGC Automotive Americas
4000 Gantz Rd Ste A (43123-4844)
PHONE.............................614 322-4580
▲ EMP: 66
SIC: 7549 1793 1799 3231 Automotive
  customizing services, nonfactory basis;
  Glass and glazing work; Glass tinting,
  architectural or automotive; Products of
  purchased glass

(G-7369)
AIM ATTACHMENTS
1720 Feddern Ave (43123-1206)
PHONE.............................614 539-3030
Dennis Hamilton, *Owner*
▼ EMP: 6 EST: 2008
SALES (est): 864.48K **Privately Held**

Web: www.aimattachments.com
SIC: 3531 Construction machinery
  attachments

(G-7370)
ALL PACK SERVICES LLC
3442 Grant Ave (43123-2513)
PHONE.............................614 935-0964
EMP: 9 EST: 2013
SALES (est): 972.03K **Privately Held**
Web: www.ieccentraloh.org
SIC: 7349 3613 Building maintenance
  services, nec; Time switches, electrical
  switchgear apparatus

(G-7371)
**AMERICAN NTRILE OPERATIONS
LLC**
Also Called: American Nitrile
3500 Southwest Blvd (43123-2244)
PHONE.............................614 425-5211
EMP: 8 EST: 2021
SALES (est): 725.62K **Privately Held**
Web: www.americannitrile.com
SIC: 3069 Medical and laboratory rubber
  sundries and related products

(G-7372)
**AMERICAS MDULAR OFF
SPECIALIST**
4423 Broadway Ste A (43123-3078)
PHONE.............................614 277-0216
Ronald Mills, *Pr*
EMP: 7 EST: 1996
SALES (est): 534.96K **Privately Held**
Web: www.americasmodular.com
SIC: 2522 5712 Office furniture, except wood
  ; Office furniture

(G-7373)
AMIR INTERNATIONAL FOODS INC
3504 Broadway (43123-1941)
PHONE.............................614 332-1742
Basel Said, *Prin*
EMP: 6 EST: 2011
SALES (est): 77.03K **Privately Held**
SIC: 2099 Food preparations, nec

(G-7374)
BOEHM INC (PA)
Also Called: Mammoth Labels & Packaging
2050 Hardy Parkway St (43123-1214)
PHONE.............................614 875-9010
Stuart Reeve, *Pr*
Michael Hutchison, *
Jonda Lacy, *
EMP: 30 EST: 1954
SQ FT: 12,000
SALES (est): 6.61MM
SALES (corp-wide): 6.61MM **Privately
Held**
Web: www.boehminc.com
SIC: 2672 2759 Labels (unprinted),
  gummed: made from purchased materials;
  Decals: printing, nsk

(G-7375)
BUCK EQUIPMENT INC
1720 Feddern Ave (43123-1206)
PHONE.............................614 539-3039
Dennis Hamilton, *CEO*
◆ EMP: 35 EST: 1934
SQ FT: 60,000
SALES (est): 5.61MM **Privately Held**
Web: www.buckequipment.com
SIC: 3531 3743 3441 5088 Logging
  equipment; Railroad equipment; Fabricated
  structural metal; Railroad equipment and
  supplies

(G-7376)
CARE INDUSTRIES
6137 Enterprise Pkwy (43123-9539)
PHONE.............................614 584-6595
Jarrod Simmons, *Prin*
EMP: 6 EST: 2016
SALES (est): 129.27K **Privately Held**
SIC: 1389 Construction, repair, and
  dismantling services

(G-7377)
CONCORD FABRICATORS INC
6511 Seeds Rd (43123-8431)
PHONE.............................614 875-2500
Gary Hammel, *Pr*
Chuck Purdom, *VP*
EMP: 23 EST: 1988
SQ FT: 21,500
SALES (est): 5.41MM **Privately Held**
Web: www.concordfab.com
SIC: 1791 3441 Structural steel erection;
  Fabricated structural metal

(G-7378)
CROWN EQUIPMENT CORPORATION
Also Called: Crown Lift Trucks
2100 Southwest Blvd (43123-1898)
PHONE.............................614 274-7700
Rusty Edwards, *Mgr*
EMP: 71
SALES (corp-wide): 7.12B **Privately Held**
Web: www.crown.com
SIC: 3537 Lift trucks, industrial: fork,
  platform, straddle, etc.
PA: Crown Equipment Corporation
  44 S Washington St
  New Bremen OH 45869
  419 629-2311

(G-7379)
CUMMINS INC
2297 Southwest Blvd Ste K (43123-1822)
P.O. Box 291989 (37229-1989)
PHONE.............................614 604-6004
Tammy Fawley, *Brnch Mgr*
EMP: 14
SALES (corp-wide): 34.1B **Publicly Held**
Web: www.cummins.com
SIC: 3519 3714 3694 3621 Internal
  combustion engines, nec; Motor vehicle
  parts and accessories; Engine electrical
  equipment; Generator sets: gasoline,
  diesel, or dual-fuel
PA: Cummins Inc.
  500 Jackson St
  Columbus IN 47201
  812 377-5000

(G-7380)
**CUSTOM INFORMATION SYSTEMS
INC**
Also Called: Clientrax Software
3347 Mcdowell Rd (43123-2907)
PHONE.............................614 875-2245
Michael Mantkowski, *Pr*
John Cantu, *VP*
EMP: 10 EST: 1987
SALES (est): 577.83K **Privately Held**
SIC: 7372 7389 Business oriented computer
  software; Business Activities at Non-
  Commercial Site

(G-7381)
DEERFIELD VENTURES INC
Also Called: Ink Well
2224 Stringtown Rd (43123-3926)
P.O. Box 305 (43123-0305)
PHONE.............................614 875-0688
David Keil, *Pr*
Anna Keil, *Sec*
EMP: 8 EST: 1982

▲ = Import ▼ = Export
◆ = Import/Export

SQ FT: 3,000
SALES (est): 995.28K **Privately Held**
Web: www.gcofficesupply.com
SIC: 2752 Offset printing

(G-7382)
DYNAMP LLC
Also Called: Dynamp
3735 Gantz Rd Ste D (43123-4849)
PHONE..........................614 871-6900
▲ EMP: 27 EST: 2003
SQ FT: 16,000
SALES (est): 5.97MM **Privately Held**
Web: www.dynamp.com
SIC: 3825 Current measuring equipment, nec

(G-7383)
EDGE ADHESIVES INC
3709 Grove City Rd (43123-3020)
PHONE..........................614 875-6343
Darren Ourth, Pr
Paul Strickler, Prin
John Thomas, Prin
Scott Hauncher, Prin
Andrew Wiegand, Prin
▲ EMP: 45 EST: 2010
SALES (est): 4.52MM **Privately Held**
Web: www.edgeadhesives.com
SIC: 2891 Adhesives

(G-7384)
EJ USA INC
1855 Feddern Ave (43123-1207)
PHONE..........................614 871-2436
Brian Hall, Mgr
EMP: 6
Web: www.ejco.com
SIC: 3321 Manhole covers, metal
HQ: Ej Usa, Inc.
301 Spring St
East Jordan MI 49727
800 874-4100

(G-7385)
ELECTR-GNRAL PLAS CORP CLUMBUS
6200 Enterprise Pkwy (43123-9286)
PHONE..........................614 871-2915
Patrick A Castro Senior, Pr
Patrick A Castro Junior, VP
EMP: 8 EST: 1961
SQ FT: 36,400
SALES (est): 4.69MM **Privately Held**
Web: www.electro-generalplastics.com
SIC: 3089 Injection molding of plastics

(G-7386)
FABCON COMPANIES LLC
3400 Jackson Pike (43123-8993)
PHONE..........................614 875-8601
Michael Lejeune, CEO
EMP: 100
SQ FT: 40,000
Web: www.fabconprecast.com
SIC: 3272 Prestressed concrete products
PA: Fabcon Companies, Llc
6111 Hwy 13 W
Savage MN 55378

(G-7387)
FORGE BIOLOGICS INC
3900 Gantz Rd (43123-4834)
PHONE..........................216 401-7611
Timothy J Miller, Pr
EMP: 7 EST: 2020
SALES (est): 14.31MM **Privately Held**
Web: www.forgebiologics.com
SIC: 2836 Biological products, except diagnostic
HQ: Ajinomoto North America Holdings, Inc.
7124 N Marine Dr

Portland OR 97203
503 505-5783

(G-7388)
GATEKEEPER PRESS LLC
2167 Stringtown Rd Ste 109 (43123-2989)
PHONE..........................866 535-0913
EMP: 11 EST: 2019
SALES (est): 155.81K **Privately Held**
Web: www.gatekeeperpress.com
SIC: 2741 Miscellaneous publishing

(G-7389)
HALCORE GROUP INC (HQ)
Also Called: Horton Emergency Vehicles
3800 Mcdowell Rd (43123-4022)
PHONE..........................614 539-8181
John Slawson, Pr
▼ EMP: 192 EST: 1997
SQ FT: 110,000
SALES (est): 82.98MM **Publicly Held**
Web: www.hortonambulance.com
SIC: 3711 Motor vehicles and car bodies
PA: Rev Group, Inc.
245 S Exec Dr Ste 100
Brookfield WI 53005

(G-7390)
HAYDEN VALLEY FOODS INC (PA)
Also Called: Tropical Nut & Fruit
3150 Urbancrest Industrial Dr (43123-1767)
PHONE..........................614 539-7233
▲ EMP: 50 EST: 1984
SALES (est): 22.9MM **Privately Held**
Web: www.haydenvalleyfoods.com
SIC: 5149 2068 2064 2034 Fruits, dried;
Salted and roasted nuts and seeds; Candy
and other confectionery products; Dried
and dehydrated fruits, vegetables and soup
mixes

(G-7391)
INSTANTWHIP-COLUMBUS INC (HQ)
3855 Marlane Dr (43123-9224)
P.O. Box 249 (43123-0249)
PHONE..........................614 871-9447
Douglas A Smith, Pr
Vinson Lewis, *
Tom G Michaelides, *
G Fredrick Smith, *
EMP: 32 EST: 1936
SQ FT: 10,300
SALES (est): 6.32MM
SALES (corp-wide): 47.03MM **Privately Held**
Web: www.instantwhip.com
SIC: 2026 5143 2023 8741 Whipped
topping, except frozen or dry mix; Dairy
products, except dried or canned; Dietary
supplements, dairy and non-dairy based;
Management services
PA: Instantwhip Foods, Inc.
2200 Cardigan Ave
Columbus OH 43215
614 488-2536

(G-7392)
INTERCO DIVISION 10 OHIO INC
3600 Brookham Dr Ste D (43123-4851)
PHONE..........................614 875-2959
EMP: 9 EST: 2018
SALES (est): 386.74K **Privately Held**
Web: www.inter-co.com
SIC: 2844 Perfumes, cosmetics and other
toilet preparations

(G-7393)
KIRK WILLIAMS COMPANY INC
2734 Home Rd (43123-1701)
PHONE..........................614 875-9023
James K Williams Junior, Pr

James K Williams Iii, Sec
EMP: 80 EST: 1949
SQ FT: 40,000
SALES (est): 17.52MM **Privately Held**
Web: www.kirkwilliamsco.com
SIC: 1711 3564 3444 Mechanical contractor;
Blowers and fans; Sheet metalwork

(G-7394)
LIBERTY TIRE RECYCLING LLC
Also Called: LIBERTY TIRE RECYCLING, LLC
3041 Jackson Pike (43123-9737)
PHONE..........................614 871-8097
Ed Kincaid, Brnch Mgr
EMP: 26
SALES (corp-wide): 494.57MM **Privately Held**
Web: www.libertytire.com
SIC: 7534 Tire retreading and repair shops
HQ: Liberty Tire Services, Llc
600 River Ave 3rd Fl
Pittsburgh PA 15212
412 562-1700

(G-7395)
LOGITECH INC
6423 Seeds Rd (43123-9524)
PHONE..........................614 871-2822
Kirk Wallace, Pr
David W Ritchie Iii, VP
▲ EMP: 20 EST: 1990
SQ FT: 32,400
SALES (est): 4.39MM **Privately Held**
Web: www.logitechconveyor.com
SIC: 3535 5084 Conveyors and conveying
equipment; Conveyor systems

(G-7396)
MAGIC DRAGON MACHINE INC
3451 Grant Ave (43123-2512)
PHONE..........................614 539-8004
Richard Burket, Pr
EMP: 6 EST: 1993
SQ FT: 4,000
SALES (est): 789.29K **Privately Held**
SIC: 3711 Automobile assembly, including
specialty automobiles

(G-7397)
MARNE PLASTICS LLC
3655 Brookham Dr Ste F (43123-4932)
PHONE..........................614 732-4666
EMP: 11 EST: 2013
SALES (est): 4.02MM **Privately Held**
Web: www.marneplastics.com
SIC: 3089 Injection molded finished plastics
products, nec

(G-7398)
MEGALIFT LLC
Also Called: Megalift
2087 Hendrix Dr (43123-1216)
PHONE..........................614 696-9086
Charles Lang, Managing Member
EMP: 7 EST: 2020
SALES (est): 1.11MM **Privately Held**
SIC: 3993 Signs and advertising specialties

(G-7399)
MESSER LLC
1699 Feddern Ave (43123-1205)
PHONE..........................614 539-2259
Judy Rogers, Mgr
EMP: 7
SALES (corp-wide): 2.29B **Privately Held**
Web: www.messeramericas.com
SIC: 2813 Industrial gases
HQ: Messer Llc
200 Smrset Corp Blvd Ste
Bridgewater NJ 08807
800 755-9277

(G-7400)
MID-OHIO SCREEN PRINT INC
4163 Kelnor Dr (43123-2960)
PHONE..........................614 875-1774
Mike Haughn, Pr
Steven Haughn, VP
EMP: 6 EST: 1977
SQ FT: 18,000
SALES (est): 239.42K **Privately Held**
SIC: 2759 Screen printing

(G-7401)
MIDWEST METAL PRODUCTS LLC
3945 Brookham Dr (43123-9741)
PHONE..........................614 539-7322
FAX: 614 539-7319
EMP: 25 EST: 1999
SALES (est): 2.58MM **Privately Held**
SIC: 3444 Sheet metalwork

(G-7402)
MOHAWK INDUSTRIES INC
3565 Urbancrest Industrial Dr (43123-1766)
PHONE..........................800 837-3812
Gary Miller, Brnch Mgr
EMP: 25
Web: www.mohawkind.com
SIC: 2273 3253 Finishers of tufted carpets
and rugs; Ceramic wall and floor tile
PA: Mohawk Industries, Inc.
160 S Industrial Blvd
Calhoun GA 30701

(G-7403)
MURRAY DISPLAY FIXTURES LTD
2300 Southwest Blvd (43123-4829)
PHONE..........................614 875-1594
Todd Murray, CEO
Kim Ellen Murray, Treas
Glenn Murray, VP
Jonathan Murray, VP
EMP: 12 EST: 2006
SQ FT: 11,000
SALES (est): 2.97MM **Privately Held**
Web: www.mdfltd.com
SIC: 2541 1751 Display fixtures, wood;
Cabinet building and installation

(G-7404)
NATIONAL WLDG TANKER REPR LLC
Also Called: National Welding
2036 Hendrix Dr (43123-1215)
PHONE..........................614 875-3399
Bryan Baker, Pr
EMP: 9 EST: 2014
SALES (est): 650.08K **Privately Held**
Web: www.nationalweld.com
SIC: 7692 7699 7389 9621 Welding repair;
Tank repair and cleaning services;
Inspection and testing services; Licensing,
inspection: transportation facilities, services

(G-7405)
NEW SABINA INDUSTRIES INC
3650 Brookham Dr Ste A (43123-4929)
PHONE..........................937 584-2433
Ken Ferrell, Brnch Mgr
EMP: 6
Web: www.nippon-seiki.co.jp
SIC: 3714 Instrument board assemblies,
motor vehicle
HQ: New Sabina Industries, Inc.
12555 Us Hwy 22 And 3
Sabina OH 45169
937 584-2433

(G-7406)
OROURKE SALES COMPANY
3319 Southwest Blvd (43123-2237)

GEOGRAPHIC

PHONE...................877 599-6548
Jeff O'rourke, *Pr*
Jake O'rourke, *COO*
EMP: 11 **EST:** 2018
SALES (est): 1.22MM **Privately Held**
Web: www.orourkesales.com
SIC: 3634 Electric household cooking
appliances

(G-7407)
OWENS CORNING SALES LLC
Also Called: Owens Corning
3750 Brookham Dr Ste K (43123-4850)
PHONE...................614 539-0830
Anne Depaaew, *Mgr*
EMP: 23
Web: www.owenscorning.com
SIC: 3296 Fiberglass insulation
HQ: Owens Corning Sales, Llc
1 Owens Corning Pkwy
Toledo OH 43659
419 248-8000

(G-7408)
PRECISE CUSTOM MILLWORK INC
6145 Enterprise Pkwy (43123-9539)
P.O. Box 1083 (43123-6083)
PHONE...................614 539-7855
Charles Caudill, *Pr*
EMP: 8 **EST:** 2001
SQ FT: 6,000
SALES (est): 231.44K **Privately Held**
SIC: 2431 Millwork

(G-7409)
PRESTRESS SERVICES INDS LLC (PA)
3400 Southwest Blvd (43123-2242)
P.O. Box 55436 (40555-5436)
PHONE...................859 299-0461
Martin Cohen, *Managing Member*
EMP: 250 **EST:** 2003
SALES (est): 44.31MM
SALES (corp-wide): 44.31MM **Privately Held**
Web: www.prestressservices.com
SIC: 3272 Concrete products, nec

(G-7410)
PVM INCORPORATED
3515 Grove City Rd (43123-3054)
PHONE...................614 871-0302
Gary Curry, *Pr*
EMP: 8 **EST:** 1985
SQ FT: 10,000
SALES (est): 802.71K **Privately Held**
SIC: 3599 Machine shop, jobbing and repair

(G-7411)
RICHARDSON SUPPLY LTD
2080 Hardy Parkway St (43123-1214)
PHONE...................614 539-3033
Sharon Fisher, *CEO*
Jeffrey W Richardson, *Pr*
EMP: 6 **EST:** 1968
SALES (est): 2.03MM **Privately Held**
Web: www.richardsonsupply.com
SIC: 2759 Screen printing

(G-7412)
RUBEX INC
Also Called: Edge Adhesives-Oh
3709 Grove City Rd (43123-3020)
PHONE...................614 875-6343
Dave Burger, *CEO*
▼ **EMP:** 9 **EST:** 2005
SALES (est): 8.21MM
SALES (corp-wide): 10.81MM **Privately Held**
Web: www.rubex-us.com
SIC: 2891 Adhesives

PA: Edge Adhesives Holdings, Inc.
5117 Northeast Pkwy
Fort Worth TX 76106
817 232-2026

(G-7413)
SHELLY MATERIALS INC
3300 Jackson Pike (43123-8875)
PHONE...................614 871-6704
Craig Ferguson, *Brnch Mgr*
EMP: 27
SALES (corp-wide): 34.95B **Privately Held**
Web: www.shellyco.com
SIC: 3273 Ready-mixed concrete
HQ: Shelly Materials, Inc.
80 Park Dr
Thornville OH 43076
740 246-6315

(G-7414)
SOUND COMMUNICATIONS INC
3474 Park St (43123-2530)
P.O. Box 1148 (43123-6148)
PHONE...................614 875-8500
Darin Cooper, *CEO*
Garry Stephenson, *
Toni Vanhorn, *
Darin Cooper, *Sec*
EMP: 25 **EST:** 1983
SQ FT: 6,000
SALES (est): 4.93MM **Privately Held**
Web: www.soundcommunications.com
SIC: 3669 7382 7338 Intercommunication systems, electric; Security systems services ; Secretarial and court reporting

(G-7415)
TAYLOR COMMUNICATIONS INC
3545 Urbancrest Industrial Dr (43123-1766)
PHONE...................937 221-3347
Wesley Thompson, *Mgr*
EMP: 13
SALES (corp-wide): 3.81B **Privately Held**
Web: www.taylor.com
SIC: 2761 Manifold business forms
HQ: Taylor Communications, Inc.
1725 Roe Crest Dr
North Mankato MN 56003
866 541-0937

(G-7416)
TIGERPOLY MANUFACTURING INC
6231 Enterprise Pkwy (43123-9271)
PHONE...................614 871-0045
Seiji Shiga, *Pr*
Michael S Crane, *
Yasuhiko Tomita, *
Reina Mito, *
▲ **EMP:** 350 **EST:** 1987
SQ FT: 196,000
SALES (est): 48.32MM **Privately Held**
Web: www.tigerpoly.com
SIC: 3089 3714 3621 3061 Blow molded finished plastics products, nec; Motor vehicle parts and accessories; Motors and generators; Mechanical rubber goods
PA: Tigers Polymer Corporation
1-4-1, Shinsenrihigashimachi
Toyonaka OSK 560-0

(G-7417)
TOSOH AMERICA INC (HQ)
3600 Gantz Rd (43123-1895)
PHONE...................614 539-8622
Jan Top, *Pr*
◆ **EMP:** 350 **EST:** 1989
SQ FT: 250,000
SALES (est): 482.13MM **Privately Held**
Web: www.tosohamerica.com

SIC: 5169 3564 5047 5052 Industrial chemicals; Blowers and fans; Diagnostic equipment, medical; Coal and other minerals and ores
PA: Tosoh Corporation
2-2-1, Yaesu
Chuo-Ku TKY 104-0

(G-7418)
TOSOH SMD INC (DH)
3600 Gantz Rd (43123-1895)
PHONE...................614 875-7912
Marten Blazic, *Pr*
▲ **EMP:** 92 **EST:** 1975
SQ FT: 250,000
SALES (est): 39.48MM **Privately Held**
Web: www.tosohsmd.com
SIC: 3674 Semiconductors and related devices
HQ: Tosoh America, Inc.
3600 Gantz Rd
Grove City OH 43123

(G-7419)
TRIMTEC SYSTEMS LTD
2455 Harrisburg Pike (43123-1453)
PHONE...................614 820-0340
EMP: 18
Web: www.trimtecfoam.com
SIC: 2431 Ornamental woodwork: cornices, mantels, etc.

(G-7420)
TURN-KEY INDUSTRIAL SVCS LLC
4512 Harrisburg Pike (43123-8940)
PHONE...................614 274-1128
Gregory Less, *Managing Member*
EMP: 52 **EST:** 2017
SALES (est): 4.38MM **Privately Held**
Web: www.turn-keyind.com
SIC: 7692 3441 Automotive welding; Building components, structural steel

(G-7421)
VANDAVA INC
Also Called: Mob Apparel
4094 Broadway (43123-3025)
PHONE...................614 277-8003
William Chaffin, *Pr*
EMP: 8 **EST:** 2014
SALES (est): 263.3K **Privately Held**
SIC: 5999 2396 Miscellaneous retail stores, nec; Screen printing on fabric articles

---

Groveport
Franklin County

(G-7422)
AMSTED INDUSTRIES INCORPORATED
Griffin Wheel
3900 Bixby Rd (43125-9510)
PHONE...................614 836-2323
Joe Cuske, *Manager*
EMP: 55
SALES (corp-wide): 3.96B **Privately Held**
Web: www.amsted.com
SIC: 3321 5088 3743 3714 Railroad car wheels and brake shoes, cast iron; Railroad equipment and supplies; Railroad equipment; Motor vehicle parts and accessories
PA: Amsted Industries Incorporated
111 S Wacker Dr Ste 4400
Chicago IL 60606
312 645-1700

(G-7423)
AVT TECHNOLOGY SOLUTIONS LLC
5350 Centerpoint Pkwy (43125-2501)
PHONE...................727 539-7429
Robert M Dutkowsky, *CEO*
EMP: 11 **EST:** 2016
SALES (est): 9.72MM
SALES (corp-wide): 58.45B **Publicly Held**
SIC: 7372 Prepackaged software
HQ: Tech Data Corporation
5350 Tech Data Dr
Clearwater FL 33760
727 539-7429

(G-7424)
BECTON DICKINSON AND COMPANY
Also Called: Carefusion
2727 London Groveport Rd (43125-9304)
PHONE...................858 617-4272
EMP: 9 **EST:** 2016
SALES (est): 1.71MM **Privately Held**
Web: www.bd.com
SIC: 3841 Surgical and medical instruments

(G-7425)
BENCHMARK EDUCATION CO LLC
6295 Commerce Center Dr Ste B (43125-1137)
PHONE...................845 215-9808
Tom Reycraft, *Pr*
EMP: 205
SALES (corp-wide): 44.92MM **Privately Held**
Web: www.benchmarkeducation.com
SIC: 2731 Book publishing
PA: Benchmark Education Company Llc
145 Huguenot St Fl 8
New Rochelle NY 10801
914 637-7200

(G-7426)
BOLTTECH MANNINGS LLC
351 Lowery Ct Ste 3 (43125-9344)
PHONE...................614 836-0021
EMP: 6
SALES (corp-wide): 47.5MM **Privately Held**
Web: www.bolttechmannings.com
SIC: 3398 Metal heat treating
PA: Bolttech Mannings Llc
103 Equity Dr
Greensburg PA 15601
724 872-4873

(G-7427)
C & R INC (PA)
5600 Clyde Moore Dr (43125-1081)
PHONE...................614 497-1130
Ronald E Murphy, *Pr*
Phillip Lee Mc Kitrick, *
Christina M Murphy, *
EMP: 47 **EST:** 1972
SALES (est): 4.03MM
SALES (corp-wide): 4.03MM **Privately Held**
Web: www.crproducts.com
SIC: 3444 7692 3443 3312 Sheet metal specialties, not stamped; Welding repair; Fabricated plate work (boiler shop); Blast furnaces and steel mills

(G-7428)
CAREISMATIC BRANDS LLC
6625 Port Rd (43125-9101)
PHONE...................561 843-8727
EMP: 8
SALES (corp-wide): 490.12MM **Privately Held**
Web: www.careismatic.com

▲ = Import ▼ = Export
◆ = Import/Export

SIC: 3143 3144 5139 Men's footwear, except athletic; Women's footwear, except athletic; Shoes
HQ: Careismatic Brands, Llc
15301 Ventura Blvd
Sherman Oaks CA 91403

(G-7429)
CAREISMATIC BRANDS LLC
6755 Port Rd (43125-9102)
PHONE................................614 497-5289
EMP: 6
SALES (corp-wide): 490.12MM Privately Held
Web: www.strategicpartners.net
SIC: 3143 3144 5139 2339 Men's footwear, except athletic; Women's footwear, except athletic; Shoes; Women's and misses' outerwear, nec
HQ: Careismatic Brands, Llc
15301 Ventura Blvd
Sherman Oaks CA 91403

(G-7430)
CREATIVE TOOL & DIE LLC
244 Main St (43125-1124)
PHONE................................614 836-0080
James Newman Junior, Pt
Anita Raisley, Pt
EMP: 6 EST: 1992
SQ FT: 2,600
SALES (est): 2.2MM Privately Held
Web: www.creativetooldie.com
SIC: 3599 Machine shop, jobbing and repair

(G-7431)
EVOQUA WATER TECHNOLOGIES LLC
6300 Commerce Center Dr (43125-1183)
PHONE................................614 491-5917
Jim Campbell, Mgr
EMP: 11
Web: www.evoqua.com
SIC: 3589 7699 Water purification equipment, household type; Cleaning services
HQ: Evoqua Water Technologies Llc
210 6th Ave Ste 3300
Pittsburgh PA 15222
724 772-0044

(G-7432)
FLOOD HELIARC INC
Also Called: Flood Heliarc
4181 Venture Pl (43125-9207)
P.O. Box 237 (43125-0237)
PHONE................................614 835-3929
Robert Flood, Pr
Suzanne Flood, Sec
EMP: 10 EST: 1984
SQ FT: 7,000
SALES (est): 2.85MM Privately Held
Web: www.floodheliarc.com
SIC: 3444 3613 3469 Sheet metal specialties, not stamped; Switchgear and switchboard apparatus; Metal stampings, nec

(G-7433)
FLUVITEX USA INC
6510 Pontius Rd (43125-7505)
PHONE................................614 610-1199
Jaume Burgell, CEO
EMP: 118 EST: 2016
SQ FT: 123,588
SALES (est): 17.13MM Privately Held
Web: www.fluvitexusa.com
SIC: 2392 Blankets, comforters and beddings
HQ: Count Indo Global Inc
8720 Red Oak Blvd Ste 528
Charlotte NC 28217
980 443-1300

(G-7434)
FRANK BRUNCKHORST COMPANY LLC
2225 Spiegel Dr (43125-9036)
PHONE................................614 662-5300
Alexander Morris, Prin
EMP: 8 EST: 2011
SALES (est): 786.41K Privately Held
SIC: 5142 2013 Meat, frozen: packaged; Frozen meats, from purchased meat

(G-7435)
FRANKLIN EQUIPMENT LLC (HQ)
4141 Hamilton Square Blvd (43125-9084)
PHONE................................614 228-2014
EMP: 48 EST: 2007
SQ FT: 20,000
SALES (est): 22.9MM
SALES (corp-wide): 15.35B Publicly Held
Web: www.franklinequipmentllc.com
SIC: 3524 5083 Lawn and garden equipment; Tractors, agricultural
PA: United Rentals, Inc.
100 Frst Stmford Pl Ste 7
Stamford CT 06902
203 622-3131

(G-7436)
GABRIEL LOGAN LLC (PA)
4141 Hamilton Square Blvd (43125-9084)
P.O. Box 446 (43123)
PHONE................................740 380-6809
Troy L Gabriel, CEO
Thomas Richardson, *
◆ EMP: 61 EST: 2002
SALES (est): 1.66MM
SALES (corp-wide): 1.66MM Privately Held
Web: www.gabriellogan.com
SIC: 2541 Display fixtures, wood

(G-7437)
GPI OHIO LLC
6300 Commerce Center Dr Ste 100 (43125-1183)
PHONE................................605 332-6721
Benjamin Graham, Pr
EMP: 10 EST: 2015
SALES (est): 21.18MM Publicly Held
Web: www.bell-inc.com
SIC: 2657 Folding paperboard boxes
HQ: Gpi South Dakota Llc
617 W Algonquin St
Sioux Falls SD 57104
605 332-6721

(G-7438)
HOME CITY ICE COMPANY
4505 S Hamilton Rd (43125-9416)
PHONE................................614 836-2877
Tony Bakes, Brnch Mgr
EMP: 13
SQ FT: 12,000
SALES (corp-wide): 100.42MM Privately Held
Web: www.homecityice.com
SIC: 5199 5999 2097 Ice, manufactured or natural; Ice; Manufactured ice
PA: The Home City Ice Company
6045 Bridgetown Rd Ste 1
Cincinnati OH 45248
513 574-1800

(G-7439)
IOSIL ENERGY CORPORATION
5700 Green Pointe Dr N Ste A (43125-1082)
EMP: 10 EST: 2010
SALES (est): 241.76K Privately Held
Web: www.iosilenergy.com

SIC: 3433 Solar heaters and collectors

(G-7440)
KEYSTONE AUTOMOTIVE INDS INC
Also Called: Autobody Supply Company
5830 Green Pointe Dr S (43125-1188)
PHONE................................614 228-4328
James Volpe, Brnch Mgr
EMP: 7
SALES (corp-wide): 14.36B Publicly Held
Web: www.finishmaster.com
SIC: 3563 5013 5198 Air and gas compressors including vacuum pumps; Automotive supplies; Paints, varnishes, and supplies
HQ: Keystone Automotive Industries, Inc.
5846 Crossings Blvd
Antioch TN 37013
615 781-5200

(G-7441)
KRAFT ELECTRICAL CONTG INC
5710 Green Pointe Dr N (43125-1185)
PHONE................................614 836-9300
EMP: 26
SALES (corp-wide): 22.8MM Privately Held
Web: www.kecc.com
SIC: 4813 3699 Telephone communication, except radio; Electrical equipment and supplies, nec
PA: Kraft Electrical Contracting, Inc.
5710 Hillside Ave
Cincinnati OH 45233
513 467-0500

(G-7442)
KUBOTA TRACTOR CORPORATION
6300 At One Kubota Way (43125-1186)
PHONE................................614 835-3800
Ted Pederson, Genl Mgr
EMP: 25
Web: www.kubota.com
SIC: 3531 Construction machinery
HQ: Kubota Tractor Corporation
1000 Kubota Dr
Grapevine TX 76051
817 756-1171

(G-7443)
LOMAR ENTERPRISES INC
Also Called: Ecc Company
5905 Green Pointe Dr S Ste G (43125-2007)
P.O. Box 55 (43125-0055)
PHONE................................614 409-9104
Lou Onders, Pr
Mark Molnar, VP
EMP: 10 EST: 1981
SQ FT: 10,000
SALES (est): 2.53MM Privately Held
SIC: 3825 3544 Test equipment for electronic and electrical circuits; Special dies, tools, jigs, and fixtures

(G-7444)
MCGILL CORPORATION (PA)
1 Mission Park (43125-1149)
PHONE................................614 829-1200
James D Mcgill, Ch Bd
Jayne F Mcgill, Sec
◆ EMP: 10 EST: 1986
SQ FT: 13,000
SALES (est): 67.2MM
SALES (corp-wide): 67.2MM Privately Held
Web: www.unitedmcgill.com
SIC: 3564 3444 5169 Precipitators, electrostatic; Ducts, sheet metal; Sealants

(G-7445)
METAL MAN INC
4681 Homer Ohio Ln Ste A (43125-9231)
PHONE................................614 830-0968
Robert Posey, Pr
Ken Gilkerson, VP
EMP: 6 EST: 1989
SALES (est): 946.2K Privately Held
SIC: 3441 Fabricated structural metal

(G-7446)
NIFCO AMERICA CORPORATION
4485 S Hamilton Rd (43125-9334)
PHONE................................614 836-8691
Allen Hofmann, Prin
EMP: 48
Web: www.nifcousa.com
SIC: 3089 Automotive parts, plastic
HQ: Nifco America Corporation
8015 Dove Pkwy
Canal Winchester OH 43110
614 920-6800

(G-7447)
PEERLESS LASER PROCESSORS INC
4353 Directors Blvd (43125-9504)
PHONE................................614 836-5790
Tim Gase, Pr
Kenneth Lloyd, VP
EMP: 15 EST: 1984
SQ FT: 35,000
SALES (est): 2.06MM
SALES (corp-wide): 9.6MM Privately Held
Web: www.peerlesssaw.com
SIC: 3699 Laser welding, drilling, and cutting equipment
PA: The Peerless Saw Company
4353 Directors Blvd
Groveport OH 43125
614 836-5790

(G-7448)
PEERLESS SAW COMPANY (PA)
4353 Directors Blvd (43125-9350)
PHONE................................614 836-5790
Steve Hartshorn, Pr
Tim Gase, *
Ken Lloyd, *
▲ EMP: 50 EST: 1931
SQ FT: 30,000
SALES (est): 9.6MM
SALES (corp-wide): 9.6MM Privately Held
Web: www.peerlesssaw.com
SIC: 3541 3425 Machine tools, metal cutting type; Saw blades, for hand or power saws

(G-7449)
PINNACLE DATA SYSTEMS INC
Also Called: Pdsi
6600 Port Rd (43125-9129)
PHONE................................614 748-1150
▲ EMP: 148
SIC: 3575 3572 7378 7373 Computer terminals; Computer auxiliary storage units; Computer maintenance and repair; Systems software development services

(G-7450)
STABER INDUSTRIES INC
4800 Homer Ohio Ln (43125-9390)
PHONE................................614 836-5995
William Staber, Pr
▲ EMP: 35 EST: 1978
SQ FT: 55,000
SALES (est): 9.21MM Privately Held
Web: www.staber.com
SIC: 3633 3444 Household laundry equipment; Sheet metalwork

(G-7451)
SUPERB BAKEHOUSE INC
4395 Marketing Pl (43125-9556)
PHONE.............................614 302-7242
Stacie Skinner, *Prin*
EMP: 10 **EST:** 2015
SALES (est): 2.23MM **Privately Held**
Web: www.lopauspoint.com
SIC: 2038 Ethnic foods, nec, frozen

(G-7452)
TD SYNNEX CORPORATION
Also Called: Td Synnex Corporation
5350 Centerpoint Pkwy (43125-2501)
PHONE.............................614 669-6889
Charles Sims, *Prin*
EMP: 29
SALES (corp-wide): 58.45B **Publicly Held**
Web: www.tdsynnex.com
SIC: 3575 Computer terminals
HQ: Tech Data Corporation
5350 Tech Data Dr
Clearwater FL 33760
727 539-7429

(G-7453)
TIMKEN COMPANY
3782 Potomac St (43125-9472)
PHONE.............................614 836-3337
James Ferguson, *Brnch Mgr*
EMP: 12
SALES (corp-wide): 4.57B **Publicly Held**
Web: www.timken.com
SIC: 3562 Ball and roller bearings
PA: The Timken Company
4500 Mount Pleasant St Nw
North Canton OH 44720
234 262-3000

(G-7454)
TRANE US INC
Also Called: Trane
6600 Port Rd Ste 200 (43125-9129)
PHONE.............................614 497-6300
Sean Strane, *Brnch Mgr*
EMP: 7
Web: www.trane.com
SIC: 3585 Refrigeration and heating
equipment
HQ: Trane U.S. Inc.
800-E Beaty St
Davidson NC 28036
704 655-4000

(G-7455)
UNITED MCGILL CORPORATION (HQ)
1 Mission Park (43125-1100)
PHONE.............................614 829-1200
James D Mcgill, *Pr*
Jayne F Mcgill, *Sec*
▲ **EMP:** 30 **EST:** 1951
SQ FT: 13,000
SALES (est): 67.2MM
SALES (corp-wide): 67.2MM **Privately Held**
Web: www.unitedmcgill.com
SIC: 3444 3564 5169 3567 Ducts, sheet
metal; Precipitators, electrostatic; Sealants;
Industrial furnaces and ovens
PA: The Mcgill Corporation
One Mission Park
Groveport OH 43125
614 829-1200

(G-7456)
VERTIV CORPORATION
Also Called: Tech Data
5350 Centerpoint Pkwy (43125-2501)
PHONE.............................614 491-9286
Giordano Albertazzi, *CEO*
EMP: 6

SALES (corp-wide): 8.01B **Publicly Held**
Web: www.vertiv.com
SIC: 3585 Refrigeration and heating
equipment
HQ: Vertiv Corporation
505 N Cleveland Ave
Westerville OH 43082
614 888-0246

(G-7457)
WATTS WATER
6201 Green Pointe Dr S (43125-7501)
PHONE.............................614 491-5143
EMP: 15 **EST:** 2017
SALES (est): 7.53MM **Privately Held**
Web: www.watts.com
SIC: 3491 Industrial valves

(G-7458)
WILLIAM R HAGUE INC
Also Called: Hague Quality Water Intl
4343 S Hamilton Rd (43125-9332)
PHONE.............................614 836-2115
Robert Hague, *Pr*
◆ **EMP:** 100 **EST:** 1960
SQ FT: 90,000
SALES (est): 4.81MM
SALES (corp-wide): 3.82B **Publicly Held**
Web: www.haguewater.com
SIC: 5999 7389 3589 Water purification
equipment; Water softener service; Water
filters and softeners, household type
PA: A. O. Smith Corporation
11270 W Park Pl Ste 170
Milwaukee WI 53224
414 359-4000

Grover Hill
Paulding County

(G-7459)
R & L TRUSS INC
17985 Road 60 (45849-9400)
P.O. Box 130 (45849-0130)
PHONE.............................419 587-3440
Ron Treece, *CEO*
Larry Pressler, *Pr*
EMP: 10 **EST:** 1991
SQ FT: 3,360
SALES (est): 656.12K **Privately Held**
Web: www.rltruss.com
SIC: 2439 Trusses, wooden roof

Gypsum
Ottawa County

(G-7460)
UNITED STATES GYPSUM COMPANY
121 S Lake St (43433)
P.O. Box 121 (43433-0121)
PHONE.............................419 734-3161
Bill Steleger, *Brnch Mgr*
EMP: 350
SALES (corp-wide): 16.93B **Privately Held**
Web: www.usg.com
SIC: 3275 Gypsum products
HQ: United States Gypsum Company
550 W Adams St
Chicago IL 60661
312 606-4000

Hamden
Vinton County

(G-7461)
CORBETT R CAUDILL CHIPPING INC
35887 State Route 324 (45634-8824)
PHONE.............................740 596-5984
Corbett R Caudill, *Pr*
Myrta Caudill, *Sec*
EMP: 6 **EST:** 1971
SALES (est): 1.28MM **Privately Held**
Web: www.caudillchipping.com
SIC: 3546 4212 Hammers, portable: electric
or pneumatic, chipping, etc.; Local trucking,
without storage

Hamilton
Butler County

(G-7462)
ADVANCED DRAINAGE SYSTEMS INC
ADS Hancor
2650 Hamilton Eaton Rd (45011-9502)
P.O. Box 718 (45012-0718)
PHONE.............................513 863-1384
Nathan Williams, *Brnch Mgr*
EMP: 100
SALES (corp-wide): 2.87B **Publicly Held**
Web: www.adspipe.com
SIC: 3084 Plastics pipe
PA: Advanced Drainage Systems, Inc.
4640 Trueman Blvd
Hilliard OH 43026
614 658-0050

(G-7463)
AMERICAN PRINTING & LITHOG CO (PA)
528 S 7th St (45011-3619)
PHONE.............................513 867-0602
Ronald Smith, *Pr*
Randolph Smith, *VP*
Richard Smith, *Sec*
EMP: 19 **EST:** 1959
SQ FT: 14,000
SALES (est): 1.67MM
SALES (corp-wide): 1.67MM **Privately Held**
SIC: 2791 2789 2752 2759 Typesetting;
Bookbinding and related work; Commercial
printing, lithographic; Commercial printing,
nec

(G-7464)
AMERICAN RUGGED ENCLOSURES INC (PA)
4 Standen Dr (45015-2208)
PHONE.............................513 942-3004
Raymond J Casey, *Pr*
Shawn Beckman, *Sec*
EMP: 12 **EST:** 1993
SQ FT: 13,500
SALES (est): 2.42MM **Privately Held**
Web: www.mlctechnologies.com
SIC: 3469 Electronic enclosures, stamped or
pressed metal

(G-7465)
AMERICAN TOOL WORKS INC
Also Called: ATW
160 Hancock Ave (45011-4351)
PHONE.............................513 844-6363
Michael Lorance, *Pr*
EMP: 19 **EST:** 1990
SALES (est): 962.09K **Privately Held**
Web: www.americantoolworks.com

SIC: 3599 Machine shop, jobbing and repair

(G-7466)
ART TECHNOLOGIES LLC
Also Called: Art Metals Group
3795 Symmes Rd (45015-1373)
PHONE.............................513 942-8800
▲ **EMP:** 60 **EST:** 1946
SQ FT: 40,000
SALES (est): 8.67MM **Privately Held**
Web: www.art-technologies.com
SIC: 3469 Stamping metal for the trade

(G-7467)
ATLAS MACHINE AND SUPPLY INC
8556 Trade Center Dr # 250 (45011-9354)
PHONE.............................502 584-7262
Sonny Welker, *Mgr*
EMP: 28
SALES (corp-wide): 31.67MM **Privately Held**
Web: www.atlasmachine.com
SIC: 5084 3599 Compressors, except air
conditioning; Machine shop, jobbing and
repair
PA: Atlas Machine And Supply, Inc.
7000 Global Dr
Louisville KY 40258
502 584-7262

(G-7468)
BARRETT PAVING MATERIALS INC (DH)
8590 Bilstein Blvd Ste 100 (45015-2206)
PHONE.............................973 533-1001
Robert Doucet, *Pr*
Robert Pomton, *VP Opers*
Fred Shelton, *CFO*
◆ **EMP:** 20 **EST:** 1903
SALES (est): 76.67MM
SALES (corp-wide): 105.44MM **Privately Held**
Web: www.barrettpaving.com
SIC: 1611 2951 4213 1799 Highway and
street paving contractor; Road materials,
bituminous (not from refineries); Trucking,
except local; Building site preparation
HQ: Barrett Industries Corporation
73 Hedqrters Plz N Twr Fl
Morristown NJ 07960

(G-7469)
BAXTER HOLDINGS INC
3370 Port Union Rd (45014-4491)
PHONE.............................513 860-3593
Robert Kelly, *CEO*
EMP: 8 **EST:** 1923
SQ FT: 32,000
SALES (est): 1.69MM **Privately Held**
SIC: 3272 3443 Steps, prefabricated
concrete; Fabricated plate work (boiler
shop)

(G-7470)
BETHART ENTERPRISES INC (PA)
Also Called: Bethart Printing Services
531 Main St (45013-3221)
PHONE.............................513 863-6161
Richard Bethart, *Pr*
EMP: 14 **EST:** 1974
SQ FT: 4,400
SALES (est): 898.75K
SALES (corp-wide): 898.75K **Privately Held**
Web: www.bethart.com
SIC: 2752 7334 Offset printing;
Photocopying and duplicating services

(G-7471)
BORKE MOLD SPECIALIST INC
9541 Glades Dr (45011-9410)
PHONE.............................513 870-8000
Fritz Borke, Pr
Patty Borke, Sec
EMP: 17 **EST:** 1990
SQ FT: 14,000
SALES (est): 2.4MM **Privately Held**
Web: www.borkemold.com
SIC: 3089 Injection molding of plastics

(G-7472)
BP 10 INC
Also Called: Bagpack
9486 Sutton Pl (45011-9698)
PHONE.............................513 346-3900
Steven Dreyer, Pr
Ronald C Dreyer, *
EMP: 40 **EST:** 1988
SQ FT: 40,000
SALES (est): 9.66MM
SALES (corp-wide): 54.78MM **Privately Held**
Web: www.flex-pack.com
SIC: 5199 2752 Packaging materials; Commercial printing, lithographic
PA: Advanced Converting Works
1500 W. Bryn Mawr Ave
Itasca IL 60143
630 285-1500

(G-7473)
BRIDGESTONE RET OPERATIONS LLC
Also Called: Firestone
33 N Brookwood Ave (45013-1209)
PHONE.............................513 868-7399
Robert Johnson, Mgr
EMP: 7
SQ FT: 5,200
Web: www.bebridgestone.com
SIC: 5531 7534 Automotive tires; Rebuilding and retreading tires
HQ: Bridgestone Retail Operations, Llc
200 4th Ave S Ste 100
Nashville TN 37201
615 937-1000

(G-7474)
BROOK & WHITTLE LIMITED
4000 Hamilton Middletown Rd (45011-2263)
PHONE.............................513 860-2457
Mark Pollard, CEO
EMP: 25
Web: www.brookandwhittle.com
SIC: 2754 2759 Commercial printing, gravure ; Commercial printing, nec
PA: Brook & Whittle Limited
20 Carter Dr
Guilford CT 06437

(G-7475)
BUTLER CNTY SURGICAL PRPTS LLC
213 Dayton St (45011-1633)
PHONE.............................513 844-2200
Richard R Roebuck, Prin
EMP: 6 **EST:** 2009
SALES (est): 138.41K **Privately Held**
SIC: 3841 Surgical and medical instruments

(G-7476)
CIMA INC
1010 Eaton Ave Ste B (45013-4684)
PHONE.............................513 382-8976
Tom Uhl, Pr
▲ **EMP:** 6 **EST:** 1992
SALES (est): 301.02K **Privately Held**

Web: www.cimaohio.com
SIC: 3561 7363 2449 Industrial pumps and parts; Temporary help service; Rectangular boxes and crates, wood

(G-7477)
CIMA INC
1010 Eaton Ave Ste B (45013-4684)
PHONE.............................513 382-8976
Thomas Uhl, Prin
EMP: 20 **EST:** 1994
SALES (est): 813.17K **Privately Held**
Web: www.cimaohio.com
SIC: 2449 2448 Wood containers, nec; Pallets, wood

(G-7478)
CINCINNATI ABRASIVE SUPPLY CO
9431 Sutton Pl (45011-9705)
PHONE.............................513 941-8866
Thomas Spinnenweber, Pr
Kathleen Spinnenweber, VP
Larry Kite, Treas
EMP: 6 **EST:** 1974
SALES (est): 1.01MM **Privately Held**
Web: www.cincinnatiabrasivesupplycompany.com
SIC: 5085 3471 Abrasives; Finishing, metals or formed products

(G-7479)
COLOR PRODUCTS INC
36 Standen Dr (45015-2210)
PHONE.............................513 860-2749
James K Krouse, Pr
EMP: 7 **EST:** 1993
SQ FT: 12,000
SALES (est): 102.52K **Privately Held**
SIC: 2865 Cyclic crudes and intermediates

(G-7480)
CONNAUGHTON WLDG & FENCE LLC
Also Called: Connaughton Welding & Fence
440 Vine St (45011-1777)
PHONE.............................513 867-0230
EMP: 6 **EST:** 1962
SQ FT: 5,000
SALES (est): 105.88K **Privately Held**
SIC: 1799 7692 3469 Fence construction; Welding repair; Ornamental metal stampings

(G-7481)
CRYOGENIC EQUIPMENT & SVCS INC
Also Called: Cesgroup
4583 Brate Dr (45011-3577)
PHONE.............................513 761-4200
Hans Vanackere, CEO
◆ **EMP:** 10 **EST:** 1998
SALES (est): 11.07MM **Privately Held**
Web: www.dsidantech.com
SIC: 3585 Refrigeration and heating equipment
PA: Dsi Dantech
Vlaswaagplein 13
Kortrijk VWV 8501

(G-7482)
CUSTOM FAB BY FISHER LLC
5009 Cincinnati Brookville Rd (45013-9210)
PHONE.............................513 738-4600
EMP: 6 **EST:** 2004
SALES (est): 208.4K **Privately Held**
SIC: 3599 Machine shop, jobbing and repair

(G-7483)
DBS STNLESS STL FBRCTORS INC
21 Standen Dr (45015-2209)

PHONE.............................513 856-9600
Nick Bauer, Genl Mgr
Russell Bowermaster, Stockholder
▲ **EMP:** 9 **EST:** 1985
SQ FT: 12,000
SALES (est): 911.11K **Privately Held**
SIC: 3444 Restaurant sheet metalwork

(G-7484)
DESCO LLC
903 Belle Ave (45015-1605)
PHONE.............................513 860-4490
Darryl Cuttell, Managing Member
EMP: 12 **EST:** 2012
SALES (est): 3.16MM **Privately Held**
Web: desco.descoindustries.com
SIC: 3612 Transformers, except electric

(G-7485)
DYNAMAT INC (PA)
Also Called: Dynamat
3042 Symmes Rd (45015-1331)
PHONE.............................513 860-5094
Mark Seist, CEO
EMP: 14 **EST:** 2020
SALES (est): 4.78MM
SALES (corp-wide): 4.78MM **Privately Held**
Web: www.dynamat.com
SIC: 3443 Baffles

(G-7486)
DYNAMIC CONTROL NORTH AMER INC (PA)
Also Called: Dynamic Control
3042 Symmes Rd (45015-1331)
PHONE.............................513 860-5094
▲ **EMP:** 16 **EST:** 1989
SQ FT: 15,000
SALES (est): 3.93MM **Privately Held**
Web: www.dynamat.com
SIC: 3443 Baffles

(G-7487)
EAGLE CHEMICALS INC
2550 Bobmeyer Rd (45015-1366)
P.O. Box 713 (45012-0713)
PHONE.............................513 868-9662
EMP: 14
SIC: 2819 Industrial inorganic chemicals, nec

(G-7488)
ELRA INDUSTRIES INC
550 S Erie Hwy (45011-4346)
PHONE.............................513 868-6228
Eldon Smith, Pr
EMP: 8 **EST:** 1977
SQ FT: 13,000
SALES (est): 750K **Privately Held**
Web: www.elra.com
SIC: 3089 Injection molding of plastics

(G-7489)
EXCEL LOADING SYSTEMS LLC
1051 Belle Ave (45015-1607)
PHONE.............................513 504-1069
EMP: 8 **EST:** 2016
SALES (est): 145.41K **Privately Held**
Web: www.excelloading.com
SIC: 3568 Joints, swivel and universal, except aircraft and auto

(G-7490)
FIN PAN INC (PA)
3255 Symmes Rd (45015-1361)
PHONE.............................513 870-9200
Elisa Schafer, Pr
Theodore Clear, VP
Louis A Beimford, Prin
Marsha G Rhodus, Prin

Theodore E Clear, Prin
◆ **EMP:** 18 **EST:** 1975
SQ FT: 40,000
SALES (est): 5.13MM
SALES (corp-wide): 5.13MM **Privately Held**
Web: www.finpan.com
SIC: 3272 Concrete products, precast, nec

(G-7491)
FUTURE FINISHES INC
40 Standen Dr (45015-2210)
PHONE.............................513 860-0020
Daniel L Brown, Pr
EMP: 6 **EST:** 1993
SQ FT: 25,000
SALES (est): 764.32K **Privately Held**
Web: www.futurefinishes.com
SIC: 3471 Plating of metals or formed products

(G-7492)
G & J PEPSI-COLA BOTTLERS INC
Also Called: Pepsi-Cola
2580 Bobmeyer Rd (45015-1394)
PHONE.............................513 896-3700
Don Chalfant, Brnch Mgr
EMP: 73
SQ FT: 50,000
SALES (corp-wide): 404.54MM **Privately Held**
Web: www.gjpepsi.com
SIC: 2086 Carbonated soft drinks, bottled and canned
PA: G & J Pepsi-Cola Bottlers Inc
9435 Wtrstone Blvd Ste 39
Cincinnati OH 45249
513 785-6060

(G-7493)
GERDAU AMERISTEEL US INC
2175 Schlichter Dr (45015-1481)
PHONE.............................513 869-7660
Mike Stanofer, Mgr
EMP: 12
Web: gerdau.com
SIC: 3312 Blast furnaces and steel mills
HQ: Gerdau Ameristeel Us Inc.
4221 W Boy Scout Blvd Ste
Tampa FL 33607
813 286-8383

(G-7494)
GL INDUSTRIES INC
Also Called: Climax Packaging Machinery
25 Standen Dr (45015-2209)
P.O. Box 18097 (45018-0097)
PHONE.............................513 874-1233
William George, Pr
EMP: 20 **EST:** 1959
SQ FT: 18,000
SALES (est): 5.03MM **Privately Held**
Web: www.climaxpackaging.com
SIC: 3565 7389 Packaging machinery; Packaging and labeling services

(G-7495)
GLANCE SOFTWARE LLC
1340 Missy Ct (45013-7601)
PHONE.............................844 383-2500
Austin Klei, Pr
EMP: 10 **EST:** 2016
SALES (est): 1.78MM **Privately Held**
Web: www.glancesoftware.com
SIC: 7372 7379 Prepackaged software; Computer related consulting services

(G-7496)
GLOBAL PACKAGING & EXPORTS INC (PA)
9166 Sutton Pl (45011-9317)

P.O. Box 1758 (45071-1758)
PHONE................................513 454-2020
Lori Mennett-jordan, *Pr*
EMP: 6 **EST:** 1980
SQ FT: 19,000
SALES (est): 1.84MM
SALES (corp-wide): 1.84MM **Privately Held**
Web: www.globalpkg.com
SIC: 2441 4783 2448 Cases, wood; Packing goods for shipping; Skids, wood

(G-7497)
GRK MANUFACTURING CO
1200 Dayton St (45011-4220)
PHONE................................513 863-3131
Gary Kilday, *Pr*
Eileen K Kilday, *
David S Kilday, *
Lori E Kilday, *
James Vicena, *
▲ **EMP:** 30 **EST:** 1917
SQ FT: 100,000
SALES (est): 2.44MM **Privately Held**
Web: www.grkmfg.com
SIC: 2511 2499 2512 Wood household furniture; Decorative wood and woodwork; Upholstered household furniture

(G-7498)
GVS INDUSTRIES INC
Also Called: Cadillac Papers
1030 Beissinger Rd (45013-9322)
PHONE................................513 851-3606
Donald Gillespie, *Pr*
Sharon Sheppard, *Off Mgr*
Ronald Green, *Stockholder*
Donald Gillespie Ii, *Stockholder*
EMP: 6 **EST:** 1991
SALES (est): 212.03K **Privately Held**
Web: www.gvs.com
SIC: 2621 3861 5113 5112 Specialty or chemically treated papers; Toners, prepared photographic (not made in chemical plants); Industrial and personal service paper; Stationery and office supplies

(G-7499)
HACKER WOOD PRODUCTS INC
2144 Jackson Rd (45011-9534)
PHONE................................513 737-4462
Chris Hacker, *Pr*
EMP: 6 **EST:** 1998
SQ FT: 2,200
SALES (est): 464.37K **Privately Held**
SIC: 2448 Pallets, wood

(G-7500)
HAMILTON BRASS & ALUM CASTINGS
706 S 8th St (45011-3753)
P.O. Box 657 (45012-0657)
EMP: 6 **EST:** 1918
SQ FT: 25,000
SALES (est): 812.49K **Privately Held**
Web: www.hamilton-ohio.com
SIC: 3364 3321 Brass and bronze die-castings; Gray and ductile iron foundries

(G-7501)
HAMILTON CUSTOM MOLDING INC
1365 Shuler Ave (45011-4567)
PHONE................................513 844-6643
Ed White, *Pr*
Dorothy White, *Sec*
EMP: 7 **EST:** 1992
SQ FT: 20,000
SALES (est): 894.32K **Privately Held**
Web: www.hamiltoncm.com

SIC: 3089 3544 Plastics containers, except foam; Special dies, tools, jigs, and fixtures

(G-7502)
HAMILTON INDUSTRIAL GRINDING INC (PA)
Also Called: Carolina Knife Services
240 N B St (45013-3105)
PHONE................................513 863-1221
▲ **EMP:** 20 **EST:** 1961
SALES (est): 2.51MM
SALES (corp-wide): 2.51MM **Privately Held**
Web: www.hamiltonknife.com
SIC: 3423 7699 Knives, agricultural or industrial; Knife, saw and tool sharpening and repair

(G-7503)
HAMILTON MACHINE SERVICES CORP
2380 Hamilton Eaton Rd (45011-9052)
PHONE................................513 895-7200
Russell Kinsey, *Prin*
EMP: 6 **EST:** 2004
SALES (est): 1.51MM **Privately Held**
Web: www.hamiltonmachine.com
SIC: 3599 Machine shop, jobbing and repair

(G-7504)
IMI REAL ESTATE LLC
600 Augspurger Rd (45011-6913)
PHONE................................513 844-8444
Randy Jones, *Brnch Mgr*
EMP: 10
SALES (corp-wide): 440.22MM **Privately Held**
Web: www.irvmat.com
SIC: 3273 Ready-mixed concrete
PA: Imi Real Estate, Llc
    8032 N State Rd 9
    Greenfield IN 46140
    317 326-3101

(G-7505)
INNOVTIVE LBLING SOLUTIONS INC
Also Called: I L S
4000 Hamilton Middletown Rd (45011-2263)
PHONE................................513 860-2457
Jay Dollries, *Pr*
Steve Wolf, *
Jeanne Wolf, *
▲ **EMP:** 65 **EST:** 1996
SQ FT: 65,000
SALES (est): 9.05MM **Privately Held**
Web: www.academiedessports.com
SIC: 2759 Labels and seals: printing, nsk

(G-7506)
INTEGRATED POWER SERVICES LLC
2175a Schlichter Dr (45015-1482)
PHONE................................513 863-8816
Jason Reynolds, *Brnch Mgr*
EMP: 28
SQ FT: 20,500
Web: www.ips.us
SIC: 7694 Electric motor repair
PA: Integrated Power Services Llc
    250 Exctive Ctr Dr Ste 20
    Greenville SC 29615

(G-7507)
J R CUSTOM UNLIMITED INC
2620 Bobmeyer Rd (45015-1306)
PHONE................................513 894-9800
James Riesenberg, *Pr*
EMP: 10 **EST:** 1999
SALES (est): 331.73K **Privately Held**

SIC: 2499 Decorative wood and woodwork

(G-7508)
KAIVAC INC
Also Called: Kaivac
2680 Van Hook Ave (45015-1583)
PHONE................................513 887-4600
Bob Robinson Senior, *Pr*
Carlene Robinson, *
Robert Toews, *
▲ **EMP:** 81 **EST:** 1998
SALES (est): 20.3MM **Privately Held**
Web: www.kaivac.com
SIC: 3589 Commercial cleaning equipment

(G-7509)
KNAPPCO CORPORATION
Also Called: Civacon
9393 Princeton Glendale Rd (45011-9707)
PHONE................................513 870-3100
John F Anderson, *CEO*
Pat Gerard, *
Dan Taylor, *
▲ **EMP:** 140 **EST:** 1975
SQ FT: 110,000
SALES (est): 24.91MM
SALES (corp-wide): 7.75B **Publicly Held**
Web: www.knappco.com
SIC: 3321 3643 3494 Manhole covers, metal ; Caps and plugs, electric: attachment; Valves and pipe fittings, nec
PA: Dover Corporation
    3005 Hghland Pkwy Ste 200
    Downers Grove IL 60515
    630 541-1540

(G-7510)
LIBERTY SPORTSWEAR LLC
5573 Eureka Dr (45011-4267)
PHONE................................513 755-8740
Mark Scott, *Owner*
EMP: 6 **EST:** 1990
SALES (est): 154.37K **Privately Held**
Web: www.hofapparel.com
SIC: 2759 Screen printing

(G-7511)
LOUS MACHINE COMPANY INC
102 Hastings Ave (45011-4708)
PHONE................................513 856-9199
G Danny Jackson, *Pr*
EMP: 10 **EST:** 1978
SQ FT: 10,000
SALES (est): 431.35K **Privately Held**
SIC: 3599 Machine shop, jobbing and repair

(G-7512)
NETUREN AMERICA CORPORATION
2995 Moser Ct (45011-5430)
PHONE................................513 863-1900
Etsla Yamamura, *CEO*
Makoto Nakahara, *Prin*
▲ **EMP:** 18 **EST:** 2007
SALES (est): 4.44MM **Privately Held**
Web: www.neturen-america.com
SIC: 3398 Metal heat treating

(G-7513)
NK MACHINE INC
1550 Pleasant Ave (45015-1035)
PHONE................................513 737-8035
Nick Emenaker, *Pr*
Edward Emenaker, *Owner*
EMP: 7 **EST:** 1987
SQ FT: 6,000
SALES (est): 1.12MM **Privately Held**
Web: www.nkmachine.com
SIC: 3599 Machine shop, jobbing and repair

(G-7514)
OBERSONS NURS & LANDSCAPES LLC
Also Called: Obersons Snow and Ice MGT
2389 Hamilton Cleves Rd (45013-9604)
PHONE................................513 687-7379
Alan Handley, *Mgr*
Chad Oberson, *
EMP: 45 **EST:** 2000
SQ FT: 7,000
SALES (est): 3.85MM **Privately Held**
Web: www.obersonsnursery.com
SIC: 0782 7349 2899 Landscape contractors ; Building maintenance services, nec; Salt

(G-7515)
OHIO HEAT TRANSFER
3400 Port Union Rd (45014-4224)
PHONE................................513 870-5323
EMP: 7
SALES (est): 451.18K **Privately Held**
Web: www.ohioheattransfer.com
SIC: 3443 Fabricated plate work (boiler shop)

(G-7516)
OLIVER HEALTHCARE PACKAGING CO
Also Called: Oliver-Tolas Healthcare Packg
3840 Symmes Rd (45015-1378)
PHONE................................513 860-6880
Heather Fletcher, *Brnch Mgr*
EMP: 222
SALES (corp-wide): 2.26B **Privately Held**
Web: www.oliverhcp.com
SIC: 2672 Chemically treated papers, made from purchased materials
HQ: Oliver Healthcare Packaging Company
    445 6th St Nw
    Grand Rapids MI 49504
    833 465-4837

(G-7517)
PLAS-TANKS INDUSTRIES INC (PA)
39 Standen Dr (45015-2209)
PHONE................................513 942-3800
J Kent Covey, *Pr*
Connie Royse, *
EMP: 38 **EST:** 1976
SQ FT: 33,000
SALES (est): 3.98MM
SALES (corp-wide): 3.98MM **Privately Held**
Web: www.plastanks.com
SIC: 3089 3564 3444 3084 Tubs, plastics (containers); Blowers and fans; Sheet metalwork; Plastics pipe

(G-7518)
PRODUCTION MANUFACTURING INC
870 Hanover St Bldg A (45011-3790)
PHONE................................513 892-2331
FAX: 513 892-0014
EMP: 25
SQ FT: 75,000
SALES (est): 6.2MM **Privately Held**
SIC: 3444 Sheet metalwork

(G-7519)
QLOG CORP
33 Standen Dr (45015-2209)
PHONE................................513 874-1211
J Robert Warden, *Pr*
Thomas Rebel, *VP*
EMP: 9 **EST:** 1980
SQ FT: 7,500
SALES (est): 445.75K **Privately Held**
Web: www.qlog.com
SIC: 8748 3679 Systems analysis or design; Electronic circuits

(G-7520)
QUALITY PUBLISHING CO
Also Called: Quality Printing & Publishing
3200 Symmes Rd (45015-1357)
PHONE..........................513 863-8210
Jane Johnson, *Pr*
David Johnson, *VP*
EMP: 10 **EST:** 1953
SQ FT: 10,000
SALES (est): 599.94K **Privately Held**
Web: www.qualitypublishingco.com
SIC: 2752 Offset printing

(G-7521)
RUBBER DUCK 4X4 INC
1622 Smith Rd (45013-8629)
PHONE..........................513 889-1735
Travis Depew, *Owner*
EMP: 6 **EST:** 2004
SALES (est): 807.17K **Privately Held**
Web: www.rubberduck4x4.com
SIC: 3714 Motor vehicle parts and
accessories

(G-7522)
SAICA PACK US LLC
Also Called: Saica
2995 Mcbride Ct (45011-5420)
PHONE..........................513 399-5602
Ramn Alejandro, *Pr*
EMP: 26 **EST:** 2020
SALES (est): 26.64MM **Privately Held**
Web: usa.saica.com
SIC: 2657 2631 Folding paperboard boxes;
Packaging board
HQ: Sociedad Anonima Industrias Celulosa
Aragonesa
Calle San Juan De La Pela 144
Zaragoza Z 50015

(G-7523)
SCHAEFER BOX & PALLET CO
11875 Paddys Run Rd (45013-9365)
PHONE..........................513 738-2500
Stanley Schaefer, *CEO*
Tod Hollifield, *
EMP: 32 **EST:** 1968
SQ FT: 45,000
SALES (est): 2.49MM **Privately Held**
Web: www.schaeferboxandpallet.com
SIC: 2449 2448 2441 Rectangular boxes
and crates, wood; Pallets, wood; Nailed
wood boxes and shook

(G-7524)
SENSUS LLC
2991 Hamilton Mason Rd (45011-5355)
PHONE..........................513 892-7100
Dan Wampler, *Managing Member*
▲ **EMP:** 12 **EST:** 1999
SQ FT: 25,000
SALES (est): 2.16MM **Privately Held**
Web: www.sensus.com
SIC: 2087 Pastes, flavoring
HQ: Synergy Flavors, Inc.
1500 Synergy Dr
Wauconda IL 60084
847 487-1011

(G-7525)
SHAPE SUPPLY INC
700 S Erie Hwy (45011-3904)
PHONE..........................513 863-6695
Eugene Lukjan, *Pr*
EMP: 7 **EST:** 1978
SQ FT: 16,000
SALES (est): 517.97K **Privately Held**
SIC: 3444 5075 Pipe, sheet metal; Warm air
heating equipment and supplies

(G-7526)
SONOSITE INC
236 High St (45011-2711)
PHONE..........................425 951-1200
EMP: 6 **EST:** 2018
SALES (est): 942.99K **Privately Held**
Web: www.sonosite.com
SIC: 3845 Electromedical equipment

(G-7527)
STAT INDUSTRIES INC
3269 Profit Dr (45014-4239)
PHONE..........................513 860-4482
Robyn Kellough, *Mgr*
EMP: 6
Web: www.statindex.com
SIC: 2675 Index cards, die-cut: made from
purchased materials
PA: Stat Industries, Inc.
137 Stone Rd
Chillicothe OH 45601

(G-7528)
**SURGICAL RECOVERY SYSTEMS
LLC**
4130 Tylersville Rd (45011-8633)
PHONE..........................513 833-6868
EMP: 50 **EST:** 2020
SALES (est): 707.92K **Privately Held**
Web: www.surgicalrecoverysystems.com
SIC: 3842 Surgical appliances and supplies

(G-7529)
**TERRY ASPHALT MATERIALS INC
(DH)**
8600 Bilstein Blvd (45015-2204)
PHONE..........................513 874-6192
Dan Koeninger, *CEO*
EMP: 25 **EST:** 2013
SALES (est): 11.54MM
SALES (corp-wide): 105.44MM **Privately
Held**
Web: www.terryasphalt.com
SIC: 5082 2952 Road construction and
maintenance machinery; Asphalt felts and
coatings
HQ: Barrett Industries Corporation
73 Hedqrters Plz N Twr Fl
Morristown NJ 07960

(G-7530)
**THE HAMILTON CASTER & MFG
COMPANY**
1637 Dixie Hwy (45011-4087)
PHONE..........................513 863-3300
▲ **EMP:** 68 **EST:** 1907
SALES (est): 9.52MM **Privately Held**
Web: www.hamiltoncaster.com
SIC: 3562 3312 Casters; Wheels

(G-7531)
**THYSSENKRUPP BILSTEIN AMER
INC (HQ)**
8685 Bilstein Blvd (45015-2205)
PHONE..........................513 881-7600
Fabian Schmahl, *Pr*
▲ **EMP:** 212 **EST:** 1972
SQ FT: 115,000
SALES (est): 460.14MM
SALES (corp-wide): 39.13B **Privately Held**
Web: www.bilstein.com
SIC: 3714 5013 Shock absorbers, motor
vehicle; Springs, shock absorbers and struts
PA: Thyssenkrupp Ag
Thyssenkrupp Allee 1
Essen NW 45143
2018440

(G-7532)
TIPCO PUNCH INC
6 Rowe Ct (45015-2211)
PHONE..........................513 874-9140
Jack Pickins, *CEO*
Scott Ellsworth, *VP*
EMP: 30 **EST:** 1973
SQ FT: 12,000
SALES (est): 4.16MM
SALES (corp-wide): 24.64MM **Privately
Held**
Web: www.tipcopunch.com
SIC: 3544 Special dies and tools
HQ: Tipco Inc
1 Coventry Rd
Brampton ON L6T 4
905 791-9811

(G-7533)
TRI-MAC MFG & SVCS CO
Also Called: Tri-Mac Mfg & Serv
860 Belle Ave (45015-1151)
PHONE..........................513 896-4445
William Bates, *Pr*
Bill Galster, *VP*
EMP: 10 **EST:** 1984
SQ FT: 40,000
SALES (est): 2.02MM **Privately Held**
Web: www.trimacmanufacturing.com
SIC: 3714 3554 5084 3549 Motor vehicle
parts and accessories; Paper industries
machinery; Trucks, industrial; Metalworking
machinery, nec

(G-7534)
TRIANGLE SIGN CO LLC
221 N B St (45013-3195)
PHONE..........................513 266-1009
Donald K Whittlesey, *Pt*
Everett Hoskins Junior, *Pt*
Tim Hoskins, *Pt*
EMP: 9 **EST:** 1920
SQ FT: 6,695
SALES (est): 293.54K **Privately Held**
Web: www.trianglesigncompany.com
SIC: 3993 7389 Neon signs; Sign painting
and lettering shop

(G-7535)
ULTRAEDIT INC
Also Called: IDM Computer Solutions
5559 Eureka Dr Ste B (45011-4267)
PHONE..........................216 464-7465
Derek Holder, *Dir*
EMP: 9
SALES (corp-wide): 249.4MM **Privately
Held**
Web: www.ultraedit.com
SIC: 7372 Prepackaged software
HQ: Ultraedit, Inc.
10801 N Mpac Expy Bldg 1
Austin TX 78759
713 523-4433

(G-7536)
VALVSYS LLC
2 Rowe Ct (45015-2211)
PHONE..........................513 870-1234
Brad Frank, *Pr*
▲ **EMP:** 8 **EST:** 2000
SALES (est): 991.59K **Privately Held**
Web: www.valvsys.com
SIC: 2812 Alkalies

(G-7537)
WALLOVER OIL HAMILTON INC
Also Called: National Oil Products
1000 Forest Ave (45015-1632)
PHONE..........................513 896-6692
George Marquis, *Ch*
EMP: 8 **EST:** 1963

SQ FT: 15,000
SALES (est): 2.5MM
SALES (corp-wide): 1.84B **Publicly Held**
SIC: 2992 Re-refining lubricating oils and
greases, nec
HQ: Wallover Enterprises Inc.
21845 Drake Rd
Strongsville OH 44149
440 238-9250

(G-7538)
WATSON GRAVEL INC (PA)
2728 Hamilton Cleves Rd (45013-9452)
PHONE..........................513 863-0070
Ronald E Watson, *Pr*
Michael T Watson, *
Janet L Meyers, *
EMP: 37 **EST:** 1970
SQ FT: 2,000
SALES (est): 4.86MM
SALES (corp-wide): 4.86MM **Privately
Held**
Web: www.watsongravel.com
SIC: 1442 Gravel mining

(G-7539)
WULCO INC
Also Called: Cima
1010 Eaton Ave Ste B # B (45013-4640)
PHONE..........................513 379-6115
Richard G Wulfeck, *Pr*
EMP: 95
Web: www.wulco.com
SIC: 5085 3599 Industrial supplies; Machine
shop, jobbing and repair
PA: Wulco, Inc.
6899 Steger Dr Ste A
Cincinnati OH 45237

Hannibal
Monroe County

(G-7540)
ORMET CORPORATION
43840 State Rte 7 (43931)
PHONE..........................740 483-1381
◆ **EMP:** 1250
Web: www.ormet.com
SIC: 3334 Primary aluminum

(G-7541)
ORMET PRIMARY ALUMINUM CORP
Also Called: Velvetflow
43840 State Rt 7 (43931)
PHONE..........................740 483-1381
Michael Tanchuk, *Pr*
▲ **EMP:** 1100 **EST:** 2015
SALES (est): 7.04MM **Privately Held**
Web: www.burnsideterminal.com
SIC: 3334 3297 Aluminum ingots and slabs;
Nonclay refractories

Harrison
Hamilton County

(G-7542)
ALLIANCE KNIFE INC
124 May Dr (45030-2024)
P.O. Box 729 (45030-0729)
PHONE..........................513 367-9000
William L Keith, *Pr*
Sharon Keith, *Sec*
◆ **EMP:** 20 **EST:** 1985
SALES (est): 2.01MM **Privately Held**
Web: www.allianceknife.com
SIC: 5085 3545 Knives, industrial; Machine
knives, metalworking

(G-7543)

BELL INDUSTRIES
9843 New Haven Rd (45030-1836)
PHONE..............................513 353-2355
Edward Vierling, *Owner*
EMP: 10 **EST:** 1933
SQ FT: 8,600
SALES (est): 889.68K **Privately Held**
Web: www.bell-ind.com
SIC: 3931 Bells (musical instruments)

(G-7544)

CATEXEL NEASE LLC
Also Called: Nease Performance Chemicals
10740 Paddys Run Rd (45030-9251)
PHONE..............................513 738-1255
Frank Canepa, *Brnch Mgr*
EMP: 60
SALES (corp-wide): 355.83K **Privately Held**
Web: www.neaseco.com
SIC: 2869 Glycol ethers
HQ: Catexel Nease Llc
9774 Windisch Rd
West Chester OH 45069

(G-7545)

CINCINNATI INCORPORATED (PA)
7420 Kilby Rd (45030-8915)
P.O. Box 11111 (45211-0111)
PHONE..............................513 367-7100
EMP: 244 **EST:** 1898
SALES (est): 48.88MM
SALES (corp-wide): 48.88MM **Privately Held**
Web: www.e-ci.com
SIC: 3549 Metalworking machinery, nec

(G-7546)

CINCINNATI TEST SYSTEMS INC (HQ)
10100 Progress Way (45030-1295)
PHONE..............................513 202-5100
Barbara A Jackson, *Prin*
Kevin Hansell, *
Joanna Moncivaiz, *
EMP: 57 **EST:** 1981
SQ FT: 25,000
SALES (est): 48.69MM
SALES (corp-wide): 287.28MM **Privately Held**
Web: www.cincinnati-test.com
SIC: 3823 Pressure measurement instruments, industrial
PA: Tasi Holdings, Inc.
40 Locke Dr Ste B
Marlborough MA 01752
513 202-5182

(G-7547)

COATING SYSTEMS INC
Also Called: C S I
150 Sales Ave (45030-1484)
PHONE..............................513 367-5600
Thomas W Ritter, *Pr*
John Ritter, *VP*
EMP: 17 **EST:** 1974
SQ FT: 20,000
SALES (est): 3MM **Privately Held**
Web: www.coatingsystems.com
SIC: 3479 Coating of metals and formed products

(G-7548)

CROWN PLASTICS CO LLC
116 May Dr (45030-2095)
PHONE..............................513 367-0238
Gary Ellerhorst, *Pr*
Gregg Ellerhorst, *
Ken Myers, *Stockholder*
Robert H Ellerhorst, *

▲ **EMP:** 52 **EST:** 1972
SQ FT: 56,000
SALES (est): 15.69MM **Privately Held**
Web: www.crownplastics.com
SIC: 2821 3081 Plastics materials and resins
; Polypropylene film and sheet

(G-7549)

DIVERSFIED LBLING SLUTIONS INC
9487 Dry Fork Rd (45030-2900)
PHONE..............................630 625-1225
EMP: 10
Web: www.teamdls.com
SIC: 2754 Commercial printing, gravure
HQ: Diversified Labeling Solutions, Inc.
1285 Hamilton Pkwy
Itasca IL 60143
630 625-1225

(G-7550)

FASTPATCH LTD
10774 Carolina Trace Rd (45030-2729)
P.O. Box 5 (45030-0005)
PHONE..............................513 367-1838
Mike Jacobs, *Pr*
EMP: 10 **EST:** 2006
SALES (est): 99.64K **Privately Held**
Web: www.fastpatch.com
SIC: 2395 Embroidery products, except Schiffli machine

(G-7551)

FEILHAUERS MACHINE SHOP INC
421 Industrial Dr (45030-2104)
PHONE..............................513 202-0545
Don Feilhauer, *Pr*
EMP: 11 **EST:** 1979
SQ FT: 8,000
SALES (est): 2.24MM **Privately Held**
Web: www.feilhauers.com
SIC: 3599 Machine shop, jobbing and repair

(G-7552)

FRONTIER SIGNS & DISPLAYS INC
525 New Biddinger Rd (45030-1252)
P.O. Box 328 (45030-0328)
PHONE..............................513 367-0813
Jack S Wuesterfeld, *Pr*
Ruth Wuesterfeld, *Sec*
EMP: 7 **EST:** 1945
SQ FT: 17,000
SALES (est): 514.47K **Privately Held**
Web: www.frontiersigns.net
SIC: 2521 2522 3993 Wood office furniture; Office furniture, except wood; Signs and advertising specialties

(G-7553)

GEOGRAPH INDUSTRIES INC
475 Industrial Dr (45030-2104)
PHONE..............................513 202-9200
George Freudiger, *Pr*
Mark Freudiger, *
George Michael Freudiger, *
EMP: 26 **EST:** 1988
SQ FT: 25,000
SALES (est): 9.72MM **Privately Held**
Web: www.geograph-ind.com
SIC: 2541 3993 2521 2522 Wood partitions and fixtures; Signs and advertising specialties; Cabinets, office: wood; Chairs, office: padded or plain: except wood

(G-7554)

HALEX ELECTRIC COMPANY (HQ)
Also Called: Halex/Scott Fetzer Company
101 Production Dr (45030-1477)
PHONE..............................800 749-3261
Gary Heeman, *Pr*
◆ **EMP:** 25 **EST:** 1985
SALES (est): 8.88MM

SALES (corp-wide): 226 **Privately Held**
Web: www.halexco.com
SIC: 3699 Electrical equipment and supplies, nec
PA: The Scott Fetzer Company
28800 Clemens Rd
Westlake OH 44145
440 892-3000

(G-7555)

HOME CITY ICE COMPANY
5709 State Rte 128 (45030)
PHONE..............................513 353-9346
Cliff Riegler, *Mgr*
EMP: 10
SALES (corp-wide): 100.42MM **Privately Held**
Web: www.homecityice.com
SIC: 2097 Manufactured ice
PA: The Home City Ice Company
6045 Bridgetown Rd Ste 1
Cincinnati OH 45248
513 574-1800

(G-7556)

JTM PROVISIONS COMPANY INC (PA)
Also Called: Jtm Food Group
200 Sales Ave (45030-1485)
PHONE..............................513 367-4900
Anthony A Maas, *Pr*
John Maas Junior, *VP*
Jerome Maas, *
Joseph Maas, *
EMP: 400 **EST:** 1963
SQ FT: 96,000
SALES (est): 177.52MM
SALES (corp-wide): 177.52MM **Privately Held**
Web: www.jtmfoodgroup.com
SIC: 2038 Frozen specialties, nec

(G-7557)

JTM PROVISIONS COMPANY INC
Also Called: Jtm Food Group
270 Industrial Dr (45030-1491)
PHONE..............................513 367-4900
Anthony A Maas, *Brnch Mgr*
EMP: 300
SALES (corp-wide): 177.52MM **Privately Held**
Web: www.jtmfoodgroup.com
SIC: 2038 Frozen specialties, nec
PA: Jtm Provisions Company, Inc.
200 Sales Ave
Harrison OH 45030
513 367-4900

(G-7558)

KAPLAN INDUSTRIES INC
Also Called: Midwest Cylinder
6255 Kilby Rd (45030-9417)
PHONE..............................856 779-8181
Dean Kaplan, *Pr*
Rita Kaplan, *
Jim Johnston, *
◆ **EMP:** 70 **EST:** 1959
SQ FT: 6,000
SALES (est): 8.95MM **Privately Held**
Web: www.kaplanindustries.com
SIC: 3491 8734 Compressed gas cylinder valves; Hydrostatic testing laboratory

(G-7559)

MAINLINE CONTRACTING LLC
10860 Paddys Run Rd (45030-9252)
P.O. Box 1072 (45012-1072)
PHONE..............................513 202-1408
Richard Strobl, *CEO*
EMP: 13 **EST:** 2008
SQ FT: 36,000

SALES (est): 2.39MM **Privately Held**
Web: www.cincinnati-crane.com
SIC: 3536 1796 Hoists, cranes, and monorails; Installing building equipment

(G-7560)

PCS PHOSPHATE COMPANY INC
10818 Paddys Run Rd (45030-9252)
PHONE..............................513 738-1261
Jack Sullivan, *Mgr*
EMP: 127
SALES (corp-wide): 29.06B **Privately Held**
SIC: 2819 Phosphates, except fertilizers: defluorinated and ammoniated
HQ: Pcs Phosphate Company, Inc.
1101 Skokie Blvd Ste 400
Northbrook IL 60062
847 849-4200

(G-7561)

POWEREX-IWATA AIR TECH INC
Also Called: Powerex
150 Production Dr (45030-1477)
PHONE..............................888 769-7979
Gary Heman, *Pr*
Charles Heman, *
Pruce Jacobs, *
▲ **EMP:** 70 **EST:** 1986
SQ FT: 75,000
SALES (est): 22.93MM
SALES (corp-wide): 226 **Privately Held**
Web: www.powerexinc.com
SIC: 3563 Air and gas compressors
PA: The Scott Fetzer Company
28800 Clemens Rd
Westlake OH 44145
440 892-3000

(G-7562)

PREMIER INK SYSTEMS INC (PA)
10420 N State St (45030-9501)
P.O. Box P.O. Box 670 (45030-0670)
PHONE..............................513 367-2300
Thomas Farmer, *Pr*
EMP: 15 **EST:** 1984
SALES (est): 14.7MM
SALES (corp-wide): 14.7MM **Privately Held**
Web: www.premierink.com
SIC: 2851 2893 2899 Lacquers, varnishes, enamels, and other coatings; Printing ink; Chemical preparations, nec

(G-7563)

PUTTMANN INDUSTRIES INC
Also Called: Atlas Dowel & Wood Products Co
320 N State St (45030-1146)
P.O. Box 327 (45030-0327)
PHONE..............................513 202-9444
Peter Puttmann, *Pr*
▲ **EMP:** 15 **EST:** 1951
SQ FT: 65,000
SALES (est): 1.72MM **Privately Held**
Web: www.atlasdowel.com
SIC: 2499 Dowels, wood

(G-7564)

QUIKRETE COMPANIES LLC
Also Called: Quikrete Cincinnati
5425 Kilby Rd (45030-8910)
PHONE..............................513 367-6135
Glen Lainhart, *Mgr*
EMP: 38
SQ FT: 21,340
Web: www.quikrete.com
SIC: 3272 3273 Dry mixture concrete; Ready-mixed concrete
HQ: The Quikrete Companies Llc
5 Concourse Pkwy Ste 1900
Atlanta GA 30328
404 634-9100

(G-7565)
R L TORBECK INDUSTRIES INC
Also Called: Torbeck Industries
355 Industrial Dr (45030-1483)
PHONE..........................513 367-0080
Richard L Torbeck Junior, *Pr*
EMP: 8 **EST:** 1975
SQ FT: 67,000
SALES (est): 919.71K **Privately Held**
Web: www.torbeckind.com
SIC: 3441 3499 3448 3444 Fabricated
structural metal; Metal household articles;
Prefabricated metal buildings and
components; Sheet metalwork

(G-7566)
SEKUWORKS LLC
Also Called: Northern Bank Note Company
9487 Dry Fork Rd (45030-2900)
PHONE..........................513 202-1210
EMP: 38
Web: www.sekuworks.com
SIC: 2754 2752 2759 Commercial printing,
gravure; Commercial printing, lithographic;
Commercial printing, nec

(G-7567)
SHIM SHACK
105 May Dr (45030-2023)
PHONE..........................877 557-3930
EMP: 9 **EST:** 2013
SALES (est): 641.49K **Privately Held**
Web: www.theshimshack.com
SIC: 3499 Shims, metal

(G-7568)
SIMPSON & SONS INC
10220 Harrison Ave (45030-1938)
PHONE..........................513 367-0152
Joseph A Simpson, *Pr*
James Simpson, *VP*
EMP: 8 **EST:** 1973
SQ FT: 10,500
SALES (est): 978.72K **Privately Held**
SIC: 4789 7692 Railroad maintenance and
repair services; Welding repair

(G-7569)
STELTER AND BRINCK INC
201 Sales Ave (45030-1472)
PHONE..........................513 367-9300
Joseph A Brinck Ii, *Pr*
Henry Stelter, *
Larry Brinck, *
Mary B Turpen, *
EMP: 35 **EST:** 1940
SQ FT: 17,000
SALES (est): 8.24MM **Privately Held**
Web: www.stelterbrinck.com
SIC: 3564 3567 3494 3433 Blowers and fans
; Industrial furnaces and ovens; Valves and
pipe fittings, nec; Heating equipment,
except electric

(G-7570)
STOP STICK LTD
Also Called: Stop Stick, Liability Company
365 Industrial Dr (45030-1498)
PHONE..........................513 202-5500
Andrew Morrison, *Pr*
Louis M Groen, *Managing Member*
▲ **EMP:** 28 **EST:** 1993
SQ FT: 10,000
SALES (est): 2.38MM **Privately Held**
Web: www.stopstick.com
SIC: 3315 Nails, spikes, brads, and similar
items

(G-7571)
WAYNE WATER SYSTEMS INC
Also Called: Wayne/Scott Fetzer Company
101 Production Dr (45030-1477)
PHONE..........................800 237-0987
Duane Johnson, *Pr*
▲ **EMP:** 200 **EST:** 1985
SQ FT: 160,000
SALES (est): 23.24MM
SALES (corp-wide): 226 **Privately Held**
Web: www.waynepumps.com
SIC: 3561 5074 Pumps, domestic: water or
sump; Water purification equipment
PA: The Scott Fetzer Company
28800 Clemens Rd
Westlake OH 44145
440 892-3000

(G-7572)
WHITEWATER PROCESSING LLC
10964 Campbell Rd (45030-8902)
PHONE..........................513 367-4133
Ryan Kopp, *Pr*
Kristin Feller, *
EMP: 100 **EST:** 1929
SQ FT: 7,500
SALES (est): 7.44MM **Privately Held**
SIC: 2015 Turkey, slaughtered and dressed

Hartford
Trumbull County

(G-7573)
STANWADE METAL PRODUCTS INC
Also Called: Stanwade Tanks and Equipment
6868 State Rt 305 (44424)
P.O. Box 10 (44424-0010)
PHONE..........................330 772-2421
EMP: 44 **EST:** 1947
SALES (est): 13.79MM **Privately Held**
Web: www.stanwade.com
SIC: 3443 5084 Fuel tanks (oil, gas, etc.),
metal plate; Petroleum industry machinery

Hartville
Stark County

(G-7574)
AMERICAN COUNTERTOPS INC
7291 Swamp St Ne (44632-9324)
P.O. Box 535 (44632-0535)
PHONE..........................330 495-1915
Jarred E Yoder, *Pr*
Cory Smith, *VP*
EMP: 35 **EST:** 2001
SQ FT: 500
SALES (est): 2.67MM **Privately Held**
Web: www.acitops.com
SIC: 2541 Counter and sink tops

(G-7575)
FIRE CONTAINMENT CONCEPTS LLC
13155 Market Ave N (44632-9065)
PHONE..........................800 877-2204
EMP: 10 **EST:** 2013
SALES (est): 273.33K **Privately Held**
Web: www.fcconcepts.com
SIC: 7389 2899 Fire protection service other
than forestry or public; Fire extinguisher
charges

(G-7576)
HARTVILLE CHOCOLATES INC
Also Called: Hartville Chocolate Factory
114 S Prospect Ave (44632-8906)
P.O. Box 1360 (44632-1360)
PHONE..........................330 877-1999
Mary L Barton, *Pr*

EMP: 7 **EST:** 1984
SQ FT: 3,200
SALES (est): 475.03K **Privately Held**
Web: www.discoverhartville.com
SIC: 2066 5441 5999 Chocolate; Candy;
Cake decorating supplies

(G-7577)
HARTVILLE LOCKER SERVICE LTD
119 Sunnyside St Sw (44632-8933)
PHONE..........................330 877-9547
James Young, *Pr*
Jill E Young, *Sec*
EMP: 8 **EST:** 1952
SQ FT: 5,500
SALES (est): 130.39K **Privately Held**
Web: www.hartvilleoh.com
SIC: 2011 Meat packing plants

(G-7578)
HERITAGE TRUCK EQUIPMENT INC
661 Powell Ave (44632-7800)
PHONE..........................330 699-4491
Eric Bontrager, *Pr*
Brian Bontrager, *
EMP: 85 **EST:** 2000
SALES (est): 16.37MM **Privately Held**
Web: www.heritagetruck.com
SIC: 3537 Trucks, tractors, loaders, carriers,
and similar equipment

(G-7579)
L C F INC
Also Called: Love Chocolate Factory
114 S Prospect Ave (44632-8906)
P.O. Box 1360 (44632-1360)
PHONE..........................330 877-3322
Robert M Barton, *Pr*
▼ **EMP:** 7 **EST:** 1986
SQ FT: 12,000
SALES (est): 696.97K **Privately Held**
Web: www.strategicimpact.com
SIC: 2066 Chocolate candy, solid

(G-7580)
**LOUISVILLE MOLDED PRODUCTS
INC**
Also Called: Lmp
13122 Duquette Ave Ne (44632-8829)
PHONE..........................330 877-9740
Robert Osolinski, *Pr*
Charles Lynn, *VP*
EMP: 6 **EST:** 1962
SQ FT: 40,000
SALES (est): 309.63K **Privately Held**
SIC: 2821 Polyurethane resins

(G-7581)
MITCHELL PIPING LLC
1101 Sunnyside St Sw (44632-9066)
PHONE..........................330 245-0258
Scott Mitchell, *Pr*
EMP: 30 **EST:** 2010
SALES (est): 2.91MM **Privately Held**
Web: www.mitchell-piping.com
SIC: 3498 Fabricated pipe and fittings

(G-7582)
RANDOLPH TOOL COMPANY INC
750 Wales Dr (44632-8852)
PHONE..........................330 877-4923
Patrick Franze, *Pr*
Lisa M Franze, *Treas*
EMP: 12 **EST:** 1968
SQ FT: 5,800
SALES (est): 2.21MM **Privately Held**
Web: www.randolphtoolco.com
SIC: 3599 3423 Machine shop, jobbing and
repair; Knives, agricultural or industrial

(G-7583)
SCANACON INCORPORATED
950 Wales Dr (44632-8856)
PHONE..........................330 877-7600
Kevin Wolf, *Pr*
Sven Hedman, *Ch Bd*
▲ **EMP:** 6 **EST:** 1995
SALES (est): 9.33MM
SALES (corp-wide): 199.07K **Privately
Held**
Web: www.scanaconus.com
SIC: 3565 Canning machinery, food
HQ: Scanacon Ab
Fagerstagatan 18b
SpAnga 163 5
856482300

(G-7584)
SCOTT PROCESS SYSTEMS INC
Also Called: Spsi
1160 Sunnyside St Sw (44632-9098)
PHONE..........................330 877-2350
Andrew Hawranick, *Pr*
◆ **EMP:** 240 **EST:** 1983
SQ FT: 100,000
SALES (est): 4.46MM
SALES (corp-wide): 82.02MM **Privately
Held**
Web: www.scottprocess.com
SIC: 3498 Pipe sections, fabricated from
purchased pipe
PA: Ansgar Industrial, Llc
6000 Fairview Rd Ste 1200
Charlotte NC 28210
866 284-1931

Haverhill
Scioto County

(G-7585)
ALTIVIA PETROCHEMICALS LLC
1019 Haverhill Ohio Furnance Rd (45636)
PHONE..........................740 532-3420
Mark Tipton, *Mgr*
EMP: 50
SALES (corp-wide): 51.15MM **Privately
Held**
Web: www.altivia.com
SIC: 2865 Phenol, alkylated and cumene
PA: Altivia Petrochemicals, Llc
1100 La St Ste 4800
Houston TX 77002
713 658-9000

Haviland
Paulding County

(G-7586)
CUSTOM ASSEMBLY INC
2952 Road 107 (45851-9638)
PHONE..........................419 622-3040
George Keysor, *Pr*
Sharon Keysor, *
Gus A Schlatter, *
Steven R Plummer, *
EMP: 50 **EST:** 1985
SQ FT: 60,000
SALES (est): 9.33MM **Privately Held**
Web: www.customassembly.net
SIC: 3751 Motorcycles, bicycles and parts

(G-7587)
DRAINAGE PRODUCTS INC
100 Main St (45851-8603)
P.O. Box 61 (45851-0061)
PHONE..........................419 622-6951
Craig A Stoller, *Pr*
Thomas Coy, *Sec*

EMP: 8 **EST:** 1978
SALES (est): 2.46MM **Privately Held**
Web: www.haviland-drainage.com
SIC: 3084 Plastics pipe

(G-7588)
HAVILAND CULVERT COMPANY
100 Main St (45851-8603)
P.O. Box 97 (45851-0097)
PHONE..............................419 622-6951
Russell W Stoller, *Pr*
Thomas A Gordon, *Sec*
EMP: 7 **EST:** 1972
SALES (est): 247.51K **Privately Held**
Web: www.haviland-drainage.com
SIC: 3272 Pipe, concrete or lined with
concrete

(G-7589)
**HAVILAND DRAINAGE PRODUCTS
CO (PA)**
100 Main St (45851-8603)
PHONE..............................800 860-6294
Russell Stoller, *Pr*
Todd Stoller, *Sec*
EMP: 17 **EST:** 1924
SQ FT: 1,000
SALES (est): 4.87MM
SALES (corp-wide): 4.87MM **Privately
Held**
Web: www.haviland-drainage.com
SIC: 3259 Drain tile, clay

(G-7590)
HAVILAND PLASTIC PRODUCTS CO
119 Main St (45851-8603)
P.O. Box 38 (45851-0038)
PHONE..............................419 622-3110
Craig Stoller, *Pr*
Todd Stoller, *
▼ **EMP:** 26 **EST:** 1995
SALES (est): 4.55MM **Privately Held**
Web: www.havilandplastics.com
SIC: 3089 Injection molding of plastics

Hayesville
Ashland County

(G-7591)
COBURN INC (PA)
636 Ashland County Rd 30 A (44838)
P.O. Box 447 (44805-0447)
PHONE..............................419 368-4051
Charles Zimmerman, *CEO*
Todd Zimmerman, *
EMP: 65 **EST:** 1966
SQ FT: 82,000
SALES (est): 4.88MM
SALES (corp-wide): 4.88MM **Privately
Held**
Web: www.rohrer.com
SIC: 2631 Container, packaging, and
boxboard

Heath
Licking County

(G-7592)
**AMERICAN VENEER EDGEBANDING
CO**
Also Called: A.V.E.C.
1700 James Pkwy (43056-4027)
PHONE..............................740 928-2700
Germany Heigtz, *Prin*
▲ **EMP:** 6 **EST:** 1997
SQ FT: 30,000
SALES (est): 3.93MM
SALES (corp-wide): 1.82B **Privately Held**

Web: www.avec-usa.com
SIC: 2435 2436 Veneer stock, hardwood;
Veneer stock, softwood
HQ: Heitz International Beteiligungs Gmbh
Maschweg 27
Melle NI

(G-7593)
ATLANTIC INERTIAL SYSTEMS INC
781 Irving Wick Dr W Ste 01 (43056-9492)
PHONE..............................740 788-3800
Al Bonacci, *Brnch Mgr*
EMP: 103
SALES (corp-wide): 80.74B **Publicly Held**
Web: www.atlanticinertial.com
SIC: 3812 Gyroscopes
HQ: Atlantic Inertial Systems Inc.
250 Knotter Dr
Cheshire CT 06410
203 250-3500

(G-7594)
BOEING COMPANY
Also Called: Boeing
801 Irving Wick Dr W (43056-1199)
PHONE..............................740 788-4000
Daniel Acassidy, *Brnch Mgr*
EMP: 25
SALES (corp-wide): 66.52B **Publicly Held**
Web: www.boeing.com
SIC: 3721 3812 Airplanes, fixed or rotary
wing; Search and navigation equipment
PA: The Boeing Company
929 Long Bridge Dr
Arlington VA 22202
703 465-3500

(G-7595)
GUSHEN AMERICA INC
701 International Dr (43056-1108)
PHONE..............................708 664-2852
Shiwei Li, *Pr*
Shiwei Li, *Managing Member*
Zulin Shi, *Sec*
EMP: 6 **EST:** 2016
SALES (est): 819.35K **Privately Held**
SIC: 2869 Perfumes, flavorings, and food
additives

(G-7596)
HARTMAN DISTRIBUTING LLC
1262 Bluejack Ln (43056-8228)
PHONE..............................740 616-7764
EMP: 84 **EST:** 2012
SALES (est): 463.79K **Privately Held**
SIC: 2759 Screen printing

(G-7597)
ISO TECHNOLOGIES INC
1870 James Pkwy (43056-4003)
PHONE..............................740 928-0084
EMP: 20
SALES (corp-wide): 6.05MM **Privately
Held**
Web: www.isotechfoam.com
SIC: 3086 Plastics foam products
PA: Iso Technologies, Inc.
200 Milliken Dr Se
Hebron OH 43025
740 928-0084

(G-7598)
KAISER ALUMINUM FAB PDTS LLC
Also Called: Kaiser Aluminum Newark Works
600 Kaiser Dr (43056-1088)
PHONE..............................740 522-1151
Eric Angermeier, *Mgr*
EMP: 250
SALES (corp-wide): 3.02B **Publicly Held**
Web: www.kaiseraluminum.com

SIC: 3355 3334 Rods, rolled, aluminum;
Primary aluminum
HQ: Kaiser Aluminum Fabricated Products,
Llc
1550 W Mcewen Dr Ste 500,
Franklin TN 37067

(G-7599)
KLARITY MEDICAL PRODUCTS LLC
600 Industrial Pkwy Ste A (43056-1636)
PHONE..............................740 788-8107
EMP: 10 **EST:** 2012
SALES (est): 2.28MM **Privately Held**
Web: www.klaritymedical.com
SIC: 3841 Surgical and medical instruments

(G-7600)
PLANT PLANT CO ✪
630 Kaiser Dr (43056-1088)
PHONE..............................303 809-9588
Aaron Matthew Tullman, *CEO*
EMP: 25 **EST:** 2024
SALES (est): 5.06MM **Privately Held**
SIC: 2099 Food preparations, nec

(G-7601)
POLYMER TECH & SVCS INC (HQ)
Also Called: Pts
1835 James Pkwy (43056-1092)
PHONE..............................740 929-5500
Sharad Thakkar, *Pr*
EMP: 10 **EST:** 2002
SQ FT: 50,000
SALES (est): 5.1MM
SALES (corp-wide): 64.91MM **Privately
Held**
Web: www.polymertechnologiesinc.com
SIC: 2611 2821 Pulp mills; Plastics materials
and resins
PA: Niche Polymer Llc
8815 Centre Pk Dr Ste 400
Columbia MD 21045
304 273-1200

(G-7602)
R D HOLDER OIL CO INC
1000 Keller Dr (43056-8055)
PHONE..............................740 522-3136
EMP: 18
SALES (corp-wide): 11.63MM **Privately
Held**
Web: www.holderoil.com
SIC: 1311 Crude petroleum and natural gas
PA: R. D. Holder Oil Co., Inc.
600 N Dayton Lakeview Rd
New Carlisle OH 45344
800 243-0432

(G-7603)
RTZ MANUFACTURING CO
12755 Fairview Rd (43056-9043)
P.O. Box 289 (43085-0289)
PHONE..............................614 848-8366
Zoe Rosser, *Pr*
Ty Rosser, *VP*
EMP: 9 **EST:** 1994
SALES (est): 3.33MM **Privately Held**
SIC: 3599 Custom machinery

(G-7604)
SAMUEL SON & CO (USA) INC
Samuel Packaging Systems Group
1455 James Pkwy (43056-4007)
PHONE..............................740 522-2500
Jay Jones, *Mgr*
EMP: 100
SALES (corp-wide): 1.54B **Privately Held**
Web: www.samuel.com

SIC: 3089 5085 5084 5199 Plastics
processing; Industrial supplies; Industrial
machinery and equipment; Packaging
materials
HQ: Samuel, Son & Co. (Usa) Inc.
1401 Davey Rd Ste 300
Woodridge IL 60517
800 323-4424

(G-7605)
XPERION E & E USA LLC
1475 James Pkwy (43056-4007)
PHONE..............................740 788-9560
Sean Ellen, *Managing Member*
EMP: 25 **EST:** 2013
SQ FT: 50,000
SALES (est): 4.8MM
SALES (corp-wide): 121.41MM **Privately
Held**
SIC: 3624 Fibers, carbon and graphite
HQ: Hexagon Purus Gmbh
Hannoversche Str. 1
Kassel HE 34134
561585490

Hebron
Licking County

(G-7606)
4W SERVICES
7901 Minecaster Rd (43025)
PHONE..............................614 554-5427
Donald White, *Owner*
EMP: 15 **EST:** 2011
SALES (est): 1.33MM **Privately Held**
SIC: 3715 8999 Semitrailers for truck tractors
; Artists and artists' studios

(G-7607)
ALLIED TUBE & CONDUIT CORP
250 Capital Dr (43025-9489)
PHONE..............................740 928-1018
Scott Shipley, *Brnch Mgr*
EMP: 10
Web: www.atkore.com
SIC: 3644 Electric conduits and fittings
HQ: Allied Tube & Conduit Corporation
16100 S Center Ave
Harvey IL 60426
708 339-1610

(G-7608)
ARMORSOURCE LLC
3600 Hebron Rd (43025-9664)
PHONE..............................740 928-0070
Yoav Kapah, *CEO*
Donald Blake, *Ex VP*
Tim Tallentire, *CFO*
▼ **EMP:** 20 **EST:** 2005
SQ FT: 120,000
SALES (est): 7.16MM **Privately Held**
Web: www.armorsource.com
SIC: 3469 Helmets, steel

(G-7609)
**BOWMAN TIRE REPR CTR BXLEY
LLC**
110 Burch St (43025-9029)
PHONE..............................740 928-7000
Jon Bowman, *Managing Member*
EMP: 6 **EST:** 2010
SALES (est): 896.82K **Privately Held**
Web: www.bowmantireandrepair.com
SIC: 5531 7538 7534 7539 Automotive tires;
General automotive repair shops; Tire
retreading and repair shops; Automotive
repair shops, nec

(G-7610)
CLEARPATH UTLITY SOLUTIONS LLC
2925 National Rd Sw (43025-9407)
PHONE..........................740 661-4240
Maureen E Riley, *Managing Member*
Rodney Riley, *Prin*
EMP: 10 **EST:** 2007
SALES (est): 3.19MM **Privately Held**
Web: www.directionaldrilling.com
SIC: 1381 Directional drilling oil and gas wells

(G-7611)
COVESTRO LLC
1111 O Neill Dr (43025-9409)
PHONE..........................740 929-2015
Lora Rand, *Mgr*
EMP: 150
SALES (corp-wide): 14.99B **Privately Held**
Web: www.covestro.com
SIC: 2822 2821 Synthetic rubber; Plastics materials and resins
HQ: Covestro Llc
1 Covestro Cir
Pittsburgh PA 15205
412 413-2000

(G-7612)
DIEBOLD NIXDORF INCORPORATED
Also Called: Midwest Division
511 Milliken Dr (43025-9657)
PHONE..........................740 928-1010
Bob Brown, *Mgr*
EMP: 200
SALES (corp-wide): 3.75B **Publicly Held**
Web: www.dieboldnixdorf.com
SIC: 3499 3578 Safes and vaults, metal; Banking machines
PA: Diebold Nixdorf, Incorporated
350 Orchard Ave Ne
North Canton OH 44720
330 490-4000

(G-7613)
DIEBOLD NIXDORF INCORPORATED
Also Called: Self-Srvice PDT Dist Shipg Ctr
1050 O Neill Dr (43025-9409)
PHONE..........................740 928-0200
EMP: 59
SALES (corp-wide): 3.75B **Publicly Held**
Web: www.dieboldnixdorf.com
SIC: 3578 Automatic teller machines (ATM)
PA: Diebold Nixdorf, Incorporated
350 Orchard Ave Ne
North Canton OH 44720
330 490-4000

(G-7614)
FOLDEDPAK INC
263 Milliken Dr (43025-9657)
PHONE..........................740 527-1090
EMP: 6 **EST:** 2015
SALES (est): 1.15MM **Privately Held**
SIC: 2675 Die-cut paper and board

(G-7615)
FORCEONE LLC
3600 Hebron Rd (43025-9664)
PHONE..........................513 939-1018
EMP: 7 **EST:** 2000
SQ FT: 17,000
SALES (est): 754.23K **Privately Held**
SIC: 3842 Bulletproof vests

(G-7616)
HARRY & DAVID OPERATIONS INC
Also Called: Harry & David
111 Enterprise Dr (43025-9201)
PHONE..........................541 864-3710

Joseph Rowland, *Pr*
EMP: 1000
Web: www.harryanddavid.com
SIC: 2099 Food preparations, nec
HQ: Harry & David Operations, Inc.
2500 S Pacific Hwy
Medford OR 97501
877 322-1200

(G-7617)
HENDRICKSON INTERNATIONAL CORP
Also Called: Hendrickson Auxiliary Axles
277 N High St (43025-8008)
PHONE..........................740 929-5600
Mike Keeler, *Genl Mgr*
EMP: 78
SALES (corp-wide): 758.84MM **Privately Held**
Web: www.hendrickson-intl.com
SIC: 3714 3493 3089 5084 Motor vehicle parts and accessories; Steel springs, except wire; Plastics containers, except foam; Industrial machinery and equipment
HQ: Hendrickson International Corporation
840 S Frontage Rd
Woodridge IL 60517

(G-7618)
HENDRICKSON USA LLC
277 N High St (43025-8008)
PHONE..........................740 929-5600
EMP: 213
SALES (corp-wide): 758.84MM **Privately Held**
Web: www.hendrickson-intl.com
SIC: 3714 Motor vehicle parts and accessories
HQ: Hendrickson Usa, L.L.C.
840 S Frontage Rd
Woodridge IL 60517

(G-7619)
INTEGRIS COMPOSITES INC
1051 O Neill Dr (43025-9409)
PHONE..........................740 928-0326
Erick Johnson, *Brnch Mgr*
EMP: 65
Web: www.integriscomposites.com
SIC: 3229 3795 8711 Yarn, fiberglass; Tanks and tank components; Engineering services
HQ: Integris Composites, Inc.
120 Cremona Dr Ste 130
Coleta CA 03117

(G-7620)
ISO TECHNOLOGIES INC (PA)
200 Milliken Dr (43025-9657)
PHONE..........................740 928-0084
Alan Benton, *Pr*
EMP: 10 **EST:** 1997
SQ FT: 20,000
SALES (est): 6.05MM
SALES (corp-wide): 6.05MM **Privately Held**
Web: www.isotechfoam.com
SIC: 3069 Foam rubber

(G-7621)
KEHO FITNESS AND NUTRITION LLC
Also Called: Bia Factory, The
660 International Dr (43025)
PHONE..........................740 587-1313
Trent Wills, *Managing Member*
EMP: 7 **EST:** 2013
SALES (est): 893.16K **Privately Held**
Web: www.thebiafactory.com
SIC: 2064 2099 Granola and muesli, bars and clusters; Food preparations, nec

(G-7622)
LEAR CORPORATION
Also Called: Renosol Seating
180 N High St (43025-9011)
P.O. Box 640 (43025-0640)
PHONE..........................740 928-4358
Jeff O'sickey, *Manager*
EMP: 71
SALES (corp-wide): 23.31B **Publicly Held**
Web: www.lear.com
SIC: 3714 Motor vehicle parts and accessories
PA: Lear Corporation
21557 Telegraph Rd
Southfield MI 48033
248 447-1500

(G-7623)
MOLDING TECHNOLOGIES LTD
Also Called: Molding Technologies
85 N. High Street (43025)
PHONE..........................740 929-2065
EMP: 10 **EST:** 2017
SQ FT: 60,000
SALES (est): 2.15MM **Privately Held**
SIC: 3089 Injection molding of plastics

(G-7624)
MOMENTIVE PERFORMANCE MTLS INC
611 O Neill Dr (43025-9680)
PHONE..........................740 928-7010
Cherly Glaton, *Mgr*
EMP: 482
Web: www.momentive.com
SIC: 2869 3479 Silicones; Coating of metals with silicon
HQ: Momentive Performance Materials Inc.
2750 Balltown Rd
Niskayuna NY 12309

(G-7625)
MPW INDUSTRIAL SVCS GROUP INC (PA)
9711 Lancaster Rd (43025-9764)
PHONE..........................740 927-8790
Monte R Black, *CEO*
Jared Black, *
Sarah D Pemberton, *
EMP: 253 **EST:** 1972
SQ FT: 24,000
SALES (est): 213.53MM
SALES (corp-wide): 213.53MM **Privately Held**
Web: www.mpwservices.com
SIC: 7349 8744 3589 Cleaning service, industrial or commercial; Facilities support services; Commercial cleaning equipment

(G-7626)
NFI INDUSTRIES INC
111 Enterprise Dr (43025-9201)
PHONE..........................740 928-9522
EMP: 10 **EST:** 2006
SALES (est): 240.22K **Privately Held**
Web: www.nfiindustries.com
SIC: 3999 Manufacturing industries, nec

(G-7627)
OHIO METAL TECHNOLOGIES INC
470 John Alford Pkwy (43025-9437)
P.O. Box 33 (43025)
PHONE..........................740 928-8288
Toshi Hara, *Pr*
Masao Segawa, *
Toshiyuki Hara, *
▲ **EMP:** 80 **EST:** 1996
SQ FT: 20,600
SALES (est): 9.18MM **Privately Held**
Web: www.ohiometal.net

SIC: 3441 Fabricated structural metal

(G-7628)
OWENS CORNING SALES LLC
Also Called: Owens Corning
341 O Neill Dr Bldg 6 (43025-9680)
P.O. Box 1477 (43025-1477)
PHONE..........................740 928-6620
Gary Jakubcin, *Brnch Mgr*
EMP: 50
SQ FT: 81,000
SIC: 3296 Fiberglass insulation
HQ: Owens Corning Sales, Llc
1 Owens Corning Pkwy
Toledo OH 43659
419 248-8000

(G-7629)
PALMER DONAVIN MANUFACTURING
1120 O Neill Dr (43025-9409)
PHONE..........................740 527-1111
EMP: 10 **EST:** 2015
SALES (est): 2.35MM **Privately Held**
Web: www.palmerdonavin.com
SIC: 3999 Manufacturing industries, nec

(G-7630)
PLASTIPAK PACKAGING INC
Also Called: Constar International
610 O Neill Dr Bldg 22 (43025-9680)
PHONE..........................740 928-4435
Brian Dunlap, *Mgr*
EMP: 103
SALES (corp-wide): 2.9B **Privately Held**
Web: www.plastipak.com
SIC: 3089 3085 Plastics containers, except foam; Plastics bottles
HQ: Plastipak Packaging, Inc.
41605 Ann Arbor Rd
Plymouth MI 48170
734 455-3600

(G-7631)
POLYMERA INC
511 Milliken Dr (43025-9657)
PHONE..........................740 527-2069
Maan Said, *Pr*
Herbert Hutchison, *Sr VP*
Jeffrey Brandt, *VP*
Matthew Kollar, *VP*
Michael Skoff, *CFO*
EMP: 9 **EST:** 2010
SALES (est): 978.47K **Privately Held**
Web: www.polymera.com
SIC: 3087 Custom compound purchased resins

(G-7632)
R R DONNELLEY & SONS COMPANY
Also Called: R R Donnelley
190 Milliken Dr (43025-9657)
PHONE..........................740 928-6110
Jeff Gebhart, *Brnch Mgr*
EMP: 280
SALES (corp-wide): 15B **Privately Held**
Web: www.rrd.com
SIC: 2759 Business forms: printing, nsk
HQ: R. R. Donnelley & Sons Company
227 W Monroe St Ste 500
Chicago IL 60606
312 326-8000

(G-7633)
RESINOID ENGINEERING CORP (PA)
251 O Neill Dr (43025-9680)
PHONE..........................740 928-6115
Clarence A Herbst Junior, *Ch*
Robert C Herbst, *
◆ **EMP:** 58 **EST:** 1939
SQ FT: 70,000

SALES (est): 12.68MM
SALES (corp-wide): 12.68MM **Privately Held**
Web: www.resinoid.com
SIC: 2821 3083 3089 Molding compounds, plastics; Laminated plastics plate and sheet ; Injection molding of plastics

(G-7634)
S R DOOR INC (PA)
Also Called: Seal-Rite Door
1120 O Neill Dr (43025-9409)
P.O. Box 2109 (43216-2109)
PHONE..............................740 927-3558
Scott A Miller, *Pr*
Glen Miller, *
EMP: 80 **EST:** 1980
SQ FT: 75,000
SALES (est): 4.37MM
SALES (corp-wide): 4.37MM **Privately Held**
Web: www.palmerdonavin.com
SIC: 2431 3442 3211 5031 Doors, wood; Metal doors; Construction glass; Lumber, plywood, and millwork

(G-7635)
SCHWEBEL BAKING COMPANY
121 O Neill Dr (43025-9680)
PHONE..............................330 783-2860
John Phillips, *Mgr*
EMP: 35
SALES (corp-wide): 71.65MM **Privately Held**
Web: www.schwebels.com
SIC: 5461 2051 Bread; Bread, cake, and related products
PA: Schwebel Baking Company
965 E Midlothian Blvd
Youngstown OH 44502
330 783-2860

(G-7636)
SMARTBILL LTD
1050 O Neill Dr (43025-9409)
PHONE..............................740 928-6909
EMP: 17 **EST:** 2001
SQ FT: 10,000
SALES (est): 2.98MM **Privately Held**
Web: www.smartbillcorp.com
SIC: 2759 Business forms: printing, nsk

(G-7637)
STATE INDUSTRIAL PRODUCTS CORP
Also Called: State Chemical Manufacturing
383 N High St (43025-9436)
PHONE..............................740 929-6370
Kale Moberg, *Brnch Mgr*
EMP: 56
SALES (corp-wide): 86.95MM **Privately Held**
Web: www.stateindustrial.com
SIC: 2841 5072 Soap: granulated, liquid, cake, flaked, or chip; Bolts, nuts, and screws
PA: State Industrial Products Corporation
5915 Lndrbrook Dr Ste 300
Cleveland OH 44124
877 747-6986

(G-7638)
SUNFIELD INC
116 Enterprise Dr (43025-9200)
PHONE..............................740 928-0405
Norio Hirotani, *Pr*
◆ **EMP:** 70 **EST:** 1993
SQ FT: 33,000
SALES (est): 24.48MM **Privately Held**
Web: www.sunfieldinc.com

SIC: 3469 Stamping metal for the trade
HQ: Ikeda Manufacturing Co., Ltd.
135-3, Nishishinmachi
Ota GNM 373-0

(G-7639)
THK MANUFACTURING AMERICA INC
471 N High St (43025-9012)
P.O. Box 759 (43025-0759)
PHONE..............................740 928-1415
Nobuyuki Maki, *Pr*
▲ **EMP:** 160 **EST:** 1997
SQ FT: 400,000
SALES (est): 48.37MM **Privately Held**
SIC: 3823 3469 Process control instruments; Machine parts, stamped or pressed metal
HQ: Thk Holdings Of America, L.L.C.
200 Commerce Dr
Schaumburg IL 60173
847 310-1111

(G-7640)
TI GROUP AUTO SYSTEMS LLC
Bundy Tubing Div
3600 Hebron Rd (43025-9664)
PHONE..............................740 929-2049
Mark Lanancusa, *Mgr*
EMP: 41
SALES (corp-wide): 26.11B **Publicly Held**
Web: www.tifluidsystems.com
SIC: 3317 3714 3498 Steel pipe and tubes; Motor vehicle parts and accessories; Fabricated pipe and fittings
HQ: Ti Group Automotive Systems, Llc
2020 Taylor Rd
Auburn Hills MI 48326
248 296-8000

(G-7641)
TRANSCENDIA INC
Also Called: Dow Chemical
3700 Hebron Rd (43025-9665)
PHONE..............................740 929-5100
Andy Maynard, *Brnch Mgr*
EMP: 112
SALES (corp-wide): 290.26MM **Privately Held**
Web: www.transcendia.com
SIC: 3081 Unsupported plastics film and sheet
PA: Transcendia, Inc.
9201 W Belmont Ave
Franklin Park IL 60131
847 678-1800

(G-7642)
TRULITE GL ALUM SOLUTIONS LLC
160 N High St (43025-9011)
P.O. Box 220 (43025-0220)
PHONE..............................740 929-2443
EMP: 60
SIC: 3211 5039 3231 Tempered glass; Exterior flat glass: plate or window; Products of purchased glass
PA: Trulite Glass & Aluminum Solutions, Llc
403 Westpark Ct Ste 201
Peachtree City GA 30009

(G-7643)
UNIPAC INC
2109 National Rd Sw (43025-9639)
PHONE..............................740 929-2000
David L De Ment, *Pr*
Chris De Ment, *Sec*
EMP: 22 **EST:** 1973
SQ FT: 50,000
SALES (est): 2.46MM **Privately Held**
Web: www.unipacinc.com

SIC: 2657 2653 Folding paperboard boxes; Boxes, corrugated: made from purchased materials

---

Hicksville
Defiance County

(G-7644)
A & P TOOL INC
Also Called: APT Manufacturing Solutions
801 Industrial Dr (43526-1174)
P.O. Box 88 (43526-0088)
PHONE..............................419 542-6681
Anthony R Nighswander, *Pr*
EMP: 30 **EST:** 1995
SALES (est): 7.53MM **Privately Held**
Web: www.aptmfg.com
SIC: 3541 3822 Machine tools, metal cutting type; Building services monitoring controls, automatic

(G-7645)
ADROIT THINKING INC
Also Called: 5-Acre Mill
10860 State Route 2 (43526-9366)
PHONE..............................419 542-9363
Tim Becker, *Pr*
Mary Becker, *VP*
EMP: 17 **EST:** 2004
SQ FT: 28,000
SALES (est): 1.68MM **Privately Held**
SIC: 2499 Laundry products, wood

(G-7646)
ARC SOLUTIONS LLC
Also Called: ARC Solutions
605 Industrial Dr (43526-1177)
P.O. Box 264 (43526-0264)
PHONE..............................419 542-9272
Dennis Vetter, *
EMP: 30 **EST:** 2001
SQ FT: 28,800
SALES (est): 2.52MM **Privately Held**
Web: www.arcsolinc.com
SIC: 7692 7699 5084 5999 Welding repair; Industrial machinery and equipment repair; Welding machinery and equipment; Welding supplies

(G-7647)
DL SCHWARTZ CO LLC
9737 State Route 49 (43526-9780)
PHONE..............................260 692-1464
EMP: 8 **EST:** 1935
SALES (est): 428.64K **Privately Held**
SIC: 5072 3441 Hardware; Fabricated structural metal

(G-7648)
MST INC
Also Called: Modern Safety Techniques
11370 Breininger Rd (43526-9339)
P.O. Box 87 (43526-0087)
PHONE..............................419 542-6645
Charles Martin, *Pr*
James M Prickett, *Prin*
EMP: 7 **EST:** 1989
SQ FT: 10,000
SALES (est): 1.26MM **Privately Held**
Web: www.modsafe.com
SIC: 3842 Respiratory protection equipment, personal

(G-7649)
NEMCO FOOD EQUIPMENT LTD (PA)
301 Meuse Argonne St (43526-1143)
P.O. Box 305 (43526-0305)
PHONE..............................419 542-7751
Kenny Moffatt, *Ch Bd*

Stanley Guilliam, *
Larry Stewart, *
▼ **EMP:** 71 **EST:** 1976
SQ FT: 50,000
SALES (est): 23.41MM
SALES (corp-wide): 23.41MM **Privately Held**
Web: www.nemcofoodequip.com
SIC: 3556 Food products machinery

(G-7650)
PARKER-HANNIFIN CORPORATION
Hydraulic Valve Div
373 Meuse Argonne St (43526-1182)
PHONE..............................419 542-6611
Andy Ross, *Brnch Mgr*
EMP: 78
SALES (corp-wide): 19.93B **Publicly Held**
Web: www.parker.com
SIC: 3492 3491 Valves, hydraulic, aircraft; Industrial valves
PA: Parker-Hannifin Corporation
6035 Parkland Blvd
Cleveland OH 44124
216 896-3000

(G-7651)
PEC BIOFUELS LLC
210 Wendell Ave (43526-1405)
PHONE..............................419 542-8210
EMP: 6 **EST:** 2006
SALES (est): 197.09K **Privately Held**
SIC: 2836 2911 Biological products, except diagnostic; Diesel fuels

(G-7652)
SABRE INDUSTRIES INC
761 W High St (43526-1052)
PHONE..............................419 542-1420
EMP: 10 **EST:** 2020
SALES (est): 2.35MM **Privately Held**
Web: www.sabreindusties.com
SIC: 3441 Fabricated structural metal

(G-7653)
TRI STATE DAIRY LLC
210 Wendell Ave (43526-1405)
P.O. Box 284 (43526-0284)
PHONE..............................419 542-8788
EMP: 9
SALES (corp-wide): 1.19MM **Privately Held**
SIC: 2022 Natural cheese
PA: Tri State Dairy Llc
9946 Fiat Rd Sw
Baltic OH 43804
330 897-5555

(G-7654)
TRIBUNE PRINTING INC
Also Called: News Tribune
147 E High St (43526-1159)
P.O. Box 303 (43526-0303)
PHONE..............................419 542-7764
Mary Ann Barth, *Pr*
EMP: 9 **EST:** 1970
SQ FT: 2,000
SALES (est): 365.61K **Privately Held**
Web: www.tribuneprintinginc.com
SIC: 2711 2752 Newspapers: publishing only, not printed on site; Commercial printing, lithographic

---

Highland Heights
Cuyahoga County

(G-7655)
C & S ASSOCIATES INC
Also Called: National Lien Digest

729 Miner Rd (44143-2117)
P.O. Box 24101 (44124-0101)
PHONE.................................440 461-9661
Mary B Cowan, *Pr*
Delores A Cowan, *
Greg Powelson, *
Bernie Cowan, *
Bernard J Cowan, *
EMP: 50 **EST:** 1974
SQ FT: 9,000
SALES (est): 9.06MM **Privately Held**
Web: www.ncscredit.com
SIC: 7322 2721 Collection agency, except
real estate; Periodicals, publishing only

(G-7656)
COTSWORKS INC (PA)
749 Miner Rd (44143-2145)
PHONE.................................440 446-8800
Ken Applebaum, *CEO*
EMP: 94 **EST:** 2006
SQ FT: 6,000
SALES (est): 14.39MM **Privately Held**
Web: www.cotsworks.com
SIC: 3661 Fiber optics communications
equipment

(G-7657)
GENVAC AEROSPACE INC
110 Alpha Park (44143-2215)
PHONE.................................440 646-9986
Gerald T Mearini, *Prin*
Gerald Mearini, *Prin*
EMP: 11 **EST:** 2006
SALES (est): 2.46MM **Privately Held**
Web: www.genvac.com
SIC: 3827 Optical instruments and lenses

(G-7658)
GOOCH & HOUSEGO (OHIO) LLC
Also Called: Clevelandcrystals
676 Alpha Dr (44143-2123)
PHONE.................................216 486-6100
Gareth Jones, *CEO*
Jon Fowler, *
Terry Scribbins, *
Andrew Boteler, *
EMP: 65 **EST:** 1973
SALES (est): 24.28MM
SALES (corp-wide): 179.95MM **Privately
Held**
Web: www.gandh.com
SIC: 3823 3827 Process control instruments;
Optical instruments and lenses
PA: Gooch & Housego Plc
Dowlish Ford
Ilminster TA19
146 025-6440

(G-7659)
**HEICO AEROSPACE PARTS CORP
(DH)**
Also Called: Flight Specialties Components
375 Alpha Park (44143-2237)
PHONE.................................954 987-6101
Luis J Morell, *Pr*
Elizabeth R Letendre, *
Carlos L Macau, *
Frank Stevens, *
EMP: 294 **EST:** 2001
SQ FT: 1,500
SALES (est): 28.91MM **Publicly Held**
Web: www.heico.com
SIC: 3724 Aircraft engines and engine parts
HQ: Heico Aerospace Corporation
3000 Taft St
Hollywood FL 33021
954 987-6101

(G-7660)
NORMAN NOBLE INC (PA)
5507 Avion Park Dr (44143-1921)
PHONE.................................216 761-5387
Lawrence Noble, *Pr*
Chris Noble, *
Dan Stefano, *
▲ **EMP:** 450 **EST:** 1962
SQ FT: 20,000
SALES (est): 42.44MM
SALES (corp-wide): 42.44MM **Privately
Held**
Web: www.nnoble.com
SIC: 3841 Instruments, microsurgical: except
electromedical

(G-7661)
OPTICAL DISPLAY ENGRG INC
375 Alpha Park (44143-2237)
PHONE.................................440 995-6555
Nicholas Wright, *Prin*
Jeremy Walker, *Prin*
EMP: 16 **EST:** 2018
SALES (est): 889.91K **Privately Held**
Web: www.heico.com
SIC: 3724 Aircraft engines and engine parts

(G-7662)
PURE FOODS LLC
675 Alpha Dr Ste E (44143-2139)
PHONE.................................303 358-8375
Anthony Stedillie, *Managing Member*
EMP: 9 **EST:** 2017
SALES (est): 265.02K **Privately Held**
SIC: 2099 Food preparations, nec

Hilliard
Franklin County

(G-7663)
ADS INTERNATIONAL INC
4640 Trueman Blvd (43026-2438)
PHONE.................................614 658-0050
EMP: 9 **EST:** 1991
SALES (est): 2.56MM
SALES (corp-wide): 2.87B **Publicly Held**
Web: www.adspipe.com
SIC: 3084 Plastics pipe
PA: Advanced Drainage Systems, Inc.
4640 Trueman Blvd
Hilliard OH 43026
614 658-0050

(G-7664)
ADS WORLDWIDE INC (HQ)
4640 Trueman Blvd (43026-2438)
PHONE.................................614 658-0050
EMP: 6 **EST:** 2015
SALES (est): 2.25MM
SALES (corp-wide): 2.87B **Publicly Held**
Web: www.adspipe.com
SIC: 3086 Plastics foam products
PA: Advanced Drainage Systems, Inc.
4640 Trueman Blvd
Hilliard OH 43026
614 658-0050

(G-7665)
ADVANCED DRAINAGE OF OHIO INC
4640 Trueman Blvd (43026-2438)
PHONE.................................614 658-0050
Franklin E Eck, *CEO*
Joseph A Chlapaty, *
EMP: 9 **EST:** 1968
SALES (est): 2.97MM
SALES (corp-wide): 2.87B **Publicly Held**
Web: www.adspipe.com
SIC: 3084 Plastics pipe
PA: Advanced Drainage Systems, Inc.

4640 Trueman Blvd
Hilliard OH 43026
614 658-0050

(G-7666)
**ADVANCED DRAINAGE SYSTEMS
INC (PA)**
Also Called: ADS
4640 Trueman Blvd (43026-2438)
PHONE.................................614 658-0050
D Scott Barbour, *Pr*
Scott A Cottrill, *Ex VP*
Kevin C Talley, *Ex VP*
Darin S Harvey, *Executive Supply Chain
Vice President*
Michael G Huebert, *VP Sls*
▼ **EMP:** 100 **EST:** 1966
SQ FT: 65,000
SALES (est): 2.87B
SALES (corp-wide): 2.87B **Publicly Held**
Web: www.adspipe.com
SIC: 3084 3086 4953 Plastics pipe; Plastics
foam products; Hazardous waste collection
and disposal

(G-7667)
AMERICAN REGENT INC
4150 Lyman Dr (43026-1230)
PHONE.................................614 436-2222
Joseph Kenneth Keller, *CEO*
EMP: 100
Web: www.americanregent.com
SIC: 2834 5122 Pharmaceutical preparations
; Pharmaceuticals
HQ: American Regent, Inc.
5 Ramsey Rd
Shirley NY 11967
631 924-4000

(G-7668)
ARES SPORTSWEAR LTD
3700 Lacon Rd Ste A (43026-2220)
PHONE.................................614 767-1950
Michael Campbell, *Managing Member*
▲ **EMP:** 55 **EST:** 1994
SALES (est): 9.4MM **Privately Held**
Web: www.areswear.com
SIC: 2759 Screen printing

(G-7669)
**ARMSTRONG WORLD INDUSTRIES
INC**
Also Called: Armstrong World
4241 Leap Rd Bldg A (43026-1125)
P.O. Box 580 (43026-0580)
PHONE.................................614 771-9307
David G Haggerty, *Mgr*
EMP: 25
SQ FT: 225,000
SALES (corp-wide): 1.45B **Publicly Held**
Web: www.armstrongceilings.com
SIC: 5713 3996 3251 Floor covering stores;
Hard surface floor coverings, nec; Brick and
structural clay tile
PA: Armstrong World Industries, Inc.
2500 Columbia Ave
Lancaster PA 17603
717 397-0611

(G-7670)
AVID LIGHTING LLC
3757 Parkway Ln (43026-1265)
PHONE.................................614 502-2843
EMP: 6 **EST:** 2019
SALES (est): 1.13MM **Privately Held**
Web: www.avidlighting.com
SIC: 3648 Lighting equipment, nec

(G-7671)
AXALT POWDE COATI SYSTE USA I
4150 Lyman Dr (43026-1230)
PHONE.................................614 921-8000
Danielle Conner, *Mgr*
EMP: 8
SALES (corp-wide): 5.28B **Publicly Held**
Web: www.axalta.com
SIC: 2851 Paints and paint additives
HQ: Axalta Powder Coating Systems Usa,
Inc.
9800 Genard Rd
Houston TX 77041

(G-7672)
AXALT POWDE COATI SYSTE USA I
4130 Lyman Dr (43026-1230)
PHONE.................................614 600-4104
EMP: 8
SALES (corp-wide): 5.28B **Publicly Held**
Web: www.axalta.com
SIC: 2851 Paints and paint additives
HQ: Axalta Powder Coating Systems Usa,
Inc.
9800 Genard Rd
Houston TX 77041

(G-7673)
**AXALTA COATING SYSTEMS USA
LLC**
4130 Lyman Dr (43026-1230)
PHONE.................................614 777-7230
EMP: 58 **EST:** 2018
SALES (est): 2.73MM **Privately Held**
Web: www.axalta.com
SIC: 3999 Manufacturing industries, nec

(G-7674)
BAESMAN GROUP INC (PA)
4477 Reynolds Dr (43026-1261)
PHONE.................................614 771-2300
EMP: 91 **EST:** 1952
SALES (est): 22.34MM
SALES (corp-wide): 22.34MM **Privately
Held**
Web: www.baesman.com
SIC: 2752 7331 2791 2789 Commercial
printing, lithographic; Direct mail advertising
services; Typesetting; Bookbinding and
related work

(G-7675)
BALMAC INC
4010 Main St (43026-1423)
PHONE.................................614 876-1295
Mark Slebodnik, *Prin*
EMP: 7 **EST:** 2010
SALES (est): 145.49K **Privately Held**
Web: www.jcccpa.com
SIC: 3829 Measuring and controlling
devices, nec

(G-7676)
BENZLE PORCELAIN COMPANY
6100 Hayden Run Rd (43026-9456)
PHONE.................................614 876-2159
Curtis M Benzle, *Pr*
EMP: 6 **EST:** 1979
SALES (est): 320K **Privately Held**
SIC: 3269 3961 Art and ornamental ware,
pottery; Costume jewelry, ex. precious
metal and semiprecious stones

(G-7677)
CITYSCAPES INTERNATIONAL INC
4200 Lyman Ct (43026-1213)
PHONE.................................614 850-2540
James Cullinan, *Pr*
EMP: 200 **EST:** 2004
SQ FT: 30,000

GEOGRAPHIC

SALES (est): 1.66MM **Privately Held**
Web: www.cityscapesinc.com
SIC: 3531 Construction machinery

(G-7678)
COLORAMICS LLC
Also Called: Mayco Colors
4077 Weaver Ct S (43026-1197)
PHONE..............................614 876-1171
◆ **EMP: 43 EST:** 1989
SQ FT: 75,000
SALES (est): 15.05MM **Privately Held**
Web: www.maycocolors.com
SIC: 2851 Paints and paint additives

(G-7679)
CUMMINS INC
4000 Lyman Dr (43026-1212)
PHONE..............................614 771-1000
Greg Bowl, *Brnch Mgr*
EMP: 10
SALES (corp-wide): 34.1B **Publicly Held**
Web: www.cummins.com
SIC: 5084 7538 3519 Engines and parts,
diesel; Diesel engine repair: automotive;
Internal combustion engines, nec
PA: Cummins Inc.
500 Jackson St
Columbus IN 47201
812 377-5000

(G-7680)
DECENT HILL PUBLISHERS LLC
Also Called: Decent Hill Press
2825 Wynneleaf St (43026-8144)
PHONE..............................216 548-1255
EMP: 6 **EST:** 2010
SALES (est): 182.81K **Privately Held**
Web: www.decenthill.com
SIC: 2731 Book music: publishing only, not
printed on site

(G-7681)
FAST SIGNS
Also Called: Fastsigns
4440 Reynolds Dr (43026-1279)
PHONE..............................614 710-1312
EMP: 14 **EST:** 2019
SALES (est): 697.8K **Privately Held**
Web: www.fastsigns.com
SIC: 3993 Signs and advertising specialties

(G-7682)
FLUID POWER SOLUTIONS LLC (PA)
4400 Edgewyn Ave (43026-1221)
PHONE..............................614 777-8954
Mike Rogers, *Managing Member*
EMP: 9 **EST:** 2000
SALES (est): 5.14MM
SALES (corp-wide): 5.14MM **Privately
Held**
Web: www.fluid-power-solutions.com
SIC: 5084 3594 Hydraulic systems
equipment and supplies; Fluid power
pumps and motors

(G-7683)
HANCOR INC (HQ)
4640 Trueman Blvd (43026-2438)
PHONE..............................614 658-0050
Steven A Anderson, *Pr*
Derek Kamp, *
William E Altermatt, *
Pat Ferren, *
John Maag, *
◆ **EMP:** 330 **EST:** 2002
SQ FT: 20,000
SALES (est): 15.08MM
SALES (corp-wide): 2.87B **Publicly Held**
Web: www.adspipe.com

SIC: 3084 3088 3089 3083 Plastics pipe;
Plastics plumbing fixtures; Septic tanks,
plastics; Laminated plastics plate and sheet
PA: Advanced Drainage Systems, Inc.
4640 Trueman Blvd
Hilliard OH 43026
614 658-0050

(G-7684)
INS ROBOTICS INC
3600 Parkway Ln (43026-1281)
PHONE..............................888 293-5325
Beth Harkins, *Managing Member*
EMP: 6 **EST:** 2009
SALES (est): 2.48MM **Privately Held**
Web: www.insrobotics.com
SIC: 3535 Conveyors and conveying
equipment

(G-7685)
JD POWER SYSTEMS LLC
Also Called: John Deere Authorized Dealer
3979 Parkway Ln (43026-1250)
PHONE..............................614 317-9394
Jeffrey D Mitchell, *Owner*
EMP: 12 **EST:** 2011
SALES (est): 1.04MM **Privately Held**
Web: www.deere.com
SIC: 3621 5082 Motors and generators;
Construction and mining machinery

(G-7686)
MID-OHIO PRODUCTS INC
4329 Reynolds Dr (43026-1261)
PHONE..............................614 771-2795
Richard Coleman Ii, *Pr*
▲ **EMP:** 56 **EST:** 1980
SQ FT: 16,000
SALES (est): 5.4MM **Privately Held**
Web: www.mid-ohioproducts.com
SIC: 3544 3444 Dies and die holders for
metal cutting, forming, die casting; Sheet
metalwork

(G-7687)
MORLAN & ASSOCIATES INC
Also Called: Flex-Core Division
4970 Scioto Darby Rd Ste D (43026-1548)
P.O. Box 6047 (43026-6047)
PHONE..............................614 889-6152
Teri Shaw, *Pr*
Donald Morlan, *
Eric Whelan, *
Amy Mcnabb, *Corporate Secretary*
▼ **EMP:** 29 **EST:** 1977
SQ FT: 15,000
SALES (est): 5.08MM **Privately Held**
Web: www.flex-core.com
SIC: 3612 Transformers, except electric

(G-7688)
MXR IMAGING INC
Also Called: Baldwin
4770 Northwest Pkwy (43026-1131)
PHONE..............................614 219-2011
Eric Cole, *Mgr*
EMP: 6
SALES (corp-wide): 109.03MM **Privately
Held**
Web: www.mxrimaging.com
SIC: 6411 2899 Medical insurance claim
processing, contract or fee basis; Chemical
supplies for foundries
PA: Mxr Imaging, Inc.
4909 Mrphy Cyn Rd Ste 120
San Diego CA 92123
858 565-4472

(G-7689)
NATIONAL SIGN SYSTEMS INC
Also Called: Advanced Visual Solutions
4200 Lyman Ct (43026-1213)
PHONE..............................614 850-2540
▼ **EMP:** 75 **EST:** 1987
SALES (est): 15.68MM **Privately Held**
Web: www.nationalsignsystems.com
SIC: 3993 3444 Signs and advertising
specialties; Metal roofing and roof drainage
equipment

(G-7690)
OGR PUBLISHING INC
Also Called: O Gauge Railroading
5825 Redsand Rd (43026-8057)
P.O. Box 218 (43026-0218)
PHONE..............................330 757-3020
Richard P Melvin, *Pr*
EMP: 7 **EST:** 2002
SQ FT: 4,000
SALES (est): 175.15K **Privately Held**
Web: www.ogaugerr.com
SIC: 2741 Miscellaneous publishing

(G-7691)
OHIO LAMINATING & BINDING INC
4364 Reynolds Dr (43026-1260)
PHONE..............................614 771-4868
Jim Ondecko, *Pr*
Jimmy R Ondecko, *
▲ **EMP:** 6 **EST:** 1987
SQ FT: 5,000
SALES (est): 391.16K **Privately Held**
Web: www.ohiolam.com
SIC: 7389 2789 2672 Laminating service;
Bookbinding and related work; Paper;
coated and laminated, nec

(G-7692)
OHIO SEMITRONICS INC
Also Called: OSI
4242 Reynolds Dr (43026-1260)
PHONE..............................614 777-1005
Warren E Bulman, *Ch Bd*
Robert A Shaw, *
◆ **EMP:** 88 **EST:** 1964
SQ FT: 49,000
SALES (est): 8.89MM **Privately Held**
Web: www.ohiosemitronics.com
SIC: 3674 3679 3663 3625 Semiconductors
and related devices; Transducers, electrical
; Radio and t.v. communications equipment;
Relays and industrial controls

(G-7693)
OPEN TEXT INC
Also Called: Open Text
3671 Ridge Mill Dr (43026-7752)
PHONE..............................614 658-3588
Anik Ganguly, *Mgr*
EMP: 50
SALES (corp-wide): 5.77B **Privately Held**
Web: www.opentext.com
SIC: 7372 Prepackaged software
HQ: Open Text Inc.
2440 Sand Hill Rd Ste 302
Menlo Park CA 94025
650 645-3000

(G-7694)
PERDATUM INC
4098 Main St (43026-1437)
PHONE..............................614 761-1578
Mark Tochtenhagen, *Pr*
Leo Renner, *CFO*
EMP: 8 **EST:** 1993
SQ FT: 2,500
SALES (est): 436.54K **Privately Held**
SIC: 7372 Prepackaged software

(G-7695)
PHANTOM TECHNOLOGY LLC
Also Called: Pool Office Manager
4179 Lyman Dr (43026-1228)
P.O. Box 893 (34991-0893)
PHONE..............................614 710-0074
EMP: 6 **EST:** 2018
SALES (est): 877.57K **Privately Held**
Web: www.poolofficemanager.com
SIC: 7372 Business oriented computer
software

(G-7696)
PHOENIX HYDRAULIC PRESSES INC
4329 Reynolds Dr (43026-1261)
P.O. Box 1048 (43065-1048)
PHONE..............................614 850-8940
Charles Sherman, *Pr*
EMP: 10 **EST:** 2003
SQ FT: 6,000
SALES (est): 727.3K **Privately Held**
Web: www.phoenixhydraulic.com
SIC: 3542 Presses: hydraulic and
pneumatic, mechanical and manual

(G-7697)
PROTO PRCSION MFG SLUTIONS LLC
Also Called: Proto Precision Fabricators
4101 Leap Rd (43026-1117)
PHONE..............................614 771-0080
Sugu Suguness, *Prin*
EMP: 13 **EST:** 2018
SALES (est): 280.55K **Privately Held**
Web: www.protoprecision.com
SIC: 3999 Manufacturing industries, nec

(G-7698)
RAGE CORPORATION (PA)
Also Called: Rage Plastics
3949 Lyman Dr (43026-1274)
P.O. Box 159 (43026-0159)
PHONE..............................614 771-4771
George Saliaris, *Pr*
Dan Saliaris, *
▲ **EMP:** 68 **EST:** 1968
SQ FT: 65,000
SALES (est): 18.57MM
SALES (corp-wide): 18.57MM **Privately
Held**
Web: www.rageplastics.com
SIC: 3089 3544 Injection molding of plastics;
Special dies, tools, jigs, and fixtures

(G-7699)
RICH PRODUCTS CORPORATION
4600 Northwest Pkwy (43026-1130)
P.O. Box 490 (43026-0490)
PHONE..............................614 771-1117
Michael Callaway, *Mgr*
EMP: 150
SALES (corp-wide): 4.81B **Privately Held**
Web: www.richs.com
SIC: 2023 2099 2051 2045 Dry, condensed
and evaporated dairy products; Food
preparations, nec; Bread, cake, and related
products; Prepared flour mixes and doughs
PA: Rich Products Corporation
1 Robert Rich Way
Buffalo NY 14213
716 878-8000

(G-7700)
S & G MANUFACTURING GROUP LLC (PA)
Also Called: S&G Distribution
4830 Northwest Pkwy (43026-1131)
PHONE..............................614 529-0100
Bret Klisares, *Managing Member*
Eric Schmidlin, *

2025 Harris Ohio
Industrial Directory

▲ = Import ▼ = Export
◆ = Import/Export

EMP: 95 EST: 1990
SQ FT: 105,500
SALES (est): 9.97MM Privately Held
Web: www.sgmgroup.com
SIC: 3441 3444 2435 2436 Fabricated
structural metal; Sheet metalwork;
Hardwood veneer and plywood; Softwood
veneer and plywood

(G-7701)
SENSOTEC LLC
Also Called: Sensorwerks
3450 Cemetery Rd (43026-8348)
PHONE..................................614 481-8616
EMP: 6 EST: 2004
SALES (est): 867.91K Privately Held
SIC: 3829 Pressure transducers

(G-7702)
STAR DYNAMICS CORPORATION
(PA)
Also Called: Aeroflex Powell
4455 Reynolds Dr (43026-1261)
PHONE..................................614 334-4510
Jerry Jost, Pr
▲ EMP: 65 EST: 1989
SQ FT: 20,000
SALES (est): 9.24MM
SALES (corp-wide): 9.24MM Privately
Held
Web: www.stardynamics.com
SIC: 3812 Search and navigation equipment

(G-7703)
STATE METAL HOSE INC
4171 Lyman Dr (43026-1228)
PHONE..................................614 527-4700
Thomas Decamp, CEO
EMP: 7 EST: 2000
SALES (est): 1.1MM Privately Held
Web: www.statemetalhose.com
SIC: 3492 7692 Hose and tube fittings and
assemblies, hydraulic/pneumatic; Welding
repair

(G-7704)
SUTPHEN TOWERS INC
4500 Sutphen Ct (43026-1296)
P.O. Box 158 (43002-0158)
PHONE..................................614 876-1262
EMP: 81 EST: 1978
SALES (est): 19.23MM Privately Held
Web: www.sutphen.com
SIC: 3713 7538 Truck bodies and parts;
Truck engine repair, except industrial

(G-7705)
TEACHERS PUBLISHING GROUP
Also Called: Essential Learning Products
4200 Parkway Ct (43026-1200)
PHONE..................................614 486-0631
Gary Meyers, Pr
Gary Meyers, CEO
Thomas Mason, Treas
▲ EMP: 10 EST: 1980
SQ FT: 36,000
SALES (est): 729.47K
SALES (corp-wide): 72.35MM Privately
Held
Web: www.biostilo.com
SIC: 7371 2731 Custom computer
programming services; Books, publishing
only
PA: Highlights For Children, Inc.
1800 Watermark Dr
Columbus OH 43215
614 486-0631

(G-7706)
TEXTILES INC
Also Called: Sales Office Rob Jordan Vp Sls
5892 Heritage Lakes Dr (43026-7617)
PHONE..................................614 529-8642
Rob Jordan, Brnch Mgr
EMP: 8
SALES (corp-wide): 700.35K Privately
Held
SIC: 2511 2599 Wood household furniture;
Hotel furniture
PA: Textiles, Inc.
23 Old Springfield Rd
London OH 43140
740 852-0782

(G-7707)
THE GUARDTOWER INC
Also Called: Shield Laminating
5514 Nike Dr (43026-9081)
PHONE..................................614 488-4311
Lynn Bartells, Pr
EMP: 10 EST: 1987
SALES (est): 561.92K Privately Held
Web: www.theguardtower.com
SIC: 3944 5945 Games, toys, and children's
vehicles; Models, toy and hobby

(G-7708)
TUBULAR TECHNIQUES INC
3025 Scioto Darby Executive Ct
(43026-8990)
PHONE..................................614 529-4130
Steve Harman, Pr
Amy Pope-harman, Sec
Tracy Stamper, Adm/Asst
EMP: 6 EST: 1972
SQ FT: 7,500
SALES (est): 848.23K Privately Held
Web: www.tubulartechniques.com
SIC: 5051 3599 Tubing, metal; Tubing,
flexible metallic

(G-7709)
VANNER HOLDINGS INC
Also Called: Vanner
4282 Reynolds Dr (43026-1260)
PHONE..................................614 771-2718
Steven Funk, Pr
Merry H Pieper, *
Chris Collet, *
◆ EMP: 55 EST: 2005
SQ FT: 20,000
SALES (est): 851K Privately Held
Web: www.vanner.com
SIC: 3629 3823 3699 3648 Inverters,
nonrotating: electrical; Process control
instruments; Electrical equipment and
supplies, nec; Lighting equipment, nec

(G-7710)
VICART PRCSION FABRICATORS INC
Also Called: Proto Precision Fabricators
4101 Leap Rd (43026-1117)
PHONE..................................614 771-0080
Arthur Handshy, Pr
EMP: 35 EST: 1988
SQ FT: 18,000
SALES (est): 2.32MM Privately Held
Web: www.protoprecision.com
SIC: 3444 Sheet metal specialties, not
stamped

(G-7711)
VT INDUSTRIES LLC
1999 Friston Blvd (43026-6038)
PHONE..................................614 804-6904
EMP: 6 EST: 2011
SALES (est): 84.89K Privately Held
SIC: 3999 Manufacturing industries, nec

(G-7712)
ZURN INDUSTRIES LLC
4501 Sutphen Ct (43026-1224)
PHONE..................................814 455-0921
Bob Armbrewster, Mgr
EMP: 10
Web: www.zurn.com
SIC: 5074 3431 Plumbing and hydronic
heating supplies; Sinks: enameled iron,
cast iron, or pressed metal
HQ: Zurn Industries, Llc
511 W Freshwater Way
Milwaukee WI 53204
855 663-9876

Hillsboro
Highland County

(G-7713)
BEAR MECHANICAL LLC
2336 State Route 131 (45133-7558)
PHONE..................................937 288-2316
Charles W Bear, Owner
▲ EMP: 8 EST: 1971
SQ FT: 8,000
SALES (est): 2.17MM Privately Held
Web: www.bearmech.com
SIC: 1711 3599 Plumbing contractors;
Machine and other job shop work

(G-7714)
BEAZER EAST INC
Plum Run Stone Division
4281 Roush Rd (45133-9147)
PHONE..................................937 364-2311
J Craig Morgan, Mgr
EMP: 35
SALES (corp-wide): 22.37B Privately Held
SIC: 3281 3273 1422 Stone, quarrying and
processing of own stone products; Ready-
mixed concrete; Crushed and broken
limestone
HQ: Beazer East, Inc.
600 River Ave Ste 200
Pittsburgh PA 15212
412 428-9407

(G-7715)
CAMECO COMMUNICATIONS LLC
Also Called: Highland County Press
128 S High St (45133-1443)
P.O. Box 849 (45133-0849)
PHONE..................................937 840-9490
Rory Ryan, Pr
Angie Matticks, VP
Rosemary Ryan, Off Mgr
EMP: 7 EST: 2009
SQ FT: 1,000
SALES (est): 183.38K Privately Held
Web: www.highlandcountypress.com
SIC: 2711 Commercial printing and
newspaper publishing combined

(G-7716)
G FORDYCE CO
210 Hobart Dr (45133-9487)
P.O. Box 309 (45133-0309)
PHONE..................................937 393-3241
Bob Wilson, Owner
EMP: 6 EST: 1980
SQ FT: 12,000
SALES (est): 2.37MM Privately Held
Web: www.gfordyce.com
SIC: 3554 Folding machines, paper

(G-7717)
HIGGINS CONSTRUCTION &
SUPPLY CO INC
Also Called: Higgins Tool Rental

3801 Us Highway 50 (45133-9178)
PHONE..................................937 364-2331
TOLL FREE: 800
EMP: 12 EST: 1959
SALES (est): 2.49MM Privately Held
SIC: 5211 3444 5031 7359 Lumber and
other building materials; Metal flooring and
siding; Building materials, exterior;
Equipment rental and leasing, nec

(G-7718)
HIGHLAND COMPUTER FORMS INC
(PA)
Also Called: R & S Data Products
1025 W Main St (45133-8219)
P.O. Box 831 (45133-0831)
PHONE..................................937 393-4215
Robert D Wilson, Pr
Philip D Wilson, *
EMP: 56 EST: 1979
SQ FT: 70,000
SALES (est): 8.53MM
SALES (corp-wide): 8.53MM Privately
Held
Web: www.hcf.com
SIC: 2752 5112 Commercial printing,
lithographic; Business forms

(G-7719)
ITW FOOD EQUIPMENT GROUP LLC
Also Called: Hobart
1495 N High St (45133-8203)
PHONE..................................937 393-4271
Bill Zinno, Mgr
EMP: 241
SALES (corp-wide): 16.11B Publicly Held
Web: www.itwweighwrap.com
SIC: 5046 3556 Restaurant equipment and
supplies, nec; Food products machinery
HQ: Itw Food Equipment Group Llc
701 S Ridge Ave
Troy OH 45374

(G-7720)
MID AMERICA TIRE OF HILLSBORO
INC
Also Called: Best One Tire of Hillsboro
108 Willetsville Pike (45133-8461)
P.O. Box 728 (45133-0728)
PHONE..................................937 393-3520
EMP: 20
SIC: 5531 7534 Automotive tires; Tire
retreading and repair shops

(G-7721)
OHIO ASPHALTIC LIMESTONE CORP
8591 Mad River Rd (45133-9451)
PHONE..................................937 364-2191
TOLL FREE: 888
Diana Jones, Pr
William C Mason, Pr
Dianna Jones, VP
EMP: 10 EST: 1935
SQ FT: 1,200
SALES (est): 3.86MM
SALES (corp-wide): 5.56MM Privately
Held
Web: www.ohio-asphaltic-limestone.com
SIC: 1422 Limestones, ground
PA: Miller-Mason Paving Co.
8591 Mad River Rd
Hillsboro OH
937 364-2369

(G-7722)
OHIO VALLEY TRUSS COMPANY (PA)
6000 Us Highway 50 (45133-7546)
P.O. Box 365 (45133)
PHONE..................................937 393-3995
Willard G Bohrer, Pr
Joann Bohrer, *

EMP: 35 **EST:** 1976
SQ FT: 12,000
SALES (est): 4.75MM
SALES (corp-wide): 4.75MM **Privately Held**
SIC: 2439 Trusses, wooden roof

(G-7723)
PAS TECHNOLOGIES INC
Also Called: Standardaero
214 Hobart Dr (45133-9487)
PHONE..............................937 840-1053
Mark Greene, *Mgr*
EMP: 100
Web: www.standardaerocomponents.com
SIC: 3724 7699 Aircraft engines and engine parts; Aircraft and heavy equipment repair services
HQ: Pas Technologies Inc.
1234 Atlantic St
North Kansas City MO 64116

(G-7724)
ROTARY FORMS PRESS INC (PA)
835 S High St (45133-9692)
PHONE..............................937 393-3426
Jon Cassner, *Pr*
Brian Cassner, *Treas*
EMP: 24 **EST:** 1952
SQ FT: 24,500
SALES (est): 223.27K
SALES (corp-wide): 223.27K **Privately Held**
Web: www.rotaryfp.com
SIC: 2761 2752 Computer forms, manifold or continuous; Commercial printing, lithographic

(G-7725)
SEAL TITE LLC
Also Called: Seal Tite
120 Moore Rd (45133-8523)
PHONE..............................937 393-4268
EMP: 100 **EST:** 2003
SQ FT: 120,000
SALES (est): 8.84MM **Privately Held**
Web: www.sealtitehvac.com
SIC: 3498 Fabricated pipe and fittings

(G-7726)
STANDARD AERO INC
214 Hobart Dr (45133-9487)
PHONE..............................937 840-1053
EMP: 79
SALES (est): 1.5MM **Privately Held**
Web: www.standardaero.com
SIC: 3599 Machine shop, jobbing and repair

(G-7727)
UNIT SETS INC
835 S High St (45133-9602)
PHONE..............................937 840-6123
Jon Cassner, *Pr*
Jon H Cassner, *
Kathy Cassner, *
Brian Cassner, *
EMP: 22 **EST:** 1972
SQ FT: 25,000
SALES (est): 98.24K
SALES (corp-wide): 223.27K **Privately Held**
Web: www.rotaryfp.com
SIC: 2761 Unit sets (manifold business forms)
PA: Rotary Forms Press, Inc.
835 S High St
Hillsboro OH 45133
937 393-3426

(G-7728)
WEASTEC INCORPORATED (HQ)
1600 N High St (45133-9400)
PHONE..............................937 393-6800
Yasusuke Sugino, *Pr*
Kiyoshi Koide, *
Bill Smith, *
Keigo Sakaguchi, *
▲ **EMP:** 222 **EST:** 1988
SQ FT: 190,000
SALES (est): 24.62MM **Privately Held**
Web: www.weastec.com
SIC: 3714 Motor vehicle electrical equipment
PA: Toyo Denso Co., Ltd.
2-10-4, Shimbashi
Minato-Ku TKY 105-0

(G-7729)
WILLIAMSON SAFE INC
5631 State Route 73 (45133-9005)
PHONE..............................937 393-9919
J Edgar Williamson, *Pr*
Bing C Williamson, *
EMP: 7 **EST:** 1979
SQ FT: 40,000
SALES (est): 442.45K **Privately Held**
SIC: 3499 Safe deposit boxes or chests, metal

Hinckley
Medina County

(G-7730)
A-KOBAK CONTAINER COMPANY INC
1701 W 130th St (44233-9586)
P.O. Box 490 (44233-0490)
PHONE..............................330 225-7791
Gerald H Dolph, *Pr*
Edward Clark, *VP*
EMP: 15 **EST:** 1963
SQ FT: 40,000
SALES (est): 4.74MM **Privately Held**
Web: www.akobak.com
SIC: 2653 Boxes, corrugated: made from purchased materials

(G-7731)
GREAT LAKES STAIR & MLLWK CO
1545 W 130th St Ste A1 (44233-9168)
P.O. Box 125 (44233-0125)
PHONE..............................330 225-2005
Tim Noonan, *Pr*
Barb Noonan, *Sec*
EMP: 7 **EST:** 1990
SQ FT: 7,500
SALES (est): 1.72MM **Privately Held**
Web: www.stair.com
SIC: 2431 5031 Staircases and stairs, wood; Doors and windows

(G-7732)
HINCKLEY WOOD PRODUCTS LTD
1545 W 130th St (44233-9121)
PHONE..............................330 220-9999
Tim Noonan, *Pr*
EMP: 6 **EST:** 2003
SALES (est): 488.07K **Privately Held**
SIC: 2431 Staircases and stairs, wood

(G-7733)
JAMAR PRECISION GRINDING CO
2661 Center Rd (44233-9562)
PHONE..............................330 220-0099
John Hatala, *Pr*
EMP: 48 **EST:** 1981
SALES (est): 4.45MM **Privately Held**
Web: web.jamargrinding.com

SIC: 3599 Machine shop, jobbing and repair

(G-7734)
L J PUBLISHING LLC
1287 Ridge Rd Ste B (44233-9288)
P.O. Box 425 (44280-0425)
PHONE..............................888 749-5994
EMP: 6 **EST:** 2011
SALES (est): 124.87K **Privately Held**
SIC: 2741 Miscellaneous publishing

(G-7735)
PEARCE INC
1935 Stone Ridge Dr (44233-9126)
PHONE..............................216 252-0550
Gerald Myatt, *Pr*
David Myatt, *VP*
Laurel Myatt, *Sec*
EMP: 11 **EST:** 1945
SALES (est): 1MM **Privately Held**
SIC: 3555 3554 3599 Printing trades machinery; Folding machines, paper; Machine shop, jobbing and repair

(G-7736)
WENTWORTH SOLUTIONS
1265 Ridge Rd (44233-9806)
P.O. Box 283 (44233-0283)
PHONE..............................440 212-7696
Sean Spigtle, *Pr*
Jessica Spittle, *Sec*
EMP: 10 **EST:** 2005
SALES (est): 947.05K **Privately Held**
Web: www.wentinc.com
SIC: 7371 7372 Computer software writing services; Prepackaged software

Hiram
Portage County

(G-7737)
DURAMAX MARINE LLC
17990 Great Lakes Pkwy (44234-9681)
PHONE..............................440 834-5400
Richard Spangler, *Pr*
◆ **EMP:** 85 **EST:** 1999
SQ FT: 65,000
SALES (est): 18.85MM **Privately Held**
Web: www.duramaxmarine.com
SIC: 3069 Medical and laboratory rubber sundries and related products

(G-7738)
GLUETREAD LLC
11684 Hayden Ave (44234-9803)
PHONE..............................800 238-9791
Andrew Auble, *Managing Member*
EMP: 13 **EST:** 2018
SALES (est): 1.23MM **Privately Held**
Web: www.gluetread.com
SIC: 3011 Retreading materials, tire

(G-7739)
GREAT LAKES CHEESE CO INC (PA)
17825 Great Lakes Pkwy (44234-9677)
P.O. Box 1806 (44234-1806)
PHONE..............................440 834-2500
Gary Vanic, *Pr*
John Epprecht, *
Albert Z Meyers, *
Marcel Dasen, *
Hans Epprecht, *
◆ **EMP:** 500 **EST:** 1958
SQ FT: 218,000
SALES (est): 491.5MM
SALES (corp-wide): 491.5MM **Privately Held**
Web: www.greatlakescheese.com

SIC: 5143 2022 Cheese; Natural cheese

(G-7740)
MANTALINE CORPORATION
Also Called: Mantaline
6969 Constance Rd (44234-3402)
PHONE..............................330 569-3147
EMP: 14
SALES (corp-wide): 39.13MM **Privately Held**
Web: www.mantalinestandardseals.com
SIC: 3061 Mechanical rubber goods
PA: Mantaline Corporation
4754 E High St
Mantua OH 44255
330 274-2264

(G-7741)
PORTAGE PACKAGING SYSTEMS INC
5933 State Route 82 (44234-9795)
P.O. Box 1776 (44234-1776)
PHONE..............................330 274-8295
Chris Taucher, *Pr*
John Taucher, *VP*
EMP: 6 **EST:** 1982
SQ FT: 30,000
SALES (est): 2.21MM **Privately Held**
Web: www.portagesystems.com
SIC: 3565 Packaging machinery

Holiday City
Williams County

(G-7742)
20/20 CUSTOM MOLDED PLAS LLC (HQ)
14620 Selwyn Dr (43543-9237)
PHONE..............................419 506-5788
Ron Ernsberger, *CEO*
Chad Adams, *Pr*
Mike Gepfert, *Ex VP*
Toby Ernsberger, *VP*
David Rupp, *Mgr*
EMP: 51 **EST:** 2000
SALES (est): 53.25MM **Privately Held**
Web: www.2020cmp.com
SIC: 3089 3086 Injection molding of plastics; Padding, foamed plastics
PA: Inteplast Group Corporation
9 Peach Tree Hill Rd
Livingston NJ 07039

Holland
Lucas County

(G-7743)
ADAMS ELEVATOR EQUIPMENT CO (DH)
Also Called: Schindler Logistics Center
1530 Timber Wolf Dr (43528-9129)
PHONE..............................847 581-2900
Robert Schreck, *CEO*
▲ **EMP:** 62 **EST:** 1930
SALES (est): 299.8K **Privately Held**
Web: www.adamselevator.com
SIC: 3312 3825 3534 5084 Locomotive wheels, rolled; Signal generators and averagers; Elevators and equipment; Materials handling machinery
HQ: Schindler Enterprises Inc.
20 Whippany Rd
Morristown NJ 07960
973 397-6500

(G-7744)
ADDITIVE METAL ALLOYS LTD
1421 Holloway Rd Ste B (43528-8647)
PHONE...............................800 687-6110
Richard Meklus, *Prin*
EMP: 8 **EST:** 2014
SQ FT: 1,100
SALES (est): 497.94K **Privately Held**
SIC: 3399 Powder, metal

(G-7745)
BAY CONTROLS LLC
1044 Hamilton Dr (43528-8210)
PHONE...............................419 891-4390
Scott Parry, *Pt*
▼ **EMP:** 30 **EST:** 1983
SALES (est): 5.7MM **Privately Held**
Web: www.baycontrols.com
SIC: 3625 Industrial controls: push button,
selector switches, pilot

(G-7746)
BOLLINGER TOOL & DIE INC
959 Hamilton Dr (43528-8211)
PHONE...............................419 866-5180
Danny N Bollinger, *Pr*
Anne Bollinger, *VP*
EMP: 7 **EST:** 1985
SQ FT: 6,700
SALES (est): 1.16MM **Privately Held**
SIC: 3544 Special dies and tools

(G-7747)
BUNTING BEARINGS LLC (PA)
1001 Holland Park Blvd (43528-9156)
P.O. Box 729 (43528-0729)
PHONE...............................419 866-7000
Keith Brown, *Ch*
Thomas Kwiatkowski, *
George Mugford, *
Dale Kucaj, *
Rick Nelson, *
▲ **EMP:** 100 **EST:** 1907
SQ FT: 94,000
SALES (est): 55MM **Privately Held**
Web: www.buntingbearings.com
SIC: 3366 3566 Brass foundry, nec; Speed
changers, drives, and gears

(G-7748)
CAMEO COUNTERTOPS INC (PA)
7723 Airport Hwy (43528-7601)
PHONE...............................419 865-6371
Brian Hudock, *Pr*
Tim Sorokin, *
EMP: 15 **EST:** 1992
SALES (est): 3.97MM **Privately Held**
Web: www.cameocountertops.com
SIC: 2541 5031 2821 Counter and sink tops;
Lumber, plywood, and millwork; Plastics
materials and resins

(G-7749)
CGS IMAGING INC
6950 Hall St (43528-9485)
PHONE...............................419 897-3000
Chuck Stranc, *CEO*
Carol Stranc, *CFO*
▲ **EMP:** 14 **EST:** 2003
SQ FT: 14,000
SALES (est): 2.56MM **Privately Held**
Web: www.cgs-imaging.com
SIC: 3993 7319 Signs and advertising
specialties; Display advertising service

(G-7750)
CLARIOS LLC
Also Called: Johnson Controls
10300 Industrial St (43528-9791)
PHONE...............................419 865-0542

Aaron Byrne, *Mgr*
EMP: 600
SALES (corp-wide): 69.83B **Privately Held**
Web: www.clarios.com
SIC: 3691 Batteries, rechargeable
HQ: Clarios, Llc
5757 N Green Bay Ave Flor
Glendale WI 53209

(G-7751)
COLBURN PATTERSON LLC (PA)
1100 S Holland Sylvania Rd (43528-8422)
PHONE...............................419 866-5544
Tony J Colburn, *Managing Member*
EMP: 6 **EST:** 1994
SALES (est): 222.57K **Privately Held**
Web: www.colburnpatterson.com
SIC: 8721 7372 Accounting services, except
auditing; Prepackaged software

(G-7752)
CREATIVE PRODUCTS INC
Also Called: CPI
1430 Kieswetter Rd (43528-9785)
PHONE...............................419 866-5501
Marvin Smith, *Pr*
EMP: 6 **EST:** 1973
SQ FT: 26,000
SALES (est): 499.05K **Privately Held**
SIC: 5023 5211 2541 Kitchen tools and
utensils, nec; Cabinets, kitchen; Wood
partitions and fixtures

(G-7753)
D & J DISTRIBUTING & MFG
Also Called: Exotica Fresheners Co
1302 Holloway Rd (43528-9538)
PHONE...............................419 865-2552
Adnan Elassir, *VP*
Adnan Elassir, *VP*
Oussama Elassir, *Pr*
◆ **EMP:** 11 **EST:** 1988
SQ FT: 45,000
SALES (est): 1.28MM **Privately Held**
Web: www.exoticafresh.com
SIC: 2842 Sanitation preparations,
disinfectants and deodorants

(G-7754)
DANA LIMITED
Also Called: Dana Supply Chain Mgmt
6201 Trust Dr (43528-8424)
PHONE...............................419 866-7253
Ron Drahelm, *Sls Dir*
EMP: 100
Web: www.dana.com
SIC: 3714 Motor vehicle parts and
accessories
HQ: Dana Limited
3939 Technology Dr
Maumee OH 43537

(G-7755)
DESIGNETICS INC (PA)
1624 Eber Rd (43528-9776)
PHONE...............................419 866-0700
Craig Williams, *Pr*
EMP: 73 **EST:** 1987
SQ FT: 20,000
SALES (est): 558K **Privately Held**
Web: www.designetics.com
SIC: 3559 3991 Automotive related
machinery; Brooms and brushes

(G-7756)
DOYLE MANUFACTURING INC
Also Called: Shamrock Molded Products
1440 Holloway Rd (43528-8608)
PHONE...............................419 865-2548
Michael A Doyle, *Pr*
Linda Doyle, *

Adrienne Sautter, *Prin*
Chad Doyle, *Prin*
Bryan Doyle, *Prin*
EMP: 70 **EST:** 1975
SQ FT: 100,000
SALES (est): 10.17MM **Privately Held**
Web: www.doyleshamrock.com
SIC: 3089 3544 Injection molding of plastics;
Special dies, tools, jigs, and fixtures

(G-7757)
DREAMSCAPE MEDIA LLC
Also Called: Dreamscape Media
1417 Timber Wolf Dr (43528-8302)
PHONE...............................877 983-7326
Bradley Rose, *Genl Mgr*
EMP: 8 **EST:** 2011
SALES (est): 559.4K **Privately Held**
Web: www.dreamscapepublishing.com
SIC: 2731 Books, publishing only

(G-7758)
DRS INDUSTRIAL LLC
1067 Hamilton Dr (43528-8165)
PHONE...............................419 861-0334
EMP: 7 **EST:** 2019
SALES (est): 1.01MM **Privately Held**
Web: www.drsinc.com
SIC: 2819 3089 Aluminum compounds;
Injection molding of plastics

(G-7759)
DRS INDUSTRIES INC
1067 Hamilton Dr (43528-8165)
PHONE...............................419 861-0334
J Peter Hottois, *Pr*
EMP: 65 **EST:** 1982
SQ FT: 28,120
SALES (est): 4.94MM **Privately Held**
Web: www.drsinc.com
SIC: 2819 3089 Aluminum compounds;
Injection molding of plastics

(G-7760)
DURA TEMP CORPORATION
949 S Mccord Rd (43528-8695)
P.O. Box 368 (43528-0368)
PHONE...............................419 866-4348
Dave Rollins, *Pr*
EMP: 13 **EST:** 1983
SQ FT: 6,000
SALES (est): 2.15MM **Privately Held**
Web: www.duratemp.com
SIC: 3559 3221 Glass making machinery,
blowing, molding, forming, etc.; Glass
containers

(G-7761)
DYNAMIC DIES INC (PA)
1705 Commerce Rd (43528-9789)
P.O. Box 576 (43528-0576)
PHONE...............................419 865-0249
EMP: 50 **EST:** 1971
SALES (est): 22.27MM
SALES (corp-wide): 22.27MM **Privately
Held**
Web: www.dynamicdies.com
SIC: 3544 3555 2796 Special dies and tools;
Printing plates; Platemaking services

(G-7762)
EDITENCOM LTD
7134 Railroad St (43528-9539)
P.O. Box 176 (43528-0176)
PHONE...............................419 865-5877
Robert Disanza, *Pr*
▲ **EMP:** 40 **EST:** 1997
SQ FT: 30,000
SALES (est): 3.66MM **Privately Held**
Web: www.tencom.com

SIC: 3812 Antennas, radar or
communications

(G-7763)
**ELECTRONIC CONCEPTS ENGRG
INC**
Also Called: E C E
1465 Timber Wolf Dr (43528-8302)
PHONE...............................419 861-9000
Karl W Swonger Junior, *CEO*
EMP: 16 **EST:** 1988
SQ FT: 17,900
SALES (est): 4.83MM **Privately Held**
Web: www.eceinc.com
SIC: 7371 8731 3728 7373 Computer
software development; Electronic research;
Aircraft assemblies, subassemblies, and
parts, nec; Computer integrated systems
design

(G-7764)
GENERIC SYSTEMS INC
10560 Geiser Rd (43528-8506)
P.O. Box 153 (43552-0153)
PHONE...............................419 841-8460
James Fletcher, *Pr*
Melinda Fletcher, *Sec*
EMP: 15 **EST:** 1996
SQ FT: 18,000
SALES (est): 1.06MM **Privately Held**
Web: www.genericfluidsystems.com
SIC: 3549 7373 7371 Assembly machines,
including robotic; Systems integration
services; Computer software development
and applications

(G-7765)
GREAT LAKES TURBINES INC
1740 Eber Rd Ste N (43528-8108)
PHONE...............................419 705-0490
Gregory Thibodeau, *
Gregory M Thibodeau, *Pr*
EMP: 7 **EST:** 2013
SALES (est): 4.82MM **Privately Held**
Web: www.glturbines.com
SIC: 3511 Turbines and turbine generator
sets

(G-7766)
HAMILTON MANUFACTURING CORP
1026 Hamilton Dr (43528-8210)
PHONE...............................419 867-4858
Robin Ritz, *CEO*
Bonnie Usborne, *
Steve Alt, *
Laura Harris, *
▲ **EMP:** 45 **EST:** 1921
SQ FT: 32,000
SALES (est): 5.39MM **Privately Held**
Web: www.hamiltonmfg.com
SIC: 3172 8711 Coin purses; Designing:
ship, boat, machine, and product

(G-7767)
HONEYBAKED FOODS INC
Also Called: Honeybaked
6145 Merger Dr (43528-8430)
P.O. Box 965 (43528-0965)
PHONE...............................567 703-0002
Dan Kurz, *Pr*
Louis Schmidt Junior, *VP*
Mary Lou Anderson, *
Craig Kurz, *
EMP: 600 **EST:** 1984
SQ FT: 103,000
SALES (est): 8.44MM **Privately Held**
Web: www.honeybaked.com
SIC: 2013 Bacon, side and sliced: from
purchased meat

(G-7768)
ICO PRODUCTS LLC
Also Called: Icomold By Fathom
6415 Angola Rd (43528-8501)
PHONE................................419 867-3900
EMP: 11
SALES (est): 3.39MM **Privately Held**
Web: www.icomold.com
SIC: 3089 Injection molding of plastics

(G-7769)
IMAGE GROUP INC
1255 Corporate Dr (43528-9590)
PHONE................................419 866-3300
Jon M Levine, *CEO*
Joel A Levine, *
Tom Herman, *
Lisa Hoverson, *
Zack Ottenstein, *
◆ **EMP:** 44 **EST:** 1989
SQ FT: 29,400
SALES (est): 11.78MM **Privately Held**
Web: www.theimagegroup.com
SIC: 2261 Screen printing of cotton
   broadwoven fabrics

(G-7770)
JML HOLDINGS INC
Also Called: Bassett Nut Company
6210 Merger Dr (43528-9593)
PHONE................................419 866-7500
Jon M Levine, *Pr*
Larry J Robbins, *VP*
Jeff Williams, *COO*
◆ **EMP:** 14 **EST:** 1928
SQ FT: 12,000
SALES (est): 1.57MM **Privately Held**
Web: www.bassettnut.com
SIC: 5441 5145 2064 Nuts; Nuts, salted or
   roasted; Popcorn balls or other treated
   popcorn products

(G-7771)
KERN-LIEBERS USA INC (HQ)
1510 Albon Rd (43528-9159)
PHONE................................419 865-2437
Lothar Bauerle, *Pr*
Hans Jocheim Steim, *
Gert Wagner, *
▲ **EMP:** 60 **EST:** 1977
SQ FT: 40,000
SALES (est): 35.39MM
SALES (corp-wide): 844.66MM **Privately
Held**
Web:
www.kern-liebers-north-america.com
SIC: 3495 3493 Mechanical springs,
   precision; Steel springs, except wire
PA: Kern Liebers Gmbh & Co. Kg
   Dr.-Kurt-Steim-Str. 35
   Schramberg BW 78713
   74225110

(G-7772)
MATHESON TRI-GAS INC
1720 Trade Rd (43528-8202)
PHONE................................419 865-8881
Craig Morton, *Mgr*
EMP: 13
SQ FT: 18,120
Web: www.mathesongas.com
SIC: 5084 2813 Welding machinery and
   equipment; Nitrogen
HQ: Matheson Tri-Gas, Inc.
   3 Mountainview Rd Ste 3 # 3
   Warren NJ 07059
   908 991-9200

(G-7773)
**NATIONAL COMPRESSOR SVCS
LLC (PA)**
10349 Industrial St (43528-9791)
P.O. Box 760 (43528-0760)
PHONE................................419 868-4980
Erik E Babcock, *Pr*
Stan Kolev, *
Gregory Jones, *
James Gordon, *
Matthew Delong, *
EMP: 39 **EST:** 2011
SQ FT: 60,000
SALES (est): 1.73MM
SALES (corp-wide): 1.73MM **Privately
Held**
Web: www.national-compressor.com
SIC: 3563 Air and gas compressors

(G-7774)
NATIONAL ILLMINATION SIGN CORP
6525 Angola Rd (43528-9651)
P.O. Box 563 (43528-0563)
PHONE................................419 866-1666
George L Jeakle, *Pr*
Neil Jeakle, *VP*
EMP: 9 **EST:** 1985
SQ FT: 18,200
SALES (est): 502.92K **Privately Held**
Web: www.nationalsignco.com
SIC: 3993 Electric signs

(G-7775)
OTTAWA RUBBER COMPANY (PA)
1600 Commerce Rd (43528-8689)
P.O. Box 553 (43528-0553)
PHONE................................419 865-1378
Mike Bugert, *Pr*
EMP: 17 **EST:** 1945
SQ FT: 12,000
SALES (est): 4.84MM
SALES (corp-wide): 4.84MM **Privately
Held**
Web: www.ottawarubber.com
SIC: 3069 Molded rubber products

(G-7776)
PATRIOT PRODUCTS INC
Also Called: Patriot Mobility
1133 Corporate Dr Ste B (43528-7405)
P.O. Box 88 (49777-0088)
PHONE................................419 865-9712
Steven Grudzien, *Pr*
EMP: 15 **EST:** 2004
SALES (est): 983.02K **Privately Held**
Web: www.dmetree.com
SIC: 3841 Surgical and medical instruments

(G-7777)
**PETERSON AMERICAN
CORPORATION**
Peterson Spring - Maumee Plant
1625 Commerce Rd (43528-9154)
PHONE................................419 867-8711
Geary Belzung, *Brnch Mgr*
EMP: 30
SQ FT: 41,400
SALES (corp-wide): 40.23MM **Privately
Held**
Web: www.pspring.com
SIC: 3496 3452 3592 3493 Miscellaneous
   fabricated wire products; Washers, metal;
   Carburetors, pistons, piston rings and
   valves; Steel springs, except wire
HQ: Peterson American Corporation
   16805 Heimbach Rd
   Three Rivers MI 49093
   248 304-7385

(G-7778)
PRECISION CUTOFF LLC
7400 Airport Hwy (43528-9545)
P.O. Box 1040 (43528-1040)
PHONE................................419 866-8000
Jim Cannaley, *Managing Member*
EMP: 11 **EST:** 1989
SQ FT: 150,000
SALES (est): 1.08MM **Privately Held**
Web: www.woodsage.com
SIC: 3441 Fabricated structural metal

(G-7779)
PRINCIPLED DYNAMICS INC
6920 Hall St (43528-9485)
PHONE................................419 351-6303
Patricia Earl, *VP*
Gene Gunderson, *Prin*
James Swartz, *Prin*
Michael W Holmes, *Prin*
Robert E Holmes, *Prin*
EMP: 8 **EST:** 2012
SALES (est): 240.13K **Privately Held**
SIC: 2834 Pharmaceutical preparations

(G-7780)
QUALITY CARE PRODUCTS LLC
Also Called: Qcp
6920 Hall St (43528-9485)
P.O. Box 1267 (43528-1267)
PHONE................................734 847-2704
James Swartz, *
EMP: 40 **EST:** 2001
SALES (est): 4.38MM **Privately Held**
Web: www.qcprx.com
SIC: 2834 Pharmaceutical preparations

(G-7781)
**RENNCO AUTOMATION SYSTEMS
INC**
971 Hamilton Dr (43528-8211)
PHONE................................419 861-2340
Mike E Owens, *Pr*
Dave Miklos, *
EMP: 30 **EST:** 1989
SQ FT: 15,000
SALES (est): 4.39MM **Privately Held**
Web: www.renncoautomation.com
SIC: 3569 Robots, assembly line: industrial
   and commercial

(G-7782)
RNM HOLDINGS INC
1810 Eber Rd Ste C (43528-7898)
PHONE................................419 867-8712
Matthew Milton, *Pr*
EMP: 12
SQ FT: 15,000
SIC: 5084 3536 Cranes, industrial; Hoists,
   cranes, and monorails
PA: Rnm Holdings, Inc.
   550 Conover Dr
   Franklin OH 45005

(G-7783)
**SCHINDLER ELEVATOR
CORPORATION**
Also Called: Schindler Elevator
1530 Timber Wolf Dr Ste B (43528-9161)
P.O. Box 960 (43528-0960)
PHONE................................419 861-5900
Mark Kershner, *Mgr*
EMP: 20
Web: www.schindler.com
SIC: 3534 7699 Elevators and equipment;
   Elevators: inspection, service, and repair
HQ: Schindler Elevator Corporation
   20 Whippany Rd
   Morristown NJ 07960
   973 397-6500

(G-7784)
SELCO INDUSTRIES INC
1590 Albon Rd Ste 1 (43528-9410)
PHONE................................419 861-0336
Seldon Hill, *Pr*
Ruby Hill, *
EMP: 10 **EST:** 1998
SQ FT: 17,000
SALES (est): 784.8K **Privately Held**
Web: www.selcoindustries.com
SIC: 2678 Papeteries and writing paper sets

(G-7785)
SPONSELLER GROUP INC (PA)
1600 Timber Wolf Dr (43528-8303)
PHONE................................419 861-3000
Harold P Sponseller, *Ch*
Keith Sponseller, *
David Nowak, *
Kevin R Nevius, *
EMP: 44 **EST:** 1973
SQ FT: 8,900
SALES (est): 9.31MM
SALES (corp-wide): 9.31MM **Privately
Held**
Web: www.sponsellergroup.com
SIC: 8711 3599 Consulting engineer;
   Machine shop, jobbing and repair

(G-7786)
TEKNI-PLEX INC
Also Called: Global Technology Center
1445 Timber Wolf Dr (43528-8302)
PHONE................................419 491-2399
Paul J Young, *CEO*
Phil Bourgeois, *VP*
EMP: 26 **EST:** 1967
SALES (est): 13.57MM **Privately Held**
Web: www.tekni-plex.com
SIC: 2679 7389 2672 Egg cartons, molded
   pulp: made from purchased material;
   Packaging and labeling services; Cloth
   lined paper: made from purchased paper

(G-7787)
TENCOM LTD
7134 Railroad St (43528-9539)
PHONE................................419 865-5877
Robert Disanza, *Prin*
Shannon Leach, *Off Mgr*
▲ **EMP:** 8 **EST:** 1997
SALES (est): 4.98MM **Privately Held**
Web: www.tencom.com
SIC: 3312 3663 Bar, rod, and wire products;
   Antennas, transmitting and communications

(G-7788)
TRANE US INC
Also Called: Ingersoll Rand
1001 Hamilton Dr (43528-8210)
PHONE................................419 491-2278
Dennis Goldsmith, *Brnch Mgr*
EMP: 17
Web: www.trane.com
SIC: 3585 Heating equipment, complete
HQ: Trane U.S. Inc.
   800-E Beaty St
   Davidson NC 28036
   704 655-4000

(G-7789)
TURBINE STANDARD LTD (PA)
1750 Eber Rd Ste A (43528-7896)
PHONE................................419 865-0355
David R Corwin, *Pr*
Patty Kops, *Contrlr*
▲ **EMP:** 9 **EST:** 2003
SALES (est): 5.12MM
SALES (corp-wide): 5.12MM **Privately
Held**
Web: www.turbinestandard.com

▲ = Import ▼ = Export
◆ = Import/Export

SIC: 3724 Aircraft engines and engine parts

(G-7790)
VINYL DESIGN CORPORATION
7856 Hill Ave (43528-9181)
PHONE..................419 283-4009
Patrick J Trompeter, *Pr*
EMP: 29 EST: 1988
SQ FT: 36,000
SALES (est): 2.53MM **Privately Held**
Web: www.vinyldesigncorp.com
SIC: 3089 5033 2452 Windows, plastics;
Siding, except wood; Prefabricated wood
buildings

(G-7791)
WOODSAGE INDUSTRIES LLC
7400 Airport Hwy (43528-9545)
P.O. Box 1040 (43528-1040)
PHONE..................419 866-8000
Daniel Brown, *Managing Member*
EMP: 7 EST: 2000
SALES (est): 949.1K **Privately Held**
Web: www.woodsage.com
SIC: 3999 Atomizers, toiletry

(G-7792)
WOODSAGE LLC
Also Called: Proveyance Group
7400 Airport Hwy (43528-9545)
P.O. Box 1040 (43528-1040)
PHONE..................419 866-8000
Tim Carpenter, *CEO*
Curtis Bowers, *
EMP: 110 EST: 2014
SQ FT: 150,000
SALES (est): 12.16MM **Privately Held**
Web: www.woodsage.com
SIC: 3317 Steel pipe and tubes

Holmesville
Holmes County

(G-7793)
ACTION COUPLING & EQP INC
8248 County Road 245 (44633-9724)
P.O. Box 99 (44633-0099)
PHONE..................330 279-4242
Scott Eliot, *Pr*
▲ EMP: 80 EST: 1991
SQ FT: 75,000
SALES (est): 11.77MM **Privately Held**
Web: www.actioncoupling.com
SIC: 3569 5087 3429 Firefighting and
related equipment; Firefighting equipment;
Hardware, nec

(G-7794)
AURIA HOLMESVILLE LLC
8281 County Road 245 (44633-9724)
PHONE..................330 279-4505
Brian Pour, *Pr*
EMP: 271 EST: 2007
SALES (est): 17.98MM
SALES (corp-wide): 19K **Privately Held**
SIC: 3714 Motor vehicle parts and
accessories
HQ: Auria Solutions Usa Inc.
26999 Cntl Pk Blvd Ste 30
Southfield MI 48076
248 728-8000

(G-7795)
HEARTLAND STAIRWAYS INC (PA)
8230 County Road 245 (44633-9724)
PHONE..................330 279-2554
Roy Hostewtler, *Pr*
EMP: 9 EST: 2000
SQ FT: 17,000

SALES (est): 902.7K
SALES (corp-wide): 902.7K **Privately Held**
Web: www.heartlandstairways.com
SIC: 3534 Elevators and moving stairways

(G-7796)
HEARTLAND STAIRWAYS INC
7964 Township Road 565 (44633-9702)
PHONE..................330 279-2554
Roy Hostewtler, *Pr*
EMP: 6
SALES (corp-wide): 902.7K **Privately Held**
Web: www.heartlandstairways.com
SIC: 2431 Millwork
PA: Heartland Stairways, Inc.
8230 County Road 245
Holmesville OH 44633
330 279-2554

(G-7797)
HOLMES REDIMIX INC
7571 State Route 83 (44633-9633)
PHONE..................330 674-0865
Daniel L Mathie, *Pr*
EMP: 20 EST: 2007
SALES (est): 4.97MM **Privately Held**
Web: www.melwaygroup.com
SIC: 1442 Construction sand and gravel

(G-7798)
HOLMES STAIR PARTS LTD
8614 Township Road 561 (44633-9706)
PHONE..................330 279-2797
Ben R Hershberger, *Owner*
EMP: 20 EST: 1997
SALES (est): 2.4MM **Privately Held**
Web: www.holmesstair.cc
SIC: 3534 Elevators and moving stairways

(G-7799)
HOLMES SUPPLY CORP
7571 State Route 83 (44633-9633)
PHONE..................330 279-2634
Steve Schlabach, *Pr*
EMP: 9 EST: 1997
SALES (est): 1.42MM **Privately Held**
Web: www.melwaygroup.com
SIC: 3299 2951 1442 Sand lime products;
Asphalt paving mixtures and blocks;
Construction sand and gravel

(G-7800)
HOLMES WHEEL SHOP INC
Also Called: American Stirrup
7969 County Road 189 (44633-9756)
P.O. Box 56 (44633-0056)
PHONE..................330 279-2891
Ronald Clark, *Pr*
Paul Stutzman, *VP*
▲ EMP: 20 EST: 1970
SQ FT: 32,000
SALES (est): 941.69K **Privately Held**
Web: www.holmeswheelshop.com
SIC: 2499 3199 Spools, reels, and pulleys:
wood; Stirrups, wood or metal

(G-7801)
INTERNATIONAL AUTOMOTIVE COMPO
8281 County Road 245 (44633-9724)
PHONE..................330 279-6557
Kim Landall, *Brnch Mgr*
EMP: 10
Web: www.iacgroup.com
SIC: 3069 Hard rubber products, nec
PA: International Automotive Components
Group North America, Inc.
27777 Frnklin Rd Ste 2000
Southfield MI 48034

(G-7802)
MILLER LOGGING INC
8373 State Route 83 (44633-9726)
P.O. Box 86 (44633-0086)
PHONE..................330 279-4721
Roy A Miller Junior, *Pr*
Barbara Miller, *VP*
Levi Miller, *Sec*
EMP: 6 EST: 1962
SALES (est): 743.16K **Privately Held**
Web: www.millerlogging.com
SIC: 2421 1629 2411 Wood chips, produced
at mill; Land clearing contractor; Logging

(G-7803)
ROTO SOLUTIONS INC
8300 County Rd 189 (44633)
PHONE..................330 279-2424
Richard Cook, *Pr*
Ralph Kirkpatrick, *
Mark Scheibe, *
EMP: 6 EST: 2006
SALES (est): 805.82K **Privately Held**
Web: www.rotosolutions.com
SIC: 3089 Injection molding of plastics

Homer
Licking County

(G-7804)
OHIO STATE PALLET CORP
2175 Broehm Rd (43027)
PHONE..................614 332-3961
Teresa Salyers, *Prin*
EMP: 6 EST: 2001
SALES (est): 572.72K **Privately Held**
Web: www.ohiostatepallet.com
SIC: 2448 Pallets, wood

Homeworth
Columbiana County

(G-7805)
HOMEWORTH FABRICATION MCH INC
23094 Georgetown Rd (44634)
P.O. Box 127 (44634-0127)
PHONE..................330 525-5459
Ronald D Matz, *Pr*
Rocco Vizzuso, *VP*
EMP: 11 EST: 1986
SQ FT: 3,000
SALES (est): 1.21MM **Privately Held**
SIC: 3823 3544 Process control instruments;
Jigs and fixtures

(G-7806)
OHIO DRILL & TOOL CO (PA)
Also Called: Homeworth Sales Service Div
23255 Georgetown Rd (44634)
P.O. Box 154 (44634-0154)
PHONE..................330 525-7717
Connie Hallman, *Pr*
George Sanor, *Ch Bd*
Daniel Matz, *VP*
Ronald D Matz, *Sec*
Dale Buckman, *Genl Mgr*
EMP: 20 EST: 1947
SQ FT: 5,000
SALES (est): 4.87MM
SALES (corp-wide): 4.87MM **Privately Held**
Web: www.ohiodrill.com
SIC: 5085 5261 3546 3545 Industrial tools;
Lawn and garden equipment; Power-driven
handtools; Machine tool accessories

(G-7807)
WAYNE A WHALEY
Also Called: Wayne Tire Service
4466 12th St (44634-9725)
PHONE..................330 525-7779
Wayne Whaley, *Prin*
EMP: 6 EST: 1989
SALES (est): 62.16K **Privately Held**
SIC: 7534 5531 Tire repair shop; Automotive
tires

Hubbard
Trumbull County

(G-7808)
BALL AROSOL SPECIALTY CONT INC
Also Called: Ball Aerosol And Specialty
Container Inc.
644 Myron St (44425-1466)
PHONE..................330 534-1903
Bernie Grilli, *Brnch Mgr*
EMP: 37
SALES (corp-wide): 11.79B **Publicly Held**
Web: www.ball.com
SIC: 3411 Food and beverage containers
HQ: Ball Aerosol And Specialty Container
Corporation
9300 W 108th Cir
Westminster CO 80021

(G-7809)
BARFECTIONS LLC
6105 W Liberty St (44425-1060)
PHONE..................330 759-3100
Mike Handel, *Contrlr*
EMP: 8
SALES (corp-wide): 10.64MM **Privately
Held**
SIC: 2064 Candy and other confectionery
products
PA: Barfections Llc
1598 Motor Inn Dr
Girard OH 44420
330 759-3100

(G-7810)
ELLWOOD ENGINEERED CASTINGS CO
7158 Hubbard Masury Rd (44425-9756)
PHONE..................330 568-3000
Pat Callihan, *Pr*
Lyda Force, *
Susan A Apel, *
◆ EMP: 135 EST: 1991
SALES (est): 22.72MM
SALES (corp-wide): 593.7MM **Privately
Held**
Web:
www.ellwoodengineeredcastings.com
SIC: 3321 3369 3322 Gray iron ingot molds,
cast; Nonferrous foundries, nec; Malleable
iron foundries
PA: Ellwood Group, Inc.
600 Commercial Ave
Ellwood City PA 16117
724 752-3680

(G-7811)
INDEPENDENCE 2 LLC
Also Called: I2
623 W Liberty St (44425-1750)
P.O. Box 40 (44425-0040)
PHONE..................800 414-0545
Ronald P Baldine, *Mng Pt*
Bonnie L Buchanan, *Pt*
Nick Ingoedue, *Pt*
▲ EMP: 10 EST: 2004
SQ FT: 10,000

SALES (est): 1.63MM **Privately Held**
Web: www.i2hardware.com
SIC: **3429** Door locks, bolts, and checks

(G-7812)
J & D STEEL SERVICE CENTER LLC
3030 Gale Dr (44425-1011)
PHONE..................................330 759-7430
EMP: 6 EST: 2003
SALES (est): 1.17MM **Privately Held**
Web: www.jdsteelservice.com
SIC: **3599** Machine shop, jobbing and repair

(G-7813)
JET STREAM INTERNATIONAL INC
644 Myron St (44425-1466)
PHONE..................................330 505-9988
Edgar B Rumble Junior, *CEO*
Edgar B Rumble Junior, *Pr*
John Isbill, *
▲ EMP: 70 EST: 2000
SALES (est): 15.47MM **Privately Held**
Web: www.jetstr.com
SIC: **3469** **3272** Metal stampings, nec;
Concrete structural support and building
material

(G-7814)
MS MURCKO & SONS LLC
8090 Chestnut Ridge Rd (44425-9718)
PHONE..................................724 854-4907
Thomas Murcko, *Prin*
Donald Murcko, *Prin*
EMP: 8 EST: 2020
SALES (est): 604.62K **Privately Held**
SIC: **3498** Fabricated pipe and fittings

(G-7815)
OHIO STEEL SHEET AND PLATE INC
7845 Chestnut Ridge Rd (44425-9702)
P.O. Box 1146 (44482-1146)
PHONE..................................800 827-2401
John Rebhan, *Pr*
Eric Rebhan, *
Mike Link, *
EMP: 45 EST: 1987
SQ FT: 320,000
SALES (est): 2.24MM **Privately Held**
Web: www.ohiosteelplate.com
SIC: **3312** **5051** **3444** Sheet or strip, steel,
hot-rolled; Metals service centers and
offices; Sheet metalwork

(G-7816)
PSK STEEL CORP
2960 Gale Dr (44425-1099)
P.O. Box 308 (44425-0308)
PHONE..................................330 759-1251
Jerry Kinast, *Pr*
Henry Kinast, *
Steven R Anderson, *
▲ EMP: 40 EST: 1962
SQ FT: 120,000
SALES (est): 9.8MM **Privately Held**
Web: www.psksteel.com
SIC: **3544** Special dies and tools

(G-7817)
TAYLOR - WINFIELD CORPORATION
Also Called: Denton & Anderson Mktg Div
3200 Innovation Place (44425)
PHONE..................................330 259-8500
John A Anderson Ii, *Ch Bd*
Michael G Marando, *
◆ EMP: 125 EST: 1882
SQ FT: 45,000
SALES (est): 4.93MM **Privately Held**
Web: www.taylor-winfield.com
SIC: **3548** **3542** **3567** Welding apparatus;
Machine tools, metal forming type;
Induction heating equipment

(G-7818)
WARREN FABRICATING CORPORATION (PA)
7845 Chestnut Ridge Rd (44425-9702)
PHONE..................................330 534-5017
Eric Rebhan, *CEO*
John C Rebhan, *
◆ EMP: 90 EST: 1967
SQ FT: 380,000
SALES (est): 24.91MM
SALES (corp-wide): 24.91MM **Privately Held**
Web: www.warfab.com
SIC: **3441** **3599** **3547** **3532** Fabricated
structural metal; Machine shop, jobbing and
repair; Rolling mill machinery; Mining
machinery

(G-7819)
YOUNGSTOWN-KENWORTH INC (PA)
Also Called: All-Line Truck Sales
7255 Hubbard Masury Rd (44425-9757)
PHONE..................................330 534-9761
Tomiel Mikes, *Pr*
Randall R Fiest, *
Geraldine Mikes, *
EMP: 18 EST: 1972
SQ FT: 14,900
SALES (est): 15.59MM
SALES (corp-wide): 15.59MM **Privately Held**
Web: www.youngstownkenworth.com
SIC: **5013** **5012** **7538** **3713** Truck parts and
accessories; Trucks, commercial; General
automotive repair shops; Truck and bus
bodies

Huber Heights
Montgomery County

(G-7820)
ENJET AERO LLC
Also Called: Enjet Aero Dayton
7700 New Carlisle Pike (45424-1512)
PHONE..................................937 878-3800
EMP: 16
SALES (est): 7.03MM **Privately Held**
Web: www.enjetaero.com
SIC: **3728** Aircraft parts and equipment, nec

(G-7821)
ENJET AERO DAYTON INC (DH)
Also Called: Enginetics Aero Space
7700 New Carlisle Pike (45424-1512)
PHONE..................................937 878-3800
Bruce Breckenridge, *CEO*
Christopher Ferraro, *CFO*
EMP: 38 EST: 1976
SQ FT: 57,000
SALES (est): 21.32MM
SALES (corp-wide): 222.67MM **Privately Held**
Web: www.enjetaero.com
SIC: **3724** **3728** **3812** **3519** Aircraft engines
and engine parts; Aircraft parts and
equipment, nec; Search and navigation
equipment; Jet propulsion engines
HQ: Enjet Aero Acquisitions Holding Inc.
9401 Indian Creek Pkwy
Overland Park KS 66210
913 717-7396

(G-7822)
MJO INDUSTRIES INC (PA)
Also Called: Hughes-Peters
8000 Technology Blvd (45424-1573)
PHONE..................................800 590-4055
EMP: 88 EST: 1923

SALES (est): 81.52MM
SALES (corp-wide): 81.52MM **Privately Held**
Web: www.hughespeters.com
SIC: **5063** **5065** **3679** Wire and cable;
Connectors, electronic; Electronic circuits

(G-7823)
MPE AEROENGINES INC
Also Called: Enginetics
7700 New Carlisle Pike (45424-1512)
PHONE..................................937 878-3800
Dale Pelfrey, *CEO*
EMP: 25 EST: 2010
SALES (est): 548.47K
SALES (corp-wide): 720.63MM **Publicly Held**
SIC: **3365** Aerospace castings, aluminum
PA: Standex International Corporation
23 Keewaydin Dr
Salem NH 03079
603 893-9701

(G-7824)
PVS PLASTICS TECHNOLOGY CORP
6290 Executive Blvd (45424-1424)
PHONE..................................937 233-4376
Juerden Frank, *Pr*
▲ EMP: 20 EST: 2004
SQ FT: 25,000
SALES (est): 16.19MM
SALES (corp-wide): 355.83K **Privately Held**
Web: www.pvs-plastics.net
SIC: **3089** Injection molding of plastics
PA: Pvs Kunststofftechnik Beteiligungsges.
Mbh
Salzstr. 20
Niedernhall BW
794091260

(G-7825)
UPDIKE SUPPLY COMPANY
Also Called: Machine Tools Supply
8241 Expansion Way (45424-6381)
PHONE..................................937 482-4000
Steve Short, *Pr*
Jeff Butts, *
Trixi Myers, *
Shane Hannan, *
Rob Johnson, *
EMP: 36 EST: 1995
SALES (est): 2.4MM **Privately Held**
SIC: **3541** Machine tools, metal cutting type

Hudson
Summit County

(G-7826)
A JC INC
Also Called: A J C Hatchet Co
5145 Hudson Dr (44236-3735)
PHONE..................................800 428-2438
Mathew Crookston, *Pr*
Thomas Crookston, *Sls Dir*
Jim R Crookston, *CFO*
▲ EMP: 15 EST: 1968
SQ FT: 10,000
SALES (est): 2.32MM **Privately Held**
Web: www.ajctools.com
SIC: **3531** **3423** **3546** **3429** Roofing
equipment; Hand and edge tools, nec;
Power-driven handtools; Hardware, nec

(G-7827)
ADVANCE MATERIALS PRODUCTS INC
Also Called: Adma Products
1890 Georgetown Rd (44236-4058)

PHONE..................................330 650-4000
Vladimir Moxson, *Pr*
Sophia Moxson, *VP*
▲ EMP: 6 EST: 1988
SQ FT: 20,000
SALES (est): 727.88K **Privately Held**
Web: www.admaproducts.com
SIC: **3339** Titanium metal, sponge and
granules

(G-7828)
ALPHA TECHNOLOGIES SVCS LLC (DH)
Also Called: Alpha
6279 Hudson Crossing Pkwy Ste 200
(44236-4350)
PHONE..................................330 745-1641
Ken Brown, *Managing Member*
Barbara Davidson, *
◆ EMP: 60 EST: 1996
SALES (est): 17.15MM
SALES (corp-wide): 528.83MM **Privately Held**
Web: www.alpha-technologies.com
SIC: **3823** **8748** Process control instruments;
Testing services
HQ: Dynisco Instruments Llc
38 Forge Pkwy
Franklin MA 02038
508 541-9400

(G-7829)
AMERICAN FIREWORKS INC
Also Called: American Fireworks
7041 Darrow Rd (44236-2254)
P.O. Box 1447 (44236)
PHONE..................................330 650-1776
Roberto Sorgi, *CEO*
EMP: 720 EST: 1964
SALES (est): 10.52MM **Privately Held**
Web: www.americanfireworks.com
SIC: **2899** Fireworks

(G-7830)
AMERICAN FIREWORKS COMPANY
7041 Darrow Rd (44236-2254)
P.O. Box 1447 (44236-0947)
PHONE..................................330 650-1776
Roberto Sorgi, *CEO*
EMP: 720 EST: 1956
SALES (est): 2.49MM **Privately Held**
SIC: **2899** Fireworks

(G-7831)
AMERICAN ULTRA SPECIALTIES INC
6855 Industrial Pkwy (44236-1158)
PHONE..................................330 656-5000
Christi Yacinski, *Pr*
William Stofey, *Stockholder*
Michaela M Stofey, *Sec*
Albert Sivillo, *Stockholder*
John Ningard Senior, *Stockholder*
EMP: 18 EST: 1979
SQ FT: 37,500
SALES (est): 3.78MM **Privately Held**
Web: www.ultraspecoil.com
SIC: **2992** **5172** Re-refining lubricating oils
and greases, nec; Lubricating oils and
greases

(G-7832)
AMF BURNS
1797 Georgetown Rd (44236-4192)
PHONE..................................330 650-6500
EMP: 7 EST: 2015
SALES (est): 648.78K **Privately Held**
Web: www.amfbrunsamerica.com
SIC: **3443** Fabricated plate work (boiler shop)

(G-7833)
ARLINGTON VALLEY FARMS LLC (PA)
5369 Hudson Dr (44236-3739)
PHONE..............................216 426-5000
EMP: 25 EST: 2010
SALES (est): 1.83MM
SALES (corp-wide): 1.83MM **Privately Held**
Web: www.arlingtonvalleyfarms.com
SIC: 2051 Bread, cake, and related products

(G-7834)
BECKER SIGNS INC
6381 Chittenden Rd Ste E9 (44236-2052)
PHONE..............................330 659-4504
Brian Becker, *Pr*
Karen Becker, *Prin*
EMP: 8 EST: 2010
SALES (est): 478.59K **Privately Held**
Web: www.beckersigns.com
SIC: 3993 5999 Signs and advertising specialties; Alarm and safety equipment stores

(G-7835)
BOXOUT LLC (PA)
Also Called: Meyerpt
6333 Hudson Crossing Pkwy (44236-4346)
PHONE..............................833 462-7746
Ron Harrington, *CEO*
◆ EMP: 103 EST: 1948
SQ FT: 50,000
SALES (est): 41.82MM
SALES (corp-wide): 41.82MM **Privately Held**
Web: www.meyerpt.com
SIC: 5122 5047 3843 8041 Vitamins and minerals; Medical and hospital equipment; Dental equipment and supplies; Offices and clinics of chiropractors

(G-7836)
CEIA USA LTD
Also Called: Ceia USA
6336 Hudson Crossing Pkwy (44236-4306)
PHONE..............................330 310-4741
Luca Cacioli, *CEO*
Alessandro Manneschi, *Managing Member**
Marco Manneschi, *Managing Member**
Luca Manneschi, *
Giovanni Manneschi, *
▲ EMP: 55 EST: 1997
SQ FT: 42,318
SALES (est): 9.83MM **Privately Held**
Web: www.ceia-usa.com
SIC: 3669 3812 3829 Metal detectors; Magnetic field detection apparatus; Magnetometers

(G-7837)
CITY VISITOR INC
Also Called: City Visitor Publications
2099 Edgeview Dr (44236-1850)
PHONE..............................216 661-6666
Rocco Dililo, *Pr*
Mark Timm, *VP*
EMP: 9 EST: 1977
SALES (est): 246.63K **Privately Held**
Web: www.eisenlab.org
SIC: 2721 Magazines: publishing only, not printed on site

(G-7838)
CLAFLIN CO
Also Called: Claflin Company
5270 Hudson Dr (44236-3738)
PHONE..............................330 650-0582
James C Claflin, *Pr*
Howard Claflin, *Pr*
EMP: 8 EST: 1973

SQ FT: 10,000
SALES (est): 748.06K **Privately Held**
Web: www.claflin.com
SIC: 3089 Injection molding of plastics

(G-7839)
CLEVELAND STEEL CONTAINER CORPORATION (PA)
100 Executive Pkwy (44236-1630)
PHONE..............................440 349-8000
◆ EMP: 24 EST: 1964
SALES (est): 165.45MM
SALES (corp-wide): 165.45MM **Privately Held**
Web: www.clevelandsteelcontainter.com
SIC: 3412 Pails, shipping: metal

(G-7840)
CLINICAL SPECIALTIES INC (HQ)
Also Called: Csi Infusion Services
6288 Hudson Crossing Pkwy (44236-4347)
PHONE..............................888 873-7888
Edward Rivalsky, *Pr*
EMP: 74 EST: 1988
SALES (est): 3.28MM **Publicly Held**
Web: www.optioncarehealth.com
SIC: 2834 Intravenous solutions
PA: Option Care Health, Inc.
3000 Lakeside Dr Ste 300n
Bannockburn IL 60015

(G-7841)
FLUID POWER INC
Also Called: Guardian Mfg.
1300 Hudson Gate Dr (44236-4401)
PHONE..............................330 653-5107
Matt Davis, *Pr*
Matthew Davis, *Ex VP*
Karen Voytek, *Off Mgr*
EMP: 12 EST: 1949
SQ FT: 12,000
SALES (est): 9.2MM
SALES (corp-wide): 11.94MM **Privately Held**
Web: www.fluidpowerohio.com
SIC: 3728 Oxygen systems, aircraft
PA: O2 Aero Acquisitions, Llc
8 Morgan Pl
Unionville CT

(G-7842)
GRIFFIN TECHNOLOGY INC
Also Called: Applied Collegiate Systems Div
50 Executive Pkwy (44236-1605)
PHONE..............................585 924-7121
Jonathan B Leiken, *Pr*
EMP: 190 EST: 1995
SALES (est): 3.5MM
SALES (corp-wide): 3.75B **Publicly Held**
SIC: 3571 3089 Mainframe computers; Identification cards, plastics
PA: Diebold Nixdorf, Incorporated
350 Orchard Ave Ne
North Canton OH 44720
330 490-4000

(G-7843)
HANDCRAFTED JEWELRY INC
Also Called: Jewelry Art
116 N Main St (44236-2827)
PHONE..............................330 650-9011
Georgianna Bojtos, *Pr*
Barbara Johnson, *VP*
EMP: 7 EST: 1977
SQ FT: 1,000
SALES (est): 384.04K **Privately Held**
Web: www.jewelryarthudson.com
SIC: 5944 5947 7699 2759 Jewelry, precious stones and precious metals; Gift shop; Customizing services; Engraving, nec

(G-7844)
HOWARD B CLAFLIN CO
Also Called: Claflin Co
5270 Hudson Dr (44236-3738)
PHONE..............................330 928-1704
Howard B Claflin, *Pr*
Bruce Claflin, *Sls Mgr*
EMP: 6 EST: 1957
SALES (est): 473.41K **Privately Held**
SIC: 2655 2599 Reels (fiber), textile: made from purchased material; Boards: planning, display, notice

(G-7845)
HUDSON EXTRUSIONS INC
1255 Norton Rd (44236-4403)
P.O. Box 255 (44236-0255)
PHONE..............................330 653-6015
Marylin Hansen, *Pr*
Dewey Hansen, *Stockholder**
EMP: 35 EST: 1956
SQ FT: 33,000
SALES (est): 4.97MM **Privately Held**
Web: www.hudsonextrusions.com
SIC: 3089 Injection molding of plastics

(G-7846)
IMPRINTS
77 Maple Dr (44236-3037)
PHONE..............................330 650-0467
William Stemple, *Owner*
EMP: 10 EST: 1983
SQ FT: 1,100
SALES (est): 274.63K **Privately Held**
SIC: 2791 Typesetting

(G-7847)
INTERNTNAL PRCSION CAST SUPS I
1570 Terex Rd (44236-4069)
PHONE..............................330 342-0407
Charlotte Joseph, *Dir*
▲ EMP: 7 EST: 2009
SQ FT: 50,000
SALES (est): 1.24MM **Privately Held**
Web: www.ipcs-uk.com
SIC: 3324 Aerospace investment castings, ferrous

(G-7848)
KOBELCO STEWART BOLLING INC
1600 Terex Rd (44236-4086)
PHONE..............................330 655-3111
Atsushi Shigeno, *Pr*
Robert Mcdermott, *Sec*
Takehiko Fujioka, *
◆ EMP: 94 EST: 1923
SQ FT: 270,000
SALES (est): 21.03MM **Privately Held**
Web: www.ksbi.com
SIC: 3559 Rubber working machinery, including tires
HQ: Kobe Steel Usa Holdings Inc.
535 Madison Ave, 5th Fl
New York NY 10022

(G-7849)
LEAK FINDER INC
6583 Wooded View Dr (44236-1068)
PHONE..............................440 735-0130
James Riffle, *Pr*
EMP: 6 EST: 2009
SQ FT: 1,000
SALES (est): 364.42K **Privately Held**
Web: www.leakfinderinc.com
SIC: 1799 1389 7389 Gas leakage detection; Pipe testing, oil field service; Inspection and testing services

(G-7850)
MABIS SHIPPING SOLUTIONS INC
Also Called: Labelmatch
126 W Streetsboro St (44236-2720)
PHONE..............................330 650-1788
Matthew Villenauve, *Pr*
Christine Villenauve, *VP*
▼ EMP: 6 EST: 1998
SQ FT: 1,900
SALES (est): 2.77MM **Privately Held**
Web: www.labelmatch.com
SIC: 2679 3579 2759 5099 Labels, paper: made from purchased material; Mailing, letter handling, and addressing machines; Financial note and certificate printing and engraving; Firearms and ammunition, except sporting

(G-7851)
MAGNUM ASSET ACQUISITION LLC
Also Called: Magnum Innovations
5675 Hudson Industrial Pkwy # 3 (44236-5012)
PHONE..............................330 915-2382
Ron Cozean, *Prin*
Maria Hughes, *
EMP: 28 EST: 2018
SALES (est): 4.04MM **Privately Held**
SIC: 3646 Fluorescent lighting fixtures, commercial

(G-7852)
METTLER FOOTWEAR INC ✪
704 Westbrook Way (44236-5221)
PHONE..............................330 703-0079
Michael Mettler, *Pr*
EMP: 6 EST: 2023
SALES (est): 3.31MM **Privately Held**
SIC: 3021 Rubber and plastics footwear

(G-7853)
NCRFORMSCOM
137 Owen Brown St (44236-2811)
PHONE..............................800 709-1938
EMP: 7 EST: 2013
SALES (est): 124.02K **Privately Held**
Web: www.ncrforms.com
SIC: 2759 Commercial printing, nec

(G-7854)
PRINTERS DEVIL INC
77 Maple Dr (44236-3037)
PHONE..............................330 650-1218
William Stemple, *Pr*
EMP: 11 EST: 1977
SQ FT: 800
SALES (est): 814.66K **Privately Held**
Web: www.printersdevilinc.com
SIC: 2752 7334 Offset printing; Photocopying and duplicating services

(G-7855)
RAMCO SPECIALTIES INC (PA)
5445 Hudson Industrial Pkwy (44236-3777)
PHONE..............................330 653-5135
Richard Malson Ii, *Pr*
Mark Gamble, *
◆ EMP: 77 EST: 1977
SQ FT: 165
SALES (est): 27.75MM
SALES (corp-wide): 27.75MM **Privately Held**
Web: www.ramcospecialties.com
SIC: 3965 3452 3714 Fasteners; Nuts, metal; Motor vehicle parts and accessories

(G-7856)
SHERWIN-WILLIAMS COMPANY
Also Called: Sherwin-Williams
5860 Darrow Rd (44236-3864)

GEOGRAPHIC

PHONE..............................330 528-0124
Mindy Malone, *Mgr*
EMP: 6
SALES (corp-wide): 23.1B **Publicly Held**
Web: www.sherwin-williams.com
SIC: 5231 2851 Paint; Paints and allied
  products
PA: The Sherwin-Williams Company
  101 W Prospect Ave
  Cleveland OH 44115
  216 566-2000

(G-7857)
SINTERED METAL INDUSTRIES INC
Also Called: Simet
1890 Georgetown Rd (44236-4058)
PHONE..............................330 650-4000
Vladimir Moxson, *Pr*
Sophia Moxson, *VP*
EMP: 10 **EST:** 1985
SALES (est): 489.68K **Privately Held**
SIC: 3441 3568 Fabricated structural metal;
  Bearings, bushings, and blocks

(G-7858)
SPECIALTY METALS PROC INC
837 Seasons Rd (44224-1027)
PHONE..............................330 656-2767
Michael Miniea, *Pr*
Becky Miniea, *Prin*
▲ **EMP:** 47 **EST:** 1996
SQ FT: 170,000
SALES (est): 14.01MM **Publicly Held**
Web: www.specialtymetalspro.com
SIC: 3541 Machine tools, metal cutting type
PA: Ryerson Holding Corporation
  227 W Monroe St Fl 27
  Chicago IL 60606

(G-7859)
STARBRIGHT LIGHTING USA LLC
Also Called: Manufacturers Repdirect Distr
5136 Darrow Rd (44236-4004)
PHONE..............................330 650-2000
Chris Bokash, *Managing Member*
EMP: 8 **EST:** 2013
SALES (est): 811.2K **Privately Held**
Web: www.starbrightlightingusa.com
SIC: 3648 Lighting equipment, nec

(G-7860)
THE LITTLE TIKES COMPANY (PA)
Also Called: Little Tikes
2180 Barlow Rd (44236-4199)
PHONE..............................330 650-3000
◆ **EMP:** 1800 **EST:** 1967
SALES (est): 58.7MM
SALES (corp-wide): 58.7MM **Privately
Held**
Web: www.littletikes.com
SIC: 3944 2519 Games, toys, and children's
  vehicles; Juvenile furniture, rattan or reed:
  padded or plain

(G-7861)
**UNIVERSAL DIRECT FULFILLMENT
CORP**
5581 Hudson Industrial Pkwy (44236-5019)
PHONE..............................330 650-5000
▲ **EMP:** 16
Web: www.universalscreenarts.com
SIC: 5961 2741 2396 Catalog and mail-order
  houses; Miscellaneous publishing;
  Automotive and apparel trimmings

(G-7862)
**WOLTERS KLUWER CLINICAL
DRUG INFORMATION INC**
1100 Terex Rd (44236-3771)
P.O. Box 1560 (21741-1560)

PHONE..............................330 650-6506
EMP: 65
Web: www.wolterskluwer.com
SIC: 2731 2791 7379 Books, publishing only
  ; Typesetting, computer controlled;
  Computer related maintenance services

Huntsville
Logan County

(G-7863)
DUFF QUARRY INC (PA)
Also Called: Duff Quarry
9042 State Route 117 (43324-9617)
P.O. Box 305 (43324-0305)
PHONE..............................937 686-2811
James E Duff, *Pr*
Scott Duff, *VP*
Sandy Duff, *Sec*
EMP: 15 **EST:** 1953
SQ FT: 26,000
SALES (est): 5.22MM
SALES (corp-wide): 5.22MM **Privately
Held**
Web: www.duffquarry.com
SIC: 1422 Crushed and broken limestone

(G-7864)
FIRE SAFETY SERVICES INC
6228 Township Road 95 (43324-9673)
PHONE..............................937 686-2000
Steven Spath, *Pr*
Marcus Taylor, *VP*
Kay Spath, *Sec*
EMP: 18 **EST:** 1962
SQ FT: 6,400
SALES (est): 4.95MM **Privately Held**
Web: www.fssohio.com
SIC: 5099 5012 5087 3999 Fire extinguishers
  ; Fire trucks; Firefighting equipment; Fire
  extinguishers, portable

(G-7865)
**RETENTION KNOB SUPPLY & MFG
CO**
4905 State Route 274 W (43324-9643)
P.O. Box 61 (43311-0061)
PHONE..............................937 686-6405
Thomas E Christen, *Pr*
Carrie Christen, *Sec*
EMP: 10 **EST:** 1981
SQ FT: 100,000
SALES (est): 1.27MM **Privately Held**
Web: www.retentionknobsupply.com
SIC: 3545 Machine tool attachments and
  accessories

Huron
Erie County

(G-7866)
AKZO NOBEL COATINGS INC
300 Sprowl Rd (44839-2636)
PHONE..............................419 433-9143
EMP: 26
SALES (corp-wide): 11.6B **Privately Held**
SIC: 2851 Paints and allied products
HQ: Akzo Nobel Coatings Inc.
  535 Marriott Dr Ste 500
  Nashville TN 37214
  440 297-5100

(G-7867)
AMERICAN PUBLISHERS LLC
Also Called: American Publishers
2401 Sawmill Pkwy (44839-2284)
PHONE..............................419 626-0623
Steven Ester, *Pr*

John Rohan Junior, *Treas*
Catherine Bostron, *
John P Loughlin, *
EMP: 100 **EST:** 1918
SALES (est): 12.72MM
SALES (corp-wide): 4.29B **Privately Held**
Web: www.american-publishers.com
SIC: 2741 Miscellaneous publishing
PA: The Hearst Corporation
  300 W 57th St
  New York NY 10019
  212 649-2000

(G-7868)
ARTHUR CORPORATION
1305 Huron Avery Rd (44839-2429)
PHONE..............................419 433-7202
Charles Hensel, *Pr*
Mark Svancara, *
EMP: 65 **EST:** 1981
SQ FT: 65,000
SALES (est): 4.87MM **Privately Held**
Web: www.arthurcorp.com
SIC: 3089 3083 Thermoformed finished
  plastics products, nec; Laminated plastics
  plate and sheet

(G-7869)
ASSEMBLY WORKS INC
Also Called: Assembly Works Matrix Automtn
1705 Sawmill Pkwy (44839-2232)
PHONE..............................419 433-5010
William E Kaman, *Pr*
Julie Smart, *Sec*
EMP: 8 **EST:** 1998
SQ FT: 10,200
SALES (est): 447.82K **Privately Held**
SIC: 3613 Panelboards and distribution
  boards, electric

(G-7870)
**CENTRAL OHIO PAPER & PACKG
INC (PA)**
Also Called: Breckenridge Paper & Packaging
2350 University Dr E (44839-9173)
PHONE..............................419 621-9239
Edward Pettegrew Junior, *Pr*
EMP: 15 **EST:** 1994
SQ FT: 12,000
SALES (est): 2.12MM **Privately Held**
SIC: 2671 Paper, coated or laminated for
  packaging

(G-7871)
DENTON ATD INC (PA)
900 Denton Dr (44839-8922)
PHONE..............................567 265-5200
Robert A Denton, *Ch*
David C Stein, *
Micheal Beebe, *
Craig Morgan, *Stockholder*
EMP: 29 **EST:** 1991
SQ FT: 16,000
SALES (est): 840.87K **Privately Held**
Web: www.humaneticsgroup.com
SIC: 3999 3821 3829 Mannequins;
  Calibration tapes, for physical testing
  machines; Measuring and controlling
  devices, nec

(G-7872)
EVERWAY LLC
2401 Sawmill Pkwy Ste 10-11
(44839-2284)
P.O. Box 550 (44839-0550)
PHONE..............................419 433-9800
Craig Powell, *Managing Member*
David Swank, *
Steve Lubowicz, *
Don Wostmann, *
EMP: 250 **EST:** 1997

SQ FT: 16,800
SALES (est): 26.36MM **Privately Held**
Web: www.n2y.com
SIC: 3999 Education aids, devices and
  supplies

(G-7873)
GEOCORP INC
9010 River Rd (44839-9523)
PHONE..............................419 433-1101
George Conrad, *Pr*
EMP: 46 **EST:** 1989
SQ FT: 6,000
SALES (est): 12.65MM **Privately Held**
Web: www.geocorpinc.com
SIC: 3823 Thermocouples, industrial
  process type

(G-7874)
**HURON CEMENT PRODUCTS
COMPANY (PA)**
Also Called: H & C Building Supplies
617 Main St (44839-2593)
PHONE..............................419 433-4161
John Caporini, *Pr*
EMP: 38 **EST:** 1914
SQ FT: 37,800
SALES (est): 1.24MM
SALES (corp-wide): 1.24MM **Privately
Held**
Web: www.terminalreadymix.com
SIC: 5032 3273 3546 3272 Cement; Ready-
  mixed concrete; Power-driven handtools;
  Concrete products, nec

(G-7875)
I 5S OF HURON INC
356 Main St (44839-1663)
PHONE..............................419 433-9075
Mike Glaser, *Prin*
EMP: 6 **EST:** 2006
SALES (est): 245.88K **Privately Held**
SIC: 2599 Bar, restaurant and cafeteria
  furniture

(G-7876)
LABEL AID INC
Also Called: Label Aid
608 Rye Beach Rd (44839-2064)
PHONE..............................419 433-2888
Darlene Crooks, *Pr*
Carl S Hanson, *
Lucille Hanson, *
Heather Feeney, *
▲ **EMP:** 32 **EST:** 1983
SQ FT: 40,000
SALES (est): 4.5MM **Privately Held**
Web: www.labelaidinc.com
SIC: 2759 2679 Labels and seals: printing,
  nsk; Labels, paper: made from purchased
  material

(G-7877)
LAKEWAY MFG INC (PA)
730 River Rd (44839-2623)
P.O. Box 486 (44839-0486)
PHONE..............................419 433-3030
Jack Kenning, *Pr*
Barbara K Straka, *
EMP: 25 **EST:** 1977
SALES (est): 2.48MM
SALES (corp-wide): 2.48MM **Privately
Held**
Web: www.lakewaymfg.com
SIC: 3567 3255 3446 3433 Industrial
  furnaces and ovens; Clay refractories;
  Architectural metalwork; Heating
  equipment, except electric

(G-7878)
LATANICK EQUIPMENT INC
720 River Rd (44839-2623)
PHONE..............................419 433-2200
Richard D Poorman, *Pr*
Richard Decker, *VP*
EMP: 20 **EST:** 1973
SQ FT: 32,000
SALES (est): 4.04MM **Privately Held**
Web: www.latanickequipment.com
SIC: 8711 3599 Designing; ship, boat, machine, and product; Custom machinery

(G-7879)
LUC ICE INC
10020 River Rd (44839-9768)
PHONE..............................419 734-2201
TOLL FREE: 800
Michael Luc, *Pr*
Paul Luc, *VP*
EMP: 7 **EST:** 1982
SALES (est): 213.42K **Privately Held**
Web: www.homecityice.com
SIC: 2097 Block ice

(G-7880)
MUDBROOK GOLF CTR AT THNDRBIRD
1609 Mudbrook Rd (44839-8905)
PHONE..............................419 433-2945
Dan Stupka, *Prin*
EMP: 6 **EST:** 2007
SALES (est): 211.81K **Privately Held**
Web: www.thunderbirdgolfcourses.com
SIC: 3949 Driving ranges, golf, electronic

(G-7881)
PITTSBURGH PAINTS CO
Glidden Professional Paint Ctr
300 Sprowl Rd (44839-2636)
PHONE..............................419 433-5664
William Radjewski, *Brnch Mgr*
EMP: 210
SALES (corp-wide): 388.64MM **Privately Held**
Web: www.ppgpaints.com
SIC: 2851 Paints and allied products
PA: The Pittsburgh Paints Co
400 Bertha Lamme Dr
Cranberry Township PA 16066
724 742-5200

(G-7882)
SEVEN LAKEWAY REFRACTORIES LLC
730 River Rd (44839-2623)
PHONE..............................419 433-3030
Leanne Pate, *Managing Member*
EMP: 16 **EST:** 2021
SALES (est): 1.27MM **Privately Held**
SIC: 3255 Tile and brick refractories, except plastic

Iberia
Morrow County

(G-7883)
GLEN-GERY CORPORATION
County Rd 9 (43325)
P.O. Box 207 (43325-0207)
PHONE..............................419 468-5002
George Robinson, *Mgr*
EMP: 37
Web: www.glengery.com
SIC: 3251 3255 Structural brick and blocks; Clay refractories
HQ: Glen-Gery Corporation
1166 Spring St
Reading PA 19610
610 374-4011

(G-7884)
RP MANUFACTURING LLC
Also Called: Dualift Hoist
3424 State Rte 309 (43325)
P.O. Box 3188 (44904-0188)
PHONE..............................419 468-5095
EMP: 6 **EST:** 2004
SQ FT: 7,000
SALES (est): 243.37K **Privately Held**
Web: www.refuseparts.com
SIC: 3536 `Hoists

(G-7885)
YIZUMI-HPM CORPORATION
Also Called: HPM North America Corp
3424 State Rt 309 (43325)
P.O. Box 210 (43325-0210)
PHONE..............................740 382-5600
Randy Clements, *Mgr*
▲ **EMP:** 25 **EST:** 2011
SALES (est): 4.05MM **Privately Held**
Web: www.hpmmachinery.com
SIC: 3542 Die casting machines
PA: Yizumi Holdings Co., Ltd.
No.22, Keyuan 3rd Road, High-Tech Zone, Shunde District
Foshan GD 52830

Independence
Cuyahoga County

(G-7886)
7SIGNAL INC (PA)
6155 Rockside Rd Ste 110 (44131-2217)
PHONE..............................216 777-2900
Thomas Barrett, *CEO*
Don Cook, *CMO**
EMP: 23 **EST:** 2011
SQ FT: 3,900
SALES (est): 3.92MM
SALES (corp-wide): 3.92MM **Privately Held**
Web: www.7signal.com
SIC: 3661 Telephone and telegraph apparatus

(G-7887)
ACCEL PERFORMANCE GROUP LLC (DH)
6100 Oak Tree Blvd Ste 200 (44131-6914)
PHONE..............................216 658-6413
Robert Tobey, *CEO*
Robert Romanelli, ***
Andrew Mazzarella, ***
◆ **EMP:** 180 **EST:** 1993
SQ FT: 200,000
SALES (est): 11.91MM
SALES (corp-wide): 602.22MM **Publicly Held**
Web: www.airsoftswat.com
SIC: 3714 5013 3053 Motor vehicle parts and accessories; Automotive supplies and parts; Gaskets; packing and sealing devices
HQ: Msdp Group Llc
1350 Pullman Dr Dock #14
El Paso TX 79936
915 857-5200

(G-7888)
AGILE GLOBAL SOLUTIONS INC
5755 Granger Rd Ste 610 (44131-1458)
PHONE..............................916 655-7745
EMP: 29
SALES (corp-wide): 4.84MM **Privately Held**
Web: www.agileglobalsolutions.com
SIC: 7372 Business oriented computer software
PA: Agile Global Solutions, Inc.

193 Blue Ravine Rd # 160
Folsom CA 95630
916 353-1780

(G-7889)
ALCAN PRIMARY PRODUCTS CORP
6055 Rockside Woods Blvd N Ste 180 (44131-2301)
◆ **EMP:** 214 **EST:** 2003
SALES (est): 2.01MM
SALES (corp-wide): 53.66B **Privately Held**
SIC: 3334 Primary aluminum
HQ: Alcan Corporation
6060 Parkland Blvd
Cleveland OH 44124

(G-7890)
CARDIOINSIGHT TECHNOLOGIES INC
Also Called: Medtronic
3 Summit Park Dr Ste 400 (44131-2582)
PHONE..............................216 274-2221
Patrick J Wethington, *Pr*
Charu Ramanathan, *CSO*
EMP: 9 **EST:** 2006
SALES (est): 1.94MM **Privately Held**
Web: www.cardioinsight.com
SIC: 3845 Electrocardiographs
PA: Medtronic Public Limited Company
Building 2 Parkmore
Galway

(G-7891)
CHECKPOINT SURGICAL INC
Also Called: Checkpoint Surgical Instrs Inc
6050 Oak Tree Blvd Ste 360 (44131-6938)
PHONE..............................216 378-9107
Leonard Cosentino, *CEO*
EMP: 55 **EST:** 2009
SALES (est): 8.64MM **Privately Held**
Web: www.checkpointsurgical.com
SIC: 3845 Electromedical equipment

(G-7892)
CHROMASCAPE LLC (PA)
Also Called: Amerimulch
7555 E Pleasant Valley Rd Ste 100 (44131-5557)
PHONE..............................330 998-7574
Joseph Majewski, *Pr*
George Chase, ***
Steve Lefkowitz, ***
◆ **EMP:** 33 **EST:** 1998
SALES (est): 80.22MM
SALES (corp-wide): 80.22MM **Privately Held**
Web: www.chromascape.com
SIC: 2816 2895 Color pigments; Carbon black

(G-7893)
CONSTRCTION AGGRGTES CORP MICH
3 Summit Park Dr Ste 700 (44131-6901)
PHONE..............................616 842-7900
Andrew D Eich, *Prin*
David Sensibar, *Pr*
Albert Fruend, *Sec*
EMP: 20 **EST:** 1982
SALES (est): 560.86K **Privately Held**
SIC: 1442 Construction sand and gravel

(G-7894)
COVIA HOLDINGS LLC (PA)
3 Summit Park Dr Ste 700 (44131-6901)
PHONE..............................800 243-9004
◆ **EMP:** 90 **EST:** 1970
SALES (est): 1.47B
SALES (corp-wide): 1.47B **Privately Held**
Web: www.coviacorp.com

SIC: 1446 Silica mining

(G-7895)
COVIA SOLUTIONS LLC (HQ)
3 Summit Park Dr Ste 700 (44131-6901)
P.O. Box 87 (44024-0087)
PHONE..............................440 214-3200
Bruno Biasiotta, *Pr*
Brian Richardson, *Ex VP*
Duncan Stuart, *Ex VP*
Rory O'donnell, *Sr VP*
Christopher Nagel, *Ex VP*
▼ **EMP:** 9 **EST:** 1986
SALES (est): 928MM
SALES (corp-wide): 1.47B **Privately Held**
Web: www.coviacorp.com
SIC: 1442 3295 Sand mining; Minerals, ground or otherwise treated
PA: Covia Holdings Llc
3 Summit Park Dr Ste 700
Independence OH 44131
800 243-9004

(G-7896)
CRH US
6925 Granger Rd (44131-1407)
PHONE..............................216 642-3920
EMP: 6 **EST:** 2018
SALES (est): 609.89K **Privately Held**
Web: www.ashgrove.com
SIC: 3531 Cement silos (batch plant)

(G-7897)
DIE-MATIC CORPORATION
201 Eastview Dr (44131-1074)
PHONE..............................216 749-4656
Louie J Zeitler, *CEO*
Jerry Zeitler, ***
John A Gorman, ***
Cynthia Graor, *Stockholder**
▲ **EMP:** 55 **EST:** 1958
SQ FT: 120,000
SALES (est): 9.42MM **Privately Held**
Web: www.die-matic.com
SIC: 3469 3544 Stamping metal for the trade ; Special dies, tools, jigs, and fixtures

(G-7898)
DUNHAM MACHINE INC
1311 E Schaaf Rd Bldg A (44131-1347)
PHONE..............................216 398-4500
Ted Pawelec, *Pr*
EMP: 9 **EST:** 1988
SQ FT: 7,500
SALES (est): 1.02MM **Privately Held**
Web: www.dunhammachine.com
SIC: 3599 Machine shop, jobbing and repair

(G-7899)
E VENTUS CORPORATION
5005 Rockside Rd (44131-2194)
PHONE..............................216 643-6840
David Brennan, *Mgr*
EMP: 6 **EST:** 2010
SALES (est): 696.84K **Privately Held**
Web: www.e-ventus.com
SIC: 7372 Prepackaged software

(G-7900)
ECOPRO SOLUTIONS LLC
5617 E Schaaf Rd (44131-1305)
PHONE..............................216 232-4040
Dennis B Angers, *Pr*
EMP: 50 **EST:** 2019
SALES (est): 4.91MM **Privately Held**
Web: www.ecopro.com
SIC: 3822 Hardware for environmental regulators

(G-7901)
EDGEWATER CAPITAL PARTNERS LP (PA)
5005 Rockside Rd Ste 1300　(44131-6806)
PHONE..............................216 292-3838
Chris Childres, *Mng Pt*
Ryan J Meany, *Pt*
Richard Schwarz, *Pt*
EMP: 8 **EST:** 1998
SQ FT: 3,200
SALES (est): 160.78MM
SALES (corp-wide): 160.78MM **Privately Held**
Web: www.edgewatercapital.com
SIC: 6799 2899　Investors, nec; Chemical supplies for foundries

(G-7902)
EPIROC USA LLC
7171 E Pleasant Valley Rd　(44131-5541)
PHONE..............................844 437-4762
EMP: 11
Web: www.epiroc.com
SIC: 3532　Drills, bits, and similar equipment
HQ: Epiroc Usa Llc
　　8001 Arista Pl Ste 400
　　Broomfield CO 80021
　　844 437-4762

(G-7903)
FIVE STAR TECHNOLOGIES LTD
6801 Brecksville Rd Ste 200　(44131-5064)
PHONE..............................216 447-9422
Gerard Weimann, *CEO*
Marilyn A Eisele, *CFO*
Timothy E Fahey, *VP*
Oleg V Kozyuk, *Chief Scientist*
EMP: 15 **EST:** 1995
SQ FT: 20,000
SALES (est): 1.33MM **Privately Held**
Web: www.fivestartech.com
SIC: 3823　Process control instruments

(G-7904)
FML TERMINAL LOGISTICS LLC (DH)
3 Summit Park Dr Ste 700　(44131-6901)
PHONE..............................440 214-3200
EMP: 10 **EST:** 2013
SALES (corp-wide): 1.47B **Privately Held**
SIC: 1442　Construction sand and gravel
HQ: Covia Solutions Llc
　　3 Summit Park Dr Ste 700
　　Independence OH 44131
　　440 214-3200

(G-7905)
GRAFTECH HOLDINGS INC
6100 Oak Tree Blvd Ste 300　(44131-6970)
PHONE..............................216 676-2000
Joel L Hawthorne, *CEO*
Erick R Asmussen, *VP*
John D Moran, *VP*
EMP: 65 **EST:** 1993
SALES (est): 14.11MM **Publicly Held**
Web: www.graftechaet.com
SIC: 1499 3624　Graphite mining; Carbon and graphite products
PA: Graftech International Ltd.
　　982 Keynote Cir
　　Brooklyn Heights OH 44131

(G-7906)
KOMATSU MINING CORP
981 Keynote Cir Ste 8　(44131-1842)
PHONE..............................216 503-5029
Edward L Doheny, *Brnch Mgr*
EMP: 101
Web: www.joyglobal.com

SIC: 3532　Mining machinery
HQ: Komatsu Mining Corp.
　　311 E Greenfield Ave
　　Milwaukee WI 53204

(G-7907)
LIQUID DEVELOPMENT COMPANY (PA)
Also Called: L D C
5708 E Schaaf Rd　(44131-1308)
PHONE..............................216 641-9366
Doug Hutchinson, *Pr*
Beldon Hutchinson, *VP*
Dawn Hutchinson, *Sec*
Lynn Hutchinson, *Treas*
▲ **EMP:** 9 **EST:** 1978
SQ FT: 18,000
SALES (est): 296.4K
SALES (corp-wide): 296.4K **Privately Held**
Web: www.ldcbrushplate.com
SIC: 2899 3559　Chemical preparations, nec; Electroplating machinery and equipment

(G-7908)
MEDTRONIC INC
Also Called: Medtronic
3 Summit Park Dr Ste 400　(44131-2582)
PHONE..............................763 526-2566
EMP: 8
Web: www.medtronic.com
SIC: 3841　Surgical and medical instruments
HQ: Medtronic, Inc.
　　710 Medtronic Pkwy
　　Minneapolis MN 55432
　　763 514-4000

(G-7909)
MILL & MOTION INC
5415 E Schaaf Rd　(44131-1335)
PHONE..............................216 524-4000
Daniel Hala, *Pr*
EMP: 12 **EST:** 1983
SQ FT: 18,000
SALES (est): 2.59MM **Privately Held**
Web: www.millmotion.com
SIC: 3599 8711　Machine shop, jobbing and repair; Designing: ship, boat, machine, and product

(G-7910)
MILL & MOTION PROPERTIES LTD
5415 E Schaaf Rd　(44131-1335)
PHONE..............................216 524-4000
Albert E Hala, *Ch Bd*
Daniel Hala, *Pr*
EMP: 12 **EST:** 1983
SALES (est): 830.95K **Privately Held**
SIC: 3824　Mechanical and electromechanical counters and devices

(G-7911)
MILLCRAFT GROUP LLC (PA)
Also Called: Deltacraft
9000 Rio Nero Dr　(44131-5502)
PHONE..............................216 441-5500
Kay Mlakar, *Ch Bd*
Charles Mlakar, *Managing Member*
David Hegeman, *CFO*
▲ **EMP:** 75 **EST:** 1995
SALES (est): 388.34MM **Privately Held**
Web: www.millcraft.com
SIC: 5111 5113 2679　Printing paper; Industrial and personal service paper; Paper products, converted, nec

(G-7912)
NIDEC AVTRON AUTOMATION CORPORATION
Also Called: Avtron Industrial Automation
7555 E Pleasant Valley Rd　(44131-5562)

PHONE..............................216 642-1230
EMP: 150
Web: www.nidec-avtron.com
SIC: 3823 3829　Process control instruments; Aircraft and motor vehicle measurement equipment

(G-7913)
OSRAM SYLVANIA INC
6400 Rockside Rd　(44131-2309)
PHONE..............................800 463-9275
EMP: 93
SALES (corp-wide): 3.9B **Privately Held**
Web: www.sylvania-automotive.com
SIC: 3641　Electric lamps
HQ: Osram Sylvania Inc.
　　200 Ballardvale St Bldg 2
　　Wilmington MA 01887
　　978 570-3000

(G-7914)
PENINSULA PUBLISHING LLC
Also Called: Plastics Machinery Magazine
2 Summit Park Dr Ste 300　(44131-2560)
PHONE..............................330 524-3359
J A Lewellenc, *CEO*
EMP: 9 **EST:** 2015
SALES (est): 726.86K **Privately Held**
SIC: 2721　Magazines: publishing and printing

(G-7915)
POLYMER ADDITIVES HOLDINGS INC (PA)
Also Called: Valtris
7500 E Pleasant Valley Rd　(44131-5536)
PHONE..............................216 875-7200
Paul Angus, *Pr*
Andy Gehrlein, *
Jim Mason, *
Steve Hughes, *Comm Vice President*
EMP: 200 **EST:** 2014
SALES (est): 465.61MM
SALES (corp-wide): 465.61MM **Privately Held**
Web: www.valtris.com
SIC: 5169 2899　Chemicals and allied products, nec; Chemical preparations, nec

(G-7916)
PRECISION METALFORMING ASSN
6363 Oak Tree Blvd　(44131-2500)
PHONE..............................216 901-8800
William E Gaskin, *CEO*
Doug Johnson, *
David C Klotz, *
Daniel E Ellashek, *
Bill Smith, *
▲ **EMP:** 41 **EST:** 1942
SQ FT: 20,000
SALES (est): 7.43MM **Privately Held**
Web: www.pma.org
SIC: 8611 2731　Trade associations; Book publishing

(G-7917)
PREFERRED SOLUTIONS INC
5000 Rockside Rd Ste 230　(44131-2178)
PHONE..............................216 642-1200
John A Stahl, *Pr*
Jack Stahl, *VP*
EMP: 14 **EST:** 1992
SALES (est): 2.28MM **Privately Held**
Web: www.preferredsolutions.net
SIC: 3089　Plastics processing

(G-7918)
QUEZ MEDIA MARKETING INC
Also Called: Quez Media
6100 Oak Tree Blvd Ste 200　(44131-2544)
PHONE..............................216 910-0202
Jose A Vasquez, *CEO*

EMP: 7 **EST:** 2009
SALES (est): 698.22K **Privately Held**
Web: www.quezmedia.com
SIC: 7374 2752 7336 7371　Computer graphics service; Offset printing; Commercial art and graphic design; Computer software systems analysis and design, custom

(G-7919)
STEIN LLC (DH)
3 Summit Park Dr Ste 425　(44131-6902)
P.O. Box 470548　(44147-0548)
PHONE..............................440 526-9301
Donald Ries, *CEO*
Marc Glasgow, *Pr*
James Conlon, *Sec*
David Holvey, *CFO*
▲ **EMP:** 15 **EST:** 1945
SALES (est): 9.71MM **Privately Held**
Web: www.steininc.com
SIC: 7629 7699 3399　Electrical repair shops; Cleaning services; Iron ore recovery from open hearth slag
HQ: Tms International, Llc
　　2835 East Carson Street
　　Pittsburgh PA 15203
　　412 678-6141

(G-7920)
STEIN HOLDINGS INC
3 Summit Park Dr Ste 425　(44131-6902)
PHONE..............................440 526-9301
EMP: 22 **EST:** 2016
SALES (est): 1.87MM **Privately Held**
Web: www.steininc.com
SIC: 2542　Partitions and fixtures, except wood

(G-7921)
THYSSENKRUPP MATERIALS NA INC
6050 Oak Tree Blvd Ste 110　(44131-6927)
PHONE..............................216 883-8100
Randy Pacelli, *Brnch Mgr*
EMP: 60
SQ FT: 65,000
SALES (corp-wide): 39.13B **Privately Held**
Web: www.thyssenkrupp-materials-na.com
SIC: 5051 3341　Steel; Secondary nonferrous metals
HQ: Thyssenkrupp Materials Na, Inc.
　　22355 W 11 Mile Rd
　　Southfield MI 48033
　　248 233-5600

(G-7922)
TRIAD CAPITAL GROUP LLC (PA)
Also Called: Special Metal Stamping
4641 Spring Rd　(44131-1021)
PHONE..............................440 236-6677
Philip Rankin, *Pr*
EMP: 7 **EST:** 2011
SALES (est): 1.08MM
SALES (corp-wide): 1.08MM **Privately Held**
Web: evenmix.com
SIC: 3441　Fabricated structural metal

(G-7923)
TROYMILL LUMBER COMPANY
7000 Granger Rd Ste 1　(44131-1462)
PHONE..............................440 632-6353
Marvin Schaefer, *Pr*
Collen Satterlee, *Mgr*
EMP: 8 **EST:** 1992
SALES (est): 644.08K **Privately Held**
Web: www.troymill.com
SIC: 2448　Pallets, wood

▲ = Import ▼ = Export
◆ = Import/Export

(G-7924)
WEDRON SILICA LLC
3 Summit Park Dr Ste 700 (44131-6901)
P.O. Box 119 (60557)
PHONE..........................815 433-2449
William Conway, *Ch*
Charles Fowler, *
Jenniffer Deckard, *
Joseph Fodo, *
David Crandall, *
EMP: 90 **EST:** 1984
SQ FT: 4,500
SALES (est): 17.45MM
SALES (corp-wide): 1.47B **Privately Held**
SIC: 1446 Industrial sand
HQ: Covia Solutions Llc
3 Summit Park Dr Ste 700
Independence OH 44131
440 214-3200

(G-7925)
WESTON BRANDS INC
7575 E Pleasant Valley Rd Ste 100
(44131-5567)
PHONE..........................800 814-4895
Michael Caspar, *Pr*
EMP: 11 **EST:** 2016
SALES (est): 229.55K **Privately Held**
Web: www.westonbrands.com
SIC: 2099 Food preparations, nec

(G-7926)
WISCONSIN INDUS SAND CO LLC
3 Summit Park Dr Ste 700 (44131-6901)
PHONE..........................715 235-0942
Jenniffer Deckard, *Managing Member*
William E Conway, *
Andrew D Eich, *
EMP: 26 **EST:** 1996
SALES (est): 11.07MM
SALES (corp-wide): 1.47B **Privately Held**
SIC: 2819 Silica compounds
HQ: Technisand, Inc.
3 Summit Park Dr Ste 700
Independence OH 44131

Irondale
Jefferson County

(G-7927)
C A JOSEPH CO
C A Joseph Machine Shop
170 Broadway St (43932)
P.O. Box 274 (43932-0274)
PHONE..........................330 532-4646
Joe Smithbower, *Mgr*
EMP: 17
SALES (corp-wide): 3.09MM **Privately
Held**
Web: www.cajoseph.com
SIC: 3599 3444 3443 3441 Machine shop,
jobbing and repair; Sheet metalwork;
Fabricated plate work (boiler shop);
Fabricated structural metal
PA: C. A. Joseph Co.
13712 Old Frdericktown Rd
East Liverpool OH 43920
330 385-6869

Ironton
Lawrence County

(G-7928)
ALLEN ENTERPRISES INC
Also Called: Tri-State Wilbert Vault Co
2900 S 9th St (45638-2844)
P.O. Box 231 (45638-0231)
PHONE..........................740 532-5913

Douglas M Allen, *Pr*
Ronald Keener, *Sec*
Gretchen A Allen, *Dir*
Robin Robison, *Contrlr*
EMP: 20 **EST:** 1928
SQ FT: 22,000
SALES (est): 2.85MM **Privately Held**
Web: www.tristatewilbert.com
SIC: 5039 3272 5087 Septic tanks; Septic
tanks, concrete; Caskets

(G-7929)
AMERICAN HYDRAULIC SVCS INC
1912 S 1st St (45638-2478)
P.O. Box 624 (41129-0624)
PHONE..........................606 739-8680
Jeremiah Fulks, *Pr*
Randall Blankenship, *
▲ **EMP:** 41 **EST:** 2001
SALES (est): 8.42MM **Privately Held**
Web: www.americanhydraulic.net
SIC: 3593 7699 Fluid power cylinders,
hydraulic or pneumatic; Hydraulic
equipment repair

(G-7930)
AMERICAS STYRENICS LLC
925 County Road 1a (45638-8687)
PHONE..........................740 302-8667
EMP: 64
SALES (corp-wide): 7.42B **Privately Held**
Web: www.amsty.com
SIC: 2821 Plastics materials and resins
HQ: Americas Styrenics Llc
24 Waterway Ave Ste 1200
The Woodlands TX 77380

(G-7931)
EMERSON NETWORK POWER
3040 S 9th St (45638-2895)
PHONE..........................614 841-8054
Steve Hassell, *Pr*
EMP: 8 **EST:** 2016
SALES (est): 1.21MM **Privately Held**
Web: www.emerson.com
SIC: 3613 3585 7629 Switchgear and
switchboard apparatus; Refrigeration and
heating equipment; Electrical repair shops

(G-7932)
PLATINUM INDUSTRIES LLC
Also Called: Platinum Industries
541 Private Road 908 (45638-8602)
PHONE..........................740 205-2041
Tim Price, *Prin*
Jim Price, *Prin*
Rob Marshall, *Prin*
EMP: 15 **EST:** 2019
SALES (est): 565.3K **Privately Held**
SIC: 3999 Manufacturing industries, nec

(G-7933)
PREMERE PRECAST PRODUCTS
317 Hecla St (45638-1370)
PHONE..........................740 533-3333
Evyian Terry, *Prin*
EMP: 6 **EST:** 2008
SALES (est): 138.08K **Privately Held**
Web: www.ohioprecast.org
SIC: 3272 Concrete products, precast, nec

(G-7934)
**ROACH WOOD PRODUCTS & PLAS
INC**
25 Township Road 328 (45638-8171)
PHONE..........................740 532-4855
Bruce Roach Senior, *CEO*
Bruce Roach Junior, *Pr*
EMP: 8 **EST:** 1984
SQ FT: 10,700
SALES (est): 1.43MM **Privately Held**

SIC: 3082 Unsupported plastics profile
shapes

(G-7935)
SWIFT MANUFACTURING CO INC
700 Lorain St (45638-1088)
PHONE..........................740 237-4405
Michael Moore, *Pr*
Zachary Moore, *VP*
EMP: 6 **EST:** 2008
SALES (est): 1.22MM **Privately Held**
Web: www.swiftmfg.net
SIC: 3339 Primary nonferrous metals, nec

(G-7936)
VERTIV CORPORATION
Also Called: Vertiv
3040 S 9th St (45638-2895)
PHONE..........................740 547-5100
Bob Walters, *Genl Mgr*
EMP: 124
SALES (corp-wide): 8.01B **Publicly Held**
Web: www.vertiv.com
SIC: 3823 Process control instruments
HQ: Vertiv Corporation
505 N Cleveland Ave
Westerville OH 43082
614 888-0246

(G-7937)
WELLS GROUP LLC
487 Gallia Pike (45638-8080)
PHONE..........................740 532-9240
Kimberly Cole, *Brnch Mgr*
EMP: 10
SALES (corp-wide): 46.35MM **Privately
Held**
Web: www.wellsgroupconcrete.com
SIC: 3273 Ready-mixed concrete
PA: The Wells Group Llc
611 W Main St
West Liberty KY 41472
606 743-3485

Jackson
Jackson County

(G-7938)
ALUCHEM OF JACKSON INC
14782 Beaver Pike (45640-9661)
PHONE..........................740 286-2455
Ronald P Zapletal, *Pr*
Ronald L Bell, *
Edward L Butera, *
EMP: 8 **EST:** 1987
SALES (est): 2.33MM **Privately Held**
Web: www.aluchem.com
SIC: 2819 Industrial inorganic chemicals, nec

(G-7939)
BELLISIO
100 E Broadway St (45640-1347)
P.O. Box 550 (45640-0550)
PHONE..........................740 286-5505
◆ **EMP:** 13 **EST:** 2008
SALES (est): 183.18K **Privately Held**
Web: www.bellisiofoods.com
SIC: 2038 Frozen specialties, nec

(G-7940)
BELLISIO FOODS INC
100 E Bdwy (45640-1347)
P.O. Box 550 (45640-0550)
PHONE..........................740 286-5505
Jeff Wilson, *Brnch Mgr*
EMP: 110
Web: www.bellisiofoods.com

SIC: 2038 2033 Dinners, frozen and
packaged; Spaghetti and other pasta
sauce; packaged in cans, jars, etc
HQ: Bellisio Foods, Inc
701 N Wash St Ste 400
Minneapolis MN 55401

(G-7941)
BRENMAR CONSTRUCTION INC
900 Morton St (45640-1089)
PHONE..........................740 286-2151
Todd Ghearing, *Pr*
Tim Ousley, *
Andy Graham, *
EMP: 60 **EST:** 1988
SQ FT: 5,000
SALES (est): 11.07MM **Privately Held**
Web: www.brenmarconstruction.com
SIC: 1542 3312 Commercial and office
building contractors; Structural shapes and
pilings, steel

(G-7942)
BROWN PUBLISHING CO INC (PA)
Also Called: Brown Publishing
1 Acy Ave Ste D (45640-9563)
P.O. Box 270 (45640-0270)
PHONE..........................740 286-2187
Roy Brown, *Pr*
EMP: 15 **EST:** 1925
SQ FT: 5,250
SALES (est): 297.6K
SALES (corp-wide): 297.6K **Privately Held**
SIC: 2711 Newspapers: publishing only, not
printed on site

(G-7943)
D G M INC
Also Called: Tow Path Ready Mix
1668 Kessinger School Rd (45640-9127)
PHONE..........................740 286-2131
Lonnie Lemaster, *Brnch Mgr*
EMP: 10
SALES (corp-wide): 12.67MM **Privately
Held**
Web: www.towpathreadymix.com
SIC: 3273 Ready-mixed concrete
PA: D. G. M., Inc.
1881 Adams Rd
Beaver OH 45613
740 226-1950

(G-7944)
ELEMETAL REFINING LLC
16064 Beaver Pike (45640-9659)
P.O. Box 605 (45640-0605)
PHONE..........................740 286-6457
EMP: 150 **EST:** 1974
SALES (est): 2.88MM
SALES (corp-wide): 103.18MM **Privately
Held**
SIC: 3341 3356 3339 Secondary precious
metals; Nonferrous rolling and drawing, nec
; Primary nonferrous metals, nec
PA: Elemetal, Llc
15850 N Dallas Pkwy
Dallas TX 75248
214 956-7600

(G-7945)
**EQUIP BUSINESS SOLUTIONS CO
(PA)**
120 Twin Oaks Dr (45640-9828)
PHONE..........................614 854-9755
Craig Lund, *Pr*
EMP: 6 **EST:** 1997
SALES (est): 2.62MM
SALES (corp-wide): 2.62MM **Privately
Held**
Web: www.equipbusinesssolutions.com

SIC: 2759 8742 5112 Commercial printing, nec; Management consulting services; Stationery and office supplies

(G-7946)
JACKSON MONUMENT INC
14 Fairmount St (45640-1409)
PHONE..............................740 286-1590
Stan Louis, *Pr*
Darryl Radliff, *Prin*
EMP: 8 EST: 1987
SALES (est): 242.13K Privately Held
Web: www.jacksonmonumentworks.com
SIC: 3272 5999 Monuments, concrete; Monuments, finished to custom order

(G-7947)
JALCO INDUSTRIES INC
330 Athens St (45640-9433)
P.O. Box 947 (45640-0947)
PHONE..............................740 286-3808
Randal L Ridge, *Pr*
Susan R Ridge, *Sec*
EMP: 10 EST: 1997
SQ FT: 10,000
SALES (est): 312.1K Privately Held
SIC: 3281 5032 Building stone products; Concrete building products

(G-7948)
MONTGOMERY MCH FABRICATION INC
206 Watts Blevins Rd (45640-9768)
P.O. Box 247 (45640-0247)
PHONE..............................740 286-2863
Carry E Montgomery, *Pr*
Bobbi D Montgomery, *
Jason Montgomery, *
Mary Montgomery, *
EMP: 35 EST: 1982
SQ FT: 20,000
SALES (est): 2.37MM Privately Held
Web:
www.montgomerymachineshop.com
SIC: 3599 Machine shop, jobbing and repair

(G-7949)
OHIO METAL PROCESSING LLC
16064 Beaver Pike (45640-9659)
PHONE..............................740 912-2057
EMP: 8 EST: 2017
SQ FT: 70,000
SALES (est): 247.56K Privately Held
Web: www.greenelyonmetals.com
SIC: 3341 5051 Secondary precious metals; Copper products

(G-7950)
OSCO INDUSTRIES INC
165 Athens St (45640-1306)
P.O. Box 327 (45640-0327)
PHONE..............................740 286-5004
Keith Denny, *Brnch Mgr*
EMP: 86
SALES (corp-wide): 32.6MM Privately Held
Web: www.oscoind.com
SIC: 3321 3322 Gray iron castings, nec; Malleable iron foundries
PA: Osco Industries, Inc.
734 11th Street
Portsmouth OH 45662
740 354-3183

(G-7951)
PHOENIX QUALITY MFG LLC
16064 Beaver Pike # 888 (45640-9659)
PHONE..............................705 279-0538
EMP: 30 EST: 2020
SALES (est): 2.45MM Privately Held

SIC: 3841 Surgical and medical instruments

(G-7952)
SPOT ON MAIN LLC
Also Called: Spot On Main Coffee Roastery
91 Harding Ave (45640-1774)
P.O. Box 364 (45640)
PHONE..............................740 285-0441
EMP: 16
SALES (corp-wide): 478.55K Privately Held
Web: www.thespotonmain.com
SIC: 2095 Coffee roasting (except by wholesale grocers)
PA: The Spot On Main Llc
298 E Main St
Jackson OH 45640
740 577-3327

(G-7953)
SPRING HLTHCARE DAGNOSTICS LLC
16064 Beaver Pike (45640-9659)
PHONE..............................866 201-9503
I Amhed, *Managing Member*
EMP: 60 EST: 2022
SALES (est): 2.78MM Privately Held
Web: www.springdiagnostic.com
SIC: 3841 Surgical and medical instruments

(G-7954)
SUMMERS ORGANIZATION LLC
Also Called: Premium Wood & Garden Products
345 E Main St Ste H (45640-1789)
P.O. Box 527 (45640-0527)
PHONE..............................740 286-1322
EMP: 20 EST: 2001
SALES (est): 578.39K Privately Held
SIC: 2873 Fertilizers: natural (organic), except compost

(G-7955)
WATERLOO COAL COMPANY INC (PA)
Also Called: Madison Mine Supply Co
235 E Main St (45640-1715)
P.O. Box 626 (45640-0626)
PHONE..............................740 286-0004
EMP: 70 EST: 1934
SALES (est): 4.69MM
SALES (corp-wide): 4.69MM Privately Held
Web: www.waterloocoal.com
SIC: 1221 1411 1459 Strip mining, bituminous; Limestone, dimension-quarrying; Clays (common) quarrying

(G-7956)
WINTERS PRODUCTS INC
Also Called: Winters Concrete
109 Athens St (45640-1306)
PHONE..............................740 286-4149
David R Michael, *Pr*
EMP: 10 EST: 1955
SQ FT: 800
SALES (est): 96.15K Privately Held
SIC: 3273 Ready-mixed concrete

Jackson Center
Shelby County

(G-7957)
A G PARTS INC
Also Called: Quality Parts
500 N Linden St (45334)
P.O. Box 757 (45334-0757)
PHONE..............................937 596-6448
Charles Cole, *Pr*

Tony Nimeyer, *VP*
EMP: 16 EST: 1972
SALES (est): 352.76K Privately Held
SIC: 3714 Motor vehicle parts and accessories

(G-7958)
AIRSTREAM INC (HQ)
1001 W Pike St (45334-6066)
P.O. Box 629 (45334-0629)
PHONE..............................937 596-6111
Robert Wheeler, *Pr*
Lawrence J Huttle, *
Peter B Orthwein, *
Wade F B Thompson, *
Dan Froehlich, *
◆ EMP: 350 EST: 1980
SQ FT: 286,000
SALES (est): 39.23K
SALES (corp-wide): 10.04B Publicly Held
Web: www.airstream.com
SIC: 3716 3792 3714 3713 Motor homes; Travel trailers and campers; Motor vehicle parts and accessories; Truck and bus bodies
PA: Thor Industries, Inc.
52700 Independence Ct
Elkhart IN 46514
574 970-7460

(G-7959)
CREATIVE PLASTICS INTL
18163 Snider Rd (45334-9734)
PHONE..............................937 596-6769
Gerald Wurm, *Pr*
Gerald B Wurm, *Pr*
Keith Korn, *VP*
Randolph Korn, *VP*
Richard Wurm, *VP*
EMP: 17 EST: 1968
SQ FT: 40,000
SALES (est): 840.47K Privately Held
Web: www.cpiforming.com
SIC: 3089 Injection molding of plastics

(G-7960)
CURLYS CUSTOM MEATS INC
315 East St (45334-5078)
PHONE..............................937 596-6518
Edward Schmerge, *Pr*
Joshua Schmerge, *Treas*
Joel Schmerge, *VP*
Jennifer Shroyer, *Sec*
EMP: 16 EST: 2005
SALES (est): 943.88K Privately Held
Web: www.curlysmeats.com
SIC: 2011 Meat packing plants

(G-7961)
DESIGN ORIGINAL INC
402 Jackson St (45334-5057)
P.O. Box 727 (45334-0727)
PHONE..............................937 596-5121
Frank E Pusey, *Pr*
Glenn A Pusey, *VP*
EMP: 16 EST: 1971
SQ FT: 25,000
SALES (est): 728.68K Privately Held
Web: www.design-original.com
SIC: 5136 5137 2396 2395 Sportswear, men's and boys'; Sportswear, women's and children's; Automotive and apparel trimmings; Pleating and stitching

(G-7962)
ELDORADO NATIONAL KANSAS INC
419 W Pike St (45334-9728)
PHONE..............................937 596-6849
Andrew Imanse, *CEO*
EMP: 197
Web: www.eldorado-bus.com

SIC: 3711 Buses, all types, assembly of
HQ: Eldorado National (Kansas), Inc.
2367 Century Dr
Goshen IN 46528

(G-7963)
EMI CORP (PA)
Also Called: E M I Plastic Equipment
801 W Pike St (45334-6037)
P.O. Box 590 (45334-0590)
PHONE..............................937 596-5511
James E Andraitis, *Pr*
Brad Wren, *
Linda Andraitis-varljen, *Treas*
▲ EMP: 85 EST: 1980
SQ FT: 80,000
SALES (est): 12.19MM
SALES (corp-wide): 12.19MM Privately Held
Web: www.emicorp.com
SIC: 3544 5084 Special dies, tools, jigs, and fixtures; Industrial machinery and equipment

(G-7964)
LACAL EQUIPMENT INC
901 W Pike St (45334-6024)
P.O. Box 757 (45334-0757)
PHONE..............................937 596-6106
Roger Dietrich, *Pr*
Tom Homan, *
Tony Niemeyer, *
Roger Detrick, *
Charles M Cole, *
▲ EMP: 50 EST: 1982
SQ FT: 14,000
SALES (est): 8.98MM
SALES (corp-wide): 46.13MM Privately Held
Web: www.lacal.com
SIC: 3714 Motor vehicle parts and accessories
PA: Jmac Inc.
200 W Ntnwide Blvd Unit 1
Columbus OH 43215
614 436-2418

(G-7965)
MASTER SWAGING INC
210 Washington St (45334-4010)
P.O. Box 550 (45334-0550)
PHONE..............................937 596-6171
Daniel Gilroy, *Pr*
Cindy Gilroy, *Prin*
EMP: 6 EST: 1960
SQ FT: 26,000
SALES (est): 632.13K Privately Held
Web: www.masterswaging.com
SIC: 3728 3599 Aircraft assemblies, subassemblies, and parts, nec; Machine shop, jobbing and repair

(G-7966)
PLASTIPAK PACKAGING INC
18015 State Route 65 (45334-9434)
P.O. Box 789 (45334-0789)
PHONE..............................937 596-6142
Willis Vetter, *Brnch Mgr*
EMP: 360
SALES (corp-wide): 2.9B Privately Held
Web: www.plastipak.com
SIC: 3085 2671 Plastics bottles; Paper; coated and laminated packaging
HQ: Plastipak Packaging, Inc.
41605 Ann Arbor Rd
Plymouth MI 48170
734 455-3600

(G-7967)
PRECISION DETAILS INC
104 Washington St (45334-1101)
P.O. Box 696 (45334-0696)

PHONE..................937 596-0068
Jeff Winemiller, *Pr*
Katie Winemiller, *VP*
EMP: 15 **EST:** 1981
SQ FT: 4,500
SALES (est): 2.14MM **Privately Held**
Web: www.precisiondetailsinc.com
SIC: 3544 Special dies and tools

Jamestown
Greene County

(G-7968)
BALL JACKETS LLC
Also Called: Just-Ink-Tees
5120 Waynesville Jamestown Rd
(45335-1542)
P.O. Box 57 (45335-0057)
PHONE..................937 572-1114
Jason Baker, *Prin*
Tara Allen, *
EMP: 25 **EST:** 2012
SALES (est): 2.26MM **Privately Held**
Web: www.justinktees.com
SIC: 2759 Screen printing

(G-7969)
TWIST INC (PA)
47 S Limestone St (45335-9501)
P.O. Box 177 (45335-0177)
PHONE..................937 675-9581
Joe W Wright, *Pr*
▲ **EMP:** 110 **EST:** 1972
SQ FT: 50,000
SALES (est): 10.89MM
SALES (corp-wide): 10.89MM **Privately Held**
Web: www.twistinc.com
SIC: 3495 3542 3469 3471 Mechanical springs, precision; Machine tools, metal forming type; Metal stampings, nec; Electroplating and plating

(G-7970)
TWIST INC
5100 Waynesville (45335)
PHONE..................937 675-9581
J Smith, *Brnch Mgr*
EMP: 9
SALES (corp-wide): 10.89MM **Privately Held**
Web: www.twistinc.com
SIC: 3495 3542 3469 Mechanical springs, precision; Machine tools, metal forming type; Metal stampings, nec
PA: Twist Inc.
47 S Limestone St
Jamestown OH 45335
937 675-9581

Jefferson
Ashtabula County

(G-7971)
ADA SOLUTIONS INC
901 Footville Richmond Rd E (44047-8627)
PHONE..................440 576-0423
David Chase, *Pr*
▼ **EMP:** 7 **EST:** 2012
SALES (est): 2.11MM **Privately Held**
SIC: 2821 Molding compounds, plastics

(G-7972)
CHUCK MEADORS PLASTICS CO
150 S Cucumber St (44047-1439)
PHONE..................440 813-4466
Chuck Meadors, *Pr*
EMP: 10 **EST:** 2005

SALES (est): 853.18K **Privately Held**
SIC: 3089 Hardware, plastics

(G-7973)
JUBA INDUSTRIES INC
126 W Jefferson St (44047-1048)
PHONE..................440 655-9960
Bruce Vance, *Prin*
EMP: 6 **EST:** 2010
SALES (est): 96.62K **Privately Held**
SIC: 3999 Manufacturing industries, nec

(G-7974)
KEN FORGING INC
1049 Griggs Rd (44047-8772)
P.O. Box 277 (44047-0277)
PHONE..................440 993-8091
Richard Kovach, *Pr*
Ken Kovach, *
EMP: 115 **EST:** 1970
SQ FT: 150,000
SALES (est): 17.45MM **Privately Held**
Web: www.kenforging.com
SIC: 3462 3544 Iron and steel forgings; Special dies and tools

(G-7975)
KING LUMINAIRE COMPANY INC (HQ)
Also Called: Stresscrete
1153 State Route 46 N (44047-8748)
P.O. Box 266 (44047-0266)
PHONE..................440 576-9073
Greg Button, *Pr*
▲ **EMP:** 45 **EST:** 1984
SQ FT: 18,000
SALES (est): 2.35MM
SALES (corp-wide): 27.42MM **Privately Held**
Web: www.scgrp.com
SIC: 3646 Ornamental lighting fixtures, commercial
PA: Stress-Crete Holdings Inc
840 Walker's Line
Burlington ON L7N 2
905 632-9301

(G-7976)
LAKE CITY PLATING LLC
108 S Sycamore St (44047-1433)
PHONE..................440 964-3555
EMP: 51
SALES (corp-wide): 22.53MM **Privately Held**
Web: www.lakecityplating.com
SIC: 3471 Electroplating of metals or formed products
PA: Lake City Plating, Llc
1701 Lake Ave
Ashtabula OH 44004
440 964-3555

(G-7977)
LAKE ERIE SHIP REPR FBRCTION L
1459 State Route 46 S (44047-9505)
PHONE..................440 228-7110
Joseph Craine, *Managing Member*
EMP: 16 **EST:** 2012
SQ FT: 4,000
SALES (est): 1.31MM **Privately Held**
SIC: 3731 3441 Shipbuilding and repairing; Fabricated structural metal

(G-7978)
METAL SALES MANUFACTURING CORP
352 E Erie St (44047-1406)
PHONE..................440 319-3779
Bill Mako, *Mgr*
EMP: 21

SQ FT: 33,000
SALES (corp-wide): 443.57MM **Privately Held**
Web: metalsales.us.com
SIC: 3444 3449 3441 2952 Siding, sheet metal; Miscellaneous metalwork; Fabricated structural metal; Asphalt felts and coatings
HQ: Metal Sales Manufacturing Corporation
545 S 3rd St Ste 200
Louisville KY 40202
502 855-4300

(G-7979)
NEXT SURFACE INC
223 S Spruce St (44047-8321)
PHONE..................440 576-0194
Rhine Blake, *CEO*
EMP: 52 **EST:** 2007
SALES (est): 7.59MM **Privately Held**
Web: www.ndci.biz
SIC: 3272 Concrete window and door components, sills and frames

(G-7980)
PICKENS PLASTICS INC
149 S Cucumber St (44047-1438)
PHONE..................440 576-4001
EMP: 9
SALES (est): 957.07K **Privately Held**
SIC: 3089 Injection molding of plastics

(G-7981)
PRESRITE CORPORATION
322 S Cucumber St (44047-1423)
P.O. Box 550 (44047-0550)
PHONE..................440 576-0015
Roy Stainfield, *Genl Mgr*
EMP: 59
SALES (corp-wide): 47.58MM **Privately Held**
Web: www.presrite.com
SIC: 3462 Iron and steel forgings
PA: Presrite Corporation
3665 E 78th St
Cleveland OH 44105
216 441-5990

(G-7982)
RMC USA INCORPORATION
149 S Cucumber St (44047-1438)
P.O. Box 127 (44047-0127)
PHONE..................440 992-4906
EMP: 90
SIC: 3089 Molding primary plastics

(G-7983)
STRESS-CRETE COMPANY
Also Called: King Luminaire
1153 State Route 46 N (44047-8748)
P.O. Box 266 (44047-0266)
PHONE..................440 576-9073
Jim Fultz, *Brnch Mgr*
EMP: 46
SALES (corp-wide): 27.42MM **Privately Held**
Web: www.scgrp.com
SIC: 3646 Commercial lighting fixtures
HQ: Stress-Crete Limited
7-840 Walker's Line
Burlington ON L7N 2
905 827-6901

(G-7984)
THE GAZETTE PRINTING CO INC (PA)
Also Called: Tribune , The
46 W Jefferson St (44047-1028)
P.O. Box 166 (44047-0166)
PHONE..................440 576-9125
Jeffrey Lampson, *Pr*

John E Lampson, *
Marilyn Lampson, *
EMP: 62 **EST:** 1876
SQ FT: 8,600
SALES (est): 5.63MM
SALES (corp-wide): 5.63MM **Privately Held**
Web: www.visitashtabulacounty.com
SIC: 2711 Newspapers, publishing and printing

(G-7985)
TMD WEK NORTH LLC
Also Called: Wek Industries
1085 Jefferson Eagleville Rd (44047-1267)
P.O. Box 167 (44047-0167)
PHONE..................440 576-6940
William Hylan, *CFO*
Kimberly Schaefer, *
EMP: 116 **EST:** 2014
SQ FT: 112,500
SALES (est): 3.56MM
SALES (corp-wide): 7.28B **Privately Held**
Web: www.tmdinc.com
SIC: 3089 Blow molded finished plastics products, nec
HQ: Toledo Molding & Die, Llc
1429 Coining Dr
Toledo OH 43612

(G-7986)
TOD THIN BRUSHES INC
1152 State Route 46 N (44047-8748)
PHONE..................440 576-6859
Michael R Oliver, *Pr*
Mildred Oliver, *Pr*
EMP: 10 **EST:** 1960
SQ FT: 2,500
SALES (est): 481.64K **Privately Held**
Web: www.todthinbrushesinc.com
SIC: 3991 Brushes, household or industrial

(G-7987)
WORTHINGTON CYLINDER CORP
863 State Route 307 E (44047-9668)
PHONE..................440 576-5847
Dan Brubaker, *Brnch Mgr*
EMP: 240
SALES (corp-wide): 1.25B **Publicly Held**
Web: www.worthingtonenterprises.com
SIC: 3316 Cold finishing of steel shapes
HQ: Worthington Cylinder Corporation
200 W Old Wilson Bridge Rd
Worthington OH 43085
614 840-3210

Jeffersonville
Fayette County

(G-7988)
TFO TECH CO LTD
Also Called: T F O
221 State St (43128-1090)
PHONE..................740 426-6381
Katsumasa Toya, *Ch*
Yoshio Saisharo, *
Kanji Endo, *
Curtis A Loveland, *
▲ **EMP:** 140 **EST:** 1988
SQ FT: 70,000
SALES (est): 29.62MM **Privately Held**
SIC: 3462 3465 3714 Automotive forgings, ferrous: crankshaft, engine, axle, etc.; Automotive stampings; Motor vehicle parts and accessories
PA: Tfo Corporation
2-16-4, Akabane
Kita-Ku TKY 115-0

Jewett
Harrison County

(G-7989)
MARKWEST ENERGY PARTNERS LP
Also Called: Hopedale Fractionation Fcilty
46700 Giacobbi Rd (43986-9553)
PHONE..................................800 730-8388
EMP: 8
Web: www.markwest.com
SIC: 1321 Fractionating natural gas liquids
HQ: Markwest Energy Partners, L.P.
1515 Arphoe St Twr 1 Ste
Denver CO 80202
303 925-9200

Johnstown
Licking County

(G-7990)
ALLIANCE CARPET CUSHION CO
143 Commerce Blvd (43031-9610)
PHONE..................................740 966-5001
Keith Anders, *Mgr*
EMP: 30
SIC: 2282 2273 Carpet yarn: twisting,
winding, or spooling; Carpets and rugs
HQ: Alliance Carpet Cushion Co
180 Church St
Torrington CT 06790
860 489-4273

(G-7991)
APEKS LLC ✪
Also Called: Apeks Supercritical
31 Greenscape Ct (43031-8007)
PHONE..................................740 809-1174
Andy Joseph, *Pr*
EMP: 20 **EST:** 2023
SQ FT: 10,000
SALES (est): 2.46MM
SALES (corp-wide): 1.31B **Publicly Held**
Web: www.apekssupercritical.com
SIC: 3542 Mechanical (pneumatic or
hydraulic) metal forming machines
PA: Gibraltar Industries, Inc.
3556 Lake Shore Rd
Buffalo NY 14219
716 826-6500

(G-7992)
BIGMAR INC
9711 Sportsman Club Rd (43031-9141)
PHONE..................................740 966-5800
John Tramontana, *Ch*
John Tramontata, *
Cynthia R May, *
Bernard Kramer, *
Philippe J H Rohrer, *
EMP: 50 **EST:** 1995
SQ FT: 8,600
SALES (est): 1MM **Privately Held**
SIC: 2834 8111 Pharmaceutical preparations
; Legal services

(G-7993)
BUCKEYE READY-MIX LLC
7720 Johnstown Alexandria Rd
(43031-9340)
PHONE..................................740 967-4801
EMP: 23
SALES (corp-wide): 21.97MM **Privately
Held**
Web: www.buckeyereadymix.com
SIC: 3273 Ready-mixed concrete
PA: Buckeye Ready-Mix, Llc
7657 Taylor Rd Sw
Reynoldsburg OH 43068

614 575-2132

(G-7994)
BUD CORP
158 Commerce Blvd (43031-9011)
PHONE..................................740 967-9992
Kelton Brown, *Prin*
EMP: 8 **EST:** 2006
SALES (est): 265.61K **Privately Held**
Web: www.budcorp.com
SIC: 1542 3444 5084 Nonresidential
construction, nec; Sheet metalwork;
Materials handling machinery

(G-7995)
CHAM COR INDUSTRIES INC
117 W Coshocton St (43031-1108)
PHONE..................................740 967-9015
Gary H Chambers Junior, *Pr*
Michael Chambers, *CEO*
Michael Bailey, *VP*
EMP: 8 **EST:** 1964
SQ FT: 6,000
SALES (est): 141.52K **Privately Held**
SIC: 2754 Job printing: gravure

(G-7996)
MUNSON MACHINE COMPANY INC
80 E College Ave (43031-1204)
P.O. Box 304 (43031-0304)
PHONE..................................740 967-6867
Leroy Thacker, *Sec*
Todd Thacker, *Pr*
EMP: 7 **EST:** 1987
SQ FT: 4,500
SALES (est): 1.29MM **Privately Held**
SIC: 3599 Machine shop, jobbing and repair

(G-7997)
PUMPCO CONCRETE PUMPING LLC
7230 Johnstown Utica Rd (43031-9406)
PHONE..................................740 809-1473
Richard Miller, *Managing Member*
EMP: 12 **EST:** 2018
SALES (est): 1.88MM **Privately Held**
Web: www.keimconcretepumping.com
SIC: 3462 Construction or mining equipment
forgings, ferrous

(G-7998)
STEEL CEILINGS INC
451 E Coshocton St (43031-9010)
PHONE..................................740 967-1063
▲ **EMP:** 24
SIC: 3324 Steel investment foundries

(G-7999)
**TECHNICAL RUBBER COMPANY
INC (PA)**
Also Called: Tech International
200 E Coshocton St (43031-1083)
P.O. Box 486 (43031-0486)
PHONE..................................740 967-9015
Dan Layne, *Pr*
Robert Overs, *
Jeff Sellers, *
Gary Armstrong, *
Nikki Layne, *
◆ **EMP:** 197 **EST:** 1939
SQ FT: 10,000
SALES (est): 29.67MM
SALES (corp-wide): 29.67MM **Privately
Held**
Web: www.trc4r.com
SIC: 3011 5014 2891 Tire sundries or tire
repair materials, rubber; Tire and tube
repair materials; Sealing compounds,
synthetic rubber or plastic

(G-8000)
TRI-TECH LABORATORIES INC
Also Called: K D C
8825 Smiths Mill Rd N (43031)
PHONE..................................740 927-2817
Pierre Prudhomme, *Pr*
EMP: 49 **EST:** 1991
SALES (est): 11.67MM **Privately Held**
SIC: 2834 Pharmaceutical preparations

(G-8001)
TRUFLEX RUBBER PRODUCTS CO
Also Called: Pang Rubber Company
200 E Coshocton St (43031-1096)
PHONE..................................740 967-9015
Pauline Chambers Yost, *Pr*
Mike Chambers, *
Cheryl Poulton, *
Robert Overs, *
EMP: 225 **EST:** 1964
SQ FT: 75,000
SALES (est): 708.48K **Privately Held**
Web: www.pangindustrial.com
SIC: 3011 3069 Tire and inner tube materials
and related products; Air-supported rubber
structures

Junction City
Perry County

(G-8002)
K-MAR STRUCTURES LLC
Also Called: Mast Mini Barn
1825 Flagdale Rd S (43748-9792)
PHONE..................................231 924-5777
Marvin Mast, *Managing Member*
EMP: 10 **EST:** 2005
SQ FT: 17,000
SALES (est): 470.32K **Privately Held**
Web: www.minibarnsonline.com
SIC: 3272 5999 Solid containing units,
concrete; Sales barn

Kalida
Putnam County

(G-8003)
B-K TOOL & DESIGN INC
480 W Main St (45853-2024)
P.O. Box 416 (45853-0416)
PHONE..................................419 532-3890
Bob Kahle, *Pr*
Kevin M Kahle, *
EMP: 80 **EST:** 1987
SQ FT: 12,000
SALES (est): 13.44MM **Privately Held**
Web: www.bktool.com
SIC: 3544 Special dies and tools

(G-8004)
KALIDA MANUFACTURING INC
801 Ottawa St (45853)
P.O. Box P.O. Box 390 (45853-0390)
PHONE..................................419 532-2026
Bruce R Henke, *Pr*
Tim Inoue, *
Sho Akimoto, *
▲ **EMP:** 250 **EST:** 1996
SQ FT: 300,000
SALES (est): 42.85MM **Privately Held**
Web: www.kalidamfg.com
SIC: 3714 Motor vehicle parts and
accessories
HQ: Kth Parts Industries, Inc.
1111 N State Rte 235
Saint Paris OH 43072
937 663-5941

(G-8005)
**REMLINGER MANUFACTURING CO
INC**
16394 Us 224 (45853)
P.O. Box 299 (45853-0299)
PHONE..................................419 532-3647
Mildred C Remlinger, *Ch Bd*
John Remlinger, *
▲ **EMP:** 32 **EST:** 1977
SQ FT: 52,000
SALES (est): 5.98MM **Privately Held**
Web: www.remlingermfg.com
SIC: 3523 Harrows: disc, spring, tine, etc.

(G-8006)
SARKA BROS MACHINING INC
607 Ottawa St (45853)
P.O. Box 316 (45853-0316)
PHONE..................................419 532-2393
Bob Allen, *Pr*
Terry Burnett, *
EMP: 8 **EST:** 1990
SQ FT: 24,000
SALES (est): 1.91MM **Privately Held**
Web: www.sarkabros.com
SIC: 3556 Food products machinery

(G-8007)
UNVERFERTH MFG CO INC (PA)
Also Called: Unverferth
601 S Broad St (45853-2108)
P.O. Box P.O. Box 357 (45853-0357)
PHONE..................................419 532-3121
R Steven Unverferth, *Pr*
Richard A Unverferth, *
Gladys Unverferth, *
Dennis Kapcar, *
Daniel Fanger, *
◆ **EMP:** 249 **EST:** 1948
SQ FT: 828,501
SALES (est): 99.99MM
SALES (corp-wide): 99.99MM **Privately
Held**
Web: www.unverferth.com
SIC: 3523 Farm machinery and equipment

Kelleys Island
Erie County

(G-8008)
KELLEYS ISLAND WINERY INC
418 Woodford Rd (43438-6616)
PHONE..................................419 746-2678
Kirt Zettler, *Pr*
Roberta Zettler, *Sec*
EMP: 8 **EST:** 1981
SQ FT: 7,000
SALES (est): 357.46K **Privately Held**
Web: www.kelleysislandwineco.com
SIC: 2084 5921 Wines; Wine

(G-8009)
KELLSTONE INC
Also Called: Kellstone
Lake Shore Drive (43438)
P.O. Box 31 (43438-0031)
PHONE..................................419 746-2396
Ralph Kunar, *Mgr*
EMP: 40
SALES (corp-wide): 7.02MM **Privately
Held**
SIC: 3281 1422 Cut stone and stone
products; Crushed and broken limestone
HQ: Kellstone, Inc.
3203 Harvard Ave
Newburgh Heights OH 44105

Kensington
Columbiana County

(G-8010)
M3 MIDSTREAM LLC
Also Called: Kensington Plant
11543 State Route 644 (44427-9717)
PHONE..................................330 223-2220
EMP: 34
SALES (corp-wide): 23.57MM **Privately Held**
Web: www.momentummidstream.com
SIC: 1382 Oil and gas exploration services
PA: M3 Midstream Llc
600 Travis St Ste 5600
Houston TX 77002
713 783-3000

(G-8011)
WILLIAM S MILLER INC
11250 Montgomery Rd (44427-9702)
P.O. Box 145 (44423-0145)
PHONE..................................330 223-1794
George Miller, *Pr*
William Miller, *CEO*
Jane Todd, *Sec*
David W Miller, *VP*
EMP: 9 **EST:** 1985
SALES (est): 1.68MM **Privately Held**
SIC: 1311 Crude petroleum production

Kent
Portage County

(G-8012)
ACCU-GRIND INC
4430 Crystal Pkwy (44240-8006)
PHONE..................................330 677-2225
Robert Sly, *Pr*
EMP: 8 **EST:** 1992
SQ FT: 4,000
SALES (est): 242.28K **Privately Held**
Web: www.maag.com
SIC: 7699 3421 Knife, saw and tool sharpening and repair; Knives: butchers', hunting, pocket, etc.

(G-8013)
ACS INDUSTRIES INC
Also Called: American Coupler Systems
2151 Mogadore Rd (44240-7201)
P.O. Box 810 (44240-0017)
PHONE..................................330 678-2511
▲ **EMP:** 95 **EST:** 1968
SALES (est): 9.36MM **Privately Held**
Web: www.acs-coupler.com
SIC: 3531 Construction machinery attachments

(G-8014)
ACTION SUPER ABRASIVE PDTS INC
945 Greenbriar Pkwy (44240-6478)
PHONE..................................330 673-7333
Joseph Haag, *Pr*
Dan Noonan, *VP*
EMP: 20 **EST:** 1985
SQ FT: 27,000
SALES (est): 2.45MM **Privately Held**
Web: www.actionsuper.com
SIC: 3291 Wheels, grinding: artificial

(G-8015)
AILES MILLWORK INC
1520 Enterprise Way (44240-7547)
PHONE..................................330 678-4300
Patrick Ailes, *Pr*
Ryan Ailes, *VP*
Margaret Ailes, *Sec*
EMP: 11 **EST:** 1975
SQ FT: 13,000
SALES (est): 1.94MM **Privately Held**
Web: www.ailesmillwork.com
SIC: 2431 2434 Millwork; Wood kitchen cabinets

(G-8016)
ALLOY EXTRUSION COMPANY
4211 Karg Industrial Pkwy (44240-6470)
PHONE..................................330 677-4946
EMP: 20
Web: www.alloyextrusion.com
SIC: 3061 8742 Mechanical rubber goods; Industrial consultant

(G-8017)
AMETEK TCHNICAL INDUS PDTS INC (HQ)
Also Called: Ametek Electromechanical Group
100 E Erie St Ste 130 (44240-3587)
PHONE..................................330 673-3451
David A Zapico, *Ch Bd*
Matt French, *
Peter Smith, *
Todd Schlegel, *
Kathryn E Sena, *
EMP: 65 **EST:** 2009
SALES (est): 29.75MM
SALES (corp-wide): 6.94B **Publicly Held**
Web: www.ametektip.com
SIC: 3621 5063 3566 Motors, electric; Motors, electric; Speed changers, drives, and gears
PA: Ametek, Inc.
1100 Cassatt Rd
Berwyn PA 19312
610 647-2121

(G-8018)
BEEMER MACHINE COMPANY INC
1530 Enterprise Way (44240-7547)
PHONE..................................330 678-3822
Edward Burch, *Pr*
EMP: 8 **EST:** 1989
SALES (est): 739.23K **Privately Held**
Web: www.beemermachine.com
SIC: 3599 Machine shop, jobbing and repair

(G-8019)
BOYCE MACHINE INC
3609 Mogadore Rd (44240-7431)
PHONE..................................330 678-3210
Shelby C Boyce, *Pr*
Patricia Boyce, *Sec*
EMP: 9 **EST:** 1988
SQ FT: 5,400
SALES (est): 1.09MM **Privately Held**
Web: www.boycemachine.com
SIC: 3599 Machine shop, jobbing and repair

(G-8020)
BRIDGESTONE RET OPERATIONS LLC
Also Called: Firestone
202 E Main St (44240-2527)
PHONE..................................330 673-1700
Thomas Shaw, *Mgr*
EMP: 7
Web: www.bridgestoneamericas.com
SIC: 5531 7534 Automotive tires; Rebuilding and retreading tires
HQ: Bridgestone Retail Operations, Llc
200 4th Ave S Ste 100
Nashville TN 37201
615 937-1000

(G-8021)
COLONIAL MACHINE COMPANY INC
1041 Mogadore Rd (44240-7534)

P.O. Box 650 (44240-0012)
PHONE..................................330 673-5859
James Rankin, *Pr*
Roy Metcalf, *
EMP: 71 **EST:** 1945
SQ FT: 35,000
SALES (est): 9.06MM **Privately Held**
Web: www.colonial-machine.com
SIC: 3544 Special dies and tools

(G-8022)
COLONIAL PATTERNS INC
920 Overholt Rd (44240-7550)
PHONE..................................330 673-6475
Martin A Meluch, *Pr*
Valent Meluch, *
▲ **EMP:** 6 **EST:** 1952
SQ FT: 4,800
SALES (est): 991.67K **Privately Held**
Web: www.colonialpatt.com
SIC: 3543 3544 Industrial patterns; Special dies, tools, jigs, and fixtures

(G-8023)
COPEN MACHINE INC
501 Dodge St (44240-3709)
PHONE..................................330 678-4598
Terry D Copen, *Pr*
EMP: 13 **EST:** 1978
SQ FT: 13,000
SALES (est): 611.5K **Privately Held**
Web: www.copenmachine.com
SIC: 3599 Machine shop, jobbing and repair

(G-8024)
D & J PRINTING INC
Also Called: Hess Print Solutions
3765 Sunnybrook Rd (44240-7443)
PHONE..................................330 678-5868
Douglas Mann, *Brnch Mgr*
EMP: 242
SALES (corp-wide): 611.15MM **Privately Held**
Web: www.sheridan.com
SIC: 2752 Offset printing
HQ: D. & J. Printing, Inc.
3323 Oak St
Brainerd MN 56401
218 829-2877

(G-8025)
DAVEY KENT INC
Also Called: Davey Drill
200 W Williams St (44240-3797)
P.O. Box 1497 (44501-1497)
PHONE..................................330 673-5400
Tom Myers, *Pr*
J Thomas Myers Ii, *CEO*
David Myers, *VP*
J Gnandt, *Sec*
Chris Cooler, *Prin*
▲ **EMP:** 20 **EST:** 1981
SQ FT: 50,000
SALES (est): 1.95MM **Privately Held**
Web: newsite.daveykent.com
SIC: 3532 Drills and drilling equipment, mining (except oil and gas)

(G-8026)
DON WARTKO CONSTRUCTION INC
Also Called: Design Concrete Surfaces
975 Tallmadge Rd (44240-6474)
PHONE..................................330 673-5252
Thomas Wartko, *Pr*
David Wartko, *
Mike Wartko, *
Doris Wartko, *
Ron Wartko, *
EMP: 60 **EST:** 1967
SQ FT: 15,000
SALES (est): 12.73MM **Privately Held**

Web: www.donwartkoconstruction.com
SIC: 1623 1794 3732 Oil and gas line and compressor station construction; Excavation work; Boatbuilding and repairing

(G-8027)
DSI MANAGEMENT HOLDINGS LLC
1597 S Water St (44240-4441)
PHONE..................................800 645-7002
John Large, *Pr*
David Kern, *Prin*
EMP: 19 **EST:** 1998
SQ FT: 2,400
SALES (est): 1.02MM **Privately Held**
Web: www.dsistream.com
SIC: 4813 1731 3661 Internet connectivity services; Fiber optic cable installation; Fiber optics communications equipment

(G-8028)
EAST END WELDING LLC
Also Called: East End Welding
357 Tallmadge Rd (44240-7201)
PHONE..................................330 677-6000
Tim Rosengarten, *CEO*
▲ **EMP:** 120 **EST:** 1967
SQ FT: 146,500
SALES (est): 2.07MM
SALES (corp-wide): 376.52MM **Privately Held**
Web: www.eastendwelding.com
SIC: 7692 3599 Welding repair; Custom machinery
PA: Connell Limited Partnership
1 Intrnational Pl 31th Fl
Boston MA 02110
617 737-2700

(G-8029)
ELBEX CORPORATION
Also Called: Elbex
300 Martinel Dr (44240-4369)
PHONE..................................330 673-3233
Edward L Bittle, *Pr*
EMP: 90 **EST:** 1991
SALES (est): 11.33MM **Privately Held**
Web: www.elbex-us.com
SIC: 3069 Medical and laboratory rubber sundries and related products

(G-8030)
EMBROIDERY NETWORK INC
Also Called: Do Duds
4693 Kent Rd (44240-5206)
PHONE..................................330 678-4887
Jennifer Cox, *Pr*
Susan W Ritchie, *VP*
Arch Ritchie, *VP*
EMP: 7 **EST:** 1990
SQ FT: 3,000
SALES (est): 110.32K **Privately Held**
Web: www.embroiderymart.com
SIC: 2395 Embroidery products, except Schiffli machine

(G-8031)
EMERGENCY PRODUCTS & RES INC
Also Called: Epr
890 W Main St (44240-2284)
PHONE..................................330 673-5003
Jerold Ramsey, *Pr*
Jim Doherty, *VP*
▲ **EMP:** 6 **EST:** 1992
SQ FT: 350,000
SALES (est): 959.36K **Privately Held**
Web: www.epandr.com
SIC: 2448 Pallets, wood

GEOGRAPHIC

(G-8032)

ENTERPRISE PLASTICS INC
838 Overholt Rd (44240-7530)
PHONE..........................330 346-0496
Martin Mulch, *Pr*
Valente Muluch, *Sec*
▲ **EMP:** 20 **EST:** 2003
SALES (est): 4.2MM **Privately Held**
Web: www.enterpriseplastics.net
SIC: 3089 Injection molding of plastics

(G-8033)

FURUKAWA ROCK DRILL USA INC
(HQ)
Also Called: Furukawa Rock Drill
805 Lake St (44240-2740)
PHONE..........................330 673-5826
Jeff Crane, *CEO*
Shoji Iguchi, *Dir*
◆ **EMP:** 15 **EST:** 1924
SQ FT: 240,000
SALES (est): 7.28MM **Privately Held**
Web: www.frdusa.com
SIC: 3533 3599 3546 Drilling tools for gas,
oil, or water wells; Machine shop, jobbing
and repair; Power-driven handtools
PA: Furukawa Co., Ltd.
2-6-4, Otemachi
Chiyoda-Ku TKY 100-0

(G-8034)

FURUKAWA ROCK DRILL USA CO
LTD (PA)
Also Called: Frd
711 Lake St (44240-2738)
PHONE..........................330 673-5826
Michael Sato, *Pr*
◆ **EMP:** 15 **EST:** 1956
SQ FT: 27,181
SALES (est): 2.4MM
SALES (corp-wide): 2.4MM **Privately Held**
Web: www.frdusa.com
SIC: 3545 3594 3546 3423 Tools and
accessories for machine tools; Fluid power
pumps and motors; Power-driven handtools
; Hand and edge tools, nec

(G-8035)

HAPCO INC
Also Called: Tarpco
390 Portage Blvd (44240-7283)
PHONE..........................330 678-9353
Charles George, *CEO*
Chuck George, *CEO*
Bernard Carpenter, *Pr*
John A Daily, *Prin*
◆ **EMP:** 11 **EST:** 1979
SQ FT: 23,000
SALES (est): 5.64MM **Privately Held**
Web: www.hapcoinc.com
SIC: 3545 5049 Diamond cutting tools for
turning, boring, burnishing, etc.; Precision
tools

(G-8036)

HUGO SAND COMPANY
7055 State Route 43 (44240-6198)
PHONE..........................216 570-1212
Dorothy Strohm, *Pr*
Sythnia Terhune, *VP*
Scott R Terhune, *VP*
EMP: 7 **EST:** 1928
SQ FT: 400
SALES (est): 448.38K **Privately Held**
SIC: 1442 Construction sand mining

(G-8037)

J B MANUFACTURING INC
4465 Crystal Pkwy (44240-8005)
PHONE..........................330 676-9744

John L Anderson, *Pr*
EMP: 8 **EST:** 1976
SQ FT: 36,000
SALES (est): 620.48K **Privately Held**
SIC: 3599 Machine shop, jobbing and repair

(G-8038)

JOS-TECH INC
852 W Main St (44240-2216)
P.O. Box 952 (44240-0019)
PHONE..........................330 678-3260
Bradford Joslyn, *Pr*
Caroline Mueller, *
David Fox, *
EMP: 25 **EST:** 1996
SALES (est): 1.97MM **Privately Held**
Web: www.jos-tech.com
SIC: 3089 Injection molding of plastics

(G-8039)

KENT ADHESIVE PRODUCTS CO
Also Called: Kapco
1000 Cherry St (44240-7501)
P.O. Box 626 (44240-0011)
PHONE..........................330 678-1626
Edward Small, *Pr*
Philip M Zavracky, *
Jenifer Codrea, *
◆ **EMP:** 80 **EST:** 1974
SQ FT: 100,000
SALES (est): 23.36MM **Privately Held**
Web: www.kapco.com
SIC: 2679 2672 2675 7389 Paper products,
converted, nec; Adhesive papers, labels, or
tapes: from purchased material; Die-cut
paper and board; Laminating service

(G-8040)

KENT DISPLAYS INC (PA)
Also Called: Improv Electronics
343 Portage Blvd (44240-9200)
PHONE..........................330 673-8784
Joel Domino, *Pr*
▲ **EMP:** 70 **EST:** 1996
SQ FT: 42,000
SALES (est): 20.18MM **Privately Held**
Web: www.kentdisplays.com
SIC: 3679 Liquid crystal displays (LCD)

(G-8041)

KENT ELASTOMER PRODUCTS INC
(HQ)
1500 Saint Clair Ave (44240-4364)
P.O. Box 668 (44240-0012)
PHONE..........................330 673-1011
Bob Oborn, *Pr*
▲ **EMP:** 101 **EST:** 1986
SQ FT: 42,000
SALES (est): 24.67MM
SALES (corp-wide): 331.16MM **Privately**
Held
Web: www.kentelastomer.com
SIC: 3069 Medical and laboratory rubber
sundries and related products
PA: Meridian Industries, Inc.
735 N Water St Ste 630
Milwaukee WI 53202
414 224-0610

(G-8042)

KENT INFORMATION SERVICES INC
6185 2nd Ave (44240-2991)
PHONE..........................330 672-2110
John H Graves, *Pr*
John Graves, *Pr*
EMP: 6 **EST:** 1994
SALES (est): 161.91K **Privately Held**
Web: www.kent.edu
SIC: 2721 8721 Periodicals; Accounting,
auditing, and bookkeeping

(G-8043)

KENT MOLD AND MANUFACTURING
CO
1190 W Main St (44240-1942)
PHONE..........................330 673-3469
Paul Ferder, *Pr*
Henry Trivelli, *
EMP: 11 **EST:** 1944
SQ FT: 35,000
SALES (est): 2.05MM **Privately Held**
Web: www.kentmold.com
SIC: 3544 Special dies and tools

(G-8044)

KENT POST ACQUISITION INC
449 Dodge St (44240-3707)
PHONE..........................330 678-6343
Michael Pollard, *Pr*
Dennis Lyell, *Pr*
Gary Lyell, *VP*
EMP: 15 **EST:** 1983
SQ FT: 12,000
SALES (est): 2.32MM **Privately Held**
Web: www.kentautomation.com
SIC: 3599 Machine shop, jobbing and repair

(G-8045)

LAND OLAKES INC
Also Called: Land O'Lakes
2001 Mogadore Rd (44240-7296)
PHONE..........................330 678-1578
Steve Sehafer, *Mgr*
EMP: 165
SALES (corp-wide): 2.89B **Privately Held**
Web: www.landolakesinc.com
SIC: 2022 Cheese; natural and processed
PA: Land O'lakes, Inc.
4001 Lexington Ave N
Arden Hills MN 55112
651 375-2222

(G-8046)

LINNEAS CANDY SUPPLIES INC (PA)
Also Called: Linnea's
4149 Karg Industrial Pkwy (44240-6425)
PHONE..........................330 678-7112
EMP: 20 **EST:** 1968
SALES (est): 19.05MM
SALES (corp-wide): 19.05MM **Privately**
Held
Web: www.linneasinc.com
SIC: 5145 5441 2672 3089 Confectionery;
Candy; Adhesive papers, labels, or tapes:
from purchased material; Injection molding
of plastics

(G-8047)

MAAG AUTOMATIK INC
Also Called: Maag Reduction Engineering
235 Progress Blvd (44240-8055)
PHONE..........................330 677-2225
EMP: 35
SALES (corp-wide): 7.75B **Publicly Held**
Web: www.maag.com
SIC: 3532 5084 Crushing, pulverizing, and
screening equipment; Pulverizing
machinery and equipment
HQ: Maag Reduction, Inc.
3700 Arco Corporate Dr
Charlotte NC 28273

(G-8048)

MAAG REDUCTION INC
235 Progress Blvd (44240-8055)
PHONE..........................704 716-9000
EMP: 27
SALES (corp-wide): 7.75B **Publicly Held**
Web: www.maag.com
SIC: 3561 Pumps and pumping equipment
HQ: Maag Reduction, Inc.
3700 Arco Corporate Dr

Charlotte NC 28273

(G-8049)

MARK GRZIANIS ST TREATS EX INC
(PA)
Also Called: Yaya's
1294 Windward Ln (44240-1895)
PHONE..........................330 414-6266
Mark Graziani, *Pr*
Wendy Graziani, *VP*
EMP: 12 **EST:** 2002
SALES (est): 1.23MM
SALES (corp-wide): 1.23MM **Privately**
Held
Web: www.streettreatsgrill.com
SIC: 5812 2035 7389 Cafeteria; Dressings,
salad: raw and cooked (except dry mixes);
Business services, nec

(G-8050)

MASTERS PRCISION MACHINING
INC
4465 Crystal Pkwy (44240-8005)
PHONE..........................330 419-1933
Kenneth Rice, *Pr*
Charlotte Rice, *CFO*
EMP: 10 **EST:** 2014
SALES (est): 3.43MM **Privately Held**
Web: www.mpmachininginc.com
SIC: 3541 Numerically controlled metal
cutting machine tools

(G-8051)

MERIDIAN INDUSTRIES INC
Also Called: Kent Elastomer Products
1500 Saint Clair Ave (44240-4364)
P.O. Box 668 (44240-0012)
PHONE..........................330 673-1011
Vann Epp Murray, *Pr*
EMP: 71
SALES (corp-wide): 331.16MM **Privately**
Held
Web: www.meridiancompanies.com
SIC: 3069 3842 3083 3082 Tubing, rubber;
Surgical appliances and supplies;
Laminated plastics plate and sheet;
Unsupported plastics profile shapes
PA: Meridian Industries, Inc.
735 N Water St Ste 630
Milwaukee WI 53202
414 224-0610

(G-8052)

METAL-MAX INC
1540 Enterprise Way (44240-7547)
PHONE..........................330 673-9926
Richard La Mancusa, *Pr*
EMP: 8 **EST:** 1999
SQ FT: 5,000
SALES (est): 991.31K **Privately Held**
SIC: 3444 Sheet metal specialties, not
stamped

(G-8053)

MICHAEL KAUFMAN COMPANIES
INC
Also Called: Educational Equipment
845 Overholt Rd (44240-7529)
P.O. Box 154 (44240-0003)
PHONE..........................330 673-4881
Michael Kaufman, *Pr*
John T Waller, *Prin*
◆ **EMP:** 12 **EST:** 1934
SQ FT: 60,000
SALES (est): 2.31MM **Privately Held**
SIC: 3281 2599 2493 2541 Blackboards,
slate; Boards: planning, display, notice;
Bulletin boards, cork; Store and office
display cases and fixtures

(G-8054)
MILLER BEARING COMPANY INC
420 Portage Blvd (44240-7285)
PHONE.............................330 678-8844
Donald A Miller, *Pr*
Julie Miller, *
EMP: 28 **EST:** 1978
SQ FT: 75,000
SALES (est): 3.6MM **Privately Held**
Web: www.millerbearing.com
SIC: 3562 Ball bearings and parts

(G-8055)
MOLD SURFACE TEXTURES INC
Also Called: MST
4485 Crystal Pkwy Ste 300 (44240-8016)
PHONE.............................330 678-8590
Joe Gendron, *Pr*
Aaron Pendergast, *Sec*
Kevin Gasaway, *Treas*
EMP: 6 **EST:** 2004
SALES (est): 502.13K **Privately Held**
Web: www.mstextures.com
SIC: 3544 Industrial molds

(G-8056)
NEWELL BRANDS INC
Also Called: Rubbermaid
212 Progress Blvd (44240-8015)
PHONE.............................330 733-1184
Amy Smith, *Brnch Mgr*
EMP: 12
SALES (corp-wide): 7.58B **Publicly Held**
Web: www.newellbrands.com
SIC: 3069 Medical and laboratory rubber
sundries and related products
PA: Newell Brands Inc.
6655 Pachtree Dunwoody Rd
Atlanta GA 30328
770 418-7000

(G-8057)
ON US LLC
315 Gougler Ave (44240-2405)
PHONE.............................330 286-3436
Ryan Cene, *Pr*
Ryan Cenc, *Managing Member*
EMP: 20 **EST:** 2017
SALES (est): 4.09MM **Privately Held**
Web: www.onus.co
SIC: 2086 Water, natural: packaged in cans,
bottles, etc.

(G-0050)
PODNAR PLASTICS INC (PA)
1510 Mogadore Rd (44240-7599)
EMP: 21 **EST:** 1977
SQ FT: 38,000
SALES (est): 2.4MM
SALES (corp-wide): 2.4MM **Privately Held**
Web: www.rez-tech-jars.com
SIC: 3089 Injection molding of plastics

(G-8059)
PODNAR PLASTICS INC
343 Portage Blvd Unit 3 (44240-9200)
PHONE.............................330 673-2255
Scott Podnar, *Pr*
EMP: 6
SALES (corp-wide): 2.4MM **Privately Held**
Web: www.rez-tech-jars.com
SIC: 3089 Molding primary plastics
PA: Podnar Plastics, Inc.
1510 Mogadore Rd
Kent OH 44240

(G-8060)
POLYMERICS INC
1540 Saint Clair Ave (44240-4364)
PHONE.............................330 677-1131

Tony Bisesi, *Contrlr*
EMP: 20
SQ FT: 26,458
SALES (corp-wide): 1.27MM **Privately Held**
Web: www.polymericsinc.com
SIC: 2899 2821 Chemical preparations, nec;
Plastics materials and resins
PA: Polymerics, Inc.
2828 2nd St
Cuyahoga Falls OH 44221
330 928-2210

(G-8061)
POST PRODUCTS INC
1600 Franklin Ave (44240-4308)
P.O. Box 777 (44240-0015)
PHONE.............................330 678-0048
Jay Mcelravy, *Pr*
Nancy Mcelravy, *Sec*
EMP: 7 **EST:** 1971
SQ FT: 6,000
SALES (est): 661.11K **Privately Held**
Web: www.postproductsinc.com
SIC: 3599 Machine shop, jobbing and repair

(G-8062)
PRESS OF OHIO INC
Also Called: Hess Print Solutions
3765 Sunnybrook Rd (44240-7443)
PHONE.............................330 678-5868
Doug Mann, *Pr*
EMP: 19 **EST:** 2013
SALES (est): 2.38MM **Privately Held**
Web: www.pressofohio.com
SIC: 2759 Commercial printing, nec

(G-8063)
PRIMAL SCREEN INC
Also Called: Alpha Strike
1021 Mason Ave (44240-2718)
PHONE.............................330 677-1766
Terry Tasker, *Pr*
Tom Diroll, *Sec*
EMP: 6 **EST:** 1995
SQ FT: 10,000
SALES (est): 567.79K **Privately Held**
Web: www.primalscreenprinting.com
SIC: 2759 Screen printing

(G-8064)
PROTO MACHINE & MFG INC
2190 State Route 59 (44240-7142)
PHONE.............................330 677-1700
Edward L Dias, *Pr*
Shelly Morgan, *Admn*
EMP: 15 **EST:** 1984
SQ FT: 10,000
SALES (est): 2.78MM **Privately Held**
Web: www.theprotoway.com
SIC: 3599 Machine shop, jobbing and repair

(G-8065)
PYRAMID MOLD & MACHINE CO INC
Also Called: Pyramid Mold & Machine
Company
222 Martinel Dr (44240-4321)
P.O. Box 634 (44240-0011)
PHONE.............................330 673-5200
Joan Siciliano, *Pr*
EMP: 9 **EST:** 1984
SQ FT: 10,000
SALES (est): 992.59K **Privately Held**
Web: www.pyramidmold-machine.com
SIC: 3544 Special dies and tools

(G-8066)
QUICK SERVICE WELDING & MCH CO
117 E Summit St (44240-3556)
PHONE.............................330 673-3818

Frank S Bowen, *Pr*
James M Bowen, *VP*
Wilma Bowen, *Sec*
EMP: 11 **EST:** 1919
SQ FT: 11,200
SALES (est): 1.21MM **Privately Held**
SIC: 7692 3599 Welding repair; Machine
shop, jobbing and repair

(G-8067)
REDUCTION ENGINEERING INC
Also Called: Accu Grind
235 Progress Blvd (44240-8055)
PHONE.............................330 677-2225
◆ **EMP:** 45
Web: www.maag.com
SIC: 5084 3532 Industrial machinery and
equipment; Crushing, pulverizing, and
screening equipment

(G-8068)
REZ-TECH CORPORATION
1510 Mogadore Rd (44240-7531)
PHONE.............................330 673-4009
Jack Podnar, *CEO*
Scott Podnar, *
Craig Podnar, *
Jeanette M Podnar, *
◆ **EMP:** 47 **EST:** 1981
SQ FT: 38,000
SALES (est): 6.64MM **Privately Held**
Web: www.rez-tech-jars.com
SIC: 3089 Injection molding of plastics

(G-8069)
ROBERT LONG MANUFACTURING CO
4192 Karg Industrial Pkwy (44240-6400)
PHONE.............................330 678-0911
Robert Long, *Pr*
EMP: 8 **EST:** 1982
SQ FT: 7,200
SALES (est): 493.3K **Privately Held**
SIC: 3599 Machine shop, jobbing and repair

(G-8070)
RON-AL MOLD & MACHINE INC
1057 Mason Ave (44240-2718)
P.O. Box 364 (44240-0007)
PHONE.............................330 673-7919
Ronald Siciliano, *Pr*
Alan Siciliano, *VP*
Rosalee Hodge, *Off Mgr*
EMP: 12 **EST:** 1980
SQ FT: 2,500
SALES (est): 2.89MM **Privately Held**
Web: www.ronalmold.com
SIC: 3544 Industrial molds

(G-8071)
ROTOLINE USA LLC
4429 Crystal Pkwy Ste B (44240-8001)
PHONE.............................330 677-3223
Alain Stpierre, *Genl Mgr*
EMP: 6 **EST:** 2013
SALES (est): 4.33MM **Privately Held**
Web: www.rotoline.com
SIC: 3524 Rototillers (garden machinery)

(G-8072)
SAGE INTEGRATION HOLDINGS LLC (PA)
4075 Karg Industrial Pkwy Ste B
(44240-6485)
P.O. Box 214 (44278-0214)
PHONE.............................330 733-8183
Eric Frasier, *CEO*
Rod Bragg, *Prin*
EMP: 36 **EST:** 2001
SALES (est): 5.43MM

SALES (corp-wide): 5.43MM **Privately
Held**
Web: www.sageintegration.com
SIC: 5065 3699 7382 Security control
equipment and systems; Security devices;
Security systems services

(G-8073)
SCHNELLER LLC (HQ)
Also Called: Polyplastex International
6019 Powdermill Rd (44240-7109)
PHONE.............................330 673-1400
Richard Organ, *Managing Member*
John Schirra, *Managing Member**
Jeffrey Frye, *Managing Member**
◆ **EMP:** 112 **EST:** 2007
SQ FT: 125,000
SALES (est): 67.4MM
SALES (corp-wide): 7.94B **Publicly Held**
Web: www.schneller.com
SIC: 2295 Resin or plastic coated fabrics
PA: Transdigm Group Incorporated
1350 Euclid Ave Ste 1600
Cleveland OH 44115
216 706-2960

(G-8074)
SCOTT MOLDERS INCORPORATED
7180 State Route 43 (44240-5940)
P.O. Box 645 (44240-0012)
PHONE.............................330 673-5777
Scott Yahner, *Pr*
EMP: 70 **EST:** 1955
SQ FT: 23,000
SALES (est): 2.77MM **Privately Held**
Web: www.scottmolders.com
SIC: 3089 2821 Thermoformed finished
plastics products, nec; Plastics materials
and resins

(G-8075)
SEAL MASTER CORPORATION
Also Called: Sealmaster
340 Martinel Dr (44240-4369)
PHONE.............................330 673-8410
Edward Bittle, *Brnch Mgr*
EMP: 50
SALES (corp-wide): 4.65MM **Privately
Held**
Web: www.sealmaster.com
SIC: 2951 Asphalt paving mixtures and
blocks
PA: Seal Master Corporation
369 Martinel Dr
Kent OH 44240
330 673-8410

(G-8076)
SEAL MASTER CORPORATION (PA)
Also Called: Sealmaster
368 Martinel Dr (44240-4368)
PHONE.............................330 673-8410
EMP: 25 **EST:** 1974
SALES (est): 4.65MM
SALES (corp-wide): 4.65MM **Privately
Held**
Web: www.sealmaster.com
SIC: 3053 Gaskets and sealing devices

(G-8077)
SELECT MACHINE INC
4125 Karg Industrial Pkwy (44240-6425)
PHONE.............................330 678-7676
Bill Sagaser, *Pr*
Douglas Beavers, *VP*
William Sagaser, *Sec*
EMP: 10 **EST:** 1994
SQ FT: 7,000
SALES (est): 1.43MM **Privately Held**

SIC: 3544 3599 Special dies, tools, jigs, and fixtures; Machine shop, jobbing and repair

(G-8078)
SEW & SEW EMBROIDERY INC
881 Tallmadge Rd Ste C (44240-6451)
P.O. Box 333 (44278-0333)
PHONE...............................330 676-1600
Andrew Coufal, *Pr*
EMP: 12 **EST:** 1997
SALES (est): 439.41K **Privately Held**
Web: www.sewandsewemb.com
SIC: 2395 7389 5199 Embroidery products, except Schiffli machine; Advertising, promotional, and trade show services; Advertising specialties

(G-8079)
SMITHERS-OASIS COMPANY
Smithers-Oasis North America
919 Marvin St (44240-2436)
P.O. Box 790 (44240-0016)
PHONE...............................330 673-5831
Robert Williams, *Brnch Mgr*
EMP: 11
SALES (corp-wide): 48.49MM **Privately Held**
Web: www.oasisfloral.com
SIC: 3086 Plastics foam products
PA: Smithers-Oasis Company
295 S Water St Ste 201
Kent OH 44240
330 945-5100

(G-8080)
SMITHERS-OASIS COMPANY (PA)
Also Called: Smithersoasis North America
295 S Water St Ste 201 (44240-3591)
PHONE...............................330 945-5100
Charles F Walton, *CEO*
Robin M Kilbride, *Pr*
◆ **EMP:** 15 **EST:** 1954
SQ FT: 7,500
SALES (est): 48.49MM
SALES (corp-wide): 48.49MM **Privately Held**
Web: www.oasisfloral.com
SIC: 3086 Packaging and shipping materials, foamed plastics

(G-8081)
SORBOTHANE INC (PA)
2144 State Route 59 (44240-7142)
PHONE...............................330 678-9444
Robert Whitlinger, *Prin*
David Church, *Pr*
EMP: 20 **EST:** 1982
SQ FT: 60,000
SALES (est): 2.3MM
SALES (corp-wide): 2.3MM **Privately Held**
Web: www.sorbothane.com
SIC: 3069 3545 3296 2821 Molded rubber products; Machine tool accessories; Mineral wool; Plastics materials and resins

(G-8082)
SOUND LABORATORY LLC ✪
109 S Water St (44240-3582)
PHONE...............................330 968-4060
EMP: 10 **EST:** 2023
SALES (est): 521.63K **Privately Held**
SIC: 3861 Sound recording and reproducing equipment, motion picture

(G-8083)
STEINERT INDUSTRIES INC
1507 Franklin Ave (44240-3770)
PHONE...............................330 678-0028
John J Steinert, *Pr*
Laura Cheges, *Sec*
EMP: 9 **EST:** 1976

SQ FT: 11,000
SALES (est): 3.45MM **Privately Held**
Web: www.steinertindustries.com
SIC: 3559 3599 Glass making machinery: blowing, molding, forming, etc.; Machine shop, jobbing and repair

(G-8084)
SUNNY BROOK PREST CONCRETE CO
3586 Sunnybrook Rd (44240-7448)
PHONE...............................330 673-7667
Joseph F Repasky Junior, *Pr*
EMP: 9 **EST:** 1979
SALES (est): 1.94MM **Privately Held**
Web: www.sunnybrookpressedconcrete.com
SIC: 3271 Architectural concrete: block, split, fluted, screen, etc.

(G-8085)
T-MAC MACHINE INC
924 Overholt Rd (44240-7551)
PHONE...............................330 673-0621
Ray Thompson, *Pr*
Ruth Thompson-asst, *Sec*
Gary Thompson, *Sec*
EMP: 7 **EST:** 1975
SQ FT: 10,400
SALES (est): 828.42K **Privately Held**
SIC: 3599 3069 Machine shop, jobbing and repair; Platens, except printers': solid or covered rubber

(G-8086)
TARPCO INC
390 Portage Blvd (44240-7283)
PHONE...............................330 677-8277
Chuck George, *Pr*
Harold A Neidlinger, *Pr*
Michael R Harrison, *VP*
EMP: 18 **EST:** 1938
SQ FT: 6,500
SALES (est): 2.58MM **Privately Held**
Web: www.tarpco.com
SIC: 2394 7359 3537 Tarpaulins, fabric: made from purchased materials; Tent and tarpaulin rental; Industrial trucks and tractors

(G-8087)
TECHNIDRILL SYSTEMS INC
429 Portage Blvd (44240-7286)
PHONE...............................330 678-9980
EMP: 36
Web: www.kays-dehoff.com
SIC: 3541 3546 3545 Drilling and boring machines; Power-driven handtools; Machine tool accessories

(G-8088)
TEMPRECISION INTL CORP (PA)
777 Stow St (44240-3429)
PHONE...............................855 891-7732
James Stull, *Pr*
EMP: 7 **EST:** 2018
SALES (est): 1.84MM
SALES (corp-wide): 1.84MM **Privately Held**
Web: www.temprecision.com
SIC: 3086 Plastics foam products

(G-8089)
THE D B HESS COMPANY
Also Called: Hess Print Solutions
3765 Sunnybrook Rd (44240-7443)
PHONE...............................330 678-5868
▲ **EMP:** 25
SIC: 2759 2789 Commercial printing, nec; Bookbinding and related work

(G-8090)
THE PRESS OF OHIO INC
Also Called: Hess Print Solutions - OH
3765 Sunnybrook Rd (44240-7443)
PHONE...............................330 678-5868
EMP: 400
SIC: 2732 Book printing

(G-8091)
TPO HESS HOLDINGS INC
Also Called: Hess Print Solutions
3765 Sunnybrook Rd (44240-7443)
PHONE...............................815 334-6140
Jerry Haywood, *CEO*
EMP: 88 **EST:** 2009
SALES (est): 3.1MM **Privately Held**
Web: www.hessprintsolutions.com
SIC: 2759 Commercial printing, nec

(G-8092)
TRANSDIGM INC
2146 State Route 59 (44240-7142)
PHONE...............................330 676-7147
Jeannette Selzer, *Brnch Mgr*
EMP: 7
SALES (corp-wide): 7.94B **Publicly Held**
Web: www.aerocontrolex.com
SIC: 2821 Plastics materials and resins
HQ: Transdigm, Inc.
1350 Euclid Ave
Cleveland OH 44115

(G-8093)
URRA CO INC
Also Called: Flynn's Tire Co
1897 State Route 59 (44240-4173)
PHONE...............................330 673-8473
Craig Hale, *Brnch Mgr*
EMP: 7
SALES (corp-wide): 9.32MM **Privately Held**
Web: www.flynnstire.com
SIC: 5531 7534 Automotive tires; Tire repair shop
PA: Urra Co. Inc.
2908 Mrcer W Middlesex Rd
West Middlesex PA 16159
724 906-8091

(G-8094)
US DEVELOPMENT CORP
Also Called: Akro-Plastics
900 W Main St (44240-2285)
PHONE...............................330 673-6900
Jerold Ramsey, *Pr*
EMP: 80 **EST:** 1985
SQ FT: 185,000
SALES (est): 5.72MM **Privately Held**
Web: www.rotomold.net
SIC: 3089 6512 Molding primary plastics; Commercial and industrial building operation

Kenton
Hardin County

(G-8095)
ATMOSPHERE ANNEALING LLC
Also Called: Aalberts Surface Technologies
1501 Raff Rd Sw (43326)
PHONE...............................330 478-0314
Saminathan Ramaswamy, *Mgr*
EMP: 65
SALES (corp-wide): 41.55MM **Privately Held**
Web: www.aalberts-ht.us
SIC: 3398 Annealing of metal
HQ: Atmosphere Annealing, Llc
209 W Mount Hope Ave # 2

Lansing MI 48910
517 485-5090

(G-8096)
BAKELITE N SUMITOMO AMER INC
13717 Us Highway 68 (43326-9302)
PHONE...............................419 675-1282
Kurt Sandy, *Brnch Mgr*
EMP: 36
Web: www.sbhpp.com
SIC: 3089 Plastics containers, except foam
HQ: Sumitomo Bakelite North America, Inc.
4400 Haggerty Hwy
Commerce Township MI 48390

(G-8097)
DUREZ CORPORATION
Also Called: Durez
13717 Us Highway 68 (43326-9302)
PHONE...............................567 295-6400
Bill Bazell, *Mgr*
EMP: 65
SQ FT: 25,000
Web: resins.sbna-inc.com
SIC: 2891 2295 2821 Adhesives, plastic; Resin or plastic coated fabrics; Plastics materials and resins
HQ: Durez Corporation
4400 Haggerty Hwy
Commerce Township MI 48390
248 313-7000

(G-8098)
GOLDEN GIANT INC
Also Called: Golden Giants Building System
13300 S Vision Dr (43326-9599)
P.O. Box 389 (43326-0389)
PHONE...............................419 674-4038
Gene A Good, *CEO*
Sharon J Good, *
Chris Richards, *
Paul N Mckinley, *Prin*
Wright Mccullough, *Prin*
EMP: 35 **EST:** 1971
SQ FT: 80,000
SALES (est): 5.12MM **Privately Held**
Web: www.goldengiant.us
SIC: 3448 Buildings, portable: prefabricated metal

(G-8099)
GOLDEN GRAPHICS LTD
Also Called: Golden Graphics
314 W Franklin St (43326-1702)
P.O. Box 208 (43326-0208)
PHONE...............................419 673-6260
EMP: 10 **EST:** 1982
SQ FT: 8,000
SALES (est): 365.3K **Privately Held**
Web: www.golden-graphics.com
SIC: 2752 7335 7336 2789 Offset printing; Commercial photography; Graphic arts and related design; Bookbinding and related work

(G-8100)
GRAPHIC PACKAGING INTL LLC
Also Called: International Paper
1300 S Main St (43326-2298)
PHONE...............................419 673-0711
Ted Riggs, *Brnch Mgr*
EMP: 375
Web: www.graphicpkg.com
SIC: 2656 2621 Cups, paper: made from purchased material; Paper mills
HQ: Graphic Packaging International, Llc
1500 Rvredge Pkwy Ste 100
Atlanta GA 30328

▲ = Import ▼ = Export
◆ = Import/Export

(G-8101)
HARDIN COUNTY PUBLISHING CO (HQ)
Also Called: Kenton Times, The
201 E Columbus St (43326-1583)
P.O. Box 230 (43326)
PHONE..................419 674-4066
Jeff Barnes, Pr
EMP: 36 **EST:** 1953
SQ FT: 9,600
SALES (est): 1.81MM
SALES (corp-wide): 3.45MM **Privately Held**
Web: www.kentontimes.com
SIC: 2711 Job printing and newspaper publishing combined
PA: Ray Barnes Newspaper Inc
201 E Columbus St # 207
Kenton OH 43326
419 674-4066

(G-8102)
KENTON IRON PRODUCTS INC (PA)
13510 S Vision Dr (43326-1592)
PHONE..................419 674-4178
Jerry Harmeyer, Pr
Michael Heyne, *
EMP: 35 **EST:** 1974
SALES (est): 840.06K
SALES (corp-wide): 840.06K **Privately Held**
Web: www.kentoniron.com
SIC: 3321 3322 Gray iron ingot molds, cast; Malleable iron foundries

(G-8103)
KENTON STRL & ORN IR WORKS
100 Cleveland Ave (43326-1706)
P.O. Box 115 (43326-0115)
PHONE..................419 674-4025
O Bud A Winzenried, Junior President
O Bud A Winzenried Junior, Pr
Barbara E Winzenried, *
Anthony K Osbun, *
EMP: 70 **EST:** 1933
SQ FT: 22,000
SALES (est): 476.55K **Privately Held**
SIC: 3449 3446 3444 3443 Miscellaneous metalwork; Architectural metalwork; Sheet metalwork; Fabricated plate work (boiler shop)

(G-8104)
MCCULLOUGH INDUSTRIES INC
13047 County Road 175 (43326-9022)
P.O. Box 222 (43326-0222)
PHONE..................419 673-0767
EMP: 25
SIC: 3537 Hoppers, end dump

(G-8105)
MCI INC
Also Called: Verizon Business
13047 County Road 175 (43326-9022)
PHONE..................800 245-9490
EMP: 19
SALES (corp-wide): 1.94B **Publicly Held**
Web: www.mcculloughind.com
SIC: 3537 Hoppers, end dump
HQ: Mci, Inc.
22901 Millcreek Blvd
Cleveland OH 44122
216 292-3800

(G-8106)
MCI INC
Also Called: McCullough Industries
13047 County Road 175 (43326-9022)
PHONE..................800 245-9490
EMP: 19
SALES (corp-wide): 1.94B **Publicly Held**

Web: www.mcculloughind.com
SIC: 3537 Hoppers, end dump
HQ: Mci, Inc.
22901 Millcreek Blvd
Cleveland OH 44122
216 292-3800

(G-8107)
MID OHIO WOOD RECYCLING INC
16289 State Route 31 (43326-8819)
PHONE..................419 673-8470
Leo Smithberger, Owner
Carla Smithberger, VP
EMP: 8 **EST:** 1993
SQ FT: 30,000
SALES (est): 359.9K **Privately Held**
SIC: 2448 Pallets, wood

(G-8108)
MOLDMAKERS INC
13608 Us Highway 68 (43326-9302)
P.O. Box 372 (43326-0372)
PHONE..................419 673-0902
Gene R Longbrake, Pr
Shari K Longbrake, Treas
EMP: 10 **EST:** 1968
SQ FT: 12,000
SALES (est): 1.03MM **Privately Held**
Web: www.moldmakersinc.com
SIC: 3544 3089 Special dies and tools; Injection molding of plastics

(G-8109)
MORTON BUILDINGS INC
14623 State Route 31 (43326-9021)
PHONE..................419 399-4549
Jeff Dawson, Mgr
EMP: 7
SALES (corp-wide): 89.89MM **Privately Held**
Web: www.mortonbuildings.com
SIC: 3448 Prefabricated metal buildings and components
PA: Morton Buildings, Inc.
252 W Adams St
Morton IL 61550
800 447-7436

(G-8110)
MORTON BUILDINGS INC
Also Called: Morton Buildings Plant
14483 State Route 31 (43326-9055)
P.O. Box 223 (43326-0223)
PHONE..................419 675-2911
Garry Shirk, Mgr
EMP: 24
SALES (corp-wide): 89.89MM **Privately Held**
Web: www.mortonbuildings.com
SIC: 3448 5039 2452 Farm and utility buildings; Prefabricated structures; Prefabricated wood buildings
PA: Morton Buildings, Inc.
252 W Adams St
Morton IL 61550
800 447-7436

(G-8111)
PLEASANT PRECISION INC
Also Called: Team Ppi
13840 Us Highway 68 (43326-9591)
PHONE..................419 675-0556
EMP: 32 **EST:** 1977
SALES (est): 6.29MM **Privately Held**
Web: www.teamppi.com
SIC: 3544 3089 Forms (molds), for foundry and plastics working machinery; Injection molding of plastics

(G-8112)
PRECISION STRIP INC
190 Bales Rd (43326-8909)
PHONE..................419 674-4186
Don Bornhorst, Brnch Mgr
EMP: 52
SALES (corp-wide): 13.84B **Publicly Held**
Web: www.precision-strip.com
SIC: 4225 3341 General warehousing and storage; Secondary nonferrous metals
HQ: Precision Strip Inc.
86 S Ohio St
Minster OH 45865
419 628-2343

(G-8113)
ROBINSON FIN MACHINES INC
13670 Us Highway 68 (43326-9302)
PHONE..................419 674-4152
Sheryl Haushalter, Pr
Ruth A Haushalter, *
David Haushalter, *
Sheryl Haushalter, VP
▲ **EMP:** 46 **EST:** 1980
SQ FT: 27,000
SALES (est): 6.53MM **Privately Held**
Web: www.robfin.com
SIC: 3444 Sheet metalwork

(G-8114)
ROUND MATE SYSTEMS
13840 Us Highway 68 (43326-9302)
PHONE..................419 675-3334
Ron Pleasant, Prin
EMP: 7 **EST:** 2007
SALES (est): 249.13K **Privately Held**
Web: www.teamppi.com
SIC: 2431 Moldings and baseboards, ornamental and trim

(G-8115)
SCIOTO SIGN CO INC
6047 Us Highway 68 (43326-9218)
PHONE..................419 673-1261
Shawn Moore, Pr
Sandra A Pruden, *
EMP: 30 **EST:** 1897
SQ FT: 52,500
SALES (est): 2.18MM **Privately Held**
Web: www.sciotosigns.com
SIC: 3993 Signs, not made in custom sign painting shops

(G-8116)
SUPERIOR MACHINE TOOL INC
13606 Us Highway 68 (43326-9302)
PHONE..................419 675-2363
Bill Clum, Pr
EMP: 10 **EST:** 1968
SQ FT: 7,200
SALES (est): 885.78K **Privately Held**
Web: www.superiormachineinc.com
SIC: 3599 Machine shop, jobbing and repair

Kettering
Montgomery County

(G-8117)
BWI CHASSIS DYNAMICS NA INC
3100 Research Blvd (45420-4022)
PHONE..................937 455-5100
Jeff Zhao, Brnch Mgr
EMP: 13
Web: www.bwigroup.com
SIC: 3714 Motor vehicle parts and accessories
HQ: Bwi Chassis Dynamics (Na), Inc.
12501 Grand River Rd
Brighton MI 48116
937 455-5308

(G-8118)
DAYTON BAG & BURLAP CO
4248 Display Ln (45429-5149)
PHONE..................419 733-7108
EMP: 21
SALES (corp-wide): 3.15MM **Privately Held**
Web: www.daybag.com
SIC: 2393 Textile bags
PA: The Dayton Bag & Burlap Co
322 Davis Ave
Dayton OH 45403
937 258-8000

(G-8119)
EASTMAN KODAK COMPANY
Also Called: Kodak
3100 Research Blvd Ste 250 (45420-4019)
PHONE..................937 259-3000
Bonnie Saravullo, Brnch Mgr
EMP: 45
SALES (corp-wide): 1.04B **Publicly Held**
Web: www.kodak.com
SIC: 3861 Photographic equipment and supplies
PA: Eastman Kodak Company
343 State St
Rochester NY 14650
800 356-3259

(G-8120)
ETI TECH LLC
3387 Woodman Dr (45429-4131)
PHONE..................937 832-4200
Matthew Eberhardt, CEO
Bill Mclendon, Pr
Jeff Hartman, Ex VP
EMP: 13 **EST:** 1996
SQ FT: 23,000
SALES (est): 4.55MM
SALES (corp-wide): 38.58MM **Privately Held**
Web: www.etitechinc.com
SIC: 3812 3679 8711 3629 Search and navigation equipment; Electronic circuits; Engineering services; Electronic generation equipment
PA: Eti Mission Controls, Llc
3387 Woodman Dr
Dayton OH 45429
937 832-4200

(G-8121)
JASPER PRINTING CO LLC
Also Called: Minuteman Press
3540 Marshall Rd (45429-4916)
PHONE..................937 294-5218
EMP: 7 **EST:** 2022
SALES (est): 1.16MM **Privately Held**
Web: chanhassen-mn.minutemanpress.com
SIC: 2752 Commercial printing, lithographic

(G-8122)
NANOSPERSE LLC
2000 Composite Dr (45420-1493)
PHONE..................937 296-5030
▼ **EMP:** 9 **EST:** 2005
SQ FT: 10,000
SALES (est): 1.85MM **Privately Held**
Web: www.nanosperse.com
SIC: 3087 2891 2851 2821 Custom compound purchased resins; Epoxy adhesives; Epoxy coatings; Epoxy resins

(G-8123)
RESONETICS LLC
Also Called: Mound Laser Photonics Center
2941 College Dr (45420-1172)
PHONE..................937 865-4070
EMP: 75

Web: www.resonetics.com
SIC: 3699 3841 Laser systems and
equipment; Medical instruments and
equipment, blood and bone work
PA: Resonetics Llc
26 Whipple St
Nashua NH 03060

(G-8124)
XERION ADVANCED BATTERY CORP
3100 Research Blvd Ste 320 (45420-4022)
PHONE.............................720 229-0697
John Busbee, *Pr*
Christopher Kolb, *Ex VP*
Paul Braun, *Prin*
Jim Thompson, *CFO*
EMP: 10 EST: 2012
SALES (est): 3.77MM Privately Held
Web: www.xerionbattery.com
SIC: 3691 Batteries, rechargeable

Kettlersville
Shelby County

(G-8125)
ROETTGER HARDWOOD INC
17066 Kettlersville Rd (45336)
P.O. Box 68 (45336-0068)
PHONE.............................937 693-6811
Viola Roettger, *Pr*
EMP: 9 EST: 1947
SQ FT: 74,000
SALES (est): 1.7MM Privately Held
SIC: 2431 2434 Millwork; Wood kitchen
cabinets

Kidron
Wayne County

(G-8126)
E P GERBER & SONS INC
Also Called: Gerber Lumber & Hardware
4918 Kidron Rd (44636)
P.O. Box 2 (44636-0002)
PHONE.............................330 857-2021
EMP: 65 EST: 1901
SALES (est): 3.85MM Privately Held
Web: www.gerberlumber.com
SIC: 5251 5211 3993 Hardware stores;
Lumber and other building materials;
Advertising novelties

(G-8127)
GERBER POULTRY LLC
5889 Kidron Rd (44636)
P.O. Box 206 (44636-0206)
PHONE.............................330 857-2731
EMP: 500 EST: 1952
SALES (est): 49.61MM Privately Held
Web: www.gerbers.com
SIC: 2015 Chicken, processed: fresh

(G-8128)
GERBER WOOD PRODUCTS INC
6075 Kidron Rd (44636)
P.O. Box 250 (44636-0250)
PHONE.............................330 857-9007
Steve Gerber, *Pr*
Eldon Gerber, *
EMP: 70 EST: 1946
SALES (est): 953.28K Privately Held
Web: www.gerberwood.com
SIC: 3993 3999 Advertising novelties;
Plaques, picture, laminated

(G-8129)
KIDRON INC
13442 Emerson Rd (44636)
P.O. Box 880 (27889-0880)
PHONE.............................330 857-3011
EMP: 500
Web: www.farmersbankgroup.com
SIC: 3713 3715 3444 Truck bodies (motor
vehicles); Trailer bodies; Sheet metalwork

Killbuck
Holmes County

(G-8130)
BAKERWELL INC (PA)
10420 County Road 620 (44637-9728)
P.O. Box 425 (44637-0425)
PHONE.............................330 276-2161
W Rex Baker, *Pr*
Robert K Baker, *CFO*
EMP: 21 EST: 1980
SQ FT: 126,000
SALES (est): 9.06MM
SALES (corp-wide): 9.06MM Privately
Held
Web: www.bakerwell.com
SIC: 1311 1389 Crude petroleum production;
Servicing oil and gas wells

(G-8131)
**BAKERWELL SERVICE RIGS INC
(HQ)**
10420 County Road 620 (44637-9728)
P.O. Box 425 (44637-0425)
PHONE.............................330 276-2161
W Rex Baker, *Pr*
Jeffrey Baker, *Sec*
Andrew Baker, *VP*
EMP: 18 EST: 1980
SALES (est): 4.82MM
SALES (corp-wide): 9.06MM Privately
Held
Web: www.bakerwell.com
SIC: 1381 Service well drilling
PA: Bakerwell, Inc.
10420 County Road 620
Killbuck OH 44637
330 276-2161

(G-8132)
CROW WORKS LLC
9595 Us-62 (44637)
PHONE.............................888 811-2769
Belinda Hughes, *CFO*
Dennis Blankemeyer, *
Denise Blankemeyer, *
EMP: 50 EST: 2010
SQ FT: 4,800
SALES (est): 13.1MM Privately Held
Web: www.crowworks.com
SIC: 2521 2599 Wood office furniture; Bar,
restaurant and cafeteria furniture

(G-8133)
SHREINER SOLE COMPANY INC
1 Taylor Dr (44637)
P.O. Box 347 (44637-0347)
PHONE.............................330 276-6135
David Shreiner, *Pr*
▲ EMP: 10 EST: 1948
SQ FT: 56,750
SALES (est): 725.7K Privately Held
Web: www.shreinerco.com
SIC: 3069 3061 Soles, boot or shoe: rubber,
composition, or fiber; Mechanical rubber
goods

(G-8134)
SPERRY & RICE LLC
1088 N Main St (44637-9504)
PHONE.............................330 276-2801
Darrell Detzler, *Brnch Mgr*
EMP: 12
Web: www.sperryrice.com
SIC: 3061 Mechanical rubber goods
PA: Sperry & Rice, Llc
1088 N Main St
Killbuck OH 44637

(G-8135)
SPERRY & RICE LLC (PA)
Also Called: Sperry & Rice
1088 N Main St (44637-9504)
PHONE.............................765 647-4141
EMP: 8 EST: 2007
SALES (est): 6.29MM Privately Held
Web: www.sperryrice.com
SIC: 3061 Mechanical rubber goods

Kimbolton
Guernsey County

(G-8136)
CALVIN W LAFFERTY
Also Called: Lafferty Chipping
72628 Hopewell Rd (43749-9586)
PHONE.............................740 498-6566
Calvin Lafferty, *Owner*
EMP: 8 EST: 1967
SALES (est): 1.32MM Privately Held
SIC: 2421 Wood chips, produced at mill

Kings Mills
Warren County

(G-8137)
SEVERN RIVER PUBLISHING LLC
P.O. Box 396 (45034-0396)
PHONE.............................703 819-4686
EMP: 6 EST: 2017
SALES (est): 127.92K Privately Held
Web: www.severnriverbooks.com
SIC: 2741 Miscellaneous publishing

Kingsville
Ashtabula County

(G-8138)
LYONS
5231 State Route 193 (44048-7713)
P.O. Box 554 (44048-0554)
PHONE.............................440 224-0676
Elijah Lyons, *Owner*
EMP: 6 EST: 2008
SALES (est): 422.48K Privately Held
SIC: 3715 Truck trailers

(G-8139)
NELSON SAND & GRAVEL INC
5720 State Route 193 (44048-9715)
P.O. Box 466 (44048-0466)
PHONE.............................440 224-0198
Thomas Nelson, *Pr*
Donna J Nelson, *Sec*
EMP: 10 EST: 1968
SQ FT: 6,000
SALES (est): 495.68K Privately Held
SIC: 1442 Common sand mining

Kinsman
Trumbull County

(G-8140)
**BAYLOFF STMPED PDTS KNSMAN
INC**
8091 State Route 5 (44428-9628)
P.O. Box 289 (44428-0289)
PHONE.............................330 876-4511
Richard Bayer, *Pr*
Kevin Jordan, *
Dan Moore, *
Dixon Morgan, *
M E Newcomer, *
EMP: 80 EST: 1948
SQ FT: 115,000
SALES (est): 7.04MM Privately Held
Web: www.bayloff.com
SIC: 3469 7692 3444 3315 Stamping metal
for the trade; Welding repair; Sheet
metalwork; Steel wire and related products

(G-8141)
MCGILL SEPTIC TANK CO
8913 State St (44428-9706)
PHONE.............................330 876-2171
Charles Mcgill, *Pr*
James Mcelhinny, *VP*
EMP: 8 EST: 1958
SQ FT: 10,000
SALES (est): 1.19MM Privately Held
SIC: 3272 2531 Concrete products, precast,
nec; Public building and related furniture

(G-8142)
R E H INC
Also Called: Hine Racing Equipment
St Rt 5 (44428)
P.O. Box 6 (44428-0006)
PHONE.............................330 876-2775
Carlon Hine, *Prin*
EMP: 7 EST: 1991
SALES (est): 190.37K Privately Held
SIC: 3462 Automotive and internal
combustion engine forgings

(G-8143)
**STRATTON CREEK WOOD WORKS
LLC**
5915 Burnett East Rd (44428-9757)
PHONE.............................330 876-0005
EMP: 11 EST: 2004
SALES (est): 859.37K Privately Held
Web: www.strattoncreek.com
SIC: 2431 Millwork

Kirtland
Lake County

(G-8144)
ESSENTIALWARE
Also Called: Global Principals
7637 Euclid Chardon Rd (44094-8724)
PHONE.............................888 975-0405
EMP: 6 EST: 2015
SALES (est): 1.98MM Privately Held
Web: www.essentialware.com
SIC: 3999 Manufacturing industries, nec

(G-8145)
KIRTLAND PLASTICS INC
7955 Euclid Chardon Rd (44094-9014)
PHONE.............................440 951-4466
Mark Di Lillo, *Pr*
EMP: 85 EST: 1961
SQ FT: 26,000
SALES (est): 2.1MM Privately Held

Web: www.endura.com
SIC: 3089 3544 Injection molded finished plastics products, nec; Special dies, tools, jigs, and fixtures

(G-8146)
WHOLESALE CHANNEL LETTERS
8603 Euclid Chardon Rd (44094-9586)
PHONE..............................440 256-3200
Dale Heigley, *Owner*
EMP: 8 EST: 1990
SALES (est): 453.62K **Privately Held**
Web: www.wholesalesigns4u.com
SIC: 3993 Neon signs

Kitts Hill
Lawrence County

(G-8147)
DAVID ADKINS LOGGING
1260 Township Road 256 (45645-8885)
PHONE..............................740 533-0297
David A Adkins, *Sec*
EMP: 6 EST: 2000
SALES (est): 65.29K **Privately Held**
SIC: 2411 Logging camps and contractors

Lagrange
Lorain County

(G-8148)
INSERVCO INC (DH)
Also Called: Staci Lagrange
110 Commerce Dr (44050-9491)
P.O. Box 106 (44050-0106)
PHONE..............................847 855-9600
Frances Bernardic, *Pr*
Mike Nargi, *VP*
Greg Hebson, *VP*
Jere Simonson, *Sec*
▲ EMP: 71 EST: 1968
SQ FT: 26,300
SALES (est): 45.79MM **Privately Held**
Web: www.vexos.com
SIC: 3679 Electronic circuits
HQ: Vexos, Inc.
   60 E 42nd St Ste 1250
   New York NY 10165
   855 711-3227

(G 8140)
LA GRANGE ELEC ASSEMBLIES CO
349 S Center St (44050-9014)
P.O. Box 555 (44050-0555)
PHONE..............................440 355-5388
W Robin Mc Clain, *Pr*
Richard M Mc Clain, *VP*
EMP: 22 EST: 1971
SQ FT: 40,000
SALES (est): 5.14MM **Privately Held**
Web: www.lagrangeelectrical.com
SIC: 3679 Harness assemblies, for electronic use: wire or cable

(G-8150)
MADER MACHINE CO INC
Also Called: Mader Dampers
422 Commerce Dr E (44050-9316)
PHONE..............................440 355-4505
Lon Zeager, *Pr*
Lon James Zeager, *
Nancy Zeager, *
EMP: 32 EST: 1963
SQ FT: 45,000
SALES (est): 2.44MM **Privately Held**
Web: www.maderdampers.com
SIC: 3822 Damper operators: pneumatic, thermostatic, electric

(G-8151)
MICRON MANUFACTURING INC
186 Commerce Dr (44050-8926)
PHONE..............................440 355-4200
Mark A Zupan, *Pr*
Anne Zupan, *
EMP: 60 EST: 1992
SQ FT: 50,000
SALES (est): 8.48MM **Privately Held**
Web: www.micronmfg.com
SIC: 3599 Machine shop, jobbing and repair

(G-8152)
NEW AGE DESIGN & TOOL INC
162 Commerce Dr (44050-8926)
PHONE..............................440 355-5400
Glen Allen, *Pr*
Donald Youngblood, *Sec*
EMP: 7 EST: 1993
SQ FT: 10,000
SALES (est): 893.59K **Privately Held**
Web: www.newagedesigntool.com
SIC: 3312 Tool and die steel

(G-8153)
PANEL MASTER LLC
191 Commerce Dr (44050-8926)
PHONE..............................440 355-4442
Ridley Watts, *Managing Member*
Cheryl Watts, *Finance*
EMP: 30 EST: 1985
SQ FT: 24,000
SALES (est): 4.65MM **Privately Held**
Web: www.panelmaster.com
SIC: 3613 3625 Control panels, electric; Relays and industrial controls

(G-8154)
TRIMLINE DIE CORPORATION
421 Commerce Dr E (44050-9316)
P.O. Box 66 (44050-0066)
PHONE..............................440 355-6900
Dave Gido, *Pr*
EMP: 20 EST: 1993
SQ FT: 10,000
SALES (est): 4.74MM
SALES (corp-wide): 22.16MM **Privately Held**
Web: www.varbroscorp.com
SIC: 3544 Special dies and tools
PA: Varbros, Llc
   16025 Brookpark Rd
   Cleveland OH 44142
   216 267-3200

(G-8155)
VEXOS INC
Also Called: Vexos Electronic Mfg Svcs
110 Commerce Dr (44050-9491)
PHONE..............................440 284-2500
John Wilkinson, *Sr VP*
EMP: 419
Web: www.vexos.com
SIC: 3672 Printed circuit boards
HQ: Vexos, Inc.
   60 E 42nd St Ste 1250
   New York NY 10165
   855 711-3227

Lakemore
Summit County

(G-8156)
ROBAN INC
1319 Main St (44250-9803)
P.O. Box 3483 (33572-1004)
PHONE..............................330 794-1059
Karen Medzi, *Pr*
EMP: 9 EST: 1972

SQ FT: 7,000
SALES (est): 220.77K **Privately Held**
Web: www.robansignage.com
SIC: 2796 7336 3479 Engraving platemaking services; Silk screen design; Etching on metals

Lakeside
Ottawa County

(G-8157)
CUSTOM CANVAS & BOAT REPR INC
Also Called: Custom Canvas & Upholstery
29 S Bridge Rd (43440-9483)
PHONE..............................419 732-3314
Shawn Harrison, *Pr*
Von Ellis, *VP*
David Walter, *Treas*
Carol Ellis, *Sec*
EMP: 6 EST: 1983
SQ FT: 4,800
SALES (est): 360.34K **Privately Held**
SIC: 2394 Liners and covers, fabric: made from purchased materials

Lakeview
Logan County

(G-8158)
UNITED TOOL AND MACHINE INC
490 N Main St (43331-9398)
P.O. Box 307 (43331-0307)
PHONE..............................937 843-5603
Gary Ginter, *Pr*
Sylvia Heintz, *Treas*
Chris Shrader, *Sec*
Shelly Ginter, *Off Mgr*
EMP: 13 EST: 1973
SQ FT: 41,000
SALES (est): 2.42MM **Privately Held**
Web: www.unitedtoolandmachineinc.com
SIC: 3599 Machine shop, jobbing and repair

Lakeville
Holmes County

(G-8159)
1200 FEET LIMITED
Also Called: Krin USA
41 County Road 2350 (44638-9614)
PHONE..............................419 827-6061
Deaunna F Morgan, *Admn*
EMP: 9 EST: 2013
SALES (est): 2.4MM **Privately Held**
SIC: 3569 Filters, general line: industrial

(G-8160)
AXLE MACHINE SERVICES LTD
41 County Road 2350 (44638-9614)
P.O. Box 117 (44611-0117)
PHONE..............................419 827-2000
Dennis Morgan, *Pt*
EMP: 7 EST: 1997
SQ FT: 5,600
SALES (est): 514.85K **Privately Held**
SIC: 3599 Machine shop, jobbing and repair

Lakewood
Cuyahoga County

(G-8161)
717 INC
Also Called: 717 Ink
13000 Athens Ave Ste 110 (44107-6256)

PHONE..............................440 925-0402
Joseph Haddad, *Pr*
EMP: 7 EST: 2010
SALES (est): 498.65K **Privately Held**
SIC: 2262 Screen printing: manmade fiber and silk broadwoven fabrics

(G-8162)
ASSOCIATED SOFTWARE CONS INC
Also Called: A S C
1101 Forest Rd (44107-1028)
PHONE..............................440 826-1010
Tim Liston, *Pr*
John H Liston, *Sec*
EMP: 17 EST: 1978
SALES (est): 2.36MM **Privately Held**
Web: www.powerlender.com
SIC: 7371 7372 Computer software systems analysis and design, custom; Prepackaged software

(G-8163)
BENSAN JEWELERS INC
Also Called: Broestl & Wallis Fine Jewelers
14410 Madison Ave (44107-4513)
PHONE..............................216 221-1434
Daniel D Wallis, *Pr*
Jeffery Broestl, *Sec*
EMP: 7 EST: 1946
SQ FT: 2,106
SALES (est): 624.57K **Privately Held**
Web: www.broestlwallis.com
SIC: 5944 3911 7631 Jewelry, precious stones and precious metals; Jewelry apparel; Jewelry repair services

(G-8164)
CARE FUSION
14414 Detroit Ave Ste 205 (44107-4473)
PHONE..............................216 521-1220
Geoffrey Sleeper, *Pr*
EMP: 6 EST: 1992
SALES (est): 953.68K **Privately Held**
SIC: 3841 Surgical and medical instruments

(G-8165)
CLEVELAND MICA CO
1360 Hird Ave (44107-3091)
PHONE..............................216 226-1360
Bruce C Burton, *Pr*
Donna Brady, *Sec*
Kevin D Burton, *Stockholder*
EMP: 10 EST: 1932
SQ FT: 16,000
SALES (est): 1.17MM **Privately Held**
Web: www.clevelandmica.com
SIC: 3299 Mica products, built-up or sheet

(G-8166)
EUCLID STEEL & WIRE INC
Also Called: ES&w
13000 Athens Ave Ste 101 (44107-6233)
PHONE..............................216 731-6744
Donald J Anzells, *Pr*
Donald J Anzells, *Pr*
Charles D Mc Bride, *Prin*
Daniel R Corcoran, *Prin*
T P Mc Mahon, *Prin*
EMP: 7 EST: 1978
SQ FT: 10,400
SALES (est): 700.07K **Privately Held**
Web: www.euclidsteel.com
SIC: 3315 Wire, steel: insulated or armored

(G-8167)
HAWTHORNE WIRE LTD
13000 Athens Ave Ste 101 (44107-6233)
PHONE..............................216 712-4747
Christopher Whiting, *Pr*
EMP: 6 EST: 2005
SALES (est): 543.02K **Privately Held**

Web: www.hawthornewire.com
SIC: 3315 Wire and fabricated wire products

(G-8168)
JOE THE PRINTER GUY LLC
1590 Parkwood Rd (44107-4739)
PHONE..............................216 651-3880
Joseph E Mchugh, *Prin*
EMP: 6
SALES (corp-wide): 251.47K **Privately Held**
SIC: 2752 Commercial printing, lithographic
PA: Joe The Printer Guy Llc
    14035 Madison Ave
    Lakewood OH 44107
    216 409-1656

(G-8169)
MCDONALDS
16407 Detroit Ave (44107-3625)
PHONE..............................216 226-7754
EMP: 11 EST: 2020
SALES (est): 57.19K **Privately Held**
Web: www.mcdonalds.com
SIC: 5813 5812 5499 2038 Drinking places; Eating places; Miscellaneous food stores; Frozen specialties, nec

(G-8170)
NEOGRAF SOLUTIONS LLC
11709 Madison Ave (44107-5230)
PHONE..............................216 529-3777
Natesh Krishnan, *CEO*
Drew Walker, *
Tony Glauser, *
Brian Bartos, *
EMP: 140 EST: 2016
SALES (est): 24.71MM
SALES (corp-wide): 160.78MM **Privately Held**
Web: www.neograf.com
SIC: 3624 Electrodes, thermal and electrolytic uses: carbon, graphite
PA: Edgewater Capital Partners, L.P.
    5005 Rockside Rd Ste 1300
    Independence OH 44131
    216 292-3838

(G-8171)
NORTON INDUSTRIES INC
1366 W 117th St (44107-3011)
PHONE..............................888 357-2345
Trisha Rhea, *Pr*
Alan Rhea, *VP*
EMP: 33 EST: 1967
SQ FT: 30,000
SALES (est): 5.64MM **Privately Held**
SIC: 3646 2541 Ceiling systems, luminous; Store fixtures, wood

(G-8172)
TRICO ENTERPRISES LLC
17717 Hilliard Rd (44107-5332)
PHONE..............................216 970-9984
EMP: 13
Web: www.tricoenterprises.com
SIC: 3553 Woodworking machinery
PA: Trico Enterprises Llc
    6430 Township Road 348
    Millersburg OH 44654

(G-8173)
WESTERN RESERVE DISTILLERS LLC
14221 Madison Ave (44107-4509)
PHONE..............................330 780-9599
Kevin Thomas, *Managing Member*
Ann Thomas, *Managing Member*
EMP: 7 EST: 2014
SALES (est): 1.85MM **Privately Held**
Web: www.westernreservedistillers.com

SIC: 2085 Distilled and blended liquors

Lancaster
Fairfield County

(G-8174)
ACCURATE MECHANICAL INC
566 Mill Park Dr (43130-7744)
PHONE..............................740 681-1332
EMP: 58
SALES (corp-wide): 21.41MM **Privately Held**
Web: www.accuratehvac.com
SIC: 5074 5063 3499 1711 Heating equipment (hydronic); Electrical supplies, nec; Aerosol valves, metal; Septic system construction
PA: Accurate Mechanical, Inc.
    3001 River Rd
    Chillicothe OH
    740 775-5005

(G-8175)
ANCHI INC
Also Called: Anchor Hocking
1115 W 5th Ave (43130-2938)
PHONE..............................740 653-2527
◆ EMP: 1500 EST: 2001
SALES (est): 38.23MM
SALES (corp-wide): 509.79MM **Privately Held**
SIC: 3231 Products of purchased glass
HQ: Anchor Hocking, Llc
    1600 Dblin Rd E Bldg Ste
    Columbus OH 43215

(G-8176)
ANCHOR HOCKING CONSMR GL CORP
1115 W 5th Ave (43130-2900)
PHONE..............................740 653-2527
Mark Eichorn, *Pr*
▼ EMP: 7 EST: 2006
SALES (est): 596.28K **Privately Held**
Web: www.anchorhocking.com
SIC: 3229 Glassware, art or decorative

(G-8177)
B & T WELDING AND MACHINE CO
423 S Mount Pleasant Ave (43130-3913)
P.O. Box 987 (43130-0987)
PHONE..............................740 687-1908
Alvin R Brown, *Pr*
Patricia Brown, *VP*
Darlene Baker, *Treas*
EMP: 6 EST: 1973
SQ FT: 8,500
SALES (est): 631.17K **Privately Held**
SIC: 3599 Machine shop, jobbing and repair

(G-8178)
BABCOCK & WILCOX COMPANY
Also Called: Babcock & Wilcox Co
2600 E Main St (43130-8490)
P.O. Box 415 (43130-0415)
PHONE..............................740 687-6500
Chris Mckeown, *Superintnt*
EMP: 48 EST: 1977
SALES (est): 17.66MM
SALES (corp-wide): 717.33MM **Publicly Held**
Web: www.babcock.com
SIC: 3511 Turbines and turbine generator sets
PA: Babcock & Wilcox Enterprises, Inc.
    1200 E Market St Ste 650
    Akron OH 44305
    330 753-4511

(G-8179)
BABCOCK & WILCOX ENTPS INC
2560 E Main St (43130-8490)
PHONE..............................740 687-4370
EMP: 22
SALES (corp-wide): 717.33MM **Publicly Held**
Web: www.babcock.com
SIC: 3511 Turbines and turbine generator sets
PA: Babcock & Wilcox Enterprises, Inc.
    1200 E Market St Ste 650
    Akron OH 44305
    330 753-4511

(G-8180)
BAINTER MACHINING COMPANY (PA)
1230 Rainbow Dr Ne (43130-1137)
PHONE..............................740 653-2422
Daniel A Bainter, *Pr*
Reda L Bainter, *Sec*
EMP: 9 EST: 1971
SQ FT: 2,000
SALES (est): 825.27K
SALES (corp-wide): 825.27K **Privately Held**
SIC: 3444 3599 Sheet metalwork; Machine shop, jobbing and repair

(G-8181)
BAINTER MACHINING COMPANY
842 N Columbus St (43130-2548)
PHONE..............................740 756-4598
Dan Bainter, *Mgr*
EMP: 12
SALES (corp-wide): 825.27K **Privately Held**
SIC: 3599 Machine shop, jobbing and repair
PA: Bainter Machining Company
    1230 Rainbow Dr Ne
    Lancaster OH 43130
    740 653-2422

(G-8182)
BUCKEYE READY-MIX LLC
Fairfield Concrete
1750 Logan Lancaster Rd Se (43130-9001)
PHONE..............................740 654-4423
Jerry Culp, *Mgr*
EMP: 28
SALES (corp-wide): 21.97MM **Privately Held**
Web: www.buckeyereadymix.com
SIC: 3273 Ready-mixed concrete
PA: Buckeye Ready-Mix, Llc
    7657 Taylor Rd Sw
    Reynoldsburg OH 43068
    614 575-2132

(G-8183)
BWX TECHNOLOGIES INC
2600 E Main St (43130-8490)
PHONE..............................740 687-4180
Dave Keller, *Brnch Mgr*
EMP: 51
Web: www.babcock.com
SIC: 3511 Turbines and turbine generator sets
PA: Bwx Technologies, Inc.
    800 Main St Fl 4
    Lynchburg VA 24504

(G-8184)
C J KRAFT ENTERPRISES INC
Also Called: Bay Packing
301 S Maple St (43130-4406)
PHONE..............................740 653-9606
Kathleen Kraft, *Pr*
David Kraft, *VP*
Karen Kraft, *Sec*

EMP: 6 EST: 1932
SQ FT: 2,000
SALES (est): 547.63K **Privately Held**
Web: www.bayfoodmarket.com
SIC: 5411 2011 5148 Grocery stores, independent; Meat packing plants; Fruits, fresh

(G-8185)
CAMERON INTERNATIONAL CORP
Also Called: Cameron Valve & Measurement
471 Quarry Rd Se (43130-8272)
PHONE..............................740 654-4260
Bill Wingard, *Brnch Mgr*
EMP: 48
Web: www.slb.com
SIC: 3533 Oil and gas field machinery
HQ: Cameron International Corporation
    1333 W Loop S Ste 1700
    Houston TX 77027

(G-8186)
CIRBA SOLUTIONS US INC (PA)
Also Called: Lithchem
265 Quarry Rd Se (43130-8271)
PHONE..............................740 653-6290
Steven Kinsbursky, *CEO*
▲ EMP: 23 EST: 2013
SALES (est): 71.88MM
SALES (corp-wide): 71.88MM **Privately Held**
Web: www.cirbasolutions.com
SIC: 2819 4953 3341 Industrial inorganic chemicals, nec; Recycling, waste materials; Recovery and refining of nonferrous metals

(G-8187)
CIRBA SOLUTIONS US INC
265 Quarry Rd Se (43130-8271)
PHONE..............................740 653-6290
Ed Green, *Brnch Mgr*
EMP: 100
SALES (corp-wide): 71.88MM **Privately Held**
Web: www.cirbasolutions.com
SIC: 3691 Batteries, rechargeable
PA: Cirba Solutions Us, Inc.
    265 Quarry Rd Se
    Lancaster OH 43130
    740 653-6290

(G-8188)
CITY OF LANCASTER
Also Called: Lancaster Municipal Gas
1424 Campground Rd (43130-9503)
PHONE..............................740 687-6670
Michael R Pettit, *Superintnt*
EMP: 46
SALES (corp-wide): 65.12MM **Privately Held**
Web: www.lancaster.k12.oh.us
SIC: 1311 4924 Crude petroleum and natural gas; Natural gas distribution
PA: City Of Lancaster
    104 E Main St
    Lancaster OH 43130
    740 687-6600

(G-8189)
CONSOLIDATED GRAPHICS INC
Also Called: Cyril-Scott Company, The
3950 Lancaster New Lexington Rd Se (43130-7899)
PHONE..............................740 654-2112
Chad Stephenson, *Pr*
EMP: 155
SALES (corp-wide): 15B **Privately Held**
Web: www.consolidatedgraphicsinc.com
SIC: 2752 Offset printing
HQ: Consolidated Graphics, Inc.
    5858 Westheimer Rd # 200

Houston TX 77057

(G-8190)
CREATIVE CABINETS LTD
1807 Snoke Rd Sw (43130-8902)
PHONE..................................740 689-0603
Jerry Meldrum, *Genl Pt*
Kenny Mitchell, *Pt*
EMP: 10 **EST:** 1996
SQ FT: 15,000
SALES (est): 965.22K **Privately Held**
SIC: 2434 Wood kitchen cabinets

(G-8191)
CROWN CLOSURES MACHINERY
1765 W Fair Ave (43130-2325)
PHONE..................................740 681-6593
John Conway, *CEO*
▲ **EMP:** 40 **EST:** 1996
SALES (est): 4.81MM
SALES (corp-wide): 11.8B **Publicly Held**
Web: www.crowncork.com
SIC: 3565 Packaging machinery
PA: Crown Holdings Inc.
  14025 Rveredge Dr Ste 300
  Tampa FL 33637
  215 698-5100

(G-8192)
CROWN CORK & SEAL USA INC
1765 W Fair Ave (43130-2325)
PHONE..................................740 681-6593
Shelia Heath, *Brnch Mgr*
EMP: 98
SALES (corp-wide): 11.8B **Publicly Held**
Web: www.crowncork.com
SIC: 3411 Metal cans
HQ: Crown Cork & Seal Usa, Inc.
  770 Township Line Rd
  Yardley PA 19067
  215 698-5100

(G-8193)
CROWN CORK & SEAL USA INC
940 Mill Park Dr (43130-9576)
PHONE..................................740 681-3000
Ed Schott, *Mgr*
EMP: 90
SALES (corp-wide): 11.8B **Publicly Held**
Web: www.crowncork.com
SIC: 3089 3466 3411 Closures, plastics;
  Closures, stamped metal; Metal cans
HQ: Crown Cork & Seal Usa, Inc.
  770 Township Line Rd
  Yardley PA 19067
  215 698-5100

(G-8194)
D K MANUFACTURING
2118 Commerce St (43130-9363)
PHONE..................................740 654-5566
Daniel Keifer, *Pr*
EMP: 8 **EST:** 2004
SALES (est): 1.57MM **Privately Held**
Web: www.dkmanufacturing.com
SIC: 3089 Injection molding of plastics

(G-8195)
DEVAULT MACHINE & MOULD CO LLC
Also Called: General Machine and Mould Co
2294 Commerce St (43130-9363)
P.O. Box 785 (43130-0785)
PHONE..................................740 654-5925
Terris E Devault, *Managing Member*
EMP: 7 **EST:** 1966
SQ FT: 5,000
SALES (est): 1.14MM **Privately Held**
Web: www.genmach.com

SIC: 3599 Machine shop, jobbing and repair

(G-8196)
DIAMOND ELECTRONICS INC
Also Called: Honeywell
1858 Cedar Hill Rd (43130-4178)
P.O. Box 415 (43130-0415)
PHONE..................................740 652-9222
George K Broady, *Ch Bd*
EMP: 9 **EST:** 1946
SQ FT: 72,000
SALES (est): 654.46K **Privately Held**
Web: www.babcock.com
SIC: 3663 Television closed circuit equipment

(G-8197)
DIAMOND POWER INTL INC
Also Called: Diamond Electronics
2530 E Main St (43130-8490)
PHONE..................................740 687-4001
Ron Burris, *Mgr*
EMP: 11
SALES (corp-wide): 717.33MM **Publicly Held**
Web: www.babcock.com
SIC: 3823 Process control instruments
HQ: Diamond Power International, Inc.
  2600 E Main St
  Lancaster OH 43130
  740 687-6500

(G-8198)
DIAMOND POWER INTL INC (DH)
Also Called: Diamond Power Specialty
2600 E Main St (43130-9366)
P.O. Box 415 (43130-0415)
PHONE..................................740 687-6500
Eileen M Competti, *Pr*
◆ **EMP:** 66 **EST:** 1903
SALES (est): 49.04MM
SALES (corp-wide): 717.33MM **Publicly Held**
Web: www.babcock.com
SIC: 3511 Turbines and turbine generator sets
HQ: The Babcock & Wilcox Company
  1200 E Market St Ste 650
  Akron OH 44305
  330 753-4511

(G-8199)
DISPATCH CONSUMER SERVICES
Also Called: Bag, The
0100 W Fair Ave (43130-9500)
PHONE..................................740 687-1893
Donna Holbrook, *Mgr*
EMP: 115
SALES (corp-wide): 48.78MM **Privately Held**
Web: www.dispatch.com
SIC: 2711 Newspapers, publishing and printing
HQ: Dispatch Consumer Services Inc
  5300 Crosswind Dr
  Columbus OH 43228
  740 548-5555

(G-8200)
DK MANUFACTURING LANCASTER INC
2118 Commerce St (43130-9363)
PHONE..................................740 654-5566
Daniel Keifer, *Pr*
EMP: 72 **EST:** 2004
SALES (est): 7.59MM
SALES (corp-wide): 15.67MM **Privately Held**
Web: www.dkmanufacturing.com
SIC: 3089 Injection molding of plastics
PA: Dak Enterprises, Inc.
  18062 Timber Trails Rd

Marysville OH 43040
740 828-3291

(G-8201)
FAIRFIELD WOOD WORKS LTD
1612 E Main St (43130-3472)
PHONE..................................740 689-1953
Ron Smith, *Pr*
Ben Smith, *VP*
Jed Smith, *VP*
EMP: 7 **EST:** 1998
SQ FT: 5,000
SALES (est): 947.44K **Privately Held**
Web: www.fairfieldwoodworks.com
SIC: 2434 2431 Wood kitchen cabinets;
  Moldings and baseboards, ornamental and trim

(G-8202)
FIMM USA INC
4155 Brook Rd Nw (43130-8317)
PHONE..................................614 568-4874
Enrico Spinelli, *Pr*
◆ **EMP:** 19 **EST:** 2010
SALES (est): 2.95MM **Privately Held**
Web: www.fimmusa.com
SIC: 3991 Brooms and brushes

(G-8203)
GHP II LLC
2893 W Fair Ave (43130-8993)
P.O. Box 600 (43130-0600)
PHONE..................................740 681-6825
Tom Gilligan, *Mgr*
EMP: 12
SQ FT: 1,300,000
SALES (corp-wide): 509.79MM **Privately Held**
SIC: 5023 3231 China; Products of purchased glass
HQ: Ghp Ii, Llc
  1115 W 5th Ave
  Lancaster OH 43130
  740 687-2500

(G-8204)
GHP II LLC (DH)
Also Called: Anchor Hocking Indus GL Div
1115 W 5th Ave (43130-2938)
PHONE..................................740 687-2500
Mark Eichorn, *CEO*
Mark Hedstrom, *
◆ **EMP:** 200 **EST:** 1905
SQ FT: 41,900
SALES (est): 7.01MM
SALES (corp-wide): 509.79MM **Privately Held**
SIC: 3229 3089 3411 3221 Tableware, glass or glass ceramic; Cups, plastics, except foam; Food and beverage containers; Food containers, glass
HQ: Anchor Hocking, Llc
  1600 Dblin Rd E Bldg Ste
  Columbus OH 43215

(G-8205)
INCESSANT SOFTWARE INC
8577 Ohio Wesleyan Ct Nw (43130-9329)
PHONE..................................614 206-2211
Al Pruden, *Pr*
EMP: 9 **EST:** 1997
SALES (est): 193.72K **Privately Held**
SIC: 7372 Prepackaged software

(G-8206)
LANCASTER METAL PRODUCTS INC
520 Slocum St (43130-2998)
PHONE..................................740 653-3421
Max Giles, *Pr*
Dorothy Giles, *VP*
Elizabeth Kilbarger, *VP*

EMP: 19 **EST:** 1950
SQ FT: 10,000
SALES (est): 3.41MM **Privately Held**
Web: www.lancastermetalproducts.com
SIC: 3599 Machine shop, jobbing and repair

(G-8207)
LANCASTER W SIDE COAL CO INC (PA)
700 Van Buren Ave (43130-2339)
PHONE..................................740 862-4713
Jerry H Fahrer, *Pr*
Mary K Cann, *VP*
Bruce Fahrer, *Treas*
William Cann, *Sec*
EMP: 10 **EST:** 1925
SQ FT: 1,600
SALES (est): 997.15K
SALES (corp-wide): 997.15K **Privately Held**
SIC: 3273 5211 5032 Ready-mixed concrete
  ; Lumber and other building materials;
  Brick, stone, and related material

(G-8208)
LOCHER INC
422 Quarry Rd Se (43130-9303)
PHONE..................................740 654-8888
Scott Locher, *Pr*
EMP: 9 **EST:** 1993
SQ FT: 2,500
SALES (est): 4.01MM **Privately Held**
Web: www.locher.com
SIC: 3599 Machine shop, jobbing and repair

(G-8209)
MARGO TOOL TECHNOLOGY INC
2616 Setter Ct Nw (43130-9151)
PHONE..................................740 653-8115
John Porter, *Pr*
Jeff Ellis, *Sec*
EMP: 10 **EST:** 1977
SQ FT: 7,500
SALES (est): 900.79K **Privately Held**
Web: www.margotool.com
SIC: 3599 Machine shop, jobbing and repair

(G-8210)
MEMAC INDUSTRIES INC
324 Quarry Rd Se (43130-8055)
P.O. Box 231 (43130-0231)
PHONE..................................740 653-4815
Carol L Figgins-clarke, *Pr*
Roger Figgins, *Dir*
Danny Clarke, *VP*
EMP: 8 **EST:** 1920
SQ FT: 5,900
SALES (est): 1.11MM **Privately Held**
Web: www.memacindustries.com
SIC: 3599 Machine shop, jobbing and repair

(G-8211)
MID-WEST FABRICATING CO
885 Mill Park Dr (43130-8061)
PHONE..................................740 277-7021
Ann Custer, *VP*
EMP: 20
SALES (corp-wide): 28.07MM **Privately Held**
Web: www.midwestfab.com
SIC: 3452 Bolts, metal
PA: Mid-West Fabricating Co.
  313 N Johns St
  Amanda OH 43102
  740 969-4411

(G-8212)
MUSTER RDU INC
1450 E Walnut St (43130-4000)
PHONE..................................614 537-5440
Darin Hadinger, *CEO*

Al Burzynski, *Pr*
Sean Curran, *Prin*
Elizabeth Mallett, *Prin*
EMP: 8 **EST:** 2020
SALES (est): 140.19K **Privately Held**
SIC: 2451 Mobile buildings: for commercial use

(G-8213)
NEIL R SCHOLL INC
54 Snoke Hill Rd Ne (43130-9315)
PHONE..........................740 653-6593
Neil R Scholl, *Pr*
Betty Scholl, *VP*
EMP: 10 **EST:** 1954
SQ FT: 2,000
SALES (est): 428.89K **Privately Held**
SIC: 3599 5084 Custom machinery; Industrial machinery and equipment

(G-8214)
NEWELL HOLDINGS DELAWARE INC
1115 W 5th Ave (43130-2938)
PHONE..........................740 681-6461
◆ **EMP:** 61
SIC: 3211 Building glass, flat

(G-8215)
NORTH END PRESS INCORPORATED
235 S Columbus St (43130-4315)
PHONE..........................740 653-6514
Richard Benadum, *Pr*
Greg Benadum, *VP*
Brad A Benadum, *VP*
EMP: 8 **EST:** 1933
SQ FT: 55,000
SALES (est): 780.9K **Privately Held**
Web: krisnorthendpress.wixsite.com
SIC: 2789 Bookbinding and related work

(G-8216)
NORWESCO INC
3111 Wilson Rd (43130-8144)
PHONE..........................740 654-6402
Darrin Dittman, *Mgr*
EMP: 12
SQ FT: 15,000
Web: www.norwesco.com
SIC: 3089 Plastics and fiberglass tanks
HQ: Norwesco, Inc.
　　2200 Commerce Blvd
　　Mound MN 55364
　　952 446-1945

(G-8217)
PRECISION CNC LLC
1858 Cedar Hill Rd (43130-4178)
PHONE..........................740 689-9009
Paul Davis, *Managing Member*
Nathan Hawkins, *
EMP: 28 **EST:** 2006
SQ FT: 10,000
SALES (est): 3.06MM **Privately Held**
Web: www.precision-cnc.com
SIC: 3599 Machine shop, jobbing and repair

(G-8218)
PRO-KLEEN INDUSTRIAL SVCS INC
Also Called: Porta-Kleen
1030 Mill Park Dr (43130-9576)
PHONE..........................740 689-1886
Monte Black, *Ch Bd*
EMP: 45 **EST:** 1995
SALES (est): 4.31MM **Privately Held**
Web: www.portakleen.com
SIC: 7359 7699 5963 3088 Portable toilet rental; Septic tank cleaning service; Bottled water delivery; Tubs (bath, shower, and laundry), plastics

(G-8219)
PROFESSIONAL SCREEN PRINTING
731 N Pierce Ave (43130-2416)
PHONE..........................740 687-0760
Jeff Uhl, *Pr*
EMP: 8 **EST:** 1987
SQ FT: 3,000
SALES (est): 285.47K **Privately Held**
Web: www.professionalscreenprintinginc.com
SIC: 7336 2752 Silk screen design; Commercial printing, lithographic

(G-8220)
QUALITY RUBBER STAMP INC
1777 Victor Rd Nw (43130-0100)
PHONE..........................614 235-2700
John J Lawler, *Pr*
EMP: 8 **EST:** 1971
SALES (est): 489.96K **Privately Held**
Web: www.qrsohio.com
SIC: 3953 3083 2396 2395 Numbering stamps, hand: rubber or metal; Plastics finished products, laminated; Screen printing on fabric articles; Embroidery and art needlework

(G-8221)
R F I
276 Bremen Rd (43130-7873)
PHONE..........................740 654-4502
Don Eiferd, *Prin*
EMP: 6 **EST:** 2008
SALES (est): 620.69K **Privately Held**
SIC: 3699 Security control equipment and systems

(G-8222)
RABLE MACHINE INC
1858 Cedar Hill Rd (43130-4178)
PHONE..........................740 689-9009
Kris Porte, *Admn*
EMP: 45 **EST:** 2021
SALES (est): 1.95MM **Privately Held**
Web: www.rablemachineinc.com
SIC: 3999 Manufacturing industries, nec

(G-8223)
SHERIDAN ONE STOP CARRYOUT INC
1510 Sheridan Dr (43130-1303)
PHONE..........................740 687-1300
Eric Molzan, *Owner*
EMP: 7 **EST:** 1981
SALES (est): 364.19K **Privately Held**
SIC: 1311 Crude petroleum and natural gas

(G-8224)
SMITH RN SHEET METAL SHOP INC
1312 Campground Rd (43130-9503)
PHONE..........................740 653-5011
Patrick Smith, *Pr*
Sue Smith, *
Mary Jo Smith, *
EMP: 11 **EST:** 1922
SQ FT: 1,800
SALES (est): 2.95MM **Privately Held**
Web: www.rnsmith.net
SIC: 3444 Sheet metalwork

(G-8225)
SOUTHSTERN MCHNING FELD SVC IN (PA)
500 Lincoln Ave (43130-4243)
PHONE..........................740 689-1147
John Treitmaier, *Pr*
EMP: 37 **EST:** 1989
SQ FT: 6,500
SALES (est): 8.35MM **Privately Held**
Web: www.semohio.com

SIC: 3599 Machine shop, jobbing and repair

(G-8226)
SRI OHIO INC
1061 Mill Park Dr (43130-9577)
PHONE..........................740 653-5800
Bonnita Heston, *Prin*
▲ **EMP:** 33 **EST:** 2010
SALES (est): 7.85MM **Privately Held**
Web: www.serigraphierichford.com
SIC: 2759 Screen printing

(G-8227)
TED M FIGGINS
Also Called: Glass City Machining and Fab
347 S Columbus St Pmb 634 (43130-4329)
PHONE..........................740 277-3750
Ted M Figgins, *Owner*
EMP: 14 **EST:** 2015
SALES (est): 450K **Privately Held**
Web: www.glasscitymachining.com
SIC: 3441 3599 Fabricated structural metal; Machine shop, jobbing and repair

(G-8228)
THE CYRIL-SCOTT COMPANY
3950 Lancaster New Lexington Rd Se (43130-7899)
PHONE..........................740 654-2112
▲ **EMP:** 150
SIC: 2759 Commercial printing, nec

(G-8229)
THORWALD HOLDINGS INC
Also Called: Martins Partitions
866 Mill Park Dr (43130-2572)
P.O. Box 102 (43112-0102)
PHONE..........................740 756-9271
Tamara Miller, *Pr*
Bruce Miller, *Treas*
EMP: 15 **EST:** 2007
SALES (est): 1.04MM **Privately Held**
SIC: 2631 Packaging board

(G-8230)
TOXCO INC
265 Quarry Rd Se (43130-8271)
PHONE..........................740 653-6290
Ed Green, *Brnch Mgr*
EMP: 23
SALES (corp-wide): 3.78MM **Privately Held**
Web: www.toxco.com
SIC: 3691 Batteries, rechargeable
PA: Toxco, Inc.
　　125 E Commercial St Ste A
　　Anaheim CA 92801
　　714 738-8516

(G-8231)
TREEHOUSE PRIVATE BRANDS INC
Also Called: Ralston Food
3775 Lancaster New Lexington Rd Se (43130-9314)
PHONE..........................740 654-8880
Andy Rohrbach, *Brnch Mgr*
EMP: 96
SALES (corp-wide): 3.35B **Publicly Held**
Web: treehousefoods2023rb.q4web.com
SIC: 2043 Cereal breakfast foods
HQ: Treehouse Private Brands, Inc.
　　2021 Spring Rd Ste 600
　　Oak Brook IL 60523

(G-8232)
TREEHOUSE PRIVATE BRANDS INC
276 Bremen Rd (43130-7873)
PHONE..........................740 654-8880
Gary Rodkin, *CEO*
EMP: 22

SALES (corp-wide): 3.35B **Publicly Held**
Web: treehousefoods2023rb.q4web.com
SIC: 2043 Cereal breakfast foods
HQ: Treehouse Private Brands, Inc.
　　2021 Spring Rd Ste 600
　　Oak Brook IL 60523

(G-8233)
ZEBCO INDUSTRIES INC
211 N Columbus St (43130-3006)
PHONE..........................740 654-4510
Kevin Stalter, *Pr*
Jill Stalter, *VP*
Madonna Christy, *Sec*
EMP: 19 **EST:** 1965
SQ FT: 128,000
SALES (est): 2.19MM **Privately Held**
Web: www.zebcoindustries.com
SIC: 3086 5113 2671 Packaging and shipping materials, foamed plastics; Industrial and personal service paper; Paper; coated and laminated packaging

---

Lansing
Belmont County

(G-8234)
VINO DI PICCIN LLC
55155 National Rd (43934)
P.O. Box 408 (43934-0408)
PHONE..........................740 738-0261
Louis Piccin, *CEO*
John Piccin, *Pr*
Sharon Acosta, *Sec*
Steve Piccin, *VP*
Nina Lenz, *VP*
EMP: 14 **EST:** 2010
SQ FT: 3,600
SALES (est): 701K **Privately Held**
Web: www.vinodipiccin.com
SIC: 2084 Wine cellars, bonded: engaged in blending wines

Latham
Pike County

(G-8235)
LATHAM LIMESTONE LLC
6424 State Route 124 (45646-9703)
PHONE..........................740 493-2677
EMP: 8 **EST:** 1960
SQ FT: 500
SALES (est): 562.7K **Privately Held**
Web: www.jrjnet.com
SIC: 1422 Limestones, ground

Latty
Paulding County

(G-8236)
AL-CO PRODUCTS INC
485 2nd St (45855)
P.O. Box 74 (45855-0074)
PHONE..........................419 399-3867
Russell W Stoller, *Pr*
John F Kohler, *VP*
Trent Stoller, *Sec*
EMP: 9 **EST:** 1968
SQ FT: 11,000
SALES (est): 1.08MM
SALES (corp-wide): 4.87MM **Privately Held**
Web: www.al-coproducts.com
SIC: 3281 3949 2821 2434 Marble, building: cut and shaped; Sporting and athletic goods, nec; Plastics materials and resins; Wood kitchen cabinets

▲ = Import ▼ = Export
◆ = Import/Export

PA: Haviland Drainage Products Co.
100 W Main St
Haviland OH 45851
800 860-6294

Laurelville
Hocking County

(G-8237)
JACK PINE STUDIO LLC
21397 State Route 180 (43135-9307)
PHONE..............................740 332-2223
EMP: 6 **EST:** 2017
SALES (est): 1.35MM **Privately Held**
Web: www.jackpinestudio.com
SIC: 3229 Pressed and blown glass, nec

(G-8238)
T & D THOMPSON INC
Also Called: Hocking Hills Hardwoods
15952 State Route 56 E (43135-9741)
P.O. Box 88 (43135-0088)
PHONE..............................740 332-8515
Terry L Thompson, *Pr*
David R Thompson, *
EMP: 10 **EST:** 1975
SQ FT: 50,000
SALES (est): 858.37K **Privately Held**
Web: www.hardwoodproducts.com
SIC: 2448 2449 2431 2426 Pallets, wood;
Wood containers, nec; Millwork; Hardwood
dimension and flooring mills

Leavittsburg
Trumbull County

(G-8239)
DENMAN TIRE CORPORATION
400 Diehl South Rd (44430-9705)
PHONE..............................330 675-4242
▲ **EMP:** 200
SIC: 3011 Pneumatic tires, all types

(G-8240)
LAURENCO SYSTEMS OF OHIO LLC
4255 W Market St (44430-9555)
P.O. Box 241 (44430-0241)
▲ **EMP:** 7 **EST:** 1992
SALES (est): 165.01K **Privately Held**
SIC: 2891 2295 Adhesives and sealants;
Waterproofing fabrics, except rubberizing

Lebanon
Warren County

(G-8241)
ADDITION MANUFACTURING TECHNOLOGIES LLC
Also Called: Addisonmckee
1637 Kingsview Dr (45036-8395)
PHONE..............................513 228-7000
▲ **EMP:** 175
Web: www.numalliance.com
SIC: 3542 3599 5084 3549 Bending
machines; Machine shop, jobbing and repair
; Industrial machinery and equipment;
Metalworking machinery, nec

(G-8242)
ADVICS MANUFACTURING OHIO INC
Also Called: Advics
1650 Kingsview Dr (45036-8390)
PHONE..............................513 932-7878
Geoff Hearsum, *Pr*
Atsuo Matsumoto, *
◆ **EMP:** 625 **EST:** 2003

SQ FT: 323,000
SALES (est): 43.26MM **Privately Held**
Web: www.advics-ohio.com
SIC: 3714 Motor vehicle brake systems and
parts
HQ: Advics North America, Inc.
1650 Kingsview Dr
Lebanon OH 45036
513 696-5450

(G-8243)
ALLEN FIELDS ASSOC INC
3525 Grant Ave Ste D (45036-6431)
PHONE..............................513 228-1010
Raymond Watson, *Owner*
EMP: 34 **EST:** 2004
SALES (est): 1.31MM **Privately Held**
Web: www.fieldselectric.com
SIC: 3699 5063 Electrical equipment and
supplies, nec; Electrical apparatus and
equipment

(G-8244)
AVID SIGNS PLUS LLC
495 Lakeside Dr (45036-1630)
PHONE..............................513 932-7446
Greg L Davis, *Admn*
EMP: 6 **EST:** 2017
SALES (est): 517.42K **Privately Held**
Web: www.avidsignsplus.com
SIC: 3993 Signs and advertising specialties

(G-8245)
AWS INDUSTRIES INC
Also Called: Tomak Precision
2600 Henkle Dr (45036-8026)
PHONE..............................513 932-7941
Alvin W Schaeper, *Pr*
Paul Balash, *
EMP: 45 **EST:** 1953
SQ FT: 20,000
SALES (est): 9.99MM **Privately Held**
Web: www.tomak.com
SIC: 3728 3841 Aircraft parts and
equipment, nec; Surgical and medical
instruments

(G-8246)
BBH HOLDINGS INC
1899 Kingsview Dr (45036-8397)
PHONE..............................513 870-3000
Mike Brunst, *Owner*
Terry Pater, *VP*
Terry Evans, *Manager*
Barry Ludwig, *Contrlr*
Kathy Henry, *Manager*
EMP: 20 **EST:** 1988
SALES (est): 2.44MM **Privately Held**
Web:
www.midwestcontainercorporation.com
SIC: 2653 Boxes, corrugated: made from
purchased materials

(G-8247)
BIG CHIEF MANUFACTURING LTD
250 Harmon Ave (45036-8800)
PHONE..............................513 934-3888
James Howe Junior, *Pt*
▲ **EMP:** 25 **EST:** 1998
SQ FT: 20,000
SALES (est): 956.11K
SALES (corp-wide): 28.72MM **Privately Held**
Web: www.bigchiefheaters.com
SIC: 3545 Machine tool accessories
HQ: Big Chief Supply Llc
5150 Big Chief Dr
Cincinnati OH 45227
513 271-7411

(G-8248)
BUNNELL HILL CONSTRUCTION INC
3000g Henkle Dr (45036-9258)
PHONE..............................513 932-6010
Kevin Scott, *Pr*
EMP: 12 **EST:** 1994
SALES (est): 1.01MM **Privately Held**
SIC: 1389 Construction, repair, and
dismantling services

(G-8249)
CLOUTH SPRENGER LLC
1425 Kingsview Dr (45036-7591)
PHONE..............................937 642-8390
▲ **EMP:** 6 **EST:** 2010
SALES (est): 5.02MM **Publicly Held**
Web: www.clouth.com
SIC: 3316 Strip, steel, razor blade, cold-
rolled: purchased hot-rolled
PA: Kadant Inc.
1 Technlogy Pk Dr Ste 210
Westford MA 01886

(G-8250)
CONTEMPRARY IMAGE LABELING INC
2034 Mckinley Blvd (45036-6425)
PHONE..............................513 583-5699
Doug Weideman, *Prin*
Doug Weideman, *Prin*
Kurt Wiedeman, *VP*
EMP: 6 **EST:** 1994
SQ FT: 18,000
SALES (est): 457.3K **Privately Held**
SIC: 2759 Labels and seals: printing, nsk

(G-8251)
D & E MACHINE CO
962 S Us Route 42 (45036-7918)
PHONE..............................513 932-2184
Kent P Coomer, *Pr*
Tim Wilkerson, *Opers Mgr*
Kimberly A Coomer, *VP*
EMP: 9 **EST:** 1990
SQ FT: 12,000
SALES (est): 2.46MM **Privately Held**
Web: www.demachine.com
SIC: 3599 Machine shop, jobbing and repair

(G-8252)
E-BEAM SERVICES INC
2775 Henkle Dr Unit B (45036-8256)
PHONE..............................513 933-0031
Dave Keenan, *Brnch Mgr*
EMP: 24
SQ FT: 129,116
SALES (corp-wide): 11.85MM **Privately Held**
Web: www.ebeamservices.com
SIC: 3699 Electronic training devices
PA: E-Beam Services, Inc.
270 Duffy Ave Ste H
Hicksville NY 11801
516 622-1422

(G-8253)
ECOLAB INC
726 E Main St Ste F (45036-1900)
PHONE..............................513 932-0830
Dan Elam, *Dist Mgr*
EMP: 8
SALES (corp-wide): 15.74B **Publicly Held**
Web: www.ecolab.com
SIC: 2842 Sanitation preparations,
disinfectants and deodorants
PA: Ecolab Inc.
1 Ecolab Pl
Saint Paul MN 55102
800 232-6522

(G-8254)
ERNST ENTERPRISES INC
4250 Columbia Rd (45036-9589)
PHONE..............................513 874-8300
Robert Himes, *Mgr*
EMP: 25
SQ FT: 2,822
SALES (corp-wide): 240.08MM **Privately Held**
Web: www.ernstconcrete.com
SIC: 3273 Ready-mixed concrete
PA: Ernst Enterprises, Inc.
993 Falls Creek Dr
Vandalia OH 45377
937 233-5555

(G-8255)
FB ACQUISITION LLC
2025 Mckinley Blvd (45036-8075)
PHONE..............................513 459-7782
Alex Weaner, *Pr*
Alexander Weaner, *
EMP: 42 **EST:** 2021
SALES (est): 515.46K **Privately Held**
SIC: 3398 3999 Annealing of metal;
Manufacturing industries, nec

(G-8256)
FECON LLC
1087b Mane Way (45036-8049)
PHONE..............................513 696-4430
John Heekin, *Pr*
EMP: 27
Web: www.fecon.com
SIC: 3523 Farm machinery and equipment
PA: Fecon, Llc
3460 Grant Dr
Lebanon OH 45036

(G-8257)
FECON LLC (PA)
3460 Grant Ave (45036-6432)
PHONE..............................513 696-4430
▲ **EMP:** 75 **EST:** 1992
SALES (est): 24.79MM **Privately Held**
Web: www.fecon.com
SIC: 3523 3531 Farm machinery and
equipment; Construction machinery

(G-8258)
GEORGE MANUFACTURING INC
160 Harmon Ave (45036-9511)
PHONE..............................513 932-1067
Erin George, *Pr*
Dan George, *Stockholder*
EMP: 15 **EST:** 1995
SQ FT: 60,000
SALES (est): 385.1K **Privately Held**
SIC: 3312 3479 3444 Pipes and tubes;
Painting, coating, and hot dipping; Sheet
metalwork

(G-8259)
GEORGE STEEL FABRICATING INC
1207 S Us Route 42 (45036-8198)
PHONE..............................513 932-2887
John George, *Pr*
Kevin Nickell, *
Brad Frost, *
EMP: 35 **EST:** 1960
SQ FT: 32,100
SALES (est): 4.87MM **Privately Held**
Web: www.georgesteel.com
SIC: 7692 3441 3599 Welding repair;
Fabricated structural metal; Machine shop,
jobbing and repair

(G-8260)
GEORGIA-PACIFIC PCPI INC
Also Called: Pax Corrugated Products, Inc.

1899 Kingsview Dr (45036-8397)
PHONE.................................513 932-9855
Stan Bernard, *CEO*
James E Cory Ii, *Pr*
EMP: 100 **EST:** 1990
SQ FT: 119,457
SALES (est): 5.71MM
SALES (corp-wide): 64.44B **Privately Held**
Web: www.welchpkg.com
SIC: 2653 Boxes, corrugated: made from purchased materials
HQ: Georgia-Pacific Llc
133 Peachtree St Ne
Atlanta GA 30303
404 652-4000

(G-8261)
GLOBAL INNOVATIVE PRODUCTS LLC
235 Harmon Ave (45036-8800)
PHONE.................................513 701-0441
Ramesh Malhotra, *Managing Member*
▲ **EMP:** 7 **EST:** 2013
SALES (est): 3.24MM **Privately Held**
Web: www.gip-edmwire.com
SIC: 3621 Electric motor and generator parts

(G-8262)
GMI COMPANIES INC (PA)
Also Called: Ghent Manufacturing
2999 Henkle Dr (45036-9260)
PHONE.................................513 932-3445
George L Leasure, *Ch*
Mary Alice Leasure, *
◆ **EMP:** 130 **EST:** 1970
SQ FT: 101,000
SALES (est): 41MM
SALES (corp-wide): 41MM **Privately Held**
Web: www.gmicompanies.com
SIC: 2531 2493 2599 2541 Blackboards, wood; Bulletin boards, wood; Boards: planning, display, notice; Showcases, except refrigerated: wood

(G-8263)
GMI COMPANIES INC
Ghent A Division GMI Companies
2999 Henkle Dr (45036-9260)
PHONE.................................513 932-3445
George L Leasure, *Pr*
EMP: 17
SALES (corp-wide): 41MM **Privately Held**
Web: www.ghent.com
SIC: 2531 2493 2599 2541 Blackboards, wood; Bulletin boards, wood; Boards: planning, display, notice; Showcases, except refrigerated: wood
PA: Gmi Companies, Inc.
2999 Henkle Dr
Lebanon OH 45036
513 932-3445

(G-8264)
GOLDEN TURTLE CHOCOLATE FCTRY
120 S Broadway St Ste 1 (45036-1729)
P.O. Box 647 (45036-0647)
PHONE.................................513 932-1990
Joy Kossouji, *Owner*
Ted Kossouji, *Pt*
EMP: 6 **EST:** 1982
SQ FT: 3,000
SALES (est): 106.18K **Privately Held**
SIC: 2066 5441 5947 Chocolate; Candy, nut, and confectionery stores; Gifts and novelties

(G-8265)
GRAFISK MASKINFABRIK AMER LLC
Also Called: Grafisk Msknfabrik-America LLC
603 Norgal Dr Ste F (45036-9382)
PHONE.................................630 432-4370

Jim Honeycutt, *Managing Member*
▲ **EMP:** 6 **EST:** 2011
SALES (est): 509.11K
SALES (corp-wide): 5.31MM **Privately Held**
Web: www.gmfinishing.com
SIC: 2759 Commercial printing, nec
PA: Grafisk Maskinfabrik A/S
Klintehoj Vange 12
Birkerod
45812300

(G-8266)
GREEN BAY PACKAGING INC
Cincinnati Division
760 Kingsview Dr (45036-9554)
PHONE.................................513 489-8700
Wayne Petersen, *Mgr*
EMP: 71
SQ FT: 103,000
SALES (corp-wide): 1.87B **Privately Held**
Web: www.gbpcoated.com
SIC: 2653 3412 Boxes, corrugated: made from purchased materials; Metal barrels, drums, and pails
PA: Green Bay Packaging Inc.
1700 N Webster Ave
Green Bay WI 54302
920 433-5111

(G-8267)
HEAT SENSOR TECHNOLOGIE LLC
Also Called: Heat & Sensor
627 Norgal Dr (45036-9275)
PHONE.................................513 228-0481
Gary Shackeford, *Managing Member*
Michelle Shackeford, *
▲ **EMP:** 53 **EST:** 2002
SQ FT: 12,000
SALES (est): 5.04MM **Privately Held**
Web: www.heatandsensortech.com
SIC: 3567 Heating units and devices, industrial: electric

(G-8268)
INX INTERNATIONAL INK CO
Also Called: INX INTERNATIONAL INK CO
350 Homan Rd (45036-1181)
PHONE.................................707 693-2990
EMP: 10
Web: www.inxinternational.com
SIC: 2893 Printing ink
HQ: Inx International Ink Co.
150 N Mrtngale Rd Ste 700
Schaumburg IL 60173
630 382-1800

(G-8269)
JBM PACKAGING COMPANY
Also Called: Jbm Packaging
2850 Henkle Dr (45036-8894)
P.O. Box 828 (45036-0828)
PHONE.................................513 933-8333
▲ **EMP:** 150 **EST:** 1985
SALES (est): 24.38MM **Privately Held**
Web: www.jbmpackaging.com
SIC: 2677 5112 Envelopes; Envelopes

(G-8270)
KADANT BLACK CLAWSON INC (HQ)
1425 Kingsview Dr (45036-7591)
PHONE.................................513 229-8100
Jonathan W Painter, *Pr*
Thomas M Obrie, *
Sandra Lambert, *
Kenny Leathers, *
◆ **EMP:** 75 **EST:** 1893
SQ FT: 26,000
SALES (est): 43.31MM **Publicly Held**
Web: fiberprocessing.kadant.com

SIC: 3554 Paper industries machinery
PA: Kadant Inc.
1 Technlogy Pk Dr Ste 210
Westford MA 01886

(G-8271)
KANDO OF CINCINNATI INC
Also Called: Franklin Brazing Met Treating
2025 Mckinley Blvd (45036-8075)
PHONE.................................513 459-7782
Timothy Mathile, *CEO*
Blake Michaels, *
EMP: 50 **EST:** 1972
SQ FT: 53,000
SALES (est): 4.6MM **Privately Held**
Web: www.franklinbrazing.com
SIC: 3398 Brazing (hardening) of metal

(G-8272)
KIRBYS AUTO AND TRUCK REPR INC
Also Called: Warren Welding and Fabrication
875 Columbus Ave (45036-1692)
PHONE.................................513 934-3999
Glen Kirby, *Pr*
Jennifer Kirby, *Sec*
EMP: 8 **EST:** 1996
SQ FT: 12,510
SALES (est): 552.18K **Privately Held**
Web: www.kirbysautorepair.com
SIC: 7538 7539 7692 General automotive repair shops; Automotive repair shops, nec; Welding repair

(G-8273)
LANGE PRECISION INC
865 S Us Route 42 (45036-7917)
PHONE.................................513 530-9500
Karl Lange, *Pr*
EMP: 15 **EST:** 1985
SALES (est): 493.26K **Privately Held**
Web: www.langeprecision.com
SIC: 3544 3599 3545 3537 Special dies and tools; Machine shop, jobbing and repair; Machine tool accessories; Industrial trucks and tractors

(G-8274)
LUCAS SUMITOMO BRAKES INC
1650 Kingsview Dr (45036-8390)
PHONE.................................513 934-0024
Paul C Hirt, *Prin*
EMP: 18 **EST:** 2005
SALES (est): 1.96MM **Privately Held**
Web: www.advics-ohio.com
SIC: 3714 5013 5015 Motor vehicle brake systems and parts; Automotive brakes; Motor vehicle parts, used

(G-8275)
MANE INC
1093 Mane Way (45036-8049)
PHONE.................................513 248-9876
EMP: 65
Web: www.mane.com
SIC: 2087 Flavoring extracts and syrups, nec
HQ: Mane, Inc.
2501 Henkle Dr
Lebanon OH 45036
513 248-9876

(G-8276)
MANE INC (DH)
Also Called: Mane Calafornia
2501 Henkle Dr (45036-7794)
PHONE.................................513 248-9876
Jean Mane, *Ch Bd*
Brad Kelley, *
◆ **EMP:** 70 **EST:** 1998
SQ FT: 70,000
SALES (est): 105.12MM **Privately Held**

Web: www.mane.com
SIC: 2087 2099 Extracts, flavoring; Food preparations, nec
HQ: Mane Usa Inc.
60 Demarest Dr
Wayne NJ 07470
973 633-5533

(G-8277)
MIX-MASTERS INC
Also Called: Jbs Industries
2726 Henkle Dr (45036-8209)
PHONE.................................513 228-2800
Scott Baeten, *Pr*
John T Hufford, *VP*
Laurie Baeten, *CFO*
EMP: 17 **EST:** 2000
SALES (est): 6.33MM **Privately Held**
Web: www.jbsindustries.com
SIC: 2841 2842 Soap and other detergents; Polishing preparations and related products

(G-8278)
NEWMAN DIAPHRAGMS LLC
964 W Main St (45036-9173)
PHONE.................................513 932-7379
David Wj Newman, *Mgr*
EMP: 20 **EST:** 2021
SALES (est): 700K **Privately Held**
Web: www.newmangasket.com
SIC: 3053 Gaskets, all materials

(G-8279)
NEWMAN SANITARY GASKET COMPANY
964 W Main St (45036-9173)
P.O. Box 222 (45036-0222)
PHONE.................................513 932-7379
David William Newman, *Pr*
Thomas Moore, *
EMP: 41 **EST:** 1973
SQ FT: 38,000
SALES (est): 3.99MM **Privately Held**
Web: www.newmangasket.com
SIC: 3053 Gaskets, all materials

(G-8280)
ONPOWER INC
3525 Grant Ave Ste A (45036-6431)
PHONE.................................513 228-2100
Larry D Davis, *Pr*
Tom Mergy, *
EMP: 27 **EST:** 2001
SQ FT: 41,350
SALES (est): 6.73MM **Privately Held**
Web: www.onpowerinc.com
SIC: 3511 8711 Gas turbines, mechanical drive; Consulting engineer

(G-8281)
OVERLY HAUTZ COMPANY
285 S West St (45036-2152)
P.O. Box 837 (45036-0837)
PHONE.................................513 932-0025
Thomas Copanas, *Pr*
Edward Bees, *
Clara Mendez Dof, *Prin*
▲ **EMP:** 50 **EST:** 1984
SQ FT: 27,000
SALES (est): 4.63MM **Privately Held**
Web: www.overlyhautz.com
SIC: 3699 Electrical equipment and supplies, nec

(G-8282)
R W LONG LUMBER & BOX CO INC
1840 Cornett Rd Ste 1 (45036-7511)
P.O. Box 678 (45036-0678)
PHONE.................................513 932-5124
Marlene Long, *Pr*
Marlene Long, *Pr*

Rodney W Long, *VP*
EMP: 16 **EST:** 1979
SQ FT: 16,200
SALES (est): 1.01MM **Privately Held**
Web: www.rwlong.com
SIC: 5031 2448 Lumber, plywood, and
millwork; Pallets, wood and wood with metal

(G-8283)
**RESTORTION PARTS UNLIMITED
INC (PA)**
Also Called: Rpui
2175 Deerfield Rd (45036-6422)
PHONE..............................513 934-0815
Mitch Williams, *CEO*
EMP: 10 **EST:** 2012
SALES (est): 9.23MM
SALES (corp-wide): 9.23MM **Privately
Held**
Web: www.rpui.com
SIC: 3714 Motor vehicle parts and
accessories

(G-8284)
RPMI PACKAGING INC
Also Called: Rpmi
3899 S Us Route 42 (45036-9530)
P.O. Box 105 (45040-0105)
PHONE..............................513 398-4040
Robert Hillerich, *Pr*
EMP: 10 **EST:** 1991
SALES (est): 2.27MM **Privately Held**
Web: www.rpmipackaging.com
SIC: 3565 Packaging machinery

(G-8285)
SCHMIDT PROGRESSIVE LLC
Also Called: Food Furniture
360 Harmon Ave (45036-8801)
P.O. Box 380 (45036-0380)
PHONE..............................513 934-2600
Julia Rodenbeck, *Managing Member*
EMP: 6 **EST:** 1998
SQ FT: 55,000
SALES (est): 2.18MM **Privately Held**
Web: www.schmidtprogressive.com
SIC: 3089 Fiberglass doors

(G-8286)
SPECTRUM TEXTILES INC
5883 Casaway Rd (45036)
PHONE..............................513 933-8346
Robin Steele, *Pr*
Jennifer Stenger, *VP*
EMP: 12 **EST:** 1995
SQ FT: 5,000
SALES (est): 414.24K **Privately Held**
SIC: 3728 Aircraft propellers and associated
equipment

(G-8287)
STC INTERNATIONAL CO LTD (PA)
1499 Shaker Run Blvd (45036-4041)
PHONE..............................561 308-6002
Frank Ferguson, *Pr*
EMP: 8 **EST:** 2010
SALES (est): 1.99MM **Privately Held**
SIC: 3541 3545 2821 Machine tools, metal
cutting type; Machine tool accessories;
Plastics materials and resins

(G-8288)
TELEMPU N HAYASHI AMER CORP
1500 Kingsview Dr (45036-8389)
PHONE..............................513 932-9319
Harry Okamoto, *Dir*
EMP: 6
Web: www.htnanorthamerica.com
SIC: 2396 Automotive trimmings, fabric

HQ: Hayashi Telempu North America
Corporation
14328 Genoa Ct
Plymouth MI 48170
734 456-5221

(G-8289)
TOTAL MAINTENANCE MGT INC
320 Harmon Ave (45036-8801)
PHONE..............................513 228-2345
Thomas Koerner, *Pr*
EMP: 6 **EST:** 2003
SQ FT: 14,700
SALES (est): 988.83K **Privately Held**
Web: www.tm2motor.com
SIC: 7694 Electric motor repair

(G-8290)
TRAMONTE & SONS LLC
3850 Welden Dr (45036-8815)
PHONE..............................513 770-5501
Michael R Tramonte Senior, *Managing
Member*
EMP: 10 **EST:** 2002
SALES (est): 459.84K **Privately Held**
Web: www.tramonteandsons.com
SIC: 8742 2084 Distribution channels
consultant; Wines

(G-8291)
TRIM PARTS INC
2175 Deerfield Rd (45036-6422)
PHONE..............................513 934-0815
Carl Chadwell, *Pr*
▲ **EMP:** 35 **EST:** 1982
SQ FT: 55,000
SALES (est): 4.12MM
SALES (corp-wide): 9.23MM **Privately
Held**
Web: www.rpui.com
SIC: 3714 3544 3429 Motor vehicle parts
and accessories; Special dies, tools, jigs,
and fixtures; Hardware, nec
PA: Restoration Parts Unlimited, Inc.
2175 Deerfield Rd
Lebanon OH 45036
513 934-0815

(G-8292)
TRUE STEP LLC
1105 S Us Route 42 (45036-9526)
PHONE..............................513 933-0933
Jeff Kenny, *CEO*
Jerry Monnin, *Pr*
EMP: 9 **EST:** 2022
SALES (est): 2.52MM **Privately Held**
Web: www.truestepllc.com
SIC: 3599 Machine shop, jobbing and repair

(G-8293)
TURTLECREEK TOWNSHIP
670 N State Route 123 (45036-7016)
PHONE..............................513 932-4080
Steven Flint, *Chief*
EMP: 12
Web: www.turtlecreektownship.org
SIC: 9199 3621 General government
administration; Generating apparatus and
parts, electrical
PA: Turtlecreek Township
670 N State Route 123
Lebanon OH 45036
513 932-4902

(G-8294)
UGN INC
201 Exploration Dr (45036)
PHONE..............................513 360-3500
Peter Anthony, *Pr*
EMP: 180
Web: www.ugn.com

SIC: 3714 Motor vehicle parts and
accessories
HQ: U.G.N., Inc.
2650 Wrrnville Rd Ste 300
Downers Grove IL 60515
773 437-2400

(G-8295)
VEGA AMERICAS INC (HQ)
Also Called: Ohmart Vega
3877 Mason Research Pkwy (45036-9435)
PHONE..............................513 272-0131
Don Jackson, *Contrlr*
Shawn Little, *
Brian Oeder, *
◆ **EMP:** 200 **EST:** 1950
SALES (est): 36.07MM
SALES (corp-wide): 2.42MM **Privately
Held**
Web: www.vega.com
SIC: 3823 Process control instruments
PA: Vega Grieshaber Kg
Am Hohenstein 113
Schiltach BW 77761
7836500

(G-8296)
VISTECH MFG SOLUTIONS LLC
265 S West St (45036-2152)
PHONE..............................513 933-9300
Dylan Roundtree, *Manager*
EMP: 10
SALES (corp-wide): 31.21MM **Privately
Held**
Web: www.vistechmfg.com
SIC: 3565 Packaging machinery
HQ: Vistech Manufacturing Solutions, Llc
1156 Scenic Dr Ste 120
Modesto CA 95350
209 544-9333

(G-8297)
WRAY PRECISION PRODUCTS INC
3650 Turtlecreek Rd (45036-9685)
PHONE..............................513 228-5000
Steven Dorgan, *Pr*
EMP: 7 **EST:** 1997
SQ FT: 12,000
SALES (est): 1.31MM **Privately Held**
SIC: 3599 Machine shop, jobbing and repair

Leesburg
Highland County

(G-8298)
CREATIVE FAB & WELDING LLC
Also Called: Valley Trailers
9691 Stafford Rd (45135-9464)
PHONE..............................937 780-5000
Cameron Dyck, *Pr*
Cameron Dyck, *Managing Member*
Mindy Wilson, *Sec*
EMP: 22 **EST:** 2008
SQ FT: 800
SALES (est): 4.91MM **Privately Held**
Web: www.cfwohio.com
SIC: 3441 7692 Fabricated structural metal;
Welding repair

(G-8299)
MASON COMPANY LLC
260 Depot Ln (45135-8438)
P.O. Box 365 (45135-0365)
PHONE..............................937 780-2321
Greg Taylor, *CEO*
EMP: 44 **EST:** 1892
SQ FT: 35,000
SALES (est): 8.56MM
SALES (corp-wide): 497.54MM **Privately
Held**

Web: www.masonco.com
SIC: 3496 Cages, wire
PA: Midmark Corporation
10170 Penny Ln Ste 300
Miamisburg OH 45342
937 528-7500

(G-8300)
MM OUTSOURCING LLC
355 S South St (45135-9473)
P.O. Box 29 (45135-0029)
PHONE..............................937 661-4300
EMP: 10 **EST:** 2017
SALES (est): 475.73K **Privately Held**
SIC: 3052 3061 4212 Automobile hose,
rubber; Automotive rubber goods
(mechanical); Local trucking, without
storage

Leetonia
Columbiana County

(G-8301)
DEIBEL INDUSTRIES LLC
Also Called: Deibel Manufacturing
41659 Esterly Dr (44431-9676)
PHONE..............................330 482-3351
Michael Goren, *Pr*
EMP: 20 **EST:** 2009
SALES (est): 4.07MM **Privately Held**
Web: www.ohiodrum.com
SIC: 3443 Fabricated plate work (boiler shop)

(G-8302)
HAMILTON POLYMERS COMPANY
Also Called: New Life Sustainable Solutions
446 Center St (44431-1242)
P.O. Box 4650 (98061-0650)
PHONE..............................484 245-4557
Munish Suri, *Pr*
Munish Suri, *Pr*
EMP: 10 **EST:** 2011
SALES (est): 1.35MM **Privately Held**
Web: www.hamiltonpolymers.com
SIC: 2821 Plastics materials and resins

(G-8303)
M K METALS
41659 Esterly Dr (44431-9676)
PHONE..............................330 482-3351
George Siembida, *Prin*
EMP: 7 **EST:** 2008
SALES (est): 96.7K **Privately Held**
SIC: 3441 Fabricated structural metal

(G-8304)
PENNEX ALUMINUM COMPANY LLC
1 Commerce Ave (44431-8720)
PHONE..............................330 427-6704
Thomas Hutchinson, *Brnch Mgr*
EMP: 189
SALES (corp-wide): 407.97MM **Privately
Held**
Web: www.pennexaluminum.com
SIC: 3354 Aluminum extruded products
HQ: Pennex Aluminum Company Llc
50 Community St
Wellsville PA 17365

(G-8305)
QUAKER CITY CONCRETE PDTS LLC
290 E High St (44431-9653)
PHONE..............................330 427-2239
Jeff Foust, *Managing Member*
EMP: 8 **EST:** 1961
SQ FT: 4,000
SALES (est): 2MM **Privately Held**
Web: www.quakercityseptictank.com

SIC: 3272 Septic tanks, concrete

Leipsic
Putnam County

(G-8306)
DILLER METALS INC
507 S Eastom St (45856-1300)
PHONE..............................419 943-3364
Pete Diller, *Pr*
EMP: 6 EST: 1994
SALES (est): 910.86K **Privately Held**
SIC: 3443 Metal parts

(G-8307)
MARS PETCARE US INC
3700 State Route 65 (45856-9231)
PHONE..............................419 943-4280
Herminio Reynoso, *Mgr*
EMP: 23
SALES (corp-wide): 42.84B **Privately Held**
Web: www.marspetcare.com
SIC: 2047 Dog food
HQ: Mars Petcare Us, Inc.
　　1676 Intl Dr 10th Fl
　　Mclean VA 22102
　　615 807-4626

(G-8308)
PATRICK PRODUCTS INC
150 S Werner St (45856-1363)
PHONE..............................419 943-4137
Robert S Patrick, *Pr*
Thomas M Patrick, *
Roger Selhorst, *
▲ **EMP:** 145 **EST:** 1999
SQ FT: 300,000
SALES (est): 8.91MM **Privately Held**
SIC: 3089 Plastics containers, except foam

(G-8309)
POET BIOREFINING - LEIPSIC LLC
Also Called: Poet Biorefining-Leipsic
3875 State Route 65 (45856-9231)
PHONE..............................419 943-7447
Jeff Lautt, *CEO*
Daniel Loveland, *
Mark Borer, *
EMP: 40 **EST:** 2005
SALES (est): 40.27MM **Privately Held**
Web: poetbiorefining-leipsic.aghost.net
SIC: 2869 Ethyl alcohol, ethanol
PA: Poet, Llc
　　4615 N Lewis Ave
　　Sioux Falls SD 57104

(G-8310)
PRECISION LASER & FORMING INC
6500 Road 5 (45856-9763)
PHONE..............................419 943-4350
Thomas Koenig, *CEO*
Howard Hermiller, *Treas*
EMP: 17 **EST:** 1998
SQ FT: 17,000
SALES (est): 1.97MM **Privately Held**
SIC: 3441 Fabricated structural metal

(G-8311)
PRO-TEC COATING COMPANY INC (PA)
5500 Pro Tec Pkwy (45856-8215)
PHONE..............................419 943-1100
Richard E Veitch, *Pr*
Brent Rosebrook, *
▲ **EMP:** 230 **EST:** 1991
SQ FT: 725,000
SALES (est): 80.31MM **Privately Held**
Web: www.proteccoating.com

SIC: 3479 Coating of metals and formed products

(G-8312)
PRO-TEC COATING COMPANY LLC
Also Called: Pro-tec Coating Company, Llc
4500 Protec Pkwy (45856)
PHONE..............................419 943-1100
Richard Veitch, *Pr*
EMP: 80
Web: www.proteccoating.com
SIC: 3479 Galvanizing of iron, steel, or end-formed products
PA: Pro-Tec Coating Company, Inc.
　　5500 Protec Pkwy
　　Leipsic OH 45856

(G-8313)
PRO-TEC COATING COMPANY LLC
Also Called: Pro-tec Coating Company, Llc
5000 Pro Tec Pkwy (45856-8212)
PHONE..............................419 943-1100
Richard Veitch, *Pr*
EMP: 80
Web: www.proteccoating.com
SIC: 3398 Annealing of metal
PA: Pro-Tec Coating Company, Inc.
　　5500 Protec Pkwy
　　Leipsic OH 45856

(G-8314)
RUHE SALES INC
5450 State Route 109 (45856-9438)
PHONE..............................419 943-3357
Marilyn Ruhe, *Pr*
Marilyn Ruhe, *Pr*
Robert G Ruhe, *VP*
EMP: 15 **EST:** 1963
SQ FT: 10,000
SALES (est): 199.91K **Privately Held**
Web: www.rsvpair.com
SIC: 0721 3721 4581 4512 Crop dusting services; Aircraft; Airports, flying fields, and services; Air transportation, scheduled

(G-8315)
WAGNER FARMS SAWMILL LTD LBLTY
13201 Road X (45856-9295)
PHONE..............................419 653-4126
James Wagner, *Pt*
Thomas Wagner, *Pt*
Steven Wagner, *Pt*
Michael Wagner, *Pt*
EMP: 6 **EST:** 1940
SALES (est): 1.05MM **Privately Held**
Web: www.wagnersawmill.info
SIC: 2421 0191 2426 Sawmills and planing mills, general; General farms, primarily crop ; Hardwood dimension and flooring mills

(G-8316)
WARD CONSTRUCTION CO (PA)
385 Oak St (45856-1358)
PHONE..............................419 943-2450
Arnold W Rosebrock, *Pr*
Daniel A Rosebrock, *VP*
Barry A Rosebrock, *VP*
Patricia A Newell, *Sec*
EMP: 12 **EST:** 1967
SALES (est): 4.7MM
SALES (corp-wide): 4.7MM **Privately Held**
Web: www.wardcompanies.com
SIC: 1611 4212 1442 1771 General contractor, highway and street construction; Local trucking, without storage; Sand mining ; Concrete work

Lewis Center
Delaware County

(G-8317)
ABRASIVE TECHNOLOGY LLC (PA)
8400 Green Meadows Dr N (43035-9453)
P.O. Box 545 (43035)
PHONE..............................740 548-4100
Loyal M Peterman Junior, *Pr*
Daryl L Peterman, *
▲ **EMP:** 200 **EST:** 1971
SQ FT: 100,000
SALES (est): 40.87MM
SALES (corp-wide): 40.87MM **Privately Held**
Web: www.abrasive-tech.com
SIC: 3291 Buffing or polishing wheels, abrasive or nonabrasive

(G-8318)
ABRASIVE TECHNOLOGY LAPIDARY
Also Called: Crystalite
8400 Green Meadows Dr N (43035-9453)
P.O. Box 545 (43035-0545)
PHONE..............................740 548-4855
Loyal M Peterman, *Pr*
EMP: 7 **EST:** 1986
SQ FT: 50,000
SALES (est): 328.52K **Privately Held**
Web: www.abrasive-tech.com
SIC: 3291 Abrasive products

(G-8319)
ABSOLUTE IMPRESSIONS INC
281 Enterprise Dr (43035-9418)
PHONE..............................614 840-0599
Keith Hamilton, *Pr*
Jeff Vigar, *VP*
EMP: 14 **EST:** 1997
SQ FT: 15,000
SALES (est): 901.58K **Privately Held**
Web: www.absoluteimpressionsinc.com
SIC: 2759 Screen printing

(G-8320)
AIRWAVES LLC
7750 Green Meadows Dr Ste A (43035-8381)
PHONE..............................740 548-1200
Kyle Kantner, *CEO*
Daniel Kaiser, *CFO*
◆ **EMP:** 250 **EST:** 2013
SQ FT: 50,000
SALES (est): 43.86MM
SALES (corp-wide): 252.15MM **Privately Held**
Web: www.airwavesinc.com
SIC: 2759 Screen printing
PA: Hybrid Promotions, Llc
　　10700 Valley View St
　　Cypress CA 90630
　　714 952-3866

(G-8321)
AMERIHUA INTL ENTPS INC
707 Radio Dr (43035-7134)
PHONE..............................740 549-0300
Stephen S Chen, *Ch Bd*
David W Chen, *VP Fin*
◆ **EMP:** 7 **EST:** 1984
SQ FT: 3,000
SALES (est): 811.61K **Privately Held**
Web: www.reddestiny.com
SIC: 5149 8742 3231 Specialty food items; Management consulting services; Christmas tree ornaments: made from purchased glass

(G-8322)
ANIME PALACE
8185 Green Meadows Dr N Ste M (43035-8771)
PHONE..............................408 858-1918
Jean Levin, *Prin*
▲ **EMP:** 7 **EST:** 2009
SALES (est): 216.61K **Privately Held**
Web: www.theanimepalace.com
SIC: 3944 5945 Games, toys, and children's vehicles; Toys and games

(G-8323)
ATS OHIO INC
Also Called: Automation Tooling Systems
7115 Green Meadows Dr (43035-9445)
PHONE..............................614 888-2344
Anthony Caputo, *CEO*
Carl Galloway, *
▼ **EMP:** 125 **EST:** 1974
SQ FT: 99,000
SALES (est): 2.8MM
SALES (corp-wide): 2.24B **Privately Held**
Web: www.atsautomation.com
SIC: 3563 Robots for industrial spraying, painting, etc.
PA: Ats Corporation
　　730 Fountain St N Bldg 3
　　Cambridge ON N3H 4
　　604 332-2666

(G-8324)
ATS SYSTEMS OREGON INC
425 Enterprise Dr (43035-9424)
PHONE..............................541 738-0932
Anthony Caputo, *CEO*
Maria Perrella, *
Stewart Mccvaig, *Sec*
▲ **EMP:** 14 **EST:** 1966
SQ FT: 85,000
SALES (est): 7.65MM
SALES (corp-wide): 2.24B **Privately Held**
Web: www.atsautomation.com
SIC: 3569 5084 Robots, assembly line: industrial and commercial; Industrial machinery and equipment
PA: Ats Corporation
　　730 Fountain St N Bldg 3
　　Cambridge ON N3H 4
　　604 332-2666

(G-8325)
BLACK BOX CORPORATION
Also Called: Black Box Network Services
255 Enterprise Dr (43035-9418)
P.O. Box 327 (43035-0327)
PHONE..............................614 825-7400
Dave Oddo, *Brnch Mgr*
EMP: 24
Web: www.blackbox.com
SIC: 3577 3679 3661 Computer peripheral equipment, nec; Electronic switches; Modems
HQ: Black Box Corporation
　　2701 N Dllas Pkwy Ste 510
　　Plano TX 75093
　　724 746-5500

(G-8326)
BTC INC
8842 Whitney Dr (43035-8297)
PHONE..............................740 549-2722
Sheldon Lambert, *Prin*
Jerold S Cook, *Prin*
EMP: 11 **EST:** 2010
SALES (est): 2.24MM **Privately Held**
Web: www.btcgps.com
SIC: 3812 Search and navigation equipment

(G-8327)
BTC TECHNOLOGY SERVICES INC
617 Carle Ave (43035-8294)
PHONE.............................740 549-2722
Sheldon Lambert, *CEO*
EMP: 6 EST: 2011
SALES (est): 496.98K **Privately Held**
SIC: 3812 Search and navigation equipment

(G-8328)
CARDINAL HEALTH INC
Also Called: Cardinal Hlth Nclear Prcsion H
850 Corduroy Rd Ste 100 (43035-3545)
PHONE.............................614 757-2863
EMP: 6
SALES (corp-wide): 226.83B **Publicly Held**
Web: www.cardinalhealth.com
SIC: 5122 5047 8741 3842 Pharmaceuticals;
Surgical equipment and supplies;
Management services; Surgical appliances
and supplies
PA: Cardinal Health, Inc.
7000 Cardinal Pl
Dublin OH 43017
614 757-5000

(G-8329)
COLUMBUS INTERNATIONAL CORP
8876 Whitney Dr (43035-8297)
PHONE.............................614 917-2274
Rajeev Kumar, *Brnch Mgr*
EMP: 10
SALES (corp-wide): 1.17MM **Privately Held**
Web: www.columbuscorp.com
SIC: 7372 Business oriented computer
software
PA: Columbus International Corporation
200 E Campus View Blvd
Columbus OH 43235
614 323-1086

(G-8330)
DINOL US INC
8500 Cotter St (43035-7138)
PHONE.............................740 548-1656
Joe Renzi, *CEO*
EMP: 50 EST: 2014
SALES (est): 2.29MM
SALES (corp-wide): 22.17B **Privately Held**
SIC: 2899 Corrosion preventive lubricant
HQ: Wurth Group Of North America Inc.
93 Grant St
Ramsey NJ 07446

(G-8331)
DISPATCH PRINTING COMPANY
Also Called: Columbus Dispatch
7801 N Central Dr (43035-3547)
P.O. Box 699 (43035-0699)
PHONE.............................740 548-5331
Don Patton, *Brnch Mgr*
EMP: 19
SALES (corp-wide): 48.78MM **Privately Held**
Web: www.dispatch.com
SIC: 2711 4833 Commercial printing and
newspaper publishing combined; Television
broadcasting stations
PA: The Dispatch Printing Company
62 E Broad St.
Columbus OH 43215
614 220-5833

(G-8332)
ELECTRONIC IMAGING SVCS INC
Also Called: Vestcom Retail Solutions
8273 Green Meadows Dr N Ste 400
(43035-7373)
PHONE.............................740 549-2487

EMP: 12
SALES (corp-wide): 8.76B **Publicly Held**
SIC: 8742 2759 Marketing consulting
services; Commercial printing, nec
HQ: Electronic Imaging Services, Inc.
2800 Cantrell Rd Ste 400
Little Rock AR 72202
501 663-0100

(G-8333)
EOI INC
Also Called: Medical Resources
8377 Green Meadows Dr N Ste C
(43035-9506)
PHONE.............................740 201-3300
Suzi Reichenbach, *CEO*
Randy Reichenbach, *VP*
Dianne Risch, *CFO*
▼ EMP: 16 EST: 1987
SQ FT: 18,000
SALES (est): 1.97MM **Privately Held**
Web: www.medicalresources.com
SIC: 5712 5021 5047 3841 Furniture stores;
Office and public building furniture; Medical
equipment and supplies; Diagnostic
apparatus, medical

(G-8334)
GILSON COMPANY INC (PA)
7975 N Central Dr (43035-9409)
P.O. Box 200 (43035-0200)
PHONE.............................740 548-7298
▲ EMP: 41 EST: 1939
SALES (est): 22.23MM
SALES (corp-wide): 22.23MM **Privately Held**
Web: www.globalgilson.com
SIC: 5049 3829 3821 Analytical instruments;
Measuring and controlling devices, nec;
Laboratory apparatus and furniture

(G-8335)
HEAT TREATING EQUIPMENT INC
8185 Green Meadows Dr N (43035-8770)
PHONE.............................740 549-3700
EMP: 50 EST: 2004
SALES (est): 312.49K **Privately Held**
SIC: 3398 Metal heat treating

(G-8336)
INDUSTRIAL SOLUTIONS INC
Also Called: I S I
8333 Green Meadows Dr N Ste A
(43035-0407)
PHONE.............................614 431-8118
James D Cooke, *Pr*
Susan Cooke, *VP*
EMP: 21 EST: 1987
SALES (est): 2.03MM **Privately Held**
Web: www.industrialsolutionsusa.com
SIC: 3613 Panelboards and distribution
boards, electric

(G-8337)
INPOWER LLC
8311 Green Meadows Dr N (43035-9451)
P.O. Box 435 (43035)
PHONE.............................740 548-0965
James D Sullivan, *Managing Member*
Patrick Sullivan, *OM*
EMP: 18 EST: 2000
SQ FT: 14,000
SALES (est): 9.3MM **Privately Held**
Web: www.inpowerelectronics.com
SIC: 3559 Electronic component making
machinery

(G-8338)
INSIDE OUTFITTERS INC
Also Called: S O S Shades
8333 Green Meadows Dr N Ste B
(43035-8497)

PHONE.............................614 798-3500
▲ EMP: 46
SIC: 5023 2591 2221 2211 Draperies;
Drapery hardware and window blinds and
shades; Draperies and drapery fabrics,
manmade fiber and silk; Draperies and
drapery fabrics, cotton

(G-8339)
INTERNATIONAL NOODLE COMPANY
341 Enterprise Dr (43035-9418)
PHONE.............................614 888-0665
Ridge Cheung, *Pr*
Jerry Cheung, *VP*
Ning Ho Cheung, *Sec*
▲ EMP: 15 EST: 1988
SQ FT: 12,000
SALES (est): 1.56MM **Privately Held**
SIC: 2098 Noodles (e.g. egg, plain, and
water), dry

(G-8340)
JBT MAREL CORPORATION
8270 Green Meadows Dr N (43035-9450)
PHONE.............................614 891-2732
Melanie Harter, *Brnch Mgr*
EMP: 28
Web: www.jbtc.com
SIC: 3823 Industrial process control
instruments
PA: Jbt Marel Corporation
70 W Madison St Ste 4400
Chicago IL 60602

(G-8341)
KW ACQUISITION INC
Also Called: Karol-Warner
7975 N Central Dr (43035-9409)
PHONE.............................740 548-7298
Trent Smith, *Pr*
EMP: 6 EST: 2016
SQ FT: 1,300
SALES (est): 584.81K **Privately Held**
Web: www.karolwarner.com
SIC: 3829 Physical property testing
equipment

(G-8342)
LUMENOMICS INC
Also Called: Inside Outfitters
8333 Green Meadows Dr N Ste B
(43035-8496)
PHONE.............................614 798-3500
Cailee 3wlhari, *VP Opers*
EMP: 46
Web: www.insideoutfitters.com
SIC: 5023 2591 2221 2211 Draperies;
Drapery hardware and window blinds and
shades; Draperies and drapery fabrics,
manmade fiber and silk; Draperies and
drapery fabrics, cotton
PA: Lumenomics, Inc.
7800 7th Ave S
Seattle WA 98108

(G-8343)
MICROCOM CORPORATION
855 Corduroy Rd (43035-1550)
PHONE.............................740 548-6262
Steven Wolfe, *CEO*
James R Larson, *
Steven Wolfe, *CFO*
David Dezse, *
▲ EMP: 24 EST: 1982
SALES (est): 4.88MM **Privately Held**
Web: www.microcomcorp.com
SIC: 3577 5111 5112 3953 Printers, computer
; Printing and writing paper; Inked ribbons;
Marking devices

(G-8344)
MULTI-PLASTICS INC (PA)
7770 N Central Dr (43035-9404)
PHONE.............................740 548-4894
John R Parsio, *Pr*
John Parsio Junior, *Ex VP*
Wesley Hall, *
Steven Parsio, *
Michael T Hickey, *
◆ EMP: 55 EST: 1979
SQ FT: 32,000
SALES (est): 107.83MM
SALES (corp-wide): 107.83MM **Privately Held**
Web: www.multi-plastics.com
SIC: 2821 Plastics materials and resins

(G-8345)
NAT2 INC (PA)
8754 Cotter St (43035-7104)
PHONE.............................614 270-2507
Shirley Bartee, *Dir*
EMP: 7 EST: 2017
SALES (est): 841.68K
SALES (corp-wide): 841.68K **Privately Held**
SIC: 2099 Food preparations, nec

(G-8346)
NEXTECH MATERIALS LTD
Also Called: Nexceris
404 Enterprise Dr (43035-9423)
PHONE.............................614 842-6606
EMP: 70 EST: 1994
SALES (est): 11.59MM **Privately Held**
Web: www.nexceris.com
SIC: 3823 3825 Industrial process
measurement equipment; Energy
measuring equipment, electrical

(G-8347)
OHIO MULCH SUPPLY INC
Also Called: Ohio Mulch
6673 Columbus Pike (43035-9010)
PHONE.............................740 548-6242
James Weber, *Pr*
EMP: 6
SALES (corp-wide): 47.86MM **Privately Held**
Web: www.ohiomulch.com
SIC: 2499 5261 Mulch or sawdust products,
wood; Garden supplies and tools, nec
PA: Ohio Mulch Supply, Inc.
1600 Universal Rd
Columbus OH 43207
614 445-4455

(G-8348)
PELTON ENVIRONMENTAL PDTS INC
8638 Cotter St (43035-7136)
PHONE.............................440 838-1221
Edward Pelton, *VP*
EMP: 8 EST: 1992
SALES (est): 4.51MM **Privately Held**
Web: www.peltonenv.com
SIC: 5074 3589 Water purification equipment
; Sewage and water treatment equipment

(G-8349)
QUINTUS TECHNOLOGIES LLC
8270 Green Meadows Dr N (43035-9450)
PHONE.............................614 891-2732
Ed Williams, *Managing Member*
EMP: 50 EST: 2014
SALES (est): 8.66MM **Privately Held**
Web: www.quintustechnologies.com
SIC: 7699 7389 3443 Industrial equipment
services; Industrial and commercial
equipment inspection service; Industrial
vessels, tanks, and containers

GEOGRAPHIC

(G-8350)
QXSOFT LLC
759 Carle Ave (43035-8293)
PHONE...................740 777-9609
Jian Shi, *Pr*
EMP: 6 **EST:** 2020
SALES (est): 2.02MM **Privately Held**
Web: www.qxcmm.com
SIC: 7372 7371 Publisher's computer
   software; Software programming
   applications

(G-8351)
RETAIL MANAGEMENT PRODUCTS
LTD
Also Called: Rxscan
8851 Whitney Dr (43035-7107)
PHONE...................740 548-1725
Max J Peoples, *Pt*
Bill Peoples, *Pt*
EMP: 8 **EST:** 1995
SALES (est): 2.05MM **Privately Held**
Web: www.rxscan.com
SIC: 7372 Business oriented computer
   software

(G-8352)
RUBBERTEC INDUSTRIAL PDTS CO
Elledge Gasket
7580 Commerce Ct (43035-9702)
PHONE...................740 657-3345
Mark Knore, *Mgr*
EMP: 8
SIC: 3053 Gaskets; packing and sealing
   devices
PA: Rubbertec Industrial Products
   Company
   7580 Commerce Ct
   Lewis Center OH 43035

(G-8353)
SARCOM INC
8337a Green Meadows Dr N (43035-9451)
PHONE...................614 854-1300
▲ **EMP:** 960
SIC: 5045 7373 7374 7372 Computers,
   peripherals, and software; Computer
   integrated systems design; Data processing
   and preparation; Prepackaged software

(G-8354)
SOLUT INC (PA)
Also Called: Solut
7787 Graphics Way (43035-8000)
PHONE...................740 549-3336
Bill Shepard, *CEO*
Scott Rechel, *Managing Member*
Erik O Neil, *VP*
Jason Kauffman, *VP*
▼ **EMP:** 47 **EST:** 2005
SALES (est): 24.3MM **Privately Held**
Web: www.gosolut.com
SIC: 2621 2656 Packaging paper; Sanitary
   food containers

(G-8355)
TESA INC
544 Enterprise Dr Ste A (43035-9704)
PHONE...................614 847-8200
John Truitt, *Pr*
EMP: 7 **EST:** 1973
SALES (est): 2.91MM **Privately Held**
Web: www.tesa-inc.com
SIC: 3612 5063 Distribution transformers,
   electric; Electrical apparatus and equipment

(G-8356)
TRACEWELL SYSTEMS INC (PA)
567 Enterprise Dr (43035-9431)
PHONE...................614 846-6175

Larry Tracewell, *Pr*
Betty Tracewell, *
Matt Tracewell, *
EMP: 57 **EST:** 1973
SQ FT: 10,000
SALES (est): 23.74MM
SALES (corp-wide): 23.74MM **Privately**
Held
Web: www.tracewell.com
SIC: 3572 3571 3728 Computer storage
   devices; Electronic computers; Aircraft
   parts and equipment, nec

(G-8357)
WIKA SENSOR TECHNLGY LP
6957 Green Meadows Dr (43035-3570)
PHONE...................614 430-0683
Bruce Yohr, *Pt*
EMP: 50 **EST:** 2008
SALES (est): 3.71MM
SALES (corp-wide): 700.85MM **Privately**
Held
Web: www.wika.com
SIC: 3823 Process control instruments
HQ: Wika Holding, Lp
   1000 Wiegand Blvd
   Lawrenceville GA 30043
   888 945-2872

Lewisburg
Preble County

(G-8358)
ANDERSON PALLET & PACKG INC
Also Called: Anderson Pallet Service
210 Western Ave (45338-9584)
P.O. Box 669 (45338-0669)
PHONE...................937 962-2614
Ross Anderson, *Pr*
Grace Anderson, *Treas*
Marc Anderson, *VP*
EMP: 6 **EST:** 1983
SQ FT: 10,000
SALES (est): 442.54K **Privately Held**
SIC: 2448 Pallets, wood

(G-8359)
D M TOOL & PLASTICS INC (PA)
4140 Us Route 40 E (45338-9506)
P.O. Box 309 (45309-0309)
PHONE...................937 962-4140
Dennis Meyer, *Pr*
Bill Meyer, *VP*
Pat Meyer, *Treas*
EMP: 18 **EST:** 1977
SQ FT: 35,000
SALES (est): 9.47MM
SALES (corp-wide): 9.47MM **Privately**
Held
SIC: 3089 3599 Injection molding of plastics;
   Machine shop, jobbing and repair

(G-8360)
LEWISBURG CONTAINER COMPANY
(DH)
275 W Clay St (45338-8107)
P.O. Box 39 (45338-0039)
PHONE...................937 962-2681
Anthony Pratt, *Pr*
Davis Kyles, *
David Wiser, *
▲ **EMP:** 235 **EST:** 1955
SQ FT: 384,000
SALES (est): 25.21MM **Privately Held**
Web: www.prattindustries.com
SIC: 2653 Boxes, corrugated: made from
   purchased materials
HQ: Pratt Properties, Inc.
   1800 Sarasot Bus Pkwy Ne
   Conyers GA 30013
   770 918-5678

(G-8361)
PRATT INDUSTRIES INC
301 W Clay St (45338-8132)
P.O. Box 220 (45338-0220)
PHONE...................937 583-4990
EMP: 10
Web: www.prattindustries.com
SIC: 2621 2653 Paper mills; Corrugated and
   solid fiber boxes
PA: Pratt Industries, Inc.
   4004 Smmit Blvd Ne Ste 10
   Atlanta GA 30319

(G-8362)
PROVIMI NORTH AMERICA INC (HQ)
Also Called: Cargill Premix and Nutrition
6571 State Route 503 N (45338-6713)
PHONE...................937 770-2400
▲ **EMP:** 253 **EST:** 1973
SALES (est): 95.97MM
SALES (corp-wide): 159.59B **Privately**
Held
Web: www.nanutrition.com
SIC: 5191 2048 Animal feeds; Prepared
   feeds, nec
PA: Cargill, Incorporated
   15407 Mcginty Rd W
   Wayzata MN 55391
   800 227-4455

(G-8363)
PROVIMI NORTH AMERICA INC
6531 State Route 503 N (45338-6713)
PHONE...................937 770-2400
Dwight Armstrong, *Pr*
EMP: 41
SALES (corp-wide): 159.59B **Privately**
Held
Web: www.provimius.com
SIC: 2048 Prepared feeds, nec
HQ: Provimi North America, Inc.
   6571 State Route 503
   Lewisburg OH 45338
   937 770-2400

(G-8364)
PROVIMI NORTH AMERICA INC
6571 State Route 503 N (45338-6713)
PHONE...................937 770-2400
EMP: 17
SALES (corp-wide): 159.59B **Privately**
Held
Web: www.provimius.com
SIC: 2048 Prepared feeds, nec
HQ: Provimi North America, Inc.
   6571 State Route 503
   Lewisburg OH 45338
   937 770-2400

Lewistown
Logan County

(G-8365)
INDUSTRIAL FARM TANK INC
10676 Township Road 80 (43333-9759)
PHONE...................937 843-2972
Pyllis Yazel, *CEO*
EMP: 25 **EST:** 1975
SQ FT: 10,000
SALES (est): 284.38K **Privately Held**
Web: www.industrialfarmtankinc.com
SIC: 3089 3443 Molding primary plastics;
   Farm storage tanks, metal plate

Lewisville
Monroe County

(G-8366)
G-R CONTRACTING INC
35479 State Route 78 (43754-7512)
PHONE...................740 567-3202
Gary A Rubel, *Pr*
Nancy Rubel, *Sec*
EMP: 10 **EST:** 1977
SALES (est): 2.47MM **Privately Held**
SIC: 1629 1311 1611 Land reclamation;
   Crude petroleum and natural gas production
   ; Highway and street construction

Lexington
Richland County

(G-8367)
CHARTER NEXT GENERATION INC
165 Industrial Dr (44904-1338)
P.O. Box 809132 (60680-9132)
PHONE...................419 884-8150
Apurva Shah, *Prin*
EMP: 128
SALES (corp-wide): 1.5B **Privately Held**
Web: www.cnginc.com
SIC: 2671 Plastic film, coated or laminated
   for packaging
PA: Charter Next Generation, Inc.
   300 N La Slle Dr Ste 1575
   Chicago IL 60654
   608 868-5757

(G-8368)
CHARTER NEXT GENERATION INC
Also Called: CNG
1450 State Route 97 (44904-9321)
PHONE...................419 884-8150
EMP: 128
SALES (corp-wide): 1.5B **Privately Held**
Web: www.cnginc.com
SIC: 2671 Plastic film, coated or laminated
   for packaging
PA: Charter Next Generation, Inc.
   300 N La Slle Dr Ste 1575
   Chicago IL 60654
   608 868-5757

(G-8369)
CHARTER NEXT GENERATION INC
235 Industrial Dr (44904-1347)
PHONE...................419 884-8150
EMP: 128
SALES (corp-wide): 1.5B **Privately Held**
Web: www.cnginc.com
SIC: 2671 Plastic film, coated or laminated
   for packaging
PA: Charter Next Generation, Inc.
   300 N La Slle Dr Ste 1575
   Chicago IL 60654
   608 868-5757

(G-8370)
CHARTER NEXT GENERATION INC
145 Frecka Dr (44904)
PHONE...................419 884-8150
EMP: 128
SALES (corp-wide): 1.5B **Privately Held**
Web: www.cnginc.com
SIC: 2671 Plastic film, coated or laminated
   for packaging
PA: Charter Next Generation, Inc.
   300 N La Slle Dr Ste 1575
   Chicago IL 60654
   608 868-5757

(G-8371)
CHARTER NEXT GENERATION INC
215 Industrial Dr (44904-1347)
PHONE..............................419 884-8150
David Frecka, *Mgr*
EMP: 128
SALES (corp-wide): 1.5B **Privately Held**
Web: www.cnginc.com
SIC: 2671 Plastic film, coated or laminated
for packaging
PA: Charter Next Generation, Inc.
300 N La Slle Dr Ste 1575
Chicago IL 60654
608 868-5757

(G-8372)
CONTACT INDUSTRIES INC
25 Industrial Dr (44904-1372)
P.O. Box 3086 (44904-0086)
PHONE..............................419 884-9788
James Arnholt, *Pr*
E R Mc Intyre, *Marketing**
EMP: 36 **EST:** 1988
SQ FT: 12,000
SALES (est): 4.73MM **Privately Held**
Web: www.contactindustriesinc.com
SIC: 3625 3825 3612 Switches, electronic
applications; Instruments to measure
electricity; Transformers, except electric

(G-8373)
ENGINEERED FILMS DIVISION INC
230 Industrial Dr (44904-1346)
PHONE..............................419 884-8150
▲ **EMP:** 100
SIC: 2673 2671 Plastic and pliofilm bags;
Plastic film, coated or laminated for
packaging

(G-8374)
STONERIDGE INC
Also Called: Hi-Stat A Stoneridge Co
345 S Mill St (44904-9573)
PHONE..............................419 884-1219
Tom Morell, *Manager*
EMP: 700
Web: www.stoneridge.com
SIC: 3714 Motor vehicle electrical equipment
PA: Stoneridge, Inc.
39675 Mckenzie Dr Ste 400
Novi MI 48377

(G-8375)
SUPPORT SVC LLC
Also Called: Support Service
25 Walnut St Ste 4 (44904-1260)
PHONE..............................419 617-0660
EMP: 7 **EST:** 2010
SQ FT: 450,000
SALES (est): 185.87K **Privately Held**
Web: www.supportsvc.com
SIC: 5531 7539 7536 8711 Auto and home
supply stores; Alternators and generators,
rebuilding and repair; Automotive glass
replacement shops; Engineering services

Liberty Center
Henry County

(G-8376)
SMITHCO DISTRIBUTING
T480 County Road 7 (43532-9721)
PHONE..............................419 367-7685
Tyler Smith, *Pr*
Tyler Smith, *Owner*
EMP: 25 **EST:** 2011
SALES (est): 844.32K **Privately Held**
Web: www.smithcodistributing.com

SIC: 8742 5099 5065 5145 Management
consulting services; Sunglasses; Mobile
telephone equipment; Candy

Liberty Township
Butler County

(G-8377)
HAMILTON JOURNAL NEWS INC
7320 Yankee Rd (45044-9168)
PHONE..............................513 863-8200
Anne Hoffman, *Pr*
EMP: 7 **EST:** 1800
SALES (est): 245.02K **Privately Held**
Web: www.journal-news.com
SIC: 2711 Commercial printing and
newspaper publishing combined

(G-8378)
QUEST SOLUTIONS GROUP LLC
8046 Green Lake Dr (45044-9474)
PHONE..............................513 703-4520
Larry Thomas, *Managing Member*
P Diana Thomas, *Managing Member*
EMP: 6 **EST:** 2008
SALES (est): 177.07K **Privately Held**
Web: www.questsolutionsgroup.com
SIC: 2891 2621 Adhesives and sealants;
Waterproof paper

(G-8379)
VARIAN MEDICAL SYSTEMS INC
7777 Yankee Rd (45044-3500)
PHONE..............................888 827-4265
Dow Wilson, *CEO*
EMP: 7
SALES (corp-wide): 84.78B **Privately Held**
Web: www.varian.com
SIC: 3845 7372 Electromedical equipment;
Prepackaged software
HQ: Varian Medical Systems, Inc.
3100 Hansen Way
Palo Alto CA 94304
650 493-4000

(G-8380)
ZELAYA STONEWORKS LLC
7590 Wyandot Ln Ste 1 (45044-9539)
PHONE..............................513 777-8030
EMP: 15 **EST:** 2006
SQ FT: 4,000
SALES (est): 958.52K **Privately Held**
Web: www.zelayastoneworks.com
SIC: 3281 Granite, cut and shaped

Liberty Twp
Butler County

(G-8381)
COFFING CORPORATION (PA)
5336 Lesourdsville West Chester Rd
(45011-9740)
PHONE..............................513 919-2813
Chris Coffing, *Pr*
EMP: 24 **EST:** 1995
SQ FT: 5,000
SALES (est): 456.26K
SALES (corp-wide): 456.26K **Privately
Held**
Web: www.coffingco.com
SIC: 7372 7389 Prepackaged software;
Business services, nec

(G-8382)
DM2018 LLC
Also Called: Dalaco
4805 Hamilton Middletown Rd Ste A
(45011-2686)

PHONE..............................513 893-5483
EMP: 7 **EST:** 1986
SQ FT: 120,000
SALES (est): 953.45K **Privately Held**
SIC: 3272 Concrete products, nec

(G-8383)
FEATHER LITE INNOVATIONS INC
Also Called: Tuf-N-Lite
4805 Hamilton Middletown Rd
(45011-2686)
PHONE..............................513 893-5483
Randy Ledford, *Genl Mgr*
EMP: 11
Web: s532643390.onlinehome.us
SIC: 3444 Concrete forms, sheet metal
PA: Feather Lite Innovations, Inc.
650 Pleasant Valley Dr
Springboro OH 45066

(G-8384)
FIXTURE DIMENSIONS INC
5660 Liberty Woods Dr (45011-9783)
PHONE..............................513 360-7512
Linda F Schaffeld, *Pr*
▼ **EMP:** 30 **EST:** 1992
SALES (est): 1.1MM **Privately Held**
Web: www.fixturedimensions.com
SIC: 2541 2431 Store and office display
cases and fixtures; Millwork

Lima
Allen County

(G-8385)
AIRWAVE COMMUNICATIONS CONS
Also Called: Cell 4less
1209 Allentown Rd (45805-2432)
P.O. Box 5216 (45802-5216)
PHONE..............................419 331-1526
Dominic Sementelli, *Pr*
Jeff Lunguy, *Ex VP*
EMP: 8 **EST:** 1985
SQ FT: 2,700
SALES (est): 219.07K **Privately Held**
SIC: 4813 4812 3577 7371 Local and long
distance telephone communications; Radio
pager (beeper) communication services;
Computer peripheral equipment, nec;
Computer software systems analysis and
design, custom

(G-8386)
ALLEN COUNTY FABRICATION INC
Also Called: A C F
999 Industry Ave (45804-4171)
PHONE..............................419 227-7447
Kevin E Hall, *Pr*
Ronald M Kennedy, *Pr*
Patricia Kennedy, *Treas*
EMP: 20 **EST:** 1992
SQ FT: 16,800
SALES (est): 4.99MM **Privately Held**
Web: www.allencountyohio.com
SIC: 3444 Sheet metal specialties, not
stamped

(G-8387)
AMERICAN BOTTLING COMPANY
Also Called: 7 Up Bottling Co
2350 Central Point Pkwy (45804-3806)
PHONE..............................419 229-7777
Mike Hoenie, *Mgr*
EMP: 53
Web: www.keurigdrpepper.com
SIC: 2086 Soft drinks: packaged in cans,
bottles, etc.
HQ: The American Bottling Company
6425 Hall Of Fame Ln

Frisco TX 75034

(G-8388)
AMERICAN TRIM LLC (HQ)
1005 W Grand Ave (45801-3429)
PHONE..............................419 228-1145
Jeffrey A Hawk, *CEO*
Rick Pfeifer, *
Leo J Hawk, *
Dana Morgan, *
◆ **EMP:** 50 **EST:** 1948
SQ FT: 15,000
SALES (est): 96.84MM
SALES (corp-wide): 445.1MM **Privately
Held**
Web: www.amtrim.com
SIC: 3469 Porcelain enameled products and
utensils
PA: Superior Metal Products, Inc.
1005 W Grand Ave
Lima OH 45801
419 228-1145

(G-8389)
BEST ONE TIRE & SVC LIMA INC (PA)
Also Called: Bandag
701 E Hanthorn Rd (45804-3823)
PHONE..............................419 229-2380
David Mitchell, *Pr*
Sheila Mitchell, *
▲ **EMP:** 45 **EST:** 1933
SQ FT: 100,000
SALES (est): 4.46MM
SALES (corp-wide): 4.46MM **Privately
Held**
Web: www.bestonetire.com
SIC: 7534 5531 5014 Tire recapping;
Automotive tires; Truck tires and tubes

(G-8390)
BETTER BRAKE PARTS INC
915 Shawnee Rd (45805-3439)
PHONE..............................419 227-0685
John Mikesell, *Pr*
Edwin F Mikesell, *
James Borgert, *
Ronald Kimmel, *
Mark Misell, *
◆ **EMP:** 40 **EST:** 1981
SALES (est): 2.06MM **Privately Held**
Web: www.betterbrake.com
SIC: 3714 Motor vehicle parts and
accessories

(G-8391)
BRANDON SCREEN PRINTING
1755 Shawnee Rd (45805-3857)
PHONE..............................419 229-9837
Robert L Liddle, *Owner*
EMP: 10 **EST:** 1972
SALES (est): 216.35K **Privately Held**
Web: www.brandonscreenprinting.net
SIC: 2396 3993 2752 Screen printing on
fabric articles; Signs and advertising
specialties; Commercial printing,
lithographic

(G-8392)
BRINKMAN LLC
Also Called: American Paint Recyclers
1524 Adak Ave (45805-3905)
PHONE..............................419 204-5934
Jeremy Brinkman, *Managing Member*
EMP: 10 **EST:** 2007
SALES (est): 208.57K **Privately Held**
SIC: 2851 5812 7359 Paints and paint
additives; Pizzeria, independent;
Equipment rental and leasing, nec

(G-8393)
BRP MANUFACTURING COMPANY
Also Called: Buckeye Rubber Products
637 N Jackson St (45801-4125)
PHONE.....................800 858-0482
Kendall House, *Pr*
Steve Pendergast, *
◆ **EMP:** 44 **EST:** 1997
SQ FT: 190,000
SALES (est): 5.09MM **Privately Held**
Web: www.brpmfg.com
SIC: 3069 3061 2822 Sheeting, rubber or
rubberized fabric; Mechanical rubber goods
; Synthetic rubber

(G-8394)
CAMERON PACKAGING INC
250 E Hanthorn Rd (45804-2344)
PHONE.....................419 222-9404
Michael Cameron, *CEO*
Bridget Cribben, *Treas*
Grant Morgenstern, *Pr*
Diane Cameron, *Sec*
▲ **EMP:** 9 **EST:** 1969
SQ FT: 56,000
SALES (est): 1.03MM **Privately Held**
Web: www.cameronpackaging.com
SIC: 2653 Boxes, corrugated: made from
purchased materials

(G-8395)
COCA-COLA CONSOLIDATED INC
Also Called: Coca-Cola
201 N Shore Dr (45801-4822)
P.O. Box 268 (45839-0268)
PHONE.....................419 422-3743
John Iafolla, *Brnch Mgr*
EMP: 9
SALES (corp-wide): 6.9B **Publicly Held**
Web: www.cokeconsolidated.com
SIC: 2086 Bottled and canned soft drinks
PA: Coca-Cola Consolidated, Inc.
4100 Coca-Cola Plz
Charlotte NC 28211
980 392-8298

(G-8396)
**CONSOLIDATED BOTTLING
COMPANY**
Also Called: Pepsi Cola Bottling Co
1750 Greely Chapel Rd (45804-4122)
PHONE.....................419 227-3541
Louis A Cira, *General Vice President*
Kenneth Frankl, *
C A Carrature, *
EMP: 160 **EST:** 1901
SQ FT: 130,000
SALES (est): 1.12MM **Privately Held**
Web: www.pepsico.com
SIC: 2086 Carbonated soft drinks, bottled
and canned

(G-8397)
CROWN GROUP CO (HQ)
Also Called: PPG Coating Services
1340 Neubrecht Rd (45801-3120)
PHONE.....................586 575-9800
Wayne Oliver, *CFO*
Jim Keena, *COO*
EMP: 26 **EST:** 2013
SALES (est): 158.55MM
SALES (corp-wide): 18.25B **Publicly Held**
Web: www.thecrowngrp.com
SIC: 3479 Coating of metals and formed
products
PA: Ppg Industries, Inc.
1 Ppg Pl
Pittsburgh PA 15272
412 434-3131

(G-8398)
CSS PUBLISHING COMPANY
5450 N Dixie Hwy (45807-9559)
P.O. Box 4503 (45802-4503)
PHONE.....................419 227-1818
Wesley T Runk, *Pr*
Elen Shockey, *
David Runk, *
Tim Runk, *VP Mktg*
EMP: 10 **EST:** 1970
SQ FT: 50,000
SALES (est): 659.42K **Privately Held**
Web: store.csspub.com
SIC: 2731 5192 Books, publishing only;
Books

(G-8399)
CUSTOM BLAST & COAT INC
Also Called: Custom Blast
1511 S Dixie Hwy (45804-1844)
PHONE.....................419 225-6024
G J Gossard, *Pr*
Bruce Dukeman, *Sec*
EMP: 8 **EST:** 2007
SALES (est): 241.98K **Privately Held**
Web: www.customblastandcoat.com
SIC: 3312 Blast furnace and related products

(G-8400)
DESTER CORPORATION (DH)
1200 E Kibby St Bldg 32 (45804-3163)
PHONE.....................419 362-8020
Stef Vandeperre, *Pr*
◆ **EMP:** 10 **EST:** 2006
SQ FT: 157,000
SALES (est): 20.03MM **Privately Held**
Web: www.desterjobs.com
SIC: 3089 Plastics containers, except foam
HQ: Gategroup Holding Ag
Sagereistrasse 20
Glattbrugg ZH 8152

(G-8401)
DESTER CORPORATION
1200 E Kibby St Bldg 6 (45804-3163)
PHONE.....................419 362-8020
Patricia Hopkins, *Pr*
EMP: 12 **EST:** 2017
SALES (est): 661.56K **Privately Held**
Web: www.gategroup.com
SIC: 3089 Plastics containers, except foam

(G-8402)
DR PEPPER SNAPPLE GROUP
Also Called: Dr Pepper
2480 Saint Johns Rd (45804-4003)
PHONE.....................419 223-0072
Larry Young, *Pr*
EMP: 8 **EST:** 2015
SALES (est): 166.36K **Privately Held**
Web: www.keurigdrpepper.com
SIC: 2086 Soft drinks: packaged in cans,
bottles, etc.

(G-8403)
DR PEPPER/SEVEN UP INC
2350 Central Point Pkwy (45804-3806)
PHONE.....................419 229-7777
Marvin Lehman, *Prin*
EMP: 14
Web: www.drpepper.com
SIC: 2086 Soft drinks: packaged in cans,
bottles, etc.
HQ: Dr Pepper/Seven Up, Inc.
6425 Hall Of Fame Ln
Frisco TX 75034
800 527-7096

(G-8404)
DUBOSE STRAPPING INC
1221 Stewart Rd (45801-3223)
P.O. Box 819 (28329-0819)
PHONE.....................419 221-0626
EMP: 28
Web: www.dubosestrapping.com
SIC: 3499 2671 Strapping, metal; Paper;
coated and laminated packaging
PA: Dubose Strapping, Inc.
906 Industrial Dr
Clinton NC 28328

(G-8405)
**ENERGY & CTRL INTEGRATORS INC
(PA)**
1130 E Albert St (45804-1614)
PHONE.....................419 222-0025
Richard M Lyons, *Pr*
Randy Alvis, *VP*
Michael Lawrence, *Sec*
EMP: 6 **EST:** 1994
SQ FT: 5,400
SALES (est): 945.48K **Privately Held**
Web: www.ecilighting.ie
SIC: 3822 Temperature controls, automatic

(G-8406)
ERNST ENTERPRISES INC
Also Called: Ernst Ready Mix Division
377 S Central Ave (45804-1301)
PHONE.....................419 222-2015
Edward Bryam, *Mgr*
EMP: 13
SALES (corp-wide): 240.08MM **Privately
Held**
Web: www.ernstconcrete.com
SIC: 5211 3275 Concrete and cinder block;
Gypsum products
PA: Ernst Enterprises, Inc.
993 Falls Creek Dr
Vandalia OH 45377
937 233-5555

(G-8407)
EZ CONCRETE SUPPLY LLC (DH)
Also Called: Aramsco Inc Plsboro NJ Rdnor P
600 S Roberts Ave (45804-3143)
PHONE.....................844 393-7699
Corey Henson, *Managing Member*
EMP: 6 **EST:** 2015
SALES (est): 1.1MM **Privately Held**
Web: www.ez-concretesupply.com
SIC: 5961 2851 3273 Tools and hardware,
mail order; Epoxy coatings; Ready-mixed
concrete
HQ: Aramsco, Inc.
Five Rdnor Corp Ctr 100 M
Radnor PA 19087
800 767-6933

(G-8408)
FORD MOTOR COMPANY
Also Called: Ford
1155 Bible Rd (45801-3193)
PHONE.....................419 226-7000
Paul A Edwards, *Brnch Mgr*
EMP: 1949
SQ FT: 2,424,360
SALES (corp-wide): 184.99B **Publicly
Held**
Web: www.ford.com
SIC: 5511 3519 Automobiles, new and used;
Internal combustion engines, nec
PA: Ford Motor Company
1 American Rd
Dearborn MI 48126
313 322-3000

(G-8409)
GASDORF TOOL AND MCH CO INC
445 N Mcdonel St (45801-4266)
PHONE.....................419 227-0103
Richard R Rapp, *Pr*
Lynn Krohn, *
EMP: 27 **EST:** 1953
SQ FT: 20,000
SALES (est): 7.69MM **Privately Held**
Web: www.gasdorf.com
SIC: 3599 3544 Custom machinery; Special
dies and tools

(G-8410)
**GENERAL DYNMICS LAND
SYSTEMS I**
Also Called: General Dynmics Lima Army
Tank
1161 Buckeye Rd (45804-1815)
PHONE.....................419 221-7000
Hank Kennedy, *Mgr*
EMP: 400
SALES (corp-wide): 47.72B **Publicly Held**
Web: www.gdls.com
SIC: 3795 Tanks, military, including factory
rebuilding
HQ: General Dynamics Land Systems Inc.
38500 Mound Rd
Sterling Heights MI 48310
586 825-4000

(G-8411)
**GROSS & SONS CUSTOM
MILLWORK**
1219 Grant St (45801-3735)
PHONE.....................419 227-0214
James H Gross, *Pr*
Debra Gross, *Treas*
EMP: 6 **EST:** 1983
SQ FT: 8,000
SALES (est): 169.31K **Privately Held**
Web: www.gross-sons.com
SIC: 2431 2541 2434 Millwork; Counter and
sink tops; Wood kitchen cabinets

(G-8412)
GUARDIAN LIMA LLC
2485 Houx Pkwy (45804-3901)
PHONE.....................567 940-9500
Don Dales, *CEO*
EMP: 34 **EST:** 2010
SALES (est): 24.31MM
SALES (corp-wide): 33.39MM **Privately
Held**
Web: www.guardianlima.com
SIC: 2869 Ethyl alcohol, ethanol
PA: Guardian Energy, Llc
4745 380th Ave
Janesville MN 56048
507 234-5000

(G-8413)
**HEAT-TREATING TECHNOLOGIES
INC**
1799 E 4th St (45804-2713)
PHONE.....................419 224-8324
Chester L Walthall, *CEO*
Richard W Deibel, *Pr*
Judith Walthall, *Sec*
EMP: 23 **EST:** 1993
SQ FT: 33,000
SALES (est): 5.37MM **Privately Held**
Web: www.httlima.com
SIC: 3398 Metal heat treating

(G-8414)
HEMMELRATH COATINGS INC
Also Called: Hemmelrath
1340 Neubrecht Rd (45801-3120)
▲ **EMP:** 10 **EST:** 2006

SALES (est): 835.45K
SALES (corp-wide): 18.25B **Publicly Held**
Web: www.ppgcoatingsservices.com
SIC: 3479 Coating of metals and formed
products
HQ: Ppg Hemmelrath Lackfabrik Gmbh
Jakob-Hemmelrath-Str. 1
Klingenberg A. Main BY 63911
93721360

(G-8415)
HIGH TECH METAL PRODUCTS LLC
1900 Garland Ave (45804-3922)
PHONE..............................419 227-9414
Jerry Neuman, *Owner*
EMP: 8 EST: 1992
SALES (est): 997.84K **Privately Held**
SIC: 3599 Machine shop, jobbing and repair

(G-8416)
HUSKY LIMA REFINERY
1150 S Metcalf St (45804-1145)
PHONE..............................419 226-2300
EMP: 44 EST: 2016
SALES (est): 11.41MM **Privately Held**
SIC: 2911 Oils, fuel

(G-8417)
HUSKY MARKETING AND SUPPLY CO
1150 S Metcalf St (45804-1145)
PHONE..............................419 993-8000
EMP: 39
SALES (corp-wide): 40.39B **Privately Held**
Web: hmsc.huskyenergy.com
SIC: 1321 Natural gas liquids
HQ: Husky Marketing And Supply Company
5550 Blazer Pkwy Ste 200
Dublin OH 43017

(G-8418)
IHEARTCOMMUNICATIONS INC
Also Called: Clear Channel
667 W Market St (45801-4603)
PHONE..............................419 223-2060
Kim Field, *Genl Mgr*
EMP: 6
Web: www.iheartmedia.com
SIC: 4832 2711 Radio broadcasting stations;
Newspapers
HQ: Iheartcommunications, Inc.
20880 Stone Oak Pkwy
San Antonio TX 78258
210 822-2828

(G-8419)
INEOS LLC (PA)
1900 Fort Amanda Rd (45804-1827)
P.O. Box 628 (45802-0628)
PHONE..............................419 226-1200
Dennis Seith, *Pr*
David Brackett, *
Gary Wallace, *
Mike Nagle, *
Tim Avery, *
▲ EMP: 76 EST: 2002
SALES (est): 41.83MM **Privately Held**
Web: www.ineos.com
SIC: 2821 Plastics materials and resins

(G-8420)
INEOS NITRILES USA LLC (DH)
1900 Fort Amanda Rd (45804-1827)
PHONE..............................281 535-6600
▲ EMP: 10 EST: 2015
SALES (est): 60MM
SALES (corp-wide): 1.38MM **Privately Held**
Web: www.ineos.com

SIC: 2821 Plastics materials and resins
HQ: Ineos Americas Llc
2600 S Shore Blvd Ste 400
League City TX 77573
281 535-4266

(G-8421)
ISP LIMA LLC
12220 S Metcalf St (45804)
PHONE..............................419 998-8700
▲ EMP: 36 EST: 2005
SALES (est): 11.61MM
SALES (corp-wide): 2.11B **Publicly Held**
SIC: 2911 Petroleum refining
HQ: Isp Chemicals Llc
455 N Main St
Calvert City KY 42029
270 395-4165

(G-8422)
JM HAMILTON GROUP INC
Also Called: Metal Coating Company
1700 Elida Rd (45805-1511)
PHONE..............................419 229-4010
Howell D Glover Junior, *Pr*
Richard W Hussey, *VP*
James I Hunt, *Prin*
John H Romey, *Prin*
Marie L Glover, *Prin*
EMP: 17 EST: 1939
SQ FT: 25,000
SALES (est): 3.09MM **Privately Held**
Web: www.metalcoatingcompany.com
SIC: 3479 3559 3471 Coating of metals and
formed products; Glass making machinery:
blowing, molding, forming, etc.; Plating and
polishing

(G-8423)
KETTLE CREATIONS LLC
651 Commerce Pkwy (45804-4033)
PHONE..............................567 940-9401
EMP: 40
SIC: 2034 Potato products, dried and
dehydrated

(G-8424)
LIMA ARMATURE WORKS INC
Also Called: Double Eagle Golf
142 E Pearl St (45801-4149)
PHONE..............................419 222-4010
TOLL FREE: 800
Rick Smith, *Pr*
James W Smith, *Ch Bd*
Margaret E Smith, *Sec*
EMP: 7 EST: 1927
SQ FT: 41,000
SALES (est): 1.01MM **Privately Held**
Web: www.limaarmature.com
SIC: 7694 5063 Electric motor repair;
Motors, electric

(G-8425)
LIMA PALLET COMPANY INC
1470 Neubrecht Rd (45801-3122)
PHONE..............................419 229-5736
Tracie Sanchez, *Pr*
Kelly Sarno, *Pers/VP*
EMP: 21 EST: 1981
SQ FT: 25,000
SALES (est): 1.83MM **Privately Held**
Web: www.limapallet.com
SIC: 2448 2441 Pallets, wood; Nailed wood
boxes and shook

(G-8426)
LIMA SHEET METAL MCH & MFG INC
Also Called: Lima Sheet Metal
1001 Bowman Rd (45804-3409)
PHONE..............................419 229-1161
Michael R Emerick, *Pr*

Thomas Emerick, *
Ann Emerick, *
EMP: 10 EST: 1974
SQ FT: 26,250
SALES (est): 3.86MM **Privately Held**
Web: www.limasheetmetal.com
SIC: 3589 3599 7349 7692 Commercial
cooking and foodwarming equipment;
Machine shop, jobbing and repair; Building
maintenance, except repairs; Welding repair

(G-8427)
LIMA SPORTING GOODS INC
1404 Allentown Rd (45805-2204)
PHONE..............................419 222-1036
David Kirian, *Pr*
EMP: 20 EST: 1976
SQ FT: 12,900
SALES (est): 2.27MM **Privately Held**
Web: www.limasportinggoods.net
SIC: 2759 5941 Screen printing; Team
sports equipment

(G-8428)
LRI POST-ACQUISITION INC (PA)
893 Shawnee Rd (45805-3437)
PHONE..............................419 227-2200
Gary Stanklus, *Pr*
Darlene Stanklus, *Sec*
▲ EMP: 23 EST: 1991
SQ FT: 12,000
SALES (est): 928.72K **Privately Held**
Web: www.leadar-roll.com
SIC: 3599 Machine shop, jobbing and repair

(G-8429)
MENARD INC
2614 N Eastown Rd (45807-1601)
PHONE..............................419 998-4348
Timothy Bart, *Mgr*
EMP: 92
SALES (corp-wide): 1.7B **Privately Held**
Web: www.menards.com
SIC: 2431 Millwork
PA: Menard, Inc.
5101 Menard Dr
Eau Claire WI 54703
715 876-2000

(G-8430)
MESSER LLC
961 Industry Ave (45804-4171)
PHONE..............................419 227-9585
EMP: 10
SALES (corp-wide): 1.63B **Privately Held**
Web: www.messeramericas.com
SIC: 2813 Industrial gases
HQ: Messer Llc
200 Smrst Corp Blvd # 7000
Bridgewater NJ 08807
800 755-9277

(G-8431)
MESSER LLC
1680 Buckeye Rd (45804-1826)
PHONE..............................419 221-5043
Stuart Emmons, *Brnch Mgr*
EMP: 34
SALES (corp-wide): 2.29B **Privately Held**
Web: www.messeramericas.com
SIC: 2813 Nitrogen
HQ: Messer Llc
200 Smrset Corp Blvd Ste
Bridgewater NJ 08807
800 755-9277

(G-8432)
METOKOTE CORPORATION (HQ)
Also Called: Ppg-Metokote
1340 Neubrecht Rd (45801-3120)
PHONE..............................419 996-7800

Jeffrey J Oravitz, *Pr*
▲ EMP: 445 EST: 1969
SQ FT: 30,000
SALES (est): 397.04MM
SALES (corp-wide): 18.25B **Publicly Held**
Web: www.ppgcoatingsservices.com
SIC: 3479 Coating of metals and formed
products
PA: Ppg Industries, Inc.
1 Ppg Pl
Pittsburgh PA 15272
412 434-3131

(G-8433)
MIDWEST COMMERCIAL MLLWK INC
514 N Union St (45801-4159)
PHONE..............................419 224-5001
Doug Coolidge, *Pr*
EMP: 12 EST: 1996
SQ FT: 15,200
SALES (est): 1.71MM **Privately Held**
Web: www.mwmill.com
SIC: 2431 Millwork

(G-8434)
MURPHY TRACTOR & EQP CO INC
Also Called: John Deere Authorized Dealer
3550 Saint Johns Rd (45804-4017)
PHONE..............................419 221-3666
Chris Cron, *Brnch Mgr*
EMP: 8
Web: www.murphytractor.com
SIC: 3531 5082 Construction machinery;
Construction and mining machinery
HQ: Murphy Tractor & Equipment Co., Inc.
5375 N Deere Rd
Park City KS 67219
855 246-9124

(G-8435)
NATIONAL LIME AND STONE CO
1314 Findlay Rd (45801-3106)
PHONE..............................419 228-3434
Nick Morris, *Mgr*
EMP: 18
SQ FT: 1,200
SALES (corp-wide): 86.85MM **Privately Held**
Web: www.natlime.com
SIC: 1422 Crushed and broken limestone
PA: The National Lime And Stone
Company
551 Lake Cascade Pkwy
Findlay OH 45840
419 422-4341

(G-8436)
P-AMERICAS LLC
Also Called: Pepsico
1750 Greely Chapel Rd (45804-4122)
PHONE..............................419 227-3541
Rob Rosser, *Mgr*
EMP: 161
SALES (corp-wide): 91.47B **Publicly Held**
Web: www.pepsico.com
SIC: 5149 2086 Soft drinks; Bottled and
canned soft drinks
HQ: P-Americas Llc
1 Pepsi Way
Somers NY 10589
336 896-5740

(G-8437)
PCS NITROGEN INC
Also Called: Arcadian Ohio
1900 Fort Amanda Rd (45804-1827)
P.O. Box 628 (45802-0628)
PHONE..............................419 226-1200
Chuck Treloar, *Mgr*
EMP: 11
SALES (corp-wide): 29.06B **Privately Held**

Web: www.nutrien.com
SIC: 2873 Nitrogen solutions (fertilizer)
HQ: Pcs Nitrogen, Inc.
500 Lake Cook Rd Ste 150
Deerfield IL 60015

(G-8438)
PPG INDUSTRIES INC
2599 Shawnee Industrial Dr (45804-2365)
PHONE...................419 331-2011
EMP: 9
SALES (corp-wide): 18.25B **Publicly Held**
Web: www.ppg.com
SIC: 2851 Paints and allied products
PA: Ppg Industries, Inc.
1 Ppg Pl
Pittsburgh PA 15272
412 434-3131

(G-8439)
PROCTER & GAMBLE MFG CO
Also Called: Procter & Gamble
3875 Reservoir Rd (45801-3302)
P.O. Box 1900 (45802)
PHONE...................419 226-5500
J G Boney, Brnch Mgr
EMP: 250
SALES (corp-wide): 84.04B **Publicly Held**
Web: us.pg.com
SIC: 2844 Perfumes, cosmetics and other
toilet preparations
HQ: The Procter & Gamble Manufacturing
Company
1 Procter And Gamble Plz
Cincinnati OH 45202
513 983-1100

(G-8440)
PROFORMA SYSTEMS ADVANTAGE
Also Called: Systems Advantage
1207 Findlay Rd (45801-3103)
PHONE...................419 224-8747
Robert Mcpheron, Pr
Michelle Mcpheron, VP
Cathy Richard, Sec
EMP: 6 EST: 1995
SALES (est): 632.87K **Privately Held**
SIC: 2759 Calendars: printing, nsk

(G-8441)
PUNCH COMPONENTS INC
505 N Cable Rd (45805-2132)
PHONE...................419 224-1242
EMP: 30
SQ FT: 50,000
SALES (est): 1.96MM **Privately Held**
SIC: 3663 3827 Television broadcasting and
communications equipment; Optical
instruments and lenses
PA: Iep Invest Nv
Noorderlaan 139
Antwerpen 2030
57226720

(G-8442)
RANDALL BEARINGS INC (DH)
Also Called: Randall
240 Jay Begg Pkwy (45804-1901)
P.O. Box 1258 (45802-1258)
PHONE...................419 223-1075
Erwin Mayr, CEO
▲ EMP: 78 EST: 1906
SALES (est): 18.42MM **Privately Held**
Web: www.randallbearings.com
SIC: 3568 3624 3366 Bearings, bushings,
and blocks; Carbon and graphite products;
Copper foundries
HQ: Wieland-Werke Ag
Graf-Arco-Str. 36
Ulm BW 89079
7319440

(G-8443)
REGAL BELOIT AMERICA INC
200 E Chapman Rd (45801-2012)
PHONE...................608 364-8800
William Conway, Manager
EMP: 38
SALES (corp-wide): 6.03B **Publicly Held**
SIC: 3621 3625 Motors and generators;
Relays and industrial controls
HQ: Regal Beloit America, Inc.
111 W Michigan St
Milwaukee WI 53203
608 364-8800

(G-8444)
RESOURCE RECYCLING INC
1596 Neubrecht Rd (45801-3124)
PHONE...................419 222-2702
Micah Hollinger, Pr
EMP: 15 EST: 2008
SALES (est): 7.65MM **Privately Held**
Web: www.resourcemulch.com
SIC: 4953 3999 4214 Recycling, waste
materials; Grinding and pulverizing of
materials, nec; Local trucking with storage

(G-8445)
RMT HOLDINGS INC
1025 Findlay Rd (45801-3171)
P.O. Box 5183 (45802-5183)
PHONE...................419 221-1168
Richard Toth, Pr
Cathi Toth, Pr
EMP: 15 EST: 1989
SQ FT: 15,000
SALES (est): 3.44MM **Privately Held**
SIC: 2789 Paper cutting

(G-8446)
RUDOLPH FOODS COMPANY INC
(PA)
Also Called: Rudolph Foods
6575 Bellefontaine Rd (45804-4415)
P.O. Box 509 (45802-0509)
PHONE...................909 383-7463
James Rudolph, Ch
John E Rudolph Senior, Ch
Richard Rudolph, *
Barbara Snyder, *
Philip Rudolph, *
◆ EMP: 160 EST: 1987
SQ FT: 110,000
SALES (est): 131.1MM
SALES (corp-wide): 131.1MM **Privately
Held**
Web: www.rudolphfoods.com
SIC: 2096 2099 Pork rinds; Food
preparations, nec

(G-8447)
SEWER RODDING EQUIPMENT CO
Also Called: Sreco Flexible
3434 S Dixie Hwy (45804-3756)
PHONE...................419 991-2065
Larry Drain, Mgr
EMP: 140
SALES (corp-wide): 2.28MM **Privately
Held**
SIC: 5032 3546 3423 Sewer pipe, clay;
Power-driven handtools; Hand and edge
tools, nec
PA: Sewer Rodding Equipment Co Inc
3217 Carter Ave
Marina Del Rey CA 90292
310 301-9009

(G-8448)
SIEFKER SAWMILL LLC
8705 W State Rd (45807-8730)
PHONE...................419 339-8523
Gary Siefker, Managing Member

EMP: 8 EST: 2019
SALES (est): 502.76K **Privately Held**
SIC: 2426 2421 Lumber, hardwood
dimension; Sawmills and planing mills,
general

(G-8449)
SIGN SOURCE USA INC
1700 S Dixie Hwy (45804-1834)
PHONE...................419 224-1130
Jeff Pisel, Pr
Sompahkoun Southibounnorath, *
Karen Hoblein, *
EMP: 55 EST: 1996
SALES (est): 8.66MM **Privately Held**
Web: www.signsourceusainc.com
SIC: 5085 3993 Signmaker equipment and
supplies; Signs and advertising specialties

(G-8450)
SIGNS OHIO INC
57 Town Sq (45801-4950)
PHONE...................419 228-7446
Bud Smith, CEO
Greg Smith, Pr
EMP: 6 EST: 2006
SALES (est): 331.8K **Privately Held**
Web: www.signsohio.com
SIC: 3993 Signs and advertising specialties

(G-8451)
SNOW PRINTING CO INC
1000 W Grand Ave Frnt (45801-3498)
PHONE...................419 229-7669
Donald L Kohl, Pr
Daniel Kohl, VP
Joyce Kohl, Sec
EMP: 10 EST: 1890
SQ FT: 4,200
SALES (est): 310.74K **Privately Held**
SIC: 2752 2759 Offset printing; Letterpress
printing

(G-8452)
SPALLINGER MILLWRIGHT SVC CO
Also Called: Spallnger Atclave Systms/US MI
1155 E Hanthorn Rd (45804-3929)
PHONE...................419 225-5830
Scott Spallinger, Pr
▲ EMP: 42 EST: 1989
SQ FT: 80,000
SALES (est): 9.61MM **Privately Held**
Web: www.spallinger.com
SIC: 3446 1796 Stairs, staircases, stair
treads: prefabricated metal; Machinery
installation

(G-8453)
SUPERIOR FORGE & STEEL CORP
(PA)
1820 Mcclain Rd (45804-1978)
PHONE...................419 222-4412
James C Markovitz, CEO
Keith Schwarz, *
◆ EMP: 92 EST: 1991
SQ FT: 350,000
SALES (est): 25.44MM **Privately Held**
Web: www.sfsrolls.com
SIC: 3316 3462 Cold finishing of steel
shapes; Iron and steel forgings

(G-8454)
SUPERIOR METAL PRODUCTS INC
(PA)
Also Called: American Trim
1005 W Grand Ave (45801-3400)
PHONE...................419 228-1145
Leo Hawk, Ch
Richard Pfeifer, *
Dana Morgan, *

◆ EMP: 50 EST: 1958
SQ FT: 15,000
SALES (est): 445.1MM
SALES (corp-wide): 445.1MM **Privately
Held**
Web: www.amtrim.com
SIC: 3429 3469 Hardware, nec; Porcelain
enameled products and utensils

(G-8455)
TELEDOOR LLC
1075 Prosperity Rd (45801-3127)
P.O. Box 316 (45853-0316)
PHONE...................419 227-3000
John Recker, Managing Member
EMP: 7 EST: 2005
SQ FT: 22,000
SALES (est): 219.67K **Privately Held**
Web: www.teledoormfg.com
SIC: 2431 Doors, wood

(G-8456)
THE419
201 W Market St (45801-4819)
PHONE...................855 451-1018
EMP: 10 EST: 2016
SALES (est): 49.41K **Privately Held**
Web: www.limalive.com
SIC: 2741 Miscellaneous publishing

(G-8457)
UNITED STATES PLASTIC CORP
Also Called: Neatlysmart
1390 Neubrecht Rd (45801-3196)
PHONE...................419 228-2242
EMP: 100 EST: 1962
SALES (est): 4MM
SALES (corp-wide): 14.65MM **Privately
Held**
Web: www.usplastic.com
SIC: 5162 3089 Plastics materials and basic
shapes; Plastics processing
HQ: Stanita Foundation
941 Fry Rd
Greenwood IN 46142
317 881-6751

(G-8458)
W T INC
Also Called: Midwest Plastics
606 N Jackson St (45801-4126)
P.O. Box 1687 (45802-1687)
PHONE...................419 224-6942
William M Taflinger, Pr
Rebecca Taflinger, VP
William S Talfinger, Treas
Stephen C Talfinger, Sec
▼ EMP: 11 EST: 1991
SQ FT: 7,500
SALES (est): 2.15MM **Privately Held**
Web: www.midwestplasticsoh.com
SIC: 3089 Injection molding of plastics

(G-8459)
WHEMCO-OHIO FOUNDRY INC
Also Called: Whemco
1600 Mcclain Rd (45804-1979)
PHONE...................419 222-2111
Charles R Novelli, Pr
Robert J Peterson, VP
Carl Maskiewicz, VP
Robert Zabelsky, Quality Vice President
Anthony J Poli, Prin
EMP: 140 EST: 1990
SALES (est): 9.95MM
SALES (corp-wide): 645.61MM **Privately
Held**
Web: www.whemco.com
SIC: 3321 3325 3322 Gray iron castings, nec
; Steel foundries, nec; Malleable iron
foundries

▲ = Import ▼ = Export
◆ = Import/Export

HQ: Whemco Inc.
5 Hot Metal St Ste 300
Pittsburgh PA 15203
412 390-2700

Lima
Auglaize County

(G-8460)
ALPLA INC
3320 Fort Shawnee Industrial Dr
(45806-1843)
PHONE..............................419 991-9484
Keith Wagner, *Brnch Mgr*
▲ EMP: 15
SALES (corp-wide): 242.12K **Privately Held**
Web: www.alpla.com
SIC: 3089 Plastics containers, except foam
HQ: Alpla Inc.
289 Hwy 155 S
Mcdonough GA 30253
770 305-7213

(G-8461)
PRECISION THRMPLSTIC CMPNNTS I
Also Called: P T C
3765 Saint Johns Rd (45806-2629)
P.O. Box 1296 (45802-1296)
PHONE..............................419 227-4500
Randy E Carter, *CEO*
◆ EMP: 100 EST: 1982
SQ FT: 62,000
SALES (est): 9.99MM **Privately Held**
Web: www.ptclima.com
SIC: 3089 Injection molding of plastics

(G-8462)
PROSTAR LLC
4610 S Dixie Hwy Ste D (45806-1821)
P.O. Box 536 (45802-0536)
PHONE..............................419 225-8806
EMP: 16 EST: 2004
SQ FT: 10,000
SALES (est): 1.22MM **Privately Held**
Web: www.prostarusa.net
SIC: 3799 Trailers and trailer equipment

Lisbon
Columbiana County

(G-8463)
ALBCO FOUNDRY INC
230 Maple St (44432-1275)
PHONE..............................330 424-7716
EMP: 10 EST: 1956
SALES (est): 2.2MM **Privately Held**
Web: www.albco.com
SIC: 3366 3369 3365 Castings (except die), nec, bronze; Zinc and zinc-base alloy castings, except die-castings; Masts, cast aluminum

(G-8464)
BRIGHTPET NUTRITION GROUP LLC (PA)
38251 Industrial Park Rd (44432-8325)
PHONE..............................330 424-1431
Matthew Golladay, *Pr*
EMP: 20 EST: 2016
SALES (est): 71.9MM
SALES (corp-wide): 71.9MM **Privately Held**
Web: www.brightpet.com
SIC: 2048 Canned pet food (except dog and cat)

(G-8465)
CCBDD
35947 State Route 172 (44432-9404)
PHONE..............................330 424-0404
EMP: 12 EST: 2017
SALES (est): 784.69K **Privately Held**
Web: www.ccbdd.net
SIC: 3999

(G-8466)
D W DICKEY AND SON INC (PA)
Also Called: D W Dickey
7896 Dickey Dr (44432-9391)
P.O. Box 189 (44432-0189)
PHONE..............................330 424-1441
Gary Neville, *Pr*
Timothy Dickey, *
David Dickey, *
Janet Blosser, *
EMP: 128 EST: 1948
SALES (est): 24.75MM
SALES (corp-wide): 24.75MM **Privately Held**
Web: www.dwdickey.com
SIC: 5169 3273 5172 Explosives; Ready-mixed concrete; Fuel oil

(G-8467)
GLOBAL-PAK INC (PA)
9636 Elkton Rd (44432-9575)
P.O. Box 89 (44415-0089)
PHONE..............................330 482-1993
James Foster, *Pr*
▲ EMP: 26 EST: 1998
SQ FT: 75,000
SALES (est): 24.3MM
SALES (corp-wide): 24.3MM **Privately Held**
Web: www.global-pak.com
SIC: 5199 2393 Packaging materials; Textile bags

(G-8468)
GRANT STREET PALLET INC
39196 Grant St (44432-9781)
P.O. Box 268 (44432-0268)
PHONE..............................330 424-0355
Kenneth Miller, *Pr*
EMP: 8 EST: 2013
SALES (est): 143K **Privately Held**
SIC: 2448 Pallets, wood

(G-8469)
HEIM SHEET METAL INC
905 N Market St (44432-1023)
PHONE..............................330 424-7820
David Belaney, *Pr*
Melinda Belaney, *Sec*
EMP: 6 EST: 1928
SALES (est): 710.36K **Privately Held**
SIC: 3444 Sheet metalwork

(G-8470)
HOUSING & EMRGNCY LGSTCS PLNNR
36905 State Route 30 (44432-9413)
PHONE..............................209 201-7511
EMP: 20 EST: 2008
SALES (est): 272.46K **Privately Held**
SIC: 3999 Manufacturing industries, nec

(G-8471)
J & J TIRE & ALIGNMENT
12649 State Route 45 (44432-9698)
PHONE..............................330 424-5200
Braine Schafer, *Owner*
EMP: 7 EST: 1977
SQ FT: 2,500
SALES (est): 638.98K **Privately Held**
SIC: 5531 7538 7534 7539 Batteries, automotive and truck; General automotive repair shops; Tire retreading and repair shops; Automotive repair shops, nec

(G-8472)
J I T PALLETS INC
39196 Grant St (44432-9781)
P.O. Box 268 (44432-0268)
PHONE..............................330 424-0355
Kenneth Miller, *Pr*
EMP: 6 EST: 2015
SALES (est): 120.47K **Privately Held**
SIC: 2448 Pallets, wood

(G-8473)
J P INDUSTRIAL PRODUCTS INC (PA)
Also Called: JP Industrial
11988 State Route 45 (44432-8625)
PHONE..............................330 424-1110
James E Pastore, *Pr*
▲ EMP: 8 EST: 1989
SQ FT: 5,000
SALES (est): 14.93MM
SALES (corp-wide): 14.93MM **Privately Held**
Web: www.jpindustrial.com
SIC: 2821 Plastics materials and resins

(G-8474)
J P INDUSTRIAL PRODUCTS INC
State Rte 518 (44432)
PHONE..............................330 424-3388
Beccy Brown, *Mgr*
EMP: 22
SALES (corp-wide): 14.93MM **Privately Held**
Web: www.jpindustrial.com
SIC: 3086 Padding, foamed plastics
PA: J. P. Industrial Products, Inc.
11988 State Route 45
Lisbon OH 44432
330 424-1110

(G-8475)
JPI COASTAL LLC
11988 State Route 45 (44432-9615)
PHONE..............................330 424-1110
EMP: 8 EST: 2014
SALES (est): 2.06MM **Privately Held**
Web: www.jpindustrial.com
SIC: 3087 Custom compound purchased resins

(G-8476)
LISBON POWDER COATING
6191 Lisbon Rd (44432-9310)
PHONE..............................234 567-1324
Gabriel W Miller, *Admn*
EMP: 6 EST: 2014
SALES (est): 88.61K **Privately Held**
SIC: 3479 Coating of metals and formed products

(G-8477)
OHIO PET FOODS INC (HQ)
38251 Industrial Park Rd (44432-8397)
PHONE..............................330 424-1431
Jim Golladay, *Pr*
Matthew Golladay, *
Travis Golladay, *
◆ EMP: 27 EST: 1978
SQ FT: 50,000
SALES (est): 12.4MM
SALES (corp-wide): 71.9MM **Privately Held**
Web: www.brightpet.com
SIC: 2048 2047 Feeds, specialty: mice, guinea pig, etc.; Dog food
PA: Brightpet Nutrition Group Llc
38251 Industrial Park Rd

Lisbon OH 44432
330 424-1431

(G-8478)
PAPER SERVICE INC
12022 Leslie Rd (44432-9531)
PHONE..............................330 227-3546
Randy Barnard, *Pr*
Dean Barnard, *VP*
EMP: 7 EST: 1968
SQ FT: 20,000
SALES (est): 650.97K **Privately Held**
Web: www.paperserviceco.com
SIC: 2621 Paper mills

(G-8479)
RL CRAIG INC
6496 State Route 45 (44432-8357)
PHONE..............................330 424-1525
Richard L Craig, *Pr*
Katheryn A Craig, *VP*
EMP: 13 EST: 1993
SQ FT: 7,600
SALES (est): 3.52MM **Privately Held**
Web: www.rlcraig.com
SIC: 3599 Machine shop, jobbing and repair

(G-8480)
WELDING IMPROVEMENT COMPANY
Also Called: Wicom Services
10070 Stookesberry Rd (44432-8639)
PHONE..............................330 424-9666
Tina Strong, *Pr*
Scott Strong, *VP*
EMP: 8 EST: 1978
SALES (est): 2.16MM **Privately Held**
Web: www.weldingimprovement.com
SIC: 3441 Fabricated structural metal

Litchfield
Medina County

(G-8481)
MEDINA FOODS INC
Also Called: Gold Rush Jerky
9706 Crow Rd (44253-9549)
PHONE..............................330 725-1390
Abdalla Nimer, *Pr*
Cathy Fobes, *
EMP: 45 EST: 1945
SQ FT: 50,000
SALES (est): 14.68MM **Privately Held**
Web: www.goldrushjerky.com
SIC: 2011 Meat packing plants

(G-8482)
PARKN MANUFACTURING LLC
8035 Norwalk Rd Ste 107 (44253-9135)
PHONE..............................330 723-8172
Willard Robert Scandlon, *CEO*
EMP: 12 EST: 1992
SQ FT: 10,000
SALES (est): 1.44MM **Privately Held**
Web: www.parkn-mfg.com
SIC: 3599 Machine shop, jobbing and repair

Lithopolis
Fairfield County

(G-8483)
LEHNER SIGNS INC
133 Salinger Dr (43136-9727)
PHONE..............................614 258-0500
Robin Owens, *Pr*
EMP: 7 EST: 1990
SALES (est): 917.1K **Privately Held**
Web: www.lehnersigns.com

SIC: 3993 Signs and advertising specialties

(G-8484)
UNITED MCGILL CORPORATION
122 E Columbus St (43136-1006)
PHONE.................................614 920-1267
EMP: 17
SALES (corp-wide): 67.2MM **Privately Held**
Web: www.unitedmcgill.com
SIC: 3589 Water filters and softeners, household type
HQ: United Mcgill Corporation
   1 Mission Park
   Groveport OH 43125
   614 829-1200

Little Hocking
Washington County

(G-8485)
AGE GRAPHICS LLC (PA)
678 Collins Rd (45742-5397)
PHONE.................................740 989-0006
EMP: 9 EST: 1997
SALES (est): 2.54MM
SALES (corp-wide): 2.54MM **Privately Held**
Web: www.cheapyardsignsage.com
SIC: 3577 Graphic displays, except graphic terminals

(G-8486)
AMERICAN BOTTLING COMPANY
871 State Route 618 (45742-5377)
PHONE.................................740 423-9230
Robert Deeds, *Prin*
EMP: 43
Web: www.keurigdrpepper.com
SIC: 2086 Soft drinks: packaged in cans, bottles, etc.
HQ: The American Bottling Company
   6425 Hall Of Fame Ln
   Frisco TX 75034

Lockbourne
Franklin County

(G-8487)
CCBCC OPERATIONS LLC
6040 Collings Dr (43137)
PHONE.................................304 203-8647
J Frank Harrison Iii, *Mgr*
EMP: 66
SALES (corp-wide): 6.9B **Publicly Held**
SIC: 2086 Bottled and canned soft drinks
HQ: Ccbcc Operations, Llc
   4100 Coca-Cola Plz
   Charlotte NC 28211
   704 364-8728

(G-8488)
CENTRAL COCA-COLA BTLG CO INC
Also Called: Coca-Cola
6040 Collings Dr (43137-3502)
PHONE.................................614 863-7200
Doug Davis, *Mgr*
EMP: 198
SALES (corp-wide): 45.75B **Publicly Held**
Web: www.coca-cola.com
SIC: 2086 Bottled and canned soft drinks
HQ: Central Coca-Cola Bottling Company, Inc.
   555 Taxter Rd Ste 550
   Elmsford NY 10523
   914 789-1100

(G-8489)
GR8 NEWS PACKAGING LLC
3657 Tradeport Ct (43137-9676)
PHONE.................................314 739-1202
Patrick Mcswain, *Managing Member*
EMP: 15 EST: 2019
SALES (est): 790.78K **Privately Held**
SIC: 2621 Molded pulp products

(G-8490)
HIKMA PHARMACEUTICALS USA INC
2130 Rohr Rd (43137-9323)
PHONE.................................732 542-1191
Michael Raya, *Mgr*
EMP: 26
SALES (corp-wide): 3.13B **Privately Held**
Web: www.hikma.com
SIC: 2834 Pharmaceutical preparations
HQ: Hikma Pharmaceuticals Usa Inc.
   200 Connell Dr 4th Fl
   Berkeley Heights NJ 07922
   908 673-1030

(G-8491)
NATIONAL LIME AND STONE CO
5911 Lockbourne Rd (43137-9256)
PHONE.................................614 497-0083
Richard Roberts, *Brnch Mgr*
EMP: 18
SQ FT: 4,032
SALES (corp-wide): 86.85MM **Privately Held**
Web: www.natlime.com
SIC: 3271 1442 Blocks, concrete or cinder: standard; Construction sand mining
PA: The National Lime And Stone Company
   551 Lake Cascade Pkwy
   Findlay OH 45840
   419 422-4341

(G-8492)
SPACE EXPLORATION TECH CORP
4555 Creekside Pkwy (43137-9287)
PHONE.................................559 593-2731
EMP: 132
SALES (corp-wide): 2.07B **Privately Held**
SIC: 3761 Guided missiles and space vehicles
PA: Space Exploration Technologies Corp.
   1 Rocket Rd
   Hawthorne CA 90250
   310 363-6000

(G-8493)
VSP LAB COLUMBUS
2605 Rohr Rd (43137-9281)
PHONE.................................614 409-8900
Ed Morris, *Prin*
EMP: 9 EST: 2003
SALES (est): 1.8MM **Privately Held**
Web: www.vspone.com
SIC: 3827 Optical instruments and lenses

(G-8494)
WHIRLPOOL CORPORATION
Also Called: Whirlpool
6241 Shook Rd (43137-9306)
PHONE.................................614 409-4340
EMP: 23
SALES (corp-wide): 16.61B **Publicly Held**
Web: www.whirlpoolcorp.com
SIC: 3585 3632 3633 Air conditioning units, complete: domestic or industrial; Refrigerators, mechanical and absorption: household; Household laundry machines, including coin-operated
PA: Whirlpool Corporation
   2000 N M-63
   Benton Harbor MI 49022
   269 923-5000

Lodi
Medina County

(G-8495)
ABC PLASTICS INC
140 West Dr (44254-1062)
P.O. Box 59 (44254-0059)
PHONE.................................330 948-3322
Barbara Lohmier, *Pr*
EMP: 40 EST: 1986
SQ FT: 66,000
SALES (est): 2.76MM **Privately Held**
Web: www.abcplasticslodi.com
SIC: 3089 Injection molded finished plastics products, nec

(G-8496)
ADVANCE BRONZE INC (PA)
139 Ohio St (44254-1047)
P.O. Box 280 (44254-0280)
PHONE.................................330 948-1231
David Del Propost, *Pr*
Tohmas Seringer, *
Jerry Shapiro, *
▲ EMP: 12 EST: 1954
SQ FT: 150,000
SALES (est): 4.23MM
SALES (corp-wide): 4.23MM **Privately Held**
Web: www.advancebronze.com
SIC: 3568 3366 Power transmission equipment, nec; Bushings and bearings

(G-8497)
ADVANCE BRONZEHUBCO DIV (HQ)
139 Ohio St (44254-1047)
PHONE.................................304 232-4414
EMP: 20 EST: 1969
SALES (est): 780.74K
SALES (corp-wide): 4.23MM **Privately Held**
Web: www.advancebronze.com
SIC: 3366 Bronze foundry, nec
PA: Advance Bronze, Inc.
   139 Ohio St
   Lodi OH 44254
   330 948-1231

(G-8498)
ALLOY FABRICATORS INC
700 Wooster St (44254-1340)
P.O. Box 37 (44254-0037)
PHONE.................................330 948-3535
Lance Yurich, *Pr*
Dan Dietrick, *Genl Mgr*
Donna Yurich Stckhdlr, *Prin*
EMP: 11 EST: 1939
SQ FT: 15,000
SALES (est): 4.24MM **Privately Held**
Web: www.alloyfab.net
SIC: 3441 Fabricated structural metal

(G-8499)
CARBON POLYMERS COMPANY
104 Lee St (44254-1056)
PHONE.................................330 948-3007
Saquib Toor, *Pr*
Pavel Smyshlyaev, *CFO*
Jay Jafar Ctrl, *Prin*
EMP: 59 EST: 2021
SALES (est): 5.51MM **Privately Held**
Web: www.carbonpolymersco.com
SIC: 3089 Pallets, plastics

(G-8500)
CROPKING INCORPORATED
134 West Dr (44254-1062)
PHONE.................................330 302-4203
Paul Brentlinger, *Pr*

Marilyn Brentlinger, *Sec*
◆ EMP: 16 EST: 1982
SQ FT: 40,000
SALES (est): 2.69MM **Privately Held**
Web: www.cropking.com
SIC: 3448 3999 Greenhouses, prefabricated metal; Hydroponic equipment

(G-8501)
FASTFEED CORPORATION
124 S Academy St (44254-1345)
PHONE.................................330 948-7333
Dan Reed, *Pr*
EMP: 6 EST: 1997
SALES (est): 2.31MM **Privately Held**
Web: www.fastfeedcorporation.com
SIC: 3441 Fabricated structural metal

(G-8502)
I-M-A ENTERPRISES INC
700 Wooster St (44254-1340)
PHONE.................................330 948-3535
Robert Yurich, *Pr*
Dennis Yurich, *VP*
Laurice Paultz, *Sec*
EMP: 10 EST: 1968
SQ FT: 1,600
SALES (est): 193.82K **Privately Held**
SIC: 3444 Sheet metal specialties, not stamped

(G-8503)
KNOTT BRAKE COMPANY
144 West Dr (44254-1062)
PHONE.................................800 566-8887
▲ EMP: 50 EST: 1987
SALES (est): 88MM **Privately Held**
Web: www.knottbrake.com
SIC: 3714 Motor vehicle brake systems and parts
PA: Knott Holding Gmbh
   Obinger Str. 17
   Eggstatt BY 83125

(G-8504)
MAGNACO INDUSTRIES INC
140 West Dr (44254-1062)
PHONE.................................216 961-3636
Ken Geith, *Pr*
Magdalaine Geith, *Sec*
EMP: 25 EST: 1974
SQ FT: 43,000
SALES (est): 268.46K **Privately Held**
SIC: 3714 7389 Motor vehicle parts and accessories; Packaging and labeling services

(G-8505)
PIONEER MACHINE INC
104 S Prospect St (44254-1313)
P.O. Box 277 (44254-0277)
PHONE.................................330 948-6500
Don Gray, *Pr*
Sherry Gray, *VP*
EMP: 6 EST: 1987
SQ FT: 8,400
SALES (est): 799.63K **Privately Held**
Web: www.communitypsychassoc.com
SIC: 3441 3599 Fabricated structural metal; Machine shop, jobbing and repair

(G-8506)
SHILLING TRANSPORT INC
9718 Avon Lake Rd (44254-9639)
PHONE.................................330 948-1105
Gary Frank, *Pr*
EMP: 7 EST: 2002
SALES (est): 580.21K **Privately Held**
SIC: 3715 Truck trailers

(G-8507)
STEPHEN ANDREWS INC
Also Called: Camelot Printing
7634 Lafayette Rd (44254-9607)
PHONE...............................330 725-2672
Stephen Andrews, *Pr*
EMP: 7 **EST:** 1978
SQ FT: 1,700
SALES (est): 207.69K **Privately Held**
Web: www.camelotprinting.com
SIC: 2759 2752 Commercial printing, nec;
Commercial printing, lithographic

Logan
Hocking County

(G-8508)
AMANDA BENT BOLT COMPANY
Also Called: Amanda Manufacturing
1120 C I C Dr (43138-9153)
P.O. Box 1027 (43138-4027)
PHONE...............................740 385-6893
Robert Gruschow, *Pr*
▲ **EMP:** 212 **EST:** 1953
SQ FT: 139,000
SALES (est): 19.52MM
SALES (corp-wide): 25.7MM **Privately Held**
Web: www.abb1.com
SIC: 3496 3452 Miscellaneous fabricated
wire products; Bolts, nuts, rivets, and
washers
PA: Deshler Group, Inc.
34450 Industrial Rd
Livonia MI 48150
734 525-9100

(G-8509)
AVT BECKETT ELEVATORS USA INC
30130 Industrial Park Dr (43138-3603)
PHONE...............................844 360-0288
Barb.Buchanan, *Pr*
EMP: 8 **EST:** 2017
SALES (est): 1.95MM **Privately Held**
Web: www.avtbeckett.com
SIC: 3534 Elevators and equipment

(G-8510)
CARBORUNDUM GRINDING WHEEL COMPANY
Also Called: Carborundum
1011 E Front St (43138-9791)
P.O. Box 759 (43138-0759)
PHONE...............................740 385-2171
▲ **EMP:** 33 **EST:** 1984
SALES (est): 1.93MM **Privately Held**
Web: www.carborundum.net
SIC: 3291 Wheels, grinding: artificial

(G-8511)
CLAY LOGAN PRODUCTS COMPANY
Also Called: Logan Foundry & Machine
201 S Walnut St (43138-1376)
PHONE...............................740 385-2184
Richard H Brandt, *Ch Bd*
William R Brandt, *
Donald Hoobler, *
William Heft, *
EMP: 80 **EST:** 1904
SQ FT: 266,000
SALES (est): 21.84MM **Privately Held**
Web: www.loganclaypipe.com
SIC: 3259 Clay sewer and drainage pipe and
tile

(G-8512)
COLUMBUS WASHBOARD COMPANY LTD
4 E Main St (43138-1221)

PHONE...............................740 380-3828
Jacqueline M Barnett, *Managing Member*
▲ **EMP:** 8 **EST:** 1926
SALES (est): 944.04K **Privately Held**
Web: www.columbuswashboard.com
SIC: 2499 Washboards, wood and part wood

(G-8513)
ENGINRED ATMSPHRIC MTGTION LLC
32919 Logan Horns Mill Rd (43138-8497)
PHONE...............................740 385-6690
David E Poling, *Prin*
Douglas Kitchen, *Prin*
David Poling, *Prin*
Shawn Maynard, *Prin*
Greg Mason, *Prin*
EMP: 8 **EST:** 2020
SALES (est): 447.31K **Privately Held**
SIC: 2842 Polishes and sanitation goods

(G-8514)
GENERAL ELECTRIC COMPANY
Also Called: GE
State Route 93 N (43138)
PHONE...............................740 385-2114
John Davis, *Brnch Mgr*
EMP: 6
SALES (corp-wide): 38.7B **Publicly Held**
Web: geaerospace.com
SIC: 3231 3229 Products of purchased glass
; Pressed and blown glass, nec
PA: General Electric Company
1 Aviation Way
Cincinnati OH 45215
617 443-3000

(G-8515)
HOCKING HLLS ENRGY WELL SVCS L
32919 Logan Horns Mill Rd (43138-8497)
PHONE...............................740 385-6690
David Poling, *Managing Member*
EMP: 7 **EST:** 2015
SALES (est): 1.38MM **Privately Held**
SIC: 1382 1381 Geophysical exploration, oil
and gas field; Drilling oil and gas wells

(G-8516)
HOCKING VALLEY CONCRETE INC (PA)
35255 Hocking Dr (43138-9482)
PHONE...............................740 385-2165
William Vaughn, *Pr*
Mark Vaughn, *VP*
David Vaughn, *VP*
EMP: 12 **EST:** 1956
SQ FT: 2,000
SALES (est): 3.78MM
SALES (corp-wide): 3.78MM **Privately Held**
Web: www.hockingvalleyconcrete.com
SIC: 3273 1442 Ready-mixed concrete;
Construction sand mining

(G-8517)
KEYNES BROS INC
1 W Front St (43138-1825)
P.O. Box 628 (43138-0628)
PHONE...............................740 385-6824
EMP: 65
Web: www.keynesbros.com
SIC: 2041 5191 Flour mills, cereal (except
rice); Feed

(G-8518)
KILBARGER CONSTRUCTION INC
Also Called: C & L Supply
450 Gallagher Ave (43138-1893)
P.O. Box 946 (43138-0946)

PHONE...............................740 385-6019
Edward Kilbarger, *CEO*
James E Kilbarger, *
Anthony Kilbarger, *
Ann Kilbarger, *
EMP: 120 **EST:** 1958
SQ FT: 2,500
SALES (est): 21.74MM **Privately Held**
Web: www.kilbarger.com
SIC: 1381 Drilling oil and gas wells

(G-8519)
LOGAN COATINGS LLC
2255 E Front St (43138-8637)
P.O. Box 202 (43138-0202)
PHONE...............................740 380-0047
James M Johnson, *Prin*
EMP: 10 **EST:** 2014
SALES (est): 2.71MM **Privately Held**
Web: www.logancoatings.com
SIC: 3479 Coating of metals and formed
products

(G-8520)
LOGAN WELDING INC
37062 Hocking Dr (43138-9465)
PHONE...............................740 385-9651
Tim Cordle, *Off Mgr*
Julie Cordle, *Off Mgr*
EMP: 6 **EST:** 1976
SQ FT: 5,100
SALES (est): 491.62K **Privately Held**
Web: www.loganweldinginc.com
SIC: 7692 Welding repair

(G-8521)
MENNEL MILLING COMPANY
Also Called: Mennel Milling Logan
1 W Front St (43138-1825)
PHONE...............................740 385-6824
Larry Hawkins, *Opers*
EMP: 37
SALES (corp-wide): 211.12MM **Privately Held**
Web: www.mennel.com
SIC: 5191 2041 Feed; Flour mills, cereal
(except rice)
PA: The Mennel Milling Company
319 S Vine St
Fostoria OH 44830
419 435-8151

(G-8522)
OSBURN ASSOCIATES INC (PA)
9383 Vanatta Rd (43138-8719)
P.O. Box 912 (43138-0912)
PHONE...............................740 385-5732
Harry Osburn, *Dir*
Donna Osburn, *Dir*
Charles A Gerken, *Dir*
▲ **EMP:** 16 **EST:** 1982
SQ FT: 39,360
SALES (est): 8.4MM
SALES (corp-wide): 8.4MM **Privately Held**
Web: www.osburns.com
SIC: 3089 5063 Fittings for pipe, plastics;
Boxes and fittings, electrical

(G-8523)
PATTONS TRCK & HVY EQP SVC INC
Also Called: K & K Auto & Truck Parts
35640 Hocking Dr (43138-9467)
P.O. Box 963 (43138-0963)
PHONE...............................740 385-4067
Paul Doug Patton, *Pr*
Troy Sanborn, *Off Mgr*
EMP: 11 **EST:** 1991
SQ FT: 3,400
SALES (est): 1.38MM **Privately Held**
Web:
www.pattonstruckandkkautoparts.com

SIC: 3599 7538 5531 Machine shop, jobbing
and repair; General automotive repair shops
; Auto and home supply stores

(G-8524)
RALPH ROBINSON INC
Also Called: Oil Enterprises
700 Ohio Ave (43138-8469)
P.O. Box 84 (43138-0084)
PHONE...............................740 385-2747
Michael Robinson, *Pr*
EMP: 6 **EST:** 1962
SQ FT: 4,700
SALES (est): 669.95K **Privately Held**
SIC: 1389 5084 Oil and gas wells: building,
repairing and dismantling; Oil refining
machinery, equipment, and supplies

(G-8525)
RAM PRODUCTS INC
19250 Unger Rd (43138-7501)
PHONE...............................614 443-4634
John Pelleriti, *Pr*
Richard Dawson, *VP*
Anne Pelleriti, *Treas*
EMP: 12 **EST:** 1980
SALES (est): 1.67MM **Privately Held**
Web: www.ramprocess.com
SIC: 3542 Presses: hydraulic and
pneumatic, mechanical and manual

(G-8526)
SIGNS UNLMTED THE GRPHIC ADVNT (PA)
Also Called: Advent Designs
21313 State Route 93 S (43138-7508)
PHONE...............................614 836-7446
Ed Zell, *Pr*
Judy Zell, *Prin*
EMP: 7 **EST:** 1972
SQ FT: 20,000
SALES (est): 482.21K **Privately Held**
SIC: 3993 7389 Signs and advertising
specialties; Design services

(G-8527)
SMEAD MANUFACTURING COMPANY
Also Called: The Smead Manufacturing
Company
851 Smead Rd (43138-9500)
PHONE...............................740 385-5601
Arthur Tripp, *Mgr*
EMP: 194
SALES (corp-wide): 70.57MM **Privately Held**
Web: www.smead.com
SIC: 2675 Folders, filing, die-cut: made from
purchased materials
PA: The Smead Manufacturing Company
Llc
600 Smead Blvd
Hastings MN 55033
651 437-4111

(G-8528)
WRIGHTS WELL SERVICE LLC
37940 Scout Rd (43138-8832)
PHONE...............................740 380-9602
Ken Wright, *Owner*
EMP: 6 **EST:** 2002
SALES (est): 261.65K **Privately Held**
Web: wrightswellservicellc.business.site
SIC: 1389 Servicing oil and gas wells

London
Madison County

(G-8529)
ADVANCED DRAINAGE SYSTEMS INC
Also Called: ADS
400 E High St (43140-9501)
PHONE.................................740 852-2980
Robert Sensabaugh, *Brnch Mgr*
EMP: 108
SALES (corp-wide): 2.87B **Publicly Held**
Web: www.adspipe.com
SIC: 3084 Plastics pipe
PA: Advanced Drainage Systems, Inc.
4640 Trueman Blvd
Hilliard OH 43026
614 658-0050

(G-8530)
ARMALY LLC
Also Called: Armaly Brands
110 W 1st St (43140-1484)
PHONE.................................740 852-3621
Annmarie Armaly, *Treas*
▼ **EMP:** 40 **EST:** 2010
SALES (est): 11.46MM
SALES (corp-wide): 25.36MM **Privately Held**
Web: www.armalybrands.com
SIC: 3089 5199 3086 Floor coverings, plastics; Sponges (animal); Plastics foam products
PA: Armaly Sponge Company
1900 Easy St
Walled Lake MI 48390
248 669-2100

(G-8531)
BODYCOTE IMT INC
443 E High St (43140-9501)
PHONE.................................740 852-5000
Chris Gattie, *Mgr*
EMP: 17
SALES (corp-wide): 959.76MM **Privately Held**
Web: www.bodycote.com
SIC: 3398 3269 Metal heat treating; Pottery household articles, except kitchen articles
HQ: Bodycote Imt, Inc.
155 River St
Andover MA 01810
978 470-0876

(G-8532)
BODYCOTE THERMAL PROC INC
Also Called: Bodycote Kolsterising
443 E High St (43140-9501)
PHONE.................................740 852-4955
Doug Ridgeway, *Genl Mgr*
EMP: 7
SALES (corp-wide): 959.76MM **Privately Held**
Web: www.bodycote.com
SIC: 3398 Metal heat treating
HQ: Bodycote Thermal Processing, Inc.
12750 Merit Dr Ste 1400
Dallas TX 75251
214 904-2420

(G-8533)
CHURCH & DWIGHT CO INC
Also Called: Arm & Hammer
110 W 1st St (43140-1484)
PHONE.................................740 852-3621
Neil Parrish, *Brnch Mgr*
EMP: 8
SALES (corp-wide): 6.11B **Publicly Held**
Web: www.churchdwight.com

SIC: 2812 Sodium bicarbonate
PA: Church & Dwight Co., Inc.
500 Charles Ewing Blvd
Ewing NJ 08628
609 806-1200

(G-8534)
CREAMER METAL PRODUCTS INC (PA)
77 S Madison Rd (43140-1444)
PHONE.................................740 852-1752
Kennison Sims, *Pt*
Scott Sims, *Pt*
EMP: 19 **EST:** 1945
SQ FT: 31,000
SALES (est): 2.66MM
SALES (corp-wide): 2.66MM **Privately Held**
Web: www.creamermetal.com
SIC: 3523 Farm machinery and equipment

(G-8535)
DEER CREEK HONEY FARMS LTD
551 E High St (43140-9304)
PHONE.................................740 852-0899
Christopher L Dunham, *Pt*
Mark L Dunham, *Pt*
Lee T Dunham, *Pt*
EMP: 8 **EST:** 1938
SQ FT: 22,000
SALES (est): 2.44MM **Privately Held**
Web: www.deercreekhoney.com
SIC: 2099 0279 Honey, strained and bottled; Apiary (bee and honey farm)

(G-8536)
GRA-MAG TRUCK INTR SYSTEMS LLC (DH)
470 E High St (43140-9303)
PHONE.................................740 490-1000
Rick Chefer, *Managing Member*
▲ **EMP:** 30 **EST:** 1998
SQ FT: 60,000
SALES (est): 16.04MM
SALES (corp-wide): 42.84B **Privately Held**
Web: www.gramag.com
SIC: 3714 Motor vehicle parts and accessories
HQ: Magna Seating Of America, Inc.
30020 Cabot Dr
Novi MI 48377

(G-8537)
INTELLIGRATED PRODUCTS LLC
475 E High St (43140-9303)
P.O. Box 899 (43140-0899)
PHONE.................................740 490-0300
▲ **EMP:** 33 **EST:** 2001
SQ FT: 210,000
SALES (est): 3.66MM
SALES (corp-wide): 38.5B **Publicly Held**
SIC: 3535 Conveyors and conveying equipment
HQ: Intelligrated Systems, Inc.
7901 Innovation Way
Mason OH 45040
866 936-7300

(G-8538)
KMAK GROUP LLC
480 E High St (43140-9303)
P.O. Box 496 (43140-0496)
PHONE.................................937 308-1023
Kevin Henry, *Managing Member*
EMP: 11 **EST:** 2009
SQ FT: 15,000
SALES (est): 2.7MM **Privately Held**
SIC: 2448 3089 Cargo containers, wood and wood with metal; Air mattresses, plastics

(G-8539)
NISSEN CHEMITEC AMERICA INC
Also Called: Nissen Chemitec America
350 E High St (43140-9773)
PHONE.................................740 852-3200
Shawn Hendrix, *Pr*
Shinya Kawakami, *
Richard Hendrix, *
Kunihiko Nagura, *
▲ **EMP:** 380 **EST:** 1988
SQ FT: 155,000
SALES (est): 38.32MM **Privately Held**
Web: www.nissenchemitec.com
SIC: 3089 Injection molding of plastics
PA: Nissen Chemitec Corporation
2-4-34, Nishiharacho
Niihama EHM 792-0

(G-8540)
O CONNOR OFFICE PDTS & PRTG
60 W High St (43140-1075)
PHONE.................................740 852-2209
Gary Feliks, *Owner*
EMP: 8 **EST:** 1942
SQ FT: 3,200
SALES (est): 386.63K **Privately Held**
SIC: 5943 2752 Office forms and supplies; Offset printing

(G-8541)
STANLEY ELECTRIC US CO INC (HQ)
420 E High St (43140-9799)
PHONE.................................740 852-5200
Shinomiya Masahiro, *Pr*
▲ **EMP:** 47 **EST:** 1981
SQ FT: 733,000
SALES (est): 260.34MM **Privately Held**
Web: www.stanleyelectricus.com
SIC: 3647 3694 3089 Automotive lighting fixtures, nec; Automotive electrical equipment, nec; Injection molding of plastics
PA: Stanley Electric Co., Ltd.
2-9-13, Nakameguro
Meguro-Ku TKY 153-0

(G-8542)
TEXTILES INC (PA)
Also Called: Jordan Young International
23 Old Springfield Rd (43140-2033)
PHONE.................................740 852-0782
Phillip Jordan, *Pr*
Catherine Jordan, *VP*
Rob Jordan, *VP*
▲ **EMP:** 6 **EST:** 1989
SQ FT: 4,000
SALES (est): 700.35K
SALES (corp-wide): 700.35K **Privately Held**
SIC: 2511 Wood household furniture

(G-8543)
WHITE TIGER INC
Also Called: White Tiger Graphics
131 S Oak St (43140-1446)
PHONE.................................740 852-4873
George Peyton, *Pr*
EMP: 14 **EST:** 1988
SQ FT: 6,000
SALES (est): 363.19K **Privately Held**
Web: www.whitetigergraphics.com
SIC: 7336 2752 5199 Graphic arts and related design; Offset printing; Advertising specialties

Lorain
Lorain County

(G-8544)
A-1 WELDING & FABRICATION
4909 Oak Point Rd (44053-1937)
PHONE.................................440 233-8474
Kenneth J Balko, *Pr*
Wayne Balko, *VP*
Holly Herbert, *Sec*
EMP: 10 **EST:** 1966
SALES (est): 837.99K **Privately Held**
Web: www.a1weldingandfabrication.net
SIC: 3443 3312 Weldments; Structural shapes and pilings, steel

(G-8545)
ACKERMAN
1138 W 19th St (44052-3834)
PHONE.................................440 246-2034
David Selent, *Pr*
EMP: 6 **EST:** 2008
SALES (est): 557.4K **Privately Held**
SIC: 3711 Snow plows (motor vehicles), assembly of

(G-8546)
BCT ALARM SERVICES INC
5064 Oberlin Ave (44053-3432)
P.O. Box 216 (44001-0216)
PHONE.................................440 669-8153
Brian J Jankowski, *Pr*
EMP: 6 **EST:** 2007
SALES (est): 753.46K **Privately Held**
Web: www.security-ohio.com
SIC: 2752 Commercial printing, lithographic

(G-8547)
BODNAR PRINTING CO INC
3480 Colorado Ave (44052-2818)
PHONE.................................440 277-8295
Ralph Woodward, *Pr*
Bonnie Woodward, *Sec*
EMP: 11 **EST:** 1948
SQ FT: 5,000
SALES (est): 2.85MM **Privately Held**
Web: www.bodnarprinting.com
SIC: 2752 Offset printing

(G-8548)
BOSCOWOOD VENTURES INC
7425 Industrial Parkway Dr (44053-2064)
PHONE.................................800 526-1816
Rosario Boscarello, *Pr*
David Boscarello, *VP*
Rosario Boscarello Senior, *Sec*
EMP: 10 **EST:** 2022
SALES (est): 2MM **Privately Held**
SIC: 2448 Wood pallets and skids

(G-8549)
CAMACO LLC
Also Called: Camaco Lorain
3400 River Industrial Park Rd (44052-2900)
PHONE.................................440 288-4444
Willie Gratzel, *Brnch Mgr*
EMP: 560
SALES (corp-wide): 494.73MM **Privately Held**
Web: www.camacollc.com
SIC: 3499 Automobile seat frames, metal
HQ: Camaco, Llc
37000 W Twlve Mile Rd Ste
Farmington Hills MI 48331
248 442-6800

▲ = Import ▼ = Export
◆ = Import/Export

(G-8550)
CERTIFIED AUTO & TRCK REPR INC
Also Called: Tom Tire & Automotive
1405 E 28th St (44055-1603)
PHONE..............................440 288-2029
Tom Hakaim, *Pr*
Pamela Hakaim, *VP*
EMP: 9 **EST:** 1982
SQ FT: 80,000
SALES (est): 504.18K **Privately Held**
Web:
www.certifiedautoandtruckrepair.com
SIC: 7538 7539 7534 General automotive
repair shops; Automotive repair shops, nec;
Tire retreading and repair shops

(G-8551)
CLEVELAND RECLAIM INDS INC (PA)
Also Called: Turtle Plastics
7400 Industrial Parkway Dr (44053-2064)
PHONE..............................440 282-4917
Thomas Norton, *Ch Bd*
Liz Demetriou, *Pr*
Carol Maier, *CFO*
Dennis Hildebrandt, *VP*
Karen Bradley, *Bd of Dir*
EMP: 9 **EST:** 1982
SQ FT: 15,000
SALES (est): 237.28K
SALES (corp-wide): 237.28K **Privately Held**
Web: www.turtleplastics.com
SIC: 3089 Floor coverings, plastics

(G-8552)
CONSUMERACQ INC (PA)
2509 N Ridge Rd E (44055-3772)
P.O. Box 823 (44052-0823)
PHONE..............................440 277-9305
Jeffrey Riddell, *Pr*
Jacqueline Riddell, *Sec*
EMP: 30 **EST:** 1982
SQ FT: 4,000
SALES (est): 2.67MM **Privately Held**
Web:
www.consumersbuilderssupply.com
SIC: 3273 5211 Ready-mixed concrete;
Lumber and other building materials

(G-8553)
CONSUMERS BUILDERS SUPPLY CO (PA)
2509 N Ridge Rd E (44055-3772)
P.O. Box 824 (44052-0824)
PHONE..............................440 277-9306
Jeffrey Riddell, *Pr*
Jacqueline Riddell, *Sec*
EMP: 6 **EST:** 1904
SALES (est): 2.52MM
SALES (corp-wide): 2.52MM **Privately Held**
Web:
www.consumersbuilderssupply.com
SIC: 3273 5211 Ready-mixed concrete;
Lumber and other building materials

(G-8554)
DAYTON HEIDELBERG DISTRG CO
Also Called: DAYTON HEIDELBERG
DISTRIBUTING CO.
5901 Baumhart Rd (44053-2012)
PHONE..............................440 989-1027
Kevin Knight, *VP*
EMP: 157
SALES (corp-wide): 2.07B **Privately Held**
Web: www.heidelbergdistributing.com
SIC: 2082 Beer (alcoholic beverage)
HQ: Dayton Heidelberg Distributing Co., Llc
3601 Dryden Rd
Moraine OH 45439
937 222-8692

(G-8555)
ERDIE INDUSTRIES INC
1205 Colorado Ave (44052-3313)
PHONE..............................440 288-0166
Jason Erdie, *Pr*
Jeffrey Erdie, *
EMP: 40 **EST:** 1983
SQ FT: 50,000
SALES (est): 4.91MM **Privately Held**
Web: www.erdie.com
SIC: 2655 Tubes, fiber or paper; made from
purchased material

(G-8556)
GLOBAL PLASTIC TECH INC
1657 Bdwy Ave (44052-3439)
PHONE..............................440 879-6045
Makki Odeh, *Pr*
EMP: 7 **EST:** 2017
SALES (est): 326.8K **Privately Held**
Web: www.global-plastic.com
SIC: 2673 Food storage and frozen food
bags, plastic

(G-8557)
H P NIELSEN INC
Also Called: Nielsen Jewelers
753 Broadway (44052-1805)
PHONE..............................440 244-4255
Carl G Nielsen, *Pr*
Krystina Nielsen, *VP*
EMP: 6 **EST:** 1877
SQ FT: 2,600
SALES (est): 282.8K **Privately Held**
Web: www.nielsenjewelers.com
SIC: 5944 3911 7631 Jewelry, precious
stones and precious metals; Jewelry,
precious metal; Jewelry repair services

(G-8558)
J & S TOOL CORPORATION
1606 W 12th St (44052-1267)
PHONE..............................216 676-8330
Vernon Justice, *Pr*
Donald Justice, *
EMP: 6 **EST:** 1958
SALES (est): 796.3K **Privately Held**
SIC: 3542 5084 3544 3541 Machine tools,
metal forming type; Machine tools and
accessories; Special dies, tools, jigs, and
fixtures; Machine tools, metal cutting type

(G-8559)
JOHNSON METALL INC
1305 Oberlin Ave (44052-1559)
PHONE..............................440 245-6826
EMP: 65
SIC: 3366 Bushings and bearings, brass
(nonmachined)

(G-8560)
JOURNAL REGISTER COMPANY
Also Called: Morning Journal, The
401 Broadway Ste B (44052-1749)
PHONE..............................440 245-6901
Jeff Sudbrook, *Branch*
EMP: 99
SALES (corp-wide): 92.91MM **Privately Held**
Web: www.morningjournal.com
SIC: 2711 5994 Newspapers, publishing and
printing; Newsstand
PA: Journal Register Company
5 Hanover Sq 25th Fl
New York NY 10005
212 257-7212

(G-8561)
KTS MET-BAR PRODUCTS INC
967 G St (44052-3329)

PHONE..............................440 288-9308
Delvis Kerns, *Pr*
EMP: 9 **EST:** 1984
SQ FT: 8,500
SALES (est): 676.37K **Privately Held**
Web: www.ktsmet-bar.com
SIC: 3451 Screw machine products

(G-8562)
KUHN FABRICATING INC
1637 E 28th St (44055-1701)
P.O. Box 1203 (44055-0203)
PHONE..............................440 277-4182
Lewis Kuhn, *Pr*
Rosemary Kuhn, *VP*
EMP: 6 **EST:** 1958
SQ FT: 18,000
SALES (est): 2.4MM **Privately Held**
Web: www.kuhnfab.com
SIC: 3444 Sheet metal specialties, not
stamped

(G-8563)
LAKE SCREEN PRINTING INC
1924 Broadway (44052-3682)
PHONE..............................440 244-5707
Ben Zientarski Junior, *Pr*
Teresa Zientarski, *VP*
Annette Zientarski, *Sec*
EMP: 8 **EST:** 1976
SQ FT: 10,000
SALES (est): 381.77K **Privately Held**
Web: www.lakescreenprinting.com
SIC: 2759 Screen printing

(G-8564)
LORAIN COUNTY AUTO SYSTEMS INC
3400 River Industrial Park Rd (44052-2900)
PHONE..............................248 442-6800
Thomas Rockwell, *CFO*
EMP: 1613
SALES (corp-wide): 494.73MM **Privately Held**
Web: www.camacollc.com
SIC: 3714 Motor vehicle engines and parts
HQ: Lorain County Automotive Systems,
Inc.
7470 Industrial Pkwy Dr
Lorain OH 44053
440 960-7470

(G-8565)
LORAIN COUNTY AUTO SYSTEMS INC (HQ)
Also Called: Lcas
7470 Industrial Parkway Dr (44053-2070)
PHONE..............................440 960-7470
Arvind Pradhan, *CEO*
Tom Rockwell, *
▲ **EMP:** 50 **EST:** 1987
SQ FT: 36,000
SALES (est): 8.42MM
SALES (corp-wide): 494.73MM **Privately Held**
Web: www.camacollc.com
SIC: 3714 Motor vehicle engines and parts
PA: P & C Group I, Inc.
37000 W 12 Mile Rd Ste 10
Farmington Hills MI 48331
248 442-6800

(G-8566)
M/W INTERNATIONAL INC
Also Called: Mwi Dmntable Office Partitions
3839 Heron Dr (44053-1597)
P.O. Box 470115 (44147-0115)
PHONE..............................440 526-6900
Joseph R Bucalo, *Pr*
Kathleen Bucalo, *Sec*
◆ **EMP:** 18 **EST:** 1996

SQ FT: 1,500
SALES (est): 766.37K **Privately Held**
Web: www.mwintl.net
SIC: 2522 Office furniture, except wood

(G-8567)
MARIOTTI PRINTING CO LLC
513 E 28th St (44055-1396)
PHONE..............................440 245-4120
Martin Mariotti, *Managing Member*
EMP: 6 **EST:** 1937
SQ FT: 15,000
SALES (est): 371.67K **Privately Held**
Web: www.mariottiprinting.com
SIC: 2752 2759 Offset printing; Letterpress
printing

(G-8568)
NATIONAL BRONZE MTLS OHIO INC
Also Called: Aviva Metals
5311 W River Rd (44055-3735)
PHONE..............................440 277-1226
Michael Greathead, *Pr*
Norman M Lazarus, *
Jill Conyer, *
Phil Meehan, *Sr VP*
▲ **EMP:** 27 **EST:** 1997
SALES (est): 11.44MM **Privately Held**
Web: www.avivametals.com
SIC: 3366 3341 5051 Copper foundries;
Secondary nonferrous metals; Copper
PA: Metchem Anstalt
C/O Feger Treuunternehmen Reg.
Vaduz

(G-8569)
NORLAB INC
Also Called: Norlab
7465 Industrial Parkway Dr (44053-2079)
P.O. Box 380 (44001-0380)
PHONE..............................440 282-5265
John Azok, *VP*
Frank Azok, *VP*
EMP: 10 **EST:** 1974
SQ FT: 10,000
SALES (est): 1.33MM **Privately Held**
Web: www.norlabdyes.com
SIC: 2819 Industrial inorganic chemicals, nec

(G-8570)
NOVEX PRODUCTS INC
2707 Toledo Ave Ste A (44055-1465)
PHONE..............................440 244-3330
Peyman Pakdel, *Pr*
▲ **EMP:** 30 **EST:** 2001
SQ FT: 30,000
SALES (est): 9.87MM **Privately Held**
Web: www.novexproducts.com
SIC: 2676 Towels, napkins, and tissue paper
products

(G-8571)
PC CAMPANA INC
3000 Leavitt Rd Frnt (44052-4167)
PHONE..............................800 321-0151
▲ **EMP:** 94
SALES (corp-wide): 4.99MM **Privately Held**
Web: www.pccampana.com
SIC: 3441 Fabricated structural metal
PA: P.C. Campana, Inc.
6155 Park Sq Dr Ste 1
Lorain OH 44053
800 321-0151

(G-8572)
PC CAMPANA INC (PA)
6155 Park Square Dr Ste 1 (44053-4145)
PHONE..............................800 321-0151
Pat Campana Junior, *Pr*
Michael Marsico, *

▲ **EMP:** 35 **EST:** 1969
SQ FT: 250,000
SALES (est): 4.99MM
SALES (corp-wide): 4.99MM **Privately Held**
Web: www.pccampana.com
SIC: 3441 Boat and barge sections, prefabricated metal

(G-8573)
PERKINS MOTOR SERVICE LTD (PA)
Also Called: Standard Welding & Lift Truck
1864 E 28th St (44055-1804)
PHONE..............................440 277-1256
EMP: 18 **EST:** 1969
SQ FT: 10,200
SALES (est): 2.03MM
SALES (corp-wide): 2.03MM **Privately Held**
SIC: 5013 5531 7692 7539 Truck parts and accessories; Truck equipment and parts; Automotive welding; Radiator repair shop, automotive

(G-8574)
PRIME INDUSTRIES INC
1817 Iowa Ave (44052-3359)
EMP: 17 **EST:** 1984
SQ FT: 53,000
SALES (est): 2.98MM **Privately Held**
SIC: 3086 3544 2821 2671 Plastics foam products; Special dies, tools, jigs, and fixtures; Plastics materials and resins; Paper; coated and laminated packaging

(G-8575)
RACEWAY PETROLEUM INC
Also Called: Raceway
3040 Oberlin Ave (44052-4563)
PHONE..............................440 989-2660
Imran Nazir, *Prin*
EMP: 6 **EST:** 2009
SALES (est): 509.42K **Privately Held**
SIC: 3644 Raceways

(G-8576)
REFRACTORY COATING TECH INC
2421 E 28th St (44055-2113)
PHONE..............................800 807-7464
EMP: 20
Web: www.refcotec.com
SIC: 3299 Insulsleeves (foundry materials)
PA: Refractory Coating Technologies, Inc.
542 Collins Blvd
Orrville OH 44667

(G-8577)
REPUBLIC ENGINEERED PRODUCTS
Also Called: Republic Steel
1807 E 28th St (44055-1803)
PHONE..............................440 277-2000
Jim Kuntz, *Pr*
EMP: 27 **EST:** 2015
SALES (est): 1.87MM **Privately Held**
Web: www.republicsteel.com
SIC: 3312 Bars, iron: made in steel mills

(G-8578)
REPUBLIC STEEL
1807 E 28th St (44055-1803)
PHONE..............................440 277-2000
Joseph Lapinsky, *Brnch Mgr*
EMP: 26
Web: www.republicsteel.com
SIC: 3312 Blast furnaces and steel mills
HQ: Republic Steel
2633 8th St
Canton OH 44704
330 438-5435

(G-8579)
ROCKWELL METALS COMPANY LLC
3709 W Erie Ave (44053-1237)
PHONE..............................440 242-2420
Chris Harrington, *Managing Member*
▲ **EMP:** 15 **EST:** 2010
SQ FT: 54,000
SALES (est): 5.04MM **Privately Held**
Web: www.rockwellmetals.com
SIC: 5051 3444 Sheets, metal; Sheet metalwork

(G-8580)
SENTINEL MANAGEMENT INC
Also Called: Semco Carbon
3000 Leavitt Rd Unit 1 (44052-4168)
PHONE..............................440 821-7372
Vincent L Thompson, *Pr*
Nancy Thompson, *
Matt Thompson, *
EMP: 28 **EST:** 1971
SALES (est): 5.76MM **Privately Held**
SIC: 3624 Carbon and graphite products

(G-8581)
SKYLIFT INC
3000 Leavitt Rd Ste 6 (44052-4166)
PHONE..............................440 960-2100
George Wojnowski, *Pr*
Nicholas Jarmoszuk, *
EMP: 52 **EST:** 2001
SQ FT: 6,000
SALES (est): 8.73MM **Privately Held**
Web: www.skyliftus.com
SIC: 3537 Cranes, industrial truck

(G-8582)
SYSCO GUEST SUPPLY LLC
7395 Industrial Parkway Dr (44052)
PHONE..............................440 960-2515
Jeff Dubois, *Mgr*
EMP: 41
SALES (corp-wide): 78.84B **Publicly Held**
Web: www.guestsupply.com
SIC: 5122 2844 5131 5139 Drugs, proprietaries, and sundries; Perfumes, cosmetics and other toilet preparations; Piece goods and notions; Footwear
HQ: Sysco Guest Supply, Llc
300 Davidson Ave
Somerset NJ 08873
732 537-2297

(G-8583)
TERMINAL READY-MIX INC
524 Colorado Ave (44052-2198)
PHONE..............................440 288-0181
Theresa Pelton, *Pr*
John Falbo, *
Diane Gale, *
Pete Falbo, *
▲ **EMP:** 45 **EST:** 1954
SQ FT: 1,000
SALES (est): 9.12MM **Privately Held**
Web: www.terminalreadymix.com
SIC: 3273 1611 Ready-mixed concrete; Highway and street paving contractor

(G-8584)
V & A PROCESS INC
2345 E 28th St (44055-2003)
PHONE..............................440 288-8137
Albert Di Luciano, *Pr*
Gilbert Rothman, *VP*
EMP: 11 **EST:** 1965
SALES (est): 3.42MM **Privately Held**
Web: www.vaprocessinc.com
SIC: 2821 Plastics materials and resins

(G-8585)
VERTIV ENERGY SYSTEMS INC
Also Called: Vertiv
1510 Kansas Ave (44052-3364)
PHONE..............................440 288-1122
◆ **EMP:** 800
SIC: 3661 3644 7629 Telephone and telegraph apparatus; Noncurrent-carrying wiring devices; Telecommunication equipment repair (except telephones)

(G-8586)
VERTIV GROUP CORPORATION
1510 Kansas Ave (44052-3364)
PHONE..............................440 288-1122
Dave Smith, *Opers Mgr*
EMP: 9
SALES (corp-wide): 8.01B **Publicly Held**
Web: www.vertiv.com
SIC: 3661 3644 7629 Telephone and telegraph apparatus; Noncurrent-carrying wiring devices; Telecommunication equipment repair (except telephones)
HQ: Vertiv Group Corporation
505 N Cleveland Ave
Westerville OH 43082
614 888-0246

(G-8587)
WS THERMAL PROCESS TECH INC
8301 W Erie Ave (44053-2090)
PHONE..............................440 385-6829
Joachin G Wunning, *Pr*
EMP: 9 **EST:** 2006
SALES (est): 818.34K **Privately Held**
Web: www.thermalprocessing.com
SIC: 3433 Gas burners, industrial

Lore City
Guernsey County

(G-8588)
BOB SUMEREL TIRE CO INC
63303 Institute Rd (43755-9754)
PHONE..............................740 432-5200
James Olden, *Mgr*
EMP: 9
SALES (corp-wide): 35.8MM **Privately Held**
Web: www.bobsumereltire.com
SIC: 5531 7534 5014 Automotive tires; Tire retreading and repair shops; Tires and tubes
PA: Bob Sumerel Tire Co., Inc.
1257 Cox Ave
Erlanger KY 41018
859 283-2700

(G-8589)
VIKING WELL SERVICE INC
64201 Wintergreen Rd (43755-9704)
PHONE..............................681 205-1999
Duke Landry, *CEO*
Shawna Pinkerton, *Sec*
EMP: 9 **EST:** 2003
SALES (est): 5.86MM **Privately Held**
Web: www.vikingwellservice.com
SIC: 1381 Service well drilling

Loudonville
Ashland County

(G-8590)
CHAD M MARSH
16104 State Route 39 (44842-9722)
PHONE..............................419 994-0587
Chad Marsh, *Prin*
EMP: 6 **EST:** 2016
SALES (est): 380.36K **Privately Held**

SIC: 2084 Wines, brandy, and brandy spirits

(G-8591)
HOCHSTETLER MILLING LLC
552 State Route 95 (44842-9611)
PHONE..............................419 368-0004
EMP: 22 **EST:** 1987
SQ FT: 13,000
SALES (est): 2.31MM **Privately Held**
Web: www.hochstetlerloghomes.com
SIC: 7389 2452 Log and lumber broker; Log cabins, prefabricated, wood

(G-8592)
OAKBRIDGE TIMBER FRAMING
9001 Township Road 461 (44842-9701)
P.O. Box 89 (44842-0089)
PHONE..............................419 994-1052
Johnny Miller, *Owner*
EMP: 6
Web: www.oakbridgetimberframing.com
SIC: 2411 Timber, cut at logging camp
PA: Oakbridge Timber Framing
20857 Earnest Rd
Howard OH 43028

(G-8593)
OHIO BIOSYSTEMS COOP INC
134 S Adams St (44842-1502)
P.O. Box 381 (44661-0381)
PHONE..............................419 980-7663
Glenn Chipner, *Pr*
EMP: 7 **EST:** 2009
SALES (est): 455.95K **Privately Held**
SIC: 2869 Industrial organic chemicals, nec

(G-8594)
SHROCK PREFAB LLC
Also Called: Shrock Engineering
614 N Spring St (44842-1038)
PHONE..............................419 994-1900
Joseph Shrock, *Managing Member*
EMP: 26 **EST:** 2008
SALES (est): 1.69MM **Privately Held**
Web: www.shrockprefab.com
SIC: 3448 Trusses and framing, prefabricated metal

(G-8595)
TRUAX PRINTING INC
425 E Haskell St (44842-1312)
PHONE..............................419 994-4166
Tom Truax, *Pr*
Bruce Truax, *
Sally Truax, *
Dan Truax; *
Zack Traux, *
EMP: 45 **EST:** 1966
SQ FT: 56,000
SALES (est): 5.38MM **Privately Held**
Web: www.truaxprinting.com
SIC: 2752 Offset printing

(G-8596)
UGLY BUNNY WINERY LLC
16104 State Route 39 (44842-9722)
PHONE..............................330 988-9057
Chad Marsh, *Managing Member*
EMP: 14 **EST:** 2017
SALES (est): 1.03MM **Privately Held**
Web:
uglybunnywinery.wpcomstaging.com
SIC: 2084 Wines

(G-8597)
YOUNGS SAND & GRAVEL CO INC
689 State Route 39 (44842)
P.O. Box 117 (44842-0117)
PHONE..............................419 994-3040
Myron Oswalt, *Pr*

EMP: 14 EST: 1946
SQ FT: 2,400
SALES (est): 1.33MM Privately Held
Web: www.youngssandandgravel.com
SIC: 1442 Construction sand and gravel

Louisville
Stark County

(G-8598)
ATI FLAT RLLED PDTS HLDNGS LLC
Also Called: ATI Flat Rolled Products
1500 W Main St (44641-2325)
PHONE...............................330 875-2244
Tony Denoi, Mgr
EMP: 10
Web: www.atimaterials.com
SIC: 3312 3471 3398 3316 Stainless steel;
  Plating and polishing; Metal heat treating;
  Cold finishing of steel shapes
HQ: Ati Flat Rolled Products Holdings, Llc
  1000 Six Ppg Pl
  Pittsburgh PA

(G-8599)
BRADLEY ENTERPRISES INC (PA)
Also Called: Family Fun
3750 Beck Ave (44641-9455)
PHONE...............................330 875-1444
Scott Cook, Pr
Terry Mckimm, VP
Pamela Halgreen, Sec
EMP: 6 EST: 1958
SQ FT: 1,500
SALES (est): 3.51MM
SALES (corp-wide): 3.51MM Privately
Held
Web: www.familyfunpools.com
SIC: 3949 5091 Swimming pools, except
  plastic; Swimming pools, equipment and
  supplies

(G-8600)
H & H QUICK MACHINE INC
7816 Edison St Ne (44641-8325)
PHONE...............................330 935-0944
Martin Hustead, Pr
Anthony Hustead, VP
EMP: 10 EST: 1997
SALES (est): 850.92K Privately Held
SIC: 3599 Machine shop, jobbing and repair

(G-8601)
H-P PRODUCTS INC
2000 W Main St (44641-2344)
PHONE...............................330 875-7193
Paul Bishop, Brnch Mgr
EMP: 172
SQ FT: 24,000
SALES (corp-wide): 47.21MM Privately
Held
Web: www.h-pproducts.com
SIC: 3498 3635 Tube fabricating (contract
  bending and shaping); Household vacuum
  cleaners
PA: H-P Products, Inc.
  512 W Gorgas St
  Louisville OH 44641
  330 875-5556

(G-8602)
H-P PRODUCTS INC (PA)
512 W Gorgas St (44641-1305)
P.O. Box 3912 (44641-3912)
PHONE...............................330 875-5556
◆ EMP: 200 EST: 1948
SALES (est): 47.21MM
SALES (corp-wide): 47.21MM Privately
Held

Web: www.h-pproducts.com
SIC: 3498 3564 3494 3354 Tube fabricating
  (contract bending and shaping); Air
  cleaning systems; Valves and pipe fittings,
  nec; Aluminum extruded products

(G-8603)
HERITAGE GROUP INC
303 S Chapel St (44641-1612)
PHONE...............................330 875-5566
John M Falk, Brnch Mgr
EMP: 3790
SALES (corp-wide): 894.43MM Privately
Held
Web: www.thgrp.com
SIC: 2951 Asphalt and asphaltic paving
  mixtures (not from refineries)
PA: Heritage Group Inc
  6320 Intech Way
  Indianapolis IN 46278
  317 872-6010

(G-8604)
HOPPEL FABRICATION SPC INC
9481 Columbus Rd Ne Ste 1 (44641-8546)
PHONE...............................330 823-5700
Steffon Hoppel, Pr
Sheryl Hoppel, VP
Renee Heilman, Treas
EMP: 10 EST: 1987
SALES (est): 914.07K Privately Held
Web: www.hoppelfab.com
SIC: 3441 Fabricated structural metal

(G-8605)
INK INC
200 S Bauman Ct (44641-1602)
P.O. Box 223 (44641-0223)
PHONE...............................330 875-4789
Bruce Leone, Pr
Jennifer Leone, VP
EMP: 6 EST: 1986
SALES (est): 171.21K Privately Held
Web: www.planetink.com
SIC: 2752 Offset printing

(G-8606)
J & L SPECIALTY STEEL INC
1500 W Main St (44641-2325)
P.O. Box 3920 (44641-3920)
PHONE...............................330 875-6200
Victor Fusco, Prin
EMP: 6 EST: 2013
SALES (est): 833.50K Privately Held
SIC: 3441 Fabricated structural metal

(G-8607)
JOHANNINGS INC
3244 S Nickelplate St (44641-9654)
PHONE...............................330 875-1706
Curtis Bates, Pr
Christy Bates, Off Mgr
EMP: 9 EST: 1964
SALES (est): 484.42K Privately Held
Web: www.johanningsinc.com
SIC: 2434 Wood kitchen cabinets

(G-8608)
MIDLAKE PRODUCTS & MFG CO
819 N Nickelplate St (44641-2455)
PHONE...............................330 875-4202
Jeffrey Rich, Pr
Jane Pukys, *
Greg Duplin, *
EMP: 60 EST: 1986
SQ FT: 28,000
SALES (est): 9.62MM Privately Held
Web: www.midlake.com
SIC: 3429 Hardware, nec

(G-8609)
MY SPLASH PAD
6565 Saint Peters Church Rd Ne
(44641-9709)
PHONE...............................330 705-1802
EMP: 6 EST: 2012
SALES (est): 792.72K Privately Held
Web: www.myportablesplashpad.com
SIC: 3999 Manufacturing industries, nec

(G-8610)
OHIO ROLL GRINDING INC
5165 Louisville St (44641-8630)
P.O. Box 7099 (44705-0099)
PHONE...............................330 453-1884
James P Robinson, Pr
Catherine Robinson, *
EMP: 26 EST: 1981
SQ FT: 14,000
SALES (est): 2.55MM Privately Held
Web: www.ohioroll.com
SIC: 3599 3471 Machine shop, jobbing and
  repair; Plating and polishing

(G-8611)
OTC SERVICES INC
1776 Constitution Ave (44641-1362)
P.O. Box 188 (44641-0188)
PHONE...............................330 871-2444
Robert Ganser Junior, CEO
▲ EMP: 80 EST: 2012
SQ FT: 98,000
SALES (est): 22MM Privately Held
Web: www.otcservices.com
SIC: 3612 Transformers, except electric

(G-8612)
PARKSITE INC
3934 Jeffries Cir (44641-7923)
PHONE...............................330 455-3782
Dennis Varn, Prin
EMP: 6 EST: 2010
SALES (est): 485.3K Privately Held
Web: www.parksite.com
SIC: 3272 Building materials, except block or
  brick: concrete

(G-8613)
**PERFORMANCE TECHNOLOGIES
LLC**
3690 Tulane Ave (44641-7960)
PHONE...............................330 875-1216
Andy Connolly, Brnch Mgr
EMP: 52
SALES (corp-wide): 5.38B Publicly Held
Web: www.patenergy.com
SIC: 1389 Oil field services, nec
HQ: Performance Technologies Llc
  3715 S Radio Rd
  El Reno OK 73036

(G-8614)
RAM INNOVATIVE TECH LLC
3969 Jeffries Cir (44641-7923)
PHONE...............................330 956-4056
EMP: 6 EST: 2012
SALES (est): 1.24MM Privately Held
Web: www.raminnovative.com
SIC: 3599 Machine shop, jobbing and repair

(G-8615)
SALCO MACHINE INC
3822 Victory Ave (44641-8601)
PHONE...............................330 456-8281
Annette Rosenverg, Pr
Susanna Saliola, Treas
John Saliol, VP
EMP: 10 EST: 1982
SQ FT: 8,900
SALES (est): 2.04MM Privately Held

Web: www.salcomachine.com
SIC: 3599 Machine shop, jobbing and repair

(G-8616)
SHERWOOD RTM CORP
4043 Beck Ave (44641-9458)
P.O. Box 211 (44641)
PHONE...............................330 875-7151
Ronald Brookes, Pr
EMP: 6 EST: 1967
SQ FT: 15,000
SALES (est): 968.41K Privately Held
Web: www.sherwoodcorp.com
SIC: 2821 3543 Plastics materials and resins
  ; Industrial patterns

(G-8617)
UNIWALL MFG CO (HQ)
3750 Beck Ave (44641-9455)
PHONE...............................330 875-1444
Scott Cook, Pr
Terry Mckimm, VP
Pamala Hellgren, Sec
EMP: 10 EST: 1958
SQ FT: 4,500
SALES (est): 235.24K
SALES (corp-wide): 3.51MM Privately
Held
Web: www.familyfunpools.com
SIC: 3949 Swimming pools, except plastic
PA: Bradley Enterprises, Inc.
  3750 Beck Ave
  Louisville OH 44641
  330 875-1444

(G-8618)
WASHITA VALLEY ENTERPRISES INC
3707 Tulane Ave Bldg 9 (44641-7949)
P.O. Box 409 (44641-0409)
PHONE...............................330 510-1568
Tiffany Midgett, Pr
EMP: 11
SALES (corp-wide): 25.26MM Privately
Held
Web: www.wvei.com
SIC: 1389 Oil consultants
PA: Washita Valley Enterprises, Inc.
  1705 Southeast 59th St
  Oklahoma City OK 73129
  405 670-5338

Loveland
Clermont County

(G-8619)
**AMANO CINCINNATI
INCORPORATED**
130 Commerce Dr (45140-7726)
PHONE...............................513 697-9000
Kash Gokli, VP
EMP: 11
SQ FT: 52,200
Web: www.amano.com
SIC: 3559 3873 3829 3625 Parking facility
  equipment and supplies; Watches, clocks,
  watchcases, and parts; Measuring and
  controlling devices, nec; Relays and
  industrial controls
HQ: Amano Cincinnati Incorporated
  29j Commerce Way
  Totowa NJ 07512
  973 403-1900

(G-8620)
AMANO USA HOLDINGS INC
130 Commerce Dr (45140-7726)
PHONE...............................973 403-1900
EMP: 8 EST: 2018
SALES (est): 5.66MM Privately Held

Web: www.amano.com
SIC: 3469 Metal stampings, nec

(G-8621)
ANDRITZ INC
6680 Miami Woods Dr (45140-6120)
PHONE..............................513 677-5620
EMP: 72
SALES (corp-wide): 1.13B Privately Held
Web: www.andritz.com
SIC: 3554 Pulp mill machinery
HQ: Andritz Inc.
5405 Windward Pkwy 100w
Alpharetta GA 30004
770 640-2500

(G-8622)
COLD JET INTERNATIONAL LLC (PA)
Also Called: Cold Jet
455 Wards Corner Rd (45140-9033)
PHONE..............................513 831-3211
Eugene L Cooke Iii, Managing Member
EMP: 80 EST: 2004
SALES (est): 2.29MM
SALES (corp-wide): 2.29MM Privately Held
Web: www.coldjet.com
SIC: 3589 2813 Commercial cleaning equipment; Dry ice, carbon dioxide (solid)

(G-8623)
CURRENT ELEC & ENRGY SOLUTIONS
Also Called: Current Electrical & Lighting
1527 State Route 28 (45140-8413)
PHONE..............................513 575-4600
Tim Driscoll, Prin
EMP: 6 EST: 2015
SALES (est): 442.43K Privately Held
SIC: 3229 3641 5063 Bulbs for electric lights; Electric lamps; Lighting fittings and accessories

(G-8624)
DVDBREW LLC
1555 Loveland Madeira Rd (45140-7804)
PHONE..............................513 677-2739
Dana Depenbrock, CEO
EMP: 10 EST: 2021
SALES (est): 63.4K Privately Held
Web: www.dvdbrew.com
SIC: 2082 Beer (alcoholic beverage)

(G-8625)
FLOWSERVE CORPORATION
Flowserve
422 Wards Corner Rd Unit F (45140-6964)
PHONE..............................513 874-6990
Brad Harrellson, Genl Mgr
EMP: 6
SALES (corp-wide): 4.56B Publicly Held
Web: www.flowserve.com
SIC: 3561 Industrial pumps and parts
PA: Flowserve Corporation
5215 N Ocnnor Blvd Ste 70
Irving TX 75039
972 443-6500

(G-8626)
GL NAUSE CO INC
1971 Phoenix Dr (45140-9241)
PHONE..............................513 722-9500
Gregory L Nause, Pr
Jodie K Nause, *
EMP: 25 EST: 1986
SQ FT: 30,000
SALES (est): 2.5MM Privately Held
Web: www.glnause.com

SIC: 3441 3443 1791 7699 Building components, structural steel; Fabricated plate work (boiler shop); Structural steel erection; Industrial equipment services

(G-8627)
GQ BUSINESS PRODUCTS INC
142 Commerce Dr (45140-7726)
PHONE..............................513 792-4750
Diana Queen, Pr
Gordon Queen, Treas
EMP: 8 EST: 1987
SALES (est): 353.17K Privately Held
Web: www.gqproducts.com
SIC: 5112 2759 5199 Business forms; Commercial printing, nec; Advertising specialties

(G-8628)
GREENLIGHT OPTICS LLC
8940 Glendale Milford Rd (45140-8908)
PHONE..............................513 247-9777
Todd Rutherford, Managing Member
Michael Okeefe, Managing Member
Bill Phillips, Managing Member
EMP: 20 EST: 2009
SQ FT: 8,000
SALES (est): 5.63MM Privately Held
Web: www.greenlightoptics.com
SIC: 3827 3089 Optical instruments and apparatus; Lenses, except optical: plastics

(G-8629)
HAECO INC (PA)
6504 Charles Snider Rd (45140-9228)
PHONE..............................513 722-1030
Jerry Henline, Pr
▲ EMP: 8 EST: 1985
SQ FT: 7,200
SALES (est): 2.35MM
SALES (corp-wide): 2.35MM Privately Held
Web: www.haeco.us
SIC: 3559 Pack-up assemblies, wheel overhaul

(G-8630)
HEULE TOOL CORPORATION
131 Commerce Dr (45140-7727)
PHONE..............................513 860-9900
Heinrich Heule, Pr
Ulf Heule, *
Gary Brown, *
EMP: 25 EST: 1988
SQ FT: 3,500
SALES (est): 2.67MM Privately Held
Web: www.heuletool.com
SIC: 3599 Machine shop, jobbing and repair
PA: Heule Werkzeug Ag
Wegenstrasse 11
Balgach SG 9436

(G-8631)
INNERWOOD & COMPANY
688 Elizabeth Ln (45140-9172)
PHONE..............................513 677-2229
J V Melink-hueber, Prin
Janine V Melink-hueber, CEO
EMP: 15 EST: 1993
SALES (est): 290.72K Privately Held
Web: www.innerwood.com
SIC: 2517 2521 Wood television and radio cabinets; Wood office filing cabinets and bookcases

(G-8632)
INTELLIGENT SIGNAL TECH INTL
Also Called: Ist International
6318 Dustywind Ln (45140-7730)
PHONE..............................614 530-4784
Sheldyn K Armstrong, Pr

Matthew Bolton, CFO
EMP: 8 EST: 1997
SQ FT: 2,500
SALES (est): 271.6K Privately Held
Web: www.intelligentsignals.com
SIC: 3669 Traffic signals, electric

(G-8633)
INTERNATIONAL PAPER COMPANY
Also Called: International Paper
6283 Tri Ridge Blvd (45140-8318)
PHONE..............................513 248-6319
EMP: 118
SALES (corp-wide): 18.62B Publicly Held
Web: www.internationalpaper.com
SIC: 2621 Paper mills
PA: International Paper Company
6400 Poplar Ave
Memphis TN 38197
901 419-7000

(G-8634)
KBC SERVICES
9993 Union Cemetery Rd (45140-7187)
PHONE..............................513 693-3743
Kevin Brown, Prin
EMP: 10 EST: 2015
SALES (est): 229.31K Privately Held
Web: www.kbcservicesllc.com
SIC: 1389 8742 Construction, repair, and dismantling services; Construction project management consultant

(G-8635)
KMGRAFX INC
Also Called: Asi Sign Systems
394 Wards Corner Rd Ste 100 (45140-8339)
PHONE..............................513 248-4100
Kimberly Moscarino, Pr
Kenneth Knarr, Treas
EMP: 8 EST: 1982
SQ FT: 2,700
SALES (est): 468.48K Privately Held
Web: www.asisignage.net
SIC: 3993 Signs and advertising specialties

(G-8636)
KROSS ACQUISITION COMPANY LLC
10690 Loveland Madeira Rd (45140-8964)
PHONE..............................513 554-0555
EMP: 30 EST: 2006
SALES (est): 4.59MM Privately Held
Web: www.basementdoctorcincy.com
SIC: 1799 7299 1389 Waterproofing; Home improvement and renovation contractor agency; Construction, repair, and dismantling services

(G-8637)
LOCKFAST LLC
107 Northeast Dr (45140-7145)
PHONE..............................800 543-7157
Ed Packer, Pr
EMP: 9 EST: 1969
SALES (est): 925.07K Privately Held
Web: www.lockfast.com
SIC: 2396 3965 3069 2672 Automotive trimmings, fabric; Tape, hook-and-eye, and snap fastener; Tape, pressure sensitive: rubber; Tape, pressure sensitive: made from purchased materials

(G-8638)
MACPRO INC
Also Called: Machine Products
1456 Fay Rd Unit B (45140-9771)
PHONE..............................513 575-3000
D Wayne Hughes, Pr
David Hughes, VP

EMP: 10 EST: 1967
SQ FT: 20,000
SALES (est): 817.82K Privately Held
Web: www.macpro1.com
SIC: 3599 Machine shop, jobbing and repair

(G-8639)
MAINSTREAM WATERJET LLC
108 Northeast Dr (45140-7144)
PHONE..............................513 683-5426
Thomas Harbin, CEO
Jayson Daus, VP
EMP: 22 EST: 2004
SQ FT: 25,000
SALES (est): 5.89MM Privately Held
Web: www.mainstreamwaterjet.com
SIC: 3599 Machine shop, jobbing and repair

(G-8640)
MATERIAL HOLDINGS INC
185 Commerce Dr (45140-7727)
PHONE..............................513 583-5500
Winfield Scott, Pr
Thomas C Hamm, Prin
Joe Schuetz, CFO
▲ EMP: 20 EST: 1999
SALES (est): 4.49MM Privately Held
Web: www.bryantpro.com
SIC: 3535 Conveyors and conveying equipment

(G-8641)
MATTR US INC
Also Called: Dsg-Canusa
173 Commerce Dr (45140-7727)
P.O. Box 498830 (45249-8830)
PHONE..............................513 683-7800
Jim Raussen N America, Sls Mgr
EMP: 25
SALES (corp-wide): 673.6MM Privately Held
Web: www.mattr.com
SIC: 3317 Steel pipe and tubes
HQ: Mattr Us Inc.
5875 N Sam Hston Pkwy E S
Houston TX 77032
281 886-2350

(G-8642)
MENARD INC
Also Called: Menards
3787 W State Route 22 3 (45140-3515)
PHONE..............................513 583-1444
Bert Marsh, Mgr
EMP: 150
SALES (corp-wide): 1.7B Privately Held
Web: www.menards.com
SIC: 2431 5211 Millwork; Lumber and other building materials
PA: Menard, Inc.
5101 Menard Dr
Eau Claire WI 54703
715 876-2000

(G-8643)
MICHAELS PRE-CAST CON PDTS INC
1917 Adams Rd (45140-7236)
PHONE..............................513 683-1292
Vernon Michael, Pr
Donald Michael, VP
Mary Jane Micheal, Sec
Vernon Jim Michael, VP
EMP: 10 EST: 1950
SQ FT: 5,000
SALES (est): 234.1K Privately Held
SIC: 5032 5999 3446 3272 Concrete building products; Concrete products, pre-cast; Architectural metalwork; Concrete products, nec

(G-8644)
PHANTOM SOUND
11865 Enyart Rd (45140-8230)
PHONE..............................513 759-4477
Howard Mc Gurdy, *Owner*
◆ **EMP: 6 EST:** 2000
SALES (est): 466.15K **Privately Held**
Web: www.phantomsound.com
SIC: 3651 5731 Speaker systems; Radio,
   television, and electronic stores

(G-8645)
PHOENIX INDS & APPARATUS INC
6466 Snider Rd Apt C (45140-9542)
PHONE..............................513 722-1085
Sheri L Nause, *Pr*
Carl D Nause, *VP*
EMP: 15 EST: 1969
SQ FT: 8,550
SALES (est): 965.57K **Privately Held**
SIC: 7692 Welding repair

(G-8646)
POWDER ALLOY CORPORATION
Also Called: Pac
9401 Union Cemetery Rd (45140-9622)
PHONE..............................513 984-4016
E Stephen Payne, *Pr*
Darlene Payne, *
Kimberly R Gatto, *
▲ **EMP: 40 EST:** 1976
SQ FT: 20,000
SALES (est): 9.9MM **Privately Held**
Web: www.powderalloy.com
SIC: 3479 1382 4911 2836 Coating of
   metals and formed products; Oil and gas
   exploration services; Electric services;
   Biological products, except diagnostic

(G-8647)
RAY MEYER SIGN COMPANY INC
8942 Glendale Milford Rd (45140-8908)
PHONE..............................513 984-5446
Ray A Meyer, *Pr*
Michael A Meyer, *
John A Meyer, *
Barbara A Meyer, *
EMP: 25 EST: 1956
SQ FT: 12,000
SALES (est): 2.99MM **Privately Held**
Web: www.raymeyersigns.com
SIC: 3993 Signs and advertising specialties

(G-8048)
ROBERDS CONVERTING CO INC
113 Northeast Dr (45140-7145)
PHONE..............................513 683-6667
James J Achberger, *Pr*
John M Achberger, *
William W Achberger, *
EMP: 38 EST: 1905
SQ FT: 72,000
SALES (est): 5.11MM **Privately Held**
Web: www.roberdsconverting.com
SIC: 2679 Paperboard products, converted,
   nec

(G-8649)
ROZZI COMPANY INC (PA)
Also Called: Rozzi Company
10059 Loveland Madeira Rd (45140-8956)
P.O. Box 5 (45140-0005)
PHONE..............................513 683-0620
Joseph Rozzi, *Pr*
Arthur Rozzi, *
Nancy Rozzi, *
▲ **EMP: 25 EST:** 1931
SALES (est): 2.18MM
SALES (corp-wide): 2.18MM **Privately
Held**
Web: www.rozzifireworks.com

SIC: 2899 Fireworks

(G-8650)
SAFE-GRAIN INC (PA)
417 Wards Corner Rd Ste B (45140-9083)
PHONE..............................513 398-2500
Scott Chant, *Pr*
EMP: 7 EST: 1954
SALES (est): 2.6MM
SALES (corp-wide): 2.6MM **Privately Held**
Web: www.safegrain.com
SIC: 3829 1731 Temperature sensors,
   except industrial process and aircraft;
   Electronic controls installation

(G-8651)
SATCO INC
457 Wards Corner Rd (45140-9027)
PHONE..............................513 707-6150
EMP: 60
SALES (corp-wide): 30.19MM **Privately
Held**
Web: www.satco-inc.com
SIC: 2448 Pallets, wood and metal
   combination
PA: Satco, Inc.
   1601 E El Segundo Blvd
   El Segundo CA 90245
   310 322-4719

(G-8652)
SCRIP-SAFE SECURITY PRODUCTS
Also Called: Scrip-Safe International
136 Commerce Dr (45140-7726)
PHONE..............................513 697-7789
Joseph E Orndorff, *Pr*
Joanne Orndorff, *Treas*
▼ **EMP: 20 EST:** 1989
SQ FT: 15,000
SALES (est): 2.16MM **Privately Held**
Web: www.parchment.com
SIC: 2752 7389 Offset printing; Printing
   broker

(G-8653)
SIGNODE INDUSTRIAL GROUP LLC
Also Called: Angleboard
396 Wards Corner Rd Ste 100
(45140-9060)
PHONE..............................513 248-2990
Shane Harrisson, *Mgr*
EMP: 120
SALES (corp-wide): 11.8B **Publicly Held**
Web: www.signode.com
SIC: 2679 2671 Paper products, converted,
   nec; Paper; coated and laminated
   packaging
HQ: Signode Industrial Group Llc
   14025 Rveredge Dr Ste 500
   Tampa FL 33637
   800 323-2464

(G-8654)
SIRRUS INC
422 Wards Corner Rd (45140-6965)
P.O. Box 53130 (45253-0130)
PHONE..............................513 448-0308
Robert Goodnight, *Pr*
▲ **EMP: 34 EST:** 2009
SALES (est): 2.42MM **Privately Held**
Web: www.sirruschemistry.com
SIC: 2891 Adhesives and sealants

(G-8655)
VALVE RELATED CONTROLS INC
Also Called: Vrc
143 Commerce Dr (45140-7727)
PHONE..............................513 677-8724
Fred Tasch, *CEO*
Ed Lester, *Pr*
▲ **EMP: 12 EST:** 1990

SQ FT: 12,000
SALES (est): 1.44MM **Privately Held**
Web: www.vrc-usa.com
SIC: 5084 3625 Industrial machinery and
   equipment; Positioning controls, electric

(G-8656)
WASHING SYSTEMS LLC (HQ)
167 Commerce Dr (45140-7727)
PHONE..............................800 272-1974
John Walroth, *CEO*
Jonathan C Dill, *
▼ **EMP: 110 EST:** 1989
SALES (est): 27.33MM **Privately Held**
Web: www.washingsystems.com
SIC: 5169 2841 Detergents; Soap and other
   detergents
PA: Kao Corporation
   1-14-10, Nihombashikayabacho
   Chuo-Ku TKY 103-0

Lowellville
Mahoning County

(G-8657)
**ALUMINUM COLOR INDUSTRIES INC
(PA)**
369 W Wood St (44436-1039)
PHONE..............................330 536-6295
Trude Stoeckel-spinosa, *Pr*
Lorna Willard, *Sec*
Tina Spinosa, *Treas*
EMP: 43 EST: 1953
SQ FT: 30,000
SALES (est): 402.67K
SALES (corp-wide): 402.67K **Privately
Held**
SIC: 3442 3471 3444 Moldings and trim,
   except automobile: metal; Finishing, metals
   or formed products; Sheet metalwork

(G-8658)
**ARS RECYCLING SYSTEMS LLC
(PA)**
Also Called: Advanced Recycling Systems
4000 Mccartney Rd (44436-9413)
PHONE..............................330 536-8210
Gus G Lyras, *Pr*
Elio Mussullo, *VP*
Victor Pallotta, *VP*
Patsy Pilorusso, *Stockholder*
FMP· 17 FST· 1991
SQ FT: 25,000
SALES (est): 9.85MM **Privately Held**
Web: www.arsrecycling.com
SIC: 7699 3559 Welding equipment repair;
   Recycling machinery

(G-8659)
**ARS RECYCLING SYSTEMS 2019
LLC**
4000 Mccartney Rd (44436-9413)
PHONE..............................330 536-8210
EMP: 20 EST: 2019
SALES (est): 2.69MM **Privately Held**
Web: www.arsrecycling.com
SIC: 3999 Manufacturing industries, nec

(G-8660)
ERNEST INDUSTRIES INC
4000 Mccartney Rd (44436-9413)
PHONE..............................937 325-9851
Michael T Stute, *Pr*
EMP: 50 EST: 1967
SALES (est): 4.9MM **Privately Held**
Web: www.ernestindustries.com
SIC: 3559 Concrete products machinery
PA: Ars Recycling Systems, Llc
   4000 Mccartney Rd

Lowellville OH 44436

(G-8661)
FALCON FOUNDRY COMPANY
96 6th St (44436-1264)
P.O. Box 301 (44436-0301)
PHONE..............................330 536-6221
Gary S Slaven, *Pr*
Lisa Mendozzi, *
William R Lopatta, *
John Lopatta, *
◆ **EMP: 90 EST:** 1953
SQ FT: 175,000
SALES (est): 8.77MM **Privately Held**
Web: www.falconfoundry.com
SIC: 3366 Castings (except die), nec, copper
   and copper-base alloy

(G-8662)
GARLAND WELDING CO INC
804 E Liberty St (44436-1266)
PHONE..............................330 536-6506
Rose Del Signore, *Pr*
Vincent Del Signore, *Prin*
Ralph Signore, *VP*
Nick Del Signore, *Sec*
Joanne Del Signore, *Sec*
EMP: 12 EST: 1962
SQ FT: 6,880
SALES (est): 3.24MM **Privately Held**
Web: www.garlandwelding.com
SIC: 3441 7692 Fabricated structural metal;
   Welding repair

(G-8663)
LYCO CORPORATION
Also Called: Pilorusso Construction Div
1089 N Hubbard Rd (44436-9737)
PHONE..............................412 973-9176
Patsy Pilorusso, *Pr*
Elio Massullo, *Owner*
W C Pilorusso, *VP*
Mike Pallotto, *VP*
EMP: 7 EST: 1947
SQ FT: 25,000
SALES (est): 494.95K **Privately Held**
Web: www.lycomfg.com
SIC: 7699 3441 Welding equipment repair;
   Fabricated structural metal

(G-8664)
RAVANA INDUSTRIES INC
6170 Center Rd (44436-9521)
PHONE..............................330 536-4015
Danette J St Vencent, *CEO*
William St Vincent, *Pr*
EMP: 8 EST: 1988
SALES (est): 317.32K **Privately Held**
SIC: 3541 3363 Machine tool replacement &
   repair parts, metal cutting types; Aluminum
   die-castings

Lower Salem
Washington County

(G-8665)
BLAIR LOGGING
30530 Lebanon Rd (45745-9733)
PHONE..............................740 934-2730
Ronald Blair, *Owner*
EMP: 6 EST: 1998
SALES (est): 96.22K **Privately Held**
SIC: 2411 Logging camps and contractors

Lucasville
Scioto County

(G-8666)
E A COX INC
11201 State Route 104 (45648-7512)
P.O. Box 819 (45648-0819)
PHONE......................740 858-4400
Forrest Arbaugh, *Pr*
EMP: 8 EST: 1970
SALES (est): 228.82K **Privately Held**
SIC: 3272 Septic tanks, concrete

(G-8667)
MAKO FINISHED PRODUCTS INC
708 Fairground Rd (45648-3507)
P.O. Box 1030 (45662-1030)
PHONE......................740 357-0839
Mark Miller, *Pr*
EMP: 25 EST: 2014
SALES (est): 869.91K **Privately Held**
Web: www.makofinishedproducts.com
SIC: 3999 Manufacturing industries, nec

(G-8668)
MICHAEL W NEWTON
Also Called: Newton's Paint & Body
768 Fairground Rd (45648-8363)
PHONE......................740 352-9334
Michael W Newton, *Owner*
Michael Newton, *Owner*
EMP: 7 EST: 1990
SQ FT: 20,000
SALES (est): 152.64K **Privately Held**
SIC: 7532 3479 Paint shop, automotive;
　Painting of metal products

(G-8669)
R & D LOGGING LLC
2218 Cramer Rd (45648-8316)
PHONE......................740 259-6127
Randall Burns, *Prin*
EMP: 6 EST: 2014
SALES (est): 169.76K **Privately Held**
SIC: 2411 Logging camps and contractors

Luckey
Wood County

(G-8670)
HIRZEL FARMS INC
20790 Bradner Rd (43443-9727)
PHONE......................419 837-2710
Lou Kozma, *Pr*
EMP: 7 EST: 1963
SALES (est): 475.7K **Privately Held**
Web: www.hirzelfarms.com
SIC: 0191 2074 General farms, primarily crop
　; Cottonseed oil mills

(G-8671)
NSG GLASS NORTH AMERICA INC
21705 Pemberville Rd (43443-9783)
PHONE......................734 755-5816
EMP: 118
SALES (corp-wide): 4.43MM **Privately
Held**
SIC: 3211 Flat glass
PA: Nsg Glass North America, Inc.
　811 Madison Ave
　Toledo OH 43604
　419 247-4800

Ludlow Falls
Miami County

(G-8672)
MARMAX MACHINE CO
Also Called: Meiring Precision
2425 S State Route 48 (45339-9792)
P.O. Box 99 (45339-0099)
PHONE......................937 698-9900
David M Shepherd, *Owner*
EMP: 7 EST: 1983
SQ FT: 7,200
SALES (est): 214.62K **Privately Held**
Web: www.marmaxmachine.com
SIC: 3599 Machine shop, jobbing and repair

Lyons
Fulton County

(G-8673)
B W GRINDING CO
Also Called: Bw Supply Co.
15048 County Rd 10-3 (43533-9713)
P.O. Box 307 (43533-0307)
PHONE......................419 923-1376
Martin Welch, *Pr*
EMP: 35 EST: 1978
SQ FT: 30,000
SALES (est): 4.73MM **Privately Held**
Web: www.bwsupplyco.com
SIC: 5085 3324 Industrial tools; Commercial
　investment castings, ferrous

(G-8674)
MCS MFG LLC
15210 County Road 10 3 (43533-9713)
PHONE......................419 923-0169
Aaron R Call, *Prin*
EMP: 7 EST: 2008
SALES (est): 469.12K **Privately Held**
Web: www.mcsmfg.com
SIC: 3999 Manufacturing industries, nec

(G-8675)
RAY-TECH INDUSTRIES LLC
15210 County Road 10 3 (43533-9713)
PHONE......................419 923-0169
Aaron Call, *Prin*
EMP: 6 EST: 2005
SALES (est): 739.85K **Privately Held**
Web: www.ray-tech-ind.com
SIC: 3599 Machine shop, jobbing and repair

Macedonia
Summit County

(G-8676)
AGS CUSTOM GRAPHICS INC
Also Called: A G S Ohio
8107 Bavaria Dr E (44056-2252)
PHONE......................330 963-7770
John Green, *Pr*
Mark Edgar, *
EMP: 74 EST: 1993
SQ FT: 70,000
SALES (est): 26.07MM
SALES (corp-wide): 15B **Privately Held**
Web: www.rrd.com
SIC: 2752 2721 3375 2791 Offset printing;
　Periodicals; Information retrieval services;
　Typesetting
HQ: R. R. Donnelley & Sons Company
　227 W Monroe St Ste 500
　Chicago IL 60606
　312 326-8000

(G-8677)
AMERICAN LIGHT METALS LLC
Also Called: Empire Die Casting Company
635 Highland Rd E (44056-2109)
PHONE......................330 908-3065
Yogen Rahangdale, *Managing Member*
EMP: 200 EST: 2013
SQ FT: 200,000
SALES (est): 22.12MM
SALES (corp-wide): 44.27MM **Privately
Held**
SIC: 3363 3364 Aluminum die-castings; Zinc
　and zinc-base alloy die-castings
HQ: Srs Die Casting Holdings, Llc
　635 Highland Rd E
　Macedonia OH 44056
　330 467-0750

(G-8678)
BILZ VIBRATION TECHNOLOGY INC
895 Highland Rd E Ste F (44056-2128)
P.O. Box 241305 (44124-8305)
PHONE......................330 468-2459
Marc A Brower, *Pr*
Bill Granchi, *VP*
▲ **EMP: 15 EST:** 2005
SQ FT: 8,000
SALES (est): 1.81MM **Privately Held**
Web: www.bilz-usa.com
SIC: 5084 3829 Machinists' precision
　measuring tools; Vibration meters,
　analyzers, and calibrators

(G-8679)
BINDTECH LLC
Also Called: Finish Line Binderies
8212 Bavaria Dr E (44056-2248)
PHONE......................615 834-0404
EMP: 57
SALES (corp-wide): 23.93MM **Privately
Held**
Web: www.bindtechinc.com
SIC: 2789 Binding only: books, pamphlets,
　magazines, etc.
HQ: Bindtech, Llc
　1232 Antioch Pike
　Nashville TN 37211
　615 834-0404

(G-8680)
BUDGET MOLDERS SUPPLY INC
8303 Corporate Park Dr (44056-2300)
PHONE......................216 367-7050
Ed Kuchar Senior, *Pr*
Ed Kuchar Junior, *VP*
Francis E Kuchar, *Sec*
Raymond A Kuchar, *OK Vice President*
EMP: 18 EST: 1987
SALES (est): 432.64K **Privately Held**
Web: www.ppe.com
SIC: 3559 Plastics working machinery

(G-8681)
**CHAMPION WIN CO CLEVELAND
LLC**
9011 Freeway Dr Ste 1 (44056-1524)
PHONE......................440 899-2562
◆ **EMP: 7 EST:** 1997
SALES (est): 2.12MM **Privately Held**
Web: www.championwindow.com
SIC: 3442 5031 Storm doors or windows,
　metal; Windows

(G-8682)
CUSTOM GRAPHICS INC
Also Called: AGS Custom Graphics
8107 Bavaria Dr E (44056-2252)
PHONE......................330 963-7770
Stan Ritter, *Pr*
EMP: 59 EST: 1977
SQ FT: 85,000

SALES (est): 990.6K
SALES (corp-wide): 15B **Privately Held**
Web: www.rrd.com
SIC: 2752 Offset printing
HQ: Consolidated Graphics, Inc.
　5858 Westheimer Rd # 200
　Houston TX 77057

(G-8683)
DESIGN MOLDED PLASTICS INC
8220 Bavaria Dr E (44056-2248)
PHONE......................330 963-4400
Jay Honsaker, *Pr*
Diane Hanson, *
Andre Burke, *
▲ **EMP: 132 EST:** 1985
SALES (est): 6.96MM **Privately Held**
Web: www.designmolded.com
SIC: 3089 Injection molded finished plastics
　products, nec

(G-8684)
**DESIGN MOLDED PRODUCTS LLC
(PA)** ✪
8220 Bavaria Dr E (44056-2248)
PHONE......................330 963-4400
Brian Schroeder, *Pr*
EMP: 17 EST: 2023
SALES (est): 15.31MM
SALES (corp-wide): 15.31MM **Privately
Held**
SIC: 3089 Injection molded finished plastics
　products, nec

(G-8685)
DESIGN MOLDED PRODUCTS LLC
8272 Bavaria Dr E (44056-2248)
PHONE......................330 963-4400
EMP: 33
SALES (corp-wide): 15.31MM **Privately
Held**
Web: www.designmolded.com
SIC: 3089 Injection molding of plastics
PA: Design Molded Products Llc
　8220 Bavaria Rd
　Macedonia OH 44056
　330 963-4400

(G-8686)
DIEMASTER TOOL & MOLD INC
895 Highland Rd E # 5 (44056-2128)
PHONE......................330 467-4281
Paul Badovick, *Pr*
Dorothy Badovick, *Sec*
EMP: 6 EST: 1966
SQ FT: 7,200
SALES (est): 2.1MM **Privately Held**
Web: www.diemaster.com
SIC: 3089 Injection molding of plastics

(G-8687)
DON BASCH JEWELERS INC
8210 Macedonia Commons Blvd Unit 36
(44056-1861)
PHONE......................330 467-2116
Don Basch, *Pr*
Denise Basch, *Sec*
EMP: 13 EST: 1979
SALES (est): 1.47MM **Privately Held**
Web: www.donbaschjewelers.com
SIC: 3911 7631 Jewelry, precious metal;
　Watch, clock, and jewelry repair

(G-8688)
EDC LIQUIDATING INC
Also Called: Empire Die Casting Co
635 Highland Rd E (44056-2109)
PHONE......................330 467-0750
▼ **EMP:** 200

▲ = Import ▼ = Export
◆ = Import/Export

SIC: 3364 3363 Zinc and zinc-base alloy die-castings; Aluminum die-castings

(G-8689)
ETS SCHAEFER LLC
8050 Highland Pointe Pkwy (44056-2147)
PHONE.....................330 468-6600
EMP: 15
SALES (corp-wide): 483.55MM **Publicly Held**
Web: www.etsschaefer.com
SIC: 3297 3433 Nonclay refractories; Heating equipment, except electric
HQ: Ets Schaefer, Llc
3700 Park E Dr Ste 300
Beachwood OH 44122
330 468-6600

(G-8690)
FEITL MANUFACTURING CO INC
8406 Bavaria Dr E (44056-2275)
PHONE.....................330 405-6600
Julius Feitl, *Pr*
EMP: 10 **EST:** 2021
SQ FT: 70,000
SALES (est): 4.7MM **Privately Held**
Web: www.pmd-inc.com
SIC: 3429 3544 3469 Hardware, nec; Special dies, tools, jigs, and fixtures; Metal stampings, nec

(G-8691)
FORTERRA PIPE & PRECAST LLC
7925 Empire Pkwy (44056-2144)
PHONE.....................330 467-7890
Sue Waters, *Brnch Mgr*
EMP: 34
Web: www.forterrabp.com
SIC: 3272 Culvert pipe, concrete
HQ: Forterra Pipe & Precast, Llc
511 E John Crptr Fwy Ste
Irving TX 75062
469 458-7973

(G-8692)
FUNCTIONAL PRODUCTS INC
8282 Bavaria Dr E (44056-2248)
PHONE.....................330 963-3060
David Devore, *Pr*
Diane Costas, *VP*
▼ **EMP:** 12 **EST:** 1984
SQ FT: 24,000
SALES (est): 1.75MM **Privately Held**
Web: www.functionalproducts.com
SIC: 2911 5172 Oils, lubricating; Lubricating oils and greases

(G-8693)
G W STEFFEN BOOKBINDERS INC
8212 Bavaria Dr E (44056-2248)
PHONE.....................330 963-0300
William Turoczy, *Pr*
Elizabeth L Turoczy, *
EMP: 50 **EST:** 1904
SQ FT: 45,000
SALES (est): 2.37MM **Privately Held**
SIC: 2789 Binding only: books, pamphlets, magazines, etc.

(G-8694)
GASPAR SERVICES LLC
Also Called: Akland Printing
7791 Capital Blvd Ste 2 (44056-2186)
PHONE.....................330 467-8292
EMP: 6 **EST:** 1984
SQ FT: 4,200
SALES (est): 471.54K **Privately Held**
SIC: 2752 Offset printing

(G-8695)
GREAT DAY IMPROVEMENTS LLC (HQ)
Also Called: Patio Enclsures Stanek Windows
700 Highland Rd E (44056-2160)
PHONE.....................267 223-1289
Drew Weinfurtner, *CEO*
Craig Cox, *
Kevin Dow, *
EMP: 265 **EST:** 2010
SALES (est): 675.05MM **Privately Held**
Web: www.greatdayimprovements.com
SIC: 3231 3448 3444 5712 Products of purchased glass; Prefabricated metal buildings; Sheet metalwork; Outdoor and garden furniture
PA: Gdic Group, Llc
1300 E 9th St Fl 20
Cleveland OH 44114

(G-8696)
IER FUJIKURA INC (PA)
Also Called: I E R Industries
8271 Bavaria Dr E (44056-2259)
PHONE.....................330 425-7121
John Elsley, *Pr*
Athur E Lange, *
▲ **EMP:** 128 **EST:** 1958
SQ FT: 60,000
SALES (est): 22.25MM **Privately Held**
Web: www.ierfujikura.com
SIC: 3069 3061 3053 2821 Molded rubber products; Mechanical rubber goods; Gaskets; packing and sealing devices; Plastics materials and resins

(G-8697)
INNOVE INC (PA)
Also Called: Sunless
8909 Freeway Dr (44056-1574)
PHONE.....................440 836-0199
Peter Van Niekerk, *CEO*
▼ **EMP:** 64 **EST:** 2000
SQ FT: 68,000
SALES (est): 24.26MM
SALES (corp-wide): 24.26MM **Privately Held**
Web: www.sunlessinc.com
SIC: 3648 2844 Sun tanning equipment, incl. tanning beds; Face creams or lotions

(G-8698)
INOVENT ENGINEERING INC
8877 Freeway Dr (44056-1506)
P.O. Box 560314 (44056-0314)
PHONE.....................330 468-0019
Brian Fenn, *Pr*
P Clark Hungerford Junior, *Pr*
Ron Fenn, *VP*
Jim Eucker, *Stockholder*
EMP: 7 **EST:** 1984
SQ FT: 7,000
SALES (est): 844.59K **Privately Held**
Web: www.inoventengineering.com
SIC: 3599 8711 Custom machinery; Professional engineer

(G-8699)
JAY DEE SERVICE CORPORATION
Also Called: Bearing & Transm Sup Co Div
1320 Highland Rd E (44056-2310)
P.O. Box 560185 (44056-0185)
PHONE.....................330 425-1546
John Zimmerman Senior, *CEO*
Constance A Zimmerman, *Pr*
John Zimmerman Junior, *VP Sls*
Alfred Palay, *Prin*
Julia Zimmerman, *Prin*
▲ **EMP:** 8 **EST:** 1979
SQ FT: 13,000
SALES (est): 8.19MM **Privately Held**

SIC: 5084 3562 Hydraulic systems equipment and supplies; Ball bearings and parts

(G-8700)
JDH HOLDINGS INC
8220 Bavaria Dr E (44056-2248)
PHONE.....................330 963-4400
▲ **EMP:** 160
SIC: 3089 Injection molded finished plastics products, nec

(G-8701)
JOSLYN MANUFACTURING COMPANY
9400 Valley View Rd (44056-2060)
PHONE.....................330 467-8111
Bret Joslyn, *Pr*
Charles B Joslyn, *
Brain Joslyn, *
▲ **EMP:** 25 **EST:** 1946
SQ FT: 105,000
SALES (est): 9.03MM **Privately Held**
Web: www.joslyn-mfg.com
SIC: 3089 Injection molding of plastics

(G-8702)
KIMPTON PRINTING & SPC CO
Also Called: Kimpton Prtg & Specialities
400 Highland Rd E (44056-2133)
PHONE.....................330 467-1640
Dale Kimpton, *Pr*
Helen Kimpton, *VP*
Don Kimpton, *VP*
EMP: 10 **EST:** 1987
SQ FT: 2,400
SALES (est): 1.08MM **Privately Held**
Web: www.kimptonprinting.com
SIC: 2752 7336 Offset printing; Silk screen design

(G-8703)
M & M CERTIFIED WELDING INC
556 Highland Rd E Ste 3 (44056-2162)
PHONE.....................330 467-1729
Matthew B Mccann, *Pr*
EMP: 10 **EST:** 1982
SQ FT: 16,000
SALES (est): 5.58MM **Privately Held**
Web: www.mmcertifiedwelding.com
SIC: 1799 7692 Welding on site; Welding repair

(G-8704)
PEI LIQUIDATION COMPANY
700 Highland Rd E (44056-2160)
PHONE.....................330 467-4267
TOLL FREE: 800
▲ **EMP:** 160
Web: www.patioenclosures.com
SIC: 3231 3448 3444 5712 Products of purchased glass; Prefabricated metal buildings; Sheet metalwork; Outdoor and garden furniture

(G-8705)
PLASTIC MATERIALS INC
775 Highland Rd E (44056-2111)
PHONE.....................330 468-5706
William Speaks, *Prin*
EMP: 25 **EST:** 2012
SALES (est): 7.21MM **Privately Held**
Web: www.plasticmaterialsinc.com
SIC: 2821 Plastics materials and resins

(G-8706)
PLASTIC PROCESS EQUIPMENT INC (PA)
Also Called: Ppe
8303 Corporate Park Dr (44056-2300)

PHONE.....................216 367-7000
Edward Kuchar, *Pr*
◆ **EMP:** 20 **EST:** 1974
SALES (est): 12.77MM
SALES (corp-wide): 12.77MM **Privately Held**
Web: www.ppe.com
SIC: 3559 5085 5084 Plastics working machinery; Industrial supplies; Industrial machinery and equipment

(G-8707)
POLY-CARB INC
9456 Freeway Dr (44056-1000)
P.O. Box 39278 (44139-0278)
PHONE.....................440 248-1223
Puneet Singh, *Pr*
▲ **EMP:** 10 **EST:** 1973
SQ FT: 55,000
SALES (est): 3.74MM
SALES (corp-wide): 42.96B **Publicly Held**
Web: www.olinpolycarb.com
SIC: 2821 Silicone resins
HQ: The Dow Chemical Company
2211 H H Dow Way
Midland MI 48674
989 636-1000

(G-8708)
POLYONE CORPORATION
POLYONE CORPORATION
775 Highland Rd E (44056-2111)
PHONE.....................330 467-8108
Kurt Walker, *Mgr*
EMP: 100
SQ FT: 18,000
Web: www.avient.com
SIC: 2821 3087 Plastics materials and resins ; Custom compound purchased resins
PA: Avient Corporation
33587 Walker Rd
Avon Lake OH 44012

(G-8709)
PRECISION REPLACEMENT LLC
9009 Freeway Dr Unit 7 (44056-1523)
PHONE.....................330 908-0410
Joseph D Lukes, *Prin*
EMP: 6 **EST:** 2004
SQ FT: 5,500
SALES (est): 933.68K **Privately Held**
SIC: 3565 5999 Vacuum packaging machinery; Electronic parts and equipment

(G-8710)
REVAIR LLC
1333 Highland Rd E Ste E (44056-2398)
PHONE.....................440 462-6100
Scott Thomason, *Managing Member*
EMP: 14 **EST:** 2014
SALES (est): 7.66MM **Privately Held**
Web: www.myrevair.com
SIC: 3634 Hair dryers, electric

(G-8711)
ROYAL CHEMICAL COMPANY LTD (HQ)
8679 Freeway Dr (44056-1535)
PHONE.....................330 467-1300
EMP: 70 **EST:** 1938
SALES (est): 86.44MM
SALES (corp-wide): 112.99MM **Privately Held**
Web: www.royalchemical.com
SIC: 2841 Soap: granulated, liquid, cake, flaked, or chip
PA: Chemical Services Group, Inc.
8679 S Freeway Dr
Macedonia OH 44056
330 467-1300

(G-8712)
SC FIRE PROTECTION LTD
Also Called: S C Fastening Systems
8531 Freeway Dr (44056-1534)
PHONE..................................330 468-3300
Scott Filips, *Pr*
Chuck Domonkos, *CEO*
▲ EMP: 7 EST: 1999
SALES (est): 514.36K **Privately Held**
SIC: 2899 Fire extinguisher charges

(G-8713)
**SILGAN DISPENSING SYSTEMS
CORP**
1244 Highland Rd E (44056-2308)
PHONE..................................330 425-4260
Kent Houser, *Pr*
George Sehringer, *
◆ EMP: 100 EST: 1973
SQ FT: 95,000
SALES (est): 21.57MM **Publicly Held**
Web: www.silgandispensing.com
SIC: 3089 Injection molding of plastics
PA: Silgan Holdings Inc.
4 Landmark Sq Ste 400
Stamford CT 06901

(G-8714)
**SRS DIE CASTING HOLDINGS LLC
(HQ)**
Also Called: Empire Diecasting
635 Highland Rd E (44056-2109)
PHONE..................................330 467-0750
EMP: 24 EST: 2013
SALES (est): 44.27MM
SALES (corp-wide): 44.27MM **Privately
Held**
Web: www.empirecastingco.com
SIC: 3363 3364 Aluminum die-castings; Zinc
and zinc-base alloy die-castings
PA: Srs Light Metals Inc.
635 Highland Rd E
Macedonia OH 44056
330 467-0750

(G-8715)
SRS LIGHT METALS INC (PA)
635 Highland Rd E (44056-2109)
PHONE..................................330 467-0750
EMP: 14 EST: 2013
SALES (est): 44.27MM
SALES (corp-wide): 44.27MM **Privately
Held**
SIC: 3363 3364 Aluminum die-castings; Zinc
and zinc-base alloy die-castings

(G-8716)
**STANDARD SIGNS INCORPORATED
(PA)**
Also Called: Lumacurve Airfield Signs
9115 Freeway Dr (44056-1543)
PHONE..................................330 467-2030
John A Messner, *Pr*
EMP: 7 EST: 1936
SQ FT: 27,000
SALES (est): 4.31MM
SALES (corp-wide): 4.31MM **Privately
Held**
Web: www.lumacurve.com
SIC: 3993 Signs, not made in custom sign
painting shops

(G-8717)
STANEK E F AND ASSOC INC
Also Called: Stanek Windows
700 Highland Rd E (44056-2160)
PHONE..................................216 341-7700
Mark Davis, *Pr*
Jerry Donatelli, *
Robert Van Schoonhaven, *

Ron Stanek, *
EMP: 120 EST: 1985
SQ FT: 35,000
SALES (est): 1.92MM **Privately Held**
Web: www.stanekwindows.com
SIC: 3089 Windows, plastics

(G-8718)
SUPERFINISHERS INC
380 Highland Rd E (44056-2139)
PHONE..................................330 467-2125
Frank Bucar, *Pr*
EMP: 7 EST: 1958
SQ FT: 5,000
SALES (est): 698.41K **Privately Held**
Web: www.superfinishers.com
SIC: 3471 3599 Finishing, metals or formed
products; Machine shop, jobbing and repair

(G-8719)
SYSTEMS PACK INC
649 Highland Rd E (44056-2109)
PHONE..................................330 467-5729
Ray Attwell, *Pr*
Dennis Kay, *
Laurene Neval, *
EMP: 30 EST: 1977
SQ FT: 62,131
SALES (est): 8.21MM **Privately Held**
Web: www.systemspackinc.com
SIC: 5199 7389 5113 2653 Packaging
materials; Packaging and labeling services;
Shipping supplies; Corrugated and solid
fiber boxes

(G-8720)
TIN WIZARD HEATING & COOLG INC
8853 Robinwood Ter (44056-2719)
PHONE..................................330 467-9826
James Plush, *Prin*
EMP: 6 EST: 2010
SALES (est): 240.79K **Privately Held**
SIC: 3356 Tin

(G-8721)
VOLENS LLC
480 Highland Rd E (44056-2106)
PHONE..................................216 544-1200
Myron Hadetskyy, *Admn*
EMP: 6 EST: 2015
SALES (est): 1.47MM **Privately Held**
SIC: 3537 5012 Industrial trucks and tractors
; Trailers for trucks, new and used

(G-8722)
WILLARD MACHINE & WELDING INC
556 Highland Rd E Ste 3 (44056-2162)
PHONE..................................330 467-0642
Margaret Willard, *Pr*
George C Willard, *VP*
EMP: 10 EST: 1971
SQ FT: 9,600
SALES (est): 759.13K **Privately Held**
SIC: 3713 7532 Specialty motor vehicle
bodies; Top and body repair and paint shops

Madison
Lake County

(G-8723)
ALLPASS CORPORATION
222 N Lake St (44057-3118)
P.O. Box 10 (44057-0010)
PHONE..................................440 998-6300
Joseph Passerell, *CEO*
David Passerell, *CEO*
Joe Passerell, *Pr*
Steve Passerell, *COO*
Mike Passerell, *VP*

▲ EMP: 12 EST: 1992
SALES (est): 2.48MM **Privately Held**
SIC: 3443 Metal parts

(G-8724)
CASK 307 LLC
7259 Warner Rd (44057-9546)
PHONE..................................440 307-9586
EMP: 12 EST: 2018
SALES (est): 279.17K **Privately Held**
Web: www.cask307.com
SIC: 2084 Wines

(G-8725)
CHALET DEBONNE VINEYARDS INC
Also Called: Chalet Debonne
7840 Doty Rd (44057-9511)
PHONE..................................440 466-3485
Anthony Paul Debevc, *Pr*
Tony J Debevc, *VP*
Beth Debevc, *Sec*
EMP: 11 EST: 1971
SQ FT: 14,000
SALES (est): 988.09K **Privately Held**
Web: www.debonne.com
SIC: 2084 Wines

(G-8726)
CHEMMASTERS INC
300 Edwards St (44057-3112)
PHONE..................................440 428-2105
Daniel Schodowski, *Pr*
Greg Myers, *VP*
Paul Murphy Cbh, *Prin*
◆ EMP: 20 EST: 1987
SQ FT: 25,000
SALES (est): 8.51MM **Privately Held**
Web: www.chemmasters.net
SIC: 2899 2891 5169 2851 Concrete curing
and hardening compounds; Sealants;
Chemicals and allied products, nec; Paints
and allied products

(G-8727)
COMPETETIVE CARBIDE INC
Also Called: Competitive Carbide
5879 Shore Dr (44057-1801)
PHONE..................................440 350-9393
Tom Cirino, *Pr*
▲ EMP: 40 EST: 1992
SALES (est): 2.49MM **Privately Held**
Web: www.archcuttingtools.com
SIC: 3541 Machine tools, metal cutting type

(G-8728)
COUNTY OF LAKE
Also Called: Waste Water Treatment Plant
7815 Cashen Rd (44057-1651)
PHONE..................................440 428-1794
Terry Rascke, *Mgr*
EMP: 10
SQ FT: 650
SALES (corp-wide): 219.71MM **Privately
Held**
Web: www.lakecountyohio.gov
SIC: 3589 Water treatment equipment,
industrial
PA: County Of Lake
105 Main St
Painesville OH 44077
440 350-2500

(G-8729)
FORZZA CORPORATION (PA)
222 N Lake St (44057-3118)
P.O. Box 10 (44057-0010)
PHONE..................................440 998-6300
Joseph C Passerell, *CEO*
Steve Passerell, *COO*
EMP: 21 EST: 2010
SALES (est): 2.48MM

SALES (corp-wide): 2.48MM **Privately
Held**
SIC: 3585 Parts for heating, cooling, and
refrigeration equipment

(G-8730)
**GREAT LAKES POWER PRODUCTS
INC (PA)**
Also Called: John Deere Authorized Dealer
1973 Great Lakes Way (44057-9569)
PHONE..................................440 951-5111
Harry Allen Junior, *CEO*
Harry L Allen Junior, *Ch Bd*
Richard J Pennza, *
David Bell, *
Sam Profio, *
▲ EMP: 60 EST: 1973
SALES (est): 40.45MM
SALES (corp-wide): 40.45MM **Privately
Held**
Web: www.glpower.com
SIC: 5085 5084 3566 Power transmission
equipment and apparatus; Materials
handling machinery; Speed changers
(power transmission equipment), except
auto

(G-8731)
LAURENTIA WINERY
6869 River Rd (44057-9008)
PHONE..................................440 296-9170
EMP: 10 EST: 2015
SALES (est): 1.02MM **Privately Held**
Web: www.laurentiawinery.com
SIC: 2084 Wines

(G-8732)
PUMPHREY MACHINE CORP
7240 N Ridge Rd (44057-2629)
P.O. Box 477 (44057-0477)
PHONE..................................440 417-0481
Herbert Pumphrey, *Pr*
EMP: 9 EST: 1989
SQ FT: 9,000
SALES (est): 686.85K **Privately Held**
Web: www.pumphreymachinecorp.com
SIC: 3599 Machine shop, jobbing and repair

(G-8733)
TOPKOTE INC
404 N Lake St (44057-3151)
PHONE..................................440 428-0525
Shane Slattman, *Prin*
EMP: 9 EST: 2006
SALES (est): 178.83K **Privately Held**
Web: www.topkote.biz
SIC: 3479 Coating of metals and formed
products

(G-8734)
UNIVERSAL SCIENTIFIC INC
6210 Campbell Dr (44057-2003)
PHONE..................................440 428-1777
Thomas W Heckman, *Pr*
Phoebe Heckman, *Sec*
EMP: 8 EST: 1985
SQ FT: 2,500
SALES (est): 479.89K **Privately Held**
Web: www.universalscientificinc.com
SIC: 3821 Laboratory equipment: fume
hoods, distillation racks, etc.

Magnolia
Stark County

(G-8735)
OLDE WOOD LTD
7557 Willowdale Ave Se (44643-9718)
PHONE..................................330 866-1441

▲ = Import ▼ = Export
◆ = Import/Export

Thomas Sancic, *CEO*
EMP: 35 **EST:** 1996
SQ FT: 70,000
SALES (est): 6.26MM **Privately Held**
Web: www.oldewoodltd.com
SIC: 3272 Building materials, except block or brick: concrete

(G-8736)
PHOENIX ASPHALT COMPANY INC
18025 Imperial Rd (44643)
PHONE..............................330 339-4935
James R Demuth, *Pr*
EMP: 6 **EST:** 2002
SALES (est): 284.62K **Privately Held**
SIC: 1442 5032 Construction sand and gravel; Sand, construction

---

Maineville
Warren County

(G-8737)
ABCO BAR & TUBE CUTNG SVC INC
7685 S State Route 48 Ste 1 (45039-8802)
PHONE..............................513 697-9487
Kris Martin, *Pr*
Jason Martin, *
EMP: 30 **EST:** 1973
SQ FT: 40,000
SALES (est): 6.82MM **Privately Held**
Web: www.abcomachining.com
SIC: 3451 3452 3599 Screw machine products; Bolts, nuts, rivets, and washers; Machine and other job shop work

(G-8738)
BAVIS FABACRAFT INC
201 Grandin Rd (45039-9762)
PHONE..............................513 677-0500
David Bavis, *Pr*
Larry Sumpter, *CEO*
Kim Coots, *CFO*
EMP: 29 **EST:** 2021
SALES (est): 1.33MM **Privately Held**
Web: www.bavis.com
SIC: 3535 2522 3552 Belt conveyor systems, general industrial use; File drawer frames: except wood; Opening machinery and equipment

(G-8739)
EMPANADAS AQUI LLC
8749 Surrey Pl (45039-9519)
PHONE..............................513 312-9566
EMP: 20 **EST:** 2020
SALES (est): 294.66K **Privately Held**
Web: www.empanadasaqui.com
SIC: 2099 Food preparations, nec

(G-8740)
FABACRAFT INC
Also Called: Fabacraft Co
201 Grandin Rd (45039-9762)
PHONE..............................513 677-0500
Edward F Bavis, *Ch Bd*
William Sieber, *
Dolly Mattingly, *
Michael Brown, *
EMP: 35 **EST:** 1958
SQ FT: 44,000
SALES (est): 3.46MM **Privately Held**
Web: www.bavis.com
SIC: 3535 Conveyors and conveying equipment

(G-8741)
MARKET READY
1129 Avalon Dr (45039-9131)
PHONE..............................513 289-9231

Dan H Letzler, *Owner*
EMP: 6 **EST:** 2013
SALES (est): 143.01K **Privately Held**
Web: www.marketreadyhs.com
SIC: 3273 Ready-mixed concrete

Malinta
Henry County

(G-8742)
GILSON SCREEN INCORPORATED
8-810 K-2 Rd (43535)
P.O. Box P.O. Box99 (43535-0199)
PHONE..............................419 256-7711
David A Cody, *Pr*
Steven J Roby, *
Trent Smith, *
James A Cody, *
Shelly Franz, *
EMP: 42 **EST:** 1961
SQ FT: 30,000
SALES (est): 7.01MM **Privately Held**
Web: www.gilsonscreen.com
SIC: 3829 3444 Testing equipment: abrasion, shearing strength, etc.; Sheet metalwork

(G-8743)
JAD MACHINE COMPANY INC
10620 County Road J (43535-9713)
PHONE..............................419 256-6332
Jim Hastedt, *Pr*
Diane Hastedt, *Sec*
EMP: 12 **EST:** 1992
SQ FT: 12,000
SALES (est): 2.51MM **Privately Held**
Web: www.jadmachine.com
SIC: 3451 Screw machine products

Malta
Morgan County

(G-8744)
E Z GROUT CORPORATION
Also Called: Ezg Manufacturing
1833 N Riverview Rd (43758-9303)
PHONE..............................740 749-3512
Damian Lang, *Pr*
Daniel Kern, *
Douglas Taylor, *
▲ **EMP:** 26 **EST:** 1008
SALES (est): 7.05MM **Privately Held**
Web: www.ezgmfg.com
SIC: 3423 3531 Masons' hand tools; Construction machinery

(G-8745)
EZ GROUT CORPORATION INC
Also Called: Ezg Manufacturing
1833 N Riverview Rd (43758-9303)
PHONE..............................740 962-2024
Damian Lang, *Owner*
EMP: 40 **EST:** 2007
SALES (est): 9.1MM **Privately Held**
Web: www.ezgmfg.com
SIC: 5082 3499 3549 Masonry equipment and supplies; Chests, fire or burglary resistive: metal; Wiredrawing and fabricating machinery and equipment, ex. die

---

Malvern
Carroll County

(G-8746)
AMERICAN AXLE & MFG INC
Also Called: AAM Mtal Frmng-Mlvern Opration
3255 Alliance Rd Nw (44644-9756)
PHONE..............................330 863-7500
EMP: 9
SALES (corp-wide): 6.12B **Publicly Held**
Web: www.aam.com
SIC: 3714 Motor vehicle parts and accessories
HQ: American Axle & Manufacturing, Inc.
One Dauch Dr
Detroit MI 48211

(G-8747)
CAMBRIDGE MILL PRODUCTS INC
6005 Alliance Rd Nw (44644-9439)
P.O. Box 490 (44644-0490)
PHONE..............................330 863-1121
Charles Lebeau Iii, *Pr*
Jerry W Morris Ii, *VP*
EMP: 7 **EST:** 1970
SQ FT: 2,400
SALES (est): 4.34MM **Privately Held**
Web: www.cambridgemillproducts.com
SIC: 2992 Oils and greases, blending and compounding

(G-8748)
COLFOR MANUFACTURING INC (DH)
3255 Alliance Rd Nw (44644-9756)
PHONE..............................330 623-7814
David Dauch, *Ch*
Michael Simonte, *Ex VP*
Alberto Satine, *Sr VP*
▲ **EMP:** 363 **EST:** 1996
SQ FT: 60,000
SALES (est): 900MM
SALES (corp-wide): 6.12B **Publicly Held**
Web: www.colformanufacturinginc.com
SIC: 3462 3599 3463 Iron and steel forgings; Machine shop, jobbing and repair; Nonferrous forgings
HQ: American Axle & Manufacturing, Inc.
One Dauch Dr
Detroit MI 48211

(G-8749)
FOR CALL INC
3255 Alliance Rd Nw (44644-9756)
PHONE..............................330 863-0404
Inacio Moriguchi, *Pr*
EMP: 6 **EST:** 1967
SALES (est): 247.71K **Privately Held**
SIC: 3462 Iron and steel forgings

(G-8750)
GBS CORP
Also Called: GBS Filing Solutions
224 Morges Rd (44644-9736)
P.O. Box 308 (44644-0308)
PHONE..............................330 863-1828
Michele Benson, *Brnch Mgr*
EMP: 116
SALES (corp-wide): 190.76MM **Privately Held**
Web: www.gbscorp.com
SIC: 2675 2752 2672 2761 Folders, filing, die-cut: made from purchased materials; Forms, business: lithographed; Adhesive papers, labels, or tapes: from purchased material; Manifold business forms
PA: Gbs Corp.
7233 Freedom Ave Nw

North Canton OH 44720
330 494-5330

(G-8751)
GORDONS GRAPHICS INC
123 S Reed Ave (44644-9496)
P.O. Box 586 (44644-0586)
PHONE..............................330 863-2322
Brad Lewis, *Pr*
Jerry Hinton, *Sec*
EMP: 7 **EST:** 1987
SQ FT: 1,500
SALES (est): 892.88K **Privately Held**
Web: www.gordonsgraphics.com
SIC: 2752 2759 5734 5943 Offset printing; Engraving, nec; Computer and software stores; Office forms and supplies

(G-8752)
PERFECT PRODUCTS COMPANY
Also Called: Aurora Balloon Company
265 Morges Rd (44644-9753)
EMP: 25 **EST:** 1971
SQ FT: 36,000
SALES (est): 305.62K **Privately Held**
SIC: 3069 Balloons, advertising and toy: rubber

Manchester
Adams County

(G-8753)
BLUE CREEK ENTERPRISES INC
401 Starks Ave Ste A (45144-1420)
PHONE..............................937 364-2920
EMP: 10
SALES (corp-wide): 37.64MM **Privately Held**
Web: www.miracllc.com
SIC: 3672 Printed circuit boards
PA: Blue Creek Enterprises, Inc.
316 N Main St
Lynchburg OH 45142

(G-8754)
HILLTOP RECREATION INC
Also Called: Hilltop Golf Course
1649 Brown Hill Rd (45144-9317)
PHONE..............................937 549-2904
Thomas D Kizer Senior, *Pr*
George Beckner, *VP*
EMP: 6 **EST:** 1970
SQ FT: 2,451,000
SALES (est): 215.48K **Privately Held**
Web: tf.click.com.cn
SIC: 7997 2099 Golf club, membership; Ready-to-eat meals, salads, and sandwiches

(G-8755)
VANCES DEPARTMENT STORE (PA)
Also Called: Vance's Wonder Store
37 E 2nd St (45144-1301)
P.O. Box 326 (45144-0326)
PHONE..............................937 549-2188
David A Scott, *Owner*
EMP: 6 **EST:** 1980
SQ FT: 5,000
SALES (est): 928.22K
SALES (corp-wide): 928.22K **Privately Held**
SIC: 5651 5661 5211 2541 Family clothing stores; Shoe stores; Lumber and other building materials; Cabinets, except refrigerated: show, display, etc.: wood

(G-8756)
VANCES DEPARTMENT STORE
Also Called: Adams County Lumber

600 Washington St (45144-1362)
PHONE.................................937 549-3033
Gregory B Scott, *Prin*
EMP: 6
SALES (corp-wide): 928.22K **Privately Held**
SIC: 5651 5661 5211 2541 Family clothing stores; Shoe stores; Lumber and other building materials; Cabinets, except refrigerated: show, display, etc.: wood
PA: Vance's Department Store
37 E 2nd St
Manchester OH 45144
937 549-2188

Mansfield
Richland County

(G-8757)
A L CALLAHAN DOOR SALES
35 Industrial Dr (44904-1372)
PHONE.................................419 884-3667
TOLL FREE: 800
Don Callahan, *Owner*
EMP: 7 **EST:** 1983
SQ FT: 3,000
SALES (est): 949.54K **Privately Held**
Web: www.callahandoors.com
SIC: 5211 7699 3699 Garage doors, sale and installation; Garage door repair; Door opening and closing devices, electrical

(G-8758)
ABLEPRINT / TOUCAN INC
26 W 6th St (44902-1068)
PHONE.................................419 522-9742
Peter Boyko, *CEO*
Janice Boyko, *Pr*
Michelle Blackledege, *VP*
EMP: 19 **EST:** 1994
SALES (est): 1.25MM **Privately Held**
Web: www.ableprint.com
SIC: 2759 Imprinting

(G-8759)
AK MANSFIELD
913 Bowman St (44903-4109)
PHONE.................................419 755-3011
Randy Hartman, *Prin*
EMP: 13 **EST:** 2007
SALES (est): 345.91K **Privately Held**
SIC: 3999 Bleaching and dyeing of sponges

(G-8760)
AMAROQ INC
Also Called: Guetle Die & Stamping
648 N Trimble Rd (44906-2002)
PHONE.................................419 747-2110
R T Mong, *Pr*
EMP: 7 **EST:** 1967
SQ FT: 8,000
SALES (est): 1.01MM **Privately Held**
Web: www.amaroqinc.com
SIC: 3469 3544 Stamping metal for the trade; Special dies, tools, jigs, and fixtures

(G-8761)
AMATROL INC
150 Industrial Dr (44904-1339)
PHONE.................................812 288-8285
EMP: 29
SALES (corp-wide): 19.54MM **Privately Held**
Web: www.amatrol.com
SIC: 3569 Robots, assembly line: industrial and commercial
PA: Amatrol Inc
2400 Centennial Blvd
Jeffersonville IN 47130

812 288-8285

(G-8762)
AMERASCREW INC
653 Lida St (44903-1242)
P.O. Box 1407 (44901-1407)
PHONE.................................419 522-2232
John R Keith, *Pr*
EMP: 21 **EST:** 1920
SQ FT: 37,000
SALES (est): 2.48MM **Privately Held**
Web: www.amerascrew.com
SIC: 3451 Screw machine products

(G-8763)
AS AMERICA INC
Also Called: American Standard Brands
41 Cairns Rd (44903-8992)
PHONE.................................419 522-4211
Kevin Oak, *Mgr*
EMP: 60
Web: www.americanstandard-us.com
SIC: 3261 3431 3281 2541 Plumbing fixtures, vitreous china; Metal sanitary ware; Cut stone and stone products; Wood partitions and fixtures
HQ: As America, Inc.
30 Knghtsbrdge Rd Ste 301
Piscataway NJ 08854

(G-8764)
AUTOMATIC PARTS
433 Springmill St (44903-7008)
P.O. Box 1505 (44901-1505)
PHONE.................................419 524-5841
Robert H Wittmer, *Pr*
David A Wittmer, *VP*
EMP: 20 **EST:** 1956
SQ FT: 17,000
SALES (est): 679.44K **Privately Held**
Web: www.automaticparts.com
SIC: 3599 Machine shop, jobbing and repair

(G-8765)
BLACK RIVER GROUP INC (PA)
Also Called: Black River Display Group
195 E 4th St (44902-1519)
PHONE.................................419 524-6699
Terry Neff, *Pr*
EMP: 47 **EST:** 1960
SQ FT: 74,000
SALES (est): 11.55MM
SALES (corp-wide): 11.55MM **Privately Held**
Web: www.blackriverconnect.com
SIC: 7311 2752 2791 2789 Advertising agencies; Commercial printing, lithographic; Typesetting; Bookbinding and related work

(G-8766)
BLEVINS METAL FABRICATION INC
Also Called: Blevins Fabrication
288 Illinois Ave S (44905-2827)
PHONE.................................419 522-6082
Lloyd T Blevins, *Pr*
EMP: 25 **EST:** 1997
SQ FT: 13,000
SALES (est): 2.62MM **Privately Held**
Web: www.blevinsfabricationcorp.com
SIC: 7692 3446 3444 3443 Welding repair; Architectural metalwork; Sheet metalwork; Fabricated plate work (boiler shop)

(G-8767)
BREITINGER COMPANY
595 Oakenwaldt St (44905-1900)
PHONE.................................419 526-4255
Milo Breitinger, *Pr*
EMP: 120 **EST:** 1954
SQ FT: 106,000
SALES (est): 9.5MM **Privately Held**

Web: www.breitingercompany.com
SIC: 3441 3469 7692 3444 Fabricated structural metal; Metal stampings, nec; Welding repair; Sheet metalwork

(G-8768)
BROST FOUNDRY COMPANY
198 Wayne St (44902-1433)
PHONE.................................419 522-1133
Chuck Horvath, *Mgr*
EMP: 22
SALES (corp-wide): 3.88MM **Privately Held**
Web: www.brostfoundry.com
SIC: 3366 Brass foundry, nec
PA: Brost Foundry Company (Inc)
2934 E 55th St
Cleveland OH 44127
216 641-1131

(G-8769)
BUCKLER INDUSTRIES INC
Also Called: National Machine Company
861 Expressview Dr (44905-1535)
P.O. Box 2127 (44905-0127)
PHONE.................................419 589-6134
Robert Buckler, *Pr*
Marianne Buckler, *
EMP: 25 **EST:** 1972
SQ FT: 100,000
SALES (est): 224.27K **Privately Held**
SIC: 2796 Platemaking services

(G-8770)
BUNTING BEARINGS LLC
153 E 5th St (44902-1407)
P.O. Box 1053 (44901-1053)
PHONE.................................419 522-3323
Kim J Keogh, *Brnch Mgr*
EMP: 49
SQ FT: 68,000
Web: www.buntingbearings.com
SIC: 3366 3568 3369 3356 Bushings and bearings, bronze (nonmachined); Power transmission equipment, nec; Nonferrous foundries, nec; Nonferrous rolling and drawing, nec
PA: Bunting Bearings, Llc
1001 Holland Park Blvd
Holland OH 43528

(G-8771)
CASE-MAUL MANUFACTURING CO
30 Harker St (44903-1395)
PHONE.................................419 524-1061
Craig Case, *Pr*
Sandra Collins, *Sec*
Debbie Johnson, *Mgr*
▲ **EMP:** 10 **EST:** 1953
SQ FT: 18,000
SALES (est): 969.09K **Privately Held**
Web: www.casemaul.com
SIC: 3599 7692 Machine shop, jobbing and repair; Welding repair

(G-8772)
CEMENT PRODUCTS INC
389 Park Ave E (44905-2896)
PHONE.................................419 524-4342
TOLL FREE: 877
Dwight Schmitz, *Pr*
Douglas Schmitz, *
Daniel Schmitz, *
EMP: 26 **EST:** 1916
SQ FT: 82,778
SALES (est): 4.24MM **Privately Held**
Web: www.cementproductsinc.com
SIC: 3271 3273 3272 Blocks, concrete or cinder: standard; Ready-mixed concrete; Concrete products, nec

(G-8773)
CENTRAL COCA-COLA BTLG CO INC
Also Called: Coca-Cola
100 Industrial Pkwy (44903-8999)
PHONE.................................419 522-2653
Mike Dewalt, *Mgr*
EMP: 49
SALES (corp-wide): 45.75B **Publicly Held**
Web: www.coca-cola.com
SIC: 2086 Bottled and canned soft drinks
HQ: Central Coca-Cola Bottling Company, Inc.
555 Taxter Rd Ste 550
Elmsford NY 10523
914 789-1100

(G-8774)
CLEANING LADY INC
190 Stewart Rd N (44905-2639)
PHONE.................................419 589-5566
Suzanne Stewart, *Pr*
EMP: 6 **EST:** 1978
SQ FT: 7,360
SALES (est): 233.31K **Privately Held**
SIC: 7349 5169 2841 Janitorial service, contract basis; Detergents; Detergents, synthetic organic or inorganic alkaline

(G-8775)
CLEVELAND-CLIFFS STEEL CORP
Also Called: Mansfield Operations
913 Bowman St (44903-4109)
P.O. Box 247 (44901-0247)
PHONE.................................419 755-3011
Robert J Pasquarelli, *Brnch Mgr*
EMP: 500
SALES (corp-wide): 19.18B **Publicly Held**
Web: www.clevelandcliffs.com
SIC: 3312 Stainless steel
HQ: Cleveland-Cliffs Steel Corporation
200 Public Sq Ste 3300
Cleveland OH 44114

(G-8776)
COMMERCIAL CUTNG GRAPHICS LLC
Also Called: Commercial Cutting
208 Central Ave (44905-2410)
PHONE.................................419 526-4800
Jeffrey A Burkhart, *
EMP: 62 **EST:** 1987
SQ FT: 45,000
SALES (est): 10.18MM **Privately Held**
Web: www.commercialcutting.com
SIC: 2675 2754 Die-cut paper and board; Commercial printing, gravure

(G-8777)
CORPAD COMPANY INC
555 Park Ave E (44905-2871)
P.O. Box 1492 (44901-1492)
PHONE.................................419 522-7818
Dane Arlen Bonecutter, *Prin*
EMP: 55 **EST:** 1980
SQ FT: 97,500
SALES (est): 11.42MM **Privately Held**
Web: www.tavens.com
SIC: 2653 Boxes, corrugated: made from purchased materials

(G-8778)
CRANE PLUMBING LLC
41 Cairns Rd (44903-8992)
PHONE.................................419 522-4211
◆ **EMP:** 1300
SIC: 3261 3431 3088 Bathroom accessories/fittings, vitreous china or earthenware; Metal sanitary ware; Shower stalls, fiberglass and plastics

▲ = Import ▼ = Export
◆ = Import/Export

(G-8779)
DALLAS DESIGN & TECHNOLOGY INC
184 Industrial Dr (44904-1339)
P.O. Box 3043 (44904-0043)
PHONE..............................419 884-9750
Mark Stevens, *Pr*
EMP: 9 **EST:** 1976
SQ FT: 8,500
SALES (est): 1.66MM **Privately Held**
Web: www.dallasdesigntech.com
SIC: 3599 Machine shop, jobbing and repair

(G-8780)
DECA MFG CO
300 S Mill St (44904-8519)
PHONE..............................419 884-0071
Hansford R Williams, *Pr*
Karen M Cashell, *VP*
Carolyn Williams, *Sec*
EMP: 15 **EST:** 1976
SQ FT: 33,000
SALES (est): 6.35MM **Privately Held**
Web: www.decamanufacturing.com
SIC: 3679 3544 3672 Harness assemblies, for electronic use: wire or cable; Industrial molds; Printed circuit boards

(G-8781)
DTE INC
110 Baird Pkwy (44903-7909)
PHONE..............................419 522-3428
Dean Russell, *Pr*
Burke Melching, *
Rob Nelson, *
EMP: 30 **EST:** 1990
SQ FT: 45,000
SALES (est): 2.43MM **Privately Held**
Web: www.dteinc.com
SIC: 7629 3661 Telephone set repair; Telephone and telegraph apparatus

(G-8782)
EAGLES NEST HOLDINGS LLC
Also Called: Sabin Robbins Paper Company
1111 N Main St (44903-9718)
PHONE..............................419 526-4123
Joe Talion, *Mgr*
EMP: 50
SIC: 2679 Paper products, converted, nec
PA: Eagles Nest Holdings, Llc
455 E 86th St
New York NY 10028

(G-8783)
ECO ENERGY INTERNATIONAL LLC
233 Park Ave E (44902-1845)
PHONE..............................419 544-5000
EMP: 35 **EST:** 2021
SALES (est): 1.01MM **Privately Held**
Web: www.ecoenergyinternational.com
SIC: 2813 Hydrogen

(G-8784)
EDGE PLASTICS INC (PA)
449 Newman St (44902-1123)
PHONE..............................419 522-6696
Shelley Fisher, *Pr*
▲ **EMP:** 150 **EST:** 1989
SQ FT: 146,000
SALES (est): 20.95MM **Privately Held**
Web: www.edgeplasticsinc.com
SIC: 3089 Injection molded finished plastics products, nec

(G-8785)
ELTOOL CORPORATION
1400 Park Ave E (44905-2989)
PHONE..............................513 723-1772
Edward Crotty, *Pr*

EMP: 7 **EST:** 1999
SALES (est): 486.71K **Privately Held**
Web: www.eltool.com
SIC: 8742 3599 5084 Marketing consulting services; Machine shop, jobbing and repair; Industrial machinery and equipment

(G-8786)
ENERGY TECHNOLOGIES INC
Also Called: E T I
219 Park Ave E (44902-1845)
PHONE..............................419 522-4444
Paul C Madden, *Pr*
John S Madden, *
EMP: 80 **EST:** 1991
SQ FT: 30,000
SALES (est): 4.37MM **Privately Held**
Web: www.ruggedsystems.com
SIC: 3629 3625 3621 Electronic generation equipment; Relays and industrial controls; Motors and generators

(G-8787)
FILL-RITE COMPANY (HQ)
600 S Airport Rd (44903-7831)
PHONE..............................419 755-1011
Scott King, *Pr*
EMP: 27 **EST:** 2022
SALES (est): 38.93MM
SALES (corp-wide): 659.67MM **Publicly Held**
Web: www.fillrite.com
SIC: 3561 Pumps and pumping equipment
PA: Gorman-Rupp Company
600 S Airport Rd
Mansfield OH 44903
419 755-1011

(G-8788)
FIVE HANDICAP INC (PA)
Also Called: Mansfield Graphics
127 N Walnut St (44902-1221)
P.O. Box 7 (44901-0007)
PHONE..............................419 525-2511
Chuck B Mccartney, *Pr*
EMP: 10 **EST:** 1929
SQ FT: 20,000
SALES (est): 1.55MM
SALES (corp-wide): 1.55MM **Privately Held**
Web: www.mansfieldgraphics.com
SIC: 3469 Stamping metal for the trade

(C-0709)
FLEET RELIEF COMPANY
550 N Main St (44902-7322)
PHONE..............................419 525-2625
George Rohaly, *Pr*
Rhonda Rohaly, *Sec*
Connie Kant, *Prin*
EMP: 8 **EST:** 1996
SALES (est): 468.37K **Privately Held**
SIC: 7534 Tire repair shop

(G-8790)
FORREST MACHINE PDTS CO LTD
Also Called: Forrest Scrw Machine
145 Industrial Dr (44904-1338)
P.O. Box 3648 (44907-0648)
PHONE..............................419 589-3774
EMP: 22 **EST:** 2009
SALES (est): 5.47MM **Privately Held**
Web: www.fmpcorp.com
SIC: 3549 3451 Metalworking machinery nec ; Screw machine products

(G-8791)
GENERAL TECHNOLOGIES INC
855 W Longview Ave (44906-2131)
P.O. Box 1726 (44901-1726)
PHONE..............................419 747-1800

Margaret Marlow, *VP*
Susan L Moran, *Prin*
▲ **EMP:** 20 **EST:** 1957
SQ FT: 40,000
SALES (est): 3.89MM **Privately Held**
Web: www.general-technologies.com
SIC: 3469 7692 3444 3443 Metal stampings, nec; Welding repair; Sheet metalwork; Fabricated plate work (boiler shop)

(G-8792)
GLOBAL ENERGY PARTNERS LLC
Also Called: Gofs
3401 State Route 13 (44904-9394)
PHONE..............................419 756-8027
Jim Jackson, *Pr*
Annette Jones, *Sec*
EMP: 23 **EST:** 2013
SALES (est): 8.66MM **Privately Held**
Web: www.globalenergypartnersllc.com
SIC: 1389 5082 1623 Oil field services, nec; Oil field equipment; Oil and gas line and compressor station construction

(G-8793)
GORMAN-RUPP COMPANY
Ipt Pumps Division
305 Bowman St (44903-1689)
P.O. Box 1217 (44901-1217)
PHONE..............................419 755-1011
James A Lomax, *Dir*
EMP: 500
SALES (corp-wide): 659.67MM **Publicly Held**
Web: www.grpumps.com
SIC: 3561 Industrial pumps and parts
PA: Gorman-Rupp Company
600 S Airport Rd
Mansfield OH 44903
419 755-1011

(G-8794)
GORMAN-RUPP COMPANY (PA)
Also Called: GORMAN-RUPP COMPANY
600 S Airport Rd (44903-7831)
P.O. Box 1217 (44901-1217)
PHONE..............................419 755-1011
Scott A King, *Pr*
Jeffrey S Gorman, *
James C Kerr, *Ex VP*
Brigette A Burnell, *Corporate Secretary*
EMP: 147 **EST:** 1934
SQ FT: 970,000
SALES (est): 660.67MM
SALES (corp-wide): 659.67MM **Publicly Held**
Web: www.gormanrupp.com
SIC: 3594 3561 Fluid power pumps and motors; Industrial pumps and parts

(G-8795)
GORMAN-RUPP COMPANY
Also Called: Warehouse
100 Rupp Rd (44903-6512)
P.O. Box 1217 (44901-1217)
PHONE..............................419 755-1245
Jeffrey Gorman, *Pr*
EMP: 8
SALES (corp-wide): 659.67MM **Publicly Held**
Web: www.gormanrupp.com
SIC: 5084 3561 Pumps and pumping equipment, nec; Pumps and pumping equipment
PA: Gorman-Rupp Company
600 S Airport Rd
Mansfield OH 44903
419 755-1011

(G-8796)
GOYAL INDUSTRIES INC
382 Park Ave E (44905-2843)
PHONE..............................419 522-7099
Prakash R Goyal, *Pr*
▲ **EMP:** 21 **EST:** 1988
SQ FT: 18,000
SALES (est): 4.94MM **Privately Held**
Web: www.goyalinc.com
SIC: 3599 3441 Machine shop, jobbing and repair; Fabricated structural metal

(G-8797)
GRASAN EQUIPMENT COMPANY INC
Also Called: Grasan Equipment Co
440 S Illinois Ave (44907-1809)
PHONE..............................419 526-4440
Marian L Eilenfeld, *Pr*
Edward Eilenfeld Junior, *VP*
David Eilenfeld, *
Scott Eilenfeld, *
▼ **EMP:** 65 **EST:** 1970
SQ FT: 62,000
SALES (est): 943.57K **Privately Held**
Web: www.grasan.com
SIC: 4953 3532 3559 3535 Recycling, waste materials; Crushers, stationary; Recycling machinery; Conveyors and conveying equipment

(G-8798)
GRAYWACKE INC
300 S Mill St (44904-8519)
PHONE..............................419 884-7014
Scott Huffman, *Pr*
Mark Huffman, *VP*
EMP: 8 **EST:** 1999
SQ FT: 14,000
SALES (est): 1.72MM **Privately Held**
Web: www.graywacke.net
SIC: 3691 Batteries, rechargeable

(G-8799)
GROWCO INC
844 Kochheiser Rd (44904-8637)
PHONE..............................419 886-4628
Jeff Mason, *Prin*
EMP: 6 **EST:** 2009
SALES (est): 190.3K **Privately Held**
SIC: 3272 Concrete products, nec

(G-8800)
HAYFORD TECHNOLOGIES INC
Also Called: Milark Industries
500 S Airport Rd (44903-8067)
PHONE..............................419 524-7627
Matt Breitinger, *Pr*
Mary Breitinger, *
Trisha Breitinger, *
Brooke Breitinger, *
EMP: 99 **EST:** 2016
SALES (est): 707.38K **Privately Held**
SIC: 3465 3469 Automotive stampings; Metal stampings, nec

(G-8801)
HERGATT MACHINE INC
2530 Pavonia Rd (44903-7807)
PHONE..............................419 589-2931
Neil N Hergatt, *Pr*
Becky Hergatt, *Sec*
EMP: 8 **EST:** 1976
SQ FT: 4,000
SALES (est): 771.94K **Privately Held**
Web: www.hergattmachine.com
SIC: 3599 Machine shop, jobbing and repair

(G-8802)
HESS INDUSTRIES LTD
108 Sawyer Pkwy (44903-6514)
PHONE..........................419 525-4000
Mark A Hess, *Pr*
Pamela Hess, *VP*
EMP: 10 **EST:** 1999
SQ FT: 12,000
SALES (est): 2.35MM **Privately Held**
Web: www.hessindltd.com
SIC: 3544 Special dies and tools

(G-8803)
HIGHPOINT FIREARMS
Also Called: Hi-Point Firearms
1015 Springmill St (44906-1571)
PHONE..........................419 747-9444
Tom Deeb, *Pr*
Shirley Deeb, *
EMP: 8 **EST:** 1988
SQ FT: 24,000
SALES (est): 3.44MM **Privately Held**
Web: www.hi-pointfirearms.com
SIC: 3484 5941 Guns (firearms) or gun
parts, 30 mm. and below; Sporting goods
and bicycle shops

(G-8804)
IDEAL ELECTRIC POWER CO
Also Called: Ideal Electric
330 E 1st St (44902-7700)
PHONE..........................419 522-3611
Jim Petersen, *Pr*
◆ **EMP:** 30 **EST:** 1903
SQ FT: 280,000
SALES (est): 7.01MM **Privately Held**
Web: www.theidealelectric.com
SIC: 3621 3613 3625 Generators and sets,
electric; Switchgear and switchgear
accessories, nec; Relays and industrial
controls

(G-8805)
IDEX CORPORATION
800 N Main St (44902-4204)
PHONE..........................419 526-7222
EMP: 7 **EST:** 2019
SALES (est): 3.17MM **Privately Held**
Web: www.sandpiperpump.com
SIC: 3561 Pumps and pumping equipment

(G-8806)
JAY INDUSTRIES INC
Also Called: Broshco Fabricated Products
1595 W Longview Ave (44906-1806)
PHONE..........................419 747-4161
Rick R Taylor, *Pr*
Josh Taylor, *
Dave Benick, *
Rodger Loesch, *
R G Taylor, *
▲ **EMP:** 930 **EST:** 1946
SQ FT: 125,000
SALES (est): 37.31MM **Privately Held**
Web: www.jayindinc.com
SIC: 2531 3089 Seats, automobile; Injection
molding of plastics

(G-8807)
JAY MID-SOUTH LLC
150 Longview Ave E (44903-4206)
PHONE..........................256 439-6600
Rick Taylor, *Managing Member*
◆ **EMP:** 9 **EST:** 2004
SQ FT: 65,000
SALES (est): 1.63MM **Privately Held**
SIC: 3499 Automobile seat frames, metal

(G-8808)
JONES POTATO CHIP CO (PA)
823 Bowman St (44903-4107)
PHONE..........................419 529-9424
Robert Jones, *Pr*
Regina Jones, *
Charles K Hellinger, *
Frederick W Jones, *
EMP: 46 **EST:** 1940
SQ FT: 50,000
SALES (est): 9.05MM
SALES (corp-wide): 9.05MM **Privately
Held**
Web: www.joneschips.com
SIC: 2096 5145 Potato chips and other
potato-based snacks; Potato chips

(G-8809)
JOTCO INC
1400 Park Ave E (44905-2989)
PHONE..........................513 721-4943
John Young, *Pr*
Vicki Young, *Sec*
EMP: 6 **EST:** 1984
SQ FT: 100,000
SALES (est): 357.3K **Privately Held**
Web: www.eltool.com
SIC: 3471 8711 3599 Finishing, metals or
formed products; Engineering services;
Machine and other job shop work

(G-8810)
KARMA METAL PRODUCTS INC
556 Caldwell Ave (44905-1401)
PHONE..........................419 524-4371
Thomas Taska, *Pr*
Ron Kocher, *VP*
Judy Taska, *Sec*
EMP: 10 **EST:** 1952
SQ FT: 6,800
SALES (est): 1.21MM **Privately Held**
Web: www.karmametalproducts.com
SIC: 3451 3545 Screw machine products;
Measuring tools and machines, machinists'
metalworking type

(G-8811)
KOKOSING MATERIALS INC
215 Oak St (44907-1439)
PHONE..........................419 522-2715
Bill Burgett, *Brnch Mgr*
EMP: 10
SALES (corp-wide): 1.17B **Privately Held**
Web: www.kokosing.biz
SIC: 2951 Asphalt and asphaltic paving
mixtures (not from refineries)
HQ: Kokosing Materials, Inc.
17531 Waterford Rd
Fredericktown OH 43019
740 694-9585

(G-8812)
LENNOX MACHINE INC
Also Called: Lennox Machine Shop
1471 Sprang Pkwy (44903-6531)
P.O. Box 1643 (44901-1643)
PHONE..........................419 525-1020
Terry L Eighinger, *Pr*
David Eighinger, *VP*
EMP: 8 **EST:** 1988
SALES (est): 969.21K **Privately Held**
SIC: 3599 Machine shop, jobbing and repair

(G-8813)
**LEXINGTON CONCRETE & SUP INC
(PA)**
362 N Trimble Rd (44906-2541)
P.O. Box 1342 (44901-1342)
PHONE..........................419 529-3232
Martin F Moritz, *Pr*
EMP: 8 **EST:** 2008

SQ FT: 260,000
SALES (est): 2.69MM **Privately Held**
Web: www.lexingtonconcreteinc.com
SIC: 3273 Ready-mixed concrete

(G-8814)
LONG VIEW STEEL CORP
1555 W Longview Ave (44906-1806)
P.O. Box P.O. Box 2839 (44906-0839)
PHONE..........................419 747-1108
David Jacko, *Pr*
EMP: 12 **EST:** 1999
SALES (est): 3.55MM **Privately Held**
SIC: 3312 Blast furnaces and steel mills

(G-8815)
MAJOR METALS COMPANY
844 Kochheiser Rd (44904-8637)
PHONE..........................419 886-4600
Jeffrey C Mason, *Pr*
Wayne Riffe, *
EMP: 30 **EST:** 1973
SQ FT: 60,000
SALES (est): 10MM **Privately Held**
Web: www.majormetals.net
SIC: 3312 5051 3317 Plate, sheet and strip,
except coated products; Iron or steel flat
products; Steel pipe and tubes

(G-8816)
MALABAR PROPERTIES LLC
Also Called: Deca Manufacturing
300 S Mill St (44904-8519)
PHONE..........................419 884-0071
Cameron Haring, *Pr*
EMP: 10 **EST:** 2018
SQ FT: 33,000
SALES (est): 1.39MM **Privately Held**
Web: www.decamanufacturing.com
SIC: 3679 Harness assemblies, for
electronic use: wire or cable

(G-8817)
MANAIRCO INC
28 Industrial Pkwy (44903-8999)
P.O. Box 111 (44901-0111)
PHONE..........................419 524-2121
Gayle Gorman Freeman, *Pr*
James C Gorman, *Ch Bd*
Joel Beinbrech, *VP*
Marjorie Gorman, *Sec*
EMP: 9 **EST:** 1953
SQ FT: 14,000
SALES (est): 460.41K **Privately Held**
Web: www.manairco.com
SIC: 3648 3645 Airport lighting fixtures:
runway approach, taxi, or ramp; Residential
lighting fixtures

(G-8818)
MANSFIELD BREW WORKS LLC
Also Called: Phoenix Brewing
131 N Diamond St (44902-1331)
PHONE..........................419 631-3153
EMP: 15 **EST:** 2013
SALES (est): 621.13K **Privately Held**
Web: www.phoenixbrewing.com
SIC: 5813 2082 Bars and lounges; Beer
(alcoholic beverage)

(G-8819)
**MANSFIELD ENGINEERED
COMPONENTS LLC**
Also Called: Assembleis Co
1776 Harrington Memorial Rd (44903-8996)
P.O. Box 1602 (44901-1602)
PHONE..........................419 524-1300
◆ **EMP:** 160 **EST:** 1987
SALES (est): 24.93MM **Privately Held**
Web: www.mansfieldec.com

SIC: 3499 Furniture parts, metal

(G-8820)
MANSFIELD INDUSTRIES INC
1776 Harrington Memorial Rd (44903-8996)
PHONE..........................419 524-1300
Otis M Cummins, *Ch*
Barry Jackenheimer, *
EMP: 15 **EST:** 1994
SALES (est): 3.6MM **Privately Held**
Web: www.mansfieldec.com
SIC: 3469 Stamping metal for the trade

(G-8821)
MATERN METAL WORKS INC
210 N Adams St (44902-1449)
P.O. Box 1686 (44901)
PHONE..........................419 529-3100
Joseph Matern, *Pr*
Reba Matern, *VP*
EMP: 10 **EST:** 1982
SQ FT: 3,600
SALES (est): 1.35MM **Privately Held**
Web: www.maternmetalworks.com
SIC: 3444 Sheet metalwork

(G-8822)
MCDANIEL PRODUCTS INC (PA)
Also Called: Automatic Parts
50 Industrial Pkwy (44903-8999)
P.O. Box 1505 (44901-1505)
PHONE..........................419 524-5841
Kevin L Mcdaniel, *Pr*
Ken Mcdaniel, *VP*
EMP: 6 **EST:** 2008
SALES (est): 3.75MM **Privately Held**
SIC: 3451 Screw machine products

(G-8823)
MCDANIEL PRODUCTS INC
Also Called: Automatic Parts
433 Springmill St (44903-7008)
P.O. Box 1505 (44901-1505)
PHONE..........................419 524-5841
Justin Constable, *Brnch Mgr*
EMP: 10
SIC: 3451 Screw machine products
PA: Mcdaniel Products, Inc.
50 Mansfield Indus Pkwy
Mansfield OH 44903

(G-8824)
MERLE NORMAN COSMETICS INC
893 Park Ave W (44906-2971)
PHONE..........................419 282-0630
EMP: 45
SALES (corp-wide): 39.64MM **Privately
Held**
Web: www.merlenorman.com
SIC: 2844 Cosmetic preparations
PA: Merle Norman Cosmetics, Inc.
9130 Bellanca Ave
Los Angeles CA 90045
310 641-3000

(G-8825)
**MICHAEL BYRNE MANUFACTURING
CO INC**
1855 Earth Boring Rd (44903-9000)
P.O. Box 444 (44901-0444)
PHONE..........................419 525-1214
EMP: 25 **EST:** 1966
SALES (est): 4.91MM **Privately Held**
Web: www.byrnegroup.com
SIC: 3531 3599 3546 3541 Tunneling
machinery; Custom machinery; Power-
driven handtools; Machine tools, metal
cutting type

▲ = Import ▼ = Export
◆ = Import/Export

(G-8826)
MIDWEST AIRCRAFT PRODUCTS CO
Also Called: Mapco
125 S Mill St (44904-9571)
P.O. Box 457 (44901-0457)
PHONE................................419 884-2164
Jeffrey Miller, *CEO*
Jerry Miller, *CEO*
▼ **EMP:** 12 **EST:** 1986
SQ FT: 25,000
SALES (est): 3.47MM **Privately Held**
Web: www.midwestaircraft.com
SIC: 3728 Aircraft parts and equipment, nec

(G-8827)
MILARK INDUSTRIES INC
520 S Airport Rd (44903-8067)
PHONE................................419 524-7627
EMP: 80
Web: www.milarkindustries.com
SIC: 3465 3469 3751 3714 Automotive stampings; Metal stampings, nec; Motorcycles, bicycles and parts; Motor vehicle parts and accessories
PA: Milark Industries, Inc.
536 S Airport Rd
Mansfield OH 44903

(G-8828)
MILARK INDUSTRIES INC (PA)
536 S Airport Rd (44903-8067)
PHONE................................419 524-7627
EMP: 94 **EST:** 1986
SALES (est): 1.84MM **Privately Held**
Web: www.milarkindustries.com
SIC: 3465 3469 3751 3714 Automotive stampings; Metal stampings, nec; Motorcycles, bicycles and parts; Motor vehicle parts and accessories

(G-8829)
MINNICH MANUFACTURING CO INC
1444 State Route 42 (44903-9509)
P.O. Box 367 (44901-0367)
PHONE................................419 903-0010
James R Minnich, *Pr*
▲ **EMP:** 25 **EST:** 1968
SQ FT: 43,000
SALES (est): 5.45MM **Privately Held**
Web: www.minnich-mfg.com
SIC: 3531 Vibrators for concrete construction

(G-8830)
MK METAL PRODUCTS ENTPS INC (PA)
Also Called: Mavericks Stainless
90 Sawyer Pkwy (44903-6514)
P.O. Box 878 (44901-0878)
PHONE................................419 756-3644
Richard L Kemp, *CEO*
J Douglas Drusbal, *
David Cole, *
EMP: 20 **EST:** 1956
SQ FT: 39,000
SALES (est): 4.44MM
SALES (corp-wide): 4.44MM **Privately Held**
Web: www.mkmetalproducts.com
SIC: 3441 Fabricated structural metal

(G-8831)
MODERN BUILDERS SUPPLY INC
85 Smith Ave (44905-2854)
PHONE................................419 526-0002
Rich Graham, *Mgr*
EMP: 21
SALES (corp-wide): 346.23MM **Privately Held**
Web: www.modernbbuilderssupply.com

SIC: 5032 3089 5033 5031 Brick, stone, and related material; Doors, folding: plastics or plastics coated fabric; Roofing, asphalt and sheet metal; Kitchen cabinets
PA: Modern Builders Supply, Inc.
3500 Phillips Ave
Toledo OH 43608
419 241-3961

(G-8832)
MORITZ CONCRETE INC
362 N Trimble Rd (44906-2541)
P.O. Box 1342 (44901-1342)
PHONE................................419 529-3232
Martin F Moritz Junior, *Pr*
James Moritz, *
Peter Moritz, *
Robert Moritz, *
Joe Moritz, *
EMP: 47 **EST:** 1950
SQ FT: 260,000
SALES (est): 4.85MM **Privately Held**
Web: www.moritzconcrete.com
SIC: 3273 Ready-mixed concrete

(G-8833)
MORITZ INTERNATIONAL INC
665 N Main St (44902-4201)
PHONE................................419 526-5222
Frank Moritz, *Pr*
Thomas R Moritz, *
EMP: 37 **EST:** 1992
SQ FT: 50,000
SALES (est): 5.38MM **Privately Held**
Web: www.moritzinternational.com
SIC: 3715 Truck trailers

(G-8834)
NANOGATE NORTH AMERICA LLC
Crestline Paint
515 Newman St (44902-1160)
P.O. Box 1527 (44901-1527)
PHONE................................419 522-7745
Steve Kunz, *Brnch Mgr*
EMP: 300
SALES (corp-wide): 193.63MM **Privately Held**
Web: www.jayindinc.com
SIC: 3714 Motor vehicle parts and accessories
HQ: Nanogate North America Llc
150 E Longview Ave
Mansfield OH 44903
419 524-3778

(G-8835)
NANOGATE NORTH AMERICA LLC
Rohr Manufacturing Div
1555 W Longview Ave (44906-1806)
PHONE................................419 747-1096
EMP: 300
SALES (corp-wide): 193.63MM **Privately Held**
Web: www.jayindinc.com
SIC: 3312 Tubes, steel and iron
HQ: Nanogate North America Llc
150 E Longview Ave
Mansfield OH 44903
419 524-3778

(G-8836)
NATIONAL PAT ANLYTICAL SYSTEMS
2090 Harrington Memorial Rd (44903-8051)
P.O. Box 20306 (43220-0306)
PHONE................................419 526-6727
John Fusco, *Pr*
EMP: 31 **EST:** 1991
SQ FT: 2,000
SALES (est): 4.98MM **Privately Held**
Web: www.npas.com

SIC: 3829 Breathalyzers

(G-8837)
NATIONAL PRIDE EQUIPMENT INC
Also Called: National Pride Equipment
905 Hickory Ln Ste 101 (44905-2873)
P.O. Box 467 (44805)
PHONE................................419 289-2886
Charles Collins, *Pr*
Richard Walter, *Sec*
EMP: 9 **EST:** 1992
SALES (est): 4.47MM **Privately Held**
Web: www.carwashsuperstore.com
SIC: 3589 5087 5046 Car washing machinery; Carwash equipment and supplies; Commercial equipment, nec

(G-8838)
NEWMAN TECHNOLOGY INC (HQ)
100 Cairns Rd (44903-8990)
PHONE................................419 525-1856
Takuji Shimizu, *Pr*
Stephen Rourke, *
Yukihisa Murata, *
▲ **EMP:** 576 **EST:** 1987
SQ FT: 450,000
SALES (est): 34.94MM **Privately Held**
Web: www.newmantech.com
SIC: 3714 3751 Mufflers (exhaust), motor vehicle; Motorcycle accessories
PA: Sankei Giken Co., Ltd.
1024-11, Niihori
Kawaguchi STM 334-0

(G-8839)
NEWSPAPER NETWORK CENTRAL OH
70 W 4th St (44903-1676)
PHONE................................419 524-3545
Tom Brennan, *Prin*
EMP: 6 **EST:** 2006
SALES (est): 149.87K **Privately Held**
SIC: 2711 Newspapers, publishing and printing

(G-8840)
NPAS INC
2090 Harrington Memorial Rd (44903-8051)
P.O. Box 20306 (43220-0306)
PHONE................................614 595-6916
Daniel Fusco, *CEO*
EMP: 11 **EST:** 2021
SALES (est): 4.75MM **Privately Held**
Web: www.npas.com
SIC: 3613 3677 3672 3625 Switchgear and switchboard apparatus; Electronic coils and transformers; Printed circuit boards; Relays and industrial controls

(G-8841)
OHIO VALLEY MANUFACTURING INC
1501 Harrington Memorial Rd (44903-8995)
PHONE................................419 522-5818
Michael C Fanello, *Pr*
John Fanello, *
Jeff Fanello, *
Steven Fanello, *
Thom Weber, *
EMP: 80 **EST:** 1999
SQ FT: 131,300
SALES (est): 9.94MM **Privately Held**
Web: www.ohiovalleymfg.com
SIC: 3469 3399 Stamping metal for the trade; Flakes, metal

(G-8842)
OHIO VLY STMPNG-ASSEMBLIES INC
500 Newman St (44902-1122)
PHONE................................419 522-0983

Todd J Flagel, *Prin*
EMP: 19 **EST:** 2002
SALES (est): 2.46MM **Privately Held**
SIC: 3297 Nonclay refractories

(G-8843)
OMEGA TEK INC
649 Old Mill Run Rd (44906-3474)
P.O. Box 185 (44875-0185)
PHONE................................419 756-9580
James C Hudson, *Pr*
Marguerite Hudson, *VP*
EMP: 6 **EST:** 1981
SALES (est): 177.45K **Privately Held**
SIC: 3625 Control circuit relays, industrial

(G-8844)
PCR RESTORATIONS INC
Also Called: Lehr Awning Co
933 W Longview Ave (44906-2133)
PHONE................................419 747-7957
Phillip E Russell, *Pr*
Debbie Russell, *VP*
EMP: 6 **EST:** 1932
SQ FT: 11,000
SALES (est): 503.81K **Privately Held**
Web: www.pcr-lehrawning.com
SIC: 2394 3089 2221 5999 Canvas awnings and canopies; Awnings, fiberglass and plastics combination; Upholstery, tapestry, and wall covering fabrics; Awnings

(G-8845)
POSM SOFTWARE LLC
2145 Millsboro Rd (44906-1336)
PHONE................................859 274-0041
Robert Katter, *Prin*
EMP: 11 **EST:** 2013
SALES (est): 2.04MM **Privately Held**
Web: www.posmsoftware.com
SIC: 7372 Prepackaged software

(G-8846)
PRINT CENTERS OF OHIO INC
36 W 3rd St (44902-1218)
PHONE................................419 526-4139
Amy Zimmerman, *Pr*
EMP: 16 **EST:** 1975
SQ FT: 12,000
SALES (est): 227.5K **Privately Held**
Web: www.jonesdigitalprintcenter.com
SIC: 2752 Offset printing

(G-8847)
RABLE MACHINE INC
30 Paragon Pkwy (44903-8074)
P.O. Box 1583 (44901-1583)
PHONE................................419 525-2255
EMP: 61 **EST:** 1956
SALES (est): 1.07MM **Privately Held**
Web: www.rablemachineinc.com
SIC: 3451 Screw machine products

(G-8848)
RICHLAND NEWHOPE INDS INC (PA)
150 E 4th St (44902-1520)
P.O. Box 916 (44901)
PHONE................................419 774-4400
Elizabeth Prather, *Ex Dir*
EMP: 250 **EST:** 1963
SQ FT: 63,000
SALES (est): 9.07MM
SALES (corp-wide): 9.07MM **Privately Held**
Web: www.rniinc.com
SIC: 0782 2448 7349 8331 Lawn and garden services; Wood pallets and skids; Building maintenance services, nec; Job training and related services

(G-8849)
RICHLAND SCREW MCH PDTS INC
531 Grant St (44903-1213)
P.O. Box 696 (44901)
PHONE..............................419 524-1272
Randall L Schoenman, *Pr*
EMP: 22 EST: 1946
SQ FT: 15,000
SALES (est): 4.32MM **Privately Held**
Web: www.richlandscrewmachine.com
SIC: 3451 Screw machine products

(G-8850)
RICHLAND SOURCE
40 W 4th St (44902-1206)
PHONE..............................419 610-2100
EMP: 24 EST: 2013
SALES (est): 335.76K **Privately Held**
Web: www.richlandsource.com
SIC: 2741 Miscellaneous publishing

(G-8851)
RUSSELL T BUNDY ASSOCIATES INC
Also Called: Pan-Glo
1711 N Main St (44903-8111)
PHONE..............................419 526-4454
William Matzke, *Mgr*
EMP: 11
SALES (corp-wide): 46.03MM **Privately Held**
Web: www.bundybakingsolutions.com
SIC: 3479 Pan glazing
PA: Russell T. Bundy Associates, Inc.
417 E Water St
Urbana OH 43078
937 652-2151

(G-8852)
SIR STEAK MACHINERY INC
40 Baird Pkwy (44903-7908)
PHONE..............................419 526-9181
James Munroe, *Pr*
Dean Schlichting, *Treas*
Richard C Biro, *VP*
Michael J Biro, *VP*
Robert S Biro, *Clerk*
EMP: 20 EST: 1948
SQ FT: 37,500
SALES (est): 4.73MM
SALES (corp-wide): 11MM **Privately Held**
SIC: 3556 Food products machinery
PA: The Biro Manufacturing Company
1114 West Main St
Marblehead OH 43440
419 798-4451

(G-8853)
SKYBOX PACKAGING LLC
Also Called: Mr Box
1275 Pollock Pkwy (44905-1374)
P.O. Box 1567 (44901-1567)
PHONE..............................419 525-7209
Marc Miller, *Pr*
EMP: 160 EST: 2001
SALES (est): 27.77MM
SALES (corp-wide): 882.33MM **Privately Held**
Web: www.skyboxpackaging.com
SIC: 3086 5199 2653 5162 Packaging and shipping materials, foamed plastics; Packaging materials; Boxes, corrugated: made from purchased materials; Plastics materials and basic shapes
PA: Atlantic Packaging Products Ltd
111 Progress Ave
Scarborough ON M1P 2
416 298-8101

(G-8854)
STEIN INC
1490 Old Bowman St (44903-8805)
PHONE..............................419 747-2611
EMP: 12 EST: 2010
SALES (est): 356.94K **Privately Held**
Web: www.steininc.com
SIC: 2431 Millwork

(G-8855)
STRASSELLS MACHINE INC
1015 Springmill St (44906-1571)
PHONE..............................419 747-1088
Michael Strassell, *Pr*
Kimberly Strassell, *VP*
EMP: 10 EST: 1987
SQ FT: 1,600
SALES (est): 1.88MM **Privately Held**
Web: www.hi-pointfirearms.net
SIC: 3599 Machine shop, jobbing and repair

(G-8856)
SUBURBANITE INC
1552 W Cook Rd (44906-3625)
PHONE..............................419 756-4390
Dan Pease, *Pr*
EMP: 6 EST: 1991
SALES (est): 128.89K **Privately Held**
SIC: 3469 5521 Automobile license tags, stamped metal; Used car dealers

(G-8857)
TAYLOR METAL PRODUCTS CO
700 Springmill St (44903-1199)
PHONE..............................419 522-3471
Richard G Taylor, *Pr*
Helen F Taylor, *
Mark Taylor, *
▲ EMP: 155 EST: 1923
SQ FT: 160,000
SALES (est): 23.12MM **Privately Held**
Web: www.tmpind.com
SIC: 3469 3465 Stamping metal for the trade ; Automotive stampings

(G-8858)
TE CONNECTIVITY CORPORATION
Cii Technologies Hartman Pdts
175 N Diamond St (44902-1004)
PHONE..............................419 521-9500
Kathy Castor, *Brnch Mgr*
EMP: 112
Web: www.te.com
SIC: 3613 3625 3812 3769 Power switching equipment; Relays, for electronic use; Search and navigation equipment; Space vehicle equipment, nec
PA: Te Connectivity Corporation
1050 Westlakes Dr
Berwyn PA 19312

(G-8859)
THE MANSFIELD STRL & ERCT CO (PA)
Also Called: Mansfield Fabricated Products
429 Park Ave E (44905-2844)
P.O. Box 427 (44901-0427)
PHONE..............................419 522-5911
Richard Gash, *Pr*
Barbara Gash, *Sec*
EMP: 16 EST: 1924
SQ FT: 60,000
SALES (est): 2.16MM
SALES (corp-wide): 2.16MM **Privately Held**
SIC: 3441 5051 Fabricated structural metal; Metals service centers and offices

(G-8860)
THORNTON POWDER COATINGS INC
2300 N Main St (44903-6703)
P.O. Box 1119 (44901-1119)
PHONE..............................419 522-7183
James Thornton, *Pr*
Dawn Thornton, *VP*
EMP: 6 EST: 1989
SQ FT: 20,000
SALES (est): 711.32K **Privately Held**
Web: www.thorntonpowdercoating.com
SIC: 3479 Coating of metals and formed products

(G-8861)
TRI-R TOOLING INC
220 Piper Rd (44905-1370)
PHONE..............................419 522-8665
Robert John, *Pr*
Rudy John, *VP*
Renee John, *Treas*
EMP: 12 EST: 1990
SQ FT: 6,500
SALES (est): 1.02MM **Privately Held**
Web: www.trirtooling.com
SIC: 3599 Machine shop, jobbing and repair

(G-8862)
UNIVERSAL CH DIRECTORIES LLC
Also Called: Photography and Publishing
1150 National Pkwy (44906-1911)
PHONE..............................419 522-5011
Jeffrey Earl Bellew, *Managing Member*
EMP: 6 EST: 2003
SALES (est): 1.04MM **Privately Held**
Web: www.ucdir.com
SIC: 7335 2759 Commercial photography; Publication printing

(G-8863)
WARREN RUPP INC
Also Called: Sandpiper
800 N Main St (44902-4209)
P.O. Box 1568 (44901-1568)
PHONE..............................419 524-8388
Joshua Stiever, *Pr*
John Carter, *
◆ EMP: 224 EST: 1986
SQ FT: 80,000
SALES (est): 30.65MM
SALES (corp-wide): 3.27B **Publicly Held**
Web: www.warrenruppinc.com
SIC: 3561 Industrial pumps and parts
PA: Idex Corporation
3100 Sanders Rd Ste 301
Northbrook IL 60062
847 498-7070

(G-8864)
WATERSOURCE LLC
1225 W Longview Ave (44906-1907)
PHONE..............................419 747-9552
Craig Bodell, *Brnch Mgr*
EMP: 7
SALES (corp-wide): 891.05K **Privately Held**
Web: www.watersourceusa.com
SIC: 3261 Plumbing fixtures, vitreous china
PA: Watersource, L.L.C.
6 Foxmoor Ct
Norwalk OH 44857
419 747-9552

(G-8865)
WEISS INDUSTRIES INC
Also Called: Weiss Metallurgical Services
2480 N Main St (44903-8555)
P.O. Box 157 (44901-0157)
PHONE..............................419 526-2480
Rudolph Weiss, *Pr*
William Heichel, *

Phyllis B Weiss, *
Maria Weiss, *
Robert Nikolaus, *
EMP: 30 EST: 1954
SQ FT: 40,000
SALES (est): 6.89MM **Privately Held**
Web: www.weissind.com
SIC: 3469 3398 3544 Metal stampings, nec; Metal heat treating; Special dies and tools

(G-8866)
WESTINGHOUSE A BRAKE TECH CORP
Also Called: Wabtec Global Services
472 Rembrandt St (44902-7015)
PHONE..............................419 526-5323
EMP: 6
Web: www.wabteccorp.com
SIC: 3743 Brakes, air and vacuum: railway
PA: Westinghouse Air Brake Technologies Corporation
30 Isabella St
Pittsburgh PA 15212

Mantua
Portage County

(G-8867)
ASSOCIATED ASSOCIATES INC
Also Called: Associated Ready Mix Concrete
9551 Elliman Rd (44255-9440)
P.O. Box 670538 (44067-0538)
PHONE..............................330 626-3300
Harold Joslin, *Pr*
Sandra Riha, *Sec*
EMP: 20 EST: 1993
SQ FT: 2,700
SALES (est): 2.34MM **Privately Held**
Web: www.associatedreadymix.com
SIC: 3273 5211 Ready-mixed concrete; Masonry materials and supplies

(G-8868)
CREATIVE PROCESSING INC
17540 Rapids Rd (44255)
P.O. Box 708 (44021-0708)
PHONE..............................440 834-4070
Daniel Piscura Junior, *Pr*
Freida Piscura, *Sec*
EMP: 8 EST: 1992
SQ FT: 10,000
SALES (est): 1.02MM **Privately Held**
Web: www.creativeprocessinginc.com
SIC: 3599 Machine shop, jobbing and repair

(G-8869)
INDUSTRIAL CONNECTIONS INC
11730 Timber Point Trl (44255-9694)
PHONE..............................330 274-2155
Wendy Carlton, *Pr*
▼ EMP: 6 EST: 1992
SQ FT: 7,000
SALES (est): 835.68K **Privately Held**
Web: www.industrialconnectionsinc.com
SIC: 5085 3492 Industrial fittings; Hose and tube fittings and assemblies, hydraulic/pneumatic

(G-8870)
LAKESIDE SAND & GRAVEL INC
3498 Frost Rd (44255-9136)
PHONE..............................330 274-2569
Larry Kotkowski, *Pr*
Ronald Kotkowski, *Sec*
EMP: 31 EST: 1954
SQ FT: 4,200
SALES (est): 4.97MM **Privately Held**
Web: www.lakesidesandgravel.com

▲ = Import ▼ = Export
◆ = Import/Export

SIC: 1442 Construction sand mining

(G-8871)
MANTALINE CORPORATION
Also Called: Transportation Group
4754 E High St (44255-9201)
PHONE..............................330 274-2264
Bryan Fink, *Mgr*
EMP: 14
SALES (corp-wide): 39.13MM **Privately Held**
Web: www.mantalinestandardseals.com
SIC: 5169 3061 Synthetic rubber; Mechanical rubber goods
PA: Mantaline Corporation
4754 E High St
Mantua OH 44255
330 274-2264

(G-8872)
MANTALINE CORPORATION (PA)
4754 E High St (44255-9201)
PHONE..............................330 274-2264
EMP: 115 **EST:** 1964
SALES (est): 39.13MM
SALES (corp-wide): 39.13MM **Privately Held**
Web: www.mantaline.com
SIC: 3061 2822 3069 Mechanical rubber goods; Synthetic rubber; Hard rubber and molded rubber products

(G-8873)
OK BRUGMANN JR & SONS INC
4083 Mennonite Rd (44255-9413)
PHONE..............................330 274-2106
Oscar Brugmann Junior, *Pr*
Gail Brugmann, *VP*
Mark Brugmann, *Prin*
EMP: 7 **EST:** 1981
SALES (est): 894.81K **Privately Held**
Web: www.okbrugmann.com
SIC: 5032 5211 3273 3272 Concrete and cinder building products; Concrete and cinder block; Ready-mixed concrete; Concrete products, nec

(G-8874)
OSCAR BRUGMANN SAND & GRAVEL
3828 Dudley Rd (44255-9426)
PHONE..............................330 274-8224
Roy Brugmann, *Pr*
Olga Van Auken, *Sec*
Joan Martin, *Sec*
EMP: 26 **EST:** 1929
SQ FT: 1,000
SALES (est): 3.38MM **Privately Held**
Web: www.obsag.com
SIC: 1442 Construction sand mining

(G-8875)
STAMM CONTRACTING COMPANY INC
4566 Orchard St (44255-9701)
P.O. Box 450 (44255-0450)
PHONE..............................330 274-8230
Hal Stamm, *Pr*
Elva Novotny, *
EMP: 17 **EST:** 1913
SQ FT: 1,500
SALES (est): 3.46MM **Privately Held**
Web: www.stammcontracting.com
SIC: 3273 1541 1542 5211 Ready-mixed concrete; Industrial buildings and warehouses; Commercial and office building contractors; Lumber and other building materials

(G-8876)
T J DAVIES COMPANY INC
11823 State Route 44 (44255-9647)
PHONE..............................440 248-5510
Sherry Davies, *CEO*
EMP: 8 **EST:** 1965
SALES (est): 2.3MM **Privately Held**
Web: www.tjdavies.com
SIC: 3999 Barber and beauty shop equipment

Maple Heights
Cuyahoga County

(G-8877)
BARNES SERVICES LLC
20677 Centuryway Rd (44137-3116)
PHONE..............................440 319-2088
Leon Barnes, *Prin*
EMP: 6
SALES (est): 408.84K **Privately Held**
SIC: 1389 Construction, repair, and dismantling services

(G-8878)
BOGGS GRAPHICS EQUIPMENT LLC
Also Called: Boggs Equipment
14901 Broadway Ave (44137-1107)
P.O. Box 544 (44065-0544)
PHONE..............................888 837-8101
Jack Boggs, *Pr*
Christopher Boggs, *VP*
▼ **EMP:** 22 **EST:** 2005
SALES (est): 3.2MM **Privately Held**
Web: www.boggsequipment.com
SIC: 3555 5084 3565 Printing presses; Printing trades machinery, equipment, and supplies; Packaging machinery

(G-8879)
CHARLES SVEC INC
Also Called: Rock Lite
5470 Dunham Rd (44137-3690)
PHONE..............................216 662-5200
Michael Svec, *Pr*
Dean Svec, *
EMP: 25 **EST:** 1906
SQ FT: 25,000
SALES (est): 2.84MM **Privately Held**
Web: www.chassvecinc.com
SIC: 3271 3272 Concrete block and brick; Concrete products, nec

(G-8880)
CLIFTON CAPITAL HOLDINGS LLC (PA)
16500 Rockside Rd (44137-4324)
PHONE..............................330 562-9000
EMP: 16 **EST:** 2016
SALES (est): 43.73MM
SALES (corp-wide): 43.73MM **Privately Held**
Web: www.cliftonsteel.com
SIC: 5051 3443 3441 Steel; Fabricated plate work (boiler shop); Fabricated structural metal

(G-8881)
CLIFTON STEEL COMPANY (HQ)
16500 Rockside Rd (44137-4324)
PHONE..............................216 662-6111
Herbert C Neides, *Pr*
Howard Feldenkris, *
Bruce Goodman, *CUST SERVCS*
◆ **EMP:** 59 **EST:** 1971
SQ FT: 160,000
SALES (est): 5.88MM
SALES (corp-wide): 43.73MM **Privately Held**

Web: www.cliftonsteel.com
SIC: 5051 3443 3398 Steel; Fabricated structural metal; Metal parts; Metal heat treating
PA: Clifton Capital Holdings, Llc
16500 Rockside Rd
Maple Heights OH 44137
330 562-9000

(G-8882)
DEWITT INC
Also Called: Non-Ferrous Heat Treating
14450 Industrial Ave N (44137-3249)
PHONE..............................216 662-0800
John Whittaker, *Pr*
Joe Frankhauser, *Treas*
EMP: 8 **EST:** 1957
SQ FT: 10,000
SALES (est): 465.89K **Privately Held**
Web: www.nonferrousheattreating.com
SIC: 3398 Metal heat treating

(G-8883)
DR Z AMPS INC
Also Called: Dr Z Amplification
17011 Broadway Ave (44137-3407)
PHONE..............................216 475-1444
Michael D Zaite, *Pr*
EMP: 10 **EST:** 1988
SQ FT: 3,500
SALES (est): 771.91K **Privately Held**
Web: www.drzamps.com
SIC: 3651 Amplifiers: radio, public address, or musical instrument

(G-8884)
INEZ ESSENTIALS LLC
5333 Cato St (44137-2627)
PHONE..............................216 701-8360
EMP: 10 **EST:** 2020
SALES (est): 145.97K **Privately Held**
SIC: 3999 Candles

(G-8885)
LAMINATED CONCEPTS INC
14300 Industrial Ave N (44137-3248)
PHONE..............................216 475-4141
Vera Dudley, *Pr*
Lisa Elliots, *VP*
EMP: 11 **EST:** 1987
SQ FT: 8,500
SALES (est): 265.44K **Privately Held**
Web: www.laminatedconcepts.com
SIC: 2341 2434 Table or counter tops, plastic laminated; Wood kitchen cabinets

(G-8886)
MAMMANA CUSTOM WOODWORKING INC
14400 Industrial Ave N (44137-3249)
PHONE..............................216 581-9059
Max Mammana, *Pr*
EMP: 25 **EST:** 1993
SQ FT: 18,000
SALES (est): 4.51MM **Privately Held**
SIC: 2434 Wood kitchen cabinets

(G-8887)
MCKINLEY PACKAGING COMPANY
16645 Granite Rd (44137-4301)
PHONE..............................216 663-3344
Charles Messina, *Brnch Mgr*
EMP: 15
Web: www.mckinleypackaging.com
SIC: 2653 Boxes, corrugated: made from purchased materials
HQ: Mckinley Packaging Company
1503 Lyndon B Jhnson Fwy
Dallas TX 75234
972 354-3600

(G-8888)
OHIO MAGNETICS INC
5400 Dunham Rd (44137-3653)
PHONE..............................216 662-8484
Thomas J Pozda, *CEO*
Randy L Greely, *
▲ **EMP:** 36 **EST:** 1917
SQ FT: 140,000
SALES (est): 8.44MM
SALES (corp-wide): 241.4MM **Privately Held**
Web: www.ohiomagnetics.com
SIC: 3499 3559 3669 3625 Magnets, permanent: metallic; Separation equipment, magnetic; Metal detectors; Relays and industrial controls
HQ: Peerless-Winsmith, Inc.
5200 Upper Mtro Pl Ste 11
Dublin OH 43017
614 526-7000

(G-8889)
OR-TEC INC
5445 Dunham Rd (44137-3673)
PHONE..............................216 475-5225
David Marriott, *Genl Mgr*
Ciaran O-mezia, *Pr*
▲ **EMP:** 9 **EST:** 1979
SALES (est): 2.23MM **Privately Held**
Web: www.or-tec.com
SIC: 3589 Water treatment equipment, industrial

(G-8890)
R & C MONUMENT COMPANY LLC
5146 Warrensville Center Rd (44137-1929)
PHONE..............................216 297-5444
Jajuan L Robinson, *Admn*
EMP: 7 **EST:** 2017
SALES (est): 197.23K **Privately Held**
Web: www.monumentsdoniphan.com
SIC: 3272 Monuments and grave markers, except terrazzo

(G-8891)
RACELITE SOUTHCOAST INC
16518 Broadway Ave (44137-2602)
P.O. Box 370076 (44137-9076)
PHONE..............................216 581-4600
James Sima, *Pr*
Maryann Sima, *Sec*
EMP: 10 **EST:** 1967
SQ FT: 5,000
SALES (est): 720K **Privately Held**
Web: www.racelitehardware.com
SIC: 3429 3732 3469 3312 Marine hardware; Boatbuilding and repairing; Metal stampings, nec; Blast furnaces and steel mills

(G-8892)
ST LAWRENCE HOLDINGS LLC
16500 Rockside Rd (44137-4324)
PHONE..............................330 562-9000
Herbert Neides, *Pr*
Jonh Zanin, *
EMP: 34 **EST:** 2017
SALES (est): 2.82MM
SALES (corp-wide): 43.73MM **Privately Held**
Web: www.stlawrencesteel.com
SIC: 5051 3443 3441 Steel; Fabricated plate work (boiler shop); Fabricated structural metal
PA: Clifton Capital Holdings, Llc
16500 Rockside Rd
Maple Heights OH 44137
330 562-9000

(G-8893)
ST LAWRENCE STEEL CORPORATION
16500 Rockside Rd (44137-4324)
PHONE..................................330 562-9000
◆ EMP: 34
Web: www.stlawrencesteel.com
SIC: 5051 3443 3441 Steel; Fabricated plate work (boiler shop); Fabricated structural metal

(G-8894)
UNITED METAL FABRICATORS INC
14301 Industrial Ave S (44137-3252)
PHONE..................................216 662-2000
Stephen B Martis, Pr
James A Martis, *
EMP: 30 EST: 1945
SQ FT: 16,500
SALES (est): 4.75MM Privately Held
Web: www.unitedmetalfabricators.com
SIC: 3441 Fabricated structural metal

Marblehead
Ottawa County

(G-8895)
BIRO MANUFACTURING COMPANY (PA)
Also Called: Biro Manufacturing Company
1114 W Main St (43440-2099)
PHONE..................................419 798-4451
Carl G Biro, Prin
Richard C Biro, *
Robert S Biro, General Vice President*
Michael J Biro, *
Teresa Marez, *
◆ EMP: 57 EST: 1986
SQ FT: 76,000
SALES (est): 11MM
SALES (corp-wide): 11MM Privately Held
Web: www.birosaw.com
SIC: 3556 Choppers, commercial, food

Marengo
Morrow County

(G-8896)
DARPRO STORAGE SOLUTIONS LLC
1089 County Road 26 (43334-3503)
PHONE..................................567 233-3190
EMP: 23 EST: 2020
SALES (est): 7.52MM
SALES (corp-wide): 6.79B Publicly Held
Web: www.mfsparts.com
SIC: 2599 Carts, restaurant equipment
PA: Darling Ingredients Inc.
5601 N Macarthur Blvd
Irving TX 75038
972 717-0300

(G-8897)
GIUSEPPES CONCESSIONS LLC
5383 Township Road 187 (43334-9783)
PHONE..................................614 554-2551
Christopher Leadbeater, Managing Member
EMP: 10 EST: 2019
SALES (est): 356.19K Privately Held
SIC: 7999 3443 Concession operator; Dumpsters, garbage

(G-8898)
MORITZ READY MIX INC
4083 Bennington Way (43334-9536)
PHONE..................................419 253-0001
Frank Moritz, CEO
EMP: 6 EST: 1933

SALES (est): 527.83K Privately Held
Web: www.moritzreadymix.com
SIC: 3273 Ready-mixed concrete

Maria Stein
Mercer County

(G-8899)
MANCO MANUFACTURING CO
2411 Rolfes Rd (45860-9708)
PHONE..................................419 925-4152
Nancy Nieberding, Pr
Patrick R Nieberding, VP
Eric Nieberding, Treas
EMP: 8 EST: 1974
SQ FT: 14,000
SALES (est): 947.32K Privately Held
Web: www.manco-mfg-co.com
SIC: 3441 Fabricated structural metal

(G-8900)
MS WELDING LLC
8070 Flyer Dr (45860-9570)
PHONE..................................419 925-4141
EMP: 9 EST: 1983
SALES (est): 620.22K Privately Held
Web: www.mswelding.com
SIC: 7692 Welding repair

Marietta
Washington County

(G-8901)
ANTERO RESOURCES CORPORATION
27841 State Route 7 (45750-9060)
PHONE..................................740 760-1000
EMP: 60
Web: www.anteroresources.com
SIC: 1382 Oil and gas exploration services
PA: Antero Resources Corporation
1615 Wynkoop St
Denver CO 80202

(G-8902)
ARTEX OIL COMPANY
2337 State Route 821 (45750-5475)
PHONE..................................740 373-3313
Arthur Rupe, CEO
Jerry James, Pr
Gene Huck, VP
EMP: 20 EST: 1995
SALES (est): 3.61MM Privately Held
Web: www.artexoil.com
SIC: 1381 Drilling oil and gas wells

(G-8903)
BD OIL GATHERING CORP
649 Mitchells Ln (45750-6865)
PHONE..................................740 374-9355
Floyd Deer Senior, Pr
Gordon J Deer, *
Floyd A Deer Junior, Dir
EMP: 29 EST: 1993
SALES (est): 4.72MM Privately Held
Web: www.bdoil.com
SIC: 1382 Oil and gas exploration services

(G-8904)
BOB LANES WELDING INC
5151 Warren Chapel Rd (45750-6537)
PHONE..................................740 373-3567
Robert Lane, Pr
Sandra Lane, Sec
EMP: 6 EST: 1976
SALES (est): 682.39K Privately Held

SIC: 1799 1623 7692 3444 Welding on site; Pipe laying construction; Welding repair; Sheet metalwork

(G-8905)
C L W INC
1201 Gilman Ave (45750-9499)
PHONE..................................740 374-8443
David Armstrong, Pr
Frederick L Burge, Sec
EMP: 9 EST: 1972
SQ FT: 7,500
SALES (est): 1.72MM Privately Held
Web: www.clwrg.com
SIC: 3444 Concrete forms, sheet metal

(G-8906)
CARON PRODUCTS AND SVCS INC
27640 State Route 7 (45750-5146)
P.O. Box 715 (45750-0715)
PHONE..................................740 373-6809
Joanna Moncivaiz, Pr
Jon F Bergen, Prin
Bob Beckelman, Prin
Spencer Krigsman, Prin
Paul Sereni, Prin
▲ EMP: 22 EST: 1985
SQ FT: 12,000
SALES (est): 7.07MM Privately Held
Web: www.caronproducts.com
SIC: 3823 3821 Temperature instruments: industrial process type; Laboratory apparatus, except heating and measuring

(G-8907)
CARPER WELL SERVICE INC
30745 State Route 7 (45750-5177)
P.O. Box 273 (45773-0273)
PHONE..................................740 374-2567
Millard E Carper, Pr
Ryan Carper, Treas
EMP: 10 EST: 1979
SQ FT: 3,500
SALES (est): 2.04MM Privately Held
SIC: 1389 Construction, repair, and dismantling services

(G-8908)
CDK PERFORATING LLC
2167 State Route 821 (45750-1196)
PHONE..................................817 862-9834
EMP: 60
SALES (corp-wide): 554.1MM Publicly Held
Web: www.nineenergyservice.com
SIC: 1389 Oil field services, nec
HQ: Cdk Perforating, Llc
6500 West Fwy Ste 600
Fort Worth TX 76116
817 945-1051

(G-8909)
CHEVRON PHLLIPS CHEM LTD PRTNR
Also Called: CHEVRON PHILLIPS CHEMICAL COMPANY LIMITED PARTNERSHIP
17401 State Route 7 (45750-7962)
P.O. Box 1000 (45750-6000)
PHONE..................................740 374-2500
Ivan Rohrer, Prin
EMP: 31
SALES (corp-wide): 7.42B Privately Held
Web: www.chevron.com
SIC: 2821 Plastics materials and resins
HQ: Chevron Phillips Chemical Company Lp
9500 Lakeside Blvd
The Woodlands TX 77381
832 813-4100

(G-8910)
COIL SPECIALTY CHEMICALS LLC
2375 Glendale Rd (45750-8038)
PHONE..................................740 236-2407
Robert Coil, Managing Member
EMP: 8 EST: 2007
SQ FT: 5,000
SALES (est): 232.2K Privately Held
Web: www.coilchem.com
SIC: 2869 Glycerin

(G-8911)
COMMUNITY ACTION PROGRAM CORP
Also Called: Community Action Wic Hlth Svc
696 Wayne St (45750-3265)
PHONE..................................740 374-8501
Kathleen Boersma, Dir
EMP: 10
SALES (corp-wide): 18.3MM Privately Held
Web: www.wmcap.org
SIC: 8399 8093 8011 2241 Community action agency; Family planning and birth control clinics; Offices and clinics of medical doctors; Wicking
PA: Community Action Program Corp, Of Washington-Morgan County Ohio, Inc
218 Putnam St
Marietta OH 45750
740 373-3745

(G-8912)
CRESCENT & SPRAGUE
1100 Greene St (45750-2413)
PHONE..................................740 373-2331
EMP: 14 EST: 2019
SALES (est): 5MM Privately Held
Web: www.crescentsprague.com
SIC: 3621 Motors and generators

(G-8913)
DIRECTIONAL ONE SVCS INC USA
2163a-1 Gwb Complex 2 Bldg 6 State Route 821 (45750)
PHONE..................................740 371-5031
Kevin Onishenko, CEO
EMP: 6 EST: 2014
SALES (est): 430.19K Privately Held
Web: www.directional1services.com
SIC: 1381 Directional drilling oil and gas wells

(G-8914)
DIVERSIFIED PRODUCTION LLC
111 Industry Rd Unit 206 (45750-9315)
P.O. Box 141 (45773-0141)
PHONE..................................740 373-8771
Martin Miller, Brnch Mgr
EMP: 142
SALES (corp-wide): 61.05MM Privately Held
Web: ir.div.energy
SIC: 1382 Oil and gas exploration services
HQ: Diversified Production Llc
4150 Blden Vlg Ave Nw Ste
Canton OH 44718

(G-8915)
EDGEWELL PERSONAL CARE COMPANY
P.O. Box 300 (45750-0300)
PHONE..................................740 374-1905
Stacy Parks, Brnch Mgr
EMP: 6
SALES (corp-wide): 2.25B Publicly Held
Web: www.edgewell.com
SIC: 3421 Razor blades and razors
PA: Edgewell Personal Care Company
6 Research Dr

Shelton CT 06484
203 944-5500

(G-8916)
ERAMET MARIETTA INC
16705 State Route 7 (45750-8519)
P.O. Box 299 (45750-0299)
PHONE.................................740 374-1000
Michel Masci, *CFO*
◆ **EMP:** 205 **EST:** 1950
SALES (est): 39.64MM
SALES (corp-wide): 3.43B **Privately Held**
Web: marietta.eramet.com
SIC: 3313 Ferroalloys
HQ: Eramet Holding Manganese
10 Bd De Grenelle
Paris 15 IDF

(G-8917)
FLEXMAG INDUSTRIES INC (DH)
Also Called: Arnold Magnetic Technologies
107 Industry Rd (45750-9355)
PHONE.................................740 373-3492
Tim Wilson, *CEO*
◆ **EMP:** 100 **EST:** 1981
SQ FT: 84,619
SALES (est): 9.9MM **Publicly Held**
Web: www.arnoldmagnetics.com
SIC: 3499 Magnets, permanent: metallic
HQ: Arnold Magnetic Technologies
Corporation
770 Linden Ave
Rochester NY 14625
585 385-9010

(G-8918)
**GANNETT STLLITE INFO NTWRK
LLC**
Also Called: Marietta Times
700 Channel Ln (45750-2342)
P.O. Box 761 (26102-0761)
PHONE.................................304 485-1891
Roger Watson, *Mgr*
EMP: 35
SALES (corp-wide): 2.51B **Publicly Held**
Web: www.mariettatimes.com
SIC: 2711 Newspapers, publishing and
printing
HQ: Gannett Satellite Information Network,
Llc
1675 Broadway Fl 23
New York NY 10019
703 854-6000

(G-8919)
GILLARD CONSTRUCTION INC
Also Called: Cypress Valley Log Homes
1308 Greene St (45750-9809)
PHONE.................................740 376-9744
John Gillard, *Pr*
Debra Gillard, *VP*
Kelly Gillard, *Sec*
Jill Wright, *Treas*
EMP: 16 **EST:** 1991
SALES (est): 2.37MM **Privately Held**
Web: www.gillardscustomcabinets.com
SIC: 1521 2434 5211 2452 General
remodeling, single-family houses; Wood
kitchen cabinets; Cabinets, kitchen; Log
cabins, prefabricated, wood

(G-8920)
GRAE-CON PROCESS PIPING LLC
300 Commerce Dr (45750-3524)
PHONE.................................740 282-6830
William Blake Junior, *Managing Member*
EMP: 32 **EST:** 2014
SALES (est): 9.57MM
SALES (corp-wide): 25.65MM **Privately
Held**
Web: www.graecon.com

SIC: 3317 Steel pipe and tubes
PA: Grae-Con Construction, Inc.
880 Kingsdale Rd
Steubenville OH 43952
740 282-6830

(G-8921)
GRIMM SCIENTIFIC INDS INC
1403 Pike St (45750-5106)
P.O. Box 2143 (45750-7143)
PHONE.................................740 374-3412
Joseph E Grimm, *Pr*
Edmund Dutton, *VP*
Jane Grimm, *Sec*
Walt Brothers, *Treas*
EMP: 10 **EST:** 1979
SQ FT: 5,000
SALES (est): 2.38MM **Privately Held**
Web: www.grimmscientific.com
SIC: 3841 Physiotherapy equipment,
electrical

(G-8922)
HAESSLY LUMBER SALES CO (PA)
25 Sheets Run Rd (45750-5186)
PHONE.................................740 373-6681
Norman E Haessly Junior, *Pr*
Steve Haessly, *
Julie Haessly, *
EMP: 55 **EST:** 1941
SQ FT: 160
SALES (est): 7.48MM
SALES (corp-wide): 7.48MM **Privately
Held**
Web: www.haesslylumber.com
SIC: 2421 2449 2448 2435 Lumber: rough,
sawed, or planed; Wood containers, nec;
Wood pallets and skids; Hardwood veneer
and plywood

(G-8923)
HI-VAC CORPORATION (PA)
117 Industry Rd (45750-9355)
PHONE.................................740 374-2306
◆ **EMP:** 135 **EST:** 1969
SALES (est): 24.31MM
SALES (corp-wide): 24.31MM **Privately
Held**
Web: www.hi-vac.com
SIC: 3589 Vacuum cleaners and sweepers,
electric: industrial

(G-8924)
INLAND HARDWOOD CORPORATION
Also Called: Inland Wood Products
25 Sheets Run Rd (45750-5186)
PHONE.................................740 373-7187
Norman E Haessly Junior, *Pr*
Julie Haessly, *Sec*
Mark Haessly, *VP*
Steve Haessly, *Treas*
EMP: 17 **EST:** 1966
SALES (est): 1.7MM
SALES (corp-wide): 7.48MM **Privately
Held**
SIC: 2448 Pallets, wood
PA: Haessly Lumber Sales Co.
25 Sheets Run Rd
Marietta OH 45750
740 373-6681

(G-8925)
KAYDEN INDUSTRIES
2167 State Route 821 (45750-1196)
PHONE.................................740 336-7801
EMP: 7 **EST:** 2015
SALES (est): 256.16K **Privately Held**
Web: www.kaydenindustries.com
SIC: 3999 Manufacturing industries, nec

(G-8926)
**MAGNUM MAGNETICS
CORPORATION (PA)**
Also Called: Magnum Inks & Coatings
801 Masonic Park Rd (45750-9357)
PHONE.................................740 373-7770
Allen Love, *Pr*
Tom Love, *
▼ **EMP:** 82 **EST:** 1991
SQ FT: 30,000
SALES (est): 21.88MM **Privately Held**
Web: www.magnummagnetics.com
SIC: 3499 Magnets, permanent: metallic

(G-8927)
**MARIETTA RESOURCES
CORPORATION**
704 Pike St (45750-3501)
PHONE.................................740 373-6305
Lynn Foster, *Pr*
EMP: 10 **EST:** 1984
SALES (est): 222.03K **Privately Held**
SIC: 1311 Crude petroleum production

(G-8928)
**MC ALARNEY POOL SPAS AND
BILLD**
Also Called: McAlarney Pols Spas Billd More
908 Pike St (45750-3505)
PHONE.................................740 373-6698
Wayne Mc Alarney, *Ex VP*
Cheryl Mcalarney, *Pr*
EMP: 15 **EST:** 1975
SQ FT: 6,500
SALES (est): 2.14MM **Privately Held**
Web: www.mcalarney.com
SIC: 5091 3949 Swimming pools, equipment
and supplies; Sporting and athletic goods,
nec

(G-8929)
MIDWAY MACHINING INC
1060 Gravel Bank Rd (45750-8370)
PHONE.................................740 373-8976
Robert L Casto, *Pr*
Gary Hendershot, *VP*
Katherine E Murphy, *Sec*
EMP: 11 **EST:** 1969
SQ FT: 3,000
SALES (est): 1.98MM **Privately Held**
Web:
www.midwaymachiningincorporated.com
SIC: 3599 Machine shop, jobbing and repair

(G-8930)
**MONDO POLYMER TECHNOLOGIES
INC (PA)**
27620 State Route 7 (45750-5146)
P.O. Box 250 (45773-0250)
PHONE.................................740 376-9396
Mark Mondo, *Pr*
Judy Mondo, *VP*
Maggie Ellis, *Genl Mgr*
EMP: 40 **EST:** 1999
SQ FT: 3,200
SALES (est): 12.11MM **Privately Held**
Web: www.mondopolymer.com
SIC: 4953 2822 Recycling, waste materials;
Synthetic rubber

(G-8931)
OHIO VALLEY ALLOY SERVICES INC
100 Westview Ave (45750-9403)
PHONE.................................740 373-1900
Randall Henthorn, *Pr*
Richard J Henthorn Junior, *VP*
▲ **EMP:** 20 **EST:** 1994
SQ FT: 2,500
SALES (est): 3.1MM **Privately Held**
Web: www.ohiovalleyalloys.com

SIC: 3312 4225 3341 Blast furnaces and
steel mills; General warehousing;
Secondary nonferrous metals

(G-8932)
OHIO VALLEY SPECIALTY COMPANY
115 Industry Rd (45750-9355)
PHONE.................................740 373-2276
Larry G Hawkins, *Pr*
Frank D Mendicino, *VP*
EMP: 12 **EST:** 1966
SQ FT: 7,000
SALES (est): 2.49MM **Privately Held**
Web: www.ovsc.com
SIC: 3339 Silicon, pure

(G-8933)
ORION ENGINEERED CARBONS LLC
1300 Blue Knob Rd (45750-8280)
PHONE.................................985 312-7406
EMP: 50
SALES (corp-wide): 2.67MM **Privately
Held**
SIC: 2895 Carbon black
HQ: Orion Engineered Carbons Llc
1700 City Plz Dr Ste 300
Spring TX 77389
832 445-3300

(G-8934)
PARDSON INC
Also Called: Bird Watcher's Digest
149 Acme St (45750-3402)
P.O. Box 3396 (47803-0396)
PHONE.................................740 373-5285
Andy Thompson, *Pr*
William Thompson Iii, *VP*
Elsa Thompson, *Treas*
EMP: 13 **EST:** 1978
SQ FT: 3,400
SALES (est): 843.05K **Privately Held**
Web: www.birdwatchersdigest.com
SIC: 2721 2731 5961 Magazines: publishing
only, not printed on site; Book publishing;
Mail order house, nec

(G-8935)
PAWNEE MAINTENANCE INC
101 Rathbone Rd (45750-1437)
P.O. Box 269 (45750-0269)
PHONE.................................740 373-6861
Ted R Szabo, *Pr*
EMP: 8 **EST:** 1990
SQ FT: 3,000
SALES (est): 2.27MM **Privately Held**
Web: www.pawneemaintenance.com
SIC: 1541 3272 Industrial buildings and
warehouses; Concrete products, nec

(G-8936)
PEN-ANN CORPORATION
Also Called: Hyde Brothers Printing Co
2343 State Route 821 Ste A (45750-5465)
P.O. Box 586 (45750-0586)
PHONE.................................740 373-2054
TOLL FREE: 800
Lewis Camp, *Pr*
David Mccullough, *Sec*
EMP: 9 **EST:** 1991
SQ FT: 5,000
SALES (est): 126.43K **Privately Held**
Web: www.hydebrothersprinting.com
SIC: 2752 Offset printing

(G-8937)
PIONEER PIPE INC
Also Called: Pioneer Group
2021 Hanna Rd (45750-8255)
PHONE.................................740 376-2400
David M Archer, *Pr*
Arlene M Archer, *

(PA)=Parent Co (HQ)=Headquarters
✪ = New Business established in last 2 years

2025 Harris Ohio
Industrial Directory

407

GEOGRAPHIC

▲ **EMP:** 600 **EST:** 1981
SQ FT: 24,800
SALES (est): 23.7MM **Privately Held**
Web: www.pioneergroup.us
SIC: 3498 1711 3443 3441 Pipe sections,
fabricated from purchased pipe; Plumbing
contractors; Fabricated plate work (boiler
shop); Fabricated structural metal

(G-8938)
PROFUSION INDUSTRIES LLC
700 Bf Goodrich Rd (45750-7849)
P.O. Box 657 (45750-0657)
PHONE.............................740 374-6400
Jon Golden, *Brnch Mgr*
EMP: 92
SALES (corp-wide): 20.85MM **Privately
Held**
Web: www.profusionindustries.com
SIC: 3081 Unsupported plastics film and
sheet
PA: Profusion Industries, Llc
822 Kumho Dr Ste 202
Fairlawn OH 44333
800 938-2858

(G-8939)
R W SIDLEY INC
105 Maple Shade Dr (45750-1158)
PHONE.............................440 224-2664
Robert Buescher, *Pr*
EMP: 8 **EST:** 1956
SALES (est): 183.41K **Privately Held**
Web: www.rwsidley.com
SIC: 3273 Ready-mixed concrete

(G-8940)
RAMPP COMPANY (PA)
20445 State Route 550 Ofc (45750-6900)
P.O. Box 608 (45750-0608)
PHONE.............................740 373-7886
Mark E Fulton, *Pr*
Charles Hall, *
Charles D Fogle, *
David Fox, *
Martin J Ramp, *
EMP: 45 **EST:** 1950
SQ FT: 50,000
SALES (est): 6.93MM
SALES (corp-wide): 6.93MM **Privately
Held**
Web: www.ramppco.com
SIC: 3533 3443 3325 Drilling tools for gas,
oil, or water wells; Crane hooks, laminated
plate; Alloy steel castings, except
investment

(G-8941)
RICHARDSON PRINTING CORP (PA)
Also Called: Zip Center, The-Division
201 Acme St (45750-3404)
P.O. Box 663 (45750-0663)
PHONE.............................800 848-9752
TOLL FREE: 800
Dennis E Valentine, *Pr*
Charles E Schwab, *
Robert Richardson Junior, *Stockholder*
▲ **EMP:** 60 **EST:** 1944
SQ FT: 100,000
SALES (est): 541.63K
SALES (corp-wide): 541.63K **Privately
Held**
Web: www.rpcprint.com
SIC: 7389 2752 Mailing and messenger
services; Offset printing

(G-8942)
SCEPTER SUPPLY LLC
1500 Greene St (45750-8044)
P.O. Box 233 (82003-0233)
PHONE.............................307 634-6074

Yon Malkuch, *VP*
EMP: 6
Web: www.sceptersupply.com
SIC: 3546 Drills and drilling tools
HQ: Scepter Supply, Llc
1912 Whitney Rd Ste B
Cheyenne WY 82007
307 634-6074

(G-8943)
SEWAH STUDIOS INC
190 Mill Creek Rd (45750-1381)
P.O. Box 298 (45750-0298)
PHONE.............................740 373-2087
Bradford Smith, *Pr*
David Smith, *VP*
EMP: 11 **EST:** 1927
SQ FT: 6,000
SALES (est): 2.31MM **Privately Held**
Web: www.sewahstudios.com
SIC: 3446 Architectural metalwork

(G-8944)
SILICON PROCESSORS INC
1988 Masonic Park Rd (45750-5402)
PHONE.............................740 373-2252
W Trent Elliott, *Pr*
David Downing, *CFO*
EMP: 6 **EST:** 2004
SALES (est): 126.63K **Privately Held**
SIC: 3339 Silicon refining (primary, over 99%
pure)

(G-8945)
SILVESCO INC
2985 State Route 26 (45750-7586)
P.O. Box 161 (45750-0161)
PHONE.............................740 373-6661
Rodney Paxton, *Pr*
Michele Paxton, *VP*
EMP: 10 **EST:** 1964
SQ FT: 11,800
SALES (est): 484.6K **Privately Held**
Web: www.silvescopallets.com
SIC: 2448 2449 Pallets, wood; Rectangular
boxes and crates, wood

(G-8946)
SKUTTLE MFG CO
Also Called: Skuttle Indoor Air Qulty Pdts
101 Margaret St (45750-9052)
PHONE.............................740 373-9169
Davis Powers, *Pr*
Debby Romick, *Sec*
▲ **EMP:** 14 **EST:** 1917
SQ FT: 96,500
SALES (est): 2.35MM **Privately Held**
Web: www.skuttle.com
SIC: 3634 3564 3822 Humidifiers, electric;
household; Filters, air: furnaces, air
conditioning equipment, etc.; Environmental
controls

(G-8947)
SOLVAY ADVANCED POLYMERS LLC
17005 State Route 7 (45750-8248)
P.O. Box 446 (45750-0446)
PHONE.............................740 373-9242
Joseph D Greulich, *Pr*
EMP: 48 **EST:** 2001
SALES (est): 10.52MM **Privately Held**
SIC: 2819 Radium, luminous compounds

(G-8948)
**SOLVAY SPCLTY POLYMERS USA
LLC**
17005 State Route 7 (45750-8248)
P.O. Box 446 (45750-0446)
PHONE.............................740 373-9242
Wally Kandell, *Brnch Mgr*
EMP: 17

SALES (corp-wide): 8.01MM **Privately
Held**
Web: www.solvay.com
SIC: 2821 Plastics materials and resins
HQ: Solvay Specialty Polymers Usa, L.L.C.
4500 Mcginnis Ferry Rd
Alpharetta GA 30005
770 772-8200

(G-8949)
SOMERVILLE MANUFACTURING INC
15 Townhall Rd (45750-5374)
PHONE.............................740 336-7847
Steve Somerville, *Pr*
Peggy Somerville, *VP*
EMP: 20 **EST:** 2013
SALES (est): 4.86MM **Privately Held**
Web: www.somervilleindustries.com
SIC: 3441 3444 7692 Fabricated structural
metal; Sheet metalwork; Welding repair

(G-8950)
STEVES VANS ACC UNLIMITED LLC
Also Called: Steve's Vans Auto Sales
221 Pike St (45750-3320)
PHONE.............................740 374-3154
TOLL FREE: 800
EMP: 9 **EST:** 1983
SQ FT: 3,700
SALES (est): 585.16K **Privately Held**
Web: www.mariettamobilityservices.com
SIC: 5511 7532 5531 5999 Vans, new and
used; Van conversion; Automotive
accessories; Technical aids for the
handicapped

(G-8951)
TEIKOKU USA INC
27881 State Route 7 (45750-9060)
PHONE.............................304 699-1156
John Cox, *Brnch Mgr*
EMP: 13
Web: www.teikokupumps.com
SIC: 3561 Pumps and pumping equipment
HQ: Teikoku Usa Inc.
959 Mearns Rd
Warminster PA 18974

(G-8952)
TENGAM PRO INC
Also Called: Magnetic Source
108 Industry Rd (45750-9355)
PHONE.............................740 373-0909
Dewayne Collins, *Brnch Mgr*
EMP: 10
SALES (corp-wide): 13.84MM **Privately
Held**
Web: www.magnetsource.com
SIC: 3499 Fire- or burglary-resistive products
PA: Tengam Pro, Inc.
1211 Atchison Ct
Castle Rock CO 80109
303 688-3966

(G-8953)
TERRA SONIC INTERNATIONAL LLC
27825 State Route 7 (45750-9060)
PHONE.............................740 374-6608
John Walsh, *Managing Member*
◆ **EMP:** 22 **EST:** 1998
SQ FT: 600,000
SALES (est): 4.95MM **Privately Held**
Web: www.terrasonicinternational.com
SIC: 1623 7353 3533 Oil and gas pipeline
construction; Oil field equipment, rental or
leasing; Oil and gas drilling rigs and
equipment

(G-8954)
**THERMO FSHER SCNTFIC ASHVLLE
L**
401 Mill Creek Rd (45750-4304)
P.O. Box 649 (45750-0649)
PHONE.............................740 373-4763
Jamie Keefer, *Brnch Mgr*
EMP: 592
SQ FT: 287
SALES (corp-wide): 42.86B **Publicly Held**
Web: www.marysittonteam.com
SIC: 3826 Analytical instruments
HQ: Thermo Fisher Scientific (Asheville) Llc
275 Aiken Rd
Asheville NC 28804
828 658-2711

(G-8955)
TKN OILFIELD SERVICES LLC
108 Woodcrest Dr (45750-1352)
PHONE.............................740 516-2583
EMP: 12 **EST:** 2018
SQ FT: 1,500
SALES (est): 1.26MM **Privately Held**
Web: www.tknoilfieldservices.com
SIC: 1389 Oil field services, nec

(G-8956)
TRIAD ENERGY CORPORATION
125 Putnam St (45750-2936)
PHONE.............................740 374-2940
Kean Weaver, *Pr*
James R Bryden, *VP*
EMP: 7 **EST:** 1956
SALES (est): 725.49K **Privately Held**
SIC: 2992 1382 Lubricating oils and greases
; Oil and gas exploration services

(G-8957)
UNITED CHART PROCESSORS INC
1461 Masonic Park Rd (45750-5393)
PHONE.............................740 373-5801
David Graham, *Pr*
Barbara Graham, *VP*
EMP: 8 **EST:** 1984
SALES (est): 964.74K **Privately Held**
Web: www.ucpgas.com
SIC: 1389 Oil field services, nec

(G-8958)
UNITED DAIRY INC
1701 Greene St (45750-7000)
PHONE.............................740 373-4121
Joseph L Carson, *Pr*
EMP: 260
SALES (corp-wide): 80.92MM **Privately
Held**
Web: www.drinkunited.com
SIC: 5451 2024 2026 Dairy products stores;
Ice cream, packaged: molded, on sticks,
etc.; Cottage cheese
PA: United Dairy, Inc.
300 N 5th St
Martins Ferry OH 43935
740 633-1451

(G-8959)
**VANGUARD PAINTS AND FINISHES
INC**
1409 Greene St (45750-9807)
P.O. Box 654 (45750-0654)
PHONE.............................740 373-5261
EMP: 22 **EST:** 1939
SALES (est): 4.32MM **Privately Held**
Web: www.vanguardpaints.com
SIC: 2851 Paints and allied products

(G-8960)
VIKING FABRICATORS INC
2021 Hanna Rd (45750-8255)

▲ = Import ▼ = Export
◆ = Import/Export

PHONE.................740 374-5246
David M Archer, *Pr*
Arlene M Archer, *
Matthew Hilverding, *
James S Huggins, *
EMP: 6 **EST:** 1988
SQ FT: 20,000
SALES (est): 913.68K **Privately Held**
Web: www.pioneerpipeinc.com
SIC: 3441 7692 3446 3443 Fabricated structural metal; Welding repair; Architectural metalwork; Fabricated plate work (boiler shop)

(G-8961)
WESTLAKE DIMEX LLC
28305 State Route 7 (45750-5151)
P.O. Box 337 (45773)
PHONE.................800 334-3776
Andy Antil, *CEO*
Dan Allan, *
▲ **EMP:** 160 **EST:** 1991
SQ FT: 224,000
SALES (est): 22.17MM **Publicly Held**
Web: www.dimexcorp.com
SIC: 6726 3089 3069 Investment offices, nec ; Plastics hardware and building products; Mats or matting, rubber, nec
PA: Westlake Corporation
2801 Post Oak Blvd Ste 60
Houston TX 77056

(G-8962)
WINSTON OIL CO INC
1 Court House Ln Ste 3 (45750-2900)
P.O. Box 754 (45750-0754)
PHONE.................740 373-9664
Deborah Cunningham, *Prin*
EMP: 7 **EST:** 2007
SALES (est): 732.5K **Privately Held**
SIC: 3569 Gas producers, generators, and other gas related equipment

(G-8963)
ZIDE SPORT SHOP OF OHIO INC
Also Called: Zide Screen Printing
118 Industry Rd (45750-9355)
PHONE.................740 373-8199
Randy Schneeberger, *Mgr*
EMP: 17
SALES (corp-wide): 2.94MM **Privately Held**
Web: www.zides.com
SIC: 2396 Screen printing on fabric articles
PA: Zide Sport Shop Of Ohio, Inc.
253 2nd St
Marietta OH 45750
740 373-6446

Marion
Marion County

(G-8964)
ALIN MACHINING COMPANY INC
Also Called: ALIN MACHINING COMPANY, INC.
875 E Mark St (43302-2748)
PHONE.................740 223-0200
Ryan Dballinger, *Brnch Mgr*
EMP: 61
SALES (corp-wide): 40.01MM **Privately Held**
Web: www.ppsvcs.com
SIC: 3511 Turbines and turbine generator sets
PA: Alin Machining Company, Llc
3131 W Soffel Ave
Melrose Park IL 60160
708 681-1043

(G-8965)
BENDER COMMUNICATIONS INC (PA)
1541 Harding Hwy E (43302-4567)
PHONE.................740 382-0000
TOLL FREE: 800
Donald L Bender, *Pr*
Dustin Bender, *VP*
Kelesta Edwards, *Sec*
Karen Bender, *Treas*
EMP: 10 **EST:** 1975
SQ FT: 2,500
SALES (est): 2.94MM
SALES (corp-wide): 2.94MM **Privately Held**
Web: www.bendercomm.com
SIC: 3669 5731 Intercommunication systems, electric; Radios, two-way, citizens band, weather, short-wave, etc.

(G-8966)
CENTRAL MACHINERY COMPANY LLC
Also Called: Cenmac Metalworks
1339 E Fairground Rd (43302-8873)
PHONE.................740 387-1289
Rod Galbreath, *Pr*
EMP: 17 **EST:** 1960
SQ FT: 25,000
SALES (est): 8.35MM **Privately Held**
Web: www.cenmacmetalworks.com
SIC: 3599 3499 Machine shop, jobbing and repair; Fire- or burglary-resistive products

(G-8967)
CENTRAL MACHINERY COMPANY LLC
116 S Main St (43302-3702)
PHONE.................740 387-1289
Charlotte R Baldauf, *Prin*
EMP: 9 **EST:** 2001
SALES (est): 124.73K **Privately Held**
SIC: 3569 General industrial machinery, nec

(G-8968)
CREATIVE DCUMENT SOLUTIONS LLC
1629 Marion Waldo Rd (43302-7425)
PHONE.................740 389-4252
Lorraine Corbin, *Prin*
EMP: 6 **EST:** 2005
SALES (est): 229.35K **Privately Held**
Web: www.creativedocumentsolutions.com
SIC: 2759 Commercial printing, nec

(G-8969)
ENVIRI CORPORATION
Also Called: Patent Construction Systems
3477 Harding Hwy E (43302-8534)
PHONE.................740 387-1150
Don Broadwater, *Brnch Mgr*
EMP: 12
SALES (corp-wide): 2.34B **Publicly Held**
Web: www.enviri.com
SIC: 3537 3536 3535 3531 Industrial trucks and tractors; Hoists, cranes, and monorails; Conveyors and conveying equipment; Construction machinery
PA: Enviri Corporation
100-120 N 18th St # 17
Philadelphia PA 19103
267 857-8715

(G-8970)
FOLKS CREATIVE PRINTERS INC
101 E George St (43302-2304)
P.O. Box 521 (43301-0521)
PHONE.................740 383-6326
Trudi E Maish, *Ch Bd*

James L Saiter, *Pr*
Linda M Maish, *Sec*
EMP: 8 **EST:** 1922
SALES (est): 847.74K **Privately Held**
Web: www.folksprinting.com
SIC: 2752 3993 2789 2759 Offset printing; Signs and advertising specialties; Bookbinding and related work; Commercial printing, nec

(G-8971)
GENERAL MACHINE & SAW COMPANY
305 Davids St (43302-4713)
P.O. Box 587 (43301-0587)
PHONE.................740 382-1104
Joseph Murphy, *Pr*
Matt Murphy, *
Beth Murphy, *
Jack Dean, *
EMP: 96 **EST:** 1980
SQ FT: 100,000
SALES (est): 9.76MM **Privately Held**
Web: www.gmsaw.com
SIC: 3441 Fabricated structural metal

(G-8972)
HIGHWAY SAFETY CORP
Also Called: HIGHWAY SAFETY CORP.
473 W Fairground St (43302-1701)
PHONE.................740 387-6991
Jim Chick, *Mgr*
EMP: 15
SALES (corp-wide): 48.78MM **Privately Held**
Web: www.highwaysafety.net
SIC: 3444 3479 Guard rails, highway: sheet metal; Galvanizing of iron, steel, or end-formed products
HQ: Highway Safety Llc
239 Commerce St
Glastonbury CT 06033
860 633-9445

(G-8973)
HILDRETH MFG LLC
1657 Cascade Dr (43302-8509)
P.O. Box 905 (43301-0905)
PHONE.................740 375-5832
EMP: 25 **EST:** 1999
SALES (est): 8.79MM **Privately Held**
Web: www.hildrethmfg.com
SIC: 3331 Blocks, copper

(G-8974)
INTERNATIONAL PAPER COMPANY
Also Called: International Paper
1600 Cascade Dr (43302-8509)
PHONE.................740 383-4061
Ron Iden, *Prin*
EMP: 40
SALES (corp-wide): 18.62B **Publicly Held**
Web: www.internationalpaper.com
SIC: 2621 Paper mills
PA: International Paper Company
6400 Poplar Ave
Memphis TN 38197
901 419-7000

(G-8975)
LAIPPLYS PRTG MKTG SLTIONS INC
270 E Center St (43302-4124)
P.O. Box 777 (43301-0777)
PHONE.................740 387-9282
Ronald E Laipply, *Pr*
Jacque Laipply, *VP*
Effie Laipply, *Sec*
EMP: 9 **EST:** 1973
SQ FT: 5,000
SALES (est): 582.28K **Privately Held**
Web: www.laipplyqprint.com

SIC: 2789 7336 7331 Bookbinding and related work; Graphic arts and related design; Direct mail advertising services

(G-8976)
MARION DOFASCO INC
686 W Fairground St (43302-1706)
PHONE.................740 382-3979
D Pether, *Prin*
EMP: 6 **EST:** 2016
SALES (est): 228.77K **Privately Held**
Web: www.ltv-copperweld.com
SIC: 3312 Blast furnaces and steel mills

(G-8977)
MARION INDUSTRIES LLC
999 Kellogg Pkwy (43302-1791)
PHONE.................740 223-0075
EMP: 753
Web: www.marionindustries.com
SIC: 3714 Motor vehicle wheels and parts

(G-8978)
MIDWEST GLYCOL SERVICES LLC
116 Lawrence Ave (43302-3346)
PHONE.................419 946-3326
Gennifer Schaefer, *CEO*
EMP: 25 **EST:** 2022
SALES (est): 1.16MM **Privately Held**
SIC: 2899 Chemical preparations, nec

(G-8979)
MILLS PARTITION COMPANY LLC
3007 Harding Hwy E Bldg 201 (43302-2575)
PHONE.................740 375-0770
Donald H Mullett, *Ch Bd*
John Kleczka, *Sec*
▲ **EMP:** 70 **EST:** 1921
SALES (est): 3.86MM
SALES (corp-wide): 2.25B **Publicly Held**
SIC: 2542 Partitions for floor attachment, prefabricated: except wood
HQ: Bradley Company, Llc
W142 N9101 Fountain Blvd
Menomonee Falls WI 53051
262 251-6000

(G-8980)
MISSION INDUSTRIAL GROUP LLC
Also Called: Drum Runner
3602 Harding Hwy E (43302-8534)
PHONE.................740 387-2287
Mark Snow, *Managing Member*
▼ **EMP:** 10 **EST:** 1947
SQ FT: 17,000
SALES (est): 1.76MM **Privately Held**
Web: www.drumrunner.com
SIC: 3599 Machine shop, jobbing and repair

(G-8981)
MOTHERSON YCHIYO US AUTO SYSTE
Also Called: US Yachiyo Inc.
1177 Kellogg Pkwy (43302-1779)
PHONE.................740 375-4687
Hiroshi Sasamoto, *Pr*
Kazuyoshi Itai, *
Tsugio Motoori, *
Yasushi Ota, *
Kazuhiro Asabuki, *
◆ **EMP:** 232 **EST:** 1999
SQ FT: 125,000
SALES (est): 23.59MM **Privately Held**
Web: www.yachiyo-of-america.com
SIC: 3795 Tanks and tank components
HQ: Motherson Yachiyo Automotive Tech Products Of America, Inc.
2285 Walcutt Rd
Columbus OH 43228

GEOGRAPHIC

(G-8982)
NACHURS ALPINE SOLUTIONS LLC (HQ)
Also Called: Nachurs Alpine Solutions Corp
421 Leader St (43302-2225)
PHONE..................................740 382-5701
Jeffrey Barnes, *Pr*
Robert Hopp, *
Reiny Packull, *
David Rose, *
▲ EMP: 25 EST: 1946
SALES (est): 114.52MM
SALES (corp-wide): 3.23B **Privately Held**
Web: www.nachurs.com
SIC: 2875 2869 2819 Fertilizers, mixing only; Industrial organic chemicals, nec; Industrial inorganic chemicals, nec
PA: Wilbur-Ellis Holdings, Inc.
345 California St Fl 27
San Francisco CA 94104
415 772-4000

(G-8983)
NATIONAL LIME AND STONE CO
700 Likens Rd (43302-8601)
P.O. Box 144 (43301-0144)
PHONE..................................740 387-3485
Scott Silver, *Mgr*
EMP: 27
SALES (corp-wide): 86.85MM **Privately Held**
Web: www.natlime.com
SIC: 1422 5999 Limestones, ground; Rock and stone specimens
PA: The National Lime And Stone Company
551 Lake Cascade Pkwy
Findlay OH 45840
419 422-4341

(G-8984)
NUCOR STEEL MARION INC
Scrap Division
400 Bartram Ave (43302-2108)
P.O. Box 1217 (43301-1217)
PHONE..................................740 383-6068
Tim Bia, *Mgr*
EMP: 20
SALES (corp-wide): 30.73B **Publicly Held**
Web: www.nucorhighway.com
SIC: 3312 5051 5093 Sheet or strip, steel, cold-rolled: own hot-rolled; Metals service centers and offices; Metal scrap and waste materials
HQ: Nucor Steel Marion, Inc.
912 Cheney Ave
Marion OH 43302
740 383-4011

(G-8985)
NUCOR STEEL MARION INC (HQ)
912 Cheney Ave (43302-6208)
P.O. Box 1801 (43301-1801)
PHONE..................................740 383-4011
◆ EMP: 375 EST: 1981
SALES (est): 59.3MM
SALES (corp-wide): 30.73B **Publicly Held**
Web: www.nucorhighway.com
SIC: 3316 3441 3312 5051 Cold finishing of steel shapes; Fabricated structural metal; Iron and steel products, hot-rolled; Iron and steel (ferrous) products
PA: Nucor Corporation
1915 Rexford Rd
Charlotte NC 28211
704 366-7000

(G-8986)
OHIO GALVANIZING LLC
467 W Fairground St (43302-1701)
PHONE..................................740 387-6474
W Patric Gregory Iii, *CEO*
Robert J West, *
EMP: 50 EST: 1994
SQ FT: 57,000
SALES (est): 2.56MM
SALES (corp-wide): 48.78MM **Privately Held**
Web: www.ohgalv.com
SIC: 3479 Coating of metals and formed products
PA: Race Rock Gp, L.L.C.
1980 Post Oak Blvd Ste 21
Houston TX 77056
832 920-1276

(G-8987)
OVERHEAD DOOR CORPORATION
Todco
1332 E Fairground Rd (43302-8505)
PHONE..................................740 383-6376
Daniel C Rengert, *Pr*
EMP: 100
Web: www.overheaddoor.com
SIC: 3442 2431 3441 Garage doors, overhead: metal; Doors, wood; Fabricated structural metal
HQ: Overhead Door Corporation
2501 S State Hwy 121 Ste
Lewisville TX 75067
469 549-7100

(G-8988)
PACIFIC HIGHWAY PRODUCTS LLC
324 Barnhart St (43302-3206)
PHONE..................................740 914-5217
EMP: 6 EST: 2018
SALES (est): 3.81MM **Privately Held**
SIC: 3699 Electrical welding equipment

(G-8989)
PISTON AUTOMOTIVE LLC
999 Kellogg Pkwy (43302-1791)
PHONE..................................740 223-0075
Robert Holloway, *Pr*
EMP: 753
SALES (corp-wide): 2.3B **Privately Held**
Web: www.pistonautomotive.com
SIC: 3714 Motor vehicle wheels and parts
HQ: Piston Automotive, L.L.C.
12723 Telegraph Rd
Redford MI 48239
313 541-8674

(G-8990)
POET BIOREFINING MARION LLC
Also Called: Poet Biorefining
1660 Hillman Ford Rd (43302-9475)
PHONE..................................740 383-4400
Rick Fox, *Mgr*
EMP: 45 EST: 2008
SALES (est): 144MM **Privately Held**
Web: poetbiorefining-marion.aghost.net
SIC: 2869 2046 Ethyl alcohol, ethanol; Corn oil products
PA: Poet, Llc
4615 N Lewis Ave
Sioux Falls SD 57104

(G-8991)
R ANTHONY ENTERPRISES LLC
2626 Whetstone River Rd S (43302-8937)
PHONE..................................419 341-0961
Rocco Piacentino, *Managing Member*
EMP: 10 EST: 2012
SQ FT: 10,000
SALES (est): 581.78K **Privately Held**
SIC: 1389 Construction, repair, and dismantling services

(G-8992)
REX WELDING INC
1410 E Center St (43302-4593)
PHONE..................................740 387-1650
Joel Plough, *Pr*
Mary E Plough, *VP*
Chris Plough, *Sec*
EMP: 10 EST: 1944
SQ FT: 9,000
SALES (est): 227.1K **Privately Held**
SIC: 5051 1791 7692 7389 Steel; Structural steel erection; Welding repair; Crane and aerial lift service

(G-8993)
RI ALTO MFG INC
1632 Cascade Dr (43302-8509)
PHONE..................................740 914-4230
Rick Mattix, *Pr*
Maryann Mattix, *Sec*
Sam Hawkins, *VP*
EMP: 19 EST: 1981
SQ FT: 9,000
SALES (est): 5.34MM **Privately Held**
Web: www.rialtomfg.com
SIC: 3599 7692 Machine shop, jobbing and repair; Welding repair

(G-8994)
ROY I KAUFMAN INC
1672 Marion Upper Sandusky Rd (43302-1531)
PHONE..................................740 382-0643
Martin T Kaufman Ii, *Dir*
Beth Kaufman, *Sec*
EMP: 8 EST: 1956
SQ FT: 12,000
SALES (est): 410.86K **Privately Held**
Web: www.kaufmancables.com
SIC: 3496 Woven wire products, nec

(G-8995)
SAKAMURA USA INC
970 Kellogg Pkwy (43302-1783)
PHONE..................................740 223-7777
Takayuki Nakano, *Pr*
Jun Kobayashi, *VP*
Naomi Taniguchi, *Treas*
▲ EMP: 14 EST: 1997
SQ FT: 10,000
SALES (est): 9.02MM **Privately Held**
Web: www.sakamura.net
SIC: 3462 Iron and steel forgings
PA: Sakamura Machine Co., Ltd.
46, Tominojo, Shimotsuya, Kumiyamacho
Kuse-Gun KYO 613-0

(G-8996)
SCHWARZ PARTNERS PACKAGING LLC
Also Called: Royal Group, The
2135 Innovation Dr (43302-8261)
PHONE..................................740 387-3700
Jeff Gorsuch, *Brnch Mgr*
EMP: 75
SALES (corp-wide): 653.03MM **Privately Held**
Web: theroyalgroup.wpengine.com
SIC: 2653 Boxes, corrugated: made from purchased materials
HQ: Schwarz Partners Packaging, Llc
10 W Carmel Dr Ste 300 In
Carmel IN 46032
317 290-1140

(G-8997)
SEMCO INC
1025 Pole Lane Rd (43302-8524)
PHONE..................................800 848-5764
Leonard Furman, *Ch*
Brett Tennar, *
Shelby Furman, *
Randy Furman, *
J Douglass Schrim, *
▲ EMP: 60 EST: 1976
SQ FT: 40,000
SALES (est): 5.85MM **Privately Held**
Web: www.semcotips.com
SIC: 3599 3366 Machine shop, jobbing and repair; Copper foundries

(G-8998)
SILVER LINE BUILDING PDTS LLC
2549 Innovation Dr (43302-8721)
PHONE..................................740 382-5595
EMP: 877
SALES (corp-wide): 5.58B **Privately Held**
Web: www.silverlinewindows.com
SIC: 3089 Composition stone, plastics
HQ: Silver Line Building Products Llc
1 Silver Line Dr
North Brunswick NJ 08902
732 435-1000

(G-8999)
SIMCOTE INC
Also Called: Simcote of Ohio Division
250 N Greenwood St (43302-3177)
PHONE..................................740 382-5000
Art Tofte, *Brnch Mgr*
EMP: 13
SALES (corp-wide): 13.08MM **Privately Held**
Web: www.simcote.com
SIC: 3479 3449 Painting, coating, and hot dipping; Miscellaneous metalwork
PA: Simcote, Inc.
1645 Red Rock Rd
Saint Paul MN 55119
651 735-9660

(G-9000)
SIMS BROS INC (PA)
Also Called: Sims Brothers Recycling
1011 S Prospect St (43302-6217)
P.O. Box 1170 (43301-1170)
PHONE..................................740 387-9041
TOLL FREE: 800
▲ EMP: 95 EST: 1965
SALES (est): 23.86MM
SALES (corp-wide): 23.86MM **Privately Held**
Web: www.simsbros.com
SIC: 5051 5013 5093 3341 Iron and steel (ferrous) products; Automotive supplies and parts; Waste paper; Secondary nonferrous metals

(G-9001)
STEAM TRBINE ALTRNTIVE RSRCES
Also Called: Star
370 W Fairground St (43302-1728)
P.O. Box 862 (43301)
PHONE..................................740 387-5535
Sue B Flaherty, *Ch Bd*
Tammy Flaherty, *
Ken Kubinski, *
Donna Macgregor Rambin, *
EMP: 45 EST: 1988
SALES (est): 4.88MM **Privately Held**
Web: www.starturbine.com
SIC: 3511 5085 Steam turbines; Industrial supplies

(G-9002)
TODCO
1295 E Fairground Rd (43302-8002)
PHONE..................................740 223-2542
Dennis Stone, *CEO*
EMP: 10 EST: 2017
SALES (est): 2.42MM **Privately Held**

Web: www.todco.com
SIC: 2431 Millwork

(G-9003)
WHIRLPOOL CORPORATION
Whirlpool
1300 Marion Agosta Rd (43302-9577)
PHONE..............................740 383-7122
Stan Kenneth, *VP*
EMP: 83
SALES (corp-wide): 16.61B **Publicly Held**
Web: www.whirlpoolcorp.com
SIC: 3633 5064 3632 Laundry dryers, household or coin-operated; Washing machines; Household refrigerators and freezers
PA: Whirlpool Corporation
2000 N M-63
Benton Harbor MI 49022
269 923-5000

(G-9004)
WILLIAMS LEATHER PRODUCTS INC
Also Called: McKinley Leather
1476 Likens Rd Ste 104 (43302-8788)
PHONE..............................740 223-1604
Derek Williams, *Pr*
EMP: 6 **EST:** 1994
SQ FT: 8,000
SALES (est): 227.49K **Privately Held**
Web: www.mckinleyleather.com
SIC: 3172 Personal leather goods, nec

(G-9005)
WILSON BOHANNAN COMPANY
Also Called: W B
621 Buckeye St (43302-6121)
P.O. Box 504 (43301-0504)
PHONE..............................740 382-3639
Howard Smith, *Pr*
Pamela Smith, *
Randy Dawson, *
Mark Williams, *
Craig Stone, *
EMP: 72 **EST:** 1860
SQ FT: 40,000
SALES (est): 8.35MM **Privately Held**
Web: www.padlocks.com
SIC: 3429 Padlocks

(G-9006)
WYANDOT USA LLC (PA)
Also Called: Wyandot Snacks
135 Wyandot Ave (43302-1338)
PHONE..............................740 383-4031
Ken Romanzi, *Managing Member*
Erich Fritz, *COO*
▲ **EMP:** 225 **EST:** 1936
SQ FT: 265,000
SALES (est): 39.05MM
SALES (corp-wide): 39.05MM **Privately Held**
Web: www.wyandotsnacks.com
SIC: 2099 Food preparations, nec

Marshallville
Wayne County

(G-9007)
MARSHALLVILLE PACKING CO INC
50 E Market St (44645-9468)
P.O. Box 276 (44645-0276)
PHONE..............................330 855-2871
Frank T Tucker, *Pr*
Jeannette Tucker, *
EMP: 7 **EST:** 1960
SQ FT: 35,000
SALES (est): 489.55K **Privately Held**
Web: www.marshallville-meats.com

SIC: 5421 5147 2013 2011 Meat markets, including freezer provisioners; Meats, fresh; Sausages and other prepared meats; Meat packing plants

(G-9008)
RUPP CONSTRUCTION INC
18228 Fulton Rd (44645-9716)
PHONE..............................330 855-2781
Gary Radabaugh, *Pr*
Dorothea Radabaugh, *Sec*
EMP: 10 **EST:** 1935
SQ FT: 20,000
SALES (est): 1.42MM **Privately Held**
Web: www.ruppconstruct.com
SIC: 1442 Construction sand and gravel

Martins Ferry
Belmont County

(G-9009)
AYERS LIMESTONE QUARRY INC
2002 Colerain Pike (43935)
P.O. Box 67 (43935-0067)
PHONE..............................740 633-2958
Thomas E Ayers Junior, *Pr*
Patricia Ayers, *Sec*
John Ayers, *VP*
EMP: 10 **EST:** 1958
SQ FT: 8,000
SALES (est): 967.61K **Privately Held**
Web: www.martinsferry.org
SIC: 1422 3274 Whiting mining, crushed and broken-quarrying; Lime

(G-9010)
LESCO INC
Also Called: Lesco Service Center
100 Picoma Rd (43935-9700)
PHONE..............................740 633-6366
Frank Damato, *Mgr*
EMP: 10
SALES (corp-wide): 4.54B **Publicly Held**
Web: www.lesco.com
SIC: 5191 2875 Limestone, agricultural; Fertilizers, mixing only
HQ: Lesco, Inc.
1385 E 36th St
Cleveland OH 44114
216 706-9250

(G-9011)
UNITED DAIRY INC (PA)
Also Called: United Dairy Company
300 N 5th St (43935-1647)
P.O. Box 280 (43935-0280)
PHONE..............................740 633-1451
Joseph M Carson Junior, *Ch*
Gary Cowell, *
Joseph L Carson, *
George Wood, *
James Carson, *
EMP: 200 **EST:** 1903
SQ FT: 20,000
SALES (est): 80.92MM
SALES (corp-wide): 80.92MM **Privately Held**
Web: www.drinkunited.com
SIC: 2026 2024 Milk processing (pasteurizing, homogenizing, bottling); Ice cream, bulk

(G-9012)
WILSON BLACKTOP CORP
915 Carlisle St Rear (43935-1511)
P.O. Box 128 (43916)
PHONE..............................740 635-3566
Dale M Wilson, *Pr*
Mark E Wilson, *VP*

Janice L Wilson, *Sec*
EMP: 15 **EST:** 1976
SQ FT: 1,000
SALES (est): 3.07MM **Privately Held**
Web: www.wilsonblacktop.com
SIC: 2951 1611 1771 Asphalt and asphaltic paving mixtures (not from refineries); Highway and street paving contractor; Blacktop (asphalt) work

Martinsville
Clinton County

(G-9013)
ROZZI COMPANY INC
6047 State Route 350 (45146-9539)
PHONE..............................513 683-0620
Matthew Sheeley, *Prin*
EMP: 15
SALES (corp-wide): 2.18MM **Privately Held**
Web: www.rozzifireworks.com
SIC: 2899 Chemical preparations, nec
PA: The Rozzi Company Inc
10059 Loveland Madeira Rd
Loveland OH 45140
513 683-0620

Marysville
Union County

(G-9014)
AMERICAN AGRITECH LLC
Also Called: Botanicare
14111 Scottslawn Rd (43040-7800)
PHONE..............................480 777-2000
◆ **EMP:** 30 **EST:** 1996
SQ FT: 21,000
SALES (est): 9.38MM
SALES (corp-wide): 3.55B **Publicly Held**
SIC: 3423 Garden and farm tools, including shovels
PA: The Scotts Miracle-Gro Company
14111 Scottslawn Rd
Marysville OH 43041
937 644-0011

(G-9015)
BUCKEYE READY-MIX LLC
838 N Main St (43040-9701)
P.O. Box 31 (43060-0031)
PHONE..............................937 642-2951
Larry Randels, *VP*
EMP: 17
SQ FT: 3,000
SALES (corp-wide): 21.97MM **Privately Held**
Web: www.buckeyereadymix.com
SIC: 3273 Ready-mixed concrete
PA: Buckeye Ready-Mix, Llc
7657 Taylor Rd Sw
Reynoldsburg OH 43068
614 575-2132

(G-9016)
CONTITECH USA LLC
Also Called: Continental Contitech
13601 Industrial Pkwy (43040-8890)
PHONE..............................937 644-8900
Ken Kontely, *Mgr*
EMP: 120
SALES (corp-wide): 42B **Privately Held**
Web: www.continental-industry.com
SIC: 5084 3399 3496 Industrial machinery and equipment; Metal fasteners; Mats and matting
HQ: Contitech Usa, Llc.
703 S Clvland Mssillon Rd

Akron OH 44333

(G-9017)
CONTRACT BLDG COMPONENTS LTD
Also Called: C B C
14540 Industrial Pkwy (43040-9595)
P.O. Box 1018 (43040-2018)
PHONE..............................937 644-0739
Jeff Coulter, *Mgr*
Steven Yoder, *VP*
EMP: 20 **EST:** 2000
SALES (est): 4.22MM **Privately Held**
Web: www.contractbuilding.com
SIC: 2439 Trusses, wooden roof

(G-9018)
DAK ENTERPRISES INC (PA)
18062 Timber Trails Rd (43040-8158)
P.O. Box 409 (43822-0409)
PHONE..............................740 828-3291
Daniel Keifer, *Pr*
EMP: 13 **EST:** 2004
SALES (est): 15.67MM
SALES (corp-wide): 15.67MM **Privately Held**
Web: www.dkmanufacturing.com
SIC: 3089 Injection molding of plastics

(G-9019)
ENGINEERED MFG & EQP CO
Also Called: E M E C
11611 Industrial Pkwy (43040-9522)
PHONE..............................937 642-7776
Raymond A Grigorenko, *Pr*
Leslie Grigorenko, *VP*
Thomas Walter, *Genl Mgr*
EMP: 8 **EST:** 1995
SQ FT: 9,000
SALES (est): 895.91K **Privately Held**
Web: www.emec.us
SIC: 3544 3699 Special dies, tools, jigs, and fixtures; Electrical equipment and supplies, nec

(G-9020)
FRANKES WOOD PRODUCTS LLC
825 Collins Ave (43040-1330)
PHONE..............................937 642-0706
William Franke, *Pr*
Michelle R Franke, *Stockholder**
Kevin Franke, *Stockholder**
Christopher S Franke, *Stockholder**
EMP: 40 **EST:** 2001
SQ FT: 93,800
SALES (est): 8.15MM **Privately Held**
Web: www.frankeswoodproducts.com
SIC: 2448 2449 2493 3061 Cargo containers, wood; Shipping cases and drums, wood: wirebound and plywood; Fiberboard, wood; Mechanical rubber goods

(G-9021)
GRAPHIC STITCH INC
169 Grove St Rm A (43040-1342)
PHONE..............................937 642-6707
Todd M Hoge, *Pr*
Karen Valentino, *Off Mgr*
EMP: 9 **EST:** 1995
SQ FT: 2,800
SALES (est): 925.89K **Privately Held**
Web: www.graphicstitch.com
SIC: 2395 2759 Embroidery products, except Schiffli machine; Commercial printing, nec

(G-9022)
GREENVILLE TECHNIOLOGY INC
15000 Industrial Pkwy (43040-9547)
PHONE..............................937 642-6744
EMP: 6 **EST:** 2015

SALES (est): 2.11MM **Privately Held**
SIC: 3089 Automotive parts, plastic

(G-9023)
HAWTHORNE GARDENING COMPANY (HQ)
Also Called: Hawthorne Gardening Co.
14111 Scottslawn Rd (43040-7800)
PHONE......................360 883-8846
James Hagedorn, *CEO*
Christopher Hagedorn, *Genl Mgr*
Michael Lukemire, *COO*
Randy Coleman, *Ex VP*
Ivan Smith, *CCO*
EMP: 21 **EST:** 2014
SALES (est): 48.43MM
SALES (corp-wide): 3.55B **Publicly Held**
Web: www.hawthorne-gardening.com
SIC: 5083 7342 3524 Lawn and garden machinery and equipment; Pest control services; Lawn and garden tractors and equipment
PA: The Scotts Miracle-Gro Company
14111 Scottslawn Rd
Marysville OH 43041
937 644-0011

(G-9024)
HAWTHORNE HYDROPONICS LLC (DH)
Also Called: Hawthorne Hydrophonics Botanic
14111 Scottslawn Rd (43040-7800)
PHONE......................888 478-6544
Christopher J Hagedorn, *Pr*
Mark Scheiwer, *VP*
Dimiter Todorov, *Sec*
Ross Haley, *Prin*
▲ **EMP:** 19 **EST:** 1997
SALES (est): 28.65MM
SALES (corp-wide): 3.55B **Publicly Held**
Web: www.hawthorne-gardening.com
SIC: 2879 5083 5084 3674 Agricultural chemicals, nec; Hydroponic equipment and supplies; Water pumps (industrial); Light emitting diodes
HQ: The Hawthorne Gardening Company
14111 Scottslawn Rd
Marysville OH 43040
360 883-8846

(G-9025)
HH ASSOCIATES US INC
14111 Scottslawn Rd (43040-7800)
PHONE......................937 644-7492
EMP: 12
Web: www.hhglobal.com
SIC: 2752 Commercial printing, lithographic
HQ: Hh Associates U.S., Inc.
203 N Lasalle St Ste 1800
Chicago IL 60601
847 987-3182

(G-9026)
HONDA DEV & MFG AMER LLC (DH)
Also Called: Marysville Auto Plant
24000 Honda Pkwy (43040-9251)
PHONE......................937 642-5000
Mitsugu Matsukawa, *Pr*
Tomomi Kosaka, *
John Adams, *
◆ **EMP:** 750 **EST:** 1978
SQ FT: 2,235,000
SALES (est): 597.39MM **Privately Held**
Web: www.honda.com
SIC: 3711 Motor vehicles and car bodies
HQ: American Honda Motor Co., Inc.
1919 Torrance Blvd
Torrance CA 90501
310 783-2000

(G-9027)
HONDA DEV & MFG AMER LLC
25000 Honda Pkwy (43040-9190)
PHONE......................937 642-5000
EMP: 500
Web: www.hondainamerica.com
SIC: 3711 Automobile assembly, including specialty automobiles
HQ: Honda Development & Manufacturing Of America, Llc
24000 Honda Pkwy
Marysville OH 43040
937 642-5000

(G-9028)
HONDA DEV & MFG AMER LLC
Also Called: Honda Support Office
19900 State Route 739 (43040-9256)
PHONE......................937 644-0724
EMP: 200
Web: www.honda.com
SIC: 5511 3711 3465 8742 Automobiles, new and used; Motor vehicles and car bodies; Automotive stampings; Training and development consultant
HQ: Honda Development & Manufacturing Of America, Llc
24000 Honda Pkwy
Marysville OH 43040
937 642-5000

(G-9029)
HONDA ENGINEERING NORTH AMERICA LLC
Also Called: Honda Engineering N Amer Inc
24000 Honda Pkwy (43040-9251)
PHONE......................937 642-5000
▲ **EMP:** 350
Web: www.hondaengineering.com
SIC: 3544 Special dies and tools

(G-9030)
HONDA TRANSMISSION MANUFACTURI
25000 Honda Pkwy (43040-9190)
PHONE......................937 843-5555
EMP: 11 **EST:** 2019
SALES (est): 4.69MM **Privately Held**
Web: www.honda.com
SIC: 3999 Manufacturing industries, nec

(G-9031)
HYPONEX CORPORATION (DH)
Also Called: Scotts- Hyponex
14111 Scottslawn Rd (43040-7800)
PHONE......................937 644-0011
James Hagedorn, *Pr*
Christopher Nagel, *
David M Brockman, *
David C Evans, *
EMP: 100 **EST:** 1980
SQ FT: 73,000
SALES (est): 105MM
SALES (corp-wide): 3.55B **Publicly Held**
Web: www.scotts.com
SIC: 2873 2875 Fertilizers: natural (organic), except compost; Fertilizers, mixing only
HQ: The Scotts Company Llc
14111 Co Hwy 105
Marysville OH 43040
937 644-0011

(G-9032)
INDUSTRIAL CERAMIC PRODUCTS INC
14401 Suntra Way (43040-9579)
PHONE......................937 642-3897
◆ **EMP:** 60 **EST:** 1936
SALES (est): 4.98MM **Privately Held**
Web: www.industrialceramic.com

SIC: 3255 3297 Clay refractories; Nonclay refractories

(G-9033)
INTERNATIONAL PAPER COMPANY
Also Called: International Paper
13307 Industrial Pkwy (43040-9589)
PHONE......................937 578-7718
EMP: 23
SALES (corp-wide): 18.62B **Publicly Held**
Web: www.internationalpaper.com
SIC: 2621 Paper mills
PA: International Paper Company
6400 Poplar Ave
Memphis TN 38197
901 419-7000

(G-9034)
LARSEN PACKAGING PRODUCTS INC
Also Called: Alpha Container
16789 Square Dr (43040-8476)
PHONE......................937 644-5511
Bill Larsen, *Brnch Mgr*
EMP: 12
Web: www.larsenpackaging.com
SIC: 2653 Boxes, corrugated: made from purchased materials
PA: Larsen Packaging Products, Inc.
1350 S River St
Batavia IL 60510

(G-9035)
LINEAR IT SOLUTIONS LLC
639 Gallop Ln (43040-7072)
PHONE......................614 306-0761
Scott Verbus, *Prin*
EMP: 11 **EST:** 2017
SALES (est): 6.63MM **Privately Held**
Web: mail1.linearit.net
SIC: 3429 Hardware, nec

(G-9036)
MAGNETIC SCREW MACHINE PDTS
23241 State Route 37 (43040-9749)
PHONE......................937 348-2807
Bryan Bayes, *Pr*
EMP: 7 **EST:** 1971
SQ FT: 16,000
SALES (est): 909.34K **Privately Held**
SIC: 3451 Screw machine products

(G-9037)
MARYSVILLE NEWSPAPER INC (PA)
Also Called: Richwood Gazette
207 N Main St (43040-1161)
P.O. Box 226 (43040-0226)
PHONE......................937 644-9111
Daniel Behrens, *Pr*
Kevin Behrens, *
EMP: 30 **EST:** 1859
SQ FT: 10,000
SALES (est): 2.38MM
SALES (corp-wide): 2.38MM **Privately Held**
Web: www.marysvillejt.com
SIC: 2711 2731 Newspapers, publishing and printing; Books, publishing and printing

(G-9038)
MARYSVILLE STEEL INC
323 E 8th St (43040)
P.O. Box 383 (43040-0383)
PHONE......................937 642-5971
Steven J Clayman, *CEO*
EMP: 31 **EST:** 1951
SQ FT: 50,000
SALES (est): 4.09MM **Privately Held**
Web: www.marysvillesteel.com

SIC: 3441 1791 5039 Fabricated structural metal; Structural steel erection; Joists

(G-9039)
MORIROKU TECHNOLOGY N AMER INC (HQ)
15000 Industrial Pkwy (43040-9547)
P.O. Box 974 (45331-0974)
PHONE......................937 548-3217
Yaf Nakao, *Pr*
William Laframboise, *VP*
Akihiko Hirano, *VP*
James Heiser, *Ex VP*
◆ **EMP:** 672 **EST:** 1986
SQ FT: 300,000
SALES (est): 103.1MM **Privately Held**
SIC: 3089 Injection molded finished plastics products, nec
PA: Moriroku Co, Ltd.
1-1-1, Minamiaoyama
Minato-Ku TKY 107-0

(G-9040)
NEW REPUBLIC INDUSTRIES LLC (PA)
Also Called: My Second Home Early Lrng Schl
497 Bridle Dr (43040-1658)
PHONE......................614 580-9927
EMP: 7 **EST:** 2018
SALES (est): 2.62MM
SALES (corp-wide): 2.62MM **Privately Held**
Web: www.advantage-ela.com
SIC: 3999 Manufacturing industries, nec

(G-9041)
PARKER-HANNIFIN CORPORATION
Hydraulic Pump Division
14249 Industrial Pkwy (43040-9504)
PHONE......................937 644-3915
Ken Theiss, *Brnch Mgr*
EMP: 46
SALES (corp-wide): 19.93B **Publicly Held**
Web: www.parker.com
SIC: 3594 3491 3679 Pumps, hydraulic power transfer; Industrial valves; Electronic circuits
PA: Parker-Hannifin Corporation
6035 Parkland Blvd
Cleveland OH 44124
216 896-3000

(G-9042)
PRECISION COATINGS SYSTEMS
948 Columbus Ave (43040-9501)
PHONE......................937 642-4727
Fred Myers Junior, *Pr*
Sherry Myers, *VP*
Wendy Myers, *VP*
Mark Myers, *VP*
EMP: 12 **EST:** 1989
SQ FT: 26,000
SALES (est): 502.18K **Privately Held**
Web: www.qtsohio.com
SIC: 3479 7532 7549 7514 Painting of metal products; Paint shop, automotive; Towing services; Rent-a-car service

(G-9043)
PREMIER PRTG CENTL OHIO LTD
16710 Square Dr (43040-9616)
PHONE......................937 642-0988
John Hubbard, *Pt*
Dan Behren, *Pt*
Jeff Barnes, *Pt*
Tom Thompson, *Pt*
Kevin Vehrens, *Pt*
EMP: 30 **EST:** 2000
SALES (est): 140.67K **Privately Held**

SIC: 2711 2752 Newspapers, publishing and printing; Commercial printing, lithographic

(G-9044)
ROD MCLELLAN COMPANY
14111 Scottslawn Rd (43040-7800)
PHONE..................................937 578-5284
Mark West, *Prin*
EMP: 8 EST: 2009
SALES (est): 2.97MM **Privately Held**
SIC: 2875 Fertilizers, mixing only

(G-9045)
SCOTTS COMPANY LLC (HQ)
Also Called: Scotts Miracle-Gro Products
14111 Co Hwy 105 (43040)
P.O. Box 418 (43040-0418)
PHONE..................................937 644-0011
James Hagedorn, *Managing Member*
Michael P Kelty, *
Christopher L Nagel, *
David M Aronowitz, *
◆ EMP: 143 EST: 1969
SALES (est): 518.89MM
SALES (corp-wide): 3.55B **Publicly Held**
Web: www.scotts.com
SIC: 2873 2874 2879 0782 Fertilizers: natural (organic), except compost; Phosphates; Fungicides, herbicides; Lawn services
PA: The Scotts Miracle-Gro Company
    14111 Scottslawn Rd
    Marysville OH 43041
    937 644-0011

(G-9046)
SCOTTS MIRACLE-GRO COMPANY (PA)
Also Called: Scotts Miracle-Gro
14111 Scottslawn Rd (43041)
PHONE..................................937 644-0011
James Hagedorn, *Ch Bd*
Nate Baxter, *Pr*
Matthew E Garth, *CAO*
Dimiter Todorov, *Corporate Secretary*
Julie Demuesy, *ETHICS*
▲ EMP: 289 EST: 1868
SALES (est): 3.55B
SALES (corp-wide): 3.55B **Publicly Held**
Web: www.scottsmiraclegro.com
SIC: 2873 7342 2879 Nitrogenous fertilizers; Pest control services; Insecticides and pesticides

(G-9047)
SCOTTS MIRACLE-GRO COMPANY
Also Called: East Chemical Plant
14101 Industrial Pkwy (43040-9591)
PHONE..................................937 578-5065
Mike Henkel, *Brnch Mgr*
EMP: 22
SALES (corp-wide): 3.55B **Publicly Held**
Web: www.scottsmiraclegro.com
SIC: 2873 2879 Fertilizers: natural (organic), except compost; Fungicides, herbicides
PA: The Scotts Miracle-Gro Company
    14111 Scottslawn Rd
    Marysville OH 43041
    937 644-0011

(G-9048)
SCOTTS TEMECULA OPERATIONS LLC
14111 Scottslawn Rd (43040-7801)
PHONE..................................800 221-1760
EMP: 9 EST: 2001
SALES (est): 5.2MM
SALES (corp-wide): 3.55B **Publicly Held**
Web: investor.scotts.com
SIC: 3524 Lawn and garden equipment
PA: The Scotts Miracle-Gro Company

14111 Scottslawn Rd
Marysville OH 43041
937 644-0011

(G-9049)
SMG GROWING MEDIA INC (HQ)
14111 Scottslawn Rd (43041-0001)
PHONE..................................937 644-0011
EMP: 12 EST: 2005
SALES (est): 17.43MM
SALES (corp-wide): 3.55B **Publicly Held**
SIC: 3524 5083 Lawn and garden equipment ; Farm and garden machinery
PA: The Scotts Miracle-Gro Company
    14111 Scottslawn Rd
    Marysville OH 43041
    937 644-0011

(G-9050)
SMGM LLC
14111 Scottslawn Rd (43040-7800)
PHONE..................................937 644-0011
EMP: 10 EST: 2004
SALES (est): 5.8MM
SALES (corp-wide): 3.55B **Publicly Held**
SIC: 2873 Nitrogenous fertilizers
PA: The Scotts Miracle-Gro Company
    14111 Scottslawn Rd
    Marysville OH 43041
    937 644-0011

(G-9051)
STRAIGHT 72 INC
Also Called: MAI Manufacturing
20078 State Route 4 (43040-9723)
PHONE..................................740 943-5730
Chris Vogelsang, *Pr*
Chris Vogelsang, *Pr*
Linda Wolf, *
EMP: 60 EST: 1995
SALES (est): 9.25MM **Privately Held**
Web: www.maimfg.com
SIC: 8711 3544 Acoustical engineering; Special dies, tools, jigs, and fixtures

(G-9052)
SUMITOMO ELC WIRG SYSTEMS INC
14800 Industrial Pkwy (43040-7507)
PHONE..................................937 642-7579
EMP: 27
Web: www.sewsus.com
SIC: 3714 5063 3694 Automotive wiring harness sets; Wire and cable; Engine electrical equipment
HQ: Sumitomo Electric Wiring Systems, Inc.
    1018 Ashley St
    Bowling Green KY 42103
    270 782-7397

(G-9053)
TOOL TECHNOLOGIES VAN DYKE
639 Clymer Rd (43040-9502)
P.O. Box 256 (43045-0256)
PHONE..................................937 349-4900
Steven Vand Yke, *Owner*
EMP: 10 EST: 1991
SQ FT: 5,000
SALES (est): 4.17MM **Privately Held**
Web: www.tooltechohio.com
SIC: 3829 3544 Measuring and controlling devices, nec; Special dies, tools, jigs, and fixtures

(G-9054)
TRIPLE ARROW INDUSTRIES INC
Also Called: Arch Polymers
13311 Industrial Pkwy (43040-9589)
PHONE..................................614 437-5588
Howard Wei, *Pr*
George Wu, *VP*
◆ EMP: 7 EST: 2010

SALES (est): 854.85K **Privately Held**
Web: www.triplearrowohio.com
SIC: 2821 5093 Plastics materials and resins ; Metal scrap and waste materials

(G-9055)
Z LINE KITCHEN AND BATH LLC (PA)
Also Called: Z Line Kitchen and Bath
916 Delaware Ave (43040-1726)
PHONE..................................614 777-5004
Andy Zuro, *CEO*
EMP: 8 EST: 2004
SQ FT: 13,000
SALES (est): 9.91MM
SALES (corp-wide): 9.91MM **Privately Held**
Web: www.zlinekitchen.com
SIC: 3444 5722 Hoods, range: sheet metal; Gas ranges

Mason
Warren County

(G-9056)
AERO FULFILLMENT SERVICES CORP (PA)
3900 Aero Dr (45040-8840)
PHONE..................................800 225-7145
Jon T Gimpel, *Pr*
Jon T Gimpel, *Pr*
Brenda Conaway, *
▲ EMP: 100 EST: 1986
SQ FT: 125,000
SALES (est): 24.72MM
SALES (corp-wide): 24.72MM **Privately Held**
Web: www.aerofulfillment.com
SIC: 4225 7374 7331 2759 General warehousing; Data processing service; Mailing service; Commercial printing, nec

(G-9057)
AEROSERV INC
201 Industrial Row Dr (45040-2600)
P.O. Box 48 (45040-0048)
PHONE..................................513 932-9227
Steve Michael, *Pr*
EMP: 10 EST: 1988
SQ FT: 14,000
SALES (est): 429.19K **Privately Held**
Web: www.aeroservinc.com
SIC: 3599 Machine shop, jobbing and repair

(G-9058)
AI LIFE LLC
Also Called: Ai Wellness
4680 Parkway Dr Ste 300 (45040-7979)
PHONE..................................513 605-1079
Adam Ross, *Managing Member*
EMP: 10 EST: 2018
SALES (est): 146.7K **Privately Held**
Web: www.aiwellness.com
SIC: 2023 Dietary supplements, dairy and non-dairy based

(G-9059)
ALPHAGRAPHICS
7288 Central Parke Blvd (45040-6776)
PHONE..................................513 204-6070
Patrick Crowley, *Pdt Mgr*
EMP: 6 EST: 2018
SALES (est): 173.81K **Privately Held**
Web: www.alphagraphics.com
SIC: 2752 Commercial printing, lithographic

(G-9060)
AMPACET CORPORATION
4705 Duke Dr Ste 400 (45040-9502)
PHONE..................................513 247-5403

EMP: 22
SALES (corp-wide): 410.74MM **Privately Held**
Web: www.ampacet.com
SIC: 2821 Plastics materials and resins
PA: Ampacet Corporation
    660 White Plins Rd Ste 36
    Tarrytown NY 10591
    914 631-6600

(G-9061)
ANDRE CORPORATION
4600 N Mason Montgomery Rd (45040-9176)
PHONE..................................574 293-0207
David Andre, *Pr*
EMP: 20 EST: 1991
SQ FT: 50,000
SALES (est): 901K **Privately Held**
SIC: 3452 3469 5085 Washers, metal; Stamping metal for the trade; Fasteners, industrial: nuts, bolts, screws, etc.

(G-9062)
APRECIA PHARMACEUTICALS LLC (HQ)
7200 Industrial Row Dr Ste 200 (45040-1386)
PHONE..................................513 984-5000
Kyle Smith, *Pr*
Chris Gilmore, *CEO*
Michael Rohlfs, *CFO*
EMP: 15 EST: 2003
SQ FT: 14,000
SALES (est): 9.17MM
SALES (corp-wide): 46.31MM **Privately Held**
Web: www.aprecia.com
SIC: 2834 Pharmaceutical preparations
PA: Prasco, Llc
    6125 Commerce Ct
    Mason OH 45040
    513 204-1100

(G-9063)
ARMOR AFTERMARKET INC
4600 N Mason Montgomery Rd Oh (45040-9176)
PHONE..................................513 923-5600
EMP: 11 EST: 2011
SALES (est): 586.47K **Privately Held**
Web: www.armoraftermarket.com
SIC: 3599 Industrial machinery, nec

(G-9064)
ARMOR CONSOLIDATED INC (PA)
4600 N Mason Montgomery Rd (45040-9176)
PHONE..................................513 923-5260
David K Schmitt, *CEO*
EMP: 510 EST: 1996
SALES (est): 2.09MM
SALES (corp-wide): 2.09MM **Privately Held**
Web: www.thearmorgroup.com
SIC: 3441 3446 3443 6719 Fabricated structural metal; Architectural metalwork; Fabricated plate work (boiler shop); Investment holding companies, except banks

(G-9065)
ARMOR METAL GROUP ELKHART INC
4600 N Mason Montgomery Rd (45040-9176)
PHONE..................................800 672-6373
Jeffrey G Stagaro, *Prin*
EMP: 13 EST: 2012
SALES (est): 2.39MM **Privately Held**
Web: www.armorcontract.com

SIC: 3444 Sheet metalwork

(G-9066)
ARMOR METAL GROUP MASON INC (HQ)
Also Called: Armormetal
4600 N Mason Montgomery Rd
(45040-9176)
PHONE.....................513 769-0700
Jeffrey G Stagnaro, *Prin*
David K Schmitt, *
Frank Ahaus, *
▲ EMP: 200 EST: 1927
SALES (est): 21.15MM **Privately Held**
Web: www.thearmorgroup.com
SIC: 3441 3446 3444 3443 Fabricated
structural metal; Architectural metalwork;
Sheet metalwork; Fabricated plate work
(boiler shop)
PA: The Armor Group, Inc.
4600 N Masn Montgomery Rd
Mason OH 45040

(G-9067)
ASHLEY F WARD INC (PA)
Also Called: Precision Tek Manufacturing
7490 Easy St (45040-9423)
PHONE.....................513 398-1414
Bill Ward, *Ch Bd*
William H Ward, *
Terry Bien, *
Brian Scalf, *
Nate Ruhenkamp, *
▲ EMP: 116 EST: 1908
SQ FT: 150,000
SALES (est): 3.38K
SALES (corp-wide): 3.38K **Privately Held**
Web: www.ashleyward.com
SIC: 3451 Screw machine products

(G-9068)
ATRICURE INC (PA)
Also Called: ATRICURE
7555 Innovation Way (45040-9695)
PHONE.....................513 755-4100
Michael H Carrel, *Pr*
B Kristine Johnson, *
Douglas J Seith, *COO*
M Andrew Wade, *Sr VP*
EMP: 1153 EST: 2000
SQ FT: 92,000
SALES (est): 465.31MM
SALES (corp-wide): 465.31MM **Publicly
Held**
Web: www.atricure.com
SIC: 3841 Surgical instruments and
apparatus

(G-9069)
BASCO MANUFACTURING COMPANY (HQ)
Also Called: Basco Shower Enclosures
7201 Snider Rd (45040-9601)
PHONE.....................513 573-1900
George Rohde Junior, *CEO*
Steve Lotz, *
G William Rohde Senior, *Ch*
◆ EMP: 174 EST: 1955
SQ FT: 80,000
SALES (est): 28.31MM **Privately Held**
Web: www.bascoshowerdoor.com
SIC: 3231 Doors, glass: made from
purchased glass
PA: Lixil Corporation
1-1-1, Nishishinagawa
Shinagawa-Ku TKY 141-0

(G-9070)
BEAUMONT MACHINE LLC
Also Called: Beaumont Machine
7697 Innovation Way Ste 1100
(45040-9605)

PHONE.....................513 701-0421
EMP: 15 EST: 1990
SQ FT: 21,000
SALES (est): 2.15MM **Privately Held**
Web: www.beaumontmachine.com
SIC: 3823 7699 Industrial process
measurement equipment; Precision
instrument repair

(G-9071)
BERRY FILM PRODUCTS CO INC (DH)
Also Called: Clopay
8585 Duke Blvd (45040-3100)
P.O. Box 959 (47706-0959)
PHONE.....................800 225-6729
Alan H Koblin, *Pr*
Tom Givens, *
◆ EMP: 100 EST: 1992
SQ FT: 35,000
SALES (est): 46.99MM **Privately Held**
Web: www.berryglobal.com
SIC: 3081 Plastics film and sheet
HQ: Berry Global, Inc.
101 Oakley St
Evansville IN 47710

(G-9072)
BODYCOTE SRFC TECH PRPERTY LLC
8118 Corporate Way Ste 201 (45040-9560)
PHONE.....................513 770-4900
Stephen Harris, *CEO*
Thomas Gibbons, *
EMP: 215 EST: 2007
SALES (est): 590.44K **Privately Held**
Web: www.bodycote.com
SIC: 3398 Metal heat treating

(G-9073)
BODYCOTE SURFACE TECH INC (DH)
Also Called: Ellison Surface Technologies
8118 Corporate Way Ste 201 (45040-9560)
PHONE.....................513 770-4922
Stephen Harris, *CEO*
Thomas Gibbons, *Pr*
EMP: 15 EST: 1986
SQ FT: 27,000
SALES (est): 26.03MM
SALES (corp-wide): 959.76MM **Privately
Held**
Web: www.bodycote.com
SIC: 3479 Coating of metals and formed
products
HQ: Bodycote Surface Technology Group,
Inc.
8118 Corp Way Ste 201
Mason OH 45040

(G-9074)
BODYCOTE SURFC TECH GROUP INC (HQ)
8118 Corporate Way Ste 201 (45040-9560)
PHONE.....................513 770-4900
Stephen Harris, *CEO*
Thomas Gibbons, *Pr*
EMP: 15 EST: 2004
SALES (est): 74.8MM
SALES (corp-wide): 959.76MM **Privately
Held**
Web: www.bodycote.com
SIC: 3479 Coating of metals and formed
products
PA: Bodycote Plc
Springwood Court
Macclesfield SK10
162 550-5300

(G-9075)
BODYCOTE SURFC TECH MEXICO LLC
8118 Corporate Way Ste 201 (45040-9560)
PHONE.....................513 770-4900
Stephen Harris, *CEO*
Thomas Gibbons, *
EMP: 130 EST: 2013
SQ FT: 13,000
SALES (est): 1.89MM
SALES (corp-wide): 959.76MM **Privately
Held**
SIC: 3398 Metal heat treating
HQ: Bodycote Surface Technology Group,
Inc.
8118 Corp Way Ste 201
Mason OH 45040

(G-9076)
CARDEN DOOR COMPANY LLC
1224 Castle Dr (45040-9433)
PHONE.....................513 459-2233
Bruce Carden, *Cncil Mbr*
John Jackson, *Cncil Mbr*
EMP: 7 EST: 1998
SQ FT: 10,000
SALES (est): 2.47MM **Privately Held**
Web: www.cardendoor.com
SIC: 2431 Doors and door parts and trim,
wood

(G-9077)
CARTER MANUFACTURING CO INC
4220 State Route 42 (45040-1931)
PHONE.....................513 398-7303
Chris Carter, *Pr*
EMP: 10 EST: 1973
SALES (est): 2.51MM **Privately Held**
Web: www.carter-mfg.com
SIC: 3544 7692 3541 Dies and die holders
for metal cutting, forming, die casting;
Welding repair; Machine tools, metal cutting
type

(G-9078)
CENGAGE LEARNING INC
770 Broadway (45036-1726)
PHONE.....................513 234-5967
EMP: 143
Web: www.cengage.com
SIC: 2731 Book publishing
HQ: Cengage Learning, Inc.
5191 Natorp Blvd
Mason OH 45040

(G-9079)
CENGAGE LEARNING INC (HQ)
Also Called: Course Technology
5191 Natorp Blvd (45040-7104)
PHONE.....................617 289-7700
Michael Hansen, *Pr*
Angela M Schilling, *
Henry Pierz, *
Kevin Stone, *Chief Sales & Marketing
Officer*
Dean D Durbin, *
◆ EMP: 60 EST: 1994
SALES (est): 1.12B **Privately Held**
Web: www.cengage.com
SIC: 2731 Books, publishing only
PA: Cengage Learning Holdings Ii, Inc.
5191 Natorp Blvd
Mason OH 45040

(G-9080)
CENGAGE LEARNING INC
Also Called: Thomson Higher Education
5191 Natorp Blvd Lowr (45040-7599)
PHONE.....................415 839-2300
Frank Talamantez, *Mgr*
EMP: 315

Web: www.cengage.com
SIC: 2731 Textbooks: publishing and printing
HQ: Cengage Learning, Inc.
5191 Natorp Blvd
Mason OH 45040

(G-9081)
CENGAGE LRNG HOLDINGS II INC (PA)
Also Called: Cengage Learning
5191 Natorp Blvd (45040-7104)
PHONE.....................617 289-7700
Michael Hansen, *CEO*
William Rieders, *
Dean D Durbin, *
Kenneth Carson, *
Brian Mulligan, *
EMP: 50 EST: 1994
SALES (est): 1.12B **Privately Held**
Web: www.cengagegroup.com
SIC: 2731 Textbooks: publishing and printing

(G-9082)
CHE HOLDINGS INC
6404 Thornberry Ct Ste 440 (45040-3502)
PHONE.....................513 770-0777
Timothy J Stillson, *Pr*
Elizabeth Stillson, *Sec*
▲ EMP: 6 EST: 1994
SQ FT: 2,121
SALES (est): 595.33K **Privately Held**
Web: www.cinheats.com
SIC: 3443 Fabricated plate work (boiler shop)

(G-9083)
CINCINNATI FAN & VENTILATOR COMPANY INC (DH)
Also Called: Cincinnati Fan
7697 Snider Rd (45040-9135)
PHONE.....................513 573-1000
EMP: 96 EST: 1956
SALES (est): 24.22MM
SALES (corp-wide): 1.83B **Privately Held**
Web: www.cincinnatifan.com
SIC: 3564 Blowing fans: industrial or
commercial
HQ: Canvas Sx, Llc
6325 Ardrey Kell Rd Ste 4
Charlotte NC 28277
980 474-3700

(G-9084)
CINCINNATI FTN SQ NEWS INC
Also Called: Fountain News
8739 S Shore Pl (45040-5044)
PHONE.....................513 421-4049
Diane Witte, *Pr*
James Witte, *VP*
Wanda Mauge, *Sec*
Vido Patel, *Mgr*
EMP: 10 EST: 1992
SQ FT: 2,200
SALES (est): 83.81K **Privately Held**
Web: www.lynchandassociates.com
SIC: 2711 Newspapers, publishing and
printing

(G-9085)
CINCINNATI INDUSTRIAL MCHY INC
4600 N Mason Montgomery Rd
(45040-9176)
PHONE.....................513 923-5600
David Williams, *Pr*
▲ EMP: 250 EST: 1943
SQ FT: 200,000
SALES (est): 98.08MM **Privately Held**
Web: www.cinind.com
SIC: 3441 Fabricated structural metal
HQ: Armor Metal Group Mason, Inc.
4600 N Masn Montgomery Rd
Mason OH 45040

(G-9086)
CINTAS CORPORATION (PA)
Also Called: Cintas
6800 Cintas Blvd (45040-9151)
P.O. Box 625737 (45262-5737)
PHONE..................................513 459-1200
Todd M Schneider, *Pr*
Scott D Farmer, *
J Michael Hansen, *Ex VP*
James N Rozakis, *Ex VP*
D Brock Denton, *Sr VP*
◆ **EMP: 1113 EST:** 1968
SALES (est): 9.6B
SALES (corp-wide): 9.6B **Publicly Held**
Web: www.cintas.com
SIC: **2326** 2337 7218 5084 Work uniforms;
Uniforms, except athletic: women's,
misses', and juniors'; Industrial uniform
supply; Safety equipment

(G-9087)
CLOPAY AMES INC (HQ)
8585 Duke Blvd (45040-3100)
PHONE..................................800 282-2260
Franklin Smith Junior, *CFO*
Gary Abyad, *Sr VP*
Ellen Shoemaker, *Sr VP*
Eugene Colleran, *Sr VP*
◆ **EMP: 231 EST:** 1889
SQ FT: 130,587
SALES (est): 935.67MM
SALES (corp-wide): 2.62B **Publicly Held**
Web: www.clopaydoor.com
SIC: **3081** 3442 2431 1796 Plastics film and
sheet; Garage doors, overhead: metal;
Garage doors, overhead, wood; Power
generating equipment installation
PA: Griffon Corporation
712 5th Ave Fl 18
New York NY 10019
212 957-5000

(G-9088)
CLOPAY CORPORATION (DH)
Also Called: Clopay Building Pdts Co Inc
8585 Duke Blvd (45040-3100)
PHONE..................................513 770-4800
Gene Colleran, *Pr*
Dan Beckley, *
Mister Pat Lohse, *VP*
◆ **EMP: 36 EST:** 1859
SQ FT: 35,000
SALES (est): 436.93MM
SALES (corp-wide): 2.62B **Publicly Held**
Web: www.clopaydoor.com
SIC: **2436** 2431 Plywood, softwood; Garage
doors, overhead, wood
HQ: Ames Clopay Inc
8585 Duke Blvd
Mason OH 45040
800 282-2260

(G-9089)
CLOROX COMPANY
Also Called: Clorox
4680 Parkway Dr Ste 130 (45040-8357)
PHONE..................................513 445-1840
Gina Kelly, *Mgr*
EMP: 6
SALES (corp-wide): 7.09B **Publicly Held**
Web: www.thecloroxcompany.com
SIC: **2842** 2812 Laundry cleaning
preparations; Chlorine, compressed or
liquefied
PA: The Clorox Company
1221 Broadway
Oakland CA 94612
510 271-7000

(G-9090)
CM PAULA COMPANY (PA)
Also Called: Geocentral
6049 Hi Tek Ct (45040-2603)
PHONE..................................513 759-7473
Charles W Mc Cullough, *Ch Bd*
Greg Ionna, *
William Creager Ii, *Ex VP*
Bill Creager, *
▲ **EMP: 25 EST:** 1958
SQ FT: 56,000
SALES (est): 12.7MM
SALES (corp-wide): 12.7MM **Privately Held**
Web: www.cmpaula.com
SIC: **3089** 2678 2499 3999 Novelties,
plastics; Stationery: made from purchased
materials; Decorative wood and woodwork;
Bric-a-brac

(G-9091)
CMC ELECTRONICS CINCINN
7500 Innovation Way (45040-9695)
PHONE..................................513 573-6316
Alan Scalf, *Engineering Staff*
EMP: 9 EST: 2015
SALES (est): 1.32MM **Privately Held**
SIC: **3679** Electronic circuits

(G-9092)
DANONE US LLC
7577 Central Parke Blvd (45040-6810)
PHONE..................................513 229-0092
George Denmen, *Mgr*
EMP: 25
SALES (corp-wide): 967.4MM **Privately Held**
Web: www.danoneawayfromhome.com
SIC: **2024** Yogurt desserts, frozen
HQ: Danone Us, Llc
1 Maple Ave
White Plains NY 10605
914 872-8400

(G-9093)
DEERFIELD MANUFACTURING INC
Also Called: Ice Industries Deerfield
320 N Mason Montgomery Rd
(45040-7528)
PHONE..................................513 398-2010
Howard Ice, *Pr*
Jeff Boger, *
Paul Bishop, *
EMP: 24 EST: 1946
SQ FT: 80,000
SALES (est): 10.41MM **Privately Held**
Web: www.iceindustries.com
SIC: **3469** Stamping metal for the trade
PA: Ice Industries, Inc.
3810 Herr Rd
Sylvania OH 43560

(G-9094)
DIGITEK CORP
3785 Marble Ridge Ln (45040-3005)
PHONE..................................513 794-3190
Marc E Brown, *Pr*
EMP: 10 EST: 2000
SALES (est): 318.1K **Privately Held**
Web: www.digitekcorp.net
SIC: **5136** 5137 2253 Uniforms, men's and
boys'; Uniforms, women's and children's; T-
shirts and tops, knit

(G-9095)
DOWN-LITE INTERNATIONAL INC (PA)
Also Called: Downlite
8153 Duke Blvd (45040-8104)
PHONE..................................513 229-3696
Joe Crawford, *CEO*

Robert Altbaier, *
Chad Altbaier, *
John G Kuhnash, *
Marvin Werthaiser, *
▲ **EMP: 230 EST:** 1983
SQ FT: 20,000
SALES (est): 49.86MM
SALES (corp-wide): 49.86MM **Privately Held**
Web: www.downlite.com
SIC: **2392** 5719 Pillows, bed: made from
purchased materials; Bedding (sheets,
blankets, spreads, and pillows)

(G-9096)
EBSCO INDUSTRIES INC
Also Called: Imagen Brands
4680 Parkway Dr Ste 200 (45040-8173)
P.O. Box 497 (45040-0497)
PHONE..................................513 398-3695
Lori Kates, *Genl Mgr*
EMP: 15
SALES (corp-wide): 3.1B **Privately Held**
Web: www.ebscoind.com
SIC: **2741** Miscellaneous publishing
PA: Ebsco Industries, Inc.
5724 Hwy 280 East
Birmingham AL 35201
205 991-6600

(G-9097)
EMPIRE PACKING COMPANY LLC
4780 Alliance Dr (45040-7832)
PHONE..................................901 948-4788
Din Kirk, *Brnch Mgr*
EMP: 800
SALES (corp-wide): 141.72MM **Privately Held**
Web: www.empirepk.com
SIC: **2011** Meat packing plants
PA: Empire Packing Company, Llc
1837 Harbor Ave
Memphis TN 38113
901 948-4788

(G-9098)
ESSILOR OF AMERICA INC
4000 Luxottica Pl (45040-8114)
PHONE..................................513 765-6000
EMP: 19
SALES (corp-wide): 7.66MM **Privately Held**
Web: www.essilorluxottica.com
SIC: **3851** Frames, lenses, and parts,
eyeglass and spectacle
HQ: Essilor Of America, Inc.
13555 N Stemmons Fwy
Dallas TX 75234

(G-9099)
EVOKES LLC
8118 Corporate Way Ste 212 (45040-9560)
PHONE..................................513 947-8433
Daniel Lincoln, *Pr*
Tony Leslie, *
EMP: 50 EST: 2015
SQ FT: 900
SALES (est): 2.19MM **Privately Held**
Web: www.evokesllc.com
SIC: **3822** 8011 Building services monitoring
controls, automatic; Surgeon

(G-9100)
FORTE INDUSTRIAL EQUIPMENT SYSTEMS INC
Also Called: Forte Industries
6037 Commerce Ct (45040-8819)
PHONE..................................513 398-2800
EMP: 32

SIC: **5084** 8711 3537 Materials handling
machinery; Consulting engineer; Industrial
trucks and tractors

(G-9101)
FRENCH TRANSIT LLC
7588 Central Parke Blvd Ste 220
(45040-6859)
PHONE..................................650 431-3959
EMP: 6 EST: 2019
SALES (est): 476.68K **Privately Held**
SIC: **2844** Perfumes, cosmetics and other
toilet preparations

(G-9102)
GATESAIR INC (HQ)
5300 Kings Island Dr Ste 101 (45040-2795)
PHONE..................................513 459-3400
Barbara Spicek, *CEO*
Joseph Mack, *
Jeff Hills, *
▲ **EMP: 80 EST:** 1922
SQ FT: 30,000
SALES (est): 34.86MM
SALES (corp-wide): 1.81B **Privately Held**
Web: www.gatesair.com
SIC: **1731** 3663 Communications
specialization; Radio broadcasting and
communications equipment
PA: The Gores Group Llc
9800 Wilshire Blvd
Beverly Hills CA 90212
310 209-3010

(G-9103)
GLOBAL LASER TEK LLC
7697 Innovation Way Ste 700 (45040-9605)
PHONE..................................513 701-0452
Dan Polto, *Dir*
EMP: 24 EST: 2014
SALES (est): 690.27K
SALES (corp-wide): 2.58MM **Privately Held**
Web: www.globallasertek.com
SIC: **3599** Machine shop, jobbing and repair
PA: Global Specialty Machines, Llc
7697 Innovation Way # 700
Mason OH 45040
513 701-0452

(G-9104)
GLOBAL SPECIALTY MACHINES LLC (PA)
7697 Innovation Way Ste 700 (45040-9605)
PHONE..................................513 701-0452
Ramesh Malhotra, *Managing Member*
Dan Polto, *Managing Member*
▲ **EMP: 15 EST:** 2012
SQ FT: 3,000
SALES (est): 2.58MM
SALES (corp-wide): 2.58MM **Privately Held**
Web: www.globalsmsas.com
SIC: **3541** Electron-discharge metal cutting
machine tools

(G-9105)
GRAHAM PACKAGING PET TECH INC
1225 Castle Dr (45040-9672)
PHONE..................................513 398-5000
Lee Banks, *Brnch Mgr*
EMP: 9
Web: www.grahampackaging.com
SIC: **3089** Buckets, plastics
HQ: Graham Packaging Pet Technologies
Inc.
700 Indian Sprng Dr Ste 1
Lancaster PA 17601

(G-9106)
GRAPHIC INFO SYSTEMS INC
7177 Central Parke Blvd (45040-7451)
P.O. Box 37958 (45222)
PHONE..............................513 948-1300
Walter Theiss, *Pr*
John Lauck, *Sec*
Edward Reilly, *Treas*
EMP: 16 **EST:** 1984
SALES (est): 5.41MM **Privately Held**
Web: www.graphicinfo.com
SIC: 2752 Offset printing

(G-9107)
HAAG-STREIT USA INC (DH)
Also Called: Reliance Medical Products
3535 Kings Mills Rd (45040-2303)
PHONE..............................513 398-3937
Ernest Cavin, *CEO*
◆ **EMP:** 85 **EST:** 1898
SQ FT: 100,000
SALES (est): 15.53MM **Privately Held**
Web: us.haag-streit.com
SIC: 3841 5048 Surgical and medical
instruments; Ophthalmic goods
HQ: Haag-Streit Holding Ag
Gartenstadtstrasse 10
Koniz BE 3098

(G-9108)
HI-TEK MANUFACTURING INC
Also Called: System EDM of Ohio
6050 Hi Tek Ct (45040-2602)
PHONE..............................513 459-1094
Cletis Jackson, *Pr*
Teresa Stang, *VP*
▲ **EMP:** 180 **EST:** 1979
SQ FT: 71,000
SALES (est): 24.94MM **Privately Held**
Web: www.hitekmfg.com
SIC: 3599 7692 3724 3714 Machine shop,
jobbing and repair; Welding repair; Aircraft
engines and engine parts; Motor vehicle
parts and accessories

(G-9109)
HONEYWELL INTERNATIONAL I
7901 Innovation Way (45040-9498)
PHONE..............................513 282-5519
EMP: 16 **EST:** 2018
SALES (est): 3.63MM **Privately Held**
SIC: 3724 Aircraft engines and engine parts

(G-9110)
IMAGINE COMMUNICATIONS CORP
Also Called: Harris Broadcast
5300 Kings Island Dr Ste 101 (45040-2668)
PHONE..............................513 459-3400
Rich Lohmueller, *Prin*
EMP: 6
SQ FT: 17,000
SALES (corp-wide): 1.81B **Privately Held**
Web: www.imaginecommunications.com
SIC: 3663 Radio broadcasting and
communications equipment
HQ: Imagine Communications Corp.
6100 Tnnyson Pkwy Ste 130
Plano TX 75024
469 803-4900

(G-9111)
INTELLIGRATED INC (HQ)
7901 Innovation Way (45040-9498)
PHONE..............................866 936-7300
Chris Cole, *CEO*
Jim Mccarthy, *Pr*
Edward Puisis, *
▲ **EMP:** 29 **EST:** 2001
SALES (est): 416.12MM
SALES (corp-wide): 38.5B **Publicly Held**
Web: automation.honeywell.com

SIC: 3535 Conveyors and conveying
equipment
PA: Honeywell International Inc.
855 S Mint St
Charlotte NC 28202
704 627-6200

(G-9112)
**INTELLIGRATED SUB HOLDINGS
INC (PA)**
7901 Innovation Way (45040-9498)
PHONE..............................513 701-7300
Chris Cole, *CEO*
EMP: 74 **EST:** 2013
SQ FT: 250,000
SALES (est): 1.66MM
SALES (corp-wide): 1.66MM **Privately
Held**
SIC: 3535 Conveyors and conveying
equipment

(G-9113)
INTELLIGRATED SYSTEMS INC (HQ)
Also Called: Honeywell Intelligrated
7901 Innovation Way (45040-9498)
PHONE..............................866 936-7300
Chris Cole, *CEO*
Jim Mccarthy, *Pr*
Ed Puisis, *CFO*
▲ **EMP:** 800 **EST:** 1996
SQ FT: 390,000
SALES (est): 529.86MM
SALES (corp-wide): 38.5B **Publicly Held**
Web: automation.honeywell.com
SIC: 3535 5084 7371 Conveyors and
conveying equipment; Industrial machinery
and equipment; Computer software
development
PA: Honeywell International Inc.
855 S Mint St
Charlotte NC 28202
704 627-6200

(G-9114)
**INTELLIGRATED SYSTEMS OHIO
LLC (DH)**
7901 Innovation Way (45040-9498)
PHONE..............................513 701-7300
TOLL FREE: 800
Jim Mccarthy, *Pr*
Stephen Ackerman, *
Stephen Causey, *
◆ **EMP:** 600 **EST:** 2010
SQ FT: 332,000
SALES (est): 105.57MM
SALES (corp-wide): 38.5B **Publicly Held**
SIC: 3535 5084 3537 Conveyors and
conveying equipment; Industrial machinery
and equipment; Palletizers and depalletizers
HQ: Intelligrated Systems, Inc.
7901 Innovation Way
Mason OH 45040
866 936-7300

(G-9115)
INTERSTATE CONTRACTORS LLC
Also Called: Ic Roofing
762 Reading Rd # G (45040-1362)
PHONE..............................513 372-5393
Jiah Jung, *
EMP: 40 **EST:** 2010
SALES (est): 2.3MM **Privately Held**
Web: www.ic-roofing.com
SIC: 8611 3444 Business associations;
Metal roofing and roof drainage equipment

(G-9116)
J W HARRIS CO INC (HQ)
Also Called: Harris Products Group, The
4501 Quality Pl (45040-1971)
PHONE..............................513 754-2000

◆ **EMP:** 252 **EST:** 1914
SALES (est): 56.36MM
SALES (corp-wide): 4.01B **Publicly Held**
Web: www.harrisproductsgroup.com
SIC: 3356 3548 2899 Solder: wire, bar, acid
core, and rosin core; Welding wire, bare
and coated; Fluxes: brazing, soldering,
galvanizing, and welding
PA: Lincoln Electric Holdings, Inc.
22801 St Clair Ave
Cleveland OH 44117
216 481-8100

(G-9117)
K & K PRECISION INC
5001 N Mason Montgomery Rd
(45040-9148)
PHONE..............................513 336-0032
David J Kappes, *Pr*
Larry G Hixson, *
Melinda Kappes, *
EMP: 38 **EST:** 1991
SALES (est): 7.82MM **Privately Held**
Web: www.kkprec.com
SIC: 3599 Machine shop, jobbing and repair

(G-9118)
KLOSTERMAN BAKING CO LLC
1130 Reading Rd (45040-9156)
PHONE..............................513 398-2707
Chip Klosterman, *Pr*
EMP: 19
SQ FT: 60,000
SALES (corp-wide): 93.13MM **Privately
Held**
Web: www.klostermanbakery.com
SIC: 2051 4225 Bakery: wholesale or
wholesale/retail combined; General
warehousing
PA: Klosterman Baking Co., Llc
2100 Litton Ln
Hebron KY 41048
513 242-1004

(G-9119)
KRAFT HEINZ FOODS COMPANY
7325 Snider Rd (45040-9601)
PHONE..............................513 339-0045
EMP: 26
SALES (corp-wide): 25.85B **Publicly Held**
Web: www.kraftheinzcompany.com
SIC: 2022 Cheese spreads, dips, pastes,
and other cheese products
HQ: Kraft Heinz Foods Company
1 Ppg Pl Ste 3400
Pittsburgh PA 15222
412 456-5700

(G-9120)
**L-3 CMMNCATIONS NOVA ENGRG
INC**
4393 Digital Way (45040-7604)
P.O. Box 16850 (84116-0850)
PHONE..............................877 282-1168
Mark Fischer, *Pr*
EMP: 19 **EST:** 1990
SQ FT: 80,000
SALES (est): 3.8MM
SALES (corp-wide): 21.32B **Publicly Held**
SIC: 8711 3663 Electrical or electronic
engineering; Carrier equipment, radio
communications
HQ: L3 Technologies, Inc.
600 3rd Ave Fl 34
New York NY 10016
321 727-9100

(G-9121)
**L3HARRIS CINCINNATI ELEC CORP
(DH)**
Also Called: Space & Sensors

7500 Innovation Way (45040-9699)
PHONE..............................513 573-6100
Patrick J Sweeney, *Ch*
Russ Walker, *
Vance King, *
Mark Dapore, *
Ed English, *
EMP: 600 **EST:** 1972
SQ FT: 230,000
SALES (est): 96.75MM
SALES (corp-wide): 21.32B **Publicly Held**
SIC: 3812 3769 3823 Detection apparatus:
electronic/magnetic field, light/heat; Space
vehicle equipment, nec; Infrared
instruments, industrial process type
HQ: L3 Technologies, Inc.
600 3rd Ave Fl 34
New York NY 10016
321 727-9100

(G-9122)
LANTEK SYSTEMS INC (DH)
5412 Courseview Dr Ste 205 (45040-2355)
PHONE..............................877 805-1028
Juan Louis Larranaga, *Pr*
Adria Iles, *Dir*
Alberto Martinez, *VP*
EMP: 6 **EST:** 1998
SQ FT: 2,750
SALES (est): 4.03MM
SALES (corp-wide): 5.75B **Privately Held**
Web: www.lantek.com
SIC: 7372 7371 5734 7373 Business
oriented computer software; Computer
software development and applications;
Computer software and accessories;
Computer system selling services
HQ: Lantek Sheet Metal Solutions Slu
Calle Ferdinand Zeppelin 2
Vitoria-Gasteiz 01510

(G-9123)
MAKINO INC (HQ)
7680 Innovation Way (45040-9695)
P.O. Box 8003 (45040-8003)
PHONE..............................513 573-7200
Donald Lane, *Pr*
Bob Henry, *
F Matsubara, *
◆ **EMP:** 356 **EST:** 1887
SQ FT: 320,000
SALES (est): 47.89MM **Privately Held**
Web: www.makino.com
SIC: 3541 Machine tools, metal cutting type
PA: Makino Milling Machine Co., Ltd.
2-3-19, Nakane
Meguro-Ku TKY 152-0

(G-9124)
MARTIN MARIETTA MATERIALS INC
Also Called: Martin Marietta Aggregates
4900 Parkway Dr (45040-8430)
PHONE..............................513 701-1120
Michael Hunt, *Prin*
EMP: 10
Web: www.martinmarietta.com
SIC: 1422 Crushed and broken limestone
PA: Martin Marietta Materials Inc
4123 Parklake Ave
Raleigh NC 27612

(G-9125)
MAUSER USA LLC
1229 Castle Dr (45040-9672)
P.O. Box 350 (45040-0350)
PHONE..............................513 398-1300
Steve Haunert, *Manager*
EMP: 90
SALES (corp-wide): 3.82B **Privately Held**
Web: www.mauserpackaging.com

SIC: 3412 Drums, shipping: metal
HQ: Mauser Usa, Llc
1515 W 22nd St Ste 1100
Oak Brook IL 60523

(G-9126)
MCC - MASON W&S (DH)
Also Called: Multi-Color
5510 Courseview Dr (45040-2366)
PHONE..................513 459-1100
Richard Spear, *CEO*
Randall Spear, *
Michael Henry, *
▲ EMP: 125 EST: 1999
SQ FT: 80,000
SALES (est): 60.39MM
SALES (corp-wide): 14.54B Privately Held
SIC: 2759 Screen printing
HQ: Multi-Color Corporation
6111 N River Rd Fl 8
Rosemont IL 60018
847 427-5354

(G-9127)
MCDONALDS
5301 Kings Island Dr (45040-2354)
PHONE..................513 336-0820
EMP: 20 EST: 2020
SALES (est): 57.19K Privately Held
Web: www.mcdonalds.com
SIC: 5813 5812 5499 2038 Drinking places;
Eating places; Miscellaneous food stores;
Frozen specialties, nec

(G-9128)
MITSUBISHI ELC AUTO AMER INC (DH)
4773 Bethany Rd (45040-8344)
PHONE..................513 573-6614
Takeo Sasaki, *Pr*
Dave Stone, *
◆ EMP: 422 EST: 1987
SQ FT: 220,000
SALES (est): 269.33MM Privately Held
Web: www.meaa-mea.com
SIC: 5511 3651 3714 Automobiles, new and
used; Household audio and video
equipment; Motor vehicle parts and
accessories
HQ: Mitsubishi Electric Us Holdings, Inc.
5900 Katella Ave Ste A
Cypress CA 90630
714 220-2500

(G-9129)
MORSE ENTERPRISES INC
Also Called: AlphaGraphics Cincinnati
6678 Tri Way Dr (45040-2605)
PHONE..................513 229-3600
Cinda Morse, *Prin*
Steven Morse, *Prin*
EMP: 7 EST: 2013
SQ FT: 3,200
SALES (est): 407.61K Privately Held
Web: www.alphagraphics.com
SIC: 2752 7334 7336 2732 Commercial
printing, lithographic; Photocopying and
duplicating services; Commercial art and
graphic design; Pamphlets: printing and
binding, not published on site

(G-9130)
MULTI-COLOR CORPORATION
5510 Courseview Dr (45040-2366)
PHONE..................513 459-3283
Bob Feldman, *Brnch Mgr*
EMP: 9
SALES (corp-wide): 14.54B Privately Held
Web: www.mcclabel.com

SIC: 2759 2679 2672 Labels and seals:
printing, nsk; Labels, paper: made from
purchased material; Labels (unprinted),
gummed: made from purchased materials
HQ: Multi-Color Corporation
6111 N River Rd Fl 8
Rosemont IL 60018
847 427-5354

(G-9131)
OAKLEY DIE & MOLD CO
Also Called: O D M
4393 Digital Way (45040-7604)
PHONE..................513 754-8500
Ernest Petrinowitsch, *CEO*
Harry Petrinowitsch, *
Peggy Braun, *
▲ EMP: 35 EST: 1948
SALES (est): 1.9MM Privately Held
Web: www.odm.com
SIC: 3599 3544 3545 Machine shop, jobbing
and repair; Industrial molds; Tools and
accessories for machine tools

(G-9132)
OMYA DISTRIBUTION LLC (DH)
4605 Duke Dr (45040-7626)
PHONE..................513 387-4600
Anthony Colak, *Pr*
EMP: 12 EST: 2010
SALES (est): 6.25MM Privately Held
Web: distribution-us.omya.com
SIC: 2819 Calcium compounds and salts,
inorganic, nec
HQ: Omya Inc.
9987 Carver Rd Ste 300
Cincinnati OH 45242
513 387-4600

(G-9133)
OMYA INDUSTRIES INC (HQ)
Also Called: Omya
4605 Duke Dr Ste 700 (45040-7626)
PHONE..................513 387-4600
Rainer Seidler, *CEO*
Patrick Preussner, *
Athanasios Katsilometes, *
Paul Thimons, *
◆ EMP: 85 EST: 1977
SALES (est): 590.06MM Privately Held
Web: distribution-us.omya.com
SIC: 1422 Crushed and broken limestone
PA: Omya Ag
Baslerstrasse 42
Oftringen AG 4665

(G-9134)
PORTION PAC INC (DH)
7325 Snider Rd (45040-9193)
PHONE..................513 398-0400
Timothy E Hoberg, *Prin*
Pete Jack, *
Jeffrey Berger, *
Leslie Boettcher, *
▼ EMP: 400 EST: 1973
SQ FT: 100,000
SALES (est): 16.45MM
SALES (corp-wide): 25.85B Publicly Held
Web: www.portionpac.com
SIC: 2033 2035 Catsup: packaged in cans,
jars, etc.; Seasonings and sauces, except
tomato and dry
HQ: Kraft Heinz Foods Company
1 Ppg Pl Ste 3400
Pittsburgh PA 15222
412 456-5700

(G-9135)
PRASCO LLC (PA)
Also Called: Prasco Laboratories
6125 Commerce Ct (45040-6723)

PHONE..................513 204-1100
Christopher H Arington, *CEO*
David Vucurevich, *
▲ EMP: 49 EST: 2002
SALES (est): 46.31MM
SALES (corp-wide): 46.31MM Privately
Held
Web: www.prasco.com
SIC: 2834 Pharmaceutical preparations

(G-9136)
PRATT (TARGET CONTAINER) INC
4700 Duke Dr Ste 140 (45040-9507)
PHONE..................513 770-0851
EMP: 22
SALES (corp-wide): 1.19MM Privately
Held
SIC: 2653 Corrugated and solid fiber boxes
PA: Pratt (Target Container), Inc.
4004 Smmit Blvd Ne Ste 10
Atlanta GA 30319
470 704-6986

(G-9137)
PRECISION QUINCY INDS INC
4600 N Mason Montgomery Rd
(45040-9176)
PHONE..................888 312-5442
Frank Ferguson, *Pr*
EMP: 300 EST: 2012
SQ FT: 315,000
SALES (est): 4.22MM Privately Held
Web: www.pqind.com
SIC: 3441 Fabricated structural metal

(G-9138)
PROCTER & GAMBLE COMPANY
Also Called: Procter & Gamble
8700 S Mason Montgomery Rd
(45040-9760)
P.O. Box 8006 (45040-8006)
PHONE..................513 622-1000
Casey Cahill, *Mgr*
EMP: 128
SALES (corp-wide): 84.04B Publicly Held
Web: us.pg.com
SIC: 2844 2676 3421 2842 Deodorants,
personal; Towels, napkins, and tissue paper
products; Razor blades and razors;
Specialty cleaning
PA: The Procter & Gamble Company
1 Procter & Gamble Plz
Cincinnati OH 45202
513 983-1100

(G-9139)
PULSE WORLDWIDE LTD
7554 Central Parke Blvd (45040-6816)
PHONE..................513 234-7829
Julie Gutterman, *Prin*
EMP: 9 EST: 2014
SALES (est): 1.07MM Privately Held
Web: www.pulseworldwide.com
SIC: 3841 Surgical and medical instruments

(G-9140)
QUEST DIAGNOSTICS INCORPORATED
Also Called: Quest Diagnostics
4690 Parkway Dr (45040-8172)
PHONE..................513 229-5500
EMP: 9
SALES (corp-wide): 9.87B Publicly Held
Web: www.questdiagnostics.com
SIC: 8071 2835 Testing laboratories;
Diagnostic substances
PA: Quest Diagnostics Incorporated
500 Plaza Dr
Secaucus NJ 07094
973 520-2700

(G-9141)
R-K ELECTRONICS INC
7405 Industrial Row Dr (45040-1301)
PHONE..................513 204-6060
John L Keller, *Pr*
Carolyn R Keller, *Ex VP*
▲ EMP: 14 EST: 1949
SQ FT: 11,200
SALES (est): 2.67MM Privately Held
Web: www.rke.com
SIC: 3625 3672 Control equipment, electric;
Wiring boards

(G-9142)
REMTEC ENGINEERING
Also Called: Mbs Acquisition
6049 Hi Tek Ct (45040-2603)
PHONE..................513 860-4299
Keith Rosnell, *CEO*
EMP: 10 EST: 1981
SQ FT: 25,000
SALES (est): 1.38MM Privately Held
Web: www.remtecautomation.com
SIC: 3569 5084 Assembly machines, non-
metalworking; Robots, industrial

(G-9143)
RHINESTAHL CORPORATION
Also Called: Rhinestahl CTS
7687 Innovation Way (45040-9695)
PHONE..................513 229-5300
EMP: 25
SALES (corp-wide): 53.91MM Privately
Held
Web: www.rhinestahl.com
SIC: 3544 Special dies, tools, jigs, and
fixtures
PA: Rhinestahl Corporation
1111 Western Row Rd
Mason OH 45040
513 489-1317

(G-9144)
RHINESTAHL CORPORATION (PA)
Also Called: Rhinestahl AMG
1111 Western Row Rd (45040-1365)
PHONE..................513 489-1317
Dieter Moeller, *Pr*
Chris Hanna, *
Dave Rettenmaier, *
Scott Crislip, *
▲ EMP: 72 EST: 1967
SQ FT: 120,000
SALES (est): 53.91MM
SALES (corp-wide): 53.91MM Privately
Held
Web: www.rhinestahl.com
SIC: 3523 Turf and grounds equipment

(G-9145)
RYSE AERO HOLDCO INC
6951 Cintas Blvd (45040-8923)
PHONE..................513 318-9907
Mick Kowitz, *CEO*
EMP: 20 EST: 2021
SALES (est): 2.28MM Privately Held
SIC: 3812 Aircraft/aerospace flight
instruments and guidance systems

(G-9146)
S&M TRUCKING LLC
5700 Gateway Ste 400 (45040-1890)
PHONE..................661 310-2585
EMP: 12 EST: 2014
SQ FT: 5,000
SALES (est): 938.04K Privately Held
SIC: 4212 3537 4424 Local trucking, without
storage; Trucks: freight, baggage, etc.:
industrial, except mining; Intercoastal
transportation, freight

(G-9147)
SALUS NORTH AMERICA INC
Also Called: Salus Enterprises North Amer
4700 Duke Dr Ste 200 (45040-9507)
PHONE..............................888 387-2587
Shen Owyang, *Pr*
Janine M Kinney, *Sec*
EMP: 13 **EST:** 2000
SALES (est): 2.26MM **Privately Held**
Web: www.braeburnonline.com
SIC: 3822 Thermostats and other
environmental sensors
HQ: Computime Group Limited
6/F Hong Kong Science Park Bldg 20e
Ph 3
Sha Tin NT

(G-9148)
SARA WOOD PHARMACEUTICALS
LLC
Also Called: Sara Wood Pharmaceuticals
4518 Margaret Ct (45040-2922)
PHONE..............................513 833-5502
Mina Pathel, *Prin*
David Schultenover, *Ofcr*
Mina Pathel, *Ofcr*
Eileen Rogers, *Ofcr*
Thomas Docherty, *COO*
EMP: 8 **EST:** 2016
SALES (est): 165.53K **Privately Held**
SIC: 2834 Solutions, pharmaceutical

(G-9149)
SEAPINE SOFTWARE INC (HQ)
6960 Cintas Blvd (45040-8922)
PHONE..............................513 754-1655
Richard Riccetti, *Pr*
Judy Test, *CFO*
Matthew Disher, *CIO*
Kelly Riccetti, *Ex VP*
EMP: 18 **EST:** 1996
SQ FT: 36,000
SALES (est): 4.98MM **Privately Held**
Web: www.perforce.com
SIC: 7371 7372 Custom computer
programming services; Operating systems
computer software
PA: Perforce Software, Inc.
400 1st Ave N Ste 400
Minneapolis MN 55401

(G-9150)
SHOALS TUBULAR INC
Also Called: Shoals Tubular
4501 Quality Pl (45040-1971)
PHONE..............................256 767-7171
Terry Cook, *Pr*
Mike Nelson, *
Lynn Cook, *
▲ **EMP:** 87 **EST:** 1989
SALES (est): 2.39MM
SALES (corp-wide): 4.01B **Publicly Held**
Web: www.seda-shoals.com
SIC: 3585 Parts for heating, cooling, and
refrigerating equipment
PA: Lincoln Electric Holdings, Inc.
22801 St Clair Ave
Cleveland OH 44117
216 481-8100

(G-9151)
SIEMENS AG
6693 Summer Field Dr (45040-7332)
PHONE..............................513 576-2451
Sivarama Nalluri, *Ofcr*
EMP: 7 **EST:** 2018
SALES (est): 635.98K **Privately Held**
Web: www.siemens.com
SIC: 3661 Telephones and telephone
apparatus

(G-9152)
SIGHTGAIN INC
Also Called: Sightgain
5325 Deerfield Blvd (45040-2511)
PHONE..............................202 494-9317
Christian Sorensen, *CEO*
EMP: 10 **EST:** 2019
SALES (est): 664.96K **Privately Held**
Web: www.sightgain.com
SIC: 7372 7373 7374 7375 Application
computer software; Computer systems
analysis and design; Computer processing
services; On-line data base information
retrieval

(G-9153)
SOUNDTRACE INC
408 4th Ave (45040-1508)
PHONE..............................513 278-5288
Matthew Reinhold, *Prin*
EMP: 12 **EST:** 2021
SALES (est): 617.89K **Privately Held**
Web: www.soundtrace.com
SIC: 3842 Hearing aids

(G-9154)
SPEAR INC
Also Called: Spear Application Systems
5510 Courseview Dr (45040-2385)
PHONE..............................513 459-1100
▲ **EMP:** 80
Web: www.spearsystem.com
SIC: 2759 Screen printing

(G-9155)
SPECIAL MACHINED COMPONENTS
7626 Easy St (45040-9424)
PHONE..............................513 459-1113
Larry Johnson, *Owner*
EMP: 9 **EST:** 1989
SQ FT: 12,000
SALES (est): 583.39K **Privately Held**
SIC: 3599 Machine shop, jobbing and repair

(G-9156)
SRI HEALTHCARE LLC
7086 Industrial Row Dr (45040-1363)
PHONE..............................513 398-6406
EMP: 7 **EST:** 1990
SALES (est): 372.1K **Privately Held**
Web: www.sri-healthcare.com
SIC: 3841 Surgical and medical instruments

(G-9157)
SUPERIOR LABEL SYSTEMS INC
(DH)
Also Called: Superior Machine Systems
7500 Industrial Row Dr (45040-1307)
PHONE..............................513 336-0825
Kenneth Kidd, *Ch Bd*
Thomas Braig, *
EMP: 275 **EST:** 1970
SQ FT: 30,000
SALES (est): 4.25MM
SALES (corp-wide): 14.54B **Privately Held**
SIC: 3565 2759 3993 3577 Labeling
machines, industrial; Flexographic printing;
Signs and advertising specialties;
Computer peripheral equipment, nec
HQ: W/S Packaging Group, Inc.
2571 S Hemlock Rd
Green Bay WI 54229
800 818-5481

(G-9158)
TELEDYNE INSTRUMENTS INC
Also Called: Teledyne Tekmar
4736 Socialville Foster Rd (45040-8265)
PHONE..............................513 229-7000
EMP: 26

SALES (corp-wide): 5.67B **Publicly Held**
Web: www.teledynelabs.com
SIC: 5049 3826 3829 3821 Laboratory
equipment, except medical or dental;
Analytical instruments; Measuring and
controlling devices, nec; Laboratory
apparatus and furniture
HQ: Teledyne Instruments, Inc.
16830 Chestnut St
City Of Industry CA 91748
626 934-1500

(G-9159)
TELEDYNE INSTRUMENTS INC
Also Called: Teledyne Leeman Labs
4736 Socialville Foster Rd (45040-8265)
PHONE..............................603 886-8400
Peter Brown, *Mgr*
EMP: 65
SALES (corp-wide): 5.67B **Publicly Held**
Web: www.teledynelabs.com
SIC: 3826 Spectrometers
HQ: Teledyne Instruments, Inc.
16830 Chestnut St
City Of Industry CA 91748
626 934-1500

(G-9160)
TELEDYNE TEKMAR COMPANY (DH)
Also Called: Tekmar-Dohrmann
4736 Socialville Foster Rd (45040-8265)
PHONE..............................513 229-7000
Robert Mehrabian, *Ch Bd*
EMP: 25 **EST:** 1972
SQ FT: 40,000
SALES (est): 18.56MM
SALES (corp-wide): 5.67B **Publicly Held**
Web: www.teledynelabs.com
SIC: 5049 3826 3829 3821 Laboratory
equipment, except medical or dental;
Analytical instruments; Measuring and
controlling devices, nec; Laboratory
apparatus and furniture
HQ: Teledyne Instruments, Inc.
16830 Chestnut St
City Of Industry CA 91748
626 934-1500

(G-9161)
THE ARMOR GROUP INC (PA)
Also Called: Armor Contract Manufacturing
4600 N Mason Montgomery Rd
(45040-9176)
PHONE..............................513 923-5260
David K Schmitt, *CEO*
Katherine D Schmitt, *
▲ **EMP:** 102 **EST:** 1927
SALES (est): 91.45MM **Privately Held**
Web: www.cinind.com
SIC: 3441 3446 3444 3443 Fabricated
structural metal; Architectural metalwork;
Sheet metalwork; Fabricated plate work
(boiler shop)

(G-9162)
TO SCALE SOFTWARE LLC
Also Called: Stack Constructyion Technology
6398 Thornberry Ct (45040-7816)
PHONE..............................513 253-0053
Phillip Ogilby, *Managing Member*
Jane Baysore, *
EMP: 35 **EST:** 2007
SALES (est): 1.63MM **Privately Held**
Web: www.stackct.com
SIC: 7372 Prepackaged software

(G-9163)
TRANSNORM SYSTEM INC
7901 Innovation Way (45040-9498)
PHONE..............................972 606-0303
Gary Cline, *CEO*

Kay Lynn Wolfe, *
▲ **EMP:** 80 **EST:** 1988
SALES (est): 2.83MM
SALES (corp-wide): 38.5B **Publicly Held**
SIC: 3535 5084 Conveyors and conveying
equipment; Conveyor systems
HQ: Transnorm System Gmbh
Forster Str. 2
Harsum NI 31177
51274020

(G-9164)
VELOCITY CONCEPT DEV GROUP
LLC (PA)
4393 Digital Way (45040-7604)
PHONE..............................513 204-2100
EMP: 6 **EST:** 2012
SALES (est): 4.25MM
SALES (corp-wide): 4.25MM **Privately**
Held
Web: www.velocityfast.com
SIC: 3999 Atomizers, toiletry

(G-9165)
VNDLY LLC
4900 Parkway Dr Ste 125 (45040-8430)
PHONE..............................513 572-2500
Shashank Saxena, *CEO*
EMP: 50 **EST:** 2017
SQ FT: 5,483
SALES (est): 4.06MM **Publicly Held**
Web: www.workday.com
SIC: 7372 7374 Application computer
software; Data processing service
PA: Workday, Inc.
6110 Stoneridge Mall Rd
Pleasanton CA 94588

(G-9166)
W/S PACKAGING GROUP INC
7400 Industrial Row Dr (45040-1302)
PHONE..............................513 459-8800
Klaus Kok, *Brnch Mgr*
EMP: 40
SALES (corp-wide): 14.54B **Privately Held**
SIC: 2759 Labels and seals: printing, nsk
HQ: W/S Packaging Group, Inc.
2571 S Hemlock Rd
Green Bay WI 54229
800 818-5481

(G-9167)
WITT INDUSTRIES INC (HQ)
Also Called: Witt Products
4600 N Mason Montgomery Rd
(45040-9176)
PHONE..............................513 871-5700
TOLL FREE: 800
Tim Harris, *Pr*
▼ **EMP:** 100 **EST:** 1974
SQ FT: 71,500
SALES (est): 5.08MM **Privately Held**
Web: www.witt.com
SIC: 3479 3469 3441 3412 Galvanizing of
iron, steel, or end-formed products;
Garbage cans, stamped and pressed metal
; Fabricated structural metal; Metal barrels,
drums, and pails
PA: The Armor Group, Inc.
4600 N Masn Montgomery Rd
Mason OH 45040

Massillon
Stark County

(G-9168)
3-D SERVICE LTD (PA)
Also Called: Magnetech
800 Nave Rd Se (44646-9476)

▲ = Import ▼ = Export
◆ = Import/Export

PHONE...................330 830-3500
Bernie Dewees, *Pr*
▲ **EMP:** 120 **EST:** 2002
SQ FT: 85,000
SALES (est): 1.02MM
SALES (corp-wide): 1.02MM **Privately Held**
Web: www.magnetech.com
SIC: 7694 7699 Electric motor repair; Industrial equipment services

(G-9169)
A & R MACHINE CO INC
13212 Vega St Sw (44647-9200)
PHONE...................330 832-4631
Rollin Shriner, *Pr*
Patsy Shriner, *VP*
EMP: 6 **EST:** 1986
SQ FT: 10,000
SALES (est): 496.39K **Privately Held**
SIC: 3599 Custom machinery

(G-9170)
A R E LOGISTICS LLC
400 Nave Rd Se (44646-8898)
PHONE...................330 327-7315
EMP: 8 **EST:** 2018
SALES (est): 2.38MM **Privately Held**
SIC: 2821 Plastics materials and resins

(G-9171)
ABP INDUCTION LLC (PA)
Also Called: A B P Induction
607 1st St Sw (44646-6729)
PHONE...................262 878-6390
Paul Decker, *Managing Member**
Frank Possinger, *
◆ **EMP:** 15 **EST:** 2005
SALES (est): 7.96MM **Privately Held**
Web: www.abpinduction.com
SIC: 3567 Industrial furnaces and ovens

(G-9172)
ARE INC
400 Nave Rd Sw (44646)
P.O. Box 1100 (44648-1100)
PHONE...................330 830-7800
EMP: 518
SIC: 3713 3714 3792 5013 Truck bodies and parts; Motor vehicle body components and frame; Travel trailers and campers; Motor vehicle supplies and new parts

(G-9173)
AVIENT CORPORATION
1675 Navarre Rd Se (44646-9607)
PHONE...................330 834-3812
Steve Strover, *Mgr*
EMP: 30
Web: www.avient.com
SIC: 2821 Plastics materials and resins
PA: Avient Corporation
33587 Walker Rd
Avon Lake OH 44012

(G-9174)
BATES PRINTING INC
150 23rd St Se (44646-7046)
PHONE...................330 833-5830
Dan Bates, *Pr*
John Bates, *Pr*
Daniel Bates, *VP*
EMP: 10 **EST:** 1913
SQ FT: 3,000
SALES (est): 342.65K **Privately Held**
Web: www.batesprinting.com
SIC: 2752 2759 Offset printing; Commercial printing, nec

(G-9175)
BRINKLEY TECHNOLOGY GROUP LLC
Also Called: Hercules Engine
2770 Erie St S (44646-7943)
PHONE...................330 830-2498
Douglas Brinkley, *Pr*
EMP: 17 **EST:** 2015
SQ FT: 34,000
SALES (est): 4.75MM **Privately Held**
Web: www.herculesmanufacturing.com
SIC: 3599 3519 3621 3694 Oil filters, internal combustion engine, except auto; Governors, diesel engine; Storage battery chargers, motor and engine generator type; Distributors, motor vehicle engine

(G-9176)
C-N-D INDUSTRIES INC
Also Called: Cnd Machine
359 State Ave Nw (44647-4269)
PHONE...................330 478-8811
Clyde Shetler, *Pr*
Don Rossbach, *
EMP: 13 **EST:** 1989
SQ FT: 28,000
SALES (est): 901.45K **Privately Held**
SIC: 3441 3599 7692 3444 Fabricated structural metal; Machine shop, jobbing and repair; Welding repair; Sheet metalwork

(G-9177)
CARBONLESS ON DEMANDCOM LLC
332 Erie St S (44646-6740)
PHONE...................330 837-8611
David Mathis, *Owner*
EMP: 19 **EST:** 1989
SALES (est): 1.63MM **Privately Held**
Web: www.carbonlessondemand.com
SIC: 2752 Offset printing

(G-9178)
CASE FARMS LLC
Also Called: Massillon Feed Mill
4001 Millennium Blvd Se (44646-9606)
PHONE...................330 832-0030
Thomas R Shelton, *Brnch Mgr*
EMP: 84
Web: www.casefarms.com
SIC: 2015 Poultry slaughtering and processing
PA: Case Farms, L.L.C.
385 Pilch Rd
Troutman NC 28166

(G-9179)
CHARTER NEXT GENERATION INC
8333 Navarre Rd Se (44646-9652)
PHONE...................330 830-6030
Kathy Bolhous, *CEO*
EMP: 128
SALES (corp-wide): 1.5B **Privately Held**
Web: www.cnginc.com
SIC: 2671 Plastic film, coated or laminated for packaging
PA: Charter Next Generation, Inc.
300 N La Slle Dr Ste 1575
Chicago IL 60654
608 868-5757

(G-9180)
COLD HEADED FAS ASSEMBLIES INC
1875 Harsh Ave Se Ste 3 (44646-7182)
P.O. Box 547 (44648-0547)
PHONE...................330 833-0800
Oscar Lee, *Pr*
Gwen Hemperly, *Sec*
▲ **EMP:** 12 **EST:** 1990

SQ FT: 30,000
SALES (est): 1.7MM **Privately Held**
SIC: 3452 3599 Bolts, metal; Machine shop, jobbing and repair

(G-9181)
CORRCHOICE CINCINNATI
777 3rd St Nw (44647-4203)
PHONE...................330 833-2884
EMP: 6 **EST:** 2019
SALES (est): 787.8K **Privately Held**
Web: www.greif.com
SIC: 2621 Wrapping and packaging papers

(G-9182)
CRACK CORN LTD
7993 Hills And Dales Rd Ne (44646-5242)
PHONE...................440 467-0108
James Alay, *Managing Member*
EMP: 10 **EST:** 2019
SALES (est): 387.14K **Privately Held**
SIC: 2096 Potato chips and similar snacks

(G-9183)
CROWN CORK & SEAL USA INC
700 16th St Se (44646-7152)
PHONE...................330 833-1011
Bernard Baumann, *Mgr*
EMP: 300
SALES (corp-wide): 11.8B **Publicly Held**
Web: www.crowncork.com
SIC: 3411 Aluminum cans
HQ: Crown Cork & Seal Usa, Inc.
770 Township Line Rd
Yardley PA 19067
215 698-5100

(G-9184)
CUSTER PRODUCTS LIMITED
1320 Sanders Ave Sw (44647-7631)
P.O. Box 2997 (44720-0997)
PHONE...................330 490-3158
Bradley Custer, *Pr*
▲ **EMP:** 15 **EST:** 1993
SQ FT: 12,500
SALES (est): 3.45MM **Privately Held**
Web: www.custerproducts.com
SIC: 3714 5013 5072 Motor vehicle parts and accessories; Motor vehicle supplies and new parts; Hardware

(G-9185)
DAVID A AND MARY A MATHIS
Also Called: D & M Printing
332 Erie St S (44646-6740)
PHONE...................330 837-8611
David A Mathis, *Owner*
EMP: 7 **EST:** 1993
SALES (est): 326.22K **Privately Held**
SIC: 2752 Offset printing

(G-9186)
DOTCENTRAL LLC
1650 Deerford Ave Sw (44647-9732)
PHONE...................330 809-0112
Daniel Swartz, *Managing Member*
EMP: 10 **EST:** 2017
SALES (est): 205.83K **Privately Held**
SIC: 2741 Internet publishing and broadcasting

(G-9187)
DW HERCULES LLC
Also Called: Hercules Engine Components
2770 Erie St S (44646-7943)
P.O. Box 451 (44648-0451)
PHONE...................330 830-2498
Doug Brinkley, *Pr*
▲ **EMP:** 9 **EST:** 1999
SQ FT: 22,000

SALES (est): 3.72MM **Privately Held**
Web: dwhercules.openfos.com
SIC: 3519 5999 Parts and accessories, internal combustion engines; Engine and motor equipment and supplies

(G-9188)
E-B DISPLAY COMPANY INC
1369 Sanders Ave Sw (44647-7632)
P.O. Box 650 (44648-0650)
PHONE...................330 833-4101
▲ **EMP:** 110 **EST:** 1952
SALES (est): 8.66MM
SALES (corp-wide): 8.66MM **Privately Held**
Web: www.ebdisplay.com
SIC: 3993 2542 Signs, not made in custom sign painting shops; Office and store showcases and display fixtures
HQ: Rotolo Industries, Inc.
1369 Sanders Ave Sw
Massillon OH

(G-9189)
E-B WIRE WORKS INC
1350 Sanders Ave Sw (44647-7631)
P.O. Box 650 (44648-0650)
PHONE...................330 833-4101
▲ **EMP:** 71 **EST:** 1989
SALES (est): 4.63MM **Privately Held**
Web: www.ebdisplay.com
SIC: 3399 Tacks, nonferrous metal or wire

(G-9190)
ENGRAVERS GALLERY & SIGN CO
10 Lincoln Way E (44646-6632)
P.O. Box 709 (44648-0709)
PHONE...................330 830-1271
Bonnie Fall, *Owner*
EMP: 6 **EST:** 1987
SQ FT: 1,600
SALES (est): 243.47K **Privately Held**
Web: nilboglin.wix.com
SIC: 3993 7389 Letters for signs, metal; Engraving service

(G-9191)
FIBERCORR MILLS LLC
670 17th St Nw (44647-5343)
P.O. Box 453 (44648-0453)
PHONE...................330 837-5151
▲ **EMP:** 77
SIC: 2679 2631 Paper products, converted, nec; Paperboard mills

(G-9192)
FRESH MARK INC (PA)
Also Called: Superior's Brand Meats
1888 Southway St Sw (44646-9429)
PHONE...................330 832-7491
Neil Genshaft, *Ch*
Tim Cranor, *
Tom Cicarella, *
David Cochenour, *
◆ **EMP:** 500 **EST:** 1932
SQ FT: 80,000
SALES (est): 1.38B
SALES (corp-wide): 1.38B **Privately Held**
Web: www.freshmark.com
SIC: 2013 5147 2011 Prepared beef products, from purchased beef; Meats and meat products; Meat packing plants

(G-9193)
GAMEDAY VISION
1147 Oberlin Ave Sw (44647-7665)
PHONE...................330 830-4550
Krista Simcic, *Pr*
EMP: 10 **EST:** 2010
SALES (est): 340.92K **Privately Held**
Web: www.gamedayvision.com

SIC: 3577 Printers and plotters

(G-9194)
GARY LAWRENCE ENTERPRISES INC
Also Called: Lawrence Machine
21 Charles Ave Sw (44646-6621)
P.O. Box 727 (44648-0727)
PHONE..............................330 833-7181
Gary Lawrence, *Pr*
Christopher Lawrence, *VP*
Eric Lawrence, *Treas*
EMP: 8 EST: 1976
SQ FT: 15,000
SALES (est): 552.92K **Privately Held**
Web: www.lawrencemachine.com
SIC: 3993 5199 Signs and advertising
specialties; Advertising specialties

(G-9195)
GERSTENSLAGER CONSTRUCTION
Also Called: Gerstenslager Hardwood Pdts
343 16th St Se (44646-7177)
PHONE..............................330 832-3604
Mike Gerstenslager, *Owner*
Myron F Gerstenslager Junior, *Owner*
EMP: 6 EST: 1958
SQ FT: 12,000
SALES (est): 330K **Privately Held**
Web: www.gerstenslagerhardwood.com
SIC: 2431 Millwork

(G-9196)
GREEN MEADOWS PAPER COMPANY
670 17th St Nw (44647-5343)
PHONE..............................330 837-5151
Scott Welch, *Prin*
Jay Frem, *
EMP: 65 EST: 2021
SALES (est): 2.59MM **Privately Held**
Web: www.gmpaperco.com
SIC: 2679 Paper products, converted, nec

(G-9197)
GREIF INC
787 Warmington Rd Se (44646-8830)
P.O. Box 675 (44648-0675)
PHONE..............................330 879-2936
Matt Sullivan, *Mgr*
EMP: 52
SALES (corp-wide): 5.45B **Publicly Held**
Web: www.greif.com
SIC: 2655 Fiber cans, drums, and similar
products
PA: Greif, Inc.
425 Winter Rd
Delaware OH 43015
740 549-6000

(G-9198)
GSDI SPECIALTY DISPERSIONS INC
Also Called: Gsdi
1675 Navarre Rd Se (44646-9607)
PHONE..............................330 848-9200
▲ EMP: 20 EST: 1980
SALES (est): 5.88MM **Publicly Held**
SIC: 2816 Color pigments
PA: Avient Corporation
33587 Walker Rd
Avon Lake OH 44012

(G-9199)
H P E INC (PA)
2025 Harsh Ave Se (44646-7127)
P.O. Box 528 (44648)
PHONE..............................330 833-3161
Robert Boley, *Pr*
Robert N Boley, *Pr*
Sandra Boley, *Sec*

EMP: 7 EST: 1979
SQ FT: 12,000
SALES (est): 504.25K
SALES (corp-wide): 504.25K **Privately Held**
Web: www.hpe--inc.com
SIC: 3533 3569 3547 3494 Oil and gas field
machinery; Gas separators (machinery);
Rolling mill machinery; Valves and pipe
fittings, nec

(G-9200)
HEINZ FOREIGN INVESTMENT CO
1301 Oberlin Ave Sw (44647-7669)
P.O. Box 15222 (15237-0222)
PHONE..............................330 837-8331
EMP: 6 EST: 2015
SALES (est): 371.38K
SALES (corp-wide): 25.85B **Publicly Held**
Web: www.kraftheinz.com
SIC: 2037 Frozen fruits and vegetables
PA: The Heinz Kraft Company
1 Ppg Pl
Pittsburgh PA 15222
412 456-5700

(G-9201)
HENDRICKS VACUUM FORMING INC
Also Called: Hvfi
3500 17th St Sw (44647-9700)
PHONE..............................330 837-2040
Robin Hendricks, *Pr*
EMP: 17 EST: 1978
SQ FT: 40,000
SALES (est): 2.72MM **Privately Held**
Web: www.hvfi.com
SIC: 3993 Electric signs

(G-9202)
HJ HEINZ COMPANY LP (DH)
Also Called: Heinz Frozen Foods
1301 Oberlin Ave Sw (44647-7669)
PHONE..............................330 837-8331
Allan Briggs, *Mng Pt*
Mike Parks, *Mgr*
Rick Uriguem, *Manager*
▲ EMP: 56 EST: 2000
SALES (est): 47.6MM
SALES (corp-wide): 25.85B **Publicly Held**
SIC: 2037 Frozen fruits and vegetables
HQ: Kraft Heinz Foods Company
1 Ppg Pl Ste 3400
Pittsburgh PA 15222
412 456-5700

(G-9203)
HUTH READY MIX & SUPPLY CO
Also Called: Huth Ready-Mix & Supply Co
501 5th St Nw (44647-5473)
P.O. Box 524 (44648-0524)
PHONE..............................330 833-4191
Roger L Huth, *Pr*
Alice H Huth, *Sec*
EMP: 9 EST: 1880
SQ FT: 3,000
SALES (est): 1.25MM **Privately Held**
SIC: 3273 5211 Ready-mixed concrete; Brick

(G-9204)
HYDRO-DYNE INC
225 Wetmore Ave Se (44646-6788)
P.O. Box 318 (44648-0318)
PHONE..............................330 832-5076
Rose Ann Dare, *Pr*
Lynn Neel, *
Sherri Mcmillen, *Mgr*
Ken Yeaman, *
Jean Holiday, *
▲ EMP: 15 EST: 1967
SQ FT: 130,000
SALES (est): 1.46MM **Privately Held**

Web: www.hydrodyneinc.com
SIC: 3585 8711 Evaporative condensers,
heat transfer equipment; Engineering
services

(G-9205)
HYDRO-THRIFT CORPORATION
Also Called: Hydrothrift
1301 Sanders Ave Sw (44647-7632)
P.O. Box 1037 (44648-1037)
PHONE..............................330 837-5141
T K Heston, *Pr*
Paul Heston, *Treas*
▼ EMP: 23 EST: 1973
SQ FT: 27,000
SALES (est): 6.3MM **Privately Held**
Web: www.hydrothrift.com
SIC: 3443 3585 Heat exchangers,
condensers, and components; Air
conditioning equipment, complete

(G-9206)
IDENTITEK SYSTEMS INC
Also Called: Adams Signs
1100 Industrial Ave Sw (44647-7608)
P.O. Box 347 (44648-0347)
PHONE..............................330 832-9844
Joseph Pugliese, *Pr*
EMP: 53 EST: 1943
SQ FT: 70,000
SALES (est): 9.74MM **Privately Held**
Web: www.adamsigns.com
SIC: 1799 3993 Sign installation and
maintenance; Signs and advertising
specialties

(G-9207)
J L R PRODUCTS INC
1212 Oberlin Ave Sw (44647-7668)
PHONE..............................330 832-9557
Matthew Radocaj, *Pr*
EMP: 6 EST: 1993
SALES (est): 1.02MM **Privately Held**
Web: www.jlrproducts.com
SIC: 3429 3568 Pulleys, metal; Pulleys,
power transmission

(G-9208)
JACODAR INC
1212 Oberlin Ave Sw (44647-7668)
PHONE..............................330 832-9557
Matthew Radocaj, *Pr*
EMP: 10 EST: 1983
SQ FT: 24,000
SALES (est): 795.9K
SALES (corp-wide): 358.52MM **Privately Held**
Web: www.jlrproducts.com
SIC: 3452 Bolts, metal
PA: Ojim, Inc.
1212 Oberlin Ave Sw
Massillon OH 44647
330 832-9557

(G-9209)
KARL KUEMMERLING INC
129 Edgewater Ave Nw (44646-3321)
EMP: 18
SIC: 5261 5083 5699 3524 Lawn and
garden equipment; Lawn and garden
machinery and equipment; Work clothing;
Lawn and garden equipment

(G-9210)
KENDEL WLDG & FABRICATION INC
1700 Navarre Rd Se (44646)
PHONE..............................330 834-2429
Bettina M Kendel, *Pr*
Donald R Kendel, *VP*
EMP: 8 EST: 1999
SALES (est): 497.09K **Privately Held**

SIC: 7692 Welding repair

(G-9211)
KENMORE CONSTRUCTION CO INC
Also Called: American Sand & Gravel Div
9500 Forty Corners Rd Nw (44646-9309)
PHONE..............................330 832-8888
Chris Scala, *Mgr*
EMP: 79
SALES (corp-wide): 44.06MM **Privately Held**
Web: www.kenmorecompanies.com
SIC: 1611 1442 General contractor, highway
and street construction; Construction sand
and gravel
PA: Kenmore Construction Co., Inc.
700 Home Ave
Akron OH 44310
330 762-8936

(G-9212)
KING MACHINE AND TOOL CO
1237 Sanders Ave Sw (44647-7684)
PHONE..............................330 833-7217
William Kapper, *Pr*
Tracy Kapper, *VP*
Kelly Kapper, *Treas*
Judith A Kapper, *Sec*
▲ EMP: 18 EST: 1949
SQ FT: 22,000
SALES (est): 2.54MM **Privately Held**
Web: www.kmtco.com
SIC: 3599 Machine shop, jobbing and repair

(G-9213)
KRAFT HEINZ COMPANY
Also Called: Kraft Heinz Company
1301 Oberlin Ave Sw (44647-7669)
PHONE..............................330 837-8331
Ken Stiffler, *Manager*
EMP: 700
SQ FT: 1,196
SALES (corp-wide): 25.85B **Publicly Held**
Web: www.kraftheinzcompany.com
SIC: 2033 2099 Tomato sauce: packaged in
cans, jars, etc.; Food preparations, nec
PA: The Heinz Kraft Company
1 Ppg Pl
Pittsburgh PA 15222
412 456-5700

(G-9214)
LAND OLAKES INC
Also Called: Land O'Lakes
8485 Navarre Rd Sw (44646-8814)
PHONE..............................330 879-2158
Gary Hauenstin, *Mgr*
EMP: 51
SALES (corp-wide): 2.89B **Privately Held**
Web: www.landolakesinc.com
SIC: 2048 5191 2047 Livestock feeds;
Animal feeds; Dog and cat food
PA: Land O'lakes, Inc.
4001 Lexington Ave N
Arden Hills MN 55112
651 375-2222

(G-9215)
LLC RING MASTERS
240 6th St Nw (44647-5413)
PHONE..............................330 832-1511
EMP: 14 EST: 2003
SQ FT: 51,000
SALES (est): 2.77MM **Privately Held**
Web: www.ring-masters.net
SIC: 3316 Cold finishing of steel shapes

(G-9216)
MAGNETECH INDUSTRIAL SVCS INC
Also Called: Miscor Group
800 Nave Rd Se (44646-9476)

PHONE..............................330 830-3500
EMP: 6
Web: www.magnetech.com
SIC: 7694 Electric motor repair
HQ: Magnetech Industrial Services, Inc.
800 Nave Rd Se
Massillon OH 44646
330 830-3500

(G-9217)
MAGNETECH INDUSTRIAL SVCS INC (DH)
Also Called: Magnetech Industrial Services
800 Nave Rd Se (44646-9476)
PHONE..............................330 830-3500
Michael P Moore, *Pr*
William Wisnieweski, *
James I Depew, *
▲ **EMP:** 80 **EST:** 2000
SALES (est): 49.48MM **Publicly Held**
Web: www.magnetech.com
SIC: 7694 Electric motor repair
HQ: Ies Subsidiary Holdings, Inc
5433 Westheimer Rd # 500
Houston TX 77056
713 860-1500

(G-9218)
MAGNETECH INDUSTRIAL SVCS INC
800 Nave Rd Se (44646-9476)
PHONE..............................330 830-3500
Mike Rice, *Brnch Mgr*
EMP: 10
Web: www.magnetech.com
SIC: 7694 7699 Electric motor repair; Industrial equipment services
HQ: Magnetech Industrial Services, Inc.
800 Nave Rd Se
Massillon OH 44646
330 830-3500

(G-9219)
MASSILLON MACHINE & DIE INC
3536 17th St Sw (44647-9211)
PHONE..............................330 833-8913
Gary Burkholder, *Pr*
EMP: 9 **EST:** 2004
SQ FT: 7,000
SALES (est): 2.12MM **Privately Held**
SIC: 3599 1799 Custom machinery; Welding on site

(G-9220)
MATCH MOLD & MACHINE INC
1100 Nova Dr Se (44646-8867)
PHONE..............................330 830-5503
Timothy V Lidderdale, *Pr*
Thomas Knipfer, *
Ruth Lidderdale, *
EMP: 7 **EST:** 1981
SALES (est): 331.51K **Privately Held**
SIC: 3544 Special dies and tools

(G-9221)
MATRIX SYS AUTO FINISHES LLC
600 Nova Dr Se (44646-8884)
PHONE..............................248 668-8135
W Kent Gardner, *Pr*
Sean Hook, *Director of Information*
EMP: 256 **EST:** 1983
SQ FT: 26,000
SALES (est): 2.2MM
SALES (corp-wide): 11.37MM **Privately Held**
Web: www.matrixsystem.com
SIC: 5198 2851 Paints; Paints and allied products
PA: Quest Specialty Chemicals, Inc.
225 Sven Farms Dr Ste 204
Charleston SC 29492
800 966-7580

(G-9222)
MEL WACKER SIGNS INC
Also Called: Wacker Sign
13076 Barrs St Sw (44647-9746)
PHONE..............................330 832-1726
TOLL FREE: 800
Bonnie Maier, *Pr*
Melville Maier, *VP*
EMP: 6 **EST:** 1975
SALES (est): 380.85K **Privately Held**
Web: www.wackersigns.com
SIC: 3993 1799 5999 Signs, not made in custom sign painting shops; Sign installation and maintenance; Flags

(G-9223)
MIDWESTERN INDUSTRIES INC (PA)
915 Oberlin Ave Sw (44648)
P.O. Box 810 (44648-0810)
PHONE..............................330 837-4203
David Weaver, *VP*
Gary A Cunningham, *
Harold J Painter, *
William J Crone, *
Laverne J Riesbeck, *
▼ **EMP:** 92 **EST:** 1961
SQ FT: 148,000
SALES (est): 18.84MM
SALES (corp-wide): 18.84MM **Privately Held**
Web: www.midwesternind.com
SIC: 3559 3496 3564 3443 Screening equipment, electric; Mesh, made from purchased wire; Blowers and fans; Fabricated plate work (boiler shop)

(G-9224)
MISCOR GROUP LTD
800 Nave Rd Se (44646-9476)
PHONE..............................330 830-3500
▲ **EMP:** 269
SIC: 7629 7539 3519 Electrical equipment repair services; Electrical services; Diesel, semi-diesel, or duel-fuel engines, including marine

(G-9225)
MPI LOGISTICS AND SERVICE INC
Also Called: M P I Logistics
1414 Industrial Ave Sw (44647-7663)
PHONE..............................330 832-5309
Richard D Miller, *Pr*
Judith A Miller, *VP*
EMP: 21 **EST:** 1980
SQ FT: 16,500
SALES (est): 4.93MM **Privately Held**
Web: www.mpitruckrepair.com
SIC: 7699 2448 4213 7549 Pallet repair; Pallets, wood; Trucking, except local; Automotive maintenance services

(G-9226)
NFM/WELDING ENGINEERS INC (PA)
Also Called: N F M
577 Oberlin Ave Sw (44647-7820)
PHONE..............................330 837-3868
Philip A Roberson, *Pr*
Ronald Pribich, *
Scott Swallen, *
Paul Roberson, *
John Roberson, *
▲ **EMP:** 140 **EST:** 1985
SQ FT: 150,000
SALES (est): 48.86MM
SALES (corp-wide): 48.86MM **Privately Held**
Web: www.nfm.net
SIC: 3599 Machine shop, jobbing and repair

(G-9227)
OMNI DIE CASTING INC
1100 Nova Dr Se (44646-8867)
PHONE..............................330 830-5500
Timothy Lidderdale, *Pr*
Derek Lidderdale, *
▲ **EMP:** 30 **EST:** 1958
SQ FT: 10,000
SALES (est): 5.55MM **Privately Held**
Web: www.omnidiecasting.com
SIC: 3363 Aluminum die-castings

(G-9228)
OMNI USA INC
1100 Nova Dr Se (44646-8867)
PHONE..............................330 830-5500
Timothy V Lidderdale, *Pr*
Theodore Buss, *
EMP: 8 **EST:** 1982
SALES (est): 1.05MM **Privately Held**
SIC: 3363 Aluminum die-castings

(G-9229)
OSTER SAND AND GRAVEL INC
Also Called: Oster Enterprises
1955 Riverside Dr Nw (44647-9300)
PHONE..............................330 833-2649
Bruce Bickel, *Mgr*
EMP: 8
SALES (corp-wide): 3.25MM **Privately Held**
Web: www.ostersandandgravelnorthcantonoh.com
SIC: 1442 1422 Construction sand and gravel; Crushed and broken limestone
PA: Oster Sand And Gravel, Inc.
5947 Whipple Ave Nw
Canton OH 44720
330 494-5472

(G-9230)
P-AMERICAS LLC
Also Called: Pepsico
815 Oberlin Ave Sw (44647-7876)
PHONE..............................330 837-4224
Jenny Plummet, *Mgr*
EMP: 31
SALES (corp-wide): 91.47B **Publicly Held**
Web: www.pepsico.com
SIC: 2086 Carbonated soft drinks, bottled and canned
HQ: P-Americas Llc
1 Pepsi Way
Somers NY 10509
336 896-5740

(G-9231)
PACE MOLD & MACHINE LLC
8225 Navarre Rd Sw (44646-8813)
P.O. Box 6 (44662-0006)
PHONE..............................330 879-1777
Marilyn Hurst, *Sec*
EMP: 6 **EST:** 1977
SQ FT: 14,000
SALES (est): 784.23K **Privately Held**
Web: www.pacemold.com
SIC: 3544 2821 3089 Forms (molds), for foundry and plastics working machinery; Molding compounds, plastics; Injection molding of plastics

(G-9232)
PER-TECH INC
113 Erie St S (44646-6649)
PHONE..............................330 833-8824
Robert Phillips, *VP*
Randall Hutsell, *
EMP: 28 **EST:** 1986
SQ FT: 90,000
SALES (est): 5.8MM **Privately Held**
Web: www.pertechinc.net

SIC: 3679 3694 Harness assemblies, for electronic use: wire or cable; Engine electrical equipment

(G-9233)
PLASTIC FORMING COMPANY INC
201 Vista Ave Se (44646-7938)
PHONE..............................330 830-5167
Mike Warth, *Mgr*
EMP: 25
SALES (corp-wide): 10.22MM **Privately Held**
Web: www.pfccases.com
SIC: 3089 3086 3161 Blow molded finished plastics products, nec; Plastics foam products; Luggage
PA: The Plastic Forming Company Inc
20 S Bradley Rd
Woodbridge CT 06525
203 397-1338

(G-9234)
POHLMAN PRECISION LLC
Also Called: Pohlman
999 Oberlin Ave Sw (44647-7661)
PHONE..............................636 537-1909
Mark Winham, *Contrlr*
EMP: 40 **EST:** 2015
SALES (est): 659.31K **Privately Held**
SIC: 3451 Screw machine products

(G-9235)
PREMIER BUILDING SOLUTIONS LLC (PA)
480 Nova Dr Se (44646-9597)
PHONE..............................330 244-2907
Derek J Miller, *Pr*
Rebecca J Miller, *VP*
▲ **EMP:** 35 **EST:** 2006
SALES (est): 22.87MM **Privately Held**
Web: www.premierbuildingsolutions.net
SIC: 2891 Adhesives

(G-9236)
R W SCREW PRODUCTS INC
999 Oberlin Ave Sw (44647-7698)
P.O. Box 310 (44648-0310)
PHONE..............................330 837-9211
James Woolley, *CEO*
Larry Longworth, *
EMP: 240 **EST:** 1948
SQ FT: 180,000
SALES (est): 22.87MM **Privately Held**
Web: www.rwscrew.com
SIC: 3451 Screw machine products

(G-9237)
RAH INVESTMENT HOLDING INC
Also Called: Electra - Cord, Inc.
1320 Sanders Ave Sw (44647-7631)
P.O. Box 1197 (44648-1197)
PHONE..............................330 832-8124
Randall A Hutsell, *Pr*
▲ **EMP:** 75 **EST:** 1980
SQ FT: 33,000
SALES (est): 3.14MM
SALES (corp-wide): 15.22B **Publicly Held**
Web: www.electracord.net
SIC: 3699 3357 Extension cords; Nonferrous wiredrawing and insulating
HQ: Tpc Wire & Cable Corp.
9600 Valley View Rd
Macedonia OH 44056

(G-9238)
RETAIN LOYALTY LLC
1250 Sanders Ave Sw (44647-7683)
P.O. Box 6088 (44706-0088)
PHONE..............................330 830-0839
Nancy Schmidt, *Pt*
Karl Schmidt, *Pt*

EMP: 7 EST: 1995
SALES (est): 952.61K **Privately Held**
Web: www.momentsusa.com
SIC: 3993 7313 7331 3555 Signs and
advertising specialties; Electronic media
advertising representatives; Direct mail
advertising services; Mats, advertising and
newspaper

(G-9239)
ROYAL DOCKS BREWING CO LLC
5646 Wales Ave Nw (44646-9096)
PHONE..............................330 353-9103
John Bikis, *Prin*
EMP: 57 **EST:** 2014
SALES (est): 3.49MM **Privately Held**
Web: www.docks.beer
SIC: 2082 Malt beverages

(G-9240)
RW SCREW LLC
999 Oberlin Ave Sw (44647-7661)
PHONE..............................330 837-9211
EMP: 26 **EST:** 2019
SALES (est): 5.98MM **Privately Held**
Web: www.rwscrew.com
SIC: 3599 Machine shop, jobbing and repair

(G-9241)
SHEARERS FOODS LLC (HQ)
Also Called: Shearer's Snacks
100 Lincoln Way E (44646-6634)
PHONE..............................800 428-6843
Mark Mcneil, *CEO*
Montgomery Pooley, *
Fritz Kohmann, *
Alan Fritts, *Corporate Controller*
C J Fraleigh, *
◆ **EMP:** 700 **EST:** 1980
SQ FT: 200,000
SALES (est): 712.7MM
SALES (corp-wide): 14.54B **Privately Held**
Web: www.shearers.com
SIC: 2096 5145 Potato chips and similar
snacks; Snack foods
PA: Clayton, Dubilier & Rice, Inc.
375 Park Ave Fl 18
New York NY 10152
212 407-5200

(G-9242)
SHEARERS FOODS LLC
Also Called: Millennium Plant
4100 Millennium Blvd Se (44646-7449)
PHONE..............................330 767-7969
EMP: 71
SALES (corp-wide): 14.54B **Privately Held**
Web: www.shearers.com
SIC: 2096 Potato chips and similar snacks
HQ: Shearer's Foods, Llc
100 Lincoln Way E
Massillon OH 44646
800 428-6843

(G-9243)
SHERWIN-WILLIAMS COMPANY
Sherwin-Williams
600 Nova Dr Se (44646-8884)
P.O. Box 709 (44648-0709)
PHONE..............................330 830-6000
Thomas M Perry, *Pr*
EMP: 192
SQ FT: 139,645
SALES (corp-wide): 23.1B **Publicly Held**
Web: www.sherwin-williams.com
SIC: 2851 3087 2842 2891 Paints and paint
additives; Custom compound purchased
resins; Stain removers; Adhesives and
sealants
PA: The Sherwin-Williams Company
101 W Prospect Ave

Cleveland OH 44115
216 566-2000

(G-9244)
SMITHERS GROUP INC
1845 Harsh Ave Se (44646-7123)
PHONE..............................330 833-8548
Michael J Hochschwender, *CEO*
EMP: 60
SALES (corp-wide): 122.64MM **Privately
Held**
Web: www.smithers.com
SIC: 3829 8734 8071 Testing equipment:
abrasion, shearing strength, etc.; Product
testing laboratory, safety or performance;
Medical laboratories
PA: The Smithers Group Inc
121 S Main St Ste 300
Akron OH 44308
330 762-7441

(G-9245)
SNACK ALLIANCE INC (DH)
100 Lincoln Way E (44646-6634)
P.O. Box 70 (97838-0070)
PHONE..............................330 767-3426
Robert Shearer, *CEO*
Fredric Kohmann, *
Scott Smith, *
Thomas Shearer, *
◆ **EMP:** 400 **EST:** 1996
SALES (est): 4.87MM
SALES (corp-wide): 14.54B **Privately Held**
Web: www.shearers.com
SIC: 2096 Potato chips and similar snacks
HQ: Shearer's Foods, Llc
100 Lincoln Way E
Massillon OH 44646
800 428-6843

(G-9246)
STERILITE CORPORATION
Also Called: Sterilite
4495 Sterilite St Se (44646-7400)
PHONE..............................330 830-2204
Dennis Forges, *Mgr*
EMP: 239
SALES (corp-wide): 430.83MM **Privately
Held**
Web: www.sterilite.com
SIC: 3089 Plastics kitchenware, tableware,
and houseware
PA: Sterilite Corporation
30 Scales Ln
Townsend MA 01469
978 597-1000

(G-9247)
**THE MASSILLON-CLEVELAND-
AKRONSIGN COMPANY**
Also Called: MCA Industries
681 1st St Sw (44646-6729)
PHONE..............................330 833-3165
EMP: 137
SIC: 3993 Signs and advertising specialties

(G-9248)
TIGER SAND & GRAVEL LLC
411 Oberlin Ave Sw (44647-7826)
PHONE..............................330 833-6325
Leenn Cush, *Off Mgr*
David M Dipietro, *Managing Member*
EMP: 10 **EST:** 2005
SALES (est): 5.02MM **Privately Held**
Web: www.massillonlogistics.com
SIC: 1442 Construction sand and gravel

(G-9249)
TOWER INDUSTRIES LTD
Also Called: Tower Countertops
2101 9th St Sw (44647-7651)

PHONE..............................330 837-2216
EMP: 43 **EST:** 1995
SQ FT: 15,000
SALES (est): 9.02MM **Privately Held**
Web: www.towersurfaces.com
SIC: 3088 Plastics plumbing fixtures

(G-9250)
U S CHEMICAL & PLASTICS
600 Nova Dr Se (44646-8884)
PHONE..............................330 830-6000
John Nelson, *Manager*
◆ **EMP:** 8 **EST:** 2015
SALES (est): 846.12K **Privately Held**
Web: www.uschem.com
SIC: 2899 Chemical preparations, nec

(G-9251)
VEHICLE SYSTEMS INC
Also Called: V S I
7130 Lutz Ave Nw (44646-9343)
PHONE..............................330 854-0535
Ervin Van Denberg, *Pr*
Vivian Vandenberg, *Sec*
Scott Vandenberg, *VP*
EMP: 7 **EST:** 1989
SALES (est): 458.21K **Privately Held**
SIC: 3714 8742 8731 Motor vehicle brake
systems and parts; Management consulting
services; Commercial physical research

(G-9252)
WASHINGTON PRODUCTS INC (PA)
1875 Harsh Ave Se Ste 1 (44646-7182)
P.O. Box 644 (44648-0644)
PHONE..............................330 837-5101
John A Boring, *Pr*
EMP: 10 **EST:** 1972
SQ FT: 30,000
SALES (est): 479.92K
SALES (corp-wide): 479.92K **Privately
Held**
Web: www.wpimass.com
SIC: 3443 3647 3429 2656 Fabricated plate
work (boiler shop); Automotive lighting
fixtures, nec; Hardware, nec; Sanitary food
containers

Masury
Trumbull County

(G-9253)
16363 SCA INC
7800 Addison Rd (44438-1207)
PHONE..............................330 448-0000
William Bilske, *Mgr*
EMP: 6
Web: www.pipelinesinc.com
SIC: 3494 1794 Line strainers, for use in
piping systems; Excavation work
PA: 16363 Sca, Inc.
16363 Saint Clair Ave
East Liverpool OH 43920

(G-9254)
CAPARO BULL MOOSE INC
Also Called: Caparo Bull Moose, Inc.
1433 Standard Ave (44438-1558)
P.O. Box 67 (44438-0067)
PHONE..............................330 448-4878
Dave Thompson, *Mgr*
EMP: 8
SALES (corp-wide): 900.8MM **Privately
Held**
Web: www.bullmoosetube.com
SIC: 3317 Steel pipe and tubes
HQ: Bull Moose Tube Company
1819 Clarkson Rd Ste 100
Chesterfield MO 63017
636 537-1249

(G-9255)
CARAPA INDUSTRIES INC
1080 Bedford Rd (44438-9707)
PHONE..............................330 307-1890
EMP: 6 **EST:** 2019
SALES (est): 279.61K **Privately Held**
SIC: 3999 Manufacturing industries, nec

(G-9256)
ROEMER INDUSTRIES INC
1555 Masury Rd (44438-1702)
PHONE..............................330 448-2000
Joseph L O'toole, *Pr*
Faith Otoole, *
EMP: 71 **EST:** 1937
SQ FT: 52,000
SALES (est): 8.82MM **Privately Held**
Web: www.roemerind.com
SIC: 3479 3469 3993 3613 Name plates:
engraved, etched, etc.; Metal stampings,
nec; Signs and advertising specialties;
Switchgear and switchboard apparatus

Maumee
Lucas County

(G-9257)
AFFYMETRIX INC
434 W Dussel Dr (43537-1685)
PHONE..............................419 887-1233
Kristin Yakimow, *Brnch Mgr*
EMP: 32
SALES (corp-wide): 42.86B **Publicly Held**
Web: www.thermofisher.com
SIC: 3826 Analytical instruments
HQ: Affymetrix, Inc.
3450 Central Expy
Santa Clara CA 95051

(G-9258)
ALSIDE INC
3510 Briarfield Blvd (43537-9504)
PHONE..............................419 865-0934
Todd Anderson, *Brnch Mgr*
EMP: 24
SALES (corp-wide): 1.18B **Privately Held**
Web: www.alside.com
SIC: 5211 5033 3089 1751 Windows, storm:
wood or metal; Siding, except wood; Siding,
plastics; Window and door (prefabricated)
installation
HQ: Alside, Inc.
3773 State Rd
Cuyahoga Falls OH 44223
330 929-1811

(G-9259)
**AMERICAN FRAME CORPORATION
(PA)**
400 Tomahawk Dr (43537-1695)
PHONE..............................419 893-5595
Laura Jajko, *Pr*
Ronald J Mickel, *
Dana Dunbar, *
Larry Haddad, *
Michael Cromly, *
▲ **EMP:** 49 **EST:** 1967
SQ FT: 33,000
SALES (est): 8.42MM
SALES (corp-wide): 8.42MM **Privately
Held**
Web: www.americanframe.com
SIC: 5961 5023 3444 7699 Mail order
house, nec; Homefurnishings; Sheet
metalwork; Picture framing, custom

(G-9260)
ANDERSONS INC
Also Called: Fabrication Division

415 Illinois Ave (43537-1705)
P.O. Box 119 (43537-0119)
PHONE..............................419 891-2930
Michael Andersons, *Brnch Mgr*
EMP: 25
SALES (corp-wide): 11.26B **Publicly Held**
Web: www.andersonsinc.com
SIC: 3599 Machine shop, jobbing and repair
PA: The Andersons Inc
 1947 Briarfield Blvd
 Maumee OH 43537
 419 893-5050

(G-9261)
ANDERSONS INC (PA)
Also Called: Andersons, The
1947 Briarfield Blvd (43537-1690)
P.O. Box 119 (43537-0119)
PHONE..............................419 893-5050
William E Krueger, *Pr*
Patrick E Bowe, *
Brian A Valentine, *Ex VP*
Christine M Castellano, *Corporate Secretary*
Sarah J Zibbel, *Chief Human Resources Officer*
EMP: 150 **EST:** 1947
SALES (est): 11.26B
SALES (corp-wide): 11.26B **Publicly Held**
Web: www.andersonsinc.com
SIC: 0723 5191 2874 4789 Crop preparation
 services for market; Farm supplies;
 Phosphate fertilizers; Railroad car repair

(G-9262)
APPLIED ENERGY TECH INC
Also Called: A E T
1720 Indian Wood Cir Ste E (43537-4000)
PHONE..............................419 537-9052
Terence Seikel, *Ch Bd*
Craig Winn, *Pr*
John Harberts, *VP*
Aaron Faust, *VP*
Terrence Seikel, *CFO*
EMP: 6 **EST:** 2009
SQ FT: 16,100
SALES (est): 555.3K **Privately Held**
Web: www.aetenergy.com
SIC: 3441 Fabricated structural metal

(G-9263)
B & B PRINTING GRAPHICS INC
Also Called: Printing Graphics
1689 Lance Pointe Rd (43537-1603)
PHONE..............................419 893-7068
Beth Stewart, *Pr*
Barney Stewart, *VP*
EMP: 10 **EST:** 1987
SQ FT: 6,000
SALES (est): 337K **Privately Held**
SIC: 2752 Offset printing

(G-9264)
BARNES GROUP INC
370 W Dussel Dr Ste A (43537-1604)
PHONE..............................419 891-9292
Tracy Allison, *Contrlr*
EMP: 172
SALES (corp-wide): 2.6B **Privately Held**
Web: www.asraymond.com
SIC: 5072 3495 Hardware; Wire springs
HQ: Barnes Group Inc.
 123 Main St
 Bristol CT 06010
 860 583-7070

(G-9265)
**BARTON-CAREY MEDICAL PDTS
INC (PA)**
1331 Conant St Ste 102 (43537-1665)
P.O. Box 421 (43552)
PHONE..............................419 887-1285

John H Mays, *Pr*
EMP: 28 **EST:** 1985
SALES (est): 1.92MM
SALES (corp-wide): 1.92MM **Privately
Held**
Web: www.bartoncarey.com
SIC: 3842 2339 2326 Clothing, fire resistant
 and protective; Women's and misses'
 outerwear, nec; Men's and boy's work
 clothing

(G-9266)
BERRY GLOBAL INC
1695 Indian Wood Cir (43537-4003)
PHONE..............................419 887-1602
Estelle Berry, *Brnch Mgr*
EMP: 6
Web: www.berryglobal.com
SIC: 3089 3081 Bottle caps, molded plastics;
 Unsupported plastics film and sheet
HQ: Berry Global, Inc.
 101 Oakley St
 Evansville IN 47710

(G-9267)
**BIONIX SAFETY TECHNOLOGIES
LTD (HQ)**
1670 Indian Wood Cir (43537-4004)
PHONE..............................419 727-0552
Andrew Milligan, *Pr*
Doctor James Huttner, *VP*
EMP: 41 **EST:** 1988
SALES (est): 1.37MM **Privately Held**
Web: www.bionix.com
SIC: 3825 3826 5084 3829 Test equipment
 for electronic and electric measurement;
 Analytical instruments; Industrial machinery
 and equipment; Measuring and controlling
 devices, nec
PA: M&H Medical Holdings, Inc.
 1670 Indian Wood Cir
 Maumee OH 43537

(G-9268)
CDC CORPORATION
1445 Holland Rd (43537-1617)
PHONE..............................715 532-5548
James M Roenitz, *Pr*
David R Sachse, *VP*
▲ **EMP:** 8 **EST:** 1971
SQ FT: 80,000
SALES (est): 920.2K **Privately Held**
SIC: 2542 Partitions and fixtures, except
 wood

(G-9269)
CDC FAB CO
1445 Holland Rd (43537-1617)
PHONE..............................419 866-7705
Peter A Dewhirst, *Prin*
EMP: 13 **EST:** 2016
SALES (est): 4.84MM **Privately Held**
SIC: 3448 Prefabricated metal buildings and
 components

(G-9270)
**DANA AUTO SYSTEMS GROUP LLC
(DH)**
3939 Technology Dr (43537-9194)
PHONE..............................419 887-3000
◆ **EMP:** 37 **EST:** 2007
SALES (est): 274.05MM **Publicly Held**
Web: www.dana.com
SIC: 3714 Motor vehicle parts and
 accessories
HQ: Dana Limited
 3939 Technology Dr
 Maumee OH 43537

(G-9271)
DANA AUTOMOTIVE MFG INC (HQ)
Also Called: Dana Automotive Aftermarket,
3939 Technology Dr (43537-9194)
PHONE..............................419 887-3000
James K Kamsickas, *CEO*
EMP: 101 **EST:** 2001
SALES (est): 9.13MM **Publicly Held**
Web: www.dana.com
SIC: 3714 Motor vehicle parts and
 accessories
PA: Dana Incorporated
 3939 Technology Dr
 Maumee OH 43537

(G-9272)
DANA BRAZIL HOLDINGS I LLC
3939 Technology Dr (43537-9194)
PHONE..............................419 887-3000
Roger Wood, *Pr*
EMP: 250 **EST:** 2004
SALES (est): 23.42MM **Publicly Held**
Web: www.dana.com
SIC: 3714 Motor vehicle parts and
 accessories
HQ: Dana World Trade Corporation
 3939 Technology Dr
 Maumee OH 43537

(G-9273)
**DANA COMMERCIAL VHCL PDTS
LLC (DH)**
Also Called: Dana
3939 Technology Dr (43537-9194)
PHONE..............................419 887-3000
◆ **EMP:** 6 **EST:** 2007
SALES (est): 34.24MM **Publicly Held**
Web: www.dana-industrial.com
SIC: 3714 Motor vehicle parts and
 accessories
HQ: Dana Heavy Vehicle Systems Group,
 Llc
 3939 Technology Dr
 Maumee OH 43537

(G-9274)
**DANA DRIVESHAFT PRODUCTS
LLC (DH)**
Also Called: Dana Driveshaft Products
3939 Technology Dr (43537-9194)
PHONE..............................419 887-3000
▲ **EMP:** 25 **EST:** 2007
SALES (est): 44.1MM **Publicly Held**
Web: www.dana.com
SIC: 3714 Motor vehicle parts and
 accessories
HQ: Dana Automotive Systems Group, Llc
 3939 Technology Dr
 Maumee OH 43537

(G-9275)
DANA GLOBAL PRODUCTS INC (DH)
3939 Technology Dr (43537-9194)
P.O. Box 1000 (43537-7000)
PHONE..............................419 887-3000
Rodney R Filcek, *Pr*
Jeffrey S Bowen, *VP*
Marc S Levin, *Sec*
Lillian Etzkorn, *Treas*
◆ **EMP:** 55 **EST:** 1999
SALES (est): 9.28MM **Publicly Held**
Web: www.dana.com
SIC: 3714 Motor vehicle parts and
 accessories
HQ: Dana Limited
 3939 Technology Dr
 Maumee OH 43537

(G-9276)
**DANA HVY VHCL SYSTEMS GROUP
LL (DH)**
Also Called: Dana Heavy Vhcl Systems Group
3939 Technology Dr (43537-9194)
PHONE..............................419 887-3000
Nick Cole, *Pr*
◆ **EMP:** 49 **EST:** 2007
SALES (est): 45.11MM **Publicly Held**
Web: www.dana.com
SIC: 3714 Motor vehicle parts and
 accessories
HQ: Dana Limited
 3939 Technology Dr
 Maumee OH 43537

(G-9277)
DANA INCORPORATED (PA)
Also Called: Dana
3939 Technology Dr (43537-9194)
P.O. Box 1000 (43537-7000)
PHONE..............................419 887-3000
R Bruce Mcdonald, *Ch Bd*
Timothy R Kraus, *Sr VP*
Douglas H Liedberg, *Sr VP*
EMP: 1058 **EST:** 1904
SALES (est): 10.28B **Publicly Held**
Web: www.dana.com
SIC: 3714 Motor vehicle parts and
 accessories

(G-9278)
DANA LIGHT AXLE MFG LLC (DH)
Also Called: Dana Light Axle Products
3939 Technology Dr (43537-9194)
PHONE..............................419 346-4528
Mark Howard, *Managing Member*
▲ **EMP:** 6 **EST:** 2007
SALES (est): 15.08MM **Publicly Held**
Web: www.dana.com
SIC: 3714 Motor vehicle parts and
 accessories
HQ: Dana Light Axle Products, Llc
 2100 W State Blvd
 Fort Wayne IN 46808

(G-9279)
DANA LIMITED
6515 Maumee Western Rd (43537-9367)
PHONE..............................419 887-3000
EMP: 48
Web: www.dana.com
SIC: 3714 Motor vehicle parts and
 accessories
HQ: Dana Limited
 3939 Technology Dr
 Maumee OH 43537

(G-9280)
DANA LIMITED
Also Called: Dana Automotive Systems
6515 Maumee Western Rd (43537-9367)
PHONE..............................419 887-3000
EMP: 39 **EST:** 2019
SALES (est): 8.87MM **Privately Held**
Web: www.dana.com
SIC: 3714 Motor vehicle parts and
 accessories

(G-9281)
DANA LIMITED
Also Called: Dana Information Technology
580 Longbow Dr (43537-1709)
P.O. Box 537 (43697-0537)
PHONE..............................419 482-2000
Al Henderson, *Mgr*
EMP: 100
Web: www.dana.com
SIC: 3714 Motor vehicle parts and
 accessories
HQ: Dana Limited

3939 Technology Dr
Maumee OH 43537

(G-9282)
DANA LIMITED (HQ)
3939 Technology Dr (43537-9194)
P.O. Box 1000 (43537-7000)
PHONE..............................419 887-3000
James Sweetnam, *Pr*
John Devine, *
Gary Convis, *Vice Chairman*
Marc S Levin, *
James Yost, *
▲ **EMP: 500 EST:** 2007
SALES (est): 1.92B **Publicly Held**
Web: www.dana.com
SIC: 3714 3053 3593 3492 Motor vehicle
parts and accessories; Gaskets and sealing
devices; Fluid power cylinders, hydraulic or
pneumatic; Control valves, fluid power:
hydraulic and pneumatic
PA: Dana Incorporated
3939 Technology Dr
Maumee OH 43537

(G-9283)
**DANA OFF HIGHWAY PRODUCTS
LLC (DH)**
Also Called: Dana
3939 Technology Dr (43537-9194)
P.O. Box 1000 (43537-7000)
PHONE..............................419 887-3000
Nick Stanage, *Pr*
◆ **EMP: 49 EST:** 2007
SALES (est): 9.55MM **Publicly Held**
Web: www.dana.com
SIC: 3714 Motor vehicle parts and
accessories
HQ: Dana Heavy Vehicle Systems Group,
Llc
3939 Technology Dr
Maumee OH 43537

(G-9284)
DANA SAC USA INC
Also Called: Dana
3939 Technology Dr (43537-9194)
PHONE..............................419 887-3550
EMP: 8 EST: 2019
SALES (est): 4.27MM **Publicly Held**
Web: www.dana.com
SIC: 3714 Motor vehicle parts and
accessories
PA: Dana Incorporated
3939 Technology Dr
Maumee OH 43537

(G-9285)
**DANA SEALING MANUFACTURING
LLC (DH)**
3939 Technology Dr (43537-9194)
▲ **EMP: 16 EST:** 2007
SALES (est): 32.94MM **Publicly Held**
Web: www.dana.com
SIC: 3714 Motor vehicle parts and
accessories
HQ: Dana Sealing Products, Llc
3939 Technology Dr
Maumee OH 43537

(G-9286)
**DANA SEALING PRODUCTS LLC
(DH)**
3939 Technology Dr (43537-9194)
P.O. Box 1000 (43537-7000)
PHONE..............................419 887-3000
▲ **EMP: 18 EST:** 2007
SALES (est): 154.52MM **Publicly Held**
Web: www.dana.com

SIC: 3714 Motor vehicle parts and
accessories
HQ: Dana Automotive Systems Group, Llc
3939 Technology Dr
Maumee OH 43537

(G-9287)
**DANA STRUCTURAL PRODUCTS
LLC (DH)**
Also Called: Dana Structural Products
3939 Technology Dr (43537-9194)
PHONE..............................419 887-3000
EMP: 6 EST: 2007
SALES (est): 5.52MM **Publicly Held**
Web: www.dana.com
SIC: 3714 Motor vehicle parts and
accessories
HQ: Dana Automotive Systems Group, Llc
3939 Technology Dr
Maumee OH 43537

(G-9288)
**DANA THERMAL PRODUCTS LLC
(DH)**
Also Called: Dana Thermal Products
3939 Technology Dr (43537-9194)
PHONE..............................419 887-3000
▲ **EMP: 13 EST:** 2007
SALES (est): 30.2MM **Publicly Held**
Web: www.dana.com
SIC: 3714 Motor vehicle parts and
accessories
HQ: Dana Automotive Systems Group, Llc
3939 Technology Dr
Maumee OH 43537

(G-9289)
**DANA WORLD TRADE
CORPORATION (DH)**
3939 Technology Dr (43537-9194)
PHONE..............................419 887-3000
Kenneth A Hiltz, *CFO*
EMP: 14 EST: 2006
SALES (est): 25.74MM **Publicly Held**
Web: www.dana.com
SIC: 3714 Motor vehicle parts and
accessories
HQ: Dana Limited
3939 Technology Dr
Maumee OH 43537

(G-9290)
DENTSPLY SIRONA INC
520 Illinois Ave (43537-1708)
PHONE..............................419 893-5672
Garyn Livecchi, *Genl Mgr*
EMP: 41
SQ FT: 4,000
SALES (corp-wide): 3.79B **Publicly Held**
Web: www.dentsplysirona.com
SIC: 3843 Teeth, artificial (not made in
dental laboratories)
PA: Dentsply Sirona Inc.
13320 Ballantyne Corp Pl
Charlotte NC 28277
844 848-0137

(G-9291)
DENTSPLY SIRONA INC
Ransom & Randolph
3535 Briarfield Blvd (43537-9383)
PHONE..............................419 865-9497
Dan Nixon, *Brnch Mgr*
EMP: 25
SALES (corp-wide): 3.79B **Publicly Held**
Web: www.dentsplysirona.com
SIC: 3844 2821 3915 3843 X-ray apparatus
and tubes; Molding compounds, plastics;
Jewelers' castings; Impression material,
dental
PA: Dentsply Sirona Inc.

13320 Ballantyne Corp Pl
Charlotte NC 28277
844 848-0137

(G-9292)
EATON AEROQUIP LLC
1660 Indian Wood Cir (43537-4004)
PHONE..............................419 891-7775
Howard Selland, *Pr*
EMP: 1373
SIC: 3052 3594 3593 3561 Rubber hose;
Fluid power pumps and motors; Fluid
power cylinders and actuators; Pumps and
pumping equipment
HQ: Eaton Aeroquip Llc
1000 Eaton Blvd
Cleveland OH 44122
440 523-5000

(G-9293)
**GENIUS SOLUTIONS ENGRG CO
(HQ)**
Also Called: Gs Engineering
6421 Monclova Rd (43537-9760)
PHONE..............................419 794-9914
Grigoriy Grinberg, *Pr*
Matthew Shade, *
EMP: 39 EST: 2004
SALES (est): 10.66MM
SALES (corp-wide): 720.63MM **Publicly
Held**
Web: www.mold-tech.com
SIC: 8711 2821 7389 Mechanical
engineering; Thermoplastic materials;
Engraving service
PA: Standex International Corporation
23 Keewaydin Dr
Salem NH 03079
603 893-9701

(G-9294)
HALL-TOLEDO INC
525 W Sophia St (43537-1847)
P.O. Box 1501 (43537-8501)
PHONE..............................419 893-4334
Andrew F Boesel, *Pr*
EMP: 10 EST: 1928
SQ FT: 5,000
SALES (est): 2.34MM **Privately Held**
Web: www.hall-toledo.com
SIC: 3546 3714 Power-driven handtools;
Motor vehicle parts and accessories
PA: Michabo Inc
525 W Sophia St
Maumee OH 43537

(G-9295)
HAMMILL MANUFACTURING CO (PA)
Also Called: Impact Cutoff Div
360 Tomahawk Dr (43537-1612)
P.O. Box 1450 (43537-8450)
PHONE..............................419 476-0789
John Hammill, *Ch Bd*
John E Hamill Junior, *Pr*
Carl Barnard, *
Robert Doubler, *
EMP: 100 EST: 1955
SQ FT: 80,000
SALES (est): 22.18MM
SALES (corp-wide): 22.18MM **Privately
Held**
Web: www.hammillmedical.com
SIC: 3842 3545 Implants, surgical; Chucks:
drill, lathe, or magnetic (machine tool
accessories)

(G-9296)
HELM INSTRUMENT COMPANY INC
361 W Dussel Dr (43537-1649)
PHONE..............................419 893-4356
Richard T Wilhelm, *Pr*

Nancy Wilhelm, *Sec*
Mary L Tice, *VP*
Michael Wilhelm, *VP*
Thomas Wilhelm, *VP*
EMP: 34 EST: 1962
SQ FT: 12,500
SALES (est): 4.42MM **Privately Held**
Web: www.helminstrument.com
SIC: 3845 3829 3625 Patient monitoring
apparatus, nec; Pulse analyzers, nuclear
monitoring; Motor starters and controllers,
electric

(G-9297)
IMAGE BY J & K LLC
Also Called: Image
1575 Henthorne Dr (43537-1372)
PHONE..............................888 667-6929
James Land Iv, *Managing Member*
EMP: 19 EST: 2006
SQ FT: 10,000
SALES (est): 967.57K **Privately Held**
SIC: 3589 7217 7349 7342 Floor washing
and polishing machines, commercial;
Carpet and upholstery cleaning; Building
and office cleaning services; Rest room
cleaning service

(G-9298)
INNOVATIVE CONTROLS CORP
6528 Weatherfield Ct (43537-9468)
PHONE..............................419 691-6684
Louis M Soltis, *Pr*
Anson F Schultz, *
EMP: 18 EST: 1974
SALES (est): 4.72MM **Privately Held**
Web: www.innovativecontrolscorp.com
SIC: 3613 3535 8711 3823 Control panels,
electric; Conveyors and conveying
equipment; Engineering services; Process
control instruments

(G-9299)
ISHIKAWA GASKET AMERICA INC
1745 Indian Wood Cir Ste 125
(43537-4167)
PHONE..............................419 353-7300
Toshio Matsuzaki, *Pr*
▲ **EMP: 10 EST:** 1992
SQ FT: 3,000
SALES (est): 936.57K **Privately Held**
Web: www.ishikawaamerica.com
SIC: 3053 Gaskets, all materials
PA: Ishikawa Gasket Co., Ltd.
2-5-5, Toranomon
Minato-Ku TKY 105-0

(G-9300)
JONES-HAMILTON CO (PA)
Also Called: Jones-Hamilton Co.
570 Longbow Dr (43537-1724)
PHONE..............................888 858-4425
Bernard D Murphy, *Pr*
Brian Brooks C.p.a., *CFO*
Charlie Wheeler, *
Kimberly Sosko C.p.a., *CAO*
◆ **EMP: 95 EST:** 1949
SALES (est): 128.65MM
SALES (corp-wide): 128.65MM **Privately
Held**
Web: www.jones-hamilton.com
SIC: 2819 Hydrochloric acid

(G-9301)
**KELLERMYER BERGENSONS SVCS
LLC**
6546 Weatherfield Ct (43537-9252)
PHONE..............................419 867-4300
Mark Minasian, *CEO*
EMP: 60
SALES (corp-wide): 620.83MM **Privately
Held**

Web: www.kbs-services.com
SIC: 3589 Commercial cleaning equipment
PA: Kellermeyer Bergensons Services, Llc
3605 Ocean Rnch Blvd Ste
Oceanside CA 92056
760 631-5111

(G-9302)
KEYSTONE AUTO GLASS INC
2255 Linden Ct (43537-2338)
PHONE..............................419 509-0497
Neal Golding, *Pr*
Alan Golding, *
Andrew K Golding, *
Brian Silver, *
EMP: 100 EST: 1953
SQ FT: 20,000
SALES (est): 590.23K **Privately Held**
SIC: 3714 7536 5531 5013 Motor vehicle parts and accessories; Automotive glass replacement shops; Auto and home supply stores; Motor vehicle supplies and new parts

(G-9303)
KUHLMAN CORPORATION (PA)
Also Called: Kuhlman Construction Products
1845 Indian Wood Cir (43537-4072)
P.O. Box 714 (43697-0714)
PHONE..............................419 897-6000
Timothy L Goligoski, *Pr*
Kenneth Kuhlman, *
Terry Schaefer, *
▲ **EMP: 32 EST:** 1901
SQ FT: 18,000
SALES (est): 42.49MM
SALES (corp-wide): 42.49MM **Privately Held**
Web: www.gerkencompanies.com
SIC: 4226 5032 3273 Special warehousing and storage, nec; Brick, stone, and related material; Ready-mixed concrete

(G-9304)
LINE DRIVE SPORTZ-LCRC LLC
2901 Key St Ste 1 (43537-2421)
PHONE..............................419 794-7150
EMP: 6 EST: 2009
SALES (est): 201.07K **Privately Held**
SIC: 3949 Sporting and athletic goods, nec

(G-9305)
M&H MEDICAL HOLDINGS INC (PA)
Also Called: Bionix Radiation Therapy
1670 Indian Wood Cir (43537-4004)
PHONE..............................419 727-8421
Andrew J Milligan, *Pr*
James J Huttner, *
Dawn Hall, *
▲ **EMP: 35 EST:** 1984
SALES (est): 4.04MM **Privately Held**
Web: www.bionix.com
SIC: 3841 3829 Surgical and medical instruments; Measuring and controlling devices, nec

(G-9306)
MAGNESIUM PRODUCTS GROUP INC
Also Called: M P G
3928 Azalea Cir (43537-9191)
PHONE..............................310 971-5799
Bradley A Hirou, *Pr*
Ronald W Banks, *Ex VP*
Steve Hubble, *COO*
EMP: 6 EST: 2008
SALES (est): 301.24K **Privately Held**
SIC: 3441 Fabricated structural metal

(G-9307)
MAUMEE ASSEMBLY & STAMPING LLC
920 Illinois Ave (43537-1716)
PHONE..............................419 304-2887
Stanley Chlebowski, *CEO*
Joseph Munren Ctrl, *Prin*
Jim Young, *
EMP: 150 EST: 2009
SQ FT: 800,000
SALES (est): 8.77MM **Privately Held**
Web: www.mastamping.com
SIC: 3469 Stamping metal for the trade

(G-9308)
MAUMEE HOSE & FITTING INC
Also Called: Maumee Hose & Belting Co
720 Illinois Ave Ste H (43537-1750)
PHONE..............................419 893-7252
James C Walsh, *Pr*
Karen Walsh, *VP*
EMP: 7 EST: 1988
SQ FT: 10,000
SALES (est): 401.53K **Privately Held**
SIC: 3429 5085 Clamps, couplings, nozzles, and other metal hose fittings; Hose, belting, and packing

(G-9309)
METAL FORMING & COINING LLC (PA)
Also Called: Netform
1007 Illinois Ave (43537-1752)
PHONE..............................419 893-8748
Tim Cripsey, *Pr*
Kurt Geisheimer, *
Paul Kessler, *
Diana Wienrich, *
EMP: 100 EST: 1953
SQ FT: 103,000
SALES (est): 20.68MM
SALES (corp-wide): 20.68MM **Privately Held**
Web: www.netform.com
SIC: 3462 Iron and steel forgings

(G-9310)
MIRROR PUBLISHING CO INC
Also Called: Mirror, The
113 W Wayne St (43537-2150)
PHONE..............................419 893-8135
Michael Mccarthy, *Pr*
EMP: 7 EST: 2007
SQ FT: 3,000
SALES (est): 776.6K **Privately Held**
Web: www.themirrornewspaper.com
SIC: 2711 Newspapers: publishing only, not printed on site

(G-9311)
MITCHS WELDING & HITCHES
802 Kingsbury St (43537-1826)
PHONE..............................419 893-3117
James Mitchell, *Pr*
EMP: 8 EST: 1980
SQ FT: 5,000
SALES (est): 771.79K **Privately Held**
Web: www.mitchsweldingandhitches.com
SIC: 3537 5561 Industrial trucks and tractors ; Recreational vehicle parts and accessories

(G-9312)
PRESTIGE STORE INTERIORS INC
427 W Dussel Dr # 209 (43537-4208)
PHONE..............................419 476-2106
Jeffrey Simenski, *Pr*
Blain Stobinski, *VP*
EMP: 6 EST: 1993
SALES (est): 680.08K **Privately Held**

SIC: 2542 Partitions and fixtures, except wood

(G-9313)
PRO-PAK INDUSTRIES INC (PA)
1125 Ford St (43537-1703)
P.O. Box 1176 (43537-8176)
PHONE..............................419 729-0751
Leo Deiger, *Pr*
Anthony Deiger, *VP*
Charles M Deiger, *Sec*
EMP: 98 EST: 1948
SALES (est): 25.21MM
SALES (corp-wide): 25.21MM **Privately Held**
Web: www.pro-pakindustries.com
SIC: 2653 Boxes, corrugated: made from purchased materials

(G-9314)
RANSOM & RANDOLPH LLC (PA)
520 Illinois Ave (43537-1708)
PHONE..............................419 865-9497
Daniel Nixon, *Pr*
EMP: 6 EST: 2021
SALES (est): 2.7MM
SALES (corp-wide): 2.7MM **Privately Held**
Web: www.ransom-randolph.com
SIC: 3365 Aerospace castings, aluminum

(G-9315)
ROLLED ALLOYS INC (PA)
6630 Monclova Rd (43537-9759)
PHONE..............................800 521-0332
Thomas Nichol, *Pr*
Dale G Kuntz, *
Linda Roemer, *
◆ **EMP: 92 EST:** 1953
SQ FT: 83,000
SALES (est): 212.62MM
SALES (corp-wide): 212.62MM **Privately Held**
Web: www.rolledalloys.com
SIC: 5051 3369 3341 3317 Steel; Nonferrous foundries, nec; Secondary nonferrous metals; Steel pipe and tubes

(G-9316)
SENATOR INTERNATIONAL INC (HQ)
Also Called: Allermuir
4111 N Jerome Rd (43537-7100)
PHONE..............................419 887-5806
Mark Brettschneider, *Pr*
▲ **EMP: 22 EST:** 2007
SALES (est): 25.94MM
SALES (corp-wide): 251.89MM **Privately Held**
Web: www.allermuir.com
SIC: 5712 2522 2521 Office furniture; Office furniture, except wood; Wood office furniture
PA: Senator International Limited
Sykeside Drive Altham Business Park
Accrington LANCS BB5 5

(G-9317)
SERVICE SPRING CORP
6615 Maumee Western Rd (43537-9368)
PHONE..............................419 867-0212
Michael Mcalear, *Brnch Mgr*
EMP: 7
SALES (corp-wide): 24.02MM **Privately Held**
Web: www.servicespring.com
SIC: 5085 3493 Industrial supplies; Steel springs, except wire
PA: Service Spring Corp.
1703 Toll Gate Dr
Maumee OH 43537
419 838-6081

(G-9318)
SERVICE SPRING CORP (PA)
1703 Toll Gate Dr (43537-1673)
PHONE..............................419 838-6081
Michael Mcalear, *CEO*
Clarence J Veigel, *
Evelyn F Veigel, *
Allen Bishop, *
▼ **EMP: 69 EST:** 1962
SQ FT: 98,000
SALES (est): 24.02MM
SALES (corp-wide): 24.02MM **Privately Held**
Web: www.servicespring.com
SIC: 3493 Steel springs, except wire

(G-9319)
SPOSIE LLC
4064 Technology Dr (43537-9738)
PHONE..............................888 977-2229
Ryan Wright, *Managing Member*
EMP: 12 EST: 2015
SQ FT: 35,000
SALES (est): 1.4MM **Privately Held**
Web: www.sposie.com
SIC: 2676 Infant and baby paper products

(G-9320)
STEPPING STONE ENTERPRISES INC
Also Called: Minuteman Press
1689 Lance Pointe Rd (43537-1603)
PHONE..............................419 472-0505
Steven Heaney, *Pr*
Ronald R Kimler, *VP*
Vicki Kimler, *Sec*
EMP: 10 EST: 1982
SALES (est): 894.5K **Privately Held**
Web: www.mmptoledo.com
SIC: 2752 Offset printing

(G-9321)
STONECO INC
Also Called: Shelley Company
1360 Ford St (43537-1733)
PHONE..............................419 893-7645
Lee Wehner, *Mgr*
EMP: 40
SALES (corp-wide): 34.95B **Privately Held**
Web: www.shellyco.com
SIC: 1422 5032 Crushed and broken limestone; Stone, crushed or broken
HQ: Stoneco, Inc.
1700 Fostoria Ave Ste 200
Findlay OH 45840
419 422-8854

(G-9322)
SUN CHEMICAL CORPORATION
Ink & Plates
1380 Ford St (43537-1733)
PHONE..............................419 891-3514
Wes Lucas, *Mgr*
EMP: 71
SQ FT: 68,000
Web: www.sunchemical.com
SIC: 2893 Printing ink
HQ: Sun Chemical Corporation
35 Waterview Blvd
Parsippany NJ 07054
973 404-6000

(G-9323)
SURFACE COMBUSTION INC (PA)
1700 Indian Wood Cir (43537-4067)
P.O. Box 428 (43537-0428)
PHONE..............................419 891-7150
William J Bernard Junior, *Pr*
Max Hoetzl, *
William B J Bernard, *Dir*
▲ **EMP: 100 EST:** 1987

SQ FT: 36,000
SALES (est): 22.27MM
SALES (corp-wide): 22.27MM **Privately Held**
Web: www.surfacecombustion.com
SIC: 3567 Industrial furnaces and ovens

(G-9324)
THE ANDERSONS CLYMERS ETHANOL LLC
1947 Briarfield Blvd (43537-1690)
P.O. Box 119 (43537-0119)
PHONE..................574 722-2627
EMP: 33
SIC: 2869 Ethyl alcohol, ethanol

(G-9325)
TIAMA AMERICAS INC
6500 Weatherfield Ct (43537-9468)
PHONE..................269 274-3107
EMP: 24 **EST:** 2015
SALES (est): 10.93MM **Privately Held**
Web: www.tiama.com
SIC: 3221 Glass containers
HQ: Tiama
215 Chemin Du Grand Revoyet
Saint-Genis-Laval ARA 69230

(G-9326)
TILT-OR-LIFT INC (PA)
124 E Dudley St (43537-3366)
P.O. Box 8728 (43537-8728)
PHONE..................419 893-6944
Dennis Rober, *Pr*
EMP: 6 **EST:** 1973
SQ FT: 1,400
SALES (est): 732.14K
SALES (corp-wide): 732.14K **Privately Held**
Web: www.tiltorlift.com
SIC: 3537 5084 Lift trucks, industrial: fork, platform, straddle, etc.; Industrial machinery and equipment

(G-9327)
TOLEDO TRANSDUCERS INC
Also Called: Toledo Integrated Systems
1345 Ford St (43537-1732)
PHONE..................419 724-4170
Mark Storer, *Pr*
Daniel N Falcone, *
Randall W Seed, *
EMP: 40 **EST:** 1976
SALES (est): 4.88MM **Privately Held**
Web: www.ttoledo.com
SIC: 3823 3829 3625 3613 Process control instruments; Measuring and controlling devices, nec; Relays and industrial controls; Switchgear and switchboard apparatus

(G-9328)
US COEXCELL INC
640 Mingo Dr (43537-1704)
PHONE..................419 897-9110
Christopher Nelson, *Pr*
Dennis Puening, *VP*
▲ **EMP:** 41 **EST:** 1991
SQ FT: 40,000
SALES (est): 13.82MM
SALES (corp-wide): 165.45MM **Privately Held**
Web: www.coexcellinc.com
SIC: 3089 Plastics containers, except foam
PA: Cleveland Steel Container Corporation
100 Executive Pkwy
Hudson OH 44236
440 349-8000

(G-9329)
VICKERS INTERNATIONAL INC
3000 Strayer Rd (43537-9529)
PHONE..................419 867-2200
Darryl F Allen, *Pr*
James Oathout, *Sec*
Gary J Findling, *Treas*
EMP: 7 **EST:** 1984
SQ FT: 21,000
SALES (est): 2.49MM **Privately Held**
SIC: 3561 3594 3491 Pumps and pumping equipment; Motors, pneumatic; Industrial valves
HQ: Eaton Corporation
1000 Eaton Blvd
Cleveland OH 44122
440 523-5000

(G-9330)
WILLIAMS CONCRETE INC
1350 Ford St (43537-1733)
PHONE..................419 893-3251
Mark Williams, *Pr*
Terry Schaefer, *VP Fin*
EMP: 30 **EST:** 2001
SALES (est): 1.24MM
SALES (corp-wide): 42.49MM **Privately Held**
Web: www.gerkencompanies.com
SIC: 3273 Ready-mixed concrete
PA: Kuhlman Corporation
1845 Indian Wood Cir
Maumee OH 43537
419 897-6000

(G-9331)
YZ ENTERPRISES INC
Also Called: Almondina Brand Biscuits
1930 Indian Wood Cir Ste 100 (43537-4001)
PHONE..................419 893-8777
Yuval N Zaliouk, *CEO*
Susan M Zaliouk, *Ex VP*
Jack Hunter, *VP*
Christopher Moody, *VP Opers*
EMP: 20 **EST:** 1990
SQ FT: 12,500
SALES (est): 4.17MM **Privately Held**
Web: www.almondina.com
SIC: 2052 Cookies

Mayfield Heights
Cuyahoga County

(G-9332)
BECK ALUMINUM ALLOYS LTD
6150 Parkland Blvd Ste 260 (44124-4103)
PHONE..................216 861-4455
EMP: 63
SIC: 3341 Secondary nonferrous metals

(G-9333)
FERRO INTERNATIONAL SVCS INC (DH)
6060 Parkland Blvd Ste 250 (44124-4225)
PHONE..................216 875-5600
EMP: 8 **EST:** 2007
SALES (est): 3MM
SALES (corp-wide): 1.88B **Privately Held**
Web: www.vibrantz.com
SIC: 2816 Color pigments
HQ: Vibrantz Corporation
6060 Prkland Blvd Ste 250
Mayfield Heights OH 44124
216 875-5600

(G-9334)
GANEDEN BIOTECH INC
Also Called: Ganeden

5800 Landerbrook Dr Ste 300 (44124-4083)
PHONE..................440 229-5200
EMP: 21
Web: www.bc30probiotic.com
SIC: 2834 Pharmaceutical preparations

(G-9335)
MATERION ADVNCED MTLS TECH SVC (HQ)
Also Called: Materion Microlectronics Svcs
6070 Parkland Blvd (44124-4191)
PHONE..................216 486-4200
Leo Linehan, *Pr*
Edward Strother, *
Christopher Eberhardt, *
▲ **EMP:** 74 **EST:** 1980
SQ FT: 16,000
SALES (est): 13.16MM **Publicly Held**
Web: www.materion.com
SIC: 3341 3559 3356 3369 Secondary nonferrous metals; Silver recovery equipment; Nonferrous rolling and drawing, nec; Nonferrous foundries, nec
PA: Materion Corporation
6070 Parkland Blvd
Mayfield Heights OH 44124

(G-9336)
MATERION BRUSH INC (HQ)
Also Called: Materion
6070 Parkland Blvd Ste 1 (44124-4191)
PHONE..................216 486-4200
Michael C Hasychak, *Pr*
▲ **EMP:** 100 **EST:** 1931
SALES (est): 376.71MM **Publicly Held**
Web: www.materion.com
SIC: 3351 3356 3264 3339 Copper and copper alloy sheet, strip, plate, and products; Nickel and nickel alloy pipe, plates, sheets, etc.; Porcelain parts for electrical devices, molded; Beryllium metal
PA: Materion Corporation
6070 Parkland Blvd
Mayfield Heights OH 44124

(G-9337)
MATERION CORPORATION (PA)
6070 Parkland Blvd (44124-4191)
PHONE..................216 486-4200
Jugal K Vijayvargiya, *Pr*
Vinod M Khilnani, *Non-Executive Chairman of the Board*
Shelly M Chadwick, *VP Fin*
Gregory R Chemnitz, *VP*
◆ **EMP:** 150 **EST:** 1931
SQ FT: 79,100
SALES (est): 1.68B **Publicly Held**
Web: www.materion.com
SIC: 3339 3351 3356 3341 Beryllium metal; Copper and copper alloy sheet, strip, plate, and products; Nickel and nickel alloy pipe, plates, sheets, etc.; Secondary precious metals

(G-9338)
NATURAL BEAUTY HC EXPRESS
6809 Mayfield Rd Apt 550 (44124-2262)
PHONE..................440 459-1776
Stacey Carlton, *Mgr*
EMP: 7 **EST:** 2010
SALES (est): 236.21K **Privately Held**
SIC: 3999 Furniture, barber and beauty shop

(G-9339)
ONX ACQUISITION LLC
Also Called: Onx Enterprise Solutions
5910 Landerbrook Dr Ste 250 (44124-6508)
PHONE..................440 569-2300
EMP: 300

SIC: 7372 7379 Business oriented computer software; Computer related consulting services

(G-9340)
PRIEST SERVICES INC (PA)
1127 Linda St 5885 Landerbrook Dr Ste 140 (44124)
PHONE..................440 333-1123
Howard E Priest, *Ch Bd*
Homer S Taft, *Pr*
Carol Kuehnle, *Prin*
Donald W Farley, *Prin*
Judy Oneacre, *Prin*
EMP: 8 **EST:** 1950
SQ FT: 40,000
SALES (est): 2.31MM
SALES (corp-wide): 2.31MM **Privately Held**
SIC: 3275 2891 2851 Gypsum products; Adhesives and sealants; Paints and allied products

(G-9341)
ROCKWELL AUTOMATION INC
1 Allen Bradley Dr (44124-6118)
PHONE..................440 646-5000
Sandra Klosowski, *Brnch Mgr*
EMP: 99
SQ FT: 156,653
Web: www.rockwellautomation.com
SIC: 3625 Electric controls and control accessories, industrial
PA: Rockwell Automation, Inc.
1201 S 2nd St
Milwaukee WI 53204

(G-9342)
TRIMBLE TRNSP ENTP SLTIONS INC (HQ)
6085 Parkland Blvd (44124-4184)
PHONE..................216 831-6606
David Wangler, *Pr*
David Mook, *
Jeffrey Ritter, *
Scott Vanselous, *
David Schildmeyer, *
EMP: 125 **EST:** 1986
SQ FT: 32,500
SALES (est): 31.84MM
SALES (corp-wide): 3.68B **Publicly Held**
Web: transportation.trimble.com
SIC: 7372 Business oriented computer software
PA: Trimble Inc.
10368 Westmoor Dr
Westminster CO 80021
720 887-6100

(G-9343)
TRUE NORTH ENERGY LLC
Also Called: Truenorth Energy
6411 Mayfield Rd (44124-3214)
PHONE..................440 442-0060
EMP: 26
SALES (corp-wide): 82.74MM **Privately Held**
Web: www.truenorthstores.com
SIC: 5541 1382 Filling stations, gasoline; Oil and gas exploration services
PA: True North Energy, Llc
10346 Brecksville Rd
Brecksville OH 44141
877 245-9336

(G-9344)
VIBRANTZ CORPORATION (DH)
Also Called: Ferro
6060 Parkland Blvd Ste 250 (44124-4225)
PHONE..................216 875-5600
Glenn Fish, *Pr*

Mark Whitney, *Ex VP*
◆ **EMP:** 90 **EST:** 1919
SALES (est): 1.13B
SALES (corp-wide): 1.88B **Privately Held**
Web: www.vibrantz.com
SIC: 2851 2816 Paints and allied products; Color pigments
HQ: Vibrantz Technologies Inc.
16945 Nrthchase Dr Ste 20
Houston TX 77060
646 747-4222

Mayfield Village
Cuyahoga County

(G-9345)
OMNI SYSTEMS LLC (PA)
701 Beta Dr (44143-2367)
PHONE..............................216 377-5160
EMP: 100 **EST:** 1990
SALES (est): 45.7MM **Privately Held**
Web: www.omnisystem.com
SIC: 2759 Flexographic printing

(G-9346)
PREFORMED LINE PRODUCTS CO (PA)
660 Beta Dr (44143-2398)
P.O. Box 91129 (44101-3129)
PHONE..............................440 461-5200
Dennis F Mckenna, *CEO*
Robert G Ruhlman, *
J Ryan Ruhlman, *
Andrew S Klaus, *CFO*
EMP: 436 **EST:** 1947
SALES (est): 593.71MM
SALES (corp-wide): 593.71MM **Publicly Held**
Web: www.plp.com
SIC: 3644 3661 1623 Pole line hardware; Fiber optics communications equipment; Water, sewer, and utility lines

(G-9347)
QUALITY ELECTRODYNAMICS LLC
6655 Beta Dr Ste 100 (44143-2380)
PHONE..............................440 638-5106
Michael P Esposito Junior, *Ch*
Albert B Ratner, *Ch*
Debbie Sun, *CFO*
EMP: 115 **EST:** 2005
SALES (est): 24.1MM **Privately Held**
Web: www.qedinnovations.com
SIC: 3841 Surgical and medical instruments
PA: Canon Inc.
3-30-2, Shimomaruko
Ota-Ku TKY 146-0

Mc Arthur
Vinton County

(G-9348)
AUSTIN POWDER COMPANY
Also Called: Red Diamond Plant
430 Powder Plant Rd (45651-8260)
P.O. Box 317 (45651-0317)
PHONE..............................740 596-5286
Keith Mills, *Mgr*
EMP: 225
SALES (corp-wide): 749.73MM **Privately Held**
Web: www.austinpowder.com
SIC: 2892 Explosives
HQ: Austin Powder Company
25800 Science Park Dr # 300
Cleveland OH 44122
216 464-2400

(G-9349)
CROWNOVER LUMBER COMPANY INC (PA)
501 Fairview Ave (45651)
P.O. Box 301 (45651-0301)
PHONE..............................740 596-5229
Lundy Crownover, *Pr*
EMP: 60 **EST:** 1959
SQ FT: 2,000
SALES (est): 4.61MM
SALES (corp-wide): 4.61MM **Privately Held**
Web: www.crownoverlumber.com
SIC: 2421 2426 Lumber: rough, sawed, or planed; Hardwood dimension and flooring mills

(G-9350)
SUPERIOR HARDWOODS OHIO INC
62581 Us Highway 50 (45651-8414)
P.O. Box 320 (45651-0320)
PHONE..............................740 596-2561
Emmett Conway, *Pr*
Emmett Conway, *Pr*
Adam Conway, *
EMP: 6 **EST:** 1979
SQ FT: 11,000
SALES (est): 747.01K **Privately Held**
Web:
www.superiorhardwoodsofohio.com
SIC: 2421 2426 Sawmills and planing mills, general; Hardwood dimension and flooring mills

Mc Clure
Henry County

(G-9351)
INDUSTRIAL FLUID MGT INC
2926 Us Highway 6 (43534-9730)
PHONE..............................419 748-7460
Richard Bennett, *Pr*
EMP: 19 **EST:** 1993
SALES (est): 10.53MM
SALES (corp-wide): 458.93MM **Privately Held**
Web: www.ifmenviro.com
SIC: 3589 Water treatment equipment, industrial
HQ: Poggemeyer Design Group, Inc.
1168 N Main St
Bowling Green OH 43402
419 244-8074

Mc Comb
Hancock County

(G-9352)
CRUSHPROOF TUBING CO (PA)
100 North St (45858-7539)
P.O. Box 668 (45858-0668)
PHONE..............................419 293-2111
Vance M Kramer Junior, *Pr*
Richard Hollington, *
EMP: 34 **EST:** 1950
SQ FT: 28,000
SALES (est): 5.73MM
SALES (corp-wide): 5.73MM **Privately Held**
Web: www.crushproof.com
SIC: 3052 2822 Rubber and plastics hose and beltings; Synthetic rubber

(G-9353)
HEARTHSIDE FOOD SOLUTIONS LLC
Also Called: Consolidated Biscuit Company
312 Rader Rd (45858-9751)

PHONE..............................419 293-2911
Robert Cummings, *Brnch Mgr*
EMP: 2500
Web: www.hearthsidefoods.com
SIC: 2052 Cookies
PA: Hearthside Food Solutions, Llc
3333 Finley Rd Ste 800
Downers Grove IL 60515

(G-9354)
K & L READY MIX INC
5511 State Route 613 (45858-9345)
PHONE..............................419 293-2937
Gary Langhals, *Dir*
EMP: 10
SALES (corp-wide): 2.68MM **Privately Held**
Web: www.kandlreadymix.com
SIC: 3273 Ready-mixed concrete
PA: K & L Ready Mix Inc
10391 State Route 15
Ottawa OH 45875
419 523-4376

Mc Cutchenville
Wyandot County

(G-9355)
BUCKYS MACHINE AND FAB LTD
8376 S County Road 47 (44844-9620)
PHONE..............................419 981-5050
EMP: 7 **EST:** 1988
SQ FT: 5,500
SALES (est): 717.12K **Privately Held**
SIC: 3599 Machine shop, jobbing and repair

Mc Dermott
Scioto County

(G-9356)
WALLER BROTHERS STONE COMPANY
744 Mcdermott Rushtown Rd (45652-8906)
P.O. Box 157 (45652-0157)
PHONE..............................740 858-1948
Frank L Waller, *Pr*
Lowell M Shope, *
EMP: 14 **EST:** 1908
SQ FT: 5,175
SALES (est): 2.5MM **Privately Held**
Web: www.wallerbrothersstone.com
SIC: 3281 3821 2511 Stone, quarrying and processing of own stone products; Laboratory apparatus and furniture; Wood household furniture

Mc Donald
Trumbull County

(G-9357)
AMROD BRIDGE & IRON LLC
105 Ohio Ave (44437-1900)
P.O. Box 749 (44501-0749)
EMP: 24 **EST:** 2005
SALES (est): 1.06MM **Privately Held**
SIC: 3441 Fabricated structural metal

(G-9358)
GENERAL ELECTRIC COMPANY
Also Called: GE
3159 Wildwood Dr (44437-1354)
P.O. Box 688 (44030-0688)
PHONE..............................440 593-1156
Jeff Adams, *Mgr*
EMP: 12
SALES (corp-wide): 38.7B **Publicly Held**

Web: geaerospace.com
SIC: 3641 5719 Electric lamps; Lighting, lamps, and accessories
PA: General Electric Company
1 Aviation Way
Cincinnati OH 45215
617 443-3000

(G-9359)
MANDREL GROUP LLC
105 Ohio Ave (44437-1900)
PHONE..............................330 881-1266
Tim Merlin, *Managing Member*
EMP: 10 **EST:** 2021
SALES (est): 6.16MM **Privately Held**
Web: www.themandrelgroup.com
SIC: 3499 Machine bases, metal

(G-9360)
MCDONALD STEEL CORPORATION (PA)
100 Ohio Ave (44437-1954)
P.O. Box 416 (44437-0416)
PHONE..............................330 530-9118
James Grasso, *Pr*
Bill Bresnahan, *Ch Bd*
Mark Pecchia, *CFO*
◆ **EMP:** 67 **EST:** 1980
SQ FT: 680,000
SALES (est): 4.98MM
SALES (corp-wide): 4.98MM **Privately Held**
Web: www.mcdonaldsteel.com
SIC: 3312 Bars and bar shapes, steel, hot-rolled

(G-9361)
STEEL & ALLOY UTILITY PDTS INC
110 Ohio Ave (44437-1900)
P.O. Box 354 (44437-0354)
PHONE..............................330 530-2220
Nathan Gallo, *Pr*
Nick Gallo, *
▼ **EMP:** 50 **EST:** 1946
SQ FT: 60,000
SALES (est): 4.61MM **Privately Held**
SIC: 3569 3443 3444 3441 Assembly machines, non-metalworking; Fabricated plate work (boiler shop); Sheet metalwork; Fabricated structural metal

Mcconnelsville
Morgan County

(G-9362)
HANN MANUFACTURING INC
4678 N State Route 60 Nw (43756-9317)
P.O. Box 400 (43758)
PHONE..............................740 962-3752
Darl Hann, *Pr*
EMP: 26 **EST:** 1995
SQ FT: 30,000
SALES (est): 3.45MM **Privately Held**
Web: www.hannmfg.com
SIC: 2531 2448 2441 Public building and related furniture; Wood pallets and skids; Nailed wood boxes and shook

(G-9363)
MAHLE ENG COMPONENTS USA INC
5130 N State Route 60 Nw (43756-9021)
PHONE..............................740 962-8004
EMP: 13
SALES (corp-wide): 3.75MM **Privately Held**
Web: us.mahle.com
SIC: 3714 Motor vehicle parts and accessories
HQ: Mahle Engine Components Usa, Inc.

1 Mahle Dr
Morristown TN 37815
248 305-8200

(G-9364)
MIBA BEARINGS US LLC
5037 N State Route 60 Nw (43756-9218)
PHONE..............................740 962-4242
F Peter Mitterbauer, *Ch Bd*
Markus Hofer, *
▲ **EMP:** 300 **EST:** 2001
SQ FT: 182,000
SALES (est): 39.28MM
SALES (corp-wide): 242.12K **Privately Held**
Web: www.miba.com
SIC: 5085 3365 3471 3511 Bearings;
　Aluminum foundries; Plating and polishing;
　Turbines and turbine generator sets
HQ: Mitterbauer Beteiligungs Gmbh
　Dr. Mitterbauer-StraBe 3
　Laakirchen 4663
　76132541

(G-9365)
MIBA SINTER USA LLC
5045 N State Route 60 Nw (43756-9640)
PHONE..............................740 962-4242
Steve Krise, *Managing Member*
▲ **EMP:** 10 **EST:** 2008
SALES (est): 10.92MM
SALES (corp-wide): 242.12K **Privately Held**
Web: www.miba.com
SIC: 3312 Sinter, iron
HQ: Mitterbauer Beteiligungs Gmbh
　Dr. Mitterbauer-StraBe 3
　Laakirchen 4663
　76132541

(G-9366)
MORGAN COUNTY PUBLISHING CO
Also Called: Morgan County Herald
25 N 5th St (43756-1200)
P.O. Box 268 (43756-0268)
PHONE..............................740 962-3377
Jack Barnes, *Pr*
EMP: 9 **EST:** 1964
SALES (est): 256.65K **Privately Held**
Web: www.mchnews.com
SIC: 2711 Newspapers, publishing and
　printing

Mechanicsburg
Champaign County

(G-9367)
MECHANICSBURG SAND & GRAVEL
5734 State Route 4 (43044-9748)
PHONE..............................937 834-2606
James Cushman, *Pr*
Charles Wibright Junior, *Sec*
EMP: 8 **EST:** 1957
SQ FT: 3,400
SALES (est): 1.41MM **Privately Held**
Web:
www.mechanicsburgsandandgravel.com
SIC: 1442 Construction sand mining

Mechanicstown
Carroll County

(G-9368)
KINGS WELDING AND FABG INC
5259 Bane Rd Ne (44651-9020)
PHONE..............................330 738-3592
Glen Richard King Senior, *Pr*
Diane Garrett, *

EMP: 6 **EST:** 1974
SQ FT: 9,500
SALES (est): 370.81K **Privately Held**
Web: www.kingswelding.net
SIC: 3599 7692 3498 3441 Machine shop,
　jobbing and repair; Welding repair;
　Fabricated pipe and fittings; Fabricated
　structural metal

Medina
Medina County

(G-9369)
3M COMPANY
Also Called: 3M
1030 Lake Rd (44256-2450)
PHONE..............................330 725-1444
Tom Gregory, *Brnch Mgr*
EMP: 64
SALES (corp-wide): 32.68B **Publicly Held**
Web: 3m.com
SIC: 2672 Tape, pressure sensitive: made
　from purchased materials
PA: 3m Company
　3m Center
　Saint Paul MN 55144
　651 733-1110

(G-9370)
AGRATI - MEDINA LLC (DH)
941 Lake Rd 955 (44256-2453)
PHONE..............................330 725-8853
Ashi Uppal, *CEO*
Jack Woodruff, *
◆ **EMP:** 146 **EST:** 1978
SALES (est): 25.65MM
SALES (corp-wide): 798.77MM **Privately Held**
Web: www.agrati.com
SIC: 3452 Screws, metal
HQ: Agrati, Inc.
　24000 S Western Ave
　Park Forest IL 60466
　704 747-1200

(G-9371)
AI ROOT COMPANY (PA)
Also Called: West Liberty Commons
623 W Liberty St (44256-2225)
PHONE..............................330 723-4359
John A Root, *Ch Bd*
Brad I Root, *
Stuart Root, *
William Fleming, *
▲ **EMP:** 190 **EST:** 1869
SQ FT: 182,000
SALES (est): 52.46MM
SALES (corp-wide): 52.46MM **Privately Held**
Web: www.rootcandles.com
SIC: 3999 3085 Candles; Plastics bottles

(G-9372)
AI ROOT COMPANY
Also Called: Root Candles
234 S State Rd (44256-2697)
PHONE..............................330 725-6677
Brad Root, *Brnch Mgr*
EMP: 22
SALES (corp-wide): 52.46MM **Privately Held**
Web: www.beeculture.com
SIC: 3999 3085 Candles; Plastics bottles
PA: The A I Root Company
　623 West Liberty St
　Medina OH 44256
　330 723-4359

(G-9373)
ALCHEM CORPORATION
525 W Liberty St (44256-2223)
PHONE..............................330 725-2436
B George Buskin, *Pr*
▲ **EMP:** 8 **EST:** 1976
SQ FT: 28,000
SALES (est): 970.54K **Privately Held**
Web: www.alchemcorp.com
SIC: 2819 Industrial inorganic chemicals, nec

(G-9374)
ALSATIAN LLC
Also Called: Sushi On The Roll
985 Boardman Aly (44256-1599)
PHONE..............................330 661-0600
EMP: 6 **EST:** 2007
SQ FT: 3,000
SALES (est): 462.19K **Privately Held**
Web: www.sushiontherollonline.com
SIC: 2048 5146 Fish food; Fish and seafoods

(G-9375)
ANCHOR LAMINA AMERICA INC
445 W Liberty St (44256-2273)
PHONE..............................330 952-1595
EMP: 14
Web: www.daytonlamina.com
SIC: 3545 Machine tool accessories
HQ: Anchor Lamina America, Inc.
　3650 S Derenzy Rd
　Bellaire MI 49615
　248 489-9122

(G-9376)
APEX SIGNS INC
Also Called: Fastsigns
2755 Medina Rd (44256-8284)
PHONE..............................330 952-2626
Ed Gonzalez, *Pr*
EMP: 6 **EST:** 2015
SALES (est): 363.35K **Privately Held**
Web: www.fastsigns.com
SIC: 3993 Signs and advertising specialties

(G-9377)
APEX SPECIALTY CO INC
620 E Smith Rd Ste E7 (44256-3650)
PHONE..............................330 725-6663
EMP: 7 **EST:** 1956
SQ FT: 3,000
SALES (est): 774.27K **Privately Held**
SIC: 3599 Machine shop, jobbing and repair

(G-9378)
AUTOMTIVE RFNISH CLOR SLTONS I
2771 Sunburst Dr (44256-6494)
PHONE..............................330 461-6067
Strath Wood, *Pr*
EMP: 50 **EST:** 2016
SALES (est): 853.04K **Privately Held**
SIC: 3999 7538 Atomizers, toiletry; General
　automotive repair shops

(G-9379)
AXON MEDICAL LLC
1484 Medina Rd Ste 117 (44256-5378)
PHONE..............................216 276-0262
Christopher Hardin, *Prin*
Joel Hawley, *Prin*
EMP: 20 **EST:** 2015
SALES (est): 809.12K **Privately Held**
SIC: 3841 3842 5047 Surgical and medical
　instruments; Surgical appliances and
　supplies; Instruments, surgical and medical

(G-9380)
BIL-JAC FOODS INC (PA)
3337 Medina Rd (44256-9631)
PHONE..............................330 722-7888

William Kelly, *Ch*
Robert Kelly, *
James Kelly, *
Ray Kelly, *
EMP: 25 **EST:** 1947
SQ FT: 6,000
SALES (est): 23.34MM
SALES (corp-wide): 23.34MM **Privately Held**
Web: www.bil-jac.com
SIC: 2047 Dog food

(G-9381)
BLASTER CORPORATION
775 W Smith Rd (44256-3556)
PHONE..............................216 901-5800
EMP: 10 **EST:** 2017
SALES (est): 6.12MM **Privately Held**
Web: www.blasterproducts.com
SIC: 2911 Petroleum refining

(G-9382)
BOND CHEMICALS INC
1154 W Smith Rd (44256-2443)
PHONE..............................330 725-5935
Thomas Goslee Junior, *Pr*
Carol Goslee, *VP*
EMP: 7 **EST:** 1960
SQ FT: 24,000
SALES (est): 494.72K **Privately Held**
Web: www.bondchemicalsinc.com
SIC: 2899 2819 Water treating compounds;
　Industrial inorganic chemicals, nec

(G-9383)
BPR-RICO EQUIPMENT INC (PA)
691 W Liberty St (44256-2225)
PHONE..............................330 723-4050
EMP: 80 **EST:** 1980
SALES (est): 22.78MM
SALES (corp-wide): 22.78MM **Privately Held**
Web: www.ricoequipment.com
SIC: 3537 Lift trucks, industrial: fork,
　platform, straddle, etc.

(G-9384)
BPR-RICO MANUFACTURING INC
Also Called: Bpr/Rico
691 W Liberty St (44256-2225)
PHONE..............................330 723-4050
Dave Mueller, *CEO*
Steve Shuck, *
Sandy Mueller, *
Kent Stelmasczuk, *
▲ **EMP:** 100 **EST:** 1987
SQ FT: 175,000
SALES (est): 21.06MM
SALES (corp-wide): 22.78MM **Privately Held**
SIC: 3537 Lift trucks, industrial: fork,
　platform, straddle, etc.
PA: Bpr-Rico Equipment, Inc.
　691 W Liberty St
　Medina OH 44256
　330 723-4050

(G-9385)
BREAKWALL PUBLISHING LLC
Also Called: Seaside Retailer
3593 Medina Rd # 117 (44256-8182)
PHONE..............................813 575-2570
EMP: 11 **EST:** 2019
SALES (est): 621.77K **Privately Held**
Web: www.seasideretailer.com
SIC: 2721 Magazines: publishing and printing

(G-9386)
BREW KETTLE STRONGSVILLE LLC
3520 Longwood Dr (44256-8400)
P.O. Box 360893 (44136-0015)

▲ = Import ▼ = Export
◆ = Import/Export

PHONE............................440 915-7074
EMP: 6 **EST:** 2013
SALES (est): 373.65K **Privately Held**
Web: www.thebrewkettle.com
SIC: 2082 Malt beverages

(G-9387)
CHICK MASTER INCUBATOR COMPANY (PA)
Also Called: Jamesway Chick Mstr Incubator
779 W Smith Rd (44256-2422)
PHONE............................330 722-5591
Robert Holzer, *CEO*
Alan Shandler, *
Michael Hurd, *
Chad Daniels, *
◆ **EMP:** 88 **EST:** 1944
SALES (est): 8.56MM
SALES (corp-wide): 8.56MM **Privately Held**
Web: www.chickmaster.com
SIC: 3523 1711 Incubators and brooders, farm; Plumbing, heating, air-conditioning

(G-9388)
CMBF PRODUCTS INC (DH)
Also Called: Cbf
920 Lake Rd (44256-2453)
PHONE............................855 403-9083
Thomas Cornelis Vanderlaan, *CEO*
▲ **EMP:** 239 **EST:** 1924
SALES (est): 71.76MM
SALES (corp-wide): 476.36MM **Privately Held**
Web: www.carlislecbf.com
SIC: 3751 Brakes, friction clutch and other: bicycle
HQ: Engineered Components And Systems, Llc
N19 W24200 Rvrwood Dr Ste
Waukesha WI 53188
262 754-7300

(G-9389)
COMMERCIAL GRINDING SVCS INC
Also Called: Cgs
1155 Industrial Pkwy Unit 1 (44258)
P.O. Box 1121 (44258)
PHONE............................330 273-5040
Kevin Thies, *CEO*
Kevin T Butas, *Pr*
EMP: 20 **EST:** 1975
SQ FT: 3,600
SALES (est): 2.59MM **Privately Held**
Web: www.cgstool.com
SIC: 3541 3545 Machine tools, metal cutting type; End mills

(G-9390)
CONTROLS INC
5204 Portside Dr (44256-5966)
P.O. Box 368 (44274-0368)
PHONE............................330 239-4345
Robert Cowen, *Pr*
Scott Izzo, *
EMP: 25 **EST:** 1990
SALES (est): 4.2MM **Privately Held**
Web: www.controlsinc.com
SIC: 3625 7389 1731 Control equipment, electric; Design services; Electronic controls installation

(G-9391)
CONVIBER INC
Also Called: Heintz Conveying Belt Service
1066 Industrial Pkwy (44256-2449)
PHONE............................330 723-6006
Rich Serrena, *Mgr*
EMP: 10
SALES (corp-wide): 10.98MM **Privately Held**

Web: www.conviber.com
SIC: 7699 3559 Rubber product repair; Rubber working machinery, including tires
PA: Conviber, Inc.
644 Garfield St
Springdale PA 15144
724 274-6300

(G-9392)
CORRPRO COMPANIES INC
Also Called: Corrosion Cntrl/Cthdic Prtctio
820 Lafayette Rd (44256-2413)
PHONE............................770 761-5400
Dean Slessas, *Rgnl Mgr*
EMP: 26
SALES (corp-wide): 1.48B **Privately Held**
Web: www.corrpro.com
SIC: 3699 8711 1799 Electrical equipment and supplies, nec; Engineering services; Corrosion control installation
HQ: Corrpro Companies, Inc.
580 Goddard Ave
Chesterfield MO 63005
636 530-8000

(G-9393)
CORRPRO COMPANIES INC
Also Called: Corrpro Waterworks
820 Lafayette Rd (44256-2413)
PHONE............................330 725-6681
George Giannakos, *Brnch Mgr*
EMP: 27
SALES (corp-wide): 1.48B **Privately Held**
Web: www.corrpro.com
SIC: 3699 8711 Electrical equipment and supplies, nec; Engineering services
HQ: Corrpro Companies, Inc.
580 Goddard Ave
Chesterfield MO 63005
636 530-8000

(G-9394)
CORRPRO COMPANIES INTL INC
820 Lafayette Rd (44256-2413)
PHONE............................330 723-5082
EMP: 16 **EST:** 2013
SALES (est): 2.16MM
SALES (corp-wide): 1.48B **Privately Held**
Web: www.madeinmedinacounty.com
SIC: 3699 Electrical equipment and supplies, nec
HQ: Insituform Technologies, Llc
17988 Edison Ave
Chesterfield MO 63005
636 530-8000

(G-9395)
DAIRY FARMERS AMERICA INC
1035 Medina Rd Ste 300 (44256-5398)
PHONE............................330 670-7800
Glenn Wallace, *Chief*
EMP: 6
SALES (corp-wide): 23.02B **Privately Held**
Web: www.dfamilk.com
SIC: 2022 2026 2021 0211 Cheese; natural and processed; Fluid milk; Creamery butter; Beef cattle feedlots
PA: Dairy Farmers Of America, Inc.
1405 N 98th St
Kansas City KS 66111
816 801-6455

(G-9396)
DIE GUYS INC
5238 Portside Dr (44256-5966)
PHONE............................330 239-3437
Jeri Potts, *CEO*
Cathy Greenwald, *Pr*
Luke Darling, *Sec*
EMP: 15 **EST:** 2000
SQ FT: 14,000

SALES (est): 2.99MM **Privately Held**
Web: www.dieguys.com
SIC: 3544 Dies, steel rule

(G-9397)
DJE MANAGEMENT CONSULTING LLC
Also Called: Shelfgenie
5590 Champion Creek Blvd (44256-8741)
PHONE............................330 760-2990
EMP: 6 **EST:** 2019
SALES (est): 692.81K **Privately Held**
Web: www.shelfgenie.com
SIC: 8748 2511 Business consulting, nec; Wood household furniture

(G-9398)
DO TECHNOLOGIES CO
667 Lafayette Rd (44256-3700)
PHONE............................330 725-4561
Douglas R Piskac, *Pr*
EMP: 10 **EST:** 1986
SQ FT: 14,700
SALES (est): 846.79K **Privately Held**
Web: directory.wadsworthchamber.com
SIC: 3599 Machine shop, jobbing and repair

(G-9399)
ENI USA R&M CO INC
740 S Progress Dr (44256-1368)
PHONE............................330 723-6457
Joe Krisky, *VP*
EMP: 10
SQ FT: 6,000
SALES (corp-wide): 101.87B **Privately Held**
Web: www.eni.com
SIC: 2992 5172 Lubricating oils and greases ; Petroleum products, nec
HQ: Eni Usa R&M Co. Inc.
299 Park Ave
New York NY 10171

(G-9400)
FACULTATIEVE TECH AMERICAS INC
Also Called: Incinerator Specialists
940 Lake Rd (44256-2453)
PHONE............................330 723-6339
Henri Keizer, *CEO*
▲ **EMP:** 25 **EST:** 1908
SALES (est): 4.19MM **Privately Held**
Web: www.facultatieve-technologies.com
SIC: 3567 Fuel-fired furnaces and ovens

(G-9401)
FALCON INDUSTRIES INC (PA)
Also Called: Falcon
180 Commerce Dr (44256-3949)
PHONE............................330 723-0099
J Don Fitzgerald, *CEO*
EMP: 27 **EST:** 1970
SQ FT: 24,000
SALES (est): 9.44MM
SALES (corp-wide): 9.44MM **Privately Held**
Web: www.falconindustries.com
SIC: 3541 3535 3444 3423 Machine tools, metal cutting type; Conveyors and conveying equipment; Sheet metalwork; Hand and edge tools, nec

(G-9402)
FASTSIGNS
Also Called: Fastsigns
2736 Medina Rd Ste 109 (44256-9660)
PHONE............................330 952-2626
EMP: 7
SALES (est): 149.13K **Privately Held**
Web: www.fastsigns.com

SIC: 3993 Signs and advertising specialties

(G-9403)
FIRE-DEX LLC (PA)
Also Called: Gear Wash
780 S Progress Dr (44256-1368)
PHONE............................330 723-0000
Bill Burke, *Managing Member*
Brett Jaffe, *CEO*
▲ **EMP:** 81 **EST:** 1983
SQ FT: 28,000
SALES (est): 3.79MM
SALES (corp-wide): 3.79MM **Privately Held**
Web: www.firedex.com
SIC: 2389 Uniforms and vestments

(G-9404)
FOM USA INCORPORATED
1065 Medina Rd Ste 800 (44256-5376)
PHONE............................234 248-4400
Daniel Donafini, *Pr*
Scott Kochevar, *VP Sls*
▲ **EMP:** 9 **EST:** 2008
SQ FT: 9,000
SALES (est): 6.76MM **Privately Held**
Web: www.fom-group.com
SIC: 3354 Aluminum extruded products
HQ: F.O.M. Industrie Srl
Via Mercadante 85/87
Cattolica RN 47841
054 183-2611

(G-9405)
FOUNDATIONS WORLDWIDE INC (PA)
Also Called: Foundations
5216 Portside Dr (44256-5966)
PHONE............................330 722-5033
Joseph A Lawlor, *Pr*
Lisa Vanadia, *VP*
◆ **EMP:** 21 **EST:** 2002
SQ FT: 60,000
SALES (est): 9.51MM
SALES (corp-wide): 9.51MM **Privately Held**
Web: www.foundations.com
SIC: 5999 2511 3944 Children's furniture, nec; Children's wood furniture; Strollers, baby (vehicle)

(G-9406)
FRICTION PRODUCTS CO
Also Called: Hawk Performance
920 Lake Rd (44256-2453)
PHONE............................330 725-4941
Chris Disantis, *CEO*
Ronald E Weinberg, *
Thomas A Gilbride, *
◆ **EMP:** 266 **EST:** 1989
SQ FT: 176,000
SALES (est): 7.4MM
SALES (corp-wide): 476.36MM **Privately Held**
Web: www.hawkperformance.com
SIC: 3728 3714 Aircraft landing assemblies and brakes; Motor vehicle brake systems and parts
HQ: Cmbf Products, Inc.
920 Lake Rd
Medina OH 44256

(G-9407)
GASKO FABRICATED PRODUCTS LLC (HQ)
4049 Ridge Rd (44256-8618)
P.O. Box 1050 (44062-1050)
PHONE............................330 239-1781
Randy Guernsey, *Pr*
Gregory Nemecek, *Pr*
Ed Bosken, *VP*

EMP: 31 EST: 1998
SQ FT: 12,000
SALES (est): 3.44MM
SALES (corp-wide): 8.29MM **Privately Held**
SIC: 3053 Gaskets, all materials
PA: Cornerstone Industrial Holdings Inc
   100 Park Pl
   Chagrin Falls OH 44022
   440 893-9144

(G-9408)
HERAEUS ELECTRO-NITE CO LLC
6469 Fenn Rd (44256-9463)
PHONE..............................330 725-1419
EMP: 6
SALES (corp-wide): 2.67MM **Privately Held**
Web: www.heraeus-group.com
SIC: 3829 3674 Thermocouples;
   Semiconductors and related devices
HQ: Heraeus Electro-Nite Co., Llc
   541 S Industrial Dr
   Hartland WI 53029
   215 944-9000

(G-9409)
HOWDEN NORTH AMERICA INC
935 Heritage Dr (44256-2404)
PHONE..............................330 721-7374
Edward Biesiada, *Brnch Mgr*
EMP: 12
SALES (corp-wide): 2.74B **Publicly Held**
Web: www.madeinmedinacounty.com
SIC: 3443 Fabricated plate work (boiler shop)
HQ: Howden North America Inc.
   2475 Grge Urban Blvd Ste
   Depew NY 14043
   330 867-8540

(G-9410)
HOWDEN NORTH AMERICA INC
411 Independence Dr (44256-2406)
PHONE..............................330 867-8540
Scott Burdett, *Mgr*
EMP: 11
SQ FT: 2,662
SALES (corp-wide): 2.74B **Publicly Held**
Web: www.chartindustries.com
SIC: 3443 Fabricated plate work (boiler shop)
HQ: Howden North America Inc.
   2475 Grge Urban Blvd Ste
   Depew NY 14043
   330 867-8540

(G-9411)
I V MILLER & SONS
940 Lafayette Rd (44256-2415)
PHONE..............................732 493-4040
George Miller, *Pr*
Jack Miller, *VP*
Juni Fraser, *Sec*
▲ EMP: 18 EST: 1949
SALES (est): 359.39K **Privately Held**
Web: www.ivmiller.com
SIC: 3479 Painting, coating, and hot dipping

(G-9412)
INNOVATION SALES LLC
803 E Washington St Ste 210 (44256-3333)
PHONE..............................330 239-0400
Pamela Blackburn, *Mgr*
EMP: 7 EST: 2002
SALES (est): 151.66K **Privately Held**
Web: www.innovationsales.net
SIC: 3291 Abrasive metal and steel products

(G-9413)
INTERACTIVE ENGINEERING CORP
884 Medina Rd (44256-9615)
PHONE..............................330 239-6888

Ming Zhang, *Pr*
▲ EMP: 25 EST: 1995
SQ FT: 200,000
SALES (est): 3.22MM **Privately Held**
Web: www.4iec.com
SIC: 8748 3672 Systems analysis and
   engineering consulting services; Printed
   circuit boards

(G-9414)
INTERNATIONAL METAL SUPPLY LLC
3995 Medina Rd Ste 200 (44256-5958)
PHONE..............................330 764-1004
EMP: 9 EST: 2016
SALES (est): 2.69MM **Privately Held**
Web: www.intmetalsupply.com
SIC: 3313 Ferroalloys

(G-9415)
JES FOODS INC (PA)
865 W Liberty St Ste 200 (44256-3938)
P.O. Box 367 (44258-0367)
PHONE..............................216 883-8987
Elaine R Freed, *Pr*
William Freed, *
EMP: 19 EST: 1992
SALES (est): 4.96MM **Privately Held**
Web: www.jesfoods.com
SIC: 2033 Canned fruits and specialties

(G-9416)
KANYA INDUSTRIES LLC
694 W Liberty St (44256-2226)
PHONE..............................330 722-5432
Paul Kanya, *Prin*
EMP: 6 EST: 2017
SALES (est): 2.54MM **Privately Held**
SIC: 3999 Manufacturing industries, nec

(G-9417)
KATHYS KRAFTS AND KOLLECTIBLES
3303 Hamilton Rd (44256-7633)
PHONE..............................423 787-3709
Kathy Hayes, *Prin*
EMP: 6 EST: 2013
SALES (est): 190.37K **Privately Held**
SIC: 2022 Natural cheese

(G-9418)
KELLY FOODS CORPORATION (PA)
Also Called: Bil-Jac Foods
3337 Medina Rd (44256-9631)
PHONE..............................330 722-8855
Robert Kelly, *Pr*
Jim Kelly, *Sec*
▼ EMP: 22 EST: 1987
SALES (est): 11.4MM
SALES (corp-wide): 11.4MM **Privately Held**
Web: www.bil-jac.com
SIC: 2048 2047 Dry pet food (except dog
   and cat); Dog and cat food

(G-9419)
KG MEDINA LLC
Also Called: Ken Ganley Kia
2925 Medina Rd (44256-9672)
PHONE..............................256 330-4273
Kenneth G Ganley, *Mgr*
EMP: 25 EST: 2019
SALES (est): 5.65MM **Privately Held**
Web: www.kenganleykia.com
SIC: 3714 Motor vehicle parts and
   accessories

(G-9420)
LEITNER FABRICATION LLC
935 Heritage Dr (44256-2404)

PHONE..............................330 721-7374
EMP: 22
SIC: 3441 Fabricated structural metal

(G-9421)
LSQ MANUFACTURING INC
1140 Industrial Pkwy (44256-2486)
PHONE..............................330 725-4905
Richard L Rauckhorst III, *Pr*
Richard L Rauckhorst Iii, *Pr*
Judith L Coffman, *VP*
EMP: 10 EST: 1946
SQ FT: 8,000
SALES (est): 1.02MM **Privately Held**
Web: www.arthurproducts.com
SIC: 3494 3563 3432 Valves and pipe
   fittings, nec; Air and gas compressors;
   Plumbing fixture fittings and trim

(G-9422)
MANSFIELD PAINT CO INC
525 W Liberty St (44256-2223)
PHONE..............................330 725-2436
George Bufkin, *CEO*
EMP: 8 EST: 1945
SQ FT: 24,000
SALES (est): 464.66K **Privately Held**
Web: www.mansfieldpaint.com
SIC: 2851 Paints: oil or alkyd vehicle or
   water thinned

(G-9423)
MEDINA COUNTY
Also Called: Medina County Recorders
144 N Broadway St Ste 117 (44256-1928)
PHONE..............................330 723-3641
Linda Hoffman, *Brnch Mgr*
EMP: 20
SALES (corp-wide): 185.57MM **Privately Held**
Web: www.medinaco.org
SIC: 3825 Recorders, oscillographic
PA: Medina County
   144 N Broadway St Rm 201
   Medina OH 44256
   330 723-3641

(G-9424)
MEDINA HNTNGTON RE GROUP II LL
635 N Huntington St (44256-1871)
PHONE..............................330 591-2777
Darrel L Seibert Ii, *Prin*
EMP: 20 EST: 2017
SALES (est): 412.4K **Privately Held**
SIC: 2711 Newspapers, publishing and
   printing

(G-9425)
MEDINA SUPPLY COMPANY
820 W Smith Rd (44256-2425)
PHONE..............................330 364-4411
Daryl Albright, *Mgr*
EMP: 81
SALES (corp-wide): 34.95B **Privately Held**
Web: www.shellyco.com
SIC: 1429 Igneus rock, crushed and broken-
   quarrying
HQ: Medina Supply Company
   230 E Smith Rd
   Medina OH 44256
   330 723-3681

(G-9426)
MEDINA SUPPLY COMPANY (DH)
230 E Smith Rd (44256-3616)
PHONE..............................330 723-3681
Jerry A Schwab, *Pr*
David Schwab, *VP*
Donna L Schwab, *Sec*
Mary Lynn Schwab, *Treas*
EMP: 20 EST: 1974

SQ FT: 2,000
SALES (est): 7.44MM
SALES (corp-wide): 34.95B **Privately Held**
Web: www.shellyco.com
SIC: 1442 3273 3281 5211 Construction
   sand and gravel; Ready-mixed concrete;
   Cut stone and stone products; Brick
HQ: Shelly Materials, Inc.
   80 Park Dr
   Thornville OH 43076
   740 246-6315

(G-9427)
MILLER PLATING LLC
940 Lafayette Rd (44256-2415)
PHONE..............................330 952-2550
Adam Anderson, *Managing Member*
EMP: 20 EST: 2019
SALES (est): 3.76MM **Privately Held**
Web: www.millerplating.net
SIC: 3471 Electroplating of metals or formed
   products

(G-9428)
MSLS GROUP LLC
Also Called: Main Street Lighting Standards
1080 Industrial Pkwy (44256-2449)
PHONE..............................330 723-4431
Bernard Mcrae, *Managing Member*
EMP: 39 EST: 2014
SALES (est): 6.8MM **Privately Held**
Web: www.mainstreetlighting.com
SIC: 3312 Fence posts, iron and steel

(G-9429)
NORTHSTAR PUBLISHING INC
437 Lafayette Rd Ste 310 (44256-2398)
P.O. Box 1166 (44258-1166)
PHONE..............................330 721-9126
Rodney Auth, *Pr*
EMP: 7 EST: 1998
SQ FT: 500
SALES (est): 129.47K **Privately Held**
Web: www.northstarpubs.com
SIC: 2741 Miscellaneous publishing

(G-9430)
OFFICE MAGIC INC (PA)
Also Called: Electrocoat
2290 Wilbur Rd (44256-8496)
PHONE..............................510 782-6100
Craig Codding, *Pr*
EMP: 14 EST: 1975
SALES (est): 221.6K
SALES (corp-wide): 221.6K **Privately Held**
Web: www.electrocoat.ws
SIC: 3479 2522 7641 2519 Painting, coating,
   and hot dipping; Office desks and tables,
   except wood; Reupholstery; Fiberglass and
   plastic furniture

(G-9431)
OPTIMUM SURGICAL
2524 Medina Rd Ste 600 (44256-5390)
PHONE..............................216 870-8526
Eric Henning, *Pr*
EMP: 10 EST: 2017
SALES (est): 450.11K **Privately Held**
Web: www.optimumsi.com
SIC: 7699 3841 Surgical instrument repair;
   Surgical instruments and apparatus

(G-9432)
OVATION PLYMR TECH ENGNRED MTL
Also Called: Optem
1030 W Smith Rd (44256-2445)
PHONE..............................330 723-5686
Delbert Henderson, *COO*
Asis Banerjie, *Pr*
▲ EMP: 23 EST: 2004

SQ FT: 55,000
SALES (est): 2.22MM **Privately Held**
Web: www.opteminc.com
SIC: 2821 Plastics materials and resins

(G-9433)
PACKAGING SPECIALTIES INC
300 Lake Rd (44256-2459)
PHONE...................................330 723-6000
Robert Syme, *Ch Bd*
James Munson, *
◆ EMP: 50 EST: 1959
SQ FT: 59,000
SALES (est): 7.15MM
SALES (corp-wide): 7.15MM **Privately Held**
Web: www.packspec.com
SIC: 3412 3411 Metal barrels, drums, and pails; Metal cans
PA: Syme, Inc.
300 Lake Rd
Medina OH 44256
330 723-6000

(G-9434)
PARK CORPORATION (PA)
Also Called: Charleston Ordnance Center
3555 Reserve Commons Dr (44256-5900)
P.O. Box 8678 (25303-0678)
PHONE...................................216 267-4870
Raymond P Park, *Ch Bd*
Daniel K Park, *
Shelva J Davis, *
Tim Geharing, *
Ricky L Bertrem, *
◆ EMP: 300 EST: 1948
SALES (est): 645.61MM
SALES (corp-wide): 645.61MM **Privately Held**
Web: www.parkcorp.com
SIC: 5084 3547 6512 7999 Industrial machinery and equipment; Rolling mill machinery; Commercial and industrial building operation; Exposition operation

(G-9435)
PLASTI-KOTE CO INC
Also Called: Valspar
1000 Lake Rd (44256-3598)
PHONE...................................330 725-4511
Richard Rompala, *Ch Bd*
◆ EMP: 250 EST: 1989
SQ FT: 145,000
SALES (est): 2.53MM
SALES (corp-wide): 23.1B **Publicly Held**
Web: www.plasti-kote.com
SIC: 2813 2992 2851 Industrial gases; Lubricating oils and greases; Paints and allied products
PA: The Sherwin-Williams Company
101 W Prospect Ave
Cleveland OH 44115
216 566-2000

(G-9436)
PLATE ENGRAVING CORPORATION
2324 Sharon Copley Rd (44256-9773)
PHONE...................................330 239-2155
James Brobeck, *Pr*
James Michael Brobeck, *Pr*
Von Brobeck, *VP*
EMP: 6 EST: 1968
SQ FT: 4,018
SALES (est): 688.16K **Privately Held**
Web: plateengravingcorp.godaddysites.com
SIC: 2796 3089 Engraving on copper, steel, wood, or rubber: printing plates; Engraving of plastics

(G-9437)
PROGRESSIVE MOLDING TECH
2620 Medina Rd (44256-8145)
PHONE...................................330 220-7030
Laird Daubenspeck, *CEO*
EMP: 8 EST: 2002
SALES (est): 1.05MM **Privately Held**
Web: www.promoldtech.com
SIC: 3089 Injection molding of plastics

(G-9438)
PUREBUTTONSCOM LLC
4930 Chippewa Rd Unit A (44256-8824)
PHONE...................................330 721-1600
EMP: 15 EST: 2005
SQ FT: 1,200
SALES (est): 2.71MM **Privately Held**
Web: www.purebuttons.com
SIC: 5131 3965 Buttons; Fasteners, buttons, needles, and pins

(G-9439)
QUALITY TOOLING SYSTEMS INC
5352 Lance Rd (44256-7521)
PHONE...................................330 722-5025
Robert F Kacic, *Prin*
Robert Kacic, *Owner*
EMP: 11 EST: 2000
SALES (est): 963.41K **Privately Held**
Web: www.qualitytoolingsystems.com
SIC: 3544 Special dies and tools

(G-9440)
RAVAGO AMERICAS LLC
Entec Polymers
5192 Lake Rd (44256-8809)
PHONE...................................330 825-2505
Mike Gasper, *Brnch Mgr*
EMP: 62
Web: www.amcopolymers.com
SIC: 2821 Plastics materials and resins
HQ: Ravago Americas Llc
1900 Smmit Twr Blvd Ste 9
Orlando FL 32810
800 262-6685

(G-9441)
REPUBLIC POWDERED METALS INC (HQ)
2628 Pearl Rd (44256-9099)
P.O. Box 777 (44258-0777)
PHONE...................................330 225-3192
Thomas Sullivan, *Ch Bd*
Frank C Sullivan, *
◆ EMP: 61 EST: 1963
SQ FT: 20,000
SALES (est): 1.29B
SALES (corp-wide): 7.34B **Publicly Held**
Web: www.rpminc.com
SIC: 2851 2891 3069 2899 Paints and allied products; Adhesives and sealants; Roofing, membrane rubber; Waterproofing compounds
PA: Rpm International Inc.
2628 Pearl Rd
Medina OH 44258
330 273-5090

(G-9442)
RPM INTERNATIONAL INC (PA)
2628 Pearl Rd (44258)
P.O. Box 777 (44258-0777)
PHONE...................................330 273-5090
Frank C Sullivan, *Ch Bd*
Russell L Gordon, *VP*
Tracy D Crandall, *CCO*
Michael J Laroche, *CAO*
Janeen B Kastner, *BENEFITS & RISK MANAGEMENT*
◆ EMP: 61 EST: 1947
SALES (est): 7.34B

SALES (corp-wide): 7.34B **Publicly Held**
Web: www.rpminc.com
SIC: 2891 3069 2899 2865 Adhesives and sealants; Roofing, membrane rubber; Waterproofing compounds; Dyes and pigments

(G-9443)
S&V INDUSTRIES INC (PA)
5054 Paramount Dr (44256-5363)
PHONE...................................330 666-1986
Senthil K Sundarapandian, *CEO*
Joan Owens, *
Mahesh Douglas, *
▲ EMP: 35 EST: 1993
SQ FT: 1,618
SALES (est): 12.47MM **Privately Held**
Web: www.svindustries.com
SIC: 5049 3089 3312 Engineers' equipment and supplies, nec; Casting of plastics; Forgings, iron and steel

(G-9444)
SAM OHT SERVICES LLC
620 E Smith Rd Enterprise Ctr Ste D (44256-2692)
PHONE...................................330 225-3117
▲ EMP: 18 EST: 2008
SQ FT: 20,000
SALES (est): 1.51MM **Privately Held**
Web: www.thomastechllc.com
SIC: 5045 3572 Computers, peripherals, and software; Computer storage devices

(G-9445)
SEALY MATTRESS MFG CO LLC
1070 Lake Rd (44256-2450)
PHONE...................................800 697-3259
Vicky Avans, *Mgr*
EMP: 25
SALES (corp-wide): 4.93B **Publicly Held**
Web: www.madeinmedinacounty.com
SIC: 2515 Mattresses, innerspring or box spring
HQ: Sealy Mattress Manufacturing Company, Llc
1000 Tempur Way
Lexington KY 40511
859 455-1000

(G-9446)
SFS GROUP USA INC
Also Called: Sfs Intec
5201 Portside Dr (44256-5966)
PHONE...................................330 239-7100
Urs Langenauer, *Genl Mgr*
EMP: 186
Web: us.sfs.com
SIC: 3714 Motor vehicle parts and accessories
HQ: Sfs Group Usa, Inc.
1045 Spring St
Wyomissing PA 19610
610 376-5751

(G-9447)
SFS INTEC INC
5201 Portside Dr (44256-5966)
PHONE...................................330 239-7100
Jens Breu, *CEO*
EMP: 20 EST: 2003
SALES (est): 5.91MM **Privately Held**
SIC: 3714 Motor vehicle parts and accessories

(G-9448)
SHELLY MATERIALS INC
820 W Smith Rd (44256-2425)
PHONE...................................330 723-3681
EMP: 18
SALES (corp-wide): 34.95B **Privately Held**

Web: www.shellyco.com
SIC: 3273 Ready-mixed concrete
HQ: Shelly Materials, Inc.
80 Park Dr
Thornville OH 43076
740 246-6315

(G-9449)
SOLUTIONS IN POLYCARBONATE LLC
6353 Norwalk Rd (44256-9455)
PHONE...................................330 572-2860
Bruce Gold, *Pr*
EMP: 9 EST: 2016
SQ FT: 24,000
SALES (est): 5.03MM **Privately Held**
Web: www.solutionsinpc.com
SIC: 3089 Windows, plastics

(G-9450)
STANDARD WLDG & STL PDTS INC
260 S State Rd (44256-2474)
P.O. Box 297 (44258-0297)
PHONE...................................330 273-2777
Christopher Coleman, *Pr*
Jack Colman, *VP*
Jayne Coleman, *Sec*
Charles Coleman, *CEO*
EMP: 10 EST: 1939
SQ FT: 30,000
SALES (est): 2.4MM **Privately Held**
Web: www.stdwelding.com
SIC: 3441 Fabricated structural metal

(G-9451)
SUPRO SPRING & WIRE FORMS INC
9085 Coon Club Rd (44256-7548)
PHONE...................................330 722-5628
Kevin Provagna, *Pr*
James Gensert, *
▲ EMP: 35 EST: 1996
SALES (est): 3.58MM **Privately Held**
Web: www.suprospring.com
SIC: 3495 Wire springs

(G-9452)
SYMATIC INC
Also Called: Ancom Business Products
803 E Washington St Ste 200 (44256-3333)
P.O. Box 150 (44212-0150)
PHONE...................................330 225-1510
Walter H Tanner, *Pr*
Cindy Holton, *
EMP: 6 EST: 1961
SALES (est): 622.14K **Privately Held**
SIC: 3579 5044 2541 2521 Paper handling machines; Office equipment; Wood partitions and fixtures; Wood office furniture

(G-9453)
SYME INC (PA)
300 Lake Rd (44256-2459)
PHONE...................................330 723-6000
Robert P Syme, *CEO*
Jim L Munson, *Pr*
EMP: 21 EST: 1976
SQ FT: 58,000
SALES (est): 7.15MM
SALES (corp-wide): 7.15MM **Privately Held**
Web: www.packspec.com
SIC: 3412 Metal barrels, drums, and pails

(G-9454)
TFP CORPORATION (PA)
Also Called: Tru-Weld Stud Welding Div
460 Lake Rd (44256-2457)
PHONE...................................330 725-7741
◆ EMP: 50 EST: 1928
SALES (est): 22.46MM
SALES (corp-wide): 22.46MM **Privately Held**

Web: www.tfpcorp.com
SIC: **3965** Fasteners

(G-9455)
THEKEN SPINE LLC
1153 Medina Rd Ste 100 (44256-5402)
PHONE.............................330 773-7677
EMP: 10
SALES (corp-wide): 2.62MM **Privately
Held**
SIC: **3842** Implants, surgical
PA: Theken Spine, Llc
　　5770 Armada Dr
　　Carlsbad CA

(G-9456)
TIGER GENERAL LLC
6867 Wooster Pike (44256-8859)
PHONE.............................330 239-4949
Mark Overholt, *Pr*
Sherry Overholt, *VP*
Mickey Manack, *VP*
EMP: 10 **EST:** 2008
SQ FT: 18,000
SALES (est): 2.06MM **Privately Held**
Web: www.tigergeneral.com
SIC: **3533 5511** Oil and gas drilling rigs and
　　equipment; Trucks, tractors, and trailers:
　　new and used

(G-9457)
TRAILER ONE INC
1030 W Liberty St (44256-1326)
PHONE.............................330 723-7474
Kenneth Smith, *Pr*
Bradley Thomas, *VP*
▼ **EMP:** 10 **EST:** 1989
SALES (est): 780.45K **Privately Held**
Web: www.traileroneinc.com
SIC: **5511 3715 7359** Trucks, tractors, and
　　trailers: new and used; Truck trailers;
　　Equipment rental and leasing, nec

(G-9458)
TROGDON PUBLISHING INC
Also Called: Ohio Standard Bread
5164 Normandy Park Dr Ste 100
(44256-5903)
PHONE.............................330 721-7678
Bruce Trogdon, *Pr*
Raymond Leroy, *
EMP: 42 **EST:** 1975
SQ FT: 6,200
SALES (est): 1.44MM **Privately Held**
Web: www.thepostnewspapers.com
SIC: **2741 2711** Guides: publishing and
　　printing; Newspapers

(G-9459)
UNISAND INCORPORATED
1097 Industrial Pkwy (44256-2448)
PHONE.............................330 722-0222
David W Bullock, *Pr*
Douglas Bullock, *
▲ **EMP:** 26 **EST:** 1990
SQ FT: 3,000
SALES (est): 4.52MM **Privately Held**
Web: www.unisand.com
SIC: **3291** Abrasive wheels and grindstones,
　　not artificial

(G-9460)
UNITED SPORT APPAREL
229 Harding St Ste B (44256-1288)
PHONE.............................330 722-0818
David A Bricker, *Owner*
EMP: 10 **EST:** 1984
SQ FT: 6,000
SALES (est): 167.27K **Privately Held**
Web: www.usacustomapparel.com

SIC: **2759** 2395 Screen printing; Embroidery
　　products, except Schiffli machine

(G-9461)
UNITED TUBE CORPORATION
960 Lake Rd (44256-2453)
PHONE.............................330 725-4196
Frank J Sadowski, *Pr*
Angelina Chaplain, *
Harvey O Yoder, *
EMP: 54 **EST:** 1945
SALES (est): 3.88MM **Privately Held**
Web: www.unitedtube.com
SIC: **3317** Tubes, wrought: welded or lock
　　joint

(G-9462)
WAN DYNAMICS INC
303 N Court St Unit 1758 (44258-5377)
P.O. Box 1758 (44258-1758)
PHONE.............................877 400-9490
Jason Valore, *Pr*
Jason Gintert, *VP*
EMP: 10 **EST:** 2016
SALES (est): 3MM **Privately Held**
Web: www.wandynamics.com
SIC: **3661** Telephone and telegraph
　　apparatus

(G-9463)
WELLMAN PRODUCTS LLC
920 Lake Rd (44256-2453)
PHONE.............................855 403-9083
Thomas Cornelis Vanderlaan, *Pr*
◆ **EMP:** 255 **EST:** 2004
SQ FT: 240,000
SALES (est): 20.55MM
SALES (corp-wide): 476.36MM **Privately
Held**
SIC: **3499** Friction material, made from
　　powdered metal
HQ: Cmbf Products, Inc.
　　920 Lake Rd
　　Medina OH 44256

(G-9464)
WERKS KRAFT ENGINEERING LLC
935 Heritage Dr (44256-2404)
PHONE.............................330 721-7374
Kris Klingmann, *Pr*
EMP: 45 **EST:** 2018
SQ FT: 60,000
SALES (est): 8.5MM **Privately Held**
Web: www.kraftwerks.com
SIC: **8711 3566 3535 3441** Engineering
　　services; Speed changers (power
　　transmission equipment), except auto;
　　Conveyors and conveying equipment;
　　Fabricated structural metal

(G-9465)
WOODBINE PRODUCTS COMPANY
Also Called: Powrkleen
915 W Smith Rd (44256-2446)
PHONE.............................330 725-0165
Phillip Navratil, *Pr*
Stephen A Kuzyk Junior, *Sec*
▲ **EMP:** 14 **EST:** 1961
SQ FT: 20,000
SALES (est): 5.73MM **Privately Held**
Web: www.woodbineproducts.com
SIC: **2842 2844** Cleaning or polishing
　　preparations, nec; Perfumes, cosmetics
　　and other toilet preparations

Medway
Clark County

(G-9466)
WAYNE CONCRETE COMPANY LLC
223 Western Dr (45341-9521)
PHONE.............................937 545-9919
Wayne Gibson, *Owner*
EMP: 10 **EST:** 1987
SALES (est): 461.92K **Privately Held**
SIC: **1442** Construction sand and gravel

Mentor
Lake County

(G-9467)
ACCURATE TECH INC
Also Called: Accurate Tech
7230 Industrial Park Blvd (44060-5316)
PHONE.............................440 951-9153
Micheal Karcic Senior, *Pr*
Micheal Karcic Junior, *VP*
EMP: 6 **EST:** 1987
SQ FT: 3,000
SALES (est): 403.22K **Privately Held**
Web: www.accuratetechinc.net
SIC: **3599** Machine shop, jobbing and repair

(G-9468)
ACO INC (DH)
Also Called: Quartz
9470 Pinecone Dr (44060-1863)
PHONE.............................440 639-7230
Derek Humphries, *CEO*
Kevin Taylor, *
Judy Brubaker, *
◆ **EMP:** 50 **EST:** 1978
SQ FT: 30,000
SALES (est): 24.84MM
SALES (corp-wide): 1.15B **Privately Held**
Web: www.acousa.com
SIC: **3272 3089 3312** Concrete products,
　　precast, nec; Plastics and fiberglass tanks;
　　Stainless steel
HQ: Severin Ahlmann Holding Gmbh
　　Am Ahlmannkai
　　Budelsdorf SH 24782
　　43313540

(G-9469)
ACTIVITIES PRESS INC
Also Called: AP Direct
7181 Industrial Park Blvd (44060-5327)
PHONE.............................440 953-1200
Graydon Bullard, *Pr*
Leroy Bridges, *
Linda Bridges, *
Martin Hilston, *
▲ **EMP:** 28 **EST:** 1947
SQ FT: 24,000
SALES (est): 4.75MM **Privately Held**
Web: www.activitiespress.com
SIC: **2752 2791 2789** Offset printing;
　　Typesetting; Bookbinding and related work

(G-9470)
ADVANCED FME PRODUCTS INC
9413 Hamilton Dr (44060-8709)
PHONE.............................440 953-0700
Thomas Nalfi, *Pr*
EMP: 6 **EST:** 2005
SALES (est): 500.82K **Privately Held**
Web: www.advsts.com
SIC: **3462** Nuclear power plant forgings,
　　ferrous

(G-9471)
AERO TECH TOOL & MOLD INC
7224 Industrial Park Blvd (44060-5316)
PHONE.............................440 942-3327
Tom Murphy, *Pr*
EMP: 6 **EST:** 1979
SQ FT: 12,000
SALES (est): 374.95K **Privately Held**
SIC: **3544 3728 3462** Industrial molds;
　　Aircraft parts and equipment, nec; Iron and
　　steel forgings

(G-9472)
AEXCEL CORPORATION (PA)
7373 Production Dr (44060-4858)
PHONE.............................440 974-3800
◆ **EMP:** 34 **EST:** 1963
SALES (est): 1.45MM
SALES (corp-wide): 1.45MM **Privately
Held**
Web: www.aexcelcorp.com
SIC: **2851** Paints and paint additives

(G-9473)
AIR POWER DYNAMICS LLC
Also Called: APD
7350 Corporate Blvd (44060-4856)
PHONE.............................440 701-2100
James Stewart, *CEO*
Boya Belasic, *
EMP: 200 **EST:** 2002
SQ FT: 73,000
SALES (est): 24.79MM
SALES (corp-wide): 1.9B **Privately Held**
Web: www.airpowerdynamics.com
SIC: **3543** Industrial patterns
PA: Consolidated Precision Products Corp.
　　1621 Euclid Ave Ste 1850
　　Cleveland OH 44115
　　216 453-4800

(G-9474)
AIR TECHNICAL INDUSTRIES INC
7501 Clover Ave (44060-5297)
PHONE.............................440 951-5191
Pero Novak, *CEO*
Vida Novak, *
◆ **EMP:** 40 **EST:** 1964
SQ FT: 80,000
SALES (est): 9.7MM **Privately Held**
Web: www.airtechnical.com
SIC: **3569 3536 3535 5084** Robots,
　　assembly line: industrial and commercial;
　　Hoists, cranes, and monorails; Bulk
　　handling conveyor systems; Materials
　　handling machinery

(G-9475)
ALB TYLER HOLDINGS INC
7255 Industrial Park Blvd Ste A
(44060-5331)
PHONE.............................440 946-7171
Art Bastulli, *Pr*
Jody Kamenshy, *VP*
Kathleen Potts, *Sec*
EMP: 9 **EST:** 1990
SQ FT: 7,500
SALES (est): 256.91K **Privately Held**
Web: www.coastaldiamond.com
SIC: **3291 5085** Abrasive products; Industrial
　　supplies

(G-9476)
ALL STATE GL BLOCK FCTRY INC
8781 East Ave (44060-4303)
PHONE.............................440 205-8410
Vince Tassone, *Pr*
Vince Tasone, *Pr*
EMP: 8 **EST:** 1995
SQ FT: 3,000
SALES (est): 703.26K **Privately Held**

▲ = Import ▼ = Export
◆ = Import/Export

SIC: **1793** 5231 3229 Glass and glazing work ; Glass; Blocks and bricks, glass

(G-9477)
ALLOY PRECISION TECH INC
6989 Lindsay Dr (44060-4928)
PHONE..................440 266-7700
Michael Canty, *CEO*
Michael Canty, *Pr*
Michele Ponsart, *
◆ **EMP: 95 EST:** 1935
SALES (est): 24.72MM **Privately Held**
Web: www.alloyprecisiontech.com
SIC: **3599** 3498 3494 Bellows, industrial: metal; Fabricated pipe and fittings; Valves and pipe fittings, nec

(G-9478)
AMERICAN HERITAGE BILLD LLC
9248 Headlands Rd (44060-1026)
PHONE..................877 998-0908
◆ **EMP: 70 EST:** 1999
SALES (est): 2.4MM **Privately Held**
Web:
www.americanheritagebilliards.com
SIC: **3949** Billiard and pool equipment and supplies, general

(G-9479)
AMERICAN METAL COATINGS INC (PA)
7700 Tyler Blvd (44060-4964)
PHONE..................216 451-3131
Konstantinos Dotsikas, *Pr*
EMP: 40 EST: 1995
SQ FT: 180,000
SALES (est): 4.38MM **Privately Held**
Web: www.americanmetal.com
SIC: **3479** Coating of metals and formed products

(G-9480)
AMERICAN STERILIZER COMPANY (PA)
5960 Heisley Rd (44060-1834)
P.O. Box 960 (44061-0960)
PHONE..................440 392-8328
▲ **EMP: 46 EST:** 2009
SALES (est): 9.95MM
SALES (corp-wide): 9.95MM **Privately Held**
Web: www.steris-ast.com
SIC: **3821** Sterilizers

(G-9481)
ANGSTROM PRECISION METALS LLC
8229 Tyler Blvd (44060-4218)
PHONE..................440 255-6700
Nagesh K Palakurthi, *CEO*
David Berg, *Genl Mgr*
Sandy Bradford, *COO*
▲ **EMP: 19 EST:** 2010
SALES (est): 1.68MM **Privately Held**
Web: www.w-pm.com
SIC: **3545** Precision tools, machinists'
PA: Angstrom Automotive Group, Llc
2000 Town Ctr Ste 100
Southfield MI 48075

(G-9482)
ANODIZING SPECIALISTS INC
7547 Tyler Blvd (44060-4869)
PHONE..................440 951-0257
David J Pecjak, *Pr*
Michael T Pecjak, *VP*
EMP: 20 EST: 1977
SQ FT: 11,000
SALES (est): 1.52MM **Privately Held**
Web: www.anodizingspecialists.com

SIC: **3471** Finishing, metals or formed products

(G-9483)
APOLLO MANUFACTURING CO LLC
7911 Enterprise Dr (44060-5311)
PHONE..................440 951-9972
Allen Sandy, *Managing Member*
Ronald Jack, *
Draga Marusic, *
EMP: 30 EST: 1989
SQ FT: 25,000
SALES (est): 5.64MM **Privately Held**
Web: www.apollo-mfg.com
SIC: **3599** Machine shop, jobbing and repair

(G-9484)
APOLLO PLASTICS INC
7555 Tyler Blvd Ste 11 (44060-4866)
PHONE..................440 951-7774
Stanley Skrbis, *Pr*
Maria Skrbis, *Sec*
EMP: 10 EST: 1973
SQ FT: 8,000
SALES (est): 954.88K **Privately Held**
Web: www.apolloplastics.net
SIC: **3544** 3089 Industrial molds; Plastics processing

(G-9485)
ARBOR INDUSTRIES INC
6830 Patterson Dr (44060-4344)
PHONE..................440 255-4720
EMP: 100 EST: 1978
SALES (est): 5.06MM **Privately Held**
Web: www.arborindustriesinc.com
SIC: **3469** Stamping metal for the trade

(G-9486)
ARCH CUTTING TLS - MENTOR LLC
9332 Pinecone Dr (44060-1861)
PHONE..................440 350-9393
EMP: 11
SALES (est): 2.61MM **Privately Held**
Web: www.archcuttingtools.com
SIC: **3541** Machine tools, metal cutting type

(G-9487)
AVALIGN - INTEGRATED LLC
7124 Industrial Park Blvd (44060-5314)
PHONE..................440 269-6984
EMP: 10 EST: 2019
SALES (est): 8.97MM **Privately Held**
Web: www.avalign.com
SIC: **3841** Surgical and medical instruments

(G-9488)
AVERY DENNISON CORPORATION
8100 Tyler Blvd (44060-4865)
PHONE..................440 534-6527
EMP: 11
SALES (corp-wide): 8.76B **Publicly Held**
Web: www.averydennison.com
SIC: **2672** Paper; coated and laminated, nec
PA: Avery Dennison Corporation
8080 Norton Pkwy
Mentor OH 44060
440 534-6000

(G-9489)
AVERY DENNISON CORPORATION (PA)
Also Called: Avery Dennison
8080 Norton Pkwy (44060-5990)
PHONE..................440 534-6000
Deon M Stander, *Pr*
Mitchell R Butier, *
Danny G Allouche, *Interim Chief Financial Officer*
Deena Baker Nel, *Chief Human Resource Officer*

Nicholas R Colisto, *CIO*
EMP: 532 EST: 1935
SALES (est): 8.76B
SALES (corp-wide): 8.76B **Publicly Held**
Web: www.averydennison.com
SIC: **2672** 3081 3497 2678 Adhesive papers, labels, or tapes: from purchased material; Unsupported plastics film and sheet; Metal foil and leaf; Notebooks: made from purchased paper

(G-9490)
AVERY DENNISON CORPORATION
Avery Dnnson Fsson Flms Div US
5750 Heisley Rd (44060-1830)
P.O. Box 8008 (44077-8008)
PHONE..................440 639-3900
Bruce J Wilson, *Brnch Mgr*
EMP: 70
SALES (corp-wide): 8.76B **Publicly Held**
Web: www.averydennison.com
SIC: **2672** 2679 3081 3497 Adhesive papers, labels, or tapes: from purchased material; Building, insulating, and packaging paper; Packing materials, plastics sheet; Metal foil and leaf
PA: Avery Dennison Corporation
8080 Norton Pkwy
Mentor OH 44060
440 534-6000

(G-9491)
AVERY DENNISON CORPORATION
7100 Lindsay Dr (44060-4923)
PHONE..................440 358-2828
Frederick Buse, *Brnch Mgr*
EMP: 75
SALES (corp-wide): 8.76B **Publicly Held**
Web: www.averydennison.com
SIC: **2672** Adhesive backed films, foams and foils
PA: Avery Dennison Corporation
8080 Norton Pkwy
Mentor OH 44060
440 534-6000

(G-9492)
AVERY DNNISON G HOLDINGS I LLC
8080 Norton Pkwy (44060-5990)
PHONE..................440 534-6000
EMP: 6 EST: 2007
SALES (est): 687.27K
SALES (corp-wide): 8.76B **Publicly Held**
Web: reflectives.averydennison.com
SIC: **2672** Adhesive papers, labels, or tapes: from purchased material
PA: Avery Dennison Corporation
8080 Norton Pkwy
Mentor OH 44060
440 534-6000

(G-9493)
BRIDGESTONE RET OPERATIONS LLC
Also Called: Firestone
7495 Mentor Ave (44060-5405)
PHONE..................440 299-6126
Nathan Tokar, *Mgr*
EMP: 10
Web: www.bridgestoneamericas.com
SIC: **5531** 7534 7538 Automotive tires; Tire retreading and repair shops; General automotive repair shops
HQ: Bridgestone Retail Operations, Llc
200 4th Ave S Ste 100
Nashville TN 37201
615 937-1000

(G-9494)
BRUMALL MANUFACTURING CORP
7850 Division Dr (44060-4874)
PHONE..................440 974-2622
Rod Brumberg, *Pr*
Yvonne Brumberg, *
▲ **EMP: 40 EST:** 1968
SQ FT: 25,000
SALES (est): 5.03MM **Privately Held**
Web: www.brumall.com
SIC: **3643** Connectors and terminals for electrical devices

(G-9495)
BURTON INDUSTRIES INC
7875 Division Dr (44060-4877)
PHONE..................440 974-1700
Christopher Burton, *Pr*
Linda Burton, *Sec*
EMP: 51 EST: 1983
SALES (est): 813.03K **Privately Held**
Web: www.burtonems.com
SIC: **3599** Machine shop, jobbing and repair

(G-9496)
BUYERS PRODUCTS COMPANY (PA)
9049 Tyler Blvd (44060-4800)
PHONE..................440 974-8888
Mark Saltzman, *Pr*
Rhonda Carder, *
◆ **EMP: 150 EST:** 1947
SQ FT: 172,000
SALES (est): 92.43MM
SALES (corp-wide): 92.43MM **Privately Held**
Web: www.buyersproducts.com
SIC: **5013** 3714 Truck parts and accessories ; Motor vehicle parts and accessories

(G-9497)
BUYERS PRODUCTS COMPANY
8120 Tyler Blvd (44060-4852)
PHONE..................440 974-8888
James Kleinman, *Brnch Mgr*
EMP: 267
SALES (corp-wide): 92.43MM **Privately Held**
Web: www.buyersproducts.com
SIC: **3465** Body parts, automobile: stamped metal
PA: Buyers Products Company
9049 Tyler Blvd
Mentor OH 44060
440 974-8888

(G-9498)
CHEMSULTANTS INTERNATIONAL INC (PA)
9079 Tyler Blvd (44060-1868)
P.O. Box 1118 (44061-1118)
PHONE..................440 974-3080
Jennifer Raj Muny, *Dir*
Keith Muny, *VP*
Judith Muny, *Sec*
EMP: 9 EST: 1986
SQ FT: 10,000
SALES (est): 4.82MM
SALES (corp-wide): 4.82MM **Privately Held**
Web: www.chemsultants.com
SIC: **3821** 8734 8742 Laboratory apparatus and furniture; Product testing laboratory, safety or performance; Industry specialist consultants

(G-9499)
CLARIOS LLC
Also Called: Johnson Controls
7780 Metric Dr (44060-4862)
PHONE..................440 205-7221
George Ells, *Brnch Mgr*

GEOGRAPHIC

EMP: 34
SALES (corp-wide): 69.83B **Privately Held**
Web: www.clarios.com
SIC: 2531 Seats, automobile
HQ: Clarios, Llc
   5757 N Green Bay Ave Flor
   Glendale WI 53209

(G-9500)
CLARK RUBBER & PLASTIC COMPANY
Also Called: Clark Rubber & Plastics
8888 East Ave (44060-4306)
P.O. Box 299 (44061)
PHONE..............................440 255-9793
Gregory Clark, *Pr*
EMP: 130 **EST:** 1970
SALES (est): 9.53MM **Privately Held**
Web: www.clarkrandp.com
SIC: 3061 3069 3089 Mechanical rubber goods; Molded rubber products; Extruded finished plastics products, nec

(G-9501)
CLEVELAND SPCLTY INSPTN SVC IN
8562 East Ave (44060-4302)
PHONE..............................440 974-1818
James Popovic, *Pr*
EMP: 11 **EST:** 1984
SQ FT: 3,200
SALES (est): 501.86K **Privately Held**
Web: www.clevelandspecialty.com
SIC: 7389 3545 Inspection and testing services; Threading tools (machine tool accessories)

(G-9502)
CLIMAX METAL PRODUCTS COMPANY
8141 Tyler Blvd (44060-4855)
PHONE..............................440 943-8898
Jerry Wheaton, *CEO*
Gerald R Wheaton, *
John T White, *
L G Knecht, *
▲ **EMP:** 65 **EST:** 1946
SQ FT: 25,000
SALES (est): 8.98MM
SALES (corp-wide): 1.56B **Publicly Held**
Web: www.climaxmetal.com
SIC: 3366 3568 Bushings and bearings; Couplings, shaft: rigid, flexible, universal joint, etc.
PA: Rbc Bearings Incorporated
   1 Tribiology Ctr
   Oxford CT 06478
   203 267-7001

(G-9503)
COMMERCIAL DOCK & DOOR INC
7653 Saint Clair Ave (44060-5235)
PHONE..............................440 951-1210
Allen A Kovar, *Pr*
Raymond M Strumbly, *VP*
Tom Liebhardt, *CFO*
EMP: 22 **EST:** 2004
SALES (est): 2.48MM **Privately Held**
Web: www.commercialdockanddoor.com
SIC: 3448 Docks, prefabricated metal

(G-9504)
CONCORD ROAD EQUIPMENT MFG LLC
8200 Tyler Blvd Ste H (44060-4250)
PHONE..............................440 357-5344
Jeffery Warfield, *Managing Member*
EMP: 40 **EST:** 2021
SALES (est): 7.2MM
SALES (corp-wide): 92.43MM **Privately Held**
Web: www.concordroadequipment.com

SIC: 3531 Road construction and maintenance machinery
PA: Buyers Products Company
   9049 Tyler Blvd
   Mentor OH 44060
   440 974-8888

(G-9505)
CORE MANUFACTURING LLC
Also Called: Core Manufacturing
8878 East Ave (44060-4306)
PHONE..............................440 946-8002
Ted Wolf, *Pr*
David Sukenik, *Dir*
Theodore Wolf, *Dir*
Richard Stark, *Dir*
EMP: 9 **EST:** 2013
SALES (est): 3.95MM **Privately Held**
Web: www.coremfg.net
SIC: 3452 Bolts, nuts, rivets, and washers

(G-9506)
CORE-TECH ENTERPRISES LLC
7850 Enterprise Dr (44060-5310)
PHONE..............................440 946-8324
EMP: 6 **EST:** 2016
SALES (est): 1.6MM **Privately Held**
Web: www.core-tech-inc.com
SIC: 3599 Machine shop, jobbing and repair

(G-9507)
CRESCENT METAL PRODUCTS INC (PA)
Also Called: Cres Cor
5925 Heisley Rd (44060-1833)
PHONE..............................440 350-1100
Clifford D Baggott, *Prin*
Rio Degennaro, *
Gregory D Baggott, *
Heather B Stewart, *
Anna Baggott, *Prin*
▲ **EMP:** 171 **EST:** 1936
SALES (est): 14.62MM
SALES (corp-wide): 14.62MM **Privately Held**
Web: www.crescor.com
SIC: 3556 3567 3537 2542 Food products machinery; Industrial furnaces and ovens; Industrial trucks and tractors; Partitions and fixtures, except wood

(G-9508)
CREST PRODUCTS INC
Also Called: Crest Aluminum Products
8287 Tyler Blvd (44060-4218)
PHONE..............................440 942-5770
John M Allin, *Pr*
Peter Antos, *Treas*
Timothy Antos, *VP*
Nancy Worden, *Sec*
EMP: 18 **EST:** 1966
SQ FT: 41,500
SALES (est): 2.42MM **Privately Held**
Web: www.crestaluminum.com
SIC: 3444 7389 Awnings, sheet metal; Metal slitting and shearing

(G-9509)
CUYAHOGA MOLDED PLASTICS CO
9351 Mercantile Dr (44060-4523)
PHONE..............................216 261-2744
Ed Zalar, *Brnch Mgr*
EMP: 7
SALES (corp-wide): 5.15MM **Privately Held**
Web: www.cuyahogaplastics.com
SIC: 3089 Injection molding of plastics
PA: Cuyahoga Molded Plastics Co (Inc)
   1265 Babbitt Rd
   Euclid OH 44132
   216 261-2744

(G-9510)
DMI MANUFACTURING INC
7177 Industrial Park Blvd (44060-5327)
PHONE..............................800 238-5384
Timothy J Doney, *Prin*
EMP: 14 **EST:** 1998
SALES (est): 2.47MM **Privately Held**
Web: www.dmiparts.com
SIC: 3433 Burners, furnaces, boilers, and stokers

(G-9511)
DRUMMOND DOLOMITE INC
Also Called: Drummond Dolomite Quarry
7954 Reynolds Rd (44060-5334)
P.O. Box 658 (44061-0658)
PHONE..............................440 942-7000
Jerome T Osborne, *Pr*
Harold T Larned, *VP*
Ilda Hayden, *Sec*
EMP: 10 **EST:** 1988
SALES (est): 456.48K **Privately Held**
SIC: 1422 Dolomite, crushed and broken-quarrying

(G-9512)
DRYCAL INC
7355 Production Dr (44060-4858)
PHONE..............................440 974-1999
Margus Sweigard, *Pr*
Lembit Sweigard, *VP*
EMP: 8 **EST:** 1969
SQ FT: 14,500
SALES (est): 554.86K **Privately Held**
Web: www.drycalinc.com
SIC: 2759 Screen printing

(G-9513)
ENTERPRISE WELDING & FABG INC
6257 Heisley Rd (44060-1887)
PHONE..............................440 354-4128
Ivan Katic, *Pr*
Slavko Katic, *
Albert R Amigoni, *
EMP: 170 **EST:** 1975
SQ FT: 100,000
SALES (est): 1.92MM **Privately Held**
Web: www.enterprisewelding.com
SIC: 3444 Sheet metalwork

(G-9514)
ENTERPRISE WELDING FBRCTN
9280 Pineneedle Dr (44060-1824)
PHONE..............................440 354-3868
Mike Katic, *Prin*
EMP: 6 **EST:** 2008
SALES (est): 920.1K **Privately Held**
Web: www.enterprisewelding.com
SIC: 3441 Fabricated structural metal

(G-9515)
FASTSIGNS
7538 Mentor Ave (44060-5418)
PHONE..............................440 954-9191
EMP: 6 **EST:** 2018
SALES (est): 149K **Privately Held**
Web: www.fastsigns.com
SIC: 3993 Signs and advertising specialties

(G-9516)
FISCHER SPECIAL TOOLING CORP
7219 Commerce Dr (44060-5307)
PHONE..............................440 951-8411
Kevin Johnson, *Pr*
Molly Johnson, *Sec*
EMP: 9 **EST:** 1959
SQ FT: 5,000
SALES (est): 1.05MM **Privately Held**
Web: www.fischerspecialtooling.com

SIC: 3544 3541 3545 Special dies, tools, jigs, and fixtures; Machine tools, metal cutting: exotic (explosive, etc.); Machine tool accessories

(G-9517)
FOCUS MANUFACTURING LLC
7770 Division Dr (44060-4860)
PHONE..............................440 946-8766
Ronald K Brehm, *Pr*
Jeff Waterman, *VP*
Richard Scebbi, *Treas*
Bruce Vanek, *Sec*
EMP: 14 **EST:** 1994
SALES (est): 5.31MM
SALES (corp-wide): 144.38MM **Privately Held**
Web: www.focusmanufacturing.com
SIC: 3679 3599 Antennas, receiving; Machine shop, jobbing and repair
HQ: Libra Industries, Llc
   7770 Division Dr
   Mentor OH 44060
   440 974-7770

(G-9518)
FORMASTERS CORPORATION
5959 Pinecone Dr (44060-1866)
PHONE..............................440 639-9206
John J Ferguson, *Pr*
EMP: 12 **EST:** 1993
SQ FT: 10,500
SALES (est): 2.24MM **Privately Held**
Web: www.formasters.com
SIC: 3469 3449 Metal stampings, nec; Custom roll formed products

(G-9519)
FRANTZ MEDICAL DEVELOPMENT LTD (PA)
7740 Metric Dr (44060-4862)
PHONE..............................440 255-1155
Mark G Frantz, *Pr*
J Paul Hanson, *VP*
EMP: 8 **EST:** 1980
SQ FT: 3,750
SALES (est): 3.67MM
SALES (corp-wide): 3.67MM **Privately Held**
Web: www.frantzgroup.com
SIC: 3841 3089 Surgical and medical instruments; Injection molding of plastics

(G-9520)
FREDON CORPORATION
8990 Tyler Blvd (44060-5368)
P.O. Box 600 (44061-0600)
PHONE..............................440 951-5200
Roger J Sustar, *CEO*
Alyson Scott, *
Chris Sustar, *
Richard Ditto, *
▼ **EMP:** 80 **EST:** 1967
SQ FT: 70,000
SALES (est): 9.89MM **Privately Held**
Web: www.fredon.com
SIC: 3599 3541 Custom machinery; Grinding machines, metalworking

(G-9521)
FULTON SIGN & DECAL INC
7144 Industrial Park Blvd (44060-5314)
PHONE..............................440 951-1515
Charles Fulton, *Pr*
Gertrude Fulton, *VP*
Robert B Fulton, *Treas*
Gary Fulton, *Genl Mgr*
EMP: 6 **EST:** 1969
SQ FT: 5,000
SALES (est): 714.15K **Privately Held**
Web: www.fultonsign.com

▲ = Import ▼ = Export
◆ = Import/Export

SIC: 2759 Screen printing

(G-9522)
G & T MANUFACTURING CO
6085 Pinecone Dr (44060-1866)
PHONE..............................440 639-7777
Gerald Cutts, *Pr*
Thomas B Cutts, *Pr*
Gerald Cutts, *VP*
Beverly Cutts, *Sec*
Pat Caticchio, *Prin*
EMP: 19 EST: 1979
SQ FT: 6,200
SALES (est): 8.83MM **Privately Held**
Web: www.gtmanufacturingco.com
SIC: 3531 3537 Aerial work platforms:
hydraulic/elec. truck/carrier mounted;
Industrial trucks and tractors

(G-9523)
GDJ INC
Also Called: Technology Explortation Pdts
7585 Tyler Blvd (44060-4869)
PHONE..............................440 975-0258
Jack Gilbert, *Pr*
Deborah Gilbert, *VP*
EMP: 6 EST: 1992
SQ FT: 6,500
SALES (est): 942.73K **Privately Held**
Web: www.gdjinc.com
SIC: 3821 Laboratory equipment: fume
hoods, distillation racks, etc.

(G-9524)
GLO-QUARTZ ELECTRIC HTR CO
INC
Also Called: Heatmax Heaters
7084 Maple St (44060-4932)
P.O. Box 358 (44061-0358)
PHONE..............................440 255-9701
George T Strokes, *Pr*
Thomas M Strokes, *
Nancy L Strokes, *
EMP: 25 EST: 1952
SQ FT: 22,000
SALES (est): 5.67MM **Privately Held**
Web: www.heatmaxheaters.com
SIC: 3567 3823 3634 3433 Heating units
and devices, industrial: electric; Process
control instruments; Electric housewares
and fans; Heating equipment, except
electric

(C 0525)
HABCO TOOL AND DEV CO INC
7725 Metric Dr (44060-4863)
PHONE..............................440 946-5546
Steven Sanders, *Pr*
EMP: 34 EST: 1955
SQ FT: 24,000
SALES (est): 4.83MM **Privately Held**
Web: www.habcotool.com
SIC: 3599 7692 Machine shop, jobbing and
repair; Welding repair

(G-9526)
HDWT HOLDINGS INC
7124 Industrial Park Blvd (44060-5314)
PHONE..............................440 269-6984
Lee Dwyer, *Prin*
Mike Watts, *
Ray Arnold, *Prin*
Gus Deangelo, *
EMP: 60 EST: 1998
SALES (est): 4.38MM **Privately Held**
Web: www.avalign.com
SIC: 3841 3842 Diagnostic apparatus,
medical; Surgical appliances and supplies

(G-9527)
HEISLEY TIRE & BRAKE INC
5893 Heisley Rd (44060-1831)
PHONE..............................440 357-9797
Ralph Gamber Junior, *Pr*
Ralph Gamber Senior, *VP*
Joan Gamber, *
Nancy Gamber, *Secretary of Treasurer**
EMP: 9 EST: 1991
SQ FT: 4,000
SALES (est): 935.5K **Privately Held**
Web: www.heisleytire.net
SIC: 7534 7538 7539 Tire repair shop;
Engine repair; Brake repair, automotive

(G-9528)
HENKEL US OPERATIONS CORP
7405 Production Dr (44060-4876)
PHONE..............................440 255-8900
Robert Kern, *Brnch Mgr*
EMP: 119
SALES (corp-wide): 22.83B **Privately Held**
Web: www.henkel.com
SIC: 2891 Adhesives
HQ: Henkel Us Operations Corporation
1 Henkel Way
Rocky Hill CT 06067
860 571-5100

(G-9529)
HIGHLAND PRODUCTS CORP
9331 Mercantile Dr (44060-4523)
PHONE..............................440 352-4777
Mark Erickson, *Pr*
Jeanne Wojciechowicz, *Sec*
EMP: 10 EST: 1992
SQ FT: 11,000
SALES (est): 884.12K **Privately Held**
Web: www.highlandproducts.com
SIC: 3599 Machine shop, jobbing and repair

(G-9530)
INDUSTRIAL QUARTZ
CORPORATION
7552 Saint Clair Ave Ste D (44060-5201)
PHONE..............................440 942-0909
Richard Intihar, *Pr*
Robert Initihar, *Genl Mgr*
▲ EMP: 12 EST: 1967
SQ FT: 10,000
SALES (est): 1.03MM **Privately Held**
Web: www.indquartz.com
SIC: 3295 3769 3677 3498 Minerals, ground
or treated; Space vehicle equipment, nec;
Electronic coils and transformers;
Fabricated pipe and fittings

(G-9531)
INDUSTRIAL THERMOSET PLAS INC
Also Called: I.T. Plastics
7675 Jenther Dr (44060-4872)
PHONE..............................440 975-0411
Jack Schriner, *Pr*
EMP: 10 EST: 1982
SQ FT: 8,000
SALES (est): 911.21K **Privately Held**
Web: www.itplastics.com
SIC: 2821 Molding compounds, plastics

(G-9532)
INNOVATIVE SPORT SURFACING
LLC
8425 Station St (44060-4924)
PHONE..............................440 205-0875
Kristen Rossi, *Managing Member*
EMP: 17 EST: 2020
SALES (est): 1.5MM **Privately Held**
Web: www.innovativesportsurfacing.com

SIC: 3069 0782 Rubber floorcoverings/mats
and wallcoverings; Turf installation
services, except artificial

(G-9533)
INTEGRA ENCLOSURES LIMITED
8989 Tyler Blvd (44060-2184)
PHONE..............................440 269-4966
EMP: 100
SALES (est): 8.77MM **Privately Held**
Web: www.integraenclosures.com
SIC: 2821 Thermoplastic materials

(G-9534)
INTERNATIONAL HYDRAULICS INC
Also Called: Ihi Connectors R
7700 Saint Clair Ave (44060-5238)
PHONE..............................440 951-7186
Charles Ridley, *Pr*
▲ EMP: 50 EST: 1981
SQ FT: 62,000
SALES (est): 9.11MM **Privately Held**
Web: www.ihiconnectors.com
SIC: 3643 Electric connectors

(G-9535)
INTERPAK INC
Also Called: Roto Mold
7278 Justin Way (44060-4881)
PHONE..............................440 974-8999
Mark Shaw, *Pr*
Tad Heyman, *
▼ EMP: 43 EST: 1993
SQ FT: 65,000
SALES (est): 4.79MM **Privately Held**
Web: www.rotomold.com
SIC: 3089 Injection molding of plastics

(G-9536)
J & C GROUP INC OF OHIO
6781 Hopkins Rd (44060-4311)
PHONE..............................440 205-9658
James Smolik, *Pr*
Christine Smolik, *Stockholder*
◆ EMP: 8 EST: 2002
SQ FT: 13,000
SALES (est): 533.6K **Privately Held**
SIC: 3651 5065 Speaker systems; TV parts
and accessories, nec

(G-9537)
J & L MANAGEMENT CORPORATION
Also Called: Kramer Printing
8634 Station St (44060-4316)
PHONE..............................440 205-1199
Leonard Kramer, *Pt*
Gerald Kramer, *Pt*
EMP: 6 EST: 1986
SQ FT: 7,000
SALES (est): 472.35K **Privately Held**
Web: www.kramercolor.com
SIC: 2752 2732 Offset printing; Book printing

(G-9538)
J & M INDUSTRIES INC
7775 Division Dr (44060-4861)
PHONE..............................440 951-1985
David Martin, *Pr*
EMP: 8 EST: 2000
SQ FT: 8,000
SALES (est): 700.88K **Privately Held**
Web: www.jmdiecasting.com
SIC: 3544 Dies and die holders for metal
cutting, forming, die casting

(G-9539)
J & P PRODUCTS INC
Also Called: Specialties Unlimited
8865 East Ave (44060-4305)
PHONE..............................440 974-2830

Paul Jonke, *Pr*
Dennis Jonke, *
EMP: 10 EST: 1971
SQ FT: 18,000
SALES (est): 898.56K **Privately Held**
SIC: 3599 Machine shop, jobbing and repair

(G-9540)
JACK WALKER PRINTING CO
Also Called: Walker Printing Co.
9517 Jackson St (44060-4515)
PHONE..............................440 352-4222
Jack G Walker, *Pr*
▲ EMP: 18 EST: 1987
SQ FT: 3,500
SALES (est): 2.12MM **Privately Held**
Web: www.walker-printing.com
SIC: 2752 2791 2789 2759 Offset printing;
Typesetting; Bookbinding and related work;
Commercial printing, nec

(G-9541)
JADE PRODUCTS INC
9309 Mercantile Dr (44060-4523)
PHONE..............................440 352-1700
John Erickson, *Pr*
Darcy Erickson, *Contrlr*
EMP: 17 EST: 1992
SQ FT: 5,500
SALES (est): 4.68MM **Privately Held**
Web: www.jadeproductsinc.com
SIC: 3599 Machine shop, jobbing and repair

(G-9542)
JJ SLEEVES INC
6850 Patterson Dr (44060-4331)
PHONE..............................440 205-1055
EMP: 8 EST: 1991
SALES (est): 553.7K **Privately Held**
SIC: 3599 Machine shop, jobbing and repair

(G-9543)
JOHN D OIL AND GAS COMPANY
7001 Center St (44060-4933)
P.O. Box 5069 (44061-5069)
PHONE..............................440 255-6325
Richard M Osborne, *Ch Bd*
Timothy P Reilly, *Pr*
Carolyn Coatoam, *CFO*
EMP: 7 EST: 1999
SALES (est): 1.22MM **Privately Held**
Web: www.johndoilandgas.com
SIC: 1382 1311 4225 Oil and gas exploration
services; Crude petroleum and natural gas
production; Warehousing, self storage

(G-9544)
JOHNSTON MFG CO INC
Also Called: J M C Rollmasters
7611 Saint Clair Ave (44060-5235)
PHONE..............................440 269-1420
Dennis Johnston, *Pr*
Marsha Johnston, *Sec*
EMP: 8 EST: 1968
SQ FT: 8,500
SALES (est): 325.72K **Privately Held**
Web: www.jmcrolls.com
SIC: 3544 Special dies and tools

(G-9545)
KAEPER MACHINE INC
8680 Twinbrook Rd (44060-4341)
PHONE..............................440 974-1010
Kye Hwang, *Pr*
Mike Kidner, *Prin*
EMP: 20 EST: 1998
SALES (est): 3.71MM **Privately Held**
Web: www.kaeper.com
SIC: 3545 3484 Precision tools, machinists';
Small arms

(G-9546)
KISH COMPANY INC (PA)
8020 Tyler Blvd Ste 100 (44060-4825)
PHONE.............................440 205-9970
John R Kish, *Pr*
Brian Richards, *VP*
◆ **EMP:** 16 **EST:** 1986
SQ FT: 4,800
SALES (est): 16.49MM
SALES (corp-wide): 16.49MM **Privately Held**
Web: www.kishcompany.com
SIC: 2816 3295 Inorganic pigments; Minerals, ground or otherwise treated

(G-9547)
L J MANUFACTURING INC
9436 Mercantile Dr (44060-1889)
PHONE.............................440 352-1979
Michael Ball, *Pr*
Darlene Ball, *Sec*
EMP: 8 **EST:** 1988
SQ FT: 10,000
SALES (est): 705.34K **Privately Held**
Web: www.ljmfg.com
SIC: 3599 Machine shop, jobbing and repair

(G-9548)
LAKE COUNTY PLATING CORP
7790 Division Dr (44060-4860)
PHONE.............................440 255-8835
Charles H Dowling, *Pr*
Janet Dowling, *VP*
EMP: 10 **EST:** 1958
SQ FT: 20,000
SALES (est): 463.54K **Privately Held**
Web: www.lakecountyplating.com
SIC: 3471 Electroplating of metals or formed products

(G-9549)
LAKE PUBLISHING INC
Also Called: Callender Group, The
9930 Johnnycake Ridge Rd (44060-6752)
PHONE.............................440 299-8500
James S Callender Junior, *Prin*
Heidi Callender, *Ofcr*
EMP: 7 **EST:** 2009
SALES (est): 170.44K **Privately Held**
Web: www.thecallendergroup.com
SIC: 2741 8748 Miscellaneous publishing; Business consulting, nec

(G-9550)
LANKO INDUSTRIES INC
7301 Industrial Park Blvd (44060-5317)
PHONE.............................440 269-1641
John Lanphier, *Pr*
Susan Lanphier, *Sec*
EMP: 8 **EST:** 1981
SQ FT: 9,000
SALES (est): 810.84K **Privately Held**
Web: www.allsaintsainslie.org.au
SIC: 3544 Wire drawing and straightening dies

(G-9551)
LECTROETCH CO
9200 Tyler Blvd (44060-1882)
PHONE.............................440 934-1249
David Badt, *Pr*
Otis Mahaffey, *Stockholder*
◆ **EMP:** 14 **EST:** 1943
SALES (est): 1.17MM **Privately Held**
Web: www.monode.com
SIC: 3953 Figures (marking devices), metal

(G-9552)
LIBRA GUAYMAS LLC
7770 Division Dr (44060-4860)

Rod Howell, *CEO*
EMP: 115 **EST:** 2019
SALES (est): 7.02MM
SALES (corp-wide): 144.38MM **Privately Held**
SIC: 3291 Abrasive metal and steel products
HQ: Libra Industries, Llc
　　7770 Division Dr
　　Mentor OH 44060
　　440 974-7770

(G-9553)
LIBRA INDUSTRIES LLC (DH)
7770 Division Dr (44060-4860)
PHONE.............................440 974-7770
Jim Kircher, *CEO*
Luis Montiel, *
EMP: 120 **EST:** 1980
SQ FT: 52,000
SALES (est): 99.39MM
SALES (corp-wide): 144.38MM **Privately Held**
Web: www.libraindustries.com
SIC: 3599 3672 Machine shop, jobbing and repair; Printed circuit boards
HQ: Gem Cw Holdings, Llc
　　1100 Superior Ave
　　Cleveland OH

(G-9554)
LINTERN CORPORATION (PA)
8685 Station St (44060-4336)
P.O. Box 90 (44061-0090)
PHONE.............................440 255-9333
Richard K Lintern, *Pr*
Ray Ohler, *Development**
◆ **EMP:** 35 **EST:** 1903
SQ FT: 22,500
SALES (est): 6.23MM
SALES (corp-wide): 6.23MM **Privately Held**
Web: www.lintern.com
SIC: 3585 3714 3648 Air conditioning units, complete: domestic or industrial; Heaters, motor vehicle; Lanterns: electric, gas, carbide, kerosene, or gasoline

(G-9555)
LITTLE MOUNTAIN PRECISION LLC
8677 Tyler Blvd (44060-4346)
PHONE.............................440 290-2903
Keith R Kraus, *Prin*
EMP: 25 **EST:** 2019
SALES (est): 3.76MM **Privately Held**
Web: www.littlemountainprecision.com
SIC: 3566 3599 Gears, power transmission, except auto; Machine and other job shop work

(G-9556)
LUMINAUD INC
8688 Tyler Blvd (44060-4348)
PHONE.............................440 255-9082
Thomas Lennox, *Pr*
Dorothy Lennox, *VP*
EMP: 7 **EST:** 1964
SQ FT: 5,000
SALES (est): 510.21K **Privately Held**
Web: www.luminaud.com
SIC: 3842 Limbs, artificial

(G-9557)
MAG-NIF INC
8820 East Ave (44060-4390)
P.O. Box 720 (44061-0720)
PHONE.............................440 255-9366
William W Knox Junior, *Ch Bd*
Jim Weiss, *
Dennis Delaat, *
▲ **EMP:** 100 **EST:** 1963

SQ FT: 180,000
SALES (est): 2.64MM **Privately Held**
Web: www.magnif.com
SIC: 3944 3089 Banks, toy; Injection molding of plastics

(G-9558)
MALISH CORPORATION (PA)
Also Called: Malish
7333 Corporate Blvd (44060-4857)
PHONE.............................440 951-5356
Jeffery J Malish, *Pr*
Fred Lombardi, *
Mark Ray, *
◆ **EMP:** 100 **EST:** 1948
SQ FT: 82,000
SALES (est): 8.57MM
SALES (corp-wide): 8.57MM **Privately Held**
Web: www.malish.com
SIC: 3991 3089 Brushes, household or industrial; Extruded finished plastics products, nec

(G-9559)
MALONE SPECIALTY INC
8900 East Ave (44060-4306)
PHONE.............................440 255-4200
Steven Malone, *Pr*
▲ **EMP:** 12 **EST:** 1982
SQ FT: 10,000
SALES (est): 1.78MM **Privately Held**
Web: www.malonespecialtyinc.com
SIC: 5013 3492 Truck parts and accessories ; Hose and tube fittings and assemblies, hydraulic/pneumatic

(G-9560)
MATRIX TOOL & MACHINE INC
7870 Division Dr (44060-4874)
PHONE.............................440 255-0300
Richard Wilson, *Pr*
George Maust, *
Alan Bockmuller, *
EMP: 24 **EST:** 1975
SQ FT: 20,000
SALES (est): 3.81MM **Privately Held**
Web: www.matrix-tool.com
SIC: 3599 3545 Custom machinery; Machine tool accessories

(G-9561)
MEDALLION LIGHTING CORPORATION
Also Called: Complements Lighting
9345 Progress Pkwy (44060-1855)
P.O. Box 51 (44061-0051)
PHONE.............................440 255-8383
William A Knuff, *Pr*
Kenneth Maclean, *
◆ **EMP:** 40 **EST:** 1982
SQ FT: 50,000
SALES (est): 2.34MM **Privately Held**
Web: www.medallionlighting.com
SIC: 3645 3641 2514 Table lamps; Electric lamps; Metal household furniture

(G-9562)
METAL SEAL & PRODUCTS INC
7333 Corporate Blvd (44060-4857)
PHONE.............................440 946-8500
EMP: 175
Web: www.metalseal.com
SIC: 3451 3471 Screw machine products; Plating and polishing

(G-9563)
METAL SEAL PRECISION LTD (PA)
8687 Tyler Blvd (44060-4346)
PHONE.............................440 255-8888
John L Habe Iv, *Pr*

Allan B Pirnat, *
Richard Sippola, *
▼ **EMP:** 72 **EST:** 2011
SQ FT: 158,000
SALES (est): 8.65MM
SALES (corp-wide): 8.65MM **Privately Held**
Web: www.metalseal.com
SIC: 3444 Sheet metalwork

(G-9564)
MICRO LABORATORIES INC
7158 Industrial Park Blvd (44060-5314)
PHONE.............................440 918-0001
Keith Kokal, *Pr*
EMP: 6 **EST:** 1987
SQ FT: 1,500
SALES (est): 2.39MM **Privately Held**
Web: www.microlabs-inc.com
SIC: 3829 8734 Measuring and controlling devices, nec; Testing laboratories

(G-9565)
MILL ROSE LABORATORIES INC
7310 Corp Blvd (44060)
PHONE.............................440 974-6730
Paul M Miller, *Pr*
Stephen W Kovalcheck Junior, *CFO*
Lawrence W Miller, *
▲ **EMP:** 40 **EST:** 1977
SQ FT: 59,000
SALES (est): 4.8MM
SALES (corp-wide): 27.19MM **Privately Held**
Web: www.millroselabs.com
SIC: 3991 5047 Brooms and brushes; Medical equipment and supplies
PA: The Mill-Rose Company
　　7995 Tyler Blvd
　　Mentor OH 44060
　　440 255-9171

(G-9566)
MILL-ROSE COMPANY (PA)
Also Called: Mill-Rose
7995 Tyler Blvd (44060-4896)
PHONE.............................440 255-9171
Paul M Miller, *Pr*
Lawrence W Miller, *
Diane Miller, *
▲ **EMP:** 160 **EST:** 1920
SQ FT: 61,000
SALES (est): 27.19MM
SALES (corp-wide): 27.19MM **Privately Held**
Web: www.millrose.com
SIC: 3841 5085 3991 3624 Surgical instruments and apparatus; Industrial supplies; Brushes, household or industrial; Carbon and graphite products

(G-9567)
MONODE MARKING PRODUCTS INC (PA)
Also Called: Lectroetch Company, The
9200 Tyler Blvd (44060-1882)
PHONE.............................440 975-8802
Tom Mackey, *Pr*
EMP: 45 **EST:** 1956
SQ FT: 15,000
SALES (est): 9.29MM
SALES (corp-wide): 9.29MM **Privately Held**
Web: www.monode.com
SIC: 3542 5084 Marking machines; Printing trades machinery, equipment, and supplies

(G-9568)
MONODE STEEL STAMP INC
7620 Tyler Blvd (44060-4853)
PHONE.............................440 975-8802

▲ = Import ▼ = Export
◆ = Import/Export

Chris Lillstrung, *Mgr*
EMP: 14
Web: www.monode.com
SIC: 3542 3469 Marking machines; Metal stampings, nec
PA: Monode Steel Stamp, Inc
149 High St
New London OH 44851

(G-9569)
MUM INDUSTRIES INC (PA)
8989 Tyler Blvd (44060-2184)
P.O. Box 1870 (44061-1870)
PHONE..................................440 269-4966
Jim Cooney, *Pr*
Chris Brizes, *
▲ **EMP:** 64 **EST:** 1996
SALES (est): 4.76MM
SALES (corp-wide): 4.76MM **Privately Held**
Web: www.mumindustries.com
SIC: 2821 Plasticizer/additive based plastic materials

(G-9570)
NEW TRANSCON LLC
Also Called: Transcon Conveyor
8824 Twinbrook Rd (44060-4335)
PHONE..................................440 255-7600
Robert W Bruml, *Managing Member*
Roger Breedlove, *
◆ **EMP:** 26 **EST:** 1959
SQ FT: 45,000
SALES (est): 5.56MM **Privately Held**
Web: www.transconconveyor.com
SIC: 3535 Belt conveyor systems, general industrial use

(G-9571)
NHVS INTERNATIONAL INC
7600 Tyler Blvd (44060-4853)
PHONE..................................440 527-8610
Sherry Richcreek, *CEO*
EMP: 325 **EST:** 2010
SQ FT: 100,000
SALES (est): 9.79MM **Privately Held**
Web: www.nhvsinternational.com
SIC: 3812 Acceleration indicators and systems components, aerospace

(G-9572)
NIFTECH INC
Also Called: Niftech Precision Race Pdts
5555 Wilson Dr (44060-1555)
PHONE..................................440 257-6018
Julie Knaus, *Pr*
Raymond Knaus, *VP*
EMP: 10 **EST:** 1983
SALES (est): 215.77K **Privately Held**
Web: www.niftech.com
SIC: 3699 Electrical equipment and supplies, nec

(G-9573)
NORTHCOAST VALVE AND GATE INC
9437 Mercantile Dr (44060-4524)
P.O. Box 901 (44096)
PHONE..................................440 392-9910
Anthony Fistek, *Pr*
EMP: 8 **EST:** 1985
SALES (est): 965.04K **Privately Held**
Web: www.ncvg.net
SIC: 3494 Valves and pipe fittings, nec

(G-9574)
NOVA METAL PRODUCTS INC
Also Called: Nova Metal Products
7500 Clover Ave (44060-5214)
PHONE..................................440 269-1741
Dan Novak, *CEO*
EMP: 20 **EST:** 2004

SALES (est): 3.81MM **Privately Held**
Web: www.novametalproducts.com
SIC: 3599 Machine shop, jobbing and repair

(G-9575)
OE EXCHANGE LLC (PA)
7750 Tyler Blvd (44060-4802)
PHONE..................................440 266-1639
EMP: 7 **EST:** 2008
SALES (est): 3.54MM
SALES (corp-wide): 3.54MM **Privately Held**
Web: www.wheelcraft.com
SIC: 3714 Wheels, motor vehicle

(G-9576)
OMEGA MACHINE & TOOL INC
7590 Jenther Dr (44060-4872)
PHONE..................................440 946-6846
Dolf Litschel, *Pr*
Ema Litschel, *VP*
EMP: 10 **EST:** 1980
SQ FT: 9,000
SALES (est): 759.3K **Privately Held**
Web: www.omegamachine.com
SIC: 3599 Machine shop, jobbing and repair

(G-9577)
OSAIR INC (PA)
7001 Center St (44060-4933)
P.O. Box 1020 (44061-1020)
PHONE..................................440 974-6500
Richard Osborne, *Pr*
Jon Magnusson, *VP*
EMP: 9 **EST:** 1963
SQ FT: 4,000
SALES (est): 6.29MM
SALES (corp-wide): 6.29MM **Privately Held**
Web: www.osairinc.com
SIC: 1381 2813 Drilling oil and gas wells; Nitrogen

(G-9578)
OSBORNE INC (PA)
7954 Reynolds Rd (44060-5334)
P.O. Box 658 (44061-0658)
PHONE..................................440 942-7000
Jerome T Osborne, *Prin*
William Mackey, *
▲ **EMP:** 25 **EST:** 1947
SQ FT: 4,500
SALES (est): 14.18MM
SALES (corp-wide): 14.18MM **Privately Held**
Web: www.osbornecompaniesinc.com
SIC: 5211 3273 3271 Lumber and other building materials; Ready-mixed concrete; Blocks, concrete or cinder: standard

(G-9579)
OSBORNE CO
7954 Reynolds Rd (44060-5334)
P.O. Box 658 (44061-0658)
PHONE..................................440 942-7000
Jerome T Osborne, *Pr*
Gerald J Smith, *
EMP: 6 **EST:** 1956
SQ FT: 4,500
SALES (est): 116.87K **Privately Held**
Web: www.osbornecompaniesinc.com
SIC: 3273 Ready-mixed concrete

(G-9580)
PAKO INC
7615 Jenther Dr (44060-4872)
PHONE..................................440 946-8030
Paul Kosir, *Pr*
▲ **EMP:** 216 **EST:** 1973
SQ FT: 142,000
SALES (est): 20.89MM **Privately Held**

Web: www.pakoinc.com
SIC: 3714 3728 3724 Motor vehicle parts and accessories; Aircraft parts and equipment, nec; Aircraft engines and engine parts

(G-9581)
PARKER PRECISION INC
8950 Tyler Blvd (44060-2185)
PHONE..................................440 951-6501
Reeve J Parker, *Pr*
Maria Parker, *VP*
EMP: 9 **EST:** 1996
SQ FT: 12,000
SALES (est): 1.14MM **Privately Held**
Web: www.parkerprecision.com
SIC: 3599 Machine shop, jobbing and repair

(G-9582)
PARKER-HANNIFIN CORPORATION
Also Called: Gas Turbine Fuel Systems
8940 Tyler Blvd (44060-2185)
PHONE..................................440 266-2300
Mark Seidel, *Brnch Mgr*
EMP: 50
SALES (corp-wide): 19.93B **Publicly Held**
Web: www.parker.com
SIC: 3594 Fluid power pumps
PA: Parker-Hannifin Corporation
6035 Parkland Blvd
Cleveland OH 44124
216 896-3000

(G-9583)
PATTERSON-BRITTON PRINTING INC
7805 Saint James Dr (44060-4067)
PHONE..................................216 781-7997
Harry Britton, *Pr*
John Britton, *VP*
EMP: 8 **EST:** 1974
SALES (est): 403.24K **Privately Held**
Web: www.pattersonbritton.com
SIC: 2752 Offset printing

(G-9584)
PCC AIRFOILS LLC
8607 Tyler Blvd (44060-4296)
PHONE..................................440 255-9770
Armand Lauzon, *Genl Mgr*
EMP: 108
SQ FT: 55,000
SALES (corp-wide): 424.23B **Publicly Held**
Web: www.pccairfoils.com
SIC: 3369 3324 3724 Castings, except die-castings, precision; Steel investment foundries; Airfoils, aircraft engine
HQ: Pcc Airfoils, Llc
3401 Entp Pkwy Ste 200
Beachwood OH 44122
216 831-3590

(G-9585)
PERFORMANCE MOTORSPORTS INC
7201 Industrial Park Blvd (44060-5315)
PHONE..................................440 951-6600
EMP: 10 **EST:** 1989
SALES (est): 470.42K **Privately Held**
Web: www.wiseco.com
SIC: 3714 Motor vehicle parts and accessories

(G-9586)
PERFORMANCE SUPERABRASIVES LLC
Also Called: Coastal Diamond
7255 Industrial Park Blvd Ste A (44060-5331)
PHONE..................................440 946-7171

Scott Kaplan, *Managing Member*
EMP: 9 **EST:** 2012
SQ FT: 5,200
SALES (est): 676.34K **Privately Held**
SIC: 3291 3545 Wheels, grinding: artificial; Wheel turning equipment, diamond point or other

(G-9587)
PLATING PROCESS SYSTEMS INC
7561 Tyler Blvd Ste 5 (44060-4867)
P.O. Box 808 (44060-0808)
▼ **EMP:** 9 **EST:** 1985
SQ FT: 9,880
SALES (est): 284.79K **Privately Held**
Web: www.platingprocess.com
SIC: 2899 Plating compounds

(G-9588)
POLYCHEM LLC (HQ)
Also Called: Greenbridge
6277 Heisley Rd (44060-1899)
PHONE..................................440 357-1500
Brian Jeckering, *CEO*
Barry Clifford, *
◆ **EMP:** 180 **EST:** 1973
SQ FT: 165,000
SALES (est): 105.3MM **Privately Held**
Web: www.polychem.com
SIC: 2671 Plastic film, coated or laminated for packaging
PA: The Sterling Group L P
9 Greenway Plz Ste 2400
Houston TX 77046

(G-9589)
POLYMER CONCEPTS INC
7555 Tyler Blvd Ste 1 (44060-4866)
PHONE..................................440 953-9605
Chris Callsen, *Pr*
▼ **EMP:** 7 **EST:** 1999
SQ FT: 6,000
SALES (est): 2.05MM **Privately Held**
Web: www.polymerconcept.com
SIC: 2821 Polyurethane resins

(G-9590)
PRECISION BENDING TECH INC (PA)
Also Called: Stam
7350 Production Dr (44060-4859)
PHONE..................................440 974-2500
William Lennon, *Pr*
EMP: 11 **EST:** 2017
SALES (est): 8.41MM
SALES (corp-wide): 8.41MM **Privately Held**
Web: www.precisionbending.com
SIC: 3498 Tube fabricating (contract bending and shaping)

(G-9591)
PRECISION METALS GROUP LLC
8687 Tyler Blvd (44060-4346)
PHONE..................................440 255-8888
EMP: 6 **EST:** 2018
SALES (est): 1.26MM **Privately Held**
Web: www.metalseal.com
SIC: 3599 Machine shop, jobbing and repair

(G-9592)
PRINCETON TOOL INC (PA)
Also Called: Princeton Precision Group
7830 Division Dr (44060-4874)
P.O. Box 508 (44061-0508)
PHONE..................................440 290-8666
Kenneth Bevington Iii, *CEO*
▲ **EMP:** 135 **EST:** 1997
SALES (est): 14.78MM
SALES (corp-wide): 14.78MM **Privately Held**
Web: www.princetontool.com

SIC: 3599 5084 Machine shop, jobbing and repair; Tool and die makers equipment

(G-9593)
PROFAC INC (PA)
Also Called: Merritt
7198 Industrial Park Blvd (44060-5328)
PHONE..............................440 942-0205
G Michael Merritt, *CEO*
Keith E Merritt, *VP*
Stephanie Cherok, *Dir Fin*
▲ EMP: 135 EST: 1972
SQ FT: 90,000
SALES (est): 23.52MM
SALES (corp-wide): 23.52MM **Privately Held**
Web: www.merrittwoodwork.com
SIC: 2431 Millwork

(G-9594)
PROFAC INC
Also Called: Merritt Woodwork
7171 Industrial Park Blvd (44060-5351)
PHONE..............................440 942-0205
EMP: 65
SALES (corp-wide): 23.52MM **Privately Held**
Web: www.merrittwoodwork.com
SIC: 2431 Millwork
PA: Profac, Inc.
7198 Industrial Prk Blvd
Mentor OH 44060
440 942-0205

(G-9595)
PROFICIENT MACHINING CO
7522 Tyler Blvd Unit B-G (44060-5450)
PHONE..............................440 942-4942
Kenneth Putman, *Pr*
Kenneth Putman Junior, *Ex VP*
Carol Putman, *Sec*
EMP: 22 EST: 1973
SQ FT: 15,000
SALES (est): 5.69MM **Privately Held**
Web: www.proficientmachining.com
SIC: 3599 Machine shop, jobbing and repair

(G-9596)
PROFICIENT PLASTICS INC
7777 Saint Clair Ave (44060-5237)
P.O. Box 5053 (44061-5053)
PHONE..............................440 205-9700
Robert W Wisen, *Pr*
EMP: 10 EST: 1997
SQ FT: 1,500
SALES (est): 883.15K **Privately Held**
Web: www.proficientplastics.com
SIC: 3089 Injection molding of plastics

(G-9597)
PROGAGE INC
Also Called: Progage
7555 Tyler Blvd Ste 6 (44060-4866)
PHONE..............................440 951-4477
Edward Vadakin, *Pr*
EMP: 19 EST: 1985
SQ FT: 14,000
SALES (est): 2.43MM **Privately Held**
Web: www.progage.com
SIC: 3544 Special dies and tools

(G-9598)
PROGRESSIVE POWDER COATING INC
7742 Tyler Blvd (44060-4802)
PHONE..............................440 974-3478
Mark Saltzman, *Pr*
Thomas Gries, *
EMP: 25 EST: 1995
SQ FT: 24,024
SALES (est): 2.1MM **Privately Held**

Web: www.progressivepowdercoating.com
SIC: 3479 Coating of metals and formed products

(G-9599)
PYROMATICS CORP (PA)
9321 Pineneedle Dr (44060-1825)
PHONE..............................440 352-3500
Andre Ezis, *CEO*
EMP: 10 EST: 1975
SQ FT: 27,000
SALES (est): 1.54MM
SALES (corp-wide): 1.54MM **Privately Held**
Web: www.pyromatics.com
SIC: 3221 3231 3297 Glass containers; Products of purchased glass; Nonclay refractories

(G-9600)
QUADREL INC
Also Called: Quadrel Labeling Systems
7670 Jenther Dr (44060-4872)
PHONE..............................440 602-4700
Lon Deckard, *Pr*
Charles Wepler, *
Joseph P Rouse, *
◆ EMP: 43 EST: 1962
SQ FT: 3,842
SALES (est): 9.75MM **Privately Held**
Web: www.quadrel.com
SIC: 3565 Labeling machines, industrial

(G-9601)
QUALITY COMPONENTS INC
8825 East Ave (44060-4305)
P.O. Box 956 (44061-0956)
PHONE..............................440 255-0606
William Dennison Senior, *Pr*
EMP: 15 EST: 1999
SQ FT: 10,000
SALES (est): 2.5MM
SALES (corp-wide): 534.79MM **Publicly Held**
Web: www.qccmfg.com
SIC: 7699 3548 Welding equipment repair; Welding and cutting apparatus and accessories, nec
HQ: Stratos International, Inc.
299 Johnson Ave Sw
Waseca MN 56093
507 833-8822

(G-9602)
QUALITY MACHINE SYSTEMS LLC
7875 Enterprise Dr (44060-5309)
PHONE..............................440 223-2217
Paul Kinczel, *Pt*
Steve Vucic, *Pt*
EMP: 8 EST: 1997
SQ FT: 10,000
SALES (est): 1.53MM **Privately Held**
Web: www.qualitymachinerysystems.com
SIC: 3599 Machine shop, jobbing and repair

(G-9603)
QUALTEK ELECTRONICS CORP
7610 Jenther Dr (44060-4872)
PHONE..............................440 951-3300
John Hallums, *Pr*
▲ EMP: 120 EST: 1979
SQ FT: 20,000
SALES (est): 9.78MM **Privately Held**
Web: www.qualtekusa.com
SIC: 3634 3643 3577 3612 Electric housewares and fans; Current-carrying wiring services; Computer peripheral equipment, nec; Transformers, except electric

(G-9604)
R J K ENTERPRISES INC
Also Called: Niftech
5565 Wilson Dr (44060-1555)
PHONE..............................440 257-6018
Raymond Knaus, *Pr*
Julie Knaus, *VP*
Ellen Cook, *VP*
EMP: 10 EST: 1977
SQ FT: 1,500
SALES (est): 78.06K **Privately Held**
SIC: 7389 3599 Design, commercial and industrial; Custom machinery

(G-9605)
R T & T MACHINING CO INC
Also Called: R T & T Machining
8195 Tyler Blvd (44060-4854)
PHONE..............................440 974-8479
F Paul Thompson, *Pr*
Ellen Thompson, *VP*
EMP: 14 EST: 1982
SQ FT: 12,000
SALES (est): 1.1MM **Privately Held**
Web: www.rttmachining.com
SIC: 3451 3599 3545 3544 Screw machine products; Machine shop, jobbing and repair ; Machine tool accessories; Special dies, tools, jigs, and fixtures

(G-9606)
RACE WINNING BRANDS INC (PA)
Also Called: Wiseco
7201 Industrial Park Blvd (44060-5315)
PHONE..............................440 951-6600
Robert Bruegging, *Pr*
Steve Boyack, *
EMP: 290 EST: 2016
SQ FT: 150,000
SALES (est): 195.05MM
SALES (corp-wide): 195.05MM **Privately Held**
Web: www.racewinningbrands.com
SIC: 3592 3714 Pistons and piston rings; Motor vehicle parts and accessories

(G-9607)
RB SIGMA LLC
6111 Heisley Rd (44060-1837)
PHONE..............................440 290-0577
EMP: 85 EST: 2016
SALES (est): 34.04MM **Privately Held**
Web: www.rbsigma.com
SIC: 8741 5047 3999 5734 Management services; Medical equipment and supplies; Barber and beauty shop equipment; Software, business and non-game

(G-9608)
RKI INC (PA)
Also Called: Roll-Kraft
8901 Tyler Blvd (44060-2184)
PHONE..............................888 953-9400
George C Gehrisch Junior, *Pr*
Sanjay Singh, *
Dennis M Langer, *
Chuck Summerhill, *
Ken Fruscella, *
EMP: 121 EST: 1964
SQ FT: 100,000
SALES (est): 19.92MM
SALES (corp-wide): 19.92MM **Privately Held**
Web: www.roll-kraft.com
SIC: 3547 Primary rolling mill equipment

(G-9609)
ROGERS DISPLAY INC (HQ)
Also Called: Rogers Company, The
7550 Tyler Blvd (44060-4868)
PHONE..............................440 951-9200

EMP: 30 EST: 1956
SALES (est): 8.15MM
SALES (corp-wide): 450.24MM **Privately Held**
Web: www.therogersco.com
SIC: 3993 2542 Displays and cutouts, window and lobby; Partitions and fixtures, except wood
PA: Nesco, Inc.
6140 Prkland Blvd Ste 110
Cleveland OH 44124
440 461-6000

(G-9610)
ROYAL PLASTICS INC
9410 Pineneedle Dr (44060-1880)
PHONE..............................440 352-1357
Gary Mcconnell, *Pr*
Bruce Usnik, *
Patricia Garner, *
▲ EMP: 225 EST: 1966
SQ FT: 135,000
SALES (est): 23.16MM **Privately Held**
Web: www.royalplastics.com
SIC: 3089 3643 Injection molding of plastics; Current-carrying wiring services

(G-9611)
RS MANUFACTURING INC
8878 East Ave (44060-4306)
PHONE..............................440 946-8002
Richard Stark Senior, *Pr*
Richard Stark Junior, *VP*
David Stark, *Stockholder*
Robyn Stark, *Stockholder*
Dee Ann Stark, *Stockholder*
EMP: 7 EST: 1975
SQ FT: 4,800
SALES (est): 415.27K **Privately Held**
SIC: 3452 Bolts, metal

(G-9612)
SEABISCUIT MOTORSPORTS INC (HQ)
7201 Industrial Park Blvd (44060-5315)
PHONE..............................440 951-6600
▲ EMP: 290 EST: 1980
SQ FT: 150,000
SALES (est): 23.52MM
SALES (corp-wide): 7.75B **Publicly Held**
Web: www.wiseco.com
SIC: 3592 3714 Pistons and piston rings; Motor vehicle parts and accessories
PA: Dover Corporation
3005 Hghland Pkwy Ste 200
Downers Grove IL 60515
630 541-1540

(G-9613)
SEMPER QUALITY INDUSTRY INC
Also Called: Mc Cartney Industries
9411 Mercantile Dr (44060-4524)
P.O. Box 1449 (44061-1449)
PHONE..............................440 352-8111
Dale B Mccartney, *Pr*
Duane Mccartney, *VP*
EMP: 8 EST: 1985
SQ FT: 12,000
SALES (est): 936.48K **Privately Held**
Web: www.semperquality.com
SIC: 1721 3479 Industrial painting; Coating of metals and formed products

(G-9614)
SGM CO INC
9000 Tyler Blvd (44060-1897)
PHONE..............................440 255-1190
Laura L Gerboth, *Pr*
Patrick L Gerboth, *
EMP: 40 EST: 1967
SQ FT: 45,000

SALES (est): 4.43MM **Privately Held**
Web: www.sgmcoinc.com
SIC: 3433 Heating equipment, except electric

(G-9615)
SHEET METAL PRODUCTS CO INC
5950 Pinecone Dr (44060-1865)
PHONE...........................440 392-9000
Joseph J Mahovlic, *CEO*
James F Saxa, *
Steven H Sneiderman, *
EMP: 25 EST: 1998
SALES (est): 2.87MM **Privately Held**
Web: www.smpohio.com
SIC: 3444 3429 Sheet metal specialties, not
  stamped; Hardware, nec
PA: The Providence Group Inc
    9290 Metcalf Rd
    Willoughby OH

(G-9616)
SMP WELDING LLC
8171 Tyler Blvd (44060-4826)
PHONE...........................440 205-9353
EMP: 12 EST: 1988
SQ FT: 10,000
SALES (est): 4.77MM **Privately Held**
Web: www.smpwelding.com
SIC: 7692 Welding repair

(G-9617)
SONOMA GRINDING MACHINING INC
9330 Progress Pkwy (44060-1859)
PHONE...........................440 918-7990
Josip Filipovic, *Pr*
EMP: 6 EST: 2004
SQ FT: 6,000
SALES (est): 2.06MM **Privately Held**
SIC: 3599 Machine shop, jobbing and repair

(G-9618)
SOUTH SHORE CONTROLS INC
9395 Pinecone Dr (44060-1862)
PHONE...........................440 259-2500
John Ovsek, *VP*
Chris Langmack, *
EMP: 45 EST: 1995
SQ FT: 22,000
SALES (est): 11.07MM **Privately Held**
Web: www.southshorecontrols.com
SIC: 3549 5084 Metalworking machinery, nec
  ; Instruments and control equipment

(G-9019)
SPANG & COMPANY
Spang Power Electronics
9305 Progress Pkwy (44060-1855)
PHONE...........................440 350-6108
Timothy J Lindey, *Div Pres*
EMP: 31
SALES (corp-wide): 42.75MM **Privately
Held**
Web: www.spang.com
SIC: 3613 3625 3674 3566 Switchgear and
  switchboard apparatus; Control equipment,
  electric; Semiconductors and related
  devices; Speed changers, drives, and gears
PA: Spang & Company
    110 Delta Dr
    Pittsburgh PA 15238
    412 963-9363

(G-9620)
SSC CONTROLS COMPANY
8909 East Ave (44060-4305)
PHONE...........................440 205-1600
James Moll, *Pr*
James E Moll, *
Brent Moll, *
▲ EMP: 25 EST: 1994
SQ FT: 8,500

SALES (est): 3.85MM **Privately Held**
Web: www.ssccontrols.com
SIC: 3625 Relays and industrial controls

(G-9621)
ST TOOL & DESIGN INC
9452 Mercantile Dr (44060-1889)
PHONE...........................440 357-1250
John Fifa, *Genl Mgr*
Tony Sisa, *Mgr*
EMP: 14 EST: 1982
SQ FT: 6,000
SALES (est): 4MM **Privately Held**
Web: www.st-tool.com
SIC: 3599 Machine shop, jobbing and repair

(G-9622)
STAM INC
Also Called: Stam
7350 Production Dr (44060-4859)
P.O. Box 951108 (44193-0005)
PHONE...........................440 974-2500
Kent Marvin, *Pr*
Brendan Anderson, *
H James Sheedy, *
▲ EMP: 45 EST: 1973
SQ FT: 28,000
SALES (est): 3.48MM
SALES (corp-wide): 8.41MM **Privately
Held**
Web: www.precisionbending.com
SIC: 3498 Tube fabricating (contract bending
  and shaping)
PA: Precision Bending Technology, Inc.
    7350 Production Dr
    Mentor OH 44060
    440 974-2500

(G-9623)
STERIS CORPORATION
Also Called: Research & Development II
5900 Heisley Rd (44060-1834)
PHONE...........................440 354-2600
EMP: 55
Web: www.steris.com
SIC: 3841 Surgical and medical instruments
HQ: Steris Corporation
    5960 Heisley Rd
    Mentor OH 44060
    440 354-2600

(G-9624)
STERIS CORPORATION (DH)
5900 Heisley Rd (44060-1834)
PHONE...........................440 354-2600
Walter Rosebrough Junior, *Pr*
Michael Tokich, *CFO*
Kathie Bardwell, *CCO*
Adam Zangerle, *Sec*
Loyal Wilson, *Prin*
◆ EMP: 843 EST: 1985
SALES (est): 1.97B **Privately Held**
Web: www.steris.com
SIC: 3842 3845 3841 Sterilizers, hospital
  and surgical; Endoscopic equipment,
  electromedical, nec; Diagnostic apparatus,
  medical
HQ: Steris Limited
    Rutherford House
    Derby DE21
    345 241-3588

(G-9625)
STERIS CORPORATION
6515 Hopkins Rd (44060-4307)
PHONE...........................330 696-9946
Les Vinney, *Mgr*
EMP: 96
Web: www.steris.com
SIC: 3842 Sterilizers, hospital and surgical
HQ: Steris Corporation

5960 Heisley Rd
Mentor OH 44060
440 354-2600

(G-9626)
STERIS CORPORATION
6100 Heisley Rd (44060-1838)
PHONE...........................440 392-8079
EMP: 79
Web: www.steris.com
SIC: 3842 Surgical appliances and supplies
HQ: Steris Corporation
    5960 Heisley Rd
    Mentor OH 44060
    440 354-2600

(G-9627)
STERIS CORPORATION
9325 Pinecone Dr (44060-1862)
P.O. Box 75044 (44101-2199)
PHONE...........................440 354-2600
EMP: 125
Web: www.steris.com
SIC: 3842 Surgical appliances and supplies
HQ: Steris Corporation
    5960 Heisley Rd
    Mentor OH 44060
    440 354-2600

(G-9628)
STRATEGIC TECHNOLOGY ENTP
5960 Heisley Rd (44060-1834)
PHONE...........................440 354-2600
Gerry Reis, *VP*
Gerry Reis, *Pr*
Les Binney, *Pr*
EMP: 8 EST: 2002
SALES (est): 696.65K **Privately Held**
Web: www.steris.com
SIC: 3821 Clinical laboratory instruments,
  except medical and dental

(G-9629)
STRATUS UNLIMITED LLC (PA)
Also Called: Mc Group
8959 Tyler Blvd (44060-2133)
PHONE...........................440 209-6200
Tim Eippert, *CEO*
Kurt Ripkey, *CRO*
Bryan Hartnett, *
▲ EMP: 185 EST: 1995
SALES (est): 134.32MM
SALES (corp-wide): 134.32MM **Privately
Held**
Web: www.stratusunlimited.com
SIC: 3993 Signs and advertising specialties

(G-9630)
**SULECKI PRECISION PRODUCTS
INC**
8785 East Ave (44060-4303)
PHONE...........................440 255-5454
Daniel Sulecki, *Pr*
John Sulecki, *VP*
David Sulecki, *Sec*
Ed Sulecki, *Pur/Dir*
EMP: 10 EST: 1988
SQ FT: 4,500
SALES (est): 1.03MM **Privately Held**
Web: www.suleckiprecision.com
SIC: 3599 3544 3444 3441 Machine shop,
  jobbing and repair; Special dies, tools, jigs,
  and fixtures; Sheet metalwork; Fabricated
  structural metal

(G-9631)
SUNSET INDUSTRIES INC
7567 Tyler Blvd (44060-4869)
PHONE...........................440 306-8284
Tony Hauptman, *Pr*
Ivan Hauptman, *

Tony Hauptman, *Sec*
Rudy Hren, *
Frank Hren, *Stockholder*
EMP: 26 EST: 1959
SQ FT: 14,500
SALES (est): 3.72MM **Privately Held**
Web: www.sunsetindustries.com
SIC: 3812 3594 3599 Search and navigation
  equipment; Fluid power pumps and motors;
  Machine shop, jobbing and repair

(G-9632)
SUTTERLIN MACHINE & TL CO INC
9445 Pineneedle Dr (44060-1827)
PHONE...........................440 357-0817
Claude Sutterlin, *Pr*
EMP: 17 EST: 1966
SQ FT: 6,000
SALES (est): 2.28MM **Privately Held**
Web: www.sutterlinmachine.com
SIC: 3544 Special dies and tools

(G-9633)
TECMARK CORPORATION
Also Called: North Shore Safety
7335 Production Dr (44060-4858)
PHONE...........................440 205-9188
EMP: 25
SALES (corp-wide): 11.1MM **Privately
Held**
Web: www.nssltd.com
SIC: 3823 Process control instruments
PA: Tecmark Corporation
    7745 Metric Dr
    Mentor OH 44060
    440 205-7600

(G-9634)
TECMARK CORPORATION (PA)
7745 Metric Dr (44060-4863)
PHONE...........................440 205-7600
Walter Swick, *CEO*
Sean Swick, *
Chuck Stein, *
Adam Stein Ctrl, *Prin*
▲ EMP: 55 EST: 1999
SQ FT: 23,000
SALES (est): 11.1MM
SALES (corp-wide): 11.1MM **Privately
Held**
Web: www.tecmarkcorp.com
SIC: 3629 3823 3643 Electronic generation
  equipment; Process control instruments;
  Current carrying wiring services

(G-9635)
TEN MFG LLC
7675 Saint Clair Ave (44060-5235)
PHONE...........................440 487-1100
Angelo Pariza, *Sole Member*
EMP: 10 EST: 2017
SALES (est): 2.01MM **Privately Held**
SIC: 3599 Machine and other job shop work

(G-9636)
TFI MANUFACTURING LLC
8989 Tyler Blvd (44060-2184)
PHONE...........................440 290-9411
EMP: 11 EST: 2018
SALES (est): 741.66K **Privately Held**
Web: www.tfi-manufacturing.com
SIC: 8711 3469 3542 Engineering services;
  Metal stampings, nec; Die casting and
  extruding machines

(G-9637)
THERMOTION CORP
Also Called: Thermotion-Madison
6520 Hopkins Rd (44060-4308)
PHONE...........................440 639-8325
Gary Swanson, *Pr*

EMP: 15 EST: 1964
SALES (est): 2.43MM Privately Held
Web: www.thermotion.com
SIC: 3625 Actuators, industrial

(G-9638)
TOTAL MANUFACTURING CO INC
7777 Saint Clair Ave (44060-5237)
P.O. Box 5053 (44061-5053)
PHONE....................................440 205-9700
Robert W Wisen, *Pr*
EMP: 22 EST: 1990
SALES (est): 4.83MM Privately Held
Web: www.totalmfg.com
SIC: 3599 Machine shop, jobbing and repair

(G-9639)
TQ MANUFACTURING COMPANY INC
7345 Production Dr (44060-4858)
PHONE....................................440 255-9000
James Klopp, *Pr*
EMP: 7 EST: 1996
SQ FT: 10,000
SALES (est): 994.83K Privately Held
Web: www.tqmfg.com
SIC: 3599 Machine shop, jobbing and repair

(G-9640)
TRAILER COMPONENT MFG INC
8120 Tyler Blvd (44060-4852)
PHONE....................................440 255-2888
James Kleinman, *Pr*
Mark Saltzman, *
Thomas Gries, *
▲ EMP: 30 EST: 1992
SQ FT: 42,000
SALES (est): 6.7MM Privately Held
SIC: 3714 3599 3537 Motor vehicle parts
and accessories; Machine and other job
shop work; Industrial trucks and tractors

(G-9641)
TRANSCAT INC
9325 Progress Pkwy (44060-1855)
PHONE....................................440 853-1907
EMP: 10
SALES (corp-wide): 259.48MM Publicly
Held
Web: www.transcat.com
SIC: 3825 Instruments to measure electricity
PA: Transcat, Inc.
35 Vantage Point Dr
Rochester NY 14624
585 352-7777

(G-9642)
TRANSFER EXPRESS INC
7650 Tyler Blvd (44060-4853)
PHONE....................................440 918-1900
Ted Stahl, *Pr*
Matt Cook, *
Jason Ziga, *
◆ EMP: 65 EST: 1990
SQ FT: 85,000
SALES (est): 8.22MM
SALES (corp-wide): 24.42MM Privately
Held
Web: www.transferexpress.com
SIC: 2759 2752 Screen printing; Transfers,
decalcomania or dry: lithographed
PA: Stahls' Inc.
25901 Jefferson Ave
Saint Clair Shores MI 48081
586 772-6161

(G-9643)
TRAVELERS CUSTOM CASE INC
7444 Tyler Blvd Ste C (44060-5402)
PHONE....................................216 621-8447
Kenneth Nosse, *Pr*
Elizabeth Nosse, *Sec*

EMP: 10 EST: 1946
SQ FT: 18,000
SALES (est): 431.16K Privately Held
Web: www.travelerscustomcase.com
SIC: 3161 Cases, carrying, nec

(G-9644)
TRENT MANUFACTURING COMPANY
7310 Corporate Blvd (44060-4856)
PHONE....................................216 391-1551
Lynn Gallatin, *Pr*
EMP: 6 EST: 1958
SALES (est): 404.46K Privately Held
Web: www.trentmfg.com
SIC: 3991 5085 Brushes, household or
industrial; Brushes, industrial

(G-9645)
TYLER HAVER INC (DH)
Also Called: W S Tyler
8570 Tyler Blvd (44060-4232)
PHONE....................................440 974-1047
Randy A Bakeberg, *Pr*
▲ EMP: 50 EST: 1998
SQ FT: 65,000
SALES (est): 10.2MM
SALES (corp-wide): 676.62MM Privately
Held
Web: www.wstyler.com
SIC: 3496 Miscellaneous fabricated wire
products
HQ: Haver & Boecker Holding Usa, Inc.
8570 Tyler Blvd
Mentor OH 44060
800 321-6188

(G-9646)
UNIQUE PACKAGING & PRINTING
9086 Goldfinch Ct (44060-1810)
P.O. Box 417 (44045-0417)
PHONE....................................440 785-6730
Robert F Bradach, *Pr*
Madeline Bradach, *VP*
EMP: 10 EST: 1972
SQ FT: 20,000
SALES (est): 127.2K Privately Held
SIC: 7389 3991 Packaging and labeling
services; Brooms and brushes

(G-9647)
**UNITED STTES ENDSCOPY GROUP
IN (DH)**
Also Called: US Endoscopy
5976 Heisley Rd (44060-1873)
PHONE....................................440 639-4494
Tony Siracusa, *CEO*
Gretchen Younker Cohen, *
Lynda Younker, *
▲ EMP: 161 EST: 1991
SQ FT: 30,000
SALES (est): 35.12MM Privately Held
Web: www.steris.com
SIC: 3841 Surgical and medical instruments
HQ: Steris Corporation
5960 Heisley Rd
Mentor OH 44060
440 354-2600

(G-9648)
VECTOR INTERNATIONAL CORP
Also Called: Vector Screenprinting & EMB
7404 Tyler Blvd (44060-5402)
PHONE....................................440 942-2002
Doug Anderson, *Pr*
EMP: 8 EST: 1988
SQ FT: 6,000
SALES (est): 442.95K Privately Held
Web: www.vectorpromo.com
SIC: 2396 2395 Screen printing on fabric
articles; Embroidery and art needlework

(G-9649)
VICON FABRICATING COMPANY LTD
7200 Justin Way (44060-4881)
PHONE....................................440 205-6700
Jeffrey Conforte, *
Anita R Seidemann, *
EMP: 35 EST: 1965
SQ FT: 40,000
SALES (est): 6.15MM Privately Held
Web: www.viconfab.com
SIC: 3441 3398 Fabricated structural metal;
Metal heat treating

(G-9650)
VISTA CREATIONS LLC
Also Called: Fastsigns
7896 Tyler Blvd (44060-4878)
PHONE....................................440 954-9191
Kimberly Hoffmann, *Prin*
EMP: 6 EST: 2019
SALES (est): 323.06K Privately Held
Web: www.vistaequitypartners.com
SIC: 3993 Signs and advertising specialties

(G-9651)
VOLK OPTICAL INC
Also Called: Volk Optical
7893 Enterprise Dr (44060-5309)
PHONE....................................440 942-6161
Jyoti Gupta, *Pr*
Gary Webel, *
▲ EMP: 70 EST: 1974
SQ FT: 18,000
SALES (est): 9.96MM
SALES (corp-wide): 2.58B Privately Held
Web: www.volk.com
SIC: 8011 3851 3827 Offices and clinics of
medical doctors; Lenses, ophthalmic;
Optical instruments and lenses
HQ: Halma Holdings Inc.
535 Sprngfeld Ave Ste 110
Summit NJ 07901
513 772-5501

(G-9652)
WILSON OPTICAL LABS INC
Also Called: North American Coating Labs
9450 Pineneedle Dr (44060-1828)
PHONE....................................440 357-7000
John H Wilson, *CEO*
Brian Wilson, *Pr*
EMP: 50 EST: 1974
SQ FT: 30,000
SALES (est): 3.99MM Privately Held
Web: www.nacl.com
SIC: 3851 3827 3229 Lens coating,
ophthalmic; Optical instruments and lenses;
Pressed and blown glass, nec

(G-9653)
WIRE SHOP INC
5959 Pinecone Dr (44060-1866)
PHONE....................................440 354-6842
John Ferguson, *Pr*
Howard Pindale, *VP*
EMP: 20 EST: 1984
SQ FT: 20,000
SALES (est): 3.12MM Privately Held
Web: www.thewireshop.com
SIC: 3544 3599 Special dies and tools;
Machine and other job shop work

(G-9654)
**WISMAR PRCSION TOLING PROD
INC**
7505 Tyler Blvd Ste 2 (44060-5416)
PHONE....................................440 296-0487
Gerald Wisen, *Prin*
Noel Martinez, *Prin*
EMP: 9 EST: 1996
SALES (est): 2.01MM Privately Held

Web: www.wismarptp.com
SIC: 3599 Machine shop, jobbing and repair

(G-9655)
YUKON INDUSTRIES INC
7665 Mentor Ave Ste 113 (44060-5409)
PHONE....................................440 478-4174
Leonard Norwood, *CEO*
EMP: 25 EST: 2008
SALES (est): 1.07MM Privately Held
SIC: 3585 Heating equipment, complete

Mentor On The Lake
Lake County

(G-9656)
AQUA PENNSYLVANIA INC
Also Called: Aqua Ohio
7748 Twilight Dr (44060-2629)
PHONE....................................440 257-6190
Bill Bowers, *Brnch Mgr*
EMP: 6
SALES (corp-wide): 2.09B Publicly Held
Web: www.aquawater.com
SIC: 5499 4941 3589 Water: distilled mineral
or spring; Water supply; Water treatment
equipment, industrial
HQ: Aqua Pennsylvania, Inc.
762 W Lancaster Ave
Bryn Mawr PA 19010
610 525-1400

(G-9657)
BLINGFLINGFOREVER LLC
7383 Dahlia Dr (44060-3121)
PHONE....................................216 215-6955
Monica Koczan, *Owner*
EMP: 7 EST: 2019
SALES (est): 246.75K Privately Held
SIC: 2339 Women's and misses' accessories

Metamora
Fulton County

(G-9658)
PARKER-HANNIFIN CORPORATION
Hydraulic Filter Division
16810 County Road 2 (43540-9714)
PHONE....................................419 644-4311
Dibyava Ghosh, *Brnch Mgr*
EMP: 150
SALES (corp-wide): 19.93B Publicly Held
Web: www.parker.com
SIC: 3594 Fluid power pumps and motors
PA: Parker-Hannifin Corporation
6035 Parkland Blvd
Cleveland OH 44124
216 896-3000

Miamisburg
Montgomery County

(G-9659)
A-1 SPRINKLER COMPANY INC
2383 Northpointe Dr (45342-2989)
PHONE....................................937 859-6198
Bill Hausmann, *CEO*
EMP: 68 EST: 1982
SQ FT: 15,000
SALES (est): 8.66MM Privately Held
Web: www.a1ssi.com
SIC: 3569 5087 Firefighting and related
equipment; Firefighting equipment

(G-9660)
ADVANCED INDUS MSRMENT SYSTEMS (PA)
Also Called: Measurement Specialties
2580 Kohnle Dr (45342-3669)
P.O. Box 341118 (45434-1118)
PHONE..................937 320-4930
David A Delph, *Pr*
▲ **EMP:** 13 **EST:** 2009
SALES (est): 4.31MM **Privately Held**
Web: www.aimsmetrology.com
SIC: 3829 Measuring and controlling devices, nec

(G-9661)
ADVANTIC BUILDING GROUP LLC
511 Byers Rd (45342-5337)
PHONE..................513 290-4796
EMP: 26 **EST:** 2021
SALES (est): 1.09MM **Privately Held**
Web: www.advanticllc.com
SIC: 1799 3543 Special trade contractors, nec; Industrial patterns

(G-9662)
AEROSEAL LLC (PA)
225 Byers Rd # 1 (45342-3614)
PHONE..................937 428-9300
Amit Gupta, *CEO*
Vijay Kollepara, *VP*
Daniel Crowe, *CFO*
Chris Gibson, *VP Mktg*
Tim Burnette, *Commercial Vice President*
▲ **EMP:** 32 **EST:** 2011
SALES (est): 14MM
SALES (corp-wide): 14MM **Privately Held**
Web: www.aeroseal.com
SIC: 8748 3679 Energy conservation consultant; Hermetic seals, for electronic equipment

(G-9663)
ALDRICH CHEMICAL
Also Called: Sigma-Aldrich
3858 Benner Rd (45342-4304)
PHONE..................937 859-1808
Diane Szydell, *Mgr*
EMP: 74
SQ FT: 30,000
SALES (corp-wide): 22.37B **Privately Held**
SIC: 2819 5084 2899 2869 Isotopes, radioactive; Chemical process equipment; Chemical preparations, nec; Industrial organic chemicals, nec
HQ: Aldrich Chemical
3050 Spruce St
Saint Louis MO 63103
314 771-5765

(G-9664)
ALEGRE INC
Also Called: Alegre Global Supply Solutions
3101 W Tech Blvd (45342-0819)
PHONE..................937 885-6786
Lilly Phillips, *Pr*
Don Phillips, *VP*
▲ **EMP:** 18 **EST:** 1992
SQ FT: 24,000
SALES (est): 6.34MM **Privately Held**
Web: www.alegreglobalsupplysolutions.com
SIC: 4225 3714 5013 General warehousing; Motor vehicle engines and parts; Automotive supplies and parts

(G-9665)
AMSIVE OH LLC
3303 W Tech Blvd (45342-0817)
PHONE..................937 885-8000
Don Landrum, *Managing Member*
Jim Wisnionski, *Managing Member*

Gordon Anderson, *Managing Member*
Mike Dolan, *Managing Member*
EMP: 70 **EST:** 1965
SQ FT: 140,000
SALES (est): 10.65MM
SALES (corp-wide): 147.04MM **Privately Held**
Web: www.amsive.com
SIC: 7331 7374 2752 Direct mail advertising services; Data processing service; Commercial printing, lithographic
HQ: Amsive Aq Llc
1224 Poinsett Hwy
Greenville SC 29609

(G-9666)
APPLEHEART INC
Also Called: Appleheart
2240 E Central Ave (45342-7601)
PHONE..................937 384-0430
Tom Robbins, *Pr*
EMP: 6 **EST:** 1990
SQ FT: 4,500
SALES (est): 317.17K **Privately Held**
Web: www.appleheartbrandingsolutions.com
SIC: 5699 2759 2395 Uniforms and work clothing; Commercial printing, nec; Embroidery products, except Schiffli machine

(G-9667)
AVERY DENNISON CORPORATION
200 Monarch Ln (45342-3639)
PHONE..................937 865-2439
EMP: 13
SALES (corp-wide): 8.76B **Publicly Held**
Web: www.averydennison.com
SIC: 2672 Adhesive papers, labels, or tapes: from purchased material
PA: Avery Dennison Corporation
8080 Norton Pkwy
Mentor OH 44060
440 534-6000

(G-9668)
BELL VAULT AND MONU WORKS INC
1019 S Main St (45342-3148)
PHONE..................937 866-2444
Timothy Bell, *Pr*
Greg Bell, *Sec*
EMP: 12 **EST:** 1928
SQ FT: 17,000
SALES (est): 2.14MM **Privately Held**
Web: www.bellvaultandmonument.com
SIC: 3272 5999 7261 3281 Burial vaults, concrete or precast terrazzo; Monuments, finished to custom order; Funeral service and crematories; Cut stone and stone products

(G-9669)
BILLERUD AMERICAS CORPORATION (HQ)
10050 Innovation Dr Ste 200 (45342-4935)
PHONE..................877 855-7243
Kevin M Kuznicki, *Sr VP*
Kevin M Kuznicki, *Sr VP*
Aaron D Haas, *
Terrance M Dyer, *Senior Vice President Human Resources*
EMP: 37 **EST:** 2006
SALES (est): 1.28B
SALES (corp-wide): 3.92B **Privately Held**
Web: www.billerud.com
SIC: 2621 Paper mills
PA: Billerud Ab (Publ)
Evenemangsgatan 17
Solna 169 7
855333500

(G-9670)
BILLERUD COMMERCIAL LLC
8540 Gander Creek Dr (45342-5439)
PHONE..................877 855-7243
Tor Lundqvist, *Managing Member*
EMP: 15 **EST:** 2021
SALES (est): 11.58MM
SALES (corp-wide): 3.92B **Privately Held**
SIC: 2621 Specialty papers
HQ: Billerud Americas Corporation
10050 Innvtion Dr Ste 200
Miamisburg OH 45342

(G-9671)
BILLERUD ESCANABA LLC
8540 Gander Creek Dr (45342-5439)
PHONE..................877 855-7243
EMP: 10 **EST:** 2016
SALES (est): 1.35MM
SALES (corp-wide): 3.92B **Privately Held**
SIC: 2621 Paper mills
PA: Billerud Ab (Publ)
Evenemangsgatan 17
Solna 169 7
855333500

(G-9672)
BILLERUD US PROD HOLDG LLC (DH)
10050 Innovation Dr Ste 200 (45342-4935)
PHONE..................877 855-7243
Mike Jackson, *CEO*
Mark A Angelson, *
Daniel A Clark, *
Jay A Epstein, *
David L Santez, *
◆ **EMP:** 380 **EST:** 2005
SALES (est): 399.66MM
SALES (corp-wide): 3.92B **Privately Held**
Web: www.billerud.com
SIC: 2621 2611 Fine paper; Pulp manufactured from waste or recycled paper
HQ: Billerud Americas Corporation
10050 Innvtion Dr Ste 200
Miamisburg OH 45342

(G-9673)
BLATCHFORD INC
Also Called: Endolite
1031 Byers Rd (45342-5487)
PHONE..................937 291-3636
Steven Blatchford, *CEO*
Chris Nolan, *
Tanya Shell, *
◆ **EMP:** 60 **EST:** 1992
SQ FT: 22,000
SALES (est): 9.6MM **Privately Held**
Web: www.blatchfordmobility.com
SIC: 3949 5999 5047 Sporting and athletic goods, nec; Orthopedic and prosthesis applications; Artificial limbs

(G-9674)
BMC GROWTH FUND LLC
2991 Newmark Dr (45342-5416)
PHONE..................937 291-4110
David Brixey, *Prin*
EMP: 162 **EST:** 2015
SALES (est): 4.88MM **Privately Held**
SIC: 2672 Paper; coated and laminated, nec

(G-9675)
BMF DEVICES INC
510 S Riverview Ave (45342-3028)
P.O. Box 1414 (45343-1414)
PHONE..................937 866-3451
Gregg A Layman, *Pr*
Gary S Layman, *VP*
Rodney G Layman, *CFO*
▲ **EMP:** 19 **EST:** 1997
SALES (est): 871.61K **Privately Held**

Web: www.bmfdevices.com
SIC: 3089 Plastics processing

(G-9676)
BRAINERD INDUSTRIES INC (PA)
680 Precision Ct (45342-6138)
P.O. Box 755 (45066)
PHONE..................937 228-0488
Gregory W Fritz, *Pr*
Rhonda Reynolds, *
EMP: 49 **EST:** 1997
SQ FT: 72,000
SALES (est): 4.98MM
SALES (corp-wide): 4.98MM **Privately Held**
Web: www.brainerdindustries.com
SIC: 3469 3993 3442 Stamping metal for the trade; Name plates: except engraved, etched, etc.: metal; Metal doors, sash, and trim

(G-9677)
BROWN CNC MACHINING INC
433 E Maple Ave (45342-2343)
PHONE..................937 865-9191
Mike Brown, *Pr*
Steve Brown, *Ex VP*
EMP: 17 **EST:** 1996
SQ FT: 20,000
SALES (est): 2.22MM **Privately Held**
SIC: 3599 Machine shop, jobbing and repair

(G-9678)
C B MFG & SLS CO INC (PA)
4455 Infirmary Rd (45342-1233)
PHONE..................937 866-5986
Charles S Biehn Junior, *CEO*
Richard Porter, *
Merle Wilberding, *
Donald M Cain, *
▲ **EMP:** 67 **EST:** 1967
SQ FT: 90,000
SALES (est): 25.37MM
SALES (corp-wide): 25.37MM **Privately Held**
Web: www.americancuttingedge.com
SIC: 5085 3423 Knives, industrial; Knives, agricultural or industrial

(G-9679)
CERTIFIED COMPARATOR PRODUCTS
2580 Kohnle Dr (45342-3669)
PHONE..................937 426-9677
Rod Murch, *Pr*
EMP: 6 **EST:** 2012
SALES (est): 928.8K **Privately Held**
Web: www.aimsmetrology.com
SIC: 5065 3545 Electronic parts and equipment, nec; Comparators (machinists' precision tools)

(G-9680)
CERTIFIED TOOL & GRINDING INC
Also Called: Ctg
4455 Infirmary Rd (45342-1233)
PHONE..................937 865-5934
Charles Biehn, *Pr*
Joseph Biehn, *VP*
▲ **EMP:** 7 **EST:** 1972
SALES (est): 882.75K
SALES (corp-wide): 882.75K **Privately Held**
Web: www.toolgrindcoat.com
SIC: 3479 Coating of metals and formed products
PA: Certified Heat Treating, Inc
4475 Infirmary Rd
Dayton OH 45449
937 866-0245

(G-9681)
CESO INC (PA)
Also Called: Ceso
3601 Rigby Rd Ste 300 (45342-5047)
PHONE..................................937 435-8584
David Oakes, *Pr*
James I Weprin, *
Kathleen Cyphert, *
EMP: 29 **EST:** 1987
SALES (est): 28.13MM
SALES (corp-wide): 28.13MM **Privately Held**
Web: www.cesoinc.com
SIC: 8711 3674 8712 Civil engineering; Light emitting diodes; Architectural services

(G-9682)
CHRISTIAN BLUE PAGES (PA)
521 Byers Rd Ste 102 (45342-5379)
PHONE..................................937 847-2583
Darrel Geis, *Pr*
EMP: 8 **EST:** 1991
SALES (est): 549.4K
SALES (corp-wide): 549.4K **Privately Held**
Web: www.christianblue.com
SIC: 2741 Directories, telephone: publishing only, not printed on site

(G-9683)
CONNECTIVE DESIGN INCORPORATED
Also Called: C D I
3010 S Tech Blvd (45342-4860)
PHONE..................................937 746-8252
Danya A Chandler, *Pr*
Mike Chandler, *VP*
EMP: 11 **EST:** 1991
SQ FT: 8,500
SALES (est): 6.12MM **Privately Held**
Web: www.connectivedesign.com
SIC: 3678 3714 3679 Electronic connectors; Automotive wiring harness sets; Harness assemblies, for electronic use: wire or cable

(G-9684)
COX NEWSPAPERS LLC
Also Called: Miamisburg News
230 S 2nd St (45342-2925)
P.O. Box 108 (45343-0108)
PHONE..................................937 866-3331
Donald J Miller, *Pr*
EMP: 10
SALES (corp-wide): 961.55MM **Privately Held**
Web: www.coxnewspapers.com
SIC: 2711 Newspapers, publishing and printing
HQ: Cox Newspapers, Inc.
6205 Pchtree Dnwody Rd N
Atlanta GA 30328

(G-9685)
CUSTOMFORMED PRODUCTS INC
Also Called: Custom Formed Products
645 Precision Ct (45342-6138)
PHONE..................................937 388-0480
Michael Schindler, *Pr*
EMP: 15 **EST:** 1973
SQ FT: 15,000
SALES (est): 2.33MM **Privately Held**
Web: www.customformedproducts.com
SIC: 2789 3469 3544 Paper cutting; Metal stampings, nec; Dies, steel rule

(G-9686)
DAY-TEC TOOL & MFG INC
4900 Lyons Rd Unit A (45342-6417)
PHONE..................................937 847-0022
Gerald Whitehead, *Pr*
Dana Whitehead, *Pr*
Joseph Baylogh, *VP*

EMP: 12 **EST:** 1985
SQ FT: 15,000
SALES (est): 883.33K **Privately Held**
Web: www.daytectool.com
SIC: 3599 Machine shop, jobbing and repair

(G-9687)
DAYTON SUPERIOR CORPORATION (DH)
1125 Byers Rd (45342-5765)
PHONE..................................937 866-0711
Mark D Carpenter, *Pr*
Daniel T Dolson, *Ex VP*
◆ **EMP:** 115 **EST:** 1924
SQ FT: 72,000
SALES (est): 467.72MM
SALES (corp-wide): 7.35B **Privately Held**
Web: www.daytonsuperior.com
SIC: 3315 3452 3462 3089 Steel wire and related products; Dowel pins, metal; Construction or mining equipment forgings, ferrous; Plastics hardware and building products
HQ: White Cap Supply Holdings, Llc
6250 Brook Hllow Pkwy Ste
Norcross GA 30071
800 944-8322

(G-9688)
DAYTON SYSTEMS GROUP INC
3003 S Tech Blvd (45342-4864)
PHONE..................................937 885-5665
Henry C Bachmann, *Pr*
Steve Cook, *VP*
Brad Bachmann, *COO*
EMP: 15 **EST:** 1993
SQ FT: 23,000
SALES (est): 1.15MM **Privately Held**
Web: www.dsgtech.com
SIC: 3599 Machine shop, jobbing and repair

(G-9689)
DAYTON WATERJET LLC
8641 Washington Church Rd (45342-4470)
P.O. Box 562 (45343-0562)
PHONE..................................937 428-0944
EMP: 7 **EST:** 2005
SALES (est): 1.26MM **Privately Held**
Web: www.daytonwaterjet.com
SIC: 1629 3599 Cutting of right-of-way; Machine and other job shop work

(G-9690)
DAYTRONIC CORPORATION (HQ)
Also Called: Daytronic
965 Capstone Cir (45342-1000)
PHONE..................................937 866-3300
Robert Bob Hart, *Pr*
EMP: 9 **EST:** 1954
SALES (est): 428.31K **Privately Held**
Web: www.daytronic.com
SIC: 3829 Measuring and controlling devices, nec
PA: Global Power Technology Inc.
191 Talmadge Rd Ste 3
Edison NJ 08817

(G-9691)
ESKO-GRAPHICS INC (HQ)
Also Called: Eskoartwork
8535 Gander Creek Dr (45342-5436)
PHONE..................................937 454-1721
Stefaan Deveen, *CEO*
Frank Mcfaden, *CFO*
James O'reilly, *Sec*
◆ **EMP:** 70 **EST:** 1997
SQ FT: 27,000
SALES (est): 24.38MM
SALES (corp-wide): 5.19B **Publicly Held**
Web: www.esko.com

SIC: 5084 7372 Printing trades machinery, equipment, and supplies; Prepackaged software
PA: Veralto Corporation
225 Wyman St Ste 250
Waltham MA 02451
781 755-3655

(G-9692)
EVENFLO COMPANY INC (DH)
Also Called: Evenflo
3131 Newmark Dr Ste 300 (45342-5400)
PHONE..................................937 415-3300
Dave Taylor, *CEO*
Peter Banat, *VP*
Josh Korth, *CFO*
David Mcgillivary, *Treas*
◆ **EMP:** 677 **EST:** 1920
SQ FT: 1,250,000
SALES (est): 272.16MM **Privately Held**
Web: www.evenflo.com
SIC: 5099 2531 Baby carriages, strollers and related products; Seats, automobile
HQ: Goodbaby International Holdings Limited
Rm 2502 25/F Tung Chiu Coml Ctr
Wan Chai HK

(G-9693)
GAYSTON CORPORATION
Also Called: Mulch Masters of Ohio
721 Richard St (45342-1840)
P.O. Box 523 (45343-0523)
PHONE..................................937 743-6050
Adam Stone, *CEO*
Andrew Sheldrick, *
◆ **EMP:** 125 **EST:** 1951
SQ FT: 280,000
SALES (est): 23.81MM **Privately Held**
Web: www.gayston.com
SIC: 1794 3999 2819 2499 Excavation and grading, building construction; Military insignia; Aluminum compounds; Mulch, wood and bark

(G-9694)
HAHN AUTOMATION GROUP US INC
10909 Industry Ln (45342-0818)
PHONE..................................937 886-3232
John C Hanna, *CEO*
Thomas Hahn, *
EMP: 60 **EST:** 1993
SQ FT: 63,000
SALES (est): 24.97MM
SALES (corp-wide): 2.62B **Privately Held**
Web: www.invotec.com
SIC: 8711 3599 Machine tool design; Custom machinery
HQ: Hahn Automation Group Holding Gmbh
Liebshausener Str. 3
Rheinbollen RP 55494
676490220

(G-9695)
HAMMELMANN CORPORATION (HQ)
436 Southpointe Dr (45342-6459)
PHONE..................................937 859-8777
Gisela Hammelmann, *VP*
Michael Goecke, *VP*
Peter Englehardt, *Sec*
▲ **EMP:** 16 **EST:** 1987
SQ FT: 10,000
SALES (est): 18.01MM **Privately Held**
Web: www.hammelmann.com
SIC: 5084 3443 Pumps and pumping equipment, nec; Fabricated plate work (boiler shop)
PA: Interpump Group Spa
Via Enrico Fermi 25
Sant'ilario D'enza RE 42049

(G-9696)
HARTZELL MFG CO LLC
2533 Technical Dr (45342-6108)
PHONE..................................937 859-5955
EMP: 36 **EST:** 1939
SQ FT: 35,000
SALES (est): 5.79MM **Privately Held**
Web: pm.drtholdingsllc.com
SIC: 3444 3479 3471 Sheet metal specialties, not stamped; Coating of metals and formed products; Plating and polishing
HQ: Drt Precision Mfg., Llc
1985 Campbell Rd
Sidney OH 45365
937 507-4308

(G-9697)
HEARTH PRODUCTS CONTROLS CO
Also Called: Galaxy Outdoor
2225 Lyons Rd (45342-4465)
PHONE..................................937 436-9800
Sean Steimle, *CEO*
Greg Stech, *General Vice President*
▲ **EMP:** 18 **EST:** 1976
SALES (est): 3.91MM **Privately Held**
Web: www.hpcfire.com
SIC: 3491 Process control regulator valves

(G-9698)
HEARTLAND PUBLICATIONS LLC
Also Called: Civitas Media
4500 Lyons Rd (45342-6447)
PHONE..................................860 664-1075
EMP: 110
SIC: 2759 Publication printing

(G-9699)
HILLTOP BASIC RESOURCES INC
Also Called: Riverbend Sand Rock and Gravel
4710 Soldiers Home W Carrollton Rd (45342-1274)
PHONE..................................937 859-3616
Mike Oliver, *Mgr*
EMP: 8
SALES (corp-wide): 49.96MM **Privately Held**
Web: www.hilltopcompanies.com
SIC: 5032 1442 Gravel; Construction sand and gravel
PA: Hilltop Basic Resources, Inc.
50 E Rvrcnter Blvd Ste 10
Covington KY 41011
513 651-5000

(G-9700)
HUFFY SPORTS WASHINGTON INC
Also Called: Gen X Sports
225 Byers Rd (45342-3614)
PHONE..................................937 865-2800
John Muskovich, *Prin*
EMP: 6 **EST:** 2004
SALES (est): 959.69K
SALES (corp-wide): 24.14MM **Privately Held**
Web: www.huffy.com
SIC: 3949 Basketball equipment and supplies, general
PA: Huffy Corporation
8877 Gander Creek Dr
Miamisburg OH 45342
800 872-2453

(G-9701)
INNOMARK COMMUNICATIONS LLC
3233 S Tech Blvd (45342-0843)
PHONE..................................937 454-5555
Rob Jones, *Mgr*
EMP: 97
SALES (corp-wide): 47.75MM **Privately Held**
Web: www.innomarkcom.com

▲ = Import ▼ = Export
◆ = Import/Export

SIC: **2752** 2789 Offset printing; Bookbinding and related work
PA: Innmark Communications Llc
420 Distribution Cir
Fairfield OH 45014
888 466-6627

(G-9702)
JASON SCHIRMER
Also Called: Deuce Shirt Customs & More
3020 S Tech Blvd (45342-4860)
PHONE..........................937 433-3023
Jason Schirmer, *Owner*
EMP: 6 EST: 2018
SALES (est): 129.53K **Privately Held**
Web: www.deuceshirts.com
SIC: **5699** 2759 Shirts, custom made; Screen printing

(G-9703)
JATRODIESEL INC
Also Called: Jatrodiesel
845 N Main St (45342-1871)
◆ EMP: 17 EST: 2004
SALES (est): 902.41K **Privately Held**
Web: www.rpsol.com
SIC: **2869** 3519 Industrial organic chemicals, nec; Diesel engine rebuilding

(G-9704)
JOHNSON MFG SYSTEMS LLC
4505 Infirmary Rd (45342-1235)
PHONE..........................937 866-4744
Tom Johnson, *Pt*
Tom Johnson, *Managing Member*
EMP: 11 EST: 2003
SQ FT: 2,500
SALES (est): 1.3MM **Privately Held**
Web: www.jms-tech.net
SIC: **3599** 3499 8711 Machine shop, jobbing and repair; Machine bases, metal; Mechanical engineering

(G-9705)
KILLER BROWNIE LTD (PA)
Also Called: Killer Brownie Company, The
2495 Technical Dr (45342-6137)
P.O. Box 751568 (45475-1568)
PHONE..........................937 535-5690
Norman C Mayne, *Managing Member*
EMP: 33 EST: 2000
SALES (est): 4.58MM
SALES (corp-wide): 4.58MM **Privately Held**
Web: www.killerbrownie.com
SIC: **2051** Bakery: wholesale or wholesale/retail combined

(G-9706)
KILLER BROWNIE LTD
Also Called: Killer Brownie Company, The
675 Precision Ct Ste A (45342-6138)
PHONE..........................937 530-8600
EMP: 59
SALES (corp-wide): 4.58MM **Privately Held**
Web: www.killerbrownie.com
SIC: **2051** Bakery: wholesale or wholesale/retail combined
PA: Killer Brownie Ltd.
2495 Technical Dr
Miamisburg OH 45342
937 535-5690

(G-9707)
KONGSBERG PRCSION CTNG SYSTEMS
1983 Byers Rd (45342-5777)
PHONE..........................937 800-2169
Matt Thackray, *General Vice President*
EMP: 10 EST: 2021

SALES (est): 5.38MM
SALES (corp-wide): 355.83K **Privately Held**
Web: www.kongsbergsystems.com
SIC: **3545** Machine tool accessories
HQ: Kongsberg Precision Cutting Systems
Belgium
Kortrijksesteenweg 1087
Ghent VOV 9051
93966967

(G-9708)
LAB-PRO INC
845 N Main St (45342-1871)
PHONE..........................937 434-9600
Joseph Jobe, *Pr*
EMP: 9 EST: 2004
SALES (est): 2.36MM **Privately Held**
Web: www.lab-pro.com
SIC: **3448** 5039 Prefabricated metal buildings and components; Prefabricated buildings

(G-9709)
LEXISNEXIS GROUP (DH)
Also Called: Lexisnexis Group
9443 Springboro Pike (45342-5490)
PHONE..........................937 865-6800
Kurt Sanford, *CEO*
Joe Eberhardt Gcno, *Prin*
▲ EMP: 162 EST: 2004
SALES (est): 359.22MM
SALES (corp-wide): 11.96B **Privately Held**
Web: www.lexisnexis.co.in
SIC: **7375** 2741 Data base information retrieval; Miscellaneous publishing
HQ: Relx Inc.
230 Park Ave Ste 700
New York NY 10169
212 309-8100

(G-9710)
MATTHEW BENDER & COMPANY INC
Also Called: Matthew Bender & Company
9443 Springboro Pike (45342-4425)
PHONE..........................518 487-3000
George Bearse, *VP*
EMP: 240
SALES (corp-wide): 11.96B **Privately Held**
Web: www.lexisnexis.com
SIC: **2721** 2731 Periodicals; Book publishing
HQ: Matthew Bender & Company, Inc.
744 Droad Ot Γl0
Newark NJ 07102
518 487-3000

(G-9711)
MDI OF OHIO INC (HQ)
Also Called: Aptyx
802 N 4th St (45342-1812)
PHONE..........................937 866-2345
John E Dempsey, *Pr*
EMP: 24 EST: 2013
SALES (est): 5.15MM
SALES (corp-wide): 36.45MM **Privately Held**
Web: www.moldeddevices.com
SIC: **3089** Injection molded finished plastics products, nec
PA: Molded Devices, Inc.
740 W Knox Rd
Tempe AZ 85284
480 785-9100

(G-9712)
METAL SHREDDERS INC
5101 Farmersville W Carrollton Rd (45342-1207)
P.O. Box 244 (45449)
PHONE..........................937 866-0777

Wilbur Cohen, *Ch*
Ken Cohen, *
EMP: 7 EST: 1971
SQ FT: 8,000
SALES (est): 558.82K **Privately Held**
SIC: **7389** 3341 Metal slitting and shearing; Secondary nonferrous metals

(G-9713)
MIAMI VALLEY PRECISION INC
1944 Byers Rd (45342-3249)
PHONE..........................937 866-1804
Michael Smith, *Pr*
Christine Smith, *Treas*
Brian Smith, *VP*
EMP: 10 EST: 1994
SALES (est): 2.38MM **Privately Held**
Web: www.miamivalleyprecision.com
SIC: **3599** Machine shop, jobbing and repair

(G-9714)
MIAMI VLY COUNTERS & SPC INC
8515 Dayton Cincinnati Pike (45342-3168)
PHONE..........................937 865-0562
Ron James, *Pr*
Robert Dennis, *VP*
EMP: 6 EST: 1997
SQ FT: 2,987
SALES (est): 1.05MM **Privately Held**
Web: www.miamivalleycounters.com
SIC: **2434** Wood kitchen cabinets

(G-9715)
MIAMI-CAST INC
901 N Main St (45342-1873)
PHONE..........................937 866-2951
George Deckebach, *Pr*
C Thomas Koehler, *VP*
Charles Koehler, *Treas*
EMP: 14 EST: 1993
SQ FT: 20,000
SALES (est): 2.76MM **Privately Held**
Web: www.miami-cast.com
SIC: **3321** Gray iron castings, nec

(G-9716)
MIAMISBURG COATING
925 N Main St (45342-1873)
PHONE..........................937 866-1323
William Sizemore, *Pt*
Opal Sizemore, *Pt*
EMP: 10 EST: 1984
SQ FT: 15,000
SALES (est): 511.27K **Privately Held**
SIC: **3479** Coating of metals and formed products

(G-9717)
MIDMARK CORPORATION (PA)
10170 Penny Ln Ste 300 (45342-5014)
PHONE..........................937 528-7500
John Baumann, *Pr*
Robert Morris, *
Mike Walker, *
Sharyl Gardner, *CAO*
Jon Wells, *CCO*
◆ EMP: 600 EST: 1915
SQ FT: 400,000
SALES (est): 497.54MM
SALES (corp-wide): 497.54MM **Privately Held**
Web: www.midmark.com
SIC: **3648** 3842 3843 2542 Lighting equipment, nec; Stretchers; Dental equipment and supplies; Partitions and fixtures, except wood

(G-9718)
MIL-MAR CENTURY CORPORATION
8641 Washington Church Rd (45342-4470)
PHONE..........................937 275-4860

Trib Tewari, *Pr*
▲ EMP: 15 EST: 1954
SALES (est): 2MM **Privately Held**
Web: www.mil-mar.net
SIC: **3599** Machine shop, jobbing and repair

(G-9719)
MJCJ HOLDINGS INC
2580 Kohnle Dr (45342-3669)
PHONE..........................937 885-0800
Mike Campbell, *Pr*
Sean Quinn, *VP*
EMP: 8 EST: 1992
SALES (est): 295.77K **Privately Held**
Web: www.msicmm.com
SIC: **7699** 8734 3559 Industrial machinery and equipment repair; Calibration and certification; Screening equipment, electric
PA: Advanced Industrial Measurement Systems, Inc.
2580 Kohnle Dr
Miamisburg OH 45342

(G-9720)
MOUND PRINTING COMPANY INC
Also Called: Promotional Spring
2455 Belvo Rd (45342-3909)
PHONE..........................937 866-2872
Wade Riggs, *Pr*
Frances Riggs, *
EMP: 25 EST: 1955
SQ FT: 30,000
SALES (est): 4.31MM **Privately Held**
Web: www.promotionalspring.com
SIC: **2752** Offset printing

(G-9721)
NEW PAGE CORPORATION
8540 Gander Creek Dr (45342-5439)
PHONE..........................877 855-7243
David J Paterson, *Pr*
EMP: 51 EST: 2016
SALES (est): 15.21MM **Privately Held**
Web: www.billerud.com
SIC: **2621** Paper mills

(G-9722)
NEWPAGE GROUP INC
8540 Gander Creek Dr (45342-5439)
PHONE..........................937 242-9500
George F Martin, *Pr*
Chan W Galbato, *
James C Tyrone, *
Daniel A Clark, *
Douglas K Cooper, *
EMP: 4500 EST: 2007
SALES (est): 14.82MM
SALES (corp-wide): 3.92B **Privately Held**
Web: www.billerud.com
SIC: **2621** Paper mills
HQ: Billerud Americas Corporation
10050 Innvtion Dr Ste 200
Miamisburg OH 45342

(G-9723)
OCM LLC
Also Called: Ohio Community Media
4500 Lyons Rd (45342-6447)
PHONE..........................937 247-2700
EMP: 264
Web: www.ohcommedia.com
SIC: **2711** Newspapers: publishing only, not printed on site

(G-9724)
OHIO GRAVURE TECHNOLOGIES INC
Also Called: Ohio Gravure Technologies
4401 Lyons Rd (45342-6456)
PHONE..........................937 439-1582
Chris Winter, *Pr*

Eric Serenius, *Pr*
▲ **EMP:** 13 **EST:** 2007
SALES (est): 2.36MM
SALES (corp-wide): 151.28MM **Privately Held**
Web: www.ohiogt.com
SIC: 2754 Commercial printing, gravure
HQ: Heliograph Holding Gmbh
　　Konrad-Zuse-Bogen 18
　　Krailling BY 82152
　　89785960

(G-9725)
ONEIL & ASSOCIATES INC (PA)
Also Called: Oneil
495 Byers Rd (45342-3798)
PHONE..............................937 865-0800
Hernan Olivas, *CEO*
Hernan Olivas, *Pr*
Joe Stevens, *
David Stackhouse, *CIO**
Cindy Schneider Ctrl, *Prin*
EMP: 176 **EST:** 1947
SQ FT: 75,000
SALES (est): 20.75MM
SALES (corp-wide): 20.75MM **Privately Held**
Web: www.oneil.com
SIC: 2741 8999 7336 Technical manuals: publishing only, not printed on site; Technical manual preparation; Commercial art and illustration

(G-9726)
PERFORMANCE WRAPS LLC
229 S 3rd St (45342-2930)
PHONE..............................937 535-2400
Andrew Banks, *CEO*
EMP: 9 **EST:** 2017
SALES (est): 786.73K **Privately Held**
Web: www.performancewraps.com
SIC: 3993 Signs and advertising specialties

(G-9727)
PIONEER AUTOMOTIVE TECH INC (DH)
10100 Innovation Dr Ste 150 (45342-0002)
PHONE..............................937 746-2293
Steven Moerner, *Pr*
Mike Honda, *
◆ **EMP:** 175 **EST:** 1981
SALES (est): 9.53MM **Privately Held**
SIC: 5013 3714 3651 Automotive supplies and parts; Motor vehicle parts and accessories; Household audio and video equipment
HQ: Pioneer North America, Inc.
　　970 W 190th St Ste 360
　　Torrance CA 90502
　　310 952-2000

(G-9728)
PRECISION IMPACTS LLC (PA)
721 Richard St (45342-1840)
PHONE..............................937 530-8254
EMP: 69 **EST:** 2021
SALES (est): 8.48MM
SALES (corp-wide): 8.48MM **Privately Held**
Web: www.gayston.com
SIC: 3449 1761 Miscellaneous metalwork; Sheet metal work, nec

(G-9729)
PRINTING SERVICE COMPANY
3233 S Tech Blvd (45342-0843)
PHONE..............................937 425-6100
William Fair, *Pr*
Paul Molyneaux, *Executive Vice President Finance & Administration**
Gary Boens, *

Rob Jones, *
Kristen Kahut, *
EMP: 70 **EST:** 1933
SQ FT: 40,000
SALES (est): 16.4MM **Privately Held**
SIC: 2752 Offset printing

(G-9730)
RELX INC
4700 Lyons Rd (45342-6453)
PHONE..............................937 865-6800
Bill Wheeler, *Mgr*
EMP: 8
SALES (corp-wide): 11.96B **Privately Held**
Web: www.lexisnexis.com
SIC: 2721 Periodicals
HQ: Relx Inc.
　　230 Park Ave Ste 700
　　New York NY 10169
　　212 309-8100

(G-9731)
RELX INC
Also Called: Lexisnexis
9333 Springboro Pike (45342-4424)
PHONE..............................937 865-6800
Doug Kaplan, *Bmch Mgr*
EMP: 128
SALES (corp-wide): 11.96B **Privately Held**
Web: www.lexisnexis.com
SIC: 2731 Books, publishing only
HQ: Relx Inc.
　　230 Park Ave Ste 700
　　New York NY 10169
　　212 309-8100

(G-9732)
RENEGADE MATERIALS CORPORATION
3363 S Tech Blvd (45342-0826)
PHONE..............................937 350-5274
Matthew Trombly, *Pr*
Vicki Hoffman, *Contrlr*
▲ **EMP:** 52 **EST:** 2006
SQ FT: 25,000
SALES (est): 24.94MM **Privately Held**
Web: www.renegadematerials.com
SIC: 2821 2891 3081 Epoxy resins; Epoxy adhesives; Plastics film and sheet
HQ: Teijin Holdings Usa Inc.
　　1 Harbor Dr Ste 200
　　Sausalito CA 94965
　　212 308-8744

(G-9733)
RETALIX INC
2490 Technical Dr (45342-6136)
PHONE..............................937 384-2277
Barry Shaked, *Pr*
Karen Weaver, *
Barry Shake, *
EMP: 8 **EST:** 1979
SQ FT: 72,000
SALES (est): 684.29K
SALES (corp-wide): 2.83B **Publicly Held**
Web: www.ncr.com
SIC: 5734 7372 Software, business and non-game; Prepackaged software
HQ: Ncr Global Ltd
　　1 Zarchin Alexander
　　Raanana 43662

(G-9734)
RTI SECUREX LLC
20 S 1st St (45342-2816)
P.O. Box 750354 (45475-0354)
PHONE..............................937 859-5290
Ted Humphrey, *Prin*
EMP: 15 **EST:** 1999
SALES (est): 555.13K **Privately Held**

SIC: 3861 Cameras and related equipment

(G-9735)
RUMFORD PAPER COMPANY
8540 Gander Creek Dr (45342-5439)
PHONE..............................937 242-9230
George F Martin, *Pr*
EMP: 7 **EST:** 2010
SALES (est): 130.15K **Privately Held**
SIC: 2621 Paper mills

(G-9736)
SGI MATRIX LLC (PA)
1041 Byers Rd (45342-5487)
PHONE..............................937 438-9033
James Young, *
Jeffrey S Young, *
John Schomburg, *
Joseph Jenkins, *
EMP: 68 **EST:** 1977
SQ FT: 12,000
SALES (est): 10.16MM
SALES (corp-wide): 10.16MM **Privately Held**
Web: www.matrixsys.com
SIC: 8711 7373 3873 Engineering services; Computer integrated systems design; Watches, clocks, watchcases, and parts

(G-9737)
SIGNATURE TECHNOLOGIES INC (DH)
Also Called: Com-Net Software Specialists
3728 Benner Rd (45342-4302)
PHONE..............................937 859-6323
Elie Geva, *Pr*
David Michaels, *
EMP: 40 **EST:** 1985
SQ FT: 25,000
SALES (est): 8.12MM
SALES (corp-wide): 11.51MM **Privately Held**
Web: www.sita.aero
SIC: 3669 3674 3577 Transportation signaling devices; Semiconductors and related devices; Computer peripheral equipment, nec
HQ: Sita Information Networking Computing Uk Limited
　　1 London Gate
　　Hayes MIDDX UB3 1

(G-9738)
SPINTECH HOLDINGS INC
Also Called: Spintech
1964 Byers Rd (45342-3249)
PHONE..............................937 912-3250
Craig Jennings, *CEO*
Craig Jennings, *Pr*
Tom Margraf, *VP*
EMP: 21 **EST:** 2010
SALES (est): 4.56MM **Privately Held**
Web: www.smarttooling.com
SIC: 3544 Special dies, tools, jigs, and fixtures

(G-9739)
STACO ENERGY PRODUCTS CO (HQ)
2425 Technical Dr (45342-6137)
PHONE..............................937 253-1191
Cary M Maguire, *Ch Bd*
Jeff Hoffman, *Pr*
Jefferey Nick, *VP*
◆ **EMP:** 6 **EST:** 1944
SALES (est): 5.73MM
SALES (corp-wide): 51.25MM **Privately Held**
Web: www.stacoenergy.com

SIC: 3677 3612 Electronic coils and transformers; Generator voltage regulators
PA: Components Corporation Of America
　　5950 Berkshire Ln # 1500
　　Dallas TX 75225
　　214 969-0166

(G-9740)
STEINER EOPTICS INC (PA)
Also Called: Sensor Technology Systems
3475 Newmark Dr (45342-5426)
PHONE..............................937 426-2341
Alan Page, *Dir*
EMP: 80 **EST:** 1991
SQ FT: 50,000
SALES (est): 7.44MM **Privately Held**
Web: www.steiner-optics.com
SIC: 8731 3851 Electronic research; Ophthalmic goods

(G-9741)
SYNAGRO MIDWEST INC
4515 Infirmary Rd (45342-1235)
PHONE..............................937 384-0669
Jim Rosendall, *VP*
EMP: 10 **EST:** 1979
SALES (est): 1.83MM **Privately Held**
SIC: 4953 2873 Recycling, waste materials; Nitrogenous fertilizers
PA: Synagro Technologies, Inc.
　　435 Williams Ct Ste 100
　　Baltimore MD 21220

(G-9742)
T&T GRAPHICS INC
2563 Technical Dr (45342-6108)
P.O. Box 690 (45343-0690)
PHONE..............................937 847-6000
EMP: 80 **EST:** 1971
SALES (est): 4.78MM
SALES (corp-wide): 23.84MM **Privately Held**
Web: www.ttgraphics.com
SIC: 3993 2759 2679 Advertising artwork; Decals: printing, nsk; Labels, paper: made from purchased material
PA: Repacorp, Inc.
　　31 Industry Park Ct
　　Tipp City OH 45371
　　937 667-8496

(G-9743)
TARK INC (PA)
9273 Byers Rd (45342-4349)
PHONE..............................937 434-6766
Joe Mccarthy, *CEO*
Jim Mccarthy, *Pr*
Donna Mccarthy, *VP*
John Basnett, *VP*
John Koverman, *Treas*
EMP: 30 **EST:** 1961
SALES (est): 9.05MM
SALES (corp-wide): 9.05MM **Privately Held**
Web: www.tarkinc.com
SIC: 3561 Pumps and pumping equipment

(G-9744)
TECH PRODUCTS CORPORATION (DH)
2215 Lyons Rd (45342-4465)
PHONE..............................937 438-1100
Dan Rork, *Pr*
A M Zimmerman, *
Hugh E Wall Junior, *Prin*
Peirce Wood, *
EMP: 11 **EST:** 1967
SQ FT: 25,000
SALES (est): 9.41MM
SALES (corp-wide): 1.46B **Privately Held**
Web: www.novibes.com

▲ = Import ▼ = Export
◆ = Import/Export

SIC: **3625** 5084 3829 3651 Noise control
  equipment; Noise control equipment;
  Measuring and controlling devices, nec;
  Household audio and video equipment
HQ: Fabreeka International Holdings, Inc.
  1023 Turnpike St
  Stoughton MA 02072
  781 341-3655

(G-9745)
TECHNICOTE INC (PA)
Also Called: Technicote
222 Mound Ave (45342-2996)
P.O. Box 188 (45343-0188)
PHONE.................................800 358-4448
Frank Gavrillos, *Pr*
Michelle Davis, *
Dorothy L Chapman, *
Michael A Ogline, *
Peggy Curtiss, *
◆ EMP: 46 EST: 1980
SALES (est): 49.86MM
SALES (corp-wide): 49.86MM **Privately
Held**
Web: www.technicote.com
SIC: **2672** Adhesive papers, labels, or tapes:
  from purchased material

(G-9746)
TELEDYNE DEFENSE ELEC LLC
Also Called: Teledyne Qptiq Eltrnic Sltions
1100 Vanguard Blvd (45342-0312)
PHONE.................................866 539-5916
Doug Benner, *Brnch Mgr*
EMP: 120
SALES (corp-wide): 5.67B **Publicly Held**
Web: www.excelitas.com
SIC: **3829** 3489 Thermometers and
  temperature sensors; Ordnance and
  accessories, nec
HQ: Teledyne Defense Electronics, Llc
  11361 Sunrise Park Dr
  Rancho Cordova CA 95742
  800 284-7007

(G-9747)
THE HOOVEN - DAYTON CORP
Also Called: H D C
511 Byers Rd (45342-5337)
P.O. Box 507 (45040-0507)
PHONE.................................937 233-4473
▲ EMP: 101
Web: www.hoovendayton.com
SIC: **2679** 2672 2671 2759 Tags and labels,
  paper; Tape, pressure sensitive: made from
  purchased materials; Paper; coated and
  laminated packaging; Labels and seals:
  printing, nsk

(G-9748)
TOAST WITH CAKE LLC
9231 Towering Pine Dr Apt L (45342-5807)
PHONE.................................937 554-5900
Sherlonda Campbell, *Managing Member*
EMP: 7
SALES (est): 222.59K **Privately Held**
SIC: **2051** Bakery products, partially cooked
  (except frozen)

(G-9749)
TOMCO MACHINING INC
10950 Industry Ln (45342-0894)
PHONE.................................937 264-1943
James W Tomasiak, *Pr*
Kathy J Tomasiak, *Ch Bd*
EMP: 20 EST: 2000
SALES (est): 3.85MM **Privately Held**
Web: www.tomcoaero.com
SIC: **3599** Machine shop, jobbing and repair

(G-9750)
TRU-FAB INC
2225 Lyons Rd (45342-4465)
PHONE.................................937 435-1733
Steven Dudley, *Pr*
Ed Parker, *VP*
EMP: 11 EST: 1977
SALES (est): 4.3MM **Privately Held**
Web: www.hpcfire.com
SIC: **3441** Fabricated structural metal

(G-9751)
VERSO PAPER INC
8540 Gander Creek Dr (45342-5439)
PHONE.................................901 369-4100
David J Paterson, *Pr*
EMP: 22
SALES (est): 5MM **Privately Held**
Web: www.billerud.com
SIC: **2621** Paper mills

(G-9752)
WAXCO INTERNATIONAL INC
Also Called: Dacraft
727 Dayton Oxford Rd (45342)
P.O. Box 147 (45343-0147)
PHONE.................................937 746-4845
Roger Wax, *Pr*
Bill Wax, *VP*
EMP: 10 EST: 1985
SALES (est): 1.03MM **Privately Held**
Web: www.dacraft.com
SIC: **3355** 1521 5211 1761 Structural
  shapes, rolled, aluminum; General
  remodeling, single-family houses; Door and
  window products; Siding contractor

(G-9753)
WOODWORKING SHOP LLC
1195 Mound Rd (45342-6715)
PHONE.................................513 330-9663
Mark Sams, *Pr*
EMP: 15 EST: 2002
SQ FT: 1,300
SALES (est): 3.17MM **Privately Held**
Web: www.thewoodworkingshop.com
SIC: **2599** 2511 3425 Cabinets, factory;
  Wood household furniture; Saws, hand:
  metalworking or woodworking

(G-9754)
WURTH ELECTRONICS ICS INC
Also Called: Wurth Elecktronik
1982 Byers Rd (45342-3249)
PHONE.................................937 415-7700
Brad Weaver, *CEO*
EMP: 27 EST: 2010
SALES (est): 21.85MM
SALES (corp-wide): 22.17B **Privately Held**
Web: www.we-online.com
SIC: **5065** 3672 Electronic parts; Printed
  circuit boards
HQ: Wurth Group Of North America Inc.
  93 Grant St
  Ramsey NJ 07446

(G-9755)
YASKAWA AMERICA INC
Motoman Robotics Division
100 Automation Way (45342-4962)
PHONE.................................937 847-6200
Steve Barhorst, *Div Pres*
EMP: 180
SQ FT: 304,815
Web: www.yaskawa.com
SIC: **7694** Armature rewinding shops
HQ: Yaskawa America, Inc.
  2121 S Norman Dr
  Waukegan IL 60085
  847 887-7000

Miamitown
Hamilton County

(G-9756)
BICKERS METAL PRODUCTS INC
5825 State Rte128 (45041)
P.O. Box 648 (45041-0648)
PHONE.................................513 353-4000
Robert C Graff, *Pr*
Roger Coffaro, *VP*
Charles Coffaro, *Stockholder*
EMP: 40 EST: 1964
SQ FT: 30,000
SALES (est): 5.65MM **Privately Held**
SIC: **3441** 3444 Fabricated structural metal;
  Sheet metalwork

(G-9757)
BROTHERS TOOL AND MFG LTD
8300 Harrison Ave (45041)
P.O. Box 89 (45041-0089)
PHONE.................................513 353-9700
Grant Schutte, *Pt*
John Schutte, *Pt*
EMP: 7 EST: 1994
SQ FT: 6,000
SALES (est): 1.62MM **Privately Held**
SIC: **3544** Special dies and tools

(G-9758)
GATEWAY CON FORMING SVCS INC
5938 Hamilton-Cleves Rd (45041)
P.O. Box 130 (45041-0130)
PHONE.................................513 353-2000
Robert Bilz, *Pr*
Tim Hughey, *
Brandon Erfman, *
Jean C Hughey, *
J Robert Hughey, *Stockholder**
EMP: 75 EST: 1960
SQ FT: 3,000
SALES (est): 11.3MM
SALES (corp-wide): 11.3MM **Privately
Held**
Web: www.gatewayconcreteforming.com
SIC: **1771** 3449 3496 3429 Foundation and
  footing contractor; Bars, concrete
  reinforcing: fabricated steel; Miscellaneous
  fabricated wire products; Hardware, nec
PA: Imcon Corp.
  5938 State Route 128
  Miamitown OH 45041
  513 353-2000

(G-9759)
JACP INC (PA)
5928 Hamilton Cleves Rd (45041)
PHONE.................................513 353-3660
Michael Baltes, *Pr*
EMP: 6 EST: 1991
SQ FT: 25,000
SALES (est): 866.82K **Privately Held**
SIC: **3541** 3443 3564 Grinding machines,
  metalworking; Tanks for tank trucks, metal
  plate; Dust or fume collecting equipment,
  industrial

(G-9760)
SEILKOP INDUSTRIES INC
A-G Tool & Die Company
5927 State Route 128 (45041-2501)
P.O. Box 250 (45041-0250)
PHONE.................................513 353-3090
Ken Seilkop, *Owner*
EMP: 13
SQ FT: 19,000
SALES (corp-wide): 19.44MM **Privately
Held**
Web: www.agtool.com

SIC: **3312** 3544 Tool and die steel; Special
  dies, tools, jigs, and fixtures
PA: Seilkop Industries, Inc.
  425 W N Bend Rd
  Cincinnati OH 45216
  513 761-1035

Miamiville
Clermont County

(G-9761)
AIM INTERNATIONAL
264 Center St (45147-4501)
PHONE.................................513 831-2938
EMP: 7 EST: 2013
SALES (est): 1.22MM **Privately Held**
Web: www.aimmro.com
SIC: **3728** Aircraft parts and equipment, nec

(G-9762)
IRVINE WOOD RECOVERY INC (PA)
110 Glendale Milford Rd (45147)
P.O. Box 110 (45147-0110)
PHONE.................................513 831-0060
Les Irvine, *Pr*
EMP: 49 EST: 1982
SQ FT: 15,000
SALES (est): 4.9MM **Privately Held**
Web: www.irvinewoodrecovery.com
SIC: **2499** Mulch, wood and bark

(G-9763)
MESSER LLC
Boc Gases
State Road 126160 Glendale-Milford Road
(45147)
PHONE.................................513 831-4742
John L Seibert, *Mgr*
EMP: 14
SALES (corp-wide): 2.29B **Privately Held**
Web: www.messeramericas.com
SIC: **2813** Nitrogen
HQ: Messer Llc
  200 Smrset Corp Blvd Ste
  Bridgewater NJ 08807
  800 755-9277

Middle Point
Van Wert County

(G-9704)
TRAVELING RECYCLE WD PDTS INC
Also Called: T&R Wood Products
19590 Bellis Rd (45863-9721)
P.O. Box 143 (45863-0143)
PHONE.................................419 968-2649
Eddy Miller, *Pr*
Scott Miller, *VP*
EMP: 6 EST: 1963
SQ FT: 13,680
SALES (est): 441.95K **Privately Held**
SIC: **2441** 2448 2449 Boxes, wood; Pallets,
  wood; Wood containers, nec

Middlebranch
Stark County

(G-9765)
HEIDELBERG MTLS US CEM LLC
8282 Middlebranch Ave Ne (44652-9006)
PHONE.................................330 499-9100
EMP: 17
SALES (corp-wide): 22.37B **Privately Held**
Web: www.heidelbergmaterials.us
SIC: **3273** Ready-mixed concrete
HQ: Heidelberg Materials Us Cement Llc

300 E John Crptr Fwy Ste
Irving TX 75062
877 534-4442

Middleburg Heights
Cuyahoga County

(G-9766)
AP SERVICES LLC
18001 Sheldon Rd (44130-2465)
PHONE..........................216 267-3200
EMP: 85 **EST:** 2010
SALES (est): 896.04K
SALES (corp-wide): 3.12B **Publicly Held**
Web: www.cwnuclear.com
SIC: 3053 Gaskets; packing and sealing
devices
PA: Curtiss-Wright Corporation
130 Harbour Pl Dr Ste 300
Davidson NC 28036
704 869-4600

(G-9767)
CLEVELAND DIE & MFG CO (PA)
Also Called: Cleveland Die & Mfg
20303 1st Ave (44130-2433)
PHONE..........................440 243-3404
Juan Chahda, *Pr*
Liliana Chahda, *VP*
◆ **EMP:** 133 **EST:** 1973
SQ FT: 165,000
SALES (est): 12.49MM
SALES (corp-wide): 12.49MM **Privately
Held**
Web: www.clevelanddie.com
SIC: 3469 3544 Stamping metal for the trade
; Special dies, tools, jigs, and fixtures

(G-9768)
COATING SYSTEMS GROUP INC
6909 Engle Rd Bldg C (44130-3473)
PHONE..........................440 816-9306
Frank Popiel, *Pr*
Dawn Kaminski, *Prin*
EMP: 10 **EST:** 2013
SALES (est): 488.08K **Privately Held**
Web: www.csginconline.com
SIC: 8711 3535 Engineering services;
Conveyors and conveying equipment

(G-9769)
**DUBOSE NAT ENRGY FAS MCHNED
PR**
18737 Sheldon Rd (44130-2472)
PHONE..........................216 362-1700
Carl Rogers, *CEO*
Martin Kossick, *Pr*
Richard Rogers, *Treas*
EMP: 18 **EST:** 2010
SALES (est): 4.15MM
SALES (corp-wide): 13.84B **Publicly Held**
Web: www.dubosenes.com
SIC: 3965 Fasteners
PA: Reliance, Inc.
16100 N 71st St Ste 400
Scottsdale AZ 85254
480 564-5700

(G-9770)
FLUKE CORPORATION
17830 Englewood Dr Ste 17 (44130-3485)
PHONE..........................440 234-4809
EMP: 13
SALES (corp-wide): 6.23B **Publicly Held**
SIC: 3823 Process control instruments
HQ: Fluke Corporation
6920 Seaway Blvd
Everett WA 98203
425 347-6100

(G-9771)
IEC INFRARED SYSTEMS INC
Also Called: IEC
7803 Freeway Cir (44130-6308)
PHONE..........................440 234-8000
Rick Pettergrew, *Pr*
EMP: 25 **EST:** 1999
SQ FT: 2,300
SALES (est): 6.79MM **Privately Held**
Web: www.iecinfrared.com
SIC: 3812 Infrared object detection
equipment

(G-9772)
IEC INFRARED SYSTEMS LLC
Also Called: IEC
7803 Freeway Cir (44130-6308)
PHONE..........................440 234-8000
Richard Pettegrew, *Managing Member*
EMP: 22 **EST:** 2013
SALES (est): 995.4K **Privately Held**
Web: www.iecinfrared.com
SIC: 7389 3826 7382 Design services;
Infrared analytical instruments; Protective
devices, security

(G-9773)
**INCORPRTED TRSTEES OF THE
GSPL**
Also Called: Union Gospel Press Division
19695 Commerce Pkwy (44130-2408)
P.O. Box 6059 (44101-1059)
PHONE..........................216 749-2100
Beryl C Bidlen, *Pr*
Reverend Lanny C Akers, *VP*
Robert Andrews, *
Vera Mc Kinney, *
EMP: 90 **EST:** 1902
SQ FT: 60,000
SALES (est): 1.72MM **Privately Held**
Web: www.uniongospelpress.com
SIC: 2721 5942 5999 8661 Periodicals,
publishing and printing; Books, religious;
Religious goods; Nonchurch religious
organizations

(G-9774)
KINETIC CONCEPTS INC
Also Called: Kci
6751 Engle Rd (44130-7951)
PHONE..........................440 234-8590
EMP: 10
SALES (corp-wide): 8.25B **Publicly Held**
Web: www.acelity.com
SIC: 3841 Surgical and medical instruments
HQ: Kinetic Concepts, Inc.
12930 W Interstate 10
San Antonio TX 78249
800 531-5346

(G-9775)
NOVA MACHINE PRODUCTS INC
Also Called: Nova
18001 Sheldon Rd (44130-2465)
PHONE..........................216 267-3200
David Linton, *CEO*
Martin R Benante, *
▲ **EMP:** 115 **EST:** 2005
SALES (est): 9.33MM
SALES (corp-wide): 3.12B **Publicly Held**
Web: www.curtisswright.com
SIC: 3452 3429 3369 3356 Bolts, metal;
Hardware, nec; Nonferrous foundries, nec;
Nonferrous rolling and drawing, nec
PA: Curtiss-Wright Corporation
130 Harbour Pl Dr Ste 300
Davidson NC 28036
704 869-4600

(G-9776)
RIVALS SPORTS GRILLE LLC
6710 Smith Rd (44130-2656)
PHONE..........................216 267-0005
EMP: 48 **EST:** 2007
SQ FT: 4,368
SALES (est): 823.19K **Privately Held**
Web: www.rivalscleveland.com
SIC: 5812 7372 Grills (eating places);
Application computer software

(G-9777)
SINICO MTM US INC
7007 Engle Rd Ste C (44130-3512)
PHONE..........................216 264-8344
Marco Barban, *Pr*
EMP: 13 **EST:** 2017
SALES (est): 1.15MM **Privately Held**
Web: www.sinico.com
SIC: 3541 Machine tools, metal cutting type
PA: Sinico Holding Srl
Via Del Progresso 28
Montebello Vicentino VI

(G-9778)
VERANTIS CORPORATION (PA)
7251 Engle Rd Ste 300 (44130-3400)
PHONE..........................440 243-0700
Don Day, *CEO*
William Jackson, *
▼ **EMP:** 30 **EST:** 2009
SALES (est): 34.07MM **Privately Held**
Web: www.verantis.com
SIC: 5075 3564 Air pollution control
equipment and supplies; Blowers and fans

Middlefield
Geauga County

(G-9779)
ALL FOAM PRODUCTS CO (PA)
Also Called: All Foam Pdts Safety Foam Proc
15005 Enterprise Way (44062-9369)
PHONE..........................330 849-3636
Darrell Mcnair, *Pr*
Marvin Steinlauf, *VP*
Debbie Irlbacker, *VP*
Shelly Silver, *Sec*
EMP: 6 **EST:** 1977
SQ FT: 3,200
SALES (est): 2.01MM
SALES (corp-wide): 2.01MM **Privately
Held**
Web: www.allfoam.com
SIC: 3086 Plastics foam products

(G-9780)
AMERICAN PLASTIC TECH INC
Also Called: A P T
15229 S State Ave (44062-9468)
P.O. Box 37 (44062-0037)
PHONE..........................440 632-5203
Joseph A Bergen, *Pr*
Duncan M Simpson Junior, *Sr VP*
Edd Hiksman, *
▲ **EMP:** 182 **EST:** 1950
SQ FT: 178,000
SALES (est): 3.12MM **Privately Held**
Web: www.universalplastics.com
SIC: 3089 3559 Injection molding of plastics;
Plastics working machinery

(G-9781)
BASETEK LLC (PA)
14975 White Rd (44062-9216)
PHONE..........................877 712-2273
Scott Sapita, *Managing Member*
EMP: 16 **EST:** 2000
SALES (est): 3.56MM

SALES (corp-wide): 3.56MM **Privately
Held**
Web: www.basetek.com
SIC: 3531 5032 Construction machinery;
Concrete and cinder block

(G-9782)
BENTRONIX CORP
14999 Madison Rd (44062-8403)
P.O. Box 1297 (44062-1297)
PHONE..........................440 632-0606
Ludmilla Benins, *Pr*
Peter Benins, *VP*
Brian Lanstrum, *VP*
EMP: 7 **EST:** 1984
SQ FT: 2,500
SALES (est): 1.51MM **Privately Held**
Web: www.bentronix.com
SIC: 3613 7629 Control panels, electric;
Electronic equipment repair

(G-9783)
CABINETWORKS GROUP MICH LLC
15535 S State Ave (44062)
PHONE..........................440 632-2547
Mike Newton, *Mgr*
EMP: 119
SALES (corp-wide): 486.01MM **Privately
Held**
Web: www.cabinetworksgroup.com
SIC: 2434 Wood kitchen cabinets
PA: Cabinetworks Group Michigan, Llc
20000 Victor Pkwy
Livonia MI 48152
734 205-4600

(G-9784)
**CABINTWRKS GROUP MDDLFIELD
LLC (HQ)**
Also Called: Kraftmaid Cabinetry
15535 S State Ave (44062)
P.O. Box 1055 (44062-1055)
PHONE..........................888 562-7744
Keith Scherzer, *Managing Member*
Andrew Rattray, *
◆ **EMP:** 2533 **EST:** 1969
SALES (est): 43.4MM
SALES (corp-wide): 532.81MM **Privately
Held**
Web: www.kraftmaid.com
SIC: 2511 2434 Wood household furniture;
Wood kitchen cabinets
PA: Cabinetworks Group, Inc.
20000 Victor Pkwy
Livonia MI 48152
734 205-4600

(G-9785)
CARTER-JONES LUMBER COMPANY
Also Called: Carter Lumber
14601 Kinsman Rd (44062-9245)
PHONE..........................440 834-8164
Lenny Barciskoi, *Mgr*
EMP: 29
SALES (corp-wide): 1.44B **Privately Held**
Web: www.carterlumber.com
SIC: 2452 5074 5211 Prefabricated
buildings, wood; Plumbing and hydronic
heating supplies; Lumber products
HQ: The Carter-Jones Lumber Company
601 Tallmadge Rd
Kent OH 44240
330 673-6100

(G-9786)
CHEM TECHNOLOGIES LTD
14875 Bonner Dr (44062-8493)
PHONE..........................440 632-9311
S James Schill, *CEO*
Randall Vancura, *
EMP: 99 **EST:** 2001

▲ = Import ▼ = Export
◆ = Import/Export

SQ FT: 120,000
SALES (est): 23.45MM **Privately Held**
Web: www.chemtechnologiesltd.com
SIC: 2819 2899 Industrial inorganic chemicals, nec; Chemical preparations, nec

(G-9787)
CHEROKEE HARDWOODS INC (PA)
Also Called: Amish Heritg WD Floors & Furn
16741 Newcomb Rd (44062-8248)
PHONE..................................440 632-0322
Wallace D Byler, *Pr*
Bill W Byler, *VP*
EMP: 6 **EST:** 1997
SQ FT: 12,500
SALES (est): 322.65K
SALES (corp-wide): 322.65K **Privately Held**
Web: www.cherokeehardwoods.com
SIC: 2421 2426 Sawmills and planing mills, general; Hardwood dimension and flooring mills

(G-9788)
CROSSCREEK PALLET CO
14530 Madison Rd (44062-9499)
PHONE..................................440 632-1940
Michael Yoder, *Owner*
EMP: 7 **EST:** 2005
SALES (est): 184.25K **Privately Held**
SIC: 2448 Pallets, wood

(G-9789)
CT SPECIALTY POLYMERS LTD
14875 Bonner Dr (44062-8493)
PHONE..................................440 632-9311
James Schill, *Prin*
EMP: 6 **EST:** 2010
SALES (est): 150K **Privately Held**
Web: www.chemtechnologiesltd.com
SIC: 2241 Rubber and elastic yarns and fabrics

(G-9790)
CUSTOM PALET MANUFACTURING
9291 N Girdle Rd (44062-9531)
PHONE..................................440 693-4603
Lester Mullet, *Owner*
EMP: 7 **EST:** 1995
SALES (est): 114.58K **Privately Held**
Web: www.lkelectric.net
SIC: 2448 Pallets, wood

(G-9791)
D MARTONE INDUSTRIES INC
Also Called: Jaco Products
15060 Madison Rd (44062-9450)
PHONE..................................440 632-5800
Frank Defino, *Pr*
David B Cathcart, *
Samuel R Martillotta, *
EMP: 30 **EST:** 1991
SQ FT: 38,000
SALES (est): 5.12MM **Privately Held**
Web: www.jacoproducts.com
SIC: 3089 Injection molding of plastics
PA: A.J.D. Holding Co.
2181 Enterprise Pkwy
Twinsburg OH 44087

(G-9792)
DRUMMOND CORPORATION
14990 Berkshire Industrial Pkwy
(44062-9390)
P.O. Box 389 (44021-0389)
PHONE..................................440 834-9660
Paul Spangler Senior, *Pr*
Paul Spangler Junior, *VP*
Joan Spangler, *VP*
EMP: 15 **EST:** 1980
SQ FT: 10,000

SALES (est): 2.03MM **Privately Held**
Web: www.drummondcorp.com
SIC: 3089 Injection molding of plastics

(G-9793)
EEI ACQUISITION CORP
Also Called: Engineered Endeavors
15175 Kinsman Rd (44062-9471)
PHONE..................................440 564-5484
Patrick Deloney, *Pr*
Gerry Truax, *
EMP: 45 **EST:** 1988
SALES (est): 4.53MM **Privately Held**
SIC: 3663 Mobile communication equipment

(G-9794)
FLAMBEAU INC
15981 Valplast St (44062-9399)
P.O. Box 97 (44062-0097)
PHONE..................................440 632-6131
Jason Sauey, *Pr*
EMP: 97
Web: www.flambeau.com
SIC: 3089 Plastics containers, except foam
HQ: Flambeau, Inc.
801 Lynn Ave
Baraboo WI 53913
800 352-6266

(G-9795)
GAS ASSIST INJCTION MLDING EXP
15285 S State Ave (44062-9468)
PHONE..................................440 632-5203
EMP: 7 **EST:** 2018
SALES (est): 137.81K **Privately Held**
Web: www.universalplastics.com
SIC: 3089 Injection molding of plastics

(G-9796)
HANS ROTHENBUHLER & SON INC
15815 Nauvoo Rd (44062-8501)
PHONE..................................440 632-6000
John Rothenbuhler, *Pr*
▲ **EMP:** 40 **EST:** 1956
SALES (est): 5.23MM **Privately Held**
Web:
www.rothenbuhlercheesemakers.com
SIC: 2022 5451 5143 2023 Natural cheese; Dairy products stores; Dairy products, except dried or canned; Dry, condensed and evaporated dairy products

(G-9797)
HARDWOOD LUMBER COMPANY INC
13813 Station Rd (44062-8728)
PHONE..................................440 834-1891
Stephen Trudic, *Pr*
EMP: 16 **EST:** 1958
SALES (est): 2.37MM **Privately Held**
Web: www.hardwood-lumber.com
SIC: 1751 2511 2541 2431 Cabinet building and installation; Wood household furniture; Counters or counter display cases, wood; Millwork

(G-9798)
HAUSER SERVICES LLC
Also Called: Hauser Landscaping
15668 Old State Rd (44062-8488)
P.O. Box 1161 (44062-1161)
PHONE..................................440 632-5126
Dave Hauser Mng, *Mgr*
Monique Hauser, *Managing Member*
EMP: 20 **EST:** 1988
SQ FT: 10,000
SALES (est): 2.6MM **Privately Held**
SIC: 2499 0781 Mulch, wood and bark; Landscape services

(G-9799)
HEXPOL CMPNDING AMRCAS MFG LLC
Also Called: Hexpol Middlefield
14910 Madison Rd (44062-8403)
PHONE..................................440 632-0901
Ken Bloom, *
Mark Ramsey, *Chief Procurement Officer*
▼ **EMP:** 185 **EST:** 1997
SQ FT: 160,000
SALES (est): 4.73MM
SALES (corp-wide): 6.47MM **Privately Held**
Web: www.hexpol.com
SIC: 3069 2891 Reclaimed rubber and specialty rubber compounds; Adhesives and sealants
HQ: Hexpol Holding Inc.
14330 Kinsman Rd
Burton OH 44021
440 834-4644

(G-9800)
HEXPOL COMPOUNDING LLC
14910 Madison Rd (44062-8403)
PHONE..................................440 632-1962
EMP: 129
SALES (corp-wide): 6.47MM **Privately Held**
Web: www.hexpol.com
SIC: 3087 Custom compound purchased resins
HQ: Hexpol Compounding Llc
14330 Kinsman Rd
Burton OH 44021
440 834-4644

(G-9801)
HK LOGGING & LUMBER LTD
16465 Farley Rd (44062-8290)
PHONE..................................440 632-1997
Henry Kuhns, *Pr*
EMP: 7 **EST:** 2004
SALES (est): 394.02K **Privately Held**
Web: www.hkloggingandlumber.com
SIC: 2411 Logging camps and contractors

(G-9802)
J K PLASTICS CO
14135 Madison Rd (44062-9763)
PHONE..................................440 632-1482
FAX: 440 632-1482
EMP: 6
SQ FT: 8,400
SALES (est): 626.67K **Privately Held**
SIC: 3089 3635 Injection molding of plastics; Household vacuum cleaners

(G-9803)
JOBAP ASSEMBLY INC
16090 Industrial Pkwy Unit 9 (44062-6302)
PHONE..................................440 632-5393
Rebecca Portman, *Pr*
Judith Mellenger, *Treas*
▲ **EMP:** 9 **EST:** 1990
SQ FT: 6,000
SALES (est): 1.61MM **Privately Held**
Web: www.jobapassembly.com
SIC: 3699 1731 Electrical equipment and supplies, nec; Electrical work

(G-9804)
JOHNSONITE INC
Also Called: Johnsonite Rubber Flooring
16035 Industrial Pkwy (44062-9386)
P.O. Box 880 (44062-0880)
PHONE..................................440 632-3441
Jeff Buttitta, *Pr*
Tom Dowling, *
▲ **EMP:** 500 **EST:** 1895
SALES (est): 8.99MM **Privately Held**

Web: commercial.tarkett.com
SIC: 3086 Carpet and rug cushions, foamed plastics
HQ: Tarkett
Tour Initiale
Puteaux IDF

(G-9805)
KRAFTMAID TRUCKING INC (PA)
16052 Industrial Pkwy (44062-9382)
P.O. Box 1055 (44062-1055)
PHONE..................................440 632-2531
EMP: 100 **EST:** 1989
SQ FT: 12,000
SALES (est): 10.48MM
SALES (corp-wide): 10.48MM **Privately Held**
Web: www.kraftmaid.com
SIC: 4813 2517 Telephone communication, except radio; Wood television and radio cabinets

(G-9806)
LA ROSE PAVING CO
16590 Nauvoo Rd (44062-9408)
P.O. Box 146 (44062-0146)
PHONE..................................440 632-0330
TOLL FREE: 888
Linda Rose, *Pr*
Jim Rose, *VP*
EMP: 8 **EST:** 1997
SALES (est): 238.01K **Privately Held**
Web: www.larosepaving.com
SIC: 2951 Paving blocks

(G-9807)
MARSH VALLEY FOREST PDTS LTD
14141 Old State Rd (44062-9740)
PHONE..................................440 632-1889
Mervin P Miller, *Pr*
Pete Miller, *Genl Pt*
EMP: 7 **EST:** 1996
SQ FT: 16,000
SALES (est): 2.12MM **Privately Held**
SIC: 2426 5211 Flooring, hardwood; Lumber products

(G-9808)
MERCURY PLASTICS LLC
15760 Madison Rd (44062-8408)
P.O. Box 989 (44062-0989)
PHONE..................................440 632-5281
EMP: 156 **EST:** 2017
SALES (est): 9.8MM
SALES (corp-wide): 7.83B **Publicly Held**
Web: www.mercury-plastics.com
SIC: 3089 Injection molding of plastics
PA: Masco Corporation
17450 College Pkwy
Livonia MI 48152
313 274-7400

(G-9809)
MIDDLEFIELD GLASS INCORPORATED
17447 Kinsman Rd (44062-9433)
P.O. Box 1266 (44062-1266)
PHONE..................................440 632-5699
Michael Lyons, *Pr*
Carol Lyons, *VP*
EMP: 6 **EST:** 1992
SQ FT: 9,000
SALES (est): 1.5MM **Privately Held**
Web: www.middlefieldglass.com
SIC: 3231 5231 Stained glass: made from purchased glass; Glass, leaded or stained

(G-9810)
MIDDLEFIELD PALLET INC
15940 Burton Windsor Rd (44062-9791)
PHONE..................................440 632-0553

Robert J Troyer, *Pr*
John A Yoder, *
EMP: 42 **EST:** 1998
SQ FT: 30,000
SALES (est): 5.5MM **Privately Held**
Web: www.middlefieldpallet.com
SIC: 2448 Pallets, wood

(G-9811)
MIDDLEFIELD PLASTICS INC
15235 Burton Windsor Rd (44062-9806)
P.O. Box 708 (44062-0708)
PHONE.................................440 834-4638
John D Fisher, *Pr*
Edward Minick, *
EMP: 45 **EST:** 1970
SQ FT: 44,000
SALES (est): 5.26MM **Privately Held**
Web: www.middlefieldplastics.com
SIC: 3089 3053 Extruded finished plastics
products, nec; Gaskets; packing and
sealing devices

(G-9812)
MIDDLFELD ORIGINAL CHEESE
COOP
Also Called: Das Deutsch Cheese
16942 Kinsman Rd (44062-9484)
P.O. Box 237 (44062-0237)
PHONE.................................440 632-5567
Eli D L Miller, *Pr*
Nevin R Byler, *General Vice President*
EMP: 11 **EST:** 1956
SQ FT: 12,000
SALES (est): 1.14MM **Privately Held**
Web: www.middlefieldohio.com
SIC: 2022 Natural cheese

(G-9813)
MOLTEN MTAL EQP INNVATIONS
LLC
Also Called: Mmei
15510 Old State Rd (44062-8208)
PHONE.................................440 632-9119
Paul Cooper, *Pr*
Kevin Doherty, *
▲ **EMP:** 28 **EST:** 2012
SALES (est): 11.13MM **Privately Held**
Web: www.mmei-inc.com
SIC: 3561 Industrial pumps and parts

(G-9814)
MULTI-WING AMERICA INC
15030 Berkshire Industrial Pkwy
(44062-9390)
P.O. Box 425 (44021)
PHONE.................................440 834-9400
Jesper Bernhoft, *Ch Bd*
Jim Crowley, *
William Crowley, *
John Crowley, *
Terese Crowley, *
▲ **EMP:** 45 **EST:** 1972
SQ FT: 27,500
SALES (est): 10.74MM **Privately Held**
Web: www.multi-wing.com
SIC: 3564 Exhaust fans: industrial or
commercial

(G-9815)
MVP PLASTICS INC (PA)
15005 Enterprise Way (44062-9369)
PHONE.................................440 834-1790
Darrell Mcnair, *Pr*
EMP: 10 **EST:** 2009
SQ FT: 5,000
SALES (est): 7.49MM **Privately Held**
Web: www.mvpplastics.com
SIC: 3089 Injection molding of plastics

(G-9816)
MVP PLASTICS SA LLC
15005 Enterprise Way (44062-9369)
PHONE.................................440 834-1790
Darell Mcnair, *CEO*
EMP: 15 **EST:** 2014
SALES (est): 5.12MM **Privately Held**
Web: www.mvpplastics.com
SIC: 3089 Injection molding of plastics
PA: Mvp Plastics, Inc.
15005 Enterprise Way
Middlefield OH 44062

(G-9817)
MYERS INDUSTRIES INC
Also Called: Dillen Products
15150 Madison Rd (44062-9495)
P.O. Box 738 (44062-0738)
PHONE.................................440 632-1006
Dexter Chumley, *Mgr*
EMP: 40
SALES (corp-wide): 836.28MM **Publicly**
Held
Web: www.myersindustries.com
SIC: 3089 3423 Injection molded finished
plastics products, nec; Hand and edge
tools, nec
PA: Myers Industries, Inc.
1293 S Main St
Akron OH 44301
330 253-5592

(G-9818)
NEFF-PERKINS COMPANY (PA)
16080 Industrial Pkwy (44062-9382)
PHONE.................................440 632-1658
▲ **EMP:** 89 **EST:** 1979
SALES (est): 1.82MM
SALES (corp-wide): 1.82MM **Privately**
Held
Web: www.neff-perkins.com
SIC: 3069 3089 Molded rubber products;
Thermoformed finished plastics products,
nec

(G-9819)
NORMANDY PRODUCTS CO
16125 Industrial Pkwy (44062-9393)
P.O. Box 52 (44062-0052)
PHONE.................................440 632-5050
Carl Arysiak, *Prin*
EMP: 60
SQ FT: 64,000
SALES (corp-wide): 8.73MM **Privately**
Held
Web: www.normandyproducts.com
SIC: 3082 3498 Tubes, unsupported plastics
; Fabricated pipe and fittings
HQ: Normandy Products Co.
1150 Freeport Rd
Pittsburgh PA 15238
412 826-1825

(G-9820)
PCKD ENTERPRISES INC
Also Called: Molten Metals
15510 Old State Rd (44062-8208)
PHONE.................................440 632-9119
Paul Cooper, *Pr*
Kevin Doherty, *VP*
Mark Andes, *Prin*
Sarah Mikash, *Prin*
▲ **EMP:** 9 **EST:** 1990
SQ FT: 16,000
SALES (est): 1.02MM **Privately Held**
Web: www.mmei-inc.com
SIC: 3561 Industrial pumps and parts

(G-9821)
PLASTIC EXTRUSION TECH LTD
15229 S State Ave (44062-9468)
P.O. Box 92 (44062-0092)
PHONE.................................440 632-5611
William E Spencer, *Pr*
Diane Spencer, *Corporate Secretary*
▼ **EMP:** 25 **EST:** 1997
SQ FT: 38,500
SALES (est): 7.55MM **Privately Held**
Web: www.plasticextrusiontech.net
SIC: 3089 Extruded finished plastics
products, nec

(G-9822)
POLYCHEM DISPERSIONS INC
16066 Industrial Pkwy (44062-9382)
PHONE.................................800 545-3530
William Nichols, *CEO*
Anthony Vanni, *
Jeff Nichols, *
EMP: 45 **EST:** 1981
SQ FT: 30,000
SALES (est): 15.32MM **Privately Held**
Web: www.dispersions.com
SIC: 2869 Industrial organic chemicals, nec

(G-9823)
RESOURCE MTL HDLG & RECYCL
INC (PA)
14970 Berkshire Industrial Pkwy
(44062-9390)
PHONE.................................440 834-0727
Josh Jones, *Pr*
Stacey Cremers, *COO*
▼ **EMP:** 20 **EST:** 1991
SQ FT: 50,000
SALES (est): 4.3MM
SALES (corp-wide): 4.3MM **Privately Held**
Web: www.extera.eco
SIC: 5099 3089 Containers: glass, metal or
plastic; Plastics containers, except foam

(G-9824)
ROTHENBUHLER CHEESE CHALET
LLC
15815 Nauvoo Rd (44062-8501)
PHONE.................................800 327-9477
EMP: 8 **EST:** 2012
SALES (est): 395.42K **Privately Held**
Web:
www.rothenbuhlercheesemakers.com
SIC: 2022 Natural cheese

(G-9825)
ROTHENBUHLER HOLDING
COMPANY
15815 Nauvoo Rd (44062-8501)
PHONE.................................440 632-6000
Ann Rothenbuhler, *Prin*
Hans Rothenbuhler, *Prin*
EMP: 8 **EST:** 1973
SALES (est): 957.54K **Privately Held**
Web:
www.rothenbuhlercheesemakers.com
SIC: 2022 Natural cheese

(G-9826)
SCHNIDER PALLET LLC
9782 Bundysburg Rd (44062-9362)
PHONE.................................440 632-5346
EMP: 9 **EST:** 2007
SALES (est): 110.14K **Privately Held**
SIC: 2448 Pallets, wood

(G-9827)
SIMON DE YOUNG CORPORATION
15010 Berkshire Industrial Pkwy
(44062-9390)
P.O. Box 217 (44062-0217)

PHONE.................................440 834-3000
Simon D Young, *Pr*
Margaret D Young, *Sec*
EMP: 8 **EST:** 1984
SALES (est): 488.62K **Privately Held**
SIC: 3552 3549 Braiding machines, textile;
Wiredrawing and fabricating machinery and
equipment, ex. die

(G-9828)
SPI LIQUIDATION INC
Also Called: Sajar Plastics, Inc.
15285 S State Ave (44062-9468)
P.O. Box 37 (44062-0037)
EMP: 100
SIC: 3089 Injection molding of plastics

(G-9829)
SUBURBAN COMMUNICATIONS INC
Also Called: Good News
14905 N State Ave (44062-9747)
P.O. Box 95 (44062-0095)
PHONE.................................440 632-0130
Thomas Henry, *Pr*
Don Cimorell, *
Neil Belcher, *
EMP: 7 **EST:** 1979
SALES (est): 221.48K **Privately Held**
Web: www.good-news.com
SIC: 2721 2741 Magazines: publishing only,
not printed on site; Miscellaneous publishing

(G-9830)
TARKETT INC
16035 Industrial Pkwy (44062-9386)
PHONE.................................800 771-7476
EMP: 12
Web: www.tarkettna.com
SIC: 3069 Flooring, rubber: tile or sheet
HQ: Tarkett, Inc.
30000 Aurora Rd
Solon OH 44139
800 899-8916

(G-9831)
TROY INNOVATIVE INSTRS INC
15111 White Rd (44062-9216)
P.O. Box 1328 (44062-1328)
PHONE.................................440 834-9567
Brett Crawford, *Pr*
Carol Cseplo, *
Randall Hampton, *
August Deangelo, *
EMP: 40 **EST:** 1992
SQ FT: 12,000
SALES (est): 5.32MM **Privately Held**
Web: www.troyinnovative.com
SIC: 3841 Medical instruments and
equipment, blood and bone work

(G-9832)
TROYMILL MANUFACTURING INC
(PA)
Also Called: Troymill Wood Products
17055 Kinsman Rd (44062-9485)
P.O. Box 306 (44062-0306)
PHONE.................................440 632-5580
Marvin Schaefer, *Pr*
Steven Belman, *VP*
Brian Schaefer, *Prin*
EMP: 12 **EST:** 1988
SQ FT: 19,500
SALES (est): 18.74MM **Privately Held**
Web: www.troymill.com
SIC: 5031 2448 Lumber, plywood, and
millwork; Wood pallets and skids

(G-9833)
TRUMBULL COUNTY HARDWOODS
9446 Bundysburg Rd (44062-9300)
PHONE.................................440 632-0555

John Betweiler, *Pt*
Rudy Detweiler, *Pt*
▼ **EMP:** 23 **EST:** 1989
SQ FT: 600
SALES (est): 2.47MM **Privately Held**
Web: www.tchardwoods.com
SIC: 2421 2426 Lumber: rough, sawed, or planed; Hardwood dimension and flooring mills

(G-9834)
UNIVERSAL POLYMER & RUBBER LTD (PA)
15730 Madison Rd (44062-8408)
P.O. Box 767 (44062-0767)
PHONE..............................440 632-1691
Joe Colebank, *Pr*
Andrew Cavanagh, *
▲ **EMP:** 109 **EST:** 1988
SQ FT: 56,000
SALES (est): 24.73MM
SALES (corp-wide): 24.73MM **Privately Held**
Web: www.universalpolymer.com
SIC: 3069 3089 Molded rubber products; Extruded finished plastics products, nec

(G-9835)
V & S SCHULER ENGINEERING INC
15175 Kinsman Rd (44062-9471)
PHONE..............................330 452-5200
Brian Miller, *Pr*
EMP: 66
SALES (corp-wide): 1.08B **Privately Held**
Web: www.vsschuler.com
SIC: 3441 Fabricated structural metal
HQ: V & S Schuler Engineering Inc
2240 Allen Ave Se
Canton OH 44707

(G-9836)
WOODCRAFT INDUSTRIES INC
Also Called: WOODCRAFT INDUSTRIES, INC.
15351 S State Ave (44062-9469)
P.O. Box 250 (44062-0250)
PHONE..............................440 632-9655
Dan Miller, *Mgr*
EMP: 37
Web: middlefield-oh.findstorenearme.us
SIC: 2434 2431 2426 Wood kitchen cabinets ; Millwork; Dimension, hardwood
HQ: Quanex Custom Components, Inc.
525 Lincoln Ave Se
Saint Cloud MN 56304
320 656-2345

(G-9837)
WOODWORKS DESIGN
9005 N Girdle Rd (44062-9502)
PHONE..............................440 693-4414
Todd Armfelt, *Prin*
EMP: 7 **EST:** 1998
SALES (est): 876.33K **Privately Held**
Web: www.woodworks-design.com
SIC: 2431 Millwork

Middletown
Butler County

(G-9838)
3D SALES & CONSULTING INC
Also Called: M R T
408 Vanderveer St (45044-4239)
PHONE..............................513 422-1198
Talbert Selby, *Pr*
David Poe, *
EMP: 25 **EST:** 2007
SQ FT: 25,000

SALES (est): 4.68MM **Privately Held**
Web: www.mrtinc.com
SIC: 3599 Machine shop, jobbing and repair

(G-9839)
AKERS PACKAGING SERVICE INC (PA)
Also Called: Akers Packaging Service Group
2820 Lefferson Rd (45044-6999)
P.O. Box 610 (45042-0610)
PHONE..............................513 422-6312
James F Akers, *Ch Bd*
William C Akers Ii, *Pr*
Michael S Akey, *
Marilyn R Akey, *
▲ **EMP:** 140 **EST:** 1963
SQ FT: 220,000
SALES (est): 74.17MM
SALES (corp-wide): 74.17MM **Privately Held**
Web: www.akers-pkg.com
SIC: 2653 Boxes, corrugated: made from purchased materials

(G-9840)
AKERS PACKAGING SOLUTIONS INC (PA)
Also Called: Akers Packaging Service Group
2820 Lefferson Rd (45044-6999)
P.O. Box 610 (45042-0610)
PHONE..............................513 422-6312
James F Akers, *Ch Bd*
William C Akers, *
Michael Shannon Akey, *
Alfred J Pedicone, *
EMP: 75 **EST:** 2014
SALES (est): 9.09MM
SALES (corp-wide): 9.09MM **Privately Held**
Web: www.akers-pkg.com
SIC: 2653 Boxes, corrugated: made from purchased materials

(G-9841)
AKKO FASTENER INC (PA)
1225 Hook Dr (45042-1734)
PHONE..............................513 489-8300
Nancy Fernandez, *Pr*
Nestor Fernandez, *VP*
▲ **EMP:** 16 **EST:** 1960
SALES (est): 1.86MM
SALES (corp-wide): 1.86MM **Privately Held**
Web: www.akkofastener.com
SIC: 3452 5072 Screws, metal; Bolts

(G-9842)
BACKYARD SCOREBOARDS LLC
Also Called: Nifty Promo Products
431 Kenridge Dr (45042-4930)
PHONE..............................513 702-6561
EMP: 9 **EST:** 2005
SQ FT: 11,000
SALES (est): 123.96K **Privately Held**
Web: www.backyardscoreboards.com
SIC: 3949 Team sports equipment

(G-9843)
CENTURY MOLD COMPANY INC
55 Wright Dr (45044-3287)
PHONE..............................513 539-9283
Ron Ricotta, *Brnch Mgr*
EMP: 6
SALES (corp-wide): 197.74MM **Privately Held**
Web: www.centurymold.com
SIC: 3089 Injection molding of plastics
PA: Century Mold Company, Inc.
25 Vantage Point Dr
Rochester NY 14624
585 352-8600

(G-9844)
CITY OF MIDDLETOWN
Also Called: Water Treatment
805 Columbia Ave (45042-1907)
PHONE..............................513 425-7781
Scott Belcher, *Mgr*
EMP: 66
SALES (corp-wide): 87.24MM **Privately Held**
Web: www.cityofmiddletown.org
SIC: 3589 4941 Water treatment equipment, industrial; Water supply
PA: City Of Middletown
One Donham Plaza
Middletown OH 45042
513 425-7766

(G-9845)
CLEVELAND-CLIFFS STEEL CORP
622 Box (45042)
PHONE..............................513 425-3593
EMP: 10
SALES (corp-wide): 19.18B **Publicly Held**
Web: www.clevelandcliffs.com
SIC: 3312 Blast furnaces and steel mills
HQ: Cleveland-Cliffs Steel Corporation
200 Public Sq Ste 3300
Cleveland OH 44114

(G-9846)
CLEVELAND-CLIFFS STEEL CORP
Also Called: Clevelnd-Clffs Mddletown Works
1801 Crawford St (45044-4572)
PHONE..............................513 425-5000
Doctor Stephen W Gilby, *Dir*
EMP: 148
SALES (corp-wide): 19.18B **Publicly Held**
Web: www.clevelandcliffs.com
SIC: 3312 Blast furnaces and steel mills
HQ: Cleveland-Cliffs Steel Corporation
200 Public Sq Ste 3300
Cleveland OH 44114

(G-9847)
CLEVELAND-CLIFFS STEEL CORP
801 Crawford St (45044-4537)
PHONE..............................513 425-3694
Brian Nuelk, *Brnch Mgr*
EMP: 298
SALES (corp-wide): 19.18B **Publicly Held**
Web: www.clevelandcliffs.com
SIC: 3312 Stainless steel
HQ: Cleveland-Cliffs Steel Corporation
200 Public Sq Ste 3300
Cleveland OH 44114

(G-9848)
COHEN BROTHERS INC (PA)
1520 14th Ave (45044-5801)
P.O. Box 957 (45044)
PHONE..............................513 422-3696
TOLL FREE: 800
Wilbur Cohen, *Ch Bd*
Kenneth Cohen, *
Donald Zulanch, *
Robert Dumes, *
Neil Cohen, *
EMP: 50 **EST:** 1924
SQ FT: 90,000
SALES (est): 96.24MM
SALES (corp-wide): 96.24MM **Privately Held**
Web: www.cohenusa.com
SIC: 5093 3441 3341 3312 Ferrous metal scrap and waste; Fabricated structural metal ; Secondary nonferrous metals; Blast furnaces and steel mills

(G-9849)
COHEN BROTHERS INC
Also Called: Cohen Brothers Inc Lafayette
1300 Lafayette Ave (45044-5913)
PHONE..............................513 217-5200
EMP: 35
SALES (corp-wide): 96.24MM **Privately Held**
Web: www.cohenusa.com
SIC: 5093 3312 3341 Ferrous metal scrap and waste; Blast furnaces and steel mills; Secondary nonferrous metals
PA: Cohen Brothers, Inc.
1520 14th Ave
Middletown OH 45044
513 422-3696

(G-9850)
CORNERSTONE BLDG BRANDS INC
2400 Yankee Rd (45044-8301)
PHONE..............................937 584-3300
EMP: 164
SALES (corp-wide): 5.58B **Privately Held**
Web: www.cornerstonebuildingbrands.com
SIC: 3448 Prefabricated metal buildings
HQ: Cornerstone Building Brands, Inc.
5020 Weston Pkwy
Cary NC 27513
281 897-7788

(G-9851)
CRANE CONSUMABLES INC
155 Wright Dr (45044-3311)
PHONE..............................513 539-9980
Robert Crane, *CEO*
EMP: 45 **EST:** 2007
SALES (est): 4.39MM **Privately Held**
Web: www.craneconsumables.com
SIC: 7389 2241 Packaging and labeling services; Labels, woven

(G-9852)
CROWN ELECTRIC ENGRG & MFG LLC
175 Edison Dr (45044-3269)
PHONE..............................513 539-7394
Chad Shell, *Managing Member*
Bruce Hack, *
▲ **EMP:** 25 **EST:** 2005
SQ FT: 48,000
SALES (est): 6.72MM **Privately Held**
Web: www.crown-electric.com
SIC: 3643 3444 Bus bars (electrical conductors); Sheet metal specialties, not stamped

(G-9853)
DAUBENMIRES PRINTING CO LLC
1527 Central Ave (45044-4135)
PHONE..............................513 425-7223
Gary Daubenmire, *Owner*
EMP: 8 **EST:** 1982
SQ FT: 4,000
SALES (est): 978.61K **Privately Held**
Web: www.daubenmiresprinting.com
SIC: 2752 2791 Offset printing; Typesetting

(G-9854)
DMK INDUSTRIES INC
1801 Made Dr (45044-8948)
PHONE..............................513 727-4549
Dennis Kuna, *Pr*
EMP: 15 **EST:** 1996
SALES (est): 3.58MM **Privately Held**
SIC: 3369 Nonferrous foundries, nec

(G-9855)
DYNAMIC DIES INC
1310 Hook Dr (45042-1712)

PHONE.................513 705-9524
EMP: 27
SALES (corp-wide): 22.27MM **Privately Held**
Web: www.dynamicdies.com
SIC: 3544 Special dies and tools
PA: Dynamic Dies, Inc.
　　1705 Commerce Rd
　　Holland OH 43528
　　419 865-0249

(G-9856)
ELECTRO-METALLICS CO
3004 Lefferson Rd (45044-6903)
PHONE.................513 423-8091
Hamilton Watkins, *Pr*
Jane M Watkins, *Sec*
EMP: 8 **EST:** 1965
SQ FT: 2,500
SALES (est): 466.43K **Privately Held**
SIC: 3471 Electroplating of metals or formed products

(G-9857)
ERNST ENTERPRISES INC
2504 S Main St (45042)
PHONE.................513 422-3651
EMP: 13
SALES (corp-wide): 240.08MM **Privately Held**
Web: www.ernstconcrete.com
SIC: 3273 Ready-mixed concrete
PA: Ernst Enterprises, Inc.
　　993 Falls Creek Dr
　　Vandalia OH 45377
　　937 233-5555

(G-9858)
ESSITY OPERATIONS WAUSAU LLC
700 Columbia Ave (45042-1931)
PHONE.................513 217-3644
Mark Hoton, *Purchasing*
EMP: 36
SALES (corp-wide): 14B **Privately Held**
SIC: 2621 Paper mills
HQ: Essity Operations Wausau Llc
　　N434 Greenville Ctr
　　Appleton WI 54914
　　920 725-7031 .

(G-9859)
ESSITY PROF HYGIENE N AMER LLC
Also Called: ESSITY PROFESSIONAL HYGIENE NORTH AMERICA LLC
700 Columbia Ave (45042-1931)
PHONE.................513 217-3644
EMP: 14
SALES (corp-wide): 14B **Privately Held**
Web: www.torkusa.com
SIC: 2621 Paper mills
HQ: Essity Professional Hygiene North America Llc
　　2929 Arch St Ste 2600
　　Philadelphia PA 19104
　　920 727-3770

(G-9860)
EVERTZ TECHNOLOGY SVC USA INC
2601 S Verity Pkwy Bldg 102 (45044-7482)
PHONE.................513 422-8400
Egon Evertz, *Pr*
▲ **EMP:** 10 **EST:** 2003
SALES (est): 2.99MM **Privately Held**
Web: www.evertz-group.com
SIC: 3325 Steel foundries, nec

(G-9861)
FLEXTRONICS INTL USA INC
6224 Windham Ct (45044-8659)
PHONE.................513 755-2500
EMP: 25

Web: www.flex.com
SIC: 3672 Printed circuit boards
HQ: Flextronics International Usa, Inc.
　　12455 Research Blvd
　　Austin TX 78759

(G-9862)
GRANGER PLASTICS CO THE
1600 Made Dr (45044-8957)
PHONE.................513 424-1955
James Cravens, *Pr*
Jack Cobb, *VP*
Jeffrey T Witschey, *Prin*
EMP: 20 **EST:** 1994
SALES (est): 2.49MM **Privately Held**
Web: www.grangerplastics.com
SIC: 3089 Injection molding of plastics

(G-9863)
GRAPHIC PACKAGING INTL LLC
Also Called: Altivity Packaging
407 Charles St (45042-2107)
PHONE.................513 424-4200
Scott Lebeau, *Mgr*
EMP: 143
Web: www.graphicpkg.com
SIC: 2631 2657 Folding boxboard; Folding paperboard boxes
HQ: Graphic Packaging International, Llc
　　1500 Rvredge Pkwy Ste 100
　　Atlanta GA 30328

(G-9864)
HY-BLAST INC
70 Enterprise Dr (45044-8925)
P.O. Box 602 (45042-0602)
PHONE.................513 424-0704
Robert Cunningham, *Pr*
Thomas Cunningham, *VP*
Betty Jane Cunningham, *Sec*
Donald Ray Cunningham, *VP*
EMP: 11 **EST:** 1981
SQ FT: 25,000
SALES (est): 1.05MM **Privately Held**
Web: www.hyblastinc.com
SIC: 1799 3471 7699 Epoxy application; Polishing, metals or formed products; Industrial equipment cleaning

(G-9865)
INJECTION ALLOYS INCORPORATED
2601 S Verity Pkwy Bldg 1 (45044-7481)
PHONE.................513 422-8819
Chris Jackson, *CEO*
Manuel Franco, *CFO*
Michelle Shockley Ctrl, *Prin*
▲ **EMP:** 10 **EST:** 2005
SALES (est): 8.13MM **Privately Held**
Web: www.injectionalloys.com
SIC: 3315 Wire and fabricated wire products
HQ: Injection Alloys Limited
　　The Way
　　Royston HERTS

(G-9866)
INTERNATIONAL PAPER COMPANY
Also Called: International Paper
912 Nelbar St (45042-2529)
PHONE.................800 473-0830
EMP: 69
SALES (corp-wide): 18.62B **Publicly Held**
Web: www.internationalpaper.com
SIC: 2621 Paper mills
PA: International Paper Company
　　6400 Poplar Ave
　　Memphis TN 38197
　　901 419-7000

(G-9867)
INTERSCOPE MANUFACTURING INC
2901 Carmody Blvd (45042-1761)
PHONE.................513 423-8866
John Michael Brill, *CEO*
◆ **EMP:** 50 **EST:** 1988
SQ FT: 175,000
SALES (est): 10.88MM **Privately Held**
Web: www.interscopemfg.com
SIC: 3599 7389 Custom machinery; Repossession service

(G-9868)
JBT MAREL CORPORATION
2601 S Verity Pkwy Bldg 13 (45044-7495)
PHONE.................513 433-2500
Keith Cripe, *Brnch Mgr*
EMP: 122
Web: www.jbtc.com
SIC: 3556 Food products machinery
PA: Jbt Marel Corporation
　　70 W Madison St Ste 4400
　　Chicago IL 60602

(G-9869)
JEFF LORI JED HOLDINGS INC
1500 S University Blvd (45044-5968)
PHONE.................513 423-0319
Jeff Pennington, *Pr*
Lori Combs, *
Jed Brubaker, *
EMP: 40 **EST:** 1982
SQ FT: 70,000
SALES (est): 9.75MM **Privately Held**
Web: www.n-stockbox.com
SIC: 2653 Boxes, corrugated: made from purchased materials

(G-9870)
JOHN H HOSKING CO
Also Called: Diamond Aluminum Co
4665 Emerald Way (45044-8966)
PHONE.................513 422-9425
James Hodde Junior, *Pr*
EMP: 6 **EST:** 1956
SQ FT: 6,725
SALES (est): 627.98K **Privately Held**
Web: www.diamond-aluminum.com
SIC: 3498 Fabricated pipe and fittings

(G-9871)
KATHOM MANUFACTURING CO INC
1301 Hook Dr (45042-3571)
PHONE.................513 868-8890
Thomas R Wells, *Pr*
EMP: 22 **EST:** 1983
SALES (est): 2.1MM **Privately Held**
Web: www.kathom.com
SIC: 3089 3643 2821 Injection molding of plastics; Current-carrying wiring services; Plastics materials and resins

(G-9872)
LUBRISOURCE INC
2900 Cincinnati Dayton Rd (45044-9313)
P.O. Box 750221 (45475-0221)
PHONE.................937 432-9292
Angela Morrow, *Pr*
Angela Morrow, *Pr*
Kevin Morrow, *VP*
EMP: 17 **EST:** 2001
SALES (est): 4.11MM **Privately Held**
Web: www.lubrisource.com
SIC: 5084 3561 1389 7699 Hydraulic systems equipment and supplies; Pumps and pumping equipment; Oil sampling service for oil companies; Industrial equipment services

(G-9873)
M-D BUILDING PRODUCTS INC
100 Westheimer Dr (45044-3242)
PHONE.................513 539-2255
Carrie Taylor-lane, *Prin*
EMP: 83
SALES (corp-wide): 216.18MM **Privately Held**
Web: www.mdteam.com
SIC: 3442 Weather strip, metal
PA: M-D Building Products, Inc.
　　4041 N Santa Fe Ave
　　Oklahoma City OK 73118
　　405 528-4411

(G-9874)
M-D BUILDING PRODUCTS INC
Also Called: M-D Metal Source
100 Westheimer Dr (45044-3242)
PHONE.................513 539-2255
Carrie Taylor, *Brnch Mgr*
EMP: 10
SALES (corp-wide): 216.18MM **Privately Held**
Web: www.mdmetalsource.com
SIC: 3354 5031 5051 3442 Aluminum extruded products; Doors, nec; Aluminum bars, rods, ingots, sheets, pipes, plates, etc.; Screens, window, metal
PA: M-D Building Products, Inc.
　　4041 N Santa Fe Ave
　　Oklahoma City OK 73118
　　405 528-4411

(G-9875)
MAGELLAN AROSPC MIDDLETOWN INC (HQ)
2320 Wedekind Dr (45042-2390)
PHONE.................513 422-2751
John Furbay, *Dir Fin*
James S Butyniec, *
EMP: 100 **EST:** 1928
SALES (est): 18.95MM
SALES (corp-wide): 569.19MM **Privately Held**
SIC: 3724 3728 Aircraft engines and engine parts; Aircraft body assemblies and parts
PA: Magellan Aerospace Corporation
　　3160 Derry Rd E
　　Mississauga ON L4T 1
　　905 677-1889

(G-9876)
MAGNUM MAGNETICS CORPORATION
Magnum Inks & Coatings
355 Wright Dr (45044-3268)
PHONE.................513 360-0790
EMP: 39
Web: www.magnuminks.com
SIC: 2893 Printing ink
PA: Magnum Magnetics Corporation
　　801 Masonic Park Rd
　　Marietta OH 45750

(G-9877)
MANUFACTURERS EQUIPMENT CO
Also Called: Meco
35 Enterprise Dr (45044-8928)
PHONE.................513 424-3573
Adam W Miller, *Pr*
J Howard Sachs, *Dir*
Frank B Carraher, *VP*
◆ **EMP:** 14 **EST:** 1910
SQ FT: 16,000
SALES (est): 3.02MM **Privately Held**
Web: www.mecoservices.com
SIC: 3496 3535 Wire chain; Belt conveyor systems, general industrial use

(G-9878)
MCINTOSH MANUFACTURING LLC
3350 Yankee Rd (45044-8927)
PHONE....................513 424-5307
▼ EMP: 55 EST: 1998
SQ FT: 60,000
SALES (est): 4.88MM
SALES (corp-wide): 35.72MM Privately
Held
Web: www.triosim.com
SIC: 3554 3312 Paper industries machinery;
Stainless steel
PA: Triosim Corporation
2111 N Sandra St
Appleton WI 54911
920 968-0800

(G-9879)
MIDDLETOWN LICENSE AGENCY INC
3232 Roosevelt Blvd (45044-6424)
P.O. Box 546 (45042-0546)
PHONE....................513 422-7225
Cristy Gamble, Pr
EMP: 6 EST: 2004
SALES (est): 366.45K Privately Held
SIC: 3469 Automobile license tags, stamped
metal

(G-9880)
MOORCHILD LLC
Also Called: Murphy's Landing Casual Dining
6 S Broad St (45044-4000)
PHONE....................513 649-8867
Linda Moorman, Managing Member
Nancy Fairchild, Managing Member
EMP: 10 EST: 2014
SALES (est): 97.94K Privately Held
Web: www.murphys-landing.com
SIC: 2599 Bar, restaurant and cafeteria
furniture

(G-9881)
NATREEOLA SOAP COMPANY LLC
2367 Bendel Dr (45044-9448)
PHONE....................513 390-2247
Angela Smith, CEO
EMP: 6 EST: 2021
SALES (est): 27.98K Privately Held
SIC: 2841 Soap and other detergents

(G-9882)
NATURAL BEAUTY PRODUCTS INC
Also Called: Decaplus
104 Charles St (45042-2139)
P.O. Box 1566 (45042-7383)
PHONE....................513 420-9400
Kenneth Alsop, Pr
David Haddix, VP
James Webb, Treas
Michelle Randall, Sec
EMP: 10 EST: 1985
SALES (est): 233.68K Privately Held
Web: www.deccaplus.com
SIC: 5999 2844 Hair care products; Hair
preparations, including shampoos

(G-9883)
PACKAGING CORPORATION AMERICA
Also Called: Pca/Middletown 353
1824 Baltimore St (45044-5902)
P.O. Box 127 (45042-0127)
PHONE....................513 424-3542
Tom Falvey, Mgr
EMP: 53
SQ FT: 200,000
SALES (corp-wide): 7.73B Publicly Held
Web: www.packagingcorp.com

SIC: 2653 Boxes, corrugated: made from
purchased materials
PA: Packaging Corporation Of America
1 N Field Ct
Lake Forest IL 60045
847 482-3000

(G-9884)
PERSONAL DEFENSE & TACTICS LLC
2200 Ernestine Dr (45042-2794)
PHONE....................513 571-7163
Matthew Burns, Prin
EMP: 6 EST: 2012
SALES (est): 136.09K Privately Held
SIC: 3812 Defense systems and equipment

(G-9885)
PHILLIPS TUBE GROUP INC
Also Called: Phillips Tube Group, LLC
2201 Trine St (45044-5766)
P.O. Box 125 (44875-0125)
PHONE....................205 338-4771
Angela Phillips, Pr
EMP: 44 EST: 2016
SQ FT: 50,000
SALES (est): 5.5MM
SALES (corp-wide): 31.79MM Privately
Held
Web: www.phillipstube.com
SIC: 3312 Pipes and tubes
PA: Phillips Mfg. And Tower Co.
5578 State Rte 61 N
Shelby OH 44875
419 347-1720

(G-9886)
PILOT CHEMICAL CORP
3439 Yankee Rd (45044-8931)
PHONE....................513 424-9700
Jeff Russell, Brnch Mgr
EMP: 217
SQ FT: 25,000
SALES (corp-wide): 126.04MM Privately
Held
Web: www.pilotchemical.com
SIC: 2841 2842 Detergents, synthetic
organic or inorganic alkaline; Polishes and
sanitation goods
HQ: Pilot Chemical Corp.
9075 Cntre Pnte Dr Ste 40
West Chester OH 45069
513 326-0600

(G-9887)
PROGRESSIVE RIBBON INC (PA)
1533 Central Ave (45044-4135)
P.O. Box 887 (45044-0887)
PHONE....................513 705-9319
Darryl Bowen, Pr
Darryl Bowen, Pr
Dan Bush, VP
EMP: 20 EST: 1983
SQ FT: 20,000
SALES (est): 584.76K
SALES (corp-wide): 584.76K Privately
Held
SIC: 3955 Ribbons, inked: typewriter, adding
machine, register, etc.

(G-9888)
QUAKER CHEMICAL CORPORATION (HQ)
Also Called: Quaker Houghton
3431 Yankee Rd (45044-8931)
PHONE....................513 422-9600
Michael Barry, Pr
Carl Mitchell, Pdt Mgr
Donald Biltz, Prin
Patrick Piccioni, Prin
D Jeffry Benoliel, Sec

▲ EMP: 43 EST: 1995
SALES (est): 28.83MM
SALES (corp-wide): 1.84B Publicly Held
Web: home.quakerhoughton.com
SIC: 2992 2899 Lubricating oils and greases
; Chemical preparations, nec
PA: Quaker Chemical Corporation
901 E Hector St
Conshohocken PA 19428
610 832-4000

(G-9889)
QUAKER HOUGHTON PA INC
3431 Yankee Rd. (45044-8931)
PHONE....................513 422-9600
EMP: 6
SALES (corp-wide): 1.84B Publicly Held
Web: home.quakerhoughton.com
SIC: 2992 Lubricating oils and greases
HQ: Quaker Houghton Pa, Inc.
901 E Hctor St One Qker P
Conshohocken PA 19428
610 832-4000

(G-9890)
REBILTCO INC
8775 Thomas Rd (45042-1233)
P.O. Box 936 (45044-0936)
PHONE....................513 424-2024
Larry Eckhardt, Pr
EMP: 6 EST: 1977
SQ FT: 25,000
SALES (est): 494.04K Privately Held
Web: www.rebiltcoincweldfab.com
SIC: 3554 Corrugating machines, paper

(G-9891)
ROAD APPLE MUSIC
65 S Main St (45044-4061)
PHONE....................513 217-4444
Edward Hall, Owner
EMP: 6 EST: 2006
SALES (est): 182.74K Privately Held
SIC: 2741 Music book and sheet music
publishing

(G-9892)
ROSS HX LLC (PA)
Also Called: Ross Hx
2722 Cincinnati Dayton Rd (45044-8960)
PHONE....................513 217-1565
Richard Ross, Pr
EMP: 32 EST: 2018
SQ FT: 9,000
SALES (est): 5.23MM
SALES (corp-wide): 5.23MM Privately
Held
Web: www.rosshx.com
SIC: 3443 Heat exchangers, plate type

(G-9893)
SHER INTERNATIONAL INC
Also Called: Sher International
2608 Oxford State Rd (45044-8910)
PHONE....................800 895-9581
Gurpreet Pabla, Pr
Gurpreet S Pabla, Pr
EMP: 15 EST: 2018
SALES (est): 4.63MM Privately Held
SIC: 3537 Trucks: freight, baggage, etc.:
industrial, except mining

(G-9894)
SPURLINO MATERIALS LLC (PA)
4000 Oxford State Rd (45044-8973)
PHONE....................513 705-0111
Jim Spurlino, Pr
EMP: 50 EST: 2000
SQ FT: 10,000
SALES (est): 1.56MM
SALES (corp-wide): 1.56MM Privately
Held

Web: www.spurlino.net
SIC: 3273 Ready-mixed concrete

(G-9895)
SUNCOKE ENERGY INC
Also Called: Mto Suncoke
3353 Yankee Rd (45044-8927)
PHONE....................513 727-5571
Frederick Henderson, Brnch Mgr
EMP: 40
Web: www.suncoke.com
SIC: 1241 Coal mining services
PA: Suncoke Energy, Inc.
1011 Wrrnville Rd Ste 600
Lisle IL 60532

(G-9896)
SUPERIOR CASTER INC
Also Called: Superior Casters
455 Wright Dr (45044-3264)
PHONE....................513 539-8980
Lilly Chang, Pr
EMP: 10 EST: 1998
SALES (est): 1.41MM Privately Held
SIC: 5072 3562 Hardware; Casters
PA: Durable U.S.A., Inc.
2801 E Abram St
Arlington TX 76010

(G-9897)
TEMPLE INLAND
912 Nelbar St (45042-2529)
PHONE....................513 425-0830
EMP: 6 EST: 2015
SALES (est): 462.85K Privately Held
SIC: 2653 Boxes, corrugated: made from
purchased materials

(G-9898)
TMS INTERNATIONAL LLC
1801 Crawford St (45044-4572)
PHONE....................513 425-6462
EMP: 15
Web: www.tmsinternational.com
SIC: 3312 Blast furnaces and steel mills
HQ: Tms International, Llc
2835 East Carson Street
Pittsburgh PA 15203
412 678-6141

(G-9899)
TMS INTERNATIONAL LLC
3018 Oxford State Rd (45044-8900)
PHONE....................513 422-4572
EMP: 32
Web: www.tmsinternational.com
SIC: 3312 Blast furnaces and steel mills
HQ: Tms International, Llc
2835 East Carson Street
Pittsburgh PA 15203
412 678-6141

(G-9900)
TOMSON STEEL COMPANY
1400 Made Dr (45044-8936)
PHONE....................513 420-8600
Stephen Lutz, Pr
Thomas Lutz, *
EMP: 25 EST: 1981
SQ FT: 94,000
SALES (est): 9.58MM Privately Held
Web: www.tomsonsteel.com
SIC: 5051 3291 Steel; Abrasive metal and
steel products

(G-9901)
VAIL RUBBER WORKS INC
Also Called: Midwest Service
605 Clark St (45042-2117)
PHONE....................513 705-2060

Donald Bown, *Brnch Mgr*
EMP: 13
SALES (corp-wide): 19.37MM **Privately Held**
Web: www.vailrubber.com
SIC: 3554 Paper industries machinery
PA: Vail Rubber Works, Inc.
　521 Langley Ave
　Saint Joseph MI 49085
　877 350-0441

(G-9902)
WATSON GRAVEL INC
2100 S Main St (45044-7345)
PHONE..............................513 422-3781
Ron Price, *Mgr*
EMP: 8
SALES (corp-wide): 4.86MM **Privately Held**
Web: www.watsongravel.com
SIC: 1442 Gravel mining
PA: Watson Gravel, Inc.
　2728 Hamilton Cleves Rd
　Hamilton OH 45013
　513 863-0070

(G-9903)
WAUSAU PAPER CORP
Also Called: Wausau Mosinee Paper
700 Columbia Ave (45042-1931)
PHONE..............................513 217-3623
Douglas Zirbel, *Mgr*
EMP: 281
SALES (corp-wide): 14B **Privately Held**
Web: www.torkusa.com
SIC: 2621 Paper mills
HQ: Wausau Paper Corp.
　2929 Arch St Ste 2600
　Philadelphia PA 19104
　866 722-8675

(G-9904)
WHITT MACHINE INC
806 Central Ave (45044-1718)
PHONE..............................513 423-7624
Dean Whitt, *Pr*
Wendy Whitt, *VP*
Angie Snarski, *Sec*
EMP: 10 **EST:** 1981
SQ FT: 35,000
SALES (est): 805.7K **Privately Held**
SIC: 3599 7692 Machine shop, jobbing and repair; Welding repair

(G-9905)
WIKOFF COLOR CORPORATION
1392 Oxford State Rd (45044-7580)
PHONE..............................513 423-0727
Bill Dishman, *Mgr*
EMP: 9
SALES (corp-wide): 92.4MM **Privately Held**
Web: www.wikoff.com
SIC: 2893 Printing ink
PA: Wikoff Color Corporation
　1886 Merrit Rd
　Fort Mill SC 29715
　803 548-2210

Midvale
Tuscarawas County

(G-9906)
AMERICAN BOTTLING COMPANY
Also Called: 7 Up Bottling Co
Old Rte #250 (44653)
P.O. Box 535 (44653-0535)
PHONE..............................740 922-5253
Nick Kazocoff, *Mgr*

EMP: 43
Web: www.keurigdrpepper.com
SIC: 2086 Soft drinks: packaged in cans, bottles, etc.
HQ: The American Bottling Company
　6425 Hall Of Fame Ln
　Frisco TX 75034

(G-9907)
AMKO SERVICE COMPANY (DH)
Also Called: Dover Cryogenics
3211 Brightwood Rd (44653)
P.O. Box 280 (44653-0280)
PHONE..............................330 364-8857
Darren Nippard, *Pr*
Duane R Yant, *Prin*
▲ **EMP:** 50 **EST:** 1965
SALES (est): 858.56K **Privately Held**
Web: www.amkotech.com
SIC: 7699 3443 7629 Tank repair and cleaning services; Cryogenic tanks, for liquids and gases; Electrical repair shops
HQ: Linde Inc.
　10 Riverview Dr
　Danbury CT 06810
　203 837-2000

(G-9908)
DOVER CONVEYOR INC
3323 Brightwood Rd (44653-1901)
P.O. Box 300 (44653-0300)
PHONE..............................740 922-9390
Joseph Coniglio, *Pr*
EMP: 25 **EST:** 1962
SQ FT: 40,000
SALES (est): 2.52MM **Privately Held**
Web: www.doverconveyor.com
SIC: 3535 3441 3532 Conveyors and conveying equipment; Fabricated structural metal; Cages, mine shaft

(G-9909)
FIBA TECHNOLOGIES INC
Also Called: Amko Service Company
3211 Brightwood Road (44653)
P.O. Box 280 (44653-0280)
PHONE..............................330 602-7300
David Ohl, *Brnch Mgr*
EMP: 10
SALES (corp-wide): 49.31MM **Privately Held**
Web: www.fibatech.com
SIC: 3443 Cryogenic tanks, for liquids and gases
PA: Fiba Technologies, Inc.
　53 Ayer Rd
　Littleton MA 01460
　508 887-7100

(G-9910)
FLEX TECHNOLOGIES INC (PA)
5479 Gundy Dr (44653)
P.O. Box 400 (44653-0400)
PHONE..............................740 922-5992
▼ **EMP:** 40 **EST:** 1964
SALES (est): 6MM
SALES (corp-wide): 6MM **Privately Held**
Web: www.flextechnologies.com
SIC: 3084 3357 3083 3089 Plastics pipe; Nonferrous wiredrawing and insulating; Laminated plastics plate and sheet; Molding primary plastics

(G-9911)
HYDRAULIC SPECIALISTS INC
5655 Gundy Dr (44653)
PHONE..............................740 922-3343
Dale Burkholder, *Pr*
Laraine Burkholder, *Sec*
EMP: 6 **EST:** 1990
SQ FT: 15,000

SALES (est): 966.47K **Privately Held**
SIC: 3443 7699 3593 Industrial vessels, tanks, and containers; Hydraulic equipment repair; Fluid power cylinders and actuators

(G-9912)
KLX ENERGY SERVICES LLC
3571 Brighwood Rd (44653)
PHONE..............................740 922-1155
EMP: 24
SALES (corp-wide): 709.3MM **Publicly Held**
Web: www.klx.com
SIC: 1389 Fishing for tools, oil and gas field
HQ: Klx Energy Services Llc
　3040 Post Oak Blvd Ste 15
　Houston TX 77056
　832 844-1015

(G-9913)
MAINTENANCE REPAIR SUPPLY INC
Also Called: Convertapax
5539 Gundy Dr (44653)
P.O. Box 540 (44653-0540)
PHONE..............................740 922-3006
Brad Mathias, *Pr*
▲ **EMP:** 6 **EST:** 1985
SQ FT: 48,000
SALES (est): 996.81K **Privately Held**
Web: www.maintenancerepairsupply.com
SIC: 5085 2821 5084 Industrial supplies; Polyesters; Plastic products machinery

---

Milan
Erie County

(G-9914)
CERTAINTEED LLC
11519 Us Highway 250 N (44846-9708)
PHONE..............................419 499-2581
Mark Hyde, *Mgr*
EMP: 247
SALES (corp-wide): 402.18MM **Privately Held**
Web: www.certainteed.com
SIC: 2952 Roofing materials
HQ: Certainteed Llc
　20 Moores Rd
　Malvern PA 19355
　800 233-8990

(G-9915)
FREUDENBERG-NOK SEALING TECH
11617 State Route 13 (44846-9725)
PHONE..............................877 331-8427
EMP: 13 **EST:** 2015
SALES (est): 5.03MM **Privately Held**
Web: www.transtec.com
SIC: 3714 Motor vehicle parts and accessories

(G-9916)
JOHNS MANVILLE CORPORATION
49 Lockwood Rd (44846-9734)
PHONE..............................419 499-1400
Brian Keyser, *Genl Mgr*
EMP: 52
SALES (corp-wide): 424.23B **Publicly Held**
Web: www.jm.com
SIC: 2952 Roofing materials
HQ: Johns Manville Corporation
　717 17th St
　Denver CO 80202
　303 978-2000

(G-9917)
PULLMAN COMPANY
Also Called: Tenneco
33 Lockwood Rd (44846-9734)
PHONE..............................419 499-2541
Casey Mcelwain, *Brnch Mgr*
EMP: 232
SALES (corp-wide): 18.04B **Privately Held**
Web: www.pullman-services.com
SIC: 3714 Shock absorbers, motor vehicle
HQ: The Pullman Company
　1 International Dr
　Monroe MI 48161
　734 243-8000

(G-9918)
SCHLESSMAN SEED CO (PA)
11513 Us Highway 250 N (44846-9708)
PHONE..............................419 499-2572
Daryl Deering, *Ch Bd*
Dave Herzer, *
EMP: 23 **EST:** 1915
SQ FT: 100,000
SALES (est): 5.5MM
SALES (corp-wide): 5.5MM **Privately Held**
Web: www.schlessman-seed.com
SIC: 5191 2075 0723 0116 Seeds: field, garden, and flower; Soybean oil mills; Crop preparation services for market; Soybeans

---

Milford
Clermont County

(G-9919)
4BLAR LLC
5948 Shallow Creek Dr (45150-1525)
PHONE..............................513 576-0441
Beth Caudell, *Prin*
EMP: 6 **EST:** 2008
SALES (est): 101.67K **Privately Held**
SIC: 2273 Carpets and rugs

(G-9920)
AB PLASTICS INC
1287 Us Route 50 (45150-9688)
PHONE..............................513 576-6333
Robert Basile, *Pr*
Kim Basille, *Sec*
EMP: 9 **EST:** 1989
SQ FT: 5,000
SALES (est): 512.61K **Privately Held**
Web: www.ab-plastics.com
SIC: 3089 Injection molding of plastics

(G-9921)
AMERICAN INSULATION TECH LLC
6071 Branch Hill Guinea Pike Ste A (45150-1567)
PHONE..............................513 733-4248
Jerome Napier, *Managing Member*
EMP: 12 **EST:** 2013
SALES (est): 744.73K **Privately Held**
Web: www.aitinsulation.com
SIC: 3296 3081 Fiberglass insulation; Film base, cellulose acetate or nitrocellulose plastics

(G-9922)
B & D MACHINISTS INC
1350 Us Route 50 (45150-9205)
PHONE..............................513 831-8588
Tonson Roy Boone Junior, *Pr*
Steven Boone, *VP*
Gary W Boone, *VP*
Velma Boone, *Sec*
EMP: 8 **EST:** 1980
SQ FT: 16,000
SALES (est): 904.28K **Privately Held**
Web: www.bdmachinists.com

SIC: **3599** Machine shop, jobbing and repair

(G-9923)
BATMAN ENTERPRISES LLC
Also Called: Commerical Roofing
931 Business 28 (45150-4918)
PHONE.....................................513 600-3079
Donna Castelluccio, *CEO*
EMP: 10 EST: 2016
SALES (est): 1.7MM Privately Held
Web: www.batsremoval.com
SIC: **3069** 1761 Roofing, membrane rubber;
Roofing, siding, and sheetmetal work

(G-9924)
BEARING PRECIOUS SEED INTL INC
(PA)
1369 Woodville Pike Unit B (45150-2260)
PHONE.....................................513 575-1706
William Duttry, *Pr*
Alan Braley, *Dir*
▼ **EMP: 6 EST:** 1973
SALES (est): 2MM Privately Held
Web: www.bpsmilford.org
SIC: **2731** Books, publishing and printing

(G-9925)
BECK STUDIOS INC
1001 Tech Dr (45150-9780)
PHONE.....................................513 831-6650
Dan L Ilhardt, *Pr*
Matthew Mullen, *VP*
Cathie Haverkamp, *Sec*
EMP: 20 EST: 1856
SQ FT: 9,000
SALES (est): 4.92MM Privately Held
Web: www.beckstudios.net
SIC: **1799** 3999 Rigging, theatrical; Stage
hardware and equipment, except lighting

(G-9926)
BREWER COMPANY (PA)
Also Called: Brewercote
25 Whitney Dr Ste 104 (45150-8400)
PHONE.....................................800 394-0017
Pinckney W Brewer, *Pr*
Michael T Dooley, *VP Fin*
Thomas P Matlock, *VP Sls*
▲ **EMP: 8 EST:** 1933
SALES (est): 12.34MM
SALES (corp-wide): 12.34MM Privately
Held
Web: www.thebrewerco.com
SIC: **2952** 0782 2951 Coating compounds,
tar; Seeding services, lawn; Asphalt paving
mixtures and blocks

(G-9927)
CALORPLAST USA LLC
1287 Us Route 50 (45150-9688)
PHONE.....................................513 576-6333
Graham Tenbrink, *Prin*
EMP: 9 EST: 2017
SALES (est): 3.3MM
SALES (corp-wide): 3.3MM Privately Held
Web: www.calorplastusa.com
SIC: **3089** Plastics hardware and building
products
PA: Magen Eco - Energy Usa, Inc
451 Prosperity Farms Rd
Ocoee FL

(G-9928)
CHRIS STEPP
Also Called: Stepp Sewing Service
927 Business 28 Unit B (45150-1948)
PHONE.....................................513 248-0822
Chris Stepp, *Owner*
EMP: 6 EST: 1975
SQ FT: 1,200
SALES (est): 215.62K Privately Held

SIC: **2395** 5651 Embroidery and art
needlework; Unisex clothing stores

(G-9929)
CINCINNATI PRINT SOLUTIONS LLC
2002 Ford Cir Ste G (45150-2748)
PHONE.....................................513 943-9500
EMP: 6 EST: 2006
SALES (est): 1.02MM Privately Held
Web: www.shamrockcompanies.net
SIC: **2752** 7334 2759 Offset printing;
Photocopying and duplicating services;
Commercial printing, nec
PA: The Shamrock Companies Inc
24090 Detroit Rd
Westlake OH 44145

(G-9930)
COMMERCIAL CNSTR GROUP LLC
Also Called: General Contractor
5902 Montclair Blvd (45150-2501)
PHONE.....................................513 722-8952
Daniel Taylor, *Pr*
EMP: 7 EST: 2000
SALES (est): 8.86MM Privately Held
Web: www.ccgmidwest.com
SIC: **1542** 1531 1389 Commercial and office
building contractors; Construction, repair,
and dismantling services

(G-9931)
CONVEYOR TECHNOLOGIES LTD
501 Techne Center Dr Ste B (45150-2796)
PHONE.....................................513 248-0663
Charles Mitchell, *Pr*
Tony Mitchell, *VP*
Tim Mitchell, *VP*
EMP: 8 EST: 1997
SQ FT: 7,000
SALES (est): 1.75MM Privately Held
Web: www.conveyortechltd.com
SIC: **3535** Conveyors and conveying
equipment

(G-9932)
CUSTOM BUILT CRATES INC
1700 Victory Park Dr (45150-1812)
EMP: 20 EST: 1997
SALES (est): 2.68MM Privately Held
Web: www.custombuiltcrates.com
SIC: **4213** 2449 7389 Trucking, except local;
Rectangular boxes and crates, wood;
Business Activities at Non-Commercial Site

(G-9933)
F & S HYDRAULICS INC
6071 Branch Hill Guinea Pike Ste B
(45150-2253)
PHONE.....................................513 575-1600
James M Foster, *Pr*
Howard E Sneed, *VP*
EMP: 7 EST: 1977
SQ FT: 4,000
SALES (est): 236.4K Privately Held
SIC: **3599** Machine shop, jobbing and repair

(G-9934)
FOUNTAIN SPECIALISTS INC
226 Main St (45150-1124)
PHONE.....................................513 831-5717
Lois Sedacca, *Pr*
Mark Sedacca, *VP*
EMP: 8 EST: 1960
SQ FT: 5,000
SALES (est): 309.75K Privately Held
Web: www.fountainspecialist.com
SIC: **5261** 3272 3499 3089 Fountains,
outdoor; Fountains, concrete; Fountains
(except drinking), metal; Plastics processing

(G-9935)
GB LIQUIDATING COMPANY INC
22 Whitney Dr (45150-9783)
PHONE.....................................513 248-7600
EMP: 22 EST: 1946
SALES (est): 412.64K Privately Held
Web: www.gordonbernard.com
SIC: **7371** 2759 2741 2752 Custom
computer programming services;
Commercial printing, nec; Miscellaneous
publishing; Calendar and card printing,
lithographic

(G-9936)
GORDON BERNARD COMPANY LLC
22 Whitney Dr (45150-9781)
PHONE.....................................513 248-7600
Robert Sherman Junior, *CEO*
EMP: 45 EST: 1944
SQ FT: 25,000
SALES (est): 4.89MM Privately Held
Web: www.gordonbernard.com
SIC: **5199** 2752 2741 Calendars;
Commercial printing, lithographic;
Miscellaneous publishing

(G-9937)
GREGG MACMILLAN
Also Called: Macmillan Graphics
2002 Ford Cir Ste A (45150-2748)
PHONE.....................................513 248-2121
Gregg Macmillan, *Owner*
Gregg J Macmillan, *CEO*
EMP: 8 EST: 1985
SQ FT: 4,000
SALES (est): 119.48K Privately Held
Web: www.macgra.com
SIC: **2752** 7336 Offset printing; Graphic arts
and related design

(G-9938)
HAMILTON SAFE CO (DH)
Also Called: Hamilton Safe Company
1030 Round Bottom Rd (45150-9740)
PHONE.....................................513 874-3733
Robert C Deluse, *Pr*
David Vanschoik, *VP*
Greg Holbrock, *Prin*
John Stroia, *Pr*
▲ **EMP: 19 EST:** 1967
SALES (est): 10.16MM
SALES (corp-wide): 1.25MM Privately
Held
web:
www.hamiltonsecuritysolutions.com
SIC: **3499** Safe deposit boxes or chests,
metal
HQ: Hamilton Products Group, Inc.
1030 Round Bottom Rd
Milford OH 45150
800 876-6066

(G-9939)
HAMILTON SECURITY PRODUCTS
CO
Also Called: Hamilton Safe
1030 Round Bottom Rd (45150-9740)
PHONE.....................................513 874-3733
Robert Leslie, *CEO*
John Haining, *
▲ **EMP: 46 EST:** 1974
SALES (est): 7.66MM
SALES (corp-wide): 1.25MM Privately
Held
Web:
www.hamiltonsecuritysolutions.com
SIC: **3499** Safe deposit boxes or chests,
metal
HQ: Gunnebo Ab
Johan Pa Gardas Gata 7
Goteborg 412 5

(G-9940)
JOURNEY SYSTEMS LLC
25 Whitney Dr Ste 100 (45150-8400)
PHONE.....................................513 831-6200
EMP: 14 EST: 2006
SQ FT: 9,875
SALES (est): 2.27MM Privately Held
Web: gov.journeysystems.com
SIC: **3571** 5045 5734 Electronic computers;
Computers, peripherals, and software;
Computer and software stores

(G-9941)
M4 KNICK LLC
55 W Techne Center Dr Ste C
(45150-8902)
PHONE.....................................513 833-2500
Shawn Little, *Managing Member*
EMP: 8 EST: 2016
SALES (est): 2.51MM Privately Held
Web: www.m4knick.com
SIC: **5065** 3829 3569 Electronic parts and
equipment, nec; Measuring and controlling
devices, nec; General industrial machinery,
nec

(G-9942)
MCCC SPORTSWEAR INC (PA)
501 Techne Center Dr (45150-2796)
PHONE.....................................513 583-9210
Marta Callahan, *Pr*
▲ **EMP: 9 EST:** 1994
SALES (est): 2.77MM Privately Held
Web: www.mccc-sportswear.com
SIC: **5137** 2395 5136 Women's and
children's clothing; Embroidery and art
needlework; Men's and boy's clothing

(G-9943)
MELINK CORPORATION
5140 River Valley Rd (45150-9108)
PHONE.....................................513 685-0958
Stephen K Melink, *Pr*
EMP: 68 EST: 1997
SQ FT: 36,000
SALES (est): 25.21MM Privately Held
Web: www.melinkcorp.com
SIC: **8711** 8748 3822 Heating and ventilation
engineering; Energy conservation
consultant; Appliance controls,except air-
conditioning and refrigeration

(G-9944)
MILFORD PRINTERS (PA)
317 Main St (45150-1125)
P.O. Box 123 (45131-0123)
PHONE.....................................513 831-6630
Robert M Heichel, *Owner*
EMP: 20 EST: 1978
SQ FT: 8,000
SALES (est): 358.02K
SALES (corp-wide): 358.02K Privately
Held
SIC: **2752** Offset printing

(G-9945)
ODOM INDUSTRIES INC
Also Called: Odom
1262 Us Route 50 (45150-9767)
PHONE.....................................513 248-0287
EMP: 50
Web: www.odomindustries.com
SIC: **3443** Tanks, standard or custom
fabricated: metal plate

(G-9946)
OVERHOFF TECHNOLOGY CORP
1160 Us Route 50 (45150-9517)
P.O. Box 182 (45150-0182)
PHONE.....................................513 248-2400

Robert Goldstein, *Pr*
EMP: 14 **EST:** 1971
SQ FT: 8,000
SALES (est): 1.95MM
SALES (corp-wide): 2.23MM **Publicly Held**
Web: www.overhoff.com
SIC: 3829 3823 Nuclear instrument modules ; Controllers, for process variables, all types
PA: Us Nuclear Corp.
7051 Eton Ave
Canoga Park CA 91303
818 296-0746

(G-9947)
PARKER-HANNIFIN CORPORATION
Also Called: Electromechanical North Amer
50 W Techne Center Dr Ste H (45150-8403)
PHONE.............................513 831-2340
Kenneth Sweet, *Brnch Mgr*
EMP: 10
SALES (corp-wide): 19.93B **Publicly Held**
Web: www.parker.com
SIC: 3577 7371 3575 3571 Computer peripheral equipment, nec; Computer software development; Computer terminals; Electronic computers
PA: Parker-Hannifin Corporation
6035 Parkland Blvd
Cleveland OH 44124
216 896-3000

(G-9948)
PPG INDUSTRIES INC
Also Called: P P G
500 Techne Center Dr (45150-2763)
PHONE.............................513 576-0360
Greg Wagner, *Mgr*
EMP: 15
SALES (corp-wide): 18.25B **Publicly Held**
Web: www.ppg.com
SIC: 2851 Shellac (protective coating)
PA: Ppg Industries, Inc.
1 Ppg Pl
Pittsburgh PA 15272
412 434-3131

(G-9949)
PRIMEX
400 Techne Center Dr Ste 104 (45150-2792)
PHONE.............................513 831-9959
Douglas Strief, *Pr*
Catherine Strief, *
EMP: 7 **EST:** 1983
SQ FT: 20,000
SALES (est): 1.43MM **Privately Held**
Web: www.primexcontrols.com
SIC: 3613 3823 3699 3625 Control panels, electric; Process control instruments; Electrical equipment and supplies, nec; Relays and industrial controls

(G-9950)
REMINGTON ENGRG MACHINING INC
5105 River Valley Rd (45150-9117)
PHONE.............................513 965-8999
Dan Mallaley, *Pr*
Valerie Mallaley, *Sec*
EMP: 6 **EST:** 1996
SQ FT: 2,500
SALES (est): 1.87MM
SALES (corp-wide): 37.78MM **Privately Held**
SIC: 3599 Machine shop, jobbing and repair
PA: Cold Jet, Llc
6283 Tri Ridge Blvd
Loveland OH 45140
513 831-3211

(G-9951)
SARDINIA CONCRETE COMPANY (PA)
911 Us Route 50 (45150-9703)
PHONE.............................513 248-0090
James Fraley, *Mng Pt*
James E Sauls Junior, *Mgr*
EMP: 40 **EST:** 2003
SQ FT: 12,500
SALES (est): 2.2MM
SALES (corp-wide): 2.2MM **Privately Held**
Web: www.sardiniareadymix.com
SIC: 3273 Ready-mixed concrete

(G-9952)
SIEMENS INDUSTRY INC
2000 Eastman Dr (45150-2712)
PHONE.............................513 576-2088
EMP: 14
SALES (corp-wide): 84.78B **Privately Held**
Web: www.siemens.com
SIC: 5311 3569 Department stores; Heaters, swimming pool: electric
HQ: Siemens Industry, Inc.
1000 Deerfield Pkwy
Buffalo Grove IL 60089
847 215-1000

(G-9953)
SILER EXCAVATION SERVICES
6025 Catherine Dr (45150-2203)
PHONE.............................513 400-8628
EMP: 40 **EST:** 2007
SALES (est): 1.02MM **Privately Held**
SIC: 1794 1389 Excavation work; Construction, repair, and dismantling services

(G-9954)
TATA AMERICA INTL CORP
Also Called: Tata Consultancy Services
1000 Summit Dr Unit 1 (45150-2724)
PHONE.............................513 677-6500
Sumanta Roy, *Rgnl Mgr*
EMP: 300
Web: www.tcs.com
SIC: 7372 7373 7371 Prepackaged software ; Computer integrated systems design; Custom computer programming services
HQ: Tata America International Corporation
101 Park Ave Fl 26
New York NY 10178
212 557-8038

(G-9955)
TRIUMPH SIGNS & CONSULTING INC
480 Milford Pkwy (45150-9104)
PHONE.............................513 576-8090
William Downey, *Pr*
EMP: 13 **EST:** 2005
SALES (est): 1.96MM **Privately Held**
Web: www.triumphsigns.com
SIC: 3993 Signs and advertising specialties

Milford Center
Union County

(G-9956)
ADVANCED TECHNOLOGY PRODUCTS INC (PA)
Also Called: A T P
190 N Mill St (43045-9765)
PHONE.............................937 349-4055
◆ **EMP:** 58 **EST:** 1990
SALES (est): 4.46MM **Privately Held**
Web: www.atp4pneumatics.com
SIC: 3052 Rubber and plastics hose and beltings

(G-9957)
FORUM WORKS LLC
77 Brown St (43045-8900)
P.O. Box 1330 (43065-1330)
PHONE.............................937 349-8685
EMP: 30 **EST:** 2019
SALES (est): 3.93MM **Privately Held**
Web: www.forumwrks.com
SIC: 2431 Millwork

(G-9958)
NUTRIEN AG SOLUTIONS INC
9972 State Route 38 (43045-9760)
PHONE.............................614 873-4253
Jason Hess, *Prin*
EMP: 6
SALES (corp-wide): 29.06B **Privately Held**
Web: www.nutrienagsolutions.com
SIC: 5261 5191 2875 Fertilizer; Fertilizers and agricultural chemicals; Fertilizers, mixing only
HQ: Nutrien Ag Solutions, Inc.
3005 Rocky Mountain Ave
Loveland CO 80538
970 685-3300

Millbury
Wood County

(G-9959)
DOUTHIT COMMUNICATIONS INC
Also Called: Metro Press
1550 Woodville Rd (43447-9619)
P.O. Box 169 (43447-0169)
PHONE.............................419 855-7465
John Szozda, *Genl Mgr*
EMP: 55
SALES (corp-wide): 9.79MM **Privately Held**
Web: www.adwriter.com
SIC: 2711 Job printing and newspaper publishing combined
PA: Douthit Communications, Inc.
520 Warren St
Sandusky OH 44870
419 625-5825

(G-9960)
ELECTRO PLASMA INCORPORATED
Also Called: Epi Global
4400 Moline Martin Rd (43447-8400)
PHONE.............................419 838-7365
EMP: 106
Web: www.epiglobal.com
SIC: 3699 Electrical equipment and supplies, nec

(G-9961)
FORMLABS OHIO INC
Also Called: Spectra Photopolymers
27800 Lemoyne Rd Ste J (43447-9683)
PHONE.............................419 837-9783
Alex Mejiritski, *Pr*
EMP: 45 **EST:** 2017
SALES (est): 12.05MM
SALES (corp-wide): 108.63MM **Privately Held**
Web: www.formlabs.com
SIC: 2899 5169 Chemical preparations, nec; Chemicals and allied products, nec
PA: Formlabs Inc.
35 Medford St Ste 201
Somerville MA 02143
617 932-5227

(G-9962)
GUARDIAN FABRICATION LLC
Also Called: Guardian Millbury
24145 W Moline Martin Rd (43447-9568)

PHONE.............................419 855-7706
EMP: 125
SALES (corp-wide): 64.44B **Privately Held**
Web: www.guardian.com
SIC: 3211 3231 Plate glass, polished and rough; Products of purchased glass
HQ: Guardian Fabrication, Llc
2300 Harmon Rd
Auburn Hills MI 48326
248 340-1800

(G-9963)
LAKE TOWNSHIP TRUSTEES
3800 Ayers Rd (43447-9745)
PHONE.............................419 836-1143
Dan Mclargin, *Mgr*
EMP: 30
Web: www.laketwpohio.com
SIC: 9111 7997 3531 City and town managers' office; Baseball club, except professional and semi-professional; Road construction and maintenance machinery
PA: Lake Township Trustees
27975 Cummings Rd
Millbury OH 43447

(G-9964)
LEVISON ENTERPRISES LLC
Also Called: Epi Global
4470 Moline Martin Rd (43447-9201)
PHONE.............................419 838-7365
David Levison, *Pr*
EMP: 25 **EST:** 2008
SQ FT: 14,000
SALES (est): 10.19MM **Privately Held**
Web: www.levisonenterprises.com
SIC: 3672 Printed circuit boards

(G-9965)
SPECTRA GROUP LIMITED INC
Also Called: Spectra Photopolymers
27800 Lemoyne Rd Ste J (43447-9683)
PHONE.............................419 837-9783
Douglas C Neckers, *Ch Bd*
Alex Mejiritski, *Pr*
EMP: 7 **EST:** 1990
SQ FT: 5,680
SALES (est): 2.37MM **Privately Held**
Web: www.sglinc.com
SIC: 2891 Adhesives

Millersburg
Holmes County

(G-9966)
AFFORDABLE BARN CO LTD
Also Called: Southern Wholesale
4260 Township Road 617 (44654-7913)
PHONE.............................330 674-3001
Robert Yoder, *Mgr*
EMP: 9 **EST:** 2012
SALES (est): 2.11MM **Privately Held**
Web: www.affordablebarncompanyltd.com
SIC: 3448 Buildings, portable: prefabricated metal

(G-9967)
AL YODER CONSTRUCTION CO
Also Called: Fairview Log Homes
3375 County Road 160 (44654-8366)
P.O. Box 275 (44690-0275)
PHONE.............................330 359-5726
Alvin A Yoder, *Pr*
Ruth Yoder, *Sec*
Sarah Troyer, *Sec*
EMP: 6
SALES (est): 430.27K **Privately Held**
Web: www.fairviewloghomes.net

SIC: **1521** 2452 New construction, single-family houses; Log cabins, prefabricated, wood

(G-9968)
ALONOVUS CORP
Also Called: Bargain Hunter
7368 County Road 623 (44654-9387)
P.O. Box 358 (44654-0358)
PHONE..................................330 674-2300
Michael Mast, *Pr*
Frances Mast, *
▲ **EMP: 27 EST:** 1973
SQ FT: 12,000
SALES (est): 1.72MM Privately Held
Web: www.alonovus.com
SIC: **2721** 7336 Periodicals, publishing only; Graphic arts and related design

(G-9969)
AMISH WEDDING FOODS INC
316 S Mad Anthony St (44654-1388)
PHONE..................................330 674-9199
EMP: 40
Web: www.liparifoods.com
SIC: **2022** 2099 2013 Cheese; natural and processed; Food preparations, nec; Sausages and other prepared meats

(G-9970)
BERLIN TRUCK CAPS & TARPS LTD
Also Called: Berlin Parts
4560 State Route 39 (44654-9600)
PHONE..................................330 893-2811
Wayne Beachy Senior, *Pt*
Wayne Beachy Junior, *Pt*
James Beachy, *Pt*
EMP: 10 **EST:** 1970
SQ FT: 12,000
SALES (est): 136.66K Privately Held
SIC: **5199** 3792 Tarpaulins; Pickup covers, canopies or caps

(G-9971)
BIJOE DEVELOPMENT INC
7188 State Rte 62 & 39 (44654)
PHONE..................................330 674-5981
William Baker, *Pr*
Joseph Cross, *
EMP: 40 **EST:** 1989
SQ FT: 4,000
SALES (est): 469.45K Privately Held
SIC: **1389** 1311 Oil field services, nec; Crude petroleum and natural gas production

(G-9972)
BUCKEYE SEATING LLC
6945 County Road 672 (44654-8350)
P.O. Box 128 (44610-0128)
PHONE..................................330 893-7700
Emanuel Weaver, *Managing Member*
EMP: 14 **EST:** 2009
SALES (est): 1MM Privately Held
Web: www.buckeyeseating.com
SIC: **2512** 2521 Chairs: upholstered on wood frames; Chairs, office: padded, upholstered, or plain: wood

(G-9973)
BUNKER HILL CHEESE CO INC
Also Called: Heinis Cheese Chalet
6005 County Road 77 (44654-9045)
PHONE..................................330 893-2131
Peter Dauwalder, *Pr*
P H C Dauwalder, *
T D Gindlesberger, *
EMP: 60 **EST:** 1935
SQ FT: 80,000
SALES (est): 9.57MM Privately Held
Web: www.bunkerhillcheese.com

(G-9974)
CANAL DOVER FURNITURE LLC
8211 Township Road 652 (44654-8341)
PHONE..................................330 359-5375
Dan Mast, *Managing Member*
▼ **EMP:** 60 **EST:** 2000
SQ FT: 60,000
SALES (est): 2.72MM Privately Held
Web: www.canaldover.com
SIC: **2511** Dining room furniture: wood

(G-9975)
CARTER-JONES LUMBER COMPANY
Carter Lumber
6139 State Route 39 (44654-8845)
PHONE..................................330 674-9060
EMP: 9
SALES (corp-wide): 1.44B Privately Held
Web: www.carterlumber.com
SIC: **5031** 5211 2439 2434 Lumber, plywood, and millwork; Lumber and other building materials; Structural wood members, nec; Wood kitchen cabinets
HQ: The Carter-Jones Lumber Company
601 Tallmadge Rd
Kent OH 44240
330 673-6100

(G-9976)
CENTOR INC
5091 County Road 120 (44654-9231)
PHONE..................................800 321-3391
Mitch Stein, *Brnch Mgr*
EMP: 150
SALES (corp-wide): 2.2B Privately Held
Web: www.centorrx.com
SIC: **2631** Container, packaging, and boxboard
HQ: Centor Inc.
1899 N Wilkinson Way
Perrysburg OH 43551
567 336-8094

(G-9977)
CHEESE HOLDINGS INC
Also Called: Troyer Cheese, Inc.
6597 County Road 625 (44654-9071)
PHONE..................................330 893-2479
James A Troyer, *Pr*
John Troyer, *Sec*
EMP: 45 **EST:** 1959
SQ FT: 59,500
SALES (est): 5.38MM
SALES (corp-wide): 320.05MM Privately Held
Web: www.liparifoods.com
SIC: **5147** 2032 5143 5149 Meats, cured or smoked; Ethnic foods, canned, jarred, etc.; Cheese; Specialty food items
PA: Lipari Foods Operating Company Llc
26661 Bunert Rd
Warren MI 48089
586 447-3500

(G-9978)
COUNTY OF HOLMES
Also Called: Holmes County Gis
75 E Clinton St Ste 112 (44654-1283)
PHONE..................................330 674-2083
Erik Parker, *Dir*
EMP: 7
SALES (corp-wide): 75.03MM Privately Held
Web: www.holmescountyauditor.org
SIC: **3999** 9111 Globes, geographical; Executive offices, Local government
PA: County Of Holmes
2 Court St Ste 14

Millersburg OH 44654
330 674-1896

(G-9979)
EUROCASE ARCHTCTRAL CBNETS MLL
6086 State Route 241 (44654-9170)
PHONE..................................330 674-0681
Garrett M Roach, *Managing Member*
EMP: 15 **EST:** 2006
SALES (est): 2.91MM Privately Held
Web: www.eurocase.biz
SIC: **3469** Architectural panels or parts, porcelain enameled

(G-9980)
FEIKERT SAND & GRAVEL CO INC
Also Called: Feikert Concrete
6971 County Road 189 (44654-9186)
PHONE..................................330 674-0038
Lynn Feikert, *Pr*
James Feikert, *VP*
John T Feikert, *Sec*
EMP: 20 **EST:** 1932
SQ FT: 6,000
SALES (est): 2.19MM Privately Held
Web: www.feikerts.com
SIC: **1442** 3273 1422 Common sand mining; Ready-mixed concrete; Crushed and broken limestone

(G-9981)
FRYBURG DOOR INC
6086 State Route 241 (44654-9170)
PHONE..................................330 674-5252
EMP: 60 **EST:** 1988
SALES (est): 4.28MM Privately Held
Web: www.fryburgdoor.com
SIC: **2431** 2435 Doors, wood; Hardwood veneer and plywood

(G-9982)
GUGGISBERG CHEESE INC (PA)
Also Called: Chalet In The Valley
5060 State Route 557 (44654-9266)
PHONE..................................330 893-2550
Richard Guggisberg, *Pr*
Diane Melloe, *
Paul A Miller, *
Rosanne Parrot, *
Cynthia Mellor, *
EMP: 26 **EST:** 1976
SQ FT: 10,000
SALES (est): 18.44MM
SALES (corp-wide): 18.44MM Privately Held
Web: www.babyswiss.com
SIC: **2022** 5812 5961 5451 Natural cheese; Eating places; Cheese, mail order; Cheese

(G-9983)
HERSHBERGER LAWN STRUCTURES
Also Called: Play Mor
8990 State Route 39 (44654-9791)
PHONE..................................330 674-3900
Paul Hershberger, *Pt*
Amos Stoltzfus Junior, *Pt*
EMP: 17 **EST:** 1992
SQ FT: 21,000
SALES (est): 2.24MM Privately Held
Web: www.playmorswingsets.com
SIC: **3944** 5941 5091 Structural toy sets; Playground equipment; Sporting and recreation goods

(G-9984)
HERSHY WAY LTD
5918 County Road 201 (44654-9294)
PHONE..................................330 893-2809

Aden Hershberger, *Pt*
Steven Hershberger, *Pt*
Jay Hershberger, *Pt*
EMP: 7 **EST:** 1972
SALES (est): 524.08K Privately Held
Web: www.hershywayltd.com
SIC: **2519** 3523 Lawn furniture, except wood, metal, stone, or concrete; Cattle feeding, handling, and watering equipment

(G-9985)
HOLMES BY-PRODUCTS CO INC
3175 Township Road 411 (44654-9176)
PHONE..................................330 893-2322
Abe Miller, *Pr*
Brian Miller, *
Mary Miller, *
▲ **EMP:** 50 **EST:** 1958
SQ FT: 15,000
SALES (est): 2.12MM Privately Held
Web: www.holmesbyproducts.com
SIC: **2077** Animal and marine fats and oils

(G-9986)
HOLMES CHEESE CO
9444 State Route 39 (44654-9764)
PHONE..................................330 674-6451
Robert J Ramseyer, *Pr*
Walter P Ramseyer, *
▲ **EMP:** 35 **EST:** 1941
SQ FT: 42,000
SALES (est): 4.47MM Privately Held
Web: www.holmescheese.com
SIC: **2022** Natural cheese

(G-9987)
HOLMES COUNTY HUB INC
Also Called: Daily Record, The
6 W Jackson St Ste C (44654-1396)
PHONE..................................330 674-1811
Cindy Hinkle, *Mgr*
EMP: 9 **EST:** 1985
SALES (est): 83.11K Privately Held
SIC: **2711** Newspapers, publishing and printing

(G-9988)
HOLMES CUSTOM MOULDING LTD
5039 County Road 120 (44654-9281)
P.O. Box 161 (44610-0161)
PHONE..................................330 893-3598
Dan Hershburg, *Managing Member*
Wayne Hershburg, *Managing Member*
Linda Hershburg, *Managing Member*
▲ **EMP:** 45 **EST:** 1992
SQ FT: 250,000
SALES (est): 5.75MM Privately Held
Web: www.hcmohio.com
SIC: **2431** Millwork

(G-9989)
HOLMES LUMBER & BLDG CTR INC (PA)
Also Called: Holmes Lumber & Supply
6139 S R 39 (44654)
PHONE..................................330 674-9060
Paul Miller, *Pr*
Harry A Shaw, *Prin*
James H Estill, *Prin*
Elmo M Estill, *Prin*
EMP: 104 **EST:** 1952
SQ FT: 16,000
SALES (est): 9.13MM
SALES (corp-wide): 9.13MM Privately Held
Web: www.holmeslumber.com
SIC: **5031** 5211 2439 2434 Lumber, plywood, and millwork; Lumber and other building materials; Structural wood members, nec; Wood kitchen cabinets

GEOGRAPHIC

(G-9990)
HOLMES MANUFACTURING
6775 County Road 624 (44654-8840)
PHONE..................................330 231-6327
Todd W Kandel, *Owner*
EMP: 6 EST: 2015
SALES (est): 370.08K **Privately Held**
Web: www.holmesmanufacturing.com
SIC: 7299 3353 Home improvement and
  renovation contractor agency; Aluminum
  sheet, plate, and foil

(G-9991)
LBC CLAY CO LLC
4501 Township Road 307 (44654-9656)
PHONE..................................330 674-0674
Larry L Clark, *Prin*
EMP: 7 EST: 2010
SALES (est): 453.63K **Privately Held**
SIC: 3251 Brick and structural clay tile

(G-9992)
LIPARI FOODS OPERATING CO LLC
Also Called: Troyer Manufacturing
6597 County Road 625 (44654-9071)
PHONE..................................330 893-2479
Jonas Yoder, *Brnch Mgr*
EMP: 40
SALES (corp-wide): 320.05MM **Privately
Held**
Web: www.liparifoods.com
SIC: 8721 2022 2099 2013 Accounting,
  auditing, and bookkeeping; Cheese; natural
  and processed; Food preparations, nec;
  Sausages and other prepared meats
  PA: Lipari Foods Operating Company Llc
    26661 Bunert Rd
    Warren MI 48089
    586 447-3500

(G-9993)
LIPARI FOODS OPERATING CO LLC
Also Called: Troyer Manufacturing
316 S Mad Anthony St (44654-1388)
PHONE..................................330 674-9199
Jonas Yoder, *Brnch Mgr*
EMP: 40
SALES (corp-wide): 320.05MM **Privately
Held**
Web: www.liparifoods.com
SIC: 2022 2099 2013 Cheese; natural and
  processed; Food preparations, nec;
  Sausages and other prepared meats
  PA: Lipari Foods Operating Company Llc
    26661 Bunert Rd
    Warren MI 48089
    586 447-3500

(G-9994)
LLC BOWMAN LEATHER
6705 Private Road 387 (44654-8249)
PHONE..................................330 893-1954
EMP: 7 EST: 2008
SALES (est): 178.79K **Privately Held**
SIC: 3199 5699 Leather goods, nec; Leather
  garments

(G-9995)
M H WOODWORKING LLC
Also Called: Buckeye Rocker
2789 County Rd Ste 600 (44654)
PHONE..................................330 893-3929
EMP: 8 EST: 2004
SALES (est): 453.68K **Privately Held**
SIC: 2431 Millwork

(G-9996)
MAC OIL FIELD SERVICE INC
7861 Township Road 306 (44654-9666)
P.O. Box 211 (44654-0211)

PHONE..................................330 674-7371
Robert G Mc Vicker Junior, *Pr*
Patricia Mc Vicker, *VP*
EMP: 9 EST: 1978
SQ FT: 1,376
SALES (est): 2.3MM **Privately Held**
SIC: 1389 4212 Oil field services, nec; Liquid
  haulage, local

(G-9997)
**MIDDLEBURY CHEESE COMPANY
LLC**
5060 State Route 557 (44654-9440)
PHONE..................................330 893-2500
EMP: 13
SALES (corp-wide): 18.44MM **Privately
Held**
Web: www.mimilk.com
SIC: 2022 Cheese spreads, dips, pastes,
  and other cheese products
  HQ: Middlebury Cheese Company, Llc
    11275 W 250 N
    Middlebury IN 46540
    574 825-9511

(G-9998)
MILLER LUMBER CO INC
7101 State Route 39 (44654-8828)
PHONE..................................330 674-0273
Myron Miller, *Pr*
Scott Miller, *Treas*
EMP: 9 EST: 1949
SQ FT: 5,000
SALES (est): 498.71K **Privately Held**
SIC: 2421 Kiln drying of lumber

(G-9999)
MILLERS STORAGE BARNS LLC
4230 State Route 39 (44654-9682)
PHONE..................................330 893-3293
Owen Miller, *Managing Member*
EMP: 6 EST: 1979
SQ FT: 15,928
SALES (est): 1.44MM **Privately Held**
Web: www.millerstoragebarns.com
SIC: 2452 Farm buildings, prefabricated or
  portable; wood

(G-10000)
MILLERSBURG ICE COMPANY
25 S Grant St (44654-1322)
PHONE..................................330 674-3016
TOLL FREE: 800
Lewis Ritchey, *Pr*
Phillip Ritchey, *VP*
EMP: 20 EST: 1936
SQ FT: 18,000
SALES (est): 1.12MM **Privately Held**
Web: www.sitestar.net
SIC: 2097 5921 Manufactured ice; Beer
  (packaged)

(G-10001)
MT EATON PALLET LTD
4761 County Road 207 (44654-9055)
PHONE..................................330 893-2986
Dwain Schlabach, *Pt*
EMP: 21 EST: 1991
SQ FT: 12,000
SALES (est): 967.13K **Privately Held**
Web: www.mteatonpallet.com
SIC: 2448 Pallets, wood

(G-10002)
MULLET CABINETS INC
6086 State Route 241 (44654-9170)
PHONE..................................330 674-9646
EMP: 100 EST: 1965
SALES (est): 4.81MM **Privately Held**
Web: www.mulletcabinet.com

SIC: 2434 Wood kitchen cabinets

(G-10003)
MULTI PRODUCTS COMPANY
7188 State Route 39 (44654-9204)
P.O. Box 1597 (76241-1597)
PHONE..................................330 674-5981
Jeff Berlin, *CEO*
William T Baker, *
Greg Guthrie, *
Bud Doty, *
◆ **EMP:** 11 EST: 1965
SQ FT: 30,000
SALES (est): 1.08MM **Privately Held**
Web: www.plungerlift.com
SIC: 3533 5084 Oil field machinery and
  equipment; Industrial machinery and
  equipment

(G-10004)
NJM FURNITURE OUTLET INC
6899 County Road 672 (44654-8349)
PHONE..................................330 893-3514
James Kandell, *Prin*
EMP: 10 EST: 1996
SALES (est): 169.88K **Privately Held**
SIC: 2512 Upholstered household furniture

(G-10005)
PRECISION GEOPHYSICAL INC (PA)
2695 State Route 83 (44654-9455)
P.O. Box 152 (44654-0152)
PHONE..................................330 674-2198
Steven Mc Crossin, *Pr*
EMP: 32 EST: 1990
SALES (est): 2.27MM **Privately Held**
Web: www.precisiongeophysical.com
SIC: 1382 Oil and gas exploration services

(G-10006)
REXAM PLC
Rexam Prescription Products
5091 County Road 120 (44654-9231)
PHONE..................................330 893-2451
Paul Arsenault, *Mgr*
EMP: 10
SALES (corp-wide): 11.79B **Publicly Held**
Web: www.ball.com
SIC: 3085 Plastics bottles
  HQ: Rexam Limited
    100 Capability Green
    Luton BEDS LU1 3

(G-10007)
ROCKWOOD PRODUCTS LTD
Also Called: Rockwood Door & Millwork
5264 Township Road 401 (44654-8740)
PHONE..................................330 893-2392
Roger Schrock, *Pt*
Roger Schrock, *Pr*
Paul Schrock, *Pt*
EMP: 30 EST: 1986
SALES (est): 2.01MM **Privately Held**
Web: www.rockwooddoor.com
SIC: 5211 2431 5031 Door and window
  products; Doors and door parts and trim,
  wood; Doors and windows

(G-10008)
SALTILLO CORPORATION (PA)
2143 Township Road 112 (44654-9410)
PHONE..................................330 674-6722
Leona Hershberger, *Pr*
David H Hershberger, *VP*
Fanie Herb Miller, *Sec*
▲ **EMP:** 6 EST: 1996
SALES (est): 1.97MM
SALES (corp-wide): 1.97MM **Privately
Held**
Web: www.saltillo.com

SIC: 3669 Intercommunication systems,
  electric

(G-10009)
SCHLABACH WOODWORKS LTD
6678 State Route 241 (44654-8826)
PHONE..................................330 674-7488
David Schlabach, *Owner*
EMP: 10 EST: 1993
SALES (est): 2MM **Privately Held**
SIC: 3996 Hard surface floor coverings, nec

(G-10010)
STAR BRITE EXPRESS CAR WA
887 S Washington St (44654-1707)
PHONE..................................330 674-0062
Rodney J Starr, *Prin*
EMP: 9 EST: 2006
SALES (est): 84.73K **Privately Held**
SIC: 2741 Miscellaneous publishing

(G-10011)
STONY HILL MIXING LTD
5526 Township Road 127 (44654-9452)
PHONE..................................330 674-0814
Mahlon Yoder, *Mgr*
Levi Yoder, *Pt*
EMP: 7 EST: 2001
SALES (est): 487.1K **Privately Held**
SIC: 2048 5191 Bird food, prepared; Feed

(G-10012)
STUTZMAN MANUFACTURING LTD
7727 Township Road 604 (44654-2352)
PHONE..................................330 674-4359
Bert L Stutzman, *Managing Member*
EMP: 6 EST: 1995
SALES (est): 938.42K **Privately Held**
SIC: 3542 7389 Nail heading machines;
  Business Activities at Non-Commercial Site

(G-10013)
TH MANUFACTURING INC
4674 County Road 120 (44654-9280)
PHONE..................................330 893-3572
Jeff Tomski, *Pr*
EMP: 9 EST: 1992
SQ FT: 60,000
SALES (est): 2.48MM **Privately Held**
Web: www.thcores.com
SIC: 3543 Industrial patterns

(G-10014)
TOPE PRINTING INC
1056 S Washington St (44654-9438)
PHONE..................................330 674-4993
John C Tope, *Pr*
Andrew P Tope, *VP*
Vanessa Tope, *Sec*
EMP: 7 EST: 1974
SQ FT: 6,000
SALES (est): 327.68K **Privately Held**
Web: www.topeprinting.com
SIC: 2752 2759 Offset printing; Letterpress
  printing

(G-10015)
TROYRIDGE MFG
3998 County Road 168 (44654-7000)
PHONE..................................330 893-7516
Norman Troyer, *Prin*
EMP: 6 EST: 2008
SALES (est): 611.47K **Privately Held**
SIC: 3999 Manufacturing industries, nec

(G-10016)
UNIVERSAL WELL SERVICES INC
11 S Washington St (44654-1341)
PHONE..................................814 333-2656
Rick Sloan, *Mgr*

EMP: 98
SALES (corp-wide): 5.38B **Publicly Held**
Web: www.patenergy.com
SIC: 1389 Oil field services, nec
HQ: Universal Well Services, Inc.
13549 S Mosiertown Rd
Meadville PA 16335
814 337-1983

(G-10017)
W H PATTEN DRILLING CO INC
6336 County Road 207 (44654-9153)
P.O. Box 10 (44654-0010)
PHONE..................330 674-3046
William H Patten Iii, *Pr*
Kim Mathie, *Sec*
William H Patten Junior, *Stockholder*
EMP: 8 EST: 1940
SQ FT: 1,200
SALES (est): 600K **Privately Held**
SIC: 1311 Crude petroleum production

(G-10018)
WALNUT CREEK PLANING LTD
5778 State Route 515 (44654-8807)
PHONE..................330 893-3244
Dwight Kratzer, *Pr*
Ken Kratzer, *
Charles Kratzer, *
◆ **EMP: 100 EST:** 1988
SQ FT: 90,000
SALES (est): 3.98MM **Privately Held**
Web: www.wcplaning.com
SIC: 5211 2421 2499 2426 Millwork and
lumber; Planing mills, nec; Decorative wood
and woodwork; Hardwood dimension and
flooring mills

(G-10019)
WEAVER LEATHER LLC (HQ)
7540 County Road 201 (44654-9296)
P.O. Box 68 (44660-0068)
PHONE..................330 674-7548
▲ **EMP: 86 EST:** 1973
SALES (est): 25.15MM
SALES (corp-wide): 472.43MM **Privately
Held**
Web: www.weaverleather.com
SIC: 3199 5199 3172 3161 Harness or
harness parts; Leather and cut stock;
Personal leather goods, nec; Luggage
PA: Blue Point Capital Partners Llc
127 Public Sq Ste 5100
Cleveland OH 44114
216 535-4700

(G-10020)
YODER LUMBER CO INC (PA)
4515 Township Road 367 (44654-8885)
PHONE..................330 893-3121
Eli J Yoder, *Pr*
Roy Yoder, *
Melvin Yoder, *
Ken Grate, *
Nathan Yoder, *
▼ **EMP: 55 EST:** 1947
SQ FT: 15,000
SALES (est): 24.4MM
SALES (corp-wide): 24.4MM **Privately
Held**
Web: www.yoderlumber.com
SIC: 2421 2448 2499 2431 Lumber: rough,
sawed, or planed; Pallets, wood; Mulch,
wood and bark; Millwork

(G-10021)
YODER LUMBER CO INC
7100 County Road 407 (44654-9628)
PHONE..................330 674-1435
Mel Yoder, *Mgr*
EMP: 55

SALES (corp-wide): 24.4MM **Privately
Held**
Web: www.yoderlumber.com
SIC: 2421 2448 Lumber: rough, sawed, or
planed; Wood pallets and skids
PA: Yoder Lumber Co., Inc.
4515 Township Rd 367
Millersburg OH 44654
330 893-3121

Millersport
Fairfield County

(G-10022)
**ATWOOD ROPE MANUFACTURING
INC**
2185 Refugee St (43046-9748)
PHONE..................614 920-0534
Curtis Dale Atwood, *CEO*
EMP: 10 EST: 2006
SALES (est): 607K **Privately Held**
Web: www.atwoodrope.com
SIC: 2298 Ropes and fiber cables

(G-10023)
HEFTY HOIST INC
Also Called: Aqua Marine Supply
2397a Refugee St (43046-9748)
P.O. Box 44 (43046-0044)
PHONE..................740 467-2515
Chet Hauck, *Pr*
▲ **EMP: 20 EST:** 1984
SQ FT: 14,000
SALES (est): 2.16MM **Privately Held**
Web: www.heftyhoist.com
SIC: 3566 Reduction gears and gear units
for turbines, except auto

(G-10024)
SCHELL SCENIC STUDIO INC
2140 Refugee St (43046-9748)
PHONE..................614 444-9550
Gustav Schell, *Pr*
Philip G Schell, *VP*
EMP: 7 EST: 1994
SQ FT: 20,000
SALES (est): 511.98K **Privately Held**
Web: www.schellscenic.com
SIC: 3999 7922 Theatrical scenery; Scenery
rental, theatrical

(G-10025)
SEE YA THERE INC
Also Called: See Ya There Vacation and Trvl
12710 W Bank Dr Ne (43046-9738)
PHONE..................614 856-9037
John J Allen, *Pr*
George Lindsey, *Treas*
Michael Hatem, *VP*
EMP: 7 EST: 1998
SQ FT: 800
SALES (est): 96.75K **Privately Held**
SIC: 2741 Newsletter publishing

(G-10026)
WELDON ICE CREAM COMPANY
2887 Canal Dr (43046-9701)
PHONE..................740 467-2400
David Pierce, *Prin*
Undet Er Mined, *Owner*
EMP: 8 EST: 1930
SQ FT: 10,800
SALES (est): 135.21K **Privately Held**
Web: www.weldons.com
SIC: 2024 Ice cream, bulk

Millersville
Sandusky County

(G-10027)
CARMEUSE LIME INC
Also Called: Carmeuse Lime & Stone
3964 County Road 41 (43435-9619)
PHONE..................419 638-2511
Mike Klenda, *Brnch Mgr*
EMP: 19
SALES (corp-wide): 2.67MM **Privately
Held**
Web: www.carmeuse.com
SIC: 1422 Crushed and broken limestone
HQ: Carmeuse Lime, Inc.
11 Stanwix St Fl 21
Pittsburgh PA 15222
412 995-5500

Mineral City
Tuscarawas County

(G-10028)
HILLTOP ENERGY INC
6978 Lindentree Rd Ne (44656-8973)
P.O. Box 395 (44656-0395)
PHONE..................330 859-2108
Brandy Caterley, *Dir*
EMP: 16
SQ FT: 3,200
SALES (corp-wide): 24.75MM **Privately
Held**
Web: www.hilltopenergy.com
SIC: 2892 2819 Explosives; Industrial
inorganic chemicals, nec
HQ: Hilltop Energy, Inc.
7896 Dickey Dr
Lisbon OH 44432
330 424-1441

Mineral Ridge
Trumbull County

(G-10029)
JMB ENERGY INC
3729 Union St (44440-9004)
PHONE..................330 505-9610
Martin G Solomon, *Pr*
Ben Z Post, *Sec*
EMP: 6 EST: 1980
SALES (est): 327.31K **Privately Held**
SIC: 1311 Crude petroleum and natural gas

(G-10030)
L B FOSTER COMPANY
Also Called: Relay Rail Div.
1193 Salt Springs Rd (44440-9318)
PHONE..................330 652-1461
Scott Calahoun, *Mgr*
EMP: 13
SQ FT: 3,000
SALES (corp-wide): 543.74MM **Publicly
Held**
Web: www.lbfoster.com
SIC: 1799 3743 Coating of metal structures
at construction site; Railroad equipment
PA: L. B. Foster Company
415 Holiday Dr Ste 100
Pittsburgh PA 15220
412 928-3400

(G-10031)
VALLEY CONTAINERS INC
3515 Union St (44440-9007)
P.O. Box 171 (44440-0171)
PHONE..................330 544-2244

Steve Hershfeldt, *Pr*
EMP: 14 EST: 1980
SQ FT: 15,000
SALES (est): 3.37MM **Privately Held**
Web: www.vcibox.com
SIC: 2653 Boxes, corrugated: made from
purchased materials

Minerva
Stark County

(G-10032)
ABRASIVE SUPPLY COMPANY INC
25240 State Route 172 (44657-9430)
PHONE..................330 894-2818
Rob Miller, *Pr*
▲ **EMP: 16 EST:** 1991
SQ FT: 16,000
SALES (est): 1.93MM **Privately Held**
Web: www.polyblast.com
SIC: 3291 Abrasive products

(G-10033)
AMERICAN AXLE & MFG INC
Also Called: Minerva Manufacturing Facility
461 Knox Ct (44657-1530)
PHONE..................330 868-5761
EMP: 57
SALES (corp-wide): 6.12B **Publicly Held**
Web: www.aam.com
SIC: 3714 Rear axle housings, motor vehicle
HQ: American Axle & Manufacturing, Inc.
One Dauch Dr
Detroit MI 48211

(G-10034)
B & H MACHINE INC
15001 Lincoln St Se (44657-8900)
P.O. Box 96 (44657-0096)
PHONE..................330 868-6425
J Timothy Bush, *Pr*
EMP: 36 EST: 1951
SQ FT: 70,000
SALES (est): 5.2MM **Privately Held**
Web: www.bhcylinders.com
SIC: 3593 3599 Fluid power cylinders,
hydraulic or pneumatic; Machine shop,
jobbing and repair

(G-10035)
**CARAUSTAR INDUS CNSMR PDTS
CRO**
Also Called: Minerva Tube Plant
460 Knox Ct (44657-1528)
PHONE..................330 868-4111
Steve Lacher, *Mgr*
EMP: 68
SQ FT: 45,000
SALES (corp-wide): 5.45B **Publicly Held**
SIC: 2655 Tubes, fiber or paper: made from
purchased material
HQ: Caraustar Industrial And Consumer
Products Group Inc
5000 Austell Powder Ste
Austell GA 30106
803 548-5100

(G-10036)
COLFOR MANUFACTURING INC
Also Called: Minerva Operations
461 Knox Ct (44657-1530)
PHONE..................330 863-0404
Tom Szymanski, *Mgr*
EMP: 328
SALES (corp-wide): 6.12B **Publicly Held**
Web: www.colformanufacturinginc.com
SIC: 3462 Iron and steel forgings
HQ: Colfor Manufacturing, Inc.
3255 Alliance Rd Nw

GEOGRAPHIC

Malvern OH 44644

(G-10037)
DUTCHCRAFT TRUSS COMPONENT INC
2212 Fox Ave Se (44657-9146)
PHONE.............................330 862-2220
Reginald Stoltzfus, *Prin*
Jennette Stolzfus, *Prin*
EMP: 7 EST: 2005
SALES (est): 2.42MM **Privately Held**
Web: www.dutchcrafttruss.com
SIC: 2439 Trusses, wooden roof

(G-10038)
GENERAL COLOR INVESTMENTS INC
Also Called: Plastic Color Division
250 Bridge St (44657-1509)
P.O. Box 7 (44657-0007)
PHONE.............................330 868-4161
Holly Gartner, *Pr*
Keith W Gartner, *
EMP: 100 EST: 1938
SQ FT: 142,800
SALES (est): 24.57MM **Privately Held**
Web: www.generalcolor.com
SIC: 2816 3087 Color pigments; Custom
compound purchased resins

(G-10039)
JERICO PLASTIC INDUSTRIES INC
250 Bridge St (44657-1509)
PHONE.............................330 868-4600
EMP: 11
SIC: 2821 Plastics materials and resins
PA: Jerico Plastic Industries, Inc.
7970 Boneta Rd
Wadsworth OH 44281

(G-10040)
KEPCOR INC
Also Called: Ssi Tiles
215 Bridge St (44657-1508)
P.O. Box 119 (44657-0119)
PHONE.............................330 868-6434
Robert B Keplinger, *Pr*
Connie Keplinger, *VP*
EMP: 10 EST: 1988
SQ FT: 121,500
SALES (est): 700K **Privately Held**
SIC: 3253 3251 Ceramic wall and floor tile;
Brick and structural clay tile

(G-10041)
MACHINE DYNAMICS & ENGRG INC
Also Called: Energy Transfer
9312 Arrow Rd Nw (44657-8742)
PHONE.............................330 868-5603
Kenneth Barkan Ii, *Pr*
Paul D Barkan, *
◆ **EMP: 75 EST:** 1984
SQ FT: 240,000
SALES (est): 9.61MM **Privately Held**
Web: www.durafintube.com
SIC: 3498 Tube fabricating (contract bending
and shaping)

(G-10042)
MINERVA DAIRY INC
Also Called: Minerva Maid
430 Radloff Ave (44657-1400)
P.O. Box 60 (44657-0060)
PHONE.............................330 868-4196
Phillip Muller, *CEO*
Phillip Muller, *Pr*
Adam Muller, *
Venae Watts, *
Steven H Lefkowitz, *
EMP: 65 EST: 1900

SQ FT: 53,000
SALES (est): 9.56MM **Privately Held**
Web: www.minervadairy.com
SIC: 2023 2021 2022 Dry, condensed and
evaporated dairy products; Creamery butter
; Processed cheese

(G-10043)
MINERVA WELDING AND FABG INC
22133 Us Route 30 (44657-9401)
P.O. Box 369 (44657-0369)
PHONE.............................330 868-7731
James A Gram, *Pr*
Stephen J Gram, *
Daniel E Gram, *
EMP: 40 EST: 1949
SQ FT: 20,000
SALES (est): 11.93MM **Privately Held**
Web: www.minervawelding.com
SIC: 5084 3599 Industrial machinery and
equipment; Machine shop, jobbing and
repair

(G-10044)
MONARCH PRODUCTS CO
105 Short St (44657-1698)
P.O. Box 118 (44657-0118)
PHONE.............................330 868-7717
Gene Mercarelli, *VP*
EMP: 9 EST: 1947
SQ FT: 16,000
SALES (est): 2.33MM **Privately Held**
SIC: 3544 Special dies and tools

(G-10045)
PCC AIRFOILS LLC
3860 Union Ave Se (44657-8944)
PHONE.............................330 868-6441
Ken Buck, *General Vice President*
EMP: 214
SQ FT: 300,000
SALES (corp-wide): 424.23B **Publicly
Held**
Web: www.pccairfoils.com
SIC: 3369 3324 Nonferrous foundries, nec;
Steel investment foundries
HQ: Pcc Airfoils, Llc
3401 Entp Pkwy Ste 200
Beachwood OH 44122
216 831-3590

(G-10046)
REGAL METAL PRODUCTS CO (PA)
3615 Union Ave Se (44657-8972)
P.O. Box 207 (44657-0207)
PHONE.............................330 868-6343
J Ted Tomak Junior, *CEO*
Mark Righetti, *
Christian Tomack, *
EMP: 38 EST: 1965
SQ FT: 125,000
SALES (est): 16MM
SALES (corp-wide): 16MM **Privately Held**
Web: www.regalmetalproducts.com
SIC: 3465 3544 Automotive stampings;
Special dies, tools, jigs, and fixtures

(G-10047)
SUMMITVILLE TILES INC
1310 Alliance Rd Nw (44657-9767)
P.O. Box 283 (44657-0283)
PHONE.............................330 868-6771
James A Miller, *Mgr*
EMP: 47
SALES (corp-wide): 4.59B **Privately Held**
Web: www.summitville.com
SIC: 3253 Floor tile, ceramic
HQ: Summitville Tiles, Inc
15364 State Rte 644
Summitville OH 43962
330 223-1511

(G-10048)
SUMMITVILLE TILES INC
Also Called: Summitville Labs
81 Arbor Rd Ne (44657-8755)
P.O. Box 90 (44657-0090)
PHONE.............................330 868-6463
Joseph Dutt, *Mgr*
EMP: 55
SALES (corp-wide): 4.59B **Privately Held**
Web: www.summitville.com
SIC: 2891 3255 2899 Epoxy adhesives; Clay
refractories; Chemical preparations, nec
HQ: Summitville Tiles, Inc
15364 State Rte 644
Summitville OH 43962
330 223-1511

(G-10049)
WESTMONT INC
3035 Union Ave Ne (44657-8667)
PHONE.............................330 862-3080
Michael Zawaski, *Pr*
EMP: 8 EST: 1978
SQ FT: 5,000
SALES (est): 499.89K **Privately Held**
Web: www.westmontinc.com
SIC: 3824 Mechanical and
electromechanical counters and devices

Mingo Junction
Jefferson County

(G-10050)
EASTERN AUTOMATED PIPING
424 State St (43938-1053)
P.O. Box 249 (43938-0249)
PHONE.............................740 535-8184
Ron Kleineke, *Owner*
▼ **EMP: 6 EST:** 2012
SALES (est): 422.85K **Privately Held**
Web:
www.easternconstructionservicesllc.com
SIC: 3499 3312 1711 1623 Fabricated metal
products, nec; Blast furnaces and steel mills
; Plumbing, heating, air-conditioning;
Pipeline construction, nsk

(G-10051)
FEX LLC (PA)
Also Called: Fex Group
1058 Commercial St (43938-1007)
PHONE.............................412 604-0400
Michael Thomas, *Managing Member*
▼ **EMP: 18 EST:** 1998
SALES (est): 4.95MM
SALES (corp-wide): 4.95MM **Privately
Held**
Web: www.fexgroup.com
SIC: 5093 8744 3341 Metal scrap and waste
materials; Environmental remediation;
Recovery and refining of nonferrous metals

(G-10052)
JSW STEEL USA OHIO INC
Also Called: Jsw USA
1500 Commercial St (43938-1096)
P.O. Box 99 (43938)
PHONE.............................740 535-8172
Mark Bush, *CEO*
Cynthia L Woolheater, *
Jonathan Shank, *
Rahul Singh, *
EMP: 347 EST: 2016
SALES (est): 78.26MM **Privately Held**
Web: www.jswsteel.us
SIC: 5051 3312 Steel; Pipes, iron and steel
PA: Jsw Steel Limited
Jsw Centre, Bandra Kurla Complex,
Mumbai MH 40005

Minster
Auglaize County

(G-10053)
ALBERT FREYTAG INC
306 Executive Dr (45865)
P.O. Box 5 (45865-0005)
PHONE.............................419 628-2018
William Freytag, *Pr*
Joseph Freytag, *
EMP: 25 EST: 1943
SQ FT: 1,200
SALES (est): 5.13MM **Privately Held**
Web: www.albertfreytaginc.com
SIC: 3441 1741 Fabricated structural metal;
Masonry and other stonework

(G-10054)
BENDCO MACHINE & TOOL INC
283 W 1st St (45865-1251)
P.O. Box 6 (45865-0006)
PHONE.............................419 628-3802
Norman Tidwell, *Pr*
Kenneth C Wolaver, *Pr*
Norman E Bud Tidwell, *Sec*
Jennifer Axe, *Mgr*
EMP: 10 EST: 1981
SQ FT: 19,500
SALES (est): 1.06MM **Privately Held**
Web: www.bendcomachine.com
SIC: 3542 3547 Bending machines; Rolling
mill machinery

(G-10055)
DANONE US LLC
216 Southgate (45865-9552)
P.O. Box 122 (45865-0122)
PHONE.............................419 628-1295
Didier Menu, *Mgr*
EMP: 390
SALES (corp-wide): 967.4MM **Privately
Held**
Web: www.dannon.com
SIC: 2024 Yogurt desserts, frozen
HQ: Danone Us, Llc
1 Maple Ave
White Plains NY 10605
914 872-8400

(G-10056)
DUCO TOOL & DIE INC
19 S Main St (45865-1349)
P.O. Box 76 (45865-0076)
PHONE.............................419 628-2031
Dale J Dues, *Pr*
Margaret Dues, *Sec*
EMP: 10 EST: 1985
SQ FT: 10,000
SALES (est): 516.12K **Privately Held**
Web: mail.nktelco.net
SIC: 3544 7692 Special dies and tools;
Welding repair

(G-10057)
FABCOR INC
Also Called: Jails Correctional Products
350 S Ohio St (45865-1272)
P.O. Box 58 (45865-0058)
PHONE.............................419 628-4428
EMP: 19 EST: 1985
SALES (est): 4.42MM **Privately Held**
Web: www.fabcor.com
SIC: 3444 3544 5021 Sheet metalwork;
Special dies, tools, jigs, and fixtures;
Furniture

(G-10058)
GLOBUS PRINTING & PACKG CO INC (PA)

1 Exec Pkwy (45865-1274)
P.O. Box 114 (45865-0114)
PHONE.....................................419 628-2381
Dennis Schmiesing, *Pr*
Tim Schmiesing, *
EMP: 68 **EST:** 1957
SQ FT: 100,000
SALES (est): 8.18MM
SALES (corp-wide): 8.18MM **Privately Held**
Web: www.globusprinting.com
SIC: 2752 Offset printing

(G-10059)
KARD WELDING INC
Also Called: Kard Bridge Products
480 Osterloh Rd (45865-9750)
P.O. Box 124 (45865-0124)
PHONE.....................................419 628-2598
Ken Osterloh, *Owner*
Doris Osterloh, *Pr*
Kenneth H Osterloh, *VP*
EMP: 20 **EST:** 1983
SQ FT: 36,360
SALES (est): 4.57MM **Privately Held**
Web: www.kardwelding.com
SIC: 3499 3443 Machine bases, metal;
Fabricated plate work (boiler shop)

(G-10060)
MACHINE CONCEPTS INC
2167 State Route 66 (45865-9401)
P.O. Box 127 (45865-0127)
PHONE.....................................419 628-3498
John Eiting, *Pr*
▲ **EMP:** 32 **EST:** 1994
SQ FT: 30,000
SALES (est): 9.49MM **Privately Held**
Web: www.machineconcepts.com
SIC: 3599 Machine shop, jobbing and repair

(G-10061)
MINSTER FARMERS COOP EXCH
Also Called: Minster Farmers Co-Op
Exchange
292 W 4th St (45865-1024)
P.O. Box 100 (45865-0100)
PHONE.....................................419 628-4705
Kevin Doseck, *Genl Mgr*
EMP: 55 **EST:** 1920
SQ FT: 4,800
SALES (est): 272.76K **Privately Held**
SIC: 5191 5153 5172 2041 Farm supplies;
Grain elevators; Engine fuels and oils; Flour
and other grain mill products

(G-10062)
NIDEC MINSTER CORPORATION (DH)
Also Called: Minster Machine
240 W 5th St (45865-1065)
P.O. Box 120 (45865)
PHONE.....................................419 628-2331
◆ **EMP:** 245 **EST:** 1901
SALES (est): 92.19MM **Privately Held**
Web: www.minster.com
SIC: 3542 3568 Presses: hydraulic and
pneumatic, mechanical and manual;
Clutches, except vehicular
HQ: Nidec Americas Holding Corporation
8050 W Florissant Ave
Saint Louis MO 63136
314 595-8000

(G-10063)
POST BUSINESS PROPERTIES INC
(PA)
205 W 4th St (45865-1062)
P.O. Box 101 (45865-0101)
PHONE.....................................419 628-2321
Jane Thompson, *Dir*
Glenn Thompson Ii, *VP*

EMP: 54 **EST:** 1948
SQ FT: 14,400
SALES (est): 9MM
SALES (corp-wide): 9MM **Privately Held**
Web: www.postprinting.com
SIC: 2759 2752 Letterpress printing; Offset
printing

(G-10064)
PROGRESS TOOL & STAMPING INC
Also Called: Progress Tool Co
207 Southgate (45865-9552)
P.O. Box 53 (45865-0053)
PHONE.....................................419 628-2384
Lee H Westerheide, *Pr*
EMP: 20 **EST:** 1968
SQ FT: 22,000
SALES (est): 3.09MM **Privately Held**
Web:
www.progresstoolandstamping.com
SIC: 3544 3469 Special dies and tools;
Metal stampings, nec

(G-10065)
SECURCOM INC
Also Called: Securcom
307 W 1st St (45865-1210)
P.O. Box 116 (45865-0116)
PHONE.....................................419 628-1049
Bill Bergman, *Pr*
Marlene Hoying, *Sec*
James R Shenk, *Prin*
EMP: 22 **EST:** 1997
SALES (est): 2.64MM **Privately Held**
Web: www.securcom.com
SIC: 5999 7382 3699 5065 Telephone and
communication equipment; Security
systems services; Security control
equipment and systems; Communication
equipment

(G-10066)
SUNRISE COOPERATIVE INC
Also Called: Minster Farmers
292 W 4th St (45865-1024)
P.O. Box 870 (43420-0870)
PHONE.....................................419 628-4705
Mike Bensman, *Brnch Mgr*
EMP: 7
SALES (corp-wide): 455.8MM **Privately Held**
Web: www.sunriseco-op.com
SIC: 5191 5153 5172 2041 Feed; Grain
elevators; Engine fuels and oils; Flour and
other grain mill products
PA: Sunrise Cooperative, Inc.
2025 W State St
Fremont OH 43420
419 332-6468

(G-10067)
TRADEMARK DESIGNS INC
17 Jackson St (45865-1144)
PHONE.....................................419 628-3897
Mark Nolan, *Pr*
Jerry Henkaline, *Sec*
EMP: 20 **EST:** 1989
SQ FT: 3,700
SALES (est): 465.45K **Privately Held**
Web: www.tmdzinc.com
SIC: 3999 Identification plates

Mogadore
Portage County

(G-10068)
AAA PLASTICS & PALLETS INC
246 N Cleveland Ave (44260-1205)
PHONE.....................................330 844-2556
Dan A Hargrove, *Pr*

EMP: 8 **EST:** 2002
SALES (est): 265.21K **Privately Held**
Web: www.aaaplasticsandpallets.com
SIC: 2448 Pallets, wood

(G-10069)
AMERIMOLD INC
595 Waterloo Rd Ste A (44260-8710)
PHONE.....................................800 950-8020
Bill Wensel, *Pr*
EMP: 6 **EST:** 1988
SQ FT: 2,000
SALES (est): 170.33K **Privately Held**
Web: www.amerimoldexpo.com
SIC: 3544 3599 Industrial molds; Machine
shop, jobbing and repair

(G-10070)
BICO AKRON INC
Also Called: Bico Steel Service Centers
3100 Gilchrist Rd (44260-1246)
PHONE.....................................330 794-1716
Michael A Ensminger, *Pr*
▲ **EMP:** 65 **EST:** 1988
SQ FT: 90,000
SALES (est): 23.91MM
SALES (corp-wide): 37.8MM **Privately Held**
Web: www.bicosteel.com
SIC: 5051 3443 Steel; Fabricated plate work
(boiler shop)
PA: Bico Buyer, Inc.
3100 Gilchrist Rd
Mogadore OH 44260
330 794-1716

(G-10071)
CORNWELL QUALITY TOOLS COMPANY
Also Called: Cornwell Quality Tools
200 N Cleveland Ave (44260-1205)
PHONE.....................................330 628-2627
Bill Nobley, *Brnch Mgr*
EMP: 76
SQ FT: 3,000
SALES (corp-wide): 55.65MM **Privately Held**
Web: www.cornwelltools.com
SIC: 3423 5085 Hand and edge tools, nec;
Industrial supplies
PA: The Cornwell Quality Tools Company
667 Seville Rd
Wadsworth OH 44281
330 330-3500

(G-10072)
DIAMOND AMERICA CORPORATION
1436 Martin Rd (44260-1558)
PHONE.....................................330 535-3330
EMP: 7
SALES (corp-wide): 6.84MM **Privately Held**
Web: www.daextrusion.com
SIC: 3544 Special dies, tools, jigs, and
fixtures
PA: Diamond America Corporation
96 E Miller Ave
Akron OH 44301
330 762-9269

(G-10073)
DNH MIXING INC
3939a Mogadore Industrial Pkwy
(44260-1224)
PHONE.....................................330 296-6327
▲ **EMP:** 50
SIC: 3069 Custom compounding of rubber
materials

(G-10074)
DUMA MEATS INC
857 Randolph Rd (44260-9343)
P.O. Box 54 (44260-0054)
PHONE.....................................330 628-3438
Dave Duma, *Pr*
Beverley Duma, *Sec*
EMP: 8 **EST:** 1972
SQ FT: 3,000
SALES (est): 1.01MM **Privately Held**
Web: www.dumameats.com
SIC: 5421 2013 Freezer provisioners, meat;
Sausages and other prepared meats

(G-10075)
EXTRUDED SLCONE PDTS GSKETS IN
3300 Gilchrist Rd (44260-1254)
PHONE.....................................330 733-0101
Joseph E Foreman, *Pr*
EMP: 48 **EST:** 1984
SALES (est): 1.41MM **Privately Held**
Web: www.esprubber.com
SIC: 3061 Mechanical rubber goods

(G-10076)
GEORGIA-PACIFIC LLC
Also Called: Georgia-Pacific
3265 Gilchrist Rd (44260-1247)
PHONE.....................................330 794-4444
Craig Mcneil, *Mgr*
EMP: 50
SALES (corp-wide): 64.44B **Privately Held**
Web: www.gp.com
SIC: 2621 Paper mills
HQ: Georgia-Pacific Llc
133 Peachtree St Ne
Atlanta GA 30303
404 652-4000

(G-10077)
HUNTERS MANUFACTURING CO INC (PA)
Also Called: Tenpoint Crossbow Technologies
1325 Waterloo Rd (44260-9608)
PHONE.....................................330 628-9245
Richard L Bednar, *CEO*
Joanna Rolenz, *
Cindy Shaffer, *Secretary IV**
Steve Bednar, *
Philip Bednar, *
▲ **EMP:** 30 **EST:** 1993
SALES (est): 14.61MM **Privately Held**
Web: www.tenpointcrossbows.com
SIC: 3949 3999 Crossbows; Cigarette
lighters, except precious metal

(G-10078)
JANORPOT LLC
3175 Gilchrist Rd (44260-1245)
PHONE.....................................330 564-0232
Norm Belliveau, *Pr*
Ron Vandiver, *
Charles Snyder, *
▲ **EMP:** 35 **EST:** 2001
SQ FT: 40,000
SALES (est): 2.81MM **Privately Held**
Web: www.summitplastic.com
SIC: 3089 Flower pots, plastics

(G-10079)
KENT ELASTOMER PRODUCTS INC
3890 Mogadore Industrial Pkwy
(44260-1223)
PHONE.....................................800 331-4762
Murrey Vanepp, *Prin*
EMP: 49
SALES (corp-wide): 331.16MM **Privately Held**
Web: www.kentelastomer.com

SIC: **3052** Rubber and plastics hose and beltings

HQ: Kent Elastomer Products, Inc.
1500 Saint Clair Ave
Kent OH 44240
330 673-1011

(G-10080)
MOORE WELL SERVICES INC
246 N Cleveland Ave (44260-1205)
P.O. Box 1399 (44224-0399)
PHONE...............................330 650-4443
Jeff Moore, *Pr*
Jeita Moore, *VP*
EMP: 19 **EST:** 1964
SQ FT: 8,000
SALES (est): 4.9MM **Privately Held**
Web: www.moorewellservices.com
SIC: **1381** Drilling oil and gas wells

(G-10081)
NEWELL BRANDS INC
Also Called: Newell Rubbermaid
3200 Gilchrist Rd (44260-1248)
PHONE...............................330 733-7771
Joe Soldano, *Brnch Mgr*
EMP: 15
SALES (corp-wide): 7.58B **Publicly Held**
Web: www.newellbrands.com
SIC: **3089** Plastics kitchenware, tableware, and houseware
PA: Newell Brands Inc.
6655 Pachtree Dunwoody Rd
Atlanta GA 30328
770 418-7000

(G-10082)
RUBBERMAID HOME PRODUCTS
Also Called: Rubbermaid
3200 Gilchrist Rd (44260-1248)
P.O. Box 1257 (61032-1257)
PHONE...............................330 733-7771
EMP: 49 **EST:** 2017
SALES (est): 25.93MM
SALES (corp-wide): 7.58B **Publicly Held**
SIC: **3089** Thermoformed finished plastics products, nec
PA: Newell Brands Inc.
6655 Pachtree Dunwoody Rd
Atlanta GA 30328
770 418-7000

(G-10083)
RUBBERMAID INCORPORATED
Rubbermaid
3200 Gilchrist Rd (44260-1248)
PHONE...............................330 733-7771
John Bias, *Mgr*
EMP: 2397
SALES (corp-wide): 7.58B **Publicly Held**
Web: www.newellbrands.com
SIC: **3089** Planters, plastics
HQ: Rubbermaid Incorporated
6655 Pachtree Dunwoody Rd
Atlanta GA 30328
888 895-2110

(G-10084)
S P E INC
Also Called: Extruded Silicone Products
3300 Gilchrist Rd (44260-1254)
P.O. Box 37 (44260-0037)
PHONE...............................330 733-0101
EMP: 33 **EST:** 1984
SALES (est): 4.39MM **Privately Held**
SIC: **3069** **2822** Rubber automotive products ; Silicone rubbers

(G-10085)
SAM AMERICAS INC
3555 Gilchrist Rd (44260-1240)
P.O. Box 8 (44260-0008)
PHONE...............................330 628-1118
Kenji Saito, *Pr*
Kaz Nakai, *

EMP: 33 **EST:** 2006
SQ FT: 60,000
SALES (est): 3.67MM **Privately Held**
Web: www.shinagawa-usa.com
SIC: **3369** Castings, except die-castings, precision
PA: Shinagawa Refractories Co., Ltd.
1-7-12, Marunouchi
Chiyoda-Ku TKY 100-0

(G-10086)
SHINAGAWA INC
Also Called: Shinagawa
3555 Gilchrist Rd (44260-1240)
P.O. Box 8 (44260-0008)
PHONE...............................330 628-1118
Keiji Saito, *Pr*
◆ **EMP:** 28 **EST:** 1993
SQ FT: 28,800
SALES (est): 7.18MM **Privately Held**
Web: www.shinagawa-usa.com
SIC: **3399** Metal powders, pastes, and flakes
PA: Shinagawa Refractories Co., Ltd.
1-7-12, Marunouchi
Chiyoda-Ku TKY 100-0

(G-10087)
SUMMIT MACHINE LTD
3991 Mogadore Rd (44260-1367)
P.O. Box 127 (44260-0127)
PHONE...............................330 628-2663
▲ **EMP:** 14 **EST:** 2001
SQ FT: 23,000
SALES (est): 2.33MM **Privately Held**
Web: www.summit-machine.com
SIC: **3599** Machine shop, jobbing and repair

(G-10088)
SUMMIT MACHINING CO LTD
3991 Mogadore Rd (44260-1367)
PHONE...............................330 628-2663
EMP: 13 **EST:** 2019
SALES (est): 1.88MM **Privately Held**
Web: www.summit-machine.com
SIC: **3599** Machine shop, jobbing and repair

(G-10089)
TIRE TREAD DEVELOPMENT INC
1460 Martin Rd (44260-1558)
PHONE...............................330 628-5666
Michael Sapp, *Pr*
EMP: 20 **EST:** 1973
SQ FT: 13,000
SALES (est): 1.8MM **Privately Held**
Web: www.tiretreaddev.com
SIC: **3089** Tires, plastics

(G-10090)
TPL HOLDINGS LLC
Also Called: Label Print Technologies, LLC
3380 Gilchrist Rd (44260-1254)
PHONE...............................800 475-4030
Jodi Westphal, *Pr*
▲ **EMP:** 25 **EST:** 2011
SALES (est): 4.82MM
SALES (corp-wide): 22.49MM **Privately Held**
Web: www.labelprinttech.com
SIC: **2752** Commercial printing, lithographic
PA: Western Shield Acquisitions Llc
3760 Klroy Arprt Way Ste
Long Beach CA 90806
310 527-6212

(G-10091)
VACUUM ELECTRIC SWITCH CO INC (PA)
3900 Mogadore Industrial Pkwy (44260-1201)
PHONE...............................330 374-5156
Cecil C Wristen, *Pr*
Sandra M Wristen, *VP*
EMP: 17 **EST:** 1998
SQ FT: 200
SALES (est): 2.41MM
SALES (corp-wide): 2.41MM **Privately Held**
Web: www.vesco.com
SIC: **3613** **7629** Switchboards and parts, power; Electronic equipment repair

(G-10092)
VERTEX INC
3956 Mogadore Industrial Pkwy (44260-1201)
PHONE...............................330 628-6230
Salvatore Brugnano, *Ch*
Ronald Mayfield, *
James Westhoff, *
Mike Ferarra, *
◆ **EMP:** 30 **EST:** 1992
SQ FT: 20,000
SALES (est): 8.63MM **Privately Held**
Web: www.vertexseals.com
SIC: **3069** **3061** **3053** Valves, hard rubber; Mechanical rubber goods; Gaskets; packing and sealing devices

(G-10093)
VESCO LLC
3900 Mogadore Industrial Pkwy (44260-1201)
PHONE...............................330 374-5156
Lance Sabados, *Pr*
EMP: 20 **EST:** 2021
SALES (est): 4.78MM **Privately Held**
Web: www.vesco.com
SIC: **3699** Electrical equipment and supplies, nec

(G-10094)
WISE EDGE LLC
Also Called: Ovs Knife Co.
491 Roland Hills Dr (44260-9796)
PHONE...............................330 208-0889
Jeffery Wise, *Pr*
Ashley Combs, *Mgr*
EMP: 7 **EST:** 2010
SALES (est): 1.23MM **Privately Held**
SIC: **3599** **3423** **3555** **3541** Grinding castings for the trade; Hand and edge tools, nec; Printing trades machinery; Machine tools, metal cutting type

---

Monroe
Butler County

(G-10095)
ALFREBRO LLC
1055 Reed Dr (45050-1725)
PHONE...............................513 539-7373
EMP: 14 **EST:** 1983
SALES (est): 6.07MM
SALES (corp-wide): 85.53B **Publicly Held**
Web: www.adm.com
SIC: **2499** **2819** Food handling and processing products, wood; Industrial inorganic chemicals, nec
HQ: Wild Flavors, Inc.
1261 Pacific Ave
Erlanger KY 41018

(G-10096)
ARKAY INDUSTRIES INC (PA)
240 American Way (45050-1202)
PHONE...............................513 360-0390
EMP: 25
SQ FT: 19,000
SALES (est): 31.59MM
SALES (corp-wide): 31.59MM **Privately Held**
SIC: **3089** **3086** Injection molding of plastics; Plastics foam products

(G-10097)
ARKAY PLASTICS ALABAMA INC (HQ)
220 American Way (45050-1202)
PHONE...............................513 360-0390
FAX: 513 539-8904
EMP: 15
SALES (est): 23.55MM
SALES (corp-wide): 31.59MM **Privately Held**
SIC: **3089** Injection molding of plastics
PA: Arkay Industries, Inc.
240 American Way
Monroe OH 45050
513 360-0390

(G-10098)
CHROME DEPOSIT CORPORATION
341 Lawton Ave (45050-1215)
P.O. Box 130 (45050-0130)
PHONE...............................513 539-8486
Dan Zimmerman, *Mgr*
EMP: 29
SALES (corp-wide): 18.05B **Publicly Held**
Web: www.chromedeposit.com
SIC: **3471** Chromium plating of metals or formed products
HQ: Chrome Deposit Corporation
6640 Melton Rd
Portage IN 46368
219 763-1571

(G-10099)
CIPTED CORP
301 Lawton Ave (45050-1215)
PHONE...............................412 829-2120
EMP: 75
SALES (est): 4.52MM **Privately Held**
SIC: **3713** **5012** Truck bodies (motor vehicles); Trucks, noncommercial

(G-10100)
CSAFE LLC
Also Called: Csafe
675 Gateway Blvd (45050-2587)
PHONE...............................513 360-7189
Patrick Schafer, *CEO*
Tom Weir, *COO*
Anthony Pishotti, *CFO*
◆ **EMP:** 8 **EST:** 1979
SALES (est): 376.57K **Privately Held**
Web: www.csafeglobal.com
SIC: **3585** Refrigeration and heating equipment

(G-10101)
DAYTON TECHNOLOGIES
351 N Garver Rd (45050-1292)
PHONE...............................513 539-5474
Darwin Brown, *Prin*
EMP: 8 **EST:** 2007
SALES (est): 734.3K **Privately Held**
SIC: **3082** Unsupported plastics profile shapes

(G-10102)
DECEUNINCK NORTH AMERICA LLC (HQ)

351 N Garver Rd (45050-1233)
PHONE....................513 539-4444
Filip Geeraert, *Pr*
▲ **EMP:** 36 **EST:** 1969
SALES (est): 95.22MM
SALES (corp-wide): 242.95MM **Privately Held**
Web: www.deceuininckna.com
SIC: 3082 Unsupported plastics profile shapes
PA: Deceuninck
Bruggesteenweg 360
Hooglede VWV 8830
51239211

(G-10103)
DIXIE MACHINERY INC
Also Called: Dixitech Cnc
845 Todhunter Rd (45050-1032)
PHONE....................513 360-0091
Devin Flowers, *Pr*
EMP: 15 **EST:** 1984
SALES (est): 6.73MM
SALES (corp-wide): 6.73MM **Privately Held**
Web: www.dixitechcnc.com
SIC: 3541 Machine tools, metal cutting type
PA: Devin Flowers, Inc.
1300 Ridenour Blvd Nw
Kennesaw GA 30152
302 521-1182

(G-10104)
DOUBLEDAY ACQUISITIONS LLC (PA)
Also Called: Acutemp
675 Gateway Blvd (45050-2587)
PHONE....................513 360-7189
Patrick Schafer, *CEO*
Nadine Siqueland, *
▲ **EMP:** 44 **EST:** 1979
SALES (est): 18.79MM
SALES (corp-wide): 18.79MM **Privately Held**
Web: www.csafeglobal.com
SIC: 3823 Temperature instruments: industrial process type

(G-10105)
FLEETCHEM LLC
651 N Garver Rd (45050-1207)
PHONE....................513 539-1111
Tj Blakemor, *Brnch Mgr*
EMP: 10
Web: www.fleetchem.com
SIC: 2045 Blended flour: from purchased flour
PA: Fleetchem, Llc
1222 Brassie Ave Ste 19
Flossmoor IL 60422

(G-10106)
G3 PACKAGING LLC
4273 Salzman Rd (45044-9741)
PHONE....................334 799-0015
Tom Gruber, *Managing Member*
EMP: 6 **EST:** 2022
SALES (est): 1MM **Privately Held**
Web: www.g3pkg.com
SIC: 3089 Plastics containers, except foam

(G-10107)
GLASS COATINGS & CONCEPTS LLC
Also Called: Gcc
300 Lawton Ave (45050-1216)
P.O. Box 130 (45050-0130)
PHONE....................513 539-5300
Lee Shepherd, *Managing Member*
▲ **EMP:** 25 **EST:** 2003
SALES (est): 9.64MM
SALES (corp-wide): 95.5MM **Privately Held**

Web: www.gcconcepts.com
SIC: 2893 3479 Printing ink; Painting, coating, and hot dipping
PA: The Shepherd Color Company
4539 Dues Dr
Cincinnati OH 45246
513 874-0714

(G-10108)
HONEY CELL INC MID WEST
6480 Hamilton Lebanon Rd (45044-9285)
PHONE....................513 360-0280
Rick Gillette, *Genl Mgr*
EMP: 27 **EST:** 1997
SQ FT: 40,000
SALES (est): 6.59MM **Privately Held**
Web: www.valleycontainer.com
SIC: 2621 Paper mills
PA: Honey Cell, Inc.
850 Union Ave
Bridgeport CT 06607

(G-10109)
HONEYCOMB MIDWEST
6480 Hamilton Lebanon Rd (45044-9285)
PHONE....................513 360-0280
EMP: 30
SALES (est): 1.8MM **Privately Held**
Web: www.valleycontainer.com
SIC: 2621 Art paper

(G-10110)
INTERACTIVE PRODUCTS CORP
5346 Roden Park Dr (45050-2504)
PHONE....................513 313-3397
Mark Comeaux, *Pr*
EMP: 6 **EST:** 1995
SQ FT: 5,000
SALES (est): 316.71K **Privately Held**
SIC: 3577 Computer peripheral equipment, nec

(G-10111)
JOURNEY ELECTRONICS CORP
902 N Garver Rd (45050-1241)
P.O. Box 465 (45050-0465)
PHONE....................513 539-9836
Michael Gorden, *Pr*
EMP: 7 **EST:** 1983
SQ FT: 3,000
SALES (est): 1.77MM **Privately Held**
Web: www.journeyelectronics.com
SIC: 3672 3823 Printed circuit boards; industrial process control instruments
PA: Gorden Inc.
3269 Blackberry Ln
Malvern PA 19355

(G-10112)
KLW PLASTICS INC (DH)
980 Deneen Ave (45050-1210)
PHONE....................513 539-2673
Kenneth M Roessler, *Pr*
Don Pearson, *CFO*
▲ **EMP:** 6 **EST:** 2004
SQ FT: 37,000
SALES (est): 3.05MM
SALES (corp-wide): 3.82B **Privately Held**
SIC: 3089 5099 Blow molded finished plastics products, nec; Containers: glass, metal or plastic
HQ: Bway Corporation
1515 W 22nd St Ste 1100
Oak Brook IL 60523

(G-10113)
LAHLOUH INC
150 Lawton Ave (45050-1212)
PHONE....................650 692-6600
EMP: 9
SALES (corp-wide): 48.85MM **Privately Held**

Web: www.lahlouh.com
SIC: 2752 Offset printing
PA: Lahlouh, Inc.
1649 Adrian Rd
Burlingame CA 94010
650 692-6600

(G-10114)
PAC WORLDWIDE CORPORATION
Also Called: Pac Manufacturing
575 Gateway Blvd (45050-2586)
PHONE....................800 535-0039
Bruce Johnson, *Mgr*
EMP: 28
Web: www.pac.com
SIC: 5112 2677 Envelopes; Envelopes
HQ: Pac Worldwide Corporation
15435 Ne 92nd St
Redmond WA 98052
425 202-4000

(G-10115)
R & L SOFTWARE LLC (PA)
Also Called: Marz Direct
421 Breaden Dr Ste 3 (45050-1575)
PHONE....................513 847-4942
EMP: 9
SQ FT: 2,500
SALES (est): 1.38MM
SALES (corp-wide): 1.38MM **Privately Held**
SIC: 7373 7372 Computer system selling services; Prepackaged software

(G-10116)
SOFTBOX SYSTEMS INC
Also Called: Csafe Passive Solutions
675 Gateway Blvd (45050-2587)
PHONE....................513 360-7189
Kevin Valentine, *Pr*
▼ **EMP:** 61 **EST:** 2007
SALES (est): 16.39MM
SALES (corp-wide): 18.79MM **Privately Held**
Web: www.softboxsystems.com
SIC: 2653 Pallets, corrugated: made from purchased materials
PA: Doubleday Acquisitions, Llc
675 Gateway Blvd
Monroe OH 45050
513 360-7189

Monrooville
Huron County

(G-10117)
BERRY GLOBAL INC
Also Called: Berry Plastics
311 Monroe St (44847-9406)
PHONE....................419 465-2291
Thomas Salmon, *Brnch Mgr*
EMP: 66
Web: www.berryglobal.com
SIC: 3089 3081 Bottle caps, molded plastics; Unsupported plastics film and sheet
HQ: Berry Global, Inc.
101 Oakley St
Evansville IN 47710

(G-10118)
BORES MANUFACTURING INC
Also Called: Bores, J F Mfg
300 Sandusky St (44847-9476)
P.O. Box 216 (44847-0216)
PHONE....................419 465-2606
Kevin Bores, *Pr*
Shirley Bores, *Sec.*
EMP: 6 **EST:** 1973
SQ FT: 9,200

SALES (est): 2.47MM **Privately Held**
Web: www.boresmfg.com
SIC: 3714 3713 Motor vehicle parts and accessories; Truck and bus bodies

(G-10119)
HBE MACHINE INCORPORATED
1100 State Route 61 N (44847-9202)
PHONE....................419 668-9426
Thomas R Hedrick, *Pr*
EMP: 6 **EST:** 1985
SQ FT: 10,000
SALES (est): 821.6K **Privately Held**
Web: www.hbemachine.com
SIC: 3599 Machine shop, jobbing and repair

(G-10120)
SCOTTRODS LLC
2512 Higbee Rd (44847-9617)
PHONE....................419 499-2705
EMP: 7 **EST:** 2007
SALES (est): 1.47MM **Privately Held**
Web: www.scottrodscustom.com
SIC: 3229 7389 3711 Glass fiber products; Business services, nec; Automobile bodies, passenger car, not including engine, etc.

(G-10121)
SMS TECHNOLOGIES INC
3531 Everingin Rd (44847-9726)
PHONE....................419 465-4175
Stanley Schug, *Pr*
Nickie Schug, *VP*
EMP: 10 **EST:** 1990
SALES (est): 926.83K **Privately Held**
SIC: 3646 Commercial lighting fixtures

(G-10122)
VENTURE PACKAGING INC
311 Monroe St (44847-9406)
PHONE....................419 465-2534
Ira Boots, *Pr*
James Kratochuil, *
John Rathbun, *
EMP: 18 **EST:** 1976
SQ FT: 112,000
SALES (est): 5.7MM **Privately Held**
SIC: 3089 Injection molded finished plastics products, nec
HQ: Berry Global, Inc.
101 Oakley St
Evansville IN 47710

(G-10123)
VENTURE PACKAGING MIDWEST INC
311 Monroe St (44847-9406)
P.O. Box 246 (44847-0246)
PHONE....................419 465-2534
Kurt Klodnick, *Prin*
EMP: 7 **EST:** 1997
SALES (est): 2.05MM **Privately Held**
SIC: 3089 Bottle caps, molded plastics
HQ: Berry Global, Inc.
101 Oakley St
Evansville IN 47710

Montgomery
Hamilton County

(G-10124)
D J KLINGLER INC
Also Called: Montgomery License Bureau
9999 Montgomery Rd (45242-5311)
PHONE....................513 891-2284
Donna Klingler, *Pr*
EMP: 6 **EST:** 1993
SALES (est): 203.66K **Privately Held**

SIC: 3469 7299 Automobile license tags,
stamped metal; Personal appearance
services

(G-10125)
VENTI-NOW
9891 Montgomery Rd Ste 302
(45242-6424)
PHONE...............513 334-3375
John Molander, *Pr*
EMP: 16 EST: 2020
SALES (est): 443.13K **Privately Held**
Web: www.venti-now.org
SIC: 3444 Ventilators, sheet metal

Montpelier
Williams County

(G-10126)
AMP PLASTICS OF OHIO LLC
1815 Magda Dr (43543-9208)
EMP: 20 EST: 2007
SALES (est): 1.92MM **Privately Held**
SIC: 3089 Injection molding of plastics

(G-10127)
CREATIVE LIQUID COATINGS INC
Also Called: CK Technologies
1701 Magda Dr (43543-9368)
PHONE...............419 485-1110
EMP: 250
Web: www.creativeliquidcoatings.com
SIC: 3089 Injection molding of plastics
PA: Creative Liquid Coatings, Inc.
2620 Marion Dr
Kendallville IN 46755

(G-10128)
DYCO MANUFACTURING INC
12708 State Route 576 (43543-9242)
PHONE...............419 485-5525
Alan M Dye, *Pr*
Wes Dye, *VP*
Crystal Tyre, *Sec*
EMP: 14 EST: 1968
SALES (est): 3.4MM **Privately Held**
Web: www.dycomfg.com
SIC: 3469 3544 Stamping metal for the trade
; Special dies and tools

(G-10129)
KIMBLE MACHINES INC
124 S Jonesville St (43543-1337)
PHONE...............419 485-8449
Robert J Kimble, *Pr*
Margaret Kimble, *Sec*
EMP: 6 EST: 1989
SQ FT: 8,200
SALES (est): 1.35MM **Privately Held**
Web: www.kimblemachines.com
SIC: 3599 Custom machinery

(G-10130)
MOORE INDUSTRIES INC
1317 Henricks Dr (43543-1951)
P.O. Box 316 (43543-0316)
PHONE...............419 485-5572
Michael Moore, *Pr*
Rebecca Moore, *
▲ EMP: 65 EST: 1980
SQ FT: 40,000
SALES (est): 8.26MM **Privately Held**
Web: www.moore-industries.com
SIC: 3089 Injection molding of plastics

(G-10131)
PIONEER INDUSTRIAL SYSTEMS
LLC (PA)
1815 Magda Dr (43543-9208)

PHONE...............419 737-9506
Todd Hendricks Senior, *Pr*
▲ EMP: 7 EST: 2003
SALES (est): 6.33MM
SALES (corp-wide): 6.33MM **Privately
Held**
Web: www.pioneerindsys.com
SIC: 3599 Machine shop, jobbing and repair

(G-10132)
POWERS AND SONS LLC (DH)
Also Called: Pioneer Frge A Div Pwers Sons
1613 Magda Dr (43543-9359)
PHONE...............419 485-3151
▲ EMP: 220 EST: 2002
SQ FT: 200,000
SALES (est): 49.5MM **Privately Held**
Web: www.powersandsonsllc.com
SIC: 3714 Motor vehicle parts and
accessories
HQ: Wanxiang (Usa) Holdings Corporation
88 Airport Rd Ste 100
Elgin IL 60123
847 622-8838

(G-10133)
RANTEK PRODUCTS LLC
1826 Magda Dr Ste A (43543-9366)
PHONE...............419 485-2421
EMP: 6 EST: 2001
SALES (est): 949.77K **Privately Held**
Web: www.rantekproducts.com
SIC: 3199 Harness or harness parts

(G-10134)
RICHMOND MACHINE CO
1528 Travis Dr (43543-9524)
PHONE...............419 485-5740
Lee Richmond, *Pr*
Robert Richmond, *
EMP: 32 EST: 1965
SQ FT: 60,000
SALES (est): 7.23MM **Privately Held**
Web:
www.richmondmachinecompany.com
SIC: 3599 3535 Custom machinery;
Conveyors and conveying equipment

(G-10135)
TOMAHAWK TOOL SUPPLY
1604 Magda Dr (43543-9206)
PHONE...............419 485-8737
Jeff Thomas, *Pr*
EMP: 9 EST: 2003
SALES (est): 675.05K **Privately Held**
Web: www.tomahawk-tool.com
SIC: 3544 Special dies and tools

(G-10136)
WINZELER COUPLINGS & MTLS LLC
910 E Main St (43543-1260)
PHONE...............419 485-3147
Joseph Folkman, *Ch Bd*
David Rauch, *CEO*
EMP: 88 EST: 2022
SALES (est): 4.52MM **Privately Held**
Web: www.winzelermfg.com
SIC: 3466 Closures, stamped metal

(G-10137)
WINZELER MANUFACTURING
COMPANY (PA) ✪
129 W Wabash St (43543-1838)
PHONE...............419 485-8147
EMP: 18 EST: 2023
SALES (est): 17.95MM
SALES (corp-wide): 17.95MM **Privately
Held**
SIC: 3492 Fluid power valves and hose
fittings

(G-10138)
WINZELER STAMPING CO (HQ)
129 W Wabash St (43543-1881)
P.O. Box 226 (43543-0226)
PHONE...............419 485-3147
▲ EMP: 50 EST: 1919
SALES (est): 17.95MM
SALES (corp-wide): 17.95MM **Privately
Held**
Web: www.winzelerstamping.com
SIC: 3429 3465 3469 3714 Clamps and
couplings, hose; Automotive stampings;
Metal stampings, nec; Motor vehicle parts
and accessories
PA: Winzeler Manufacturing Company
129 W Wabash St
Montpelier OH 43543
419 485-8147

Montville
Geauga County

(G-10139)
5 S INC
9755 Plank Rd (44064-9712)
P.O. Box 188 (44064-0188)
PHONE...............440 968-0212
Tom Sparks, *Pr*
EMP: 7 EST: 2005
SALES (est): 1.25MM **Privately Held**
Web: www.5scomponents.com
SIC: 3599 Machine shop, jobbing and repair

Moraine
Montgomery County

(G-10140)
3249 INC
3249 Dryden Rd (45439-1423)
PHONE...............937 294-5692
Lisa S Pierce, *Prin*
EMP: 11 EST: 2005
SALES (est): 1.18MM **Privately Held**
Web: www.empowermfg.com
SIC: 3599 Machine shop, jobbing and repair

(G-10141)
3JD INC
Also Called: Stone Center of Dayton
2823 Northlawn Ave (45439-1645)
PHONE...............513 324-9655
Jerry Berkemeyer, *Prin*
▲ EMP: 15 EST: 2011
SALES (est): 922.21K **Privately Held**
SIC: 2541 Counter and sink tops

(G-10142)
ACUTEMP THERMAL SYSTEMS
2900 Dryden Rd (45439-1618)
PHONE...............937 312-0114
Marshall Griffin, *CFO*
EMP: 11 EST: 2012
SALES (est): 1.62MM **Privately Held**
Web: www.csafeglobal.com
SIC: 3822 Temperature controls, automatic

(G-10143)
AEROSPACE LLC
Also Called: Aerospace Logistics
3300 Encrete Ln (45439-1944)
PHONE...............937 561-1104
EMP: 10 EST: 2015
SALES (est): 498.55K **Privately Held**
SIC: 3728 Aircraft parts and equipment, nec

(G-10144)
ALLIED SHIPPING AND PACKAGING
SUPPLIES INC
Also Called: ASAP
3681 Vance Rd (45439-7940)
PHONE...............937 222-7422
EMP: 13 EST: 1981
SALES (est): 2.69MM **Privately Held**
Web: www.asapi.com
SIC: 5085 5162 7822 3086 Industrial
supplies; Plastics materials and basic
shapes; Video tapes, recorded: wholesale;
Plastics foam products

(G-10145)
AMERICAN THERMAL INSTRS INC
(PA)
2400 E River Rd (45439-1530)
PHONE...............937 429-2114
Marvin L Kidd, *CEO*
Timothy Riazzi, *
Trent Matthews, *
EMP: 25 EST: 1981
SALES (est): 4.73MM
SALES (corp-wide): 4.73MM **Privately
Held**
Web: www.americanthermal.com
SIC: 3829 Measuring and controlling
devices, nec

(G-10146)
ANDRIN ENTERPRISES INC
Also Called: Mmp Printing
3350 Kettering Blvd (45439-2011)
PHONE...............937 276-7794
Gary Luther, *Pr*
Shannon Luther, *VP*
EMP: 12 EST: 1979
SQ FT: 5,000
SALES (est): 144.31K **Privately Held**
SIC: 2752 2791 2789 Offset printing;
Typesetting; Bookbinding and related work

(G-10147)
ANGELS LANDING INC
Also Called: Compass
3430 S Dixie Dr Ste 301 (45439-2316)
PHONE...............513 687-3681
John Riedl, *Prin*
Dan Jackson, *CFO*
▲ EMP: 6 EST: 2004
SQ FT: 2,000
SALES (est): 121.42K **Privately Held**
SIC: 2514 Juvenile furniture, household:
metal

(G-10148)
BARRETT PAVING MATERIALS INC
2701 W Dorothy Ln (45439-1864)
PHONE...............937 293-9033
Jim Shaver, *Brnch Mgr*
EMP: 10
SALES (corp-wide): 105.44MM **Privately
Held**
Web: www.barrettpaving.com
SIC: 3273 Ready-mixed concrete
HQ: Barrett Paving Materials Inc.
8590 Bilstein Blvd
Hamilton OH 45015
973 533-1001

(G-10149)
BAYARD INC
2621 Dryden Rd Ste 300 (45439-1600)
PHONE...............937 293-1415
John P Koize, *Prin*
EMP: 81
Web: www.bayardinc.com
SIC: 2759 Publication printing
HQ: Bayard, Inc.

▲ = Import ▼ = Export
◆ = Import/Export

977 Hartford Tpke Unit A
Waterford CT 06385

(G-10150)
BERRY INVESTMENTS INC
3055 Kettering Blvd Ste 418 (45439-1900)
PHONE..............................937 293-0398
John W Berry Junior, *CEO*
William T Lincoln, *Pr*
EMP: 6 **EST:** 1983
SQ FT: 2,500
SALES (est): 475.74K **Privately Held**
SIC: 5091 3679 Sporting and recreation
goods; Microwave components

(G-10151)
BRAVO LLC (HQ)
Also Called: Bravo Pet Foods
2425 W Dorothy Ln (45439-1827)
PHONE..............................866 922-9222
David J Bogner, *Managing Member*
EMP: 17 **EST:** 2022
SALES (est): 25.08MM
SALES (corp-wide): 71.9MM **Privately Held**
Web: www.bravorawdiet.com
SIC: 2047 Dog food
PA: Brightpet Nutrition Group Llc
38251 Industrial Park Rd
Lisbon OH 44432
330 424-1431

(G-10152)
BRONT MACHINING INC
2601 W Dorothy Ln (45439-1831)
PHONE..............................937 228-4551
Gary Warlaumont, *Pr*
Brian Warlaumont, *VP*
EMP: 22 **EST:** 1975
SQ FT: 25,000
SALES (est): 3.49MM **Privately Held**
Web: www.brontmachine.com
SIC: 3451 3599 Screw machine products;
Machine shop, jobbing and repair

(G-10153)
BWI NORTH AMERICA INC (DH)
Also Called: Bwi Group
2586 E River Rd (45439-1514)
PHONE..............................614 394-5983
Zhong Wang, *Pr*
Zijian Zhao, *Dir*
▲ **EMP:** 20 **EST:** 2009
SQ FT: 00,000
SALES (est): 44.28MM **Privately Held**
Web: www.bwigroup.com
SIC: 3714 Motor vehicle parts and
accessories
HQ: Bwi (Beijing) Limited
No.85 Puan Road, Doudian Town,
Fangshan District
Beijing BJ 10240

(G-10154)
CARAUSTAR INDUSTRIES INC
2601 E River Rd (45439-1533)
PHONE..............................937 298-9969
Bill Theado, *Genl Mgr*
EMP: 38
SALES (corp-wide): 5.45B **Publicly Held**
Web: www.greif.com
SIC: 2655 Fiber cans, drums, and similar
products
HQ: Caraustar Industries, Inc.
5000 Astell Pwdr Sprng Rd
Austell GA 30106
770 948-3101

(G-10155)
DAPSCO
3110 Kettering Blvd (45439-1972)
PHONE..............................937 294-5331
Richard Schwartz, *Prin*
EMP: 12 **EST:** 2010
SALES (est): 1.9MM **Privately Held**
SIC: 3571 Electronic computers

(G-10156)
DAYTON BRICK COMPANY INC
Also Called: D & M Welding
2300 Arbor Blvd (45439-1724)
PHONE..............................937 293-4189
Jeffrey Mccarroll, *Pr*
Jeffrey Mc Carroll, *Pr*
Brian Mc Carroll, *Sec*
Justin Mccarroll, *Opers Mgr*
EMP: 15 **EST:** 1921
SQ FT: 15,000
SALES (est): 2.16MM **Privately Held**
Web: www.dmweldingusa.com
SIC: 7692 Welding repair

(G-10157)
DMAX LTD (DH)
Also Called: Dmax
3100 Dryden Rd (45439-1622)
PHONE..............................937 425-9700
Lawrence R Sessoms, *Prin*
Susumu Hosoi, *
◆ **EMP:** 98 **EST:** 1998
SQ FT: 700,000
SALES (est): 27.94MM **Publicly Held**
Web: www.dmaxengines.com
SIC: 3519 Engines, diesel and semi-diesel
or dual-fuel
HQ: General Motors Llc
300 Rnaissance Ctr Ste L1
Detroit MI 48243

(G-10158)
DRYDEN SHAFTS LLC
3249 Dryden Rd (45439-1423)
PHONE..............................937 365-7420
Eli Liechty, *Managing Member*
EMP: 30 **EST:** 2017
SALES (est): 15.07MM **Privately Held**
Web: www.empowermfg.com
SIC: 3568 Power transmission equipment,
nec

(G-10159)
ELECTRIPACK LLC
2985 Springboro W (45439-1713)
PHONE..............................937 433-2602
Jeanne Wright, *CEO*
◆ **EMP:** 40 **EST:** 2002
SALES (est): 7.13MM **Privately Held**
Web: www.electripack.com
SIC: 3694 Harness wiring sets, internal
combustion engines

(G-10160)
ENTING WATER CONDITIONING INC (PA)
Also Called: Superior Water Conditioning Co
3211 Dryden Rd Frnt (45439-1400)
PHONE..............................937 294-5100
TOLL FREE: 800
Mel Entingh, *CEO*
Dan Entingh, *
Doris Entingh, *
Karen Entingh, *
▲ **EMP:** 31 **EST:** 1965
SQ FT: 43,440
SALES (est): 2.44MM
SALES (corp-wide): 2.44MM **Privately Held**
Web: www.enting.com

SIC: 3589 5999 5074 Water filters and
softeners, household type; Water
purification equipment; Water purification
equipment

(G-10161)
ERNST METAL TECHNOLOGIES LLC
3031 Dryden Rd (45439-1619)
PHONE..............................937 434-3133
Neil Cordonnier, *Pr*
EMP: 82
SALES (corp-wide): 130.82MM **Privately Held**
Web: www.ernst.de
SIC: 3469 Stamping metal for the trade
HQ: Ernst Metal Technologies Llc
2920 Kreitzer Rd
Dayton OH 45439

(G-10162)
EXTREME MICROBIAL TECH LLC
Also Called: Extreme Microbial Technologies
2800 E River Rd (45439-1538)
PHONE..............................844 885-0088
Randall Mount, *Managing Member*
EMP: 21 **EST:** 2016
SALES (est): 2.25MM **Privately Held**
Web: www.extrememicrobial.com
SIC: 1799 3564 Decontamination services;
Air purification equipment

(G-10163)
F & G TOOL AND DIE CO (PA)
3024 Dryden Rd (45439-1690)
PHONE..............................937 294-1405
Jeff Johnson, *Pr*
Gary M Fischer, *
Ed Scharer, *
EMP: 44 **EST:** 1948
SQ FT: 60,000
SALES (est): 8.79MM
SALES (corp-wide): 8.79MM **Privately Held**
Web: www.fgtool.com
SIC: 3544 3599 Special dies and tools;
Custom machinery

(G-10164)
FUYAO GLASS AMERICA INC (HQ)
800 Fuyao Ave (45439-7500)
PHONE..............................937 496-5777
Zuogui Xie, *Pr*
Tim Reynolds, *
EMP: 306 **EST:** 2014
SALES (est): 126.65MM **Privately Held**
Web: www.fuyaousa.com
SIC: 3231 5013 Products of purchased glass
; Automobile glass
PA: Fuyao Glass Industry Group Co., Ltd.
Fuyao Industrial Area 1
Fuqing FJ 35030

(G-10165)
GLOBAL GAUGE CORPORATION
3200 Kettering Blvd (45439-1926)
PHONE..............................937 254-3500
William Mccormick, *Pr*
Tim Mccormick, *Pr*
Giovanni Adduci, *Sec*
EMP: 20 **EST:** 1999
SQ FT: 45,000
SALES (est): 4.6MM **Privately Held**
Web: www.globalgauge.com
SIC: 3829 Gauging instruments, thickness
ultrasonic

(G-10166)
GRAY AMERICA CORP (PA)
3050 Dryden Rd (45439-1620)
PHONE..............................937 293-9313
◆ **EMP:** 24 **EST:** 1946

SALES (est): 38.29MM
SALES (corp-wide): 38.29MM **Privately Held**
Web: www.grayamerica.com
SIC: 3312 3452 Blast furnaces and steel mills
; Bolts, metal

(G-10167)
HARCO MANUFACTURING GROUP LLC (PA)
3535 Kettering Blvd (45439-2014)
PHONE..............................937 528-5000
Christina Harris, *
▲ **EMP:** 150 **EST:** 2006
SQ FT: 300,000
SALES (est): 23.04MM **Privately Held**
Web: www.harcoonline.com
SIC: 3714 Motor vehicle brake systems and
parts

(G-10168)
HARCO MANUFACTURING GROUP LLC
3535 Kettering Blvd # 200 (45439-2014)
PHONE..............................937 528-5000
Tom Mc Nulty, *Brnch Mgr*
EMP: 150
Web: www.harcoonline.com
SIC: 3714 Motor vehicle brake systems and
parts
PA: Harco Manufacturing Group, Llc
3535 Kettering Blvd
Moraine OH 45439

(G-10169)
HEADING4WARD INVESTMENT CO (PA)
Also Called: Miracle
2425 W Dorothy Ln (45439-1827)
PHONE..............................937 293-9994
William M Sherk Junior, *Pr*
◆ **EMP:** 66 **EST:** 1988
SQ FT: 11,500
SALES (est): 14.31MM **Privately Held**
Web: www.bngmiraclepet.com
SIC: 3999 0752 5999 Pet supplies; Animal
specialty services; Pet supplies

(G-10170)
INSIGNIA SIGNS INC
2265 Dryden Rd (45439-1737)
PHONE..............................937 866-2341
Rick Dobson, *Pr*
Dan Mcbride, *Prin*
EMP: 8 **EST:** 2009
SALES (est): 669.31K **Privately Held**
Web: www.imagineinsignia.com
SIC: 3993 7336 Electric signs; Graphic arts
and related design

(G-10171)
JENA TOOL INC
5219 Springboro Pike (45439-2970)
PHONE..............................937 296-1122
George J Derr, *Ch*
EMP: 74 **EST:** 1968
SQ FT: 45,000
SALES (est): 9.11MM **Privately Held**
Web: www.jenatool.com
SIC: 3544 Special dies and tools

(G-10172)
KRAMER GRAPHICS INC
2408 W Dorothy Ln (45439-1828)
PHONE..............................937 296-9600
Mary Lou Kramer, *Ch*
John Kramer Junior, *Pr*
Kelley Kramer, *
▲ **EMP:** 50 **EST:** 1978
SALES (est): 3.41MM

SALES (corp-wide): 4.9MM **Privately Held**
Web: www.outdoorimagepop.com
SIC: **2752** Offset printing
PA: Outdoor Image, Llc
    3400 Rivergreen Ct # 100
    Duluth GA 30096
    770 817-9517

(G-10173)
L&H THREADED RODS CORP
3050 Dryden Rd (45439-1620)
PHONE..............................937 294-6666
John C Gray, *Pr*
Jeff Schroder, *
▲ **EMP:** 125 **EST:** 1986
SQ FT: 45,000
SALES (est): 9.38MM
SALES (corp-wide): 38.29MM **Privately Held**
Web: www.lhrods.com
SIC: **3312** Rods, iron and steel: made in steel mills
PA: Gray America Corp.
    3050 Dryden Rd
    Moraine OH 45439
    937 293-9313

(G-10174)
LASTAR INC
3555 Kettering Blvd (45439-2014)
PHONE..............................937 224-0639
▲ **EMP:** 420
SIC: **3678** Electronic connectors

(G-10175)
MAR-CON TOOL COMPANY
2301 Arbor Blvd (45439-1788)
PHONE..............................937 299-2244
Gene A Hamrick, *Pr*
Gene A Hamrick, *Pr*
Jeff Hamrick, *
Jim Hamrick, *
Gene Hamrick, *
EMP: 25 **EST:** 1959
SQ FT: 15,500
SALES (est): 2.86MM **Privately Held**
Web: www.marcontool.com
SIC: **3599 3728 3544** Machine shop, jobbing and repair; Aircraft parts and equipment, nec; Special dies, tools, jigs, and fixtures

(G-10176)
MCON INDS INC (HQ)
Also Called: Miller Consolidated Inds Inc
2221 Arbor Blvd (45439-1521)
PHONE..............................937 294-2681
Thomas Miller, *CEO*
Kelly Henderson, *
EMP: 49 **EST:** 1982
SQ FT: 55,000
SALES (est): 14.76MM
SALES (corp-wide): 22.74MM **Privately Held**
Web: www.millerconsolidated.com
SIC: **5051 3398** Steel; Metal heat treating
PA: Wilse, Inc.
    938 W County Road 250 S
    Greensburg IN

(G-10177)
METALLURGICAL SERVICE INC
2221 Arbor Blvd (45439-1575)
PHONE..............................937 294-2681
William R Miller, *Ch Bd*
Robert Miller, *VP*
Thomas Miller, *VP*
Alice L Miller, *Sec*
EMP: 12 **EST:** 1942
SQ FT: 45,000
SALES (est): 2.38MM
SALES (corp-wide): 22.74MM **Privately Held**

SIC: **3398** Metal heat treating
HQ: Mcon Inds, Inc.
    2221 Arbor Blvd
    Moraine OH 45439
    937 294-2681

(G-10178)
METRO FLEX INC
3304 Encrete Ln (45439-1944)
PHONE..............................937 299-5360
Scot Terry, *CEO*
Charleston Cline, *Sec*
EMP: 8 **EST:** 2003
SALES (est): 496.85K **Privately Held**
Web: www.mfplates.com
SIC: **2759** Screen printing

(G-10179)
MIDWEST MUFFLER PROS & MORE
3061 Dryden Rd (45439-1619)
PHONE..............................937 293-2450
Brian Madden, *Pr*
EMP: 6 **EST:** 2014
SALES (est): 233.29K **Privately Held**
Web: www.midwestmufflerpros.com
SIC: **7539 3714** Automotive repair shops, nec ; Mufflers (exhaust), motor vehicle

(G-10180)
PERFORMNCE PLYMR SOLUTIONS INC
Also Called: Proof RES Advnced Cmpsites Div
2711 Lance Dr (45409-1519)
PHONE..............................937 298-3713
Larry Murphy, *CEO*
David B Curliss, *Pr*
Jason Lincoln, *VP*
▲ **EMP:** 14 **EST:** 2002
SQ FT: 25,000
SALES (est): 2.96MM **Privately Held**
SIC: **8733 8731 8711 2821** Scientific research agency; Commercial research laboratory; Mechanical engineering; Plastics materials and resins
PA: Proof Research, Inc.
    10 Western Village Ln
    Columbia Falls MT 59912

(G-10181)
PFLAUM PUBLISHING GROUP
3055 Kettering Blvd Ste 100 (45439-1989)
PHONE..............................937 293-1415
EMP: 8 **EST:** 2010
SALES (est): 178.84K **Privately Held**
Web: www.pflaumweeklies.com
SIC: **2741** Miscellaneous publishing

(G-10182)
PJL ENTERPRISE INC (DH)
Also Called: Peter LI Education Group
3055 Kettering Blvd Ste 100 (45439-1989)
PHONE..............................937 293-1415
Peter J Li, *Pr*
EMP: 65 **EST:** 1971
SQ FT: 17,500
SALES (est): 1.28MM **Privately Held**
SIC: **2741** Miscellaneous publishing
HQ: Bayard, Inc.
    977 Hartford Tpke Unit A
    Waterford CT 06385

(G-10183)
PJL ENTERPRISE INC
2019 Springboro W (45439-1665)
PHONE..............................937 293-1415
Peter Li, *Pr*
EMP: 11
SIC: **2721** Magazines: publishing only, not printed on site
HQ: Pjl Enterprise, Inc.

3055 Kettering Blvd # 100
Moraine OH 45439
937 293-1415

(G-10184)
PLACECRETE INC
2475 Arbor Blvd (45439-1776)
PHONE..............................937 298-2121
Donald L Phlipot, *Pr*
EMP: 7 **EST:** 1966
SQ FT: 17,000
SALES (est): 920.71K **Privately Held**
SIC: **3273** Ready-mixed concrete

(G-10185)
POLAR INC
2297 N Moraine Dr (45439-1507)
P.O. Box 2995 (46515-2995)
PHONE..............................937 297-0911
Robert J Crawford, *Pr*
Shaery Eilon, *Acctg Mgr*
▼ **EMP:** 10 **EST:** 1955
SQ FT: 3,000
SALES (est): 483.4K **Privately Held**
SIC: **5169 5172 2841** Industrial chemicals; Petroleum products, nec; Soap and other detergents

(G-10186)
PREMIER INV CAST GROUP LLC
3034 Dryden Rd (45439-1620)
PHONE..............................937 299-7333
Harry Greenhouse, *Pt*
Peter Tur, *
EMP: 35 **EST:** 2017
SALES (est): 3.63MM **Privately Held**
Web: www.bimac.com
SIC: **3325** Steel foundries, nec

(G-10187)
PRINTING EXPRESS
3350 Kettering Blvd (45439-2011)
PHONE..............................937 276-7794
James Armstrong, *Owner*
EMP: 6 **EST:** 1989
SALES (est): 142.59K **Privately Held**
Web: www.printingexpressdayton.com
SIC: **2752** Offset printing

(G-10188)
PROMATCH SOLUTIONS LLC
2251 Arbor Blvd (45439-1521)
PHONE..............................877 299-0185
Jeffrey R Relick, *Pr*
EMP: 15 **EST:** 1992
SQ FT: 11,500
SALES (est): 577.14K **Privately Held**
SIC: **2741 7375 2789 2752** Micropublishing; Information retrieval services; Bookbinding and related work; Commercial printing, lithographic

(G-10189)
RACK PROCESSING COMPANY INC (PA)
2350 Arbor Blvd (45439-1760)
PHONE..............................937 294-1911
Craig Coy, *Pr*
Kevyn Coy, *
H Singer, *Prin*
EMP: 50 **EST:** 1948
SQ FT: 24,000
SALES (est): 8.83MM
SALES (corp-wide): 8.83MM **Privately Held**
Web: www.rackprocessing.com
SIC: **2542 3471** Partitions and fixtures, except wood; Plating and polishing

(G-10190)
RACK PROCESSING COMPANY INC
Also Called: Pique Stripping Division
2350 Arbor Blvd (45439-1760)
PHONE..............................937 294-1911
Dan Grammer, *Brnch Mgr*
EMP: 35
SALES (corp-wide): 8.83MM **Privately Held**
Web: www.rackprocessing.com
SIC: **3471 3479 2542** Electroplating of metals or formed products; Coating of metals with plastic or resins; Racks, merchandise display or storage: except wood
PA: Rack Processing Company, Inc.
    2350 Arbor Blvd
    Moraine OH 45439
    937 294-1911

(G-10191)
ROLLING ENTERPRISES INC
Also Called: Cat-Wood Metalworks
2701 Lance Dr (45409-1519)
PHONE..............................937 866-4917
August Rolling, *Pr*
August Jay Rolling, *
EMP: 36 **EST:** 1994
SALES (est): 8.15MM **Privately Held**
Web: www.cat-wood.com
SIC: **3599** Machine shop, jobbing and repair

(G-10192)
SNYDER CONCRETE PRODUCTS INC (PA)
Also Called: Snyder Brick and Block
2301 W Dorothy Ln (45439-1825)
PHONE..............................937 885-5176
Lee E Snyder, *CEO*
Mark Snyder, *
Julie Flory, *
▲ **EMP:** 25 **EST:** 1949
SQ FT: 50,000
SALES (est): 24.02MM
SALES (corp-wide): 24.02MM **Privately Held**
Web: www.snyderonline.com
SIC: **5032 3271 3272** Brick, except refractory ; Blocks, concrete or cinder: standard; Concrete products, nec

(G-10193)
SOUTHPAW ENTERPRISES INC
2350 Dryden Rd (45439-1736)
P.O. Box 1047 (45401-1047)
PHONE..............................937 252-7676
Frank Howard, *Pr*
Paul Lauzau, *
▼ **EMP:** 34 **EST:** 1975
SQ FT: 37,500
SALES (est): 9.76MM **Privately Held**
Web: www.southpaw.com
SIC: **3842** Technical aids for the handicapped

(G-10194)
TAILORED SYSTEMS INC
Also Called: Vibrodyne Division
2853 Springboro W (45439-2045)
PHONE..............................937 299-3900
Joseph Riess, *Pr*
John Riess, *VP*
Ron Logan, *Sec*
Karen Berry, *Asst Tr*
EMP: 7 **EST:** 1982
SQ FT: 12,000
SALES (est): 487.38K **Privately Held**
Web: www.vibrodyne.com
SIC: **3541 3599** Deburring machines; Machine shop, jobbing and repair

(G-10195)
THE WAGNER-SMITH COMPANY
3201 Encrete Ln (45439-1903)
P.O. Box 127 (45401-0127)
PHONE....................................866 338-0398
EMP: 490 **EST:** 1917
SALES (est): 16.61MM
SALES (corp-wide): 1.76B **Publicly Held**
Web: www.wagnersmith.com
SIC: 1731 3531 5082 7353 General
electrical contractor; Construction
machinery; Construction and mining
machinery; Heavy construction equipment
rental
HQ: Mdu Construction Services Group, Inc.
1150 W Century Ave
Bismarck ND 58503
701 530-1000

(G-10196)
TYLER TECHNOLOGIES INC
1 Tyler Way (45439-7503)
PHONE....................................800 800-2581
EMP: 19
SALES (corp-wide): 2.14B **Publicly Held**
Web: www.tylertech.com
SIC: 7372 Prepackaged software
PA: Tyler Technologies, Inc.
5101 Tennyson Pkwy
Plano TX 75024
972 713-3700

(G-10197)
VAGABOND CREATIONS INC
2560 Lance Dr (45409-1512)
P.O. Box 292854 (45429-8854)
PHONE....................................937 298-1124
George F Stanley Junior, *Pr*
EMP: 6 **EST:** 1955
SQ FT: 20,700
SALES (est): 141.04K **Privately Held**
Web: www.vagabondcreations.com
SIC: 2759 2771 Stationery: printing, nsk;
Greeting cards

Moreland Hills
Cuyahoga County

(G-10198)
BOWS BARRETTES & BAUBLES
4180 Chagrin River Rd (44022-1111)
PHONE................................440 247-2697
Cherrie Miller, *Owner*
EMP: 10 **EST:** 1985
SALES (est): 331.24K **Privately Held**
SIC: 2353 Hats, trimmed: women's, misses',
and children's

Morral
Marion County

(G-10199)
J-LENCO INC
664 N High St (43337)
P.O. Box 346 (43332-0346)
PHONE....................................740 499-2260
Edward P Murphy, *Pr*
Nancy Murphy, *
Thomas A Frericks, *
▲ **EMP:** 14 **EST:** 1973
SALES (est): 4.82MM **Privately Held**
Web: www.jlenco.com
SIC: 3543 Industrial patterns

Morristown
Belmont County

(G-10200)
BUCKEYE BRAKE MFG INC
40168 National Rd W (43759)
P.O. Box 676 (43950-0676)
PHONE....................................740 782-1379
Greg Beckett, *Pr*
EMP: 10 **EST:** 1996
SALES (est): 791.13K **Privately Held**
SIC: 3714 Motor vehicle brake systems and
parts

Morrow
Warren County

(G-10201)
ACTION MACHINE & MFG INC
6788 E Us Highway 22 And 3 (45152-9713)
PHONE....................................513 899-3889
Delores Nadine Hartman, *Pr*
Daryl Hartman, *VP*
Nick Hartman, *Sec*
EMP: 8 **EST:** 1963
SQ FT: 14,000
SALES (est): 582.97K **Privately Held**
SIC: 3599 Machine shop, jobbing and repair

(G-10202)
MORROW GRAVEL COMPANY INC
Also Called: Valley Asphalt
4850 Stubbs Mills Rd (45152-8340)
PHONE....................................513 899-2000
Rick Dostal, *Superintnt*
EMP: 11
SALES (corp-wide): 21.28MM **Privately
Held**
Web: www.jrjnet.com
SIC: 1442 Gravel mining
PA: Morrow Gravel Company Inc
11641 Mosteller Rd
Cincinnati OH 45241
513 771-0820

(G-10203)
VALLEY ASPHALT CORPORATION
Also Called: Morrow Gravel
4850 Stubbs Mills Rd (45152-8340)
PHONE....................................513 381-0652
Bob Hayton, *Mgr*
EMP: 8
SALES (corp-wide): 225.16MM **Privately
Held**
Web: www.jrjnet.com
SIC: 2951 Asphalt paving mixtures and
blocks
HQ: Valley Asphalt Corporation
11641 Mosteller Rd
Cincinnati OH 45241
513 771-0820

(G-10204)
VALLEY MACHINE TOOL INC
9773 Morrow Cozaddale Rd (45152-8589)
PHONE....................................513 899-2737
Larry R Wilson, *Pr*
Ralph Wilson, *
Douglas Wilson, *
EMP: 40 **EST:** 1967
SQ FT: 11,000
SALES (est): 3.73MM **Privately Held**
SIC: 3599 7692 Machine shop, jobbing and
repair; Welding repair

Mount Cory
Hancock County

(G-10205)
SNAPS INC
2557 Township Road 35 (45868-9701)
PHONE....................................419 477-5100
Nancy Ruppright, *Pr*
Gary Ruppright, *VP*
EMP: 6 **EST:** 1993
SALES (est): 73.42K **Privately Held**
Web: www.costumers.com
SIC: 2389 Theatrical costumes

Mount Eaton
Wayne County

(G-10206)
DUTCH QUALITY STONE INC
18012 Dover Rd (44659)
P.O. Box 308 (44659-0308)
PHONE....................................877 359-7866
Travis Hostetler, *Pr*
▲ **EMP:** 100 **EST:** 1996
SQ FT: 40,000
SALES (est): 16.28MM **Privately Held**
Web: www.dutchqualitystone.com
SIC: 3281 Cut stone and stone products
HQ: Headwaters Incorporated
10701 S Rver Front Pkwy
South Jordan UT 84095

(G-10207)
FLEX TECHNOLOGIES INC
Also Called: Mount Eaton Division
16183 East Main St (44659)
P.O. Box 223 (44659-0223)
PHONE....................................330 359-5415
Jim Eichel, *Mgr*
EMP: 52
SALES (corp-wide): 6MM **Privately Held**
Web: www.flextechnologies.com
SIC: 3089 3714 3694 3564 Injection molding
of plastics; Motor vehicle parts and
accessories; Engine electrical equipment;
Blowers and fans
PA: Flex Technologies, Inc.
5479 Gundy Dr
Midvale OH 44653
740 922-5992

(G-10208)
**QUALITY BLOCK & SUPPLY INC
(DH)**
Rte 250 (44659)
PHONE....................................330 364-4411
Jerry A Schwab, *Pr*
David Schwab, *
Donna Schwab, *
Mary Lynn Hites, *Treas*
EMP: 27 **EST:** 1973
SQ FT: 4,000
SALES (est): 388.28K
SALES (corp-wide): 34.95B **Privately Held**
SIC: 3271 3273 5032 Blocks, concrete or
cinder: standard; Ready-mixed concrete;
Concrete and cinder block
HQ: Schwab Industries, Inc.
2301 Progress St
Dover OH 44622
330 364-4411

Mount Gilead
Morrow County

(G-10209)
CONSOLIDATED GAS COOP INC
5255 State Route 95 (43338-9763)
P.O. Box 111 (43338-0111)
PHONE....................................419 946-6600
Nancy Salyer, *CFO*
EMP: 6 **EST:** 2001
SALES (est): 559.15K **Privately Held**
Web: www.consolidated.coop
SIC: 1321 Propane (natural) production

(G-10210)
HIRT PUBLISHING CO INC
Also Called: Marrow County Sentinel
245 Neal Ave Ste A (43338-9372)
P.O. Box 149 (43338-0149)
PHONE....................................419 946-3010
Vicki Taylor, *Mgr*
EMP: 38
SALES (corp-wide): 880.44K **Privately
Held**
Web: www.putnamsentinel.com
SIC: 2711 5999 Newspapers, publishing and
printing; Rubber stamps
PA: Hirt Publishing Co, Inc
224 E Main St
Ottawa OH 45875
419 523-5709

(G-10211)
LILLY INDUSTRIES INC (PA)
Also Called: Lightning Bolt Fastners
6437 County Road 20 (43338-9624)
PHONE....................................419 946-7908
Phil Lilly, *Pr*
Alvin Lilly, *VP*
EMP: 20 **EST:** 1972
SQ FT: 8,000
SALES (est): 3.7MM
SALES (corp-wide): 3.7MM **Privately Held**
Web: 1gj.7ec.myftpupload.com
SIC: 3441 Fabricated structural metal

(G-10212)
LUBRICATION SPECIALTIES LLC
3975 Morrow Meadows Dr (43338-7512)
PHONE....................................800 341-6516
Chris Gabrelick, *Pr*
EMP: 24 **EST:** 1997
SALES (est): 790.65K
SALES (corp-wide): 77.18MM **Privately
Held**
Web: www.lubricationspecialties.com
SIC: 7549 2992 Lubrication service,
automotive; Lubricating oils and greases
PA: Gold Eagle Co.
4400 S Kildare Ave
Chicago IL 60632
773 376-4400

Mount Hope
Holmes County

(G-10213)
GMI HOLDINGS INC (DH)
Also Called: Genie Company, The
1 Door Dr (44660-2503)
P.O. Box 67 (44660-0067)
PHONE....................................800 354-3643
Mike Kridel, *Pr*
Craig Smith, *
◆ **EMP:** 350 **EST:** 1990
SQ FT: 230,000
SALES (est): 56.71MM **Privately Held**
Web: www.geniecompany.com

SIC: **5064** 3699 Vacuum cleaners, nec; Door opening and closing devices, electrical
HQ: Overhead Door Corporation
2501 S State Hwy 121 Ste
Lewisville TX 75067
469 549-7100

(G-10214)
HOPE HOLDINGS INC
1 Door Dr (44660-2503)
P.O. Box 67 (44660-0067)
PHONE....................................330 674-7015
EMP: 6 EST: 1990
SALES (est): 311.21K **Privately Held**
Web: www.geniecompany.com
SIC: **2431** 3442 Garage doors, overhead, wood; Garage doors, overhead: metal

---

Mount Orab
Brown County

(G-10215)
CINCINNATI DOWEL & WD PDTS CO
135 Oak St (45154-9090)
PHONE....................................937 444-2502
William Streight, *Pr*
◆ EMP: 25 EST: 1925
SQ FT: 2,400
SALES (est): 1.72MM **Privately Held**
Web: www.cincinnatidowel.com
SIC: **2499** Dowels, wood

(G-10216)
CINDOCO WOOD PRODUCTS CO
Also Called: Craftwood
410 Mount Clifton Dr (45154-9353)
PHONE....................................937 444-2504
Melissa Hacker, *Pr*
EMP: 6 EST: 2006
SALES (est): 904.29K **Privately Held**
Web: www.cindoco.com
SIC: **5099** 2431 Wood and wood by-products; Millwork

(G-10217)
HAWKLINE NEVADA LLC
200 Front St (45154-8964)
PHONE....................................937 444-4295
Larry Danna, *
▲ EMP: 6 EST: 2006
SQ FT: 150,000
SALES (est): 682.77K **Privately Held**
SIC: **3523** 3799 Cabs, tractors, and agricultural machinery; Trailers and trailer equipment

(G-10218)
LUXUS PRODUCTS LLC
Also Called: Luxus Arms
222 Homan Way (45154-8269)
P.O. Box 11 (45154-0011)
PHONE....................................937 444-6500
Clay Barker, *Prin*
EMP: 6 EST: 2009
SALES (est): 347.2K **Privately Held**
Web: www.hmdefense.com
SIC: **2491** Structural lumber and timber, treated wood

(G-10219)
MILACRON PLAS TECH GROUP LLC
418 W Main St (45154-9596)
PHONE....................................937 444-2532
James Kinzie, *Genl Mgr*
EMP: 621
Web: www.milacron.com
SIC: **3544** Forms (molds), for foundry and plastics working machinery

HQ: Milacron Plastics Technologies Group Llc
4165 Half Acre Rd
Batavia OH 45103

(G-10220)
NET BRAZE LLC
351 Apple St (45154-8565)
PHONE....................................937 444-1444
▲ EMP: 18
SIC: **2899** Fluxes: brazing, soldering, galvanizing, and welding

(G-10221)
PRECISION WELDING & MFG INC (PA)
101 Day Rd (45154-8924)
P.O. Box 369 (45154-0369)
PHONE....................................937 444-6925
Daniel L Fischer, *Pr*
EMP: 10 EST: 1994
SQ FT: 20,000
SALES (est): 737.06K **Privately Held**
Web: www.precisionweldingcorp.net
SIC: **7692** Welding repair

(G-10222)
PRO-TECH MANUFACTURING INC
14944 Hillcrest Rd (45154-8513)
PHONE....................................937 444-6484
Patrick Gregory, *Pr*
Jeff Roades, *VP*
EMP: 10 EST: 1994
SQ FT: 9,000
SALES (est): 973.47K **Privately Held**
SIC: **3544** Special dies and tools

(G-10223)
WEDCO LLC
Also Called: Bardwell Winery
716 N High St (45154-8349)
P.O. Box 391 (45154-0391)
PHONE....................................513 309-0781
Roy R Weddle, *Managing Member*
Roy R Weddle, *Pr*
Gayle Weddle, *VP*
EMP: 6 EST: 2005
SALES (est): 92.96K **Privately Held**
SIC: **6531** 2082 5182 Real estate brokers and agents; Brewers' grain; Wine

(G-10224)
X-MIL INC
220 Homan Way (45154-8269)
P.O. Box 452 (45154-0452)
PHONE....................................937 444-1323
Steven E Seibert, *Pr*
Joel Scott Dalton, *VP*
Angie Kreidler, *Sec*
EMP: 20 EST: 1998
SALES (est): 3.18MM **Privately Held**
Web: www.x-mil.com
SIC: **3599** Machine shop, jobbing and repair

Mount Perry
Perry County

(G-10225)
MT PERRY FOODS INC
5705 State Route 204 Ne (43760-9734)
P.O. Box 404 (43086-0404)
PHONE....................................740 743-3890
Reg Martin, *Pr*
EMP: 75 EST: 2000
SALES (est): 8.68MM **Privately Held**
Web: www.mtperryfoods.com
SIC: **2499** Food handling and processing products, wood

(G-10226)
SCHEIDERS FOODS LLC (PA)
5705 State Route 204 Ne (43760-9734)
PHONE....................................740 404-6641
Jeff Cormell, *Managing Member*
EMP: 10 EST: 2021
SALES (est): 937.47K
SALES (corp-wide): 937.47K **Privately Held**
SIC: **2051** Bakery: wholesale or wholesale/retail combined

Mount Sterling
Madison County

(G-10227)
CPI INDUSTRIAL CO
299 Yankeetown St (43143-9410)
P.O. Box 235 (43143-0235)
PHONE....................................614 445-0800
Mark Owens, *Pr*
Mark T Owens, *Pr*
Susan Flannigan, *Sec*
EMP: 22 EST: 1988
SALES (est): 7.83MM **Privately Held**
Web: www.epoxyfloors.com
SIC: **2851** Epoxy coatings

(G-10228)
FURNISS CORPORATION LTD
15812 State Route 56 W (43143-9532)
P.O. Box 128 (43143-0128)
PHONE....................................614 871-1470
Andy Furniss, *Mng Pt*
EMP: 19 EST: 1997
SQ FT: 27,000
SALES (est): 3.01MM **Privately Held**
Web: www.furnisscorp.com
SIC: **3845** Electromedical apparatus

(G-10229)
STEPHENS PIPE & STEEL LLC
10732 Schadel Ln (43143-9731)
P.O. Box 237 (43143-0237)
PHONE....................................740 869-2257
Rick Redman, *Prin*
EMP: 185
Web: www.spsfence.com
SIC: **3523** 3496 3494 3446 Farm machinery and equipment; Miscellaneous fabricated wire products; Valves and pipe fittings, nec; Architectural metalwork
HQ: Stephens Pipe & Steel, Llc
2224 E Hwy 619
Russell Springs KY 42642
270 866-3331

(G-10230)
WATERSHED MANGEMENT LLC
Also Called: Nancy Blanket
10460 State Route 56 Se (43143-9429)
P.O. Box 126 (43143-0126)
PHONE....................................740 852-5607
EMP: 10 EST: 1998
SALES (est): 346.16K **Privately Held**
Web: www.nancysblankets.com
SIC: **5023** 2399 Blankets; Aprons, breast (harness)

(G-10231)
WILLOWWOOD GLOBAL LLC (PA)
Also Called: Ohio Willow Wood Company, The
15441 Scioto Darby Rd (43143-9036)
P.O. Box 130 (43143-0130)
PHONE....................................740 869-3377
Mahesh Mansukhani, *CEO*
Ryan Arbogast, *Pr*
Daniel Rubin, *COO*
◆ EMP: 154 EST: 1907

SQ FT: 90,000
SALES (est): 25MM
SALES (corp-wide): 25MM **Privately Held**
Web: www.willowwood.com
SIC: **3842** Limbs, artificial

Mount Vernon
Knox County

(G-10232)
AMG INDUSTRIES INC
300 Commerce Dr (43050-4642)
PHONE....................................740 397-4044
EMP: 10 EST: 2018
SALES (est): 1.18MM **Privately Held**
Web: www.amgindustries.com
SIC: **3999** Manufacturing industries, nec

(G-10233)
AMG INDUSTRIES LLC
200 Commerce Dr (43050-4699)
PHONE....................................740 397-4044
David J Mcelroy, *Pr*
Mike Miller, *
Kim Rose, *
Dennis Mcelroy, *Ex VP*
EMP: 100 EST: 1904
SQ FT: 120,000
SALES (est): 22.97MM **Privately Held**
Web: www.amgindustries.com
SIC: **3469** Metal stampings, nec
PA: Reserve Group Management Company
3560 W Market St Ste 300
Akron OH 44333

(G-10234)
AMG PRODUCTS LLC ✪
1375 Newark Rd (43050-4779)
PHONE....................................614 507-7749
Douglas Spangler, *Managing Member*
EMP: 16 EST: 2023
SALES (est): 2.4MM **Privately Held**
Web: www.amgproductsllc.com
SIC: **3053** Gaskets; packing and sealing devices

(G-10235)
ARIEL CORPORATION
8405 Blackjack Rd (43050-2781)
PHONE....................................740 397-0311
EMP: 14
SALES (corp-wide): 170.79MM **Privately Held**
Web: www.arielcorp.com
SIC: **3563** Air and gas compressors
PA: Ariel Corporation
35 Blackjack Rd
Mount Vernon OH 43050
740 397-0311

(G-10236)
ARIEL CORPORATION (PA)
35 Blackjack Road Ext (43050-9482)
PHONE....................................740 397-0311
◆ EMP: 198 EST: 1966
SALES (est): 170.79MM
SALES (corp-wide): 170.79MM **Privately Held**
Web: www.arielcorp.com
SIC: **3563** Air and gas compressors including vacuum pumps

(G-10237)
BRIDGESTONE RET OPERATIONS LLC
Also Called: Firestone
855 Coshocton Ave Ste 21 (43050-1975)
PHONE....................................740 397-5601
Robert Stauffer, *Mgr*

▲ = Import ▼ = Export
◆ = Import/Export

EMP: 10
SQ FT: 9,200
Web: www.bridgestoneamericas.com
SIC: 5531 7534 Automotive tires; Tire repair shop
HQ: Bridgestone Retail Operations, Llc
200 4th Ave S Ste 100
Nashville TN 37201
615 937-1000

(G-10238)
CAPITAL CITY OIL INC
Also Called: American Energy Pdts Inc Ind
375 Columbus Rd (43050-4427)
PHONE....................740 397-4483
Roy Bailey, *Pr*
EMP: 6 EST: 1995
SALES (est): 1.56MM **Privately Held**
Web: www.capitalcityusedoil.com
SIC: 2911 4953 Oils, fuel; Refuse systems

(G-10239)
CENTRAL OHIO FABRICATORS LLC
105 Progress Dr (43050-4772)
PHONE....................740 393-3892
EMP: 16 EST: 1984
SQ FT: 22,000
SALES (est): 2.14MM **Privately Held**
Web: www.centralohiofab.com
SIC: 3441 Fabricated structural metal

(G-10240)
CITY OF MOUNT VERNON
Also Called: Water & Waste Water Dept.
1550 Old Delaware Rd (43050-8631)
PHONE....................740 393-9508
Judie Scott, *Admn*
EMP: 8
Web: www.mountvernonohio.org
SIC: 2899 Water treating compounds
PA: City Of Mount Vernon
40 Public Sq Ste 206
Mount Vernon OH 43050
740 393-9520

(G-10241)
COYNE GRAPHIC FINISHING INC
Also Called: Coyne Finishing
1301 Newark Rd (43050-4730)
PHONE....................740 397-6232
Robert Coyne, *Ch*
Kevin Coyne, *
Alice Ann Coyne, *
EMP: 20 EST: 1920
SQ FT: 57,000
SALES (est): 5.67MM **Privately Held**
Web: www.coynefinishing.com
SIC: 7336 2752 Graphic arts and related design; Commercial printing, lithographic

(G-10242)
DIVERSIFIED PRODUCTS & SVCS
1250 Vernonview Dr (43050-1447)
PHONE....................740 393-6202
Louis Ohara, *Dir*
EMP: 16 EST: 1982
SALES (est): 261.46K **Privately Held**
SIC: 5199 2541 2511 Packaging materials; Wood partitions and fixtures; Wood household furniture

(G-10243)
DOWN HOME
Also Called: Down Home Leather
9 N Main St (43050-3203)
PHONE....................740 393-1186
Laurel Lee Wagoner, *Owner*
EMP: 8 EST: 1971
SQ FT: 5,000
SALES (est): 191.39K **Privately Held**
Web: www.downhomeleather.com

SIC: 5947 3172 Gift shop; Personal leather goods, nec

(G-10244)
ELLIS BROTHERS INC UPG
14220 Parrott Ext (43050-4500)
PHONE....................740 397-9191
EMP: 12 EST: 2019
SALES (est): 2.72MM **Privately Held**
Web: www.ellisbros.net
SIC: 3273 Ready-mixed concrete

(G-10245)
INTERNATIONAL PAPER COMPANY
International Paper
8800 Granville Rd (43050-9192)
PHONE....................740 397-5215
Mark Smith, *Brnch Mgr*
EMP: 152
SALES (corp-wide): 18.62B **Publicly Held**
Web: www.internationalpaper.com
SIC: 2621 Paper mills
PA: International Paper Company
6400 Poplar Ave
Memphis TN 38197
901 419-7000

(G-10246)
JELD-WEN INC
Also Called: Jeld-Wen Windows
1201 Newark Rd (43050-4728)
PHONE....................740 397-1144
Brad Hunter, *Mgr*
EMP: 189
Web: www.jeld-wen.ca
SIC: 2431 Doors, wood
HQ: Jeld-Wen, Inc.
2645 Silver Crescent Dr
Charlotte NC 28273
800 535-3936

(G-10247)
JELD-WEN INC
335 Commerce Dr (43050-4643)
PHONE....................740 397-3403
Ted Schnormeier, *Brnch Mgr*
EMP: 8
Web: www.jeld-wen.com
SIC: 2431 Doors, wood
HQ: Jeld-Wen, Inc.
2645 Silver Crescent Dr
Charlotte NC 28273
800 535-3936

(G-10248)
KNOX MACHINE & TOOL
250 Columbus Rd (43050-4428)
PHONE....................740 392-3133
Korby Bricker, *Pr*
Trent Hauke, *Sec*
EMP: 9 EST: 1994
SALES (est): 706.41K **Privately Held**
SIC: 3599 Machine shop, jobbing and repair

(G-10249)
MACK INDUSTRIES INC
400 Howard St (43050-3547)
PHONE....................740 393-1121
EMP: 17
SALES (corp-wide): 86.93MM **Privately Held**
Web: www.mackconcrete.com
SIC: 3272 Burial vaults, concrete or precast terrazzo
PA: Mack Industries, Inc.
1321 Indus Pkwy N Ste 500
Brunswick OH 44212
330 460-7005

(G-10250)
MARKT LLC
314 W Burgess St (43050-2353)
PHONE....................740 397-5900
Taylor Todd, *Admn*
EMP: 7 EST: 2012
SALES (est): 297.58K **Privately Held**
Web: www.marktapparel.com
SIC: 5699 2395 2759 Uniforms and work clothing; Embroidery and art needlework; Screen printing

(G-10251)
MAUSER USA LLC
219 Commerce Dr (43050-4645)
PHONE....................740 397-1762
Chuck Sesco, *Mgr*
EMP: 62
SALES (corp-wide): 3.82B **Privately Held**
Web: www.mauserpackaging.com
SIC: 5085 3412 Packing, industrial; Metal barrels, drums, and pails
HQ: Mauser Usa, Llc
1515 W 22nd St Ste 1100
Oak Brook IL 60523

(G-10252)
MOHAWK MANUFACTURING INC
306 E Gambier St (43050-3514)
PHONE....................860 632-2345
Walter Nacey, *Pr*
EMP: 8 EST: 1996
SALES (est): 235.45K **Privately Held**
SIC: 3469 Stamping metal for the trade

(G-10253)
MOUNT VERNON PACKAGING INC
135 Progress Dr (43050-4772)
P.O. Box 950 (43050-0950)
PHONE....................740 397-3221
Donald Nuce, *Pr*
Margo Nuce, *VP*
EMP: 10 EST: 1971
SALES (est): 9.58MM **Privately Held**
Web: www.mountvernonpackaging.com
SIC: 2653 Boxes, corrugated: made from purchased materials

(G-10254)
MT VERNON MACHINE & TOOL INC
Also Called: Mount Vernon Steel
8585 Blackjack Road Ext (43050-2782)
PHONE....................740 397-0311
EMP: 50
Web: www.mltwmachine.com
SIC: 3599 5999 Machine shop, jobbing and repair; Welding supplies

(G-10255)
OWENS CORNING SALES LLC
Also Called: Owens Corning
100 Blackjack Road Ext (43050-9194)
PHONE....................614 399-3915
Bob Demory, *Mgr*
EMP: 23
SIC: 2621 3296 Building paper, insulation; Mineral wool
HQ: Owens Corning Sales, Llc
1 Owens Corning Pkwy
Toledo OH 43659
419 248-8000

(G-10256)
PACS INDUSTRIES INC
8405 Blackjack Road Ext (43050-2781)
PHONE....................740 397-5021
▲ **EMP:** 100
SIC: 3613 3823 Switchgear and switchgear accessories, nec; Process control instruments

(G-10257)
PAGE ONE GROUP
10 E Vine St Ste C (43050-3244)
PHONE....................740 397-4240
Jana Burson, *Pt*
EMP: 7 EST: 1944
SQ FT: 800
SALES (est): 362.88K **Privately Held**
Web: www.pageonegroup.net
SIC: 2752 8742 Offset printing; Marketing consulting services

(G-10258)
PERFORMACE DIESEL INC
16901 Mcvay Rd (43050)
PHONE....................740 392-3693
Stephen Harsany, *Pr*
Angel Harsany, *Sec*
EMP: 10 EST: 1991
SQ FT: 7,000
SALES (est): 994.86K **Privately Held**
Web: www.purrformancediesel.com
SIC: 3519 Diesel engine rebuilding

(G-10259)
POTEMKIN INDUSTRIES INC (PA)
8043 Columbus Rd (43050-9358)
PHONE....................740 397-4888
Horst Krajenski, *Pr*
Debbie Hamilton, *
EMP: 19 EST: 1980
SQ FT: 14,000
SALES (est): 3.7MM
SALES (corp-wide): 3.7MM **Privately Held**
Web: www.global-compression.com
SIC: 3563 Air and gas compressors including vacuum pumps

(G-10260)
PRINTING ARTS PRESS INC
8028 Newark Rd (43050-8155)
P.O. Box 431 (43050-0431)
PHONE....................740 397-6106
Robert Vogt, *Pr*
Rhonda Gherman, *Ex Dir*
Charles Gherman, *Mgr*
EMP: 10 EST: 1945
SQ FT: 15,000
SALES (est): 480.56K **Privately Held**
Web:
printingartspress.secureprintorder.com
SIC: 2752 2791 Offset printing; Typesetting

(G-10261)
PROGRSSIVE COMMUNICATIONS CORP
Also Called: Mount Vernon News
18 E Vine St (43050-3226)
P.O. Box 791 (43050-0791)
PHONE....................740 397-5333
Kay H Culbertson, *Pr*
Michelle L Hartman, *
Elizabeth Lutwick, *
EMP: 17 EST: 1838
SQ FT: 30,000
SALES (est): 425.66K **Privately Held**
Web: www.mountvernonnews.com
SIC: 2711 2752 2791 Commercial printing and newspaper publishing combined; Offset printing; Typesetting

(G-10262)
REPLEX MIRROR COMPANY
Also Called: Replex Plastics
11 Mount Vernon Ave (43050-4163)
PHONE....................740 397-5535
Mark Schuetz, *Pr*
◆ **EMP:** 21 EST: 1991
SQ FT: 100,000
SALES (est): 4.77MM **Privately Held**
Web: www.replex.com

(PA)=Parent Co (HQ)=Headquarters
✪ = New Business established in last 2 years

SIC: 3089 Thermoformed finished plastics products, nec

(G-10263)
ROLLS-ROYCE ENERGY SYSTEMS INC
105 N Sandusky St (43050-2447)
PHONE..............................703 834-1700
◆ **EMP:** 1000
SIC: 3511 5084 8711 Turbines and turbine generator sets; Compressors, except air conditioning; Engineering services

(G-10264)
ROYAL METAL PRODUCTS LLC
Also Called: Heating & Cooling Products
325 Commerce Dr (43050-4643)
PHONE..............................740 397-8842
Don Smith, *Genl Mgr*
EMP: 160
SALES (corp-wide): 223.79MM **Privately Held**
Web: www.johnsoncontrols.com
SIC: 3444 3585 3312 Sheet metalwork; Refrigeration and heating equipment; Blast furnaces and steel mills
HQ: Royal Metal Products, Llc
100 Royal Way
Temple GA 30179

(G-10265)
SIEMENS ENERGY INC
Also Called: Siemens Power and Gas
105 N Sandusky St (43050-2447)
PHONE..............................740 504-1947
Steven Charles Conner, *CEO*
EMP: 7
SALES (corp-wide): 38.48B **Privately Held**
Web: www.siemens.com
SIC: 3511 Steam turbines
HQ: Siemens Energy, Inc.
4400 N Alafaya Trl
Orlando FL 32826
407 736-2000

(G-10266)
STRAWSER STEEL DRUM OHIO LTD
219 Commerce Dr (43050-4645)
PHONE..............................614 856-5982
Brad Strawser, *Genl Pt*
EMP: 25 **EST:** 1985
SQ FT: 70,000
SALES (est): 2.92MM **Privately Held**
SIC: 3412 Metal barrels, drums, and pails

(G-10267)
UNITED PRECAST INC
400 Howard St (43050-3547)
PHONE..............................740 393-1121
TOLL FREE: 800
John P Ellis, *Genl Mgr*
John D Ellis, *
George Ellis, *Stockholder*
Linda Ellis, *Stockholder*
EMP: 226 **EST:** 1970
SQ FT: 4,000
SALES (est): 1.59MM **Privately Held**
Web: www.unitedprecast.net
SIC: 3272 Concrete products, precast, nec

(G-10268)
VER-MAC INDUSTRIES INC
100 Progress Dr (43050-4700)
PHONE..............................740 397-6511
Dennis Mcelroy, *Pr*
Mitch Durbin, *
William D Heichel, *
▲ **EMP:** 40 **EST:** 1985
SQ FT: 26,000
SALES (est): 4.65MM **Privately Held**
Web: www.ver-macindustries.com

SIC: 3599 3496 3449 Machine shop, jobbing and repair; Miscellaneous fabricated wire products; Miscellaneous metalwork

Mount Victory
Hardin County

(G-10269)
NATURES HEALTH FOOD LLC
21561 County Road 190 (43340-8827)
PHONE..............................419 260-9265
Tony Siebeneck, *Managing Member*
EMP: 11 **EST:** 2016
SALES (est): 500K **Privately Held**
SIC: 5149 2099 7389 Honey; Maple syrup; Business services, nec

(G-10270)
RAVENWORKS DEER SKIN
34477 Shertzer Rd (43340-9615)
P.O. Box 6 (43340-0006)
PHONE..............................937 354-5151
Charles Harris, *Pt*
Nina Harris, *Pt*
EMP: 6 **EST:** 1970
SALES (est): 139.99K **Privately Held**
SIC: 3171 3172 Women's handbags and purses; Personal leather goods, nec

Munroe Falls
Summit County

(G-10271)
M S B MACHINE INC
36 Castle Dr (44262-1602)
PHONE..............................330 686-7740
Jim Burkart, *Pr*
EMP: 6 **EST:** 2004
SQ FT: 3,880
SALES (est): 491.57K **Privately Held**
Web: www.msbmachine.com
SIC: 3599 Machine shop, jobbing and repair

(G-10272)
SONOCO PRODUCTS COMPANY
59 N Main St (44262-1064)
P.O. Box 217 (44262-0217)
PHONE..............................330 688-8247
John Parman, *Mgr*
EMP: 42
SALES (corp-wide): 5.31B **Publicly Held**
Web: www.sonoco.com
SIC: 2631 2655 Paperboard mills; Fiber cans, drums, and similar products
PA: Sonoco Products Company
1 N 2nd St
Hartsville SC 29550
843 383-7000

(G-10273)
SUPERIOR MOLD & DIE CO
449 N Main St (44262-1007)
PHONE..............................330 688-8251
Richard Yamokoski, *Pr*
Richard Yamokoski, *Pr*
Gale Young, *
Jeffery Yamokoski, *
EMP: 13 **EST:** 1943
SQ FT: 43,000
SALES (est): 2.98MM **Privately Held**
Web: www.s-m-d.us
SIC: 3544 3599 Industrial molds; Machine shop, jobbing and repair

Napoleon
Henry County

(G-10274)
ADVANCED DRAINAGE SYSTEMS INC
1075 Independence Dr (43545-9717)
PHONE..............................419 599-9565
Jason Hartland, *Mgr*
EMP: 30
SQ FT: 14,000
SALES (corp-wide): 2.87B **Publicly Held**
Web: www.adspipe.com
SIC: 3084 3083 Plastics pipe; Laminated plastics plate and sheet
PA: Advanced Drainage Systems, Inc.
4640 Trueman Blvd
Hilliard OH 43026
614 658-0050

(G-10275)
C&C FABRICATION LLC
13226 County Road R (43545-5966)
PHONE..............................419 592-1408
Jade Shank, *Admn*
EMP: 23 **EST:** 2017
SALES (est): 4.76MM **Privately Held**
SIC: 3441 Fabricated structural metal

(G-10276)
CARSON INDUSTRIES LLC
1675 Industrial Dr (43545-9734)
PHONE..............................419 592-2309
Rich Gordinier, *Prin*
EMP: 6 **EST:** 2009
SALES (est): 611.48K **Privately Held**
SIC: 3089 Injection molding of plastics

(G-10277)
CUSTAR STONE CO
9072 County Road 424 (43545-9732)
P.O. Box 607 (43545-0607)
PHONE..............................419 669-4327
Brent Gerken, *Pr*
Mike Gerken, *VP*
Jon Myers, *Sec*
Julian Gerken, *Stockholder*
EMP: 26 **EST:** 1994
SQ FT: 3,000
SALES (est): 6.24MM **Privately Held**
Web: www.gerkencompanies.com
SIC: 1422 Crushed and broken limestone

(G-10278)
DEFIANCE STAMPING CO
800 Independence Dr (43545-9192)
PHONE..............................419 782-5781
Tony Stuart, *Pr*
Joe Harmon, *
Dennis Maude, *
Brian Callan, *
▲ **EMP:** 65 **EST:** 1927
SQ FT: 60,000
SALES (est): 9.32MM
SALES (corp-wide): 96.62MM **Publicly Held**
Web: www.defiancestamping.com
SIC: 3469 Stamping metal for the trade
HQ: Defiance Integrated Technologies, Inc.
800 Independence Dr
Napoleon OH 43545

(G-10279)
FORKLIFT SOLUTIONS LLC
425 Oxford St (43545-2068)
PHONE..............................419 717-9496
Ernie Franz, *Prin*
EMP: 7 **EST:** 2016
SALES (est): 62.68K **Privately Held**

SIC: 3537 Forklift trucks

(G-10280)
GAZETTE PUBLISHING COMPANY
Also Called: Fulton County Expositor
595 E Riverview Ave (43545-1865)
P.O. Box 376 (43567-0376)
PHONE..............................419 335-2010
Janice May, *Mgr*
EMP: 69
SALES (corp-wide): 4.39MM **Privately Held**
Web: www.northwestsignal.net
SIC: 7313 5994 2711 Newspaper advertising representative; Newsstand; Newspapers
PA: The Gazette Publishing Company
42 S Main St
Oberlin OH 44074
419 483-4190

(G-10281)
GERKEN MATERIALS INC (PA)
9072 County Road 424 (43545-9732)
P.O. Box 607 (43545-0607)
PHONE..............................419 533-2421
EMP: 50 **EST:** 1959
SALES (est): 51.86MM
SALES (corp-wide): 51.86MM **Privately Held**
Web: www.gerkencompanies.com
SIC: 1611 2951 Highway and street paving contractor; Asphalt and asphaltic paving mixtures (not from refineries)

(G-10282)
GILSON MACHINE & TOOL CO INC
529 Freedom Dr (43545-5945)
PHONE..............................419 592-2911
William E Gilson Junior, *Pr*
Glen Gilson, *Sec*
EMP: 20 **EST:** 1946
SQ FT: 11,000
SALES (est): 3.44MM **Privately Held**
Web: www.gilsonmachine.com
SIC: 3599 7692 3549 3544 Machine shop, jobbing and repair; Welding repair; Metalworking machinery, nec; Special dies, tools, jigs, and fixtures

(G-10283)
HIGH PRODUCTION TECHNOLOGY LLC
13068 County Road R (43545-5964)
PHONE..............................419 599-1511
Marlow Witt, *Brnch Mgr*
EMP: 8
Web: www.automaticfeed.com
SIC: 3542 Machine tools, metal forming type
HQ: High Production Technology, Llc
476 E Riverview Ave
Napoleon OH 43545
419 591-7000

(G-10284)
HIGH PRODUCTION TECHNOLOGY LLC (DH)
476 E Riverview Ave (43545-1855)
PHONE..............................419 591-7000
EMP: 15 **EST:** 1997
SQ FT: 6,000
SALES (est): 2.16MM **Privately Held**
Web: www.automaticfeed.com
SIC: 3542 3441 Presses: hydraulic and pneumatic, mechanical and manual; Fabricated structural metal
HQ: Nidec Automatic Feed Company
476 E Riverview Ave
Napoleon OH 43545
419 592-0050

(G-10285)
HOLGATE METAL FAB INC
555 Independence Dr (43545-9656)
PHONE...............................419 599-2000
Jeff Spangler, *Pr*
Denise Spangler, *VP*
EMP: 15 **EST:** 1987
SQ FT: 16,000
SALES (est): 2.27MM **Privately Held**
Web: www.holgatemetalfab.com
SIC: 1711 1761 3444 3441 Boiler
maintenance contractor; Sheet metal work,
nec; Sheet metalwork; Fabricated structural
metal

(G-10286)
HP2G LLC
403 N Hill St (43545-9215)
P.O. Box 165 (43545-0165)
PHONE...............................419 906-1525
Sheila Kay, *VP*
Jen Rodgers, *Contrlr*
EMP: 8 **EST:** 2009
SALES (est): 560.22K **Privately Held**
Web: www.hp2g.com
SIC: 3714 Motor vehicle parts and
accessories

(G-10287)
INNOVATIVE TOOL & DIE INC
1700 Industrial Dr (43545-9282)
PHONE...............................419 599-0492
Loren Sonnenberg, *Pr*
Larry Huber, *Sec*
EMP: 8 **EST:** 1992
SQ FT: 5,000
SALES (est): 961.92K **Privately Held**
Web: www.innovative-tool.com
SIC: 3544 3599 Special dies and tools;
Machine and other job shop work

(G-10288)
ISOFOTON NORTH AMERICA INC
800 Independence Dr (43545-9192)
PHONE...............................419 591-4330
▲ **EMP:** 10 **EST:** 2011
SALES (est): 1.16MM **Privately Held**
SIC: 3674 Solar cells

(G-10289)
KOESTER CORPORATION (PA)
813 N Perry St (43545-1521)
PHONE...............................419 599-0291
Michael Koester, *Pr*
Jeanette Spiller, *
EMP: 40 **EST:** 1970
SQ FT: 40,000
SALES (est): 9.57MM
SALES (corp-wide): 9.57MM **Privately
Held**
Web: www.koester-corp.com
SIC: 3569 3823 3613 Lubricating equipment;
Pressure measurement instruments,
industrial; Control panels, electric

(G-10290)
M & S AG SOLUTIONS LLC
Also Called: Paul Martin and Sons
755 American Rd (43545-6301)
PHONE...............................419 598-8675
Doug Martin, *Managing Member*
EMP: 13 **EST:** 2015
SALES (est): 603.11K **Privately Held**
Web: www.martinequipment.net
SIC: 5999 3523 Farm equipment and
supplies; Farm machinery and equipment

(G-10291)
MIDWEST WOOD TRIM INC
1650 Commerce Dr (43545-6726)

PHONE...............................419 592-3389
Brad Westhoven, *Pr*
Eugene Westhoven, *
EMP: 35 **EST:** 1984
SQ FT: 40,000
SALES (est): 319.54K **Privately Held**
SIC: 2431 Moldings, wood: unfinished and
prefinished

(G-10292)
MUSTANG PRINTING
Also Called: Turkeyfoot Printing
119 W Washington St (43545-1739)
P.O. Box 413 (43567-0413)
PHONE...............................419 592-2746
Jerry Dehnbostel, *Pr*
EMP: 10
SQ FT: 4,800
SALES (est): 509.78K **Privately Held**
SIC: 2759 Commercial printing, nec
HQ: Mustang Corporation
229 N Fulton St
Wauseon OH
419 335-9070

(G-10293)
NAPOLEON MACHINE LLC
476 E Riverview Ave (43545-1855)
PHONE...............................419 591-7010
EMP: 35 **EST:** 2010
SALES (est): 5.42MM **Privately Held**
Web: www.napoleonmachine.com
SIC: 1721 3599 Commercial painting;
Machine and other job shop work

(G-10294)
OLDCASTLE INFRASTRUCTURE INC
1675 Industrial Dr (43545-9734)
PHONE...............................419 592-2309
EMP: 35
SALES (corp-wide): 34.95B **Privately Held**
Web: www.oldcastleinfrastructure.com
SIC: 3272 Concrete products, nec
HQ: Oldcastle Infrastructure, Inc.
7000 Central Pkwy Ste 800
Atlanta GA 30328
770 270-5000

(G-10295)
PANDROL INC
25 Interstate Dr (43545-9714)
P.O. Box 69 (43545-0069)
PHONE...............................419 592-5050
David C Barrett Junior, *Prin*
◆ **EMP:** 43 **EST:** 1983
SQ FT: 60,000
SALES (est): 9.76MM
SALES (corp-wide): 2.67MM **Privately
Held**
Web: www.pandrol.com
SIC: 3355 Rails, rolled and drawn, aluminum
HQ: Delachaux Sa
307 Rue D'estienne D'orves
Colombes IDF 92700
146881500

(G-10296)
PULLMAN COMPANY
Also Called: Tenneco
11800 County Road 424 (43545-5778)
PHONE...............................419 592-2055
Tom Weaver, *Brnch Mgr*
EMP: 204
SQ FT: 220,000
SALES (corp-wide): 18.04B **Privately Held**
Web: www.tenneco.com
SIC: 3714 Motor vehicle engines and parts
HQ: The Pullman Company
1 International Dr
Monroe MI 48161
734 243-8000

(G-10297)
RETTIG FAMILY PALLETS INC
12484 State Route 110 (43545-9340)
PHONE...............................419 439-0776
Robert Rettig, *Pr*
EMP: 10 **EST:** 2000
SQ FT: 30,000
SALES (est): 191.03K **Privately Held**
SIC: 2448 Pallets, wood

(G-10298)
**RSV WLDING FBRCTION MCHNING
IN**
M063 County Road 12 (43545-9366)
P.O. Box 430 (43545-0430)
PHONE...............................419 592-0993
Ralph F Vocke, *Pr*
Randy Vocke, *VP*
Steve Vocke, *Sec*
EMP: 10 **EST:** 1979
SQ FT: 10,400
SALES (est): 734.28K **Privately Held**
SIC: 3441 7692 Fabricated structural metal;
Welding repair

Nashport
Muskingum County

(G-10299)
HANBY FARMS INC
10790 Newark Rd (43830-9066)
P.O. Box 97 (43830-0097)
PHONE...............................740 763-3554
Ralph Hanby, *Pr*
Doug Hanby, *
David R Hanby, *
Carol Hanby, *
EMP: 40 **EST:** 1960
SQ FT: 10,000
SALES (est): 4.72MM **Privately Held**
Web: www.performancefeed.com
SIC: 2048 5153 5191 Livestock feeds; Corn;
Fertilizer and fertilizer materials

(G-10300)
HERITAGE COOPERATIVE INC
10790 Newark Rd (43830-9066)
PHONE...............................740 828-2215
EMP: 13
Web: www.heritagecooperative.com
SIC: 2032 2099 Canned specialties; Food
preparations, nec
PA: Heritage Cooperative, Inc.
59 Greif Pkwy Ste 200
Delaware OH 43015

(G-10301)
MUSCLE FEAST LLC (PA)
1320 Boston Rd (43830-9603)
PHONE...............................740 877-8808
▲ **EMP:** 10 **EST:** 2009
SQ FT: 16,000
SALES (est): 3.52MM **Privately Held**
Web: www.musclefeast.com
SIC: 5149 2023 Health foods; Dietary
supplements, dairy and non-dairy based

Navarre
Stark County

(G-10302)
B & S TRANSPORT INC (PA)
11325 Lawndell Rd Sw (44662-8804)
P.O. Box 2678 (44720-0678)
PHONE...............................330 767-4319
Ronald Harris, *Pr*
Irvin Jackson, *VP*

EMP: 9 **EST:** 1977
SQ FT: 6,000
SALES (est): 435.37K
SALES (corp-wide): 435.37K **Privately
Held**
SIC: 3011 5014 5052 5045 Tires and inner
tubes; Tires and tubes; Coal and other
minerals and ores; Computers, peripherals,
and software

(G-10303)
FAR CORNER
13189 Mount Eaton St Sw (44662-9476)
P.O. Box 92 (44613-0092)
PHONE...............................330 767-3734
EMP: 6
SALES (est): 452.61K **Privately Held**
Web: www.farcorner-online.com
SIC: 2752 Commercial printing, lithographic

(G-10304)
GOJO INDUSTRIES INC
4676 Erie Ave Sw (44662-9658)
PHONE...............................330 255-6000
EMP: 7
SALES (corp-wide): 802.21MM **Privately
Held**
Web: www.gojo.com
SIC: 2842 Polishes and sanitation goods
PA: Gojo Industries, Inc.
1 Gojo Plz Ste 500
Akron OH 44311
330 255-6000

(G-10305)
IMAGINE THIS RENOVATIONS
4220 Alabama Ave Sw (44662-9618)
PHONE...............................330 833-6739
Scott Miller, *Prin*
EMP: 8 **EST:** 2009
SALES (est): 369.2K **Privately Held**
SIC: 2759 Commercial printing, nec

(G-10306)
MASSILLON CONTAINER CO
49 Ohio St Sw (44662-1183)
PHONE...............................330 879-5653
EMP: 46 **EST:** 1949
SALES (est): 11.1MM
SALES (corp-wide): 11.1MM **Privately
Held**
Web: www.vailpkg.com
SIC: 2653 Corrugated and solid fiber boxes
PA: Vail Industries, Inc.
49 Ohio St Sw
Navarre OH
330 879-5653

(G-10307)
**MILLER WELDMASTER
CORPORATION (PA)**
4220 Alabama Ave Sw (44662-9618)
PHONE...............................330 833-6739
Brent Nussbaum, *Pr*
Jeff Dimos, *
◆ **EMP:** 88 **EST:** 1973
SQ FT: 20,000
SALES (est): 10.5MM
SALES (corp-wide): 10.5MM **Privately
Held**
Web: www.weldmaster.com
SIC: 3548 Welding and cutting apparatus
and accessories, nec

(G-10308)
MYSTA EQUIPMENT CO
6434 Werstler Ave Sw (44662-9140)
PHONE...............................330 879-5353
Stanley Josefczyk, *Owner*
EMP: 6 **EST:** 1983
SALES (est): 352.51K **Privately Held**

SIC: 3599 Machine and other job shop work

(G-10309)
OWENS CORNING
9318 Erie Ave Sw (44662-9448)
PHONE....................419 248-8000
Jeannie Bender, *VP*
EMP: 6
Web: www.owenscorning.com
SIC: 3296 Fiberglass insulation
PA: Owens Corning
1 Owens Corning Pkwy
Toledo OH 43659

(G-10310)
PERENNIAL VINEYARDS LLC
11877 Poorman St Sw (44662-9683)
PHONE....................330 832-3677
Damon Leeman, *Owner*
EMP: 10 EST: 2002
SQ FT: 10,000
SALES (est): 127.8K **Privately Held**
Web: www.perennialvineyards.com
SIC: 2084 Wines

(G-10311)
PREMIER PALLET AND RECYCL INC
11361 Lawndell Rd Sw (44662-8804)
P.O. Box 31 (44613-0031)
PHONE....................330 767-2221
Pete Grove, *Pr*
EMP: 7 EST: 2004
SALES (est): 493.4K **Privately Held**
Web: www.premierpallet.net
SIC: 2448 Pallets, wood

(G-10312)
PT METALS LLC
10384 Navarre Rd Sw (44662-9462)
PHONE....................330 767-3003
Paul Miller, *
EMP: 25 EST: 2019
SALES (est): 572.48K **Privately Held**
Web: www.pt-metals.com
SIC: 3699 Laser welding, drilling, and cutting
equipment

(G-10313)
RC INDUSTRIES INC
Also Called: Mid's Spaghetti Sauce
620 Main St N (44662-8556)
P.O. Box 5 (44662-0005)
PHONE....................330 879-5486
Scott Ricketts, *Pr*
Steve Cress, *
EMP: 25 EST: 1964
SQ FT: 10,000
SALES (est): 5.94MM **Privately Held**
Web: www.midssauce.com
SIC: 2033 2035 Spaghetti and other pasta
sauce: packaged in cans, jars, etc; Pickles,
sauces, and salad dressings

(G-10314)
TERYDON INC
7260 Erie Ave Sw (44662-8807)
PHONE....................330 879-2448
Terry Gromes Senior, *Pr*
EMP: 7 EST: 1994
SQ FT: 800
SALES (est): 3.2MM
SALES (corp-wide): 28.3MM **Privately
Held**
Web: www.stoneagetools.com
SIC: 3599 Custom machinery
PA: Stoneage, Inc.
466 S Skylane Dr
Durango CO 81303
970 259-2869

Negley
Columbiana County

(G-10315)
MAGNECO/METREL INC
51365 State Route 154 (44441-9728)
P.O. Box 176 (44441-0176)
PHONE....................330 426-9468
Paul Painter, *Brnch Mgr*
EMP: 107
SALES (corp-wide): 45.46MM **Privately
Held**
Web: www.magneco-metrel.com
SIC: 3255 3297 Clay refractories; Nonclay
refractories
PA: Magneco/Metrel, Inc.
740 Waukegan Rd Ste 212
Deerfield IL 60015
630 543-6660

(G-10316)
X L SAND AND GRAVEL CO
9289 Jackman Rd (44441)
P.O. Box 255 (44441-0255)
PHONE....................330 426-9876
Raymond Lansberry, *Pr*
James Lansberry, *Treas*
EMP: 7 EST: 1969
SQ FT: 1,000
SALES (est): 2.49MM **Privately Held**
Web: www.xlsandandgravel.com
SIC: 1442 Common sand mining

Nelsonville
Athens County

(G-10317)
GEORGIA-BOOT INC
Also Called: Durango Boot
39 E Canal St (45764-1247)
PHONE....................740 753-1951
Gerald M Cohn, *CEO*
Thomas R Morrison, *Pr*
EMP: 100 EST: 1937
SALES (est): 3.14MM **Privately Held**
Web: www.georgiaboot.com
SIC: 5139 3144 3143 3021 Shoes; Women's
footwear, except athletic; Men's footwear,
except athletic; Rubber and plastics
footwear

(G-10318)
MCDONALDS
21 Watkins St (45764-1459)
PHONE....................740 753-4018
EMP: 10 EST: 2020
SALES (est): 286.04K **Privately Held**
Web: www.mcdonalds.com
SIC: 5813 5812 5499 2038 Drinking places;
Eating places; Miscellaneous food stores;
Frozen specialties, nec

(G-10319)
**MILOS WHOLE WORLD GOURMET
LLC**
296 S Harper St (45764-1600)
PHONE....................740 589-6456
Jonathan Leal, *Managing Member*
EMP: 9 EST: 2003
SALES (est): 4.49MM **Privately Held**
Web: www.miloswholeworld.com
SIC: 1541 2033 Food products
manufacturing or packing plant construction
; Canned fruits and specialties

(G-10320)
ROCKY BRANDS INC (PA)
Also Called: Gore-Tex
39 E Canal St (45764-1247)
PHONE....................740 753-1951
Jason Brooks, *Ch Bd*
Thomas D Robertson, *CFO*
Byron Wortham, *Sr VP*
Curtis A Loveland, *
EMP: 211 EST: 1932
SQ FT: 24,400
SALES (est): 453.77MM
SALES (corp-wide): 453.77MM **Publicly
Held**
Web: www.rockybrands.com
SIC: 3143 3144 2329 2331 Men's footwear,
except athletic; Women's footwear, except
athletic; Men's and boys' sportswear and
athletic clothing; Women's and misses'
blouses and shirts

(G-10321)
STARR MACHINE INC
226 Sylvania Ave (45764)
PHONE....................740 753-0184
Brian Kasler, *Pr*
EMP: 24 EST: 2000
SQ FT: 34,000
SALES (est): 611.62K **Privately Held**
Web: www.starrmachine.com
SIC: 3599 Machine shop, jobbing and repair

(G-10322)
US FOOTWEAR HOLDINGS LLC
39 E Canal St (45764-1247)
PHONE....................740 753-9100
Jason S Brooks, *Managing Member*
EMP: 121 EST: 2020
SALES (est): 4.76MM
SALES (corp-wide): 453.77MM **Publicly
Held**
SIC: 5139 3021 Footwear; Rubber and
plastics footwear
PA: Rocky Brands, Inc.
39 E Canal St
Nelsonville OH 45764
740 753-1951

Nevada
Wyandot County

(G-10323)
SHOOT-A-WAY INC
7157 County Highway 134 (44849-9753)
PHONE....................419 294-4654
John Joseph, *Pr*
EMP: 10 EST: 1990
SALES (est): 2.45MM **Privately Held**
Web: www.shootaway.com
SIC: 5699 3949 7389 Sports apparel; Team
sports equipment; Advertising, promotional,
and trade show services

(G-10324)
STIGER PRE CAST INC
17793 State Highway 231 (44849-9710)
PHONE....................740 482-2313
TOLL FREE: 800
Jim Riedlinger, *Pr*
Eva Mae Riedlinger, *VP*
Cathy Scheffler, *Sec*
EMP: 8 EST: 1943
SQ FT: 2,200
SALES (est): 605.38K **Privately Held**
Web: www.stigerprecast.com
SIC: 3272 3271 Septic tanks, concrete;
Blocks, concrete or cinder: standard

New Albany
Franklin County

(G-10325)
ALENE CANDLES MIDWEST LLC
8860 Smiths Mill Rd Ste 100 (43054-6654)
PHONE....................614 933-4005
EMP: 10 EST: 2011
SALES (est): 4.53MM **Privately Held**
Web: www.alene.com
SIC: 3999 Candles

(G-10326)
AMERICAN REGENT INC
6610 New Albany Rd E (43054-8730)
PHONE....................614 436-2222
Joseph Kenneth Keller, *CEO*
EMP: 98
Web: www.americanregent.com
SIC: 2834 Pharmaceutical preparations
HQ: American Regent, Inc.
5 Ramsey Rd
Shirley NY 11967
631 924-4000

(G-10327)
AMGEN INC
4150 Ganton Pkwy (43054-3522)
PHONE....................805 447-1000
Bob Bradway, *CEO*
EMP: 17
SALES (corp-wide): 33.42B **Publicly Held**
Web: www.amgen.com
SIC: 2834 Adrenal pharmaceutical
preparations
PA: Amgen Inc.
1 Amgen Center Dr
Thousand Oaks CA 91320
805 447-1000

(G-10328)
ANOMATIC CORPORATION (DH)
Also Called: Anomatic Opportunity
8880 Innovation Campus Way
(43054-6651)
PHONE....................740 522-2203
William B Rusch, *Pr*
Scott L Rusch, *
◆ EMP: 42 EST: 1974
SQ FT: 65,000
SALES (est): 45.17MM
SALES (corp-wide): 833.11MM **Privately
Held**
Web: www.anomatic.com
SIC: 3471 3469 2396 Anodizing (plating) of
metals or formed products; Metal
stampings, nec; Automotive and apparel
trimmings
HQ: Thyssen'sche Handelsgesellschaft Mit
Beschrankter Haftung
Dohne 54
Mulheim An Der Ruhr NW 45468
208992180

(G-10329)
ARCHITECTURAL BUSSTRUT CORP
4311 Brompton Ct (43054-8982)
PHONE....................614 933-8695
EMP: 10
Web: www.busstrut.com
SIC: 3648 5063 Lighting fixtures, except
electric: residential; Lighting fixtures
PA: Architectural Busstrut Corp.
4787 Roberts Rd
Columbus OH 43228

(G-10330)
**AROMAIR FINE FRAGRANCE
COMPANY**

8860 Smiths Mill Rd Ste 500 (43054-6653)
PHONE..................614 984-2900
Nicholas Whitley, *CEO*
Richard Nihei, *
EMP: 500 **EST:** 2010
SALES (est): 43.26MM
SALES (corp-wide): 6.19B **Privately Held**
Web: www.aromair.com
SIC: 2842 Cleaning or polishing
preparations, nec
HQ: Kdc Us Holdings, Inc.
Park 80 W Plz Ii 250 Phle
Saddle Brook NJ 07663

(G-10331)
AXIUM PACKAGING LLC (PA)
Also Called: Axium Plastics
9005 Smiths Mill Rd (43054-6650)
PHONE..................614 706-5955
EMP: 685 **EST:** 2011
SALES (est): 218.65MM **Privately Held**
Web: www.axiumpackaging.com
SIC: 3089 Plastics containers, except foam

(G-10332)
BOCCHI LABORATORIES OHIO LLC
9200 Smiths Mill Rd N (43054-6703)
PHONE..................614 741-7458
Edward Gotch, *CEO*
Wayne Byrne, *
EMP: 300 **EST:** 2014
SQ FT: 125,000
SALES (est): 18.96MM
SALES (corp-wide): 174.55MM **Privately Held**
Web: www.bocchilabs.com
SIC: 2844 Toilet preparations
PA: Bright Holdco, Llc
9002 Smith's Mill Rd N
New Albany OH 43054
614 741-7458

(G-10333)
BRIGHT HOLDCO LLC (PA)
Also Called: Bright Innovation Labs
9002 Smiths Mill Rd (43054-6647)
PHONE..................614 741-7458
Edward Gotch, *CEO*
Wayne Byrne, *CFO*
EMP: 102 **EST:** 2018
SALES (est): 174.55MM
SALES (corp-wide): 174.55MM **Privately Held**
Web: www.brightinnovationlabs.com
SIC: 2844 Face creams or lotions

(G-10334)
CCL LABEL INC
8600 Innovation Campus Way W
(43054-7550)
PHONE..................856 273-0700
EMP: 40
SALES (corp-wide): 4.84B **Privately Held**
Web: www.cclind.com
SIC: 2759 Labels and seals: printing, nsk
HQ: Ccl Label, Inc.
161 Worcester Rd Ste 603
Framingham MA 01701
508 872-4511

(G-10335)
CENTRAL OHIO MET STMPING FBRCT
4361 Brompton Ct (43054-8982)
P.O. Box 307776 (43230-7776)
PHONE..................614 861-3332
John Davidson, *Pr*
Lawrence Davidson, *
Pennie Davidson, *
EMP: 25 **EST:** 1986
SALES (est): 2.18MM **Privately Held**

Web:
www.centralohiometalstamping.com
SIC: 3469 Stamping metal for the trade

(G-10336)
COMMERCIAL VEHICLE GROUP INC (PA)
Also Called: Cvg
7800 Walton Pkwy (43054-8482)
PHONE..................614 289-5360
James R Ray Junior, *Pr*
Robert Griffin, *Ch Bd*
Andy Cheung, *Ex VP*
Scott Reed, *COO*
EMP: 391 **EST:** 2000
SALES (est): 723.36MM
SALES (corp-wide): 723.36MM **Publicly Held**
Web: www.cvgrp.com
SIC: 3694 2531 Automotive electrical
equipment, nec; Seats, automobile

(G-10337)
CUSTOM METAL PRODUCTS INC
Also Called: Do All Sheet Metal
5037 Babbitt Rd (43054-8301)
P.O. Box 149 (43054-0149)
PHONE..................614 855-2263
Sheri Brock, *Pr*
EMP: 10 **EST:** 2007
SQ FT: 24,000
SALES (est): 2.48MM **Privately Held**
SIC: 3444 Metal housings, enclosures,
casings, and other containers

(G-10338)
CVG NATIONAL SEATING CO LLC
Also Called: C V G
7800 Walton Pkwy (43054-8482)
PHONE..................219 872-7295
James Ray, *Pr*
▲ **EMP:** 10 **EST:** 1976
SALES (est): 6.45MM
SALES (corp-wide): 723.36MM **Publicly Held**
Web: www.cvgrp.com
SIC: 3714 5012 Motor vehicle parts and
accessories; Trucks, commercial
PA: Commercial Vehicle Group, Inc.
7800 Walton Pkwy
New Albany OH 43054
614 289-5360

(G-10339)
DESCO CORPORATION (PA)
7795 Walton Pkwy Ste 175 (43054-0002)
PHONE..................614 888-8855
Arnold B Siemer, *Pr*
Thomas Villano, *VP*
Russell M Gertmenian, *Sec*
Roger Bailey, *Treas*
Barbara J Siemer, *Sec*
EMP: 9 **EST:** 1975
SQ FT: 5,500
SALES (est): 90.88MM
SALES (corp-wide): 90.88MM **Privately Held**
Web: www.descocorporation.com
SIC: 3442 3825 3643 3531 Window and
door frames; Instruments to measure
electricity; Current-carrying wiring services;
Construction machinery

(G-10340)
FAITH GUIDING CAFE LLC
Also Called: Renegade Candle Company
5195 Hampsted Village Center Way
(43054-8331)
PHONE..................614 245-8451
Kathy Lavan, *Managing Member*
▲ **EMP:** 10 **EST:** 2010

SALES (est): 743.79K **Privately Held**
Web: www.renegadecandles.com
SIC: 3999 8742 Candles; General
management consultant

(G-10341)
FORM5 PROSTHETICS INC
6560 New Albany Condit Rd (43054-9734)
PHONE..................614 226-1141
Aaron Westbrook, *CEO*
EMP: 11 **EST:** 2017
SALES (est): 301.15K **Privately Held**
Web: www.form5.org
SIC: 3842 Prosthetic appliances

(G-10342)
JANOVA LLC
7570 N Goodrich Sq (43054-8983)
PHONE..................614 638-6785
Brian Lusenhop, *Product Management Vice-President*
EMP: 6 **EST:** 2010
SALES (est): 500.38K **Privately Held**
Web: www.janova.us
SIC: 7372 Application computer software

(G-10343)
KDC ONE
8825 Smiths Mill Rd (43054-6649)
PHONE..................614 984-2871
EMP: 9
SALES (est): 518.28K **Privately Held**
Web: www.kdc-one.com
SIC: 2844 Cosmetic preparations

(G-10344)
KDC US HOLDINGS INC
Also Called: Kdc Innovation
8825 Smiths Mill Rd (43054-6649)
PHONE..................614 656-1130
Matt Unger, *VP*
EMP: 445
SALES (corp-wide): 6.19B **Privately Held**
SIC: 2834 Pharmaceutical preparations
HQ: Kdc Us Holdings, Inc.
Park 80 W Plz Ii 250 Phle
Saddle Brook NJ 07663

(G-10345)
MALIK MEDIA LLC
7591 Lambton Park Rd (43054-8513)
PHONE..................614 933-0328
Samuel Malik, *Prin*
EMP: 6 **EST:** 2016
SALES (est): 197.4K **Privately Held**
Web: www.thinknotable.com
SIC: 7319 2752 8742 7336 Advertising, nec;
Commercial printing, lithographic;
Marketing consulting services; Commercial
art and graphic design

(G-10346)
MUELLER ELECTRIC COMPANY INC
7795 Walton Pkwy Ste 175 (43054-0002)
PHONE..................614 888-8855
Rodger Bailey, *CEO*
EMP: 6 **EST:** 2011
SALES (est): 302.51K **Privately Held**
Web: www.descocorporation.com
SIC: 3679 3678 3825 Harness assemblies,
for electronic use: wire or cable; Electronic
connectors; Test equipment for electronic
and electric measurement

(G-10347)
OHIO CRAFTED MALT HOUSE LLC
7775 Walton Pkwy (43054-8202)
PHONE..................614 961-7805
EMP: 7 **EST:** 2019
SALES (est): 1.36MM **Privately Held**

SIC: 2083 Barley malt

(G-10348)
OHIO HD VIDEO
1355 Bingham Mills Dr (43054-9414)
PHONE..................614 656-1162
Scott Handle, *Owner*
EMP: 11 **EST:** 2010
SALES (est): 143K **Privately Held**
Web: www.ohdstudios.com
SIC: 7841 3651 3861 Video tape rental;
Household audio and video equipment;
Photographic equipment and supplies

(G-10349)
OWENS FOODS INC
8111 Smiths Mill Rd (43054-1183)
EMP: 290
Web: www.owenssausage.com
SIC: 2013 Sausages and related products,
from purchased meat

(G-10350)
SHADOW HOLDINGS LLC (HQ)
Also Called: Bocchi Laboratories
9200 Smiths Mill Rd N (43054-6703)
PHONE..................614 741-7458
Ed Gotch, *Managing Member*
EMP: 354 **EST:** 2007
SQ FT: 88,500
SALES (est): 105.71MM
SALES (corp-wide): 174.55MM **Privately Held**
Web: www.brightinnovationlabs.com
SIC: 2844 Perfumes, cosmetics and other
toilet preparations
PA: Bright Holdco, Llc
9002 Smith's Mill Rd N
New Albany OH 43054
614 741-7458

(G-10351)
STICKTITE LENSES LLC
5195 Hampsted Village Center Way
(43054-8331)
PHONE..................571 276-9508
EMP: 10 **EST:** 2022
SALES (est): 1.02MM **Privately Held**
SIC: 3851 3827 Lenses, ophthalmic; Optical
instruments and lenses

(G-10352)
TRIM SYSTEMS OPERATING CORP (HQ)
Also Called: Cvg Trim Systems
7800 Walton Pkwy (43054-8482)
PHONE..................614 289-5360
Gerald L Armstrong, *Pr*
▲ **EMP:** 80 **EST:** 1997
SALES (est): 30.84MM
SALES (corp-wide): 723.36MM **Publicly Held**
Web: www.cvgrp.com
SIC: 3714 Motor vehicle parts and
accessories
PA: Commercial Vehicle Group, Inc.
7800 Walton Pkwy
New Albany OH 43054
614 289-5360

(G-10353)
VEEPAK OH LLC
Also Called: Voyant Beauty
9040 Smiths Mill Rd (43054-6647)
PHONE..................740 927-9002
Gene Sturino, *Prin*
EMP: 10 **EST:** 1991
SALES (est): 1.89MM **Privately Held**
Web: www.voyantbeauty.com

SIC: 2844 Cosmetic preparations

(G-10354)
VERIANO FINE FOODS SPIRITS LTD
5175 Zarley St Ste A (43054)
P.O. Box 617 (43054-0617)
PHONE................................614 745-7705
EMP: 15 EST: 2009
SQ FT: 10,000
SALES (est): 732.89K **Privately Held**
Web: www.buytessora.com
SIC: 2085 5182 Distilled and blended liquors
; Liquor

New Boston
Scioto County

(G-10355)
A & M REFRACTORIES INC
202 West Ave (45662-4946)
PHONE................................740 456-8020
Michael Cartee, *Pr*
Richard Bobst, *VP*
EMP: 20 EST: 1991
SQ FT: 60,000
SALES (est): 2.5MM **Privately Held**
Web: 212571.refwin.com
SIC: 3297 Nonclay refractories

New Bremen
Auglaize County

(G-10356)
AUGLAIZE ERIE MACHINE COMPANY
07148 Quellhorst Rd (45869-9632)
P.O. Box 72 (45869-0072)
PHONE................................419 629-2068
Tom W Slife, *Pr*
Elaine Slife, *
EMP: 30 EST: 1978
SQ FT: 7,500
SALES (est): 4.21MM **Privately Held**
Web: www.aemcnc.com
SIC: 3599 Machine shop, jobbing and repair

(G-10357)
CROWN CREDIT COMPANY
44 S Washington St (45869-1288)
P.O. Box 640352 (45264-0352)
PHONE................................419 629-2311
James Dicke Iii, *Pr*
EMP: 17 EST: 1980
SQ FT: 2,492
SALES (est): 4.5MM
SALES (corp-wide): 7.12B **Privately Held**
SIC: 3537 Lift trucks, industrial: fork,
platform, straddle, etc.
PA: Crown Equipment Corporation
44 S Washington St
New Bremen OH 45869
419 629-2311

(G-10358)
CROWN EQUIPMENT CORPORATION (PA)
Also Called: Crown Lift Trucks
44 S Washington St (45869-1288)
PHONE................................419 629-2311
James F Dicke Ii, *Ch*
James F Dicke Iii, *Pr*
Craig D Seitz, *VP*
Bradley L Smith, *Asst Tr*
John Tate, *Sr VP*
◆ EMP: 5434 EST: 1947
SQ FT: 25,000
SALES (est): 7.12B
SALES (corp-wide): 7.12B **Privately Held**
Web: www.crown.com

(G-10359)
CROWN EQUIPMENT CORPORATION
Also Called: Crown Lift Trucks
624 W Monroe St (45869-1351)
PHONE................................419 629-2311
David Obringer, *Brnch Mgr*
EMP: 21
SALES (corp-wide): 7.12B **Privately Held**
Web: www.crown.com
SIC: 3537 Lift trucks, industrial: fork,
platform, straddle, etc.
PA: Crown Equipment Corporation
44 S Washington St
New Bremen OH 45869
419 629-2311

(G-10360)
CROWN EQUIPMENT CORPORATION
Also Called: Crown Lift Trucks
510 W Monroe St (45869-1300)
PHONE................................419 629-2311
EMP: 25
SALES (corp-wide): 7.12B **Privately Held**
Web: www.crown.com
SIC: 3537 Lift trucks, industrial: fork,
platform, straddle, etc.
PA: Crown Equipment Corporation
44 S Washington St
New Bremen OH 45869
419 629-2311

(G-10361)
KINNINGER PROD WLDG CO INC
710 Kuenzel Dr (45869-9699)
P.O. Box 33 (45869-0033)
PHONE................................419 629-3491
Kevin Thobe, *Pr*
Cheryl Thobe, *
Donna Thobe, *
EMP: 53 EST: 1966
SQ FT: 54,000
SALES (est): 2.3MM **Privately Held**
Web: www.kinningerwelding.com
SIC: 7692 Welding repair

(G-10362)
MARKETING ESSENTIALS LLC
14 N Washington St (45869-1150)
P.O. Box 114 (45869-0114)
PHONE................................419 629-0080
EMP: 50 EST: 2009
SALES (est): 460.52K **Privately Held**
Web: www.mktgessentials.com
SIC: 8743 2741 2721 2711 Public relations
and publicity; Internet publishing and
broadcasting; Magazines: publishing only,
not printed on site; Newspapers: publishing
only, not printed on site

(G-10363)
NEW BREMEN MACHINE & TOOL CO
705 Kuenzel Dr (45869-8600)
P.O. Box 22 (45885)
PHONE................................419 629-3295
Joan Leffel, *CEO*
Jay Bergman, *
Randy Bergman, *
Robert Roth, *
EMP: 25 EST: 1928
SQ FT: 45,000
SALES (est): 4.12MM **Privately Held**
Web: www.newbremenmachine.com
SIC: 3469 3544 Metal stampings, nec;
Special dies and tools

(G-10364)
NUPCO INC
06561 County Road 66a (45869-9800)
PHONE................................419 629-2259
Luke Wilker, *Pr*
Virginia Dickie, *VP*
EMP: 6 EST: 1946
SQ FT: 3,750
SALES (est): 1.93MM **Privately Held**
Web: www.nupcoplastictubing.com
SIC: 3084 Plastics pipe

(G-10365)
PRECISION REFLEX INC
710 Streine Dr (45869-8608)
P.O. Box 95 (45869-0095)
PHONE................................419 629-2603
N David Dunlap, *Pr*
Mary Dunlap, *Sec*
EMP: 6 EST: 1978
SQ FT: 2,100
SALES (est): 963.62K **Privately Held**
Web: www.precisionreflex.com
SIC: 3599 2796 7692 Machine shop, jobbing
and repair; Engraving on copper, steel,
wood, or rubber: printing plates; Welding
repair

(G-10366)
SAFEWAY PACKAGING INC (PA)
300 White Mountain Dr (45869-8621)
PHONE................................419 629-3200
Kevin Manor, *Pr*
Ralph Stoner, *
EMP: 29 EST: 1984
SQ FT: 100,000
SALES (est): 18.29MM
SALES (corp-wide): 18.29MM **Privately
Held**
Web: www.opuspkg.com
SIC: 2653 2673 2671 2631 Boxes,
corrugated: made from purchased materials
; Bags: plastic, laminated, and coated;
Paper; coated and laminated packaging;
Paperboard mills

(G-10367)
THIEMAN QUALITY METAL FAB INC
05140 Dicke Rd (45869-9750)
P.O. Box 45 (45869-0045)
PHONE................................419 629-2612
Terry Marsee, *Contrlr*
EMP: 80 EST: 1951
SQ FT: 90,000
SALES (est): 9.79MM **Privately Held**
Web: www.thieman.com
SIC: 3441 Fabricated structural metal

(G-10368)
VISIONMARK NAMEPLATE CO LLC
100 White Mountain Dr (45869-8626)
P.O. Box 280 (45871-0280)
PHONE................................419 977-3131
Jerry Merges, *Pr*
Mark Nolan, *
EMP: 27 EST: 2014
SQ FT: 20,000
SALES (est): 2.45MM **Privately Held**
Web: www.vmnameplate.com
SIC: 3479 Name plates: engraved, etched,
etc.

New Carlisle
Clark County

(G-10369)
CARLISLE PLASTICS COMPANY
320 Ohio Ave (45344-1630)
P.O. Box 146 (45344-0146)
PHONE................................937 845-9411
Cynthia A Thomas, *Pr*
James Thomas, *Sec*
EMP: 7 EST: 1958
SQ FT: 12,000
SALES (est): 511.06K **Privately Held**
Web: www.carlisleplastics.com
SIC: 2821 3089 Polyvinyl chloride resins,
PVC; Injection molding of plastics

(G-10370)
CUSTOM THREADING SYSTEMS LLC
Also Called: A Plus Machining & Tooling
1833 N Dayton Lakeview Rd (45344-9501)
PHONE................................937 846-1405
EMP: 7 EST: 2007
SALES (est): 779.93K **Privately Held**
SIC: 3554 Paper industries machinery

(G-10371)
HIGH TECH CASTINGS
12170 Milton Carlisle Rd (45344-9701)
P.O. Box 486 (45344-0486)
PHONE................................937 845-1204
Stephanie Partlow, *Prin*
EMP: 9 EST: 2012
SALES (est): 2.11MM **Privately Held**
Web: www.htc-inc.com
SIC: 3366 Copper foundries

(G-10372)
HTCI CO
12170 Milton Carlisle Rd (45344-9701)
P.O. Box 486 (45344-0486)
PHONE................................937 845-1204
Kevin King, *Pr*
Deborah Jenkins, *Sec*
EMP: 18 EST: 2003
SALES (est): 5.73MM **Privately Held**
Web: www.htc-inc.com
SIC: 3365 Aerospace castings, aluminum

(G-10373)
KAFFENBARGER TRUCK EQP CO (PA)
10991 Ballentine Pike (45344-9533)
PHONE................................937 845-3804
Larry Kaffenbarger, *Pr*
Edward W Dunn, *
Everett L Kaffenbarger, *
◆ EMP: 110 EST: 1961
SALES (est): 22.65MM
SALES (corp-wide): 22.65MM **Privately
Held**
Web: www.knapheide.com
SIC: 3713 5013 Truck bodies (motor
vehicles); Truck parts and accessories

(G-10374)
KRAM PRECISION MACHINING INC
1751 Dalton Dr (45344-2309)
PHONE................................937 849-1301
Greg Flory, *Pr*
Douglas Flory, *Treas*
▲ EMP: 6 EST: 1984
SQ FT: 6,000
SALES (est): 242.59K **Privately Held**
Web: www.kramprecision.com
SIC: 3599 Machine shop, jobbing and repair

(G-10375)
MAD RIVER STEEL LTD
Also Called: Mad River Steel Company
2141 N Dayton Lakeview Rd (45344-9578)
P.O. Box 411 (45344-0411)
PHONE................................937 845-4046
John Bobo, *Pr*
EMP: 8 EST: 1994
SQ FT: 10,200

2025 Harris Ohio
Industrial Directory

▲ = Import ▼ = Export
◆ = Import/Export

SALES (est): 1.06MM **Privately Held**
SIC: 3441 Building components, structural steel

(G-10376)
NCT TECHNOLOGIES GROUP INC (PA)
Also Called: Nct Technologies Group
7867 W National Rd (45344-8268)
P.O. Box 37 (45344-0037)
PHONE....................937 882-6800
Andrew Flora, *Pr*
Curtis Flora, *VP*
EMP: 13 **EST:** 1951
SQ FT: 7,500
SALES (est): 5.43MM
SALES (corp-wide): 5.43MM **Privately Held**
Web: www.ncttech.com
SIC: 3441 Fabricated structural metal

(G-10377)
NUMERICS UNLIMITED INC
1700 Dalton Dr (45344-2307)
PHONE....................937 849-0100
Wayne Atkins, *Pr*
EMP: 22 **EST:** 1970
SQ FT: 15,000
SALES (est): 2.35MM **Privately Held**
Web: www.numericsunlimited.com
SIC: 3544 Industrial molds

(G-10378)
PATTON ALUMINUM PRODUCTS INC
65 Quick Rd (45344-9253)
PHONE....................937 845-9404
Edward E Patton, *Pr*
EMP: 15 **EST:** 1965
SQ FT: 14,000
SALES (est): 2.12MM **Privately Held**
Web: www.pattonaluminum.com
SIC: 3354 3448 Shapes, extruded aluminum, nec; Screen enclosures

(G-10379)
PFI PRECISION INC
Also Called: Pfi Precision Machining
2011 N Dayton Lakeview Rd (45344-9550)
PHONE....................937 845-3563
Colleen Janek, *Pr*
▲ **EMP:** 30 **EST:** 1966
SQ FT: 16,000
SALES (est): 6.29MM **Privately Held**
Web: www.pfiprecision.com
SIC: 3451 Screw machine products

(G-10380)
STONYRIDGE INC
570 S Dayton Lakeview Rd (45344-2129)
PHONE....................937 845-9482
James B Gastineau, *Pr*
Kathy K Abney, *Sec*
EMP: 10 **EST:** 1984
SQ FT: 2,000
SALES (est): 392.52K **Privately Held**
Web: www.stonyridge.com
SIC: 6531 6552 3089 Real estate brokers and agents; Subdividers and developers, nec; Plastics hardware and building products

(G-10381)
TAYLOR TOOL & DIE INC
306 N Main St (45344-1839)
PHONE....................937 845-1491
Michael L Taylor, *Pr*
Jim Elrod, *VP*
Vern Young, *Sec*
EMP: 7 **EST:** 1982
SQ FT: 3,900
SALES (est): 1.7MM **Privately Held**

Web: www.taylortoolanddie.com
SIC: 3544 Special dies and tools

(G-10382)
TETRA MOLD & TOOL INC
51 Quick Rd (45344-9294)
PHONE....................937 845-1651
Brent Hughes, *Pr*
Ronald L Hughes, *
Arleen Hughes, *
EMP: 25 **EST:** 1966
SQ FT: 10,000
SALES (est): 8.24MM **Privately Held**
Web: www.tetramold.com
SIC: 3089 3544 3714 Injection molding of plastics; Special dies, tools, jigs, and fixtures; Motor vehicle parts and accessories

(G-10383)
VANSCOYK SHEET METAL CORP
475 Quick Rd (45344-9255)
PHONE....................937 845-0581
David Van Scoyk, *Pr*
Wilma Van Skoyk, *VP*
David Van Skoyk, *Sec*
EMP: 7 **EST:** 1960
SQ FT: 10,000
SALES (est): 946.74K **Privately Held**
Web: www.vanscoykssheetmetal.com
SIC: 3441 Fabricated structural metal

New Concord
Muskingum County

(G-10384)
3-B WELDING LTD
2580 Holmes Rd (43762-9537)
PHONE....................740 819-4329
Wilmer Knowlton Iii, *Managing Member*
EMP: 9 **EST:** 2001
SALES (est): 572.95K **Privately Held**
Web: www.3-bwelding.com
SIC: 7692 Welding repair

(G-10385)
CARBONLESS CUT SHEET FORMS INC
1948 John Glenn Hwy (43762-9485)
PHONE....................740 826-1700
Jason Killiany, *Pr*
EMP: 18 **EST:** 1991
SQ FT: 6,000
SALES (est): 2.29MM **Privately Held**
Web: www.cacsf.com
SIC: 2759 5722 Business forms: printing, nsk; Vacuum cleaners

(G-10386)
CERNER CORPORATION
Also Called: Resource Systems
140 S Friendship Dr (43762-9453)
PHONE....................740 826-7678
EMP: 76
SALES (corp-wide): 52.96B **Publicly Held**
Web: www.oracle.com
SIC: 7372 7371 Home entertainment computer software; Custom computer programming services
HQ: Cerner Corporation
8779 Hillcrest Rd
Kansas City MO 64138
816 221-1024

(G-10387)
TK GAS SERVICES INC
2303 John Glenn Hwy (43762-9310)
PHONE....................740 826-0303
Ted Korte, *Pr*

Jill Pattison, *
EMP: 50 **EST:** 1991
SQ FT: 4,000
SALES (est): 2.43MM **Privately Held**
Web: www.tkautoservice.com
SIC: 1389 4212 4213 Oil field services, nec; Local trucking, without storage; Trucking, except local

New Franklin
Summit County

(G-10388)
CLINTON MACHINE CO INC
6270 Van Buren Rd (44216-9743)
P.O. Box 280 (44216-0280)
PHONE....................330 882-2060
Joe Podnar, *CEO*
Delores C Gregory, *Prin*
John D Judge, *Prin*
Ashley Podnar, *Dir*
Mark Podnar, *Managing Member*
▲ **EMP:** 10 **EST:** 1969
SALES (est): 1.3MM **Privately Held**
Web: www.clintonmachineco.com
SIC: 3599 Machine shop, jobbing and repair

(G-10389)
G & J EXTRUSIONS INC
1580 Turkeyfoot Lake Rd (44203-4852)
P.O. Box 275 (49745-0275)
PHONE....................330 753-0162
Garry Dumbauld, *Pr*
Julie Dumbauld, *VP*
EMP: 6 **EST:** 1987
SQ FT: 10,000
SALES (est): 500.18K **Privately Held**
Web: www.gjextrude.com
SIC: 3089 Injection molding of plastics

(G-10390)
MARTINS STEEL FABRICATION INC
2115 Center Rd (44216-8807)
PHONE....................330 882-4311
Jason Darrah, *
Beverly Martin, *VP*
EMP: 20 **EST:** 1990
SQ FT: 6,000
SALES (est): 3.78MM **Privately Held**
Web: www.martins-steel.com
SIC: 3441 Fabricated structural metal

(G-10391)
OHIO PLASTICS & BELTING CO LLC
6140 Manchester Rd (44319-4615)
P.O. Box 593 (44028-0593)
PHONE....................330 882-6764
John David Satink, *Owner*
EMP: 6 **EST:** 1995
SALES (est): 218.88K **Privately Held**
Web: www.ohioplastics.us
SIC: 2821 Plastics materials and resins

(G-10392)
PHILLIPS MCH & STAMPING CORP
5290 S Main St (44319-4997)
PHONE....................330 882-6714
Wilda Phillips, *Pr*
Craig Phillips, *VP*
EMP: 8 **EST:** 1939
SQ FT: 16,000
SALES (est): 961.39K **Privately Held**
Web: www.phillipsstamping.com
SIC: 3469 3544 Stamping metal for the trade; Special dies and tools

(G-10393)
PORTABLE CRUSHING LLC
4237 State Park Dr (44319-3444)

PHONE....................330 618-5251
Timothy D Carr, *Prin*
EMP: 7 **EST:** 2013
SALES (est): 4.76MM **Privately Held**
SIC: 1442 Construction sand and gravel

(G-10394)
RUBBER ASSOCIATES INC
1522 Turkeyfoot Lake Rd (44203-4898)
PHONE....................330 745-2186
Eugene Fiocca, *Pr*
Ronald Allan, *
Kris Fiocca, *
◆ **EMP:** 100 **EST:** 1952
SQ FT: 76,000
SALES (est): 3.43MM **Privately Held**
Web: www.rubberassociates.com
SIC: 3069 Molded rubber products

(G-10395)
TEMPERATURE CONTROLS CO INC
5729 Dailey Rd (44319-5111)
P.O. Box 7665 (44306-0665)
PHONE....................330 773-6633
John Kerr, *Ch*
Robert J Kerr Senior, *Ch*
John Kerr, *Pr*
James Mc Clarnon, *VP*
Laura Kerr, *Sec*
EMP: 15 **EST:** 1952
SALES (est): 915.45K **Privately Held**
Web: www.tempcontrolco.com
SIC: 1711 7692 Mechanical contractor; Welding repair

New Hampshire
Auglaize County

(G-10396)
BETHEL ENGINEERING AND EQP INC
Also Called: Bethel Engineering
13830 Mcbeth Rd (45870)
P.O. Box 67 (45870-0067)
PHONE....................419 568-1100
David Whitaker, *Pr*
Kathy Whitaker, *
EMP: 35 **EST:** 1996
SQ FT: 51,000
SALES (est): 6.68MM **Privately Held**
Web: www.bethelengr.com
SIC: 3559 3441 Paint making machinery; Fabricated structural metal

New Holland
Pickaway County

(G-10397)
BEVERLY DOVE INC
43 E Front St (43145-9662)
P.O. Box 125 (43145-0125)
PHONE....................740 495-5200
John Berker, *Pr*
Beverly Berker, *VP*
EMP: 7 **EST:** 1993
SQ FT: 7,000
SALES (est): 565.06K **Privately Held**
Web: www.gutterhangers.net
SIC: 3469 3541 Metal stampings, nec; Machine tools, metal cutting type

GEOGRAPHIC

New Knoxville
Auglaize County

(G-10398)
HOGE LUMBER COMPANY (PA)
Also Called: Hoge Brush
701 S Main St State (45871)
PHONE..............................419 753-2263
John H Hoge, *Pr*
Bruce L Hoge, *
Clark T Froning, *
Jack R Hoge, *
▲ **EMP:** 34 **EST:** 1904
SQ FT: 400,000
SALES (est): 4.4MM
SALES (corp-wide): 4.4MM **Privately Held**
Web: www.hoge.com
SIC: 3448 1521 2521 Prefabricated metal
   buildings and components; New
   construction, single-family houses;
   Cabinets, office: wood

New Lebanon
Montgomery County

(G-10399)
B & B GEAR AND MACHINE CO INC
440 W Main St (45345-1426)
PHONE..............................937 687-1771
Jennifer Brinson, *Pr*
Kevin Brinson, *Pr*
Jennifer Brinson, *Owner*
EMP: 22 **EST:** 1976
SQ FT: 15,000
SALES (est): 4.93MM **Privately Held**
Web: www.bbgearmachine.com
SIC: 3566 3599 Gears, power transmission,
   except auto; Machine shop, jobbing and
   repair

(G-10400)
MARTIN WELDING LLC (PA)
1472 W Main St (45345-9772)
PHONE..............................937 687-3602
EMP: 10 **EST:** 1989
SALES (est): 1MM **Privately Held**
Web: www.martinwelding.com
SIC: 7692 Welding repair

New Lexington
Perry County

(G-10401)
**COOPER-STANDARD AUTOMOTIVE
INC**
Cooper
2378 State Route 345 Ne (43764-9617)
PHONE..............................740 342-3523
Mister B Dickens, *Brnch Mgr*
EMP: 83
SQ FT: 80,000
SALES (corp-wide): 2.73B **Publicly Held**
Web: www.cooperstandard.com
SIC: 3714 3443 Motor vehicle brake systems
   and parts; Heat exchangers, condensers,
   and components
HQ: Cooper-Standard Automotive Inc.
   40300 Traditions Dr
   Northville MI 48168
   248 596-5900

(G-10402)
HOCKING VALLEY CONCRETE INC
1500 Commerce Dr (43764-9432)
PHONE..............................740 342-1948
William Laughn, *Prin*

EMP: 8
SALES (corp-wide): 3.78MM **Privately
Held**
Web: www.hockingvalleyconcrete.com
SIC: 3273 Ready-mixed concrete
PA: Hocking Valley Concrete, Inc.
   35255 Hocking Dr
   Logan OH 43138
   740 385-2165

(G-10403)
LORI HOLDING CO (PA)
Also Called: Siemer Distributing
1400 Commerce Dr (43764-9500)
PHONE..............................740 342-3230
Joseph A Siemer Iii, *Pr*
EMP: 30 **EST:** 1980
SALES (est): 2.53MM
SALES (corp-wide): 2.53MM **Privately
Held**
Web: www.siemermeats.com
SIC: 5147 5143 5199 5142 Meats, fresh;
   Cheese; Ice, manufactured or natural;
   Packaged frozen goods

(G-10404)
LUDOWICI ROOF TILE INC
4757 Tile Plant Rd Se (43764-9630)
P.O. Box 69 (43764-0069)
PHONE..............................740 342-1995
Herve Gastinel, *Pr*
Guillaume Latil, *
◆ **EMP:** 80 **EST:** 1989
SQ FT: 100,000
SALES (est): 21.07MM
SALES (corp-wide): 4.59B **Privately Held**
Web: www.ludowici.com
SIC: 3272 Concrete products, nec
HQ: Terreal
   13-17
   Suresnes IDF 92150

(G-10405)
PERRY COUNTY TRIBUNE
Also Called: Tribune Shopping News, The
399 Lincoln Park Dr Ste A (43764-1078)
P.O. Box 312 (43764-0312)
PHONE..............................740 342-4121
Deb Hutmire, *Genl Mgr*
EMP: 10 **EST:** 1975
SALES (est): 105.61K **Privately Held**
Web: www.perrytribune.com
SIC: 2711 6512 Newspapers, publishing and
   printing; Property operation, retail
   establishment

(G-10406)
R & D HILLTOP LUMBER INC
2126 State Route 93 Se (43764-9666)
PHONE..............................740 342-3051
Russell Howdyshell, *Pr*
Polly Howdyshell, *VP*
EMP: 25 **EST:** 1952
SQ FT: 8,000
SALES (est): 2.48MM **Privately Held**
Web: www.rdhilltoplumber.com
SIC: 2421 Lumber: rough, sawed, or planed

(G-10407)
**SOUTHEASTERN SHAFTING MFG
INC**
402 W Broadway St (43764-1007)
P.O. Box 168 (43764-0168)
PHONE..............................740 342-4629
Scott Jones Senior, *Pr*
Theresa M Jones, *Sec*
EMP: 18 **EST:** 1983
SALES (est): 2.27MM **Privately Held**
Web: www.seshafting.com

SIC: 3568 3599 Collars, shaft (power
   transmission equipment); Machine shop,
   jobbing and repair

(G-10408)
STAR ENGINEERING LLC ✪
701 Madison St (43764-1086)
P.O. Box 71 (43764-0071)
PHONE..............................740 342-3514
Bill Mooney, *CEO*
Christopher Mooney, *
William J Mooney, *
Daniel P Mooney, *
John Mooney, *
EMP: 35 **EST:** 2024
SQ FT: 36,000
SALES (est): 10.98MM **Privately Held**
Web: www.starengineering.com
SIC: 3567 Ceramic kilns and furnaces

(G-10409)
TERREAL NORTH AMERICA LLC
4757 Tile Plant Rd Se (43764-9630)
P.O. Box 309 (43764-0309)
PHONE..............................888 582-9052
Herve Gastinel, *Managing Member*
EMP: 175 **EST:** 2007
SALES (est): 785.42K **Privately Held**
Web: www.terrealna.com
SIC: 3259 Roofing tile, clay

New London
Huron County

(G-10410)
APPLIED AUTOMATION ENTP INC
24 Cedar St (44851-1218)
PHONE..............................419 929-2428
Timothy Hedrick, *Pr*
Vaughn Lucal, *Treas*
Stephan Pabst, *Sec*
EMP: 16 **EST:** 2000
SQ FT: 15,000
SALES (est): 2.9MM **Privately Held**
Web: www.automationent.com
SIC: 3541 Chucking machines, automatic

(G-10411)
FIRELANDS FABRICATION
201 N Main St (44851-1015)
PHONE..............................419 929-0680
EMP: 10 **EST:** 2013
SALES (est): 2.55MM **Privately Held**
Web: www.firelandsfab.com
SIC: 3441 Fabricated structural metal

(G-10412)
KENT WATER SPORTS LLC (PA)
Also Called: Kent Outdoors
433 Park Ave (44851-1177)
PHONE..............................419 929-7021
Ken Meidell, *CEO*
J Robert Tipton, *
John Clark, *
Brian Zaletel, *
Marlene Sipp, *
▲ **EMP:** 100 **EST:** 1959
SQ FT: 25,000
SALES (est): 92.97MM
SALES (corp-wide): 92.97MM **Privately
Held**
Web: www.kentoutdoors.com
SIC: 3949 Water sports equipment

(G-10413)
MONODE MARKING PRODUCTS INC
Also Called: Waldorf Marking Devices
149 High St (44851-1118)
PHONE..............................419 929-0346

Thomas Mackey, *Pr*
EMP: 10
SALES (corp-wide): 9.29MM **Privately
Held**
Web: www.monode.com
SIC: 3542 3953 Marking machines; Marking
   devices
PA: Monode Marking Products, Inc.
   9200 Tyler Blvd
   Mentor OH 44060
   440 975-8802

(G-10414)
RANKIN MFG INC
201 N Main St (44851-1015)
PHONE..............................419 929-8338
Eric Rankine, *Pr*
Michael Rankine, *Sec*
EMP: 9 **EST:** 1987
SQ FT: 52,500
SALES (est): 789.03K **Privately Held**
SIC: 3441 3799 3599 Fabricated structural
   metal; Trailers and trailer equipment;
   Machine and other job shop work

(G-10415)
ROERIG MACHINE
27348 State Route 511 (44851-9667)
PHONE..............................440 647-4718
William Roerig, *Pt*
Ron Roerig, *Pt*
EMP: 6 **EST:** 1986
SALES (est): 233K **Privately Held**
SIC: 3599 Machine shop, jobbing and repair

(G-10416)
SDG NEWS GROUP INC
Also Called: Firelands Farmer, The
43 E Main St (44851-1213)
P.O. Box 647 (44875-0647)
PHONE..............................419 929-3411
Scott Glove, *Pr*
Scott Gove, *Pr*
EMP: 10 **EST:** 1970
SALES (est): 93.5K **Privately Held**
Web: www.sdgnewsgroup.com
SIC: 2711 2752 Newspapers: publishing
   only, not printed on site; Commercial
   printing, lithographic

(G-10417)
THOMAS CREATIVE APPAREL INC
1 Harmony Pl (44851-1248)
PHONE..............................419 929-1506
Vickie Hall, *Pr*
EMP: 6 **EST:** 1972
SQ FT: 14,000
SALES (est): 779.16K **Privately Held**
Web: www.thomasrobes.com
SIC: 2384 2389 2353 Robes and dressing
   gowns; Lodge costumes; Hats, caps, and
   millinery

(G-10418)
**TIERRA-DERCO INTERNATIONAL
LLC**
40 S Main St (44851-1138)
PHONE..............................419 929-2240
Heath White, *Mgr*
EMP: 7
Web: www.tdibrands.com
SIC: 3524 Lawn and garden equipment
PA: Tierra-Derco International, Llc
   1000 S St Charles St
   Jasper IN 47546

(G-10419)
TIP PRODUCTS INC
106 Industrial Dr (44851-9111)
PHONE..............................216 252-2535
Dave Finley, *CEO*

Rhonda Gielow, *
Michelle Pellerin, *
EMP: 23 **EST:** 1965
SQ FT: 10,000
SALES (est): 2.17MM **Privately Held**
Web: www.tipproducts.com
SIC: 3643 3699 Cord connectors, electric;
Electrical equipment and supplies, nec

New Madison
Darke County

(G-10420)
ERNIE GREEN INDUSTRIES INC
Also Called: Eg Industries
1855 State Rd Ste 121n (45346)
PHONE..............................614 219-1423
EMP: 30
SALES (corp-wide): 86.16MM **Privately
Held**
Web: www.epcmfg.com
SIC: 3714 Motor vehicle wheels and parts
PA: Ernie Green Industries, Inc.
1785 Big Hill Rd
Dayton OH 45439
614 219-1423

(G-10421)
FLORIDA PRODUCTION ENGRG INC
Ernie Green Industries
1855 State Route 121 N (45346-9716)
PHONE..............................937 996-4361
Eric Opicka, *Mgr*
EMP: 90
SALES (corp-wide): 86.16MM **Privately
Held**
SIC: 3465 3714 3429 Moldings or trim,
automobile: stamped metal; Motor vehicle
parts and accessories; Hardware, nec
HQ: Florida Production Engineering, Inc.
2 E Tower Cir
Ormond Beach FL 32174
386 677-2566

(G-10422)
**LUDY GREENHOUSE MFG CORP
(PA)**
122 Railroad St (45346-5016)
P.O. Box 141 (45346-0141)
PHONE..............................800 255-5839
Stephan A Scantland, *Pr*
Deborah Scantland, *
EMP: 58 **EST:** 1957
SQ FT: 2,500
SALES (est): 2.59MM
SALES (corp-wide): 2.59MM **Privately
Held**
Web: www.ludy.com
SIC: 1542 3448 Greenhouse construction;
Greenhouses, prefabricated metal

New Matamoras
Washington County

(G-10423)
**CREIGHTON SPORTS CENTER INC
(PA)**
205 Broadway Ave (45767-1193)
P.O. Box 400 (45767-0400)
PHONE..............................740 865-2521
Bill Creighton, *Pr*
Chris Creighton, *VP*
Pam Creighton, *Sec*
EMP: 7 **EST:** 1984
SQ FT: 2,400
SALES (est): 244.13K
SALES (corp-wide): 244.13K **Privately
Held**

SIC: 3949 Sporting and athletic goods, nec

New Middletown
Mahoning County

(G-10424)
HITCH-HIKER MFG INC
10065 Rapp Rd (44442-9753)
PHONE..............................330 542-3052
Jeffrey Swartz, *Pr*
Holly Swartz, *VP*
EMP: 11 **EST:** 1973
SQ FT: 38,000
SALES (est): 2.17MM **Privately Held**
Web: www.hitch-hikermfg.com
SIC: 3799 Boat trailers

New Paris
Preble County

(G-10425)
ARNETT TOOL INC
217 W Main St (45347-1109)
P.O. Box 40 (45347-0040)
PHONE..............................937 437-0361
M James Arnett, *Pr*
Leatrice J Arnett, *Sec*
EMP: 7 **EST:** 1979
SQ FT: 4,800
SALES (est): 323.08K **Privately Held**
SIC: 3544 Special dies and tools

(G-10426)
DYNAMIC PLASTICS INC
Also Called: H & H Sailcraft
8207 H W Rd (45347-9241)
PHONE..............................937 437-7261
Paul Hemker, *Pr*
Heide Hemker, *Sec*
EMP: 8 **EST:** 1969
SQ FT: 20,000
SALES (est): 463.49K **Privately Held**
Web:
dynamicplasticsinc.centurylinksite.net
SIC: 3089 3732 3531 5551 Injection molding
of plastics; Sailboats, building and repairing
; Construction machinery; Boat dealers

(G-10427)
TRUCKS & PARTS OF TAMPA LLC
Also Called: Truck & Parts of Ohio
9206 Us Route 40 W (45347-1537)
P.O. Box 2 (45314-0002)
PHONE..............................937 437-0377
TOLL FREE: 800
Paul Guhl, *Brnch Mgr*
EMP: 25
SALES (corp-wide): 21.23MM **Privately
Held**
Web: www.trucksandparts.com
SIC: 5521 5531 3714 3713 Pickups and
vans, used; Truck equipment and parts;
Motor vehicle parts and accessories; Truck
and bus bodies
PA: Trucks & Parts Of Tampa, Llc
1015 S 50th St
Tampa FL 33619
813 247-6637

New Philadelphia
Tuscarawas County

(G-10428)
1914 MI INC
Marsh Chalk Board Co Div
1117 Bowers Ave Nw (44663-4129)

P.O. Box 1000 (44663-5100)
PHONE..............................330 308-8667
Brian Marsh, *Mgr*
EMP: 32
SALES (corp-wide): 7.5MM **Privately Held**
Web:
www.asi-visualdisplayproducts.com
SIC: 2431 5211 5943 3281 Millwork; Planing
mill products and lumber; School supplies;
Cut stone and stone products
PA: 1914 Mi, Inc.
2301 E High Ave
New Philadelphia OH 44663
800 426-4244

(G-10429)
1914 MI INC (PA)
2301 E High Ave (44663-3327)
P.O. Box 1000 (44663-5100)
PHONE..............................800 426-4244
▲ **EMP:** 68 **EST:** 1914
SALES (est): 7.5MM
SALES (corp-wide): 7.5MM **Privately Held**
Web:
www.asi-visualdisplayproducts.com
SIC: 2431 2531 2493 Trim, wood;
Blackboards, wood; Bulletin boards, wood

(G-10430)
AQUABLUE INCORPORATED
1776 Tech Park Dr Ne (44663-9410)
P.O. Box 446 (44663-0446)
PHONE..............................330 343-0220
Don Whittingham, *Pr*
EMP: 8 **EST:** 2005
SALES (est): 531.5K **Privately Held**
Web: www.aquabluechemical.com
SIC: 2899 5169 Water treating compounds;
Chemicals and allied products, nec

(G-10431)
ASI VISUAL DISPLAY PDTS INC ✪
Also Called: A S I
2301 E High Ave (44663-3327)
PHONE..............................330 308-8667
Petter Rolla, *Pr*
EMP: 25 **EST:** 2024
SALES (est): 6.33MM **Privately Held**
Web: www.asigroup.us
SIC: 3993 Signs and advertising specialties

(G-10432)
BATTLE MOTORS INC
1061 Reiser Ave Se (44663-3348)
PHONE..............................888 328-5443
Michael W Patterson, *CEO*
Oliver F Weilandt, *
Jill Cilmi, *
EMP: 126 **EST:** 2020
SALES (est): 27.38MM **Privately Held**
Web: www.cranecarrier.com
SIC: 3621 5999 Motors and generators;
Engine and motor equipment and supplies

(G-10433)
**BROWN WOOD PRODUCTS
COMPANY**
7783 Crooked Run Rd Sw (44663-6411)
PHONE..............................330 339-8000
Todd Dennison, *Mgr*
EMP: 8
SALES (corp-wide): 4.1MM **Privately Held**
Web: www.brownwoodinc.com
SIC: 2499 Decorative wood and woodwork
PA: Brown Wood Products Company
7040 N Lawndale Ave
Lincolnwood IL 60712
847 673-4780

(G-10434)
BULK CARRIER TRNSP EQP CO
2743 Brightwood Rd Se (44663-6773)
PHONE..............................330 339-3333
Richard S Hartrick, *Pr*
Marcia Hartrick, *
EMP: 7 **EST:** 1976
SALES (est): 943.43K **Privately Held**
Web: www.bcte.com
SIC: 5012 2519 Trailers for trucks, new and
used; Household furniture, except wood or
metal: upholstered

(G-10435)
BULK CARRIERS SERVICE INC
Also Called: Bcte
2743 Brightwood Rd Se (44663-6773)
PHONE..............................330 339-3333
Richard Hartrick, *Pr*
Doug Milburn, *VP*
EMP: 7 **EST:** 1995
SALES (est): 861.12K **Privately Held**
Web: www.bcte.com
SIC: 3799 4789 5084 Recreational vehicles;
Passenger train services; Engines and
transportation equipment

(G-10436)
CASTINGS USA INC
2061 Brightwood Rd Se (44663-7724)
P.O. Box 202 (44653-0202)
PHONE..............................330 339-3611
Gregory M Dean, *Pr*
Terry Yahard, *Sec*
EMP: 7 **EST:** 1974
SQ FT: 8,000
SALES (est): 2.29MM **Privately Held**
Web: www.reymondproducts.com
SIC: 3321 3325 Gray iron castings, nec;
Steel foundries, nec

(G-10437)
CHEMSPEC LTD
419 Tuscarawas Ave Nw (44663-1538)
PHONE..............................330 364-4422
EMP: 18
SALES (corp-wide): 166.77K **Privately
Held**
Web: www.safic-alcan.com
SIC: 2891 Adhesives and sealants
HQ: Chemspec, Ltd.
4450 Blden Vlg St Nw Ste
Canton OH 44718
330 896-0355

(G-10438)
COOPER-STANDARD HOLDINGS INC
1776 Tech Park Dr Ne Ste 221
(44663-9410)
PHONE..............................800 683-0676
EMP: 7
SALES (corp-wide): 2.73B **Publicly Held**
Web: www.cooperstandard.com
SIC: 3069 Molded rubber products
PA: Cooper-Standard Holdings Inc.
40300 Traditions Dr
Northville MI 48168
248 596-5900

(G-10439)
COPLEY OHIO NEWSPAPERS INC
Also Called: Times Reporter/Midwest Offset
629 Wabash Ave Nw (44663-4145)
P.O. Box 9901 (44711-0901)
PHONE..............................330 364-5577
Kevin Kampman, *Publisher*
EMP: 183
SALES (corp-wide): 2.51B **Publicly Held**
Web: www.cantonrep.com

SIC: 2711 2752 7313 2791 Commercial printing and newspaper publishing combined; Offset printing; Newspaper advertising representative; Typesetting
HQ: Copley Ohio Newspapers Inc
500 Market Ave S
Canton OH 44702
585 598-0030

(G-10440)
CRANE CARRIER COMPANY LLC (HQ)
1951 Reiser Ave Se (44663-3348)
PHONE..............................918 286-2889
Randy Rollins, *Pr*
EMP: 145 **EST:** 1973
SALES (est): 53.5MM
SALES (corp-wide): 53.5MM **Privately Held**
Web: www.battlemotors.com
SIC: 5013 3713 Truck parts and accessories ; Truck bodies and parts
PA: Battle Motors, Inc.
612 Hampton Dr Ste B
Venice CA 90291
562 536-3614

(G-10441)
CRANE CARRIER HOLDINGS LLC
1951 Reiser Ave Se (44663-3348)
PHONE..............................918 286-2889
EMP: 150 **EST:** 2018
Web: www.cranecarrier.com
SIC: 6719 5013 3713 Investment holding companies, except banks; Truck parts and accessories; Truck bodies and parts

(G-10442)
DENNEY PLASTICS MACHINING LLC
149 Stonecreek Rd Nw (44663-6902)
PHONE..............................330 308-5300
EMP: 24 **EST:** 1988
SALES (est): 4.83MM **Privately Held**
Web: www.denneyplastics.com
SIC: 3089 Injection molding of plastics

(G-10443)
DRJ WELDING SERVICES LLC
936 Front Ave Sw (44663-2090)
PHONE..............................740 229-7428
Dillon Cox, *Prin*
EMP: 6 **EST:** 2017
SALES (est): 943.75K **Privately Held**
SIC: 7692 Welding repair

(G-10444)
ELLIS LAUNDRY AND LIN SUP INC
213 8th Street Ext Sw (44663-2088)
PHONE..............................330 339-4941
Katherine Ellis, *Pr*
Jerry Ellis, *Sec*
EMP: 6 **EST:** 2003
SALES (est): 506.83K **Privately Held**
SIC: 3582 Ironers, commercial laundry and drycleaning

(G-10445)
FENTON BROS ELECTRIC CO
Also Called: Fenton's Festival of Lights
235 Ray Ave Ne (44663-2813)
P.O. Box 996 (44663-0996)
PHONE..............................330 343-0093
Tom Fenton, *Pr*
Dennis Fenton, *
Chris Fenton, *
Brian Fenton, *
Harold E Fenton, *Stockholder**
EMP: 30 **EST:** 1947
SQ FT: 37,000
SALES (est): 10.81MM **Privately Held**
Web: www.fentonbrotherselectric.com

SIC: 5063 7694 Electrical supplies, nec; Electric motor repair

(G-10446)
FRANTZ GRINDING CO
1879 E High Ave (44663-3238)
P.O. Box 408 (44663-0408)
PHONE..............................330 343-8689
Joe M Frantz, *Pr*
Kay Frantz, *Sec*
EMP: 6 **EST:** 1946
SQ FT: 11,400
SALES (est): 650.34K **Privately Held**
SIC: 3599 Machine shop, jobbing and repair

(G-10447)
FREEPORT PRESS INC (PA)
2127 Reiser Ave Se (44663-3331)
P.O. Box 198 (43973-0198)
PHONE..............................330 308-3300
David G Pilcher, *Pr*
EMP: 149 **EST:** 1880
SQ FT: 36,000
SALES (est): 52.88MM
SALES (corp-wide): 52.88MM **Privately Held**
Web: www.freeportpress.com
SIC: 2752 Offset printing

(G-10448)
GRADALL INDUSTRIES LLC (DH)
Also Called: Gradall
406 Mill Ave Sw (44663-3870)
PHONE..............................330 339-2211
Joseph H Keller, *
Daniel Kaltenbaugh, *
▲ **EMP:** 87 **EST:** 1992
SQ FT: 429,320
SALES (est): 55.71MM
SALES (corp-wide): 1.63B **Publicly Held**
Web: www.gradall.com
SIC: 3537 3531 Industrial trucks and tractors ; Construction machinery
HQ: Alamo Group (Usa) Inc.
1627 East Walnut Street
Seguin TX 78155
830 379-1480

(G-10449)
HYDRAULIC PARTS STORE INC
145 1st Dr Ne (44663-2857)
P.O. Box 808 (44663-0808)
PHONE..............................330 364-6667
Robert M Henning Senior, *Pr*
EMP: 6 **EST:** 1983
SQ FT: 25,000
SALES (est): 526.85K **Privately Held**
SIC: 5084 3594 3593 3492 Hydraulic systems equipment and supplies; Fluid power pumps and motors; Fluid power cylinders and actuators; Fluid power valves and hose fittings

(G-10450)
J & D MINING INC
3497 University Dr Ne (44663-6711)
PHONE..............................330 339-4935
John R Demuth, *Pr*
James R Demuth, *
EMP: 6 **EST:** 1981
SQ FT: 1,000
SALES (est): 352.73K **Privately Held**
SIC: 1221 Bituminous coal surface mining

(G-10451)
KAY-ZEE INC
1279 Crestview Ave Sw (44663-9642)
P.O. Box 95 (44663-0095)
PHONE..............................330 339-1268
John Stratton, *Pr*
Kathryn Stratton, *VP*

EMP: 7 **EST:** 1962
SALES (est): 853.66K **Privately Held**
Web: www.kayzeeinc.net
SIC: 3861 Lens shades, camera

(G-10452)
KIMBLE CUSTOM CHASSIS COMPANY
Also Called: Kimble Manufacturing Company
1951 Reiser Ave Se (44663-3348)
PHONE..............................877 546-2537
James C Cahill, *Pr*
Jim Moberg, *
Gregory Stohler, *
Philip Keegan, *
Brian Shepherd, *
▲ **EMP:** 100 **EST:** 2006
SQ FT: 100,000
SALES (est): 9.35MM
SALES (corp-wide): 97.77MM **Privately Held**
SIC: 3713 Truck bodies and parts
PA: Hines Corporation
1218 E Pontaluna Rd Ste B
Spring Lake MI 49456
231 799-6240

(G-10453)
KIMBLE MIXER COMPANY
Also Called: Hines Specialty Vehicle Group
1951 Reiser Ave Se (44663-3348)
PHONE..............................330 308-6700
James C Cahill, *Pr*
Scott Johnson, *
▲ **EMP:** 75 **EST:** 1995
SQ FT: 100,000
SALES (est): 22.68MM
SALES (corp-wide): 97.77MM **Privately Held**
SIC: 3713 Cement mixer bodies
PA: Hines Corporation
1218 E Pontaluna Rd Ste B
Spring Lake MI 49456
231 799-6240

(G-10454)
LAUREN INTERNATIONAL LTD (PA)
143 Garland Dr Sw (44663-6300)
PHONE..............................234 303-2400
Kevin E Gray, *Pr*
David Gingrich, *
◆ **EMP:** 200 **EST:** 1965
SALES (est): 24.6MM
SALES (corp-wide): 24.6MM **Privately Held**
Web: www.laureninternational.com
SIC: 3069 Molded rubber products

(G-10455)
LAUREN MANUFACTURING
2228 Reiser Ave Se (44663-3345)
PHONE..............................330 339-3373
EMP: 83 **EST:** 2019
SALES (est): 5.34MM **Privately Held**
Web: www.cooperstandard.com
SIC: 3999 Manufacturing industries, nec

(G-10456)
M R TRAILER SALES INC
1565 Steele Hill Rd Nw (44663-6503)
P.O. Box 562 (44622-0562)
PHONE..............................330 339-7701
Roger Rostad, *Pr*
Sharon Rostad, *Pr*
Don Rostad, *Dir*
Roger Rostad, *VP*
EMP: 8 **EST:** 1993
SALES (est): 431.1K **Privately Held**
Web: www.mrtrailersales.com

SIC: 5012 5599 3441 3715 Trailers for passenger vehicles; Utility trailers; Fabricated structural metal; Trailers or vans for transporting horses

(G-10457)
MID-AMERICA PACKAGING LLC
2127 Reiser Ave Se (44663-3331)
PHONE..............................330 963-4199
▲ **EMP:** 650
SIC: 2674 Bags: uncoated paper and multiwall

(G-10458)
MILLER PRODUCTS INC
Also Called: Beech Engineering & Mfg
642 Wabash Ave Nw (44663-4146)
P.O. Box 947 (44663-0947)
PHONE..............................330 308-5934
Naomi Downend, *Genl Mgr*
EMP: 35
SALES (corp-wide): 70.41MM **Privately Held**
Web: www.mpilabels.com
SIC: 3537 3535 Industrial trucks and tractors ; Conveyors and conveying equipment
PA: Miller Products, Inc.
450 Courtney Rd
Sebring OH 44672
330 938-2134

(G-10459)
MILLER STUDIO INC
734 Fair Ave Nw (44663-1589)
P.O. Box 997 (44663-0997)
PHONE..............................330 339-1100
Naomi Downend, *Pr*
Jeff Miller, *
John A Basiletti, *
▲ **EMP:** 7 **EST:** 1934
SALES (est): 4.69MM
SALES (corp-wide): 70.41MM **Privately Held**
Web: www.miller-studio.com
SIC: 2672 3452 3429 Adhesive papers, labels, or tapes: from purchased material; Bolts, nuts, rivets, and washers; Hardware, nec
PA: Miller Products, Inc.
450 Courtney Rd
Sebring OH 44672
330 938-2134

(G-10460)
MPS MANUFACTURING COMPANY LLC
326 Pearl Ave Ne (44663-3918)
PHONE..............................330 343-1435
EMP: 6 **EST:** 2004
SALES (est): 1.19MM **Privately Held**
Web: www.mpsco.com
SIC: 3999 Barber and beauty shop equipment

(G-10461)
OAKTREE WIRELINE LLC
1825 E High Ave (44663-3280)
PHONE..............................330 352-7250
EMP: 9 **EST:** 2013
SQ FT: 3,000
SALES (est): 861.82K **Privately Held**
SIC: 1389 Well logging

(G-10462)
PRO A V OF OHIO
Also Called: Better Banner Printing
120 6th Dr Sw (44663-2020)
PHONE..............................877 812-5350
EMP: 6
SALES (est): 440.96K **Privately Held**
Web: www.proavofohio.com

SIC: 3993 Signs and advertising specialties

(G-10463)
R & J CYLINDER & MACHINE INC
464 Robinson Dr Se (44663-3336)
PHONE.....................330 364-8263
Ronald Sandy, *Pr*
Jeffrey Shepherd, *
Don Sandy, *Stockholder*
EMP: 53 **EST:** 1990
SQ FT: 33,500
SALES (est): 9.81MM **Privately Held**
Web: www.rjcylinder.com
SIC: 3593 3599 Fluid power cylinders, hydraulic or pneumatic; Machine and other job shop work

(G-10464)
REYMOND PRODUCTS INTL INC
2066 Brightwood Rd Se (44663-7724)
P.O. Box 202 (44653-0202)
PHONE.....................330 339-3583
Greg Dean, *Pr*
▲ **EMP:** 20 **EST:** 1948
SQ FT: 15,000
SALES (est): 3.17MM **Privately Held**
Web: www.reymondproducts.com
SIC: 3599 3544 Machine shop, jobbing and repair; Special dies, tools, jigs, and fixtures

(G-10465)
RICH INDUSTRIES INC
2384 Brightwood Rd Se (44663-6772)
PHONE.....................330 339-4113
Jeffrey Contini, *Pr*
William Arnold, *
Jeffrey Contini, *Ex VP*
Anthony Contini, *
Scott Trammell, *
▲ **EMP:** 50 **EST:** 1971
SQ FT: 28,000
SALES (est): 9.66MM **Privately Held**
Web: www.richindustriesinc.com
SIC: 2389 2393 2326 Disposable garments and accessories; Textile bags; Men's and boy's work clothing

(G-10466)
TGS INDUSTRIES INC
406 Mill Ave Sw (44663-3835)
PHONE.....................330 339-2211
▼ **EMP:** 33
SIC: 3531 Excavators: cable, clamshell, crane, derrick, dragline, etc.

(G-10467)
TOLLOTI PIPE LLC
102 Barnhill Rd Se (44663-8864)
P.O. Box 129 (44683-0129)
PHONE.....................330 364-6627
Kyle Miller, *Prin*
EMP: 11 **EST:** 2011
SALES (est): 3.61MM **Privately Held**
Web: www.zuwy.com
SIC: 3084 Plastics pipe

(G-10468)
TOLLOTI PLASTIC PIPE INC (PA)
102 Barnhill Rd Se (44663-8864)
P.O. Box 508 (44663-0508)
PHONE.....................330 364-6627
Theodore Tolloti, *Pr*
Doris Tolloti, *
John Tolloti, *
EMP: 38 **EST:** 1963
SQ FT: 5,000
SALES (est): 4.8MM
SALES (corp-wide): 4.8MM **Privately Held**
SIC: 3084 Plastics pipe

(G-10469)
UNDER PRESSURE SYSTEMS INC
322 North Ave Ne (44663-2714)
P.O. Box 266 (43021-0266)
PHONE.....................330 602-4466
Cynthia J Valentine, *Pr*
EMP: 9 **EST:** 1998
SQ FT: 10,000
SALES (est): 2.4MM **Privately Held**
Web: www.underpressuresystemsllc.com
SIC: 3589 Water treatment equipment, industrial

New Riegel
Seneca County

(G-10470)
JUNO ENTERPRISES LLC
Also Called: Lucius Fence and Decking
8146 Us Highway 224 (44853-9729)
PHONE.....................419 448-9350
EMP: 6 **EST:** 2020
SALES (est): 1.84MM **Privately Held**
SIC: 2499 Fencing, docks, and other outdoor wood structural products

(G-10471)
TR BOES HOLDINGS INC
Also Called: Boes, Wilbert J
14 N Perry St (44853-9776)
P.O. Box 237 (44853-0237)
PHONE.....................419 595-2255
Wilbert J Boes, *Pr*
Hildegarde Boes, *Prin*
Tom Boes, *VP*
Richard Boes, *Sec*
EMP: 12 **EST:** 1953
SQ FT: 4,500
SALES (est): 281.3K **Privately Held**
Web: www.newriegelcafe.com
SIC: 5812 2011 Barbecue restaurant; Meat packing plants

New Springfield
Mahoning County

(G-10472)
D & D MINING CO INC
3379 E Garfield Rd (44443-9743)
PHONE.....................330 549-0127
Donald Thompson, *Pr*
David Thompson, *VP*
EMP: 10 **EST:** 1972
SQ FT: 1,000
SALES (est): 239.1K **Privately Held**
SIC: 1221 Bituminous coal and lignite-surface mining

(G-10473)
EXTENDIT COMPANY
14150 Beaver Springfield Rd (44443-9773)
PHONE.....................330 743-4343
Henry M Garlick, *Pr*
EMP: 6 **EST:** 1966
SALES (est): 385.69K **Privately Held**
Web: www.extenditco.com
SIC: 2951 Asphalt paving mixtures and blocks

(G-10474)
THOMPSON BROS MINING CO
Also Called: Thompson Brothers Mining
3379 E Garfield Rd (44443-9743)
PHONE.....................330 549-3979
Don Thompson, *Pr*
Dave Thompson, *VP*
EMP: 10 **EST:** 1947

SQ FT: 1,000
SALES (est): 159.42K **Privately Held**
SIC: 1221 Strip mining, bituminous

New Vienna
Clinton County

(G-10475)
PALM HARBOR HOMES INC
11004 State Route 28 (45159-9516)
PHONE.....................937 725-9465
EMP: 6 **EST:** 2011
SALES (est): 117.89K **Privately Held**
SIC: 2451 Mobile homes, personal or private use

(G-10476)
WELLS MANUFACTURING LLC
280 W Main St (45159-5024)
P.O. Box 325 (45159-0325)
PHONE.....................937 987-2481
Glenn Douglas, *VP Opers*
Grant Douglas, *Pr*
James J Hughes Iii, *Prin*
EMP: 10 **EST:** 1945
SQ FT: 100,000
SALES (est): 167.05K **Privately Held**
Web: www.wellsmfgco.com
SIC: 3944 Games, toys, and children's vehicles

New Washington
Crawford County

(G-10477)
C E WHITE CO (HQ)
417 N Kibler St (44854-9426)
P.O. Box 308 (44854-0308)
PHONE.....................419 492-2157
Tony Everett, *Pr*
Bob Knapp, *
▲ **EMP:** 47 **EST:** 1937
SQ FT: 65,000
SALES (est): 7.79MM
SALES (corp-wide): 430.3MM **Privately Held**
Web: www.hsmtransportation.com
SIC: 2531 Seats, miscellaneous public conveyances
PA: Hickory Springs Manufacturing Company
235 2nd Ave Nw
Hickory NC 28601
828 328-2201

(G-10478)
CREST BENDING INC
108 John St (44854-9702)
P.O. Box 458 (44854-0458)
PHONE.....................419 492-2108
Robert E Studer, *Pr*
EMP: 45 **EST:** 1966
SQ FT: 50,000
SALES (est): 2.31MM **Privately Held**
Web: www.crestbending.com
SIC: 3312 7692 3498 3317 Tubes, steel and iron; Welding repair; Fabricated pipe and fittings; Steel pipe and tubes

(G-10479)
HERALD INC
625 S Kibler St (44854-9541)
P.O. Box 367 (44854-0367)
PHONE.....................419 492-2133
Suzanne Stump, *CEO*
EMP: 35 **EST:** 2010
SALES (est): 5.99MM **Privately Held**
Web: www.theheraldinc.com

SIC: 2752 Offset printing

(G-10480)
MANSFIELD BRASS & ALUMINUM CORPORATION
Also Called: Mansfield Castings
636 S Center St (44854-9417)
PHONE.....................419 492-2154
EMP: 55
Web: www.mansfield-castings.com
SIC: 3365 Aluminum foundries

(G-10481)
NEW MANSFIELD BRASS & ALUM CO
636 S Center St (44854-9711)
PHONE.....................419 492-2166
Russell Nelson, *Pr*
EMP: 9 **EST:** 2013
SALES (est): 2.96MM **Privately Held**
Web: www.mansfield-castings.com
SIC: 3365 Aluminum and aluminum-based alloy castings

(G-10482)
OHIO FOAM CORPORATION
529 S Kibler St (44854-9524)
P.O. Box 61 (44820-0061)
PHONE.....................419 492-2151
Diane Swartzmiller, *Prin*
EMP: 10
SQ FT: 15,000
SALES (corp-wide): 8.08MM **Privately Held**
Web: www.ohiofoam.com
SIC: 3069 2821 Foam rubber; Plastics materials and resins
PA: Ohio Foam Corporation
820 Plymouth St
Bucyrus OH 44820
419 563-0399

(G-10483)
STUMPS CONVERTING INC
742 W Mansfield St (44854-9449)
PHONE.....................419 492-2542
Suzanne Stump, *Pr*
Dave Q Stump, *VP*
EMP: 10 **EST:** 1991
SALES (est): 473.15K **Privately Held**
SIC: 2679 5149 Paper products, converted, nec; Syrups, except for fountain use

(G-10484)
WURMS WOODWORKING COMPANY
Also Called: Gr Golf
725 W Mansfield St (44854-9449)
P.O. Box 275 (44854-0275)
PHONE.....................419 492-2184
Gerald B Wurm, *Pr*
Richard Wurm, *
Mary Wurm, *
Valerie Sanderson, *
EMP: 44 **EST:** 1947
SQ FT: 60,000
SALES (est): 7.54MM **Privately Held**
Web: www.wurmsproducts.com
SIC: 2499 2531 3082 3083 Furniture inlays (veneers); Vehicle furniture; Unsupported plastics profile shapes; Laminated plastics plate and sheet

New Waterford
Columbiana County

(G-10485)
CENTURY CONTAINER LLC (HQ)
5331 State Route 7 (44445-9787)
PHONE.....................330 457-2367

Mark Brothers, *Pr*
EMP: 10 **EST:** 2014
SALES (est): 9.19MM **Privately Held**
Web:
www.centurycontainercorporation.com
SIC: 3089 Plastics containers, except foam
PA: Thorworks Industries, Inc.
2520 Campbell St
Sandusky OH 44870

(G-10486)
CENTURY CONTAINER CORPORATION
5331 State Route 7 (44445-9787)
PHONE..................................330 457-2367
▼ **EMP:** 155
SIC: 3089 Plastics containers, except foam

(G-10487)
CIC OLD CORPORATION
5331 State Route 7 (44445-9787)
PHONE..................................330 457-2367
Don R Brothers, *CEO*
Jill Brothers, *
Roland Brothers, *
William G Houser, *
Budd Brothers, *
EMP: 25 **EST:** 1944
SQ FT: 100,000
SALES (est): 1.03MM **Privately Held**
Web:
www.centuryindustriescorporation.com
SIC: 2891 2952 Sealants; Asphalt felts and coatings

(G-10488)
MAJESTIC MANUFACTURING INC
4536 State Route 7 (44445-9785)
P.O. Box 128 (44445-0128)
PHONE..................................330 457-2447
Vince Kudler, *Pr*
Jeff Kudler, *VP*
Chris Kudler, *Prin*
Linda Kudler, *Prin*
◆ **EMP:** 20 **EST:** 1971
SQ FT: 68,000
SALES (est): 2.48MM **Privately Held**
Web: www.majesticrides.com
SIC: 3599 5087 Carnival machines and equipment, amusement park, nec; Carnival and amusement park equipment

Newark
Licking County

(G-10489)
ACUITY BRANDS LIGHTING INC
214 Oakwood Ave (43055-6716)
PHONE..................................740 349-4343
Steve Hummel, *Manager*
EMP: 94
SALES (corp-wide): 3.84B **Publicly Held**
Web: lithonia.acuitybrands.com
SIC: 3646 3648 3645 3612 Commercial lighting fixtures; Lighting equipment, nec; Residential lighting fixtures; Transformers, except electric
HQ: Acuity Brands Lighting, Inc.
1170 Pchtree St Ne Ste 23
Atlanta GA 30309

(G-10490)
AMPACET CORPORATION
1855 James Pkwy (43056-1092)
PHONE..................................740 929-5521
Jim Edge, *Brnch Mgr*
EMP: 112
SALES (corp-wide): 410.74MM **Privately Held**
Web: www.ampacet.com

SIC: 2869 2816 Industrial organic chemicals, nec; Inorganic pigments
PA: Ampacet Corporation
660 White Plins Rd Ste 36
Tarrytown NY 10591
914 631-6600

(G-10491)
ANOMATIC CORPORATION
1650 Tamarack Rd (43055-1359)
PHONE..................................740 522-2203
Chris Wilson, *Brnch Mgr*
EMP: 500
SALES (corp-wide): 833.11MM **Privately Held**
Web: www.anomatic.com
SIC: 3471 Anodizing (plating) of metals or formed products
HQ: Anomatic Corporation
8880 Innvation Campus Way
New Albany OH 43054
740 522-2203

(G-10492)
ARBORIS LLC
1780 Tamarack Rd (43055-1359)
PHONE..................................740 522-9350
Tom Lindow, *Brnch Mgr*
EMP: 29
SALES (corp-wide): 27.08MM **Privately Held**
Web: www.arboris-us.com
SIC: 2819 Chemicals, high purity: refined from technical grade
PA: Arboris, Llc
1101 W Lathrop Ave
Savannah GA 31415
912 238-6355

(G-10493)
ASHCRAFT MACHINE & SUPPLY INC
185 Wilson St (43055-4099)
PHONE..................................740 349-8110
Larry G Ashcraft, *Pr*
Jerry Ashcraft, *Pr*
John Balster, *Off Mgr*
Mike Ashcraft, *VP*
EMP: 12 **EST:** 1949
SQ FT: 15,000
SALES (est): 2.1MM **Privately Held**
Web: www.ashcraftmachine.com
SIC: 3599 Machine shop, jobbing and repair

(G-10494)
BOWERSTON SHALE COMPANY
1329 Seven Hills Rd (43055-8964)
PHONE..................................740 763-3921
Beth Hillyer, *Mgr*
EMP: 150
SQ FT: 100,000
SALES (corp-wide): 23.2MM **Privately Held**
Web: www.bowerstonshale.com
SIC: 3251 Brick clay: common face, glazed, vitrified, or hollow
PA: Bowerston Shale Company (Inc)
515 Main St
Bowerston OH 44695
740 269-2921

(G-10495)
BTR ENTERPRISES LLC
7371 Stewart Rd (43055-9667)
PHONE..................................740 975-2526
Brandon T Reece, *Prin*
EMP: 6 **EST:** 2008
SALES (est): 92.2K **Privately Held**
SIC: 3482 Small arms ammunition

(G-10496)
BURDENS MACHINE & WELDING INC
94 S 5th St (43055-5302)
P.O. Box 177 (43058-0177)
PHONE..................................740 345-9246
Donald Burden Senior, *Pr*
Donald Burden Junior, *VP*
Darrell Burden, *VP*
Robert Burden, *Sec*
EMP: 7 **EST:** 1977
SQ FT: 4,400
SALES (est): 508.15K **Privately Held**
SIC: 1799 3599 Welding on site; Machine shop, jobbing and repair

(G-10497)
CITY OF NEWARK
Also Called: Newark Water Plant
164 Waterworks Rd (43055-6057)
PHONE..................................740 349-6765
Steve Rhodes, *Mgr*
EMP: 49
SALES (corp-wide): 56.96MM **Privately Held**
Web: www.newarkohio.gov
SIC: 3561 Pumps, domestic: water or sump
PA: City Of Newark
40 W Main St
Newark OH 43055
740 670-7512

(G-10498)
COLUMBUS ROOF TRUSSES INC
Also Called: Central Ohio Bldg Components
400 Marne Dr (43055-8817)
PHONE..................................740 763-3000
EMP: 10
SALES (corp-wide): 4.12MM **Privately Held**
SIC: 2439 Trusses, wooden roof
PA: Columbus Roof Trusses, Inc.
2525 Fisher Rd
Columbus OH 43204
614 272-6464

(G-10499)
CONTOUR FORMING INC
215 Oakwood Ave (43055-6751)
P.O. Box 727 (43058-0727)
PHONE..................................740 345-9777
Terrie Lee Hill, *Pr*
Garrie Hill, *VP Mfg*
Tracie Hill, *VP Sls*
EMP: 18 **EST:** 1955
SQ FT: 100,000
SALES (est): 4.2MM **Privately Held**
SIC: 3356 3315 3444 3469 Nonferrous rolling and drawing, nec; Steel wire and related products; Sheet metalwork; Metal stampings, nec

(G-10500)
ELKHEAD GAS & OIL CO
12163 Marne Rd (43055-8810)
PHONE..................................740 763-3966
Maurice Dale Chapin, *Pr*
Michael Chapin, *VP*
James Chapin, *Sec*
EMP: 6 **EST:** 1964
SQ FT: 1,000
SALES (est): 1.04MM **Privately Held**
Web: www.elkheadgasandoilco.com
SIC: 1382 1311 Oil and gas exploration services; Crude petroleum production

(G-10501)
EQUIPMENT GUYS INC
185 Westgate Dr (43055-9313)
PHONE..................................614 871-9220
Matthew A Purdy, *Pr*
EMP: 11 **EST:** 1995

SALES (est): 976.33K **Privately Held**
Web: www.equipmentguys.com
SIC: 3949 5084 Dumbbells and other weightlifting equipment; Industrial machinery and equipment

(G-10502)
FGS-WI LLC
37 S Park Pl (43055-5505)
PHONE..................................630 375-8597
Michael Mumphrey, *Prin*
EMP: 21
SALES (corp-wide): 143.76MM **Privately Held**
Web: www.fgs.com
SIC: 2752 Offset printing
HQ: Fgs-Wi, Llc
1101 S Janesville St
Milton WI 53563
608 373-6500

(G-10503)
GEMCO MACHINE & TOOL INC
88 Decrow Ave (43055-3870)
PHONE..................................740 344-3111
Steve Hays, *Pr*
Faye Hays, *Sec*
EMP: 10 **EST:** 1981
SQ FT: 8,500
SALES (est): 875.58K **Privately Held**
Web: www.gemcomachine.com
SIC: 3599 Machine shop, jobbing and repair

(G-10504)
GOLF GALAXY GOLFWORKS INC
Also Called: Golfworks, The
4820 Jacksontown Rd (43056-9377)
P.O. Box 3008 (43058-3008)
PHONE..................................740 328-4193
Mark Mccormick, *CEO*
Jerry Datz, *
Mark Wilson, *
Richard C Nordvoid, *
▲ **EMP:** 150 **EST:** 1974
SQ FT: 80,000
SALES (est): 7.96MM
SALES (corp-wide): 13.44B **Publicly Held**
Web: www.golfworks.com
SIC: 5091 2731 3949 5941 Golf equipment; Books, publishing only; Golf equipment; Golf, tennis, and ski shops
HQ: Golf Galaxy, Llc
345 Ct St
Coraopolis PA 15108

(G-10505)
GRANVILLE MILLING CO
Also Called: Granville Milling Drive-Thru
145 N Cedar St (43055-6705)
PHONE..................................740 345-1305
Trent Smith, *Mgr*
EMP: 6
SALES (corp-wide): 2.34MM **Privately Held**
Web: www.granvillemilling.net
SIC: 2048 5191 Prepared feeds, nec; Animal feeds
PA: Granville Milling Co.
400 S Main St
Granville OH 43023
740 587-0221

(G-10506)
HOLOPHANE CORPORATION
Also Called: Unique Solutions
515 Mckinley Ave (43055-6737)
PHONE..................................740 349-4194
Richard Peterson, *Mgr*
EMP: 10
SALES (corp-wide): 3.84B **Publicly Held**
Web: holophane.acuitybrands.com

SIC: **3646** Commercial lighting fixtures
HQ: Holophane Corporation
3825 Columbus Rd Bldg A
Granville OH 43023

(G-10507)
**HOPE TIMBER & MARKETING
GROUP (PA)**
Also Called: Wood Recovery
141 Union St (43055-3976)
P.O. Box 502 (43023-0502)
PHONE.................................740 344-1788
Thomas J Harvey, *Pr*
Deborah L Harvey, *Ch*
EMP: 18 EST: 1993
SQ FT: 40,000
SALES (est): 2.43MM **Privately Held**
Web: www.hopetimbermulch.com
SIC: **2499** 2448 Mulch or sawdust products,
wood; Pallets, wood

(G-10508)
HOPE TIMBER MULCH LLC
141 Union St (43055-3976)
P.O. Box 502 (43023-0502)
PHONE.................................740 344-1788
Thomas Harvey, *Pr*
Deborah L Harvey, *Ex VP*
EMP: 6 EST: 2005
SQ FT: 20,000
SALES (est): 742.42K **Privately Held**
Web: www.hopetimbermulch.com
SIC: **2499** Mulch or sawdust products, wood

(G-10509)
HOPE TIMBER PALLET RECYCL LLC
Also Called: Hope Timber
141 Union St (43055-3976)
P.O. Box 502 (43023-0502)
PHONE.................................740 344-1788
Thomas J Harvey, *Pr*
▼ EMP: 21 EST: 2005
SALES (est): 4.64MM **Privately Held**
Web: www.hopetimbermulch.com
SIC: **2448** 4953 Pallets, wood; Recycling,
waste materials

(G-10510)
I G BRENNER INC
Also Called: Brenner International
1806 Stonewall Dr (43055-1652)
PHONE.................................740 345-8845
Robert M Fitzgerald, *Pr*
Jennifer Fitzgerald, *Sec*
EMP: 10 EST: 1950
SALES (est): 219.48K **Privately Held**
Web: www.igbint.com
SIC: **3599** Machine shop, jobbing and repair

(G-10511)
INNS HOLDINGS LTD
29 W Locust St (43055-5510)
PHONE.................................740 345-3700
EMP: 11 EST: 2017
SALES (est): 289.45K **Privately Held**
SIC: **7011** 3571 Inns; Personal computers
(microcomputers)

(G-10512)
INTERNATIONAL PAPER COMPANY
Also Called: International Paper
1851 Tamarack Rd (43055-1350)
PHONE.................................740 522-3123
Bill Hartshorn, *Genl Mgr*
EMP: 178
SALES (corp-wide): 18.62B **Publicly Held**
Web: www.internationalpaper.com
SIC: **2653** Boxes, corrugated: made from
purchased materials
PA: International Paper Company
6400 Poplar Ave

Memphis TN 38197
901 419-7000

(G-10513)
KEL-PAR CO INC
85 S Williams St (43055-3926)
P.O. Box 749 (43058-0749)
PHONE.................................740 344-2627
Lawrence M Kellenbarger, *Ch*
Michael L Kellenbarger, *Pr*
EMP: 12 EST: 1963
SQ FT: 25,000
SALES (est): 249.61K **Privately Held**
SIC: **1711** 1542 7692 3441 Mechanical
contractor; Commercial and office building,
new construction; Welding repair;
Fabricated structural metal

(G-10514)
KINGSPAN INSULATION LLC
Dyplast Products
1010 Brice St (43055-6893)
PHONE.................................800 433-5551
Vincent Fuster, *Genl Mgr*
EMP: 57
Web: technical.kingspaninsulation.us
SIC: **3086** 5033 Insulation or cushioning
material, foamed plastics; Roofing and
siding materials
HQ: Kingspan Insulation Llc
12501 Nw 38th Ave
Miami FL 33054
305 921-0100

(G-10515)
KREAGER CO LLC
1045 Brice St (43055-6890)
PHONE.................................740 345-1605
Judson Kreager, *Owner*
EMP: 7 EST: 1983
SQ FT: 2,000
SALES (est): 757.72K **Privately Held**
Web: www.kreagercompany.com
SIC: **2434** Wood kitchen cabinets

(G-10516)
L & T COLLINS INC
Also Called: Minuteman of Heath
44 S 4th St (43055-5436)
PHONE.................................740 345-4494
Timothy M Collins, *Pr*
Laura Collins, *CFO*
EMP: 6 EST: 2003
SQ FT: 12,500
SALES (est): 703.86K **Privately Held**
Web: www.mpnewark.com
SIC: **2752** Offset printing

(G-10517)
M & H SCREEN PRINTING
1486 Hebron Rd (43056-1035)
PHONE.................................740 522-1957
Douglas Moore, *Pt*
Laurie Moore, *Pt*
Stan Hall, *Pt*
EMP: 6 EST: 1988
SQ FT: 4,000
SALES (est): 228.4K **Privately Held**
Web: www.mandhscreenprinting.com
SIC: **2759** Screen printing

(G-10518)
M & R PHILLIPS ENTERPRISES
Also Called: Serappers Gallery
6242 Jacksontown Rd (43056-8303)
PHONE.................................740 323-0580
Mary Phillips, *Pr*
Rick Phillips, *Sec*
EMP: 10 EST: 2006
SALES (est): 398.22K **Privately Held**

SIC: **2782** Scrapbooks, albums, and diaries

(G-10519)
MICHALEK MANUFACTURING LLC
160 Obannon Ave (43055-6743)
PHONE.................................740 763-0910
EMP: 9 EST: 2022
SALES (est): 1MM **Privately Held**
Web: www.michalekmanufacturing.com
SIC: **3599** Machine shop, jobbing and repair

(G-10520)
MID OHIO WOOD PRODUCTS INC
535 Franklin Ave (43056-1610)
PHONE.................................740 323-0427
Jay Parkinson, *Pr*
Nancy Parkinson, *
EMP: 6 EST: 1982
SQ FT: 16,000
SALES (est): 454.87K **Privately Held**
SIC: **2448** 2426 Pallets, wood; Hardwood
dimension and flooring mills

(G-10521)
MIDWEST MENU MATE INC
Also Called: Midwest Marketing
1065 Lizabeth Cir (43056-1626)
PHONE.................................740 323-2599
Galiun Riggs, *Pr*
EMP: 10 EST: 1992
SALES (est): 580K **Privately Held**
SIC: **2741** 7336 Atlas, map, and guide
publishing; Commercial art and graphic
design

(G-10522)
MODERN WELDING CO OHIO INC
1 Modern Way (43055-3921)
P.O. Box 4430 (43058-4430)
PHONE.................................740 344-9425
TOLL FREE: 800
John W Jones, *Pr*
Doug Rothert, *VP*
Jerry Waller, *VP*
James M Ruth, *Ex VP*
EMP: 30 EST: 1932
SQ FT: 52,000
SALES (est): 9.06MM
SALES (corp-wide): 122.85MM **Privately
Held**
Web: www.modweldco.com
SIC: **3443** 5051 Tanks, lined: metal plate;
Metals service centers and offices
PA: Modern Welding Company, Inc.
2880 New Hartford Rd
Owensboro KY 42303
270 685-4400

(G-10523)
MYFOOTSHOPCOM LLC
1159 Cherry Valley Rd Se (43055-9321)
P.O. Box 456 (43023-0456)
PHONE.................................740 522-5681
Jeff A Oster, *Pr*
Thalia Oster, *CEO*
EMP: 6 EST: 2001
SALES (est): 641.68K **Privately Held**
Web: www.myfootshop.com
SIC: **3842** Braces, elastic

(G-10524)
**NATIONAL GAS & OIL
CORPORATION (DH)**
Also Called: Permian Oil & Gas Division
1500 Granville Rd (43055-1500)
P.O. Box 4970 (43058-4970)
PHONE.................................740 344-2102
William Sullivan Junior, *Ch Bd*
Patrick J Mc Gonagle, *Pr*
Todd P Ware, *VP*
Gordon M King, *VP*

EMP: 36 EST: 1941
SQ FT: 10,000
SALES (est): 43.95MM
SALES (corp-wide): 69.21MM **Privately
Held**
Web: www.theenergycoop.com
SIC: **4922** 4924 4932 4911 Natural gas
transmission; Natural gas distribution; Gas
and other services combined; Electric
services
HQ: National Gas & Oil Company Inc
1500 Granville Rd
Newark OH 43055
740 344-2102

(G-10525)
**NEW WORLD ENERGY RESOURCES
(PA)**
1500 Granville Rd (43055-1536)
PHONE.................................740 344-4087
John Manczak, *CEO*
EMP: 13 EST: 2001
SALES (est): 13.4MM
SALES (corp-wide): 13.4MM **Privately
Held**
SIC: **1382** Geological exploration, oil and
gas field

(G-10526)
OHIO RIVER VALLEY CABINET
4 Waterworks Rd (43055-6060)
PHONE.................................740 975-8846
Bob Bachmann, *Owner*
EMP: 6 EST: 1994
SALES (est): 248.34K **Privately Held**
SIC: **2434** Wood kitchen cabinets

(G-10527)
OWENS CRNING INSLTING SYSTM
400 Case Ave (43055-5805)
P.O. Box 3012 (43058-3012)
PHONE.................................740 328-2300
Fred Ramquist, *Brnch Mgr*
EMP: 803
SIC: **3296** Fiberglass insulation
HQ: Owens Corning Insulating Systems, Llc
1 Owens Corning Pkwy
Toledo OH 43659
419 248-8000

(G-10528)
**PACKAGING CORPORATION
AMERICA**
Also Called: PCA/Newark 365
205 S 21st St (43055-3879)
P.O. Box 4610 (43058-4610)
PHONE.................................740 344-1126
Pom Watson, *Brnch Mgr*
EMP: 115
SALES (corp-wide): 7.73B **Publicly Held**
Web: www.packagingcorp.com
SIC: **2653** Boxes, corrugated: made from
purchased materials
PA: Packaging Corporation Of America
1 N Field Ct
Lake Forest IL 60045
847 482-3000

(G-10529)
PRESTON
42 Sandalwood Dr (43055-9233)
PHONE.................................740 788-8208
Judith Preston, *Prin*
EMP: 7 EST: 2011
SALES (est): 2.55MM **Privately Held**
SIC: **3545** Collars (machine tool accessories)

(G-10530)
PUGHS DESIGNER JEWELERS INC
12 W Main St (43055-5504)

PHONE..............................740 344-9259
Kevin Pugh, *Pr*
EMP: 8 **EST:** 1990
SALES (est): 553.82K **Privately Held**
Web: www.pughsdesignerjewelers.com
SIC: 5944 3961 7389 7631 Jewelry, precious
stones and precious metals; Costume
jewelry; Appraisers, except real estate;
Jewelry repair services

(G-10531)
QUANTUM
400 Case Ave (43055-5805)
PHONE..............................740 328-2548
EMP: 18 **EST:** 2012
SALES (est): 345.84K **Privately Held**
SIC: 3572 Computer storage devices

(G-10532)
**RYANS NEWARK LEADER EX PRTG
CO**
Also Called: Leader Printing
56 Westgate Dr (43055-9313)
P.O. Box 4902 (43058-4902)
PHONE..............................740 522-2149
Andrew T Ryan, *Pr*
Gary Ryan, *Treas*
EMP: 10 **EST:** 1895
SQ FT: 9,600
SALES (est): 480.22K **Privately Held**
Web: www.leaderprinting1895.com
SIC: 2752 2791 2789 2759 Offset printing;
Typesetting; Bookbinding and related work;
Commercial printing, nec

(G-10533)
SPECTRUM ADHESIVES INC
11047 Lambs Ln (43055-9779)
PHONE..............................740 763-2886
Kent Pitcher, *Pr*
EMP: 7
SALES (corp-wide): 8.06MM **Privately
Held**
Web: www.spectrumadhesives.com
SIC: 2891 Glue
PA: Spectrum Adhesives, Inc.
5611 Universal Dr
Memphis TN 38118
901 795-1943

(G-10534)
STRATEGIC MATERIALS INC
101 S Arch St (43055-6202)
P.O. Box 816 (43058-0816)
PHONE..............................740 349-9523
Michael Back, *Brnch Mgr*
EMP: 6
SALES (corp-wide): 118.92MM **Privately
Held**
Web: www.smi.com
SIC: 3231 Products of purchased glass
HQ: Strategic Materials, Inc.
17220 Katy Fwy Ste 150
Houston TX 77094

(G-10535)
TECTUM INC
105 S 6th St (43055-4908)
P.O. Box 3002 (43058-3002)
PHONE..............................740 345-9691
Michael Massaro, *Pr*
Wayne Chester, *Marketing*
Stephen M Mihaly, *Stockholder*
John M Scott, *Stockholder*
◆ **EMP:** 120 **EST:** 1979
SQ FT: 100,000
SALES (est): 25.82MM
SALES (corp-wide): 1.45B **Publicly Held**
Web: www.tectum.com
SIC: 2493 3444 3296 Fiberboard, wood;
Sheet metalwork; Mineral wool

PA: Armstrong World Industries, Inc.
2500 Columbia Ave
Lancaster PA 17603
717 397-0611

(G-10536)
TRAFFIC CNTRL SGNLS SIGNS & MA
Also Called: City of Newark
1195 E Main St (43055-8869)
PHONE..............................740 670-7763
Gary Snavely, *Dir*
EMP: 7 **EST:** 2007
SALES (est): 552.72K **Privately Held**
Web: www.newarkohio.gov
SIC: 3993 Signs and advertising specialties

(G-10537)
UNIVERSAL PRODUCTION CORP
1776 Tamarack Rd (43055-1359)
PHONE..............................740 522-1147
Klaus Krajewski, *Pr*
◆ **EMP:** 11 **EST:** 1993
SQ FT: 98,000
SALES (est): 2.12MM **Privately Held**
Web: www.alink.com
SIC: 2436 Softwood veneer and plywood

(G-10538)
UNIVERSAL VENEER MILL CORP
1776 Tamarack Rd (43055-1384)
PHONE..............................740 522-1147
Klaus Krajewski, *Pr*
William Cooper, *
EMP: 180 **EST:** 1978
SQ FT: 75,000
SALES (est): 10.91MM **Privately Held**
Web: www.alink.com
SIC: 2435 Hardwood veneer and plywood

(G-10539)
**UNIVERSAL VENEER SALES CORP
(PA)**
1776 Tamarack Rd (43055-1384)
PHONE..............................740 522-1147
Klaus Krajewski, *Pr*
◆ **EMP:** 186 **EST:** 1993
SQ FT: 75,000
SALES (est): 3.05MM **Privately Held**
Web: www.alink.com
SIC: 2435 Veneer stock, hardwood

Newburgh Heights
Cuyahoga County

(G-10540)
DOREX LLC
4420 Gamma Ave (44105-3160)
PHONE..............................216 271-7064
Roman Lasocinski, *Prin*
EMP: 6 **EST:** 2010
SALES (est): 101.3K **Privately Held**
Web: www.dorex.com
SIC: 2392 Cushions and pillows

(G-10541)
FIRTH RIXSON INC
1616 Harvard Ave Ste 53 (44105-3040)
PHONE..............................860 760-1040
▲ **EMP:** 63
SIC: 3462 Iron and steel forgings

(G-10542)
H GOODMAN INC
Also Called: White Dove Mattress
3201 Harvard Ave (44105-3060)
PHONE..............................216 341-0200
Bruce Goodman, *Pr*
Henry J Goodman, *Ch*
▲ **EMP:** 90 **EST:** 1916

SQ FT: 270,000
SALES (est): 3.98MM **Privately Held**
Web: www.whitedoveusa.com
SIC: 2515 2512 Mattresses and foundations;
Upholstered household furniture

(G-10543)
HOWMET AEROSPACE INC
Also Called: HOWMET AEROSPACE INC
1600 Harvard Ave (44105-3040)
PHONE..............................216 641-3600
Ian Murray, *Mgr*
EMP: 1200
SALES (corp-wide): 7.43B **Publicly Held**
Web: www.howmet.com
SIC: 3463 3321 Aluminum forgings; Gray
and ductile iron foundries
PA: Howmet Aerospace Inc.
201 Isabella St Ste 200
Pittsburgh PA 15212
412 553-1950

(G-10544)
**HOWMET ALUMINUM CASTING INC
(HQ)**
Also Called: Sigma Div
1600 Harvard Ave (44105-3040)
PHONE..............................216 641-4340
Raymond B Mitchell, *Pr*
EMP: 50 **EST:** 1989
SQ FT: 10,000
SALES (est): 24.54MM
SALES (corp-wide): 7.43B **Publicly Held**
Web: www.howmet.com
SIC: 3365 Aerospace castings, aluminum
PA: Howmet Aerospace Inc.
201 Isabella St Ste 200
Pittsburgh PA 15212
412 553-1950

(G-10545)
MCGEAN-ROHCO INC
2910 Harvard Ave (44105-3010)
PHONE..............................216 441-4900
Kerry May, *Brnch Mgr*
EMP: 9
SQ FT: 350,000
SALES (corp-wide): 41.26MM **Privately
Held**
Web: www.mcgean.com
SIC: 2899 2819 3471 2842 Chemical
preparations, nec; Industrial inorganic
chemicals, nec; Plating and polishing;
Polishes and sanitation goods
PA: Mcgean-Rohco, Inc.
2910 Harvard Ave
Cleveland OH 44105
216 441-4900

(G-10546)
PARK-OHIO INDUSTRIES INC
Also Called: Ohio Crankshaft Div
3800 Harvard Ave (44105-3208)
PHONE..............................216 341-2300
Felix Parorick, *Prin*
EMP: 150
SQ FT: 427,000
SALES (corp-wide): 1.66B **Publicly Held**
Web: www.ohio-crankshaft.com
SIC: 3714 Camshafts, motor vehicle
HQ: Park-Ohio Industries, Inc.
6065 Parkland Blvd
Cleveland OH 44124
440 947-2000

Newbury
Geauga County

(G-10547)
BOGGS RECYCLING INC
12355 Kinsman Rd Unit J (44065-9620)
P.O. Box 576 (44021-0576)
PHONE..............................800 837-8101
Kimberly Boggs, *Pr*
Christopher A Boggs, *Prin*
EMP: 8 **EST:** 2004
SQ FT: 10,000
SALES (est): 939.68K **Privately Held**
Web: www.boggsrecycling.com
SIC: 3334 Primary aluminum

(G-10548)
CREATIVE MOLD AND MACHINE INC
10385 Kinsman Rd (44065-9701)
P.O. Box 323 (44065-0323)
PHONE..............................440 338-5146
Ray Lyons, *Pr*
Greg Davis, *
Mishal Dedeck, *General Vice President*
EMP: 25 **EST:** 1987
SQ FT: 39,000
SALES (est): 2.02MM **Privately Held**
Web: www.creativemoldandmachine.com
SIC: 7692 3599 Welding repair; Machine
shop, jobbing and repair

(G-10549)
DAN ALLEN SURGICAL LLC
Also Called: D. A. Surgical
11110 Kinsman Rd Unit 10 (44065-8604)
P.O. Box 189 (44065)
PHONE..............................800 261-9953
Robert Dan Allen, *Pr*
EMP: 14 **EST:** 2014
SALES (est): 2.67MM **Privately Held**
Web: www.da-surgical.com
SIC: 8062 3842 General medical and
surgical hospitals; Surgical appliances and
supplies

(G-10550)
ENGINEERED ENDEAVORS INC
10975 Kinsman Rd (44065-9787)
PHONE..............................440 564-5484
EMP: 21
SIC: 3663 Mobile communication equipment

(G-10551)
GEAUGA CONCRETE INC
10509 Kinsman Rd (44065-9803)
P.O. Box 249 (44045-0249)
PHONE..............................440 338-4915
Hal Larned, *Pr*
EMP: 10 **EST:** 1981
SALES (est): 1.38MM
SALES (corp-wide): 3.62MM **Privately
Held**
Web: geauga.oh.gov
SIC: 3273 Ready-mixed concrete
PA: Osborne Concrete & Stone Co.
1 Williams St
Grand River OH 44045
440 357-5562

(G-10552)
GREEN VISION MATERIALS INC
11220 Kinsman Rd (44065-9676)
PHONE..............................440 564-5500
Beau Gibney, *Owner*
EMP: 15 **EST:** 2010
SALES (est): 2.89MM **Privately Held**
Web: www.greenvisionmaterials.com

▲ = Import ▼ = Export
◆ = Import/Export

SIC: **4953** 3271 Recycling, waste materials;
Blocks, concrete: landscape or retaining
wall

(G-10553)
HF GROUP LLC
Also Called: General Book Binding
12375 Kinsman Rd (44065-9684)
PHONE..............................440 729-9411
Jim Bratton, *Brnch Mgr*
EMP: 177
Web: www.hfgroup.com
SIC: **2789** Bookbinding and related work
PA: Hf Group, Llc
400 Arora Cmmons Cir Unit
Aurora OH 44202

(G-10554)
HF GROUP LLC
12375 Kinsman Rd (44065-9684)
PHONE..............................440 729-9411
Terry Hymas, *Brnch Mgr*
EMP: 197
Web: www.hfgroup.com
SIC: **2732** Books, printing and binding
PA: Hf Group, Llc
400 Arora Cmmons Cir Unit
Aurora OH 44202

(G-10555)
INTELACOMM INC
12375 Kinsman Rd (44065-9684)
P.O. Box 332 (44065-0332)
PHONE..............................888 610-9250
Robert Ruckstuh, *CEO*
Robert R Ruckstuhl, *CEO*
EMP: 6 **EST:** 2016
SALES (est): 150K **Privately Held**
Web: www.intelacomm.com
SIC: **2741** Internet publishing and
broadcasting

(G-10556)
KINETICO INCORPORATED (HQ)
10845 Kinsman Rd (44065-8702)
PHONE..............................440 564-9111
◆ **EMP:** 287 **EST:** 1970
SALES (est): 100.81MM
SALES (corp-wide): 267.31MM **Privately
Held**
Web: www.kinetico.com
SIC: **3589** 5074 6799 Water treatment
equipment, industrial; Water heaters and
purification equipment, Investors, nec
PA: Axel Johnson Inc.
155 Spring St Fl 6
New York NY 10012
646 291-2445

(G-10557)
NEWBURY SNDBLST & PNTG INC
9992 Kinsman Rd (44065)
P.O. Box 378 (44065-0378)
PHONE..............................440 564-7204
Nelson Peterson, *Pr*
Pamela Peterson, *Sec*
EMP: 7 **EST:** 1976
SQ FT: 25,000
SALES (est): 373.77K **Privately Held**
SIC: **3471** 7532 Sand blasting of metal parts;
Paint shop, automotive

(G-10558)
NEWBURY WOODWORKS
10958 Kinsman Rd Unit 2 (44065-8602)
PHONE..............................440 564-5273
Aloysius Hoenigman Junior, *Owner*
EMP: 7 **EST:** 1996
SQ FT: 8,000
SALES (est): 248.75K **Privately Held**

SIC: **5712** 2499 Cabinet work, custom;
Decorative wood and woodwork

(G-10559)
OREILLY EQUIPMENT LLC
14555 Ravenna Rd (44065-9513)
PHONE..............................440 564-1234
EMP: 6 **EST:** 2002
SQ FT: 6,000
SALES (est): 482.63K **Privately Held**
Web: www.oreillyequipment.com
SIC: **5599** 3714 Utility trailers; Ice scrapers
and window brushes, motor vehicle

(G-10560)
PADCO INDUSTRIES LLC
Also Called: Dem Manufacturing
10357 Kinsman Rd Unit D (44065-8700)
PHONE..............................440 564-7160
Craig Padula, *Pr*
Craig Padula, *Managing Member*
▲ **EMP:** 40 **EST:** 2018
SALES (est): 8.91MM **Privately Held**
Web: www.dem-mfg.com
SIC: **8711** 3089 3599 Engineering services;
Injection molding of plastics; Electrical
discharge machining (EDM)

(G-10561)
R W SIDLEY INCORPORATED
10688 Kinsman Rd (44065-9761)
P.O. Box 208 (44065-0208)
PHONE..............................440 564-2221
Dan Craver, *Brnch Mgr*
EMP: 21
SALES (corp-wide): 43.09MM **Privately
Held**
Web: www.rwsidley.com
SIC: **3273** 3272 3271 1442 Ready-mixed
concrete; Concrete products, nec; Concrete
block and brick; Construction sand and
gravel
PA: R. W. Sidley Incorporated
436 Casement Ave
Painesville OH 44077
440 352-9343

(G-10562)
RALSTON INSTRUMENTS LLC
15035 Cross Creek Pkwy (44065-9726)
P.O. Box 340 (44072-0340)
PHONE..............................440 564-1430
Griffin Ralston, *CEO*
Douglas Ralston, *Managing Member*
Corey Ralston, *
EMP: 25 **EST:** 1968
SALES (est): 4.61MM **Privately Held**
Web: www.ralstoninst.com
SIC: **3829** Measuring and controlling
devices, nec

(G-10563)
SAINT-GOBAIN CERAMICS PLAS INC
Also Called: Saint Gobain Crystals
12359 Kinsman Rd (44065-9620)
PHONE..............................440 542-2712
Tom Kinisky, *Pr*
EMP: 500 **EST:** 1951
SALES (est): 5.8MM
SALES (corp-wide): 402.18MM **Privately
Held**
SIC: **3674** Semiconductors and related
devices
PA: Compagnie De Saint-Gobain
Tour Saint-Gobain
Courbevoie IDF 92400
140880316

(G-10564)
SAINT-GOBAIN CERAMICS PLAS INC
12345 Kinsman Rd (44065-9620)
PHONE..............................440 564-8000
Tom Kinisky, *Mgr*
EMP: 124
SALES (corp-wide): 402.18MM **Privately
Held**
Web: www.saint-gobain.com
SIC: **2819** Industrial inorganic chemicals, nec
HQ: Saint-Gobain Ceramics & Plastics, Inc.
3840 Fishcreek Rd
Stow OH 44224

(G-10565)
UNITED ROLLER CO LLC
14910 Cross Creek Pkwy (44065-9788)
PHONE..............................440 564-9698
EMP: 14 **EST:** 2002
SQ FT: 13,500
SALES (est): 414.93K **Privately Held**
Web: www.united-roller.com
SIC: **3069** Rolls, solid or covered rubber

Newcomerstown
Tuscarawas County

(G-10566)
31 INC
Also Called: Extra Seal
100 Enterprise Dr (43832-9242)
P.O. Box 278 (43832-0278)
PHONE..............................800 438-3302
Charles Muhs, *Pr*
Robert Hendry, *
◆ **EMP:** 100 **EST:** 1961
SQ FT: 130,000
SALES (est): 10.03MM **Privately Held**
Web: www.31inc.com
SIC: **3011** 3714 Tire sundries or tire repair
materials, rubber; Tire valve cores

(G-10567)
ACCURATE PRODUCTS COMPANY
98 Elizabeth St (43832-1432)
P.O. Box 106 (43832-0106)
PHONE..............................740 498-7202
Clark H Smith, *Pr*
R Clark Smith, *VP*
EMP: 6 **EST:** 1946
SALES (est): 300.48K **Privately Held**
SIC: **3366** Castings (except die), nec, brass

(G-10568)
ANNIN & CO
Also Called: ANNIN & CO.
100 State Route 258 (43832-8831)
PHONE..............................740 498-5008
Vane Scott, *Mgr*
EMP: 30
SALES (corp-wide): 52.62MM **Privately
Held**
Web: www.annin.com
SIC: **2399** Banners, pennants, and flags
PA: Annin & Co., Inc.
430 Mountain Ave
New Providence NJ 07974
973 228-9400

(G-10569)
BUCKEYE BOP LLC
Also Called: Buckeye Blow Out Preventer
401 Enterprise Dr (43832-9239)
PHONE..............................740 498-9898
EMP: 10 **EST:** 2011
SALES (est): 1MM **Privately Held**
Web: www.buckbop.com
SIC: **3564** 3592 5719 Blowers and fans;
Valves; Brushes

(G-10570)
H3D TOOL CORPORATION
Also Called: High Definition Tooling
295 Enterprise Dr (43832-8954)
P.O. Box 314 (43832-0314)
PHONE..............................740 498-5181
Gary Dyer, *Pr*
Chris Dyer, *
EMP: 48 **EST:** 1994
SQ FT: 20,000
SALES (est): 4.93MM **Privately Held**
Web: www.h3dtool.com
SIC: **3545** 5085 Diamond cutting tools for
turning, boring, burnishing, etc.; Industrial
supplies

(G-10571)
HERCO INC
295 Enterprise Dr (43832-8954)
P.O. Box 314 (43832-0314)
PHONE..............................740 498-5181
Gary Dyer, *Pr*
Chris Dyer, *
EMP: 6 **EST:** 1968
SQ FT: 20,000
SALES (est): 485.34K **Privately Held**
Web: www.h3dtool.com
SIC: **3541** Machine tools, metal cutting type

(G-10572)
KURZ-KASCH INC (DH)
Also Called: Kurz-Kasch
199 E State St (43832-1468)
PHONE..............................740 498-8343
Chad Merkel, *CEO*
Jack Senn, *
▲ **EMP:** 30 **EST:** 1916
SQ FT: 6,000
SALES (est): 12.5MM
SALES (corp-wide): 99.89MM **Privately
Held**
Web: www.kurz-kasch.com
SIC: **3089** 3677 Thermoformed finished
plastics products, nec; Electronic coils and
transformers
HQ: Prettl Manufacturing Corporation
1721 White Horse Rd
Greenville SC 29605
864 220-1010

(G-10573)
OAK POINTE LEGACY LLC
96 New Pace Rd (43832-1287)
PHONE..............................740 498-9820
EMP: 26 **EST:** 2007
SALES (est): 2.82MM **Privately Held**
Web: www.stairpartsandmore.com
SIC: **2431** Millwork

(G-10574)
**PARAGON INTGRTED SVCS GROUP
LL**
Also Called: Paragon Integrated Svcs Group
200 Enterprise Dr (43832-8954)
PHONE..............................724 639-5126
EMP: 22
SALES (corp-wide): 2.86MM **Privately
Held**
Web: www.paragonisg.com
SIC: **1389** Oil field services, nec
PA: Paragon Integrated Services Group Llc
825 Town Cntry Ln Ste 120
Houston TX 77024
740 492-0190

(G-10575)
SIMONA BOLTARON INC
Also Called: A Simona Group Company
1 General St (43832-1230)
PHONE..............................740 498-5900
Lawrence J Schorr, *CEO*

GEOGRAPHIC

Dean Li, *CFO*
◆ **EMP:** 100 **EST:** 2004
SQ FT: 175,000
SALES (est): 23.82MM **Privately Held**
Web: www.boltaron.com
SIC: 3081 2891 Film base, cellulose acetate or nitrocellulose plastics; Adhesives and sealants

Newton Falls
Trumbull County

(G-10576)
AMERICAN MOLDED PLASTICS INC
3876 Newton Falls Bailey Rd (44444-9746)
P.O. Box 434 (44444-0434)
PHONE.............................330 872-3838
Ray Allen, *Pr*
Bertha Allen, *VP*
EMP: 10 **EST:** 1989
SQ FT: 6,000
SALES (est): 1.06MM **Privately Held**
Web: www.americanmoldedplastic.com
SIC: 3089 Injection molding of plastics

(G-10577)
BAR PROCESSING CORPORATION
1000 Windham Rd (44444-9586)
P.O. Box 280 (44444-0280)
PHONE.............................330 872-0914
Jack Stacky, *Mgr*
EMP: 14
SALES (corp-wide): 20.62MM **Privately Held**
Web: www.barprocessingcorp.com
SIC: 3471 3316 Finishing, metals or formed products; Cold finishing of steel shapes
HQ: Bar Processing Corporation
     26601 W Huron River Dr
     Flat Rock MI 48134
     734 782-4454

(G-10578)
KENS HIS & HERS SHOP INC
Also Called: Positive Images
5 S Milton Blvd Ste C (44444-1780)
PHONE.............................330 872-3190
Doug Cochran, *Pr*
Dawn Cochran, *VP*
EMP: 6 **EST:** 1976
SQ FT: 5,200
SALES (est): 183.46K **Privately Held**
Web: www.positiveimagesdirect.com
SIC: 2759 2395 Screen printing; Embroidery and art needlework

(G-10579)
LUXAIRE CUSHION CO
2410 S Center St (44444-9408)
PHONE.............................330 872-0995
Alan E Rathbun Junior, *Pr*
Steve Fackelman, *VP*
EMP: 10 **EST:** 1946
SQ FT: 55,000
SALES (est): 588.59K **Privately Held**
Web: www.luxairefoamworks.com
SIC: 2393 Cushions, except spring and carpet: purchased materials

(G-10580)
QUALITY SWITCH INC
715 Arlington Blvd (44444-8765)
P.O. Box 250 (44444-0250)
PHONE.............................330 872-5707
Russell Sewell, *Pr*
Rick Sewell, *
Laura Whitmore, *
EMP: 29 **EST:** 1974
SQ FT: 31,200

SALES (est): 4.41MM **Privately Held**
Web: www.qualityswitch.com
SIC: 3679 Electronic switches

(G-10581)
TRANSCO RAILWAY PRODUCTS INC
2310 S Center St (44444-9406)
PHONE.............................330 872-0934
Robert Ewing, *Mgr*
EMP: 41
SQ FT: 100,000
SALES (corp-wide): 424.23B **Publicly Held**
Web: www.transcorailway.com
SIC: 3441 3743 Fabricated structural metal; Railroad equipment
HQ: Transco Railway Products Inc.
     200 Nrth Lslle St Lobby 5
     Chicago IL 60601
     312 427-2818

(G-10582)
VENTURE PLASTICS INC (PA)
Also Called: V P
4000 Warren Ravenna Rd (44444-8704)
P.O. Box P.O. Box 249 (44444-0249)
PHONE.............................330 872-5774
Kenneth M Groff, *CEO*
J Stephen Trapp, *
Bryon Osborne, *
James Smith, *
Gary Flattum, *
◆ **EMP:** 115 **EST:** 1969
SQ FT: 60,000
SALES (est): 40.38MM
SALES (corp-wide): 40.38MM **Privately Held**
Web: www.ventureplastics.com
SIC: 3089 Injection molding of plastics

Newtown
Hamilton County

(G-10583)
BRAIN BREW VENTURES 30 INC
3849 Edwards Rd (45244-2408)
PHONE.............................513 310-6374
Doug Hall, *CEO*
EMP: 10 **EST:** 2012
SALES (est): 977.44K **Privately Held**
Web: www.brainbrewwhiskey.com
SIC: 6799 2085 Venture capital companies; Bourbon whiskey

Niles
Trumbull County

(G-10584)
BRT EXTRUSIONS INC
Also Called: Building Rlationships Together
1818 N Main St Unit 1 (44446-1285)
P.O. Box 309 (44446-0309)
PHONE.............................330 544-0177
Roy Smith, *Pr*
William Fusco, *
EMP: 220 **EST:** 2004
SQ FT: 92,000
SALES (est): 21.86MM **Privately Held**
Web: www.brtextrusions.com
SIC: 3354 Aluminum extruded products

(G-10585)
CHIEFFOS FROZEN FOODS INC
406 S Main St (44446-1454)
PHONE.............................330 652-1222
Richard Yannucci, *Pr*
EMP: 8 **EST:** 1970
SQ FT: 7,200

SALES (est): 241.44K **Privately Held**
Web: www.chieffopasta.com
SIC: 2099 Food preparations, nec

(G-10586)
CLEVELAND STEEL CONTAINER CORP
412 Mason St (44446-2349)
PHONE.............................330 544-2271
Chistopher Page, *Owner*
EMP: 31
SALES (corp-wide): 165.45MM **Privately Held**
Web: www.cscpails.com
SIC: 3412 Barrels, shipping: metal
PA: Cleveland Steel Container Corporation
     100 Executive Pkwy
     Hudson OH 44236
     440 349-8000

(G-10587)
DINESOL PLASTICS INC
Also Called: Dinesol Plastics
195 E Park Ave (44446-2352)
P.O. Box 470 (44446-0470)
PHONE.............................330 544-7171
Robert Hendricks Junior, *Pr*
Kenneth Fibus, *
Kenneth Leonard, *
Michael Janak, *
▲ **EMP:** 150 **EST:** 1976
SQ FT: 380,000
SALES (est): 150MM **Privately Held**
Web: www.dinesol.com
SIC: 3089 Injection molding of plastics

(G-10588)
FAULL & SON LLC
515 Holford Ave (44446-1796)
P.O. Box 627 (44446-0627)
PHONE.............................330 652-4341
James K Faull, *Prin*
EMP: 10 **EST:** 1949
SQ FT: 16,000
SALES (est): 905.62K **Privately Held**
Web: www.faullandson.com
SIC: 3469 3544 3498 3429 Stamping metal for the trade; Special dies and tools; Fabricated pipe and fittings; Hardware, nec

(G-10589)
HOWLAND MACHINE CORP
947 Summit Ave (44446-3612)
PHONE.............................330 544-4029
Bruce V Dewey, *Pr*
EMP: 20 **EST:** 1989
SQ FT: 22,000
SALES (est): 2.81MM **Privately Held**
Web: www.hmcmachinetech.com
SIC: 3599 Machine shop, jobbing and repair

(G-10590)
HOWMET AEROSPACE INC
1000 Warren Ave (44446-1168)
PHONE.............................330 544-7633
EMP: 48
SALES (corp-wide): 7.43B **Publicly Held**
Web: www.howmet.com
SIC: 3355 3353 3463 Aluminum rolling and drawing, nec; Aluminum sheet and strip; Aluminum forgings
PA: Howmet Aerospace Inc.
     201 Isabella St Ste 200
     Pittsburgh PA 15212
     412 553-1950

(G-10591)
INTERNTNAL TCHNCAL PLYMR SYSTE
Also Called: Itps

852 Ann Ave (44446-2924)
P.O. Box 111 (44446-0111)
PHONE.............................330 505-1218
Samuel H Berkowitz, *CEO*
Richard L Goodman, *Pr*
▲ **EMP:** 23 **EST:** 1994
SQ FT: 5,000
SALES (est): 4.23MM **Privately Held**
Web: www.itps-inc.com
SIC: 2821 Plastics materials and resins

(G-10592)
IRONICS INC
750 S Main St (44446-1372)
P.O. Box 292 (44446)
PHONE.............................330 652-0583
Pete Tominey Junior, *Pr*
Mary Jane Tominey, *Stockholder*
EMP: 9 **EST:** 1974
SQ FT: 10,000
SALES (est): 958.47K **Privately Held**
SIC: 2816 3295 Iron oxide pigments (ochers, siennas, umbers); Blast furnace slag

(G-10593)
J A MCMAHON INCORPORATED
6 E Park Ave (44446-5020)
PHONE.............................330 652-2588
John A Mcmahon Iii, *Pr*
EMP: 26 **EST:** 1945
SQ FT: 32,000
SALES (est): 3.33MM **Privately Held**
Web: www.jamcmahon.com
SIC: 3441 Building components, structural steel

(G-10594)
KRONER PUBLICATIONS INC (PA)
1123 W Park Ave (44446-1188)
P.O. Box 150 (44446-0150)
PHONE.............................330 544-5500
John Kroner Senior, *Pr*
EMP: 30 **EST:** 1994
SALES (est): 1.7MM **Privately Held**
Web: www.thereviewnewspapers.com
SIC: 2711 Commercial printing and newspaper publishing combined

(G-10595)
NILES BUILDING PRODUCTS COMPANY (PA)
1600 Hunter Ave (44446-1644)
P.O. Box 662 (44446-0662)
PHONE.............................330 544-0880
EMP: 17 **EST:** 1973
SALES (est): 4.34MM
SALES (corp-wide): 4.34MM **Privately Held**
Web: www.nilesbldg.com
SIC: 3441 3442 Building components, structural steel; Metal doors, sash, and trim

(G-10596)
NILES MANUFACTURING & FINSHG
465 Walnut St (44446-2374)
PHONE.............................330 544-0402
Robert Hendricks, *Pr*
EMP: 110 **EST:** 1984
SQ FT: 150,000
SALES (est): 9.58MM **Privately Held**
SIC: 3469 3479 3471 3444 Stamping metal for the trade; Coating of metals and formed products; Plating and polishing; Sheet metalwork

(G-10597)
NILES MIRROR & GLASS INC
234 Robbins Ave Ste 1 (44446-1769)
PHONE.............................330 652-6277
Robert Leonard, *CEO*
Rick Leonard, *Pr*

Laurie Paden, *Sec*
EMP: 20 **EST:** 1997
SQ FT: 17,000
SALES (est): 624.42K **Privately Held**
SIC: 5231 1793 3211 Glass; Glass and glazing work; Insulating glass, sealed units

(G-10598)
NILES ROLL SERVICE INC (PA)
704 Warren Ave (44446-1643)
P.O. Box 86 (44446-0086)
PHONE....................330 544-0026
Timothy L Boggs, *Pr*
Beverly Boggs, *Sec*
EMP: 11 **EST:** 1993
SQ FT: 4,964
SALES (est): 1.67MM **Privately Held**
Web: www.nilesrollservice.com
SIC: 3069 Roll coverings, rubber

(G-10599)
NMC METALS INC (PA)
Also Called: Niles Expanded Metals & Plas
310 N Pleasant Ave (44446-1173)
P.O. Box 231 (44446-0231)
PHONE....................330 652-2501
▲ **EMP:** 48 **EST:** 1985
SALES (est): 4.88MM
SALES (corp-wide): 4.88MM **Privately Held**
Web: www.nilesexpandedmetals.com
SIC: 3449 Lath, expanded metal

(G-10600)
PHILLIPS MANUFACTURING CO
504 Walnut St (44446-2961)
PHONE....................330 652-4335
Steve Dalrymple, *Brnch Mgr*
EMP: 60
SALES (corp-wide): 43.4MM **Privately Held**
Web: www.phillipsmfg.com
SIC: 3442 3444 3541 Metal doors, sash, and trim; Sheet metalwork; Machine tools, metal cutting type
PA: Phillips Manufacturing Co.
4949 S 30th St
Omaha NE 68107
402 339-3800

(G-10601)
REED MINERALS LLC
412 Mckees Ln (44446-1373)
PHONE....................216 652-2002
Brian Tucker, *Pr*
EMP: 28
SALES (corp-wide): 23.88MM **Privately Held**
SIC: 3295 Minerals, ground or treated
PA: Reed Minerals, Llc
350 Poplar Church Rd
Camp Hill PA 17011
888 733-3646

(G-10602)
RMI TITANIUM COMPANY LLC
Also Called: Rti
2000 Warren Ave (44446-1148)
PHONE....................330 544-9470
EMP: 178
SALES (corp-wide): 7.43B **Publicly Held**
Web: www.howmet.com
SIC: 3441 Fabricated structural metal
HQ: Rmi Titanium Company, Llc
1000 Warren Ave
Niles OH 44446
330 652-9952

(G-10603)
RMI TITANIUM COMPANY LLC
Rti Hermitage
1000 Warren Ave (44446-1168)
PHONE....................330 652-9955
Paul Mandell, *Brnch Mgr*
EMP: 9
SALES (corp-wide): 7.43B **Publicly Held**
SIC: 3356 Titanium
HQ: Rmi Titanium Company, Llc
1000 Warren Ave
Niles OH 44446
330 652-9952

(G-10604)
RMI TITANIUM COMPANY LLC (HQ)
Also Called: Rti Niles
1000 Warren Ave (44446-1168)
PHONE....................330 652-9952
Dawn S Hickton, *Pr*
John H Odle, *Ex VP*
Lawrence W Jacobs, *VP*
◆ **EMP:** 20 **EST:** 1998
SQ FT: 677,605
SALES (est): 462.73MM
SALES (corp-wide): 7.43B **Publicly Held**
SIC: 3399 3356 1741 3533 Powder, metal; Titanium; Masonry and other stonework; Oil and gas drilling rigs and equipment
PA: Howmet Aerospace Inc.
201 Isabella St Ste 200
Pittsburgh PA 15212
412 553-1950

(G-10605)
RTI ALLOYS
1000 Warren Ave (44446-1168)
PHONE....................330 652-9952
Robert G Helwig, *Admn*
▲ **EMP:** 6 **EST:** 2013
SALES (est): 472.37K **Privately Held**
SIC: 3312 Blast furnaces and steel mills

(G-10606)
RTI INTERNATIONAL METALS INC
Also Called: Alcoa Titanium Engineered Pdts
1000 Warren Ave (44446-1168)
◆ **EMP:** 2575
SIC: 3356 3441 Titanium; Fabricated structural metal

(G-10607)
TRAICHAL CONSTRUCTION COMPANY (PA)
Also Called: Warren Door
332 Plant St (44446-1895)
P.O. Box 70 (44446-0070)
PHONE....................800 255-3667
Edward Traichal, *Pr*
EMP: 26 **EST:** 1937
SQ FT: 15,000
SALES (est): 3.39MM
SALES (corp-wide): 3.39MM **Privately Held**
Web: www.warrendoor.com
SIC: 3442 1751 5199 5031 Metal doors; Window and door installation and erection; Advertising specialties; Doors and windows

(G-10608)
VANEX TUBE CORPORATION
301 Mckees Ln Ste 2 (44446-1374)
PHONE....................330 544-9500
EMP: 70 **EST:** 1985
SALES (est): 2.15MM **Privately Held**
Web: www.vanextubecorp.com
SIC: 3498 3321 Tube fabricating (contract bending and shaping); Gray and ductile iron foundries

(G-10609)
WEST & BARKER INC
950 Summit Ave (44446-3693)
PHONE....................330 652-9923
Samuel M Barker Iii, *Pr*
Suzanne Leone, *VP*
June Barker, *Sec*
EMP: 15 **EST:** 1971
SQ FT: 106,000
SALES (est): 2.44MM **Privately Held**
Web: www.westandbarker.com
SIC: 3089 2396 3069 3714 Plastics hardware and building products; Automotive and apparel trimmings; Thread, rubber; Motor vehicle parts and accessories

(G-10610)
WHEATLAND TUBE LLC
Also Called: Wheatland Tube Company
1800 Hunter Ave (44446-1671)
PHONE....................724 342-6851
Mark Bahrey, *Brnch Mgr*
EMP: 133
Web: www.wheatland.com
SIC: 3317 3312 5051 Steel pipe and tubes; Blast furnaces and steel mills; Iron and steel (ferrous) products
HQ: Wheatland Tube, Llc
1 Council Ave
Wheatland PA 16161
800 257-8182

(G-10611)
YAR CORPORATION
406 S Main St (44446-1454)
PHONE....................330 652-1222
Richard A Yannucci, *Pr*
EMP: 7 **EST:** 2005
SALES (est): 170.62K **Privately Held**
SIC: 2098 Macaroni and spaghetti

North Baltimore
Wood County

(G-10612)
AUTOMATED BLDG COMPONENTS INC (PA)
2359 Grant Rd (45872-9662)
PHONE....................419 257-2152
Harold L Mccarty, *CEO*
Marshal Mccarty, *Pr*
Jennifer Buckingham, *Stockholder*
EMP: 30 **EST:** 1973
SQ FT: 10,000
SALES (est): 17.1MM
SALES (corp-wide): 17.1MM **Privately Held**
Web: www.abctruss.com
SIC: 2421 2439 2541 2435 Building and structural materials, wood; Trusses, wooden roof; Wood partitions and fixtures; Hardwood veneer and plywood

(G-10613)
KEYSTONE FOODS LLC
Equity Group-Ohio Div
2208 Grant Rd (45872-9663)
P.O. Box 307 (45872-0307)
PHONE....................419 257-2341
Steven Alberts, *Mgr*
EMP: 250
SQ FT: 60,000
SALES (corp-wide): 53.31B **Publicly Held**
Web: www.tysonfoods.com
SIC: 2013 Sausages and other prepared meats
HQ: Keystone Foods Llc
905 Airport Rd Ste 400
West Chester PA 19380
610 667-6700

(G-10614)
MID-WOOD INC
Also Called: True Value
101 E State St (45872-1358)
PHONE....................419 257-3331
Joe Smith, *Mgr*
EMP: 10
SALES (corp-wide): 16.88MM **Privately Held**
Web: www.mid-wood.com
SIC: 5153 5261 5251 5531 Grains; Fertilizer; Hardware stores; Automotive tires
PA: Mid-Wood, Inc.
12965 Defiance Pike
Cygnet OH
419 352-5231

(G-10615)
NATIONAL BEEF OHIO LLC
2208 Grant Rd (45872-9663)
PHONE....................800 449-2333
Bret G Wilson, *Managing Member*
EMP: 185 **EST:** 2018
SALES (est): 10.84MM **Privately Held**
Web: www.nationalbeef.com
SIC: 2011 Boxed beef, from meat slaughtered on site
HQ: National Beef Packing Company, L.L.C.
12200 N Ambssdor Dr Ste 5
Kansas City MO 64163
800 449-2333

(G-10616)
NATIONAL BEEF PACKING CO LLC
2208 Grant Rd (45872-9663)
PHONE....................419 257-5500
EMP: 1135
Web: www.nationalbeef.com
SIC: 2011 Meat packing plants
HQ: National Beef Packing Company, L.L.C.
12200 N Ambssdor Dr Ste 5
Kansas City MO 64163
800 449-2333

(G-10617)
OHIO BEEF USA LLC
2208 Grant Rd (45872-9663)
PHONE....................419 257-5536
EMP: 7 **EST:** 2019
SALES (est): 1.69MM **Privately Held**
Web: www.nationalbeef.com
SIC: 2011 Meat packing plants

(G-10618)
TEIJIN AUTOMOTIVE TECH INC
Also Called: CSP North Baltimore
100 S Poe Rd (45872-9551)
PHONE....................419 257-2231
Gary Dickson, *Brnch Mgr*
EMP: 251
Web: www.teijinautomotive.com
SIC: 3089 3714 Injection molding of plastics; Motor vehicle parts and accessories
HQ: Teijin Automotive Technologies, Inc.
255 Rex Blvd
Auburn Hills MI 48326
248 237-7800

(G-10619)
THE D S BROWN COMPANY (HQ)
300 E Cherry St (45872-1227)
P.O. Box 158 (45872-0158)
PHONE....................419 257-3561
◆ **EMP:** 220 **EST:** 1992
SALES (est): 45.98MM
SALES (corp-wide): 1.31B **Publicly Held**
Web: www.dsbrown.com
SIC: 3061 3441 5032 Mechanical rubber goods; Fabricated structural metal for bridges; Paving materials
PA: Gibraltar Industries, Inc.

GEOGRAPHIC

3556 Lake Shore Rd
Buffalo NY 14219
716 826-6500

North Bend
Hamilton County

(G-10620)
HAMMERSMITH BROS INVSTMNTS INC
Also Called: Baleco International
3200 State Line Rd (45052-9731)
P.O. Box 11331 (45211)
PHONE..............................513 353-3000
E Bernard Haviland, *Pr*
▲ **EMP:** 20 **EST:** 1958
SQ FT: 72,000
SALES (est): 2.58MM
SALES (corp-wide): 83.25MM **Privately Held**
Web: www.baleco.com
SIC: 5091 3589 Swimming pools, equipment and supplies; Swimming pool filter and water conditioning systems
PA: Haviland Enterprises, Inc.
421 Ann St Nw
Grand Rapids MI 49504
616 361-6691

(G-10621)
ROYSTER-CLARK INC
10743 Brower Rd (45052-9761)
P.O. Box 158 (45052-0158)
PHONE..............................513 941-4100
Bill Chockran, *Prin*
EMP: 6 **EST:** 2010
SALES (est): 298.94K **Privately Held**
Web: www.trammo.com
SIC: 2873 Nitrogenous fertilizers

(G-10622)
WERNKE WLDG & STL ERECTION CO
3150 State Line Rd (45052-9731)
PHONE..............................513 353-4173
Jeff Wernke, *Pr*
James Wernke, *Ch*
Jerry Wernke, *VP*
John Wernke, *Sec*
EMP: 14 **EST:** 1968
SQ FT: 4,800
SALES (est): 2.76MM **Privately Held**
Web: www.wernkesteel.com
SIC: 1791 3441 Iron work, structural; Fabricated structural metal

North Benton
Portage County

(G-10623)
PAUL J TATULINSKI LTD
1595 W Main St (44449)
P.O. Box 382 (44449-0382)
PHONE..............................330 584-8251
Paul J Tatulinski, *Pr*
EMP: 10 **EST:** 1999
SQ FT: 4,704
SALES (est): 223.07K **Privately Held**
SIC: 3053 Gaskets, all materials

(G-10624)
THEISS UAV SOLUTIONS LLC
10881 Johnson Rd (44449-9652)
P.O. Box 1086 (44460-8086)
PHONE..............................330 584-2070
Chad Kapper, *Pr*
Richard Theiss, *Pdt Mgr*
EMP: 8 **EST:** 1992

SQ FT: 4,600
SALES (est): 3.51MM
SALES (corp-wide): 24.6MM **Privately Held**
Web: www.theissuav.com
SIC: 3721 7363 Aircraft; Pilot service, aviation
PA: Lauren International, Ltd.
143 Garland Dr Sw
New Philadelphia OH 44663
234 303-2400

North Bloomfield
Trumbull County

(G-10625)
NORDEN MFG LLC
4210 Kinsman Rd Nw (44450-9710)
PHONE..............................440 693-4630
EMP: 37 **EST:** 1992
SALES (est): 5.49MM **Privately Held**
Web: www.nordenmfg.com
SIC: 3523 Farm machinery and equipment

North Canton
Stark County

(G-10626)
A STUCKI COMPANY
5335 Mayfair Rd (44720-1532)
PHONE..............................412 424-0560
Tom Seccombe, *Genl Mgr*
EMP: 74
SALES (corp-wide): 454.72MM **Privately Held**
Web: www.stucki.com
SIC: 3743 Railroad equipment
HQ: A. Stucki Company
360 Wright Brothers Dr
Moon Township PA 15108
412 424-0560

(G-10627)
AIRSOURCES INC
950 Honeysuckle Cir Ne (44720-9838)
PHONE..............................610 983-0102
Betty Scott, *Pr*
EMP: 6 **EST:** 1989
SALES (est): 159.12K **Privately Held**
SIC: 3444 Sheet metalwork

(G-10628)
ASC INDUSTRIES INC (DH)
Also Called: ASC
2100 International Pkwy (44720-1373)
PHONE..............................800 253-6009
David Peace, *CEO*
◆ **EMP:** 95 **EST:** 1976
SQ FT: 200,000
SALES (est): 49.63MM
SALES (corp-wide): 7.28B **Privately Held**
Web: www.ascindustries.com
SIC: 3714 Water pump, motor vehicle
HQ: Specialty Pumps Group, Inc.
127 Public Sq Ste 5110
Cleveland OH 44114
216 589-0198

(G-10629)
BALL CORPORATION
3075 Brookline Rd (44720-1526)
PHONE..............................330 244-2313
EMP: 10
SALES (corp-wide): 11.79B **Publicly Held**
Web: www.ball.com
SIC: 3411 Food and beverage containers
PA: Ball Corporation
9200 W 108th Cir

Westminster CO 80021
303 469-3131

(G-10630)
BIRO MANUFACTURING COMPANY
6658 Promway Ave Nw (44720-7316)
PHONE..............................419 798-4451
Sharon Edwards, *Mgr*
EMP: 10
SALES (corp-wide): 11MM **Privately Held**
Web: www.birosaw.com
SIC: 3556 Food products machinery
PA: The Biro Manufacturing Company
1114 West Main St
Marblehead OH 43440
419 798-4451

(G-10631)
CALVERT WIRE & CABLE CORP
4276 Strausser Street, Applegrove Ext (44720-7114)
PHONE..............................330 494-3248
Steve Hilson, *Mgr*
EMP: 26
Web: www.wesco.com
SIC: 3357 Nonferrous wiredrawing and insulating
HQ: Calvert Wire & Cable Corporation
17909 Clvland Pkwy Ste 18
Cleveland OH 44142
216 433-7600

(G-10632)
CANTON ELEVATOR INC
2575 Greensburg Rd (44720-1419)
PHONE..............................330 833-3600
Robert A Kazar, *CEO*
Michael J Paschke, *
◆ **EMP:** 75 **EST:** 2018
SQ FT: 80,000
SALES (est): 19.31MM **Privately Held**
Web: acim.nidec.com
SIC: 3534 3537 Elevators and equipment; Industrial trucks and tractors
HQ: Nidec Motor Corporation
8050 W Florissant Ave
Saint Louis MO 63136

(G-10633)
DELTA MEDIA GROUP INC
7015 Sunset Strip Ave Nw (44720-7078)
PHONE..............................330 493-0350
Noel England, *Pr*
EMP: 68 **EST:** 2000
SALES (est): 4.4MM **Privately Held**
Web: www.deltagroup.com
SIC: 7372 Application computer software

(G-10634)
DIEBOLD NIXDORF INCORPORATED
Also Called: Diebold
334 Orchard Ave Ne (44720-2556)
P.O. Box 3077 (44720-8077)
PHONE..............................336 662-1115
EMP: 56
SALES (corp-wide): 3.75B **Publicly Held**
Web: www.dieboldnixdorf.com
SIC: 3578 Calculating and accounting equipment
PA: Diebold Nixdorf, Incorporated
350 Orchard Ave Ne
North Canton OH 44720
330 490-4000

(G-10635)
DIEBOLD NIXDORF INCORPORATED (PA)
Also Called: Diebold Nixdorf
350 Orchard Ave Ne (44720-2556)
P.O. Box 3077 (44720-8077)
PHONE..............................330 490-4000

Octavio Marquez, *Pr*
Patrick J Byrne, *Non-Executive Chairman of the Board*
Thomas S Timko, *CAO*
Elizabeth C Radigan, *CLO*
Kathleen Creech, *CPO*
EMP: 1049 **EST:** 1859
SALES (est): 3.75B
SALES (corp-wide): 3.75B **Publicly Held**
Web: www.dieboldnixdorf.com
SIC: 3578 3699 Automatic teller machines (ATM); Security control equipment and systems; Safes and vaults, metal

(G-10636)
DOCUMENT CONCEPTS INC
Also Called: Office Furniture Solution
607 S Main St # A (44720-3002)
PHONE..............................330 575-5685
Tim Barr, *Pr*
Terry A Moore, *
EMP: 11 **EST:** 2002
SQ FT: 15,000
SALES (est): 1.28MM **Privately Held**
Web: www.document-concepts.com
SIC: 2752 Offset printing

(G-10637)
DUNCAN PRESS CORPORATION
5122 Strausser St Nw (44720-5545)
PHONE..............................330 477-4529
Richard Kempthorn, *Pr*
Scott Duncan, *VP*
Jed Parker, *VP*
EMP: 21 **EST:** 1958
SALES (est): 3.62MM **Privately Held**
Web: www.duncanpress-inc.com
SIC: 2752 Offset printing

(G-10638)
FANNIE MAY CONFECTIONS INC
5353 Lauby Rd (44720-1572)
PHONE..............................330 494-0833
Terry Michell, *Pr*
EMP: 800 **EST:** 2004
SALES (est): 39.25MM
SALES (corp-wide): 369.96MM **Privately Held**
Web: www.fanniemay.com
SIC: 5441 2066 Candy; Chocolate bars, solid
HQ: Fannie May Confections Brands, Inc.
9 W Washington St
Chicago IL 60602
330 494-0833

(G-10639)
FIVES BRONX INC
Also Called: Bronx Taylor Wilson
8817 Pleasantwood Ave Nw (44720-4759)
PHONE..............................330 244-1960
Brian Lombardi, *CEO*
Dave Macneilll, *
Curt Sabin, *
◆ **EMP:** 70 **EST:** 1988
SQ FT: 10,000
SALES (est): 10.61MM
SALES (corp-wide): 1.92MM **Privately Held**
Web: www.fivesgroup.com
SIC: 3547 Finishing equipment, rolling mill
HQ: Fives
3 Rue Drouot
Paris IDF 75009
145237575

(G-10640)
FLUID AUTOMATION INC
8400 Port Jackson Ave Nw (44720-5464)
PHONE..............................248 912-1970
Lance H Daby, *Pr*

Leon L Daby, *VP*
Beverly Daby, *Sec*
EMP: 29 **EST:** 1974
SQ FT: 16,000
SALES (est): 534.95K **Privately Held**
Web: www.graco.com
SIC: 3561 3569 Industrial pumps and parts; Liquid automation machinery and equipment

(G-10641)
GBS CORP (PA)
Also Called: GBS Filing Solutions
7233 Freedom Ave Nw (44720-7123)
P.O. Box 2340 (44720-0340)
PHONE..............................330 494-5330
Eugene Calabria, *CEO*
Eugene Calabria, *Pr*
Laurence Merriman, *
Michele Benson, *
Michael Merriman, *
▲ **EMP:** 150 **EST:** 1971
SQ FT: 115,000
SALES (est): 190.76MM
SALES (corp-wide): 190.76MM **Privately Held**
Web: www.gbscorp.com
SIC: 2675 2672 2761 2759 Folders, filing, die-cut: made from purchased materials; Labels (unprinted), gummed: made from purchased materials; Manifold business forms; Commercial printing, nec

(G-10642)
GLASCRAFT INC
8400 Port Jackson Ave Nw (44720-5464)
PHONE..............................330 966-3000
Morris Wheeler, *Pr*
Byron Bradley, *
EMP: 9 **EST:** 1959
SQ FT: 51,200
SALES (est): 2.07MM
SALES (corp-wide): 2.11B **Publicly Held**
Web: www.graco.com
SIC: 3563 Spraying outfits: metals, paints, and chemicals (compressor)
PA: Graco Inc.
88 11th Ave Ne
Minneapolis MN 55413
612 623-6000

(G-10643)
GOODRICH CORPORATION
6051 N Airport Dr (44720)
PHONE..............................330 374-2358
Jeremy Henry, *Brnch Mgr*
EMP: 6
SALES (corp-wide): 80.74B **Publicly Held**
Web: www.goodrichdeicing.com
SIC: 3728 Aircraft parts and equipment, nec
HQ: Goodrich Corporation
2730 W Tyvola Rd
Charlotte NC 28217
704 423-7000

(G-10644)
GRACO OHIO INC (HQ)
Also Called: Liquid Control
8400 Port Jackson Ave Nw (44720-5464)
PHONE..............................330 494-1313
William C Schiltz, *Ch Bd*
Kenneth Jacobs, *
Barbara Schiltz, *
Ronald W Dougherty, *
▲ **EMP:** 100 **EST:** 1978
SQ FT: 73,000
SALES (est): 29.39MM
SALES (corp-wide): 2.11B **Publicly Held**
Web: www.graco.com
SIC: 3824 3586 5251 Predetermining counters; Measuring and dispensing pumps ; Pumps and pumping equipment

PA: Graco Inc.
88 11th Ave Ne
Minneapolis MN 55413
612 623-6000

(G-10645)
HARRY LONDON CANDIES INC (DH)
Also Called: Harry London Chocolates
5353 Lauby Rd (44720-1572)
PHONE..............................330 494-0833
Terry Michell, *Pr*
Ed Seibolt, *
Matthew J Anderson, *
▲ **EMP:** 25 **EST:** 1922
SQ FT: 200,000
SALES (est): 45.64MM
SALES (corp-wide): 369.96MM **Privately Held**
Web: 88652-us.all.biz
SIC: 2066 5441 Chocolate and cocoa products; Candy
HQ: Fannie May Confections Brands, Inc.
9 W Washington St
Chicago IL 60602
330 494-0833

(G-10646)
HENDRICKSON USA LLC
9260 Pleasantwood Ave Nw (44720-9006)
PHONE..............................630 910-2800
EMP: 124
SALES (corp-wide): 758.84MM **Privately Held**
Web: www.hendrickson-intl.com
SIC: 3714 Motor vehicle parts and accessories
HQ: Hendrickson Usa, L.L.C.
840 S Frontage Rd
Woodridge IL 60517

(G-10647)
IMPERIAL ELECTRIC COMPANY
2575 Greensburg Rd (44720-1419)
PHONE..............................330 734-3600
David Molnar, *Pr*
Mark Schoolcraft, *
◆ **EMP:** 270 **EST:** 1889
SALES (est): 21.45MM **Privately Held**
Web: acim.nidec.com
SIC: 3621 Motors, electric
HQ: Nidec Motor Corporation
8050 W Florissant Ave
Saint Louis MO 63136

(G-10648)
KIRK KEY INTERLOCK COMPANY LLC
9048 Meridian Cir Nw (44720-8387)
PHONE..............................330 833-8223
James G Owens, *Managing Member*
▼ **EMP:** 47 **EST:** 1932
SQ FT: 26,000
SALES (est): 12.16MM
SALES (corp-wide): 2.58B **Privately Held**
Web: www.sentricsafetygroup.com
SIC: 3429 5063 Keys, locks, and related hardware; Electrical apparatus and equipment
PA: Halma Public Limited Company
Misbourne Court
Amersham BUCKS HP7 0
149 472-1111

(G-10649)
LT ENTERPRISES OF OHIO LLC
334 Orchard Ave Ne (44720-2556)
PHONE..............................330 526-6908
▲ **EMP:** 24 **EST:** 2005
SALES (est): 474.38K **Privately Held**
SIC: 3444 Sheet metalwork

(G-10650)
MCF INDUSTRIES
1206 N Main St (44720-1926)
P.O. Box 2747 (44720-0747)
PHONE..............................330 526-6337
Jon Graham, *Pr*
EMP: 7 **EST:** 2017
SALES (est): 2.26MM **Privately Held**
Web: www.mcf-ind.com
SIC: 3599 Machine shop, jobbing and repair

(G-10651)
MICROPLEX INC
7568 Whipple Ave Nw (44720-6922)
PHONE..............................330 498-0600
Valerie Walters, *Pr*
John Walters, *
Jon Harst, *
Susan Harst, *
EMP: 30 **EST:** 1985
SQ FT: 12,000
SALES (est): 4.55MM **Privately Held**
Web: www.microplex-inc.com
SIC: 3496 3679 5045 Cable, uninsulated wire: made from purchased wire; Harness assemblies, for electronic use: wire or cable ; Computer peripheral equipment

(G-10652)
MOHLER LUMBER COMPANY
4214 Portage St Nw (44720-7399)
PHONE..............................330 499-5461
Jennifer Hamilton, *Ch Bd*
Richard Rohrer, *Ch Bd*
Willidam Leed, *Pr*
Jed Rohrer, *VP*
Gary Leed, *Sec*
EMP: 20 **EST:** 1911
SQ FT: 8,320
SALES (est): 4.73MM **Privately Held**
Web: www.mohlerlumber.com
SIC: 2435 5211 2421 2426 Hardwood veneer and plywood; Millwork and lumber; Sawmills and planing mills, general; Hardwood dimension and flooring mills

(G-10653)
MOTION MOBILITY & DESIGN INC
6490 Promler St Nw (44720-7625)
PHONE..............................330 244-9723
Paul V Pettini, *Pr*
Steve Williams, *VP*
EMP: 11 **EST:** 1999
SQ FT: 12,000
SALES (est): 4.26MM **Privately Held**
Web: www.motionmobility.com
SIC: 3842 Braces, elastic

(G-10654)
MRO BUILT LLC
Also Called: Mro Built, Inc.
6410 Promway Ave Nw (44720-7622)
PHONE..............................330 526-0555
Alfred A Olivieri, *Pr*
Dean Olivieri, *
Virginia Olivieri, *
Timothy Feller, *
EMP: 75 **EST:** 1977
SQ FT: 55,000
SALES (est): 8.42MM
SALES (corp-wide): 48.19MM **Privately Held**
Web: www.mrobuilt.com
SIC: 2599 2542 2434 Cabinets, factory; Partitions and fixtures, except wood; Wood kitchen cabinets
PA: Fred Olivieri Construction Company
6315 Promway Ave Nw
North Canton OH 44720
330 494-1007

(G-10655)
MYERS POWER PRODUCTS INC (PA)
Also Called: Myers FSI
219 E Maple St Ste 100/200e (44720-2586)
PHONE..............................330 834-3200
Diana Grootonk, *CEO*
◆ **EMP:** 130 **EST:** 2003
SQ FT: 40,000
SALES (est): 172.09MM
SALES (corp-wide): 172.09MM **Privately Held**
Web: www.myerspower.com
SIC: 3613 Switchgear and switchboard apparatus

(G-10656)
NATIONAL LIME AND STONE CO
5377 Lauby Rd (44720-1523)
PHONE..............................330 966-4836
Dave Webere, *Prin*
EMP: 18
SALES (corp-wide): 86.85MM **Privately Held**
Web: www.natlime.com
SIC: 1422 Crushed and broken limestone
PA: The National Lime And Stone Company
551 Lake Cascade Pkwy
Findlay OH 45840
419 422-4341

(G-10657)
PAARLO PLASTICS INC
7720 Tim Ave Nw (44720-6955)
P.O. Box 2556 (44720-0556)
PHONE..............................330 494-3798
James D Park, *Pr*
▲ **EMP:** 65 **EST:** 1981
SQ FT: 80,000
SALES (est): 3.95MM **Privately Held**
Web: www.paarloplastics.com
SIC: 3089 Blow molded finished plastics products, nec

(G-10658)
POLYMER PACKAGING INC (PA)
7755 Freedom Ave Nw (44720-6905)
PHONE..............................330 832-2000
Larry L Lanham, *CEO*
Chris Thomazin, *
William D Lanham, *
Jeffrey S Davis, *
◆ **EMP:** 86 **EST:** 1986
SALES (est): 23.83MM
SALES (corp-wide): 23.83MM **Privately Held**
Web: www.polymerpkg.com
SIC: 5113 5162 2621 2821 Paper, wrapping or coarse, and products; Plastics products, nec; Wrapping and packaging papers; Plastics materials and resins

(G-10659)
PORTAGE ELECTRIC PRODUCTS INC
Also Called: Pepi
7700 Freedom Ave Nw (44720-6906)
P.O. Box 2170 (44720-0170)
PHONE..............................330 499-2727
Brandon Wehl, *Ch Bd*
Omar R Givler, *
Allyson Wehl, *
Ray Kolesar, *
Edward J Zink, *
▲ **EMP:** 220 **EST:** 1963
SQ FT: 11,000
SALES (est): 23.77MM **Privately Held**
Web: www.pepiusa.com

SIC: 3822 3829 Appliance controls,except air-conditioning and refrigeration; Measuring and controlling devices, nec

(G-10660)
POWELL ELECTRICAL SYSTEMS INC
Also Called: Pemco North Canton Division
8967 Pleasantwood Ave Nw (44721-4761)
PHONE..................................330 966-1750
Bob Gens, *Brnch Mgr*
EMP: 92
SQ FT: 41,600
SALES (corp-wide): 1.01B **Publicly Held**
Web: www.powellind.com
SIC: 3678 5063 3699 Electronic connectors; Electrical apparatus and equipment; Electrical equipment and supplies, nec
HQ: Powell Electrical Systems, Inc.
8550 Mosley Rd
Houston TX 77075
713 944-6900

(G-10661)
R R R DEVELOPMENT CO (PA)
8817 Pleasantwood Ave Nw (44720-4759)
PHONE..................................330 966-8855
Ronald Dillard, *Pr*
Thomas Dillard, *
Robert Irwin, *
▲ EMP: 80 EST: 1982
SALES (est): 9.84MM
SALES (corp-wide): 9.84MM **Privately Held**
Web: www.rrrdev.com
SIC: 3599 Machine shop, jobbing and repair

(G-10662)
RADON ELIMINATOR LLC
5046 Stoney Creek Ln (44720-1000)
PHONE..................................330 844-0703
EMP: 11 EST: 2015
SALES (est): 877.74K **Privately Held**
Web: www.radoneliminator.com
SIC: 1389 8744 8748 1731 Construction, repair, and dismantling services; Environmental remediation; Environmental consultant; Environmental system control installation

(G-10663)
RAIL BEARING SERVICE LLC
Also Called: Rail Bearing Service Inc
4500 Mount Pleasant St Nw (44720-5450)
P.O. Box 6929 (44706-0929)
PHONE..................................234 262-3000
Mervyn Cronje, *Contrlr*
EMP: 350 EST: 1973
SQ FT: 6,000
SALES (est): 7.07MM
SALES (corp-wide): 4.57B **Publicly Held**
Web: www.timken.com
SIC: 3568 Railroad car journal bearings
PA: The Timken Company
4500 Mount Pleasant St Nw
North Canton OH 44720
234 262-3000

(G-10664)
RLD TRANSPORTATION LLC
3060 Brookline Rd (44720-1527)
PHONE..................................234 334-7777
John Dimariangeli, *Pr*
EMP: 15 EST: 2016
SALES (est): 692.35K **Privately Held**
SIC: 3523 Farm machinery and equipment

(G-10665)
ROBIN INDUSTRIES INC (PA)
Also Called: Elastotec Div
6500 Rockside Rd Ste 230 (44720)
PHONE..................................216 631-7000

▲ EMP: 12 EST: 1947
SALES (est): 74.78MM
SALES (corp-wide): 74.78MM **Privately Held**
Web: www.robin-industries.com
SIC: 3069 3061 Molded rubber products; Mechanical rubber goods

(G-10666)
RTX CORPORATION
6051 W Airport Dr (44721-1447)
PHONE..................................330 784-5477
EMP: 268
SALES (corp-wide): 80.74B **Publicly Held**
Web: www.rtx.com
SIC: 3585 Refrigeration and heating equipment
PA: Rtx Corporation
1000 Wilson Blvd
Arlington VA 22209
781 522-3000

(G-10667)
SCHWEBEL BAKING COMPANY
Also Called: Schwebel Bkg Co N Canton Agcy
7382 Whipple Ave Nw (44721-7140)
PHONE..................................330 926-9410
EMP: 12
SALES (corp-wide): 71.65MM **Privately Held**
Web: www.schwebels.com
SIC: 2051 Bread, cake, and related products
PA: Schwebel Baking Company
965 E Midlothian Blvd
Youngstown OH 44502
330 783-2860

(G-10668)
SECO MACHINE INC
5335 Mayfair Rd (44720-1532)
PHONE..................................330 499-2150
Mary Seccombe, *Pr*
Delano F Rossio, *
Richard Seccombe, *
Annette M Rossio, *
EMP: 30 EST: 1985
SALES (est): 4.21MM **Privately Held**
Web: www.secomachine.com
SIC: 3599 Machine shop, jobbing and repair

(G-10669)
STANDARD ENGINEERING GROUP INC
3516 Highland Park Nw (44720-4532)
PHONE..................................330 494-4300
Ronald Schlemmer, *Pr*
William Simmons, *VP*
◆ EMP: 6 EST: 2000
SALES (est): 3.39MM **Privately Held**
Web: www.standardengineeringgroup.com
SIC: 3544 Special dies and tools

(G-10670)
STARK INDUSTRIAL LLC
5103 Stoneham Rd (44720-1540)
P.O. Box 3030 (44720-8030)
PHONE..................................330 966-8108
Samuel Wilkof, *Pr*
Ray Wilkof, *
▼ EMP: 40 EST: 1959
SQ FT: 25,000
SALES (est): 4.42MM **Privately Held**
Web: www.starkindustrial.com
SIC: 3599 Machine shop, jobbing and repair

(G-10671)
TEST MEASUREMENT SYSTEMS INC
9073 Pleasantwood Ave Nw (44720-4763)
PHONE..................................888 867-4872
John W Jobe, *Prin*

EMP: 7 EST: 2015
SALES (est): 2.09MM **Privately Held**
Web: www.tmsi-usa.com
SIC: 3569 General industrial machinery, nec

(G-10672)
THERMTROL CORPORATION
Also Called: Thermtrol
8914 Pleasantwood Ave Nw (44720-4762)
PHONE..................................330 497-4148
Mark Jeffries Senior, *Pr*
Mark Jeffries Senior, *Pr*
Mark A Jeffries Junior, *Ex VP*
John Komer, *
David Lett, *
◆ EMP: 800 EST: 1986
SQ FT: 24,000
SALES (est): 25.3MM **Privately Held**
Web: www.thermtrol.com
SIC: 3679 3822 Harness assemblies, for electronic use: wire or cable; Thermostats and other environmental sensors

(G-10673)
TIMKEN COMPANY (PA)
Also Called: Timken
4500 Mount Pleasant St Nw (44720-5450)
P.O. Box 6929 (44720)
PHONE..................................234 262-3000
Richard G Kyle, *Interim Chief Executive Officer*
John M Timken Junior, *Ch Bd*
Philip D Fracassa, *Ex VP*
Hansal N Patel, *VP*
Christopher A Coughlin, *Ex VP*
◆ EMP: 1335 EST: 1899
SALES (est): 4.57B
SALES (corp-wide): 4.57B **Publicly Held**
Web: www.timken.com
SIC: 3562 5085 Ball and roller bearings; Bearings, bushings, wheels, and gears

(G-10674)
TIMKEN NEWCO I LLC
4500 Mount Pleasant St Nw (44720-5450)
PHONE..................................234 262-3000
EMP: 7 EST: 2016
SALES (est): 1.56MM
SALES (corp-wide): 4.57B **Publicly Held**
Web: www.timken.com
SIC: 3562 3566 3568 Ball and roller bearings ; Gears, power transmission, except auto; Power transmission equipment, nec
PA: The Timken Company
4500 Mount Pleasant St Nw
North Canton OH 44720
234 262-3000

(G-10675)
TIMKEN RECEIVABLES CORPORATION
4500 Mount Pleasant St Nw (44720-5450)
PHONE..................................234 262-3000
Glenn Eisenberg, *Pr*
EMP: 11 EST: 2010
SALES (est): 897.2K
SALES (corp-wide): 4.57B **Publicly Held**
Web: www.timken.com
SIC: 3312 Blast furnaces and steel mills
PA: The Timken Company
4500 Mount Pleasant St Nw
North Canton OH 44720
234 262-3000

(G-10676)
TMSI LLC (HQ)
Also Called: Tmsi
8817 Pleasantwood Ave Nw (44720-4759)
P.O. Box 5414 (44334)
PHONE..................................888 867-4872
Gerald R Potts, *Pr*

◆ EMP: 14 EST: 1991
SALES (est): 8.26MM **Privately Held**
Web: www.tmsi-usa.com
SIC: 5013 3825 Testing equipment, electrical: automotive; Instruments to measure electricity
PA: Mesnac Co.,Ltd.
No. 43 Zhengzhou Road
Qingdao SD 26604

(G-10677)
TRI - FLEX OF OHIO INC (PA)
2701 Applegrove St Nw (44720-6213)
PHONE..................................330 705-7084
Paul R Lioi, *Prin*
Paul Lili, *Pr*
EMP: 6 EST: 2011
SALES (est): 2.24MM
SALES (corp-wide): 2.24MM **Privately Held**
SIC: 3365 Machinery castings, aluminum

(G-10678)
TRISTAN RUBBER MOLDING INC (PA)
7255 Whipple Ave Nw (44720-7137)
PHONE..................................330 499-4055
Peter Fritz, *Pr*
Christina Fritz, *VP*
Larry W Ball, *Prin*
EMP: 15 EST: 1995
SQ FT: 20,000
SALES (est): 1.12MM **Privately Held**
SIC: 3069 Molded rubber products

(G-10679)
UCI INTERNATIONAL LLC (DH)
2100 International Pkwy (44720-1373)
PHONE..................................330 899-0340
Bruce Zorich, *CEO*
Nathan Iles, *CFO*
Keith A Zar, *VP*
Curtis Draper, *S&M/VP*
Mike Malady, *Pers/VP*
▲ EMP: 22 EST: 2006
SALES (est): 473.45MM
SALES (corp-wide): 7.28B **Privately Held**
Web: www.uciholdings.com
SIC: 3714 Motor vehicle parts and accessories
HQ: Uci International Holdings, Inc.
2100 International Pkwy
North Canton OH 44720
330 899-0340

(G-10680)
UPL INTERNATIONAL INC
Also Called: Universal Plastics
7661 Freedom Ave Nw (44720-6903)
PHONE..................................330 433-2860
Jeffrey Scarpitti, *Pr*
Wade Scarpitti, *
EMP: 15 EST: 1976
SQ FT: 18,000
SALES (est): 4.6MM **Privately Held**
SIC: 3089 5162 Injection molding of plastics; Plastics products, nec

(G-10681)
WILLIAMS PARTNERS LP
7235 Whipple Ave Nw (44720-7101)
PHONE..................................330 414-6201
Travis Bonine, *Brnch Mgr*
EMP: 94
SALES (corp-wide): 10.5B **Publicly Held**
Web: www.williams.com
SIC: 1311 Natural gas production
HQ: Williams Partners L.P.
1 Williams Ctr Bsmt 2
Tulsa OK 74172

▲ = Import ▼ = Export
◆ = Import/Export

North Jackson
Mahoning County

(G-10682)
AMERICAN PLASTECH LLC
11635 Mahoning Ave (44451-9688)
P.O. Box 399 (44451-0399)
PHONE................................330 538-0576
Rick Amato, *Managing Member*
EMP: 6 **EST:** 2016
SALES (est): 397.65K **Privately Held**
SIC: 2431 Windows and window parts and trim, wood

(G-10683)
BCI AND V INVESTMENTS INC
11675 Mahoning Ave (44451-9688)
P.O. Box 698 (44451-0698)
PHONE................................330 538-0660
Harold Bartels, *Pr*
Randy Vegso, *
EMP: 6 **EST:** 1987
SQ FT: 26,000
SALES (est): 489.14K **Privately Held**
SIC: 2821 3356 Vinyl resins, nec; Nonferrous rolling and drawing, nec

(G-10684)
CANFIELD MANUFACTURING CO INC
Also Called: Wilson Specialties
489 Rosemont Rd (44451-9717)
PHONE................................330 533-3333
M J Stewart, *CEO*
Mary Mc Mahon, *Off Mgr*
EMP: 7 **EST:** 1800
SQ FT: 20,000
SALES (est): 90.18K **Privately Held**
SIC: 2426 2499 Lumber, hardwood dimension; Handles, wood

(G-10685)
CLEVELAND CORETEC INC
Also Called: Ttm
12080 Debartolo Dr (44451-9642)
PHONE................................314 727-2087
Jonathan Schofield, *Prin*
EMP: 6 **EST:** 2012
SALES (est): 2.17MM **Privately Held**
SIC: 3672 Printed circuit boards

(G-10686)
DDI NORTH JACKSON CORP
12080 Debartolo Dr (44451-9642)
P.O. Box 216 (44451-0216)
PHONE................................330 538-3900
Mark Curry, *CEO*
EMP: 8 **EST:** 2014
SALES (est): 425.73K **Privately Held**
SIC: 3672 Printed circuit boards

(G-10687)
EXTRUDEX ALUMINUM INC
12051 Mahoning Ave (44451-9617)
P.O. Box 697 (44451-0697)
PHONE................................330 538-4444
Andrew Gucciardi, *Pr*
▲ **EMP:** 120 **EST:** 1998
SQ FT: 110,000
SALES (est): 48.97MM
SALES (corp-wide): 4.08MM **Privately Held**
Web: www.extrudex.com
SIC: 3354 Aluminum extruded products
PA: Extrudex Aluminum Corp
411 Chrislea Rd
Woodbridge ON L4L 8
416 745-4444

(G-10688)
GRINDING EQUIPMENT & MCHY LLC
5417 S Salem Warren Rd (44451-9705)
PHONE................................330 747-2313
James Johnson, *Pr*
Tracy Gross, *Off Mgr*
EMP: 13 **EST:** 1982
SALES (est): 1.3MM **Privately Held**
Web: www.gem-usa.com
SIC: 3599 Machine shop, jobbing and repair

(G-10689)
INNOVAR SYSTEMS LIMITED
12155 Commissioner Dr (44451-9640)
P.O. Box 486 (44451-0486)
PHONE................................330 538-3942
John Frano, *CEO*
Paul Graff, *
Scott Yakubek, *
EMP: 35 **EST:** 2003
SQ FT: 15,000
SALES (est): 4.37MM **Privately Held**
Web: www.innovarsystems.com
SIC: 3699 Laser welding, drilling, and cutting equipment

(G-10690)
JOHN ZIDIAN COMPANY
382 Rosemont Rd (44451-9631)
PHONE................................330 965-8455
EMP: 19
SALES (corp-wide): 8.86MM **Privately Held**
Web: www.giarussa.com
SIC: 2032 Italian foods, nec: packaged in cans, jars, etc.
PA: John Zidian Company
574 Mcclurg Rd
Youngstown OH 44512
330 743-6050

(G-10691)
OHIO CUSTOM DIES LLC
293 Rosemont Rd (44451-9632)
P.O. Box 428 (44451-0428)
PHONE................................330 538-3396
EMP: 15 **EST:** 2020
SALES (est): 3.59MM **Privately Held**
Web: www.ohiocustomdies.com
SIC: 3544 Special dies and tools

(G-10692)
OHIO SPECIALTY DIES LLC
293 Rosemont Rd (44451-9632)
P.O. Box 428 (44451-0428)
PHONE................................330 538-3396
Joseph P Baco, *Managing Member*
EMP: 16 **EST:** 2011
SQ FT: 4,000
SALES (est): 1.05MM **Privately Held**
Web: www.ohiospecialtydies.com
SIC: 3544 Special dies and tools

(G-10693)
PMC SYSTEMS LIMITED
12155 Commissioner Dr (44451-9640)
P.O. Box 486 (44451-0486)
PHONE................................330 538-2268
John Frano, *Pr*
Paul Graff, *
EMP: 30 **EST:** 1983
SQ FT: 3,000
SALES (est): 5.03MM **Privately Held**
Web: www.pmcsystems.com
SIC: 3625 8711 Electric controls and control accessories, industrial; Electrical or electronic engineering

(G-10694)
SOVEREIGN CIRCUITS INC
12080 Debartolo Dr (44451-9642)
P.O. Box 216 (44451-0216)
PHONE................................330 538-3900
Robert Buss, *Prin*
EMP: 6 **EST:** 2014
SALES (est): 1.05MM **Privately Held**
Web: www.sovereign-circuits.com
SIC: 3679 Electronic circuits

(G-10695)
STAMPED STEEL PRODUCTS INC
151 S Bailey Rd (44451-9636)
P.O. Box 5224 (44514-0224)
PHONE................................330 538-3951
William Robinson Junior, *Pr*
Micheal D Geiger, *Sec*
EMP: 11 **EST:** 2001
SQ FT: 59,000
SALES (est): 2.17MM **Privately Held**
SIC: 3469 5051 Stamping metal for the trade ; Stampings, metal

(G-10696)
TTM TECHNOLOGIES INC
12080 Debartolo Dr (44451-9642)
PHONE................................330 538-3900
EMP: 11
SALES (corp-wide): 2.44B **Publicly Held**
Web: www.ttm.com
SIC: 3672 Printed circuit boards
PA: Ttm Technologies, Inc.
200 Sndpointe Ave Ste 400
Santa Ana CA 92707
714 327-3000

(G-10697)
TTM TECHNOLOGIES NORTH AMERICA LLC
Also Called: Ttm Technologies
12080 Debartolo Dr (44451-9642)
P.O. Box 216 (44451-0216)
PHONE................................330 572-3400
EMP: 60
SIC: 3672 Printed circuit boards

(G-10698)
VINYL PROFILES ACQUISITION LLC
11675 Mahoning Ave (44451-9688)
P.O. Box 698 (44451-0698)
PHONE................................330 538-0660
Randy Vegso, *Pr*
EMP: 18 **EST:** 2009
SALES (est): 4.34MM **Privately Held**
Web: www.vinylprofilesinc.com
SIC: 3089 Injection molding of plastics

(G-10699)
VINYLTECH INC
11635 Mahoning Ave (44451-9688)
P.O. Box 127 (44451-0127)
PHONE................................330 538-0369
Rick Amato, *Pr*
Mike Buchanan, *VP*
EMP: 10 **EST:** 1995
SALES (est): 2.27MM **Privately Held**
SIC: 3544 Forms (molds), for foundry and plastics working machinery

North Kingsville
Ashtabula County

(G-10700)
WHOLESALE IMPRINTS INC
Also Called: Ringer Screen Print
6259 Hewitt Lane (44068)
P.O. Box 507 (44068-0507)
PHONE................................440 224-3527
John Ringer, *Prin*
EMP: 40 **EST:** 2013
SALES (est): 5.15MM **Privately Held**
Web: www.ringer-wholesaleimprints.net
SIC: 2395 2396 Embroidery and art needlework; Fabric printing and stamping

North Lawrence
Stark County

(G-10701)
KELBLYS RIFLE RANGE INC
Also Called: Kelbly's
7222 Dalton Fox Lake Rd (44666-9543)
PHONE................................330 683-4674
George Kelbly Senior, *Pr*
James Kelbly, *VP*
George Kelbly Junior, *VP*
Karen Kelbly, *Sec*
EMP: 8 **EST:** 1970
SALES (est): 2.42MM **Privately Held**
Web: www.kelbly.com
SIC: 3484 7999 Rifles or rifle parts, 30 mm. and below; Shooting range operation

(G-10702)
SJK MACHINE LLC
Also Called: McGuire Machine
1862 Ben Fulton Rd (44666-9722)
PHONE................................330 868-3072
EMP: 14 **EST:** 2019
SALES (est): 1.1MM **Privately Held**
SIC: 3545 Precision tools, machinists'

(G-10703)
US TUBULAR PRODUCTS INC
Also Called: Benmit Division
14852 Lincoln Way W (44666)
PHONE................................330 832-1734
Jeffrey J Cunningham, *Pr*
Brian Cunningham, *
Connye Cunningham, *
EMP: 60 **EST:** 1973
SQ FT: 100,000
SALES (est): 2.52MM **Privately Held**
Web: www.benmit.com
SIC: 8734 3498 Hydrostatic testing laboratory ; Tube fabricating (contract bending and shaping)

North Lima
Mahoning County

(G-10704)
BIRD EQUIPMENT LLC
Also Called: Specialty Fab
11950 South Ave (44452-9744)
PHONE................................330 549-1004
Joe Colletti, *Pr*
Brian Dwyer, *
EMP: 28 **EST:** 1995
SQ FT: 49,500
SALES (est): 4.33MM
SALES (corp-wide): 90.88MM **Privately Held**
Web: www.birdequipmentllc.com
SIC: 3441 Fabricated structural metal
PA: Desco Corporation
7795 Walton Pkwy Ste 175
New Albany OH 43054
614 888-8855

(G-10705)
COBRA MOTORCYCLES MFG
11511 Springfield Rd (44452-9755)
PHONE................................330 207-3844
Bud Maimone, *Pr*
▲ **EMP:** 7 **EST:** 1994

SALES (est): 481.19K **Privately Held**
SIC: 3751 Motorcycles and related parts

(G-10706)
COMMERCIAL MINERALS INC
10900 South Ave (44452-9792)
P.O. Box 217 (44452-0217)
PHONE..................................330 549-2165
Thomas Mackall, *Pr*
Melanie Dunn, *Treas*
EMP: 6 **EST:** 1981
SQ FT: 6,000
SALES (est): 243.9K **Privately Held**
SIC: 1221 Bituminous coal surface mining

(G-10707)
DUO-CORP
280 Miley Rd (44452-8581)
P.O. Box 313 (44452-0313)
PHONE..................................330 549-2149
William G Kinkade, *CEO*
Bradley W Kinkade, *
Stephen De Capua, *
Diane Kinkade, *
EMP: 14 **EST:** 1977
SQ FT: 70,000
SALES (est): 3.12MM **Privately Held**
Web: www.duo-corp.com
SIC: 3089 3442 Windows, plastics; Screen
and storm doors and windows

(G-10708)
INDUSTRIAL PAPER SHREDDERS INC
12037 South Ave (44452-9742)
PHONE..................................888 637-4733
EMP: 14 **EST:** 1983
SALES (est): 198.57K **Privately Held**
Web: www.industrial-shredders.com
SIC: 3541 Machine tools, metal cutting type

(G-10709)
KTSDI LLC
801 E Middletown Rd (44452-9761)
PHONE..................................330 783-2000
Ken Timmings, *Prin*
Bryon Gotham, *Acctnt*
EMP: 7 **EST:** 2009
SALES (est): 1.05MM **Privately Held**
Web: www.ktsdi.com
SIC: 8748 3714 Business consulting, nec;
Axle housings and shafts, motor vehicle

(G-10710)
PRECISION ASSEMBLIES INC
Also Called: Firestone Machine
11233 South Ave (44452-9731)
PHONE..................................330 549-2630
David Mcdevitt, *Pr*
David Mc Devitt, *Pr*
EMP: 10 **EST:** 1968
SQ FT: 12,200
SALES (est): 161.75K **Privately Held**
SIC: 3599 7692 7629 3523 Machine shop,
jobbing and repair; Welding repair;
Electrical repair shops; Farm machinery
and equipment

(G-10711)
PRINT FACTORY PLL
Also Called: Poland Print Shop
11471 South Ave (44452-9772)
P.O. Box 312 (44452-0312)
PHONE..................................330 549-9640
John Primm, *Pt*
Doris Primm, *Pt*
EMP: 7 **EST:** 1999
SALES (est): 1.05MM **Privately Held**
Web: www.printfactorypll.com
SIC: 2752 Offset printing

(G-10712)
QC LLC
730 Miley Rd (44452-8587)
PHONE..................................847 682-9072
Renato Prestes, *Mgr*
EMP: 20
SALES (corp-wide): 4.71B **Privately Held**
SIC: 2819 Iron (ferric/ferrous) compounds or
salts
HQ: Qc Llc
1001 Winstead Dr Ste 480
Cary NC 27513
800 883-0010

(G-10713)
R A M PLASTICS CO INC
11401 South Ave (44452-9772)
P.O. Box 402 (44452-0402)
PHONE..................................330 549-3107
Richard Mallory, *Pr*
EMP: 7 **EST:** 1975
SQ FT: 20,000
SALES (est): 2.14MM **Privately Held**
SIC: 3089 Injection molding of plastics

(G-10714)
STERLING MINING CORPORATION (HQ)
10900 South Ave (44452-9792)
P.O. Box 217 (44452-0217)
PHONE..................................330 549-2165
W Thomas Mackall, *Pr*
Denise Mackall, *Treas*
EMP: 12 **EST:** 1991
SQ FT: 6,000
SALES (est): 4.45MM
SALES (corp-wide): 23.82MM **Privately Held**
Web: www.efccfamily.com
SIC: 1222 Bituminous coal-underground
mining
PA: The East Fairfield Coal Co
10900 South Ave
North Lima OH
330 549-2165

(G-10715)
TRAVIS PRODUCTS MFG INC
80 Eastgate Dr (44452-8563)
PHONE..................................234 759-3741
Joseph Soltesiz, *Prin*
EMP: 6 **EST:** 2007
SALES (est): 177.06K **Privately Held**
SIC: 3999 Manufacturing industries, nec

North Olmsted
Cuyahoga County

(G-10716)
AMERICAN RAMP SYSTEMS
4327 Coe Ave (44070-2820)
PHONE..................................440 336-4988
Martha Wright, *Prin*
EMP: 7 **EST:** 2005
SALES (est): 134.28K **Privately Held**
SIC: 3448 Prefabricated metal buildings and
components

(G-10717)
ANAHEIM MANUFACTURING COMPANY
Also Called: Waste King
25300 Al Moen Dr (44070-5619)
P.O. Box 4146 (92803-4146)
PHONE..................................800 767-6293
Steve Lattman, *Pr*
Robert A Schneider, *VP*
▲ **EMP:** 50 **EST:** 1991
SALES (est): 3.74MM

SALES (corp-wide): 4.61B **Publicly Held**
Web: www.wasteking.com
SIC: 3639 Garbage disposal units, household
HQ: Moen Incorporated
25300 Al Moen Dr
North Olmsted OH 44070
800 289-6636

(G-10718)
BIANCHI USA INC
Also Called: Keyline
31336 Industrial Pkwy Ste 3 (44070-6335)
PHONE..................................440 801-1083
Scott Hinton, *Pr*
▲ **EMP:** 15 **EST:** 2002
SALES (est): 7.21MM **Privately Held**
Web: www.bianchi1770usa.com
SIC: 3429 Keys and key blanks
HQ: Keyline Spa
Via Camillo Bianchi 2
Conegliano TV 31015

(G-10719)
BTA OF MOTORCARS INC
27500 Lorain Rd (44070-4038)
PHONE..................................440 716-1000
Gary Tamerlano, *Prin*
EMP: 7 **EST:** 2007
SALES (est): 357.53K **Privately Held**
Web: www.btacollision.com
SIC: 3479 Painting of metal products

(G-10720)
CLASSIC COATINGS
6074 Pebblebrook Ln (44070-4566)
PHONE..................................330 421-3703
EMP: 6 **EST:** 2012
SALES (est): 101.23K **Privately Held**
SIC: 3479 Coating of metals and formed
products

(G-10721)
FRAGAPANE BAKERIES INC (PA)
Also Called: Fragapane Bakery & Deli
28625 Lorain Rd (44070-4009)
PHONE..................................440 779-6050
John Fragapane, *Pr*
Nick Fragapane, *VP*
Rose Fragapane, *Sec*
Victoria Fragapane, *Treas*
EMP: 8 **EST:** 1971
SQ FT: 4,000
SALES (est): 622.87K
SALES (corp-wide): 622.87K **Privately Held**
Web: www.fragapanebakeries.com
SIC: 5411 5461 2051 Delicatessen stores;
Retail bakeries; Bread, cake, and related
products

(G-10722)
MOEN INCORPORATED (HQ)
Also Called: Moen
25300 Al Moen Dr (44070-5619)
PHONE..................................800 289-6636
◆ **EMP:** 20 **EST:** 1969
SALES (est): 153.12MM
SALES (corp-wide): 4.61B **Publicly Held**
Web: www.moen.com
SIC: 3432 Plumbers' brass goods: drain
cocks, faucets, spigots, etc.
PA: Fortune Brands Innovations, Inc.
520 Lake Cook Rd
Deerfield IL 60015
847 484-4400

North Ridgeville
Lorain County

(G-10723)
ALANOD WESTLAKE METAL IND INC
36696 Sugar Ridge Rd (44039-3832)
PHONE..................................440 327-8184
John R Johnston Junior, *Pr*
Franke Lee, *Pr*
Greg Seeley, *Sec*
James Gula, *VP*
◆ **EMP:** 21 **EST:** 1970
SQ FT: 80,000
SALES (est): 22.96MM
SALES (corp-wide): 77.24MM **Privately
Held**
Web: www.alanod-westlake.com
SIC: 5051 3354 Aluminum bars, rods, ingots,
sheets, pipes, plates, etc.; Aluminum
extruded products
PA: Alanod Gmbh & Co. Kg
Egerstr. 12
Ennepetal NW 58256
233 398-6500

(G-10724)
AMERICAN EGLE PRPRTY PRSRVTION
Also Called: 1 & 1 Property Preservation
39050 Center Ridge Rd (44039-2742)
PHONE..................................855 440-6938
John Davis, *Ex Dir*
Jodi Sanders, *Prin*
John Davis, *Prin*
EMP: 8 **EST:** 2012
SALES (est): 262.75K **Privately Held**
Web:
www.americaneaglepropertypreservation.com
SIC: 1389 1522 7299 8742 Construction,
repair, and dismantling services;
Residential construction, nec; Home
improvement and renovation contractor
agency; Management consulting services

(G-10725)
BECKETT AIR INCORPORATED (PA)
Also Called: PM Motor Fan Blade Company
37850 Taylor Pkwy (44039-3600)
P.O. Box 1236 (44036-1236)
PHONE..................................440 327-9999
Jonathan M Beckett, *CEO*
John D Beckett, *
▲ **EMP:** 88 **EST:** 1988
SALES (est): 24.31MM
SALES (corp-wide): 24.31MM **Privately
Held**
Web: www.beckettair.com
SIC: 3433 3585 3564 Heating equipment,
except electric; Refrigeration and heating
equipment; Blowers and fans

(G-10726)
BECKETT GAS INC (HQ)
Also Called: Beckett Thermal Solutions
38000 Taylor Pkwy (44039-3645)
P.O. Box 4037 (44036-4037)
PHONE..................................440 327-3141
Morrison J Carter, *Pr*
John D Beckett, *
Kevin A Beckett, *
▼ **EMP:** 45 **EST:** 1988
SQ FT: 140,000
SALES (est): 77.04MM
SALES (corp-wide): 77.04MM **Privately
Held**
Web: www.beckettgas.com
SIC: 3433 Burners, furnaces, boilers, and
stokers
PA: R.W. Beckett Corporation
38251 Center Ridge Rd

▲ = Import ▼ = Export
◆ = Import/Export

North Ridgeville OH 44039
440 327-1060

(G-10727)
BIOTHANE COATED WEBBING CORP
34655 Mills Rd (44039-1843)
PHONE....................440 327-0485
Frank Boron, *Pr*
▲ **EMP:** 35 **EST:** 1976
SQ FT: 25,000
SALES (est): 1.22MM **Privately Held**
Web: www.biothane.us
SIC: 2295 3083 2821 Resin or plastic coated fabrics; Laminated plastics plate and sheet; Plastics materials and resins

(G-10728)
CUYAHOGA VENDING CO INC
Also Called: Cuyahoga Group, The
39405 Taylor Pkwy (44035-6264)
PHONE....................440 353-9595
TOLL FREE: 800
EMP: 128
SALES (corp-wide): 7.88MM **Privately Held**
Web: www.cuyahogagroup.com
SIC: 7359 2099 Vending machine rental; Food preparations, nec
PA: Cuyahoga Vending Co., Inc.
14250 Industrial Ave S # 104
Maple Heights OH 44137
216 663-1457

(G-10729)
DRECO INC
7887 Root Rd (44039-4013)
P.O. Box 39328 (44039-0328)
PHONE....................440 327-6021
H T Ammerman, *Prin*
Christopher A Draudt, *Pr*
Russell Draudt, *Pr*
Harry Miller, *Dir Fin*
Harold F Ellsworth, *Prin*
▲ **EMP:** 130 **EST:** 1932
SQ FT: 135,000
SALES (est): 6.16MM **Privately Held**
Web: www.drecoinc.com
SIC: 3089 Injection molding of plastics

(G-10730)
FATE INDUSTRIES INC
36682 Sugar Ridge Rd (44039-3832)
PHONE....................440 327-1770
Rick Fate, *Pr*
Julie Fate, *Sec*
EMP: 8 **EST:** 1987
SQ FT: 2,800
SALES (est): 617.42K **Privately Held**
SIC: 3599 Machine shop, jobbing and repair

(G-10731)
FROHOCK-STEWART INC
39400 Taylor Pkwy (44035-6263)
PHONE....................440 329-6000
Gerald B Blouch, *Pr*
▲ **EMP:** 40 **EST:** 1954
SALES (est): 1.14MM
SALES (corp-wide): 741.73MM **Privately Held**
SIC: 3842 Surgical appliances and supplies
PA: Invacare Corporation
1 Invacare Way
Elyria OH 44035
440 329-6000

(G-10732)
GREENFIELD SOLAR CORP
7881 Root Rd (44039-4013)
PHONE....................216 535-9200
Neil Sater, *Pr*
EMP: 7 **EST:** 2009

SALES (est): 228.48K **Privately Held**
Web: www.greenfieldsolar.com
SIC: 3674 Semiconductors and related devices

(G-10733)
H & S DISTRIBUTING INC
Also Called: Team Cobra Products
35478 Lorain Rd (44039-4461)
PHONE....................800 336-7784
Robert Shaffer, *Ch Bd*
▲ **EMP:** 8 **EST:** 1980
SQ FT: 11,000
SALES (est): 188.84K **Privately Held**
Web: www.cobraproducts.com
SIC: 5091 3949 Bowling equipment; Bowling equipment and supplies

(G-10734)
HOISTECH LLC
32960 Fern Tree Ln (44039-2304)
PHONE....................440 327-5379
EMP: 6 **EST:** 2010
SALES (est): 88.97K **Privately Held**
Web: www.hoistech.ie
SIC: 3949 Sporting and athletic goods, nec

(G-10735)
IMPACT INDUSTRIES INC
5120 Mills Industrial Pkwy (44039-1958)
PHONE....................440 327-2360
William Nestor, *Pr*
Leslie Nestor, *
EMP: 13 **EST:** 1977
SQ FT: 25,000
SALES (est): 4.33MM **Privately Held**
Web: www.impactindustries.com
SIC: 3469 3544 Stamping metal for the trade ; Special dies and tools

(G-10736)
INVACARE CORPORATION
Also Called: Invacare Hme
38683 Taylor Pkwy (44035-6200)
PHONE....................440 329-6000
Brad Kushner, *Brnch Mgr*
EMP: 10
SALES (corp-wide): 741.73MM **Privately Held**
Web: global.invacare.com
SIC: 3842 Surgical appliances and supplies
PA: Invacare Corporation
1 Invacare Way
Elyria OH 44035
440 329-6000

(G-10737)
JBC TECHNOLOGIES INC (PA)
7887 Bliss Pkwy (44039-3475)
PHONE....................440 327-4522
Joe Bliss, *
▲ **EMP:** 66 **EST:** 1986
SALES (est): 24.77MM **Privately Held**
Web: www.jbc-tech.com
SIC: 3053 Gaskets, all materials

(G-10738)
KALT MANUFACTURING COMPANY
36700 Sugar Ridge Rd (44039-3800)
PHONE....................440 327-2102
Joseph W Kalt, *Pr*
Jeanne M Kalt, *Treas*
Ann C Kalt, *Asst Tr*
Gayle A Bangs, *Sec*
▲ **EMP:** 54 **EST:** 1967
SQ FT: 60,000
SALES (est): 6.97MM **Privately Held**
Web: www.kaltmfg.com

SIC: 3544 3545 3549 3599 Special dies and tools; Machine tool accessories; Metalworking machinery, nec; Machine shop, jobbing and repair

(G-10739)
LORAIN RLED DIE PDTS INDUS SUP
6287 Lear Nagle Rd Ste 4 (44039-3369)
PHONE....................440 281-8607
Roger Galippo, *Pr*
EMP: 6 **EST:** 1995
SQ FT: 2,800
SALES (est): 692.23K **Privately Held**
Web: www.lorainindie.com
SIC: 3544 Dies, steel rule

(G-10740)
METAL MARKER MANUFACTURING CO
Also Called: Metal Marker Manufacturing
6225 Lear Nagle Rd (44039-3223)
PHONE....................440 327-2300
David Primrose, *Pr*
William Primrose, *Pr*
EMP: 10 **EST:** 1923
SQ FT: 16,000
SALES (est): 2.84MM **Privately Held**
Web: www.metalmarkermfg.com
SIC: 3953 Marking devices

(G-10741)
NORLAKE MANUFACTURING COMPANY (PA)
Also Called: Norlake
39301 Taylor Pkwy (44035-6272)
P.O. Box 215 (44036-0215)
PHONE....................440 353-3200
James Markus, *Pr*
Daryl Jackson, *
▼ **EMP:** 90 **EST:** 1963
SQ FT: 50,000
SALES (est): 2.96MM
SALES (corp-wide): 2.96MM **Privately Held**
Web: www.norlakemfg.com
SIC: 3677 3714 3612 Transformers power supply, electronic type; Motor vehicle parts and accessories; Transformers, except electric

(G-10742)
PLRS LEGACY INC
38830 Taylor Pkwy (44039)
PHONE....................440 365-7333
Paul Reichlin, *Pr*
Yvonne D Reichlin, *
R Stephen Laux, *
EMP: 15 **EST:** 1986
SQ FT: 11,000
SALES (est): 2.86MM **Privately Held**
Web: www.contourprecisionmilling.com
SIC: 3545 3544 Machine tool accessories; Special dies and tools

(G-10743)
PROTECTIVE INDUSTRIAL POLYMERS
7875 Bliss Pkwy (44039-3475)
PHONE....................440 327-0015
Patrick Scudder, *Pr*
Tom Vath, *Dir*
Sean Walsh, *Mktg Mgr*
Don Batke, *Opers Mgr*
Craig Scudder, *Dir Fin*
EMP: 10 **EST:** 2008
SALES (est): 3.1MM **Privately Held**
Web:
www.protectiveindustrialpolymers.com

SIC: 1771 2515 2822 8741 Flooring contractor; Mattresses, containing felt, foam rubber, urethane, etc.; Ethylene-propylene rubbers, EPDM polymers; Construction management

(G-10744)
PURITAS METAL PRODUCTS INC
39097 Center Ridge Rd (44039-2741)
PHONE....................440 353-1917
Richard Cook, *CEO*
EMP: 6 **EST:** 1950
SALES (est): 1.05MM **Privately Held**
Web: www.puritasmetal.com
SIC: 3441 Fabricated structural metal

(G-10745)
RAVEN CONCEALMENT SYSTEMS LLC
7889 Root Rd (44039-4013)
PHONE....................440 508-9000
Michael Goerlick, *Managing Member*
John Chapman, *
Dotson Burton, *
Kelly Laurence, *
EMP: 45 **EST:** 2008
SALES (est): 2.63MM **Privately Held**
Web: www.rcsgear.com
SIC: 5399 3949 3089 Army-Navy goods stores; Cases, gun and rod (sporting equipment); Injection molding of plastics

(G-10746)
REFURB-WORLD LLC
33888 Center Ridge Rd (44039-3257)
PHONE....................440 471-9030
EMP: 32 **EST:** 2017
SALES (est): 2.46MM **Privately Held**
Web: www.refurb-world.com
SIC: 3549 Assembly machines, including robotic

(G-10747)
RHENIUM ALLOYS INC (PA)
Also Called: Rhenium Alloys
38683 Taylor Pkwy (44035-6200)
PHONE....................440 365-7388
Mike Prokop, *Pr*
▲ **EMP:** 41 **EST:** 1994
SQ FT: 35,500
SALES (est): 6.43MM
SALES (corp-wide): 6.43MM **Privately Held**
Web: www.rhenium.com
SIC: 3313 3356 3498 3339 Electrometallurgical products; Tungsten, basic shapes; Fabricated pipe and fittings; Primary nonferrous metals, nec

(G-10748)
ROCK HARD INDUSTRIES LLC
Also Called: New Stone Age
34555 Mills Rd (44039-1841)
PHONE....................440 327-3077
Matt Kerns, *CEO*
Krissy Kerns, *Pr*
EMP: 9 **EST:** 2019
SALES (est): 4.35MM **Privately Held**
SIC: 3441 Fabricated structural metal

(G-10749)
RW BECKETT CORPORATION (PA)
38251 Center Ridge Rd (44039-2895)
P.O. Box 1289 (44036-1289)
PHONE....................440 327-1060
Kevin Beckett, *Pr*
Peter Duffield, *
▲ **EMP:** 193 **EST:** 1937
SQ FT: 40,000
SALES (est): 77.04MM
SALES (corp-wide): 77.04MM **Privately Held**

Web: www.beckettcorp.com
SIC: 3433 Oil burners, domestic or industrial

(G-10750)
TANGO PRODUCTS INC
4915 Mills Industrial Pkwy (44039-1953)
PHONE....................................440 353-2605
Timothy E Bennett, *Pr*
EMP: 6 EST: 2005
SQ FT: 2,800
SALES (est): 490.88K **Privately Held**
Web: www.teb-mfg.com
SIC: 3999 Barber and beauty shop
  equipment

(G-10751)
TDS-BF/LS HOLDINGS INC
38900 Taylor Industrial Pkwy (44039)
PHONE....................................440 327-5800
Leonard Sikora, *Pr*
William T Flickinger, *
EMP: 28 EST: 1976
SQ FT: 60,000
SALES (est): 171.12K **Privately Held**
SIC: 3444 3469 3599 3479 Sheet metalwork
  ; Metal stampings, nec; Machine shop,
  jobbing and repair; Painting of metal
  products

(G-10752)
US REFRACTORY PRODUCTS LLC
7660 Race Rd (44039-3612)
PHONE....................................440 386-4580
Gary M Demarco, *Managing Member*
William Drake, *
◆ EMP: 25 EST: 2009
SQ FT: 30,000
SALES (est): 7.84MM **Privately Held**
Web: www.usrefractory.com
SIC: 3297 Nonclay refractories

(G-10753)
WOLFF BROS SUPPLY INC
38777 Taylor Industrial Pkwy (44035)
PHONE....................................440 327-1650
EMP: 15
SALES (corp-wide): 119.09MM **Privately Held**
Web: www.wolffbros.com
SIC: 3432 5074 5722 Plumbing fixture
  fittings and trim; Plumbing fittings and
  supplies; Air conditioning room units, self-
  contained
PA: Wolff Bros. Supply, Inc.
  6078 Wolff Rd
  Medina OH 44256
  330 725-3451

North Royalton
Cuyahoga County

(G-10754)
AMCLO GROUP INC
Also Called: Amclo
9721 York Alpha Dr (44133-3505)
PHONE....................................216 791-8400
William Harkins, *Pr*
Karl Morganthaler, *
EMP: 11 EST: 1985
SQ FT: 39,000
SALES (est): 1.81MM **Privately Held**
Web: www.amclo.com
SIC: 3469 3089 Stamping metal for the trade
  ; Injection molding of plastics

(G-10755)
BEST EQUIPMENT CO INC
12620 York Delta Dr (44133-3559)
PHONE....................................440 237-3515

Mike Dahlman, *Managing Member*
EMP: 20
SALES (corp-wide): 23.33MM **Privately Held**
Web: www.bestequipmentco.com
SIC: 3589 Sewer cleaning equipment, power
PA: Best Equipment Co Inc
  5550 Poindexter Dr
  Indianapolis IN 46235
  317 823-3050

(G-10756)
CARDINAL PRODUCTS INC
11929 Abbey Rd Ste D (44133-2664)
PHONE....................................440 237-8280
Janet Stanley, *Pr*
EMP: 8 EST: 1989
SQ FT: 10,000
SALES (est): 947.73K **Privately Held**
Web: www.cardinalproductsinc.com
SIC: 3089 Injection molding of plastics

(G-10757)
COMM STEEL INC
8043 Corporate Cir Ste 2 (44133-1279)
PHONE....................................216 881-4600
Eddie B Perkins, *Pr*
Michael Ciofani, *
Robert J Ciofani, *
EMP: 50 EST: 1991
SQ FT: 130,000
SALES (est): 702.54K **Privately Held**
SIC: 3441 Fabricated structural metal

(G-10758)
CONWAY GREENE CO INC
17325 Parkside Dr (44133-5413)
PHONE....................................440 230-2627
Barry Conway, *Pr*
Evalyn Greene, *Prin*
EMP: 7 EST: 1994
SALES (est): 251.61K **Privately Held**
Web: www.conwaygreene.com
SIC: 2731 Book publishing

(G-10759)
EAGLE PRECISION PRODUCTS LLC
13800 Progress Pkwy Ste J (44133-4354)
PHONE....................................440 582-9393
Bruce Reger, *Managing Member*
Joshua Reger, *VP*
EMP: 9 EST: 1979
SQ FT: 18,000
SALES (est): 2.36MM **Privately Held**
Web: www.eagleprecisionproducts.com
SIC: 3469 3544 Stamping metal for the trade
  ; Special dies and tools

(G-10760)
ENVIRNMNTAL CMPLIANCE TECH LLC
Also Called: Ect
13953 Progress Pkwy (44133-4305)
PHONE....................................216 634-0400
Sendos Mohammad, *Mgr*
EMP: 10 EST: 2004
SALES (est): 1.8MM **Privately Held**
Web: www.ecttesting.com
SIC: 1799 4959 3826 Petroleum storage
  tanks, pumping and draining;
  Environmental cleanup services;
  Environmental testing equipment

(G-10761)
FRESHLY PRESERVED LLC
11798 York Rd (44133-2857)
PHONE....................................440 523-1099
Linda Saadeh, *Managing Member*
EMP: 6 EST: 2019
SALES (est): 246.53K **Privately Held**
Web: www.freshlypreserved.com

SIC: 2099 Food preparations, nec

(G-10762)
G & P CONSTRUCTION LLC
10139 Royalton Rd Ste D (44133-4473)
PHONE....................................855 494-4830
Nicholas Gorey, *Managing Member*
EMP: 50 EST: 2019
SALES (est): 7.16MM **Privately Held**
Web: www.gandpconstruction.com
SIC: 5046 5084 1791 2542 Shelving,
  commercial and industrial; Industrial
  machinery and equipment; Structural steel
  erection; Shelving angles or slotted bars,
  except wood

(G-10763)
GARDELLA JEWELRY LLC
Also Called: Earth Dreams Jewelry
7432 Julia Dr (44133-3715)
PHONE....................................440 877-9261
Jacqueline Magyar, *COO*
EMP: 6 EST: 2011
SALES (est): 395.01K **Privately Held**
Web: www.naturedevajewelry.com
SIC: 3961 Jewelry apparel, non-precious
  metals

(G-10764)
H & D STEEL SERVICE INC
Also Called: H & D Steel Service Center
9960 York Alpha Dr (44133-3588)
PHONE....................................800 666-3390
Raymond Gary Schreiber, *Ch Bd*
Joseph Bubba, *
James P Schreiber, *
Joseph A Cachat, *
R M Jones, *
▲ EMP: 50 EST: 1972
SQ FT: 125,000
SALES (est): 9.96MM **Privately Held**
Web: www.hdsteel.com
SIC: 5051 3541 5085 Iron or steel flat
  products; Home workshop machine tools,
  metalworking; Industrial tools

(G-10765)
INDUCTION TOOLING INC
12510 York Delta Dr (44133-3543)
PHONE....................................440 237-0711
William Stuehr, *Pr*
EMP: 15 EST: 1976
SQ FT: 25,000
SALES (est): 4.33MM **Privately Held**
Web: www.inductiontooling.com
SIC: 3567 Induction heating equipment

(G-10766)
INDUSTRIAL PARTS DEPOT LLC
Also Called: I P D
11266 Royalton Rd (44133-4474)
PHONE....................................440 237-9164
Jeff Guiliano, *Brnch Mgr*
EMP: 6
SALES (corp-wide): 44.12MM **Privately Held**
Web: www.ipdparts.com
SIC: 3519 5084 Parts and accessories,
  internal combustion engines; Engines and
  parts, diesel
HQ: Industrial Parts Depot, Llc
  1550 Charles Willard St
  Carson CA 90746
  310 530-1900

(G-10767)
INTEGRANT LLC
12315 York Delta Dr (44133-3544)
PHONE....................................440 628-9550
Ty Shirley, *Managing Member*
EMP: 7 EST: 2016

SALES (est): 247.56K **Privately Held**
Web: www.integrantllc.com
SIC: 2392 Household furnishings, nec

(G-10768)
KENT CORPORATION
9601 York Alpha Dr (44133-3503)
PHONE....................................440 582-3400
Dean Costello, *CEO*
David Tsai, *
Mark Costello, *
◆ EMP: 31 EST: 1971
SQ FT: 22,000
SALES (est): 8.13MM **Privately Held**
Web: www.kentcorporation.com
SIC: 3549 Coiling machinery

(G-10769)
KRENZ PRECISION MACHINING INC
9801 York Alpha Dr (44133-3507)
PHONE....................................440 237-1800
Richard Krenz Junior, *Pr*
Alfred Krist, *
Paul Krenz, *
Adam Krenz, *
EMP: 65 EST: 1967
SQ FT: 35,000
SALES (est): 4.14MM **Privately Held**
Web: www.krenzkristmachine.com
SIC: 3599 Machine shop, jobbing and repair

(G-10770)
LASZERAY TECHNOLOGY LLC
12315 York Delta Dr (44133-3544)
PHONE....................................440 582-8430
Greg Clark, *CEO*
Steve Patton, *
▲ EMP: 81 EST: 1997
SQ FT: 60,000
SALES (est): 11.25MM **Privately Held**
Web: www.laszeray.com
SIC: 3089 3544 Injection molding of plastics;
  Special dies, tools, jigs, and fixtures

(G-10771)
LUNAR TOOL & MOLD INC
9860 York Alpha Dr (44133-3586)
PHONE....................................440 237-2141
Friedrich Hoffman Junior, *Pr*
EMP: 23 EST: 1965
SQ FT: 20,000
SALES (est): 1.87MM **Privately Held**
Web: www.lunarmold.com
SIC: 3544 7692 Special dies and tools;
  Welding repair

(G-10772)
MAY CONVEYOR INC
9981 York Theta Dr (44133-3545)
PHONE....................................440 237-8012
Leonard May, *Pr*
Matias Dost, *VP*
▲ EMP: 6 EST: 1973
SQ FT: 55,000
SALES (est): 488.58K **Privately Held**
Web: www.mayconveyor.com
SIC: 3496 Conveyor belts

(G-10773)
MAY INDUSTRIES OF OHIO INC
9981 York Theta Dr (44133-3545)
PHONE....................................440 237-8012
EMP: 35 EST: 1973
SALES (est): 4.89MM **Privately Held**
Web: www.mayind.com
SIC: 3544 3469 3444 Special dies and tools;
  Stamping metal for the trade; Sheet
  metalwork

▲ = Import ▼ = Export
◆ = Import/Export

(G-10774)
MDF TOOL CORPORATION
Also Called: Mdf Tool
10166 Royalton Rd (44133-4427)
PHONE...............................440 237-2277
John Bunjevac, *CEO*
Larry Jackson, *Pr*
EMP: 10 **EST:** 1980
SQ FT: 8,000
SALES (est): 1.23MM **Privately Held**
Web: www.mdftool.com
SIC: 3544 3545 Special dies and tools;
   Machine tool accessories

(G-10775)
MPP LEGACY INC
9940 York Alpha Dr (44133-3510)
PHONE...............................440 237-9500
Jim Diamond, *Pr*
EMP: 10 **EST:** 1991
SQ FT: 25,000
SALES (est): 858.22K **Privately Held**
Web: www.seatbeltsforpallets.com
SIC: 2296 Fabric for reinforcing industrial
   belting

(G-10776)
NEXT GERENATION CRIMPING
Also Called: N G C
9880 York Alpha Dr (44133-3508)
PHONE...............................440 237-6300
Fred Krist, *Pt*
EMP: 8 **EST:** 1999
SALES (est): 384.25K **Privately Held**
SIC: 3432 Plumbing fixture fittings and trim

(G-10777)
NU-TOOL INDUSTRIES INC
9920 York Alpha Dr (44133-3510)
PHONE...............................440 237-9240
Bruce Thompson, *Pr*
Daniel Worthington, *VP*
Richard Kuper, *VP*
EMP: 14 **EST:** 1954
SQ FT: 8,000
SALES (est): 2.5MM **Privately Held**
Web: www.nutoolind.com
SIC: 3599 Machine shop, jobbing and repair

(G-10778)
OAK INDUSTRIAL INC
12955 York Delta Dr Ste G (44133-3550)
PHONE...............................440 263-2780
Michael Johns, *CEO*
Russ Karla, *COO*
EMP: 7 **EST:** 2010
SQ FT: 5,000
SALES (est): 628.26K **Privately Held**
SIC: 3599 Machine and other job shop work

(G-10779)
OSI ENVIRONMENTAL LLC
Also Called: Oil Skimmers
12800 York Rd (44133-3683)
P.O. Box 33092 (44133)
PHONE...............................440 237-4600
William R Townsend, *Pr*
William R Townsend, *Pr*
Jim Petrucci, *VP*
EMP: 22 **EST:** 1964
SQ FT: 100,000
SALES (est): 6.29MM **Privately Held**
Web: www.oilskim.com
SIC: 3569 3564 3533 3443 Filters; Blowers
   and fans; Oil and gas field machinery;
   Fabricated plate work (boiler shop)

(G-10780)
PRECISION CUT FABRICATING INC
9921 York Alpha Dr (44133-3509)

PHONE...............................440 877-1260
Brian Wendling, *Pr*
EMP: 14 **EST:** 1999
SALES (est): 1.01MM **Privately Held**
SIC: 7389 3312 Scrap steel cutting; Sheet or
   strip, steel, hot-rolled

(G-10781)
ROYAL WIRE PRODUCTS INC (PA)
13450 York Delta Dr (44133-3584)
PHONE...............................440 237-8787
William F Peshina, *Pr*
Paige Peshina, *
William Nelson, *
▲ **EMP:** 60 **EST:** 1953
SQ FT: 35,000
SALES (est): 9.01MM
SALES (corp-wide): 9.01MM **Privately
Held**
Web: www.royalwire.com
SIC: 3496 Cages, wire

(G-10782)
**ROYALTON ARCHTCTRAL
FBRICATION**
13155 York Delta Dr (44133-3522)
PHONE...............................440 582-0400
Stefan Winkler, *Pr*
EMP: 13 **EST:** 1992
SQ FT: 10,000
SALES (est): 1.18MM **Privately Held**
Web: www.rafpanels.com
SIC: 3444 3446 Sheet metalwork;
   Architectural metalwork

(G-10783)
RUSS JR ENTERPRISES INC
6165 Royalton Rd (44133-4918)
PHONE...............................440 237-4642
Russell J Sposit Junior, *CEO*
EMP: 11 **EST:** 2007
SALES (est): 525.07K **Privately Held**
SIC: 3589 Car washing machinery

(G-10784)
S & D ARCHITECTURAL METALS
12955 York Delta Dr (44133-3534)
PHONE...............................440 582-2560
Cynthia Blessing, *Pr*
Keith Blessing, *VP*
EMP: 7 **EST:** 2001
SALES (est): 1.34MM **Privately Held**
SIC: 3444 Sheet metalwork

(G-10785)
SYMBOL TOOL & DIE INC
11000 Industrial First Ave (44133-2678)
PHONE...............................440 582-5989
Jon Ardelian, *Pr*
EMP: 6 **EST:** 1992
SQ FT: 4,000
SALES (est): 604.3K **Privately Held**
SIC: 3544 Special dies and tools

(G-10786)
TRAVELERS VACATION GUIDE
10143 Royalton Rd (44133-4470)
P.O. Box 33547 (44133-0547)
PHONE...............................440 582-4949
Pam Voigt, *Pr*
EMP: 7 **EST:** 1984
SQ FT: 1,400
SALES (est): 183.17K **Privately Held**
Web: www.guidestudio.com
SIC: 2711 Newspapers: publishing only, not
   printed on site

(G-10787)
UNIVERSAL NORTH INC
Also Called: Universal Creative Concepts

10143 Royalton Rd Ste E (44133-4463)
PHONE...............................440 230-1366
John P Yurik, *CEO*
Jeffrey Yurik, *Pr*
Amy Ehrbar, *VP*
EMP: 11 **EST:** 1991
SQ FT: 1,800
SALES (est): 941.31K **Privately Held**
Web: www.uccpromo.com
SIC: 2759 Commercial printing, nec

(G-10788)
VALLEY TOOL & DIE INC (PA)
Also Called: Valco Division
10020 York Theta Dr (44133-3581)
PHONE...............................440 237-0160
Adolf Eisenloeffel, *Pr*
Phillip S Eisenloeffel, *VP*
Ernst Peters, *Prin*
Helmut Eisenloeffel, *Prin*
EMP: 65 **EST:** 1968
SQ FT: 54,000
SALES (est): 4.1MM
SALES (corp-wide): 4.1MM **Privately Held**
Web: www.valcocleve.com
SIC: 3451 3465 3542 3452 Screw machine
   products; Automotive stampings; Machine
   tools, metal forming type; Bolts, nuts, rivets,
   and washers

(G-10789)
WHITE MACHINE INC
9621 York Alpha Dr Side (44133-3594)
PHONE...............................440 237-3282
Larry White, *Pr*
Ronald White, *Ex VP*
Ruth White, *VP*
EMP: 8 **EST:** 1971
SQ FT: 7,600
SALES (est): 962.65K **Privately Held**
SIC: 3599 3728 3544 Machine shop, jobbing
   and repair; Aircraft parts and equipment,
   nec; Special dies, tools, jigs, and fixtures

(G-10790)
X-TREME FINISHES INC
Also Called: Line-X of Akron/Medina
4821 Brookhaven Dr (44133-6486)
PHONE...............................330 474-0614
Tawny R Zajc, *Prin*
EMP: 10 **EST:** 2013
SALES (est): 475.22K **Privately Held**
Web: www.x-tremefinishes.com
SIC: 3479 2851 1752 7549 Etching and
   engraving; Epoxy coatings; Access flooring
   system installation; Undercoating/
   rustproofing cars

Northfield
Summit County

(G-10791)
AKLAND PRINTING
145 W Aurora Rd (44067-2082)
PHONE...............................330 467-8292
EMP: 12 **EST:** 2019
SALES (est): 176.68K **Privately Held**
Web: www.aklandprinting.com
SIC: 2752 Offset printing

(G-10792)
BULK HANDLING EQUIPMENT CO
28 W Aurora Rd (44067-2073)
P.O. Box 670855 (44067-0855)
PHONE...............................330 468-5703
Joseph Stakes, *Pr*
Joanne Stakes, *VP*
Mary Anne Stakes, *Sec*
EMP: 7 **EST:** 1985

SALES (est): 745.65K **Privately Held**
Web: www.bulkhand.com
SIC: 3535 Bulk handling conveyor systems

(G-10793)
GENERAL DIE CASTERS INC
6212 Akron Peninsula Rd (44067)
PHONE...............................330 467-6700
Tom Lenin, *Brnch Mgr*
EMP: 55
SQ FT: 45,136
SALES (corp-wide): 22.95MM **Privately
Held**
Web: www.generaldie.com
SIC: 3363 3364 Aluminum die-castings; Zinc
   and zinc-base alloy die-castings
HQ: General Die Casters, Inc.
   2150 Highland Rd
   Twinsburg OH 44087
   330 678-2528

(G-10794)
HY-KO PRODUCTS COMPANY LLC
60 Meadow Ln (44067-1415)
PHONE...............................330 467-7446
Michael Bass, *Managing Member*
Michael Bass, *Pr*
EMP: 14 **EST:** 2020
SALES (est): 929.74K
SALES (corp-wide): 44.41MM **Privately
Held**
Web: www.hy-ko.com
SIC: 3993 Signs and advertising specialties
PA: Midwest Fastener Corp.
   9031 Shaver Rd
   Portage MI 49024
   269 327-6917

(G-10795)
LITTLE BUSY BEEZ ERLY LRNG CHL
10578 Northfield Rd (44067-1245)
PHONE...............................216 477-1965
EMP: 7
SALES (est): 1.54MM **Privately Held**
SIC: 3999 Education aids, devices and
   supplies

(G-10796)
NOR-FAB INC
Also Called: Metalcraft Industries
231 Beechwood Dr (44067-1905)
PHONE...............................330 467-6580
Gerald C Papile, *Pr*
EMP: 7 **EST:** 1974
SQ FT: 7,500
SALES (est): 225K **Privately Held**
SIC: 2542 Partitions for floor attachment,
   prefabricated: except wood

(G-10797)
STEVES SPORTS INC
10333 Northfield Rd Unit 136 (44067-1443)
PHONE...............................440 735-0044
Steve Baraona, *Owner*
EMP: 6 **EST:** 2010
SALES (est): 505.56K **Privately Held**
SIC: 2759 Screen printing

(G-10798)
TERMINAL EQUIPMENT INDS INC
64 Privet Ln (44067-2883)
PHONE...............................330 468-0322
Ernest Pugh, *Pr*
Priscilla Pugh, *Treas*
EMP: 6 **EST:** 1977
SQ FT: 1,100
SALES (est): 485.1K **Privately Held**
Web: www.accucutinc.com
SIC: 3542 Machine tools, metal forming type

(G-10799)
WEATHER KING HEATING & AC
51 Meadow Ln Ste E (44067-1475)
PHONE..........................330 908-0281
Raj Rai, *Pr*
EMP: 6 **EST:** 2000
SALES (est): 957.54K **Privately Held**
Web: www.weatherking1.com
SIC: 1711 3433 5075 3564 Warm air heating
and air conditioning contractor; Boilers, low-
pressure heating: steam or hot water; Air
conditioning and ventilation equipment and
supplies; Filters, air: furnaces, air
conditioning equipment, etc.

(G-10800)
WEST 6TH PRODUCTS COMPANY
(PA)
60 Meadow Ln (44067-1415)
PHONE..........................330 467-7446
▲ **EMP:** 92 **EST:** 1949
SALES (est): 9.19MM
SALES (corp-wide): 9.19MM **Privately**
Held
Web: www.hy-ko.com
SIC: 3993 3822 Signs and advertising
specialties; Hardware for environmental
regulators

Northwood
Wood County

(G-10801)
ADIENT US LLC
7560 Arbor Dr (43619-7500)
PHONE..........................419 662-4900
Jeffrey Ryan Arnold, *Brnch Mgr*
EMP: 250
Web: www.adient.com
SIC: 3714 Motor vehicle parts and
accessories
HQ: Adient Us Llc
49200 Halyard Dr
Plymouth MI 48170
734 254-5000

(G-10802)
AMERICAN COLD FORGE LLC
5650 Woodville Rd (43619-2322)
PHONE..........................419 836-1062
Dave Huber, *Pr*
Jeffrey Leverenz, *
EMP: 29 **EST:** 2009
SALES (est): 4.79MM **Privately Held**
Web: www.americancoldforge.com
SIC: 5531 3462 3463 Automotive parts;
Automotive and internal combustion engine
forgings; Automotive forgings, nonferrous

(G-10803)
HIRZEL CANNING COMPANY (PA)
Also Called: Dei Fratelli
411 Lemoyne Rd (43619-1699)
PHONE..........................419 693-0531
Karl A Hirzel Junior, *Pr*
Joseph R Hirzel, *
William J Hirzel, *
▲ **EMP:** 25 **EST:** 1923
SQ FT: 250,000
SALES (est): 64.46MM
SALES (corp-wide): 64.46MM **Privately**
Held
Web: www.deifratelli.com
SIC: 2033 8611 2034 Tomato products,
packaged in cans, jars, etc.; Business
associations; Dried and dehydrated fruits,
vegetables and soup mixes

(G-10804)
HOT GRAPHIC SERVICES INC
Also Called: H.O.t
2595 Tracy Rd (43619-1004)
P.O. Box 307 (43697-0307)
PHONE..........................419 242-7000
Gregory D Shapiro, *Pr*
Flora I Shapiro, *
Myron Shapiro, *
Norman Shapiro, *
EMP: 30 **EST:** 1976
SQ FT: 11,000
SALES (est): 8.44MM **Privately Held**
Web: www.hotgraphics.us
SIC: 2791 2752 Photocomposition, for the
printing trade; Offset printing

(G-10805)
NORPLAS INDUSTRIES INC (DH)
Also Called: Magna
7825 Caple Blvd (43619-1070)
PHONE..........................419 662-3200
Seetarama Kotagiri, *Pr*
Graham Burrow, *
Patrick W D Mccann, *CFO*
Bruce R Cluney, *CLO*
◆ **EMP:** 242 **EST:** 1997
SQ FT: 450,000
SALES (est): 370.48MM
SALES (corp-wide): 42.84B **Privately Held**
Web: www.norplas.com
SIC: 3714 Motor vehicle parts and
accessories
HQ: Magna Exteriors Of America, Inc.
750 Tower Dr
Troy MI 48098
248 631-1100

(G-10806)
OAKLEY INDS SUB ASSMBLY DIV IN
6317 Fairfield Dr (43619-7508)
PHONE..........................419 661-8888
Dick Schmeltz, *Pr*
EMP: 26
SALES (corp-wide): 33.2MM **Privately**
Held
Web: www.oakleysubassembly.com
SIC: 3714 Motor vehicle body components
and frame
PA: Oakley Industries Sub Assembly
Division, Inc.
4333 Matthew
Flint MI 48507
810 720-4444

(G-10807)
OBR COOLING TOWERS LLC
Also Called: Obr Cooling Companies
2845 Crane Way (43619-1098)
PHONE..........................419 243-3443
Philip Poll, *
Brad Barefoot, *
EMP: 45 **EST:** 1984
SALES (est): 13.28MM **Privately Held**
Web: www.obrcoolingtowers.com
SIC: 7699 3444 Industrial equipment services
; Cooling towers, sheet metal

(G-10808)
PILKINGTON NORTH AMERICA INC
2401 E Broadway St (43619-1318)
PHONE..........................800 547-9280
Dan Lubelski, *Brnch Mgr*
EMP: 125
Web: www.pilkington.com
SIC: 3211 Flat glass
HQ: Pilkington North America, Inc.
811 Madison Ave
Toledo OH 43604
419 247-3731

(G-10809)
TOLEDO METAL FINISHING INC
Also Called: Toledo Deburring Co
7880 Caple Blvd (43619-1099)
PHONE..........................419 661-1422
Robert E Van Schoick Junior, *Pr*
EMP: 8 **EST:** 1962
SQ FT: 18,000
SALES (est): 686.37K **Privately Held**
Web: www.deburringcompany.com
SIC: 3471 Finishing, metals or formed
products

(G-10810)
TORBOT GROUP INC
Also Called: Jobskin Division
3461 Curtice Rd (43619-1639)
PHONE..........................419 724-1475
Greg Johnson, *Brnch Mgr*
EMP: 12
SALES (corp-wide): 2.51MM **Privately**
Held
Web: www.torbot.com
SIC: 3841 Surgical and medical instruments
PA: Torbot Group, Inc.
1367 Elmwood Ave
Cranston RI 02910
401 780-8737

(G-10811)
TURNER CONCRETE PRODUCTS
2121 Tracy Rd (43619-1324)
PHONE..........................419 662-9007
Steve Turner, *Pr*
EMP: 6 **EST:** 2005
SALES (est): 243.84K **Privately Held**
Web: www.turnerconcreteproducts.com
SIC: 3273 Ready-mixed concrete

(G-10812)
TURNER VAULT CO
2121 Tracy Rd (43619-1324)
PHONE..........................419 537-1133
Steven Turner, *Pr*
EMP: 27 **EST:** 1958
SALES (est): 4.86MM **Privately Held**
Web: www.turnervault.com
SIC: 3272 Burial vaults, concrete or precast
terrazzo

(G-10813)
WESCO DISTRIBUTION INC
Also Called: Wesco Distribution
6519 Fairfield Dr (43619-7507)
PHONE..........................419 666-1670
Chad Marrison, *Brnch Mgr*
EMP: 13
Web: www.wesco.com
SIC: 5085 3699 Industrial supplies; Electrical
equipment and supplies, nec
HQ: Wesco Distribution, Inc.
225 W Stn Sq Dr Ste 700
Pittsburgh PA 15219

(G-10814)
WHITAKER FINISHING LLC
2707 Tracy Rd (43619-1050)
PHONE..........................419 666-7746
Greg Heminger, *Pr*
▲ **EMP:** 20 **EST:** 2009
SALES (est): 2.45MM **Privately Held**
Web: www.whitakerfinishing.com
SIC: 3471 Electroplating of metals or formed
products

(G-10815)
YANFENG INTL AUTO TECH US I LL
Also Called: Johnson Contrls Authorized Dlr
7560 Arbor Dr (43619-7500)
PHONE..........................419 662-4905

Keith Wandell, *Pr*
EMP: 46
Web: www.johnsoncontrols.com
SIC: 2531 5075 Public building and related
furniture; Warm air heating and air
conditioning
HQ: Yanfeng International Automotive
Technology Us I Llc
41935 W 12 Mile Rd
Novi MI 48377
248 319-7333

Norton
Summit County

(G-10816)
ACCENT MANUFACTURING INC (PA)
Also Called: Accent Showroom & Design Ctr
1026 Gardner Blvd (44203-6670)
PHONE..........................330 724-7704
Timothy Bush, *CEO*
Tim Bush, *Pr*
Anthony Piatko, *Sls Mgr*
Tom Baum, *Manager*
Betty Bush, *Sec*
EMP: 18 **EST:** 1962
SQ FT: 12,500
SALES (est): 1.38MM
SALES (corp-wide): 1.38MM **Privately**
Held
Web: www.accentcustommarble.com
SIC: 1751 3433 3431 3261 Cabinet building
and installation; Heating equipment, except
electric; Metal sanitary ware; Vitreous
plumbing fixtures

(G-10817)
ACE READY MIX CONCRETE CO INC
3826 Summit Rd (44203-5380)
PHONE..........................330 745-8125
Clifford Perren, *VP*
EMP: 10 **EST:** 1995
SALES (est): 174.09K **Privately Held**
Web: www.esticocomputerservice.com
SIC: 3273 Ready-mixed concrete

(G-10818)
ALBERTS SCREEN PRINT INC
Also Called: Albert Screenprint
3704 Summit Rd (44203-5318)
P.O. Box 1041 (44203-9441)
PHONE..........................330 753-7559
Albert Falkenstein Senior, *Ch Bd*
Margaret Falkenstein, *
Albert S Falkenstein, *
▲ **EMP:** 115 **EST:** 1962
SQ FT: 103,000
SALES (est): 18.99MM **Privately Held**
Web: www.albertinc.com
SIC: 2759 3993 2752 Screen printing; Signs
and advertising specialties; Commercial
printing, lithographic

(G-10819)
CJ DANNEMILLER CO
5300 S Hametown Rd (44203-6126)
PHONE..........................330 825-7808
EMP: 21 **EST:** 1935
SALES (est): 9.83MM **Privately Held**
Web: www.cjdannemiller.com
SIC: 5113 5145 2099 2096 Industrial and
personal service paper; Nuts, salted or
roasted; Food preparations, nec; Potato
chips and similar snacks

(G-10820)
E L STONE COMPANY
Also Called: Stonecote
2998 Eastern Rd (44203-3902)

P.O. Box 1012 (44203-9412)
PHONE..............................330 825-4565
Elma Micire, *VP*
Mark Micire, *
EMP: 50 **EST:** 1955
SQ FT: 135,000
SALES (est): 7.54MM **Privately Held**
Web: www.elstone.com
SIC: 3479 3471 Aluminum coating of metal
   products; Plating and polishing

(G-10821)
ETKO MACHINE INC
2796 Barber Rd (44203-1002)
P.O. Box 710 (44203-0710)
PHONE..............................330 745-4033
Julius J Koroshazi, *Pr*
George J Koroshazi, *VP*
Etelka Koroshazi, *Sec*
EMP: 9 **EST:** 1969
SQ FT: 4,000
SALES (est): 680.16K **Privately Held**
Web: www.etko.com
SIC: 3599 Machine shop, jobbing and repair

(G-10822)
FISHER SAND & GRAVEL INC
Also Called: Flesher Sand & Gravel
3322 Clark Mill Rd (44203-1028)
PHONE..............................330 745-9239
James Fisher, *Pr*
EMP: 7 **EST:** 1968
SQ FT: 3,888
SALES (est): 763.83K **Privately Held**
SIC: 1442 Construction sand and gravel

(G-10823)
**ICP ADHESIVES AND SEALANTS
INC (HQ)**
2775 Barber Rd (44203-1001)
P.O. Box 1078 (44203-9478)
PHONE..............................330 753-4585
Stefan Miczka, *Ch*
Stefan Gantenbein, *Pr*
Ron Kozak, *Treas*
▲ **EMP:** 41 **EST:** 1985
SQ FT: 45,000
SALES (est): 47.08MM
SALES (corp-wide): 639.69MM **Privately
Held**
Web: www.icpadhesives.com
SIC: 3086 2891 3296 2821 Plastics foam
   products; Sealants; Mineral wool; Plastics
   materials and resins
PA: Innovative Chemical Products Group,
   Llc
   150 Dascomb Rd
   Andover MA 01810
   978 623-9980

(G-10824)
J E DOYLE COMPANY
Also Called: Doyle Systems
5186 New Haven Cir (44203-4671)
PHONE..............................330 564-0743
Joseph M Lynch, *Pr*
▲ **EMP:** 13 **EST:** 1922
SQ FT: 10,000
SALES (est): 2.08MM **Privately Held**
Web: www.doylesystems.com
SIC: 3554 Paper industries machinery

(G-10825)
KDA MANUFACTURING LLC
5221 S Cleveland Massillon Rd
(44203-7819)
PHONE..............................330 590-7431
EMP: 15 **EST:** 2011
SALES (est): 2.94MM **Privately Held**
Web: www.kdamanufacturing.com

SIC: 3312 7692 3599 Stainless steel;
   Welding repair; Machine and other job shop
   work

(G-10826)
SDK ASSOCIATES INC
Also Called: Custom Control Specialists
2044 Wadsworth Rd Unit B (44203-5306)
P.O. Box 4054 (44321-0054)
PHONE..............................330 745-3648
Scott Fausneaucht, *Pr*
Deborah Fausneaucht, *VP*
EMP: 7 **EST:** 1996
SQ FT: 2,700
SALES (est): 342.96K **Privately Held**
SIC: 3625 Motor control centers

(G-10827)
SPZ MACHINE COMPANY INC
2871 Newpark Dr (44203-1047)
PHONE..............................330 848-3286
Peter Zarkovacki, *Owner*
David Scott Zarkovacki, *VP*
EMP: 8 **EST:** 1978
SQ FT: 50,000
SALES (est): 1.66MM **Privately Held**
Web: www.spzmachine.net
SIC: 3599 Machine shop, jobbing and repair

(G-10828)
WAGNER MACHINE INC
5151 Wooster Rd W (44203-6261)
PHONE..............................330 706-0700
Michael Wagner, *CEO*
Michael Wagner, *Pr*
Courtney Wagner, *
▲ **EMP:** 35 **EST:** 1957
SQ FT: 20,000
SALES (est): 3.65MM **Privately Held**
Web: www.wagnermachine.com
SIC: 3599 Machine shop, jobbing and repair

Norwalk
Huron County

(G-10829)
AVIENT CORPORATION
80 N West St (44857-1239)
PHONE..............................419 668-4844
Gary Weaver, *Brnch Mgr*
EMP: 70
Web: www.avient.com
SIC: 2865 3087 2851 2816 Dyes and
   pigments; Custom compound purchased
   resins; Paints and allied products; Inorganic
   pigments
PA: Avient Corporation
   33587 Walker Rd
   Avon Lake OH 44012

(G-10830)
BENNETT ELECTRIC INC
211 Republic St (44857-1157)
PHONE..............................800 874-5405
Daniel L Stewart, *Pr*
Charles Avarello, *VP*
Jean Stewart, *Sec*
EMP: 14 **EST:** 1925
SQ FT: 15,000
SALES (est): 8.51MM **Privately Held**
Web: www.bennett-electric.com
SIC: 5063 7694 Motors, electric; Electric
   motor repair

(G-10831)
BROOKER BROS FORGING CO INC
102 Jefferson St (44857-1969)
P.O. Box 498 (44857-0498)
PHONE..............................419 668-2535

Rickard E Brooker, *Pr*
EMP: 20 **EST:** 1946
SQ FT: 16,000
SALES (est): 950.87K **Privately Held**
Web: www.brookerbrosforging.com
SIC: 3462 Iron and steel forgings

(G-10832)
CASE MAUL CLAMPS INC
69 N West St (44857-1213)
P.O. Box 605 (44857-0605)
PHONE..............................419 668-6563
James R Maul, *Pr*
Doctor Peggy Maul, *VP*
▲ **EMP:** 6 **EST:** 1994
SALES (est): 1.42MM **Privately Held**
Web: www.case-maul.com
SIC: 3429 Clamps, metal

(G-10833)
CRAZEWELD LLC
1563 Johnson Rd (44857-9769)
PHONE..............................419 210-3668
Joshua Ott, *CEO*
EMP: 9 **EST:** 2019
SALES (est): 689.3K **Privately Held**
Web: www.crazeweld.com
SIC: 1711 1799 7692 1623 Plumbing,
   heating, air-conditioning; Welding on site;
   Welding repair; Pipe laying construction

(G-10834)
CUSTOM METAL WORKS INC (PA)
193 Akron Rd (44857-1665)
PHONE..............................419 668-7831
Lawrence A Skinn, *Pr*
Cynthia Skinn, *Sec*
L Andrew Skinn, *VP*
Bradley Skinn, *VP*
EMP: 14 **EST:** 1981
SQ FT: 19,400
SALES (est): 1.66MM
SALES (corp-wide): 1.66MM **Privately
Held**
Web: www.custommetal-inc.com
SIC: 7699 3599 3429 Industrial machinery
   and equipment repair; Machine shop,
   jobbing and repair; Hardware, nec

(G-10835)
DAN-MAR COMPANY INC
Also Called: Danmarco
200 Bluegrass Dr E (44857-1169)
PHONE..............................419 660-8830
James D Heckelman, *Pr*
Margaret Heckelman, *
Nancy Heckelman, *
EMP: 26 **EST:** 1972
SQ FT: 50,000
SALES (est): 7.28MM **Privately Held**
Web: www.danmarco.com
SIC: 3674 3629 Solid state electronic
   devices, nec; Blasting machines, electrical

(G-10836)
DURABLE CORPORATION
75 N Pleasant St (44857-1218)
P.O. Box 290 (44857-0290)
PHONE..............................800 537-1603
Jon M Anderson, *CEO*
Tom Secor, *
Marcia Norris, *
▲ **EMP:** 60 **EST:** 1923
SQ FT: 3,000
SALES (est): 9.9MM **Privately Held**
Web: www.durablecorp.com
SIC: 3069 2273 5013 Mats or matting,
   rubber, nec; Mats and matting; Bumpers

(G-10837)
EXTOL OF OHIO INC (PA)
208 Republic St (44857-1185)
PHONE..............................419 668-2072
Robin L Degraff, *Pr*
Mergie Simon, *
◆ **EMP:** 17 **EST:** 1990
SQ FT: 45,000
SALES (est): 1.6MM **Privately Held**
Web: www.extolohio.com
SIC: 3296 Insulation: rock wool, slag, and
   silica minerals

(G-10838)
EXTOL OF OHIO INC
208 Republic St (44857-1185)
PHONE..............................419 668-2072
Robin L Degraff, *Pr*
Brian Eisenhower, *
Robert Baldwin, *
Margie Simon, *
EMP: 18 **EST:** 1985
SQ FT: 45,000
SALES (est): 1.13MM **Privately Held**
Web: www.extolohio.com
SIC: 3086 Plastics foam products
PA: Extol Of Ohio, Inc.
   208 Republic St
   Norwalk OH 44857

(G-10839)
FABRIWELD CORPORATION (PA)
405 Industrial Pkwy (44857-3101)
PHONE..............................419 668-3358
Christopher C Price, *Pr*
Faith A Price, *
R David Smith, *
▲ **EMP:** 21 **EST:** 1989
SQ FT: 100,000
SALES (est): 23.02MM **Privately Held**
Web: www.fabriweldcorporation.com
SIC: 3599 Machine shop, jobbing and repair

(G-10840)
FABRIWELD CORPORATION
360 Eastpark Dr (44857-9500)
PHONE..............................419 663-0279
EMP: 48
Web: www.fabriweldcorporation.com
SIC: 3599 Machine shop, jobbing and repair
PA: Fabriweld Corporation
   405 Industrial Pkwy
   Norwalk OH 44857

(G-10841)
FAIR PUBLISHING HOUSE INC
15 Schauss Ave (44857-1851)
P.O. Box 350 (44857-0350)
PHONE..............................419 668-3746
Charles Doyle, *Pr*
Kevin F Doyle, *
EMP: 27 **EST:** 1880
SQ FT: 25,000
SALES (est): 3.02MM
SALES (corp-wide): 5.18MM **Privately
Held**
Web: www.fairpublishing.com
SIC: 2759 3993 2752 Imprinting; Signs and
   advertising specialties; Commercial
   printing, lithographic
PA: Rotary Printing Company
   15 Schauss Ave
   Norwalk OH 44857
   419 668-4821

(G-10842)
**GFL ENVIRONMENTAL SVCS USA
INC**
4376 State Route 601 (44857-9128)
PHONE..............................281 486-4182
Patrick Dovigi, *Brnch Mgr*

G
E
O
G
R
A
P
H
I
C

EMP: 46
SALES (corp-wide): 5.6B **Privately Held**
SIC: 2911 Petroleum refining
HQ: Gfl Environmental Services Usa, Inc.
　18927 Hckry Creek Dr Ste
　Mokena IL 60448
　866 579-6900

(G-10843)
GOODLEVEL ENTERPRISES LLC
(PA)
Also Called: Maple City Rubber Company,
The
55 Newton St (44857-1200)
PHONE.................419 668-8261
Michael Will, *Managing Member*
EMP: 6 **EST:** 2016
SALES (est): 3.2MM
SALES (corp-wide): 3.2MM **Privately Held**
SIC: 3069 Balloons, advertising and toy:
　rubber

(G-10844)
GRAPHIC PACKAGING INTL LLC
209 Republic St (44857-1157)
PHONE.................419 668-1006
Darrin Carlson, *Mgr*
EMP: 40
Web: www.americraft.com
SIC: 2657 Food containers, folding: made
　from purchased material
HQ: Graphic Packaging International, Llc
　1500 Rvredge Pkwy Ste 100
　Atlanta GA 30328

(G-10845)
GYRUS ACMI LP
Also Called: Olympus Surgical Technologies
93 N Pleasant St (44857-1218)
PHONE.................419 668-8201
Tom Motta, *Brnch Mgr*
EMP: 85
SQ FT: 55,000
Web: medical.olympusamerica.com
SIC: 3841 3845 Surgical and medical
　instruments; Electromedical equipment
HQ: Gyrus Acmi, L.P.
　9600 Louisiana Ave N
　Minneapolis MN 55445
　763 416-3000

(G-10846)
HEN HOUSE INC
Also Called: Ditz Designs
100 N West St (44857-1273)
P.O. Box 586 (44857-0586)
PHONE.................419 663-3377
Robert Ludwig, *Pr*
Joyce Ditz, *
Jon Ditz, *
Deborah Ludwig, *
◆ **EMP:** 8 **EST:** 1980
SQ FT: 37,000
SALES (est): 601.74K **Privately Held**
Web: www.ditzdesigns.com
SIC: 2511 Stools, household: wood

(G-10847)
HERALD REFLECTOR INC (PA)
Also Called: Norwalk Reflector
61 E Monroe St (44857-1532)
P.O. Box 71 (44857-0071)
PHONE.................419 668-3771
David Rau, *Pr*
Alice Rau, *
EMP: 50 **EST:** 1829
SQ FT: 10,000
SALES (est): 1.35MM
SALES (corp-wide): 1.35MM **Privately Held**
Web: www.norwalkreflector.com

SIC: 2711 Commercial printing and
　newspaper publishing combined

(G-10848)
INTELLIWORKS HT LLC
61 Saint Marys St (44857-1841)
P.O. Box 899 (44857-0899)
PHONE.................419 660-9050
Dave Nunez, *Prin*
▲ **EMP:** 6 **EST:** 2007
SALES (est): 2.85MM **Privately Held**
Web: www.intelliworksht.com
SIC: 3559 Sewing machines and
　attachments, industrial, nec

(G-10849)
KUHLMAN INSTRUMENT COMPANY
54 Summit St (44857-2134)
P.O. Box 468 (44857-0468)
PHONE.................419 668-9533
Mark Lacy, *CEO*
EMP: 6 **EST:** 1959
SQ FT: 5,000
SALES (est): 888.48K **Privately Held**
Web: www.kuhlmaninstrument.com
SIC: 3823 Process control instruments

(G-10850)
LESCH BOAT COVER CANVAS CO
LLC
43 1/2 Saint Marys St (44857-1809)
PHONE.................419 668-6374
Daniel Lesch, *Prin*
EMP: 6 **EST:** 1968
SQ FT: 3,000
SALES (est): 163.39K **Privately Held**
Web: www.leschcanvas.com
SIC: 2394 2396 Tarpaulins, fabric: made
　from purchased materials; Automotive
　trimmings, fabric

(G-10851)
LINK TO SUCCESS INC
Also Called: Harknessservices
23 Stoutenburg Dr (44857-2354)
PHONE.................888 959-4203
Tara Harkness, *CEO*
EMP: 6 **EST:** 2010
SALES (est): 409.41K **Privately Held**
Web: www.harknesservices.com
SIC: 7349 8742 2899 7389 Exhaust hood or
　fan cleaning; Management consulting
　services; Fire extinguisher charges;
　Business Activities at Non-Commercial Site

(G-10852)
MCR OF NORWALK INC
Also Called: Maple City Rubber Co
55 Newton St (44857-1200)
PHONE.................419 668-8261
Michael Kilbane, *Pr*
Paul Bennett, *
Willam Chandler, *
▲ **EMP:** 44 **EST:** 1915
SQ FT: 104,000
SALES (est): 5.27MM **Privately Held**
Web: www.tuftexballoons.com
SIC: 3069 Balloons, advertising and toy:
　rubber

(G-10853)
MOTO-ELECTRIC INC
262 Cleveland Rd (44857-9024)
PHONE.................419 668-7894
Nicholas Mccall, *Pr*
EMP: 8 **EST:** 1981
SQ FT: 8,000
SALES (est): 903.36K **Privately Held**
Web: www.moto-electric.com

SIC: 7694 5063 Electric motor repair;
　Motors, electric

(G-10854)
NEW HORIZONS BAKING CO LLC
(PA)
211 Woodlawn Ave (44857-2276)
PHONE.................419 668-8226
Ronald Jones, *Pr*
Tilmon F Brown, *
Trina Bediako, *
Robert Creighton, *
John Widman, *
EMP: 220 **EST:** 1965
SQ FT: 4,526
SALES (est): 48.97MM
SALES (corp-wide): 48.97MM **Privately
Held**
Web: www.newhorizonsbaking.com
SIC: 2051 Buns, bread type: fresh or frozen

(G-10855)
NORTH RIDGE ENTERPRISES INC
62 Firelands Blvd (44857-2423)
PHONE.................440 965-5300
William Bodde, *CEO*
David Bodde, *Pr*
Robert Bodde, *VP*
EMP: 17 **EST:** 1983
SALES (est): 1.93MM **Privately Held**
SIC: 3599 Machine shop, jobbing and repair

(G-10856)
NORWALK CONCRETE INDS INC (PA)
80 Commerce Dr (44857-9003)
P.O. Box 563 (44857-0563)
PHONE.................419 668-8167
TOLL FREE: 800
John A Lendrum, *Pr*
Jeffrey S Malcolm, *
Edward Ciersezwski, *
Kathleen Leak, *
▲ **EMP:** 40 **EST:** 1906
SALES (est): 10.14MM
SALES (corp-wide): 10.14MM **Privately
Held**
Web: www.nciprecast.com
SIC: 3272 Concrete products, precast, nec

(G-10857)
NORWALK WASTEWATER EQP CO
Also Called: Norweco
220 Republic St (44857-1156)
P.O. Box 410 (44857-0410)
PHONE.................419 668-4471
Gregory Graves, *Pr*
Jan Graves, *
Michele Graves, *
◆ **EMP:** 71 **EST:** 1906
SQ FT: 70,000
SALES (est): 1.21MM **Privately Held**
Web: www.norweco.com
SIC: 3589 Water treatment equipment,
　industrial

(G-10858)
OGDEN NEWS PUBLISHING OHIO
INC
Also Called: Norwalk Reflector
34 E Main St (44857-1515)
PHONE.................567 743-9843
Joe Centers, *Brnch Mgr*
EMP: 45
Web: www.ogdennews.com
SIC: 2711 Newspapers: publishing only, not
　printed on site
HQ: Ogden News Publishing Of Ohio, Inc.
　314 W Market St
　Sandusky OH 44870
　419 625-5500

(G-10859)
PRECAST PRODUCTS LLC
Also Called: Norwalk Precast Molds, Inc.
205 Industrial Pkwy (44857-3105)
P.O. Box 293 (44857-0293)
PHONE.................419 668-1639
Jan Graves, *Pr*
Gregory D Graves, *Pr*
EMP: 20 **EST:** 1984
SQ FT: 75,000
SALES (est): 3.3MM **Privately Held**
Web: www.norwalkprecastmolds.com
SIC: 3544 Industrial molds

(G-10860)
R & D EQUIPMENT INC
206 Republic St (44857-1185)
PHONE.................419 668-8439
George Gilbert, *Pr*
Chuck Plumb, *VP*
▲ **EMP:** 15 **EST:** 1977
SQ FT: 18,000
SALES (est): 4.6MM **Privately Held**
Web: www.rndequip.com
SIC: 3555 Printing trades machinery

(G-10861)
SC STRATEGIC SOLUTIONS LLC
600 Industrial Pkwy (44857-3103)
PHONE.................567 424-6054
Chad Stein, *Managing Member*
EMP: 151 **EST:** 2007
SALES (est): 12.5MM **Privately Held**
Web: www.scstrategicsolutions.com
SIC: 7372 7374 Application computer
　software; Data processing and preparation

(G-10862)
SOLID DIMENSIONS INC
Also Called: Solid Dimensions Line
720 Townline Road 151 (44857-9535)
PHONE.................419 663-1134
Tim Parcher, *Pr*
Darla Parcher, *VP*
▲ **EMP:** 9 **EST:** 1994
SALES (est): 935.68K **Privately Held**
Web: www.soliddimensions.com
SIC: 2499 Engraved wood products

(G-10863)
WILLIAM DAUCH CONCRETE
COMPANY (PA)
84 Cleveland Rd (44857-9020)
P.O. Box 204 (44857-0204)
PHONE.................419 668-4458
William Dauch, *Pr*
Mona E Dauch, *Sec*
EMP: 15 **EST:** 1966
SQ FT: 2,000
SALES (est): 9.78MM
SALES (corp-wide): 9.78MM **Privately
Held**
Web: www.dauchconcrete.com
SIC: 5032 3273 3272 3271 Brick, stone, and
　related material; Ready-mixed concrete;
　Concrete products, nec; Concrete block
　and brick

Norwich
Muskingum County

(G-10864)
LUMI-LITE CANDLE COMPANY
Also Called: Lumi Craft
102 Sundale Rd (43767-9717)
P.O. Box 97 (43767-0097)
PHONE.................740 872-3248
William W Wilson, *Ch*
George Pappas, *

▲ = Import ▼ = Export
◆ = Import/Export

Tina Bales, *
Pete Pappas, *
▲ **EMP:** 100 **EST:** 1957
SQ FT: 50,000
SALES (est): 934.48K **Privately Held**
Web: www.cakecandle.com
SIC: 3999 Candles

(G-10865)
UNITED CANDLE COMPANY LLC
102 N Sundale Rd (43767-9766)
PHONE..............................740 872-3248
EMP: 8 **EST:** 2019
SALES (est): 2.26MM **Privately Held**
SIC: 3999 Candles

Norwood
Hamilton County

(G-10866)
BLT INC
Also Called: Uptown Graphics
2834 Highland Ave (45212-2410)
PHONE..............................513 631-5050
Ronald Bush, *Pr*
Luigi Lavalle, *VP*
EMP: 13 **EST:** 1986
SQ FT: 8,000
SALES (est): 919.67K **Privately Held**
Web: www.queencityprinting.com
SIC: 2752 3083 2791 Offset printing;
   Plastics finished products, laminated;
   Typesetting

(G-10867)
COX INTERIOR INC
4080 Webster Ave (45212-2706)
PHONE..............................270 789-3129
Robert Mears, *Brnch Mgr*
EMP: 10
SALES (corp-wide): 44.6MM **Privately
Held**
Web: www.coxinterior.com
SIC: 2431 Moldings, wood: unfinished and
   prefinished
HQ: Cox Interior, Inc.
   1751 Old Columbia Rd
   Campbellsville KY 42718
   270 789-3129

(G-10868)
EMD MILLIPORE CORPORATION
2909 Highland Ave (45212-2411)
PHONE..............................513 631-0445
Michael Mulligan, *VP*
EMP: 150
SQ FT: 100,000
SALES (corp-wide): 22.37B **Privately Held**
Web: www.emdmillipore.com
SIC: 8731 3295 2899 2842 Biotechnical
   research, commercial; Minerals, ground or
   treated; Chemical preparations, nec;
   Polishes and sanitation goods
HQ: Emd Millipore Corporation
   400 Summit Dr
   Burlington MA 01803
   800 645-5476

(G-10869)
NAMOH OHIO HOLDINGS INC (PA)
Also Called: Neider, F A Co
5612 Carthage Ave (45212-1028)
P.O. Box 76548 (41076-0548)
◆ **EMP:** 9 **EST:** 1916
SQ FT: 170,000
SALES (est): 3.45MM
SALES (corp-wide): 3.45MM **Privately
Held**
Web: www.auveco.com

SIC: 3465 5013 3714 3452 Automotive
   stampings; Automotive stampings; Motor
   vehicle parts and accessories; Bolts, nuts,
   rivets, and washers

(G-10870)
PALLET SPECS PLUS LLC
1701 Mills Ave (45212-2825)
P.O. Box 15236 (45215-0236)
PHONE..............................513 351-3200
Scott M Senter, *Pr*
Jason Catron, *COO*
EMP: 10 **EST:** 2015
SQ FT: 20,000
SALES (est): 917.99K **Privately Held**
Web: www.palletspecsplus.com
SIC: 2448 Pallets, wood

(G-10871)
SHEPHERD MATERIAL SCIENCE CO
(PA)
4900 Beech St (45212-2316)
PHONE..............................513 731-1110
Thomas L Shepherd, *Pr*
EMP: 25 **EST:** 2010
SALES (est): 107.5MM
SALES (corp-wide): 107.5MM **Privately
Held**
Web: www.shepchem.com
SIC: 2819 2869 Metal salts and compounds
   except sodium, potassium, aluminum;
   Industrial organic chemicals, nec

(G-10872)
SHEPHERD WIDNES LTD
4900 Beech St (45212-2316)
PHONE..............................513 731-1110
▲ **EMP:** 55
SIC: 2819 Industrial inorganic chemicals, nec

(G-10873)
SIEMENS INDUSTRY INC
Also Called: Motors & Drives Division
4620 Forest Ave (45212-3306)
PHONE..............................513 841-3100
Joerg Ernst, *Mgr*
EMP: 200
SQ FT: 550,000
SALES (corp-wide): 84.78B **Privately Held**
Web: www.siemens.com
SIC: 3621 Motors, electric
HQ: Siemens Industry, Inc.
   1000 Deerfield Pkwy
   Buffalo Grove IL 60089
   847 215-1000

(G-10874)
THE SHEPHERD CHEMICAL
COMPANY (HQ)
4900 Beech St (45212-2398)
PHONE..............................513 731-1110
◆ **EMP:** 175 **EST:** 1916
SALES (est): 42.82MM
SALES (corp-wide): 107.5MM **Privately
Held**
Web: www.shepchem.com
SIC: 2819 2869 Metal salts and compounds
   except sodium, potassium, aluminum;
   Laboratory chemicals, organic
PA: The Shepherd Material Science
   Company
   4900 Beech St
   Norwood OH 45212
   513 731-1110

Nova
Ashland County

(G-10875)
AMPTECH MACHINING & WELDING
910 County Road 40 (44859-9723)
PHONE..............................419 652-3444
Dana White, *Owner*
EMP: 9 **EST:** 2005
SALES (est): 190.07K **Privately Held**
Web: www.amptechwelding.com
SIC: 7692 Welding repair

(G-10876)
DANA WHITE MACHINING WLDG INC
910 County Road 40 (44859-9723)
PHONE..............................419 652-3444
Dana White, *Pr*
Tammy White, *Sec*
EMP: 6 **EST:** 1994
SQ FT: 1,000
SALES (est): 246.38K **Privately Held**
Web: www.amptechwelding.com
SIC: 7692 Welding repair

(G-10877)
GRAPHITE SALES INC (PA)
220 Township Road 791 (44859-9703)
P.O. Box 23009 (44023-0009)
PHONE..............................419 652-3388
Kevin Burmeister, *CEO*
Michael Slabe, *CFO*
◆ **EMP:** 15 **EST:** 1979
SQ FT: 16,000
SALES (est): 9.69MM
SALES (corp-wide): 9.69MM **Privately
Held**
Web: www.graphitesales.com
SIC: 3624 Electrodes, thermal and
   electrolytic uses: carbon, graphite

(G-10878)
ULTRABUILT PLAY SYSTEMS INC
1114 Us Highway 224 (44859-9773)
PHONE..............................419 652-2294
Stephen Bennet, *Pr*
EMP: 10 **EST:** 1995
SQ FT: 6,200
SALES (est): 168.1K **Privately Held**
Web: www.ultrabuilt.com
SIC: 3949 2541 Playground equipment;
   Display fixtures, wood

Novelty
Geauga County

(G-10879)
ASM INTERNATIONAL
9639 Kinsman Rd (44073-0002)
PHONE..............................440 338-5151
Thomas Dudley, *CEO*
Navin Manjooran, *
▲ **EMP:** 80 **EST:** 1913
SQ FT: 55,000
SALES (est): 8.93MM **Privately Held**
Web: www.asminternational.org
SIC: 2731 2721 7389 7999 Books,
   publishing only; Periodicals, publishing only
   ; Advertising, promotional, and trade show
   services; Exhibition operation

(G-10880)
BAMF WELDING & FABRICATION
LLC
9988 Kinsman Rd (44072-9316)
P.O. Box 335 (44065-0335)
PHONE..............................440 862-8286

Connor Roberts, *Managing Member*
EMP: 7 **EST:** 2020
SALES (est): 82.17K **Privately Held**
Web: www.arc-houndwelding.com
SIC: 7692 Welding repair

Oak Harbor
Ottawa County

(G-10881)
ACPO LTD
Also Called: Acpo
8035 W Lake Winds Dr (43449-8903)
P.O. Box 418 (43449)
PHONE..............................419 898-8273
▲ **EMP:** 85 **EST:** 1988
SALES (est): 22.57MM
SALES (corp-wide): 8.76B **Publicly Held**
Web: label.averydennison.com
SIC: 2672 Adhesive papers, labels, or tapes:
   from purchased material
PA: Avery Dennison Corporation
   8080 Norton Pkwy
   Mentor OH 44060
   440 534-6000

(G-10882)
AVERY DENNISON CORPORATION
8035 W Lake Winds Dr (43449-8903)
PHONE..............................419 898-8273
EMP: 10
SALES (est): 2.44MM **Privately Held**
Web: label.averydennison.com
SIC: 2672 Paper; coated and laminated, nec

(G-10883)
AYLING AND REICHERT CO
CONSENT
411 S Railroad St (43449-1053)
P.O. Box 389 (43449-0389)
PHONE..............................419 898-2471
Robert G Wilson, *Pr*
Robert G Wilson, *Pr*
Evelyn Wilson, *
EMP: 9 **EST:** 1926
SQ FT: 23,000
SALES (est): 1.65MM **Privately Held**
Web: www.aylingreichert.com
SIC: 3469 3561 3443 Metal stampings, nec;
   Industrial pumps and parts; Floating covers,
   metal plate

(G-10884)
C NELSON MFG CO
Also Called: Nelson
265 N Lake Winds Pkwy (43449-9012)
PHONE..............................419 898-3305
Kelley Smith, *Pr*
◆ **EMP:** 36 **EST:** 1898
SQ FT: 1,200
SALES (est): 4.81MM **Privately Held**
Web: www.cnelson.com
SIC: 3585 Refrigeration and heating
   equipment

(G-10885)
DAVIS FABRICATORS INC
15765 W State Route 2 (43449-9488)
PHONE..............................419 898-5297
Todd Davis, *CEO*
Walter Davis, *Pr*
Sandra Davis, *VP*
EMP: 20 **EST:** 1983
SQ FT: 25,000
SALES (est): 2.34MM **Privately Held**
Web: www.davisfabricators.com
SIC: 3441 Fabricated structural metal

(G-10886)
NORTHERN MANUFACTURING CO INC
150 N Lake Winds Pkwy (43449-8921)
PHONE..................................419 898-2821
Quintin Smith, *Pr*
Harry Bethel, *
Joe Bodner, *
Paul Schmitt, *
▲ **EMP:** 145 **EST:** 1951
SQ FT: 120,000
SALES (est): 14.12MM **Privately Held**
Web: www.northernmfg.com
SIC: 3441 Fabricated structural metal

Oak Hill
Jackson County

(G-10887)
DALE R ADKINS
Also Called: Adkins, Dale Logging
106 Smith St (45656-9705)
P.O. Box 151 (45656-0151)
PHONE..................................740 682-7312
Dale R Adkins, *Owner*
Dale Adkins, *Owner*
EMP: 6 **EST:** 1973
SALES (est): 95.14K **Privately Held**
SIC: 2411 4212 7389 Logging; Lumber (log) trucking, local; Log and lumber broker

(G-10888)
H & H INDUSTRIES INC
5400 State Route 93 (45656-8552)
PHONE..................................740 682-7721
Noah Hickman, *Pr*
Lisa Hickman, *
EMP: 70 **EST:** 2000
SALES (est): 7.08MM **Privately Held**
Web: www.hhindustriesinc.com
SIC: 3011 Retreading materials, tire

(G-10889)
KCS CLEANING SERVICE
7550 State Route 93 (45656-9359)
PHONE..................................740 418-5479
Kathleen Strickland, *Prin*
EMP: 10 **EST:** 2009
SALES (est): 89.27K **Privately Held**
SIC: 2842 Polishes and sanitation goods

(G-10890)
LEE SAYLOR LOGGING LLC
565 Cress Rd (45656-9423)
PHONE..................................740 682-0479
Garrett Saylor, *Prin*
EMP: 6 **EST:** 2016
SALES (est): 674.13K **Privately Held**
Web: www.saylorlogging.com
SIC: 2411 Wooden logs

(G-10891)
NOCK AND SON COMPANY
4138 Monroe Hollow Rd (45656-8995)
P.O. Box 196 (45656-0196)
PHONE..................................740 682-7741
Hayden Hammond, *Mgr*
EMP: 15
SALES (corp-wide): 4.41MM **Privately Held**
Web: www.nockandson.com
SIC: 3255 Clay refractories
PA: The Nock And Son Company
27320 W Oviatt Rd
Cleveland OH 44140
440 871-5525

(G-10892)
PLIBRICO COMPANY LLC
1627 Pyro Rd (45656-9311)
PHONE..................................740 682-7755
Patrick Barry, *CEO*
EMP: 13
Web: www.plibrico.com
SIC: 3297 Brick refractories
PA: Plibrico Company, Llc
1935 Techny Rd Unit 16
Northbrook IL 60062

(G-10893)
RESCO PRODUCTS INC
Cedar Heights Clay Division
3542 State Route 93 (45656-8548)
P.O. Box 295 (45656-0295)
PHONE..................................740 682-7794
Linda Simpson, *Mgr*
EMP: 6
Web: www.rescoproducts.com
SIC: 3255 3297 3251 Ladle brick, clay; Nonclay refractories; Brick and structural clay tile
HQ: Resco Products, Inc.
1 Robinson Plz Ste 300
Pittsburgh PA 15205
412 494-4491

(G-10894)
ROMAR METAL FABRICATING INC
201 Zane Oak Rd (45656-9742)
PHONE..................................740 682-7731
Wayne R Newsom, *Pr*
EMP: 6 **EST:** 1983
SQ FT: 3,700
SALES (est): 681.21K **Privately Held**
SIC: 3441 7692 3444 Fabricated structural metal; Welding repair; Sheet metalwork

Oakwood
Montgomery County

(G-10895)
AQUAPRO SYSTEMS LLC
223 Telford Ave (45419-3222)
PHONE..................................877 278-2797
Charles Murphy, *Pr*
EMP: 15 **EST:** 2004
SALES (est): 4.54MM **Privately Held**
Web:
SIC: 3589 3569 Swimming pool filter and water conditioning systems; Heaters, swimming pool: electric

Oakwood
Paulding County

(G-10896)
COOPER FARMS INC (PA)
22348 Road 140 (45873-9303)
P.O. Box 339 (45846-0339)
PHONE..................................419 594-3325
James R Cooper, *Pr*
Gary A Cooper, *
Dianne L Cooper, *
Anada E Cooper, *
Neil Diller, *
EMP: 100 **EST:** 1940
SQ FT: 38,000
SALES (est): 94.7MM
SALES (corp-wide): 94.7MM **Privately Held**
Web: www.cooperfarms.com
SIC: 2048 5191 Poultry feeds; Feed

(G-10897)
COOPER HATCHERY INC (PA)
Also Called: Cooper Farms
22348 Road 140 (45873-9303)
PHONE..................................419 594-3325
James R Cooper, *CEO*
Gary A Cooper, *
Dianne Cooper, *
Anada E Cooper, *
Janice Fiely, *
EMP: 225 **EST:** 1934
SQ FT: 47,000
SALES (est): 112.29MM
SALES (corp-wide): 112.29MM **Privately Held**
SIC: 0254 0253 2015 5153 Poultry hatcheries; Turkey farm; Turkey, processed, nsk; Grains

(G-10898)
MANSFIELD WELDING SERVICE LLC
20027 State Route 613 (45873-9437)
PHONE..................................419 594-2738
Randy Mansfield, *Managing Member*
EMP: 7 **EST:** 1990
SALES (est): 2.83MM **Privately Held**
Web: www.mansfieldwelding.com
SIC: 3499 3548 Machine bases, metal; Welding apparatus

(G-10899)
ROBERTS MANUFACTURING CO INC
24338 Road 148 (45873-9115)
PHONE..................................419 594-2712
Brian Bauer, *Pr*
Chuck Behrens, *
Brian Miller, *
Margaret Hopkins, *Stockholder*
Ronald E Bauer, *Stockholder*
▲ **EMP:** 50 **EST:** 1952
SQ FT: 15,000
SALES (est): 7.37MM **Privately Held**
Web: www.robertsmanufacturing.net
SIC: 3599 Machine shop, jobbing and repair

(G-10900)
STONECO INC
13762 Road 179 (45873-9012)
PHONE..................................419 393-2555
Rick Welch, *Superintnt*
EMP: 45
SALES (corp-wide): 34.95B **Privately Held**
Web: www.shellyco.com
SIC: 1422 2951 Crushed and broken limestone; Asphalt paving mixtures and blocks
HQ: Stoneco, Inc.
1700 Fostoria Ave Ste 200
Findlay OH 45840
419 422-8854

(G-10901)
TOOLING CONNECTION INC
State Rte 66 N Ste 12603 (45873)
P.O. Box 238 (45873-0238)
PHONE..................................419 594-3339
Klee Dangler, *Pr*
EMP: 9 **EST:** 1981
SQ FT: 12,000
SALES (est): 201.24K **Privately Held**
Web: www.toolingconnection.com
SIC: 3541 3544 Machine tools, metal cutting type; Special dies and tools

Oakwood Village
Cuyahoga County

(G-10902)
AGMET METALS INC
7800 Medusa Rd (44146-5549)
PHONE..................................440 439-7400
Dana J Cassidy, *CEO*
Timothy A Andel, *CFO*
EMP: 31 **EST:** 1981
SALES (est): 4.38MM **Privately Held**
Web: www.agmetmetals.com
SIC: 3559 Recycling machinery

(G-10903)
CABINET CONCEPTS INC
Also Called: Custom Millwork Designs
590 Golden Oak Pkwy Unit B (44146-6502)
PHONE..................................440 232-4644
Karen Torrence, *Pr*
James Torrence, *VP*
EMP: 7 **EST:** 1989
SQ FT: 4,000
SALES (est): 872.3K **Privately Held**
Web: www.custommillworkcmd.com
SIC: 2434 Wood kitchen cabinets

(G-10904)
CLASSIC LAMINATIONS INC
7703 First Pl Ste B (44146-6730)
PHONE..................................440 735-1333
James Tidd, *Pr*
Donna Tidd, *Sec*
EMP: 25 **EST:** 1976
SQ FT: 3,800
SALES (est): 2.32MM **Privately Held**
Web: www.classiclaminations.com
SIC: 3089 2789 Laminating of plastics; Bookbinding and related work

(G-10905)
EXECUTIVE SWEETS EAST INC
7603 First Pl (44146-6703)
PHONE..................................440 359-9866
Jeffrey Williamson, *Pr*
Sandy Williamson, *Treas*
EMP: 7 **EST:** 1979
SQ FT: 1,300
SALES (est): 80.45K **Privately Held**
Web: www.executivesweets.com
SIC: 2064 2066 Chocolate candy, except solid chocolate; Chocolate and cocoa products

(G-10906)
GOOD NUTRITION LLC
Also Called: Good Greens
7710 First Pl (44146-6717)
PHONE..................................216 534-6617
John Huff, *CEO*
Bill Ross, *Ch*
Natalie Alesci, *Treas*
EMP: 10 **EST:** 2015
SQ FT: 3,000
SALES (est): 246.9K **Privately Held**
SIC: 2064 Granola and muesli, bars and clusters

(G-10907)
N-MOLECULAR INC
Also Called: Sofie
7650 First Pl Ste B (44146-6732)
PHONE..................................440 439-5356
Kenneth Smithmier, *CEO*
EMP: 15
SALES (corp-wide): 4.41MM **Privately Held**
SIC: 2834 Pharmaceutical preparations
PA: N-Molecular, Inc.

▲ = Import ▼ = Export
◆ = Import/Export

21000 Atl Blvd Ste 730
Dulles VA 20166
703 547-8161

(G-10908)
OAKWOOD LABORATORIES LLC
(PA)
7670 First Pl Ste A (44146-6721)
PHONE..........................440 359-0000
Jeffery Fehn, *CEO*
Edward C Smith, *Ch Bd*
Mark T Smith, *Pr*
Bc Thanoo, *VP*
EMP: 20 **EST:** 1997
SQ FT: 15,000
SALES (est): 19.43MM
SALES (corp-wide): 19.43MM **Privately
Held**
Web: www.oakwoodlabs.com
SIC: 2834 Pharmaceutical preparations

(G-10909)
STATUS MENS ACCESSORIES
7650 First Pl Ste F (44146-6732)
P.O. Box 35515 (44135-0515)
PHONE..........................440 786-9394
Scott Weger, *Pr*
Lee Schloss, *VP*
Mark Schloss, *VP*
▲ **EMP:** 6 **EST:** 2004
SALES (est): 416.84K **Privately Held**
SIC: 2389 Men's miscellaneous accessories

(G-10910)
THERMO FISHER SCIENTIFIC INC
Also Called: Remel Products
1 Thermo Fisher Way (44146-6536)
PHONE..........................800 871-8909
EMP: 24
SALES (corp-wide): 42.86B **Publicly Held**
Web: www.thermofisher.com
SIC: 5047 2835 3841 Diagnostic equipment,
medical; Diagnostic substances; Surgical
and medical instruments
PA: Thermo Fisher Scientific Inc.
168 3rd Ave
Waltham MA 02451
781 622-1000

(G-10911)
VIEWRAY INC (PA)
2 Thermo Fisher Way (44146-6536)
PHONE..........................440 703-3210
Paul Ziegler, *CEO*
Daniel Moore, *Ch Bd*
Cassie Mahar, *Interim Chief Financial
Officer*
Martin Fuzz, *CMO*
James F Dempsey, *CSO*
▲ **EMP:** 51 **EST:** 2004
SALES (est): 102.21MM
SALES (corp-wide): 102.21MM **Publicly
Held**
Web: www.viewray.com
SIC: 3845 5047 Electromedical equipment;
Therapy equipment

(G-10912)
VIEWRAY TECHNOLOGIES INC (HQ)
2 Thermo Fisher Way (44146-6536)
PHONE..........................440 703-3210
Scott Drake, *CEO*
William W Wells, *Pr*
Shar Matin, *COO*
James Alecxih, *Chief Commercial Officer*
EMP: 15 **EST:** 2007
SALES (est): 22.91MM
SALES (corp-wide): 102.21MM **Publicly
Held**
Web: www.viewray.com

SIC: 3845 Electromedical equipment
PA: Viewray, Inc.
2 Thermo Fisher Way
Oakwood Village OH 44146
440 703-3210

(G-10913)
WELDON PUMP LLC
Also Called: Weldon Pump
640 Golden Oak Pkwy (44146-6504)
PHONE..........................440 232-2282
Kent Kelly, *CEO*
Jeffrey Kelly, *
Jennifer Kelly, *
EMP: 28 **EST:** 2015
SQ FT: 16,000
SALES (est): 2.5MM **Privately Held**
Web: www.weldonpumps.com
SIC: 3694 3728 3795 9661 Distributors,
motor vehicle engine; R and D by manuf.,
aircraft parts and auxiliary equipment;
Tanks and tank components; Space
research and technology

Oberlin
Lorain County

(G-10914)
ATLAS MACHINE PRODUCTS CO
Also Called: Atlas Portable Space Solutions
44800 Us Highway 20 (44074-9702)
PHONE..........................216 228-3688
N Medley, *Pr*
William Slabe, *VP Mfg*
Ed Medley, *Sec*
EMP: 7 **EST:** 1952
SALES (est): 460.45K **Privately Held**
SIC: 3451 Screw machine products

(G-10915)
BIG PRODUCTIONS INC
45300b Us Highway 20 (44074-9262)
PHONE..........................440 775-0015
Joanne Douglas, *Pr*
EMP: 6 **EST:** 1997
SQ FT: 7,000
SALES (est): 216.91K **Privately Held**
Web: www.bigproductionsinc.com
SIC: 2299 Jute and flax textile products

(G-10916)
EAST OBERLIN CABINETS LLC
13184 Hale Rd (44074-9741)
PHONE..........................440 775-1166
Dennis Luttrell, *Owner*
EMP: 7 **EST:** 1976
SALES (est): 290.53K **Privately Held**
Web: www.eastoberlincabinets.com
SIC: 2511 2434 Silverware chests: wood;
Vanities, bathroom: wood

(G-10917)
GAZETTE PUBLISHING COMPANY
(PA)
Also Called: Bellevue Gazette
42 S Main St (44074-1627)
P.O. Box 309 (44811-0309)
PHONE..........................419 483-4190
Donald Reiderman, *Prin*
Donald Reiderman, *Pur/VP*
Greg Callaghan, *
Rick Miller, *
EMP: 45 **EST:** 1867
SQ FT: 6,000
SALES (est): 4.39MM
SALES (corp-wide): 4.39MM **Privately
Held**
Web: www.northwestsignal.net

SIC: 2711 2791 2752 Newspapers,
publishing and printing; Typesetting;
Commercial printing, lithographic

(G-10918)
HYDRO TUBE ENTERPRISES INC
(PA)
137 Artino St (44074-1265)
PHONE..........................440 774-1022
Mike Prokop, *Pr*
Thomas E Hamel, *
Richard Cooks, *
▲ **EMP:** 70 **EST:** 1922
SQ FT: 67,000
SALES (est): 22.56MM
SALES (corp-wide): 22.56MM **Privately
Held**
Web: www.hydrotube.com
SIC: 3498 Tube fabricating (contract bending
and shaping)

(G-10919)
JB POLYMERS INC
55 S Main St Pmb 204 (44074-1626)
PHONE..........................216 941-7041
John Busa, *Pr*
EMP: 9 **EST:** 1995
SQ FT: 40,000
SALES (est): 485.96K **Privately Held**
Web: www.jbpolymers.com
SIC: 2821 Plastics materials and resins

(G-10920)
R R DONNELLEY & SONS COMPANY
Also Called: R & S Label
450 Sterns Rd (44074-1209)
PHONE..........................440 774-2101
Jake Martin, *Mgr*
EMP: 100
SQ FT: 23,141
SALES (corp-wide): 15B **Privately Held**
Web: www.rrd.com
SIC: 2752 2759 2672 2761 Commercial
printing, lithographic; Letterpress printing;
Paper; coated and laminated, nec;
Continuous forms, office and business
HQ: R. R. Donnelley & Sons Company
227 W Monroe St Ste 500
Chicago IL 60606
312 326-8000

Obetz
Franklin County

(G-10921)
CAPITOL CITY TRAILERS INC
3960 Groveport Rd (43207-5127)
PHONE..........................614 491-2616
Buck Stewart, *Pr*
Tim Stewart, *
EMP: 58 **EST:** 1994
SQ FT: 20,000
SALES (est): 3.76MM **Privately Held**
Web: www.capitolcitytrailers.com
SIC: 7539 3792 Trailer repair; Travel trailers
and campers

(G-10922)
CENTRAL ALUMINUM COMPANY
LLC
2045 Broehm Rd (43207-5206)
P.O. Box 624 (43023-0624)
PHONE..........................614 491-5700
Lee Grove, *Genl Mgr*
EMP: 50 **EST:** 1963
SQ FT: 94,000
SALES (est): 10.01MM **Privately Held**
Web: www.centralaluminum.com

SIC: 3354 3479 Aluminum extruded products
; Painting, coating, and hot dipping
PA: Gdic Group, Llc
1300 E 9th St Fl 20
Cleveland OH 44114

(G-10923)
CHERYL & CO
4465 Industrial Center Dr (43207-4589)
PHONE..........................614 776-1500
Jodi Dixon, *Brnch Mgr*
EMP: 17
Web: www.cheryls.com
SIC: 2052 2066 Cookies and crackers;
Chocolate and cocoa products
HQ: Cheryl & Co.
646 Mccorkle Blvd
Westerville OH 43082
614 776-1500

(G-10924)
MASONS SAND AND GRAVEL CO
2385 Rathmell Rd (43207-4835)
PHONE..........................614 491-3611
George C Smith, *Pr*
EMP: 9 **EST:** 1951
SQ FT: 3,000
SALES (est): 850.74K **Privately Held**
Web: www.masonssandandgravel.com
SIC: 1442 Construction sand mining

(G-10925)
NATIONAL BEVERAGE CORP
Also Called: Shasta Beverges
4685 Groveport Rd (43207-5216)
PHONE..........................614 491-5415
Monte Hale, *Mgr*
EMP: 10
SALES (corp-wide): 1.19B **Publicly Held**
Web: www.nationalbeverage.com
SIC: 2086 Soft drinks: packaged in cans,
bottles, etc.
PA: National Beverage Corp.
8050 Sw 10th St Ste 4000
Plantation FL 33324
954 581-0922

(G-10926)
SHASTA BEVERAGES INC
Also Called: National Beverage
4685 Groveport Rd (43207-5295)
PHONE..........................614 491-5415
Monty Hale, *Mgr*
EMP: 60
SALES (corp-wide): 1.19B **Publicly Held**
Web: www.shastapop.com
SIC: 2086 Soft drinks: packaged in cans,
bottles, etc.
HQ: Shasta Beverages, Inc.
26901 Indl Blvd
Hayward CA 94545
954 581-0922

Okeana
Butler County

(G-10927)
CHRISNIK INC
7461 Cincinnati Brookville Rd (45053-9780)
P.O. Box 516 (45061-0516)
PHONE..........................513 738-2920
Robert Zaenkert, *Pr*
EMP: 6 **EST:** 1996
SQ FT: 10,000
SALES (est): 576.94K **Privately Held**
Web: www.chrisnik.com
SIC: 3423 5072 Masons' hand tools;
Hardware

G
E
O
G
R
A
P
H
I
C

(G-10928)
CUSTOM FABRICATION BY FISHER
100 Weaver Rd (45053-9711)
PHONE...................513 738-4600
Rodney Fisher, *Prin*
EMP: 7 **EST:** 2008
SALES (est): 582.22K **Privately Held**
SIC: 3499 Novelties and giftware, including
trophies

(G-10929)
WAVY TICKET LLC
3748 State Line Rd (45053-9506)
PHONE...................513 827-0886
Stephen Mann, *Managing Member*
EMP: 40 **EST:** 2020
SALES (est): 694.83K **Privately Held**
SIC: 3599 Amusement park equipment

(G-10930)
WHITMAN CORPORATION
2530 Joyce Ln (45053-9746)
PHONE...................513 541-3223
TOLL FREE: 888
James Erhardt, *Pr*
Susan Erhardt, *VP*
EMP: 6 **EST:** 1931
SQ FT: 8,016
SALES (est): 105.16K
SALES (corp-wide): 91.47B **Publicly Held**
Web: www.whitcorp.com
SIC: 3161 3199 Cases, carrying, nec;
Saddles or parts
PA: Pepsico, Inc.
700 Anderson Hill Rd
Purchase NY 10577
914 253-2000

(G-10931)
**ZAENKERT SRVYING ESSNTIALS
INC**
7461a Cincinnati Brookville Rd
(45053-9780)
PHONE...................513 738-2917
Robert Zaenkert, *Pr*
Michelle Zaenkert, *VP*
EMP: 8 **EST:** 1986
SQ FT: 2,100
SALES (est): 482.2K **Privately Held**
Web: www.hardwoodstakes.com
SIC: 2499 5049 5211 Surveyors' stakes,
wood; Surveyor's instruments; Lumber and
other building materials

Okolona
Henry County

(G-10932)
REPUBLIC MILLS INC
Also Called: Hudson Feeds
888 School St (43545-9246)
PHONE...................419 758-3511
William H Koon Ii, *Pr*
Vivian A Koon, *Stockholder*
Ronald Wingfield, *Sec*
Andrea Gillespie, *VP*
Richard Lange, *Genl Mgr*
▼ **EMP:** 10 **EST:** 1995
SQ FT: 30,000
SALES (est): 2.38MM **Privately Held**
Web: www.republicmills.com
SIC: 2048 5191 Livestock feeds; Feed

Old Fort
Seneca County

(G-10933)
CHURCH & DWIGHT CO INC
2501 E County Rd 34 (44861)
P.O. Box 122 (44861-0122)
PHONE...................419 992-4244
Bruce Neeley, *Brnch Mgr*
EMP: 8
SALES (corp-wide): 6.11B **Publicly Held**
Web: www.churchdwight.com
SIC: 2812 Sodium bicarbonate
PA: Church & Dwight Co., Inc.
500 Charles Ewing Blvd
Ewing NJ 08628
609 806-1200

(G-10934)
M & B ASPHALT COMPANY INC
Also Called: Maple Grove Stone
1525 W County Road 42 (44861)
P.O. Box 136 (44861-0136)
PHONE...................419 992-4236
EMP: 9
SALES (corp-wide): 10.04MM **Privately
Held**
Web: www.mgqinc.com
SIC: 3273 Ready-mixed concrete
PA: M. & B. Asphalt Company, Inc.
1525 W Seneca Cnty Rd 42
Tiffin OH 44883
419 992-4235

Olmsted Falls
Cuyahoga County

(G-10935)
ADAMS AUTOMATIC INC
26070 N Depot St (44138-1647)
P.O. Box 38156 (44138-0156)
PHONE...................440 235-4416
Edward Bond, *Pr*
Eric Dales, *Pr*
Adria Bond, *VP*
EMP: 10 **EST:** 1952
SQ FT: 7,200
SALES (est): 2.23MM **Privately Held**
Web: www.adamsautomaticinc.com
SIC: 3451 Screw machine products

(G-10936)
AFFILIATED METAL INDUSTRIES INC
Also Called: A M I
25600 Chapin St (44138-2782)
PHONE...................440 235-3345
EMP: 12 **EST:** 1959
SALES (est): 808.37K **Privately Held**
Web: www.affiliatedmetal.com
SIC: 1791 3444 Structural steel erection;
Sheet metalwork

(G-10937)
BELL TIRE CO (PA)
Also Called: Almira Tire & Supply Div
27003 Oakwood Cir Apt 107 (44138-3507)
PHONE...................440 234-8022
Charles Russo, *VP*
Geraldine Russo, *Pr*
Joseph Russo, *Sec*
EMP: 11 **EST:** 1964
SQ FT: 75,000
SALES (est): 241.1K
SALES (corp-wide): 241.1K **Privately Held**
SIC: 5014 5531 7534 Automobile tires and
tubes; Automotive tires; Rebuilding and
retreading tires

(G-10938)
BLUE RIDGE PAPER PRODUCTS LLC
Also Called: Dairy Pak Div
7920 Mapleway Dr (44138-1626)
PHONE...................440 235-7200
Dave Lewallen, *Brnch Mgr*
EMP: 38
SQ FT: 161,146
SALES (corp-wide): 26.11B **Publicly Held**
Web: www.pactivevergreen.com
SIC: 2621 Fine paper
HQ: Blue Ridge Paper Products Llc
41 Main St
Canton NC 28716
828 454-0676

(G-10939)
BROCK CORPORATION (PA)
26000 Sprague Rd (44138-2743)
P.O. Box 38159 (44138-0159)
PHONE...................440 235-1806
Brock Walls, *Pr*
Linda D Walls, *VP*
EMP: 8 **EST:** 1979
SQ FT: 3,400
SALES (est): 973.63K
SALES (corp-wide): 973.63K **Privately
Held**
SIC: 3273 Ready-mixed concrete

(G-10940)
GERGEL-KELLEM COMPANY INC
Also Called: Watt Printers
8707 Forest View Dr (44138-2347)
P.O. Box 38381 (44138-0381)
PHONE...................216 398-2000
John Gergel, *Pr*
Mike Nakonek, *
EMP: 60 **EST:** 1893
SALES (est): 1.13MM **Privately Held**
SIC: 2752 Offset printing

(G-10941)
THERMAFAB ALLOY INC
25367 Water St (44138-2015)
PHONE...................216 861-0540
George M Donnelly, *CEO*
Gilbert Sherman, *
Daniel P Conway, *
EMP: 9 **EST:** 1930
SQ FT: 58,000
SALES (est): 2.55MM **Privately Held**
SIC: 3087 Custom compound purchased
resins

(G-10942)
**VITA-MIX MANUFACTURING
CORPORATION (PA)**
Also Called: Vitamix
8615 Usher Rd (44138-2199)
PHONE...................440 235-4840
◆ **EMP:** 237 **EST:** 1921
SALES (est): 55.76MM
SALES (corp-wide): 55.76MM **Privately
Held**
Web: www.vitamix.com
SIC: 3634 Electric housewares and fans

(G-10943)
WESTVIEW CONCRETE CORP (PA)
26000 Sprague Rd (44138-2743)
P.O. Box 38159 (44138-0159)
PHONE...................440 235-1800
EMP: 50 **EST:** 1957
SALES (est): 4.8MM
SALES (corp-wide): 4.8MM **Privately Held**
Web: www.westviewconcrete.com
SIC: 3273 5211 Ready-mixed concrete;
Masonry materials and supplies

Olmsted Twp
Cuyahoga County

(G-10944)
**AMERICAN WIRE & CABLE
COMPANY (PA)**
7951 Bronson Rd (44138-1088)
PHONE...................440 235-1140
Richard M Mcclain, *Pr*
Kim R Mcclain, *VP*
▲ **EMP:** 30 **EST:** 1955
SQ FT: 80,000
SALES (est): 9.93MM
SALES (corp-wide): 9.93MM **Privately
Held**
Web: www.americanwireandcable.com
SIC: 3357 3351 3315 Nonferrous
wiredrawing and insulating; Wire, copper
and copper alloy; Steel wire and related
products

(G-10945)
EAVAN CORP
8580 Evergreen Trl Apt 207 (44138-4282)
PHONE...................216 401-8619
EMP: 10
SALES (est): 1.28MM **Privately Held**
SIC: 1389 7389 Construction, repair, and
dismantling services; Business services,
nec

(G-10946)
JONES INDUSTRIES LLC
Also Called: Holding Company
8543 Evergreen Trl (44138-8126)
PHONE...................440 810-1251
Dina Jones, *CEO*
EMP: 12 **EST:** 2008
SALES (est): 191.67K **Privately Held**
SIC: 3999 Manufacturing industries, nec

Ontario
Richland County

(G-10947)
C & F TIRE & TRUCK REPAIR
Also Called: C&F Truck & Tire Service
3646 Mary Lou Ln S (44906-1015)
PHONE...................419 526-1412
Nancy C Franks, *Owner*
EMP: 7 **EST:** 1971
SQ FT: 5,000
SALES (est): 115.15K **Privately Held**
SIC: 5531 7538 7534 7539 Automotive tires;
General automotive repair shops; Tire
retreading and repair shops; Automotive
repair shops, nec

(G-10948)
COLE TOOL & DIE COMPANY
Also Called: Oil Tooling and Stamping
466 State Rte 314 N (44903-6555)
P.O. Box 150 (44862-0150)
PHONE...................419 522-1272
Alan D Cole, *CEO*
Dave Harmon, *
EMP: 40 **EST:** 1953
SQ FT: 28,000
SALES (est): 5.23MM **Privately Held**
Web: www.coletool.com
SIC: 3544 3469 3465 Special dies and tools;
Metal stampings, nec; Automotive
stampings

(G-10949)
EMERSON PROCESS MANAGEMENT
Also Called: Shafer Valve Company

2500 Park Ave W (44906-1235)
PHONE..............................419 529-4311
EMP: 43
SALES (corp-wide): 17.49B **Publicly Held**
Web: www.emersonprocess.com
SIC: 3594 3593 Fluid power pumps and motors; Fluid power actuators, hydraulic or pneumatic
HQ: Emerson Process Management Valve Automation, Inc.
8100 W Florissant Ave
Saint Louis MO 63136
314 553-2000

(G-10950)
NCF CIM FABRICATORS LLC
1310 W 4th St (44906-1828)
PHONE..............................863 425-1000
EMP: 30 **EST:** 2019
SALES (est): 1.15MM **Privately Held**
SIC: 3449 Bars, concrete reinforcing: fabricated steel

(G-10951)
OXYRASE INC
3000 Park Ave W (44906-1050)
P.O. Box 1345 (44901-1345)
PHONE..............................419 589-8800
Casey Zace, *Pr*
EMP: 10 **EST:** 1986
SQ FT: 7,000
SALES (est): 4.69MM **Privately Held**
Web: www.oxyrase.com
SIC: 2869 Enzymes

(G-10952)
P R MACHINE WORKS INC
1825 Nussbaum Pkwy (44906-2360)
PHONE..............................419 529-5748
Mark Romanchuk, *Pr*
Mark J Romanchuk, *
▲ **EMP:** 75 **EST:** 1964
SQ FT: 14,100
SALES (est): 9.18MM **Privately Held**
Web: www.prmachineworks.com
SIC: 3599 1531 Machine shop, jobbing and repair

(G-10953)
UNISPORT INC
Also Called: Johnny Johnson Sports
2254 Stumbo Rd (44906-3804)
PHONE..............................419 529-4727
H Kim Baird, *Pr*
Todd Baird, *VP*
EMP: 10 **EST:** 1987
SALES (est): 384.4K **Privately Held**
Web: www.uni-sport.com
SIC: 5136 5137 5699 2759 Sportswear, men's and boys'; Sportswear, women's and children's; Sports apparel; Screen printing

(G-10954)
WHITE MULE COMPANY
2420 W 4th St (44906-1207)
PHONE..............................740 382-9008
Steve Ritchey, *Pr*
Debby Ritchey, *Sec*
EMP: 21 **EST:** 1925
SQ FT: 15,000
SALES (est): 2.31MM **Privately Held**
Web: www.whitemuleco.com
SIC: 3714 1791 Trailer hitches, motor vehicle ; Iron work, structural

Oregon
Lucas County

(G-10955)
ABC APPLIANCE INC
Also Called: ABC
3012 Navarre Ave (43616-3308)
PHONE..............................419 693-4414
J R Pruss, *Mgr*
EMP: 20
SALES (corp-wide): 400.19MM **Privately Held**
Web: www.abcwarehouse.com
SIC: 3639 5722 5731 5065 Major kitchen appliances, except refrigerators and stoves; Vacuum cleaners; High fidelity stereo equipment; Telephone equipment
PA: Abc Appliance, Inc.
1 W Silverdome Indus Pk
Pontiac MI 48343
248 335-4222

(G-10956)
AECOM ENERGY & CNSTR INC
Also Called: Washington Group
4001 Cedar Point Rd (43616-1310)
P.O. Box 696 (43697-0696)
PHONE..............................419 698-6277
EMP: 8
SALES (corp-wide): 16.11B **Publicly Held**
Web: www.aecom.com
SIC: 1542 2911 Nonresidential construction, nec; Petroleum refining
HQ: Amentum Environment & Energy, Inc.
106 Newberry St Sw
Aiken SC 29801
213 593-8100

(G-10957)
AUTONEUM NORTH AMERICA INC
Also Called: Rieter Automotive-Oregon Plant
645 N Lallendorf Rd (43616-1334)
PHONE..............................419 693-0511
Gordon Shaw, *Brnch Mgr*
EMP: 350
SQ FT: 150,000
Web: www.autoneum.com
SIC: 3625 3714 3444 3296 Relays and industrial controls; Motor vehicle parts and accessories; Sheet metalwork; Mineral wool
HQ: Autoneum North America, Inc.
34705 W 12 Mile Rd Ste 10
Farmington Hills MI 48331
248 848-0100

(G-10958)
AUTONEUM NORTH AMERICA INC
4131 Spartan Dr (43616-1300)
PHONE..............................419 690-8924
EMP: 70
Web: www.autoneum.com
SIC: 3714 Motor vehicle parts and accessories
HQ: Autoneum North America, Inc.
34705 W 12 Mile Rd Ste 10
Farmington Hills MI 48331
248 848-0100

(G-10959)
BP PRODUCTS NORTH AMERICA INC
4001 Cedar Point Rd (43616-1310)
PHONE..............................419 698-6400
EMP: 10 **EST:** 1922
SALES (est): 3.2MM **Privately Held**
SIC: 1311 Crude petroleum and natural gas

(G-10960)
CARAUSTAR INDUS CNSMR PDTS GRO
Also Called: Caraustar
4031 Spartan Dr (43616-1355)
PHONE..............................419 690-0524
James Armstrong, *Mgr*
EMP: 54
SQ FT: 40,000
SALES (corp-wide): 5.45B **Publicly Held**
SIC: 2655 Tubes, fiber or paper: made from purchased material
HQ: Caraustar Industrial And Consumer Products Group Inc
5000 Austell Powder Ste
Austell GA 30106
803 548-5100

(G-10961)
FOUTY & COMPANY INC
5003 Bayshore Rd (43616-4478)
P.O. Box 167544 (43616-7544)
PHONE..............................419 693-0017
Marion L Fouty, *Pr*
Ken Fouty, *Pr*
▲ **EMP:** 20 **EST:** 1966
SQ FT: 20,000
SALES (est): 2.29MM **Privately Held**
Web: www.foutywaterjet.com
SIC: 5085 3053 Rubber goods, mechanical; Gaskets, all materials

(G-10962)
LINDE INC
Also Called: Praxair
3742 Cedar Point Rd (43616-1302)
PHONE..............................419 698-8005
Bill Engberg, *Mgr*
EMP: 8
Web: www.lindeus.com
SIC: 2813 Industrial gases
HQ: Linde Inc.
10 Riverview Dr
Danbury CT 06810
203 837-2000

(G-10963)
MARSULEX INC
1400 Otter Creek Rd (43616-1232)
PHONE..............................419 698-8181
EMP: 28
SIC: 2819 Sulfuric acid, oleum

(G-10964)
MR EMBLEM INC
3209 Navarre Ave (43616-3311)
PHONE..............................419 697-1888
Pat Slygh, *CEO*
EMP: 7 **EST:** 1987
SQ FT: 3,600
SALES (est): 385.76K **Privately Held**
Web: www.mremblem.com
SIC: 2395 2396 5199 Embroidery and art needlework; Screen printing on fabric articles; Advertising specialties

(G-10965)
PBF HOLDING COMPANY LLC
1819 Woodville Rd (43616-3159)
PHONE..............................419 698-6600
EMP: 55
SALES (corp-wide): 33.12B **Publicly Held**
Web: www.pbfenergy.com
SIC: 2911 Petroleum refining
HQ: Pbf Holding Company Llc
1 Sylvan Way Fl 2
Parsippany NJ 07054

(G-10966)
PSC 272 TRC PBF
1819 Woodville Rd (43616-3159)
PHONE..............................419 466-7129
EMP: 43 **EST:** 2019
SALES (est): 2.4MM **Privately Held**
Web: www.pbfenergy.com
SIC: 2911 Petroleum refining

(G-10967)
RBM ENVIRONMENTAL & CNSTR INC
4526 Bayshore Rd (43616-1035)
PHONE..............................419 693-5840
Bob J Petty, *Pr*
Mike S Petty, *
EMP: 8 **EST:** 1989
SALES (est): 939.72K **Privately Held**
SIC: 1794 7699 7692 3498 Excavation and grading, building construction; Tank and boiler cleaning service; Welding repair; Fabricated pipe and fittings

(G-10968)
SNOWS WOOD SHOP INC (PA)
7220 Brown Rd (43616-5805)
PHONE..............................419 836-3805
Vernon Snow, *Pr*
Minda Snow, *Sec*
Kurt Snow, *VP*
EMP: 21 **EST:** 1983
SQ FT: 10,380
SALES (est): 777.37K **Privately Held**
Web: www.snowswoodshop.com
SIC: 2434 1751 Wood kitchen cabinets; Cabinet and finish carpentry

(G-10969)
TOLEDO ALFALFA MILLS INC
861 S Stadium Rd (43616-5898)
PHONE..............................419 836-3705
Kathryn Lumbrezes, *Pr*
Becky Lumbrezer-box, *Sec*
Gary Lumbrezer, *VP*
EMP: 8 **EST:** 1940
SQ FT: 6,000
SALES (est): 2.1MM **Privately Held**
SIC: 2048 Alfalfa or alfalfa meal, prepared as animal feed

Orient
Pickaway County

(G-10970)
B & B INDUSTRIES INC
7001 Harrisburg Pike (43146-9468)
PHONE..............................614 871-3883
Bernard Harwood, *Owner*
EMP: 9 **EST:** 2016
SALES (est): 1.44MM **Privately Held**
Web: www.bandbindustries.com
SIC: 3799 Golf carts, powered

(G-10971)
KMJ LEASING LTD
Also Called: B & B Industries
7001 Harrisburg Pike (43146-9468)
PHONE..............................614 871-3883
Mary A Harwood, *
EMP: 8 **EST:** 1971
SQ FT: 5,000
SALES (est): 905.24K **Privately Held**
SIC: 4213 3799 Contract haulers; Golf carts, powered

Orrville
Wayne County

(G-10972)
ACCURATE ELECTRONICS INC
169 S Main St (44667-1801)
P.O. Box 900 (44667-0900)
PHONE..............................330 682-7015
Jeffrey Evans, *CEO*
EMP: 11 **EST:** 1952
SQ FT: 6,000
SALES (est): 1.52MM
SALES (corp-wide): 40.96MM **Privately Held**
SIC: 3679 3621 3812 3672 Electronic circuits ; Generators and sets, electric; Search and navigation equipment; Printed circuit boards
PA: The Will-Burt Company
401 Collins Blvd
Orrville OH 44667
330 682-7015

(G-10973)
AT&F ADVANCED METALS LLC
95 N Swinehart Rd (44667-9532)
PHONE..............................330 684-1122
Michael Ripich, *Pr*
EMP: 12
SALES (corp-wide): 5.04MM **Privately Held**
Web: www.atfco.com
SIC: 3446 Railings, prefabricated metal
PA: At&f Advanced Metals Llc
12314 Elmwood Ave
Cleveland OH 44111
330 684-1122

(G-10974)
BEKAERT CORPORATION
Also Called: Bekaert Orrville
510 Collins Blvd (44667-9796)
PHONE..............................330 683-5060
Andrew Whited, *Manager*
EMP: 15
SALES (corp-wide): 530.91MM **Privately Held**
Web: fencing.bekaert.com
SIC: 3496 Miscellaneous fabricated wire products
HQ: Bekaert Corporation
4300 Wldwood Pkwy Ste 100
Atlanta GA 30339
330 867-3325

(G-10975)
BEKAERT CORPORATION
Also Called: Contours
322 E Pine St (44667-1853)
PHONE..............................330 683-5060
Otto Simmerman, *Prin*
EMP: 49
SQ FT: 260,000
SALES (corp-wide): 530.91MM **Privately Held**
Web: fencing.bekaert.com
SIC: 3315 3316 3398 3479 Wire and fabricated wire products; Cold-rolled strip or wire; Metal heat treating; Coating of metals and formed products
HQ: Bekaert Corporation
4300 Wldwood Pkwy Ste 100
Atlanta GA 30339
330 867-3325

(G-10976)
CHEMSPEC USA LLC
9287 Smucker Rd (44667-9795)
PHONE..............................330 669-8512
Ron Snow, *Pr*

Michael Hall, *
▼ **EMP:** 60 **EST:** 2016
SALES (est): 20.01MM
SALES (corp-wide): 5.28B **Publicly Held**
SIC: 2851 Paints and paint additives
HQ: Axalta Coating Systems, Llc
50 Applied Bnk Blvd Ste 3
Glen Mills PA 19342
855 547-1461

(G-10977)
CHEMSPEC USA INC
9287 Smucker Rd (44667-9795)
PHONE..............................330 669-8512
▲ **EMP:** 54 **EST:** 1975
SALES (est): 2.63MM
SALES (corp-wide): 5.28B **Publicly Held**
Web: www.bodyshopbusiness.com
SIC: 2819 2851 2891 5013 Catalysts, chemical; Lacquer: bases, dopes, thinner; Adhesives; Motor vehicle supplies and new parts
PA: Axalta Coating Systems Ltd.
1050 Constitution Ave
Philadelphia PA 19112
855 547-1461

(G-10978)
COUNTRY SALES & SERVICE LLC
255 Tracy Bridge Rd (44667-9383)
PHONE..............................330 683-2500
EMP: 15 **EST:** 2004
SALES (est): 2.81MM **Privately Held**
Web: www.countrysalesandservice.com
SIC: 3519 5999 5084 Engines, diesel and semi-diesel or dual-fuel; Engine and motor equipment and supplies; Industrial machinery and equipment

(G-10979)
CROSSBRIDGE MKTG & MEDIA INC
1645 N Main St (44667-9171)
PHONE..............................330 682-5066
Eric Badertscher, *Pr*
Brittany Armentrout, *Dist Mgr*
EMP: 8 **EST:** 1960
SALES (est): 2.19MM **Privately Held**
Web: www.orrvilleprinting.com
SIC: 2752 2791 2789 Offset printing; Typesetting; Bookbinding and related work

(G-10980)
FERRO CORPORATION
FERRO CORPORATION
1560 N Main St (44667-9170)
P.O. Box 602 (44667-0602)
PHONE..............................330 682-8015
Kenneth Ackerman, *Brnch Mgr*
EMP: 38
SALES (corp-wide): 1.88B **Privately Held**
Web: www.vibrantz.com
SIC: 2865 Cyclic crudes and intermediates
HQ: Vibrantz Corporation
6060 Prkland Blvd Ste 250
Mayfield Heights OH 44124
216 875-5600

(G-10981)
FOLGER COFFEE COMPANY (HQ)
Also Called: Folgers
1 Strawberry Ln (44667-1241)
PHONE..............................800 937-9745
Susan Arnold, *Pr*
Alan G Lafley, *Pr*
Joseph H Etter, *Sr VP*
C C Daley Junior, *VP*
G W Price, *VP*
▲ **EMP:** 15 **EST:** 1850
SQ FT: 1,600,000
SALES (est): 211.29MM
SALES (corp-wide): 8.18B **Publicly Held**

Web: www.folgerscoffee.com
SIC: 2095 Coffee roasting (except by wholesale grocers)
PA: The J M Smucker Company
1 Strawberry Ln
Orrville OH 44667
330 682-3000

(G-10982)
GERBER FARM DIVISION LLC
133 Collins Blvd (44667-9074)
P.O. Box 206 (44636-0206)
PHONE..............................800 362-7381
John R Metzger, *Pr*
EMP: 7 **EST:** 2012
SALES (est): 2.49MM **Privately Held**
Web: www.gerbers.com
SIC: 2015 Chicken, processed: fresh

(G-10983)
HEAT EXCHANGE APPLIED TECH INC
150b Allen Ave (44667-9021)
PHONE..............................330 682-4328
Bharat Patel, *Pr*
EMP: 10 **EST:** 1983
SQ FT: 19,000
SALES (est): 2.29MM **Privately Held**
Web: www.heat-voss.com
SIC: 3443 Fabricated plate work (boiler shop)

(G-10984)
HOSTESS BRANDS INC (HQ)
Also Called: Hostess
1 Strawberry Ln (44667-1241)
PHONE..............................816 701-4600
John P Brase, *Pr*
Tucker H Marshall, *CFO*
Nadeem S Ali, *VP*
Peter O Farah, *Asst VP*
EMP: 51 **EST:** 2015
SALES (est): 1.36B
SALES (corp-wide): 8.18B **Publicly Held**
Web: www.hostessbrands.com
SIC: 2051 5461 Bread, cake, and related products; Cakes
PA: The J M Smucker Company
1 Strawberry Ln
Orrville OH 44667
330 682-3000

(G-10985)
HOSTESS BRANDS LLC (DH)
1 Strawberry Ln (44667-1241)
P.O. Box 419593 (64111)
PHONE..............................816 701-4600
William Toler, *Pr*
Thomas Peterson, *
Michael Cramer, *CAO*
Andrew Jacobs, *Chief Customer Officer*
Stuart Wilcox, *
EMP: 75 **EST:** 2013
SALES (est): 266.56MM
SALES (corp-wide): 8.18B **Publicly Held**
Web: www.hostessbrands.com
SIC: 2051 Bread, all types (white, wheat, rye, etc); fresh or frozen
HQ: Hostess Brands, Inc.
1 Strawberry Ln
Orrville OH 44667
816 701-4600

(G-10986)
IMEX BZ LLC
142 N Linden Ave Apt 502 (44667-1497)
PHONE..............................786 866-8798
Roger Taylor, *CEO*
Roger Taylor, *Managing Member*
EMP: 13 **EST:** 2015
SALES (est): 11.65MM **Privately Held**
Web: www.imexbz.com

SIC: 5099 4783 5141 5031 Logs, hewn ties, posts, and poles; Containerization of goods for shipping; Groceries, general line; Building materials, exterior
PA: Imex Inc
74 Bella Vista
Belize City

(G-10987)
J M SMUCKER COMPANY (PA)
Also Called: Smucker's
1 Strawberry Ln (44667-1298)
PHONE..............................330 682-3000
Mark T Smucker, *Ch Bd*
Mark T Smucker, *Ch Bd*
John P Brase, *COO*
Tucker H Marshall, *CFO*
Jeannette L Knudsen, *Legal*
◆ **EMP:** 1700 **EST:** 1897
SALES (est): 8.18B
SALES (corp-wide): 8.18B **Publicly Held**
Web: www.jmsmucker.com
SIC: 2033 2099 2023 2087 Jams, jellies, and preserves, packaged in cans, jars, etc.; Syrups; Canned milk, whole; Beverage bases, concentrates, syrups, powders and mixes

(G-10988)
JLG INDUSTRIES INC
2927 E Paradise Street Ext (44667-9628)
PHONE..............................330 684-0132
EMP: 50
SALES (corp-wide): 10.73B **Publicly Held**
Web: www.jlg.com
SIC: 3531 Construction machinery
HQ: Jlg Industries, Inc.
1 Jlg Dr
Mc Connellsburg PA 17233
717 485-5161

(G-10989)
JLG INDUSTRIES INC
600 E Chestnut St (44667-1951)
PHONE..............................330 684-0200
Wade Jones, *Brnch Mgr*
EMP: 53
SALES (corp-wide): 10.73B **Publicly Held**
Web: www.jlg.com
SIC: 3531 Construction machinery
HQ: Jlg Industries, Inc.
1 Jlg Dr
Mc Connellsburg PA 17233
717 485-5161

(G-10990)
JM SMUCKER LLC (HQ)
1 Strawberry Ln (44667-1298)
PHONE..............................330 682-3000
Mark T Smucker, *CEO*
EMP: 100 **EST:** 2002
SALES (est): 311.19MM
SALES (corp-wide): 8.18B **Publicly Held**
Web: www.smuckers.com
SIC: 5149 2047 Specialty food items; Dog food
PA: The J M Smucker Company
1 Strawberry Ln
Orrville OH 44667
330 682-3000

(G-10991)
KNUDSEN & SONS INC
1 Strawberry Ln (44667-1241)
PHONE..............................330 682-3000
EMP: 6
SALES (est): 1.35MM
SALES (corp-wide): 8.18B **Publicly Held**
SIC: 2033 Fruit juices: concentrated, hot pack
PA: The J M Smucker Company

1 Strawberry Ln
Orrville OH 44667
330 682-3000

(G-10992)
LAST ARROW MANUFACTURING LLC
8991 Lincoln Way E (44667-9336)
PHONE...................330 683-7777
EMP: 67 **EST:** 1974
SALES (est): 12.1MM **Privately Held**
Web: www.lastarrowmfg.com
SIC: 3599 Custom machinery

(G-10993)
LETTERGRAPHICS INC
400 W Market St (44667-1823)
P.O. Box 613 (44667-0613)
PHONE...................330 683-3903
Frank Wessels, *Pr*
Jim R Webster, *CEO*
EMP: 8 **EST:** 1976
SQ FT: 1,500
SALES (est): 965.87K **Privately Held**
Web: www.lettergraphicsinc.com
SIC: 3993 Electric signs

(G-10994)
MCELROY CONTRACT PACKAGING INC
301 Collins Blvd (44667-9727)
P.O. Box 608 (44667-0608)
PHONE...................330 682-2155
Larry Mcelroy, *Pr*
Steve Mcelroy, *VP*
Judie Mcelroy, *Sec*
Lorrie Mendenhall, *Mgr*
EMP: 15 **EST:** 1978
SQ FT: 14,500
SALES (est): 4.59MM **Privately Held**
Web: www.mcelroypackaging.com
SIC: 4783 2675 2653 Packing goods for shipping; Die-cut paper and board; Pads, corrugated: made from purchased materials

(G-10995)
MONARCH PLASTIC INC
516 Jefferson Ave (44667-1811)
P.O. Box 262 (44667-0262)
PHONE...................330 683-0822
Larry R Caskey, *Pr*
Debra Caskey, *VP*
EMP: 12 **EST:** 1979
SQ FT: 10,000
SALES (est): 383.81K **Privately Held**
SIC: 3711 3714 Automobile bodies, passenger car, not including engine, etc.; Motor vehicle parts and accessories

(G-10996)
MOOG INC
1701 N Main St (44667-9172)
PHONE...................330 682-0010
Douglas Steiner, *Prin*
EMP: 42
SALES (corp-wide): 3.32B **Publicly Held**
Web: www.moog.com
SIC: 8731 3593 Engineering laboratory, except testing; Fluid power cylinders and actuators
PA: Moog Inc.
400 Jamison Rd
Elma NY 14059
716 652-2000

(G-10997)
NATIONAL PATTERN MFGCO
1200 N Main St (44667-1017)
P.O. Box 58 (44667-0058)
PHONE...................330 682-6871

Anthony J Yonto, *Pr*
Anthony A Nicholas, *Pr*
Robert C Nicholas, *Sec*
EMP: 10 **EST:** 1952
SALES (est): 923.14K
SALES (corp-wide): 20.96MM **Privately Held**
Web: www.qcfoundry.com
SIC: 3544 3543 Dies, plastics forming; Foundry patternmaking
PA: Quality Castings Company
1200 N Main St
Orrville OH 44667
330 682-6010

(G-10998)
NU PET COMPANY (HQ)
1 Strawberry Ln (44667-1241)
PHONE...................330 682-3000
Barry C Dunaway, *Pr*
EMP: 45 **EST:** 2018
SALES (corp-wide): 8.18B **Publicly Held**
Web: www.jmsmucker.com
SIC: 2099 2033 2023 2087 Syrups; Jams, jellies, and preserves, packaged in cans, jars, etc.; Canned milk, whole; Beverage bases, concentrates, syrups, powders and mixes
PA: The J M Smucker Company
1 Strawberry Ln
Orrville OH 44667
330 682-3000

(G-10999)
ORRVILLE BRONZE & ALUMINUM CO
Central Ct (44667)
P.O. Box 216 (44667-0216)
PHONE...................330 682-4015
Robert R Cairnie II, *Pr*
Robert R Cairnie Ii, *Pr*
Hillary Cairnie, *VP*
Mark Cairnie, *VP*
EMP: 20 **EST:** 1934
SQ FT: 27,000
SALES (est): 600.43K **Privately Held**
Web: www.orrville.com
SIC: 3366 Castings (except die), nec, copper and copper-base alloy

(G-11000)
ORRVILLE TRUCKING & GRADING CO (PA)
475 Orr St (44667-9764)
P.O. Box 220 (44667-0220)
PHONE...................330 682-4010
Auvil Richmond, *Pr*
John H Wilson, *
EMP: 50 **EST:** 1953
SQ FT: 15,000
SALES (est): 6.2MM
SALES (corp-wide): 6.2MM **Privately Held**
Web: www.orrvilletrucking.com
SIC: 3273 3272 5031 Ready-mixed concrete ; Concrete products, nec; Building materials, exterior

(G-11001)
ORRVILON INC
1400 Dairy Ln (44667-2505)
PHONE...................330 684-9400
K P Singh, *Pr*
Alan Soler, *
Frank Bongrazio, *
▲ **EMP:** 110 **EST:** 2009
SQ FT: 350,000
SALES (est): 25.05MM
SALES (corp-wide): 681.48MM **Privately Held**
Web: www.holtecinternational.com

SIC: 3354 3442 Aluminum extruded products ; Metal doors
PA: Holtec International
1001 N Us Hwy 1
Jupiter FL 33477
561 745-7772

(G-11002)
PURINA MILLS LLC
Also Called: Purina Mills
635 Collins Blvd (44667-9796)
PHONE...................330 682-1951
Ken Fchwarzrock, *Mgr*
EMP: 9
SALES (corp-wide): 2.89B **Privately Held**
Web: www.purina-mills.com
SIC: 2047 Dog and cat food
HQ: Purina Mills, Llc
555 Mryvlle Univ Dr Ste 2
Saint Louis MO 63141

(G-11003)
QUALITY CASTINGS COMPANY (PA)
1200 N Main St (44667-1017)
P.O. Box 58 (44667-0058)
PHONE...................330 682-6010
Matt Nicholas, *Pr*
Di Ck Nicholas, *CEO*
Richard Nicholas, *
David Yonto, *
Anthony A Nicholas, *
EMP: 290 **EST:** 1927
SALES (est): 20.96MM
SALES (corp-wide): 20.96MM **Privately Held**
Web: www.qcfoundry.com
SIC: 3321 Gray iron castings, nec

(G-11004)
ROBURA INC
Also Called: Robura, Inc.
3328 S Kohler Rd (44667-9604)
PHONE...................330 857-7404
Albert Lehman, *Brnch Mgr*
EMP: 6
SALES (corp-wide): 21.4MM **Privately Held**
Web: www.lehmans.com
SIC: 2431 Exterior and ornamental woodwork and trim
PA: Robura, Llc
4779 Kidron Road
Dalton OH 44618
800 438 5346

(G-11005)
S & W EXPRESS INC
8849 Lincoln Way E (44667-9335)
PHONE...................330 683-2747
Ivan Hoshstetler, *Pr*
EMP: 8 **EST:** 1988
SALES (est): 361.27K **Privately Held**
Web: www.swoodpallet.com
SIC: 2448 Pallets, wood

(G-11006)
SCHANTZ ORGAN COMPANY (PA)
Also Called: Schantz Custom Woodworking
626 S Walnut St (44667-2238)
P.O. Box 156 (44667-0156)
PHONE...................330 682-6065
Victor B Schantz, *Pr*
Jeff Dexter, *
Eric Gastier, *
EMP: 19 **EST:** 1873
SQ FT: 45,600
SALES (est): 40.91K
SALES (corp-wide): 40.91K **Privately Held**
Web: www.schantzorgan.com
SIC: 3931 Organs, all types: pipe, reed, hand, electronic, etc.

(G-11007)
SCOTTS MIRACLE-GRO COMPANY
1220 Schrock Rd (44667-9582)
PHONE...................330 684-0421
Ark Dish, *Brnch Mgr*
EMP: 6
SALES (corp-wide): 3.55B **Publicly Held**
Web: www.scottsmiraclegro.com
SIC: 2873 Nitrogenous fertilizers
PA: The Scotts Miracle-Gro Company
14111 Scottslawn Rd
Marysville OH 43041
937 644-0011

(G-11008)
SMITHFOODS INC (HQ)
1381 Dairy Ln (44667-2503)
P.O. Box 87 (44667-0087)
PHONE...................330 683-8710
Nathan Schmid, *CEO*
Amy Miller, *Sec*
EMP: 25 **EST:** 2016
SALES (est): 46.27MM
SALES (corp-wide): 1.63B **Privately Held**
Web: www.smithfoods.com
SIC: 2026 2024 Fluid milk; Ice cream and frozen deserts
PA: Prairie Farms Dairy, Inc.
3744 Staunton Rd
Edwardsville IL 62025
618 659-5700

(G-11009)
SMUCKER FOODSERVICE INC
1 Strawberry Ln (44667-1241)
PHONE...................877 858-3855
EMP: 8 **EST:** 2019
SALES (est): 2.86MM
SALES (corp-wide): 8.18B **Publicly Held**
Web: www.smuckerawayfromhome.com
SIC: 2033 Jams, jellies, and preserves, packaged in cans, jars, etc.
PA: The J M Smucker Company
1 Strawberry Ln
Orrville OH 44667
330 682-3000

(G-11010)
SMUCKER INTERNATIONAL INC
Also Called: Smucker's
1 Strawberry Ln (44667-1241)
PHONE...................330 682-3000
Tim Smucker, *Ch Bd*
Richard Smucker, *CEO*
Vince Byrd, *VP*
▼ **EMP:** 11 **EST:** 1988
SALES (est): 4.94MM
SALES (corp-wide): 8.18B **Publicly Held**
Web: www.smuckers.com
SIC: 2033 2099 2086 Canned fruits and specialties; Syrups; Bottled and canned soft drinks
PA: The J M Smucker Company
1 Strawberry Ln
Orrville OH 44667
330 682-3000

(G-11011)
SMUCKER MANUFACTURING INC
1 Strawberry Ln (44667-1298)
P.O. Box 280 (44667-0280)
PHONE...................888 550-9555
Peter Farah, *Pr*
EMP: 6 **EST:** 2012
SALES (est): 3.37MM
SALES (corp-wide): 8.18B **Publicly Held**
Web: www.jmsmucker.com
SIC: 2033 Jams, jellies, and preserves, packaged in cans, jars, etc.
PA: The J M Smucker Company
1 Strawberry Ln

Orrville OH 44667
330 682-3000

(G-11012)
SMUCKER NATURAL FOODS INC
Strawberry Lane (44667)
P.O. Box 280 (44667-0280)
PHONE..............................330 682-3000
H Wagstaff, *Brnch Mgr*
EMP: 825
SALES (corp-wide): 8.18B **Publicly Held**
Web: www.jmsmucker.com
SIC: 2086 Bottled and canned soft drinks
HQ: Smucker Natural Foods, Inc.
37 Speedway Ave
Chico CA 95928
530 899-5000

(G-11013)
SMUCKER RETAIL FOODS INC
333 Wadsworth Rd (44667-9214)
PHONE..............................330 684-1500
EMP: 18
SALES (corp-wide): 8.18B **Publicly Held**
SIC: 2033 Jams, jellies, and preserves,
packaged in cans, jars, etc.
HQ: Smucker Retail Foods, Inc.
1 Strawberry Lane
Orrville OH 44667
330 682-3000

(G-11014)
SOUTHWOOD PALLET LLC
8849 Lincoln Way E (44667-9335)
PHONE..............................330 682-3747
EMP: 65 **EST:** 2022
SALES (est): 1.88MM **Privately Held**
Web: www.swoodpallet.com
SIC: 2448 7389 Wood pallets and skids; Log
and lumber broker

(G-11015)
UNITED INDUSTRIES
INCORPORATED
Also Called: Spectrum Brands
2308 S Crown Hill Rd (44667-9556)
PHONE..............................330 682-5010
Tonya Scheibel, *Brnch Mgr*
EMP: 100
SALES (corp-wide): 91.49MM **Privately
Held**
Web: www.unitedindustries.com
SIC: 5191 2875 Fertilizers and agricultural
chemicals; Fertilizers, mixing only
PA: United Industries, Incorporated
55 Produce Row
Saint Louis MO 63102
314 621-9440

(G-11016)
VENTURE PRODUCTS INC
500 Venture Dr (44667-2508)
P.O. Box 148 (44667-0148)
PHONE..............................330 683-0075
▲ **EMP:** 70 **EST:** 1988
SALES (est): 24.84MM
SALES (corp-wide): 4.58B **Publicly Held**
Web: www.ventrac.com
SIC: 3524 Lawn and garden tractors and
equipment
PA: The Toro Company
8111 Lyndale Ave S
Bloomington MN 55420
952 888-8801

(G-11017)
VIBRANTZ TECHNOLOGIES INC
1560 N Main St (44667-9170)
P.O. Box 602 (44667-0602)
PHONE..............................330 765-4378
EMP: 7

SALES (corp-wide): 1.88B **Privately Held**
Web: www.vibrantz.com
SIC: 2869 Industrial organic chemicals, nec
HQ: Vibrantz Technologies Inc.
16945 Nrthchase Dr Ste 20
Houston TX 77060
646 747-4222

(G-11018)
WILL-BURT COMPANY (PA)
401 Collins Blvd (44667-9752)
P.O. Box 900 (44667-0900)
PHONE..............................330 682-7015
Richard Lewin, *CEO*
Jeffrey Evans, *
Bruce Inzetta, *
Dan Plumly, *
▲ **EMP:** 196 **EST:** 1918
SALES (est): 40.96MM
SALES (corp-wide): 40.96MM **Privately
Held**
Web: www.willburt.com
SIC: 3599 5039 3443 3449 Machine shop,
jobbing and repair; Prefabricated structures
; Fabricated plate work (boiler shop);
Miscellaneous metalwork

(G-11019)
WILL-BURT COMPANY
312 Collins Blvd (44667-9727)
P.O. Box 900 (44667-0900)
PHONE..............................330 682-7015
Jeffrey O Evans, *Mgr*
EMP: 16
SALES (corp-wide): 40.96MM **Privately
Held**
Web: www.willburt.com
SIC: 3443 3449 3599 5039 Fabricated plate
work (boiler shop); Miscellaneous metalwork
; Machine shop, jobbing and repair;
Prefabricated structures
PA: The Will-Burt Company
401 Collins Blvd
Orrville OH 44667
330 682-7015

Orwell
Ashtabula County

(G-11020)
**CABINTWRKS GROUP MDDLFIELD
LLC**
Also Called: Kraftmaid Cabinetry
150 Grand Valley Ave (44076-9419)
P.O. Box 1055 (44062-1055)
PHONE..............................440 437-8537
Paul Schamrock, *Mgr*
EMP: 163
SALES (corp-wide): 532.81MM **Privately
Held**
Web: www.kraftmaid.com
SIC: 2431 2434 Doors, wood; Wood kitchen
cabinets
HQ: Cabinetworks Group Middlefield, Llc
15535 S State Ave
Middlefield OH 44062
888 562-7744

(G-11021)
HSP BEDDING SOLUTIONS LLC
243 Staley Rd (44076-8381)
P.O. Box 459 (44076-0459)
PHONE..............................440 437-4425
Eli Schnucker, *Managing Member*
EMP: 26 **EST:** 2015
SALES (est): 4.81MM **Privately Held**
SIC: 2515 Mattresses and bedsprings

(G-11022)
KENNAMETAL INC
180 Penniman Rd (44076-9500)
P.O. Box 2609 (44005-2609)
PHONE..............................440 437-5131
David Orth, *Mgr*
EMP: 57
SALES (corp-wide): 2.05B **Publicly Held**
Web: www.kennametal.com
SIC: 3545 Cutting tools for machine tools
PA: Kennametal Inc.
525 Wlliam Penn Pl Ste 33
Pittsburgh PA 15219
412 248-8000

(G-11023)
LOCK JOINT TUBE OHIO LLC
Also Called: Welded Tubes
135 Penniman Rd (44076-9557)
PHONE..............................210 278-3757
Ted Lerman, *Pr*
Joe Frandanisa, *
Peter Modelski, *
EMP: 172 **EST:** 2020
SALES (est): 24.41MM **Privately Held**
Web: www.weldedtubes.com
SIC: 3317 Welded pipe and tubes
HQ: Lock Joint Tube Llc
515 W Ireland Rd
South Bend IN 46614

(G-11024)
LSP TUBES INC
Also Called: Welded Tubes, Inc.
135 Penniman Rd (44076-9557)
P.O. Box 175 (44076-0175)
PHONE..............................216 378-2092
▲ **EMP:** 92
Web: www.weldedtubes.com
SIC: 3317 Tubes, wrought: welded or lock
joint

(G-11025)
QUALITY DESIGN MACHINING INC
64 Penniman Rd (44076-9557)
PHONE..............................440 352-7290
Robert Fletcher, *Pr*
EMP: 8 **EST:** 1990
SALES (est): 795.67K **Privately Held**
Web: www.qualitydesignmachining.com
SIC: 3599 Machine shop, jobbing and repair

Osgood
Darke County

(G-11026)
DYNAMIC WELD CORPORATION
Also Called: Dynamic Weld
242 North St (45351-1003)
P.O. Box 127 (45351-0127)
PHONE..............................419 582-2900
Harry Heitkamp, *Pr*
Gene Niekamp, *Prin*
Ernie Davenport, *Prin*
Steve Wilker, *Prin*
Sue Heitkamp, *Prin*
EMP: 44 **EST:** 1981
SQ FT: 35,000
SALES (est): 4.66MM **Privately Held**
Web: www.dynamicweld.com
SIC: 3444 7692 Sheet metalwork; Welding
repair

Ostrander
Delaware County

(G-11027)
KLM MANUFACTURING CO INC
56 Huston St (43061-9618)
PHONE..............................740 666-5171
K Leroy Moore, *Pr*
EMP: 6 **EST:** 1971
SQ FT: 5,000
SALES (est): 1.44MM **Privately Held**
Web: www.klmmfg.com
SIC: 3541 Machine tools, metal cutting type

(G-11028)
LIBERTY DIE CAST MOLDS INC
57 2nd St (43061-9441)
P.O. Box 2 (43061-0002)
PHONE..............................740 666-7492
Kenny L Nicol, *Pr*
Duane C Glick, *VP*
Jack Fryman, *Sec*
EMP: 15 **EST:** 1984
SQ FT: 6,544
SALES (est): 2.61MM **Privately Held**
Web: www.libertydiecastmolds.com
SIC: 3544 Industrial molds

(G-11029)
SHELLY MATERIALS INC
8328 Watkins Rd (43061-9311)
PHONE..............................740 666-5841
Keith Siler, *VP*
EMP: 36
SALES (corp-wide): 34.95B **Privately Held**
Web: www.shellyco.com
SIC: 2951 1611 3274 1422 Asphalt and
asphaltic paving mixtures (not from
refineries); Surfacing and paving; Lime;
Crushed and broken limestone
HQ: Shelly Materials, Inc.
80 Park Dr
Thornville OH 43076
740 246-6315

Ottawa
Putnam County

(G-11030)
BROOKHILL CENTER INDS INC
7989 State Route 108 (45875-9678)
PHONE..............................419 876-3932
Bill Unterbink, *Pr*
EMP: 115 **EST:** 1972
SQ FT: 16,000
SALES (est): 1.63MM **Privately Held**
Web: www.brookhillind.com
SIC: 8331 2448 Sheltered workshop; Wood
pallets and skids

(G-11031)
CUSTOM WOODWORKING INC
214 S Main St (45875-9416)
PHONE..............................419 456-3330
Jerry Hovest, *Pr*
EMP: 9 **EST:** 1991
SALES (est): 278.7K **Privately Held**
Web: www.customwoodworking214.com
SIC: 2434 Wood kitchen cabinets

(G-11032)
D4 INDUSTRIES INC
685 Woodland Dr (45875-8627)
PHONE..............................419 523-9555
James Bibler, *Pr*
EMP: 7 **EST:** 1994
SQ FT: 5,000
SALES (est): 880K **Privately Held**

SIC: 3714 3366 Motor vehicle parts and accessories; Bushings and bearings, brass (nonmachined)

(G-11033)
DRAINAGE PIPE & FITTINGS LLC
450 Tile Company St (45875-9217)
PHONE..............................419 538-6337
Floyd T Meyer, *Admn*
Crystal Solano, *Prin*
Floyd Tony Meyer, *Prin*
EMP: 8 EST: 2012
SALES (est): 843.96K Privately Held
SIC: 3494 Pipe fittings

(G-11034)
HIRZEL CANNING COMPANY
Ottawa Foods, Div of
325 E Williamstown Rd (45875-1802)
PHONE..............................419 523-3225
Karl E Hirzel, *Manager*
EMP: 7
SALES (corp-wide): 64.46MM Privately Held
Web: www.deifratelli.com
SIC: 2033 Tomato products, packaged in cans, jars, etc.
PA: Hirzel Canning Company
411 Lemoyne Rd
Northwood OH 43619
419 693-0531

(G-11035)
INDUSTRIAL MILLWRIGHT SVCS LLC
1024 Heritage Trl (45875-8521)
PHONE..............................419 523-9147
Duane Greear, *Managing Member*
Lisa Greear, *
EMP: 28 EST: 2003
SALES (est): 3.16MM Privately Held
Web: www.industrialmillwrightservices.com
SIC: 1796 3449 Millwright; Bars, concrete reinforcing: fabricated steel

(G-11036)
JB MACHINING CONCEPTS LLC
995 Sugar Mill Dr (45875-8526)
PHONE..............................419 523-0096
John Blankemeyer, *Sole Member*
Alexander Blankemeyer, *Engg Mgr*
EMP: 8 EST: 2007
SQ FT: 18,000
SALES (est): 1.41MM Privately Held
Web: www.jbmachiningconcepts.com
SIC: 3646 3645 Commercial lighting fixtures; Residential lighting fixtures

(G-11037)
K & L READY MIX INC (PA)
10391 State Route 15 (45875-8641)
P.O. Box 325 (45875-0325)
PHONE..............................419 523-4376
Ron Kahle Junior, *Pr*
EMP: 19 EST: 1975
SQ FT: 12,000
SALES (est): 2.68MM
SALES (corp-wide): 2.68MM Privately Held
Web: www.kandlreadymix.com
SIC: 3273 Ready-mixed concrete

(G-11038)
MC ELWAIN INDUSTRIES INC
17941 Road L (45875-9455)
PHONE..............................419 532-3126
Amelia Mcelwain, *Pr*
EMP: 14 EST: 1983
SALES (est): 1.11MM Privately Held
Web: www.mcelwainind.com

SIC: 7692 3441 Welding repair; Building components, structural steel

(G-11039)
NELSON MANUFACTURING COMPANY
6448 State Route 224 (45875-9789)
PHONE..............................419 523-5321
Anthony Niese, *Pr*
Chad Stall, *
Amy Niese, *
▼ EMP: 80 EST: 1947
SQ FT: 46,000
SALES (est): 9.23MM Privately Held
Web: www.nelsontrailers.com
SIC: 3715 7539 Semitrailers for truck tractors; Trailer repair

(G-11040)
OTTAWA DEFENSE LOGISTICS LLC
804 N Pratt St (45875-1556)
P.O. Box 468 (45875-0468)
PHONE..............................419 596-3202
Barb Rieman, *Managing Member*
EMP: 10 EST: 2006
SALES (est): 168.26K Privately Held
Web: www.ottawadefenselogistics.com
SIC: 7692 Welding repair

(G-11041)
PALPAC INDUSTRIES INC
610 N Agner St (45875-1533)
P.O. Box 109 (45875-0109)
PHONE..............................419 523-3230
Danny E Meyer, *Pr*
Mike Meyer, *Treas*
EMP: 18 EST: 1968
SQ FT: 62,000
SALES (est): 3.13MM Privately Held
Web: www.palpacindustries.com
SIC: 3089 3086 Molding primary plastics; Plastics foam products

(G-11042)
PHANTASM DSGNS SPRTSN MORE LTD
112 W Main St (45875-1722)
PHONE..............................419 538-6737
Don Huber, *Owner*
EMP: 9 EST: 1978
SALES (est): 283.42K Privately Held
Web: www.phantasmdesigns.com
SIC: 2262 2261 2395 7336 Screen printing: manmade fiber and silk broadwoven fabrics; Screen printing of cotton broadwoven fabrics; Embroidery and art needlework; Graphic arts and related design

(G-11043)
PUTNAM AGGREGATES CO
7053 Road M (45875-9754)
PHONE..............................419 523-6004
Barbara Shroyer, *Technical Staff*
EMP: 6 EST: 2012
SALES (est): 448.46K Privately Held
Web: www.putnamaggregates.com
SIC: 1442 Construction sand and gravel

(G-11044)
R K INDUSTRIES INC
725 N Locust St (45875-1466)
P.O. Box 306 (45875-0306)
PHONE..............................419 523-5001
Ann Woodyard, *Pr*
Kimberly French, *Sec*
Barry Woodyard, *Mfg Mgr*
Joe Maag, *VP*
▲ EMP: 85 EST: 1983
SQ FT: 45,000
SALES (est): 6.1MM Privately Held

Web: www.rkindustries.org
SIC: 7692 3465 Automotive welding; Automotive stampings

(G-11045)
SILGAN PLASTICS LLC
Also Called: Silgan
690 Woodland Dr (45875-8627)
PHONE..............................419 523-3737
Russ Zervais, *Pr*
EMP: 199
Web: www.silganplastics.com
SIC: 3089 Plastics containers, except foam
HQ: Silgan Plastics Llc
14515 N Oter 40 Rd Ste 21
Chesterfield MO 63017
800 274-5426

(G-11046)
STEEL TECHNOLOGIES LLC
740 E Williamstown Rd (45875-1873)
PHONE..............................419 523-5199
Rick Furber, *Mgr*
EMP: 50
Web: www.steeltechnologies.com
SIC: 3312 Sheet or strip, steel, cold-rolled: own hot-rolled
HQ: Steel Technologies Llc
700 N Hrstbrne Pkwy Ste 4
Louisville KY 40222
502 245-2110

(G-11047)
STERLING INDUSTRIES INC
740 E Main St (45875-2029)
PHONE..............................419 523-3788
Marilyn Kulhman, *Pr*
Keith Kuhlman, *VP*
EMP: 10 EST: 1967
SQ FT: 9,600
SALES (est): 214.94K Privately Held
Web: www.sterlingindustries.com
SIC: 2441 2448 Boxes, wood; Pallets, wood

(G-11048)
STOEPFEL DRILLING CO
12245 State Route 115 (45875-9488)
PHONE..............................419 532-3307
John H Stoepfel Junior, *Pt*
Roger Winkle, *Pt*
EMP: 7 EST: 1954
SQ FT: 6,000
SALES (est): 1.51MM Privately Held
SIC: 1481 1781 Mine and quarry services, nonmetallic minerals; Water well drilling

(G-11049)
VERHOFF ALFALFA MILLS INC (PA)
Also Called: Alfa Green Supreme
1188 Sugar Mill Dr (45875-8518)
PHONE..............................419 523-4767
Scott Verhoff, *Pr*
Donald Verhoff, *Pr*
Judith Fullenkamp, *Sec*
Darwin Verhoff, *VP*
▼ EMP: 7 EST: 1940
SQ FT: 500
SALES (est): 1.21MM
SALES (corp-wide): 1.21MM Privately Held
Web: www.alfagreensupreme.com
SIC: 0723 2048 Crop preparation services for market; Alfalfa or alfalfa meal, prepared as animal feed

(G-11050)
WARREN PRINTING & OFF PDTS INC
250 E Main St (45875-1944)
P.O. Box 229 (45875-0229)
PHONE..............................419 523-3635
Robert E Warren Junior, *Pr*

EMP: 10 EST: 1966
SALES (est): 972.38K Privately Held
Web: www.warrenprint.com
SIC: 2752 2759 5943 2679 Offset printing; Flexographic printing; Office forms and supplies; Tags and labels, paper

Ottoville
Putnam County

(G-11051)
ACME MACHINE AUTOMATICS INC
Also Called: Global Precision Parts
111 Progressive Dr (45876)
P.O. Box 579 (45876-0579)
PHONE..............................419 453-0010
Randy Mueller, *Pr*
▲ EMP: 25 EST: 1993
SQ FT: 62,500
SALES (est): 3.92MM Privately Held
Web: www.globalprecisionpartsinc.com
SIC: 3451 3484 Screw machine products; Small arms
PA: Kriegel Holding Company, Inc.
7600 Us Rte 127
Van Wert OH 45891

(G-11052)
ATALYS OTTOVILLE LLC (HQ)
14223 Rd 24 (45876)
P.O. Box P.O. Box 278 (45876-0278)
PHONE..............................419 453-3376
EMP: 49 EST: 1962
SALES (est): 16.45MM
SALES (corp-wide): 21.85MM Privately Held
Web: www.schnipke.com
SIC: 3545 Tools and accessories for machine tools
PA: Atalys, Llc
1667 Emerson St
Rochester NY 14606
585 647-2300

(G-11053)
CREATIVE EDGE CBNETS WDWKG LLC
188 Nw Canal St (45876-8743)
P.O. Box 330 (45876-0330)
PHONE..............................419 453-3416
Craig Brinkman, *Managing Member*
EMP: 6 EST: 2014
SALES (est): 479.61K Privately Held
Web: www.creativeedgecabinets.com
SIC: 2434 Wood kitchen cabinets

(G-11054)
H & M MACHINE SHOP INC
290 State Route 189 (45876-8802)
P.O. Box 207 (45876-0207)
PHONE..............................419 453-3414
Todd Horstman, *Pr*
Diane Horstman, *VP*
Roger A Horstman, *Sec*
EMP: 16 EST: 1975
SQ FT: 50,000
SALES (est): 3.92MM Privately Held
Web: www.hmmachineshop.com
SIC: 3599 Machine shop, jobbing and repair

(G-11055)
M & W TRAILERS INC
525 East Main St (45876)
P.O. Box 519 (45876-0519)
PHONE..............................419 453-3331
Kenneth Markward, *Pr*
Thomas Markward, *VP*
Scott Markward, *Sec*
Elenor Wannemacher, *Prin*

Elmer A Markward, *Prin*
EMP: 10 **EST:** 1956
SQ FT: 10,000
SALES (est): 373.89K **Privately Held**
Web: www.mandwtrailersohio.com
SIC: 7539 3715 5012 7538 Trailer repair; Truck trailers; Trailers for trucks, new and used; General truck repair

(G-11056)
MILLER PRECISION MANUFACTURING INDUSTRIES INC
131 Progressive Dr (45876)
P.O. Box 489 (45876-0489)
PHONE...............................419 453-3251
EMP: 100 **EST:** 1988
SALES (est): 17.03MM **Privately Held**
Web: www.millerprecision.com
SIC: 3599 Machine shop, jobbing and repair

(G-11057)
PROGRESSIVE STAMPING INC
200 Progressive Dr (45876)
P.O. Box 549 (45876-0549)
PHONE...............................419 453-1111
Lloyd Miller, *Pr*
◆ **EMP:** 250 **EST:** 1999
SALES (est): 23.48MM **Privately Held**
Web: www.midwayproducts.com
SIC: 3469 Metal stampings, nec
PA: Midway Products Group, Inc.
One Lyman E Hoyt Dr
Monroe MI 48161

Otway
Scioto County

(G-11058)
BLANKENSHIP LOGGING LLC
433 Curtis Smith Rd (45657-8936)
PHONE...............................740 372-3833
Harold Blankenship, *Owner*
EMP: 6 **EST:** 2000
SALES (est): 400K **Privately Held**
SIC: 2411 Logging camps and contractors

(G-11059)
COX WOOD PRODUCT INC
5715 State Route 348 (45657-9231)
PHONE...............................740 372-4735
Shelby Kratzer, *Pr*
Eric Kratzer, *VP*
EMP: 10 **EST:** 1950
SALES (est): 115.67K **Privately Held**
SIC: 2448 5211 Pallets, wood; Planing mill products and lumber

Overpeck
Butler County

(G-11060)
MIAMI ICE MACHINE INC
4251 Riverside Dr (45055)
P.O. Box 145 (45055-0145)
PHONE...............................513 863-6707
EMP: 6 **EST:** 2019
SALES (est): 487.86K **Privately Held**
Web: www.miamimachine.com
SIC: 3541 Milling machines

(G-11061)
MIAMI MACHINE CORPORATION
4251 Riverside Dr (45055)
P.O. Box 145 (45055-0145)
PHONE...............................513 863-6707
▲ **EMP:** 17
Web: www.miamimachine.com

SIC: 3554 Paper mill machinery: plating, slitting, waxing, etc.

Oxford
Butler County

(G-11062)
COX NEWSPAPERS LLC
Also Called: Oxford Press
30 W Park Pl Uppr Uppr (45056-2658)
PHONE...............................513 523-4139
Ann Hoffman, *Prin*
EMP: 7
SALES (corp-wide): 961.55MM **Privately Held**
Web: www.coxenterprises.com
SIC: 2711 Newspapers, publishing and printing
HQ: Cox Newspapers, Inc.
6205 Pchtree Dnwody Rd N
Atlanta GA 30328

(G-11063)
LETTERMAN PRINTING INC
316 S College Ave (45056-2225)
PHONE...............................513 523-1111
Jon C Rupel, *Pr*
Rhonda Rupel, *Sec*
EMP: 8 **EST:** 1991
SQ FT: 1,500
SALES (est): 145.92K **Privately Held**
Web: www.oxfordcopy.com
SIC: 2752 2759 Offset printing; Commercial printing, nec

(G-11064)
SCHNEIDER ELECTRIC USA INC
Also Called: Schneider Electric
5735 College Corner Pike (45056-9715)
PHONE...............................513 523-4171
Thomsa Mcdonald, *Brnch Mgr*
EMP: 500
SALES (corp-wide): 1.09K **Privately Held**
Web: www.se.com
SIC: 3699 3677 3612 3357 Electrical equipment and supplies, nec; Electronic coils and transformers; Transformers, except electric; Nonferrous wiredrawing and insulating
HQ: Schneider Electric Usa, Inc.
1 Boston Pl Ste 2700
Boston MA 02108
617 904-9422

(G-11065)
WILD BERRY INCENSE INC
Also Called: Wild Berry Incense Factory
5475 College Corner Pike (45056-1010)
PHONE...............................513 523-8583
Mark Biales, *Pr*
Roger Atkin, *VP*
▲ **EMP:** 19 **EST:** 1992
SQ FT: 20,000
SALES (est): 7.33MM **Privately Held**
Web: www.wild-berry.com
SIC: 2899 5947 Incense; Novelties

Painesville
Lake County

(G-11066)
ACCURATE METAL MACHINING INC
Also Called: Accurate
882 Callendar Blvd (44077-1218)
PHONE...............................440 350-8225
John Racic, *Pr*
Eva Szantho, *
Gabriel Loiczly, *

Thomas Loiczly, *
EMP: 250 **EST:** 1976
SQ FT: 15,000
SALES (est): 20.19MM **Publicly Held**
Web: www.accuratemetalmachining.com
SIC: 3599 Machine shop, jobbing and repair
HQ: Heico Flight Support Corp.
3000 Taft St
Hollywood FL 33021
954 987-4000

(G-11067)
ATRA METAL SPINNING INC
572 S Saint Clair St (44077-3637)
P.O. Box 731 (44077-0731)
PHONE...............................440 354-9525
Carl Dixon, *Pr*
Greg Shirk, *VP*
James Dixon, *Sec*
EMP: 10 **EST:** 1981
SQ FT: 22,000
SALES (est): 2.5MM **Privately Held**
SIC: 3469 Stamping metal for the trade

(G-11068)
AVERY DENNISON CORPORATION
670 Hardy Rd (44077-4573)
PHONE...............................440 358-3466
Linda E Chandler, *Brnch Mgr*
EMP: 152
SALES (corp-wide): 8.76B **Publicly Held**
Web: www.averydennison.com
SIC: 2672 Paper; coated and laminated, nec
PA: Avery Dennison Corporation
8080 Norton Pkwy
Mentor OH 44060
440 534-6000

(G-11069)
AVERY DENNISON CORPORATION
Avery Dennison - Pff
250 Chester St Bldg 3 (44077-4129)
PHONE...............................440 358-2564
Rick Olszewski, *Brnch Mgr*
EMP: 300
SALES (corp-wide): 8.76B **Publicly Held**
Web: www.averydennison.com
SIC: 2672 2891 Adhesive papers, labels, or tapes: from purchased material; Adhesives and sealants
PA: Avery Dennison Corporation
8080 Norton Pkwy
Mentor OH 44060
440 534-6000

(G-11070)
BRUCE HIGH PERFORMANCE TRAN
1 High Tech Ave (44077-3701)
PHONE...............................440 357-8964
Laurie Dibiase, *Prin*
EMP: 9 **EST:** 2013
SALES (est): 2.22MM **Privately Held**
Web: www.brucetransporters.com
SIC: 3715 Truck trailers

(G-11071)
CASCADE UNLIMITED LLC
2510 Hale Rd (44077-4926)
PHONE...............................440 352-7995
EMP: 6 **EST:** 2016
SALES (est): 910.88K **Privately Held**
Web: www.cascadeunlimited.com
SIC: 3599 Machine shop, jobbing and repair

(G-11072)
COE MANUFACTURING COMPANY (HQ)
Also Called: Automated Systems Div
70 W Erie St Ste 150 (44077-3279)
PHONE...............................440 352-9381
Shawn Casey, *CEO*

John Kucharik, *
Jim Wojtila, *
Jeffrey Darbut, *
Harry P Coe, *
EMP: 27 **EST:** 1901
SQ FT: 300,000
SALES (est): 4.66MM
SALES (corp-wide): 307.59MM **Privately Held**
SIC: 3531 3553 Construction machinery; Presses for making particleboard, hardboard, plywood, etc.
PA: Usnr, Llc
1981 Schurman Way
Woodland WA 98674
360 225-8267

(G-11073)
CONCORD ROAD EQUIPMENT MFG INC
348 Chester St (44077-4154)
P.O. Box 772 (44077-0772)
PHONE...............................440 357-5344
Glen Warfield, *Pr*
Jeffrey Warfield, *
EMP: 31 **EST:** 1975
SALES (est): 4.38MM **Privately Held**
Web: www.concordroadequipment.com
SIC: 3531 Road construction and maintenance machinery

(G-11074)
CONNECTORS UNLIMITED INC (PA)
1359 W Jackson St (44077-1341)
PHONE...............................440 357-1161
Martin Ignasiak, *Pr*
Don Barber, *Sec*
Ralph Victor, *Treas*
▲ **EMP:** 22 **EST:** 1997
SALES (est): 436.2K
SALES (corp-wide): 436.2K **Privately Held**
Web: my.connectorsunlimited.com
SIC: 3357 3678 Nonferrous wiredrawing and insulating; Electronic connectors

(G-11075)
CUSTOM DESIGN CABINETS & TOPS
Also Called: Custom Design Kitchen & Bath
379 Fountain Ave (44077-1209)
PHONE...............................440 639-9900
George Lehtonen, *Pr*
Kaarina Lehtonen, *VP*
EMP: 8
SQ FT: 11,000
SALES (est): 138.83K **Privately Held**
SIC: 5031 2541 Kitchen cabinets; Cabinets, except refrigerated: show, display, etc.: wood

(G-11076)
DE NORA NORTH AMERICA INC
7590 Discovery Ln (44077-9190)
PHONE...............................440 357-4000
Luciano Iacopetti, *CEO*
▲ **EMP:** 7 **EST:** 1998
SQ FT: 70,000
SALES (est): 1.58MM
SALES (corp-wide): 930.89MM **Privately Held**
SIC: 3589 Water treatment equipment, industrial
HQ: Oronzio De Nora International B.V.
Basisweg 10
Amsterdam NH 1043
205214777

(G-11077)
DE NORA TECH LLC
Also Called: Warehouse
7661 Crile Rdunit 1 Bldg 2 (44077)
PHONE...............................440 285-0368

▲ = Import ▼ = Export
◆ = Import/Export

Karen Farinatzi, *Superintnt*
EMP: 7
SALES (corp-wide): 930.89MM **Privately Held**
Web: business.painesvilleohchamber.org
SIC: 3589 Water treatment equipment, industrial
HQ: De Nora Tech, Llc
7590 Discovery Ln
Painesville OH 44077
440 710-5334

(G-11078)
DE NORA TECH LLC (DH)
7590 Discovery Ln (44077-9190)
PHONE....................440 710-5334
Paolo Dellacha, *CEO*
Frank J Mcgorty, *COO*
Assunta Rossi, *
Angelo Ferrari, *
◆ **EMP:** 80 **EST:** 1982
SQ FT: 20,000
SALES (est): 30.6MM
SALES (corp-wide): 930.89MM **Privately Held**
Web: business.painesvilleohchamber.org
SIC: 3624 3589 7359 Electrodes, thermal and electrolytic uses: carbon, graphite; Sewage and water treatment equipment; Equipment rental and leasing, nec
HQ: Industrie De Nora Spa
Via Leonardo Bistolfi 35
Milano MI 20134

(G-11079)
DESIGNER CNTEMPORARY LAMINATES
1700 Sheffield Ter (44077-4765)
PHONE....................440 946-8207
Robert Krauss, *Pr*
EMP: 8 **EST:** 1985
SALES (est): 540.17K **Privately Held**
Web: www.dclweb.net
SIC: 3083 2541 Plastics finished products, laminated; Cabinets, except refrigerated: show, display, etc.: wood

(G-11080)
DUKES AEROSPACE INC
Also Called: Aero Fluid Products
313 Gillett St (44077-2918)
PHONE....................818 998-9811
Greg Rufus, *CEO*
James Riley, *
EMP: 79 **EST:** 2009
SALES (est): 19.92MM
SALES (corp-wide): 7.94B **Publicly Held**
Web: www.aerofluidproducts.com
SIC: 3728 Aircraft parts and equipment, nec
HQ: Transdigm, Inc.
1350 Euclid Ave
Cleveland OH 44115

(G-11081)
DYNA-FLEX INC
1000 Bacon Rd (44077-4637)
PHONE....................440 946-9424
James D'amico, *Pr*
Barbara D'amico, *VP*
Michael J D'amico, *Sec*
Laura Curtis, *Treas*
Bob Ritchie, *Genl Mgr*
▲ **EMP:** 10 **EST:** 1995
SALES (est): 1MM **Privately Held**
Web: www.dynaflexinc.com
SIC: 3492 Hose and tube couplings, hydraulic/pneumatic

(G-11082)
ECKART AMERICA CORPORATION (DH)
Also Called: Eckart Aluminum
830 E Erie St (44077-4453)
P.O. Box 747 (44077-0747)
PHONE....................440 954-7600
Anthony J Ameo Junior, *Pr*
Thomas Meola, *
◆ **EMP:** 100 **EST:** 1997
SALES (est): 53.63MM
SALES (corp-wide): 4.44B **Privately Held**
Web: www.eckart.net
SIC: 3399 2893 2816 Powder, metal; Printing ink; Inorganic pigments
HQ: Eckart Beteiligungs Gmbh
Guntersthal 4
Hartenstein BY 91235
9152770

(G-11083)
EVOLVE SOLUTIONS LLC
1 High Tech Ave (44077-3701)
PHONE....................440 357-8964
EMP: 30 **EST:** 2019
SALES (est): 2.44MM **Privately Held**
Web: www.evolvetransporters.com
SIC: 3312 Plate, steel

(G-11084)
EXECUTIVE WINGS INC
13550 Carter Rd (44077-9171)
PHONE....................440 254-1812
Michael Toman, *Owner*
EMP: 8 **EST:** 2001
SALES (est): 193.31K **Privately Held**
SIC: 3721 Aircraft

(G-11085)
EXTRUDEX LIMITED PARTNERSHIP (PA)
Also Called: Extrudex
310 Figgie Dr (44077-3028)
PHONE....................440 352-7101
George Humphrey, *Genl.Pt*
George Humphrey, *Pr*
Tod Oliva, *Pt*
EMP: 34 **EST:** 1980
SQ FT: 27,120
SALES (est): 5.7MM **Privately Held**
Web: www.extrudex.net
SIC: 3089 3524 3431 Extruded finished plastics products, nec; Lawn and garden equipment; Metal sanitary ware

(G-11086)
FARETEC INC
1610 W Jackson St Unit 6 (44077-1388)
PHONE....................440 350-9510
Tod C R Sackett, *Pr*
George Sackett, *Sec*
Constance Sackett, *Treas*
▲ **EMP:** 10 **EST:** 1991
SQ FT: 7,000
SALES (est): 879.28K **Privately Held**
Web: www.faretec.com
SIC: 3842 5047 Braces, orthopedic; Medical equipment and supplies

(G-11087)
FIRST FRANCIS COMPANY INC (HQ)
Also Called: Federal Hose Manufacturing
25 Florence Ave (44077-1103)
PHONE....................440 352-8927
Ron George, *Pr*
EMP: 27 **EST:** 1997
SALES (est): 27.73MM
SALES (corp-wide): 150.2MM **Publicly Held**
Web: www.federalhose.com

SIC: 5085 3599 3444 3429 Hose, belting, and packing; Hose, flexible metallic; Sheet metalwork; Hardware, nec
PA: Crawford United Corporation
10514 Dupont Ave Ste 200
Cleveland OH 44108
216 243-2614

(G-11088)
GENESIS LAMP CORP
375 N Saint Clair St (44077-4053)
PHONE....................440 354-0095
Edward C Zukowski, *Pr*
Margaret Zukowski, *Sec*
Donna Williams, *Sec*
▲ **EMP:** 15 **EST:** 1979
SQ FT: 6,400
SALES (est): 4.2MM **Privately Held**
Web: www.genesislamp.com
SIC: 3646 3648 Commercial lighting fixtures; Lighting equipment, nec

(G-11089)
GRAND-ROCK COMPANY INC
395 Fountain Ave (44077-1209)
PHONE....................440 639-2000
William H Stoneman, *Pr*
Gerard Arth, *
▲ **EMP:** 50 **EST:** 1972
SQ FT: 52,000
SALES (est): 9.98MM **Privately Held**
Web: www.grandrock.com
SIC: 3714 3621 2531 Motor vehicle parts and accessories; Motors and generators; Public building and related furniture

(G-11090)
GREAT LAKES GLASSWERKS INC
360 W Prospect St (44077-3258)
PHONE....................440 358-0460
Richard Chaykowsky, *Pr*
Julie Patterson, *VP*
John Wolfe, *Sec*
▲ **EMP:** 7 **EST:** 1997
SQ FT: 10,000
SALES (est): 884.8K **Privately Held**
Web: www.quartzsupply.com
SIC: 3679 Electronic circuits

(G-11091)
GUYER PRECISION INC
280 W Prospect St (44077-3256)
PHONE....................440 354-8024
Thomas Guyer, *Pr*
EMP: 11 **EST:** 1997
SQ FT: 12,500
SALES (est): 2.56MM **Privately Held**
Web: www.guyerprecision.com
SIC: 3599 Machine shop, jobbing and repair

(G-11092)
HARDY INDUSTRIAL TECH LLC
Also Called: H I T
679 Hardy Rd (44077-4574)
PHONE....................440 350-6300
Eric Lofquist, *CEO*
Scott Forster, *
▲ **EMP:** 71 **EST:** 2002
SALES (est): 2.62MM
SALES (corp-wide): 8.39MM **Privately Held**
SIC: 2869 Fuels
PA: Magnus International Group, Inc.
679 Hardy Rd
Painesville OH 44077
216 592-8355

(G-11093)
HEALTH SENSE INC
Also Called: Healthsense
433 S State St (44077-3533)

PHONE....................440 354-8057
Stephen Musgrave, *Pr*
EMP: 8 **EST:** 1982
SQ FT: 2,500
SALES (est): 141.94K **Privately Held**
SIC: 8299 8742 2711 Educational services; Hospital and health services consultant; Newspapers: publishing only, not printed on site

(G-11094)
HIGH TECH PRFMCE TRLRS INC
1 High Tech Ave (44077-3701)
PHONE....................440 357-8964
Bruce C Hanusosky, *Pr*
Judy Hanusosky, *
Caity Hanusosky, *
Steve Lewis, *
Adam Olenchick, *
EMP: 32 **EST:** 1982
SQ FT: 84,000
SALES (est): 4MM **Privately Held**
Web: www.brucetransporters.com
SIC: 3715 Truck trailers

(G-11095)
IMAX INDUSTRIES INC
117 W Walnut Ave (44077-2925)
PHONE....................440 639-0242
Mike Miller, *Pr*
EMP: 10 **EST:** 1994
SALES (est): 2.86MM **Privately Held**
Web: www.imaxindustries.com
SIC: 8711 3548 Engineering services; Welding apparatus

(G-11096)
LBL LITHOGRAPHERS INC (PA)
Also Called: L B L Printing
365 W Prospect St (44077-3259)
PHONE....................440 350-0106
Lawrence Gidley, *CEO*
Brian Gidley, *Pr*
Lois Gidley, *Sec*
EMP: 7 **EST:** 1975
SQ FT: 4,500
SALES (est): 2.9MM
SALES (corp-wide): 2.9MM **Privately Held**
Web: www.lblprinting.com
SIC: 2752 Offset printing

(G-11097)
MAGNUS INTERNATIONAL GROUP INC (PA)
679 Hardy Rd (44077-4574)
PHONE....................216 592-8355
Eric Lofquist, *Prin*
Theresa M Paicic, *Pr*
Scott Forster, *VP*
John Malloy, *CFO*
Sharon Stefan, *Contrlr*
▲ **EMP:** 8 **EST:** 2007
SALES (est): 8.39MM
SALES (corp-wide): 8.39MM **Privately Held**
Web: dolphin.pcij.org
SIC: 4953 2048 2992 Recycling, waste materials; Prepared feeds, nec; Rust arresting compounds, animal or vegetable oil base

(G-11098)
MATPLUS LTD
Also Called: Matplus
76 Burton St (44077-3011)
PHONE....................440 352-7201
Jeffrey M Bednar, *Pr*
▲ **EMP:** 8 **EST:** 2004
SALES (est): 4.9MM **Privately Held**
Web: www.matplusinc.com

SIC: 3842 Orthopedic appliances

(G-11099)
MCNEIL INDUSTRIES INC
835 Richmond Rd Ste 2 (44077-1143)
PHONE..................440 951-7756
Randall J Mcneil, *Pr*
▲ **EMP:** 30 **EST:** 1986
SQ FT: 18,000
SALES (est): 5.68MM **Privately Held**
Web: www.mcneilindustries.com
SIC: 3366 5085 Bushings and bearings;
Seals, industrial

(G-11100)
OBRON ATLANTIC CORPORATION
Also Called: Eckart America
830 E Erie St (44077-4453)
P.O. Box 747 (44077-0747)
PHONE..................440 954-7600
Anthony Ameo, *Pr*
Mark Wallace, *
EMP: 60 **EST:** 1912
SALES (est): 3.74MM
SALES (corp-wide): 4.44B **Privately Held**
SIC: 2816 3399 Metallic and mineral
pigments, nec; Powder, metal
HQ: Eckart America Corporation
830 E Erie St
Painesville OH 44077
440 954-7600

(G-11101)
OHIO ASSOCIATED ENTPS LLC
Also Called: Meritech
72 Corwin Dr (44077-1802)
PHONE..................440 354-3148
John T Venaleck, *Brnch Mgr*
EMP: 12
SALES (corp-wide): 34.19MM **Privately
Held**
Web: www.meritec.com
SIC: 3678 3544 3469 3357 Electronic
connectors; Special dies, tools, jigs, and
fixtures; Metal stampings, nec;
Communication wire
PA: Ohio Associated Enterprises Llc
1382 W Jackson St
Painesville OH 44077
440 354-2106

(G-11102)
OHIO ASSOCIATED ENTPS LLC
Also Called: Omnitec
1359 W Jackson St (44077-1341)
P.O. Box 110 (44077-0110)
PHONE..................440 354-3148
James T Walch, *Brnch Mgr*
EMP: 49
SQ FT: 25,000
SALES (corp-wide): 34.19MM **Privately
Held**
Web: www.meritec.com
SIC: 3643 Electric connectors
PA: Ohio Associated Enterprises Llc
1382 W Jackson St
Painesville OH 44077
440 354-2106

(G-11103)
PATH TECHNOLOGIES INC
437 W Prospect St (44077-3269)
PHONE..................440 358-1500
David Princic, *Pr*
Mike Princic, *Stockholder*
Dorothy Princic, *Stockholder*
Barbara Sespico, *Stockholder*
EMP: 8 **EST:** 1986
SQ FT: 7,000
SALES (est): 940.71K **Privately Held**
Web: www.path-tech.com

SIC: 3599 Machine shop, jobbing and repair

(G-11104)
PCC AIRFOILS LLC
870 Renaissance Pkwy (44077-1287)
PHONE..................440 350-6150
EMP: 105
SALES (corp-wide): 424.23B **Publicly
Held**
Web: www.pccairfoils.com
SIC: 3369 Nonferrous foundries, nec
HQ: Pcc Airfoils, Llc
3401 Entp Pkwy Ste 200
Beachwood OH 44122
216 831-3590

(G-11105)
PET PROCESSORS LLC
1350 Bacon Rd (44077-4781)
PHONE..................440 354-4321
Gary Laughlin, *Dir*
▲ **EMP:** 77 **EST:** 1986
SQ FT: 350,000
SALES (est): 18.21MM **Privately Held**
Web: www.petus.com
SIC: 2821 Polyesters
PA: Diefenthal Holdings, Llc
1750 South Ln Ste 1
Mandeville LA 70471

(G-11106)
PRECISION CASTPARTS CORP
Also Called: PCC
870 Renaissance Pkwy (44077-1287)
PHONE..................440 350-6150
EMP: 10
SALES (corp-wide): 424.23B **Publicly
Held**
Web: www.precast.com
SIC: 3324 3369 3724 3511 Steel investment
foundries; Nonferrous foundries, nec;
Aircraft engines and engine parts; Turbines
and turbine generator sets
HQ: Precision Castparts Corp.
5885 Meadows Rd Ste 620
Lake Oswego OR 97035
503 946-4800

(G-11107)
QNNECT LLC (PA)
1382 W Jackson St (44077-1306)
PHONE..................864 275-8970
Kevin Perhamus, *Managing Member*
EMP: 6 **EST:** 2022
SALES (est): 5.06MM
SALES (corp-wide): 5.06MM **Privately
Held**
Web: www.qnnectnow.com
SIC: 3678 Electronic connectors

(G-11108)
R W SIDLEY INCORPORATED
Mining & Materials Division
436 Casement Ave (44077-3817)
P.O. Box 70 (44086-0070)
PHONE..................440 352-9343
Bob Buscher, *Pr*
EMP: 28
SALES (corp-wide): 43.09MM **Privately
Held**
Web: www.rwsidley.com
SIC: 1422 Cement rock, crushed and broken-
quarrying
PA: R. W. Sidley Incorporated
436 Casement Ave
Painesville OH 44077
440 352-9343

(G-11109)
R W SIDLEY INCORPORATED (PA)
Also Called: R. W. Sidley
436 Casement Ave (44077-3817)
P.O. Box 70 (44086-0070)
PHONE..................440 352-9343
Robert C Sidley, *Ch Bd*
Robert J Buescher, *
Dan Kennedy, *
Kevin Campany, *
Iola Black, *
▲ **EMP:** 30 **EST:** 1933
SQ FT: 10,000
SALES (est): 43.09MM
SALES (corp-wide): 43.09MM **Privately
Held**
Web: www.rwsidley.com
SIC: 1771 3299 Concrete work; Blocks and
brick, sand lime

(G-11110)
RUFF NEON & LIGHTING MAINT INC
295 W Prospect St (44077-3257)
PHONE..................440 350-6267
Thomas A Ruff, *Pr*
EMP: 10 **EST:** 1991
SALES (est): 2.5MM **Privately Held**
Web: www.ruffneonsign.com
SIC: 3993 Neon signs

(G-11111)
STAFAST PRODUCTS INC (PA)
Also Called: Stafast West
505 Lakeshore Blvd (44077-1197)
PHONE..................440 357-5546
Donald S Selle, *Pr*
Joan Selle, *
Stephen Selle, *
Christian Selle, *
Daniel Selle, *
◆ **EMP:** 40 **EST:** 1958
SQ FT: 20,600
SALES (est): 26.13MM
SALES (corp-wide): 26.13MM **Privately
Held**
Web: shop.stafast.com
SIC: 5085 3452 Fasteners, industrial: nuts,
bolts, screws, etc.; Bolts, nuts, rivets, and
washers

(G-11112)
T&T MACHINE INC
892 Callendar Blvd (44077-1218)
PHONE..................440 354-0605
Tony Padovic, *Pr*
Dan Padovic, *VP*
EMP: 14 **EST:** 1993
SQ FT: 13,000
SALES (est): 3.03MM
SALES (corp-wide): 3.03MM **Privately
Held**
Web: www.tandtmachineinc.com
SIC: 3599 Machine shop, jobbing and repair
PA: Precision Manufacturing Enterprise, Llc
3645 Sw 4th St
Miami FL

(G-11113)
**TECHNICAL GLASS PRODUCTS INC
(PA)**
881 Callendar Blvd (44077-1218)
PHONE..................440 639-6399
Jim Horvath, *Pr*
Robert Singer, *VP*
Halle Ricciardo, *Sec*
▲ **EMP:** 12 **EST:** 1990
SQ FT: 10,500
SALES (est): 3.31MM **Privately Held**
Web: www.technicalglass.com
SIC: 3229 Pressed and blown glass, nec

(G-11114)
TEKRAFT INDUSTRIES INC
244 Latimore St (44077-3903)
PHONE..................440 352-8321
Terrence Tekavec, *Pr*
Victor Tekavec, *Stockholder*
EMP: 8 **EST:** 1988
SQ FT: 3,500
SALES (est): 883.46K **Privately Held**
SIC: 3599 Machine shop, jobbing and repair

(G-11115)
TESSA PRECISION PRODUCT INC
850 Callendar Blvd (44077-1218)
PHONE..................440 392-3470
Paul Battaglia, *Pr*
Erika Battaglia, *
EMP: 50 **EST:** 1981
SQ FT: 25,000
SALES (est): 4.72MM **Privately Held**
Web: www.tessaprecision.com
SIC: 3599 3545 Machine shop, jobbing and
repair; Precision tools, machinists'

(G-11116)
THE DYSON CORPORATION
Also Called: Domestic Nut
53 Freedom Rd (44077-1200)
PHONE..................440 946-3500
◆ **EMP:** 125 **EST:** 1992
SALES (est): 24.03MM **Privately Held**
Web: www.dysoncorp.com
SIC: 3452 5085 Nuts, metal; Industrial
supplies

(G-11117)
THE LUBRIZOL CORPORATION
Also Called: Lubrizol Production Plant
155 Freedom Rd (44077-1234)
PHONE..................440 357-7064
Tanya Travis, *Mgr*
EMP: 127
SQ FT: 1,524
SALES (corp-wide): 424.23B **Publicly
Held**
Web: www.lubrizol.com
SIC: 2899 2992 Chemical preparations, nec;
Rust arresting compounds, animal or
vegetable oil base
HQ: The Lubrizol Corporation
29400 Lakeland Blvd
Wickliffe OH 44092
440 943-4200

(G-11118)
THIRION BROTHERS EQP CO LLC
Also Called: Tbec
340 W Prospect St (44077-3258)
P.O. Box 1392 (44077-7317)
PHONE..................440 357-8004
EMP: 6 **EST:** 2005
SQ FT: 1,015
SALES (est): 246.96K **Privately Held**
SIC: 3694 7699 5082 Distributors, motor
vehicle engine; Pumps and pumping
equipment repair; General construction
machinery and equipment

(G-11119)
TRANSDIGM INC
Aero Fluid Products
313 Gillett St (44077-2918)
PHONE..................440 352-6182
Jennifer Griffin Managing, *Brnch Mgr*
EMP: 40
SALES (corp-wide): 7.94B **Publicly Held**
Web: www.transdigm.com
SIC: 3561 Pumps and pumping equipment
HQ: Transdigm, Inc.
1350 Euclid Ave
Cleveland OH 44115

▲ = Import ▼ = Export
◆ = Import/Export

(G-11120)
TWIN RVERS TECH - PNSVILLE LLC
Also Called: Twin Rivers Technologies Mfg
679 Hardy Rd (44077-4574)
PHONE..................................440 350-6300
Paul J Angelico, *Managing Member*
EMP: 8 **EST:** 2003
SALES (est): 626.81K **Privately Held**
SIC: 2869 Industrial organic chemicals, nec

(G-11121)
VERSITEC MANUFACTURING INC
152 Elevator Ave (44077-3610)
PHONE..................................440 354-4283
Royce Reinhart, *Pr*
Mark Neal, *VP*
EMP: 18 **EST:** 2000
SQ FT: 3,600
SALES (est): 4.61MM **Privately Held**
Web: www.versitecinc.com
SIC: 3672 Printed circuit boards

(G-11122)
VISION PRESS INC
1634 W Jackson St (44077-1312)
P.O. Box 1308 (44077-8308)
PHONE..................................440 357-6362
Douglas Advey, *Pr*
Ronald Advey, *VP*
EMP: 6 **EST:** 1995
SALES (est): 341.47K **Privately Held**
Web: www.provisionimpressions.com
SIC: 2752 Offset printing

(G-11123)
XPONET INC
Also Called: Mold Tech
20 Elberta Rd (44077-1231)
PHONE..................................440 354-6617
Ralph Victor, *Ch Bd*
Don Barber, *
EMP: 7 **EST:** 1984
SQ FT: 25,000
SALES (est): 829.53K **Privately Held**
Web: www.moldtech.com
SIC: 3357 3678 3643 3577 Communication
wire; Electronic connectors; Current-
carrying wiring services; Computer
peripheral equipment, nec

(G-11124)
**YOKOHAMA INDS AMRICAS OHIO
INC**
474 Newell St (44077-1254)
P.O. Box 1370 (44077)
PHONE..................................440 352-3321
Yoshisa Makabayopshi, *Pr*
Don Patt, *
Larry Tremaglio, *
▲ **EMP:** 92 **EST:** 1937
SQ FT: 132,000
SALES (est): 4.95MM **Privately Held**
Web: www.yokohamaiaohio.com
SIC: 3069 Molded rubber products
HQ: Yokohama Corporation Of North
America
1 Macarthur Pl
Santa Ana CA 92707

(G-11125)
YOKOHAMA TIRE CORPORATION
Also Called: S A S Rubber
474 Newell St (44077-1254)
PHONE..................................440 352-3321
Donald A Patt, *Prin*
EMP: 89
SQ FT: 50,000
Web: www.y-yokohama.com
SIC: 3061 Mechanical rubber goods

PA: Yokohama Rubber Company, Limited,
The
2-1, Oiwake
Hiratsuka KNG 254-0

Parkman
Geauga County

(G-11126)
CNC PRECISION MACHINE INC
18360 Industrial Cir (44080)
P.O. Box 739 (44080-0739)
PHONE..................................440 548-3880
Alex Szkoe, *Pr*
EMP: 63 **EST:** 2003
SALES (est): 9.75MM **Privately Held**
Web: www.cncprecisionmachineinc.com
SIC: 3599 Machine shop, jobbing and repair

(G-11127)
MONTVILLE PLASTICS & RBR LLC
Also Called: Iron Horse Engineering
15567 Main Market Rd (44080)
P.O. Box 527 (44080-0527)
PHONE..................................440 548-2005
Jay Roberts, *Managing Member*
Tracie Roberts, *
EMP: 55 **EST:** 2014
SQ FT: 50,000
SALES (est): 7.81MM **Privately Held**
Web: www.montvilleplastics.com
SIC: 3089 Injection molding of plastics

(G-11128)
**MONTVILLE PLASTICS & RUBBER
INC**
Also Called: Montville Plastics
15567 Main Market Rd (44080)
P.O. Box 527 (44080-0527)
PHONE..................................440 548-3211
EMP: 45
SIC: 3089 Extruded finished plastics
products, nec

Parma
Cuyahoga County

(G-11129)
AMAC ENTERPRISES INC (PA)
5909 W 130th St (44130-1040)
PHONE..................................216 362-1880
George Chimples, *Ch Bd*
Constantine Chimples, *
Thomas Chimples, *
Janet Chimples, *
Lee Lettie, *
▲ **EMP:** 112 **EST:** 1951
SQ FT: 190,000
SALES (est): 5.32MM
SALES (corp-wide): 5.32MM **Privately
Held**
Web: www.amacent.com
SIC: 3398 3471 Metal heat treating;
Finishing, metals or formed products

(G-11130)
FDC MACHINE REPAIR INC
5585 Venture Dr (44130-9300)
PHONE..................................216 362-1082
Fred Di Censo, *Pr*
Ferdinando Di Censo, *
Maria Di Censo, *
EMP: 30 **EST:** 1985
SQ FT: 32,000
SALES (est): 5.38MM **Privately Held**
Web: www.fdcmachine.com
SIC: 3599 Machine shop, jobbing and repair

(G-11131)
FERGUSON ENTERPRISES LLC
2415 Brookpark Rd (44134-1404)
PHONE..................................216 635-2493
EMP: 6
SALES (corp-wide): 29.73B **Privately Held**
Web: www.ferguson.com
SIC: 5074 3432 Plumbing fittings and
supplies; Plumbing fixture fittings and trim
HQ: Ferguson Enterprises, Llc
751 Lakefront Cmns
Newport News VA 23606
757 874-7795

(G-11132)
GES GRAPHITE INC (PA)
Also Called: G E S
12300 Snow Rd (44130-1001)
PHONE..................................216 658-6660
Keith Kearney, *CEO*
Baker Kearney, *
Hunter Kearney, *
◆ **EMP:** 31 **EST:** 1985
SQ FT: 100,000
SALES (est): 13.9MM **Privately Held**
Web: www.ges-agm.com
SIC: 5085 3624 Industrial supplies; Carbon
and graphite products

(G-11133)
OSG-STERLING DIE INC
12502 Plaza Dr (44130-1045)
PHONE..................................216 267-1300
Denise L Lucas, *Prin*
▲ **EMP:** 10 **EST:** 2004
SALES (est): 4.05MM **Privately Held**
Web: www.osgtool.com
SIC: 3545 Cutting tools for machine tools
HQ: Osg Usa, Inc.
620 Stetson Ave
Saint Charles IL 60174
800 837-2223

(G-11134)
PAULIN INDUSTRIES INC
12400 Plaza Dr U 1 (44130-1057)
PHONE..................................216 433-7633
▲ **EMP:** 23
SIC: 5072 3452 Hardware; Bolts, nuts,
rivets, and washers

(G-11135)
SAIRAM OIL INC
4610 Milford Ave (44134-2122)
PHONE..................................440 289-8232
Himal Patel, *Prin*
EMP: 6 **EST:** 2016
SALES (est): 87.69K **Privately Held**
SIC: 1311 Crude petroleum and natural gas

(G-11136)
TRISOURCE EXHIBITS
12400 Plaza Dr Ste 1 (44130-1057)
PHONE..................................800 229-8600
EMP: 20 **EST:** 2016
SALES (est): 504.34K **Privately Held**
SIC: 7819 3999 Visual effects production;
Preparation of slides and exhibits

Pataskala
Licking County

(G-11137)
**BEST LIGHTING PRODUCTS INC
(HQ)**
Also Called: Best Lighting Products
1213 Etna Pkwy (43062-8041)
PHONE..................................740 964-1198
Jeffrey S Katz, *CEO*

George Jue, *
◆ **EMP:** 55 **EST:** 1997
SQ FT: 60,000
SALES (est): 44.25MM **Privately Held**
Web: www.bestlighting.net
SIC: 5063 3646 Electrical apparatus and
equipment; Commercial lighting fixtures
PA: Corinthian Capital Group, Llc
601 Lexington Ave Rm 5901
New York NY 10022

(G-11138)
EXCELSIOR PRINTING CO
1014 Putnam Rd Sw (43062-9754)
PHONE..................................740 927-2934
David Fannon, *Pr*
Melissa Fannon, *VP*
EMP: 9 **EST:** 1986
SQ FT: 8,200
SALES (est): 235.35K **Privately Held**
SIC: 2752 Offset printing

(G-11139)
GT TIRE SERVICE INC
Also Called: G T Automotive Service Center
15 W Broad St (43062-9647)
P.O. Box 296 (43062-0296)
PHONE..................................740 927-7226
Gary Townsend, *Pr*
EMP: 7 **EST:** 1988
SALES (est): 741.64K **Privately Held**
Web: www.gttires.net
SIC: 7534 5014 Tire repair shop; Tires and
tubes

(G-11140)
ILLUMINATE USA LLC ✪
3600 Etna Pkwy (43062-3506)
PHONE..................................614 598-9742
Frank Zhu, *CEO*
Kurt Wagner, *
EMP: 1609 **EST:** 2023
SQ FT: 1,100,000
SALES (est): 4.19MM **Privately Held**
Web: www.illuminateusa.com
SIC: 3674 Semiconductors and related
devices

(G-11141)
**JOULES ANGSTROM UV PRTG INKS
C (PA)**
104 Heritage Dr (43062-8042)
PHONE..................................740 964-9113
Patrick I Carlisle, *Pr*
Richard Klonowski, *Stockholder*
Norris Duncan, *Stockholder*
EMP: 24 **EST:** 1999
SQ FT: 30,000
SALES (est): 4.58MM
SALES (corp-wide): 4.58MM **Privately
Held**
Web: www.joulesangstrom.com
SIC: 2893 Printing ink

(G-11142)
KARS OHIO LLC
6359 Summit Rd Sw (43062-8763)
P.O. Box 34 (43073-0034)
PHONE..................................614 655-1099
EMP: 8 **EST:** 2014
SALES (est): 242.99K **Privately Held**
SIC: 2851 3479 1721 1629 Undercoatings,
paint; Painting of metal products; Industrial
painting; Blasting contractor, except
building demolition

(G-11143)
KNOX ENERGY INC (PA)
11872 Worthington Rd Nw (43062-9770)
P.O. Box 705 (43054-0705)
PHONE..................................740 927-6731

Mark Jordan, *Pr*
EMP: 17 **EST:** 1998
SALES (est): 4.65MM
SALES (corp-wide): 4.65MM **Privately Held**
Web: www.knoxenergy.com
SIC: 1382 Oil and gas exploration services

(G-11144)
OHIO STEEL INDUSTRIES INC
Also Called: Structural Steel Fabrication
13792 Broad St Sw (43062-9189)
P.O. Box 197 (43073-0197)
PHONE................................740 927-9500
Robet Eaton, *Brnch Mgr*
EMP: 75
SQ FT: 200,000
SALES (corp-wide): 16.31MM **Privately Held**
Web: www.osiplastics.com
SIC: 3441 Fabricated structural metal
PA: Ohio Steel Industries, Inc.
　　2575 Ferris Rd
　　Columbus OH 43224
　　614 471-4800

(G-11145)
PATASKALA POST
Also Called: Heartland Communications Div
190 E Broad St Ste 2 # E (43062-7106)
P.O. Box 722 (43062-0722)
PHONE................................740 964-6226
Randall Almendinger, *Owner*
EMP: 10 **EST:** 1999
SALES (est): 206.45K **Privately Held**
Web: www.hayesoffices.com
SIC: 2711 Newspapers, publishing and printing

(G-11146)
REDHAWK ENERGY SYSTEMS LLC
10340 Palmer Rd Sw (43062-9449)
P.O. Box 36 (43018-0036)
PHONE................................740 927-8244
Thomas J Ulrich, *Managing Member*
EMP: 6 **EST:** 2003
SQ FT: 5,000
SALES (est): 2.25MM **Privately Held**
Web: www.redhawkenergy.net
SIC: 3674 Solar cells

(G-11147)
RIDGE CORPORATION (PA)
1201 Etna Pkwy (43062-8041)
PHONE................................614 421-7434
Gary A Grandominico, *CEO*
▲ **EMP:** 90 **EST:** 1994
SALES (est): 18.48MM
SALES (corp-wide): 18.48MM **Privately Held**
Web: www.ridgecorp.com
SIC: 3443 Liners/lining

(G-11148)
RONA ENTERPRISES INC
30 W Broad St (43062-8180)
P.O. Box 1498 (43062-1498)
PHONE................................740 927-9971
Ronald A Thomas, *Pr*
EMP: 9 **EST:** 1969
SQ FT: 1,500
SALES (est): 1.24MM **Privately Held**
Web: www.ronahomes.com
SIC: 2452 6531 Prefabricated wood buildings
　; Real estate agents and managers

(G-11149)
RYDER ENGRAVING INC
1029 Hazelton Etna Rd Sw (43062-8528)
PHONE................................740 927-7193
Jill Gosnell, *Pr*

Chris Gosnell, *Sec*
EMP: 6 **EST:** 1972
SALES (est): 489.46K **Privately Held**
Web: www.ryderengraving.com
SIC: 3479 7389 Name plates: engraved, etched, etc.; Engraving service

(G-11150)
SCIOTO READY MIX LLC
6214 Taylor Rd Sw (43062-8885)
PHONE................................740 924-9273
Steve Edmond, *
EMP: 60 **EST:** 2005
SALES (est): 4.62MM **Privately Held**
Web: www.sciotoreadymix.com
SIC: 5211 3273 Cement; Ready-mixed concrete

(G-11151)
SMI HOLDINGS INC
Also Called: Screen Machine
10685 Columbus Pkwy (43062-7421)
PHONE................................740 927-3464
Bernard Cohen, *Ch*
Steven Cohen, *
Douglas Cohen, *
La June Cohen, *
◆ **EMP:** 100 **EST:** 1966
SALES (est): 1.68MM **Privately Held**
Web: www.screenmachine.com
SIC: 2752 Offset and photolithographic printing

Patriot
Gallia County

(G-11152)
TWISTED VINE FAMILY VINYRD LLC
1375 Carter Rd (45658-8808)
P.O. Box 705 (45631-0705)
PHONE................................740 256-1923
EMP: 8 **EST:** 2017
SALES (est): 127.69K **Privately Held**
Web: www.twistedvinefamilyvineyard.com
SIC: 2084 Wines

Paulding
Paulding County

(G-11153)
BAUGHMAN TILE COMPANY
8516 Road 137 (45879-9753)
PHONE................................800 837-3160
TOLL FREE: 800
Gene A Baughman, *Pr*
Eric Baughman, *
Brad Baughman, *
Mary A Baughman, *
EMP: 100 **EST:** 1883
SQ FT: 100,000
SALES (est): 9.5MM **Privately Held**
Web: www.baughmantile.com
SIC: 3084 3259 Plastics pipe; Clay sewer and drainage pipe and tile

(G-11154)
DELPHOS HERALD INC
Paulding Progress
113 S Williams St (45879-1429)
P.O. Box 180 (45879-0180)
PHONE................................419 399-4015
Doug Nutter, *Mgr*
EMP: 7
SQ FT: 7,000
SALES (corp-wide): 8.87MM **Privately Held**
Web: www.delphosherald.com

SIC: 2711 Newspapers, publishing and printing
PA: Herald Delphos Inc
　　405 N Main St
　　Delphos OH 45833
　　419 695-0015

(G-11155)
HERBERT E ORR COMPANY INC
335 W Wall St (45879-1163)
P.O. Box 209 (45879-0209)
PHONE................................419 399-4866
Greg Johnson, *Pr*
Donna J Garman, *Treas*
Ken Metzger, *
EMP: 125 **EST:** 1952
SQ FT: 48,000
SALES (est): 9.44MM **Privately Held**
Web: www.heorr.com
SIC: 5013 3479 Wheels, motor vehicle; Painting of metal products

(G-11156)
HOLCIM (US) INC
11435 Road 176 (45879-8834)
P.O. Box 160 (45879-0160)
PHONE................................419 399-4861
Geoff Fehr, *Mgr*
EMP: 105
Web: www.holcim.us
SIC: 3241 Cement, hydraulic
HQ: Holcim (Us) Inc.
　　8700 W Bryn Mawr Ave Ste
　　Chicago IL 60631

(G-11157)
INSOURCE TECHNOLOGIES INC
12124 Road 111 (45879-9000)
PHONE................................419 399-3600
Kenneth Manz, *Pr*
Roger Manz, *
▲ **EMP:** 170 **EST:** 1997
SQ FT: 11,500
SALES (est): 42.61MM **Privately Held**
Web: www.insource.tech
SIC: 3699 Electrical equipment and supplies, nec

(G-11158)
LAPHAM-HICKEY STEEL CORP
815 W Gasser Rd (45879-8765)
PHONE................................419 399-4803
Douglas Fiske, *Brnch Mgr*
EMP: 53
SQ FT: 400,000
SALES (corp-wide): 235.89MM **Privately Held**
Web: www.lapham-hickey.com
SIC: 3316 3398 Cold finishing of steel shapes; Metal heat treating
PA: Lapham-Hickey Steel Corp.
　　5500 W 73rd St
　　Bedford Park IL 60638
　　708 496-6111

(G-11159)
NASG SEATING PAULDING LLC
810 W Gasser Rd (45879-8770)
PHONE................................419 399-4500
EMP: 17 **EST:** 2019
SALES (est): 7.8MM **Privately Held**
Web: www.nasg.net
SIC: 3465 Automotive stampings

(G-11160)
OHIO MIRROR TECHNOLOGIES INC (PA)
114 W Jackson St (45879-1264)
P.O. Box 223 (45879)
PHONE................................419 399-5903
Dennis R Krick, *Pr*

Tom Krick, *Treas*
Janet Krick Prein, *Prin*
EMP: 14 **EST:** 1975
SQ FT: 2,700
SALES (est): 703.76K
SALES (corp-wide): 703.76K **Privately Held**
SIC: 3231 Products of purchased glass

(G-11161)
P C WORKSHOP INC
900 W Caroline St (45879-1381)
P.O. Box 390 (45879-0390)
PHONE................................419 399-4805
Megan Sierra, *CEO*
Brenda Miller, *Dir*
EMP: 6 **EST:** 1977
SALES (est): 1.71MM **Privately Held**
Web: www.pcworkshop.org
SIC: 7389 3711 Document and office record destruction; Automobile assembly, including specialty automobiles

(G-11162)
SPARTECH LLC
Also Called: Spartech Plastics
925 W Gasser Rd (45879-8765)
P.O. Box 420 (45879)
PHONE................................419 399-4050
Julie A Mcalindon, *Mgr*
EMP: 73
SALES (corp-wide): 344.31MM **Privately Held**
Web: www.spartech.com
SIC: 3081 3089 3083 Unsupported plastics film and sheet; Extruded finished plastics products, nec; Laminated plastics plate and sheet
PA: Spartech Llc
　　11650 Lkeside Crossing Ct
　　Saint Louis MO 63146
　　314 569-7400

Payne
Paulding County

(G-11163)
GORDON TOOL INC
1301 State Route 49 (45880-9727)
PHONE................................419 263-3151
William J Gordon, *Pr*
Lori Gordon, *Sec*
EMP: 15 **EST:** 1988
SQ FT: 15,625
SALES (est): 892.33K **Privately Held**
Web: www.gordontool.com
SIC: 5251 3544 Tools; Special dies, tools, jigs, and fixtures

(G-11164)
LIPPERT COMPONENTS INC
407 N Maple St (45880-9021)
PHONE................................574 537-8900
EMP: 9
SALES (corp-wide): 3.74B **Publicly Held**
Web: corporate.lippert.com
SIC: 3711 3469 3714 Chassis, motor vehicle; Stamping metal for the trade; Metal roofing and roof drainage equipment; Motor vehicle parts and accessories
HQ: Lippert Components, Inc.
　　3501 County Rd 6 E
　　Elkhart IN 46514
　　574 535-1125

(G-11165)
TAYLOR PRODUCTS INC
230 S Laura St (45880-9094)
P.O. Box 77 (45880-0077)

▲ = Import　▼ = Export
◆ = Import/Export

PHONE................419 263-2313
Denise Reed, *Prin*
EMP: 21
SALES (corp-wide): 200K **Privately Held**
Web: www.taylormadeproducts.com
SIC: 3231 Products of purchased glass
PA: Taylor Products Inc
66 Kingsboro Ave
Gloversville NY 12078
518 773-9312

(G-11166)
TAYLOR PRODUCTS INC
Also Called: Taylor Made Glass Systems
407 N Maple St (45880-9021)
PHONE................419 263-2313
John Ori, *Mgr*
EMP: 21
SALES (corp-wide): 200K **Privately Held**
Web: www.taylormadeproducts.com
SIC: 3231 3211 Products of purchased glass
; Flat glass
PA: Taylor Products Inc
66 Kingsboro Ave
Gloversville NY 12078
518 773-9312

(G-11167)
WILDCAT CREEK FARMS INC
Also Called: Wildcat Creek Popcorn
4633 Road 94 (45880-9124)
PHONE................419 263-2549
Don Benschneider, *Pr*
Dave Yenser, *VP*
Marge Yenser, *Sec*
EMP: 6 **EST:** 1980
SQ FT: 4,320
SALES (est): 202.91K **Privately Held**
Web: www.wildcatcreekpopcorn.com
SIC: 2099 0111 0119 0115 Popcorn,
packaged: except already popped; Wheat;
Popcorn farm; Corn

Peebles
Adams County

(G-11168)
G P MANUFACTURING INC
376 Buckeye St (45660-1114)
P.O. Box 265 (45660-0265)
PHONE................937 544-3190
EMP: 6
SQ FT: 7,500
SALES (est): 302.5K **Privately Held**
SIC: 3537 Containers (metal), air cargo

(G-11169)
HEIDELBERG MATERIALS US INC
Also Called: Hanson Aggrgates Plum Run
Quar
848 Plum Run Rd (45660-9706)
Rural Route 1 Box 11a (45660)
PHONE................937 587-2671
EMP: 48
SALES (corp-wide): 22.37B **Privately Held**
Web: www.heidelbergmaterials.us
SIC: 3273 Ready-mixed concrete
HQ: Heidelberg Materials Us, Inc.
300 E John Carpenter Fwy
Irving TX 75062

(G-11170)
J MCCOY LUMBER CO LTD (PA)
6 N Main St (45660-1243)
P.O. Box 306 (45660-0306)
PHONE................937 587-3423
Jack Mccoy, *Owner*
EMP: 13 **EST:** 1978
SQ FT: 2,400

SALES (est): 3.9MM
SALES (corp-wide): 3.9MM **Privately Held**
Web: www.jmccoylumber.com
SIC: 5031 2426 2431 Lumber: rough,
dressed, and finished; Dimension,
hardwood; Moldings, wood: unfinished and
prefinished

(G-11171)
PEEBLES MESSENGER NEWSPAPER
58 S Main St (45660-1189)
PHONE................937 587-1451
Pamela Syroney, *Owner*
EMP: 8 **EST:** 2003
SALES (est): 106.34K **Privately Held**
Web: peeblesmessenger.weebly.com
SIC: 2711 Newspapers: publishing only, not
printed on site

(G-11172)
SCHROCK JOHN
Also Called: Wheat Ridge Pallet & Lumber
99 Fugate Rd (45660-9144)
PHONE................937 544-8457
John Schrock, *Owner*
Melissa Black, *Acctnt*
EMP: 9 **EST:** 1984
SALES (est): 226.75K **Privately Held**
SIC: 2448 Pallets, wood

(G-11173)
SOUTHERN OHIO LUMBER LLC
Also Called: Southern Ohio Lumber
11855 State Route 73 (45660-9556)
P.O. Box 145 (43085-0145)
PHONE................614 436-4472
EMP: 8 **EST:** 1995
SQ FT: 25,000
SALES (est): 2.29MM **Privately Held**
Web: www.southernohiolumber.com
SIC: 2448 Pallets, wood

Pemberville
Wood County

(G-11174)
COUNTYLINE CO-OP INC (PA)
425 E Front St (43450-7039)
P.O. Box C (43450-0430)
PHONE................419 287-3241
Donald Kline, *Pr*
Robert Schroder, *VP*
Thomas Sieving, *Sec*
Robert Rahrig, *Genl Mgr*
EMP: 10 **EST:** 1916
SQ FT: 10,000
SALES (est): 4.98MM
SALES (corp-wide): 4.98MM **Privately Held**
Web: www.countylinecoop.com
SIC: 5153 5191 2875 2041 Grains; Farm
supplies; Fertilizers, mixing only; Flour and
other grain mill products

(G-11175)
HIRZEL CANNING COMPANY
Pemberville Foods
115 Columbus St (43450-7029)
P.O. Box D (43450-0431)
PHONE................419 287-3288
Joseph Hirzel, *Mgr*
EMP: 7
SALES (corp-wide): 64.46MM **Privately Held**
Web: www.deifratelli.com
SIC: 2033 Tomato products, packaged in
cans, jars, etc.
PA: Hirzel Canning Company
411 Lemoyne Rd

Northwood OH 43619
419 693-0531

(G-11176)
JA ACQUISITION CORP
Also Called: Hercules Stamping Co
850 W Front St (43450-9703)
P.O. Box F (43450-0433)
PHONE................419 287-3223
Wes Walters, *Pr*
James Gale, *Pr*
James Akers, *Ch Bd*
EMP: 10 **EST:** 1992
SQ FT: 30,000
SALES (est): 1.62MM **Privately Held**
Web: www.universalmetalproducts.com
SIC: 3465 3469 Automotive stampings;
Metal stampings, nec

(G-11177)
NATIONWIDE BELTING SLS SVC LLC (PA)
504 E Front St (43450-9655)
P.O. Box 128 (43430)
PHONE................419 287-7092
Rj Evans, *Managing Member*
EMP: 25 **EST:** 2017
SALES (est): 11.74MM
SALES (corp-wide): 11.74MM **Privately Held**
Web: www.nbeltingss.com
SIC: 2399 Belting and belt products

(G-11178)
UNIVERSAL METAL PRODUCTS INC
850 W Front St (43450-9703)
P.O. Box F (43450-0433)
PHONE................419 287-3223
EMP: 42
SALES (corp-wide): 23.57MM **Privately Held**
Web: www.universalmetalproducts.com
SIC: 3469 Stamping metal for the trade
PA: Universal Metal Products, Inc.
29980 Lakeland Blvd
Wickliffe OH 44092
440 943-3040

Peninsula
Summit County

(G-11179)
A & C WELDING INC
80 Cuyahoga Falls Industrial Pkwy
(44264-9568)
PHONE................330 762-4777
Carl Lamancusa, *Pr*
Michael Lamancusa, *
Timothy Gorbach, *
EMP: 25 **EST:** 1980
SALES (est): 4.46MM **Privately Held**
Web: www.acweld.com
SIC: 3444 7692 Sheet metalwork; Welding
repair

(G-11180)
ANSCO MACHINE COMPANY
60 Cuyahoga Falls Industrial Pkwy
(44264-9568)
PHONE................330 929-8181
Michael D Sterling, *Pr*
▲ **EMP:** 45 **EST:** 1991
SQ FT: 48,000
SALES (est): 10.53MM **Privately Held**
Web: www.anscomachine.com
SIC: 3599 Machine shop, jobbing and repair

(G-11181)
CENTER FOR INQUIRY INC
6413 Riverview Rd (44264-9624)
PHONE................330 671-7192
Bill Stalker, *Prin*
EMP: 6 **EST:** 2005
SALES (est): 68.74K **Privately Held**
SIC: 2721 Periodicals

(G-11182)
EAGLE ELASTOMER INC
70 Cuyahoga Falls Industrial Pkwy
(44264-9568)
P.O. Box 939 (44223-0939)
PHONE................330 923-7070
Gene H Mckenna, *Prin*
Neil X Mc Hale, *
Regan Mc Hale, *
Vertina Ashling, *
EMP: 45 **EST:** 1983
SQ FT: 26,000
SALES (est): 10.84MM **Privately Held**
Web: www.eagleelastomer.com
SIC: 3069 2821 Tubing, rubber; Plastics
materials and resins

(G-11183)
PREFORMED LINE PRODUCTS CO
Also Called: Pilot Plastics
200 Cuyahoga Falls Industrial Pkwy
(44264-9572)
PHONE................330 920-1718
Robert G Ruhlman, *Pr*
EMP: 14
SALES (corp-wide): 593.71MM **Publicly Held**
Web: www.plp.com
SIC: 3089 Injection molding of plastics
PA: Preformed Line Products Company
660 Beta Dr
Mayfield Village OH 44143
440 461-5200

(G-11184)
TERRY LUMBER AND SUPPLY CO
1710 Mill St W (44264-9701)
P.O. Box 216 (44264-0216)
PHONE................330 659-6800
James Montaquilla, *VP*
Judy Lahoski, *Sec*
John Lahoski, *Mgr*
EMP: 11 **EST:** 1940
SQ FT: 20,000
SALES (est): 2.61MM **Privately Held**
Web: www.terrylumbersupply.com
SIC: 5251 5211 2448 2449 Hardware stores;
Lumber and other building materials;
Pallets, wood; Rectangular boxes and
crates, wood

(G-11185)
WCCV FLOOR COVERINGS LLC (PA)
4535 State Rd (44264-9799)
PHONE................330 688-0114
John F Martin, *Pr*
EMP: 16 **EST:** 1994
SALES (est): 3.22MM
SALES (corp-wide): 3.22MM **Privately Held**
Web: www.wccv.com
SIC: 5713 3253 Floor covering stores;
Ceramic wall and floor tile

(G-11186)
WHOLECYCLE INC
Also Called: State 8 Motorcycle & Atv
100 Cuyahoga Falls Industrial Pkwy
(44264-9569)
PHONE................330 929-8123
R Kirk Compton, *Pr*
Paul Compton, *

GEOGRAPHIC

Gar Compton, *
◆ **EMP:** 40 **EST:** 1990
SQ FT: 25,000
SALES (est): 7.78MM **Privately Held**
Web: www.state8.com
SIC: 5012 5571 3799 Motorcycles;
Motorcycles; All terrain vehicles (ATV)

(G-11187)
WINE MILL
4964 Akron Cleveland Rd (44264-9513)
PHONE.............................234 571-2594
P Cunningham, *Genl Pt*
Patrick Cunningham, *Genl Pt*
EMP: 6 **EST:** 2014
SALES (est): 333.26K **Privately Held**
Web: www.thewinemill.com
SIC: 2084 Wines

(G-11188)
X44 CORP
Also Called: MBA Design
1601 Mill St W (44264-9798)
PHONE.............................330 657-2335
Steve Phillips, *Pr*
EMP: 10 **EST:** 1990
SQ FT: 2,800
SALES (est): 581.38K **Privately Held**
Web: www.mbadesigngroup.com
SIC: 2434 Wood kitchen cabinets

Pepper Pike
Cuyahoga County

(G-11189)
SURGICAL THEATER INC
30559 Pinetree Rd Ste 206 (44124-5919)
PHONE.............................216 452-2177
Alon Zuckerman, *Pr*
Jeff Witherite, *
Alon Geri, *
Guy Geri, *
▼ **EMP:** 37 **EST:** 2019
SALES (est): 4.05MM **Privately Held**
Web: www.surgicaltheater.com
SIC: 3841 Surgical and medical instruments

Perry
Lake County

(G-11190)
ALL WRIGHT ENTERPRISES LLC
Fidanza Performance
4285 Main St (44081-9635)
PHONE.............................440 259-5656
Jeffrey Jenkins, *Pr*
EMP: 9
SALES (corp-wide): 921.15K **Privately Held**
Web: www.fidanza.com
SIC: 5013 3714 Clutches; Gears, motor vehicle
PA: All Wright Enterprises, Llc
5 Bisbee Ct Ste 109-313
Santa Fe NM 87508
440 259-5656

(G-11191)
CHEROKEE MANUFACTURING LLC
3891 Shepard Rd (44081-9633)
PHONE.............................800 777-5030
EMP: 9 **EST:** 2011
SALES (est): 2.01MM **Privately Held**
SIC: 3315 Baskets, steel wire

(G-11192)
GREAT LAKES POWER SERVICE CO
Also Called: John Deere Authorized Dealer
3691 Shepard Rd (44081-9694)
PHONE.............................440 259-0025
Harry Allen, *Owner*
EMP: 19
SALES (corp-wide): 23.26MM **Privately Held**
Web: www.glpower.com
SIC: 3699 5082 Laser welding, drilling, and cutting equipment; Construction and mining machinery
PA: Great Lakes Power Service Co.
1973 Great Lakes Way
Madison OH 44057
440 951-5111

(G-11193)
JOINING METALS INC
3314 Blackmore Rd (44081-9320)
PHONE.............................440 259-1790
Jeff Beckwith, *Pr*
EMP: 12 **EST:** 2007
SALES (est): 2.61MM **Privately Held**
Web: www.joining-metals.com
SIC: 3444 Sheet metalwork

(G-11194)
LUTHER MACHINE INC
4604 Davis Rd (44081-9667)
PHONE.............................440 259-5014
Loraine Oliver, *Pr*
EMP: 6 **EST:** 1995
SALES (est): 388.44K **Privately Held**
SIC: 3545 Machine tool accessories

(G-11195)
MACDIVITT RUBBER COMPANY LLC
3291 Center Rd (44081-9589)
P.O. Box 129 (44081-0129)
PHONE.............................440 259-5937
Bob Mcdivitt, *Pr*
EMP: 20 **EST:** 1993
SQ FT: 20,000
SALES (est): 4.45MM **Privately Held**
Web: www.macdivittrubber.com
SIC: 3061 3069 Mechanical rubber goods; Molded rubber products

(G-11196)
MASTER CARBIDE TOOLS COMPANY
Also Called: Mastertech Diamond Products Co
3529 Lane Rd Ext (44081-9549)
PHONE.............................440 352-1112
Thomas Frakes, *Pr*
Cynthia Frakes, *VP*
EMP: 16 **EST:** 1946
SALES (est): 4.66MM **Privately Held**
Web: www.mastertechdiamond.com
SIC: 3545 Cutting tools for machine tools

(G-11197)
PRECISION CONVEYOR TECHNOLOGY
Also Called: Pct Industries
3785 Ln Rd (44081)
PHONE.............................440 352-6100
Robert J Eder, *Pr*
Carol Eder, *Sec*
EMP: 15 **EST:** 1990
SQ FT: 15,000
SALES (est): 1.99MM **Privately Held**
Web: www.precisionconveyor.com
SIC: 3535 3586 Conveyors and conveying equipment; Measuring and dispensing pumps

(G-11198)
PRECISION POLYMER CASTING
4304 Maple St Ste 3 (44081-8659)
PHONE.............................440 205-1900
Terry Capuano, *Owner*
David Rabatin, *Prin*
▼ **EMP:** 10 **EST:** 1988
SQ FT: 24,000
SALES (est): 1.83MM **Privately Held**
Web: www.precisionpolymercasting.com
SIC: 3089 Casting of plastics

(G-11199)
TCE INTERNATIONAL LTD
Also Called: Cutting Edge Nameplate Company
4843 N Ridge Rd (44081-9767)
PHONE.............................800 962-2376
Deborah J Fellows, *CEO*
Joseph J Fellows, *Pr*
▼ **EMP:** 15 **EST:** 1998
SQ FT: 20,000
SALES (est): 2.36MM **Privately Held**
Web: www.cuttingedgeinc.com
SIC: 3479 3993 2752 2671 Etching and engraving; Signs and advertising specialties ; Commercial printing, lithographic; Paper; coated and laminated packaging

(G-11200)
TT ELECTRONICS INTEGRATED MANUFACTURING SERVICES INC
Also Called: TT Electronics IMS
3700 Lane Rd Ext (44081-9563)
PHONE.............................440 352-8961
◆ **EMP:** 300 **EST:** 1976
SALES (est): 46.12MM
SALES (corp-wide): 660.59MM **Privately Held**
Web: www.ttelectronics.com
SIC: 3625 5731 Motor controls, electric; Consumer electronic equipment, nec
PA: Tt Electronics Plc
4th Floor St. Andrews House
Woking GU21
193 282-5300

Perrysburg
Wood County

(G-11201)
ADR FUEL INC
353 Elm St (43551-2177)
PHONE.............................419 872-2178
Glen Hefflinger, *Prin*
EMP: 6 **EST:** 2010
SALES (est): 603.83K **Privately Held**
SIC: 2869 Fuels

(G-11202)
AMERICAN STEEL TREATING INC
29200 Glenwood Rd (43551-3025)
PHONE.............................419 874-2044
Roy Waits, *CEO*
Jeff Blanker, *
EMP: 65 **EST:** 1988
SALES (est): 4.47MM **Privately Held**
Web: www.americansteeltreating.com
SIC: 3398 Metal heat treating

(G-11203)
AMPP INCORPORATED
Also Called: Ampp
28271 Cedar Park Blvd Ste 5 (43551-4883)
PHONE.............................419 666-4747
Daniel A Worline, *Prin*
▲ **EMP:** 200 **EST:** 1984
SQ FT: 53,000
SALES (est): 8.38MM

SALES (corp-wide): 24.11MM **Privately Held**
SIC: 3444 Sheet metalwork
PA: T.L. Industries, Inc.
28271 Cedar Park Blvd # 8
Perrysburg OH 43551
419 666-8144

(G-11204)
B & B BOX COMPANY INC
26490 Southpoint Rd (43551-1370)
PHONE.............................419 872-5600
Gregory B Hammer, *Pr*
EMP: 18 **EST:** 1959
SQ FT: 32,500
SALES (est): 5.85MM **Privately Held**
Web: www.b-n-bbox.com
SIC: 2653 Boxes, corrugated: made from purchased materials

(G-11205)
BOTTOMLINE INK CORPORATION
Also Called: Blink Marketing Logistics
7829 Ponderosa Rd (43551-4854)
PHONE.............................419 897-8000
Nicholas J Cron, *Prin*
Mike Davison, *
▲ **EMP:** 29 **EST:** 1991
SQ FT: 58,000
SALES (est): 8.37MM **Privately Held**
Web: www.alwaysblink.com
SIC: 2759 5199 Advertising literature: printing, nsk; Advertising specialties

(G-11206)
BPREX HALTHCARE BROOKVILLE INC (DH)
Also Called: Rexam Closure Systems
1899 N Wilkinson Way (43551-1685)
PHONE.............................847 541-9700
Steve Wirrig, *CEO*
◆ **EMP:** 135 **EST:** 1987
SALES (est): 29.1MM **Privately Held**
SIC: 3089 Caps, plastics
HQ: Berry Global, Inc.
101 Oakley St
Evansville IN 47710

(G-11207)
BRR BEAR LTD
Also Called: Coolseal USA
232 J St (43551-4416)
PHONE.............................419 666-1111
Mike Jaeck, *CFO*
Tim Wisnewski, *CFO*
Tab Hinkle, *Managing Member*
EMP: 16 **EST:** 2009
SALES (est): 6.81MM **Privately Held**
Web: www.coolsealusa.com
SIC: 3081 3083 Packing materials, plastics sheet; Laminated plastics plate and sheet
PA: Inteplast Group Corporation
9 Peach Tree Hill Rd
Livingston NJ 07039

(G-11208)
CAMEO INC
995 3rd St - Ampoint (43551-4355)
P.O. Box 535 (43697-0535)
PHONE.............................419 661-9611
E Lee Ison, *Pr*
Brandon Ison, *
◆ **EMP:** 7 **EST:** 1940
SALES (est): 485.77K **Privately Held**
Web: www.cameo.com
SIC: 2844 Perfumes, cosmetics and other toilet preparations

▲ = Import ▼ = Export
◆ = Import/Export

(G-11209)
CARDINAL AGGREGATE INC
8026 Fremont Pike (43551-9733)
PHONE.................................419 872-4380
Mark Murray, *CEO*
Philip Bisel, *VP Opers*
EMP: 13 **EST:** 2005
SALES (est): 2.58MM **Privately Held**
Web: www.cardinalaggregate.com
SIC: 3281 Stone, quarrying and processing of own stone products

(G-11210)
CENTOR INC (HQ)
1899 N Wilkinson Way (43551-1685)
P.O. Box 446 (43552-0446)
PHONE.................................567 336-8094
Ben Scheu, *Pr*
EMP: 13 **EST:** 1987
SALES (est): 40.39MM
SALES (corp-wide): 2.2B **Privately Held**
Web: www.centorrx.com
SIC: 2631 Container, packaging, and boxboard
PA: Gerresheimer Ag
Klaus-Bungert-Str. 4
Dusseldorf NW 40468
211618100

(G-11211)
CHAMPION WINDOW CO OF TOLEDO
7546 Ponderosa Rd Ste A (43551-5637)
PHONE.................................419 841-0154
Toby Tokes, *Pr*
Ed Levine, *
EMP: 6 **EST:** 1953
SALES (est): 486.98K **Privately Held**
Web: www.championwindow.com
SIC: 5211 3444 3442 3231 Doors, storm: wood or metal; Sheet metalwork; Metal doors, sash, and trim; Products of purchased glass

(G-11212)
CUTTING EDGE COUNTERTOPS INC (PA)
1300 Flagship Dr (43551-1375)
PHONE.................................419 873-9500
Doug Heerdegen, *Pr*
Jeff Erickson, *COO*
Jon Cousino, *Prin*
Rob Loughridge, *Prin*
◆ **EMP:** 40 **EST:** 2004
SQ FT: 24,000
SALES (est): 38.37MM **Privately Held**
Web: www.cectops.com
SIC: 3281 1743 Granite, cut and shaped; Marble installation, interior

(G-11213)
DCO LLC (DH)
900 E Boundary St Ste 8a (43551-2406)
PHONE.................................419 931-9086
Joe Stancati, *Managing Member*
Bricy Stringham, *
◆ **EMP:** 31 **EST:** 1904
SALES (est): 25.11MM **Publicly Held**
SIC: 3751 8741 Motor scooters and parts; Financial management for business
HQ: Enstar Holdings (Us) Llc
150 2nd Ave N Fl 3
Saint Petersburg FL 33701
727 217-2900

(G-11214)
DELAFOIL PENNSYLVANIA INC
Also Called: Delafoil
1775 Progress Dr (43551-2014)
PHONE.................................610 327-9565
James Cash, *Pr*
EMP: 6 **EST:** 1979

SQ FT: 35,000
SALES (est): 248.76K **Privately Held**
SIC: 3444 3469 Sheet metalwork; Metal stampings, nec

(G-11215)
DEPOT DIRECT INC
Also Called: Kenakore Solutions
487 J St (43551-4303)
PHONE.................................419 661-1233
▲ **EMP:** 42
Web: www.kenakoresolutions.com
SIC: 5084 7389 2741 Hydraulic systems equipment and supplies; Printing broker; Miscellaneous publishing

(G-11216)
DILLIN ENGINEERED SYSTEMS CORP
8030 Broadstone Rd (43551-4856)
PHONE.................................419 666-6789
David A Smith, *Pr*
EMP: 50 **EST:** 2000
SQ FT: 40,000
SALES (est): 9.64MM **Privately Held**
Web: www.dillin.net
SIC: 8711 3535 Mechanical engineering; Conveyors and conveying equipment

(G-11217)
DRIFTER MARINE INC
28271 Cedar Park Blvd Ste 6 (43551-3846)
PHONE.................................419 666-8144
Jon B Liebenthal, *Prin*
▲ **EMP:** 8 **EST:** 2010
SALES (est): 898.13K **Privately Held**
Web: www.driftermarine.com
SIC: 2399 Fishing nets

(G-11218)
ENCOMPASS ATMTN ENGRG TECH LLC
622 Eckel Rd (43551-1202)
P.O. Box 2912 (43606-0912)
PHONE.................................419 873-0000
EMP: 10 **EST:** 2001
SQ FT: 3,200
SALES (est): 992.08K **Privately Held**
SIC: 3823 Process control instruments

(G-11219)
EPRAD INC
Also Called: Eprad
28271 Cedar Park Blvd Ste 1 (43551-3846)
PHONE.................................419 666-3266
Ham-hi Lee, *Pr*
Theodore Steschulte, *VP*
Joseph L Young, *VP*
EMP: 8 **EST:** 1985
SQ FT: 2,000
SALES (est): 8.92K **Privately Held**
Web: www.eprad.com
SIC: 3861 3651 Motion picture apparatus and equipment; Household audio and video equipment

(G-11220)
FCA US LLC
Toledo Machining Plant
8000 Chrysler Dr (43551-4813)
PHONE.................................419 661-3500
David Arndt, *Prin*
EMP: 391
Web: www.stellantis.com
SIC: 3714 Motor vehicle transmissions, drive assemblies, and parts
HQ: Fca Us Llc
1130 Tienken Ct Ste 104
Rochester Hills MI 48306

(G-11221)
FINALE PRODUCTS INC
Also Called: Car Brite
301 Walnut St (43551-1456)
PHONE.................................419 874-2662
Alex Deedis, *Pr*
Robert Gibson, *VP*
Sharon Gibson, *VP*
Tim Gibson, *VP*
EMP: 8 **EST:** 1980
SQ FT: 25,600
SALES (est): 383.06K **Privately Held**
SIC: 2842 5013 5531 5169 Polishes and sanitation goods; Automotive supplies; Auto and home supply stores; Chemicals and allied products, nec

(G-11222)
FIRST SOLAR INC
Also Called: First Solar Electric
28101 Cedar Park Blvd (43551-4871)
P.O. Box 1032 (43697-1032)
PHONE.................................419 661-1478
Michele Youngdale, *Brnch Mgr*
EMP: 12
Web: www.firstsolar.com
SIC: 3674 3433 Solar cells; Heating equipment, except electric
PA: First Solar, Inc.
350 W Wash St Ste 600
Tempe AZ 85281

(G-11223)
FRAZIER MACHINE AND PROD INC
26489 Southpoint Rd (43551-1371)
PHONE.................................419 874-7321
Jeffrey B Frazier, *Pr*
Boyd M Frazier Junior, *CEO*
EMP: 23 **EST:** 1971
SQ FT: 18,000
SALES (est): 4.68MM **Privately Held**
Web: www.fraziermachine.com
SIC: 3599 3541 Machine shop, jobbing and repair; Machine tools, metal cutting type

(G-11224)
FRESH PRODUCTS LLC
30600 Oregon Rd (43551-4544)
PHONE.................................419 531-9741
Robert B Brown, *Pr*
Doug Brown, *
◆ **EMP:** 55 **EST:** 1971
SQ FT: 48,000
SALES (est): 9.64MM **Privately Held**
Web: www.freshproducts.com
SIC: 2842 Deodorants, nonpersonal

(G-11225)
GLASSLINE CORPORATION (PA)
Also Called: Secure Pak
28905 Glenwood Rd (43551-3020)
P.O. Box 147 (43552-0147)
PHONE.................................419 666-9712
Tom S Ziems, *Pr*
◆ **EMP:** 40 **EST:** 1970
SQ FT: 90,125
SALES (est): 24.85MM
SALES (corp-wide): 24.85MM **Privately Held**
Web: www.glassline.com
SIC: 3545 3565 3535 3541 Diamond dressing and wheel crushing attachments; Bottling machinery: filling, capping, labeling; Conveyors and conveying equipment; Machine tools, metal cutting type

(G-11226)
GLASSTECH INC (PA)
995 4th St (43551-4389)
PHONE.................................419 661-9500
Mark D Christman, *Pr*

Ken Wetmore, *
Diane Tymiak, *
◆ **EMP:** 112 **EST:** 1971
SQ FT: 80,000
SALES (est): 23.45MM
SALES (corp-wide): 23.45MM **Privately Held**
Web: www.glasstech.com
SIC: 3211 3229 3231 Tempered glass; Glass tubes and tubing; Glass sheet bent: made from purchased glass

(G-11227)
GREENWAY HOME PRODUCTS INC
1270 Flagship Dr (43551-1381)
◆ **EMP:** 12 **EST:** 2005
SALES (est): 239.89K **Privately Held**
SIC: 5023 2511 Homefurnishings; Wood household furniture

(G-11228)
HIAB USA INC (HQ)
12233 Williams Rd (43551-6802)
PHONE.................................419 482-6000
Roland Sunden, *Pr*
Lennart Brelin, *
Doug Heerdegen, *
◆ **EMP:** 70 **EST:** 1962
SQ FT: 56,000
SALES (est): 119.54MM **Privately Held**
Web: www.hiab.com
SIC: 5084 3536 Cranes, industrial; Cranes, industrial plant
PA: Hiab Oyj
Itamerenkatu 25
Helsinki 00180

(G-11229)
HINKLE MANUFACTURING INC
348 5th St (43551-4922)
P.O. Box 60210 (43460-0210)
PHONE.................................419 666-5550
EMP: 96
SIC: 3086 2653 Packaging and shipping materials, foamed plastics; Corrugated boxes, partitions, display items, sheets, and pad

(G-11230)
IMCO CARBIDE TOOL INC
Also Called: Toledo Cutting Tools
28170 Cedar Park Blvd (43551-4872)
PHONE.................................419 661-6313
Perry L Osburn, *Ch Bd*
Matthew S Osburn, *
Julie Whitlow, *
EMP: 90 **EST:** 1977
SQ FT: 25,000
SALES (est): 2.12MM **Privately Held**
Web: www.imcousa.com
SIC: 5084 3545 Machine tools and accessories; Tools and accessories for machine tools

(G-11231)
INNERAPPS LLC
Also Called: Identity Syncronizer
28350 Kensington Ln Ste 200 (43551-4174)
PHONE.................................419 467-3110
EMP: 8 **EST:** 2009
SALES (est): 513.18K **Privately Held**
Web: www.idsync.com
SIC: 7372 Business oriented computer software

(G-11232)
JERL MACHINE INC
11140 Avenue Rd (43551-2825)
PHONE.................................419 873-0270
Carol Coe, *CEO*

Linda Hetrick, *
Kristi Coe, *
Jayson Coy, *
EMP: 61 **EST:** 1974
SQ FT: 76,000
SALES (est): 8.09MM **Privately Held**
Web: www.jerl.com
SIC: 7692 3599 Welding repair; Machine shop, jobbing and repair

(G-11233)
KIEMLE-HANKINS COMPANY (PA)
Also Called: Kiemle-Hankins
94 H St (43551-4497)
P.O. Box 507 (43697-0507)
PHONE.............................419 661-2430
Stephen Martindale, *Ch*
Tim Martindale, *
Jeffrey Lee, *
EMP: 50 **EST:** 1928
SQ FT: 50,000
SALES (est): 14.06MM
SALES (corp-wide): 14.06MM **Privately Held**
Web: www.kiemlehankins.com
SIC: 7694 7629 3699 Electric motor repair; Electrical equipment repair services; Electrical equipment and supplies, nec

(G-11234)
LAKO TOOL & MANUFACTURING INC
7400 Ponderosa Rd (43551-4857)
P.O. Box 425 (43552-0425)
PHONE.............................419 662-5256
Larry E Smith, *Pr*
▲ **EMP:** 15 **EST:** 1974
SQ FT: 6,500
SALES (est): 3.2MM **Privately Held**
Web: www.lakotool.com
SIC: 3544 Special dies and tools

(G-11235)
LYONDLLBSELL ADVNCED PLYMERS I
12600 Eckel Rd (43551-1204)
PHONE.............................419 872-1408
EMP: 64
Web: www.lyondellbasell.com
SIC: 2821 Plastics materials and resins
HQ: Lyondellbasell Advanced Polymers Inc.
1221 Mckinney St Ste 300
Houston TX 77010
713 309-7200

(G-11236)
MAGNA VISUAL INC
28271 Cedar Park Blvd Ste 1 (43551-3846)
PHONE.............................314 843-9000
Diane Bishop, *Pr*
Diane Crews, *
John Wilson, *
▲ **EMP:** 50 **EST:** 1961
SALES (est): 5.01MM **Privately Held**
Web: www.magnavisual.com
SIC: 3089 3993 3953 2396 Injection molded finished plastics products, nec; Signs and advertising specialties; Marking devices; Automotive and apparel trimmings

(G-11237)
MARSHAS BUCKEYES LLC
25631 Fort Meigs Rd Ste E (43551-2098)
PHONE.............................419 872-7666
Marsha E Smith, *Managing Member*
EMP: 22 **EST:** 1985
SALES (est): 2.1MM **Privately Held**
Web: www.marshasbuckeyes.com
SIC: 2064 Candy and other confectionery products

(G-11238)
MASTER CHEMICAL CORPORATION (PA)
Also Called: Master Fluid Solutions
501 W Boundary St (43551-1200)
PHONE.............................419 874-7902
Mike Mchenry, *CEO*
Joe H Wright, *
Kyle R Stoffer, *
◆ **EMP:** 92 **EST:** 1951
SQ FT: 100,000
SALES (est): 41.26MM
SALES (corp-wide): 41.26MM **Privately Held**
Web: www.masterfluids.com
SIC: 2899 Chemical preparations, nec

(G-11239)
MICC MANUFACTURING CORPORATION
26695 Eckel Rd (43551-1209)
PHONE.............................567 331-0101
Fadi Nahhas, *CEO*
EMP: 6 **EST:** 2016
SALES (est): 469.52K **Privately Held**
Web: www.micccorp.com
SIC: 3443 Fabricated plate work (boiler shop)

(G-11240)
NATIONWIDE CHEMICAL PRODUCTS
24851 E Broadway Rd (43551-8947)
PHONE.............................419 714-7075
Joe Bassett, *Prin*
EMP: 6 **EST:** 2012
SALES (est): 204.61K **Privately Held**
Web: www.ncpprokill.com
SIC: 2869 Laboratory chemicals, organic

(G-11241)
NEW WASTE CONCEPTS INC
26624 Glenwood Rd (43551-4846)
PHONE.............................877 736-6924
Milton F Knight, *CEO*
Allan Wolf, *VP*
EMP: 10 **EST:** 1987
SQ FT: 5,000
SALES (est): 4.54MM **Privately Held**
Web: www.nwci.com
SIC: 2842 Sanitation preparations

(G-11242)
NEXT WAVE AUTOMATION LLC
600 W Boundary St (43551-1264)
PHONE.............................419 491-4520
Tim Owens, *Pr*
▲ **EMP:** 24 **EST:** 2007
SALES (est): 9.32MM **Privately Held**
Web: www.nextwaveautomation.com
SIC: 3599 Machine and other job shop work

(G-11243)
NORTHWOOD INDUSTRIES INC
7650 Ponderosa Rd (43551-4861)
PHONE.............................419 666-2100
Kurt Miller, *Pr*
EMP: 18 **EST:** 1968
SALES (est): 3.82MM **Privately Held**
Web: www.nwindustries.com
SIC: 3469 3541 7699 8711 Machine parts, stamped or pressed metal; Machine tools, metal cutting type; Industrial equipment services; Designing: ship, boat, machine, and product

(G-11244)
O-I GLASS INC (PA)
Also Called: O-I
1 Michael Owens Way (43551-2999)
PHONE.............................567 336-5000
Gordon J Hardie, *CEO*

John Humphrey, *Ch Bd*
John A Haudrich, *Sr VP*
Arnaud Aujouannet, *Chief Sales & Marketing Officer*
Darrow A Abrahams, *Corporate Secretary*
EMP: 118 **EST:** 1903
SALES (est): 6.53B
SALES (corp-wide): 6.53B **Publicly Held**
Web: www.o-i.com
SIC: 3221 Glass containers

(G-11245)
ODYSSEY MACHINE COMPANY LTD
26675 Eckel Rd # 5 (43551-1209)
PHONE.............................419 455-6621
Ronald Leroux, *Pr*
EMP: 7 **EST:** 2005
SALES (est): 1.12MM **Privately Held**
Web: www.odymac.com
SIC: 3599 7699 Custom machinery; Industrial machinery and equipment repair

(G-11246)
OHIO TABLE PAD COMPANY (PA)
Also Called: Ohio Table Pad Co Georgia Div
350 3 Meadows Dr (43551-3138)
P.O. Box 914 (43552-0914)
PHONE.............................419 872-6400
Christopher P Krauser, *Pr*
Jeffrey Lavoy, *VP*
Stephen R Krauser, *Stockholder*
Della B Bricker, *Prin*
N E Bricker, *Prin*
▲ **EMP:** 12 **EST:** 1923
SQ FT: 15,000
SALES (est): 2.49MM
SALES (corp-wide): 2.49MM **Privately Held**
SIC: 2299 5712 3949 2392 Felts and felt products; Furniture stores; Sporting and athletic goods, nec; Household furnishings, nec

(G-11247)
OHIO TABLE PAD COMPANY
Also Called: Southern Division
350 3 Meadows Dr (43551-3138)
P.O. Box 914 (43552-0914)
PHONE.............................419 872-6400
Don Unger, *Brnch Mgr*
EMP: 9
SALES (corp-wide): 2.49MM **Privately Held**
SIC: 2392 Pads and padding, table: except asbestos, felt, or rattan
PA: The Ohio Table Pad Company
350 3 Meadows Dr
Perrysburg OH 43551
419 872-6400

(G-11248)
OHIO TABLE PAD OF INDIANA
350 3 Meadows Dr (43551-3138)
PHONE.............................419 872-6400
Stephen Krauser, *Pr*
Christopher Krauser, *
Jeffrey Lavoy, *
▲ **EMP:** 54 **EST:** 1963
SQ FT: 15,000
SALES (est): 485.42K
SALES (corp-wide): 2.49MM **Privately Held**
SIC: 2299 Wool felts, pressed or needle loom
PA: The Ohio Table Pad Company
350 3 Meadows Dr
Perrysburg OH 43551
419 872-6400

(G-11249)
OLDCASTLE BUILDINGENVELOPE INC

291 M St (43551-4409)
PHONE.............................800 537-4064
Scott Switzer, *Brnch Mgr*
EMP: 152
SALES (corp-wide): 4.41B **Privately Held**
Web: www.obe.com
SIC: 3231 5231 Tempered glass: made from purchased glass; Glass
HQ: Oldcastle Buildingenvelope, Inc.
5005 Lyndon B Jhnson Fwy
Dallas TX 75244
214 273-3400

(G-11250)
ONIX CORPORATION
27100 Oakmead Dr (43551-2670)
PHONE.............................800 844-0076
Richard Allen, *Pr*
Charles Verhoff, *
Todd Mroczkowski, *
John Halderman, *
▲ **EMP:** 37 **EST:** 2006
SALES (est): 1.58MM **Privately Held**
Web: www.theonixcorp.com
SIC: 3433 Heating equipment, except electric

(G-11251)
ORBIS CORPORATION
Also Called: Hinkle Manufacturing
232 J St (43551-4416)
PHONE.............................262 560-5000
Jeff Wolens, *Brnch Mgr*
EMP: 96
SALES (corp-wide): 1.94B **Privately Held**
Web: www.orbiscorporation.com
SIC: 3086 2653 Packaging and shipping materials, foamed plastics; Corrugated boxes, partitions, display items, sheets, and pad
HQ: Orbis Corporation
1055 Corporate Ctr Dr
Oconomowoc WI 53066
262 560-5000

(G-11252)
OWENS-BROCKWAY GLASS CONT INC (DH)
Also Called: Owens-Brockway Glass Cntrs
1 Michael Owens Way (43551-2999)
PHONE.............................567 336-8449
Mister Albert P L Stroucken, *Ch*
Steve Mccracken, *CEO*
Mathew Longthorne, *Pr*
Steve Bramlage, *Sr VP*
Jim Baehren, *Sr VP*
◆ **EMP:** 250 **EST:** 1987
SQ FT: 900,000
SALES (est): 1.02B
SALES (corp-wide): 6.53B **Publicly Held**
Web: www.owens-brockway.com
SIC: 3221 Glass containers
HQ: Owens-Brockway Packaging, Inc.
1 Michael Owens Way
Perrysburg OH 43551

(G-11253)
OWENS-ILLINOIS GENERAL INC
Also Called: O-1
1 Michael Owens Way (43551-2999)
PHONE.............................567 336-5000
Al Stroucken, *CEO*
Thomas L Young, *
Ed Snyder, *
David G Van Hooser, *
Jim Baehren, *
▲ **EMP:** 550 **EST:** 1987
SQ FT: 900,000
SALES (est): 12.21MM
SALES (corp-wide): 6.53B **Publicly Held**
Web: www.o-i.com
SIC: 3221 Glass containers

HQ: Paddock Enterprises, Llc
1 Michael Owens Way Plz 2
Perrysburg OH 43551
567 336-5000

(G-11254)
OWENS-ILLINOIS GROUP INC (HQ)
1 Michael Owens Way (43551-2999)
PHONE....................567 336-5000
Albert P L Stroucken, *Ch Bd*
Stephen P Bramlage Junior, *CAO*
James W Baehren, *
Paul A Jarrell, *
◆ EMP: 60 EST: 1903
SALES (est): 1.02B
SALES (corp-wide): 6.53B Publicly Held
Web: www.o-i.com
SIC: 3221 Glass containers
PA: O-I Glass, Inc.
1 Michael Owens Way
Perrysburg OH 43551
567 336-5000

(G-11255)
OWENS-ILLINOIS INC
Also Called: Oi
1 Michael Owens Way (43551-2999)
PHONE....................567 336-5000
EMP: 26500
SIC: 3221 Glass containers

(G-11256)
PADDOCK ENTERPRISES LLC (HQ)
1 Michael Owens Way 2 (43551-2999)
PHONE....................567 336-5000
EMP: 37 EST: 2019
SALES (est): 57.72MM
SALES (corp-wide): 6.53B Publicly Held
SIC: 3221 Glass containers
PA: O-I Glass, Inc.
1 Michael Owens Way
Perrysburg OH 43551
567 336-5000

(G-11257)
PALLET WORLD INC
8272 Fremont Pike (43551-9705)
PHONE....................419 874-9333
Timothy Welch, *Pr*
Ken Welch, *
EMP: 26 EST: 1992
SQ FT: 3,000
SALES (est): 3.34MM Privately Held
Web: www.palletworldinc.com
SIC: 2448 Pallets, wood

(G-11258)
PRECISION BUSINESS SOLUTIONS
668 1st St (43551-4480)
PHONE....................419 661-8700
EMP: 10 EST: 2021
SALES (est): 879.81K Privately Held
Web: www.precisionbussol.com
SIC: 2759 Commercial printing, nec

(G-11259)
REACTIVE RESIN PRODUCTS CO
327 5th St (43551-4919)
PHONE....................419 666-6119
Jeff Freiburger, *Pr*
Robert L Hinkle, *
Joe Leonard, *
▲ EMP: 15 EST: 1988
SQ FT: 150,000
SALES (est): 4.01MM Privately Held
Web: www.rrp-mfg.com
SIC: 3565 3714 3089 Packaging machinery;
Motor vehicle parts and accessories;
Synthetic resin finished products, nec

(G-11260)
SATELYTICS INC
6330 Levis Commons Blvd (43551-7272)
PHONE....................419 372-0160
Jim Harpen, *Genl Mgr*
Milt Baker, *Pr*
Gail Nader, *Mgr*
EMP: 8 EST: 2009
SALES (est): 1.08MM Privately Held
Web: www.satelytics.com
SIC: 3826 Environmental testing equipment

(G-11261)
SCHUTZ CONTAINER SYSTEMS INC
2105 S Wilkinson Way (43551-1599)
PHONE....................419 872-2477
Pat Gillespe, *Brnch Mgr*
EMP: 80
SALES (corp-wide): 3.08B Privately Held
Web: www.schuetz-packaging.net
SIC: 2448 Cargo containers, wood and
metal combination
HQ: Schutz Container Systems, Inc.
200 Aspen Hill Rd
Branchburg NJ 08876

(G-11262)
SHRADER TIRE & OIL INC
Also Called: Shrader Tire Oil Fleet Tire S
3511 Genoa Rd (43551-9703)
PHONE....................419 420-8435
Bryan Fields, *Mgr*
EMP: 6
SALES (corp-wide): 97.58MM Privately
Held
Web: www.shradertireandoil.com
SIC: 5531 7534 Automotive tires; Tire
retreading and repair shops
PA: Shrader Tire & Oil, Inc.
2045 W Sylvania Ave Ste 51
Toledo OH 43613
419 472-2128

(G-11263)
**SYSTEM PACKAGING OF
GLASSLINE**
28905 Glenwood Rd (43551-3020)
P.O. Box 147 (43552-0147)
PHONE....................419 666-9712
Tom Wims, *Pr*
EMP: 91 EST: 1992
SALES (est): 1.54MM
SALES (corp-wide): 24.85MM Privately
Held
Web: www.glassline.com
SIC: 3565 Packaging machinery
PA: Glassline Corporation
28905 Glenwood Rd
Perrysburg OH 43551
419 666-9712

(G-11264)
TARPSTOP LLC (PA)
12000 Williams Rd (43551-6809)
P.O. Box 5760 (43613-0760)
PHONE....................419 873-7867
Andrew M Knepper, *Managing Member*
Ken Weschae, *
▲ EMP: 18 EST: 2001
SALES (est): 17.94MM
SALES (corp-wide): 17.94MM Privately
Held
Web: www.tarpstop.com
SIC: 3713 Truck and bus bodies

(G-11265)
TBK HOLDINGS LLC (PA)
232 J St (43551-4416)
PHONE....................313 584-0400
EMP: 8 EST: 1971
SALES (est): 2.52MM

SALES (corp-wide): 2.52MM Privately
Held
SIC: 3089 Plastics containers, except foam

(G-11266)
TECH DYNAMICS INC
361 D St Ste B (43551-5645)
PHONE....................419 666-1666
John W Zimmerman, *Pr*
David G Fielding, *VP*
EMP: 11 EST: 1984
SQ FT: 18,000
SALES (est): 3.38MM Privately Held
Web: www.techdynamics.us
SIC: 3441 Fabricated structural metal

(G-11267)
TECHNEGLAS INC
Also Called: TECHNEGLAS, INC.
25875 Dixie Hwy Bldg 52 (43551-1918)
PHONE....................419 873-2000
Leyshon Townsend, *Brnch Mgr*
EMP: 49
Web: www.techneglas.com
SIC: 3229 Glass tubes and tubing
HQ: Techneglas Llc
2100 N Wilkinson Way
Perrysburg OH 43551
419 873-2000

(G-11268)
TECHNEGLAS LLC (HQ)
2100 N Wilkinson Way (43551-1598)
PHONE....................419 873-2000
Jeffrey T Lowry, *Pr*
▲ EMP: 10 EST: 1988
SQ FT: 18,000
SALES (est): 7.53MM Privately Held
Web: www.techneglas.com
SIC: 3479 3674 Coating of metals with
plastic or resins; Silicon wafers, chemically
doped
PA: Nippon Electric Glass Co., Ltd.
2-7-1, Seiran
Otsu SGA 520-0

(G-11269)
TECHNICAL GLASS PRODUCTS INC
7460 Ponderosa Rd (43551-4857)
PHONE....................425 396-8420
Joseph Murray, *Pr*
EMP: 16 EST: 2013
SALES (est): 3.81MM Privately Held
Web: www.fireglass.com
SIC: 3229 Scientific glassware

(G-11270)
TEREX UTILITIES INC
Also Called: Toledo Division
25661 Fort Meigs Rd Ste A (43551-2018)
PHONE....................419 470-8408
Don Elliott, *Brnch Mgr*
EMP: 10
SALES (corp-wide): 5.13B Publicly Held
Web: www.terex.com
SIC: 3531 Construction machinery
HQ: Terex Utilities, Inc.
301 Merritt 7
Norwalk CT 06851
203 222-7170

(G-11271)
TINY LION MUSIC GROUPS
Also Called: Groovemaster Music
144 E 5th St (43551-2235)
PHONE....................419 874-7353
Gaylord Richardson, *Owner*
EMP: 8 EST: 1992
SALES (est): 81.07K Privately Held
SIC: 2741 7389 Miscellaneous publishing;
Music recording producer

(G-11272)
TL INDUSTRIES INC (PA)
28271 Cedar Park Blvd Ste 8 (43551-4883)
PHONE....................419 666-8144
Joseph Young, *Pr*
Joseph Young, *VP*
Theodore Stetschulte, *
EMP: 105 EST: 1970
SALES (est): 24.11MM
SALES (corp-wide): 24.11MM Privately
Held
Web: www.tlindustries.com
SIC: 8711 3444 3629 3679 Electrical or
electronic engineering; Sheet metalwork;
Battery chargers, rectifying or nonrotating;
Loads, electronic

(G-11273)
TMT INC
Also Called: Tmt Logistics
655 D St (43551-4908)
P.O. Box 408 (43552-0408)
PHONE....................419 592-1041
Tony Marks, *Pr*
EMP: 8 EST: 2000
SALES (est): 211.31K Privately Held
SIC: 4789 3999 Railroad maintenance and
repair services; Dock equipment and
supplies, industrial

(G-11274)
TOLEDO ELECTROMOTIVE INC
28765 White Rd (43551-3657)
PHONE....................419 874-7751
Tony Palumbo, *Pr*
EMP: 6 EST: 1995
SALES (est): 343.59K Privately Held
SIC: 3625 Motor controls, electric

(G-11275)
TOLEDO SOLAR INC
1775 Progress Dr (43551-2014)
PHONE....................567 202-4145
Mark Hartel, *CEO*
Mark Haddad, *CFO*
EMP: 12 EST: 2019
SQ FT: 300,000
SALES (est): 7.82MM Privately Held
Web: www.toledo-solar.com
SIC: 3674 Solar cells

(G-11276)
TOLEDO TARP SERVICE INC
Also Called: Wilcox Awning & Sign
3273 Genoa Rd (43551-9703)
PHONE....................419 837-5098
EMP: 20
Web: www.toledotarp.com
SIC: 2394 5085 Tarpaulins, fabric: made
from purchased materials; Industrial
supplies

(G-11277)
UNIVERSAL HYDRAULIK USA CORP
25651 Fort Meigs Rd (43551-2076)
PHONE....................419 873-6340
Michael Uhl, *CEO*
Ral Uhl, *CFO*
EMP: 7 EST: 2014
SQ FT: 4,500
SALES (est): 2.54MM
SALES (corp-wide): 16.81MM Privately
Held
Web: www.universalhydraulik-usa.com
SIC: 3443 Heat exchangers: coolers (after,
inter), condensers, etc.
PA: "universal Hydraulik Gmbh"
Siemensstr. 33
Neu-Anspach HE 61267
608194180

(G-11278)
WALKER TOOL & MACHINE COMPANY
7700 Ponderosa Rd (43551-4851)
PHONE....................................419 661-8000
Tarry F Beard, *Pr*
Larry L Beard, *Sec*
EMP: 13 EST: 1941
SQ FT: 18,500
SALES (est): 2.04MM **Privately Held**
Web: www.walkertoolandmachine.com
SIC: 3544 Special dies and tools

(G-11279)
WELCH PUBLISHING CO (PA)
Also Called: Perrysburg Messenger-Journal
117 E 2nd St (43551-2102)
P.O. Box 267 (43552-0267)
PHONE....................................419 874-2528
Matt H Welch, *Pr*
EMP: 20 EST: 1852
SQ FT: 6,000
SALES (est): 2.43MM
SALES (corp-wide): 2.43MM **Privately Held**
Web: www.vaulthealth.fit
SIC: 2711 2721 7375 2752 Job printing and newspaper publishing combined; Periodicals; Information retrieval services; Commercial printing, lithographic

(G-11280)
WHELCO INDUSTRIAL LTD
28210 Cedar Park Blvd (43551-4865)
PHONE....................................419 385-4627
EMP: 51 EST: 1992
SQ FT: 12,000
SALES (est): 7.31MM **Privately Held**
Web: www.whelco.com
SIC: 7694 Electric motor repair

(G-11281)
WONDERLY TRUCKING & EXCVTG LLC
3939 Fremont Pike (43551-9176)
PHONE....................................419 837-6294
Chad Wonderly, *Managing Member*
EMP: 10 EST: 2012
SALES (est): 2.57MM **Privately Held**
Web: www.dandkexcavating.net
SIC: 4212 3531 Timber trucking, local; Plows: construction, excavating, and grading

Perrysville
Ashland County

(G-11282)
MANSFIELD PLUMBING PDTS LLC (HQ)
1430 George Rd (44864)
P.O. Box 334 (44805-0334)
PHONE....................................419 938-5211
Jim Morando, *Pr*
◆ EMP: 600 EST: 1929
SQ FT: 700,000
SALES (est): 47.6MM **Privately Held**
Web: www.mansfieldplumbing.com
SIC: 3261 3463 3088 3431 Vitreous plumbing fixtures; Plumbing fixture forgings, nonferrous; Plastics plumbing fixtures; Bathtubs: enameled iron, cast iron, or pressed metal
PA: Organizacion Corona S A
Calle 100 8 A 55 Torre C Piso 9
Bogota DC

(G-11283)
S & S AGGREGATES INC
Also Called: Shelly & Sands Zanesville OH
4540 State Route 39 (44864-9600)
PHONE....................................419 938-5604
Kent Ewers, *Mgr*
EMP: 131
SALES (corp-wide): 433.35MM **Privately Held**
Web: www.shellyandsands.com
SIC: 1442 Construction sand mining
HQ: S & S Aggregates, Inc
3570 S River Rd
Zanesville OH 43701
740 453-0721

Pettisville
Fulton County

(G-11284)
M & R REDI MIX INC (PA)
521 Commercial St (43553-6016)
P.O. Box 53273 (43553-0273)
PHONE....................................419 445-7771
Kurt Nofziger, *Pr*
Connie Nofziger, *VP*
EMP: 20 EST: 1966
SQ FT: 2,000
SALES (est): 3.22MM
SALES (corp-wide): 3.22MM **Privately Held**
Web: www.gerkencompanies.com
SIC: 3273 4212 Ready-mixed concrete; Local trucking, without storage

(G-11285)
PETTISVILLE GRAIN CO (PA)
Also Called: Pgc Feeds
18251 County Road D-E (43553)
P.O. Box 53009 (43553-0009)
PHONE....................................419 446-2547
Neil E Rupp, *Pr*
James L Rufenacht, *Prin*
Corwin D Rufenacht, *Prin*
EMP: 21 EST: 1953
SALES (est): 21.22K
SALES (corp-wide): 21.22K **Privately Held**
Web: www.pettisvillegrain.com
SIC: 5153 5999 2048 2041 Grain elevators; Feed and farm supply; Prepared feeds, nec ; Flour and other grain mill products

(G-11286)
PETTISVILLE MEATS INCORPORATED
3082 Main St (43553)
P.O. Box 53148 (43553-0148)
PHONE....................................419 445-0921
Steve Mc Intosh, *Pr*
EMP: 10 EST: 1967
SQ FT: 7,500
SALES (est): 467.12K **Privately Held**
SIC: 2013 4222 5421 Sausages and other prepared meats; Storage, frozen or refrigerated goods; Meat markets, including freezer provisioners

Pickerington
Fairfield County

(G-11287)
ASHTON LLC (PA)
77 E Columbus St (43147-1382)
PHONE....................................336 447-4951
Billy Whitehurst, *Managing Member*
EMP: 14 EST: 2011
SALES (est): 2.14MM
SALES (corp-wide): 2.14MM **Privately Held**

Web: www.ashtonus.com
SIC: 2759 Screen printing

(G-11288)
ASHTON LLC
Also Called: Ashton Custom Prtg & Gift Sp
77 E Columbus St (43147-1382)
PHONE....................................614 833-4165
EMP: 11
SALES (corp-wide): 2.14MM **Privately Held**
Web: www.ashtonus.com
SIC: 2759 Screen printing
PA: Ashton Llc
77 E Columbus St
Pickerington OH 43147
336 447-4951

(G-11289)
BAGGALLINI INC
13405 Yarmouth Dr (43147-8493)
PHONE....................................800 448-8753
Devon Pike, *Pr*
▼ EMP: 16 EST: 2011
SALES (est): 1.61MM
SALES (corp-wide): 144.54MM **Privately Held**
Web: www.baggallini.com
SIC: 2393 5199 5948 Bags and containers, except sleeping bags: textile; Bags, textile; Luggage and leather goods stores
HQ: R. G. Barry Corporation
13405 Yarmouth Dr
Pickerington OH 43147
614 864-6400

(G-11290)
BRAND5 LLC
106 Cool Spring Ct (43147-8094)
PHONE....................................614 920-9254
EMP: 11 EST: 2006
SALES (est): 117.31K **Privately Held**
SIC: 2844 Perfumes, cosmetics and other toilet preparations

(G-11291)
CBUS INC
Also Called: N2 Publishing
13799 Nantucket Ave (43147-9315)
PHONE....................................614 327-6971
Mike Matheny, *Prin*
EMP: 10 EST: 2017
SALES (est): 1.09MM **Privately Held**
Web: www.strollmag.com
SIC: 2741 Miscellaneous publishing

(G-11292)
CLEMENS LICENSE AGENCY
12825 Wheaton Ave (43147-8591)
PHONE....................................614 288-8007
Jennifer Clemens, *Owner*
EMP: 7 EST: 1993
SALES (est): 531.02K **Privately Held**
SIC: 3469 Automobile license tags, stamped metal

(G-11293)
ECHO MOBILE SOLUTIONS LLC
108 Leasure Dr (43147-8001)
PHONE....................................614 282-3756
Trent Mcmurray, *CEO*
EMP: 6 EST: 2012
SALES (est): 203.54K **Privately Held**
Web: www.echocardreader.com
SIC: 7372 7389 Business oriented computer software; Business services, nec

(G-11294)
EVOQUA WATER TECHNOLOGIES LLC

Also Called: US Filter
1154 Hill Rd N (43147-8876)
PHONE....................................614 861-5440
Tim Swansonsn, *Mgr*
EMP: 6
Web: www.evoqua.com
SIC: 3569 Filters
HQ: Evoqua Water Technologies Llc
210 6th Ave Ste 3300
Pittsburgh PA 15222
724 772-0044

(G-11295)
LOVE YUEH LLC
9126 Calverton Ter (43147-8178)
PHONE....................................614 408-8677
Erica King, *Managing Member*
EMP: 7
SALES (est): 242.16K **Privately Held**
SIC: 3942 7389 Clothing, doll; Business services, nec

(G-11296)
MIRION TECHNOLOGIES IST CORP
12954 Stonecreek Dr Ste C (43147-8840)
PHONE....................................614 367-2050
Daniel Messer, *Brnch Mgr*
EMP: 85
SALES (corp-wide): 860.8MM **Publicly Held**
SIC: 3559 Kilns
HQ: Mirion Technologies (Ist) Corporation
315 Dniel Zenker Dr # 204
Horseheads NY 14845
607 562-4300

(G-11297)
PRECISION CNC
192 Fox Glen Dr E (43147-7896)
PHONE....................................614 496-1048
EMP: 6 EST: 2018
SALES (est): 44.06K **Privately Held**
Web: www.proficientmachining.com
SIC: 3599 Machine shop, jobbing and repair

(G-11298)
R G BARRY CORPORATION
Also Called: Dearfoams Div
13405 Yarmouth Dr (43147-8493)
PHONE....................................212 244-3145
Howard Eisenberg, *Mgr*
EMP: 10
SALES (corp-wide): 144.54MM **Privately Held**
Web: www.rgbarry.com
SIC: 3142 House slippers
HQ: R. G. Barry Corporation
13405 Yarmouth Dr
Pickerington OH 43147
614 864-6400

(G-11299)
READY 2 RIDE TRNSP LLC
12435 Thoroughbred Dr (43147-8343)
PHONE....................................614 207-2683
Latarsha Bratton, *Pr*
Latarsha Pritchard, *Managing Member*
EMP: 9 EST: 2019
SALES (est): 575.1K **Privately Held**
SIC: 3743 Freight cars and equipment

(G-11300)
RJM STAMPING CO
9151 Cotswold Dr (43147-9335)
PHONE....................................614 443-1191
Laura L Lloyd, *Pr*
Floyd Lloyd, *VP*
EMP: 12 EST: 1983
SALES (est): 1MM **Privately Held**
Web: www.rjmstamping.com

▲ = Import ▼ = Export
◆ = Import/Export

SIC: 3469 Stamping metal for the trade

(G-11301)
SWEET PERSUASIONS LLC
9636 Circle Dr (43147-9650)
PHONE..................................614 216-9052
Melissa Lewis, *Prin*
EMP: 8 **EST:** 2010
SALES (est): 376.92K Privately Held
SIC: 2051 Bakery: wholesale or wholesale/
retail combined

(G-11302)
VAN DYKE CUSTOM IRON INC
700 Janice Ln (43147-2034)
PHONE..................................614 860-9300
John Van Dyke, *Pr*
Darrell Van Dyke, *VP*
Michael Van Dyke, *VP Opers*
EMP: 6 **EST:** 1970
SALES (est): 247.61K Privately Held
SIC: 1521 3446 General remodeling, single-
family houses; Architectural metalwork

Pierpont
Ashtabula County

(G-11303)
**A W TAYLOR LUMBER
INCORPORATED**
1114 State Route 7 S (44082-9643)
PHONE..................................440 577-1889
Allen Taylor, *Pr*
Maryjo Taylor, *Prin*
Angela Taylor, *VP*
EMP: 7 **EST:** 1983
SALES (est): 883K Privately Held
Web: www.robertsfabrication.com
SIC: 2448 Pallets, wood

(G-11304)
COMPLETE ENERGY SERVICES INC
7338 Us Route 6 (44082-9725)
PHONE..................................440 577-1070
Gary Lauer, *Pt*
EMP: 14 **EST:** 2012
SALES (est): 4.04MM Privately Held
Web: www.cesinc.com
SIC: 1389 Oil field services, nec

(G-11305)
COMPLETE ENERGY SERVICES
7338 Us Route 6 (44082-9725)
PHONE..................................440 576-6000
David Beule, *Prin*
EMP: 12 **EST:** 2010
SALES (est): 297.46K Privately Held
SIC: 1389 Oil field services, nec

Piketon
Pike County

(G-11306)
CENTRUS ENERGY CORP
Also Called: American Centrifuge Plant
3930 Us Highway 23 Anx (45661-9113)
PHONE..................................740 897-2217
Angie Duduit, *Public Affairs Manager*
EMP: 53
SALES (corp-wide): 442MM Publicly Held
Web: www.centrusenergy.com
SIC: 1094 Uranium ore mining, nec
PA: Centrus Energy Corp.
    6901 Rockledge Dr Ste 800
    Bethesda MD 20817
    301 564-3200

(G-11307)
GLATFELTER CORPORATION
Also Called: GLATFELTER CORPORATION
200 Schuster Rd (45661-9687)
PHONE..................................740 289-5100
Robert Browm, *Brnch Mgr*
EMP: 7
SALES (corp-wide): 1.39B Publicly Held
Web: www.glatfelter.com
SIC: 2621 Paper mills
PA: Magnera Corporation
    9335 Hrris Crners Pkwy St
    Charlotte NC 28269
    866 744-7380

(G-11308)
JIM NIER CONSTRUCTION INC (PA)
Also Called: Jnc,
340 Bailey Chapel Rd (45661-9673)
PHONE..................................740 289-3925
Della Nier, *Pr*
Jim Nier, *VP*
EMP: 20 **EST:** 1984
SQ FT: 7,000
SALES (est): 1.93MM Privately Held
SIC: 1761 3444 1542 1541 Sheet metal
work, nec; Sheet metalwork; Nonresidential
construction, nec; Industrial buildings and
warehouses

(G-11309)
NO NAME LUMBER LLC
165 No Name Rd (45661-9736)
PHONE..................................740 289-3722
Marty Moore, *Prin*
EMP: 6 **EST:** 2006
SALES (est): 363.3K Privately Held
SIC: 2421 Sawmills and planing mills,
general

(G-11310)
OHIO VALLEY VENEER INC
165 No Name Rd (45661-9736)
PHONE..................................740 289-4979
EMP: 12
Web: www.ohiovalleyveneer.com
SIC: 2426 Lumber, hardwood dimension
PA: Ohio Valley Veneer, Inc.
    16523 State Route 124
    Piketon OH 45661

(G-11311)
OHIO VALLEY VENEER INC (PA)
Also Called: Ohio Valley Veneer Co
16523 State Route 124 (45661-9728)
PHONE..................................740 493-2901
Gregory P Bergethon, *Pr*
▼ **EMP:** 25 **EST:** 1990
SALES (est): 8.4MM Privately Held
Web: www.ohiovalleyveneer.com
SIC: 2426 2435 2421 Lumber, hardwood
dimension; Hardwood veneer and plywood;
Sawmills and planing mills, general

(G-11312)
OVERHEAD DOOR OF PIKE COUNTY
Also Called: Custom Hitch & Trailer
4237 Us Highway 23 (45661-9703)
PHONE..................................740 289-3925
James Nier, *Owner*
Della Nier, *Owner*
EMP: 7 **EST:** 1994
SALES (est): 865.55K Privately Held
Web: www.overheaddoorpike.com
SIC: 3442 5531 5031 1751 Garage doors,
overhead: metal; Trailer hitches, automotive
; Lumber, plywood, and millwork; Carpentry
work

(G-11313)
S&R LUMBER LLC
207 Sugar Run Rd (45661-9740)
P.O. Box 275 (45642-0275)
PHONE..................................740 352-6135
Paul Henderson, *Managing Member*
EMP: 16 **EST:** 2018
SQ FT: 1,524,600
SALES (est): 1.7MM Privately Held
SIC: 2421 Lumber: rough, sawed, or planed

(G-11314)
SYNERGY MANUFACTURING LLC
4239 Us Highway 23 (45661-9703)
PHONE..................................740 352-5933
EMP: 25 **EST:** 2016
SALES (est): 1.35MM Privately Held
SIC: 3089 Injection molding of plastics

(G-11315)
TAYLOR LUMBER WORLDWIDE INC
Also Called: Taylor Lumber
16523 State Route 124 (45661-9728)
P.O. Box 279 (45652-0279)
PHONE..................................740 259-6222
Edward Robbins, *Pr*
Greg Lute, *
Shery Spriggs, *
▼ **EMP:** 132 **EST:** 1882
SALES (est): 4.91MM Privately Held
SIC: 2421 Sawmills and planing mills,
general

(G-11316)
WOOLDRIDGE LUMBER CO
3264 Laurel Ridge Rd (45661-9620)
PHONE..................................740 289-4912
Mick Wooldridge, *Pt*
Dora Ransey, *Sec*
Mick Woodridge, *Pt*
EMP: 6 **EST:** 1971
SQ FT: 6,000
SALES (est): 248.16K Privately Held
SIC: 2421 Sawmills and planing mills,
general

Pioneer
Williams County

(G-11317)
ALTENLOH BRINCK & CO US INC
302 Clark St (43554-7902)
PHONE..................................419 737-2381
EMP: 38
SALES (corp-wide): 341.65MM Privately
Held
Web: www.spax.us
SIC: 3452 Screws, metal
HQ: Altenloh, Brinck & Co. Us, Inc.
    2105 Williams Co Rd 12c
    Bryan OH 43506

(G-11318)
ARTESIAN OF PIONEER INC (PA)
50 Industrial Ave (43554)
P.O. Box 247 (43554-0247)
PHONE..................................419 737-2352
EMP: 15 **EST:** 1960
SALES (est): 5.15MM
SALES (corp-wide): 5.15MM Privately
Held
Web: www.aopwater.com
SIC: 1629 3589 Waste water and sewage
treatment plant construction; Sewage and
water treatment equipment

(G-11319)
DONGAN ELECTRIC MFG CO
Pioneer Transformer Company
500 Cedar St (43554-7874)
PHONE..................................419 737-2304
EMP: 6
SALES (corp-wide): 6.66MM Privately
Held
Web: www.dongan.com
SIC: 3612 Machine tool transformers
PA: Dongan Electric Manufacturing Co Inc
    34760 Garfield Ave
    Fraser MI 48026
    313 567-8500

(G-11320)
FINISHING DEPARTMENT
201 Ohio St (43554-7934)
PHONE..................................419 737-3334
EMP: 11 **EST:** 2015
SALES (est): 85.9K Privately Held
Web: www.finishingdepartment.com
SIC: 3479 Coating of metals and formed
products

(G-11321)
HUDSON LEATHER LTD
Also Called: Hudson Leather Co
14700 State Route 15 (43554-9765)
PHONE..................................419 485-8531
EMP: 7 **EST:** 1994
SQ FT: 10,000
SALES (est): 168.07K Privately Held
Web: www.hudsonleather.com
SIC: 3131 5139 5661 Footwear cut stock;
Boots; Men's boots

(G-11322)
NN METAL STAMPINGS LLC (PA)
Also Called: Pennant
510 S Maple St (43554-7956)
P.O. Box 248 (43554-0248)
PHONE..................................419 737-2311
Rob Harger, *Pr*
Nelson Melillo, *
Larry Martin, *
EMP: 25 **EST:** 1976
SQ FT: 60,000
SALES (est): 4.82MM
SALES (corp-wide): 4.82MM Privately
Held
Web: www.nnmetalstampings.com
SIC: 3469 3544 3465 Electronic enclosures,
stamped or pressed metal; Special dies,
tools, jigs, and fixtures; Automotive
stampings

(G-11323)
PIONEER CUSTOM COATING LLC
255 Industrial Ave Bldg D (43554-9510)
P.O. Box 337 (43554-0337)
PHONE..................................419 737-3152
Deniss Sentle, *Managing Member*
Dennis Sentle, *Managing Member*
Merry Sentle, *Managing Member*
EMP: 9 **EST:** 2001
SQ FT: 2,400
SALES (est): 458.93K Privately Held
SIC: 3479 Coating of metals and formed
products

(G-11324)
PIONEER CUSTOM MOLDING INC
3 Kexon Dr (43554-9200)
P.O. Box 463 (43554-0463)
PHONE..................................419 737-3252
Terry Hendricks, *CEO*
David Roth, *
Bill Peterson, *
EMP: 23 **EST:** 1997
SQ FT: 22,500

SALES (est): 2.56MM **Privately Held**
SIC: **3089** Injection molding of plastics

(G-11325)
POWERS AND SONS LLC
Also Called: Pioneer Forge Div
101 Industrial Ave (43554)
P.O. Box 598 (43554-0598)
PHONE.............................419 737-2373
Jeffrey Wilson, *Brnch Mgr*
EMP: 7
Web: www.powersandsonsllc.com
SIC: **3462 3714 3463** Iron and steel forgings;
   Motor vehicle parts and accessories;
   Nonferrous forgings
HQ: Powers And Sons, Llc
   1613 Magda Dr
   Montpelier OH 43543
   419 485-3151

(G-11326)
PREMIERE CON SOLUTIONS LLC
Also Called: Con-Cure
508 Cedar St (43554-7874)
P.O. Box 157 (43554-0157)
PHONE.............................419 737-9808
Douglas C Wittler, *Managing Member*
EMP: 13 EST: 2004
SQ FT: 100,000
SALES (est): 2.1MM **Privately Held**
Web: www.concure.com
SIC: **3272** Concrete products, nec

(G-11327)
RAPID MACHINE INC
610 N State St (43554-9506)
P.O. Box 365 (43554-0365)
PHONE.............................419 737-2377
Jim F Spangler, *Pr*
Jennifer Wines, *Sec*
EMP: 12 EST: 1978
SQ FT: 10,000
SALES (est): 1.01MM **Privately Held**
Web: www.rapidmachineinc.com
SIC: **3544 3541 3469 3444** Special dies,
   tools, jigs, and fixtures; Grinding, polishing,
   buffing, lapping, and honing machines;
   Metal stampings, nec; Sheet metalwork

(G-11328)
REIFEL INDUSTRIES INC
201 Ohio St (43554-7934)
P.O. Box 909 (43554-0909)
PHONE.............................419 737-2138
Thomas Reifel, *Pr*
M Kathleen Reifel, *
Louis Reifel, *
▲ EMP: 65 EST: 1984
SQ FT: 60,000
SALES (est): 9.89MM **Privately Held**
Web: www.reifel.com
SIC: **3479 3471** Coating of metals and
   formed products; Plating and polishing

(G-11329)
RELIABLE METAL BUILDINGS LLC
16570 Us Highway 20ns (43554-9614)
PHONE.............................419 737-1300
EMP: 6 EST: 2017
SALES (est): 3.23MM **Privately Held**
Web: www.reliablemetalbuildingsllc.com
SIC: **3448** Prefabricated metal buildings and
   components

(G-11330)
TOLEDO TOOL AND DIE CO INC
2 Kexon Dr (43554-9200)
PHONE.............................419 476-9066
EMP: 11
SALES (corp-wide): 42.17MM **Privately
Held**

Web: www.toledotool.com
SIC: **3544** Special dies and tools
PA: Toledo Tool And Die Company, Inc.
   105 W Alexis Rd
   Toledo OH 43612
   419 476-4422

(G-11331)
UNIVERSAL INDUSTRIAL PDTS INC
1 Coreway Dr (43554)
P.O. Box 628 (43554-0628)
PHONE.............................419 737-9584
Neil Marko, *Pr*
Randy Herriman, *Treas*
▲ EMP: 18 EST: 1947
SQ FT: 86,000
SALES (est): 7.22MM **Privately Held**
Web:
www.universalindustrialproducts.com
SIC: **3429** Hardware, nec

Piqua
Miami County

(G-11332)
AESTHETIC FINISHERS INC
1502 S Main St (45356-8319)
PHONE.............................937 778-8777
Sally Coomer, *CEO*
William Coomer Iii, *VP*
EMP: 35 EST: 1992
SQ FT: 72,000
SALES (est): 3.12MM **Privately Held**
Web: www.afipowder.com
SIC: **3479** Coating of metals and formed
   products

(G-11333)
ALLIED COATING CORPORATION
220 Fox Dr (45356-9271)
PHONE.............................937 615-0391
Greg Flanary, *Pr*
Karen Flanary, *VP*
EMP: 10 EST: 1994
SALES (est): 824.23K **Privately Held**
Web: www.alliedcoating.net
SIC: **3479** Coating of metals and formed
   products

(G-11334)
APEX ALUMINUM DIE CAST CO INC
8877 Sherry Dr (45356-9111)
P.O. Box 617 (45356-0617)
PHONE.............................937 773-0432
EMP: 50 EST: 1980
SALES (est): 9.31MM **Privately Held**
Web: www.apexdiecasting.com
SIC: **3363 3369** Aluminum die-castings;
   Nonferrous foundries, nec

(G-11335)
ATLANTIC WELDING LLC
1708 Commerce Dr (45356-2602)
PHONE.............................937 570-5094
Zachary Walker, *Managing Member*
EMP: 11 EST: 2021
SALES (est): 2.4MM **Privately Held**
Web: www.atlanticweldingservices.com
SIC: **1629 3317 1791 1541** Oil refinery
   construction; Welded pipe and tubes;
   Structural steel erection; Industrial buildings
   and warehouses

(G-11336)
ATLANTIS SPORTSWEAR INC
Also Called: College Issue
344 Fox Dr (45356-8298)
PHONE.............................937 773-0680
David Scott Reardon, *

David Scott Reardon, *
Gail Reardon, *
▲ EMP: 35 EST: 1985
SQ FT: 65,000
SALES (est): 4.35MM **Privately Held**
Web: www.atlantissports.com
SIC: **2261 2395 2396** Screen printing of
   cotton broadwoven fabrics; Emblems,
   embroidered; Automotive and apparel
   trimmings

(G-11337)
BORNHORST MOTOR SERVICE INC
Also Called: Electric Motor Service
8270 N Dixie Dr (45356-8636)
P.O. Box 110 (45356-0110)
PHONE.............................937 773-0426
Regina Owen, *Pr*
EMP: 8 EST: 1955
SQ FT: 6,000
SALES (est): 464.01K **Privately Held**
SIC: **7694 5063** Electric motor repair;
   Motors, electric

(G-11338)
C A P INDUSTRIES INC
Also Called: Custom Aerosol Packaging
543 Staunton St (45356-3947)
P.O. Box 1411 (45356-1011)
PHONE.............................937 773-1824
Robert A Heckman, *Pr*
Eric Heckman, *VP*
Mary Heckman, *Sec*
▲ EMP: 17 EST: 1969
SQ FT: 33,000
SALES (est): 981.41K **Privately Held**
SIC: **7389 2813 5198** Packaging and
   labeling services; Aerosols; Paints

(G-11339)
CRANE PUMPS & SYSTEMS INC
Also Called: Crane Pumps & Systems, Inc.
1950 Covington Ave (45356-2636)
PHONE.............................937 778-8947
Roy Speigle, *Brnch Mgr*
EMP: 28
SALES (corp-wide): 2.13B **Publicly Held**
Web: www.cranepumps.com
SIC: **3561** Pumps, domestic: water or sump
HQ: Crane Pumps & Systems, Llc
   420 3rd St
   Piqua OH 45356
   937 773-2442

(G-11340)
CRANE PUMPS & SYSTEMS INC
Also Called: Pacific Valve
420 3rd St (45356-3918)
PHONE.............................937 773-2442
Allan Oak, *Brnch Mgr*
EMP: 17
SALES (corp-wide): 2.13B **Publicly Held**
Web: www.cranepumps.com
SIC: **5085 3494** Valves and fittings; Valves
   and pipe fittings, nec
HQ: Crane Pumps & Systems, Llc
   420 3rd St
   Piqua OH 45356
   937 773-2442

(G-11341)
CRANE PUMPS & SYSTEMS LLC
(HQ)
420 3rd St (45356-3918)
PHONE.............................937 773-2442
Jim Lavish, *Pr*
◆ EMP: 20 EST: 1982
SQ FT: 120,000
SALES (est): 24.02MM
SALES (corp-wide): 2.13B **Publicly Held**
Web: www.cranepumps.com

SIC: **3561** Industrial pumps and parts
PA: Crane Company
   100 1st Stmford Pl Ste 40
   Stamford CT 06902
   203 363-7300

(G-11342)
CRAYEX CORPORATION (PA)
1747 Commerce Dr (45356-2601)
P.O. Box 1673 (45356-4673)
PHONE.............................937 773-7000
▼ EMP: 65 EST: 1972
SALES (est): 19.86MM
SALES (corp-wide): 19.86MM **Privately
Held**
Web: www.crayex.com
SIC: **2671 2673 3081** Plastic film, coated or
   laminated for packaging; Plastic bags:
   made from purchased materials;
   Unsupported plastics film and sheet

(G-11343)
DARKE PRECISION INC
291 Fox Dr (45356-9265)
P.O. Box 746 (45331-0746)
PHONE.............................937 548-2232
Harold Young, *Pr*
Randy Young, *Sec*
Roger Young, *Prin*
EMP: 7 EST: 1984
SQ FT: 4,800
SALES (est): 826.13K **Privately Held**
SIC: **3544** Special dies and tools

(G-11344)
DENIZEN INC
130 Fox Dr (45356-9269)
PHONE.............................937 615-9561
John H Reynolds, *Pr*
◆ EMP: 12 EST: 1996
SQ FT: 21,000
SALES (est): 5.18MM **Privately Held**
Web: www.denizeninc.com
SIC: **2241 5033** Electric insulating tapes and
   braids, except plastic; Insulation materials

(G-11345)
DYNA-VAC PLASTICS INC
921 S Downing St (45356-3823)
P.O. Box 614 (45356-0614)
PHONE.............................937 773-0092
Scott Lade, *Pr*
Richard Lade, *Prin*
Sandra Lade, *Sec*
EMP: 6 EST: 1985
SQ FT: 18,000
SALES (est): 594K **Privately Held**
SIC: **3089** Injection molding of plastics

(G-11346)
EPSILYTE HOLDINGS LLC
Also Called: Compounded Eps
555 E Statler Rd (45356-9227)
PHONE.............................937 778-9500
Matt Cox, *Brnch Mgr*
EMP: 75
SALES (corp-wide): 5.45MM **Privately
Held**
Web: www.epsilyte.com
SIC: **2821 5162** Polystyrene resins; Resins
PA: Epsilyte Holdings Llc
   1330 Lake Robbins Dr # 310
   The Woodlands TX 77380
   815 224-1525

(G-11347)
FORREST ENTERPRISES INC
Also Called: Forre Sports Accessories
510 W Statler Rd (45356-8281)
P.O. Box 244 (45356-0244)
PHONE.............................937 773-1714

James C Reynolds, *Pr*
Staton C Reynolds, *Pr*
Curtis Reynolds, *Treas*
▲ **EMP:** 11 **EST:** 1955
SQ FT: 6,500
SALES (est): 1.22MM **Privately Held**
Web: www.4sportsus.com
SIC: 4783 3949 3089 Packing and crating; Sporting and athletic goods, nec; Blister or bubble formed packaging, plastics

(G-11348)
HAMPSHIRE CO
9225 State Route 66 (45356-8700)
P.O. Box 1195 (45356-1195)
PHONE..............................937 773-3493
Thomas F Hampshire, *Pr*
Robert Mikolajewski, *
Dorothy M Hampshire, *
EMP: 11 **EST:** 1957
SQ FT: 50,000
SALES (est): 1.11MM **Privately Held**
Web: www.hampshirecabinetry.com
SIC: 2434 Vanities, bathroom: wood

(G-11349)
HARMONY SYSTEMS AND SVC INC
1711 Commerce Dr (45356-2601)
PHONE..............................937 778-1082
Edward Adams, *CEO*
Nellie Adams, *
Hugh Wall, *
▲ **EMP:** 70 **EST:** 1994
SQ FT: 110,000
SALES (est): 9.98MM **Privately Held**
Web: www.harmonysysandsvc.com
SIC: 3089 Injection molding of plastics

(G-11350)
HARTZELL FAN INC (PA)
910 S Downing St (45356-3824)
PHONE..............................937 773-7411
James Robert Hartzell, *Ch Bd*
Jeff Bannister Hartzell, *CEO*
George Atkinson, *Pr*
Thomas Gustafson, *VP*
Jane Farley, *Sec*
◆ **EMP:** 145 **EST:** 1927
SQ FT: 196,000
SALES (est): 23.92MM
SALES (corp-wide): 23.92MM **Privately Held**
Web: www.hartzellairmovement.com
SIC: 3564 3433 Blowers and fans; Heating equipment, except electric

(G-11351)
HARTZELL HARDWOODS INC (PA)
1025 S Roosevelt Ave (45356-3713)
P.O. Box 919 (45356-0919)
PHONE..............................937 773-7054
James Robert Hartzell, *Ch Bd*
Jeffery Bannister, *
Kelly Hostetter, *
Jane Osborn, *
▼ **EMP:** 65 **EST:** 1928
SQ FT: 275,000
SALES (est): 20.89MM
SALES (corp-wide): 20.89MM **Privately Held**
Web: www.hartzellhardwoods.com
SIC: 5031 2421 2426 Lumber: rough, dressed, and finished; Sawmills and planing mills, general; Hardwood dimension and flooring mills

(G-11352)
HARTZELL INDUSTRIES INC (PA)
1025 S Roosevelt Ave (45356-3713)
P.O. Box 919 (45356-0919)
PHONE..............................937 773-6295

James Robert Hartzell, *Ch Bd*
Jeff Bannister, *CEO*
Chris Oliss, *CFO*
Michael Bardo, *Pr*
Jane Farley, *Sec*
EMP: 13 **EST:** 1964
SQ FT: 20,000
SALES (est): 11.08MM
SALES (corp-wide): 11.08MM **Privately Held**
Web: www.hartzellairmovement.com
SIC: 2435 6719 Veneer stock, hardwood; Personal holding companies, except banks

(G-11353)
HARTZELL PROPELLER INC (HQ)
Also Called: Whirlwind Propellers
1 Propeller Pl (45356-2656)
PHONE..............................937 778-4200
Joseph Brown, *Pr*
James Brown Iii, *Prin*
Jj Frigge, *
Bruce C Hanke, *
Robert G Allenbaugh, *
◆ **EMP:** 250 **EST:** 1987
SQ FT: 175,000
SALES (est): 31.59MM
SALES (corp-wide): 1.27B **Privately Held**
Web: www.hartzellprop.com
SIC: 3728 Aircraft propellers and associated equipment
PA: Arcline Investment Management Lp
4 Embrcadero Ctr Ste 3460
San Francisco CA 94111
415 801-4570

(G-11354)
HOBART BROTHERS LLC
8585 Industry Park Dr (45356-9511)
PHONE..............................937 332-5953
Jim Schwepeji, *Prin*
EMP: 147
SALES (corp-wide): 16.11B **Publicly Held**
Web: www.hobartbrothers.com
SIC: 3548 Welding apparatus
HQ: Hobart Brothers Llc
101 Trade Sq E
Troy OH 45373
937 332-5439

(G-11355)
HOBART LLC
Also Called: P M I Food Equipment Group
8616 Industry Park Dr (45356-0611)
P.O. Box 702 (45356-0702)
PHONE..............................937 332-2797
Dean Ramaeker, *Mgr*
EMP: 59
SALES (corp-wide): 16.11B **Publicly Held**
Web: www.hobartcorp.com
SIC: 3589 3556 3596 3585 Dishwashing machines, commercial; Food products machinery; Weighing machines and apparatus; Refrigeration equipment, complete
HQ: Hobart Llc
701 S Ridge Ave
Troy OH 45373

(G-11356)
INDUSTRY PRODUCTS CO (PA)
500 W Statler Rd (45356-8281)
PHONE..............................937 778-0585
Linda Cleveland, *Pr*
▲ **EMP:** 366 **EST:** 1966
SQ FT: 335,000
SALES (est): 19.81MM
SALES (corp-wide): 19.81MM **Privately Held**
Web: www.industryproductsco.com

SIC: 7692 3053 3714 3544 Automotive welding; Gaskets, all materials; Motor vehicle parts and accessories; Special dies, tools, jigs, and fixtures

(G-11357)
ISAIAH INDUSTRIES INC
9234 Country Club Rd (45356-9513)
PHONE..............................937 778-2246
Donald E Miller, *Brnch Mgr*
EMP: 8
SALES (corp-wide): 4.71MM **Privately Held**
Web: www.isaiahindustries.com
SIC: 3354 Aluminum extruded products
PA: Isaiah Industries, Inc.
8510 Industry Park Dr
Piqua OH 45356
937 773-9840

(G-11358)
ISAIAH INDUSTRIES INC (PA)
Also Called: Classic Metal Roofing Systems
8510 Industry Park Dr (45356-8535)
P.O. Box 701 (45356-0701)
PHONE..............................937 773-9840
Todd Miller, *CEO*
◆ **EMP:** 49 **EST:** 1980
SQ FT: 5,000
SALES (est): 4.71MM
SALES (corp-wide): 4.71MM **Privately Held**
Web: www.isaiahindustries.com
SIC: 3354 3444 2952 Aluminum extruded products; Sheet metalwork; Asphalt felts and coatings

(G-11359)
J & D WOOD LTD
Also Called: J&D Wood Enterprises
401 S College St (45356-3429)
PHONE..............................937 778-9663
Joe A Kinsella, *Pr*
Douglas Kinsella, *VP*
EMP: 7 **EST:** 1982
SQ FT: 12,000
SALES (est): 120.19K **Privately Held**
Web: www.qualitypinebedding.com
SIC: 2499 Trophy bases, wood

(G-11360)
J M MOLD INC
1707 Commerce Dr (45356-2601)
PHONE..............................937 778-0011
Kriss Scheer, *Pr*
Robert P Scheer, *Pr*
EMP: 8 **EST:** 1966
SQ FT: 9,600
SALES (est): 359.34K **Privately Held**
Web: www.jmmoldinc.com
SIC: 3544 Industrial molds

(G-11361)
JACKSON TUBE SERVICE INC (PA)
8210 Industry Park Dr (45356-8536)
P.O. Box 1650 (45356-4650)
PHONE..............................937 773-8550
Robert W Jackson, *CEO*
Marcus Sergy, *
▲ **EMP:** 127 **EST:** 1972
SQ FT: 75,000
SALES (est): 22.55MM
SALES (corp-wide): 22.55MM **Privately Held**
Web: www.446design.com
SIC: 3317 Steel pipe and tubes

(G-11362)
K B MACHINE & TOOL INC
1500 S Main St (45356-8319)
P.O. Box 426 (45356-0426)

PHONE..............................937 773-1624
Kenneth G Bricker, *Pr*
Joyce K Bricker, *Sec*
Miki Bricker, *VP*
EMP: 9 **EST:** 1972
SQ FT: 9,500
SALES (est): 931.33K **Privately Held**
SIC: 3544 Special dies and tools

(G-11363)
LITTLE PRINTING COMPANY
Also Called: Quality Forms
4317 W Us Route 36 (45356-9334)
P.O. Box 1176 (45356-1176)
PHONE..............................937 773-4595
Tom Kinnison, *Pr*
L J Bertke, *VP*
EMP: 7 **EST:** 1953
SQ FT: 54,000
SALES (est): 590.88K **Privately Held**
Web: www.qualforms.com
SIC: 2752 Offset printing

(G-11364)
MAKERS SUPPLY LLC
6665 N Spiker Rd (45356-9333)
PHONE..............................937 203-8245
Garrett Burgoon, *Managing Member*
EMP: 6 **EST:** 2021
SALES (est): 1.52MM **Privately Held**
Web: www.makerssply.com
SIC: 5093 2448 Scrap and waste materials; Wood pallets and skids

(G-11365)
MARK KNUPP MUFFLER & TIRE INC
950 S College St (45356-3700)
PHONE..............................937 773-1334
Mark Knupp, *Pr*
Rosemary Knupp, *Sec*
EMP: 7 **EST:** 1987
SQ FT: 9,000
SALES (est): 588.43K **Privately Held**
Web: www.markknupp.com
SIC: 5531 7533 7534 7539 Automotive parts ; Muffler shop, sale or repair and installation ; Tire repair shop; Brake repair, automotive

(G-11366)
MIAMI SPECIALTIES INC
Also Called: M C D Plastics & Manufacturing
172 Robert M Davis Pkwy (45356-8338)
PHONE..............................937 778-1850
Joann Howell, *Pr*
Robb Howell Iii, *VP*
EMP: 7 **EST:** 1993
SQ FT: 10,000
SALES (est): 869.12K **Privately Held**
Web: www.mcdplastics.com
SIC: 3089 Injection molding of plastics

(G-11367)
NICKS PLATING CO
6980 Free Rd (45356-9279)
P.O. Box 337 (45356-0337)
PHONE..............................937 773-3175
Duane Penrod, *Pr*
EMP: 10 **EST:** 1973
SQ FT: 4,500
SALES (est): 476.68K **Privately Held**
Web: www.nicksplating.com
SIC: 3471 Electroplating of metals or formed products

(G-11368)
NITTO INC
220 Fox Dr (45356-9271)
PHONE..............................937 773-4820
EMP: 87
Web: www.nitto.com

SIC: 3714 Motor vehicle parts and accessories
HQ: Nitto, Inc.
400 Frank W Burr Blvd Ste
Teaneck NJ 07666
732 901-7905

(G-11369)
NITTO INC
1620 S Main St (45356-8320)
PHONE..................................937 773-4820
▲ EMP: 118
Web: www.nitto.com
SIC: 3714 Motor vehicle parts and accessories
HQ: Nitto, Inc.
400 Frank W Burr Blvd Ste
Teaneck NJ 07666
732 901-7905

(G-11370)
P & R SPECIALTY INC
1835 W High St (45356-9399)
P.O. Box 741 (45356-0741)
PHONE..................................937 773-0263
Greg Blankenship, Pr
Pat Kiernan, *
Alissa Blankenship, *
Mike Koon, *
Vincent Reidy, *
▲ EMP: 35 EST: 1982
SQ FT: 47,500
SALES (est): 8.38MM Privately Held
Web: www.prspecialty.com
SIC: 2499 3053 2675 2631 Spools, wood; Gaskets, all materials; Paper die-cutting; Paperboard mills

(G-11371)
PALSTAR INC
9676 Looney Rd (45356-8800)
P.O. Box 1136 (45356-1136)
PHONE..................................937 773-6255
Paul Hrivnak, Pr
Donald Keffler, VP
Eva Hrivnak, Treas
EMP: 16 EST: 1985
SQ FT: 4,000
SALES (est): 2.3MM Privately Held
Web: www.palstar.com
SIC: 3825 Signal generators and averagers

(G-11372)
PERFECTO INDUSTRIES INC
1729 W High St (45356-9300)
PHONE..................................937 778-1900
Harvey Howard, Brnch Mgr
EMP: 45
SALES (corp-wide): 12.96MM Privately Held
Web: www.perfectoindustries.com
SIC: 3547 3549 3599 3537 Rolling mill machinery; Coiling machinery; Custom machinery; Industrial trucks and tractors
PA: Perfecto Industries, Inc.
1567 Calkins Dr
Gaylord MI 49735
989 732-2941

(G-11373)
PIQUA CHAMPION FOUNDRY INC
Also Called: Piqua
918 S Main St (45356-3858)
P.O. Box 716 (45356-0716)
EMP: 6 EST: 1974
SQ FT: 35,000
SALES (est): 825.01K Privately Held
Web: www.piquadreamchasers.com
SIC: 3321 Gray iron castings, nec

(G-11374)
PIQUA CHOCOLATE COMPANY INC (PA)
Also Called: Winans Chocolate and Coffee
310 Spring St (45356-2334)
PHONE..................................937 773-1981
Joe Reiser, Pr
EMP: 9 EST: 1993
SQ FT: 2,000
SALES (est): 5.28MM
SALES (corp-wide): 5.28MM Privately Held
Web: www.winanschocolate.com
SIC: 5441 5947 2064 Candy; Greeting cards ; Candy and other confectionery products

(G-11375)
PIQUA EMERY CUTTER & FNDRY CO
Also Called: Piqua Emery Foundry
821 S Downing St (45356-3821)
PHONE..................................937 773-4134
Stephen Mikolajewski, Pr
Helen Mikolajewski, *
Roger Mclain, VP
EMP: 54 EST: 1934
SQ FT: 54,000
SALES (est): 1.66MM Privately Held
Web: www.piquaemery.com
SIC: 3365 3369 3366 Aluminum and aluminum-based alloy castings; Nonferrous foundries, nec; Castings (except die), nec, bronze

(G-11376)
PIQUA GRANITE & MARBLE CO INC (PA)
Also Called: Classic Monuments
123 N Main St (45356-2311)
PHONE..................................937 773-2000
TOLL FREE: 800
Pat Obara, Pr
Steve Supinger, VP
EMP: 9 EST: 1882
SQ FT: 18,000
SALES (est): 211.67K
SALES (corp-wide): 211.67K Privately Held
Web: www.classicmonuments.com
SIC: 5999 5032 3281 Monuments, finished to custom order; Granite building stone; Marble, building: cut and shaped

(G-11377)
PIQUA MATERIALS INC
Also Called: Piqua Mineral Division
1750 W Statler Rd (45356-9264)
PHONE..................................937 773-4824
John Harris, Brnch Mgr
EMP: 79
SQ FT: 16,808
Web: www.piquamaterials.com
SIC: 1422 3274 Limestones, ground; Lime
PA: Piqua Materials, Inc.
11641 Mosteller Rd Ste 1
Cincinnati OH 45241

(G-11378)
PIQUA PAPER BOX COMPANY
616 Covington Ave (45356-3205)
P.O. Box 814 (45356-0814)
PHONE..................................937 773-0313
TOLL FREE: 800
Brian T Gleason, Pr
Frank J Gleason Junior, Ch Bd
Eugene Elsass, *
▲ EMP: 35 EST: 1908
SQ FT: 85,000
SALES (est): 2.28MM Privately Held
Web: www.piquapaperbox.com
SIC: 2653 Boxes, corrugated: made from purchased materials

(G-11379)
POLYSOURCE LLC
Also Called: Epsilyte
555 E Statler Rd (45356-9227)
PHONE..................................937 778-9500
David Shainberg, Pr
EMP: 26 EST: 2021
SALES (est): 8.53MM Privately Held
Web: www.polysource.net
SIC: 3089 Injection molding of plastics

(G-11380)
PROTO-MOLD PRODUCTS CO INC
1750 Commerce Dr (45356-2699)
PHONE..................................937 778-1959
Graig Flintcraft, Pr
Craig Flitcraft, *
EMP: 25 EST: 1979
SQ FT: 50,000
SALES (est): 1.42MM Privately Held
Web: www.protomoldproducts.com
SIC: 3089 Injection molding of plastics

(G-11381)
QUEEN EXHIBITS LLC
1707 Commerce Dr (45356-2601)
PHONE..................................937 615-6051
Walter Foster Queen, Prin
EMP: 8 EST: 2019
SALES (est): 589.15K Privately Held
Web: www.queenexhibits.com
SIC: 3993 Signs and advertising specialties

(G-11382)
RETTERBUSH FIBERGLASS CORP
719 Long St (45356-9262)
P.O. Box 207 (45356-0207)
PHONE..................................937 778-1936
Bryan Retterbush, Pr
EMP: 25 EST: 1976
SQ FT: 32,000
SALES (est): 2.18MM Privately Held
Web: www.retterbushfiberglass.com
SIC: 3089 Injection molding of plastics

(G-11383)
RV XPRESS INC
501 East St (45356-3930)
PHONE..................................937 418-0127
Michael T Mcgahan, Prin
Glenn Mckinney, Pr
EMP: 8 EST: 2007
SALES (est): 424.46K Privately Held
SIC: 3799 Recreational vehicles

(G-11384)
SKULD LLC
918 S Main St (45356-3858)
P.O. Box 973 (45501-0973)
PHONE..................................330 423-7339
Sarah Jordan, CEO
Sarah Jordan, Mgr
EMP: 20 EST: 2015
SALES (est): 2.83MM Privately Held
Web: www.skuldllc.com
SIC: 3321 3365 3812 3559 Gray and ductile iron foundries; Aluminum foundries; Defense systems and equipment; Foundry machinery and equipment

(G-11385)
SMYRNA READY MIX CONCRETE LLC
Also Called: Srm Concrete
8395 Piqua Lockington Rd (45356-9701)
PHONE..................................937 773-0841
Dick Hoying, Brnch Mgr
EMP: 77
SALES (corp-wide): 513.05MM Privately Held

Web: www.smyrnareadymix.com
SIC: 3273 Ready-mixed concrete
PA: Smyrna Ready Mix Concrete, Llc
1000 Hollingshead Cir
Murfreesboro TN 37129
615 355-1028

(G-11386)
TAILWIND TECHNOLOGIES INC (PA)
1 Propeller Pl (45356-2655)
PHONE..................................937 778-4200
James W Brown Iii, Pr
Matthew L Jesch, CFO
Joseph W Brown, Prin
Michael J Piscatella, Prin
EMP: 569 EST: 1988
SALES (est): 61.26MM Privately Held
Web: www.tailwindtechnologiesinc.com
SIC: 3356 Titanium

(G-11387)
TEMPO MANUFACTURING COMPANY
Also Called: Tempo Trophy Mfg
727 E Ash St (45356-2411)
P.O. Box 718 (45356-0718)
PHONE..................................937 773-6613
Robert Elrod, Pr
Patricia Elrod, VP
EMP: 8 EST: 1946
SQ FT: 30,000
SALES (est): 323.61K Privately Held
SIC: 3914 Trophies, nsk

(G-11388)
US KONDO CORPORATION
233 1st St (45356-4005)
PHONE..................................937 916-3045
Koshin Shimasaki, Pr
▲ EMP: 12 EST: 2009
SALES (est): 1.03MM Privately Held
Web: www.uskondo.com
SIC: 3714 Motor vehicle parts and accessories

Plain City
Madison County

(G-11389)
44TOOLSCOM
7640 Commerce Pl (43064-9222)
PHONE..................................614 873-4800
George R Lewis, Prin
EMP: 7 EST: 2011
SALES (est): 1.4MM Privately Held
Web: www.44tools.com
SIC: 3861 Motion picture film

(G-11390)
ACTIVE AERATION SYSTEMS INC
7245 Industrial Pkwy (43064-9487)
PHONE..................................614 873-3626
Deborah Wade, CEO
John Graves, Pr
Patty Hoke, VP
EMP: 6 EST: 1985
SALES (est): 735.85K Privately Held
SIC: 5046 5039 3589 Commercial equipment, nec; Septic tanks; Sewage treatment equipment

(G-11391)
ADVANCED GAUGING TECH LLC
Also Called: Intense Enterprises
8430 Estates Ct (43064-8015)
PHONE..................................936 443-7129
Scott Cook, Pr
EMP: 11 EST: 1997
SALES (est): 2.14MM Privately Held
Web: www.advgauging.com

SIC: 3829 Physical property testing equipment

(G-11392)
ADVANCED GREEN TECH INC
8059 Corporate Blvd Ste A (43064-8070)
PHONE...................614 397-8130
Christopher Brossia, *VP*
EMP: 6 EST: 2012
SALES (est): 210K **Privately Held**
SIC: 8999 3589 2096 5084 Scientific consulting; Water treatment equipment, industrial; Potato chips and other potato-based snacks; Pulp (wood) manufacturing machinery

(G-11393)
ALTRASERV LLC
Also Called: Brio Coffee Co
8495 Estates Ct (43064-8083)
P.O. Box 355 (43017-0355)
PHONE...................614 889-2500
Dorothy Moran, *Pr*
Tom Moran, *VP*
EMP: 6 EST: 2008
SALES (est): 622.86K **Privately Held**
Web: www.altraserv.com
SIC: 2095 Roasted coffee

(G-11394)
APPLIED EXPERIENCE LLC
7780 Corporate Blvd Ste 82 (43064-3598)
P.O. Box 61 (43017-0061)
PHONE...................614 943-2970
Matthew Schrader, *Prin*
George Catlin, *Prin*
Christopher Brandon, *Prin*
Kedar Kapoor, *Prin*
Michael Krull, *Prin*
EMP: 7 EST: 2015
SALES (est): 477.1K **Privately Held**
Web: www.appliedxp.com
SIC: 7389 7373 8711 3599 Drafting service, except temporary help; Computer integrated systems design; Engineering services; Machine and other job shop work

(G-11395)
AUTOTOOL INC
7875 Corporate Blvd (43064-8045)
PHONE...................614 733-0222
Bassam Homsi, *Pr*
EMP: 38 EST: 1994
0Q FT: 40,000
SALES (est): 11.9MM **Privately Held**
Web: www.autotoolinc.com
SIC: 3559 Automotive related machinery

(G-11396)
BAHLER MEDICAL INC
Also Called: Venture Medical
8910 Warner Rd (43064-9467)
PHONE...................614 873-7600
Michael Bahler, *Pr*
EMP: 6 EST: 1987
SALES (est): 2.43MM **Privately Held**
SIC: 3842 Implants, surgical

(G-11397)
BEACHY BARNS LTD
8720 Amish Pike (43064-9538)
PHONE...................614 873-4193
TOLL FREE: 800
EMP: 12 EST: 1981
SQ FT: 7,500
SALES (est): 941.72K **Privately Held**
Web: www.beachybarns.com
SIC: 2452 1542 Prefabricated wood buildings; Garage construction

(G-11398)
BINDERY & SPC PRESSWORKS INC
Also Called: Pressworks
351 W Bigelow Ave (43064-1152)
PHONE...................614 873-4623
Dick Izzard, *Pr*
Betty Izzard, *
Mark Izzard, *
Doug Izzard, *
Tami Roberts, *
EMP: 74 EST: 1978
SQ FT: 42,000
SALES (est): 9.62MM **Privately Held**
Web: www.pressworks.us
SIC: 2791 7331 2759 2789 Typesetting; Mailing service; Commercial printing, nec; Bookbinding and related work

(G-11399)
BROOKS PASTRIES INC
8205 Estates Pkwy Ste F (43064-8018)
PHONE...................614 274-4880
Donald Wess Senior, *Pr*
Margret Wess, *VP*
EMP: 8
SALES (est): 221.06K **Privately Held**
SIC: 2051 5461 Bread, all types (white, wheat, rye, etc); fresh or frozen; Bread

(G-11400)
BUILDING BLOCK PERFORMANCE LLC
7920 Corporate Blvd Ste C (43064-9275)
PHONE...................614 918-7476
Kamyron A White, *Managing Member*
EMP: 6 EST: 2014
SALES (est): 125.21K **Privately Held**
SIC: 7999 7372 Physical fitness instruction; Application computer software

(G-11401)
COM-FAB INC
4657 Price Hilliards Rd (43064-8838)
PHONE...................740 857-1107
Jim Sheehy, *Pr*
EMP: 22 EST: 1970
SQ FT: 20,000
SALES (est): 2.65MM **Privately Held**
Web: www.comfab-inc.com
SIC: 3441 Fabricated structural metal

(G-11402)
DARBY CREEK MILLWORK LLC
10001 Plain City Georgesville Rd Ne (43064-8958)
PHONE...................614 873-3267
Ivan Beachy, *Owner*
EMP: 7 EST: 1990
SQ FT: 8,000
SALES (est): 213.76K **Privately Held**
Web: www.darbymillworks.com
SIC: 2431 Doors, wood

(G-11403)
DELAWARE PAINT COMPANY LTD
Also Called: Ohio Brush Works
8455 Rausch Dr (43064-8064)
PHONE...................740 368-9981
Pete Newton, *Pr*
Phillip Hopkins, *VP*
EMP: 15 EST: 2001
SQ FT: 12,000
SALES (est): 3.6MM **Privately Held**
Web: www.delawarepaintco.com
SIC: 3991 Brooms

(G-11404)
DISTINCTIVE MARBLE & GRAN INC
7635 Commerce Pl (43064-9223)
PHONE...................614 760-0003

Chris Schnetzler, *Pr*
Kathy Schnetzler, *Prin*
▲ EMP: 10 EST: 2001
SALES (est): 1.54MM **Privately Held**
Web: www.distinctivemarbleandgranite.com
SIC: 1743 3281 Marble installation, interior; Curbing, granite or stone

(G-11405)
DRIVETRAIN USA INC
Also Called: Cryogenic Technical Services
8445 Rausch Dr (43064-8064)
P.O. Box 3787 (43016-0406)
PHONE...................614 733-0940
John Canfield, *Pr*
EMP: 10 EST: 2008
SQ FT: 40,000
SALES (est): 439.42K **Privately Held**
SIC: 3679 Cryogenic cooling devices for infrared detectors, masers

(G-11406)
ECOCHEM ALTERNATIVE FUELS LLC
7304 Town St (43064-9483)
PHONE...................614 764-3835
Joshua Koch, *Pt*
Joshua Koch, *CEO*
EMP: 35 EST: 2011
SALES (est): 7.91MM **Privately Held**
Web: www.hpcdfuel.com
SIC: 2869 Fuels

(G-11407)
ELASTOSTAR RUBBER CORP
8475 Rausch Dr (43064-8064)
PHONE...................614 841-4400
Ghanshyam Dungarani, *Sls Mgr*
EMP: 20 EST: 2013
SALES (est): 2.28MM **Privately Held**
Web: www.elastostar.com
SIC: 3069 Medical and laboratory rubber sundries and related products

(G-11408)
FORGEO LLC
8260 Estates Pkwy (43064-8409)
PHONE...................614 873-7030
Gregg P Simpson, *Managing Member*
EMP: 20 EST: 1995
SQ FT: 30,000
SALES (est): 8.19MM **Privately Held**
web: www.ohiolaser.com
SIC: 3499 Welding tips, heat resistant: metal

(G-11409)
FRIESEN TRANSFER LTD
9280 Iams Rd (43064-9108)
PHONE...................614 873-5672
Klaas Friesen, *Pr*
EMP: 6 EST: 1979
SALES (est): 661.96K **Privately Held**
SIC: 3713 0115 0111 Dump truck bodies; Corn; Wheat

(G-11410)
GOLF CAR COMPANY INC
8899 Memorial Dr (43064-8636)
PHONE...................614 873-1055
William Mead, *Pr*
EMP: 6 EST: 2000
SALES (est): 656.55K **Privately Held**
Web: www.nationalcarts.com
SIC: 3949 7359 5599 Sporting and athletic goods, nec; Stores and yards equipment rental; Golf cart, powered

(G-11411)
KML ACQUISITIONS LTD
10325 Spicebrush Dr (43064-2608)
PHONE...................614 732-9777
EMP: 6 EST: 2001
SALES (est): 86.38K **Privately Held**
SIC: 2711 Commercial printing and newspaper publishing combined

(G-11412)
KNB TOOLS OF AMERICA INC
8440 Rausch Dr (43064-8047)
PHONE...................614 733-0400
Toshihiko Kawanobe, *CEO*
▲ EMP: 10 EST: 2003
SALES (est): 1.63MM **Privately Held**
Web: www.knb-tools.com
SIC: 3545 Cutting tools for machine tools

(G-11413)
KREMA GROUP INC
Also Called: Crazy Richards
8415 Rausch Dr (43064-8064)
P.O. Box 715 (43017-0815)
PHONE...................614 889-4824
Kimberly Wernli, *Pr*
Craig Sonksen, *Pr*
Joanna Carroll, *CFO*
Chris Wernli, *CEO*
Richard Sonksen, *Prin*
EMP: 10 EST: 2001
SALES (est): 2.47MM
SALES (corp-wide): 3.9MM **Privately Held**
Web: www.crazyrichards.com
SIC: 2099 Peanut butter
PA: Krema Products Inc.
45 N High St
Dublin OH 43017
614 889-4824

(G-11414)
MIDWEST RETAIL SERVICES INC
7920 Industrial Pkwy (43064-9376)
PHONE...................800 576-7577
Matthew Ray, *Pr*
EMP: 14 EST: 1994
SALES (est): 12.97MM **Privately Held**
Web: www.midwestretailservices.com
SIC: 2542 Partitions and fixtures, except wood

(G-11415)
MILLER CABINET LTD
6217 Converse Huff Rd (43064-9185)
PHONE...................614 873-4221
TOLL FREE: 800
EMP: 10 EST: 2006
SALES (est): 811.48K **Privately Held**
Web: www.millercabinets.com
SIC: 5722 2541 2521 2511 Kitchens, complete (sinks, cabinets, etc.); Cabinets, except refrigerated: show, display, etc.: wood; Wood office furniture; Wood household furniture

(G-11416)
OTP HOLDING LLC
Also Called: Pk Controls
8000 Corporate Blvd (43064-9220)
PHONE...................614 733-0979
Matthew Patel, *Brnch Mgr*
EMP: 43
SALES (corp-wide): 1.04B **Privately Held**
Web: www.otcindustrial.com
SIC: 3625 Relays and industrial controls
HQ: Otp Holding Llc
1900 Jetway Blvd
Columbus OH 43219
614 342-6123

(G-11417)
QUILTING INC (PA)
Also Called: Mattress Mart
7600 Industrial Pkwy (43064-9468)
PHONE..............................614 504-5971
Ben Tiburzio, *Pr*
▲ **EMP: 55 EST: 1984**
SQ FT: 85,000
SALES (est): 1.07MM Privately Held
SIC: 2515 Mattresses, innerspring or box spring

(G-11418)
STI LIQUIDATION INC
7710 Corporate Blvd (43064-9214)
PHONE..............................614 733-0099
Carrie Perini, *Pr*
EMP: 20 EST: 1979
SQ FT: 6,000
SALES (est): 4.88MM Privately Held
Web: www.silverthreadsinc.com
SIC: 2211 7389 2392 2391 Draperies and drapery fabrics, cotton; Interior designer; Household furnishings, nec; Curtains and draperies

(G-11419)
SUPERIOR PLASTICS INC (PA)
8175 Business Way (43064-9216)
PHONE..............................614 733-0307
◆ **EMP: 20 EST: 1997**
SALES (est): 4.93MM
SALES (corp-wide): 4.93MM Privately Held
Web: www.superiorplasticsinc.com
SIC: 3089 Injection molding of plastics

(G-11420)
SUPERIOR PLASTICS INC
8163 Business Way (43064-9216)
PHONE..............................614 733-0307
EMP: 15
SALES (corp-wide): 4.93MM Privately Held
Web: www.superiorplasticsinc.com
SIC: 3089 Molding primary plastics
PA: Superior Plastics Inc.
8175 Business Way
Plain City OH 43064
614 733-0307

(G-11421)
TOTAL TENNIS INC
321 W Bigelow Ave (43064-7101)
PHONE..............................614 504-7446
EMP: 6 EST: 2017
SALES (est): 2.36MM Privately Held
Web: www.totaltennisinc.com
SIC: 3949 Sporting and athletic goods, nec

(G-11422)
TUFFCO SAND AND GRAVEL INC
8195 Old State Route 161 (43064-8991)
P.O. Box 399 (43040-0399)
PHONE..............................614 873-3977
Bruce Valentino, *Pr*
Charles Lewis, *Pr*
EMP: 6 EST: 1989
SALES (est): 970.89K Privately Held
SIC: 1442 Construction sand and gravel

(G-11423)
UNITED ROTARY BRUSH INC
8150 Business Way (43064-9209)
PHONE..............................937 644-3515
Bruce Davis, *Mgr*
EMP: 23
SQ FT: 63,820
SALES (corp-wide): 48.68MM Privately Held

Web: www.united-rotary.com
SIC: 3991 Brushes, household or industrial
PA: United Rotary Brush Corporation
510 W Frontier Ln
Olathe KS 66061
913 888-8450

(G-11424)
VELOCYS INC
8520 Warner Rd (43064-3561)
PHONE..............................614 733-3300
David Pummell, *CEO*
Susan Robertson, *
Doctor Paul F Schubert, *COO*
EMP: 60 EST: 2000
SALES (est): 9.43MM
SALES (corp-wide): 2.12MM Privately Held
Web: www.velocys.com
SIC: 8731 3559 Commercial physical research; Sewing machines and hat and zipper making machinery
HQ: Velocys Limited
Regus
Oxford OXON
186 580-0821

(G-11425)
VISTA COMMUNITY CHURCH
8500 Memorial Dr Ste C (43064-8051)
P.O. Box 3278 (43016-0128)
PHONE..............................614 718-2294
EMP: 10 EST: 2006
SALES (est): 931.43K Privately Held
Web: www.vistacommunitychurch.org
SIC: 7372 8661 Application computer software; Religious organizations

(G-11426)
W OF OHIO INC (PA)
Also Called: Skiff Craft
225 Guy St (43064-1160)
P.O. Box 115 (43064-0115)
PHONE..............................614 873-4664
Gabriel Jabbour, *Pr*
EMP: 6 EST: 1996
SALES (est): 497.54K
SALES (corp-wide): 497.54K Privately Held
SIC: 3732 Boatbuilding and repairing

(G-11427)
WHITMER WOODWORKS INC
8490 Carters Mill Rd (43064-9116)
PHONE..............................614 873-1196
Jerry Whitmer, *Pr*
Don Whitmer, *Treas*
EMP: 7 EST: 1990
SALES (est): 944.03K Privately Held
Web: www.whitmerwoodworks.com
SIC: 2431 Millwork

(G-11428)
WORLD RESOURCE SOLUTONS CORP
8485 Estates Ct (43064-8015)
PHONE..............................614 733-3737
Thomas Warner, *Pr*
▲ **EMP: 7 EST: 2002**
SQ FT: 3,750
SALES (est): 966.34K Privately Held
Web: www.wrstool.biz
SIC: 3089 Injection molding of plastics

(G-11429)
WRIGHT ENRICHMENT INCORPORATED
Also Called: Wright Group, The
8000 Memorial Dr (43064-9007)
PHONE..............................337 783-3096

EMP: 12
SALES (corp-wide): 19.71MM Privately Held
Web: www.thewrightgroup.net
SIC: 2834 Vitamin preparations
PA: Wright Enrichment, Incorporated
201 Energy Pkwy Ste 100
Lafayette LA 70508
337 783-3096

(G-11430)
YONEZAWA USA INC
7920 Corporate Blvd Ste A (43064-9275)
PHONE..............................614 799-2210
Shunichi Aoki, *Pr*
EMP: 11 EST: 2014
SALES (est): 2.51MM Privately Held
SIC: 3577 Computer peripheral equipment, nec

Pleasant Hill
Miami County

(G-11431)
CD SOLUTIONS INC
100 W Monument St (45359-9669)
P.O. Box 536 (45359-0536)
PHONE..............................937 676-2376
Jerald Warner, *Pr*
EMP: 8 EST: 1992
SQ FT: 10,000
SALES (est): 531.2K Privately Held
Web: www.cds.com
SIC: 7374 3695 5099 Service bureau, computer; Magnetic and optical recording media; Compact discs

---

Pleasant Plain
Warren County

(G-11432)
HARTZ MOUNTAIN CORPORATION
Also Called: L M Animal Farms
5374 Long Spurling Rd (45162-9256)
P.O. Box 57 (45162-0057)
PHONE..............................513 877-2131
Larry Mohrfield, *Brnch Mgr*
EMP: 75
Web: www.hartz.com
SIC: 2047 3999 2048 Cat food; Pet supplies; Prepared feeds, nec
HQ: The Hartz Mountain Corporation
400 Plaza Dr
Secaucus NJ 07094
800 275-1414

Plymouth
Huron County

(G-11433)
POWER SHELF LLC
500 Industrial Park Dr (44865)
PHONE..............................419 775-6125
EMP: 8 EST: 2008
SQ FT: 15,000
SALES (est): 654.76K Privately Held
Web: www.buypowershelf.com
SIC: 3644 Noncurrent-carrying wiring devices

Poland
Mahoning County

(G-11434)
ACME COMPANY
Also Called: Acme

9495 Harvard Blvd (44514-3369)
PHONE..............................330 758-2313
Carmine Zarlenga Junior, *Pr*
John M Newman, *
EMP: 60 EST: 1934
SQ FT: 10,000
SALES (est): 5.92MM Privately Held
Web: www.theacmecompany.com
SIC: 5032 3423 1422 3295 Sand, construction; Hand and edge tools, nec; Crushed and broken limestone; Minerals, ground or treated

(G-11435)
CULTURED MARBLE INC
213 N Main St (44514-1662)
PHONE..............................330 549-2282
Todd Worsencroft, *Pr*
David Worsencroft, *Pr*
Arthur D Worsencroft, *Sec*
EMP: 8 EST: 1970
SALES (est): 201.39K Privately Held
SIC: 3299 3088 Synthetic stones, for gem stones and industrial use; Plastics plumbing fixtures

(G-11436)
FLEX FAB LLC
3267 Olde Winter Trl (44514-2893)
PHONE..............................330 757-8720
Joseph Whiteside, *Prin*
EMP: 6 EST: 2018
SALES (est): 735.46K Privately Held
Web: www.flex.com
SIC: 3672 Printed circuit boards

Pomeroy
Meigs County

(G-11437)
FACEMYER LUMBER CO INC (PA)
31940 Bailey Run Rd (45769-9301)
P.O. Box 227 (45760-0227)
PHONE..............................740 992-5965
Eugene Facemyer, *Ch Bd*
Dennis Facemyer Junior, *VP*
Leslie Facemyer, *Sec*
▼ **EMP: 18 EST: 1967**
SQ FT: 1,500
SALES (est): 1.36MM
SALES (corp-wide): 1.36MM Privately Held
Web: www.facemyerlumber.com
SIC: 2421 2411 Custom sawmill; Veneer logs

(G-11438)
SNOWVILLE CREAMERY LLC
32623 State Route 143 (45769-9695)
PHONE..............................740 698-2301
Warren Taylor, *Managing Member*
EMP: 20 EST: 2003
SALES (est): 5.14MM Privately Held
Web: www.snowvillecreamery.com
SIC: 5143 2026 Dairy products, except dried or canned; Fluid milk

---

Port Clinton
Ottawa County

(G-11439)
ARES INC
818 Front St Lake Erie Business Park (43452)
PHONE..............................419 635-2175
Herb Roder, *Pr*
Ann Yamrick, *
EMP: 56 EST: 1971
SQ FT: 60,000

SALES (est): 2.5MM **Privately Held**
Web: www.aresinc.net
SIC: 3443 3482 3484 3489 Fabricated plate
work (boiler shop); Small arms ammunition;
Small arms; Ordnance and accessories, nec

(G-11440)
D & L EXCAVATING LTD
969 N Rymers Rd (43452-9437)
PHONE..............................419 271-0635
Darryl Trent, *Prin*
EMP: 6 **EST:** 2016
SALES (est): 679.11K **Privately Held**
SIC: 3531 Buckets, excavating: clamshell,
concrete, dragline, etc.

(G-11441)
**FELLHAUER MECHANICAL
SYSTEMS**
Also Called: Fellhauer In-Focus
2435 E Gill Rd (43452-2555)
PHONE..............................419 734-3674
John Fellhauer, *Pr*
EMP: 40 **EST:** 2003
SALES (est): 1.12MM **Privately Held**
SIC: 1711 7382 3651 Mechanical contractor;
Security systems services; Household
audio and video equipment

(G-11442)
**FENNER DUNLOP PORT CLINTON
LLC**
Also Called: Fenner Dnlop Engnred Cnvyor Sl
5225 W Lakeshore Dr Ste 320
(43452-9412)
PHONE..............................419 635-2191
Cassandra Pan, *Pr*
Bill Mooney, *CFO*
Ben Ficklen, *Sec*
▲ **EMP:** 115 **EST:** 1985
SQ FT: 200,000
SALES (est): 23.32MM
SALES (corp-wide): 1.95B **Privately Held**
SIC: 3535 Bucket type conveyor systems
HQ: Fenner Dunlop Americas, Llc
200 Crprate Ctr Dr Ste 22
Coraopolis PA 15108

(G-11443)
GREAT LAKES POPCORN COMPANY
60 Madison St (43452-1102)
PHONE..............................419 732-3080
Bill Yuhasz, *Pr*
EMP: 6 **EST:** 2000
SQ FT: 4,000
SALES (est): 225.38K **Privately Held**
Web: www.greatlakespopcorn.com
SIC: 2099 2064 5441 Popcorn, packaged:
except already popped; Nuts, glace; Candy,
nut, and confectionery stores

(G-11444)
LAKECRAFT INC (PA)
Also Called: Lakecraft
1010 W Lakeshore Dr (43452-9564)
PHONE..............................419 734-2828
Samuel J Conte, *Pr*
EMP: 6 **EST:** 1940
SQ FT: 15,000
SALES (est): 2.82MM
SALES (corp-wide): 2.82MM **Privately
Held**
Web: www.lakecraft.com
SIC: 3599 7692 3561 Machine shop, jobbing
and repair; Welding repair; Pumps,
domestic: water or sump

(G-11445)
**LOADMASTER TRAILER COMPANY
LTD**

Also Called: Loadmaster Trailers Mfg
2354 East Harbor Rd (43452-1517)
PHONE..............................419 732-3434
Gary Straw, *Pr*
Diane Straw, *Pr*
EMP: 13 **EST:** 1983
SQ FT: 12,000
SALES (est): 3.73MM **Privately Held**
Web: www.loadmasterboattrailer.com
SIC: 3799 7699 Boat trailers; Nautical repair
services

(G-11446)
NAUTICAL NEEDLE LLC
2853 East Harbor Rd Ste B (43452-2679)
PHONE..............................419 732-2990
Ronda Renz, *Pt*
Jan Ford, *Pt*
EMP: 6 **EST:** 2003
SALES (est): 121.03K **Privately Held**
Web: www.thenauticalneedle.com
SIC: 2392 Comforters and quilts: made from
purchased materials

(G-11447)
**PORT CLINTON MANUFACTURING
LLC**
328 W Perry St (43452-1035)
P.O. Box 220 (43452-0220)
PHONE..............................419 734-2141
Daniel Stott, *Pr*
Jane Stott, *
EMP: 25 **EST:** 1928
SQ FT: 67,000
SALES (est): 4.36MM **Privately Held**
Web: www.pcmfg.net
SIC: 3451 Screw machine products

(G-11448)
PRECISION MACHINE & TOOL CO
142 W Wilcox Rd (43452-2366)
PHONE..............................419 334-8405
Ken Ambrozy, *Pr*
Carolyn Ambrozy, *Sec*
EMP: 7 **EST:** 1979
SALES (est): 566.83K **Privately Held**
Web: www.pmtcompany.com
SIC: 3599 Machine shop, jobbing and repair

(G-11449)
QUIKSTIR INC
Also Called: Quikspray
2105 W Lakeshore Dr (43452-9485)
P.O. Box 327 (43452-0327)
PHONE..............................419 732-2601
Thomas P Mc Ritchie, *Pr*
T Park Mc Ritchie, *Sec*
EMP: 8 **EST:** 1954
SQ FT: 6,000
SALES (est): 2.31MM **Privately Held**
Web: www.quikspray.com
SIC: 3561 3563 3531 Pumps and pumping
equipment; Spraying outfits: metals, paints,
and chemicals (compressor); Mixers, nec:
ore, plaster, slag, sand, mortar, etc.

(G-11450)
QUINAMI LLC
Also Called: Gideon Owen Wine
3845 E Wine Cellar Rd (43452-3704)
PHONE..............................419 797-4445
EMP: 6 **EST:** 2019
SALES (est): 1.18MM **Privately Held**
Web: www.gideonowenwine.com
SIC: 2084 Wines

(G-11451)
REXLES INC
Also Called: Plastiform Tool & Die
1850 W Lakeshore Dr (43452-9091)
P.O. Box 26 (43452-0026)

PHONE..............................419 732-8188
Rex Montgomery, *Pr*
Leslie Rister, *Sec*
EMP: 6 **EST:** 1988
SQ FT: 1,122
SALES (est): 886.39K **Privately Held**
SIC: 3089 Plastics processing

(G-11452)
SCHAFFNER PUBLICATION INC
Also Called: Beacon, The
4340 Mckenna Ln (43452-2809)
P.O. Box 176 (43452)
PHONE..............................419 732-2154
John Schaffner, *Pr*
Mary Alice Schaffner, *VP*
Malisha Mcnabb, *Genl Mgr*
Tina Britt, *Off Mgr*
EMP: 6 **EST:** 1982
SQ FT: 4,000
SALES (est): 399.55K **Privately Held**
Web: www.thebeacon.net
SIC: 2711 Newspapers, publishing and
printing

(G-11453)
TACK-ANEW INC
Also Called: Brands' Marina
451 W Lakeshore Dr. (43452-9478)
PHONE..............................419 734-4212
Dalton Brand, *Pr*
EMP: 8 **EST:** 1971
SQ FT: 15,000
SALES (est): 446.98K **Privately Held**
Web: www.brandsmarina.com
SIC: 4493 3731 Boat yards, storage and
incidental repair; Shipbuilding and repairing

Port Jefferson
Shelby County

(G-11454)
**MCCRARY METAL POLISHING CO
INC**
Also Called: McCrary
207 Pasco Montra Rd (45360)
P.O. Box 190 (45360-0190)
PHONE..............................937 492-1979
James P Mccrary Junior, *Pr*
Shirley Mc Crary, *VP*
▲ **EMP:** 12 **EST:** 1967
SQ FT: 4,800
SALES (est): 2.49MM **Privately Held**
Web: www.mccrarymetalpolishing.com
SIC: 3599 4225 2842 Machine shop, jobbing
and repair; Warehousing, self storage;
Metal polish

Port Washington
Tuscarawas County

(G-11455)
BATES METAL PRODUCTS INC
403 E Mn St (43837)
P.O. Box 68 (43837-0068)
PHONE..............................740 498-8371
James A Bates, *Pr*
Terry L Bates, *
Betty Bates, *
EMP: 60 **EST:** 1956
SQ FT: 106,500
SALES (est): 7.41MM **Privately Held**
Web: www.batesmetal.com
SIC: 4783 2542 3993 3469 Packing and
crating; Racks, merchandise display or
storage: except wood; Signs and
advertising specialties; Metal stampings,
nec

(G-11456)
DESIGNER STONE CO
303 E Main St (43837-9704)
PHONE..............................740 492-1300
Darren Galbraith, *Pr*
Lisa Massner, *Sec*
▲ **EMP:** 8 **EST:** 2006
SALES (est): 949.17K **Privately Held**
Web: www.thedesignerstoneco.com
SIC: 1411 Granite dimension stone

Portage
Wood County

(G-11457)
J D HYDRAULIC INC
Rte 25 (43451)
P.O. Box 188 (43451-0188)
PHONE..............................419 686-5234
James Simon, *Pr*
EMP: 6 **EST:** 1974
SQ FT: 12,000
SALES (est): 1.14MM **Privately Held**
SIC: 3593 Fluid power cylinders, hydraulic or
pneumatic

(G-11458)
LABORIE ENTERPRISES LLC
Also Called: Laborie Enterprises
10892 S Dixie Hwy (43451-9798)
PHONE..............................419 686-6245
Larry C Smith, *Pt*
Douglas Laborie, *Pt*
Ronald Laborie, *Pt*
Edith Laborie, *Pt*
EMP: 7 **EST:** 1991
SQ FT: 10,000
SALES (est): 331.58K **Privately Held**
Web: www.laborieenterprises.com
SIC: 5211 2431 Millwork and lumber;
Moldings, wood: unfinished and prefinished

(G-11459)
MORLOCK ASPHALT LTD
9362 Mermill Rd (43451-9729)
PHONE..............................419 419-4772
Tony Morlock, *Managing Member*
EMP: 10 **EST:** 1995
SALES (est): 1.95MM **Privately Held**
Web: www.morlockasphaltltd.com
SIC: 1611 3541 Surfacing and paving;
Milling machines

(G-11460)
PALMER BROS TRANSIT MIX CON
Also Called: Precision Aggregates
12580 Greensburg Pike (43451-9755)
PHONE..............................419 686-2366
Will Smelts, *Mgr*
EMP: 10
SALES (corp-wide): 5.86MM **Privately
Held**
SIC: 3273 5032 Ready-mixed concrete;
Stone, crushed or broken
PA: Palmer Bros Transit Mix Concrete Inc
12205 E Gypsy Lane Rd
Bowling Green OH 43402
419 352-4681

(G-11461)
STONECO INC
11580 S Dixie Hwy (43451-9756)
PHONE..............................419 686-3311
Lee Wehner, *Mgr*
EMP: 7
SALES (corp-wide): 34.95B **Privately Held**
Web: www.shellyco.com
SIC: 1422 Crushed and broken limestone
HQ: Stoneco, Inc.

GEOGRAPHIC

1700 Fostoria Ave Ste 200
Findlay OH 45840
419 422-8854

Portland
Meigs County

(G-11462)
CRAIG SAYLOR
53020 State Route 124 (45770-9768)
PHONE..............................740 352-8363
Craig Saylor, *Prin*
EMP: 7 **EST:** 2013
SALES (est): 144.94K **Privately Held**
Web: www.saylorlogging.com
SIC: 2411 Logging camps and contractors

Portsmouth
Scioto County

(G-11463)
AIRGAS USA LLC
1411 Robinson Ave (45662-3508)
PHONE..............................740 353-5710
Andrew R Cichocki, *Pr*
EMP: 8
SALES (corp-wide): 114.13MM **Privately Held**
SIC: 5084 3599 Welding machinery and equipment; Machine shop, jobbing and repair
HQ: Airgas Usa, Llc
259 N Rdnor Chster Rd Ste
Radnor PA 19087
216 642-6600

(G-11464)
COCA-COLA CONSOLIDATED INC
Also Called: Coca-Cola
5050 Old Scioto Trl (45662-6461)
PHONE..............................740 353-3133
Tony Burns, *Prin*
EMP: 180
SALES (corp-wide): 6.9B **Publicly Held**
Web: www.cokeconsolidated.com
SIC: 2086 Bottled and canned soft drinks
PA: Coca-Cola Consolidated, Inc.
4100 Coca-Cola Plz
Charlotte NC 28211
980 392-8298

(G-11465)
EVANS FOOD GROUP LTD
406 Barklow Extension Rd (45662-3599)
PHONE..............................626 636-8110
Byron Hernandez, *Mgr*
EMP: 14
SALES (corp-wide): 421.61MM **Privately Held**
Web: www.benestarbrands.com
SIC: 2096 Pork rinds
HQ: Evans Food Group Ltd.
4118 S Halsted St
Chicago IL 60609
773 254-7400

(G-11466)
EVANS FOOD GROUP LTD
2310 8th St (45662-4740)
PHONE..............................740 285-3078
EMP: 7
SALES (corp-wide): 421.61MM **Privately Held**
Web: www.benestarbrands.com
SIC: 2096 Pork rinds
HQ: Evans Food Group Ltd.
4118 S Halsted St
Chicago IL 60609
773 254-7400

(G-11467)
GRACIE PLUM INVESTMENTS INC
Also Called: Gracie Plum Investments
609 2nd St Unit 2 (45662-3974)
PHONE..............................740 355-9029
Francesca G Hartop, *CEO*
▼ **EMP:** 27 **EST:** 1999
SQ FT: 3,150
SALES (est): 4.67MM **Privately Held**
Web: www.atp4health.com
SIC: 7372 7374 7371 Application computer software; Data processing and preparation; Custom computer programming services

(G-11468)
KSA LIMITED PARTNERSHIP
6501 Pershing Ave (45662-7502)
PHONE..............................740 776-3238
Frank Anderson Iii, *Pt*
Tom Lodeman, *Pt*
EMP: 8 **EST:** 1992
SALES (est): 162.09K **Privately Held**
SIC: 3272 Ties, railroad: concrete

(G-11469)
MCGOVNEY READY MIX INC
Also Called: McGovney River Terminal
55 River Ave (45662-4712)
P.O. Box 510 (45662-0510)
PHONE..............................740 353-4111
TOLL FREE: 800
Carolyn Kegley, *Pr*
David Kegley, *VP*
Debra Coburn, *Sec*
EMP: 9 **EST:** 1964
SQ FT: 1,200
SALES (est): 494.75K **Privately Held**
Web: www.mcgovney.com
SIC: 3273 Ready-mixed concrete

(G-11470)
MITCHELL BROS TIRE RTREAD SVC
Also Called: Mitchell Brothers Retread Svc
1205 Findlay St (45662-3449)
P.O. Box 1506 (45662-1506)
PHONE..............................740 353-1551
Mark Mitchell, *Pt*
Dennis Mitchell, *Pt*
Randy Mitchell, *Pt*
EMP: 7 **EST:** 1961
SALES (est): 514.65K **Privately Held**
SIC: 7534 5531 Tire recapping; Automotive tires

(G-11471)
MITCHELLACE INC (PA)
830 Murray St (45662-4515)
P.O. Box 89 (45662-0089)
PHONE..............................740 354-2813
Steven Keating, *Pr*
Kerry W Keating, *
Tom Keating, *
Mitchell Keating, *
◆ **EMP:** 74 **EST:** 1902
SQ FT: 365,000
SALES (est): 2.02MM
SALES (corp-wide): 2.02MM **Privately Held**
Web: www.mitchellace.com
SIC: 2241 Shoe laces, except leather

(G-11472)
NORTH SHORE PRINTING LLC
1105 Gallia St (45662-4142)
PHONE..............................740 876-9066
Jason Whisman, *Managing Member*
EMP: 6 **EST:** 2020
SALES (est): 246.04K **Privately Held**
Web: www.northshoreohio.com

SIC: 2752 7389 Commercial printing, lithographic; Business Activities at Non-Commercial Site

(G-11473)
OSCO INDUSTRIES INC (PA)
Also Called: Portsmouth Division
734 11th St (45662-3407)
P.O. Box 1388 (45662-1388)
PHONE..............................740 354-3183
William J Burke, *Ch Bd*
John M Burke, *
Jeffrey A Burke, *
Philip L Vetter, *
Keith Denny, *
◆ **EMP:** 285 **EST:** 1872
SQ FT: 150,000
SALES (est): 32.6MM
SALES (corp-wide): 32.6MM **Privately Held**
Web: www.oscoind.com
SIC: 3321 Gray iron castings, nec

(G-11474)
PORTSMOUTH BLOCK INC
Also Called: Portsmouth Block & Brick
2700 Gallia St (45662-4807)
PHONE..............................740 353-4113
Glenn Coriell, *Pr*
Mildred Coriell, *Sec*
Kevin Coriell, *VP*
EMP: 14 **EST:** 1930
SQ FT: 100,000
SALES (est): 2.19MM **Privately Held**
Web: www.portsmouthblock.com
SIC: 3271 5211 Blocks, concrete or cinder: standard; Lumber and other building materials

(G-11475)
ROCLA CONCRETE TIE INC
Also Called: ROCLA CONCRETE TIE, INC
6501 Pershing Ave (45662-7502)
PHONE..............................740 776-3238
EMP: 32
SALES (corp-wide): 144.19K **Privately Held**
Web: www.vossloh-north-america.com
SIC: 3272 Concrete products, nec
HQ: Rocla Concrete Tie, Inc.
1819 Denver W Dr Ste 450
Lakewood CO 80401

(G-11476)
SAVORY FOODS INC
2240 6th St (45662-4787)
P.O. Box 1604 (45662-1604)
PHONE..............................740 354-6655
James Speak, *Pr*
EMP: 58 **EST:** 1946
SQ FT: 40,000
SALES (est): 4.88MM
SALES (corp-wide): 421.61MM **Privately Held**
Web: www.savoryfoods.com
SIC: 2099 Food preparations, nec
HQ: Evans Food Group Ltd.
4118 S Halsted St
Chicago IL 60609
773 254-7400

(G-11477)
SOLE CHOICE INC
2415 Scioto Trl (45662-2536)
P.O. Box 89 (45662-0089)
PHONE..............................740 354-2813
Nelson K Smith, *Ch*
Ryan B Bouts, *
Bryan K Davis, *
Mark Harner, *Stockholder*
David Kuhn, *Stockholder*

▲ **EMP:** 30 **EST:** 2009
SALES (est): 1.97MM **Privately Held**
Web: www.solechoiceinc.com
SIC: 2241 Shoe laces, except leather

(G-11478)
SOUTHERN OHIO VAULT CO INC
Also Called: Sovac
502 Shale Dr (45662)
P.O. Box 418 (45662-0418)
PHONE..............................740 456-5898
Jerry Russell Senior, *Pr*
EMP: 9 **EST:** 1984
SALES (est): 278.16K **Privately Held**
SIC: 3272 Burial vaults, concrete or precast terrazzo

(G-11479)
TOM BARBOUR AUTO PARTS INC (PA)
Also Called: Barbour Auto Parts
915 11th St (45662-3410)
PHONE..............................740 354-4654
Josephine Keating, *Pr*
EMP: 12 **EST:** 1956
SQ FT: 12,000
SALES (est): 2.43MM
SALES (corp-wide): 2.43MM **Privately Held**
Web: www.barbourauto.com
SIC: 5531 3599 Automotive parts; Machine shop, jobbing and repair

(G-11480)
YOST LABS INC
630 2nd St (45662-3902)
PHONE..............................740 876-4936
Lowell Morrison, *CFO*
Greg Merrill, *Prin*
EMP: 11 **EST:** 2016
SALES (est): 1.22MM **Privately Held**
Web: www.yostlabs.com
SIC: 3812 Search and navigation equipment

Powell
Delaware County

(G-11481)
ADVANCED INDUS MACHINING INC (PA)
3982 Powell Rd Ste 218 (43065-7662)
PHONE..............................614 596-4183
Morgan Koth, *Pr*
EMP: 10 **EST:** 2003
SQ FT: 3,600
SALES (est): 513.24K
SALES (corp-wide): 513.24K **Privately Held**
Web: www.aimmach.com
SIC: 1629 3599 Industrial plant construction; Amusement park equipment

(G-11482)
BUILDING CTRL INTEGRATORS LLC (PA)
Also Called: B C I
383 N Liberty St (43065-8388)
PHONE..............................614 334-3300
EMP: 31 **EST:** 2000
SQ FT: 20,000
SALES (est): 8.5MM
SALES (corp-wide): 8.5MM **Privately Held**
Web: www.bcicontrols.com
SIC: 3822 Temperature controls, automatic

(G-11483)
CARBONKLEAN LLC
24 Village Pointe Dr (43065-7760)
PHONE..............................614 980-9515

▲ = Import ▼ = Export
◆ = Import/Export

EMP: 7 **EST:** 2015
SQ FT: 5,000
SALES (est): 519.05K **Privately Held**
Web: www.carbonklean.com
SIC: 2842 Specialty cleaning

(G-11484)
CARDIAC ANALYTICS LLC
5683 Liberty Rd N (43065-8996)
PHONE..................................614 314-1332
Dan Mcfarland, *Pr*
EMP: 10 **EST:** 2010
SALES (est): 369.09K **Privately Held**
SIC: 3845 Electromedical equipment

(G-11485)
CONTINENTAL GL SLS & INV GROUP
Also Called: Continental Group
315 Ashmoore Cir W (43065-7486)
P.O. Box 1764 (43065-1764)
PHONE..................................614 679-1201
Sean Snyder, *Pt*
Chris Snyder, *Pt*
▲ **EMP:** 8 **EST:** 1998
SQ FT: 100,000
SALES (est): 2.74MM **Privately Held**
Web: www.cgsi.co
SIC: 3441 7011 3211 Fabricated structural
metal; Hotels; Structural glass

(G-11486)
D-TERRA SOLUTIONS LLC
35 Clairedan Dr (43065-8064)
PHONE..................................614 450-1040
Denis Bruncak, *CEO*
▲ **EMP:** 7 **EST:** 2012
SALES (est): 2MM **Privately Held**
Web: www.dterrasolutions.com
SIC: 3714 Motor vehicle parts and
accessories

(G-11487)
EYESCIENCE LABS LLC
Also Called: Eyescience
493 Village Park Dr (43065-6605)
PHONE..................................614 885-7100
Jeffrey Northup, *Managing Member*
EMP: 7 **EST:** 2007
SQ FT: 7,000
SALES (est): 448.53K **Privately Held**
Web: www.basicbrandsinc.com
SIC: 2834 Vitamin preparations

(G-11488)
GFS CHEMICALS INC (PA)
Also Called: GFS Chemicals
155 Hidden Ravines Dr (43065-9928)
P.O. Box 245 (43065-0245)
PHONE..................................740 881-5501
J Steel Hutchinson, *CEO*
J Steel Hutchinson, *Pr*
Darrell A Hutchinson, *Dir*
M Robert Pierron, *VP*
Edward Reusch, *CFO*
◆ **EMP:** 20 **EST:** 1928
SQ FT: 125,000
SALES (est): 25.94MM
SALES (corp-wide): 25.94MM **Privately**
Held
Web: www.gfschemicals.com
SIC: 2819 2899 2869 2812 Chemicals,
reagent grade: refined from technical grade
; Chemical preparations, nec; Industrial
organic chemicals, nec; Alkalies and
chlorine

(G-11489)
IKIRISKA LLC
16 Village Pointe Dr (43065-7760)
PHONE..................................614 389-8994
EMP: 10 **EST:** 2020

SALES (est): 253.16K **Privately Held**
Web:
ikiriska-custom-curtains.business.site
SIC: 2391 Curtains and draperies

(G-11490)
MERISTEM CROP PRFMCE GROUP
LLC
489 Village Park Dr (43065-6610)
PHONE..................................833 637-4783
Stephanie Graham, *CEO*
David Schumacher, *CCO**
EMP: 50 **EST:** 2020
SALES (est): 5.32MM **Privately Held**
Web: www.meristemag.com
SIC: 2879 Agricultural chemicals, nec

(G-11491)
METAL PRODUCTS COMPANY (PA)
Also Called: Stamtex Metal Stampings
9455 Concord Rd (43065-8968)
PHONE..................................330 652-2558
Philip Frankle, *Pr*
EMP: 40 **EST:** 1921
SALES (est): 2.01MM
SALES (corp-wide): 2.01MM **Privately**
Held
Web: www.stamtexmp.com
SIC: 3469 Stamping metal for the trade

(G-11492)
MORGAN WOOD PRODUCTS INC
9761 Fairway Dr (43065-6947)
P.O. Box 177 (43065-0177)
PHONE..................................614 336-4000
Luke Reinstetle, *Pr*
◆ **EMP:** 12 **EST:** 2002
SQ FT: 4,000
SALES (est): 4.88MM
SALES (corp-wide): 8.98MM **Privately**
Held
Web: www.morganwood.org
SIC: 2448 Pallets, wood
PA: Evening Post Group, Llc
39 Broad St
Charleston SC 29401
843 867-2990

(G-11493)
NEW PATH INTERNATIONAL LLC
1476 Manning Pkwy Ste A (43065-7295)
PHONE..................................614 410-3974
Damon Canfield, *Managing Member*
Nell Macivor, *
◆ **EMP:** 15 **EST:** 1989
SQ FT: 13,000
SALES (est): 1.42MM **Privately Held**
Web: www.npi.com
SIC: 3639 8711 7389 Major kitchen
appliances, except refrigerators and stoves;
Engineering services; Design, commercial
and industrial

(G-11494)
SAWMILL 9721 LLC
9721 Sawmill Rd (43065-6613)
PHONE..................................614 937-4400
Jason Lusk, *Prin*
EMP: 6 **EST:** 2017
SALES (est): 105.64K **Privately Held**
SIC: 2421 Sawmills and planing mills,
general

(G-11495)
SUMMIT ONLINE PRODUCTS LLC
Also Called: Massageblocks.com
3982 Powell Rd Ste 137 (43065-7662)
PHONE..................................800 326-1972
Thomas W Turner, *Managing Member*
EMP: 6 **EST:** 2011
SALES (est): 307.6K **Privately Held**

Web: www.summitonlineproducts.com
SIC: 3841 Surgical and medical instruments

(G-11496)
VILLAGE CONTROLS LLC
9349 Westview Dr (43065-5097)
PHONE..................................614 600-8880
Dan Boggess, *Pr*
EMP: 10 **EST:** 2019
SALES (est): 1.45MM **Privately Held**
Web: www.villagecontrols.com
SIC: 3625 1731 Control equipment, electric;
Lighting contractor

Powhatan Point
Belmont County

(G-11497)
COAL SERVICES INC
Also Called: Coal Services Group
155 Highway 7 S (43942-1033)
PHONE..................................740 795-5220
Don Gentry, *Pr*
Robert Moore, *
Michael O Mckown, *Prin*
EMP: 355 **EST:** 1999
SALES (est): 778.83K
SALES (corp-wide): 4.34B **Privately Held**
SIC: 8741 8711 1231 1222 Management
services; Engineering services; Anthracite
mining; Bituminous coal-underground
mining
HQ: The American Coal Company
9085 Highway 34 N
Galatia IL 62935
618 268-6311

(G-11498)
UTAHAMERICAN ENERGY INC
153 Highway 7 S (43942-1033)
P.O. Box 910 (84520-0910)
PHONE..................................435 888-4000
David Hibbs, *Brnch Mgr*
EMP: 138
SALES (corp-wide): 4.34B **Privately Held**
SIC: 1222 Bituminous coal-underground
mining
HQ: Utahamerican Energy, Inc.
45 W Sego Lily Dr Ste 401
Sandy UT 84070
435 888-4000

Proctorville
Lawrence County

(G-11499)
SUPERIOR MARINE WAYS INC
5852 County Rd 1 Suoth Pt (45669)
P.O. Box 519 (45669-0519)
PHONE..................................740 894-6224
Dale Manns, *Mgr*
EMP: 130
SALES (corp-wide): 7.52MM **Privately**
Held
Web: www.superiormarineinc.com
SIC: 3731 7699 Barges, building and
repairing; Boat repair
PA: Superior Marine Ways, Inc.
5852 County Road 1
South Point OH 45680
740 894-6224

(G-11500)
TRI-STATE PLATING & POLISHING
187 Township Road 1204 (45669-8688)
PHONE..................................304 529-2579
Edison Adkins, *Pr*
Laura L Adkins, *VP*

Joseph Adkins, *Genl Mgr*
EMP: 6 **EST:** 1963
SQ FT: 300
SALES (est): 372.98K **Privately Held**
SIC: 3471 7692 Electroplating of metals or
formed products; Welding repair

Prospect
Marion County

(G-11501)
FLEMING CONSTRUCTION CO
Also Called: Scioto Sand & Gravel
5298 Marion Marysville Rd (43342-9342)
P.O. Box 31 (43301-0031)
PHONE..................................740 494-2177
Gerald E Fleming, *Pr*
Sonya Fleming, *
EMP: 6 **EST:** 1965
SQ FT: 2,400
SALES (est): 418.5K **Privately Held**
Web:
www.flemingconstructioncompany.com
SIC: 1542 1541 1623 1442 Commercial and
office building, new construction; Industrial
buildings, new construction, nec; Sewer line
construction; Gravel mining

(G-11502)
HERCULES INDUSTRIES INC
7194 Prospect Delaware Rd (43342-7505)
P.O. Box 197 (43342-0197)
PHONE..................................740 494-2620
Keith Popovich, *Pr*
Jean Meyer, *
▲ **EMP:** 23 **EST:** 1969
SQ FT: 18,380
SALES (est): 4.14MM **Privately Held**
Web: www.herculock.com
SIC: 3429 Padlocks
PA: Scientific Forming Technologies
Corporation
2545 Farmers Dr Ste 200
Columbus OH 43235

Quaker City
Guernsey County

(G-11503)
B&D WATER INC
60478 Fairground Rd (43773-2501)
P.O. Box 329 (81323-0329)
PHONE..................................330 771-3318
Tabitha Lassen, *Prin*
EMP: 28 **EST:** 2017
SALES (est): 3.55MM **Privately Held**
Web: bd-water-inc.business.site
SIC: 2842 Sweeping compounds, oil or
water absorbent, clay or sawdust

Racine
Meigs County

(G-11504)
J D DRILLING COMPANY
107 S 3rd St (45771-9552)
P.O. Box 369 (45771-0369)
PHONE..................................740 949-2512
James E Diddle, *Pr*
EMP: 7 **EST:** 1975
SQ FT: 6,000
SALES (est): 1.12MM **Privately Held**
SIC: 1381 Drilling oil and gas wells

(G-11505)
MARIETTA MARTIN MATERIALS INC
Also Called: Martin Marietta Aggregates
50427 State Route 124 (45771-9082)
PHONE......................................740 247-2211
John Bentz, Genl Mgr
EMP: 6
Web: www.martinmarietta.com
SIC: 1422 Crushed and broken limestone
PA: Martin Marietta Materials Inc
　4123 Parklake Ave
　Raleigh NC 27612

(G-11506)
SHELLY MATERIALS INC
49947 State Route 338 (45771)
PHONE......................................740 247-2311
Michael Gard, Mgr
EMP: 10
SALES (corp-wide): 34.95B Privately Held
Web: www.shellyco.com
SIC: 4492 1442 Tugboat service;
　Construction sand and gravel
HQ: Shelly Materials, Inc.
　80 Park Dr
　Thornville OH 43076
　740 246-6315

Radnor
Delaware County

(G-11507)
TIM CALVIN ACCESS CONTROLS
Also Called: Tim Calvin Enterprises
7585 Taway Rd (43066-9711)
PHONE......................................740 494-4200
Tim Calvin, Pr
Renee Calvin, VP
EMP: 8 EST: 1992
SQ FT: 240
SALES (est): 938.57K Privately Held
Web: www.calvininc.com
SIC: 3446 Architectural metalwork

(G-11508)
ULTERIOR PRODUCTS LLC
3142 N Section Line Rd (43066-9774)
P.O. Box 759 (43026-0759)
PHONE......................................614 441-9465
Kurt Nienberg, Pr
EMP: 6 EST: 2013
SALES (est): 2.22MM Privately Held
Web: www.ulteriorproducts.com
SIC: 3535 Unit handling conveying systems

Randolph
Portage County

(G-11509)
EAST MANUFACTURING CORPORATION
Also Called: EAST MANUFACTURING CORPORATION
3865 Waterloo Rd (44265-9802)
PHONE......................................330 325-9921
Torie Tollman, Mgr
EMP: 239
Web: www.eastmfg.com
SIC: 3715 Trailer bodies
HQ: East Trailers Llc
　1871 State Rt 44
　Randolph OH 44265
　330 325-9921

(G-11510)
EAST TRAILERS LLC (DH)
1871 State Rt 44 (44265)

P.O. Box 277 (44265-0277)
PHONE......................................330 325-9921
Chris Olson, CEO
David De Poincy, Pr
Robert J Bruce, VP
Donald C Pecano, CFO
Mark T Tate, Sec
▼ EMP: 39 EST: 1968
SQ FT: 350,000
SALES (est): 37.46MM Privately Held
Web: www.eastmfg.com
SIC: 3715 5013 7539 Trailer bodies; Truck
　parts and accessories; Automotive repair
　shops, nec
HQ: Fultra, S.A.P.I. De C.V.
　Miguel Aleman No.1000
　Guadalupe NLE 67110

Ravenna
Portage County

(G-11511)
A C WILLIAMS CO INC (PA)
Also Called: Lake Metals
700 N Walnut St (44266-2300)
PHONE......................................330 296-6110
Dale E Mccoy, Pr
Barbara Cramer, *
EMP: 23 EST: 1944
SQ FT: 65,000
SALES (est): 4.11MM
SALES (corp-wide): 4.11MM Privately
Held
Web: www.litemetals.com
SIC: 3369 3321 Magnesium and magnes.-
　base alloy castings, exc. die-casting; Gray
　iron castings, nec

(G-11512)
ACE PRODUCTS & CONSULTING LLC
6800 N Chestnut St Ste 3 (44266-3927)
PHONE......................................330 577-4088
EMP: 10 EST: 2014
SALES (est): 2.52MM Privately Held
Web: www.ace-laboratories.com
SIC: 3069 Acid bottles, rubber

(G-11513)
AIR CRAFT WHEELS LLC
700 N Walnut St (44266-2372)
PHONE......................................440 937-7903
Dale Mccoy, Pr
EMP: 9 EST: 2004
SALES (est): 977.28K Privately Held
Web: www.aircraftwheels.net
SIC: 3356 3365 3369 Magnesium; Aluminum
　foundries; Nonferrous foundries, nec

(G-11514)
ALLEN AIRCRAFT PRODUCTS INC
312 E Lake St (44266-3428)
P.O. Box 951146 (44193-0005)
PHONE......................................330 296-9621
Kevin Barbeck, Brnch Mgr
EMP: 44
SALES (corp-wide): 17MM Privately Held
Web: www.allenaircraft.com
SIC: 3728 3471 Aircraft parts and
　equipment, nec; Plating and polishing
PA: Allen Aircraft Products, Inc.
　6168 Woodbine Ave
　Ravenna OH 44266
　330 296-9621

(G-11515)
ALLEN AIRCRAFT PRODUCTS INC
Also Called: Metal Finishing Divison
4879 Newton Falls Rd (44266-9673)

P.O. Box 1211 (44266-1211)
PHONE......................................330 296-1531
Roger Rollison, Brnch Mgr
EMP: 44
SALES (corp-wide): 17MM Privately Held
Web: www.allenaircraft.com
SIC: 3471 Finishing, metals or formed
　products
PA: Allen Aircraft Products, Inc.
　6168 Woodbine Ave
　Ravenna OH 44266
　330 296-9621

(G-11516)
ALLEN AIRCRAFT PRODUCTS INC (PA)
6168 Woodbine Rd (44266-9665)
P.O. Box 1211 (44266-1211)
PHONE......................................330 296-9621
▲ EMP: 60 EST: 1947
SALES (est): 17MM
SALES (corp-wide): 17MM Privately Held
Web: www.allenaircraft.com
SIC: 3728 3471 5531 Aircraft parts and
　equipment, nec; Anodizing (plating) of
　metals or formed products; Auto and home
　supply stores

(G-11517)
BECK ENERGY CORPORATION
160 N Chestnut St (44266-2256)
P.O. Box 1070 (44266-1070)
PHONE......................................330 297-6891
Raymond Beck, Pr
EMP: 24 EST: 1971
SQ FT: 4,000
SALES (est): 5.9MM Privately Held
Web: www.beckenergycorp.com
SIC: 1382 Oil and gas exploration services

(G-11518)
BECK SAND & GRAVEL INC
2820 Webb Rd (44266-9459)
PHONE......................................330 626-3863
Rod Wenrich, Pr
Dan Lostoski, VP
EMP: 9 EST: 1950
SQ FT: 3,200
SALES (est): 1.08MM Privately Held
Web: www.becksand.com
SIC: 1442 Gravel mining

(G-11519)
BOLLARI/DAVIS INC
5292 S Prospect St (44266-9032)
P.O. Box 609 (44266-0609)
PHONE......................................330 296-4445
David Stonestreet, Pr
EMP: 10 EST: 1958
SQ FT: 13,000
SALES (est): 233.6K Privately Held
Web: www.bollaridavis.com
SIC: 3599 Machine shop, jobbing and repair

(G-11520)
CATACEL CORP
785 N Freedom St (44266-2469)
EMP: 11
Web: www.catacel.com
SIC: 3823 Combustion control instruments

(G-11521)
CITY OF RAVENNA
Also Called: Waste Water Plant, The
3722 Hommon Rd (44266-3543)
PHONE......................................330 296-5214
Michael Lacivita, Mgr
EMP: 9
Web: www.ravennaoh.gov

SIC: 4952 3589 Sewerage systems; Sewage
　treatment equipment
PA: City Of Ravenna
　210 Park Way
　Ravenna OH 44266
　330 296-3864

(G-11522)
COLONIAL RUBBER COMPANY (PA)
706 Oakwood St (44266-2138)
P.O. Box 111 (44266-0111)
PHONE......................................330 296-2831
Dale P Fosnight, Pr
Wayne Slack, *
Wayne H Wise, *
Alan D Fosnight, *
EMP: 50 EST: 1937
SQ FT: 55,000
SALES (est): 862.7K
SALES (corp-wide): 862.7K Privately Held
SIC: 3061 3069 Mechanical rubber goods;
　Hard rubber and molded rubber products

(G-11523)
DURACOTE CORPORATION
350 N Diamond St (44266-2155)
P.O. Box 1209 (44266-1209)
PHONE......................................330 296-9600
Jack Pallay, CEO
Tim Pallay, *
▼ EMP: 40 EST: 1947
SQ FT: 143,000
SALES (est): 10.82MM Privately Held
Web: www.duracote.com
SIC: 3083 2295 3082 2261 Laminated
　plastics plate and sheet; Resin or plastic
　coated fabrics; Unsupported plastics profile
　shapes; Finishing plants, cotton

(G-11524)
ENDURO RUBBER COMPANY
685 S Chestnut St (44266-3068)
P.O. Box 752 (44266-0752)
PHONE......................................330 296-9603
Jerry Stuver, Pr
Neal A Stuver, VP
Luanne Stuver, VP
EMP: 9 EST: 1946
SQ FT: 24,000
SALES (est): 915.27K Privately Held
Web: www.endurorubber.com
SIC: 3069 Molded rubber products

(G-11525)
G GRAFTON MACHINE & RUBBER
640 Cleveland Rd (44266-2021)
PHONE......................................330 297-1062
Montgomery Grafton, Pr
EMP: 10 EST: 1969
SQ FT: 17,500
SALES (est): 585.42K Privately Held
Web: www.graftonmachine.com
SIC: 3599 3069 Machine shop, jobbing and
　repair; Hard rubber and molded rubber
　products

(G-11526)
GENERAL ALUMINUM MFG COMPANY
5159 S Prospect St (44266-9031)
PHONE......................................330 297-1020
EMP: 20
SALES (corp-wide): 1.44B Publicly Held
Web: www.generalaluminum.com
SIC: 3365 3369 Aluminum and aluminum-
　based alloy castings; Nonferrous foundries,
　nec
HQ: General Aluminum Mfg. Company
　5159 S Prospect St
　Ravenna OH 44266
　330 297-1225

(G-11527)
GENERAL ALUMINUM MFG LLC (HQ)
Also Called: Gamco
5159 S Prospect St (44266-9031)
PHONE................................330 297-1225
Steve Case, *Pr*
Kevin Kaminsky, *
Craig Schlauch, *
Gary Mclaughlin, *Sls Dir*
◆ **EMP:** 84 **EST:** 1981
SALES (est): 46.31MM **Privately Held**
Web: www.generalaluminum.com
SIC: 3365 3369 Aluminum and aluminum-
based alloy castings; Nonferrous foundries,
nec
PA: Angstrom Automotive Group, Llc
2000 Town Ctr Ste 100
Southfield MI 48075

(G-11528)
HYTECH SILICONE PRODUCTS INC
6112 Knapp Rd (44266-8876)
PHONE................................330 297-1888
John Roberts, *Pr*
EMP: 6 **EST:** 1987
SQ FT: 2,450
SALES (est): 470.53K **Privately Held**
Web: www.hytechproducts.com
SIC: 3069 Molded rubber products

(G-11529)
LAAD SIGN & LIGHTING INC
3097 State Route 59 (44266-1653)
PHONE................................330 379-2297
Linda Nichols, *Pr*
EMP: 10 **EST:** 2013
SALES (est): 1.49MM **Privately Held**
Web: www.laadsignandlighting.com
SIC: 3993 Signs and advertising specialties

(G-11530)
LG CHEM OHIO PETROCHEMICAL INC
310 Rayann Pkwy (44266-3904)
PHONE................................470 792-5127
Samantha Ritter, *CEO*
EMP: 12 **EST:** 2021
SALES (est): 10.75MM **Privately Held**
SIC: 2899 Oils and essential oils

(G-11531)
LITE MAGNESIUM PRODUCTS INC
700 N Walnut St (44266-2372)
PHONE................................330 296-6110
Arun Jeldi, *CEO*
Arun Jeldi, *Pr*
EMP: 70 **EST:** 2020
SALES (est): 1.27MM **Privately Held**
Web: www.litemagnesium.com
SIC: 3369 3812 3621 Aerospace castings,
nonferrous: except aluminum; Defense
systems and equipment; Motor housings

(G-11532)
LITE METALS COMPANY
700 N Walnut St (44266-2372)
PHONE................................330 296-6110
Dale E Mc Coy, *Pr*
Barbara Cramer, *
EMP: 35 **EST:** 1973
SQ FT: 65,000
SALES (est): 4.11MM
SALES (corp-wide): 4.11MM **Privately Held**
Web: www.litemetals.com
SIC: 3369 3356 3365 Nonferrous foundries,
nec; Magnesium; Aluminum foundries
PA: A C Williams Co Inc
700 N Walnut St
Ravenna OH 44266
330 296-6110

(G-11533)
MONTGOMERYS PALLET SERVICE INC
7937 State Route 44 (44266-9781)
PHONE................................330 297-6677
Teresa Montgomery, *Pr*
William Montgomery, *VP*
EMP: 7 **EST:** 1992
SALES (est): 457.56K **Privately Held**
Web:
www.montgomeryspalletservice.com
SIC: 2448 4953 Pallets, wood; Refuse
collection and disposal services

(G-11534)
NICHOLS MOLD INC
222 W Lake St (44266-3651)
PHONE................................330 297-9719
Edward Nichols, *Pr*
Nancy Nichols, *Sec*
EMP: 6 **EST:** 1972
SQ FT: 4,000
SALES (est): 605K **Privately Held**
Web: www.nicholsmold.com
SIC: 3544 3599 Industrial molds; Machine
shop, jobbing and repair

(G-11535)
PERFORMANCE ELASTOMERS CORPORATION
Also Called: Performance Elastomers
7162 State Route 88 (44266-9189)
PHONE................................330 297-2255
EMP: 81 **EST:** 1992
SALES (est): 14.36MM
SALES (corp-wide): 1.05B **Privately Held**
Web: www.performanceelastomers.com
SIC: 3061 Mechanical rubber goods
HQ: Pexco, Llc
1600 Birchwood Ave
Des Plaines IL 60018
847 296-5511

(G-11536)
QUIKRETE COMPANIES LLC
Also Called: Quikrete of Cleveland
2693 Lake Rockwell Rd (44266-8041)
PHONE................................330 296-6080
Tim Ryon, *Mgr*
EMP: 30
SQ FT: 48,000
Web: www.quikrete.com
SIC: 3272 5211 3273 3241 Dry mixture
concrete; Masonry materials and supplies;
Ready-mixed concrete; Cement, hydraulic
HQ: The Quikrete Companies Llc
5 Concourse Pkwy Ste 1900
Atlanta GA 30328
404 634-9100

(G-11537)
R W MACHINE & TOOL INC
7944 State Route 44 (44266-9781)
PHONE................................330 296-5211
Alan Wilbur, *CEO*
Michael Jenkins, *
Karen Wilbur, *
Mike Jenkins, *
▲ **EMP:** 12 **EST:** 1983
SQ FT: 17,500
SALES (est): 3.08MM **Privately Held**
Web: www.rwmachinetool.com
SIC: 3599 Machine shop, jobbing and repair

(G-11538)
SAINT-GOBAIN PRFMCE PLAS CORP
335 N Diamond St (44266-2153)
PHONE................................330 296-9948
Ron Bauer, *Genl Mgr*
EMP: 130
SALES (corp-wide): 402.18MM **Privately Held**

Web: plastics.saint-gobain.com
SIC: 2821 Plastics materials and resins
HQ: Saint-Gobain Performance Plastics
Corporation
20 Moores Rd
Malvern PA 19355
440 836-6900

(G-11539)
SCHAEFFER METAL PRODUCTS INC
357 Commerce St (44266-2422)
PHONE................................330 296-6226
Jack W Schaeffer Junior, *Pr*
Patricia Nock, *Sec*
EMP: 7 **EST:** 1971
SQ FT: 42,000
SALES (est): 499.26K **Privately Held**
Web: www.schaeffermetal.com
SIC: 7699 3443 Tank repair; Fabricated plate
work (boiler shop)

(G-11540)
SCIENTIFIC PLASTICS LTD
7154 State Route 88 (44266-9189)
PHONE................................305 557-3737
Bernardo Perafan, *Mgr*
◆ **EMP:** 10 **EST:** 2001
SALES (est): 681.24K **Privately Held**
Web: www.astraproductsltd.com
SIC: 3089 Injection molded finished plastics
products, nec

(G-11541)
SIX C FABRICATION INC
5245 S Prospect St (44266-9032)
PHONE................................330 296-5594
EMP: 305
SALES (corp-wide): 2.69MM **Privately Held**
Web: www.sixcfab.com
SIC: 3495 Wire springs
PA: Six C Fabrication, Inc.
349 Thomas Mill Rd
Winnfield LA 71483
318 628-2764

(G-11542)
SPECTRUM DISPERSIONS INC
225 W Lake St (44266-3650)
P.O. Box 805 (44266-0805)
PHONE................................330 296-0600
Gary Klemm, *Pr*
Gregory Klemm, *VP*
Timothy Klemm, *
▲ **EMP:** 15 **EST:** 1979
SQ FT: 70,000
SALES (est): 4.97MM **Privately Held**
Web: www.spectrumcustom.com
SIC: 2865 2816 2851 Color pigments,
organic; Color pigments; Paints and paint
additives

(G-11543)
SPRINGSEAL INC
800 Enterprise Pkwy (44266-8061)
PHONE................................330 626-0673
Mark Knapp, *Pr*
EMP: 12 **EST:** 2004
SQ FT: 10,000
SALES (est): 5.08MM **Privately Held**
Web: www.springsealinc.com
SIC: 3089 Injection molding of plastics

(G-11544)
STA-WARM ELECTRIC COMPANY
553 N Chestnut St (44266-2217)
P.O. Box 150 (44266-0150)
PHONE................................330 296-6461
John Snell, *Pr*
Brian Borthwick, *VP*
Linda Barns, *Mgr*

EMP: 10 **EST:** 1920
SQ FT: 25,000
SALES (est): 2.13MM **Privately Held**
Web: www.sta-warm.com
SIC: 3443 Fabricated plate work (boiler shop)

(G-11545)
TARPED OUT INC
Also Called: Mountain Tarp
4442 State Route 14 (44266-8741)
PHONE................................330 325-7722
Marc Campitelli, *Brnch Mgr*
EMP: 28
Web: www.mountaintarp.com
SIC: 2394 Awnings, fabric: made from
purchased materials
HQ: Tarped Out, Inc.
1002 N 15th St
Middlesboro KY 40965

(G-11546)
TREXLER RUBBER CO INC (PA)
503 N Diamond St (44266-2113)
P.O. Box 667 (44266-0667)
PHONE................................330 296-9677
Jack W Schaefer, *Pr*
EMP: 20 **EST:** 1953
SQ FT: 26,000
SALES (est): 2.07MM
SALES (corp-wide): 2.07MM **Privately Held**
Web: www.trexlerrubber.com
SIC: 3069 2851 3544 Latex, foamed;
Polyurethane coatings; Special dies, tools,
jigs, and fixtures

(G-11547)
TRUE INDUSTRIES INC
Also Called: Cleveland Punch and Die Co
666 Pratt St (44266-3161)
P.O. Box 769 (44266-0769)
PHONE................................330 296-4342
Kyle Brown, *Pr*
Dan Brown, *
Ryan Brodie, *
EMP: 50 **EST:** 1880
SQ FT: 70,000
SALES (est): 9.9MM **Privately Held**
Web: www.clevelandpunch.com
SIC: 3544 Special dies and tools

(G-11548)
W POLE CONTRACTING INC
4188 State Route 14 (44266-8739)
PHONE................................330 325-7177
Wade Pol, *Pr*
Christine Pol, *Treas*
EMP: 10 **EST:** 1987
SALES (est): 1MM **Privately Held**
SIC: 1389 Oil field services, nec

(G-11549)
WESCO MACHINE INC
2304 Roberts Journey (44266-7809)
PHONE................................330 688-6973
De Etta Connelly, *Pr*
Ronald Connelly, *VP Opers*
EMP: 17 **EST:** 1974
SALES (est): 2.46MM **Privately Held**
Web: www.wesco-machine.com
SIC: 3599 3559 Machine shop, jobbing and
repair; Plastics working machinery

(G-11550)
WESTROCK RKT LLC
Also Called: Rock Tenn
975 N Freedom St (44266-2465)
PHONE................................330 296-5155
EMP: 32
Web: www.westrock.com

SIC: 2653 Boxes, corrugated: made from purchased materials
HQ: Westrock Rkt, Llc
1000 Abernathy Rd Ste 125
Atlanta GA 30328
770 448-2193

Rawson
Hancock County

(G-11551)
DNC HYDRAULICS LLC
5219 County Road 313 (45881-9650)
PHONE..............................419 963-2800
EMP: 12 EST: 1991
SALES (est): 2.52MM Privately Held
Web: www.dnchydraulics.com
SIC: 7699 3492 Industrial machinery and equipment repair; Control valves, fluid power: hydraulic and pneumatic

Rayland
Jefferson County

(G-11552)
SHELLY AND SANDS INC
Also Called: Tri-State Asphalt Co
1731 Old State Route 7 (43943-7962)
P.O. Box 66 (43943-0066)
PHONE..............................740 859-2104
TOLL FREE: 800
Mark Haverty, Genl Mgr
EMP: 44
SALES (corp-wide): 433.35MM Privately Held
Web: www.shellyandsands.com
SIC: 2951 1542 Asphalt paving mixtures and blocks; Nonresidential construction, nec
PA: Shelly And Sands, Inc.
3570 S River Rd
Zanesville OH 43701
740 453-0721

Raymond
Union County

(G-11553)
NATURE PURE LLC (PA)
26586 State Route 739 (43067-9763)
PHONE..............................937 358-2364
Kurt Lausecker, Managing Member
EMP: 15 EST: 2007
SALES (est): 2.57MM Privately Held
Web: www.naturepure.us
SIC: 0252 2048 Started pullet farm; Poultry feeds

Reynoldsburg
Franklin County

(G-11554)
ADVANCED INTEGRATION LLC
Also Called: Advint
6880 Tussing Rd (43068-4101)
PHONE..............................614 863-2433
Paul Salopek, CEO
Paul R Salopek, *
John C Albert, *
EMP: 32 EST: 1999
SQ FT: 6,000
SALES (est): 15.4MM Privately Held
Web: www.advint.com
SIC: 3825 Test equipment for electronic and electric measurement

(G-11555)
ALBANY SCREEN PRINTING LLC
7049 Trillium Ln (43068-4832)
P.O. Box 80 (43004-0080)
PHONE..............................614 585-3279
Winter Adams, Pr
EMP: 15 EST: 2006
SALES (est): 529.5K Privately Held
SIC: 2759 2395 Screen printing; Embroidery and art needlework

(G-11556)
B B & H TOOL COMPANY
7719 Taylor Rd Sw (43068-9626)
P.O. Box 100 (43026-0100)
PHONE..............................614 868-8634
Mousa Aframian, Owner
EMP: 8 EST: 1971
SQ FT: 8,000
SALES (est): 2.29MM Privately Held
Web: www.bbhtool.com
SIC: 3599 Machine shop, jobbing and repair

(G-11557)
BATH & BODY WORKS LLC (HQ)
Also Called: Bath & Body Works
7 Limited Pkwy E (43068-5300)
PHONE..............................614 856-6000
Nicholas Coe, CEO
Julie Rosen, *
Timothy B Lyons, *
Kenneth B Gilman, *
Patrick Hectorne, *
◆ EMP: 336 EST: 1990
SALES (est): 1.06B
SALES (corp-wide): 7.31B Publicly Held
Web: www.bathandbodyworks.com
SIC: 5999 2844 Toiletries, cosmetics, and perfumes; Perfumes, cosmetics and other toilet preparations
PA: Bath & Body Works, Inc.
3 Limited Pkwy
Columbus OH 43230
614 415-7000

(G-11558)
BEAUTYAVENUES LLC (HQ)
Also Called: Bath and Body Works
7 Limited Pkwy E (43068-5300)
PHONE..............................614 856-6000
Charles Mcguigan, CEO
◆ EMP: 13 EST: 2005
SALES (est): 15.42MM
SALES (corp-wide): 7.31B Publicly Held
SIC: 5999 5122 2844 Toiletries, and perfumes; Perfumes; Face creams or lotions
PA: Bath & Body Works, Inc.
3 Limited Pkwy
Columbus OH 43230
614 415-7000

(G-11559)
BOB SUMEREL TIRE COMPANY INC
67 Klema Dr N Ste D (43068-6814)
PHONE..............................740 927-2811
Todd Sumerel, Pr
Bob Sumerel, CEO
EMP: 6 EST: 1993
SQ FT: 4,000
SALES (est): 213.68K Privately Held
Web: www.bobsumereltire.com
SIC: 5531 5014 7534 Automotive tires; Tires and tubes; Tire repair shop

(G-11560)
BRIDGESTONE RET OPERATIONS LLC
Also Called: Firestone
7085 E Main St (43068-2011)
PHONE..............................614 861-7994

James Thompson, Mgr
EMP: 7
Web: www.bridgestoneamericas.com
SIC: 5531 7534 Automotive tires; Rebuilding and retreading tires
HQ: Bridgestone Retail Operations, Llc
200 4th Ave S Ste 100
Nashville TN 37201
615 937-1000

(G-11561)
BUCKEYE READY-MIX LLC (PA)
Also Called: Buckeye Building Products
7657 Taylor Rd Sw (43068-9626)
P.O. Box 164119 (43216-4119)
PHONE..............................614 575-2132
Tom Murphy, *
Larry Randles, *
EMP: 50 EST: 1999
SQ FT: 10,000
SALES (est): 21.97MM
SALES (corp-wide): 21.97MM Privately Held
Web: www.buckeyereadymix.com
SIC: 3273 Ready-mixed concrete

(G-11562)
CHRISTIAN MISSIONARY ALLIANCE (PA)
Also Called: Alliance, The
6421 E Main St (43068-2378)
P.O. Box 35000 (80935-3500)
PHONE..............................380 208-6200
John Stumbo, Pr
Gary Benedict, *
Kenneth Baldes, *
EMP: 150 EST: 1880
SQ FT: 59,000
SALES (est): 10.05MM
SALES (corp-wide): 10.05MM Privately Held
Web: www.cmalliance.org
SIC: 8661 2731 5942 Miscellaneous denomination church; Books, publishing only; Books, religious

(G-11563)
COLUMBUS GRAPHICS INC
7295 Rickly St (43068-2513)
PHONE..............................614 577-9360
William Stewart Iii, Pr
EMP: 7 EST: 1981
SQ FT: 8,000
SALES (est): 711.11K Privately Held
Web: www.columbusgraphics.net
SIC: 3993 Signs and advertising specialties

(G-11564)
DAIFUKU AMERICA CORPORATION (DH)
6700 Tussing Rd (43068-5083)
PHONE..............................614 863-1888
Satoru Otani, Pr
Tatsuo Inoue, *
John Doychich, *
Ken Hamel, *
Akihiko Nishimura, *
▲ EMP: 150 EST: 1983
SQ FT: 70,000
SALES (est): 43.35MM Privately Held
Web: www.daifuku.com
SIC: 3535 Conveyors and conveying equipment
HQ: Daifuku North America Inc.
30100 Cabot Dr
Novi MI 48377
248 553-1000

(G-11565)
DIMENSIONAL METALS INC (PA)
Also Called: D M I
58 Klema Dr N (43068-9691)
PHONE..............................740 927-3633
Stephen C Wissman, CEO
Phillip Gastaldo, *
Steven Gastaldo, *
EMP: 43 EST: 1988
SQ FT: 34,000
SALES (est): 9.56MM Privately Held
Web: www.dmimetals.com
SIC: 1761 3444 3531 Sheet metal work, nec; Sheet metalwork; Roofing equipment

(G-11566)
DYNALAB EMS INC
555 Lancaster Ave (43068)
PHONE..............................614 866-9999
Gary James, Pr
Charles Arbuckle, *
▲ EMP: 113 EST: 2008
SALES (est): 11.2MM
SALES (corp-wide): 41.06MM Privately Held
Web: www.dynalabems.com
SIC: 3679 Electronic circuits
PA: Dynalab, Inc.
555 Lancaster Ave
Reynoldsburg OH 43068
614 866-9999

(G-11567)
DYNALAB FF INC
555 Lancaster Ave (43068-1128)
PHONE..............................614 866-9999
Gary James, Pr
Charles Arbuckle, Sec
▲ EMP: 72 EST: 2008
SALES (est): 12.36MM
SALES (corp-wide): 41.06MM Privately Held
Web: www.dynalabems.com
SIC: 3679 Electronic circuits
PA: Dynalab, Inc.
555 Lancaster Ave
Reynoldsburg OH 43068
614 866-9999

(G-11568)
DYNALAB INC (PA)
555 Lancaster Ave (43068-1128)
PHONE..............................614 866-9999
▲ EMP: 95 EST: 1984
SALES (est): 41.06MM
SALES (corp-wide): 41.06MM Privately Held
Web: www.dynalabems.com
SIC: 3679 3678 3672 3661 Harness assemblies, for electronic use: wire or cable ; Electronic connectors; Printed circuit boards; Telephone and telegraph apparatus

(G-11569)
FARBER SPECIALTY VEHICLES INC
7052 Americana Pkwy (43068-4117)
PHONE..............................614 863-6470
Ken Farber, Pr
Nick Farber, *
John Farber, *
◆ EMP: 110 EST: 1975
SQ FT: 60,000
SALES (est): 9.32MM Privately Held
Web: www.farberspecialty.com
SIC: 3711 Automobile assembly, including specialty automobiles

(G-11570)
FRAME WAREHOUSE
7502 E Main St (43068-1208)
PHONE..............................614 861-4582

Jeff Christian, *Owner*
EMP: 6 **EST:** 1964
SALES (est): 236.08K **Privately Held**
Web:
www.theoriginalframewarehouse.com
SIC: 2499 2752 3499 Picture and mirror frames, wood; Posters, lithographed; Picture frames, metal

(G-11571)
FREDRICK WELDING & MACHINING
6840 Americana Pkwy (43068-4113)
PHONE..........................614 866-9650
Fred Williams, *Pr*
Tammy Corriveau, *VP*
John Corriveau, *VP*
Lillian Joyce Williams, *Sec*
EMP: 6 **EST:** 1973
SQ FT: 18,750
SALES (est): 799.51K **Privately Held**
Web: www.fredrickwelding.com
SIC: 3599 7692 Machine shop, jobbing and repair; Welding repair

(G-11572)
INTEGRITY GROUP CONSULTING INC
Also Called: Igc Software
6432 E Main St Ste 201 (43068-2369)
PHONE..........................614 759-9148
Brian Ferguson, *Pr*
EMP: 10 **EST:** 1999
SALES (est): 2.2MM
SALES (corp-wide): 12.69MM **Privately Held**
SIC: 7372 Business oriented computer software
HQ: Movehq Inc.
3440 Hollenberg Dr
Bridgeton MO 63044
614 759-9148

(G-11573)
KENYETTA BAGBY ENTERPRISE LLC
6629 Penick Dr (43068-2836)
PHONE..........................614 584-3426
Kenyetta Bagby, *Pr*
EMP: 10 **EST:** 2007
SALES (est): 498.77K **Privately Held**
SIC: 2754 8741 6531 7929 Business form and card printing, gravure; Management services; Real estate agents and managers ; Entertainment service

(G-11574)
MMELO BTQ CONFECTIONERS LLC
6475 E Main St Ste 128 (43068-7320)
PHONE..........................614 822-9530
Michelle Allen, *Managing Member*
EMP: 7 **EST:** 2017
SALES (est): 493.81K **Privately Held**
Web: www.mmelo.co
SIC: 2066 2052 Chocolate candy, solid; Cookies and crackers

(G-11575)
MULCH MANUFACTURING INC (HQ)
Also Called: Cypress Court
6747 Taylor Rd Sw (43068-9649)
PHONE..........................614 864-4004
▲ **EMP:** 40 **EST:** 1985
SALES (est): 23.4MM
SALES (corp-wide): 96.96MM **Privately Held**
Web: www.mulchmfg.com
SIC: 2499 Mulch, wood and bark
PA: Sustainablegreen Team, Ltd.
24200 County Road 561
Astatula FL 34705
407 886-8733

(G-11576)
OHIO STATE INSTITUTE FIN INC
Also Called: Ohio Select Imprinted Fabrics
7394 E Main St (43068-2166)
P.O. Box 1645 (43068)
PHONE..........................614 861-8811
Eleanor J Martin, *CEO*
Robert Martin, *Pr*
EMP: 8 **EST:** 1970
SQ FT: 1,600
SALES (est): 485.23K **Privately Held**
Web: www.ohioselect.com
SIC: 2396 5199 Screen printing on fabric articles; Advertising specialties

(G-11577)
OHIOS BEST JUICE COMPANY LLC
299 Pathfinder Dr Ste 103 (43068-4804)
PHONE..........................440 258-0834
EMP: 11 **EST:** 2020
SALES (est): 462.07K **Privately Held**
SIC: 2037 Frozen fruits and vegetables

(G-11578)
PRECISION POLYMERS INC
6919 Americana Pkwy (43068-4116)
PHONE..........................614 322-9951
Andrew Wood, *Pr*
EMP: 20 **EST:** 2000
SQ FT: 17,500
SALES (est): 2.49MM **Privately Held**
Web: www.precisionpolymers.com
SIC: 3089 Injection molding of plastics

(G-11579)
READY RIGS LLC
2321 Taylor Park Dr (43068-8052)
PHONE..........................740 963-9203
EMP: 10 **EST:** 2021
SALES (est): 1.41MM **Privately Held**
SIC: 3537 Trucks: freight, baggage, etc.: industrial, except mining

(G-11580)
SNOOK ADVERTISING AL PUBLISHER
Also Called: Snook Al Advertising/Publisher
1567 Alar Ave (43068-2601)
P.O. Box 1 (43068-0001)
PHONE..........................614 866-3333
Don T Iles, *Owner*
Audrey Iles, *CEO*
EMP: 10 **EST:** 1968
SQ FT: 1,479
SALES (est): 488.99K **Privately Held**
Web: www.groveportinfo.com
SIC: 2741 Directories, nec: publishing only, not printed on site

(G-11581)
STREAMLINE MEDIA & PUBG LLC
2699 Prendergast Pl (43068-5218)
PHONE..........................614 822-1817
EMP: 6 **EST:** 2020
SALES (est): 50K **Privately Held**
SIC: 2711 Newspapers, publishing and printing

(G-11582)
TOWN CNTRY TECHNICAL SVCS INC
Also Called: Keytel Systems
6200 Eastgreen Blvd (43068-3442)
PHONE..........................614 866-7700
Kristopher Haley, *Pr*
EMP: 10 **EST:** 1983
SQ FT: 4,000
SALES (est): 2.68MM **Privately Held**
Web: www.keytelsystems.com

SIC: 7629 5999 1731 7373
Telecommunication equipment repair (except telephones); Telephone equipment and systems; Computer installation; Local area network (LAN) systems integrator

(G-11583)
TS TECH AMERICAS INC (HQ)
8458 E Broad St (43068-9749)
PHONE..........................614 575-4100
Minoru Maeda, *Pr*
Jason J Ma, *Ex VP*
Takayuki Taniuchi, *
Hiroshi Suzuki, *
▲ **EMP:** 350 **EST:** 2013
SALES (est): 337.17MM **Privately Held**
Web: www.tstech.com
SIC: 5099 2396 Child restraint seats, automotive; Automotive trimmings, fabric
PA: Ts Tech Co., Ltd.
3-7-27, Sakaecho
Asaka STM 351-0

(G-11584)
TS TECH USA CORPORATION (DH)
8400 E Broad St (43068-9749)
PHONE..........................614 577-1088
Kazuhiso Saito, *Pr*
Hideo Mizusawa, *
Rudy Claming, *
▲ **EMP:** 388 **EST:** 1994
SQ FT: 244,000
SALES (est): 45.05MM **Privately Held**
Web: www.tstech.com
SIC: 3714 Motor vehicle body components and frame
HQ: Ts Tech Americas, Inc.
8458 E Broad St
Reynoldsburg OH 43068
614 575-4100

(G-11585)
TWO GRNDMTHERS GOURMET KIT LLC
9127 Firstgate Dr (43068-9596)
PHONE..........................614 746-0888
Vicky Moore, *Owner*
Ven Jackson, *Owner*
EMP: 6 **EST:** 2009
SALES (est): 289.54K **Privately Held**
SIC: 2033 Canned fruits and specialties

(G-11586)
VS SERVICE COMPANY LLC
Also Called: Victorias Secret Service Co
4 Limited Pkwy E (43068-5300)
PHONE..........................614 415-2348
EMP: 1845 **EST:** 1986
SALES (est): 5.45MM
SALES (corp-wide): 6.23B **Publicly Held**
SIC: 2341 Women's and children's underwear
PA: Victoria's Secret & Co.
4 Limited Pkwy E
Reynoldsburg OH 43068
614 577-7000

Richfield
Summit County

(G-11587)
ALLEGA CONCRETE CORP
5146 Allega Way (44286-9817)
PHONE..........................216 447-0814
John Allega, *Pr*
Joe Allega, *
Jim Allega, *
Jeffrey Wallis, *
EMP: 35 **EST:** 1990

SALES (est): 2.05MM **Privately Held**
Web: www.allega.com
SIC: 3273 Ready-mixed concrete

(G-11588)
CISCO SYSTEMS INC
Also Called: Cisco Systems
4125 Highlander Pkwy (44286-9085)
PHONE..........................330 523-2000
Michael Wyss, *Brnch Mgr*
EMP: 7
SALES (corp-wide): 53.8B **Publicly Held**
Web: www.cisco.com
SIC: 3577 Data conversion equipment, media-to-media: computer
PA: Cisco Systems, Inc.
170 W Tasman Dr
San Jose CA 95134
408 526-4000

(G-11589)
CLEVELAND-CLIFFS COLUMBUS LLC (DH)
4020 Kinross Lakes Pkwy Ste 101 (44286-9249)
PHONE..........................614 492-6800
▲ **EMP:** 102 **EST:** 2003
SALES (est): 49.4MM
SALES (corp-wide): 19.18B **Publicly Held**
SIC: 3479 3471 3398 Galvanizing of iron, steel, or end-formed products; Plating and polishing; Metal heat treating
HQ: Cleveland-Cliffs Steel Llc
1 S Dearborn St Fl 19
Chicago IL 60603
312 346-0300

(G-11590)
DENTAL CERAMICS INC
3404 Brecksville Rd (44286-9662)
PHONE..........................330 523-5240
John Lavicka, *Pr*
EMP: 24 **EST:** 1963
SALES (est): 6.43MM **Privately Held**
Web: www.dentalceramicsusa.com
SIC: 8072 3843 Crown and bridge production ; Dental equipment and supplies

(G-11591)
EXIT 11 TRUCK TIRE SERVICE INC
5219 Brecksville Rd Ste B (44286-9697)
PHONE..........................330 659-6372
James Smith Junior, *Pr*
EMP: 9 **EST:** 1981
SQ FT: 8,000
SALES (est): 2.42MM **Privately Held**
Web: www.exit11trucktire.com
SIC: 5531 7534 Automotive tires; Tire repair shop

(G-11592)
FAWCETT CO INC
3863 Congress Pkwy (44286-9745)
PHONE..........................330 659-4187
Jack Grace, *Pr*
EMP: 7 **EST:** 1946
SQ FT: 16,000
SALES (est): 922.81K **Privately Held**
Web: www.fawcettco.com
SIC: 3559 7699 Paint making machinery; Industrial machinery and equipment repair

(G-11593)
FRONTIER TANK CENTER INC
3800 Congress Pkwy (44286-9745)
P.O. Box 460 (44286-0460)
PHONE..........................330 659-3888
James S Hollabaugh, *Pr*
Mary Hollabaugh, *
EMP: 9 **EST:** 1988
SQ FT: 25,000

SALES (est): 1.38MM **Privately Held**
Web: www.frontiertrailersales.com
SIC: **7699** 5013 3714 Tank repair; Trailer
parts and accessories; Motor vehicle body
components and frame

(G-11594)
GOPOWERX INC
3850 Sawbridge Dr Unit 24 (44286-9260)
PHONE....................................440 707-6029
Neil Sater, *Pr*
EMP: 36 EST: 2010
SALES (est): 3.49MM **Privately Held**
SIC: **5211** 3674 Solar heating equipment;
Semiconductors and related devices
PA: Mh Gopower Company Limited
6-2, Luke 3rd Rd.,
Kaohsiung City

(G-11595)
PAK MASTER LLC
3778 Timberlake Dr (44286-9187)
PHONE....................................330 523-5319
Peter Biierg, *Managing Member*
EMP: 50 EST: 2016
SQ FT: 100,000
SALES (est): 4.18MM
SALES (corp-wide): 142.34MM **Privately
Held**
SIC: **3565** Packaging machinery
HQ: Switchback Group, Inc.
5638 Transportation Blvd
Cleveland OH 44125

(G-11596)
PREMIER FARNELL CORP (HQ)
4180 Highlander Pkwy (44286-9352)
PHONE....................................330 659-0459
◆ EMP: 55 EST: 1996
SALES (est): 1.39B
SALES (corp-wide): 23.76B **Publicly Held**
Web: www.farnell.com
SIC: **3451** Screw machine products
PA: Avnet, Inc.
2211 S 47th St
Phoenix AZ 85034
480 643-2000

(G-11597)
**PREMIER FARNELL HOLDING INC
(DH)**
4180 Highlander Pkwy (44286-9352)
PHONE....................................330 523-4273
Dan Hill, *Pr*
Joseph R Daprile, *VP*
Paul M Barlak, *Treas*
Steven Webb, *VP*
◆ EMP: 20 EST: 1998
SQ FT: 35,000
SALES (est): 5.38MM
SALES (corp-wide): 23.76B **Publicly Held**
Web: www.summit4success.com
SIC: **5065** 5046 Electronic parts and
equipment, nec; Nozzles, fire fighting
HQ: Element14 Us Holdings Inc
4180 Highlander Pkwy
Richfield OH 44286
330 523-4280

(G-11598)
RAYHAVEN GROUP INC
Also Called: Rayhaven Group
3842 Congress Pkwy Ste A (44286-9745)
PHONE....................................330 659-3183
Robert Rickenbacker, *Mgr*
EMP: 6
Web: www.rayhaven.com
SIC: **3448** 5046 5084 Prefabricated metal
buildings; Commercial equipment, nec;
Heat exchange equipment, industrial
PA: Rayhaven Group, Inc.

35901 Schoolcraft Rd
Livonia MI 48150

(G-11599)
SCRIPTYPE PUBLISHING INC
Also Called: Broadview Journal, The
4300 W Streetsboro Rd (44286-9796)
PHONE....................................330 659-0303
Sue Serdinak, *Pr*
EMP: 19 EST: 1978
SQ FT: 5,708
SALES (est): 367.39K **Privately Held**
Web: www.scriptype.com
SIC: **2741** Miscellaneous publishing

(G-11600)
SENSIBLE PRODUCTS INC
3857 Brecksville Rd (44286-9634)
PHONE....................................330 659-4212
Philip Mclean, *Pr*
Brittany Mclean, *VP*
EMP: 9 EST: 1984
SALES (est): 904.13K **Privately Held**
Web: www.senpro.net
SIC: **3429** Nozzles, fire fighting

(G-11601)
SMC CORPORATION OF AMERICA
4160 Highlander Pkwy Ste 200
(44286-9082)
PHONE....................................330 659-2006
Scott Chonko, *Brnch Mgr*
EMP: 14
Web: www.smcusa.com
SIC: **3625** 3492 Actuators, industrial; Control
valves, fluid power: hydraulic and pneumatic
HQ: Smc Corporation Of America
10100 Smc Blvd
Noblesville IN 46060
317 899-4440

(G-11602)
**SNAP-ON BUSINESS SOLUTIONS
INC (HQ)**
4025 Kinross Lakes Pkwy (44286-9371)
PHONE....................................330 659-1600
Timothy Chambers, *Pr*
Michael Maddison, *
EMP: 300 EST: 1987
SQ FT: 88,000
SALES (est): 32.93MM
SALES (corp-wide): 5.11B **Publicly Held**
Web: sbs.snapon.com
SIC: **7372** Business oriented computer
software
PA: Snap-On Incorporated
2801 80th St
Kenosha WI 53143
262 656-5200

(G-11603)
TAYLOR COMMUNICATIONS INC
4125 Highlander Pkwy Ste 230
(44286-9085)
PHONE....................................216 265-1800
Ray Taylor, *Mgr*
EMP: 19
SALES (corp-wide): 3.81B **Privately Held**
Web: www.taylor.com
SIC: **2761** Manifold business forms
HQ: Taylor Communications, Inc.
1725 Roe Crest Dr
North Mankato MN 56003
866 541-0937

Richmond
Jefferson County

(G-11604)
MC CONNELLS MARKET
Also Called: McConnell's Farm Market
2189 State Route 43 (43944-7980)
PHONE....................................740 765-4300
Kenneth Mc Connell, *Pt*
James Mc Connell, *Pt*
EMP: 6 EST: 1953
SALES (est): 653.13K **Privately Held**
Web: www.mcconnellsmarket.com
SIC: **2011** 5421 Meat packing plants; Meat
markets, including freezer provisioners

(G-11605)
SIGN AMERICA INCORPORATED
3887 State Route 43 (43944-7912)
P.O. Box 396 (43944-0396)
PHONE....................................740 765-5555
Judith A Hilty, *Pr*
Scott Hilty Junior, *VP*
John Bray, *Sec*
EMP: 9 EST: 1986
SQ FT: 6,000
SALES (est): 2.21MM **Privately Held**
Web: www.signamericainc.com
SIC: **5046** 3993 Signs, electrical; Signs and
advertising specialties

Richmond Dale
Ross County

(G-11606)
APPALACHIA FREEZE DRY CO LLC
✪
659 Jackson St (45673-9705)
PHONE....................................740 412-0169
Kristen Howard, *Admn*
Kristen Howard, *Managing Member*
EMP: 10 EST: 2023
SALES (est): 485.96K **Privately Held**
SIC: **2034** 2064 7389 Dried and dehydrated
fruits, vegetables and soup mixes; Candy
and other confectionery products; Business
Activities at Non-Commercial Site

Richmond Heights
Cuyahoga County

(G-11607)
AVIATION CMPNENT SOLUTIONS INC
26451 Curtiss Wright Pkwy Ste 106
(44143-4410)
PHONE....................................440 295-6590
Joe Klinehamer, *Pr*
EMP: 15 EST: 2006
SALES (est): 5MM **Privately Held**
Web: www.acs-parts.com
SIC: **3728** Aircraft parts and equipment, nec

(G-11608)
BODIED BEAUTIES LLC
4820 Geraldine Rd (44143-2832)
PHONE....................................216 971-1155
EMP: 9 EST: 2020
SALES (est): 173.22K **Privately Held**
SIC: **2339** Women's and misses' athletic
clothing and sportswear

(G-11609)
CCP INDUSTRIES INC
Also Called: Ccp Industries
26301 Curtiss Wright Pkwy Ste 200
(44143-1454)

P.O. Box 6500 (44101-1500)
PHONE....................................216 535-4227
▼ EMP: 400
SIC: **5169** 2392 2297 2273 Specialty
cleaning and sanitation preparations;
Household furnishings, nec; Nonwoven
fabrics; Carpets and rugs

(G-11610)
JC CARTER LLC (DH)
Also Called: JC Carter Nozzles
26451 Curtiss Wright Pkwy Ste 106
(44143-4410)
PHONE....................................440 569-1818
▲ EMP: 8 EST: 2007
SALES (est): 3.86MM **Privately Held**
Web: www.jccarternozzles.com
SIC: **3559** Cryogenic machinery, industrial
HQ: Atlas Copco Mafi-Trench Company Llc
3037 Industrial Pkwy
Santa Maria CA 93455

(G-11611)
**MOMENTIVE PERFORMANCE MTLS
INC**
Also Called: Momentive Performance Mtls
24400 Highland Rd (44143-2503)
PHONE....................................440 878-5705
EMP: 147
Web: www.momentivetech.com
SIC: **2869** 3479 Silicones; Coating of metals
with silicon
HQ: Momentive Performance Materials Inc.
2750 Balltown Rd
Niskayuna NY 12309

(G-11612)
R & H ENTERPRISES LLC
Also Called: Rh Enterprises
4933 Karen Isle Dr (44143-1412)
PHONE....................................216 702-4449
Ryan Hoover, *Managing Member*
EMP: 6 EST: 2008
SALES (est): 252.71K **Privately Held**
SIC: **7372** 7389 Application computer
software; Business services, nec

(G-11613)
TZ ACQUISITION CORP
Also Called: Tranzonic Companies
26301 Curtiss Wright Pkwy 2nd Fl
(44143-4413)
PHONE....................................216 535-4300
Kenneth Vuylsteke, *Prin*
Thomas S Friedl, *
◆ EMP: 14 EST: 1997
SQ FT: 22,000
SALES (est): 863.61K **Privately Held**
SIC: **2211** 2326 2842 2262 Scrub cloths;
Work garments, except raincoats:
waterproof; Sanitation preparations,
disinfectants and deodorants; Napping:
manmade fiber and silk broadwoven fabrics

Richwood
Union County

(G-11614)
CREATIVE FABRICATION LTD
20110 Predmore Rd (43344-9014)
PHONE....................................740 262-5789
John Hughes, *Managing Member*
EMP: 7 EST: 2009
SALES (est): 443.58K **Privately Held**
Web: www.creativefabrication.org
SIC: **7692** 7389 Welding repair; Business
services, nec

2025 Harris Ohio
Industrial Directory
▲ = Import ▼ = Export
◆ = Import/Export

Ridgeville Corners
Henry County

(G-11615)
NASG AUTO-SEAT TEC LLC
19911 County Rd T (43555)
PHONE................................419 359-5954
David Vondeylen, *Managing Member*
EMP: 30 **EST:** 2013
SALES (est): 1.09MM **Privately Held**
SIC: 3469 Stamping metal for the trade

(G-11616)
NASG STING RDGVLLE CORNERS LLC (HQ)
Also Called: Alex Products, Inc.
19911 County Rd T (43555)
P.O. Box 326 (43555-0326)
PHONE................................419 267-5240
Dave Von Deylen, *Pr*
Gary Crider, *
▲ **EMP:** 300 **EST:** 1973
SQ FT: 150,000
SALES (est): 21.22MM
SALES (corp-wide): 250.69MM **Privately Held**
Web: www.alexproducts.cc
SIC: 3599 Machine shop, jobbing and repair
PA: Nasg Realty, Llc
119 Kirby Dr
Portland TN 37148
615 323-0500

Rio Grande
Gallia County

(G-11617)
INLAND PRODUCTS INC
Also Called: Galipols Reduction Co
P.O. Box 337 (45674-0337)
PHONE................................740 245-5514
Mark Dickson, *Mgr*
EMP: 15
SALES (corp-wide): 2.56MM **Privately Held**
SIC: 2077 Grease rendering, inedible
PA: Inland Products, Inc.
599 Frank Rd
Columbus OH 43223
614 443-3425

Ripley
Brown County

(G-11618)
GLENRO INC
133 N 3rd St (45167-1114)
PHONE................................606 564-4778
EMP: 7
SALES (corp-wide): 11.36MM **Privately Held**
Web: www.glenro.com
SIC: 3567 Heating units and devices, industrial: electric
PA: Glenro, Inc.
39 Mcbride Ave
Paterson NJ 07501
973 279-5900

(G-11619)
RIPLEY METALWORKS LLC
111 Waterworks Rd (45167-1456)
PHONE................................937 392-4992
Michael Walkup, *Genl Pt*
EMP: 45 **EST:** 1992
SQ FT: 75,000
SALES (est): 9.3MM **Privately Held**
Web: www.ripleymetalworks.com
SIC: 3441 Fabricated structural metal

Risingsun
Wood County

(G-11620)
WELLS INC
8176 Us Highway 23 (43457-9629)
P.O. Box 9 (43457-0009)
PHONE................................419 457-2611
Steffen Wellstein, *Pr*
Steffen R Wellstein, *Pr*
EMP: 10 **EST:** 1967
SQ FT: 15,000
SALES (est): 949.26K **Privately Held**
Web: www.wellsfargoadvisors.com
SIC: 3494 Well adapters

Rittman
Wayne County

(G-11621)
FASTFORMINGCOM LLC
300 Morning Star Dr (44270-9644)
PHONE................................330 927-3277
James Reedy, *Pr*
EMP: 12 **EST:** 1999
SQ FT: 12,000
SALES (est): 1.87MM **Privately Held**
Web: www.fastforming.com
SIC: 3089 Injection molding of plastics

(G-11622)
IMPERIAL FAMILY INC
80 Industrial St (44270-1508)
P.O. Box 375 (44270)
PHONE................................330 927-5065
Walter Staiger, *Pr*
John Klein, *
Genevieve Staiger, *
Eugene Staiger, *
Susan Klein, *
EMP: 55 **EST:** 1960
SQ FT: 60,000
SALES (est): 9MM **Privately Held**
Web: www.ip-inc.com
SIC: 3089 Injection molding of plastics

(G-11623)
J & O PLASTICS INC
12475 Sheets Rd (44270-9730)
PHONE................................330 927-3169
Oscar Gross, *Pr*
Edgar Gross, *
Christine Gross, *
EMP: 50 **EST:** 1982
SQ FT: 90,000
SALES (est): 7.82MM **Privately Held**
Web: www.jandoplastics.com
SIC: 3089 Injection molding of plastics

(G-11624)
LUKE ENGINEERING & MFG CORP
11 Pipestone Rd (44270-9729)
PHONE................................330 925-3344
Pam Craig, *Mgr*
EMP: 20
SALES (corp-wide): 4.76MM **Privately Held**
Web: www.lukeeng.com
SIC: 3471 Electroplating of metals or formed products
PA: Luke Engineering & Mfg Corp
456 South Blvd
Wadsworth OH 44281
330 335-1501

(G-11625)
MORTON SALT INC
151 Industrial Ave (44270-1593)
PHONE................................330 925-3015
Mark Wallace, *Brnch Mgr*
EMP: 150
SALES (corp-wide): 3.82B **Privately Held**
Web: www.mortonsalt.com
SIC: 5149 2899 Salt, edible; Chemical preparations, nec
HQ: Morton Salt, Inc.
444 W Lake St Ste 3000
Chicago IL 60606

(G-11626)
PFI DISPLAYS INC (PA)
Also Called: Promotional Fixtures
40 Industrial St (44270-1525)
P.O. Box 508 (44270-0508) .
PHONE................................330 925-9015
Vincent Tricomi, *Ch Bd*
Anthony R Tricomi, *
James Tricomi, *
Carol Tricomi, *
Robert J Kapitan, *
EMP: 39 **EST:** 1970
SQ FT: 70,000
SALES (est): 3.9MM
SALES (corp-wide): 3.9MM **Privately Held**
Web: www.pfidisplays.com
SIC: 3993 2541 2542 Displays and cutouts, window and lobby; Store and office display cases and fixtures; Partitions and fixtures, except wood

(G-11627)
RITTMAN INC
Also Called: Mull Iron
10 Mull Dr (44270-9777)
PHONE................................330 927-6855
Chester Mull Junior, *Pr*
William Mull, *
Beth Mull, *
Richard J Wendelken, *
Robert A O'neil, *Prin*
EMP: 60 **EST:** 1983
SQ FT: 34,000
SALES (est): 9.33MM **Privately Held**
Web: www.mulliron.net
SIC: 3441 1791 Fabricated structural metal; Structural steel erection

(G-11628)
3WI33 WOODCRAFT INC
15 Industrial St (44270-1507)
PHONE................................330 925-1807
Ken Maibach, *Pr*
Dave Rufener, *
EMP: 30 **EST:** 1981
SQ FT: 45,000
SALES (est): 6.97MM **Privately Held**
Web: www.swisswoodcraft.com
SIC: 2431 Doors, wood

Rock Creek
Ashtabula County

(G-11629)
DAVID BIXEL
Also Called: Hartsgrove Machine
2683 State Route 534 (44084-9340)
PHONE................................440 474-4410
David Bixel, *Owner*
EMP: 14 **EST:** 2001
SALES (est): 1.87MM **Privately Held**
Web: www.hartsgrovemachine.com
SIC: 3599 Machine shop, jobbing and repair

Rockford
Mercer County

(G-11630)
FREMONT COMPANY
Also Called: Fremont
150 Hickory St (45882-9264)
PHONE................................419 363-2924
James Gibson, *Mgr*
EMP: 40
SALES (corp-wide): 51.18MM **Privately Held**
Web: www.fremontcompany.com
SIC: 2033 2099 2035 Fruit juices: packaged in cans, jars, etc.; Food preparations, nec; Pickles, sauces, and salad dressings
PA: The Fremont Company
802 N Front St
Fremont OH 43420
419 334-8995

(G-11631)
WORLD CONNECTIONS CORPS
10803 Erastus Durbin Rd (45882-9654)
PHONE................................419 363-2681
Llloyd Linton, *Pr*
EMP: 6 **EST:** 2001
SALES (est): 261.36K **Privately Held**
SIC: 3081 Vinyl film and sheet

Rocky River
Cuyahoga County

(G-11632)
CANVUS INC
18500 Lake Rd (44116-1744)
P.O. Box 16543 (44116)
PHONE................................216 340-7500
Alex Kowalski, *Pr*
EMP: 50 **EST:** 2022
SALES (est): 9.21MM **Privately Held**
SIC: 3511 Turbines and turbine generator sets

(G-11633)
CRUISIN TIMES MAGAZINE
20545 Center Ridge Rd Ste LI40 (44116-3441)
P.O. Box 27247 (19118-0247)
PHONE................................440 331-4615
John Shapiro, *Prin*
EMP: 7 **EST:** 2008
SALES (est): 189.86K **Privately Held**
Web: www.cruisintimesmagazine.com
SIC: 5994 2721 Magazine stand; Magazines: publishing and printing

(G-11634)
GREAT LAKES MFG GROUP LTD
19035 Old Detroit Rd (44116-1710)
PHONE................................440 391-8266
Andrew E Drumm, *Pt*
Thomas Mc Neill, *Pt*
EMP: 7 **EST:** 2016
SALES (est): 948.95K **Privately Held**
Web: www.glmfg.com
SIC: 3312 8748 Stainless steel; Systems analysis and engineering consulting services

(G-11635)
OPAL DIAMOND LLC
20033 Detroit Rd N Ridge Annex 2nd.Fl (44116-2400)
PHONE................................330 653-5876
William Mitchell, *Pr*
Michael Reilly, *Ex VP*
Henry Ng, *VP*

GEOGRAPHIC

EMP: 7 EST: 2015
SQ FT: 2,000
SALES (est): 611.59K Privately Held
SIC: 2875 Compost

(G-11636)
P S GRAPHICS INC
20284 Orchard Grove Ave (44116-3527)
PHONE..............................440 356-9656
Nancy Vedda, Pr
Phil Vedda, VP
EMP: 6 EST: 1969
SQ FT: 4,000
SALES (est): 193.39K Privately Held
SIC: 2759 Screen printing

(G-11637)
PAMEE LLC
18500 Lake Rd (44116-1744)
PHONE..............................216 232-9255
EMP: 50 EST: 2020
SALES (est): 1.78MM Privately Held
Web: www.pamee.com
SIC: 7372 Prepackaged software

(G-11638)
ROCKY RIVER BREWING CO
21290 Center Ridge Rd (44116-3204)
PHONE..............................440 895-2739
Gary Cintron, Owner
EMP: 8 EST: 1997
SQ FT: 4,000
SALES (est): 914.87K Privately Held
Web: www.rockyriverbrewco.com
SIC: 2082 5813 5812 Malt beverages;
  Drinking places; Eating places

(G-11639)
SCRATCH OFF WORKS LLC
19537 Lake Rd (44116-1858)
PHONE..............................440 333-4302
EMP: 8 EST: 1993
SALES (est): 558.27K Privately Held
Web: www.scratchoffworks.com
SIC: 2752 Offset printing

(G-11640)
SYNTEC LLC
20525 Center Ridge Rd Ste 512
(44116-3447)
PHONE..............................440 229-6262
Maximillian Fisher, Managing Member
EMP: 10 EST: 2010
SALES (est): 4.18MM Privately Held
Web: www.syntecdental.com
SIC: 7372 7373 7379 Business oriented
  computer software; Computer integrated
  systems design; Computer related
  maintenance services

(G-11641)
ZULLIX LLC
18500 Lake Rd (44116-1744)
PHONE..............................440 536-9300
EMP: 30 EST: 2021
SALES (est): 2.68MM Privately Held
SIC: 7372 Application computer software

Rogers
Columbiana County

(G-11642)
PAUL R LIPP & SON INC
47563 Pancake Clarkson Rd (44455-9723)
PHONE..............................330 227-9614
Gregory A Lipp, Pr
Paul R Lipp, VP
Lauren Lipp, Sec
EMP: 10 EST: 1964

SALES (est): 527.15K Privately Held
Web: www.prlipp.com
SIC: 1794 3273 Excavation and grading;
  building construction; Ready-mixed concrete

(G-11643)
STEELCON LLC
47161 Oh-558 (44455)
PHONE..............................330 457-4003
Ronald Allen Hodge, Managing Member
EMP: 37 EST: 2007
SALES (est): 11.67MM Privately Held
Web: www.steelcon.co
SIC: 3441 Building components, structural
  steel

Rome
Ashtabula County

(G-11644)
J AARON WEAVER
Also Called: Indian Creek Structures
5759 Us Highway 6 (44085-9634)
PHONE..............................440 474-9185
J Aaron Weaver, Owner
EMP: 6 EST: 2015
SQ FT: 2,400
SALES (est): 144.45K Privately Held
Web: www.indiancreekstructure.com
SIC: 2452 Prefabricated wood buildings

(G-11645)
MSC INDUSTRIES INC
5131 Ireland Rd (44085-9812)
P.O. Box 200 (44064-0200)
PHONE..............................440 474-8788
John M Husek, Pr
Mary C Husek, Sec
EMP: 6 EST: 1987
SQ FT: 4,000
SALES (est): 789.91K Privately Held
SIC: 3545 3469 Tools and accessories for
  machine tools; Machine parts, stamped or
  pressed metal

Rootstown
Portage County

(G-11646)
A TO Z PAPER BOX COMPANY
4477 Tallmadge Rd (44272-9610)
PHONE..............................330 325-8722
Douglas Eatinger, Pr
EMP: 9 EST: 1962
SQ FT: 3,600
SALES (est): 767.52K Privately Held
SIC: 2652 5113 2759 Filing boxes,
  paperboard: made from purchased
  materials; Bags, paper and disposable
  plastic; Commercial printing, nec

(G-11647)
**BARREL RUN CRSSING WNERY
VNYRD**
Also Called: Brx
3272 Industry Rd (44272-9775)
PHONE..............................330 325-1075
Nick M Miller, Pr
EMP: 6 EST: 2010
SALES (est): 71.03K Privately Held
Web: www.barrelrunwinery.com
SIC: 2084 Wines

(G-11648)
JET RUBBER COMPANY
4457 Tallmadge Rd (44272-9610)
PHONE..............................330 325-1821

Franklin R Brubaker, Prin
Karen Crooks, *
EMP: 43 EST: 1954
SQ FT: 20,000
SALES (est): 3.95MM Privately Held
Web: www.jetrubber.com
SIC: 3069 3053 3533 5085 Molded rubber
  products; Gaskets; packing and sealing
  devices; Gas field machinery and equipment
  ; Rubber goods, mechanical

(G-11649)
MINERS TRACTOR SALES INC (PA)
Also Called: Miner's Bishop Tractor Sales
6941 Tallmadge Rd (44272-9758)
PHONE..............................330 325-9914
Stephen Miner, CEO
Craig M Stephens, Pr
EMP: 10 EST: 2006
SALES (est): 2MM
SALES (corp-wide): 2MM Privately Held
Web: www.edinburgtractor.com
SIC: 3537 5999 Industrial trucks and tractors
  ; Farm tractors

(G-11650)
MONITOR MOLD & MACHINE CO
3393 Industry Rd (44272-9505)
P.O. Box 396 (44272-0396)
PHONE..............................330 697-7800
Phillip Warlop, Pr
EMP: 10 EST: 1980
SQ FT: 12,000
SALES (est): 860.2K Privately Held
SIC: 3544 Industrial molds

(G-11651)
NUEVUE SOLUTIONS INC
4209 State Route 44 D-134 (44272-9698)
PHONE..............................440 836-4772
William Mccroskey, Pr
James Sacher, Prin
EMP: 6 EST: 2016
SALES (est): 228.76K Privately Held
Web: www.nuevuesolutions.com
SIC: 3841 Surgical and medical instruments

(G-11652)
SINGLETON REELS INC
4612 Lynn Rd (44272-9710)
PHONE..............................330 274-2961
Scott Hamilton, Pr
EMP: 20 EST: 1972
SALES (est): 4.29MM Privately Held
Web: www.singletonreels.com
SIC: 2499 Reels, plywood

Roseville
Muskingum County

(G-11653)
CLAY BURLEY PRODUCTS CO (PA)
455 Gordon St (43777-1110)
P.O. Box 35 (43777-0035)
PHONE..............................740 452-3633
Peter Petratsas, Pr
▲ EMP: 50 EST: 1922
SQ FT: 180,000
SALES (est): 4.82MM
SALES (corp-wide): 4.82MM Privately
Held
Web: www.burleyclay.com
SIC: 3269 5032 Stoneware pottery products;
  Ceramic wall and floor tile, nec

(G-11654)
TRADEWINDS PRIN TWEAR
35 E Athens Rd (43777-1212)
P.O. Box 813 (43702-0813)

PHONE..............................740 214-5005
Tom Erdico, Owner
EMP: 6 EST: 2011
SALES (est): 249.38K Privately Held
Web: www.tradewindsprintwear.com
SIC: 2752 Offset printing

Rossburg
Darke County

(G-11655)
CAL-MAINE FOODS INC
3078 Washington Rd (45362-9500)
PHONE..............................937 337-9576
Leonard Kropp, Genl Mgr
EMP: 67
SALES (corp-wide): 2.33B Publicly Held
Web: www.calmainefoods.com
SIC: 0252 2015 Chicken eggs; Poultry
  slaughtering and processing
PA: Cal-Maine Foods, Inc.
  1052 Hghland Clny Pkwy St
  Ridgeland MS 39157
  601 948-6813

Rossford
Wood County

(G-11656)
ELECTRO PRIME ASSEMBLY INC
63 Dixie Hwy Ste 7 (43460-1264)
PHONE..............................419 476-0100
Fred Busch, Pr
John Lauffer, VP Fin
James E Wilson, VP Mfg
Kevin Meade, VP
EMP: 7 EST: 1997
SALES (est): 147.64K Privately Held
Web: www.electroprime.com
SIC: 3471 Electroplating of metals or formed
  products

(G-11657)
HUNGER HYDRAULICS CC LTD
Also Called: Hunger Industrial Complex
63 Dixie Hwy Ste 1 (43460-1270)
P.O. Box 37 (43460-0037)
PHONE..............................419 666-4510
Walter Hunger, Pr
▲ EMP: 12 EST: 1996
SALES (est): 4.93MM Privately Held
Web: www.hunger-hydraulics.com
SIC: 3593 7699 Fluid power cylinders,
  hydraulic or pneumatic; Hydraulic
  equipment repair
HQ: Walter Hunger International
  Gesellschaft Mit Beschrankter Haftung
  Alfred-Nobel-Str. 26
  Wurzburg BY 97080
  931900970

(G-11658)
IC-FLUID POWER INC
63 Dixie Hwy (43460-1269)
PHONE..............................419 661-8811
Bernd Hunger, Pr
Armin Hunger, Pr
▲ EMP: 10 EST: 1989
SQ FT: 15,000
SALES (est): 10.75MM Privately Held
Web: www.icfluid.com
SIC: 5084 3593 7699 3492 Hydraulic
  systems equipment and supplies; Fluid
  power cylinders and actuators; Hydraulic
  equipment repair; Fluid power valves and
  hose fittings

▲ = Import ▼ = Export
◆ = Import/Export

(G-11659)
INDUSTRIAL POWER SYSTEMS INC
Also Called: I P S
146 Dixie Hwy (43460-1215)
PHONE..............................419 531-3121
Kevin D Gray, *CEO*
Jeremiah Johnson, *
Tim Grosteffon, *
Mike Williams, *
Kirk Guy, *
EMP: 300 EST: 1985
SQ FT: 20,000
SALES (est): 57.74MM **Privately Held**
Web: www.ipscontractor.com
SIC: 1711 3498 1731 1796 Mechanical
contractor; Coils, pipe: fabricated from
purchased pipe; General electrical
contractor; Millwright

(G-11660)
PILKINGTON NORTH AMERICA INC
Also Called: Pilington Libbey-Owens-Ford Co
140 Dixie Hwy (43460-1215)
PHONE..............................419 247-3211
Dick Altman, *Mgr*
EMP: 360
SQ FT: 3,000,000
Web: www.pilkington.com
SIC: 3211 3231 Float glass; Products of
purchased glass
HQ: Pilkington North America, Inc.
811 Madison Ave
Toledo OH 43604
419 247-3731

(G-11661)
RADOCY INC
30652 East River Rd (43551-3441)
P.O. Box 67 (43460-0067)
PHONE..............................419 666-4400
Thomas Bradley, *Pr*
Paul F Radocy, *Stockholder*
EMP: 15 EST: 1940
SQ FT: 18,000
SALES (est): 2.11MM **Privately Held**
Web: www.radocy.com
SIC: 3536 3594 3566 Cranes, industrial plant
; Fluid power pumps and motors; Speed
changers, drives, and gears

(G-11662)
RSW TECHNOLOGIES LLC
135 Dixie Hwy (43460-1241)
PHONE..............................419 662-8100
▲ **EMP: 17 EST:** 2007
SALES (est): 2.76MM **Privately Held**
Web: www.rswtechnologies.com
SIC: 3823 Process control instruments

(G-11663)
SASHA ELECTRONICS INC
Also Called: Digital Technologies
135 Dixie Hwy (43460-1241)
PHONE..............................419 662-8100
William R Wumer Junior, *Pr*
▲ **EMP: 7 EST:** 1982
SQ FT: 20,000
SALES (est): 344.44K **Privately Held**
Web: www.rswtechnologies.com
SIC: 7629 3822 Electronic equipment repair;
Energy cutoff controls, residential or
commercial types

(G-11664)
WELCH PUBLISHING CO
215 Osborne St (43460-1238)
PHONE..............................419 666-5344
John Welch, *VP*
EMP: 7
SQ FT: 1,167
SALES (corp-wide): 2.43MM **Privately
Held**

Web: www.perrysburg.com
SIC: 2711 Newspapers: publishing only, not
printed on site
PA: Welch Publishing Co.
117 E 2nd St
Perrysburg OH 43551
419 874-2528

Rushsylvania
Logan County

(G-11665)
DAYTON SUPERIOR CORPORATION
Also Called: Roberts Screw Products
270 Rush St (43347-2502)
PHONE..............................937 682-4015
Allan Kerns, *Brnch Mgr*
EMP: 19
SALES (corp-wide): 7.35B **Privately Held**
Web: www.daytonsuperior.com
SIC: 3429 Hardware, nec
HQ: Dayton Superior Corporation
1125 Byers Rd
Miamisburg OH 45342
937 866-0711

(G-11666)
**ROBERTS MACHINE PRODUCTS
LLC**
270 Rush St (43347-2502)
P.O. Box 210 (43347-0210)
PHONE..............................937 682-4015
Mike Stapleton, *Prin*
Kelli Phillips, *Mgr*
EMP: 11 EST: 2010
SALES (est): 3.49MM **Privately Held**
Web: www.robertsmachineproducts.com
SIC: 3559 3599 Ammunition and explosives,
loading machinery; Machine shop, jobbing
and repair

Russells Point
Logan County

(G-11667)
HONDA DEV & MFG AMER LLC
6964 State Route 235 N (43348-9703)
PHONE..............................937 843-5555
EMP: 935
Web: www.hondainamerica.com
SIC: 3714 Motor vehicle parts and
accessories
HQ: Honda Development & Manufacturing
Of America, Llc
24000 Honda Pkwy
Marysville OH 43040
937 642-5000

(G-11668)
**HONDA TRANSMISSION
MANUFACTURING OF AMERICA INC**
6964 State Route 235 N (43348-9703)
P.O. Box 2200 (90509-2200)
PHONE..............................937 843-5555
▲ **EMP:** 1200
Web: www.honda.com
SIC: 3714 Wheels, motor vehicle

(G-11669)
INDIAN LAKE SHOPPERS EDGE
204 1/2 Lincoln Blvd (43348-9681)
P.O. Box 38 (43348-0038)
PHONE..............................937 843-6600
Art Shellenbarger, *Pt*
Miriam Shellenbarger, *Pt*
EMP: 9 EST: 1988
SALES (est): 75.9K **Privately Held**
Web: www.myshoppersedge.com

SIC: 2711 Newspapers: publishing only, not
printed on site

(G-11670)
WEST OHIO TOOL CO
7311 World Class Dr (43348-9593)
P.O. Box 1457 (43348-1457)
PHONE..............................937 842-6688
Kerry Buchenroth, *Pr*
EMP: 13 EST: 1989
SALES (est): 1.6MM **Privately Held**
Web: www.westohiotool.com
SIC: 3541 Machine tools, metal cutting type

(G-11671)
WORLD CLASS PLASTICS INC
7695 State Route 708 (43348-9506)
PHONE..............................937 843-3003
Steven L Buchenroth, *CEO*
Mark Seeley, *
Scott Wisniewski, *
▲ **EMP: 80 EST:** 1994
SQ FT: 42,000
SALES (est): 23.02MM **Privately Held**
Web: www.worldclassplastics.com
SIC: 3089 Injection molding of plastics

Russia
Shelby County

(G-11672)
ABRASIVE SOURCE INC
211 W Main St (45363-9678)
P.O. Box 369 (45363-0369)
PHONE..............................937 526-9753
Kenneth W Whetstone, *Pr*
Diana J Whetstone, *VP*
EMP: 10 EST: 1994
SQ FT: 1,600
SALES (est): 493.89K **Privately Held**
Web: www.abrasivesource.com
SIC: 3291 Abrasive products

(G-11673)
**FRANCIS MANUFACTURING
COMPANY**
500 E Mn St (45363)
P.O. Box 400 (45363-0400)
PHONE..............................937 526-4551
William T Francis, *Pr*
Thomas V Francis, *
William T Francis, *Pr*
David J Francis, *
EMP: 125 EST: 1946
SQ FT: 145,000
SALES (est): 4.77MM **Privately Held**
Web: www.francismanufacturing.com
SIC: 3369 3365 Nonferrous foundries, nec;
Aluminum foundries

(G-11674)
FRANCIS-SCHULZE CO
3880 Rangeline Rd (45363-9711)
P.O. Box 245 (45363-0245)
PHONE..............................937 295-3941
Ralph Schulze, *Pr*
Rita Schulze, *
EMP: 17 EST: 1943
SQ FT: 50,000
SALES (est): 2.47MM **Privately Held**
Web: www.francisschulze.com
SIC: 3442 5031 Metal doors; Building
materials, exterior

(G-11675)
L & J CABLE INC
102 Industrial Dr (45363-7501)
P.O. Box 61 (45363-0061)
PHONE..............................937 526-9445

Doug Francis, *Pr*
Linda Francis, *VP*
▲ **EMP: 20 EST:** 1980
SALES (est): 1.31MM **Privately Held**
SIC: 3679 Harness assemblies, for
electronic use: wire or cable

(G-11676)
OREILLY PRECISION PDTS INC
Also Called: O'Reilly Precision Tool
560 E Main St (45363-9806)
PHONE..............................937 526-4677
Jeffrey O'reilly, *Pr*
Craig Martin, *
Shane Borchers, *
EMP: 35 EST: 1984
SALES (est): 5.28MM **Privately Held**
Web: www.oreillymts.com
SIC: 3312 3599 3541 Tool and die steel;
Amusement park equipment; Grinding
machines, metalworking

(G-11677)
PRODUCTION SUPPORT INC
105 Francis St (45363-9692)
P.O. Box 457 (45363-0457)
PHONE..............................937 526-3897
Linda Grogean, *Pr*
EMP: 15 EST: 1985
SALES (est): 929.98K **Privately Held**
Web: www.productionsupportinc.com
SIC: 7389 3441 Packaging and labeling
services; Fabricated structural metal

(G-11678)
**WESTERN OHIO TECHNOLOGIES
LLC**
105 Commerce Dr (45363-8788)
P.O. Box 15 (45363-0015)
PHONE..............................937 947-8810
Stephen Smith, *Managing Member*
EMP: 6 EST: 2017
SALES (est): 594.4K **Privately Held**
Web: www.wohtech.com
SIC: 3469 3544 Metal stampings, nec; Die
sets for metal stamping (presses)

Sabina
Clinton County

(G-11679)
MIKE SELLS POTATO CHIP CO
155 N College St (45169-1103)
PHONE..............................937 228-9400
Barry Wilson, *Admn*
EMP: 69
SALES (corp-wide): 34.32MM **Privately
Held**
Web: www.mikesells.com
SIC: 2096 Potato chips and similar snacks
HQ: Mike-Sell's Potato Chip Co.
333 Leo St
Dayton OH 45404
937 228-9400

(G-11680)
NEW SABINA INDUSTRIES INC (HQ)
12555 Us Highway 22 And 3 (45169-9463)
P.O. Box 8 (45169-0008)
PHONE..............................937 584-2433
Kazu Kishi, *Pr*
▲ **EMP: 37 EST:** 1986
SQ FT: 150,000
SALES (est): 49.36MM **Privately Held**
Web: www.nsna.com
SIC: 3714 Instrument board assemblies,
motor vehicle
PA: Nippon Seiki Co., Ltd.
2-2-34, Higashizao

GEOGRAPHIC

Nagaoka NIG 940-0

(G-11681)
PENNANT COMPANIES (PA)
12381 Us Highway 22 And 3 (45169-9304)
PHONE..............................614 451-1782
Chuck Foster, *CEO*
Chuck Foster, *Ch Bd*
Larry Martin, *
EMP: 24 **EST:** 1999
SALES (est): 23.93MM
SALES (corp-wide): 23.93MM **Privately Held**
Web: www.pennant-us.com
SIC: 3465 Moldings or trim, automobile: stamped metal

(G-11682)
PENNANT MOLDINGS INC
12381 Us Highway 22 And 3 (45169-9304)
PHONE..............................937 584-5411
Kurt Walterhouse, *Pr*
Charles E Foster, *
Larry R Martin, *
EMP: 200 **EST:** 1966
SALES (est): 23.93MM
SALES (corp-wide): 23.93MM **Privately Held**
Web: www.pennant-us.com
SIC: 3469 3444 Stamping metal for the trade ; Sheet metalwork
PA: Pennant Companies
12381 Us Highway 22 And 3
Sabina OH 45169
614 451-1782

(G-11683)
PREMIER FEEDS LLC (HQ)
292 N Howard St (45169-1110)
PHONE..............................937 584-2411
Christopher V Meter, *Sec*
EMP: 7 **EST:** 1955
SQ FT: 60,000
SALES (est): 20.28MM
SALES (corp-wide): 20.65MM **Privately Held**
Web: www.premiersolutions.net
SIC: 2048 5261 5153 2041 Prepared feeds, nec; Fertilizer; Grains; Flour and other grain mill products
PA: Sabina Farmers Exchange, Inc.
292 N Howard St
Sabina OH 45169
937 584-6528

(G-11684)
PREMIER GRAIN LLC (PA)
1 Solutions Ave (45169-7500)
PHONE..............................937 584-6552
John Heinz, *VP*
EMP: 6
SALES (est): 764.62K
SALES (corp-wide): 764.62K **Privately Held**
Web: www.premiergrainllc.com
SIC: 2048 Prepared feeds, nec

Saint Clairsville
Belmont County

(G-11685)
AMERICAN CNSLD NTRAL RSRCES IN (PA)
46226 National Rd (43950-8742)
PHONE..............................740 338-3100
EMP: 22 **EST:** 2020
SALES (est): 76.93MM
SALES (corp-wide): 76.93MM **Privately Held**

Web: www.acnrinc.com
SIC: 1241 Coal mining exploration and test boring

(G-11686)
AMERICAN COAL COMPANY
46226 National Rd (43950-8742)
PHONE..............................740 338-3334
Chris Newport, *Brnch Mgr*
EMP: 71
SALES (corp-wide): 4.34B **Privately Held**
SIC: 1241 Coal mining services
HQ: The American Coal Company
9085 Highway 34 N
Galatia IL 62935
618 268-6311

(G-11687)
AUSTIN POWDER COMPANY
74200 Edwards Rd (43950-9510)
PHONE..............................740 968-1555
Dave Ferri, *Mgr*
EMP: 8
SALES (corp-wide): 749.73MM **Privately Held**
Web: www.austinpowder.com
SIC: 2892 Explosives
HQ: Austin Powder Company
25800 Science Park Dr # 300
Cleveland OH 44122
216 464-2400

(G-11688)
BELCO WORKS INC
Also Called: BELCO WORKS
68425 Hammond Rd (43950-8783)
PHONE..............................740 695-0500
Anne Haning, *CEO*
EMP: 94 **EST:** 1966
SQ FT: 5,000
SALES (est): 4.09MM **Privately Held**
Web: www.belcoworks.com
SIC: 8331 3993 3931 2448 Sheltered workshop; Signs and advertising specialties ; Musical instruments; Wood pallets and skids

(G-11689)
COAL RESOURCES INC (PA)
46226 National Rd (43950-8742)
PHONE..............................216 765-1240
Robert E Murray, *CEO*
Robert D Moore, *
EMP: 23 **EST:** 1988
SALES (est): 56.84MM **Privately Held**
SIC: 1221 Bituminous coal and lignite-surface mining

(G-11690)
D LEWIS INC
Also Called: Bill's Counter Tops
52235 National Rd (43950-9306)
PHONE..............................740 695-2615
David Lewis, *Pr*
EMP: 6 **EST:** 1971
SQ FT: 5,000
SALES (est): 455.08K **Privately Held**
Web: www.dlewis.com
SIC: 2542 2541 2434 Cabinets: show, display, or storage: except wood; Wood partitions and fixtures; Wood kitchen cabinets

(G-11691)
FORTIS ENERGY SERVICES INC
66999 Executive Dr (43950-7402)
PHONE..............................248 283-7100
EMP: 51
SALES (corp-wide): 24.85MM **Privately Held**
Web: www.fortisenergyservices.com

SIC: 1381 Drilling oil and gas wells
PA: Fortis Energy Services, Inc.
2844 Livernois Rd
Troy MI 48099
248 283-7100

(G-11692)
FRANKLIN COUNTY COAL COMPANY
46226 National Rd (43950-8742)
PHONE..............................740 338-3100
Robert E Murray, *CEO*
EMP: 206 **EST:** 2019
SALES (est): 5.92MM
SALES (corp-wide): 4.34B **Privately Held**
SIC: 1221 Bituminous coal and lignite-surface mining
HQ: Murray American Energy, Inc.
46226 National Rd
Saint Clairsville OH 43950
740 338-3100

(G-11693)
HARRISON COUNTY COAL COMPANY (HQ)
46226 National Rd (43950-8742)
PHONE..............................740 338-3100
Robert E Murray, *CEO*
EMP: 17 **EST:** 2014
SALES (est): 15.61MM
SALES (corp-wide): 76.93MM **Privately Held**
Web: www.acnrinc.com
SIC: 1221 Bituminous coal and lignite-surface mining
PA: American Consolidated Natural Resources, Inc.
46226 National Rd
Saint Clairsville OH 43950
740 338-3100

(G-11694)
KENAMERICAN RESOURCES INC
46226 National Rd (43950-8742)
PHONE..............................740 338-3100
Bob Sandidge, *Pr*
Robert E Murray, *Dir*
Randy L Wiles, *VP*
James R Turner, *Treas*
Michael O Mckown, *Sec*
EMP: 165 **EST:** 1994
SALES (est): 10.43MM **Privately Held**
SIC: 1222 Bituminous coal-underground mining
HQ: Mill Creek Mining Company
46226 National Rd
Saint Clairsville OH 43950

(G-11695)
MARIETTA COAL CO (PA)
67705 Friends Church Rd (43950-9500)
P.O. Box 2 (43950-0002)
PHONE..............................740 695-2197
George Nicolozakes, *Ch*
Paul Gill, *
John Nicolozakes, *
EMP: 50 **EST:** 1946
SQ FT: 4,300
SALES (est): 783.41K
SALES (corp-wide): 783.41K **Privately Held**
SIC: 1221 Surface mining, bituminous, nec

(G-11696)
MARION CNTY COAL RESOURCES INC
46226 National Rd (43950-8742)
PHONE..............................740 338-3100
Robert Putsock, *Dir*
EMP: 6 **EST:** 2020
SALES (est): 1.91MM **Privately Held**

SIC: 3312 Coal gas, derived from chemical recovery coke ovens

(G-11697)
MARION COUNTY COAL COMPANY
46226 National Rd (43950-8742)
PHONE..............................740 338-3100
Robert E Murray, *Pr*
EMP: 77 **EST:** 2013
SALES (est): 16.85MM
SALES (corp-wide): 76.93MM **Privately Held**
SIC: 3312 2865 Coal tar crudes, derived from chemical recovery coke ovens; Coal tar: crudes, intermediates, and distillates
PA: American Consolidated Natural Resources, Inc.
46226 National Rd
Saint Clairsville OH 43950
740 338-3100

(G-11698)
MARSHALL CNTY COAL RSURCES INC
Also Called: American Cnsld Ntral Rsrces In
46226 National Rd (43950-8742)
PHONE..............................740 338-3100
EMP: 18 **EST:** 2020
SALES (est): 3.1MM
SALES (corp-wide): 76.93MM **Privately Held**
Web: www.acnrinc.com
SIC: 1241 Bituminous coal mining services, contract basis
PA: American Consolidated Natural Resources, Inc.
46226 National Rd
Saint Clairsville OH 43950
740 338-3100

(G-11699)
MCELROY COAL COMPANY (DH)
46226 National Rd (43950-8742)
PHONE..............................724 485-4000
Robert D Moore, *CEO*
P B Lilly, *Pr*
J N Magro, *VP*
EMP: 12 **EST:** 1987
SQ FT: 150,000
SALES (est): 5.47MM
SALES (corp-wide): 4.34B **Privately Held**
SIC: 1221 Bituminous coal surface mining
HQ: Consolidation Coal Company Inc
1000 Consol Energy Dr
Canonsburg PA 15317
740 338-3100

(G-11700)
MEIGS COUNTY COAL COMPANY
46226 National Rd (43950-8742)
PHONE..............................740 338-3100
Robert E Murray, *CEO*
EMP: 206 **EST:** 2013
SALES (est): 1.98MM
SALES (corp-wide): 4.34B **Privately Held**
SIC: 1221 Bituminous coal and lignite-surface mining
HQ: Murray American Energy, Inc.
46226 National Rd
Saint Clairsville OH 43950
740 338-3100

(G-11701)
MUHLENBERG COUNTY COAL CO LLC
46226 National Rd (43950-8742)
PHONE..............................740 338-3100
Robert E Murray, *CEO*
EMP: 63 **EST:** 2018
SALES (est): 22.49MM
SALES (corp-wide): 4.34B **Privately Held**

▲ = Import ▼ = Export
◆ = Import/Export

SIC: **1221** Bituminous coal and lignite-
surface mining
HQ: Western Kentucky Consolidated
Resources, Llc
46226 National Rd
Saint Clairsville OH 43950
740 338-3100

(G-11702)
MURRAY AMERICAN ENERGY INC
(DH)
46226 National Rd (43950-8742)
PHONE............................740 338-3100
Robert E Murray, *Pr*
Robert D Moore, *VP*
Jason D Witt, *Sec*
Michael D Loiacono, *Treas*
EMP: **129** EST: 2013
SALES (est): 43.1MM
SALES (corp-wide): **4.34B** **Privately Held**
SIC: **1221** Bituminous coal surface mining
HQ: Ohio Valley Resources, Inc.
29325 Chgrin Blvd Ste 300
Beachwood OH 44122
216 765-1240

(G-11703)
MURRAY KENTUCKY ENERGY INC
(HQ)
46226 National Rd (43950-8742)
PHONE............................740 338-3100
Robert E Murray, *CEO*
EMP: **10** EST: 2018
SALES (est): 70.05MM
SALES (corp-wide): **4.34B** **Privately Held**
SIC: **1222** Bituminous coal-underground
mining
PA: Murray Energy Corporation
46226 National Rd St
Saint Clairsville OH 43950
740 338-3100

(G-11704)
NOMAC DRILLING LLC
67090 Executive Dr (43950-8473)
PHONE............................724 324-2205
Mark Hughes, *Brnch Mgr*
EMP: **216**
SALES (corp-wide): **5.38B** **Publicly Held**
Web: www.patenergy.com
SIC: **1381** Drilling oil and gas wells
HQ: Nomac Drilling, L.L.C.
3400 S Radio Rd
El Reno OK 73036
405 422-2754

(G-11705)
OHIO HEAT TRANSFER LTD
66721 Executive Dr (43950-8474)
PHONE............................877 633-0391
Mark E Epure, *Managing Member*
▲ EMP: **13** EST: 2003
SALES (est): 2.73MM **Privately Held**
Web: www.ohioheattransfer.com
SIC: **3443** Heat exchangers: coolers (after,
inter), condensers, etc.

(G-11706)
OHIO VALLEY COAL COMPANY
46226 National Rd (43950-8742)
PHONE............................740 926-1351
Robert E Murray, *CEO*
Robert D Moore, *
Michael O Mckown, *Sr VP*
John R Forrelli, *
Ryan M Murray C, *Pr*
EMP: **400** EST: 1969
SQ FT: 40,380
SALES (est): 17.56MM
SALES (corp-wide): **4.34B** **Privately Held**

SIC: **1241** Coal mining services
HQ: Ohio Valley Resources, Inc.
29325 Chgrin Blvd Ste 300
Beachwood OH 44122
216 765-1240

(G-11707)
PROSPECT ROCK LLC
98 N Market St Ste 4 (43950-1274)
PHONE............................740 512-0542
EMP: **10** EST: 2021
SALES (est): 150K **Privately Held**
SIC: **1389** 7389 Roustabout service;
Business Activities at Non-Commercial Site

(G-11708)
RAYLE COAL CO
67705 Friends Church Rd (43950-9500)
P.O. Box 2 (43950-0002)
PHONE............................740 695-2197
George Nicolozakes, *Ch*
John Nicolozakes, *Pr*
EMP: **15** EST: 1974
SQ FT: 4,300
SALES (est): 216.11K **Privately Held**
SIC: **1221** 4491 Surface mining, bituminous,
nec; Marine cargo handling

(G-11709)
RIESBECK FOOD MARKETS INC
Also Called: Reisbeck Fd Mkts St Clirsville
104 Plaza Dr (43950-8736)
P.O. Box 707 (43950-0707)
PHONE............................740 695-3401
Dennis Kasprowski, *Brnch Mgr*
EMP: **125**
SALES (corp-wide): 84.33MM **Privately
Held**
Web: www.riesbeckfoods.com
SIC: **5411** 5912 5421 2051 Supermarkets,
chain; Drug stores and proprietary stores;
Meat and fish markets; Bread, cake, and
related products
PA: Riesbeck Food Markets, Inc.
48661 National Rd
Saint Clairsville OH 43950
740 695-7050

(G-11710)
SIDWELL MATERIALS INC
72607 Gun Club Rd (43950-8637)
PHONE............................740 968-4313
Jeffrey Sidwell, *Pr*
EMP: **15** EST: 2013
SALES (est): 346.91K **Privately Held**
Web: www.sidwellmaterials.com
SIC: **3273** Ready-mixed concrete

(G-11711)
STEIN-PALMER PRINTING CO
1 Westwood Dr Unit 202 (43950-1053)
PHONE............................740 633-3894
Thomas R Palmer, *Owner*
EMP: **8** EST: 1916
SQ FT: 2,500
SALES (est): 102.98K **Privately Held**
SIC: **2752** Offset printing

(G-11712)
STRATA MINE SERVICES INC
68000 Bayberry Dr Unit 103 (43950-8102)
PHONE............................740 695-6880
Jeff Hamrick, *VP*
EMP: **7** EST: 2006
SALES (est): 1.16MM **Privately Held**
SIC: **3532** Mining machinery

(G-11713)
STRATA MINE SERVICES LLC
67925 Bayberry Dr (43950-9132)

PHONE............................740 695-0488
EMP: **13**
SALES (est): 1.04MM **Privately Held**
SIC: **1241** Mine preparation services

(G-11714)
WASHINGTON COUNTY COAL
COMPANY
46226 National Rd (43950-8742)
PHONE............................740 338-3100
Robert D Moore, *CEO*
EMP: **274** EST: 2013
SALES (est): 2.76MM
SALES (corp-wide): **4.34B** **Privately Held**
SIC: **1221** Bituminous coal surface mining
HQ: Murray American Energy, Inc.
46226 National Rd
Saint Clairsville OH 43950
740 338-3100

(G-11715)
WESTERN KENTUCKY COAL CO LLC
46226 National Rd (43950-8742)
PHONE............................740 338-3334
EMP: **54** EST: 2018
SALES (est): 9.39MM
SALES (corp-wide): **4.34B** **Privately Held**
SIC: **1081** Metal mining services
HQ: Western Kentucky Consolidated
Resources, Llc
46226 National Rd
Saint Clairsville OH 43950
740 338-3100

(G-11716)
WESTERN KY CNSLD RESOURCES
LLC (DH)
46226 National Rd (43950-8742)
PHONE............................740 338-3100
EMP: **8** EST: 2018
SALES (est): 70.05MM
SALES (corp-wide): **4.34B** **Privately Held**
SIC: **1241** Coal mining services
HQ: Western Kentucky Resources
Financing, Llc
46226 National Rd
Saint Clairsville OH 43950
740 338-3100

(G-11717)
WESTERN KY COAL RESOURCES
LLC (DH)
46226 National Rd (43950-8742)
PHONE............................740 338-3100
EMP: **25** EST: 2018
SALES (est): 70.05MM
SALES (corp-wide): **4.34B** **Privately Held**
SIC: **1222** Bituminous coal-underground
mining
HQ: Murray Kentucky Energy, Inc.
46226 National Rd W
Saint Clairsville OH 43950
740 338-3100

(G-11718)
WESTERN KY RESOURCES FING
LLC (DH)
46226 National Rd (43950-8742)
PHONE............................740 338-3100
EMP: **8** EST: 2018
SALES (est): 70.05MM
SALES (corp-wide): **4.34B** **Privately Held**
SIC: **1241** Coal mining services
HQ: Western Kentucky Coal Resources, Llc
46226 National Rd
Saint Clairsville OH 43950
740 338-3100

(G-11719)
WHEELING COFFEE & SPICE CO
117 Pinecrest Dr (43950-1446)
PHONE............................304 232-0141
Mary Ann Lokmer, *Pr*
Stephanie Ann Lokmer, *VP*
EMP: **10** EST: 1914
SALES (est): 165.22K **Privately Held**
Web: www.wheelingcoffeeco.com
SIC: **2095** 5149 Coffee roasting (except by
wholesale grocers); Canned goods: fruit,
vegetables, seafood, meats, etc.

Saint Henry
Mercer County

(G-11720)
BECKMAN & GAST COMPANY (PA)
282 W Kremer Hoying Rd (45883-9617)
P.O. Box 307 (45883-0307)
PHONE............................419 678-4195
William C Gast, *Pr*
Karl J Gast, *VP*
Paul Moorman, *Sec*
EMP: **15** EST: 1927
SQ FT: 65,000
SALES (est): 5.82MM
SALES (corp-wide): **5.82MM** **Privately
Held**
Web: www.beckmangast.com
SIC: **2032** 2033 Beans, without meat:
packaged in cans, jars, etc.; Tomato
products, packaged in cans, jars, etc.

(G-11721)
HI-TECH WIRE INC
Also Called: Hi-Tech Wire & Manufacturing
631 E Washington St (45883-9683)
PHONE............................419 678-8376
Bill Hemmelgarn, *Pr*
Susan Hemmelgarn, *
EMP: **57** EST: 1991
SQ FT: 30,000
SALES (est): 5.97MM **Privately Held**
Web: www.hi-techwire.com
SIC: **3544** Special dies and tools

(G-11722)
ITR MANUFACTURING LLC
811 Ash St (45883-9826)
PHONE............................419 763-1493
Chris Borgerding, *Managing Member*
EMP: **10** EST: 2014
SQ FT: 2,400
SALES (est): 3.68MM **Privately Held**
Web: www.itrmanufacturing.com
SIC: **3553** Furniture makers machinery,
woodworking

(G-11723)
R & R FABRICATIONS INC
601 E Washington St (45883-9824)
P.O. Box P.O. Box 500 (45883-0500)
PHONE............................419 678-4831
EMP: **24** EST: 1986
SALES (est): 4.93MM **Privately Held**
Web: www.rrfabrications.com
SIC: **2541** Wood partitions and fixtures

(G-11724)
ST HENRY TILE CO INC (PA)
Also Called: Richmond Builders Supply
281 W Washington St (45883-9663)
P.O. Box 318 (45883-0318)
PHONE............................419 678-4841
Bob Homan, *Pr*
Robert Homan, *
Eugene Subler, *
Mike Homan, *

G
E
O
G
R
A
P
H
I
C

Robert Bruns, *Stockholder**
EMP: 35 **EST:** 1960
SQ FT: 7,600
SALES (est): 8.27MM
SALES (corp-wide): 8.27MM **Privately Held**
Web: www.sthenrytileco.com
SIC: 3271 5211 3273 Blocks, concrete or cinder: standard; Masonry materials and supplies; Ready-mixed concrete

(G-11725)
TEGR INC
191 N Eastern Ave (45883-9707)
P.O. Box 310 (45883-0310)
PHONE...........................419 678-4991
Tim Knapke, *Ex VP*
Jack Meizlish, *Pr*
Rick Meizlish, *VP*
Brent Meizlish, *Treas*
Mark Stimer, *VP*
EMP: 24 **EST:** 1996
SQ FT: 20,000
SALES (est): 3.92MM **Publicly Held**
Web: www.tru-edge.com
SIC: 3599 Machine shop, jobbing and repair
HQ: Bis (Oh) Incorporated.
3989 Groves Rd
Columbus OH 43232
614 864-8400

(G-11726)
V H COOPER & CO INC
Also Called: Cooper Farms
1 Cooper Farm Dr (45883-9556)
PHONE...........................419 678-4853
Jim Cooper, *Prin*
EMP: 625
SALES (corp-wide): 112.29MM **Privately Held**
Web: www.cooperfarms.com
SIC: 2011 Sausages, from meat slaughtered on site
HQ: V. H. Cooper & Co, Inc
2321 State Route 49
Fort Recovery OH 45846

(G-11727)
V H COOPER & CO INC
Cooper Processing of St Henry
1 Cooper Farm Dr (45883-9556)
PHONE...........................419 678-4853
Dale Hart, *Mgr*
EMP: 625
SALES (corp-wide): 112.29MM **Privately Held**
SIC: 2015 2011 Turkey, processed, nsk; Meat packing plants
HQ: V. H. Cooper & Co, Inc
2321 State Route 49
Fort Recovery OH 45846

Saint Louisville
Licking County

(G-11728)
C GREEN & SONS INCORPORATED
Also Called: 64 Metals
9020 Mount Vernon Rd (43071-9672)
PHONE...........................740 745-2998
EMP: 18 **EST:** 1998
SALES (est): 1.27MM **Privately Held**
Web: www.lifespanbuildings.com
SIC: 2952 3448 Siding materials; Trusses and framing, prefabricated metal

(G-11729)
KOKOSING MATERIALS INC
9134 Mount Vernon Rd (43071-9637)

PHONE...........................740 745-3341
Tom Nethers, *Prin*
EMP: 12
SALES (corp-wide): 1.17B **Privately Held**
Web: www.kokosing.biz
SIC: 2951 Asphalt and asphaltic paving mixtures (not from refineries)
HQ: Kokosing Materials, Inc.
17531 Waterford Rd
Fredericktown OH 43019
740 694-9585

Saint Marys
Auglaize County

(G-11730)
ADIENT US LLC
1111 Mckinley Rd (45885-1816)
PHONE...........................419 394-7800
EMP: 32
Web: www.adient.com
SIC: 3714 Motor vehicle parts and accessories
HQ: Adient Us Llc
49200 Halyard Dr
Plymouth MI 48170
734 254-5000

(G-11731)
BEHRCO INC
Also Called: Unique Awards & Signs
1865 Celina Rd (45885-1219)
PHONE...........................419 394-1612
Gerry Schetter, *Pr*
Julia Haehn, *VP*
Tom Crast, *Sec*
EMP: 6 **EST:** 1991
SQ FT: 3,000
SALES (est): 136.84K **Privately Held**
Web: www.uniqueas.org
SIC: 3914 3993 5094 5046 Trophies, plated (all metals); Electric signs; Trophies; Neon signs

(G-11732)
BEST INC
State Rte 116 (45885)
P.O. Box 775 (45885-0775)
PHONE...........................419 394-2745
Richard Brock, *Pr*
Kaye Brock, *Sec*
EMP: 6 **EST:** 1981
SQ FT: 12,050
SALES (est): 141.96K **Privately Held**
Web: www.bestoficinasvirtuales.com
SIC: 3599 Machine shop, jobbing and repair

(G-11733)
BEST PERFORMANCE INC
14381 State Route 116 (45885-9226)
P.O. Box 238 (45885-0238)
PHONE...........................419 394-2299
Eric Brock, *Pr*
EMP: 6 **EST:** 1984
SQ FT: 34,000
SALES (est): 800K **Privately Held**
Web: www.bestperformanceinc.com
SIC: 3599 Machine shop, jobbing and repair

(G-11734)
BRW TOOL INC
502 Scott St (45885-1862)
P.O. Box 417 (45885-0417)
PHONE...........................419 394-3371
Ray Barber, *Pr*
EMP: 14 **EST:** 1966
SQ FT: 50,000
SALES (est): 1.02MM **Privately Held**
Web: www.brwtool.com

SIC: 3469 3544 Metal stampings, nec; Special dies and tools

(G-11735)
CARGILL INCORPORATED
Also Called: Cargill
1400 Mckinley Rd (45885-1821)
P.O. Box B (45885)
PHONE...........................419 394-3374
Brent Marquis, *Brnch Mgr*
EMP: 7
SALES (corp-wide): 159.59B **Privately Held**
Web: www.cargill.com
SIC: 2047 2048 Dog and cat food; Prepared feeds, nec
PA: Cargill, Incorporated
15407 Mcginty Rd W
Wayzata MN 55391
800 227-4455

(G-11736)
CONAG INC
Also Called: Con-AG
16672 County Road 66a (45885-9212)
PHONE...........................419 394-8870
Robert Hirschfeld, *Pr*
Lee Kuck, *
John Hirschfeld, *
EMP: 6 **EST:** 1979
SALES (est): 950.55K **Privately Held**
Web: www.conag.com
SIC: 1422 Limestones, ground

(G-11737)
FLUIDPOWER ASSEMBLY INC
313 S Park Dr (45885-9689)
PHONE...........................419 394-7486
Ronald E Langston, *Pr*
Eric Langston, *Sec*
Ruth Langston, *VP*
Mark Langston, *VP*
EMP: 6 **EST:** 1984
SQ FT: 6,000
SALES (est): 462.93K **Privately Held**
Web: www.hypowerequipment.com
SIC: 3542 3511 Riveting machines; Turbines and turbine generator sets

(G-11738)
HORIZON OHIO PUBLICATIONS INC (HQ)
Also Called: Evening Leader, The
102 E Spring St (45885-2310)
PHONE...........................419 394-7414
Todd Boit, *Pr*
Roland Mc Bride, *Ex VP*
EMP: 17 **EST:** 1905
SQ FT: 8,000
SALES (est): 1.7MM
SALES (corp-wide): 12.26MM **Privately Held**
Web: www.theeveningleader.com
SIC: 2711 Commercial printing and newspaper publishing combined
PA: Horizon Publications, Inc.
1120 N Carbon St Ste 100
Marion IL 62959
618 993-1711

(G-11739)
JOHNSON CONTROLS INC
Also Called: Johnson Controls
1111 Mckinley Rd (45885-1816)
PHONE...........................414 524-1200
Rob Luebke, *Prin*
EMP: 6 **EST:** 2016
SALES (est): 564.46K **Privately Held**
SIC: 3714 Motor vehicle parts and accessories

(G-11740)
KOSEI ST MARYS CORPORATION
1100 Mckinley Rd (45885-1815)
PHONE...........................419 394-7840
Tomonori Okuyama, *Pr*
Douglas Kramer, *
Shunkichi Kamiya, *
Bruce Sakamoto, *
Randy Wendel, *
▲ **EMP:** 681 **EST:** 1987
SQ FT: 470,000
SALES (est): 45.84MM **Privately Held**
Web: www.koseina.com
SIC: 3714 Wheels, motor vehicle
PA: Gyoseishoshi Okuda Tomiko Jimusho
3-5-5, Sayamadai
Sayama STM

(G-11741)
LIETTE L & S EXPRESS LLC
2286 Celina Rd (45885-1226)
P.O. Box 726 (45885-0726)
PHONE...........................419 394-7077
Gregory D Liette, *Prin*
EMP: 6 **EST:** 2004
SQ FT: 4,910
SALES (est): 232.11K **Privately Held**
SIC: 2741 Miscellaneous publishing

(G-11742)
MERCER TOOL CORPORATION
311 S Park Dr (45885-9689)
PHONE...........................419 394-7277
Donald Gladish, *Pr*
EMP: 25 **EST:** 1989
SQ FT: 21,000
SALES (est): 449.08K **Privately Held**
SIC: 3312 Tool and die steel and alloys

(G-11743)
MUROTECH OHIO CORPORATION
Also Called: M T O
550 Mckinley Rd (45885-1803)
P.O. Box 716 (45885-0716)
PHONE...........................419 394-6529
Naonobu Kemmoku, *Pr*
▲ **EMP:** 120 **EST:** 1998
SQ FT: 30,000
SALES (est): 24.11MM **Privately Held**
Web: www.murotech.com
SIC: 3465 Body parts, automobile: stamped metal
PA: Muro Corporation
7-1, Kiyoharakogyodanchi
Utsunomiya TCG 321-3

(G-11744)
OLD CLASSIC DELIGHT INC
Also Called: Classic Delight
310 S Park Dr (45885-9688)
P.O. Box 367 (45885-0367)
PHONE...........................419 394-7955
Jim Clough, *Pr*
EMP: 55 **EST:** 1987
SQ FT: 18,800
SALES (est): 8.76MM **Privately Held**
Web: www.classicdelight.com
SIC: 2099 Food preparations, nec

(G-11745)
OLD SMO INC
323 S Park Dr (45885-9689)
PHONE...........................419 394-3346
Colston L Dine Chb@, *Brnch Mgr*
EMP: 7
SALES (corp-wide): 9.82MM **Privately Held**
Web: www.stmfoundry.com
SIC: 3321 Gray and ductile iron foundries
PA: Old Smo, Inc.
405 E South St

▲ = Import ▼ = Export
◆ = Import/Export

Saint Marys OH 45885
419 394-3346

(G-11746)
OLD SMO INC (PA)
405 E South St (45885-2540)
PHONE..............................419 394-3346
Angela Dine Molaskey, *CEO*
Colston L Dine, *
Mark Dine, *
Ronald S Stumphauzer, *
James Perts, *
EMP: 127 **EST:** 1984
SQ FT: 180,000
SALES (est): 9.82MM
SALES (corp-wide): 9.82MM **Privately Held**
Web: www.stmfoundry.com
SIC: 3321 3369 3322 Gray iron castings, nec ; Nonferrous foundries, nec; Malleable iron foundries

(G-11747)
OMNI MANUFACTURING INC (PA)
901 Mckinley Rd (45885-1812)
P.O. Box 179 (45885-0179)
PHONE..............................419 394-7424
Wayne L Freewalt, *Pr*
▲ **EMP:** 100 **EST:** 1982
SQ FT: 190,000
SALES (est): 23.03MM
SALES (corp-wide): 23.03MM **Privately Held**
Web: www.omnimfg.com
SIC: 3469 3479 3544 Stamping metal for the trade; Coating of metals and formed products; Special dies and tools

(G-11748)
OMNI MANUFACTURING INC
220 Cleveland Ave (45885-1706)
PHONE..............................419 394-7424
Wayne Freewalt, *Mgr*
EMP: 13
SALES (corp-wide): 23.03MM **Privately Held**
Web: www.omnimfg.com
SIC: 3469 3479 3544 Stamping metal for the trade; Coating of metals and formed products; Special dies and tools
PA: Omni Manufacturing, Inc.
901 Mckinley Rd
Saint Marys OH 45885
419 394-7424

(G-11749)
PRO-PET LLC
1601 Mckinley Rd (45885-1864)
P.O. Box 369 (45885-0369)
PHONE..............................419 394-3374
Jim Wiegmann, *Pr*
Greg Wolking, *
◆ **EMP:** 93 **EST:** 1996
SQ FT: 5,000
SALES (est): 4.91MM
SALES (corp-wide): 159.59B **Privately Held**
SIC: 2047 2048 4212 7389 Cat food; Prepared feeds, nec; Animal and farm product transportation services; Packaging and labeling services
PA: Cargill, Incorporated
15407 Mcginty Rd W
Wayzata MN 55391
800 227-4455

(G-11750)
QUALITY READY MIX INC (PA)
16672 County Road 66a (45885-9212)
PHONE..............................419 394-8870
TOLL FREE: 800

Robert E Hirschfeld, *Pr*
John Hirschfeld, *VP*
Lee Kuck, *Sec*
EMP: 10 **EST:** 1931
SQ FT: 2,000
SALES (est): 2.15MM
SALES (corp-wide): 2.15MM **Privately Held**
Web: www.qrmconcrete.com
SIC: 3273 Ready-mixed concrete

(G-11751)
RELIABLE PRODUCTS CO
315 S Park Dr (45885-9689)
PHONE..............................419 394-5854
Wayne Steineman, *Pr*
Kristine Ranly, *Sec*
EMP: 8 **EST:** 1973
SQ FT: 10,000
SALES (est): 953.75K **Privately Held**
SIC: 3541 Machine tools, metal cutting type

(G-11752)
SETEX INC
1111 Mckinley Rd (45885-1816)
PHONE..............................419 394-7800
Mister Yamada, *Pr*
Shinichirou Shirahama, *
Robert Bowlin, *
▲ **EMP:** 470 **EST:** 1987
SQ FT: 168,000
SALES (est): 35MM **Privately Held**
Web: www.setexinc.net
SIC: 2531 Seats, automobile

(G-11753)
TAIYO AMERICA INC (HQ)
1702 E Spring St (45885-2460)
PHONE..............................419 300-8811
Takuji Maekawa, *Pr*
▲ **EMP:** 10 **EST:** 1986
SQ FT: 50,000
SALES (est): 1.29MM **Privately Held**
Web: www.taiyo-america.com
SIC: 5084 3492 Hydraulic systems equipment and supplies; Fluid power valves for aircraft
PA: Taiyo,Ltd.
2-6-8, Bingomachi, Chuo-Ku
Osaka OSK 541-0

(G-11754)
WEBER READY MIX INC
10072 County Road 66a (45885-9212)
PHONE..............................419 394-9097
Marc Bader, *VP*
EMP: 25 **EST:** 2016
SALES (est): 397.06K **Privately Held**
SIC: 3273 Ready-mixed concrete

Saint Paris
Champaign County

(G-11755)
ALL OHIO WELDING INC
3833 State Route 235 N (43072-9536)
PHONE..............................937 663-7116
Charles Grimes, *Pr*
Julie A Grimes, *Prin*
EMP: 7 **EST:** 2015
SALES (est): 387.37K **Privately Held**
Web: www.allohiowelding.com
SIC: 1799 3499 7692 Welding on site; Fire- or burglary-resistive products; Welding repair

(G-11756)
BHI TRANSITION INC
8801 Us Highway 36 (43072-9358)

PHONE..............................937 663-4152
Bryce Hill, *Mgr*
EMP: 47
Web: www.brycehill.com
SIC: 3273 Ready-mixed concrete
PA: Bhi Transition, Inc.
2301 Sheridan Ave
Springfield OH 45505

(G-11757)
CAM MACHINE INC
513 S Springfield St (43072-9410)
PHONE..............................937 663-5000
Douglas Macy, *Pr*
EMP: 29 **EST:** 1980
SALES (est): 1.65MM **Privately Held**
SIC: 3599 Machine shop, jobbing and repair

(G-11758)
KTH PARTS INDUSTRIES INC (HQ)
1111 State Route 235 N (43072-9680)
P.O. Box 940 (43072-0940)
PHONE..............................937 663-5941
Toshio Inoue, *Pr*
Sanichi Kanai, *
Fumio Takeuchi, *
◆ **EMP:** 770 **EST:** 1984
SQ FT: 811,500
SALES (est): 102.99MM **Privately Held**
Web: www.kth.net
SIC: 3714 Motor vehicle parts and accessories
PA: H-One Co.,Ltd.
1-11-5, Sakuragicho, Omiya-Ku
Saitama STM 330-0

(G-11759)
RUNKLES SAWMILL LLC
2534 Dialton Rd (43072-9423)
PHONE..............................937 663-0115
Steve Runkle, *Managing Member*
EMP: 7 **EST:** 2004
SALES (est): 142K **Privately Held**
SIC: 2421 Sawmills and planing mills, general

Salem
Columbiana County

(G-11760)
ACCU-TEK TOOL & DIE INC
1390 Allen Rd Bldg 1 (44460-1003)
PHONE..............................330 726-1946
James A Kutchel, *Pr*
Gary Sebrell, *VP*
EMP: 8 **EST:** 1990
SQ FT: 12,000
SALES (est): 1.12MM **Privately Held**
Web: www.accutektoolanddie.com
SIC: 3544 3354 Special dies and tools; Aluminum extruded products

(G-11761)
ADVANTAGE MACHINE SHOP
777 S Ellsworth Ave (44460-3781)
PHONE..............................330 337-8377
Vic Jones, *Owner*
EMP: 6 **EST:** 2005
SALES (est): 1.79MM **Privately Held**
SIC: 3599 Machine shop, jobbing and repair

(G-11762)
AS AMERICA INC
605 S Ellsworth Ave (44460-3743)
PHONE..............................330 332-9954
Jay Gould, *Pr*
EMP: 13
Web: www.americanstandard-us.com

SIC: 3261 3432 Vitreous plumbing fixtures; Plumbing fixture fittings and trim
HQ: As America, Inc.
30 Knghtsbrdge Rd Ste 301
Piscataway NJ 08854

(G-11763)
BARCLAY MACHINE INC
Also Called: Barclay Rolls
650 S Bdwy Ave (44460-3795)
PHONE..............................330 337-9541
Jeff Cushman, *Pr*
EMP: 16 **EST:** 1898
SALES (est): 3.45MM **Privately Held**
Web: www.barclayrolls.com
SIC: 3542 Machine tools, metal forming type

(G-11764)
BUTECH INC
633 S Broadway Ave (44460-3795)
PHONE..............................330 337-0000
Matt Joing, *Prin*
EMP: 76
SALES (corp-wide): 24.17MM **Privately Held**
Web: www.butechbliss.com
SIC: 3541 Machine tools, metal cutting type
PA: Butech Inc.
550 S Ellsworth Ave
Salem OH 44460
330 337-0000

(G-11765)
BUTECH INC
Also Called: Butech Bliss
240 Pennsylvania Ave (44460-2733)
PHONE..............................330 337-0000
EMP: 76
SALES (corp-wide): 24.17MM **Privately Held**
SIC: 3541 Machine tools, metal cutting type
PA: Butech Inc.
550 S Ellsworth Ave
Salem OH 44460
330 337-0000

(G-11766)
BUTECH INC (PA)
Also Called: Butech Bliss
550 S Ellsworth Ave (44460-3067)
PHONE..............................330 337-0000
▲ **EMP:** 97 **EST:** 1985
SALES (est): 24.17MM
SALES (corp-wide): 24.17MM **Privately Held**
Web: www.butechbliss.com
SIC: 3541 Machine tools, metal cutting type

(G-11767)
CARDINAL PUMPS EXCHANGERS INC (DH)
Also Called: Unifin Chesapeake
1425 Quaker Ct (44460-1008)
PHONE..............................330 332-8558
Manny A Agostinho, *Pr*
Ed Shapiro, *Genl Mgr*
Matthew Flamini, *VP*
Jeanne R Hernandez, *Treas*
▲ **EMP:** 15 **EST:** 2007
SALES (est): 3.79MM **Publicly Held**
Web: 3326-us.all.biz
SIC: 3443 Heat exchangers, condensers, and components
HQ: Wabtec Components Llc
30 Isabella St
Pittsburgh PA 15212
412 825-1000

(G-11768)

CASTRUCTION COMPANY INC
1588 Salem Pkwy (44460-1071)
PHONE..............................330 332-9622
Benjamine R Brown, *Pr*
Shannon Brown, *VP*
EMP: 12 **EST:** 1965
SQ FT: 9,600
SALES (est): 912.29K **Privately Held**
Web: www.castruction.com
SIC: 3297 Cement refractories

(G-11769)

CHAPPELL-ZIMMERMAN INC
641 Olive St (44460-4219)
P.O. Box 94 (44460-0094)
PHONE..............................330 337-8711
Chris Chappell, *Pr*
EMP: 14 **EST:** 1946
SQ FT: 2,000
SALES (est): 971.74K **Privately Held**
Web: www.czconcrete.com
SIC: 3273 5999 Ready-mixed concrete;
Alcoholic beverage making equipment and
supplies

(G-11770)

CHURCH-BUDGET ENVELOPE COMPANY
271 S Ellsworth Ave (44460-3071)
P.O. Box 420 (44460-0420)
PHONE..............................800 446-9780
James A Pidgeon Junior, *Pr*
EMP: 48 **EST:** 1917
SQ FT: 60,000
SALES (est): 4.38MM **Privately Held**
Web: www.churchbudget.com
SIC: 2677 Envelopes

(G-11771)

CMI INDUSTRY AMERICAS INC (DH)
435 W Wilson St (44460-2767)
PHONE..............................330 332-4661
Rob Johnson, *Ch Bd*
Patricia Simonsic, *
▲ **EMP:** 100 **EST:** 1923
SQ FT: 250,000
SALES (est): 24.4MM
SALES (corp-wide): 250.72K **Privately Held**
SIC: 3567 Metal melting furnaces, industrial:
electric
HQ: John Cockerill Traction
Avenue Georges Pirson 12
Manage WHT 7170
64521631

(G-11772)

COMPCO QUAKER MFG INC
187 Georgetown Rd (44460-2009)
PHONE..............................330 482-0200
Gregory Smith, *Ch Bd*
Richard Kamperman, *
Richard Fryda, *
Joe Irwin, *
EMP: 37 **EST:** 2017
SALES (est): 5.18MM
SALES (corp-wide): 27.79MM **Privately Held**
Web: www.cqlmfg.com
SIC: 3469 3544 3465 3599 Metal stampings,
nec; Special dies and tools; Automotive
stampings; Machine and other job shop
work
HQ: Compco Columbiana Company
400 W Railroad St Ste 1
Columbiana OH 44408
330 482-0200

(G-11773)

CQL MFG LLC
187 Georgetown Rd (44460-2009)
PHONE..............................330 482-5846
EMP: 100 **EST:** 2021
SALES (est): 25MM **Privately Held**
SIC: 3469 Ornamental metal stampings

(G-11774)

CTM INTEGRATION INCORPORATED
1318 Quaker Cir (44460-1051)
P.O. Box 589 (44460-0589)
PHONE..............................330 332-1800
Thomas C Rumsey, *Pr*
Dan Mc Laughlin, *
EMP: 36 **EST:** 1980
SQ FT: 30,000
SALES (est): 4.91MM **Privately Held**
Web: www.ctmlabelingsystems.com
SIC: 3565 5084 3549 Packaging machinery;
Industrial machinery and equipment;
Metalworking machinery, nec

(G-11775)

CTM LABELING SYSTEMS
1318 Quaker Cir (44460-1051)
PHONE..............................330 332-1800
EMP: 23 **EST:** 2018
SALES (est): 9.15MM **Privately Held**
Web: www.ctmlabelingsystems.com
SIC: 3565 Packaging machinery

(G-11776)

DILCO INDUSTRIES INC
300 Benton Rd (44460-2029)
PHONE..............................330 337-6732
Robert Dillon Junior, *Pr*
Kathy Dillion, *Sec*
EMP: 9 **EST:** 1987
SQ FT: 14,000
SALES (est): 954.45K **Privately Held**
Web: www.dilcoind.com
SIC: 3599 Machine shop, jobbing and repair

(G-11777)

ETL PERFORMANCE PRODUCTS INC
1717 Pennsylvania Ave (44460-2781)
PHONE..............................234 575-7226
Xiangdong Liu, *Pr*
EMP: 8 **EST:** 2017
SQ FT: 4,000
SALES (est): 859.58K **Privately Held**
Web: www.etlperformance.com
SIC: 3429 Clamps, metal

(G-11778)

EVERFLOW EASTERN PARTNERS LP
Also Called: Strawn Oil Field Service
29093 Salem Alliance Rd (44460-9706)
PHONE..............................330 537-3863
Richard Strawn, *Brnch Mgr*
EMP: 6
SIC: 1389 Oil field services, nec
PA: Everflow Eastern Partners, L.P.
585 W Main St
Canfield OH 44406

(G-11779)

FIRESTONE LASER AND MFG LLC
14000 W Middletown Rd (44460-9184)
PHONE..............................330 337-9551
Richard Kamperman, *Managing Member*
Gregory Smith, *Managing Member*
Rick Fryda, *Managing Member*
Tom Spivak, *Managing Member*
EMP: 25 **EST:** 1954
SALES (est): 2.43MM **Privately Held**
SIC: 3444 Sheet metalwork

(G-11780)

FLATIRON CRANE OPER CO LLC
Also Called: Simmers Crane Design & Svcs
1134 Salem Pkwy (44460-1063)
PHONE..............................330 332-3300
Mark Bilali, *Brnch Mgr*
EMP: 234
SALES (corp-wide): 88.41MM **Privately Held**
Web: www.flatironcrane.com
SIC: 3536 Hoists, cranes, and monorails
PA: Flatiron Crane Operating Company Llc
11 Vanguard Dr
Reading PA 19606
610 582-7203

(G-11781)

FRESH MARK INC
1735 S Lincoln Ave (44460-4203)
PHONE..............................330 332-8508
Steve Smith, *Brnch Mgr*
EMP: 650
SQ FT: 125,000
SALES (corp-wide): 1.38B **Privately Held**
Web: www.freshmark.com
SIC: 2011 2013 Meat packing plants;
Sausages and other prepared meats
PA: Fresh Mark, Inc.
1888 Southway St Sw
Massillon OH 44646
330 832-7491

(G-11782)

GORDON BROTHERS BTLG GROUP INC
776 N Ellsworth Ave (44460-1600)
P.O. Box 63 (44436-0063)
PHONE..............................330 337-8754
Edward P Ned Jones Iii, *Ch*
Frank Tombo, *Prin*
Scott P Jones, *Pr*
EMP: 6 **EST:** 2004
SALES (est): 243.25K **Privately Held**
Web: www.gordonbroswater.com
SIC: 2086 Bottled and canned soft drinks

(G-11783)

GRID INDUSTRIAL HEATING INC
1108 Salem Pkwy (44460-1063)
P.O. Box 950 (44460-0950)
PHONE..............................330 332-9931
Donald Stamp, *Pr*
EMP: 7 **EST:** 1985
SQ FT: 20,000
SALES (est): 497.55K **Privately Held**
Web: www.gridheating.com
SIC: 3433 1711 Steam heating apparatus;
Plumbing, heating, air-conditioning

(G-11784)

HALTEC CORPORATION
32585 N Price Rd (44460-9517)
P.O. Box 1180 (44460-8180)
PHONE..............................330 222-1501
Thomas Moyer, *Pr*
Edward Russell, *
Mike Russell, *
David Caruso, *
Frank Bezon, *
◆ **EMP:** 116 **EST:** 1985
SQ FT: 65,000
SALES (est): 17.49MM **Privately Held**
Web: www.haltec.com
SIC: 3714 Tire valve cores

(G-11785)

HAZENSTAB MACHINE INC
1575 Salem Pkwy (44460-1072)
PHONE..............................330 337-1865
James Hazenstab Junior, *Pr*
▲ **EMP:** 7 **EST:** 1977

SQ FT: 12,000
SALES (est): 968.17K **Privately Held**
Web: www.hazenstabmachine.com
SIC: 3599 Machine shop, jobbing and repair

(G-11786)

HOWMET AEROSPACE INC
Also Called: Howmet Aerospace Inc
32585 N Price Rd (44460-9513)
P.O. Box 1180 (44460-8180)
PHONE..............................330 222-1501
Edward Russell, *Brnch Mgr*
EMP: 70
SALES (corp-wide): 7.43B **Publicly Held**
Web: www.howmet.com
SIC: 3353 Aluminum sheet and strip
PA: Howmet Aerospace Inc.
201 Isabella St Ste 200
Pittsburgh PA 15212
412 553-1950

(G-11787)

HUNT VALVE ACTUATOR LLC
1913 E State St (44460-2491)
PHONE..............................330 337-9535
Charles Ferrer, *
EMP: 80 **EST:** 2017
SQ FT: 50,000
SALES (est): 4.64MM **Privately Held**
Web: www.fairbanksmorsedefense.com
SIC: 3593 Fluid power actuators, hydraulic
or pneumatic

(G-11788)

HUNT VALVE COMPANY INC (DH)
1913 E State St (44460-2491)
PHONE..............................330 337-9535
▲ **EMP:** 72 **EST:** 1919
SALES (est): 73.85MM
SALES (corp-wide): 1.27B **Privately Held**
Web: www.fairbanksmorsedefense.com
SIC: 3492 Control valves, fluid power:
hydraulic and pneumatic
HQ: Valveco Inc.
251 Little Falls Dr
Wilmington DE 19808

(G-11789)

INTERSTATE PUMP COMPANY INC (PA)
33370 Winona Rd (44460-9000)
P.O. Box 109 (44460-0109)
PHONE..............................330 222-1006
EMP: 7 **EST:** 1939
SALES (est): 2.02MM **Privately Held**
Web: www.interstatepump.com
SIC: 5084 5085 3561 Pumps and pumping
equipment, nec; Filters, industrial; Pumps
and pumping equipment

(G-11790)

JOHN KRIZAY INC
1777 Pennsylvania Ave (44460-2781)
P.O. Box 974 (44460-0974)
PHONE..............................330 332-5607
William Stratton, *Pr*
Linda Horsall, *
▲ **EMP:** 12 **EST:** 1968
SQ FT: 12,000
SALES (est): 3.04MM **Privately Held**
Web: www.jkrizay.com
SIC: 3229 Art, decorative and novelty
glassware

(G-11791)

JOSEPH SABATINO
Also Called: Sabatino Cabinet
1834 Depot Rd (44460-4359)
PHONE..............................330 332-5879
Joseph Sabatino, *Owner*
EMP: 6 **EST:** 1990

SQ FT: 8,500
SALES (est): 246.37K **Privately Held**
Web: www.sabatinocabinet.com
SIC: 1751 2491 Carpentry work; Millwork, treated wood

(G-11792)
KORFF HOLDINGS LLC
Also Called: Quaker City Casting
310 E Euclid Ave (44460-3778)
PHONE...................................330 332-1566
Geoffrey Korff, *Pr*
Jason Korff, *
Ronald H Lasko, *
▲ EMP: 120 EST: 1932
SALES (est): 6.28MM **Privately Held**
Web: www.quakercitycastings.com
SIC: 3325 3321 Steel foundries, nec; Gray and ductile iron foundries

(G-11793)
LASENOR USA LLC
600 Snyder Rd (44460-4260)
PHONE...................................800 754-1228
Jeff Simmons, *Mgr*
EMP: 10 EST: 2019
SALES (est): 2.83MM **Privately Held**
Web: www.lasenor.com
SIC: 2099 Emulsifiers, food
HQ: Lasenor Emul Sl
Carretera Abrera-Manresa
Olesa De Montserrat B 08640

(G-11794)
LIFT-TECH INTERNATIONAL INC
240 Pennsylvania Ave (44460-2733)
PHONE...................................330 424-7248
▲ EMP: 345
SIC: 3536 Hoists

(G-11795)
LOWRY TOOL & DIE INC
986 Salem Pkwy (44460-1059)
PHONE...................................330 332-1722
Robert Lowry, *Pr*
EMP: 14 EST: 1966
SQ FT: 10,000
SALES (est): 2.2MM **Privately Held**
Web: www.lowrytd.com
SIC: 3544 Special dies and tools

(G-11796)
LYLE PRINTING & PUBLISHING CO (PA)
Also Called: Farm & Dairy
185 E State St (44460-2842)
P.O. Box 38 (44460-0038)
PHONE...................................330 337-3419
Jordan Roberts, *CEO*
Scot Darling, *
Tom Darling, *
EMP: 50 EST: 1890
SQ FT: 12,500
SALES (est): 2.14MM
SALES (corp-wide): 2.14MM **Privately Held**
Web: www.lyleprinting.com
SIC: 2721 2752 2759 Trade journals: publishing only, not printed on site; Offset printing; Letterpress printing

(G-11797)
MAC MANUFACTURING INC
1453 Allen Rd (44460-1004)
PHONE...................................330 829-1680
Cora Mcdonald, *Brnch Mgr*
EMP: 104
Web: www.mactrailer.com
SIC: 3715 5012 Truck trailers; Trailers for trucks, new and used
HQ: Mac Manufacturing, Inc.

14599 Commerce St
Alliance OH 44601

(G-11798)
METAL & WIRE PRODUCTS COMPANY
1069 Salem Pkwy (44460-1062)
PHONE...................................330 332-1015
EMP: 14
Web: www.metalandwire.com
SIC: 3469 Stamping metal for the trade
PA: Metal & Wire Products Company Inc
1065 Salem Pkwy
Salem OH 44460

(G-11799)
METAL & WIRE PRODUCTS COMPANY (PA)
1065 Salem Pkwy (44460-1062)
PHONE...................................330 332-9448
Vincent M Cianciola, *Pr*
Timothy J Cianciola, *
Jeffrey T Cianciola, *
Mary Ann Franko, *
EMP: 50 EST: 1981
SQ FT: 62,000
SALES (est): 8.65MM **Privately Held**
Web: www.metalandwire.com
SIC: 3469 3542 3544 Stamping metal for the trade; Machine tools, metal forming type; Special dies, tools, jigs, and fixtures

(G-11800)
MILLER-HOLZWARTH INC
450 W Pershing St (44460-2752)
PHONE...................................330 342-7224
EMP: 60 EST: 1955
SALES (est): 4.44MM **Privately Held**
Web: www.millerholzwarth.com
SIC: 3827 3861 3231 Periscopes; Photographic equipment and supplies; Products of purchased glass

(G-11801)
MILSEK FURNITURE POLISH INC
1351 Quaker Cir (44460-1006)
PHONE...................................330 542-2700
Chris Herubin, *CEO*
Chris Ruben, *Pr*
Dan Bender, *Sec*
EMP: 6 EST: 2006
SQ FT: 2,080
SALES (est): 517.9K **Privately Held**
Web: www.milsek.com
SIC: 2842 Polishes and sanitation goods

(G-11802)
MM INDUSTRIES INC
Also Called: Vorti-Siv
36135 Salem Grange Rd (44460-9442)
P.O. Box 720 (44460)
PHONE...................................330 332-5947
Barbara Maroscher, *Pr*
Victor Maroscher, *
Art Maroscher, *
▲ EMP: 30 EST: 1967
SQ FT: 10,000
SALES (est): 3.79MM **Privately Held**
Web: www.vorti-siv.com
SIC: 3559 Screening equipment, electric

(G-11803)
MOORE MR SPECIALTY COMPANY
1050 Pennsylvania Ave (44460)
P.O. Box 107 (44460-0107)
PHONE...................................330 332-1229
Robert N Moore, *Pr*
Martha Moore, *VP*
EMP: 8 EST: 1966
SQ FT: 5,000

SALES (est): 707.32K **Privately Held**
SIC: 3443 Fabricated plate work (boiler shop)

(G-11804)
PIMA VALVE LLC
1913 E State St (44460-2422)
PHONE...................................330 337-9535
George Whittier, *Pr*
EMP: 59 EST: 1967
SQ FT: 38,000
SALES (est): 3.49MM
SALES (corp-wide): 1.27B **Privately Held**
Web: www.fairbanksmorsedefense.com
SIC: 3494 3491 3492 Valves and pipe fittings, nec; Industrial valves; Fluid power valves and hose fittings
HQ: Hunt Valve Company, Inc.
1913 E State St
Salem OH 44460
330 337-9535

(G-11805)
POLLOCK RESEARCH & DESIGN INC
Simmers Crane Design & Svc Co
1134 Salem Pkwy (44460-1063)
PHONE...................................330 332-3300
Randy L Stull, *Mgr*
EMP: 45
SALES (corp-wide): 88.41MM **Privately Held**
Web: www.readingcrane.com
SIC: 8711 7389 7353 3531 Civil engineering; Crane and aerial lift service; Heavy construction equipment rental; Industrial trucks and tractors
HQ: Pollock Research & Design, Inc.
11 Vanguard Dr
Reading PA 19606
610 582-7203

(G-11806)
QUAKER CITY CASTINGS INC
310 E Euclid Ave (44460-3778)
PHONE...................................330 332-1566
Colby Collier, *Ch Bd*
Phillip Jones, *
Mike Mazzarino, *
EMP: 775 EST: 1966
SALES (est): 4.94MM **Privately Held**
Web: www.quakercitycastings.com
SIC: 3321 3325 3312 3592 Gray iron castings, nec; Alloy steel castings, except investment; Stainless steel; Pistons and piston rings

(G-11807)
QUAKER MFG CORP
Also Called: Quaker Mfg
187 Georgetown Rd (44460-2009)
PHONE...................................330 332-4631
▲ EMP: 115
Web: www.cqlmfg.com
SIC: 3469 3544 3465 3599 Metal stampings, nec; Special dies and tools; Automotive stampings; Machine and other job shop work

(G-11808)
QUALITY FABRICATED METALS INC
14000 W Middletown Rd (44460-9184)
EMP: 10 EST: 1987
SQ FT: 42,000
SALES (est): 1.48MM **Privately Held**
Web: www.fabricatedmetals.com
SIC: 3469 1799 Stamping metal for the trade ; Welding on site

(G-11809)
REDEX INDUSTRIES INC (PA)
Also Called: Udderly Smooth
1176 Salem Pkwy (44460-1063)

P.O. Box 939 (44460-0939)
PHONE...................................330 332-9800
William C Kennedy, *Pr*
William C Kennedy, *Pr*
Margaret Kennedy, *Sec*
EMP: 16 EST: 1976
SQ FT: 24,000
SALES (est): 5.47MM
SALES (corp-wide): 5.47MM **Privately Held**
Web: www.udderlysmooth.com
SIC: 2844 Face creams or lotions

(G-11810)
SALEM MILL & CABINET CO
1455 Quaker Cir (44460-1054)
P.O. Box 1072 (44460-8072)
PHONE...................................330 337-9568
Steven W Kastenhuber, *Pr*
EMP: 6 EST: 1986
SQ FT: 6,000
SALES (est): 472.84K **Privately Held**
SIC: 5211 2431 2434 Lumber products; Millwork; Wood kitchen cabinets

(G-11811)
SALEM WELDING & SUPPLY COMPANY
475 Prospect St (44460-2618)
P.O. Box 386 (44460-0386)
PHONE...................................330 332-4517
Frederick Baker Senior, *Pr*
Frederick Baker Junior, *VP*
Anna Baker, *Sec*
EMP: 9 EST: 1975
SQ FT: 15,200
SALES (est): 843.22K **Privately Held**
Web: www.salemweldingco.com
SIC: 7692 5084 Welding repair; Welding machinery and equipment

(G-11812)
SIMMONS FEED & SUPPLY LLC
Also Called: Simmons Grain Company
600 Snyder Rd (44460-4260)
PHONE...................................800 754-1228
Jeffrey Simmons, *Pr*
▲ EMP: 20 EST: 1982
SQ FT: 10,000
SALES (est): 5.17MM **Privately Held**
Web: www.simmonsgrain.com
SIC: 5153 3556 Grains; Oilseed crushing and extracting machinery

(G-11813)
SLATER ROAD MILLS INC
11000 Youngstown Salem Rd (44460-9654)
P.O. Box 1083 (44460-8083)
PHONE...................................330 332-9951
EMP: 25 EST: 1986
SALES (est): 356.22K **Privately Held**
Web: www.lehmannmills.com
SIC: 3541 7699 3552 Milling machines; Industrial equipment services; Textile machinery

(G-11814)
THE LABEL TEAM INC
1251 Quaker Cir (44460-1050)
PHONE...................................330 332-1067
Dean J Mcdaniel, *Pr*
Paula Mcdaniel, *VP*
EMP: 15 EST: 1998
SQ FT: 11,400
SALES (est): 2.14MM **Privately Held**
Web: www.thelabelteam.net
SIC: 2759 Labels and seals: printing, nsk

(G-11815)
TRI-FAB INC
10372 W South Range Rd (44460-9621)
P.O. Box 310 (44460-0310)
PHONE....................................330 337-3425
Samuel Lippiatt, *Pr*
EMP: 32 **EST:** 1979
SQ FT: 44,000
SALES (est): 4.15M **Privately Held**
SIC: 3644 3441 3444 Fuse boxes, electric;
  Fabricated structural metal; Sheet
  metalwork

(G-11816)
TURNER MACHINE CO
1433 Salem Pkwy (44460-1070)
PHONE....................................330 332-5821
Jacob O Kamm, *Pr*
Patricia Simonsic, *Treas*
EMP: 7 **EST:** 1943
SALES (est): 1.06M **Privately Held**
Web: 044df3b.netsolhost.com
SIC: 3599 3547 3542 Machine shop, jobbing
  and repair; Rolling mill machinery; Machine
  tools, metal forming type

(G-11817)
VIC MAROSCHER
36135 Salem Grange Rd (44460-9442)
P.O. Box 720 (44460-0720)
PHONE....................................330 332-4958
Vic Maroscher, *Owner*
EMP: 10 **EST:** 2009
SALES (est): 127.56K **Privately Held**
Web: www.vorti-siv.com
SIC: 3999 Manufacturing industries, nec

Salineville
Columbiana County

(G-11818)
M3 MIDSTREAM LLC
Also Called: Salineville Office
10 E Main St (43945-1134)
PHONE....................................330 679-5580
EMP: 34
SALES (corp-wide): 23.57M **Privately
Held**
Web: www.momentummidstream.com
SIC: 1382 Oil and gas exploration services
PA: M3 Midstream Llc
  600 Travis St Ste 5600
  Houston TX 77002
  713 783-3000

Sandusky
Erie County

(G-11819)
ACH LLC
Also Called: Ach Sandusky Plastics
3020 Tiffin Ave (44870-5352)
PHONE....................................419 621-5748
Andy Short, *Prin*
▲ **EMP:** 8 **EST:** 2008
SALES (est): 1.35M **Privately Held**
SIC: 3714 Motor vehicle parts and
  accessories

(G-11820)
AHNER FABRICATING & SHTMTL INC
2001 E Perkins Ave (44870-5130)
PHONE....................................419 626-6641
Mark Ahner, *Pr*
Timothy Ahner, *
EMP: 24 **EST:** 1984
SQ FT: 7,000
SALES (est): 4.35M **Privately Held**

Web: www.ahner-industrial.com
SIC: 3444 3914 5049 Sheet metal
  specialties, not stamped; Carving sets,
  stainless steel; Precision tools

(G-11821)
AMERICAN COLORS INC (PA)
4602 Timber Commons Dr (44870-7189)
P.O. Box 397 (44871-0397)
PHONE....................................419 621-4000
◆ **EMP:** 50 **EST:** 1975
SALES (est): 26.65MM
SALES (corp-wide): 26.65MM **Privately
Held**
Web: www.americancolors.com
SIC: 2816 Color pigments

(G-11822)
AMERICAN QUALITY STRIPPING INC
1750 5th St (44870-1301)
PHONE....................................419 625-6288
Tim Finneran, *Pr*
Richard Finneran, *
EMP: 30 **EST:** 1987
SQ FT: 16,000
SALES (est): 4.95MM **Privately Held**
Web: www.americanqualitystripping.com
SIC: 3471 3398 Finishing, metals or formed
  products; Metal heat treating

(G-11823)
**BRIDGESTONE RET OPERATIONS
LLC**
Also Called: Firestone
4320 Milan Rd (44870-5836)
PHONE....................................419 625-6571
Richard Oliver, *Mgr*
EMP: 6
Web: www.bridgestoneamericas.com
SIC: 5531 7534 7538 Automotive tires; Tire
  retreading and repair shops; General
  automotive repair shops
HQ: Bridgestone Retail Operations, Llc
  200 4th Ave S Ste 100
  Nashville TN 37201
  615 937-1000

(G-11824)
**BUDERER DRUG COMPANY INC
(PA)**
633 Hancock St (44870-3603)
PHONE....................................419 627-2800
Matthew Buderer, *VP*
James Buderer, *Pr*
EMP: 25 **EST:** 2014
SQ FT: 5,000
SALES (est): 5.37MM
SALES (corp-wide): 5.37MM **Privately
Held**
Web: www.budererdrug.com
SIC: 5122 2834 Drugs and drug proprietaries
  ; Proprietary drug products

(G-11825)
BUSCH & THIEM INC
1316 Cleveland Rd (44870-4271)
P.O. Box 1088 (44871-1088)
PHONE....................................419 625-7515
C A Busch, *Pr*
James R Kellam, *Sec*
EMP: 20 **EST:** 1926
SQ FT: 45,000
SALES (est): 3.3MM **Privately Held**
Web: www.buschthiem.com
SIC: 2542 3993 3496 3444 Racks,
  merchandise display or storage: except
  wood; Signs and advertising specialties;
  Miscellaneous fabricated wire products;
  Sheet metalwork

(G-11826)
CANTELLI BLOCK AND BRICK INC
1602 Milan Rd (44870-4116)
PHONE....................................419 433-0102
Raymond J Cantelli, *Pr*
Anita Cantelli, *
Adriana Cantelli, *
Ray A Cantelli, *
EMP: 25 **EST:** 1923
SALES (est): 474.49K **Privately Held**
SIC: 3271 Blocks, concrete or cinder:
  standard

(G-11827)
CHEFS GARDEN INC
1104 Scheid Rd (44870-8355)
PHONE....................................419 433-4947
Barbara Jones, *Pr*
Bob L Jones, *
Lee Jones, *
Robert N Jones, *
EMP: 130 **EST:** 1981
SQ FT: 1,684
SALES (est): 23.67MM **Privately Held**
Web: www.chefs-garden.com
SIC: 2099 5148 0161 Ready-to-eat meals,
  salads, and sandwiches; Fresh fruits and
  vegetables; Market garden

(G-11828)
**DOUTHIT COMMUNICATIONS INC
(PA)**
Also Called: Photo Journals
520 Warren St (44870-2958)
P.O. Box 760 (44871-0760)
PHONE....................................419 625-5825
H Kenneth Iii, *Pr*
Harold K Douthit, *
Joanne Kraine, *
EMP: 75 **EST:** 1956
SQ FT: 12,000
SALES (est): 9.79MM
SALES (corp-wide): 9.79MM **Privately
Held**
Web: www.westlifenews.com
SIC: 2711 2741 Job printing and newspaper
  publishing combined; Miscellaneous
  publishing

(G-11829)
EDSAL SANDUSKY CORPORATION
Also Called: EDSAL SANDUSKY
CORPORATION
117 E Washington Row (44870-2629)
PHONE....................................419 626-5465
EMP: 34
SALES (corp-wide): 9.99MM **Privately
Held**
Web: www.sanduskycabinets.com
SIC: 2522 Cabinets, office: except wood
PA: Edsal Sandusky Llc
  1555 W 44th St
  Chicago IL 60609
  773 475-3000

(G-11830)
ENCORE INDUSTRIES INC
319 Howard Dr (44870-8607)
PHONE....................................419 626-8000
Timothy Rathbun, *Brnch Mgr*
EMP: 125
SALES (corp-wide): 816.52K **Privately
Held**
SIC: 3089 3559 3841 3411 Injection molded
  finished plastics products, nec; Plastics
  working machinery; Surgical and medical
  instruments; Metal cans
HQ: Encore Industries, Inc.
  725 Water St
  Cambridge OH 43725
  419 626-8000

(G-11831)
**ENCORE PLASTICS SOUTHEAST
LLC**
319 Howard Dr (44870-8607)
PHONE....................................419 626-8000
Craig Rathbun, *Prin*
EMP: 10 **EST:** 2011
SALES (est): 147.21K **Privately Held**
SIC: 3089 Plastics products, nec

(G-11832)
ENTRATECH SYSTEMS LLC (PA)
Also Called: Entratech Systems
202 Fox Rd (44870-8363)
PHONE....................................419 433-7683
EMP: 9 **EST:** 1982
SQ FT: 14,000
SALES (est): 1.32MM
SALES (corp-wide): 1.32MM **Privately
Held**
Web: www.entratech.com
SIC: 7539 3714 Electrical services; Filters:
  oil, fuel, and air, motor vehicle

(G-11833)
EQUINOX ENTERPRISES LLC
Also Called: A & L Metal Processing
1920 George St (44870-1739)
P.O. Box 1367 (44871-1367)
PHONE....................................419 627-0022
EMP: 7 **EST:** 1991
SQ FT: 25,000
SALES (est): 967.47K **Privately Held**
Web: www.almetalprocessing.com
SIC: 3471 Electroplating of metals or formed
  products

(G-11834)
ETHIMA INC
Also Called: Universal Clay Products
1528 First St (44870-3902)
PHONE....................................419 626-4912
Doctor Vimal Kumar, *Pr*
EMP: 55 **EST:** 1993
SQ FT: 80,000
SALES (est): 335.91K **Privately Held**
SIC: 3264 3255 3295 3444 Insulators,
  electrical: porcelain; Foundry refractories,
  clay; Minerals, ground or treated; Sheet
  metalwork

(G-11835)
GARY L GAST
Also Called: Ohio Wood Fabrication
2024 Campbell St (44870-4890)
PHONE....................................419 626-5915
Gary L Gast, *Owner*
EMP: 6 **EST:** 1991
SQ FT: 3,600
SALES (est): 63.57K **Privately Held**
SIC: 2541 Cabinets, except refrigerated:
  show, display, etc.: wood

(G-11836)
GENERAL FABRICATIONS CORP
7777 Milan Rd (44870-6413)
P.O. Box 2461 (44871-2461)
PHONE....................................419 625-6055
Chester Boraski, *Pr*
Carol Boraski, *
EMP: 42 **EST:** 1982
SQ FT: 10,000
SALES (est): 9.07MM **Privately Held**
Web: www.gfcfinishing.com
SIC: 3559 3563 Paint making machinery; Air
  and gas compressors

(G-11837)
**GUNDLACH SHEET METAL WORKS
INC (PA)**

Also Called: Honeywell Authorized Dealer
910 Columbus Ave (44870-3594)
PHONE..............................419 626-4525
Terry W Gundlach, *Ch*
Roger M Gundlach, *
Terry Kette, *
Andrew Gundluch, *
EMP: 33 **EST:** 1889
SQ FT: 17,000
SALES (est): 10.52MM
SALES (corp-wide): 10.52MM **Privately Held**
Web: www.gundlachsheetmetal.com
SIC: 1711 3444 Warm air heating and air conditioning contractor; Sheet metalwork

(G-11838)
HK COOPERATIVE INC
Also Called: HK Coprative Inc/J H Routh Pkg
4413 W Bogart Rd (44870-9648)
PHONE..............................419 626-2551
Jeff Wall, *Prin*
Paul Kalmbach, *Prin*
Blake Holden, *Prin*
EMP: 6 **EST:** 2020
SALES (est): 1.24MM **Privately Held**
Web: www.routhpacking.com
SIC: 2011 Meat packing plants

(G-11839)
HULL READY MIX CONCRETE INC
Also Called: Hull Builders Supply
4419 Tiffin Ave (44870-9645)
P.O. Box 823 (44052-0823)
PHONE..............................419 625-8070
Jeffery Riddell, *Pr*
EMP: 10 **EST:** 1999
SALES (est): 175.71K **Privately Held**
Web: www.buildersupply.com
SIC: 3273 4212 1611 7359 Ready-mixed concrete; Truck rental with drivers; Highway and street construction; Industrial truck rental

(G-11840)
IMAGINE BAKING BUYER LLC ✪
1034 Hancock St (44870-3616)
PHONE..............................419 502-9000
Maria Hibler, *Contrlr*
EMP: 18 **EST:** 2024
SALES (est): 1.15MM **Privately Held**
SIC: 2052 Bakery products, dry

(G-11841)
INDISPENSER LTD
520 Warren St (44870-2958)
P.O. Box 760 (44871-0760)
PHONE..............................419 625-5825
Harold Douthit, *Prin*
EMP: 45 **EST:** 1999
SALES (est): 384.5K **Privately Held**
SIC: 3999 Advertising display products

(G-11842)
INDUSTRIAL NUT CORP
1425 Tiffin Ave (44870-2054)
PHONE..............................419 625-8543
William Springer, *Pr*
John E Moffitt, *
James B Springer, *
John William Springer Iii, *VP*
▲ **EMP:** 54 **EST:** 1908
SQ FT: 100,000
SALES (est): 9.21MM **Privately Held**
Web: www.industrialnut.com
SIC: 3452 Nuts, metal

(G-11843)
ISAAC FOSTER MACK CO (PA)
Also Called: Sandusky Newspaper Group
314 W Market St (44870-2410)

PHONE..............................419 625-5500
Dudley A White Junior, *Ch Bd*
David A Rau, *
Susan E White, *
EMP: 140 **EST:** 1822
SQ FT: 45,000
SALES (est): 37.57MM
SALES (corp-wide): 37.57MM **Privately Held**
Web: www.sanduskyregister.com
SIC: 4832 2711 2752 Radio broadcasting stations; Newspapers; Commercial printing, lithographic

(G-11844)
J H ROUTH PACKING COMPANY
4413 W Bogart Rd (44870-6415)
P.O. Box 2253 (44871-2253)
PHONE..............................419 626-2251
EMP: 300 **EST:** 1947
SALES (est): 22.7MM **Privately Held**
Web: www.routhpacking.com
SIC: 2011 Meat packing plants

(G-11845)
JAMAC INC
422 Buchanan St (44870-4700)
PHONE..............................419 625-9790
Mark Mc Gory, *Pr*
Elaine Mc Gory, *VP*
Blake Mc Gory, *Sec*
James G Mc Gory Junior, *Treas*
James G Mc Gory Senior, *Stockholder*
▼ **EMP:** 21 **EST:** 1983
SQ FT: 10,000
SALES (est): 1.3MM **Privately Held**
Web: www.jamac.com
SIC: 2759 Labels and seals: printing, nsk

(G-11846)
JBT MAREL CORPORATION
Also Called: Jbt Foodtech
1622 First St (44870-3902)
PHONE..............................419 626-0304
Larry Martin, *Brnch Mgr*
EMP: 260
Web: www.jbtc.com
SIC: 3556 Food products machinery
PA: Jbt Marel Corporation
70 W Madison St Ste 4400
Chicago IL 60602

(G-11847)
KELKO MANUFACTURING LLC
Also Called: Kelko Products
2110 George St (44870-1743)
PHONE..............................419 626-2571
Matthew Varndell, *
EMP: 30 **EST:** 2019
SALES (est): 1.26MM **Privately Held**
SIC: 3452 Bolts, nuts, rivets, and washers

(G-11848)
KYKLOS BEARING INTERNATIONAL LLC
Also Called: K B I
2509 Hayes Ave (44870-5359)
PHONE..............................419 627-7000
▲ **EMP:** 900
SIC: 3714 Bearings, motor vehicle

(G-11849)
LAKE SHORE GRAPHIC INDS INC
2111 Cleveland Rd (44870-4412)
PHONE..............................419 626-8631
Craig H Stahl, *CEO*
William E Stahl, *Ch*
EMP: 7 **EST:** 1979
SALES (est): 243.05K **Privately Held**
SIC: 2752 Offset printing

(G-11850)
LEWCO INC (PA)
706 Lane St (44870-3846)
PHONE..............................419 625-4014
Ronald Guerra, *Pr*
Gerald Guerra, *
◆ **EMP:** 234 **EST:** 1967
SQ FT: 135,000
SALES (est): 58.23MM
SALES (corp-wide): 58.23MM **Privately Held**
Web: www.lewcoinc.com
SIC: 3535 3567 Bulk handling conveyor systems; Heating units and devices, industrial: electric

(G-11851)
LONZ WINERY LLC
Also Called: Specialty Wine-Spirits
917 Bardshar Rd (44870-1507)
PHONE..............................419 625-5474
Claudio Salvador, *Pr*
▲ **EMP:** 21 **EST:** 2002
SALES (est): 2.13MM **Privately Held**
Web: www.firelandswinery.com
SIC: 2084 Wines

(G-11852)
LORIS PRINTING INC
Also Called: Loris Printing & Party Center
2111 Cleveland Rd (44870-4412)
PHONE..............................419 626-6648
Joseph Loris, *Pr*
Kathy Loris, *Sec*
EMP: 7 **EST:** 1966
SALES (est): 2.44MM **Privately Held**
Web: www.lorisprinting.net
SIC: 2759 2752 7299 Screen printing; Commercial printing, lithographic; Facility rental and party planning services

(G-11853)
MAAGS AUTOMOTIVE & MCH INC
Also Called: Maag's Automotive
1640 Columbus Ave (44870-3542)
PHONE..............................419 626-1539
Robert Maag, *Pr*
EMP: 9 **EST:** 1976
SQ FT: 1,500
SALES (est): 700.28K **Privately Held**
SIC: 3519 7538 7539 3714 Diesel engine rebuilding; Engine rebuilding: automotive; Automotive repair shops, nec; Motor vehicle parts and accessories

(G-11854)
MACHINE APPLICATIONS CORP
Also Called: Mac Instruments
3410 Tiffin Ave (44870-9752)
PHONE..............................419 621-2322
James G Weit, *Pr*
Karen Weit, *Sec*
EMP: 7 **EST:** 1990
SQ FT: 1,672
SALES (est): 2.46MM **Privately Held**
Web: www.macinstruments.com
SIC: 3823 Process control instruments

(G-11855)
MACK IRON WORKS COMPANY
124 Warren St (44870-2823)
PHONE..............................419 626-3712
John O Bacon, *Pr*
Peter P Kowalski Junior, *VP*
EMP: 40 **EST:** 1901
SQ FT: 63,000
SALES (est): 9.42MM **Privately Held**
Web: www.mackiron.com

SIC: 3494 3444 3443 3446 Valves and pipe fittings, nec; Sheet metalwork; Fabricated plate work (boiler shop); Stairs, staircases, stair treads: prefabricated metal

(G-11856)
MARK ADVERTISING AGENCY INC
1600 5th St (44870-1300)
P.O. Box 413 (44871-0413)
PHONE..............................419 626-9000
Joe Wesnitzer, *CEO*
Shelly Cook, *Pr*
Shirley Wesnitzer, *VP*
EMP: 15 **EST:** 1965
SQ FT: 8,000
SALES (est): 1.83MM **Privately Held**
Web: www.markadvertising.com
SIC: 2752 7311 Offset printing; Advertising agencies

(G-11857)
MECCAS LOUNGE LLC
2614 Pioneer Trl Apt 606 (44870-5148)
PHONE..............................419 239-6918
EMP: 7 **EST:** 2021
SALES (est): 150K **Privately Held**
SIC: 2599 Food wagons, restaurant

(G-11858)
METALTEK INTERNATIONAL INC
Also Called: Metaltek International
615 W Market St (44870-2413)
PHONE..............................419 626-5340
EMP: 90
Web: www.metaltek.com
SIC: 3366 Copper foundries
PA: Metaltek International, Inc.
905 E St Paul Ave
Waukesha WI 53188

(G-11859)
MH & SON MACHINING & WLDG CO
210 W Perkins Ave Ste 10 (44870-9005)
PHONE..............................419 621-0690
Mark A Howard, *Pr*
Kim M Howard, *VP*
EMP: 6 **EST:** 2002
SQ FT: 2,000
SALES (est): 906.12K **Privately Held**
Web: www.mhandson.com
SIC: 3599 1799 Machine shop, jobbing and repair; Welding on site

(G-11860)
MIELKE FURNITURE REPAIR INC
3209 Columbus Ave (44870-5595)
PHONE..............................419 625-4572
Daniel H Mielke, *Pr*
Allan R Mielke, *VP*
Christine Mielke, *Sec*
EMP: 8 **EST:** 1947
SQ FT: 2,800
SALES (est): 378.53K **Privately Held**
Web: www.mielkefurniture.com
SIC: 7641 2511 Furniture refinishing; Wood household furniture

(G-11861)
OGDEN NEWS PUBLISHING OHIO INC (DH)
Also Called: Courier, The
314 W Market St (44870-2410)
PHONE..............................419 625-5500
Bob Nutting, *CEO*
EMP: 30 **EST:** 1997
SALES (est): 2MM **Privately Held**
Web: www.ogdennews.com
SIC: 2711 Newspapers: publishing only, not printed on site
HQ: The Ogden Newspapers Inc
1500 Main St

Wheeling WV 26003
304 233-0100

(G-11862)
OKAMOTO SANDUSKY MFG LLC
Also Called: Okamoto USA
3130 W Monroe St (44870-1811)
PHONE..............................419 626-1633
Yoshiyuki Okamoto, *Pr*
▲ **EMP:** 100 **EST:** 2007
SALES (est): 20.47MM **Privately Held**
Web: www.okamotosandusky.com
SIC: 3069 Bibs, vulcanized rubber or
rubberized fabric
PA: Okamoto Industries,Inc.
3-27-12, Hongo
Bunkyo-Ku TKY 113-0

(G-11863)
P & T PRODUCTS INC
472 Industrial Pkwy (44870-5883)
PHONE..............................419 621-1966
Paul Todd, *Pr*
Jennifer Fildley, *VP*
Susan K Todd, *Sec*
EMP: 20 **EST:** 1988
SQ FT: 20,000
SALES (est): 1.77MM **Privately Held**
Web: www.p-tproductsinc.com
SIC: 2891 Sealants

(G-11864)
PARK PRESS DIRECT
2143 Sherman St (44870-4714)
P.O. Box 2311 (44871-2311)
PHONE..............................419 626-4426
Slate Kessler, *Prin*
Scott Bowlers, *Prin*
EMP: 9 **EST:** 2015
SALES (est): 96.57K **Privately Held**
Web: www.parkpressdirect.com
SIC: 2752 7389 Offset printing; Business
Activities at Non-Commercial Site

(G-11865)
PEERLESS STOVE & MFG CO
Also Called: Peerless Prof Cooking Eqp
334 Harrison St (44870)
P.O. Box 859 (44871-0859)
PHONE..............................419 625-4514
Brian R Huntley, *Pr*
EMP: 10 **EST:** 1916
SQ FT: 40,000
SALES (est): 3.15MM **Privately Held**
Web: www.peerlessovens.com
SIC: 3556 Food products machinery

(G-11866)
POLYNT COMPOSITES USA INC
1321 First St (44870-3901)
PHONE..............................816 391-6000
Scott Bechtel, *Mgr*
EMP: 34
SALES (corp-wide): 2.59B **Privately Held**
Web: www.polynt.com
SIC: 2834 2842 2851 2821 Emulsions,
pharmaceutical; Polishes and sanitation
goods; Paints and allied products;
Polyesters
HQ: Polynt Composites Usa Inc.
99 E Cottage Ave
Carpentersville IL 60110

(G-11867)
**SANDUSKY FABRICATING & SLS
INC (PA)**
Also Called: San-Fab Conveyor and Automtn
2000 Superior St (44870-1824)
P.O. Box 2190 (44871-2190)
PHONE..............................419 626-4465
Timothy H Shenigo, *Pr*

EMP: 23 **EST:** 1954
SQ FT: 85,000
SALES (est): 1.73MM
SALES (corp-wide): 1.73MM **Privately
Held**
Web: www.sanfab.com
SIC: 3535 Conveyors and conveying
equipment

(G-11868)
SANDUSKY INTERNATIONAL INC
Also Called: CARONDELET FOUNDRY
510 W Water St (44870)
PHONE..............................419 626-5340
Edward R Ryan, *CEO*
Richard A Hargrave, *
◆ **EMP:** 200 **EST:** 1904
SQ FT: 500,000
SALES (est): 81.06K **Privately Held**
Web: www.metaltek.com
SIC: 3325 3369 Alloy steel castings, except
investment; Castings, except die-castings,
precision
PA: Metaltek International, Inc.
905 E St Paul Ave
Waukesha WI 53188

(G-11869)
SANDUSKY MACHINE & TOOL INC
2223 Tiffin Ave (44870-1994)
PHONE..............................419 626-8359
Walter Schaufler, *Ch Bd*
James Schaufler, *Pr*
EMP: 8 **EST:** 1966
SQ FT: 17,600
SALES (est): 2.11MM **Privately Held**
SIC: 3599 Machine shop, jobbing and repair

(G-11870)
**SANDUSKY PACKAGING
CORPORATION**
2016 George St (44870-1797)
P.O. Box Po Box2217 (44871)
PHONE..............................419 626-8520
Randall A Johnson, *Pr*
Greg Norman, *
EMP: 49 **EST:** 1965
SQ FT: 75,000
SALES (est): 10MM **Privately Held**
Web: www.sanduskypackaging.com
SIC: 2652 2657 Setup paperboard boxes;
Folding paperboard boxes

(G-11871)
SCHWAB MACHINE INC
3120 Venice Rd (44870-1886)
PHONE..............................419 626-0245
Robert Schwab, *Pr*
James Mcmahon, *VP*
EMP: 6 **EST:** 1946
SQ FT: 9,600
SALES (est): 587.81K **Privately Held**
Web: www.schwabmachine.com
SIC: 3599 Machine shop, jobbing and repair

(G-11872)
SPOERR PRECAST CONCRETE INC
2020 Caldwell St (44870-4874)
PHONE..............................419 625-9132
TOLL FREE: 800
William R Shank, *Pr*
William Shank, *Pr*
Robert Shank, *Research Vice President*
EMP: 11 **EST:** 1933
SQ FT: 18,000
SALES (est): 975.13K **Privately Held**
Web: www.spoerrprecast.com
SIC: 3272 Concrete products, precast, nec

(G-11873)
**SUPERIOR STREET HOLDING INC
(PA)**
2105 Superior St (44870-1825)
PHONE..............................419 626-5757
Bill Niggemyer, *Pr*
▲ **EMP:** 47 **EST:** 1930
SQ FT: 20,000
SALES (est): 8.64MM
SALES (corp-wide): 8.64MM **Privately
Held**
Web: www.decko.com
SIC: 2064 Cake ornaments, confectionery

(G-11874)
SUPERIOR STREET HOLDING INC
2020 Superior St (44870-1824)
PHONE..............................419 626-5757
Bill Niggemyer, *Brnch Mgr*
EMP: 18
SALES (corp-wide): 8.64MM **Privately
Held**
Web: www.decko.com
SIC: 2064 Cake ornaments, confectionery
PA: Superior Street Holding, Inc.
2105 Superior St
Sandusky OH 44870
419 626-5757

(G-11875)
THERMOCOLOR LLC (DH)
Also Called: Rhetech Colors
2901 W Monroe St (44870-1810)
PHONE..............................419 626-5677
EMP: 25 **EST:** 1986
SQ FT: 30,000
SALES (est): 9.43MM
SALES (corp-wide): 6.47MM **Privately
Held**
Web: www.rhetechcolors.com
SIC: 2821 Plastics materials and resins
HQ: Hexpol Holding Inc.
14330 Kinsman Rd
Burton OH 44021
440 834-4644

(G-11876)
THORWORKS INDUSTRIES INC (PA)
Also Called: Sealmaster
2520 Campbell St (44870-5309)
P.O. Box 2218 (44870)
PHONE..............................419 626-4375
David Thorson, *Pr*
Larry Mullins, *
◆ **EMP:** 110 **EST:** 1985
SQ FT: 80,000
SALES (est): 88.97MM **Privately Held**
Web: www.thorworks.com
SIC: 2951 3531 2952 2891 Asphalt paving
mixtures and blocks; Construction
machinery; Asphalt felts and coatings;
Adhesives and sealants

(G-11877)
TOFT DAIRY INC
3717 Venice Rd (44870-1640)
P.O. Box 2558 (44871-2558)
PHONE..............................419 625-4376
TOLL FREE: 800
Eugene H Meisler, *Pr*
Carl Meisler, *
Nicholas Catri, *
Thomas E Meisler, *
Charles M Meisler, *
EMP: 52 **EST:** 1900
SQ FT: 94,000
SALES (est): 9.5MM **Privately Held**
Web: www.toftdairy.com
SIC: 2026 2024 Milk processing
(pasteurizing, homogenizing, bottling); Ice
cream and ice milk

(G-11878)
TUNE TOWN CAR AUDIO
Also Called: Tune Town
2345 E Perkins Ave (44870-5176)
PHONE..............................419 627-1100
TOLL FREE: 877
Mark Myers, *Owner*
EMP: 7 **EST:** 1994
SQ FT: 4,800
SALES (est): 126.98K **Privately Held**
Web: www.tune-town.com
SIC: 5731 3651 High fidelity stereo
equipment; Household audio and video
equipment

(G-11879)
UNION FABRICATING AND MCH CO
3427 Venice Rd (44870-1766)
PHONE..............................419 626-5963
TOLL FREE: 800
Alden V Lake, *CEO*
Mary Lake, *Sec*
Daniel Lake, *Pr*
Jeffrey Lake, *VP*
EMP: 7 **EST:** 1965
SALES (est): 177.19K **Privately Held**
SIC: 3441 Fabricated structural metal

(G-11880)
UNIVERSAL DSIGN FBRICATION LLC
Also Called: Fabrication and Welding
7319 Portland Rd (44870-9672)
PHONE..............................419 202-5269
John Eckhardt, *Managing Member*
EMP: 10 **EST:** 2018
SALES (est): 1MM **Privately Held**
Web:
www.universaldesignandfabrication.com
SIC: 7389 1531 1799 3443 Design services;
Welding on site; Weldments

(G-11881)
US TSUBAKI POWER TRANSM LLC
Also Called: Engineering Chain Div
1010 Edgewater Ave (44870-1601)
PHONE..............................419 626-4560
Myron Timmer, *VP*
EMP: 180
Web: www.ustsubaki.com
SIC: 5049 3568 3714 3462 Engineers'
equipment and supplies, nec; Chain, power
transmission; Motor vehicle parts and
accessories; Iron and steel forgings
HQ: U.S. Tsubaki Power Transmission Llc
301 E Marquardt Dr
Wheeling IL 60090
847 459-9500

(G-11882)
VENTRA SANDUSKY LLC
3020 Tiffin Ave (44870-5352)
PHONE..............................419 627-3600
▲ **EMP:** 244 **EST:** 2007
SALES (est): 21.26MM
SALES (corp-wide): 1.57B **Privately Held**
Web: www.ventra.com
SIC: 3822 3714 Environmental controls;
Motor vehicle parts and accessories
PA: Flex-N-Gate Llc
1306 E University Ave
Urbana IL 61802
217 384-6600

(G-11883)
WAGNER QUARRIES COMPANY
Also Called: Hanson Aggregates
4203 Milan Rd (44870-5880)
PHONE..............................419 625-8141
Chuck Cashan, *Mgr*
EMP: 21 **EST:** 1912
SQ FT: 2,400

2025 Harris Ohio
Industrial Directory

▲ = Import ▼ = Export
◆ = Import/Export

SALES (est): 1.91MM **Privately Held**
Web: www.wagnerquarry.com
SIC: 1422 Limestones, ground

Sarahsville
Noble County

(G-11884)
BIEDENBACH LOGGING
48443 Seneca Lake Rd (43779-9732)
PHONE....................740 732-6477
John Biedenbach, *Pt*
EMP: 6 EST: 1978
SALES (est): 121.23K **Privately Held**
SIC: 2411 1629 Logging camps and contractors; Earthmoving contractor

Sardinia
Brown County

(G-11885)
MANNINGS PACKING CO
100 College Ave (45171-7500)
P.O. Box 23 (45171-0023)
PHONE....................937 446-3278
Gregory Thomas Manning, *Pt*
Robert Manning, *Pt*
EMP: 8 EST: 1950
SQ FT: 5,000
SALES (est): 947.1K **Privately Held**
Web: www.manningpacking.com
SIC: 2011 Meat packing plants

(G-11886)
SARDINIA READY MIX INC
9 Oakdale Ave (45171)
P.O. Box 53 (45171-0053)
PHONE....................937 446-2523
David Taylor, *Pr*
Charles Taylor, *VP*
Cheryl Taylor, *Sec*
EMP: 22 EST: 1951
SQ FT: 2,000
SALES (est): 1.79MM **Privately Held**
Web: www.sardiniareadymix.com
SIC: 3273 Ready-mixed concrete

Sardis
Monroe County

(G-11887)
APPALACHIAN OILFIELD SVCS LLC
34602 State Route 7 (43946-8704)
P.O. Box 430 (45767-0430)
PHONE....................337 216-0066
EMP: 18 EST: 2015
SALES (est): 6.91MM **Privately Held**
SIC: 1389 Oil field services, nec

Scio
Harrison County

(G-11888)
M3 MIDSTREAM LLC
Also Called: Harrison Hub
37950 Crimm Rd (43988-8761)
PHONE....................740 945-1170
EMP: 34
SALES (corp-wide): 23.57MM **Privately Held**
Web: www.momentummidstream.com
SIC: 1382 Oil and gas exploration services
PA: M3 Midstream Llc
600 Travis St Ste 5600
Houston TX 77002

713 783-3000

Seaman
Adams County

(G-11889)
ALL WAYS GREEN LAWN & TURF LLC
1856 Greenbrier Rd (45679-9552)
PHONE....................937 763-4766
EMP: 7 EST: 2008
SALES (est): 235.84K **Privately Held**
SIC: 2875 0781 Fertilizers, mixing only; Landscape services

Sebring
Mahoning County

(G-11890)
AMERICANA GLASS CO INC
356 E Maryland Ave (44672-1518)
P.O. Box 310 (44672-0310)
PHONE....................330 938-6135
Joan Mercer, *Pr*
James Puckett, *Sec*
EMP: 10 EST: 1966
SQ FT: 7,500
SALES (est): 836.71K
SALES (corp-wide): 1.3MM **Privately Held**
SIC: 3231 3262 Decorated glassware: chipped, engraved, etched, etc.; Vitreous china table and kitchenware
PA: Americana Art China Co., Inc.
316 Manito Trl
Mercer PA 16137
330 938-6133

(G-11891)
APEX CONTROL SYSTEMS INC
751 N Johnson Rd (44672-1011)
P.O. Box 66 (44672-0066)
PHONE....................330 938-2588
EMP: 65 EST: 1992
SALES (est): 7.93MM **Privately Held**
Web: www.apexcontrol.com
SIC: 3625 8748 3676 3643 Electric controls and control accessories, industrial; Business consulting, nec; Electronic resistors; Current-carrying wiring services

(G-11892)
BINOS INC
700 W Ohio Ave (44672-1003)
PHONE....................330 938-0888
Bryan Rohrer, *CEO*
EMP: 8
SALES (est): 803.63K **Privately Held**
SIC: 3556 5812 Food products machinery; Pizza restaurants

(G-11893)
CIRCLE MACHINE ROLLS INC
245 W Kentucky Ave (44672-1909)
PHONE....................330 938-9010
Peter Kuhlmann, *Pr*
Ken Kuhlmann, *
Brenda Reed, *
▲ EMP: 27 EST: 1965
SQ FT: 15,000
SALES (est): 4.35MM **Privately Held**
Web: www.rollsbycircle.com
SIC: 3599 3547 Machine shop, jobbing and repair; Rolling mill machinery

(G-11894)
FOUNDRY SAND SERVICE LLC
20455 Lake Park Blvd (44672-1771)

P.O. Box 262 (44672-0262)
PHONE....................330 823-6152
Jim Budd, *Dir*
EMP: 10 EST: 2015
SALES (est): 3.07MM **Privately Held**
Web: www.foundrysands.com
SIC: 1442 Construction sand and gravel

(G-11895)
JF MARTT AND ASSOCIATES INC
501 N Johnson Rd (44672-1007)
P.O. Box 10 (44672-0010)
PHONE....................330 938-4000
Judson Martt, *Pr*
Frank Tluchowski, *VP*
EMP: 15 EST: 1989
SQ FT: 12,000
SALES (est): 867.8K **Privately Held**
Web: www.jfmartt.com
SIC: 7699 3599 Industrial machinery and equipment repair; Custom machinery

(G-11896)
M PI LABEL SYSTEMS
450 Courtney Rd (44672-1339)
P.O. Box 70 (44672-0070)
PHONE....................330 938-2134
Randy Kocher, *Pr*
Carson Mc Neely, *Pr*
Donald J Mcdanial, *Pr*
Joe Skiba, *Treas*
EMP: 6 EST: 1991
SALES (est): 120.22K **Privately Held**
Web: www.mpilabels.com
SIC: 2759 2754 3565 Labels and seals: printing, nsk; Labels: gravure printing; Labeling machines, industrial

(G-11897)
MILLER PRODUCTS INC (PA)
Also Called: M P I Label Systems
450 Courtney Rd (44672-1339)
P.O. Box 70 (44672-0070)
PHONE....................330 938-2134
EMP: 160 EST: 1968
SALES (est): 70.41MM
SALES (corp-wide): 70.41MM **Privately Held**
Web: www.mpilabels.com
SIC: 2672 Adhesive papers, labels, or tapes: from purchased material

(G-11898)
MODERN CHINA COMPANY INC (PA)
550 E Ohio Ave (44672-1642)
P.O. Box 309 (44672)
PHONE....................330 938-6104
Debbie Grindley, *Pr*
EMP: 35 EST: 1959
SQ FT: 27,000
SALES (est): 1.66MM
SALES (corp-wide): 1.66MM **Privately Held**
Web: www.modernchinasouv.com
SIC: 5947 3229 3263 Souvenirs; Glassware, art or decorative; Semivitreous table and kitchenware

(G-11899)
MPI LABELS OF BALTIMORE INC (HQ)
Also Called: Mpi Label Systems.
450 Courtney Rd (44672-1339)
P.O. Box 70 (44672-0070)
PHONE....................330 938-2134
Randy L Kocher, *Pr*
Elvin Barnit, *Pr*
Carson Mc Neely, *Pr*
Donald Mcdanial, *Pr*
EMP: 45 EST: 2010
SQ FT: 110,000

SALES (est): 8.3MM
SALES (corp-wide): 70.41MM **Privately Held**
Web: www.mpilabels.com
SIC: 2759 2754 3565 Labels and seals: printing, nsk; Labels: gravure printing; Labeling machines, industrial
PA: Miller Products, Inc.
450 Courtney Rd
Sebring OH 44672
330 938-2134

(G-11900)
REFRACTORY SPECIALTIES INC
Also Called: Unifrax Sebring S Operations
230 W California Ave (44672-1920)
PHONE....................330 938-2101
Richard F Wilk Junior, *Pr*
Suhas Patil, *
Jim Vaughn, *
▲ EMP: 49 EST: 1992
SQ FT: 55,000
SALES (est): 3.71MM **Privately Held**
Web: www.unifrax.com
SIC: 3296 3823 3297 Mineral wool; Process control instruments; Graphite refractories: carbon bond or ceramic bond
PA: Unifrax Holding Llc
600 Riverwalk Pkwy
Tonawanda NY 14150

(G-11901)
SALEM-REPUBLIC RUBBER COMPANY
475 W California Ave (44672-1922)
P.O. Box 339 (44672-0339)
PHONE....................877 425-5079
Drew Ney, *Pr*
▲ EMP: 47 EST: 1972
SQ FT: 180,000
SALES (est): 9.12MM **Privately Held**
Web: www.salem-republic.com
SIC: 3052 3069 Rubber hose; Rubberized fabrics

(G-11902)
SEBRING FLUID POWER CORP
513 N Johnson Rd (44672-1007)
P.O. Box 6 (44672-0006)
PHONE....................330 938-9984
Paul Mc Guire, *Pr*
Stan Ware, *Treas*
EMP: 7 EST: 1986
SQ FT: 10,000
SALES (est): 472.35K **Privately Held**
SIC: 3599 3593 Machine shop, jobbing and repair; Fluid power cylinders and actuators

(G-11903)
TRUCUT INCORPORATED (PA)
1145 Allied Dr (44672-1355)
PHONE....................330 938-9806
David Gano, *Pr*
Larry Grossi, *Ex VP*
▲ EMP: 53 EST: 1968
SQ FT: 85,000
SALES (est): 7.66MM
SALES (corp-wide): 7.66MM **Privately Held**
Web: www.trucut.com
SIC: 3544 3542 3469 3613 Special dies and tools; Machine tools, metal forming type; Metal stampings, nec; Control panels, electric

(G-11904)
UNITED DIE & MFG SALES CO
100 S 17th St (44672-1914)
P.O. Box 38 (44672-0038)
PHONE....................330 938-6141
Gary Close, *Pr*

GEOGRAPHIC

Dennis Close, *
EMP: 30 **EST:** 1951
SQ FT: 40,000
SALES (est): 2.44MM **Privately Held**
Web: www.uniteddiemfg.com
SIC: 3429 3469 Hardware, nec; Stamping metal for the trade

(G-11905)
VACUFORM INC
500 Courtney Rd (44672-1349)
P.O. Box 117 (44672-0117)
PHONE................................330 938-9674
Michael Hubbs, *VP*
▲ **EMP:** 35 **EST:** 1998
SQ FT: 50,000
SALES (est): 2.85MM **Privately Held**
Web: lbsp.click.com.cn
SIC: 3297 Nonclay refractories
HQ: Unifrax I Llc
　　600 Rverwalk Pkwy Ste 120
　　Tonawanda NY 14150

Senecaville
Guernsey County

(G-11906)
PAUL YODER
13051 Deerfield Rd (43780-9406)
PHONE................................740 439-5811
Paul Yoder, *Owner*
EMP: 6 **EST:** 1998
SQ FT: 6,500
SALES (est): 487.83K **Privately Held**
Web: www.yoderbuilding.com
SIC: 2542 Cabinets: show, display, or storage: except wood

Seven Mile
Butler County

(G-11907)
ENCORE PRECAST LLC
416 W Ritter (45062)
P.O. Box 380 (45062-0380)
PHONE................................513 726-5678
Charles Ehlers, *Prin*
EMP: 64 **EST:** 2001
SALES (est): 6.44MM **Privately Held**
Web: www.encoreprecastllc.com
SIC: 3272 5032 5211 Septic tanks, concrete; Concrete and cinder building products; Concrete and cinder block

Seville
Medina County

(G-11908)
4-B WOOD SPECIALTIES INC
Also Called: 4-B Wood Custom Cabinets
255 W Greenwich Rd (44273-8876)
PHONE................................330 769-2188
Kurt E Grassell, *Pr*
Tracy Romanotto, *Off Mgr*
EMP: 8 **EST:** 1976
SQ FT: 17,000
SALES (est): 767.5K **Privately Held**
Web: www.4bwood.com
SIC: 2434 Wood kitchen cabinets

(G-11909)
ALLIED POLYMERS
21 Mill St (44273-9164)
P.O. Box 154 (44273-0154)
PHONE................................330 975-4200
Edward Joseph, *Pt*

Edward Jospeh, *Pt*
EMP: 8 **EST:** 1992
SALES (est): 253.84K **Privately Held**
SIC: 2822 Ethylene-propylene rubbers, EPDM polymers

(G-11910)
BENCHMARK CRAFTSMAN INC
Also Called: Benchmark Craftsmen
4700 Greenwich Rd (44273-8848)
PHONE................................866 313-4700
Nathan Sublett, *Pr*
EMP: 30 **EST:** 2002
SALES (est): 2.67MM **Privately Held**
Web: benchmark.us.com
SIC: 7389 3993 Exhibit construction by industrial contractors; Displays and cutouts, window and lobby

(G-11911)
BLAIR RUBBER COMPANY
5020 Enterprise Pkwy (44273-8960)
PHONE................................330 769-5583
John M Glenn, *CEO*
◆ **EMP:** 65 **EST:** 1981
SQ FT: 50,000
SALES (est): 13.43MM
SALES (corp-wide): 1.26B **Privately Held**
Web: www.blairrubber.com
SIC: 3069 3535 Linings, vulcanizable rubber; Belt conveyor systems, general industrial use
HQ: Goldis Enterprises, Inc.
　　120 Hay Rd
　　Wilmington DE 19809
　　302 764-3100

(G-11912)
BLAIR SALES INC
Also Called: Blair Rubber
5020 Enterprise Pkwy (44273-8960)
PHONE................................330 769-5586
Yedidia Koschitzky, *Pr*
EMP: 67 **EST:** 2017
SALES (est): 1.78MM **Privately Held**
Web: www.blairrubber.com
SIC: 2822 Silicone rubbers

(G-11913)
BLEACHTECH LLC
320 Ryan Rd (44273-9109)
PHONE................................216 921-1980
Richard Immerman, *Managing Member*
Richard Immerman, *Pr*
Benjamin Calkins, *
EMP: 25 **EST:** 2002
SALES (est): 8.71MM **Privately Held**
Web: www.bleachtech.com
SIC: 7349 2819 5169 Chemical cleaning services; Bleaching powder, lime bleaching compounds; Chemicals and allied products, nec

(G-11914)
BOB SUMEREL TIRE CO INC
8692 Lake Rd (44273-9000)
PHONE................................330 769-9092
Jason Negray, *Brnch Mgr*
EMP: 11
SALES (corp-wide): 35.8MM **Privately Held**
Web: www.bobsumereltire.com
SIC: 5531 7534 7537 7538 Automotive tires; Tire retreading and repair shops; Automotive transmission repair shops; General automotive repair shops
PA: Bob Sumerel Tire Co., Inc.
　　1257 Cox Ave
　　Erlanger KY 41018
　　859 283-2700

(G-11915)
COLOR PROCESS INC
8760 Guilford Rd (44273-9341)
PHONE................................440 268-7100
Mark Ingham, *Pr*
Jim Greiner, *
EMP: 25 **EST:** 1959
SALES (est): 5.26MM **Privately Held**
Web: www.colorprocess.info
SIC: 2752 Offset printing

(G-11916)
COMDESS COMPANY INC
8733 Wooster Pike Rd (44273-9363)
P.O. Box 91 (44273-0091)
PHONE................................330 769-2094
Sam Mandich, *Pr*
▲ **EMP:** 13 **EST:** 1981
SQ FT: 25,000
SALES (est): 1.03MM **Privately Held**
Web: www.comdess.com
SIC: 3089 Thermoformed finished plastics products, nec

(G-11917)
HYLOAD INC (DH)
5020 Enterprise Pkwy (44273-8960)
PHONE................................330 336-6604
Dave Jentzsch, *Pr*
▼ **EMP:** 7 **EST:** 1982
SQ FT: 40,000
SALES (est): 3.51MM
SALES (corp-wide): 10.93MM **Privately Held**
Web: www.hyload.com
SIC: 3069 2952 Roofing, membrane rubber; Asphalt felts and coatings
HQ: Iko Holdings Limited
　　Carthusian Ct
　　London EC1M

(G-11918)
ISLAND DELIGHTS INC
240 W Greenwich Rd (44273-8878)
P.O. Box 187 (44273-0187)
PHONE................................866 887-4100
James Murray, *Pr*
Greg Miller, *VP*
EMP: 8 **EST:** 2009
SQ FT: 12,000
SALES (est): 449.9K **Privately Held**
Web: www.islanddelights.com
SIC: 5441 2064 Candy; Candy and other confectionery products

(G-11919)
JJ SEVILLE LLC
Also Called: Seville Bronze
22 Milton St (44273-9316)
P.O. Box 45 (44273-0045)
PHONE................................330 769-2071
Tim Steele, *Managing Member*
EMP: 25 **EST:** 2009
SALES (est): 5.47MM **Privately Held**
Web: www.sevillebronze.com
SIC: 3351 Bronze rolling and drawing

(G-11920)
RUBICON RUBBER LLC ✪
276 W Greenwich Rd (44273-8881)
P.O. Box 13697 (44398)
PHONE................................234 678-0078
Vincent Del Medico, *Pr*
Vincent Del Medico, *Managing Member*
EMP: 12 **EST:** 2023
SALES (est): 1.01MM **Privately Held**
SIC: 8731 3069 Environmental research; Linings, vulcanizable rubber

(G-11921)
STELLAR GROUP INC
4935 Enterprise Pkwy (44273-8930)
PHONE................................330 769-8484
Dennis Rowbotham, *Contrlr*
EMP: 13 **EST:** 2017
SALES (est): 4.73MM **Privately Held**
Web: www.stellargroupinc.com
SIC: 2899 Corrosion preventive lubricant

Shadyside
Belmont County

(G-11922)
KNIGHT MANUFACTURING CO INC
Also Called: Belmont Stamping
E 40th St (43947)
P.O. Box 98 (43947-0098)
PHONE................................740 676-5516
David Knight, *Mgr*
EMP: 6
SALES (corp-wide): 2.19MM **Privately Held**
Web: www.belmontstamping.com
SIC: 3444 3469 3589 Sheet metalwork; Metal stampings, nec; Garbage disposers and compactors, commercial
PA: Knight Manufacturing Co Inc
　　399 E 40th St
　　Shadyside OH 43947
　　740 676-9532

(G-11923)
KNIGHT MANUFACTURING CO INC (PA)
399 E 40th St (43947-1206)
P.O. Box 27 (43947-0027)
PHONE................................740 676-9532
David Knight, *Pr*
EMP: 10 **EST:** 1935
SQ FT: 140,000
SALES (est): 2.19MM
SALES (corp-wide): 2.19MM **Privately Held**
SIC: 3599 3469 Machine shop, jobbing and repair; Boxes: tool, lunch, mail, etc.: stamped metal

(G-11924)
NEW CUT TOOL AND MFG CORP
1 New Cut Road (43947)
P.O. Box 8 (43947-0008)
PHONE................................740 676-1666
Michael Koonce, *Pr*
Cynthia Badia, *VP*
EMP: 10 **EST:** 1979
SQ FT: 2,700
SALES (est): 1.86MM **Privately Held**
SIC: 3599 Machine shop, jobbing and repair

Shaker Heights
Cuyahoga County

(G-11925)
ACORN TECHNOLOGY CORPORATION
3176 Morley Rd (44122-2862)
PHONE................................216 663-1244
Lalana Green, *Pr*
Robert Green, *VP*
EMP: 20 **EST:** 1993
SALES (est): 2.2MM **Privately Held**
Web: www.acorntechnology.com
SIC: 3613 5063 3634 3429 Panel and distribution boards and other related apparatus; Electrical apparatus and equipment; Ceiling fans; Aircraft & marine hardware, inc. pulleys & similar items

▲ = Import ▼ = Export
◆ = Import/Export

(G-11926)
BAKER STORE EQUIPMENT COMPANY
23449 Laurerdale Rd (44122-2106)
EMP: 10 **EST:** 1956
SALES (est): 539.42K **Privately Held**
Web: www.bakerstorequip.com
SIC: 2541 Store fixtures, wood

(G-11927)
C-MOLD INC
22251 Mccauley Rd (44122-2713)
EMP: 25 **EST:** 1993
SQ FT: 21,500
SALES (est): 1.05MM **Privately Held**
Web: www.cmold.net
SIC: 3089 Injection molding of plastics

(G-11928)
CELLULAR TECHNOLOGY LIMITED
Also Called: Ctl Analyzers
20521 Chagrin Blvd Ste 200 (44122-5301)
PHONE..................216 791-5084
EMP: 40 **EST:** 1998
SQ FT: 30,000
SALES (est): 3.75MM **Privately Held**
Web: www.immunospot.com
SIC: 8071 3821 Medical laboratories;
Clinical laboratory instruments, except
medical and dental

(G-11929)
CTL ANALYZERS LLC (PA)
Also Called: Cellular Technology Ltd
20521 Chagrin Blvd Ste 200 (44122-5350)
PHONE..................216 791-5084
Magdalana Terry-lehmann, *Co-Treasurer*
EMP: 47 **EST:** 1999
SALES (est): 5MM **Privately Held**
Web: www.immunospot.com
SIC: 3845 Electromedical equipment

(G-11930)
FULLGOSPEL PUBLISHING
16781 Chagrin Blvd Ste 134 (44120-3721)
P.O. Box 201331 (44120-8105)
PHONE..................216 339-1973
Kathy Brown, *Owner*
EMP: 10 **EST:** 2018
SALES (est): 162.93K **Privately Held**
Web: www.fullgospelpublishing.com
SIC: 2741 Miscellaneous publishing

(G-11931)
MODEL MEDICAL LLC
3429 Lee Rd Apt 12 (44120-3652)
PHONE..................216 972-0573
EMP: 10 **EST:** 2020
SALES (est): 111.55K **Privately Held**
SIC: 2326 Medical and hospital uniforms,
men's

(G-11932)
PURUSHEALTH LLC
3558 Lee Rd (44120-5123)
PHONE..................800 601-0580
John Huff, *CEO*
EMP: 11 **EST:** 2011
SALES (est): 395.04K **Privately Held**
SIC: 2099 Food preparations, nec

Shandon
Butler County

(G-11933)
CARTESSA CORP
4825 Cincinnati Brookville Rd (45063-5000)
P.O. Box 190 (45063-0190)

PHONE..................513 738-4477
Darryl Kristof, *Pr*
Kathleen Kristof, *VP*
▼ **EMP:** 16 **EST:** 1975
SQ FT: 5,000
SALES (est): 3.15MM **Privately Held**
Web: www.cartessa.com
SIC: 3672 5065 Printed circuit boards;
Electronic parts and equipment, nec

(G-11934)
DIAMOND TRAILERS INC
Also Called: Diamond Heavy Haul
5045 Cincinnati-Brookville Rd (45063)
P.O. Box 146 (45063-0146)
PHONE..................513 738-4500
Steven J Engel, *Pr*
Tonya Engel, *Prin*
EMP: 6 **EST:** 1997
SQ FT: 92,000
SALES (est): 2.46MM **Privately Held**
Web: www.diamondheavyhaul.com
SIC: 3715 Truck trailers

(G-11935)
TRI STATE EQUIPMENT COMPANY
5009 Cincinnati-Brookville Rd (45063)
P.O. Box 155 (45063-0155)
PHONE..................513 738-7227
Kevin Hughes, *Pr*
EMP: 6 **EST:** 1973
SQ FT: 5,000
SALES (est): 330.77K **Privately Held**
SIC: 5084 7699 7359 3563 Industrial
machinery and equipment; Aircraft and
heavy equipment repair services;
Equipment rental and leasing, nec;
Spraying outfits: metals, paints, and
chemicals (compressor)

Sharon Center
Medina County

(G-11936)
ATC LEGACY INC
Also Called: Aerotorque Corporation
1441 Wolf Creek Trail (44274)
P.O. Box 305 (44274-0305)
PHONE..................330 590-8105
David Heidenreich, *Pr*
Doug Herr, *Genl Mgr*
EMP: 6 **EST:** 2007
SALES (est): 868.26K
SALES (corp-wide): 4.57B **Publicly Held**
Web: www.pttech.com
SIC: 3566 Speed changers, drives, and
gears
HQ: Ebog Legacy, Inc.
1441 Wolf Creek Trl
Sharon Center OH 44274
330 239-4933

(G-11937)
BEAUFORT RFD INC
1420 Wolf Creek Trl (44274)
P.O. Box 359 (44274-0359)
PHONE..................330 239-4331
David Abbott, *Pr*
Jerald Chunat, *VP*
Roseann Ziraks, *Sec*
D J Wilman, *Asst VP*
Doug Baxter, *Ch*
▲ **EMP:** 17 **EST:** 1996
SQ FT: 62,000
SALES (est): 10.2MM **Privately Held**
Web: www.rfdbeaufortmarine.com
SIC: 3842 Life preservers, except cork and
inflatable
HQ: Survitec Group (Usa), Inc.
1420 Wolfcreek Trl

Sharon Center OH 44274

(G-11938)
CAREY COLOR INC
6835 Ridge Rd (44274)
PHONE..................330 239-1835
Gary Moravcik, *Pr*
Russell Kotalac, *VP*
Ebert Libbey, *Quality Control*
EMP: 60 **EST:** 1978
SQ FT: 19,000
SALES (est): 3.97MM **Privately Held**
Web: www.careyweb.com
SIC: 2759 Commercial printing, nec

(G-11939)
CELL-O-CORE CO
6935 Ridge Rd (44274-7000)
P.O. Box 342 (44274-0342)
PHONE..................330 239-4370
Lino Abram, *CEO*
David C Nelson, *
Craig Cook, *
Tom Allen, *
▲ **EMP:** 50 **EST:** 1941
SQ FT: 50,000
SALES (est): 9.8MM **Privately Held**
Web: www.cellocore.com
SIC: 3089 Extruded finished plastics
products, nec

(G-11940)
EBOG LEGACY INC (HQ)
Also Called: Ebo Group, Inc.
1441 Wolf Creek Trail (44274)
P.O. Box 305 (44274-0305)
PHONE..................330 239-4933
Keith Nichols, *CEO*
David Given, *Ch Bd*
EMP: 96 **EST:** 1977
SQ FT: 12,200
SALES (est): 18.19MM
SALES (corp-wide): 4.57B **Publicly Held**
Web: www.ebogroupinc.com
SIC: 3568 3542 3714 3566 Clutches, except
vehicular; Brakes, metal forming; Motor
vehicle parts and accessories; Speed
changers, drives, and gears
PA: The Timken Company
4500 Mount Pleasant St Nw
North Canton OH 44720
234 262-3000

(G-11941)
GROENEVELD-BEKA USA INC (HQ)
Also Called: Groenveld Lbrction Sltions Inc
1441 Wolf Creek Trl (44274)
PHONE..................330 225-4949
Tim Wynia, *CEO*
Henk Groeneveld, *Pr*
Graham Keltie, *CFO*
▲ **EMP:** 7 **EST:** 1992
SQ FT: 8,000
SALES (est): 14.08MM
SALES (corp-wide): 4.57B **Publicly Held**
Web: www.groeneveld-beka.com
SIC: 5084 5172 2992 Instruments and
control equipment; Lubricating oils and
greases; Brake fluid (hydraulic): made from
purchased materials
PA: The Timken Company
4500 Mount Pleasant St Nw
North Canton OH 44720
234 262-3000

(G-11942)
SHARON MANUFACTURING INC
6867 Ridge Rd (44274)
P.O. Box 119 (44274-0119)
PHONE..................330 239-1561
John Beres, *Pr*

Tom Klimchak, *Opers Mgr*
EMP: 20 **EST:** 1970
SQ FT: 22,000
SALES (est): 2.46MM **Privately Held**
Web: www.sharonmfg.net
SIC: 3443 3441 Metal parts; Fabricated
structural metal

(G-11943)
SURVITEC GROUP (USA) INC (DH)
1420 Wolfcreek Trl (44274)
P.O. Box 359 (44274-0359)
PHONE..................330 239-4331
David Abbott, *Pr*
Gerald Chunat, *VP*
Roseann Ziraks, *Sec*
D J Wilman, *Asst VP*
Doug Baxter, *Ch*
▼ **EMP:** 9 **EST:** 2006
SALES (est): 31.34MM **Privately Held**
SIC: 3069 Pontoons, rubber
HQ: Survitec Group Limited
Aviator Industrial Park
Ellesmere Port CH65
151 670-9009

(G-11944)
TILT 15 INC
1440 Wolf Creek Trl (44274)
PHONE..................330 239-4192
James Ankoviak, *Pr*
Tom Lorick, *
Dan Sharpe, *
Kc Corbett-chaney, *CFO*
▲ **EMP:** 97 **EST:** 1993
SALES (est): 2.9MM **Privately Held**
SIC: 3842 Surgical appliances and supplies
PA: Winco Mfg., Llc
5516 Sw 1st Ln
Ocala FL 34474

Sharonville
Hamilton County

(G-11945)
ARI PHOENIX INC (PA)
11163 Woodward Ln (45241-1856)
PHONE..................513 229-3750
Gareth Hudson, *CEO*
Christopher Jones, *
James Mock, *
EMP: 27 **EST:** 2015
SALES (est): 9.76MM
SALES (corp-wide): 9.76MM **Privately
Held**
Web: www.ari-hetra.com
SIC: 3536 3564 Hoists; Exhaust fans:
industrial or commercial

(G-11946)
KUTOL PRODUCTS COMPANY INC (PA)
100 Partnership Way (45241-1571)
PHONE..................513 527-5500
Joseph W Rhodenbaugh, *Pr*
Tom Rhodenbaugh, *VP*
Brandon Jones, *Pr*
John Rhodenbaugh, *Vice President Elect*
▲ **EMP:** 82 **EST:** 1912
SQ FT: 160,000
SALES (est): 6.78MM
SALES (corp-wide): 6.78MM **Privately
Held**
Web: www.kutol.com
SIC: 2841 Soap: granulated, liquid, cake,
flaked, or chip

(G-11947)
KUTOL PRODUCTS COMPANY INC
11955 Enterprise Dr (45241-1513)
PHONE...............................513 527-5500
EMP: 58
SALES (corp-wide): 6.78MM **Privately Held**
Web: www.kutol.com
SIC: **2841** Soap: granulated, liquid, cake, flaked, or chip
PA: Kutol Products Company, Inc.
100 Partnership Way
Sharonville OH 45241
513 527-5500

(G-11948)
SAFRAN USA INC
300 E Business Way (45241-2384)
PHONE...............................513 247-7000
EMP: 178
SALES (corp-wide): 940.23MM **Privately Held**
Web: www.safran-group.com
SIC: **3621** Motors and generators
HQ: Safran Usa, Inc.
700 South Wash St Ste 320
Alexandria VA 22314
703 351-9898

(G-11949)
USUI INTERNATIONAL CORPORATION
88 Partnership Way (45241-1507)
PHONE...............................513 448-0410
Haruyasu Ito, *Pr*
EMP: 230
Web: www.usuiusa.com
SIC: **3714** Connecting rods, motor vehicle engine
HQ: Usui International Corporation
44780 Helm St
Plymouth MI 48170
734 354-3626

(G-11950)
WORKHORSE GROUP INC (PA)
3600 Park 42 Dr Ste 160e (45241-4039)
PHONE...............................888 646-5205
Richard F Dauch, *CEO*
Raymond J Chess, *Ch Bd*
Robert M Ginnan, *CFO*
Kerry K Roraff, *Chief Human Resources Officer*
EMP: 51 EST: 2007
SALES (est): 6.62MM **Publicly Held**
Web: www.workhorse.com
SIC: **3714** Motor vehicle parts and accessories

(G-11951)
WORKHORSE TECHNOLOGIES INC
3600 Park 42 Dr Ste 160 (45241-4039)
PHONE...............................888 646-5205
Richard Dauch, *CEO*
Martin J Rucidlo, *Pr*
Julio C Rodriguez, *CFO*
EMP: 45 EST: 2007
SALES (est): 2.08MM **Publicly Held**
Web: www.workhorse.com
SIC: **3711** 3714 Motor vehicles and car bodies; Motor vehicle parts and accessories
PA: Workhorse Group Inc.
3600 Park 42 Dr Ste 160e
Sharonville OH 45241

Shawnee
Perry County

(G-11952)
SUPERIOR FIBERS INC
9702 Iron Point Rd Se (43782-9723)
P.O. Box 478 (26547-0478)
PHONE...............................740 394-2491
Robert Williams, *Dir*
EMP: 345
SALES (corp-wide): 7.82MM **Privately Held**
Web: www.superiorfibers.com
SIC: **3089** Awnings, fiberglass and plastics combination
PA: Superior Fibers, Inc.
1333 Corporate Dr #350
Irving TX 75038
972 600-9953

Sheffield Lake
Lorain County

(G-11953)
ADVANCED WLDG FABRICATION INC (PA)
821 Lafayette Blvd (44054-1432)
PHONE...............................440 724-9165
Scott J Cornelius Senior, *Pr*
Scott J Cornelius Junior, *VP*
EMP: 11 EST: 2004
SALES (est): 361.24K
SALES (corp-wide): 361.24K **Privately Held**
SIC: **7692** Welding repair

(G-11954)
JD INDOOR COMFORT INC
Also Called: J D Indoor Comfort Duct Clg
4040 Colorado Ave (44054-2512)
PHONE...............................440 949-8758
James Sustersic, *Pr*
EMP: 13 EST: 1994
SALES (est): 2.44MM **Privately Held**
Web: www.jdindoorcomfort.com
SIC: **3585** 1711 Air conditioning equipment, complete; Plumbing, heating, air-conditioning

Sheffield Village
Lorain County

(G-11955)
ADI MACHINING INC
Also Called: Advanced Design Industries
4686 French Creek Rd (44054-2716)
PHONE...............................440 277-4141
Leonard Jungbluth, *Pr*
Jerome R Winiasz, *Prin*
EMP: 9 EST: 1980
SQ FT: 2,500
SALES (est): 748.21K **Privately Held**
Web: www.advanceddesignindustries.com
SIC: **3599** Machine shop, jobbing and repair

(G-11956)
ADVANCED DESIGN INDUSTRIES INC
Also Called: ADI
4686 French Creek Rd (44054-2716)
PHONE...............................440 277-4141
Jerome Winiasz, *Pr*
Thomas Winiasz, *
Edward J Winiasz, *
R G Brooks Junior, *Prin*

▲ EMP: 12 EST: 1955
SQ FT: 27,000
SALES (est): 3.1MM **Privately Held**
Web: www.advanceddesignindustries.com
SIC: **3569** 3599 8711 Robots, assembly line: industrial and commercial; Machine shop, jobbing and repair; Designing: ship, boat, machine, and product

(G-11957)
BENKO PRODUCTS INC
Also Called: Environmental Products Div
5350 Evergreen Pkwy (44054-2446)
PHONE...............................440 934-2180
John Benko, *Pr*
Robert Benko, *VP*
▼ EMP: 23 EST: 1983
SQ FT: 30,000
SALES (est): 10.65MM **Privately Held**
Web: www.benkoproducts.com
SIC: **3534** 3567 3448 2542 Elevators and moving stairways; Industrial furnaces and ovens; Prefabricated metal buildings and components; Partitions and fixtures, except wood

(G-11958)
GREEN IMPRESSIONS LLC
842 Abbe Rd (44054-2302)
PHONE...............................440 240-8508
Joseph Schill, *Prin*
Joseph Schill, *Pr*
James P Louth, *
EMP: 62 EST: 2011
SALES (est): 6.46MM **Privately Held**
Web: www.mygreenimpressions.com
SIC: **7349** 0782 0781 4959 Building maintenance services, nec; Lawn and garden services; Landscape services; Snowplowing

(G-11959)
HKM DRECT MKT CMMNICATIONS INC
Also Called: H K M Drect Mktg Cmmunications
2931 Abbe Rd (44054-2424)
PHONE...............................440 934-3060
Joann Tomasheski, *Mgr*
EMP: 18
SALES (corp-wide): 26.5MM **Privately Held**
Web: www.hkmdirectmarket.com
SIC: **2759** Commercial printing, nec
PA: Hkm Direct Market Communications, Inc.
5501 Cass Ave
Cleveland OH 44102
800 860-4456

(G-11960)
MAGNA SEATING AMERICA INC
Also Called: Intier Sting Systems-Lordstown
3637 Mallard Run (44054-2848)
PHONE...............................330 824-3101
Sean Ewing, *Brnch Mgr*
EMP: 108
SALES (corp-wide): 42.84B **Privately Held**
Web: www.magna.com
SIC: **3714** 2531 Motor vehicle parts and accessories; Seats, automobile
HQ: Magna Seating Of America, Inc.
30020 Cabot Dr
Novi MI 48377

(G-11961)
OLDCASTLE APG MIDWEST INC
Also Called: Sheffield Oldcastle
5190 Oster Rd (44054-1566)
PHONE...............................440 949-1815

Jim Jergins, *Mgr*
EMP: 25
SALES (corp-wide): 34.95B **Privately Held**
Web: www.northfieldblock.com
SIC: **3272** Concrete products, precast, nec
HQ: Oldcastle Apg Midwest, Inc.
400 Prmter Ctr Terr Ste 1
Atlanta GA 30346
770 804-3363

(G-11962)
PROTO-VEST INC
5462 Walnut Ridge Ln (44054-2487)
PHONE...............................623 872-3495
Richard Flores, *Pr*
Lucian Mac Mcelroy, *Ch Bd*
EMP: 18 EST: 1985
SALES (est): 2.33MM **Privately Held**
Web: www.protovest.com
SIC: **3589** Car washing machinery

(G-11963)
ROBBINS INDUSTRIAL FRNC CO INC
3739 Colorado Ave (44054-2505)
PHONE...............................440 949-2292
Michael K Robbins, *Pr*
EMP: 11 EST: 2006
SALES (est): 1.4MM **Privately Held**
SIC: **3567** Industrial furnaces and ovens

(G-11964)
SHEFFIELD METALS CLEVELAND LLC (PA)
Also Called: Sheffield Metals International
5467 Evergreen Pkwy (44054-2400)
PHONE...............................800 283-5262
Michael Blake, *Pr*
▼ EMP: 10 EST: 2004
SALES (est): 1.59MM **Privately Held**
Web: www.sheffieldmetals.com
SIC: **3444** Sheet metalwork

(G-11965)
SHEFFIELD METALS INTL INC
5467 Evergreen Pkwy (44054-2400)
PHONE...............................440 934-8500
Mike Blake, *Pr*
David Mielcusny, *Genl Mgr*
Jill Wilson, *Prin*
▼ EMP: 23 EST: 1998
SALES (est): 1.16MM **Privately Held**
Web: www.mazzellacompanies.com
SIC: **3496** Miscellaneous fabricated wire products
PA: Sheffield Metals Cleveland Llc
5467 Evergreen Pkwy
Sheffield Village OH 44054

Shelby
Richland County

(G-11966)
ARCELRMTTAL TBLAR PDTS SHLBY L
Also Called: Arcelormittal Tubular Pdts USA
132 W Main St (44875-1471)
PHONE...............................419 347-2424
Edward Vore, *CEO*
EMP: 631 EST: 2005
SALES (est): 49.37MM
SALES (corp-wide): 2.74B **Privately Held**
Web: www.arcelormittal-oh.com
SIC: **3317** 3321 Steel pipe and tubes; Gray and ductile iron foundries
HQ: Arcelormittal Tubular Products Usa Llc
4 Gateway Ctr
Pittsburgh PA 15222
419 342-1200

(G-11967)
ARCELRMTTAL TBLAR PDTS USA LLC
132 W Main St (44875-1471)
PHONE..............................419 347-2424
EMP: 2255
SALES (corp-wide): 2.74B **Privately Held**
Web: www.arcelormittal-oh.com
SIC: 3317 Steel pipe and tubes
HQ: Arcelormittal Tubular Products Usa Llc
4 Gateway Ctr
Pittsburgh PA 15222
419 342-1200

(G-11968)
COOPER ENTERPRISES INC
89 Curtis Dr (44875-8400)
P.O. Box 50 (44875-0050)
PHONE..............................419 347-5232
EMP: 70 EST: 1965
SALES (est): 23.45MM **Privately Held**
Web: www.cooperenterprises.com
SIC: 5087 2452 Service establishment
equipment; Prefabricated wood buildings

(G-11969)
CUSTOM CONTROL TECH LLC
Also Called: CCT
4469 Funk Rd (44875-9701)
PHONE..............................419 342-5593
EMP: 9 EST: 2007
SALES (est): 3.02MM **Privately Held**
Web: www.cct-llc.com
SIC: 3449 Miscellaneous metalwork

(G-11970)
GB FABRICATION COMPANY
2510 Taylortown Rd (44875-8836)
PHONE..............................419 347-1835
Dave Groff, *Brnch Mgr*
EMP: 34
SALES (corp-wide): 69.43MM **Privately Held**
Web: www.gbmfg.com
SIC: 3469 3441 Metal stampings, nec;
Fabricated structural metal
HQ: Gb Fabrication Company
60 Scott St
Shiloh OH 44878
419 896-3191

(G-11971)
MTD PRODUCTS INC
Also Called: M T D Service Division
305 Mansfield Ave (44875-1884)
PHONE..............................419 342-6455
Jayson Goth, *Mgr*
EMP: 250
SALES (corp-wide): 15.37B **Publicly Held**
Web: www.mtdparts.com
SIC: 3524 Lawn and garden equipment
HQ: Mtd Products Inc
5965 Grafton Rd
Valley City OH 44280
330 225-2600

(G-11972)
PHILLIPS MFG AND TOWER CO (PA)
Also Called: Shelby Welded Tube Div
5578 State Route 61 N (44875-9564)
P.O. Box 125 (44875-0125)
PHONE..............................419 347-1720
Angela Phillip, *CEO*
Theresa Wallace, *
EMP: 85 EST: 1970
SQ FT: 90,000
SALES (est): 31.79MM
SALES (corp-wide): 31.79MM **Privately Held**
Web: www.phillipstube.com

SIC: 3312 3498 3317 7692 Tubes, steel and
iron; Fabricated pipe and fittings; Steel pipe
and tubes; Welding repair

(G-11973)
PREMIER TANNING & NUTRITION
35 Mansfield Ave (44875-1322)
PHONE..............................419 342-6259
Jeff Tronewett, *Owner*
EMP: 6 EST: 2001
SALES (est): 179.93K **Privately Held**
SIC: 7299 3111 5499 Tanning salon; Leather
tanning and finishing; Health and dietetic
food stores

(G-11974)
R S HANLINE AND CO INC (PA)
Also Called: Hanline Fresh
17 Republic Ave (44875-2142)
P.O. Box 494 (44875-0494)
PHONE..............................419 347-8077
▲ EMP: 115 EST: 1986
SALES (est): 41.64MM
SALES (corp-wide): 41.64MM **Privately Held**
Web: www.rshanline.com
SIC: 5141 2099 Groceries, general line;
Food preparations, nec

Sherrodsville
Carroll County

(G-11975)
KARON C ENOLD
Also Called: Coen Grinding
45 Monroe St (44675)
PHONE..............................740 269-3475
Walt Enold, *Owner*
EMP: 20 EST: 1975
SALES (est): 202.81K **Privately Held**
SIC: 7629 7699 3599 Aircraft electrical
equipment repair; Aircraft and heavy
equipment repair services; Amusement
park equipment

Sherwood
Defiance County

(G-11976)
QUALITY MACHINING AND MFG INC
14168 State Route 18 (43556-9774)
PHONE..............................419 899-2543
Amber C Yochum, *Pr*
▲ EMP: 17 EST: 1993
SQ FT: 25,000
SALES (est): 1.07MM **Privately Held**
Web: www.qmfittings.com
SIC: 3492 3451 3599 Fluid power valves
and hose fittings; Screw machine products;
Machine and other job shop work

Shiloh
Richland County

(G-11977)
GB FABRICATION COMPANY (HQ)
60 Scott St (44878-8712)
P.O. Box 8 (43515-0008)
PHONE..............................419 896-3191
EMP: 66 EST: 2014
SALES (est): 20.17MM
SALES (corp-wide): 69.43MM **Privately Held**
Web: www.gbmfg.com
SIC: 3469 Metal stampings, nec
PA: Gb Manufacturing Company

1120 E Main St
Delta OH 43515
419 822-5323

(G-11978)
LAKESIDE CABINS LTD
7389 State Route 13 N (44878-8945)
PHONE..............................419 896-2299
Ellis Zimmerman, *Prin*
Allis Zim, *Pt*
EMP: 7 EST: 2005
SALES (est): 1.36MM **Privately Held**
Web: www.mylakesidecabins.com
SIC: 2522 Filing boxes, cabinets, and cases:
except wood

(G-11979)
LEON NEWSWANGER
Also Called: Newswanger Machine
7828 Planktown North Rd (44878-8906)
PHONE..............................419 896-3336
Leon Newswanger, *Owner*
EMP: 15 EST: 1989
SQ FT: 3,500
SALES (est): 2.38MM **Privately Held**
SIC: 3599 1799 Machine shop, jobbing and
repair; Welding on site

(G-11980)
VOISARD MANUFACTURING INC
60 Scott St (44878-8712)
P.O. Box 296 (44878-0296)
PHONE..............................419 896-3191
EMP: 100
Web: m.gbfab.com
SIC: 3469 Metal stampings, nec

Shreve
Wayne County

(G-11981)
GROWERS CHOICE LTD
5505 S Elyria Rd (44676-9567)
PHONE..............................330 262-8754
Charles R Wood, *Pt*
EMP: 6 EST: 2007
SALES (est): 482.44K **Privately Held**
Web: www.growersc.com
SIC: 2499 Wood products, nec

(G-11982)
HYPONEX CORPORATION
Also Called: Scotts- Hyponex
3875 S Elyria Rd (44676-9529)
PHONE..............................330 262-1300
Dennis Tafoya, *Brnch Mgr*
EMP: 214
SALES (corp-wide): 3.55B **Publicly Held**
Web: www.suntreksolar.com
SIC: 2873 2875 Fertilizers: natural (organic),
except compost; Compost
HQ: Hyponex Corporation
14111 Scottslawn Rd
Marysville OH 43040
937 644-0011

(G-11983)
I CERCO INC (PA)
Also Called: Diamonite Plant
453 W Mcconkey St (44676-9741)
PHONE..............................330 567-2145
Byron Anderson, *Pr*
◆ EMP: 157 EST: 2003
SQ FT: 160,000
SALES (est): 24.08MM
SALES (corp-wide): 24.08MM **Privately Held**
Web: www.cercocorp.com

SIC: 3567 Ceramic kilns and furnaces

(G-11984)
L N BRUT MANUFACTURING CO
7300 State Route 754 (44676-9450)
PHONE..............................330 833-9045
Lynn Neiss, *Pr*
Dolores J Schmidt, *Sec*
EMP: 8 EST: 1975
SALES (est): 625.44K **Privately Held**
Web: www.brutmfg.com
SIC: 3589 Sandblasting equipment

(G-11985)
RED HEAD BRASS INC
643 Legion Dr (44676-9271)
PHONE..............................330 567-2903
EMP: 17 EST: 1972
SALES (est): 2.31MM **Privately Held**
Web: www.redheadbrass.com
SIC: 3545 3569 Tools and accessories for
machine tools; Firefighting and related
equipment

(G-11986)
RHBA ACQUISITIONS LLC
Also Called: Red Head Brass
643 Legion Dr (44676-9271)
P.O. Box 566 (44676-0566)
PHONE..............................330 567-2903
Edwin Dumire, *
▲ EMP: 60 EST: 2002
SQ FT: 80,000
SALES (est): 9.93MM **Privately Held**
Web: www.redheadbrass.com
SIC: 3569 Firefighting and related equipment

(G-11987)
SCOTS
3875 S Elyria Rd (44676-9529)
PHONE..............................215 370-9498
EMP: 7 EST: 2017
SALES (est): 1.23MM **Privately Held**
Web: www.suntreksolar.com
SIC: 1499 Miscellaneous nonmetallic
minerals, except fuels

Sidney
Shelby County

(G-11988)
1157 DESIGNCONCEPTS LLC
210 S Lester Ave (45365-7057)
PHONE..............................937 497-1157
Evelyn Flock, *Managing Member*
EMP: 12 EST: 2007
SALES (est): 2.23MM **Privately Held**
Web: www.11fiftyseven.com
SIC: 3993 Advertising artwork

(G-11989)
A & B MACHINE INC
2040 Commerce Dr (45365-9393)
P.O. Box 540 (45365-0540)
PHONE..............................937 492-8662
Marc Gilardi, *Pr*
Robert L Alexander, *
Jimmy Alexander, *
EMP: 32 EST: 1988
SQ FT: 22,500
SALES (est): 2.53MM **Privately Held**
Web: www.aandbmachine.com
SIC: 3599 Machine shop, jobbing and repair

(G-11990)
ADVANCED COMPOSITES INC (DH)
Also Called: Sidney Plant
1062 S 4th Ave (45365-8977)
PHONE..............................937 575-9800

Seiji Oshima, *Pr*
Yoichi Kawai, *
Richard Lake, *
Robert Brown, *
▲ **EMP:** 220 **EST:** 1986
SQ FT: 128,000
SALES (est): 81.39MM **Privately Held**
Web: www.advcmp.com
SIC: 3082 3087 Unsupported plastics profile shapes; Custom compound purchased resins
HQ: Mitsui Chemicals America, Inc.
1 N Lexington Ave Ste 850
White Plains NY 10601

(G-11991)
AMERICAN TRIM LLC
1501 Michigan St Ste 1 (45365-3500)
PHONE.............................419 228-1145
Mike Caughell, *Mgr*
EMP: 600
SALES (corp-wide): 445.1MM **Privately Held**
Web: www.amtrim.com
SIC: 3469 3465 Metal stampings, nec; Moldings or trim, automobile: stamped metal
HQ: American Trim, L.L.C.
1005 W Grand Ave
Lima OH 45801

(G-11992)
AMOS MEDIA COMPANY (PA)
Also Called: Coin World
1660 Campbell Rd Ste A (45365-2480)
P.O. Box 4129 (45365)
PHONE.............................937 498-2121
Rick Amos, *Ch Bd*
Bruce Boyd, *
John O Amos, *
▲ **EMP:** 200 **EST:** 1876
SQ FT: 90,000
SALES (est): 11.24MM
SALES (corp-wide): 11.24MM **Privately Held**
Web: www.amosmedia.com
SIC: 2796 7389 2741 2721 Platemaking services; Appraisers, except real estate; Miscellaneous publishing; Magazines: publishing only, not printed on site

(G-11993)
ANKIM ENTERPRISES INCORPORATED
2005 Campbell Rd (45365-2474)
P.O. Box 569 (43311-0569)
PHONE.............................937 599-1121
Stan Wright, *Pr*
Clara Wright, *VP*
EMP: 7 **EST:** 1985
SQ FT: 24,000
SALES (est): 1.55MM **Privately Held**
Web: www.everydaytech.com
SIC: 3678 3679 Electronic connectors; Harness assemblies, for electronic use: wire or cable

(G-11994)
AURIA SIDNEY LLC
2000 Schlater Dr (45365-8904)
PHONE.............................937 492-1225
Brian Pour, *Pr*
Brian K Pour, *
EMP: 262 **EST:** 2007
SALES (est): 17.84MM
SALES (corp-wide): 19K **Privately Held**
SIC: 3714 Motor vehicle parts and accessories
HQ: Auria Solutions Usa Inc.
26999 Cntl Pk Blvd Ste 30
Southfield MI 48076
248 728-8000

(G-11995)
BAMAL CORP
2580 Ross St (45365-8848)
PHONE.............................937 492-9484
EMP: 9 **EST:** 2019
SALES (est): 4.16MM **Privately Held**
Web: www.bamal.com
SIC: 3965 Fasteners

(G-11996)
BAUMFOLDER CORPORATION (DH)
1660 Campbell Rd (45365-2480)
PHONE.............................937 492-1281
Janice Benanzer, *Pr*
◆ **EMP:** 44 **EST:** 1917
SQ FT: 125,000
SALES (est): 10MM
SALES (corp-wide): 2.6B **Privately Held**
Web: www.baumfolder.com
SIC: 3579 7389 3554 Binding machines, plastic and adhesive; Packaging and labeling services; Folding machines, paper
HQ: Heidelberg Americas Inc
1000 Gutenberg Dr Nw
Kennesaw GA 30144

(G-11997)
BELL INDUSTRIAL SERVICES LLC
1553 Target Dr (45365-7330)
PHONE.............................937 507-9193
Larry Bell, *Pr*
EMP: 15 **EST:** 2014
SALES (est): 480.21K **Privately Held**
Web: www.bellindustrialservice.com
SIC: 7623 3589 Refrigeration service and repair; Service industry machinery, nec

(G-11998)
BLUE SKIES OPERATING CORP
1661 Saint Marys Rd (45365-9395)
PHONE.............................877 330-2354
Kristin Hicks, *Mgr*
EMP: 19
SALES (corp-wide): 3.67MM **Privately Held**
SIC: 3441 Fabricated structural metal
PA: Blue Skies Operating Corporation
2375 Kensington Dr
Columbus OH 43221
877 330-2354

(G-11999)
CARGILL INCORPORATED
Cargill
701 S Vandemark Rd (45365-8959)
PHONE.............................937 497-4848
Jason Brewer, *Mgr*
EMP: 10
SALES (corp-wide): 159.59B **Privately Held**
Web: www.cargill.com
SIC: 2048 Prepared feeds, nec
PA: Cargill, Incorporated
15407 Mcginty Rd W
Wayzata MN 55391
800 227-4455

(G-12000)
CARGILL INCORPORATED
Cargill
2400 Industrial Dr (45365-8952)
PHONE.............................937 498-4555
Shane Soloman, *Mgr*
EMP: 60
SALES (corp-wide): 159.59B **Privately Held**
Web: www.cargill.com
SIC: 2075 2077 Soybean oil mills; Animal and marine fats and oils
PA: Cargill, Incorporated
15407 Mcginty Rd W

Wayzata MN 55391
800 227-4455

(G-12001)
CARS AND PARTS MAGAZINE
911 S Vandemark Rd (45365-8974)
P.O. Box 4129 (45365-4129)
PHONE.............................937 498-0803
Bruce Boyd, *Pr*
EMP: 98 **EST:** 1978
SALES (est): 514.26K
SALES (corp-wide): 11.24MM **Privately Held**
Web: www.carsandparts.com
SIC: 2721 5521 Magazines: publishing and printing; Used car dealers
PA: Amos Media Company
1660 Campbell Rd Ste A
Sidney OH 45365
937 498-2121

(G-12002)
CONFORM AUTOMOTIVE LLC
1630 Ferguson Ct (45365-9398)
PHONE.............................937 492-2708
Danielle Boisbert, *Contrlr*
EMP: 259
Web: www.conformgroup.com
SIC: 2396 3429 2221 Automotive trimmings, fabric; Hardware, nec; Broadwoven fabric mills, manmade
PA: Conform Automotive, Llc
32500 Telg Rd Ste 207
Bingham Farms MI 48025

(G-12003)
COPELAND ACCESS + INC
1675 Campbell Rd (45365-2479)
P.O. Box 669 (45365-0669)
PHONE.............................937 498-3802
Clinton Clay, *Prin*
Jan Burns, *Asst VP*
◆ **EMP:** 10 **EST:** 1986
SALES (est): 8.72MM
SALES (corp-wide): 572.67MM **Privately Held**
Web: www.copeland.com
SIC: 3823 Process control instruments
HQ: Copeland Lp
1675 W Campbell Rd
Sidney OH 45365
937 498-3011

(G-12004)
COPELAND CORPORATION
1675 W Campbell Rd (45365-2493)
PHONE.............................937 498-3011
Rene Betance, *Managing Member*
EMP: 15 **EST:** 2007
SALES (est): 4.39MM **Privately Held**
Web: www.copeland.com
SIC: 3585 Compressors for refrigeration and air conditioning equipment

(G-12005)
COPELAND LP (HQ)
1675 W Campbell Rd (45365-2493)
P.O. Box 4309 (45365)
PHONE.............................937 498-3011
Ross B Shuster, *CEO*
Paul Lundstrom, *
Marjorie Wallman, *
Art Gabbard, *
Tom Croone, *
◆ **EMP:** 1500 **EST:** 2006
SQ FT: 807,000
SALES (est): 482.91MM
SALES (corp-wide): 572.67MM **Privately Held**
Web: www.copeland.com

SIC: 3585 Compressors for refrigeration and air conditioning equipment
PA: Jv Holdings Emerald L P
8100 W Florissant Ave
Saint Louis MO 63136
314 553-2000

(G-12006)
COPELAND LP
Condensing Unit Division
756 Brooklyn Ave (45365-9401)
P.O. Box 669 (45365-0669)
PHONE.............................937 498-3011
Tom Croone, *VP*
EMP: 322
SALES (corp-wide): 572.67MM **Privately Held**
Web: www.copeland.com
SIC: 3585 Condensers, refrigeration
HQ: Copeland Lp
1675 W Campbell Rd
Sidney OH 45365
937 498-3011

(G-12007)
COPELAND LP
Design Services Network
1351 N Vandemark Rd (45365-3501)
P.O. Box 669 (45365-0669)
PHONE.............................937 498-3587
Thomas Crone, *Genl Mgr*
EMP: 285
SALES (corp-wide): 572.67MM **Privately Held**
Web: www.copeland.com
SIC: 3585 Condensers, refrigeration
HQ: Copeland Lp
1675 W Campbell Rd
Sidney OH 45365
937 498-3011

(G-12008)
COPELAND SCROLL COMPRESSORS LP (DH)
1675 Campbell Rd (45365-2479)
P.O. Box 669 (45365)
PHONE.............................937 498-3066
Michael Zwayer, *Pt*
▲ **EMP:** 6 **EST:** 2010
SALES (est): 22.51MM
SALES (corp-wide): 572.67MM **Privately Held**
Web: www.copeland.com
SIC: 3823 Process control instruments
HQ: Copeland Lp
1675 W Campbell Rd
Sidney OH 45365
937 498-3011

(G-12009)
COPERION FOOD EQUIPMENT LLC (DH)
Also Called: Peerless Food Equipment LLC
500 S Vandemark Rd (45365-8991)
PHONE.............................937 492-4158
Ron Howard, *Managing Member*
Nicholas Farrell, *Asst VP*
EMP: 35 **EST:** 2022
SALES (est): 2.26MM **Publicly Held**
Web: www.peerlessfood.com
SIC: 3556 Bakery machinery
HQ: K-Tron Investment Co.
300 Delaware Ave Ste 900
Wilmington DE

(G-12010)
DAMAR PRODUCTS INC
516 Park St (45365-1346)
PHONE.............................937 492-9023
Don Alexander, *Pr*
EMP: 13

▲ = Import ▼ = Export
◆ = Import/Export

SALES (corp-wide): 1.67MM **Privately Held**
SIC: 2448 2441 Pallets, wood; Boxes, wood
PA: Damar Products, Inc.
    17222 State Rte 47 E
    Sidney OH 45365
    937 492-9023

(G-12011)
DETAILED MACHINING INC
2490 Ross St (45365-8834)
PHONE....................937 492-1264
John Bertsch, *CEO*
EMP: 42 EST: 1997
SQ FT: 42,000
SALES (est): 8.9MM **Privately Held**
Web: www.detailedmachining.com
SIC: 3599 Machine shop, jobbing and repair

(G-12012)
DIGITAL SIGN GRAPHICS INC
837 Saint Marys Ave (45365-1359)
PHONE....................937 492-9550
Larry Bell, *CEO*
EMP: 7 EST: 1999
SALES (est): 185.12K **Privately Held**
Web: www.digitalsigngraphics.com
SIC: 3993 Signs and advertising specialties

(G-12013)
DRT AEROSPACE LLC (HQ)
1950 Campbell Rd (45365-2413)
PHONE....................937 492-6121
EMP: 25 EST: 2013
SQ FT: 36,000
SALES (est): 31.02MM **Privately Held**
Web: www.drtpowersystems.com
SIC: 3728 3724 R and D by manuf., aircraft
    parts and auxiliary equipment; Aircraft
    engines and engine parts
PA: Drt Holdings, Llc
    618 Greenmount Blvd
    Dayton OH 45419

(G-12014)
DRT PRECISION MFG LLC (HQ)
1985 Campbell Rd (45365-2412)
PHONE....................937 507-4308
EMP: 36 EST: 2016
SALES (est): 14.92MM **Privately Held**
Web: pm.drtholdingsllc.com
SIC: 3599 Machine shop, jobbing and repair
PA: Drt Holdings, Llc
    618 Greenmount Blvd
    Dayton OH 45419

(G-12015)
EDGEWELL PERSONAL CARE LLC
1810 Progress Way (45365-8961)
PHONE....................937 492-1057
Eric Simmons, *Brnch Mgr*
EMP: 175
SALES (corp-wide): 2.25B **Publicly Held**
Web: www.edgewell.com
SIC: 2844 Shaving preparations
HQ: Edgewell Personal Care, Llc
    1350 Tmbrlake Mnor Pkwy S
    Chesterfield MO 63017
    314 594-1900

(G-12016)
ELECTRO CONTROLS INC
1625 Ferguson Ct (45365-9398)
P.O. Box 539 (45365-0539)
PHONE....................866 497-1717
Tim Geise, *Pr*
EMP: 45 EST: 2000
SALES (est): 4.64MM **Privately Held**
Web: www.electro-controls.com
SIC: 3613 Control panels, electric

(G-12017)
EMERSON COMMERCIAL RESIDE
1675 Campbell Rd (45365-2479)
PHONE....................937 493-2828
EMP: 26 EST: 2018
SALES (est): 7.09MM **Privately Held**
Web: www.copeland.com
SIC: 3823 Process control instruments

(G-12018)
EVERYDAY TECHNOLOGIES INC
324 Adams St Bldg 1 (45365-2328)
PHONE....................937 497-7774
Scott Perry, *Brnch Mgr*
EMP: 11
SALES (corp-wide): 9.96MM **Privately Held**
Web: www.everydaytech.com
SIC: 3444 1761 Sheet metalwork; Sheet
    metal work, nec
PA: Everyday Technologies, Inc.
    2005 Campbell Rd
    Sidney OH 45365
    937 492-4171

(G-12019)
EVERYDAY TECHNOLOGIES INC (PA)
2005 Campbell Rd (45365-2474)
PHONE....................937 492-4171
EMP: 48 EST: 1929
SALES (est): 9.96MM
SALES (corp-wide): 9.96MM **Privately Held**
Web: www.everydaytech.com
SIC: 3444 Sheet metalwork

(G-12020)
FRESHWAY FOODS COMPANY INC (DH)
Also Called: Fresh and Limited
601 Stolle Ave (45365-8895)
PHONE....................937 498-4664
Frank Gilardi Junior, *Ch Bd*
Phil Gilardi, *Pr*
Devon Beer, *CFO*
EMP: 100 EST: 1988
SQ FT: 90,000
SALES (est): 19.77MM **Publicly Held**
Web: www.freshwayfoods.com
SIC: 5148 2099 Vegetables, fresh; Food
    preparations, nec
HQ: Us Foods, Inc.
    9399 W Higgins Rd Ste 500
    Rosemont IL 60018

(G-12021)
G DENVER AND CO LLC
Also Called: Leroi Compressors
211 E Russell Rd (45365-1732)
PHONE....................937 498-2555
Richard Wall, *Mgr*
EMP: 25
SALES (corp-wide): 7.24B **Publicly Held**
Web: www.gardnerdenver.com
SIC: 3563 Air and gas compressors
HQ: G. Denver And Co., Llc
    800-A Beaty St
    Davidson NC 28036

(G-12022)
HEXA AMERICAS INC
1150 S Vandemark Rd (45365-3571)
PHONE....................937 497-7900
Hideaki Tanaka, *Pr*
Takuro Miyamoto, *
John Marcum, *
▲ **EMP: 40 EST:** 2005
SALES (est): 10.72MM **Privately Held**
Web: www.hexa-chem.co.jp
SIC: 2821 Protein plastics

(G-12023)
HOLLOWAY SPORTSWEAR INC (DH)
2633 Campbell Rd (45365-8837)
PHONE....................937 497-7575
◆ **EMP: 100 EST:** 1946
SALES (est): 18.3MM **Privately Held**
SIC: 2329 2339 2392 Men's and boys'
    leather, wool and down-filled outerwear;
    Women's and misses' outerwear, nec;
    Blankets: made from purchased materials
HQ: Augusta Sportswear, Inc.
    425 Park W Dr
    Grovetown GA 30813
    800 237-6695

(G-12024)
HYDRO ALUMINUM FAYETTEVILLE
401 N Stolle Ave (45365-7806)
PHONE....................937 492-9194
Eddie Smith, *Prin*
EMP: 6 EST: 2007
SALES (est): 2.06MM **Privately Held**
SIC: 3354 Aluminum extruded products

(G-12025)
HYDRO EXTRUSION USA LLC
401 N Stolle Ave (45365-7806)
PHONE....................888 935-5759
Brent Taylor, *Brnch Mgr*
EMP: 175
Web: www.hydro.com
SIC: 3465 3479 Automotive stampings;
    Painting of metal products
HQ: Hydro Extrusion Usa, Llc
    6250 N River Rd Ste 5000
    Rosemont IL 60018

(G-12026)
IVEX PROTECTIVE PACKAGING LLC (PA)
456 Stolle Ave (45365-8846)
P.O. Box 4699 (45365-4699)
PHONE....................937 498-9298
Paul Gaulin, *Pr*
Tom Trauscht, *
▼ **EMP: 25 EST:** 2005
SALES (est): 10.2MM
SALES (corp-wide): 10.2MM **Privately Held**
Web: www.ivexpackaging.com
SIC: 3086 2429 Plastics foam products;
    Wrappers, excelsior

(G-12027)
KSE MANUFACTURING
175 S Lester Ave (45365-7044)
PHONE....................937 409-9831
EMP: 6 EST: 2012
SALES (est): 3.28MM **Privately Held**
SIC: 3369 Nonferrous foundries, nec

(G-12028)
L & F PRODUCTS
1810 Progress Way (45365-8961)
PHONE....................937 498-4710
Charles Jacoby, *Prin*
EMP: 7 EST: 2010
SALES (est): 142.12K **Privately Held**
SIC: 2679 Paper products, converted, nec

(G-12029)
L & W INVESTMENTS INC
2005 Campbell Rd (45365-2474)
PHONE....................937 492-4171
Cody Lee, *CEO*
EMP: 85 EST: 2020
SALES (est): 4.75MM **Privately Held**
SIC: 3444 Sheet metalwork

(G-12030)
LASERFAB TECHNOLOGIES INC
2339 Industrial Dr (45365-8100)
P.O. Box 4812 (45365-4812)
PHONE....................937 493-0800
Jamie Ellis, *Pr*
Jeff Beigel, *Treas*
EMP: 12 EST: 2004
SQ FT: 22,000
SALES (est): 2.74MM **Privately Held**
Web: www.laserfabtech.com
SIC: 3441 Fabricated structural metal

(G-12031)
LOCHARD INC
Also Called: Do It Best
903 Wapakoneta Ave (45365-1409)
P.O. Box 260 (45365-0260)
PHONE....................937 492-8811
Michael Lochard, *Pr*
Donald W Lochard, *
EMP: 75 EST: 1945
SQ FT: 44,500
SALES (est): 9.53MM **Privately Held**
Web:
www.lochardplumbingheatingandcooling.com
SIC: 1711 5251 3599 Mechanical contractor;
    Hardware stores; Machine and other job
    shop work

(G-12032)
MASTELLER ELECTRIC MOTOR SVC
122 Lane St (45365-2323)
PHONE....................937 492-8500
Fred Masteller, *Owner*
EMP: 6 EST: 1960
SQ FT: 5,000
SALES (est): 598.69K **Privately Held**
Web: www.mastellerelectric.com
SIC: 7694 5063 Electric motor repair;
    Motors, electric

(G-12033)
MECHANICAL GALV-PLATING CORP
933 Oak Ave (45365-1374)
P.O. Box 56 (45365-0056)
PHONE....................937 492-3143
Tim Baker, *Pr*
John Garmhausen, *
Susan A Baker, *
▲ **EMP: 45 EST:** 1981
SQ FT: 40,000
SALES (est): 4.78MM **Privately Held**
Web: www.mgpcorp.com
SIC: 3471 Electroplating of metals or formed
    products

(G-12034)
MIAMI VALLEY POLISHING LLC
211 S Lester Ave (45365-7058)
PHONE....................937 615-9353
Matthew Powers, *Prin*
EMP: 14 EST: 2008
SALES (est): 1.69MM **Privately Held**
Web: www.mvpolishing.net
SIC: 3471 Electroplating of metals or formed
    products

(G-12035)
MITSUBISHI ELC AUTOMTN INC
213 N Ohio Ave (45365-2711)
PHONE....................937 492-3058
Melynda Rowlett, *Pr*
EMP: 20
Web: www.mitsubishi-motors.com
SIC: 5511 5084 3699 Automobiles, new and
    used; Conveyor systems; Electrical
    equipment and supplies, nec
HQ: Mitsubishi Electric Automation, Inc.
    500 Corporate Woods Pkwy
    Vernon Hills IL 60061

(G-12036)

NORCOLD LLC (HQ)
1440 N Vandemark Rd (45365-3548)
P.O. Box 1285 (48106-1285)
PHONE....................800 543-1219
◆ **EMP: 8 EST:** 1960
SQ FT: 150,000
SALES (est): 9.51MM
SALES (corp-wide): 96.67MM **Privately Held**
Web: www.norcold.com
SIC: 3632 Refrigerators, mechanical and absorption: household
PA: Thetford Llc
7101 Jackson Rd
Ann Arbor MI 48103
734 769-6000

(G-12037)

P&THE MFG ACQUISITION LLC
Also Called: Ross Aluminum
815 Oak Ave (45365-1339)
P.O. Box 4487 (45365-4487)
PHONE....................937 492-4134
Pancho Hall, *CEO*
Raybon White, *CFO*
Jason Pawel, *Pr*
EMP: 57 **EST:** 2022
SALES (est): 4MM **Privately Held**
SIC: 3334 Primary aluminum

(G-12038)

PEERLESS FOODS INC
Also Called: Peerless Foods Equipment
500 S Vandemark Rd (45365-8991)
PHONE....................937 492-4158
Robert L Zielsdorf, *CEO*
Dane A Belden, *
Matthew J Zielsdorf, *
Robert F Zielsdorf, *Parts Vice President*
Thomas Seving, *
◆ **EMP:** 62 **EST:** 1913
SQ FT: 130,000
SALES (est): 17.29MM **Publicly Held**
Web: www.peerlessfood.com
SIC: 3556 Bakery machinery
PA: Hillenbrand, Inc.
1 Batesville Blvd
Batesville IN 47006

(G-12039)

PLAYTEX MANUFACTURING INC
1905 Progress Way (45365-8114)
PHONE....................937 498-4710
EMP: 38
SALES (corp-wide): 2.25B **Publicly Held**
SIC: 2676 Sanitary paper products
HQ: Playtex Manufacturing, Inc.
50 N Dupont Hwy
Dover DE 19901
302 678-6000

(G-12040)

POLYFILL LLC
960 N Vandemark Rd (45365-3508)
PHONE....................937 493-0041
Dan T Moore, *Managing Member*
Richard Sczerowski, *Contrlr*
Ralph Fearnley, *Genl Mgr*
▲ **EMP:** 40 **EST:** 2009
SQ FT: 50,000
SALES (est): 5.19MM **Privately Held**
Web: www.polyfillproducts.com
SIC: 3089 Automotive parts, plastic

(G-12041)

PREFERRED PRINTING (PA)
3700 Michigan St (45365-7018)
PHONE....................937 492-6961
Gil Bornhorst, *Owner*
EMP: 6 **EST:** 1983

SQ FT: 2,800
SALES (est): 175.04K
SALES (corp-wide): 175.04K **Privately Held**
Web: www.printingisus.com
SIC: 2752 Offset printing

(G-12042)

QUALITY STEEL FABRICATION
2500 Fair Rd (45365-7523)
P.O. Box 905 (45365-0905)
PHONE....................937 492-9503
Robert P Brunswick, *Pr*
Ted Daniel, *VP Opers*
EMP: 15 **EST:** 2002
SQ FT: 25,000
SALES (est): 2.33MM **Privately Held**
Web: www.qsfab.com
SIC: 3441 3444 Fabricated structural metal; Sheet metalwork

(G-12043)

RELIABLE CASTINGS CORPORATION
1521 W Michigan St (45365-2498)
P.O. Box 829 (45365-0829)
PHONE....................937 497-5217
Tom Abney, *Mgr*
EMP: 75
SQ FT: 40,000
SALES (corp-wide): 15.32MM **Privately Held**
Web: www.reliablecastings.com
SIC: 3363 3369 3365 Aluminum die-castings; Nonferrous foundries, nec; Aluminum foundries
PA: Reliable Castings Corporation
3530 Spring Grove Ave
Cincinnati OH 45223
513 541-2627

(G-12044)

RING CONTAINER TECH LLC
603 Oak Ave (45365-1335)
PHONE....................937 492-0961
Dennis W Koerner, *VP*
EMP: 16
SALES (corp-wide): 1.06B **Privately Held**
Web: www.ringcontainer.com
SIC: 3085 Plastics bottles
HQ: Ring Container Technologies, Llc.
1 Industrial Park
Oakland TN 38060
800 280-7464

(G-12045)

ROE TRANSPORTATION ENTPS INC
3680 Michigan St (45365-9086)
PHONE....................937 497-7161
Chad Roe, *Prin*
EMP: 7 **EST:** 2009
SQ FT: 7,400
SALES (est): 2.39MM **Privately Held**
Web: www.roeenterprisesinc.com
SIC: 2875 2499 4212 4953 Potting soil, mixed; Mulch or sawdust products, wood; Dump truck haulage; Recycling, waste materials

(G-12046)

ROSS ALUMINUM CASTINGS LLC
815 Oak Ave (45365-1317)
P.O. Box 4489 (45365)
PHONE....................937 492-4134
Mike Francis, *Managing Member*
Robert Wyehl, *
Bob Clements, *
▲ **EMP:** 165 **EST:** 2006
SQ FT: 250,000
SALES (est): 8.85MM
SALES (corp-wide): 8.85MM **Privately Held**

Web: www.rossal.com
SIC: 3365 3543 3369 Aluminum and aluminum-based alloy castings; Industrial patterns; Nonferrous foundries, nec
PA: Advanced Metals Group, L.L.C.
114 S Valley Rd
Paoli PA 19301
610 408-8006

(G-12047)

ROSS CASTING & INNOVATION LLC
Also Called: Rci
402 S Kuther Rd (45365-8870)
P.O. Box 89 (45365-0089)
PHONE....................937 497-4500
Sampath Ramesh, *Pr*
Wayne Thompson, *
Robert Zangri, *
Brad Hohenstein, *
▲ **EMP:** 350 **EST:** 1999
SQ FT: 120,000
SALES (est): 19.21MM **Privately Held**
Web: www.rciwheels.com
SIC: 3363 Aluminum die-castings
HQ: Abi-Showatech (India) Private Limited
Stoneacre, No 67,
Chennai TN 60002

(G-12048)

SCHINDLER ELEVATOR CORPORATION
Also Called: Schindler
920 S Vandemark Rd (45365-8140)
PHONE....................937 492-3186
Philip L Warnecke, *Mgr*
EMP: 150
SQ FT: 35,000
Web: www.schindler.com
SIC: 3534 Elevators and equipment
HQ: Schindler Elevator Corporation
20 Whippany Rd
Morristown NJ 07960
973 397-6500

(G-12049)

SCHWANS MAMA ROSASS LLC (DH)
Also Called: Mama Rosas's
1910 Fair Rd (45365-8906)
PHONE....................937 498-4511
EMP: 249 **EST:** 2006
SQ FT: 160,000
SALES (est): 39.69MM **Privately Held**
SIC: 2038 Pizza, frozen
HQ: Schwan's Company
115 W College Dr
Marshall MN 56258
507 532-3274

(G-12050)

SCHWARZ PARTNERS PACKAGING LLC
Royal Group, The
2450 Campbell Rd (45365-7533)
PHONE....................317 290-1140
Jim Freisthler, *Brnch Mgr*
EMP: 15
SALES (corp-wide): 653.03MM **Privately Held**
Web: theroyalgroup.wpengine.com
SIC: 2653 3412 2671 Boxes, corrugated: made from purchased materials; Metal barrels, drums, and pails; Paper; coated and laminated packaging
HQ: Schwarz Partners Packaging, Llc
10 W Carmel Dr Ste 300 In
Carmel IN 46032
317 290-1140

(G-12051)

SELMCO METAL FABRICATORS INC
1615 Ferguson Ct (45365-9398)
P.O. Box 4368 (45365-4368)
PHONE....................937 498-1331
Tim Cotterman, *Pr*
Ron Jones, *Sec*
EMP: 13 **EST:** 1997
SQ FT: 25,000
SALES (est): 2.9MM **Privately Held**
Web: www.selmcometalfabricators.com
SIC: 3444 Sheet metal specialties, not stamped

(G-12052)

SHAFFER METAL FAB INC
2031 Commerce Dr (45365-9393)
P.O. Box 523 (45365-0523)
PHONE....................937 492-1384
Michael R Shaffer, *Prin*
Steve Shaffer, *Prin*
EMP: 34 **EST:** 1992
SQ FT: 45,000
SALES (est): 8.21MM **Privately Held**
Web: www.shaffermetalfab.com
SIC: 3441 3444 Fabricated structural metal; Sheet metalwork

(G-12053)

SIDNEY MANUFACTURING COMPANY
405 N Main Ave (45365-2345)
P.O. Box 380 (45365-0380)
PHONE....................937 492-4154
Jon F Baker, *Pr*
Steven Baker, *
▼ **EMP:** 30 **EST:** 1966
SQ FT: 125,000
SALES (est): 4.3MM **Privately Held**
Web: www.sidneymfg.com
SIC: 3556 3444 Food products machinery; Sheet metalwork

(G-12054)

SPONSELLER GROUP INC
1516 Target Dr (45365-7332)
PHONE....................937 492-9949
Ken Hensworth, *Mgr*
EMP: 6
SALES (corp-wide): 9.31MM **Privately Held**
Web: www.sponsellergroup.com
SIC: 8711 3599 Consulting engineer; Machine shop, jobbing and repair
PA: Sponseller Group, Inc.
1600 Timber Wolf Dr
Holland OH 43528
419 861-3000

(G-12055)

STD LIQUIDATION INC
1950 Campbell Rd (45365-2413)
P.O. Box 849 (45365-0849)
PHONE....................937 492-6121
EMP: 104
SIC: 3599 3544 Machine and other job shop work; Special dies, tools, jigs, and fixtures

(G-12056)

STOLLE MACHINERY COMPANY LLC
Also Called: Stolle Machinery-Sidney
2900 Campbell Rd (45365-8864)
PHONE....................937 497-5400
Greg Butcher, *Mgr*
EMP: 125
SALES (corp-wide): 492.99MM **Privately Held**
Web: www.stollemachinery.com

SIC: 3469 2759 3542 Stamping metal for the trade; Commercial printing, nec; Machine tools, metal forming type
PA: Stolle Machinery Company, Llc
6949 S Potomac St
Centennial CO 80112
303 708-9044

(G-12057)
THERMOSEAL INC (PA)
Also Called: Klinger Thermoseal
2350 Campbell Rd (45365-9573)
PHONE...................................937 498-2222
◆ EMP: 7 EST: 1994
SALES (est): 4.87MM
SALES (corp-wide): 4.87MM Privately Held
Web: www.klinger-thermoseal.com
SIC: 3053 Gasket materials

(G-12058)
VALENCE INDUSTRIAL LLC ✿
Also Called: Valence Industrial
1661 Saint Marys Rd (45365-9395)
PHONE...................................877 330-2354
EMP: 35 EST: 2023
SALES (est): 5.39MM Privately Held
Web: www.valenceindustrial.com
SIC: 3531 5082 Construction machinery; Mining machinery and equipment, except petroleum

(G-12059)
VMI LIQUIDATING INC
2309 Industrial Dr (45365-8100)
P.O. Box 4129 (45365-4129)
PHONE...................................937 492-3100
▲ EMP: 40
SIC: 3993 Name plates: except engraved, etched, etc.: metal

(G-12060)
WAPPOO WOOD PRODUCTS INC
Also Called: Interntnal Pckg Pallets Crates
12877 Kirkwood Rd (45365-8102)
PHONE...................................937 492-1166
Thomas G Baker, Ch Bd
T Adam Baker, *
Gary O'connor, Prin
Matthew Baker, *
EMP: 40 EST: 1980
SQ FT: 21,800
SALES (est): 8.15MM Privately Held
Web: www.wappoowood.com
SIC: 5031 2435 2436 2421 Lumber: rough, dressed, and finished; Hardwood veneer and plywood; Softwood veneer and plywood ; Sawmills and planing mills, general

(G-12061)
WESTERN OHIO CUT STONE LTD
1130 Dingman Slagle Rd (45365-9102)
P.O. Box 419 (45365-0419)
PHONE...................................937 492-4722
Thomas Milligan, Managing Member
EMP: 15 EST: 1995
SALES (est): 1.5MM Privately Held
Web: www.westernohiocutstone.com
SIC: 3281 Cut stone and stone products

(G-12062)
WIPE OUT ENTERPRISES INC
6523 Dawson Rd (45365-8672)
PHONE...................................937 497-9473
Dave Waesch, Owner
EMP: 7 EST: 2002
SALES (est): 686.98K Privately Held
Web: www.wipeoutenterprises.com
SIC: 3599 Machine shop, jobbing and repair

Silver Lake
Summit County

(G-12063)
AVTEK INTERNATIONAL INC
2867 Lakeland Pkwy (44224-2918)
PHONE...................................330 633-7500
Thomas Milan, Pr
▲ EMP: 6 EST: 2001
SALES (est): 462.9K Privately Held
Web: www.avtekintl.net
SIC: 3651 Household audio equipment

Smithville
Wayne County

(G-12064)
BOVILLE INDUS COATINGS INC
7459 Leichty Rd (44677-9708)
P.O. Box 487 (44677-0487)
PHONE...................................330 669-8558
Larry Boville Senior, Pr
Larry Boville Junior, VP
EMP: 25 EST: 1996
SQ FT: 30,000
SALES (est): 2.01MM Privately Held
Web: www.boville.com
SIC: 3471 3479 Sand blasting of metal parts; Coating of metals and formed products

(G-12065)
FLYING DUTCHMAN INC
6631 Egypt Rd (44677-9774)
PHONE...................................330 669-2297
James Lepley, CEO
Gary Lepley, Pr
Esther Lepley, Assistant Chief Executive Officer
Kevin Lepley, VP
John Waltman, Sec
EMP: 7 EST: 1970
SQ FT: 3,600
SALES (est): 2.2MM Privately Held
Web: www.flyingd.com
SIC: 3523 Silo fillers and unloaders

(G-12066)
MK METAL PRODUCTS INC
Maverick Stainless Fabrication
301 W Prospect St (44677-9516)
PHONE...................................330 669-2631
Richard L Kemp, CEO
EMP: 15
SALES (corp-wide): 4.44MM Privately Held
Web: www.mkmetalproducts.com
SIC: 3441 Fabricated structural metal
PA: Mk Metal Products Enterprises, Inc.
90 Sawyer Pkwy
Mansfield OH 44903
419 756-3644

(G-12067)
RAY C SPROSTY BAG CO INC
Also Called: Sprosty
5857 Applecreek Rd (44677-9715)
P.O. Box 186 (44677-0186)
PHONE...................................330 669-0045
EMP: 10 EST: 1941
SALES (est): 3.97MM Privately Held
Web: www.sprostybag.com
SIC: 5113 2759 Bags, paper and disposable plastic; Bags, plastic: printing, nsk

(G-12068)
RIVERVIEW INDUS WD PDTS INC (PA)

179 S Gilbert Dr (44677)
P.O. Box 408 (44677-0408)
PHONE...................................330 669-8509
Michael Meenan, Pr
EMP: 9 EST: 1988
SQ FT: 17,000
SALES (est): 6.22MM Privately Held
Web: www.riverviewpallet.com
SIC: 2448 Pallets, wood

(G-12069)
RIVERVIEW TRANSPORT LLC
Also Called: Riverview Transport, Inc.
179 Gilbert Dr (44677)
P.O. Box 408 (44677-0408)
PHONE...................................330 669-8509
EMP: 21 EST: 2012
SALES (est): 912.44K Privately Held
Web: www.riverviewpallet.com
SIC: 2448 Pallets, wood
PA: Riverview Industrial Wood Products, Inc.
179 S Gilbert Dr
Smithville OH 44677

(G-12070)
TYLER GRAIN & FERTILIZER CO
3388 Eby Rd (44677-9785)
PHONE...................................330 669-2341
Walter F Tyler Junior, Pr
William A Tyler, VP
Mildred Tyler, Sec
Nick Franks, Genl Mgr
EMP: 10 EST: 1860
SQ FT: 18,000
SALES (est): 4.99MM Privately Held
Web: www.tylersfertilizer.com
SIC: 2875 5191 8748 Fertilizers, mixing only; Chemicals, agricultural; Agricultural consultant

Solon
Cuyahoga County

(G-12071)
911CELLULAR LLC
6001 Cochran Rd Ste 200 (44139-3325)
PHONE...................................216 283-6100
Chad Salahshour, Managing Member
EMP: 15 EST: 2013
SALES (est): 929.58K Privately Held
Web: www.911cellular.com
SIC: 4812 7372 Cellular telephone services; Application computer software

(G-12072)
ACLARA TECHNOLOGIES LLC
30400 Solon Rd (44139-3416)
PHONE...................................440 528-7200
Gary Moore, Brnch Mgr
EMP: 10
SALES (corp-wide): 5.63B Publicly Held
Web: www.hubbell.com
SIC: 3824 3825 3829 7371 Mechanical and e lectromechanical counters and devices; Instruments to measure electricity; Measuring and controlling devices, nec; Custom computer programming services
HQ: Aclara Technologies Llc
77 West Port Plz Ste 500
Saint Louis MO 63146
314 895-6400

(G-12073)
ADVANCED LIGHTING TECH LLC (PA)
6675 Parkland Blvd Ste 100 (44139-4345)
PHONE...................................888 440-2358
Sabu Krishnan, Pr

Michael Knight, CFO
◆ EMP: 74 EST: 1995
SALES (est): 96.72MM Privately Held
Web: www.adlt.com
SIC: 3645 3641 3646 3648 Residential lighting fixtures; Electric lamps and parts for generalized applications; Commercial lighting fixtures; Lighting equipment, nec

(G-12074)
AEROSPACE MAINT SOLUTIONS LLC
29401 Ambina Dr (44139-3953)
PHONE...................................440 729-7703
John Dooley, Pr
John P Dooley, Managing Member*
Thomas Dooley, *
Andrea Rillahan, *
Denette Ditmer, *
▲ EMP: 27 EST: 2005
SQ FT: 7,500
SALES (est): 4.85MM Privately Held
Web: www.aerospacellc.com
SIC: 3728 Aircraft parts and equipment, nec

(G-12075)
ALLEN GRAPHICS INC
Also Called: Printing Partners
27100 Richmond Rd Ste 6 (44139-1030)
PHONE...................................440 349-4100
Donald J Allen, Pr
EMP: 9 EST: 1976
SQ FT: 5,000
SALES (est): 535.94K Privately Held
Web: www.allengraphics.com
SIC: 2752 2789 Offset printing; Bookbinding and related work

(G-12076)
ALLOY WELDING & FABRICATING
30340 Solon Industrial Pkwy Ste B (44139-4358)
PHONE...................................440 914-0650
William Kelly, Pr
EMP: 10 EST: 1979
SQ FT: 12,000
SALES (est): 2.38MM Privately Held
SIC: 3441 Fabricated structural metal

(G-12077)
ALLTECH MED SYSTEMS AMER INC
28900 Fountain Pkwy Ste B (44139-4383)
PHONE...................................440 424-2240
Mark Zou, Pr
William Joliat, *
Don Russell, *
Sandra Ritchie, Finance*
▼ EMP: 39 EST: 2004
SALES (est): 4.48MM Privately Held
Web: www.alltechms.com
SIC: 3845 Magnetic resonance imaging device, nuclear

(G-12078)
AMERICAN PLATINUM DOOR LLC
Also Called: Construction
30335 Solon Industrial Pkwy (44139-4325)
PHONE...................................440 497-6213
Anthony Lorello, Managing Member
EMP: 6 EST: 2019
SALES (est): 1.69MM Privately Held
Web: www.apdoorandgate.com
SIC: 5021 5211 3088 1751 Lockers; Home centers; Bathroom fixtures, plastics; Garage door, installation or erection

(G-12079)
AMERICAN RUBBER PDTS CO INC
30775 Solon Industrial Pkwy (44139-4338)
PHONE...................................440 461-0900
Doug Kaufman, Pr

GEOGRAPHIC

EMP: 8 **EST:** 1999
SALES (est): 401.36K **Privately Held**
SIC: 3069 Molded rubber products

(G-12080)
ASPHALT FABRICS & SPECIALTIES
7710 Bond St (44139-5312)
PHONE..........................440 786-1077
Brian Reed, *Pr*
EMP: 20 **EST:** 2002
SALES (est): 2.84MM **Privately Held**
Web: www.asphaltfabrics.com
SIC: 2951 Asphalt paving mixtures and
blocks

(G-12081)
B D G WRAP-TITE INC (PA)
Also Called: Wrap-Tite
6200 Cochran Rd (44139-3308)
PHONE..........................440 349-5400
Suresh Bafna, *CEO*
Sunil Daga, *
◆ **EMP:** 40 **EST:** 2004
SQ FT: 89,000
SALES (est): 11.08MM
SALES (corp-wide): 11.08MM **Privately
Held**
Web: www.wraptite.com
SIC: 3069 5199 Film, rubber; Leather goods,
except footwear, gloves, luggage, belting

(G-12082)
BARDONS & OLIVER INC (PA)
5800 Harper Rd (44139-1833)
PHONE..........................440 498-5800
William Beattie, *Pr*
Heath Oliver, *
James S Dalton, *
Richard Moscarino, *
Brett Baldi, *
▲ **EMP:** 120 **EST:** 1891
SQ FT: 94,000
SALES (est): 8.92MM
SALES (corp-wide): 8.92MM **Privately
Held**
Web: www.bardonsoliver.com
SIC: 3549 3541 3547 3599 Metalworking
machinery, nec; Lathes, metal cutting and
polishing; Finishing equipment, rolling mill;
Machine and other job shop work

(G-12083)
BARUDAN AMERICA INC (HQ)
Also Called: Barudan
30901 Carter St Frnt A (44139-4384)
PHONE..........................440 248-8770
Ted Yamaue, *Ch Bd*
Shin Hasegawa, *Pr*
Robert Stone, *VP*
Kevin H Hrabak, *Treas*
◆ **EMP:** 12 **EST:** 1985
SQ FT: 34,970
SALES (est): 37.36MM **Privately Held**
Web: www.barudanamerica.com
SIC: 3552 Embroidery machines
PA: Barudan Co., Ltd.
20, Azatsukakoshi, Josuiji
Ichinomiya AIC 491-0

(G-12084)
BIRD ELECTRONIC CORPORATION
30303 Aurora Rd (44139-2743)
PHONE..........................440 248-1200
Terrence Grant, *Pr*
Dennis Morgan, *
Thomas L Kuklo, *General Vice President**
▲ **EMP:** 235 **EST:** 1942
SQ FT: 80,000
SALES (est): 23.2MM **Privately Held**
Web: www.birdrf.com

SIC: 3825 Test equipment for electronic and
electric measurement
PA: Bird Technologies Group Inc.
30303 Aurora Rd
Solon OH 44139

(G-12085)
**BIRD TECHNOLOGIES GROUP INC
(PA)**
30303 Aurora Rd (44139-2743)
PHONE..........................440 248-1200
Mark I Johnson, *Pr*
Dennis Morgan, *CFO*
Terrence C Grant, *VP*
Thomas L Kuklo, *VP*
Edward J Bartos Junior, *VP*
EMP: 165 **EST:** 1995
SQ FT: 12,000
SALES (est): 41.86MM **Privately Held**
Web: www.birdrf.com
SIC: 3825 3669 Test equipment for
electronic and electric measurement;
Intercommunication systems, electric

(G-12086)
BLUE COLLAR M LLC
Also Called: Colbleu Vodka
31005 Bainbridge Rd Ste 2 (44139-6401)
PHONE..........................216 209-5666
Ralph Faulkner, *Managing Member*
EMP: 12 **EST:** 2017
SALES (est): 750K **Privately Held**
SIC: 2085 5182 Vodka (alcoholic beverage);
Liquor

(G-12087)
BOWES MANUFACTURING INC
Also Called: Tungsten and Capital
30340 Solon Industrial Pkwy Ste B
(44139-4343)
PHONE..........................216 378-2110
Zelda Stutz, *Pr*
EMP: 13 **EST:** 1974
SQ FT: 30,000
SALES (est): 2.53MM **Privately Held**
Web: www.bowesmfg.com
SIC: 3568 3452 3494 3429 Couplings, shaft:
rigid, flexible, universal joint, etc.; Bolts,
metal; Valves and pipe fittings, nec; Clamps
and couplings, hose

(G-12088)
BRADLEY STONE INDUSTRIES LLC
30801 Carter St (44139-3517)
PHONE..........................440 519-3277
EMP: 18 **EST:** 1996
SALES (est): 3.94MM **Privately Held**
Web: www.bradley-stone.com
SIC: 1423 Crushed and broken granite

(G-12089)
BRAZE SOLUTIONS LLC
6850 Cochran Rd (44139-4336)
PHONE..........................440 349-5100
Gregory Greenspan, *Managing Member*
▲ **EMP:** 16 **EST:** 2007
SALES (est): 1.86MM **Privately Held**
Web: www.brazesolutions.com
SIC: 8711 7692 Engineering services;
Brazing

(G-12090)
BREAKER TECHNOLOGY INC
30625 Solon Industrial Pkwy (44139-4389)
PHONE..........................440 248-7168
EMP: 19
SALES (corp-wide): 927.43K **Privately
Held**
Web: www.astecindustries.com

SIC: 3532 5084 1629 Mining machinery;
Hydraulic systems equipment and supplies;
Trenching contractor
PA: Breaker Technology, Inc.
86470 Franklin Blvd
Eugene OR 97405
951 369-0878

(G-12091)
CARDPAK INCORPORATED
29601 Solon Rd (44139-3451)
PHONE..........................440 542-3100
EMP: 130
SIC: 2657 2752 Folding paperboard boxes;
Commercial printing, lithographic

(G-12092)
**CEQUENT CONSUMER PRODUCTS
INC**
Also Called: Cequent Consumer Products
29000 Aurora Rd Ste 2 (44139-7202)
P.O. Box 673071 (48267-3071)
PHONE..........................440 498-0001
◆ **EMP:** 85
SIC: 5531 3714 Automotive accessories;
Motor vehicle parts and accessories

(G-12093)
CHANNEL PRODUCTS INC (PA)
30700 Solon Industrial Pkwy (44139-4333)
PHONE..........................440 423-0113
Teresa Hack, *Pr*
Wayne Monaco, *
James Becker, *Prin*
Suzanne French, *Prin*
Steve Marrero, *Prin*
▲ **EMP:** 70 **EST:** 1972
SQ FT: 50,000
SALES (est): 9.09MM
SALES (corp-wide): 9.09MM **Privately
Held**
Web: www.channelproducts.com
SIC: 7363 3679 3643 3625 Manpower pools;
Electronic circuits; Current-carrying wiring
services; Relays and industrial controls

(G-12094)
CHRISTOPHER TOOL & MFG CO
30500 Carter St Frnt (44139-3580)
PHONE..........................440 248-8080
Patrick Christopher, *CEO*
Steve Fonash, *Pr*
Larry Walker, *VP*
Craig Peck, *VP Opers*
Karen Christopher, *Sec*
EMP: 102 **EST:** 1953
SQ FT: 48,500
SALES (est): 23.54MM **Privately Held**
Web: www.christophertool.com
SIC: 3599 Machine shop, jobbing and repair

(G-12095)
CMC PHARMACEUTICALS INC (PA)
Also Called: CMC Consulting
30625 Solon Rd Ste G (44139-3473)
PHONE..........................216 600-9430
Mike Radomsky, *Pr*
EMP: 6 **EST:** 2014
SQ FT: 1,000
SALES (est): 2.3MM
SALES (corp-wide): 2.3MM **Privately Held**
Web: www.cmcpharm.com
SIC: 2834 Druggists' preparations
(pharmaceuticals)

(G-12096)
CO-AX TECHNOLOGY INC
30301 Emerald Valley Pkwy (44139-4394)
PHONE..........................440 914-9200
Gholam Hosein Varghai, *Pr*
Hassan Varghai, *

EMP: 250 **EST:** 1993
SQ FT: 22,000
SALES (est): 22.01MM **Privately Held**
Web: www.coaxinc.com
SIC: 3672 3679 Printed circuit boards;
Harness assemblies, for electronic use:
wire or cable

(G-12097)
COCHRAN 6573 LLC
6573 Cochran Rd Ste I (44139-3972)
PHONE..........................440 349-4900
Carr F Briggs, *Managing Member*
▲ **EMP:** 15 **EST:** 2006
SALES (est): 880.61K **Privately Held**
Web: www.cadaudio.com
SIC: 3651 Microphones

(G-12098)
**COPERION PROCESS SOLUTIONS
LLC**
30825 Aurora Rd # 150 (44139-2733)
PHONE..........................513 576-9200
Graham Cooper, *Brnch Mgr*
EMP: 10
Web: fpm.coperion.com
SIC: 3535 3564 5084 Pneumatic tube
conveyor systems; Dust or fume collecting
equipment, industrial; Pneumatic tools and
equipment
HQ: Coperion Process Solutions Llc
7901 Nw 107th Ter
Kansas City MO 64153
816 891-9300

(G-12099)
DANDI ENTERPRISES INC
Also Called: Dunkin' Donuts
6353 Som Center Rd (44139-2914)
PHONE..........................419 516-9070
Lonnie Weiser, *Pr*
EMP: 9 **EST:** 1996
SALES (est): 253.44K **Privately Held**
Web: www.dunkindonuts.com
SIC: 5461 2051 Doughnuts; Doughnuts,
except frozen

(G-12100)
**DEMAG CRANES & COMPONENTS
CORP (DH)**
Also Called: Terex USA
6675 Parkland Blvd Ste 200 (44139-4345)
P.O. Box 39245 (44139-0245)
PHONE..........................440 248-2400
Martin Marincic, *Pr*
Steve Mayes, *
Todd Robenson, *
Bernard D'ambrosi, *Dir*
◆ **EMP:** 200 **EST:** 1965
SQ FT: 87,000
SALES (est): 37.49MM **Privately Held**
Web: www.demagcranes.com
SIC: 3536 Cranes, industrial plant
HQ: Konecranes, Inc.
4401 Gateway Blvd
Springfield OH 45502

(G-12101)
DOCMANN PRINTING & ASSOC INC
5275 Naiman Pkwy Ste E (44139-1033)
PHONE..........................440 975-1775
Todd Brichmann, *Pr*
James E Docherty, *VP*
EMP: 7 **EST:** 1992
SQ FT: 14,000
SALES (est): 538.73K **Privately Held**
Web: www.docmann.com
SIC: 2752 Offset printing

(G-12102)
E B P INC
Also Called: Epic Steel
29125 Hall St (44139-3909)
PHONE..................................216 241-2550
Dan Fremont, *Pr*
Neff Fremont, *
Mark Fremont, *
Arthur M Hemlock, *
Robert M Lustig, *
EMP: 29 EST: 1963
SALES (est): 3.42MM Privately Held
Web: www.epicsteel.com
SIC: 3441 3446 3444 Fabricated structural metal; Architectural metalwork; Sheet metalwork

(G-12103)
ELECTROVATIONS INC
30333 Emerald Valley Pkwy (44139-4394)
PHONE..................................330 274-3558
R Charles Vermerris, *Pr*
EMP: 7 EST: 1987
SALES (est): 337.01K Privately Held
SIC: 8711 7389 3357 Electrical or electronic engineering; Design, commercial and industrial; Nonferrous wiredrawing and insulating

(G-12104)
EMBEDDED PLANET INC
31225 Bainbridge Rd Ste N (44139-2293)
PHONE..................................216 245-4180
Mark Leopold, *CEO*
Mark Lowdermilk, *CEO*
Timothy J Callahan, *Ch Bd*
EMP: 15 EST: 1997
SALES (est): 2.69MM Privately Held
Web: www.embeddedplanet.com
SIC: 7371 3577 Computer software development; Computer peripheral equipment, nec

(G-12105)
ERICO INC
34600 Solon Rd (44139-2695)
PHONE..................................440 248-0100
George H Vincent, *Pr*
Larry Fisher, *
◆ EMP: 27 EST: 1995
SALES (est): 7.64MM Privately Held
Web: www.nvent.com
SIC: 3644 Noncurrent-carrying wiring devices

(G-12106)
ERICO GLOBAL COMPANY
31700 Solon Rd (44139-3532)
PHONE..................................440 248-0100
EMP: 8 EST: 2006
SALES (est): 1.88MM Privately Held
Web: www.nvent.com
SIC: 3699 Electrical equipment and supplies, nec
PA: Nvent Electric Public Limited Company
10 Earlsfort Terrace
Dublin D02T3

(G-12107)
ERICO INTERNATIONAL CORP
34600 Solon Rd (44139-2631)
PHONE..................................440 248-0100
Steve Rohacz, *Brnch Mgr*
EMP: 400
Web: www.nvent.com
SIC: 3441 3965 Fabricated structural metal; Fasteners
HQ: Erico International Corporation
1665 Utica Ave Ste 700
Saint Louis Park MN 55416
440 349-2630

(G-12108)
ET&F FASTENING SYSTEMS INC
29019 Solon Rd (44139-3440)
PHONE..................................800 248-2376
John C Tillman, *Pr*
John C Tillman, *Pr*
Dave Nolan, *VP*
▲ EMP: 6 EST: 1984
SQ FT: 15,000
SALES (est): 895.99K Privately Held
Web: www.etf-fastening.com
SIC: 3965 3546 5085 Fasteners; Power-driven handtools; Fasteners, industrial: nuts, bolts, screws, etc.

(G-12109)
ETCHED METAL COMPANY
30200 Solon Industrial Pkwy (44139-4311)
PHONE..................................440 248-0240
Scott Nameth, *Prin*
Mike Mcdivitt, *Prin*
▲ EMP: 45 EST: 1928
SQ FT: 27,500
SALES (est): 3.59MM Privately Held
Web: www.etched-metal.com
SIC: 3479 3613 3596 3993 Name plates: engraved, etched, etc.; Control panels, electric; Scales and balances, except laboratory; Signs and advertising specialties

(G-12110)
FD ROLLS CORP
Also Called: Fd Machinery
30400 Solon Industrial Pkwy (44139-4328)
PHONE..................................216 916-1922
EMP: 6 EST: 2015
SALES (est): 4.18MM Privately Held
Web: www.fdmachinery.com
SIC: 3317 Steel pipe and tubes
PA: Dalian Field Heavy Machinery Manufacturing Co., Ltd.
No.1, Jinma Road, Technology & Economy Development Zone, Tiexi D
Dalian LN 11620

(G-12111)
FINDAWAY WORLD LLC (PA)
31999 Aurora Rd (44139-2853)
PHONE..................................440 893-0808
Mitch Kroll, *CEO*
▲ EMP: 47 EST: 2004
SALES (est): 3.55MM Privately Held
Web: www.playaway.com
SIC: 5999 8031 3009 5192 Audio-visual equipment and supplies; Job training and related services; Visual communication systems; Periodicals

(G-12112)
FIRE FROM ICE VENTURES LLC
30333 Emerald Valley Pkwy (44139-4394)
PHONE..................................419 944-6705
▲ EMP: 10 EST: 1998
SQ FT: 13,500
SALES (est): 1.47MM Privately Held
SIC: 3585 Refrigeration and heating equipment
PA: The Providence Group Inc
9290 Metcalf Rd
Willoughby OH

(G-12113)
FLUKE BIOMEDICAL LLC (DH)
28775 Aurora Rd (44139-1837)
PHONE..................................440 248-9300
James Lico, *Pr*
▲ EMP: 120 EST: 1999
SALES (est): 8.4MM
SALES (corp-wide): 6.23B Publicly Held
Web: www.flukebiomedical.com

SIC: 3829 Nuclear radiation and testing apparatus
HQ: Fluke Electronics Corporation
6920 Seaway Blvd
Everett WA 98203
425 347-6100

(G-12114)
FOLIO PHOTONICS INC
6864 Cochran Rd (44139-4336)
PHONE..................................440 420-4500
Kenneth Singer, *Ex Dir*
EMP: 10 EST: 2012
SQ FT: 9,500
SALES (est): 5.04MM Privately Held
Web: www.foliophotonics.com
SIC: 3695 Optical disks and tape, blank

(G-12115)
GLAVIN INDUSTRIES INC
Also Called: Glavin Specialty Co
6835 Cochran Rd Ste A (44139-3927)
P.O. Box 391316 (44139-8316)
PHONE..................................440 349-0049
Daniel Glavin, *CEO*
David H Glavin, *
Julia S Glavin, *
EMP: 25 EST: 1986
SQ FT: 23,000
SALES (est): 10.95MM Privately Held
Web: www.glavinid.com
SIC: 5084 3993 2759 Industrial machinery and equipment; Signs and advertising specialties; Screen printing

(G-12116)
GLENRIDGE MACHINE CO
37435 Fawn Path Dr (44139-2507)
PHONE..................................440 975-1055
▲ EMP: 33
Web: www.glenridgemachine.com
SIC: 3599 7692 Machine shop, jobbing and repair; Welding repair

(G-12117)
GLOBAL TBM COMPANY (HQ)
Also Called: Robbins Company, The
29100 Hall St (44139-3932)
PHONE..................................440 248-3303
Lok Home, *Pr*
◆ EMP: 150 EST: 2020
SQ FT: 79,000
SALES (est): 44.08MM Privately Held
Web: www.robbinstbm.com
SIC: 3535 3541 3531 Unit handling conveying systems; Drilling and boring machines; Tunneling machinery
PA: Northern Heavy Industries Group Co., Ltd.
No.16, Kaifa Higway, Economic Tehnology Development Zone
Shenyang LN 11002

(G-12118)
GRAPHIC PACKAGING INTL LLC
Also Called: Altivity Packaging
6385 Cochran Rd (44139-3961)
PHONE..................................440 248-4370
Mary Turk, *Brnch Mgr*
EMP: 237
Web: www.graphicpkg.com
SIC: 2631 2657 Folding boxboard; Folding paperboard boxes
HQ: Graphic Packaging International, Llc
1500 Rvredge Pkwy Ste 100
Atlanta GA 30328

(G-12119)
HAB INC
Also Called: Hab Computer Services
28925 Fountain Pkwy (44139-4356)

P.O. Box 1 (54602-0001)
PHONE..................................608 785-7650
Michael Juran, *Pr*
EMP: 6 EST: 1985
SALES (est): 677.38K
SALES (corp-wide): 20.23K Privately Held
Web: www.mrisoftware.com
SIC: 7371 7372 Computer software development and applications; Prepackaged software
PA: Mri Software Llc
28925 Fountain Pkwy
Solon OH 44139
800 321-8770

(G-12120)
HDT EP INC
30500 Aurora Rd Ste 100 (44139-2776)
PHONE..................................216 438-6111
EMP: 200
SIC: 3585 3564 3433 Air conditioning units, complete: domestic or industrial; Filters, air: furnaces, air conditioning equipment, etc.; Heating equipment, except electric

(G-12121)
HDT EXPEDITIONARY SYSTEMS INC (HQ)
30500 Aurora Rd Ste 100 (44139-2776)
PHONE..................................216 438-6111
Sean Bond, *Pr*
Rita Thomas, *
Barry Sullivan, *
▲ EMP: 34 EST: 1981
SQ FT: 172,000
SALES (est): 134.52MM Privately Held
Web: www.hdtglobal.com
SIC: 2393 2394 Canvas bags; Canvas and related products
PA: Hunter Defense Technologies, Inc.
30500 Aurora Rd Ste 100
Solon OH 44139

(G-12122)
HDT TACTICAL SYSTEMS INC
30525 Aurora Rd (44139-2739)
PHONE..................................216 438-6111
▲ EMP: 200
SIC: 3569 3714 Filters; Heaters, motor vehicle

(G-12123)
HOSTAR INTERNATIONAL INC (PA)
31005 Solon Rd (44139-3436)
PHONE..................................440 564-5362
Claudia Berg, *Pr*
Todd Bush, *Pr*
Adam Wodka, *VP*
Ron Vitale, *Ex VP*
Dolores Lapalio, *VP*
EMP: 11 EST: 1988
SALES (est): 4.13MM
SALES (corp-wide): 4.13MM Privately Held
Web: www.hostar.com
SIC: 3535 Unit handling conveying systems

(G-12124)
HUNTER DEFENSE TECH INC (PA)
Also Called: Hdt Global
30500 Aurora Rd Ste 100 (44139-2776)
PHONE..................................216 438-6111
Vincent Buffa, *Pr*
Greg Miller, *
Carl Pates, *
Barry Sullivan, *
▼ EMP: 50 EST: 2000
SQ FT: 26,000
SALES (est): 416.26MM Privately Held
Web: www.hdtglobal.com

SIC: **3433** 3569 3822 8331 Room and wall
heaters, including radiators; Filters;
Environmental controls; Sheltered workshop

(G-12125)
HUNTER ENVIRONMENTAL CORP
Also Called: Hunter Manufacturing Company
30525 Aurora Rd (44139-2739)
PHONE.............................440 248-6111
Eugene Strine, *CEO*
EMP: 27 EST: 2016
SALES (est): 1.96MM Privately Held
Web: www.hdtglobal.com
SIC: **3564** Filters, air: furnaces, air
conditioning equipment, etc.

(G-12126)
ILLINOIS TOOL WORKS INC
Also Called: Permatex
6875 Parkland Blvd (44139-4377)
PHONE.............................440 914-3100
Krista Bursott, *Contrlr*
EMP: 75
SQ FT: 2,500
SALES (corp-wide): 16.11B Publicly Held
Web: www.itw.com
SIC: **2819** 2992 2899 2891 Industrial
inorganic chemicals, nec; Lubricating oils
and greases; Chemical preparations, nec;
Adhesives and sealants
PA: Illinois Tool Works Inc.
155 Harlem Ave
Glenview IL 60025
847 724-7500

(G-12127)
INNOCOMP
33195 Wagon Wheel Dr (44139-2368)
PHONE.............................440 248-5104
Jeri Lynn Hoffman, *Pt*
Robert Cecil, *Pt*
Craig Gruber, *Pt*
EMP: 7 EST: 1983
SQ FT: 3,500
SALES (est): 329.72K Privately Held
Web: www.innocomp.com
SIC: **3679** Voice controls

(G-12128)
INTELLIGENT MOBILE SUPPORT INC
28420 Blue Pond Trl (44139-1582)
PHONE.............................888 980-9119
John Steidley, *CEO*
EMP: 13 EST: 2010
SALES (est): 1.26MM Privately Held
Web: www.imobilesupport.com
SIC: **7372** Prepackaged software

(G-12129)
JEFFERSON SMURFIT CORPORATION
6385 Cochran Rd (44139-3961)
PHONE.............................440 248-4370
Lisa Porter, *Genl Mgr*
EMP: 7 EST: 2010
SALES (est): 147.6K Privately Held
SIC: **2657** Folding paperboard boxes

(G-12130)
JERPBAK-BAYLESS CO
34150 Solon Rd (44139-2623)
P.O. Box 39157 (44139-0157)
PHONE.............................440 248-5387
J Scott Jerpbak, *Pr*
Jean Hentemann, *
EMP: 30 EST: 1944
SQ FT: 40,000
SALES (est): 5.85MM Privately Held
Web: www.jerpbakbayless.com

SIC: **3599** Machine shop, jobbing and repair

(G-12131)
JOHNSONITE INC
Also Called: Tarkett USA
30000 Aurora Rd (44139-2728)
PHONE.............................440 543-8916
▲ EMP: 450
SIC: **3069** 3089 Floor coverings, rubber;
Floor coverings, plastics

(G-12132)
JOY GLOBAL UNDERGROUND MIN LLC
Also Called: Bedford Gear
6160 Cochran Rd (44139-3306)
PHONE.............................440 248-7970
Ed Doheny, *Brnch Mgr*
▲ EMP: 140
SIC: **3532** Mining machinery
HQ: Joy Global Underground Mining Llc
40 Pennwood Pl Ste 100
Warrendale PA 15086
724 779-4500

(G-12133)
JTM PRODUCTS INC
Also Called: J T M
31025 Carter St (44139-3521)
PHONE.............................440 287-2302
Daniel Schodowski, *Pr*
Greg Myers, *VP*
Brian F Murphy, *Prin*
EMP: 22 EST: 1991
SQ FT: 75,000
SALES (est): 2.14MM Privately Held
Web: www.jtmproducts.com
SIC: **2992** 2841 3053 Oils and greases,
blending and compounding; Soap:
granulated, liquid, cake, flaked, or chip;
Packing: steam engines, pipe joints, air
compressors, etc.

(G-12134)
KANAN ENTERPRISES INC (PA)
Also Called: King Nut Companies
31900 Solon Rd (44139-3536)
PHONE.............................440 248-8484
Martin Kanan, *Pr*
Michael Kanan, *
Matthew Kanan, *
◆ EMP: 198 EST: 1927
SQ FT: 250,000
SALES (est): 40.11MM
SALES (corp-wide): 40.11MM Privately Held
Web: www.kingnut.com
SIC: **2068** 2034 Nuts: dried, dehydrated,
salted or roasted; Fruits, dried or
dehydrated, except freeze-dried

(G-12135)
KANAN ENTERPRISES INC
Also Called: King Nut Companies
30600 Carter St (44139-3503)
PHONE.............................440 248-8484
EMP: 82
SALES (corp-wide): 40.11MM Privately Held
Web: www.kingnut.com
SIC: **2068** 2034 Nuts: dried, dehydrated,
salted or roasted; Fruits, dried or
dehydrated, except freeze-dried
PA: Kanan Enterprises, Inc.
31900 Solon Rd
Solon OH 44139
440 248-8484

(G-12136)
KANAN ENTERPRISES INC
Also Called: King Nut Companies, Plant 2
6401 Davis Industrial Pkwy (44139-3566)
PHONE.............................440 349-0719
EMP: 10
SQ FT: 84,130
SALES (corp-wide): 40.11MM Privately
Held
Web: www.kingnut.com
SIC: **2068** 2034 Nuts: dried, dehydrated,
salted or roasted; Fruits, dried or
dehydrated, except freeze-dried
PA: Kanan Enterprises, Inc.
31900 Solon Rd
Solon OH 44139
440 248-8484

(G-12137)
KEITHLEY INSTRUMENTS LLC (DH)
28775 Aurora Rd (44139-1891)
PHONE.............................440 248-0400
Joseph P Keithley, *Pr*
Linda C Rae, *
Mark J Plush, *
Daniel A Faia, *SUPPORT**
Larry L Pendergrass, *New Product
Development Vice President**
▲ EMP: 99 EST: 1946
SQ FT: 125,000
SALES (est): 50.28MM
SALES (corp-wide): 6.23B Publicly Held
Web: www.tek.com
SIC: **3823** 7371 3825 Computer interface
equipment, for industrial process control;
Computer software development; Test
equipment for electronic and electric
measurement
HQ: Tektronix, Inc.
13725 Sw Karl Braun Dr
Beaverton OR 97077
800 833-9200

(G-12138)
KENNAMETAL INC
6865 Cochran Rd (44139-4398)
PHONE.............................440 349-5151
Brian Maglosky, *Mgr*
EMP: 110
SQ FT: 1,500
SALES (corp-wide): 2.05B Publicly Held
Web: www.kennametal.com
SIC: **3545** 3532 Tool holders; Mining
machinery
PA: Kennametal Inc.
525 Wlliam Penn Pl Ste 33
Pittsburgh PA 15219
412 248-8000

(G-12139)
KICHLER LIGHTING LLC (DH)
Also Called: Kichler Lighting
30455 Solon Rd (44139-3415)
P.O. Box 318010 (44131)
PHONE.............................216 573-1000
Vijay Shankar, *Pr*
◆ EMP: 500 EST: 1938
SQ FT: 630,000
SALES (est): 97.96MM
SALES (corp-wide): 539.53MM Privately
Held
Web: www.kichler.com
SIC: **3645** 3648 3641 Residential lighting
fixtures; Lighting equipment, nec; Electric
lamps
HQ: Kingswood Capital Management, L.P.
11111 Snta Mnica Blvd Ste
Los Angeles CA 90025
424 744-8238

(G-12140)
KYNTRONICS INC (PA)
6565 Davis Industrial Pkwy Ste R
(44139-3560)
PHONE.............................440 220-5990
Wayne Foley, *Pr*
EMP: 16 EST: 2013
SALES (est): 5.07MM
SALES (corp-wide): 5.07MM Privately
Held
Web: www.kyntronics.com
SIC: **3593** Fluid power actuators, hydraulic
or pneumatic

(G-12141)
LATTICE COMPOSITES LLC
29001 Solon Rd Unit S (44139-3469)
PHONE.............................440 759-2082
Ruchir Shanbhag, *CEO*
EMP: 19 EST: 2012
SALES (est): 1.09MM Privately Held
Web: www.latticecomposites.com
SIC: **2821** Epoxy resins

(G-12142)
LINK SYSTEMS INC
Also Called: Prolease
28925 Fountain Pkwy (44139-4356)
PHONE.............................800 321-8770
Patrick Ghilani, *Pr*
John Ensign, *Sec*
Roman Telerman, *Treas*
EMP: 15 EST: 1992
SALES (est): 554.31K
SALES (corp-wide): 20.23K Privately Held
Web: www.proleasesoftware.com
SIC: **7371** 7372 7379 7389 Computer
software development; Business oriented
computer software; Computer related
consulting services
PA: Mri Software Llc
28925 Fountain Pkwy
Solon OH 44139
800 321-8770

(G-12143)
MADISON ELECTRIC PRODUCTS INC (HQ)
30575 Bainbridge Rd Ste 130 (44139-2200)
PHONE.............................216 391-7776
Brad Wiandt, *Pr*
Rob Fisher, *
▲ EMP: 37 EST: 1988
SALES (est): 4.46MM
SALES (corp-wide): 584.3MM Privately
Held
Web: www.southwire.com
SIC: **3644** Electric conduits and fittings
PA: Southwire Company, Llc
One Southwire Dr
Carrollton GA 30119
770 832-4242

(G-12144)
MAJESTIC TOOL AND MACHINE INC
30700 Carter St Ste C (44139-3585)
PHONE.............................440 248-5058
Walter Krueger, *
Todd Krueger, *
Kurt Krueger, *
EMP: 8 EST: 1973
SQ FT: 30,000
SALES (est): 1.6MM Privately Held
Web: www.majestictool.com
SIC: **3599** 7692 3544 Machine shop, jobbing
and repair; Welding repair; Special dies,
tools, jigs, and fixtures

(G-12145)
MEDICAL QUANT USA INC
Also Called: Multi Radiance Medical
6521 Davis Industrial Pkwy (44139-3549)
PHONE................................440 542-0761
Max Kanarsky, *Pr*
Galina Marqova, *CFO*
EMP: 14 **EST:** 2004
SALES (est): 3.88MM **Privately Held**
Web: www.multiradiance.com
SIC: 3841 Surgical and medical instruments

(G-12146)
MERCURY IRON AND STEEL CO
Also Called: Misco Refractometer
6275 Cochran Rd (44139-3316)
PHONE................................440 349-1500
Michael Rainer, *Pr*
EMP: 14 **EST:** 1949
SQ FT: 6,000
SALES (est): 4.94MM **Privately Held**
Web: www.misco.com
SIC: 8711 3827 3443 3441 Industrial engineers; Optical instruments and lenses; Plate work for the metalworking trade; Fabricated structural metal

(G-12147)
MERCURY MACHINE CO
30250 Carter St (44139-3500)
PHONE................................440 349-3222
Jonathon Petrenchik, *Pr*
EMP: 67 **EST:** 1954
SQ FT: 10,000
SALES (est): 8.73MM **Privately Held**
Web: www.mercurymachine.com
SIC: 3324 3544 Steel investment foundries; Industrial molds

(G-12148)
METAULLICS SYSTEMS LP
Also Called: Metaullics Systems
31935 Aurora Rd (44139-2717)
PHONE................................509 926-6212
▲ **EMP:** 133
SIC: 3569 3624 3295 3561 Filters, general line: industrial; Carbon and graphite products; Graphite, natural: ground, pulverized, refined, or blended; Pumps and pumping equipment

(G-12149)
MFS SUPPLY LLC (PA)
31100 Solon Rd Ste 16 (44139-3463)
PHONE................................800 607-0541
Jeff Muencz, *CFO*
Michael Halpern, *Managing Member**
◆ **EMP:** 62 **EST:** 2006
SALES (est): 24.37MM **Privately Held**
Web: www.mfssupply.com
SIC: 2542 Postal lock boxes, mail racks, and related products

(G-12150)
MICHAEL W HYES DESGR GOLDSMITH
Also Called: Hayes, Michael Designer
28200 Miles Rd Unit F (44139-6915)
PHONE................................440 519-0889
Michael Hayes, *CEO*
Marcy Hayes, *VP*
EMP: 7 **EST:** 1978
SQ FT: 1,250
SALES (est): 305.28K **Privately Held**
Web: www.michaelwhayes.com
SIC: 3911 5944 7631 Jewelry, precious metal ; Jewelry stores; Jewelry repair services

(G-12151)
MICROPLEX PRINTWARE CORP
30300 Solon Industrial Pkwy Ste E
(44139-4382)
PHONE................................440 374-2424
Andre Fedak, *Pr*
▲ **EMP:** 11 **EST:** 1998
SALES (est): 959.66K **Privately Held**
Web: www.microplex-usa.com
SIC: 2759 Laser printing

(G-12152)
MILLWOOD INC
30311 Emerald Valley Pkwy Ste 300
(44139-4339)
PHONE................................440 914-0540
Vern Walker, *Brnch Mgr*
EMP: 58
Web: www.millwoodinc.com
SIC: 2448 Pallets, wood
PA: Millwood, Inc.
3708 International Blvd
Vienna OH 44473

(G-12153)
MOTIONSOURCE INTERNATIONAL LLC
31200 Solon Rd Ste 7 (44139-3583)
PHONE................................440 287-7037
Charles Hautala, *Pr*
Doug Karpowicz, *Prin*
EMP: 10 **EST:** 2012
SQ FT: 4,000
SALES (est): 4.89MM **Privately Held**
Web: www.motionsource1.com
SIC: 3569 5084 5013 Lubrication equipment, industrial; Pumps and pumping equipment, nec; Pumps, oil and gas

(G-12154)
MP BIOMEDICALS LLC
29525 Fountain Pkwy (44139-4351)
PHONE................................440 337-1200
Dragon Kraojovic, *Brnch Mgr*
EMP: 130
SALES (corp-wide): 601.99MM **Privately Held**
Web: www.mpbio.com
SIC: 8731 2869 2834 8071 Biological research; Enzymes; Pharmaceutical preparations; Medical laboratories
HQ: Mp Biomedicals, Llc
6 Thomas
Irvine CA 92618
949 833-2500

(G-12155)
MUSTARD SEED HEALTH FD MKT INC
6025 Kruse Dr Ste 100 (44139-2378)
PHONE................................440 519-3663
Margaret Kanfer-nabors, *Ch Bd*
EMP: 35
SALES (corp-wide): 12.12MM **Privately Held**
Web: www.mustardseedmarket.com
SIC: 5499 7299 5812 2051 Gourmet food stores; Banquet hall facilities; Caterers; Bread, cake, and related products
PA: Mustard Seed Health Food Market, Inc.
3885 Medina Rd
Akron OH 44333
330 666-7333

(G-12156)
MYTEE PRODUCTS INC
Also Called: Mytee
30701 Carter St (44139-3515)
PHONE................................888 705-8277
Vick Agarwalla, *Pr*

Prabhav Agarwalla, *
▲ **EMP:** 51 **EST:** 2003
SALES (est): 11.71MM **Privately Held**
Web: www.myteeproducts.com
SIC: 5013 2824 Truck parts and accessories ; Vinyl fibers

(G-12157)
NESTLE PREPARED FOODS COMPANY
5750 Harper Rd (44139-1831)
PHONE................................440 349-5757
C Wayne Partin, *Pr*
EMP: 477
Web: www.nestle.com
SIC: 2038 5411 2037 Frozen specialties, nec ; Grocery stores; Frozen fruits and vegetables
HQ: Nestle Prepared Foods Company
30003 Bainbridge Rd
Solon OH 44139
440 248-3600

(G-12158)
NESTLE PREPARED FOODS COMPANY (DH)
Also Called: Nestle
30003 Bainbridge Rd (44139-2290)
P.O. Box P.O. Box 2178 (18703-2178)
PHONE................................440 248-3600
Laurent Freixe, *CEO*
David H Jennings, *
James M Biggar, *
Charles Werner, *
James H Ball, *
▲ **EMP:** 1910 **EST:** 1969
SQ FT: 250,000
SALES (est): 479.51MM **Privately Held**
Web: www.nestle.com
SIC: 2038 5411 2037 Dinners, frozen and packaged; Grocery stores; Vegetables, quick frozen & cold pack, excl. potato products
HQ: The Stouffer Corporation
30003 Bainbridge Rd
Solon OH 44139
440 349-5757

(G-12159)
NESTLE USA INC
Nestle Business Services
30003 Bainbridge Rd (44139-2290)
PHONE................................440 349-5757
Jim Triskett, *Mgr*
EMP: 287
Web: www.nestleusa.com
SIC: 2023 Evaporated milk
HQ: Nestle Usa, Inc.
1812 N Moore St
Arlington VA 22209
800 225-2270

(G-12160)
NESTLE USA INC
Also Called: Nestle Brands Company
30000 Bainbridge Rd (44139-2206)
PHONE................................440 264-6600
Cheryl Lavine, *Prin*
EMP: 380
Web: www.nestleusa.com
SIC: 2023 Evaporated milk
HQ: Nestle Usa, Inc.
1812 N Moore St
Arlington VA 22209
800 225-2270

(G-12161)
NESTLE USA INC
30500 Bainbridge Rd (44139-2216)
PHONE................................440 349-5757
EMP: 107

Web: www.nestleusa.com
SIC: 3556 Food products machinery
HQ: Nestle Usa, Inc.
1812 N Moore St
Arlington VA 22209
800 225-2270

(G-12162)
NVENT MANAGEMENT COMPANY
6800 Arnold Miller Pkwy (44139-4364)
PHONE................................440 248-0100
EMP: 625
Web: www.nvent.com
SIC: 3444 Sheet metalwork
HQ: Nvent Management Company
1665 Utica Ave Ste 700
Saint Louis Park MN 55416
763 204-7700

(G-12163)
OAKWOOD LABORATORIES LLC
27070 Miles Rd (44139-1162)
PHONE................................440 505-2011
Shritin Shah, *Brnch Mgr*
EMP: 60
SALES (corp-wide): 19.43MM **Privately Held**
Web: www.oakwoodlabs.com
SIC: 2834 Vitamin, nutrient, and hematinic preparations for human use
PA: Oakwood Laboratories, L.L.C.
7670 First Pl Ste A
Oakwood Village OH 44146
440 359-0000

(G-12164)
OHIO LUMEX CO INC
30350 Bruce Industrial Pkwy (44139-3938)
PHONE................................440 264-2500
Joseph Siperstein, *Pr*
EMP: 49 **EST:** 1998
SQ FT: 4,000
SALES (est): 8.89MM **Privately Held**
Web: www.ohiolumex.com
SIC: 3826 8734 Analytical instruments; Testing laboratories

(G-12165)
OSB SOFTWARE INC
6240 Som Center Rd Ste 230 (44139-2950)
PHONE................................440 542-9145
Steven Wiser, *Pr*
EMP: 8 **EST:** 2003
SALES (est): 2.11MM **Privately Held**
Web: www.specializedbusinesssoftware.com
SIC: 7372 Business oriented computer software

(G-12166)
PDI GROUND SUPPORT SYSTEMS INC
Also Called: Pdi Group, The
6225 Cochran Rd (44139-3315)
PHONE................................216 271-7344
Irwin G Haber, *Ch*
Ida S Haber, *
▲ **EMP:** 60 **EST:** 1992
SQ FT: 110,000
SALES (est): 10.85MM **Privately Held**
Web: www.thepdigroup.com
SIC: 3714 3715 Axle housings and shafts, motor vehicle; Semitrailers for missile transportation

(G-12167)
PENTAIR
34600 Solon Rd (44139-2631)
PHONE................................440 248-0100
EMP: 46 **EST:** 2017
SALES (est): 6.57MM **Privately Held**

Web: www.pentair.com
SIC: 3561 Pumps and pumping equipment

(G-12168)
PLAS-MAC CORP
30250 Carter St (44139-3506)
PHONE..............................440 349-3222
Jonathon Petrenchik, *Pr*
EMP: 100 EST: 1980
SQ FT: 33,000
SALES (est): 4.94MM **Privately Held**
Web: www.plasmaccorp.com
SIC: 3543 3599 Foundry patternmaking; Air
intake filters, internal combustion engine,
except auto

(G-12169)
PRECISION BRUSH CO
6700 Parkland Blvd (44139-4341)
PHONE..............................440 542-9600
James C Benjamin, *Pr*
EMP: 14 EST: 1950
SQ FT: 11,000
SALES (est): 2.42MM **Privately Held**
Web: www.precisionbrush.com
SIC: 3991 Brushes, household or industrial

(G-12170)
PTMJ ENTERPRISES INC
32000 Aurora Rd (44139-2875)
P.O. Box 391437 (44139-8437)
PHONE..............................440 543-8000
Peter Joyce, *Pr*
▲ EMP: 16 EST: 1980
SALES (est): 6.82MM **Privately Held**
Web: www.signumdisplays.com
SIC: 2541 1799 Display fixtures, wood;
Closet organizers, installation and design

(G-12171)
R & D NESTLE CENTER INC
5750 Harper Rd (44139-1831)
PHONE..............................440 349-5757
EMP: 102
Web: www.nestle.com
SIC: 2038 Frozen specialties, nec
HQ: R & D Nestle Center Inc
809 Collins Ave
Marysville OH 43040
937 642-7015

(G-12172)
RADIX WIRE & CABLE LLC
Also Called: Radix Wire
30333 Emerald Valley Pkwy (44139-4394)
PHONE..............................216 731-9191
Steve Demko, *VP Fin*
EMP: 71 EST: 2013
SALES (est): 9MM **Privately Held**
Web: www.radix-wire.com
SIC: 2298 3312 3315 Ropes and fiber cables
; Wire products, steel or iron; Wire and
fabricated wire products

(G-12173)
RADIX WIRE CO (PA)
Also Called: Radix Wire Company, The
30333 Emerald Valley Pkwy (44139-4394)
PHONE..............................216 731-9191
Keith D Nootbaar, *Pr*
Marylou Vermerris, *
Jim Schaefer, *
Brain Bukovec, *
EMP: 60 EST: 1944
SALES (est): 20.56MM
SALES (corp-wide): 20.56MM **Privately
Held**
Web: www.radix-wire.com
SIC: 3357 5051 Nonferrous wiredrawing and
insulating; Cable, wire

(G-12174)
RADIX WIRE CO
30333 Emerald Valley Pkwy (44139-4394)
PHONE..............................216 731-9191
Bill Toll, *Mgr*
EMP: 17
SALES (corp-wide): 20.56MM **Privately
Held**
Web: www.radix-wire.com
SIC: 3357 Nonferrous wiredrawing and
insulating
PA: Radix Wire Co
30333 Emerald Valley Pkwy
Solon OH 44139
216 731-9191

(G-12175)
REPUBLIC STEEL WIRE PROC LLC
31000 Solon Rd (44139-3467)
PHONE..............................440 996-0740
Larry Braun, *Genl Mgr*
Jim Phillips, *Genl Mgr*
▲ EMP: 25 EST: 2010
SALES (est): 23.9MM **Privately Held**
Web: www.republicsteel.com
SIC: 3315 Steel wire and related products
HQ: Republic Steel
2633 8th St
Canton OH 44704
330 438-5435

(G-12176)
RTSI LLC
6161 Cochran Rd Ste G (44139-3324)
PHONE..............................440 542-3066
Vikki Velimesis, *Genl Mgr*
EMP: 7 EST: 2013
SALES (est): 3.04MM **Privately Held**
Web: www.rtsillc.com
SIC: 3451 Screw machine products
PA: Kirkwood Holding Inc.
1239 Rockside Rd
Cleveland OH 44134

(G-12177)
SAGEQUEST LLC
31500 Bainbridge Rd Ste 1 (44139-2289)
PHONE..............................216 896-7243
EMP: 86
Web: www.sage-quest.com
SIC: 3663 Mobile communication equipment

(G-12178)
SAINT-GOBAIN PRFMCE PLAS CORP
31500 Solon Rd (44139-3528)
PHONE..............................440 836-6900
EMP: 328
SALES (corp-wide): 402.18MM **Privately
Held**
Web: www.saint-gobain.com
SIC: 3089 3053 Thermoformed finished
plastics products, nec; Gaskets; packing
and sealing devices
HQ: Saint-Gobain Performance Plastics
Corporation
20 Moores Rd
Malvern PA 19355
440 836-6900

(G-12179)
SCHWEBEL BAKING COMPANY
Also Called: Schwebel Baking Co-Solon Bky
6250 Camp Industrial Rd (44139-2750)
PHONE..............................440 248-1500
Grant West, *Mgr*
EMP: 150
SALES (corp-wide): 71.65MM **Privately
Held**
Web: www.myschwebels.com

SIC: 5461 5149 2051 Bread; Groceries and
related products, nec; Bread, cake, and
related products
PA: Schwebel Baking Company
965 E Midlothian Blvd
Youngstown OH 44502
330 783-2860

(G-12180)
SENSICAL INC
Also Called: Unitus
31115 Aurora Rd (44139-2701)
PHONE..............................216 641-1141
John F Haas, *Pr*
James Haas, *
▲ EMP: 55 EST: 1978
SQ FT: 45,000
SALES (est): 9.7MM **Privately Held**
Web: www.sensical.com
SIC: 3993 2752 2672 2759 Signs and
advertising specialties; Commercial
printing, lithographic; Paper; coated and
laminated, nec; Promotional printing

(G-12181)
SK WELLMAN CORP
Also Called: Wellman Friction Products
6180 Cochran Rd (44139-3314)
PHONE..............................440 528-4000
▲ EMP: 250
SIC: 3499 Friction material, made from
powdered metal

(G-12182)
**SKIDMORE-WILHELM MFG
COMPANY**
Also Called: Columbia Industries
30340 Solon Industrial Pkwy Ste B
(44139-4343)
PHONE..............................216 481-4774
John Obrayan, *Pr*
Kathleen Wilhelm, *Stockholder*
John Wilhelm, *Stockholder*
Joanne Hoffman, *Corporate Secretary*
▲ EMP: 8 EST: 1944
SQ FT: 15,000
SALES (est): 2.34MM **Privately Held**
Web: www.skidmore-wilhelm.com
SIC: 3728 3829 3825 3593 Aircraft parts and
equipment, nec; Torsion testing equipment;
Instruments to measure electricity; Fluid
power cylinders and actuators

(G-12183)
SOLON SPECIALTY WIRE CO
30000 Solon Rd (44139-3408)
PHONE..............................440 248-7600
Dave Haffenr, *CEO*
▲ EMP: 25 EST: 2002
SQ FT: 180,000
SALES (est): 9.09MM **Privately Held**
SIC: 3315 Wire, ferrous/iron

(G-12184)
SOURCE3MEDIA INC
6470 Som Center Rd (44139-4214)
PHONE..............................330 467-9003
Gary Began, *Pr*
Ronald S Marshek, *
◆ EMP: 35 EST: 1967
SALES (est): 8.75MM **Privately Held**
Web: www.source3media.com
SIC: 2752 Offset printing

(G-12185)
STOCK FAIRFIELD CORPORATION
Also Called: Stock Equipment Company
30825 Aurora Rd # 150 (44139-2733)
PHONE..............................440 543-6000
Robert Ciavarella, *Pr*
EMP: 170 EST: 2007

SALES (est): 15.46MM **Publicly Held**
Web: www.schenckprocess.com
SIC: 5063 8711 3535 3823 Power
transmission equipment, electric; Electrical
or electronic engineering; Conveyors and
conveying equipment; Process control
instruments
HQ: Coperion Process Solutions Llc
7901 Nw 107th Ter
Kansas City MO 64153
816 891-9300

(G-12186)
STOUFFER CORPORATION (DH)
30003 Bainbridge Rd (44139-2205)
PHONE..............................440 349-5757
Peter Knox, *Prin*
▲ EMP: 8 EST: 1912
SQ FT: 124,000
SALES (est): 477.29MM **Privately Held**
Web: www.goodnes.com
SIC: 2038 Dinners, frozen and packaged
HQ: Tsc Holdings, Inc.
800 N Brand Blvd
Glendale CA 91203
818 549-6000

(G-12187)
SWAGELOK COMPANY
Also Called: Corporate Raw Materials
31400 Aurora Rd (44139-2708)
PHONE..............................440 248-4600
EMP: 6
SALES (corp-wide): 881.02MM **Privately
Held**
Web: www.aldvalve.com
SIC: 3491 Pressure valves and regulators,
industrial
PA: Swagelok Company
29500 Solon Rd
Solon OH 44139
440 248-4600

(G-12188)
SWAGELOK COMPANY (PA)
29500 Solon Rd (44139-3474)
PHONE..............................440 248-4600
Thomas F Lozick, *Ch*
James Cavoli, *
Chris Miklich, *
◆ EMP: 900 EST: 1947
SALES (est): 881.02MM
SALES (corp-wide): 881.02MM **Privately
Held**
Web: www.aldvalve.com
SIC: 3494 3491 3599 Pipe fittings; Pressure
valves and regulators, industrial; Machine
shop, jobbing and repair

(G-12189)
SWAGELOK COMPANY
6100 Cochran Rd (44139-3311)
PHONE..............................440 349-5652
Nancy Brown, *Brnch Mgr*
EMP: 34
SALES (corp-wide): 881.02MM **Privately
Held**
Web: cleveland.swagelok.com
SIC: 3494 3491 3599 3498 Pipe fittings;
Pressure valves and regulators, industrial;
Machine shop, jobbing and repair;
Fabricated pipe and fittings
PA: Swagelok Company
29500 Solon Rd
Solon OH 44139
440 248-4600

(G-12190)
SWAGELOK COMPANY
Also Called: Crawford Computer Center
29495 F A Lennon Dr (44139-2764)

PHONE.................440 349-5836
Arthur Anton, *Prin*
EMP: 25
SALES (corp-wide): 881.02MM **Privately Held**
Web: www.aldvalve.com
SIC: 3494 3491 3599 3594 Pipe fittings; Pressure valves and regulators, industrial; Machine shop, jobbing and repair; Fluid power pumps and motors
PA: Swagelok Company
29500 Solon Rd
Solon OH 44139
440 248-4600

(G-12191)
SWAGELOK COMPANY
29495 F A Lennon Dr (44139-2764)
PHONE.................440 349-5934
Nick Lubar, *Mgr*
EMP: 100
SALES (corp-wide): 881.02MM **Privately Held**
Web: www.swagelok.com
SIC: 5051 3593 3498 3494 Tubing, metal; Fluid power cylinders and actuators; Fabricated pipe and fittings; Valves and pipe fittings, nec
PA: Swagelok Company
29500 Solon Rd
Solon OH 44139
440 248-4600

(G-12192)
TARKETT INC (DH)
Also Called: Tarkett North America
30000 Aurora Rd (44139-2728)
PHONE.................800 899-8916
Jeff Fenwick, *CEO*
Jack Lee, *
Peter De Bonis, *
Christer Hiller, *
▲ **EMP:** 99 **EST:** 1981
SQ FT: 5,000
SALES (est): 421.66MM **Privately Held**
Web: www.tarketthome.com
SIC: 3069 Flooring, rubber: tile or sheet
HQ: Tarkett Inc
1001 Rue Yamaska E
Farnham QC J2N 1
450 293-3173

(G-12193)
TARKETT USA INC (DH)
Also Called: Johnsonite
30000 Aurora Rd (44139-2728)
PHONE.................877 827-5388
Jeff Fenwick, *Pr*
Nicolas Carre, *
EMP: 250 **EST:** 1996
SALES (est): 301.17MM **Privately Held**
Web: www.tarkett-group.com
SIC: 3253 Ceramic wall and floor tile
HQ: Tarkett
Tour Initiale
Puteaux IDF

(G-12194)
TECHNOLOGY HOUSE LTD
30700 Carter St (44139-3568)
PHONE.................440 248-3025
EMP: 91
Web: www.tth.com
SIC: 3599 Machine shop, jobbing and repair
PA: The Technology House Ltd
10036 Aurora-Hudson Rd
Streetsboro OH 44241

(G-12195)
TECHTRON SYSTEMS INC
29500 Fountain Pkwy (44139-4350)

PHONE.................440 505-2990
Paul Teel Junior, *Pr*
John Teel, *Stockholder**
Tina Sudlow, *Stockholder**
Pam Teel, *
▲ **EMP:** 50 **EST:** 1971
SQ FT: 38,000
SALES (est): 14.08MM **Privately Held**
Web: www.techtronsys.com
SIC: 3672 Printed circuit boards

(G-12196)
TEKTRONIX INC
Also Called: Tektronix
28775 Aurora Rd (44139-1837)
PHONE.................440 248-0400
EMP: 6
SALES (corp-wide): 6.23B **Publicly Held**
Web: www.tek.com
SIC: 3825 Instruments to measure electricity
HQ: Tektronix, Inc.
13725 Sw Karl Braun Dr
Beaverton OR 97077
800 833-9200

(G-12197)
TEXAS TILE MANUFACTURING LLC
30000 Aurora Rd (44139-2728)
PHONE.................713 869-5811
Gilles De Beaumont, *Pr*
Lee James, *VP*
Tom Dowling, *Treas*
Anthony Matti, *Dir*
▲ **EMP:** 9 **EST:** 2005
SALES (est): 705.88K **Privately Held**
SIC: 3292 Tile, vinyl asbestos

(G-12198)
TIMEKEEPING SYSTEMS INC
30700 Bainbridge Rd Ste H (44139-6403)
PHONE.................216 595-0890
George Markwitz, *Pr*
Barry Markwitz, *VP*
▲ **EMP:** 11 **EST:** 1986
SALES (est): 6.35MM **Privately Held**
Web: www.guard1.com
SIC: 7371 8711 7372 3577 Custom computer programming services; Engineering services; Prepackaged software; Computer peripheral equipment, nec

(G-12199)
TRITON GLOBAL PRODUCTS INC
Also Called: Triton Products
30700 Carter St Ste D (44139-3585)
PHONE.................440 248-5480
Antony Demarco, *Pr*
Scott Hanslik, *Account Executive*
▲ **EMP:** 18 **EST:** 2000
SQ FT: 38,000
SALES (est): 3.44MM **Privately Held**
Web: www.tritonproducts.com
SIC: 3429 Hangers, wall hardware

(G-12200)
TWINSOURCE LLC
32333 Aurora Rd Ste 50 (44139-2851)
PHONE.................440 248-6800
Fred Tamjidi, *Managing Member*
EMP: 10 **EST:** 1999
SQ FT: 1,500
SALES (est): 1.97MM **Privately Held**
Web: www.twinsource.net
SIC: 3625 Switches, electronic applications

(G-12201)
VALTRONIC TECHNOLOGY INC
29200 Fountain Pkwy (44139-4347)
PHONE.................440 349-1239
Martin Zimmermann, *CEO*

Jay Wimer, *
Donald Styblo, *
Sbastien Robert, *
EMP: 68 **EST:** 1986
SQ FT: 26,000
SALES (est): 23.23MM **Privately Held**
Web: www.valtronic.com
SIC: 3672 Printed circuit boards
PA: Valtronic Technologies (Holding) Sa
Route De Bonport 2
Le Lieu VD 1345

(G-12202)
VERSATILE AUTOMATION TECH LTD
Also Called: VA Technology
30355 Solon Industrial Pkwy (44139-4325)
PHONE.................440 589-6700
James Byrne, *Pr*
▲ **EMP:** 6 **EST:** 1993
SQ FT: 1,300
SALES (est): 5.59MM **Privately Held**
SIC: 3569 5084 Robots, assembly line: industrial and commercial; Robots, industrial
PA: V A Technology Limited
Versatile Technology Centre
Telford TF7 4

(G-12203)
VR ASSETS LLC
5265 Naiman Pkwy Ste J (44139-1013)
PHONE.................440 600-2963
Valeri Sakhanevitch, *Pr*
EMP: 8 **EST:** 2015
SALES (est): 410.96K **Privately Held**
Web: www.vrassets.us
SIC: 5045 7379 7378 3571 Computers, peripherals, and software; Computer related services, nec; Computer maintenance and repair; Electronic computers

(G-12204)
VWR CHEMICALS LLC (DH)
28600 Fountain Pkwy (44139-4314)
PHONE.................800 448-4442
Michael Stubblefield, *CEO*
▲ **EMP:** 30 **EST:** 1967
SALES (est): 23.31MM
SALES (corp-wide): 6.78B **Publicly Held**
SIC: 2819 Industrial inorganic chemicals, nec
HQ: Vwr Funding, Inc.
100 W Matsonford Rd Ste 1
Radnor PA 19087

(G-12205)
VWR PART OF AVANTOR (DH)
Also Called: Amresco, LLC
28600 Fountain Pkwy (44139-4314)
PHONE.................440 349-1199
▲ **EMP:** 39 **EST:** 1976
SALES (est): 16.76MM
SALES (corp-wide): 6.78B **Publicly Held**
SIC: 2833 Medicinals and botanicals
HQ: Vwr International, Llc
100 Mtsnford Rd Bldg 1 St
Radnor PA 19087
610 386-1700

(G-12206)
WALLEYE INVESTMENTS LTD
6750 Arnold Miller Pkwy (44139-4363)
PHONE.................440 564-7210
Willard E Frissell, *Managing Member*
EMP: 8 **EST:** 2004
SALES (est): 226.26K **Privately Held**
SIC: 3089 Injection molding of plastics

(G-12207)
WATER & WASTE WATER EQP CO
32100 Solon Rd Ste 101a (44139-3584)
PHONE.................440 542-0972

Walter Senney, *Pr*
EMP: 7 **EST:** 1978
SALES (est): 247.73K **Privately Held**
Web: www.wwe-co.com
SIC: 3589 Water treatment equipment, industrial

(G-12208)
WILLIAM J BERGEN & CO
Also Called: Bergen, W J & Co
32520 Arthur Rd (44139-4503)
PHONE.................440 248-6132
William J Bergen, *Owner*
EMP: 9 **EST:** 1979
SQ FT: 3,500
SALES (est): 292.94K **Privately Held**
SIC: 5112 2752 2759 Business forms; Offset printing; Letterpress printing

(G-12209)
XCHANGING
31500 Solon Rd (44139-3528)
PHONE.................440 914-2000
William White, *VP*
EMP: 6 **EST:** 2017
SALES (est): 696.15K **Privately Held**
SIC: 7372 Prepackaged software

Somerset
Perry County

(G-12210)
RHODES MANUFACTURING CO INC
7045 Buckeye Valley Rd Ne (43783-9709)
PHONE.................740 743-2614
Douglas L Rhodes, *Pr*
Brian Rhodes, *VP*
EMP: 20 **EST:** 1977
SQ FT: 6,000
SALES (est): 2.5MM **Privately Held**
Web: www.rhodesmfg.com
SIC: 3443 Industrial vessels, tanks, and containers

(G-12211)
SCHMELZER INDUSTRIES INC
7970 Wesley Chapel Rd Ne (43783-9737)
P.O. Box 249 (43783-0249)
PHONE.................740 743-2866
Jean Schmelzer, *Pr*
Monica Schmelzer, *
Timothy Schmelzer, *VP*
EMP: 25 **EST:** 1984
SQ FT: 23,700
SALES (est): 3.96MM **Privately Held**
Web: www.siveils.com
SIC: 2221 5999 Fiberglass fabrics; Fiberglass materials, except insulation

Somerton
Belmont County

(G-12212)
STUMPTOWN LBR PALLET MILLS LTD
55613 Washington St (43713-9794)
PHONE.................740 757-2275
EMP: 8 **EST:** 1995
SQ FT: 1,300
SALES (est): 761.31K **Privately Held**
Web: www.dixxeephoto.com
SIC: 2448 Pallets, wood

South Charleston
Clark County

(G-12213)
BUCKEYE DIAMOND LOGISTICS INC (PA)
Also Called: Bdl Supply
15 Sprague Rd (45368-9644)
PHONE....................................937 462-8361
Samuel J Mc Adow Junior, *Pr*
John Mcadow, *VP*
Marianne Hinson, *
EMP: 120 **EST:** 1969
SALES (est): 20.8MM
SALES (corp-wide): 20.8MM **Privately Held**
Web: www.bdlsupply.com
SIC: 2448 2441 Pallets, wood; Boxes, wood

(G-12214)
WOODFORD LOGISTICS
15 Sprague Rd (45368-9644)
PHONE....................................513 417-8453
Steven L Means, *Prin*
EMP: 9 **EST:** 2010
SQ FT: 60,000
SALES (est): 408.54K **Privately Held**
Web: www.woodfordlogistics.com
SIC: 2448 Pallets, wood

(G-12215)
YAMADA NORTH AMERICA INC
Also Called: Yotec
9000 Columbus Cincinnati Rd
(45368-9406)
P.O. Box Y (45368-0825)
PHONE....................................937 462-7111
Kiyoshi Osawa, *Pr*
William Mallory, *
John C Beeler, *
▲ **EMP:** 350 **EST:** 1946
SQ FT: 110,000
SALES (est): 29.21MM **Privately Held**
Web: www.yamadanorthamerica.com
SIC: 3714 3621 Motor vehicle steering
systems and parts; Rotors, for motors
PA: Yamada Manufacturing Co., Ltd.
2-1296, Kobayashicho
Isesaki GNM 379-2

South Euclid
Cuyahoga County

(G-12216)
AEROCONTROLEX GROUP INC
Also Called: Aerocontrolex
4223 Monticello Blvd (44121-2814)
PHONE....................................216 291-6025
Chris Swartz, *Pr*
EMP: 99 **EST:** 1954
SQ FT: 55,000
SALES (est): 21.51MM
SALES (corp-wide): 7.94B **Publicly Held**
Web: www.aerocontrolex.com
SIC: 3492 5084 3594 Valves, hydraulic,
aircraft; Industrial machinery and equipment
; Fluid power pumps and motors
HQ: Transdigm, Inc.
1350 Euclid Ave
Cleveland OH 44115

(G-12217)
AGRICOOL VEG & FRUITS LLC
310 S Green Rd (44121-2323)
PHONE....................................310 625-0024
EMP: 8 **EST:** 2020
SALES (est): 179.26K **Privately Held**

SIC: 2033 Vegetables and vegetable
products, in cans, jars, etc.

(G-12218)
AS CLEAN AS IT GETS OFF BRKROO
4099 Lowden Rd (44121-2314)
PHONE....................................216 256-1143
EMP: 26 **EST:** 2020
SALES (est): 1.05MM **Privately Held**
SIC: 3589 7389 Commercial cleaning
equipment; Business Activities at Non-
Commercial Site

(G-12219)
EJ USA INC
4160 Glenridge Rd (44121-2802)
PHONE....................................216 692-3001
Richard Humkes Junior, *Brnch Mgr*
EMP: 19
SQ FT: 11,397
Web: www.ejco.com
SIC: 3321 3322 Gray iron castings, nec;
Malleable iron foundries
HQ: Ej Usa, Inc.
301 Spring St
East Jordan MI 49727
800 874-4100

South Lebanon
Warren County

(G-12220)
OHIO FLEXIBLE PACKAGING CO
512 S Main St (45065-1441)
PHONE....................................513 494-1800
Larry Lehman, *Pr*
Juith Lehman, *Sec*
Frank Remmey, *VP*
EMP: 11 **EST:** 1984
SQ FT: 10,000
SALES (est): 983.89K **Privately Held**
Web: www.ohioflex.com
SIC: 2759 Flexographic printing

South Point
Lawrence County

(G-12221)
ALPHA CONTROL LLC
Also Called: Alpha Control Fabg & Mfg
1042 County Road 60 (45680-7465)
P.O. Box 1036 (45680-1036)
PHONE....................................740 377-3400
Greg Joseph, *Pr*
EMP: 35 **EST:** 2010
SQ FT: 60,000
SALES (est): 2.16MM **Privately Held**
Web: www.alphacontrolfab.com
SIC: 3441 Fabricated structural metal

(G-12222)
AMERICAN BOTTLING COMPANY
2531 County Road 1 (45680-7879)
PHONE....................................740 377-4371
Rick Hannon, *Mgr*
EMP: 75
Web: www.keurigdrpepper.com
SIC: 2086 Soft drinks: packaged in cans,
bottles, etc.
HQ: The American Bottling Company
6425 Hall Of Fame Ln
Frisco TX 75034

(G-12223)
ENGINES INC OF OHIO
101 Commerce Dr (45680-8457)
P.O. Box 428 (45680-0428)
PHONE....................................740 377-9874

Carl C Grover, *Pr*
David W Sanders, *
Daniel T Yon, *
EMP: 29 **EST:** 2005
SQ FT: 100,000
SALES (est): 4.89MM **Privately Held**
Web: www.engines-inc.com
SIC: 3321 3325 3743 3532 Railroad car
wheels and brake shoes, cast iron; Railroad
car wheels, cast steel; Interurban cars and
car equipment; Mining machinery

(G-12224)
JENNMAR MCSWEENEY LLC
235 Commerce Dr (45680-8465)
PHONE....................................740 377-3354
Joe Mcsweeney, *CEO*
Frank Calandra, *Pr*
Sandra Blackburn, *VP*
▲ **EMP:** 140 **EST:** 2013
SQ FT: 30,900
SALES (est): 3.25MM
SALES (corp-wide): 568.6MM **Privately
Held**
SIC: 3532 3531 Bits, except oil and gas field
tools, rock; Blades for graders, scrapers,
dozers, and snow plows
PA: Jennmar Holdings, Llc
258 Kappa Dr
Pittsburgh PA 15238
412 963-9071

(G-12225)
KINOLY SIGNS
Also Called: Sign-A-Rama
2485 County Road 1 (45680-7879)
PHONE....................................740 451-7446
EMP: 6 **EST:** 2017
SALES (est): 1.36MM **Privately Held**
Web: www.signarama.com
SIC: 3993 Signs and advertising specialties

(G-12226)
MCGINNIS INC (HQ)
502 2nd St E (45680-9446)
P.O. Box 534 (45680-0534)
PHONE....................................740 377-4391
Rickey Lee Griffith, *Pr*
Bruce D Mcginnis, *CEO*
Bill Jessie, *
D Dwaine Stephens, *
EMP: 193 **EST:** 1971
SQ FT: 5,000
SALES (est): 24.65MM **Privately Held**
Web: www.mcnational.com
SIC: 4491 3731 Marine cargo handling;
Barges, building and repairing
PA: Mcnational, Inc.
502 2nd St E
South Point OH 45680

(G-12227)
MCNATIONAL INC (PA)
502 2nd St E (45680-9446)
P.O. Box 534 (45680-0534)
PHONE....................................740 377-4391
Rick Griffith, *Pr*
C Clayton Johnson, *
C Barry Gipson, *
Bruce D Mcginnis, *CEO*
EMP: 97 **EST:** 1988
SQ FT: 5,000
SALES (est): 76.09MM **Privately Held**
Web: www.mcnational.com
SIC: 3731 7699 4491 Barges, building and
repairing; Aircraft and heavy equipment
repair services; Marine cargo handling

(G-12228)
MCSWEENEYS INC
235 Commerce Dr (45680-8465)

PHONE....................................740 894-3353
▲ **EMP:** 140
SIC: 3532 3531 Bits, except oil and gas field
tools, rock; Blades for graders, scrapers,
dozers, and snow plows

(G-12229)
PRECISIONS PAINT SYSTEMS LLC
5852 County Road 1 (45680-7420)
PHONE....................................740 894-6224
Michael Manns, *CEO*
EMP: 10 **EST:** 2015
SALES (est): 944.61K **Privately Held**
SIC: 2851 Marine paints

(G-12230)
PYRO-CHEM CORPORATION
Also Called: Better Foam Insulation
2491 County Road 1 (45680-7879)
P.O. Box 884 (45680-0884)
PHONE....................................740 377-2244
Joseph P Smith, *Pr*
Gailene M Smith, *Sec*
EMP: 14 **EST:** 1978
SQ FT: 12,000
SALES (est): 2.17MM **Privately Held**
SIC: 2899 Fire retardant chemicals

South Webster
Scioto County

(G-12231)
MAE MATERIALS LLC
8336 Bennett School House Rd
(45682-9029)
PHONE....................................740 778-2242
Mark Allard, *Managing Member*
EMP: 23 **EST:** 2012
SQ FT: 108,900
SALES (est): 593.78K **Privately Held**
SIC: 2951 Asphalt paving mixtures and
blocks

South Zanesville
Muskingum County

(G-12232)
COCONIS FURNITURE INC (PA)
4 S Maysville Ave (43701-7401)
PHONE....................................740 452-1231
▲ **EMP:** 45 **EST:** 1927
SALES (est): 7.74MM
SALES (corp-wide): 7.74MM **Privately
Held**
Web: www.coconisfurniture.com
SIC: 5712 2515 Furniture stores; Mattresses
and bedsprings

Spencer
Medina County

(G-12233)
ALTA MIRA CORPORATION
Also Called: Spencer Forge & Manufacturing
225 N Main St (44275-9759)
PHONE....................................330 648-2461
Laurence E Rich, *Pr*
Deborah Rich, *
EMP: 65 **EST:** 1986
SQ FT: 83,000
SALES (est): 9.99MM **Privately Held**
Web: www.spencerforge.com
SIC: 3714 3462 Axles, motor vehicle; Iron
and steel forgings

▲ = Import ▼ = Export
◆ = Import/Export

(G-12234)
NICK KOSTECKI EXCAVATING INC
10644 Chatham Rd (44275-9333)
PHONE..................................330 242-0706
Leah A Kostecki, *Pr*
EMP: 26 **EST:** 2007
SALES (est): 1.72MM **Privately Held**
SIC: 3531 Plows: construction, excavating, and grading

(G-12235)
SPENCER FEED & SUPPLY LLC
227 N Main St (44275-9759)
PHONE..................................330 648-2111
EMP: 11 **EST:** 2016
SALES (est): 1.04MM **Privately Held**
Web: www.spencerfeed.com
SIC: 5251 2048 0782 Hardware stores; Livestock feeds; Garden services

(G-12236)
SPENCER MANUFACTURING COMPANY INC
Also Called: Spencer Forge & Manufacturing
225 N Main St (44275-9759)
P.O. Box 68 (44275-0068)
PHONE..................................330 648-2461
EMP: 70
Web: www.spencerforge.com
SIC: 3714 3542 Axles, motor vehicle; Machine tools, metal forming type

Spencerville
Allen County

(G-12237)
D&D INGREDIENT DISTRS INC
Also Called: D&D Ingredients LLC
1610 S Acadia Rd (45887-9517)
PHONE..................................419 692-2667
Arnold Miller, *Pr*
Ted Williams, *COO*
EMP: 78 **EST:** 1988
SALES (est): 1.1MM **Privately Held**
SIC: 2048 Cereal-, grain-, and seed-based feeds

(G-12238)
OHIO DECORATIVE PRODUCTS LLC
(PA)
220 S Elizabeth St (45887-1315)
P.O. Box 126 (45887-0126)
PHONE..................................419 647-9033
Charles D Moeller, *Pr*
Rick Moeller, *
Candace Moeller, *
Donald L Jerwers, *
George J Bowers, *
◆ **EMP:** 135 **EST:** 1970
SQ FT: 5,000
SALES (est): 3.59MM
SALES (corp-wide): 3.59MM **Privately Held**
SIC: 3086 3369 3471 3363 Plastics foam products; Zinc and zinc-base alloy castings, except die-castings; Plating and polishing; Aluminum die-castings

(G-12239)
PFP HOLDINGS LLC
220 S Elizabeth St (45887-1315)
P.O. Box 126 (45887-0126)
PHONE..................................419 647-4191
◆ **EMP:** 750
SIC: 3069 5199 Foam rubber; Foam rubber

(G-12240)
S I DISTRIBUTING INC
Also Called: Holland Grills Distributing
13540 Spencerville Rd (45887-9525)
PHONE..................................419 647-4909
Dave Durgei, *Pr*
Todd Keysor, *Prin*
▲ **EMP:** 13 **EST:** 1993
SQ FT: 22,000
SALES (est): 2.74MM **Privately Held**
Web: www.sidist.com
SIC: 3523 5083 5023 Cabs, tractors, and agricultural machinery; Agricultural machinery and equipment; Grills, barbecue

Spring Valley
Greene County

(G-12241)
ADVANCED TELEMETRICS INTL
Also Called: A T I
2361 Darnell Dr (45370-8708)
PHONE..................................937 862-6948
Phillip Merrill, *Pr*
EMP: 11 **EST:** 1987
SQ FT: 3,000
SALES (est): 2.33MM **Privately Held**
Web: www.atitelemetry.com
SIC: 3829 Measuring and controlling devices, nec

(G-12242)
PMRSERVICES LLC ✪
Also Called: Millwright
2543 Us Route 42 (45370-9811)
PHONE..................................937 219-0062
Michael King, *CEO*
Michael King, *Managing Member*
EMP: 11 **EST:** 2024
SALES (est): 521.64K **Privately Held**
Web: pmrservicesllc.com
SIC: 1796 1799 7692 7389 Machinery dismantling; Welding on site; Welding repair ; Business Activities at Non-Commercial Site

(G-12243)
SAILORS TAILOR INC
Also Called: Bean Bag City
1480 Spring Valley Painters Rd (45370-9701)
PHONE..................................937 862-7781
Robert Rowland, *Pr*
Sandra Rowland, *Mgr*
EMP: 10 **EST:** 1972
SQ FT: 2,400
SALES (est): 482.83K **Privately Held**
Web: www.beanbag.com
SIC: 2394 2519 5712 5551 Liners and covers, fabric: made from purchased materials; Household furniture, except wood or metal: upholstered; Furniture stores ; Marine supplies and equipment

Springboro
Warren County

(G-12244)
ADVANCED ENGRG SOLUTIONS INC
Also Called: Aesi
250 Advanced Dr (45066-1802)
PHONE..................................937 743-6900
Khang D.o.s., *Pr*
Thomas J Harrington, *
▲ **EMP:** 70 **EST:** 1995
SQ FT: 44,000
SALES (est): 7.27MM **Privately Held**
Web: www.advancedinternational.com

SIC: 8711 3544 Consulting engineer; Special dies, tools, jigs, and fixtures

(G-12245)
ADVANCED INTR SOLUTIONS INC
250 Advanced Dr (45066-1802)
PHONE..................................937 550-0065
Jeffrey S Senney, *Prin*
Khang D.o.s., *VP*
▲ **EMP:** 48 **EST:** 2005
SALES (est): 6.08MM **Privately Held**
Web: www.advancedinternational.com
SIC: 3544 Special dies, tools, jigs, and fixtures

(G-12246)
ALFONS HAAR INC
150 Advanced Dr (45066-1800)
PHONE..................................937 560-2031
Thomas Haar, *Pr*
Bernd Haar, *
◆ **EMP:** 31 **EST:** 1993
SQ FT: 5,000
SALES (est): 8.64MM
SALES (corp-wide): 63.34MM **Privately Held**
Web: www.alfons-haar.us
SIC: 5084 3599 8711 Packaging machinery and equipment; Custom machinery; Engineering services
PA: Alfons Haar Maschinenbau Gmbh & Co. Kg
Fangdieckstr. 67
Hamburg HH 22547
40833910

(G-12247)
BLUE FIN ENVIRONMENTAL LLC
8753 Sycamore Trails Dr (45066-9664)
PHONE..................................330 415-6010
Heather Moorman, *Prin*
Bob Hellman, *CFO*
EMP: 6 **EST:** 2019
SALES (est): 162.51K **Privately Held**
SIC: 1389 Construction, repair, and dismantling services

(G-12248)
BUCKEYE FABRICATING COMPANY
245 S Pioneer Blvd (45066-1180)
PHONE..................................937 746-9822
Richard K Macaulay, *Pr*
Teri Macaulay, *
▼ **EMP:** 33 **EST:** 1963
SQ FT: 20,000
SALES (est): 7.29MM
SALES (corp-wide): 47.46MM **Privately Held**
Web: www.buckeyefabricating.com
SIC: 3443 Tanks, standard or custom fabricated: metal plate
PA: Lt Corporation, Inc.
2914 Hwy 61
Cleveland MS 38732
800 345-2495

(G-12249)
COACH TOOL & DIE LLC
235 S Pioneer Blvd (45066-1180)
PHONE..................................937 890-4716
Dave Hollon, *Pr*
Gregg Kopp, *VP*
EMP: 6 **EST:** 1998
SALES (est): 1.02MM **Privately Held**
Web: www.coachtoolinc.com
SIC: 3544 Special dies and tools

(G-12250)
DIGILUBE SYSTEMS INC
216 E Mill St (45066-1614)
PHONE..................................937 748-2209

David Hamilton, *Pr*
EMP: 10 **EST:** 1981
SQ FT: 5,000
SALES (est): 4.99MM **Privately Held**
Web: www.digilube.com
SIC: 3569 2992 5084 5172 Lubricating equipment; Oils and greases, blending and compounding; Conveyor systems; Lubricating oils and greases

(G-12251)
EPLUNO LLC
420 Heatherwoode Cir (45066-1528)
PHONE..................................800 249-5275
EMP: 17 **EST:** 2012
SALES (est): 1.42MM **Privately Held**
Web: www.epluno.com
SIC: 2326 Men's and boy's work clothing

(G-12252)
FEATHER LITE INNOVATIONS INC
(PA)
Also Called: Tuf-N-Lite
650 Pleasant Valley Dr (45066-3026)
PHONE..................................937 743-9008
Dallas Meyers, *Pr*
Brent Cox, *VP*
▲ **EMP:** 20 **EST:** 1995
SALES (est): 1.57MM **Privately Held**
Web: www.tuf-n-lite.com
SIC: 3444 5211 Concrete forms, sheet metal ; Masonry materials and supplies

(G-12253)
GENERAL DYNAMICS-OTS INC
Also Called: General Dynamics
200 S Pioneer Blvd (45066-1179)
PHONE..................................937 746-8500
Anne-marie Stanley, *Dir*
EMP: 178
SQ FT: 220,000
SALES (corp-wide): 47.72B **Publicly Held**
Web: www.gd-ots.com
SIC: 3728 Aircraft parts and equipment, nec
HQ: General Dynamics-Ots, Inc.
100 Carillon Pkwy Ste 100
Saint Petersburg FL 33716
727 578-8100

(G-12254)
GRAPHIC SYSTEMS SERVICES INC
Also Called: G S S
400 S Pioneer Blvd (45066-3001)
PHONE..................................937 746-0708
Daniel L Green, *Pr*
John Sillies, *
EMP: 41 **EST:** 1995
SQ FT: 100,000
SALES (est): 12.55MM
SALES (corp-wide): 1.04B **Publicly Held**
Web: www.didde.com
SIC: 7699 3555 Industrial equipment services ; Printing presses
PA: Eastman Kodak Company
343 State St
Rochester NY 14650
800 356-3259

(G-12255)
HIGH CONCRETE GROUP LLC
95 Mound Park Dr (45066-2402)
PHONE..................................937 748-2412
Dennis Nemenz, *Brnch Mgr*
EMP: 255
SALES (corp-wide): 658.1MM **Privately Held**
Web: www.highconcrete.com
SIC: 3272 Concrete structural support and building material
HQ: High Concrete Group Llc
125 Denver Rd

Denver PA 17517
717 735-1060

(G-12256)
JK DIGITAL PUBLISHING LLC
Also Called: Greyden Press
20 Heatherwoode Cir (45066-1500)
P.O. Box 224 (44652-0224)
PHONE.....................937 299-0185
EMP: 7 **EST:** 1991
SQ FT: 7,500
SALES (est): 153.48K **Privately Held**
SIC: 2752 3652 Commercial printing, lithographic; Compact laser discs, prerecorded

(G-12257)
KASKELL MANUFACTURING INC
Also Called: Kaskell
240 Hiawatha Trl (45066-3010)
P.O. Box 83 (45305-0083)
PHONE.....................937 704-9700
Diane W Harris, *Pr*
Brian Harris, *VP*
EMP: 10 **EST:** 1996
SQ FT: 4,500
SALES (est): 1.38MM **Privately Held**
Web: www.kaskellmfg.com
SIC: 3599 Machine shop, jobbing and repair

(G-12258)
KELCHNER INC (DH)
50 Advanced Dr (45066-1805)
PHONE.....................937 704-9890
Todd Kelchner, *CEO*
Troy Norvell, *
EMP: 92 **EST:** 1948
SQ FT: 8,600
SALES (est): 45.41MM
SALES (corp-wide): 5.9B **Privately Held**
Web: www.kelchner.com
SIC: 1794 1389 Excavation work; Mud service, oil field drilling
HQ: Wood Group Uk Limited
Sir Ian Wood House
Aberdeen AB12
122 450-0400

(G-12259)
MACHINED GLASS SPECIALIST INC
245 Hiawatha Trl (45066-3011)
PHONE.....................937 743-6166
David Behm, *Pr*
Melanie Behm, *Sec*
Maurice Vines, *Genl Mgr*
EMP: 6 **EST:** 1989
SQ FT: 9,000
SALES (est): 896.96K **Privately Held**
Web: www.mgsfusedquartz.com
SIC: 5039 3211 Glass construction materials ; Tempered glass

(G-12260)
MOUND TECHNOLOGIES INC
25 Mound Park Dr (45066-2402)
PHONE.....................937 748-2937
Thomas Miller, *Pr*
John Barger, *
Shelia A Campbell, *
EMP: 45 **EST:** 2003
SQ FT: 40,000
SALES (est): 29.52MM
SALES (corp-wide): 54.68MM **Privately Held**
Web: www.moundtechnologies.com
SIC: 3441 1791 3446 Building components, structural steel; Structural steel erection; Gates, ornamental metal
PA: Heartland, Inc.
1005 N 19th St
Middlesboro KY 40965

606 248-7323

(G-12261)
NO RINSE LABORATORIES LLC
Also Called: Cleanlife Products
868 Pleasant Valley Dr (45066-1159)
PHONE.....................937 746-7357
EMP: 7 **EST:** 1948
SQ FT: 6,000
SALES (est): 4.21MM **Privately Held**
Web: www.cleanlifeproducts.com
SIC: 2836 Veterinary biological products

(G-12262)
OHIO TOOL & JIG GRIND INC
6948 Clearview Ct (45066-7000)
PHONE.....................937 415-0692
David A Brinker, *Pr*
EMP: 7 **EST:** 1999
SALES (est): 427.85K **Privately Held**
Web: www.otjg.org
SIC: 3544 Special dies, tools, jigs, and fixtures

(G-12263)
PHYMET INC
75 N Pioneer Blvd (45066-3055)
PHONE.....................937 743-8061
Amy Minck Lachman, *Pr*
EMP: 17 **EST:** 1986
SQ FT: 12,500
SALES (est): 2.94MM **Privately Held**
Web: www.micropoly.com
SIC: 2992 8734 Oils and greases, blending and compounding; Metallurgical testing laboratory

(G-12264)
PSIX LLC
Also Called: Paper Systems Incorporated
185 S Pioneer Blvd (45066-3045)
P.O. Box 150 (45066-0150)
PHONE.....................937 746-6841
Bryan Eovaldi, *Pr*
EMP: 100 **EST:** 2018
SALES (est): 10.55MM **Privately Held**
Web: www.papersystems.com
SIC: 2679 Paper products, converted, nec

(G-12265)
QUICK TECH BUSINESS FORMS INC
408 Sharts Dr (45066-3000)
P.O. Box 607 (45066-0607)
PHONE.....................937 743-5952
Kevin Gilliam, *Mgr*
Chris Felker, *
Linda Felker, *
EMP: 8 **EST:** 1990
SALES (est): 520.17K **Privately Held**
SIC: 2759 3999 Financial note and certificate printing and engraving; Barber and beauty shop equipment

(G-12266)
QUICK TECH GRAPHICS INC
408 Sharts Dr Frnt (45066-3021)
P.O. Box 607 (45066-0607)
PHONE.....................937 743-5952
Christopher H Felker, *Pr*
Linda Felker, *
EMP: 17 **EST:** 1990
SQ FT: 15,000
SALES (est): 4.73MM **Privately Held**
Web: www.quicktechgraphics.com
SIC: 2761 5943 2791 2782 Manifold business forms; Office forms and supplies; Typesetting; Blankbooks and looseleaf binders

(G-12267)
SAFE HAVEN BRANDS LLC
Also Called: DK Bicycles
217 S Pioneer Blvd (45066-1183)
PHONE.....................937 550-9407
EMP: 14 **EST:** 2015
SALES (est): 4.54MM **Privately Held**
SIC: 3751 Bicycles and related parts

(G-12268)
SUNSTAR ENGRG AMERICAS INC (HQ)
Also Called: Sunstar
85 S Pioneer Blvd (45066-3039)
PHONE.....................937 746-8575
Yoshikazu Kuwahara, *Pr*
▲ **EMP:** 32 **EST:** 1993
SQ FT: 28,000
SALES (est): 49.33MM **Privately Held**
Web: www.sunstar-braking.com
SIC: 3751 2891 Motorcycles and related parts; Adhesives
PA: Starlecs Inc.
3-1, Asahimachi
Takatsuki OSK 569-1

(G-12269)
THALER MACHINE COMPANY LLC
216 Tahlequah Trl (45066-3052)
P.O. Box 430 (45066-0430)
PHONE.....................937 550-2400
▲ **EMP:** 135 **EST:** 1952
SALES (est): 22.04MM
SALES (corp-wide): 24.55MM **Privately Held**
Web: www.thalermachine.com
SIC: 3545 Precision measuring tools
PA: Thaler Machine Holdings, Llc
216 Tahlequah Trl
Springboro OH 45066
937 550-2400

(G-12270)
THALER MACHINE HOLDINGS LLC (PA)
216 Tahlequah Trl (45066-3052)
P.O. Box 430 (45066-0430)
PHONE.....................937 550-2400
Greg Donson, *CEO*
EMP: 12 **EST:** 2019
SQ FT: 22,000
SALES (est): 24.55MM
SALES (corp-wide): 24.55MM **Privately Held**
Web: www.thalermachine.com
SIC: 3545 Precision measuring tools

(G-12271)
TOOLING ZONE INC
285 S Pioneer Blvd (45066-1180)
PHONE.....................937 550-4180
Steven D liams, *Pr*
EMP: 30 **EST:** 1995
SQ FT: 9,000
SALES (est): 6.07MM **Privately Held**
Web: www.toolingzone.com
SIC: 3544 Special dies and tools

(G-12272)
TREBNICK SYSTEMS LLC
Also Called: Trebnick Tags and Labels
215 S Pioneer Blvd (45066-1180)
PHONE.....................937 743-1550
Gregg Trebnick, *CEO*
Linda Trebnick, *
Aaron Trebnick, *
◆ **EMP:** 29 **EST:** 1986
SQ FT: 24,480
SALES (est): 9.53MM **Privately Held**
Web: www.trebnick.com

SIC: 2752 2759 Tags, lithographed; Bags, plastic: printing, nsk

---

Springdale
Hamilton County

(G-12273)
GE AVIATION SYSTEMS LLC
Also Called: GE Aviation
183 Progress Pl (45246-1717)
PHONE.....................620 218-5237
David Joyce, *CEO*
EMP: 34
SALES (corp-wide): 38.7B **Publicly Held**
Web: www.geaerospace.com
SIC: 3313 Alloys, additive, except copper: not made in blast furnaces
HQ: Ge Aviation Systems Llc
1 Neumann Way
Cincinnati OH 45215
937 898-9600

Springfield
Clark County

(G-12274)
A & E POWDER COATING LTD
1511 Sheridan Ave (45505-2257)
P.O. Box 1226 (45501-1226)
PHONE.....................937 525-3750
Edward Leventhal, *Pr*
EMP: 7 **EST:** 2000
SALES (est): 906.93K **Privately Held**
Web: www.aepowdercoating.com
SIC: 3479 Coating of metals and formed products

(G-12275)
ACCURIDE CORPORATION
4800 Gateway Blvd (45502-8818)
PHONE.....................937 323-9669
EMP: 12
Web: www.accuridecorp.com
SIC: 3714 Wheels, motor vehicle
HQ: Accuride Corporation
38777 6 Mile Rd Ste 410
Livonia MI 48152
812 962-5000

(G-12276)
ACE TRANSFER COMPANY
1020 Hometown St (45504-2055)
PHONE.....................937 398-1103
David J Shaw, *Pr*
EMP: 6 **EST:** 1994
SALES (est): 444.98K **Privately Held**
Web: www.acetransco.com
SIC: 2759 Screen printing

(G-12277)
AKZO NOBEL COATINGS INC
1550 Progress Rd (45505-4456)
PHONE.....................937 322-2671
Ron Cecil, *Mgr*
EMP: 30
SALES (corp-wide): 11.6B **Privately Held**
SIC: 2851 Paints: oil or alkyd vehicle or water thinned
HQ: Akzo Nobel Coatings Inc.
535 Marriott Dr Ste 500
Nashville TN 37214
440 297-5100

(G-12278)
ALL-IN NUTRITIONALS LLC
5060 S Charleston Pike (45502-6315)
PHONE.....................888 400-0333
Lindsey Duncan, *CEO*

EMP: 10 **EST:** 2018
SALES (est): 513.24K **Privately Held**
Web: www.allinnutritionals.com
SIC: 2023 Dietary supplements, dairy and non-dairy based

(G-12279)
AMCAN STAIR & RAIL LLC
20 Zischler St (45504-2853)
PHONE.................................937 781-3084
Mike Edmondson, *Prin*
EMP: 7 **EST:** 2001
SALES (est): 1.19MM **Privately Held**
Web: www.amcanstairandrail.com
SIC: 2431 Staircases and stairs, wood

(G-12280)
AOT LLC
Also Called: Aot Inc.
4800 Gateway Blvd (45502-8818)
PHONE.................................937 323-9669
Richard F Dauch, *CEO*
EMP: 11 **EST:** 1991
SQ FT: 136,000
SALES (est): 3.58MM **Privately Held**
Web: www.accuridecorp.com
SIC: 3559 Pack-up assemblies, wheel overhaul
HQ: Accuride Corporation
   38777 6 Mile Rd Ste 410
   Livonia MI 48152
   812 962-5000

(G-12281)
APPETZERS R US ST EATS 2 GO LL
2019 Ontario Ave (45505-4733)
PHONE.................................937 460-1470
EMP: 6 **EST:** 2021
SALES (est): 236.34K **Privately Held**
SIC: 2599 7389 Food wagons, restaurant; Business services, nec

(G-12282)
ARCTECH FABRICATING INC (PA)
1317 Lagonda Ave (45503-4001)
P.O. Box 1447 (45501-1447)
PHONE.................................937 525-9353
James C Roberts Ii, *Pr*
Tina Roberts, *
Leonard Mcconnaghey, *CEO*
EMP: 29 **EST:** 1992
SQ FT: 13,200
SALES (est): 6.23MM **Privately Held**
Web: www.arctechfabricating.com
SIC: 7692 3441 Welding repair; Fabricated structural metal

(G-12283)
ARMOLOY OF OHIO INC
1950 E Leffel Ln (45505-4623)
P.O. Box 996 (45501-0996)
PHONE.................................937 323-8702
Steven Neely, *Pr*
EMP: 16 **EST:** 1976
SQ FT: 10,000
SALES (est): 1.58MM **Privately Held**
Web: www.armoloyofohio.com
SIC: 3479 Coating of metals and formed products

(G-12284)
BAN INC
Also Called: Harwood Screw Products
619 S Belmont Ave (45505-2325)
P.O. Box 194 (45501-0194)
PHONE.................................937 325-5539
Bruce Lloyd, *Pr*
Douglas R Lloyd, *
Neita Lloyd, *
EMP: 25 **EST:** 1947
SQ FT: 9,000

SALES (est): 285.48K **Privately Held**
SIC: 3451 Screw machine products

(G-12285)
BAY BUSINESS FORMS INC
1803 W Columbia St (45504-2903)
PHONE.................................937 322-3000
Paulette Bay, *Pr*
Robert E Troop, *CEO*
EMP: 12 **EST:** 1974
SQ FT: 22,000
SALES (est): 896.4K **Privately Held**
SIC: 5112 2752 Business forms; Offset printing
PA: The Shamrock Companies Inc
   24090 Detroit Rd
   Westlake OH 44145

(G-12286)
BRIDGESTONE RET OPERATIONS LLC
Also Called: Firestone
1475 Upper Valley Pike (45504-4023)
PHONE.................................937 325-4638
David Weeks, *Mgr*
EMP: 10
Web: www.bridgestoneamericas.com
SIC: 5531 7534 Automotive tires; Tire retreading and repair shops
HQ: Bridgestone Retail Operations, Llc
   200 4th Ave S Ste 100
   Nashville TN 37201
   615 937-1000

(G-12287)
CASCADE CORPORATION
2501 Sheridan Ave (45505-2519)
P.O. Box 20187 (97294-0187)
PHONE.................................937 327-0300
Rodney Hitman, *Brnch Mgr*
EMP: 33
Web: www.cascorp.com
SIC: 3537 3713 3593 Trucks, tractors, loaders, carriers, and similar equipment; Truck and bus bodies; Fluid power cylinders and actuators
HQ: Cascade Corporation
   2201 Ne 201st Ave
   Fairview OR 97024
   503 669-6300

(G-12288)
CAVE TOOL & MFG INC
20 Walnut St (45505-1145)
PHONE.................................937 324-0662
Gilbert R Cave, *Pr*
Carrie Cave, *VP*
EMP: 10 **EST:** 1967
SQ FT: 26,000
SALES (est): 246.25K **Privately Held**
SIC: 3599 Machine shop, jobbing and repair

(G-12289)
CES NATIONWIDE
567 E Leffel Ln (45505-4748)
PHONE.................................937 322-0771
John Lewis, *Prin*
EMP: 7 **EST:** 2009
SALES (est): 529.5K **Privately Held**
SIC: 3699 3634 5063 Electrical equipment and supplies, nec; Electric housewares and fans; Electrical supplies, nec

(G-12290)
CHAMPION COMPANY
Also Called: Champion
1100 Kenton St (45505-3136)
PHONE.................................937 324-5681
Bob Rizer, *Genl Mgr*
EMP: 8
SALES (corp-wide): 10.59MM **Privately Held**

Web: www.thechampioncompany.com
SIC: 3412 Metal barrels, drums, and pails
PA: The Champion Company
   400 Harrison St
   Springfield OH 45505
   937 324-5681

(G-12291)
CHAMPION COMPANY (PA)
Also Called: Champion Companies, The
400 Harrison St (45505-2067)
P.O. Box 967 (45501-0967)
PHONE.................................937 324-5681
Aristides Gianakopoulos, *Pr*
Benjamin G Devoe, *
EMP: 60 **EST:** 1878
SQ FT: 165,000
SALES (est): 10.59MM
SALES (corp-wide): 10.59MM **Privately Held**
Web: www.championgse.com
SIC: 2869 3412 Embalming fluids; Metal barrels, drums, and pails

(G-12292)
COLBY PROPERTIES LLC
2071 N Bechtle Ave (45504-1583)
PHONE.................................937 390-0816
EMP: 6 **EST:** 2002
SALES (est): 565.21K **Privately Held**
Web: www.privatelendingmadeeasy.com
SIC: 3999 Education aids, devices and supplies

(G-12293)
COMPTONS PRECISION MACHINE
Also Called: Eastern Enterprise
224 Dayton Ave (45506-1206)
P.O. Box 2614 (45501-2614)
PHONE.................................937 325-9139
John Compton, *Pr*
Denise Compton, *Sec*
EMP: 12 **EST:** 1981
SQ FT: 11,000
SALES (est): 1.65MM **Privately Held**
SIC: 3599 7692 Machine shop, jobbing and repair; Welding repair

(G-12294)
CORROTEC INC
1125 W North St (45504-2713)
PHONE.................................937 325-3585
David A Stratton, *CEO*
Aristides G Gianakopoulos, *
John C Stratton, *
Walter A Wildman, *
EMP: 25 **EST:** 1981
SQ FT: 28,500
SALES (est): 9.84MM **Privately Held**
Web: www.corrotec.com
SIC: 3559 7699 3479 3625 Electroplating machinery and equipment; Tank repair; Coating of metals with plastic or resins; Electric controls and control accessories, industrial

(G-12295)
CRANE PRO SERVICES
4401 Gateway Blvd (45502-9339)
PHONE.................................937 525-5555
George Berner, *Engr*
EMP: 8 **EST:** 2015
SALES (est): 1.12MM **Privately Held**
Web: www.konecranes.com
SIC: 3536 Hoists, cranes, and monorails

(G-12296)
CROWNING FOOD COMPANY
Also Called: Wober Muster
1966 Commerce Cir (45504-2012)
P.O. Box 388 (45501-0388)

PHONE.................................937 323-4699
Ray Woeber, *Owner*
◆ **EMP:** 85 **EST:** 1905
SALES (est): 8.03MM **Privately Held**
Web: www.woebermustard.com
SIC: 2035 Pickles, sauces, and salad dressings

(G-12297)
CUSTOM RECAPPING INC
Also Called: Custom Tire
126 Linden Ave (45505-1015)
PHONE.................................937 324-4331
Brian W House, *Pr*
Carolyn House, *Sec*
EMP: 6 **EST:** 1954
SQ FT: 10,000
SALES (est): 241.64K **Privately Held**
Web: www.customtire.biz
SIC: 5531 7534 Automotive tires; Tire recapping

(G-12298)
DEARTH RESOURCES INC (PA)
Also Called: Hill Bryce Concrete
2301 Sheridan Ave (45505-2515)
P.O. Box 1043 (45501-1043)
PHONE.................................937 325-0651
Debra Grimes, *Pr*
EMP: 6 **EST:** 1934
SQ FT: 20,000
SALES (est): 282.14K
SALES (corp-wide): 282.14K **Privately Held**
Web: www.brycehill.com
SIC: 3273 3271 5211 Ready-mixed concrete ; Blocks, concrete or cinder: standard; Lumber and other building materials

(G-12299)
DEARTH RESOURCES INC
8801 State Route 36 (45501)
P.O. Box 1043 (45501-1043)
PHONE.................................937 663-4171
Debra Grimes, *Pr*
EMP: 8
SALES (corp-wide): 282.14K **Privately Held**
Web: www.brycehill.com
SIC: 3273 3271 Ready-mixed concrete; Blocks, concrete or cinder: standard
PA: Dearth Resources, Inc.
   2301 Sheridan Ave
   Springfield OH 45505
   937 325-0651

(G-12300)
DELILLE OXYGEN COMPANY
1101 W Columbia St (45504-2846)
PHONE.................................937 325-9595
Mike Lee, *Mgr*
EMP: 8
SALES (corp-wide): 25.83MM **Privately Held**
Web: www.delille.com
SIC: 2813 5084 Industrial gases; Welding machinery and equipment
PA: Delille Oxygen Company
   772 Marion Rd
   Columbus OH 43207
   614 444-1177

(G-12301)
DEMMY SAND AND GRAVEL LLC
4324 Fairfield Pike (45502-9707)
EMP: 25 **EST:** 1944
SALES (est): 850.99K **Privately Held**
SIC: 1442 0115 0119 0111 Common sand mining; Corn; Bean (dry field and seed) farm ; Wheat

(G-12302)
DILLON MANUFACTURING INC
2115 Progress Rd (45505-4470)
PHONE..............................937 325-8482
Joseph Shouvlin, *Pr*
EMP: 19 **EST:** 1953
SQ FT: 15,000
SALES (est): 2.7MM **Privately Held**
Web: www.dillonmfg.com
SIC: 3599 Machine shop, jobbing and repair

(G-12303)
DOLE FRESH VEGETABLES INC
Also Called: Dole
600 Benjamin Dr (45502-8860)
PHONE..............................937 525-4300
Lenny Pelifian, *Brnch Mgr*
EMP: 190
SALES (corp-wide): 3.83B **Privately Held**
Web: www.dole.com
SIC: 5148 2099 Fruits, fresh; Food
preparations, nec
HQ: Dole Fresh Vegetables, Inc.
2959 Salinas Hwy
Monterey CA 93940

(G-12304)
**DUPLEX MILL & MANUFACTURING
CO**
Also Called: Kelly Duplex
415 Sigler St (45506-1144)
P.O. Box 1266 (45501-1266)
PHONE..............................937 325-5555
Eric W Wise, *Pr*
Frederick Wise, *VP*
EMP: 20 **EST:** 1908
SQ FT: 50,000
SALES (est): 2.26MM **Privately Held**
Web: www.dmmc.com
SIC: 3535 3531 Conveyors and conveying
equipment; Mixers, nec: ore, plaster, slag,
sand, mortar, etc.

(G-12305)
ECHO THERM LLC
2755 Columbus Rd (45503-3203)
PHONE..............................937 322-5972
EMP: 13 **EST:** 2020
SALES (est): 600K **Privately Held**
Web: www.echotherminc.com
SIC: 3829 Thermometers, liquid-in-glass and
bimetal type

(G-12306)
ELECTRIC EEL MFG CO INC
501 W Leffel Ln (45506-3529)
P.O. Box 419 (45501-0419)
PHONE..............................937 323-4644
David Hale, *CEO*
Thomas H Hale, *
▲ **EMP:** 38 **EST:** 1968
SQ FT: 21,000
SALES (est): 4.92MM **Privately Held**
Web: www.electriceel.com
SIC: 3423 3589 Hand and edge tools, nec;
Sewer cleaning equipment, power

(G-12307)
ERNEST INDUSTRIES INC
Also Called: Kelly-Creswell Company
1221 Groop Rd (45504-3829)
PHONE..............................937 325-9851
EMP: 11 **EST:** 1995
SALES (est): 2.65MM **Privately Held**
Web: www.ernestindustries.com
SIC: 3563 Air and gas compressors

(G-12308)
ESTERLINE & SONS MFG CO LLC
6508 Old Clifton Rd (45502-8474)

PHONE..............................937 265-5278
John Maurer, *Managing Member*
▲ **EMP:** 22 **EST:** 1957
SQ FT: 1,500
SALES (est): 4.58MM **Privately Held**
Web: www.esterlineandsons.com
SIC: 3599 Machine shop, jobbing and repair

(G-12309)
EVER ROLL SPECIALTIES CO
3988 Lawrenceville Dr (45504-4499)
PHONE..............................937 964-1302
John Hadley, *CEO*
Edwin J Kohl, *
I Scott Wallace, *
▲ **EMP:** 24 **EST:** 1945
SQ FT: 43,000
SALES (est): 4.89MM **Privately Held**
Web: www.ever-roll.com
SIC: 3498 3496 Tube fabricating (contract
bending and shaping); Miscellaneous
fabricated wire products

(G-12310)
FAMILY PACKAGING INC (PA)
504 W Euclid Ave (45506-2010)
PHONE..............................937 325-4106
Janet Kennedy, *Pr*
James Miles, *VP*
EMP: 6 **EST:** 1992
SQ FT: 47,000
SALES (est): 2.06MM **Privately Held**
SIC: 2653 Boxes, corrugated: made from
purchased materials

(G-12311)
FINK MEAT COMPANY INC
2475 Troy Rd (45504-4233)
P.O. Box 1281 (45501-1281)
PHONE..............................937 390-2750
William Craig Minter, *Pr*
Douglas Minter, *VP*
EMP: 7 **EST:** 1921
SQ FT: 8,600
SALES (est): 677.17K **Privately Held**
Web: www.finkmeatco.com
SIC: 5147 2013 Meats, fresh; Luncheon
meat, from purchased meat

(G-12312)
FLASHIONS SPORTSWEAR LTD
1002 N Bechtle Ave (45504-2008)
PHONE..............................937 323-5885
Ronald Turner, *Genl Pt*
Bethany Turner, *Pt*
EMP: 9 **EST:** 1987
SQ FT: 4,000
SALES (est): 512.9K **Privately Held**
Web: www.flashions.com
SIC: 5199 2262 Advertising specialties;
Screen printing: manmade fiber and silk
broadwoven fabrics

(G-12313)
FLUID QUIP KS LLC
1940 S Yellow Springs St Ste 2
(45506-3048)
PHONE..............................937 324-0352
Danai Brooks, *CEO*
Mark Schneider, *Ex VP*
EMP: 55 **EST:** 2021
SALES (est): 5.33MM
SALES (corp-wide): 92.18MM **Privately
Held**
Web: www.fluidquip.com
SIC: 2046 Wet corn milling
PA: Komline-Sanderson Corporation
12 Holland Ave
Peapack NJ 07977
908 234-1000

(G-12314)
FQ SALE INC (PA)
1940 S Yellow Springs St (45506-3000)
PHONE..............................937 324-0352
Andy Franko, *Pr*
Andy Franko, *Pr*
John Mcblane, *VP*
Robert Patton, *
◆ **EMP:** 26 **EST:** 1987
SQ FT: 50,000
SALES (est): 5.73MM
SALES (corp-wide): 5.73MM **Privately
Held**
Web: www.fluidquip.com
SIC: 3554 Pulp mill machinery

(G-12315)
**GRAPHIC PAPER PRODUCTS CORP
(HQ)**
Also Called: Miller Printing Co
6069 Yeazell Rd (45502-9216)
P.O. Box 1666 (45501-1666)
PHONE..............................937 325-5503
Jeanne Lampe, *Pr*
EMP: 82 **EST:** 1891
SALES (est): 14.74MM **Privately Held**
SIC: 2754 2752 2652 2653 Job printing:
gravure; Commercial printing, lithographic;
Setup paperboard boxes; Boxes,
corrugated: made from purchased materials
PA: Patented Acquisition Corporation
2490 Cross Pointe Dr
Miamisburg OH 45342

(G-12316)
HALLMARK INDUSTRIES INC (PA)
Also Called: Miller, Jim Furniture
2233 N Limestone St (45503-2635)
PHONE..............................937 864-7378
James Odell Miller, *Pr*
Diane E Miller, *
EMP: 25 **EST:** 1972
SQ FT: 54,000
SALES (est): 530.92K
SALES (corp-wide): 530.92K **Privately
Held**
Web: www.hallmarkind.com
SIC: 2512 5712 Living room furniture:
upholstered on wood frames; Furniture
stores

(G-12317)
HAYS FABRICATING & WELDING INC
633 E Leffel Ln (45505-4750)
PHONE..............................937 325-0031
Clayton Hays, *Pr*
EMP: 27 **EST:** 1975
SQ FT: 25,000
SALES (est): 4.04MM **Privately Held**
Web: www.haysfab.com
SIC: 3441 3555 Fabricated structural metal;
Plates, metal: engravers'

(G-12318)
HDI LANDING GEAR USA INC (DH)
663 Montgomery Ave (45506-1847)
PHONE..............................937 325-1586
Frederick Gagne, *Ex Dir*
Frederick Gagne, *Pr*
William Michalski, *
EMP: 100 **EST:** 2008
SALES (est): 97.02MM **Privately Held**
Web: www.herouxdevtek.com
SIC: 3728 Alighting (landing gear)
assemblies, aircraft
HQ: Heroux-Devtek Inc. - Kitchener Division
1111 Saint-Charles St W Suite 600
West Tower
Longueuil QC J4K 5
450 679-5450

(G-12319)
HEAT TREATING INC (PA)
1762 W Pleasant St (45506-1128)
PHONE..............................937 325-3121
Chester L Walthall, *Pr*
Judith A Walthall, *
Michael Trimble, *
Keith Thue, *Quality Vice President*
EMP: 29 **EST:** 1959
SQ FT: 33,000
SALES (est): 2.27MM
SALES (corp-wide): 2.27MM **Privately
Held**
Web: www.heattreating.com
SIC: 3398 Metal heat treating

(G-12320)
HEF USA CORPORATION (PA)
2015 Progress Rd (45505-4472)
PHONE..............................937 323-2556
Kenneth Metzgar, *Prin*
▲ **EMP:** 8 **EST:** 1993
SALES (est): 3.91MM **Privately Held**
Web: www.hefusa.net
SIC: 3826 Surface area analyzers

(G-12321)
HEROUX-DEVTEK INC
Also Called: Heroux-Devtek Springfield
663 Montgomery Ave (45506-1847)
PHONE..............................937 325-1586
Gilles Labbe, *Pr*
EMP: 19 **EST:** 2010
SALES (est): 5.15MM **Privately Held**
Web: www.herouxdevtek.com
SIC: 3728 Aircraft parts and equipment, nec
HQ: Heroux-Devtek Inc. - Kitchener Division
1111 Saint-Charles St W Suite 600
West Tower
Longueuil QC J4K 5
450 679-5450

(G-12322)
HILLTOP BASIC RESOURCES INC
Enon Washed Sand & Gravel Div
1665 Enon Rd (45502-9102)
PHONE..............................937 882-6357
Jack Blair, *Prin*
EMP: 8
SALES (corp-wide): 49.96MM **Privately
Held**
Web: www.hilltopcompanies.com
SIC: 1771 1442 Concrete work; Construction
sand and gravel
PA: Hilltop Basic Resources, Inc.
50 E Rvrcnter Blvd Ste 10
Covington KY 41011
513 651-5000

(G-12323)
HOLMES W & SONS PRINTING
Also Called: Holmes Printing
401 E Columbia St (45503-4214)
P.O. Box 2300 (45501-2300)
PHONE..............................937 325-1509
William W Holmes, *Pr*
EMP: 6 **EST:** 1974
SQ FT: 2,500
SALES (est): 323.05K **Privately Held**
Web: www.thinkholmes.com
SIC: 2752 Offset printing

(G-12324)
**HORIZON INDUSTRIES
CORPORATION**
1801 W Columbia St (45504-2903)
PHONE..............................937 323-0801
John Neiswinger, *Pr*
Richard Koehler, *VP*
EMP: 9 **EST:** 1990
SQ FT: 15,000

SALES (est): 493.03K **Privately Held**
Web: www.horizonindustriescorp.com
SIC: 3544 Special dies and tools

(G-12325)
HORNER INDUSTRIAL SERVICES INC
Also Called: Scherer Industrial Group
5330 Prosperity Dr (45502-9074)
PHONE......................937 390-6667
Michael Harper, *Dir*
EMP: 11
SALES (corp-wide): 21.85MM **Privately Held**
Web: www.hornerindustrial.com
SIC: 5063 7694 Motors, electric; Electric motor repair
PA: Horner Industrial Services, Inc.
1521 E Washington St
Indianapolis IN 46201
317 639-4261

(G-12326)
HOUSTON MACHINE PRODUCTS INC
1065 W Leffel Ln (45506-3555)
PHONE......................937 322-8022
Sandra White, *Pr*
EMP: 30 EST: 1970
SQ FT: 35,000
SALES (est): 2.26MM **Privately Held**
Web: www.houstonmachine.com
SIC: 3599 3541 3451 Machine shop, jobbing and repair; Machine tools, metal cutting type; Screw machine products

(G-12327)
HUGO BOSCA COMPANY INC (PA)
Also Called: Bosca Accesories
1905 W Jefferson St (45506-1117)
P.O. Box 777 (45501-0777)
PHONE......................937 323-5523
Christopher B Bosca, *Pr*
D'orsi Bosca, *VP Sls*
Dick Rabe, *CFO*
Cathy Gainer, *COO*
Brian Janetski, *Prin*
▲ EMP: 19 EST: 1911
SQ FT: 48,000
SALES (est): 1.12MM
SALES (corp-wide): 1.12MM **Privately Held**
Web: www.bosca.com
SIC: 3171 3172 Handbags, women's; Wallets

(G-12328)
INTERNATIONAL MOTORS LLC
Also Called: Navistar
6125 Urbana Rd (45502-9279)
P.O. Box 600 (45501)
PHONE......................937 390-4776
Barry Laughlin, *Mgr*
EMP: 130
SALES (corp-wide): 343.33B **Privately Held**
Web: www.navistar.com
SIC: 3711 Truck and tractor truck assembly
HQ: International Motors, Llc
2701 International Dr
Lisle IL 60532
331 332-5000

(G-12329)
INTERNATIONAL MOTORS LLC
Navistar
811 N Murray St (45503-3733)
PHONE......................937 561-3315
Tom Tullis, *Genl Mgr*
EMP: 32
SALES (corp-wide): 343.33B **Privately Held**
Web: www.internationaltrucks.com

SIC: 3711 Truck and tractor truck assembly
HQ: International Motors, Llc
2701 International Dr
Lisle IL 60532
331 332-5000

(G-12330)
INTERTAPE POLYMER CORP
Also Called: Maiweave
1800 E Pleasant St (45505-3316)
PHONE......................704 279-3011
EMP: 25
SQ FT: 85,000
SALES (corp-wide): 623.56MM **Privately Held**
Web: www.itape.com
SIC: 3081 Unsupported plastics film and sheet
HQ: Intertape Polymer Corp.
100 Paramount Dr Ste 300
Sarasota FL 34232
888 898-7834

(G-12331)
JMAC INC
Also Called: A Division of Jmci
2020 Progress Rd (45505-4472)
PHONE......................937 346-0800
Teresa Homer, *Brnch Mgr*
EMP: 28
SALES (corp-wide): 46.13MM **Privately Held**
SIC: 3469 Metal stampings, nec
PA: Jmac Inc.
200 W Ntnwide Blvd Unit 1
Columbus OH 43215
614 436-2418

(G-12332)
JMS INDUSTRIES INC
Also Called: JMS Composites
3240 E National Rd (45505-1524)
P.O. Box 507 (45501-0507)
PHONE......................937 325-3502
Manjit Nagra, *CEO*
Jennifer Nagra, *VP*
▲ EMP: 14 EST: 1967
SQ FT: 27,000
SALES (est): 5.76MM **Privately Held**
Web: www.jmscomposites.com
SIC: 2821 Molding compounds, plastics

(G-12333)
K K TOOL CO
115 S Center St (45502-1203)
P.O. Box 995 (45501-0995)
PHONE......................937 325-1373
John Koehler, *Pr*
Donald Koehler, *
Edward Kurt Koehler, *
Teresa Koehler Yancey, *
Kristopher Kent Koehler, *
EMP: 25 EST: 1972
SALES (est): 2.89MM **Privately Held**
Web: www.kktool.net
SIC: 3599 3999 Machine shop, jobbing and repair; Barber and beauty shop equipment

(G-12334)
K WM BEACH MFG CO INC
4655 Urbana Rd (45502-9503)
PHONE......................937 399-3838
William R Beach, *CEO*
Bret L Beach, *
EMP: 200 EST: 1945
SQ FT: 125,000
SALES (est): 9.28MM **Privately Held**
Web: www.kwmbeach.com
SIC: 3053 3714 Gaskets, all materials; Motor vehicle parts and accessories

(G-12335)
KCI HOLDING USA INC (DH)
4401 Gateway Blvd (45502-9339)
PHONE......................937 525-5533
Bernie D'ambrosi, *Sr VP*
Guy Shumaker, *
Amy Corbisier, *
Todd Robenson, *
Steve Mayes, *
◆ EMP: 150 EST: 1993
SALES (est): 23.52MM **Privately Held**
Web: www.konecranes.com
SIC: 3536 Cranes, industrial plant
HQ: Konecranes Finance Oy
Koneenkatu 8
HyvinkAA 05830

(G-12336)
KEYAH INTERNATIONAL TRDG LLC (PA)
4655 Urbana Rd (45502-9503)
PHONE......................937 399-3140
Brett L Beach, *Pr*
Jo Anna Kipp-beach, *CEO*
▲ EMP: 20 EST: 2000
SQ FT: 30,000
SALES (est): 4.72MM
SALES (corp-wide): 4.72MM **Privately Held**
Web: www.keyahint.com
SIC: 2675 Die-cut paper and board

(G-12337)
KONECRANES INC
Also Called: Americas Components
4505 Gateway Blvd (45502-8863)
PHONE......................937 328-5100
Troy Posts, *Mgr*
EMP: 50
Web: www.konecranes.com
SIC: 3536 Cranes, industrial plant
HQ: Konecranes, Inc.
4401 Gateway Blvd
Springfield OH 45502

(G-12338)
KONECRANES INC (HQ)
4401 Gateway Blvd (45502-9339)
PHONE......................937 525-5533
Rob Smith, *CEO*
Pekka Lundmark, *
Steve Kosir, *
Bernard D'ambrosi Junior, *VP*
Guy Shumaker, *
◆ EMP: 279 EST: 1910
SQ FT: 17,000
SALES (est): 733.09MM **Privately Held**
Web: www.konecranes.com
SIC: 3536 Cranes, industrial plant
PA: Konecranes Oyj
Koneenkatu 8
HyvinkAA 05800

(G-12339)
KONTRON AMERICA INCORPORATED
Also Called: Hartmann Electronic
202 N Limestone St (45503-4246)
P.O. Box 1585 (45501-1585)
PHONE......................937 324-2420
Andreas Ruben, *Admn*
Andreas Ruben, *Pr*
Folker Hemmann, *Treas*
◆ EMP: 7 EST: 1997
SQ FT: 3,990
SALES (est): 2.45MM **Privately Held**
Web: www.wiener-us.com
SIC: 5065 3679 Electronic parts; Power supplies, all types: static

(G-12340)
KRAFFT AND ASSOCIATES INC
991 W Leffel Ln (45506-3537)
P.O. Box 1292 (45501-1292)
PHONE......................937 325-4671
William F Krafft, *Pr*
Gretchen Krafft, *Sec*
EMP: 8 EST: 1966
SQ FT: 20,000
SALES (est): 1.3MM **Privately Held**
Web: www.krafftandassociates.com
SIC: 3599 Machine shop, jobbing and repair

(G-12341)
KREIDER CORP
400 Harrison St (45505-2067)
PHONE......................937 325-8787
Aristides Gianakopoulas, *Pr*
James Gianakopoulas, *
Walt Wildeman, *
John Patton, *
EMP: 66 EST: 1952
SALES (est): 935.46K **Privately Held**
Web: www.kreidercorp.com
SIC: 3469 3544 Stamping metal for the trade; Special dies, tools, jigs, and fixtures

(G-12342)
LAGONDA INVESTMENTS III INC
2145 Airpark Dr (45502-7931)
P.O. Box 1511 (45501)
PHONE......................937 325-7305
Greg Gearhart, *Pr*
EMP: 15 EST: 1983
SQ FT: 44,000
SALES (est): 3.51MM
SALES (corp-wide): 1.08B **Privately Held**
Web: www.unitedfiberglass.com
SIC: 3644 Electric conduits and fittings
PA: Hill & Smith Plc
Westhaven House
Solihull W MIDLANDS B90 4
121 704-7430

(G-12343)
M & H FABRICATING CO INC
823 Mound St (45505-1132)
P.O. Box 1248 (45501-1248)
PHONE......................937 325-8708
Michael Duramus, *Mgr*
EMP: 6
SALES (corp-wide): 958.28K **Privately Held**
SIC: 3443 Tanks, standard or custom fabricated: metal plate
PA: M & H Fabricating Co Inc
717 Mound St
Springfield OH 45505
937 325-8708

(G-12344)
M & H FABRICATING CO INC (PA)
717 Mound St (45505-1130)
P.O. Box 1248 (45501-1248)
PHONE......................937 325-8708
Michael C De Ramus, *Pr*
EMP: 10 EST: 1970
SQ FT: 6,000
SALES (est): 958.28K
SALES (corp-wide): 958.28K **Privately Held**
SIC: 3441 Fabricated structural metal

(G-12345)
MACRAY CO LLC
100 W North St (45504-2547)
PHONE......................937 325-1726
Robert Yingst, *Managing Member*
EMP: 6 EST: 1986
SQ FT: 17,600
SALES (est): 929.42K **Privately Held**

Web: www.macraycompany.com
SIC: 3993 1799 5099 Signs and advertising
specialties; Sign installation and
maintenance; Signs, except electric

(G-12346)
**MADER ELC MTR PWR
TRNSMSSONS L**
205 E Main St (45503-4221)
P.O. Box 626 (45501-0626)
PHONE.....................937 325-5576
Bret Eric Mader, *Managing Member*
EMP: 7 EST: 1952
SQ FT: 20,000
SALES (est): 9.26MM **Privately Held**
Web: www.maderelectric.com
SIC: 5063 7694 Motors, electric; Electric
motor repair

(G-12347)
MAI-WEAVE LLC
1800 E Pleasant St (45505-3316)
PHONE.....................937 322-1698
▲ EMP: 75
SIC: 3081 Packing materials, plastics sheet

(G-12348)
**MCGREGOR METAL NATIONAL
WORKS LLC**
5573 W National Rd (45504-3218)
P.O. Box 1343 (45501)
PHONE.....................937 882-6347
EMP: 50 EST: 1945
SALES (est): 4.6MM **Privately Held**
Web: www.mcgregormetal.com
SIC: 3451 Screw machine products

(G-12349)
**MCGREGOR MTAL INNSFLLEN
WRKS L**
Also Called: (Mcgregor Metal Yellow Springs
Works Llc, Springfield, OH)
1305 Innisfallen Ave (45506-1827)
P.O. Box 1103 (45501-1103)
PHONE.....................937 322-3880
Dan Mcgregor, *Ch*
James Mcgregor, *Pr*
Dwight Kent, *
Seth Powers, *
James Doyle, *
EMP: 120 EST: 1999
SQ FT: 140,000
SALES (est): 14.05MM
SALES (corp-wide): 49.08MM **Privately
Held**
Web: www.mcgregormetal.com
SIC: 3469 Stamping metal for the trade
PA: Mcgregor Metal Yellow Springs Works
Llc
2100 S Yellow Springs St
Springfield OH 45506
937 325-5561

(G-12350)
**MCGREGOR MTAL LEFFEL WORKS
LLC**
900 W Leffel Ln (45506-3538)
P.O. Box 1103 (45501)
PHONE.....................937 325-5561
Daniel Mcgregor, *Pr*
Dane A Belden, *
Hugh Barnett, *
▲ EMP: 60 EST: 1991
SQ FT: 44,000
SALES (est): 8.68MM
SALES (corp-wide): 49.08MM **Privately
Held**
Web: www.mcgregormetal.com
SIC: 7692 Automotive welding

PA: Mcgregor Metal Yellow Springs Works
Llc
2100 S Yellow Springs St
Springfield OH 45506
937 325-5561

(G-12351)
**MCGREGOR MTAL YLLOW SPRNG
WRKS (PA)**
Also Called: McGregor Metalworking
2100 S Yellow Springs St (45506-3354)
P.O. Box 1103 (45501)
PHONE.....................937 325-5561
Jamie Mcgregor, *CEO*
Tom Wright, *
Dwight Kent, *
Pete Dane, *
▲ EMP: 90 EST: 1939
SQ FT: 98,000
SALES (est): 49.08MM
SALES (corp-wide): 49.08MM **Privately
Held**
Web: www.mcgregormetal.com
SIC: 3568 3544 3451 3429 Power
transmission equipment, nec; Special dies,
tools, jigs, and fixtures; Screw machine
products; Hardware, nec

(G-12352)
METAL STAMPINGS UNLIMITED INC
552 W Johnny Lytle Ave (45506-2679)
PHONE.....................937 328-0206
Edward Anderson, *Pr*
Roger Evilsizor, *VP*
EMP: 10 EST: 1996
SQ FT: 12,000
SALES (est): 859.08K **Privately Held**
SIC: 3469 Stamping metal for the trade

(G-12353)
METALTEK INDUSTRIES INC
829 Pauline St (45503-3815)
P.O. Box 479 (45501-0479)
PHONE.....................937 342-1750
Charles J Muscato, *Pr*
Charles K Muscato, *VP*
EMP: 14 EST: 1950
SALES (est): 2.45MM **Privately Held**
SIC: 2842 3479 Rust removers; Bonderizing
of metal or metal products

(G-12354)
MULLER ENGINE & MACHINE CO
Also Called: Miller Engine & Machine Co
1414 S Yellow Springs St (45506-2545)
PHONE.....................937 322-1861
Ginnie Mullen, *Owner*
EMP: 7 EST: 1952
SQ FT: 10,000
SALES (est): 468.33K **Privately Held**
Web: www.millerengine.com
SIC: 3511 3599 Wheels, water; Machine
shop, jobbing and repair

(G-12355)
MUNCY CORPORATION
2020 Progress Rd (45505-4472)
PHONE.....................937 346-0800
Michael A Priest, *Pr*
EMP: 86 EST: 2005
SALES (est): 9.19MM
SALES (corp-wide): 46.13MM **Privately
Held**
Web: www.muncycorp.com
SIC: 3465 Automotive stampings
PA: Jmac Inc.
200 W Ntnwide Blvd Unit 1
Columbus OH 43215
614 436-2418

(G-12356)
NATIONAL STAIR CORP
20 Zischler St (45504-2853)
P.O. Box 1261 (45501-1261)
PHONE.....................937 325-1347
John Druckenbroad, *Pr*
Mike Earl, *Sec*
Larry Houck, *VP*
EMP: 8 EST: 1988
SQ FT: 11,000
SALES (est): 821.81K **Privately Held**
Web: www.nationalstair.com
SIC: 3446 Architectural metalwork

(G-12357)
NEHER BURIAL VAULT COMPANY
Also Called: Burial Vaults By Neher
1903 Saint Paris Pike (45504-1299)
PHONE.....................937 399-4494
Doreen Pinney, *Pr*
Gary W Pinney, *VP*
EMP: 7 EST: 1939
SQ FT: 5,500
SALES (est): 928.77K **Privately Held**
SIC: 3272 Burial vaults, concrete or precast
terrazzo

(G-12358)
OS KELLY CORPORATION
318 E North St (45503-4298)
P.O. Box 1267 (45501-1267)
PHONE.....................937 322-4921
Theodore Golba, *VP*
▲ EMP: 42 EST: 1890
SQ FT: 110,000
SALES (est): 8.31MM
SALES (corp-wide): 478.63MM **Privately
Held**
SIC: 3321 Gray iron castings, nec
HQ: Steinway, Inc.
1 Steinway Pl
Long Island City NY 11105
718 721-2600

(G-12359)
**PARKER TRUTEC INCORPORATED
(HQ)**
Also Called: Parker Trutec
4700 Gateway Blvd (45502-8817)
PHONE.....................937 323-8833
Keiko Satomi, *Ch Bd*
Yutaka Satomi, *Pr*
Joseph Gummel, *
▲ EMP: 80 EST: 1991
SQ FT: 80,000
SALES (est): 67.5MM **Privately Held**
Web: www.parkertrutec.com
SIC: 3398 3479 Metal heat treating;
Painting, coating, and hot dipping
PA: Nihon Parkerizing Co., Ltd.
2-16-8, Nihombashi
Chuo-Ku TKY 103-0

(G-12360)
PENTAFLEX INC
4981 Gateway Blvd (45502-8867)
PHONE.....................937 325-5551
Dave Arndt, *Pr*
Julie Mcgregor, *Treas*
Walter Wildman, *
◆ EMP: 110 EST: 1972
SQ FT: 146,000
SALES (est): 21.51MM **Privately Held**
Web: www.pentaflex.com
SIC: 3469 7692 Stamping metal for the trade
; Welding repair

(G-12361)
PEPSI-COLA METRO BTLG CO INC
Also Called: Pepsi-Cola
233 Dayton Ave (45506-1205)

PHONE.....................937 328-6750
Phyllis Beach, *Rgnl Mgr*
EMP: 6
SALES (corp-wide): 91.47B **Publicly Held**
Web: www.pepsico.com
SIC: 2086 Carbonated soft drinks, bottled
and canned
HQ: Pepsi-Cola Metropolitan Bottling
Company, Inc.
700 Anderson Hill Rd
Purchase NY 10577
914 767-6000

(G-12362)
PHOENIX SAFETY OUTFITTERS LLC
19 S Fostoria Ave (45505-1404)
P.O. Box 20445 (43220-0445)
PHONE.....................614 361-0544
EMP: 9 EST: 2007
SALES (est): 6.07MM **Privately Held**
Web: www.phoenixoutfitters.com
SIC: 3569 Assembly machines, non-
metalworking

(G-12363)
PIECO INC
Also Called: Superior Trims Springfield Div
5225 Prosperity Dr (45502-9540)
PHONE.....................937 399-5100
Bob Banghle, *Brnch Mgr*
EMP: 65
SALES (corp-wide): 37.77MM **Privately
Held**
Web: www.pieco.com
SIC: 2396 Automotive trimmings, fabric
PA: Pieco, Inc.
2151 Industrial Dr
Findlay OH 45840
419 422-5335

(G-12364)
PRATT (JET CORR) INC
Also Called: Pratt Industries USA
1515 Baker Rd (45504-4501)
PHONE.....................937 390-7100
Michael Day, *Genl Mgr*
EMP: 1585
Web: www.prattindustries.com
SIC: 2653 Boxes, corrugated: made from
purchased materials
HQ: Pratt (Jet Corr), Inc.
1800 Sarasota Bus Pkwy Ne
Conyers GA 30013
770 929-1300

(G-12365)
PRESS TECHNOLOGY & MFG INC
1401 Fotler St (45504-2051)
PHONE.....................937 327-0755
George Berner, *Pr*
▲ EMP: 8 EST: 1992
SQ FT: 30,000
SALES (est): 1.97MM **Privately Held**
Web: www.presstechnology.com
SIC: 3554 Paper mill machinery: plating,
slitting, waxing, etc.

(G-12366)
RAINBOW INDUSTRIES INC
Also Called: Rainbow Tarp
5975 E National Rd (45505-1854)
P.O. Box 506 (45369-0506)
PHONE.....................937 323-6493
F Vernon Mccoy, *CEO*
Evelyn Mccoy, *Treas*
Joe Schmid, *Pr*
▲ EMP: 7 EST: 1894
SQ FT: 6,000
SALES (est): 389.86K **Privately Held**
Web: www.rainbowindustries.com

▲ = Import ▼ = Export
◆ = Import/Export

SIC: 2394 5999 7359 Tarpaulins, fabric: made from purchased materials; Tents; Tent and tarpaulin rental

(G-12367)
REBECCA BENSTON
Also Called: Higher Ground Ministries
2130 W Possum Rd (45506-2814)
PHONE..........................937 360-0669
Rebecca Benston, *Owner*
EMP: 15 EST: 2013
SALES (est): 280.17K **Privately Held**
Web:
www.highergroundbooksandmedia.com
SIC: 2731 Books, publishing only

(G-12368)
REITER DAIRY LLC DEAN FOODS
1941 Commerce Cir (45504-2011)
PHONE..........................937 323-5777
EMP: 6 EST: 2017
SALES (est): 224.51K **Privately Held**
Web: www.dfamilk.com
SIC: 2026 Fluid milk

(G-12369)
REITER DAIRY OF AKRON INC
Also Called: Reiter Dairy
1961 Commerce Cir (45504-2081)
PHONE..........................937 323-5777
EMP: 30
SIC: 2026 Milk processing (pasteurizing, homogenizing, bottling)

(G-12370)
REMINGTON STEEL INC
1120 S Burnett Rd (45505-3408)
P.O. Box 1491 (45501-1491)
PHONE..........................937 322-2414
▲ EMP: 59
SIC: 5051 3714 Steel; Clutches, motor vehicle

(G-12371)
SCHULERS BAKERY INC (PA)
1911 S Limestone St (45505-4045)
PHONE..........................937 323-4154
Theodore Schuler, *Pr*
Larry Schuler, *
Daniel Edward Schuler, *
EMP: 30 EST: 1937
SALES (est): 2.46MM
SALES (corp-wide): 2.46MM **Privately Held**
Web: www.schulersbakery.com
SIC: 5461 2052 2051 Doughnuts; Cookies and crackers; Bread, cake, and related products

(G-12372)
SHELLY MATERIALS INC
4301 S Charleston Pike (45502-9376)
PHONE..........................937 325-7386
Todd Palmer, *Mgr*
EMP: 9
SALES (corp-wide): 34.95B **Privately Held**
Web: www.shellyco.com
SIC: 3273 Ready-mixed concrete
HQ: Shelly Materials, Inc.
80 Park Dr
Thornville OH 43076
740 246-6315

(G-12373)
SILFEX INC
1000 Titus Rd (45502-9307)
PHONE..........................937 324-2487
Kit Armstrong, *Genl Mgr*
EMP: 436
SALES (corp-wide): 14.91B **Publicly Held**

Web: www.silfex.com
SIC: 3674 Semiconductors and related devices
HQ: Silfex, Inc.
950 S Franklin St
Eaton OH 45320

(G-12374)
SONIC DRIVE-IN
40 S Tuttle Rd (45505-1552)
PHONE..........................937 717-6917
EMP: 6 EST: 1953
SALES (est): 83.06K **Privately Held**
Web: www.sonicdrivein.com
SIC: 5812 2038 Drive-in restaurant; Frozen specialties, nec

(G-12375)
SPRADLIN BROS WELDING CO
2131 Quality Ln (45505-3625)
PHONE..........................800 219-2182
Jeffery Spradlin, *Pr*
Mike Spradlin, *VP*
Tammi Spradlin, *Sec*
Rhonda Spradlin, *Treas*
EMP: 17 EST: 1962
SQ FT: 25,500
SALES (est): 3.23MM **Privately Held**
Web: www.weldedparts.com
SIC: 1799 7692 3444 3443 Ornamental metal work; Welding repair; Sheet metalwork; Fabricated plate work (boiler shop)

(G-12376)
SPRINGFIELD NEWSPAPERS INC
Also Called: Springfield News Sun
137 E Main St (45502-1363)
PHONE..........................937 323-5533
Ben Mclaughlin, *Editor*
EMP: 10 EST: 1904
SQ FT: 76,268
SALES (est): 1.01MM
SALES (corp-wide): 16.61B **Privately Held**
Web: www.springfieldnewssun.com
SIC: 2711 Job printing and newspaper publishing combined
PA: Cox Enterprises, Inc.
6205a Pchtree Dunwoody Rd
Atlanta GA 30328
678 645-0000

(G-12377)
SPRINGFIELD PLASTICS INC
15 N Bechtle Ave (45504-2897)
PHONE..........................937 322-6071
Frederick B Becker, *Pr*
Janet Becker, *Sec*
EMP: 15
SQ FT: 24,000
SALES (est): 2.28MM **Privately Held**
Web: www.spi-oh.com
SIC: 3089 Injection molding of plastics

(G-12378)
STALDER SPRING WORKS INC
2345 Springfield Xenia Rd (45506-3994)
PHONE..........................937 322-6120
Damon D Kaufman, *Pr*
Dana Kaufman, *VP*
Corella Kaufman, *Sec*
Dennis Kaufman, *Stockholder*
▲ EMP: 9 EST: 1945
SQ FT: 18,000
SALES (est): 811.43K **Privately Held**
Web: www.stalderspring.com
SIC: 3495 Mechanical springs, precision

(G-12379)
STEWART MANUFACTURING CORP
5230 Prosperity Dr (45502-7503)
PHONE..........................937 390-3333
James S Stewart, *Pr*
Suzanne S Collins, *VP*
EMP: 10 EST: 1974
SQ FT: 18,000
SALES (est): 3MM **Privately Held**
SIC: 3823 Differential pressure instruments, industrial process type

(G-12380)
STRIDE OUT RNCH N RODEO SP LLC
4122 Laybourne Rd (45505-3616)
PHONE..........................937 539-1537
Michael Hess, *CEO*
EMP: 11 EST: 2017
SALES (est): 750K **Privately Held**
Web: www.strideoutworld.com
SIC: 3559 Boots, shoes, and leather working machinery

(G-12381)
SWEET MANUFACTURING COMPANY
2000 E Leffel Ln (45505-4625)
P.O. Box 1086 (45501-1086)
PHONE..........................937 325-1511
Alicia Sweet-hupp, *Pr*
Alan D Sweet, *
◆ EMP: 40 EST: 1955
SQ FT: 75,000
SALES (est): 9.06MM **Privately Held**
Web: www.sweetmfg.com
SIC: 3535 3523 3534 3537 Conveyors and conveying equipment; Elevators, farm; Elevators and equipment; Industrial trucks and tractors

(G-12382)
TAC INDUSTRIES INC (PA)
2160 Old Selma Rd (45505-4600)
PHONE..........................937 328-5200
James Zahora, *CEO*
Michael Ahern, *
EMP: 280 EST: 1960
SQ FT: 52,800
SALES (est): 9.77MM
SALES (corp-wide): 9.77MM **Privately Held**
Web: www.tacind.com
SIC: 8741 2399 8331 Management services; Nets, launderers and dyers; Work experience center

(G-12383)
TAYLOR MANUFACTURING CO INC
1101 W Main St (45504-2899)
PHONE..........................937 322-8622
Christopher Taylor, *Pr*
Robert B Taylor, *Pr*
Mildred B Taylor, *Sec*
EMP: 15 EST: 1939
SQ FT: 18,000
SALES (est): 2.32MM **Privately Held**
Web: www.taylor-mfg.com
SIC: 3728 Aircraft parts and equipment, nec

(G-12384)
TECHNIQUES SURFACES USA INC
2015 Progress Rd (45505-4472)
PHONE..........................937 323-2556
Alain Charlois, *Pr*
Kenneth Metzgar, *Dir*
EMP: 7 EST: 2008
SALES (est): 3.91MM **Privately Held**
Web: www.hefusa.net
SIC: 3398 Metal heat treating
PA: H.E.F. Usa Corporation
2015 Progress Rd
Springfield OH 45505

(G-12385)
TED BOLLE MILLWORK INC
2834 Hustead Rd (45502-7909)
P.O. Box 82 (45387-0082)
PHONE..........................937 325-8779
EMP: 10 EST: 1953
SALES (est): 2.47MM **Privately Held**
Web: www.bollemillwork.com
SIC: 2431 Millwork

(G-12386)
TEIKURO CORPORATION
4500 Gateway Blvd (45502-8815)
PHONE..........................937 327-3955
Mike Houseman, *Mgr*
EMP: 43
Web: www.teikuro.com
SIC: 3471 Electroplating of metals or formed products
HQ: Teikuro Corporation
101a Clay St Ste 128
San Francisco CA 94111
415 273-2650

(G-12387)
TINKER OMEGA SINTO LLC
2424 Columbus Rd (45503-3549)
P.O. Box 328 (45501-0328)
PHONE..........................937 322-2272
William F Tinker Junior, *Managing Member*
▲ EMP: 29 EST: 2001
SQ FT: 54,000
SALES (est): 5.47MM **Privately Held**
Web: www.tinkeromega.com
SIC: 3555 Type casting, founding, or melting machines

(G-12388)
TOMCO TOOL INC
203 S Wittenberg Ave (45506-1646)
PHONE..........................937 322-5768
Bryan Stewart, *Pr*
Mark Stewart, *Sec*
Richard Wheeler, *VP*
Patfy Stewart, *Mgr*
EMP: 7 EST: 1970
SQ FT: 18,000
SALES (est): 369.75K **Privately Held**
Web: www.tomco-tool.com
SIC: 3545 3544 Tools and accessories for machine tools; Special dies, tools, jigs, and fixtures

(G-12389)
TOOL TECH LLC
4901 Urbana Rd (45502-9069)
PHONE..........................614 893-5876
Matt Mcgreevy, *Prin*
Kevin Kroos, *
Kevin Seibert, *
Doug Hanaway, *
Don Gamble, *
EMP: 38 EST: 2017
SALES (est): 4.61MM **Privately Held**
Web: www.tooltech.com
SIC: 3544 Special dies, tools, jigs, and fixtures

(G-12390)
TURN-ALL MACHINE & GEAR CO
5499 Tremont Ln (45502-7522)
P.O. Box 448 (45501-0448)
PHONE..........................937 342-8710
Carl Power, *Pr*
Jane Power, *VP*
EMP: 11 EST: 1972
SALES (est): 3.64MM **Privately Held**
Web: www.turn-all.com
SIC: 3599 Machine shop, jobbing and repair

(G-12391)
VALCO INDUSTRIES LLC
625 Burt St (45505-3266)
P.O. Box 1226 (45501-1226)
PHONE..............................937 399-7400
Edward H Leventhal, *Pr*
EMP: 35 **EST:** 1974
SQ FT: 44,000
SALES (est): 7.38MM **Privately Held**
Web: www.valco-ind.com
SIC: 3713 3441 3465 Truck cabs, for motor
   vehicles; Fabricated structural metal; Body
   parts, automobile: stamped metal

(G-12392)
WESTFIELD STEEL INC
Also Called: Remington Steel
1120 S Burnett Rd (45505-3408)
PHONE..............................937 322-2414
Frank Bair, *Brnch Mgr*
EMP: 60
SALES (corp-wide): 86.07MM **Privately
Held**
Web: www.westfieldsteel.com
SIC: 5051 3714 Steel; Clutches, motor
   vehicle
PA: Westfield Steel Inc
   530 W State Road 32
   Westfield IN 46074
   317 896-5587

(G-12393)
WETSU GROUP INC
125 W North St (45504-2546)
P.O. Box 1985 (45501)
PHONE..............................937 324-9353
Charles Ingle, *Pr*
Jay Greenland, *VP*
EMP: 15 **EST:** 1993
SQ FT: 1,200
SALES (est): 2.84MM **Privately Held**
Web: www.wetsumfg.com
SIC: 3679 Harness assemblies, for
   electronic use: wire or cable

(G-12394)
WOEBER MUSTARD MFG CO (PA)
1966 Commerce Cir (45504-2012)
P.O. Box 388 (45501-0388)
PHONE..............................937 323-6281
Raymond Woeber, *Pr*
Richard E Woeber, *VP*
Gloria Woeber, *Sec*
D I C K Woeber, *VP*
Rick Schmidt, *VP*
◆ **EMP:** 126 **EST:** 1972
SQ FT: 40,000
SALES (est): 2.9MM
SALES (corp-wide): 2.9MM **Privately Held**
Web: www.woebermustard.com
SIC: 2099 2035 Vinegar; Mustard, prepared
   (wet)

(G-12395)
WOEBER MUSTARD MFG CO
5103 Urbana Rd (45502-9277)
PHONE..............................937 342-9601
Ray Woeber, *Pr*
▼ **EMP:** 115
SALES (corp-wide): 2.9MM **Privately Held**
SIC: 2099 Food preparations, nec
PA: Woeber Mustard Manufacturing
   Company
   1966 Commerce Cir
   Springfield OH 45504
   937 323-6281

(G-12396)
WOODROW MANUFACTURING CO
4300 River Rd (45502-7517)
P.O. Box 1567 (45501-1567)

PHONE..............................937 399-9333
John K Woodrow, *Pr*
Patrick T Mcatee, *VP*
EMP: 20 **EST:** 1964
SQ FT: 26,000
SALES (est): 1.13MM **Privately Held**
Web: www.woodrowcorp.com
SIC: 7336 3479 2752 2396 Silk screen
   design; Etching on metals; Commercial
   printing, lithographic; Automotive and
   apparel trimmings

(G-12397)
YOST SUPERIOR CO
300 S Center St Ste 1 (45501)
P.O. Box 1487 (45501)
PHONE..............................937 323-7591
Bert D Barnes, *Ch Bd*
Gary Dickerhoff, *
David Deerwester, *
▼ **EMP:** 50 **EST:** 1924
SQ FT: 47,000
SALES (est): 4.29MM **Privately Held**
Web: www.yostsuperior.com
SIC: 3495 3496 Mechanical springs,
   precision; Miscellaneous fabricated wire
   products

Sterling
Wayne County

(G-12398)
MJC ENTERPRISE INC
7820 Blough Rd (44276-9734)
P.O. Box 182 (44677-0182)
PHONE..............................330 669-3744
Lynn Bolens, *Pr*
EMP: 9 **EST:** 1991
SQ FT: 1,352
SALES (est): 652.11K **Privately Held**
Web: www.mjc-enterprises.com
SIC: 2448 Pallets, wood

Steubenville
Jefferson County

(G-12399)
ATV INSIDER
742 Sunshine Park Rd (43953-7134)
PHONE..............................740 282-7102
EMP: 6 **EST:** 2007
SALES (est): 119.28K **Privately Held**
SIC: 2721 Periodicals, publishing only

(G-12400)
BARIUM & CHEMICALS INC
515 Kingsdale Rd (43952-4321)
P.O. Box 218 (43952-5218)
PHONE..............................740 282-9776
▲ **EMP:** 30 **EST:** 1916
SALES (est): 9.18MM **Privately Held**
Web: www.bariumchemicals.com
SIC: 2819 Barium compounds

(G-12401)
BULLY TOOLS INC
14 Technology Way (43952-7079)
PHONE..............................740 282-5834
Mark Gracy, *Pr*
EMP: 35 **EST:** 2002
SALES (est): 4.64MM **Privately Held**
Web: www.bullytools.com
SIC: 3423 Hand and edge tools, nec

(G-12402)
**DIETRICH VON HLDBRAND LGACY
PR**

1235 University Blvd (43952-1792)
PHONE..............................703 496-7821
John Crosby, *Dir*
EMP: 7 **EST:** 2004
SALES (est): 473.17K **Privately Held**
Web: www.hildebrandproject.org
SIC: 2759 8299 Commercial printing, nec;
   Educational services

(G-12403)
**FORT STBEN BURIAL ESTATES
ASSN**
Also Called: ROBERTS BROTHERS
801 Canton Rd (43953-4109)
PHONE..............................740 266-6101
Kirk Roberts, *Pt*
EMP: 6 **EST:** 1937
SALES (est): 261.59K **Privately Held**
Web: www.harrisonpaintsupply.com
SIC: 6553 3272 Cemeteries, real estate
   operation; Burial vaults, concrete or precast
   terrazzo

(G-12404)
JEFFCO SHELTERED WORKSHOP
256 John Scott Hwy (43952-3001)
PHONE..............................740 264-4608
Mikel Michalik, *Ex Dir*
EMP: 7 **EST:** 1973
SQ FT: 15,000
SALES (est): 289.34K **Privately Held**
SIC: 8331 8322 2511 Vocational training
   agency; Refugee service; Wood household
   furniture

(G-12405)
**LT WRIGHT HANDCRAFTED KNIFE
CO**
130 Warren Ln Unit B (43953-3758)
PHONE..............................740 317-1404
Leonard T Wright, *Pr*
EMP: 10 **EST:** 2014
SALES (est): 674.59K **Privately Held**
Web: www.ltwrightknives.com
SIC: 3421 Knives: butchers', hunting,
   pocket, etc.

(G-12406)
MEYER PRODUCTS LLC
324 N 7th St (43952-2249)
PHONE..............................216 486-1313
Andrew Outcalt, *Pr*
◆ **EMP:** 86 **EST:** 2004
SALES (est): 9.5MM
SALES (corp-wide): 11.53MM **Privately
Held**
Web: www.meyerproducts.com
SIC: 3531 Blades for graders, scrapers,
   dozers, and snow plows
PA: The Louis Berkman Company
   600 Grant St Ste 3230
   Pittsburgh PA 15219
   740 283-3722

(G-12407)
NATIONAL COLLOID COMPANY
11 Technology Way (43952-7079)
P.O. Box 309 (43952-5309)
PHONE..............................740 282-1171
Michael Barber Junior, *Pr*
▲ **EMP:** 25 **EST:** 1938
SQ FT: 45,000
SALES (est): 2.16MM **Privately Held**
Web: www.natcoll.com
SIC: 2869 5169 2899 2842 Industrial organic
   chemicals, nec; Caustic soda; Chemical
   preparations, nec; Polishes and sanitation
   goods

(G-12408)
OGDEN NEWSPAPERS INC
Also Called: Weirton Daily Times, The
401 Herald Sq (43952-2059)
PHONE..............................304 748-0606
Tammie Macintosh, *Mgr*
EMP: 52
Web: www.ogdennews.com
SIC: 2711 Newspapers: publishing only, not
   printed on site
HQ: The Ogden Newspapers Inc
   1500 Main St
   Wheeling WV 26003
   304 233-0100

(G-12409)
P-AMERICAS LLC
Also Called: Pepsico
729 Main St (43953-3867)
PHONE..............................740 266-6121
Mark Heil, *Mgr*
EMP: 21
SALES (corp-wide): 91.47B **Publicly Held**
Web: www.pepsico.com
SIC: 2086 Carbonated soft drinks, bottled
   and canned
HQ: P-Americas Llc
   1 Pepsi Way
   Somers NY 10589
   336 896-5740

(G-12410)
RUSSELL HUNT
Also Called: Russel Hunt Total Land Care
175 Detmar Rd (43953-7170)
P.O. Box 126 (43952-5126)
PHONE..............................740 264-1196
Russell Hunt, *Prin*
Russell Hunt, *Owner*
EMP: 10 **EST:** 2005
SALES (est): 325.99K **Privately Held**
Web: www.totallawncare.net
SIC: 0782 3524 Landscape contractors;
   Snowblowers and throwers, residential

(G-12411)
SIGNS LIMITED LLC
356 Technology Way (43952-7079)
PHONE..............................740 282-7715
EMP: 7 **EST:** 2009
SALES (est): 491.03K **Privately Held**
Web: www.signsunlimitedusa.com
SIC: 3993 Electric signs

(G-12412)
SUNNEST SERVICE LLC
619 Slack St (43952-2821)
P.O. Box 16484 (92623)
PHONE..............................740 283-2815
▲ **EMP:** 25 **EST:** 2009
SALES (est): 929.11K **Privately Held**
SIC: 2514 Metal lawn and garden furniture

(G-12413)
**TRI-STATE PUBLISHING COMPANY
(PA)**
Also Called: Tri-State Printing
157 N 3rd St (43952-2118)
P.O. Box 1119 (43952-6119)
PHONE..............................740 283-3686
TOLL FREE: 800
Richard S Pflug, *Pr*
Dawna L Mccabe, *Sec*
EMP: 21 **EST:** 1953
SQ FT: 11,000
SALES (est): 2.22MM
SALES (corp-wide): 2.22MM **Privately
Held**
Web: www.tristateprintingco.com
SIC: 2752 Offset printing

Stow
Summit County

(G-12414)
ACE PLASTICS COMPANY
122 E Tuscarawas Ave (44224)
PHONE..............................330 928-7720
Peggy Lyn Assaly, *Pr*
Joe Vereecken, *Pr*
EMP: 7 **EST:** 1947
SQ FT: 4,000
SALES (est): 324.08K **Privately Held**
Web: www.aceframes.com
SIC: 3499 5199 Novelties and giftware,
including trophies; Advertising specialties

(G-12415)
ADVANCE TRANS INC ✪
4833 Darrow Rd Ste 105 (44224-1411)
PHONE..............................330 572-0390
Oscar Brown, *Prin*
EMP: 11 **EST:** 2023
SALES (est): 4.62MM **Privately Held**
SIC: 3537 Trucks, tractors, loaders, carriers,
and similar equipment

(G-12416)
ADVANCED ENGRG & MFG CO INC
5026 Hudson Dr Ste D (44224-7100)
PHONE..............................330 686-9911
Bob Hanna, *Pr*
Paul Christ, *VP*
Jill Hanna, *Stockholder*
Gail Christ, *Stockholder*
EMP: 10 **EST:** 1994
SQ FT: 1,250
SALES (est): 1.37MM **Privately Held**
Web:
www.advancedengineeringmfg.com
SIC: 3599 Machine shop, jobbing and repair

(G-12417)
ALGIX LLC
3916 Clock Pointe Trl Ste 103
(44224-2932)
PHONE..............................706 207-3425
EMP: 6 **EST:** 2011
SALES (est): 438.48K **Privately Held**
SIC: 2836 Biological products, except
diagnostic

(G-12418)
ANDERSON INTERNATIONAL CORP
4545 Boyce Pkwy (44224-1770)
PHONE..............................216 641-1112
Len Trocano, *Pr*
Stephen C Ellis, *
Gary Pace, *
Kathleen O'hearn, *Treas*
◆ **EMP:** 90 **EST:** 1888
SQ FT: 100,000
SALES (est): 22.71MM
SALES (corp-wide): 22.71MM **Privately
Held**
Web: www.andersonintl.com
SIC: 3559 3556 Rubber working machinery,
including tires; Meat, poultry, and seafood
processing machinery
PA: Kimbell Inc
420 Throckmorton St # 710
Fort Worth TX 76102
817 332-6104

(G-12419)
AUBURN METAL PROCESSING LLC
(PA)
4550 Darrow Rd (44224-1804)
PHONE..............................315 253-2565
▼ **EMP:** 7 **EST:** 2003

SALES (est): 4.17MM
SALES (corp-wide): 4.17MM **Privately
Held**
Web: www.reserve-group.com
SIC: 3444 Forming machine work, sheet
metal

(G-12420)
AUSTIN TAPE AND LABEL INC
3350 Cavalier Trl (44224-4906)
PHONE..............................330 928-7999
James Burkle Junior, *Pr*
Darrell K Floyd, *
EMP: 54 **EST:** 1976
SQ FT: 11,000
SALES (est): 4.91MM **Privately Held**
Web: www.austintape.com
SIC: 2672 2759 2671 Tape, pressure
sensitive: made from purchased materials;
Commercial printing, nec; Paper; coated
and laminated packaging

(G-12421)
BAKER MCMILLEN CO (PA)
Also Called: Crook Miller Company
3688 Wyoga Lake Rd (44224-4987)
PHONE..............................330 923-8300
William L Kimmerle, *Pr*
◆ **EMP:** 55 **EST:** 1874
SQ FT: 65,000
SALES (est): 9.43MM
SALES (corp-wide): 9.43MM **Privately
Held**
Web: www.summit-growth.com
SIC: 2499 Carved and turned wood

(G-12422)
BLAZE TECHNICAL SERVICES INC
1445 Commerce Dr (44224-1709)
PHONE..............................330 923-0409
Ralph Hickman, *Pr*
Brian Hickman, *
EMP: 24 **EST:** 1996
SQ FT: 5,000
SALES (est): 4.95MM **Privately Held**
Web: www.blazeprobes.com
SIC: 3829 Thermocouples

(G-12423)
CHANDLER MACHINE COMPANY
Also Called: Chandler Mch & Prod Gear & Bro
4960 Hudson Dr (44224-1789)
PHONE..............................330 688-7615
Jeffery H Capple, *Pr*
EMP: 9 **EST:** 1940
SQ FT: 2,400
SALES (est): 1.89MM **Privately Held**
Web: www.chandlermachineco.com
SIC: 3599 Machine shop, jobbing and repair

(G-12424)
CHANDLER MACHINE COMPANY
4960 Hudson Dr (44224-1789)
PHONE..............................330 688-5585
Jeffery Capple, *Pr*
EMP: 21 **EST:** 1962
SQ FT: 2,400
SALES (est): 1.16MM **Privately Held**
Web: www.chandlergearmachining.com
SIC: 3599 Machine shop, jobbing and repair

(G-12425)
CONQUEST INDUSTRIES INC
4488 Allen Rd (44224-1051)
PHONE..............................330 926-9236
Tom Fares, *Prin*
Harry Frederick, *
EMP: 14 **EST:** 1994
SALES (est): 3.48MM **Privately Held**
Web: www.irbfmanufacturing.com

SIC: 3599 Machine shop, jobbing and repair

(G-12426)
DES MACHINE SERVICES INC
4115 Baird Rd (44224-3603)
PHONE..............................330 633-6897
William M Smith, *Pr*
Debora Smith, *VP*
EMP: 9 **EST:** 2005
SALES (est): 978.57K **Privately Held**
Web: www.desmachine.com
SIC: 3599 Machine shop, jobbing and repair

(G-12427)
ELECTROMOTIVE INC (PA)
4880 Hudson Dr (44224-1708)
PHONE..............................330 688-6494
Michael Piglia, *CEO*
Jeffrey Bissell, *CFO*
EMP: 50 **EST:** 1970
SALES (est): 56.37MM
SALES (corp-wide): 56.37MM **Privately
Held**
Web: www.electromotive.com
SIC: 3679 3677 Solenoids for electronic
applications; Electronic coils and
transformers

(G-12428)
ELECTRONIC PRINTING PDTS INC
Also Called: Laser Label Technologies
4560 Darrow Rd (44224-1888)
PHONE..............................800 882-4050
James Peruzzi, *Pr*
James W Ransom, *
Jerry S Krempa, *
Ted F Unton, *
Sheri H Edison, *
EMP: 32 **EST:** 2014
SQ FT: 30,000
SALES (est): 3.71MM **Privately Held**
Web: www.lltlabels.com
SIC: 2752 Commercial printing, lithographic
HQ: Morgan Adhesives Company, Llc
4560 Darrow Rd
Stow OH 44224
330 688-1111

(G-12429)
ESTERLE MOLD & MACHINE CO INC
(PA)
Also Called: Plastics Division
1539 Commerce Dr (44224-1783)
PHONE..............................330 686-1685
Richard Esterle, *Pr*
Adam Esterle, *
Kathleen Sawyer, *
Carol Esterle, *
EMP: 45 **EST:** 1976
SQ FT: 18,100
SALES (est): 9.68MM
SALES (corp-wide): 9.68MM **Privately
Held**
Web: www.esterle.com
SIC: 3498 3599 3544 Fabricated pipe and
fittings; Machine shop, jobbing and repair;
Industrial molds

(G-12430)
FALLS FILTRATION TECH INC
115 E Steels Corners Rd (44224-4919)
PHONE..............................330 928-4100
Tom Page, *Pr*
Lou Scalise, *
EMP: 35 **EST:** 2004
SALES (est): 9.76MM **Privately Held**
Web: www.fallsfti.com
SIC: 3569 Filters, general line: industrial

(G-12431)
FERRY INDUSTRIES INC
Also Called: Ferry & Quintax
4445 Allen Rd Ste A (44224-1058)
PHONE..............................330 920-9200
Adam Covington, *Pr*
Courtney Mahan, *
◆ **EMP:** 77 **EST:** 1927
SQ FT: 70,000
SALES (est): 8.8MM **Privately Held**
Web: www.ferryindustries.com
SIC: 3599 3829 Custom machinery;
Measuring and controlling devices, nec

(G-12432)
FLEXOTECH GRAPHICS INC (PA)
4830 Hudson Dr (44224-1703)
PHONE..............................330 929-4743
Cris Apley, *Pr*
EMP: 10 **EST:** 1997
SQ FT: 6,500
SALES (est): 538.21K
SALES (corp-wide): 538.21K **Privately
Held**
Web: www.flexotech.com
SIC: 3555 Printing plates

(G-12433)
GLI HOLDINGS INC (PA)
Also Called: Gli
4246 Hudson Dr (44224-2251)
PHONE..............................216 651-1500
James R Schultz, *Ch*
James R Schultz, *Ch*
Scot D Adkins, *
Anthony Sanson, *
Robert J Schultz, *
▲ **EMP:** 90 **EST:** 1931
SALES (est): 5.23MM
SALES (corp-wide): 5.23MM **Privately
Held**
Web: www.gll.com
SIC: 2752 2796 2789 Offset printing;
Lithographic plates, positives or negatives;
Bookbinding and related work

(G-12434)
GLI HOLDINGS INC
GL Direct
4484 Allen Rd (44224-1051)
PHONE..............................440 892-7760
Neal Gallagher, *Mgr*
EMP: 65
SALES (corp-wide): 5.23MM **Privately
Held**
Web: www.gll.com
SIC: 2752 2796 Offset printing; Lithographic
plates, positives or negatives
PA: Gli Holdings, Inc.
4246 Hudson Dr
Stow OH 44224
216 651-1500

(G-12435)
GOJO INDUSTRIES INC
1366 Commerce Dr (44224-1737)
PHONE..............................330 255-6525
EMP: 6
SALES (corp-wide): 802.21MM **Privately
Held**
Web: www.gojo.com
SIC: 2842 3586 2844 Polishes and
sanitation goods; Measuring and
dispensing pumps; Perfumes, cosmetics
and other toilet preparations
PA: Gojo Industries, Inc.
1 Gojo Plz Ste 500
Akron OH 44311
330 255-6000

G
E
O
G
R
A
P
H
I
C

(G-12436)
HYDRAULIC MANIFOLDS USA LLC
Also Called: Selling Precision
4540 Boyce Pkwy (44224-1769)
PHONE..............................973 728-1214
Nimit Patel, *Managing Member*
EMP: 30 EST: 2017
SALES (est): 9.54MM **Privately Held**
Web: www.hydraulicmanifoldsusa.com
SIC: 5084 5085 3492 Hydraulic systems
   equipment and supplies; Hydraulic and
   pneumatic pistons and valves; Valves,
   hydraulic, aircraft

(G-12437)
LASPINA TOOL AND DIE INC
4282 Hudson Dr (44224-2251)
PHONE..............................330 923-9996
Timothy P Laspina, *Owner*
EMP: 19 EST: 1996
SQ FT: 8,500
SALES (est): 2.8MM **Privately Held**
Web: www.laspinatd.com
SIC: 3544 3599 Special dies and tools;
   Machine shop, jobbing and repair

(G-12438)
LEVAN ENTERPRISES INC (PA)
Also Called: R F Cook Manufacturing Co
4585 Allen Rd (44224-1035)
PHONE..............................330 923-9797
Peter H Levan, *Pr*
Carolyn G Levan, *
EMP: 25 EST: 1986
SQ FT: 18,000
SALES (est): 4.29MM
SALES (corp-wide): 4.29MM **Privately
Held**
Web: www.rfcook.com
SIC: 3541 3542 3545 3544 Machine tools,
   metal cutting type; Machine tools, metal
   forming type; Precision tools, machinists';
   Special dies, tools, jigs, and fixtures

(G-12439)
MACTAC AMERICAS LLC (DH)
Also Called: Mactac
4560 Darrow Rd (44224-1898)
PHONE..............................800 762-2822
Ed Laforge, *Pr*
EMP: 80 EST: 2015
SQ FT: 559,400
SALES (est): 517.01MM **Privately Held**
Web: www.mactac.com
SIC: 2891 Adhesives and sealants
HQ: Lintec Usa Holding, Inc.
   4560 Darrow Rd
   Stow OH 44224

(G-12440)
MATCO TOOLS CORPORATION (HQ)
Also Called: Matco Tools
4403 Allen Rd (44224-1096)
P.O. Box 1429 (44224-0429)
PHONE..............................330 929-4949
Mike Dwyer, *Pr*
Raymond Michaud, *
▲ EMP: 400 EST: 1953
SALES (est): 134.73MM
SALES (corp-wide): 2.98B **Publicly Held**
Web: www.matcotools.com
SIC: 5013 5072 3469 3423 Tools and
   equipment, automotive; Hardware; Metal
   stampings, nec; Hand and edge tools, nec
PA: Vontier Corporation
   5438 Wade Pk Blvd Ste 600
   Raleigh NC 27607
   984 275-6000

(G-12441)
MORGAN ADHESIVES COMPANY LLC (DH)
Also Called: Mactac
4560 Darrow Rd (44224-1898)
PHONE..............................330 688-1111
◆ EMP: 500 EST: 1959
SQ FT: 559,400
SALES (est): 473.98MM **Privately Held**
Web: www.mactac.com
SIC: 2891 3565 2672 2823 Adhesives;
   Labeling machines, industrial; Adhesive
   papers, labels, or tapes: from purchased
   material; Cellulosic manmade fibers
HQ: Mactac Americas, Llc
   4560 Darrow Rd
   Stow OH 44224
   800 762-2822

(G-12442)
MURRUBBER TECHNOLOGIES INC
1350 Commerce Dr (44224-1737)
P.O. Box 1328 (44224)
EMP: 40 EST: 1986
SQ FT: 50,000
SALES (est): 4.97MM **Privately Held**
Web: www.murrubber.com
SIC: 3069 2241 Reclaimed rubber and
   specialty rubber compounds; Rubber and
   elastic yarns and fabrics

(G-12443)
NATIONAL AEROSPACE PROC LLC
1330 Commerce Dr (44224-1737)
PHONE..............................234 900-6497
Mike Piglia, *Prin*
Michael Fabrizio, *Prin*
EMP: 8 EST: 2020
SALES (est): 1.34MM **Privately Held**
Web: www.naprocessing.com
SIC: 3471 Electroplating of metals or formed
   products

(G-12444)
NATIONAL AVIATION PRODUCTS INC (DH)
4880 Hudson Dr (44224-1708)
PHONE..............................330 688-6494
Peter Piglia, *Ch Bd*
Thomas G Knoll, *Prin*
EMP: 8 EST: 1999
SALES (est): 10.03MM
SALES (corp-wide): 56.37MM **Privately
Held**
Web: www.nmgaerospace.com
SIC: 3599 3492 Machine shop, jobbing and
   repair; Control valves, fluid power: hydraulic
   and pneumatic
HQ: National Machine Company
   4880 Hudson Dr
   Stow OH 44224
   330 688-6494

(G-12445)
NATIONAL MACHINE CO
Also Called: NATIONAL MACHINE CO (INC)
1330 Commerce Dr (44224-1737)
PHONE..............................330 688-2584
Tom Huntsman, *Mgr*
EMP: 7
SALES (corp-wide): 56.37MM **Privately
Held**
Web: www.nmgaerospace.com
SIC: 3545 3599 Sockets (machine tool
   accessories); Machine shop, jobbing and
   repair
HQ: National Machine Company
   4880 Hudson Dr
   Stow OH 44224
   330 688-6494

(G-12446)
NATIONAL MACHINE COMPANY (HQ)
Also Called: Nmg Aerospace
4880 Hudson Dr (44224-1799)
PHONE..............................330 688-6494
Darryl Piglia, *CEO*
Bill Anop, *
Jeffrey Bissell, *
▲ EMP: 250 EST: 1967
SQ FT: 80,000
SALES (est): 43.21MM
SALES (corp-wide): 56.37MM **Privately
Held**
Web: www.nmgaerospace.com
SIC: 3599 3492 Machine shop, jobbing and
   repair; Control valves, fluid power: hydraulic
   and pneumatic
PA: Electromotive, Inc.
   4880 Hudson Dr
   Stow OH 44224
   330 688-6494

(G-12447)
NORDEC INC
900 Hampshire Rd (44224-1113)
PHONE..............................330 940-3700
Christine A Snyder, *Pr*
Jason D Sudbrink, *
Jeffrey L Smith, *Product Vice President*
William L Snyder, *Stockholder*
EMP: 60 EST: 1962
SQ FT: 50,000
SALES (est): 11.29MM **Privately Held**
Web: www.nordecinc.com
SIC: 2759 2675 Screen printing; Die-cut
   paper and board

(G-12448)
OSMANS PIES INC
3678 Elm Rd (44224-3954)
PHONE..............................330 607-9083
Ethel Osman, *Pr*
Terry Osman, *
Cheryl Osman Crowe, *
EMP: 30 EST: 1949
SQ FT: 3,500
SALES (est): 257.26K **Privately Held**
SIC: 5461 5149 2052 2051 Retail bakeries;
   Bakery products; Cookies and crackers;
   Bread, cake, and related products

(G-12449)
POLAR PRODUCTS INC
3380 Cavalier Trl (44224-4906)
PHONE..............................330 253-9973
Jacob Graessle, *Pr*
William S Graessle, *
▲ EMP: 24 EST: 1984
SQ FT: 10,000
SALES (est): 2.21MM **Privately Held**
Web: www.polarproducts.com
SIC: 2833 8041 Medicinal chemicals; Offices
   and clinics of chiropractors

(G-12450)
POLYSTAR INC
1676 Commerce Dr (44224-1731)
PHONE..............................330 963-5100
David Huston, *CEO*
EMP: 14 EST: 1992
SQ FT: 3,500
SALES (est): 14.27MM **Privately Held**
Web: www.polystarcontainment.com
SIC: 2655 Containers, laminated phenolic
   and vulcanized fiber

(G-12451)
PRINT-DIGITAL INCORPORATED
Also Called: Print Digital
4688 Darrow Rd (44224-1819)
PHONE..............................330 686-5945

Marvin Weber, *Pr*
Eric Weber, *VP*
EMP: 9 EST: 1984
SQ FT: 4,500
SALES (est): 499.87K **Privately Held**
Web: www.printdigitalinc.com
SIC: 2752 7334 2789 2761 Offset printing;
   Photocopying and duplicating services;
   Bookbinding and related work; Manifold
   business forms

(G-12452)
PROCESS DYNAMICS INC
1659 Commerce Dr (44224-1730)
PHONE..............................330 686-2597
Robert Lay, *Pr*
EMP: 7 EST: 2001
SALES (est): 1.04MM **Privately Held**
Web: www.pdiheattransfer.com
SIC: 5084 3561 3443 7699 Heat exchange
   equipment, industrial; Industrial pumps and
   parts; Industrial vessels, tanks, and
   containers; Industrial equipment cleaning

(G-12453)
RAY COMMUNICATIONS INC
Also Called: Raytec Systems
1337 Commerce Dr Ste 11 (44224-1758)
PHONE..............................330 686-0226
Richard A Yarnell, *Pr*
EMP: 9 EST: 1986
SQ FT: 2,400
SALES (est): 2.02MM **Privately Held**
Web: www.raytecsystems.com
SIC: 5065 2542 5999 Communication
   equipment; Telephone booths: except wood
   ; Telephone equipment and systems

(G-12454)
RECORD PUBLISHING CO
Also Called: Weekly Division
1619 Commerce Dr (44224-1730)
P.O. Box 5199 (44240-5199)
PHONE..............................330 688-0088
Richard M Sekella, *Genl Mgr*
EMP: 54
SQ FT: 6,600
SALES (corp-wide): 38.43MM **Privately
Held**
Web: www.record-courier.com
SIC: 2711 Newspapers, publishing and
   printing
HQ: Record Publishing Co
   1050 W Main St
   Kent OH 44240
   330 541-9400

(G-12455)
SADLER CORPORATION
4600 Hudson Dr (44224-1704)
PHONE..............................330 688-0009
Kathleen Kathy Sadler, *CEO*
Ronald L Sadler, *Pr*
EMP: 7 EST: 1980
SQ FT: 14,000
SALES (est): 1.23MM **Privately Held**
Web: www.sadlercorporation.com
SIC: 3599 3469 Machine shop, jobbing and
   repair; Stamping metal for the trade

(G-12456)
SAINT-GOBAIN CERAMICS PLAS INC
Also Called: Saint-Gobain Norpro
3840 Fishcreek Rd (44224-4306)
PHONE..............................330 673-5860
EMP: 92
SALES (corp-wide): 402.18MM **Privately
Held**
Web: www.saint-gobain.com

SIC: 2819 3679 3544 3297 Industrial
inorganic chemicals, nec; Electronic crystals
; Special dies and tools; Nonclay
refractories
HQ: Saint-Gobain Ceramics & Plastics, Inc.
3840 Fishcreek Rd
Stow OH 44224

(G-12457)
**SAINT-GOBAIN CERAMICS PLAS
INC (DH)**
Also Called: Corhart Refractories
3840 Fishcreek Rd (44224-4306)
P.O. Box 15137 (01606)
PHONE..................610 893-6000
Benoit Bazin, *CEO*
M Shawn Puccio, *
Timothy Feagans, *
▲ **EMP:** 3000 **EST:** 1951
SALES (est): 452.97MM
SALES (corp-wide): 402.18MM **Privately
Held**
Web: www.saint-gobain.com
SIC: 2819 3679 3544 3297 Industrial
inorganic chemicals, nec; Electronic crystals
; Special dies and tools; Nonclay
refractories
HQ: Saint-Gobain Corporation
20 Moores Rd
Malvern PA 19355

(G-12458)
SAINT-GOBAIN NORPRO CORP (HQ)
3840 Fishcreek Rd (44224-4306)
PHONE..................330 673-5860
Antonio Vilela, *Pr*
Joseph H Menendez, *
◆ **EMP:** 126 **EST:** 1991
SALES (est): 47.2MM
SALES (corp-wide): 402.18MM **Privately
Held**
Web: norpro.saint-gobain.com
SIC: 3533 5211 Oil and gas field machinery;
Tile, ceramic
PA: Compagnie De Saint-Gobain
Tour Saint-Gobain
Courbevoie IDF 92400
140880316

(G-12459)
SCOTT BADER INC
4280 Hudson Dr (44224-2251)
P.O. Box 115 (27028)
PHONE..................330 920 4410
Nick Padfield, *Pr*
▲ **EMP:** 8 **EST:** 1992
SQ FT: 5,500
SALES (est): 24.05MM
SALES (corp-wide): 342.21MM **Privately
Held**
Web: www.scottbader.com
SIC: 2821 Plastics materials and resins
HQ: Scott Bader Company Limited
Wollaston Hall, Wollaston
Wellingborough NORTHANTS NN29
193 366-3100

(G-12460)
SELLING PRECISION INC
4540 Boyce Pkwy (44224-1769)
PHONE..................973 728-1214
William Calcagno Junior, *Pr*
Kenneth Calcagno, *
EMP: 35 **EST:** 1971
SALES (est): 682.61K **Privately Held**
Web: www.hydraulicmanifoldsusa.com
SIC: 3498 Manifolds, pipe: fabricated from
purchased pipe

(G-12461)
SPIRAL BRUSHES INC
1355 Commerce Dr (44224-1751)
PHONE..................330 686-2861
Ernest R Preston Iii, *Pr*
Laura B Preston, *
◆ **EMP:** 30 **EST:** 1939
SQ FT: 25,000
SALES (est): 5.87MM **Privately Held**
Web: www.spiralbrushes.com
SIC: 3991 Brushes, household or industrial

(G-12462)
SPIROL SHIM CORPORATION (DH)
321 Remington Rd (44224-4915)
PHONE..................330 920-3655
Jeffrey Koehl, *CEO*
Ken Hagen, *Pr*
EMP: 25 **EST:** 2018
SALES (est): 81.7K
SALES (corp-wide): 48.64MM **Privately
Held**
Web: www.spirol.com
SIC: 3469 Stamping metal for the trade
HQ: Spirol International Corporation
30 Rock Ave
Danielson CT 06239
860 774-8571

(G-12463)
STEEL PRODUCTS CORP AKRON
2288 Samira Rd (44224-3404)
PHONE..................330 688-6633
William E Welsh, *Pr*
William Mac Cracken, *Ch Bd*
Lou Nelson, *VP*
EMP: 22 **EST:** 1950
SQ FT: 100,000
SALES (est): 880.49K **Privately Held**
SIC: 3599 Machine shop, jobbing and repair

(G-12464)
STERIS INSTRUMENT MGT SVCS INC
Also Called: Spectrum Surgical Instruments
4575 Hudson Dr (44224-1725)
PHONE..................800 783-9251
Rick Costello, *Brnch Mgr*
EMP: 140
Web: www.steris-ims.com
SIC: 3841 Surgical and medical instruments
HQ: Steris Instrument Management
Services, Inc.
3316 2nd Ave N
Birmingham AL 35222

(G-12465)
STERIS-IMS
4575 Hudson Dr (44224-1725)
PHONE..................330 686-4557
EMP: 8 **EST:** 2019
SALES (est): 2.42MM **Privately Held**
Web: www.steris-ims.com
SIC: 3842 Surgical appliances and supplies

(G-12466)
TRAXIUM LLC
Also Called: Printing Concepts
4246 Hudson Dr (44224-2251)
PHONE..................330 572-8200
Frank Tuzzio, *
Devin Gilespie, *
Tiffani Gerber, *
EMP: 49 **EST:** 1977
SQ FT: 45,000
SALES (est): 13.31MM **Privately Held**
Web: www.printingconcepts.com
SIC: 7331 2789 2752 2759 Direct mail
advertising services; Bookbinding and
related work; Offset printing; Letterpress
printing

(G-12467)
TUFFY PAD COMPANY
454 Seasons Rd (44224-1020)
P.O. Box 1302 (44224-0302)
PHONE..................330 688-0043
Joseph M Burks, *Pr*
Margaret Burks, *Sec*
Debbie Burks, *Treas*
EMP: 10 **EST:** 1958
SQ FT: 15,000
SALES (est): 477.28K **Privately Held**
Web: www.tuffypad.com
SIC: 3949 Pads: football, basketball, soccer,
lacrosse, etc.

(G-12468)
TWIN SISTERS PRODUCTIONS LLC
4710 Hudson Dr (44224-1706)
PHONE..................330 631-0361
▲ **EMP:** 40
Web: www.twinsisters.com
SIC: 3999 5092 5961 7389 Education aids,
devices and supplies; Toys and hobby
goods and supplies; Educational supplies
and equipment, mail order; Music recording
producer

(G-12469)
VALV-TROL LLC
1340 Commerce Dr (44224-1737)
P.O. Box 2259 (44224-1000)
PHONE..................330 686-2800
Kevin Gray, *Pr*
Kenneth R Ingram, *Pr*
Richard Houck, *VP*
Marjorie Ingram, *Ch Bd*
EMP: 10 **EST:** 1947
SQ FT: 10,000
SALES (est): 2.56MM **Privately Held**
Web: www.valv-trol.com
SIC: 3492 3592 3491 5084 Control valves,
fluid power: hydraulic and pneumatic;
Valves; Industrial valves; Industrial
machinery and equipment

(G-12470)
VEOLIA WTS SYSTEMS USA INC
Also Called: General Ionics
887 Hampshire Rd Ste I (44224-1122)
PHONE..................330 929-1639
Ron Mettler, *Mgr*
EMP: 10
Web: www.suezwatertechnologies.com
SIC: 3589 Water treatment equipment,
industrial
HQ: Veolia Wts Systems Usa, Inc.
3600 Horizon Blvd Ste 100
Trevose PA 19053
866 439-2837

(G-12471)
VMI AMERICAS INC (HQ)
4670 Allen Rd (44224-1042)
PHONE..................330 929-6800
Auke Diaster, *Pr*
▲ **EMP:** 26 **EST:** 1983
SQ FT: 65,000
SALES (est): 20.2MM
SALES (corp-wide): 1.89B **Privately Held**
Web: www.vmi-group.com
SIC: 3565 3544 Packaging machinery;
Special dies, tools, jigs, and fixtures
PA: Tkh Group N.V.
Spinnerstraat 15
Haaksbergen OV 7481
535732900

(G-12472)
WOLFE GRINDING INC
4582 Allen Rd (44224-1091)
PHONE..................330 929-6677

Larry W Wolfe, *Pr*
Phyllis Wolfe, *VP*
EMP: 6 **EST:** 1971
SQ FT: 48,750
SALES (est): 685.66K **Privately Held**
SIC: 3599 Machine shop, jobbing and repair

(G-12473)
WRAYCO INDUSTRIES INC
858 Seasons Rd (44224-1071)
PHONE..................330 688-5617
▲ **EMP:** 106
Web: www.wrayco.com
SIC: 3441 Fabricated structural metal

(G-12474)
WRAYCO MANUFACTURING IN
5010 Hudson Dr (44224-1797)
PHONE..................330 688-5617
EMP: 16 **EST:** 2019
SALES (est): 1.05MM **Privately Held**
SIC: 3999 Manufacturing industries, nec

Strasburg
Tuscarawas County

(G-12475)
ALRON
805 Margo Dr Sw (44680-9792)
PHONE..................330 477-3405
Ron Gritzam, *Pt*
Allen Knotz, *Pt*
EMP: 8 **EST:** 2004
SALES (est): 74.27K **Privately Held**
Web: www.alroncustomfabrication.com
SIC: 2295 Metallizing of fabrics

(G-12476)
B A MALCUIT RACING INC
Also Called: Malcuit Racing Engines
707 S Wooster Ave (44680-9702)
P.O. Box 166 (44680-0166)
PHONE..................330 878-7111
Mark Malcuit, *Pr*
Brad Malcuit, *VP*
EMP: 8 **EST:** 1984
SQ FT: 30,000
SALES (est): 359.52K **Privately Held**
SIC: 3519 3714 Internal combustion
engines, nec; Motor vehicle parts and
accessories

(G-12477)
BEACH CITY LUMBER LLC
5177 Austin Ln Nw (44680-9109)
PHONE..................330 878-4097
Paul Weaver, *Owner*
EMP: 7 **EST:** 1986
SQ FT: 5,000
SALES (est): 253.9K **Privately Held**
SIC: 2421 Lumber: rough, sawed, or planed

(G-12478)
**GREEN RDCED EMSSONS NETWRK
LLC**
Also Called: Gre'n Disc
5029 Hilltop Dr Nw (44680-9069)
PHONE..................330 340-0941
EMP: 8 **EST:** 2010
SALES (est): 425.19K **Privately Held**
SIC: 3714 Motor vehicle parts and
accessories

(G-12479)
KLEEN TEST PRODUCTS CORP
216 12th St Ne (44680-9752)
PHONE..................330 878-5586
Bill Ahlborn, *Brnch Mgr*
EMP: 255

SALES (corp-wide): 331.16MM **Privately Held**
Web: www.kleentest.com
SIC: 2842 Cleaning or polishing preparations, nec
HQ: Kleen Test Products Corporation
1611 Sunset Rd
Port Washington WI 53074
262 284-6600

(G-12480)
LEIDEN CABINET COMPANY LLC
1230 Hensel Ave Ne (44680-9779)
PHONE..................330 425-8555
Dave Marusa, *Mgr*
EMP: 7
SALES (corp-wide): 8.38MM **Privately Held**
Web: www.leidencompany.com
SIC: 5046 2541 Store fixtures; Wood partitions and fixtures
PA: Leiden Cabinet Company, Llc
2385 Edison Blvd
Twinsburg OH 44087
330 425-8555

(G-12481)
LINCOLN MANUFACTURING INC
Also Called: LINCOLN MANUFACTURING, INC.
310 Railroad Ave Se (44680-1235)
PHONE..................330 878-7772
Eric Ward, *Pr*
EMP: 17
SALES (corp-wide): 35.55MM **Privately Held**
Web: www.lincolnmanufacturing.com
SIC: 3999 Barber and beauty shop equipment
PA: Lincoln Manufacturing, Llc
31209 Fm 2978 Rd
Magnolia TX 77354
281 252-9494

(G-12482)
TREMCAR USA INC
436 12th St Ne (44680-9760)
PHONE..................330 878-7708
Daniel Tremblay, *Pr*
Marie Marquis, *
▲ **EMP:** 57 **EST:** 1998
SQ FT: 35,000
SALES (est): 11.47MM
SALES (corp-wide): 2.1MM **Privately Held**
Web: www.tremcar.com
SIC: 3711 Motor vehicles and car bodies
HQ: Tremcar Inc
790 Av Montrichard
Saint-Jean-Sur-Richelieu QC J2X 5
450 347-7822

(G-12483)
UNITED HARDWOODS LTD
5508 Hilltop Dr Nw (44680-9117)
PHONE..................330 878-9510
Norm Shetler, *Prin*
EMP: 9 **EST:** 2006
SALES (est): 445.84K **Privately Held**
Web: www.unitedhardwoodsltd.com
SIC: 2421 Custom sawmill

Streetsboro
Portage County

(G-12484)
ACCURATE FAB LLC
1400 Miller Pkwy (44241-4640)
PHONE..................330 562-3140
EMP: 6 **EST:** 2005

SALES (est): 2.03MM **Privately Held**
Web: www.acsteel.net
SIC: 3441 Ship sections, prefabricated metal

(G-12485)
AGRATRONIX LLC
1790 Miller Pkwy (44241-4633)
PHONE..................330 562-2222
Gerald Stephens, *Managing Member*
▲ **EMP:** 30 **EST:** 2007
SALES (est): 9.75MM **Privately Held**
Web: www.agratronix.com
SIC: 5039 3699 3446 Wire fence, gates, and accessories; Electric fence chargers; Fences, gates, posts, and flagpoles

(G-12486)
ALACRIANT INC (PA)
1760 Miller Pkwy (44241-4611)
PHONE..................330 562-7191
Jeff Berkes, *Pr*
James Berkes, *
Ken Quinn, *
EMP: 55 **EST:** 1997
SQ FT: 72,000
SALES (est): 31.82MM
SALES (corp-wide): 31.82MM **Privately Held**
Web: www.alacriant.com
SIC: 3499 Strapping, metal

(G-12487)
ALACRIANT INC
2500 Crane Centre Dr (44241-5072)
PHONE..................330 562-7191
Andrew Stanford, *Mgr*
EMP: 30
SALES (corp-wide): 31.82MM **Privately Held**
Web: www.alacriant.com
SIC: 3499 Strapping, metal
PA: Alacriant Inc.
1760 Miller Pkwy
Streetsboro OH 44241
330 562-7191

(G-12488)
AURORA PLASTICS LLC (HQ)
Also Called: Aurora Material Solutions
9280 Jefferson St (44241-3966)
PHONE..................330 422-0700
Darrell Hughes, *Pr*
Mike Klein, *
Matthew Kuwatch, *Development**
Steve Harrigan, *
Melissa Neiberlein, *
▲ **EMP:** 30 **EST:** 1997
SALES (est): 106.83MM **Privately Held**
Web: www.auroramaterialsolutions.com
SIC: 2821 3087 Polyvinyl chloride resins, PVC; Custom compound purchased resins
PA: Nautic Partners, Llc
50 Kennedy Plz Fl 12
Providence RI 02903

(G-12489)
AUTOMATED LASER FABRICATION CO
1 Singer Dr (44241)
PHONE..................330 562-7200
Paul Y Shapiro, *Pr*
EMP: 6 **EST:** 2003
SALES (est): 352.54K **Privately Held**
SIC: 3441 Fabricated structural metal

(G-12490)
AUTOMATED PACKAGING SYSTEMS LLC (HQ)
10175 Philipp Pkwy (44241-4041)
PHONE..................330 528-2000

▲ **EMP:** 250 **EST:** 1963
SALES (est): 67.96MM
SALES (corp-wide): 5.39B **Publicly Held**
Web: www.autobag.co.nz
SIC: 3081 3565 Packing materials, plastics sheet; Packaging machinery
PA: Sealed Air Corporation
2415 Cascade Pointe Blvd
Charlotte NC 28208
980 221-3235

(G-12491)
AUTOMATED PACKG SYSTEMS INC
Also Called: AUTOMATED PACKAGING SYSTEMS, INC.
600 Mondial Pkwy (44241-5211)
PHONE..................330 626-2313
Bernard Lerner, *CEO*
EMP: 6
SQ FT: 173,000
SALES (corp-wide): 5.39B **Publicly Held**
Web: www.autobag.com
SIC: 3081 3565 Packing materials, plastics sheet; Packaging machinery
HQ: Automated Packaging Systems, Llc
10175 Philipp Pkwy
Streetsboro OH 44241
330 528-2000

(G-12492)
BERRY GLOBAL INC
1275 Ethan Ave (44241-4977)
PHONE..................330 896-6700
Robert Maltarich, *Mgr*
EMP: 15
Web: www.berryglobal.com
SIC: 3089 Bottle caps, molded plastics
HQ: Berry Global, Inc.
101 Oakley St
Evansville IN 47710

(G-12493)
CLEVELAND STEEL CONTAINER CORP
10048 Aurora Hudson Rd (44241-1636)
PHONE..................330 656-5600
Roger Mayle, *Genl Mgr*
EMP: 27
SALES (corp-wide): 165.45MM **Privately Held**
Web: www.cscpails.com
SIC: 3412 3411 Pails, shipping: metal; Metal cans
PA: Cleveland Steel Container Corporation
100 Executive Pkwy
Hudson OH 44236
440 349-8000

(G-12494)
COMMERCIAL TURF PRODUCTS LTD
1777 Miller Pkwy (44241-4634)
PHONE..................330 995-7000
Mike Sobera, *Genl Mgr*
EMP: 15 **EST:** 1997
SQ FT: 177,000
SALES (est): 3.25MM
SALES (corp-wide): 15.37B **Publicly Held**
SIC: 3524 Lawn and garden equipment
HQ: Mtd Products Inc
5965 Grafton Rd
Valley City OH 44280
330 225-2600

(G-12495)
DAVIS MACHINE PRODUCTS INC
74 Sapphire Ln (44241-4128)
PHONE..................440 474-0247
William G Davis, *Pr*
EMP: 6 **EST:** 1972
SQ FT: 7,200

SALES (est): 189.66K **Privately Held**
SIC: 3599 Machine shop, jobbing and repair

(G-12496)
DELTA SYSTEMS INC
1734 Frost Rd (44241-5008)
P.O. Box 2459 (44241-0459)
PHONE..................330 626-2811
Joey Arnold, *Pr*
Michael R Jeziorski, *
Mark J Fechtel, *
Dean Barry, *
◆ **EMP:** 252 **EST:** 1971
SQ FT: 137,000
SALES (est): 24.26MM **Privately Held**
Web: www.deltasystemsinc.com
SIC: 3613 3625 Switchgear and switchboard apparatus; Relays and industrial controls

(G-12497)
DELUXE CORPORATION
Also Called: Deluxe Business Systems
10030 Philipp Pkwy (44241-4708)
PHONE..................330 342-1500
Robin Lebine, *Prin*
EMP: 54
SALES (corp-wide): 2.12B **Publicly Held**
Web: www.deluxe.com
SIC: 2782 Blankbooks and looseleaf binders
PA: Deluxe Corporation
801 Marquette Ave
Minneapolis MN 55402
651 483-7111

(G-12498)
DRC ACQUISITION INC
Also Called: David Round Company, The
10200 Wellman Rd (44241-1615)
PHONE..................330 656-1600
Bradley R Young, *Pr*
▲ **EMP:** 27 **EST:** 1869
SQ FT: 30,000
SALES (est): 5.73MM **Privately Held**
Web: www.davidround.com
SIC: 3536 3531 Hoists; Winches

(G-12499)
DUDICK INC
1818 Miller Pkwy (44241-5067)
PHONE..................330 562-1970
EMP: 46 **EST:** 2007
SALES (est): 5.01MM **Privately Held**
Web: www.dudick.com
SIC: 3429 Furniture, builders' and other household hardware

(G-12500)
EBCO INC
Also Called: Protectoplas Div
3500 Crane Centre Dr (44241-5074)
PHONE..................330 562-8265
EMP: 20 **EST:** 1972
SALES (est): 2.53MM **Privately Held**
Web: www.protectoplas.com
SIC: 3089 3714 Plastics containers, except foam; Motor vehicle parts and accessories

(G-12501)
EPG INC (DH)
1780 Miller Pkwy (44241-4633)
PHONE..................330 995-9725
Michael Orazen Junior, *Pr*
Michael Scanlon, *VP*
Smith Mckee, *VP Opers*
Gabriel Orazen, *VP*
EMP: 13 **EST:** 1983
SQ FT: 46,000
SALES (est): 4.79MM
SALES (corp-wide): 60.4MM **Privately Held**
Web: www.dudick.com

SIC: 3053 3061 Gaskets, all materials;
Mechanical rubber goods
HQ: Trelleborg Corporation
200 Veterans Blvd Ste 3
South Haven MI 49090
269 639-9891

(G-12502)
GORELL ENTERPRISES INC (DH)
Also Called: Gorell Windows & Doors
10250 Philipp Pkwy (44241-4765)
PHONE.............................724 465-1800
Wayne C Gorell, *Ch Bd*
Brian Zimmerman, *
Michael A Rempel, *
Arnold S Levitt, *
EMP: 360 EST: 1993
SQ FT: 240,000
SALES (est): 5.76MM
SALES (corp-wide): 5.58B Privately Held
SIC: 3089 5031 Plastics hardware and
building products; Doors and windows
HQ: Soft-Lite L.L.C.
10250 Phillip Pkwy
Streetsboro OH 44241
330 528-3400

(G-12503)
HP ENTERPRISE INC
Also Called: Jolly Pats
10008 State Route 43 (44241-4940)
PHONE.............................800 232-7950
Rob Miavitz, *Pr*
Brenda Miavitz, *Sec*
◆ EMP: 22 EST: 1976
SQ FT: 20,000
SALES (est): 4.84MM Privately Held
Web: www.horsemenspride.com
SIC: 3089 Extruded finished plastics
products, nec

(G-12504)
HUDSON HINES HILL COMPANY
1818 Miller Pkwy (44241-5067)
PHONE.............................330 562-1970
Tom Dudick, *Pr*
EMP: 55 EST: 1982
SALES (est): 3.19MM Privately Held
Web: www.dudick.com
SIC: 2851 Lacquers, varnishes, enamels,
and other coatings

(G-12505)
INTERNATIONAL PAPER COMPANY
Also Called: International Paper
700 Mondial Pkwy (44241-4511)
PHONE.............................330 626-7300
Chuck Bakaitis, *Brnch Mgr*
EMP: 53
SALES (corp-wide): 18.62B Publicly Held
Web: www.internationalpaper.com
SIC: 2653 Boxes, corrugated: made from
purchased materials
PA: International Paper Company
6400 Poplar Ave
Memphis TN 38197
901 419-7000

(G-12506)
**INTERNTNAL CUTNG SOLUTIONS
INC**
Also Called: I C S
1790 Hannum Dr (44241-5131)
PHONE.............................440 786-1700
James Syvertsen, *Pr*
Terry Syvertsen, *VP*
Nancy Syvertsen, *Sec*
Patricia Syvertsen, *Treas*
EMP: 9 EST: 2005
SQ FT: 40,000
SALES (est): 534.38K Privately Held

Web:
internationalcuttingsolutions.blogspot.com
SIC: 3465 3841 Automotive stampings;
Surgical and medical instruments

(G-12507)
JOSEPH INDUSTRIES INC
Also Called: BUCKEYE FASTENERS
COMPANY
10039 Aurora Hudson Rd (44241-1600)
PHONE.............................330 528-0091
Clyde Faust, *Pr*
Linda Kerekes, *
▲ EMP: 52 EST: 1969
SQ FT: 76,260
SALES (est): 7.05MM
SALES (corp-wide): 46.16MM Privately
Held
Web: www.joseph.com
SIC: 3714 5084 3713 3566 Motor vehicle
parts and accessories; Lift trucks and parts;
Truck and bus bodies; Speed changers,
drives, and gears
PA: Fastener Industries, Inc.
1 Berea Commons Ste 209
Berea OH 44017
440 243-0034

(G-12508)
LANGE GRINDING & MACHINING INC
10165 Philipp Pkwy (44241-4706)
PHONE.............................330 463-3500
Richard C Lange, *Pr*
EMP: 23 EST: 1989
SQ FT: 30,000
SALES (est): 2.09MM Privately Held
Web: www.langegrinding.com
SIC: 3599 Machine shop, jobbing and repair

(G-12509)
METALFAB GROUP
10145 Philipp Pkwy (44241-5099)
PHONE.............................440 543-6234
EMP: 7 EST: 2016
SALES (est): 750.81K Privately Held
Web: www.metalfabgroup.com
SIC: 3441 3443 3444 3449 Fabricated
structural metal; Fabricated plate work
(boiler shop); Sheet metalwork;
Miscellaneous metalwork

(G-12510)
**MICRO-PISE MSRMENT SYSTEMS
LLC**
Also Called: Ametek Micro-Poise
Measurement
555 Mondial Pkwy (44241-4510)
P.O. Box 1869 (44309-1869)
PHONE.............................330 541-9100
Steve Harris, *Managing Member*
Kenneth Garvey, *Managing Member*
◆ EMP: 250 EST: 2007
SALES (est): 51.47MM
SALES (corp-wide): 6.94B Publicly Held
Web: www.micropoise.com
SIC: 3559 Automotive maintenance
equipment
PA: Ametek, Inc.
1100 Cassatt Rd
Berwyn PA 19312
610 647-2121

(G-12511)
MM SERVICE
8936 State Route 14 (44241-5605)
PHONE.............................330 626-2520
David Phillips, *Owner*
EMP: 6 EST: 2002
SQ FT: 10,000
SALES (est): 694.82K Privately Held

SIC: 3524 Lawn and garden equipment

(G-12512)
MOJONNIER USA LLC
10325 State Route 43 Ste N (44241-4945)
PHONE.............................844 665-6664
Matt Brinn, *Mgr*
EMP: 24 EST: 2015
SALES (est): 5.8MM Privately Held
Web: www.mojonnier.com
SIC: 3556 Beverage machinery

(G-12513)
NATURAL ESSENTIALS INC (PA)
Also Called: Bulk Apothecary
1830 Miller Pkwy (44241-5067)
PHONE.............................330 562-8022
Gary Pellegrino, *Pr*
◆ EMP: 158 EST: 1992
SQ FT: 17,000
SALES (est): 22.31MM Privately Held
Web: www.naturalessentialsinc.com
SIC: 2844 2899 Cosmetic preparations; Oils
and essential oils

(G-12514)
**NORTHCOAST ENVIRONMENTAL
LABS**
10100 Wellman Rd (44241-1613)
PHONE.............................330 342-3377
Timothy Spevak, *Pr*
Dave Morehead, *VP*
Fred Pratt, *VP*
John Lawrence, *VP*
EMP: 8 EST: 1994
SQ FT: 3,000
SALES (est): 964.74K Privately Held
SIC: 3826 8731 Environmental testing
equipment; Commercial physical research

(G-12515)
PERMCO INC
1500 Frost Rd (44241-5004)
P.O. Box 2068 (44241-0068)
PHONE.............................330 626-2801
Robert L Shell Junior, *Ch*
Bernard Shell, *
Robert L Shell Iii, *COO*
Phillip Todd Shell, *
Lena Shell, *
▲ EMP: 110 EST: 1964
SALES (est): 2.36MM
SALES (corp-wide): 24.34MM Privately
Held
Web: www.permco.com
SIC: 3594 Fluid power pumps and motors
PA: Guyan International, Inc.
5 Nichols Dr
Barboursville WV 25504
304 733-1029

(G-12516)
PETROX INC
10005 Ellsworth Rd (44241-1608)
PHONE.............................330 653-5526
Benjamin Cart, *Pr*
Mark Depew, *VP*
EMP: 10 EST: 1986
SALES (est): 3.11MM Privately Held
SIC: 1389 5082 Oil field services, nec; Oil
field equipment

(G-12517)
PM GRAPHICS INC
10170 Philipp Pkwy (44241-4705)
PHONE.............................330 650-0861
Paul W Mc Ghee Ii, *Pr*
Christine Mcghee, *Sec*
Robert Davis, *
EMP: 50 EST: 1959
SQ FT: 35,000

SALES (est): 8.17MM Privately Held
Web: www.pmgraphics.com
SIC: 2752 Offset printing

(G-12518)
R R DONNELLEY & SONS COMPANY
Also Called: R R Donnelley
10400 Danner Dr (44241-5070)
PHONE.............................330 562-5250
John Augustiniak, *Mgr*
EMP: 51
SALES (corp-wide): 15B Privately Held
Web: www.rrd.com
SIC: 2752 Commercial printing, lithographic
HQ: R. R. Donnelley & Sons Company
227 W Monroe St Ste 500
Chicago IL 60606
312 326-8000

(G-12519)
RB&W MANUFACTURING LLC (HQ)
10080 Wellman Rd (44241-1611)
PHONE.............................234 380-8540
Craig Cowan, *Pr*
▲ EMP: 9 EST: 1998
SALES (est): 9.13MM
SALES (corp-wide): 1.66B Publicly Held
Web: www.rbwmfg.com
SIC: 5085 3452 3469 Fasteners, industrial:
nuts, bolts, screws, etc.; Bolts, nuts, rivets,
and washers; Stamping metal for the trade
PA: Park-Ohio Holdings Corp.
6065 Parkland Blvd
Cleveland OH 44124
440 947-2000

(G-12520)
READY FIELD SOLUTIONS LLC
1240 Ethan Ave (44241-4976)
PHONE.............................330 562-0550
EMP: 24 EST: 2016
SALES (est): 4.91MM Privately Held
Web: www.readyfieldsolutions.com
SIC: 3271 Blocks, concrete: landscape or
retaining wall

(G-12521)
S TOYS HOLDINGS LLC
10010 Aurora Hudson Rd (44241-1621)
PHONE.............................330 656-0440
Jack Bresics, *CEO*
Jim Smith, *CFO*
James Schaefer, *COO*
✿ EMP: 900 EST: 2006
SALES (est): 1.21MM Privately Held
Web: www.step2.com
SIC: 3944 3089 Games, toys, and children's
vehicles; Plastics containers, except foam

(G-12522)
SAFEGUARD TECHNOLOGY INC
Also Called: Safeguard
1460 Miller Pkwy (44241-4640)
PHONE.............................330 995-5200
William Kosinski, *Pr*
▲ EMP: 33 EST: 1992
SQ FT: 20,510
SALES (est): 5.45MM Privately Held
Web: www.safeguard-technology.com
SIC: 3069 Stair treads, rubber

(G-12523)
**SELAS HEAT TECHNOLOGY CO LLC
(HQ)**
11012 Aurora Hudson Rd (44241-1629)
PHONE.............................800 523-6500
David S Bovenizer, *CEO*
▲ EMP: 28 EST: 2005
SALES (est): 21.9MM
SALES (corp-wide): 41.96MM Privately
Held

Web: www.selas.com
SIC: 3433 3255 3823 3564 Heating equipment, except electric; Clay refractories ; Process control instruments; Blowers and fans
PA: Lionheart Holdings Llc
54 Friends Ln Ste 125
Newtown PA 18940
215 283-8400

(G-12524)
SPECTRUM MACHINE INC (PA)
1668 Frost Rd (44241-5006)
PHONE..............................330 626-3666
Kevin Lamb, *Pr*
Timothy Lamb, *VP*
Todd Lamb, *Sec*
EMP: 15 **EST:** 1987
SQ FT: 31,000
SALES (est): 5.04MM
SALES (corp-wide): 5.04MM **Privately Held**
Web: www.spectrummachine.com
SIC: 3545 3469 3599 Machine tool accessories; Machine parts, stamped or pressed metal; Machine shop, jobbing and repair

(G-12525)
STEP2 COMPANY LLC (HQ)
Also Called: Step 2
10010 Aurora Hudson Rd (44241-1621)
PHONE..............................866 429-5200
Cody Fox, *CEO*
◆ **EMP:** 500 **EST:** 2006
SQ FT: 400,000
SALES (est): 76.09MM **Privately Held**
Web: www.step2.com
SIC: 3089 3944 3423 Molding primary plastics; Games, toys, and children's vehicles; Hand and edge tools, nec
PA: Step2 Discovery, Llc
3001 N Rouse Ave
Pittsburg KS 66762

(G-12526)
TECHNOLOGY HOUSE LTD
10036 Aurora Hudson Rd (44241-1640)
PHONE..............................440 248-3025
EMP: 15 **EST:** 2008
SALES (est): 3.39MM **Privately Held**
Web: www.tth.com
SIC: 3721 3559 Aircraft; Robots, molding and forming plastics

(G-12527)
TECHNOLOGY HOUSE LTD (PA)
Also Called: North Cape Manufacturing
10036 Aurora Hudson Rd (44241-1640)
PHONE..............................440 248-3025
▲ **EMP:** 8 **EST:** 1996
SQ FT: 14,000
SALES (est): 16.26MM **Privately Held**
Web: www.tth.com
SIC: 8711 3544 3369 Industrial engineers; Special dies, tools, jigs, and fixtures; Nonferrous foundries, nec

(G-12528)
TELCON LLC
1677 Miller Pkwy (44241-4635)
PHONE..............................330 562-5566
EMP: 75 **EST:** 1987
SQ FT: 56,000
SALES (est): 1.15MM **Privately Held**
Web: www.telcon.us
SIC: 3599 3369 Machine shop, jobbing and repair; Nonferrous foundries, nec

(G-12529)
VIKING FORGE LLC
4500 Crane Centre Dr (44241-5080)
PHONE..............................330 562-3366
EMP: 131 **EST:** 2018
SALES (est): 33.75MM
SALES (corp-wide): 33.75MM **Privately Held**
Web: www.viking-forge.com
SIC: 3462 Iron and steel forgings
PA: Forge Holding, Llc
4500 Crane Centre Dr
Streetsboro OH 44241
330 562-3366

(G-12530)
WALTCO LIFT CORP (PA)
1777 Miller Pkwy (44241-4634)
P.O. Box P.O. Box 354 (44278)
PHONE..............................330 633-9191
Dave Hammes, *Sr Mgr*
◆ **EMP:** 120 **EST:** 1960
SQ FT: 70,000
SALES (est): 24.73MM
SALES (corp-wide): 24.73MM **Privately Held**
Web: www.hiab.com
SIC: 3537 3593 Industrial trucks and tractors ; Fluid power cylinders, hydraulic or pneumatic

---

Strongsville
Cuyahoga County

(G-12531)
ACTION INDUSTRIES LTD (PA)
Also Called: Action
13325 Darice Pkwy (44149-3819)
PHONE..............................216 252-7800
John E Marron, *Pr*
Guenter Plamper, *Sec*
▲ **EMP:** 8 **EST:** 1980
SQ FT: 25,000
SALES (est): 5.19MM
SALES (corp-wide): 5.19MM **Privately Held**
Web: www.action-ind.com
SIC: 3699 2431 Door opening and closing devices, electrical; Weather strip, wood

(G-12532)
ADVANCED TECH UTILIZATION CO
Also Called: Advanced Technology
12005 Prospect Rd Unit 1 (44149-2935)
P.O. Box 360461 (44136-0008)
PHONE..............................440 238-3770
Terry Yamrick, *Owner*
EMP: 10 **EST:** 1967
SQ FT: 2,500
SALES (est): 435.13K **Privately Held**
Web: www.newandusedmachines.com
SIC: 3542 5084 Rebuilt machine tools, metal forming types; Metalworking machinery

(G-12533)
AKZO NOBEL PAINTS LLC
Also Called: Glidden Professional Paint Ctr
8381 Pearl Rd (44136-1637)
P.O. Box 3200 (15230-3200)
PHONE..............................440 297-8000
◆ **EMP:** 5000
SIC: 2851 2891 Paints and paint additives; Adhesives

(G-12534)
ALBION INDUSTRIES INC
20246 Progress Dr (44149-3296)
PHONE..............................440 238-1955
Ralph Holstein, *Pr*

Caroline Holstein, *
Roman T Keenen, *
◆ **EMP:** 30 **EST:** 1971
SQ FT: 21,000
SALES (est): 2.5MM **Privately Held**
Web: www.albioncasters.com
SIC: 2514 Frames for box springs or bedsprings: metal

(G-12535)
ALPHAGRAPHICS 507 INC
Also Called: AlphaGraphics
14765 Pearl Rd (44136-5003)
PHONE..............................440 878-9700
Rob Kammer, *Pr*
EMP: 6 **EST:** 1999
SQ FT: 3,000
SALES (est): 247.64K **Privately Held**
Web: www.alphagraphics.com
SIC: 2752 Commercial printing, lithographic

(G-12536)
AMERICAN WATER SERVICES INC
17449 W Sprague Rd (44136-1666)
PHONE..............................440 243-9840
Rick Meloy, *Proj Mgr*
EMP: 7
SALES (est): 517.37K **Privately Held**
SIC: 3823 4941 Water quality monitoring and control systems; Water supply

(G-12537)
APPH WICHITA INC
Also Called: Apph
15900 Foltz Pkwy (44149-5531)
PHONE..............................316 943-5752
Mike Meshey, *Pr*
Jon Sharrock, *
▲ **EMP:** 50 **EST:** 1959
SALES (est): 490.01K **Privately Held**
SIC: 7699 3594 3728 Aircraft and heavy equipment repair services; Fluid power pumps and motors; Aircraft parts and equipment, nec
HQ: Heroux-Devtek Inc. - Kitchener Division
1111 Saint-Charles St W Suite 600
West Tower
Longueuil QC J4K 5
450 679-5450

(G-12538)
ARMATURE COIL EQUIPMENT INC
Also Called: Ace Equipment Company
22269 Horseshoe Ln (44149-9256)
PHONE..............................216 267-6366
Robert F Heran, *Pr*
Jean Heran, *Sec*
EMP: 12 **EST:** 1919
SALES (est): 2.18MM **Privately Held**
Web: www.armaturecoil.com
SIC: 3549 3567 Coil winding machines for springs; Industrial furnaces and ovens

(G-12539)
ATLANTIC TOOL & DIE COMPANY (PA)
19963 Progress Dr (44149-3299)
PHONE..............................440 238-6931
Frank Mehwald, *Pr*
Mike Mehwald, *
◆ **EMP:** 240 **EST:** 1947
SQ FT: 110,000
SALES (est): 96.49MM
SALES (corp-wide): 96.49MM **Privately Held**
Web: www.atlantictool.com
SIC: 3469 3544 Stamping metal for the trade ; Special dies, tools, jigs, and fixtures

(G-12540)
AUTO TECHNOLOGY COMPANY
20026 Progress Dr (44149-3214)
PHONE..............................440 572-7800
Kevin A Smith, *Pr*
Walter Senney, *VP*
EMP: 15 **EST:** 1999
SQ FT: 50,000
SALES (est): 2.62MM **Privately Held**
Web: www.autotechnology.com
SIC: 3826 Environmental testing equipment

(G-12541)
AUTOMATED MFG SOLUTIONS INC
Also Called: AMS
19706 Progress Dr (44149-3208)
PHONE..............................440 878-3711
David Minney, *Pr*
Thomas P Setele, *Pr*
Mark Ogorzaly, *OF OPTN*
EMP: 18 **EST:** 2002
SQ FT: 8,000
SALES (est): 6.33MM **Privately Held**
Web: www.automfgsolutions.com
SIC: 3599 Machine shop, jobbing and repair

(G-12542)
AUTOWAX INC
15015 Foltz Pkwy (44149-4728)
PHONE..............................440 334-4417
Alina Baron, *CEO*
James Baron, *VP*
EMP: 6 **EST:** 2012
SALES (est): 1.61MM **Privately Held**
Web: www.autowaxinc.com
SIC: 3711 Motor vehicles and car bodies

(G-12543)
AVERY DENNISON CORPORATION
17700 Foltz Pkwy (44149-5536)
PHONE..............................440 878-7000
Gary Murphy, *Mgr*
EMP: 400
SALES (corp-wide): 8.76B **Publicly Held**
Web: www.averydennison.com
SIC: 2672 Adhesive papers, labels, or tapes: from purchased material
PA: Avery Dennison Corporation
8080 Norton Pkwy
Mentor OH 44060
440 534-6000

(G-12544)
BEARINGS MANUFACTURING COMPANY (PA)
Also Called: BMC
15157 Foltz Pkwy (44149-4730)
PHONE..............................440 846-5517
Steve Sivo, *Pr*
Jeff Walls, *
EMP: 17 **EST:** 2001
SALES (est): 9.73MM
SALES (corp-wide): 9.73MM **Privately Held**
Web: www.bmcbearing.com
SIC: 3562 5085 Ball bearings and parts; Bearings, bushings, wheels, and gears

(G-12545)
BLUE CRESCENT ENTERPRISES INC
Also Called: AlphaGraphics Strongsville
17295 Foltz Pkwy Ste B (44149-5568)
P.O. Box 360379 (44136-0036)
PHONE..............................440 878-9700
Saleh Afif Alafifi, *Pr*
EMP: 7 **EST:** 2016
SQ FT: 3,800
SALES (est): 1.21MM **Privately Held**
Web: www.alphagraphics.com

▲ = Import ▼ = Export
◆ = Import/Export

SIC: 2752 Commercial printing, lithographic

(G-12546)
BREW KETTLE INC
Also Called: Ringneck Brewing Company
8377 Pearl Rd (44136-1637)
PHONE......................440 234-8788
Chris J Mckim, *Pr*
EMP: 11 EST: 1995
SQ FT: 3,500
SALES (est): 771.4K **Privately Held**
Web: www.thebrewkettle.com
SIC: 2082 5149 Beer (alcoholic beverage);
Groceries and related products, nec

(G-12547)
CARDINAL MACHINE COMPANY
14459 Foltz Pkwy (44149-4797)
PHONE......................440 238-7050
Richard Z Kaszei, *CEO*
Greg Kaszei, *Pr*
EMP: 8 EST: 1974
SQ FT: 10,000
SALES (est): 959K **Privately Held**
Web: www.cardinalmachine.biz
SIC: 3599 Machine shop, jobbing and repair

(G-12548)
CCL LABEL INC
Also Called: CCL Design
17890 Foltz Pkwy (44149-5503)
PHONE......................440 878-7000
John Walsh, *Brnch Mgr*
EMP: 80
SALES (corp-wide): 4.84B **Privately Held**
Web: www.cclind.com
SIC: 2672 3081 3497 2678 Adhesive
papers, labels, or tapes: from purchased
material; Unsupported plastics film and
sheet; Metal foil and leaf; Notebooks: made
from purchased paper
HQ: Ccl Label, Inc.
161 Worcester Rd Ste 603
Framingham MA 01701
508 872-4511

(G-12549)
CCL LABEL INC
Also Called: CCL Design Electronics
17700 Foltz Pkwy (44149-5536)
PHONE......................440 878-7277
Patrick Thomas, *Brnch Mgr*
EMP: 350
SALES (corp-wide): 4.84B **Privately Held**
Web: www.cclind.com
SIC: 2759 Labels and seals: printing, nsk
HQ: Ccl Label, Inc.
161 Worcester Rd Ste 603
Framingham MA 01701
508 872-4511

(G-12550)
CLARK-RELIANCE LLC (PA)
Also Called: Jerguson
16633 Foltz Pkwy (44149-5597)
PHONE......................440 572-1500
Matthew P Figgie Junior, *Ch Bd*
Rick Solon, *
Mike Pressnell, *
◆ EMP: 155 EST: 1884
SQ FT: 93,000
SALES (est): 21.26MM
SALES (corp-wide): 21.26MM **Privately Held**
Web: www.clarkreliance.com
SIC: 3823 3491 Industrial process control
instruments; Process control regulator
valves

(G-12551)
CUSTOM IMPRINT
19573 Progress Dr (44149-3203)
PHONE......................440 238-4488
Ed Rebish, *Owner*
EMP: 10 EST: 1999
SALES (est): 84.34K **Privately Held**
Web: www.customimprint.com
SIC: 2752 Commercial printing, lithographic

(G-12552)
CYLINDERS AND VALVES INC
20811 Westwood Dr (44149-3999)
P.O. Box 360555 (44136-0010)
PHONE......................440 238-7343
James P Gardner Iii, *Pr*
Katherine Frederick, *Mgr*
EMP: 8 EST: 1958
SQ FT: 7,500
SALES (est): 4.13MM **Privately Held**
Web: www.cylval.com
SIC: 3594 3593 3494 Motors: hydraulic, fluid
power, or air; Fluid power cylinders and
actuators; Valves and pipe fittings, nec

(G-12553)
DEDICATED INDUSTRIES INC (PA)
Also Called: Hinchcliff Products
13550 Falling Water Rd Ste 105
(44136-4348)
P.O. Box 386 (26287-0386)
PHONE......................440 238-5200
Jay D Phillips, *Pr*
EMP: 76 EST: 1923
SQ FT: 100,000
SALES (est): 5.62MM **Privately Held**
Web: www.hinchcliffproducts.com
SIC: 2448 2449 Pallets, wood; Wood
containers, nec

(G-12554)
DONPRINT INC
Also Called: Worldmark
17700 Foltz Pkwy (44149-5536)
PHONE......................847 573-7777
▲ EMP: 36
SIC: 2759 Labels and seals: printing, nsk

(G-12555)
DUPLI-SYSTEMS INC
Also Called: Ohio Cut Sheet
8260 Dow Cir (44136-1762)
PHONE......................440 234-9415
Bud Eldridge, *CEO*
Randy Eldridge, *
Todd Eldridge, *
Dave Griffith, *
EMP: 125 EST: 1955
SALES (est): 3.93MM **Privately Held**
Web: www.dupli-systems.com
SIC: 2759 2754 2782 2761 Commercial
printing, nec; Forms, business: gravure
printing; Blankbooks and looseleaf binders;
Manifold business forms

(G-12556)
DUROX COMPANY
12312 Alameda Dr (44149-3023)
PHONE......................440 238-5350
Richard A Mathes, *Sec*
▲ EMP: 70 EST: 1953
SQ FT: 50,000
SALES (est): 3.37MM **Publicly Held**
Web: www.mechanicalrubber.com
SIC: 3053 Gaskets, all materials
HQ: Wabtec Components Llc
30 Isabella St
Pittsburgh PA 15212
412 825-1000

(G-12557)
EFFICIENT MACHINE PDTS CORP
12133 Alameda Dr (44149-3018)
PHONE......................440 268-0205
Ted Imbrogno, *Pr*
EMP: 40 EST: 1962
SQ FT: 31,000
SALES (est): 4.94MM **Privately Held**
Web: www.efficientm.com
SIC: 3599 Machine shop, jobbing and repair

(G-12558)
ERNST FLOW INDUSTRIES LLC
16633 Foltz Pkwy (44149-5513)
PHONE......................732 938-5641
Roger Ernst, *Pr*
Eugene Ernst Junior, *Treas*
John Ernst, *VP*
EMP: 14 EST: 1962
SQ FT: 9,000
SALES (est): 2.94MM
SALES (corp-wide): 21.26MM **Privately Held**
Web: www.ernstflow.com
SIC: 3823 3824 Flow instruments, industrial
process type; Water meters
PA: Clark-Reliance Llc
16633 Foltz Pkwy
Strongsville OH 44149
440 572-1500

(G-12559)
FOUNDATION SOFTWARE LLC (PA)
17999 Foltz Pkwy (44149-5565)
PHONE......................330 220-8383
Fred Ode, *CEO*
Kathleen Ode, *Sec*
Paul Noonan, *CGO*
EMP: 479 EST: 1985
SQ FT: 16,000
SALES (est): 33.65MM
SALES (corp-wide): 33.65MM **Privately Held**
Web: www.foundationsoft.com
SIC: 7372 7371 Prepackaged software;
Software programming applications

(G-12560)
GRAPHTECH COMMUNICATIONS INC
19001 Bennington Dr (44136-8229)
PHONE......................216 676-1020
Stephen L Adamson, *Pr*
William Kall, *VP*
EMP: 10 EST: 1977
SALES (est): 943.25K **Privately Held**
Web:
www.graphtechcommunications.com
SIC: 2752 Offset printing

(G-12561)
GREAT LAKES BREWING CO
13675 Darice Pkwy (44149-3823)
PHONE......................216 771-4404
EMP: 40
SALES (corp-wide): 24.22MM **Privately Held**
Web: www.greatlakesbrewing.com
SIC: 2082 Malt beverages
PA: The Great Lakes Brewing Co
2516 Market Ave
Cleveland OH 44113
216 771-4404

(G-12562)
GUARANTEE SPECIALTIES INC
Also Called: Garvin Industries Div
21693 Drake Rd (44149-6614)
P.O. Box 360247 (44136-0005)
PHONE......................216 451-9744
Armando E Pages, *Pr*
Carol Braunschweig, *

▲ EMP: 9 EST: 1916
SQ FT: 75,000
SALES (est): 780.21K **Privately Held**
SIC: 3463 3465 3469 Plumbing fixture
forgings, nonferrous; Automotive stampings
; Stamping metal for the trade

(G-12563)
HDI LANDING GEAR USA INC
Also Called: Heroux Devtek Landing Gear Div
663 Montgomery Ave (44149-5531)
PHONE......................937 325-1586
Frederick Gagne, *Pr*
EMP: 50
SQ FT: 115,000
Web: www.herouxdevtek.com
SIC: 3728 Alighting (landing gear)
assemblies, aircraft
HQ: Hdi Landing Gear Usa Inc.
663 Montgomery Ave
Springfield OH 45506

(G-12564)
HUGHES CORPORATION (PA)
Also Called: Weschler Instruments
16900 Foltz Pkwy (44149-5520)
PHONE......................440 238-2550
Paul Layne, *CEO*
David E Hughes, *
Douglas Hughes, *
Michael F Dorman, *
Esther Carpenter, *
EMP: 30 EST: 1941
SQ FT: 11,500
SALES (est): 26.85MM
SALES (corp-wide): 26.85MM **Privately Held**
Web: www.weschler.com
SIC: 5063 3825 Electrical apparatus and
equipment; Instruments to measure
electricity

(G-12565)
HUMPHREY POPCORN COMPANY (PA)
11606 Pearl Rd (44136-3320)
P.O. Box 23003 (44123-0003)
PHONE......................216 662-6629
Micheal Prokop, *Pr*
Dudley Humphrey, *Pr*
Elizabeth Humphrey, *VP*
EMP: 10 EST: 1897
SQ FT: 11,000
SALES (est): 941.49K
SALES (corp-wide): 941.49K **Privately Held**
Web: www.humphreycompany.com
SIC: 0191 2064 5145 General farms,
primarily crop; Popcorn balls or other
treated popcorn products; Popcorn and
supplies

(G-12566)
IMPERIAL DIE & MFG CO
22930 Royalton Rd (44149-3842)
PHONE......................440 268-9080
Ronald Lapossy, *Pr*
Kenneth Lapossy, *Treas*
EMP: 8 EST: 1959
SQ FT: 20,000
SALES (est): 1.09MM **Privately Held**
Web: www.imperialdiemfg.com
SIC: 3469 3544 Stamping metal for the trade
; Special dies and tools

(G-12567)
INFINIUM WALL SYSTEMS INC
21000 Infinium Way (44149-5000)
PHONE......................440 572-5000
Shawn Gaffney, *Pr*
Caryn Gaffney, *Stockholder*

▼ **EMP:** 30 **EST:** 2003
SALES (est): 16.6MM **Privately Held**
Web: www.infiniumwalls.com
SIC: 2522 Office furniture, except wood

(G-12568)
INSTRUMENTORS INC
22077 Drake Rd (44149-6606)
PHONE..............................440 238-3430
Robert A Heinrich, *Pr*
James R Heinrich, *VP*
Elvera Heinrich, *Sec*
EMP: 6 **EST:** 1973
SQ FT: 10,000
SALES (est): 959.98K **Privately Held**
Web: www.instrumentorsinc.com
SIC: 3829 7699 5084 Measuring and
controlling devices, nec; Scientific
equipment repair service; Instruments and
control equipment

(G-12569)
KALINICH FENCE COMPANY INC
12223 Prospect Rd (44149-2994)
PHONE..............................440 238-6127
Mike Kalinich Senior, *Pr*
Mike Kalinich Junior, *VP*
Erma Kalinich, *Sec*
EMP: 18 **EST:** 1918
SQ FT: 33,000
SALES (est): 2.42MM **Privately Held**
Web: www.kalinichfenceco.com
SIC: 2499 Fencing, wood

(G-12570)
LEES GRINDING INC
15620 Foltz Pkwy (44149-4741)
P.O. Box 360169 (44136-0003)
PHONE..............................440 572-4610
Nick D Papanikolaou, *Pr*
EMP: 30 **EST:** 1961
SQ FT: 20,000
SALES (est): 5.53MM **Privately Held**
Web: www.leesgrinding.com
SIC: 3599 Machine shop, jobbing and repair

(G-12571)
LITEHOUSE PRODUCTS LLC (PA)
Also Called: Litehouse Pools & Spas
10883 Pearl Rd Ste 301 (44136-3359)
PHONE..............................440 638-2350
▲ **EMP:** 50 **EST:** 2004
SALES (est): 22.56MM
SALES (corp-wide): 22.56MM **Privately
Held**
Web: www.litehouse.com
SIC: 5091 3949 5999 5712 Swimming pools,
equipment and supplies; Water sports
equipment; Swimming pools, above ground
; Outdoor and garden furniture

(G-12572)
LUMITEX INC (PA)
Also Called: Lumitex
8443 Dow Cir (44136-1796)
PHONE..............................440 243-8401
Peter W Broer, *Pr*
Thomas E Walden, *
Richard D Gridley, *
Maynard H Murch V, *Dir*
▲ **EMP:** 90 **EST:** 1985
SQ FT: 19,000
SALES (est): 9.28MM
SALES (corp-wide): 9.28MM **Privately
Held**
Web: www.lumitex.com
SIC: 3646 3641 3648 3845 Commercial
lighting fixtures; Electric lamps; Lighting
equipment, nec; Electromedical equipment

(G-12573)
MECHANICAL RUBBER OHIO LLC
12312 Alameda Dr (44149-3023)
PHONE..............................845 986-2271
Cedric Glasper, *Pr*
EMP: 22 **EST:** 2020
SALES (est): 1.48MM **Privately Held**
Web: www.mechanicalrubber.com
SIC: 3053 Gaskets, all materials
PA: Mechanical Rubber Products
Company, Inc.
77 Forester Ave Ste 1
Warwick NY 10990

(G-12574)
MOMENTIVE PERF MTRLS QUARTZ
22557 Lunn Rd (44149-4871)
PHONE..............................408 436-6221
▲ **EMP:** 9 **EST:** 2008
SALES (est): 498.18K **Privately Held**
Web: www.momentivetech.com
SIC: 2869 Industrial organic chemicals, nec

(G-12575)
MOMENTIVE PRFMCE MTLS QRTZ
INC (HQ)
Also Called: Momentive Technologies
22557 Lunn Rd (44149-4871)
PHONE..............................440 878-5700
Philip Rose, *Pr*
Ryan Croskey, *
◆ **EMP:** 50 **EST:** 1996
SALES (est): 161.67MM
SALES (corp-wide): 365MM **Privately
Held**
Web: www.momentivetech.com
SIC: 2869 3479 3446 3297 Silicones;
Coating of metals with silicon; Architectural
metalwork; Nonclay refractories
PA: Momq Holding Company
22557 W Lunn Rd
Strongsville OH 44149
440 878-5700

(G-12576)
MOMQ HOLDING COMPANY (PA)
22557 Lunn Rd (44149-4871)
PHONE..............................440 878-5700
Philip Rose, *Pr*
Jp Park, *VP*
Ryan Croskey, *
Daniel Fashimpaur, *
Dale Brosky, *Tax Director*
EMP: 950 **EST:** 2019
SALES (est): 365MM
SALES (corp-wide): 365MM **Privately
Held**
SIC: 3299 Tubing for electrical purposes,
quartz

(G-12577)
MUELLER ART COVER & BINDING
CO
12005 Alameda Dr (44149-3016)
PHONE..............................440 238-3303
TOLL FREE: 888
Edmond Mueller, *Pr*
EMP: 45 **EST:** 1932
SQ FT: 38,000
SALES (est): 269.71K **Privately Held**
Web: www.muellerartcover.com
SIC: 2782 7336 Looseleaf binders and
devices; Graphic arts and related design

(G-12578)
NEWBERRY WOOD ENTERPRISES
INC (PA)
12223 Prospect Rd (44149-2939)
PHONE..............................440 238-6127
Mike Kalinich, *Pr*

EMP: 9 **EST:** 1983
SQ FT: 25,000
SALES (est): 1.89MM
SALES (corp-wide): 1.89MM **Privately
Held**
SIC: 2421 Custom sawmill

(G-12579)
NPL HOMECARE LLC
13500 Darice Pkwy Ste A (44149-3840)
PHONE..............................440 365-8581
TOLL FREE: 800
David Haynes, *Pr*
John T Thaler, *
Joyce A Thaler, *
Carol G Thaler, *
EMP: 36 **EST:** 1993
SALES (est): 12.34MM **Privately Held**
Web: www.nplhomemedical.com
SIC: 3842 Wheelchairs

(G-12580)
NUTRO CORPORATION
Also Called: Nutro Machinery
11515 Alameda Dr (44149-3006)
PHONE..............................440 572-3800
Mark Rooney, *Pr*
George Wharton, *
Lisa Stanton, *
EMP: 55 **EST:** 1951
SQ FT: 65,000
SALES (est): 7.1MM **Privately Held**
Web: www.nutroinc.com
SIC: 3569 3559 Liquid automation
machinery and equipment; Paint making
machinery

(G-12581)
NUTRO INC
11515 Alameda Dr (44149-3006)
PHONE..............................440 572-3800
Mark Rooney, *Prin*
Christian Nuesser, *
EMP: 31 **EST:** 2008
SALES (est): 7.26MM
SALES (corp-wide): 56.51MM **Privately
Held**
Web: www.nutro.com
SIC: 3559 3251 Paint making machinery;
Ceramic glazed brick, clay
PA: Venjakob Maschinenbau Gmbh & Co.
Kg
Augsburger Str. 2-6
Rheda-Wiedenbruck NW 33378
524296030

(G-12582)
OHIO CLLBRTIVE LRNG SLTONS
INC (PA)
Also Called: Smart Solutions
17171 Golden Star Dr (44136-7666)
PHONE..............................216 595-5289
Anand Julka, *Pr*
▲ **EMP:** 50 **EST:** 1983
SALES (est): 9.5MM
SALES (corp-wide): 9.5MM **Privately Held**
SIC: 7372 8741 Business oriented computer
software; Business management

(G-12583)
OUTOTEC OYJ
Also Called: Outotec North America
11288 Alameda Dr (44149-3037)
PHONE..............................440 783-3336
Tim Robinson, *Brnch Mgr*
EMP: 65
Web:
mntstoprdgz2lxjekdcd7e.z6.web.core.window
s.net
SIC: 3441 Fabricated structural metal
PA: Metso Oyj

Rauhalanpuisto 9
Espoo 02230

(G-12584)
PA MA INC
Also Called: Pama Tool & Die
11288 Alameda Dr (44149-3037)
P.O. Box 361459 (44136-0025)
PHONE..............................440 846-3799
Ron Pansil, *Pr*
Donna Pansil, *VP*
Danuta Pansil, *Treas*
EMP: 7 **EST:** 1985
SQ FT: 8,000
SALES (est): 1.21MM **Privately Held**
SIC: 3544 Special dies and tools

(G-12585)
PIPE LINE DEVELOPMENT
COMPANY
Also Called: Plidco Ppline Repr Ppline Mint
11792 Alameda Dr (44149-3011)
PHONE..............................440 871-5700
Kimberly Smith, *Pr*
Dave Pincura, *
◆ **EMP:** 96 **EST:** 1949
SQ FT: 70,000
SALES (est): 20.69MM **Privately Held**
Web: www.plidco.com
SIC: 3498 Pipe fittings, fabricated from
purchased pipe

(G-12586)
PITTSBURGH PAINTS CO
Glidden Professional Paint Ctr
16651 W Sprague Rd (44136-1757)
PHONE..............................440 826-5100
Patricia Starrett, *Mgr*
EMP: 434
SALES (corp-wide): 388.64MM **Privately
Held**
Web: www.ppgpaints.com
SIC: 2851 Paints and allied products
PA: The Pittsburgh Paints Co
400 Bertha Lamme Dr
Cranberry Township PA 16066
724 742-5200

(G-12587)
PPG ARCHITECTURAL COATINGS
LLC
Also Called: Synteko
15885 W Sprague Rd (44136-1772)
PHONE..............................440 297-8000
▼ **EMP:** 92
SIC: 2851 2899 2891 2861 Paints and paint
additives; Chemical preparations, nec;
Adhesives and sealants; Gum and wood
chemicals

(G-12588)
PPG INDUSTRIES INC
Also Called: Powder Coatings
19699 Progress Dr (44149-3298)
PHONE..............................440 572-2800
William Shaw, *Brnch Mgr*
EMP: 100
SALES (corp-wide): 18.25B **Publicly Held**
Web: www.ppg.com
SIC: 2851 Paints and allied products
PA: Ppg Industries, Inc.
1 Ppg Pl
Pittsburgh PA 15272
412 434-3131

(G-12589)
PPG INDUSTRIES OHIO INC
Also Called: PPG AF US
9699 Progress Dr (44149)
PHONE..............................440 572-6777

▲ = Import ▼ = Export
◆ = Import/Export

EMP: 66
SALES (corp-wide): 18.25B **Publicly Held**
Web: www.ppg.com
SIC: 2851 Paints and paint additives
HQ: Ppg Industries Ohio, Inc.
3800 West 143rd St
Cleveland OH 44111
216 671-0050

(G-12590)
PRECISION PRODUCTION LLC
Also Called: Precision Production
8250 Dow Cir (44136-1762)
PHONE..........................216 252-0372
Craig Cook, *Pr*
Mathew A Carson, *
Bryon N Shafer, *
▲ **EMP:** 40 **EST:** 1978
SQ FT: 38,000
SALES (est): 6.41MM **Privately Held**
Web: www.precisionproduction.com
SIC: 3599 Machine shop, jobbing and repair

(G-12591)
R M TOOL & DIE INC
19768 Progress Dr (44149-3208)
PHONE..........................440 238-6459
Mike Regian, *CEO*
EMP: 12 **EST:** 1991
SQ FT: 25,000
SALES (est): 1.42MM **Privately Held**
Web: www.rmtoolinc.com
SIC: 3544 Special dies and tools

(G-12592)
RAFTER EQUIPMENT COMPANY LLC
12430 Alameda Dr (44149-3025)
PHONE..........................440 572-3700
Walter Krenz, *Pr*
Paul Rohde, *
▲ **EMP:** 30 **EST:** 1917
SQ FT: 22,500
SALES (est): 5.31MM **Privately Held**
Web: www.rafterequipment.com
SIC: 3542 3549 3547 3541 Machine tools, metal forming type; Metalworking machinery, nec; Rolling mill machinery; Machine tools, metal cutting type

(G-12593)
ROBERT E MCGRATH INC
Also Called: Olympia Candies
11606 Pearl Rd (44136-3320)
PHONE..........................440 572-7747
EMP: 19 **EST:** 1911
SQ FT: 15,000
SALES (est): 3.78MM **Privately Held**
Web: www.olympiasweettreats.com
SIC: 5145 5441 2096 2066 Candy; Candy; Potato chips and similar snacks; Chocolate and cocoa products

(G-12594)
SCEPTER PUBLISHERS
21510 Drake Rd (44149-6617)
P.O. Box 360694 (44136)
PHONE..........................212 354-0670
Robert Singerline, *Pr*
John Powers, *Sls Mgr*
EMP: 7 **EST:** 1952
SQ FT: 700
SALES (est): 2.14MM **Privately Held**
Web: www.scepterpublishers.org
SIC: 2731 Books, publishing only

(G-12595)
SCHWEBEL BAKING COMPANY
22626 Royalton Rd (44149-3838)
PHONE..........................440 846-1921
Steve Leach, *Mgr*

EMP: 12
SALES (corp-wide): 71.65MM **Privately Held**
Web: www.schwebels.com
SIC: 2051 Bakery: wholesale or wholesale/retail combined
PA: Schwebel Baking Company
965 E Midlothian Blvd
Youngstown OH 44502
330 783-2860

(G-12596)
SENTRO TECH CORPORATION
21294 Drake Rd (44149-6623)
PHONE..........................440 260-0364
Neil Zhu, *Mgr*
▲ **EMP:** 7 **EST:** 1997
SALES (est): 2.29MM **Privately Held**
Web: www.sentrotech.com
SIC: 3567 Industrial furnaces and ovens

(G-12597)
SEVILLE SAND & GRAVEL INC
12663 Bristol Ln (44149-9240)
P.O. Box 360 (44254-0360)
PHONE..........................330 948-0168
FAX: 330 948-4186
EMP: 22 **EST:** 1958
SQ FT: 600
SALES (est): 2MM **Privately Held**
Web: www.sevsg.com
SIC: 1442 Construction sand mining

(G-12598)
SGL CARBON TECHNIC LLC
21945 Drake Rd (44149-6608)
PHONE..........................440 572-3600
Ken Manning, *Pr*
▼ **EMP:** 36 **EST:** 2004
SQ FT: 46,004
SALES (est): 16.14MM
SALES (corp-wide): 1.09B **Privately Held**
Web: www.sglcarbon.com
SIC: 3443 Fabricated plate work (boiler shop)
PA: Sgl Carbon Se
Sohnleinstr. 8
Wiesbaden HE 65201
61160290

(G-12599)
SHEIBAN JEWELRY INC
16938 Pearl Rd (44136-6053)
PHONE..........................440 238-0616
Tony Sheiban, *Pr*
EMP: 10 **EST:** 1976
SQ FT: 3,300
SALES (est): 1.9MM **Privately Held**
Web: www.sheibanjewelers.com
SIC: 5094 5944 7631 3911 Jewelry; Jewelry, precious stones and precious metals; Watch, clock, and jewelry repair; Jewelry, precious metal

(G-12600)
SHERWIN-WILLIAMS COMPANY
Also Called: Sherwin-Williams
11410 Alameda Dr (44149-3005)
PHONE..........................440 846-4328
Blair Lacour, *Pr*
EMP: 17
SQ FT: 24,150
SALES (corp-wide): 23.1B **Publicly Held**
Web: www.sherwin-williams.com
SIC: 5231 2851 Paint; Paints and allied products
PA: The Sherwin-Williams Company
101 W Prospect Ave
Cleveland OH 44115
216 566-2000

(G-12601)
SLY INC (PA)
8300 Dow Cir Ste 600 (44136-6607)
PHONE..........................800 334-2957
E D Davis, *Prin*
Sidney C Vessy, *Prin*
W C Bruce, *Prin*
W C Sly, *Prin*
W W Sly, *Prin*
EMP: 50 **EST:** 1874
SQ FT: 36,000
SALES (est): 21.62MM
SALES (corp-wide): 21.62MM **Privately Held**
Web: www.slyinc.com
SIC: 3564 Dust or fume collecting equipment, industrial

(G-12602)
SOLUTION INDUSTRIES LLC
21555 Drake Rd (44149-6616)
PHONE..........................440 816-9500
John Radel, *Pr*
▲ **EMP:** 11 **EST:** 2014
SALES (est): 1.45MM **Privately Held**
Web: www.solutionind.com
SIC: 3965 Fasteners, buttons, needles, and pins

(G-12603)
SPARTRONICS STRONGSVILLE INC
22740 Lunn Rd (44149-4899)
PHONE..........................440 878-4630
Paul Fraipont, *Pr*
Greg Kelble, *
EMP: 59 **EST:** 2006
SALES (est): 10.78MM
SALES (corp-wide): 810.86MM **Privately Held**
Web: www.spartronics.com
SIC: 3841 Surgical and medical instruments
HQ: Spartronics Watertown, Llc
2920 Kelly Ave
Watertown SD 57201

(G-12604)
SPIEGELBERG MANUFACTURING INC (HQ)
Also Called: Stud Welding Associates
12200 Alameda Dr (44149-3050)
PHONE..........................440 324-3042
▲ **EMP:** 51 **EST:** 1984
SALES (est): 17.64MM
SALES (corp-wide): 15.62B **Publicly Held**
Web: www.proweldinternational.com
SIC: 3548 Welding apparatus
PA: Stanley Black & Decker, Inc.
1000 Stanley Dr
New Britain CT 06053
860 225-5111

(G-12605)
STEFRA INC
Also Called: E & E Parts Machining
18021 Cliffside Dr (44136-4256)
PHONE..........................440 846-8240
Frank Ungerer, *Pr*
Steve Pucha, *VP*
Colleen Ungerer, *CEO*
EMP: 7 **EST:** 1966
SQ FT: 2,900
SALES (est): 265.11K **Privately Held**
SIC: 3599 Machine shop, jobbing and repair

(G-12606)
STELFAST LLC (HQ)
22979 Stelfast Pkwy (44149-5561)
PHONE..........................440 879-0077
Bill Nikitis, *CEO*
Simmi Sakhuja, *
◆ **EMP:** 32 **EST:** 1972

SQ FT: 85,000
SALES (est): 22.18MM
SALES (corp-wide): 103.69MM **Privately Held**
Web: www.stelfast.com
SIC: 3452 3965 Bolts, metal; Fasteners
PA: Lindstrom, Llc
2950 100th Ct Ne
Blaine MN 55449
763 780-4200

(G-12607)
STUD WELDING ASSOCIATES INC
Also Called: Stud Welding
12200 Alameda Dr (44149-3021)
PHONE..........................440 783-3160
▼ **EMP:** 70
SIC: 5085 3496 1799 Fasteners, industrial: nuts, bolts, screws, etc.; Clips and fasteners, made from purchased wire; Welding on site

(G-12608)
SWEETIES OLYMPIA TREATS LLC
11606 Pearl Rd (44136-3320)
PHONE..........................440 572-7747
Robert Mcgrath, *Pr*
EMP: 18 **EST:** 2022
SALES (est): 2.31MM
SALES (corp-wide): 14.22MM **Privately Held**
Web: www.olympiasweettreats.com
SIC: 5145 5441 2096 2066 Candy; Candy; Potato chips and similar snacks; Chocolate and cocoa products
PA: Brookpark Holdings Llc
6770 Brookpark Rd
Cleveland OH 44129
216 739-2244

(G-12609)
TADD SPRING CO INC
15060 Foltz Pkwy (44149-4729)
PHONE..........................440 572-1313
Mark Anguilano, *Pr*
EMP: 6 **EST:** 1962
SQ FT: 5,000
SALES (est): 957.52K **Privately Held**
Web: www.taddspring.com
SIC: 3495 3493 Precision springs; Steel springs, except wire

(G-12610)
TRANSCENDIA INC
22889 Lunn Rd (44149-4800)
P.O. Box 368003 (44136-9703)
PHONE..........................440 638-2000
James Carlin, *Brnch Mgr*
EMP: 80
SQ FT: 25,000
SALES (corp-wide): 290.26MM **Privately Held**
Web: www.transcendia.com
SIC: 3081 Unsupported plastics film and sheet
PA: Transcendia, Inc.
9201 W Belmont Ave
Franklin Park IL 60131
847 678-1800

(G-12611)
TSW INDUSTRIES INC
14960 Foltz Pkwy (44149-4727)
PHONE..........................440 572-7200
Tich Wan, *Pr*
Lee Wan, *
▲ **EMP:** 30 **EST:** 1981
SQ FT: 41,000
SALES (est): 3.92MM **Privately Held**
Web: www.tswindustries.com

SIC: **3599** Machine shop, jobbing and repair

(G-12612)
WALLOVER ENTERPRISES INC (DH)
21845 Drake Rd (44149-6610)
PHONE..............................440 238-9250
George M Marquis, *Pr*
William C Cutri, *
EMP: 30 **EST:** 1863
SQ FT: 28,000
SALES (est): 20.33MM
SALES (corp-wide): 1.84B **Publicly Held**
SIC: **2992 8734** Oils and greases, blending
and compounding; Product testing
laboratories
HQ: Quaker Houghton Pa, Inc.
901 E Hctor St One Qker P
Conshohocken PA 19428
610 832-4000

(G-12613)
WALLOVER OIL COMPANY INC (DH)
Also Called: Woco
21845 Drake Rd (44149-6610)
PHONE..............................440 238-9250
Michael F Barry, *Ch Bd*
Mary Dean Hall, *VP*
◆ **EMP:** 33 **EST:** 1835
SQ FT: 28,000
SALES (est): 17.83MM
SALES (corp-wide): 1.84B **Publicly Held**
Web: www.walloveroil.com
SIC: **2992 2841** Oils and greases, blending
and compounding; Soap and other
detergents
HQ: Wallover Enterprises Inc.
21845 Drake Rd
Strongsville OH 44149
440 238-9250

(G-12614)
WESTERN RESERVE SLEEVE INC
22360 Royalton Rd (44149-3826)
P.O. Box 361310 (44136-0022)
PHONE..............................440 238-8850
Scott Gilbert, *Pr*
Sharon Gilbert, *Sec*
EMP: 6 **EST:** 1993
SALES (est): 1.93MM **Privately Held**
Web: www.a-roo.com
SIC: **3081** Packing materials, plastics sheet

Struthers
Mahoning County

(G-12615)
ADD-A-TRAP LLC
488 Como St (44471-1237)
PHONE..............................330 750-0417
Robert N Davenport, *CEO*
Ray Hassay, *Pr*
Allan Stratron, *COO*
EMP: 6 **EST:** 2001
SALES (est): 391.62K **Privately Held**
Web: www.addatrap.com
SIC: **3088** Plastics plumbing fixtures

(G-12616)
ASTRO ALUMINUM ENTERPRISES INC
65 Main St (44471-1942)
P.O. Box 208 (44471-0208)
PHONE..............................330 755-1414
Paul Cene, *Pr*
James Dibacco, *
EMP: 7 **EST:** 1994
SALES (est): 252K **Privately Held**
Web: www.astroshapes.com

SIC: **3354** Aluminum extruded products

(G-12617)
ASTRO-COATINGS INC
65 Main St (44471-1942)
P.O. Box 208 (44471-0208)
PHONE..............................330 755-1414
Paul Cene, *Pr*
Jim Di Bacco, *
Robert Cene Junior, *VP*
EMP: 7 **EST:** 1986
SQ FT: 25,000
SALES (est): 455.17K **Privately Held**
Web: www.astroshapes.com
SIC: **3354** Aluminum extruded products

(G-12618)
GIANNIOS CANDY CO INC (PA)
430 Youngstown Poland Rd (44471-1058)
PHONE..............................330 755-7000
John G Giannios, *Pr*
EMP: 49 **EST:** 1910
SQ FT: 28,000
SALES (est): 9.44MM
SALES (corp-wide): 9.44MM **Privately Held**
Web: www.giannioscandy.com
SIC: **2066 2064** Chocolate candy, solid;
Candy and other confectionery products

(G-12619)
KURTZ TOOL & DIE CO INC
164 State St (44471-1956)
P.O. Box 116 (44471-0116)
PHONE..............................330 755-7723
Robert Kurtz Junior, *Pr*
Robert Kurtz Senior, *Stockholder*
EMP: 6 **EST:** 1960
SALES (est): 822.46K **Privately Held**
SIC: **3544** Die sets for metal stamping
(presses)

(G-12620)
QUALITY BAR INC
17 Union Ste 7 (44471-1964)
PHONE..............................330 755-0000
Donald A Casey, *Ch Bd*
Carrie Casey, *Pr*
EMP: 29 **EST:** 1995
SALES (est): 456.37K
SALES (corp-wide): 3.83MM **Privately Held**
SIC: **3312** Stainless steel
PA: Casey Equipment Corporation
275 Kappa Dr
Pittsburgh PA 15238
412 963-1111

Stryker
Williams County

(G-12621)
DALTON CORPORATION
310 Ellis St (43557-9329)
P.O. Box 2600 (43557-2600)
PHONE..............................419 682-6328
Alan Sheets, *Mgr*
EMP: 42
SALES (corp-wide): 7.28B **Privately Held**
Web: www.daltoncorporation.com
SIC: **3625** Industrial controls: push button,
selector switches, pilot
HQ: The Dalton Corporation
1900 E Jefferson St
Warsaw IN 46580
574 267-8111

(G-12622)
DALTON STRYKER MCHINING FCILTY
310 Ellis St (43557-9329)
PHONE..............................419 682-6328
Joe Derita, *Pr*
Ron Schmucker, *
EMP: 138 **EST:** 1988
SALES (est): 1.79MM
SALES (corp-wide): 841.88MM **Privately Held**
Web: www.daltoncorporation.com
SIC: **3599** Machine shop, jobbing and repair
HQ: Neenah Foundry Company
2121 Brooks Ave
Neenah WI 54956
920 725-7000

(G-12623)
FRANKS SAWMILL INC
Rd 1950 (43557)
P.O. Box 4600 (43557-4600)
PHONE..............................419 682-3831
Dave Frank, *Pr*
Mike Meyer, *Sec*
EMP: 10 **EST:** 1958
SQ FT: 8,000
SALES (est): 290.66K **Privately Held**
SIC: **2448** Pallets, wood

(G-12624)
LYONDLLBSELL ADVNCED PLYMERS I
103 Railroad Ave (43557-9492)
PHONE..............................419 682-3311
Jeff Miccichi, *Mgr*
EMP: 93
SQ FT: 54,000
Web: www.lyondellbasell.com
SIC: **2865 2851 2821 2816** Color pigments,
organic; Lacquers, varnishes, enamels, and
other coatings; Plastics materials and resins
; Inorganic pigments
HQ: Lyondellbasell Advanced Polymers Inc.
1221 Mckinney St Ste 300
Houston TX 77010
713 309-7200

(G-12625)
OHIO TIMBERLAND PRODUCTS INC
102 Railroad Ave (43557-9533)
P.O. Box 330 (43557-0330)
PHONE..............................419 682-6322
Mike Burkholder, *Pr*
Harley Burkholder, *VP*
Donna Burkholder, *Sec*
EMP: 10 **EST:** 1996
SQ FT: 15,000
SALES (est): 465.42K **Privately Held**
Web: www.ohiotimberland.com
SIC: **2411** Poles, posts, and pilings:
untreated wood

(G-12626)
QUADCO REHABILITATION CTR INC (PA)
Also Called: Northwest Products
427 N Defiance St (43557-9472)
PHONE..............................419 682-1011
Bruce Abell, *Ex Dir*
EMP: 199 **EST:** 1967
SQ FT: 24,000
SALES (est): 1.27MM
SALES (corp-wide): 1.27MM **Privately Held**
Web: www.quadcorehab.org
SIC: **8331 2448 2441** Vocational
rehabilitation agency; Wood pallets and
skids; Nailed wood boxes and shook

(G-12627)
SAUDER MANUFACTURING CO
Also Called: Stryker Plant
201 Horton St (43557-9310)
P.O. Box 110 (43557-0110)
PHONE..............................419 682-3061
Luther Gautsche, *VP*
EMP: 97
SQ FT: 46,000
SALES (corp-wide): 543.69MM **Privately Held**
Web: www.saudermfg.com
SIC: **2531 2521** Chairs, portable folding;
Wood office furniture
HQ: Sauder Manufacturing Co.
930 W Barre Rd
Archbold OH 43502
419 445-7670

(G-12628)
WILLIAMS PORK CO OP
18487 County Road F (43557-9306)
PHONE..............................419 682-9022
Paul Kalmbach, *Pr*
EMP: 9 **EST:** 1997
SALES (est): 100.25K **Privately Held**
SIC: **2013** Pork, cured: from purchased meat

Sugar Grove
Fairfield County

(G-12629)
COMMERCIAL MUSIC SERVICE CO
Also Called: Chime Master Systems
6312 Goss Rd (43155-9610)
PHONE..............................740 746-8500
Jeffrey A Crook, *Pr*
▼ **EMP:** 8 **EST:** 1959
SALES (est): 993.07K **Privately Held**
Web: www.chimemaster.com
SIC: **3931** Bells (musical instruments)

(G-12630)
WARTHMAN DRILLING INC
7525 Lancaster Logan Rd (43155)
P.O. Box 360 (43155-0360)
PHONE..............................740 746-9950
Steven Warthman, *Pr*
EMP: 6 **EST:** 1965
SALES (est): 713.85K **Privately Held**
Web: www.warthmandrillinginc.com
SIC: **1781 1381** Servicing, water wells;
Drilling oil and gas wells

Sugarcreek
Tuscarawas County

(G-12631)
ARCHER-DANIELS-MIDLAND COMPANY
Also Called: ADM
554 Pleasant Valley Rd Nw (44681-7800)
P.O. Box 486 (44681-0486)
PHONE..............................330 852-3025
Doug Miller, *Brnch Mgr*
EMP: 7
SQ FT: 12,000
SALES (corp-wide): 85.53B **Publicly Held**
Web: www.adm.com
SIC: **2048** Prepared feeds, nec
PA: Archer-Daniels-Midland Company
77 W Wacker Dr Ste 4600
Chicago IL 60601
312 634-8100

▲ = Import ▼ = Export
◆ = Import/Export

(G-12632)
BELDEN BRICK COMPANY LLC
Also Called: Plant 8
700 Edelweiss Dr Ne (44681-9501)
P.O. Box 430 (44681-0430)
PHONE.............................330 456-0031
Doug Mutchelknaus, *Prin*
EMP: 68
SALES (corp-wide): 113.08MM **Privately Held**
Web: www.beldenbrick.com
SIC: 3251 3271 Structural brick and blocks; Brick, concrete
HQ: The Belden Brick Company Llc
700 Tuscarawas St W Uppr
Canton OH 44702
330 456-0031

(G-12633)
BELDEN BRICK COMPANY LLC
Also Called: Belden Brick Plant 3
690 Dover Rd Ne (44681-7683)
P.O. Box 20910 (44701-0910)
PHONE.............................330 265-2030
Rick Hicks, *Mgr*
EMP: 57
SALES (corp-wide): 113.08MM **Privately Held**
Web: www.beldenbrick.com
SIC: 3251 3271 Structural brick and blocks; Brick, concrete
HQ: The Belden Brick Company Llc
700 Tuscarawas St W Uppr
Canton OH 44702
330 456-0031

(G-12634)
CARLISLE OAK
3872 Township Road 162 (44681-9621)
PHONE.............................330 852-8734
David Miller, *Owner*
EMP: 7 **EST:** 1991
SALES (est): 359.4K **Privately Held**
SIC: 2511 Wood household furniture

(G-12635)
CARLISLE PRTG WALNUT CREEK LTD
2673 Township Road 421 (44681-9486)
PHONE.............................330 852-9922
Marcus Wengerd, *Pr*
EMP: 35 **EST:** 1992
SALES (est): 6.53MM **Privately Held**
Web: www.carlisleprinting.com
SIC: 2621 2791 Catalog, magazine, and newsprint papers; Typesetting

(G-12636)
CENTURY COMPONENTS LLC
1691 Sr-39 (44681)
PHONE.............................330 852-3610
Chad B Yoder, *VP*
EMP: 6 **EST:** 2019
SALES (est): 338.47K **Privately Held**
SIC: 2434 Wood kitchen cabinets

(G-12637)
EAGLE MACHINERY & SUPPLY INC
422 Dutch Valley Dr Ne (44681-7517)
PHONE.............................330 852-1300
Kirk Spillman, *Pr*
Lori Spillman, *Sec*
▲ **EMP:** 21 **EST:** 2003
SQ FT: 20,000
SALES (est): 4.89MM **Privately Held**
Web: www.eaglemachines.com
SIC: 3541 Machine tool replacement & repair parts, metal cutting types

(G-12638)
FARMERSTOWN MEATS
2933 Township Road 163 (44681-9635)
PHONE.............................330 897-7972
Lucille Gingerich, *Owner*
Raymond Gingerich, *Owner*
EMP: 6 **EST:** 1982
SALES (est): 361.8K **Privately Held**
SIC: 2011 Meat packing plants

(G-12639)
JACOB & LEVIS LTD
1689 State Route 39 (44681-9666)
PHONE.............................330 852-7600
EMP: 6 **EST:** 2015
SALES (est): 667.04K **Privately Held**
Web: www.jacobandlevis.com
SIC: 2434 Wood kitchen cabinets

(G-12640)
L & M MINERAL CO
2010 County Road 144 (44681-9439)
PHONE.............................330 852-3696
John E Ling Junior, *Pr*
Merle Mullet, *Treas*
EMP: 8 **EST:** 1954
SALES (est): 634.48K **Privately Held**
Web: www.andrew-wright.net
SIC: 1459 1221 Clays (common) quarrying; Bituminous coal and lignite-surface mining

(G-12641)
MIDDAUGH ENTERPRISES INC
Also Called: Idea Works
211 Yoder Ave Ne (44681)
P.O. Box 400 (44681-0400)
PHONE.............................330 852-2471
Steven Middaugh, *Pr*
L Wade Middaugh, *VP*
Jeri Middaugh, *Sec*
EMP: 6 **EST:** 1956
SQ FT: 8,500
SALES (est): 993.35K **Privately Held**
Web: www.middaughprinters.com
SIC: 2752 2759 Offset printing; Imprinting

(G-12642)
MILLER MANUFACTURING INC
Also Called: Miller Wood Design
2705 Shetler Rd Nw (44681-7604)
P.O. Box 425 (44681-0425)
PHONE.............................330 852-0689
Raymond Miller, *Pr*
▼ **EMP:** 6 **EST:** 1993
SALES (est): 292.52K **Privately Held**
SIC: 2493 2499 2435 2431 Particleboard, plastic laminated; Decorative wood and woodwork; Hardwood veneer and plywood; Millwork

(G-12643)
MULLET ENTERPRISES INC (PA)
Also Called: Tmk Farm Service
138 2nd St Nw (44681-7824)
P.O. Box 278 (44681-0278)
PHONE.............................330 852-4681
Larry Tietje, *Pr*
Raymond Mullet, *VP*
▼ **EMP:** 8 **EST:** 2008
SQ FT: 34,000
SALES (est): 3.97MM
SALES (corp-wide): 3.97MM **Privately Held**
SIC: 5153 2041 Grain elevators; Flour and other grain mill products

(G-12644)
PALLET DISTRIBUTORS INC
Also Called: Scenic Wood Products
10343 Copperhead Rd Nw (44681-7768)
PHONE.............................330 852-3531
Martin Troyer, *Genl Mgr*
EMP: 28
Web: www.epalletinc.com
SIC: 2448 Pallets, wood
PA: Pallet Distributors, Inc.
14701 Detroit Ave Ste 750
Lakewood OH 44107

(G-12645)
PLEASANT VALLEY READY MIX INC
559 Pleasant Valley Rd Nw (44681-7800)
P.O. Box 436 (44681-0436)
PHONE.............................330 852-2613
Daniel O Miller, *Pr*
EMP: 10 **EST:** 1989
SQ FT: 3,000
SALES (est): 415.56K **Privately Held**
SIC: 3273 5211 Ready-mixed concrete; Masonry materials and supplies

(G-12646)
PROVIA HOLDINGS INC (PA)
Also Called: Provia - Heritage Stone
2150 State Route 39 (44681-9201)
PHONE.............................330 852-4711
Bill Mullet, *Prin*
Brian Miller, *
Larry Troyer, *
Willis Schlabach, *
Phil Wengerd, *
EMP: 180 **EST:** 1972
SQ FT: 280,000
SALES (est): 100.7MM
SALES (corp-wide): 100.7MM **Privately Held**
Web: www.provia.com
SIC: 3442 5031 Metal doors; Door frames, all materials

(G-12647)
RNR ENTERPRISES LLC
1361 County Road 108 (44681-9631)
PHONE.............................330 852-3022
EMP: 10 **EST:** 1998
SALES (est): 1.45MM **Privately Held**
Web: www.rnrenterprisesltd.com
SIC: 2511 Wood household furniture

(G-12648)
RUBIX LLC
2310 Township Road 444 (44681-9466)
PHONE.............................330 577-8249
Josie Miller, *Managing Member*
EMP: 6 **EST:** 2021
SALES (est): 885.29K **Privately Held**
SIC: 3825 Instruments to measure electricity

(G-12649)
SCHLABACH PRINTERS LLC
Also Called: Schlabach Printers
798 State Route 93 Nw (44681-7726)
PHONE.............................330 852-4687
Dan Miller, *Pt*
EMP: 20 **EST:** 1979
SQ FT: 3,500
SALES (est): 3.75MM **Privately Held**
Web: www.schlabachprinters.com
SIC: 2759 2752 Screen printing; Commercial printing, lithographic

(G-12650)
SKYLINE CORPORATION
Also Called: SKYLINE CORPORATION
580 Mill St Nw (44681-9561)
PHONE.............................330 852-2483
Bruce Monteith, *Mgr*
EMP: 136
SQ FT: 100,000
SALES (corp-wide): 2.02B **Publicly Held**
Web: www.skylinehomes.com

SIC: 2451 3448 2452 Mobile homes; Prefabricated metal buildings and components; Prefabricated wood buildings
PA: Champion Homes, Inc.
755 W Big Bevr Rd Ste 100
Troy MI 48084
248 614-8211

(G-12651)
SUGARCREEK SHAVINGS LLC
3121 Winklepleck Rd Nw (44681-7656)
PHONE.............................330 763-4239
Ruth Troyer, *Prin*
EMP: 9 **EST:** 2012
SALES (est): 675.01K **Privately Held**
Web: www.sugarcreekshavings.com
SIC: 2421 Sawdust and shavings

(G-12652)
SUPERB INDUSTRIES INC
330 3rd St Nw (44681-9310)
P.O. Box 708 (44681)
PHONE.............................330 852-0500
John Miller, *Pr*
Susan Miller, *
▲ **EMP:** 75 **EST:** 1986
SQ FT: 50,000
SALES (est): 9.64MM **Privately Held**
Web: www.superbindustries.com
SIC: 3625 3491 Control equipment, electric; Valves, automatic control

(G-12653)
SWP LEGACY LTD
10143 Copperhead Rd Nw (44681-7770)
P.O. Box 396 (44681-0396)
PHONE.............................330 340-9663
Paul Monaco, *
EMP: 55 **EST:** 1996
SALES (est): 3.67MM **Privately Held**
SIC: 2448 Pallets, wood

(G-12654)
TRUPOINT PRODUCTS LLC
Uknown (44681)
P.O. Box 72 (44687-0072)
PHONE.............................330 204-3302
Myron Miller, *Owner*
EMP: 10 **EST:** 2015
SALES (est): 613.11K **Privately Held**
SIC: 3312 3495 Wire products, steel or iron; Wire springs

(G-12655)
TUSCO HARDWOODS LLC
Also Called: M & M Hardwoods
10887 Gerber Valley Rd Nw (44681-7932)
PHONE.............................330 852-4281
EMP: 9 **EST:** 1966
SQ FT: 10,000
SALES (est): 750.31K **Privately Held**
SIC: 2448 2421 Wood pallets and skids; Sawmills and planing mills, general

(G-12656)
WEAVER BARNS LTD
1696 State Route 39 (44681-9666)
PHONE.............................330 852-2103
Jonathan Beachy, *Contrlr*
Michael Troyer, *Off Mgr*
EMP: 10 **EST:** 1993
SALES (est): 1.35MM **Privately Held**
Web: www.weaverbarns.com
SIC: 2452 Prefabricated buildings, wood

(G-12657)
WEAVERS FURNITURE LTD
Also Called: Weaver Craft of Sugarcreek
7011 Old Route 39 Nw (44681-7968)
PHONE.............................330 852-2701

Wayne Weaver, *Owner*
▲ **EMP:** 17 **EST:** 1992
SQ FT: 42,000
SALES (est): 6.29MM **Privately Held**
Web: www.weaverfurniturestore.com
SIC: 2512 5023 Upholstered household
　furniture; Homefurnishings

(G-12658)
YODER LUMBER CO INC
3799 County Road 70 (44681-9426)
PHONE......................330 893-3131
Paul Dow, *Brnch Mgr*
EMP: 47
SALES (corp-wide): 24.4MM **Privately
Held**
Web: www.yoderlumber.com
SIC: 5211 2435 2426 2421 Planing mill
　products and lumber; Hardwood veneer
　and plywood; Hardwood dimension and
　flooring mills; Sawmills and planing mills,
　general
PA: Yoder Lumber Co., Inc.
　4515 Township Rd 367
　Millersburg OH 44654
　330 893-3121

Sullivan
Ashland County

(G-12659)
J L CUSTOM WOODWORKING LLC
587 Us-224 (44880)
PHONE......................419 704-5181
Christina Gonzales, *Managing Member*
EMP: 8 **EST:** 2018
SALES (est): 490.28K **Privately Held**
Web: www.jlcabinetry.com
SIC: 2434 Wood kitchen cabinets

Summerfield
Noble County

(G-12660)
MARKWEST ENERGY PARTNERS LP
Also Called: Seneca Processing Facility
26645 Zep Rd E (43788-9505)
PHONE......................740 838-1434
EMP: 11
Web: www.markwest.com
SIC: 4922 1389 1321 Pipelines, natural gas;
　Gas compressing (natural gas) at the fields;
　Fractionating natural gas liquids
HQ: Markwest Energy Partners, L.P.
　1515 Arphoe St Twr 1 Ste
　Denver CO 80202
　303 925-9200

Summitville
Columbiana County

(G-12661)
SUMMITVILLE TILES INC (DH)
Also Called: Summitville Laboratories
15364 State Rte 644 (43962)
P.O. Box 73 (43962-0073)
PHONE......................330 223-1511
▲ **EMP:** 30 **EST:** 1995
SALES (est): 35.54MM
SALES (corp-wide): 4.59B **Privately Held**
Web: www.summitville.com
SIC: 3253 Mosaic tile, glazed and unglazed:
　ceramic
HQ: General Shale Brick, Inc.
　3015 Bristol Hwy
　Johnson City TN 37601
　423 282-4661

Sunbury
Delaware County

(G-12662)
BRY-AIR INC
10793 E State Route 37 (43074-9311)
PHONE......................740 965-2974
Mel Meyers, *Pr*
Doug Howery, *
◆ **EMP:** 43 **EST:** 1964
SQ FT: 40,000
SALES (est): 9.61MM **Privately Held**
Web: www.bry-air.com
SIC: 3585 3826 3535 3823 Dehumidifiers
　electric, except portable; Environmental
　testing equipment; Conveyors and
　conveying equipment; Process control
　instruments

(G-12663)
DUFFEE FINISHING INC
4860 N County Line Rd (43074-8305)
PHONE......................740 965-4848
Nancy Duffee, *VP*
EMP: 8 **EST:** 1967
SQ FT: 20,000
SALES (est): 573.93K **Privately Held**
Web: www.duffeefinishing.com
SIC: 3479 3399 Painting of metal products;
　Powder, metal

(G-12664)
EN-HANCED PRODUCTS INC
14111 Chambers Rd (43074-8361)
PHONE......................614 882-7400
James M Hance, *Pr*
EMP: 7 **EST:** 2001
SALES (est): 498.63K **Privately Held**
Web: www.en-hancedproducts.com
SIC: 3443 Fabricated plate work (boiler shop)

(G-12665)
GERLING AND ASSOCIATES INC
200 Kintner Pkwy (43074-9320)
PHONE......................740 965-2888
Fred Gerling, *Pr*
◆ **EMP:** 80 **EST:** 1988
SALES (est): 5.73MM **Privately Held**
Web: www.gerlinggroup.com
SIC: 3711 Mobile lounges (motor vehicle),
　assembly of

(G-12666)
HITACHI ASTEMO AMERICAS INC
707 W Cherry St (43074-9595)
PHONE......................740 965-1133
EMP: 335
Web: www.hitachi-automotive.us
SIC: 3694 Alternators, automotive
HQ: Hitachi Astemo Americas, Inc.
　955 Warwick Rd
　Harrodsburg KY 40330
　859 734-9451

(G-12667)
ICC SYSTEMS INC
5665 Blue Church Rd Ste 202
(43074-9695)
PHONE......................614 524-0299
Harold Arnette, *Pr*
EMP: 6 **EST:** 1992
SALES (est): 312.19K **Privately Held**
SIC: 7372 Prepackaged software

(G-12668)
KRISTA MESSER
15301 E State Route 37 (43074-9634)
PHONE......................734 459-1952
Krista Messer, *Prin*

EMP: 6 **EST:** 2010
SALES (est): 97.15K **Privately Held**
SIC: 3443 Fabricated plate work (boiler shop)

(G-12669)
NELSON TOOL CORPORATION
388 N County Line Rd (43074-9004)
PHONE......................740 965-1894
Michael Nelson, *Pr*
EMP: 14 **EST:** 1979
SQ FT: 18,200
SALES (est): 3.28MM **Privately Held**
SIC: 3544 Special dies and tools

(G-12670)
OBERFIELDS LLC
471 Kintner Pkwy (43074-8978)
PHONE......................740 369-7644
Bruce Loris, *Pr*
EMP: 22
SQ FT: 833
SALES (corp-wide): 21.04MM **Privately
Held**
Web: www.oberfields.com
SIC: 3272 Concrete products, precast, nec
HQ: Oberfield's, Llc
　528 London Rd
　Delaware OH 43015
　740 369-7644

(G-12671)
OHASHI TECHNICA USA INC (HQ)
111 Burrer Dr (43074-9323)
PHONE......................740 965-5115
Mamoru Shibasaki, *Prin*
Hikaru Tateiwa, *
▲ **EMP:** 50 **EST:** 1987
SQ FT: 110,000
SALES (est): 26.4MM **Privately Held**
Web: www.ohashiusa.com
SIC: 5013 5072 3452 Automotive supplies
　and parts; Hardware; Bolts, nuts, rivets,
　and washers
PA: Ohashi Technica Inc.
　4-3-13, Toranomon
　Minato-Ku TKY 105-0

(G-12672)
OHASHI TECHNICA USA MFG INC
99 Burrer Dr (43074-9319)
PHONE......................740 965-9002
Hikaru Tateiwa, *Pr*
Nobuya Moritani, *Sec*
▲ **EMP:** 18 **EST:** 1994
SQ FT: 60,000
SALES (est): 2.73MM **Privately Held**
SIC: 3965 Fasteners
HQ: Ohashi Technica U.S.A. Inc.
　111 Burrer Dr
　Sunbury OH 43074
　740 965-5115

(G-12673)
OMEGA ENGINEERING INC
Also Called: Omegadyne
149 Stelzer Ct (43074-8528)
PHONE......................740 965-9340
Dennis Guy, *Brnch Mgr*
EMP: 50
SALES (corp-wide): 1.27B **Privately Held**
Web: www.omega.com
SIC: 3829 3679 3825 Pressure transducers;
　Loads, electronic; Instruments to measure
　electricity
HQ: Omega Engineering, Inc.
　800 Cnnctcut Ave Ste 5n01
　Norwalk CT 06854
　203 359-1660

(G-12674)
OMEGADYNE INC
Also Called: Omegadyne
149 Stelzer Ct (43074-8528)
PHONE......................740 965-9340
EMP: 65
SIC: 3829 3679 3825 Pressure transducers;
　Loads, electronic; Instruments to measure
　electricity

(G-12675)
**RUSSELL T BUNDY ASSOCIATES
INC**
Also Called: American Pan Company
601 W Cherry St (43074-9803)
PHONE......................740 965-3008
Brad Moore, *Mgr*
EMP: 9
SALES (corp-wide): 46.03MM **Privately
Held**
Web: www.bundybakingsolutions.com
SIC: 3479 Coating of metals and formed
　products
PA: Russell T. Bundy Associates, Inc.
　417 E Water St
　Urbana OH 43078
　937 652-2151

Swanton
Fulton County

(G-12676)
AMBROSIA INC
Also Called: Swan Creek Candle Co.
395 W Airport Hwy (43558-1445)
P.O. Box 239 (43558-0239)
PHONE......................419 825-3896
Ann Albright, *Pr*
EMP: 7
SALES (corp-wide): 5.17MM **Privately
Held**
Web: www.swancreekcandle.com
SIC: 3999 Candles
PA: Ambrosia, Inc.
　395 W Airport Hwy
　Swanton OH 43558
　419 825-1151

(G-12677)
AMBROSIA INC
1680 Us Highway 20a (43558-8663)
PHONE......................734 529-5024
Jean B Duet, *Brnch Mgr*
EMP: 7
SALES (corp-wide): 5.17MM **Privately
Held**
Web: www.swancreekcandle.com
SIC: 3999 Candles
PA: Ambrosia, Inc.
　395 W Airport Hwy
　Swanton OH 43558
　419 825-1151

(G-12678)
AQUABLOK LTD
230 W Airport Hwy (43558-1471)
PHONE......................419 402-4170
John Collins, *COO*
EMP: 7
SALES (corp-wide): 6.61MM **Privately
Held**
Web: www.aquablok.com
SIC: 3299 Nonmetallic mineral statuary and
　other decorative products
PA: Aquablok, Ltd.
　175 Woodland Ave
　Swanton OH 43558
　419 825-1325

▲ = Import ▼ = Export
◆ = Import/Export

(G-12679)
AQUABLOK LTD (PA)
175 Woodland Ave Ste A (43558-1026)
PHONE..............................419 825-1325
John Hall, *Pr*
EMP: 11 **EST:** 1999
SALES (est): 6.61MM
SALES (corp-wide): 6.61MM **Privately Held**
Web: www.aquablok.com
SIC: 3299 3295 Nonmetallic mineral statuary and other decorative products; Minerals, ground or treated

(G-12680)
COLUMBUS JACK CORPORATION
Also Called: Columbus Jack Regent
1 Air Cargo Pkwy E (43558-9490)
PHONE..............................614 443-7492
Paul Schwarzbaum, *CEO*
John Cattell, *
▲ **EMP:** 25 **EST:** 1992
SQ FT: 50,000
SALES (est): 9.72MM
SALES (corp-wide): 1.17B **Privately Held**
Web: www.columbusjack.com
SIC: 3542 3728 Presses: hydraulic and pneumatic, mechanical and manual; Aircraft body and wing assemblies and parts
HQ: Tronair, Inc.
1 Air Cargo Pkwy E
Swanton OH 43558
419 866-6301

(G-12681)
DAE HOLDINGS LLC
Also Called: Dae Industries
1 Air Cargo Pkwy E (43558-9490)
PHONE..............................419 866-6301
Paul Schwarzbaum, *CEO*
John Cattell, *CFO*
EMP: 30 **EST:** 1984
SALES (est): 4.98MM
SALES (corp-wide): 1.17B **Privately Held**
Web: www.daeind.com
SIC: 3441 3444 Fabricated structural metal; Sheet metalwork
HQ: Tronair, Inc.
1 Air Cargo Pkwy E
Swanton OH 43558
419 866-6301

(G-12682)
DATCOMEDIA LLC
1 Air Cargo Pkwy E (43558-9490)
PHONE..............................419 866-6301
Paul Schwarzbaum, *CEO*
John Cattell, *CFO*
EMP: 6 **EST:** 2008
SALES (est): 1.28MM
SALES (corp-wide): 1.17B **Privately Held**
Web: www.datcomedia.com
SIC: 7372 7371 Prepackaged software; Custom computer programming services
HQ: Tronair, Inc.
1 Air Cargo Pkwy E
Swanton OH 43558
419 866-6301

(G-12683)
EAGLE INDUSTRIAL TRUCK MFG LLC
Also Called: Eagle Tugs
1 Air Cargo Pkwy E (43558-9490)
PHONE..............................419 866-6301
Paul Schwarzbaum, *CEO*
John Cattell, *CFO*
◆ **EMP:** 20 **EST:** 2000
SQ FT: 70,000
SALES (est): 4.12MM
SALES (corp-wide): 1.17B **Privately Held**

Web: www.eagletugs.com
SIC: 5085 3537 Industrial supplies; Industrial trucks and tractors
HQ: Tronair, Inc.
1 Air Cargo Pkwy E
Swanton OH 43558
419 866-6301

(G-12684)
GRAND AIRE INC (PA)
11777 W Airport Service Rd (43558-9387)
PHONE..............................419 861-6700
Zachary Cheema, *CEO*
EMP: 20 **EST:** 1998
SQ FT: 57,000
SALES (est): 5.85MM
SALES (corp-wide): 5.85MM **Privately Held**
Web: www.grandaire.com
SIC: 4522 5172 4512 4581 Air cargo carriers, nonscheduled; Petroleum products, nec; Air transportation, scheduled ; Airports, flying fields, and services

(G-12685)
GSE PRODUCTION AND SUPPORT LLC (DH)
Also Called: GSE Spares
1 Air Cargo Pkwy E (43558-9490)
PHONE..............................419 866-6301
Paul Schwarzbaum, *Managing Member*
John Cattell, *CFO*
▲ **EMP:** 6 **EST:** 1994
SQ FT: 5,000
SALES (est): 4.29MM
SALES (corp-wide): 1.17B **Privately Held**
Web: www.tronair.com
SIC: 3728 3542 Aircraft body and wing assemblies and parts; Presses: hydraulic and pneumatic, mechanical and manual
HQ: Tronair, Inc.
1 Air Cargo Pkwy E
Swanton OH 43558
419 866-6301

(G-12686)
MAGNA SEATING AMERICA INC
Also Called: Chemical Technologies
428 Church St (43558-1113)
PHONE..............................419 410-4780
EMP: 48
SALES (corp-wide): 42.84B **Privately Held**
Web: www.magna.com
SIC: 3714 Motor vehicle parts and accessories
HQ: Magna Seating Of America, Inc.
30020 Cabot Dr
Novi MI 48377

(G-12687)
MALABAR
Also Called: Malabar International
1 Air Cargo Pkwy E (43558-9490)
PHONE..............................419 866-6301
EMP: 25 **EST:** 1937
SALES (est): 3.57MM
SALES (corp-wide): 1.17B **Privately Held**
Web: www.malabar.com
SIC: 3728 3829 3492 3799 Aircraft parts and equipment, nec; Testers for checking hydraulic controls on aircraft; Fluid power valves for aircraft; Trailers and trailer equipment
HQ: Tronair, Inc.
1 Air Cargo Pkwy E
Swanton OH 43558
419 866-6301

(G-12688)
MLB MOLDED URETHANE PDTS LLC
1680 Us Highway 20a (43558-8663)
P.O. Box 464 (43552-0464)
PHONE..............................419 825-9140
EMP: 9 **EST:** 2004
SQ FT: 15,000
SALES (est): 1.27MM **Privately Held**
Web: www.mlbproducts.net
SIC: 3086 Plastics foam products

(G-12689)
OWENS CORNING SALES LLC
Also Called: Owens Corning
11451 W Airport Service Rd (43558-9389)
PHONE..............................419 248-5751
Roger G Waddill, *Brnch Mgr*
EMP: 9
SIC: 3296 Fiberglass insulation
HQ: Owens Corning Sales, Llc
1 Owens Corning Pkwy
Toledo OH 43659
419 248-8000

(G-12690)
PJS CORRUGATED INC
2330 Us Highway 20 (43558-8649)
PHONE..............................419 644-3383
Michael Iozzo, *Pr*
Joseph Iozzo, *VP*
Priscilla Iozzo, *Sec*
EMP: 10 **EST:** 1992
SQ FT: 10,000
SALES (est): 4.81MM **Privately Held**
SIC: 2653 Boxes, corrugated: made from purchased materials

(G-12691)
SCOTTDEL CUSHION INC
400 Church St (43558-1199)
PHONE..............................419 825-0432
Kevin Thornton, *CEO*
Scott Carson, *
▲ **EMP:** 45 **EST:** 1943
SQ FT: 185,000
SALES (est): 4.77MM **Privately Held**
Web: www.scottdel.com
SIC: 3086 Carpet and rug cushions, foamed plastics

(G-12692)
SOARING SOFTWARE SOLUTIONS INC
110 W Airport Hwy Ste 1 (43558-1446)
PHONE..............................419 442-7676
Richard Lederman, *Pr*
EMP: 13 **EST:** 1998
SALES (est): 930.22K **Privately Held**
Web: www.soaringsoftware.com
SIC: 7371 7372 Computer software systems analysis and design, custom; Prepackaged software

(G-12693)
SPINAL BALANCE INC
11360 S Airfield Rd (43558-7900)
PHONE..............................419 530-5935
Anand Agarwal, *CEO*
Arthur Karas, *Sec*
EMP: 8 **EST:** 2013
SALES (est): 1.23MM **Privately Held**
Web: www.confelicityspine.com
SIC: 3842 Implants, surgical

(G-12694)
SWANTON WLDG MACHINING CO INC (PA)
407 Bdwy Ave (43558-1341)
PHONE..............................419 826-4816
Norm D Zeiter, *CEO*

Chuck Morgan, *
Kevin Thornton, *
Jeff Gyurasics, *
Constance Zeiter, *
EMP: 80 **EST:** 1956
SQ FT: 314,000
SALES (est): 2.26MM
SALES (corp-wide): 2.26MM **Privately Held**
Web: www.swantonweld.com
SIC: 3446 3444 3443 3599 Architectural metalwork; Sheet metalwork; Fabricated plate work (boiler shop); Machine and other job shop work

(G-12695)
TOLEDO JET CENTER LLC (PA)
Also Called: Toledo Express
11591 W Airport Service Rd (43558-9618)
PHONE..............................419 866-9050
Alan R Carsten, *Managing Member*
Bill Pribe, *Genl Mgr*
Mindy Leppala, *Genl Mgr*
William Pribe, *Genl Mgr*
EMP: 9 **EST:** 2009
SALES (est): 2.97MM **Privately Held**
Web: www.toledojet.com
SIC: 3721 4581 Aircraft; Aircraft maintenance and repair services

(G-12696)
TRI-COUNTY BLOCK AND BRICK INC
1628 Us Highway 20a (43558-8662)
PHONE..............................419 826-7060
TOLL FREE: 800
Roger L Cooley, *Pr*
Karen Cooley, *
Carl Kuhlman, *
Roberta E Cooley, *
EMP: 35 **EST:** 1953
SQ FT: 4,160
SALES (est): 4.81MM **Privately Held**
Web: www.tricountyblock.com
SIC: 5211 3271 Lumber and other building materials; Blocks, concrete or cinder: standard

(G-12697)
TRONAIR INC (DH)
1 Air Cargo Pkwy E (43558-9490)
PHONE..............................419 866-6301
Howard Jones, *CEO*
John Cattell, *
◆ **EMP:** 81 **EST:** 1972
SQ FT: 80,000
SALES (est): 90MM
SALES (corp-wide): 1.17B **Privately Held**
Web: www.tronair.com
SIC: 3728 Aircraft parts and equipment, nec
HQ: Tronair Parent, Inc.
1 Air Cargo Pkwy E
Swanton OH 43558
419 866-6301

(G-12698)
WILLYS INC
Also Called: Willy's Fresh Salsa
11305 W Airport Service Rd (43558-9390)
PHONE..............................419 823-3200
Dennis Dickey, *Pr*
EMP: 16 **EST:** 2003
SQ FT: 6,000
SALES (est): 2.1MM **Privately Held**
Web: www.willyssalsa.com
SIC: 2099 Food preparations, nec

Sycamore
Wyandot County

(G-12699)
CREATIVE PLASTIC CONCEPTS LLC (HQ)
206 S Griffith St (44882-9694)
PHONE.................................419 927-9588
▲ EMP: 17 EST: 2013
SALES (est): 19.46MM
SALES (corp-wide): 778.2MM **Privately Held**
Web: www.americanplasticsllc.com
SIC: 2499 5085 Clothes drying frames, racks and reels, wood; Bins and containers, storage
PA: Jansan Acquisition, Llc
    11840 Wstline Indus Dr St
    Saint Louis MO 63146
    314 656-4321

Sylvania
Lucas County

(G-12700)
AD-SENSATIONS INC
3315 Centennial Rd Ste A (43560-9397)
P.O. Box 411 (43560-0411)
PHONE.................................419 841-5395
Gary Sears, *Pr*
EMP: 14 EST: 1989
SQ FT: 5,000
SALES (est): 226.84K **Privately Held**
Web: www.wavehunter.com
SIC: 2759 5199 Promotional printing; Calendars

(G-12701)
ADVANCE PRODUCTS
6041 Angleview Dr (43560-1209)
PHONE.................................419 882-8117
David Frantz, *Owner*
James Frantz, *Owner*
EMP: 10 EST: 1947
SALES (est): 490.2K **Privately Held**
SIC: 3571 3999 Computers, digital, analog or hybrid; Models, except toy

(G-12702)
BOBBART INDUSTRIES INC
Also Called: American Custom Industries
5035 Alexis Rd Ste 1 (43560-1637)
PHONE.................................419 350-5477
Bart Lea, *Pr*
Laura Lea, *Sec*
EMP: 8 EST: 1968
SQ FT: 45,000
SALES (est): 1.9MM **Privately Held**
SIC: 3711 3082 7532 3714 Motor vehicles and car bodies; Unsupported plastics profile shapes; Top and body repair and paint shops; Motor vehicle parts and accessories

(G-12703)
CSW INC
3545 Silica Rd Unit E (43560-9889)
PHONE.................................413 589-1311
Jeffrey Francis, *Prin*
EMP: 29
SALES (corp-wide): 18.05MM **Privately Held**
Web: www.cswgraphics.com
SIC: 2796 3544 Platemaking services; Dies, steel rule
PA: Csw, Inc.
    45 Tyburski Rd
    Ludlow MA 01056

413 589-1311

(G-12704)
DON-ELL CORPORATION (PA)
Also Called: X M C Division
8450 Central Ave (43560-9747)
P.O. Box 351480 (43635-1480)
PHONE.................................419 841-7114
Donald R Sell, *Ch Bd*
Robert N Sell, *
EMP: 25 EST: 1956
SQ FT: 12,000
SALES (est): 5.87MM
SALES (corp-wide): 5.87MM **Privately Held**
SIC: 3679 3089 Electronic switches; Molding primary plastics

(G-12705)
DON-ELL CORPORATION
Also Called: X M C
8456 Central Ave (43560-9747)
PHONE.................................419 841-7114
Jim Krumm, *Mgr*
EMP: 8
SALES (corp-wide): 5.87MM **Privately Held**
SIC: 3089 Injection molding of plastics
PA: Don-Ell Corporation
    8450 Central Ave
    Sylvania OH 43560
    419 841-7114

(G-12706)
DURA MAGNETICS INC
5500 Schultz Dr (43560-2384)
PHONE.................................419 882-0591
Donald C Kuchers, *CEO*
Robert M Csortos, *Pr*
Catherine A Kuchers, *Sec*
▲ EMP: 17 EST: 1961
SQ FT: 15,000
SALES (est): 4.42MM **Privately Held**
Web: www.duramag.com
SIC: 5084 3499 Industrial machinery and equipment; Magnets, permanent: metallic

(G-12707)
GRENADA STAMPING ASSEMBLY INC (HQ)
Also Called: Ice Industries Grenada
3810 Herr Rd (43560-8925)
PHONE.................................419 842-3600
Jeffrey Snavely, *Prin*
EMP: 25 EST: 2006
SALES (est): 12.72MM **Privately Held**
Web: www.iceindustries.com
SIC: 3469 Stamping metal for the trade
PA: Ice Industries, Inc.
    3810 Herr Rd
    Sylvania OH 43560

(G-12708)
HEIDELBERG MTLS MDWEST AGG INC
8130 Brint Rd (43560-9719)
PHONE.................................419 882-0123
Ron Tipton, *Brnch Mgr*
EMP: 10
SALES (corp-wide): 22.37B **Privately Held**
SIC: 1422 Crushed and broken limestone
HQ: Heidelberg Materials Midwest Agg, Inc.
    300 E John Crptr Fwy Ste
    Irving TX

(G-12709)
HEIDELBERG MTLS US CEM LLC
8130 Brint Rd (43560-9719)
PHONE.................................972 653-5500
EMP: 9

SALES (corp-wide): 22.37B **Privately Held**
Web: www.heidelbergmaterials.us
SIC: 3273 Ready-mixed concrete
HQ: Heidelberg Materials Us Cement Llc
    300 E John Crptr Fwy Ste
    Irving TX 75062
    877 534-4442

(G-12710)
ICE INDUSTRIES INC (PA)
3810 Herr Rd (43560-8925)
PHONE.................................419 842-3600
Howard E Ice Junior, *CEO*
Paul Bishop, *
Jeff Boger, *
Bennett Bishop, *
Steve Doseck, *
▲ EMP: 26 EST: 2002
SQ FT: 10,000
SALES (est): 121MM **Privately Held**
Web: www.iceindustries.com
SIC: 3469 Stamping metal for the trade

(G-12711)
ICE INDUSTRIES COLUMBUS INC
3810 Herr Rd (43560-8925)
PHONE.................................614 475-3853
EMP: 30
Web: www.iceindustries.com
SIC: 3441 Fabricated structural metal

(G-12712)
INNOVATIVE HANDLING LLC
7755 Sylvania Ave (43560-9518)
PHONE.................................419 882-7480
EMP: 20 EST: 1981
SQ FT: 30,000
SALES (est): 4.47MM **Privately Held**
Web: www.innovativehandling.com
SIC: 3535 5084 Conveyors and conveying equipment; Materials handling machinery

(G-12713)
INTEGRATED RESOURCES INC
7901 Sylvania Ave (43560-9732)
PHONE.................................419 885-7122
Scott Stansley, *Pr*
Richard Stansley Junior, *Sec*
EMP: 40 EST: 1989
SQ FT: 10,000
SALES (est): 692.55K **Privately Held**
SIC: 3273 8741 Ready-mixed concrete; Management services

(G-12714)
KEVIN K TIDD
Also Called: Arrow Print & Copy
5505 Roan Rd (43560-2306)
PHONE.................................419 885-5603
Kevin K Tidd, *Owner*
EMP: 6 EST: 1985
SQ FT: 3,500
SALES (est): 1.35MM **Privately Held**
Web: www.arrowprint.com
SIC: 2752 2791 2789 Offset printing; Typesetting; Bookbinding and related work

(G-12715)
MICHIGAN SILKSCREEN INC
5354 Whiteford Rd (43560-2520)
PHONE.................................419 885-1163
Michael Schnaidt, *Pr*
Brenda Schnaidt, *VP*
EMP: 8 EST: 1977
SQ FT: 2,500
SALES (est): 153.19K **Privately Held**
SIC: 2396 Screen printing on fabric articles

(G-12716)
MOLD SHOP INC
8520 Central Ave (43560-9748)
PHONE.................................419 829-2041
Lan Wagner, *Pr*
Donna Wagner, *VP*
EMP: 10 EST: 1965
SQ FT: 12,000
SALES (est): 1.1MM **Privately Held**
Web: www.usmolds.com
SIC: 3544 Special dies and tools

(G-12717)
MOORE CHROME PRODUCTS COMPANY
Also Called: Moore Metal Finishing
3525 Silica Rd (43560-9814)
PHONE.................................419 843-3510
Scott W Backus, *Pr*
Scott Backus, *Pr*
Mary Huth, *VP*
Larry Huth, *VP*
EMP: 7 EST: 1930
SQ FT: 24,000
SALES (est): 862.79K **Privately Held**
SIC: 3471 Electroplating of metals or formed products

(G-12718)
NABCO ENTRANCES INC
Also Called: Nabco Entrances
3407 Silica Rd (43560-9539)
PHONE.................................419 842-0484
EMP: 14
Web: www.nabcoentrances.com
SIC: 3699 Electrical equipment and supplies, nec
HQ: Nabco Entrances, Inc.
    S82w18717 Gemini Dr
    Muskego WI 53150
    262 679-7532

(G-12719)
NEXT SPECIALTY RESINS INC (PA)
Also Called: Next Resins
3315 Centennial Rd Ste J (43560-9419)
P.O. Box 365 (49220-0365)
PHONE.................................419 843-4600
Rajiv H Naik, *Pr*
Saurabh H Naik, *VP*
◆ EMP: 30 EST: 1996
SALES (est): 3.31MM **Privately Held**
Web: www.nextresins.com
SIC: 2821 Melamine resins, melamine-formaldehyde

(G-12720)
NORTHERN CONCRETE PIPE INC
3756 Centennial Rd (43560-9734)
PHONE.................................419 841-3361
Jeff Levon, *Prin*
EMP: 10
SALES (corp-wide): 23.97MM **Privately Held**
Web: www.ncp-inc.com
SIC: 3272 Pipe, concrete or lined with concrete
PA: Northern Concrete Pipe, Inc.
    401 Kelton St
    Bay City MI 48706
    989 892-3545

(G-12721)
PIERCE SIGNS & DISPLAYS INC
Also Called: Pierce Signs
5648 Bent Oak Rd (43560-1103)
PHONE.................................408 292-3500
John Hopson, *Pr*
Nannette Hopson, *Sec*
EMP: 9 EST: 1980
SALES (est): 333.52K **Privately Held**

Web: www.piercesigns.com
SIC: **3993** Signs and advertising specialties

(G-12722)
SELECT MATTRESS CO INC
8125 Kevin Ln (43560-1097)
PHONE......................419 244-3645
Ruben R Gonzalez Senior, *Pr*
Ruben Gonzalez, *Pr*
Jorge Gonalez, *Sec*
Arthur Rios, *Treas*
Jose Gonzalez, *VP*
EMP: 13 **EST:** 1991
SQ FT: 41,000
SALES (est): 224.34K **Privately Held**
SIC: **2515** Mattresses and foundations

(G-12723)
SHARONCO INC
Also Called: Sylvan Studio
5651 Main St (43560-1929)
PHONE......................419 882-3443
Scott Stampflmeier, *Pr*
Scott Stampfomeier, *Prin*
EMP: 8 **EST:** 2013
SALES (est): 1.33MM **Privately Held**
Web: www.sylvanstudio.com
SIC: **3499** **5094** Novelties and giftware,
   including trophies; Trophies

(G-12724)
**STANSLEY MINERAL RESOURCES
INC (PA)**
3793 Silica Rd # B (43560-9814)
PHONE......................419 843-2813
Rick Stansley, *CEO*
Jeff Stansley, *
Richard Stansley Junior, *Sec*
Mandy Billau, *
EMP: 35 **EST:** 1978
SQ FT: 10,000
SALES (est): 4.76MM
SALES (corp-wide): 4.76MM **Privately
Held**
SIC: **1442** Gravel mining

(G-12725)
SYLVAN STUDIOS INC
5651 Main St (43560-1929)
P.O. Box 59 (43560-0059)
PHONE......................419 882-3423
Terry E Crandell, *Pr*
EMP: 7 **EST:** 1959
SQ FT: 5,000
SALES (est): 569.81K **Privately Held**
Web: www.sylvanstudio.com
SIC: **2396** **7336** Ribbons and bows, cut and
   sewed; Commercial art and graphic design

(G-12726)
SYLVANIA ADVANTAGE
5655 Main St Apt 1 (43560-6907)
PHONE......................419 725-2695
EMP: 6 **EST:** 2020
SALES (est): 96.08K **Privately Held**
Web: sylvanianews.wpcomstaging.com
SIC: **2711** Newspapers, publishing and
   printing

(G-12727)
SYLVANIA MOSE LDGE NO 1579 LYA
Also Called: SYLVANIA MOOSE LODGE
1579
6072 Main St (43560-1266)
PHONE......................419 885-4953
Gary Muter, *Admn*
EMP: 13 **EST:** 1977
SALES (est): 1.93MM **Privately Held**
Web: www.sylvaniamoose.org

SIC: **8641** **7372** Fraternal associations;
   Application computer software

(G-12728)
TGM HOLDINGS COMPANY
Also Called: Toledo Grmtor Blffton Mtr Wrks
5439 Roan Rd (43560-2304)
PHONE......................419 885-3769
John Toth, *Pr*
EMP: 8 **EST:** 1948
SQ FT: 35,000
SALES (est): 2.29MM **Privately Held**
Web: www.toledogear.com
SIC: **3566** Gears, power transmission,
   except auto

Tallmadge
Summit County

(G-12729)
**AKRON GASKET & PACKG ENTPS
INC**
445 Northeast Ave (44278-1444)
PHONE......................330 633-3742
Carter Ray, *CEO*
Craig Ray, *Pr*
Matthew Ray, *VP*
▲ **EMP:** 19 **EST:** 1974
SQ FT: 40,000
SALES (est): 1.53MM **Privately Held**
Web: www.akron-gasket.com
SIC: **3053** Gaskets, all materials

(G-12730)
AMERICANA DEVELOPMENT INC
Also Called: Martin Wheel
342 West Ave (44278-2113)
PHONE......................330 633-3278
Jimmy Yang, *Pr*
EMP: 100
Web: www.kendatire.com
SIC: **3714** **3011** Motor vehicle wheels and
   parts; Pneumatic tires, all types
PA: Americana Development, Inc.
   7095 Americana Pkwy
   Reynoldsburg OH 43068

(G-12731)
CHEMIONICS CORPORATION
390 Munroe Falls Rd (44278-3399)
PHONE......................330 733-8834
John Blackfan, *Genl Mgr*
Jim Ferguson, *
Mike Schmidt, *
▲ **EMP:** 32 **EST:** 1978
SQ FT: 80,000
SALES (est): 11.58MM
SALES (corp-wide): 202.63K **Privately
Held**
Web: www.chemionics.com
SIC: **2869** **3069** **3087** **2821** Plasticizers,
   organic: cyclic and acyclic; Reclaimed
   rubber and specialty rubber compounds;
   Custom compound purchased resins;
   Plastics materials and resins
HQ: Protech Powder Coatings, Inc.
   21 Audrey Pl
   Fairfield NJ 07004

(G-12732)
CIRCLE MOLD INCORPORATED
Also Called: Circle Mold & Machine Co
85 S Thomas Rd (44278-2107)
P.O. Box 513 (44278-0513)
PHONE......................330 633-7017
Edward A Siciliano, *CEO*
Edward T Siciliano, *Pr*
Agnes Siciliano, *Sec*
EMP: 18 **EST:** 1966

SQ FT: 12,000
SALES (est): 2.71MM **Privately Held**
Web: www.circlemold.com
SIC: **3599** Machine shop, jobbing and repair

(G-12733)
CLS FINISHING INC
409 Munroe Falls Rd (44278-3339)
P.O. Box 239 (44278-0239)
PHONE......................330 784-4134
Steven Kenneth Geer, *Pr*
EMP: 10 **EST:** 1990
SALES (est): 835.56K **Privately Held**
Web: www.clsfinishing.com
SIC: **3479** Coating of metals and formed
   products

(G-12734)
E Z MACHINE INC
298 Northeast Ave (44278-1428)
PHONE......................330 784-3363
Eugene Zemlanfky, *Pr*
EMP: 8 **EST:** 1988
SALES (est): 370.71K **Privately Held**
SIC: **3599** Machine shop, jobbing and repair

(G-12735)
GREEN TECHNOLOGIES OHIO LLC
460 Tacoma Ave Ste B (44278-2756)
PHONE......................330 630-3350
EMP: 8 **EST:** 2013
SALES (est): 728.55K **Privately Held**
Web: www.greentechofohio.com
SIC: **3053** Gaskets, all materials

(G-12736)
HERMAN MACHINE INC
298 Northeast Ave (44278-1494)
PHONE......................330 633-3261
Suzanne E Rickards, *Pr*
EMP: 10 **EST:** 1919
SALES (est): 3.95MM **Privately Held**
Web: www.hermanmachine.net
SIC: **3599** **7389** **3429** Machine shop, jobbing
   and repair; Grinding, precision: commercial
   or industrial; Clamps, metal

(G-12737)
INDUSTRIAL CTRL DSIGN MINT INC
Also Called: Industrial Ctrl Design & Maint
311 Geneva Ave (44278-2702)
PHONE......................330 785-9840
David M Brown Junior, *Pr*
Jon Coles, *VP*
EMP: 10 **EST:** 1999
SQ FT: 14,000
SALES (est): 3.56MM **Privately Held**
Web: www.icdminc.com
SIC: **3613** **7699** **5063** Control panels, electric
   ; Engine repair and replacement, non-
   automotive; Switchboards

(G-12738)
KARG CORPORATION
241 Southwest Ave (44278-2239)
P.O. Box 197 (44278-0197)
PHONE......................330 633-4916
Michael Karg, *Pr*
EMP: 17 **EST:** 1947
SQ FT: 40,000
SALES (est): 3.15MM **Privately Held**
Web: www.kargcorp.com
SIC: **3552** Braiding machines, textile

(G-12739)
MANUFACTURING CONCEPTS
409 Munroe Falls Rd (44278-3339)
P.O. Box 493 (44278-0493)
PHONE......................330 784-9054
Nancy Minne, *Pt*

Sue Brown, *CFO*
Mike Cast, *Mgr*
EMP: 8 **EST:** 2001
SQ FT: 14,500
SALES (est): 646.06K **Privately Held**
SIC: **3599** Machine shop, jobbing and repair

(G-12740)
MARIK SPRING INC
121 Northeast Ave (44278-1947)
PHONE......................330 564-0617
Greg A Bedrick, *Pr*
EMP: 25 **EST:** 1954
SQ FT: 35,000
SALES (est): 4.45MM **Privately Held**
Web: www.marikteam.com
SIC: **3493** **3496** Flat springs, sheet or strip
   stock; Miscellaneous fabricated wire
   products

(G-12741)
MIDWEST FABRICATIONS INC
516 Commerce St (44278-2132)
P.O. Box 399 (44278-0399)
PHONE......................330 633-0191
Robert E Parsons, *Pr*
Timothy Parsons, *
Barbara Parsons, *
EMP: 10 **EST:** 1979
SQ FT: 9,000
SALES (est): 3.48MM **Privately Held**
SIC: **3444** Sheet metal specialties, not
   stamped

(G-12742)
NORTHCOAST WOODCRAFT INC
939 Treat Blvd (44278-2637)
PHONE......................330 677-1189
Sandra Whited, *Pr*
EMP: 8 **EST:** 2011
SALES (est): 795.22K **Privately Held**
Web: www.northcoastwoodcraft.com
SIC: **3553** Cabinet makers' machinery

(G-12743)
NORTHEAST COATINGS INC
415 Munroe Falls Rd (44278-3339)
PHONE......................330 784-7773
Rod Fisher, *Pr*
Chad Fisher, *Mng Pt*
EMP: 6 **EST:** 1991
SQ FT: 12,000
SALES (est): 544.4K **Privately Held**
web: www.necoatings.com
SIC: **3479** Coating of metals and formed
   products

(G-12744)
OWENS CORNING SALES LLC
Owens Corning
170 South Ave (44278-2813)
PHONE......................330 634-0460
Richard W Hooper, *Manager*
EMP: 112
SIC: **3275** **3086** Gypsum products; Plastics
   foam products
HQ: Owens Corning Sales, Llc
   1 Owens Corning Pkwy
   Toledo OH 43659
   419 248-8000

(G-12745)
OWENS CORNING SALES LLC
Also Called: Owens Corning
275 Southwest Ave (44278-2232)
PHONE......................330 633-6735
Joe Brackman, *Brnch Mgr*
EMP: 10
SQ FT: 300

G
E
O
G
R
A
P
H
I
C

SIC: 8711 8731 2821 Building construction consultant; Commercial physical research; Plastics materials and resins
HQ: Owens Corning Sales, Llc
　　1 Owens Corning Pkwy
　　Toledo OH 43659
　　419 248-8000

(G-12746)
P & P MOLD & DIE INC
1034 S Munroe Rd (44278-3336)
PHONE............................330 784-8333
Mary Jean Putra, *Pr*
William Putra, *Treas*
Emil Putra, *Sec*
EMP: 17 EST: 1985
SQ FT: 6,000
SALES (est): 3.28MM **Privately Held**
SIC: 3599 Machine shop, jobbing and repair

(G-12747)
PROMOLD INC
Also Called: Promold Gauer
487 Commerce St (44278-2134)
PHONE............................330 633-3532
Stefan K Schler, *Pr*
Mary Ann Schler, *VP*
EMP: 10 EST: 1977
SQ FT: 9,000
SALES (est): 1.64MM **Privately Held**
Web: www.gauermold.com
SIC: 3089 Injection molding of plastics

(G-12748)
RHOADS PRINT CENTER INC
Also Called: Copy Print
564 Washburn Rd (44278-2620)
PHONE............................330 678-2042
Richard M Rhoads, *Pr*
Jill Rhoads, *Sec*
EMP: 8 EST: 1971
SALES (est): 1.7MM **Privately Held**
Web: www.copyprinttoday.com
SIC: 2752 7334 Offset printing; Photocopying and duplicating services

(G-12749)
SGB USA INC (DH)
180 South Ave (44278-2813)
P.O. Box 188 (80403)
PHONE............................330 472-1187
Robert Ganser Junior, *Pr*
Asad Jawaid, *VP*
Denise Morgan, *Sec*
◆ **EMP: 8 EST:** 2009
SQ FT: 12,500
SALES (est): 9.97MM **Privately Held**
Web: www.sgbusa.com
SIC: 3612 Autotransformers, electric (power transformers)
HQ: Starkstrom - Geratebau Gesellschaft Mit Beschrankter Haftung
　　Ohmstr. 10
　　Regensburg BY 93055
　　94178410

(G-12750)
STEERE ENTERPRISES INC
303 Tacoma Ave (44278-2716)
PHONE............................330 633-4926
Mark Stahl, *Brnch Mgr*
EMP: 102
SALES (corp-wide): 25.46MM **Privately Held**
Web: www.steere.com
SIC: 3089 Injection molding of plastics
PA: Steere Enterprises, Inc.
　　285 Commerce St
　　Tallmadge OH 44278
　　330 633-4926

(G-12751)
STEERE ENTERPRISES INC (PA)
285 Commerce St (44278-2140)
PHONE............................330 633-4926
▲ **EMP: 98 EST:** 1949
SALES (est): 25.46MM
SALES (corp-wide): 25.46MM **Privately Held**
Web: www.steere.com
SIC: 3089 3714 Plastics processing; Motor vehicle parts and accessories

(G-12752)
STORETEK ENGINEERING INC
399 Commerce St (44278-2134)
PHONE............................330 294-0678
Jim Crews, *Pr*
EMP: 22 EST: 2008
SALES (est): 4.96MM **Privately Held**
Web: www.storetekeng.com
SIC: 8711 3559 Consulting engineer; Electronic component making machinery

(G-12753)
SUNSET GOLF LLC
71 West Ave Ste 6 (44278-2236)
P.O. Box 89 (44842-0089)
PHONE............................419 994-5563
Dan Dieghan, *
▲ **EMP: 6 EST:** 1987
SQ FT: 40,000
SALES (est): 411.79K **Privately Held**
SIC: 3949 5941 Golf equipment; Sporting goods and bicycle shops

(G-12754)
TOTAL ENGINE AIRFLOW
285 West Ave (44278-2118)
PHONE............................330 634-2155
Brian Tooley, *Owner*
Brian Tooley, *Prin*
EMP: 6 EST: 2008
SALES (est): 556.37K **Privately Held**
Web: www.totalengineairflow.com
SIC: 3714 Motor vehicle parts and accessories

(G-12755)
TRANS-FOAM INC
Also Called: Cutting Edge Roofing Products
281 Southwest Ave (44278-2232)
PHONE............................330 630-9444
Todd Jordan, *Pr*
EMP: 9 EST: 2000
SALES (est): 1.08MM **Privately Held**
Web: www.jordanpower.com
SIC: 3086 Insulation or cushioning material, foamed plastics

(G-12756)
UNITED DENTAL LABORATORIES (PA)
261 South Ave (44278-2819)
P.O. Box 418 (44278)
PHONE............................330 253-1810
Richard Delapa Junior, *Pr*
EMP: 35 EST: 1923
SQ FT: 15,000
SALES (est): 2.67MM
SALES (corp-wide): 2.67MM **Privately Held**
Web: www.uniteddentallabs.com
SIC: 8072 3843 Denture production; Dental equipment and supplies

(G-12757)
UNIVERSAL POLYMER & RUBBER LTD
Also Called: Universal Rubber & Plastics
165 Northeast Ave (44278-1450)

PHONE............................330 633-1666
EMP: 14
SALES (corp-wide): 24.73MM **Privately Held**
Web: www.universalpolymer.com
SIC: 3069 Molded rubber products
PA: Universal Polymer & Rubber, Ltd.
　　15730 Madison Rd
　　Middlefield OH 44062
　　440 632-1691

(G-12758)
VERSATILE MACHINE
402 Commerce St (44278-2135)
PHONE............................330 618-9895
Darren George, *Owner*
EMP: 8 EST: 2011
SALES (est): 1.68MM **Privately Held**
SIC: 3599 Machine shop, jobbing and repair

(G-12759)
WHOLE SHOP INC
181 S Thomas Rd (44278-2752)
PHONE............................330 630-5305
Nancie Scott, *Pr*
◆ **EMP: 19 EST:** 1974
SQ FT: 27,000
SALES (est): 5MM **Privately Held**
Web: www.wholeshopinc.com
SIC: 3441 7389 Fabricated structural metal; Metal cutting services

---

The Plains
Athens County

(G-12760)
TYJEN INC
Also Called: Slater Builders Supply
8 Slater Dr (45780-1321)
PHONE............................740 797-4064
Mark Vaughn, *Pr*
EMP: 9
SALES (corp-wide): 1.56MM **Privately Held**
Web: www.hockingvalleyconcrete.com
SIC: 3271 Blocks, concrete or cinder: standard
PA: Tyjen, Inc.
　　35255 Hocking Dr
　　Logan OH 43138
　　740 380-3215

(G-12761)
WATTS ANTENNA COMPANY
70 N Plains Rd Ste H (45780-1156)
PHONE............................740 797-9380
John Johnson, *Pr*
EMP: 7 EST: 1978
SALES (est): 589.93K **Privately Held**
Web: www.wattsantenna.com
SIC: 3812 3663 Search and navigation equipment; Antennas, transmitting and communications

---

Thompson
Geauga County

(G-12762)
R W SIDLEY INCORPORATED
Also Called: Sidley Truck & Equipment
7123 Madison Rd (44086-9775)
P.O. Box 10 (44086-0010)
PHONE............................440 298-3232
Rob Sidley, *Mgr*
EMP: 58
SALES (corp-wide): 43.09MM **Privately Held**
Web: www.rwsidley.com

SIC: 3273 Ready-mixed concrete
PA: R. W. Sidley Incorporated
　　436 Casement Ave
　　Painesville OH 44077
　　440 352-9343

(G-12763)
R W SIDLEY INCORPORATED
Sidley Contracting
6900 Madison Rd (44086-9774)
P.O. Box 70 (44086-0070)
PHONE............................440 298-3232
Ray Kennedy, *Mgr*
EMP: 104
SQ FT: 3,000
SALES (corp-wide): 43.09MM **Privately Held**
Web: www.rwsidley.com
SIC: 1799 5032 3272 Erection and dismantling of forms for poured concrete; Limestone; Concrete products, nec
PA: R. W. Sidley Incorporated
　　436 Casement Ave
　　Painesville OH 44077
　　440 352-9343

(G-12764)
SLABE
8000 Plank Rd (44086-9537)
PHONE............................440 298-3693
David Slabe, *Prin*
EMP: 6 EST: 2007
SALES (est): 135.25K **Privately Held**
Web: www.slabemachine.com
SIC: 3599 Machine shop, jobbing and repair

Thornville
Perry County

(G-12765)
BUCKEYE LAKE WINERY
13750 Rosewood Dr Ne (43076-8117)
PHONE............................614 439-7576
Tracy Higginbotham, *Prin*
EMP: 16 EST: 2013
SALES (est): 892.49K **Privately Held**
Web: www.buckeyelakewinery.com
SIC: 2084 Wines

(G-12766)
JAY TEES LLC
8941 Somerset Rd (43076-9654)
PHONE............................740 405-1579
Jay Tees, *Prin*
EMP: 37
SIC: 2752 Commercial printing, lithographic
PA: Jay Tees L.L.C.
　　5227 National Rd Se
　　Hebron OH 43025

(G-12767)
RE CONNORS CONSTRUCTION LTD
13352 Forrest Rd Ne (43076-9164)
PHONE............................740 644-0261
EMP: 9 EST: 2014
SALES (est): 518.14K **Privately Held**
SIC: 1771 1761 3271 7389 Concrete work; Roofing, siding, and sheetmetal work; Concrete block and brick; Business Activities at Non-Commercial Site

(G-12768)
ROCKS GENERAL MAINTENANCE LLC
10019 Jacksontown Rd (43076-8802)
PHONE............................740 323-4711
EMP: 7 EST: 2005
SALES (est): 447.67K **Privately Held**

▲ = Import ▼ = Export
◆ = Import/Export

SIC: 3498 Piping systems for pulp, paper, and chemical industries

(G-12769)
SHELLY MATERIALS INC
8775 Blackbird Ln (43076-9515)
PHONE................................740 246-5009
Larry Shively, *VP*
EMP: 36
SALES (corp-wide): 34.95B **Privately Held**
Web: www.shellyco.com
SIC: 2951 Asphalt paving mixtures and blocks
HQ: Shelly Materials, Inc.
   80 Park Dr
   Thornville OH 43076
   740 246-6315

(G-12770)
SHELLY MATERIALS INC (DH)
Also Called: Shelly Company, The
80 Park Dr (43076-9397)
P.O. Box 266 (43076-0266)
PHONE................................740 246-6315
John Power, *Pr*
Ted Lemon, *
Doug Radabaugh N, *Sec*
EMP: 100 EST: 1938
SALES (est): 461.47MM
SALES (corp-wide): 34.95B **Privately Held**
Web: www.shellyco.com
SIC: 1422 1442 2951 4492 Crushed and broken limestone; Construction sand and gravel; Concrete, asphaltic (not from refineries); Tugboat service
HQ: Shelly Company
   80 Park Dr
   Thornville OH 43076
   740 246-6315

Thurman
Gallia County

(G-12771)
S & J LUMBER COMPANY LLC
Also Called: S & J Lumber
3667 Garners Ford Rd (45685-9301)
PHONE................................740 245-5804
John Smith, *Owner*
EMP: 13 EST: 1980
SQ FT: 3,000
SALES (est): 2.03MM **Privately Held**
SIC: 2421 Sawmills and planing mills, general

Tiffin
Seneca County

(G-12772)
AGRATI - TIFFIN LLC
1988 S County Road 593 (44883-9275)
PHONE................................419 447-2221
Philip Johnson, *CEO*
EMP: 54 EST: 2007
SALES (est): 10.47MM
SALES (corp-wide): 798.77MM **Privately Held**
Web: www.agrati.com
SIC: 3452 Screws, metal
HQ: Agrati - Park Forest, Llc
   24000 S Western Ave
   Park Forest IL 60466
   708 228-5193

(G-12773)
AMERICAN ARMATURE CORPORATION
980 S Morgan Ave (44883-2534)

PHONE................................419 448-1926
Stephen Bell, *Pr*
EMP: 7 EST: 1982
SQ FT: 3,600
SALES (est): 236.54K **Privately Held**
SIC: 7694 5999 3621 Electric motor repair; Motors, electric; Motors and generators

(G-12774)
AMERICAN FINE SINTER CO LTD
957 N Maule Rd (44883)
PHONE................................419 443-8880
Toshiya Yamaguchi, *Pr*
Yoshito Tanaka, *Ex VP*
▲ EMP: 125 EST: 2001
SQ FT: 80,000
SALES (est): 24.3MM **Privately Held**
Web: www.afsus.com
SIC: 3519 Parts and accessories, internal combustion engines
PA: Fine Sinter Co., Ltd.
   1189-11, Nishinohora, Akechicho
   Kasugai AIC 480-0

(G-12775)
ARNOLD MACHINE INC
Also Called: Arnold Machine
19 Heritage Dr (44883-9503)
PHONE................................419 443-1818
Zachary W Arnold, *Pr*
EMP: 13 EST: 1994
SQ FT: 22,000
SALES (est): 6.39MM **Privately Held**
Web: www.arnoldmachine.com
SIC: 3599 Machine shop, jobbing and repair

(G-12776)
B J PALLETT
324 4th Ave (44883-1227)
PHONE................................419 447-9665
Bernard Breidenbach Junior, *Owner*
EMP: 9 EST: 1986
SQ FT: 27,500
SALES (est): 968.9K **Privately Held**
SIC: 2448 Pallets, wood

(G-12777)
BALLREICH BROS INC
Also Called: Ballreichs Potato Chips Snacks
186 Ohio Ave (44883-1746)
PHONE................................419 447-1814
EMP: 105
Web: www.ballreich.com
SIC: 2096 2099 4226 Potato chips and other potato-based snacks; Food preparations, nec; Special warehousing and storage, nec

(G-12778)
BSFC LLC (HQ)
186 Ohio Ave (44883-1746)
PHONE................................419 447-1814
Thomas Miller, *Pr*
EMP: 55 EST: 2019
SALES (est): 7.91MM
SALES (corp-wide): 21.21MM **Privately Held**
Web: www.ballreich.com
SIC: 2096 Potato chips and similar snacks
PA: Grippo Foods, Inc.
   6750 Colerain Ave
   Cincinnati OH 45239
   513 923-1900

(G-12779)
CARMEUSE LIME INC
1967 W County Rd 42 (44883)
PHONE................................419 986-2000
Amy Kuhn, *Brnch Mgr*
EMP: 13
SALES (corp-wide): 2.67MM **Privately Held**

Web: www.carmeuse.com
SIC: 1422 Agricultural limestone, ground
HQ: Carmeuse Lime, Inc.
   11 Stanwix St Fl 21
   Pittsburgh PA 15222
   412 995-5500

(G-12780)
CCP NEWCO LLC
1780 S County Road 1 (44883-8800)
PHONE................................419 448-1700
Robert Guerra, *CEO*
EMP: 478
SALES (corp-wide): 778.2MM **Privately Held**
Web: www.continentalcommercialproducts.com
SIC: 3089 Injection molding of plastics
HQ: Ccp Newco Llc
   11840 Wstline Indus Dr St
   Saint Louis MO 63146
   314 656-4301

(G-12781)
CUSTOM MACHINE INC
3315 W Township Road 158 (44883-9453)
PHONE................................419 986-5122
David Hammer, *Pr*
Jeffery Hammer, *
Phyllis Hammer, *
EMP: 20 EST: 1979
SQ FT: 19,200
SALES (est): 4.8MM **Privately Held**
Web: www.custom-machine-inc.com
SIC: 3544 3599 7692 Special dies and tools; Machine shop, jobbing and repair; Welding repair

(G-12782)
DOREL HOME FURNISHINGS INC
Also Called: Ameriwood Industries
458 2nd Ave (44883-9358)
PHONE................................419 447-7448
Rick Jackson, *Pr*
EMP: 67
SALES (corp-wide): 1.39B **Privately Held**
Web: www.dorel.com
SIC: 2511 Console tables: wood
HQ: Dorel Home Furnishings, Inc.
   410 E 1st St S
   Wright City MO 63390
   636 745-3351

(G 12783)
E SYSTEMS DESIGN & AUTOMTN INC
226 Heritage Dr (44883-9504)
P.O. Box 158 (44883-0158)
PHONE................................419 443-0220
Don Bagent, *Pr*
Brenda Bagent, *Treas*
EMP: 8 EST: 1994
SQ FT: 9,000
SALES (est): 241.94K **Privately Held**
Web: www.esystems-usa.com
SIC: 3599 Machine shop, jobbing and repair

(G-12784)
FRY FOODS INC
99 Maule Rd (44883-9400)
P.O. Box 837 (44883-0837)
PHONE................................419 448-0831
Norman Fry, *Pr*
Beverly Fry, *
Philip Fry, *
Jerry Kaufman, *
David Fry, *
▼ EMP: 50 EST: 1961
SQ FT: 40,000
SALES (est): 8.34MM **Privately Held**
Web: www.fryfoods.com

SIC: 2038 2033 Snacks, incl. onion rings, cheese sticks, etc.; Canned fruits and specialties

(G-12785)
JOHNS WELDING & TOWING INC
850 N County Road 11 (44883-9415)
PHONE................................419 447-8937
Joseph Keller, *Pr*
James Keller, *VP*
EMP: 8 EST: 1956
SQ FT: 20,000
SALES (est): 837.85K **Privately Held**
Web: www.johnsweldingandtowing.com
SIC: 7549 7692 Towing services; Welding repair

(G-12786)
LAMINATE TECHNOLOGIES INC (PA)
Also Called: Lam Tech
161 Maule Rd (44883-9400)
PHONE................................800 231-2523
Frederick E Zoeller, *Pr*
A Louise Zoeller, *
Allan Funkhouser, *
▲ EMP: 55 EST: 1985
SQ FT: 80,000
SALES (est): 49.27MM
SALES (corp-wide): 49.27MM **Privately Held**
Web: www.lamtech.net
SIC: 2439 2891 2672 Structural wood members, nec; Adhesives and sealants; Paper; coated and laminated, nec

(G-12787)
M & B ASPHALT COMPANY INC (PA)
1525 W County Road 42 (44883-8457)
P.O. Box 130 (44861-0130)
PHONE................................419 992-4235
EMP: 15 EST: 1946
SALES (est): 10.04MM
SALES (corp-wide): 10.04MM **Privately Held**
Web: www.mgqinc.com
SIC: 1429 2951 1611 2952 Grits mining (crushed stone); Asphalt and asphaltic paving mixtures (not from refineries); Highway and street paving contractor; Asphalt felts and coatings

(G-12788)
M G Q INC
Also Called: Maple Grove Companies
1525 W County Road 42 (44883-8457)
P.O. Box 130 (44861-0130)
PHONE................................419 992-4236
Lynn Radabaugh, *Pr*
Tim Bell, *
Lynn Radabaugh, *VP*
Bob Chesebro, *
Bruce Chubb, *
▲ EMP: 34 EST: 1999
SALES (est): 8.94MM **Privately Held**
Web: www.mgqinc.com
SIC: 4214 1481 Local trucking with storage; Mine and quarry services, nonmetallic minerals

(G-12789)
MACHINE TOOL DESIGN & FAB LLC
226 Heritage Dr (44883-9504)
PHONE................................419 435-7676
Christopher Eastman, *Managing Member*
EMP: 19 EST: 2016
SALES (est): 4.87MM
SALES (corp-wide): 5.34MM **Privately Held**
Web: www.para-port.com

SIC: **7699** 3544 3441 Metal reshaping and replating services; Special dies and tools; Fabricated structural metal
PA: Eastman Holding Llc
1185 W Parkway Blvd
Aurora OH 44202
419 435-7676

(G-12790)
MAPLE GROVE MATERIALS INC
1525 W City Rd Ste 42 (44883)
P.O. Box 136 (44861-0136)
PHONE.............................419 992-4235
Tim Bell, *Pr*
Lynn O Radabaugh, *VP*
Robert Chesebro, *Sec*
EMP: 9 EST: 1984
SQ FT: 2,000
SALES (est): 956.22K
SALES (corp-wide): 10.04MM **Privately Held**
Web: www.mgqinc.com
SIC: **3281** Limestone, cut and shaped
PA: M. & B. Asphalt Company, Inc.
1525 W Seneca Cnty Rd 42
Tiffin OH 44883
419 992-4235

(G-12791)
ML ADVERTISING & DESIGN LLC
Also Called: Mlad Graphic Design Services
185 Jefferson St (44883-2865)
PHONE.............................419 447-6523
Mark A Levans, *Managing Member*
EMP: 6 EST: 1999
SQ FT: 3,000
SALES (est): 577.29K **Privately Held**
Web: www.mlad.com
SIC: **7336** 2759 Graphic arts and related design; Commercial printing, nec

(G-12792)
NATIONAL MACHINERY LLC (HQ)
161 Greenfield St (44883-2471)
PHONE.............................419 447-5211
◆ EMP: 310 EST: 2002
SQ FT: 650,000
SALES (est): 89.25MM
SALES (corp-wide): 159.97MM **Privately Held**
Web: www.nationalmachinery.com
SIC: **3599** Machine shop, jobbing and repair
PA: Nm Group Global, Llc
161 Greenfield St
Tiffin OH 44883
419 447-5211

(G-12793)
NMGG CTG LLC (HQ)
Also Called: Cleaning Technologies Grp
161 Greenfield St (44883-2499)
PHONE.............................419 447-5211
Andrew H Kalnow, *CEO*
Robert J Foster, *CFO*
EMP: 101 EST: 2006
SALES (est): 49.84MM
SALES (corp-wide): 159.97MM **Privately Held**
Web: www.nationalmachinery.com
SIC: **3569** 3541 Blast cleaning equipment, dustless; Ultrasonic metal cutting machine tools
PA: Nm Group Global, Llc
161 Greenfield St
Tiffin OH 44883
419 447-5211

(G-12794)
OGDEN NEWSPAPERS OHIO INC
Also Called: Advertiser-Tribune, The
320 Nelson St (44883-8956)

P.O. Box 778 (44883-0778)
PHONE.............................419 448-3200
Chris Dixon, *Dir*
David Frisch, *Dir*
EMP: 17 EST: 1991
SALES (est): 463.69K **Privately Held**
Web: www.advertiser-tribune.com
SIC: **2711** Newspapers, publishing and printing

(G-12795)
OHIO INDUSTRIAL COATING CORP
880 S Bon Aire Ave (44883-2581)
PHONE.............................567 230-6719
Zech Cunningham, *Prin*
EMP: 6 EST: 2015
SALES (est): 135.84K **Privately Held**
SIC: **3479** Metal coating and allied services

(G-12796)
QUICK TAB II INC (PA)
241 Heritage Dr (44883-9504)
P.O. Box 723 (44883-0723)
PHONE.............................419 448-6622
Chuck Daughenbaugn, *CEO*
Charles Eingle, *
Mike Daughenbaugh, *
▼ EMP: 64 EST: 1992
SQ FT: 30,000
SALES (est): 8.45MM **Privately Held**
Web: www.qt2.com
SIC: **2752** 5112 2791 2789 Forms, business: lithographed; Stationery and office supplies; Typesetting; Bookbinding and related work

(G-12797)
SARKA SHTMTL & FABRICATION INC
Also Called: Sarka Conveyor
70 Clinton Ave (44883-1620)
PHONE.............................419 447-4377
Kendall T Parker, *Pr*
Larry D Sarka, *Stockholder*
EMP: 22 EST: 1985
SQ FT: 11,000
SALES (est): 685.4K **Privately Held**
Web: www.sarkaconveyors.com
SIC: **3444** Sheet metalwork

(G-12798)
SEISLOVE VAULT & SEPTIC TANKS
Also Called: Seislove Brial Vlts Sptic Tnks
2168 S State Route 100 (44883-3699)
PHONE.............................419 447-5473
P David Seislove, *Pr*
EMP: 7 EST: 1946
SQ FT: 13,000
SALES (est): 481.13K **Privately Held**
Web: www.seislovesinc.com
SIC: **3272** Burial vaults, concrete or precast terrazzo

(G-12799)
SENECA ENVIRONMENTAL PRODUCTS INC
1685 S County Road 1 (44883-9746)
PHONE.............................419 447-1282
EMP: 40
SIC: **3443** 3625 3564 Tanks, standard or custom fabricated: metal plate; Noise control equipment; Purification and dust collection equipment

(G-12800)
SENECA SHEET METAL COMPANY
Also Called: Sheet Metal Fabricator
277 Water St (44883-1698)
PHONE.............................419 447-8434
Robert J Fulton, *Pr*
George H Wells, *VP*
EMP: 10 EST: 1966
SQ FT: 55,000

SALES (est): 2.31MM **Privately Held**
Web: www.senecasheetmetal.com
SIC: **3444** 1761 Sheet metal specialties, not stamped; Sheet metal work, nec

(G-12801)
TAIHO CORPORATION OF AMERICA
Also Called: Taiho
194 Heritage Dr (44883-9503)
PHONE.............................419 443-1645
Shigeki Awazu, *Pr*
Karl Kortlandt, *
Mike Shannaberger, *
◆ EMP: 120 EST: 1981
SQ FT: 140
SALES (est): 24.87MM **Privately Held**
Web: www.taihousa.com
SIC: **3714** 3585 3568 Air conditioner parts, motor vehicle; Refrigeration and heating equipment; Power transmission equipment, nec
PA: Taiho Kogyo Co., Ltd.
3-65, Midorigaoka
Toyota AIC 471-0

(G-12802)
TIFFIN FOUNDRY & MACHINE INC
423 W Adams St (44883-9284)
P.O. Box 37 (44883-0037)
PHONE.............................419 447-3991
Steven Sobol, *Pr*
Melvin A Jones, *
EMP: 35 EST: 2004
SQ FT: 45,000
SALES (est): 4.49MM **Privately Held**
Web: www.tiffinfoundry.com
SIC: **3592** 3599 3322 3325 Carburetors, pistons, piston rings and valves; Machine shop, jobbing and repair; Malleable iron foundries; Steel foundries, nec

(G-12803)
TIFFIN METAL PRODUCTS CO (PA)
450 Wall St (44883-1366)
PHONE.............................419 447-8414
Richard S Harrison, *Pr*
Richard M Wyka, *
Ron Myers, *
Michael R Reser, *
Timothy Demith, *
▼ EMP: 97 EST: 1903
SQ FT: 120,000
SALES (est): 19.71MM
SALES (corp-wide): 19.71MM **Privately Held**
Web: www.steelesolutions.com
SIC: **2599** 2542 2531 2522 Boards: planning, display, notice; Lockers (not refrigerated): except wood; Public building and related furniture; Office furniture, except wood

(G-12804)
TIFFIN PAPER COMPANY (PA)
Also Called: TPC Food Service
401 Wall St (44883-1351)
P.O. Box 129 (44883-0129)
PHONE.............................419 447-2121
Thomas M Maiberger, *Pr*
Tony Paulus, *
Kevin Maiberger, *
EMP: 40 EST: 1963
SQ FT: 40,000
SALES (est): 3.61MM
SALES (corp-wide): 3.61MM **Privately Held**
Web: www.tpcfoodservice.com
SIC: **5149** 2064 Groceries and related products, nec; Candy and other confectionery products

(G-12805)
TIFFIN SCENIC STUDIOS INC (PA)
Also Called: Atlantic and Prfmce Rigging
146 Riverside Dr (44883-1644)
P.O. Box 39 (44883-0039)
PHONE.............................800 445-1546
Brad Hossler, *Pr*
Steve Maiberger, *
Steve Everhart, *
EMP: 33 EST: 1901
SQ FT: 24,000
SALES (est): 6.63MM
SALES (corp-wide): 6.63MM **Privately Held**
Web: www.tiffinscenic.com
SIC: **2391** 3999 Draperies, plastic and textile: from purchased materials; Stage hardware and equipment, except lighting

(G-12806)
TOLEDO MOLDING & DIE LLC
1441 Maule Rd (44883-9130)
PHONE.............................419 443-9031
Dave Spott, *Mgr*
EMP: 215
SALES (corp-wide): 7.28B **Privately Held**
Web: www.tmdinc.com
SIC: **3089** Automotive parts, plastic
HQ: Toledo Molding & Die, Llc
1429 Coining Dr
Toledo OH 43612

(G-12807)
VIEWPOINT GRAPHIC DESIGN
132 S Washington St (44883-2840)
PHONE.............................419 447-6073
Pete Krupp, *Owner*
EMP: 6 EST: 1985
SQ FT: 5,000
SALES (est): 484.59K **Privately Held**
Web: www.viewpointtiffin.com
SIC: **2759** Screen printing

(G-12808)
WEBSTER INDUSTRIES INC (PA)
Also Called: Webster Manufacturing Company
325 Hall St (44883-1471)
PHONE.............................419 447-8232
Andrew J Felter, *Pr*
Fredric C Spurck, *
Nicholas D Spurck, *
Dean Bogner, *
Steven Hickey, *
◆ EMP: 295 EST: 1876
SQ FT: 250,000
SALES (est): 76.75MM
SALES (corp-wide): 76.75MM **Privately Held**
Web: www.websterchain.com
SIC: **3535** Bulk handling conveyor systems

Tiltonsville
Jefferson County

(G-12809)
CROFT & SON MFG INC
509 Highland Ave (43963-1110)
P.O. Box 66 (43963-0066)
PHONE.............................740 859-2200
Samuel E Croft, *Pr*
Shirley Pielech, *Sec*
Kathy Lester, *Sec*
EMP: 6 EST: 1977
SQ FT: 3,600
SALES (est): 644.63K **Privately Held**
SIC: **3599** Machine shop, jobbing and repair

(G-12810)
WALDEN INDUSTRIES INC
Also Called: Belot Concrete Block
101 Walden Ave (43963-1130)
P.O. Box 68 (43963-0068)
PHONE................................740 633-5971
TOLL FREE: 800
John Belot, *Pr*
EMP: 20 **EST:** 1995
SALES (est): 2.02MM **Privately Held**
Web: www.waldenindustries.com
SIC: 3273 Ready-mixed concrete

Tipp City
Miami County

(G-12811)
A & B FOUNDRY LLC
Also Called: A&B Fndry McHning Fabrications
4754 Us Route 40 (45371-9481)
PHONE................................937 412-1900
EMP: 11
SALES (corp-wide): 5.94MM **Privately Held**
Web: www.abfoundry.com
SIC: 3559 Foundry machinery and equipment
PA: A & B Foundry Llc
835 N Main St
Franklin OH 45005
937 369-3007

(G-12812)
ABBOTT LABORATORIES
1 Abbott Park Way (45371-1285)
PHONE................................937 503-3405
▲ **EMP:** 15
SALES (corp-wide): 41.95B **Publicly Held**
Web: www.abbottnutrition.com
SIC: 2834 Pharmaceutical preparations
PA: Abbott Laboratories
100 Abbott Park Rd
Abbott Park IL 60064
224 667-6100

(G-12813)
ACCU-TOOL INC
9765 Julie Ct (45371-9000)
P.O. Box 440 (45371-0440)
PHONE................................937 667-5878
Dale Howard, *Pr*
Patricia Howard, *VP*
EMP: 8 **EST:** 1983
SQ FT: 7,500
SALES (est): 412.29K **Privately Held**
Web: www.accu-tool.com
SIC: 3544 3599 Special dies and tools;
Machine shop, jobbing and repair

(G-12814)
ACON INC
11408 Dogleg Rd (45371-9516)
PHONE................................513 276-2111
Thomas Mescher, *Pr*
EMP: 7 **EST:** 1970
SQ FT: 12,000
SALES (est): 591.73K **Privately Held**
Web: www.aconinc.net
SIC: 3625 Noise control equipment

(G-12815)
ALPINE GAGE INC
7677 Winding Way S (45371-9169)
PHONE................................937 669-8665
Dennis Tresslar, *Pr*
EMP: 6 **EST:** 2002
SALES (est): 1.2MM **Privately Held**
Web: www.alpinegage.com
SIC: 3544 Special dies and tools

(G-12816)
B S F INC
320b S 5th St (45371-1625)
PHONE................................937 890-6121
Tim Boocher, *Mgr*
EMP: 10
SALES (corp-wide): 2.47MM **Privately Held**
Web: www.bsfinc.net
SIC: 3498 3568 3599 Couplings, pipe:
fabricated from purchased pipe; Couplings,
shaft: rigid, flexible, universal joint, etc.;
Machine shop, jobbing and repair
PA: B S F, Inc.
8895 N Dixie Dr
Dayton OH 45414
937 890-6121

(G-12817)
CANINE CREATIONS INC
120b W Broadway St # A (45371-1638)
PHONE................................937 667-8576
Robin Riedel, *Prin*
Robert Reidel, *Owner*
EMP: 7 **EST:** 2004
SALES (est): 179.41K **Privately Held**
Web: www.canine-creations.net
SIC: 0752 3999 Grooming services, pet and
animal specialties; Pet supplies

(G-12818)
CAPTOR CORPORATION
5040 S County Road 25a (45371-2899)
PHONE................................937 667-8484
Donald Cooper, *Ch*
D Scott Timms, *
Carolyn Kiser, *
Tom Dysinger, *Corporate Secretary**
EMP: 85 **EST:** 1965
SQ FT: 35,000
SALES (est): 18.44MM **Privately Held**
Web: www.captorcorp.com
SIC: 3679 Electronic circuits

(G-12819)
CASE CRAFTERS INC
211 S 1st St (45371-1705)
PHONE................................937 667-9473
Dan Paugh, *Pr*
Steven Paugh, *VP*
EMP: 8 **EST:** 1992
SQ FT: 9,200
SALES (est): 955.8K **Privately Held**
Web: www.casecraftersinc.com
SIC: 2541 1751 Cabinets, except
refrigerated: show, display, etc.: wood;
Cabinet and finish carpentry

(G-12820)
CHART-TECH TOOL INC
4060 Lisa Dr (45371-9499)
P.O. Box 477 (45371)
PHONE................................937 667-3543
Eugene Crompton, *Pr*
Lee Scheidweiler, *VP*
EMP: 10 **EST:** 1965
SQ FT: 30,000
SALES (est): 1.67MM **Privately Held**
Web: www.ctti-inc.com
SIC: 3541 3545 3544 Machine tools, metal
cutting type; Gauges (machine tool
accessories); Special dies, tools, jigs, and
fixtures

(G-12821)
CONCRETE SEALANTS INC
Also Called: Conseal
9325 State Route 201 (45371-8524)
PHONE................................937 845-8776
Howard E Wingert, *Pr*
Cynthia Wingert, *

◆ **EMP:** 50 **EST:** 1970
SQ FT: 100,000
SALES (est): 9.73MM **Privately Held**
Web: www.conseal.com
SIC: 3053 2891 2821 2822 Gaskets; packing
and sealing devices; Sealants; Plastics
materials and resins; Synthetic rubber

(G-12822)
DAP PRODUCTS INC
Also Called: Darusta Woodlife Division
875 N 3rd St (45371-3053)
PHONE................................937 667-4461
Gary Williams, *Brnch Mgr*
EMP: 72
SALES (corp-wide): 7.34B **Publicly Held**
Web: www.dap.com
SIC: 2891 2851 Caulking compounds; Paints
and paint additives
HQ: Dap Products Inc.
2400 Boston St Ste 200
Baltimore MD 21224
800 543-3840

(G-12823)
DUNCAN TOOL INC
9790 Julie Ct (45371-9000)
PHONE................................937 667-9364
Sandra L Duncan, *Pr*
Dave Duncan, *VP*
▲ **EMP:** 10 **EST:** 1992
SQ FT: 5,500
SALES (est): 1.64MM **Privately Held**
Web: www.duncantool.com
SIC: 3544 3599 Special dies and tools;
Machine shop, jobbing and repair

(G-12824)
**ENVIRNMENT CTRL STHWEST OHIO
I**
7939 S County Road 25a (45371-9107)
PHONE................................937 669-9900
EMP: 19 **EST:** 2012
SALES (est): 2.96MM **Privately Held**
Web: www.environmentcontrol.com
SIC: 3822 Environmental controls

(G-12825)
FIELD STONE INC
2750 Us Route 40 (45371-9230)
PHONE................................937 898-3236
Paul Carmack, *Pr*
◆ **EMP:** 8 **EST:** 1973
SQ FT: 18,000
SALES (est): 1.1MM **Privately Held**
SIC: 3586 3432 Gasoline pumps, measuring
or dispensing; Plumbing fixture fittings and
trim

(G-12826)
G & M PRECISION MACHINING INC
9785 Wildcat Rd (45371-9421)
PHONE................................937 667-1443
Lori Galovics, *Pr*
Joe Galovics, *Pr*
EMP: 6 **EST:** 1992
SQ FT: 10,000
SALES (est): 832.47K **Privately Held**
Web: g-m-precision-machining.hub.biz
SIC: 3599 Machine shop, jobbing and repair

(G-12827)
HIGH-TEC INDUSTRIAL SERVICES ✪
15 Industry Park Ct (45371-3060)
PHONE................................937 667-1772
Christopher Griffin, *Pr*
Daniel Whitlock, *VP*
Kyle Packer, *Sec*
EMP: 60 **EST:** 2023
SQ FT: 11,000
SALES (est): 8.16MM **Privately Held**

SIC: 1799 7349 3589 Construction site
cleanup; Building and office cleaning
services; Commercial cleaning equipment

(G-12828)
INDIAN CREEK FABRICATORS INC
1350 Commerce Park Dr (45371-3323)
PHONE................................937 667-7214
Andrea Dakin, *Pr*
Michael Dakin, *
EMP: 50 **EST:** 1986
SQ FT: 65,000
SALES (est): 4.26MM **Privately Held**
Web: www.indiancreekfab.com
SIC: 3446 3444 3443 3441 Architectural
metalwork; Sheet metalwork; Fabricated
plate work (boiler shop); Fabricated
structural metal

(G-12829)
J & L WOOD PRODUCTS INC (PA)
155 Lightner Rd (45371-9296)
P.O. Box 69 (45371-0069)
PHONE................................937 667-4064
Jeffrey Herzog, *Pr*
Kevin Mcclurg, *VP*
▲ **EMP:** 32 **EST:** 1968
SQ FT: 30,000
SALES (est): 4.54MM
SALES (corp-wide): 4.54MM **Privately
Held**
Web: www.jlwoodproducts.com
SIC: 2448 2441 2449 Pallets, wood; Nailed
wood boxes and shook; Rectangular boxes
and crates, wood

(G-12830)
METEOR CREATIVE INC (DH)
1414 Commerce Park Dr (45371-2845)
PHONE................................800 273-1535
Thorsten Conrad, *VP*
EMP: 20 **EST:** 2021
SALES (est): 48.36MM
SALES (corp-wide): 355.83K **Privately
Held**
Web: www.meteor-creative.com
SIC: 3089 Extruded finished plastics
products, nec
HQ: Meteor Group Gmbh
Gabrielenstr. 9
Munchen BY 80636
89262048400

(G-12831)
MORE MANUFACTURING LLC
4025 Lisa Dr Ste A (45371-9462)
PHONE................................937 233-3898
Matt Lovelace, *Managing Member*
EMP: 12 **EST:** 2007
SQ FT: 6,000
SALES (est): 3.86MM **Privately Held**
Web: www.moremfg.com
SIC: 3541 Machine tool replacement &
repair parts, metal cutting types

(G-12832)
MUTUAL TOOL LLC
1350 Commerce Park Dr (45371-3323)
PHONE................................937 667-5818
EMP: 11 **EST:** 2004
SQ FT: 31,200
SALES (est): 2.13MM **Privately Held**
Web: www.indiancreekfab.com
SIC: 3599 3544 Machine shop, jobbing and
repair; Special dies, tools, jigs, and fixtures

(G-12833)
ODAWARA AUTOMATION INC
4805 S County Road 25a (45371-2900)
PHONE................................937 667-8433
Takayuki Tsugawa, *CEO*

Christopher Spejna, *Pr*
▲ **EMP:** 37 **EST:** 1971
SQ FT: 51,000
SALES (est): 9.41MM **Privately Held**
Web: www.odawara.com
SIC: 3599 Custom machinery
PA: Odawara Engineering Co.,Ltd.
  1577, Matsudasoryo, Matsudamachi
  Ashigara Kami-Gun KNG 258-0

(G-12834)
PDQ TECHNOLOGIES INC
2500 Us Route 40 (45371-9131)
PHONE...............937 274-4958
Robert Adams, *Admn*
EMP: 9 **EST:** 1989
SALES (est): 1.7MM **Privately Held**
SIC: 3599 Machine shop, jobbing and repair

(G-12835)
PECO HOLDINGS CORP (PA)
6555 S State Route 202 (45371-9094)
PHONE...............937 667-5705
Michael Van Haaren, *Pr*
James Zahora, *VP*
William Rosenberg, *CFO*
EMP: 56 **EST:** 2005
SALES (est): 9.52MM **Privately Held**
SIC: 3599 3548 3549 Machine shop, jobbing
  and repair; Welding apparatus; Assembly
  machines, including robotic

(G-12836)
PRECISION STRIP INC
315 Park Ave (45371-1887)
PHONE...............937 667-6255
Jerry Huber, *Mgr*
EMP: 52
SQ FT: 3,080
SALES (corp-wide): 13.84B **Publicly Held**
Web: www.precision-strip.com
SIC: 4225 3312 General warehousing and
  storage; Blast furnaces and steel mills
HQ: Precision Strip Inc.
  86 S Ohio St
  Minster OH 45865
  419 628-2343

(G-12837)
PROCESS EQP CO WLDG SVCS LLC
Also Called: Peco Welding Services LLC
319 S 1st St (45371-1707)
PHONE...............937 667-4451
Michael Loughman, *Managing Member*
EMP: 6 **EST:** 2018
SALES (est): 270.63K **Privately Held**
SIC: 7692 Automotive welding

(G-12838)
**PROCESS EQUIPMENT CO TIPP
CITY (HQ)**
Also Called: Process Equipment Company
319 S 1st St (45371-1707)
PHONE...............937 667-5705
Michael V Haaren, *Pr*
James Zahora, *
William Rosenberg, *
▲ **EMP:** 37 **EST:** 1945
SALES (est): 4.73MM **Privately Held**
SIC: 3599 3548 3549 Machine shop, jobbing
  and repair; Welding apparatus; Assembly
  machines, including robotic
PA: Peco Holdings Corp.
  6555 S State Route 202
  Tipp City OH 45371

(G-12839)
PROTO PLASTICS INC
316 Park Ave (45371-1894)
PHONE...............937 667-8416
Thomas A Gagnon, *Pr*

Thomas Gagnon, *
Sue Gagnon, *
▲ **EMP:** 42 **EST:** 1969
SQ FT: 62,000
SALES (est): 4.91MM **Privately Held**
Web: www.protoplastics.com
SIC: 3089 3544 Injection molding of plastics;
  Special dies, tools, jigs, and fixtures

(G-12840)
REGAL BELOIT AMERICA INC
Also Called: Regal
531 N 4th St (45371-1857)
PHONE...............937 667-2431
Steve O'brien, *Brnch Mgr*
EMP: 231
SALES (corp-wide): 6.03B **Publicly Held**
SIC: 3621 Motors, electric
HQ: Regal Beloit America, Inc.
  111 W Michigan St
  Milwaukee WI 53203
  608 364-8800

(G-12841)
REPACORP INC (PA)
Also Called: Presto Labels
31 Industry Park Ct (45371-3060)
PHONE...............937 667-8496
EMP: 71 **EST:** 1974
SALES (est): 23.84MM
SALES (corp-wide): 23.84MM **Privately
Held**
Web: www.repacorp.com
SIC: 2759 Commercial printing, nec

(G-12842)
RPG INDUSTRIES INC
3571 Ginghamsburg Frederick Rd
(45371-9652)
P.O. Box 233 (45383-0233)
PHONE...............937 698-9801
Robert Ginsburg, *Pr*
EMP: 6 **EST:** 1995
SQ FT: 3,600
SALES (est): 1.27MM **Privately Held**
Web: www.rpgindustries.com
SIC: 3599 Machine shop, jobbing and repair

(G-12843)
SINBON USA LLC
4265 Gibson Dr (45371-9452)
PHONE...............937 667-8999
Chun-yu Chen, *CEO*
EMP: 35 **EST:** 2017
SALES (est): 11.16MM **Privately Held**
SIC: 3679 Antennas, receiving

(G-12844)
SK MOLD & TOOL INC (PA)
955 N 3rd St (45371-3055)
PHONE...............937 339-0299
Samuel K Kingrey, *Pr*
Keith Kingrey, *
Vince Hinde, *
EMP: 45 **EST:** 1983
SQ FT: 76,500
SALES (est): 5.68MM
SALES (corp-wide): 5.68MM **Privately
Held**
Web: www.skmold.com
SIC: 3544 3599 Special dies and tools;
  Machine shop, jobbing and repair

(G-12845)
SLONE GEAR INTERNATIONAL INC
207 S 1st St (45371-1705)
P.O. Box 292528 (45429-0528)
PHONE...............507 401-4327
Brian Slone, *VP Opers*
EMP: 7
SALES (corp-wide): 1.3MM **Privately Held**

Web: www.slonegear.com
SIC: 3823 Industrial process measurement
  equipment
PA: Slone Gear International, Inc
  2154 Liberty Rd
  New Carlisle OH 45344
  937 478-1595

(G-12846)
SP3 WINCO LLC
Also Called: Winco Industries, Inc.
835 N Hyatt St (45371-1558)
P.O. Box 70 (45371-0070)
PHONE...............937 667-4476
EMP: 20 **EST:** 1961
SALES (est): 1.6MM **Privately Held**
SIC: 3545 Drills (machine tool accessories)
PA: Sp3 Cutting Tools, Inc.
  835 N Hyatt St
  Tipp City OH 45371

(G-12847)
TECH MOLD AND TOOL CO
4333 Lisa Dr (45371-9463)
PHONE...............937 667-8851
Dan Isenbarger, *Pr*
Arlene Isenbarger, *Sec*
EMP: 7 **EST:** 1975
SQ FT: 5,100
SALES (est): 650.16K **Privately Held**
SIC: 3544 Special dies and tools

(G-12848)
TRIMBLE INC
Also Called: Trimble Engineering & Cnstr
4450 Gibson Dr (45371-9461)
PHONE...............937 233-8921
EMP: 17
SALES (corp-wide): 3.68B **Publicly Held**
Web: www.trimble.com
SIC: 3812 Navigational systems and
  instruments
PA: Trimble Inc.
  10368 Westmoor Dr
  Westminster CO 80021
  720 887-6100

(G-12849)
TROPHY NUT CO (PA)
320 N 2nd St (45371-1960)
P.O. Box 199 (45371-0199)
PHONE...............937 667-8478
Gerald J Allen, *CEO*
Robert J Bollinger, *
Robert N Wilke, *
David Henning, *
◆ **EMP:** 49 **EST:** 1968
SQ FT: 85,000
SALES (est): 31.94MM
SALES (corp-wide): 31.94MM **Privately
Held**
Web: www.trophynut.com
SIC: 2068 5441 Nuts: dried, dehydrated,
  salted or roasted; Nuts

(G-12850)
TROPHY NUT CO
1567 Harmony Dr (45371-3319)
P.O. Box 199 (45371-0199)
PHONE...............937 669-5513
Bob Loy, *Mgr*
EMP: 6
SALES (corp-wide): 31.94MM **Privately
Held**
Web: www.trophynut.com
SIC: 2068 Nuts: dried, dehydrated, salted or
  roasted
PA: Trophy Nut Co.
  320 N 2nd St
  Tipp City OH 45371
  937 667-8478

(G-12851)
UDECX LLC
320 N 4th St (45371-1803)
PHONE...............877 698-3329
John Van Leeuwen, *CEO*
Patrick Bertke, *Dir*
EMP: 6 **EST:** 2010
SQ FT: 2,200
SALES (est): 1.33MM **Privately Held**
Web: www.udecx.com
SIC: 3089 Floor coverings, plastics

(G-12852)
VISION PROJECTS INC
1350 Commerce Park Dr (45371-3323)
PHONE...............937 667-8648
George J Minarcek, *CEO*
Chris Dakin, *Treas*
EMP: 6 **EST:** 2003
SQ FT: 20,000
SALES (est): 164.47K **Privately Held**
Web: www.indiancreekfab.com
SIC: 3599 Machine shop, jobbing and repair

(G-12853)
VSCORP LLC
4754 Us Route 40 (45371-9481)
PHONE...............937 305-3562
EMP: 15 **EST:** 2017
SALES (est): 1MM **Privately Held**
SIC: 3441 Fabricated structural metal

(G-12854)
**WENRICK MACHINE AND TOOL
CORP**
Also Called: Wenrick Machine
4685 Us Route 40 (45371-8339)
PHONE...............937 667-7307
Tom Wenrick, *Pr*
Betty Wenrick, *Sec*
EMP: 10 **EST:** 1987
SQ FT: 8,000
SALES (est): 779.12K **Privately Held**
Web: www.wenrickmachine.com
SIC: 3599 7692 Machine shop, jobbing and
  repair; Welding repair

(G-12855)
WPC SUCCESSOR INC
Also Called: Weldcraft Products Co
6555 Oh 202 (45371)
P.O. Box 122 (45404-0122)
PHONE...............937 233-6141
Nancy Massey, *Pr*
EMP: 12 **EST:** 1953
SALES (est): 2.65MM **Privately Held**
SIC: 3499 7692 Machine bases, metal;
  Welding repair

Tippecanoe
Harrison County

(G-12856)
EXCO RESOURCES LLC
3618 Fallen Timber Rd Se (44699-9650)
PHONE...............740 254-4061
EMP: 16
SALES (corp-wide): 394.03MM **Privately
Held**
SIC: 1311 Crude petroleum and natural gas
  production
HQ: Exco Resources, Llc
  12377 Merit Dr Ste 1700
  Montoursville PA 17754

(G-12857)
GARDNER LUMBER COMPANY INC
5805 Laurel Creek Rd Se (44699-9661)
PHONE...............740 254-4664

Richard Gardner, *Pr*
Harvey Gardner, *VP*
EMP: 10 **EST:** 1938
SALES (est): 411.64K **Privately Held**
SIC: 2421 2448 5154 Sawmills and planing
mills, general; Pallets, wood; Cattle

(G-12858)
GRAY-EERING LTD
3158 Sandy Ridge Rd Se (44699-9657)
PHONE..................740 498-8816
Glenn Gray, *Pt*
Jay Gray, *Pt*
Lainard Gray, *Pt*
Sandra K Gray, *Sec*
EMP: 7 **EST:** 1978
SALES (est): 2.11MM **Privately Held**
Web: www.grayeering.com
SIC: 3535 3536 3534 Conveyors and
conveying equipment; Mine hoists;
Elevators and equipment

Toledo
Lucas County

(G-12859)
A & B TOOL & MANUFACTURING
2921 South Ave (43609-1327)
PHONE..................419 382-0215
Timothy J Adams, *Pr*
EMP: 7 **EST:** 1966
SQ FT: 8,000
SALES (est): 138.98K **Privately Held**
SIC: 3544 Special dies and tools

(G-12860)
A&M CHEESE CO
253 Waggoner Blvd (43612-1952)
PHONE..................419 476-8369
Michael J Sofo, *Pr*
Antonio Sofo, *
Joseph J Sofo Junior, *VP*
EMP: 53 **EST:** 1981
SQ FT: 190,000
SALES (est): 3.95MM **Privately Held**
Web: www.amcheese.com
SIC: 2022 Natural cheese

(G-12861)
ABBOTT TOOL INC
Also Called: ATI
405 Dura Ave (43612-2619)
PHONE..................419 476-6742
Arthur Stange, *VP*
Leonard Livecchi, *
Karle Stange, *
EMP: 20 **EST:** 1973
SQ FT: 12,000
SALES (est): 3.86MM **Privately Held**
Web: www.abbotttool.com
SIC: 3469 7692 Machine parts, stamped or
pressed metal; Welding repair

(G-12862)
ABUTILON COMPANY INC
Also Called: Abco Services
701 N Westwood Ave (43607-3559)
PHONE..................419 536-6123
Steven Zimmerman, *CEO*
Steve Zimmerman, *CEO*
EMP: 18 **EST:** 1991
SQ FT: 13,000
SALES (est): 2.6MM **Privately Held**
Web: www.abcotruckequipment.com
SIC: 5531 7538 3713 Auto and truck
equipment and parts; General automotive
repair shops; Truck and bus bodies

(G-12863)
ACCUSHRED LLC
1114 W Central Ave (43610-1061)
PHONE..................419 244-7473
Nate Segall, *Pr*
Barry Gudelman, *VP*
EMP: 16 **EST:** 2002
SALES (est): 2.38MM **Privately Held**
Web: www.accushred.net
SIC: 3589 Shredders, industrial and
commercial

(G-12864)
**ADAMS STREET PUBLISHING CO
INC**
Also Called: Toledo City Paper
1120 Adams St (43604-5509)
PHONE..................419 244-9859
Collette Jacobs, *Pr*
Marck Jacobs, *CEO*
EMP: 22 **EST:** 1992
SQ FT: 4,268
SALES (est): 954.41K **Privately Held**
Web: www.adamsstreetpublishing.com
SIC: 2721 Magazines: publishing only, not
printed on site

(G-12865)
ADVANCED INCENTIVES INC
1732 W Alexis Rd (43613-2349)
PHONE..................419 471-9088
James Williams, *Pr*
Rose Williams, *Sec*
Brian Williams, *VP*
EMP: 6 **EST:** 1993
SQ FT: 1,800
SALES (est): 368.97K **Privately Held**
Web: www.advancedincentives.com
SIC: 2759 Screen printing

(G-12866)
ADVANTAGE MOLD INC
525 N Wheeling St (43605-1337)
PHONE..................419 691-5676
Larry J Bolander, *Pr*
EMP: 8 **EST:** 1999
SQ FT: 13,000
SALES (est): 1.05MM **Privately Held**
Web: www.advantage-mold.com
SIC: 3089 Injection molding of plastics

(G-12867)
AIR-TECH MECHANICAL INC
4444 Monroe St (43613-4732)
PHONE..................419 292-0074
EMP: 6 **EST:** 2014
SALES (est): 777.44K **Privately Held**
Web: www.airtechtoledo.com
SIC: 3443 1711 Cooling towers, metal plate;
Heating and air conditioning contractors

(G-12868)
AIRTEX INDUSTRIES LLC
Also Called: Pumps Group
6056 Deer Park Ct (43614-6000)
PHONE..................330 899-0340
David Peace, *CEO*
EMP: 16 **EST:** 2005
SALES (est): 2.47MM
SALES (corp-wide): 7.28B **Privately Held**
SIC: 3714 Motor vehicle parts and
accessories
HQ: Uci-Airtex Holdings, Inc.
6056 Deer Park Ct
Toledo OH 43614
330 899-0340

(G-12869)
ALLEN INDUSTRIES INC
7844 W Central Ave (43617-1530)

PHONE..................567 408-7538
EMP: 78
SALES (corp-wide): 51.31MM **Privately
Held**
Web: www.allenindustries.com
SIC: 3993 Electric signs
PA: Allen Industries, Inc.
6434 Burnt Poplar Rd
Greensboro NC 27409
336 668-2791

(G-12870)
ALLIED MASK AND TOOLING INC
6051 Telegraph Rd Ste 6 (43612-4573)
P.O. Box 639 (48182-0639)
PHONE..................419 470-2555
Mike Murray, *Pr*
EMP: 9 **EST:** 1998
SQ FT: 3,600
SALES (est): 218.33K **Privately Held**
Web: www.alliedmask.com
SIC: 3599 3356 3444 3542 Machine shop,
jobbing and repair; Nickel; Sheet metalwork
; Electroforming machines

(G-12871)
ALRO STEEL CORPORATION
3003 Airport Hwy (43609-1405)
P.O. Box 964 (43697-0964)
PHONE..................,419 720-5300
Keith Daly, *Mgr*
EMP: 57
SALES (corp-wide): 3.04B **Privately Held**
Web: www.alro.com
SIC: 5051 5085 5162 3444 Steel; Industrial
supplies; Plastics materials, nec; Sheet
metalwork
PA: Alro Steel Corporation
3100 E High St
Jackson MI 49203
517 787-5500

(G-12872)
AMCRAFT INC
Also Called: Amcraft Manufacturing
5144 Enterprise Blvd (43612-3807)
PHONE..................419 729-7900
David R Frank, *Pr*
▼ **EMP:** 8 **EST:** 1966
SQ FT: 6,000
SALES (est): 914.75K **Privately Held**
Web: www.amcraftinc.com
SIC: 3423 3544 3469 Hand and edge tools,
nec; Special dies and tools; Metal
stampings, nec

(G-12873)
AMERICAN BOTTLING COMPANY
7 Up Bottling Co of Toledo
224 N Byrne Rd (43607-2605)
PHONE..................419 535-0777
Jeff Lark, *Mgr*
EMP: 78
Web: www.keurigdrpepper.com
SIC: 2086 Soft drinks: packaged in cans,
bottles, etc.
HQ: The American Bottling Company
6425 Hall Of Fame Ln
Frisco TX 75034

(G-12874)
AMERICAN CANVAS PRODUCTS INC
2925 South Ave (43609-1327)
PHONE..................419 382-8450
Richard W Jockett, *Pr*
EMP: 6 **EST:** 1994
SQ FT: 6,000
SALES (est): 488.77K **Privately Held**
Web: www.northstarproductsinc.com
SIC: 2394 Convertible tops, canvas or boat:
from purchased materials

(G-12875)
**AMERICAN MANUFACTURING INC
(PA)**
2375 Dorr St Ste F (43607-3407)
PHONE..................419 531-9471
Charles P Gotberg, *Pr*
▲ **EMP:** 10 **EST:** 1971
SALES (est): 7.27MM
SALES (corp-wide): 7.27MM **Privately
Held**
Web:
www.buyamericanmanufacturing.com
SIC: 3441 Fabricated structural metal

(G-12876)
**AMERICAN MNFCTRING OPRTONS
INC**
1931 E Manhattan Blvd (43608-1534)
PHONE..................419 269-1560
Jonathan R Saul, *Pr*
EMP: 8 **EST:** 2004
SALES (est): 974.97K **Privately Held**
SIC: 3715 Truck trailers

(G-12877)
AMERICAN POSTS LLC
810 Chicago St (43611-3609)
PHONE..................419 720-0652
David Feniger, *Managing Member*
EMP: 60 **EST:** 2005
SALES (est): 11.04MM
SALES (corp-wide): 62.42MM **Privately
Held**
Web: www.americanposts.com
SIC: 5051 3312 Steel; Rods, iron and steel:
made in steel mills
PA: Northwestern Holding, Llc
805 Chicago St
Toledo OH 43611
419 726-0850

(G-12878)
AMERICAN STEEL ASSOD PDTS INC
2375 Dorr St Ste F (43607-3407)
PHONE..................419 531-9471
Charles P Gotberg, *Pr*
EMP: 90 **EST:** 1995
SALES (est): 7.27MM
SALES (corp-wide): 7.27MM **Privately
Held**
Web:
www.buyamericanmanufacturing.com
SIC: 3441 Fabricated structural metal
PA: American Manufacturing, Inc.
2375 Dorr St Ste F
Toledo OH 43607
419 531-9471

(G-12879)
AMERICAN TOOL AND DIE INC
2024 Champlain St (43611-3700)
PHONE..................419 726-5394
Richard J Russell Junior, *Pr*
Gerald Russell, *VP*
Paul Philabaum, *VP*
EMP: 15 **EST:** 1963
SQ FT: 20,000
SALES (est): 2.13MM **Privately Held**
Web: www.americantoolanddieinc.com
SIC: 3469 3544 Stamping metal for the trade
; Special dies, tools, jigs, and fixtures

(G-12880)
ANDERSONS INC
125 Edwin Dr (43609-2669)
PHONE..................419 243-6800
EMP: 6
SALES (est): 298.74K **Privately Held**
Web: www.andersonsinc.com
SIC: 2873 Fertilizers: natural (organic),
except compost

(G-12881)
ANDERSONS INC
801 S Reynolds Rd (43615-6309)
PHONE..............................419 536-0460
Bill Kale, *Mgr*
EMP: 7
SALES (corp-wide): 11.26B **Publicly Held**
Web: www.andersonsinc.com
SIC: 0723 5191 2874 4789 Crop preparation
  services for market; Farm supplies;
  Phosphatic fertilizers; Railroad car repair
PA: The Andersons Inc
  1947 Briarfield Blvd
  Maumee OH 43537
  419 893-5050

(G-12882)
APEX BOLT & MACHINE COMPANY
Also Called: Apex Metal Fabricating & Mch
5324 Enterprise Blvd (43612-3870)
PHONE..............................419 729-3741
William G Foradas, *Ch Bd*
Michael S Petree, *
Luanna M Foradas, *
EMP: 39 EST: 1973
SQ FT: 51,000
SALES (est): 4.87MM **Privately Held**
Web: www.apexfab.net
SIC: 3441 Fabricated structural metal

(G-12883)
ARBOR FOODS INC
3332 Saint Lawrence Dr Bldg C
(43605-1046)
PHONE..............................419 698-4442
Mark S Flegenheimer, *Pr*
Sheila Severn, *Contrlr*
EMP: 50 EST: 2016
SALES (est): 2.23MM **Privately Held**
Web: www.streamlinefoods.com
SIC: 3556 Mixers, commercial, food

(G-12884)
ARCHER-DANIELS-MIDLAND COMPANY
Also Called: ADM
1308 Miami St (43605-3354)
PHONE..............................419 705-3292
Dan Hines, *Prin*
EMP: 9
SALES (corp-wide): 85.53B **Publicly Held**
Web: www.adm.com
SIC: 2041 2048 Flour and other grain mill
  products; Prepared feeds, nec
PA: Archer-Daniels-Midland Company
  77 W Wacker Dr Ste 4600
  Chicago IL 60601
  312 634-8100

(G-12885)
ARCLIN USA LLC
6175 American Rd (43612-3901)
PHONE..............................419 726-5013
Warren Shunk, *Manager*
EMP: 10
SALES (corp-wide): 136.26MM **Privately Held**
Web: www.arclin.com
SIC: 2891 2821 Adhesives and sealants;
  Plastics materials and resins
PA: Arclin Usa Llc
  1150 Sanctuary Pkwy
  Alpharetta GA 30009
  678 999-2100

(G-12886)
ARLINGTON RACK & PACKAGING CO
6120 N Detroit Ave (43612-4810)
P.O. Box 12207 (43612-0207)

PHONE..............................419 476-7700
Michael A Flaum, *Pr*
Harley Kripke, *Ch*
Mark Hahm, *VP*
EMP: 8 EST: 1990
SQ FT: 110,000
SALES (est): 999.07K **Privately Held**
Web: www.racksandpackaging.com
SIC: 3714 3086 Motor vehicle parts and
  accessories; Packaging and shipping
  materials, foamed plastics

(G-12887)
ART IRON INC
860 Curtis St (43609-2304)
P.O. Box 964 (43697-0964)
PHONE..............................419 241-1261
TOLL FREE: 800
▲ EMP: 70 EST: 1927
SALES (est): 2.2MM **Privately Held**
Web: www.artiron.com
SIC: 3441 3446 Fabricated structural metal;
  Architectural metalwork

(G-12888)
AUNT MINNIES FOOD SERVICES INC
702 Searles Rd (43607-2847)
PHONE..............................419 872-4396
Claudia Brown, *Pr*
Minnie Sebree, *Pr*
EMP: 12 EST: 2000
SQ FT: 6,000
SALES (est): 335.99K **Privately Held**
SIC: 2038 Breakfasts, frozen and packaged

(G-12889)
AUTOTEC CORPORATION
Also Called: Autotec Systems
6155 Brent Dr (43611-1083)
PHONE..............................419 885-2529
Thomas P Ballay, *Pr*
Thomas P Ballay, *Pr*
Jim Proffitt, *VP*
James Mihaly, *CFO*
EMP: 20 EST: 1979
SQ FT: 23,000
SALES (est): 9.26MM **Privately Held**
Web: www.autotecinc.com
SIC: 8711 3544 3599 Designing: ship, boat,
  machine, and product; Special dies, tools,
  jigs, and fixtures; Custom machinery

(G-12890)
AXALTA
1930 Tremainsville Rd (43613-5200)
PHONE..............................855 629-2582
EMP: 8 EST: 2019
SALES (est): 638.24K **Privately Held**
Web: www.axalta.com
SIC: 2834 Pharmaceutical preparations

(G-12891)
AXIOM ENGINEERED SYSTEMS LLC (PA)
1 Seagate Fl 27 (43604-1558)
PHONE..............................416 435-7313
EMP: 12 EST: 2019
SALES (est): 3.48MM
SALES (corp-wide): 3.48MM **Privately Held**
Web: www.axiomgroup.ca
SIC: 3089 Injection molding of plastics

(G-12892)
BANNER MATTRESS CO INC
Also Called: Banner Mattress & Furniture Co
2544 N Reynolds Rd (43615-2820)
PHONE..............................419 324-7181
▲ EMP: 85
Web: www.bannermattress.com

SIC: 5712 2515 Mattresses; Mattresses and
  bedsprings

(G-12893)
BASILIUS INC
4338 South Ave (43615-6236)
PHONE..............................419 536-5810
Scott Basilius, *Pr*
Dave Keiser, *
▲ EMP: 33 EST: 1940
SQ FT: 52,000
SALES (est): 4.88MM **Privately Held**
Web: www.basilius.com
SIC: 3544 Forms (molds), for foundry and
  plastics working machinery

(G-12894)
BEAUTE ASYLUM LLC
2011 Glendale Ave (43614-2802)
PHONE..............................419 377-9933
EMP: 10 EST: 2013
SALES (est): 80K **Privately Held**
Web: www.beauteasylum.com
SIC: 7231 3999 5087 Hairdressers;
  Fingernails, artificial; Beauty salon and
  barber shop equipment and supplies

(G-12895)
BELL BINDERS LLC
320 21st St (43604-5037)
P.O. Box 313 (43697-0313)
PHONE..............................419 242-3201
EMP: 15 EST: 1954
SALES (est): 911.8K **Privately Held**
Web: www.bellbinders.com
SIC: 2782 3089 Looseleaf binders and
  devices; Laminating of plastics

(G-12896)
BERNARD ENGRAVING CORP
414 N Erie St Ste 100 (43604-5625)
P.O. Box 320034 (06825-0034)
PHONE..............................419 478-5610
Jerry Moore, *Mgr*
EMP: 11 EST: 1992
SQ FT: 10,000
SALES (est): 90.93K **Privately Held**
Web: www.bernardengraving.com
SIC: 3111 3089 Die-cutting of leather;
  Injection molding of plastics

(G-12897)
BISON LEATHER CO
7409 W Central Ave (43617-1122)
PHONE..............................419 517-1737
Barry Cody, *CEO*
EMP: 6 EST: 2004
SALES (est): 51.86K **Privately Held**
Web: www.bisonleathertoledo.com
SIC: 3172 Personal leather goods, nec

(G-12898)
BLOCK COMMUNICATIONS INC (PA)
Also Called: BCI
405 Madison Ave Ste 2100 (43604-1224)
PHONE..............................419 724-6212
Jodi Miehls, *Pr*
Karen Block Johnese, *Ch Bd*
Jodi Miehls, *Pr*
Walter H Carstensen, *Pr*
John R Block, *V Ch Bd*
EMP: 14 EST: 1965
SQ FT: 64,100
SALES (est): 461.93MM
SALES (corp-wide): 461.93MM **Privately Held**
Web: www.blockcommunications.com
SIC: 4841 4833 2711 Cable television
  services; Television broadcasting stations;
  Newspapers, publishing and printing

(G-12899)
BOBCO ENTERPRISES INC
Also Called: Taylor Mtl Hdlg & Conveyor
2910 Glanzman Rd (43614-3955)
P.O. Box 39 (43560-0039)
PHONE..............................419 867-3560
TOLL FREE: 888
Robert Cordrey, *Pr*
EMP: 12 EST: 2002
SQ FT: 40,000
SALES (est): 4.59MM **Privately Held**
Web: www.taylormhc.com
SIC: 5084 3536 3535 Materials handling
  machinery; Hoists, cranes, and monorails;
  Conveyors and conveying equipment

(G-12900)
BOLLIN & SONS INC
Also Called: Bollin Label Systems
6001 Brent Dr (43611-1090)
PHONE..............................419 693-6573
Mark D Bollin, *Pr*
Chris Younkman, *
EMP: 40 EST: 1969
SQ FT: 21,000
SALES (est): 14.54MM **Privately Held**
Web: www.bollin.com
SIC: 5084 7389 2851 2759 Packaging
  machinery and equipment; Design services;
  Paints and allied products; Commercial
  printing, nec

(G-12901)
BP PRODUCTS NORTH AMERICA INC
B P Exploration
2450 Hill Ave (43607-3609)
P.O. Box 932 (43697-0932)
PHONE..............................419 537-9540
Jim Brahier, *Brnch Mgr*
EMP: 44
SQ FT: 11,485
SALES (corp-wide): 161.06B **Privately Held**
Web: www.bp.com
SIC: 2911 Petroleum refining
HQ: Bp Products North America Inc.
  501 Westlake Park Blvd
  Houston TX 77079
  281 366-2000

(G-12902)
BPREX PLASTIC PACKAGING INC (DH)
Also Called: Rexam Plastic Packaging
1 Seagate (43604-1558)
PHONE..............................419 247-5000
Joseph Lemieux, *CEO*
Lisa Hysko, *Prin*
Kenneth Hicks, *Prin*
EMP: 10 EST: 1987
SALES (est): 4.77MM **Privately Held**
SIC: 3089 3221 Plastics containers, except
  foam; Food containers, glass
HQ: Berry Global, Inc.
  101 Oakley St
  Evansville IN 47710

(G-12903)
BPREX PLASTIC SERVICES CO INC
Also Called: Specialty Packg Licensing Ltd
1 Seagate (43604-1563)
PHONE..............................419 247-5000
Joseph Lemieux, *CEO*
EMP: 7 EST: 1985
SALES (est): 2.31MM **Privately Held**
SIC: 3081 Unsupported plastics film and
  sheet
HQ: Berry Global, Inc.
  101 Oakley St
  Evansville IN 47710

(G-12904)
BRAIN CHILD PRODUCTS LLC
146 Main St (43605-2067)
PHONE..............................419 698-4020
EMP: 12 **EST:** 2005
SALES (est): 425.87K **Privately Held**
SIC: 2822 Silicone rubbers

(G-12905)
BROOKS MANUFACTURING
1102 N Summit St (43604-1816)
PHONE..............................419 244-1777
Michael Brooks, *Owner*
EMP: 9 **EST:** 1968
SQ FT: 5,000
SALES (est): 138.18K **Privately Held**
SIC: 3931 3592 3824 Brass instruments and parts; Valves; Water meters

(G-12906)
BRYAN DIE-CAST PRODUCTS LTD
4 Seagate Ste 803 (43604-2608)
PHONE..............................419 252-6208
Chad R Baker, *Prin*
EMP: 6 **EST:** 2012
SALES (est): 126.53K **Privately Held**
Web: www.bryandiecast.com
SIC: 3544 Special dies and tools

(G-12907)
BTW LLC
2226 Greenlawn Dr (43614-5120)
PHONE..............................419 382-4443
Paul Long, *Pr*
EMP: 8 **EST:** 1998
SALES (est): 168.09K **Privately Held**
Web: www.btw.com
SIC: 2679 5012 Wrappers, paper (unprinted): made from purchased material; Automobiles and other motor vehicles

(G-12908)
BUILDER TECH WHOLESALE LLC
Also Called: Builder Tech Windows
2931 South Ave (43609-1327)
PHONE..............................419 535-7606
EMP: 8 **EST:** 2000
SQ FT: 6,000
SALES (est): 806.3K **Privately Held**
SIC: 3089 Windows, plastics

(G-12909)
CAKE IN A CUP INC
6801 W Central Ave Ste B (43617-0400)
PHONE..............................419 491-1104
Lori Jacobs, *Prin*
Dana Iliev, *Prin*
EMP: 6 **EST:** 2007
SALES (est): 671.27K **Privately Held**
Web: www.cakeinacup.com
SIC: 5461 2051 Cakes; Cakes, bakery: except frozen

(G-12910)
CANBERRA CORPORATION
3610 N Holland Sylvania Rd (43615-1099)
PHONE..............................419 724-4300
R Bruce Yacko, *Pr*
James C Lower, *
William Schneck, *
◆ **EMP:** 205 **EST:** 1964
SQ FT: 220,000
SALES (est): 28.28MM **Privately Held**
Web: www.canberracorp.com
SIC: 2842 Cleaning or polishing preparations, nec

(G-12911)
CAPITAL TIRE INC
Also Called: Beitner Tire

516 E Hudson St (43608-1229)
PHONE..............................330 364-4731
EMP: 21
SALES (corp-wide): 79.32MM **Privately Held**
Web: www.capitaltire.com
SIC: 7534 5531 Tire retreading and repair shops; Automotive tires
PA: Capital Tire, Inc.
7001 Integrity Dr
Rossford OH 43460
419 241-5111

(G-12912)
CDH LIQUIDATION INC
Also Called: Custom Deco
1343 Miami St (43605-3313)
PHONE..............................419 720-4096
EMP: 33
SIC: 3231 Products of purchased glass

(G-12913)
CENTRAL COCA-COLA BTLG CO INC
Also Called: Coca-Cola
3970 Catawba St (43612-1404)
PHONE..............................419 476-6622
Paul Kenny, *Mgr*
EMP: 129
SALES (corp-wide): 45.75B **Publicly Held**
Web: www.coca-cola.com
SIC: 2086 2087 5149 Bottled and canned soft drinks; Syrups, drink; Groceries and related products, nec
HQ: Central Coca-Cola Bottling Company, Inc.
555 Taxter Rd Ste 550
Elmsford NY 10523
914 789-1100

(G-12914)
CHAMPION LABORATORIES INC
6056 Deer Park Ct (43614-6000)
PHONE..............................330 899-0340
EMP: 8
SALES (corp-wide): 7.28B **Privately Held**
Web: www.champlabs.com
SIC: 3714 Filters: oil, fuel, and air, motor vehicle
HQ: Champion Laboratories, Inc.
200 S 4th St
Albion IL 62806
618 445-6011

(G-12915)
CHAMPION SPARK PLUG COMPANY
900 Upton Ave (43607-3727)
PHONE..............................419 535-2567
Richard Keller, *Pr*
▲ **EMP:** 72 **EST:** 1907
SQ FT: 15,000
SALES (est): 2.72MM
SALES (corp-wide): 18.04B **Privately Held**
Web: www.championautoparts.com
SIC: 3714 Motor vehicle parts and accessories
HQ: Tenneco Inc.
15701 Technology Dr
Northville MI 48168
248 849-1290

(G-12916)
CHANTILLY DEVELOPMENT CORP
Acme Specialty Mfg Co
3101 Monroe St (43606-4605)
P.O. Box 2510 (43606-0510)
PHONE..............................419 243-8109
Robert T Skilliter Junior, *Prin*
EMP: 20
SQ FT: 70,000
SALES (corp-wide): 4.98MM **Privately Held**

Web: www.acmespecialty.com
SIC: 3714 3231 3429 3221 Frames, motor vehicle; Mirrored glass; Hardware, nec; Glass containers
PA: Chantilly Development Corp
Wollaston Rd
Unionville PA
419 243-8109

(G-12917)
CHASE SIGN & LIGHTING SVC INC
5924 American Rd E (43612-3950)
PHONE..............................567 128-3444
EMP: 6 **EST:** 2015
SALES (est): 354.76K **Privately Held**
Web: www.chasesign.net
SIC: 3993 Signs and advertising specialties

(G-12918)
CHEM-SALES INC
Also Called: C S I
3860 Dorr St (43607-1003)
P.O. Box 351684 (43635-1684)
EMP: 12 **EST:** 1980
SALES (est): 551.75K **Privately Held**
Web: www.chemsalesinc.com
SIC: 2869 5087 5169 Industrial organic chemicals, nec; Janitors' supplies; Chemicals and allied products, nec

(G-12919)
CHEMPACE CORPORATION
339 Arco Dr (43607-2908)
PHONE..............................419 535-0101
Richard Shall, *Pr*
Ralph E Wooddell, *Sec*
Terry W O'neill, *VP*
Sue Klotz, *Contrlr*
▲ **EMP:** 18 **EST:** 1968
SQ FT: 12,500
SALES (est): 4.37MM **Privately Held**
Web: www.chempace.com
SIC: 2842 Cleaning or polishing preparations, nec

(G-12920)
CHINA ENTERPRISES INC
Also Called: Chang Audio
5151 Monroe St (43623-3462)
PHONE..............................419 885-1485
Stella Lee, *Pr*
Michael Chang, *Ex VP*
EMP: 7 **EST:** 1991
SALES (est): 188.07K **Privately Held**
SIC: 3651 Household audio equipment

(G-12921)
CLAMPS INC
5960 American Rd E (43612-3966)
PHONE..............................419 729-2141
Jd Riker, *CEO*
J D Riker, *
Jeanne E Graham, *
Kelly Smith, *
Tom Shackelford, *
EMP: 25 **EST:** 1957
SQ FT: 67,000
SALES (est): 4.91MM **Privately Held**
Web: www.clampsinc.com
SIC: 3496 Miscellaneous fabricated wire products

(G-12922)
CLAYCOR INC
Also Called: Denbro Plastics Company
5924 American Rd E (43612-3950)
PHONE..............................419 318-7290
Jack Mckisson, *Pr*
EMP: 10 **EST:** 1964
SQ FT: 10,000
SALES (est): 248.14K **Privately Held**

Web: www.koesterchiropracticcenter.com
SIC: 3089 Injection molding of plastics

(G-12923)
CLEAR IMAGES LLC
121 11th St (43604-5829)
PHONE..............................419 241-9347
Frank Ozanski, *Managing Member*
EMP: 9 **EST:** 2003
SALES (est): 604.98K **Privately Held**
Web: www.clearimagestoledo.com
SIC: 2759 Screen printing

(G-12924)
CLINTON FOUNDRY LTD
1202 W Bancroft St (43606-4631)
PHONE..............................419 243-6885
James D Heninger, *Prin*
EMP: 10 **EST:** 1997
SQ FT: 4,500
SALES (est): 252.8K **Privately Held**
Web:
www.clinton-patternandfoundry.com
SIC: 3543 Industrial patterns

(G-12925)
CLINTON PATTERN WORKS INC
1215 W Bancroft St (43606-4632)
PHONE..............................419 243-0855
James D Heninger, *Pr*
Timothy Heninger, *VP*
EMP: 6 **EST:** 1941
SQ FT: 25,000
SALES (est): 1MM **Privately Held**
Web:
www.clinton-patternandfoundry.com
SIC: 3543 Industrial patterns

(G-12926)
CM SLICECHIEF CO
Also Called: Slicechief
3333 Maple St (43608-1147)
PHONE..............................419 241-7647
Susan L Brown, *Pr*
Barbara Cairl, *Sec*
EMP: 9 **EST:** 1946
SQ FT: 18,000
SALES (est): 257.32K **Privately Held**
SIC: 3556 Slicers, commercial, food

(G-12927)
COLE ORTHOTICS PROSTHETIC CTR
723 Phillips Ave Bldg F (43612-1351)
PHONE..............................419 476-4248
Daniel P Cole, *Owner*
EMP: 6 **EST:** 1920
SQ FT: 8,000
SALES (est): 972.88K **Privately Held**
Web: www.leimkuehleroandp.com
SIC: 3842 Braces, orthopedic

(G-12928)
COMFORT LINE LTD
Also Called: Fiber Frame
5500 Enterprise Blvd (43612-3815)
PHONE..............................419 729-8520
Daniel J La Valley, *Pr*
Richard G La Valley, *
Dianne Tankoos, *
◆ **EMP:** 100 **EST:** 1959
SQ FT: 200,000
SALES (est): 9.95MM **Privately Held**
Web: www.fiberframe.com
SIC: 3089 Windows, plastics

(G-12929)
CONFORMING MATRIX CORPORATION

6255 Suder Ave (43611-1022)
PHONE..........................419 729-3777
Albert J Spelker, *Pr*
Ella Mae Macarthur, *
H E Macarthur, *
Chad Mccomas, *CFO*
EMP: 40 **EST:** 1939
SQ FT: 38,000
SALES (est): 2.39MM **Privately Held**
SIC: 3559 3544 Metal finishing equipment
for plating, etc.; Special dies, tools, jigs,
and fixtures

(G-12930)
CONNECTRONICS CORP (DH)
Also Called: Wiremax A Heico Company
2745 Avondale Ave (43607-3232)
P.O. Box 3355 (43607-0355)
PHONE..........................419 537-0020
Thomas Ricketts, *CEO*
Thomas L Ricketts, *
Lex Potter, *
Al Mocek, *
Judith W Vetter, *
EMP: 50 **EST:** 1988
SQ FT: 25,000
SALES (est): 9.28MM **Publicly Held**
Web: www.connectronicscorp.com
SIC: 3678 3643 Electronic connectors;
Connectors and terminals for electrical
devices
HQ: Heico Electronic Technologies Corp.
3000 Taft St
Hollywood FL 33021
954 987-6101

(G-12931)
CONSUMER GUILD FOODS INC
5035 Enterprise Blvd (43612-3839)
PHONE..........................419 726-3406
Wilbur R Ascham, *Pr*
Robert J Petrick, *VP*
Ann Ascham, *Sec*
EMP: 6 **EST:** 1966
SQ FT: 14,500
SALES (est): 381.92K **Privately Held**
SIC: 2035 Dressings, salad: raw and cooked
(except dry mixes)

(G-12932)
CONTAINER GRAPHICS CORP
305 Ryder Rd (43607-3105)
PHONE..........................419 531-5133
Bill Beaker, *Brnch Mgr*
EMP: 33
SQ FT: 24,200
SALES (corp-wide): 3.99MM **Privately
Held**
Web: www.containergraphics.com
SIC: 7336 3545 3944 Graphic arts and
related design; Cutting tools for machine
tools; Dice and dice cups
PA: Container Graphics Corp.
114 Ednbrgh S Drv Ste 104
Cary NC 27511
919 481-4200

(G-12933)
CROWN CORK & SEAL USA INC
5201 Enterprise Blvd (43612-3808)
PHONE..........................419 727-8201
Willaim Lahner, *Mgr*
EMP: 143
SALES (corp-wide): 11.8B **Publicly Held**
Web: www.crowncork.com
SIC: 3411 Metal cans
HQ: Crown Cork & Seal Usa, Inc.
770 Township Line Rd
Yardley PA 19067
215 698-5100

(G-12934)
CULAINE INC
Also Called: Cpg Printing & Graphics
1036 W Laskey Rd (43612-3030)
PHONE..........................419 345-4984
Mike Cutcher, *Pr*
Elaine R Cutcher, *VP*
EMP: 6 **EST:** 1970
SQ FT: 4,000
SALES (est): 205.23K **Privately Held**
SIC: 2759 2752 Commercial printing, nec;
Commercial printing, lithographic

(G-12935)
CUSTOM DECO LLC
1345 Miami St (43605-3313)
PHONE..........................419 698-2900
Michelle Schkeryantz, *Managing Member*
EMP: 22 **EST:** 2018
SALES (est): 618.33K **Privately Held**
SIC: 2759 Screen printing

(G-12936)
**DAKKOTA INTEGRATED SYSTEMS
LLC**
315 Matzinger Rd Unit G (43612-2626)
PHONE..........................517 694-6500
James Horwath, *Contrlr*
EMP: 26
SQ FT: 65,000
SALES (corp-wide): 242.26MM **Privately
Held**
Web: www.dakkota.com
SIC: 3711 Automobile assembly, including
specialty automobiles
PA: Dakkota Integrated Systems, Llc
123 Brghton Lk Rd Ste 202
Brighton MI 48116
517 694-6500

(G-12937)
DANA
3044 Jeep Pkwy (43610-1072)
PHONE..........................419 887-3000
EMP: 21 **EST:** 2019
SALES (est): 7.39MM **Privately Held**
Web: www.dana.com
SIC: 3714 Motor vehicle parts and
accessories

(G-12938)
DANA LIGHT AXLE MFG LLC
Also Called: Toledo Driveline
3044 Jeep Pkwy (43610-1072)
PHONE..........................419 887-3000
EMP: 300
SQ FT: 100,000
Web: www.dana.com
SIC: 3714 Motor vehicle parts and
accessories
HQ: Dana Light Axle Manufacturing, Llc
3939 Technology Dr
Maumee OH 43537

(G-12939)
DECO TOOLS INC
1541 Coining Dr (43612-2978)
PHONE..........................419 476-9321
Mike Bollenbacher, *Pr*
EMP: 25 **EST:** 1955
SQ FT: 30,000
SALES (est): 4.65MM **Privately Held**
Web: www.decotools.com
SIC: 3563 3991 3842 2672 Spraying outfits:
metals, paints, and chemicals (compressor)
; Brooms and brushes; Surgical appliances
and supplies; Paper; coated and laminated,
nec

(G-12940)
**DECOMA SYSTEMS INTEGRATION
GRO**
Also Called: Team Systems
1800 Nathan Dr (43611-1091)
PHONE..........................419 324-3387
Belinda Stronach, *CEO*
EMP: 100 **EST:** 2005
SALES (est): 21.86MM
SALES (corp-wide): 42.84B **Privately Held**
SIC: 3465 Body parts, automobile: stamped
metal
PA: Magna International Inc
337 Magna Dr
Aurora ON L4G 7
905 726-2462

(G-12941)
DECORATIVE PANELS INTL INC (DH)
Also Called: D P I
2900 Hill Ave (43607-2929)
PHONE..........................419 535-5921
Tim Clark, *Pr*
Allen Steiber, *Contrlr*
▼ **EMP:** 75 **EST:** 2004
SQ FT: 225,000
SALES (est): 53.46MM **Privately Held**
Web: www.decpanels.com
SIC: 2421 Sawmills and planing mills,
general
HQ: As America, Inc.
30 Knghtsbrdge Rd Ste 301
Piscataway NJ 08854

(G-12942)
DETROIT TOLEDO FIBER LLC
1245 E Manhattan Blvd (43608-1549)
PHONE..........................248 647-0400
Steven Philips, *Pr*
Gary Stanis, *CFO*
EMP: 10 **EST:** 2012
SALES (est): 1.1MM **Privately Held**
SIC: 3714 Motor vehicle engines and parts
PA: Conform Automotive, Llc
32500 Telg Rd Ste 207
Bingham Farms MI 48025

(G-12943)
DFA DAIRY BRANDS ICE CREAM LLC
4117 Fitch Rd (43613-4007)
PHONE..........................419 473-9621
Randy Bevier, *Mgr*
EMP: 331
SALES (corp-wide): 23.02B **Privately Held**
Web: www.dfamilk.com
SIC: 2026 Fluid milk
HQ: Dfa Dairy Brands Ice Cream, Llc
1405 N 98th St
Kansas City KS 66111
816 801-6455

(G-12944)
DISMAT CORPORATION
336 N Westwood Ave (43607-3343)
PHONE..........................419 531-8963
John A Donofrio, *Pr*
EMP: 6 **EST:** 1945
SQ FT: 12,000
SALES (est): 508.9K **Privately Held**
Web: www.mckays-seasoning.com
SIC: 2099 Food preparations, nec

(G-12945)
DIVERSEY TASKI INC (PA) ◎
3115 Frenchmens Rd (43607-2918)
PHONE..........................419 531-2121
Tracy Long, *Pr*
EMP: 32 **EST:** 2023
SALES (est): 32.02MM
SALES (corp-wide): 32.02MM **Privately
Held**

Web: www.taski.com
SIC: 3589 Floor washing and polishing
machines, commercial

(G-12946)
ELAIRE CORPORATION
7944 W Central Ave Ste 10 (43617-1550)
PHONE..........................419 843-2192
Mark Neeley, *Pr*
EMP: 8 **EST:** 2011
SALES (est): 878.51K **Privately Held**
Web: www.elairecorp.com
SIC: 3999 Manufacturing industries, nec

(G-12947)
ELDEN DRAPERIES OF TOLEDO INC
1845 N Reynolds Rd (43615-3531)
PHONE..........................419 535-1909
Betsy Grubb, *Pr*
Gary Grubb, *VP*
EMP: 10
SQ FT: 6,000
SALES (est): 885.45K **Privately Held**
Web: www.eldenblinds.com
SIC: 2391 5714 Draperies, plastic and
textile: from purchased materials; Draperies

(G-12948)
ELECTRO PRIME GROUP LLC
Also Called: Electro Prime
4510 Lint Ave Ste B (43612-2658)
PHONE..........................419 476-0100
John L Lauffer, *Managing Member*
Kevin Meade, *
▲ **EMP:** 40 **EST:** 2005
SQ FT: 20,100
SALES (est): 7.17MM **Privately Held**
Web: www.electroprime.com
SIC: 3711 Motor vehicles and car bodies

(G-12949)
ELEMENT MACHINERY LLC
4801 Bennett Rd (43612-2531)
PHONE..........................855 447-7648
Benjamin Mcgilvery, *CEO*
Samuel Mcgilvery 40, *Pr*
Joseph Box, *VP*
EMP: 6 **EST:** 2015
SQ FT: 20,000
SALES (est): 2.77MM **Privately Held**
Web: www.elementmachinery.com
SIC: 3547 Rolling mill machinery

(G-12950)
**ELEVATOR CNCEPTS BY WURTEC
LLC**
6200 Brent Dr (43611-1081)
PHONE..........................734 246-4700
Douglas Scott, *Pr*
Leigh Gaither, *VP*
▲ **EMP:** 10 **EST:** 1985
SQ FT: 10,000
SALES (est): 1.63MM
SALES (corp-wide): 33.89MM **Privately
Held**
Web: www.wurtec.com
SIC: 3534 Elevators and equipment
PA: Wurtec, Incorporated
6200 Brent Dr
Toledo OH 43611
419 726-1066

(G-12951)
**EMSSONS FAURECIA CTRL
SYSTEMS (DH)**
543 Matzinger Rd (43612-2638)
PHONE..........................812 341-2000
David Degraaf, *Pr*
Mark Stidham, *
Christophe Schmidt, *

▲ **EMP:** 130 **EST:** 1988
SQ FT: 40,000
SALES (est): 218.01MM
SALES (corp-wide): 92.81MM **Privately Held**
SIC: 3714 5013 Mufflers (exhaust), motor vehicle; Motor vehicle supplies and new parts
HQ: Faurecia Emissions Control Technologies Usa, Llc
2800 High Meadow Cir
Auburn Hills MI 48326

(G-12952)
ENDURA PRODUCTS LLC
1 Owens Corning Pkwy (43659-1000)
PHONE..........................419 248-8911
EMP: 18
SIC: 3429 Builders' hardware
HQ: Endura Products, Llc
8817 W Market St
Colfax NC 27235
336 668-2472

(G-12953)
ENGINEERED IMAGING LLC
110 E Woodruff Ave (43604-5226)
PHONE..........................419 255-1283
EMP: 15 **EST:** 2021
SALES (est): 3MM **Privately Held**
Web: www.engineeredimaging.com
SIC: 2759 Commercial printing, nec

(G-12954)
ENNIS INC
Tennessee Business Forms
4444 N Detroit Ave (43612-1978)
PHONE..........................800 537-8648
Tina Furgason, *Brnch Mgr*
EMP: 33
SALES (corp-wide): 420.11MM **Publicly Held**
Web: www.printxcel.com
SIC: 2752 Commercial printing, lithographic
PA: Ennis, Inc.
2441 Presidential Pkwy
Midlothian TX 76065
972 775-9801

(G-12955)
ERD SPECIALTY GRAPHICS INC
3250 Monroe St (43606-4550)
PHONE..........................419 242-9545
Steve Crouse, *Pr*
EMP: 9 **EST:** 1934
SQ FT: 19,500
SALES (est): 456.94K **Privately Held**
Web: erdspecialtygraphics.imprintableapparel.com
SIC: 2759 7389 3554 2396 Screen printing; Printers' services: folding, collating, etc.; Die cutting and stamping machinery, paper converting; Fabric printing and stamping

(G-12956)
ERIE STEEL LTD
5540 Jackman Rd (43613-2330)
PHONE..........................419 478-3743
Pat Flynn, *Pr*
EMP: 50 **EST:** 2004
SALES (est): 5.02MM **Privately Held**
Web: www.erie.com
SIC: 3398 Metal heat treating

(G-12957)
ESTONE GROUP LLC
Also Called: Wholesale and Manufacturer
2900 Carskaddon Ave # 200 (43606-1601)
PHONE..........................888 653-2246
Bing Li, *CEO*
EMP: 20 **EST:** 2011

SALES (est): 1.01MM **Privately Held**
Web: www.estonetech.com
SIC: 8748 3663 Business consulting, nec; Mobile communication equipment

(G-12958)
EXCO ENGINEERING USA INC (HQ)
Also Called: Edco Tool & Die
5244 Enterprise Blvd (43612-3874)
PHONE..........................419 726-1595
Jai Singh, *Pr*
Paul Riganelli, *
◆ **EMP:** 45 **EST:** 1955
SQ FT: 50,000
SALES (est): 24.62MM
SALES (corp-wide): 473.72MM **Privately Held**
Web: www.excoengusa.com
SIC: 3544 Special dies and tools
PA: Exco Technologies Limited
130 Spy Crt Fl 2
Markham ON L3R 5
905 477-3065

(G-12959)
EXOTHERMICS
5040 Enterprise Blvd (43612-3840)
PHONE..........................419 729-9726
Rich Lattanzi, *Prin*
Matthew Nozemack, *Prin*
Kelly Gonzales, *
Lach Perks, *
▲ **EMP:** 25 **EST:** 1976
SQ FT: 38,000
SALES (est): 2.33MM
SALES (corp-wide): 38.5B **Publicly Held**
SIC: 3443 Heat exchangers, condensers, and components
HQ: Eclipse, Inc.
201 E 18th St
Muncie IN 47302

(G-12960)
EXP FUELS INC
3070 Airport Hwy (43609-1406)
PHONE..........................419 382-7713
Victor Safadi, *Prin*
EMP: 6 **EST:** 2012
SALES (est): 178.31K **Privately Held**
SIC: 2869 Fuels

(G-12961)
FENNER DUNLOP (TOLEDO) LLC
146 S Westwood Ave (43607-2948)
P.O. Box 441 (43697-0441)
PHONE..........................419 531-5300
Cassandra Pan, *
Bill Mooney, *
Ben Ficklen, *
▲ **EMP:** 16 **EST:** 2001
SQ FT: 100,000
SALES (est): 3.37MM
SALES (corp-wide): 1.95B **Privately Held**
SIC: 3052 Rubber belting
HQ: Fenner Dunlop Americas, Llc
200 Crprate Ctr Dr Ste 22
Coraopolis PA 15108

(G-12962)
FENWICK GALLERY OF FINE ARTS (PA)
Also Called: Fenwick Frame Shppe Art Gllery
3433 W Alexis Rd Frnt (43623-1400)
PHONE..........................419 475-1651
Beverly A Freshour, *Pr*
EMP: 6
SQ FT: 3,000
SALES (est): 137.23K
SALES (corp-wide): 137.23K **Privately Held**

SIC: 5999 2499 Art dealers; Picture and mirror frames, wood

(G-12963)
FIBREBOARD CORPORATION (DH)
1 Owens Corning Pkwy (43659-1000)
PHONE..........................419 248-8000
David T Brown, *Pr*
Michael Thaman, *
▲ **EMP:** 200 **EST:** 1917
SALES (est): 24.49MM **Publicly Held**
SIC: 3089 3272 3296 Siding, plastics; Cast stone, concrete; Mineral wool insulation products
HQ: Owens Corning Sales, Llc
1 Owens Corning Pkwy
Toledo OH 43659
419 248-8000

(G-12964)
FINISHING BRANDS HOLDINGS INC
Also Called: Finishing Brands
320 Phillips Ave (43612-1467)
PHONE..........................260 665-8800
▼ **EMP:** 190
SIC: 3563 Spraying outfits: metals, paints, and chemicals (compressor)

(G-12965)
FISKE BROTHERS REFINING CO
1500 Oakdale Ave (43605-3843)
P.O. Box 8038 (43605-0038)
PHONE..........................419 691-2491
William Kuhlman, *Mgr*
EMP: 60
SQ FT: 30,000
SALES (corp-wide): 45.18MM **Privately Held**
Web: www.lubriplate.com
SIC: 2992 2077 Re-refining lubricating oils and greases, nec; Animal and marine fats and oils
PA: Fiske Brothers Refining Co Inc
129 Lockwood St
Newark NJ 07105
973 589-9150

(G-12966)
FLYNN INC
5540 Jackman Rd (43613-2330)
PHONE..........................419 478-3743
Patrick Flynn, *Pr*
Mary Schira, *
EMP: 9 **EST:** 1961
SALES (est): 1.6MM **Privately Held**
Web: www.erie.com
SIC: 3398 Metal heat treating

(G-12967)
FORKLIFT TIRE EAST MICH INC
4934 Lewis Ave (43612-2825)
P.O. Box 235 (48066-0235)
PHONE..........................586 771-1330
Michael Fogel Iii, *Pr*
EMP: 10 **EST:** 1992
SALES (est): 134.38K **Privately Held**
Web: tiremaxx.jambestone.com
SIC: 5014 7534 Tires and tubes; Tire repair shop

(G-12968)
FOSTER CANNING INC
6725 W Central Ave Ste T (43617-1154)
P.O. Box 30 (43545-0030)
PHONE..........................419 841-6755
Martin Davidson, *Pr*
Martin Davidson, *Sls Dir*
EMP: 40 **EST:** 1939
SQ FT: 100,000
SALES (est): 197.38K **Privately Held**

SIC: 2033 2047 Tomato products, packaged in cans, jars, etc.; Dog food

(G-12969)
FRITZIE FREEZE INC
5137 N Summit St Unit 1 (43611-2754)
PHONE..........................419 727-0818
Chris Schwind, *Prin*
EMP: 6 **EST:** 2007
SALES (est): 251.08K **Privately Held**
Web: fritzie-freeze-inc.edan.io
SIC: 2024 Ice cream, bulk

(G-12970)
FULTON EQUIPMENT CO (PA)
823 Hamilton St (43607-4477)
PHONE..........................419 290-5393
Richard G Paul Junior, *Pr*
EMP: 16 **EST:** 1989
SQ FT: 8,000
SALES (est): 465.9K **Privately Held**
SIC: 3441 3444 3443 Fabricated structural metal; Sheet metalwork; Fabricated plate work (boiler shop)

(G-12971)
G H CUTTER SERVICES INC
6203 N Detroit Ave (43612-4818)
PHONE..........................419 476-0476
Gene Hodapp, *Pr*
Mary Hodapp, *Sec*
EMP: 9 **EST:** 1988
SALES (est): 698.35K **Privately Held**
Web: www.ghcutters.com
SIC: 3599 7389 Machine shop, jobbing and repair; Grinding, precision: commercial or industrial

(G-12972)
GARDNER SIGNS INC (PA)
3800 Airport Hwy (43615-7106)
PHONE..........................419 385-6669
Weston L Gardner Junior, *CEO*
Scott Gardner, *Pr*
EMP: 17 **EST:** 1945
SQ FT: 13,000
SALES (est): 2.61MM
SALES (corp-wide): 2.61MM **Privately Held**
Web: www.gardnersigns.com
SIC: 3993 Electric signs

(G-12973)
GDY INSTALLATIONS INC
Also Called: GDY INSTALLATIONS INC
302 Arco Dr (43607-2907)
PHONE..........................419 467-0036
Gary Young, *Brnch Mgr*
EMP: 10
SQ FT: 8,430
Web: www.gdyinstallations.com
SIC: 3272 Furniture, church: concrete
PA: Gdy Installations, Inc.
2226 Linden Ct
Maumee OH 43537

(G-12974)
GENERAL MILLS INC
Also Called: General Mills
1250 W Laskey Rd (43612-2935)
PHONE..........................419 269-3100
Ann Bombrys, *Brnch Mgr*
EMP: 10
SALES (corp-wide): 19.86B **Publicly Held**
Web: www.generalmills.com
SIC: 2043 Wheat flakes: prepared as cereal breakfast food
PA: General Mills, Inc.
1 General Mills Blvd
Minneapolis MN 55426
763 764-7600

(G-12975)
GIANT INDUSTRIES INC
900 N Westwood Ave (43607-3261)
PHONE..............................419 531-4600
Raymond Simon, *CEO*
Edward Simon, *
Wolfgang Drescher, *
▲ EMP: 40 EST: 1990
SQ FT: 83,000
SALES (est): 15.95MM **Publicly Held**
Web: www.giantpumps.com
SIC: 3581 3589 5084 3594 Automatic
vending machines; Car washing machinery;
Pumps and pumping equipment, nec; Fluid
power pumps and motors
PA: Marathon Petroleum Corporation
539 S Main St
Findlay OH 45840

(G-12976)
GOTTFRIED MEDICAL INC
2920 Centennial Rd (43617-1833)
P.O. Box 8966 (43623)
PHONE..............................419 474-2973
Brent Gottfried, *Pr*
Pauline Gottfried, *VP*
Lisa King, *Sec*
EMP: 11 EST: 1980
SALES (est): 207.18K **Privately Held**
Web: www.gottfriedmedical.com
SIC: 3842 Orthopedic appliances

(G-12977)
GREGGS SPECIALTY SERVICES
Also Called: Ch Enterprises
306 Dura Ave (43612-2618)
PHONE..............................419 478-0803
Matthew Haocomb, *Pr*
EMP: 10 EST: 1985
SQ FT: 20,000
SALES (est): 223.24K **Privately Held**
Web: www.browdersflorist.com
SIC: 7692 7539 7629 Welding repair; Trailer
repair; Electrical repair shops

(G-12978)
GT TECHNOLOGIES INC
Also Called: Gt Technlgies Tledo Operations
99 N Fearing Blvd (43607-3602)
PHONE..............................419 324-7300
Daniel Brinker, *Pr*
EMP: 100
SALES (corp-wide): 283.29MM **Privately
Held**
Web: www.gttechnologies.com
SIC: 3714 3469 3465 Motor vehicle engines
and parts; Metal stampings, nec;
Automotive stampings
PA: Gt Technologies, Inc.
5859 E Executive Dr
Westland MI 48185
734 467-8371

(G-12979)
**GWS LEVI UP HOME SOLUTIONS
LLC**
6020 W Bancroft St Unit 350061
(43615-3200)
PHONE..............................419 667-6041
EMP: 25 EST: 1985
SALES (est): 341.13K **Privately Held**
Web: www.toledogeneralcontractor.com
SIC: 1521 1389 General remodeling, single-
family houses; Construction, repair, and
dismantling services

(G-12980)
H&M MACHINE & TOOL LLC
3823 Seiss Ave (43612-1316)
PHONE..............................419 776-9220
John Miller, *Managing Member*

Mike Whatley, *VP*
EMP: 22 EST: 2008
SALES (est): 2.49MM **Privately Held**
Web: www.handmmachine.com
SIC: 3544 3543 Industrial molds; Industrial
patterns

(G-12981)
H2FLOW CONTROLS INC
7629 New West Rd (43617-4201)
PHONE..............................419 841-7774
Paul Hackett, *CEO*
David Atkins, *VP*
Russel Weiss, *VP*
EMP: 6 EST: 1998
SALES (est): 7.02MM **Privately Held**
Web: www.h2flow.net
SIC: 5065 3823 Security control equipment
and systems; Process control instruments

(G-12982)
HA-INTERNATIONAL LLC
4243 South Ave (43615-6233)
PHONE..............................419 537-0096
Michael Hohol, *Brnch Mgr*
EMP: 30
SQ FT: 62,680
SALES (corp-wide): 167.14K **Privately
Held**
Web: www.ha-international.com
SIC: 2869 3582 2992 Industrial organic
chemicals, nec; Commercial laundry
equipment; Lubricating oils and greases
HQ: Ha-International, Llc
630 Oakmont Ln
Westmont IL 60559
630 575-5700

(G-12983)
**HAFNERS HRDWOOD CONNECTION
LLC**
Also Called: Hardwood Connection, The
2845 111th St (43611-2826)
PHONE..............................419 726-4828
Todd Hafner, *Managing Member*
EMP: 6 EST: 1993
SQ FT: 5,600
SALES (est): 180.7K **Privately Held**
SIC: 3999 7389 Plaques, picture, laminated;
Engraving service

(G-12984)
**HALE PERFORMANCE COATINGS
INC**
2282 Albion St (43606-4523)
PHONE..............................419 244-6451
Frederick M Deye, *Pr*
Carol Lambrecht, *
G C Scharfy, *
J C Straub, *
R A Jefferies Junior, *Prin*
EMP: 42 EST: 1966
SQ FT: 14,700
SALES (est): 3.94MM **Privately Held**
Web:
www.haleperformancecoatings.com
SIC: 3471 3544 Chromium plating of metals
or formed products; Special dies, tools, jigs,
and fixtures

(G-12985)
HAMMILL MANUFACTURING CO
Co-Op Tool
1517 Coining Dr (43612-2930)
PHONE..............................419 476-9125
Jeff Mack, *Div Mgr*
EMP: 50
SALES (corp-wide): 22.18MM **Privately
Held**
Web: www.productionworkholding.com

SIC: 3599 Machine shop, jobbing and repair
PA: Hammill Manufacturing Co.
360 Tomahawk Dr
Maumee OH 43537
419 476-0789

(G-12986)
HANSEN-MUELLER CO
1800 N Water St (43611)
PHONE..............................419 729-5535
Mike Burget, *Mgr*
EMP: 7
SALES (corp-wide): 111.32MM **Privately
Held**
Web: www.hansenmueller.com
SIC: 5153 2041 Grains; Flour and other
grain mill products
PA: Hansen-Mueller Co.
13321 Cal St Ste 100
Omaha NE 68164
402 491-3385

(G-12987)
HAYES BROS ORNA IR WORKS INC
1830 N Reynolds Rd (43615-3530)
PHONE..............................419 531-1491
Gary M Hayes, *Pr*
Patrick Hayes, *VP*
Douglas C Hayes, *Treas*
Gregory M Hayes, *Sec*
EMP: 10 EST: 1946
SQ FT: 10,000
SALES (est): 468.61K **Privately Held**
Web: www.hayesbrosiron.com
SIC: 3446 Railings, prefabricated metal

(G-12988)
HEARN PLATING CO LTD
3184 Bellevue Rd (43606-1801)
PHONE..............................419 473-9773
John D Drumheller, *Managing Member*
EMP: 12 EST: 1902
SQ FT: 6,400
SALES (est): 2.08MM **Privately Held**
Web: www.hearnplatingcompany.com
SIC: 3471 3599 Electroplating of metals or
formed products; Amusement park
equipment

(G-12989)
HECKS DIRECT MAIL & PRTG SVC
Also Called: Heck's Diamond Printing
202 W Florence Ave (43605-3304)
P.O. Box 543 (43697-0543)
PHONE..............................419 661-6028
Cosino Trina, *VP*
EMP: 22
SALES (corp-wide): 2.58MM **Privately
Held**
Web: www.hecksprinting.com
SIC: 2752 7331 5192 Offset and
photolithographic printing; Direct mail
advertising services; Books, periodicals,
and newspapers
PA: Hecks Direct Mail And Printing
Service, Inc.
417 Main St
Toledo OH 43605
419 697-3505

(G-12990)
**HECKS DIRECT MAIL PRTG SVC INC
(PA)**
417 Main St (43605-2057)
P.O. Box 543 (43697-0543)
PHONE..............................419 697-3505
Edward Heck, *CEO*
▲ EMP: 18 EST: 1943
SQ FT: 30,000
SALES (est): 2.58MM
SALES (corp-wide): 2.58MM **Privately
Held**

Web: www.hecksprinting.com
SIC: 7331 2752 2791 2789 Addressing
service; Offset printing; Typesetting;
Bookbinding and related work

(G-12991)
HEDGES SELECTIVE TL & PROD INC
Also Called: Select Tool & Production
702 W Laskey Rd (43612-3209)
PHONE..............................419 478-8670
Jeffrey Lachapelle, *Pr*
Jeff Lachatelle, *Pr*
Kathy Lachatelle, *VP*
EMP: 7 EST: 1972
SQ FT: 15,048
SALES (est): 1.75MM **Privately Held**
Web: www.selecttoolanddie.com
SIC: 3544 Special dies and tools

(G-12992)
**HEIDTMAN STEEL PRODUCTS INC
(HQ)**
Also Called: Heidtman Steel
2401 Front St (43605-1199)
PHONE..............................419 691-4646
John C Bates Senior, *Ch*
Tim Berra, *Pr*
Mark Ridenour, *CFO*
Mike Kruse, *VP*
John Bates Junior, *Ex VP*
▲ EMP: 45 EST: 1954
SQ FT: 15,000
SALES (est): 218.59MM
SALES (corp-wide): 230.06MM **Privately
Held**
Web: www.heidtman.com
SIC: 3316 3312 Strip, steel, cold-rolled, nec:
from purchased hot-rolled,; Sheet or strip,
steel, hot-rolled
PA: Centaur, Inc.
2401 Front St
Toledo OH 43605
419 469-8000

(G-12993)
HILL JOHN
Also Called: R J Displays
3019 E Manhattan Blvd (43611-1714)
PHONE..............................419 727-8666
John R Hill, *Owner*
EMP: 15 EST: 1992
SQ FT: 15,000
SALES (est): 461.3K **Privately Held**
Web: www.rjmachining.com
SIC: 3993 Displays and cutouts, window and
lobby

(G-12994)
HOLLAND ENGRAVING COMPANY
Also Called: Holland Engineering Co
7340 Dorr St (43615-4112)
PHONE..............................419 865-2765
Martin Hartkopf, *Pr*
EMP: 9 EST: 1939
SQ FT: 15,600
SALES (est): 2.23MM **Privately Held**
Web: www.holland-eng.com
SIC: 3544 Special dies and tools

(G-12995)
HOOVER & WELLS INC
Also Called: Rez Stone
2011 Seaman St (43605-1908)
PHONE..............................419 691-9220
Margaret Hoover, *Ch Bd*
John Corsini, *
James Mc Collum, *
Barbara Corsini, *
Lisa Pudlicki, *
EMP: 120 EST: 1978
SQ FT: 23,448

▲ = Import ▼ = Export
◆ = Import/Export

SALES (est): 32.54MM **Privately Held**
Web: www.hooverwells.com
SIC: **1752** 2891 2851 Wood floor installation and refinishing; Adhesives and sealants; Paints and allied products

(G-12996)
HORWITZ & PINTIS CO
1604 Tracy St (43605-3426)
P.O. Box 60257 (43460-0257)
PHONE...............419 666-2220
Steve Horwitz, *Pr*
Phyllis Horwitz, *Sec*
EMP: 15 EST: 1904
SQ FT: 20,000
SALES (est): 3.62MM **Privately Held**
SIC: **5085** 3412 2655 Drums, new or reconditioned; Metal barrels, drums, and pails; Fiber cans, drums, and similar products

(G-12997)
HP INDUSTRIES INC
400 E State Line Rd (43614-4779)
PHONE...............419 478-0695
Scott Dubuc, *Pr*
Mark Dubuc, *
EMP: 30 EST: 1922
SQ FT: 11,000
SALES (est): 2.3MM **Privately Held**
Web: www.hotgraphics.us
SIC: **2752** 2791 2789 2759 Offset printing; Typesetting; Bookbinding and related work; Commercial printing, nec

(G-12998)
IBIDLTD-BLUE GREEN ENERGY
1456 N Summit St (43604)
PHONE...............909 547-5160
Garry Inwood, *Brnch Mgr*
EMP: 10
SALES (corp-wide): 118.44K **Privately Held**
Web: www.internationalbrandidltd.com
SIC: **2869** Industrial organic chemicals, nec
PA: Ibidltd-Blue Green Energy
6659 Schaefer Rd Ste 110
Dearborn MI 48126
909 547-5160

(G-12999)
IGNIO SYSTEMS LLC
444 W Laskey Rd Ste V (43612-3460)
PHONE...............419 708-0503
EMP: 6 EST: 2013
SALES (est): 2.04MM **Privately Held**
Web: www.igniosystems.com
SIC: **3821** 3625 3822 5063 Ovens, laboratory; Motor controls, electric; Temperature controls, automatic; Boxes and fittings, electrical

(G-13000)
IMPAC HI-PERFORMANCE MACHINING
5515 Enterprise Blvd (43612-3814)
PHONE...............419 726-7100
Gerald R Nastachowski, *Owner*
Chris Nastachowski, *Mgr*
EMP: 6 EST: 1971
SQ FT: 6,000
SALES (est): 300K **Privately Held**
SIC: **3599** Machine shop, jobbing and repair

(G-13001)
IMPACT PRODUCTS LLC
2840 Centennial Rd (43617-1898)
PHONE...............419 841-2891
Terry Neal, *Pr*
Laura Marcero, *
◆ EMP: 139 EST: 2001

SQ FT: 155,000
SALES (est): 27.49MM
SALES (corp-wide): 523.82MM **Privately Held**
Web: www.impact-products.com
SIC: **5087** 5084 2392 3089 Janitors' supplies ; Safety equipment; Mops, floor and dust; Buckets, plastics
PA: The Tranzonic Companies
26301 Crtiss Wrght Pkwy S
Cleveland OH 44143
216 535-4300

(G-13002)
INDEPENDENT POWER CONS INC
6051 Telegraph Rd Ste 19 (43612-4560)
PHONE...............419 476-8383
David Denner, *Pr*
Michael W Denner, *VP*
Patricia M Denner, *Sec*
EMP: 7 EST: 1982
SALES (est): 802.92K **Privately Held**
Web: www.ipctoledo.com
SIC: **3469** Machine parts, stamped or pressed metal

(G-13003)
INDUSTRIAL SCREEN PRCESS SVC I (PA)
Also Called: Isps
17 17th St (43604-6708)
P.O. Box 593 (43697-0593)
PHONE...............419 255-4900
Thomas V Cutcher Senior, *Pr*
Thomas V Cutcher Ii, *VP*
Sharon Cutcher, *Sec*
EMP: 15 EST: 1979
SQ FT: 53,000
SALES (est): 3.15MM **Privately Held**
Web: www.ispsinc.com
SIC: **2759** 7373 Screen printing; Computer-aided design (CAD) systems service

(G-13004)
INITIAL DESIGNS INC
Also Called: Seaway Enterprises
2453 Tremainsville Rd Unit 2 (43613-3438)
PHONE...............419 475-3900
Robert W Stauffer, *Pr*
Carole S Stauffer, *Sec*
EMP: 6 EST: 1986
SQ FT: 13,000
SALES (est): 153.76K **Privately Held**
Web: www.initial-design.com
SIC: **2395** Embroidery products, except Schiffli machine

(G-13005)
INNOMARK GROUP LLC
1218 Madison Ave (43604-5540)
PHONE...............419 720-8102
Mohamad Awad, *Managing Member*
EMP: 8
SALES (est): 1.43MM **Privately Held**
SIC: **3993** Signs and advertising specialties

(G-13006)
INSTA PLAK INC (PA)
Also Called: Insta-Plak
5025 Dorr St (43615-3855)
PHONE...............419 537-1555
Rexford E Hardin D.d.s., *CEO*
Stephen R Hardin, *Pr*
James Byrd, *VP*
Betty Hardin, *Sec*
EMP: 8 EST: 1985
SQ FT: 7,800
SALES (est): 736.65K
SALES (corp-wide): 736.65K **Privately Held**
Web: www.instaplak.com

SIC: **2499** 3993 Decorative wood and woodwork; Signs, not made in custom sign painting shops

(G-13007)
INTERTEC CORPORATION (PA)
3400 Exec Pkwy (43606)
PHONE...............419 537-9711
George B Seifried, *Pr*
Darrel G Howard, *Sec*
Scott A Slater, *VP Fin*
◆ EMP: 10 EST: 1978
SQ FT: 1,000
SALES (est): 4.24MM
SALES (corp-wide): 4.24MM **Privately Held**
Web: www.intertecsystems.com
SIC: **3559** 1796 3523 Glass making machinery: blowing, molding, forming, etc.; Machinery installation; Farm machinery and equipment

(G-13008)
INVESTORS UNITED INC (PA)
Also Called: Tiger Lebanese Bakery
4215 Monroe St (43606-1975)
PHONE...............419 473-8942
Abdul Hammuda, *Pr*
Abdul Shamamit, *Sec*
EMP: 8 EST: 1973
SQ FT: 4,500
SALES (est): 1.07MM
SALES (corp-wide): 1.07MM **Privately Held**
Web: www.tigerbakery.com
SIC: **5461** 5411 2051 Bread; Delicatessen stores; Bakery, for home service delivery

(G-13009)
IPS TREATMENTS INC
3254 Hill Ave (43607-2911)
PHONE...............419 241-5955
Fred Pinto, *Pr*
Manit Vichitchot, *VP*
EMP: 9 EST: 1994
SQ FT: 16,000
SALES (est): 219.28K **Privately Held**
SIC: **3471** Cleaning, polishing, and finishing

(G-13010)
IRONHEAD FABG & CONTG INC
2245 Front St (43605-1231)
PHONE...............419 690-0000
Anthony Lamantia, *Pr*
Kathy Lamantia, *
EMP: 6 EST: 2002
SQ FT: 33,500
SALES (est): 500.75K **Privately Held**
Web: www.ironheadfab.com
SIC: **3441** Fabricated structural metal

(G-13011)
IRONHEAD MARINE INC
2245 Front St (43605-1231)
PHONE...............419 690-0000
Kathy Lamantia, *CFO*
EMP: 20 EST: 2008
SALES (est): 1.33MM **Privately Held**
Web: www.ironheadmarine.com
SIC: **3731** Shipbuilding and repairing

(G-13012)
J & S INDUSTRIAL MCH PDTS INC
123 Oakdale Ave (43605-3322)
PHONE...............419 691-1380
Nancy Colyer, *Prin*
Donald R Colyer, *
Elton E Bowland, *
John Sehr, *
George Bowland, *
EMP: 21 EST: 1946

SQ FT: 32,000
SALES (est): 2.26MM **Privately Held**
Web: www.jsindustrialmachine.com
SIC: **3559** 7692 Glass making machinery: blowing, molding, forming, etc.; Welding repair

(G-13013)
JUPMODE
2022 Adams St (43604-4432)
PHONE...............419 318-2029
EMP: 22 EST: 2017
SALES (est): 684.47K **Privately Held**
Web: www.jupmode.com
SIC: **2759** Screen printing

(G-13014)
JUSTINS DELIGHT LLC
101 W Park St (43608-1727)
PHONE...............567 234-3575
Danielle Bryant, *Managing Member*
EMP: 6
SALES (est): 212.01K **Privately Held**
SIC: **2599** Food wagons, restaurant

(G-13015)
KAPIOS LLC
Also Called: Kapios Health
2865 N Reynolds Rd Ste 220d (43615-2100)
PHONE...............567 661-0772
Justin Hammerling, *CEO*
EMP: 6 EST: 2017
SALES (est): 480.77K **Privately Held**
Web: www.kapioshealth.com
SIC: **7372** 8099 Business oriented computer software; Health and allied services, nec

(G-13016)
KASPER ENTERPRISES INC
Also Called: Harmon Sign Company
7844 W Central Ave (43617-1530)
PHONE...............419 841-6656
Daniel C Kasper, *Ch Bd*
Jeff Kasper, *Pr*
John E Wagoner, *Prin*
EMP: 7 EST: 1937
SQ FT: 55,430
SALES (est): 1.95MM
SALES (corp-wide): 51.31MM **Privately Held**
Web: www.harmonsign.com
SIC: **3993** Neon signs
PA: Allen Industries, Inc.
6434 Burnt Poplar Rd
Greensboro NC 27409
336 668-2791

(G-13017)
KAY TOLEDO TAG INC
6050 Benore Rd (43612-3906)
P.O. Box 5038 (43611-0038)
PHONE...............419 729-5479
Dan Kay, *Pr*
EMP: 96 EST: 1973
SQ FT: 87,000
SALES (est): 7.58MM
SALES (corp-wide): 420.11MM **Publicly Held**
Web: www.kaytag.com
SIC: **2752** 2679 2759 2671 Offset printing; Tags and labels, paper; Commercial printing, nec; Paper; coated and laminated packaging
PA: Ennis, Inc.
2441 Presidential Pkwy
Midlothian TX 76065
972 775-9801

G
E
O
G
R
A
P
H
I
C

(G-13018)
KEYSTONE PRESS INC
1801 Broadway St (43609-3290)
P.O. Box 9183 (43697-9183)
PHONE...419 243-7326
Paul A Schultz, *CEO*
David P Schultz, *Pr*
Andrew C Schultz, *VP*
Elizabeth Schultz, *Sec*
EMP: 8 **EST:** 1921
SQ FT: 9,000
SALES (est): 418.67K **Privately Held**
Web: www.keystonepresstoledo.com
SIC: 2752 2759 2796 2791 Offset printing;
    Letterpress printing; Platemaking services;
    Typesetting

(G-13019)
KITCHEN DESIGNS PLUS INC
2725 N Reynolds Rd (43615-2031)
PHONE...419 536-6605
Pat Mckimmy, *Pr*
EMP: 6 **EST:** 1962
SQ FT: 6,000
SALES (est): 697.43K **Privately Held**
Web: www.kitchendesignplus.com
SIC: 5031 2434 Kitchen cabinets; Wood
    kitchen cabinets

(G-13020)
KNIGHT INDUSTRIES CORP
5949 Telegraph Rd (43612-4548)
PHONE...419 478-8550
Kevin Ebeid, *VP*
Carrie Ebeid, *
EMP: 10 **EST:** 1986
SQ FT: 104,000
SALES (est): 1.53MM **Privately Held**
Web: www.artist-choice.com
SIC: 3211 Picture glass

(G-13021)
KONECRANES INC
Also Called: Crane Pro Services
2221 Tedrow Rd (43614-3860)
PHONE...419 382-7575
Terri Dietrich, *Mgr*
EMP: 10
Web: www.konecranes.com
SIC: 3536 Hoists, cranes, and monorails
HQ: Konecranes, Inc.
    4401 Gateway Blvd
    Springfield OH 45502

(G-13022)
KUHLMAN CORPORATION
444 Kuhlman Dr (43609-2629)
PHONE...419 321-1670
Dwayne Palmer, *Brnch Mgr*
EMP: 18
SALES (corp-wide): 42.49MM **Privately
Held**
Web: www.gerkencompanies.com
SIC: 3273 Ready-mixed concrete
PA: Kuhlman Corporation
    1845 Indian Wood Cir
    Maumee OH 43537
    419 897-6000

(G-13023)
KUHLMAN ENGINEERING CO
840 Champlain St (43604-3643)
PHONE...419 243-2196
Phil Kolling, *Pr*
Norman Kuhlman, *VP*
EMP: 10 **EST:** 1916
SQ FT: 7,500
SALES (est): 868.05K **Privately Held**
SIC: 3444 Sheet metal specialties, not
    stamped

(G-13024)
**KUKA TLEDO PRDCTION OPRTONS
LL**
3770 Stickney Ave (43608-1310)
PHONE...419 727-5500
Lawrence A Drake, *CEO*
Paul Ambros, *
Larry Drake, *
Jake Ladouceur, *
EMP: 247 **EST:** 2004
SALES (est): 7.78MM **Privately Held**
Web: www.kuka.com
SIC: 3713 Truck and bus bodies
HQ: Kuka Systems Gmbh
    BlucherstraBe 144
    Augsburg BY 86165
    8217970

(G-13025)
KYLE MEDIA INC
Also Called: Great Lakes Scuttlebutt
7862 W Central Ave Ste F (43617-1549)
P.O. Box 351417 (43635-1417)
PHONE...877 775-2538
Erik Kyle, *Pr*
Erik R Kyle, *CEO*
EMP: 15 **EST:** 1992
SALES (est): 550.16K **Privately Held**
Web: www.greatlakesscuttlebutt.com
SIC: 8999 2721 7311 7313 Writing for
    publication; Periodicals, publishing and
    printing; Advertising consultant; Magazine
    advertising representative

(G-13026)
LA PERLA INC (PA)
Also Called: Tortilla Factory
2742 Hill Ave (43607-2926)
PHONE...419 534-2074
TOLL FREE: 800
Santiago Martinez, *Pr*
EMP: 8 **EST:** 1963
SQ FT: 8,000
SALES (est): 871.18K
SALES (corp-wide): 871.18K **Privately
Held**
Web: www.laperla.com
SIC: 2099 5141 Tortillas, fresh or refrigerated
    ; Groceries, general line

(G-13027)
LA PRENSA PUBLICATIONS INC
Also Called: Aztlan Communications
616 Adams St (43604-1420)
PHONE...419 870-6565
Becky Mc Queen, *Prin*
EMP: 6 **EST:** 1989
SALES (est): 456.72K **Privately Held**
Web: www.laprensatoledo.com
SIC: 2711 Newspapers: publishing only, not
    printed on site

(G-13028)
LBA CUSTOM PRINTING
207 Arco Dr (43607-2906)
P.O. Box 352679 (43635-2679)
PHONE...419 535-3151
Brett Bullock, *Prin*
EMP: 6 **EST:** 2008
SALES (est): 120.4K **Privately Held**
Web: www.metzgers.com
SIC: 2752 Offset printing

(G-13029)
LED LIGHTING CENTER INC (PA)
Also Called: Optimal Led
5500 Enterprise Blvd (43612-3815)
PHONE...714 271-2633
Steven James, *CEO*
▲ **EMP:** 9 **EST:** 2013
SALES (est): 1.41MM

SALES (corp-wide): 1.41MM **Privately
Held**
Web: www.optimalled.com
SIC: 3646 3645 Commercial lighting fixtures;
    Residential lighting fixtures

(G-13030)
LED LIGHTING CENTER LLC
Also Called: Optimalled
5500 Enterprise Blvd (43612-3815)
PHONE...888 988-6533
EMP: 11 **EST:** 2015
SALES (est): 786.25K
SALES (corp-wide): 2.09MM **Privately
Held**
SIC: 3646 3645 Commercial lighting fixtures;
    Residential lighting fixtures
PA: Led Lighting Center Inc.
    5500 Enterprise Blvd
    Toledo OH 43612
    714 271-2633

(G-13031)
LEE WILLIAMS MEATS INC (PA)
3002 131st St (43611-2329)
PHONE...419 729-3893
Barry L Williams, *Pr*
Richard W Boldt, *
Mary Jo Cramer, *
Margaret Williams, *
EMP: 25 **EST:** 1955
SQ FT: 3,096
SALES (est): 2.43MM
SALES (corp-wide): 2.43MM **Privately
Held**
Web: www.houseofmeats.com
SIC: 5421 2013 Meat markets, including
    freezer provisioners; Sausages and other
    prepared meats

(G-13032)
LEMSCO INC
Also Called: Lemsco-Girkins
2056 Canton Ave (43620-1945)
PHONE...419 242-4005
Richard J Baldwin, *Pr*
Richard Baldwin, *Pr*
Barbara Baldwin, *Sec*
EMP: 8 **EST:** 1947
SQ FT: 11,000
SALES (est): 544.41K **Privately Held**
Web: www.lemsco.com
SIC: 7694 5999 Electric motor repair;
    Motors, electric

(G-13033)
LIBBEY GLASS LLC (HQ)
Also Called: Libbey
300 Madison Ave (43604-2634)
P.O. Box 919 (43699)
PHONE...419 325-2100
Michael P Bauer, *CEO*
Richard Reynolds, *
Ken Boerger, *
Daniel P Ibele, *
Susan A Kovach, *
◆ **EMP:** 200 **EST:** 1987
SALES (est): 482.56MM **Privately Held**
Web: www.libbey.com
SIC: 3229 3231 Tableware, glass or glass
    ceramic; Products of purchased glass
PA: Libbey Inc.
    300 Madison Ave
    Toledo OH 43604

(G-13034)
LIBBEY GLASS LLC
Also Called: Libbey America
940 Ash St (43611-3846)
PHONE...419 727-2211
Steve Felix, *Brnch Mgr*

EMP: 100
Web: www.libbey.com
SIC: 3229 3421 3262 Tableware, glass or
    glass ceramic; Cutlery; Vitreous china table
    and kitchenware
HQ: Libbey Glass Llc
    300 Madison Ave
    Toledo OH 43604
    419 325-2100

(G-13035)
LIBBEY INC (PA)
Also Called: Libbey
300 Madison Ave (43604-2634)
P.O. Box 919 (43699-0919)
PHONE...419 325-2100
Michael P Bauer, *CEO*
William A Foley, *Non-Executive Chairman
    of the Board*
Juan Amezquita, *
James C Burmeister, *
Jennifer Molnar, *Chief Human Resources
    Officer*
▼ **EMP:** 200 **EST:** 1818
SALES (est): 785.6MM **Privately Held**
Web: www.libbey.com
SIC: 3229 3262 Glass furnishings and
    accessories; Tableware, vitreous china

(G-13036)
LILY ANN CABINETS
2939 Douglas Rd (43606-3502)
PHONE...419 360-2455
Chuck Bennett, *Pr*
EMP: 10 **EST:** 2018
SALES (est): 582.73K **Privately Held**
Web: www.lilyanncabinets.com
SIC: 2434 Wood kitchen cabinets

(G-13037)
LINDE GAS & EQUIPMENT INC
Also Called: Praxair
6055 Brent Dr (43611-1084)
PHONE...419 729-7732
EMP: 22
Web: www.lindeus.com
SIC: 2813 Industrial gases
HQ: Linde Gas & Equipment Inc.
    10 Riverview Dr
    Danbury CT 06810
    844 445-4633

(G-13038)
LITHIUM INNOVATIONS CO LLC
3171 N Republic Blvd Ste 101
(43615-1515)
PHONE...419 725-3525
Ford B Cauffiel, *Managing Member*
◆ **EMP:** 6 **EST:** 2010
SALES (est): 223.95K **Privately Held**
Web: www.liinnovations.com
SIC: 2819 Lithium compounds, inorganic

(G-13039)
LOVE LAUGH & LAUNDRY
Also Called: Love. Laugh. Laundry.
5333 Secor Rd (43623-2407)
PHONE...567 377-1951
Brandi Hopson, *CEO*
EMP: 6 **EST:** 2018
SALES (est): 180.32K **Privately Held**
SIC: 5999 5641 2331 5169 Miscellaneous
    retail stores, nec; Children's wear;
    Women's and misses' blouses and shirts;
    Detergents and soaps, except specialty
    cleaning

(G-13040)
LRBG CHEMICALS USA INC
2112 Sylvan Ave (43606-4767)
P.O. Box 2570 (43606-0570)

▲ = Import ▼ = Export
◆ = Import/Export

PHONE..............................419 244-5856
James Bennett, *Managing Member*
James Bennett, *VP*
EMP: 30 **EST:** 2018
SQ FT: 70,000
SALES (est): 6.07MM **Privately Held**
Web: www.lrbgchemicals.com
SIC: 2821 Plastics materials and resins

(G-13041)
LUBRIPLATE LUBRICANTS COMPANY
1500 Oakdale Ave (43605-3843)
PHONE..............................419 691-2491
EMP: 7 **EST:** 2017
SALES (est): 928.38K **Privately Held**
Web: www.lubriplate.com
SIC: 5172 2992 Lubricating oils and greases ; Lubricating oils and greases

(G-13042)
LWHS LTD
Also Called: Bata Plastics
2145 Tedrow Rd (43614-3827)
PHONE..............................419 407-5454
EMP: 13
Web: www.bataplastics.com
SIC: 3083 Laminated plastics plate and sheet
PA: Lwhs, Ltd.
1001 40th St Se
Grand Rapids MI 49508

(G-13043)
M&D MACHINE LLC
Also Called: Machine Shop
42 W Sylvania Ave (43612-1445)
PHONE..............................419 214-0201
EMP: 6 **EST:** 2013
SALES (est): 2.29MM **Privately Held**
Web: www.mdmachineusa.com
SIC: 3599 Machine shop, jobbing and repair

(G-13044)
MAGIC WOK INC (PA)
Also Called: Magic Wok Enterprises
3352 W Laskey Rd (43623-4030)
PHONE..............................419 531-1818
Sutas Pipatjarasgit, *Pr*
Nucharee Pipatjarasgit, *Sec*
EMP: 7 **EST:** 1983
SQ FT: 580
SALES (est): 1.03MM
SALES (corp-wide): 1.03MM **Privately Held**
Web: www.magicwok.com
SIC: 5812 2032 Chinese restaurant; Ethnic foods, canned, jarred, etc.

(G-13045)
MAGNA MODULAR SYSTEMS LLC (DH)
Also Called: T.E.A.M. Systems
1800 Jason St (43611)
PHONE..............................419 324-3387
Grahhame Burrow, *CEO*
Keith Mcmahon, *Genl Mgr*
Michael Hanson, *
▲ **EMP:** 70 **EST:** 2005
SQ FT: 140,000
SALES (est): 47.22MM
SALES (corp-wide): 42.84B **Privately Held**
Web: www.magna.com
SIC: 3714 Motor vehicle body components and frame
HQ: Magna Exteriors Of America, Inc.
750 Tower Dr
Troy MI 48098
248 631-1100

(G-13046)
MALLORY PATTERN WORKS INC
5340 Enterprise Blvd (43612-3811)
PHONE..............................419 726-8001
Al Antoine, *Pr*
Janice Mallory, *Treas*
Shirley Peschel, *Sec*
EMP: 6 **EST:** 1960
SQ FT: 6,000
SALES (est): 726.63K **Privately Held**
Web: www.mallorypatternworks.com
SIC: 3544 3469 Industrial molds; Patterns on metal

(G-13047)
MAUMEE BAY BREWING COMPANY
27 Broadway St Ste A (43604-8701)
PHONE..............................419 243-1253
Patricia Appold, *Pr*
EMP: 50 **EST:** 1993
SQ FT: 5,000
SALES (est): 2.39MM **Privately Held**
Web: www.mbaybrew.com
SIC: 5812 2082 Chicken restaurant; Beer (alcoholic beverage)

(G-13048)
MAUMEE MACHINE & TOOL CORP
2960 South Ave (43609-1328)
PHONE..............................419 385-2501
Bruce M Denman, *Pr*
Bruce M Denman, *VP*
Patrick T Denman, *VP*
John S Buescher, *General Vice President*
EMP: 20 **EST:** 1966
SALES (est): 926K **Privately Held**
SIC: 3451 5072 Screw machine products; Screws

(G-13049)
MAUMEE PATTERN COMPANY
1019 Hazelwood St (43605-3248)
PHONE..............................419 693-4968
H Jeffrey Neuman, *Pr*
Mark Neuman, *
Alice Neuman, *
EMP: 29 **EST:** 1915
SQ FT: 13,000
SALES (est): 2.37MM **Privately Held**
Web: www.maumeepattern.com
SIC: 3543 3544 Industrial patterns; Industrial molds

(G-13050)
MAUMEE VALLEY FABRICATORS INC
Also Called: Escher Division
4801 Bennett Rd (43612-2531)
PHONE..............................419 476-1411
Patrick Copeland, *Pr*
EMP: 25 **EST:** 1978
SQ FT: 54,000
SALES (est): 5.19MM **Privately Held**
Web: www.maumeevalleyfab.com
SIC: 3441 Fabricated structural metal

(G-13051)
MELDRUM MECHANICAL SERVICES
4455 South Ave (43615-6416)
PHONE..............................419 535-3500
Brent R Meldrum Junior, *Pr*
EMP: 10 **EST:** 2001
SALES (est): 2.94MM **Privately Held**
Web: www.meldrum-mechanical.com
SIC: 3599 Machine shop, jobbing and repair

(G-13052)
MELNOR GRAPHICS LLC
5225 Telegraph Rd (43612-3570)
PHONE..............................419 476-8808
EMP: 27 **EST:** 2016

SALES (est): 1.46MM **Privately Held**
SIC: 2759 Circulars: printing, nsk

(G-13053)
METZGERS
150 Arco Dr (43607-2903)
PHONE..............................419 861-8611
John Luscombe, *VP*
Todd Beringer, *S&M/VP*
Andrea Ohrt, *CFO*
Tom Metzger, *CEO*
EMP: 62 **EST:** 2014
SALES (est): 2.98MM **Privately Held**
Web: www.metzgers.com
SIC: 2752 Offset printing

(G-13054)
MIDTOWN PALLET & RECYCLING INC
1987 Hawthorne St (43606)
P.O. Box 95 (43542-0095)
PHONE..............................419 241-1311
Rita Stang, *Pr*
EMP: 8 **EST:** 1993
SQ FT: 10,000
SALES (est): 1.06MM **Privately Held**
Web: www.midtownpallet.com
SIC: 2448 Pallets, wood

(G-13055)
MIDWEST DIE SUPPLY COMPANY
6240 American Rd Ste A (43612-3925)
PHONE..............................419 729-7141
David Brezinski, *Pr*
EMP: 9 **EST:** 1948
SQ FT: 5,000
SALES (est): 459.04K **Privately Held**
Web: www.midwestdie.com
SIC: 3599 Machine shop, jobbing and repair

(G-13056)
MJB TOLEDO INC (HQ)
Also Called: National Super Service Co
3115 Frenchmens Rd (43607-2918)
PHONE..............................419 531-2121
Mark Bevington, *Pr*
◆ **EMP:** 100 **EST:** 1911
SQ FT: 160,000
SALES (est): 22.09MM
SALES (corp-wide): 32.02MM **Privately Held**
Web: www.nss.com
SIC: 3589 Floor washing and polishing machines, commercial
PA: Diversey Taski, Inc.
3115 Frenchmens Rd
Toledo OH 43607
419 531-2121

(G-13057)
MMP TOLEDO
5847 Secor Rd (43623-1421)
PHONE..............................419 472-0505
Steven Heaney, *Pr*
Teresa Heaney, *Prin*
EMP: 6 **EST:** 1980
SQ FT: 1,500
SALES (est): 146.51K **Privately Held**
Web: www.mmptoledo.com
SIC: 2752 Offset printing

(G-13058)
MODERN BUILDERS SUPPLY INC (PA)
Also Called: Polaris Technologies
3500 Phillips Ave (43608-1070)
P.O. Box 80025 (43608-0025)
PHONE..............................419 241-3961
Kevin Leggett, *CEO*
Larry Leggett, *

G Taylor Evans Iii, *Treas*
Eric Leggett, *
Jack Marstellar, *
EMP: 200 **EST:** 1944
SQ FT: 40,000
SALES (est): 346.23MM
SALES (corp-wide): 346.23MM **Privately Held**
Web: www.modernbuilderssupply.com
SIC: 3089 5032 3446 3442 Windows, plastics ; Brick, stone, and related material; Architectural metalwork; Metal doors, sash, and trim

(G-13059)
MON-SAY CORP
Also Called: Ergocan
2735 Dorr St (43607-3240)
P.O. Box 8487 (43623-0487)
PHONE..............................419 720-0163
Terry Netterfield, *Pr*
▲ **EMP:** 7 **EST:** 1987
SQ FT: 22,000
SALES (est): 1.67MM **Privately Held**
Web: www.ergocan.com
SIC: 3089 Bowl covers, plastics

(G-13060)
MOSSING MACHINE AND TOOL INC
5225 Telegraph Rd (43612-3570)
PHONE..............................419 476-5657
Dave S Mossing, *Pr*
EMP: 8 **EST:** 1981
SQ FT: 8,000
SALES (est): 698.86K **Privately Held**
Web: www.hvacwichitaks.com
SIC: 3599 Machine shop, jobbing and repair

(G-13061)
N-VIRO INTERNATIONAL CORP
Also Called: N-Viro
2254 Centennial Rd (43617-1870)
P.O. Box 8770 (43623-0770)
PHONE..............................419 535-6374
Timothy R Kasmoch, *Ch Bd*
Robert W Bohmer, *Ex VP*
James K Mchugh, *CFO*
EMP: 10 **EST:** 1979
SALES (est): 1.28MM **Privately Held**
Web: www.nviro.com
SIC: 3589 4959 Water treatment equipment, industrial; Sanitary services, nec

(G-13062)
NEW DIE INC
2828 E Manhattan Blvd (43611-1710)
PHONE..............................419 726-7581
Richard A Pack, *Pr*
Terry Cousino, *VP*
Donald R Cousino, *VP*
Ken Coss, *VP*
James David, *VP*
EMP: 22 **EST:** 1996
SQ FT: 7,500
SALES (est): 2.61MM **Privately Held**
SIC: 3544 Special dies and tools

(G-13063)
NORTH TOLEDO GRAPHICS LLC
Also Called: Nt
5225 Telegraph Rd (43612-3570)
PHONE..............................419 476-8808
Shirleen Kistner, *Managing Member*
Melanie Tremonti, *
EMP: 95 **EST:** 2004
SQ FT: 210,000
SALES (est): 2.14MM **Privately Held**
Web: www.northtoledographics.com
SIC: 2752 Offset printing

(G-13064)
NORTHCOAST PMM LLC
Also Called: Blink Print & Mail
4725 Southbridge Rd (43623-3123)
PHONE...................................419 540-8667
Thomas J Pruss, *Managing Member*
EMP: 10 EST: 2017
SALES (est): 174.08K **Privately Held**
SIC: 7331 2752 Mailing service; Commercial
printing, lithographic

(G-13065)
NSG GLASS NORTH AMERICA INC
(PA)
811 Madison Ave (43604-5684)
PHONE...................................419 247-4800
Richard A Altman, *Pr*
Gary J Roser, *Sec*
EMP: 32 EST: 2018
SQ FT: 4,000
SALES (est): 4.43MM
SALES (corp-wide): 4.43MM **Privately
Held**
SIC: 3211 Flat glass

(G-13066)
NTA GRAPHICS INC
5225 Telegraph Rd (43612-3547)
PHONE...................................419 476-8808
Gregory Tremonti, *Pr*
David Tremonti, *
Gail Shaffer, *
EMP: 6 EST: 1984
SQ FT: 163,000
SALES (est): 217.2K **Privately Held**
Web: www.ntagraphics.com
SIC: 2752 Offset printing

(G-13067)
OASIS MDITERRANEAN CUISINE INC
1520 W Laskey Rd (43612-2914)
P.O. Box 8881 (43623)
PHONE...................................419 269-1459
Francois Hashem, *Pr*
▲ EMP: 32 EST: 1985
SQ FT: 30,000
SALES (est): 4MM **Privately Held**
Web: www.omcfood.com
SIC: 2099 2032 Dips, except cheese and
sour cream based; Canned specialties

(G-13068)
OBARS MACHINE AND TOOL
COMPANY (PA)
Also Called: Obars Welding & Fabg Div
115 N Westwood Ave # 125 (43607-3341)
PHONE...................................419 535-6307
Greg Obarski, *Pr*
Alvin R Obarski, *
Jeffrey R Obarski, *
Michael Webber, *
EMP: 41 EST: 1946
SQ FT: 30,000
SALES (est): 3.99MM
SALES (corp-wide): 3.99MM **Privately
Held**
Web: www.obarsmachine.com
SIC: 3451 3541 3545 Screw machine
products; Machine tools, metal cutting type;
Machine tool accessories

(G-13069)
OCCV1 INC
1 Owens Corning Prkwy (43659-1000)
PHONE...................................419 248-8000
EMP: 9 EST: 2017
SALES (est): 1MM **Publicly Held**
SIC: 3272 Concrete products, nec
PA: Owens Corning
1 Owens Corning Pkwy

Toledo OH 43659

(G-13070)
OCCV2 LLC
1 Owens Corning Prkwy (43659-1000)
PHONE...................................419 248-8000
EMP: 6 EST: 2017
SALES (est): 868.42K **Publicly Held**
SIC: 3299 Nonmetallic mineral products,
PA: Owens Corning
1 Owens Corning Pkwy
Toledo OH 43659

(G-13071)
OFF CONTACT INC
Also Called: Off Contact Productions
4756 W Bancroft St (43615-3902)
PHONE...................................419 255-5546
Allen Schall, *Pr*
▲ EMP: 10 EST: 1988
SQ FT: 9,600
SALES (est): 675.65K **Privately Held**
Web: www.offcontact.com
SIC: 2759 5084 Screen printing; Industrial
machinery and equipment

(G-13072)
OHIO BLENDERS INC (PA)
Also Called: Alfagreen Supreme
2404 N Summit St (43611-3599)
PHONE...................................419 726-2655
Ken Vaupel, *CEO*
Donald Verhoff, *Pr*
Ronald Yarnell, *VP*
Becky Lumbrezer-box, *Sec*
EMP: 10 EST: 1960
SQ FT: 6,000
SALES (est): 7.85MM
SALES (corp-wide): 7.85MM **Privately
Held**
Web: ohioblenders.tripod.com
SIC: 2048 2047 Prepared feeds, nec; Dog
and cat food

(G-13073)
OHIO BUILDING RESTORATION INC
(PA)
830 Mill St (43609-2448)
PHONE...................................419 244-7372
Duane Haas, *Pr*
Duane W Haas, *Pr*
John Hall, *VP*
Debra Haas, *Sec*
EMP: 22 EST: 1949
SQ FT: 6,500
SALES (est): 2.42MM
SALES (corp-wide): 2.42MM **Privately
Held**
Web: www.ohiobr.com
SIC: 1741 1721 1799 1389 Tuckpointing or
restoration; Exterior commercial painting
contractor; Waterproofing; Construction,
repair, and dismantling services

(G-13074)
OHIO MODULE MANUFACTURING
COMPANY LLC
Also Called: M N A
3900 Stickney Ave (43608-1314)
PHONE...................................419 729-6700
◆ EMP: 706
SIC: 3711 Chassis, motor vehicle

(G-13075)
OHIO STEEL PROCESSING LLC
Also Called: Ohio Pickling & Processing
1149 Campbell St (43607-4467)
PHONE...................................419 241-9601
Sergei Kuznetsov, *Managing Member*
EMP: 90 EST: 2020

SALES (est): 2.38MM **Privately Held**
Web: www.ohiopickling.com
SIC: 3312 Blast furnaces and steel mills

(G-13076)
OHIO TRANSITIONAL MCH & TL INC
3940 Castener St (43612-1402)
PHONE...................................419 476-0820
Marten Whalen, *Pr*
EMP: 7 EST: 1984
SQ FT: 5,000
SALES (est): 904.6K **Privately Held**
Web: ohiotransitional.wixsite.com
SIC: 3599 Machine shop, jobbing and repair

(G-13077)
ONESOURCE WATER LLC
Also Called: Pure Water Technology NW Ohio
812 Warehouse Rd Ste F (43615-6476)
PHONE...................................866 917-7873
Jim Kasch, *Brnch Mgr*
EMP: 15
SALES (corp-wide): 1.77MM **Privately
Held**
SIC: 3589 Swimming pool filter and water
conditioning systems
PA: Onesource Water, Llc
3175 Bass Pro Dr
Grapevine TX 76051
866 917-7873

(G-13078)
ONLINE MEGA SELLERS CORP (PA)
Also Called: Distinct Advantage Cabinetry
4236 W Alexis Rd (43623-1255)
PHONE...................................888 384-6468
Timothy Baker, *Pr*
Craig Poupard, *VP*
EMP: 8 EST: 2013
SQ FT: 250,000
SALES (est): 1.06MM
SALES (corp-wide): 1.06MM **Privately
Held**
Web:
www.kitchenandbathroomcabinets.com
SIC: 2434 7371 7373 Wood kitchen cabinets
; Computer software systems analysis and
design, custom; Systems software
development services

(G-13079)
OPC INC
419 N Reynolds Rd (43615-5221)
PHONE...................................419 531-2222
Anne M Cole, *Prin*
EMP: 8 EST: 1992
SALES (est): 331.37K **Privately Held**
SIC: 3842 Braces, orthopedic

(G-13080)
OPP DISSOLUTION LLC
Also Called: Opp
1149 Campbell St (43607-4467)
PHONE...................................419 241-9601
Sergei Kuznetsov, *Managing Member*
Mike Balk, *
▲ EMP: 70 EST: 1999
SALES (est): 14.91MM
SALES (corp-wide): 221.96MM **Privately
Held**
Web: www.ohiopickling.com
SIC: 3312 Blast furnaces and steel mills
PA: Mnp Corporation
44225 Utica Rd
Utica MI 48317
586 254-1320

(G-13081)
OSTEONOVUS INC
1510 N Westwood Ave Ste 1080
(43606-8202)

PHONE...................................419 530-5940
Anand Agarwal, *Pr*
EMP: 10 EST: 2013
SALES (est): 2.1MM **Privately Held**
Web: www.osteonovus.com
SIC: 3842 Grafts, artificial: for surgery

(G-13082)
OSTEONOVUS INC
1510 N Westwood Ave # 2040
(43606-8202)
PHONE...................................419 530-5940
EMP: 7
SALES (est): 283.16K **Privately Held**
Web: www.osteonovus.com
SIC: 3842 Grafts, artificial: for surgery

(G-13083)
OVERHEAD INC
Also Called: Overhead Door Company
340 New Towne Square Dr (43612-4606)
PHONE...................................419 476-0300
Michael Huss, *Mgr*
EMP: 7
SQ FT: 11,470
SALES (corp-wide): 10.68MM **Privately
Held**
Web: www.overheadinc.com
SIC: 3442 5719 5211 Metal doors, sash, and
trim; Fireplace equipment and accessories;
Garage doors, sale and installation
PA: Overhead Inc.
340 New Towne Square Dr
Toledo OH 43612
419 476-7811

(G-13084)
OWENS CORNING (PA)
Also Called: Owens Corning Pink
1 Owens Corning Pkwy (43659-0001)
PHONE...................................419 248-8000
Brian D Chambers, *Ch Bd*
Todd W Fister, *Ex VP*
Paula Russell, *Chief Human Resources
Officer*
Jose L Mendez-andino, *Research &
Development*
Gina A Beredo, *Corporate Secretary*
◆ EMP: 1000 EST: 1938
SQ FT: 400,000
SALES (est): 10.97B **Publicly Held**
Web: www.owenscorning.com
SIC: 3292 2519 Asbestos products;
Fiberglass and plastic furniture

(G-13085)
OWENS CORNING CORP SVCS LLC
1 Owens Corning Pkwy (43659-0001)
PHONE...................................419 248-8000
Brian Chamber, *CEO*
EMP: 17 EST: 2019
SALES (est): 25.51MM **Publicly Held**
Web: www.owenscorning.com
SIC: 3292 Asbestos products
PA: Owens Corning
1 Owens Corning Pkwy
Toledo OH 43659

(G-13086)
OWENS CORNING HT INC
Owens Corning World Headquar
(43659-0001)
PHONE...................................419 248-8000
EMP: 7 EST: 2016
SALES (est): 1.25MM **Publicly Held**
Web: careers.owenscorning.com
SIC: 3229 Glass fibers, textile
HQ: Owens Corning Sales, Llc
1 Owens Corning Pkwy
Toledo OH 43659
419 248-8000

(G-13087)
OWENS CORNING ROOFG & ASP LLC (HQ)
Also Called: Trumbull Asphalt
1 Owens Corning Pkwy (43659-1000)
PHONE...................................877 858-3855
EMP: 30 EST: 2019
SALES (est): 52.57MM **Publicly Held**
SIC: 3296 Fiberglass insulation
PA: Owens Corning
1 Owens Corning Pkwy
Toledo OH 43659

(G-13088)
OWENS CORNING SALES LLC (HQ)
1 Owens Corning Pkwy (43659-0001)
P.O. Box 13950 (27709-3950)
PHONE...................................419 248-8000
Brian Chambers, *Pr*
Stephen K Krull, *VP*
David L Johns, *VP*
◆ EMP: 1000 EST: 2006
SQ FT: 400,000
SALES (est): 1.9B **Publicly Held**
SIC: 3296 2952 3229 3089 Fiberglass
insulation; Asphalt felts and coatings; Glass
fibers, textile; Windows, plastics
PA: Owens Corning
1 Owens Corning Pkwy
Toledo OH 43659

(G-13089)
OWENS CRNING TCHNCAL FBRICS LL
1 Owens Corning Pkwy (43659-1000)
PHONE...................................419 248-5535
EMP: 7 EST: 2012
SALES (est): 2.03MM **Publicly Held**
SIC: 3292 Asbestos products
PA: Owens Corning
1 Owens Corning Pkwy
Toledo OH 43659

(G-13090)
P & J INDUSTRIES INC (PA)
4934 Lewis Ave (43612-2825)
P.O. Box 6918 (43612-0918)
PHONE...................................419 726-2675
James E Powers Junior, *Pr*
Marguerite M Powers, *
▼ EMP: 120 EST: 1980
SALES (est): 1.62MM
SALES (corp-wide): 1.62MM **Privately Held**
Web: www.pjind.com
SIC: 3471 Electroplating of metals or formed
products

(G-13091)
PB FBRCTION MECH CONTRS CORP
750 W Laskey Rd (43612-3209)
PHONE...................................419 478-4869
Charles W Bailey, *Pr*
Hubert Backes, *VP*
EMP: 11 EST: 1986
SQ FT: 6,000
SALES (est): 3.56MM **Privately Held**
Web: www.pbfabrication.com
SIC: 3535 3444 3443 3441 Conveyors and
conveying equipment; Sheet metalwork;
Fabricated plate work (boiler shop);
Fabricated structural metal

(G-13092)
PEAK ELECTRIC INC
Also Called: Peak Electric
320 N Byrne Rd (43607-2607)
PHONE...................................419 726-4848
Milton Mcintyre, *Pr*
Lenora Mcintyre, *VP*

Rhys Petee, *Prin*
EMP: 10 EST: 2000
SALES (est): 855.14K **Privately Held**
Web: www.peakelectrictoledo.com
SIC: 3612 5063 Transformers, except electric
; Electrical apparatus and equipment

(G-13093)
PEPSI-COLA METRO BTLG CO INC
Also Called: Pepsico
3245 Hill Ave (43607-2936)
PHONE...................................419 534-2186
Michael Hill, *Brnch Mgr*
EMP: 75
SALES (corp-wide): 91.47B **Publicly Held**
Web: www.pepsico.com
SIC: 2086 Carbonated soft drinks, bottled
and canned
HQ: Pepsi-Cola Metropolitan Bottling
Company, Inc.
700 Anderson Hill Rd
Purchase NY 10577
914 767-6000

(G-13094)
PERFORMANCE PACKAGING INC
5219 Telegraph Rd (43612-3570)
PHONE...................................419 478-8805
Frank Duval, *Pr*
Scott Ruetz, *VP*
▲ EMP: 10 EST: 2006
SALES (est): 921.6K **Privately Held**
Web: www.perfpack.com
SIC: 7389 7319 4225 2759 Labeling bottles,
cans, cartons, etc.; Display advertising
service; General warehousing and storage;
Labels and seals: printing, nsk

(G-13095)
PERSTORP POLYOLS INC
600 Matzinger Rd (43612-2695)
PHONE...................................419 729-5448
David Wolf, *Pr*
Larry Fioritto, *
◆ EMP: 109 EST: 1983
SQ FT: 3,000
SALES (est): 62.85MM **Privately Held**
Web: www.perstorp.com
SIC: 2819 2851 2821 Elements; Paints and
allied products; Plastics materials and resins
HQ: Perstorp Ab
Perstorp Industripark
Perstorp 284 8
43538000

(G-13096)
PEXCO PACKAGING CORP
795 Berdan Ave (43610-1065)
P.O. Box 118 (43537-0118)
PHONE...................................419 470-5935
Bill Buri, *Pr*
Dennis Taylor, *
Thomas Jesionowski, *
EMP: 35 EST: 1950
SQ FT: 64,000
SALES (est): 3.68MM **Privately Held**
Web: www.pexcopkg.com
SIC: 2673 3082 3081 2759 Plastic bags:
made from purchased materials;
Unsupported plastics profile shapes;
Unsupported plastics film and sheet;
Commercial printing, nec

(G-13097)
PILKINGTON HOLDINGS INC (DH)
Also Called: P H I
811 Madison Ave Fl 1 (43604-5688)
P.O. Box 799 (43697-0799)
◆ EMP: 300 EST: 1982
SQ FT: 217,000
SALES (est): 1.32B **Privately Held**

Web: www.pilkington.com
SIC: 3211 Flat glass
HQ: Pilkington Group Limited
Group Taxation Department European
Technical Centre
Ormskirk LANCS L40 5
169550000

(G-13098)
PILKINGTON NORTH AMERICA INC (DH)
811 Madison Ave Fl 3 (43604-5688)
P.O. Box 799 (43697-0799)
PHONE...................................419 247-3731
Richard Altman, *Pr*
◆ EMP: 99 EST: 1986
SALES (est): 1.32B **Privately Held**
Web: www.pilkington.com
SIC: 3211 Construction glass
HQ: Pilkington Holdings Inc.
811 Madison Ave Fl 1
Toledo OH 43604

(G-13099)
PISTON AUTOMOTIVE LLC
Also Called: Piston Group
1212 E Alexis Rd (43612-3974)
PHONE...................................419 464-0250
EMP: 1005
SALES (corp-wide): 2.3B **Privately Held**
Web: www.pistonautomotive.com
SIC: 3714 Motor vehicle parts and
accessories
HQ: Piston Automotive, L.L.C.
12723 Telegraph Rd
Redford MI 48239
313 541-8674

(G-13100)
PITTSBURGH CORNING LLC (HQ)
Also Called: Pittsbrgh Crning Corp Asb Per
1 Owens Corning Pkwy (43659-1000)
P.O. Box 1032 (19899-1032)
PHONE...................................724 327-6100
James R Kane, *Pr*
◆ EMP: 490 EST: 1937
SALES (est): 5.76MM **Publicly Held**
Web: www.owenscorning.com
SIC: 3229 Pressed and blown glass, nec
PA: Owens Corning
1 Owens Corning Pkwy
Toledo OH 43659

(G-13101)
PLABELL RUBBER PRODUCTS CORP (PA)
300 S Saint Clair St # 324 (43604-8846)
PHONE...................................419 691-5878
John Jaksetic, *Pr*
Jim Farkas, *VP*
Randy Reif, *Sec*
EMP: 22 EST: 1993
SQ FT: 40,000
SALES (est): 977.77K **Privately Held**
SIC: 3069 3061 Molded rubber products;
Mechanical rubber goods

(G-13102)
POWERBUFF INC
1001 Brown Ave (43607-3942)
PHONE...................................419 241-2156
Walter C Anderson, *Pr*
EMP: 11 EST: 1994
SQ FT: 50,000
SALES (est): 508.98K **Privately Held**
SIC: 3589 Floor washing and polishing
machines, commercial

(G-13103)
PRINT ALL INC
Also Called: A I M Specialists
380 S Erie St (43604-4634)
PHONE...................................419 534-2880
Ann M Fago, *Pr*
Irene Fago, *VP*
EMP: 6 EST: 1989
SQ FT: 7,500
SALES (est): 175.74K **Privately Held**
Web: www.aimspecialists.com
SIC: 2752 7331 Offset printing; Mailing
service

(G-13104)
PROJECTS DESIGNED & BUILT
Also Called: PD&b
5949 American Rd E (43612-3950)
PHONE...................................419 726-7400
Ken Martin, *Pr*
▼ EMP: 21 EST: 1998
SQ FT: 16,000
SALES (est): 4.96MM **Privately Held**
Web: www.pdbinc.com
SIC: 8742 3599 8711 3499 Automation and
robotics consultant; Custom machinery;
Mechanical engineering; Machine bases,
metal

(G-13105)
QUALITY TOOL COMPANY
Also Called: Quality Stamping
577 Mel Simon Dr (43612-4729)
P.O. Box 3320 (43702)
PHONE...................................419 476-8228
James G Pasch, *Pr*
Michael Pasch, *VP*
EMP: 20 EST: 1954
SQ FT: 48,000
SALES (est): 5.41MM **Privately Held**
Web: www.qualitytool.com
SIC: 3469 3312 Stamping metal for the trade
; Tool and die steel

(G-13106)
QUIKRETE COMPANIES LLC
873 Western Ave (43609-2774)
PHONE...................................419 241-1148
Becky Garner, *Mgr*
EMP: 19
SQ FT: 10,700
Web: www.quikrete.com
SIC: 3272 3241 Dry mixture concrete;
Cement, hydraulic
HQ: The Quikrete Companies Llc
5 Concourse Pkwy Ste 1900
Atlanta GA 30328
404 634-9100

(G-13107)
R & D CUSTOM MACHINE & TL INC
5961 American Rd E (43612-3950)
PHONE...................................419 727-1700
David Skomer, *Pr*
EMP: 25 EST: 1982
SQ FT: 16,800
SALES (est): 2.95MM **Privately Held**
Web: www.rdcustommachine.com
SIC: 3599 Machine shop, jobbing and repair

(G-13108)
RADCO FIRE PROTECTION INC
444 W Laskey Rd Ste S (43612-3460)
PHONE...................................419 476-0102
Douglas W Ward, *Pr*
EMP: 7 EST: 1985
SQ FT: 1,800
SALES (est): 524.1K **Privately Held**
SIC: 3569 Sprinkler systems, fire: automatic

(G-13109)
RADCO INDUSTRIES INC
3226 Frenchmens Rd (43607-2996)
PHONE......................419 531-4731
Richard Anderson, *Pr*
Mary Anderson, *VP*
◆ EMP: 11 EST: 1962
SQ FT: 28,000
SALES (est): 2.46MM **Privately Held**
Web: www.radcoindustries.com
SIC: 3599 Machine shop, jobbing and repair

(G-13110)
RAKA CORPORATION
Also Called: Lockrey Manufacturing
203 Matzinger Rd (43612-2624)
PHONE......................419 476-6572
Don Vollmar, *CEO*
Mark A Makulinski, *
EMP: 78 EST: 1953
SQ FT: 75,000
SALES (est): 9.08MM **Privately Held**
Web: www.lockreymanufacturing.com
SIC: 3451 3444 Screw machine products;
Sheet metalwork

(G-13111)
REA POLISHING INC
1606 W Laskey Rd (43612-2916)
PHONE......................419 470-0216
Jay Rea Senior, *Pr*
Jay Rea Junior, *Sec*
Tracy Rea, *Off Mgr*
EMP: 61 EST: 1995
SQ FT: 19,600
SALES (est): 2.05MM **Privately Held**
SIC: 3471 Finishing, metals or formed
products

(G-13112)
RIKER PRODUCTS INC
4901 Stickney Ave (43612-3716)
P.O. Box 6976 (43612-0976)
PHONE......................419 729-1626
Mark Foster, *CEO*
Gary Frye, *
Rollie Bauer, *
Michael Jaeck, *
▼ EMP: 88 EST: 1932
SQ FT: 250,000
SALES (est): 8.49MM **Privately Held**
Web: www.rikerprod.com
SIC: 3714 3498 Mufflers (exhaust), motor
vehicle; Fabricated pipe and fittings

(G-13113)
RIVER EAST CUSTOM CABINETS INC
221 S Saint Clair St (43602)
PHONE......................419 244-3226
Joe Weiser, *Pr*
John Weiser, *VP*
EMP: 9 EST: 1984
SQ FT: 15,000
SALES (est): 2.31MM **Privately Held**
Web: www.rivereastcabinets.com
SIC: 5712 2434 Cabinet work, custom;
Wood kitchen cabinets

(G-13114)
RIVERSIDE MARINE INDS INC
Also Called: H Hansen Industries
2824 N Summit St (43611-3425)
PHONE......................419 729-1621
Tony La Mantia, *Pr*
Larry Ansler, *
Jerry Norton, *
EMP: 60 EST: 1924
SQ FT: 30,000
SALES (est): 8.33MM **Privately Held**
Web: www.hansenind.com

SIC: 3599 Machine shop, jobbing and repair

(G-13115)
RLM FABRICATING INC
4801 Bennett Rd (43612-2531)
PHONE......................419 729-6130
Michael Reser, *Pr*
Patrick Copeland, *
EMP: 30 EST: 2006
SALES (est): 1.45MM **Privately Held**
Web: www.maumeevalleyfab.com
SIC: 3441 Fabricated structural metal

(G-13116)
ROBERT BECKER IMPRESSIONS INC
4646 Angola Rd (43615-6407)
PHONE......................419 385-5303
Robert O Becker, *Pr*
Jennie Becker, *VP*
EMP: 12 EST: 1976
SQ FT: 9,000
SALES (est): 943.7K **Privately Held**
Web: www.beckerimpressions.com
SIC: 7334 5044 2752 Blueprinting service;
Blueprinting equipment; Offset printing

(G-13117)
ROCKET VENTURES LLC
300 Madison Ave Ste 270 (43604-1568)
PHONE......................419 530-6083
EMP: 12 EST: 2017
SALES (est): 1.86MM **Privately Held**
Web: www.rocketventures.org
SIC: 3229 Pressed and blown glass, nec

(G-13118)
ROGAR INTERNATIONAL INC
Also Called: N M Hansen Machine and Tool
4015 Dewey St (43612-1415)
P.O. Box 6938 (43612-0938)
PHONE......................419 476-5500
Ronnie W Clark, *CEO*
Roger Burditt, *VP*
James V Schindler, *Sec*
R Ken Clark, *Treas*
EMP: 15 EST: 1909
SQ FT: 30,000
SALES (est): 2.47MM **Privately Held**
Web: www.nmhansen.com
SIC: 3599 Machine shop, jobbing and repair

(G-13119)
RONFELDT MANUFACTURING LLC (HQ)
Also Called: Ice Industries Ronfeldt
2345 S Byrne Rd (43614-5107)
PHONE......................419 382-5641
Howard Ice, *Managing Member*
Paul Bishop, *Pr*
Jeff Boger, *CFO*
EMP: 17 EST: 2007
SALES (est): 31.02MM **Privately Held**
Web: www.iceindusties.com
SIC: 3469 Stamping metal for the trade
PA: Ice Industries, Inc.
3810 Herr Rd
Sylvania OH 43560

(G-13120)
SABCO INDUSTRIES INC
5242 Angola Rd Ste 150 (43615-6334)
PHONE......................419 531-5347
Robert Sulier, *Pr*
John Pershing, *
▲ EMP: 28 EST: 1961
SALES (est): 247.78K **Privately Held**
SIC: 7699 5085 3993 3412 Tank repair and
cleaning services; Barrels, new or
reconditioned; Signs and advertising
specialties; Metal barrels, drums, and pails

(G-13121)
SANDWISCH ENTERPRISES INC (PA)
1644 Campbell St (43607-4381)
PHONE......................419 944-6446
Daniel Sandwisch, *CEO*
Peter James Harvey, *Pr*
William Harvey, *VP*
Elizabeth Harvey, *Sec*
EMP: 8 EST: 1978
SQ FT: 14,000
SALES (est): 352.71K
SALES (corp-wide): 352.71K **Privately Held**
Web: www.sandwischx.com
SIC: 3471 7389 4213 Finishing, metals or
formed products; Grinding, precision:
commercial or industrial; Trucking, except
local

(G-13122)
SAXON PRODUCTS INC
2283 Fulton St (43620-1272)
PHONE......................419 241-6771
Edward L Poling, *Pr*
Tony Berezowski, *VP*
Mary Mazziotti, *Sec*
▲ EMP: 9 EST: 1961
SQ FT: 20,000
SALES (est): 389.93K **Privately Held**
Web: www.saxonproducts.com
SIC: 3496 Miscellaneous fabricated wire
products

(G-13123)
SEAPORT MOLD & CASTING COMPANY
1309 W Bancroft St (43606-4634)
PHONE......................419 243-1422
Michael A Kumor, *Pr*
Fred Kumor, *VP*
EMP: 7 EST: 1946
SQ FT: 15,000
SALES (est): 765.78K **Privately Held**
SIC: 3369 3543 Nonferrous foundries, nec;
Industrial patterns

(G-13124)
SEAWAY PATTERN MFG INC
5749 Angola Rd (43615-6319)
PHONE......................419 865-5724
Richard Johnston, *Pr*
EMP: 17 EST: 1962
SQ FT: 30,000
SALES (est): 4.75MM **Privately Held**
Web: www.seawaypatterninc.com
SIC: 3543 3544 Industrial patterns; Industrial
molds

(G-13125)
SEM-COM COMPANY INC (PA)
1040 N Westwood Ave (43607-3263)
P.O. Box 8428 (43623-0428)
PHONE......................419 537-8813
Lawrence V Pfaender, *Ch*
Michael V Pfaender, *Pr*
Johann Manning, *Sec*
James Pfaender, *VP*
William Garrett, *VP*
EMP: 11 EST: 1984
SQ FT: 22,500
SALES (est): 488.5K
SALES (corp-wide): 488.5K **Privately Held**
Web: www.sem-com.com
SIC: 3231 2891 3229 Products of purchased
glass; Adhesives and sealants; Fiber optics
strands

(G-13126)
SENECA PETROLEUM CO INC
1441 Woodville Rd (43605-3233)
PHONE......................419 691-3581
Dean Friend, *Mgr*
EMP: 15
SALES (corp-wide): 9.47MM **Privately Held**
SIC: 2951 2911 Asphalt and asphaltic paving
mixtures (not from refineries); Petroleum
refining
PA: Seneca Petroleum Co., Inc.
13301 Cicero Ave
Crestwood IL 60418
708 396-1100

(G-13127)
SENECA PETROLEUM CO INC
2563 Front St (43605-1153)
PHONE......................419 691-3581
Dean Friend, *Brnch Mgr*
EMP: 12
SALES (corp-wide): 9.47MM **Privately Held**
SIC: 2911 1611 Asphalt or asphaltic
materials, made in refineries; Highway and
street construction
PA: Seneca Petroleum Co., Inc.
13301 Cicero Ave
Crestwood IL 60418
708 396-1100

(G-13128)
SFC GRAPHICS CLEVELAND LTD
Also Called: Sfc Graphic Arts Div
110 E Woodruff Ave (43604-5226)
P.O. Box 877 (43697-0877)
PHONE......................419 255-1283
Tom Clark, *CEO*
Paul Clark, *
EMP: 10 EST: 1982
SQ FT: 15,000
SALES (est): 879.93K **Privately Held**
Web: www.engineeredimaging.com
SIC: 2752 Offset printing

(G-13129)
SHELAR INC
5335 Enterprise Blvd (43612-3810)
PHONE......................419 729-9756
Fred Shelar, *Pr*
Dennis Krout, *VP*
▲ EMP: 140 EST: 1987
SQ FT: 70,000
SALES (est): 24.7MM **Privately Held**
Web: www.sterlingpipeandtube.com
SIC: 3317 Steel pipe and tubes

(G-13130)
SHELLY MATERIALS INC
Also Called: Shelly Liquid Division
352 George Hardy Dr (43605-1063)
PHONE......................740 246-6315
John Power, *Pr*
EMP: 27
SALES (corp-wide): 34.95B **Privately Held**
Web: www.shellyco.com
SIC: 1422 Crushed and broken limestone
HQ: Shelly Materials, Inc.
80 Park Dr
Thornville OH 43076
740 246-6315

(G-13131)
SIGMA TUBE COMPANY
Also Called: Sterling Pipe & Tube
1050 Progress Ave (43612-9800)
PHONE......................419 729-9756
EMP: 15 EST: 2000
SALES (est): 1.43MM **Privately Held**

SIC: 3312 Pipes and tubes

(G-13132)
SILLY BRANDZ GLOBAL LLC
148 Main St (43605-2067)
PHONE..................................419 697-8324
EMP: 52 **EST:** 2009
SQ FT: 10,000
SALES (est): 3.26MM **Privately Held**
SIC: 3961 3085 2396 3999 Keychains,
except precious metal; Plastics bottles;
Sweat bands, hat and cap: made from
purchased materials; Identification tags,
except paper

(G-13133)
SOJOURNERS TRUTH INC
7 E Bancroft St (43620-1916)
PHONE..................................419 243-0007
Fletcher Word, *Pr*
EMP: 10 **EST:** 2013
SALES (est): 365.7K **Privately Held**
Web: wordpress.thetruthtoledo.com
SIC: 2711 Newspapers, publishing and
printing

(G-13134)
STONECO INC
352 George Hardy Dr (43605-1063)
PHONE..................................419 693-3933
William Hodges, *Mgr*
EMP: 9
SALES (corp-wide): 34.95B **Privately Held**
Web: www.shellyco.com
SIC: 2951 Paving mixtures
HQ: Stoneco, Inc.
1700 Fostoria Ave Ste 200
Findlay OH 45840
419 422-8854

(G-13135)
SUNSHINE PRODUCTS
760 Warehouse Rd Ste O (43615-6455)
P.O. Box 350786 (43635-0786)
PHONE..................................303 478-4913
Del Short, *Prin*
EMP: 7 **EST:** 2006
SALES (est): 191.18K **Privately Held**
Web: www.sunshine.org
SIC: 3915 Jewelers' materials and lapidary
work

(G-13136)
SUPERIOR IMPRESSIONS INC
327 12th St (43604-7531)
PHONE..................................419 244-8676
Douglas A Shelton, *Pr*
EMP: 8 **EST:** 1967
SQ FT: 6,000
SALES (est): 352.85K **Privately Held**
Web: www.superiorimpressions.com
SIC: 2752 Offset printing

(G-13137)
SUPERIOR PACKAGING
2930 Airport Hwy (43609-1404)
PHONE..................................419 380-3335
Steve Davis, *Owner*
EMP: 10 **EST:** 2007
SALES (est): 959.71K **Privately Held**
Web: www.dunnagebags.com
SIC: 3629 Electronic generation equipment

(G-13138)
SYRACUSE CHINA LLC (DH)
Also Called: Syracuse China Company
300 Madison Ave (43604-1561)
P.O. Box 10060 (43699-0060)
PHONE..................................419 325-2100
Michael P Bauer, *CEO*

◆ **EMP:** 225 **EST:** 1995
SQ FT: 50,000
SALES (est): 5.94MM **Privately Held**
SIC: 2711 Newspapers, publishing and
printing
HQ: Libbey Glass Llc
300 Madison Ave
Toledo OH 43604
419 325-2100

(G-13139)
TAFT TOOL & PRODUCTION CO
756 S Byrne Rd Ste 1 (43609-1088)
PHONE..................................419 385-2576
Rose Tavtigian, *VP*
Paul Sneider, *Genl Mgr*
EMP: 10 **EST:** 1948
SQ FT: 13,000
SALES (est): 255.55K **Privately Held**
SIC: 3544 3545 7699 Special dies and tools;
Gauges (machine tool accessories);
Industrial machinery and equipment repair

(G-13140)
TELEX COMMUNICATIONS INC
Also Called: Toledo Business Journals
5660 Southwyck Blvd Ste 150
(43614-1504)
P.O. Box 1206 (43537-8206)
PHONE..................................419 865-0972
Sanford Lubin, *Pr*
EMP: 13 **EST:** 1986
SALES (est): 203.19K **Privately Held**
Web: www.toledobiz.com
SIC: 8742 2721 8748 Industry specialist
consultants; Periodicals; Communications
consulting

(G-13141)
TEMBEC BTLSR INC
2112 Sylvan Ave (43606-4767)
P.O. Box 2570 (43606-0570)
PHONE..................................419 244-5856
James M Lopez, *Pr*
Lawrence Rowley, *
Dan Wozniak, *
◆ **EMP:** 32 **EST:** 1902
SQ FT: 84,000
SALES (est): 2.85MM
SALES (corp-wide): 1.63B **Publicly Held**
Web: www.lrbgchemicals.com
SIC: 2821 5169 Plastics materials and resins
; Industrial chemicals
HQ: Tembec Inc.
100-4 Place Ville-Marie
Montreal QC H3B 2
514 871-0137

(G-13142)
THERMAFIBER INC (HQ)
1 Owens Corning Pkwy (43659-1000)
PHONE..................................260 563-2111
Austin Hess, *Pr*
Jonathan Lyons, *
Gregory Greenberg, *
Douglas E Mays, *
James Kuhens, *
◆ **EMP:** 93 **EST:** 1997
SQ FT: 3,000
SALES (est): 3.38MM **Publicly Held**
Web: www.highriseinsulation.com
SIC: 3296 Fiberglass insulation
PA: Owens Corning
1 Owens Corning Pkwy
Toledo OH 43659

(G-13143)
TJ METZGERS INC
Also Called: Metzgers
207 Arco Dr (43607-2906)
PHONE..................................419 861-8611

Anthony Metzger, *CEO*
Thomas H Metzger, *
EMP: 72 **EST:** 1976
SQ FT: 63,146
SALES (est): 13.39MM **Privately Held**
Web: www.metzgers.com
SIC: 2789 2791 7335 2752 Bookbinding and
related work; Photocomposition, for the
printing trade; Color separation,
photographic and movie film; Offset printing

(G-13144)
TM MACHINE & TOOL INC
521 Mel Simon Dr (43612-4726)
PHONE..................................419 478-0310
Karyn Weeks, *Pr*
EMP: 8 **EST:** 1984
SQ FT: 20,000
SALES (est): 1.04MM **Privately Held**
Web: www.tmmachineandtool.com
SIC: 3544 3599 Special dies and tools;
Machine shop, jobbing and repair

(G-13145)
TMD INC
4 E Laskey Rd (43612-3517)
PHONE..................................419 476-4581
Joe Pirrone, *Brnch Mgr*
EMP: 110
SALES (corp-wide): 2.63MM **Privately
Held**
Web: www.tmdinc.com
SIC: 3544 Special dies, tools, jigs, and
fixtures
PA: Tmd, Inc.
1429 Coining Dr
Toledo OH 43612
419 470-3950

(G-13146)
TNT SOLID SOLUTIONS LLC
6120 N Detroit Ave (43612-4810)
PHONE..................................419 262-6228
Beth Godfrey, *Prin*
EMP: 11 **EST:** 2017
SALES (est): 2.96MM **Privately Held**
Web: www.tntsolidsolutions.com
SIC: 3444 Sheet metalwork

(G-13147)
TOLCO CORPORATION (PA)
Also Called: Tolco
1920 Linwood Ave (43604-5293)
PHONE..................................419 241-1113
George L Notarianni, *Pr*
◆ **EMP:** 48 **EST:** 1961
SQ FT: 30,000
SALES (est): 21.61MM
SALES (corp-wide): 21.61MM **Privately
Held**
Web: www.tolcocorp.com
SIC: 5085 3563 3586 3561 Bottler supplies;
Spraying outfits: metals, paints, and
chemicals (compressor); Measuring and
dispensing pumps; Pumps and pumping
equipment

(G-13148)
TOLEDO BLADE COMPANY
541 N Superior St (43660-0002)
P.O. Box 921 (43697-0921)
PHONE..................................419 724-6000
Joseph H Zerbey Iv, *Pr*
EMP: 423 **EST:** 1985
SALES (est): 9.48MM
SALES (corp-wide): 461.93MM **Privately
Held**
Web: www.toledoblade.com
SIC: 2711 Commercial printing and
newspaper publishing combined
PA: Block Communications, Inc.

405 Madison Ave Ste 2100
Toledo OH 43604
419 724-6212

(G-13149)
TOLEDO CONTROLS
3550 Maxwell Rd (43606-1921)
PHONE..................................419 474-2537
Leslie J Declercq Junior, *Prin*
EMP: 7 **EST:** 2012
SALES (est): 45.59K **Privately Held**
Web: www.ttoledo.com
SIC: 3823 Process control instruments

(G-13150)
TOLEDO CUT STONE INC
Also Called: Tri-State Archtctural Panl Sls
4011 South Ave (43615-6229)
PHONE..................................419 531-1623
Ted Piel, *Pr*
Kendal Piel, *VP*
Richard Szczepaniak, *Sec*
EMP: 11 **EST:** 1906
SQ FT: 16,400
SALES (est): 245.41K **Privately Held**
SIC: 3281 5032 Building stone products;
Building stone

(G-13151)
TOLEDO ENGINEERING CO INC (PA)
Also Called: Teco
3400 Executive Pkwy (43606-1364)
P.O. Box 2927 (43606-0927)
PHONE..................................419 537-9711
Scott A Slater, *Ch*
Todd Seifried, *
Christopher J Hoyle, *
◆ **EMP:** 75 **EST:** 1929
SQ FT: 50,000
SALES (est): 43.55MM
SALES (corp-wide): 43.55MM **Privately
Held**
Web: www.teco.com
SIC: 3559 Glass making machinery: blowing,
molding, forming, etc.

(G-13152)
**TOLEDO METAL SPINNING
COMPANY**
1819 Clinton St (43607-1600)
PHONE..................................419 535-5931
Kenneth F Fankhauser, *Pr*
Eric S Fankhauser, *
Craig B Fankhauser, *
▼ **EMP:** 35 **EST:** 1929
SQ FT: 100,000
SALES (est): 11.31MM **Privately Held**
Web: www.toledometalspinning.com
SIC: 3469 3443 Spinning metal for the trade;
Cylinders, pressure: metal plate

(G-13153)
TOLEDO MOLDING & DIE LLC (DH)
Also Called: Tmd
1429 Coining Dr (43612-2932)
PHONE..................................419 470-3950
Nilesh Soni, *Managing Member*
Robert Briggs, *Managing Member*
Justin Cousino, *
◆ **EMP:** 60 **EST:** 1989
SQ FT: 35,000
SALES (est): 389.13MM
SALES (corp-wide): 7.28B **Privately Held**
Web: www.tmdinc.com
SIC: 3544 3089 Special dies, tools, jigs, and
fixtures; Injection molded finished plastics
products, nec
HQ: Apc Parent, Llc
127 Public Sq Ste 5110
Cleveland OH 44114
216 589-0198

(G-13154)
TOLEDO MOLDING & DIE LLC
4 E Laskey Rd (43612-3517)
PHONE...................................419 476-0581
Joe Pirrone, *Mgr*
EMP: 136
SALES (corp-wide): 7.28B **Privately Held**
Web: www.tmdinc.com
SIC: 3089 3544 Injection molded finished
plastics products, nec; Special dies, tools,
jigs, and fixtures
HQ: Toledo Molding & Die, Llc
1429 Coining Dr
Toledo OH 43612

(G-13155)
TOLEDO OPTICAL LABORATORY INC
Also Called: Toledo Optical
1201 Jefferson Ave (43604-5836)
P.O. Box 2028 (43603-2028)
PHONE...................................419 248-3384
Irland Tashima, *Pr*
Jeffrey Seymenski, *
Toshi Kadowaki, *
EMP: 6 **EST:** 1947
SQ FT: 10,000
SALES (est): 489.4K **Privately Held**
Web: www.walmanoptical.com
SIC: 3851 5048 Eyeglasses, lenses and
frames; Lenses, ophthalmic

(G-13156)
TOLEDO PRO FIBERGLASS INC
210 Wade St (43604-8852)
PHONE...................................419 241-9390
Don Jardine, *VP*
EMP: 8 **EST:** 1989
SQ FT: 24,000
SALES (est): 108.81K **Privately Held**
Web: www.toledocustomfiberglass.com
SIC: 5999 3714 3711 3089 Fiberglass
materials, except insulation; Motor vehicle
parts and accessories; Motor vehicles and
car bodies; Fiberglass doors

(G-13157)
TOLEDO SIGN COMPANY INC (PA)
2021 Adams St (43604-5431)
PHONE...................................419 244-4444
Brad Heil, *Pr*
Brian Heil Junior, *VP*
EMP: 22 **EST:** 1914
SQ FT: 34,000
SALES (est): 2.37MM
SALES (corp-wide): 2.37MM **Privately
Held**
Web: www.toledosign.com
SIC: 3993 Signs and advertising specialties

(G-13158)
TOLEDO SPIRITS COMPANY LLC
1301 N Summit St (43604-1819)
PHONE...................................419 704-3705
Andrew Newby, *Admn*
EMP: 15 **EST:** 2014
SALES (est): 2.19MM **Privately Held**
Web: www.toledospirits.com
SIC: 5921 2085 Wine; Applejack (alcoholic
beverage)

(G-13159)
TOLEDO TICKET COMPANY
3963 Catawba St (43612-1492)
P.O. Box 6876 (43612-0876)
PHONE...................................419 476-5424
Roy L Carter, *Ch*
Roy L Carter, *Pr*
Robin G Carter, *
EMP: 50 **EST:** 1910
SQ FT: 50,000
SALES (est): 5.42MM **Privately Held**

Web: www.toledoticket.com
SIC: 2752 2759 Tickets, lithographed;
Commercial printing, nec

(G-13160)
TOLEDO TOOL AND DIE CO INC
5639 Telegraph Rd (43612-3632)
PHONE...................................419 476-4422
John Vanbelle, *Brnch Mgr*
EMP: 11
SALES (corp-wide): 42.17MM **Privately
Held**
Web: www.toledotool.com
SIC: 3469 3544 Metal stampings, nec;
Special dies, tools, jigs, and fixtures
PA: Toledo Tool And Die Company, Inc.
105 W Alexis Rd
Toledo OH 43612
419 476-4422

(G-13161)
TOLEDO TOOL AND DIE CO INC (PA)
Also Called: Toledo Tool & Die
105 W Alexis Rd (43612-3603)
PHONE...................................419 476-4422
Anthony Kujawa Iii, *CEO*
John Hrovatich, *
▲ **EMP:** 232 **EST:** 1940
SQ FT: 60,000
SALES (est): 42.17MM
SALES (corp-wide): 42.17MM **Privately
Held**
Web: www.toledotool.com
SIC: 3469 3544 Stamping metal for the trade
; Special dies, tools, jigs, and fixtures

(G-13162)
TOLEDO WINDOW & AWNING INC
3035 W Sylvania Ave (43613-4135)
PHONE...................................419 474-3396
Dennis Whitaker, *Pr*
Dawn Whitaker, *VP*
EMP: 11 **EST:** 1950
SQ FT: 2,600
SALES (est): 847.69K **Privately Held**
Web: www.toledowindow.org
SIC: 3444 5031 5211 Awnings, sheet metal;
Doors and windows; Doors, storm: wood or
metal

(G-13163)
TOOLING & COMPONENTS CORP
Also Called: Toolcomp
5261 Tractor Rd (43612-3439)
PHONE...................................419 478-9122
David Gonzalez, *Pr*
Ezekiel Gonzalez, *VP*
EMP: 12 **EST:** 1993
SQ FT: 5,900
SALES (est): 1.06MM **Privately Held**
Web: www.toolcomp.com
SIC: 3599 3544 Machine shop, jobbing and
repair; Special dies, tools, jigs, and fixtures

(G-13164)
TOTH INDUSTRIES INC
5102 Enterprise Blvd (43612-3897)
PHONE...................................419 729-4669
Richard Toth, *Pr*
EMP: 70 **EST:** 1955
SQ FT: 40,000
SALES (est): 9.69MM **Privately Held**
Web: www.tothindustries.com
SIC: 3599 3594 Machine shop, jobbing and
repair; Fluid power pumps and motors

(G-13165)
TPAM INC
5915 Jason St (43611-1088)
PHONE...................................567 315-8694
Tomohisa Sugiura, *Pr*

Doryo Iwanaga, *
EMP: 25 **EST:** 2015
SALES (est): 19.51MM **Privately Held**
SIC: 5012 3711 Automobiles; Motor vehicles
and car bodies
PA: Topia Co.,Ltd.
1477-1, Ichinomiyacho
Suzuka MIE 513-0

(G-13166)
TRU-FORM STEEL & WIRE INC
5509 Telegraph Rd (43612-2662)
PHONE...................................765 348-5001
Jeffrey Tuttle, *Brnch Mgr*
EMP: 20
SALES (corp-wide): 4.75MM **Privately
Held**
Web: www.tru-formsteel.com
SIC: 3315 3441 Steel wire and related
products; Fabricated structural metal
PA: Tru-Form Steel & Wire, Inc.
1204 Gilkey Ave
Hartford City IN 47348
765 348-5001

(G-13167)
TWISTER CLEANING TECH INC
3115 Frenchmens Rd (43607-2918)
PHONE...................................865 521-3976
Mats Franzen, *Prin*
EMP: 9 **EST:** 2011
SALES (est): 477.2K **Privately Held**
Web: www.twisterpad.com
SIC: 2392 Mops, floor and dust

(G-13168)
UNITED COMPONENTS LLC (DH)
Also Called: UCI
6056 Deer Park Ct (43614-6000)
PHONE...................................330 899-0340
David Peace, *CEO*
Mark P Blaufuss, *
Michael G Malady, *
Keith A Zar, *
David L Squier, *
◆ **EMP:** 50 **EST:** 2003
SALES (est): 473.45MM
SALES (corp-wide): 7.28B **Privately Held**
SIC: 3714 Motor vehicle parts and
accessories
HQ: Uci International, Llc
2100 International Pkwy
North Canton OH 44720

(G-13169)
UNIVERSAL URETHANE PDTS INC
410 1st St (43605-2002)
P.O. Box 50617 (43605-0617)
PHONE...................................419 693-7400
Harry G Conrad, *CEO*
Jeffrey A Conrad, *
Scott Conrad, *
EMP: 55 **EST:** 1973
SQ FT: 32,000
SALES (est): 5MM **Privately Held**
Web: www.universalurethane.com
SIC: 3069 3312 3061 2851 Molded rubber
products; Blast furnaces and steel mills;
Mechanical rubber goods; Paints and allied
products

(G-13170)
UNIVERSITY OF TOLEDO
University of Toledo Press
2801 W Bancroft St (43606-3390)
PHONE...................................419 530-2311
EMP: 11
SALES (corp-wide): 888.64MM **Privately
Held**
Web: www.utoledo.edu

SIC: 2731 Books, publishing only
PA: The University Of Toledo
2801 W Bancroft St
Toledo OH 43606
419 530-4636

(G-13171)
UNLIMITED MACHINE AND TOOL
LLC
5139 Tractor Rd Ste C (43612-3432)
PHONE...................................419 269-1730
Tom Mccloskey, *Managing Member*
EMP: 15 **EST:** 2004
SQ FT: 6,000
SALES (est): 3.15MM **Privately Held**
Web: www.unlimmachtool.com
SIC: 3544 3312 Special dies and tools; Tool
and die steel and alloys

(G-13172)
V M SYSTEMS INC
3125 Hill Ave (43607-2987)
PHONE...................................419 535-1044
Craig Gabel, *Pr*
Ronald H Gabel, *
Trent Bloomfield, *
Kenneth J Gabel, *
EMP: 100 **EST:** 1973
SQ FT: 24,000
SALES (est): 24.71MM **Privately Held**
Web: www.vmsystemsinc.com
SIC: 1711 3444 Warm air heating and air
conditioning contractor; Sheet metalwork

(G-13173)
VALLEY PLASTICS COMPANY INC
399 Phillips Ave (43612-1349)
PHONE...................................419 666-2349
Walter Norris, *CEO*
EMP: 40 **EST:** 1975
SALES (est): 2.05MM **Privately Held**
Web: www.valleyplasticsinc.com
SIC: 3089 2542 Injection molding of plastics;
Partitions and fixtures, except wood

(G-13174)
VIKING PAPER COMPANY (PA)
5148 Stickney Ave (43612-3721)
PHONE...................................419 729-4951
J Anthony Mooter, *Pr*
Robert Walker, *
EMP: 46 **EST:** 1986
SQ FT: 60,000
SALES (est): 24.19MM
SALES (corp-wide): 24.19MM **Privately
Held**
Web: www.packpros.net
SIC: 2653 Boxes, corrugated: made from
purchased materials

(G-13175)
VINTAGE AUTOMOTIVE ELC INC
Also Called: Vintage Heating and Air
3335 Mcgregor Ln (43623-1917)
PHONE...................................419 472-9349
Jacquelyn Crozier, *Pr*
John Crozier, *VP*
EMP: 10 **EST:** 1974
SQ FT: 4,000
SALES (est): 425.23K **Privately Held**
Web: www.vintageautotoledo.com
SIC: 1711 7539 5013 5531 Plumbing,
heating, air-conditioning; Electrical services
; Automotive supplies and parts; Auto and
home supply stores

(G-13176)
WALL TECHNOLOGY INC
1 Owens Corning Pkwy (43659-1000)
PHONE...................................715 532-5548
Johna Ryan, *Sec*

▲ = Import ▼ = Export
◆ = Import/Export

EMP: 7 EST: 2001
SALES (est): 262.49K Privately Held
SIC: 3446 3275 Acoustical suspension systems, metal; Gypsum products

(G-13177)
WEST EQUIPMENT COMPANY INC (PA)
1545 E Broadway St (43605-3852)
PHONE..............................419 698-1601
TOLL FREE: 800
Paul Erdmann, *Pr*
Bernard Erdmann, *CEO*
Paul Erdmann, *Pr*
Chad Erdmann, *VP*
Kristi Erdmann, *Prin*
EMP: 6 EST: 1952
SQ FT: 7,200
SALES (est): 13.75MM
SALES (corp-wide): 13.75MM Privately Held
Web: www.thewestequipment.com
SIC: 5082 7699 7359 3496 General construction machinery and equipment; Construction equipment repair; Equipment rental and leasing, nec; Slings, lifting: made from purchased wire

(G-13178)
WESTROCK COMMERCIAL LLC
1635 Coining Dr (43612-2906)
PHONE..............................419 476-9101
EMP: 31
SIC: 5112 2752 Stationery and office supplies; Commercial printing, lithographic
HQ: Westrock Commercial, Llc
501 S 5th St
Richmond VA 23219
804 444-1000

(G-13179)
WIREMAX LTD
705 Wamba Ave (43607-3252)
P.O. Box 3336 (43607-0336)
PHONE..............................419 531-9500
Al Mocek, *Pr*
Mark Robinson, *Mgr*
EMP: 6 EST: 1995
SQ FT: 8,000
SALES (est): 429.89K Privately Held
Web: www.wiremax.com
SIC: 3357 Nonferrous wiredrawing and insulating

(G-13180)
WURTEC MANUFACTURING SERVICE
6200 Brent Dr (43611-1081)
PHONE..............................419 726-1066
Steven P Wurth, *Pr*
Jane A Wurth, *Sec*
▲ **EMP: 20 EST: 1995**
SQ FT: 26,000
SALES (est): 2.32MM Privately Held
Web: www.wurtec.com
SIC: 3544 3993 Special dies, tools, jigs, and fixtures; Signs, not made in custom sign painting shops

(G-13181)
XUNLIGHT CORPORATION
3145 Nebraska Ave (43607-3102)
PHONE..............................419 469-8600
▲ **EMP: 60**
Web: www.xunlight.com
SIC: 3433 Solar heaters and collectors

(G-13182)
YARDER MANUFACTURING COMPANY (PA)

722 Phillips Ave (43612-1333)
P.O. Box 6886 (43612-0886)
PHONE..............................419 476-3933
Richard W Yarder, *Pr*
Matt Yarder, *
Maryann Bailey, *
Amy Conlan, *
EMP: 49 EST: 1930
SQ FT: 55,000
SALES (est): 7.86MM
SALES (corp-wide): 7.86MM Privately Held
Web: www.yardermfg.com
SIC: 3499 Boxes for packing and shipping, metal

(G-13183)
ZF ACTIVE SAFETY & ELEC US LLC
5915 Jason St (43611-1088)
PHONE..............................419 726-5599
Dennis Burke, *Brnch Mgr*
EMP: 32
SALES (corp-wide): 144.19K Privately Held
SIC: 3714 Motor vehicle parts and accessories
HQ: Zf Active Safety & Electronics Us Llc
15811 Centennial Dr
Northville MI 48168
765 429-1936

(G-13184)
ZIE BART RHINO LININGS TOLEDO
Also Called: Rhino Linings
3343 N Holland Sylvania Rd (43615-1409)
PHONE..............................419 841-2886
Keith Tucker, *Owner*
EMP: 6 EST: 1991
SALES (est): 452.83K Privately Held
SIC: 3713 Truck beds

Toronto
Jefferson County

(G-13185)
EXPRESS ENERGY SVCS OPER LP
1515 Franklin St (43964-1029)
PHONE..............................740 337-4530
EMP: 31
SALES (corp-wide): 91.34MM Privately Held
Web: www.brhas.com
SIC: 1389 Oil field services, nec
PA: Express Energy Services Operating, Lp
3547 Fm 236
Victoria TX 77905
713 625-7400

(G-13186)
RIDGE MACHINE & WELDING CO
1015 Railroad St (43964-1115)
P.O. Box 190 (43964-0190)
PHONE..............................740 537-2821
David Artman, *Pr*
J Curtis Artman, *VP*
Debbie Artman, *Sec*
EMP: 6 EST: 1950
SQ FT: 27,600
SALES (est): 826.8K Privately Held
Web: www.ridgemachineandwelding.com
SIC: 3599 7692 3398 Machine shop, jobbing and repair; Welding repair; Metal heat treating

(G-13187)
TITANIUM METALS CORPORATION
Also Called: Timet Toronto
100 Titanium Way (43964-1990)
P.O. Box 309 (43964-0309)

PHONE..............................740 537-1571
Steve Wright, *Brnch Mgr*
EMP: 527
SALES (corp-wide): 424.23B Publicly Held
Web: www.timet.com
SIC: 3566 3356 Speed changers, drives, and gears; Nonferrous rolling and drawing, nec
HQ: Titanium Metals Corporation
4832 Richmond Rd Ste 100
Warrensville Heights OH 44128
740 537-5600

(G-13188)
VALLEY CONVERTING CO INC (PA)
Also Called: Valley
405 Daniels St (43964-1343)
P.O. Box 279 (43964-0279)
PHONE..............................740 537-2152
Gino Biasi, *Ch Bd*
Michael D Biasi, *
▼ **EMP: 50 EST: 1973**
SQ FT: 107,500
SALES (est): 5.26MM
SALES (corp-wide): 5.26MM Privately Held
Web: www.valleyconverting.com
SIC: 2631 Cardboard

Tremont City
Clark County

(G-13189)
MIKE LOPPE
Also Called: Kutrite Manufacturing
2 W Main St (45372)
P.O. Box 186 (45372-0186)
PHONE..............................937 969-8102
Mike Loppe, *Owner*
EMP: 10 EST: 1983
SQ FT: 5,500
SALES (est): 995.27K Privately Held
SIC: 3599 7692 3444 Machine shop, jobbing and repair; Welding repair; Sheet metalwork

Trenton
Butler County

(G-13190)
BC MACHINE SERVICES CORP
3104 Wayne Madison Rd (45067-9746)
PHONE..............................513 428-0327
Ryan Curry, *Pr*
EMP: 7 EST: 2015
SALES (est): 1.77MM Privately Held
Web: www.bc-machine.com
SIC: 3599 Machine shop, jobbing and repair

(G-13191)
BIDWELL FAMILY CORPORATION (HQ)
400 E State St (45067-1549)
PHONE..............................513 988-6351
Arthur W Bidwell, *CEO*
Martin J Bidwell, *
Johnie Adams, *
Ann F Bidwell, *
Douglas J Howell, *
EMP: 125 EST: 1974
SQ FT: 100,000
SALES (est): 22.27MM
SALES (corp-wide): 526.16MM Privately Held
Web: www.shapecorp.com
SIC: 3354 Aluminum extruded products
PA: Shape Corp.
1900 Hayes St

Grand Haven MI 49417
616 846-8700

(G-13192)
EVERSHARPE-DEBURRING TOOL CO
10 Baltimore Ave (45067-1513)
PHONE..............................513 988-6240
David Huff, *Pr*
Bernice Huff, *Sec*
Roger Sprinkle, *VP*
EMP: 8 EST: 1961
SQ FT: 2,400
SALES (est): 205.64K Privately Held
Web: www.eversharpe.com
SIC: 7699 3545 Knife, saw and tool sharpening and repair; Machine tool accessories

(G-13193)
MIILER BREWING COMPANY
2525 Wayne Madison Rd (45067-9799)
PHONE..............................513 896-9200
Wayne Mccauley, *Prin*
EMP: 24 EST: 2010
SALES (est): 2.08MM Privately Held
SIC: 2082 Beer (alcoholic beverage)

(G-13194)
MOLSON COORS BEV CO USA LLC
2525 Wayne Madison Rd (45067-9768)
P.O. Box 168 (45067-0168)
PHONE..............................513 896-9200
Dennis Puffer, *Brnch Mgr*
EMP: 104
SALES (corp-wide): 11.63B Publicly Held
Web: www.molsoncoors.com
SIC: 2082 Beer (alcoholic beverage)
HQ: Molson Coors Beverage Company Usa Llc
250 S Wacker Dr Ste 800
Chicago IL 60606
312 496-2700

Trotwood
Montgomery County

(G-13195)
CROWNME COIL CARE LLC
Also Called: Arcani Coil Care
4910 Denlinger Rd (45426-2014)
PHONE..............................037 707 2070
Jerricha Richardson, *Managing Member*
EMP: 18 EST: 2017
SALES (est): 6MM Privately Held
Web: arcani.square.site
SIC: 3999 Hair and hair-based products

(G-13196)
KASEL ENGINEERING LLC
5911 Wolf Creek Pike (45426-2439)
PHONE..............................937 854-8875
EMP: 8 EST: 2001
SQ FT: 8,000
SALES (est): 587.43K Privately Held
Web: www.kaselengineering.com
SIC: 3556 Slicers, commercial, food

(G-13197)
TROTWOOD CORPORATION
11 N Broadway St (45426-3594)
PHONE..............................937 854-3047
Bruce J Flora, *Pr*
Lucille Flora, *
Thomas E Flora, *
EMP: 6 EST: 1932
SQ FT: 30,000
SALES (est): 612.65K Privately Held
Web: www.stryver.com

GEOGRAPHIC

SIC: 3599 Machine shop, jobbing and repair

Troy
Miami County

(G-13198)
3 SIGMA LLC
1985 W Stanfield Rd (45373-2330)
PHONE....................................937 440-3400
Tony Rowley, *Pr*
EMP: 82 **EST:** 1980
SALES (est): 2.92MM
SALES (corp-wide): 79.1MM **Privately Held**
Web: www.3sigma.cc
SIC: 2672 Paper; coated and laminated, nec
PA: Duraco Specialty Tapes Llc
7400 W Industrial Dr
Forest Park IL 60130
866 800-0775

(G-13199)
AMERICAN ADVNCED ASSMBLIES LLC
37 Harolds Way (45373-4098)
PHONE....................................937 339-6267
Thomas B Fay, *Pr*
EMP: 28 **EST:** 2011
SALES (est): 4.26MM **Privately Held**
Web: www.aaassemblies.com
SIC: 3679 Harness assemblies, for electronic use: wire or cable

(G-13200)
AMETEK INC
Also Called: Ametek Presto Light Power
66 Industry Ct Ste F (45373-2560)
PHONE....................................937 440-0800
Patrick Williams, *Prin*
EMP: 10
SALES (corp-wide): 6.94B **Publicly Held**
Web: www.ametek.com
SIC: 5063 3699 Batteries; Electrical equipment and supplies, nec
PA: Ametek, Inc.
1100 Cassatt Rd
Berwyn PA 19312
610 647-2121

(G-13201)
ARC ABRASIVES INC
Also Called: A R C
2131 Corporate Dr (45373-1067)
P.O. Box 10 (45373-0010)
PHONE....................................800 888-4885
Anthony H Stayman, *CEO*
Anthony Stayman, *
▲ **EMP:** 76 **EST:** 1960
SALES (est): 22.04MM **Privately Held**
Web: www.arcabrasives.com
SIC: 5085 3291 2296 Abrasives; Abrasive products; Tire cord and fabrics

(G-13202)
AZTECH PRINTING & PROMOTIONS
402 E Main St (45373-3413)
PHONE....................................937 339-0100
Charles Lobaugh, *Prin*
EMP: 6 **EST:** 2007
SALES (est): 90.78K **Privately Held**
Web: www.aztechprinting.com
SIC: 2759 5734 7319 7334 Screen printing; Printers and plotters: computers; Sample distribution; Photocopying and duplicating services

(G-13203)
BRASSGATE INDUSTRIES INC
650 Olympic Dr (45373-2306)

PHONE....................................937 339-2192
Douglas W Tyger, *Prin*
EMP: 6 **EST:** 2016
SALES (est): 579.42K **Privately Held**
SIC: 3544 Die sets for metal stamping (presses)

(G-13204)
CHARACTERS INC
190 Peters Ave Ste A (45373-3995)
PHONE....................................937 335-1976
Esther Marko, *Pr*
Jason Marko, *VP*
EMP: 9 **EST:** 1961
SQ FT: 8,000
SALES (est): 426.3K **Privately Held**
SIC: 2791 Typesetting

(G-13205)
CITY OF TROY
Also Called: Troy Water Treatment Plant
300 E Staunton Rd (45373-2105)
PHONE....................................937 339-4826
Tim Ray, *Superintnt*
EMP: 10
SALES (corp-wide): 47.69MM **Privately Held**
Web: www.troyohio.gov
SIC: 3589 4941 Sewage and water treatment equipment; Water supply
PA: City Of Troy
100 S Market St
Troy OH 45373
937 335-2224

(G-13206)
CONAGRA FODS PCKAGED FOODS LLC
801 Dye Mill Rd (45373-4223)
PHONE....................................937 440-2800
Scott Adkins, *Brnch Mgr*
EMP: 30
SALES (corp-wide): 12.05B **Publicly Held**
SIC: 2099 Food preparations, nec
HQ: Conagra Foods Packaged Foods, Llc
1 Conagra Dr
Omaha NE 68102

(G-13207)
CROWE MANUFACTURING SERVICES
Also Called: King of The Road
2731 Walnut Ridge Dr (45373-4562)
PHONE....................................800 831-1893
Jamie King, *CEO*
Rob Haviland, *
Robert King, *
EMP: 6 **EST:** 1967
SQ FT: 140,000
SALES (est): 629.24K **Privately Held**
SIC: 3599 3544 Machine and other job shop work; Special dies, tools, jigs, and fixtures

(G-13208)
DARE ELECTRONICS INC
3245 S County Road 25a (45373-9384)
P.O. Box 419 (45373-0419)
PHONE....................................937 335-0031
Karen Beagle, *Pr*
EMP: 50 **EST:** 1976
SQ FT: 28,750
SALES (est): 4.83MM **Privately Held**
Web: www.dareelectronics.com
SIC: 3679 3651 Power supplies, all types: static; Amplifiers: radio, public address, or musical instrument

(G-13209)
DAYTON SUPERIOR PDTS CO INC
1370 Lytle Rd (45373-9401)

PHONE....................................937 332-1930
Daniel P Gleason, *Pr*
Frank Gleason Junior, *Ch Bd*
▲ **EMP:** 8 **EST:** 1959
SQ FT: 15,000
SALES (est): 1.07MM **Privately Held**
Web: www.daytonsuperiorproducts.com
SIC: 3568 Power transmission equipment, nec

(G-13210)
DELTECH POLYMERS LLC
1250 Union St (45373-4118)
PHONE....................................937 339-3150
Robert Elefante, *Ch Bd*
EMP: 8 **EST:** 1990
SQ FT: 435,600
SALES (est): 10.84MM
SALES (corp-wide): 107.44MM **Privately Held**
Web: www.deltech.com
SIC: 3087 2821 Custom compound purchased resins; Polystyrene resins
PA: Deltech Llc
11911 Scenic Hwy
Baton Rouge LA 70807
225 775-0150

(G-13211)
DESIGN TECHNOLOGIES & MFG CO
Also Called: Des Tech
2000 Corporate Dr (45373-1069)
PHONE....................................937 335-0757
D Jeffrey Meredith, *Pr*
William Leffel, *VP*
Debbie Meredith, *Sec*
Marilyn J Freeman, *Prin*
John E Fulker, *Prin*
EMP: 18 **EST:** 1984
SQ FT: 32,000
SALES (est): 3.55MM **Privately Held**
Web: www.destechmfg.com
SIC: 3599 Machine shop, jobbing and repair

(G-13212)
ERNST ENTERPRISES INC
Troy Ready Mix
805 Union St (45373-4109)
PHONE....................................937 339-6249
Dwayne Littlejohn, *Mgr*
EMP: 13
SQ FT: 7,446
SALES (corp-wide): 240.08MM **Privately Held**
Web: www.ernstconcrete.com
SIC: 3273 Ready-mixed concrete
PA: Ernst Enterprises, Inc.
993 Falls Creek Dr
Vandalia OH 45377
937 233-5555

(G-13213)
EVENFLO COMPANY INC
1801 W Main St (45373-2303)
PHONE....................................937 773-3971
Rick Frank, *Brnch Mgr*
EMP: 100
Web: www.evenflo.com
SIC: 2519 3944 Fiberglass and plastic furniture; Child restraint seats, automotive
HQ: Evenflo Company, Inc.
3131 Newmark Dr
Miamisburg OH 45342

(G-13214)
F&P AMERICA MFG INC (HQ)
2101 Corporate Dr (45373-1076)
PHONE....................................937 339-0212
Masafumi Yamano, *Pr*
Akihide Fukuda, *
Hirp Enomoto, *

▲ **EMP:** 27 **EST:** 1993
SQ FT: 400,000
SALES (est): 163.74MM **Privately Held**
Web: www.fandp.com
SIC: 3714 Motor vehicle steering systems and parts
PA: F-Tech Inc.
19, Shobuchoshowanuma
Kuki STM 346-0

(G-13215)
FREDS SIGN SERVICE INC
3055 S County Road 25a (45373-9341)
PHONE....................................937 335-1901
Bruce Haas, *Pr*
Kathy Hutson, *Sec*
Eloise Haas, *Treas*
EMP: 8 **EST:** 1960
SQ FT: 4,000
SALES (est): 174.63K **Privately Held**
SIC: 7389 3993 Sign painting and lettering shop; Signs, not made in custom sign painting shops

(G-13216)
FREUDENBERG-NOK GENERAL PARTNR
Also Called: Freudenberg-Nok Sealing Tech
1275 Archer Dr (45373-3841)
P.O. Box 844 (51301-0844)
PHONE....................................937 335-3306
Larry Heimilghton, *Mgr*
EMP: 30
SALES (corp-wide): 12.96B **Privately Held**
Web: www.freudenberg.com
SIC: 2821 Plastics materials and resins
HQ: Freudenberg-Nok General Partnership
47774 W Anchor Ct
Plymouth MI 48170
734 451-0020

(G-13217)
FTECH R&D NORTH AMERICA INC (HQ)
1191 Horizon West Ct (45373-7560)
PHONE....................................937 339-2777
Bing Liu, *COO*
Eldon H Kakuda, *
▲ **EMP:** 25 **EST:** 2003
SQ FT: 50,000
SALES (est): 18.86MM **Privately Held**
Web: www.fandp.com
SIC: 8731 3714 Commercial physical research; Motor vehicle parts and accessories
PA: F-Tech Inc.
19, Shobuchoshowanuma
Kuki STM 346-0

(G-13218)
GOKOH CORPORATION (HQ)
1280 Archer Dr (45373-3842)
PHONE....................................937 339-4977
Shuji Hioki, *Pr*
Parker Bailey, *VP*
T Hioki Stkldr, *Prin*
M Fujita Stkldr, *Prin*
Heiju Hashimoto, *Prin*
▲ **EMP:** 13 **EST:** 1987
SQ FT: 16,000
SALES (est): 9.47MM **Privately Held**
Web: www.gokoh.us
SIC: 5085 5084 3544 3559 Industrial supplies; Industrial machinery and equipment; Special dies and tools; Foundry machinery and equipment
PA: Goko Sangyo Co., Ltd.
1-2-2, Higashiryoke
Kawaguchi STM 332-0

(G-13219)
GOODRICH CORPORATION
Also Called: Collins Aerospace
101 Waco St (45373-3872)
PHONE..............................937 339-3811
EMP: 750
SALES (corp-wide): 80.74B **Publicly Held**
Web: www.collinsaerospace.com
SIC: 3721 3714 3728 Aircraft; Wheels, motor
  vehicle; Aircraft landing assemblies and
  brakes
HQ: Goodrich Corporation
   2730 W Tyvola Rd
   Charlotte NC 28217
   704 423-7000

(G-13220)
GOODRICH CORPORATION
101 Walton St (45373)
P.O. Box 304 (45373-0304)
PHONE..............................216 429-4378
EMP: 15
SALES (corp-wide): 80.74B **Publicly Held**
Web: www.collinsaerospace.com
SIC: 3728 Aircraft parts and equipment, nec
HQ: Goodrich Corporation
   2730 W Tyvola Rd
   Charlotte NC 28217
   704 423-7000

(G-13221)
HAWKINS MACHINE SHOP INC
1112 Race Dr (45373-4228)
PHONE..............................937 335-8737
Dorothy Haulmanmiller, *Pr*
Jeff Haulman, *Sec*
EMP: 8 **EST:** 1988
SQ FT: 11,000
SALES (est): 469.95K **Privately Held**
SIC: 3599 Machine shop, jobbing and repair

(G-13222)
HOBART BROTHERS LLC (HQ)
Also Called: ITW Hobart Brothers
101 Trade Sq E (45373-2488)
PHONE..............................937 332-5439
Sundaram Nagarajan, *VP*
Grant Harvey, *General Vice President*
S E Hobart, *
◆ **EMP:** 600 **EST:** 1917
SQ FT: 1,000,000
SALES (est): 94.3MM
SALES (corp-wide): 16.11B **Publicly Held**
Web: www.hobartbrothers.com
SIC: 3548 3537 Welding apparatus;
  Industrial trucks and tractors
PA: Illinois Tool Works Inc.
   155 Harlem Ave
   Glenview IL 60025
   847 724-7500

(G-13223)
HOBART BROTHERS LLC
1260 Brukner Dr (45373-3843)
PHONE..............................937 332-5023
EMP: 114
SALES (corp-wide): 16.11B **Publicly Held**
Web: www.hobartbrothers.com
SIC: 3548 Welding apparatus
HQ: Hobart Brothers Llc
   101 Trade Sq E
   Troy OH 45373
   937 332-5439

(G-13224)
HOBART CABINET COMPANY
1100 Wayne St Ste 1 (45373-3074)
PHONE..............................937 335-4666
Martin E Hobart, *Pr*
EMP: 9 **EST:** 1907
SALES (est): 542.48K **Privately Held**

Web: www.hobartcabinet.com
SIC: 2522 Office bookcases, wallcases and
  partitions, except wood

(G-13225)
HOBART LLC
Also Called: Engineering Dept
401 S Market St (45373-3330)
PHONE..............................937 332-3000
Gary Banks, *Mgr*
EMP: 31
SALES (corp-wide): 16.11B **Publicly Held**
Web: www.hobartcorp.com
SIC: 3589 3556 3596 3585 Dishwashing
  machines, commercial; Food products
  machinery; Weighing machines and
  apparatus; Refrigeration equipment,
  complete
HQ: Hobart Llc
   701 S Ridge Ave
   Troy OH 45373

(G-13226)
HOBART LLC (DH)
Also Called: Hobart
701 S Ridge Ave (45373-5501)
P.O. Box 3001 (45374)
PHONE..............................937 332-3000
▲ **EMP:** 100 **EST:** 1897
SALES (est): 466.47MM
SALES (corp-wide): 16.11B **Publicly Held**
Web: www.hobartcorp.com
SIC: 3589 3556 3596 3585 Dishwashing
  machines, commercial; Food products
  machinery; Weighing machines and
  apparatus; Refrigeration equipment,
  complete
HQ: Itw Food Equipment Group Llc
   701 S Ridge Ave
   Troy OH 45374

(G-13227)
ILLINOIS TOOL WORKS INC
Also Called: ITW Hobart
750 Lincoln Ave (45373-3137)
PHONE..............................937 332-2839
Bob Freef, *Genl Mgr*
EMP: 25
SALES (corp-wide): 16.11B **Publicly Held**
Web: www.itw.com
SIC: 3089 Injection molded finished plastics
  products, nec
PA: Illinois Tool Works Inc.
   155 Harlem Ave
   Glenview IL 60025
   847 724-7500

(G-13228)
**INDEPENDENT MACHINE & WLDG
INC**
710 Boone Dr (45373-9343)
PHONE..............................937 339-7330
Glenn Reed, *Pr*
Dale F Deaton, *VP*
Carol Owens, *Treas*
EMP: 6 **EST:** 2000
SALES (est): 453.62K **Privately Held**
SIC: 3599 7692 Machine shop, jobbing and
  repair; Welding repair

(G-13229)
INTEGRITY INDUSTRIAL EQUIPMENT
18 E Water St (45373-3435)
P.O. Box 1040 (45373-8040)
PHONE..............................937 335-5658
Jose Lopez, *Prin*
EMP: 7 **EST:** 2014
SALES (est): 482.15K **Privately Held**
SIC: 3599 Industrial machinery, nec

(G-13230)
ISHMAEL PRECISION TOOL CORP
Also Called: Iptc
55 Industry Ct (45373-2368)
PHONE..............................937 335-8070
Larry R Ishmael, *Pr*
Larry Ishmael, *Pr*
Robert Ishmael, *VP*
Isaiah Wilmoth, *Prin*
Jackie Mathes, *Prin*
▲ **EMP:** 20 **EST:** 1978
SQ FT: 32,000
SALES (est): 2.33MM **Privately Held**
Web: www.ishmaelcorp.com
SIC: 3544 Special dies and tools

(G-13231)
**ITW FOOD EQUIPMENT GROUP LLC
(HQ)**
Also Called: Hobart
701 S Ridge Ave (45374-0001)
PHONE..............................937 332-2396
Harold B Smith, *CEO*
Tom Szafranski, *
Chris O Herlihy, *
Axel Beck, *
◆ **EMP:** 1100 **EST:** 2002
SALES (est): 1.58B
SALES (corp-wide): 16.11B **Publicly Held**
Web: www.itwfoodequipment.com
SIC: 5046 3556 Restaurant equipment and
  supplies, nec; Food products machinery
PA: Illinois Tool Works Inc.
   155 Harlem Ave
   Glenview IL 60025
   847 724-7500

(G-13232)
JAYNA INC (PA)
15 Marybill Dr S (45373-1033)
PHONE..............................937 335-8922
Damaroo Shah, *Pr*
Mayank Shah, *
EMP: 47 **EST:** 1988
SQ FT: 40,000
SALES (est): 3.6MM
SALES (corp-wide): 3.6MM **Privately Held**
Web: www.jaynainc.com
SIC: 3599 Machine shop, jobbing and repair

(G-13233)
KERBER SHEETMETAL WORKS INC
Also Called: Ksm Metal Fabrications
104 Foss Way (45373-1430)
PHONE..............................937 339-6366
Kathleen Kerber, *Pr*
EMP: 18 **EST:** 1979
SQ FT: 27,000
SALES (est): 2.14MM **Privately Held**
Web: www.ksmmetalfabrication.com
SIC: 3444 Ducts, sheet metal

(G-13234)
KNAPKE CABINETS INC
2 E Main St (45373-3202)
PHONE..............................937 335-8383
Bernie Knapke, *Pr*
EMP: 35 **EST:** 2001
SALES (est): 210.22K **Privately Held**
Web: www.knapkecabinets.com
SIC: 2434 1521 Wood kitchen cabinets;
  General remodeling, single-family houses

(G-13235)
KSM METAL FABRICATION
104 Foss Way (45373-1430)
PHONE..............................937 339-6366
Kathy Kerber, *Pr*
EMP: 10 **EST:** 2014
SALES (est): 2.86MM **Privately Held**
Web: www.ksmmetalfabrication.com

SIC: 3499 Fabricated metal products, nec

(G-13236)
LEGACY STWR LLC
1040 S Dorset Rd (45373-4708)
PHONE..............................937 440-2505
Dennis J Miller, *CEO*
John V Handelsman, *
William Diederich, *
Michael Vanhaaren, *
Karen Benanzer, *
EMP: 90 **EST:** 2016
SQ FT: 1,250
SALES (est): 14.95MM **Privately Held**
Web: www.stlwtr.com
SIC: 3599 Machine and other job shop work

(G-13237)
LUKENS INC
1040 S Dorset Rd (45373-4708)
PHONE..............................937 440-2500
Bill Diederich, *Prin*
Bill Diederich, *CEO*
Michael Van Haaren, *
EMP: 90 **EST:** 1958
SQ FT: 70,000
SALES (est): 5.13MM **Privately Held**
SIC: 3544 Special dies and tools

(G-13238)
**MADER AUTOMOTIVE CENTER INC
(PA)**
Also Called: Bushong Auto Service
225 S Walnut St (45373-3532)
PHONE..............................937 339-2681
Dan Mader, *Pr*
EMP: 15 **EST:** 1966
SQ FT: 18,000
SALES (est): 247.62K
SALES (corp-wide): 247.62K **Privately
Held**
SIC: 5013 5531 3599 Automotive supplies
  and parts; Automotive parts; Machine shop,
  jobbing and repair

(G-13239)
MARIETTA MARTIN MATERIALS INC
Also Called: Troy Sand and Gravel
250 Dye Mill Rd (45373-4280)
PHONE..............................937 335-8313
Darrell Sparks, *Mgr*
EMP: 7
Web: www.martinmarietta.com
SIC: 1422 Crushed and broken limestone
PA: Martin Marietta Materials Inc
   4123 Parklake Ave
   Raleigh NC 27612

(G-13240)
MEDWAY TOOL CORP
2100 Corporate Dr (45373-1085)
PHONE..............................937 335-7717
Tom Drake, *Pr*
EMP: 8 **EST:** 1974
SQ FT: 15,000
SALES (est): 1.79MM **Privately Held**
SIC: 3599 3545 3544 3444 Machine shop,
  jobbing and repair; Machine tool
  accessories; Special dies, tools, jigs, and
  fixtures; Sheet metalwork

(G-13241)
MICROPOWER GROUP US INC
150 Marybill Dr S (45373-1053)
PHONE..............................937 606-2793
Torbjorn Gustafsson, *CEO*
EMP: 6 **EST:** 2021
SALES (est): 560.03K
SALES (corp-wide): 4.99MM **Privately
Held**

SIC: 3691 Storage batteries
PA: Micropower Group Ab
Gullhallavagen 20c
VAxjo 352 5

(G-13242)
MICROPOWER LLC
150 Marybill Dr S (45373-1053)
PHONE.....................937 606-2793
Torbjorn Gustafsson, *CEO*
EMP: 6 EST: 2021
SALES (est): 3.7MM
SALES (corp-wide): 4.99MM **Privately Held**
SIC: 3691 Storage batteries
PA: Micropower Group Ab
Gullhallavagen 20c
VAxjo 352 5

(G-13243)
NOVACEL INC
421 Union St (45373-4151)
PHONE.....................937 335-5611
Tim Shank, *Brnch Mgr*
EMP: 160
Web: www.novacelinc.com
SIC: 2671 Paper; coated and laminated packaging
HQ: Novacel, Inc.
21 3rd St
Palmer MA 01069
413 283-3468

(G-13244)
NOVACEL PRFMCE COATINGS INC
421 Union St (45373-4151)
PHONE.....................937 552-4932
David Bullard, *Pr*
◆ EMP: 100 EST: 2000
SALES (est): 4.26MM **Privately Held**
Web: www.novacel-solutions.com
SIC: 2672 Coated paper, except photographic, carbon, or abrasive
HQ: Novacel
27 Rue Du Docteur Emile Bataille
Deville-Les-Rouen NOR 76250
232827232

(G-13245)
OHIO NEWSPAPERS INC
Also Called: Dayton Daily News
131 S Market St (45373-3324)
PHONE.....................937 335-3997
Doudlas Franklin, *CEO*
EMP: 179
SALES (corp-wide): 961.55MM **Privately Held**
Web: www.cmglocalsolutions.com
SIC: 2711 Newspapers, publishing and printing
HQ: Ohio Newspapers, Inc.
1611 S Main St
Dayton OH 45409
937 225-2000

(G-13246)
PAINTED HILL INV GROUP INC
Also Called: Western Ohio Graphics
402 E Main St (45373-3413)
PHONE.....................937 339-1756
Anthony W Cockerham, *Pr*
EMP: 10 EST: 1977
SQ FT: 13,000
SALES (est): 474.18K **Privately Held**
SIC: 2752 2396 3993 2759 Offset printing; Screen printing on fabric articles; Signs and advertising specialties; Screen printing

(G-13247)
PEAK FOODS LLC
1903 W Main St (45373-1165)
PHONE.....................937 440-0707
Steve Vogel, *
Jeff White, *Branch*
EMP: 65 EST: 2000
SQ FT: 5,500
SALES (est): 20.66MM
SALES (corp-wide): 41.65MM **Privately Held**
Web: www.peakfoods.com
SIC: 2026 Whipped topping, except frozen or dry mix
PA: Oppenheimer Companies, Inc.
877 W Main St Ste 700
Boise ID 83702
208 342-7771

(G-13248)
R & D MACHINE INC
1204 S Crawford St (45373-4134)
PHONE.....................937 339-2545
Daniel Daffner, *Pr*
Pam Daffner, *Owner*
EMP: 15 EST: 1994
SALES (est): 956.4K **Privately Held**
Web: www.randdmachine.com
SIC: 3312 Tool and die steel

(G-13249)
RAYMATH COMPANY
Also Called: Raymath
2323 W State Route 55 (45373-9234)
PHONE.....................937 335-1860
Greg Lefevre, *Pr*
James M Ruef, *
William Moore, *
▲ EMP: 140 EST: 1982
SQ FT: 50,000
SALES (est): 22.36MM **Privately Held**
Web: www.raymath.com
SIC: 3544 3444 Special dies and tools; Sheet metalwork

(G-13250)
ROSS SPECIAL PRODUCTS INC
2500 W State Route 55 (45373-9511)
PHONE.....................937 335-8406
Dave Pollard, *Pr*
EMP: 17 EST: 1984
SQ FT: 13,000
SALES (est): 2.1MM **Privately Held**
SIC: 3089 3544 Injection molding of plastics; Forms (molds), for foundry and plastics working machinery

(G-13251)
RT INDUSTRIES INC (PA)
Also Called: CHAMPION INDUSTRIES DIV
110 Foss Way (45373-1430)
PHONE.....................937 335-5784
Ann Hinkle, *Superintnt*
Karen Mayer, *Superintnt*
EMP: 6 EST: 1974
SQ FT: 18,000
SALES (est): 3.32MM
SALES (corp-wide): 3.32MM **Privately Held**
Web: www.rtindustries.org
SIC: 3579 8331 7349 2789 Paper cutters, trimmers, and punches; Sheltered workshop ; Janitorial service, contract basis; Bookbinding and related work

(G-13252)
SC LIQUIDATION COMPANY LLC (DH)
Also Called: Spinnaker Coating
550 Summit Ave (45373-3047)
PHONE.....................937 332-6500

Louis Guzzetti Junior, *CEO*
George Fuehrer, *
Stuart Postle, *Sr VP*
Perry Schiller, *Sr VP*
Kevin Ahlfeld, *VP*
▲ EMP: 100 EST: 2002
SALES (est): 43.03MM **Privately Held**
Web: www.spinps.com
SIC: 2621 Paper mills
HQ: Mactac Americas, Llc
4560 Darrow Rd
Stow OH 44224
800 762-2822

(G-13253)
SEGNA INC
1316 Barnhart Rd Ste 1316 (45373-9510)
PHONE.....................937 335-6700
Junichi Yakahi, *Pr*
◆ EMP: 15 EST: 2001
SQ FT: 2,100
SALES (est): 2.08MM **Privately Held**
Web: segna.segglobal.com
SIC: 3559 Automotive maintenance equipment

(G-13254)
SEW-EURODRIVE INC
2001 W Main St (45373-1018)
PHONE.....................937 335-0036
Gene Hart, *Mgr*
EMP: 100
SQ FT: 32,400
SALES (corp-wide): 4.27B **Privately Held**
Web: www.seweurodrive.com
SIC: 3566 3714 3699 Gears, power transmission, except auto; Motor vehicle parts and accessories; Electrical equipment and supplies, nec
HQ: Sew-Eurodrive, Inc.
1295 Old Spartanburg Hwy
Lyman SC 29365
864 439-7537

(G-13255)
SK MOLD & TOOL INC
2120 Corporate Dr (45373-1085)
P.O. Box 495 (45373-0495)
PHONE.....................937 339-0299
Vince Hinde, *Brnch Mgr*
EMP: 20
SALES (corp-wide): 5.68MM **Privately Held**
Web: www.skmold.com
SIC: 3544 3599 Special dies and tools; Machine shop, jobbing and repair
PA: Sk Mold & Tool Inc.
955 N 3rd St
Tipp City OH 45371
937 339-0299

(G-13256)
SLIMLINE SURGICAL DEVICES LLC
Also Called: Canyon Run Engineering
1990 W Stanfield Rd (45373-2329)
PHONE.....................937 335-0496
Gary Ward, *Pr*
Amy Ward, *Prin*
Carly Witmer, *Prin*
EMP: 7 EST: 2015
SALES (est): 3.57MM **Privately Held**
Web: www.crengtech.com
SIC: 3599 Machine shop, jobbing and repair

(G-13257)
SNYDER CONCRETE PRODUCTS INC
Also Called: Snyder Brick & Block
3246 N County Road 25a (45373-9404)
PHONE.....................937 339-7577
Babs Martin, *Mgr*

EMP: 8
SALES (corp-wide): 24.02MM **Privately Held**
Web: www.snyderonline.com
SIC: 5032 3271 5211 5039 Brick, except refractory; Blocks, concrete or cinder: standard; Brick; Glass construction materials
PA: Snyder Concrete Products, Inc.
2301 W Dorothy Ln
Moraine OH 45439
937 885-5176

(G-13258)
SPINNKER PRSSURE SNSTIVE PDTS
550 Summit Ave (45373-3075)
PHONE.....................800 543-9452
EMP: 7 EST: 2021
SALES (est): 542.79K **Privately Held**
SIC: 2621 Paper mills

(G-13259)
STULL WOODWORKS INC
Also Called: Wood Working
155 Marybill Dr S (45373-1054)
PHONE.....................937 698-8181
Brian Stull, *Pr*
Sandy Stull, *
EMP: 45 EST: 1992
SALES (est): 4.31MM **Privately Held**
Web: www.stullwoodworks.com
SIC: 2431 Woodwork, interior and ornamental, nec

(G-13260)
VISION MANUFACTURING INC
513 Garfield Ave (45373-3113)
P.O. Box 267 (45373-0267)
PHONE.....................937 332-1801
Jerry Hicks, *Owner*
EMP: 6 EST: 1993
SALES (est): 1.86MM **Privately Held**
SIC: 3599 Machine shop, jobbing and repair

(G-13261)
YASKAWA AMERICA INC
1050 S Dorset Rd (45373-4708)
PHONE.....................937 440-2600
Craig Jenninings, *Brnch Mgr*
EMP: 130
Web: www.yaskawa.com
SIC: 3569 Robots, assembly line: industrial and commercial
HQ: Yaskawa America, Inc.
2121 S Norman Dr
Waukegan IL 60085
847 887-7000

Tuppers Plains
Meigs County

(G-13262)
REMRAM RECOVERY LLC (PA)
49705 East Park Dr (45783)
P.O. Box 189 (45783-0189)
PHONE.....................740 667-0092
Ray Maxson, *Managing Member*
EMP: 10 EST: 2005
SQ FT: 36,000
SALES (est): 1.39MM **Privately Held**
Web: www.remramrecovery.com
SIC: 3089 Panels, building: plastics, nec

(G-13263)
WECAN FABRICATORS LLC
49425 E Park Dr (45783-9000)
P.O. Box 159 (45783-0159)
PHONE.....................740 667-0731
Jeffrey Cox, *Managing Member*

EMP: 8 EST: 2002
SQ FT: 4,000
SALES (est): 893.08K Privately Held
SIC: 3441 Fabricated structural metal

Twinsburg
Summit County

(G-13264)
48 HR BOOKS INC
1909 Summit Commerce Park
(44087-2371)
PHONE..............................330 374-6917
James Fulton, *Pr*
▼ EMP: 20 EST: 2007
SALES (est): 2.44MM Privately Held
Web: www.48hrbooks.com
SIC: 2741 Miscellaneous publishing

(G-13265)
A E WILSON HOLDINGS INC
Also Called: Quest Service Labs
2307 E Aurora Rd (44087-1958)
PHONE..............................330 405-0316
Al Wilson, *Pr*
EMP: 8 EST: 2001
SALES (est): 206.75K Privately Held
Web: www.questservicelabs.com
SIC: 2759 Commercial printing, nec

(G-13266)
A SIGN ABOVE INC
8982 Dutton Dr (44087-1929)
PHONE..............................330 425-7832
William A Geschke, *Pr*
EMP: 12 EST: 1992
SQ FT: 12,000
SALES (est): 824.7K Privately Held
Web: www.a-sign-above.com
SIC: 3993 7319 Signs and advertising
specialties; Display advertising service

(G-13267)
ACE AMERICAN WIRE DIE CO
9041 Dutton Dr (44087-1930)
PHONE..............................330 425-7269
Linda Hohl, *Pr*
EMP: 10 EST: 1998
SQ FT: 10,000
SALES (est): 1.16MM Privately Held
SIC: 3544 Special dies and tools

(G-13268)
ACHILLES AEROSPACE PDTS INC
Also Called: Achilles Aerospace Products
2100 Enterprise Pkwy (44087-2212)
PHONE..............................330 425-8444
David L Hoyack, *Pr*
J Michael Corfias, *Contrlr*
EMP: 22 EST: 1989
SQ FT: 20,000
SALES (est): 5.03MM Privately Held
Web: www.achillesaerospace.com
SIC: 3728 Aircraft body and wing assemblies
and parts

(G-13269)
ADAPTALL AMERICA INC
9047 Dutton Dr (44087-1930)
PHONE..............................330 425-4114
C Lane Wood, *Pr*
EMP: 16 EST: 2002
SALES (est): 3.31MM Privately Held
Web: www.adaptall.com
SIC: 3494 Pipe fittings

(G-13270)
AIRGAS USA LLC
9155 Dutton Dr (44087-1956)
PHONE..............................440 232-6397
Todd Testa, *Brnch Mgr*
EMP: 6
SALES (corp-wide): 114.13MM Privately
Held
Web: www.airgas.com
SIC: 5169 5084 5085 2813 Industrial gases;
Welding machinery and equipment;
Welding supplies; Industrial gases
HQ: Airgas Usa, Llc
259 N Rdnor Chster Rd Ste
Radnor PA 19087
216 642-6600

(G-13271)
AJD HOLDING CO (PA)
2181 Enterprise Pkwy (44087-2211)
PHONE..............................330 405-4477
Frank Defino, *Pr*
Leonard Defino, *
EMP: 60 EST: 1994
SQ FT: 55,000
SALES (est): 40.17MM Privately Held
Web: www.ajdholding.com
SIC: 3469 3544 3315 3537 Stamping metal
for the trade; Special dies, tools, jigs, and
fixtures; Wire and fabricated wire products;
Tractors, used in plants, docks,terminals,
etc.: industrial

(G-13272)
ALLIED CORPORATION INC
8920 Canyon Falls Blvd Ste 120
(44087-1990)
PHONE..............................330 425-7861
Dan Mongomery, *Pr*
EMP: 16 EST: 1948
SQ FT: 500
SALES (est): 7.98MM
SALES (corp-wide): 34.95B Privately Held
Web: us.rs-online.com
SIC: 2951 5032 Asphalt paving mixtures and
blocks; Sand, construction
HQ: Shelly Company
80 Park Dr
Thornville OH 43076
740 246-6315

(G-13273)
ALLIED SEPARATION TECH INC
Also Called: Allied Supplied Company
2300 E Enterprise Pkwy (44087-2349)
PHONE..............................704 736-0420
Mike Williams, *Pr*
Lori Williams, *
EMP: 6 EST: 2002
SALES (est): 317.19K Privately Held
SIC: 3714 3564 Oil strainers, motor vehicle;
Air purification equipment

(G-13274)
ALLIED SEPARATION TECH INC (PA)
Also Called: Air Supply Co
2300 E Enterprise Pkwy (44087-2349)
PHONE..............................704 732-8034
Michael E Williams, *Pr*
Lorrie Williams, *VP*
▲ EMP: 33 EST: 2009
SALES (est): 708.32K
SALES (corp-wide): 708.32K Privately
Held
SIC: 3569 Filters

(G-13275)
AMERICAN AXLE & MFG INC
8001 Bavaria Rd (44087-2261)
PHONE..............................330 486-3200
EMP: 108

SALES (corp-wide): 6.12B Publicly Held
Web: www.aam.com
SIC: 3714 Motor vehicle parts and
accessories
HQ: American Axle & Manufacturing, Inc.
One Dauch Dr
Detroit MI 48211

(G-13276)
AUTOMATION SOFTWARE & ENGRG (PA)
9321 Ravenna Rd Ste A (44087-2461)
PHONE..............................330 405-2990
Kenneth Hutchison, *Pr*
EMP: 15 EST: 1990
SQ FT: 6,000
SALES (est): 2.56MM Privately Held
SIC: 7372 Prepackaged software

(G-13277)
BADLIME PROMO AND APPAREL LLC
2146 E Aurora Rd (44087-1924)
PHONE..............................330 425-7100
EMP: 10 EST: 2018
SALES (est): 52.94K Privately Held
Web: www.badlime.com
SIC: 2759 Screen printing

(G-13278)
BAUTEC N TECHNOFORM AMER INC
1755 Enterprise Pkwy Ste 300
(44087-2277)
PHONE..............................330 487-6600
Albert Stankus, *Genl Mgr*
▲ EMP: 30 EST: 2006
SALES (est): 9.47MM Privately Held
Web: www.technoform.com
SIC: 2431 Windows and window parts and
trim, wood

(G-13279)
BESSAMAIRE SALES INC
1869 E Aurora Rd Ste 700 (44087-2500)
PHONE..............................440 439-1200
William Sullivan, *Pr*
EMP: 23 EST: 1953
SQ FT: 50,000
SALES (est): 2.26MM Privately Held
Web: www.bessamaire.com
SIC: 3585 Refrigeration and heating
equipment

(G-13280)
BESSAMAIRE SALES INTL LLC
1869 E Aurora Rd (44087-1998)
PHONE..............................800 321-5992
EMP: 15
SALES (est): 463.03K Privately Held
SIC: 3433 Heating equipment, except electric

(G-13281)
BIRD CONTROL INTERNATIONAL
1393 Highland Rd (44087-2213)
PHONE..............................330 425-2377
Jack Polnick, *Dir*
Stanley Baker, *Pr*
Benjamin Baker, *VP*
EMP: 6 EST: 1982
SALES (est): 239.5K Privately Held
SIC: 2879 2899 Pesticides, agricultural or
household; Chemical preparations, nec

(G-13282)
BOCK COMPANY LLC
Also Called: Bock Lighting
2476 Edison Blvd (44087-2340)
PHONE..............................216 912-7050
▲ EMP: 6 EST: 2009
SALES (est): 3.67MM Privately Held

Web: www.bocklighting.com
SIC: 3646 Commercial lighting fixtures

(G-13283)
C C M WIRE INC
Also Called: Wrwp
1920 Case Pkwy S (44087-2358)
PHONE..............................330 425-3421
▲ EMP: 11 EST: 1988
SALES (est): 976.41K Privately Held
SIC: 3496 3679 3694 3678 Miscellaneous
fabricated wire products; Harness
assemblies, for electronic use: wire or cable
; Engine electrical equipment; Electronic
connectors

(G-13284)
CANADUS POWER SYSTEMS LLC
9347 Ravenna Rd Ste A (44087-2463)
PHONE..............................216 831-6600
EMP: 10 EST: 2000
SQ FT: 1,000
SALES (est): 929.69K Privately Held
Web: www.canadus.com
SIC: 3678 Electronic connectors

(G-13285)
CENTRAL COCA-COLA BTLG CO INC
Also Called: Coca-Cola
1882 Highland Rd (44087-2223)
PHONE..............................330 425-4401
Rick Bodzenski, *Mgr*
EMP: 225
SALES (corp-wide): 45.75B Publicly Held
Web: www.coca-cola.com
SIC: 2086 Bottled and canned soft drinks
HQ: Central Coca-Cola Bottling Company,
Inc.
555 Taxter Rd Ste 550
Elmsford NY 10523
914 789-1100

(G-13286)
CHURCHILL STEEL PLATE LTD
7851 Bavaria Rd (44087-2263)
PHONE..............................330 425-9000
Jim Stevenson, *Pr*
James M Fleming V Pes, *Treas*
Kirk Mooney, *
EMP: 48 EST: 2013
SQ FT: 120,000
SALES (est): 8.31MM Privately Held
Web: www.churchillsteelplate.com
SIC: 3312 Plate, steel

(G-13287)
CLEVELAND ELECTRIC LABS CO (PA)
Also Called: Cleveland Electric Labs
1776 Enterprise Pkwy (44087-2246)
PHONE..............................800 447-2207
Jack Allan Lieske, *Pr*
Val Jean Lieske, *
Rebecca Lieske, *
C M Lemmon, *
EMP: 42 EST: 1920
SQ FT: 30,000
SALES (est): 5.97MM
SALES (corp-wide): 5.97MM Privately
Held
Web: www.clevelandelectriclabs.com
SIC: 3823 7699 Thermocouples, industrial
process type; Professional instrument
repair services

(G-13288)
COMTEC INCORPORATED
1800 Enterprise Pkwy (44087-2269)
PHONE..............................330 425-8102
Kenneth Drummond, *Pr*
EMP: 12 EST: 1973

SQ FT: 10,200
SALES (est): 2.12MM **Privately Held**
Web: www.comtecinc.com
SIC: 3823 3625 8711 Computer interface equipment, for industrial process control; Relays and industrial controls; Engineering services

(G-13289)
CONTRACTORS STEEL COMPANY
8383 Boyle Pkwy (44087-2236)
PHONE..............................330 425-3050
. Mitch Kubasek, *Mgr*
EMP: 74
SQ FT: 58,000
SALES (corp-wide): 486.04MM **Privately Held**
Web: www.upgllc.com
SIC: 5051 3498 3312 Steel; Fabricated pipe and fittings; Blast furnaces and steel mills
HQ: Contractors Steel Company
48649 Schooner St
Van Buren Twp MI 48111
734 464-4000

(G-13290)
CURTISS-WRIGHT SURFC TECH LLC
1652 Highland Rd (44087-2219)
PHONE..............................330 425-1490
Lynn Bamford, *Brnch Mgr*
EMP: 14
SALES (corp-wide): 3.12B **Publicly Held**
Web: www.cwst.com
SIC: 3398 Metal heat treating
HQ: Curtiss-Wright Surface Technologies Llc
80 E Rte 4 Ste 310
Paramus NJ 07652
201 843-7800

(G-13291)
DAY-GLO COLOR CORP
1570 Highland Rd (44087-2217)
PHONE..............................216 391-7070
Joe Shaw, *Mgr*
EMP: 15
SQ FT: 33,500
SALES (corp-wide): 7.34B **Publicly Held**
Web: www.dayglo.com
SIC: 2816 Inorganic pigments
HQ: Day-Glo Color Corp.
4515 St Clair Ave
Cleveland OH 44103
216 391-7070

(G-13292)
DESCO EQUIPMENT CORP
1903 Case Pkwy (44087-2343)
PHONE..............................330 405-1581
Leo E Henry, *Pr*
Barbara Krane, *VP*
Gene A Gilbert, *Sec*
▲ **EMP:** 15 **EST:** 1985
SQ FT: 50,000
SALES (est): 3.69MM
SALES (corp-wide): 24.31MM **Privately Held**
Web: www.descomachine.com
SIC: 3555 Printing presses
PA: Apex Machine Company
3000 Ne 12th Ter
Oakland Park FL 33334
954 563-0209

(G-13293)
DESCO MACHINE COMPANY LLC
1903 Case Pkwy (44087-2343)
PHONE..............................330 405-5181
EMP: 7 **EST:** 2016
SALES (est): 2.88MM **Privately Held**
Web: www.descomachine.com

SIC: 3999 Manufacturing industries, nec

(G-13294)
DF SUPPLY INC
Also Called: Df Supply
8500 Hadden Rd (44087-2114)
PHONE..............................330 650-9226
John Ridley, *Pr*
George H Mitchell, *
John Ridley, *VP*
◆ **EMP:** 38 **EST:** 1982
SQ FT: 10,000
SALES (est): 11.02MM **Privately Held**
Web: www.dfsupplyinc.com
SIC: 5031 5211 3499 1731 Fencing, wood; Fencing; Barricades, metal; Access control systems specialization

(G-13295)
DIRECT DIGITAL GRAPHICS INC
1716 Enterprise Pkwy (44087-2204)
PHONE..............................330 405-3770
Mike Boswell, *Pr*
Kimberly Boswell, *Off Mgr*
EMP: 8 **EST:** 1996
SQ FT: 14,000
SALES (est): 778.66K **Privately Held**
SIC: 2752 Offset printing

(G-13296)
DIXON VALVE & COUPLING CO LLC
1900 Enterprise Pkwy (44087-2296)
PHONE..............................330 425-3000
Louis Young, *Mgr*
EMP: 10
SALES (corp-wide): 439.82MM **Privately Held**
Web: www.dixonvalve.com
SIC: 3492 5085 Fluid power valves and hose fittings; Hose, belting, and packing
HQ: Dixon Valve & Coupling Company, Llc
1 Dixon Sq
Chestertown MD 21620

(G-13297)
DRG HYDRAULICS INC
1900 Case Pkwy S (44087-2358)
PHONE..............................216 663-9747
Don I Stetner, *Pr*
▲ **EMP:** 35 **EST:** 1986
SALES (est): 2.26MM **Privately Held**
Web: www.drghydraulics.com
SIC: 3542 3559 Presses: hydraulic and pneumatic, mechanical and manual; Plastics working machinery

(G-13298)
ELECTRO-MAGWAVE INC
Also Called: E M Wave
2241 Pinnacle Pkwy (44087-5300)
PHONE..............................216 453-1160
Frank Kim Goryance, *Pr*
Anthony Zupancic, *VP Opers*
EMP: 7 **EST:** 2007
SALES (est): 2.36MM **Privately Held**
Web: www.emwaveinc.com
SIC: 3663 Antennas, transmitting and communications

(G-13299)
EPI OF CLEVELAND INC
Also Called: Engineered Products
2224 E Enterprise Pkwy (44087-2393)
PHONE..............................330 468-2872
Robert Knazek, *VP*
EMP: 8
SALES (corp-wide): 7.39MM **Privately Held**
Web: www.epimetal.com

SIC: 3441 5051 Fabricated structural metal; Metals service centers and offices
HQ: E.P.I. Of Cleveland, Inc.
2224 E Enterprise Pkwy
Twinsburg OH 44087
330 468-2872

(G-13300)
ESSILOR LABORATORIES AMER INC
Also Called: Bell Optical
9221 Ravenna Rd # 3 (44087-2472)
P.O. Box 620 (44087-0620)
PHONE..............................330 425-3003
EMP: 8
SALES (corp-wide): 1.42MM **Privately Held**
SIC: 3851 Eyeglasses, lenses and frames
HQ: Essilor Laboratories Of America, Inc.
13515 N Stemmons Fwy
Dallas TX 75234
972 241-4141

(G-13301)
FABRICATING SOLUTIONS INC
7920 Bavaria Rd (44087-2252)
PHONE..............................330 486-0998
Dewey Lockwood, *Pr*
EMP: 14 **EST:** 2003
SALES (est): 5.64MM **Privately Held**
Web: www.fab-solution.com
SIC: 3499 3444 Fire- or burglary-resistive products; Sheet metalwork

(G-13302)
FACIL NORTH AMERICA INC (HQ)
Also Called: Streetsboro Operations
2242 Pinnacle Pkwy Ste 100 (44087-5301)
PHONE..............................330 487-2500
Rene Achten, *CEO*
Daniel Michiels, *
◆ **EMP:** 210 **EST:** 1967
SQ FT: 150,000
SALES (est): 63.91MM
SALES (corp-wide): 10.07MM **Privately Held**
Web: www.facil.be
SIC: 5072 3452 5085 Nuts (hardware); Nuts, metal; Fasteners, industrial: nuts, bolts, screws, etc.
PA: Facil Corporate
Geleenlaan 20
Genk VLI 3600
89410450

(G-13303)
FERRUM INDUSTRIES INC (HQ)
1831 Highland Rd (44087-2222)
P.O. Box 360230 (44136-0004)
PHONE..............................440 519-1768
Steve Joseph, *Pr*
Don Moreno, *VP*
▲ **EMP:** 6 **EST:** 2001
SALES (est): 807.36K
SALES (corp-wide): 4.17MM **Privately Held**
Web: www.ferrum.net
SIC: 2899 Metal treating compounds
PA: Auburn Metal Processing, Llc
4550 Darrow Rd
Stow OH 44224
315 253-2565

(G-13304)
FONTAINE PIECIAK ENGRG INC
2300 E Enterprise Pkwy (44087-2349)
PHONE..............................413 592-2273
David Pieciak, *Pr*
Roger Fontaine, *VP*
EMP: 8 **EST:** 1942
SQ FT: 20,000
SALES (est): 990.82K **Privately Held**

SIC: 3677 Filtration devices, electronic

(G-13305)
FREEDOM USA INC
Also Called: Avadirect.com
2045 Midway Dr (44087-1933)
PHONE..............................216 503-6374
Alex Sonis, *CEO*
EMP: 35 **EST:** 2000
SQ FT: 8,000
SALES (est): 7.98MM **Privately Held**
Web: www.avadirect.com
SIC: 3572 7373 7379 3575 Computer storage devices; Systems engineering, computer related; Computer related maintenance services; Computer terminals

(G-13306)
FUCHS LUBRICANTS CO
Also Called: Fuchs Franklin Div
8036 Bavaria Rd (44087-2262)
PHONE..............................330 963-0400
Kipp Kofsky, *Brnch Mgr*
EMP: 12
SALES (corp-wide): 3.73B **Privately Held**
Web: www.fuchs.com
SIC: 4225 2992 2899 2851 General warehousing and storage; Lubricating oils and greases; Chemical preparations, nec; Paints and allied products
HQ: Fuchs Lubricants Co.
17050 Lathrop Ave
Harvey IL 60426
708 333-8900

(G-13307)
GANZCORP INVESTMENTS INC
Also Called: Mustang Dynamometer
2300 Pinnacle Pkwy (44087-2368)
PHONE..............................330 963-5400
Dean Ganzhorn, *Prin*
Dean K Ganzhorn, *
Donald W Ganzhorn Junior, *Ex VP*
◆ **EMP:** 35 **EST:** 1986
SQ FT: 82,000
SALES (est): 9.7MM **Privately Held**
Web: www.mustangdyne.com
SIC: 3559 Automotive related machinery

(G-13308)
GE VERNOVA INTERNATIONAL LLC
Also Called: GE
8941 Dutton Dr (44087-1939)
PHONE..............................330 963-2066
Jeffrey Pack, *Mgr*
EMP: 7
SALES (corp-wide): 34.94B **Publicly Held**
Web: www.ge.com
SIC: 5084 3561 Compressors, except air conditioning; Pumps, oil well and field
HQ: Ge Vernova International Llc
58 Charles St
Cambridge MA 02141
617 443-3000

(G-13309)
GED HOLDINGS INC
9280 Dutton Dr (44087-1967)
PHONE..............................330 963-5401
William Weaver, *Pr*
EMP: 8 **EST:** 2000
SALES (est): 1.32MM **Privately Held**
Web: www.gedusa.com
SIC: 3559 3549 5084 Glass making machinery: blowing, molding, forming, etc.; Cutting and slitting machinery; Industrial machinery and equipment

▲ = Import ▼ = Export
◆ = Import/Export

(G-13310)
GENERAL DIE CASTERS INC (HQ)
2150 Highland Rd (44087-2229)
PHONE..............................330 678-2528
Brian Lennon, *CEO*
Tim Foley, *
▲ EMP: 40 EST: 1957
SQ FT: 31,000
SALES (est): 22.95MM
SALES (corp-wide): 22.95MM **Privately Held**
Web: www.generaldie.com
SIC: 3364 3363 3544 3369 Zinc and zinc-base alloy die-castings; Aluminum die-castings; Special dies, tools, jigs, and fixtures; Nonferrous foundries, nec
PA: Wolny Enterprises Inc.
12400 S Lombard Ln
Alsip IL 60803
708 388-4914

(G-13311)
GENERAL ELECTRIC COMPANY
Also Called: GE
8499 Darrow Rd (44087-2309)
PHONE..............................330 425-3755
J E Breen, *Prin*
EMP: 6
SALES (corp-wide): 38.7B **Publicly Held**
Web: geaerospace.com
SIC: 1311 Crude petroleum and natural gas
PA: General Electric Company
1 Aviation Way
Cincinnati OH 45215
617 443-3000

(G-13312)
GREAT LAKES FASTENERS INC (PA)
Also Called: Great Lakes Fasteners & Sup Co
2204 E Enterprise Pkwy (44087-2356)
PHONE..............................330 425-4488
Kevin Weidinger, *Pr*
Kevin Weidinger, *Pr*
Tim Umberger, *VP*
▲ EMP: 21 EST: 2010
SALES (est): 9.3MM
SALES (corp-wide): 9.3MM **Privately Held**
Web: www.glfus.com
SIC: 5085 3452 Fasteners, industrial: nuts, bolts, screws, etc.; Bolts, nuts, rivets, and washers

(G-13313)
H B CHEMICAL CORPORATION (DH)
1665 Enterprise Pkwy (44087-2243)
PHONE..............................330 920-8023
▲ EMP: 8 EST: 1986
SALES (est): 8.93MM **Privately Held**
Web: www.hbchemical.com
SIC: 2899 Chemical preparations, nec
HQ: Ravago Chemical Distribution, Inc.
1900 Smmit Twr Blvd Ste 9
Orlando FL 32810
630 665-3085

(G-13314)
HANA TECHNOLOGIES INC
2061 Case Pkwy S (44087-2361)
PHONE..............................330 405-4600
John Erdmann, *Pr*
David Tsing, *
Edward M Stiles Iii, *VP*
D Scott Worthington, *
Paul R Brown Junior, *VP*
▲ EMP: 60 EST: 1999
SQ FT: 24,000
SALES (est): 15.43MM **Privately Held**
Web: www.hana.family
SIC: 3825 Instruments to measure electricity
PA: Hana Microelectronics Group
65/98 Soi Vibhavadi-Rangsit 64 Yaek 2

Lak Si 10210

(G-13315)
HC COMPANIES INC (HQ)
Also Called: Pro Cal
2450 Edison Blvd Ste 3 (44087-4335)
P.O. Box 738 (44062-0738)
PHONE..............................440 632-3333
Chris Koscho, *Pr*
John Landefeld, *
▲ EMP: 40 EST: 2015
SQ FT: 11,000
SALES (est): 159.67MM **Privately Held**
Web: www.hc-companies.com
SIC: 3089 5261 Planters, plastics; Lawn and garden supplies
PA: Platinum Equity, Llc
360 N Crescent Dr Bldg S
Beverly Hills CA 90210

(G-13316)
HGI HOLDINGS INC
Also Called: Edgepark Medical Supplies
1810 Summit Commerce Park (44087-2300)
PHONE..............................330 963-6996
◆ EMP: 950
SIC: 3841 Hypodermic needles and syringes

(G-13317)
HYDROMOTIVE ENGINEERING CO
9261 Ravenna Rd Bldg B1 (44087-2470)
PHONE..............................330 425-4266
Tom Bucknell, *Owner*
EMP: 6 EST: 1979
SQ FT: 8,000
SALES (est): 895.68K **Privately Held**
Web: www.hydromotive.com
SIC: 3429 5088 5551 Marine hardware; Marine supplies; Marine supplies and equipment

(G-13318)
IBYCORP
Also Called: Ibycorp Tool & Die
8968 Dutton Dr (44087-1929)
PHONE..............................330 425-8226
Steven Hamori, *Pr*
Violet Hamori, *Sec*
EMP: 6 EST: 1975
SQ FT: 10,000
SALES (est): 440.26K **Privately Held**
SIC: 3544 Special dies and tools

(G-13319)
ICM DISTRIBUTING COMPANY INC
Also Called: Inventory Controlled Mdsg
1755 Enterprise Pkwy Ste 200 (44087-2277)
PHONE..............................234 212-3030
Harry Singer, *Pr*
Phillip B Singer, *
▼ EMP: 35 EST: 2006
SQ FT: 80,000
SALES (est): 21.99MM
SALES (corp-wide): 22.92MM **Privately Held**
Web: www.icmint.com
SIC: 5049 5092 5199 5122 School supplies; Toys, nec; General merchandise, non-durable; Hair preparations
PA: Sandusco, Inc.
1755 Entp Pkwy Ste 200
Twinsburg OH 44087
440 357-5964

(G-13320)
INDUSTRIAL MOLD INC
Also Called: Industrial Prfctn Mold & Mch
2057 E Aurora Rd (44087-1938)
PHONE..............................330 425-7374

David Kuhary, *Pr*
EMP: 24 EST: 1988
SQ FT: 8,600
SALES (est): 2.46MM **Privately Held**
Web: www.industrialmold.com
SIC: 3544 5085 3354 Forms (molds), for foundry and plastics working machinery; Industrial supplies; Aluminum extruded products

(G-13321)
JH INDUSTRIES INC
Also Called: Copperloy
1981 E Aurora Rd (44087-1919)
PHONE..............................330 963-4105
John J Hallack, *Pr*
Jacqueline Hallack, *
Dale Doherty, *
EMP: 30 EST: 1952
SQ FT: 70,000
SALES (est): 5.77MM **Privately Held**
Web: www.copperloy.com
SIC: 3599 3448 3537 3444 Machine shop, jobbing and repair; Ramps, prefabricated metal; Industrial trucks and tractors; Sheet metalwork

(G-13322)
KELTEC INC (PA)
Also Called: Keltec-Technolab
2300 E Enterprise Pkwy (44087-2349)
PHONE..............................330 425-3100
Edward Kaiser, *Pr*
Dolores Kaiser, *
◆ EMP: 74 EST: 1982
SQ FT: 100,000
SALES (est): 15.26MM
SALES (corp-wide): 15.26MM **Privately Held**
Web: www.keltecinc.com
SIC: 3569 Separators for steam, gas, vapor, or air (machinery)

(G-13323)
KING FORGE AND MACHINE COMPANY
Also Called: King Force & Machine
8250 Boyle Pkwy (44087-2234)
PHONE..............................330 963-0600
Raymond W King Junior, *Pr*
EMP: 10 EST: 1992
SQ FT: 10,000
SALES (est): 235.23K **Privately Held**
SIC: 3462 Flange, valve, and pipe fitting forgings, ferrous

(G-13324)
KING-INDIANA FORGE INC
8250 Boyle Pkwy (44087-2234)
PHONE..............................330 425-4250
Raymond W King Junior, *Pr*
EMP: 8 EST: 1993
SQ FT: 250,000
SALES (est): 1.57MM
SALES (corp-wide): 24.28MM **Privately Held**
SIC: 3462 Iron and steel forgings
PA: Ssp Fittings Corp.
8250 Boyle Pkwy
Twinsburg OH 44087
330 425-4250

(G-13325)
KIWI PROMOTIONAL AP & PRTG CO
Also Called: Inc., K.I.W.I.
2170 E Aurora Rd (44087-1924)
PHONE..............................330 487-5115
Mark Candle, *Pr*
Paul Steels, *
EMP: 37 EST: 1987
SQ FT: 28,000

SALES (est): 2.34MM **Privately Held**
Web: www.kiwipromotional.com
SIC: 2396 2395 Screen printing on fabric articles; Embroidery products, except Schiffli machine

(G-13326)
KRISS KREATIONS
Also Called: Edible Arrangement
9224 Darrow Rd (44087-1897)
PHONE..............................330 405-6102
Kristine Brownfield, *Owner*
EMP: 6 EST: 2003
SALES (est): 517.96K **Privately Held**
Web: www.ediblearrangements.com
SIC: 3523 5999 Shakers, tree: nuts, fruits, etc.; Alarm and safety equipment stores

(G-13327)
L J STAR INCORPORATED
2396 Edison Blvd (44087-2376)
P.O. Box 1116 (44087-9116)
PHONE..............................330 405-3040
David Star, *Pr*
Leonard J Star, *Ch*
Joel Feldman, *COO*
▲ EMP: 20 EST: 1991
SQ FT: 10,000
SALES (est): 5.58MM **Privately Held**
Web: www.ljstar.com
SIC: 3823 Flow instruments, industrial process type

(G-13328)
LEGACY SUPPLIES INC
8252 Darrow Rd Ste E (44087-2392)
P.O. Box 1173 (44087-9173)
PHONE..............................330 405-4565
Mike Corcelli, *Pr*
Frank Corcelli, *VP*
EMP: 10 EST: 1998
SALES (est): 911.96K **Privately Held**
SIC: 3694 5013 Distributors, motor vehicle engine; Motor vehicle supplies and new parts

(G-13329)
LEIDEN CABINET CO
1842 Enterprise Pkwy (44087-2289)
PHONE..............................330 425-8555
EMP: 6 EST: 2017
SALES (est): 53.79K **Privately Held**
Web: www.leidencompany.com
SIC: 2434 Wood kitchen cabinets

(G-13330)
LEIDEN CABINET COMPANY LLC (PA)
Also Called: Leiden Company
2385 Edison Blvd (44087-2376)
PHONE..............................330 425-8555
Melissa Hale, *Pr*
Michael Hopp, *
Michael Schmidt, *Head OF Accounting*
EMP: 83 EST: 1940
SQ FT: 210,000
SALES (est): 8.38MM
SALES (corp-wide): 8.38MM **Privately Held**
Web: www.leidencompany.com
SIC: 2541 Store fixtures, wood

(G-13331)
LEXINGTON RUBBER GROUP INC (PA)
Also Called: Qsr
1700 Highland Rd (44087-2221)
P.O. Box 1030 (44087-9030)
PHONE..............................330 425-8472
Randy Ross, *CEO*

Dennis Welhouse, *
▲ EMP: 29 EST: 1988
SQ FT: 110,000
SALES (est): 67.09MM Privately Held
SIC: 3069 Hard rubber and molded rubber
products

(G-13332)
LINDE GAS USA LLC
2045 E Aurora Rd (44087-2280)
PHONE...........................330 425-3989
Jim Lawrence, Prin
EMP: 9 EST: 2006
SALES (est): 987.96K Privately Held
SIC: 2813 Industrial gases

(G-13333)
LINEAR ASICS INC
2061 Case Pkwy S (44087-2361)
PHONE...........................330 474-3920
Mike Ward, CEO
EMP: 8 EST: 2016
SQ FT: 2,000
SALES (est): 4.7MM Privately Held
Web: www.linearasics.com
SIC: 3674 Semiconductors and related
devices

(G-13334)
MARSAM METALFAB INC
1870 Enterprise Pkwy (44087-2206)
PHONE...........................330 405-1520
Mark Brownfield, Pr
EMP: 25 EST: 1990
SQ FT: 30,000
SALES (est): 7.04MM Privately Held
Web: www.marsamfab.com
SIC: 1799 3441 7692 3444 Welding on site;
Fabricated structural metal; Welding repair;
Sheet metalwork

(G-13335)
MATHESON TRI-GAS INC
Also Called: Matheson Gas Products
1650 Enterprise Pkwy (44087-2202)
PHONE...........................330 425-4407
Les Gibson, Mgr
EMP: 29
SQ FT: 7,226
Web: www.mathesongas.com
SIC: 2813 5084 Industrial gases; Welding
machinery and equipment
HQ: Matheson Tri-Gas, Inc.
3 Mountainview Rd Ste 3 # 3
Warren NJ 07059
908 991-9200

(G-13336)
MAVAL INDUSTRIES LLC (PA)
Also Called: Maval Manufacturing
1555 Enterprise Pkwy (44087-2239)
PHONE...........................330 405-1600
John Dougherty, Pr
Dale Lumby, *
◆ EMP: 137 EST: 1986
SQ FT: 88,000
SALES (est): 24.87MM
SALES (corp-wide): 24.87MM Privately
Held
Web: www.mavalgear.com
SIC: 3714 8711 Power steering equipment,
motor vehicle; Consulting engineer

(G-13337)
MCFLUSION INC
2112 Case Pkwy Ste 8 (44087-2378)
PHONE...........................800 341-8616
Ole Madsen, Pr
▲ EMP: 8 EST: 2010
SALES (est): 2.42MM Privately Held
Web: www.mcflusion.com

SIC: 3559 Pharmaceutical machinery

(G-13338)
MEDINA SUPPLY COMPANY
Also Called: Medina Supply Co
1516 Highland Rd (44087-2217)
PHONE...........................330 425-0752
Lowell Perry, Mgr
EMP: 68
SQ FT: 18,612
SALES (corp-wide): 34.95B Privately Held
Web: www.shellyco.com
SIC: 3273 Ready-mixed concrete
HQ: Medina Supply Company
230 E Smith Rd
Medina OH 44256
330 723-3681

(G-13339)
**METAL IMPROVEMENT COMPANY
LLC**
1652 Highland Rd (44087-2219)
PHONE...........................330 425-1490
Matt Heschel, Mgr
EMP: 28
SALES (corp-wide): 3.12B Publicly Held
Web: www.curtisswright.com
SIC: 3398 Shot peening (treating steel to
reduce fatigue)
HQ: Metal Improvement Company, Llc
80 Route 4 E Ste 310
Paramus NJ 07652
201 843-7800

(G-13340)
METALLIC RESOURCES INC
2368 E Enterprise Pkwy (44087-2349)
P.O. Box 368 (44087-0368)
PHONE...........................330 425-3155
Stan Rothschild, Pr
William Griffith, *
▲ EMP: 32 EST: 1979
SQ FT: 26,000
SALES (est): 11.21MM Privately Held
Web: www.metallicresources.com
SIC: 3356 3339 Solder: wire, bar, acid core,
and rosin core; Precious metals
PA: Metallic Solders De Mexico, S. De R.L.
De C.V.
Norte 7 No. 35-A
Matamoros TAM 87494

(G-13341)
**MILES RUBBER & PACKING
COMPANY (PA)**
9020 Dutton Dr (44087-1994)
PHONE...........................330 425-3888
James M Smith, Pr
Larry Lempke, *
Janet Schickler, *
K J Ertle, *
EMP: 25 EST: 1952
SQ FT: 27,800
SALES (est): 4.71MM
SALES (corp-wide): 4.71MM Privately
Held
Web: www.milesrubber.com
SIC: 3053 3069 Gaskets, all materials;
Sponge rubber and sponge rubber products

(G-13342)
MOLD-RITE PLASTICS LLC
2300 Highland Rd (44087-2232)
PHONE...........................330 405-7739
EMP: 147
SALES (corp-wide): 73.82MM Privately
Held
Web: www.mrpsolutions.com
SIC: 3089 Injection molding of plastics
PA: Mold-Rite Plastics, Llc
100 N Field Dr Ste 100

Lake Forest IL 60045
518 849-8431

(G-13343)
MOLD-RITE PLASTICS LLC
2222 Highland Rd (44087-2231)
PHONE...........................330 405-7739
EMP: 147
SALES (corp-wide): 73.82MM Privately
Held
Web: www.mrpsolutions.com
SIC: 3089 Closures, plastics
PA: Mold-Rite Plastics, Llc
100 N Field Dr Ste 100
Lake Forest IL 60045
518 849-8431

(G-13344)
**MORGAN ADVANCED CERAMICS
INC**
Also Called: Morgan Advanced Materials
2181 Pinnacle Pkwy (44087-2365)
PHONE...........................330 405-1033
EMP: 28
SALES (corp-wide): 1.39B Privately Held
Web:
www.morgantechnicalceramics.com
SIC: 2899 Chemical preparations, nec
HQ: Morgan Advanced Ceramics, Inc.
2425 Whipple Rd
Hayward CA 94544

(G-13345)
NATIONAL POWER COATING OHIO
2020 Case Pkwy (44087-2344)
PHONE...........................330 405-5587
William D Amato, Pr
EMP: 6 EST: 1972
SALES (est): 495.38K Privately Held
Web: www.nationalpowdercoating.com
SIC: 3479 Coating of metals and formed
products

(G-13346)
**OLIVER PRINTING & PACKG CO LLC
(HQ)**
Also Called: Oliver Inc.
1760 Enterprise Pkwy (44087-2204)
PHONE...........................330 425-7890
Mark Mcelhinny, Pr
Stephen Ernst, *
EMP: 60 EST: 1952
SQ FT: 21,000
SALES (est): 42.74MM
SALES (corp-wide): 196.73MM Privately
Held
Web: www.oliverinc.com
SIC: 2752 Offset printing
PA: Oliver Printing And Packaging, Inc.
10 Gilpin Ave
Hauppauge NY 11788
631 234-1400

(G-13347)
OLIVER STEEL PLATE CO
7851 Bavaria Rd (44087-2263)
PHONE...........................330 425-7000
▲ EMP: 65
SIC: 5051 3444 3443 3398 Metals service
centers and offices; Sheet metalwork;
Fabricated plate work (boiler shop); Metal
heat treating

(G-13348)
P3 INFRASTRUCTURE INC
2146 Entp Pkwy Ste C (44087)
PHONE...........................330 408-9504
EMP: 12 EST: 2017
SALES (est): 424.48K Privately Held
Web: www.p3-i.com

SIC: 2851 Paints, asphalt or bituminous

(G-13349)
PARAGON ROBOTICS LLC
2234 E Enterprise Pkwy (44087-2393)
PHONE...........................216 313-9299
EMP: 25 EST: 2006
SALES (est): 1.45MM Privately Held
Web: www.paragonrobotics.com
SIC: 3695 Computer software tape and
disks: blank, rigid, and floppy

(G-13350)
PARO SERVICES CO (PA)
1755 Enterprise Pkwy Ste 100
(44087-2277)
PHONE...........................330 467-1300
Daniel N Zelman, Pr
Edward J Kubek Junior, VP
Nick La Magna, VP
Brian Mccue, COO
▲ EMP: 10 EST: 1998
SQ FT: 60,000
SALES (est): 4.3MM
SALES (corp-wide): 4.3MM Privately Held
SIC: 7349 2842 Cleaning service, industrial
or commercial; Cleaning or polishing
preparations, nec

(G-13351)
PENN MACHINE COMPANY LLC
2182 E Aurora Rd (44087-1924)
PHONE...........................814 288-1547
EMP: 56
SQ FT: 27,000
SALES (corp-wide): 424.23B Publicly
Held
Web: www.pennmach.com
SIC: 3568 3532 3462 Power transmission
equipment, nec; Mining machinery; Iron
and steel forgings
HQ: Penn Machine Company Llc
106 Station St
Johnstown PA 15905

(G-13352)
PEPPERL + FUCHS INC (DH)
1600 Enterprise Pkwy (44087-2245)
PHONE...........................330 425-3555
Wolfgang Mueller, Pr
▲ EMP: 130 EST: 1983
SQ FT: 55,050
SALES (est): 47.61MM
SALES (corp-wide): 1.01B Privately Held
Web: pepperl-fuchs.com
SIC: 5065 3625 3822 3674 Electronic parts
and equipment, nec; Relays and industrial
controls; Environmental controls;
Semiconductors and related devices
HQ: Pepperl + Fuchs Enterprises, Inc.
1600 Enterprise Pkwy
Twinsburg OH 44087
330 425-3555

(G-13353)
PEPSI-COLA METRO BTLG CO INC
Also Called: Pepsi-Cola
1999 Enterprise Pkwy (44087-2253)
PHONE...........................330 425-8236
Charlie Powers, Mgr
EMP: 107
SALES (corp-wide): 91.47B Publicly Held
Web: www.pepsico.com
SIC: 2086 5149 Bottled and canned soft
drinks; Groceries and related products, nec
HQ: Pepsi-Cola Metropolitan Bottling
Company, Inc.
700 Anderson Hill Rd
Purchase NY 10577
914 767-6000

(G-13354)
PEPSI-COLA METRO BTLG CO INC
Also Called: Pepsico
1999 Enterprise Pkwy (44087-2253)
PHONE..............................330 963-5300
Charlie Powers, *Brnch Mgr*
EMP: 9
SALES (corp-wide): 91.47B **Publicly Held**
Web: www.pepsico.com
SIC: 2086 Carbonated soft drinks, bottled and canned
HQ: Pepsi-Cola Metropolitan Bottling Company, Inc.
700 Anderson Hill Rd
Purchase NY 10577
914 767-6000

(G-13355)
PERRY WELDING SERVICE INC
2075 Case Pkwy S (44087-2361)
PHONE..............................330 425-2211
Jerry Perry, *Pr*
Margo Perry, *VP*
EMP: 14 **EST:** 1974
SQ FT: 12,000
SALES (est): 2.67MM **Privately Held**
Web: www.perrywelding.com
SIC: 3599 3469 7692 3544 Custom machinery; Machine parts, stamped or pressed metal; Welding repair; Special dies, tools, jigs, and fixtures

(G-13356)
PHOENIX MTAL SLS FBRCATION LLC
Also Called: Manufacturing
2201 Pinnacle Pkwy Ste A (44087-2479)
P.O. Box 476 (44202-0476)
PHONE..............................330 562-0585
Scott Holman, *Pr*
Scott Holman, *Managing Member*
EMP: 10 **EST:** 2010
SALES (est): 1.87MM **Privately Held**
Web: www.pmsaf.com
SIC: 3441 Fabricated structural metal

(G-13357)
PLATING PERCEPTIONS INC
8815 Herrick Rd (44087-2417)
P.O. Box 81 (44087-0081)
PHONE..............................330 425-4180
Randall Bauer, *Pr*
James Konicek, *VP*
EMP: 9 **EST:** 1988
SQ FT: 8,000
SALES (est): 915.15K **Privately Held**
Web: www.platingperceptions.com
SIC: 3471 Plating of metals or formed products

(G-13358)
PRECISION GEAR LLC
1900 Midway Dr (44087-1957)
PHONE..............................330 487-0888
EMP: 76 **EST:** 1970
SALES (est): 17.71MM
SALES (corp-wide): 6.03B **Publicly Held**
SIC: 3566 Speed changers, drives, and gears
HQ: Rexnord Industries, Llc
111 W Michigan St
Milwaukee WI 53203
414 643-3000

(G-13359)
PREMIER SHOT COMPANY
1666 Enterprise Pkwy (44087-2202)
PHONE..............................330 405-0583
Bob Gillespie, *Pr*
▲ **EMP:** 6 **EST:** 1987
SQ FT: 10,000

SALES (est): 2.1MM **Privately Held**
Web: www.premiershot.com
SIC: 3482 Shot, steel (ammunition)

(G-13360)
PRODUCTION TL CO CLEVELAND INC
Also Called: Assembly Tool Specialists
9002 Dutton Dr (44087-1931)
PHONE..............................330 425-4466
Jackie Ahrens, *CEO*
Ronald T Carpenter, *Pr*
EMP: 18 **EST:** 1940
SQ FT: 3,800
SALES (est): 2.44MM **Privately Held**
Web: www.assytool.com
SIC: 3999 Barber and beauty shop equipment

(G-13361)
Q HOLDING COMPANY (HQ)
Also Called: Q Holding Mexico
1700 Highland Rd (44087-2221)
PHONE..............................440 903-1827
Mauricio Arellano, *CEO*
Roy Showman, *
▲ **EMP:** 385 **EST:** 1966
SQ FT: 41,000
SALES (est): 40.67MM
SALES (corp-wide): 5.01B **Privately Held**
Web: www.qco.net
SIC: 3061 Mechanical rubber goods
PA: 3i Group Plc
1 Knightsbridge
London SW1X
207 975-3131

(G-13362)
QUEST SERVICE LABS INC
2307 E Aurora Rd Unit B10 (44087-1958)
PHONE..............................330 405-0316
Al Wilson, *Prin*
EMP: 6 **EST:** 2009
SALES (est): 648.88K **Privately Held**
Web: www.questservicelabs.com
SIC: 2759 Commercial printing, nec

(G-13363)
R A HAMED INTERNATIONAL INC
Also Called: Scott Thomas Furniture
8400 Darrow Rd (44087-2375)
PHONE..............................330 247-0190
Rosemary Hamed, *Pr*
Scott Hamed, *VP*
◆ **EMP:** 7 **EST:** 1977
SQ FT: 19,000
SALES (est): 335.04K **Privately Held**
SIC: 2511 Wood household furniture

(G-13364)
RAVAGO CHEMICAL DIST INC
Also Called: H B Chemical
1665 Enterprise Pkwy (44087-2243)
PHONE..............................330 920-8023
James Duffy, *Pr*
EMP: 38
Web: www.hbchemical.com
SIC: 2899 Chemical preparations, nec
HQ: Ravago Chemical Distribution, Inc.
1900 Smmit Twr Blvd Ste 9
Orlando FL 32810
630 665-3085

(G-13365)
REUTER-STOKES LLC
8499 Darrow Rd Ste 1 (44087-2398)
PHONE..............................330 425-3755
Leo Zanderschur, *Pr*
◆ **EMP:** 260 **EST:** 1956
SQ FT: 110,000
SALES (est): 24.1MM

SALES (corp-wide): 27.83B **Publicly Held**
SIC: 3829 3826 3823 3812 Nuclear radiation and testing apparatus; Environmental testing equipment; Process control instruments; Search and navigation equipment
PA: Baker Hughes Company
575 N Dar Ashford Rd Ste
Houston TX 77079
713 439-8600

(G-13366)
RHEACO BUILDERS INC
1941 E Aurora Rd (44087-1919)
PHONE..............................330 425-3090
George Rheaco, *Pr*
EMP: 6 **EST:** 1989
SALES (est): 405.83K **Privately Held**
Web: www.rheacoinc.com
SIC: 2434 Wood kitchen cabinets

(G-13367)
RO-MAI INDUSTRIES INC
1605 Enterprise Pkwy (44087-2201)
P.O. Box 366 (44087-0366)
PHONE..............................330 425-9090
Robert Maier, *Pr*
Robert Maier, *Pr*
▲ **EMP:** 30 **EST:** 1984
SQ FT: 26,000
SALES (est): 200.37K **Privately Held**
Web: www.saundersengineering.com
SIC: 3089 Injection molding of plastics

(G-13368)
ROCKWELL AUTOMATION INC
8440 Darrow Rd (44087-2310)
P.O. Box 2167 (53201-2167)
PHONE..............................330 425-3211
Mark Todd, *Brnch Mgr*
EMP: 400
Web: www.rockwellautomation.com
SIC: 3625 Control equipment, electric
PA: Rockwell Automation, Inc.
1201 S 2nd St
Milwaukee WI 53204

(G-13369)
ROYAL CHEMICAL COMPANY LTD
1755 Enterprise Pkwy Ste 100 (44087-2277)
PHONE..............................330 467-1300
Eric Cubec, *CFO*
EMP: 15
SALES (corp-wide): 112.99MM **Privately Held**
Web: www.royalchemical.com
SIC: 2841 Soap: granulated, liquid, cake, flaked, or chip
HQ: Royal Chemical Company, Ltd.
8679 South Freeway Dr
Macedonia OH 44056
330 467-1300

(G-13370)
RTD ELECTRONICS INC
1632 Enterprise Pkwy Ste D (44087-2281)
P.O. Box 560192 (44056-0192)
PHONE..............................330 487-0716
Terry L Kellhofer, *Pr*
EMP: 7 **EST:** 2008
SQ FT: 4,000
SALES (est): 1.26MM **Privately Held**
Web: www.rtdelectronicsinc.com
SIC: 3679 Harness assemblies, for electronic use: wire or cable

(G-13371)
S A OMA-U INC
9329 Ravenna Rd Ste A (44087-2457)
PHONE..............................330 487-0602

Mauro Nava, *Pr*
Maria Pia Nava, *VP*
Clara Maria Nava, *Treas*
Antonio Villa, *Genl Mgr*
▲ **EMP:** 6 **EST:** 1996
SQ FT: 2,860
SALES (est): 498.61K **Privately Held**
Web: www.omabraid.it
SIC: 3549 3552 Wiredrawing and fabricating machinery and equipment, ex. die; Braiding machines, textile

(G-13372)
S&B METAL PDTS TWINSBURG LLC (PA)
2060 Case Pkwy (44087-2344)
PHONE..............................330 487-5790
Paul Balliette, *Ch*
Cindy Balliette, *
Stephen Campbell, *
▼ **EMP:** 49 **EST:** 1974
SQ FT: 25,000
SALES (est): 4.31MM
SALES (corp-wide): 4.31MM **Privately Held**
Web: www.sbmetal.com
SIC: 3444 Sheet metal specialties, not stamped

(G-13373)
S-TEK INC (PA)
2095 Midway Dr (44087-1933)
P.O. Box 27 (45371-0027)
PHONE..............................440 439-8232
David Lepore, *Pr*
Bob Smith, *Sec*
Fred B Holzworth, *Ex VP*
▲ **EMP:** 7 **EST:** 1988
SALES (est): 966.76K **Privately Held**
Web: www.stek-inc.com
SIC: 3679 3826 5065 Liquid crystal displays (LCD); Magnetic resonance imaging apparatus; Radio and television equipment and parts

(G-13374)
SCHAFFER GRINDING CO INC
8470 Chamberlin Rd (44087-2085)
PHONE..............................323 724-4476
Chet Schaffer, *Brnch Mgr*
EMP: 15
SQ FT: 10,000
SALES (corp-wide): 16.24MM **Privately Held**
Web: www.schaffergrinding.com
SIC: 3599 Machine shop, jobbing and repair
PA: Schaffer Grinding Co., Inc.
848 S Maple Ave
Montebello CA
323 724-4476

(G-13375)
SCIENTIFIC MOLDING CORP LTD
Also Called: SMC Ltd Product Design & Dev
2374 Edison Blvd (44087-2376)
PHONE..............................330 342-7800
EMP: 6
SALES (corp-wide): 444.76MM **Privately Held**
SIC: 3841 Surgical and medical instruments
PA: Scientific Molding Corporation, Ltd.
330 Smc Dr
Somerset WI 54025
715 247-3500

(G-13376)
SCRATCH-OFF SYSTEMS INC
2457 Edison Blvd (44087-2340)
PHONE..............................216 649-7800
Daniel Ogorek, *Pr*
Michael Hazelwood, *Prin*

Robert F Collett, *Prin*
▼ **EMP:** 20 **EST:** 1998
SALES (est): 7.43MM **Privately Held**
Web: www.scratchoff.com
SIC: 2679 5112 2759 2754　Labels, paper:
made from purchased material; Stationery
and office supplies; Labels and seals:
printing, nsk; Labels: gravure printing

(G-13377)
SEMTORQ INC
Also Called: Nucam
1780 Enterprise Pkwy (44087-2255)
P.O. Box 895 (44087-0895)
PHONE...............................330 487-0600
Greg Lanham, *Dir Opers*
Joseph Seme Junior, *Pr*
Christina Seme, *Sec*
▲ **EMP:** 12 **EST:** 1956
SQ FT: 40,000
SALES (est): 3.11MM **Privately Held**
Web: www.semtorq.com
SIC: 3549 7692 3594 3548　Assembly
machines, including robotic; Welding repair;
Fluid power pumps and motors; Welding
apparatus

(G-13378)
SHELLY MATERIALS INC
1749 Highland Rd (44087-2220)
PHONE...............................330 963-5180
EMP: 18
SALES (corp-wide): 34.95B **Privately Held**
Web: www.shellyco.com
SIC: 3273　Ready-mixed concrete
HQ: Shelly Materials, Inc.
80 Park Dr
Thornville OH 43076
740 246-6315

(G-13379)
SSP FITTINGS CORP (PA)
Also Called: SSP
8250 Boyle Pkwy (44087-2200)
PHONE...............................330 425-4250
Jeffrey E King, *CEO*
Betsy S King, *
David B King, *
O F Douglas, *
F B Douglas, *
▲ **EMP:** 100 **EST:** 1926
SQ FT: 165,000
SALES (est): 24.28MM
SALES (corp-wide): 24.28MM **Privately
Held**
Web: www.myssp.com
SIC: 3494 5085 3498 3492　Pipe fittings;
Industrial supplies; Fabricated pipe and
fittings; Fluid power valves and hose fittings

(G-13380)
STEWART ACQUISITION LLC (PA)
Also Called: Cima Plastics Group
2146 Enterprise Pkwy (44087-2272)
PHONE...............................330 963-0322
▲ **EMP:** 50 **EST:** 1975
SQ FT: 44,000
SALES (est): 2.6MM
SALES (corp-wide): 2.6MM **Privately Held**
Web: www.cimaplastics.com
SIC: 3089　Injection molding of plastics

(G-13381)
SUMMIT AVIONICS INC
2225 E Enterprise Pkwy # 1a (44087-2347)
PHONE...............................330 425-1440
Michael Tartamella, *Pr*
EMP: 9 **EST:** 2001
SQ FT: 14,000
SALES (est): 2.35MM **Privately Held**
Web: www.summitavionics.com

SIC: 3728　Aircraft parts and equipment, nec

(G-13382)
TAC MATERIALS INC
Also Called: Quality Synthetic Rubber Co
1700 Highland Rd (44087-2221)
P.O. Box 1030 (44087-9030)
PHONE...............................330 425-8472
▲ **EMP:** 250 **EST:** 1966
SALES (est): 22.06MM **Privately Held**
SIC: 3061　Mechanical rubber goods
HQ: Datwyler Schweiz Ag
Militarstrasse 7
Schattdorf UR 6467

(G-13383)
TCH INDUSTRIES INCORPORATED
2307 E Aurora Rd (44087-1952)
PHONE...............................330 487-5155
Ted Hoaglin, *Pr*
Bill Harr, *VP*
Kathy Hoaglin, *CFO*
Bryan Hoaglin, *VP*
▲ **EMP:** 18 **EST:** 1983
SQ FT: 20,000
SALES (est): 10.7MM **Privately Held**
Web: www.tchindustries.com
SIC: 5085 3494　Industrial tools; Pipe fittings

(G-13384)
**TECHNOFORM GL INSUL N AMER
INC**
1755 Enterprise Pkwy Ste 300
(44087-2277)
PHONE...............................330 487-6600
Albert Stankus, *Pr*
▲ **EMP:** 30 **EST:** 2003
SQ FT: 50,000
SALES (est): 9.7MM
SALES (corp-wide): 372.38MM **Privately
Held**
Web: www.technoform.com
SIC: 3429　Hardware, nec
HQ: Technoform Bautec Holding Gmbh
Max-Planck-Str. 6
Lohfelden HE 34253
561 958-3300

(G-13385)
TLG COCHRAN INC (PA)
2026 Summit Commerce Park
(44087-2374)
PHONE...............................440 914-1122
Steven Wake, *Pr*
Joel Hammer, *
Marinko Milos, *
▲ **EMP:** 25 **EST:** 1956
SALES (est): 12.14MM
SALES (corp-wide): 12.14MM **Privately
Held**
Web: www.gltproducts.com
SIC: 2821 5033 5131 5085　Polyvinylidene
chloride resins; Insulation materials; Tape,
textile; Industrial supplies

(G-13386)
TRI COUNTY CONCRETE INC (PA)
9423 Darrow Rd (44087-1415)
P.O. Box 665 (44087-0665)
PHONE...............................330 425-4464
Tony Farenacci, *Pr*
Fred Farenacci, *VP*
EMP: 19 **EST:** 1964
SQ FT: 62,000
SALES (est): 3.06MM
SALES (corp-wide): 3.06MM **Privately
Held**
Web: www.tricountyconcrete.com
SIC: 3273 3272 1442　Ready-mixed concrete
; Concrete products, nec; Construction
sand and gravel

(G-13387)
TRIONIX RESEARCH LAB INC
8037 Bavaria Rd (44087-2261)
PHONE...............................330 425-9055
Doctor Chun Bin Lim, *Pr*
EMP: 6 **EST:** 1986
SQ FT: 150,000
SALES (est): 890.51K **Privately Held**
SIC: 3844　Nuclear irradiation equipment

(G-13388)
TWIN VENTURES INC
2457 Edison Blvd (44087-2340)
PHONE...............................330 405-3838
Dave Potts, *Pr*
EMP: 15 **EST:** 1996
SALES (est): 951.46K **Privately Held**
SIC: 3452 5072　Bolts, nuts, rivets, and
washers; Hardware

(G-13389)
UNIVERSAL ELECTRONICS INC
1864 Enterprise Pkwy Ste B (44087-2268)
PHONE...............................330 487-1110
Brian Dean, *Mgr*
EMP: 6
Web: www.uei.com
SIC: 3651　Video triggers (remote control TV
devices)
PA: Universal Electronics Inc.
15147 N Scttsdale Rd Ste
Scottsdale AZ 85254

(G-13390)
UNIVERSAL RACK & EQP CO INC
Also Called: Universal Coatings Division
8511 Tower Dr (44087-2088)
PHONE...............................330 963-6776
Ken Palik, *Pr*
John Palik, *
▲ **EMP:** 8 **EST:** 1961
SQ FT: 40,000
SALES (est): 1.08MM **Privately Held**
SIC: 3479 3559 3443　Coating of metals with
plastic or resins; Electroplating machinery
and equipment; Fabricated plate work
(boiler shop)

(G-13391)
US FITTINGS INC
2182 E Aurora Rd (44087-1924)
P.O. Box 746 (44087-0746)
PHONE...............................234 212-9420
Richard K Raymond, *Pr*
EMP: 15 **EST:** 2013
SQ FT: 1,500
SALES (est): 2.42MM **Privately Held**
SIC: 3494　Pipe fittings

(G-13392)
VISIMAX TECHNOLOGIES INC
9177 Dutton Dr Ste 2 (44087-1981)
PHONE...............................330 405-8330
Dane Clark, *Pr*
Melanie Clark, *VP*
Christopher Murphy, *CEO*
EMP: 21 **EST:** 2000
SALES (est): 2.18MM **Privately Held**
Web: www.visimaxtechnologies.com
SIC: 3479　Coating of metals and formed
products

(G-13393)
**VISUAL MARKING SYSTEMS INC
(PA)**
2097 E Aurora Rd (44087-1979)
PHONE...............................330 425-7100
EMP: 97 **EST:** 1963
SALES (est): 18.52MM
SALES (corp-wide): 18.52MM **Privately
Held**

Web: www.vmsinc.com
SIC: 2752 3993 3953 2759　Decals,
lithographed; Signs and advertising
specialties; Marking devices; Commercial
printing, nec

(G-13394)
WEATHERCHEM CORPORATION
2222 Highland Rd (44087-2295)
P.O. Box 1150 (44087-9150)
PHONE...............................330 425-4206
◆ **EMP:** 90 **EST:** 1944
SALES (est): 9.96MM
SALES (corp-wide): 20.83MM **Privately
Held**
Web: www.mrpcap.com
SIC: 3089　Injection molding of plastics
PA: Weatherhead Industries, Inc.
25825 Science Park Dr # 255
Cleveland OH
330 425-4206

(G-13395)
WEDGE PRODUCTS INC
2181 Enterprise Pkwy (44087-2211)
PHONE...............................330 405-4477
Anthony J Defino, *Pr*
Frank Defino, *
Leonard Defino, *
Mary Defino, *
▲ **EMP:** 300 **EST:** 1925
SQ FT: 55,000
SALES (est): 7.27MM **Privately Held**
Web: www.wedgeproducts.com
SIC: 3469 3643　Stamping metal for the trade
; Current-carrying wiring services
PA: A.J.D. Holding Co.
2181 Enterprise Pkwy
Twinsburg OH 44087

(G-13396)
WITTUR USA INC
Also Called: Tyler Elevator Products
7852 Bavaria Rd (44087-2260)
PHONE...............................216 524-0100
Roberto Zappa, *Pr*
Stefano Girardi, *
Giorgio Scarabello, *
◆ **EMP:** 35 **EST:** 1959
SQ FT: 35,000
SALES (est): 13.42MM
SALES (corp-wide): 18MM **Privately Held**
Web: www.wittur.com
SIC: 3534　Elevators and equipment
HQ: Sematic Spa
Via Pastrengo 9
Seriate BG 24068

(G-13397)
WORLDCLASS PROCESSING CORP
1400 Enterprise Pkwy (44087-2242)
EMP: 39 **EST:** 2000
SQ FT: 250,000
SALES (est): 322.34K
SALES (corp-wide): 1.54B **Privately Held**
SIC: 3479　Etching and engraving
PA: Samuel, Son & Co., Limited
1900 Ironoak Way
Oakville ON L6H 0
905 279-5460

(G-13398)
**WORTHNGTON SMUEL COIL PROC
LLC (HQ)**
Also Called: Samuel Steel Pickling Company
1400 Enterprise Pkwy (44087-2242)
PHONE...............................330 963-3777
Rick Snyder, *Prin*
EMP: 45 **EST:** 1989
SQ FT: 115,000
SALES (est): 10.19MM

SALES (corp-wide): 3.43B **Publicly Held**
Web: www.samuelsteelpickling.com
SIC: **7389** 5051 3471 3398 Metal slitting and shearing; Metals service centers and offices ; Plating and polishing; Metal heat treating
PA: Worthington Steel, Inc.
100 Old Wilson Bridge Rd
Columbus OH 43085
614 840-3462

(G-13399)
WRWP LLC
Also Called: Western Reserve Wire Products
1920 Case Pkwy S (44087-2358)
PHONE..............................330 425-3421
Kevin Miller, *Managing Member*
EMP: 70 EST: 2014
SALES (est): 9.15MM **Privately Held**
Web: www.wrwp.com
SIC: **3496** Miscellaneous fabricated wire products

(G-13400)
ZINKAN ENTERPRISES INC (PA)
1919 Case Pkwy (44087-2343)
PHONE..............................330 487-1500
Thomas W Mccrystal, *Prin*
Mister Lou Koenig, *Prin*
◆ EMP: 10 EST: 1982
SQ FT: 15,000
SALES (est): 13.54MM
SALES (corp-wide): 13.54MM **Privately Held**
Web: www.getchemready.com
SIC: **2899** Chemical preparations, nec

Uhrichsville
Tuscarawas County

(G-13401)
ARMSTRONG CUSTOM MOULDING INC
6408 State Route 800 Se (44683-6302)
PHONE..............................740 922-5931
Todd Armstrong, *Pr*
James B Armstrong Junior, *Treas*
James B Armstrong Senior, *Sec*
EMP: 6 EST: 1996
SALES (est): 88.22K **Privately Held**
SIC: **2431** 2426 Moldings and baseboards, ornamental and trim; Hardwood dimension and flooring mills

(G-13402)
CAROLINA STAIR SUPPLY INC (PA)
316 Herrick St (44683-2123)
PHONE..............................740 922-3333
Clair Edwards, *Pr*
▲ EMP: 20 EST: 1979
SQ FT: 2,000
SALES (est): 4.5MM **Privately Held**
Web: www.carolinastair.com
SIC: **2431** Staircases and stairs, wood

(G-13403)
FABOHIO INC
521 E 7th St (44683-1613)
P.O. Box 434 (44683-0434)
PHONE..............................740 922-4233
Kurt Shelley, *CEO*
EMP: 20 EST: 1963
SQ FT: 22,500
SALES (est): 7.64MM
SALES (corp-wide): 23.2MM **Privately Held**
Web: www.fabohio.com
SIC: **3089** Injection molding of plastics
PA: Bowerston Shale Company (Inc)
515 Main St

Bowerston OH 44695
740 269-2921

(G-13404)
NOVELIS ALR RECYCLING OHIO LLC
Also Called: Imco Recycling
7335 Newport Rd Se (44683-6368)
PHONE..............................740 922-2373
Sean M Stack, *CEO*
Robert R Holian, *
▲ EMP: 164 EST: 1992
SALES (est): 8.21MM **Privately Held**
Web: www.novelis.com
SIC: **3341** 4953 Aluminum smelting and refining (secondary); Recycling, waste materials
HQ: Novelis Inc.
3550 Pchtree Rd Ne Ste 11
Atlanta GA 30326

(G-13405)
SEALCO INC
Also Called: Sealco
6566 Superior Rd Se (44683-7487)
P.O. Box 307 (44683-0307)
PHONE..............................740 922-4122
Elmer Mcclave, *Pr*
Todd Mcclave, *VP*
▲ EMP: 6 EST: 1974
SALES (est): 198.1K **Privately Held**
Web: www.superiorclay.com
SIC: **2499** 2448 Plugs, wood; Pallets, wood

(G-13406)
SEYEKCUB INC
615 W 4th St (44683-2007)
PHONE..............................330 324-1394
Robert L Drummond Junior, *Pr*
EMP: 8 EST: 2006
SQ FT: 10,000
SALES (est): 1.42MM **Privately Held**
Web: www.seyekcubaluminum.com
SIC: **3363** Aluminum die-castings

(G-13407)
STEBBINS ENGINEERING & MFG CO
Also Called: Semco Ceramics
4778 Belden Dr Se (44683-1078)
P.O. Box 90 (44683-0090)
PHONE..............................740 922-3012
Cliff Mcpherson, *Genl Mgr*
EMP: 8
SALES (corp-wide): 38.62MM **Privately Held**
Web: www.stebbinseng.com
SIC: **3253** 3255 3251 Ceramic wall and floor tile; Clay refractories; Brick and structural clay tile
PA: The Stebbins Engineering And Manufacturing Company
363 Eastern Blvd
Watertown NY 13601
315 782-3000

(G-13408)
SUPERIOR CLAY CORPORATION
6566 Superior Rd Se (44683-7487)
P.O. Box 352 (44683-0352)
PHONE..............................740 922-4122
Elmer W Mcclave Iii, *Pr*
Joe Berni, *
◆ EMP: 75 EST: 1936
SQ FT: 190,000
SALES (est): 9.9MM **Privately Held**
Web: www.superiorclay.com
SIC: **3259** 8611 Sewer pipe or fittings, clay; Business associations

(G-13409)
UHRICHSVILLE CARBIDE INC
410 N Water St (44683-1849)
PHONE..............................740 922-9197
Bob Septer, *Pr*
Karen Septer, *Sec*
EMP: 17 EST: 1983
SALES (est): 2.4MM **Privately Held**
Web: www.uhrichsvillecarbide.com
SIC: **3545** 5072 7699 3546 Cutting tools for machine tools; Saw blades; Knife, saw and tool sharpening and repair; Power-driven handtools

Union
Montgomery County

(G-13410)
NEW DAWN LABS LLC
102 S Main St (45322-3343)
PHONE..............................203 675-5644
EMP: 10 EST: 2019
SQ FT: 6,000
SALES (est): 1.17MM **Privately Held**
Web: www.newdawnlabs.io
SIC: **3577** 8711 Input/output equipment, computer; Electrical or electronic engineering

(G-13411)
PROCTER & GAMBLE DISTRG LLC
Also Called: Procter & Gamble
1800 Union Airpark Blvd (45377-2560)
P.O. Box 2628 (27216-2628)
PHONE..............................937 387-5189
Robert Fix, *Genl Mgr*
EMP: 127
SALES (corp-wide): 84.04B **Publicly Held**
SIC: **2841** Soap and other detergents
HQ: Procter & Gamble Distributing Llc
1 Procter And Gamble Plz
Cincinnati OH 45202
513 983-1100

(G-13412)
TE-CO INC
100 Quinter Farm Rd (45322-9705)
PHONE..............................937 836-0961
EMP: 18 EST: 2018
SALES (est): 3.39MM **Privately Held**
Web: www.te-co.com
SIC: **3545** Machine tool attachments and accessories

Union City
Darke County

(G-13413)
CAL-MAINE FOODS INC
1039 Zumbrum Rd (45390-8646)
PHONE..............................937 968-4874
Chuck Jenkins, *Brnch Mgr*
EMP: 10
SALES (corp-wide): 2.33B **Publicly Held**
Web: www.calmainefoods.com
SIC: **0252** 2015 Chicken eggs; Eggs, processed: frozen
PA: Cal-Maine Foods, Inc.
1052 Hghland Clny Pkwy St
Ridgeland MS 39157
601 948-6813

(G-13414)
CAST METALS TECHNOLOGY INC
305 Se Deerfield Rd (45390-9072)
PHONE..............................937 968-5460
Ryan Olney, *Mgr*
EMP: 47

Web: www.cm-tec.com
SIC: **3365** Aluminum and aluminum-based alloy castings
PA: Cast Metals Technology, Inc.
550 Liberty Rd
Delaware OH 43015

(G-13415)
HOG SLAT INCORPORATED
200 N Grandview St (45390-9069)
PHONE..............................937 968-3890
EMP: 25
SALES (corp-wide): 451.86MM **Privately Held**
Web: www.hogslat.com
SIC: **3523** Farm machinery and equipment
PA: Hog Slat, Incorporated
206 Fayetteville St
Newton Grove NC 28366
800 949-4647

Uniontown
Stark County

(G-13416)
AMERITECH PUBLISHING INC
Also Called: SBC
1530 Corporate Woods Pkwy Ste 100 (44685-6707)
PHONE..............................330 896-6037
Kim Gergel, *Mgr*
EMP: 1328
SALES (corp-wide): 122.34B **Publicly Held**
SIC: **2741** Miscellaneous publishing
HQ: Ameritech Publishing, Inc.
23500 Northwestern Hwy
Southfield MI

(G-13417)
BBM FAIRWAY INC
Also Called: Modern Time Dealer
3515 Massillon Rd Ste 200 (44685-6113)
PHONE..............................330 899-2200
Greg Smith, *Brnch Mgr*
EMP: 9
SALES (corp-wide): 7.75MM **Privately Held**
Web: www.bobit.com
SIC: **2721** Magazines: publishing only, not printed on site
PA: Bbm Fairway, Inc.
3520 Challenger St
Torrance CA 90503

(G-13418)
DIEBOLD NIXDORF INCORPORATED
3792 Boettler Oaks Dr Ste A (44685-7733)
PHONE..............................330 899-1300
Gerrard B Schmid, *Pr*
EMP: 6
SALES (corp-wide): 3.75B **Publicly Held**
Web: www.dieboldnixdorf.com
SIC: **3578** Banking machines
PA: Diebold Nixdorf, Incorporated
350 Orchard Ave Ne
North Canton OH 44720
330 490-4000

(G-13419)
ENVIRONMENTAL CHEMICAL CORP
2167 Prestwick Dr (44685-8840)
P.O. Box 20110 (44701-0110)
PHONE..............................330 453-5200
Richard Morena, *Pr*
Thomas Wucinich, *VP*
EMP: 12 EST: 1973
SQ FT: 4,830
SALES (est): 821.86K **Privately Held**

Web: www.environmentalchemical.com
SIC: 5169 2842 2899 Chemicals, industrial
and heavy; Polishes and sanitation goods;
Chemical preparations, nec

(G-13420)
HIGH-TECH MOLD & MACHINE INC
3771 Tabs Dr (44685-9563)
PHONE.............................330 896-4466
Anthony Klisan Junior, *Pr*
Connie Klisan, *VP Fin*
Stephanie Klisan, *VP*
EMP: 15 EST: 1984
SQ FT: 15,000
SALES (est): 1.99MM **Privately Held**
Web: www.hightechmold.com
SIC: 3544 3599 Industrial molds; Machine
shop, jobbing and repair

(G-13421)
KOVATCH CASTINGS INC
Also Called: Kovatch Castings
3743 Tabs Dr (44685-9563)
PHONE.............................330 896-9944
Douglas Kovatch, *CEO*
Douglas Kovatch, *Pr*
Frank E Lysiak, *
◆ EMP: 183 EST: 1976
SQ FT: 65,000
SALES (est): 24.74MM **Privately Held**
Web: www.kovatchcastings.com
SIC: 3324 3369 3366 3365 Commercial
investment castings, ferrous; Nonferrous
foundries, nec; Copper foundries;
Aluminum foundries

(G-13422)
LIBERTY OUTDOORS LLC
Also Called: Liberty Outdoors
1519 Boettler Rd Ste A (44685-8391)
PHONE.............................330 791-3149
EMP: 10 EST: 2017
SALES (est): 2.62MM **Privately Held**
Web: www.golibertyoutdoors.com
SIC: 3714 Trailer hitches, motor vehicle

(G-13423)
MCAFEE TOOL & DIE INC
1717 Boettler Rd (44685-9588)
PHONE.............................330 896-9555
Gary Mc Afee, *Pr*
Michael J Francek Junior, *VP*
Tracee Gates, *Stockholder*
Wendy Mcafee, *Stockholder*
EMP: 41 EST: 1977
SQ FT: 40,000
SALES (est): 5.68MM **Privately Held**
Web: www.mcafeetool.com
SIC: 3544 3469 Die sets for metal stamping
(presses); Metal stampings, nec

(G-13424)
PLASTIC CARD INC (PA)
Also Called: Rainbow Printing
3711 Boettler Oaks Dr (44685-7733)
PHONE.............................330 896-5555
Kenneth Thompson, *Pr*
Thomas Thompson, *
Rich Krauth, *
▲ EMP: 60 EST: 1978
SQ FT: 24,000
SALES (est): 1.11MM
SALES (corp-wide): 1.11MM **Privately
Held**
Web: www.rainbow-printing.com
SIC: 2396 Printing and embossing on
plastics fabric articles

(G-13425)
PLASTICARDS INC (PA)
Also Called: Rainbow Printing
3711 Boettler Oaks Dr (44685-7733)
PHONE.............................330 896-5555
Kenneth Thompson, *Pr*
Patty Lou Thompson, *
Rich Crowft, *
EMP: 46 EST: 1976
SQ FT: 20,000
SALES (est): 1.31MM
SALES (corp-wide): 1.31MM **Privately
Held**
Web: www.rainbow-printing.com
SIC: 3089 Identification cards, plastics

(G-13426)
STEERAMERICA INC
Also Called: Steer America
1525 Corporate Woods Pkwy Ste 500
(44685-7883)
PHONE.............................330 563-4407
R Padmanabhan, *Ch*
Satish Padmanabhan, *Pr*
Babu Padmanabhan, *Dir*
Uttam Kumar Bhageria, *CFO*
Dipak Chattara, *Ch*
▲ EMP: 13 EST: 2008
SQ FT: 10,000
SALES (est): 5.93MM **Privately Held**
Web: www.steerworld.com
SIC: 3452 Bolts, nuts, rivets, and washers
PA: Steer Engineering Private Limited
No.290, 4th Main, 4th Phase
Bengaluru KA 56005

(G-13427)
TKM PRINT SOLUTIONS INC
3455 Forest Lake Dr (44685-8131)
PHONE.............................330 237-4029
Dalton Wayne, *Pr*
EMP: 18 EST: 2008
SALES (est): 4.74MM **Privately Held**
Web: www.discovertkm.com
SIC: 2752 Offset printing

(G-13428)
UNIONTOWN SEPTIC TANKS INC
2781 Raber Rd (44685-8125)
PHONE.............................330 699-3386
James N Kungle, *Pr*
Jeff Kungle, *VP*
EMP: 10 EST: 1965
SALES (est): 940.21K **Privately Held**
Web: www.uniontownseptictank.com
SIC: 3272 Concrete products, precast, nec

(G-13429)
XTREME OUTDOORS LLC
1519 Boettler Rd Ste A (44685-8391)
PHONE.............................330 731-4137
EMP: 40 EST: 2019
SQ FT: 2,400
SALES (est): 8.96MM **Privately Held**
Web: www.goxtoutdoors.com
SIC: 3792 Travel trailers and campers

Upper Arlington
Franklin County

(G-13430)
DAILY GROWLER INC
2812 Fishinger Rd (43221-1129)
P.O. Box 218455 (43221-8455)
PHONE.............................614 656-2337
EMP: 6 EST: 2012
SALES (est): 113.66K **Privately Held**
Web: www.thedailygrowler.com

SIC: 2711 Newspapers, publishing and
printing

(G-13431)
INDUSTRIAL MFG CO INTL LLC
3366 Riverside Dr Ste 103 (43221-1734)
PHONE.............................440 838-4555
EMP: 7 EST: 2005
SALES (est): 1.08MM
SALES (corp-wide): 459.42MM **Privately
Held**
Web: www.mfgco.com
SIC: 2542 Lockers (not refrigerated): except
wood
PA: Summa Holdings, Inc.
8223 Brcksvlle Rd Ste 100
Cleveland OH 44141
440 838-4700

(G-13432)
**REMINGTON PRODUCTS COMPANY
(PA)**
Also Called: Foundation Wellness
3366 Riverside Dr Ste 103 (43221-1734)
P.O. Box 506 (44282)
PHONE.............................330 335-1571
Rhonda Newman, *CEO*
Jeff Wert, *
C Kevin Mccomas, *CFO*
▲ EMP: 91 EST: 1930
SQ FT: 102,000
SALES (est): 24.41MM
SALES (corp-wide): 24.41MM **Privately
Held**
Web: www.foundationwellness.com
SIC: 3069 3131 Boot or shoe products,
rubber; Footwear cut stock

Upper Sandusky
Wyandot County

(G-13433)
ARCHEM AMERICA INC (DH)
245 Commerce Way (43351-9079)
PHONE.............................419 294-6304
Satoru Kusano, *CEO*
EMP: 19 EST: 2022
SALES (est): 7.97MM **Privately Held**
Web: www.archem.inc
SIC: 3069 Foam rubber
HQ: Archem Inc.
1-2-70, Konan
Minato-Ku TKY 108-0

(G-13434)
**ASSA ABLOY ENTRNCE SYSTEMS
HLA**
Also Called: Dover Roller Shutters
295 Commerce Way (43351-9079)
P.O. Box 420 (43351)
PHONE.............................419 294-3373
Ray Van Gunten, *Pr*
Matthew Baxter, *
◆ EMP: 60 EST: 1991
SQ FT: 37,500
SALES (est): 9.46MM **Privately Held**
Web: www.diamonddoor.com
SIC: 3442 Metal doors

(G-13435)
BECA HOUSE COFFEE LLC
965 E Wyandot Ave (43351-9638)
PHONE.............................419 731-4961
Heather Jackson, *Owner*
Heather Jackson, *Pr*
Steve Jackson, *Prin*
EMP: 6 EST: 2011
SALES (est): 251.34K **Privately Held**
Web: www.becahouse.com

SIC: 5812 2095 Coffee shop; Coffee
roasting (except by wholesale grocers)

(G-13436)
**CUSTOM GL SLTONS UPPER
SNDSKY**
12688 State Highway 67 (43351-9411)
PHONE.............................419 294-4921
EMP: 500 EST: 2013
SALES (est): 92.25MM
SALES (corp-wide): 118.85MM **Privately
Held**
Web: www.customglasssolutions.com
SIC: 3231 Laminated glass: made from
purchased glass
PA: Custom Glass Solutions, Llc
12688 State Highway 67
Upper Sandusky OH 43351
248 340-1800

(G-13437)
**CUSTOM GLASS SOLUTIONS LLC
(PA)**
12688 State Highway 67 (43351-9411)
PHONE.............................248 340-1800
Matthew J Dietrich, *CEO*
David B Jaffe, *Sec*
Gary Greene, *Treas*
EMP: 21 EST: 2006
SALES (est): 118.85MM
SALES (corp-wide): 118.85MM **Privately
Held**
Web: www.customglasssolutions.com
SIC: 3211 Flat glass

(G-13438)
DAILY CHIEF UNION
111 W Wyandot Ave (43351-1367)
P.O. Box 180 (43351-0180)
PHONE.............................419 294-2331
Jack L Barnes, *Pr*
Charles G Barnes, *Sec*
Tom Martin, *Mgr*
EMP: 14 EST: 1879
SQ FT: 3,000
SALES (est): 965.05K
SALES (corp-wide): 3.45MM **Privately
Held**
Web: www.dailychiefunion.com
SIC: 2711 Commercial printing and
newspaper publishing combined
HQ: Hardin County Publishing Co.
201 E Columbus St
Kenton OH 43326
419 674-4066

(G-13439)
DESIGN AND FABRICATION INC
400 Malabar Dr (43351-9747)
P.O. Box 218 (43351-0218)
PHONE.............................419 294-2414
Mike Reamer, *Pr*
Cathy Reamer, *Sec*
EMP: 7 EST: 1994
SQ FT: 7,200
SALES (est): 836.11K **Privately Held**
Web: www.designandfab.com
SIC: 3599 Machine shop, jobbing and repair

(G-13440)
**ENGINEERED WIRE PRODUCTS INC
(DH)**
1200 N Warpole St (43351-9093)
P.O. Box 313 (43351-0313)
PHONE.............................419 294-3817
Grafton Redfren, *VP Sls*
Bradley W Evers, *
▲ EMP: 101 EST: 1994
SALES (est): 27.89MM **Privately Held**
Web: www.kci-corp.com

(G-13440) *(partial)*

SIC: 3496 3315 Miscellaneous fabricated
wire products; Steel wire and related
products
HQ: Keystone Consolidated Industries, Inc.
5430 Lyndon B Jhnson Fwy
Dallas TX 75240
800 441-0308

(G-13441)
FAIRBORN USA INC (PA)
205 Broadview St (43351-9628)
P.O. Box 151 (43351-0151)
PHONE....................................419 294-4987
EMP: 47 EST: 1976
SALES (est): 22.73MM
SALES (corp-wide): 22.73MM **Privately
Held**
Web: www.fairbornusa.com
SIC: 3448 Docks, prefabricated metal

(G-13442)
HANDY TWINE KNIFE CO
5676 County Highway 330 (43351-9772)
P.O. Box 146 (43351-0146)
PHONE....................................419 294-3424
Lynn L Getz, *Pr*
John Tschantz, *VP*
Brian Caldwell, *Sec*
EMP: 9 EST: 1912
SQ FT: 1,000
SALES (est): 798.17K **Privately Held**
Web: www.handysafetyknife.com
SIC: 3423 5719 Knives, agricultural or
industrial; Cutlery

(G-13443)
KALMBACH FEEDS INC (PA)
Also Called: Kalmbach
7148 State Highway 199 (43351-9359)
PHONE....................................419 294-3838
Paul Kalmbach, *CEO*
Paul Kalmbach Junior, *Pr*
Jeff Neal, *Marketing**
Andy Bishop, *EXCELLENCE**
Eric Bernstein, *
▲ EMP: 200 EST: 1963
SALES (est): 241.82MM
SALES (corp-wide): 241.82MM **Privately
Held**
Web: www.kalmbachfeeds.com
SIC: 2048 Livestock feeds

(G-13444)
KASAI NORTH AMERICA INC
1111 N Warpole St (43351-9094)
PHONE....................................419 209-0399
Sam Kennedy, *VP*
EMP: 172
Web: www.kasai-na.com
SIC: 3465 3714 Moldings or trim,
automobile: stamped metal; Motor vehicle
parts and accessories
HQ: Kasai North America, Inc.
1225 Garrison Dr
Murfreesboro TN 37129
615 546-6040

(G-13445)
KIRBY AND SONS INC
Also Called: Kirby Sand & Gravel
4876 County Highway 43 (43351-9155)
PHONE....................................419 927-2260
Gene Kirby, *Pr*
Franklin Kirby, *VP*
Judi Kirby, *Sec*
EMP: 12 EST: 1973
SALES (est): 2.59MM **Privately Held**
Web: www.kirbysand.com
SIC: 1442 4212 Common sand mining;
Dump truck haulage

(G-13446)
LIQUI-BOX CORPORATION
519 Raybestos Dr (43351-9666)
PHONE....................................419 294-3884
Roger Schultz, *Brnch Mgr*
EMP: 24
SQ FT: 42,000
SALES (corp-wide): 5.39B **Publicly Held**
Web: www.liquibox.com
SIC: 3089 3544 Molding primary plastics;
Forms (molds), for foundry and plastics
working machinery
HQ: Liqui-Box Corporation
2415 Cascade Pointe Blvd
Charlotte NC 28208
804 325-1400

(G-13447)
MAR-METAL MFG INC
Also Called: Fanci Forms
420 N Warpole St (43351-9301)
P.O. Box 37 (43351-0037)
PHONE....................................419 447-1102
Floyd Marshall, *Pr*
Craig Marshall, *
EMP: 6 EST: 1969
SQ FT: 28,000
SALES (est): 481.36K **Privately Held**
SIC: 3544 Special dies and tools

(G-13448)
MENNEL MILLING COMPANY
Also Called: Farm Elevator
7097 County Highway 47 (43351-9190)
PHONE....................................419 294-2337
EMP: 15
SALES (corp-wide): 211.12MM **Privately
Held**
Web: www.mennel.com
SIC: 2041 Flour
PA: The Mennel Milling Company
319 S Vine St
Fostoria OH 44830
419 435-8151

(G-13449)
NEW EEZY-GRO INC
Also Called: Golden Eagle
9841 County Highway 49 (43351-9662)
PHONE....................................419 927-6110
Joseph Fox, *Brnch Mgr*
EMP: 17
SALES (corp-wide): 11.26B **Publicly Held**
Web: www.eezygro.com
SIC: 2819 5261 Calcium compounds and
salts, inorganic, nec; Fertilizer
HQ: New Eezy-Gro Inc.
1947 Briarfield Blvd
Maumee OH
419 893-5050

(G-13450)
NJF MANUFACTURING LLC
7387 Township Highway 104 (43351-9353)
PHONE....................................419 294-0400
Nathan Frey, *Managing Member*
EMP: 9 EST: 2017
SALES (est): 1.62MM **Privately Held**
Web: www.freyshowpengates.com
SIC: 3999 Manufacturing industries, nec

(G-13451)
OLEN CORPORATION
6326 County Highway 61 (43351-9749)
PHONE....................................419 294-2611
John Miller, *Brnch Mgr*
EMP: 10
SALES (corp-wide): 32.6MM **Privately
Held**
Web: www.kokosing.biz

SIC: 3273 5032 Ready-mixed concrete;
Stone, crushed or broken
PA: The Olen Corporation
4755 S High St
Columbus OH 43207
614 491-1515

(G-13452)
OVERHEAD DOOR CORPORATION
Also Called: Todco
781 Rt 30w (43351)
PHONE....................................419 294-3874
Mike Traxler, *Mgr*
EMP: 10
Web: www.overheaddoor.com
SIC: 3442 3448 2431 Garage doors,
overhead: metal; Ramps, prefabricated
metal; Doors, wood
HQ: Overhead Door Corporation
2501 S State Hwy 121 Ste
Lewisville TX 75067
469 549-7100

(G-13453)
PROSPIRA AMERICA CORPORATION
235 Commerce Way (43351-9079)
P.O. Box 450 (43351-0450)
PHONE....................................419 294-6989
Greg Ickes, *Brnch Mgr*
EMP: 100
Web: www.prospira.us
SIC: 3061 Automotive rubber goods
(mechanical)
HQ: Prospira America Corporation
2030 Production Dr
Findlay OH 45839
419 423-9552

(G-13454)
REK ASSOCIATES LLC
11218 County Highway 44 (43351-9056)
PHONE....................................419 294-3838
EMP: 15 EST: 2017
SALES (est): 479.31K **Privately Held**
SIC: 2048 Prepared feeds, nec

(G-13455)
SCHMIDT MACHINE COMPANY
Also Called: S M C
7013 State Highway 199 (43351-9347)
PHONE....................................419 294-3814
TOLL FREE: 800
Bill Junior, *Pr*
Randy F Schmidt, *
Kevin Schmidt, *
Darlene Mooney, *
Dorothy M Schmidt, *
EMP: 50 EST: 1935
SQ FT: 2,500
SALES (est): 5.11MM **Privately Held**
Web: www.schmidtmachine.com
SIC: 3599 7692 5083 Machine shop, jobbing
and repair; Welding repair; Farm equipment
parts and supplies

(G-13456)
WANNEMACHER ENTERPRISES INC
Also Called: Wannemacher Packaging
422 W Guthrie Dr (43351-1154)
PHONE....................................419 771-1101
Jerry Jackson, *Dir*
Sally Buchholz, *Dir*
EMP: 10 EST: 2012
SALES (est): 113.05K **Privately Held**
SIC: 2099 Food preparations, nec

Urbana
Champaign County

(G-13457)
AMERICAN PAN COMPANY (PA)
Also Called: Durashield
417 E Water St (43078-2178)
P.O. Box 628 (43078-0628)
PHONE....................................937 652-3232
Gilbert Bundy, *Pr*
Jason Tingley, *
Michael Cornelis, *
Curt Marino, *
◆ EMP: 120 EST: 1985
SQ FT: 55,800
SALES (est): 42.9MM
SALES (corp-wide): 42.9MM **Privately
Held**
Web: www.americanpan.com
SIC: 3556 Food products machinery

(G-13458)
CHRIS HAUGHEY
Also Called: Cupboard Distributing
1463 S Us Highway 68 (43078-8478)
PHONE....................................937 652-3338
Chris Haughey, *Owner*
EMP: 9 EST: 1987
SALES (est): 201.04K **Privately Held**
Web: www.cdwood.com
SIC: 2511 Unassembled or unfinished
furniture, household: wood

(G-13459)
CMT MACHINING & FABG LLC
1411 Kennard Kingscreek Rd (43078-9505)
P.O. Box 28 (43078-0028)
PHONE....................................937 652-3740
EMP: 14 EST: 1958
SQ FT: 22,000
SALES (est): 615.72K **Privately Held**
Web: www.cmt-usa.com
SIC: 1761 7692 3599 3544 Sheet metal
work, nec; Welding repair; Machine shop,
jobbing and repair; Jigs and fixtures

(G-13460)
COLEPAK LLC
1030 S Edgewood Ave (43078-9694)
P.O. Box 650 (43078)
PHONE....................................937 652-3910
Ole Rosgaard, *Pr*
EMP: 58 EST: 1987
SQ FT: 113,000
SALES (est): 2.09MM
SALES (corp-wide): 5.45B **Publicly Held**
Web: www.colepak.com
SIC: 2653 2671 Partitions, solid fiber: made
from purchased materials; Paper; coated
and laminated packaging
PA: Greif, Inc.
425 Winter Rd
Delaware OH 43015
740 549-6000

(G-13461)
DESMOND-STEPHAN MFGCOMPANY
121 W Water St (43078-2048)
P.O. Box 30 (43078-0030)
PHONE....................................937 653-7181
Robert B Mcconnell, *Pr*
EMP: 24 EST: 1898
SQ FT: 30,000
SALES (est): 2.45MM **Privately Held**
Web: www.desmond-stephan.com
SIC: 3541 Machine tools, metal cutting type

(G-13462)
GRIMES AEROSPACE COMPANY (HQ)
Also Called: Honeywell
550 State Route 55 (43078-9496)
P.O. Box 247 (43078-0247)
PHONE...................................937 484-2000
▲ EMP: 800 EST: 1986
SALES (est): 27.4MM
SALES (corp-wide): 38.5B Publicly Held
SIC: 3728 3647 3646 3645 Aircraft parts and
equipment, nec; Vehicular lighting
equipment; Commercial lighting fixtures;
Residential lighting fixtures
PA: Honeywell International Inc.
855 S Mint St
Charlotte NC 28202
704 627-6200

(G-13463)
GRIMES AEROSPACE COMPANY
Also Called: Honeywell Lightning & Elec
515 N Russell St (43078-1330)
P.O. Box 247 (43078-0247)
PHONE...................................937 484-2000
Ron King, *Mgr*
EMP: 74
SALES (corp-wide): 38.5B Publicly Held
SIC: 3728 Aircraft parts and equipment, nec
HQ: Grimes Aerospace Company
550 State Route 55
Urbana OH 43078
937 484-2000

(G-13464)
GRIMES AEROSPACE COMPANY
Also Called: Honeywell
550 State Route 55 (43078-9482)
PHONE...................................937 484-2001
Bruce Blagg, *Brnch Mgr*
EMP: 74
SALES (corp-wide): 38.5B Publicly Held
SIC: 5088 7699 3812 3769 Aircraft and
parts, nec; Aircraft and heavy equipment
repair services; Search and navigation
equipment; Space vehicle equipment, nec
HQ: Grimes Aerospace Company
550 State Route 55
Urbana OH 43078
937 484-2000

(G-13465)
HALL COMPANY
420 E Water St (43078-2163)
P.O. Box 727 (43078-0727)
PHONE...................................937 652-1376
Kyle J Hall, *Pr*
James A Hall, *
Carol A Hall, *
Richard J Walser, *
William D Hall Junior, *Asst Tr*
EMP: 47 EST: 1954
SQ FT: 38,500
SALES (est): 4.75MM Privately Held
Web: www.hallco.com
SIC: 3679 3993 3471 3444 Electronic
switches; Signs and advertising specialties;
Plating and polishing; Sheet metalwork

(G-13466)
HONEYWELL INTERNATIONAL INC
Honeywell
550 State Route 55 (43078-9482)
P.O. Box 247 (43078-0247)
PHONE...................................937 484-2000
Randy Marker, *Mgr*
EMP: 800
SALES (corp-wide): 38.5B Publicly Held
Web: www.honeywell.com

SIC: 3812 3669 3491 3699 Aircraft control
systems, electronic; Fire alarm apparatus,
electric; Gas valves and parts, industrial;
Security control equipment and systems
PA: Honeywell International Inc.
855 S Mint St
Charlotte NC 28202
704 627-6200

(G-13467)
HUGHEY & PHILLIPS LLC
240 W Twain Ave (43078-1059)
PHONE...................................937 652-3500
Jeff Jacobs, *VP*
Steve Schneider, *
EMP: 50 EST: 2009
SALES (est): 4MM Privately Held
Web: www.hugheyandphillips.com
SIC: 3648 Lighting equipment, nec

(G-13468)
IPL DAYTON INC
1765 W County Line Rd (43078-8476)
P.O. Box 1468 (45501)
PHONE...................................937 969-7000
◆ EMP: 190 EST: 1969
SALES (est): 20.19MM
SALES (corp-wide): 816.52K Privately
Held
Web: www.techii.com
SIC: 3089 Injection molding of plastics
HQ: Plastiques Ipl Inc
1155 Boul Rene-Levesque O Bureau
4100
Montreal QC H3B 3
418 789-2880

(G-13469)
J RETTENMAIER USA LP
1228 Muzzy Rd (43078-9685)
PHONE...................................937 652-2101
Dave Mcgill, *Brnch Mgr*
EMP: 91
SALES (corp-wide): 355.83K Privately
Held
Web: www.jrsusa.com
SIC: 2823 2299 Cellulosic manmade fibers;
Flock (recovered textile fibers)
HQ: J. Rettenmaier Usa Lp
16369 Us Highwy 131 S
Schoolcraft MI 49087
269 679-2340

(G-13470)
JACK WALTERS & SONS CORP
Also Called: Walters Buildings
5045 N Us Highway 68 (43078-9315)
PHONE...................................937 653-8986
Jerry Kauffman, *Mgr*
EMP: 31
SALES (corp-wide): 23.33MM Privately
Held
Web: www.waltersbuildings.com
SIC: 3448 Buildings, portable: prefabricated
metal
PA: Jack Walters & Sons, Corp.
6600 Midland Ct
Allenton WI 53002
262 629-5521

(G-13471)
JOE REES WELDING
326 W Twain Ave (43078-1061)
PHONE...................................937 652-4067
Joe Rees, *Owner*
Joe Rees, *Prin*
EMP: 6 EST: 1991
SALES (est): 850.24K Privately Held
Web: www.joereeswelding.com
SIC: 3441 Fabricated structural metal

(G-13472)
KOENIG EQUIPMENT INC
Also Called: John Deere Authorized Dealer
3130 E Us Highway 36 (43078-9736)
PHONE...................................937 653-5281
Dale Griest, *Mgr*
EMP: 13
SALES (corp-wide): 49.19MM Privately
Held
Web: www.koenigequipment.com
SIC: 3524 5082 Lawn and garden equipment
; Construction and mining machinery
PA: Koenig Equipment, Inc.
15213 State Route 274
Botkins OH 45306
937 693-5000

(G-13473)
MARSHALL PLASTICS INC
590 S Edgewood Ave (43078-2603)
P.O. Box 38126 (43078-8126)
PHONE...................................937 653-4740
Henry Taylor, *Pr*
Richard T Ricketts, *Prin*
EMP: 9 EST: 2002
SALES (est): 991.38K Privately Held
SIC: 3089 Injection molding of plastics

(G-13474)
MUMFORDS POTATO CHIPS & DELI
Also Called: Mumford's Potato Chip
325 N Main St (43078-1605)
PHONE...................................937 653-3491
Randy Leopard, *Pt*
Marilyn Leopard, *Pt*
EMP: 9 EST: 1932
SQ FT: 12,000
SALES (est): 426.43K Privately Held
Web:
www.mumfordspotatochipsanddeli.com
SIC: 2096 5411 Potato chips and other
potato-based snacks; Delicatessen stores

(G-13475)
ORBIS CORPORATION
200 Elm St (43078-1975)
PHONE...................................937 652-1361
EMP: 280
SALES (corp-wide): 1.94B Privately Held
Web: www.orbiscorporation.com
SIC: 3089 Synthetic resin finished products,
nec
HQ: Orbis Corporation
1055 Corporate Ctr Dr
Oconomowoc WI 53066
262 560-5000

(G-13476)
PARKER TRUTEC INCORPORATED
Also Called: Nihon Company
4795 Upper Valley Pike (43078-9295)
PHONE...................................937 653-8500
Michael Kleiber, *Genl Mgr*
EMP: 90
Web: www.parkertrutec.com
SIC: 3479 3471 2899 2851 Painting of metal
products; Plating and polishing; Chemical
preparations, nec; Paints and allied
products
HQ: Parker Trutec Incorporated
4700 Gateway Blvd
Springfield OH 45502
937 323-8833

(G-13477)
SARICA MANUFACTURING COMPANY
Also Called: Sarica
240 W Twain Ave (43078-1059)
PHONE...................................937 484-4030
Steven M Schneider, *Managing Member*

Amy Wolf, *
Constance Schneider, *
EMP: 40 EST: 2005
SQ FT: 30,000
SALES (est): 9.76MM Privately Held
Web: www.saricamfg.com
SIC: 3629 Electronic generation equipment

(G-13478)
TRIAGE ORTHO GROUP
Also Called: Imperial Orthodontics
132 Lafayette Ave (43078-1420)
P.O. Box 549 (43078-0549)
PHONE...................................937 653-6431
Vincent Gonzalez, *Owner*
Sandra Gonzalez, *Mgr*
EMP: 7 EST: 1982
SQ FT: 8,900
SALES (est): 186.41K Privately Held
Web: www.honeysucklecreations.com
SIC: 5047 2396 Dentists' professional
supplies; Screen printing on fabric articles

(G-13479)
TRULIL INC
Also Called: J W P
625 S Edgewood Ave (43078-8600)
PHONE...................................937 652-1242
Clayton W Rose Junior, *Prin*
Lilli A Johnson, *
▼ EMP: 210 EST: 1970
SQ FT: 133,000
SALES (est): 21.97MM Privately Held
Web: www.jwp-inc.com
SIC: 3714 Air brakes, motor vehicle

(G-13480)
ULTRA-MET COMPANY
120 Fyffe St (43078-1106)
PHONE...................................937 653-7133
Brent Sheerer, *Pr*
EMP: 11 EST: 2015
SALES (est): 6.12MM Privately Held
Web: www.ultra-met.com
SIC: 1311 5013 5047 8711 Crude petroleum
and natural gas; Automotive engines and
engine parts; Instruments, surgical and
medical; Aviation and/or aeronautical
engineering

(G-13481)
ULTRA-MET COMPANY
Also Called: Ultra-Met
720 N Main St (43078-1102)
PHONE...................................937 653-7133
Brent Sheerer, *Pr*
Bill Glaser, *
Jeff Hartshorn, *
Jeff Fox, *
◆ EMP: 95 EST: 1964
SQ FT: 50,000
SALES (est): 9.77MM Privately Held
Web: www.ultra-met.com
SIC: 3599 Machine shop, jobbing and repair

Urbancrest
Franklin County

(G-13482)
AMSOIL INC
3389 Urbancrest Industrial Dr (43123-1783)
PHONE...................................614 274-9851
Scott Davis, *Mgr*
EMP: 8
SALES (corp-wide): 240.81MM Privately
Held
Web: kadanoil.shopamsoil.com

SIC: 2992 3589 2873 3714 Lubricating oils and greases; Water filters and softeners, household type; Fertilizers: natural (organic), except compost; Motor vehicle parts and accessories
PA: Amsoil Inc.
925 Tower Ave
Superior WI 54880
715 392-7101

(G-13483)
PILKINGTON NORTH AMERICA INC
3440 Centerpoint Dr (43123-1794)
PHONE..................419 247-3731
Richard Frampton, *Brnch Mgr*
EMP: 223
Web: www.pilkington.com
SIC: 3211 Construction glass
HQ: Pilkington North America, Inc.
811 Madison Ave
Toledo OH 43604
419 247-3731

(G-13484)
TAYLOR COMMUNICATIONS INC
3125 Lewis Centre Way (43123-1784)
PHONE..................614 277-7500
Jeff Wise, *Brnch Mgr*
EMP: 38
SALES (corp-wide): 3.81B Privately Held
Web: www.taylor.com
SIC: 2759 Commercial printing, nec
HQ: Taylor Communications, Inc.
1725 Roe Crest Dr
North Mankato MN 56003
866 541-0937

Utica
Licking County

(G-13485)
ACUITY BRANDS LIGHTING INC
Holophane
140 Carey St (43080-9004)
P.O. Box 535 (43080-0535)
PHONE..................740 892-2011
Kim Lombardi, *Brnch Mgr*
EMP: 120
SALES (corp-wide): 3.84B Publicly Held
Web: lithonia.acuitybrands.com
SIC: 3646 Commercial lighting fixtures
HQ: Acuity Brands Lighting, Inc.
1170 Pchtree St Ne Ste 23
Atlanta GA 30309

(G-13486)
CARDINAL CT COMPANY
140 Carey St (43080-9004)
PHONE..................740 892-2324
EMP: 30
SALES (corp-wide): 1B Privately Held
Web: www.cardinalcorp.com
SIC: 3211 Tempered glass
HQ: Cardinal Ct Company
775 Pririe Ctr Dr Ste 200
Eden Prairie MN 55344

(G-13487)
CARDINAL GLASS INDUSTRIES INC
140 Carey St (43080-9004)
PHONE..................740 892-2324
Roger D O'shaughnessy, *Brnch Mgr*
EMP: 30
SALES (corp-wide): 1B Privately Held
Web: www.cardinalcorp.com
SIC: 3211 Tempered glass
PA: Cardinal Glass Industries Inc
775 Pririe Ctr Dr Ste 200
Eden Prairie MN 55344

952 229-2600

(G-13488)
VELVET ICE CREAM COMPANY (PA)
Also Called: Ye Olde Mille Shoppe
11324 Mount Vernon Rd (43080-7703)
P.O. Box 588 (43080-0588)
PHONE..................740 892-3921
EMP: 60 EST: 1960
SALES (est): 21.87MM
SALES (corp-wide): 21.87MM Privately Held
Web: www.velveticecream.com
SIC: 2024 8412 5812 5947 Ice cream, bulk; Museum; American restaurant; Gift shop

Valley City
Medina County

(G-13489)
ARNOLD CORPORATION
Also Called: Arnold Company
5965 Grafton Rd (44280-9329)
P.O. Box 368022 (44136-9722)
PHONE..................330 225-2600
◆ EMP: 107
SIC: 5083 3524 Lawn and garden machinery and equipment; Lawn and garden mowers and accessories

(G-13490)
AUTOMATION TOOL & DIE INC
5576 Innovation Dr (44280-9368)
PHONE..................330 225-8336
William E Bennett, *Pr*
James R Bennett, *
EMP: 70 EST: 1974
SQ FT: 32,000
SALES (est): 9.46MM Privately Held
Web: www.automationtd.com
SIC: 3544 Special dies and tools

(G-13491)
BOEHM PRESSED STEEL COMPANY
5440 Wegman Dr (44280-9707)
PHONE..................330 220-8000
Ted Mcquade, *Pr*
William Reis, *
EMP: 50 EST: 1977
SQ FT: 41,000
SALES (est): 9.73MM Privately Held
Web: www.boehmstampings.com
SIC: 3469 Stamping metal for the trade

(G-13492)
CON-BELT INC
5656 Innovation Dr (44280-9370)
PHONE..................330 273-2003
Marc Zeitler, *Pr*
EMP: 13 EST: 1991
SALES (est): 2.2MM Privately Held
Web: www.conbelt.com
SIC: 3535 Conveyors and conveying equipment

(G-13493)
CSM CONCEPTS LLC
6450 Grafton Rd (44280-9762)
PHONE..................330 483-1320
Gordon J Petkosh, *Managing Member*
EMP: 12 EST: 2010
SALES (est): 1.11MM Privately Held
Web: www.csmconceptsllc.com
SIC: 2542 Office and store showcases and display fixtures

(G-13494)
CUB CADET CORPORATION SALES
614 Liverpool Dr (44280-9717)
P.O. Box 368023 (44280)
PHONE..................330 273-4550
Curtis E Moll, *Ch Bd*
David Hessler, *
James M Milinski, *
▲ EMP: 53 EST: 1981
SQ FT: 185,000
SALES (est): 1.14MM
SALES (corp-wide): 15.37B Publicly Held
Web: www.cubcadet.com
SIC: 3524 Grass catchers, lawn mower
HQ: Mtd Products Inc
5965 Grafton Rd
Valley City OH 44280
330 225-2600

(G-13495)
EMH INC (PA)
Also Called: Engineered Material Handling
550 Crane Dr (44280-9361)
PHONE..................330 220-8600
Edis Hazne, *Pr*
Dave Comiono, *
◆ EMP: 60 EST: 1988
SQ FT: 65,000
SALES (est): 7.69MM
SALES (corp-wide): 7.69MM Privately Held
Web: www.emhcranes.com
SIC: 3441 3536 Fabricated structural metal; Cranes and monorail systems

(G-13496)
FUSERASHI INTL TECH INC
Also Called: F I T
5401 Innovation Dr (44280-9353)
PHONE..................330 273-0140
Mamoru Shimada, *Prin*
◆ EMP: 22 EST: 1996
SQ FT: 200,000
SALES (est): 9.21MM Privately Held
Web: www.fitinc.net
SIC: 3714 Motor vehicle parts and accessories
PA: Fuserashi Co., Ltd.
11-74, Takaida
Higashi-Osaka OSK 577-0

(G-13497)
GREENFIELD DIE & MFG CORP (HQ)
Also Called: Canton Manufacturing
880 Steel Dr (44280-9736)
PHONE..................734 454-4000
James Fanello, *Pr*
Lillian Etzkorn, *VP*
EMP: 10 EST: 1955
SALES (est): 5.66MM Privately Held
SIC: 3544 3469 Special dies and tools; Metal stampings, nec
PA: Shl Liquidation Industries Inc.
880 Steel Dr
Valley City OH 44280

(G-13498)
GROUPER ACQUISITION CO LLC
Also Called: Shiloh Industries
880 Steel Dr (44280-9736)
PHONE..................248 299-7500
EMP: 94
SALES (corp-wide): 67.44MM Privately Held
Web: www.durashiloh.com
SIC: 3465 Automotive stampings
HQ: Grouper Acquisition Company, Llc
1780 Pond Run
Auburn Hills MI 48326
248 299-7500

(G-13499)
HY-PRODUCTION LLC
6000 Grafton Rd (44280-9330)
PHONE..................330 273-2400
William Kneebusch, *Ch Bd*
Mathew Roach, *
Keith Koprowski, *
▲ EMP: 124 EST: 1966
SQ FT: 60,000
SALES (est): 23.64MM
SALES (corp-wide): 94.39MM Privately Held
Web: www.hy-production.com
SIC: 3519 3492 3451 3594 Engines, diesel and semi-diesel or dual-fuel; Control valves, fluid power: hydraulic and pneumatic; Screw machine products; Fluid power pumps and motors
HQ: Kksp Precision Machining, Llc
1688 Glen Ellyn Rd
Glendale Heights IL 60139
630 260-1735

(G-13500)
JOSEPH ADAMS CORP
5740 Grafton Rd (44280-9327)
P.O. Box 583 (44280-0583)
PHONE..................330 225-9125
Patrick Adams, *Pr*
▲ EMP: 10 EST: 1948
SQ FT: 100,000
SALES (est): 820.26K Privately Held
Web: www.josephadamscorp.com
SIC: 2087 2833 Flavoring extracts and syrups, nec; Botanical products, medicinal: ground, graded, or milled

(G-13501)
KRISDALE INC
Also Called: Krisdale
649 Marks Rd (44280-9774)
PHONE..................330 225-2392
Glenn D Phelan, *Pr*
EMP: 6 EST: 1965
SALES (est): 384.49K Privately Held
SIC: 3544 Jigs and fixtures

(G-13502)
LIVERPOOL TOWNSHIP
6700 Center Rd (44280-9435)
P.O. Box 381 (44280-0381)
PHONE..................330 483-4747
EMP: 9
SIC: 3531 9111 Road construction and maintenance machinery; Mayors' office
PA: Liverpool Township
6801 School St
Valley City OH 44280
330 483-3102

(G-13503)
MACK CONCRETE INDUSTRIES INC (HQ)
201 Columbia Rd (44280-9706)
P.O. Box 335 (44280-0335)
PHONE..................330 483-3111
Richard W Mack, *Pr*
Betsy Mack, *Pr*
Jim Thompson, *VP*
Barbara Mack, *Sec*
EMP: 12 EST: 1932
SQ FT: 20,000
SALES (est): 9.95MM
SALES (corp-wide): 86.93MM Privately Held
Web: www.mackconcrete.com
SIC: 3272 Concrete products, precast, nec
PA: Mack Industries, Inc.
1321 Indus Pkwy N Ste 500
Brunswick OH 44212
330 460-7005

(G-13504)
MACK INDUSTRIES PA INC (HQ)
201 Columbia Rd (44280-9706)
P.O. Box 335 (44280-0335)
PHONE................................330 483-3111
Betsy Mack, *Pr*
Barbara Mack, *
EMP: 100 **EST:** 1952
SQ FT: 7,000
SALES (est): 7.77MM
SALES (corp-wide): 86.93MM **Privately Held**
Web: www.mackconcrete.com
SIC: 3272 Concrete products, precast, nec
PA: Mack Industries, Inc.
　　1321 Indus Pkwy N Ste 500
　　Brunswick OH 44212
　　330 460-7005

(G-13505)
MIXED LOGIC LLC
5907 E Law Rd (44280-9770)
PHONE................................440 826-1676
Kevin Borrowman, *Managing Member*
EMP: 7 **EST:** 2000
SALES (est): 354.76K **Privately Held**
SIC: 3699 5999 Electric sound equipment;
　　Electronic parts and equipment

(G-13506)
MODERN TRANSMISSION DEV CO
5903 Grafton Rd (44280-9329)
▲ **EMP:** 250 **EST:** 1994
SALES (est): 2.75MM
SALES (corp-wide): 15.37B **Publicly Held**
SIC: 3714 Motor vehicle transmissions, drive
　　assemblies, and parts
HQ: Mtd Products Inc
　　5965 Grafton Rd
　　Valley City OH 44280
　　330 225-2600

(G-13507)
MTD CONSUMER GROUP INC (DH)
5965 Grafton Rd (44280-9329)
PHONE................................330 225-2600
Steven E Pryatel, *Prin*
▼ **EMP:** 146 **EST:** 1999
SALES (est): 48.5MM
SALES (corp-wide): 15.37B **Publicly Held**
SIC: 3524 Lawn and garden tractors and
　　equipment
HQ: Mtd Products Inc
　　5965 Grafton Rd
　　Valley City OH 44280
　　330 225-2600

(G-13508)
MTD HOLDINGS INC (HQ)
5965 Grafton Rd (44280-9329)
P.O. Box 368022 (44136)
PHONE................................330 225-2600
Curtis E Moll, *CEO*
Jeff Deuch, *
◆ **EMP:** 500 **EST:** 1946
SALES (est): 1.84B
SALES (corp-wide): 15.37B **Publicly Held**
Web: www.mtdparts.com
SIC: 3544 6141 3469 3524 Special dies and
　　tools; Financing: automobiles, furniture,
　　etc., not a deposit bank; Metal stampings,
　　nec; Lawn and garden equipment
PA: Stanley Black & Decker, Inc.
　　1000 Stanley Dr
　　New Britain CT 06053
　　860 225-5111

(G-13509)
MTD INTERNATIONAL OPERATIONS (DH)
5965 Grafton Rd (44280-9329)

PHONE................................330 225-2600
Robert T Moll, *Pr*
EMP: 9 **EST:** 2003
SALES (est): 937.42K
SALES (corp-wide): 15.37B **Publicly Held**
SIC: 3524 Lawn and garden equipment
HQ: Mtd Holdings Inc
　　5965 Grafton Rd
　　Valley City OH 44280
　　330 225-2600

(G-13510)
MTD PRODUCTS INC (DH)
5965 Grafton Rd (44280-9329)
P.O. Box 368022 (44136-9722)
PHONE................................330 225-2600
Robert T Moll, *Ch*
Jeffery Deuch, *
Michael Griffith, *
◆ **EMP:** 500 **EST:** 1932
SQ FT: 180,000
SALES (est): 1.84B
SALES (corp-wide): 15.37B **Publicly Held**
Web: www.mtdparts.com
SIC: 3524 Lawn and garden equipment
HQ: Mtd Holdings Inc
　　5965 Grafton Rd
　　Valley City OH 44280
　　330 225-2600

(G-13511)
MTD PRODUCTS INC
Also Called: Mtd Consumer Products Supply
5903 Grafton Rd (44280-9329)
P.O. Box 368022 (44136-9722)
PHONE................................330 225-1940
EMP: 241
SALES (corp-wide): 15.37B **Publicly Held**
Web: www.mtdparts.com
SIC: 3524 Lawn and garden equipment
HQ: Mtd Products Inc
　　5965 Grafton Rd
　　Valley City OH 44280
　　330 225-2600

(G-13512)
MTD PRODUCTS INC
Industrial Plastics Co Div
680 Liverpool Dr (44280-9717)
P.O. Box 360585 (44136-0045)
PHONE................................330 225-9127
Mark Tyson, *Prin*
EMP: 101
SQ FT: 90,000
SALES (corp-wide): 15.37B **Publicly Held**
Web: www.mtdparts.com
SIC: 3524 Lawnmowers, residential: hand or
　　power
HQ: Mtd Products Inc
　　5965 Grafton Rd
　　Valley City OH 44280
　　330 225-2600

(G-13513)
NORTHLAKE STEEL CORPORATION
5455 Wegman Dr (44280-9707)
PHONE................................330 220-7717
William K Bissett, *CEO*
Craig O Curie, *
◆ **EMP:** 80 **EST:** 1977
SQ FT: 82,000
SALES (est): 8.96MM **Privately Held**
Web: www.northlakesteel.com
SIC: 3398 3312 Annealing of metal; Bar, rod,
　　and wire products

(G-13514)
RAF ACQUISITION CO
Also Called: Republic Anode Fabricators
5478 Grafton Rd (44280-9719)
PHONE................................440 572-5999

Mike Horonzy, *Pr*
EMP: 22 **EST:** 1932
SQ FT: 20,000
SALES (est): 3.1MM **Privately Held**
Web: www.republicanode.com
SIC: 3471 3479 Chromium plating of metals
　　or formed products; Coating of metals and
　　formed products

(G-13515)
SCHAEFFLER GROUP USA INC
5370 Wegman Dr (44280-9700)
PHONE................................800 274-5001
EMP: 43
SALES (corp-wide): 72.7B **Privately Held**
Web: www.schaeffler.us
SIC: 3562 Ball and roller bearings
HQ: Schaeffler Group Usa Inc.
　　308 Springhill Farm Rd
　　Fort Mill SC 29715
　　803 548-8500

(G-13516)
SHILOH INDUSTRIES INC
Ohio Welded Blank
5569 Innovation Dr (44280-9369)
PHONE................................330 558-2000
Daniel Brown, *Brnch Mgr*
EMP: 600
Web: www.durashiloh.com
SIC: 3465 Automotive stampings
PA: Shl Liquidation Industries Inc.
　　880 Steel Dr
　　Valley City OH 44280

(G-13517)
SHL LIQUIDATION INDUSTRIES INC (PA)
Also Called: Shiloh Industries
880 Steel Dr (44280-9736)
PHONE................................330 558-2600
Mike Putz, *CEO*
◆ **EMP:** 541 **EST:** 1950
SALES (est): 66.56MM **Privately Held**
Web: www.durashiloh.com
SIC: 3465 3469 3544 Automotive stampings;
　　Metal stampings, nec; Special dies and
　　tools

(G-13518)
SHL LIQUIDATION LIVERPOOL INC
Also Called: Liverpool-Coil-Processing
880 Steel Dr (44280-9736)
PHONE................................330 558-2600
James Fanello, *Pr*
EMP: 31 **EST:** 2001
SALES (est): 6.84MM **Privately Held**
Web: www.durashiloh.com
SIC: 3469 Metal stampings, nec

(G-13519)
SHL LIQUIDATION MEDINA INC (PA)
Also Called: Shiloh Inds Inc Mdina Blnking
5580 Wegman Dr (44280-9321)
EMP: 150 **EST:** 1986
SQ FT: 200,000
SALES (est): 4.8MM
SALES (corp-wide): 4.8MM **Privately Held**
SIC: 3325 3469 3545 Steel foundries, nec;
　　Metal stampings, nec; Machine tool
　　accessories

(G-13520)
SHL LIQUIDATION MFG LLC (HQ)
880 Steel Dr (44280-9736)
PHONE................................330 558-2600
Thomas Dugan, *Managing Member*
Lillian Etzkorn, *
EMP: 50 **EST:** 2014
SALES (est): 44.85MM **Privately Held**
Web: www.durashiloh.com

SIC: 3465 Automotive stampings
PA: Shl Liquidation Industries Inc.
　　880 Steel Dr
　　Valley City OH 44280

(G-13521)
TWB COMPANY LLC
5569 Innovation Dr (44280-9369)
PHONE................................330 558-2026
Jeff Malik, *Brnch Mgr*
EMP: 27
SALES (corp-wide): 3.43B **Publicly Held**
Web: www.twbcompany.com
SIC: 3465 Automotive stampings
HQ: Twb Company, L.L.C.
　　1600 Nadeau Rd
　　Monroe MI 48162

(G-13522)
WELSER PROFILE NORTH AMER LLC (DH)
5535 Wegman Dr (44280-9321)
PHONE................................330 225-2500
William Johnson Iii, *Managing Member*
EMP: 33 **EST:** 2020
SALES (est): 2.75MM
SALES (corp-wide): 242.12K **Privately Held**
Web: www.welser.com
SIC: 3449 Custom roll formed products
HQ: Welser Profile Beteiligungs Gmbh
　　Prochenberg 24a
　　Ybbsitz 3341
　　74438000

(G-13523)
ZION INDUSTRIES INC (PA)
6229 Grafton Rd (44280-9312)
PHONE................................330 483-4650
Bob Puls, *Pr*
Micheal Laheta, *
Randy Lane, *
Dorothy Puls, *
EMP: 48 **EST:** 1977
SQ FT: 16,600
SALES (est): 10.21MM
SALES (corp-wide): 10.21MM **Privately Held**
Web: www.zioninduction.com
SIC: 3398 Brazing (hardening) of metal

Van Buren
Hancock County

(G-13524)
BENA INC
1390 Township Road 229 (45889-9603)
P.O. Box 77 (45889-0077)
PHONE................................419 299-3313
Gary Benjamin, *Prin*
Gary Benjamin, *Pr*
Keith Benjamin, *VP*
Barbara Benjamin, *Sec*
EMP: 9 **EST:** 1962
SQ FT: 5,000
SALES (est): 299.86K **Privately Held**
Web: www.benainc.com
SIC: 3089 Injection molding of plastics

Van Wert
Van Wert County

(G-13525)
ADVANCED BIOLOGICAL MKTG INC
Also Called: Agrauxine By Lesaffre
375 Bonnewitz Ave (45891-1101)
P.O. Box 222 (45891-0222)
PHONE................................419 232-2461

Hugo Bony, *CEO*
▲ **EMP:** 25 **EST:** 2000
SQ FT: 3,500
SALES (est): 7.74MM **Privately Held**
Web: www.agrauxine.us
SIC: 2879 0116 Insecticides and pesticides; Soybeans

(G-13526)
ALLIANCE AUTOMATION LLC
1100 John Brown Rd (45891-9184)
PHONE..................................419 238-2520
▲ **EMP:** 80 **EST:** 2004
SALES (est): 18.17MM **Privately Held**
Web: www.allianceautomation.com
SIC: 3599 Custom machinery

(G-13527)
BARKMAN HONEY LLC
550 Bonnewitz Ave (45891-1188)
PHONE..................................620 947-3173
Brent Barkman, *Brnch Mgr*
EMP: 18
SALES (corp-wide): 25.69MM **Privately Held**
SIC: 2099 Food preparations, nec
PA: Barkman Honey, Llc
120 Santa Fe St
Hillsboro KS 67063
620 947-3173

(G-13528)
BRAUN INDUSTRIES INC
1170 Production Dr (45891-9391)
PHONE..................................419 232-7020
TOLL FREE: 800
Kim Braun, *Pr*
Scott Braun, *
Dale A Schroeder, *
Gary Kohls, *
Jill Cilmi, *
EMP: 270 **EST:** 1959
SQ FT: 160,000
SALES (est): 17.33MM **Privately Held**
Web: www.braunambulances.com
SIC: 3711 Ambulances (motor vehicles), assembly of

(G-13529)
COOL MACHINES INC
740 Fox Rd (45891-2441)
PHONE..................................419 232-4871
David Krendl, *Pr*
Carlos Usuda, *VP*
Andrew Schulte, *Sec*
EMP: 14 **EST:** 2006
SQ FT: 40,000
SALES (est): 2.44MM **Privately Held**
Web: www.coolmachines.com
SIC: 3532 Mining machinery

(G-13530)
COOPER FOODS
Also Called: Cooper Farms Cooked Meat
6893 Us Route 127 (45891-9601)
PHONE..................................419 232-2440
Paula Fleming, *Prin*
EMP: 20 **EST:** 2009
SALES (est): 8.01MM **Privately Held**
Web: www.cooperfarms.com
SIC: 2015 Poultry slaughtering and processing

(G-13531)
COOPER HATCHERY INC
Also Called: Cooper Farms Cooked Meats
6793 Us Route 127 (45891-9601)
PHONE..................................419 238-4869
Eric Ludwig, *Brnch Mgr*
EMP: 130
SALES (corp-wide): 112.29MM **Privately Held**

Web: www.cooperfarms.com
SIC: 2015 Poultry slaughtering and processing
PA: Cooper Hatchery, Inc.
22348 Rd 140
Oakwood OH 45873
419 594-3325

(G-13532)
CQT KENNEDY LLC
Also Called: CORNWELL QUALITY TOOLS
1260 Industrial Dr (45891-2433)
PHONE..................................419 238-2442
Raymond Moeller, *Pr*
Robert Studenic, *Sec*
David Nist, *Treas*
EMP: 95 **EST:** 2016
SQ FT: 190,000
SALES (est): 3.86MM
SALES (corp-wide): 55.65MM **Privately Held**
Web: www.buykennedy.com
SIC: 3469 3841 Boxes: tool, lunch, mail, etc.: stamped metal; Surgical and medical instruments
PA: The Cornwell Quality Tools Company
667 Seville Rd
Wadsworth OH 44281
330 336-3506

(G-13533)
DANFOSS POWER SOLUTIONS II LLC
Also Called: Danfoss
1225 W Main St (45891-9362)
PHONE..................................419 238-1190
Joshua Wood, *Brnch Mgr*
EMP: 13
SALES (corp-wide): 10.26B **Privately Held**
SIC: 3542 3594 3052 3492 Crimping machinery, metal; Fluid power pumps; Rubber hose; Hose and tube fittings and assemblies, hydraulic/pneumatic
HQ: Danfoss Power Solutions Ii, Llc
2800 E 13th St
Ames IA 50010
515 239-6000

(G-13534)
EATON CORPORATION
Also Called: Mobile Operations
1225 W Main St (45891-9362)
PHONE..................................419 238-1190
Carey Welker, *Brnch Mgr*
EMP: 900
Web: www.dix-eaton.com
SIC: 3052 3429 Rubber hose; Clamps and couplings, hose
HQ: Eaton Corporation
1000 Eaton Blvd
Cleveland OH 44122
440 523-5000

(G-13535)
EISENHAUER MFG CO LLC
409 Center St (45891-1135)
P.O. Box 390 (45891-0390)
PHONE..................................419 238-0081
EMP: 73 **EST:** 1944
SQ FT: 50,000
SALES (est): 2.61MM **Privately Held**
Web: www.eisenhauermfg.com
SIC: 3469 3412 3411 2396 Stamping metal for the trade; Metal barrels, drums, and pails ; Metal cans; Automotive trimmings, fabric

(G-13536)
GREIF INC
975 Glenn St (45891-2331)
PHONE..................................419 238-0565
Doug Benner, *Mgr*

EMP: 48
SALES (corp-wide): 5.45B **Publicly Held**
Web: www.greif.com
SIC: 2655 Drums, fiber: made from purchased material
PA: Greif, Inc.
425 Winter Rd
Delaware OH 43015
740 549-6000

(G-13537)
HOLLYWOOD DANCE JAMS
8402 Hoaglin Center Rd (45891-9672)
PHONE..................................419 234-0746
Kim Hohman, *Prin*
EMP: 6 **EST:** 2015
SALES (est): 50.24K **Privately Held**
SIC: 2499 Wood products, nec

(G-13538)
KAM MANUFACTURING INC
1197 Grill Rd (45891-9387)
P.O. Box 407 (45891-0407)
PHONE..................................419 238-6037
Kim Adams, *Owner*
▲ **EMP:** 150 **EST:** 1985
SQ FT: 5,500
SALES (est): 3.67MM **Privately Held**
Web: www.kammfg.com
SIC: 2331 2329 3161 Women's and misses' blouses and shirts; Men's and boys' sportswear and athletic clothing; Luggage

(G-13539)
KMC HOLDINGS LLC
Also Called: Kennedy Manufacturing
1260 Industrial Dr (45891-2433)
PHONE..................................419 238-2442
▲ **EMP:** 130
Web: www.buykennedy.com
SIC: 3841 3469 5021 Surgical and medical instruments; Boxes: tool, lunch, mail, etc.: stamped metal; Racks

(G-13540)
LEESBURG LOOMS INCORPORATED
Also Called: Leesburg Loom & Supply
201 N Cherry St (45891-1210)
PHONE..................................419 238-2738
Jim Myers, *Pr*
EMP: 7 **EST:** 1988
SQ FT: 90,000
SALES (est): 692.8K **Privately Held**
Web: www.totalrug.com
SIC: 3552 Fabric forming machinery and equipment

(G-13541)
LEY INDUSTRIES INC
121 S Walnut St (45891-1720)
P.O. Box 191 (45891-0191)
PHONE..................................419 238-6742
Watson N Ley, *Pr*
Esther Ley, *VP*
Watson N Ley Prestreas, *Prin*
EMP: 6 **EST:** 1948
SQ FT: 32,000
SALES (est): 206.27K **Privately Held**
SIC: 3523 Farm machinery and equipment

(G-13542)
MEK VAN WERT INC
595 Fox Rd (45891-2457)
PHONE..................................419 203-4902
Javier Alcaba Berastegui, *CEO*
▼ **EMP:** 8 **EST:** 2017
SALES (est): 223.7K **Privately Held**
SIC: 3341 Secondary precious metals

(G-13543)
NATIONAL DOOR AND TRIM INC
1189 Grill Rd (45891-9386)
P.O. Box 278 (45874)
PHONE..................................419 238-9345
Thomas Turnwald, *Pr*
Rick Anderson, *
T Turnwald, *
Cory Michaud, *
▲ **EMP:** 48 **EST:** 1978
SQ FT: 50,000
SALES (est): 5.17MM **Privately Held**
Web: www.national-door.com
SIC: 2431 Millwork

(G-13544)
RIDGE TOWNSHIP STONE QUARRY
16905 Middle Point Rd (45891-9771)
PHONE..................................419 968-2222
Roger Davis, *Pr*
EMP: 7 **EST:** 1914
SALES (est): 1.13MM **Privately Held**
Web: www.ridgetownshipquarry.com
SIC: 1422 5032 Crushed and broken limestone; Stone, crushed or broken

(G-13545)
TECUMSEH PACKG SOLUTIONS INC
Also Called: Van Wert Division
1275 Industrial Dr (45891-2432)
PHONE..................................419 238-1122
James Robideau, *Brnch Mgr*
EMP: 15
SALES (corp-wide): 11.03MM **Privately Held**
Web: www.akers-pkg.com
SIC: 2653 Boxes, corrugated: made from purchased materials
PA: Tecumseh Packaging Solutions, Inc.
707 S Evans St
Tecumseh MI 49286
517 423-2126

(G-13546)
TEIJIN AUTOMOTIVE TECH INC
Also Called: CSP Van Wert
1276 Industrial Dr (45891-2433)
PHONE..................................419 238-4628
Tom Harth, *Brnch Mgr*
EMP: 285
Web: www.teijinautomotive.com
SIC: 3089 3714 Injection molding of plastics; Motor vehicle parts and accessories
HQ: Teijin Automotive Technologies, Inc.
255 Rex Blvd
Auburn Hills MI 48326
248 237-7800

(G-13547)
UNIVERSAL LETTERING INC
Also Called: Universal Lettering Company
1197 Grill Rd # B (45891-9387)
P.O. Box 1055 (45891-6055)
PHONE..................................419 238-9320
Mark Hoops, *Pr*
▲ **EMP:** 10 **EST:** 1990
SQ FT: 20,400
SALES (est): 935.06K **Privately Held**
Web: www.universallettering.com
SIC: 2339 2329 Women's and misses' jackets and coats, except sportswear; Men's and boys' leather, wool and down-filled outerwear

Vandalia
Montgomery County

(G-13548)
ADARE PHARMACEUTICALS INC
(DH)
845 Center Dr (45377-3129)
PHONE...................937 898-9669
John Fraher, *CEO*
▲ **EMP:** 167 **EST:** 1980
SQ FT: 870,000
SALES (est): 44.57MM
SALES (corp-wide): 3.76B **Publicly Held**
Web: www.adarepharmasolutions.com
SIC: 2834 Pharmaceutical preparations
HQ: Tpg Capital Management, L.P.
301 Commerce St Ste 3300
Fort Worth TX 76102

(G-13549)
ALL SRVICE PLASTIC MOLDING INC
(PA)
850 Falls Creek Dr (45377-8600)
PHONE...................937 890-0322
Joseph Minneman, *CEO*
Joseph Kavalauskas, *
Joe Kavalauskas, *
Gary Deaton, *
Frank Maus, *
▲ **EMP:** 80 **EST:** 1984
SALES (est): 24.44MM
SALES (corp-wide): 24.44MM **Privately Held**
Web: www.mincogroup.com
SIC: 3089 Injection molding of plastics

(G-13550)
BALANCING COMPANY INC (PA)
898 Center Dr (45377-3130)
P.O. Box 490 (45377-0490)
PHONE...................937 898-9111
Michael Belcher, *CEO*
Michael W Belcher, *
Jack Boeke, *
EMP: 28 **EST:** 1967
SQ FT: 53,000
SALES (est): 2.58MM
SALES (corp-wide): 2.58MM **Privately Held**
Web: www.balco.com
SIC: 3599 8734 3544 Machine shop, jobbing and repair; Testing laboratories; Special dies, tools, jigs, and fixtures

(G-13551)
BOSTON STOKER INC (PA)
Also Called: Boston Stoker
10855 Engle Rd (45377-9439)
P.O. Box 548 (45377-0548)
PHONE...................937 890-6401
Henry Dean, *Pr*
Donald M Dean, *Pr*
Sally Dean, *Sec*
EMP: 11 **EST:** 1973
SALES (est): 5.02MM
SALES (corp-wide): 5.02MM **Privately Held**
Web: www.bostonstoker.com
SIC: 2095 5499 5993 Coffee roasting (except by wholesale grocers); Coffee; Tobacco stores and stands

(G-13552)
CROWN EQUIPMENT CORPORATION
Also Called: Crown Lift Trucks
750 Center Dr (45377-3128)
P.O. Box 400 (45377-0400)
PHONE...................937 454-7545
Lauren Robins, *Brnch Mgr*

EMP: 58
SALES (corp-wide): 7.12B **Privately Held**
Web: www.crown.com
SIC: 3537 Lift trucks, industrial: fork, platform, straddle, etc.
PA: Crown Equipment Corporation
44 S Washington St
New Bremen OH 45869
419 629-2311

(G-13553)
CROWN SOLUTIONS CO LLC
Also Called: Crown Solutions
913 Industrial Park Dr (45377-3115)
PHONE...................937 890-4075
EMP: 200
SIC: 8711 3589 Consulting engineer; Water treatment equipment, industrial

(G-13554)
DATWYLER SLING SLTIONS USA INC
Also Called: Columbia
875 Center Dr (45377-3129)
PHONE...................937 387-2800
Brian Bueltel, *Sls Dir*
Mark Bueltel, *Site Accounts Manager*
◆ **EMP:** 67 **EST:** 1985
SQ FT: 100,000
SALES (est): 11.43MM **Privately Held**
Web: www.datwyler.com
SIC: 5085 3069 3061 Seals, industrial; Molded rubber products; Mechanical rubber goods
HQ: Keystone Holdings, Inc.
875 Center Dr
Vandalia OH 45377

(G-13555)
ENERGIZER GLOBAL AUTO CARE
2800 Concorde Dr (45377-3300)
PHONE...................937 742-4500
EMP: 9 **EST:** 2022
SALES (est): 1.74MM **Privately Held**
Web: www.energizerholdings.com
SIC: 3421 Cutlery

(G-13556)
ERNST ENTERPRISES INC (PA)
Also Called: Ernst Concrete
993 Falls Creek Dr (45377-9686)
PHONE...................937 233-5555
John C Ernst Junior, *Pr*
David Ernst, *VP*
Dan Ernst, *Stockholder*
Bob Hines, *Prin*
EMP: 20 **EST:** 1946
SALES (est): 240.08MM
SALES (corp-wide): 240.08MM **Privately Held**
Web: www.ernstconcrete.com
SIC: 3273 Ready-mixed concrete

(G-13557)
EXHIBIT CONCEPTS INC (PA)
700 Crossroads Ct (45377-9675)
PHONE...................937 890-7000
▼ **EMP:** 90 **EST:** 1978
SALES (est): 13.21MM
SALES (corp-wide): 13.21MM **Privately Held**
Web: www.exhibitconcepts.com
SIC: 7389 5032 2435 Exhibit construction by industrial contractors; Brick, stone, and related material; Hardwood veneer and plywood

(G-13558)
GE AVIATION SYSTEMS LLC
GE Aviation
740 E National Rd (45377-3062)
PHONE...................937 898-5881

Victor Bonneau, *Brnch Mgr*
EMP: 300
SALES (corp-wide): 38.7B **Publicly Held**
Web: www.geaerospace.com
SIC: 3728 Aircraft parts and equipment, nec
HQ: Ge Aviation Systems Llc
1 Neumann Way
Cincinnati OH 45215
937 898-9600

(G-13559)
HERAEUS EPURIO LLC
970 Industrial Park Dr (45377-3116)
PHONE...................937 264-1000
Jrgen Heraeus, *Ch*
Robert Housman, *
Ram B Sharma, *
Santosh K Gupta, *
▲ **EMP:** 31 **EST:** 2012
SQ FT: 28,000
SALES (est): 21.72MM
SALES (corp-wide): 2.67MM **Privately Held**
Web: www.heraeus-group.com
SIC: 2869 2819 8731 Industrial organic chemicals, nec; Chemicals, high purity: refined from technical grade; Chemical laboratory, except testing
HQ: Heraeus Holding Gesellschaft Mit Beschrankter Haftung
Heraeusstr. 12-14
Hanau HE 63450
6181350

(G-13560)
HIGH TECH ELASTOMERS INC (PA)
885 Scholz Dr (45377-3121)
PHONE...................937 236-6575
James W Back, *Pr*
Vicki Back, *VP*
▲ **EMP:** 21 **EST:** 1996
SQ FT: 5,000
SALES (est): 2.94MM **Privately Held**
Web: www.htei.com
SIC: 3479 2822 Bonderizing of metal or metal products; Synthetic rubber

(G-13561)
INDUSTRIAL FIBERGLASS SPC INC
Also Called: Fiber Systems
896 Foxfire Trl (45377-2554)
PHONE...................937 222-9000
Theodore Morton, *Ch Bd*
Janice Morton, *
Valerie Cline, *
Karen Ramsey, *
Melanie Shockey, *
EMP: 35 **EST:** 1978
SALES (est): 4.47MM **Privately Held**
Web: www.ifs-frp.com
SIC: 3229 1799 Glass fiber products; Service station equipment installation, maint., and repair

(G-13562)
INNOVATIVE PLASTIC MOLDERS LLC
10451 Dog Leg Rd Ste 200 (45377-7502)
PHONE...................937 898-3775
Brian O' Leary, *Managing Member*
EMP: 50 **EST:** 2003
SQ FT: 12,800
SALES (est): 8.45MM **Privately Held**
Web: www.ipmolders.com
SIC: 3544 3089 Special dies, tools, jigs, and fixtures; Injection molding of plastics

(G-13563)
INTEVA PRODUCTS LLC
Inteva - Vandalia Engrg Ctr
707 Crossroads Ct (45377-9675)

P.O. Box 5051 (45377-5051)
PHONE...................937 280-8500
EMP: 115
SALES (corp-wide): 3.26B **Privately Held**
Web: www.intevaproducts.com
SIC: 3714 Motor vehicle parts and accessories
HQ: Inteva Products, Llc
1401 Crooks Rd Ste 100
Troy MI 48084

(G-13564)
JB PAVERS AND HARDSCAPES LLC
812 E National Rd (45377-3016)
PHONE...................937 454-1145
Jim Bliss, *Prin*
EMP: 7 **EST:** 2012
SALES (est): 1.97MM **Privately Held**
Web: www.jbmulchco.com
SIC: 3531 Pavers

(G-13565)
MAC ITS LLC (PA)
Also Called: Compass Electronics Solutions
1625 Fieldstone Way (45377-9317)
PHONE...................937 454-0722
EMP: 8 **EST:** 2017
SALES (est): 8.63MM
SALES (corp-wide): 8.63MM **Privately Held**
Web: www.mac-cable.com
SIC: 3355 Aluminum wire and cable

(G-13566)
MAHLE BEHR DAYTON LLC
250 Northwoods Blvd Bldg 47 (45377-9694)
PHONE...................937 356-2001
Clayton Brown, *Manager*
EMP: 398
SALES (corp-wide): 3.75MM **Privately Held**
SIC: 3714 Motor vehicle parts and accessories
HQ: Mahle Behr Dayton L.L.C.
1600 Webster St
Dayton OH 45404
937 369-2900

(G-13567)
MAHLE BEHR USA INC
Also Called: Delphi
250 Northwoods Blvd Bldg 47 (45377-9694)
PHONE...................937 356-2001
Clayton Brown, *Brnch Mgr*
EMP: 176
SALES (corp-wide): 3.75MM **Privately Held**
SIC: 3714 Motor vehicle parts and accessories
HQ: Mahle Behr Usa Inc.
2700 Daley Dr
Troy MI 48083
248 743-3700

(G-13568)
MANUFCTRED ASSEMBLIES CORP LLC
1625 Fieldstone Way (45377-9317)
PHONE...................937 454-0722
EMP: 14 **EST:** 2021
SALES (est): 1.82MM **Privately Held**
Web: www.mac-cable.com
SIC: 3999 Manufacturing industries, nec

(G-13569)
MASONITE CORPORATION
3250 Old Springfield Rd Ste 1 (45377-9599)
PHONE...................937 454-9207

2025 Harris Ohio
Industrial Directory

▲ = Import ▼ = Export
◆ = Import/Export

EMP: 247
Web: www.masonite.com
SIC: 2431 Doors, wood
HQ: Masonite Corporation
1242 E 5th Ave
Tampa FL 33605
800 663-3667

(G-13570)
MASONITE INTERNATIONAL CORP
875 Center Dr (45377-3129)
PHONE..................................937 454-9308
Geroge Henderson, *Pr*
EMP: 10
Web: www.masonite.com
SIC: 3441 3442 Fabricated structural metal;
Metal doors, sash, and trim
HQ: Masonite International Corporation
1242 E 5th Ave
Tampa FL 33605
813 877-2726

(G-13571)
MICROFINISH LLC
Also Called: Microfinish
865 Scholz Dr (45377-3121)
PHONE..................................937 264-1598
Dan O'connor, *Pr*
Bill J Jernigan, *
EMP: 60 EST: 1984
SQ FT: 8,000
SALES (est): 3.02MM
SALES (corp-wide): 325MM **Privately Held**
Web: www.microfinishusa.com
SIC: 3471 Electroplating of metals or formed products
HQ: Gnap, Llc
9000 Byron Cmmrce Dr Sw S
Byron Center MI 49315
616 583-5000

(G-13572)
MINCO TOOL AND MOLD INC
Also Called: Minco Group
900 Falls Creek Dr (45377-9685)
PHONE..................................937 890-0322
EMP: 27
SALES (corp-wide): 9.39MM **Privately Held**
Web: www.mincogroup.com
SIC: 3312 Blast furnaces and steel mills
PA: Minco Tool And Mold Inc.
5690 Webster St
Dayton OH 45414
937 890-7905

(G-13573)
MURPHY TRACTOR & EQP CO INC
Also Called: John Deere Authorized Dealer
1015 Industrial Park Dr (45377-3117)
PHONE..................................937 898-4198
Chris Cron, *Mgr*
EMP: 8
Web: www.murphytractor.com
SIC: 3531 5082 Construction machinery;
Construction and mining machinery
HQ: Murphy Tractor & Equipment Co., Inc.
5375 N Deere Rd
Park City KS 67219
855 246-9124

(G-13574)
NIMERS & WOODY II INC (PA)
Also Called: M A C
1625 Fieldstone Way (45377-9317)
PHONE..................................937 454-0722
▲ EMP: 173 EST: 1976
SALES (est): 4.89MM
SALES (corp-wide): 4.89MM **Privately Held**

Web: www.mac-cable.com
SIC: 3699 3679 Electrical equipment
and supplies, nec; Cable; wire; Harness
assemblies, for electronic use: wire or cable

(G-13575)
PARLEX USA LLC (DH)
801 Scholz Dr (45377-3121)
P.O. Box 427 (45377-0427)
PHONE..................................937 898-3621
Gary Wright, *Pr*
▲ EMP: 21 EST: 1970
SQ FT: 130,000
SALES (est): 9.1MM **Privately Held**
SIC: 3672 Wiring boards
HQ: Johnson Electric North America, Inc.
47660 Halyard
Plymouth MI 48170
734 392-5300

(G-13576)
SAIA-BURGESS LCC
Also Called: Ledex & Dormeyer Products
801 Scholz Dr (45377-3121)
PHONE..................................937 898-3621
Christopher Hasson, *Pr*
Gavin Fielden, *
Gordon Penman, *
Joel Philhours, *
▲ EMP: 100 EST: 2000
SQ FT: 105,000
SALES (est): 23.53MM **Privately Held**
SIC: 3714 3643 Motor vehicle parts and
accessories; Electric switches
HQ: Johnson Electric North America, Inc.
47660 Halyard
Plymouth MI 48170
734 392-5300

(G-13577)
SINBON OHIO LLC
Also Called: C & C Industries
815 S Brown School Rd (45377-9632)
PHONE..................................937 415-2070
Michael Seibert, *Prin*
Michael Seibert, *Managing Member*
Cindy Seibert, *
EMP: 135 EST: 1986
SQ FT: 40,000
SALES (est): 13.64MM **Privately Held**
SIC: 3672 Printed circuit boards

(G-13578)
SMYRNA READY MIX CONCRETE LLC
555 Old Springfield Rd (45377-9359)
PHONE..................................937 698-7229
Scott Besecker, *Brnch Mgr*
EMP: 172
SALES (corp-wide): 513.05MM **Privately Held**
Web: www.smyrnareadymix.com
SIC: 3273 Ready-mixed concrete
PA: Smyrna Ready Mix Concrete, Llc
1000 Hollingshead Cir
Murfreesboro TN 37129
615 355-1028

(G-13579)
TRIBORO QUILT MFG CORP
Also Called: TRIBORO QUILT
MANUFACTURING CORPORATION
303 Corporate Center Dr Ste 108
(45377-1171)
PHONE..................................937 222-2132
Mindy Esmond, *Prin*
EMP: 10
SALES (corp-wide): 2.87MM **Privately Held**
SIC: 3999 Atomizers, toiletry
PA: Cuddletime, Inc.

172 S Broadway
White Plains NY 10605
914 428-7551

(G-13580)
UNIBILT INDUSTRIES INC
8005 Johnson Station Rd (45377-8617)
P.O. Box 373 (45377-0373)
PHONE..................................937 890-7570
Douglas Scholz, *Pr*
Sharon Scholz, *
EMP: 50 EST: 1969
SQ FT: 80,000
SALES (est): 5.01MM **Privately Held**
Web: www.unibiltcustomhomes.com
SIC: 2452 Modular homes, prefabricated,
wood

(G-13581)
VALMAC INDUSTRIES INC
825 Scholz Dr (45377-3121)
PHONE..................................937 890-5558
EMP: 21 EST: 1985
SALES (est): 2.56MM **Privately Held**
Web: www.valmacind.com
SIC: 3599 Machine and other job shop work

(G-13582)
VANDALIA MASSAGE THERAPY
147 W National Rd (45377-1934)
PHONE..................................937 890-8660
Rick Phillips, *Pt*
EMP: 7 EST: 1998
SALES (est): 158.35K **Privately Held**
Web: www.miamivalleymassage.com
SIC: 3999 7299 Massage machines, electric;
barber and beauty shops; Massage parlor

(G-13583)
WENTWORTH MOLD INC ELECTRA
Also Called: Electraform Industries Div
852 Scholz Dr (45377-3122)
PHONE..................................937 898-8460
Walter T Kuskowski, *CEO*
Tim Bright, *
Brian Karns, *
Ted W Kuskowski, *
Jeffrey D Barclay, *
▲ EMP: 60 EST: 1999
SQ FT: 65,000
SALES (est): 10.48MM **Privately Held**
Web: www.electraform.com
SIC: 3544 3559 Forms (molds), for foundry
and plastics working machinery; Plastics
working machinery

(G-13584)
ZED INDUSTRIES INC
3580 Lightner Rd (45377-9735)
P.O. Box 458 (45377-0458)
PHONE..................................937 667-8407
Dave Zelnick, *Ch*
Peter Zelnick, *
Mark Zelnick, *
Helen Zelnick, *
EMP: 70 EST: 1969
SQ FT: 30,000
SALES (est): 4.3MM **Privately Held**
Web: www.zedindustries.com
SIC: 3559 Plastics working machinery

Vanlue
Hancock County

(G-13585)
D & H MEATS INC
400 Blanchard St (45890-8702)
P.O. Box 213 (45890-0213)
PHONE..................................419 387-7767

Jared Fry, *Pr*
EMP: 7 EST: 1976
SALES (est): 434.64K **Privately Held**
SIC: 2011 5421 Meat packing plants; Meat
and fish markets

Venedocia
Van Wert County

(G-13586)
KRENDL RACK CO INC
18413 Haver Rd (45894-9420)
PHONE..................................419 667-4800
Tony Laman, *Pr*
Chris Koverman, *VP*
Jeff Koverman, *Treas*
Robin Laman, *Sec*
EMP: 8 EST: 1953
SQ FT: 12,000
SALES (est): 463.86K **Privately Held**
Web: www.krendlrack.com
SIC: 3471 5051 Electroplating and plating;
Plates, metal

(G-13587)
OHIO ELECTRO-POLISHING CO INC
15085 Main St (45894-9645)
PHONE..................................419 667-2281
Marty Koenig, *Pr*
Randall Koenig, *VP*
James Koenig, *Sec*
EMP: 6 EST: 1963
SQ FT: 15,000
SALES (est): 479.84K **Privately Held**
Web: www.venedocia.org
SIC: 3471 Electroplating of metals or formed
products

Vermilion
Erie County

(G-13588)
ARCHITCTRAL INDUS MET FNSHG LL
Also Called: A & I Metal Finishing
1091 Sunnyside Rd (44089-2759)
PHONE..................................440 963-0410
EMP: 15 EST: 2004
SALES (est): 3.26MM **Privately Held**
Web: www.aimetalfinishing.com
SIC: 3479 Coating of metals and formed
products

(G-13589)
COLEYS INC
Also Called: Cnc Machining
1775 Liberty Ave (44089-2510)
P.O. Box 830 (44089-0830)
PHONE..................................440 967-5630
Kenneth L Mc Daniel, *Pr*
Geraldine Mc Daniel, *
Maynard Coleman, *
Robert J Fetterman, *
EMP: 33 EST: 1968
SQ FT: 25,000
SALES (est): 8.55MM **Privately Held**
Web: www.coleys.com
SIC: 3599 Machine shop, jobbing and repair

(G-13590)
IRG OPERATING LLC
Also Called: Cleveland Quarries
850 W River Rd (44089-1530)
PHONE..................................440 963-4008
Zach Carpenter, *Managing Member*
EMP: 36 EST: 2007
SALES (est): 4.92MM **Privately Held**
Web: www.clevelandquarries.com

SIC: 1411 Sandstone, dimension-quarrying

Verona
Preble County

(G-13591)
KEYSTONE COOPERATIVE INC
Also Called: Verona Agriculture Center
141 S Commerce St (45378-5014)
P.O. Box 682 (45378-0682)
PHONE....................................937 884-5526
Rick Clark, *Mgr*
EMP: 8
SALES (corp-wide): 487.68MM **Privately Held**
Web: www.keystonecoop.com
SIC: 2873 2879 5261 5153 Nitrogenous
fertilizers; Agricultural chemicals, nec;
Fertilizer; Grain elevators
PA: Keystone Cooperative, Inc.
770 N High School
Indianapolis IN 46214
800 525-0272

Versailles
Darke County

(G-13592)
ASPEN MACHINE AND PLASTICS
257 Baker Rd (45380-9317)
PHONE....................................937 526-4644
John Moran, *Pr*
Mary Moran, *Sec*
EMP: 7 EST: 2004
SALES (est): 528.52K **Privately Held**
SIC: 3599 Machine shop, jobbing and repair

(G-13593)
COTA INTERNATIONAL INC
67 Industrial Pkwy (45380-9759)
PHONE....................................937 526-5520
Linda Cota, *Pr*
Sandra Cota, *VP*
Phillip Cota, *Sec*
Craig Cota, *Treas*
▲ **EMP:** 7 EST: 2003
SQ FT: 5,000
SALES (est): 1.9MM **Privately Held**
Web: www.cotainternational.com
SIC: 3713 5065 Truck bodies and parts;
Communication equipment

(G-13594)
DIRECT WIRE SERVICE LLP
100 Subler Dr (45380-9788)
PHONE....................................937 526-4447
Eric Barloge, *Mng Pt*
Dave Berger, *Mng Pt*
EMP: 8 EST: 2004
SQ FT: 6,000
SALES (est): 962.32K **Privately Held**
Web: www.directtoolingconcepts.com
SIC: 3544 Special dies and tools

(G-13595)
G & C RAW LLC
Also Called: G & C Raw Dog Food
225 N West St (45380-1359)
PHONE....................................937 827-0010
Cathy Manning, *Managing Member*
EMP: 9 EST: 2012
SQ FT: 1,800
SALES (est): 1.06MM **Privately Held**
Web: www.gandcrawdogfood.com
SIC: 2047 Dog food

(G-13596)
INSPIRTEC LLC
10203 Christian Rd (45380-9580)
P.O. Box 215 (45322-0215)
PHONE....................................614 571-7130
EMP: 6 EST: 2019
SALES (est): 917.15K **Privately Held**
SIC: 2873 Fertilizers: natural (organic),
except compost

(G-13597)
J & K PALLET INC
30 Subler Dr (45380-9782)
PHONE....................................937 526-5117
John Shardo, *Pr*
Jerry Shardo, *VP*
EMP: 6 EST: 1989
SQ FT: 24,000
SALES (est): 432.45K **Privately Held**
SIC: 2448 Pallets, wood

(G-13598)
KAMPS INC
Also Called: Pallets-Fam-In-place-packaging
10709 Reed Rd (45380-9701)
PHONE....................................937 526-9333
Nick Schaller, *Brnch Mgr*
EMP: 216
SALES (corp-wide): 771.73MM **Privately Held**
Web: www.kampspallets.com
SIC: 2448 Pallets, wood
HQ: Kamps, Inc.
665 Seward Ave Nw Ste 301
Grand Rapids MI 49504
616 453-9676

(G-13599)
KNAPKE CUSTOM CABINETRY LTD
Also Called: Knapke Custom Cabinetry
9306 Kelch Rd (45380-9679)
PHONE....................................937 459-8866
EMP: 7 EST: 1992
SQ FT: 8,800
SALES (est): 467.59K **Privately Held**
Web: www.knapkekitchensandbaths.com
SIC: 2434 Wood kitchen cabinets

(G-13600)
MIDMARK CORPORATION
60 Vista Dr (45380-9310)
PHONE....................................937 526-3662
EMP: 8
SALES (corp-wide): 497.54MM **Privately Held**
Web: www.midmark.com
SIC: 3648 3842 3843 2542 Lighting
equipment, nec; Stretchers; Dental
equipment and supplies; Partitions and
fixtures, except wood
PA: Midmark Corporation
10170 Penny Ln Ste 300
Miamisburg OH 45342
937 528-7500

(G-13601)
MIDMARK CORPORATION
160 Industrial Pkwy (45380-9757)
PHONE....................................937 526-8387
Anne Eiting Klamar, *Prin*
EMP: 22
SALES (corp-wide): 497.54MM **Privately Held**
Web: www.midmark.com
SIC: 3648 Lighting equipment, nec
PA: Midmark Corporation
10170 Penny Ln Ste 300
Miamisburg OH 45342
937 528-7500

(G-13602)
PRECISION FAB PRODUCTS INC
10061 Old State Route 121 (45380-9586)
P.O. Box 256 (45380-0256)
PHONE....................................937 526-5681
Eric D Miller, *CEO*
Cindy Miller, *Pr*
David Miller, *Treas*
EMP: 6 EST: 1985
SQ FT: 40,000
SALES (est): 822.46K **Privately Held**
Web: www.pfpfoam.com
SIC: 3069 5712 Foam rubber; Furniture
stores

(G-13603)
VERSAILLES BUILDING SUPPLY
741 N Center St (45380-1512)
P.O. Box 236 (45380-0236)
PHONE....................................937 526-3238
Richard P Huelsman, *Pr*
EMP: 7 EST: 1948
SQ FT: 14,000
SALES (est): 148.78K **Privately Held**
Web: www.versaillesohio.cc
SIC: 2431 Doors, wood

(G-13604)
VPP INDUSTRIES INC
960 E Main St (45380-1555)
P.O. Box 53 (45380-0053)
PHONE....................................937 526-3775
Vernon Monnin, *Pr*
Jane Monnin, *VP*
EMP: 10 EST: 1925
SQ FT: 9,600
SALES (est): 2.2MM **Privately Held**
Web: www.vppind.com
SIC: 2752 Offset printing

(G-13605)
WEAVER BROS INC (PA)
Also Called: Tri County Eggs
895 E Main St (45380-1561)
P.O. Box 333 (45380-0333)
PHONE....................................937 526-3907
Timothy John Weaver, *Pr*
Kreg Kohli, *
Audrey Weaver, *
Geo L Weaver, *
John D Weaver, *
▲ **EMP:** 60 EST: 1931
SQ FT: 20,000
SALES (est): 24.19MM
SALES (corp-wide): 24.19MM **Privately Held**
Web: www.weavereggs.com
SIC: 0252 5143 2015 Chicken eggs; Dairy
products, except dried or canned; Poultry
slaughtering and processing

(G-13606)
WINERY AT WILCOX INC
6572 State Route 47 (45380-9551)
PHONE....................................937 526-3232
Ralph M Williams, *Admn*
EMP: 7
Web: www.wineryatwilcox.com
SIC: 2084 Wines
PA: The Winery At Wilcox Inc
1867 Mefferts Run Rd
Wilcox PA 15870

Vienna
Trumbull County

(G-13607)
APTIV SERVICES US LLC
Also Called: Delphi

3400 Aero Park Dr (44473-8704)
P.O. Box 431 (44486-0001)
PHONE....................................330 367-6000
Ken Ellsworth, *Brnch Mgr*
EMP: 120
SALES (corp-wide): 20.05B **Privately Held**
Web: www.aptiv.com
SIC: 3714 Motor vehicle parts and
accessories
HQ: Aptiv Services Us, Llc
5725 Innovation Dr
Troy MI 48098

(G-13608)
**CLARKWSTERN DTRICH BLDG
SYSTEM**
1455 Ridge Rd (44473-9702)
PHONE....................................330 372-4014
Terry Westerman, *Brnch Mgr*
EMP: 62
SALES (corp-wide): 1.25B **Publicly Held**
Web: www.clarkdietrich.com
SIC: 3441 Fabricated structural metal
HQ: Clarkwestern Dietrich Building
Systems Llc
9050 Cntre Pnte Dr Ste 40
West Chester OH 45069

(G-13609)
KUNDEL INDUSTRIES INC (PA)
Also Called: Kundel
1510 Ridge Rd (44473-9704)
P.O. Box 4686 (44515-0686)
PHONE....................................330 469-6147
▲ **EMP:** 59 EST: 1987
SALES (est): 7.11MM
SALES (corp-wide): 7.11MM **Privately Held**
Web: www.kundel.com
SIC: 3531 3536 3444 Construction
machinery; Hoists, cranes, and monorails;
Sheet metalwork

(G-13610)
**LATROBE SPCIALTY MTLS DIST INC
(HQ)**
1551 Vienna Pkwy (44473-8703)
PHONE....................................330 609-5137
Gregory A Pratt, *Ch Bd*
Timothy R Armstrong, *
Thomas F Cramsey, *
James D Dee, *
Matthew S Enoch, *
◆ **EMP:** 80 EST: 1996
SQ FT: 189,000
SALES (est): 22.1MM
SALES (corp-wide): 2.76B **Publicly Held**
SIC: 3312 5051 Stainless steel; Steel
PA: Carpenter Technology Corporation
1735 Market St Fl 15
Philadelphia PA 19103
610 208-2000

(G-13611)
LITCO CORNER PROTECTION LLC
Also Called: Litco Cornerguard, LLC
1000 Tuscarawas St E (44473)
PHONE....................................330 539-5433
Lionel Trebilcock, *Managing Member*
EMP: 15 EST: 2021
SALES (est): 1.5MM
SALES (corp-wide): 22.35MM **Privately Held**
Web: www.litcomfg.com
SIC: 2653 Corrugated and solid fiber boxes
PA: Litco International, Inc.
1 Litco Dr
Vienna OH 44473
330 539-5433

(G-13612)
LITCO INTERNATIONAL INC (PA)
1 Litco Dr (44473-9600)
P.O. Box 150 (44473-0150)
PHONE...................................330 539-5433
Lionel Trebilcock, *CEO*
Gary Trebilcock, *
Gary Sharon, *
◆ **EMP:** 94 **EST:** 1962
SQ FT: 13,000
SALES (est): 22.35MM
SALES (corp-wide): 22.35MM **Privately Held**
Web: www.litco.com
SIC: 2448 5031 Pallets, wood; Particleboard

(G-13613)
MACK INDUSTRIES PA INC
2207 Sodom Hutchings Rd Ne
(44473-9716)
PHONE...................................330 638-7680
Ron Hoover, *Mgr*
EMP: 73
SALES (corp-wide): 86.93MM **Privately Held**
Web: www.mackconcrete.com
SIC: 3589 3272 Sewage treatment equipment; Concrete products, nec
HQ: Mack Industries Of Pennsylvania, Inc.
201 Columbia Rd
Valley City OH 44280
330 483-3111

(G-13614)
MILLWOOD INC
Liberty Industries
1328 Ridge Rd (44473-9702)
PHONE...................................330 609-0220
Ronald C Ringness, *Sr VP*
EMP: 61
Web: www.millwoodinc.com
SIC: 2448 Pallets, wood
PA: Millwood, Inc.
3708 International Blvd
Vienna OH 44473

(G-13615)
MILLWOOD NATURAL LLC
3708 International Blvd (44473-9796)
PHONE...................................330 393-4400
Lionel Trebilcock, *Pt*
EMP: 12 **EST:** 2013
SALES (est): 2.8MM **Privately Held**
Web: www.millwoodinc.com
SIC: 3565 4731 Packaging machinery; Freight transportation arrangement
PA: Millwood, Inc.
3708 International Blvd
Vienna OH 44473

(G-13616)
PROCESS INNOVATIONS INC
4219 King Graves Rd (44473-9708)
P.O. Box 25 (44418-0025)
PHONE...................................330 856-5192
Robert S Crow, *Pr*
EMP: 6 **EST:** 1988
SQ FT: 6,000
SALES (est): 2.1MM **Privately Held**
Web: www.heatshrinkequipment.com
SIC: 3569 8711 Robots, assembly line: industrial and commercial; Engineering services

(G-13617)
RIVERSIDE STEEL INC
3102 Warren Sharon Rd (44473-9521)
PHONE...................................330 856-5299
John Radu Junior, *Pr*
John Radu Senior, *Ch*
Catherine Radu, *Sec*

▼ **EMP:** 11 **EST:** 1966
SQ FT: 38,000
SALES (est): 2.27MM **Privately Held**
Web: www.riverside-steel.com
SIC: 3441 Fabricated structural metal

(G-13618)
STARR FABRICATING INC
4175 Warren Sharon Rd (44473-9524)
PHONE...................................330 394-9891
Thomas B Smith, *Pr*
EMP: 77 **EST:** 1965
SALES (est): 2.26MM **Privately Held**
Web: www.starrmfg.com
SIC: 3441 3564 3496 3444 Fabricated structural metal; Blowers and fans; Miscellaneous fabricated wire products; Sheet metalwork

---

Vincent
Washington County

(G-13619)
BLANEY HARDWOODS OHIO INC
425 Timberline Dr (45784-5615)
PHONE...................................740 678-8288
Randal Blaney, *Pr*
James Blaney, *
EMP: 100 **EST:** 1978
SQ FT: 3,000
SALES (est): 1.9MM **Privately Held**
SIC: 2421 Kiln drying of lumber

(G-13620)
DECKER DRILLING INC
11565 State Route 676 (45784-5636)
PHONE...................................740 749-3939
Dean Decker, *Pr*
Pat Decker, *
EMP: 9 **EST:** 1999
SALES (est): 954.77K **Privately Held**
Web: www.deckerdrilling.com
SIC: 1381 Redrilling oil and gas wells

(G-13621)
HENDRICKSON
1051 Windy Ridge Rd (45784-5226)
PHONE...................................740 678-8033
Clyde Hendrickson, *Prin*
EMP: 7 **EST:** 2010
SALES (est): 264.69K **Privately Held**
Web: www.hendrickson-intl.com
SIC: 3714 Motor vehicle parts and accessories

(G-13622)
MICRO MACHINE WORKS INC
8900 State Route 339 (45784-5411)
P.O. Box 70 (45712-0070)
PHONE...................................740 678-8471
Linn Yost, *Pr*
Dan Anstatt, *Mgr*
David Yost, *Mgr*
EMP: 17 **EST:** 1992
SQ FT: 6,592
SALES (est): 2.36MM **Privately Held**
SIC: 3599 Machine shop, jobbing and repair

Vinton
Gallia County

(G-13623)
IVI MINING GROUP LTD
72116 Grey Rd (45686-8410)
P.O. Box 1101 (45640-7101)
PHONE...................................740 418-7745
Jesse Sizemore, *Ch Bd*
EMP: 7 **EST:** 2014

SQ FT: 5,000
SALES (est): 349.7K **Privately Held**
SIC: 1041 1221 1222 Placer gold mining; Bituminous coal surface mining; Bituminous coal-underground mining

(G-13624)
STEELIAL WLDG MET FBRCTION INC
Also Called: Steelial Cnstr Met Fabrication
70764 State Route 124 (45686-8545)
PHONE...................................740 669-5300
Larry Allen Hedrick Junior, *Pr*
Krista Lynnete Hedrick, *
EMP: 32 **EST:** 1998
SQ FT: 40,000
SALES (est): 11.71MM **Privately Held**
Web: www.steelial.com
SIC: 1623 3441 3444 Pipe laying construction; Fabricated structural metal; Sheet metalwork

---

Wadsworth
Medina County

(G-13625)
ACCEL GROUP INC (PA)
325 Quadral Dr (44281-9571)
PHONE...................................330 336-0317
James Terranova, *Pr*
▲ **EMP:** 84 **EST:** 1980
SQ FT: 191,000
SALES (est): 19.69MM
SALES (corp-wide): 19.69MM **Privately Held**
Web: www.accelgrp.com
SIC: 2542 Partitions and fixtures, except wood

(G-13626)
ADVANCED PLASTICS INC
590 Corporate Pkwy (44281-8398)
PHONE...................................330 336-6681
Phil Nye, *Pr*
John Davis, *VP*
EMP: 11 **EST:** 1999
SQ FT: 12,000
SALES (est): 2.69MM **Privately Held**
Web: www.advancedplastics.net
SIC: 3089 Injection molding of plastics

(G-13627)
AKRON PRODUCTS COMPANY
6600 Ridge Rd (44281-9743)
PHONE...................................330 576-1750
Chester Marshall Junior, *CEO*
EMP: 75 **EST:** 1945
SQ FT: 45,000
SALES (est): 4.74MM **Privately Held**
Web: www.akronproducts.com
SIC: 3446 Fences or posts, ornamental iron or steel

(G-13628)
AL FE HEAT TREATING-OHIO INC
979 Seville Rd (44281-8316)
PHONE...................................330 336-0211
Steve Turner, *Mgr*
EMP: 20
Web: www.aalberts-ht.us
SIC: 3398 Metal heat treating
PA: Al Fe Heat Treating-Ohio, Inc
209 W Mount Hope Ave # 1
Lansing MI 48910

(G-13629)
BMCA INSULATION PRODUCTS INC
270 Main St (44281-1446)
PHONE...................................330 335-2501
Harley Cummings, *Mgr*

EMP: 12
SALES (corp-wide): 6.35B **Privately Held**
SIC: 2493 Insulation and roofing material, reconstituted wood
HQ: Bmca Insulation Products Inc.
1361 Alps Rd
Wayne NJ

(G-13630)
CELL-O-CORE CO
276 College St (44281-1575)
PHONE...................................800 239-4370
Craig Cook, *Pr*
EMP: 6 **EST:** 1962
SALES (est): 644.12K **Privately Held**
Web: www.cellocore.com
SIC: 3089 Plastics containers, except foam

(G-13631)
CLAMPCO PRODUCTS INC (PA)
Also Called: Clampco
1743 Wall Rd (44281-9558)
PHONE...................................330 336-8857
James R Venner, *Pr*
Linda Venner, *
◆ **EMP:** 182 **EST:** 1971
SQ FT: 54,000
SALES (est): 24.95MM
SALES (corp-wide): 24.95MM **Privately Held**
Web: www.clampco.com
SIC: 3429 Clamps, metal

(G-13632)
COUNTER CONCEPTS INC
124 Townes End Dr (44281-8484)
PHONE...................................330 848-4848
Shawn Green, *Pr*
Dave Bartlett, *Sls Mgr*
EMP: 10 **EST:** 1993
SALES (est): 366.58K **Privately Held**
Web: www.counterconceptsinc.com
SIC: 2541 3083 5211 Counters or counter display cases, wood; Plastics finished products, laminated; Lumber and other building materials

(G-13633)
CUSTOM SPORSTWEAR IMPRINTS LLC
238 High St (44281-1861)
PHONE...................................330 335-8326
EMP: 9 **EST:** 1981
SQ FT: 3,000
SALES (est): 323.49K **Privately Held**
SIC: 5199 2759 7389 Advertising specialties; Screen printing; Embroidery advertising

(G-13634)
D & J ELECTRIC MOTOR REPAIR CO
Also Called: Ohio Belt Control Supply Co
1734 Wall Rd Office (44281-8356)
PHONE...................................330 336-4343
David Zuchniak, *Pr*
John Zuchniak, *VP*
EMP: 10 **EST:** 1973
SQ FT: 20,000
SALES (est): 471.41K **Privately Held**
SIC: 5013 7694 7629 1731 Automotive servicing equipment; Electric motor repair; Electrical equipment repair services; General electrical contractor

(G-13635)
DESHEA PRINTING COMPANY
Also Called: Aldridge Folders
924 Seville Rd (44281-8316)
PHONE...................................330 336-7601
Sherri Gasser, *Pr*
EMP: 6 **EST:** 2015
SALES (est): 148.8K **Privately Held**

Web: www.aldridgefolders.com
SIC: 2752 Photo-offset printing

(G-13636)
E D M STAR-ONE INC
6831 Ridge Rd (44281-8590)
PHONE..................................440 647-0600
Howard White, *Pr*
Samuel White, *VP*
Michael White, *Treas*
Timothy White, *Sec*
EMP: 10 EST: 1989
SALES (est): 804.76K **Privately Held**
Web: www.advancedresources.us
SIC: 3599 Machine shop, jobbing and repair

(G-13637)
EBNER FURNACES INC
Also Called: Ebnerfab
224 Quadral Dr (44281-8327)
PHONE..................................330 335-2311
Robert Ebner, *Pr*
Ralph Myers, *
◆ EMP: 80 EST: 1986
SQ FT: 150,000
SALES (est): 19.38MM
SALES (corp-wide): 271.47MM **Privately
Held**
Web: www.ebnerfab.com
SIC: 3567 3444 3433 3441 Industrial
furnaces and ovens; Sheet metalwork;
Heating equipment, except electric;
Fabricated structural metal
HQ: Ebner Verwaltung Gmbh
Ebner-Platz 1
Leonding 4060
73268680

(G-13638)
FIVES ST CORP
1 Park Centre Dr Ste 210 (44281-9482)
PHONE..................................234 217-9070
Daniel Balcer, *Pr*
▲ EMP: 21 EST: 2010
SQ FT: 7,000
SALES (est): 12.43MM
SALES (corp-wide): 1.92MM **Privately
Held**
Web: www.fivesgroup.com
SIC: 3531 Construction machinery
HQ: Fives Stein
108 A 112
Maisons-Alfort IDF 94700

(G-13639)
FRONT POCKET INNOVATIONS LLC
471 E Bergey St Ste C (44281-2097)
PHONE..................................330 441-2365
Graig Davis, *CEO*
EMP: 7 EST: 2015
SALES (est): 414.89K **Privately Held**
Web: www.theneomag.com
SIC: 5531 3949 3999 Automotive
accessories; Sporting and athletic goods,
nec; Manufacturing industries, nec

(G-13640)
GOLDSMITH & EGGLETON INC
300 1st St (44281-2084)
PHONE..................................330 336-6616
▲ EMP: 18
Web: www.goldsmith-eggleton.com
SIC: 2821 3069 5169 Plastics materials and
resins; Reclaimed rubber (reworked by
manufacturing processes); Synthetic rubber

(G-13641)
GOLDSMITH & EGGLETON LLC
300 1st St (44281-2084)
PHONE..................................203 855-6000
David Derhagopian, *Managing Member*

▲ EMP: 18 EST: 2012
SALES (est): 8.37MM **Privately Held**
Web: www.goldsmith-eggleton.com
SIC: 2821 3069 5169 Plastics materials and
resins; Reclaimed rubber (reworked by
manufacturing processes); Synthetic rubber
PA: Ravago Holdings America, Inc.
1900 Smmit Twr Blvd Ste 9
Orlando FL 32810

(G-13642)
H & S TOOL INC
715 Weber Dr (44281-9550)
P.O. Box 393 (44282-0393)
PHONE..................................330 335-1536
Mark W Hillestad, *Pr*
EMP: 19 EST: 1972
SQ FT: 12,500
SALES (est): 2.29MM **Privately Held**
Web: www.climaxportable.com
SIC: 3545 Tools and accessories for
machine tools

(G-13643)
HUTNIK COMPANY
Also Called: Ohio Engineering and Mfg Co
350 State St Ste 5 (44281-2417)
PHONE..................................330 336-9700
Victor Hutnik, *Pr*
Debra Hutnik, *VP*
EMP: 6 EST: 1994
SQ FT: 5,000
SALES (est): 647.56K **Privately Held**
Web: www.ohioengr.com
SIC: 3599 3443 7389 Machine shop, jobbing
and repair; Cylinders, pressure: metal plate;
Design, commercial and industrial

(G-13644)
J C WHITLAM MANUFACTURING CO
200 W Walnut St (44281-1379)
P.O. Box 380 (44282-0380)
PHONE..................................330 334-2524
◆ EMP: 22 EST: 1900
SALES (est): 9.37MM **Privately Held**
Web: www.jcwhitlam.com
SIC: 2891 2899 2851 2992 Adhesives and
sealants; Chemical preparations, nec;
Enamels, nec; Lubricating oils and greases

(G-13645)
**JERICO PLASTIC INDUSTRIES INC
(PA)**
Also Called: Jerico Industries
7970 Boneta Rd (44281-8406)
PHONE..................................330 868-4600
Steve Copeland, *Pr*
Brenda Copeland, *VP*
EMP: 20 EST: 1996
SQ FT: 53,000
SALES (est): 8.52MM **Privately Held**
Web: www.jericoplastic.com
SIC: 2821 Plastics materials and resins

(G-13646)
KEELER ENTERPRISES INC
Also Called: Aldridge Folders
924 Seville Rd (44281-8316)
PHONE..................................330 336-7601
Fred Keeler, *Pr*
Daniel Mills, *VP*
Sheri Gasser, *Treas*
EMP: 8 EST: 1974
SQ FT: 10,000
SALES (est): 264.8K **Privately Held**
Web: www.aldridgefolders.com
SIC: 2675 2678 Folders, filing, die-cut: made
from purchased materials; Stationery
products

(G-13647)
KRAMER & KIEFER INC
Also Called: Medina Tool & Die
2662 Valley Side Ave (44281-9233)
P.O. Box 24 (44258-0024)
PHONE..................................330 336-8742
Clayton Kramer, *Pr*
Robert Kiefer, *VP*
EMP: 6 EST: 1950
SQ FT: 6,500
SALES (est): 490.79K **Privately Held**
SIC: 3544 Special dies and tools

(G-13648)
LABELTEK INC
985 Seville Rd (44281-8316)
PHONE..................................330 335-3110
EMP: 58
SIC: 2759 Labels and seals: printing, nsk

(G-13649)
**LUKE ENGINEERING & MFG CORP
(PA)**
Also Called: Luke Engineering & Mfg
456 South Blvd (44281-2032)
P.O. Box 478 (44282-0478)
PHONE..................................330 335-1501
Fred P Hayduk, *Pr*
Chris Jurey, *
◆ EMP: 40 EST: 1946
SQ FT: 37,000
SALES (est): 4.76MM
SALES (corp-wide): 4.76MM **Privately
Held**
Web: www.lukeeng.com
SIC: 3471 3559 Anodizing (plating) of metals
or formed products; Metal finishing
equipment for plating, etc.

(G-13650)
MICHAEL DAY ENTERPRISES LLC
9774 Trease Rd (44281-9557)
P.O. Box 151 (44282-0151)
PHONE..................................330 335-5100
Michael F Day, *Pr*
EMP: 20 EST: 2010
SALES (est): 7.3MM **Privately Held**
Web: www.mdayinc.com
SIC: 2821 Molding compounds, plastics

(G-13651)
MILLER PRODUCTS INC
Mpi Label Systems Div
985 Seville Rd (44281-8316)
PHONE..................................330 335-3110
Randy L Kocher, *Pr*
EMP: 14
SALES (corp-wide): 70.41MM **Privately
Held**
Web: www.mpilabels.com
SIC: 2759 Labels and seals: printing, nsk
PA: Miller Products, Inc.
450 Courtney Rd
Sebring OH 44672
330 938-2134

(G-13652)
MILLER PRODUCTS INC
Also Called: M P I Labeltek
985 Seville Rd (44281-8316)
PHONE..................................330 335-3110
Ronald Nagy, *Brnch Mgr*
EMP: 58
SALES (corp-wide): 70.41MM **Privately
Held**
Web: www.mpilabels.com
SIC: 2759 Labels and seals: printing, nsk
PA: Miller Products, Inc.
450 Courtney Rd
Sebring OH 44672
330 938-2134

(G-13653)
MYERS INDUSTRIES INC
Akro-Mils
250 Seville Rd (44281-1020)
P.O. Box 989 (44309-0989)
PHONE..................................330 336-6621
Gary Taylor, *Mgr*
EMP: 101
SQ FT: 10,000
SALES (corp-wide): 836.28MM **Publicly
Held**
Web: www.myersindustries.com
SIC: 3052 3069 3443 2542 Automobile
hose, rubber; Rubber automotive products;
Fabricated plate work (boiler shop);
Partitions and fixtures, except wood
PA: Myers Industries, Inc.
1293 S Main St
Akron OH 44301
330 253-5592

(G-13654)
NELSON COMPANIES ONE LLC
Also Called: Cell-O-Core
6935 Ridge Rd (44281)
PHONE..................................330 239-4370
EMP: 28 EST: 1945
SALES (est): 1.02MM **Privately Held**
SIC: 3069 2656 5013 Balloons, advertising
and toy: rubber; Straws, drinking: made
from purchased material; Automotive
supplies

(G-13655)
NO BURN INC
1255 High St Ste 200 (44281-8262)
PHONE..................................330 336-1500
William Kish, *Pr*
EMP: 8 EST: 1998
SQ FT: 4,000
SALES (est): 11.85MM **Privately Held**
Web: www.noburn.com
SIC: 2899 Fire retardant chemicals

(G-13656)
P C M CO (PA)
291 W Bergey St (44281-1334)
P.O. Box 479 (44282-0479)
PHONE..................................330 336-8040
Duane Coffman, *Pr*
Brannon Riley, *
Paul Bebout, *
Seng Sisouphanah, *
Emma Momchilov, *Stockholder*
EMP: 37 EST: 1965
SALES (est): 742.72K
SALES (corp-wide): 742.72K **Privately
Held**
SIC: 3365 Aluminum and aluminum-based
alloy castings

(G-13657)
PARKER-HANNIFIN CORPORATION
Also Called: Ips
135 Quadral Dr (44281-8326)
PHONE..................................330 335-6740
Barbara Mccall, *Brnch Mgr*
EMP: 6
SALES (corp-wide): 19.93B **Publicly Held**
Web: www.parker.com
SIC: 3569 Lubricating systems, centralized
PA: Parker-Hannifin Corporation
6035 Parkland Blvd
Cleveland OH 44124
216 896-3000

(G-13658)
PARKER-HANNIFIN CORPORATION
Also Called: Electromechanical North Amer
135 Quadral Dr (44281-8326)
PHONE..................................330 336-3511

Kenneth Sweet, *Brnch Mgr*
EMP: 8
SALES (corp-wide): 19.93B **Publicly Held**
Web: www.parker.com
SIC: 3599 3535 3496 3469 Machine shop, jobbing and repair; Conveyors and conveying equipment; Miscellaneous fabricated wire products; Metal stampings, nec
PA: Parker-Hannifin Corporation
6035 Parkland Blvd
Cleveland OH 44124
216 896-3000

(G-13659)
PARKER-HANNIFIN CORPORATION
Pneumatic North America
135 Quadral Dr (44281-8326)
PHONE..............................330 336-3511
Bill Treacy, *Brnch Mgr*
EMP: 139
SALES (corp-wide): 19.93B **Publicly Held**
Web: www.parker.com
SIC: 3621 3643 3593 Electric motor and generator parts; Current-carrying wiring services; Fluid power cylinders and actuators
PA: Parker-Hannifin Corporation
6035 Parkland Blvd
Cleveland OH 44124
216 896-3000

(G-13660)
PLASTICS -R- UNIQUE INC
330 Grandview Ave (44281-1161)
PHONE..............................330 334-4820
Kenneth R Boersma, *Pr*
EMP: 30 **EST:** 1988
SQ FT: 12,300
SALES (est): 5.29MM **Privately Held**
Web: www.plasticsrunique.com
SIC: 3089 5162 Plastics containers, except foam; Plastics materials, nec

(G-13661)
PREMIUM BALLOON ACC INC
Also Called: Premium Balloon Accessories
6935 Ridge Rd (44281-9706)
P.O. Box 352 (44274-0352)
PHONE..............................330 239-4547
David Nelson, *Pr*
◆ **EMP:** 7 **EST:** 1945
SALES (est): 2.29MM **Privately Held**
Web: www.premiumballoon.com
SIC: 3089 Plastics containers, except foam

(G-13662)
PT TECH LLC (HQ)
1441 Wolf Creek Trl (44281-9742)
P.O. Box 305 (44281)
PHONE..............................330 239-4933
EMP: 98 **EST:** 1978
SQ FT: 45,000
SALES (est): 10.55MM
SALES (corp-wide): 4.57B **Publicly Held**
Web: www.pttech.com
SIC: 3714 Clutches, motor vehicle
PA: The Timken Company
4500 Mount Pleasant St Nw
North Canton OH 44720
234 262-3000

(G-13663)
QUALIFORM INC
689 Weber Dr (44281-9550)
PHONE..............................330 336-6777
Andy Antonino, *Pr*
EMP: 40 **EST:** 1976
SQ FT: 17,000
SALES (est): 2.83MM **Privately Held**
Web: www.qualiformrubbermolding.com

SIC: 3069 3544 3061 Molded rubber products; Special dies, tools, jigs, and fixtures; Mechanical rubber goods

(G-13664)
QUALITY REPRODUCTIONS INC
Also Called: Fine Lines
127 Hartman Rd (44281-9402)
PHONE..............................330 335-5000
Bob Grosser, *Pr*
EMP: 9 **EST:** 1985
SQ FT: 7,000
SALES (est): 2.19MM **Privately Held**
Web: www.sstubes.com
SIC: 3714 Motor vehicle parts and accessories

(G-13665)
RADICI PLASTICS USA INC (DH)
960 Seville Rd (44281-8316)
PHONE..............................330 336-7611
Angelo Radici, *Pr*
Danilo Micheletti, *
Mattia Imberti, *
◆ **EMP:** 26 **EST:** 1989
SQ FT: 235,000
SALES (est): 20.01MM **Privately Held**
Web: www.radicigroup.com
SIC: 3087 3089 Custom compound purchased resins; Plastics processing
HQ: Radici Novacips Spa
Via Bedeschi 20
Chignolo D'isola BG 24040
035 499-7689

(G-13666)
RAYDAR INC OF OHIO
1734 Wall Rd Ste B (44281-8354)
PHONE..............................330 334-6111
Daniel Broadbent, *VP*
Angelo Savakis, *Sec*
EMP: 8 **EST:** 1995
SALES (est): 783.38K **Privately Held**
SIC: 3069 Molded rubber products

(G-13667)
RBA INC
487 College St (44281-1105)
PHONE..............................330 336-6700
Robert Bault, *Pr*
Jane Haugh, *Sec*
EMP: 8 **EST:** 1974
SQ FT: 7,000
SALES (est): 194.55K **Privately Held**
SIC: 2752 7336 Offset printing; Graphic arts and related design

(G-13668)
ROHRER CORPORATION (HQ)
Also Called: Gateway Printing
717 Seville Rd (44282)
P.O. Box 1009 (44282)
PHONE..............................330 335-1541
Tim Swanson, *CEO*
Robert Stopar, *
Chris Rautner, *Chief Human Resource Officer*
Dan Petschke, *
▲ **EMP:** 170 **EST:** 1953
SQ FT: 169,000
SALES (est): 122.41MM **Privately Held**
Web: www.rohrer.com
SIC: 3089 2675 Blister or bubble formed packaging, plastics; Die-cut paper and board
PA: Wellspring Capital Management Llc
605 3rd Ave Fl 44
New York NY 10158

(G-13669)
RUBBER CITY INDUSTRIES INC
471 E Bergey St (44281-2097)
PHONE..............................330 990-9641
Robert Price, *Prin*
EMP: 7 **EST:** 2011
SALES (est): 782.61K **Privately Held**
Web: www.rubbercityindustries.com
SIC: 3999 Manufacturing industries, nec

(G-13670)
SATTLER COMPANIES INC
Also Called: Sattler Machine Products
1455 Wolf Creek Trl (44281-9742)
P.O. Box 306 (44274-0306)
PHONE..............................330 239-2552
David Sattler, *Pr*
David F Raynor, *Prin*
▲ **EMP:** 18 **EST:** 1972
SQ FT: 22,600
SALES (est): 2.96MM **Privately Held**
Web: www.sattlermachine.com
SIC: 3599 Machine shop, jobbing and repair

(G-13671)
SOPREMA USA INC (HQ)
310 Quadral Dr (44281-9571)
PHONE..............................330 334-0066
Pierre Bindschedler, *Pr*
Gilbert Lorenzo, *
Steven P Goetz, *
J Bret Treier, *
EMP: 30 **EST:** 1991
SALES (est): 74.09MM
SALES (corp-wide): 5.01B **Privately Held**
Web: www.soprema.us
SIC: 3069 Roofing, membrane rubber
PA: Holding Soprema
15 Rue De Saint-Nazaire
Strasbourg 67100

(G-13672)
SROUFE HEALTHCARE PRODUCTS LLC
961 Seville Rd (44281-8316)
P.O. Box 347 (46767-0347)
PHONE..............................260 894-4171
▲ **EMP:** 8 **EST:** 1974
SQ FT: 76,800
SALES (est): 750.94K **Privately Held**
SIC: 3842 2396 Orthopedic appliances; Screen printing on fabric articles

(G-13673)
STABLE STEP LLC
Also Called: Powersteps
961 Seville Rd (44281-8316)
PHONE..............................800 491-1571
EMP: 150 **EST:** 2015
SALES (est): 5.06MM **Privately Held**
SIC: 3842 5047 5999 Foot appliances, orthopedic; Orthopedic equipment and supplies; Orthopedic and prosthesis applications

(G-13674)
THE CORNWELL QUALITY TOOLS COMPANY (PA)
Also Called: Cornwell Quality Tools
667 Seville Rd (44281-1077)
PHONE..............................330 336-3506
▲ **EMP:** 80 **EST:** 1919
SALES (est): 55.65MM
SALES (corp-wide): 55.65MM **Privately Held**
Web: www.cornwelltools.com
SIC: 5085 3423 6794 Industrial supplies; Mechanics' hand tools; Franchises, selling or licensing

(G-13675)
TORSION CONTROL PRODUCTS INC
1441 Wolf Creek Trl (44281-9742)
PHONE..............................248 537-1900
Timothy A Thane, *Pr*
EMP: 19 **EST:** 1987
SALES (est): 4.56MM
SALES (corp-wide): 4.57B **Publicly Held**
Web: www.torsioncontrol.com
SIC: 3714 8711 Transmission housings or parts, motor vehicle; Engineering services
PA: The Timken Company
4500 Mount Pleasant St Nw
North Canton OH 44720
234 262-3000

(G-13676)
WARNER FABRICATING INC
7812 Hartman Rd (44281-8744)
PHONE..............................330 848-3191
James Warner, *CEO*
Mark Warner, *Pr*
EMP: 10 **EST:** 1977
SQ FT: 12,000
SALES (est): 872.31K **Privately Held**
SIC: 3444 Sheet metalwork

(G-13677)
WESTERN ROTO ENGRAVERS INC
Also Called: Wre Color Tech
668 Seville Rd (44281-1080)
PHONE..............................330 336-7636
Dean Ellebruch, *Mgr*
EMP: 37
SQ FT: 11,000
SALES (corp-wide): 12.93MM **Privately Held**
Web: www.wrecolor.com
SIC: 2754 2791 2759 Rotogravure printing; Typesetting; Commercial printing, nec
PA: Western Roto Engravers, Incorporated
533 Banner Ave
Greensboro NC 27401
336 275-9821

Wakeman
Huron County

(G-13678)
CAMMANN INC
7105 State Route 60 (44889-8510)
P.O. Box 210 (44816)
PHONE..............................440 965-4051
Henry Cammann, *CEO*
Henry Cammann, *Pr*
Fred W Cammann Iv, *VP*
▲ **EMP:** 10 **EST:** 1946
SALES (est): 2.74MM **Privately Held**
Web: www.cammann.com
SIC: 3559 3823 3624 3549 Chemical machinery and equipment; Process control instruments; Carbon and graphite products; Metalworking machinery, nec

(G-13679)
CUSTOM CHASSIS INC
52826 State Route 303 (44889-9537)
PHONE..............................440 839-5574
Matthew Tipple, *Pr*
Jack Schartman, *Sec*
Michael Huhn, *VP*
▲ **EMP:** 9 **EST:** 1990
SQ FT: 13,000
SALES (est): 246.35K **Privately Held**
Web: www.customchassisinc.com
SIC: 3711 Chassis, motor vehicle

(G-13680)
DURAFLOW INDUSTRIES INC
15706 Garfield Rd (44889-8439)
PHONE......................................440 965-5047
Mark Sliman, *Prin*
EMP: 8 **EST:** 2009
SALES (est): 940.73K **Privately Held**
Web: www.duraflowindustries.com
SIC: 3999 Barber and beauty shop
equipment

(G-13681)
KRAUSHER MACHINING INC
4267 Butler Rd (44889-8212)
PHONE......................................440 839-2828
Dale K Krausher, *Pr*
Barbara Krausher, *VP*
EMP: 8 **EST:** 1970
SQ FT: 10,000
SALES (est): 503.09K **Privately Held**
Web: www.krausher.com
SIC: 3451 Screw machine products

(G-13682)
M A HARRISON MFG CO INC
14307 State Route 113 (44889-8320)
PHONE......................................440 965-4306
Chad A Harrison, *Pr*
Walter Denham, *CFO*
James Harrison, *Ch*
Keith Harris, *VP*
EMP: 20 **EST:** 1938
SQ FT: 1,544
SALES (est): 1.57MM **Privately Held**
Web: www.maharrisonmfg.com
SIC: 3545 3366 Precision tools, machinists';
Castings (except die), nec, copper and
copper-base alloy

Walbridge
Wood County

(G-13683)
CLEVELND-CLFFS TBLAR
CMPNNTS L (DH)
30400 E Broadway St (43465-9568)
PHONE......................................419 661-4150
Clifford Smith, *Pr*
Angela Stojkov, *
Brian Bishop, *
Erik Anderson, *
Denise Caruso, *
◆ **EMP:** 92 **EST:** 2001
SQ FT: 330,000
SALES (est): 35.64MM
SALES (corp-wide): 19.18B **Publicly Held**
Web: www.clevelandcliffs.com
SIC: 3317 Steel pipe and tubes
HQ: Cleveland-Cliffs Steel Corporation
200 Public Sq Ste 3300
Cleveland OH 44114

(G-13684)
GREAT LAKES WINDOW INC
30499 Tracy Rd (43465-9794)
P.O. Box 1896 (43603-1896)
PHONE......................................419 666-5555
Lynn Morstadt, *Pr*
EMP: 600 **EST:** 1981
SQ FT: 170,000
SALES (est): 9.7MM
SALES (corp-wide): 5.58B **Privately Held**
Web: www.greatlakeswindow.com
SIC: 3089 5211 Windows, plastics; Lumber
and other building materials
HQ: Ply Gem Industries, Inc.
5020 Weston Pkwy Ste 400
Cary NC 27513
919 677-3900

(G-13685)
MATERIAL SCIENCES
CORPORATION
Also Called: Walbridge Coatings
30610 E Broadway St (43465-9561)
PHONE......................................419 661-5905
Jeff Ramsay, *Manager*
EMP: 100
SQ FT: 266,000
SALES (corp-wide): 107.19MM **Privately Held**
Web: www.materialsciencescorp.com
SIC: 3479 Coating of metals and formed
products
PA: Material Sciences Corporation
6855 Commerce Blvd
Canton MI 48187
734 207-4444

(G-13686)
MSC WALBRIDGE COATINGS INC
Also Called: Walbridge Coatings
30610 E Broadway St (43465-9791)
PHONE......................................419 666-6130
Patrick Murley, *CEO*
EMP: 120 **EST:** 1971
SQ FT: 400,000
SALES (est): 12.33MM
SALES (corp-wide): 107.19MM **Privately Held**
Web: www.materialsciencescorp.com
SIC: 3316 3479 Cold finishing of steel
shapes; Galvanizing of iron, steel, or end-
formed products
PA: Material Sciences Corporation
6855 Commerce Blvd
Canton MI 48187
734 207-4444

(G-13687)
RIVERSIDE MCH & AUTOMTN INC
Also Called: Assembly Division
28701 E Broadway St (43465-9625)
PHONE......................................419 855-8308
Denny Meyer, *Mgr*
EMP: 7
Web: www.riverside-machine.com
SIC: 3549 Assembly machines, including
robotic
PA: Riverside Machine & Automation, Inc.
1240 N Genoa Clay Ctr Rd
Genoa OH 43430

(G-13688)
ROCK EM SOCK EM RETRO LLC (PA)
5902 Moline Martin Rd (43465-9421)
PHONE......................................419 575-9309
Kayla Minniear, *Prin*
EMP: 6 **EST:** 2016
SALES (est): 105.16K
SALES (corp-wide): 105.16K **Privately Held**
Web: www.rockemsockemretro.com
SIC: 2252 Socks

(G-13689)
WESTERN STATES ENVELOPE CO
Also Called: Western States Envelope Label
6859 Commodore Dr (43465-9765)
PHONE......................................419 666-7480
Shelly Hinkle, *Mgr*
EMP: 50
SALES (corp-wide): 97.93MM **Privately Held**
Web: www.wsel.com
SIC: 5112 2677 Envelopes; Envelopes
PA: Western States Envelope Company
4480 N 132 St
Butler WI 53007
262 781-5540

Waldo
Marion County

(G-13690)
NWP MANUFACTURING INC
Also Called: N W P Manufacturing
2862 County Road 146 (43356-9122)
PHONE......................................419 894-6871
John E Werner Iii, *Pr*
John Werner, *Pr*
Jerry Keiesel, *VP*
EMP: 10 **EST:** 1989
SQ FT: 36,000
SALES (est): 234.6K **Privately Held**
SIC: 2842 2448 Sweeping compounds, oil or
water absorbent, clay or sawdust; Pallets,
wood

(G-13691)
OHIGRO INC (PA)
6720 Gillette Rd (43356-9105)
P.O. Box 196 (43356-0196)
PHONE......................................740 726-2429
Jerry Ward, *Pr*
Jerry A Ward, *Pr*
James H Ward, *VP*
Jeffrey Ward, *Treas*
EMP: 20 **EST:** 1965
SQ FT: 9,600
SALES (est): 9.87MM
SALES (corp-wide): 9.87MM **Privately Held**
Web: www.ohigro.com
SIC: 5191 5261 2875 0723 Fertilizer and
fertilizer materials; Fertilizer; Fertilizers,
mixing only; Crop preparation services for
market

Walhonding
Coshocton County

(G-13692)
DUGAN DRILLING INC
27238 New Guilford Rd (43843-9612)
P.O. Box 91 (43005-0091)
PHONE......................................740 668-3811
Guy E Dugan, *Pr*
Linda Dugan, *Sec*
EMP: 9 **EST:** 1980
SALES (est): 402.44K **Privately Held**
SIC: 1381 Drilling oil and gas wells

Walnut Creek
Holmes County

(G-13693)
COBLENTZ FAMILY BRANDS INC
(PA)
Also Called: Coblentz Chocolate Co
4917 State Rte 515 (44687)
P.O. Box 86 (44687-0086)
PHONE......................................330 893-2995
Jason Coblentz, *Pr*
EMP: 25 **EST:** 1987
SQ FT: 2,000
SALES (est): 2.63MM **Privately Held**
Web: www.coblentzchocolates.com
SIC: 2064 2066 5149 5441 Chocolate
covered dates; Chocolate candy, solid;
Chocolate; Candy

(G-13694)
MAST FARM SERVICE LTD
3585 State Rte 39 (44687)
P.O. Box 142 (44687-0142)
PHONE......................................330 893-2972

Eli Mast Junior, *Owner*
Joy Yutzy, *Prin*
EMP: 13 **EST:** 1986
SALES (est): 3.76MM **Privately Held**
Web: www.mastfarmservice.com
SIC: 3499 Fire- or burglary-resistive products

(G-13695)
STITCHES USA LLC
3149 State Rte 39 (44687)
P.O. Box 724 (44681-0724)
PHONE......................................330 852-0500
EMP: 15 **EST:** 2002
SALES (est): 1.08MM **Privately Held**
Web: www.stitchesusa.com
SIC: 2211 Decorative trim and specialty
fabrics, including twist weave

Walton Hills
Cuyahoga County

(G-13696)
CONTROLLIX CORPORATION
Also Called: Walton Hills
21415 Alexander Rd (44146-5512)
PHONE......................................440 232-8757
John Kelly, *CEO*
EMP: 15 **EST:** 1985
SQ FT: 18,000
SALES (est): 5.33MM **Privately Held**
Web: www.controllix.com
SIC: 3625 5063 Industrial electrical relays
and switches; Electrical apparatus and
equipment

(G-13697)
DUNHAM PRODUCTS INC
7400 Northfield Rd (44146-6108)
PHONE......................................440 232-0885
Joseph F Klukan, *CEO*
Rosemary Klukan, *Sec*
Jay Maslanka, *Mgr*
Sarah Johnson, *Mgr*
EMP: 15 **EST:** 1946
SQ FT: 7,700
SALES (est): 3.42MM **Privately Held**
Web: www.dunhamproducts.com
SIC: 3451 Screw machine products

(G-13698)
INTIGRAL INC (PA)
Also Called: Est
7850 Northfield Rd (44146-5523)
PHONE......................................440 439-0980
Jason Thomas, *Pr*
Richard Dietrich, *
Edmond Leopold, *
Dick Dietrich, *
Jim Prete, *
▲ **EMP:** 200 **EST:** 1987
SQ FT: 158,000
SALES (est): 21.07MM
SALES (corp-wide): 21.07MM **Privately Held**
Web: www.intigral.com
SIC: 3231 Insulating glass: made from
purchased glass

(G-13699)
MASON STRUCTURAL STEEL LLC
7500 Northfield Rd (44146-6187)
PHONE......................................440 439-1040
Scott Berlin, *Pr*
Scott Polster, *VP*
Doug Shymske, *COO*
EMP: 27 **EST:** 2017
SALES (est): 4.42MM **Privately Held**
Web: www.masonsteel.com

SIC: **3441** 5031 5074 Fabricated structural
metal; Doors and windows; Fireplaces,
prefabricated

(G-13700)
MEADOR SUPPLY COMPANY INC
20437 Hannan Pkwy Ste 5 (44146-5384)
P.O. Box 668 (44087-0668)
PHONE............................330 405-4403
Audrey Kadusky, *Pr*
Don Kadusky, *VP*
EMP: 10 **EST:** 1998
SALES (est): 3.43MM **Privately Held**
Web: www.meadorsupply.co
SIC: **3491** Industrial valves

(G-13701)
MSSI GROUP INC
Also Called: Mason Steel
7500 Northfield Rd (44146-6110)
PHONE............................440 439-1040
Leonard N Polster, *CEO*
Keith Polster, *
J Moldaver, *
Joseph Patchan, *
Sol W Wyman, *
EMP: 100 **EST:** 1958
SQ FT: 75,000
SALES (est): 7.24MM **Privately Held**
Web: www.masonsteel.com
SIC: **3441** 5031 5074 Fabricated structural
metal; Doors and windows; Fireplaces,
prefabricated

(G-13702)
REA ELEKTRONIK INC
7307 Young Dr Ste B (44146-5385)
PHONE............................440 232-0555
Ray Turchi, *Pr*
▲ **EMP:** 11 **EST:** 2000
SQ FT: 5,400
SALES (est): 4.02MM **Privately Held**
Web: www.rea-jet.com
SIC: **3953** 5112 Marking devices; Marking
devices

(G-13703)
**TRANSTAR HOLDING COMPANY
LLC (PA)**
7350 Young Dr (44146-5357)
PHONE............................800 359-3339
Neil Sethi, *Pr*
Monte Ahuja, *Ch*
Jeffrey R Marshall, *VP*
Joseph Levanduski, *COO*
Anna Gluck, *Chief Human Resource Officer*
EMP: 6 **EST:** 2005
SALES (est): 719.56MM **Privately Held**
Web: www.transtarholding.com
SIC: **3444** 3281 2952 Metal roofing and roof
drainage equipment; Cut stone and stone
products; Asphalt felts and coatings

(G-13704)
VALTRIS SPECIALTY CHEMICALS
7050 Krick Rd (44146-4416)
PHONE............................216 875-7200
EMP: 11 **EST:** 2022
SALES (est): 1.01MM **Privately Held**
Web: www.valtris.com
SIC: **2899** Chemical preparations, nec

Wapakoneta
Auglaize County

(G-13705)
AMERICAN TRIM LLC
713 Maple St (45895-2323)
PHONE............................419 738-9664

Mike Staddon, *Brnch Mgr*
EMP: 111
SALES (corp-wide): 445.1MM **Privately
Held**
Web: www.amtrim.com
SIC: **3469** Porcelain enameled products and
utensils
HQ: American Trim, L.L.C.
1005 W Grand Ave
Lima OH 45801

(G-13706)
BENCHMARK PRECISION FAB INC
Also Called: Benchmark Prcision Fabrication
18692 Moulton Fort Amanda Rd
(45895-7836)
PHONE............................419 647-2003
Jon Neuman, *Pr*
James Michael, *Sec*
Robert Fissel, *VP*
EMP: 20 **EST:** 1997
SQ FT: 122,000
SALES (est): 433.96K **Privately Held**
SIC: **3441** Fabricated structural metal

(G-13707)
**BORNHORST PRINTING COMPANY
INC**
10139 County Road 25a (45895-8360)
PHONE............................419 738-5901
Glenn Bornhorst, *Pr*
Terri Bornhorst, *Sec*
EMP: 7 **EST:** 1957
SQ FT: 5,200
SALES (est): 491.05K **Privately Held**
Web: www.bornhorstprinting.com
SIC: **2752** Offset printing

(G-13708)
BRADY RUCK COMPANY
Also Called: Apex Bag Company
253 Indl Dr (45895)
PHONE............................419 738-5126
▲ **EMP:** 20
Web: www.apexbag.com
SIC: **2674** Bags: uncoated paper and
multiwall

(G-13709)
EVERYDAY TECHNOLOGIES INC
751 Industrial Dr (45895-9200)
PHONE............................419 739-6104
Michael Toal, *Brnch Mgr*
EMP: 11
SALES (corp-wide): 9.96MM **Privately
Held**
Web: www.everydaytech.com
SIC: **3444** Sheet metalwork
PA: Everyday Technologies, Inc.
2005 Campbell Rd
Sidney OH 45365
937 492-4171

(G-13710)
FENIX LLC (HQ)
820 Willipie St (45895-9201)
PHONE............................419 739-3400
Steven Wray, *Pr*
Kevin G Shumaker, *VP*
Douglas Stearns, *VP Sls*
▲ **EMP:** 13 **EST:** 2004
SQ FT: 141,000
SALES (est): 6.96MM **Privately Held**
Web: www.fenixllc.com
SIC: **3315** Wire products, ferrous/iron: made
in wiredrawing plants
PA: The Seneca Wire Group Inc
820 Willipie St
Wapakoneta OH 45895

(G-13711)
**G A WINTZER AND SON COMPANY
(PA)**
204 W Auglaize St (45895-1460)
P.O. Box 406 (45895-0406)
PHONE............................419 739-4900
EMP: 15 **EST:** 1848
SALES (est): 17.95MM
SALES (corp-wide): 17.95MM **Privately
Held**
Web: www.gawintzer.com
SIC: **2048** 5159 Feeds from meat and from
meat and vegetable meals; Hides

(G-13712)
G A WINTZER AND SON COMPANY
12279 S Dixey Hwy (45895)
P.O. Box 406 (45895-0406)
PHONE............................419 739-4913
Jim Keack, *Genl Mgr*
EMP: 70
SALES (corp-wide): 17.95MM **Privately
Held**
Web: www.gawintzer.com
SIC: **2048** Feeds from meat and from meat
and vegetable meals
PA: G. A. Wintzer And Son Company
204 W Auglaize St.
Wapakoneta OH 45895
419 739-4900

(G-13713)
**GATEWAY PACKAGING COMPANY
LLC**
Also Called: Apex Bag Company
253 Indl Dr (45895)
PHONE............................419 738-5126
EMP: 20
SALES (corp-wide): 1.58B **Privately Held**
Web: www.proampac.com
SIC: **2674** Bags: uncoated paper and
multiwall
HQ: Gateway Packaging Company Llc
605 Tn-76
White House TN 37188

(G-13714)
GRAYS ORANGE BARN INC
14286 State Route 196 (45895-8630)
PHONE............................419 568-2718
Timothy Gray, *Pr*
Glen Wagner, *Sec*
EMP: 7 **EST:** 1965
SALES (est): 179.12K **Privately Held**
SIC: **5431** 5451 2099 5148 Fruit stands or
markets; Cheese; Spices, including grinding
; Fruits, fresh

(G-13715)
HORIZON OHIO PUBLICATIONS INC
Also Called: Shelby County Review
520 Industrial Dr (45895-9200)
P.O. Box 389 (45895-0389)
PHONE............................419 738-2128
Deb Wez, *Brnch Mgr*
EMP: 51
SALES (corp-wide): 12.26MM **Privately
Held**
Web: www.theeveningleader.com
SIC: **2711** 2759 2752 Commercial printing
and newspaper publishing combined;
Commercial printing, nec; Commercial
printing, lithographic
HQ: Horizon Ohio Publications Inc
102 E Spring St
Saint Marys OH 45885
419 394-7414

(G-13716)
INGREDIA INC
Also Called: I D I
625 Commerce Rd (45895-8265)
P.O. Box 144 (45822)
PHONE............................419 738-4060
Gilles Desgrousilliers, *CEO*
Sandrine Delory, *Treas*
◆ **EMP:** 23 **EST:** 2006
SQ FT: 39,000
SALES (est): 9.83MM
SALES (corp-wide): 227.84MM **Privately
Held**
Web: www.ingredia.com
SIC: **2023** Dry, condensed and evaporated
dairy products
HQ: Ingredia
51 Avenue Fernand Lobbedez
Arras HDF 62000
321238000

(G-13717)
JEWETT SUPPLY
Also Called: Barlamy Supply
607 N Water St (45895-9379)
PHONE............................419 738-9882
Rife Jewett, *Pt*
Lori Jewett, *Pt*
Lynn Jewett, *Pt*
Lisa Hardeman, *Pt*
Barbara Young, *Pt*
EMP: 7 **EST:** 1968
SQ FT: 768
SALES (est): 106.36K **Privately Held**
SIC: **2499** Handles, poles, dowels and
stakes: wood

(G-13718)
KINSTLE TRUCK & AUTO SVC INC
Also Called: Kinstle Strlng/Wstern Star Trc
1770 Wapakoneta Fisher Rd (45895-9799)
P.O. Box 1986 (45895-0986)
PHONE............................419 738-7493
TOLL FREE: 888
J Michael Kinstle, *Pr*
Barbara Kinstle, *Sec*
EMP: 6 **EST:** 1981
SQ FT: 10,500
SALES (est): 880.39K **Privately Held**
SIC: **5012** 5511 7538 3519 Truck tractors;
Trucks, tractors, and trailers: new and used
; Truck engine repair, except industrial;
Engines, diesel and semi-diesel or dual-fuel

(G-13719)
KN RUBBER LLC (HQ)
Also Called: Koneta Rubber
1400 Lunar Dr (45895-9796)
P.O. Box 150 (45895-0150)
PHONE............................419 739-4200
Rex Mouland, *Contrlr*
◆ **EMP:** 155 **EST:** 1986
SQ FT: 165,000
SALES (est): 5.39MM
SALES (corp-wide): 537.58MM **Privately
Held**
Web: www.knrubber.com
SIC: **3069** Rubber automotive products
PA: Kinderhook Industries, Llc
505 5th Ave Fl 25
New York NY 10017
212 201-6780

(G-13720)
KONETA INC
1400 Lunar Dr (45895-9796)
P.O. Box 150 (45895-0150)
PHONE............................419 739-4200
Christopher Keogh, *CEO*
Corwynne Carruthers, *
Thomas Tuttle, *

◆ **EMP:** 90 **EST:** 2007
SALES (est): 4.63MM **Privately Held**
Web: www.koneteinc.com
SIC: 3061 Automotive rubber goods
(mechanical)

(G-13721)
MIDWEST COMPOSITES LLC
302 Krein Ave (45895-2375)
PHONE..................419 738-2431
EMP: 10 **EST:** 2011
SALES (est): 1.46MM **Privately Held**
SIC: 2231 3229 Upholstery fabrics, wool;
Glass fiber products

(G-13722)
MIDWEST ELASTOMERS INC
Also Called: MEI
700 Industrial Dr (45895-9200)
P.O. Box 412 (45895-0412)
PHONE..................419 738-8844
George Wight, *Pr*
Ron Clark, *
Barbara Link, *
Sue Hunsacker, *
Evan Piland, *
◆ **EMP:** 65 **EST:** 1986
SQ FT: 56,000
SALES (est): 10.89MM **Privately Held**
Web: www.midwestelastomers.com
SIC: 2822 3069 Synthetic rubber; Reclaimed
rubber (reworked by manufacturing
processes)

(G-13723)
MIDWEST METAL FABRICATORS
712 Maple St (45895-2324)
PHONE..................419 739-7077
EMP: 11 **EST:** 2005
SALES (est): 1.95MM **Privately Held**
Web: www.mw-metal.com
SIC: 3444 Sheet metalwork

(G-13724)
MIDWEST METAL FABRICATORS LTD
712 Maple St (45895-2324)
PHONE..................419 739-7077
Verne E Peake, *Pt*
John Neumann, *Pt*
Jason Neumann, *Pt*
EMP: 10 **EST:** 2001
SQ FT: 15,500
SALES (est): 1.5MM **Privately Held**
Web: www.midwestmetalfab.com
SIC: 3444 Sheet metal specialties, not
stamped

(G-13725)
MIDWEST SPECIALTIES INC
Also Called: Flexarm
705 Commerce Rd (45895-8555)
PHONE..................800 837-2503
Nicholas I Kennedy, *CEO*
Penny Kentosh, *
EMP: 70 **EST:** 1967
SALES (est): 5.17MM **Privately Held**
Web: www.flexmachinetools.com
SIC: 3541 3271 3599 Tapping machines;
Concrete block and brick; Machine shop,
jobbing and repair

(G-13726)
NATIONAL LIME AND STONE CO
18430 Main Street Rd (45895-9400)
PHONE..................419 657-6745
Shaun Place, *Mgr*
EMP: 9
SALES (corp-wide): 86.85MM **Privately
Held**
Web: www.natlime.com

SIC: 1422 3281 Crushed and broken
limestone; Limestone, cut and shaped
PA: The National Lime And Stone
Company
551 Lake Cascade Pkwy
Findlay OH 45840
419 422-4341

(G-13727)
PRATT PAPER (OH) LLC
602 Leon Pratt Dr (45895-9548)
PHONE..................567 320-3353
Anthony Pratt, *Ch*
Brian Mcpheely, *CEO*
EMP: 75 **EST:** 2018
SALES (est): 97.48MM **Privately Held**
SIC: 2621 4953 Paper mills; Recycling,
waste materials

(G-13728)
T & S MACHINE INC
712 Maple St (45895-2324)
P.O. Box 579 (45876-0579)
PHONE..................419 453-2101
David Kriegel, *Pr*
William G Petty, *Pr*
Todd Kriegel, *VP*
EMP: 6 **EST:** 1984
SQ FT: 2,129
SALES (est): 248.12K **Privately Held**
SIC: 3599 Machine shop, jobbing and repair

(G-13729)
VMAXX INC
323 Commerce Rd (45895-8373)
P.O. Box 36 (44622-0036)
PHONE..................419 738-4044
Mark Meyer, *VP*
Darren Meyer, *Pr*
Scott Stiles, *Treas*
EMP: 10 **EST:** 2001
SQ FT: 20,000
SALES (est): 497.01K **Privately Held**
Web: www.vmaxx.biz
SIC: 3542 Extruding machines (machine
tools), metal

(G-13730)
WHITE FEATHER FOODS INC
Also Called: Whitefeather Foods
13845 Cemetery Rd (45895-8479)
P.O. Box 365 (45895-0365)
PHONE..................419 738-8975
Stephen L Hengstler, *Pr*
Dave Jeanneret, *Contrlr*
EMP: 6 **EST:** 1983
SQ FT: 5,000
SALES (est): 456.84K **Privately Held**
Web: store.rudolphfoods.com
SIC: 2096 2099 Pork rinds; Food
preparations, nec

Warren
Trumbull County

(G-13731)
ADS MACHINERY CORP
1201 Vine Ave Ne Ste 1 (44483-3834)
P.O. Box 1027 (44482-1027)
PHONE..................330 399-3601
Dale Minton, *Pr*
K Ramalingham, *
Patricia S Beil, *
EMP: 75 **EST:** 1956
SQ FT: 57,000
SALES (est): 4.46MM **Privately Held**
Web: www.adsmachinery.com
SIC: 3549 3547 Metalworking machinery, nec
; Rolling mill machinery

(G-13732)
**AJAX TOCCO MAGNETHERMIC
CORP (HQ)**
1745 Overland Ave Ne (44483-2860)
PHONE..................800 547-1527
Thomas Illencik, *Pr*
Steven White, *
◆ **EMP:** 200 **EST:** 2002
SQ FT: 200,000
SALES (est): 12.24MM
SALES (corp-wide): 1.66B **Publicly Held**
Web: www.ajaxtocco.com
SIC: 3567 7699 3612 Metal melting
furnaces, industrial: electric; Industrial
machinery and equipment repair; Electric
furnace transformers
PA: Park-Ohio Holdings Corp.
6065 Parkland Blvd
Cleveland OH 44124
440 947-2000

(G-13733)
ALPHABET INC (HQ)
8640 E Market St (44484-2346)
PHONE..................330 856-3366
Mark Tervalon, *Pr*
Michael Jocola, *
Cloyd Abruzzo, *
EMP: 100 **EST:** 1977
SALES (est): 15.11MM **Publicly Held**
SIC: 3679 Electronic circuits
PA: Stoneridge, Inc.
39675 Mckenzie Dr Ste 400
Novi MI 48377

(G-13734)
AM WARREN LLC
Also Called: Arcelormittal Warren
2234 Main Ave. S.W. (44481)
PHONE..................330 841-2800
Lou Schorsch, *CEO*
Jeff Foster, *Genl Mgr*
EMP: 8 **EST:** 2010
SALES (est): 574.27K **Privately Held**
SIC: 3312 Blast furnaces and steel mills

(G-13735)
AMERICAN STEEL & ALLOYS LLC
4000 Mahoning Ave Nw (44483-1924)
PHONE..................330 847-0487
Mordechai Korf, *Prin*
EMP: 6 **EST:** 2005
SALES (est): 406.49K **Privately Held**
SIC: 3312 Tool and die steel and alloys

(G-13736)
**AMERICAN WAY MANUFACTURING
INC**
1871 Henn Pkwy Sw (44481-8659)
PHONE..................330 824-2353
Robert E Platt, *Pr*
▼ **EMP:** 27 **EST:** 1995
SALES (est): 2.31MM **Privately Held**
SIC: 3089 Fences, gates, and accessories:
plastics

(G-13737)
AML INDUSTRIES INC
520 Pine Ave Se Ste 1 (44483-5763)
P.O. Box 4110 (44482-4110)
PHONE..................330 399-5000
David Gurska, *CEO*
▲ **EMP:** 26 **EST:** 1989
SQ FT: 30,000
SALES (est): 6.75MM **Privately Held**
Web: www.amlube.com
SIC: 2992 Lubricating oils

(G-13738)
APTIV SERVICES US LLC
Also Called: Delphi Pckard Eea - Wrren Plan
1265 N River Rd Ne (44483-2352)
PHONE..................330 373-7614
Robert Douce, *Brnch Mgr*
EMP: 74
SQ FT: 189,000
SALES (corp-wide): 20.05B **Privately Held**
Web: www.aptiv.com
SIC: 2821 Plastics materials and resins
HQ: Aptiv Services Us, Llc
5725 Innovation Dr
Troy MI 48098

(G-13739)
APTIV SERVICES US LLC
Also Called: S&Ps
1265 N River Rd Ne # Fr11 (44483-2352)
PHONE..................330 373-3568
Stephanie Pennel, *Brnch Mgr*
EMP: 1271
SALES (corp-wide): 20.05B **Privately Held**
Web: www.aptiv.com
SIC: 3465 Body parts, automobile: stamped
metal
HQ: Aptiv Services Us, Llc
5725 Innovation Dr
Troy MI 48098

(G-13740)
APTIV SERVICES US LLC
Also Called: Delphi
1265 N River Rd Ne (44483-2352)
PHONE..................330 505-3150
Bill Coates, *Brnch Mgr*
EMP: 561
SALES (corp-wide): 20.05B **Privately Held**
Web: www.aptiv.com
SIC: 3714 Motor vehicle parts and
accessories
HQ: Aptiv Services Us, Llc
5725 Innovation Dr
Troy MI 48098

(G-13741)
APTIV SERVICES US LLC
Also Called: Delphi
4551 Research Pkwy Nw (44483-1973)
PHONE..................330 306-1000
Robert Seidler, *Dir*
EMP: 400
SALES (corp-wide): 20.05B **Privately Held**
Web: www.aptiv.com
SIC: 3714 Air conditioner parts, motor vehicle
HQ: Aptiv Services Us, Llc
5725 Innovation Dr
Troy MI 48098

(G-13742)
ASTRO TECHNICAL SERVICES INC
2401 Parkman Rd Nw (44485-1758)
PHONE..................330 394-4747
Myron Watts, *Ch Bd*
Michael Watts, *Pr*
Martin Watts, *VP*
EMP: 23 **EST:** 1990
SALES (est): 2.35MM
SALES (corp-wide): 24.29MM **Privately
Held**
Web: www.warrendb.com
SIC: 3599 Custom machinery
PA: Astro Manufacturing & Design, Inc.
34459 Curtis Blvd
Eastlake OH 44095
888 215-1746

(G-13743)
BLOOM INDUSTRIES INC
Also Called: Incredible Plastics
1052 Mahoney Ave Nw (44483)

PHONE............330 898-3878
Ted E Bloom, *Pr*
EMP: 9 **EST:** 1957
SQ FT: 95,000
SALES (est): 1.84MM **Privately Held**
Web: www.bloomindustries.com
SIC: 3089 3544 Injection molding of plastics; Special dies, tools, jigs, and fixtures

(G-13744)
BRIDGESTONE RET OPERATIONS LLC
Also Called: Firestone
370 High St Ne (44481-1222)
PHONE............724 346-2621
Thomas Mossor, *Mgr*
EMP: 8
Web: www.bridgestoneamericas.com
SIC: 5531 7534 Automotive tires; Rebuilding and retreading tires
HQ: Bridgestone Retail Operations, Llc
200 4th Ave S Ste 100
Nashville TN 37201
615 937-1000

(G-13745)
BUCKEYE MEDICAL TECH LLC
405 Niles Cortland Rd Se Ste 202 (44484-2460)
PHONE............330 719-9868
EMP: 7 **EST:** 2009
SALES (est): 520.44K **Privately Held**
Web: www.anatotemp.com
SIC: 3841 Surgical and medical instruments

(G-13746)
BUDDY BACKYARD INC
140 Dana St Ne (44483-3845)
PHONE............800 837-9353
Jan Kiftler, *Pr*
▲ **EMP:** 25 **EST:** 1992
SALES (est): 2.33MM **Privately Held**
Web: www.realgaragelife.com
SIC: 3559 Automotive related machinery

(G-13747)
BWI EAGLE LLC
655 N River Rd Nw (44483-2254)
PHONE............724 283-4681
David Festog, *Pr*
▲ **EMP:** 20 **EST:** 1988
SALES (est): 2.44MM
SALES (corp-wide): 472.89MM **Privately Held**
Web: www.bwieagle.com
SIC: 3625 Switches, electronic applications
HQ: Cattron Holdings, Inc
655 N River Rd Nw Ste A
Warren OH 44483
234 806-0018

(G-13748)
CATTRON HOLDINGS INC (HQ)
655 N River Rd Nw Ste A (44483-2254)
PHONE............234 806-0018
Ryan Wooten, *CEO*
Martin Rapp, *
Michael Pearson, *
EMP: 24 **EST:** 1959
SALES (est): 17.43MM
SALES (corp-wide): 472.89MM **Privately Held**
Web: www.cattron.com
SIC: 3625 7622 5065 5063 Relays and industrial controls; Communication equipment repair; Communication equipment; Electric alarms and signaling equipment
PA: Harbour Group Ltd.
7733 Forsyth Blvd Fl 23
Saint Louis MO 63105

314 727-5550

(G-13749)
CATTRON NORTH AMERICA INC (DH)
Also Called: Remtron
655 N River Rd Nw Ste A (44483-2254)
PHONE............234 806-0018
Ryan Wooten, *Pr*
Brian D'angelo, *CFO*
Mike Santoni, *Treas*
◆ **EMP:** 19 **EST:** 1973
SQ FT: 25,000
SALES (est): 7.89MM
SALES (corp-wide): 472.89MM **Privately Held**
Web: www.cattron.com
SIC: 3625 Relays and industrial controls
HQ: Cattron Holdings, Inc
655 N River Rd Nw Ste A
Warren OH 44483
234 806-0018

(G-13750)
CDH CUSTOM ROLL FORM LLC
1300 Phoenix Rd Ne (44483-2851)
PHONE............330 984-0555
Jack Pacalo, *Pr*
EMP: 35 **EST:** 2019
SALES (est): 2.93MM **Privately Held**
Web: www.cdhrollform.com
SIC: 3449 Custom roll formed products

(G-13751)
CHARLES MFG CO
3021 Sferra Ave Nw (44483-2268)
PHONE............330 395-3490
David Frazier, *Pr*
Christine M Frazier, *Sec*
EMP: 13 **EST:** 1982
SQ FT: 10,000
SALES (est): 2.12MM **Privately Held**
Web: www.charlesmfg.com
SIC: 3441 5039 Fabricated structural metal; Architectural metalwork

(G-13752)
CLARKWESTERN DIETRICH BUILDING
Also Called: Clark Dietrich Building
1985 N River Rd Ne (44483-2527)
PHONE............330 372-5564
Bill Courtney, *Managing Member*
EMP: 62
SALES (corp-wide): 1.25B **Publicly Held**
Web: www.clarkdietrich.com
SIC: 3444 8711 3081 Studs and joists, sheet metal; Engineering services; Vinyl film and sheet
HQ: Clarkwestern Dietrich Building Systems Llc
9050 Cntre Pnte Dr Ste 40
West Chester OH 45069

(G-13753)
COLOR 3 EMBROIDERY INC
2927 Mahoning Ave Nw (44483-2027)
P.O. Box 870 (44482)
PHONE............330 652-9495
Traci Miller, *Pr*
Don Wiley, *VP*
EMP: 8 **EST:** 1995
SALES (est): 900.13K **Privately Held**
Web: www.color3.com
SIC: 2395 Embroidery products, except Schiffli machine

(G-13754)
COMPUTER STITCH DESIGNS INC
1414 Henn Hyde Rd Ne (44484-1227)

PHONE............330 856-7826
Sam Argeras, *Pr*
Donna Mc Guire, *Sec*
Darlene Argeras, *Treas*
EMP: 6 **EST:** 1986
SALES (est): 124.18K **Privately Held**
Web: www.computerstitch.com
SIC: 2395 Embroidery products, except Schiffli machine

(G-13755)
CONDO INCORPORATED
3869 Niles Rd Se (44484-3548)
PHONE............330 609-6021
John Condoleon, *CEO*
EMP: 55 **EST:** 1989
SQ FT: 40,000
SALES (est): 2.49MM **Privately Held**
Web: www.warrenprecision.net
SIC: 3451 Screw machine products

(G-13756)
CURRENT INC
455 N River Rd Nw (44483-2250)
PHONE............330 392-5151
Todd Buratti, *CEO*
EMP: 8
SALES (corp-wide): 4.94MM **Privately Held**
Web: www.currentcomposites.com
SIC: 2821 Thermosetting materials
PA: Current, Inc.
30 Tyler Street Ext
East Haven CT 06512
203 469-1337

(G-13757)
DASHER LAWLESS AUTOMATION LLC
310 Dana St Ne (44483-3850)
PHONE............855 755-7275
EMP: 28 **EST:** 2010
SALES (est): 2.44MM **Privately Held**
Web: www.autoparkit.com
SIC: 7521 7389 3534 Automobile storage garage; Design services; Automobile elevators

(G-13758)
DIAMOND OILFIELD TECH LLC
106 E Market St Fl 2 (44481-1151)
P.O. Box 328 (44482-0328)
PHONE............234 806-4185
Matthew Kleese, *Managing Member*
Peter Karousis, *Managing Member*
EMP: 7 **EST:** 2012
SALES (est): 2.39MM **Privately Held**
SIC: 1389 Oil consultants

(G-13759)
DRAKE MANUFACTURING LLC (PA)
Also Called: Drake Manufacturing
4371 N Leavitt Rd Nw (44485-1199)
PHONE............330 847-7291
John Lirong Hu, *Pr*
David Tang, *
EMP: 35 **EST:** 2017
SALES (est): 10.49MM
SALES (corp-wide): 10.49MM **Privately Held**
Web: www.drakemfg.com
SIC: 3599 Machine shop, jobbing and repair

(G-13760)
DRAKE MANUFACTURING SERVICES CO
4371 N Leavitt Rd Nw (44485-1199)
PHONE............330 847-7291
◆ **EMP:** 90

SIC: 3541 Machine tool replacement & repair parts, metal cutting types

(G-13761)
DYBROOK PRODUCTS INC
5232 Tod Ave Sw Ste 23 (44481-8728)
P.O. Box 1050 (44062-1050)
PHONE............330 392-7665
EMP: 35
Web: www.dybrook.com
SIC: 3061 Mechanical rubber goods

(G-13762)
ENGINEERED WIRE PRODUCTS INC
3121 W Market St (44485-3070)
PHONE............330 469-6958
John Bankol, *Mgr*
EMP: 48
Web: www.kci-corp.com
SIC: 3496 Miscellaneous fabricated wire products
HQ: Engineered Wire Products, Inc.
1200 N Warpole St
Upper Sandusky OH 43351

(G-13763)
ENVIRI CORPORATION
Enviri
101 Tidewater St Ne (44483-2434)
PHONE............330 372-1781
Brian Conlon, *Brnch Mgr*
EMP: 11
SALES (corp-wide): 2.34B **Publicly Held**
Web: www.enviri.com
SIC: 2816 2899 Metallic and mineral pigments, nec; Chemical preparations, nec
PA: Enviri Corporation
100-120 N 18th St # 17
Philadelphia PA 19103
267 857-8715

(G-13764)
EVERETT INDUSTRIES LLC
3601 Larchmont Ave Ne (44483-2447)
PHONE............330 372-3700
James Vosmik, *Managing Member*
EMP: 24 **EST:** 2017
SQ FT: 25,000
SALES (est): 4.76MM **Privately Held**
Web: www.everettindustries.com
SIC: 3291 Abrasive wheels and grindstones, not artificial

(G-13765)
FLEX-STRUT INC
2900 Commonwealth Ave Ne (44483-2831)
PHONE............330 372-9999
Dale H Gebhardt, *Pr*
Larry Mears, *
Mark Mirini, *
EMP: 75 **EST:** 1994
SQ FT: 52,000
SALES (est): 7.24MM **Privately Held**
Web: www.flexstrut.com
SIC: 3441 3429 Fabricated structural metal; Hardware, nec

(G-13766)
FOXCONN EV SYSTEM LLC
2300 Hallock Young Rd Sw (44481-9238)
PHONE............234 285-4001
Young Liu, *CEO*
EMP: 400 **EST:** 2021
SALES (est): 35.39MM **Privately Held**
Web: www.fevsys.com
SIC: 3711 Motor vehicles and car bodies
PA: Hon Hai Precision Industry Co., Ltd.
No. 2, Ziyou St.
New Taipei City TAP 23640

GEOGRAPHIC

(G-13767)
GENERAL ELECTRIC COMPANY
Also Called: GE
1210 Park (44483)
PHONE..............................330 373-1400
David Martin, *Brnch Mgr*
EMP: 8
SALES (corp-wide): 38.7B **Publicly Held**
Web: geaerospace.com
SIC: 3641 3648 3229 Lamps, sealed beam;
Lighting equipment, nec; Pressed and
blown glass, nec
PA: General Electric Company
1 Aviation Way
Cincinnati OH 45215
617 443-3000

(G-13768)
GENERAL MOTORS LLC
Also Called: General Motors
2369 Ellsworth Bailey Rd Sw (44481-9235)
PHONE..............................330 824-5840
John Donahoe, *Mgr*
EMP: 178
Web: www.gm.com
SIC: 5511 3714 Automobiles, new and used;
Motor vehicle parts and accessories
HQ: General Motors Llc
300 Rnaissance Ctr Ste L1
Detroit MI 48243

(G-13769)
GLENWOOD ERECTORS INC
251 Durst Dr Nw (44483-1164)
PHONE..............................330 652-9616
Linda L Trunick, *Pr*
Michael E Trunick, *VP*
EMP: 7 **EST:** 1980
SALES (est): 345.48K **Privately Held**
SIC: 3441 Fabricated structural metal

(G-13770)
GLUNT INDUSTRIES INC
319 N River Rd Nw (44483-2248)
PHONE..............................330 399-7585
Asaf Salama, *CEO*
Dennis Glunt, *
Harold Glunt, *
Stuart Gladstone, *
Gary Shells, *
▲ **EMP:** 125 **EST:** 1971
SQ FT: 150,000
SALES (est): 27MM **Privately Held**
Web: www.glunt.com
SIC: 3599 3549 3444 Machine shop, jobbing
and repair; Metalworking machinery, nec;
Sheet metalwork

(G-13771)
**HKM DRECT MKT CMMNICATIONS
INC**
387 Chestnut Ave Ne (44483-5856)
PHONE..............................330 395-9538
James Jastatt, *Prin*
EMP: 17
SALES (corp-wide): 26.5MM **Privately
Held**
Web: www.hkmdirectmarket.com
SIC: 2759 Commercial printing, nec
PA: Hkm Direct Market Communications,
Inc.
5501 Cass Ave
Cleveland OH 44102
800 860-4456

(G-13772)
INCREDIBLE SOLUTIONS INC
1052 Mahoning Ave Nw (44483-4622)
PHONE..............................330 898-3878
Ted Bloom, *CEO*
▲ **EMP:** 16 **EST:** 2005

SALES (est): 2.98MM **Privately Held**
Web: www.incrediblesolutionsinc.com
SIC: 2821 Molding compounds, plastics

(G-13773)
J W GOSS COMPANY (PA)
Also Called: Reds Auto Glass Shop
410 South St Sw (44483-5737)
P.O. Box 1066 (44482-1066)
PHONE..............................330 395-0739
George W Goss, *Pr*
Judith L Goss, *VP*
EMP: 14 **EST:** 1941
SQ FT: 20,000
SALES (est): 768.36K
SALES (corp-wide): 768.36K **Privately
Held**
Web: www.mirracoclips.com
SIC: 7536 3429 Automotive glass
replacement shops; Hangers, wall hardware

(G-13774)
J-WELL SERVICE INC
6345 Tod Ave Sw (44481-9738)
PHONE..............................330 824-2718
James T Adams, *Pr*
Gerald Bowser, *VP*
Maxine Adams, *Sec*
EMP: 9 **EST:** 1987
SALES (est): 260.6K **Privately Held**
SIC: 1389 Oil and gas wells: building,
repairing and dismantling

(G-13775)
JB INDUSTRIES LTD (PA)
160 Clifton Dr Ne Ste 4 (44484-1820)
PHONE..............................330 856-4587
EMP: 14 **EST:** 1989
SQ FT: 1,800
SALES (est): 754.31K **Privately Held**
Web: www.jb-industries.com
SIC: 8711 3599 Industrial engineers;
Machine shop, jobbing and repair

(G-13776)
LAIRD TECHNOLOGIES INC
655 N River Rd Nw (44483-2254)
PHONE..............................234 806-0105
EMP: 21
SALES (corp-wide): 12.39B **Publicly Held**
Web: www.lairdtech.com
SIC: 3443 Nuclear shielding, metal plate
HQ: Laird Technologies, Inc.
16401 Swngley Rdge Rd Ste
Chesterfield MO 63017
636 898-6000

(G-13777)
LITCO MANUFACTURING LLC
1512 Phoenix Rd Ne (44483-2855)
P.O. Box 150 (44473-0150)
PHONE..............................330 539-5433
Lionel F Trebilcock, *CEO*
Gary Tredilcock, *COO*
Raymond W Snider, *Prin*
▲ **EMP:** 17 **EST:** 2005
SALES (est): 4.87MM
SALES (corp-wide): 22.35MM **Privately
Held**
Web: www.litco.com
SIC: 2448 Pallets, wood
PA: Litco International, Inc.
1 Litco Dr
Vienna OH 44473
330 539-5433

(G-13778)
LRB TOOL & DIE LTD
3303 Parkman Rd Nw (44481-9142)
PHONE..............................330 898-5783
George Pearce, *Managing Member*

Lee Ann Westenselder, *Sec*
EMP: 10 **EST:** 2001
SALES (est): 2.2MM **Privately Held**
Web: www.lrbtool.com
SIC: 3544 Special dies and tools

(G-13779)
MACPHERSON ENGINEERING INC
Also Called: Macpherson & Company
2809 Mahoning Ave Nw (44483-2025)
P.O. Box 92 (44017-0092)
PHONE..............................440 243-6565
Bruce Mcpherson, *Pr*
EMP: 9 **EST:** 1965
SALES (est): 2.35MM **Privately Held**
Web: www.macphersonglass.com
SIC: 3231 Reflecting glass

(G-13780)
MAGNEFORCE INC
155 Shaffer Dr Ne (44484-1842)
P.O. Box 8508 (44484-0508)
PHONE..............................330 856-9300
Richard Miller, *Pr*
David Miller, *VP*
EMP: 10 **EST:** 1988
SQ FT: 5,900
SALES (est): 2.43MM **Privately Held**
Web: www.magneforce.com
SIC: 3567 Induction heating equipment

(G-13781)
MATALCO (US) INC
5120 Tod Ave Sw (44481-9748)
PHONE..............................234 806-0600
EMP: 22
SALES (corp-wide): 10.75MM **Privately
Held**
Web: www.matalco.com
SIC: 3363 Aluminum die-castings
HQ: Matalco (U.S.), Inc.
4420 Louisville St
Canton OH 44705

(G-13782)
MESSER LLC
2000 Pine Ave Se (44483-6550)
PHONE..............................330 394-4541
EMP: 6
SALES (corp-wide): 1.45B **Privately Held**
SIC: 2813 Nitrogen
HQ: Messer Llc
200 Somerset Corp Blvd # 7000
Bridgewater NJ 08807
908 464-8100

(G-13783)
MSSK MANUFACTURING INC
400 Dietz Rd Ne (44483-2708)
P.O. Box 30 (44482-0030)
PHONE..............................330 393-6624
Murray Miller, *Pr*
Julian Lehman, *
Ken Miller, *
▲ **EMP:** 11 **EST:** 1994
SQ FT: 16,000
SALES (est): 1.04MM **Privately Held**
SIC: 3432 3433 5074 Plumbing fixture
fittings and trim; Heating equipment, except
electric; Plumbing and hydronic heating
supplies

(G-13784)
NOVELIS CORPORATION
390 Griswold St Ne (44483-2738)
P.O. Box 1151 (44482-1151)
PHONE..............................330 841-3456
Mervyn W Bell, *Brnch Mgr*
EMP: 93
Web: www.novelis.com

SIC: 3355 3353 Aluminum rolling and
drawing, nec; Aluminum sheet, plate, and
foil
HQ: Novelis Corporation
3550 Pchtree Rd Ne Ste 11
Atlanta GA 30326
404 760-4000

(G-13785)
OAKES FOUNDRY INC
700 Bronze Rd Ne (44483-2720)
PHONE..............................330 372-4010
Grant Oakes, *Pr*
EMP: 21 **EST:** 1929
SQ FT: 2,000
SALES (est): 2.68MM **Privately Held**
Web: www.oakesfoundry.com
SIC: 3366 Castings (except die), nec, bronze

(G-13786)
OHIO STAR FORGE CO (HQ)
3991 Mahoning Ave Nw (44483-1934)
P.O. Box 430 (44482)
PHONE..............................330 847-6360
William J Orbach, *CEO*
Ken Saito, *
▲ **EMP:** 24 **EST:** 1988
SQ FT: 150,000
SALES (est): 24.73MM **Privately Held**
Web: www.ohiostarforge.com
SIC: 3462 Iron and steel forgings
PA: Daido Steel Co., Ltd.
1-1-10, Higashisakura, Higashi-Ku
Nagoya AIC 461-0

(G-13787)
OHIO TRAILER INC
1899 Tod Ave Sw (44485-4221)
PHONE..............................330 392-4444
John Miller, *Pr*
EMP: 8 **EST:** 1996
SQ FT: 20,000
SALES (est): 840.5K **Privately Held**
Web: www.ohiotrailercompany.com
SIC: 5231 7692 7538 3444 Paint, glass, and
wallpaper stores; Welding repair; General
automotive repair shops; Sheet metalwork

(G-13788)
ORTHOTICS PRSTHTICS RHBLTTION
Also Called: Billock, John N Cpo
700 Howland Wilson Rd Se (44484-2512)
PHONE..............................330 856-2553
John N Billock, *Executive Clinical Director*
John N Billock, *Executive Clinical Director*
EMP: 8 **EST:** 1975
SQ FT: 9,000
SALES (est): 617.07K **Privately Held**
Web: www.oandpcentre.com
SIC: 3842 8011 Braces, orthopedic; Offices
and clinics of medical doctors

(G-13789)
PHOENIX TOOL COMPANY
1351 Phoenix Rd Ne (44483-2899)
PHONE..............................330 372-4627
Eric Fredenburg, *Pr*
Jeff Copeland, *VP*
Joel Fredenburg, *Treas*
EMP: 8 **EST:** 1949
SQ FT: 5,000
SALES (est): 993.52K **Privately Held**
Web: www.phoenixtoolcompany.com
SIC: 3544 Special dies and tools

(G-13790)
POLIMEROS USA LLC
Also Called: Rotopolymers
1052 Mahoning Ave Nw (44483-4622)
PHONE..............................216 591-0175
Ron Davis, *Contrlr*

▲ = Import ▼ = Export
◆ = Import/Export

Jose Antonio Gomez Godoy, *Genl Mgr*
EMP: 8 **EST:** 2012
SALES (est): 15.15MM **Privately Held**
Web: www.polimerosusa.com
SIC: 2821 Plastics materials and resins

(G-13791)
PRINTERS EDGE INC
4965 Mahoning Ave Nw (44483-1405)
PHONE.................................330 372-2232
George M Rogers, *Pr*
▲ **EMP:** 10 **EST:** 1992
SQ FT: 11,000
SALES (est): 881.29K **Privately Held**
Web: www.printersedge.com
SIC: 2752 Commercial printing, lithographic

(G-13792)
R W SIDLEY INCORPORATED
425 N River Rd Nw (44483-2250)
PHONE.................................330 392-2721
Rich Kaye, *Mgr*
EMP: 21
SALES (corp-wide): 43.09MM **Privately
Held**
Web: www.rwsidley.com
SIC: 3273 Ready-mixed concrete
PA: R. W. Sidley Incorporated
436 Casement Ave
Painesville OH 44077
440 352-9343

(G-13793)
**REINFORCEMENT SYSTEMS OF
OHIO LLC**
Also Called: Merksteijn
3121 W Market St (44485-3070)
PHONE.................................330 469-6958
▲ **EMP:** 8
SIC: 3315 Wire and fabricated wire products

(G-13794)
ROTOPOLYMERS
1052 Mahoning Ave Nw (44483-4622)
PHONE.................................216 645-0333
Jose A Gomez Godoy, *Prin*
EMP: 9 **EST:** 2016
SALES (est): 1.41MM **Privately Held**
Web: www.rotopolymers.com
SIC: 2821 Plastics materials and resins

(G-13795)
RSL LLC
1160 Paige Ave Ne (44483-3838)
PHONE.................................330 392-8900
Bo Campbell, *Mgr*
EMP: 23
SALES (corp-wide): 278.4MM **Privately
Held**
Web: www.rslinc.com
SIC: 2431 3089 3211 3442 Door frames,
wood; Composition stone, plastics; Flat
glass; Sash, door or window: metal
HQ: Rsl Llc
3092 English Creek Ave
Egg Harbor Township NJ 08234
609 484-1600

(G-13796)
RULTRACT INC
8598 Kimblewick Ln Ne (44484-2066)
PHONE.................................330 856-9808
Janice Rullo, *Pr*
EMP: 8 **EST:** 1994
SALES (est): 203.49K **Privately Held**
Web: www.rultract.com
SIC: 3841 Surgical and medical instruments

(G-13797)
SCHAEFER EQUIPMENT INC
1590 Phoenix Rd Ne (44483-2896)
PHONE.................................330 372-4006
Rich Barnhart, *CEO*
Barry Anderson, *VP*
▲ **EMP:** 80 **EST:** 1914
SQ FT: 101,000
SALES (est): 23.29MM **Publicly Held**
SIC: 3462 Railroad wheels, axles, frogs, or
other equipment: forged
HQ: Wabtec Corporation
30 Isabella St
Pittsburgh PA 15212

(G-13798)
STADIUM GROW LIGHTING INC
Also Called: Sgl
108 Main Ave Sw Ste 500 (44481-1010)
PHONE.................................855 346-9403
Nico Van Vuuren, *CEO*
EMP: 7 **EST:** 2019
SALES (est): 1.1MM **Privately Held**
SIC: 3648 Outdoor lighting equipment

(G-13799)
SUPERIOR WALLS OF OHIO INC
Also Called: Superior Walls
1401 Pine Ave Se (44483-6532)
PHONE.................................330 393-4101
George Schuler, *Pr*
▼ **EMP:** 60 **EST:** 1997
SQ FT: 60,000
SALES (est): 384.58K **Privately Held**
Web: www.superiorwalls.com
SIC: 1791 3272 Precast concrete structural
framing or panels, placing of; Concrete
products, nec

(G-13800)
TECNOCAP LLC
Also Called: Warren Metal Lithography
2100 Griswold Street Ext Ne (44483-2750)
PHONE.................................330 392-7222
Brian Bates, *Mgr*
EMP: 155
Web: www.tecnocapclosures.com
SIC: 3354 2752 Aluminum extruded products
; Lithographing on metal
HQ: Tecnocap Llc
1701 Wheeling Ave
Glen Dale WV 26038
304 845-3402

(G-13801)
THERM-O-LINK INC
Also Called: Vulkor
621 Dana St Ne Ste 5 (44483-3976)
PHONE.................................330 393-7600
John Mullen, *Mgr*
EMP: 7
SQ FT: 18,000
SALES (corp-wide): 23.71MM **Privately
Held**
Web: www.tolwire.com
SIC: 3357 Nonferrous wiredrawing and
insulating
PA: Therm-O-Link, Inc.
10513 Freedom St
Garrettsville OH 44231
330 527-2124

(G-13802)
TRUMBULL CEMENT PRODUCTS CO
2185 Larchmont Ave Ne (44483-2894)
PHONE.................................330 372-4342
Jeffrey Carbone, *Pr*
Darla Carbone, *Sec*
Julie Carbone, *Treas*
EMP: 6 **EST:** 1922
SQ FT: 5,000

SALES (est): 466.89K **Privately Held**
Web:
www.trumbullcementproductscompanyinc.co
m
SIC: 3271 5211 5032 Blocks, concrete or
cinder: standard; Lumber and other building
materials; Brick, stone, and related material

(G-13803)
TRUMBULL MOBILE MEALS
323 E Market St (44481-1207)
PHONE.................................330 394-2538
Sandra Mathews, *Ex Dir*
EMP: 10 **EST:** 1999
SQ FT: 3,567
SALES (est): 518.46K **Privately Held**
Web: www.trumbullmobilemeals.org
SIC: 8322 2051 Meal delivery program;
Bakery, for home service delivery

(G-13804)
ULTIMATE PRINTING INC
6090 Mahoning Ave Nw Ste C
(44481-9495)
PHONE.................................330 847-2941
Richard Wilms, *Pr*
William Pugh, *VP*
EMP: 6 **EST:** 1991
SQ FT: 3,000
SALES (est): 267.75K **Privately Held**
SIC: 2752 Offset printing

(G-13805)
ULTIUM CELLS HOLDINGS LLC
7400 Tod Ave Sw (44481-9627)
PHONE.................................313 818-6324
Kee Eun, *Pr*
EMP: 165 **EST:** 2022
SALES (est): 2.55MM **Privately Held**
SIC: 3692 Dry cell batteries, single or
multiple cell

(G-13806)
ULTIUM CELLS LLC (HQ)
7400 Tod Ave Sw (44481-9627)
PHONE.................................313 818-6324
Kee Eun, *Pr*
Lincoln Shomer, *
EMP: 110 **EST:** 2020
SALES (est): 56.66MM **Publicly Held**
Web: www.ultiumcell.com
SIC: 3692 Dry cell batteries, single or
multiple cell
PA: General Motors Company
300 Renaissance Ctr
Detroit MI 48243

(G-13807)
UNITED REFRACTORIES INC
1929 Larchmont Ave Ne (44483-3507)
PHONE.................................330 372-3716
◆ **EMP:** 30
SIC: 3255 3272 Clay refractories; Concrete
products, precast, nec

(G-13808)
VINDICATOR
240 Franklin St Se (44483-5711)
PHONE.................................330 841-1600
EMP: 6 **EST:** 2019
SALES (est): 154.19K **Privately Held**
Web: www.vindy.com
SIC: 2711 Newspapers, publishing and
printing

(G-13809)
VULKOR INCORPORATED (PA)
621 Dana St Ne Ste V (44483-3976)
P.O. Box 6 (44482-0006)
PHONE.................................330 393-7600

David J Campbell, *Pr*
Ronald M Krisher, *Stockholder**
Richard Thompson, *Stockholder**
EMP: 24 **EST:** 1992
SQ FT: 780
SALES (est): 4.78MM **Privately Held**
SIC: 3357 Nonferrous wiredrawing and
insulating

(G-13810)
**WARREN CONCRETE AND SUPPLY
CO**
1113 Parkman Rd Nw (44485-2497)
P.O. Box 1408 (44482-1408)
PHONE.................................330 393-1581
Harry N Hamilton, *Pr*
David H Hamilton, *Pr*
Harry N Hamilton, *Sec*
Richard Hamilton, *VP*
James Hamilton, *VP*
EMP: 6 **EST:** 1921
SQ FT: 2,000
SALES (est): 339.9K **Privately Held**
Web: www.warrenconcrete.com
SIC: 3273 5211 5032 Ready-mixed concrete
; Lumber and other building materials;
Brick, stone, and related material

(G-13811)
WARREN SCREW MACHINE INC
3869 Niles Rd Se (44484-3548)
PHONE.................................330 609-6020
John Condoleon, *Pr*
EMP: 10 **EST:** 1983
SALES (est): 2.45MM **Privately Held**
Web: www.warrenprecision.net
SIC: 3599 Machine shop, jobbing and repair

(G-13812)
WARREN STEEL HOLDINGS LLC
4000 Mahoning Ave Nw (44483-1924)
PHONE.................................330 847-0487
◆ **EMP:** 290
Web: www.warrensteelholdings.com
SIC: 3567 Electrical furnaces, ovens, &
heating devices, exc.induction

(G-13813)
WELD-ACTION COMPANY INC
2100 N River Rd Ne (44483-2598)
PHONE.................................330 372-1063
Todd Huna, *Pr*
EMP: 6 **EST:** 1960
SQ FT: 7,158
SALES (est): 2.29MM **Privately Held**
Web: www.weldaction.com
SIC: 5084 3548 Welding machinery and
equipment; Welding and cutting apparatus
and accessories, nec

(G-13814)
WHEATLAND TUBE LLC
Also Called: Wheatland Tube Company
901 Dietz Rd Ne (44483-2700)
PHONE.................................330 372-6611
Teri Aljoe, *Brnch Mgr*
EMP: 193
Web: www.wheatland.com
SIC: 3312 3317 Blast furnaces and steel mills
; Steel pipe and tubes
HQ: Wheatland Tube, Llc
1 Council Ave
Wheatland PA 16161
800 257-8182

Warrensville Heights
Cuyahoga County

(G-13815)
B & F MANUFACTURING CO
19050 Cranwood Pkwy (44128-4047)
PHONE.....................216 518-0333
Marsha Kutsikovich, *Pr*
EMP: 10 **EST:** 1989
SQ FT: 10,000
SALES (est): 966.55K **Privately Held**
SIC: 3599 Machine shop, jobbing and repair

(G-13816)
CHAGRIN VALLEY CUSTOM FURN LLC
26309 Miles Rd Ste 6 (44128-5945)
PHONE.....................440 591-5511
EMP: 7
SALES (corp-wide): 182.94K **Privately Held**
Web:
www.chagrinvalleycustomfurniture.com
SIC: 2521 5712 Desks, office: wood; Furniture stores
PA: Chagrin Valley Custom Furniture Llc
7425 Edwards Lndg
Chagrin Falls OH 44023
216 591-5511

(G-13817)
CHARLES HUFFMAN & ASSOCIATES
19214 Gladstone Rd (44122-6626)
PHONE.....................216 295-0850
Charles Huffman, *Mgr*
EMP: 6
SALES (corp-wide): 82.5K **Privately Held**
Web: www.mediafundsuperpac.com
SIC: 2759 Commercial printing, nec
PA: Charles Huffman & Associates
17325 Euclid Ave Ste 4002
Cleveland OH 44112
216 295-0850

(G-13818)
GINOS AWARDS INC
Also Called: Gino's Jewelers & Trophy Mfrs
4701 Richmond Rd Ste 200 (44128-5994)
PHONE.....................216 831-6565
Gino Zavarella, *Pr*
▲ **EMP:** 50 **EST:** 1950
SQ FT: 30,000
SALES (est): 8.05MM **Privately Held**
Web: www.ginosonline.com
SIC: 3911 3993 3914 Jewelry, precious metal ; Signs and advertising specialties; Trophies, nsk

(G-13819)
WHITMORE PRODUCTIONS INC
Also Called: Whitmore's Bbq
20209 Harvard Ave (44122-6808)
PHONE.....................216 752-3960
Virgil Whitmore, *Pr*
Vance Whitmore, *VP*
Kim Whitmore, *Sec*
Esther Whitmore, *Treas*
EMP: 6 **EST:** 1987
SQ FT: 1,500
SALES (est): 386.79K **Privately Held**
Web: www.whitmoreproductions.com
SIC: 2099 Sauces: dry mixes

Washington Court Hou
Fayette County

(G-13820)
COURTHOUSE MANUFACTURING LLC
Also Called: Chappell Door Company
1730 Washington Avenue, Solar Lane (43160)
PHONE.....................740 335-2727
Wayne Gooley, *Managing Member*
EMP: 38 **EST:** 1955
SQ FT: 84,000
SALES (est): 2.88MM **Privately Held**
Web: www.chappelldoor.net
SIC: 2431 Doors, wood

(G-13821)
HALLIDAY HOLDINGS INC
1544 Old Us 35 Se (43160-8624)
P.O. Box 700 (43160-0700)
PHONE.....................740 335-1430
John Halliday, *Pr*
William Halliday Ii, *VP*
EMP: 40 **EST:** 1947
SQ FT: 50,000
SALES (est): 8.81MM **Privately Held**
Web: www.hallidaylumber.com
SIC: 2448 2426 Pallets, wood; Dimension, hardwood

(G-13822)
PLASTILENE INC
1010 Mead St (43160-9310)
PHONE.....................614 592-8699
Guillermo Umana, *CEO*
Stefano Pacini, *Pr*
Gian Luca Fiori, *Treas*
Gabriel Jaramillo, *Sec*
EMP: 14 **EST:** 2021
SALES (est): 4.73MM **Privately Held**
Web: en.grupoplastilene.com
SIC: 2761 Manifold business forms
PA: Plastilene Sas
Carrera 4 58 66 Zona Industrial
Cazuca Entrada 1
Soacha CUN

(G-13823)
STARK TRUSS COMPANY INC
2000 Landmark Blvd (43160)
P.O. Box 8 (43160-0008)
PHONE.....................740 335-4156
Jeff Coulter, *Brnch Mgr*
EMP: 51
SQ FT: 12,000
SALES (corp-wide): 90.76MM **Privately Held**
Web: www.starktruss.com
SIC: 2439 Trusses, wooden roof
PA: Stark Truss Company, Inc.
109 Miles Ave Sw
Canton OH 44710
330 478-2100

(G-13824)
YUSA CORPORATION (HQ)
151 Jamison Rd Nw (43160-9504)
PHONE.....................740 335-0335
Takeyoshi Usui, *Pr*
Nobuyuki Tateno, *
Yoshiji Iwamoto, *
▲ **EMP:** 37 **EST:** 1987
SQ FT: 250,000
SALES (est): 58.2MM **Privately Held**
Web: www.yusa-oh.com
SIC: 3069 Rubber covered motor mounting rings (rubber bonded)
PA: Yamashita Rubber Co., Ltd.

1239, Kamekubo
Fujimino STM 356-0

Waterford
Washington County

(G-13825)
AIR HEATER SEAL COMPANY INC
93 Sunset Ln (45786)
P.O. Box 8 (45786-0008)
PHONE.....................740 984-2146
Randy Townsend, *Owner*
Mable Townsend, *Sec*
EMP: 23 **EST:** 1989
SQ FT: 4,500
SALES (est): 3.31MM **Privately Held**
Web: www.airheaterseal.com
SIC: 3053 3441 Gaskets; packing and sealing devices; Fabricated structural metal

(G-13826)
FERROGLOBE USA MTLLURGICAL INC (DH)
Also Called: Globe Specialty Metals
1595 Sparling Rd (45786-6104)
P.O. Box 157 County Rd 32 (45715)
PHONE.....................740 984-2361
Alan Kestenbaum, *Ch*
Jeff Bradley, *
Marlin Perkins, *
Stuart Eizenstat, *
Franklin Lavin, *
◆ **EMP:** 141 **EST:** 1871
SALES (est): 180.88MM
SALES (corp-wide): 1.65B **Privately Held**
Web: www.globemetallurgical.com
SIC: 3339 3313 2819 Silicon refining (primary, over 99% pure); Ferrosilicon, not made in blast furnaces; Industrial inorganic chemicals, nec
HQ: Globe Specialty Metals, Inc.
600 Brickell Ave Ste 310
Miami FL 33131

(G-13827)
LAMINATE SHOP
1145 Klinger Rd (45786-5347)
P.O. Box 1218 (45750-6218)
PHONE.....................740 749-3536
Tim Strahler, *Pr*
EMP: 10 **EST:** 1986
SQ FT: 25,000
SALES (est): 434.01K **Privately Held**
Web: www.thelaminateshopinc.com
SIC: 3083 5211 1799 Laminated plastics plate and sheet; Cabinets, kitchen; Counter top installation

(G-13828)
MALTA DYNAMICS LLC (PA)
405 Watertown Rd (45786-5248)
PHONE.....................740 749-3512
Damian Lang, *CEO*
Douglas Taylor, *CFO*
Ken Hebert, *Stockholder*
EMP: 11 **EST:** 2015
SALES (est): 2.4MM
SALES (corp-wide): 2.4MM **Privately Held**
Web: www.maltadynamics.com
SIC: 3531 3821 3851 4581 Winches; Incubators, laboratory; Ophthalmic goods; Aircraft maintenance and repair services

(G-13829)
VALLEY LIST LLC
11 Watertown Rd Unit C (45786-5282)
PHONE.....................740 760-6411
EMP: 9 **EST:** 2017
SALES (est): 61.92K **Privately Held**

Web: www.thevalleylist.com
SIC: 7379 3823 7389 Online services technology consultants; Programmers, process type; Design services

Waterville
Lucas County

(G-13830)
AQUILA PHARMATECH LLC
8225 Farnsworth Rd Ste A7 (43566-9781)
PHONE.....................419 386-2527
Han Chen, *Managing Member*
EMP: 6 **EST:** 2009
SALES (est): 227.21K **Privately Held**
Web: www.aquilapharmatech.com
SIC: 3559 Chemical machinery and equipment

(G-13831)
CARRUTH STUDIO INC (PA)
1178 Farnsworth Rd (43566-1074)
PHONE.....................419 878-3060
George Carruth, *Pr*
Debbie Carruth, *Sec*
EMP: 13 **EST:** 1983
SQ FT: 13,600
SALES (est): 2.33MM
SALES (corp-wide): 2.33MM **Privately Held**
Web: www.carruthstudio.com
SIC: 3269 3272 Art and ornamental ware, pottery; Concrete products, nec

(G-13832)
CRUM MANUFACTURING INC
1265 Waterville Monclova Rd (43566-1067)
PHONE.....................419 878-9779
Ernest Crum Junior, *Pr*
EMP: 25 **EST:** 1984
SQ FT: 23,000
SALES (est): 2.19MM **Privately Held**
Web: www.crummfg.com
SIC: 3544 3599 3462 Special dies, tools, jigs, and fixtures; Machine and other job shop work; Automotive forgings, ferrous: crankshaft, engine, axle, etc.

(G-13833)
FURNACE TECHNOLOGIES INC
Also Called: Furn Tech
1070 Disher Dr (43566-1079)
PHONE.....................419 878-2100
Tim Fisher, *Pr*
EMP: 6 **EST:** 1985
SALES (est): 776.29K **Privately Held**
Web: www.thermeq.com
SIC: 3567 Heating units and devices, industrial: electric

(G-13834)
HEIDELBERG MTLS MDWEST AGG INC
600 S River Rd (43566-9754)
P.O. Box 49 (43566-0049)
PHONE.....................419 878-2006
Paul Carbaugh, *Brnch Mgr*
EMP: 9
SALES (corp-wide): 22.37B **Privately Held**
SIC: 2951 Asphalt and asphaltic paving mixtures (not from refineries)
HQ: Heidelberg Materials Midwest Agg, Inc.
300 E John Crptr Fwy Ste
Irving TX

(G-13835)
JOHNS MANVILLE CORPORATION
7500 Dutch Rd (43566-9731)
PHONE.....................419 878-8111

▲ = Import ▼ = Export
◆ = Import/Export

Rhonda Francis, *Prin*
EMP: 108
SALES (corp-wide): 424.23B **Publicly Held**
Web: www.jm.com
SIC: 3296 3297 3229 2273 Fiberglass insulation; Nonclay refractories; Pressed and blown glass, nec; Carpets and rugs
HQ: Johns Manville Corporation
717 17th St
Denver CO 80202
303 978-2000

(G-13836)
JOHNS MANVILLE CORPORATION
6050 N River Rd (43566-9611)
PHONE....................419 878-8112
Mary Rhinehart, *Brnch Mgr*
EMP: 57
SALES (corp-wide): 424.23B **Publicly Held**
Web: www.jm.com
SIC: 3296 Fiberglass insulation
HQ: Johns Manville Corporation
717 17th St
Denver CO 80202
303 978-2000

(G-13837)
KAUFMAN ENGINEERED SYSTEMS INC
1260 Waterville Monclova Rd (43566-1066)
PHONE....................419 878-9727
Andrew J Quinn, *Pr*
Charles R Kaufman, *
Robert J Kaufman, *
EMP: 72 **EST:** 1957
SQ FT: 66,250
SALES (est): 19.54MM **Privately Held**
Web: www.kaufmanengsys.com
SIC: 3567 3565 Industrial furnaces and ovens; Packaging machinery

(G-13838)
LABCRAFT INC
Also Called: Furntech
1070 Disher Dr (43566-1079)
PHONE....................419 878-4400
Ernest Seeman, *Pr*
EMP: 25 **EST:** 1997
SALES (est): 2.84MM **Privately Held**
Web: www.thermeq.com
SIC: 3499 Machine bases, metal

(G-13839)
MAUMEE VALLEY MEMORIALS INC (DH)
Also Called: Americraft Bronze Co
111 Anthony Wayne Trl (43566-1373)
P.O. Box 289 (43566-0289)
PHONE....................419 878-9030
Richard Kimball, *Pr*
EMP: 12
SQ FT: 2,500
SALES (est): 708.63K
SALES (corp-wide): 1.5MM **Privately Held**
Web: www.ohiomonuments.com
SIC: 5999 3281 Monuments, finished to custom order; Cut stone and stone products
HQ: Swenson Granite Company Llc
369 N State St
Concord NH 03301
603 225-4322

(G-13840)
REEBAR DIE CASTING INC
1177 Farnsworth Rd (43566-1036)
PHONE....................419 878-7591
Byron G Reed, *Pr*
Joyce Reed, *Sec*
Byron David Reed, *VP*

EMP: 15 **EST:** 1972
SQ FT: 22,000
SALES (est): 2.3MM **Privately Held**
Web: www.reebardiecasting.com
SIC: 3364 3089 Zinc and zinc-base alloy die-castings; Injection molded finished plastics products, nec

(G-13841)
RIMER ENTERPRISES INC
Also Called: Kelic
916 Rimer Dr (43566-1019)
P.O. Box 27 (43566-0027)
PHONE....................419 878-8156
Chuck Meyers, *Pr*
Eric Nathe, *
▲ **EMP:** 30 **EST:** 1967
SQ FT: 25,000
SALES (est): 4.74MM **Privately Held**
Web: www.rimerinc.com
SIC: 3324 Commercial investment castings, ferrous

(G-13842)
SEAGATE PLASTICS COMPANY LLC (PA)
Also Called: Seagate Plastics
1110 Disher Dr (43566-1256)
PHONE....................419 878-5010
Kevin Fink, *Pr*
▲ **EMP:** 39 **EST:** 1987
SQ FT: 50,000
SALES: 9.4MM
SALES (corp-wide): 9.4MM **Privately Held**
Web: www.seagateplastics.com
SIC: 3089 Injection molding of plastics

(G-13843)
T J F INC
Also Called: Thermeq Co
1070 Disher Dr (43566-1079)
PHONE....................419 878-4400
Ernest Seeman, *Dir*
EMP: 16 **EST:** 1988
SALES (est): 4.85MM **Privately Held**
Web: www.thermeq.com
SIC: 3585 3433 3449 3567 Refrigeration and heating equipment; Heating equipment, except electric; Miscellaneous metalwork; Industrial furnaces and ovens

(G-13844)
WATERVILLE SHEET METAL CO INC
1210 Waterville Monclova Rd (43566-1000)
PHONE....................419 878-5050
Ron Kelso, *Pr*
EMP: 6 **EST:** 1981
SQ FT: 12,000
SALES (est): 2.21MM **Privately Held**
Web: www.watervillesheetmetalco.com
SIC: 3444 Sheet metal specialties, not stamped

Wauseon
Fulton County

(G-13845)
ARC METAL STAMPING LLC
Also Called: Kecy Metal Technologies
447 E Walnut St (43567-1278)
PHONE....................517 448-8954
EMP: 90 **EST:** 2014
SALES (est): 3.97MM **Privately Held**
SIC: 3469 Stamping metal for the trade

(G-13846)
BUSSE KNIFE CO
Also Called: Busse Combat Knives
11651 County Road 12 (43567-9622)

PHONE....................419 923-6471
Jerry Busse, *Pr*
EMP: 7 **EST:** 1984
SQ FT: 37,000
SALES (est): 1.92MM **Privately Held**
Web: www.bussecombat.com
SIC: 3421 Knife blades and blanks

(G-13847)
CORNERSTONE WAUSEON INC
Also Called: Wauseon Machine & Mfg
995 Enterprise Ave (43567-9333)
PHONE....................419 337-0940
Ryan Anair, *CEO*
Peter Paras Junior, *VP*
Matthew Bombick, *
Ellen Hadymon, *
EMP: 190 **EST:** 2013
SALES (est): 20.24MM **Privately Held**
Web: www.wauseonmachine.com
SIC: 3441 3559 7629 3547 Fabricated structural metal; Automotive related machinery; Electrical repair shops; Rolling mill machinery

(G-13848)
E & J DEMARK INC
Also Called: Demark
1115 N Ottokee St (43567-1911)
P.O. Box 416 (43567-0416)
PHONE....................419 337-5866
J Edwin Hecock, *Pr*
Boonie L Hecock, *
EMP: 33 **EST:** 1984
SQ FT: 29,000
SALES (est): 4.17MM **Privately Held**
Web: www.ejdemark.com
SIC: 3545 3599 Machine tool accessories; Machine shop, jobbing and repair

(G-13849)
FULTON INDUSTRIES LLC ✪
Also Called: Fulton Industries
135 E Linfoot St (43567-1000)
PHONE....................419 270-3937
Tyler Pilmore, *Managing Member*
Tayler Pilmore, *
Heather Newman, *
Jim Bauman, *
EMP: 55 **EST:** 2024
SALES (est): 1.56MM **Privately Held**
SIC: 3648 3465 Flashlights; Automotive stampings

(G-13850)
HAAS DOOR COMPANY
320 Sycamore St (43567-1100)
PHONE....................419 337-9900
Edward Nofziger, *Pr*
Carol Nofziger, *
EMP: 200 **EST:** 1971
SQ FT: 150,000
SALES (est): 2.3MM **Privately Held**
Web: www.haasdoor.com
SIC: 3442 Garage doors, overhead: metal

(G-13851)
HILL MANUFACTURING INC
318 W Chestnut St (43567-1369)
P.O. Box 241 (43567-0241)
PHONE....................419 335-5006
Marion Hill, *Pr*
Carl T Hill, *
▲ **EMP:** 50 **EST:** 1948
SQ FT: 55,000
SALES (est): 3.98MM **Privately Held**
Web: www.hillmfginc.com
SIC: 3469 Stamping metal for the trade

(G-13852)
INTERNTNAL AUTO CMPNNTS GROUP
555 W Linfoot St (43567-9558)
PHONE....................419 335-1000
EMP: 86
Web: www.iacgroup.com
SIC: 3714 Motor vehicle parts and accessories
PA: International Automotive Components Group North America, Inc.
27777 Frnklin Rd Ste 2000
Southfield MI 48034

(G-13853)
INTERNTNAL AUTO CMPNNTS GROUP
Also Called: Automotive Industries Division
555 W Linfoot St (43567-9558)
PHONE....................419 433-5653
EMP: 700
Web: www.iacgroup.com
SIC: 3089 3714 3429 3229 Injection molded finished plastics products, nec; Motor vehicle parts and accessories; Hardware, nec; Pressed and blown glass, nec
PA: International Automotive Components Group North America, Inc.
27777 Frnklin Rd Ste 2000
Southfield MI 48034

(G-13854)
LATROBE SPECIALTY MTLS CO LLC
14614 County Road H (43567-9796)
PHONE....................419 335-8010
Cheryl Bookheimer, *Brnch Mgr*
EMP: 25
SALES (corp-wide): 2.76B **Publicly Held**
Web: www.latrobefoundry.com
SIC: 3312 Tool and die steel
HQ: Latrobe Specialty Metals Company, Llc
2626 Ligonier St
Latrobe PA 15650
724 537-7711

(G-13855)
LEAR CORPORATION
Also Called: Sheridan Mfg
447 E Walnut St (43567-1278)
PHONE....................419 335-6010
Cary Wood, *Brnch Mgr*
EMP: 37
SQ FT: 80,000
SALES (corp-wide): 23.31B **Publicly Held**
Web: www.lear.com
SIC: 3714 Motor vehicle parts and accessories
PA: Lear Corporation
21557 Telegraph Rd
Southfield MI 48033
248 447-1500

(G-13856)
MULTI CAST LLC
225 E Linfoot St (43567-1007)
PHONE....................419 335-0010
Mike Schnipke, *Managing Member*
EMP: 37 **EST:** 1930
SQ FT: 42,500
SALES (est): 4.47MM **Privately Held**
Web: www.aluminumsandcastingsfoundry.com
SIC: 3365 Aluminum and aluminum-based alloy castings

(G-13857)
NOFZIGER DOOR SALES INC (PA)
Also Called: Haas Doors
320 Sycamore St (43567-1100)
PHONE....................419 337-9900
Edward L Nofziger, *Pr*

Carol Nofziger, *
▼ EMP: 173 EST: 1938
SQ FT: 200,000
SALES (est): 28.62MM
SALES (corp-wide): 28.62MM **Privately Held**
Web:
www.archboldohiogaragedoors.com
SIC: 3442 1751 5211 Metal doors; Garage door, installation or erection; Doors, wood or metal, except storm

(G-13858)
PERFECTION FINISHERS INC
1151 N Ottokee St (43567-1911)
PHONE..............................419 337-8015
Gerald Haack, CEO
EMP: 25 EST: 1986
SQ FT: 80,000
SALES (est): 2.44MM **Privately Held**
Web: www.perfectionfinishers.com
SIC: 3479 Coating of metals with plastic or resins

(G-13859)
STAMP & FLASH INC (PA)
Also Called: Fulton
135 E Linfoot St (43567-1005)
P.O. Box 377 (43567-0377)
PHONE..............................419 335-3015
John Razzano, Pr
Glenn Badenhop, *
Kim Griggs, *
Ned Griggs, *
Robert E Swanson, *
EMP: 69 EST: 1979
SQ FT: 170,000
SALES (est): 5MM
SALES (corp-wide): 5MM **Privately Held**
Web: www.fultonindoh.com
SIC: 3469 3648 Stamping metal for the trade ; Flashlights

(G-13860)
UNLIMTED RCOVERY SOLUTIONS LLC
2701 S Eberd Rd Ste B (43567)
PHONE..............................419 868-4888
EMP: 45 EST: 2010
SALES (est): 917.6K **Privately Held**
SIC: 3713 Dump truck bodies

(G-13861)
WAUSEON SILO & COAL COMPANY
Also Called: Wauseon Precast
535 Wood St (43567-1248)
P.O. Box 395 (43567-0395)
EMP: 10 EST: 1910
SQ FT: 41,000
SALES (est): 222.94K **Privately Held**
SIC: 3272 5251 Catch basin covers, concrete ; Builders' hardware

(G-13862)
WYSE INDUSTRIAL CARTS INC
10510 County Road 12 (43567-9237)
PHONE..............................419 923-7353
Gene Wyse, Pr
Randy Wyse, VP
EMP: 8 EST: 1996
SQ FT: 20,000
SALES (est): 2.02MM **Privately Held**
Web: www.wysecarts.com
SIC: 3448 Ramps, prefabricated metal

Waverly
Pike County

(G-13863)
BEAZER EAST INC
9978 State Route 220 (45690-9012)
PHONE..............................740 947-4677
William H Chattin, Brnch Mgr
EMP: 11
SALES (corp-wide): 22.37B **Privately Held**
SIC: 3273 Ready-mixed concrete
HQ: Beazer East, Inc.
600 River Ave Ste 200
Pittsburgh PA 15212
412 428-9407

(G-13864)
CLARKSVILLE STAVE & VENEER CO
Also Called: Woodco US
9329 State Route 220 Ste A (45690-9189)
PHONE..............................740 947-4159
Ben Nathan, Pr
Todd Nathan, VP
Glenda Nathan, Sec
◆ EMP: 10 EST: 1978
SALES (est): 491.5K **Privately Held**
SIC: 2421 Sawmills and planing mills, general

(G-13865)
GEO-TECH POLYMERS LLC
479 Industrial Park Dr (45690-1199)
P.O. Box 61 (48347-0061)
PHONE..............................614 797-2300
▼ EMP: 17 EST: 2000
SALES (est): 7.03MM **Privately Held**
SIC: 2821 Plastics materials and resins
PA: Vns Federal Services, Llc
1571 Shyville Rd
Piketon OH 45661

(G-13866)
KIRCHHOFF AUTO WAVERLY INC (DH)
611 W 2nd St (45690-9701)
PHONE..............................740 947-7763
Dennis Berry, CEO
▲ EMP: 10 EST: 2009
SALES (est): 35.06MM
SALES (corp-wide): 1.95B **Privately Held**
SIC: 3465 Automotive stampings
HQ: Kirchhoff Automotive Se
Stefanstr. 2
Iserlohn NW 58638
237182000

(G-13867)
MILLS PRIDE PREMIER INC
423 Hopewell Rd (45690-9801)
PHONE..............................740 941-1300
EMP: 9 EST: 2014
SALES (est): 497.52K **Privately Held**
SIC: 2434 Wood kitchen cabinets

(G-13868)
MILLTREE LUMBER HOLDINGS
535 Coal Dock Rd (45690-9799)
PHONE..............................740 226-2090
Terry Marr, Prin
EMP: 9 EST: 2014
SALES (est): 566.52K **Privately Held**
Web: www.millwoodinc.com
SIC: 2448 Pallets, wood

(G-13869)
MILLWOOD INC
535 Coal Dock Rd (45690-9799)
PHONE..............................740 226-2090
Terry Robbins, Pr

EMP: 35
Web: www.millwoodinc.com
SIC: 2448 Pallets, wood
PA: Millwood, Inc.
3708 International Blvd
Vienna OH 44473

(G-13870)
NEWS WATCHMAN & PAPER
Also Called: Acm Ohio
860 W Emmitt Ave Ste 5 (45690-1080)
P.O. Box 151 (45690-0151)
PHONE..............................740 947-2149
Norman Guilliland, Prin
Carrie Humble, Prin
EMP: 10 EST: 2005
SALES (est): 80.76K **Privately Held**
Web: www.newswatchman.com
SIC: 2711 7313 Newspapers, publishing and printing; Newspaper advertising representative

(G-13871)
OAK CHIPS INC
Also Called: O C I
9329 State Route 220 Ste A (45690-9189)
PHONE..............................740 947-4159
Edward Todd Nathan, Pr
◆ EMP: 49 EST: 2014
SALES (est): 5.03MM **Privately Held**
Web: www.oakchipsinc.com
SIC: 2448 2861 Pallets, wood; Wood extract products

(G-13872)
PERFORMANX SPECIALTY CHEM LLC
479 Industrial Park Dr (45690-1199)
PHONE..............................614 300-7001
Kim Pellock, Brnch Mgr
EMP: 6
SALES (corp-wide): 935.36K **Privately Held**
Web: www.stepan.com
SIC: 2834 Pharmaceutical preparations
PA: Performanx Specialty Chemicals, Llc
300 Westdale Ave
Westerville OH 43082
614 300-7001

(G-13873)
ROBERT A MALONE
Also Called: PC Treats
450 State Route 551 (45690-9613)
PHONE..............................740 947-2859
Robert Malone, Owner
EMP: 10 EST: 1989
SALES (est): 159.21K **Privately Held**
SIC: 2064 Candy and other confectionery products

(G-13874)
THIRD MILLENNIUM MATERIALS LLC
Also Called: Tmm
974 Prosperity Rd (45690-8938)
PHONE..............................740 947-1023
EMP: 6 EST: 2009
SALES (est): 458.05K **Privately Held**
Web: www.tmmaterials.com
SIC: 3399 Primary metal products

Waynesburg
Stark County

(G-13875)
BAUGHMAN MACHINE & WELD SP INC
6498 June Rd Nw (44688-9433)
PHONE..............................330 866-9243

Paul Baughman, Pr
John Baughaman, VP
Kathy Miller, Treas
EMP: 8 EST: 1977
SQ FT: 960
SALES (est): 218.32K **Privately Held**
SIC: 7692 Welding repair

(G-13876)
E & M LIBERTY WELDING INC
141 James St (44688-9313)
PHONE..............................330 866-2338
Mark Crowe, Pr
Earl Ecenbarger, VP
EMP: 8 EST: 2004
SALES (est): 50K **Privately Held**
SIC: 7692 1711 Welding repair; Boiler and furnace contractors

Waynesfield
Auglaize County

(G-13877)
ACA MILLWORKS INC
Also Called: Old West Woods
16330 Waynesfield Rd (45896-9618)
P.O. Box 367 (45896-0367)
PHONE..............................419 339-7600
Holly Bowersock, Prin
EMP: 11 EST: 2002
SALES (est): 1.59MM **Privately Held**
Web: www.oldwestwoods.com
SIC: 2431 Millwork

(G-13878)
INDUSTRIAL PAINT & STRIP INC
1000 Commerce Ct (45896-8415)
P.O. Box 967 (43138-0967)
PHONE..............................419 568-2222
Richard W Libby, Pr
Donna J Libby, *
EMP: 35 EST: 2000
SQ FT: 13,500
SALES (est): 704.96K **Privately Held**
Web: www.ipswest.com
SIC: 3471 Plating and polishing

Waynesville
Warren County

(G-13879)
JOHN PURDUM
Also Called: Brass Lantern Antiques
100 S Main St (45068-8954)
P.O. Box 597 (45068-0597)
PHONE..............................513 897-9686
John Purdum, Owner
EMP: 6 EST: 1970
SQ FT: 3,720
SALES (est): 307.39K **Privately Held**
Web: www.waynesvilleshops.com
SIC: 5932 5399 2519 7011 Antiques; Country general stores; Household furniture, except wood or metal: upholstered ; Hotels and motels

(G-13880)
MK WELDING & FABRICATION INC
1824 E Lower Springboro Rd (45068-9531)
PHONE..............................937 603-4430
C Alan Edinger, Pr
EMP: 7 EST: 1989
SALES (est): 180.7K **Privately Held**
Web: www.mkweld.com
SIC: 7692 Welding repair

(G-13881)
OUTHOUSE PAPER ETC INC
319 Collett Rd (45068-9306)
P.O. Box 101 (45177-0101)
PHONE....................................937 382-2800
Shelley Taylor, *Pr*
EMP: 6 **EST:** 2004
SQ FT: 3,250
SALES (est): 77.81K **Privately Held**
SIC: 2679 Paperboard products, converted,
nec

(G-13882)
PATRICK M DAVIDSON
Also Called: Davidson Meat Processing Plant
6490 Corwin Ave (45068-9722)
PHONE....................................513 897-2971
Patrick M Davidson, *Owner*
EMP: 6 **EST:** 1961
SQ FT: 3,000
SALES (est): 422K **Privately Held**
Web: www.davidsonmeatprocessing.com
SIC: 0751 2013 2011 Slaughtering: custom
livestock services; Sausages and other
prepared meats; Meat packing plants

Wellington
Lorain County

(G-13883)
BILLINGTON COMPANY INC
143 Erie St (44090-1206)
P.O. Box 156 (44090-0156)
PHONE....................................440 647-3039
Mark Lupico, *Pr*
EMP: 20 **EST:** 1945
SQ FT: 8,500
SALES (est): 1.62MM **Privately Held**
SIC: 3444 Sheet metalwork

(G-13884)
CLEVELAND CITY FORGE INC
46950 State Route 18 (44090-9791)
PHONE....................................440 647-5400
Richard Kovach, *Pr*
Kenneth Kovach, *
Drew Maddock, *
EMP: 40 **EST:** 1887
SQ FT: 200,000
SALES (est): 4.15MM **Privately Held**
Web: www.clevelandcityforge.com
SIC: 3441 Fabricated structural metal

(G-13885)
EDWARD W DANIEL LLC
46950 State Route 18 Ste B (44090-9791)
PHONE....................................440 647-1960
Ken Wrona, *
Stuart W Cordell, *
EMP: 15 **EST:** 1922
SQ FT: 75,000
SALES (est): 3.23MM **Privately Held**
Web: www.ewdaniel.com
SIC: 3429 5085 3494 3463 Hardware, nec;
Industrial supplies; Valves and pipe fittings,
nec; Nonferrous forgings

(G-13886)
EXPERT CRANE INC
Also Called: Expert Crane
720 Shiloh Ave (44090-1190)
PHONE....................................216 451-9900
James C Doty, *Pr*
Rebecca Doty, *
EMP: 66 **EST:** 1977
SALES (est): 1.3MM **Privately Held**
Web: www.expertcrane.com

SIC: 3536 7699 1796 5084 Hoists, cranes,
and monorails; Industrial machinery and
equipment repair; Machinery installation;
Cranes, industrial

(G-13887)
FIVE STAR FABRICATION LLC
18308 Quarry Rd (44090-9460)
PHONE....................................440 666-0427
Matthew Kennedy, *CEO*
EMP: 11 **EST:** 2018
SALES (est): 456.36K **Privately Held**
Web: www.weldandfabnow.com
SIC: 3999 Manufacturing industries, nec

(G-13888)
FOREST CITY TECHNOLOGIES INC
Also Called: Forest City Technologies
232 Maple St (44090-1164)
P.O. Box 86 (44090-0086)
PHONE....................................440 647-2115
Chuck Shilleg, *Mgr*
EMP: 148
SALES (corp-wide): 36.52MM **Privately
Held**
Web: www.forestcitytech.com
SIC: 3053 Gaskets and sealing devices
PA: Forest City Technologies, Inc.
299 Clay St
Wellington OH 44090
440 647-2115

(G-13889)
FOREST CITY TECHNOLOGIES INC
Also Called: Forest City Tech Plant 4
401 Magyar St (44090-1278)
P.O. Box 86 (44090-0086)
PHONE....................................440 647-2115
Bob Nelson, *Genl Mgr*
EMP: 148
SALES (corp-wide): 36.52MM **Privately
Held**
Web: www.forestcitytech.com
SIC: 3053 Gasket materials
PA: Forest City Technologies, Inc.
299 Clay St
Wellington OH 44090
440 647-2115

(G-13890)
FOREST CITY TECHNOLOGIES INC
Also Called: Adelphia
299 Clay St (44090-1128)
P.O. Box 86 (44090-0086)
PHONE....................................440 647-2115
Buzz Bernning, *Mgr*
EMP: 148
SALES (corp-wide): 36.52MM **Privately
Held**
Web: www.forestcitytech.com
SIC: 3053 Gasket materials
PA: Forest City Technologies, Inc.
299 Clay St
Wellington OH 44090
440 647-2115

(G-13891)
FOREST CITY TECHNOLOGIES INC
(PA)
299 Clay St (44090-1128)
P.O. Box 86 (44090-0086)
PHONE....................................440 647-2115
John D Cloud, *Pr*
John D Cloud Senior, *Pr*
David Snowball, *
▲ **EMP:** 430 **EST:** 1955
SQ FT: 50,000
SALES (est): 36.52MM
SALES (corp-wide): 36.52MM **Privately
Held**
Web: www.forestcitytech.com

SIC: 3053 Gaskets, all materials

(G-13892)
GROUPER ACQUISITION CO LLC
Also Called: Shiloh Industries
350 Maple St (44090-1171)
PHONE....................................330 558-2600
James Winning, *Brnch Mgr*
EMP: 150
SALES (corp-wide): 67.44MM **Privately
Held**
Web: www.durashiloh.com
SIC: 3465 Automotive stampings
HQ: Grouper Acquisition Company, Llc
1780 Pond Run
Auburn Hills MI 48326
248 299-7500

(G-13893)
KALRON LLC
143 Erie St (44090-1206)
P.O. Box 156 (44090-0156)
PHONE....................................440 647-3039
Todd Markus, *Pr*
EMP: 20 **EST:** 2008
SALES (est): 2.96MM
SALES (corp-wide): 2.96MM **Privately
Held**
Web: www.kalronllc.com
SIC: 3444 Sheet metalwork
PA: Norlake Manufacturing Company
39301 Taylor Pkwy
North Ridgeville OH 44035
440 353-3200

(G-13894)
KALRON LLC
775 Shiloh Ave (44090-1190)
PHONE....................................440 647-3039
EMP: 8 **EST:** 2019
SALES (est): 3.85MM **Privately Held**
Web: www.kalronllc.com
SIC: 3444 Sheet metalwork

(G-13895)
KTS EQUIPMENT INC
Also Called: Ford
47117 State Route 18 (44090-9264)
PHONE....................................440 647-2015
Jill Sheparovich, *Pr*
Lawrence Krystowski, *
Ronald Krystowski, *
Richard Krystowski, *
Jim Mclaughlin, *VP*
EMP: 24 **EST:** 1945
SQ FT: 15,000
SALES (est): 6MM **Privately Held**
Web: www.ktsequipment.com
SIC: 3523 Farm machinery and equipment

(G-13896)
MOHR STAMPING INC
22038 Fairgrounds Rd (44090-9266)
P.O. Box 87 (44090-0087)
PHONE....................................440 647-4316
▼ **EMP:** 32 **EST:** 1967
SALES (est): 17.67MM **Privately Held**
Web: www.mohrstamping.com
SIC: 3469 3544 Metal stampings, nec;
Special dies, tools, jigs, and fixtures

(G-13897)
NN INC
125 Bennett St (44090-1202)
PHONE....................................440 647-4711
EMP: 33
SALES (corp-wide): 464.29MM **Publicly
Held**
Web: www.nninc.com
SIC: 3562 Ball bearings and parts
PA: Nn, Inc.

6210 Ardrey Kell Rd Ste 1
Charlotte NC 28277
980 264-4300

(G-13898)
**NN AUTOCAM PRECISION
COMPONENT**
125 Bennett St (44090-1202)
PHONE....................................440 647-4711
EMP: 19 **EST:** 2016
SALES (est): 3.07MM **Privately Held**
Web: www.nninc.com
SIC: 3599 Machine shop, jobbing and repair

(G-13899)
PRECISION FITTINGS LLC
709 N Main St (44090-1089)
PHONE....................................440 647-4143
Christopher H Lake, *Pr*
▲ **EMP:** 49 **EST:** 1947
SQ FT: 65,000
SALES (est): 9.36MM **Privately Held**
Web: www.precisionfittings.com
SIC: 3452 3451 3498 Bolts, nuts, rivets, and
washers; Screw machine products;
Fabricated pipe and fittings

(G-13900)
ROCHESTER MANUFACTURING INC
Also Called: Electroburr
24765 Quarry Rd (44090-9293)
PHONE....................................440 647-2463
Scott Frombaugh, *Pr*
David Younglas, *CEO*
EMP: 16 **EST:** 1978
SQ FT: 14,000
SALES (est): 2.67MM **Privately Held**
Web: www.rochestermfg.com
SIC: 3599 Machine shop, jobbing and repair

(G-13901)
SHL LIQUIDATION INDUSTRIES INC
Also Called: Shiloh Inds Wellington Mfg Div
350 Maple St (44090-1171)
PHONE....................................440 647-2100
Sri Perumal, *Brnch Mgr*
EMP: 81
Web: www.durashiloh.com
SIC: 3469 Stamping metal for the trade
PA: Shl Liquidation Industries Inc.
880 Steel Dr
Valley City OH 44280

(G-13902)
WHIRLAWAY CORPORATION
125 Bennett St (44090-1202)
PHONE....................................440 647-4711
Thomas G Zupan, *Prin*
EMP: 88
SALES (corp-wide): 464.29MM **Publicly
Held**
Web: www.nninc.com
SIC: 3714 3451 Motor vehicle parts and
accessories; Screw machine products
HQ: Whirlaway Corporation
720 Shiloh Ave
Wellington OH 44090
440 647-4711

(G-13903)
WHIRLAWAY CORPORATION
Whirlaway Cincinatti, A Div Nn
125 Bennett St (44090-1202)
PHONE....................................440 647-4711
Richard Eichmann, *Brnch Mgr*
EMP: 88
SALES (corp-wide): 464.29MM **Publicly
Held**
Web: www.nninc.com

SIC: 3714 3451 Motor vehicle parts and
accessories; Screw machine products
HQ: Whirlaway Corporation
720 Shiloh Ave
Wellington OH 44090
440 647-4711

(G-13904)
WHIRLAWAY CORPORATION (HQ)
720 Shiloh Ave (44090-1190)
PHONE................................440 647-4711
James R Widders, *VP*
Roderick R Baty, *
▲ **EMP:** 175 **EST:** 1973
SALES (est): 20.97MM
SALES (corp-wide): 464.29MM **Publicly
Held**
Web: www.nninc.com
SIC: 3714 3451 3469 Motor vehicle brake
systems and parts; Screw machine products
; Appliance parts, porcelain enameled
PA: Nn, Inc.
6210 Ardrey Kell Rd Ste 1
Charlotte NC 28277
980 264-4300

Wellston
Jackson County

(G-13905)
BROWN-FORMAN CORPORATION
Also Called: Blue Grass Cooperage - Jackson
468 Salem Church Rd (45692)
P.O. Box 528 (45640-0528)
PHONE................................740 384-3027
James Gulley, *Brnch Mgr*
EMP: 9
SALES (corp-wide): 4.18B **Publicly Held**
Web: www.brown-forman.com
SIC: 2429 2449 Cooperage stock products:
staves, headings, hoops, etc.; Wood
containers, nec
PA: Brown-Forman Corporation
850 Dixie Hwy
Louisville KY 40210
502 585-1100

(G-13906)
GEM BEVERAGES INC
106 E 11th St (45692-1713)
PHONE................................740 384-2411
Rex Holzapfel, *Pr*
EMP: 14 **EST:** 1995
SALES (est): 1.48MM **Privately Held**
Web: www.gembeverages.com
SIC: 2086 Soft drinks: packaged in cans,
bottles, etc.

(G-13907)
GENERAL MILLS INC
Also Called: General Mills
2403 S Pennsylvania Ave (45692-9503)
P.O. Box 151 (45692-0151)
PHONE................................740 286-2170
Byron Walters, *Dir*
EMP: 64
SALES (corp-wide): 19.86B **Publicly Held**
Web: www.generalmills.com
SIC: 2043 Cereal breakfast foods
PA: General Mills, Inc.
1 General Mills Blvd
Minneapolis MN 55426
763 764-7600

(G-13908)
JOHNSONS FIRE EQUIPMENT CO
Also Called: Johnsons Emrgncy Vhcl Slutions
20213 State Route 93 (45692-9739)
P.O. Box 339 (26164-0339)

PHONE................................740 357-4916
Tony Johnson, *Pr*
Steven Dill, *Pr*
Ernie O Dill Junior, *VP*
Marjorie Dill, *Sec*
EMP: 14 **EST:** 1966
SQ FT: 15,000
SALES (est): 718.31K **Privately Held**
Web: www.johnsonsfire.com
SIC: 5999 5087 3569 Fire extinguishers;
Firefighting equipment; Firefighting
apparatus

(G-13909)
PILLSBURY COMPANY LLC
Also Called: Pillsbury
2403 S Pennsylvania Ave (45692-9503)
P.O. Box 151 (45692-0151)
PHONE................................740 286-2170
Tim Dill, *Mgr*
EMP: 99
SALES (corp-wide): 19.86B **Publicly Held**
Web: www.pillsbury.com
SIC: 2041 2033 Flour and other grain mill
products; Canned fruits and specialties
HQ: The Pillsbury Company Llc
1 General Mills Blvd
Minneapolis MN 55426

(G-13910)
**SUPERIOR HARDWOODS OHIO INC
(PA)**
134 Wellston Industrial Park Rd
(45692-6500)
P.O. Box 606 (45692-0606)
PHONE................................740 384-5677
Emmett Conway Junior, *Pr*
EMP: 60 **EST:** 1983
SALES (est): 8.88MM
SALES (corp-wide): 8.88MM **Privately
Held**
Web: www.shlumber.com
SIC: 2421 2426 Sawmills and planing mills,
general; Hardwood dimension and flooring
mills

(G-13911)
WELLSTON AEROSOL MFG CO
105 W A St (45692-1113)
P.O. Box 326 (45692-0326)
PHONE................................740 384-2320
Norma Lockard, *Pr*
Dan Lockard Junior, *VP*
EMP: 7 **EST:** 1957
SALES (est): 1.61MM **Privately Held**
SIC: 2813 Aerosols

Wellsville
Columbiana County

(G-13912)
**CIMBAR PERFORMANCE MNRL WV
LLC**
2400 Clark Ave (43968-1070)
PHONE................................330 532-2034
EMP: 24 **EST:** 2011
SALES (est): 3.63MM
SALES (corp-wide): 86.16MM **Privately
Held**
Web: www.cimbar.com
SIC: 3295 Minerals, ground or otherwise
treated
PA: United Minerals And Properties, Inc.
49-O Jackson Lake Rd
Chatsworth GA 30705
770 387-0319

(G-13913)
QUALITY LIQUID FEEDS INC
2402 Clark Ave (43968-1070)
P.O. Box 402 (43968-0402)
PHONE................................330 532-4635
Darin Porter, *Mgr*
EMP: 10
SALES (corp-wide): 150.71MM **Privately
Held**
Web: www.qlf.com
SIC: 2048 Prepared feeds, nec
PA: Quality Liquid Feeds, Inc.
3586 Hwy 23 N
Dodgeville WI 53533
608 935-2345

(G-13914)
STEVENSON MFG CO
Also Called: Stevco
1 1st St (43968-1781)
P.O. Box 135 (43968-0135)
PHONE................................330 532-1581
Timothy Lynch, *Pr*
Todd Lynch, *VP*
EMP: 8 **EST:** 1800
SQ FT: 115,000
SALES (est): 587.69K **Privately Held**
SIC: 3541 3599 Grinding machines,
metalworking; Machine shop, jobbing and
repair

(G-13915)
YELLOW CREEK CASTING CO INC
18141 Fife Coal Rd (43968-9760)
PHONE................................330 532-4608
Ron Kelly, *Pr*
Lois Kelly, *Treas*
Gerald Kelly, *Sales Process Controller*
Sandra Brown, *Sec*
Jeanne Kelly, *Treas*
EMP: 8 **EST:** 1985
SQ FT: 4,500
SALES (est): 1.25MM **Privately Held**
Web: www.yellowcreekcasting.com
SIC: 3321 3322 Gray iron castings, nec;
Malleable iron foundries

West Alexandria
Preble County

(G-13916)
AMS GLOBAL LTD
119 E Dayton St (45381-1209)
P.O. Box 746 (45378-0746)
PHONE................................937 620-1036
Terrence Brennan, *Pt*
Anna Matthews, *Pt*
EMP: 6 **EST:** 2012
SQ FT: 10,000
SALES (est): 826.74K **Privately Held**
SIC: 3089 Plastics processing

(G-13917)
CLEARY MACHINE COMPANY INC
4858 Us Route 35 E (45381-8316)
PHONE................................937 839-4278
Paul Kasperski, *Pr*
EMP: 21 **EST:** 1997
SQ FT: 24,000
SALES (est): 4.29MM **Privately Held**
Web: www.clearymachine.com
SIC: 3599 Machine shop, jobbing and repair

(G-13918)
DDP SPECIALTY ELECTRONIC MA
10 Electric St (45381-1212)
PHONE................................937 839-4612
EMP: 6
SALES (corp-wide): 12.39B **Publicly Held**

SIC: 2821 2869 2891 3569 Plastics
materials and resins; Industrial organic
chemicals, nec; Adhesives and sealants;
Filters
HQ: Ddp Specialty Electronic Materials Us
5, Llc
400 Arcola Rd
Collegeville PA

(G-13919)
DOW CHEMICAL COMPANY
Also Called: Dow Chemical
10 Electric St (45381-1299)
PHONE................................937 839-4612
David Kistner, *Dir*
EMP: 15
SALES (corp-wide): 42.96B **Publicly Held**
Web: corporate.dow.com
SIC: 2821 Plastics materials and resins
HQ: The Dow Chemical Company
2211 H H Dow Way
Midland MI 48674
989 636-1000

(G-13920)
KIMMATT CORP
Also Called: Best Glass
4459 Preble County Line Rd S
(45381-9567)
PHONE................................937 228-3811
Susan Ballweg, *Pr*
Larry Ballweg, *Treas*
Matthew Ballweg, *VP*
EMP: 8 **EST:** 1975
SALES (est): 467.8K **Privately Held**
SIC: 1793 3496 3231 Glass and glazing work
; Screening, woven wire: made from
purchased wire; Strengthened or reinforced
glass

(G-13921)
REXARC INTERNATIONAL INC
35 E 3rd St (45381-1231)
P.O. Box 7 (45381-0007)
PHONE................................937 839-4604
Robert Moyer, *CEO*
Joseph R Smith, *
James P Bowman, *
Galen Woodhouse, *
Ann C Smith, *
◆ **EMP:** 25 **EST:** 1916
SQ FT: 96,000
SALES (est): 6.43MM **Privately Held**
Web: www.rexarc.com
SIC: 3498 3548 3569 Manifolds, pipe:
fabricated from purchased pipe; Gas
welding equipment; Gas generators

(G-13922)
**TWIN VALLEY METALCRAFT ASM
LLC**
Also Called: Twin Valley Metalcraft
4739 Enterprise Rd (45381-9518)
PHONE................................937 787-4634
EMP: 6 **EST:** 2004
SQ FT: 7,000
SALES (est): 719.02K **Privately Held**
Web: www.twinvalleymetalcraft.com
SIC: 3451 3429 3599 Screw machine
products; Aircraft hardware; Machine shop,
jobbing and repair

(G-13923)
WEBERS BODY & FRAME INC
2017 State Route 503 N (45381-9701)
PHONE................................937 839-5946
David P Weber, *Pr*
EMP: 9 **EST:** 1982
SALES (est): 248.83K **Privately Held**
Web: www.webersbf.com

▲ = Import ▼ = Export
◆ = Import/Export

SIC: 7532 7536 7692 Body shop, automotive
; Automotive glass replacement shops;
Welding repair

(G-13924)
WYSONG GRAVEL CO INC (PA)
Also Called: Camden Ready Mix
2332 State Route 503 N (45381)
P.O. Box 5 (45381-0005)
PHONE.....................937 456-4539
John D Wysong, *Pr*
Carroll Wysong, *VP*
EMP: 10 EST: 1922
SQ FT: 1,500
SALES (est): 5.51MM
SALES (corp-wide): 5.51MM **Privately
Held**
Web: www.preblecountystorage.com
SIC: 1442 Gravel mining

(G-13925)
WYSONG GRAVEL CO INC
2032 State Route 503 N (45381-9701)
PHONE.....................937 839-5497
Carroll Wysong, *VP*
EMP: 9
SALES (corp-wide): 5.51MM **Privately
Held**
Web: www.preblecountystorage.com
SIC: 1442 Gravel mining
PA: Wysong Gravel Co Inc
2332 State Route 503 N
West Alexandria OH 45381
937 456-4539

West Carrollton
Montgomery County

(G-13926)
APPVION INC (PA)
1030 W Alex Bell Rd (45449-1923)
PHONE.....................937 859-8262
EMP: 6 EST: 1982
SALES (est): 415.72K
SALES (corp-wide): 415.72K **Privately
Held**
SIC: 2621 Paper mills

(G-13927)
DOMTAR CORPORATION
Also Called: West Carrollton Mfg Fcilty
820 S Alex Rd (45449-2106)
PHONE.....................937 859-8262
EMP: 37
Web: www.domtar.com
SIC: 2621 Paper mills
HQ: Domtar Corporation
234 Kingsley Park Dr
Fort Mill SC 29715
803 802-7500

(G-13928)
DOMTAR CORPORATION
1030 W Alex Bell Rd (45449-1923)
PHONE.....................937 859-8261
Mark Ferguson, *Mgr*
EMP: 400
Web: www.domtar.com
SIC: 2672 2621 Coated paper, except
photographic, carbon, or abrasive; Paper
mills
HQ: Domtar Corporation
234 Kingsley Park Dr
Fort Mill SC 29715
803 802-7500

(G-13929)
FOURTEEN VENTURES GROUP LLC
3131 W Alex Bell Rd (45449-2832)

PHONE.....................937 866-2341
Richard Dobson, *Managing Member*
EMP: 8 EST: 2014
SALES (est): 758.88K **Privately Held**
SIC: 3993 Signs and advertising specialties

(G-13930)
N2 PUBLISHING
3634 Watertower Ln Ste 4 (45449-4050)
PHONE.....................937 641-8277
Clint Hardman, *VP*
EMP: 11 EST: 2017
SALES (est): 91.24K **Privately Held**
Web: www.strollmag.com
SIC: 2741 Miscellaneous publishing

(G-13931)
PLUG POWER INC
219 S Alex Rd (45449-1910)
PHONE.....................518 605-5703
EMP: 8
SALES (corp-wide): 628.81MM **Publicly
Held**
Web: www.plugpower.com
SIC: 3629 3674 5541 Electrochemical
generators (fuel cells); Fuel cells, solid state
; Gasoline service stations
PA: Plug Power Inc.
125 Vista Blvd
Slingerlands NY 12159
518 782-7700

(G-13932)
**WEST CARROLLTON CONVERTING
INC**
400 E Dixie Dr (45449-1827)
PHONE.....................937 859-3621
Pierce J Lonergan, *Pr*
Alan P Berens, *
◆ EMP: 14 EST: 1989
SALES (est): 420.94K **Privately Held**
Web: www.westcarrollton.org
SIC: 2621 Paper mills

(G-13933)
**WEST CRRLLTON PRCHMENT
CNVRTIN**
400 E Dixie Dr (45449-1827)
PHONE.....................513 594-3341
Cameron Lonergan, *Pr*
EMP: 25 EST: 2013
SALES (est): 8.21MM **Privately Held**
Web: www.wcpconv.com
SIC: 2759 Flexographic printing

West Chester
Butler County

(G-13934)
ACCUFAB INC
9059 Sutton Pl (45011-9316)
P.O. Box 62433 (45262-0433)
PHONE.....................513 942-1929
Jim Morgan, *CEO*
Lori Oursler, *Pr*
EMP: 7 EST: 1990
SQ FT: 6,500
SALES (est): 3.69MM **Privately Held**
Web: www.cincy-accufab.com
SIC: 3444 Sheet metalwork

(G-13935)
ACE MANUFACTURING COMPANY
Also Called: Ace Sanitary
5219 Muhlhauser Rd (45011-9327)
PHONE.....................513 541-2490
Charles H Tobias Junior, *Prin*
Donald A Schenck, *
M R Fredwest, *

▲ EMP: 32 EST: 1944
SALES (est): 6.82MM **Privately Held**
Web: www.acesanitary.com
SIC: 3599 3492 Hose, flexible metallic; Hose
and tube fittings and assemblies, hydraulic/
pneumatic

(G-13936)
**ADVANCED TECHNICAL PDTS SUP
CO**
6186 Centre Park Dr (45069-3868)
PHONE.....................513 851-6858
Ben Conner, *Pr*
Timothy Conner, *VP*
EMP: 10 EST: 1986
SQ FT: 15,000
SALES (est): 2.63MM **Privately Held**
Web: www.advancedtechnicalprod.com
SIC: 3479 Coating of metals and formed
products

(G-13937)
ALLGAIER PROCESS TECHNOLOGY
Also Called: Almo Process Technology
9780 Windisch Rd (45069-3808)
PHONE.....................513 402-2566
Tom Schroeder, *Pr*
Dixon F Miller, *Prin*
▲ EMP: 6 EST: 2010
SALES (est): 2.63MM **Privately Held**
Web: www.allgaierprocess.com
SIC: 3443 3535 Separators, industrial
process: metal plate; Bolt conveyor
systems, general industrial use

(G-13938)
AMYLIN OHIO
8814 Trade Port Dr (45011-8661)
PHONE.....................512 592-8710
EMP: 22 EST: 2015
SALES (est): 2.32MM **Privately Held**
SIC: 2834 Pharmaceutical preparations

(G-13939)
ANOTEX INDUSTRIES INC
4914 Rialto Rd (45069-2927)
PHONE.....................513 860-1165
Diem Pham, *Pr*
Vinh Pham, *VP*
Thao Pham, *Stockholder*
Dominic Pham, *Admn Mgr*
EMP: 7 EST: 1989
SQ FT: 6,000
SALES (est): 1.15MM **Privately Held**
SIC: 3471 Finishing, metals or formed
products

(G-13940)
AP TECH GROUP INC
5130 Rialto Rd (45069-2923)
PHONE.....................513 761-8111
James Heimert, *Pr*
Albert C Heimert, *VP*
▼ EMP: 15 EST: 2004
SALES (est): 7.03MM **Privately Held**
Web: www.aptechgroup.com
SIC: 2899 Water treating compounds

(G-13941)
AQUA TECHNOLOGY GROUP LLC
8104 Beckett Center Dr (45069-5015)
PHONE.....................513 298-1183
EMP: 8 EST: 2010
SQ FT: 15,428
SALES (est): 1.04MM **Privately Held**
Web: www.aquatechnologygroup.com
SIC: 7363 5085 3823 3824 Industrial help
service; Industrial supplies; Industrial
process control instruments; Fluid meters
and counting devices

(G-13942)
ARNOLD GAUGE CO INC (PA)
9823 Harwood Ct (45014-7588)
PHONE.....................877 942-4243
Michael Bruns, *Pr*
EMP: 10 EST: 1918
SQ FT: 10,000
SALES (est): 2.55MM
SALES (corp-wide): 2.55MM **Privately
Held**
Web: www.arnoldgauge.com
SIC: 3545 Gauges (machine tool
accessories)

(G-13943)
ASLAN WORLDWIDE
8583 Rupp Farm Dr (45069-4526)
PHONE.....................513 671-0671
Josh Stebbins, *Prin*
EMP: 10 EST: 2008
SALES (est): 299.09K **Privately Held**
Web: www.aslanworldwide.com
SIC: 2441 Boxes, wood

(G-13944)
**ASTRAZENECA
PHARMACEUTICALS LP**
8814 Trade Port Dr (45011-8661)
PHONE.....................513 645-2600
Alejandra Sargent, *Brnch Mgr*
EMP: 99
SALES (corp-wide): 54.07B **Privately Held**
Web: www.astrazeneca.com
SIC: 2834 Pharmaceutical preparations
HQ: Astrazeneca Pharmaceuticals Lp
1800 Concord Pike
Wilmington DE 19850

(G-13945)
**BAE SYSTEMS SURVIVABILITY
SYSTEMS LLC**
9113 Le Saint Dr (45014-5453)
PHONE.....................513 881-9800
◆ EMP: 589
SIC: 3711 Motor vehicles and car bodies

(G-13946)
BARNES GROUP INC
Also Called: Windsor Airmotive
9826 Crescent Park Dr (45069-3800)
PHONE.....................513 779-6888
Jerry Bach, *Brnch Mgr*
EMP: 16
SALES (corp-wide): 2.6B **Privately Held**
Web: www.lifeatbarnes.com
SIC: 3724 Aircraft engines and engine parts
HQ: Barnes Group Inc.
123 Main St
Bristol CT 06010
860 583-7070

(G-13947)
BARNES GROUP INC
Mro Division
9826 Crescent Park Dr (45069-3800)
PHONE.....................513 779-6888
EMP: 54
SALES (corp-wide): 2.6B **Privately Held**
Web: www.barnesaero.com
SIC: 3728 Aircraft parts and equipment, nec
HQ: Barnes Group Inc.
123 Main St
Bristol CT 06010
860 583-7070

(G-13948)
BELANGER INC (DH)
9393 Princeton Glendale Rd (45011-9707)
PHONE.....................517 870-3206
Kevin Long, *Pr*

Peter Bellin, *VP*
EMP: 65 **EST:** 2018
SALES (est): 33.51MM
SALES (corp-wide): 7.75B **Publicly Held**
Web: www.opwglobal.com
SIC: 3291 3589 Abrasive products; Commercial cooking and foodwarming equipment
HQ: Revod Corporation
1403 Foulk Rd
Wilmington DE 19803

(G-13949)
BENCHMARK LAND MANAGEMENT LLC
9431 Butler Warren Rd (45069)
PHONE..............................513 310-7850
Diana E Honerlaw, *Prin*
EMP: 8 **EST:** 2012
SALES (est): 410.3K **Privately Held**
Web: www.benchmarklm.com
SIC: 0781 3271 0782 Landscape planning services; Blocks, concrete: landscape or retaining wall; Landscape contractors

(G-13950)
BESI MANUFACTURING INC
9445 Sutton Pl (45011-9705)
PHONE..............................513 874-1460
EMP: 7
SALES (corp-wide): 9.74MM **Privately Held**
Web: www.besi-inc.com
SIC: 2399 Seat covers, automobile
PA: Besi Manufacturing Inc
9087 Sutton Pl
West Chester OH 45011
513 874-0232

(G-13951)
BESI MANUFACTURING INC (PA)
9087 Sutton Pl (45011-9316)
PHONE..............................513 874-0232
William Moore, *Pr*
Sue Weaver, *
Tom Moore, *
Dave Moore, *
▲ **EMP:** 24 **EST:** 1974
SQ FT: 17,500
SALES (est): 9.74MM
SALES (corp-wide): 9.74MM **Privately Held**
Web: www.besi-inc.com
SIC: 2399 Seat covers, automobile

(G-13952)
BILLERUD AMERICAS CORPORATION
Also Called: Verso Paper
9025 Centre Pointe Dr (45069-4984)
PHONE..............................901 369-4105
Tom Huber, *Mgr*
EMP: 58
SALES (corp-wide): 3.92B **Privately Held**
Web: www.billerud.com
SIC: 2653 2656 2631 2611 Boxes, corrugated: made from purchased materials ; Food containers (liquid tight), including milk cartons; Container, packaging, and boxboard; Pulp mills
HQ: Billerud Americas Corporation
10050 Innvtion Dr Ste 200
Miamisburg OH 45342

(G-13953)
CABINET AND GRANITE DEPOT LLC
8730 N Pavillion (45069-4894)
PHONE..............................513 874-2100
EMP: 10 **EST:** 2012
SALES (est): 492.64K **Privately Held**
Web: www.granitecincinnati.com

SIC: 2434 Wood kitchen cabinets

(G-13954)
CARDINAL HEALTH 414 LLC
9866 Windisch Rd Bldg 3 (45069-3806)
PHONE..............................513 759-1900
Tommy Ward, *Brnch Mgr*
EMP: 9
SALES (corp-wide): 226.83B **Publicly Held**
SIC: 2834 2835 Pharmaceutical preparations ; Radioactive diagnostic substances
HQ: Cardinal Health 414, Llc
7000 Cardinal Pl
Dublin OH 43017
614 757-5000

(G-13955)
CATEXEL NEASE LLC (DH)
Also Called: Nease Performance Chemicals
9774 Windisch Rd (45069-3808)
PHONE..............................513 587-2800
◆ **EMP:** 10 **EST:** 2005
SALES (est): 36.01MM
SALES (corp-wide): 355.83K **Privately Held**
Web: www.neaseco.com
SIC: 2869 Industrial organic chemicals, nec
HQ: Wp Mannheim Gmbh
Sandhofer Str. 96
Mannheim BW 68305

(G-13956)
CBN WESTSIDE HOLDINGS INC
Also Called: TSS Technologies
8800 Global Way (45069-7070)
PHONE..............................513 772-7000
D Brock Denton, *Prin*
Brent Nichols, *Prin*
EMP: 24 **EST:** 2001
SALES (est): 1.65MM **Privately Held**
SIC: 3599 Machine shop, jobbing and repair

(G-13957)
CBN WESTSIDE TECHNOLOGIES INC
Also Called: TSS Technologies
8800 Global Way (45069-7070)
PHONE..............................513 772-7000
Brent Nichols, *Pr*
Charles B Nichols Junior, *VP*
Mark Nichols, *
Scott Nichols, *
Leila B Nichols, *
▲ **EMP:** 400 **EST:** 1948
SQ FT: 75,000
SALES (est): 2.37MM **Privately Held**
SIC: 3599 8711 Machine shop, jobbing and repair; Mechanical engineering

(G-13958)
CEDAR ELEC HOLDINGS CORP
5440 W Chester Rd (45069-2950)
PHONE..............................773 804-6288
Dave Smidebush, *Brnch Mgr*
EMP: 70
SALES (corp-wide): 58.61MM **Privately Held**
Web: www.cedarelectronics.com
SIC: 3812 5013 5015 Navigational systems and instruments; Tools and equipment, automotive; Automotive supplies, used: wholesale and retail
PA: Cedar Electronics Holdings Corp.
1701 Golf Rd Ste 3-900
Rolling Meadows IL 60008
800 964-3138

(G-13959)
CFM INTERNATIONAL INC (PA)
6440 Aviation Way (45069-4546)
P.O. Box 15514 (45246)

PHONE..............................513 552-2787
Gael Meheust, *Pr*
Cedric Goubet, *Ex VP*
Kevin Fewell, *CFO*
Raymond Scodellaro, *VP*
Maria Deacon, *VP*
EMP: 42 **EST:** 1975
SALES (est): 8.65MM
SALES (corp-wide): 8.65MM **Privately Held**
Web: www.cfmaeroengines.com
SIC: 3724 Aircraft engines and engine parts

(G-13960)
CHEMINSTRUMENTS INC
Also Called: Chemical Instruments
510 Commercial Dr (45014-7593)
PHONE..............................513 860-1598
Keith Muny, *Mgr*
EMP: 7
Web: www.cheminstruments.com
SIC: 3821 Chemical laboratory apparatus, nec
PA: Cheminstruments, Inc.
510 Commercial Dr
West Chester OH 45014

(G-13961)
CHEMINSTRUMENTS INC (PA)
510 Commercial Dr (45014-7593)
PHONE..............................513 860-1598
Richard Muny, *Pr*
Keith Muny, *VP*
▲ **EMP:** 8 **EST:** 1992
SQ FT: 15,000
SALES (est): 2.16MM **Privately Held**
Web: www.cheminstruments.com
SIC: 3829 Measuring and controlling devices, nec

(G-13962)
CHEMSULTANTS INTERNATIONAL INC
Also Called: Chem Instruments
510 Commercial Dr (45014-7593)
PHONE..............................513 860-1598
Keith Muny, *Mgr*
EMP: 7
SALES (corp-wide): 4.82MM **Privately Held**
Web: www.chemsultants.com
SIC: 3821 Laboratory apparatus and furniture
PA: Chemsultants International, Inc.
9079 Tyler Blvd
Mentor OH 44060
440 974-3080

(G-13963)
CINCINNATI PRECISION MCHY INC
9083 Sutton Pl (45011-9316)
PHONE..............................513 860-4133
Pam Ison, *Pr*
Dina Schnitzer, *Sec*
EMP: 9 **EST:** 1992
SQ FT: 4,800
SALES (est): 914.4K **Privately Held**
Web: www.cpmfab.com
SIC: 3599 Machine shop, jobbing and repair

(G-13964)
CIP INTERNATIONAL INC
Also Called: Commercial Interior Products
9575 Le Saint Dr (45014-5447)
PHONE..............................513 874-9925
Thomas Huff, *CEO*
Thomas Huff, *Ch Bd*
Kathleen Huff, *
Mark Elminger, *
Jay Voss, *
◆ **EMP:** 83 **EST:** 1975
SQ FT: 140,000

SALES (est): 10.95MM **Privately Held**
Web: www.cipretail.com
SIC: 7389 2541 Interior designer; Store fixtures, wood

(G-13965)
CLARITY RETAIL SERVICES LLC
Also Called: Jkrg Construction Services
5115 Excello Ct (45069-3091)
PHONE..............................513 800-9369
James R Gavigan, *Pr*
Lance H Madden, *
EMP: 75 **EST:** 2015
SQ FT: 3,200
SALES (est): 5.48MM **Privately Held**
Web: www.clarity-retail.com
SIC: 7389 8742 3999 3577 Interior designer; Sales (including sales management) consultant; Barber and beauty shop equipment; Graphic displays, except graphic terminals

(G-13966)
CLARKWSTERN DTRICH BLDG SYSTEM (HQ)
Also Called: Clarkdietrich
9050 Centre Pointe Dr Ste 400 (45069-4875)
PHONE..............................513 870-1100
Bill Courtney, *CEO*
William Courtney, *
▼ **EMP:** 110 **EST:** 2011
SQ FT: 80,000
SALES (est): 118.64MM
SALES (corp-wide): 1.25B **Publicly Held**
Web: www.clarkdietrich.com
SIC: 3444 8711 3081 Studs and joists, sheet metal; Engineering services; Vinyl film and sheet
PA: Worthington Enterprises, Inc.
200 W Wlson Bridge Rd
Worthington OH 43085
614 438-3210

(G-13967)
CLEVELND-CLFFS TLING STMPING H (DH)
9227 Centre Pointe Dr (45069-4822)
PHONE..............................519 969-4632
Brian Bishop, *CEO*
EMP: 16 **EST:** 2013
SALES (est): 99.96MM
SALES (corp-wide): 19.18B **Publicly Held**
Web: www.clevelandcliffs.com
SIC: 3465 Body parts, automobile: stamped metal
HQ: Cleveland-Cliffs Investments Inc.
9227 Centre Pointe Dr
West Chester OH 45069
513 425-5163

(G-13968)
CLEVELND-CLFFS TOLING STAMPING (DH)
9227 Centre Pointe Dr (45069-4822)
PHONE..............................216 694-5700
Brian Bishop, *CEO*
EMP: 238 **EST:** 1999
SALES (est): 99.96MM
SALES (corp-wide): 19.18B **Publicly Held**
Web: www.clevelandcliffs.com
SIC: 3465 Body parts, automobile: stamped metal
HQ: Cleveland-Cliffs Tooling And Stamping Holdings Llc
9227 Centere Pointe Dr
West Chester OH 45069
519 969-4632

▲ = Import ▼ = Export
◆ = Import/Export

(G-13969)
CONTECH BRIDGE SOLUTIONS LLC (DH)
Also Called: Bridgetek
9025 Centre Pointe Dr Ste 400
(45069-9700)
PHONE....................513 645-7000
Michael M Rafi, *Prin*
EMP: 15 EST: 1994
SQ FT: 1,440
SALES (est): 17.37MM **Privately Held**
Web: www.conteches.com
SIC: 3443 Fabricated plate work (boiler shop)
HQ: Contech Engineered Solutions Llc
9025 Centre Pointe Dr # 400
West Chester OH 45069
513 645-7000

(G-13970)
CONTECH CNSTR PDTS HLDINGS INC
9025 Centre Pointe Dr Ste 400
(45069-9700)
PHONE....................513 645-7000
Ronald Keating, *Prin*
EMP: 1483 EST: 2012
SALES (est): 12.03MM **Privately Held**
Web: www.conteches.com
SIC: 3443 Fabricated plate work (boiler shop)
HQ: Apax Partners Us, Llc
601 Lexington Ave Fl 53
New York NY 10022

(G-13971)
CONTECH ENGNERED SOLUTIONS INC
9025 Centre Pointe Dr Ste 400
(45069-9700)
PHONE....................513 645-7000
Michael Rafi, *Pr*
Jim Waters, *
J Paul Allen, *
EMP: 1300 EST: 2012
SALES (est): 14.88MM **Privately Held**
Web: www.conteches.com
SIC: 3084 3317 3441 3443 Plastics pipe; Steel pipe and tubes; Fabricated structural metal; Fabricated plate work (boiler shop)
PA: Quikrete Holdings, Inc.
5 Concourse Pkwy Ste 1900
Atlanta GA 30328

(G-13972)
CONTECH ENGNERED SOLUTIONS LLC (HQ)
9025 Centre Pointe Dr Ste 400
(45069-9700)
PHONE....................513 645-7000
Mike Rafi, *Pr*
Jeffrey S Lee, *Sr VP*
Mo Heshmati, *SUPPLY CHAIN*
Steve R Spanagel, *Sls Dir*
Vernon B Cameron, *DRAINAGE Technology*
◆ EMP: 150 EST: 1986
SQ FT: 75,000
SALES (est): 480.41MM **Privately Held**
Web: www.conteches.com
SIC: 3444 3084 3317 3441 Sheet metalwork ; Plastics pipe; Steel pipe and tubes; Fabricated structural metal
PA: Quikrete Holdings, Inc.
5 Concourse Pkwy Ste 1900
Atlanta GA 30328

(G-13973)
CONTECH STRMWTER SOLUTIONS LLC
9025 Centre Pointe Dr Ste 400
(45069-9700)
PHONE....................513 645-7000

Rick Stepien, *Pr*
Rebecca H Appenzeller, *Sec*
EMP: 8 EST: 2005
SALES (est): 5.73MM **Privately Held**
Web: www.conteches.com
SIC: 3677 Filtration devices, electronic
HQ: Contech Engineered Solutions Llc
9025 Centre Pointe Dr # 400
West Chester OH 45069
513 645-7000

(G-13974)
CONTROL INTERFACE INC
517 Commercial Dr (45014-7594)
PHONE....................513 874-2062
Tom Osborn, *Pr*
▲ EMP: 8 EST: 1986
SQ FT: 5,000
SALES (est): 2.46MM **Privately Held**
Web: www.controlinterface.com
SIC: 3613 Control panels, electric

(G-13975)
CORNERSTONE BRANDS INC
Also Called: Grandinroad Catalog
5568 W Chester Rd (45069-2914)
PHONE....................866 668-5962
David Cleavinger, *Brnch Mgr*
EMP: 7
Web: www.cornerstonefitnessohio.com
SIC: 3199 Dog furnishings: collars, leashes, muzzles, etc.: leather
HQ: Cornerstone Brands, Inc.
5568 West Chester Rd
West Chester OH 45069
513 603-1000

(G-13976)
CR HOLDING INC
9100 Centre Pointe Dr Ste 200
(45069-4856)
PHONE....................513 860-5039
Richard Owen, *CEO*
John Samoya, *
EMP: 82 EST: 2006
SQ FT: 5,000
SALES (est): 1.96MM **Publicly Held**
SIC: 2841 Soap: granulated, liquid, cake, flaked, or chip
PA: Ares Capital Corporation
245 Park Ave Fl 44
New York NY 10167

(G-13977)
CRANE 1 SERVICES INC (HQ)
9075 Centre Pointe Dr Ste 130
(45069-4805)
PHONE....................937 704-9900
Matt Biskaduros, *Pr*
Joseph Schivone, *CFO*
EMP: 21 EST: 2007
SALES (est): 73.21MM
SALES (corp-wide): 333.76MM **Privately Held**
Web: www.crane1.com
SIC: 3536 Cranes and monorail systems
PA: L Squared Capital Partners Llc
3434 Via Lido Ste 300
Newport Beach CA 92663
949 398-0168

(G-13978)
CRANE TRAINING USA INC
7908 Cincinnati Dayton Rd Ste H
(45069-6629)
PHONE....................513 755-2177
Alan Stein, *Pr*
Sandy Stein, *VP*
EMP: 6 EST: 1991
SALES (est): 512.21K **Privately Held**
Web: www.cranetraining.com

SIC: 3536 Hoists, cranes, and monorails

(G-13979)
CRYOVAC LLC
7410 Union Centre Blvd (45014-2286)
PHONE....................513 771-7770
Sharon Drysdale, *Mgr*
EMP: 10
SALES (corp-wide): 5.39B **Publicly Held**
Web: www.sealedair.com
SIC: 3086 Packaging and shipping materials, foamed plastics
HQ: Cryovac, Llc
2415 Cascade Pointe Blvd
Charlotte NC 28208
980 430-7000

(G-13980)
CUSTOM MILLCRAFT CORP
9092 Le Saint Dr (45014-2241)
PHONE....................513 874-7080
Jody Corbett, *Pr*
EMP: 25 EST: 1983
SQ FT: 56,000
SALES (est): 7MM **Privately Held**
Web: www.custommillcraft.com
SIC: 2521 2522 2542 Cabinets, office: wood; Office furniture, except wood; Partitions and fixtures, except wood

(G-13981)
DA PRECISION PRODUCTS INC
Also Called: Manufacturing
9052 Goldpark Dr (45011-9764)
PHONE....................513 459-1113
Daniel Adams, *CEO*
EMP: 10 EST: 2018
SALES (est): 388.06K **Privately Held**
Web: www.daprecision.com
SIC: 8711 3531 3545 3499 Engineering services; Construction machinery; Precision tools, machinists'; Machine bases, metal

(G-13982)
DEE SIGN CO (PA)
Also Called: Diversified Sign
6163 Allen Rd (45069-3855)
PHONE....................513 779-3333
Braden R Huenefeld, *Ch Bd*
Craig Dixon, *
Joe Kolks, *
◆ EMP: 23 EST: 1967
SQ FT: 125,000
SALES (est): 6.1MM
SALES (corp-wide): 6.1MM **Privately Held**
Web: www.deesign.com
SIC: 3993 Signs, not made in custom sign painting shops

(G-13983)
DEE SIGN USA LLC
6163 Allen Rd (45069-3855)
PHONE....................513 779-3333
Braden R Huenefeld, *Managing Member*
EMP: 14 EST: 2009
SALES (est): 1.28MM **Privately Held**
Web: www.deesign.com
SIC: 3993 Signs and advertising specialties

(G-13984)
DMG MORI USA INC
9415 Meridian Way (45069-6525)
PHONE....................440 546-7088
EMP: 10
Web: en.dmgmori.com
SIC: 3541 Machine tools, metal cutting type
HQ: Dmg Mori Usa, Inc.
2400 Huntington Blvd
Hoffman Estates IL 60192
847 593-5400

(G-13985)
DOVER CORPORATION
9393 Princeton Glendale Rd (45011-9707)
PHONE....................513 870-3206
EMP: 52
SALES (corp-wide): 7.75B **Publicly Held**
Web: www.dovercorporation.com
SIC: 3632 Household refrigerators and freezers
PA: Dover Corporation
3005 Hghland Pkwy Ste 200
Downers Grove IL 60515
630 541-1540

(G-13986)
DREDGER LLC
5698 Sage Meadow Ct (45069-5547)
PHONE....................513 507-8774
William Mahlock, *Prin*
EMP: 6 EST: 2016
SALES (est): 58.77K **Privately Held**
Web: www.dredge.com
SIC: 3731 Shipbuilding and repairing

(G-13987)
DRT HOLDINGS LLC
9025 Centre Pointe Dr Ste 120
(45069-4987)
PHONE....................937 297-6676
EMP: 8 EST: 2008
SALES (est): 1.62MM **Privately Held**
SIC: 3411 Metal cans

(G-13988)
DWYER COMPANIES INC (PA)
Also Called: Dwyer Concrete Lifting
6083 Schumacher Park Dr (45069-4812)
PHONE....................513 777-0998
EMP: 60 EST: 1984
SALES (est): 2.51MM
SALES (corp-wide): 2.51MM **Privately Held**
Web: www.thedwyercompany.com
SIC: 3441 Fabricated structural metal

(G-13989)
EAGLE COMPOSITES LLC
8494 Firebird Dr (45014-2273)
PHONE....................513 330-6108
EMP: 6 EST: 2018
SALES (est): 5.36MM **Privately Held**
Web: www.eagle-composites.com
SIC: 3829 Fuel totalizers, aircraft engine

(G-13990)
EATON CORPORATION
9902 Windisch Rd (45069-3804)
PHONE....................513 387-2000
Chris Kuzak, *Admn*
EMP: 35
Web: www.dix-eaton.com
SIC: 3613 Power circuit breakers
HQ: Eaton Corporation
1000 Eaton Blvd
Cleveland OH 44122
440 523-5000

(G-13991)
EAZYTRADE INC (PA)
Also Called: Eazytrade
9743 Crescent Park Dr (45069-3893)
PHONE....................513 257-9189
Toan Phu, *Pr*
EMP: 9 EST: 2014
SALES (est): 10MM
SALES (corp-wide): 10MM **Privately Held**
SIC: 3825 Internal combustion engine analyzers, to test electronics

(G-13992)
EAZYTRADE INC
7503 Overglen Dr (45069-9383)
PHONE...........................513 257-9189
Toan Phu, *Pr*
EMP: 7
SALES (corp-wide): 10MM **Privately Held**
SIC: 3825 Internal combustion engine
analyzers, to test electronics
PA: Eazytrade Inc
9743 Crescent Park Dr
West Chester OH 45069
513 257-9189

(G-13993)
ENVIRONMENTAL SAMPLE
TECHNOLOGY INC
503 Commercial Dr (45014-7594)
PHONE...........................513 642-0100
EMP: 49
SIC: 3826 Analytical instruments

(G-13994)
EROSION CONTROL PRODUCTS
CORP
9281 Le Saint Dr (45014-5464)
PHONE...........................302 815-6500
Kirc Horne, *Genl Mgr*
EMP: 12 EST: 2019
SALES (est): 2.35MM **Privately Held**
SIC: 3524 5999 Lawn and garden equipment
; Farm equipment and supplies
PA: Dhg Inc.
9281 Le Saint Dr
West Chester OH

(G-13995)
ESCORT INC
5440 W Chester Rd (45069-9004)
PHONE...........................513 870-8500
Chris Cowger, *CEO*
Mark Carrm, *
Gail Babirr, *
▲ EMP: 250 EST: 1997
SQ FT: 32,000
SALES (est): 13.67MM
SALES (corp-wide): 58.61MM **Privately**
Held
Web: www.escortradar.com
SIC: 3812 Radar systems and equipment
PA: Cedar Electronics Holdings Corp.
1701 Golf Rd Ste 3-900
Rolling Meadows IL 60008
800 964-3138

(G-13996)
F A TECH CORP
9065 Sutton Pl (45011-9316)
PHONE...........................513 942-1920
Michael Michimi, *CEO*
EMP: 11 EST: 1994
SALES (est): 1.02MM **Privately Held**
Web: www.brazer.com
SIC: 3599 Machine shop, jobbing and repair

(G-13997)
FINN CORPORATION (HQ)
9281 Le Saint Dr (45014-5464)
PHONE...........................513 874-2818
◆ EMP: 47 EST: 1936
SALES (est): 15.77MM **Privately Held**
Web: www.finncorp.com
SIC: 3524 3523 Lawn and garden equipment
; Farm machinery and equipment
PA: Dhg Inc.
9281 Le Saint Dr
West Chester OH

(G-13998)
FISHER CONTROLS INTL LLC
5453 W Chester Rd (45069-2963)
PHONE...........................513 285-6000
EMP: 12
SALES (corp-wide): 17.49B **Publicly Held**
SIC: 3823 Process control instruments
HQ: Fisher Controls International Llc
205 S Center St
Marshalltown IA 50158
641 754-3011

(G-13999)
FLINT GROUP US LLC
8660 Jacquemin Dr (45069-5055)
PHONE...........................513 552-7232
EMP: 7
SALES (corp-wide): 1.91B **Privately Held**
Web: www.flintgrp.com
SIC: 2865 Color pigments, organic
PA: Flint Group Us Llc
17177 N Lrel Pk Dr Ste 30
Livonia MI 48152
734 781-4600

(G-14000)
FOAM CONCEPTS & DESIGN INC
4602 Mulhauser Rd W Chester Township
(45069-9708)
PHONE...........................513 860-5589
Jeff Labermeier, *Pr*
EMP: 19 EST: 1989
SQ FT: 40,500
SALES (est): 1.75MM **Privately Held**
SIC: 3086 Packaging and shipping
materials, foamed plastics

(G-14001)
FRECON TECHNOLOGIES INC
9319 Princeton Glendale Rd (45011-9707)
PHONE...........................513 874-8981
Fred J Pfirrmann, *CEO*
▲ EMP: 12 EST: 1983
SQ FT: 6,000
SALES (est): 2.16MM **Privately Held**
Web: www.frecontechnologies.com
SIC: 3545 Machine tool attachments and
accessories

(G-14002)
G F FRANK AND SONS INC
9075 Le Saint Dr (45014-2242)
PHONE...........................513 870-9075
George P Frank, *Pr*
John Frank, *VP*
Mark Frank, *VP*
EMP: 15 EST: 1948
SQ FT: 40,000
SALES (est): 3.17MM **Privately Held**
Web: www.gffrankandsons.com
SIC: 3556 3599 Food products machinery;
Machine shop, jobbing and repair

(G-14003)
GE ADDITIVE LLC
5115 Excello Ct (45069-3091)
PHONE...........................513 341-0597
EMP: 17 EST: 2018
SALES (est): 8.04MM
SALES (corp-wide): 38.7B **Publicly Held**
Web: www.ge.com
SIC: 3825 Instruments to measure electricity
HQ: Ge Aviation Systems Llc
1 Neumann Way
Cincinnati OH 45215
937 898-9600

(G-14004)
GE AVIATION SYSTEMS LLC
Also Called: GE Aviation

7831 Ashford Glen Ct (45069-1614)
PHONE...........................513 786-4555
EMP: 10
SALES (corp-wide): 38.7B **Publicly Held**
Web: www.geaerospace.com
SIC: 3812 Aircraft control systems, electronic
HQ: Ge Aviation Systems Llc
1 Neumann Way
Cincinnati OH 45215
937 898-9600

(G-14005)
GE AVIATION SYSTEMS LLC
Also Called: Rapid Quality Manufacturing
5223 Muhlhauser Rd (45011-9327)
PHONE...........................513 889-5150
James C Taylor, *Brnch Mgr*
EMP: 8
SALES (corp-wide): 38.7B **Publicly Held**
Web: www.geaerospace.com
SIC: 3313 Alloys, additive, except copper:
not made in blast furnaces
HQ: Ge Aviation Systems Llc
1 Neumann Way
Cincinnati OH 45215
937 898-9600

(G-14006)
GE HONDA AERO ENGINES LLC
9050 Centre Pointe Dr Ste 200
(45069-6767)
PHONE...........................513 552-4322
Bill Dwyer, *CEO*
Steven J Shaknaitis, *Pr*
Jun Yanada, *Ex VP*
Adam Endress, *CFO*
Menelik Mel Solomon, *Dir*
EMP: 11 EST: 2005
SALES (est): 1.31MM **Privately Held**
Web: www.gehonda.com
SIC: 3519 Parts and accessories, internal
combustion engines

(G-14007)
GEDICO INTERNATIONAL INC
Also Called: Largemachining.com
5337 Crossbridge Dr (45069-1631)
PHONE...........................937 274-2167
George E Dorin, *Pr*
Donald J Smith, *VP*
EMP: 7 EST: 1945
SALES (est): 233.5K **Privately Held**
Web: www.gedico.com
SIC: 3555 3599 Printing trades machinery;
Machine shop, jobbing and repair

(G-14008)
GENERAL ELECTRIC COMPANY
Also Called: GE Additive
8556 Trade Center Dr Ste 100
(45011-9354)
PHONE...........................513 341-0214
David Handler, *Brnch Mgr*
EMP: 200
SALES (corp-wide): 38.7B **Publicly Held**
Web: geaerospace.com
SIC: 3541 Machine tools, metal cutting type
PA: General Electric Company
1 Aviation Way
Cincinnati OH 45215
617 443-3000

(G-14009)
GENERAL ELECTRIC COMPANY
Also Called: GE
9701 Windisch Rd (45069-3827)
PHONE...........................714 668-0951
EMP: 17
SALES (corp-wide): 38.7B **Publicly Held**
Web: geaerospace.com

SIC: 3699 Electrical equipment and supplies,
nec
PA: General Electric Company
1 Aviation Way
Cincinnati OH 45215
617 443-3000

(G-14010)
GEORGIA-PACIFIC LLC
Also Called: Georgia-Pacific
9048 Port Union Rialto Rd (45069-3254)
PHONE...........................513 942-4800
Jeff Holsom, *Mgr*
EMP: 25
SALES (corp-wide): 64.44B **Privately Held**
Web: www.gp.com
SIC: 2621 Paper mills
HQ: Georgia-Pacific Llc
133 Peachtree St Ne
Atlanta GA 30303
404 652-4000

(G-14011)
GLOBAL PARTNERS USA CO INC
7544 Bermuda Trce (45069-6324)
PHONE...........................513 276-4981
Rudy Shephard, *Prin*
EMP: 6 EST: 2012
SALES (est): 87.83K **Privately Held**
Web: www.globalpartners.com.hk
SIC: 3953 Stationery embossers, personal

(G-14012)
GRAPHEL CORPORATION
Also Called: Carbon Products
6115 Centre Park Dr (45069-3869)
PHONE...........................513 779-6166
David Trinkley, *Pr*
Mark Grammer, *
EMP: 140 EST: 1965
SQ FT: 35,000
SALES (est): 23.29MM **Privately Held**
Web: www.graphel.com
SIC: 5052 3599 3624 Coal and other
minerals and ores; Machine shop, jobbing
and repair; Electrodes, thermal and
electrolytic uses: carbon, graphite

(G-14013)
HARD SURFACE TECHNOLOGY INC
Also Called: L W G Finishing
9461 Le Saint Dr (45014-5447)
PHONE...........................513 860-1156
Dan Green, *Pr*
Ray Acree, *Stockholder*
Frank Mc Farland, *Stockholder*
EMP: 9 EST: 1988
SQ FT: 10,000
SALES (est): 749.54K **Privately Held**
SIC: 3599 Machine shop, jobbing and repair

(G-14014)
HYDRO SYSTEMS COMPANY
9393 Princeton Glendale Rd (45011-9707)
PHONE...........................513 271-8800
EMP: 10 EST: 1998
SALES (est): 1.28MM **Privately Held**
Web: www.hydrosystemsco.com
SIC: 3559 Chemical machinery and
equipment

(G-14015)
IOT DIAGNOSTICS LLC
9361 Allen Rd (45069-3846)
P.O. Box 42414 (45242-0414)
PHONE...........................844 786-7631
Jeremy Drury, *Pr*
EMP: 7 EST: 2017
SALES (est): 618.54K **Privately Held**
Web: www.iotdiag.com

▲ = Import ▼ = Export
◆ = Import/Export

SIC: 7372 Application computer software

(G-14016)
IT XCEL CONSULTING LLC
Also Called: Xgs.it
7112 Office Park Dr (45069-2261)
PHONE................................513 847-8261
Dennis Hollstegge, *Managing Member*
EMP: 15 EST: 2005
SQ FT: 1,880
SALES (est): 7.5MM **Privately Held**
Web: www.xgsit.com
SIC: 2752 7379 Commercial printing,
lithographic; Computer related consulting
services

(G-14017)
J & K CABINETRY INC
8800 Global Way # 200 (45069-7070)
PHONE................................513 860-3461
Zhi Wei Huang, *Admn*
EMP: 7 EST: 2014
SALES (est): 260.46K **Privately Held**
Web: www.jkcabinetohio.com
SIC: 2434 Wood kitchen cabinets

(G-14018)
KAO USA INC
Also Called: K A O Brands
8778 Le Saint Dr (45014-2260)
PHONE................................513 341-2630
EMP: 23
Web: www.kao.com
SIC: 2844 Cosmetic preparations
HQ: Kao Usa Inc.
2535 Spring Grove Ave
Cincinnati OH 45214
513 421-1400

(G-14019)
KC ROBOTICS INC
9000 Le Saint Dr (45014-2241)
PHONE................................513 860-4442
Kyle Carrier, *CEO*
Kenneth P Carrier Junior, *Pr*
Constance M Carrier, *
◆ EMP: 26 EST: 1989
SQ FT: 18,000
SALES (est): 10.18MM **Privately Held**
Web: www.kcrobotics.com
SIC: 3569 7373 Robots, assembly line:
industrial and commercial; Systems
integration services

(G-14020)
KIDD PROPERTIES LLC
Also Called: Lacrema Coffee Company
9085 Sutton Pl (45011-9316)
PHONE................................513 779-6278
EMP: 7 EST: 2005
SALES (est): 295.11K **Privately Held**
SIC: 2095 Roasted coffee

(G-14021)
KOPCO GRAPHICS INC (PA)
9750 Crescent Park Dr (45069-3894)
PHONE................................513 874-7230
EMP: 30 EST: 1989
SALES (est): 4.97MM **Privately Held**
Web: www.fortissolutionsgroup.com
SIC: 5199 2759 Packaging materials;
Flexographic printing

(G-14022)
LEGEND METAL AND RUBBER LLC
9388 Sutton Pl (45011-9702)
PHONE................................513 874-8020
Daniel B Cunningham, *Managing Member*
EMP: 11 EST: 2004
SALES (est): 393.41K **Privately Held**

Web: www.longstanton.com
SIC: 3599 Machine shop, jobbing and repair

(G-14023)
LEM PRODUCTS HOLDING LLC (PA)
Also Called: L.E.M. Products
4440 Muhlhauser Rd Ste 300 (45011-9767)
PHONE................................513 202-1188
Hill Kohnen, *CEO*
▲ EMP: 20 EST: 1991
SALES (est): 8.78MM **Privately Held**
Web: www.lemproducts.com
SIC: 3556 3949 Cutting, chopping, grinding,
mixing, and similar machinery; Hunting
equipment

(G-14024)
LONG-STANTON MFG COMPANY
9388 Sutton Pl (45011-9702)
PHONE................................513 874-8020
Daniel B Cunningham, *Pr*
Tom Kachovec, *
Tim Hershey, *
▲ EMP: 50 EST: 1862
SQ FT: 66,000
SALES (est): 4.52MM **Privately Held**
Web: www.longstanton.com
SIC: 3444 7692 3469 3544 Sheet metalwork
; Welding repair; Metal stampings, nec;
Special dies, tools, jigs, and fixtures

(G-14025)
LOST TECHNOLOGY LLP
Also Called: Lost Tech
9501 Woodland Hills Dr (45011-9300)
P.O. Box 8257 (45069-8257)
PHONE................................513 685-0054
Larry Hansonsmith Parnter, *Prin*
EMP: 7 EST: 2002
SALES (est): 184.24K **Privately Held**
SIC: 7372 Educational computer software

(G-14026)
MARTIN MARIETTA MATERIALS INC
Also Called: Martin Marietta Aggragate
9277 Centre Pointe Dr Ste 250
(45069-4844)
P.O. Box 30013 (27622-0013)
PHONE................................513 701-1140
Harry Charles, *Mgr*
EMP: 11
Web: www.martinmarietta.com
SIC: 1423 1422 3295 3297 Crushed and
broken granite; Crushed and broken
limestone; Magnesite, crude: ground,
calcined, or dead-burned; Nonclay
refractories
PA: Martin Marietta Materials Inc
4123 Parklake Ave
Raleigh NC 27612

(G-14027)
MARTIN-BROWER COMPANY LLC
Also Called: Distribution Center
4260 Port Union Rd (45011-9768)
PHONE................................513 773-2301
Ryan Rozen, *Genl Mgr*
EMP: 163
Web: www.martinbrower.us
SIC: 2013 2015 5087 Frozen meats, from
purchased meat; Poultry, processed: frozen
; Restaurant supplies
HQ: The Martin-Brower Company L L C
6250 N River Rd Ste 9000
Rosemont IL 60018
847 227-6500

(G-14028)
MERCHANTS METALS LLC
Also Called: Meadow Burke Products
8760 Global Way Bldg 1 (45069-7066)

PHONE................................513 942-0268
Debbie Humbert, *Genl Mgr*
EMP: 42
SALES (corp-wide): 1.09B **Privately Held**
Web: www.merchantsmetals.com
SIC: 3496 Miscellaneous fabricated wire
products
HQ: Merchants Metals Llc
3 Ravinia Dr Ste 1750
Atlanta GA 30346
770 741-0300

(G-14029)
MIDWEST SEA SALT COMPANY INC
8694 Rite Track Way (45069-7022)
PHONE................................513 770-9177
Warren Watson, *Pr*
EMP: 10 EST: 2012
SALES (est): 897.83K **Privately Held**
Web: www.midwestseasaltcompany.com
SIC: 2844 5122 5999 5961 Cosmetic
preparations; Cosmetics, perfumes, and
hair products; Toiletries, cosmetics, and
perfumes; Cosmetics and perfumes, mail
order

(G-14030)
MILLWOOD INC
4438 Muhlhauser Rd Ste 100 (45011-9776)
PHONE................................513 860-4567
Antonio Delgado, *Brnch Mgr*
EMP: 50
Web: www.millwoodinc.com
SIC: 3565 5084 Packaging machinery;
Packaging machinery and equipment
PA: Millwood, Inc.
3708 International Blvd
Vienna OH 44473

(G-14031)
MODEL GRAPHICS& MEDIA INC
Also Called: Model Graphics
2614 Crescentville Rd (45069-3819)
PHONE................................513 541-2355
Steve Fleissner, *Pr*
Barb Fleissner, *
EMP: 48 EST: 1984
SQ FT: 38,000
SALES (est): 4.82MM **Privately Held**
Web: www.modelgraphicsinc.com
SIC: 2759 Labels and seals: printing, nsk

(G-14032)
MULTI FITTINGS CORPORATION
Also Called: Lasaint Logistics
4507 Le Saint Ct (45014-5486)
PHONE................................513 942-9910
Thomas Torokvei, *Ch Bd*
Paul Graddon, *
C Masse, *
▲ EMP: 156 EST: 1983
SALES (est): 3.72MM
SALES (corp-wide): 8.01MM **Privately
Held**
Web: www.multifittings.com
SIC: 3432 4226 Plumbing fixture fittings and
trim; Special warehousing and storage, nec
HQ: Ipex Inc
1425 North Service Rd E Suite 3
Oakville ON L6H 1
289 881-0120

(G-14033)
NIKKE KUREHA AMERICA CO LTD
Also Called: Tk America
4591 Brate Dr (45011-3849)
PHONE................................513 771-6788
Ikuo Takeuchi, *CEO*
Taizo Ono, *CFO*
Seiji Yamazoe, *Genl Mgr*
▲ EMP: 9 EST: 1994

SALES (est): 2.97MM **Privately Held**
Web: www.tkamerica.com
SIC: 2297 Nonwoven fabrics
HQ: Kureha Ltd.
255, Oka
Ritto SGA 520-3

(G-14034)
NUTRITIONAL MEDICINALS LLC
Also Called: Functional Formularies
9277 Centre Pointe Dr Ste 220
(45069-4844)
PHONE................................937 433-4673
Marc Gibeley, *CEO*
Namrata Maquire, *CFO*
Brian Mcgee, *COO*
EMP: 12 EST: 2006
SALES (est): 2MM
SALES (corp-wide): 967.4MM **Privately
Held**
Web: www.functionalformularies.com
SIC: 2833 8011 Organic medicinal
chemicals: bulk, uncompounded; Offices
and clinics of medical doctors
PA: Danone
17 Boulevard Haussmann
Paris IDF 75009
149485000

(G-14035)
OATS OVERNIGHT INC
7757 Union Centre Blvd Ste 400
(45011-3693)
PHONE................................602 492-1751
EMP: 96
SALES (corp-wide): 56.88MM **Privately
Held**
Web: www.oatsovernight.com
SIC: 5963 2038 Direct selling establishments
; Breakfasts, frozen and packaged
PA: Oats Overnight, Inc.
4121 E Cotton Center Blvd
Phoenix AZ 85040
602 492-1751

(G-14036)
OHIO ALUMINUM CHEMICALS LLC
4544 Muhlhauser Rd (45011-9708)
PHONE................................513 860-3842
EMP: 6 EST: 2006
SALES (est): 453.42K **Privately Held**
SIC: 2899 Chemical preparations, nec

(G-14037)
OHIO EAGLE DISTRIBUTING LLC
9300 Allen Rd (45069-3847)
PHONE................................513 539-8483
John W Saputo, *Prin*
EMP: 41 EST: 2015
SALES (est): 4.7MM **Privately Held**
Web: www.ohioeagle.com
SIC: 2086 5921 Tea, iced: packaged in cans,
bottles, etc.; Wine and beer

(G-14038)
OMER J SMITH INC
Also Called: Paper Products Company
9112 Le Saint Dr (45014-5452)
PHONE................................513 921-4717
Dennis J Smith, *Pr*
Denny J Smith Ii, *VP*
Mary C Smith, *
▲ EMP: 30 EST: 1932
SQ FT: 80,000
SALES (est): 4.23MM **Privately Held**
Web: www.paperproductscompany.com
SIC: 2653 Boxes, corrugated: made from
purchased materials

(G-14039)
OPW ENGINEERED SYSTEMS INC (DH)
9393 Princeton Glendale Rd (45011-9707)
PHONE..............................888 771-9438
Robert B Nicholson Iii, *CEO*
Tim Warning, *
Mike Krauser, *
▲ EMP: 23 EST: 2007
SALES (est): 4.95MM
SALES (corp-wide): 7.75B Publicly Held
Web: www.enerdine.com
SIC: 3494 3825 3625 3568 Valves and pipe
   fittings, nec; Instruments to measure
   electricity; Relays and industrial controls;
   Power transmission equipment, nec
HQ: Opw Fluid Transfer Group
   4304 Mattox Rd
   Kansas City MO 64150

(G-14040)
OPW FUELING COMPONENTS INC (HQ)
Also Called: Opw Engineered Systems
9393 Princeton Glendale Rd (45011-9707)
PHONE..............................800 422-2525
David Crouse, *Pr*
◆ EMP: 95 EST: 2007
SALES (est): 109.13MM
SALES (corp-wide): 7.75B Publicly Held
Web: www.opwglobal.com
SIC: 2899 Fuel treating compounds
PA: Dover Corporation
   3005 Hghland Pkwy Ste 200
   Downers Grove IL 60515
   630 541-1540

(G-14041)
PARKER-HANNIFIN CORPORATION
9050 Centre Pointe Dr Ste 310
(45069-2941)
PHONE..............................513 847-1758
Rick Stumpf, *Brnch Mgr*
EMP: 9
SALES (corp-wide): 19.93B Publicly Held
Web: www.parker.com
SIC: 3594 Fluid power pumps and motors
PA: Parker-Hannifin Corporation
   6035 Parkland Blvd
   Cleveland OH 44124
   216 896-3000

(G-14042)
PATRIOT ARMORED SYSTEMS LLC
Also Called: Patriot Armor
9113 Le Saint Dr (45014-5453)
PHONE..............................413 637-1060
EMP: 19
Web: www.pasarmor.com
SIC: 3231 Products of purchased glass
PA: Patriot Armored Systems, Llc
   140 Crystal St
   Lenox Dale MA 01242

(G-14043)
PHASE ARRAY COMPANY LLC
9472 Meridian Way (45069-6527)
PHONE..............................513 785-0801
Dominique Braconnier, *Managing Member*
◆ EMP: 7 EST: 2017
SALES (est): 2.02MM Privately Held
Web: www.thephasedarraycompany.com
SIC: 3577 7379 Computer peripheral
   equipment, nec; Computer related
   consulting services

(G-14044)
PHOENIX DOOR SYSTEMS INC (PA)
7390 Union Centre Blvd (45014-2287)
PHONE..............................513 492-8213

Mike Hegner, *CEO*
EMP: 27 EST: 2019
SALES (est): 1.64MM
SALES (corp-wide): 1.64MM Privately
Held
Web: www.phoenixdoorsystems.com
SIC: 3442 Metal doors, sash, and trim

(G-14045)
PILOT CHEMICAL COMPANY OHIO (PA)
Also Called: Pilot Chemical Company
9075 Centre Pointe Dr Ste 400
(45069-4891)
PHONE..............................513 326-0600
Mike Clark, *CEO*
Glynn E Goertzen, *
Susan K Leslie, *
Christian Maclver, *
Derek Houck, *
◆ EMP: 30 EST: 1952
SALES (est): 126.04MM
SALES (corp-wide): 126.04MM Privately
Held
Web: www.pilotchemical.com
SIC: 2843 2841 Finishing agents;
   Detergents, synthetic organic or inorganic
   alkaline

(G-14046)
PILOT CHEMICAL CORP (HQ)
9075 Centre Pointe Dr Ste 400
(45069-4891)
PHONE..............................513 326-0600
Pamela R Butcher, *Pr*
Susan K Leslie, *
Mike Clark, *
◆ EMP: 108 EST: 1961
SALES (est): 89.2MM
SALES (corp-wide): 126.04MM Privately
Held
Web: www.pilotchemical.com
SIC: 2841 2843 Detergents, synthetic
   organic or inorganic alkaline; Surface active
   agents
PA: Pilot Chemical Company Of Ohio
   9075 Cntre Pnte Dr Ste 40
   West Chester OH 45069
   513 326-0600

(G-14047)
PILOT POLYMER TECHNOLOGIES
9075 Centre Pointe Dr Ste 400
(45069-4891)
PHONE..............................412 735-4799
Patrick Mccarthy, *CEO*
EMP: 8 EST: 2006
SALES (est): 545.77K
SALES (corp-wide): 126.04MM Privately
Held
Web: www.pilotchemical.com
SIC: 2821 Plastics materials and resins
PA: Pilot Chemical Company Of Ohio
   9075 Cntre Pnte Dr Ste 40
   West Chester OH 45069
   513 326-0600

(G-14048)
PIONEER LABELS INC
Also Called: Datamax Oneil Printer Supplies
9290 Le Saint Dr (45014-5454)
PHONE..............................618 546-5418
Paul Sindoni, *Pr*
Christian Lefort, *
Carter Williams, *
John Yuncza, *
▼ EMP: 105 EST: 1984
SALES (est): 944.73K
SALES (corp-wide): 38.5B Publicly Held

SIC: 2754 2672 2671 Labels: gravure printing
   ; Paper; coated and laminated, nec; Paper;
   coated and laminated packaging
HQ: Datamax-O'neil Corporation
   4501 Pkwy Commerce Blvd
   Orlando FL 32808

(G-14049)
PIPE PRODUCTS INC
5122 Rialto Rd (45069-2923)
P.O. Box 2778 (23609-0778)
PHONE..............................513 587-7532
▲ EMP: 150
SIC: 5051 3498 5085 Pipe and tubing, steel;
   Pipe fittings, fabricated from purchased pipe
   ; Valves and fittings

(G-14050)
POLE/ZERO LLC
Also Called: Pole/Zero Acquisition, Inc.
5558 Union Centre Dr (45069-4821)
PHONE..............................513 870-9060
Ronald Ruppersburg, *Pr*
EMP: 180 EST: 1990
SQ FT: 50,000
SALES (est): 48.88MM
SALES (corp-wide): 7.75B Publicly Held
Web: www.mpgdover.com
SIC: 3663 Radio and television switching
   equipment
PA: Dover Corporation
   3005 Hghland Pkwy Ste 200
   Downers Grove IL 60515
   630 541-1540

(G-14051)
POLYMET CORPORATION
7397 Union Centre Blvd (45014-2288)
PHONE..............................513 874-3586
Bill Mosier, *Pr*
Thomas J Dagenback, *
▲ EMP: 45 EST: 1967
SQ FT: 47,000
SALES (est): 9.06MM Privately Held
Web: www.polymet.us
SIC: 3496 3548 3341 3315 Miscellaneous
   fabricated wire products; Welding apparatus
   ; Secondary nonferrous metals; Steel wire
   and related products

(G-14052)
PRECISION DIE & STAMPING INC
9800 Harwood Ct (45014-7589)
PHONE..............................513 942-8220
Greg Johnson, *Pr*
Mike Stephens, *Prin*
EMP: 8 EST: 1999
SQ FT: 6,500
SALES (est): 732.97K Privately Held
Web:
www.precisiondieandstamping.com
SIC: 3544 Special dies and tools

(G-14053)
PREMIER CONSTRUCTION COMPANY
7092 Champions Ln (45069-4679)
PHONE..............................513 874-2611
Jan Gilkey, *Pr*
EMP: 6 EST: 1959
SALES (est): 579.99K Privately Held
Web: www.premierconstructionco.com
SIC: 5031 1751 2452 Lumber: rough,
   dressed, and finished; Carpentry work;
   Panels and sections, prefabricated, wood

(G-14054)
PROCTER & GAMBLE COMPANY
Also Called: Procter & Gamble
8256 Union Centre Blvd (45069-7056)
PHONE..............................513 634-9600

Pam Dunnon, *Brnch Mgr*
EMP: 205
SALES (corp-wide): 84.04B Publicly Held
Web: us.pg.com
SIC: 2844 2676 3421 2842 Deodorants,
   personal; Towels, napkins, and tissue paper
   products; Razor blades and razors;
   Specialty cleaning
PA: The Procter & Gamble Company
   1 Procter & Gamble Plz
   Cincinnati OH 45202
   513 983-1100

(G-14055)
PROCTER & GAMBLE COMPANY
Also Called: Procter & Gamble
8611 Beckett Rd (45069-4868)
PHONE..............................513 634-9110
Ken Litteken, *Mgr*
EMP: 205
SALES (corp-wide): 84.04B Publicly Held
Web: us.pg.com
SIC: 2844 2676 3421 2842 Deodorants,
   personal; Towels, napkins, and tissue paper
   products; Razor blades and razors;
   Specialty cleaning
PA: The Procter & Gamble Company
   1 Procter & Gamble Plz
   Cincinnati OH 45202
   513 983-1100

(G-14056)
PTS PRFSSNAL TECHNICAL SVC INC
Also Called: Est Analytical
503 Commercial Dr (45014-7594)
PHONE..............................513 642-0111
James R Murphy, *CEO*
Justin Murphy, *
Scott Bornemann, *
EMP: 52 EST: 1995
SQ FT: 12,000
SALES (est): 9.47MM Privately Held
Web: www.estanalytical.com
SIC: 3826 Analytical instruments

(G-14057)
QUALITURN INC
9081 Le Saint Dr (45014-2242)
PHONE..............................513 868-3333
Mike Barber, *Pr*
EMP: 24 EST: 1988
SQ FT: 1,500
SALES (est): 5.84MM Privately Held
Web: www.qualiturn-cnc.com
SIC: 3599 Machine shop, jobbing and repair

(G-14058)
QUASONIX INC (PA)
Also Called: Quasonix
6025 Schumacher Park Dr (45069-4812)
PHONE..............................513 942-1287
Terrance Hill, *Pr*
Pamela S Hill, *
EMP: 37 EST: 2002
SQ FT: 15,000
SALES (est): 22.04MM
SALES (corp-wide): 22.04MM Privately
Held
Web: www.quasonix.com
SIC: 5065 3663 3812 3669 Communication
   equipment; Airborne radio communications
   equipment; Antennas, radar or
   communications; Intercommunication
   systems, electric

(G-14059)
QUEEN CITY POLYMERS INC (PA)
6101 Schumacher Park Dr (45069-3818)
PHONE..............................513 779-0990
James M Powers, *Pr*
James L Powers, *

GEOGRAPHIC

EMP: 40 **EST:** 1982
SQ FT: 33,000
SALES (est): 6.7MM
SALES (corp-wide): 6.7MM **Privately Held**
Web: www.qcpinc.net
SIC: 3089 5162 Injection molding of plastics; Plastics products, nec

(G-14060)
R L INDUSTRIES INC
9355 Le Saint Dr (45014-5458)
PHONE............................513 874-2800
John R Gierl, *Prin*
EMP: 75 **EST:** 1962
SALES (est): 1.37MM
SALES (corp-wide): 1.54MM **Privately Held**
Web: www.rl-industries.com
SIC: 3089 Plastics and fiberglass tanks
PA: R L Holdings, Inc.
9355 Le Saint Dr
Fairfield OH 45014
513 874-2800

(G-14061)
R R DONNELLEY & SONS COMPANY
Also Called: RR Donnelley
8720 Global Way (45069-7066)
PHONE............................513 552-1512
Brad Hull, *Mgr*
EMP: 7
SALES (corp-wide): 15B **Privately Held**
Web: www.rrd.com
SIC: 2759 Commercial printing, nec
HQ: R. R. Donnelley & Sons Company
227 W Monroe St Ste 500
Chicago IL 60606
312 326-8000

(G-14062)
R R DONNELLEY & SONS COMPANY
8740 Global Way (45069-7066)
PHONE............................513 870-4040
EMP: 20
SALES (corp-wide): 15B **Privately Held**
Web: www.rrd.com
SIC: 2657 Folding paperboard boxes
HQ: R. R. Donnelley & Sons Company
227 W Monroe St Ste 500
Chicago IL 60606
312 326-8000

(G-14063)
REPUBLIC WIRE INC
5525 Union Centre Dr (45069-4820)
PHONE............................513 860-1800
Ron Rosenbeck, *CEO*
Mark Huelsebusch, *
◆ **EMP:** 75 **EST:** 1981
SQ FT: 175,000
SALES (est): 1.99MM **Privately Held**
Web: www.republicwire.com
SIC: 3351 3315 Wire, copper and copper alloy; Steel wire and related products

(G-14064)
RESILIENCE US INC
8814 Trade Port Dr (45011-8661)
PHONE............................513 645-2600
Joshua Matson, *Brnch Mgr*
EMP: 470
SALES (corp-wide): 400.95MM **Privately Held**
Web: www.resilience.com
SIC: 2834 Pharmaceutical preparations
HQ: Resilience Us, Inc.
3115 Mrryfeld Row Ste 200
San Diego CA 92121
984 202-0854

(G-14065)
RESPONSIBLE PRODUCTS LIMITED
6101 Schumacher Park Dr (45069-3818)
PHONE............................888 988-6627
Nathan Sedgwick, *Managing Member*
EMP: 14 **EST:** 2018
SALES (est): 3.65MM **Privately Held**
Web: www.responsibleproducts.com
SIC: 5113 2671 Boxes and containers; Paper; coated and laminated packaging

(G-14066)
RETTERBUSH GRAPHICS PACKG CORP
6392 Gano Rd (45069-4809)
PHONE............................513 779-4466
Joseph Retterbush, *Pr*
Denny Meador, *VP*
EMP: 9 **EST:** 1995
SALES (est): 1MM **Privately Held**
Web: www.retterbushcorp.com
SIC: 2671 2754 Paper, coated or laminated for packaging; Labels: gravure printing

(G-14067)
REV38 LLC
8888 Beckett Rd (45069-2902)
PHONE............................937 572-4000
Erick Carlson, *Brnch Mgr*
EMP: 6
SALES (corp-wide): 1.61MM **Privately Held**
SIC: 3663 Radio and t.v. communications equipment
PA: Rev38 Llc
131 Waterstone Dr
Franklin OH 45005
937 269-9641

(G-14068)
RITE TRACK EQUIPMENT SERVICES LLC (PA)
Also Called: Rite Track
8655 Rite Track Way (45069-7064)
PHONE............................513 881-7820
EMP: 56 **EST:** 1993
SALES (est): 23.37MM **Privately Held**
Web: www.ritetrack.com
SIC: 3559 Semiconductor manufacturing machinery

(G-14069)
ROBERT ROTHSCHILD FARM LLC
Also Called: Robert Rothschild Market Cafe
9958 Crescent Park Dr (45069-3895)
P.O. Box 767 (43078-0767)
PHONE............................855 969-8050
◆ **EMP:** 18 **EST:** 2005
SQ FT: 45,000
SALES (est): 2MM **Privately Held**
Web: www.robertrothschild.com
SIC: 0171 2035 2033 2032 Raspberry farm; Pickles, sauces, and salad dressings; Canned fruits and specialties; Canned specialties

(G-14070)
ROCKWELL AUTOMATION INC
9355 Allen Rd (45069-3846)
PHONE............................513 942-9828
Jim Sell, *Mgr*
EMP: 46
SQ FT: 16,000
Web: www.rockwellautomation.com
SIC: 3625 Relays and industrial controls
PA: Rockwell Automation, Inc.
1201 S 2nd St
Milwaukee WI 53204

(G-14071)
ROTO-DIE COMPANY INC
Also Called: Roto Met Rice
4430 Mulhauser Rd (45011-9708)
PHONE............................513 942-3500
Mike Frazer, *Mgr*
EMP: 6
SALES (corp-wide): 40.81MM **Privately Held**
Web: www.maxcessintl.com
SIC: 3544 Special dies and tools
PA: Roto-Die Company, Inc.
800 Howerton Ln
Eureka MO 63025
636 587-3600

(G-14072)
SAFEWAY SAFETY STEP LLC
Also Called: Cleancut
5242 Rialto Rd (45069-2921)
PHONE............................513 942-7837
EMP: 10 **EST:** 2000
SALES (est): 5.38MM **Privately Held**
Web: www.safewaystep.com
SIC: 3088 Tubs (bath, shower, and laundry), plastics

(G-14073)
SCHNEIDER ELECTRIC USA INC
Also Called: Schneider Electric
9870 Crescent Park Dr (45069-3800)
PHONE............................513 777-4445
Jim Newcomb, *Mgr*
EMP: 75
SALES (corp-wide): 1.09K **Privately Held**
Web: www.se.com
SIC: 3613 3643 3612 3823 Switchgear and switchboard apparatus; Bus bars (electrical conductors); Power transformers, electric; Controllers, for process variables, all types
HQ: Schneider Electric Usa, Inc.
1 Boston Pl Ste 2700
Boston MA 02108
617 904-9422

(G-14074)
SENTRILOCK LLC
7701 Service Center Dr (45069-2440)
PHONE............................513 618-5800
Scott R Fisher, *Managing Member*
John G Wenker, *
EMP: 185 **EST:** 2003
SQ FT: 7,000
SALES (est): 24.05MM **Privately Held**
Web: www.sentrilock.com
SIC: 3679 Electronic circuits

(G-14075)
SEPPI M SPA
8880 Beckett Rd (45011)
PHONE............................513 443-6339
Pierluigi Defant, *CEO*
EMP: 6
SALES (corp-wide): 33.03MM **Privately Held**
Web: www.seppi.com
SIC: 3523 Cabs, tractors, and agricultural machinery
PA: Seppi M. Spa
Via Trento 111
Mezzolombardo TN 38017
04611787500

(G-14076)
STERLING COATING
9048 Port Union Rialto Rd (45069-3254)
PHONE............................513 942-4900
Craig Lowe, *Genl Mgr*
EMP: 6 **EST:** 2014
SALES (est): 104.83K **Privately Held**

SIC: 3479 Etching and engraving

(G-14077)
STOROPACK INC
4600 Brate Dr (45011-3558)
PHONE............................513 874-0314
EMP: 11
SALES (corp-wide): 655.85MM **Privately Held**
Web: www.storopack.us
SIC: 5199 3086 2671 Packaging materials; Packaging and shipping materials, foamed plastics; Paper; coated and laminated packaging
HQ: Storopack, Inc.
4758 Devitt Dr
Cincinnati OH 45246
513 874-0314

(G-14078)
SUMMIT CONTAINER CORPORATION (PA)
8080 Beckett Center Dr Ste 203 (45069-5026)
PHONE............................719 481-8400
Adam C Walker, *CEO*
Dave Johnson, *
EMP: 13 **EST:** 1984
SALES (est): 3.04MM
SALES (corp-wide): 3.04MM **Privately Held**
Web: www.1teamsummit.com
SIC: 2653 Boxes, corrugated: made from purchased materials

(G-14079)
SUMMIT PACKAGING SOLUTIONS LLC (PA)
8080 Beckett Center Dr Ste 203 (45069-5026)
PHONE............................719 481-8400
Adam Walker, *CEO*
EMP: 12 **EST:** 2015
SALES (est): 17.45MM
SALES (corp-wide): 17.45MM **Privately Held**
Web: www.1teamsummit.com
SIC: 2631 Container, packaging, and boxboard

(G-14080)
SYSTECON LLC
6121 Schumacher Park Dr (45069-3818)
PHONE............................513 777-7722
Martin P Tierney, *Pr*
Alice Edwards, *Contrlr*
EMP: 85 **EST:** 1949
SQ FT: 60,000
SALES (est): 9.98MM
SALES (corp-wide): 58.86B **Privately Held**
Web: www.systecon.com
SIC: 3561 Pumps and pumping equipment
HQ: Engie North America Inc.
1360 Post Oak Blvd Ste 40
Houston TX 77056
713 636-1900

(G-14081)
TENACITY MANUFACTURING COMPANY
4455 Mulhauser Rd (45011-9788)
P.O. Box 15006 (45215-0006)
PHONE............................513 821-0201
Layne Meader, *Pr*
Tim Baumgardner, *Treas*
Jerry Crowder, *Product Vice President*
EMP: 8 **EST:** 1905
SQ FT: 36,500
SALES (est): 1.18MM
SALES (corp-wide): 8.51MM **Privately Held**

Web: www.tenacitymfg.com
SIC: 3469 2782 Machine parts, stamped or
　pressed metal; Looseleaf binders and
　devices
PA: Kofile Products, Inc.
　6480 Enduro Dr
　Washington MO 63090
　636 239-0140

(G-14082)
THREE BOND INTERNATIONAL INC
(DH)
6184 Schumacher Park Dr (45069-4802)
PHONE...................513 779-7300
Kazunori Shibayama, *Pr*
▲ **EMP:** 60 **EST:** 1987
SALES (est): 42MM **Privately Held**
Web: www.threebond.com
SIC: 2891 Adhesives
HQ: Threebond Co., Ltd.
　4-3-3, Minamiosawa
　Hachioji TKY 192-0

(G-14083)
TOTAL LIFE SAFETY LLC
Also Called: Atech Fire Services
6228 Centre Park Dr Ste C (45069-4825)
PHONE...................866 955-2318
Douglas Patterson, *Pr*
Douglas Patterson, *Managing Member*
EMP: 13 **EST:** 2020
SALES (est): 2MM **Privately Held**
SIC: 3669 5063 7389 7382 Fire detection
　systems, electric; Fire alarm systems; Fire
　extinguisher servicing; Fire alarm
　maintenance and monitoring

(G-14084)
TREY CORRUGATED INC
9048 Port Union Rialto Rd (45069-3254)
PHONE...................513 942-4800
Tim Cossey, *Pr*
EMP: 74 **EST:** 1984
SALES (est): 2.54MM
SALES (corp-wide): 64.44B **Privately Held**
SIC: 2653 Boxes, corrugated: made from
　purchased materials
HQ: Georgia-Pacific Corrugated Iii Llc
　5645 W 82nd St
　Indianapolis IN 46278

(G-14085)
TRUECHOICEPACK CORP
9565 Cincinnati Columbus Rd
(45069-4242)
PHONE...................937 630-3832
Heena Rathore, *Pr*
Rakesh Rathore, *CSO*
EMP: 15 **EST:** 2013
SALES (est): 7.77MM
SALES (corp-wide): 9.52MM **Privately
Held**
Web: www.truechoicepack.com
SIC: 3089 3086 5113 Blister or bubble
　formed packaging, plastics; Packaging and
　shipping materials, foamed plastics;
　Disposable plates, cups, napkins, and
　eating utensils
PA: Che International Group, Llc
　255 E 5th St Ste 1900
　Cincinnati OH 45202
　513 229-7595

(G-14086)
TUCKER PRINTERS INC
8740 Global Way (45069-7066)
PHONE...................585 359-3030
Joe R Davis, *CEO*
Daniel A Tucker, *
EMP: 82 **EST:** 1997
SALES (est): 575.66K

SALES (corp-wide): 15B **Privately Held**
SIC: 2752 Offset printing
HQ: Consolidated Graphics, Inc.
　5858 Westheimer Rd # 200
　Houston TX 77057

(G-14087)
TVH PARTS CO
Also Called: C-Tech Industries
8756 Global Way (45069-7066)
PHONE...................877 755-7311
EMP: 18
SALES (corp-wide): 2.67MM **Privately
Held**
Web: www.tvh.com
SIC: 3625 Relays and industrial controls
HQ: Tvh Parts Co.
　16355 S Lone Elm Rd
　Olathe KS 66062
　913 829-1000

(G-14088)
UPA TECHNOLOGY INC
8963 Cincinnati Columbus Rd
(45069-3513)
P.O. Box 1755 (45071-1755)
PHONE...................513 755-1380
Michael Justice, *Pr*
Susan Justice, *VP*
◆ **EMP:** 11 **EST:** 1987
SQ FT: 4,500
SALES (est): 824.25K **Privately Held**
Web: www.upa.com
SIC: 3829 7699 Measuring and controlling
　devices, nec; Professional instrument repair
　services

(G-14089)
USUI INTERNATIONAL
CORPORATION
Also Called: UIC West Chester Plant
8748 Jacquemin Dr Ste 100 (45069-4999)
PHONE...................734 354-3626
Devon Thompson, *Opers*
EMP: 100
Web: www.usuiusa.com
SIC: 3714 Motor vehicle parts and
　accessories
HQ: Usui International Corporation
　44780 Helm St
　Plymouth MI 48170
　734 354-3626

(G-14090)
VINTAGE WINE DISTRIBUTOR INC
9422 Meridian Way (45069-6527)
PHONE...................513 443-4300
EMP: 10
SALES (corp-wide): 9.67MM **Privately
Held**
Web: www.vintwine.com
SIC: 2084 Wines
PA: Vintage Wine Distributor, Inc.
　6555 Davis Indus Pkwy
　Solon OH 44139
　440 248-1750

(G-14091)
WARFIGHTER FCSED LOGISTICS
INC
8800 Global Way Ste 100a (45069-7070)
PHONE...................740 513-4692
Darrell Kem, *Pr*
EMP: 20
SALES (corp-wide): 1.94MM **Privately
Held**
Web:
www.warfighterfocusedlogistics.com
SIC: 3711 3724 Military motor vehicle
　assembly; Lubricating systems, aircraft
PA: Warfighter Focused Logistics Inc.

936 Nw 1st St
Fort Lauderdale FL 33311
740 513-4692

(G-14092)
WESTROCK CONVERTING LLC
9266 Meridian Way (45069-6521)
PHONE...................513 860-0225
EMP: 21
Web: www.smurfitwestrock.com
SIC: 2653 Boxes, corrugated: made from
　purchased materials
HQ: Westrock Converting, Llc
　1000 Abernathy Rd Ste 125
　Atlanta GA 30328
　770 448-2193

(G-14093)
WESTROCK RKT LLC
Also Called: Rocktenn Merchandising Display
9245 Meridian Way (45069-6523)
PHONE...................513 860-5546
Bob Akers, *Ltd Pt*
EMP: 103
Web: www.westrock.com
SIC: 2653 Boxes, corrugated: made from
　purchased materials
HQ: Westrock Rkt, Llc
　1000 Abernathy Rd Ste 125
　Atlanta GA 30328
　770 448-2193

(G-14094)
YKK AP AMERICA INC
Also Called: YKK USA
8748 Jacquemin Dr Ste 400 (45069-4999)
PHONE...................513 942-7200
Phil Blizzard, *Mgr*
EMP: 27
Web: www.ykkap.com
SIC: 3442 3449 Sash, door or window: metal
　; Curtain wall, metal
HQ: Ykk Ap America Inc.
　101 Mretta St Nw Ste 2100
　Atlanta GA 30303

(G-14095)
YOCKEY GROUP INC
9053 Le Saint Dr (45014-2242)
PHONE...................513 860-9053
A James Yockey, *Pr*
EMP: 6 **EST:** 1998
SALES (est): 176.13K **Privately Held**
SIC: 2759 Commercial printing, nec

West Chester
Hamilton County

(G-14096)
ACTION SPECIALTY PACKAGING
LLC (DH)
4758 Devitt Dr (45246-1106)
◆ **EMP:** 8 **EST:** 2004
SQ FT: 30,000
SALES (est): 4.27MM
SALES (corp-wide): 655.85MM **Privately
Held**
SIC: 2621 2631 2653 Kraft wrapping paper;
　Container, packaging, and boxboard;
　Boxes, corrugated: made from purchased
　materials
HQ: Storopack, Inc.
　4758 Devitt Dr
　Cincinnati OH 45246
　513 874-0314

(G-14097)
ADVANCEPIERRE FOODS INC (DH)
Also Called: Tyson

9990 Princeton Glendale Rd (45246-1116)
PHONE...................513 874-8741
Tom Hayes, *Pr*
John Tyson, *
Dennis Leatherby, *
▲ **EMP:** 300 **EST:** 2008
SALES (est): 497.96MM
SALES (corp-wide): 53.31B **Publicly Held**
Web: www.advancepierrefood.com
SIC: 2013 2015 Prepared beef products,
　from purchased beef; Chicken, processed,
　nsk
HQ: Advancepierre Foods Holdings, Inc.
　9990 Prnceton Glendale Rd
　West Chester OH 45246

(G-14098)
ADVANCPERRE FOODS HOLDINGS
INC (HQ)
Also Called: Advancepierre
9990 Princeton Glendale Rd (45246-1116)
PHONE...................513 428-5699
Donnie D King, *Pr*
EMP: 68 **EST:** 2008
SALES (est): 933.68MM
SALES (corp-wide): 53.31B **Publicly Held**
Web: investors.advancepierre.com
SIC: 2099 2013 Sandwiches, assembled
　and packaged: for wholesale market;
　Sausages and other prepared meats
PA: Tyson Foods, Inc.
　2200 W Don Tyson Pkwy
　Springdale AR 72762
　479 290-4000

(G-14099)
AGEAN MARBLE MANUFACTURING
INC
9756 Princeton Glendale Rd (45246-1015)
PHONE...................513 874-1475
Gary Bolte, *Ch*
Lois Bolte, *Sec*
Chris Bolte, *VP*
EMP: 7 **EST:** 1946
SQ FT: 26,000
SALES (est): 915.2K **Privately Held**
Web: www.agean.com
SIC: 3272 5211 5091 3431 Art marble,
　concrete; Bathroom fixtures, equipment and
　supplies; Spa equipment and supplies;
　Metal sanitary ware

(G-14100)
AJJ ENTERPRISES LLC
10073 Commerce Park Dr (45246-1333)
PHONE...................513 755-9562
Jason Wahl, *Managing Member*
▲ **EMP:** 10 **EST:** 2007
SALES (est): 1.36MM **Privately Held**
Web: www.ajjcornhole.com
SIC: 3944 Games, toys, and children's
　vehicles

(G-14101)
AMERICAN BUSINESS FORMS INC
Also Called: American Solutions For Bus
10000 International Blvd (45246-4839)
PHONE...................513 312-2522
EMP: 26
SALES (corp-wide): 110.34MM **Privately
Held**
Web: home.americanbus.com
SIC: 5112 5199 2759 Business forms;
　Advertising specialties; Promotional printing
PA: American Business Forms, Inc.
　31 E Minnesota Ave
　Glenwood MN 56334
　320 634-5471

▲ = Import ▼ = Export
◆ = Import/Export

(G-14102)
ANEST IWATA USA INC
10148 Commerce Park Dr (45246-1336)
PHONE....................513 755-3100
Hiroki Nishida, *Pr*
▲ **EMP:** 10 **EST:** 1994
SQ FT: 4,800
SALES (est): 4.3MM **Privately Held**
Web: www.anestiwata.com
SIC: **3479** 5013 Painting, coating, and hot
dipping; Motor vehicle supplies and new
parts
PA: Anest Iwata Corporation
3176, Shinyoshidacho, Kohoku-Ku
Yokohama KNG 223-0

(G-14103)
APF LEGACY SUBS LLC (DH)
9990 Princeton Glendale Rd (45246-1116)
PHONE....................513 682-7173
EMP: 46 **EST:** 1993
SALES (est): 2.9MM
SALES (corp-wide): 53.31B **Publicly Held**
SIC: **2099** Food preparations, nec
HQ: Advancepierre Foods, Inc.
9990 Prnceton Glendale Rd
West Chester OH 45246
513 874-8741

(G-14104)
ARCH CUTNG TLS CINCINNATI LLC
133 Circle Freeway Dr (45246-1203)
PHONE....................513 851-6363
Steven Long, *Pr*
EMP: 15 **EST:** 2022
SALES (est): 1.13MM **Privately Held**
Web: www.archcuttingtools.com
SIC: **3545** Drill bits, metalworking

(G-14105)
ATMOS360 INC
Also Called: Atmos 360 A Systems Solutions
4690 Interstate Dr Ste A (45246-1142)
PHONE....................513 772-4777
EMP: 45 **EST:** 1989
SALES (est): 4.75MM **Privately Held**
Web: www.atmos360.com
SIC: **8711** 3565 3564 Consulting engineer;
Packaging machinery; Blowers and fans

(G-14106)
BAXTERS NORTH AMERICA INC
Also Called: Wornick Company, The
9756 International Blvd (45246-4854)
PHONE....................513 552-7718
◆ **EMP:** 53
SALES (corp-wide): 477.56MM **Privately
Held**
Web: www.baxtersna.com
SIC: **2032** Baby foods, including meats:
packaged in cans, jars, etc.
HQ: Baxters North America, Inc.
4700 Creek Rd
Cincinnati OH 45242
513 552-7485

(G-14107)
BEIERSDORF INC
5232 E Provident Dr (45246-1040)
PHONE....................513 682-7300
Jim Kenton, *Brnch Mgr*
EMP: 168
SALES (corp-wide): 13.75B **Privately Held**
Web: www.beiersdorfusa.com
SIC: **2844** 5122 3842 2841 Face creams or
lotions; Antiseptics; Bandages and
dressings; Soap: granulated, liquid, cake,
flaked, or chip
HQ: Beiersdorf, Inc.
301 Tresser Blvd
Stamford CT 06901
203 563-5800

(G-14108)
BUILDING CTRL INTEGRATORS LLC
10174 International Blvd (45246-4846)
PHONE....................513 860-9600
David Milar, *Genl Mgr*
EMP: 7
SALES (corp-wide): 8.5MM **Privately Held**
Web: www.bcicontrols.com
SIC: **3822** Temperature controls, automatic
PA: Building Control Integrators, Llc
383 N Liberty St
Powell OH 43065
614 334-3300

(G-14109)
BUZZ SEATING INC (PA)
4774 Interstate Dr (45246-1112)
P.O. Box 31379 (45231-0379)
PHONE....................877 263-5737
Dan Ohara, *Pr*
▲ **EMP:** 7 **EST:** 2003
SQ FT: 12,982
SALES (est): 3.43MM
SALES (corp-wide): 3.43MM **Privately
Held**
Web: www.buzzseating.com
SIC: **2521** Chairs, office: padded,
upholstered, or plain: wood

(G-14110)
CHASE INDUSTRIES INC
10021 Commerce Park Dr (45246-1333)
PHONE....................513 603-2936
EMP: 21 **EST:** 2018
SALES (est): 2.52MM **Privately Held**
Web: www.chasedoors.com
SIC: **3442** Metal doors, sash, and trim

(G-14111)
CLARKE FIRE PRTECTION PDTS INC
133 Circle Freeway Dr (45246-1203)
PHONE....................513 771-2200
EMP: 10
SALES (corp-wide): 225.9MM **Privately
Held**
Web: www.clarkepowerservices.com
SIC: **3519** Diesel, semi-diesel, or duel-fuel
engines, including marine
HQ: Clarke Fire Protection Products, Inc.
3133 E Kemper Rd
Cincinnati OH 45241

(G-14112)
CTL-AEROSPACE INC
9970 International Blvd (45246-4852)
PHONE....................513 874-7900
Jc Owen, *Pr*
EMP: 20
SALES (corp-wide): 47.06MM **Privately
Held**
Web: www.ctlaerospace.com
SIC: **3728** Aircraft parts and equipment, nec
PA: Ctl-Aerospace, Inc.
5616 Spellmire Dr
Cincinnati OH 45246
513 874-7900

(G-14113)
D C CONTROLS LLC
Also Called: Coffey and Associates
4836 Duff Dr Ste E (45246-1194)
PHONE....................513 225-0813
David A Coffey, *Managing Member*
EMP: 7 **EST:** 2007
SALES (est): 1.03MM **Privately Held**
Web: www.dccontrols.net
SIC: **3315** Wire and fabricated wire products

(G-14114)
E2 MERCHANDISING INC
9706 Inter Ocean Dr (45246-1028)
PHONE....................513 860-5444
Chris Kin, *Pr*
▼ **EMP:** 20 **EST:** 2010
SALES (est): 2.33MM **Privately Held**
Web: www.e2merch.com
SIC: **2542** Racks, merchandise display or
storage: except wood

(G-14115)
EFFOX-FLEXTOR-MADER INC (HQ)
9759 Inter Ocean Dr (45246-1027)
PHONE....................513 874-8915
L James Zeager, *CEO*
EMP: 11 **EST:** 2020
SALES (est): 30.72MM **Publicly Held**
Web: www.efmequipment.com
SIC: **3564** Purification and dust collection
equipment
PA: Ceco Environmental Corp.
5080 Spectrum Dr Ste 800e
Addison TX 75001

(G-14116)
ELIASON CORPORATION
10021 Commerce Park Dr (45246-1333)
PHONE....................800 828-3655
EMP: 33
SALES (corp-wide): 1.01B **Privately Held**
Web: www.eliasoncorp.com
SIC: **3442** 3089 Metal doors; Plastics
containers, except foam
HQ: Eliason Corporation
9229 Shaver Rd
Portage MI 49024
269 327-7003

(G-14117)
EMPIRE PACKING COMPANY LP
Also Called: Cincinnatti Processing
113 Circle Freeway Dr (45246-1203)
PHONE....................513 942-5400
Dennis Hioghmas, *Genl Mgr*
EMP: 60
SALES (corp-wide): 141.72MM **Privately
Held**
Web: www.ledbetterfoods.com
SIC: **5147** 2013 2011 Meats, fresh;
Sausages and other prepared meats; Meat
packing plants
PA: Empire Packing Company, Llc
1837 Harbor Ave
Memphis TN 38113
901 948-4788

(G-14118)
FEDERALEAGLE LLC
Also Called: Eagle Coach Company
64 Circle Freeway Dr (45246-1202)
PHONE....................513 797-4100
Steven Bentley, *Pr*
Daan Kore, *
EMP: 80 **EST:** 1985
SALES (est): 13.12MM
SALES (corp-wide): 1.62B **Privately Held**
Web: www.federaleaglecoach.com
SIC: **3711** Hearses (motor vehicles),
assembly of
PA: J. B. Poindexter & Co., Inc.
600 Travis St Ste 400
Houston TX 77002
713 655-9800

(G-14119)
FIRE-END & CROKER CORP
Also Called: FIRE-END & CROKER CORP.
4690 Interstate Dr Ste P (45246-1142)
PHONE....................513 870-0517
Bob Orth, *Genl Mgr*

EMP: 37
SALES (corp-wide): 23.73MM **Privately
Held**
Web: www.croker.com
SIC: **3699** Fire control or bombing
equipment, electronic
HQ: Fire End & Croker Corp.
7 Westchester Plz Ste 267
Elmsford NY 10523
914 592-3640

(G-14120)
FKI LOGISTEX AUTOMATION INC
10045 International Blvd (45246-4845)
PHONE....................513 881-5251
▲ **EMP:** 700
SIC: **3535** Conveyors and conveying
equipment

(G-14121)
FRUTAROM USA HOLDING INC
5404 Duff Dr (45246-1323)
PHONE....................201 861-9500
Ori Yehudai, *CEO*
Alon Granot, *CFO*
Amos Anatot, *Ex VP*
EMP: 6 **EST:** 2002
SALES (est): 1.51MM
SALES (corp-wide): 11.48B **Publicly Held**
SIC: **2869** Flavors or flavoring materials,
synthetic
HQ: Frutarom Usa Inc.
5404 Duff Dr
Cincinnati OH 45246
513 870-4900

(G-14122)
FRUTAROM USA INC
9930 Commerce Park Dr (45246-1332)
PHONE....................513 870-4900
EMP: 7
SALES (corp-wide): 11.48B **Publicly Held**
SIC: **2099** Spices, including grinding
HQ: Frutarom Usa Inc.
5404 Duff Dr
Cincinnati OH 45246
513 870-4900

(G-14123)
GREENWORLD ENTERPRISES INC
Also Called: Focal Point Communications
61 Circle Freeway Dr (45246-1201)
PHONE....................800 525-6999
Joe Shooner, *CEO*
EMP: 6 **EST:** 1982
SQ FT: 3,600
SALES (est): 208.87K **Privately Held**
Web: www.growpro.com
SIC: **2711** Newspapers, publishing and
printing

(G-14124)
HANSEN SCAFFOLDING LLC (PA)
193 Circle Freeway Dr (45246-1203)
PHONE....................513 574-9000
Aaron Hansen, *Pr*
Jennifer Mcdonald, *Off Mgr*
EMP: 14 **EST:** 1986
SQ FT: 22,000
SALES (est): 2.17MM
SALES (corp-wide): 2.17MM **Privately
Held**
Web: www.hansenscaffolding.com
SIC: **7359** 3446 Equipment rental and
leasing, nec; Scaffolds, mobile or
stationary: metal

(G-14125)
HORNER INDUSTRIAL SERVICES INC
4721 Interstate Dr (45246-1111)
PHONE....................513 874-8722

TOLL FREE: 800
Mark Wolma, *VP*
EMP: 7
SALES (corp-wide): 21.85MM **Privately Held**
Web: www.hornerindustrial.com
SIC: 7694 Armature rewinding shops
PA: Horner Industrial Services, Inc.
1521 E Washington St
Indianapolis IN 46201
317 639-4261

(G-14126)
HYDROTECH INC (PA)
Also Called: Enpro
10052 Commerce Park Dr (45246-1338)
PHONE..............................888 651-5712
◆ **EMP:** 51 **EST:** 1967
SALES (est): 23.23MM
SALES (corp-wide): 23.23MM **Privately Held**
Web: www.hydrotech.com
SIC: 5084 3492 Industrial machinery and equipment; Control valves, fluid power: hydraulic and pneumatic

(G-14127)
INTELLIGRATED INC
10045 International Blvd (45246-4845)
PHONE..............................513 874-0788
Cindy Lynies, *Brnch Mgr*
EMP: 2457
SALES (corp-wide): 38.5B **Publicly Held**
Web: sps.honeywell.com
SIC: 3535 5084 7371 Conveyors and conveying equipment; Industrial machinery and equipment; Custom computer programming services
HQ: Intelligrated, Inc.
7901 Innovation Way
Mason OH 45040
866 936-7300

(G-14128)
INTELLIGRATED SYSTEMS LLC
9842 International Blvd (45246-4852)
PHONE..............................513 701-7300
Bryan Jones, *
Ed Puisis, *
Jim Mcknight, *Sr VP*
EMP: 2300 **EST:** 2001
SQ FT: 260,000
SALES (est): 27.07MM
SALES (corp-wide): 38.5B **Publicly Held**
SIC: 3535 5084 7371 Conveyors and conveying equipment; Materials handling machinery; Computer software development
HQ: Intelligrated Systems, Inc.
7901 Innovation Way
Mason OH 45040
866 936-7300

(G-14129)
INTELLIGRATED SYSTEMS OHIO LLC
Also Called: Fki Logistex
10045 International Blvd (45246-4845)
PHONE..............................513 682-6600
Doug Westman, *Dir*
EMP: 8
SALES (corp-wide): 38.5B **Publicly Held**
SIC: 3535 Conveyors and conveying equipment
HQ: Intelligrated Systems Of Ohio, Llc
7901 Innovation Way
Mason OH 45040
513 701-7300

(G-14130)
KONECRANES INC
Also Called: Crane Pro Services
4866 Duff Dr (45246-1150)
PHONE..............................513 755-2800
Barb Rothert, *Admn*
EMP: 32
Web: www.konecranes.com
SIC: 3536 Hoists, cranes, and monorails
HQ: Konecranes, Inc.
4401 Gateway Blvd
Springfield OH 45502

(G-14131)
MAGNUM PIERING INC
156 Circle Freeway Dr (45246-1204)
PHONE..............................513 759-3348
Brian Dwyer, *Pr*
Bill Bonekemper, *
Sharon Appelman, *
EMP: 30 **EST:** 2000
SALES (est): 2.51MM
SALES (corp-wide): 2.51MM **Privately Held**
Web: www.magnumpiering.com
SIC: 3441 3561 Fabricated structural metal; Pumps and pumping equipment
PA: Dwyer Companies, Inc.
6083 Schumacher Park Dr
West Chester OH 45069
513 777-0998

(G-14132)
MCNERNEY & ASSOCIATES LLC (PA)
Also Called: P J McNerney & Associates
5443 Duff Dr (45246-1323)
PHONE..............................513 241-9951
Patrick Mcnerney, *Mgr*
Patrick J Mcnerney, *Pr*
Jan Mcnerney, *VP*
◆ **EMP:** 42 **EST:** 1983
SALES (est): 8.95MM
SALES (corp-wide): 8.95MM **Privately Held**
Web: www.pjmcnerney.com
SIC: 2752 4783 Offset printing; Packing goods for shipping

(G-14133)
MICROTEK FINISHING LLC
5579 Spellmire Dr (45246-4841)
PHONE..............................513 766-5600
▲ **EMP:** 22 **EST:** 2009
SQ FT: 5,000
SALES (est): 9.07MM **Privately Held**
Web: www.mmptechnology.com
SIC: 3471 Polishing, metals or formed products
PA: Binc Industries Sa
Route De Geneve 7
Commugny VD 1291

(G-14134)
NORTHROP GRUMMAN SYSTEMS CORP
460 W Crescentville Rd (45246-1221)
PHONE..............................513 881-3296
Patricia A Newby, *Brnch Mgr*
EMP: 270
Web: www.northropgrumman.com
SIC: 3812 Search and navigation equipment
HQ: Northrop Grumman Systems Corporation
2980 Fairview Park Dr
Falls Church VA 22042
703 280-2900

(G-14135)
OCTAL EXTRUSION CORP
5399 E Provident Dr (45246-1044)
PHONE..............................513 881-6100
Joe Barenberg, *CEO*
Cameron Warren, *
EMP: 60 **EST:** 2014
SQ FT: 130,000
SALES (est): 57.42MM **Privately Held**
Web: www.alpekpolyester.com
SIC: 2671 Paper, coated or laminated for packaging
PA: Octal Holding
Al Rawaq Building Salalah Free Zone
Muscat MA 112

(G-14136)
PF MANAGEMENT INC
Also Called: Pfmi
9990 Princeton Glendale Rd (45246-1116)
PHONE..............................513 874-8741
Norbert E Woodhams, *Pr*
EMP: 7 **EST:** 1970
SQ FT: 220,000
SALES (est): 1.17MM **Privately Held**
SIC: 8741 2015 2051 Management services; Chicken slaughtering and processing; Bread, cake, and related products
HQ: Pierre Holding Corp
9990 Prnceton Glendale Rd
West Chester OH 45246

(G-14137)
PIERRE HOLDING CORP (HQ)
9990 Princeton Glendale Rd (45246-1116)
PHONE..............................513 874-8741
Norbert E Wooadhams, *Pr*
Robert C Naylor, *Marketing*
Joseph W Meyers, *CFO*
EMP: 7 **EST:** 2004
SQ FT: 220,000
SALES (est): 4.28MM **Privately Held**
SIC: 2013 2015 2051 Prepared beef products, from purchased beef; Chicken slaughtering and processing; Bread, cake, and related products
PA: Madison Dearborn Partners Iv Lp
3 1st Nat Plz Ste 3800
Chicago IL 60602

(G-14138)
POWERSONIC INDUSTRIES LLC
5406 Spellmire Dr (45246-4842)
P.O. Box 6506 (45206-0506)
PHONE..............................513 429-2329
Jason Rampersand, *Pr*
▲ **EMP:** 25 **EST:** 2014
SALES (est): 9.03MM **Privately Held**
Web: www.powersonic.net
SIC: 3571 Electronic computers

(G-14139)
PROFESSIONAL CASE INC
Also Called: PCI
4954 Provident Dr (45246-1021)
PHONE..............................513 682-2520
Thomas Brown, *Pr*
Erin Biel, *VP*
EMP: 10 **EST:** 1978
SQ FT: 7,000
SALES (est): 231.52K **Privately Held**
Web: www.professionalcase.com
SIC: 3161 Cases, carrying, nec

(G-14140)
QUALITY ENVELOPE INC
9792 Inter Ocean Dr (45246-1028)
P.O. Box 40862 (45240-0862)
PHONE..............................513 942-7578
Robert Lester, *Pr*
Rick Doxtator, *VP*

Jeffery Leatherwood Senior, *Sec*
EMP: 6 **EST:** 2002
SALES (est): 1.02MM **Privately Held**
SIC: 2677 Envelopes

(G-14141)
ROOFING ANNEX LLC
4866 Duff Dr Ste E (45246-1151)
PHONE..............................513 942-0555
Chad Janisch, *CEO*
Joey Michels, *VP*
Stephen Michels, *Sec*
EMP: 7 **EST:** 2010
SQ FT: 4,000
SALES (est): 408.32K **Privately Held**
Web: www.roofingannex.com
SIC: 5031 1761 3444 Windows; Roofing, siding, and sheetmetal work; Gutters, sheet metal

(G-14142)
RUSSELL CAST STONE INC
Also Called: Continental Cast Stone East
4600 Devitt Dr (45246-1104)
PHONE..............................856 753-4000
William Russell Iii, *CEO*
EMP: 58 **EST:** 1999
SALES (est): 5.38MM **Privately Held**
Web: www.russellstone.com
SIC: 3272 Concrete products, nec

(G-14143)
SERVICE EXPRESS LLC
10004 International Blvd (45246-4839)
PHONE..............................513 942-6170
EMP: 11
SIC: 2741 Miscellaneous publishing
PA: Service Express, Llc
3854 Broadmoor Ave Se # 101
Grand Rapids MI 49546

(G-14144)
SEXTON INDUSTRIAL INC
366 Circle Freeway Dr (45246-1208)
PHONE..............................513 530-5555
Abbe Sexton, *Pr*
Ron Sexton, *
Dan Towne, *
EMP: 150 **EST:** 1998
SQ FT: 85,000
SALES (est): 14.04MM **Privately Held**
Web: www.artisanmechanical.com
SIC: 1711 3443 Mechanical contractor; Industrial vessels, tanks, and containers

(G-14145)
SIEB & MEYER AMERICA INC
Also Called: Sieb & Meyer America USA
4884 Duff Dr Ste D (45246-1195)
PHONE..............................513 563-0860
John Endras, *Genl Mgr*
EMP: 10 **EST:** 1996
SALES (est): 3.44MM
SALES (corp-wide): 9.65MM **Privately Held**
Web: www.sieb-meyerusa.com
SIC: 3625 5063 Relays and industrial controls; Electrical apparatus and equipment
PA: First Tool Corp.
612 Linden Ave
Dayton OH 45403
937 254-6197

(G-14146)
SL ENDMILLS INC
133 Circle Freeway Dr (45246-1203)
PHONE..............................513 851-6363
Steven Long, *Pr*
Nancy Long, *Sec*
EMP: 15 **EST:** 1982

▲ = Import ▼ = Export
◆ = Import/Export

SQ FT: 5,000
SALES (est): 2.09MM **Privately Held**
Web: www.customcarbidecutter.com
SIC: 3545 Machine tool accessories

(G-14147)
SLUSH PUPPIE
44 Carnegie Way (45246-1224)
PHONE................................513 771-0940
Will Radcliff, *Ch Bd*
Dan Keating, *
Robert Schwartz, *
▲ EMP: 6 EST: 1970
SQ FT: 40,000
SALES (est): 115.78K **Privately Held**
Web: www.slushpuppie.com
SIC: 2087 5078 Syrups, drink; Soda fountain
equipment, refrigerated

(G-14148)
SONOCO PRODUCTS COMPANY
Sonoco Consumer Products
4633 Dues Dr (45246-1008)
PHONE................................513 870-3985
Lowern Laster, *Mgr*
EMP: 29
SALES (corp-wide): 5.31B **Publicly Held**
Web: www.sonoco.com
SIC: 2655 2656 Cans, composite: foil-fiber
and other: from purchased fiber; Sanitary
food containers
PA: Sonoco Products Company
1 N 2nd St
Hartsville SC 29550
843 383-7000

(G-14149)
STAR DISTRIBUTION AND MFG LLC
Also Called: Star Manufacturring
10179 Commerce Park Dr (45246-1335)
PHONE................................513 860-3573
Mario Listo, *Pr*
Bob Hinkle, *
EMP: 48 EST: 2009
SALES (est): 8.33MM **Privately Held**
Web: www.starmanufacture.com
SIC: 3613 8711 8742 Control panels, electric
; Engineering services; Management
engineering

(G-14150)
STOLLE MILK BIOLOGICS INC
4735 Devitt Dr (45246-1105)
PHONE................................513 489-7997
Con F Sterling Junior, *CEO*
Doctor Robert Stohrer, *Research Vice
President*
▲ EMP: 8 EST: 1986
SQ FT: 1,000
SALES (est): 921.39K **Privately Held**
Web: www.smbiologics.com
SIC: 2023 Powdered milk

(G-14151)
**SUPERIOR IMAGE EMBROIDERY
LLC**
10152 International Blvd (45246-4846)
PHONE................................513 991-7543
EMP: 8
SALES (est): 348.11K **Privately Held**
Web: www.si-embroidery.com
SIC: 2395 Embroidery and art needlework

(G-14152)
TEKTRONIX INC
Also Called: Tektronix
9639 Inter Ocean Dr (45246-1029)
PHONE................................248 305-5200
Mike Kitchen, *Mgr*
EMP: 16
SALES (corp-wide): 6.23B **Publicly Held**

Web: www.tek.com
SIC: 3825 7699 Instruments to measure
electricity; Laboratory instrument repair
HQ: Tektronix, Inc.
13725 Sw Karl Braun Dr
Beaverton OR 97077
800 833-9200

(G-14153)
THE RANSOHOFF COMPANY
4933 Provident Dr (45246-1020)
PHONE................................513 870-0100
EMP: 120
Web: www.ctgclean.com
SIC: 3569 3541 Blast cleaning equipment,
dustless; Deburring machines

(G-14154)
THERMO FISHER SCIENTIFIC INC
Also Called: Ppd
10085 International Blvd (45246-4845)
PHONE................................513 659-7945
EMP: 10
SALES (corp-wide): 42.86B **Publicly Held**
Web: www.thermofisher.com
SIC: 3826 Analytical instruments
PA: Thermo Fisher Scientific Inc.
168 3rd Ave
Waltham MA 02451
781 622-1000

(G-14155)
TITANS PACKAGING LLC ✪
33 Circle Freeway Dr (45246-1201)
PHONE................................513 449-0014
Kody Shumate, *Prin*
EMP: 11 EST: 2023
SALES (est): 1.77MM **Privately Held**
SIC: 3565 Packaging machinery

(G-14156)
TSK AMERICA CO LTD
9668 Inter Ocean Dr (45246-1030)
PHONE................................513 942-4002
Takeshi Takeuchi, *Pr*
▲ EMP: 10 EST: 1995
SALES (est): 307.1K **Privately Held**
Web: www.tsklmb.com
SIC: 3568 5051 3562 Bearings, bushings,
and blocks; Metals service centers and
offices; Ball bearings and parts

(G-14157)
UNIVAR SOLUTIONS USA LLC
4600 Dues Dr (45246-1009)
PHONE................................513 714-5264
Gary Southern, *Brnch Mgr*
EMP: 25
SQ FT: 129,100
SALES (corp-wide): 11.48B **Privately Held**
Web: www.univarsolutions.com
SIC: 5169 2819 2869 2899 Industrial
chemicals; Industrial inorganic chemicals,
nec; Industrial organic chemicals, nec;
Chemical preparations, nec
HQ: Univar Solutions Usa Llc
3075 Hghland Pkwy Ste 200
Downers Grove IL 60515
331 777-6000

(G-14158)
VALCO MELTON INC
497 Circle Freeway Dr Ste 490
(45246-1257)
PHONE................................513 874-6550
Austin Koehler, *Prin*
▲ EMP: 43 EST: 2012
SALES (est): 3.71MM
SALES (corp-wide): 23.19MM **Privately
Held**
Web: www.valcomelton.com

SIC: 3663 Radio and t.v. communications
equipment
PA: Valco Cincinnati, Inc.
411 Circle Freeway Dr
Cincinnati OH 45246
513 874-6550

West Farmington
Trumbull County

(G-14159)
MILLERTECH ENERGY SOLUTIONS
Also Called: Lester Miller, Owner
17795 Farmington Rd (44491-9625)
PHONE................................855 629-5484
Lester Miller, *Pr*
EMP: 15 EST: 2016
SALES (est): 1.16MM **Privately Held**
SIC: 3691 Batteries, rechargeable

West Jefferson
Madison County

(G-14160)
BUCKEYE READY-MIX LLC
6600 State Route 29 (43162-8700)
PHONE................................614 879-6316
Don Harsh, *Brnch Mgr*
EMP: 7
SALES (corp-wide): 21.97MM **Privately
Held**
Web: www.buckeyereadymix.com
SIC: 3273 Ready-mixed concrete
PA: Buckeye Ready-Mix, Llc
7657 Taylor Rd Sw
Reynoldsburg OH 43068
614 575-2132

(G-14161)
**CONDUIT PIPE PRODUCTS
COMPANY**
1501 W Main St (43162-9627)
PHONE................................614 879-9114
John Rodgers, *Pr*
Tim Mcghee, *Prin*
EMP: 60 EST: 2002
SALES (est): 15.86MM
SALES (corp-wide): 40.11MM **Privately
Held**
Web: www.phoenixforge.com
SIC: 3317 Steel pipe and tubes
PA: The Phoenix Forge Group Llc
1020 Macarthur Rd
Reading PA 19605
800 234-8665

(G-14162)
JEFFERSON INDUSTRIES CORP (HQ)
Also Called: J I C
6670 State Route 29 (43162-9677)
PHONE................................614 879-5300
Shiro Shimokagi, *Pr*
Kazuhiko Hara, *
Steve Yoder, *
Hassan Saadat, *
Curtis A Loveland, *
▲ EMP: 114 EST: 1988
SQ FT: 370,000
SALES (est): 45.22MM **Privately Held**
Web: www.jic-ohio.com
SIC: 3711 Chassis, motor vehicle
PA: G-Tekt Corporation
1-11-20, Sakuragicho, Omiya-Ku
Saitama STM 330-0

(G-14163)
KELLANOVA
Also Called: Kellog
125 Enterprise Pkwy (43162-9414)
PHONE................................614 879-9659
Richard Emerson, *Prin*
EMP: 13
SALES (corp-wide): 12.75B **Publicly Held**
Web: www.kellanova.com
SIC: 2043 Cereal breakfast foods
PA: Kellanova
412 N Wells St
Chicago IL 60654
269 961-2000

(G-14164)
MEDLINE INDUSTRIES LP
1040 Enterprise Pkwy (43162-9424)
PHONE................................614 879-9728
EMP: 29
SALES (corp-wide): 7.75B **Privately Held**
Web: www.medline.com
SIC: 3842 Surgical appliances and supplies
PA: Medline Industries, Lp
3 Lakes Dr
Northfield IL 60093
800 633-5463

(G-14165)
**MENASHA PACKAGING COMPANY
LLC**
Also Called: Menasha
131 Enterprise Pkwy (43162-9414)
PHONE................................614 202-4084
Ken Pauly, *Brnch Mgr*
EMP: 28
SALES (corp-wide): 1.94B **Privately Held**
Web: www.menasha.com
SIC: 2653 Boxes, corrugated: made from
purchased materials
HQ: Menasha Packaging Company, Llc
1645 Bergstrom Rd
Neenah WI 54956
920 751-1000

(G-14166)
PHOENIX FORGE GROUP LLC
Capitol Manufacturing Division
1501 W Main St (43162-9627)
PHONE................................800 848-6125
David R Halman, *Brnch Mgr*
EMP: 329
SALES (corp-wide): 40.11MM **Privately
Held**
Web: www.phoenixforge.com
SIC: 3498 Pipe fittings, fabricated from
purchased pipe
PA: The Phoenix Forge Group Llc
1020 Macarthur Rd
Reading PA 19605
800 234-8665

(G-14167)
TARKETT INC
1050 Gateway Park Dr (43162-9612)
P.O. Box 880 (44062-0880)
PHONE................................614 349-1565
EMP: 14
Web: www.tarkettna.com
SIC: 3069 Flooring, rubber: tile or sheet
HQ: Tarkett, Inc.
30000 Aurora Rd
Solon OH 44139
800 899-8916

(G-14168)
TOAGOSEI AMERICA INC
Also Called: Krazy Glue
1450 W Main St (43162-9730)
PHONE................................614 718-3855
Tatsuo Mishio, *Pr*

Toshio Nakao, *
▲ **EMP:** 100 **EST:** 1989
SQ FT: 64,000
SALES (est): 22.25MM **Privately Held**
Web: www.aronalpha.net
SIC: 5169 2891 Chemicals and allied
products, nec; Adhesives
PA: Toagosei Co., Ltd.
1-14-1, Nishishimbashi
Minato-Ku TKY 105-0

West Lafayette
Coshocton County

(G-14169)
CABOT LUMBER INC
304 E Union Ave (43845-1250)
P.O. Box 101 (43845-0101)
PHONE.............................740 545-7109
Donald Cabot, *Pr*
Dennis E Cabot, *Treas*
Kenneth Cabot, *Sec*
EMP: 9 **EST:** 1970
SQ FT: 14,000
SALES (est): 947.67K **Privately Held**
SIC: 5031 2448 Lumber: rough, dressed,
and finished; Pallets, wood

(G-14170)
GLENN RAVENS WINERY
56183 County Road 143 (43845-3502)
PHONE.............................740 545-1000
Bob Guilliams, *Prin*
EMP: 8 **EST:** 2003
SALES (est): 1.07MM **Privately Held**
Web: www.ravensglenn.com
SIC: 2084 5812 Wines; Italian restaurant

(G-14171)
**JONES METAL PRODUCTS CO LLC
(PA)**
200 N Center St (43845-1270)
P.O. Box 179 (43845-0179)
PHONE.............................740 545-6381
Daniel P Erb Iii, *Pr*
Marion M Sutton, *
Michael G Baker, *
Carole M Loos, *
EMP: 48 **EST:** 1923
SQ FT: 140,000
SALES (est): 9.84MM
SALES (corp-wide): 9.84MM **Privately
Held**
Web: www.jmpforming.com
SIC: 3842 3444 3469 Surgical appliances
and supplies; Forming machine work, sheet
metal; Metal stampings, nec

(G-14172)
**JONES METAL PRODUCTS
COMPANY**
Jones-Zylon Company
305 N Center St (43845-1001)
PHONE.............................740 545-6341
EMP: 40
SALES (corp-wide): 11MM **Privately Held**
SIC: 5047 3842 Hospital equipment and
supplies, nec; Surgical appliances and
supplies
PA: Jones Metal Products Company Llc
200 N Center St
West Lafayette OH 43845
740 545-6381

(G-14173)
JONESZYLON COMPANY LLC
300 N Center St (43845-1002)
P.O. Box 149 (43845-0149)
PHONE.............................740 545-6341

Robert Zachrich, *Pr*
Tracey Zachrich, *Prin*
EMP: 9 **EST:** 2014
SQ FT: 20,000
SALES (est): 2.66MM **Privately Held**
Web: www.joneszylon.com
SIC: 3089 5046 Plastics kitchenware,
tableware, and houseware; Food warming
equipment

(G-14174)
**YANKEE WIRE CLOTH PRODUCTS
INC**
221 W Main St (43845-1103)
P.O. Box 58 (43845-0058)
PHONE.............................740 545-9129
William D Timmons, *Pr*
Mary Timmons, *
EMP: 15 **EST:** 1963
SQ FT: 35,000
SALES (est): 2.3MM **Privately Held**
Web: www.yankeewire.com
SIC: 3496 Screening, woven wire: made
from purchased wire

West Liberty
Logan County

(G-14175)
HOLDREN BROTHERS INC
301 Runkle St (43357-9476)
P.O. Box 459 (43357-0459)
PHONE.............................937 465-7050
Shirley Holdren, *Pr*
EMP: 10 **EST:** 1939
SQ FT: 4,800
SALES (est): 741.88K **Privately Held**
Web: www.holdrenbrothers.com
SIC: 3599 3589 7692 3549 Machine shop,
jobbing and repair; Commercial cleaning
equipment; Welding repair; Metalworking
machinery, nec

(G-14176)
MARIES CANDIES LLC
Also Called: Marie's Candies
311 Zanesfield Rd (43357-9563)
P.O. Box 766 (43357-0766)
PHONE.............................937 465-3061
EMP: 6 **EST:** 1956
SQ FT: 4,100
SALES (est): 964.22K **Privately Held**
Web: www.mariescandies.com
SIC: 2064 5441 Candy bars, including
chocolate covered bars; Candy

West Manchester
Preble County

(G-14177)
ROWE PREMIX INC
10107 Us Rr 127 N (45382)
P.O. Box 205 (45382-0205)
PHONE.............................937 678-9015
Gene Rowe, *Pr*
Sharon Rowe, *VP*
EMP: 6 **EST:** 1979
SQ FT: 5,000
SALES (est): 467.67K **Privately Held**
SIC: 2048 Feed premixes

West Mansfield
Logan County

(G-14178)
DAYLAY EGG FARM INC
11177 Township Road 133 (43358-9709)
PHONE.............................937 355-6531
Kurt Lausecker, *Pr*
▲ **EMP:** 135 **EST:** 1978
SQ FT: 3,200
SALES (est): 673.93K **Privately Held**
SIC: 0252 2015 Chicken eggs; Poultry
slaughtering and processing

(G-14179)
M & M CONCEPTS INC
Also Called: Cmg Company Plant 2
2633 State Route 292 (43358-9523)
PHONE.............................937 355-1115
Thomas P Mcgrady, *Pr*
Alexa Mcgrady, *Sec*
Kris Carpenter, *Treas*
Larry Vermillion, *VP*
EMP: 8 **EST:** 2001
SQ FT: 14,000
SALES (est): 966.06K **Privately Held**
Web: www.cmgcompany.net
SIC: 7692 Welding repair

(G-14180)
NATURE PURE LLC
26560 Storms Rd (43358-9662)
P.O. Box 127 (43067-0127)
PHONE.............................937 358-2364
Kurt Lausecker, *CEO*
EMP: 23
Web: www.naturepure.us
SIC: 0252 2015 Chicken eggs; Egg
processing
PA: Nature Pure Llc
26586 State Route 739
Raymond OH 43067

(G-14181)
SHELLY MATERIALS INC
20620 Spangler Rd (43358-9653)
PHONE.............................937 358-2224
EMP: 7 **EST:** 2019
SALES (est): 136.95K **Privately Held**
SIC: 3281 Cut stone and stone products

West Milton
Miami County

(G-14182)
ERNST ENTERPRISES INC
Also Called: Ernst Concrete
7850 S Karns Rd (45383-9743)
PHONE.............................937 233-7777
John Ernst, *Pr*
EMP: 12
SALES (corp-wide): 240.08MM **Privately
Held**
Web: www.ernstconcrete.com
SIC: 3273 5032 Ready-mixed concrete;
Concrete mixtures
PA: Ernst Enterprises, Inc.
993 Falls Creek Dr
Vandalia OH 45377
937 233-5555

(G-14183)
MIAMI GRAPHICS SERVICES INC
225 N Jay St (45383-1706)
P.O. Box 194 (45383-0194)
PHONE.............................937 698-4013
Norma Parmenter, *Pr*
Charles Parmenter, *VP*

EMP: 10 **EST:** 1977
SQ FT: 8,500
SALES (est): 180.77K **Privately Held**
SIC: 2759 Commercial printing, nec

(G-14184)
OLD MASON WINERY INC
4199 S Iddings Rd (45383-8741)
PHONE.............................937 698-1122
Jeff Clark, *Pr*
Donna Clarke, *VP*
EMP: 9 **EST:** 2013
SALES (est): 457.58K **Privately Held**
Web: www.oldmason.com
SIC: 2084 Wines

(G-14185)
ROBERTSON CABINETS INC
1090 S Main St (45383-1365)
PHONE.............................937 698-3755
William Robertson Senior, *Ch Bd*
Jeff Yantis, *Pr*
Judith Robertson, *VP*
EMP: 8 **EST:** 1979
SQ FT: 22,000
SALES (est): 546.23K **Privately Held**
Web: www.robertsoncabinets.com
SIC: 2541 2431 Cabinets, except
refrigerated: show, display, etc.: wood;
Millwork

West Salem
Wayne County

(G-14186)
CENSTAR COATINGS INC
11829 Jeffrey Rd (44287-9219)
PHONE.............................330 723-8000
Jim Feterle, *Pr*
EMP: 6 **EST:** 2012
SQ FT: 6,000
SALES (est): 305.19K **Privately Held**
SIC: 3069 Sheeting, rubber or rubberized
fabric

(G-14187)
CHARLES MACHINE WORKS INC
Also Called: American Augers
135 State Route 42 (44287-9130)
PHONE.............................800 324-4930
EMP: 100
SALES (corp-wide): 4.58B **Publicly Held**
Web: www.thecharlesmachineworks.com
SIC: 3532 Auger mining equipment
HQ: The Charles Machine Works Inc
1959 W Fir Ave
Perry OK 73077
580 681-8994

(G-14188)
JOHNSON BROS RUBBER CO (PA)
42 W Buckeye St (44287-9747)
P.O. Box 812 (44287-0812)
PHONE.............................419 853-4122
Lawrence G Cooke, *Pr*
Eric Vail, *
◆ **EMP:** 100 **EST:** 1947
SQ FT: 70,000
SALES (est): 9.56MM
SALES (corp-wide): 9.56MM **Privately
Held**
Web:
www.johnsonbrosrubbercompany.com
SIC: 5199 3061 Foams and rubber;
Mechanical rubber goods

(G-14189)
PAROBEK TRUCKING CO
192 State Route 42 (44287-9130)

PHONE..................419 869-7500
Keigm Parobek, *Owner*
EMP: 6 **EST:** 1984
SALES (est): 520.47K **Privately Held**
SIC: 3537 4213 4212 Industrial trucks and
tractors; Trucking, except local; Local
trucking, without storage

West Union
Adams County

(G-14190)
DINSMORE INC
Also Called: Purvis Milling Co
11780 State Route 41 (45693-8025)
PHONE..................937 544-3332
Ron Dinsmore, *Pr*
Diane Dinsmore, *Sec*
EMP: 8 **EST:** 1989
SQ FT: 12,000
SALES (est): 497.76K **Privately Held**
Web: www.dinsmore.com
SIC: 3524 5999 Lawn and garden equipment
; Feed and farm supply

West Unity
Williams County

(G-14191)
AGB LLC
15188 Us Highway 127 (43570-9502)
PHONE..................419 924-5216
EMP: 7 **EST:** 2000
SALES (est): 2.27MM **Privately Held**
SIC: 3469 Stamping metal for the trade

(G-14192)
BENVIC TRINITY LLC (DH)
Also Called: Chemres Trinity
600 Oak St (43570-9545)
PHONE..................609 520-0000
EMP: 15 **EST:** 2021
SALES (est): 32.54MM
SALES (corp-wide): 355.83K **Privately
Held**
Web: www.benvic.com
SIC: 2821 Plastics materials and resins
HQ: Benvic Us Holdings, Inc.
103 Carnegie Ctr Ste 100
Princeton NJ 08540
609 520-0000

(G-14193)
CONVERSION TECH INTL INC
700 Oak St (43570-9457)
PHONE..................419 924-5566
Chester Cromwell, *Pr*
Jason Cromwell, *
▲ **EMP:** 33 **EST:** 1999
SQ FT: 130,000
SALES (est): 4.7MM **Privately Held**
Web: www.conversiontechnologies.com
SIC: 2891 7389 Adhesives; Laminating
service

(G-14194)
H K K MACHINING CO
1201 Oak St (43570-9435)
PHONE..................419 924-5116
Duane E King, *Pr*
Sharon King, *VP*
EMP: 20 **EST:** 1966
SQ FT: 23,500
SALES (est): 4MM **Privately Held**
Web: www.hkkmach.com
SIC: 3599 Machine shop, jobbing and repair

(G-14195)
HARDLINE INTERNATIONAL INC
Also Called: Rimm Kleen Systems
1107 Oak St (43570-9429)
PHONE..................419 924-9556
Robert Warmingham, *Pr*
EMP: 10 **EST:** 1980
SQ FT: 12,000
SALES (est): 922.97K **Privately Held**
Web: www.rimmkleensystems.com
SIC: 3479 Aluminum coating of metal
products

(G-14196)
KAMCO INDUSTRIES INC (HQ)
1001 E Jackson St (43570-9414)
PHONE..................419 924-5511
Joe Tubbs, *VP*
Bryan Barshel, *
◆ **EMP:** 370 **EST:** 1987
SQ FT: 160,000
SALES (est): 99.7MM **Privately Held**
Web: www.kumi-na.com
SIC: 3089 Injection molded finished plastics
products, nec
PA: Kumi Kasei Co., Ltd.
6-13-10, Sotokanda
Chiyoda-Ku TKY 101-0

(G-14197)
PR-WELD & MANUFACTURING LTD
18258 County Road H50 (43570-9750)
PHONE..................419 633-9204
Roy Rigg, *Pt*
Paul Rigg, *Pt*
EMP: 7 **EST:** 2003
SALES (est): 980.06K **Privately Held**
Web: pr-weld.webnode.page
SIC: 7692 Welding repair

(G-14198)
TRINITY SPECIALTY COMPOUNDING INC
600 Oak St (43570-9545)
P.O. Box 247 (43570-0247)
PHONE..................419 924-9090
EMP: 19
SIC: 3089 Plastics processing

(G-14199)
VISION COLOR LLC
214 S Defiance St (43570-9620)
P.O. Box 264 (43570-0264)
PHONE..................419 924-9450
EMP: 8 **EST:** 2002
SALES (est): 6.22MM **Privately Held**
Web: www.visioncolorllc.com
SIC: 3089 Injection molding of plastics
HQ: Tosaf, Inc.
330 Southridge Pkwy
Bessemer City NC 28016
980 533-3000

Westerville
Delaware County

(G-14200)
A-STAR TRANSPORTATION COMPANY
470 Olde Worthington Rd Ste 200
(43082-9127)
PHONE..................708 300-0067
Maryna Kniazieva, *CEO*
Maryna Kniazieva, *Pr*
EMP: 22 **EST:** 2020
SALES (est): 3.71MM **Privately Held**
SIC: 3537 Trucks, tractors, loaders, carriers,
and similar equipment

(G-14201)
ABB INC
Also Called: A B B Electric Systems
579 Executive Campus Dr Frnt
(43082-9801)
PHONE..................614 818-6300
John Strachan, *Brnch Mgr*
EMP: 10
Web: www.abb.com
SIC: 3612 3613 Transformers, except electric
; Switchgear and switchboard apparatus
HQ: Abb Inc.
305 Gregson Dr
Cary NC 27511

(G-14202)
AMERICAN CERAMIC SOCIETY (PA)
470 Olde Worthington Rd Ste 200
(43082-9127)
PHONE..................614 890-4700
Mark Mecklenborg, *CEO*
Michael Johnson, *CFO*
EMP: 29 **EST:** 1905
SQ FT: 10,126
SALES (est): 8.75MM
SALES (corp-wide): 8.75MM **Privately
Held**
Web: www.ceramics.org
SIC: 2721 8621 Periodicals, publishing and
printing; Scientific membership association

(G-14203)
ANGELIC BAKEHOUSE LLC
Also Called: Angelic Bakehouse, Inc.
380 Polaris Pkwy Ste 110 (43082-0003)
PHONE..................414 312-7300
Jennifer Marino, *Pr*
James Marino, *
EMP: 50 **EST:** 2009
SALES (est): 2.38MM
SALES (corp-wide): 7.01MM **Privately
Held**
Web: www.angelicbakehouse.com
SIC: 5461 2051 Bread; Bread, all types
(white, wheat, rye, etc); fresh or frozen
PA: Legacy Bakehouse Llc
N8 W 22100 Johnson Dr
Waukesha WI 53186
262 547-2447

(G-14204)
BRIGHTSTAR PROPANE & FUELS
Also Called: Guttman Oil
6190 Frost Rd (43082-9027)
PHONE..................614 891-8395
Richard Guttman, *Pr*
EMP: 7 **EST:** 2014
SALES (est): 472.82K **Privately Held**
Web: www.brightstarpropane.com
SIC: 5984 1389 2869 Propane gas, bottled;
Construction, repair, and dismantling
services; Fuels

(G-14205)
CAYOSOFT INC (PA)
470 Olde Worthington Rd Ste 200
(43082-8985)
P.O. Box 711 (43216-0711)
PHONE..................614 423-6718
Robert J Bobel, *CEO*
EMP: 15 **EST:** 2013
SALES (est): 2.3MM
SALES (corp-wide): 2.3MM **Privately Held**
Web: www.cayosoft.com
SIC: 7372 Business oriented computer
software

(G-14206)
CENTURY GRAPHICS INC
9101 Hawthorne Pt (43082-9231)
PHONE..................614 895-7698

Richard Bonham, *Pr*
EMP: 7 **EST:** 1968
SQ FT: 26,000
SALES (est): 155.15K **Privately Held**
Web: www.centurygraphics.com
SIC: 2796 2789 2759 2752 Platemaking
services; Bookbinding and related work;
Commercial printing, nec; Offset printing

(G-14207)
DERN TROPHIES CORP
Also Called: Dern Trophy Mfg
6225 Frost Rd (43082-9027)
PHONE..................614 895-3260
Ronald M Spohn, *Pr*
B Thomas Dern, *VP*
▲ **EMP:** 6 **EST:** 1963
SQ FT: 20,000
SALES (est): 474.15K **Privately Held**
Web: www.marcoawardsgroup.com
SIC: 3499 5094 3993 Trophies, metal,
except silver; Trophies; Signs and
advertising specialties

(G-14208)
ENERGY LABS LLC (DH)
Also Called: E L I
505 N Cleveland Ave (43082-7130)
PHONE..................619 671-0100
Ray Irani, *Pr*
▲ **EMP:** 400 **EST:** 1974
SQ FT: 150,000
SALES (est): 3.86MM
SALES (corp-wide): 8.01B **Publicly Held**
Web: energylabs.vertiv.com
SIC: 3585 Heating and air conditioning
combination units
HQ: Vertiv Corporation
505 N Cleveland Ave
Westerville OH 43082
614 888-0246

(G-14209)
EWEBSCHEDULE
180 Commerce Park Dr (43082-6067)
PHONE..................614 882-0726
EMP: 7 **EST:** 2012
SALES (est): 93.13K **Privately Held**
Web: www.abcsrcm.com
SIC: 7372 Prepackaged software

(G-14210)
FARAH JEWELERS INC
5965 Medallion Dr E (43082-9059)
PHONE..................614 438-6140
Eli Hannoush, *Pr*
EMP: 6 **EST:** 1996
SALES (est): 484.21K **Privately Held**
Web: www.farahjewelers.net
SIC: 3911 5944 Jewelry mountings and
trimmings; Jewelry stores

(G-14211)
GARAGE SCENES LTD
Also Called: Ready For Flight
7385 State Route 3 Unit 112 (43082-8654)
PHONE..................614 407-6094
Greg Rogers, *Managing Member*
EMP: 19 **EST:** 2005
SALES (est): 731.13K **Privately Held**
Web: www.garagescenes.com
SIC: 3663 Digital encoders

(G-14212)
HARRIS MACKESSY & BRENNAN INC
Also Called: Hmb Information Sys Developers
570 Polaris Pkwy Ste 200 (43082-7901)
PHONE..................614 221-6831
Thomas Harris, *Pr*
Tom Harris, *

GEOGRAPHIC

Mark Buchy, *
John Mackessy, *
EMP: 150 **EST:** 1994
SQ FT: 9,000
SALES (est): 6.13MM **Privately Held**
Web: www.cgi.com
SIC: 8742 3577 Management consulting services; Decoders, computer peripheral equipment

(G-14213)
IDENTITY GROUP LLC
6111c Maxtown Rd (43082-9051)
PHONE..............................614 337-6167
EMP: 7 **EST:** 2002
SALES (est): 975.1K **Privately Held**
Web: www.identitygroupllc.com
SIC: 5112 5136 5199 2741 Pens and/or pencils; Uniforms, men's and boys'; Advertising specialties; Catalogs: publishing and printing

(G-14214)
IMT DEFENSE CORP
Also Called: IMT Defense
5386 Club Dr (43082-8312)
PHONE..............................614 891-8812
Remo Assini, *Pr*
James Hacking, *Ch Bd*
EMP: 7 **EST:** 2004
SALES (est): 210.86K **Privately Held**
Web: www.imtdefence.com
SIC: 3812 Defense systems and equipment

(G-14215)
JBW SYSTEMS INC
5840 Chandler Ct (43082-9254)
P.O. Box 1530 (43086-1530)
PHONE..............................614 882-5008
James Watkins, *Pr*
Billie L Watkins, *VP*
EMP: 10 **EST:** 1981
SQ FT: 5,000
SALES (est): 909.63K **Privately Held**
Web: www.jbwsystems.com
SIC: 3559 3531 Chemical machinery and equipment; Construction machinery

(G-14216)
JST LLC
6240 Frost Rd Ste C (43082-9027)
PHONE..............................614 423-7815
Susan Testaguzza, *Managing Member*
James Testaguzza, *Managing Member*
EMP: 7 **EST:** 2011
SALES (est): 447.88K **Privately Held**
SIC: 7372 Educational computer software

(G-14217)
LAKE SHORE CRYOTRONICS INC (PA)
480 Olde Worthington Rd (43082-8954)
PHONE..............................614 891-2243
Michael S Swartz, *Pr*
John M Swartz, *
Philip R Swinehart, *
Karen Lint, *
Ed Maloof, *
EMP: 98 **EST:** 1968
SQ FT: 60,000
SALES (est): 18.48MM
SALES (corp-wide): 18.48MM **Privately Held**
Web: www.lakeshore.com
SIC: 3823 3679 3812 3825 Process control instruments; Cryogenic cooling devices for infrared detectors, masers; Search and navigation equipment; Measuring instruments and meters, electric

(G-14218)
LANCASTER COLONY CORPORATION (PA)
380 Polaris Pkwy Ste 400 (43082-8069)
PHONE..............................614 224-7141
David A Ciesinski, *Pr*
Alan F Harris, *
Thomas K Pigott, *VP*
◆ **EMP:** 25 **EST:** 1961
SALES (est): 1.87B
SALES (corp-wide): 1.87B **Publicly Held**
Web: www.lancastercolony.com
SIC: 2035 2038 Dressings, salad: raw and cooked (except dry mixes); Frozen specialties, nec

(G-14219)
LANCASTER GLASS CORPORATION
380 Polaris Pkwy Ste 400 (43082-8069)
PHONE..............................614 224-7141
EMP: 106 **EST:** 2019
SALES (est): 712.93K
SALES (corp-wide): 1.87B **Publicly Held**
Web: www.lancasterglasscorp.com
SIC: 2035 Dressings, salad: raw and cooked (except dry mixes)
PA: Lancaster Colony Corporation
380 Polaris Pkwy Ste 400
Westerville OH 43082
614 224-7141

(G-14220)
LIEBERT FIELD SERVICES INC
Also Called: Emerson Network Power System
610 Executive Campus Dr (43082-8870)
P.O. Box 29186 (43229-0186)
PHONE..............................614 841-5763
Lisa Hunt, *Mgr*
EMP: 47 **EST:** 2001
SALES (est): 7.53MM
SALES (corp-wide): 8.01B **Publicly Held**
Web: www.vertiv.com
SIC: 3823 Process control instruments
HQ: Vertiv Corporation
505 N Cleveland Ave
Westerville OH 43082
614 888-0246

(G-14221)
MAC TOOLS INC
505 N Cleveland Ave Ste 200 (43082-7130)
P.O. Box 50400 (46250-0400)
PHONE..............................614 755-7039
EMP: 20
SIC: 3699 Door opening and closing devices, electrical

(G-14222)
MCNISH CORPORATION
Also Called: E & I
214 Hoff Rd Unit M (43082-7157)
PHONE..............................614 899-2282
Glenn E Meek, *Brnch Mgr*
EMP: 7
SALES (corp-wide): 21.29MM **Privately Held**
Web: www.walker-process.com
SIC: 3589 Water treatment equipment, industrial
PA: Mcnish Corporation
840 N Russell Ave
Aurora IL 60506
630 892-7921

(G-14223)
NEW YORK FROZEN FOODS INC
Mamma Bella Foods
380 Polaris Pkwy Ste 400 (43082-8069)
PHONE..............................626 338-3000
Bob Willist, *Brnch Mgr*
EMP: 50

SALES (corp-wide): 1.87B **Publicly Held**
SIC: 2051 Buns, bread type: fresh or frozen
HQ: New York Frozen Foods, Inc.
25900 Fargo Ave
Bedford OH 44146
216 292-5655

(G-14224)
NEW YORK FROZEN FOODS INC
380 Polaris Pkwy Ste 400 (43082-8069)
P.O. Box 297737 (43229-7737)
PHONE..............................614 846-2232
Thomas E Moloney, *Brnch Mgr*
EMP: 10
SALES (corp-wide): 1.87B **Publicly Held**
SIC: 3421 Table and food cutlery, including butchers'
HQ: New York Frozen Foods, Inc.
25900 Fargo Ave
Bedford OH 44146
216 292-5655

(G-14225)
OCTOPUS EXPRESS INC
470 Olde Worthington Rd (43082-8985)
PHONE..............................614 412-1222
Matluba Ibragimova, *Prin*
EMP: 20 **EST:** 2020
SALES (est): 800K **Privately Held**
SIC: 3537 Trucks, tractors, loaders, carriers, and similar equipment

(G-14226)
ORTON EDWARD JR CRMIC FNDATION
6991 S Old 3c Hwy (43082-9026)
P.O. Box 2760 (43086-2760)
PHONE..............................614 895-2663
Jonathan Hinton, *Ch Bd*
Richard R Stedman Attorney, *Prin*
J Gary Childress, *Secretary General**
Doctor James Williams, *Trst*
Doctor Stephen Freiman, *Trst*
▼ **EMP:** 31 **EST:** 1896
SQ FT: 34,260
SALES (est): 7.35MM **Privately Held**
Web: www.ortonceramic.com
SIC: 3269 3826 3825 8748 Cones, pyrometric: earthenware; Analytical instruments; Instruments to measure electricity; Testing services

(G-14227)
PYROS PHARMACEUTICALS INC
470 Olde Worthington Rd Ste 200 (43082-9127)
PHONE..............................201 743-9468
Michael Smith, *CEO*
Edwin Urrutia, *
EMP: 35 **EST:** 2017
SALES (est): 1.39MM **Privately Held**
Web: www.pyrospharma.com
SIC: 2834 Pharmaceutical preparations

(G-14228)
QUADRIGA AMERICAS LLC (PA)
480 Olde Worthington Rd Ste 350 (43082-8954)
PHONE..............................614 890-6090
Roger Taylor, *CEO*
▼ **EMP:** 7 **EST:** 2009
SQ FT: 5,000
SALES (est): 484.9K
SALES (corp-wide): 484.9K **Privately Held**
SIC: 2741 Internet publishing and broadcasting

(G-14229)
REFLEXIS SYSTEMS INC
579 Executive Campus Dr Ste 310 (43082-9801)

PHONE..............................614 948-1931
EMP: 194
SALES (corp-wide): 4.98B **Publicly Held**
Web: www.zebra.com
SIC: 3577 Computer peripheral equipment, nec
HQ: Reflexis Systems, Inc.
3 Allied Dr Ste 400
Dedham MA 02026
781 493-3400

(G-14230)
REVOLUTION GROUP INC
670 Meridian Way (43082-7648)
PHONE..............................614 212-1111
Richard Snide, *Pr*
Polly Clavijo, *
EMP: 80 **EST:** 1995
SALES (est): 9.04MM **Privately Held**
Web: www.revolutiongroup.com
SIC: 7379 7372 4813 8741 Computer related consulting services; Prepackaged software; Internet connectivity services; Management services

(G-14231)
ROOF MAXX TECHNOLOGIES LLC
Also Called: Roof Maxx
7385 State Route 3 (43082-8654)
PHONE..............................855 766-3629
Michael Feazel, *CEO*
Michael Feazel, *Managing Member*
Todd Feazel, *
Amy Koch, *
EMP: 40 **EST:** 2017
SALES (est): 5.77MM **Privately Held**
Web: www.roofmaxx.com
SIC: 2952 Asphalt felts and coatings

(G-14232)
S&L FLEET SERVICES INC
670 Meridian Way Ste 252 (43082-2306)
PHONE..............................740 549-2722
Sheldon Lambert, *CEO*
EMP: 20 **EST:** 2017
SALES (est): 1.19MM **Privately Held**
SIC: 3812 Search and navigation equipment

(G-14233)
SISTER SCHBRTS HMMADE RLLS INC (DH)
Also Called: Sister Schubert's
380 Polaris Pkwy Ste 400 (43082-8069)
P.O. Box 112 (36049-0112)
PHONE..............................334 335-2232
Patricia W Schubert, *Pr*
George Barns, *
▲ **EMP:** 250 **EST:** 1993
SQ FT: 55,000
SALES (est): 24.5MM
SALES (corp-wide): 1.87B **Publicly Held**
Web: www.sisterschuberts.com
SIC: 2051 Breads, rolls, and buns
HQ: T.Marzetti Company
380 Polaris Pkwy Ste 400
Westerville OH 43082
614 846-2232

(G-14234)
SKLADANY ENTERPRISES INC
Also Called: Skladany Printing Center
695 Mccorkle Blvd (43082)
PHONE..............................614 823-6882
Thomas Skladany, *Pr*
Debbie Skladany, *VP*
Michael Niezgoda, *VP Sls*
EMP: 8 **EST:** 1982
SALES (est): 1.05MM **Privately Held**
Web: www.skladany.com
SIC: 2752 Offset printing

(G-14235)
STATUS SOLUTIONS LLC
Also Called: Status Solutions
999 County Line Rd W # A (43082-7237)
PHONE................................434 296-1789
EMP: 80 EST: 2001
SALES (est): 9.8MM **Privately Held**
Web: www.statussolutions.com
SIC: 3669 5063 Emergency alarms; Alarm systems, nec

(G-14236)
THERM-O-DISC INCORPORATED (HQ)
Also Called: Sensience
570 Polaris Pkwy Ste 500 (43082-8649)
PHONE................................419 525-8500
Kay Ellen Thurman, *CEO*
Loretta M Tanner, *
William M Van Cleve, *
▲ EMP: 900 EST: 1968
SALES (est): 493.93MM
SALES (corp-wide): 493.93MM **Privately Held**
Web: www.sensience.com
SIC: 3822 3823 Built-in thermostats, filled system and bimetal types; Process control instruments
PA: Sensience, Inc.
30 Rockefeller Plz Fl 54th
New York NY 10112
419 525-8500

(G-14237)
TMARZETTI COMPANY (HQ)
Also Called: Inn Maid Products
380 Polaris Pkwy Ste 400 (43082-8069)
P.O. Box 297737 (43229)
PHONE................................614 846-2232
David Ciesinski, *Pr*
Luis Viso Csco, *Prin*
◆ EMP: 147 EST: 1927
SQ FT: 28,000
SALES (est): 927.01MM
SALES (corp-wide): 1.87B **Publicly Held**
Web: www.tmarzetticompany.com
SIC: 2035 2098 Dressings, salad: raw and cooked (except dry mixes); Noodles (e.g. egg, plain, and water), dry
PA: Lancaster Colony Corporation
380 Polaris Pkwy Ste 400
Westerville OH 43082
614 224-7141

(G-14238)
TRIMCO
7265 Park Bend Dr (43082-8659)
PHONE................................614 679-3931
EMP: 7 EST: 2010
SALES (est): 100K **Privately Held**
Web: www.trimcohardware.com
SIC: 2431 Millwork

(G-14239)
VERTIV CORPORATION (DH)
Also Called: Geist
505 N Cleveland Ave (43082-7130)
P.O. Box 29186 (43229)
PHONE................................614 888-0246
Giordano Albertazzi, *CEO*
David Fallon, *CFO*
Jason Forcier, *Ex VP*
◆ EMP: 1300 EST: 1965
SQ FT: 330,000
SALES (est): 1.3B
SALES (corp-wide): 8.01B **Publicly Held**
Web: www.vertiv.com
SIC: 3585 3613 7629 Air conditioning equipment, complete; Regulators, power; Electronic equipment repair
HQ: Vertiv Group Corporation

505 N Cleveland Ave
Westerville OH 43082
614 888-0246

(G-14240)
VERTIV GROUP CORPORATION (DH)
Also Called: Vertiv Co.
505 N Cleveland Ave (43082-7130)
PHONE................................614 888-0246
Frank P Simpkins, *VP*
Matthew S Dean, *
Stephen H Liang, *GLOBAL TELECOM AND ASIA PACIFIC*
Michael Neeley, *
Eva M Kalawski, *
EMP: 1000 EST: 2016
SALES (est): 2.02B
SALES (corp-wide): 8.01B **Publicly Held**
Web: www.vertiv.com
SIC: 3585 3679 Air conditioning units, complete: domestic or industrial; Power supplies, all types: static
HQ: Vertiv Holdings, Llc
1050 Dearborn Dr
Columbus OH 43085
614 888-0246

(G-14241)
VERTIV HOLDINGS CO (PA)
Also Called: Vertiv
505 N Cleveland Ave (43082-7130)
PHONE................................614 888-0246
Giordano Albertazzi, *CEO*
David M Cote, *Ex Ch Bd*
Stephen Liang, *Ex VP*
David J Fallon, *CFO*
Stephanie L Gill, *CLO*
EMP: 189 EST: 2016
SALES (est): 8.01B
SALES (corp-wide): 8.01B **Publicly Held**
Web: www.vertiv.com
SIC: 3679 Electronic loads and power supplies

(G-14242)
WORTHINGTON CYLINDER CORP
333 Maxtown Rd (43082-8757)
PHONE................................614 840-3800
Robert Kotarba, *Brnch Mgr*
EMP: 141
SQ FT: 12,880
SALES (corp-wide): 1.25B **Publicly Held**
Web: www.worthingtonenterprises.com
SIC: 3443 Cylinders, pressure: metal plate
HQ: Worthington Cylinder Corporation
200 W Old Wlson Bridge Rd
Worthington OH 43085
614 840-3210

Westerville
Franklin County

(G-14243)
ASSETWATCH INC
Also Called: Nikola Labs
60 Collegeview Rd (43081-1429)
PHONE................................844 464-5652
Will Zell, *Pr*
EMP: 140 EST: 2015
SALES (est): 9.29MM **Privately Held**
Web: www.nikola.tech
SIC: 3823 Process control instruments

(G-14244)
AVCOM SMT INC
213 E Broadway Ave (43081-1656)
P.O. Box 1516 (43086-1516)
PHONE................................614 882-8176
Paul Wiese, *Pr*

Barbara Wiese, *VP*
EMP: 12 EST: 1970
SQ FT: 10,000
SALES (est): 4.58MM **Privately Held**
Web: www.avcomsmt.com
SIC: 3672 Printed circuit boards

(G-14245)
AXIOM TOOL GROUP INC
270 Broad St (43081-1604)
PHONE................................844 642-4902
Scott Leichtling, *CEO*
EMP: 7 EST: 2014
SALES (est): 3.45MM
SALES (corp-wide): 28.65MM **Privately Held**
Web: www.axiomprecision.com
SIC: 3553 Woodworking machinery
PA: Jpw Industries Inc.
427 New Sanford Rd
La Vergne TN 37086
615 793-8900

(G-14246)
BLF ENTERPRISES INC
Also Called: Great Harvest Bread
445 S State St (43081-2956)
PHONE................................937 642-6425
Bruce Fowler, *Pr*
Linda Fowler, *Sec*
EMP: 10 EST: 1993
SQ FT: 2,000
SALES (est): 358.81K **Privately Held**
Web: www.greatharvestwesterville.com
SIC: 5461 2052 2051 Bread; Cookies and crackers; Bread, cake, and related products

(G-14247)
BLUELOGOS INC
Also Called: Sullivan Company, The
130 Graphic Way (43081-2360)
PHONE................................614 898-9971
David Duhl, *Pr*
EMP: 17 EST: 2005
SQ FT: 5,760
SALES (est): 928.53K **Privately Held**
Web: www.wearbrandmatters.com
SIC: 2759 5699 5199 Screen printing; Customized clothing and apparel; Advertising specialties

(G-14248)
BUFFALO ABRASIVES INC
1093 Smoke Burr Dr (43081-4542)
PHONE................................614 891-6450
Timothy J Wagner, *Prin*
EMP: 45
SALES (corp-wide): 21.57MM **Privately Held**
Web: www.buffaloabrasives.com
SIC: 3291 Abrasive products
HQ: Buffalo Abrasives, Inc.
960 Erie Ave
North Tonawanda NY 14120
716 693-3856

(G-14249)
CATALYSIS ADDITIVE TOOLING LLC
190 Heatherdown Dr (43081-2868)
PHONE................................614 715-3674
Darrell Stafford, *Managing Member*
EMP: 8 EST: 2017
SALES (est): 1.92MM **Privately Held**
Web: www.catalysis3d.com
SIC: 3544 Forms (molds), for foundry and plastics working machinery

(G-14250)
COLUMBUS PRESCR REHABILITATION
Also Called: The Mobility Store

975 Eastwind Dr Ste 155 (43081-3344)
PHONE................................614 294-1600
Mark A Witchey, *Pr*
Jack A Witchey, *Sec*
EMP: 6 EST: 1990
SQ FT: 50,000
SALES (est): 668.78K **Privately Held**
SIC: 3842 7352 Wheelchairs; Medical equipment rental

(G-14251)
CURV IMAGING LLC
Also Called: Curv Imaging
841 Green Crest Dr (43081-2838)
P.O. Box 360641 (43236-0641)
PHONE................................614 890-2878
EMP: 6 EST: 2004
SALES (est): 2.37MM **Privately Held**
Web: www.curvimaging.com
SIC: 2752 Offset printing

(G-14252)
DAIKIN APPLIED AMERICAS INC
192 Heatherdown Dr (43081-2868)
PHONE................................614 351-9862
Dale Matheny, *Brnch Mgr*
EMP: 9
Web: www.daikinapplied.com
SIC: 3585 5075 Refrigeration and heating equipment; Warm air heating and air conditioning
HQ: Daikin Applied Americas Inc.
13600 Industrial Pk Blvd
Minneapolis MN 55441
763 553-5330

(G-14253)
DARIFILL INC
750 Green Crest Dr (43081-2837)
PHONE................................614 890-3274
Steve Aspery, *Pr*
Eric Rousculp, *VP*
Jack Spencer, *VP*
▲ EMP: 18 EST: 2003
SALES (est): 8.79MM **Privately Held**
Web: www.darifill.com
SIC: 3565 Packaging machinery

(G-14254)
DAVID CHOJNACKI
Also Called: Mandrax Technologies
5471 Camlin Pl E (43081-8527)
PHONE................................303 905-1918
David Chojnacki, *Owner*
EMP: 22 EST: 2014
SQ FT: 3,800
SALES (est): 318.23K **Privately Held**
SIC: 7379 7373 8711 3663 Computer related consulting services; Computer systems analysis and design; Consulting engineer; Space satellite communications equipment

(G-14255)
DEDRONE DEFENSE INC
525 W Schrock Rd (43081-8966)
PHONE................................614 948-2002
Phillip Pitsky, *Pr*
Alex Morrow, *VP*
EMP: 11 EST: 2019
SALES (est): 575.18K **Privately Held**
SIC: 3812 Radar systems and equipment

(G-14256)
DJMC PARTNERS INC
Also Called: Fastsigns
654 Brooksedge Blvd Ste A (43081-2962)
PHONE................................614 890-3821
Danell Mcginley, *Prin*
EMP: 9 EST: 2016
SALES (est): 1.65MM **Privately Held**
Web: www.fastsigns.com

GEOGRAPHIC

SIC: 3993 Signs and advertising specialties

(G-14257)
DSC SUPPLY COMPANY LLC
237 E Broadway Ave Ste A (43081-1646)
P.O. Box 2125 (43086-2125)
PHONE..............................614 891-1100
Nikki Anderson, *Pr*
EMP: 7 EST: 2003
SALES (est): 472.82K **Privately Held**
Web: www.dscdredge.com
SIC: 2759 Commercial printing, nec

(G-14258)
ELAN DESIGNS INC
10 E Schrock Rd # 110 (43081-2915)
PHONE..............................614 985-5600
Nelia Anderson, *Pr*
Neilia Anderson, *Pr*
▲ EMP: 6 EST: 1997
SALES (est): 702.91K **Privately Held**
SIC: 3524 Lawn and garden equipment

(G-14259)
EMROID ME
6065 Shreven Dr (43081-8261)
PHONE..............................614 789-1898
Joe Vulpio, *Owner*
EMP: 6 EST: 2005
SALES (est): 103.01K **Privately Held**
SIC: 2395 Embroidery products, except
Schiffli machine

(G-14260)
GLOBAL SECURITY TECH INC
132 Dorchester Sq S Ste 200 (43081-7310)
PHONE..............................614 890-6400
Greg Kyle, *Prin*
EMP: 9 EST: 2000
SALES (est): 249.22K **Privately Held**
Web: www.gstisecurity.com
SIC: 3699 Security control equipment and
systems

(G-14261)
GRACE JUICE COMPANY LLC
6318 E Dublin Granville Rd (43081-8705)
PHONE..............................614 398-6879
Leslie Burgie, *Prin*
EMP: 14 EST: 2017
SALES (est): 821.85K **Privately Held**
SIC: 5149 2599 5812 Juices; Food wagons,
restaurant; Eating places

(G-14262)
H G SCHNEIDER COMPANY
291 Broad St (43081-1603)
PHONE..............................614 882-6944
Constance Schneider, *Pr*
Harold Schneider, *VP*
EMP: 6 EST: 1968
SALES (est): 465.49K **Privately Held**
Web: www.unikixspringpins.com
SIC: 3544 Special dies and tools

(G-14263)
HIGHRISE CREATIVE LLC ✪
Also Called: Fastsigns
654 Brooksedge Blvd Ste A (43081-2962)
PHONE..............................614 890-3821
Jacob Ellzey, *Managing Member*
EMP: 11 EST: 2023
SALES (est): 2.46MM **Privately Held**
Web: www.fastsigns.com
SIC: 3993 Signs and advertising specialties

(G-14264)
IMAGE PRINT INC
6019 Jamesport Dr (43081-7925)
PHONE..............................614 776-3985

Alan Lang, *Genl Mgr*
EMP: 6 EST: 2009
SALES (est): 415.62K **Privately Held**
Web: www.imageprintweb.com
SIC: 2752 Offset printing

(G-14265)
INDUSTRIAL FABRICATORS INC
265 E Broadway Ave (43081-1646)
PHONE..............................614 882-7423
Frederick R Landig Junior, *Pr*
Frederick Landig Senior, *Pr*
EMP: 38 EST: 1964
SQ FT: 98,000
SALES (est): 4.18MM **Privately Held**
Web: www.ifab.com
SIC: 3444 Sheet metalwork

(G-14266)
JEG ASSOCIATES INC
Also Called: Jeg Associates
509 S Otterbein Ave Ste 7 (43081-2951)
P.O. Box 277 (43086-0277)
PHONE..............................614 882-1295
John Gibson Senior, *Pr*
EMP: 6 EST: 1985
SALES (est): 1.18MM **Privately Held**
Web: www.jegplastics.com
SIC: 2821 Plastics materials and resins

(G-14267)
JOHNSON CONTROLS INC
Also Called: Johnson Controls
835 Green Crest Dr (43081-2838)
PHONE..............................614 895-6600
Stephen Carter, *Brnch Mgr*
EMP: 72
Web: www.johnsoncontrols.com
SIC: 2531 Seats, automobile
HQ: Johnson Controls, Inc.
5757 N Green Bay Ave
Milwaukee WI 53209
866 496-1999

(G-14268)
MES PAINTING & GRAPHICS LTD
8298 Harlem Rd (43081-9565)
PHONE..............................614 496-1696
Michael Scherl, *Managing Member*
EMP: 42 EST: 1994
SALES (est): 2.49MM **Privately Held**
Web: www.mespaintingandgraphics.com
SIC: 1721 3993 Commercial painting; Signs
and advertising specialties

(G-14269)
MES PAINTING AND GRAPHICS
8298 Harlem Rd (43081-9565)
PHONE..............................614 496-1696
EMP: 7 EST: 1994
SALES (est): 100.94K **Privately Held**
Web: www.mespaintingandgraphics.com
SIC: 1721 3993 1799 Painting and paper
hanging; Signs and advertising specialties;
Epoxy application

(G-14270)
MICRO INDUSTRIES CORPORATION
(PA)
8399 Green Meadows Dr N (43081)
PHONE..............................740 548-7878
Michael Curran, *Pr*
John Curran, *
William Jackson, *
Amanda Curran, *
EMP: 67 EST: 1979
SQ FT: 52,000
SALES (est): 2.38MM
SALES (corp-wide): 2.38MM **Privately
Held**
Web: www.microindustries.com

SIC: 8711 3674 Engineering services;
Semiconductor circuit networks

(G-14271)
MONTGOMERY ELLIS LLC
Also Called: Goddess Maintenance Company
4151 Executive Pkwy Ste 300
(43081-3871)
PHONE..............................614 226-7976
Amanda Mason, *CEO*
Lauren Vesler, *
EMP: 200 EST: 2019
SALES (est): 2.63MM **Privately Held**
SIC: 2844 5122 5999 Cosmetic preparations
; Cosmetics, perfumes, and hair products;
Toiletries, cosmetics, and perfumes

(G-14272)
OHIO SHELTERALL INC
Also Called: Moore Outdoor Sign Craftsman
6060 Westerville Rd (43081-4048)
PHONE..............................614 882-1110
Steve P Moore, *Pr*
Tom Moore, *VP*
Dave Moore, *Sec*
Ellen Moore, *Treas*
EMP: 10 EST: 1962
SALES (est): 647.84K **Privately Held**
Web: www.mooresigns.biz
SIC: 7312 7389 7338 3993 Outdoor
advertising services; Sign painting and
lettering shop; Secretarial and typing service
; Signs and advertising specialties

(G-14273)
OPTIMUM SYSTEM PRODUCTS INC
(PA)
Also Called: Optimum Graphics
921 Eastwind Dr Ste 133 (43081-3363)
PHONE..............................614 885-4464
John Martin, *CEO*
Dorothy Martin, *
EMP: 40 EST: 1985
SQ FT: 75,000
SALES (est): 903.18K
SALES (corp-wide): 903.18K **Privately
Held**
Web: www.optimumcompanies.com
SIC: 2752 5112 Business form and card
printing, lithographic; Business forms

(G-14274)
ROBIN ENTERPRISES COMPANY
111 N Otterbein Ave (43081-5703)
P.O. Box 6180 (43086-6180)
PHONE..............................614 891-0250
Brad Hance, *Pr*
EMP: 120 EST: 1966
SQ FT: 90,000
SALES (est): 21.3MM **Privately Held**
Web: www.robinent.com
SIC: 2752 2789 2791 Offset printing;
Bookbinding and related work; Typesetting

(G-14275)
SHAWADI LLC
20 S State St Ste B (43081-2105)
PHONE..............................614 839-0698
Andrew Piper, *Managing Member*
Milton A Puckett, *
EMP: 23 EST: 2007
SALES (est): 285.1K **Privately Held**
Web: www.javacentral.coffee
SIC: 5812 2095 Cafe; Coffee roasting
(except by wholesale grocers)

(G-14276)
TACOMA ENERGY LLC
697 Green Crest Dr (43081-2848)
P.O. Box 1528 (43086)
PHONE..............................614 899-8990

EMP: 105 EST: 2009
SALES (est): 3.75MM **Privately Held**
Web: tacomaenergy.org
SIC: 8731 3825 Energy research; Electrical
energy measuring equipment

(G-14277)
TECHNIPRINT INC
Also Called: Inkwell, The
515 S State St (43081-2921)
PHONE..............................614 899-1403
Pat Patel, *Pr*
Diane L Burchetp-patel, *Sec*
EMP: 10 EST: 1988
SQ FT: 1,800
SALES (est): 142.88K **Privately Held**
Web: www.theinkwellusa.com
SIC: 2752 7334 Commercial printing,
lithographic; Photocopying and duplicating
services

(G-14278)
THOMAS TOOL & MOLD COMPANY
271 Broad St (43081-1603)
PHONE..............................614 890-4978
James W Thomas, *Pr*
James P Thomas, *VP*
▲ EMP: 11 EST: 1989
SQ FT: 7,500
SALES (est): 1.83MM **Privately Held**
Web: www.ttmco.com
SIC: 3089 Injection molding of plastics

(G-14279)
VESCO MEDICAL LLC
60 Collegeview Rd Ste 144 (43081-1429)
PHONE..............................614 914-5991
Thomas Hancock, *Brnch Mgr*
EMP: 11
SALES (corp-wide): 1.95MM **Privately
Held**
Web: www.vescomedical.com
SIC: 3841 Surgical and medical instruments
PA: Vesco Medical, Llc
7795 Walton Pkwy Ste 165
New Albany OH 43054
614 914-5991

(G-14280)
WES-GARDE COMPONENTS GROUP
INC
300 Enterprise Dr (43081)
PHONE..............................614 885-0319
Joe Jeenan, *Genl Mgr*
EMP: 6
SALES (corp-wide): 52.94MM **Privately
Held**
Web: www.wesgarde.com
SIC: 5065 3625 5063 Electronic parts;
Switches, electric power; Switches, except
electronic, nec
PA: Wes-Garde Components Group, Inc.
2820 Drane Field Rd
Lakeland FL 33811
863 644-7564

(G-14281)
WEST-CAMP PRESS INC (PA)
39 Collegeview Rd (43081-1463)
PHONE..............................614 882-2378
Ed Evina, *Prin*
Dave Mars, *
▲ EMP: 75 EST: 1961
SQ FT: 55,000
SALES (est): 24.84MM
SALES (corp-wide): 24.84MM **Privately
Held**
Web: www.westcamppress.com
SIC: 2752 2796 2791 2789 Offset printing;
Platemaking services; Typesetting;
Bookbinding and related work

▲ = Import ▼ = Export
◆ = Import/Export

(G-14282)
YESPRESS GRAPHICS LLC
515 S State St (43081-2921)
PHONE.................................614 899-1403
Sunir Patel, *Prin*
EMP: 7 **EST:** 2010
SALES (est): 1.67MM **Privately Held**
Web: www.yespress.com
SIC: 2752 Offset printing

Westlake
Cuyahoga County

(G-14283)
ACME DUPLICATING CO INC
Also Called: Acme Printing
1565 Greenleaf Cir (44145-2609)
PHONE.................................216 241-1241
Donald Sebold, *Owner*
EMP: 7 **EST:** 1934
SQ FT: 3,300
SALES (est): 179.44K **Privately Held**
Web: www.namepads.com
SIC: 2752 Offset printing

(G-14284)
AEROCASE INCORPORATED
Also Called: Odell Electronic Cleaning Stns
1061 Bradley Rd (44145-1044)
PHONE.................................440 617-9294
John Koniarczyk, *Pr*
Deborah Koniarczyk, *VP*
EMP: 10 **EST:** 1997
SALES (est): 999.26K **Privately Held**
Web: www.aerocaseinc.com
SIC: 3089 2441 Cases, plastics; Cases, wood

(G-14285)
ALUMINUM LINE PRODUCTS COMPANY (PA)
Also Called: Alpco
24460 Sperry Cir (44145-1591)
PHONE.................................440 835-8880
Richard A Daniel, *Pr*
James E Guerin, *
Gregory P Thompson, *
Ray Avramovich, *
David Lyster, *
◆ **EMP:** 100 **EST:** 1960
SQ FT: 100,000
SALES (est): 18.04MM
SALES (corp-wide): 18.04MM **Privately Held**
Web: www.aluminumline.com
SIC: 5051 3365 3999 Steel; Aluminum foundries; Barber and beauty shop equipment

(G-14286)
AMERICAN LAWYERS CO INC (PA)
Also Called: American Lawyers Quarterly
853 Westpoint Pkwy Ste 710 (44145-1546)
P.O. Box 45300 (44145)
PHONE.................................440 333-5190
Thomas W Hamilton, *Ex VP*
Edward D Familo, *Pr*
EMP: 11 **EST:** 1899
SQ FT: 4,000
SALES (est): 423.77K
SALES (corp-wide): 423.77K **Privately Held**
Web: www.alqlist.com
SIC: 2721 Periodicals, publishing only

(G-14287)
AMERICAN OFFICE SERVICES INC
30257 Clemens Rd Ste C (44145-1004)
PHONE.................................440 899-6888
Scott Ashbrook, *CEO*
Scott C Ashbrook, *Pr*
Margo L Ashbrook, *VP*
EMP: 6 **EST:** 1991
SQ FT: 8,000
SALES (est): 1.72MM **Privately Held**
Web: www.americanofficeservices.com
SIC: 7641 2531 Office furniture repair and maintenance; Stadium seating

(G-14288)
AMERICAN TCHNICAL COATINGS INC
Also Called: A T C
28045 Ranney Pkwy (44145-1144)
PHONE.................................440 401-2270
Charles Inglefield, *Pr*
EMP: 6 **EST:** 2003
SALES (est): 966.61K **Privately Held**
Web: www.atcmaterials.com
SIC: 3479 Coating of metals and formed products

(G-14289)
APPLIED MARKETING SERVICES INC (HQ)
Also Called: Medical & Home Health
28825 Ranney Pkwy (44145-1173)
PHONE.................................440 716-9962
David J Marquard, *Pr*
David J Marquard Ii, *Pr*
C V Guggenviller, *
▲ **EMP:** 23 **EST:** 1993
SQ FT: 20,000
SALES (est): 8.66MM
SALES (corp-wide): 25.9MM **Privately Held**
Web: www.applied-inc.com
SIC: 3569 8742 Gas producers, generators, and other gas related equipment; Marketing consulting services
PA: Oxygo Hq Florida Llc
2200 Principal Row
Orlando FL 32837
866 234-1692

(G-14290)
BAY CORPORATION
867 Canterbury Rd (44145-1486)
PHONE.................................440 835-2212
EMP: 24 **EST:** 1979
SALES (est): 4.32MM **Privately Held**
Web: www.baycorporation.com
SIC: 3089 3494 Fittings for pipe, plastics; Valves and pipe fittings, nec

(G-14291)
BAY STATE POLYMER DISTRIBUTION INC
Also Called: Bay State Polymer
27540 Detroit Rd Ste 102 (44145-2299)
P.O. Box 40055 (44140-0055)
PHONE.................................440 892-8500
◆ **EMP:** 15
SIC: 5162 3087 Resins, synthetic; Custom compound purchased resins

(G-14292)
BLACK BOX CORPORATION
Also Called: Black Box Network Services
26100 1st St (44145-1478)
PHONE.................................855 324-9909
EMP: 6
Web: www.blackbox.com
SIC: 3577 3679 3661 5045 Computer peripheral equipment, nec; Electronic switches; Modems; Computer peripheral equipment
HQ: Black Box Corporation
2701 N Dllas Pkwy Ste 510
Plano TX 75093
724 746-5500

(G-14293)
BONNE BELL INC
Also Called: Bonne Bell Company, The
1006 Crocker Rd (44145-1031)
PHONE.................................440 835-2440
EMP: 203
SIC: 2844 Cosmetic preparations

(G-14294)
BONNE BELL LLC (PA)
1006 Crocker Rd (44145-1094)
PHONE.................................440 835-2440
Jess A Bell Junior, *Managing Member*
◆ **EMP:** 8 **EST:** 1927
SQ FT: 40,000
SALES (est): 3.03MM
SALES (corp-wide): 3.03MM **Privately Held**
Web: www.aspirebrands.com
SIC: 2844 Cosmetic preparations

(G-14295)
BORCHERS AMERICAS INC (HQ)
Also Called: Om Group
811 Sharon Dr (44145-1522)
PHONE.................................440 899-2950
Devlin Riley, *CEO*
◆ **EMP:** 60 **EST:** 1946
SQ FT: 30,000
SALES (est): 45.3MM
SALES (corp-wide): 1.69B **Privately Held**
Web: www.borchers.com
SIC: 8731 2819 2899 2992 Commercial physical research; Industrial inorganic chemicals, nec; Chemical preparations, nec ; Lubricating oils and greases
PA: Milliken & Company
920 Milliken Rd
Spartanburg SC 29303
864 503-2020

(G-14296)
CENTURY TOOL & STAMPING CO
24600 Center Ridge Rd Ste 140 (44145-5679)
PHONE.................................216 241-2032
Todd Guist, *Pr*
William Guist Junior, *Pr*
William Guist Lii, *Treas*
James Vespoli, *Treas*
Cathy Hoy, *Sec*
EMP: 6 **EST:** 1950
SALES (est): 412K **Privately Held**
SIC: 3599 Machine shop, jobbing and repair

(G-14297)
CHEM-MATERIALS INC
Also Called: Chem-Materials Co
24700 Center Ridge Rd Ste 280 (44145-5606)
PHONE.................................440 455-9465
Philip J Haagensen, *Pr*
▲ **EMP:** 15 **EST:** 1987
SQ FT: 2,000
SALES (est): 9.48MM **Privately Held**
Web: www.chem-materials.com
SIC: 2821 Plastics materials and resins

(G-14298)
DIAMOND RESERVE INC
Also Called: National Diamond Tl & Coating
801 Sharon Dr (44145-1522)
PHONE.................................440 892-7877
Tom Abersold, *Pr*
William Pastis, *CEO*
EMP: 10 **EST:** 1980
SQ FT: 2,000
SALES (est): 1.77MM **Privately Held**
Web: www.nationaldiamondtool.com
SIC: 3545 Diamond cutting tools for turning, boring, burnishing, etc.

(G-14299)
DOME DRILLING COMPANY (PA)
Also Called: Dome Resources
2001 Crocker Rd Ste 420 (44145-6967)
PHONE.................................440 892-9434
Jon O Newton, *Pr*
James E Gessel, *VP*
Noreen C Mc Kinney, *VP Opers*
John James Carney, *Sec*
James A Carney, *Treas*
EMP: 6 **EST:** 1981
SQ FT: 1,200
SALES (est): 652.24K
SALES (corp-wide): 652.24K **Privately Held**
Web: www.sinetek.com
SIC: 1311 1382 Crude petroleum production; Oil and gas exploration services

(G-14300)
ELEVEN 10 LLC
975 Bassett Rd Ste B (44145-1171)
PHONE.................................888 216-4049
EMP: 15 **EST:** 2010
SALES (est): 2.5MM **Privately Held**
Web: www.1110gear.com
SIC: 3842 5199 First aid, snake bite, and burn kits; First aid supplies

(G-14301)
ENERGIZER MANUFACTURING INC
25225 Detroit Rd (44145-2536)
EMP: 10
SALES (corp-wide): 2.89B **Publicly Held**
Web: www.energizerholdings.com
SIC: 3691 Alkaline cell storage batteries
HQ: Energizer Manufacturing, Inc.
8235 Forsyth Blvd
Saint Louis MO 63105
314 985-2000

(G-14302)
G I PLASTEK INC
24700 Center Ridge Rd Ste 8 (44145-5636)
PHONE.................................440 230-1942
Charles Lagasse Junior, *CEO*
Shelly Trochemenko, *Treas*
EMP: 7 **EST:** 1995
SQ FT: 3,000
SALES (est): 395.95K **Privately Held**
SIC: 3089 Plastics processing

(G-14303)
GC CONTROLS INC
Also Called: Eurotherm
30311 Clemens Rd (44145-1023)
P.O. Box 450799 (44145-0617)
PHONE.................................440 779-4777
Bob Roberts, *Pr*
Joanne Albers, *Treas*
Gary Albers, *Dir*
EMP: 7 **EST:** 1987
SALES (est): 590.7K **Privately Held**
Web: www.gccontrols.net
SIC: 3625 Industrial controls: push button, selector switches, pilot

(G-14304)
GEON PERFORMANCE SOLUTIONS LLC (HQ)
25777 Detroit Rd Ste 200 (44145-2484)
P.O. Box 90 (44012)
PHONE.................................800 438-4366
Tracy Garrison, *Managing Member*
EMP: 10 **EST:** 2019
SALES (est): 501.65MM **Privately Held**
Web: www.geon.com
SIC: 2822 3084 Ethylene-propylene rubbers, EPDM polymers; Plastics pipe
PA: Sk Capital Partners, L.P.
430 Park Ave Fl 18

New York NY 10022

(G-14305)
HENKEL US OPERATIONS CORP
Also Called: Loctite
26235 1st St (44145-1439)
PHONE...................................440 250-7700
James Heginbotham, *Brnch Mgr*
EMP: 98
SALES (corp-wide): 22.83B Privately Held
Web: www.henkel.com
SIC: 2891 Adhesives and sealants
HQ: Henkel Us Operations Corporation
1 Henkel Way
Rocky Hill CT 06067
860 571-5100

(G-14306)
HMS INDUSTRIES LLC
Also Called: HMS Industries
27995 Ranney Pkwy (44145-1178)
PHONE...................................440 899-0001
Biri Saluja, *Managing Member*
▲ EMP: 17 EST: 2001
SQ FT: 10,000
SALES (est): 5.8MM Privately Held
Web: www.hms-ind.com
SIC: 3562 5085 Roller bearings and parts;
Industrial supplies

(G-14307)
HYLAND SOFTWARE INC (HQ)
Also Called: Onbase
28105 Clemens Rd (44145-1100)
PHONE...................................440 788-5000
Jitesh Ghai, *CEO*
Nancy Person, *
Ed Mcquiston, *CCO*
John Phelan, *CPO**
Noreen Kilbane, *CAO**
EMP: 1800 EST: 1991
SQ FT: 150,000
SALES (est): 409.59MM
SALES (corp-wide): 486.2MM Privately
Held
Web: www.hyland.com
SIC: 7372 Application computer software
PA: Thoma Cressey Bravo, Inc.
300 N La Slle Dr Ste 4350
Chicago IL 60654
312 254-3300

(G-14308)
ICONIC LABS LLC
Also Called: Ic Scientific Solutions
909 Canterbury Rd Ste G (44145-7212)
PHONE...................................216 759-4040
Travis Bennett Mng Mbtr, *Prin*
EMP: 14 EST: 2016
SQ FT: 3,000
SALES (est): 984.37K Privately Held
Web: www.icscientificsolutions.com
SIC: 8731 3565 3479 Engineering
laboratory, except testing; Bottling and
canning machinery; Coating of metals with
silicon

(G-14309)
IIOT WORLD LLC
25985 Rustic Ln (44145-5480)
PHONE...................................440 715-0564
EMP: 7 EST: 2017
SALES (est): 429.52K Privately Held
Web: www.iiot-world.com
SIC: 2711 Newspapers: publishing only, not
printed on site

(G-14310)
IMCD US LLC (HQ)
Also Called: Hs Services
2 Equity Way Ste 210 (44145-1050)

PHONE...................................216 228-8900
Jean-paul Scheepens, *Pr*
John L Mastrantoni, *
Thomas V Valkenburg, *
Bruce D Jarosz, *
Vlad Miller, *
▲ EMP: 46 EST: 1978
SALES (est): 227.45MM Privately Held
Web: www.imcdus.com
SIC: 2834 5169 5191 Pharmaceutical
preparations; Chemicals and allied
products, nec; Chemicals, agricultural
PA: Imcd N.V.
Wilhelminaplein 32
Rotterdam ZH

(G-14311)
INNOVTIVE CNFCTION SLTIONS LLC
Also Called: Phillips Syrup
28025 Ranney Pkwy (44145-1159)
PHONE...................................440 835-8001
EMP: 7 EST: 2014
SALES (est): 943.75K Privately Held
SIC: 2087 Syrups, drink

(G-14312)
KAEDEN PUBLISHING
Also Called: Kaeden Books
24700 Center Ridge Rd Ste 170
(44145-5668)
P.O. Box 16190 (44116-0190)
PHONE...................................440 617-1400
Craig Urmston, *Pr*
Kathleen Urmston, *VP*
▲ EMP: 6 EST: 1991
SQ FT: 7,500
SALES (est): 475.02K Privately Held
Web: www.kaeden.com
SIC: 2741 Miscellaneous publishing

(G-14313)
LS STARRETT COMPANY
Webber Gage Div
24500 Detroit Rd (44145-2580)
PHONE...................................440 835-0005
EMP: 80
SQ FT: 35,000
SALES (corp-wide): 2.37B Privately Held
Web: www.starrett.com
SIC: 3545 3829 3823 Gauge blocks;
Measuring and controlling devices, nec;
Process control instruments
HQ: The L S Starrett Company
121 Crescent St
Athol MA 01331
978 249-3551

(G-14314)
MARLIN THERMOCOUPLE WIRE INC
847 Canterbury Rd (44145-1420)
PHONE...................................440 835-1950
Allen Tymkewicz, *CEO*
Vivian Coticchia, *
Andy Gehrisch, *
▲ EMP: 24 EST: 1952
SQ FT: 46,000
SALES (est): 3.98MM Privately Held
Web: www.marlintcwire.com
SIC: 3315 Wire, steel: insulated or armored

(G-14315)
MOMENTUM FLEET MGT GROUP INC
24481 Detroit Rd (44145-1580)
PHONE...................................440 759-2219
Jack Pyros, *Pr*
EMP: 56 EST: 2005
SALES (est): 2.41MM Privately Held
Web: www.momentumgroups.com
SIC: 8741 6159 3699 Management services;
Automobile finance leasing; Electrical
equipment and supplies, nec

(G-14316)
MYERS AND LASCH INC
2530 Wyndgate Ct (44145-2994)
PHONE...................................440 235-2050
Phil Puhala, *Owner*
Mike Marhefka, *VP*
EMP: 6 EST: 1962
SALES (est): 463.08K Privately Held
Web: www.myers-lasch.com
SIC: 3993 Displays and cutouts, window and
lobby

(G-14317)
NORDSON CORPORATION (PA)
Also Called: Nordson
28601 Clemens Rd (44145-1119)
PHONE...................................440 892-1580
Sundaram Nagarajan, *Pr*
Victor L Richey Junior, *Ch Bd*
Daniel R Hopgood, *Ex VP*
Jennifer L Mcdonough, *Ex VP*
James E Devries, *Ex VP*
EMP: 1314 EST: 1909
SQ FT: 20,000
SALES (est): 2.69B
SALES (corp-wide): 2.69B Publicly Held
Web: www.nordson.com
SIC: 3563 Spraying outfits: metals, paints,
and chemicals (compressor)

(G-14318)
NORDSON MEDICAL CORPORATION
28601 Clemens Rd (44145-1119)
PHONE...................................440 892-1580
Michael F Hilton, *Pr*
EMP: 75 EST: 2010
SALES (est): 4.93MM
SALES (corp-wide): 2.69B Publicly Held
Web: www.nordson.com
SIC: 3563 Air and gas compressors
PA: Nordson Corporation
28601 Clemens Rd
Westlake OH 44145
440 892-1580

(G-14319)
PAPYRUS-RECYCLED GREETINGS INC
1 American Blvd (44145-8151)
PHONE...................................773 348-6410
Leonard Levine, *CFO*
Philip Friedmann, *VP*
Michael Keiser, *VP*
▲ EMP: 56 EST: 1972
SALES (est): 2.15MM
SALES (corp-wide): 14.54B Privately Held
Web:
aggreetingsgateway.amgreetings.com
SIC: 2771 5199 Greeting cards; Gifts and
novelties
HQ: American Greetings Corporation
1 American Blvd
Cleveland OH 44145
216 252-7300

(G-14320)
PARTY ANIMAL INC
909 Crocker Rd (44145-1030)
PHONE...................................440 471-1030
Bryan Cantrall, *Pr*
Bryan Cantrall, *CEO*
Phyllis Cantrall, *VP*
▲ EMP: 15 EST: 1989
SQ FT: 3,800
SALES (est): 11.03MM Privately Held
Web: www.partyanimalinc.com
SIC: 2399 5092 Banners, made from fabric;
Toys and games

(G-14321)
PDQ PRINTING SERVICE
29003 Brockway Dr (44145-5212)
PHONE...................................216 241-5443
Dorry Smotzer, *Owner*
EMP: 10 EST: 1963
SALES (est): 423.06K Privately Held
Web: www.pdqprintingandlabel.com
SIC: 2752 Offset printing

(G-14322)
PENGUIN ENTERPRISES INC
Also Called: PS Copy
869 Canterbury Rd Ste 2 (44145-1492)
PHONE...................................440 899-5112
Jim Seman, *Pr*
EMP: 35 EST: 1984
SALES (est): 2.15MM Privately Held
SIC: 2796 2791 2789 2759 Platemaking
services; Typesetting; Bookbinding and
related work; Commercial printing, nec

(G-14323)
PHILLIPS SYRUP LLC
28025 Ranney Pkwy (44145-1159)
PHONE...................................440 835-8001
Jim Kanner, *Managing Member*
EMP: 17 EST: 2003
SALES (est): 4.55MM Privately Held
Web: www.phillipssyrup.com
SIC: 2087 Flavoring extracts and syrups, nec

(G-14324)
PINES MANUFACTURING INC (PA)
Also Called: Pines Technology
29100 Lakeland Blvd (44145)
PHONE...................................440 835-5553
Ian Williamson, *Pr*
Donald Rebar, *Ch Bd*
▲ EMP: 45 EST: 1993
SQ FT: 48,000
SALES (est): 3.19MM Privately Held
Web: www.pines-eng.com
SIC: 5084 3542 3549 3547 Industrial
machinery and equipment; Bending
machines; Metalworking machinery, nec;
Rolling mill machinery

(G-14325)
Q-LAB CORPORATION (PA)
Also Called: Q-Lab
800 Canterbury Rd (44145-1419)
PHONE...................................440 835-8700
Douglas M Grossman, *Pr*
Gary Simecek, *
Ron Roberts, *
Brad Reis, *
Kirk Wilhelm, *
▲ EMP: 53 EST: 1964
SQ FT: 150,000
SALES (est): 31.35MM
SALES (corp-wide): 31.35MM Privately
Held
Web: www.q-lab.com
SIC: 3823 3829 3826 Process control
instruments; Measuring and controlling
devices, nec; Analytical instruments

(G-14326)
R AND J CORPORATION
Also Called: Haynes Manufacturing Company
24142 Detroit Rd (44145-1515)
PHONE...................................440 871-6009
Beth Kloos, *Pr*
Timothy Kloos, *VP*
EMP: 42 EST: 1902
SQ FT: 23,000
SALES (est): 9.47MM Privately Held
Web: www.haynesmfg.com

▲ = Import ▼ = Export
◆ = Import/Export

SIC: 3556 5084 7389 3053 Food products machinery; Food industry machinery; Design, commercial and industrial; Gaskets; packing and sealing devices

(G-14327)
RECTOR INC
Also Called: Profiles In Diversity Journal
1991 Crocker Rd Ste 320 (44145-6971)
P.O. Box 45605 (44145-0605)
PHONE...............................440 892-0444
Jim Rector, *Pr*
EMP: 7 **EST:** 1991
SQ FT: 1,000
SALES (est) 239.65K **Privately Held**
Web: www.diversityjournal.com
SIC: 2721 Magazines: publishing only, not printed on site

(G-14328)
RISK INDUSTRIES LLC
Also Called: Pines Technology
30505 Clemens Rd (44145-1000)
PHONE...............................440 835-5553
EMP: 70
Web: www.pines-eng.com
SIC: 3542 Machine tools, metal forming type

(G-14329)
S J T ENTERPRISES INC
28045 Ranney Pkwy Ste B (44145-1144)
PHONE...............................440 617-1100
Timothy J Smith, *Pr*
▲ **EMP:** 22 **EST:** 1985
SQ FT: 17,000
SALES (est): 2.43MM **Privately Held**
Web: www.sjtent.com
SIC: 2741 Miscellaneous publishing

(G-14330)
SANGRAF INTERNATIONAL INC
159 Crocker Park Blvd Ste 100
(44145-8137)
PHONE...............................216 543-3288
Xiu Qin Hou, *Prin*
▲ **EMP:** 6 **EST:** 2012
SALES (est): 3.57MM **Privately Held**
Web: www.sangrafintl.com
SIC: 3624 Electrodes, thermal and electrolytic uses: carbon, graphite
HQ: Henan Sanli Carbon Products Co., Ltd.
North Side Of Xiaotun Village, Baiquan Town, Xijiao Development
Xinxiang HA 45363

(G-14331)
SARASOTA QUALITY PRODUCTS
27330 Center Ridge Rd (44145-3957)
PHONE...............................440 899-9820
James Schilens, *Pr*
▲ **EMP:** 8 **EST:** 1991
SALES (est): 345.2K **Privately Held**
Web: www.sarasotaqp.com
SIC: 3429 Hardware, nec

(G-14332)
SEST INC
24509 Annie Ln (44145-4144)
PHONE...............................440 777-9777
Ashwin Shah, *Pr*
EMP: 10 **EST:** 1997
SQ FT: 1,000
SALES (est): 474.81K **Privately Held**
Web: www.sestinc.com
SIC: 8711 7373 7372 7371 Consulting engineer; Computer-aided engineering (CAE) systems service; Application computer software; Computer software development and applications

(G-14333)
SHAMROCK COMPANIES INC (PA)
Also Called: Shamrock Acquisition Company
24090 Detroit Rd (44145-1513)
P.O. Box 450980 (44145-0623)
PHONE...............................440 899-9510
Tim Connor, *CEO*
Gary A Lesjak, *
Dave Fechter, *
▲ **EMP:** 65 **EST:** 1982
SQ FT: 42,500
SALES (est): 87.67MM **Privately Held**
Web: www.shamrockcompanies.net
SIC: 5112 5199 7336 7389 Business forms; Advertising specialties; Art design services; Brokers' services

(G-14334)
SHELBY COMPANY
865 Canterbury Rd (44145-1496)
PHONE...............................440 871-9901
Richard J Rapacz, *Pr*
EMP: 33 **EST:** 1923
SQ FT: 50,000
SALES (est): 6.66MM **Privately Held**
Web: www.shelbycompany.com
SIC: 2657 2653 Folding paperboard boxes; Display items, corrugated: made from purchased materials

(G-14335)
SPECTRE SENSORS INC
2392 Georgia Dr (44145-5806)
PHONE...............................440 250-0372
Glen Keller, *Ch Bd*
John Keller, *Pr*
EMP: 9 **EST:** 2002
SALES (est): 469.52K **Privately Held**
Web: www.spectresensors.com
SIC: 3612 Electronic meter transformers

(G-14336)
STAR METAL PRODUCTS CO INC
30405 Clemens Rd (44145-1018)
PHONE...............................440 899-7000
John C Murray, *CEO*
Eleanor V Murray, *
Arthur Stenzel, *
Mary C Reidy, *
Rita A Dunham, *
EMP: 110 **EST:** 1958
SQ FT: 24,000
SALES (est): 4.97MM **Privately Held**
Web: www.starmetalproducts.com
SIC: 3599 Machine shop, jobbing and repair

(G-14337)
STRUERS INC (DH)
24766 Detroit Rd (44145-2525)
PHONE...............................440 871-0071
Bente Freiberg, *Pr*
Christopher Sopko, *
Steen Jensen, *
◆ **EMP:** 58 **EST:** 1875
SALES (est): 6.66MM **Privately Held**
Web: www.struers.com
SIC: 3829 Measuring and controlling devices, nec
HQ: Struers Aps
Pederstrupvej 84
Ballerup 2750
44600800

(G-14338)
SURILI COUTURE LLC
29961 Persimmon Dr (44145-5103)
PHONE...............................440 600-1456
EMP: 14 **EST:** 2016
SALES (est): 2.67MM **Privately Held**
Web: www.surilicouture.com

SIC: 2335 Bridal and formal gowns

(G-14339)
THERM-ALL INC (PA)
Also Called: Therm-All
830 Canterbury Rd Ste A (44145-1403)
PHONE...............................440 779-9494
Robert Smigel, *Pr*
Ann Sliwa, *Prin*
Dennis Kaczmarek, *VP*
Linda Smigel, *Sec*
Richard Sobiech, *CFO*
EMP: 20 **EST:** 1981
SQ FT: 56,000
SALES (est): 17.78MM
SALES (corp-wide): 17.78MM **Privately Held**
Web: www.therm-all.com
SIC: 3211 Building glass, flat

(G-14340)
TLC PRODUCTS INC
Also Called: TLC Products
26100 1st St (44145-1478)
P.O. Box 45301 (44145-0301)
PHONE...............................216 472-3030
John Wong, *CEO*
▲ **EMP:** 10 **EST:** 1996
SALES (est): 886.94K **Privately Held**
Web: www.tlc-products.com
SIC: 3999 2879 Barber and beauty shop equipment; Agricultural chemicals, nec

(G-14341)
TOLI VAULT
2035 Crocker Rd Ste 103 (44145-1996)
PHONE...............................866 998-8654
Matt Pfleging, *Prin*
EMP: 7 **EST:** 2012
SALES (est): 138.99K **Privately Held**
SIC: 3272 Burial vaults, concrete or precast terrazzo

(G-14342)
VISION GRAPHIX INC
Also Called: AlphaGraphics Westlake
29275 Clemens Rd (44145-1002)
PHONE...............................440 835-6540
Jeff Brant, *Pr*
Jeff Brant Junior, *Pr*
EMP: 6 **EST:** 1992
SQ FT: 4,000
SALES (est): 1.04MM **Privately Held**
Web: www.alphagraphics.com
SIC: 2752 3993 Commercial printing, lithographic; Advertising artwork

(G-14343)
WESTERN/SCOTT FETZER COMPANY (HQ)
28800 Clemens Rd (44145-1134)
PHONE...............................440 892-3000
Kenneth Semelsberger, *Ch Bd*
Robert D Mcbride, *Pr*
John Gretta, *Treas*
◆ **EMP:** 45 **EST:** 1985
SALES (est): 42.39MM
SALES (corp-wide): 226 **Privately Held**
Web: www.westernenterpises.com
SIC: 2813 Oxygen, compressed or liquefied
PA: The Scott Fetzer Company
28800 Clemens Rd
Westlake OH 44145
440 892-3000

(G-14344)
WESTERN/SCOTT FETZER COMPANY
Also Called: Western Enterprises
875 Bassett Rd (44145-1142)

PHONE...............................440 871-2160
Gary Heeman, *Brnch Mgr*
EMP: 250
SALES (corp-wide): 226 **Privately Held**
Web: www.westernenterprises.com
SIC: 3635 Household vacuum cleaners
HQ: Western/Scott Fetzer Company
28800 Clemens Rd
Westlake OH 44145

(G-14345)
WESTSHORE METAL FINISHING LLC
26891 Kenley Ct (44145-1456)
PHONE...............................440 892-0774
Richard J Holton, *Prin*
EMP: 6 **EST:** 2010
SALES (est): 112.26K **Privately Held**
SIC: 3471 Cleaning, polishing, and finishing

(G-14346)
WORLD BOOK COMPANY
Also Called: World Book/Scott Fetzer Co
28800 Clemens Rd (44145-1134)
PHONE...............................440 892-3000
Robert Mcbride, *CEO*
William Stephans, *
Trish Scanlon, *
John Gretta, *
EMP: 4904 **EST:** 1985
SQ FT: 2,000
SALES (est): 998.51K
SALES (corp-wide): 424.23B **Publicly Held**
Web: www.scottfetzer.com
SIC: 2731 2741 5961 Textbooks: publishing only, not printed on site; Atlases: publishing only, not printed on site; Books, mail order (except book clubs)
HQ: Bhsf Inc.
1440 Kiewit Plz
Omaha NE 68131

Weston
Wood County

(G-14347)
CRESSET CHEMICAL CO INC (PA)
13255 Main St (43569-9544)
P.O. Box 367 (43569-0367)
PHONE...............................419 669-2041
George F Baty, *Ch Bd*
Mike Baty, *Pr*
▼ **EMP:** 10 **EST:** 1946
SQ FT: 2,000
SALES (est): 5.57MM
SALES (corp-wide): 5.57MM **Privately Held**
Web: www.cresset.com
SIC: 2899 2841 Chemical preparations, nec; Soap and other detergents

(G-14348)
CRESSET CHEMICAL CO INC
13490 Silver St (43569-9522)
PHONE...............................419 669-2041
George Baty, *Mgr*
EMP: 10
SALES (corp-wide): 5.57MM **Privately Held**
Web: www.cresset.com
SIC: 2899 Chemical preparations, nec
PA: Cresset Chemical Co Inc
13255 Main St
Weston OH 43569
419 669-2041

(G-14349)
MCM PRECISION CASTINGS INC
13133 Beech St (43569-9516)

PHONE..............................419 669-3226
Donald Marion, *Pr*
EMP: 20 **EST:** 1992
SQ FT: 7,896
SALES (est): 4.29MM **Privately Held**
Web: www.mcmprecision.com
SIC: 3369 Castings, except die-castings, precision

(G-14350)
VITAKRAFT SUN SEED INC
20584 Long Judson Rd (43569-9639)
P.O. Box 33 (43402-0033)
PHONE..............................419 832-1641
Brent Weinmann, *Pr*
▲ **EMP:** 60 **EST:** 2001
SQ FT: 50,000
SALES (est): 14.33MM **Privately Held**
Web: www.vitakraftsunseed.com
SIC: 2048 2047 Bird food, prepared; Dog and cat food

Wharton
Wyandot County

(G-14351)
MENNEL MILLING COMPANY
Also Called: Wharton Grain
110 Railroad St (43359)
PHONE..............................419 458-3041
Larry Hawkins, *Mgr*
EMP: 8
SALES (corp-wide): 211.12MM **Privately Held**
Web: www.mennel.com
SIC: 2041 2048 Flour; Prepared feeds, nec
PA: The Mennel Milling Company
319 S Vine St
Fostoria OH 44830
419 435-8151

Wheelersburg
Scioto County

(G-14352)
CONNIES CANDLES
9103 Ohio River Rd (45694-1927)
P.O. Box 97 (45694-0097)
PHONE..............................740 574-1224
Connie Potters, *Owner*
EMP: 6 **EST:** 1997
SALES (est): 134.99K **Privately Held**
Web: www.conniescandles.com
SIC: 3999 Candles

(G-14353)
GREG BLUME
Also Called: Trophy's Unlimited
7459 Ohio River Rd (45694)
P.O. Box 388 (45694-0388)
PHONE..............................740 574-2308
Greg Blume, *Owner*
EMP: 6 **EST:** 1987
SALES (est): 94.6K **Privately Held**
SIC: 5999 2791 2789 2752 Trophies and plaques; Typesetting; Bookbinding and related work; Offset printing

(G-14354)
TRI-AMERICA CONTRACTORS INC (PA)
1664 State Route 522 (45694-7828)
PHONE..............................740 574-0148
Scott Taylor, *Pr*
Teresa Smith, *
EMP: 37 **EST:** 1997
SQ FT: 34,000
SALES (est): 9.42MM

SALES (corp-wide): 9.42MM **Privately Held**
Web: www.triaminc.com
SIC: 3498 3441 1629 Fabricated pipe and fittings; Fabricated structural metal; Industrial plant construction

(G-14355)
TRI-AMERICA CONTRACTORS INC
Also Called: Tri-America Contractors
1664 State Route 522 (45694-7828)
PHONE..............................740 574-0148
Teresa Smith, *Brnch Mgr*
EMP: 14
SALES (corp-wide): 9.42MM **Privately Held**
Web: www.triaminc.com
SIC: 3498 Fabricated pipe and fittings
PA: Tri-America Contractors, Inc.
1664 State Route 522
Wheelersburg OH 45694
740 574-0148

Whipple
Washington County

(G-14356)
FULL CIRCLE OIL FIELD SVCS INC
7585 State Route 821 (45788-5164)
PHONE..............................740 371-5422
Mitch Fouss, *Prin*
Danny Warren, *Prin*
Renee Warren, *Prin*
EMP: 8 **EST:** 2011
SALES (est): 2.11MM **Privately Held**
Web: www.fcofs.com
SIC: 1389 Oil field services, nec

Whitehouse
Lucas County

(G-14357)
BASF CORPORATION
Coatings & Colorants Division
6125 Industrial Pkwy (43571-9595)
P.O. Box 2757 (43571-0757)
PHONE..............................419 877-5308
Kenneth Terry, *Dir*
EMP: 136
SQ FT: 20,000
SALES (corp-wide): 69.01B **Privately Held**
Web: www.basf.com
SIC: 2869 Industrial organic chemicals, nec
HQ: Basf Corporation
100 Park Ave
Florham Park NJ 07932
800 962-7831

(G-14358)
BITTERSWEET INC (PA)
Also Called: BITTERSWEET FARMS
12660 Archbold Whitehouse Rd (43571-9534)
PHONE..............................419 875-6986
Vicki Obee-hilty, *Ex Dir*
EMP: 70 **EST:** 1977
SQ FT: 20,000
SALES (est): 7.93MM
SALES (corp-wide): 7.93MM **Privately Held**
Web: www.bittersweetfarms.org
SIC: 8361 2032 8052 Mentally handicapped home; Canned specialties; Intermediate care facilities

(G-14359)
DEWESOFT LLC
Also Called: Dewesoft

10730 Logan St (43571-9697)
PHONE..............................855 339-3669
Andrew Nowicki, *CEO*
EMP: 60 **EST:** 2012
SALES (est): 13.94MM **Privately Held**
Web: www.dewesoft.com
SIC: 7373 3825 Systems software development services; Instruments to measure electricity
HQ: Dewesoft D.O.O.
Gabrsko 11a
Trbovlje 1420

(G-14360)
GENERAL INTL PWR PDTS LLC
6243 Industrial Pkwy (43571-9594)
PHONE..............................419 877-5234
Craig Valentine, *Pr*
EMP: 26 **EST:** 2014
SALES (est): 3.91MM
SALES (corp-wide): 7.04MM **Privately Held**
Web: www.gipowerproducts.com
SIC: 3553 Woodworking machinery
PA: Dmt Holdings, Inc.
1201 Pacific Ave Ste 600
Tacoma WA 98402
253 545-0015

(G-14361)
GL HELLER CO INC
6246 Industrial Pkwy (43571-9594)
PHONE..............................419 877-5122
Gary Lee Heller, *Pr*
M Jean Heller, *Sec*
EMP: 14 **EST:** 1972
SQ FT: 17,000
SALES (est): 1.03MM **Privately Held**
Web: www.glheller.com
SIC: 3599 Machine shop, jobbing and repair

(G-14362)
KWD AUTOMOTIVE INC
Also Called: Catstrap
6700 Cemetery Rd (43571-9014)
PHONE..............................419 344-8232
Thomas J Birsen, *Pr*
EMP: 6 **EST:** 2015
SALES (est): 998.08K **Privately Held**
Web: www.catstrap.net
SIC: 3714 Motor vehicle parts and accessories

(G-14363)
PROHOS INC
10755 Logan St (43571-9698)
PHONE..............................419 877-0153
William A Green, *Pr*
Joan Green, *Sec*
Kevin Green, *VP*
EMP: 9 **EST:** 1983
SQ FT: 18,000
SALES (est): 2.13MM **Privately Held**
Web: www.prohos-inc.com
SIC: 3599 Machine shop, jobbing and repair

(G-14364)
PROHOS MANUFACTURING CO INC
10755 Logan St (43571-9698)
PHONE..............................419 877-0153
William Green, *Pr*
Joan Green, *Sec*
EMP: 8 **EST:** 1983
SQ FT: 18,000
SALES (est): 371.44K **Privately Held**
Web: www.prohos-inc.com
SIC: 3599 Machine shop, jobbing and repair

Wickliffe
Lake County

(G-14365)
ALL POINTS PRINTING INC
1330 Lloyd Rd (44092-2318)
PHONE..............................440 585-1125
Allen R Paden, *Pr*
Alan J Weber, *VP*
Catherine Weber, *Sec*
Louise Paden, *Treas*
EMP: 6 **EST:** 1954
SQ FT: 3,500
SALES (est): 86.31K **Privately Held**
SIC: 2759 2752 Letterpress printing; Offset printing

(G-14366)
AMERICAN CONTROLS INC
1340 Lloyd Rd (44092-2381)
PHONE..............................440 944-9735
▲ **EMP:** 20
Web: www.american-controls.com
SIC: 3613 8711 Control panels, electric; Electrical or electronic engineering

(G-14367)
BAR PROCESSING CORPORATION
1271 E 289th St (44092-2358)
PHONE..............................440 943-0094
Fritz Michalk, *Mgr*
EMP: 10
SALES (corp-wide): 20.62MM **Privately Held**
Web: www.barprocessingcorp.com
SIC: 3443 Process vessels, industrial: metal plate
HQ: Bar Processing Corporation
26601 W Huron River Dr
Flat Rock MI 48134
734 782-4454

(G-14368)
BREWER COMPANY
30060 Lakeland Blvd (44092-1745)
PHONE..............................440 944-3800
S Choromanski, *Genl Mgr*
EMP: 8
SQ FT: 73,188
SALES (corp-wide): 12.34MM **Privately Held**
Web: www.thebrewerco.com
SIC: 2952 Coating compounds, tar
PA: The Brewer Company
25 Whitney Dr Ste 104
Milford OH 45150
800 394-0017

(G-14369)
CHEMTOOL INCORPORATED (DH)
Also Called: Tenaxoltechnologies
29400 Lakeland Blvd (44092-2201)
PHONE..............................815 957-4140
Charles Robinson, *Pr*
◆ **EMP:** 125 **EST:** 1963
SALES (est): 22.36MM
SALES (corp-wide): 424.23B **Publicly Held**
Web: www.lubrizol.com
SIC: 2899 2842 2841 2992 Rust resisting compounds; Polishes and sanitation goods; Soap and other detergents; Cutting oils, blending: made from purchased materials
HQ: The Lubrizol Corporation
29400 Lakeland Blvd
Wickliffe OH 44092
440 943-4200

(G-14370)
CJ SALT WORLD
29149 Euclid Ave (44092-2467)
PHONE..............................440 343-5661
Clayton Williams, *Prin*
EMP: 8 **EST:** 2013
SALES (est): 132.94K **Privately Held**
SIC: 2899 Salt

(G-14371)
CLEVELAND SPECIAL TOOL INC
1351 E 286th St (44092-2505)
PHONE..............................440 944-1600
Jim Treblas, *Pr*
EMP: 10 **EST:** 1966
SQ FT: 6,000
SALES (est): 2.26MM **Privately Held**
SIC: 3599 Machine shop, jobbing and repair

(G-14372)
CP CHEMICALS GROUP LP
Also Called: CP Trading Group
28960 Lakeland Blvd (44092-2370)
PHONE..............................440 833-3000
Joseph Patrick Iii, *Pr*
EMP: 6 **EST:** 2009
SALES (est): 382.59K **Privately Held**
Web: www.cpchemicalsgroup.com
SIC: 2899 Chemical preparations, nec

(G-14373)
CUSTOM CYCLE ACC MFG DSTRG INC
29110 Anderson Rd (44092-2395)
PHONE..............................440 585-2200
Elizabeth Huntington, *Pr*
Rose Marie Parker, *VP*
EMP: 15 **EST:** 1954
SQ FT: 22,000
SALES (est): 338.26K **Privately Held**
SIC: 3751 Motorcycle accessories

(G-14374)
DSM INDUSTRIES INC
1340 E 289th St (44092-2304)
PHONE..............................440 585-1100
Scott Soble, *Pr*
▲ **EMP:** 16 **EST:** 1944
SQ FT: 106,000
SALES (est): 2.32MM **Privately Held**
Web: www.diamondshine.com
SIC: 2841 Soap: granulated, liquid, cake, flaked, or chip

(G-14375)
EUCLID SPRING CO
30006 Lakeland Blvd (44092-1745)
PHONE..............................440 943-3213
James L Marsey, *Pr*
James L Marsey, *Prin*
William J Marsey, *VP*
EMP: 22 **EST:** 1950
SQ FT: 7,000
SALES (est): 2.34MM **Privately Held**
Web: www.euclidspring.com
SIC: 3495 Wire springs

(G-14376)
GREAT LAKES CRUSHING LTD
30831 Euclid Ave (44092-1042)
PHONE..............................440 944-5500
Mark M Belich, *Managing Member*
Mark M Belich, *Genl Pt*
EMP: 60 **EST:** 1996
SQ FT: 10,000
SALES (est): 8.63MM **Privately Held**
Web: www.glcrushing.com

SIC: 7359 1623 1629 1611 Equipment rental and leasing, nec; Underground utilities contractor; Land clearing contractor; Grading

(G-14377)
HAWTHORNE TOOL LLC
1340 Lloyd Rd Ste C (44092-2381)
PHONE..............................440 516-1891
Dominic Rega, *Pr*
EMP: 10 **EST:** 2004
SALES (est): 319.45K **Privately Held**
SIC: 3544 Dies and die holders for metal cutting, forming, die casting

(G-14378)
HI TECMETAL GROUP INC (PA)
Also Called: Hydro-Vac
28910 Lakeland Blvd (44092-2321)
PHONE..............................216 881-8100
Terence Profughi, *Pr*
Cole Coe, *VP*
Gregory Hercil, *VP*
Harold Baron, *Prin*
Mary Finley, *Prin*
EMP: 20 **EST:** 1943
SALES (est): 9.44MM
SALES (corp-wide): 9.44MM **Privately Held**
Web: www.htgmetals.com
SIC: 3398 7692 Brazing (hardening) of metal ; Welding repair

(G-14379)
KERRY INC
29136 Norman Ave (44092-2341)
PHONE..............................440 229-5200
EMP: 21
Web: www.kerry.com
SIC: 2099 Food preparations, nec
HQ: Kerry Inc.
3400 Millington Rd
Beloit WI 53511
608 363-1200

(G-14380)
LINDE GAS & EQUIPMENT INC
Also Called: Praxair
1140 Lloyd Rd (44092-2314)
PHONE..............................440 944-8844
Don Mocarski, *Mgr*
EMP: 6
Web: www.lindeus.com
SIC: 2813 Industrial gases
HQ: Linde Gas & Equipment Inc.
10 Riverview Dr
Danbury CT 06810
844 445-4633

(G-14381)
LUBRIZOL HOLDINGS LLC
29400 Lakeland Blvd (44092-2201)
PHONE..............................440 943-4200
EMP: 10 **EST:** 2015
SALES (est): 6.08MM
SALES (corp-wide): 424.23B **Publicly Held**
Web: www.lubrizol.com
SIC: 2899 Chemical preparations, nec
HQ: The Lubrizol Corporation
29400 Lakeland Blvd
Wickliffe OH 44092
440 943-4200

(G-14382)
MATTEO ALUMINUM INC
1261 E 289th St (44092-2367)
PHONE..............................440 585-5213
Steve Matteo, *Pr*
EMP: 20 **EST:** 1984
SQ FT: 25,444

SALES (est): 2.22MM **Privately Held**
Web: www.matteoaluminum.com
SIC: 3444 3449 Gutters, sheet metal; Miscellaneous metalwork

(G-14383)
MULTI LAPPING SERVICE INC
30032 Lakeland Blvd (44092-1745)
PHONE..............................440 944-7592
Donna Wohr, *Pr*
Michael Adkins, *VP*
Enos Adkins Iii, *VP*
EMP: 6 **EST:** 1972
SQ FT: 72,000
SALES (est): 2.37MM **Privately Held**
SIC: 3829 Whole body counters, nuclear

(G-14384)
NOVEON FCC INC
29400 Lakeland Blvd (44092-2201)
PHONE..............................440 943-4200
Charles P Cooley Iii, *Sr VP*
▼ **EMP:** 13 **EST:** 1992
SALES (est): 6.95MM
SALES (corp-wide): 424.23B **Publicly Held**
SIC: 2869 2899 Industrial organic chemicals, nec; Chemical preparations, nec
HQ: The Lubrizol Corporation
29400 Lakeland Blvd
Wickliffe OH 44092
440 943-4200

(G-14385)
OHIO MOULDING CORPORATION (HQ)
30396 Lakeland Blvd (44092-1798)
PHONE..............................440 944-2100
▲ **EMP:** 20 **EST:** 1946
SALES (est): 42.47MM **Privately Held**
Web: www.omcoform.com
SIC: 3449 Miscellaneous metalwork
PA: Omco Holdings, Inc.
30396 Lakeland Blvd
Wickliffe OH 44092

(G-14386)
OMCO HOLDINGS INC (PA)
30396 Lakeland Blvd (44092-1798)
PHONE..............................440 944-2100
Ben Yorks, *Ch Bd*
Gary Schuster, *Pr*
Floyd Trouten, *Sec*
Clint Cassese, *Treas*
EMP: 38 **EST:** 2000
SALES (est): 45.54MM **Privately Held**
Web: www.omcoform.com
SIC: 3441 Fabricated structural metal

(G-14387)
P O MCINTIRE COMPANY (PA)
29191 Anderson Rd (44092-2357)
PHONE..............................440 269-1848
James Goglin, *Pr*
Scott Goglin, *
EMP: 27 **EST:** 1938
SQ FT: 12,000
SALES (est): 2.04MM
SALES (corp-wide): 2.04MM **Privately Held**
Web: www.pomcintire.com
SIC: 3545 3544 Cutting tools for machine tools; Jigs and fixtures

(G-14388)
PARKER-HANNIFIN CORPORATION
IHP Division
30240 Lakeland Blvd (44092-1797)
PHONE..............................704 637-1190
Terry Mcgee, *Brnch Mgr*
EMP: 8

SALES (corp-wide): 19.93B **Publicly Held**
Web: www.parker.com
SIC: 3052 3429 Rubber hose; Hardware, nec
PA: Parker-Hannifin Corporation
6035 Parkland Blvd
Cleveland OH 44124
216 896-3000

(G-14389)
PARKER-HANNIFIN CORPORATION
Hose Products Div
30240 Lakeland Blvd (44092-1797)
PHONE..............................440 943-5700
Lonnie Gallup, *Brnch Mgr*
EMP: 271
SQ FT: 145,000
SALES (corp-wide): 19.93B **Publicly Held**
Web: www.parker.com
SIC: 3714 3492 Motor vehicle parts and accessories; Fluid power valves and hose fittings
PA: Parker-Hannifin Corporation
6035 Parkland Blvd
Cleveland OH 44124
216 896-3000

(G-14390)
PCC CERAMIC GROUP 1
1470 E 289th St (44092-2306)
PHONE..............................440 516-3672
Daren Kennedy, *VP*
EMP: 9 **EST:** 2007
SALES (est): 549.59K **Privately Held**
Web: www.pccairfoils.com
SIC: 3253 Floor tile, ceramic

(G-14391)
PMC INDUSTRIES CORP
Also Called: A Park Ohio Company
29100 Lakeland Blvd (44092-2323)
PHONE..............................440 943-3300
Edward K Novak, *VP*
▲ **EMP:** 85 **EST:** 1912
SQ FT: 125,000
SALES (est): 5.69MM
SALES (corp-wide): 1.66B **Publicly Held**
Web: www.pmc-colinet.com
SIC: 3317 Steel pipe and tubes
HQ: Park-Ohio Industries, Inc.
6065 Parkland Blvd
Cleveland OH 44124
440 947-2000

(G-14392)
PRECISION MCHNING CNNCTION LLC
Also Called: P M C
29100 Lakeland Blvd (44092-2323)
PHONE..............................440 943-3300
EMP: 10 **EST:** 1999
SALES (est): 2.19MM
SALES (corp-wide): 1.66B **Publicly Held**
SIC: 3494 Valves and pipe fittings, nec
PA: Park-Ohio Holdings Corp.
6065 Parkland Blvd
Cleveland OH 44124
440 947-2000

(G-14393)
REGAL DIAMOND PRODUCTS CORP
1405 E 286th St (44092-2506)
P.O. Box 198 (44092-0198)
PHONE..............................440 944-7700
Steve Brewer, *Pr*
▼ **EMP:** 15 **EST:** 1958
SQ FT: 16,500
SALES (est): 2.45MM **Privately Held**
Web: www.regaldiamond.com

SIC: 3291 3545 3425 Abrasive wheels and grindstones, not artificial; Cutting tools for machine tools; Saw blades and handsaws

(G-14394)
RESEARCH ABRASIVE PRODUCTS INC
1400 E 286th St (44092-2507)
PHONE...........................440 944-3200
Ken Dixon Senior, *Pr*
Ken Dixon Junior, *VP*
Margaret Tripp, *
EMP: 40 **EST:** 1971
SQ FT: 32,000
SALES (est): 2.7MM **Privately Held**
Web: www.researchabrasive.com
SIC: 3291 Wheels, abrasive

(G-14395)
THE LUBRIZOL CORPORATION (HQ)
Also Called: Lubricant Additives
29400 Lakeland Blvd (44092-2298)
PHONE...........................440 943-4200
Rebecca Liebert, *CEO*
Deb Langer, *
Jason Sussman, *CLO*
◆ **EMP:** 1300 **EST:** 1928
SALES (est): 833.21MM
SALES (corp-wide): 424.23B **Publicly Held**
Web: www.lubrizol.com
SIC: 2899 2869 Oil treating compounds; Industrial organic chemicals, nec
PA: Berkshire Hathaway Inc.
   3555 Farnam St Ste 1440
   Omaha NE 68131
   402 346-1400

(G-14396)
THERMAL TREATMENT CENTER INC (HQ)
Also Called: Nettleton Steel Treating Div
28910 Lakeland Blvd (44092-2321)
PHONE...........................216 881-8100
Carmen Paponitti, *Pr*
Jack Luck, *
Louise Profughi, *
EMP: 35 **EST:** 1945
SALES (est): 2.49MM
SALES (corp-wide): 9.44MM **Privately Held**
Web: www.htgmetals.com
SIC: 3398 8711 Metal heat treating; Engineering services
PA: Hi Tecmetal Group, Inc.
   28910 Lakeland Blvd
   Wickliffe OH 44092
   216 881-8100

(G-14397)
TRULINE INDUSTRIES INC
1400 Silver St (44092-1944)
P.O. Box 227 (44092-0227)
PHONE...........................440 729-0140
Court Durkalski, *CEO*
Frank Durkalski, *
Stuart Watson, *
Joan Durkalski, *
EMP: 52 **EST:** 1939
SQ FT: 24,000
SALES (est): 9.55MM **Privately Held**
Web: www.trulineind.com
SIC: 3728 Aircraft parts and equipment, nec

(G-14398)
UNITED HYDRAULICS
29627 Lakeland Blvd (44092-2203)
P.O. Box 17 (44092-0017)
PHONE...........................440 585-0906
John Birkic, *Pr*
EMP: 6 **EST:** 2002

SALES (est): 507.85K **Privately Held**
Web: www.unitedhyd.com
SIC: 3593 5084 Fluid power cylinders, hydraulic or pneumatic; Industrial machinery and equipment

(G-14399)
UNIVERSAL METAL PRODUCTS INC (PA)
Also Called: Hercules
29980 Lakeland Blvd (44092-1744)
P.O. Box 130 (44092-0130)
PHONE...........................440 943-3040
Hugh S Seaholm, *CEO*
▲ **EMP:** 140 **EST:** 1946
SQ FT: 15,000
SALES (est): 23.57MM
SALES (corp-wide): 23.57MM **Privately Held**
Web: www.universalmetalproducts.com
SIC: 3469 Stamping metal for the trade

(G-14400)
USM PRECISION PRODUCTS INC
Also Called: U S M
1340 Lloyd Rd Ste D (44092-2381)
PHONE...........................440 975-8600
EMP: 100
SIC: 3451 Screw machine products

Willard
Huron County

(G-14401)
CAROLS ULTRA STITCH & VARIETY
122 S Myrtle Ave (44890-1425)
PHONE...........................419 935-8991
Carol Barnett, *Owner*
EMP: 8 **EST:** 1980
SQ FT: 4,000
SALES (est): 220.43K **Privately Held**
Web: www.carolsultrastitch.com
SIC: 5699 2395 Customized clothing and apparel; Embroidery products, except Schiffli machine

(G-14402)
GUARDIAN MANUFACTURING CO LLC
Also Called: Guardian Gloves
302 S Conwell Ave (44890-9525)
PHONE...........................419 933-2711
Gene Lamoreaux, *Pr*
Ron Vanderpool, *
▲ **EMP:** 25 **EST:** 1993
SQ FT: 100,000
SALES (est): 4.92MM **Privately Held**
Web: www.guardian-mfg.com
SIC: 3069 3842 Medical and laboratory rubber sundries and related products; Surgical appliances and supplies

(G-14403)
LSC COMMUNICATIONS INC
Also Called: Manufacturing Division
1145 S Conwell Ave (44890-9392)
PHONE...........................419 935-0111
Robert Gospodarek, *Mgr*
EMP: 980
SALES (corp-wide): 8.23B **Privately Held**
Web: www.lsccom.com
SIC: 2741 2732 2759 2752 Directories, nec: publishing and printing; Books, printing only ; Commercial printing, nec; Commercial printing, lithographic
HQ: Lsc Communications, Inc.
   4101 Winfield Rd
   Warrenville IL 60555
   844 572-5720

(G-14404)
MCDONALDS
207 E Walton St (44890-9103)
PHONE...........................419 935-1414
EMP: 17 **EST:** 2020
SALES (est): 105.63K **Privately Held**
Web: www.mcdonalds.com
SIC: 5813 5812 5499 2038 Drinking places; Eating places; Miscellaneous food stores; Frozen specialties, nec

(G-14405)
MTD PRODUCTS INC
810 Theo Moll Dr (44890-9293)
PHONE...........................419 951-9779
EMP: 9
SALES (corp-wide): 15.37B **Publicly Held**
Web: www.mtdparts.com
SIC: 3524 Lawn and garden equipment
HQ: Mtd Products Inc
   5965 Grafton Rd
   Valley City OH 44280
   330 225-2600

(G-14406)
MTD PRODUCTS INC
Midwest Industries
979 S Conwell Ave (44890-9301)
PHONE...........................419 935-6611
Rob Fox, *Genl Mgr*
EMP: 800
SQ FT: 480,000
SALES (corp-wide): 15.37B **Publicly Held**
Web: www.mtdparts.com
SIC: 3524 Lawn and garden mowers and accessories
HQ: Mtd Products Inc
   5965 Grafton Rd
   Valley City OH 44280
   330 225-2600

(G-14407)
PEPPERIDGE FARM INCORPORATED
3320 State Route 103 E (44890-9777)
PHONE...........................419 933-2611
George Litvak, *Brnch Mgr*
EMP: 9
SALES (corp-wide): 9.64B **Publicly Held**
Web: www.pepperidgefarm.com
SIC: 5461 2052 2099 2053 Retail bakeries; Cookies; Bread crumbs, except made in bakeries; Frozen bakery products, except bread
HQ: Pepperidge Farm, Incorporated
   1 Campbell Pl
   Camden NJ 08103
   800 257-8443

Williamsburg
Clermont County

(G-14408)
DUALITE INC (PA)
1 Dualite Ln (45176-1121)
PHONE...........................513 724-7100
▲ **EMP:** 230 **EST:** 1947
SALES (est): 2.56MM
SALES (corp-wide): 2.56MM **Privately Held**
Web: www.dualite.com
SIC: 3993 Signs and advertising specialties

(G-14409)
G & L MACHINING INC
299 N 3rd St (45176-8101)
PHONE...........................513 724-2600
Gary Abrams, *Pr*
Leslie Abrams, *VP*
EMP: 8 **EST:** 1997

SQ FT: 4,000
SALES (est): 458.9K **Privately Held**
Web: www.glmachining.com
SIC: 3599 Machine shop, jobbing and repair

(G-14410)
W&W ROCK SAND AND GRAVEL
1451 Maple Grove Rd (45176-9636)
P.O. Box 640 (45176-0640)
PHONE...........................513 266-3708
Rick A Wuebold, *Prin*
EMP: 6 **EST:** 2009
SALES (est): 401.95K **Privately Held**
SIC: 1442 Construction sand and gravel

Williston
Ottawa County

(G-14411)
DURIVAGE PATTERN AND MFG INC
20522 State Route 579 W (43468)
P.O. Box 337 (43468-0337)
PHONE...........................419 836-8655
Gary Durivage, *Pr*
Larry Durivage, *
Ron Miller, *
Gretchen Durivage, *
EMP: 21 **EST:** 1969
SQ FT: 24,000
SALES (est): 369.58K **Privately Held**
Web: www.durivagepattern.com
SIC: 3469 3544 3369 3365 Patterns on metal ; Industrial molds; Nonferrous foundries, nec ; Aluminum foundries

---

Willoughby
Lake County

(G-14412)
2E ASSOCIATES INC
38363 Airport Pkwy (44094-7562)
PHONE...........................440 975-9955
Kevin Ensinger, *Pr*
James L Ensinger, *
Donnell Ensinger, *
Harry Cook, *
Lewis E Janek, *
EMP: 25 **EST:** 1929
SQ FT: 48,000
SALES (est): 12.33MM **Privately Held**
Web: www.power-packconveyor.com
SIC: 5084 3531 3535 Industrial machinery and equipment; Road construction and maintenance machinery; Unit handling conveying systems

(G-14413)
ACE GRINDING CO INC
37518 N Industrial Pkwy (44094-6279)
PHONE...........................440 951-6760
Brian Danolfo, *Pr*
EMP: 6 **EST:** 1956
SQ FT: 12,000
SALES (est): 529.14K **Privately Held**
Web: www.acegrinding.com
SIC: 3599 Machine shop, jobbing and repair

(G-14414)
ADVANCED RV LLC
4590 Hamann Pkwy (44094-5630)
PHONE...........................440 283-0405
Mike Neundorfer, *Pr*
EMP: 25 **EST:** 2012
SALES (est): 4.61MM **Privately Held**
Web: www.advanced-rv.com
SIC: 3716 7519 7532 Motor homes; Motor home rental; Mobile home and trailer repair

(G-14415)
ALD GROUP LLC
34201 Melinz Pkwy Unit A (44095-4018)
P.O. Box 435 Locklie Dr (44143)
PHONE..............................440 942-9800
Don Difonzo, *Managing Member*
EMP: 6 **EST:** 2000
SQ FT: 10,000
SALES (est): 1.65MM **Privately Held**
Web: www.aldgroup.net
SIC: 3541 Machine tool replacement &
repair parts, metal cutting types

(G-14416)
ALEXY METALS LTD
4610 Hamann Pkwy (44094-5632)
PHONE..............................216 410-8661
Grayson Alexy, *Managing Member*
EMP: 12 **EST:** 2005
SALES (est): 907.91K **Privately Held**
Web: www.alexymetals.com
SIC: 7692 3356 3339 Brazing; Precious
metals; Silver refining (primary)

(G-14417)
AMD FABRICATORS INC
4580 Beidler Rd (44094-4602)
PHONE..............................440 946-8855
Michael Watts, *Pr*
EMP: 17 **EST:** 1986
SQ FT: 50,000
SALES (est): 3.92MM **Privately Held**
SIC: 3444 Sheet metalwork

(G-14418)
AMETCO MANUFACTURING CORP
4326 Hamann Pkwy (44094-5626)
P.O. Box 1210 (44096-1210)
PHONE..............................440 951-4300
Steve G Mitrovich, *Pr*
Greg Mitrovich, *
Rona Mitrovich, *
▲ **EMP:** 38 **EST:** 1966
SQ FT: 85,000
SALES (est): 4.67MM **Privately Held**
Web: www.ametco.com
SIC: 3441 3496 Fabricated structural metal;
Miscellaneous fabricated wire products

(G-14419)
AMFM INC
Also Called: Omegaone
38373 Pelton Rd (44094-7719)
PHONE..............................440 953-4545
John Ducharme, *Pr*
▲ **EMP:** 18 **EST:** 1987
SALES (est): 2.21MM
SALES (corp-wide): 472.89MM **Privately
Held**
Web: www.omega1.com
SIC: 3492 Fluid power valves and hose
fittings
HQ: Shf, Inc.
4861 S Sam Houston Pkwy E
Houston TX 77048
832 456-2000

(G-14420)
ANDERSON BROTHERS ENTPS INC
38180 Airport Pkwy (44094-8021)
PHONE..............................440 269-3920
H W Domeck, *Pr*
Tenneth Anderson, *Pr*
Theresa Inman, *Contrlr*
EMP: 20 **EST:** 1945
SQ FT: 52,000
SALES (est): 2.55MM
SALES (corp-wide): 51.18MM **Privately
Held**
Web: www.paisleyfarmfoods.com

SIC: 2035 Pickles, sauces, and salad
dressings
PA: The Fremont Company
802 N Front St
Fremont OH 43420
419 334-8995

(G-14421)
API PATTERN WORKS INC
4456 Hamann Pkwy (44094-5628)
PHONE..............................440 269-1766
Jesse Baden, *Pr*
Michael Scanlon, *
EMP: 11 **EST:** 1997
SQ FT: 20,000
SALES (est): 1.18MM **Privately Held**
Web: www.olympusaero.com
SIC: 3543 Industrial patterns

(G-14422)
APOLLO PRODUCTS INC
4456 Hamann Pkwy (44094-5628)
PHONE..............................440 269-8551
Jess Baden, *Pr*
Michael Scanlon, *Sec*
EMP: 15 **EST:** 1994
SQ FT: 5,000
SALES (est): 2.48MM **Privately Held**
Web: www.olympusaero.com
SIC: 3544 3545 Special dies and tools;
Machine tool accessories

(G-14423)
APOLLO WELDING & FABG INC (PA)
35600 Curtis Blvd (44095-4109)
PHONE..............................440 942-0227
John Ivan Turkalj, *Pr*
Doug Barth, *VP*
Mary Turkalj, *Sec*
EMP: 20 **EST:** 1987
SQ FT: 25,000
SALES (est): 2.29MM
SALES (corp-wide): 2.29MM **Privately
Held**
Web: www.apollowelding.com
SIC: 7692 Welding repair

(G-14424)
APR TOOL INC
4712 Beidler Rd Ste A (44094-4604)
PHONE..............................440 946-0393
Robert Zietz, *Pr*
John Zeitz, *VP*
EMP: 9 **EST:** 19/4
SQ FT: 3,200
SALES (est): 216.3K **Privately Held**
Web: www.aprtool.com
SIC: 3599 3544 Machine shop, jobbing and
repair; Dies and die holders for metal
cutting, forming, die casting

(G-14425)
AQUA LILY PRODUCTS LLC
4505 Beidler Rd (44094-4646)
PHONE..............................951 322-0981
EMP: 8
SALES (corp-wide): 805.9K **Privately Held**
Web: www.aqualilypad.com
SIC: 3086 Padding, foamed plastics
PA: Aqua Lily Products, Llc
1806 Conant St
Elkhart IN 46516
951 246-9610

(G-14426)
AREM CO
Also Called: Jaytee Division
34188 Euclid Ave (44094-3319)
PHONE..............................440 974-6740
Bob Myotte, *Pr*
Jack Kurant, *Sec*

Becky Uyesugi, *VP*
EMP: 6 **EST:** 1981
SALES (est): 996.75K **Privately Held**
Web: www.aremtube.com
SIC: 3498 3949 3354 3471 Fabricated pipe
and fittings; Sporting and athletic goods, nec
; Aluminum extruded products; Plating and
polishing

(G-14427)
ARTISTIC FINISHES INC
38357 Apollo Pkwy (44094-7723)
PHONE..............................440 951-7850
Michael Credico, *Pr*
Robert Fine, *VP*
Bonnie Credico, *Sec*
EMP: 6 **EST:** 1977
SALES (est): 627.65K **Privately Held**
Web: www.artisticfinishes.com
SIC: 2541 2511 Store fixtures, wood; Wood
household furniture

(G-14428)
ASCENDTECH INC
4772 E 355th St (44094-4632)
PHONE..............................216 458-1101
Igor Lapinskiy, *Pr*
EMP: 35 **EST:** 2002
SALES (est): 1.65MM **Privately Held**
Web: www.ascendtech.us
SIC: 5045 7379 3571 7378 Computer
peripheral equipment; Computer related
maintenance services; Electronic computers
; Computer peripheral equipment repair and
maintenance

(G-14429)
B V GRINDING MACHINING INC
1438 E 363rd St (44095-4136)
PHONE..............................440 918-1884
Ivica Ivan Begovic, *Pr*
EMP: 8 **EST:** 1999
SALES (est): 587.14K **Privately Held**
SIC: 3541 Grinding machines, metalworking

(G-14430)
BESCAST INC
4600 E 355th St (44094-4699)
PHONE..............................440 946-5300
Russ Gallagher, *Pr*
John W Gallagher, *
Tim Brown, *
David M Brown, *
▲ **EMP:** 1/0 **EST:** 1945
SQ FT: 85,000
SALES (est): 24.72MM **Privately Held**
Web: www.bescast.com
SIC: 3324 Aerospace investment castings,
ferrous

(G-14431)
BIS PRINTING
35401 Euclid Ave (44094-4557)
PHONE..............................440 951-2606
Tom Sturnilo, *Owner*
EMP: 6 **EST:** 2013
SALES (est): 102.5K **Privately Held**
SIC: 2752 Offset printing

(G-14432)
BOWDEN MANUFACTURING CORP
4590 Beidler Rd (44094-4682)
PHONE..............................440 946-1770
EMP: 45 **EST:** 1952
SALES (est): 5.42MM **Privately Held**
Web: www.bowdenmfg.com
SIC: 3599 3841 3714 3561 Machine shop,
jobbing and repair; Surgical and medical
instruments; Motor vehicle parts and
accessories; Pumps and pumping
equipment

(G-14433)
BRANDTS CANDIES INC
1238 Lost Nation Rd (44094-7325)
PHONE..............................440 942-1016
Theodore Prindle, *Pr*
EMP: 7 **EST:** 1948
SQ FT: 3,000
SALES (est): 129.17K **Privately Held**
Web: www.brandtschocolates.com
SIC: 5441 2066 Candy; Chocolate and
cocoa products

(G-14434)
BRIGHTGUY INC
38205b Stevens Blvd (44094-6239)
PHONE..............................440 942-8318
Gregory Atwell, *Pr*
Tina Fram, *S&M/VP*
EMP: 6 **EST:** 1998
SALES (est): 2.28MM **Privately Held**
Web: www.brightguy.com
SIC: 3648 Lighting equipment, nec

(G-14435)
BRONCO MACHINE INC
38411 Apollo Pkwy (44094-7725)
PHONE..............................440 951-5015
Michael Bronaka, *Pr*
Ann Turpin, *VP*
Diana Bronaka, *Treas*
EMP: 10 **EST:** 1962
SQ FT: 6,000
SALES (est): 954.81K **Privately Held**
Web: www.broncomachine.com
SIC: 3599 Machine shop, jobbing and repair

(G-14436)
BULLSEYE DART SHOPPE INC
Also Called: Bullseye
950c Erie Rd (44095-1811)
PHONE..............................440 951-9277
Thomas Nazarak, *Pr*
▲ **EMP:** 8 **EST:** 1983
SQ FT: 14,000
SALES (est): 229.61K **Privately Held**
SIC: 3949 Billiard and pool equipment and
supplies, general

(G-14437)
CAST NYLONS CO LTD (PA)
Also Called: Cast Nylons
4300 Hamann Pkwy (44094-5626)
P.O. Box 901507 (44094)
PHONE..............................440 269-2300
EMP: 70 **EST:** 1979
SALES (est): 10.37MM
SALES (corp-wide): 10.37MM **Privately
Held**
Web: www.castnylon.com
SIC: 2824 Nylon fibers

(G-14438)
CENTRAL COCA-COLA BTLG CO INC
Also Called: Coca-Cola
4800 E 355th St (44094-4634)
PHONE..............................440 269-1433
Valerie Nobacco, *Mgr*
EMP: 35
SALES (corp-wide): 45.75B **Publicly Held**
Web: www.coca-cola.com
SIC: 2086 Bottled and canned soft drinks
HQ: Central Coca-Cola Bottling Company,
Inc.
555 Taxter Rd Ste 550
Elmsford NY 10523
914 789-1100

(G-14439)
COIT TOOL COMPANY INC
38134 Western Pkwy Ste 3 (44094-8094)

PHONE.................................440 946-3377
Russell P Bliss, *Pr*
Judy Arnold, *Mgr*
EMP: 10 **EST:** 1961
SQ FT: 6,400
SALES (est): 312.54K **Privately Held**
Web: www.coittool.com
SIC: 3599 Machine shop, jobbing and repair

(G-14440)
COMMERCIAL ANODIZING CO
38387 Apollo Pkwy (44094-7791)
PHONE.................................440 942-8384
Mark S Swetel, *Pr*
Shirley Swetel, *Sec*
EMP: 14 **EST:** 1963
SQ FT: 20,000
SALES (est): 1.28MM **Privately Held**
SIC: 3471 Anodizing (plating) of metals or
formed products

(G-14441)
CONN-SELMER INC
Also Called: Eastlake Mfg Facility
34199 Curtis Blvd (44095-4008)
PHONE.................................440 946-6100
Robert Stone, *Mgr*
EMP: 125
SQ FT: 140,000
SALES (corp-wide): 478.63MM **Privately
Held**
Web: www.connselmer.com
SIC: 3931 Guitars and parts, electric and
nonelectric
HQ: Conn-Selmer, Inc.
600 Industrial Pkwy
Elkhart IN 46516
574 522-1675

(G-14442)
CORTEST INC (PA)
Also Called: Cortest
38322 Apollo Pkwy (44094-7724)
PHONE.................................440 942-1235
Allen F Denzine, *Pr*
Marsha Denzine, *Sec*
EMP: 10 **EST:** 1977
SQ FT: 10,000
SALES (est): 2.36MM
SALES (corp-wide): 2.36MM **Privately
Held**
Web: www.cortest.com
SIC: 3821 5084 Laboratory apparatus and
furniture; Industrial machinery and
equipment

(G-14443)
COUNTY OF LAKE
Also Called: Lake Cnty Dprtmntal Rtrdtion D
2100 Joseph Lloyd Pkwy (44094-8032)
PHONE.................................440 269-2193
Gary Metelko, *Dir*
EMP: 13
SALES (corp-wide): 219.71MM **Privately
Held**
Web: www.lakebdd.org
SIC: 8322 8331 3441 Individual and family
services; Job training and related services;
Fabricated structural metal
PA: County Of Lake
105 Main St
Painesville OH 44077
440 350-2500

(G-14444)
D&D QUALITY MACHINING CO INC
36495 Reading Ave Ste 1 (44094-8243)
PHONE.................................440 942-2772
Zarko Duvnjak, *Pr*
EMP: 8 **EST:** 1993
SALES (est): 973.66K **Privately Held**

Web: www.ddqualitymachining.com
SIC: 3599 Machine shop, jobbing and repair

(G-14445)
DAI CERAMICS LLC
38240 Airport Pkwy (44094-8023)
PHONE.................................440 946-6964
Richard Ruggerio, *Pr*
EMP: 65 **EST:** 1986
SQ FT: 40,000
SALES (est): 4.98MM
SALES (corp-wide): 2.67MM **Privately
Held**
Web: www.daiceramics.com
SIC: 3253 Ceramic wall and floor tile
HQ: Ceramtec North America Llc
One Technology Pl
Laurens SC 29360
864 682-3215

(G-14446)
DEMILTA SAND AND GRAVEL INC
921 Erie Rd (44095-1812)
PHONE.................................440 942-2015
Nick De Milta, *Pr*
Joe De Milta, *VP*
EMP: 11 **EST:** 1979
SQ FT: 1,800
SALES (est): 1.45MM **Privately Held**
Web: www.demiltasand.com
SIC: 1442 4212 Common sand mining; Local
trucking, without storage

(G-14447)
DM MACHINE CO
38338 Apollo Pkwy Ste 1a (44094-7770)
PHONE.................................440 946-0771
Duane Mcintire, *Pr*
Michael Mcintire, *VP*
Dennis Mcintire, *Sec*
EMP: 8 **EST:** 1973
SQ FT: 9,200
SALES (est): 317.07K **Privately Held**
SIC: 3599 Machine shop, jobbing and repair

(G-14448)
DMI MANUFACTURING INC
4780 Beidler Rd (44094-4604)
PHONE.................................440 975-8645
EMP: 10 **EST:** 2019
SALES (est): 716K **Privately Held**
Web: www.dmiparts.com
SIC: 3433 Heating equipment, except electric

(G-14449)
DMS INC
37121 Euclid Ave Ste 1 (44094-5671)
PHONE.................................440 951-9838
Ben Ulrich, *Pr*
Al Pasquale, *
◆ **EMP:** 105 **EST:** 1976
SQ FT: 1,200
SALES (est): 358.84K **Privately Held**
SIC: 8742 8711 3316 Management
consulting services; Engineering services;
Cold finishing of steel shapes

(G-14450)
DUKE GRAPHICS INC
Also Called: Duke Printing
33212 Lakeland Blvd (44095-5205)
PHONE.................................440 946-0606
Blake A Leduc, *Pr*
Thomas Chubb, *
EMP: 33 **EST:** 1974
SQ FT: 24,000
SALES (est): 4.67MM **Privately Held**
Web: www.dukeprint.com
SIC: 2752 Offset printing

(G-14451)
DUKE MANUFACTURING INC
38205 Western Pkwy (44094-7591)
PHONE.................................440 942-6537
Jeff Newmark, *Pr*
Robert Zaucha, *
▲ **EMP:** 26 **EST:** 1967
SQ FT: 18,000
SALES (est): 4.7MM **Privately Held**
Web: www.duke-mfg.com
SIC: 3599 Machine shop, jobbing and repair

(G-14452)
DYOUNG ENTERPRISE INC
Also Called: Budzar Industries
38241 Willoughby Pkwy (44094-7582)
PHONE.................................440 918-0505
Charles Kenyon, *Pr*
Joel Maganza, *
▲ **EMP:** 110 **EST:** 1976
SQ FT: 50,000
SALES (est): 19.16MM **Privately Held**
SIC: 3585 3822 3823 3634 Refrigeration and
heating equipment; Environmental controls;
Temperature instruments: industrial process
type; Electric housewares and fans

(G-14453)
EAGLE WELDING & FABG INC
Also Called: Eagle Welding
1766 Joseph Lloyd Pkwy (44094-8028)
PHONE.................................440 946-0692
Mareo Paulic, *
Nick Paulic, *VP*
Milan Paulic, *Treas*
William Schwenner, *Sec*
EMP: 20 **EST:** 1988
SQ FT: 15,500
SALES (est): 2.89MM **Privately Held**
Web: www.eagle-welding.com
SIC: 3443 3699 7692 3444 Fabricated plate
work (boiler shop); Laser systems and
equipment; Welding repair; Sheet metalwork

(G-14454)
**EASTLAKE MACHINE PRODUCTS
LLC**
1956 Joseph Lloyd Pkwy (44094-8030)
PHONE.................................440 953-1014
Ivan Saric, *Pr*
Richard Moroscak, *
Sandra Saric, *
EMP: 8 **EST:** 1980
SQ FT: 14,000
SALES (est): 2.49MM **Privately Held**
SIC: 3599 3451 Machine shop, jobbing and
repair; Screw machine products

(G-14455)
EATON CORPORATION
Eastlake Office
34899 Curtis Blvd (44095-4002)
PHONE.................................216 523-5000
Doug Koch, *Mgr*
EMP: 10
Web: www.eatonfamilycu.com
SIC: 3714 5084 Hydraulic fluid power
pumps, for auto steering mechanism;
Hydraulic systems equipment and supplies
HQ: Eaton Corporation
1000 Eaton Blvd
Cleveland OH 44122
440 523-5000

(G-14456)
ERICSON MANUFACTURING CO
4323 Hamann Pkwy (44094-5669)
PHONE.................................440 951-8000
John Ericson Iii, *Pr*
◆ **EMP:** 94 **EST:** 1918
SQ FT: 25,000

SALES (est): 39.39MM **Privately Held**
Web: www.ericson.com
SIC: 3643 3648 Electric connectors; Lighting
equipment, nec

(G-14457)
FAITH TOOL AND MFG INC
36575 Reading Ave (44094-8210)
PHONE.................................440 951-5934
Robert Levak, *Prin*
Donna Levak, *VP*
EMP: 8 **EST:** 1976
SALES (est): 2.25MM **Privately Held**
Web: www.ftmeng.com
SIC: 3544 Special dies and tools

(G-14458)
FEEDALL INC
38379 Pelton Rd (44094-7719)
PHONE.................................440 942-8100
Roger W Winslow Junior, *Pr*
Michael J O'brien, *Sec*
EMP: 12 **EST:** 1946
SQ FT: 15,300
SALES (est): 2.21MM **Privately Held**
Web: www.feedall.com
SIC: 3535 3545 Conveyors and conveying
equipment; Hopper feed devices

(G-14459)
FIRST MACHINE & TOOL CORP
38181 Airport Pkwy (44094-8038)
PHONE.................................440 269-8644
Mladen Laush, *Pr*
Herman Lackner, *VP*
EMP: 6 **EST:** 1982
SQ FT: 5,600
SALES (est): 1.47MM **Privately Held**
Web: www.firstmachinegages.com
SIC: 3544 Special dies and tools

(G-14460)
FUSION INCORPORATED (PA)
4658 E 355th St (44094-4630)
PHONE.................................440 946-3300
▲ **EMP:** 85 **EST:** 1932
SALES (est): 16.73MM
SALES (corp-wide): 16.73MM **Privately
Held**
Web: www.fusion-inc.com
SIC: 3548 3356 3398 3341 Soldering
equipment, except hand soldering irons;
Solder: wire, bar, acid core, and rosin core;
Metal heat treating; Secondary nonferrous
metals

(G-14461)
G-M-I INC
4822 E 355th St (44094-4634)
PHONE.................................440 953-8811
Donald J Restly, *Pr*
Carol L Restly, *Sec*
EMP: 9 **EST:** 1979
SQ FT: 9,200
SALES (est): 491.41K **Privately Held**
Web: www.gmigaskets.com
SIC: 3053 Gaskets, all materials

(G-14462)
GEARTEC INC
4245 Hamann Pkwy (44094-5623)
PHONE.................................440 953-3900
John Grazia, *Pr*
▲ **EMP:** 26 **EST:** 2011
SQ FT: 35,000
SALES (est): 5.74MM
SALES (corp-wide): 334.72MM **Privately
Held**
Web: www.geartec.com
SIC: 3566 Gears, power transmission,
except auto

HQ: The Electric Materials Company
50 S Washington St
North East PA 16428
814 725-9621

(G-14463)
GENERAL PRECISION CORPORATION
4553 Beidler Rd (44094-4646)
PHONE..............................440 951-9380
Allen Ernst, *Pr*
EMP: 7 **EST:** 1972
SALES (est): 490.7K **Privately Held**
Web: www.generalprecisioncorp.com
SIC: 8711 3365 Engineering services; Machinery castings, aluminum

(G-14464)
HEISLER TOOL COMPANY
38228 Western Pkwy (44094-7590)
PHONE..............................440 951-2424
Timothy M Mccord, *Pr*
Susan Mccord, *VP*
EMP: 15 **EST:** 1986
SQ FT: 22,000
SALES (est): 4.06MM **Privately Held**
Web: www.heislertool.com
SIC: 3599 3549 Custom machinery; Metalworking machinery, nec

(G-14465)
HUDCO MANUFACTURING INC
38250 Western Pkwy (44094-7590)
PHONE..............................440 951-4040
Donald M Hudak, *Pr*
Joan L Hudak, *Sec*
▲ **EMP:** 8 **EST:** 1981
SQ FT: 6,000
SALES (est): 976.12K **Privately Held**
Web: www.hudcomfg.com
SIC: 3531 Rock crushing machinery, portable

(G-14466)
HYDRAULIC PRODUCTS INC
4540 Beidler Rd (44094-4602)
PHONE..............................440 946-4575
Joseph Focareto, *Pr*
▲ **EMP:** 8 **EST:** 1972
SALES (est): 720.18K **Privately Held**
SIC: 3593 7699 3594 Fluid power cylinders, hydraulic or pneumatic; Hydraulic equipment repair; Fluid power pumps and motors

(G-14467)
IDENTIPHOTO CO LTD
1810 Joseph Lloyd Pkwy (44094-8042)
PHONE..............................440 306-9000
▲ **EMP:** 17 **EST:** 1971
SALES (est): 3.94MM **Privately Held**
Web: www.identiphoto.com
SIC: 5043 5045 3999 Photographic equipment and supplies; Computers, peripherals, and software; Identification badges and insignia

(G-14468)
IMAGING SCIENCES LLC
38174 Willoughby Pkwy (44094-7580)
PHONE..............................440 975-9640
Geoffrey R Brown, *Pr*
Geoffrey Brown, *Pr*
EMP: 9 **EST:** 2003
SQ FT: 18,000
SALES (est): 908.49K **Privately Held**
Web: www.imaging-sciences.com
SIC: 3211 Construction glass

(G-14469)
INTEGRA ENCLOSURES INC (PA)
Also Called: Integra
7750 Pyler Blvd (44094)
P.O. Box 1870 (44061-1870)
PHONE..............................440 269-4966
Jim Mcwilliams, *Pr*
EMP: 8 **EST:** 2000
SQ FT: 30,000
SALES (est): 1.86MM
SALES (corp-wide): 1.86MM **Privately Held**
Web: www.integraenclosures.com
SIC: 3089 Injection molding of plastics

(G-14470)
INTELITOOL MFG SVCS INC
36335 Reading Ave Ste 4 (44094-8200)
PHONE..............................440 953-1071
Gary Struna, *Pr*
William Tulloch, *Sr VP*
EMP: 6 **EST:** 1994
SQ FT: 10,500
SALES (est): 237.18K **Privately Held**
Web: www.intelitoolinc.com
SIC: 3544 Special dies and tools

(G-14471)
INTERLAKE STAMPING OHIO INC
4732 E 355th St (44094-4632)
PHONE..............................440 942-0800
Lisa M Habe, *Pr*
Dan Valentino, *
Mark Groenstein, *
Liz Tolbert, *
EMP: 40 **EST:** 1957
SQ FT: 36,000
SALES (est): 8.78MM
SALES (corp-wide): 24.2MM **Privately Held**
Web: www.interlakestamping.com
SIC: 3469 Stamping metal for the trade
PA: Interlake Industries, Inc.
4732 E 355th St
Willoughby OH 44094
440 942-0800

(G-14472)
JBM TECHNOLOGIES OF OHIO LLC
4515 Glenbrook Rd (44094-8215)
PHONE..............................216 264-1270
John Watkins, *Managing Member*
EMP: 6 **EST:** 2020
SALES (est): 335.85K **Privately Held**
SIC: 3545 Machine tool accessories

(G-14473)
JOURNAL REGISTER COMPANY
Journal, The
36625 Vine St (44094-6367)
PHONE..............................440 951-0000
Stephen Roszczyk, *Prin*
EMP: 396
SALES (corp-wide): 92.91MM **Privately Held**
Web: www.journalregisteroffset.com
SIC: 2711 Newspapers, publishing and printing
PA: Journal Register Company
5 Hanover Sq 25th Fl
New York NY 10005
212 257-7212

(G-14474)
KALCOR COATINGS COMPANY
37721 Stevens Blvd (44094-6231)
PHONE..............................440 946-4700
Cori Zucker, *Pr*
Don Mihalik, *
Kal Zucker, *CIO*
▲ **EMP:** 25 **EST:** 1961

SQ FT: 55,000
SALES (est): 9.11MM **Privately Held**
Web: www.kalcor.com
SIC: 2851 Paints and paint additives

(G-14475)
KEB INDUSTRIES INC
2166 Joseph Lloyd Pkwy (44094-8032)
PHONE..............................440 953-4623
Brad Butler, *Pr*
EMP: 8 **EST:** 2003
SQ FT: 6,500
SALES (est): 2.17MM **Privately Held**
Web: www.kebkollets.com
SIC: 3545 Precision tools, machinists'

(G-14476)
KELLY ARSPC THRMAL SYSTEMS LLC
Also Called: Kaps
1625 Lost Nation Rd (44094-8189)
PHONE..............................440 951-4744
Kent Kelly, *
EMP: 28 **EST:** 2005
SALES (est): 5.2MM **Privately Held**
Web: www.kellyaero.com
SIC: 3728 Aircraft parts and equipment, nec
PA: Tailwind Technologies Inc.
1 Propeller Pl
Piqua OH 45356

(G-14477)
KENNEDY GROUP INCORPORATED (HQ)
38601 Kennedy Pkwy (44094-7395)
PHONE..............................440 951-7660
Pat Kennedy, *CEO*
Todd Kennedy, *
Michael R Kennedy, *
Mary Lou Kennedy, *
Jerry Kish, *
▲ **EMP:** 83 **EST:** 1974
SQ FT: 80,000
SALES (est): 18.21MM **Privately Held**
Web: www.kennedygrp.com
SIC: 2679 2673 3089 3565 Tags and labels, paper; Bags: plastic, laminated, and coated; Plastics containers, except foam; Packaging machinery
PA: Inovar Packaging Group, Llc
9001 Sterling St
Irving TX 75063

(G-14478)
KOTTLER METAL PRODUCTS CO INC
1595 Lost Nation Rd (44094-7329)
PHONE..............................440 946-7473
Barry Feldman, *Pr*
Harold Feldman, *
Jeff Gray, *
▲ **EMP:** 25 **EST:** 1915
SALES (est): 5.26MM
SALES (corp-wide): 23.32MM **Privately Held**
Web: www.kottlermetal.com
SIC: 3498 3441 7692 3547 Pipe sections, fabricated from purchased pipe; Fabricated structural metal; Welding repair; Rolling mill machinery
PA: Pkdw Equity Partners, Llc
412 Chapel Harbor Dr
Pittsburgh PA 15238
412 586-7651

(G-14479)
LABEL TECHNIQUE SOUTHEAST LLC
38601 Kennedy Pkwy (44094-7395)
PHONE..............................440 951-7660

EMP: 16 **EST:** 1979
SQ FT: 12,000
SALES (est): 2.23MM **Privately Held**
SIC: 2759 2672 2679 Labels and seals: printing, nsk; Paper; coated and laminated, nec; Labels, paper: made from purchased material
HQ: The Kennedy Group Incorporated
38601 Kennedy Pkwy
Willoughby OH 44094
440 951-7660

(G-14480)
LAKE COMMUNITY NEWS
Also Called: Painesville Pride
36081 Lake Shore Blvd Ste 5 (44095-1554)
P.O. Box 814 (44255-0814)
PHONE..............................440 946-2577
Deanne Nelisse, *Pr*
EMP: 7 **EST:** 1987
SALES (est): 57.52K **Privately Held**
Web: www.lakecommunitynewsohio.com
SIC: 2711 Newspapers, publishing and printing

(G-14481)
LANDERWOOD INDUSTRIES INC
4245 Hamann Pkwy (44094-5623)
PHONE..............................440 233-4234
EMP: 23 **EST:** 1997
SQ FT: 30,000
SALES (est): 704.99K **Privately Held**
SIC: 3462 Gears, forged steel

(G-14482)
LANGA TOOL & MACHINE INC
36430 Reading Ave Ste 1 (44094-8220)
PHONE..............................440 953-1138
William Langa, *Pr*
EMP: 7 **EST:** 1979
SQ FT: 7,000
SALES (est): 711.09K **Privately Held**
Web: www.langatool.com
SIC: 3599 Machine shop, jobbing and repair

(G-14483)
LOKRING TECHNOLOGY LLC
38376 Apollo Pkwy (44094-7724)
PHONE..............................440 942-0880
Bill Lennon, *Pr*
▲ **EMP:** 119 **EST:** 2003
SALES (est): 23.13MM **Privately Held**
Web: www.lokring.com
SIC: 3312 Pipes and tubes

(G-14484)
MAGNUS ENGINEERED EQP LLC
4500 Beidler Rd (44094-4602)
PHONE..............................440 942-8488
William Martin, *Pr*
Jeffrey Mendrala, *CFO*
EMP: 25 **EST:** 2016
SQ FT: 38,000
SALES (est): 4.54MM **Privately Held**
Web: www.magnusequipment.com
SIC: 3452 Bolts, nuts, rivets, and washers

(G-14485)
MAR-BAL PULTRUSION INC
38310 Apollo Pkwy (44094-7724)
PHONE..............................440 953-0456
Allen J Goryance, *Pr*
James Gortance, *VP*
EMP: 10 **EST:** 1974
SQ FT: 10,000
SALES (est): 1.02MM **Privately Held**
Web: www.marbalpultrusion.com
SIC: 2519 Furniture, household: glass, fiberglass, and plastic

(G-14486)
MEISTER MEDIA WORLDWIDE INC (PA)
Also Called: Meister Media Worldwide
4420 Sherwin Rd Ste 4 (44094-7995)
PHONE.................................440 942-2000
Gary T Fitzgerald, *Ch Bd*
Steven L Siemborski, *Vice Chairman**
William J Miller Ii *Prinpl, Prin*
K Elliott Nowels, *
Cynthia Gorman, *
EMP: 100 **EST:** 1932
SQ FT: 29,000
SALES (est): 8.06MM
SALES (corp-wide): 8.06MM **Privately Held**
Web: www.meistermedia.com
SIC: 2721 Magazines: publishing only, not printed on site

(G-14487)
MELINZ INDUSTRIES INC (PA)
Also Called: Riverview Raquetball Club
34099 Melinz Pkwy Unit D (44095-4001)
PHONE.................................440 946-3512
Adolph Melinz, *Pr*
Nancy Sloat, *Sec*
Jeff Sloat, *Treas*
EMP: 10 **EST:** 1974
SQ FT: 11,000
SALES (est): 312.28K
SALES (corp-wide): 312.28K **Privately Held**
SIC: 7999 3599 Racquetball club, non-membership; Machine and other job shop work

(G-14488)
METAL SEAL PRECISION LTD
4369 Hamann Pkwy (44094-5625)
PHONE.................................440 255-8888
John L Habe, *Brnch Mgr*
EMP: 128
SALES (corp-wide): 8.65MM **Privately Held**
Web: www.metalseal.com
SIC: 3444 Sheet metalwork
PA: Metal Seal Precision, Ltd.
    8687 Tyler Blvd
    Mentor OH 44060
    440 255-8888

(G-14489)
MID-WEST FORGE CORPORATION (PA)
2778 Som Center Rd Ste 200 (44094-9152)
PHONE.................................216 481-3030
Robert I Gale Iii, *Ch Bd*
Michael Sherwin, *V Ch Bd*
Paul C Gum, *Pr*
Robert W Dems, *VP*
John T Webster, *CUST SERV*
EMP: 150 **EST:** 1925
SQ FT: 165,000
SALES (est): 21.82MM
SALES (corp-wide): 21.82MM **Privately Held**
Web: www.mid-westforge.com
SIC: 3462 Iron and steel forgings

(G-14490)
MILLENNIUM MACHINE TECH LLC
38323 Apollo Pkwy Ste 7 (44094-7761)
PHONE.................................440 269-8080
Jeffrey J Downs, *Managing Member*
EMP: 6 **EST:** 2004
SALES (est): 1.44MM **Privately Held**
SIC: 3599 Machine shop, jobbing and repair

(G-14491)
MOMENTIVE PERFORMANCE MTLS INC
4901 Campbell Rd (44094-3366)
PHONE.................................740 929-8732
EMP: 123
Web: www.momentivetech.com
SIC: 2869 Industrial organic chemicals, nec
HQ: Momentive Performance Materials Inc.
    2750 Balltown Rd
    Niskayuna NY 12309

(G-14492)
NATIONAL ROLLER DIE INC
4750 Beidler Rd Unit 4 (44094-4663)
PHONE.................................440 951-3850
Will Corral, *Pr*
Jeff Watt, *Superintnt*
Kelly Johnson, *CEO*
EMP: 10 **EST:** 2002
SALES (est): 239.54K **Privately Held**
Web: www.nrdi.net
SIC: 3544 Special dies and tools

(G-14493)
NEUNDORFER INC
Also Called: Neundorfer Engineering Service
4590 Hamann Pkwy (44094-5691)
PHONE.................................440 942-8990
Michael Neundorfer, *CEO*
EMP: 23 **EST:** 1958
SQ FT: 38,000
SALES (est): 4.24MM **Privately Held**
Web: www.neundorfer.com
SIC: 8711 3564 Pollution control engineering; Precipitators, electrostatic

(G-14494)
NEWAY STAMPING & MFG INC
4820 E 345th St (44094-4607)
P.O. Box 1023 (44096-1023)
PHONE.................................440 951-8500
Adam Bowden, *Pr*
Jason H Bowden, *
Matthew J Bowden, *
EMP: 85 **EST:** 1970
SQ FT: 15,000
SALES (est): 9.79MM **Privately Held**
Web: www.newaystamping.com
SIC: 3469 3544 Stamping metal for the trade; Special dies, tools, jigs, and fixtures

(G-14495)
NORBAR TORQUE TOOLS INC
36400 Biltmore Pl (44094-8221)
PHONE.................................440 953-1175
Keith Daiber, *Pr*
Bernice Daiber, *Sec*
Terry Daiber, *VP*
▲ **EMP:** 12 **EST:** 1962
SQ FT: 5,000
SALES (est): 4.65MM
SALES (corp-wide): 5.11B **Publicly Held**
Web: www.norbar.com
SIC: 5072 3423 Hand tools; Wrenches, hand tools
PA: Snap-On Incorporated
    2801 80th St
    Kenosha WI 53143
    262 656-5200

(G-14496)
NORTHEASTERN RFRGN CORP
38274 Western Pkwy (44094-7590)
PHONE.................................440 942-7676
Carol A Primozic, *Pr*
James A Primozic, *VP*
EMP: 20 **EST:** 1976
SQ FT: 11,000
SALES (est): 5.62MM **Privately Held**
SIC: 3585 1711 7623 Refrigeration equipment, complete; Heating and air conditioning contractors; Refrigeration repair service

(G-14497)
NRC INC
Also Called: Northeastern Process Cooling
38160 Western Pkwy (44094-7588)
PHONE.................................440 975-9449
Randolph J Primozic, *Pr*
Patricia A Primozic, *
EMP: 30 **EST:** 1998
SALES (est): 4.81MM **Privately Held**
Web: www.nrcinc.net
SIC: 3585 Refrigeration equipment, complete

(G-14498)
NUPRO COMPANY
4800 E 345th St (44094-4607)
PHONE.................................440 951-9729
F J Callahan Junior, *Ch Bd*
William Cosgrove, *
EMP: 21 **EST:** 1956
SQ FT: 60,000
SALES (est): 1.44MM
SALES (corp-wide): 881.02MM **Privately Held**
Web: www.swagelok.com
SIC: 3494 3569 3564 3491 Valves and pipe fittings, nec; Filters, general line: industrial; Blowers and fans; Industrial valves
PA: Swagelok Company
    29500 Solon Rd
    Solon OH 44139
    440 248-4600

(G-14499)
OHIO BROACH & MACHINE COMPANY
35264 Topps Industrial Pkwy (44094-4684)
PHONE.................................440 946-1040
Charles P Van De, *Mother*
Christopher C Van De, *Mother*
Richard Van De, *Mother*
Neil Van De, *Mother*
James L Lutz, *
▼ **EMP:** 34 **EST:** 1956
SQ FT: 52,000
SALES (est): 4.35MM **Privately Held**
Web: www.ohiobroach.com
SIC: 3541 7699 3545 3599 Broaching machines; Knife, saw and tool sharpening and repair; Machine tool accessories; Machine shop, jobbing and repair

(G-14500)
OHIO CARBON BLANK INC
38403 Pelton Rd (44094-7721)
PHONE.................................440 953-9302
Scott Boncha, *Pr*
EMP: 20 **EST:** 1980
SQ FT: 2,000
SALES (est): 2.38MM **Privately Held**
Web: www.ohiocarbonblank.com
SIC: 3624 Carbon and graphite products

(G-14501)
OMEGA 1 INC
38373 Pelton Rd (44094-7719)
PHONE.................................216 663-8424
Richard Profant, *Pr*
EMP: 10 **EST:** 1989
SALES (est): 2.13MM **Privately Held**
Web: www.omega1.com
SIC: 3492 5051 Hose and tube fittings and assemblies, hydraulic/pneumatic; Metals service centers and offices

(G-14502)
ORANGE BLOSSOM PRESS INC
38005 Brown Ave (44094-5836)
P.O. Box 93417 (44101-5417)
PHONE.................................216 781-8655
Greg Patt, *Pr*
John O'hara, *VP*
Donna Lirrivee-cohen, *Sec*
EMP: 8 **EST:** 1976
SQ FT: 6,000
SALES (est): 126.31K **Privately Held**
Web: www.orangeblossompress.com
SIC: 2752 2791 2789 Offset printing; Typesetting; Bookbinding and related work

(G-14503)
PACE CONSOLIDATED INC (PA)
Also Called: Pace Engineering
4800 Beidler Rd (44094-4605)
PHONE.................................440 942-1234
Craig Wallace, *CEO*
Randy Murphy, *
◆ **EMP:** 95 **EST:** 1976
SQ FT: 120,000
SALES (est): 10.2MM
SALES (corp-wide): 10.2MM **Privately Held**
Web: www.paceparts.net
SIC: 3531 Construction machinery

(G-14504)
PACE ENGINEERING INC
4800 Beidler Rd (44094-4605)
PHONE.................................440 942-1234
Craig R Wallace, *CEO*
EMP: 105 **EST:** 1963
SQ FT: 120,000
SALES (est): 516.3K
SALES (corp-wide): 10.2MM **Privately Held**
Web: www.paceparts.net
SIC: 3531 Construction machinery
PA: Pace Consolidated, Inc.
    4800 Beidler Rd
    Willoughby OH 44094
    440 942-1234

(G-14505)
PAULO PRODUCTS COMPANY
Also Called: American Brzing Div Paulo Pdts
4428 Hamann Pkwy (44094-5628)
PHONE.................................440 942-0153
Bob Muto, *Brnch Mgr*
EMP: 38
SALES (corp-wide): 52.44MM **Privately Held**
Web: www.paulo.com
SIC: 7692 1799 Brazing; Coating of concrete structures with plastic
PA: Paulo Products Company
    5711 West Park Ave
    Saint Louis MO 63110
    314 647-7500

(G-14506)
PHIL-MATIC SCREW PRODUCTS INC
1457 E 357th St (44095-4127)
P.O. Box 1178 (44096-1178)
PHONE.................................440 942-7290
Larry E Phillis, *Pr*
Fraser Young, *VP*
Richard Phillis, *VP*
EMP: 10 **EST:** 1962
SQ FT: 11,300
SALES (est): 1.29MM **Privately Held**
Web: www.philmatic.com
SIC: 3599 Machine shop, jobbing and repair

(G-14507)
PMC GAGE INC (PA)
Also Called: PMC Lonestar
38383 Willoughby Pkwy (44094-7585)
PHONE..............................440 953-1672
Nicholas Bosworth, *CEO*
Ann Gross, *
EMP: 43 EST: 1999
SALES (est): 9.33MM
SALES (corp-wide): 9.33MM **Privately Held**
Web: www.pmcgagecompanies.com
SIC: 3545 3826 3829 Measuring tools and machines, machinists' metalworking type; Analytical instruments; Measuring and controlling devices, nec

(G-14508)
POLYFLEX LLC
Also Called: Polyflex
4803 E 345th St (44094-4606)
PHONE..............................440 946-0758
EMP: 10 EST: 2005
SALES (est): 656.63K **Privately Held**
Web: www.polyflexonline.com
SIC: 3089 Plastics containers, except foam

(G-14509)
PRECISE TOOL & DIE COMPANY INC
38128 Willoughby Pkwy (44094-7580)
PHONE..............................440 951-9173
Steve Hunyadi, *CEO*
Eva Pinkerton, *
Elizabeth Hunyadi, *
▲ **EMP: 35 EST:** 1969
SQ FT: 22,000
SALES (est): 4.96MM **Privately Held**
Web: www.ptd-inc.com
SIC: 3599 Machine shop, jobbing and repair

(G-14510)
PROGRESSIVE SUPPLY LLC
38601 Kennedy Pkwy (44094-7395)
PHONE..............................570 688-9636
EMP: 6 EST: 1981
SQ FT: 10,000
SALES (est): 828.06K **Privately Held**
SIC: 2672 Tape, pressure sensitive: made from purchased materials

(G-14511)
PUBLIC SAFETY OHIO DEPARTMENT
Also Called: Ross County License Bureau
31517 Vine St (44095-3561)
PHONE..............................440 943-5545
Cynthia Marfisi, *Genl Mgr*
EMP: 6
SALES (corp-wide): 85.52MM **Privately Held**
Web: publicsafety.ohio.gov
SIC: 3469 9221 Automobile license tags, stamped metal; Police protection
HQ: Ohio Department Of Public Safety
1970 West Broad St Fl 5
Columbus OH 43223

(G-14512)
QUALITY CNC MACHINING INC
38195 Airport Pkwy (44094-8038)
PHONE..............................440 953-0723
Joseph Katic, *Pr*
EMP: 25 EST: 1988
SQ FT: 8,000
SALES (est): 4.01MM **Privately Held**
Web: www.qualitycnc.com
SIC: 3599 Machine shop, jobbing and repair

(G-14513)
QUALITY SPECIALISTS INC
Also Called: Www.slidepartsexpress.com
1428 E 363rd St (44095-4136)
PHONE..............................440 946-9129
Kenneth Bateman, *Pr*
Rosemary Bateman, *VP*
EMP: 8 EST: 1979
SQ FT: 6,000
SALES (est): 312.41K **Privately Held**
SIC: 3544 3599 Special dies and tools; Custom machinery

(G-14514)
QUALTECH TECHNOLOGIES INC
1685b Joseph Lloyd Pkwy (44094-8044)
PHONE..............................440 946-8081
Dave Vance, *Pr*
▲ **EMP: 50 EST:** 2002
SQ FT: 18,000
SALES (est): 9.88MM **Privately Held**
Web: www.qualtechinc.com
SIC: 3699 3672 Electrical equipment and supplies, nec; Printed circuit boards

(G-14515)
R & F FRANCHISE GROUP LLC
37333 Euclid Ave (44094-5617)
PHONE..............................440 942-7140
John Frech, *Prin*
EMP: 6 EST: 2010
SALES (est): 994.88K **Privately Held**
Web: www.paninisgrill.com
SIC: 3421 Table and food cutlery, including butchers'

(G-14516)
REID ASSET MANAGEMENT COMPANY
Also Called: Magnus Equipment
4500 Beidler Rd (44094-4602)
PHONE..............................440 942-8488
Scott Miller, *Brnch Mgr*
EMP: 25
SALES (corp-wide): 3.09MM **Privately Held**
Web: www.magnusequipment.com
SIC: 2842 Polishes and sanitation goods
PA: Reid Asset Management Company
9555 Rockside Rd Ste 350
Cleveland OH 44125
216 642-3223

(G-14517)
RIMECO PRODUCTS INC
2002 Joseph Lloyd Pkwy (44094-8032)
PHONE..............................440 918-1220
Valentine Ribic, *Pr*
John Ribic, *VP*
EMP: 20 EST: 1992
SQ FT: 12,000
SALES (est): 5.47MM **Privately Held**
Web: www.rimecoproducts.com
SIC: 3599 Machine shop, jobbing and repair

(G-14518)
RINOS WOODWORKING SHOP INC
36475 Biltmore Pl (44094-8222)
PHONE..............................440 946-1718
Rino Ritosa, *Pr*
▲ **EMP: 19 EST:** 1982
SQ FT: 15,000
SALES (est): 2.06MM **Privately Held**
Web: www.rinoswoodworking.com
SIC: 2541 2431 Cabinets, except refrigerated: show, display, etc.: wood; Millwork

(G-14519)
RISE HOLDINGS LLC
Also Called: All-Craft Wellman Products
4839 E 345th St (44094-4606)
PHONE..............................440 946-9646
Gil Wellman, *Pr*
EMP: 15 EST: 1902
SQ FT: 8,000
SALES (est): 969.6K **Privately Held**
Web: www.acwellman.com
SIC: 3953 3499 Letters (marking devices), metal; Tablets, bronze or other metal

(G-14520)
SAWYER TECHNICAL MATERIALS LLC (HQ)
Also Called: Sawyer Crystal Systems
35400 Lakeland Blvd (44095-5304)
PHONE..............................440 951-8770
Kelly Scott, *Managing Member*
Fred Taylor, *Managing Member*
▲ **EMP: 35 EST:** 1957
SQ FT: 100,000
SALES (est): 4.32MM **Privately Held**
Web: www.sawyerllc.com
SIC: 3679 3471 Quartz crystals, for electronic application; Plating and polishing
PA: Foreasia Corporation
Taipei City TAP

(G-14521)
SCHEEL PUBLISHING LLC
5900 Som Center Rd (44094-3086)
PHONE..............................216 731-8616
J Scheel, *Prin*
EMP: 23 EST: 2008
SALES (est): 391.2K **Privately Held**
Web: www.commercialacademy.com
SIC: 2741 Miscellaneous publishing

(G-14522)
SERVICE STAMPINGS INC
4700 Hamann Pkwy (44094-5616)
PHONE..............................440 946-2330
Christopher T Reid, *Pr*
Thurston Reid, *
Jefferey J Campbell, *Treasurer Finance*
Robert A Stohlman, *
Donald Bowen, *
EMP: 31 EST: 1956
SQ FT: 28,000
SALES (est): 7.23MM **Privately Held**
Web: www.servicestampings.com
SIC: 3469 Stamping metal for the trade

(G-14523)
SFM CORP
4530 Hamann Pkwy (44094-5630)
PHONE..............................440 951-5500
Fred J G Mika, *Pr*
Scott M Mika, *
Fred G Mika, *
EMP: 45 EST: 1939
SQ FT: 78,000
SALES (est): 786.07K **Privately Held**
Web: www.mikafab.com
SIC: 3444 Sheet metal specialties, not stamped

(G-14524)
SHAFTS MFG
1585 E 361st St Unit G1 (44095-5329)
PHONE..............................440 942-6012
Berndy Heckelmann, *Prin*
EMP: 8 EST: 2007
SALES (est): 253.77K **Privately Held**
Web: www.tylertreeservicecompany.net
SIC: 3999 Manufacturing industries, nec

(G-14525)
SHERBROOKE CORPORATION
36490 Reading Ave (44094-8207)
P.O. Box 689 (44096-0689)
PHONE..............................440 942-3520
Randy Spoth, *Pr*
Laura Krus, *Sec*
Nancy Spoth, *Treas*
EMP: 22 EST: 1993
SQ FT: 9,000
SALES (est): 2.36MM **Privately Held**
Web: www.sherbrookemetals.com
SIC: 3624 3823 3548 Electrodes, thermal and electrolytic uses: carbon, graphite; Process control instruments; Welding apparatus

(G-14526)
SHERBROOKE METALS
37552 N Industrial Pkwy (44094-6214)
PHONE..............................440 542-3066
Nancy Spoth, *Treas*
EMP: 6 EST: 2018
SALES (est): 242.68K **Privately Held**
Web: www.sherbrookemetals.com
SIC: 3548 Welding apparatus

(G-14527)
SKINNER MACHINING CO
38127 Willoughby Pkwy (44094-7581)
PHONE..............................216 486-6636
Walter B Harwood, *Pr*
EMP: 8 EST: 1962
SALES (est): 3.98MM
SALES (corp-wide): 3.98MM **Privately Held**
SIC: 3599 Electrical discharge machining (EDM)
PA: J W Harwood Co
18001 Roseland Rd
Cleveland OH 44112
216 531-6230

(G-14528)
SKRL DIE CASTING INC
34580 Lakeland Blvd (44095-5221)
PHONE..............................440 946-7200
Sandra Szuch, *Pr*
EMP: 10 EST: 1967
SQ FT: 30,000
SALES (est): 459.07K **Privately Held**
Web: www.skrltool.com
SIC: 3544 Special dies and tools

(G-14529)
SLABE MACHINE PRODUCTS LLC
4659 Hamann Pkwy (44094-5631)
PHONE..............................440 946-6555
Edward Slabe Junior, *Pr*
Brendan Slabe, *
Christopher Slabe, *
Judith Slabe, *
▲ **EMP: 100 EST:** 1942
SQ FT: 58,000
SALES (est): 24.15MM **Privately Held**
Web: www.slabemachine.com
SIC: 3599 Machine shop, jobbing and repair

(G-14530)
SLOAT INC
34099 Melinz Pkwy Unit A (44095-4001)
PHONE..............................440 951-9554
Jeff Sloat, *Pr*
EMP: 6 EST: 1993
SALES (est): 266.56K **Privately Held**
SIC: 2892 Primary explosives, fuses and detonators

(G-14531)
SPENCE TECHNOLOGIES INC
Also Called: R.W.
4752 Topps Industrial Pkwy (44094-4636)
PHONE..............................440 946-3035
William Spence, *Pr*
EMP: 18 **EST:** 1976
SQ FT: 10,320
SALES (est): 3.07MM **Privately Held**
Web: www.spencetechnologies.com
SIC: 3599 Machine shop, jobbing and repair

(G-14532)
STEEL TECHNOLOGIES LLC
Steel Technologies Ohio
2220 Joseph Lloyd Pkwy (44094-8034)
PHONE..............................440 946-8666
Rick Furber, *VP*
EMP: 51
Web: www.steeltechnologies.com
SIC: 3312 Blast furnaces and steel mills
HQ: Steel Technologies Llc
700 N Hrstbrne Pkwy Ste 4
Louisville KY 40222
502 245-2110

(G-14533)
STICKER CORPORATION
37941 Elm St (44094-6207)
PHONE..............................440 942-4700
Douglas Reighart, *Brnch Mgr*
EMP: 7
SALES (corp-wide): 2.6MM **Privately Held**
Web: www.stickercorp.com
SIC: 3441 Fabricated structural metal
PA: Sticker Corporation
37877 Elm St
Willoughby OH 44094
440 946-2100

(G-14534)
STICKER CORPORATION (PA)
Also Called: Reighart Steel Products
37877 Elm St (44094-6243)
PHONE..............................440 946-2100
Douglas Reighart, *Pr*
EMP: 11 **EST:** 1947
SQ FT: 18,000
SALES (est): 2.6MM
SALES (corp-wide): 2.6MM **Privately Held**
Web: www.stickercorp.com
SIC: 3585 3549 3547 3443 Heating
equipment, complete; Metalworking
machinery, nec; Rolling mill machinery;
Fabricated plate work (boiler shop)

(G-14535)
STRONG-COAT LLC
4420 Sherwin Rd (44094-7994)
PHONE..............................440 299-2068
James Small, *Prin*
EMP: 6 **EST:** 2015
SALES (est): 753.43K **Privately Held**
SIC: 2851 Paints and allied products

(G-14536)
T C SERVICE CO
Also Called: Top Cat Air Tools
38285 Pelton Rd (44094-7740)
PHONE..............................440 954-7500
Edgar G Henry, *Pr*
M Anne Henry, *
Valeria S Henry, *
Gerald J Henry, *
EMP: 40 **EST:** 1962
SQ FT: 60,000
SALES (est): 9.88MM **Privately Held**
Web: www.tcservice.com
SIC: 3546 Power-driven handtools

(G-14537)
TABLOX INC
4821 E 345th St (44094-4606)
PHONE..............................440 953-1951
Dana Talcott, *Pr*
Pam Cleverly, *VP*
EMP: 9 **EST:** 1968
SQ FT: 16,000
SALES (est): 490.79K **Privately Held**
Web: www.tablox.com
SIC: 3471 Electroplating of metals or formed
products

(G-14538)
TELLING INDUSTRIES LLC (PA)
4420 Sherwin Rd Ste 4 (44094-7995)
PHONE..............................440 974-3370
Edward Slish, *Managing Member*
◆ **EMP:** 10 **EST:** 2004
SQ FT: 400,000
SALES (est): 24.7MM
SALES (corp-wide): 24.7MM **Privately
Held**
Web: www.tellingindustries.com
SIC: 3316 Bars, steel, cold finished, from
purchased hot-rolled

(G-14539)
TETRAD ELECTRONICS INC (PA)
2048 Joseph Lloyd Pkwy (44094-8032)
PHONE..............................440 946-6443
Ronald K Brehm, *Pr*
Jeffrey Waterman, *
Bruce Vanek, *
Richard Scebbi, *
EMP: 61 **EST:** 1983
SQ FT: 14,000
SALES (est): 1.68MM
SALES (corp-wide): 1.68MM **Privately
Held**
Web: www.tetradelec.com
SIC: 3672 Printed circuit boards

(G-14540)
TOKU AMERICA INC
Also Called: Striker Hydraulic Breakers
3900 Ben Hur Ave Ste 3 (44094-6398)
PHONE..............................440 954-9923
David Nakamura, *Pr*
Akinori Kihara, *Sec*
▲ **EMP:** 13 **EST:** 2010
SQ FT: 15,000
SALES (est): 9.49MM **Privately Held**
Web: www.toku-america.com
SIC: 3531 Crushers, portable
PA: Toku Pneumatic Co.,Ltd.
4-3-4, Katakasu, Hakata-Ku
Fukuoka FUK 812-0

(G-14541)
TOM RICHARDS INC (PA)
Also Called: Process Technology
38809 Mentor Ave (44094-7932)
PHONE..............................440 974-1300
Jody Richards, *Pr*
Leslie N Thomas, *
▲ **EMP:** 101 **EST:** 1978
SQ FT: 72,000
SALES (est): 35.04MM
SALES (corp-wide): 35.04MM **Privately
Held**
Web: www.processtechnology.com
SIC: 3559 Metal finishing equipment for
plating, etc.

(G-14542)
TOM THUMB CLIP CO INC
36300 Lakeland Blvd Unit 2 (44095-5313)
P.O. Box 709 (44096-0709)
PHONE..............................440 953-9606
Jennifer Baxter, *Pr*

June Baxter, *VP*
EMP: 10 **EST:** 1947
SALES (est): 490.89K **Privately Held**
SIC: 3496 Clips and fasteners, made from
purchased wire

(G-14543)
TRU-FAB TECHNOLOGY INC
34820 Lakeland Blvd (44095-5224)
PHONE..............................440 954-9760
John J Stegh, *Pr*
Connie Stegh, *Treas*
EMP: 10 **EST:** 1995
SQ FT: 15,000
SALES (est): 4.35MM **Privately Held**
Web: www.trufab.com
SIC: 3599 7692 Custom machinery; Welding
repair

(G-14544)
TRUCAST INC
4382 Hamann Pkwy (44094-5683)
PHONE..............................440 942-4923
Jesse Baden, *Pr*
EMP: 60 **EST:** 1996
SQ FT: 20,000
SALES (est): 4.88MM **Privately Held**
Web: www.olympusaero.com
SIC: 3599 Machine shop, jobbing and repair

(G-14545)
TRV LLC
4860 E 345th St (44094-4607)
PHONE..............................440 951-7722
Peter Kolaric, *Pr*
Tom Kolaric, *
Victoria Kolaric, *
EMP: 30 **EST:** 1985
SALES (est): 5.02MM **Privately Held**
SIC: 3599 Machine shop, jobbing and repair

(G-14546)
TWO M PRECISION CO INC
Also Called: United Hydraulics
1747 Joseph Lloyd Pkwy Unit 3
(44094-8067)
PHONE..............................440 946-2120
Mate Brkic, *Pr*
Nate Brkic, *
Doris Brkic, *
EMP: 45 **EST:** 1978
SQ FT: 35,000
SALES (est): 3.28MM **Privately Held**
Web: www.twomprecision.com
SIC: 3599 3569 7692 Machine shop, jobbing
and repair; Filter elements, fluid, hydraulic
line; Welding repair

(G-14547)
U S MOLDING MACHINERY CO INC
38294 Pelton Rd (44094-7765)
PHONE..............................440 918-1701
Zac Cohen, *Pr*
Jerry Harper, *
Robert Luck, *
Bill Sprowls, *
EMP: 28 **EST:** 1980
SQ FT: 12,500
SALES (est): 2.13MM **Privately Held**
Web: www.usmolding.com
SIC: 3089 7699 Injection molding of plastics;
Industrial equipment services

(G-14548)
UNIVERSAL J&Z MACHINE LLC
4781 E 355th St (44094-4631)
PHONE..............................216 486-2220
Joseph Grman, *
EMP: 24 **EST:** 1994
SQ FT: 5,000
SALES (est): 4.59MM **Privately Held**

Web: www.universaljzmachine.com
SIC: 3599 Machine shop, jobbing and repair

(G-14549)
WEYBRIDGE LLC
Also Called: Mika Metal Fabricating
4530 Hamann Pkwy (44094-5630)
PHONE..............................440 951-5500
Benjamin Scott Shelfer, *Ch*
Ryan Thomas, *Pr*
EMP: 30 **EST:** 2020
SALES (est): 4.66MM **Privately Held**
Web: www.mikafab.com
SIC: 3444 Sheet metal specialties, not
stamped

(G-14550)
**WILLOUGHBY BREWING COMPANY
LLC**
4057 Erie St (44094-7804)
P.O. Box 946 (44096-0946)
PHONE..............................440 975-0202
Jeremy Banhoron, *Managing Member*
EMP: 6 **EST:** 1996
SQ FT: 1,200
SALES (est): 979.6K **Privately Held**
Web: www.willoughbybrewing.com
SIC: 2082 5812 Beer (alcoholic beverage);
Eating places

(G-14551)
WILLOUGHBY PRINTING CO INC
37946 Elm St (44094-6287)
PHONE..............................440 946-0800
Michael Yutzy, *Pr*
Randi Yutzy, *Mgr*
EMP: 8 **EST:** 1950
SQ FT: 4,800
SALES (est): 670.19K **Privately Held**
Web: www.willoughbyprinting.com
SIC: 2752 Offset printing

(G-14552)
**WINTER EQUIPMENT COMPANY
INCORPORATED**
1900 Joseph Lloyd Pkwy (44094-8030)
PHONE..............................440 946-8377
◆ **EMP:** 25 **EST:** 1983
SALES (est): 9.63MM **Privately Held**
Web: www.winterequipment.com
SIC: 3531 5082 Snow plow attachments;
Road construction equipment

(G-14553)
Z & Z MANUFACTURING INC
4765 E 355th St (44094-4631)
PHONE..............................440 953-2800
Tom Zovko, *Pr*
EMP: 18 **EST:** 1980
SQ FT: 20,000
SALES (est): 1.81MM **Privately Held**
Web: www.z-zmfg.com
SIC: 3599 Machine shop, jobbing and repair

(G-14554)
ZERO-D PRODUCTS INC
Also Called: Akron Jewelry Rubber
37939 Stevens Blvd (44094-6235)
PHONE..............................440 942-5005
William W Mull, *Pr*
Robert J Beausoleil, *VP*
James R Dillhoefer, *Sec*
EMP: 6 **EST:** 1984
SALES (est): 482.49K **Privately Held**
Web: www.zerodproducts.com
SIC: 3915 Jewelers' findings and materials

Willoughby Hills
Lake County

(G-14555)
ATLANTIC CO
26651 Curtiss Wright Pkwy (44092-2832)
PHONE.............................440 944-8988
F Joseph Callahan, *Ch Bd*
William Cosgrove, *
Thomas Janock, *
EMP: 19 EST: 1959
SQ FT: 30,000
SALES (est): 883.51K
SALES (corp-wide): 881.02MM **Privately Held**
SIC: 3432 Plumbing fixture fittings and trim
PA: Swagelok Company
29500 Solon Rd
Solon OH 44139
440 248-4600

(G-14556)
CARBON WEB PRINT LLC
38033 Dodds Hill Dr (44094-9660)
PHONE.............................216 402-3504
Mitchell Mclaughlin, *Prin*
EMP: 28 EST: 2017
SALES (est): 238.18K **Privately Held**
Web: www.carbonweb.co
SIC: 2752 Offset printing

(G-14557)
CHAGRIN VLY STL ERECTORS INC
Also Called: Ruple Trucking
2278 River Rd (44094-9685)
PHONE.............................440 975-1556
Victoria Ruple, *Pr*
John Ruple, *Pr*
EMP: 13 EST: 1993
SQ FT: 10,040
SALES (est): 2.04MM **Privately Held**
SIC: 3441 1791 4213 1796 Fabricated structural metal; Structural steel erection; Trucking, except local; Machine moving and rigging

(G-14558)
EUCLID DESIGN AND MFG INC
2895 Millgate Dr (44094-9778)
PHONE.............................440 942-0066
Don Nemeth, *Pr*
EMP: 10 EST: 1972
SALES (est): 499.63K **Privately Held**
SIC: 3544 Special dies and tools

(G-14559)
EUCLID WELDING COMPANY INC
29956 White Rd (44092-1373)
P.O. Box 202 (44092-0202)
PHONE.............................216 289-0714
John Varljen, *Pr*
EMP: 10 EST: 1972
SQ FT: 26,000
SALES (est): 706.71K **Privately Held**
SIC: 1799 3441 3599 Welding on site; Fabricated structural metal; Machine shop, jobbing and repair

(G-14560)
MICRO PRODUCTS CO INC
26653 Curtiss Wright Pkwy (44092-2832)
PHONE.............................440 943-0258
Arthur Anton, *Pr*
Frank Roddy, *
Ernie Mansour, *
EMP: 25 EST: 1981
SQ FT: 10,000
SALES (est): 699.88K
SALES (corp-wide): 881.02MM **Privately Held**

SIC: 3471 7389 Plating of metals or formed products; Grinding, precision: commercial or industrial
PA: Swagelok Company
29500 Solon Rd
Solon OH 44139
440 248-4600

(G-14561)
NEUROS MEDICAL INC
35010 Chardon Rd Ste 210 (44094-9011)
PHONE.............................440 951-2565
David Veino, *Pr*
Alan Kaganov, *Ch Bd*
Zach Stassen, *CFO*
EMP: 8 EST: 2008
SQ FT: 4,275
SALES (est): 1.55MM **Privately Held**
Web: www.neurosmedical.com
SIC: 3845 Electromedical equipment

(G-14562)
PRODUCE PACKAGING INC
27853 Chardon Rd (44092-2703)
PHONE.............................216 391-6129
Greg Fritz, *Pr*
Jerome Fritz, *
Bill Ramos, *
Bill Weinmann, *
EMP: 150 EST: 1994
SALES (est): 17.56MM
SALES (corp-wide): 17.56MM **Privately Held**
Web: www.ppifresh.net
SIC: 2099 5148 4222 Food preparations, nec ; Fresh fruits and vegetables; Refrigerated warehousing and storage
PA: Great Lakes Packers, Inc.
400 Great Lakes Pkwy
Bellevue OH 44811
419 483-2956

(G-14563)
SUPERIOR ENERGY GROUP LTD
34469 Scotch Ln Apt 4 (44094-2987)
PHONE.............................216 282-4440
EMP: 25 EST: 2020
SALES (est): 780.46K **Privately Held**
Web: www.superiorenergy.com
SIC: 1389 Oil field services, nec

(G-14564)
SWAGELOK COMPANY
Also Called: Swagelok Co
26653 Curtiss Wright Pkwy (44092-2832)
P.O. Box 31300 (44131-0300)
PHONE.............................440 248-4600
EMP: 47
SALES (corp-wide): 881.02MM **Privately Held**
Web: www.swagelok.com
SIC: 3491 3599 Pressure valves and regulators, industrial; Machine shop, jobbing and repair
PA: Swagelok Company
29500 Solon Rd
Solon OH 44139
440 248-4600

Willowick
Lake County

(G-14565)
CHIPS MANUFACTURING INC
260 E 312th St (44095-3666)
PHONE.............................440 946-3666
Frank Cipriano, *Pr*
EMP: 9 EST: 1991
SALES (est): 722.3K **Privately Held**

SIC: 3599 Machine shop, jobbing and repair

(G-14566)
EMES SUPPLY LLC
35622 Vine St (44095-3150)
PHONE.............................216 400-8025
EMP: 7 EST: 2015
SALES (est): 947.34K **Privately Held**
Web: www.emessupply.com
SIC: 2842 Cleaning or polishing preparations, nec

(G-14567)
STAKES MANUFACTURING LLC
Also Called: Stakes Mfg
34440 Vine St (44095-5114)
PHONE.............................216 245-4752
Vincent Bartozzi, *CEO*
Vince Bartozzi, *
Jed Seifert, *
Abhinav Somani, *
EMP: 99 EST: 2019
SQ FT: 40,000
SALES (est): 13.05MM **Privately Held**
Web: www.stakesmfg.com
SIC: 3953 2396 Screens, textile printing; Screen printing on fabric articles

(G-14568)
SUELOS SWEETZ LLC
35560 Vine St (44095-3148)
PHONE.............................440 478-1301
Jordan Anderson, *Managing Member*
EMP: 7 EST: 2020
SALES (est): 32K **Privately Held**
SIC: 2051 Bakery products, partially cooked (except frozen)

Wilmington
Clinton County

(G-14569)
ABBOTT IMAGE SOLUTIONS LLC
185 Park Dr Ste A (45177-2890)
PHONE.............................937 382-6677
Greg Abbott, *Owner*
EMP: 13 EST: 2012
SALES (est): 1.29MM **Privately Held**
Web: www.abbottis.com
SIC: 3993 Signs and advertising specialties

(C-14570)
AHRESTY WILMINGTON CORPORATION
2627 S South St (45177-2926)
PHONE.............................937 382-6112
Kenichi Nonaka, *Pr*
Justin Rummer, *
▲ EMP: 378 EST: 1988
SQ FT: 334,000
SALES (est): 42.91MM **Privately Held**
Web: www.ahresty.com
SIC: 3363 Aluminum die-castings
PA: Ahresty Corporation
1-2, Nakahara, Mitsuyacho
Toyohashi AIC 441-3

(G-14571)
ALKERMES INC
265 Olinger Cir (45177-2484)
PHONE.............................937 382-5642
Barry Thrift, *Brnch Mgr*
EMP: 40
SQ FT: 12,000
Web: www.alkermes.com
SIC: 2834 Pharmaceutical preparations
HQ: Alkermes, Inc.
900 Winter St
Waltham MA 02451
781 609-6000

(G-14572)
B&M UNDERGROUND LLC
1403 Gurneyville Rd (45177-8300)
PHONE.............................740 505-3096
Kevin Peelle, *Prin*
EMP: 6 EST: 2018
SALES (est): 2.25MM **Privately Held**
SIC: 3999 Manufacturing industries, nec

(G-14573)
BARBARA A LIEURANCE
180 E Sugartree St (45177-2333)
PHONE.............................937 382-2864
Barbara Lieurance, *Prin*
EMP: 6 EST: 2010
SALES (est): 88.62K **Privately Held**
SIC: 3469 Automobile license tags, stamped metal

(G-14574)
BUSH SPECIALTY VEHICLES INC
80 Park Dr (45177-2038)
PHONE.............................937 382-5502
Larry Vanover, *VP*
EMP: 15 EST: 1971
SALES (est): 5.82MM **Privately Held**
Web: www.bushspecialtyvehicles.com
SIC: 3713 Specialty motor vehicle bodies

(G-14575)
CHAMPION BRIDGE COMPANY
261 E Sugartree St (45177-2316)
PHONE.............................937 382-2521
Randy Dell, *Pr*
Gale Gerard, *VP*
EMP: 20 EST: 1934
SQ FT: 30,000
SALES (est): 2.56MM **Privately Held**
Web: www.championbridgecompany.com
SIC: 3441 Fabricated structural metal

(G-14576)
COX PRINTING COMPANY
Also Called: Cox Painting
1087 Wayne Rd (45177-2024)
P.O. Box 263 (45039-0263)
PHONE.............................937 382-2312
Pamela Olds, *Pr*
Ramona Cox, *Sec*
Frank A Cox, *Cnslt*
EMP: 7 EST: 1949
SQ FT: 2,600
SALES (est): 170.69K **Privately Held**
SIC: 2752 2759 2789 Offset printing; Letterpress printing; Bookbinding and related work

(G-14577)
CPG INTERNATIONAL LLC
Also Called: Timbertech
894 Prairie Rd (45177-8847)
PHONE.............................937 655-8766
EMP: 260
SALES (corp-wide): 1.44B **Publicly Held**
Web: www.timbertech.com
SIC: 3089 Plastics hardware and building products
HQ: The Azek Group Llc
1330 W Fulton St Ste 350
Chicago IL 60607
570 558-8000

(G-14578)
CUSTOM MOLDED PRODUCTS LLC
92 Grant St (45177-2324)
PHONE.............................937 382-1070
▲ EMP: 84 EST: 1999
SQ FT: 11,000
SALES (est): 7.71MM **Privately Held**

Web: www.custommolded.com
SIC: 3089 Injection molding of plastics

(G-14579)
ESSENTIAL PROVISIONS LLC
292 Inwood Rd (45177-8355)
PHONE................................937 271-0381
Robin Gentry Mcgee, *Pt*
Robin Mcgee, *Managing Member*
Namrata Maguire, *CFO*
EMP: 8 EST: 2022
SALES (est): 261.43K **Privately Held**
SIC: 2099 7389 Food preparations, nec;
Business Activities at Non-Commercial Site

(G-14580)
FERNO-WASHINGTON INC (PA)
Also Called: Ferno
70 Weil Way (45177-9300)
PHONE................................877 733-0911
Joseph Bourgraf, *Pr*
Elroy Bourgraf, *
◆ EMP: 243 EST: 1955
SQ FT: 212,000
SALES (est): 45.1MM
SALES (corp-wide): 45.1MM **Privately Held**
Web: www.ferno.com
SIC: 5047 3842 Medical equipment and
supplies; Splints, pneumatic and wood

(G-14581)
FORTIS PLASTICS LLC
185 Park Dr (45177-2891)
PHONE................................937 382-0966
Bob Sheriean, *Prin*
EMP: 7 EST: 2010
SALES (est): 544.32K **Privately Held**
SIC: 3089 Molding primary plastics

(G-14582)
GCI METALS INC
259 Olinger Cir (45177-2484)
PHONE................................937 835-7123
Kimberly Smallwood, *Pr*
EMP: 13 EST: 2013
SALES (est): 3.14MM **Privately Held**
Web: gcimetals.wixsite.com
SIC: 3499 Fabricated metal products, nec

(G-14583)
HALE MANUFACTURING LLC
1065 Wayne Rd (45177-2024)
PHONE................................937 382-2127
David Hale, *Pr*
David Hale, *Pt*
EMP: 10 EST: 1947
SQ FT: 10,000
SALES (est): 991.51K **Privately Held**
Web: www.halemfg.com
SIC: 3599 Machine shop, jobbing and repair

(G-14584)
HOOD PACKAGING CORPORATION
Also Called: Southern Bag
1961 Rombach Ave (45177-1997)
P.O. Box 745 (45177-0745)
PHONE................................937 382-6681
Bill Terrill, *Brnch Mgr*
EMP: 200
SQ FT: 150,000
Web: www.hoodpkg.com
SIC: 2674 2673 Shipping bags or sacks,
including multiwall and heavy duty; Bags:
plastic, laminated, and coated
HQ: Hood Packaging Corporation
25 Woodgreen Pl
Madison MS 39110
601 853-7260

(G-14585)
ORANGE FRAZER PRESS INC
37 1/2 W Main St (45177-2236)
P.O. Box 214 (45177-0214)
PHONE................................937 382-3196
Marcy Hawley, *Pr*
John Baskin, *VP*
EMP: 7 EST: 1987
SQ FT: 2,000
SALES (est): 361.86K **Privately Held**
Web: www.orangefrazer.com
SIC: 2741 Miscellaneous publishing

(G-14586)
TIMBERTECH LIMITED
Also Called: Timbertech
894 Prairie Rd (45177-8847)
PHONE................................937 655-8766
◆ EMP: 260
SIC: 3089 Plastics hardware and building
products

(G-14587)
TOTAL BAKING SOLUTIONS LLC
474 S Nelson Ave (45177-2037)
EMP: 20 EST: 2010
SQ FT: 120,000
SALES (est): 1.56MM **Privately Held**
Web: www.allfoodequip.com
SIC: 3556 Ovens, bakery

(G-14588)
TRI STATE MEDIA LLC
325 Davids Dr (45177-2431)
PHONE................................513 933-0101
John Clary, *Pr*
EMP: 15 EST: 2001
SQ FT: 10,500
SALES (est): 9.31MM **Privately Held**
Web: www.tri-statemedia.com
SIC: 2679 Labels, paper: made from
purchased material

(G-14589)
VECTOR ELECTROMAGNETICS LLC
1245 Airport Rd (45177-9389)
PHONE................................937 478-5904
Errol English, *Prin*
EMP: 10 EST: 2013
SALES (est): 988.22K **Privately Held**
Web: www.vector-em.com
SIC: 8711 3812 Electrical or electronic
engineering; Defense systems and
equipment

(G-14590)
WILMINGTON FOREST PRODUCTS
5562 S Us Highway 68 (45177-7112)
PHONE................................937 382-7813
Thomas D Driscoll, *Pr*
Mary B Driscoll, *VP*
EMP: 6 EST: 1979
SQ FT: 7,500
SALES (est): 202.49K **Privately Held**
SIC: 2421 Sawmills and planing mills,
general

(G-14591)
WILMINGTON PRCSION MCHNNG INC
Also Called: Wilmington Precision Machining
397 Starbuck Rd (45177-8875)
PHONE................................937 382-3700
Steve Garrison, *Pr*
David D Clay, *
Clifton Hamilton, *
EMP: 24 EST: 1996
SQ FT: 9,000
SALES (est): 5.23MM **Privately Held**
Web: www.wpm-inc.net

SIC: 3544 Special dies and tools

Wilmot
Stark County

(G-14592)
AMISH DOOR INC (PA)
Also Called: Amish Door Restaurant
1210 Winesburg St (44689)
P.O. Box 215 (44689-0215)
PHONE................................330 359-5464
Milo Miller, *Pr*
Yvonne Torrence, *
Katherine Miller, *Stockholder*
Eric Gerber, *
EMP: 155 EST: 1957
SQ FT: 7,500
SALES (est): 3.19MM
SALES (corp-wide): 3.19MM **Privately Held**
Web: www.amishdoor.com
SIC: 5947 5812 7011 2051 Gift shop;
Restaurant, family: independent; Hotels
and motels; Bread, cake, and related
products

(G-14593)
COSMO PLASTICS COMPANY
Also Called: Cosmo Plastics Co
211 Winesburg St (44689-9616)
P.O. Box 157 (44689-0157)
PHONE................................330 359-5429
Vicky Wartcentruber, *Mgr*
EMP: 56
SQ FT: 12,000
SALES (corp-wide): 33.37K **Privately Held**
Web: www.cosmocorp.com
SIC: 3089 Injection molding of plastics
HQ: Cosmo Plastics Company
30201 Aurora Rd
Cleveland OH 44139
440 498-7500

(G-14594)
DAVID E EASTERDAY AND CO INC
Also Called: Easterday & Co
1225 Us Route 62 Unit C (44689-9628)
PHONE................................330 359-0700
David E Easterday, *Pr*
Valeria Easterday, *Sec*
EMP: 12 EST: 1972
SQ FT: 40,000
SALES (est): 4.42MM **Privately Held**
Web: www.woodwrightfinish.com
SIC: 2851 Varnishes, nec

(G-14595)
TREVOR CLATTERBUCK
Also Called: Wholesome Valley Farm
927 Us Route 62 (44689-9610)
PHONE................................330 359-2129
Trevor Clatterbuck, *Owner*
Derek Suhoski, *Owner*
EMP: 6 EST: 2017
SALES (est): 251.11K **Privately Held**
Web: www.wholesomevalleyfarm.com
SIC: 0191 2032 2033 General farms,
primarily crop; Canned specialties; Canned
fruits and specialties

(G-14596)
WEAVER LUMBER CO
1925 Us Route 62 (44689-9604)
PHONE................................330 359-5091
Robert Weaver, *Owner*
EMP: 6 EST: 1981
SALES (est): 362.18K **Privately Held**
Web: www.weaver-lumber.com
SIC: 2421 Custom sawmill

Winchester
Adams County

(G-14597)
CANTRELL RFINERY SLS TRNSP INC
18856 State Route 136 (45697-9793)
P.O. Box 175 (45697-0175)
PHONE................................937 695-0318
Robert Cantrell, *Pr*
EMP: 7 EST: 2008
SALES (est): 2.42MM **Privately Held**
SIC: 3559 Petroleum refinery equipment

(G-14598)
HEIDELBERG MATERIALS US INC
Also Called: Hanson Aggregates Eagle
Quarry
13526 Overstake Rd (45697-9644)
PHONE................................937 442-6009
EMP: 48
SALES (corp-wide): 22.37B **Privately Held**
Web: www.heidelbergmaterials.us
SIC: 3273 Ready-mixed concrete
HQ: Heidelberg Materials Us, Inc.
300 E John Carpenter Fwy
Irving TX 75062

(G-14599)
N & W MACHINING & FABG INC
8 Mathias Rd (45697-9727)
PHONE................................937 695-5582
Junior Nesbitt, *Pr*
Julene Nesbitt, *Sec*
EMP: 9 EST: 1996
SQ FT: 10,000
SALES (est): 1.5MM **Privately Held**
Web: www.go-to-low-cost-insurance.com
SIC: 3599 Machine shop, jobbing and repair

Windham
Portage County

(G-14600)
GEAUGA HIGHWAY CO
9215 State Route 303 (44288-1012)
PHONE................................440 834-4580
John Bojec, *Pr*
EMP: 10 EST: 2021
SALES (est): 2.83MM **Privately Held**
Web: www.geaugahighway.com
SIC: 3531 7389 Asphalt plant, including
gravel-mix type; Business Activities at Non-
Commercial Site

Windsor
Ashtabula County

(G-14601)
HERSHBERGER MANUFACTURING
Also Called: Eagle Hardwoods
7584 Rockwood Rd (44099-9741)
P.O. Box 336 (44099-0336)
PHONE................................440 272-5555
John Hershberger, *Owner*
EMP: 20 EST: 1989
SQ FT: 6,500
SALES (est): 939.4K **Privately Held**
Web: www.hershbergermfg.com
SIC: 2448 4212 Pallets, wood; Local
trucking, without storage

(G-14602)
HILLSIDE PALLET LTD
8552 Cox Rd (44099-9729)
PHONE................................440 272-5425
Norman Byler, *Pt*

Timothy Miller, *Pt*
EMP: 7 **EST:** 2002
SALES (est): 114.48K **Privately Held**
Web: www.mokanauto.com
SIC: 2448 Pallets, wood

(G-14603)
S HOLLEY LUMBER LLC
7143 Noble Rd (44099-9750)
PHONE.................................440 272-5315
EMP: 6 **EST:** 2008
SALES (est): 160.36K **Privately Held**
Web: www.sholleylumber.com
SIC: 2431 2421 Millwork; Lumber stacking or
sticking

Winesburg
Holmes County

(G-14604)
9444 OHIO HOLDING CO
1658 Us Route 62 E (44690)
P.O. Box 181 (44690-0181)
PHONE.................................330 359-6291
Robert Ramseyer, *Pr*
▲ **EMP:** 45 **EST:** 1997
SQ FT: 5,500
SALES (est): 892.74K **Privately Held**
SIC: 2022 Natural cheese

(G-14605)
CASE FARMS OF OHIO INC
Also Called: Case Farms Chicken
1818 County Rd 160 (44690)
P.O. Box 185 (44690-0185)
PHONE.................................330 359-7141
EMP: 125
Web: www.casefarms.com
SIC: 2015 2011 Poultry slaughtering and
processing; Meat packing plants

(G-14606)
CASE FARMS PROCESSING INC
1818 County Rd 160 (44690)
PHONE.................................330 455-0241
Michael Popwycz, *Brnch Mgr*
EMP: 33
SALES (corp-wide): 117.64MM **Privately
Held**
SIC: 2015 Poultry slaughtering and
processing
HQ: Case Farms Processing, Inc
385 Pilch Rd
Troutman NC 28166

(G-14607)
MERIDIAN INDUSTRIES INC
Also Called: Kent Elastomer Products
7369 Peabody Kent Rd (44690)
P.O. Box 186 (44690-0186)
PHONE.................................330 359-5447
Robert Oborn, *Brnch Mgr*
EMP: 75
SALES (corp-wide): 331.16MM **Privately
Held**
Web: www.meridiancompanies.com
SIC: 3069 3949 Tubing, rubber; Sporting
and athletic goods, nec
PA: Meridian Industries, Inc.
735 N Water St Ste 630
Milwaukee WI 53202
414 224-0610

(G-14608)
ROBIN INDUSTRIES INC
Also Called: Holmco Division
7227 State Route 515 (44690)
P.O. Box 188 (44690-0188)
PHONE.................................330 359-5418

Paul Rogers, *Prin*
EMP: 68
SALES (corp-wide): 74.78MM **Privately
Held**
Web: www.robin-industries.com
SIC: 3069 3061 Molded rubber products;
Mechanical rubber goods
PA: Robin Industries, Inc.
8562 Port Jackson Ave Nw
North Canton OH 44720
216 631-7000

(G-14609)
WINESBURG MEATS INC
2181 Us Route 62 (44690-9001)
P.O. Box 202 (44690-0202)
PHONE.................................330 359-5092
Marion Pacula, *Pr*
EMP: 8 **EST:** 1959
SQ FT: 5,500
SALES (est): 963.93K **Privately Held**
Web: www.winesburg-meats.com
SIC: 2011 5421 Meat packing plants; Meat
markets, including freezer provisioners

Wintersville
Jefferson County

(G-14610)
ANTHONY MINING CO INC
72 Airport Rd (43953-9204)
P.O. Box 1298 (43952-6298)
PHONE.................................740 282-5301
Albert Carapellotti, *Pr*
Michael Carapellotti, *Sec*
EMP: 6 **EST:** 1957
SQ FT: 1,000
SALES (est): 620.14K **Privately Held**
SIC: 6512 1221 Nonresidential building
operators; Bituminous coal and lignite-
surface mining

(G-14611)
ARM (USA) INC
1506 Fernwood Rd (43953-7640)
PHONE.................................740 264-6599
Eric Bates, *CEO*
Eric Bates, *Ch Bd*
Mike Gill, *
◆ **EMP:** 50 **EST:** 1996
SALES (est): 8.95MM **Privately Held**
Web: www.armrides.com
SIC: 3599 Amusement park equipment

Woodsfield
Monroe County

(G-14612)
HEARTLAND RETREADERS INC
103 N Sycamore St (43793-1031)
P.O. Box 386 (43793-0386)
PHONE.................................740 472-0558
Craig Freeman, *Pr*
EMP: 11 **EST:** 1975
SQ FT: 7,500
SALES (est): 147.49K **Privately Held**
SIC: 7534 Rebuilding and retreading tires

(G-14613)
J C L S ENTERPRISES LLC
Also Called: Sew It Seams
742 Lewisville Rd (43793-9061)
P.O. Box 150 (43793-0150)
PHONE.................................740 472-0314
EMP: 7 **EST:** 1986
SALES (est): 85.85K **Privately Held**

SIC: 2331 2321 Blouses, women's and
juniors': made from purchased material;
Sport shirts, men's and boys': from
purchased materials

(G-14614)
KEMPS ACE HARDWARE INC
Also Called: True Value
218 State Rte 78 (43793)
P.O. Box 30 (43793-0030)
PHONE.................................740 472-1651
Walter L Kemp, *Pr*
Sally Kemp, *VP*
Charles Orum, *Sec*
EMP: 17 **EST:** 1974
SQ FT: 12,000
SALES (est): 2.01MM **Privately Held**
Web: www.truevalue.com
SIC: 5251 2421 Hardware stores; Lumber:
rough, sawed, or planed

(G-14615)
OHIO MADE TIRES LLC
47063 Black Walnut Pkwy (43793-9521)
PHONE.................................740 421-4934
Steven Georgilig, *Managing Member*
Steven Georgilis, *Managing Member*
EMP: 8 **EST:** 2010
SALES (est): 99.17K **Privately Held**
SIC: 7534 Tire retreading and repair shops

Woodville
Sandusky County

(G-14616)
CHIPPEWA TOOL AND MFG CO
1101 Oak St (43469-9792)
P.O. Box 158 (43469-0158)
PHONE.................................419 849-2790
Jim Kusian, *Pr*
EMP: 10 **EST:** 1965
SQ FT: 8,600
SALES (est): 1.49MM **Privately Held**
Web: www.chippewatool.com
SIC: 3545 3544 Precision tools, machinists';
Special dies and tools

Wooster
Wayne County

(G-1401T)
ABS MATERIALS INC
Also Called: AMC
1909 Old Mansfield Rd Ste C (44691-9474)
PHONE.................................330 234-7999
J Gary Mcdaniel, *CEO*
Stephen Spoonamore, *
Graham Evans, *
Glenn Johnso, *
Marcene Tesmer, *
EMP: 69 **EST:** 2008
SALES (est): 1.93MM **Privately Held**
Web: www.absmaterials.com
SIC: 2869 Industrial organic chemicals, nec

(G-14618)
**ADVANCED DRAINAGE SYSTEMS
INC**
3113 W Old Lincoln Way (44691-3262)
PHONE.................................330 264-4949
Barry Girvin, *Mgr*
EMP: 20
SALES (corp-wide): 2.87B **Publicly Held**
Web: www.adspipe.com
SIC: 3084 3083 Plastics pipe; Laminated
plastics plate and sheet
PA: Advanced Drainage Systems, Inc.
4640 Trueman Blvd

Hilliard OH 43026
614 658-0050

(G-14619)
AKRON BRASS COMPANY
1615 Old Mansfield Rd (44691-7211)
PHONE.................................800 228-1161
EMP: 23
SALES (corp-wide): 3.27B **Publicly Held**
Web: www.akronbrass.com
SIC: 3647 Vehicular lighting equipment
HQ: Akron Brass Company
343 Venture Blvd
Wooster OH 44691

(G-14620)
AKRON BRASS COMPANY (DH)
343 Venture Blvd (44691-7564)
P.O. Box 86 (44691-0086)
PHONE.................................330 264-5678
Sean Tillinghast, *Pr*
Richard Wuescher, *
Steven Webb, *
Mark Whiteling, *
Joseph R Daprile, *
◆ **EMP:** 325 **EST:** 1988
SQ FT: 20,000
SALES (est): 49.32MM
SALES (corp-wide): 3.27B **Publicly Held**
Web: www.akronbrass.com
SIC: 3647 3699 Vehicular lighting equipment
; Electrical equipment and supplies, nec
HQ: Akron Brass Holding Corp.
343 Venture Blvd
Wooster OH 44691
330 264-5678

(G-14621)
ALAN MANUFACTURING INC
3927 E Lincoln Way (44691-8997)
P.O. Box 24875 (44124-0875)
PHONE.................................330 262-1555
Richard Bluestone, *Pr*
▲ **EMP:** 36 **EST:** 1993
SQ FT: 110,000
SALES (est): 2.25MM **Privately Held**
Web: www.alanmfg.com
SIC: 3444 3822 1711 1761 Sheet metalwork;
Environmental controls; Plumbing, heating,
air-conditioning; Roofing, siding, and
sheetmetal work

(G-14622)
ALBRIGHT RADIATOR INC
Also Called: Albright Radiator
331 N Hillcrest Dr (44691-3722)
P.O. Box 214 (44691-0214)
PHONE.................................330 264-8886
TOLL FREE: 800
Dave Albright, *Pr*
Scott Albright, *Sec*
EMP: 6 **EST:** 1928
SQ FT: 4,000
SALES (est): 555.73K **Privately Held**
Web: www.albrightwelding.com
SIC: 7539 7692 3714 Radiator repair shop,
automotive; Welding repair; Radiators and
radiator shells and cores, motor vehicle

(G-14623)
**ARTIFLEX MANUFACTURING INC
(HQ)**
Also Called: Gerstco Division
1425 E Bowman St (44691-3185)
PHONE.................................330 262-2015
Erin Hoffmann, *CEO*
Erik Egerer, *
Greg Wolf, *
◆ **EMP:** 428 **EST:** 2011
SQ FT: 1,200,000
SALES (est): 177.37MM

SALES (corp-wide): 177.37MM **Privately Held**
Web: www.artiflexmfg.com
SIC: 3465 3469 Body parts, automobile: stamped metal; Metal stampings, nec
PA: Its-H Holdings, Llc
731 Broadway Ave Nw
Grand Rapids MI 49504
616 459-8285

(G-14624)
BAUER CORPORATION (PA)
Also Called: Bauer Ladder
2540 Progress Dr (44691-7970)
PHONE....................800 321-4760
Mark Mcconnell, *Pr*
Ward Mcconnel, *Ch*
Norman Miller Stkldr, *Prin*
John Vasichko, *
EMP: 30 **EST:** 1916
SQ FT: 71,500
SALES (est): 9.35MM **Privately Held**
Web: www.bauerladder.com
SIC: 5082 3499 3446 3441 Ladders; Metal ladders; Architectural metalwork; Fabricated structural metal

(G-14625)
BC INVESTMENT CORPORATION
1505 E Bowman St (44691-3128)
P.O. Box 165 (44691-0165)
PHONE....................330 262-3070
Norman L Miller Junior, *Pr*
EMP: 120 **EST:** 1990
SQ FT: 72,500
SALES (est): 1.38MM **Privately Held**
Web: wooster-oh.ohio-pages.com
SIC: 2499 3499 4213 3089 Ladders and stepladders, wood; Metal ladders; Trucking, except local; Plastics processing

(G-14626)
BISHOP WELL SERVICES CORP
416 N Bauer Rd (44691-8626)
P.O. Box 511 (44691-0511)
PHONE....................330 264-2023
EMP: 9 **EST:** 1992
SQ FT: 6,000
SALES (est): 541.35K **Privately Held**
SIC: 1389 Oil field services, nec

(G-14627)
BOSCH REXROTH CORPORATION
Mannesmann Rexroth
290 E Milltown Rd (44691-6113)
P.O. Box 394 (44691-0394)
PHONE....................330 263-3300
Mike Bickel, *Brnch Mgr*
EMP: 159
SALES (corp-wide): 391.51MM **Privately Held**
Web: www.boschrexroth-us.com
SIC: 3594 3494 3491 Pumps, hydraulic power transfer; Expansion joints, pipe; Industrial valves
HQ: Bosch Rexroth Corporation
14001 S Lkes Dr S Pt Bus
Charlotte NC 28273
704 583-4338

(G-14628)
BUCKEYE CORRUGATED INC
Also Called: Buckeye Container Division
3350 Long Rd (44691-7953)
PHONE....................330 264-6336
Jack Nebesky, *Brnch Mgr*
EMP: 66
SALES (corp-wide): 1.1B **Privately Held**
Web: www.bcipkg.com
SIC: 2653 Boxes, corrugated: made from purchased materials

PA: Buckeye Corrugated, Inc.
822 Kumho Dr Ste 400
Fairlawn OH 44333
330 576-0590

(G-14629)
BUCKEYE OIL PRODUCING CO
544 E Liberty St (44691-3602)
P.O. Box 129 (44691-0129)
PHONE....................330 264-8847
Adam Briggs, *CEO*
Mark Lytle, *Pr*
Steve Sigler, *VP*
EMP: 15 **EST:** 1961
SQ FT: 10,000
SALES (est): 2.09MM **Privately Held**
Web: www.buckeyeoilinc.com
SIC: 1311 1381 Crude petroleum production; Drilling oil and gas wells

(G-14630)
BUILT-RITE BOX & CRATE INC
608 Freedlander Rd (44691-4704)
P.O. Box 1051 (44691-7051)
PHONE....................330 263-0936
John C Meenan, *Pr*
Dave Schaeufele, *VP*
Jodie L Meenan, *Sec*
EMP: 25 **EST:** 1986
SQ FT: 10,000
SALES (est): 2.34MM **Privately Held**
Web: www.builtritebox.com
SIC: 2441 2448 Boxes, wood; Skids, wood

(G-14631)
CLARK-FOWLER ENTERPRISES INC
Also Called: Clark-Fowler Elc Mtr & Sups
510 W Henry St (44691-4773)
PHONE....................330 262-0906
Don Clark, *Pr*
Douglas Fowler, *
Jerry L Clark, *
EMP: 24 **EST:** 1995
SQ FT: 5,000
SALES (est): 4.54MM **Privately Held**
Web: www.clarkfowlerelectric.com
SIC: 7694 5063 Electric motor repair; Motors, electric

(G-14632)
CROWN DIV OF ALLEN GR
1654 Old Mansfield Rd (44691-7211)
PHONE....................330 263-4919
Michael Hooper, *Prin*
EMP: 7 **EST:** 2007
SALES (est): 100.33K **Privately Held**
SIC: 3714 Motor vehicle parts and accessories

(G-14633)
DAISY BRAND LLC
3049 Daisy Way (44691-9819)
PHONE....................330 202-4410
David M Sokolsky, *Managing Member*
EMP: 18
SALES (corp-wide): 211.05MM **Privately Held**
Web: www.daisybrand.com
SIC: 2026 Milk processing (pasteurizing, homogenizing, bottling)
PA: Daisy Brand, Llc
12750 Merit Dr Ste 600
Dallas TX 75251
972 726-0800

(G-14634)
DBW FIBER CORPORATION
1720 Enterprise Corporation (44691)
P.O. Box 61108 (29419-1108)
◆ **EMP:** 73 **EST:** 2006
SQ FT: 37,500

SALES (est): 1.3MM **Privately Held**
Web: www.dbw.de
SIC: 3714 Exhaust systems and parts, motor vehicle

(G-14635)
DRAGON PRODUCTS LLC
3310 Columbus Rd (44691-9134)
PHONE....................330 345-3968
Charles Baker, *Brnch Mgr*
EMP: 40
Web: www.dragonproducts.com
SIC: 3531 3537 Construction machinery; Industrial trucks and tractors
HQ: Dragon Products, Llc
1655 Louisiana St
Beaumont TX 77701
409 833-2665

(G-14636)
E-PAK MANUFACTURING LLC (PA)
1109 Pittsburgh Ave (44691-3805)
P.O. Box 269 (44691-0269)
PHONE....................330 264-0825
Bryan Mullet, *Managing Member*
▼ **EMP:** 40 **EST:** 2008
SQ FT: 12,000
SALES (est): 8.78MM
SALES (corp-wide): 8.78MM **Privately Held**
Web: www.epakmanufacturing.com
SIC: 3443 3441 Dumpsters, garbage; Fabricated structural metal

(G-14637)
FEW ATMTIVE GL APPLCATIONS INC
1720 Enterprise Pkwy (44691-7946)
PHONE....................234 249-1880
Morgan Durst, *Contrlr*
▲ **EMP:** 100 **EST:** 2011
SQ FT: 12,000
SALES (est): 9.47MM **Privately Held**
Web: www.few-group.com
SIC: 3089 Windshields, plastics

(G-14638)
FRANKLIN GAS & OIL COMPANY LLC
1615 W Old Lincoln Way (44691-3329)
P.O. Box 1005 (44691-7005)
PHONE....................330 264-8739
James C Morgan, *Managing Member*
EMP: 7 **EST:** 1957
SQ FT: 4,000
SALES (est): 1.19MM **Privately Held**
SIC: 1311 Crude petroleum production

(G-14639)
FRITO-LAY NORTH AMERICA INC
Also Called: Frito-Lay
1626 Old Mansfield Rd (44691-9056)
PHONE....................972 334-7000
Mark Vantrease, *Brnch Mgr*
EMP: 76
SALES (corp-wide): 91.47B **Publicly Held**
Web: www.fritolayemployment.com
SIC: 2099 2096 Food preparations, nec; Potato chips and similar snacks
HQ: Frito-Lay North America, Inc.
7701 Legacy Dr
Plano TX 75024

(G-14640)
G & S BAR AND WIRE LLC
4000 E Lincoln Way (44691-8600)
PHONE....................260 747-4154
EMP: 45 **EST:** 2018
SALES (est): 5.79MM **Privately Held**
Web: www.barandwire.com

SIC: 3315 Steel wire and related products

(G-14641)
G & S TITANIUM INC
4000 E Lincoln Way (44691-8600)
P.O. Box 1107 (44691-7081)
PHONE....................330 263-0564
◆ **EMP:** 50 **EST:** 1979
SALES (est): 5.02MM **Privately Held**
Web: www.barandwire.com
SIC: 3441 3496 3444 3356 Fabricated structural metal; Miscellaneous fabricated wire products; Sheet metalwork; Nonferrous rolling and drawing, nec

(G-14642)
GDC INC
1700 Old Mansfield Rd (44691-7212)
PHONE....................574 533-3128
Lonnie Abney, *COO*
EMP: 10
SALES (corp-wide): 35.06MM **Privately Held**
Web: www.gdc-corp.com
SIC: 2822 2869 2891 3069 Synthetic rubber; Perfumes, flavorings, and food additives; Adhesives and sealants; Medical and laboratory rubber sundries and related products
PA: Gdc, Inc.
815 Logan St
Goshen IN 46528
574 533-3128

(G-14643)
GLOBAL BODY & EQUIPMENT CO
Also Called: C & C Metal Products
2061 Sylvan Rd (44691-3849)
P.O. Box 857 (44691-0857)
PHONE....................330 264-6640
Robert Lapsley, *Pr*
Bob Lapsley, *
EMP: 100 **EST:** 2002
SALES (est): 2.51MM **Privately Held**
Web: www.globalbodyusa.com
SIC: 3441 Fabricated structural metal

(G-14644)
GREEN ENERGY INC
4489 E Lincoln Way (44691-8602)
PHONE....................330 262-5112
Stephen R Gessel, *Pr*
James E Gessel, *VP*
Debra J Falde, *Sec*
Carl Robert Gessel, *Asst Tr*
EMP: 7 **EST:** 1983
SQ FT: 3,700
SALES (est): 994.89K **Privately Held**
Web: www.paradiseadventures-kansas.com
SIC: 1311 Crude petroleum production

(G-14645)
GREEN FIELD FARMS CO-OP (PA)
6464 Fredericksburg Rd (44691-9422)
PHONE....................330 263-0246
Leon Wengerd, *CEO*
James Swartzentruber, *CFO*
EMP: 7 **EST:** 2003
SALES (est): 2.07MM **Privately Held**
Web: www.gffarms.com
SIC: 0191 2026 5191 General farms, primarily crop; Fluid milk; Farm supplies

(G-14646)
GRT UTILICORP INC
9268 Ashland Rd (44691-9235)
PHONE....................330 264-8444
Rod Zimmermen, *Pr*
Rod Zimmerman, *Pr*
Thomas Funk, *VP*

▲ = Import ▼ = Export
◆ = Import/Export

▲ **EMP: 20 EST:** 1985
SQ FT: 7,840
SALES (est): 5.4MM **Privately Held**
Web: www.grtutilicorp.com
SIC: 3541 5084 Drilling and boring machines
; Industrial machine parts

(G-14647)
H & H EQUIPMENT INC
Also Called: Snyder Hot Shot
6247 Ashland Rd (44691-9233)
PHONE......................330 264-5400
Gerald Snyder, *Pr*
EMP: 6 **EST:** 1971
SQ FT: 8,400
SALES (est): 963.19K **Privately Held**
SIC: 3715 Truck trailers

(G-14648)
HACKWORTH ELECTRIC MOTORS INC
500 E Henry St (44691-1195)
PHONE......................330 345-6049
TOLL FREE: 800
Jeffery Hackworth, *Pr*
Jeffery Hackworth, *Pr*
Brenda Hackworth, *VP*
EMP: 9 **EST:** 1977
SALES (est): 4.32MM **Privately Held**
Web: www.hackworthelectricmotors.com
SIC: 5063 7694 Motors, electric; Electric
motor repair

(G-14649)
HYDAC TECHNOLOGY CORP
4265 E Lincoln Way Unit C (44691-8666)
PHONE......................610 266-0100
Matthias Mueller, *Pr*
▲ **EMP:** 12 **EST:** 2010
SALES (est): 1.89MM **Privately Held**
Web: www.hydac.com
SIC: 3492 Fluid power valves and hose
fittings

(G-14650)
INGREDIENT INNOVATIONS INTL CO
Also Called: 3i Solutions
146 S Bever St (44691-4326)
PHONE......................330 262-4440
Charles Brain, *Pr*
EMP: 7 **EST:** 1997
SQ FT: 12,000
SALES (est): 4MM **Publicly Held**
Web: www.3isolutions.com
SIC: 2099 Food preparations, nec
PA: Nu Skin Enterprises, Inc.
75 W Center St
Provo UT 84601

(G-14651)
INTERNATIONAL PAPER COMPANY
International Paper
689 Palmer St (44691-3197)
P.O. Box 1047 (44691-7045)
PHONE......................330 264-1322
Jim Gracey, *Genl Mgr*
EMP: 92
SALES (corp-wide): 18.62B **Publicly Held**
Web: www.internationalpaper.com
SIC: 2653 Boxes, corrugated: made from
purchased materials
PA: International Paper Company
6400 Poplar Ave
Memphis TN 38197
901 419-7000

(G-14652)
IRON GATE INDUSTRIES LLC
Also Called: Morrison Custom Welding
1435 S Honeytown Rd (44691-8914)
PHONE......................330 264-0626

Michael Goren, *Pr*
EMP: 24 **EST:** 1996
SQ FT: 37,000
SALES (est): 4.44MM **Privately Held**
Web: www.morrisonwelding.com
SIC: 3441 Fabricated structural metal for
bridges

(G-14653)
IVIES WHOLISTIC DYNAMICS
2390 Cardinal Ct Apt D (44691-2060)
PHONE......................216 469-3103
Ivie Sorkin, *Prin*
EMP: 8 **EST:** 2016
SALES (est): 44.62K **Privately Held**
Web: www.metal-dynamics.com
SIC: 3441 Fabricated structural metal

(G-14654)
JAMES R SMAIL INC
2285 Eagle Pass Ste B (44691-5349)
P.O. Box 1157 (44691-7082)
PHONE......................330 264-7500
James R Smail, *Pr*
Mark A Sparr, *VP*
EMP: 7 **EST:** 1972
SALES (est): 910.6K **Privately Held**
SIC: 1381 Drilling oil and gas wells

(G-14655)
JNP GROUP LLC
449 Freedlander Rd (44691-4734)
P.O. Box 1022 (44691-7022)
PHONE......................800 735-9645
James Pooler, *Pr*
EMP: 12 **EST:** 2010
SALES (est): 720.9K **Privately Held**
SIC: 3585 7389 Refrigeration and heating
equipment; Business Activities at Non-
Commercial Site

(G-14656)
JRB FAMILY HOLDINGS INC
4255 E Lincoln Way (44691-8601)
◆ **EMP:** 169
Web: www.morbark.com
SIC: 3531 Forestry related equipment

(G-14657)
KENOIL INC
1537 Blachleyville Rd (44691-9752)
P.O. Box 1085 (44691-7081)
PHONE......................330 262-1144
Steve Fleisher, *VP*
EMP: 6 **EST:** 1982
SALES (est): 478.58K **Privately Held**
Web: www.kenoil.net
SIC: 1311 Crude petroleum and natural gas
production

(G-14658)
KETMAN CORPORATION
Also Called: Wooster Book Company, The
205 W Liberty St (44691-4831)
PHONE......................330 262-1688
David Wiesenberg, *Pr*
Carol A Rueger, *Sec*
EMP: 8 **EST:** 1991
SQ FT: 7,500
SALES (est): 122.93K **Privately Held**
Web: www.woosterbook.com
SIC: 5942 2731 8742 Comic books; Books,
publishing only; Industry specialist
consultants

(G-14659)
KORDA MANUFACTURING LLC
3927 E Lincoln Way (44691-8997)
PHONE......................330 262-1555
Dan Korda, *Pr*

EMP: 13 **EST:** 1994
SALES (est): 4.86MM **Privately Held**
Web: www.alanmfg.com
SIC: 3444 Sheet metalwork

(G-14660)
LINCOLN WAY VINEYARDS INC
9050 W Old Lincoln Way (44691-7504)
PHONE......................330 804-9463
James Borton, *Pr*
EMP: 10 **EST:** 2008
SALES (est): 760.89K **Privately Held**
Web: www.lincolnwayvineyards.com
SIC: 2084 Wine cellars, bonded: engaged in
blending wines

(G-14661)
LUK CLUTCH SYSTEMS LLC (DH)
Also Called: Luk Clutch Systems
3401 Old Airport Rd (44691-9544)
PHONE......................330 264-4383
◆ **EMP:** 44 **EST:** 1977
SQ FT: 400,000
SALES (est): 24.58MM
SALES (corp-wide): 72.7B **Privately Held**
Web: www.schaeffler.de
SIC: 3568 3566 3714 Power transmission
equipment, nec; Speed changers, drives,
and gears; Clutches, motor vehicle
HQ: Schaeffler Transmission, Llc.
3401 Old Airport Rd
Wooster OH 44691
330 264-4383

(G-14662)
MAGNI-POWER COMPANY (PA)
Also Called: Magni Fab & Magnetic
5511 E Lincoln Way (44691-8607)
P.O. Box 122 (44691-0122)
PHONE......................330 264-3637
EMP: 90 **EST:** 1948
SALES (est): 24.62MM
SALES (corp-wide): 24.62MM **Privately
Held**
Web: www.magnipower.com
SIC: 3441 Fabricated structural metal

(G-14663)
MAINTENANCE + INC
1051 W Liberty St (44691-3307)
P.O. Box 408 (44691-0408)
PHONE......................330 264-6262
William Neckermann, *Pr*
Robert Huebner, *Dir Opers*
◆ **EMP:** 12 **EST:** 1977
SQ FT: 10,000
SALES (est): 2.27MM **Privately Held**
Web: www.maintinc.com
SIC: 2951 Asphalt and asphaltic paving
mixtures (not from refineries)

(G-14664)
MCCANN TOOL & DIE INC
Also Called: J R Tool & Die
3230 Columbus Rd (44691-8430)
PHONE......................330 264-8820
Jess R Mccann Senior, *Pr*
J R Mccann Junior, *VP*
Nellie Mccann, *Sec*
EMP: 6 **EST:** 1982
SQ FT: 6,500
SALES (est): 699.68K **Privately Held**
SIC: 3599 3089 Machine shop, jobbing and
repair; Injection molding of plastics

(G-14665)
METROMEDIA TECHNOLOGIES INC
1061 Venture Blvd (44691-9358)
PHONE......................330 264-2501
Ralph Degliotta, *Mgr*
EMP: 80

SALES (corp-wide): 10.3MM **Privately
Held**
Web: www.mmt.com
SIC: 3993 Signs, not made in custom sign
painting shops
PA: Metromedia Technologies, Inc.
810 7th Ave Fl 29
New York NY 10019
212 273-2100

(G-14666)
MORBARK LLC
4255 E Lincoln Way (44691-8669)
PHONE......................330 264-8699
Dave Herr, *CEO*
EMP: 175
SALES (corp-wide): 1.63B **Publicly Held**
Web: www.morbark.com
SIC: 3531 Forestry related equipment
HQ: Morbark, Llc
8507 S Winn Rd
Winn MI 48896
989 866-2381

(G-14667)
MORTON BUILDINGS INC
1055 Columbus Avenue Ext (44691-9701)
PHONE......................330 345-6188
Gary Schodorf, *Mgr*
EMP: 20
SALES (corp-wide): 89.89MM **Privately
Held**
Web: www.mortonbuildings.com
SIC: 3448 5039 Buildings, portable:
prefabricated metal; Prefabricated
structures
PA: Morton Buildings, Inc.
252 W Adams St
Morton IL 61550
800 447-7436

(G-14668)
MURR CORPORATION
Also Called: Murr Printing and Graphics
201 N Buckeye St (44691-3501)
PHONE......................330 264-2223
TOLL FREE: 800
Joseph F Murr, *Pr*
EMP: 9 **EST:** 1980
SQ FT: 5,800
SALES (est): 763.65K **Privately Held**
Web: www.murrprinting.com
SIC: 2752 5943 Offset printing; Office forms
and supplies

(G-14669)
NORTH CENTRAL CON DESIGNS INC
Also Called: Nccd
3331 E Lincoln Way (44691-3762)
PHONE......................419 606-1908
Daniel Zawacki, *Pr*
Mike Wiseman, *VP Opers*
Lori Crum, *Sec*
EMP: 7 **EST:** 2005
SALES (est): 107.69K **Privately Held**
SIC: 3271 1741 Blocks, concrete: insulating;
Concrete block masonry laying

(G-14670)
NORTH EAST FUEL INC
3927 Cleveland Rd (44691-1223)
PHONE......................330 264-4454
Timothy E Miller, *Prin*
EMP: 6 **EST:** 2013
SALES (est): 219.48K **Privately Held**
SIC: 2869 Fuels

(G-14671)
NORTHEAST TUBULAR INC
426 S Grant St (44691-4712)
P.O. Box 114 (44676-0114)

PHONE..............................330 567-2690
Jeffery W Edington, *Prin*
Paul W Wright, *Prin*
EMP: 6 **EST:** 1989
SALES (est): 127.05K **Privately Held**
SIC: 2241 Hose fabric, tubular

(G-14672)
PRAIRIE LANE CORPORATION
Also Called: Prairie Lane Gravel Co
4489 Prairie Ln (44691-9442)
P.O. Box 233 (44691-0233)
PHONE..............................330 262-3322
Ralph Miller, *Pr*
James Lanham, *Sec*
EMP: 7 **EST:** 1954
SQ FT: 2,400
SALES (est): 713.27K **Privately Held**
Web: www.prairielanelakepark.com
SIC: 1442 7032 6519 Construction sand and
gravel; Sporting and recreational camps;
Farm land leasing

(G-14673)
PRENTKE ROMICH COMPANY (PA)
Also Called: Prc-Saltillo
1022 Heyl Rd (44691-9744)
PHONE..............................330 262-1984
Dave Hershberger, *CEO*
Barry Romich, *
Jan Hughes, *
Lee Miller, *
EMP: 130 **EST:** 1966
SQ FT: 8,000
SALES (est): 40.16MM
SALES (corp-wide): 40.16MM **Privately
Held**
Web: www.prentrom.com
SIC: 3442 Metal doors, sash, and trim

(G-14674)
RBB SYSTEMS INC
1909 Old Mansfield Rd Ste A (44691-9474)
PHONE..............................330 263-4502
Bruce Hendrick, *Pr*
Michele Hendrick, *
Richard L Beery, *
EMP: 135 **EST:** 1973
SQ FT: 20,000
SALES (est): 12.14MM **Privately Held**
Web: www.rbbsystems.com
SIC: 3625 Relays and industrial controls

(G-14675)
RDM EQUIPMENT COMPANY INC
1141 Mechanicsburg Rd (44691-2778)
P.O. Box 169 (44691-0169)
PHONE..............................330 264-8808
Dee Vaidya, *Pr*
Neil Vaidya, *VP*
Mary Vaidya, *VP*
EMP: 12 **EST:** 1966
SQ FT: 10,000
SALES (est): 1.77MM **Privately Held**
Web: www.rdmequipment.com
SIC: 1389 Oil field services, nec

(G-14676)
RICELAND CABINET INC
326 N Hillcrest Dr Ste A (44691-3745)
PHONE..............................330 601-1071
Leroy Miller, *Pr*
Myron Miller, *
David A Miller, *
Paul A Miller, *
Wanda Mullet, *
EMP: 92 **EST:** 1979
SQ FT: 24,220
SALES (est): 5.03MM **Privately Held**
Web: www.ricelandcabinet.com

SIC: 2434 3281 2541 Wood kitchen cabinets
; Cut stone and stone products; Wood
partitions and fixtures

(G-14677)
RICELAND CABINET CORPORATION
326 N Hillcrest Dr Ste A (44691-3745)
PHONE..............................330 601-1071
Kit Carin, *Prin*
EMP: 9 **EST:** 2006
SALES (est): 1.14MM **Privately Held**
Web: www.ricelandcabinet.com
SIC: 2434 Wood kitchen cabinets

(G-14678)
RS&B INDUSTRIES LLC
1147 Akron Rd (44691-2501)
PHONE..............................330 255-6000
EMP: 25 **EST:** 2015
SALES (est): 4.38MM **Privately Held**
SIC: 3999 Manufacturing industries, nec

(G-14679)
SCHAEFFLER GROUP USA INC
3571 Old Airport Rd (44691-7951)
PHONE..............................330 202-6752
EMP: 26
SALES (corp-wide): 72.7B **Privately Held**
SIC: 3562 Ball and roller bearings
HQ: Schaeffler Group Usa Inc.
308 Springhill Farm Rd
Fort Mill SC 29715
803 548-8500

(G-14680)
**SCHAEFFLER TRANSM SYSTEMS
LLC**
3177 Old Airport Rd (44691-9520)
PHONE..............................330 202-6212
EMP: 895
SALES (corp-wide): 72.7B **Privately Held**
Web: www.schaeffler.us
SIC: 3714 3566 Motor vehicle parts and
accessories; Speed changers, drives, and
gears
HQ: Schaeffler Transmission Systems, Llc
3401 Old Airport Rd
Wooster OH 44691
330 264-4383

(G-14681)
**SCHAEFFLER TRANSM SYSTEMS
LLC (DH)**
3401 Old Airport Rd (44691-9581)
PHONE..............................330 264-4383
Marc Mcgrath, *Regional Chief Executive
Officer*
◆ **EMP:** 30 **EST:** 2004
SALES (est): 96.83MM
SALES (corp-wide): 72.7B **Privately Held**
Web: www.schaeffler.us
SIC: 3714 3566 Motor vehicle parts and
accessories; Speed changers, drives, and
gears
HQ: Schaeffler Transmission, Llc.
3401 Old Airport Rd
Wooster OH 44691
330 264-4383

(G-14682)
**SCHAEFFLER TRANSMISSION LLC
(DH)**
3401 Old Airport Rd (44691-9581)
PHONE..............................330 264-4383
Klaus Rosenfeld, *CEO*
Marc Mcgrath, *Pr*
Ashi Uppal, *
▲ **EMP:** 252 **EST:** 2004
SALES (est): 447.99MM
SALES (corp-wide): 72.7B **Privately Held**

Web: www.schaeffler.us
SIC: 3714 Motor vehicle engines and parts
HQ: Schaeffler Group Usa Inc.
308 Springhill Farm Rd
Fort Mill SC 29715
803 548-8500

(G-14683)
SCOT INDUSTRIES INC
6578 Ashland Rd (44691-9233)
P.O. Box 1106 (44691-7081)
PHONE..............................330 262-7585
Robert G Gralinski, *Mgr*
EMP: 113
SQ FT: 2,018
SALES (corp-wide): 113.56MM **Privately
Held**
Web: www.scotindustries.com
SIC: 5051 7389 3498 3471 Steel; Metal
cutting services; Fabricated pipe and fittings
; Plating and polishing
PA: Scot Industries, Inc.
3756 F M 250 N
Lone Star TX 75668
903 639-2551

(G-14684)
SEAMAN CORPORATION (PA)
1000 Venture Blvd (44691-9358)
PHONE..............................330 262-1111
Richard N Seaman, *Ch Bd*
John Crum, *
Terrance Link, *
◆ **EMP:** 130 **EST:** 1951
SQ FT: 90,000
SALES (est): 128.86MM
SALES (corp-wide): 128.86MM **Privately
Held**
Web: www.seamancorp.com
SIC: 2221 Nylon broadwoven fabrics

(G-14685)
SHEARER FARM INC
Also Called: John Deere Authorized Dealer
7762 Cleveland Rd (44691-7700)
PHONE..............................330 345-9023
EMP: 140
Web: www.agprocompanies.com
SIC: 3523 5082 Fertilizing machinery, farm;
Construction and mining machinery

(G-14686)
SIGN DESIGN WOOSTER INC
Also Called: Sign Design
1537 W Old Lincoln Way (44691-3327)
PHONE..............................330 262-8838
Ken Stiffler, *Pr*
Stephanie Stiffler, *Sec*
EMP: 8 **EST:** 1981
SQ FT: 2,000
SALES (est): 936.47K **Privately Held**
Web: www.signdesignwooster.com
SIC: 3993 Signs, not made in custom sign
painting shops

(G-14687)
SMITHVILLE MFG CO
6563 Cleveland Rd (44691-9690)
P.O. Box 258 (44677-0258)
PHONE..............................330 345-5818
Allen Nayman, *Pr*
EMP: 10 **EST:** 1972
SQ FT: 624
SALES (est): 3.46MM **Privately Held**
Web: www.smithvillemfg.com
SIC: 3469 3544 Stamping metal for the trade
; Special dies and tools

(G-14688)
SPEED NORTH AMERICA INC
1700a Old Mansfield Rd (44691-7212)
P.O. Box 79 (44691-0079)
PHONE..............................330 202-7775
Emmanuel Legrand, *Pr*
◆ **EMP:** 38 **EST:** 2007
SALES (est): 12.7MM **Privately Held**
Web: www.speedgroupe.com
SIC: 3524 Hedge trimmers, electric
HQ: Tecomec Srl
Strada Della Mirandola 11
Reggio Nell'emilia RE 42124
052 295-9001

(G-14689)
**STAHL/SCOTT FETZER COMPANY
(HQ)**
Also Called: Arbortech
3201 W Old Lincoln Way (44691-3258)
PHONE..............................800 277-8245
Craig Aszkler, *Pr*
Bob Businger, *
Patricia Scanoln, *
W W T Stephens, *
EMP: 105 **EST:** 1955
SQ FT: 70,000
SALES (est): 23.66MM
SALES (corp-wide): 226 **Privately Held**
Web: www.stahltruckbodies.com
SIC: 3715 Trailer bodies
PA: The Scott Fetzer Company
28800 Clemens Rd
Westlake OH 44145
440 892-3000

(G-14690)
TEKFOR INC
Also Called: Tekfor USA
3690 Long Rd (44691-7962)
PHONE..............................330 202-7420
Kevin Weldi, *Pr*
▲ **EMP:** 265 **EST:** 2001
SQ FT: 100,000
SALES (est): 33.62MM
SALES (corp-wide): 6.12B **Publicly Held**
Web: www.aam.com
SIC: 3462 Automotive forgings, ferrous:
crankshaft, engine, axle, etc.
PA: American Axle & Manufacturing
Holdings, Inc.
1 Dauch Dr
Detroit MI 48211
313 758-2000

(G-14691)
**THE WOOSTER BRUSH COMPANY
(PA)**
604 Madison Ave (44691-4796)
P.O. Box 6010 (44691-6010)
PHONE..............................330 264-4440
◆ **EMP:** 238 **EST:** 1851
SALES (est): 36.31MM
SALES (corp-wide): 36.31MM **Privately
Held**
Web: www.woosterbrush.com
SIC: 3991 Paint and varnish brushes

(G-14692)
TRICOR INDUSTRIAL INC (PA)
Also Called: Tricor Metals
3225 W Old Lincoln Way (44691-3258)
P.O. Box 752 (44691-0752)
PHONE..............................330 264-3299
Nancy A Stitzlein, *CEO*
Michael D Stitzlein, *
◆ **EMP:** 77 **EST:** 1977
SQ FT: 140,000
SALES (est): 46.32MM
SALES (corp-wide): 46.32MM **Privately
Held**

▲ = Import ▼ = Export
◆ = Import/Export

Web: www.tricormetals.com
SIC: **5085** 5169 3444 5051 Fasteners, industrial: nuts, bolts, screws, etc.; Chemicals and allied products, nec; Sheet metalwork; Metals service centers and offices

(G-14693)
TROYER SIGNS INCORPORATED
2740 S Honeytown Rd (44691-8980)
PHONE..................330 263-1400
Maynard Troyer, *Pr*
Lydian Troyer, *Sec*
EMP: 6 EST: 1981
SALES (est): 496.29K **Privately Held**
Web: www.troyersigns.com
SIC: **3993** Signs and advertising specialties

(G-14694)
UNITED TITANIUM INC (PA)
Also Called: United Titanium
3450 Old Airport Rd (44691-9581)
PHONE..................330 264-2111
C Michael Reardon, *Pr*
Charlie Gray, *General Vice President**
▲ EMP: 117 EST: 1962
SQ FT: 150,000
SALES (est): 17.65MM
SALES (corp-wide): 17.65MM **Privately Held**
Web: www.unitedtitanium.com
SIC: **3452** Bolts, nuts, rivets, and washers

(G-14695)
VIB-ISO LLC
Also Called: Vib-ISO
449 Freedlander Rd (44691-4734)
P.O. Box 1022 (44691-7022)
PHONE..................800 735-9645
James Pooler, *Managing Member*
EMP: 12 EST: 2012
SALES (est): 1.08MM **Privately Held**
SIC: **3822** Environmental controls

(G-14696)
WAYNE COUNTY RUBBER INC
1205 E Bowman St (44691-3182)
PHONE..................330 264-5553
Laurie Schang, *Pr*
Arnie Berkowitz, *
EMP: 30 EST: 1991
SQ FT: 170,000
SALES (est): 2.05MM **Privately Held**
Web: www.waynecountyrubber.com
SIC: **2822** 3069 Synthetic rubber; Custom compounding of rubber materials

(G-14697)
WHITE JEWELERS INC
516 N Bever St Apt 1 (44691-6201)
PHONE..................330 264-3324
Heather Maxwell, *Owner*
EMP: 6 EST: 1928
SALES (est): 324.79K **Privately Held**
Web: www.whitejewelers.net
SIC: **5944** 7631 3911 Jewelry, precious stones and precious metals; Watch repair; Jewelry, precious metal

(G-14698)
WOOSTER ABRUZZI COMPANY (PA)
3310 Columbus Rd (44691-9134)
PHONE..................330 345-3968
Doug Drughal, *Pr*
Bill Stanton, *Stockholder*
EMP: 21 EST: 2010
SQ FT: 14,000
SALES (est): 1.88MM **Privately Held**

SIC: **1389** 3444 4212 Construction, repair, and dismantling services; Sheet metalwork; Local trucking, without storage

(G-14699)
WOOSTER BRUSH COMPANY
2550 Daisy Way (44691-9826)
PHONE..................330 264-4440
EMP: 342
SALES (corp-wide): 36.31MM **Privately Held**
SIC: **3991** Brooms and brushes
PA: The Wooster Brush Company
604 Madison Ave
Wooster OH 44691
330 264-4440

(G-14700)
WOOSTER DAILY RECORD INC LLC (HQ)
Also Called: Farmer Hub
212 E Liberty St (44691-4348)
P.O. Box 918 (44691-0918)
PHONE..................330 264-1125
TOLL FREE: 800
Charles Dix, *Pr*
David E Dix, *
Robert C Dix Junior, *VP*
G Charles Dix Ii, *Treas*
Timothy V Dix, *
EMP: 120 EST: 1890
SQ FT: 25,000
SALES (est): 1.28MM
SALES (corp-wide): 38.43MM **Privately Held**
Web: www.the-daily-record.com
SIC: **2711** Commercial printing and newspaper publishing combined
PA: Dix 1898, Inc.
212 E Liberty St
Wooster OH
330 264-3511

(G-14701)
WOOSTER PRODUCTS INC (PA)
1000 Spruce St (44691-4682)
P.O. Box 6005 (44691-6005)
PHONE..................330 264-2844
G K Jim Arora, *Pr*
Doctor Urmil Arora, *VP*
▼ EMP: 70 EST: 1921
SQ FT: 100,000
SALES (est): 10.93MM
SALES (corp-wide): 10.93MM **Privately Held**
Web: www.woosterproducts.com
SIC: **3446** 2851 Stairs, staircases, stair treads: prefabricated metal; Paints and allied products

(G-14702)
WOOSTER PRODUCTS INC
Also Called: Plant 2
1000 Spruce St (44691-4682)
P.O. Box 6005 (44691-6005)
PHONE..................330 264-2854
Adrienne Rodgers, *Brnch Mgr*
EMP: 10
SALES (corp-wide): 10.93MM **Privately Held**
Web: www.woosterproducts.com
SIC: **3446** Stairs, staircases, stair treads: prefabricated metal
PA: Wooster Products Inc
1000 Spruce St
Wooster OH 44691
330 264-2844

(G-14703)
WORTHINGTON CYLINDER CORP
899 Venture Blvd (44691-7521)
PHONE..................330 262-1762
EMP: 82
SALES (corp-wide): 1.25B **Publicly Held**
Web: www.worthingtonenterprises.com
SIC: **3443** Cylinders, pressure: metal plate
HQ: Worthington Cylinder Corporation
200 W Old Wlson Bridge Rd
Worthington OH 43085
614 840-3210

Worthington
Franklin County

(G-14704)
ALL A CART MANUFACTURING INC
870 High St Ste 15 (43085-4139)
PHONE..................614 443-5544
Jeff Morris, *Pr*
▼ EMP: 15 EST: 1972
SALES (est): 2.47MM **Privately Held**
Web: www.allacart.com
SIC: **3715** Truck trailers

(G-14705)
CGAS EXPLORATION INC (HQ)
110 E Wilson Bridge Rd Ste 250 (43085-2317)
PHONE..................614 436-4631
Kenneth Kirk, *Pr*
John Erwin, *CFO*
William Grubaugh, *Ex VP*
EMP: 10 EST: 1946
SQ FT: 27,500
SALES (est): 3.79MM
SALES (corp-wide): 7.98MM **Privately Held**
SIC: **1311** 1382 Crude petroleum production; Oil and gas exploration services
PA: Cgas Inc
110 E Wilson Bridge Rd # 250
Worthington OH 43085
614 975-4697

(G-14706)
CGAS INC (PA)
110 E Wilson Bridge Rd Ste 250 (43085-2317)
PHONE..................614 975-4697
Kenneth Kirk, *Pr*
William Grubaugh, *Ex VP*
John O Erwin, *CFO*
EMP: 6 EST: 1972
SQ FT: 36,000
SALES (est): 7.98MM
SALES (corp-wide): 7.98MM **Privately Held**
SIC: **1311** Crude petroleum production

(G-14707)
CHETTAPARTNERS LLC ✪
105 W Wilson Bridge Rd Ste 180 (43085-2686)
PHONE..................614 368-7600
Marc Chetta, *Managing Member*
EMP: 6 EST: 2023
SALES (est): 1.31MM **Privately Held**
SIC: **7372** Prepackaged software

(G-14708)
DIETRICH INDUSTRIES INC (HQ)
200 W Old Wilson Bridge Rd (43085-2247)
PHONE..................800 873-2604
John E Roberts, *Pr*
Samuel Depasquale, *
Dale T Brinkman, *
Richard F Berdik, *

Andy Rose, *
▼ EMP: 86 EST: 1959
SALES (est): 14.53MM
SALES (corp-wide): 1.25B **Publicly Held**
SIC: **3441** Fabricated structural metal
PA: Worthington Enterprises, Inc.
200 W Old Wlson Bridge Rd
Worthington OH 43085
614 438-3210

(G-14709)
ELEVENTH CANDLE CO
559 High St (43085-4132)
PHONE..................614 530-4853
Amber Runyon, *Prin*
EMP: 6 EST: 2018
SALES (est): 219.54K **Privately Held**
Web: www.eleventhcandleco.com
SIC: **3999** Candles

(G-14710)
FIBERTECH NETWORKS
720 Lakeview Plaza Blvd (43085-4733)
PHONE..................614 436-3565
David Burch, *Prin*
EMP: 8 EST: 2010
SALES (est): 499.36K **Privately Held**
SIC: **3089** Plastics products, nec

(G-14711)
HANNIBAL COMPANY INC
Also Called: Heartland Bread & Roll
6536 Proprietors Rd (43085-3233)
PHONE..................614 846-5060
Rebecca Henderson, *Pr*
EMP: 10 EST: 1991
SALES (est): 355.9K **Privately Held**
Web: www.hannibal.de
SIC: **2051** Breads, rolls, and buns

(G-14712)
HDR POWER SYSTEMS LLC
Also Called: Ametek HDR Power Systems
530 Lakeview Plaza Blvd Ste C (43085-4710)
PHONE..................614 308-5500
▲ EMP: 10 EST: 1981
SALES (est): 5.79MM
SALES (corp-wide): 6.94B **Publicly Held**
Web: www.hdrpower.com
SIC: **3629** Power conversion units, a.c. to d.c.: static-electric
HQ: Solidstate Controls, Llc
875 Dearborn Dr
Columbus OH 43085
614 846-7500

(G-14713)
IDEAL INTEGRATIONS LLC
Also Called: Thinkcsc
7420 Worthington Galena Rd (43085-1528)
PHONE..................614 786-7100
Kurt Camealy, *Technical Vice President*
EMP: 22
SALES (corp-wide): 25.46MM **Privately Held**
Web: www.idealintegrations.net
SIC: **7372** Business oriented computer software
PA: Ideal Integrations, Llc
800 Regis Ave
Pittsburgh PA 15236
412 349-6680

(G-14714)
IGLOO PRESS LLC
39 W New England Ave (43085-3535)
PHONE..................614 787-5528
Ian Brown, *Prin*
EMP: 6 EST: 2012
SALES (est): 424.81K **Privately Held**

GEOGRAPHIC

Web: www.iglooletterpress.com
SIC: 2741 Miscellaneous publishing

(G-14715)
INNERACTIV INC
Also Called: Inneractiv
7000 N High St (43085-2500)
PHONE.................................888 798-7792
Jim Mazotas, Pt
Jay Jayanthan, CEO
James Mazotas, VP
EMP: 15 EST: 2019
SALES (est): 3.09MM Privately Held
SIC: 7372 Prepackaged software

(G-14716)
INTRISM INC
6969 Worthington Galena Rd Ste J
(43085-2322)
PHONE.................................614 787-4631
Kyle Vandeveer, Pr
EMP: 6 EST: 2015
SALES (est): 499.65K Privately Held
Web: www.intrism.com
SIC: 2499 5945 Engraved wood products;
Toys and games

(G-14717)
KNAPE INDUSTRIES INC
6592 Proprietors Rd (43085-3233)
PHONE.................................614 885-3016
John Knape, Pr
Joyce Knape, VP
EMP: 22 EST: 1970
SQ FT: 14,000
SALES (est): 4.39MM Privately Held
Web: www.knapeindustries.com
SIC: 3599 Machine shop, jobbing and repair

(G-14718)
MAXX IRON LLC
287 E North St (43085-3207)
PHONE.................................614 753-9697
Mary Johnson, Prin
EMP: 7 EST: 2015
SALES (est): 729.12K Privately Held
SIC: 3462 Iron and steel forgings

(G-14719)
METTLER-TOLEDO LLC
Also Called: Toledo Scales & Systems
720 Dearborn Park Ln (43085-5703)
P.O. Box 999 (43085-0999)
PHONE.................................614 438-4511
Gary Wilkins, Mgr
EMP: 58
SALES (corp-wide): 3.87B Publicly Held
Web: www.mt.com
SIC: 3596 Industrial scales
HQ: Mettler-Toledo, Llc
1900 Polaris Pkwy Fl 6
Columbus OH 43240
614 438-4511

(G-14720)
METTLER-TOLEDO LLC
Toledo Scales & Systems
1150 Dearborn Dr (43085-4766)
PHONE.................................614 438-4390
Todd Manifold, Genl Mgr
EMP: 200
SALES (corp-wide): 3.87B Publicly Held
Web: www.mt.com
SIC: 3596 Industrial scales
HQ: Mettler-Toledo, Llc
1900 Polaris Pkwy Fl 6
Columbus OH 43240
614 438-4511

(G-14721)
MIDDLETON ENTERPRISES INC
7100 N High St (43085-2316)
PHONE.................................614 885-2514
Richard O Chakroff, Pr
Barbara M Chakroff, Sec
Christopher Norman, VP
EMP: 7 EST: 1954
SQ FT: 4,000
SALES (est): 664.89K Privately Held
SIC: 3728 Aircraft parts and equipment, nec

(G-14722)
NOXGEAR LLC
966 Proprietors Rd (43085-3152)
PHONE.................................937 317-0199
Simon Curran, CEO
EMP: 9
SALES (corp-wide): 1.48MM Privately
Held
Web: www.noxgear.com
SIC: 2329 Vests (suede, leatherette, etc.),
sport: men's and boys'
PA: Noxgear, Llc
2264 Green Island Dr
Columbus OH 43228
937 248-1860

(G-14723)
QUALITY CUSTOM SIGNS LLC
651 Lakeview Plaza Blvd Ste F
(43085-4774)
PHONE.................................614 580-7233
EMP: 6 EST: 2019
SALES (est): 3.66MM Privately Held
Web: www.qcsigns.net
SIC: 3993 Signs and advertising specialties

(G-14724)
RECYCLED SYSTEMS FURNITURE INC
Also Called: Rsfi Office Furniture
401 E Wilson Bridge Rd (43085-2320)
PHONE.................................614 880-9110
Ron Morris, Pr
Jim Ellison, *
EMP: 25 EST: 1992
SQ FT: 100,000
SALES (est): 2.38MM Privately Held
Web:
www.officefurniturecolumbusohio.com
SIC: 7641 5712 2522 Office furniture repair
and maintenance; Office furniture; Office
furniture, except wood

(G-14725)
SPORTS IMPORTS INCORPORATED
6950 Worthington Galena Rd (43085-2580)
P.O. Box 21040 (43221-0040)
PHONE.................................614 771-0246
Brad Underwood, Pr
Susan K Dunlap, Ch
Cyndie Dunlap, Ch Bd
◆ EMP: 19 EST: 1976
SALES (est): 3.05MM Privately Held
Web: www.sportsimports.com
SIC: 3949 Sporting and athletic goods, nec

(G-14726)
SWAGG PRODUCTIONS2015LLC
Also Called: Gmerecords
628 Arborway Ct (43085-4801)
P.O. Box 47 (43109-0047)
PHONE.................................614 601-7414
Travis Mcdaniels, Managing Member
EMP: 12 EST: 2015
SALES (est): 211.71K Privately Held

SIC: 2731 7819 7929 7389 Book music:
publishing and printing; Sound effects and
music production, motion picture;
Entertainers and entertainment groups;
Business services, nec

(G-14727)
THE SHARON COMPANIES LTD
200 W Old Wilson Bridge Rd (43085-2247)
P.O. Box 2168 (97208-2168)
PHONE.................................614 438-3210
EMP: 140
SIC: 3446 Stairs, staircases, stair treads:
prefabricated metal

(G-14728)
WELLPOINT
6740 N High St (43085-2512)
PHONE.................................614 771-9600
EMP: 7 EST: 2019
SALES (est): 1.23MM Privately Held
SIC: 3531 Wellpoint systems

(G-14729)
WHEMPYS CORP
6969 Worthington Galena Rd Ste P
(43085-2322)
PHONE.................................614 888-6670
David Reed, Pr
Kathy Reed, Sec
Eugene Reed, Mgr
EMP: 9 EST: 1980
SQ FT: 2,000
SALES (est): 402.18K Privately Held
Web: www.whempys.com
SIC: 5719 1711 7349 1741 Fireplace
equipment and accessories; Heating
systems repair and maintenance; Chimney
cleaning; Chimney construction and
maintenance

(G-14730)
WORTHINGTON CYLINDER CORP (HQ)
Also Called: Worthington Cylinder
200 W Old Wilson Bridge Rd (43085-2247)
PHONE.................................614 840-3210
Carol L Barnum, Prin
Jim Knox, *
◆ EMP: 185 EST: 1982
SQ FT: 125,000
SALES (est): 158.5MM
SALES (corp-wide): 1.25B Publicly Held
Web: www.worthingtonenterprises.com
SIC: 3443 Cylinders, pressure: metal plate
PA: Worthington Enterprises, Inc.
200 W Old Wlson Bridge Rd
Worthington OH 43085
614 438-3210

(G-14731)
WORTHINGTON ENTERPRISES INC (PA)
Also Called: WORTHINGTON
200 W Old Wilson Bridge Rd (43085-2247)
PHONE.................................614 438-3210
Joseph Hayek, Pr
John Blystone, Ofcr
Geoffrey G Gilmore, Ex VP
Joseph B Hayek, VP
Patrick J Kennedy, VP
◆ EMP: 250 EST: 1955
SALES (est): 1.25B
SALES (corp-wide): 1.25B Publicly Held
Web: www.worthingtonenterprises.com
SIC: 3449 3325 Fabricated bar joists and
concrete reinforcing bars; Alloy steel
castings, except investment

(G-14732)
WORTHINGTON STEEL COMPANY (PA)
Also Called: Worthington Steel
100 W Old Wilson Bridge Rd (43085-2255)
PHONE.................................800 944-2255
John H Mc Connell, Ch Bd
Dale T Brinkman, Sec
Mark A Russell, Pr
Andy Rose, CFO
◆ EMP: 309 EST: 1992
SALES (est): 259.87MM
SALES (corp-wide): 259.87MM Privately
Held
Web: www.worthingtonsteel.com
SIC: 3316 3471 3312 Cold-rolled strip or wire
; Electroplating and plating; Chemicals and
other products derived from coking

(G-14733)
WORTHNGTON STL MEXICO SA DE CV
200 W Old Wlson Bridge Rd (43085-2247)
PHONE.................................800 944-2255
EMP: 6
SALES (est): 95.29K Privately Held
SIC: 3316 Strip, steel, cold-rolled, nec: from
purchased hot-rolled,

Wshngtn Ct Hs
Fayette County

(G-14734)
ALL-AMERICAN FIRE EQP INC
Also Called: All American Fire Equiptment
5101 Us Highway 22 Sw (43160-9695)
PHONE.................................800 972-6035
Jeff Vossler, Pr
EMP: 10
Web: www.allamericanfire.us
SIC: 5099 3569 Safety equipment and
supplies; Firefighting and related equipment
PA: All-American Fire Equipment, Inc.
85 Kiwanavista Ln
Ona WV 25545

(G-14735)
BRASS BULL 1 LLC
Also Called: Print Shop, The
1020 Leesburg Ave (43160-1272)
PHONE.................................740 335-8030
EMP: 6 EST: 1974
SQ FT: 6,500
SALES (est): 508.5K Privately Held
Web: www.theprintshopwch.com
SIC: 2752 2791 2759 2396 Offset printing;
Typesetting; Commercial printing, nec;
Automotive and apparel trimmings

(G-14736)
CRESTAR CRUSTS INC
Also Called: Crestar Foods
1104 Clinton Ave (43160-1215)
PHONE.................................740 335-4813
Richard Hayward, Pr
Dan Walsh, *
EMP: 10 EST: 1998
SQ FT: 120,000
SALES (est): 1.34MM
SALES (corp-wide): 2.04MM Privately
Held
SIC: 2041 Pizza dough, prepared
HQ: Richelieu Foods, Inc.
120 W Palatine Rd
Wheeling IL 60090
781 786-6800

▲ = Import ▼ = Export
◆ = Import/Export

(G-14737)
DOMTAR PAPER COMPANY LLC
1803 Lowes Blvd (43160-8611)
PHONE..............................740 333-0003
Sue Wiggins, *Brnch Mgr*
EMP: 261
Web: www.domtar.com
SIC: 2621 Paper mills
HQ: Domtar Paper Company, Llc
234 Kingsley Park Dr
Fort Mill SC 29715

(G-14738)
DOUG MARINE MOTORS INC
1120 Clinton Ave (43160-1215)
P.O. Box 1042 (43160-8042)
PHONE..............................740 335-3700
Doug Marine, *Pr*
Bill D Marine, *
EMP: 15 **EST:** 1984
SQ FT: 8,000
SALES (est): 2.05MM Privately Held
Web: www.dougmarinemotors.net
SIC: 5511 7538 5531 5012 Automobiles,
new and used; General automotive repair
shops; Auto and home supply stores;
Automobiles and other motor vehicles

(G-14739)
FIBER -TECH INDUSTRIES INC
2000 Kenskill Ave (43160-9311)
PHONE..............................740 335-9400
Harris Armstrong, *CEO*
Jerry Kroll, *
Wayne Durnin, *
Robert Pfeifer, *
EMP: 75 **EST:** 1983
SQ FT: 180,000
SALES (est): 431.79K
SALES (corp-wide): 1.04MM Privately
Held
Web: www.fiber-tech.net
SIC: 3089 Air mattresses, plastics
PA: Celstar Group, Inc.
40 N Main St Ste 1730
Dayton OH 45423
740 335-9400

(G-14740)
**FIBERGLASS TECHNOLOGY INDS
INC**
2000 Kenskill Ave (43160-9311)
PHONE..............................740 335-9400
EMP: 30
SALES (corp-wide): 1.04MM Privately
Held
Web: www.fiber-tech.net
SIC: 3089 Panels, building: plastics, nec
HQ: Fiberglass Technology Industries, Inc.
3808 N Sullivan Rd # 31
Spokane Valley WA 99216
509 928-8880

(G-14741)
J K PRECAST LLC
1001 Armbrust Ave (43160-2457)
PHONE..............................740 335-2188
James E Kimmey, *Owner*
EMP: 8 **EST:** 2000
SQ FT: 20,500
SALES (est): 347.94K Privately Held
Web: www.jkprecast.com
SIC: 3272 3089 Septic tanks, concrete;
Septic tanks, plastics

(G-14742)
**QUALITEE DESIGN SPORTSWEAR
CO (PA)**
1270 Us Highway 22 Nw Ste 9
(43160-9187)

PHONE..............................740 333-8337
Jim Evans, *CEO*
Todd Evans, *Pr*
EMP: 10 **EST:** 1992
SQ FT: 6,500
SALES (est): 990.82K Privately Held
Web: www.qualiteedesign.com
SIC: 7336 2395 5999 2759 Silk screen
design; Embroidery and art needlework;
Trophies and plaques; Screen printing

(G-14743)
RAM MACHINING INC
806 Delaware St (43160-1552)
PHONE..............................740 333-5522
Rick Miller, *Pr*
Barb Massie, *Sec*
EMP: 6 **EST:** 1992
SALES (est): 508.95K Privately Held
SIC: 3599 Machine shop, jobbing and repair

(G-14744)
RICHELIEU FOODS INC
1104 Clinton Ave (43160-1278)
PHONE..............................740 335-4813
Richard Hayward, *Prin*
EMP: 21 **EST:** 2012
SALES (est): 2.06MM Privately Held
Web: www.richelieufoods.com
SIC: 2099 Food preparations, nec

(G-14745)
RITEN INDUSTRIES INCORPORATED
1100 Lakeview Ave (43160-1037)
P.O. Box 340 (43160-0340)
PHONE..............................740 335-5353
Andrew Lachelt, *Pr*
John E Lachat, *Stockholder*
EMP: 40 **EST:** 1933
SQ FT: 28,500
SALES (est): 3.95MM Privately Held
Web: www.riten.com
SIC: 3545 Machine tool attachments and
accessories

(G-14746)
SISTERS TANNING INC
Also Called: Sisters Tanning
1568 State Route 41 Ne (43160-9400)
PHONE..............................740 636-0303
Debbie Wolff, *Pr*
EMP: 6 **EST:** 1995
SALES (est): 240K Privately Held
SIC: 7299 3111 Tanning salon; Leather
tanning and finishing

(G-14747)
SOUTH CENTRAL INDUSTRIAL LLC
1825 Old Us 35 Se (43160-3500)
PHONE..............................740 333-5401
EMP: 17 **EST:** 2011
SQ FT: 60,000
SALES (est): 2.79MM
SALES (corp-wide): 54.68MM Privately
Held
Web: www.sciohio.com
SIC: 3441 Fabricated structural metal
PA: Heartland, Inc.
1005 N 19th St
Middlesboro KY 40965
606 248-7323

(G-14748)
TONYS WLDG & FABRICATION LLC
2305 Robinson Rd Se (43160-8675)
PHONE..............................740 333-4000
Linda Borland, *Prin*
EMP: 10 **EST:** 2015
SALES (est): 2.39MM Privately Held
Web: www.twfabrication.com
SIC: 7692 Welding repair

(G-14749)
WCH MOLDING LLC
1850 Lowes Blvd (43160-8611)
PHONE..............................740 335-6320
Gene J Kuzma, *Pr*
Jeff Kuzma, *VP*
EMP: 20 **EST:** 2004
SALES (est): 5.98MM
SALES (corp-wide): 6.96MM Privately
Held
SIC: 3089 Molding primary plastics
PA: Gk Packaging, Inc.
7680 Commerce Pl
Plain City OH 43064
614 873-3900

(G-14750)
WCR INCORPORATED
809 Delaware St (43160-1551)
PHONE..............................740 333-3448
EMP: 10
SALES (corp-wide): 43.23MM Privately
Held
Web: www.wcrhx.com
SIC: 3443 Heat exchangers, plate type
PA: Wcr Incorporated
2377 Cmmrce Ctr Blvd Ste
Fairborn OH 45324
937 223-0703

(G-14751)
WEYERHAEUSER COMPANY
Also Called: Washington Crt Hse Converting
1803 Lowes Blvd (43160-8611)
PHONE..............................740 335-4480
Jim Fink, *Mgr*
EMP: 7
SALES (corp-wide): 7.12B Publicly Held
Web: www.weyerhaeuser.com
SIC: 2653 Boxes, corrugated: made from
purchased materials
PA: Weyerhaeuser Company
220 Occidental Ave S
Seattle WA 98104
206 539-3000

Xenia
Greene County

(G-14752)
ACTION AIR & HYDRAULICS INC
1087 Bellbrook Ave (45385-4011)
P.O. Box 655 (45385-0655)
PHONE..............................937 372-8614
Peter J Pacier, *CEO*
Pat Minnela, *Sec*
EMP: 6 **EST:** 1983
SQ FT: 2,500
SALES (est): 498.61K Privately Held
SIC: 3822 Energy cutoff controls, residential
or commercial types

(G-14753)
BARCO INC
Presentation & Simulation Div
600 Bellbrook Ave (45385-4053)
PHONE..............................937 372-7579
Al Herman, *Brnch Mgr*
EMP: 21
SALES (corp-wide): 735.93MM Privately
Held
Web: www.barco.com
SIC: 3663 8731 Radio and t.v.
communications equipment; Electronic
research
HQ: Barco, Inc.
3059 Prmiere Pkwy Ste 400
Duluth GA 30097

(G-14754)
BEF FOODS INC
Also Called: Bob Evans
640 Birch Rd (45385-7600)
P.O. Box 44 (45385-0044)
PHONE..............................937 372-4493
Tom Sefton, *Mgr*
EMP: 206
SQ FT: 3,000
Web: www.bobevansgrocery.com
SIC: 2011 Sausages, from meat slaughtered
on site
HQ: Bef Foods, Inc.
8200 Walton Pkwy
New Albany OH 43054
614 492-7700

(G-14755)
BESTWOOD CABINETRY LLC
117 W Main St (45385-2914)
PHONE..............................937 661-9621
Anthony Hinzman, *Prin*
EMP: 6 **EST:** 2017
SALES (est): 58.05K Privately Held
SIC: 2434 Wood kitchen cabinets

(G-14756)
BURKE PRODUCTS INC
1355 Enterprise Ln (45385-6504)
PHONE..............................937 372-3516
Aaron Bakhshi, *Pr*
Shiv Bakhshi, *Pr*
Aaron Bakshi, *VP*
▲ **EMP:** 20 **EST:** 1966
SQ FT: 10,000
SALES (est): 7.98MM Privately Held
Web: www.burkeproducts.com
SIC: 3674 3599 Solid state electronic
devices, nec; Machine shop, jobbing and
repair

(G-14757)
CIL ISOTOPE SEPARATIONS LLC
1689 Burnett Dr (45385-5691)
PHONE..............................937 376-5413
Joel Bradley, *CEO*
Peter Dodwell, *Pr*
Maureen Duffy, *VP*
Steve Igo, *VP*
▲ **EMP:** 10 **EST:** 2006
SQ FT: 8,000
SALES (est): 31.67MM Privately Held
Web: www.isotope.com
SIC: 2819 Industrial inorganic chemicals, nec
HQ: Otsuka Pharmaceutical Co., Ltd.
2-16-4, Konan
Minato-Ku TKY 108-0

(G-14758)
CITY OF XENIA
Also Called: Xenia City Water Treatment Div
1831 Us Route 68 N (45385-9547)
PHONE..............................937 376-7269
Roger Beehler, *Brnch Mgr*
EMP: 36
SALES (corp-wide): 31.32MM Privately
Held
Web: ci.xenia.oh.us
SIC: 3589 Water treatment equipment,
industrial
PA: City Of Xenia
107 East Main St
Xenia OH 45385
937 376-7232

(G-14759)
CLARKSVILLE STAVE & LBR CO LTD
2808 Jasper Rd (45385-9425)
PHONE..............................937 376-4618
Martha Valentine, *Pr*
Chuck Valentine, *VP*

Charles Valentine, *VP*
EMP: 9 **EST:** 1970
SQ FT: 10,800
SALES (est): 785.22K **Privately Held**
Web: www.clarksvillestave.com
SIC: 2421 5031 5211 Lumber: rough, sawed, or planed; Lumber: rough, dressed, and finished; Lumber products

(G-14760)
CUSTOM MFG SOLUTIONS INC (PA)
479 Bellbrook Ave (45385-3639)
P.O. Box 840 (45385-0840)
PHONE.................................937 372-0777
Mike Collinsworth, *Pr*
Raj Soin, *CEO*
EMP: 50 **EST:** 1989
SQ FT: 82,000
SALES (est): 1.89MM
SALES (corp-wide): 1.89MM **Privately Held**
Web: www.cusmfgsol.com
SIC: 3599 Machine shop, jobbing and repair

(G-14761)
D & J MACHINE SHOP
1296 S Patton St (45385-5672)
PHONE.................................937 256-2730
Chuck Lehman, *Owner*
EMP: 6 **EST:** 1966
SALES (est): 797.44K **Privately Held**
SIC: 3599 Machine shop, jobbing and repair

(G-14762)
DESTIN DIE CASTING LLC
851 Bellbrook Ave (45385-4057)
PHONE.................................937 347-1111
EMP: 45 **EST:** 2014
SALES (est): 3.68MM **Privately Held**
Web: www.krdiecasting.com
SIC: 3363 Aluminum die-castings
PA: American Metal Technologies Llc
8213 Durand Ave
Sturtevant WI 53177

(G-14763)
DISCOUNT SMOKES & GIFTS XENIA
37 E Main St (45385-3201)
PHONE.................................937 372-0259
William Lampiasi, *Pr*
EMP: 6 **EST:** 2008
SALES (est): 1.4MM **Privately Held**
Web: www.xeniasmokeshop.com
SIC: 2111 Cigarettes

(G-14764)
FAIRBORN CEMENT COMPANY LLC
3250 Linebaugh Rd (45385-8567)
PHONE.................................937 879-8393
Gerald Essl, *Pr*
Ray Meier, *
EMP: 110 **EST:** 2016
SALES (est): 27.18MM
SALES (corp-wide): 2.15B **Publicly Held**
Web: www.fairborncement.com
SIC: 3241 Natural cement
PA: Eagle Materials Inc.
5960 Berkshire Ln Ste 900
Dallas TX 75225
214 432-2000

(G-14765)
IDIALOGS LLC
121 Pawleys Plantation Ct (45385-9120)
PHONE.................................937 372-2890
EMP: 8 **EST:** 2012
SALES (est): 658.75K **Privately Held**
Web: www.idialogs.com
SIC: 7372 Application computer software

(G-14766)
JADE TOOL COMPANY
1280 Burnett Dr (45385-5687)
PHONE.................................937 376-4740
Jeff Sakalaskas, *Pr*
Dan Baker, *Sec*
EMP: 9 **EST:** 1969
SQ FT: 3,600
SALES (est): 982.69K **Privately Held**
Web: www.jadetoolco.com
SIC: 3599 Machine shop, jobbing and repair

(G-14767)
JCL EQUIPMENT CO INC
915 Trumbull St (45385-3644)
P.O. Box 396 (45385-0396)
PHONE.................................937 374-1010
Jim Lunay, *Pr*
EMP: 9 **EST:** 1991
SQ FT: 23,000
SALES (est): 1.69MM **Privately Held**
Web: www.jclequipment.com
SIC: 3531 5084 Road construction and maintenance machinery; Industrial machinery and equipment

(G-14768)
KOTOBUKI-RELIABLE DIE CASTING INC
851 Bellbrook Ave (45385-4057)
PHONE.................................937 347-1111
EMP: 23
SIC: 3542 Die casting machines

(G-14769)
LIMING PRINTING INC
Also Called: Screenplay Printing
1450 S Patton St (45385-7406)
PHONE.................................937 374-2646
Brian Liming, *Pr*
Alan Liming, *VP*
EMP: 10 **EST:** 1985
SQ FT: 6,700
SALES (est): 457.97K **Privately Held**
Web: www.screenplayprinting.com
SIC: 2752 2759 7336 2791 Offset printing; Commercial printing, nec; Silk screen design; Typesetting

(G-14770)
MAHLE BEHR USA INC
1003 Bellbrook Ave (45385-4011)
PHONE.................................937 369-2610
EMP: 6 **EST:** 1993
SALES (est): 246.75K **Privately Held**
SIC: 3585 3443 Refrigeration and heating equipment; Fabricated plate work (boiler shop)

(G-14771)
MRL MATERIALS RESOURCES LLC
Also Called: Mrl
123 Fairground Rd (45385-9543)
P.O. Box 341091 (45434-1091)
PHONE.................................937 531-6657
EMP: 40 **EST:** 2009
SALES (est): 1.92MM **Privately Held**
Web: www.icmrl.net
SIC: 8999 8734 3812 8711 Scientific consulting; Metallurgical testing laboratory; Defense systems and equipment; Engineering services

(G-14772)
NATIONAL CARTON & COATING COMPANY
1439 Lavelle Dr (45385-5679)
PHONE.................................937 347-1042
EMP: 80
Web: www.nationalcarton.com

SIC: 2631 Packaging board

(G-14773)
OHTA PRESS US INC
1125 S Patton St (45385-5671)
PHONE.................................937 374-3382
Shigeki Ikuta, *Pr*
▲ **EMP:** 15 **EST:** 1996
SQ FT: 12,000
SALES (est): 2.31MM **Privately Held**
Web: www.xegc.org
SIC: 3714 Motor vehicle parts and accessories

(G-14774)
SAVE EDGE INC
Also Called: Save Edge USA
360 W Church St (45385-2948)
PHONE.................................937 376-8268
George Whyde, *Pr*
▲ **EMP:** 25 **EST:** 1975
SALES (est): 2.64MM **Privately Held**
Web: www.saveedge.com
SIC: 5085 7699 3423 3315 Industrial tools; Knife, saw and tool sharpening and repair; Hand and edge tools, nec; Steel wire and related products

(G-14775)
STEINBARGER PRECISION CNC INC
634 Cincinnati Ave (45385-5013)
PHONE.................................937 376-0322
Steve Steinbarger, *Pr*
EMP: 6 **EST:** 2006
SQ FT: 1,000
SALES (est): 872.35K **Privately Held**
Web: www.spcncinc.com
SIC: 3599 Machine shop, jobbing and repair

(G-14776)
SUPERION INC
1285 S Patton St (45385-5673)
PHONE.................................937 374-0033
Alton Choiniere, *Pr*
Masaru Yokokawa, *
▲ **EMP:** 40 **EST:** 1990
SQ FT: 12,000
SALES (est): 2.83MM **Privately Held**
Web: www.alliedmachine.com
SIC: 3423 3541 3545 3425 Knives, agricultural or industrial; Machine tools, metal cutting type; Machine tool accessories; Saw blades and handsaws
PA: Sanyo Tool Mfg,Co, Ltd.
3-6-21, Osaki
Shinagawa-Ku TKY 141-0

(G-14777)
TDL TOOL INC
1296 S Patton St (45385-5672)
PHONE.................................937 374-0055
Steve Mangan, *Pr*
Dan Mangan, *VP*
▼ **EMP:** 15 **EST:** 1992
SQ FT: 2,000
SALES (est): 3.59MM **Privately Held**
Web: www.tdltool.com
SIC: 3599 Machine shop, jobbing and repair

(G-14778)
THIRD WAVE WATER LLC
251 Bellbrook Ave (45385-3635)
PHONE.................................855 590-4500
Taylor Minor, *CEO*
EMP: 12 **EST:** 2016
SQ FT: 400
SALES (est): 332.48K **Privately Held**
Web: www.thirdwavewater.com
SIC: 2087 Beverage bases

(G-14779)
TIMAC MANUFACTURING COMPANY
825 Bellbrook Ave (45385-4076)
P.O. Box 329 (45385-0329)
PHONE.................................937 372-3305
Tim Mcintire, *Pr*
EMP: 6 **EST:** 1978
SQ FT: 5,000
SALES (est): 697.55K **Privately Held**
Web: www.timacspring.com
SIC: 3495 Wire springs

(G-14780)
TJAR INNOVATIONS LLC
1004 Cincinnati Ave (45385-9353)
P.O. Box 357 (45385-0357)
PHONE.................................937 347-1999
Tony Arsenault, *VP*
EMP: 12 **EST:** 2001
SALES (est): 2.47MM **Privately Held**
Web: www.tjarinnovations.com
SIC: 3089 Injection molding of plastics

(G-14781)
TREALITY SVS LLC (PA)
600 Bellbrook Ave (45385-4053)
PHONE.................................937 372-7579
Mark Saturno, *VP*
EMP: 45 **EST:** 2014
SQ FT: 200,000
SALES (est): 9.98MM
SALES (corp-wide): 9.98MM **Privately Held**
Web: www.trealitysvs.com
SIC: 3577 Computer peripheral equipment, nec

(G-14782)
TRIAD GOVERNMENTAL SYSTEMS
358 S Monroe St (45385-3442)
PHONE.................................937 376-5446
Tod A Rapp, *Pr*
EMP: 10 **EST:** 1983
SALES (est): 469.36K **Privately Held**
Web: www.triadgsi.net
SIC: 7371 7372 Computer software development; Prepackaged software

(G-14783)
WA HAMMOND DRIERITE CO LTD
138 Dayton Ave (45385-2830)
P.O. Box 460 (45385-0460)
PHONE.................................937 376-2927
Joan L Hammond, *Pt*
James F Hammond, *Pt*
EMP: 21 **EST:** 1932
SQ FT: 80,000
SALES (est): 3.94MM **Privately Held**
Web: secure.drierite.com
SIC: 2819 Industrial inorganic chemicals, nec

(G-14784)
WADES WOODWORKING INC
1427 Bellbrook Ave (45385-4064)
PHONE.................................937 374-6470
Wade A Smith, *Pr*
EMP: 10 **EST:** 1987
SQ FT: 13,000
SALES (est): 535.12K **Privately Held**
Web: www.wadeswoodworking.com
SIC: 1751 2599 Cabinet building and installation; Cabinets, factory

(G-14785)
WESTWOOD FINISHING COMPANY
1118 Neeld Dr (45385-1423)
PHONE.................................937 837-1488
Lavern Meyer, *Owner*
EMP: 6 **EST:** 1950
SALES (est): 896.11K **Privately Held**

Web: www.westwoodfinishingcompany.com
SIC: 3479 Coating of metals and formed products

Yellow Springs
Greene County

(G-14786)
BENNETT & BENNETT INC (PA)
888 Dayton St (45387-1777)
PHONE..................937 324-1100
Bill Bennett, *Pr*
Michelle Bennett, *Treas*
EMP: 6 EST: 1991
SALES (est): 1.61MM Privately Held
Web: www.4bennett.com
SIC: 3679 Static power supply converters for electronic applications

(G-14787)
BUSHWORKS INCORPORATED
1280 Grinnell Dr Unit 1 (45387-2099)
PHONE..................937 767-1713
John Bush, *Pr*
EMP: 8 EST: 1975
SALES (est): 121.41K Privately Held
Web: www.bushworks.net
SIC: 2499 Woodenware, kitchen and household

(G-14788)
ERTEL PUBLISHING INC
Also Called: Antique Power
506 S High St (45387-1576)
P.O. Box 838 (45387-0838)
PHONE..................937 767-1433
Patrick W Ertel, *Pr*
EMP: 9 EST: 1988
SALES (est): 905.51K Privately Held
Web: www.ertelpublishing.com
SIC: 2721 Magazines: publishing and printing

(G-14789)
MIAMI VALLEY EDUCTL CMPT ASSN
Also Called: Mveca
888 Dayton St Unit 102 (45387-1778)
PHONE..................937 767-1468
Thor Sage, *Dir*
Sue Welsh, *Sec*
Gary Bosserman, *Dir*
EMP: 13 EST: 1980
SALES (est): 1.04MM Privately Held
Web: www.mveca.org
SIC: 7372 7374 Prepackaged software; Computer time-sharing

(G-14790)
MORRIS BEAN & COMPANY
777 E Hyde Rd (45387-9726)
PHONE..................937 767-7301
Edward Myers, *Pr*
William Magro, *
Lawrence E Kleinschnitz, *
EMP: 175 EST: 1932
SQ FT: 185,000
SALES (est): 24.74MM Privately Held
Web: www.morrisbean.com
SIC: 3365 3769 3369 Aluminum and aluminum-based alloy castings; Space vehicle equipment, nec; Nonferrous foundries, nec

(G-14791)
VERNAY MANUFACTURING INC (HQ)
120 E South College St (45387-1623)
PHONE..................404 994-2000
Thomas Allen, *CEO*
Hugh Barnett, *Sec*
▲ EMP: 22 EST: 1979

SQ FT: 40,000
SALES (est): 13.93MM
SALES (corp-wide): 38.49MM Privately Held
Web: www.vernay.com
SIC: 3069 Molded rubber products
PA: Vernay Laboratories, Inc.
1005 Virginia Ave Ste 320
Atlanta GA 30354
404 994-2000

(G-14792)
XYLEM INC
Also Called: Ysi
1700 Brannum Ln Ste 1725 (45387-1106)
PHONE..................937 767-7241
Russel Meinka, *Brnch Mgr*
EMP: 58
Web: www.xylem.com
SIC: 3823 Process control instruments
PA: Xylem Inc.
301 Water St Se Ste 200
Washington DC 20003

(G-14793)
YELLOW SPRINGS POTTERY LLC
222 Xenia Ave Ste 1 (45387-1866)
PHONE..................937 767-1666
Janet Murie, *Prin*
Marcia Cochran, *Prin*
Jerry Davis, *Prin*
Kim Kramer, *Prin*
Eliza Bush, *Prin*
EMP: 10 EST: 2003
SALES (est): 189.11K Privately Held
Web: www.yellowspringspottery.com
SIC: 5023 3269 Pottery; Pottery products, nec

(G-14794)
YOUNGS JERSEY DAIRY INC
Also Called: Golden Jersey Inn
6880 Springfield Xenia Rd (45387-9610)
PHONE..................937 325-0629
C Daniel Young, *CEO*
C Robert Young, *
William H Young, *
Debra Whittaker, *
EMP: 300 EST: 1964
SQ FT: 35,000
SALES (est): 4.85MM Privately Held
Web: www.youngsdairy.com
SIC: 5812 5451 5947 7999 Ice cream stands or dairy bars; Dairy products stores; Gift shop; Golf driving range

(G-14795)
YSI ENVIRONMENTAL INC
Also Called: Xylem Ysi, A Xylem Brand
1725 Brannum Ln (45387-1107)
PHONE..................937 767-7241
Richard Omlor, *Pr*
EMP: 50 EST: 2000
SALES (est): 4.49MM Privately Held
Web: www.ysi.com
SIC: 3826 Analytical instruments

(G-14796)
YSI INCORPORATED (HQ)
Also Called: Yellow Springs International
1700 Brannum Ln # 1725 (45387-1106)
PHONE..................937 767-7241
Richard J Omlor, *Pr*
Leon Erdman, *
Gayle Rominger, *
◆ EMP: 100 EST: 1948
SQ FT: 120,000
SALES (est): 41.4MM Publicly Held
Web: www.ysi.com

SIC: 3826 3823 3841 Water testing apparatus; Process control instruments; Diagnostic apparatus, medical
PA: Xylem Inc.
301 Water St Se Ste 200
Washington DC 20003

Yorkshire
Darke County

(G-14797)
WINNER CORPORATION (PA)
Also Called: Winner's Meat Service
8544 State Route 705 (45388-9784)
P.O. Box 39 (45351-0039)
PHONE..................419 582-4321
Brian K Winner, *Pr*
Alan Winner, *
Terrance Winner, *
Ted Winner, *
Jay Winner, *
EMP: 40 EST: 1928
SQ FT: 6,500
SALES (est): 33.94MM
SALES (corp-wide): 33.94MM Privately Held
Web: www.winnersmeats.com
SIC: 0213 0751 5154 5147 Hog feedlot; Slaughtering: custom livestock services; Hogs; Meats and meat products

Yorkville
Jefferson County

(G-14798)
OHIO COATINGS COMPANY
2100 Tin Plate Pl (43971-1053)
PHONE..................740 859-5500
James Tennant, *Pr*
Yong Sig Bin, *
EMP: 73 EST: 1993
SQ FT: 134,000
SALES (est): 1.35MM Privately Held
Web: www.ohiocoatingscompany.com
SIC: 3479 Coating of metals and formed products

Youngstown
Mahoning County

(G-14799)
1062 TECHNOLOGIES INC
Also Called: Center Street Technologies
1062 Ohio Works Dr (44510-1077)
PHONE..................303 453-9251
Michael Garvey, *CEO*
Charles George, *CFO*
EMP: 6 EST: 2016
SALES (est): 3.3MM Privately Held
Web: www.centerstreettech.com
SIC: 3531 Construction machinery

(G-14800)
4S COMPANY
3730 Mahoning Ave (44515-3020)
PHONE..................330 792-5518
Debra Woodford, *Pr*
EMP: 10 EST: 2006
SALES (est): 275.05K Privately Held
Web: www.foursco.com
SIC: 3999 Manufacturing industries, nec

(G-14801)
A1 INDUSTRIAL PAINTING INC
894 Coitsville Hubbard Rd (44505-4635)
P.O. Box 509 (44405-0509)

PHONE..................330 750-9441
Jack Maillis, *Pr*
EMP: 50 EST: 2008
SALES (est): 4.4MM Privately Held
Web: www.a1industrialpainting.com
SIC: 1721 1389 Industrial painting; Construction, repair, and dismantling services

(G-14802)
ABI ORTHTC/PROSTHETIC LABS LTD
930 Trailwood Dr (44512-5007)
PHONE..................330 758-1143
EMP: 23 EST: 1978
SALES (est): 396.45K
SALES (corp-wide): 1.12B Privately Held
SIC: 3842 Braces, orthopedic
PA: Hanger, Inc.
10910 Domain Dr Ste 300
Austin TX 78758
512 777-3800

(G-14803)
ACCUFORM MANUFACTURING INC
2750 Intertech Dr (44509-4023)
PHONE..................330 797-9291
Bob Hockenberry, *Pr*
Thomas Manos, *
EMP: 32 EST: 1989
SQ FT: 1,056
SALES (est): 2.37MM Privately Held
Web: www.accuformprecision.com
SIC: 3599 3543 3544 Machine shop, jobbing and repair; Foundry patternmaking; Special dies, tools, jigs, and fixtures

(G-14804)
ACE LUMBER COMPANY
1039 Poland Ave (44502-2138)
P.O. Box 508 (44501-0508)
PHONE..................330 744-3167
Herbert Soss, *Pr*
Diann Zenda, *Stockholder*
Susan Soss, *Stockholder*
Julie Soss, *Stockholder*
EMP: 13 EST: 1941
SQ FT: 300,000
SALES (est): 18.95MM Privately Held
Web: www.acelumberco.com
SIC: 2431 5211 Millwork; Lumber products

(G-14805)
ACID DEVELOPMENT LLC
5700 Patriot Blvd (44515-1170)
PHONE..................330 502-4164
EMP: 6 EST: 2011
SALES (est): 102.2K Privately Held
SIC: 1389 Acidizing wells

(G-14806)
ACME STEAK & SEAFOOD INC
31 Bissell Ave (44505-2707)
P.O. Box 688 (44501-0688)
PHONE..................330 270-8000
Michael A Mike Iii, *Pr*
EMP: 10 EST: 1947
SALES (est): 2.33MM Privately Held
Web: www.acmesteak.com
SIC: 5146 5113 5149 5147 Seafoods; Disposable plates, cups, napkins, and eating utensils; Canned goods: fruit, vegetables, seafood, meats, etc.; Meats, fresh

(G-14807)
ACMI LLC
229 N Four Mile Run Rd Ste A (44515-3051)
PHONE..................330 501-0728
Josh Hillard, *Managing Member*

EMP: 9 EST: 2012
SALES (est): 898.45K Privately Held
SIC: 3441 Fabricated structural metal

(G-14808)
ALLIED CONSOLIDATED INDS INC (PA)
2100 Poland Ave (44502-2751)
PHONE...................................330 744-0808
John Ramun, Pr
Louise Ramun, *
EMP: 104 EST: 1985
SQ FT: 24,000
SALES (est): 10.37MM Privately Held
Web: www.aed.cc
SIC: 3535 3531 Conveyors and conveying equipment; Construction machinery

(G-14809)
ALLIED INDUSTRIAL DEV CORP
Also Called: Allied Erecting & Dismantling
2100 Poland Ave (44502-2751)
PHONE...................................724 346-1984
John Ramun, Pr
EMP: 28 EST: 1985
SQ FT: 24,000
SALES (est): 2.44MM Privately Held
Web: www.alliedgator.com
SIC: 3531 Construction machinery
PA: Allied Consolidated Industries, Inc.
　　2100 Poland Ave
　　Youngstown OH 44502

(G-14810)
ALUMO EXTRUSIONS AND MFG CO
3749 Mahoning Ave Ste 2 (44515-3052)
PHONE...................................330 779-3333
Frank Moulin, Pr
John Moulin, VP
Rose Palermo, Sec
EMP: 20 EST: 1975
SQ FT: 66,000
SALES (est): 1.49MM Privately Held
Web: www.brucewardlaw.com
SIC: 5039 5031 3089 Doors, sliding; Doors, garage; Doors, folding: plastics or plastics coated fabric

(G-14811)
AMERICAN PAPER GROUP INC
Also Called: American Paper Products Co Div
8401 Southern Blvd (44512-6709)
P.O. Box 3120 (44513-3120)
PHONE...................................330 758-4545
Thomas W Pietrocini, Ch Bd
Don Allevach, *
EMP: 400 EST: 1915
SQ FT: 95,000
SALES (est): 3.46MM Privately Held
SIC: 2677 7331 Envelopes; Mailing service

(G-14812)
AMERICAN ROLL FORMED PDTS CORP (DH)
Also Called: Arf
3805 Hendricks Rd Ste A (44515-1536)
PHONE...................................440 352-0753
Rob Touzalin, Pr
Jeff Laturell, *
▼ EMP: 102 EST: 1960
SQ FT: 70,000
SALES (est): 8.36MM
SALES (corp-wide): 99.27MM Privately Held
Web: www.hynesindustries.com
SIC: 3498 3449 Fabricated pipe and fittings; Custom roll formed products
HQ: Hynes Holding Company
　　3805 Henricks Rd
　　Youngstown OH 44515
　　330 799-3221

(G-14813)
AMTECH TOOL & MACHINE INC
100 Mcclurg Rd (44512-6738)
PHONE...................................330 758-8215
Fred Coss, Pr
EMP: 9 EST: 1984
SQ FT: 6,200
SALES (est): 2.02MM Privately Held
SIC: 3544 3599 3441 Special dies and tools; Machine shop, jobbing and repair; Fabricated structural metal

(G-14814)
AMTHOR STEEL INC
5019 Belmont Ave (44505-1019)
PHONE...................................330 759-0200
George Ohlin, Mgr
EMP: 7
SALES (corp-wide): 4.89MM Privately Held
Web: www.amthorsteel.com
SIC: 3312 Blast furnaces and steel mills
PA: Amthor Steel, Inc.
　　1717 Gaskell Ave
　　Erie PA 16503
　　814 452-4700

(G-14815)
ANATOMICAL CONCEPTS INC
1399 E Western Reserve Rd (44514-5224)
PHONE...................................330 757-3569
William W De Toro, Pr
Richard A Riffle, VP
William W Detoro, Pr
EMP: 14 EST: 1990
SQ FT: 1,600
SALES (est): 2.55MM Privately Held
Web: www.anatomicalconceptsinc.com
SIC: 3842 Braces, orthopedic

(G-14816)
AZTEC MANUFACTURING INC
4325 Simon Rd (44512-1327)
PHONE...................................330 783-9747
James J Rutana, Dir
Damian P Degenova, Dir
Maria E Rutana, Dir
EMP: 20 EST: 1992
SQ FT: 6,000
SALES (est): 2.3MM Privately Held
Web: www.aztecmetalfab.com
SIC: 3365 3444 Aluminum foundries; Sheet metalwork

(G-14817)
BAKER PLASTICS INC
900 Mahoning Ave (44502-1488)
PHONE...................................330 743-3142
Bonnie Baker, Pr
Robert E Baker, Ch
Ruth Luarde, Sec
EMP: 7 EST: 1946
SQ FT: 15,000
SALES (est): 884.27K Privately Held
Web: www.bakerplastics.com
SIC: 3089 3993 5099 5046 Novelties, plastics; Signs and advertising specialties; Novelties, durable; Store fixtures and display equipment

(G-14818)
BARFECTIONS LLC
4718 Belmont Ave (44505-1014)
PHONE...................................330 759-3100
Mike Handel, Contrlr
EMP: 8
SALES (corp-wide): 10.64MM Privately Held
SIC: 2064 Candy and other confectionery products
PA: Barfections Llc

1598 Motor Inn Dr
Girard OH 44420
330 759-3100

(G-14819)
BERLIN INDUSTRIES INC
Also Called: Berlin Inds Protector Pdts
1275 Boardman Poland Rd Ste 1 (44514-3911)
PHONE...................................330 549-2100
Scott Gorley, Pr
EMP: 19 EST: 1985
SQ FT: 35,000
SALES (est): 1.82MM Privately Held
SIC: 2834 5047 Veterinary pharmaceutical preparations; Veterinarians' equipment and supplies
PA: Kobayashi Pharmaceutical Co.,Ltd.
　　4-4-10, Doshomachi, Chuo-Ku
　　Osaka OSK 541-0

(G-14820)
BLACK LION PRODUCTS LLC
3710 Hendricks Rd (44515-1537)
PHONE...................................234 232-3680
Antonio Campana, Managing Member
Mia Richardson, *
EMP: 25 EST: 2009
SQ FT: 250,000
SALES (est): 3.39MM Privately Held
Web: www.blpmfg.com
SIC: 3441 Fabricated structural metal

(G-14821)
BOARDMAN MOLDED INTL LLC
1110 Thalia Ave (44512-1825)
PHONE...................................800 233-4575
Ron Kessler, Managing Member
EMP: 113 EST: 2007
SALES (est): 2.26MM
SALES (corp-wide): 25MM Privately Held
Web: www.boardmanmolded.com
SIC: 3089 Injection molding of plastics
PA: Boardman Molded Products, Inc.
　　1110 Thalia Ave
　　Youngstown OH 44512
　　330 788-2400

(G-14822)
BOARDMAN MOLDED PRODUCTS INC (PA)
1110 Thalia Ave (44512-1825)
P.O. Box 1858 (44501-1858)
PHONE...................................330 788-2400
Ken Palmman, CEO
Daniel A Kessler, *
◆ EMP: 87 EST: 1978
SQ FT: 85,000
SALES (est): 25MM
SALES (corp-wide): 25MM Privately Held
Web: www.boardmanmolded.com
SIC: 3089 3466 3429 2273 Injection molding of plastics; Crowns and closures; Hardware, nec; Carpets and rugs

(G-14823)
BOLTECH INCORPORATED
1201 Crescent St (44502-1303)
P.O. Box 749 (44501-0749)
PHONE...................................330 746-6881
Alex Benyo, Pr
Brian Benyo, VP
C R Pallante, Prin
EMP: 9 EST: 1998
SQ FT: 6,500
SALES (est): 1.58MM Privately Held
Web: www.brilex.com
SIC: 3537 Trucks, tractors, loaders, carriers, and similar equipment

(G-14824)
BRENTWOOD ORIGINALS INC
1309 N Meridian Rd (44509-1099)
PHONE...................................330 793-2255
Tim Domer, Brnch Mgr
EMP: 78
SQ FT: 130,000
SALES (corp-wide): 175MM Privately Held
Web: www.brentwoodoriginals.com
SIC: 2392 Pillows, bed: made from purchased materials
PA: Brentwood Originals, Inc.
　　3780 Klroy Arprt Way Ste
　　Long Beach CA 90806
　　310 637-6804

(G-14825)
BRIDGESTONE RET OPERATIONS LLC
Also Called: Firestone
7401 Market St Rear (44512-5624)
PHONE...................................330 758-0921
Anthony Sangialosi, Mgr
EMP: 9
Web: www.bridgestoneamericas.com
SIC: 5531 7534 Automotive tires; Rebuilding and retreading tires
HQ: Bridgestone Retail Operations, Llc
　　200 4th Ave S Ste 100
　　Nashville TN 37201
　　615 937-1000

(G-14826)
BRIDGESTONE RET OPERATIONS LLC
Also Called: Firestone
3335 Belmont Ave (44505-1805)
PHONE...................................330 759-3697
Robert Kephart, Mgr
EMP: 7
SQ FT: 4,600
Web: www.bridgestoneamericas.com
SIC: 5531 7534 Automotive tires; Rebuilding and retreading tires
HQ: Bridgestone Retail Operations, Llc
　　200 4th Ave S Ste 100
　　Nashville TN 37201
　　615 937-1000

(G-14827)
BRILEX INDUSTRIES INC (PA)
Also Called: Brilex Tech Services
1201 Crescent St (44502-1303)
P.O. Box 749 (44501-0749)
PHONE...................................330 744-1114
Doyle Hopper, CEO
Brian Benyo, *
Alex M Benyo, *
▲ EMP: 59 EST: 1996
SQ FT: 54,000
SALES (est): 48.27MM Privately Held
Web: www.brilex.com
SIC: 3441 3542 3549 Fabricated structural metal; Machine tools, metal forming type; Metalworking machinery, nec

(G-14828)
BROCKER MACHINE INC
1530 Poland Ave (44502-2147)
PHONE...................................330 744-5858
Brad Brocker, Pr
EMP: 19 EST: 1994
SQ FT: 10,000
SALES (est): 1.76MM Privately Held
Web: www.brockermachine.com
SIC: 3599 Machine shop, jobbing and repair

(G-14829)
BUDS SIGN SHOP INC
892 Mahoning Ave (44502-1414)
PHONE..............................330 744-5555
Robert Perkins, *Pr*
Barbara Perkins, *VP*
EMP: 10 **EST:** 1980
SQ FT: 10,000
SALES (est): 406.21K **Privately Held**
Web: www.budsignshop.com
SIC: 3993 Signs, not made in custom sign
painting shops

(G-14830)
BUSINESS JOURNAL
25 E Boardman St Ste 306 (44503-1803)
P.O. Box 714 (44501-0714)
PHONE..............................330 744-5023
Jeff Leo Herrmann, *CEO*
Andrea Wood, *Ch Bd*
EMP: 22 **EST:** 1984
SQ FT: 2,700
SALES (est): 935.1K **Privately Held**
Web: www.businessjournaldaily.com
SIC: 2711 Newspapers, publishing and
printing

(G-14831)
CARNEY PLASTICS INC
1010 W Rayen Ave (44502-1317)
PHONE..............................330 746-8273
Sean Carney, *Pr*
▲ **EMP:** 9 **EST:** 1986
SALES (est): 967.27K **Privately Held**
Web: www.carneyplastics.com
SIC: 3089 5162 Injection molding of plastics;
Plastics products, nec

(G-14832)
CCA YOUNGSTOWN
2240 Hubbard Rd (44505-3157)
PHONE..............................615 263-3000
EMP: 8 **EST:** 2011
SALES (est): 218.76K **Privately Held**
SIC: 7372 Business oriented computer
software

(G-14833)
CENTRAL COCA-COLA BTLG CO INC
Also Called: Coca-Cola
531 E Indianola Ave (44502-2319)
PHONE..............................330 783-1982
John Flynt, *Brnch Mgr*
EMP: 40
SALES (corp-wide): 45.75B **Publicly Held**
Web: www.coca-cola.com
SIC: 2086 Bottled and canned soft drinks
HQ: Central Coca-Cola Bottling Company,
Inc.
555 Taxter Rd Ste 550
Elmsford NY 10523
914 789-1100

(G-14834)
CENTRAL-1-OPTICAL LLC
6981 Southern Blvd Ste B (44512-4657)
PHONE..............................330 783-9660
Lloyd Yazbek, *Pr*
Linda B Yazbek, *
Richard J Thomas, *
Pamela A Thomas, *
Joyce Fiersdorf, *
▲ **EMP:** 80 **EST:** 1996
SQ FT: 10,000
SALES (est): 6.94MM **Privately Held**
Web: www.centraloneoptical.com
SIC: 3851 5995 Eyeglasses, lenses and
frames; Optical goods stores

(G-14835)
CITY CONCRETE LLC
151 Old Division St (44510)
PHONE..............................330 743-2825
Gary Carrocce, *Brnch Mgr*
EMP: 19
SALES (corp-wide): 2.04MM **Privately
Held**
SIC: 3273 Ready-mixed concrete
PA: City Concrete, L.L.C
4075 Shallow Creek Dr
Struthers OH

(G-14836)
**CITY MACHINE TECHNOLOGIES INC
(PA)**
773 W Rayen Ave (44502-1112)
P.O. Box 1466 (44501-1466)
PHONE..............................330 747-2639
Michael J Kovach, *Pr*
Claudia Kovach, *Sec*
EMP: 18 **EST:** 1986
SQ FT: 17,000
SALES (est): 8.05MM
SALES (corp-wide): 8.05MM **Privately
Held**
Web: www.cmtcompanies.com
SIC: 3621 7694 3599 7692 Motors and
generators; Armature rewinding shops;
Machine shop, jobbing and repair; Welding
repair

(G-14837)
CITY PRINTING CO INC
122 Oak Hill Ave (44502-1428)
PHONE..............................330 747-5691
Joseph A Valentini, *Pr*
EMP: 10 **EST:** 1920
SQ FT: 11,000
SALES (est): 944.79K **Privately Held**
Web: www.cityprinting.com
SIC: 2752 Offset printing

(G-14838)
CLASSIC OPTICAL LABS INC
3710 Belmont Ave (44505-1406)
P.O. Box 1341 (44501-1341)
PHONE..............................330 759-8245
Dawn Friedkin, *Pr*
▲ **EMP:** 195 **EST:** 1987
SQ FT: 30,000
SALES (est): 8.47MM **Privately Held**
Web: www.classicoptical.com
SIC: 3851 Ophthalmic goods

(G-14839)
CLIMATE PROS LLC
52 E Myrtle Ave (44507-1268)
PHONE..............................330 744-2732
Roy Guerrieri, *Brnch Mgr*
EMP: 99
Web: www.hattenbach.com
SIC: 5078 1711 2434 2541 Commercial
refrigeration equipment; Refrigeration
contractor; Wood kitchen cabinets;
Cabinets, except refrigerated: show,
display, etc.: wood
PA: Climate Pros, Llc
2190 Gladstone Ct Ste E
Glendale Heights IL 60139

(G-14840)
CORONADO STEEL CO
2360 Funston Dr (44510-1399)
PHONE..............................330 744-1143
EMP: 44 **EST:** 1958
SALES (est): 5.3MM **Privately Held**
Web: www.coronadosteel.com
SIC: 3325 Alloy steel castings, except
investment

(G-14841)
CRAFCO INC
912 Salt Springs Rd (44509-1171)
PHONE..............................330 270-3034
John Perry, *Brnch Mgr*
EMP: 17
SALES (corp-wide): 1.44B **Privately Held**
Web: www.crafco.com
SIC: 2951 Asphalt paving mixtures and
blocks
HQ: Crafco, Inc.
6165 W Detroit St
Chandler AZ 85226
602 276-0406

(G-14842)
CROWES CABINETS INC
590 E Western Reserve Rd Bldg 8
(44514-3386)
PHONE..............................330 729-9911
Diane Crowe, *Pr*
EMP: 20 **EST:** 1978
SQ FT: 6,000
SALES (est): 3.73MM **Privately Held**
Web: www.crowescabinets.com
SIC: 2434 Wood kitchen cabinets

(G-14843)
CUBBISON COMPANY (PA)
380 Victoria Rd (44515-2054)
PHONE..............................330 793-2481
Timothy Merrifield, *Pr*
EMP: 54 **EST:** 1971
SQ FT: 27,000
SALES (est): 8.02MM
SALES (corp-wide): 8.02MM **Privately
Held**
Web: www.cubbison.com
SIC: 3469 3993 3479 Metal stampings, nec;
Name plates: except engraved, etched,
etc.: metal; Etching and engraving

(G-14844)
**CUSTOM TARPAULIN PRODUCTS
INC**
8095 Southern Blvd (44512-6336)
PHONE..............................330 758-1801
Brian Robinson, *VP*
Beth Robinson, *Sec*
EMP: 10 **EST:** 1990
SALES (est): 933.23K **Privately Held**
Web: www.customtarpaulin.com
SIC: 2394 Tarpaulins, fabric: made from
purchased materials

(G-14845)
DA INVESTMENTS INC
4605 Lake Park Rd (44512-1814)
PHONE..............................330 781-6100
Thomas E Hutch Junior, *Pr*
EMP: 90 **EST:** 1986
SQ FT: 32,000
SALES (est): 3.02MM **Privately Held**
SIC: 3354 3444 Aluminum extruded products
; Sheet metalwork

(G-14846)
DE KAY FABRICATORS INC
295 S Meridian Rd (44509-2924)
PHONE..............................330 793-0826
Bryan Kennedy, *Pr*
EMP: 8 **EST:** 1975
SQ FT: 10,000
SALES (est): 739.16K **Privately Held**
SIC: 3498 Tube fabricating (contract bending
and shaping)

(G-14847)
**DEARING COMPRESSOR AND PUMP
COMPANY (PA)**
3974 Simon Rd (44501)
P.O. Box 6044 (44501)
PHONE..............................330 783-2258
EMP: 32 **EST:** 1945
SALES (est): 19.44MM
SALES (corp-wide): 19.44MM **Privately
Held**
Web: www.dearingcomp.com
SIC: 7699 7359 5084 5085 Compressor
repair; Equipment rental and leasing, nec;
Compressors, except air conditioning;
Industrial supplies

(G-14848)
DINESOL BUILDING PRODUCTS LTD
168 N Meridian Rd (44509-2036)
PHONE..............................330 270-0212
Michael Janak, *Sec*
Kenneth Leonard, *VP*
C Kenneth Fibus, *Ch*
EMP: 20 **EST:** 2002
SALES (est): 2MM **Privately Held**
SIC: 3089 Shutters, plastics

(G-14849)
**DR PEPPER BOTTLERS
ASSOCIATES**
Also Called: Dr Pepper
500 Pepsi Pl (44502-1432)
PHONE..............................330 746-7651
Danny Rittenberry, *Prin*
EMP: 9 **EST:** 2010
SALES (est): 141.55K **Privately Held**
Web: www.drpepper.com
SIC: 2086 Soft drinks: packaged in cans,
bottles, etc.

(G-14850)
**DUCA MANUFACTURING &
CONSULTING INC (PA)**
761 Mcclurg Rd (44512-6428)
PHONE..............................330 758-0828
▲ **EMP:** 28 **EST:** 1978
SALES (est): 1.97MM
SALES (corp-wide): 1.97MM **Privately
Held**
Web: www.ducamfg.com
SIC: 3567 3677 3498 Metal melting
furnaces, industrial: electric; Electronic coils
and transformers; Fabricated pipe and
fittings

(G-14851)
DUCA MFG & CONSULTING INC
697 Mcclurg Rd (44512-6408)
PHONE..............................330 726-7175
EMP: 7
SALES (corp-wide): 1.97MM **Privately
Held**
Web: www.ducamfg.com
SIC: 3567 Industrial furnaces and ovens
PA: Duca Manufacturing & Consulting, Inc.
761 Mcclurg Rd
Youngstown OH 44512
330 758-0828

(G-14852)
EJ USA INC
4150 Simon Rd (44512-1322)
PHONE..............................330 782-3900
Bill Denidovich, *Mgr*
EMP: 19
Web: www.ejco.com
SIC: 3449 3321 Custom roll formed products
; Manhole covers, metal
HQ: Ej Usa, Inc.
301 Spring St
East Jordan MI 49727
800 874-4100

(G-14853)
EPCO EXTRUSION PAINTING CO
4605 Lake Park Rd (44512-1814)
PHONE..............................330 781-6100
Thomas E Hutch Junior, *Pr*
EMP: 32 **EST:** 1989
SALES (est): 991.18K **Privately Held**
SIC: 3479 Aluminum coating of metal
products

(G-14854)
FALMER SCREW PDTS & MFG INC
690 Mcclurg Rd (44512-6407)
PHONE..............................330 758-0593
Rick Dravecky, *Pr*
Joseph Dravecky, *VP*
George Dravecky, *Sec*
EMP: 15 **EST:** 1947
SQ FT: 30,000
SALES (est): 2.41MM **Privately Held**
Web: www.falmerinc.com
SIC: 3599 3451 Machine shop, jobbing and
repair; Screw machine products

(G-14855)
FIRELINE INC (PA)
Also Called: Fireline Tcon
300 Andrews Ave (44505-3061)
PHONE..............................330 743-1164
Barbara Burley, *Pr*
Ed Ress, *
David Holmquist, *
Gloria Jones, *
◆ **EMP:** 119 **EST:** 1967
SQ FT: 85,000
SALES (est): 23.23MM
SALES (corp-wide): 23.23MM **Privately
Held**
Web: www.firelineinc.com
SIC: 3299 Nonmetallic mineral statuary and
other decorative products

(G-14856)
FOOD 4 YOUR SOUL
3957 S Schenley Ave (44511-3428)
PHONE..............................330 402-4073
Michelle White, *Owner*
EMP: 10 **EST:** 2009
SALES (est): 266.49K **Privately Held**
SIC: 2099 Food preparations, nec

(G-14857)
FORGE INDUSTRIES INC (PA)
4450 Market St (44512-1512)
P.O. Box 3465 (44513)
PHONE..............................330 960-2468
Mike Fryt, *CEO*
Michael Benowitz, *
Derek Scheefer, *
Zoltan Erkozics, *
▲ **EMP:** 1250 **EST:** 1900
SQ FT: 1,500
SALES (est): 1.51B
SALES (corp-wide): 1.51B **Privately Held**
SIC: 5085 3566 3599 3531 Bearings; Gears,
power transmission, except auto; Machine
shop, jobbing and repair; Road construction
and maintenance machinery

(G-14858)
FSCREATIONS CORPORATION (HQ)
Also Called: Einstruction Corporation
255 W Federal St (44503-1207)
PHONE..............................330 746-3015
Rich Fennessy, *CEO*
Tim Torno, *
▲ **EMP:** 100 **EST:** 1982
SQ FT: 8,000
SALES (est): 9.51MM
SALES (corp-wide): 35.75MM **Privately
Held**

Web: www.echo360.com
SIC: 7371 7379 5045 7372 Computer
software development; Computer related
consulting services; Computers,
peripherals, and software; Prepackaged
software
PA: Turning Technologies, Llc
6000 Mahoning Ave Ste 254
Youngstown OH 44515
330 746-3015

(G-14859)
FSQPRONET LLC
1152 Verona Ave (44506-1054)
PHONE..............................330 942-6014
EMP: 10
SALES (est): 410.32K **Privately Held**
SIC: 7389 2741 Business Activities at Non-
Commercial Site; Miscellaneous publishing

(G-14860)
GARVEY CORPORATION
Also Called: M7 Technologies
1019 Ohio Works Dr (44510-1078)
PHONE..............................330 779-0700
Michael S Garvey, *Pr*
Jeanette Garvey, *
EMP: 35 **EST:** 1979
SQ FT: 20,000
SALES (est): 6.54MM **Privately Held**
Web: www.m7tek.com
SIC: 3599 Machine shop, jobbing and repair

(G-14861)
GASSER CHAIR CO INC (PA)
4136 Logan Way (44505-1797)
PHONE..............................330 534-2234
Gary L Gasser, *CEO*
Mark E Gasser, *
Evelyn Mihin, *COO*
▲ **EMP:** 25 **EST:** 1947
SQ FT: 22,000
SALES (est): 24.66MM
SALES (corp-wide): 24.66MM **Privately
Held**
Web: www.gasserchair.com
SIC: 2531 2521 Chairs, table and arm;
Chairs, office: padded, upholstered, or
plain: wood

(G-14862)
GASSER CHAIR CO INC
Also Called: Production Div
2457 Logan Ave (44505-2550)
PHONE..............................330 759-2234
Frank Joy, *VP*
EMP: 53
SALES (corp-wide): 24.66MM **Privately
Held**
Web: www.gasserchair.com
SIC: 2531 2522 2521 2511 Chairs, table and
arm; Office furniture, except wood; Wood
office furniture; Wood household furniture
PA: Gasser Chair Co., Inc.
4136 Logan Way
Youngstown OH 44505
330 534-2234

(G-14863)
GEI OF COLUMBIANA INC
4040 Lake Park Rd (44512-1801)
PHONE..............................330 783-0270
Michael C Schuler, *Pr*
EMP: 22 **EST:** 2000
SALES (est): 469.11K **Privately Held**
SIC: 3354 3471 Shapes, extruded
aluminum, nec; Polishing, metals or formed
products

(G-14864)
GENERAL EXTRUSIONS INTL LLC ✪
4040 Lake Park Rd (44512-1801)
PHONE..............................330 783-0270
Gilles Teste, *CEO*
EMP: 170 **EST:** 2023
SALES (est): 22.12MM **Privately Held**
SIC: 3354 3471 Shapes, extruded
aluminum, nec; Polishing, metals or formed
products

(G-14865)
GENEVA LIBERTY STEEL LTD (PA)
Also Called: Genmak Geneva Liberty
947 Martin Luther King Jr Blvd
(44502-1106)
P.O. Box 6124 (44501-6124)
PHONE..............................330 740-0103
EMP: 40 **EST:** 2002
SQ FT: 85,000
SALES (est): 49.39MM
SALES (corp-wide): 49.39MM **Privately
Held**
Web: www.genevaliberty.com
SIC: 3316 7389 Strip, steel, flat bright, cold-
rolled: purchased hot-rolled; Scrap steel
cutting

(G-14866)
GEORGE A MITCHELL COMPANY
Also Called: Mitchell
557 Mcclurg Rd (44512-6443)
P.O. Box 3727 (44513-3727)
PHONE..............................330 758-5777
George A Mitchell, *Pr*
Paul F Russo, *VP*
Mark A Mitchell, *VP*
Patricia Jasinski, *Sec*
▼ **EMP:** 20 **EST:** 1963
SQ FT: 22,000
SALES (est): 2.48MM **Privately Held**
Web: www.mitchellmachinery.com
SIC: 3542 3541 3547 Extruding machines
(machine tools), metal; Machine tools,
metal cutting type; Rolling mill machinery

(G-14867)
GERM-BUSTERS SOLUTIONS LLC
3649 Northwood Ave (44511-2603)
PHONE..............................330 610-0480
EMP: 7 **EST:** 2020
SALES (est): 150K **Privately Held**
SIC: 2842 Polishes and sanitation goods

(G-14868)
GL INTERNATIONAL LLC
Also Called: Gli Pool Products
215 Sinter Ct (44510-1076)
PHONE..............................330 744-8812
Gary Crandall, *Managing Member*
Larry Schwimmer, *
▲ **EMP:** 130 **EST:** 2006
SALES (est): 21.55MM **Privately Held**
Web: www.glipoolproducts.com
SIC: 3949 Swimming pools, plastic

(G-14869)
**GOODYEAR TIRE & RUBBER
COMPANY**
Also Called: Goodyear
3651 Belmont Ave (44505-1490)
PHONE..............................330 759-9343
Jim March, *Mgr*
EMP: 8
SALES (corp-wide): 18.88B **Publicly Held**
Web: www.goodyear.com
SIC: 5531 7534 Automotive tires; Tire repair
shop
PA: The Goodyear Tire & Rubber Company
200 Innovation Way
Akron OH 44316

330 796-2121

(G-14870)
GREAT LAKES TELCOM LTD (PA)
Also Called: Broadband Hospitality
590 E Western Reserve Rd Bldg 9c
(44514-3389)
PHONE..............................330 629-8848
Vincenzo Lucci Junior, *CEO*
EMP: 30 **EST:** 1998
SQ FT: 9,200
SALES (est): 28.97MM **Privately Held**
Web: www.broadbandhospitality.com
SIC: 3663 4813 1623 1731 Satellites,
communications; Internet connectivity
services; Telephone and communication
line construction; Telephone and telephone
equipment installation

(G-14871)
GRENGA MACHINE & WELDING
56 Wayne Ave (44502-1938)
PHONE..............................330 743-1113
Joe Grenga, *Owner*
EMP: 10 **EST:** 1963
SQ FT: 30,000
SALES (est): 393.59K **Privately Held**
SIC: 5051 5084 3599 3443 Steel; Industrial
machinery and equipment; Machine shop,
jobbing and repair; Fabricated plate work
(boiler shop)

(G-14872)
GUNDERSON RAIL SERVICES LLC
Also Called: Greenbrier Rail Services
3710 Hendricks Rd Bldg 2a (44515-1537)
PHONE..............................330 792-6521
Adam Strysseler, *Mgr*
EMP: 60
SALES (corp-wide): 3.54B **Publicly Held**
Web: www.gbrx.com
SIC: 3743 3444 3441 Railroad equipment;
Sheet metalwork; Fabricated structural
metal
HQ: Gunderson Rail Services Llc
One Cntrpointe Dr Ste 200
Lake Oswego OR 97035
503 684-7000

(G-14873)
HYNES HOLDING COMPANY (HQ)
Also Called: Hynes Industries
3805 Hendricks Rd (44515-1536)
P.O. Box 3805 (44513-3805)
PHONE..............................330 799-3221
Rick C Organ, *CEO*
Ryan R Day, *CFO*
Robert T Moe, *COO*
Mike Giabattista, *CPO*
EMP: 7 **EST:** 2014
SALES (est): 18.82MM
SALES (corp-wide): 99.27MM **Privately
Held**
SIC: 3449 Custom roll formed products
PA: Hynes Industries, Inc.
3805 Hendricks Rd
Youngstown OH 44515
800 321-9257

(G-14874)
HYNES INDUSTRIES INC (PA)
3805 Hendricks Rd (44515-3046)
PHONE..............................800 321-9257
Rick Organ, *CEO*
Robert Moe, *
Ryan Day, *
Mike Giabattista, *CPO**
George Droder, *CCO**
▲ **EMP:** 54 **EST:** 1965
SQ FT: 154,000
SALES (est): 99.27MM

▲ = Import ▼ = Export
◆ = Import/Export

SALES (corp-wide): 99.27MM **Privately Held**
Web: www.hynesindustries.com
SIC: 3441 3316 3449 Fabricated structural metal; Wire, flat, cold-rolled strip: not made in hot-rolled mills; Custom roll formed products

(G-14875)
IMDS CORPORATION
Also Called: Imds Corporate
935 Augusta Dr (44512-7923)
PHONE....................................330 219-4299
Robert A Hill Junior, *Pr*
EMP: 10 **EST:** 1991
SQ FT: 18,600
SALES (est): 421.66K **Privately Held**
Web: www.imds-ohio.com
SIC: 3599 8711 Machine shop, jobbing and repair; Industrial engineers

(G-14876)
INDUSTRIAL MILL MAINTENANCE
1609 Wilson Ave Ste 2 (44506-1838)
P.O. Box 1465 (44501-1465)
PHONE....................................330 746-1155
Michael Mccarthy Senior, *Pr*
Kathy Mccarthy, *VP*
EMP: 18 **EST:** 1991
SQ FT: 5,600
SALES (est): 2.85MM **Privately Held**
SIC: 3471 1721 3444 3441 Sand blasting of metal parts; Industrial painting; Sheet metalwork; Fabricated structural metal

(G-14877)
INTIGRAL INC
45 Karago Ave (44512-5950)
PHONE....................................440 439-0980
Michael Mchugh, *Mgr*
EMP: 9
SALES (corp-wide): 21.07MM **Privately Held**
Web: www.intigral.com
SIC: 3231 Insulating glass: made from purchased glass
PA: Intigral, Inc.
7850 Northfield Rd
Walton Hills OH 44146
440 439-0980

(G-14878)
IRON CITY WOOD PRODUCTS INC
900 Albert St (44505-2908)
PHONE....................................330 755-2772
David S Muslovski, *Pr*
Denise Muslovski, *
EMP: 48 **EST:** 1988
SQ FT: 2,560
SALES (est): 6.05MM **Privately Held**
Web: www.icpallets.com
SIC: 2448 Pallets, wood

(G-14879)
JAMEN TOOL & DIE CO (PA)
Also Called: Truex Tool & Die Div
4450 Lake Park Rd (44512-1809)
PHONE....................................330 788-6521
Carmen P Chicone Senior, *Pr*
Antonette Chicone, *VP*
Paul Chicone, *Sec*
Carmen Chicone Junior, *Stockholder*
EMP: 19 **EST:** 1965
SQ FT: 5,000
SALES (est): 2.41MM
SALES (corp-wide): 2.41MM **Privately Held**
SIC: 3544 Extrusion dies

(G-14880)
JAMEN TOOL & DIE CO
Also Called: Mor-X Plastics
914 E Indianola Ave (44502-2674)
PHONE....................................330 782-6731
Bob Marcum, *Mgr*
EMP: 28
SALES (corp-wide): 2.41MM **Privately Held**
SIC: 3544 Industrial molds
PA: Jamen Tool & Die Co.
4450 Lake Park Rd
Youngstown OH 44512
330 788-6521

(G-14881)
JAMESTOWN INDUSTRIES INC
650 N Meridian Rd Ste 3 (44509-1245)
PHONE....................................330 779-0670
Clark Babb, *Mgr*
EMP: 60
SQ FT: 32,000
SALES (corp-wide): 2.35MM **Privately Held**
Web: www.jamestown-inc.com
SIC: 3493 Steel springs, except wire
PA: Jamestown Industries, Inc.
2210 Arbor Blvd Ste 99
Moraine OH 45439
937 643-9401

(G-14882)
JILCO LLC ✪
P.O. Box 4596 (44515-0596)
PHONE....................................330 270-9780
EMP: 6 **EST:** 2024
SALES (est): 925.27K **Privately Held**
SIC: 3541 Machine tools, metal cutting type

(G-14883)
JOHN ZIDIAN COMPANY (PA)
Also Called: Zidian Specialty Foods
574 Mcclurg Rd (44512-6405)
PHONE....................................330 743-6050
Tom Zidian, *CEO*
Harry Shood, *CFO*
▲ **EMP:** 20 **EST:** 2011
SALES (est): 8.86MM
SALES (corp-wide): 8.86MM **Privately Held**
Web: www.giarussa.com
SIC: 2032 Italian foods, nec: packaged in cans, jars, etc.

(G-14884)
JOHNSON CONTROLS INC
Also Called: Johnson Controls
1044 N Meridian Rd Ste A (44509-1070)
PHONE....................................330 270-4385
Edward Dunkerley, *Mgr*
EMP: 21
Web: www.johnsoncontrols.com
SIC: 2531 Seats, automobile
HQ: Johnson Controls, Inc.
5757 N Green Bay Ave
Milwaukee WI 53209
866 496-1999

(G-14885)
KIRALY TOOL AND DIE INC
1250 Crescent St (44502-1303)
PHONE....................................330 744-5773
Steve Kiraly, *Pr*
Shari Kiraly, *VP*
EMP: 10 **EST:** 1999
SQ FT: 9,500
SALES (est): 4.54MM **Privately Held**
Web: www.kiralytool.com
SIC: 3542 3544 Machine tools, metal forming type; Special dies, tools, jigs, and fixtures

(G-14886)
LAKE PARK TOOL & MACHINE LLC
Also Called: Lake Park Tool & Machine
1221 Velma Ct (44512-1829)
PHONE....................................330 788-2437
Oscar Lund, *Pr*
Susanne Wildner, *Prin*
Dave Cornelius, *Prin*
EMP: 13 **EST:** 2015
SALES (est): 3.41MM **Privately Held**
Web: www.lakepark.com
SIC: 3599 Machine shop, jobbing and repair

(G-14887)
LARICCIAS ITALIAN FOODS INC
7438 Southern Blvd (44512-5629)
PHONE....................................330 729-0222
Tessa Lariccia, *Pr*
Michael Allegretto, *VP*
EMP: 10 **EST:** 1910
SQ FT: 4,000
SALES (est): 208.77K **Privately Held**
Web:
www.laricciasitalianmarketplace.com
SIC: 5411 2098 2035 Grocery stores, independent; Macaroni and spaghetti; Pickles, sauces, and salad dressings

(G-14888)
LIBERTY PATTERN AND MOLD INC
1131 Meadowbrook Ave (44512-1822)
PHONE....................................330 788-9463
John Plaskett, *Pr*
EMP: 7 **EST:** 1917
SQ FT: 4,800
SALES (est): 646.59K **Privately Held**
Web: www.libpattern.com
SIC: 3543 Industrial patterns

(G-14889)
LUMENFORCE LED LLC ✪
5411 Market St (44512-2615)
PHONE....................................330 330-8962
James Rosen, *Managing Member*
EMP: 35 **EST:** 2023
SALES (est): 1.91MM **Privately Held**
SIC: 3646 Commercial lighting fixtures

(G-14890)
M F Y INC
Also Called: Youngstown Metal Fabricating
1640 Wilson Ave (44506 1839)
PHONE....................................330 747-1334
Andrew Weaver Junior, *Pr*
EMP: 15 **EST:** 1972
SQ FT: 35,000
SALES (est): 1.91MM **Privately Held**
Web: www.youngstownmetalfab.com
SIC: 3446 Stairs, staircases, stair treads: prefabricated metal

(G-14891)
M I P INC
701 Jones St (44502-2160)
P.O. Box 5467 (44514-0467)
PHONE....................................330 744-0215
Richard B Weaver Junior, *Pr*
Melvin Weaver Junior, *Pr*
Leigh Marsden, *Pr*
Linda Weaver, *VP*
Russel W Brown, *VP*
EMP: 19 **EST:** 1974
SQ FT: 50,000
SALES (est): 2.01MM **Privately Held**
Web: www.mipplating.com
SIC: 3471 Electroplating of metals or formed products

(G-14892)
MACTON CORPORATION
3200 Innovation Pl (44509-4025)
PHONE....................................330 259-8555
Peter Mcgonagle, *Pr*
Thomas E Young Senior, *VP*
Paul Spicer, *VP*
John C Shepherd, *VP*
Steve Schumacher, *VP*
▼ **EMP:** 60 **EST:** 1947
SALES (est): 2.05MM
SALES (corp-wide): 20MM **Privately Held**
Web: www.macton.com
SIC: 3537 Industrial trucks and tractors
PA: Bbm Railway Equipment, Llc
3200 Innovation Pl
Youngstown OH 44509
330 259-8555

(G-14893)
MAGNETIC ANALYSIS CORPORATION
Also Called: Mac Mfg and Test Facilities
675 Mcclurg Rd (44512-6408)
PHONE....................................330 758-1367
Manuel Morales, *Manager*
EMP: 8
SQ FT: 19,000
SALES (corp-wide): 25MM **Privately Held**
Web: www.mac-ndt.com
SIC: 3829 Testing equipment: abrasion, shearing strength, etc.
PA: Magnetic Analysis Corporation
103 Fairview Park Dr
Elmsford NY 10523
914 530-2000

(G-14894)
MAK FABRICATING INC
1609 Wilson Ave (44506-1838)
P.O. Box 212 (44501-0212)
PHONE....................................330 747-0040
Dan Maccarthy, *Pr*
EMP: 10 **EST:** 1997
SQ FT: 54,000
SALES (est): 465.39K **Privately Held**
SIC: 3499 Fire- or burglary-resistive products

(G-14895)
MCDONALDS
1709 S Raccoon Rd (44515-4702)
PHONE....................................330 792-0527
EMP: 12 **EST:** 2019
SALES (est): 57.19K **Privately Held**
Web: www.mcdonalds.com
SIC: 5813 5812 5499 2038 Drinking places; Eating places; Miscellaneous food stores; Frozen specialties, nec

(G-14896)
MCHENRY INDUSTRIES INC
85 Victoria Rd (44515-2023)
PHONE....................................330 799-8930
Robert P Willison, *Pr*
Ronald Musilli, *
Ron Musilli Senior, *Pr*
Ron Musilli Junior, *VP*
EMP: 24 **EST:** 1964
SQ FT: 20,000
SALES (est): 9.79MM **Privately Held**
Web: www.mchenryindustries.com
SIC: 3083 3315 Thermoplastics laminates: rods, tubes, plates, and sheet; Steel wire and related products

(G-14897)
MEDIAJACKED SOUND STUDIO LLC
2903 Mahoning Ave (44509-2633)
PHONE....................................330 391-3123
Emanuel Valentin, *Managing Member*
EMP: 6 **EST:** 2022

SALES (est): 369.8K **Privately Held**
SIC: **3861** Sound recording and reproducing
equipment, motion picture

(G-14898)
MERIDIAN ARTS AND GRAPHICS
16 Belgrade St (44505-1818)
PHONE..............................330 759-9099
Ted Webb, *Pr*
Robert Millham, *VP*
Cheryl Millham, *Sec*
EMP: 6 EST: 1993
SQ FT: 10,000
SALES (est): 240.89K **Privately Held**
Web: www.rsi.biz
SIC: **7336 2752** Art design services;
Lithographing on metal

(G-14899)
MICROMD
790 Boardman Canfield Rd (44512-4385)
PHONE..............................850 217-7412
Brian Batchler, *Pdt Mgr*
EMP: 6 EST: 2017
SALES (est): 2MM **Privately Held**
Web: www.micromd.com
SIC: **3841** Surgical and medical instruments

(G-14900)
MID-STATE SALES INC
Also Called: Youngstown Rubber Products
519 N Meridian Rd (44509-1227)
P.O. Box 1377 (44501-1377)
PHONE..............................330 744-2158
TOLL FREE: 800
James B Tomaino, *Mgr*
EMP: 8
SALES (corp-wide): 10.43MM **Privately
Held**
Web: www.midstate-sales.com
SIC: **5085 3492** Rubber goods, mechanical;
Hose and tube fittings and assemblies,
hydraulic/pneumatic
PA: Mid-State Sales, Inc.
1101 Gahanna Pkwy
Columbus OH 43230
614 864-1811

(G-14901)
MIKES TRANSM & AUTO SVC LLC ✪
202 S Meridian Rd (44509-2923)
PHONE..............................330 799-8266
Steve P Decost, *CEO*
Steve P Decost, *Managing Member*
EMP: 10 EST: 2023
SALES (est): 146.17K **Privately Held**
Web: www.mikestransmissionauto.com
SIC: **1731 7549 3559 7537** General
electrical contractor; High performance auto
repair and service; Automotive
maintenance equipment; Automotive
transmission repair shops

(G-14902)
MORDIES INC
Also Called: Tri-R Dies
556 Bev Rd (44512-6420)
PHONE..............................330 758-8050
Benjamin Morucci, *Pr*
Mary Morucci, *Sec*
EMP: 14 EST: 1978
SQ FT: 6,000
SALES (est): 1.16MM **Privately Held**
Web: www.trirdies.com
SIC: **3544** Extrusion dies

(G-14903)
NATIONAL TOOL & EQUIPMENT INC
60 Karago Ave (44512-5949)
PHONE..............................330 629-8665
James Simon Junior, *CEO*

Alex Simon, *Sec*
Anthony Vross, *Pr*
James Simon Senior Stkldr, *Prin*
EMP: 10 EST: 1993
SQ FT: 8,000
SALES (est): 320.08K **Privately Held**
SIC: **7699 5084 5072 5251** Engine repair
and replacement, non-automotive; Fans,
industrial; Hand tools; Tools

(G-14904)
NOMIS PUBLICATIONS INC
Also Called: Boardman Printing
8570 Foxwood Ct (44514-4301)
P.O. Box 5159 (44514-0159)
PHONE..............................330 965-2380
Lucille Mc Guire, *Pr*
Margaret Rouzzo, *Sec*
Kim Graham, *VP*
EMP: 15 EST: 1974
SQ FT: 7,000
SALES (est): 1.96MM **Privately Held**
Web: www.boardmanprinting.com
SIC: **2741 2711 2752 2759** Directories, nec:
publishing only, not printed on site;
Newspapers: publishing only, not printed on
site; Offset printing; Commercial printing,
nec

(G-14905)
NORTHEAST FABRICATORS LLC
365 E Boardman St (44503-1829)
P.O. Box 629 (44501-0629)
PHONE..............................330 747-3484
EMP: 20
Web: www.northeastfabricators.com
SIC: **3443** Weldments

(G-14906)
OHIO FOAM CORPORATION
1201 Ameritech Blvd (44509-4022)
PHONE..............................330 799-4553
Jerry Mouser, *Brnch Mgr*
EMP: 24
SALES (corp-wide): 8.08MM **Privately
Held**
Web: www.ohiofoam.com
SIC: **3069** Foam rubber
PA: Ohio Foam Corporation
820 Plymouth St
Bucyrus OH 44820
419 563-0399

(G-14907)
P & L HEAT TRTING GRINDING INC
313 E Wood St (44503-1691)
PHONE..............................330 746-1339
William H Pociask, *Pr*
Helen Premec, *
EMP: 20 EST: 1978
SQ FT: 16,000
SALES (est): 2.37MM **Privately Held**
Web: www.plheattreating.com
SIC: **3398 3599 3471** Metal heat treating;
Grinding castings for the trade; Plating and
polishing

(G-14908)
P & L METALCRAFTS LLC
Also Called: Metalcrafts
1050 Ohio Works Dr (44510-1077)
PHONE..............................330 793-2178
John Lyras, *Managing Member*
▲ EMP: 12 EST: 2013
SALES (est): 4.48MM **Privately Held**
Web: www.metalcraftsyng.com
SIC: **3446 3444 3441** Ornamental metalwork
; Sheet metalwork; Fabricated structural
metal

(G-14909)
P & L PRECISION GRINDING LLC
948 Poland Ave (44502-2137)
PHONE..............................330 746-8081
EMP: 11 EST: 2009
SQ FT: 15,000
SALES (est): 1MM **Privately Held**
SIC: **7699 7389 3398** Knife, saw and tool
sharpening and repair; Grinding, precision:
commercial or industrial; Metal heat treating

(G-14910)
P-AMERICAS LLC
Also Called: Pepsico
500 Pepsi Pl (44502-1432)
PHONE..............................330 746-7652
Richard Plant, *Mgr*
EMP: 38
SALES (corp-wide): 91.47B **Publicly Held**
Web: www.pepsico.com
SIC: **2086 5149 4225** Carbonated soft
drinks, bottled and canned; Groceries and
related products, nec; General warehousing
and storage
HQ: P-Americas Llc
1 Pepsi Way
Somers NY 10589
336 896-5740

(G-14911)
PANELMATIC INC
Also Called: Panelmatic Youngstown
1125 Meadowbrook Ave (44512-1884)
PHONE..............................330 782-8007
Gary M Urso, *Brnch Mgr*
EMP: 29
SALES (corp-wide): 56.9MM **Privately
Held**
Web: www.panelmatic.com
SIC: **3613 8711** Control panels, electric;
Designing: ship, boat, machine, and product
PA: Panelmatic, Inc.
6806 Willowbrook Park
Houston TX 77066
888 757-1957

(G-14912)
PANELMATIC YOUNGSTOWN INC
1125 Meadowbrook Ave (44512-1884)
PHONE..............................330 782-8007
Richard Leach, *Pr*
David D Adamson, *
▼ EMP: 40 EST: 1976
SQ FT: 44,000
SALES (est): 2.89MM
SALES (corp-wide): 56.9MM **Privately
Held**
Web: www.panelmatic.com
SIC: **3613** Control panels, electric
PA: Panelmatic, Inc.
6806 Willowbrook Park
Houston TX 77066
888 757-1957

(G-14913)
**PARK PLC PRNTG CPYG & DGTL
IMG**
3410 Canfield Rd Ste B (44511-2713)
PHONE..............................330 799-1739
Kay F Probst, *Pr*
EMP: 6 EST: 2007
SALES (est): 60.59K **Privately Held**
SIC: **2759** Commercial printing, nec

(G-14914)
PARKER-HANNIFIN CORPORATION
1911 Logan Ave (44505-2673)
PHONE..............................330 740-8366
Michael Wood, *Prin*
EMP: 8
SALES (corp-wide): 19.93B **Publicly Held**

Web: www.parker.com
SIC: **3594** Fluid power pumps
PA: Parker-Hannifin Corporation
6035 Parkland Blvd
Cleveland OH 44124
216 896-3000

(G-14915)
PAUL SHOVLIN
Also Called: Pauls Tire Company
807 Mulberry Ln (44512-2364)
PHONE..............................330 757-0032
Paul Shovlin, *Owner*
EMP: 6 EST: 1970
SALES (est): 87.34K **Privately Held**
SIC: **5531 7534 7389** Automotive tires; Tire
repair shop; Business Activities at Non-
Commercial Site

(G-14916)
**PHANTOM FIREWORKS WSTN REG
LLC**
Also Called: Phantom Fireworks
2445 Belmont Ave (44505-2405)
PHONE..............................330 746-1064
EMP: 6
SALES (est): 3.15MM **Privately Held**
Web: www.fireworks.com
SIC: **2899** Fireworks

(G-14917)
PLY-TRIM INC (PA)
550 N Meridian Rd (44509-1226)
PHONE..............................330 799-7876
Harry Hoffman, *Ch Bd*
Kathleen Hoffman, *Ch Bd*
EMP: 21 EST: 1981
SQ FT: 48,000
SALES (est): 2.14MM
SALES (corp-wide): 2.14MM **Privately
Held**
Web: www.plytrim.com
SIC: **2431** Millwork

(G-14918)
POLY TEC EAST INC
550 N Meridian Rd (44509-1226)
PHONE..............................330 799-7876
▲ EMP: 8
SALES (est): 531.06K **Privately Held**
SIC: **3083** Laminated plastics sheets

(G-14919)
POLYTECH COMPONENT CORP
8469 Southern Blvd (44512-6709)
PHONE..............................330 726-3235
Paul Colby, *Pr*
Robert Barber, *VP*
Michael Durina, *VP*
William White, *Treas*
Ilene Colby, *Sec*
EMP: 6 EST: 1990
SQ FT: 6,000
SALES (est): 122.43K **Privately Held**
SIC: **3599** Machine shop, jobbing and repair

(G-14920)
PRESSED COFFEE BAR & EATERY
215 Lincoln Ave (44503-1013)
PHONE..............................330 746-8030
EMP: 7 EST: 2015
SALES (est): 140.1K **Privately Held**
Web:
www.pressedcoffeebarandeatery.com
SIC: **2741** Miscellaneous publishing

(G-14921)
PROUT BOILER HTG & WLDG INC
3124 Temple St (44510-1048)
PHONE..............................330 744-0293

▲ = Import ▼ = Export
◆ = Import/Export

Wes Prout, *Pr*
Richard Dalleske, *
Donald Raybuck, *
Linda Prout, *Stockholder**
EMP: 50 **EST:** 1945
SQ FT: 3,000
SALES (est): 7.94MM **Privately Held**
Web: www.proutboiler.com
SIC: 1711 7692 3443 Boiler maintenance contractor; Welding repair; Fabricated plate work (boiler shop)

(G-14922)
R & M FLUID POWER INC
7953 Southern Blvd (44512-6091)
PHONE................................330 758-2766
Robert Gustafson Senior, *Ch Bd*
Robert Gustafson Ii, *VP*
Melissa Ricciardi, *
Jennifer Kenetz, *
EMP: 25 **EST:** 1978
SQ FT: 40,000
SALES (est): 8.44MM **Privately Held**
Web: www.rmfluidpower.com
SIC: 3593 5084 Fluid power cylinders, hydraulic or pneumatic; Hydraulic systems equipment and supplies

(G-14923)
R W SIDLEY INCORPORATED
3424 Oregon Ave (44509-1075)
PHONE................................330 793-7374
Gary Hawkins, *Mgr*
EMP: 21
SALES (corp-wide): 43.09MM **Privately Held**
Web: www.rwsidley.com
SIC: 5032 3273 Brick, stone, and related material; Ready-mixed concrete
PA: R. W. Sidley Incorporated
436 Casement Ave
Painesville OH 44077
440 352-9343

(G-14924)
RL SMITH GRAPHICS LLC
Also Called: Rl Smith Graphics
493 Bev Rd Bldg 7b (44512-6459)
PHONE................................330 629-8616
Ronald L Smith, *Managing Member*
EMP: 8 **EST:** 2010
SALES (est): 935.27K **Privately Held**
Web: www.rlsmithgraphics.com
SIC: 2752 Commercial printing, lithographic

(G-14925)
RNW HOLDINGS INC
200 Division Street Ext (44510-1000)
P.O. Box 478 (44501-0478)
PHONE................................330 792-0600
Major Hammond, *Brnch Mgr*
EMP: 42
SIC: 5093 1795 3341 Scrap and waste materials; Wrecking and demolition work; Secondary nonferrous metals
HQ: Rnw Holdings, Inc.
26949 Chagrin Blvd # 305
Cleveland OH 44122
216 831-0510

(G-14926)
ROMLINE EXPRESS LLC
1572 Brownlee Ave (44514-1010)
PHONE................................234 855-1905
Stefan Ciuhulescu, *Prin*
EMP: 6 **EST:** 2014
SALES (est): 191.39K **Privately Held**
SIC: 2541 Wood partitions and fixtures

(G-14927)
RUSCO PRODUCTS INC
Also Called: Rusco Design Center
423 E Western Reserve Rd (44514-3350)
PHONE................................330 758-0378
William R Bryson, *Pr*
Patricia Bryson, *Sec*
EMP: 6 **EST:** 1942
SALES (est): 266.52K **Privately Held**
Web: www.rusco.com
SIC: 1799 2541 Kitchen and bathroom remodeling; Table or counter tops, plastic laminated

(G-14928)
SCHWEBEL BAKING COMPANY (PA)
965 E Midlothian Blvd (44502-2869)
P.O. Box 6013 (44502)
PHONE................................330 783-2860
Paul Schwebel, *Pr*
Alyson Winick, *
David Alter, *
EMP: 450 **EST:** 1906
SQ FT: 125,000
SALES (est): 71.65MM
SALES (corp-wide): 71.65MM **Privately Held**
Web: www.schwebels.com
SIC: 2051 Bread, cake, and related products

(G-14929)
SCHWEBEL BAKING COMPANY
920 E Midlothian Blvd (44502-2838)
PHONE................................330 783-2860
EMP: 24
SALES (corp-wide): 71.65MM **Privately Held**
Web: www.schwebels.com
SIC: 2051 Bread, cake, and related products
PA: Schwebel Baking Company
965 E Midlothian Blvd
Youngstown OH 44502
330 783-2860

(G-14930)
SDMK LLC
Also Called: Fastsigns
7340 Market St (44512-5610)
PHONE................................330 965-0970
Marc Sikora, *Pr*
Kevin Sikora, *VP*
EMP: 6 **EST:** 2016
SALES (est): 1.67MM **Privately Held**
Web: www.fastsigns.com
SIC: 3993 Signs and advertising specialties

(G-14931)
SID-MAR FOODS INC
1481 South Ave Ste 182 (44502-2239)
PHONE................................330 743-0112
Charlie Brown, *Pr*
Richard Seidler, *CEO*
EMP: 7 **EST:** 1992
SQ FT: 7,000
SALES (est): 467.87K **Privately Held**
SIC: 2015 Poultry slaughtering and processing

(G-14932)
SIMON ROOFING AND SHTMTL CORP (PA)
Also Called: Simon Roofing
70 Karago Ave (44512-5949)
P.O. Box 951109 (44193-0005)
PHONE................................330 629-7392
Stephen Manser, *Pr*
Rocco Augustine, *VP*
Alex J Simon Junior, *CFO*
EMP: 105 **EST:** 1900
SQ FT: 30,000
SALES (est): 58.54MM

SALES (corp-wide): 58.54MM **Privately Held**
Web: www.simonroofing.com
SIC: 1761 2952 Roofing contractor; Asphalt felts and coatings

(G-14933)
SIT INC
Also Called: Step In Time
1305 Boardman Canfield Rd (44512-4034)
P.O. Box 3725 (44513-3725)
PHONE................................330 758-8468
Geri Slavin, *Pr*
EMP: 25 **EST:** 1992
SQ FT: 3,500
SALES (est): 2.02MM **Privately Held**
SIC: 2759 2395 Screen printing; Embroidery products, except Schiffli machine

(G-14934)
SOLAR ARTS GRAPHIC DESIGNS
824 Tod Ave (44502-1326)
PHONE................................330 744-0535
Daniel Klingensmith, *Pr*
Catherine Klingensmith, *VP*
EMP: 6 **EST:** 1977
SALES (est): 207.53K **Privately Held**
Web: www.solar-arts.com
SIC: 2396 5199 Printing and embossing on plastics fabric articles; Advertising specialties

(G-14935)
SPACELINKS ENTERPRISES INC
1110 Thalia Ave (44512-1825)
PHONE................................330 788-2401
Daniel Kessler, *Pr*
Jamie Bill, *Stockholder*
Samantha Cessker, *Stockholder*
Seth Kessler, *Stockholder*
EMP: 24 **EST:** 1995
SQ FT: 90,000
SALES (est): 791.04K **Privately Held**
Web: www.spacelinks1.com
SIC: 2273 Mats and matting

(G-14936)
SPECIALTY SWITCH COMPANY LLC
Also Called: Specialty Trans Components
525 Mcclurg Rd (44512-6406)
PHONE................................330 427-3000
Terry Turvey, *Pr*
▲ **EMP:** 15 **EST:** 1986
SQ FT: 7,000
SALES (est): 2.34MM **Privately Held**
Web: www.transformercomponents.com
SIC: 3679 5063 Electronic switches; Electrical apparatus and equipment

(G-14937)
SPECTRUM METAL FINISHING INC
535 Bev Rd (44512-6490)
PHONE................................330 758-8358
Neil Chrisman, *Pr*
Thomas Hutch, *
▼ **EMP:** 57 **EST:** 1964
SQ FT: 60,000
SALES (est): 9.95MM **Privately Held**
Web: www.spectrummetal.com
SIC: 3471 Finishing, metals or formed products

(G-14938)
SPIREX CORPORATION
375 Victoria Rd Ste 1 (44515-2053)
PHONE................................330 726-1166
▲ **EMP:** 200
Web: www.valleyextreme.com

SIC: 3599 3535 3494 3443 Machine shop, jobbing and repair; Conveyors and conveying equipment; Valves and pipe fittings, nec; Fabricated plate work (boiler shop)

(G-14939)
SR PRODUCTS
70 Karago Ave (44512-5949)
PHONE................................330 998-6500
Steve Harnish, *Pr*
Stephen Duke, *CFO*
EMP: 10 **EST:** 2014
SALES (est): 2.3MM **Privately Held**
Web: www.simonroofing.com
SIC: 2952 Asphalt felts and coatings

(G-14940)
STAR MANUFACTURING LLC
Also Called: Commercial Metal Forming
1775 Logan Ave (44505-2622)
PHONE................................330 740-8300
Michael Conglose, *CEO*
Jim Petrides, *
EMP: 148 **EST:** 2016
SALES (est): 48.26MM
SALES (corp-wide): 48.26MM **Privately Held**
SIC: 3272 Tanks, concrete
PA: Ce Star Holdings, Llc
1775 Logan Ave
Youngstown OH 44505
800 826-5867

(G-14941)
STEEL FORMING INC
Also Called: Commercial Metal Forming
1775 Logan Ave (44505-2622)
P.O. Box 599 (44501-0599)
PHONE................................714 532-6321
◆ **EMP:** 203
Web: www.cmforming.com
SIC: 3469 Metal stampings, nec

(G-14942)
T C REDI MIX YOUNGSTOWN INC (PA)
2400 Poland Ave (44502-2782)
PHONE................................330 755-2143
Sherry Andrews, *Pr*
Sandra Raider, *VP*
Susan Kirkwood, *Sec*
EMP: 20 **EST:** 1974
SQ FT: 3,000
SALES (est): 4.12MM
SALES (corp-wide): 4.12MM **Privately Held**
Web: t-c-redi-mix-inc.hub.biz
SIC: 3273 5211 Ready-mixed concrete; Lumber and other building materials

(G-14943)
TAYLOR-WINFIELD TECH INC
Also Called: Taylor Winfield Indus Wldg Eqp
3200 Innovation Pl (44509-4025)
P.O. Box 779 (44509)
PHONE................................330 259-8500
Doyle Hopper, *CEO*
Alex Benyo, *
Brian Benyo, *
EMP: 100 **EST:** 2010
SQ FT: 25,000
SALES (est): 26.28MM **Privately Held**
Web: www.taylor-winfield.com
SIC: 3548 Welding apparatus
PA: Brilex Industries, Inc.
1201 Crescent St
Youngstown OH 44502

(G-14944)
TEH INVESTMENTS INC
Also Called: Aerolite
4605 Lake Park Rd (44512-1814)
PHONE...................................330 782-1127
Thomas E Hutch Junior, *Pr*
David Camacci, *
John D Hutch, *
Paul J Hutch, *
Thomas E Hutch, *
EMP: 90 EST: 1953
SQ FT: 200,000
SALES (est): 4.43MM Privately Held
Web: www.aeroext.com
SIC: 3354 3444 Shapes, extruded
aluminum, nec; Sheet metalwork

(G-14945)
THE FLORAND COMPANY
4404 Lake Park Rd (44512-1809)
PHONE...................................330 747-8986
Andrew Hirt, *Pr*
Kevin Carney, *VP*
Florence Hirt, *Treas*
EMP: 8 EST: 1989
SALES (est): 953.9K Privately Held
Web: www.florand.com
SIC: 3312 Plate, sheet and strip, except
coated products

(G-14946)
THE VINDICATOR PRINTING COMPANY (PA)
107 Vindicator Sq (44503-1136)
P.O. Box 780 (44501-0780)
PHONE...................................330 747-1471
EMP: 320 EST: 1869
SALES (est): 5.16MM
SALES (corp-wide): 5.16MM Privately
Held
Web: www.vindy.com
SIC: 2711 Newspapers, publishing and
printing

(G-14947)
TIMEKAP INC
Also Called: Timekap Indus Sls Svc & Mch
2315 Belmont Ave (44505-2404)
PHONE...................................330 747-2122
Patrick Chrystal, *Pr*
Scott Lawrence, *VP*
EMP: 6 EST: 1994
SQ FT: 15,000
SALES (est): 220K Privately Held
SIC: 3599 Machine shop, jobbing and repair

(G-14948)
TMI INC
6475 Victoria East Rd (44515-2051)
P.O. Box 4596 (44515-0596)
PHONE...................................330 270-9780
Michael J Myhal Junior, *Pr*
Rebecca Myhal, *
▼ EMP: 28 EST: 1984
SQ FT: 30,000
SALES (est): 4.79MM Privately Held
Web: www.teamtmi.com
SIC: 3069 Molded rubber products

(G-14949)
TRAFFIC DETECTORS & SIGNS INC
Also Called: Traffic Detectors & Signs
7521 Forest Hill Ave (44514-2635)
PHONE...................................330 707-9060
Leila M Meris, *Prin*
EMP: 6 EST: 2003
SALES (est): 1.66MM Privately Held
SIC: 1611 3993 Highway signs and
guardrails; Signs and advertising specialties

(G-14950)
TRANSIT FITTINGS N AMER INC
295 S Meridian Rd (44509-2924)
PHONE...................................330 797-2516
Admiral Jeff Fox, *Prin*
EMP: 6 EST: 2019
SALES (est): 750K Privately Held
SIC: 3711 Bus and other large specialty
vehicle assembly

(G-14951)
TRANSIT SITTINGS OF NA
295 S Meridian Rd (44509-2924)
PHONE...................................330 797-2516
Wayne Donitzen, *Off Mgr*
EMP: 6 EST: 1999
SALES (est): 391.93K Privately Held
SIC: 3498 Fabricated pipe and fittings

(G-14952)
TRIVIUM ALUM PACKG USA CORP (DH)
1 Performance Pl (44502-2082)
PHONE...................................330 744-2267
Michael Mapes, *CEO*
Delfin Gibert, *
Brenda Oman, *
▲ EMP: 31 EST: 1992
SQ FT: 476,000
SALES (est): 80.14MM
SALES (corp-wide): 6.8B Privately Held
Web: www.triviumpackaging.com
SIC: 3411 3354 Aluminum cans; Aluminum
extruded products
HQ: Trivium Packaging B.V.
Schiphol Boulevard 149
Luchthaven Schiphol NH

(G-14953)
TRUMBULL MANUFACTURING INC
3850 Hendricks Rd (44515-1528)
PHONE...................................330 270-7888
Sam H Miller, *CEO*
Michael W Rosenberg, *Prin*
EMP: 22 EST: 1922
SALES (est): 1.97MM Privately Held
Web: www.trumbull-mfg.com
SIC: 3589 Water treatment equipment,
industrial

(G-14954)
TURNING TECHNOLOGIES LLC (PA)
6000 Mahoning Ave (44515-2225)
PHONE...................................330 746-3015
Mike Broderick, *Managing Member*
Dave Kauer, *
Doctor Tina Rooks, *Sr VP*
Kevin Owens, *
Sheila Hura, *
◆ EMP: 95 EST: 2002
SALES (est): 35.75MM
SALES (corp-wide): 35.75MM Privately
Held
Web: www.echo360.com
SIC: 7372 Business oriented computer
software

(G-14955)
U S WEATHERFORD L P
1100 Performance Pl (44502-4001)
PHONE...................................330 746-2502
EMP: 164
Web: www.weatherford.com
SIC: 1389 Oil field services, nec
HQ: U S Weatherford L P
1221 Evangeline Thruway
Broussard LA 70518
337 347-5300

(G-14956)
V & M STAR LP
2669 Martin Luther King Jr Blvd
(44510-1033)
PHONE...................................330 742-6300
Brian R Colquhoun, *Prin*
▲ EMP: 11 EST: 2012
SALES (est): 2.42MM Privately Held
Web: www.vmtubes.net
SIC: 3061 Oil and gas field machinery
rubber goods (mechanical)

(G-14957)
VALLOUREC STAR LP (HQ)
2669 Martin Luther King Jr Blvd
(44510-1062)
PHONE...................................330 742-6300
Edouard Guinotte, *Ch Bd*
Olivier Mallet, *CEO*
Pascal Braquehais, *MIDDLE EAST ASIA*
Philippe Carlier, *Senior Vice President
Technology*
Franois Curie, *Pers/VP*
▲ EMP: 139 EST: 2002
SALES (est): 215.37MM
SALES (corp-wide): 4.93MM Privately
Held
Web: www.vallourec.com
SIC: 3317 Pipes, seamless steel
PA: Vallourec
12 Rue De La Verrerie
Meudon IDF 92190
149093500

(G-14958)
VAM USA LLC
1053 Ohio Works Dr (44510-1078)
PHONE...................................330 742-3130
EMP: 21 EST: 2012
SALES (est): 4.65MM Privately Held
Web: www.vam-usa.com
SIC: 1389 Oil field services, nec

(G-14959)
VARCO LP
Also Called: Tuboscope
2669 Martin Luther King Jr Blvd
(44510-1062)
P.O. Box 2185 (44504-0185)
PHONE...................................330 746-2922
Brad Michlok, *Mgr*
EMP: 27
SALES (corp-wide): 8.87B Publicly Held
Web: www.nov.com
SIC: 1389 Testing, measuring, surveying,
and analysis services
HQ: Varco, L.P.
2835 Holmes Rd
Houston TX 77051
713 799-5272

(G-14960)
VETERANS REPRESENTATIVE CO LLC
1584 Tamarisk Trl (44514-3632)
PHONE...................................330 779-0768
EMP: 10 EST: 2006
SQ FT: 800
SALES (est): 198.35K Privately Held
Web: www.veteranrepco.com
SIC: 2522 Chairs, office: padded or plain:
except wood

(G-14961)
VICTOR ORGAN COMPANY
5340 Mahoning Ave (44515-2415)
PHONE...................................330 792-1321
Victor Marsilo, *Owner*
EMP: 8 EST: 1987
SQ FT: 6,500
SALES (est): 496.81K Privately Held
SIC: 3931 7699 Organs, all types: pipe,
reed, hand, electronic, etc.; Organ tuning
and repair

(G-14962)
VINDICATOR PRINTING COMPANY
Also Called: Wfmj-Tv21
101 W Boardman St (44503-1305)
P.O. Box 689 (44501-0689)
PHONE...................................330 744-8611
John Grdic, *Mgr*
EMP: 36
SALES (corp-wide): 5.16MM Privately
Held
Web: www.vindy.com
SIC: 2711 Newspapers, publishing and
printing
PA: The Vindicator Printing Company
107 Vindicator Sq
Youngstown OH 44503
330 747-1471

(G-14963)
VINYL TOOL & DIE COMPANY
1144 Meadowbrook Ave (44512-1821)
PHONE...................................330 782-0254
Paul Chicone, *Pr*
Carmen Chicone Senior, *VP*
Carmen Chicone Junior, *Sec*
EMP: 6 EST: 1988
SALES (est): 355.04K Privately Held
Web: www.vinyltoolanddie.com
SIC: 3544 Extrusion dies

(G-14964)
VINYLUME PRODUCTS INC
3745 Hendricks Rd (44515-1500)
PHONE...................................330 799-2000
Jack M White, *CEO*
Orlando White, *
Helen White, *
EMP: 13 EST: 1964
SQ FT: 200,000
SALES (est): 2.43MM Privately Held
Web: www.vinylumewindows.com
SIC: 3089 3442 3211 Window frames and
sash, plastics; Metal doors, sash, and trim;
Flat glass

(G-14965)
W B BECHERER INC
Also Called: Modernfold
7905 Southern Blvd (44512-6025)
P.O. Box 3186 (44513-3186)
PHONE...................................330 758-6616
William B Becherer Senior, *Pr*
William B Becherer Junior, *Treas*
Bruce Becherer, *Sec*
EMP: 9 EST: 1950
SQ FT: 4,000
SALES (est): 1.13MM Privately Held
Web: www.rmcks.org
SIC: 2542 Partitions and fixtures, except
wood

(G-14966)
WARRIOR IMPORTS INC
Also Called: Hardcore Offroad Tires
112 S Meridian Rd (44509-2640)
PHONE...................................954 935-5536
Ray Starr, *Pr*
Corey Burt, *Prin*
▲ EMP: 20 EST: 2001
SQ FT: 100,000
SALES (est): 1.42MM Privately Held
Web: www.warriorimport.com
SIC: 3262 Vitreous china table and
kitchenware

(G-14967)
YOUNGSTOWN BOLT & SUPPLY CO
340 N Meridian Rd (44509-1246)
PHONE..............................330 799-3201
Al Fedorisin, *Pr*
Lorraine Fedorisin, *VP*
EMP: 6 **EST:** 1981
SQ FT: 20,000
SALES (est): 437.99K **Privately Held**
Web: www.youngstownbolt.com
SIC: 5085 3965 Fasteners, industrial: nuts, bolts, screws, etc.; Fasteners

(G-14968)
YOUNGSTOWN CURVE FORM INC
1102 Rigby St (44506-1500)
PHONE..............................330 744-3028
Frank Laskay, *Pr*
EMP: 10 **EST:** 1964
SQ FT: 7,800
SALES (est): 303.93K **Privately Held**
SIC: 5031 2541 Building materials, interior; Table or counter tops, plastic laminated

(G-14969)
YOUNGSTOWN FENCE INCORPORATED
235 E Indianola Ave (44507-1546)
PHONE..............................330 788-8110
Frank J Mikitaw, *Pr*
Suzanne Mikitaw, *VP*
EMP: 6 **EST:** 1943
SQ FT: 34,000
SALES (est): 745.67K **Privately Held**
Web: www.youngstownfence.com
SIC: 1799 5211 2499 Fence construction; Fencing; Fencing, wood

(G-14970)
YOUNGSTOWN HARD CHROME PLTG GR
8451 Southern Blvd (44512-6709)
P.O. Box 3508 (44513-3508)
PHONE..............................330 758-9721
Richard S Mccarthy, *Pr*
Daniel J Mccarthy, *VP*
EMP: 28 **EST:** 1962
SQ FT: 35,000
SALES (est): 2.49MM **Privately Held**
Web: www.youngstownhardchrome.com
SIC: 3471 3599 Chromium plating of metals or formed products; Grinding castings for the trade

(G-14971)
YOUNGSTOWN HEAT TRTING NTRDING
1118 Meadowbrook Ave (44512-1821)
PHONE..............................330 788-3025
Carmen P Chicone Senior, *Pr*
EMP: 6 **EST:** 1973
SQ FT: 5,000
SALES (est): 171.29K **Privately Held**
SIC: 3398 Annealing of metal

(G-14972)
YOUNGSTOWN LETTER SHOP INC
3650 Connecticut Ave (44515-3000)
PHONE..............................330 793-4935
Jean Tuscano, *Pr*
EMP: 9 **EST:** 1920
SALES (est): 2.43MM **Privately Held**
Web: www.ylssites.com
SIC: 7331 2752 7521 Mailing service; Offset printing; Parking garage

(G-14973)
YOUNGSTOWN PLASTIC TOOLING (PA)
1209 Velma Ct (44512-1829)

PHONE..............................330 782-7222
Donald J Liga, *Pr*
Janet Liga, *
EMP: 15 **EST:** 1984
SQ FT: 20,000
SALES (est): 2.37MM
SALES (corp-wide): 2.37MM **Privately Held**
Web: www.yptm.com
SIC: 3559 8711 Plastics working machinery; Machine tool design

(G-14974)
YOUNGSTOWN PRE-PRESS INC
3691 Leharps Dr (44515-1437)
P.O. Box 2375 (44509)
PHONE..............................330 793-3690
Kenneth Slater, *Pr*
Gary P Dobrindt, *VP*
Brian Dickens, *Sec*
EMP: 6 **EST:** 1995
SQ FT: 4,000
SALES (est): 477.65K **Privately Held**
SIC: 7336 2752 Graphic arts and related design; Lithographing on metal

(G-14975)
YOUNGSTOWN SHADE & ALUM LLC
Also Called: Richards Intrors Bldg Cmpnents
3335 South Ave (44502-2407)
P.O. Box 8627 (44484-0627)
PHONE..............................330 782-2373
Richard Gula, *Owner*
EMP: 8 **EST:** 1947
SQ FT: 15,000
SALES (est): 654.47K **Privately Held**
SIC: 1542 2591 3444 3442 Commercial and office buildings, renovation and repair; Venetian blinds; Awnings, sheet metal; Metal doors, sash, and trim

(G-14976)
YOUNGSTOWN SPECIALTY MTLS INC
571 Andrews Ave (44505-3064)
PHONE..............................330 259-1110
Frank Wadlinger, *CEO*
Michael Miklus, *VP*
Richard Wadlinger, *CFO*
EMP: 8 **EST:** 2001
SQ FT: 20,000
SALES (est): 2MM **Privately Held**
Web: www.yngspecmetals.com
SIC: 3053 5051 Gaskets, packing and sealing devices; Steel

(G-14977)
YOUNGSTOWN TOOL & DIE COMPANY
2572 Salt Springs Rd (44509-1030)
PHONE..............................330 747-4464
Fred Fisher, *Pr*
EMP: 62 **EST:** 1961
SALES (est): 3.76MM **Privately Held**
Web: www.youngstowntool.com
SIC: 3544 3354 Special dies and tools; Aluminum extruded products

(G-14978)
YOUNGSTOWN TUBE CO
401 Andrews Ave (44505-3062)
PHONE..............................330 743-7414
William Veri, *Pr*
EMP: 30 **EST:** 1991
SQ FT: 93,000
SALES (est): 4.36MM **Privately Held**
Web: www.youngstowntube.com
SIC: 3312 Pipes, iron and steel

Zaleski
Vinton County

(G-14979)
LMP MACHINE LLC
115 E Chestnut St (45698)
P.O. Box 255 (45698-0255)
PHONE..............................740 596-4559
EMP: 9 **EST:** 1968
SQ FT: 4,800
SALES (est): 994.26K **Privately Held**
Web: www.sledgehammerpulling.com
SIC: 3599 Machine shop, jobbing and repair

Zanesville
Muskingum County

(G-14980)
5 BS INC (PA)
Also Called: B-Wear Sportswear
1000 5 Bs Dr (43701-7630)
P.O. Box 520 (43702-0520)
PHONE..............................740 454-8453
Todd Biles, *Pr*
Paula Moore, *
John Klies, *
Chris Nash, *
Leland Biles, *
▲ **EMP:** 250 **EST:** 1969
SQ FT: 170,000
SALES (est): 2.21MM
SALES (corp-wide): 2.21MM **Privately Held**
Web: www.5bs.com
SIC: 2339 2395 Athletic clothing: women's, misses', and juniors'; Embroidery products, except Schiffli machine

(G-14981)
ACE TRUCK EQUIPMENT CO
1130 Newark Rd (43701-2619)
P.O. Box 2605 (43702-2605)
PHONE..............................740 453-0551
David Beitzel, *Pr*
Robert D Beitzel, *CEO*
Dora Beitzel, *Sec*
EMP: 21 **EST:** 1955
SQ FT: 30,500
SALES (est): 2.78MM **Privately Held**
Web: www.acetruck.net
SIC: 3531 5012 3713 Truck equipment and parts; Truck bodies; Truck and bus bodies

(G-14982)
ADAMS BROS CONCRETE PDTS LTD
3401 East Pike (43701-8419)
PHONE..............................740 452-7566
Scott M Zemba, *Admn*
EMP: 20 **EST:** 2009
SALES (est): 2.95MM **Privately Held**
Web: www.adamsbrosconcrete.com
SIC: 3273 Ready-mixed concrete

(G-14983)
ADAMS BROTHERS INC
1501 Woodlawn Ave (43701-5955)
P.O. Box 27 (43702-0027)
PHONE..............................740 819-0323
William Adams Iv, *Pr*
Nancy Adams, *VP*
Katie Brown, *Treas*
EMP: 7 **EST:** 1908
SALES (est): 1.2MM **Privately Held**
Web: www.adamsbrosconcrete.com
SIC: 3273 5211 Ready-mixed concrete; Lumber and other building materials

(G-14984)
AJ ENTERPRISE LLC
1915 Hoge Ave (43701-2125)
PHONE..............................740 231-2205
Cory Mcgilton, *Prin*
EMP: 15 **EST:** 2019
SALES (est): 4.91MM **Privately Held**
Web: www.ajenterprise.net
SIC: 1389 Oil and gas field services, nec

(G-14985)
ALFRED NICKLES BAKERY INC
Also Called: Nickles Bakery 45
1147 Newark Rd (43701-2618)
PHONE..............................740 453-6522
Les Bell, *Genl Mgr*
EMP: 45
SALES (corp-wide): 112.69MM **Privately Held**
Web: www.nicklesbakery.com
SIC: 2051 5461 Bakery: wholesale or wholesale/retail combined; Retail bakeries
PA: Alfred Nickles Bakery, Inc.
26 Main St N
Navarre OH 44662
330 879-5635

(G-14986)
ALLIED MACHINE WORKS INC
120 Graham St (43701-3100)
PHONE..............................740 454-2534
Richard J Straker, *Pr*
Patricia Folden, *Prin*
EMP: 8 **EST:** 1964
SQ FT: 56,058
SALES (est): 772.37K **Privately Held**
SIC: 3599 7629 3533 Machine shop, jobbing and repair; Electrical repair shops; Oil and gas field machinery

(G-14987)
ANCHOR GLASS CONTAINER CORP
Zanesville Mould Division
1206 Brandywine Blvd Ste C (43701-1731)
PHONE..............................740 452-2743
Steve Brock, *Brnch Mgr*
EMP: 71
Web: www.anchorglass.com
SIC: 3321 3221 3544 Gray iron ingot molds, cast; Glass containers; Special dies, tools, jigs, and fixtures
PA: Anchor Glass Container Corporation
3001 N Rcky Pt Dr E Ste 3
Tampa FL 33607

(G-14988)
AXION INTERNATIONAL HOLDINGS INC
4005 All American Way (43701-7251)
PHONE..............................740 452-2500
EMP: 120
Web: www.axionsi.com
SIC: 3089 Prefabricated plastics buildings

(G-14989)
AXION INTERNATIONAL INC
4005 All American Way (43701-7306)
PHONE..............................740 452-2500
EMP: 6
Web: www.axionsi.com
SIC: 5084 3089 Recycling machinery and equipment; Plastics hardware and building products

(G-14990)
AXION STRL INNOVATIONS LLC (PA)
1100 Brandywine Blvd Ste H (43701-7303)
P.O. Box 3508 (43702)
PHONE..............................740 452-2500
Allen Kronstadt, *Managing Member*

Claude Brown, *Managing Member*
Matt Elli, *Managing Member*
Dave Crane, *Managing Member*
EMP: 17 **EST:** 2015
SALES (est): 1.64MM
SALES (corp-wide): 1.64MM **Privately Held**
Web: www.axionsi.com
SIC: 3089 Extruded finished plastics products, nec

(G-14991)
BALLAS EGG PRODUCTS CORP
40 N 2nd St (43701-3402)
P.O. Box 2217 (43702-2217)
PHONE..............................614 453-0386
Leonard Ballas, *Pr*
Joseph G Saliba, *VP*
Craig Ballas, *
▼ **EMP:** 100 **EST:** 1961
SQ FT: 200,000
SALES (est): 4.69MM **Privately Held**
Web: www.wabashvalleyeggs.com
SIC: 2015 5144 Egg processing; Eggs

(G-14992)
BARNES ADVERTISING CORPORATION
1580 Fairview Rd (43701-0934)
P.O. Box 277 (43702-0277)
PHONE..............................740 453-6836
TOLL FREE: 800
Maryjane Shackelford, *Pr*
John Barnes, *VP*
EMP: 18 **EST:** 1916
SALES (est): 915.57K **Privately Held**
Web: www.barnesadvertisingcorp.com
SIC: 7312 3993 Billboard advertising; Signs and advertising specialties

(G-14993)
BATTERY UNLIMITED
1080 Linden Ave (43701-2952)
PHONE..............................740 452-5030
Kent Curry, *Owner*
EMP: 6 **EST:** 1985
SALES (est): 232.02K **Privately Held**
Web: www.batteriesunlimitedohio.com
SIC: 5063 5531 5999 7699 Batteries; Batteries, automotive and truck; Batteries, non-automotive; Battery service and repair

(G-14994)
BE PRODUCTS INC
Also Called: Ballas Egg Products
40 N 2nd St (43701-3402)
P.O. Box 2217 (43702-2217)
PHONE..............................740 453-0386
Criag Ballas, *Pr*
Craig Ballas, *Pr*
Leonard Ballas, *VP*
EMP: 9 **EST:** 1928
SQ FT: 125,000
SALES (est): 755.81K **Privately Held**
Web: www.wabashvalleyeggs.com
SIC: 2015 Egg processing

(G-14995)
BILCO COMPANY
3400 Jim Granger Dr (43701-7231)
PHONE..............................740 455-9020
Charles Chirdon, *Pr*
EMP: 50
Web: www.bilco.com
SIC: 3442 3272 Metal doors; Areaways, basement window: concrete
HQ: The Bilco Company
37 Water St
West Haven CT 06516
203 934-6363

(G-14996)
BIMBO QSR US LLC
750 Airport Rd (43701-9694)
P.O. Box 256 (43017-0256)
PHONE..............................740 562-4188
David Marion, *Brnch Mgr*
EMP: 8
Web: www.bimboqsr.com
SIC: 2051 Bakery: wholesale or wholesale/retail combined
HQ: Bimbo Qsr Us, Llc
1801 W 31st Pl
Chicago IL 60608
773 376-4444

(G-14997)
BISHOP MACHINE TOOL & DIE
Also Called: Bishop Machine Shop
2304 Hoge Ave (43701-2166)
PHONE..............................740 453-8818
Robert L Bishop, *Pt*
John R Bishop, *Pt*
Alva Bishop Junior, *Mgr*
EMP: 10 **EST:** 1964
SQ FT: 2,000
SALES (est): 415.9K **Privately Held**
Web: www.sprintermarking.com
SIC: 3599 3953 Machine shop, jobbing and repair; Marking devices

(G-14998)
BLOOMER CANDY CO
3610 National Rd (43701-8812)
P.O. Box 3450 (43702-3450)
PHONE..............................740 452-7501
William S Barry, *Pr*
Teresa Young-barry, *Sec*
Tom Barry, *
Pat Barry, *
Robert Barry, *
EMP: 130 **EST:** 1893
SQ FT: 150,000
SALES (est): 2.26MM **Privately Held**
Web: www.bloomercandy.com
SIC: 5145 2064 Confectionery; Candy and other confectionery products

(G-14999)
BOB SUMEREL TIRE CO INC
1140 Newark Rd (43701-2619)
PHONE..............................740 454-9728
Steve Dickerson, *Brnch Mgr*
EMP: 7
SALES (corp-wide): 35.8MM **Privately Held**
Web: www.bobsumereltire.com
SIC: 7534 5531 Tire retreading and repair shops; Automotive tires
PA: Bob Sumerel Tire Co., Inc.
1257 Cox Ave
Erlanger KY 41018
859 283-2700

(G-15000)
BUCKEYE COMPANIES (PA)
999 Zane St (43701-3863)
P.O. Box 1480 (43702-1480)
PHONE..............................740 452-3641
C E Straker, *Pr*
M Dean Cole, *
Stephen R Straker, *
EMP: 31 **EST:** 1982
SALES (est): 3.98MM
SALES (corp-wide): 3.98MM **Privately Held**
Web: www.thebuckeyecompanies.com
SIC: 3533 5083 Drill rigs; Agricultural machinery and equipment

(G-15001)
BUCKEYE ENERGY RESOURCES INC
Also Called: Seth Enterprises
999 Zane St (43701-3863)
PHONE..............................740 452-9506
C E Staker, *Ch*
Stephen Straker, *Pr*
M Dean Cole, *Sec*
Charles E Straker, *CEO*
EMP: 6 **EST:** 1981
SALES (est): 708.81K
SALES (corp-wide): 3.98MM **Privately Held**
Web: www.sethenterprises.com
SIC: 4213 1311 Trucking, except local; Crude petroleum and natural gas
PA: Buckeye Companies
999 Zane St
Zanesville OH 43701
740 452-3641

(G-15002)
BUCKINGHAM COAL COMPANY LLC
11 N 4th St (43701-3409)
P.O. Box 340 (43702-0340)
EMP: 80 **EST:** 1994
SALES (est): 1.75MM
SALES (corp-wide): 449.53MM **Privately Held**
SIC: 1221 Bituminous coal and lignite-surface mining
HQ: Wcc Land Holding Company, Inc.
9540 Maroon Cir Unit 300
Englewood CO 80112
855 922-6463

(G-15003)
CAMERON DRILLING CO INC
3636 Adamsville Rd (43701-6954)
PHONE..............................740 453-3300
James H Cameron, *Pr*
Richard M Cameron, *VP*
EMP: 7 **EST:** 1966
SQ FT: 3,000
SALES (est): 693.96K **Privately Held**
SIC: 1311 Crude petroleum production

(G-15004)
CARL RITTBERGER SR INC
1900 Lutz Ln (43701-9260)
PHONE..............................740 452-2767
TOLL FREE: 800
Andrew Rittberger, *Pr*
Pauline Butler, *
EMP: 27 **EST:** 1910
SQ FT: 100,000
SALES (est): 5.9MM **Privately Held**
Web: www.rittbergers.com
SIC: 2013 2011 Sausages and other prepared meats; Meat packing plants

(G-15005)
CASTING SOLUTIONS LLC
2345 Licking Rd (43701-2728)
P.O. Box 3148 (43702-3148)
PHONE..............................740 452-9371
Jeremiah Clegg, *Pr*
EMP: 106 **EST:** 2001
SALES (est): 9.84MM
SALES (corp-wide): 240.55MM **Publicly Held**
Web: www.castingsolutions.com
SIC: 3321 Gray iron castings, nec
PA: Burnham Holdings, Inc.
1241 Harrisburg Pike
Lancaster PA 17604
717 390-7800

(G-15006)
CENTRAL COCA-COLA BTLG CO INC
Also Called: Coca-Cola
154 S 7th St (43701-4332)
PHONE..............................740 452-3608
Dave Llewellen, *Mgr*
EMP: 33
SALES (corp-wide): 45.75B **Publicly Held**
Web: www.coca-cola.com
SIC: 2086 Bottled and canned soft drinks
HQ: Central Coca-Cola Bottling Company, Inc.
555 Taxter Rd Ste 550
Elmsford NY 10523
914 789-1100

(G-15007)
CENTRAL OHIO BANDAG LP
Also Called: Bandag
1600 S Point Dr (43701-7366)
PHONE..............................740 454-9728
Steven Dickerson, *Pt*
Wayne Anderson, *
Bob Sumerel, *
EMP: 11 **EST:** 1971
SQ FT: 19,000
SALES (est): 1.01MM **Privately Held**
Web: www.bobsumereltire.com
SIC: 7534 5014 Tire recapping; Truck tires and tubes

(G-15008)
CONNS POTATO CHIP CO INC (PA)
1805 Kemper Ct (43701-4634)
PHONE..............................740 452-4615
Monte Hunter, *Pr*
Thomas George Senior, *VP*
EMP: 30 **EST:** 1952
SQ FT: 100,000
SALES (est): 9.37MM
SALES (corp-wide): 9.37MM **Privately Held**
Web: www.connschips.com
SIC: 2096 5963 Potato chips and other potato-based snacks; Snacks, direct sales

(G-15009)
CREATIVE PACKAGING LLC
1781 Kemper Ct (43701-4606)
P.O. Box 305 (43702-0305)
PHONE..............................740 452-8497
Keith Imhoff, *Managing Member*
EMP: 48 **EST:** 1978
SQ FT: 125,000
SALES (est): 1.9MM **Privately Held**
Web: www.creativepkg.com
SIC: 2653 2671 Boxes, corrugated: made from purchased materials; Paper; coated and laminated packaging

(G-15010)
DMV CORPORATION
1024 Military Rd (43701-1343)
P.O. Box 878 (43702-0878)
PHONE..............................740 452-4787
Allan Patterson, *Pr*
EMP: 9 **EST:** 1968
SQ FT: 1,500
SALES (est): 2.13MM **Privately Held**
Web: www.dmvcorp.com
SIC: 3851 Ophthalmic goods

(G-15011)
DOW CAMERON OIL & GAS LLC
5555 Eden Park Dr (43701-7052)
PHONE..............................740 452-1568
EMP: 8 **EST:** 2003
SALES (est): 1.33MM **Privately Held**
Web: www.dowcameronoilgas.com
SIC: 1389 Oil and gas wells: building, repairing and dismantling

(G-15012)
ECLIPSE RESOURCES - OHIO LLC
4900 Boggs Rd (43701-9491)
P.O. Box 910 (43702-0910)
PHONE..............................740 452-4503
Benjamin W Hulburt, *Managing Member*
Christopher K Hulburt, *
Thomas S Liberatore, *
Brian Panetta, *
Bryan M Moody, *
EMP: 119 **EST:** 2013
SALES (est): 1.97MM **Publicly Held**
SIC: 1381 Drilling oil and gas wells
HQ: Eclipse Resources I, Lp
122 W John Crptr Fwy Ste
Irving TX 75039
814 308-9754

(G-15013)
FINELINE IMPRINTS INC
516 State St (43701-3237)
P.O. Box 2688 (43702-2688)
PHONE..............................740 453-1083
TOLL FREE: 800
Robert Kessler, *Pr*
EMP: 9 **EST:** 1982
SQ FT: 12,000
SALES (est): 231.42K **Privately Held**
Web: www.finelineimprints.com
SIC: 5999 2396 3993 2395 Trophies and
plaques; Screen printing on fabric articles;
Signs and advertising specialties; Pleating
and stitching

(G-15014)
FLOW-LINER SYSTEMS LTD
4830 Northpointe Dr (43701-7273)
PHONE..............................800 348-0020
Jeff Tanner, *CEO*
▲ **EMP:** 25 **EST:** 2000
SQ FT: 30,000
SALES (est): 4.86MM **Privately Held**
Web: www.flow-liner.com
SIC: 1799 3443 Protective lining installation,
underground (sewage, etc.); Liners/lining

(G-15015)
FORMATION CEMENTING INC
1800 Timber Port Dr (43701)
P.O. Box 2667 (43702-2667)
PHONE..............................740 453-6926
Brian G Jasper, *Pr*
Rae Anne Jasper, *Sec*
EMP: 7 **EST:** 1979
SQ FT: 500
SALES (est): 818.53K **Privately Held**
SIC: 1389 Oil and gas wells: building,
repairing and dismantling

(G-15016)
FRANKLIN PRINTING COMPANY
Also Called: Franklin's Printing
984 Beverly Ave (43701-1413)
PHONE..............................740 452-6375
Everett Jackson Junior, *Pr*
Alice Lucille Jackson, *Sec*
EMP: 10 **EST:** 1949
SQ FT: 7,000
SALES (est): 466.89K **Privately Held**
Web: www.franklinprinting.us
SIC: 2752 7331 2791 2789 Offset printing;
Addressing service; Typesetting;
Bookbinding and related work

(G-15017)
G & J PEPSI-COLA BOTTLERS INC
Also Called: Pepsico
336 N Sixth St (43701)
PHONE..............................740 354-9191
TOLL FREE: 800
Rick Stone, *Brnch Mgr*

EMP: 41
SALES (corp-wide): 404.54MM **Privately
Held**
Web: www.gjpepsi.com
SIC: 2086 5149 Carbonated soft drinks,
bottled and canned; Groceries and related
products, nec
PA: G & J Pepsi-Cola Bottlers Inc
9435 Wtrstone Blvd Ste 39
Cincinnati OH 45249
513 785-6060

(G-15018)
HALLIBURTON ENERGY SVCS INC
4999 E Pointe Dr (43701-7680)
PHONE..............................740 617-2917
EMP: 13
Web: www.halliburton.com
SIC: 1389 Oil field services, nec
HQ: Halliburton Energy Services, Inc.
3000 N Sam Houston Pkwy E
Houston TX 77032
281 871-4000

(G-15019)
HANNON COMPANY
Electric Motor & Service Co
218 Adams St (43701-4902)
P.O. Box 667 (43702-0667)
PHONE..............................740 453-0527
Michael Arrasmith, *Brnch Mgr*
EMP: 15
SALES (corp-wide): 23.88MM **Privately
Held**
Web: www.hannonelectric.com
SIC: 7694 7699 5063 Electric motor repair;
Welding equipment repair; Motors, electric
PA: The Hannon Company
1605 Waynesburg Rd Se
Canton OH 44707
330 456-4728

(G-15020)
HYDRO SUPPLY CO
3112 East Pike (43701-8975)
PHONE..............................740 454-3842
Charles William Kimble, *Pr*
Judy K Kimble, *Sec*
EMP: 9 **EST:** 1983
SQ FT: 6,500
SALES (est): 1.6MM **Privately Held**
SIC: 5084 7699 3599 Hydraulic systems
equipment and supplies; Industrial
machinery and equipment repair; Machine
shop, jobbing and repair

(G-15021)
IG WATTEEUW USA LLC
1000 Linden Ave (43701-3098)
PHONE..............................740 588-1722
▲ **EMP:** 11 **EST:** 2013
SQ FT: 51,946
SALES (est): 8.74MM
SALES (corp-wide): 833.11K **Privately
Held**
Web: www.igwpower.com
SIC: 3714 5085 Gears, motor vehicle; Gears
HQ: Ig Watteeuw International
Kampveldstraat 51
Oostkamp VWV 8020
50826907

(G-15022)
IGW USA
1000 Linden Ave (43701-3098)
PHONE..............................740 588-1722
EMP: 7 **EST:** 2019
SALES (est): 2.91MM **Privately Held**
Web: www.igwpower.com
SIC: 3714 Motor vehicle parts and
accessories

(G-15023)
J A B WELDING SERVICE INC
Also Called: Bakers Welding
2820 S River Rd (43701-7184)
PHONE..............................740 453-5868
Jeffrey A Baker, *Pr*
Cyndy Baker, *VP*
EMP: 28 **EST:** 1984
SQ FT: 20,000
SALES (est): 1.35MM **Privately Held**
Web:
jab-welding-service-inc-in-zanesville-
oh.cityfos.com
SIC: 7692 Welding repair

(G-15024)
KELLANOVA
Also Called: Kellog
1675 Fairview Rd (43701-5168)
PHONE..............................740 453-5501
Gary Pilnick, *Owner*
EMP: 103
SALES (corp-wide): 12.75B **Publicly Held**
Web: www.kellanova.com
SIC: 2043 Cereal breakfast foods
PA: Kellanova
412 N Wells St
Chicago IL 60654
269 961-2000

(G-15025)
KESSLER SIGN COMPANY (PA)
Also Called: Kessler Outdoor Advertising
2669 National Rd (43701-8257)
P.O. Box 785 (43702-0785)
PHONE..............................740 453-0668
TOLL FREE: 800
Robert Kessler, *CEO*
Adam Kessler, *
Rodger Kessler, *
David Kessler, *
Elaine Kessler-kuntz, *Treas*
EMP: 50 **EST:** 1971
SQ FT: 25,000
SALES (est): 5.11MM
SALES (corp-wide): 5.11MM **Privately
Held**
Web: www.kesslersignco.com
SIC: 3993 7312 Signs, not made in custom
sign painting shops; Outdoor advertising
services

(G-15026)
MAR-ZANE INC (IIQ)
Also Called: Mar-Zane Materials
3570 S River Rd (43701-7731)
P.O. Box 1585 (43702-1585)
PHONE..............................740 453-0721
Gerald N Little, *Pr*
Wade Hamm, *VP*
EMP: 12 **EST:** 1963
SQ FT: 5,000
SALES (est): 10.01MM
SALES (corp-wide): 433.35MM **Privately
Held**
Web: www.shellyandsands.com
SIC: 2951 Asphalt paving mixtures and
blocks
PA: Shelly And Sands, Inc.
3570 S River Rd
Zanesville OH 43701
740 453-0721

(G-15027)
MCCLELLAND INC (PA)
Also Called: O K Coal & Concrete
98 E La Salle St (43701-6281)
P.O. Box 1815 (43702-1815)
PHONE..............................740 452-3036
Joe Mc Clelland, *Pr*
Jack Mc Clelland, *

Richard Mc Clelland, *
Gala Lemon, *
EMP: 25 **EST:** 1934
SQ FT: 1,500
SALES (est): 4.33MM
SALES (corp-wide): 4.33MM **Privately
Held**
Web: www.okcoalandconcrete.com
SIC: 3273 7992 1442 Ready-mixed concrete
; Public golf courses; Construction sand
and gravel

(G-15028)
MICHAEL ZAKANY LLC
Also Called: Jose Madrid Salsa
601 Putnam Ave (43701-5504)
P.O. Box 1061 (43702-1061)
PHONE..............................740 221-3934
Michael Zakany, *Pr*
EMP: 8 **EST:** 1989
SQ FT: 300
SALES (est): 1.13MM **Privately Held**
Web: www.josemadridsalsa.com
SIC: 2035 5149 Pickles, sauces, and salad
dressings; Seasonings, sauces, and
extracts
PA: Unique Pizza And Subs Corp
302 W Otterman St
Greensburg PA 15601

(G-15029)
**MOCK WOODWORKING COMPANY
LLC**
4400 West Pike (43701-9208)
PHONE..............................740 452-2701
Douglas F Mock, *Managing Member*
EMP: 44 **EST:** 1954
SQ FT: 46,000
SALES (est): 7.01MM **Privately Held**
Web: www.mockwoodworking.com
SIC: 2434 2541 2531 Wood kitchen cabinets
; Office fixtures, wood; Public building and
related furniture

(G-15030)
MUSKINGUM TIRE COMPANY INC
758 Putnam Ave (43701-5544)
PHONE..............................740 453-8473
Mark Todd, *Pr*
Holly Todd, *VP*
EMP: 6 **EST:** 1984
SQ FT: 2,000
SALES (est): 153.97K **Privately Held**
Web: www.muskingumcofair.com
SIC: 5531 7534 Automotive tires; Tire repair
shop

(G-15031)
NEFF MACHINERY AND SUPPLIES
Also Called: Neff Parts
112 S Shawnee Ave (43701-6221)
P.O. Box 1822 (43702-1822)
PHONE..............................740 454-0128
Robert Neff, *Pr*
EMP: 6 **EST:** 1988
SQ FT: 20,000
SALES (est): 1.2MM **Privately Held**
Web: www.neffsince1931.com
SIC: 3599 5084 5013 Machine and other job
shop work; Machine tools and accessories;
Motor vehicle supplies and new parts

(G-15032)
**NESTLE PURINA PETCARE
COMPANY**
5 N 2nd St (43701-3402)
P.O. Box 38 (43702-0038)
PHONE..............................740 454-8575
Dante Benincasa, *Mgr*
EMP: 137
Web: www.purina.com

SIC: 2047 Dog and cat food
HQ: Nestle Purina Petcare Company
　800 Chouteau Ave
　Saint Louis MO 63102
　314 982-1000

(G-15033)
NEW BLOOMER CANDY COMPANY LLC
1445 Deercreek Dr (43701-7233)
PHONE......................740 452-7501
Mike Montgomery, *
Tom Barry, *
EMP: 40 **EST:** 2009
SALES (est): 3.41MM **Privately Held**
Web: 3304-us.all.biz
SIC: 2064 Chocolate candy, except solid chocolate

(G-15034)
NEW WAYNE INC
Also Called: Wayne Manufacturing
1555 Ritchey Pkwy (43701-7050)
PHONE......................740 453-3454
Michael Higgins, *Pr*
Kurt Paul, *VP*
Mike Paul, *CFO*
EMP: 8 **EST:** 1953
SQ FT: 40,000
SALES (est): 1.02MM **Privately Held**
Web: www.waynemanufacturing.net
SIC: 3441 3443 Fabricated structural metal; Fabricated plate work (boiler shop)

(G-15035)
OMCO USA LLC
1000 Linden Ave (43701-3098)
PHONE......................740 588-1722
Teresa Reef, *Prin*
▲ **EMP:** 18 **EST:** 2005
SALES (est): 4.36MM **Privately Held**
Web: www.omcomould.com
SIC: 3559 Ammunition and explosives, loading machinery

(G-15036)
OWENS-BROCKWAY GLASS CONT INC
OWENS-BROCKWAY GLASS CONTAINER, INC.
1700 State St (43701-3116)
PHONE......................740 455-4516
John Elliot, *Brnch Mgr*
EMP: 41
SALES (corp-wide): 6.53B **Publicly Held**
Web: www.o-i.com
SIC: 3221 Glass containers
HQ: Owens-Brockway Glass Container Inc.
　One Michael Owens Way
　Perrysburg OH 43551

(G-15037)
OXFORD MINING COMPANY INC
1855 Kemper Ct (43701-4634)
PHONE......................740 588-0190
Joe Douglas, *Brnch Mgr*
EMP: 124
SALES (corp-wide): 449.53MM **Privately Held**
SIC: 1221 Bituminous coal and lignite-surface mining
HQ: Oxford Mining Company, Inc.
　544 Chestnut St
　Coshocton OH 43812
　740 622-6302

(G-15038)
PATRIOT STAINLESS WELDING
1555 Fairview Rd (43701-8889)
PHONE......................740 297-6040

EMP: 6 **EST:** 2020
SALES (est): 2.34MM **Privately Held**
Web: www.gopatriot.us
SIC: 7692 Welding repair

(G-15039)
PHILLIPS MEAT PROCESSING LLC
2790 Ridge Rd (43701-7873)
PHONE......................740 453-3337
Dale Phillips, *Owner*
EMP: 10 **EST:** 1999
SALES (est): 944.28K **Privately Held**
Web: www.phillipsmeats.com
SIC: 2011 Meat packing plants

(G-15040)
PLASKOLITE LLC
1175 5 Bs Dr (43701-7376)
PHONE......................740 450-1109
Mark Gringley, *Brnch Mgr*
EMP: 228
SALES (corp-wide): 542.25MM **Privately Held**
Web: www.plaskolite.com
SIC: 2821 3083 Acrylic resins; Laminated plastics sheets
PA: Plaskolite, Llc
　400 W Ntnwide Blvd Ste 40
　Columbus OH 43215
　614 294-3281

(G-15041)
PORTERS WELDING INC (PA)
601 Linden Ave (43701-3397)
PHONE......................740 452-4181
Virginia Porter, *Pr*
Daryl Porter, *VP*
Kimberly Browning, *Sec*
EMP: 9 **EST:** 1944
SQ FT: 70,000
SALES (est): 2.8MM
SALES (corp-wide): 2.8MM **Privately Held**
SIC: 3441 Fabricated structural metal

(G-15042)
PRECISION FABG & STAMPING INC
1755 Kemper Ct (43701-4606)
P.O. Box 2065 (43702-2065)
PHONE......................740 453-7310
Charlie Sode, *Pr*
Christine Sode, *Sec*
EMP: 9 **EST:** 1984
SQ FT: 10,000
SALES (est): 989.88K **Privately Held**
Web: www.precisionfabricating.com
SIC: 3441 Fabricated structural metal

(G-15043)
PRECISION WLDG INSTLLATION LLC
Also Called: Precision Wldg & Installation
3445 Church Hill Rd (43701-8479)
PHONE......................740 995-0613
Steven Crumbaker Junior, *Owner*
EMP: 18 **EST:** 2012
SALES (est): 943.04K **Privately Held**
Web: www.pwiohio.com
SIC: 1541 3441 1542 Steel building construction; Fabricated structural metal; Commercial and office buildings, prefabricated erection

(G-15044)
PRODUCERS SERVICE CORPORATION
109 Graham St (43701-3103)
P.O. Box 2277 (43702-2277)
PHONE......................740 454-6253
EMP: 98 **EST:** 1981
SALES (est): 9.21MM **Privately Held**

SIC: 1389 Hydraulic fracturing wells
PA: Psc Holdings, Inc.
　109 Graham St
　Zanesville OH 43701

(G-15045)
PSC HOLDINGS INC (PA)
109 Graham St (43701-3103)
P.O. Box 2277 (43702-2277)
PHONE......................740 454-6253
Dan Pottmeyer, *Prin*
Kelly Hartman, *Prin*
Jim Rose, *Prin*
Debbie Armstrong, *Sec*
EMP: 6 **EST:** 2008
SALES (est): 12.17MM **Privately Held**
SIC: 1389 Hydraulic fracturing wells

(G-15046)
S & S AGGREGATES INC (HQ)
3570 S River Rd (43701-7731)
P.O. Box 1585 (43702-1585)
PHONE......................740 453-0721
Gerald Little, *Pr*
Wade Hamm, *Ex VP*
EMP: 13 **EST:** 1923
SQ FT: 15,000
SALES (est): 4.2MM
SALES (corp-wide): 433.35MM **Privately Held**
Web: www.shellyandsands.com
SIC: 1442 3272 3271 Sand mining; Concrete products, nec; Concrete block and brick
PA: Shelly And Sands, Inc.
　3570 S River Rd
　Zanesville OH 43701
　740 453-0721

(G-15047)
SHELLY AND SANDS INC (PA)
3570 S River Rd (43701-9052)
P.O. Box 1585 (43702-1585)
PHONE......................740 453-0721
Richard H Mcclelland, *Pr*
Larry E Young, *VP*
Gerald N Little, *Pr*
EMP: 12 **EST:** 1942
SQ FT: 5,000
SALES (est): 433.35MM
SALES (corp-wide): 433.35MM **Privately Held**
Web: www.shellyandsands.com
SIC: 5541 1442 2951 Filling stations, gasoline; Construction sand mining; Asphalt and asphaltic paving mixtures (not from refineries)

(G-15048)
SHIRLEY KS LLC
1150 Newark Rd (43701-2619)
PHONE......................740 331-7934
Robert Zachrich, *CEO*
Renee Coll, *Pr*
EMP: 6 **EST:** 2020
SALES (est): 2.19MM **Privately Held**
Web: www.shirleyks.com
SIC: 3089 Plastics products, nec

(G-15049)
SHIRLEY KS STORAGE TRAYS LLC
1150 Newark Rd (43701-2619)
P.O. Box 2519 (43702-2519)
PHONE......................740 868-8140
EMP: 8 **EST:** 2013
SALES (est): 2.76MM **Privately Held**
Web: www.shirleyks.com
SIC: 3089 Plastics containers, except foam

(G-15050)
SIDWELL MATERIALS INC
4200 Maysville Pike (43701-9372)
P.O. Box 192 (43791-0192)
PHONE......................740 849-2422
Jeffrey R Sidwell, *Pr*
EMP: 130 **EST:** 1992
SALES (est): 11.07MM **Privately Held**
Web: www.sidwellmaterials.com
SIC: 1795 4953 2951 1422 Demolition, buildings and other structures; Rubbish collection and disposal; Asphalt paving mixtures and blocks; Crushed and broken limestone

(G-15051)
SPRINTER MARKING INC
1805 Chandlersville Rd (43701-4644)
PHONE......................740 453-1000
Bob Bishop, *Pr*
Al Bishop, *Sec*
John Bishop, *Treas*
EMP: 7 **EST:** 1989
SQ FT: 6,000
SALES (est): 987.13K **Privately Held**
Web: www.sprintermarking.com
SIC: 3953 Date stamps, hand: rubber or metal

(G-15052)
SWINGLE COUNTERTOPS
18 Beaumont St (43701-3134)
PHONE......................740 454-7368
Jodie Swingle, *Pr*
EMP: 10
SALES (est): 294.69K **Privately Held**
Web: www.swinglecountertops.com
SIC: 2541 1799 Table or counter tops, plastic laminated; Counter top installation

(G-15053)
US WATER COMPANY LLC
Also Called: Culligan
1115 Newark Rd (43701-2618)
PHONE......................740 453-0604
Richard Dovenbarger, *Mgr*
EMP: 9
SALES (corp-wide): 4.02MM **Privately Held**
Web: www.culliganwatercolumbus.com
SIC: 5999 7389 2899 5074 Water purification equipment; Water softener service; Water treating compounds; Plumbing and hydronic heating supplies
PA: U.S. Water Company, Llc
　270 W Palatine Rd
　Wheeling IL 60090
　815 526-3375

(G-15054)
WHITE MACHINE & MFG CO (PA)
120 Graham St (43701-3100)
PHONE......................740 453-5451
Kenneth F Vlah, *Pr*
EMP: 18 **EST:** 1955
SQ FT: 20,000
SALES (est): 2.29MM
SALES (corp-wide): 2.29MM **Privately Held**
SIC: 3599 3441 Machine shop, jobbing and repair; Fabricated structural metal

(G-15055)
WORTHINGTON FOODS INC
1675 Fairview Rd (43701-5168)
PHONE......................740 453-5501
Jackie Minarik, *Prin*
▲ **EMP:** 87 **EST:** 1967
SALES (est): 1.42MM
SALES (corp-wide): 12.75B **Publicly Held**

SIC: 2038 Frozen specialties, nec
PA: Kellanova
412 N Wells St
Chicago IL 60654
269 961-2000

(G-15056)
Y CITY RECYCLING LLC
4005 All American Way (43701-7306)
PHONE..............................740 452-2500
Brian Coll, *CEO*
Matt Elli, *
EMP: 6 **EST:** 2012
SALES (est): 2.13MM **Privately Held**
SIC: 3089 Plastics processing

(G-15057)
ZANESVILLE FABRICATORS INC
2981 E Military Rd (43701-1654)
P.O. Box 1816 (43702-1816)
PHONE..............................740 452-2439
Joseph E Nash, *Pr*
EMP: 7 **EST:** 1978
SALES (est): 312.64K **Privately Held**
Web: www.zanesvillefabricators.com
SIC: 2541 Counter and sink tops

(G-15058)
ZANESVILLE PALLET CO INC
2235 Licking Rd (43701-2728)
P.O. Box 2757 (43702-2757)
PHONE..............................740 454-3700
TOLL FREE: 800
Lee Gunnels, *Pr*
Zane Lambert, *VP*
EMP: 10 **EST:** 1993
SALES (est): 935.51K **Privately Held**
Web: www.zanesvillepallet.com
SIC: 2448 Pallets, wood

SIC NO	PRODUCT

A

3291 Abrasive products
8721 Accounting, auditing, and bookkeeping
2891 Adhesives and sealants
7322 Adjustment and collection services
7311 Advertising agencies
7319 Advertising, nec
2879 Agricultural chemicals, nec
3563 Air and gas compressors
4522 Air transportation, nonscheduled
4512 Air transportation, scheduled
3721 Aircraft
3724 Aircraft engines and engine parts
3728 Aircraft parts and equipment, nec
4581 Airports, flying fields, and services
2812 Alkalies and chlorine
3363 Aluminum die-castings
3354 Aluminum extruded products
3365 Aluminum foundries
3355 Aluminum rolling and drawing, nec
3353 Aluminum sheet, plate, and foil
3483 Ammunition, except for small arms, nec
7999 Amusement and recreation, nec
3826 Analytical instruments
2077 Animal and marine fats and oils
0279 Animal specialties, nec
0752 Animal specialty services
1231 Anthracite mining
2389 Apparel and accessories, nec
3446 Architectural metalwork
8712 Architectural services
7694 Armature rewinding shops
3292 Asbestos products
2952 Asphalt felts and coatings
2951 Asphalt paving mixtures and blocks
5531 Auto and home supply stores
7533 Auto exhaust system repair shops
3581 Automatic vending machines
7521 Automobile parking
5012 Automobiles and other motor vehicles
2396 Automotive and apparel trimmings
5599 Automotive dealers, nec
7536 Automotive glass replacement shops
7539 Automotive repair shops, nec
7549 Automotive services, nec
3465 Automotive stampings
7537 Automotive transmission repair shops

B

2673 Bags: plastic, laminated, and coated
2674 Bags: uncoated paper and multiwall
3562 Ball and roller bearings
7241 Barber shops
7231 Beauty shops
0211 Beef cattle feedlots
5181 Beer and ale
2063 Beet sugar
0171 Berry crops
2836 Biological products, except diagnostic
1221 Bituminous coal and lignite-surface mining
1222 Bituminous coal-underground mining
2782 Blankbooks and looseleaf binders
3312 Blast furnaces and steel mills
3564 Blowers and fans
5551 Boat dealers
3732 Boatbuilding and repairing
3452 Bolts, nuts, rivets, and washers
2732 Book printing
2731 Book publishing
5942 Book stores
2789 Bookbinding and related work
5192 Books, periodicals, and newspapers
2086 Bottled and canned soft drinks
7933 Bowling centers
2051 Bread, cake, and related products
3251 Brick and structural clay tile

5032 Brick, stone, and related material
1622 Bridge, tunnel, and elevated highway
2211 Broadwoven fabric mills, cotton
2221 Broadwoven fabric mills, manmade
2231 Broadwoven fabric mills, wool
3991 Brooms and brushes
7349 Building maintenance services, nec
3995 Burial caskets
8611 Business associations
8748 Business consulting, nec
7389 Business services, nec

C

4841 Cable and other pay television services
3578 Calculating and accounting equipment
2064 Candy and other confectionery products
5441 Candy, nut, and confectionery stores
2033 Canned fruits and specialties
2032 Canned specialties
2394 Canvas and related products
3624 Carbon and graphite products
2895 Carbon black
3955 Carbon paper and inked ribbons
3592 Carburetors, pistons, rings, valves
1751 Carpentry work
7217 Carpet and upholstery cleaning
2273 Carpets and rugs
0119 Cash grains, nec
5961 Catalog and mail-order houses
2823 Cellulosic manmade fibers
3241 Cement, hydraulic
6553 Cemetery subdividers and developers
3253 Ceramic wall and floor tile
2043 Cereal breakfast foods
2022 Cheese; natural and processed
1479 Chemical and fertilizer mining
2899 Chemical preparations, nec
5169 Chemicals and allied products, nec
2131 Chewing and smoking tobacco
0252 Chicken eggs
8351 Child day care services
5641 Children's and infants' wear stores
2066 Chocolate and cocoa products
2111 Cigarettes
8641 Civic and social associations
1459 Clay and related minerals, nec
3255 Clay refractories
5052 Coal and other minerals and ores
1241 Coal mining services
2295 Coated fabrics, not rubberized
7993 Coin-operated amusement devices
3316 Cold finishing of steel shapes
7336 Commercial art and graphic design
5046 Commercial equipment, nec
3582 Commercial laundry equipment
3646 Commercial lighting fixtures
8732 Commercial nonphysical research
7335 Commercial photography
8731 Commercial physical research
2754 Commercial printing, gravure
2752 Commercial printing, lithographic
2759 Commercial printing, nec
4899 Communication services, nec
3669 Communications equipment, nec
5734 Computer and software stores
7376 Computer facilities management
7373 Computer integrated systems design
7378 Computer maintenance and repair
3577 Computer peripheral equipment, nec
7379 Computer related services, nec
7377 Computer rental and leasing
3572 Computer storage devices
3575 Computer terminals
5045 Computers, peripherals, and software
3271 Concrete block and brick
3272 Concrete products, nec

1771 Concrete work
5145 Confectionery
5082 Construction and mining machinery
3531 Construction machinery
5039 Construction materials, nec
1442 Construction sand and gravel
2679 Converted paper products, nec
3535 Conveyors and conveying equipment
2052 Cookies and crackers
3366 Copper foundries
3351 Copper rolling and drawing
2298 Cordage and twine
0115 Corn
2653 Corrugated and solid fiber boxes
3961 Costume jewelry
0724 Cotton ginning
2074 Cottonseed oil mills
4215 Courier services, except by air
2021 Creamery butter
0721 Crop planting and protection
0723 Crop preparation services for market
3466 Crowns and closures
1311 Crude petroleum and natural gas
4612 Crude petroleum pipelines
1423 Crushed and broken granite
1422 Crushed and broken limestone
1429 Crushed and broken stone, nec
3643 Current-carrying wiring devices
2391 Curtains and draperies
3087 Custom compound purchased resins
7371 Custom computer programming services
3281 Cut stone and stone products
3421 Cutlery
2865 Cyclic crudes and intermediates

D

0241 Dairy farms
5451 Dairy products stores
5143 Dairy products, except dried or canned
7374 Data processing and preparation
8243 Data processing schools
4424 Deep sea domestic transportation of freight
2034 Dehydrated fruits, vegetables, soups
3843 Dental equipment and supplies
8072 Dental laboratories
5311 Department stores
2835 Diagnostic substances
2675 Die-cut paper and board
1411 Dimension stone
7331 Direct mail advertising services
5963 Direct selling establishments
7342 Disinfecting and pest control services
2085 Distilled and blended liquors
2047 Dog and cat food
3942 Dolls and stuffed toys
5714 Drapery and upholstery stores
2591 Drapery hardware and blinds and shades
1381 Drilling oil and gas wells
5813 Drinking places
5912 Drug stores and proprietary stores
5122 Drugs, proprietaries, and sundries
2023 Dry, condensed, evaporated products
5099 Durable goods, nec

E

5812 Eating places
2079 Edible fats and oils
3634 Electric housewares and fans
3641 Electric lamps
4911 Electric services
5063 Electrical apparatus and equipment
5064 Electrical appliances, television and radio
3699 Electrical equipment and supplies, nec
3629 Electrical industrial apparatus
7629 Electrical repair shops
1731 Electrical work

SIC

SIC NO	PRODUCT
3845	Electromedical equipment
3313	Electrometallurgical products
3675	Electronic capacitors
3677	Electronic coils and transformers
3679	Electronic components, nec
3571	Electronic computers
3678	Electronic connectors
5065	Electronic parts and equipment, nec
3676	Electronic resistors
8211	Elementary and secondary schools
3534	Elevators and moving stairways
3694	Engine electrical equipment
8711	Engineering services
7929	Entertainers and entertainment groups
2677	Envelopes
3822	Environmental controls
7359	Equipment rental and leasing, nec
1794	Excavation work
9111	Executive offices
2892	Explosives

F

SIC NO	PRODUCT
2381	Fabric dress and work gloves
3499	Fabricated metal products, nec
3498	Fabricated pipe and fittings
3443	Fabricated plate work (boiler shop)
3069	Fabricated rubber products, nec
3441	Fabricated structural metal
2399	Fabricated textile products, nec
8744	Facilities support services
5651	Family clothing stores
5083	Farm and garden machinery
3523	Farm machinery and equipment
4221	Farm product warehousing and storage
5191	Farm supplies
5159	Farm-product raw materials, nec
3965	Fasteners, buttons, needles, and pins
1061	Ferroalloy ores, except vanadium
2875	Fertilizers, mixing only
2655	Fiber cans, drums, and similar products
0139	Field crops, except cash grain
2261	Finishing plants, cotton
2262	Finishing plants, manmade
5146	Fish and seafoods
3211	Flat glass
2087	Flavoring extracts and syrups, nec
5713	Floor covering stores
1752	Floor laying and floor work, nec
5992	Florists
2041	Flour and other grain mill products
5193	Flowers and florists supplies
3824	Fluid meters and counting devices
2026	Fluid milk
3593	Fluid power cylinders and actuators
3594	Fluid power pumps and motors
3492	Fluid power valves and hose fittings
2657	Folding paperboard boxes
2099	Food preparations, nec
3556	Food products machinery
5139	Footwear
3131	Footwear cut stock
4731	Freight transportation arrangement
5148	Fresh fruits and vegetables
2053	Frozen bakery products, except bread
2037	Frozen fruits and vegetables
2038	Frozen specialties, nec
5431	Fruit and vegetable markets
5983	Fuel oil dealers
7261	Funeral service and crematories
2371	Fur goods
5021	Furniture
2599	Furniture and fixtures, nec
5712	Furniture stores

G

SIC NO	PRODUCT
3944	Games, toys, and children's vehicles
7212	Garment pressing and cleaners' agents
4932	Gas and other services combined
4923	Gas transmission and distribution
3053	Gaskets; packing and sealing devices
5541	Gasoline service stations
7538	General automotive repair shops

SIC NO	PRODUCT
0191	General farms, primarily crop
9199	General government, nec
3569	General industrial machinery,
8062	General medical and surgical hospitals
4225	General warehousing and storage
5947	Gift, novelty, and souvenir shop
2361	Girl's and children's dresses, blouses
1793	Glass and glazing work
3221	Glass containers
1041	Gold ores
5153	Grain and field beans
0172	Grapes
3321	Gray and ductile iron foundries
2771	Greeting cards
5149	Groceries and related products, nec
5141	Groceries, general line
5411	Grocery stores
3761	Guided missiles and space vehicles
2861	Gum and wood chemicals
3275	Gypsum products

H

SIC NO	PRODUCT
3423	Hand and edge tools, nec
3996	Hard surface floor coverings, nec
5072	Hardware
5251	Hardware stores
3429	Hardware, nec
2426	Hardwood dimension and flooring mills
2435	Hardwood veneer and plywood
2353	Hats, caps, and millinery
8099	Health and allied services, nec
3433	Heating equipment, except electric
7353	Heavy construction equipment rental
1629	Heavy construction, nec
7363	Help supply services
1611	Highway and street construction
5945	Hobby, toy, and game shops
0213	Hogs
3536	Hoists, cranes, and monorails
6719	Holding companies, nec
5023	Homefurnishings
2252	Hosiery, nec
7011	Hotels and motels
3142	House slippers
5722	Household appliance stores
3639	Household appliances, nec
3651	Household audio and video equipment
3631	Household cooking equipment
2392	Household furnishings, nec
2519	Household furniture, nec
3633	Household laundry equipment
3632	Household refrigerators and freezers
3635	Household vacuum cleaners

I

SIC NO	PRODUCT
2024	Ice cream and frozen deserts
8322	Individual and family services
5113	Industrial and personal service paper
1541	Industrial buildings and warehouses
3567	Industrial furnaces and ovens
2813	Industrial gases
2819	Industrial inorganic chemicals, nec
7218	Industrial launderers
5084	Industrial machinery and equipment
3599	Industrial machinery, nec
2869	Industrial organic chemicals, nec
3543	Industrial patterns
1446	Industrial sand
5085	Industrial supplies
3537	Industrial trucks and tractors
3491	Industrial valves
7375	Information retrieval services
2816	Inorganic pigments
1796	Installing building equipment
3825	Instruments to measure electricity
6411	Insurance agents, brokers, and service
8052	Intermediate care facilities
3519	Internal combustion engines, nec
6282	Investment advice
6726	Investment offices, nec
6799	Investors, nec
3462	Iron and steel forgings

SIC NO	PRODUCT
1011	Iron ores

J

SIC NO	PRODUCT
3915	Jewelers' materials and lapidary work
5094	Jewelry and precious stones
5944	Jewelry stores
3911	Jewelry, precious metal
8331	Job training and related services
8222	Junior colleges

K

SIC NO	PRODUCT
2253	Knit outerwear mills
2259	Knitting mills, nec

L

SIC NO	PRODUCT
3821	Laboratory apparatus and furniture
2258	Lace and warp knit fabric mills
3083	Laminated plastics plate and sheet
0781	Landscape counseling and planning
3524	Lawn and garden equipment
0782	Lawn and garden services
1031	Lead and zinc ores
3952	Lead pencils and art goods
3151	Leather gloves and mittens
3199	Leather goods, nec
3111	Leather tanning and finishing
8111	Legal services
6311	Life insurance
3648	Lighting equipment, nec
3274	Lime
7213	Linen supply
5984	Liquefied petroleum gas dealers
5921	Liquor stores
5154	Livestock
0751	Livestock services, except veterinary
4214	Local trucking with storage
4212	Local trucking, without storage
2411	Logging
2992	Lubricating oils and greases
3161	Luggage
5948	Luggage and leather goods stores
5211	Lumber and other building materials
5031	Lumber, plywood, and millwork

M

SIC NO	PRODUCT
2098	Macaroni and spaghetti
3545	Machine tool accessories
3541	Machine tools, metal cutting type
3542	Machine tools, metal forming type
3695	Magnetic and optical recording media
3322	Malleable iron foundries
2083	Malt
2082	Malt beverages
8742	Management consulting services
8741	Management services
2761	Manifold business forms
2097	Manufactured ice
3999	Manufacturing industries, nec
4493	Marinas
4491	Marine cargo handling
3953	Marking devices
1741	Masonry and other stonework
2515	Mattresses and bedsprings
3829	Measuring and controlling devices, nec
3586	Measuring and dispensing pumps
5421	Meat and fish markets
2011	Meat packing plants
5147	Meats and meat products
3061	Mechanical rubber goods
5047	Medical and hospital equipment
7352	Medical equipment rental
8071	Medical laboratories
2833	Medicinals and botanicals
8699	Membership organizations, nec
7997	Membership sports and recreation clubs
7041	Membership-basis organization hotels
5136	Men's and boy's clothing
2329	Men's and boy's clothing, nec
2321	Men's and boy's furnishings
2311	Men's and boy's suits and coats
2326	Men's and boy's work clothing
5611	Men's and boys' clothing stores

SIC NO	PRODUCT
3143	Men's footwear, except athletic
3412	Metal barrels, drums, and pails
3411	Metal cans
3479	Metal coating and allied services
3442	Metal doors, sash, and trim
3497	Metal foil and leaf
3398	Metal heat treating
2514	Metal household furniture
1081	Metal mining services
3431	Metal sanitary ware
3469	Metal stampings, nec
5051	Metals service centers and offices
3549	Metalworking machinery, nec
2431	Millwork
3296	Mineral wool
3295	Minerals, ground or treated
3532	Mining machinery
5699	Miscellaneous apparel and accessories
6159	Miscellaneous business credit
3496	Miscellaneous fabricated wire products
5499	Miscellaneous food stores
5399	Miscellaneous general merchandise
5719	Miscellaneous homefurnishings
3449	Miscellaneous metalwork
1499	Miscellaneous nonmetallic mining
7299	Miscellaneous personal services
2741	Miscellaneous publishing
5999	Miscellaneous retail stores, nec
6515	Mobile home site operators
2451	Mobile homes
7822	Motion picture and tape distribution
7812	Motion picture and video production
3716	Motor homes
3714	Motor vehicle parts and accessories
5015	Motor vehicle parts, used
5013	Motor vehicle supplies and new parts
3711	Motor vehicles and car bodies
5571	Motorcycle dealers
3751	Motorcycles, bicycles, and parts
3621	Motors and generators
8412	Museums and art galleries
5736	Musical instrument stores
3931	Musical instruments

N

SIC NO	PRODUCT
2441	Nailed wood boxes and shook
2241	Narrow fabric mills
9711	National security
4924	Natural gas distribution
1321	Natural gas liquids
4922	Natural gas transmission
5511	New and used car dealers
5994	News dealers and newsstands
7383	News syndicates
2711	Newspapers
2873	Nitrogenous fertilizers
3297	Nonclay refractories
8733	Noncommercial research organizations
3644	Noncurrent-carrying wiring devices
5199	Nondurable goods, nec
3364	Nonferrous die-castings except aluminum
3463	Nonferrous forgings
3369	Nonferrous foundries, nec
3356	Nonferrous rolling and drawing, nec
3357	Nonferrous wiredrawing and insulating
3299	Nonmetallic mineral products,
1481	Nonmetallic mineral services
6512	Nonresidential building operators
1542	Nonresidential construction, nec
2297	Nonwoven fabrics

O

SIC NO	PRODUCT
5044	Office equipment
2522	Office furniture, except wood
3579	Office machines, nec
8041	Offices and clinics of chiropractors
8011	Offices and clinics of medical doctors
8049	Offices of health practitioner
1382	Oil and gas exploration services
3533	Oil and gas field machinery
1389	Oil and gas field services, nec
1531	Operative builders

SIC NO	PRODUCT
3851	Ophthalmic goods
3048	Ophthalmic goods
5995	Optical goods stores
3827	Optical instruments and lenses
3489	Ordnance and accessories, nec
2824	Organic fibers, noncellulosic
0783	Ornamental shrub and tree services
7312	Outdoor advertising services

P

SIC NO	PRODUCT
5142	Packaged frozen goods
3565	Packaging machinery
4783	Packing and crating
5231	Paint, glass, and wallpaper stores
1721	Painting and paper hanging
2851	Paints and allied products
5198	Paints, varnishes, and supplies
3554	Paper industries machinery
2621	Paper mills
2671	Paper; coated and laminated packaging
2672	Paper; coated and laminated, nec
2631	Paperboard mills
2542	Partitions and fixtures, except wood
7514	Passenger car rental
6794	Patent owners and lessors
2721	Periodicals
6141	Personal credit institutions
3172	Personal leather goods, nec
2999	Petroleum and coal products, nec
5171	Petroleum bulk stations and terminals
5172	Petroleum products, nec
2911	Petroleum refining
2834	Pharmaceutical preparations
2874	Phosphatic fertilizers
7334	Photocopying and duplicating services
7384	Photofinish laboratories
3861	Photographic equipment and supplies
5043	Photographic equipment and supplies
2035	Pickles, sauces, and salad dressings
5131	Piece goods and notions
1742	Plastering, drywall, and insulation
3085	Plastics bottles
3086	Plastics foam products
5162	Plastics materials and basic shapes
2821	Plastics materials and resins
3084	Plastics pipe
3088	Plastics plumbing fixtures
3089	Plastics products, nec
2796	Platemaking services
3471	Plating and polishing
2395	Pleating and stitching
5074	Plumbing and hydronic heating supplies
3432	Plumbing fixture fittings and trim
1711	Plumbing, heating, air-conditioning
9221	Police protection
2842	Polishes and sanitation goods
3264	Porcelain electrical supplies
2096	Potato chips and similar snacks
3269	Pottery products, nec
5144	Poultry and poultry products
0254	Poultry hatcheries
2015	Poultry slaughtering and processing
3568	Power transmission equipment, nec
3546	Power-driven handtools
3448	Prefabricated metal buildings
2452	Prefabricated wood buildings
7372	Prepackaged software
2048	Prepared feeds, nec
2045	Prepared flour mixes and doughs
3652	Prerecorded records and tapes
3229	Pressed and blown glass, nec
3334	Primary aluminum
3692	Primary batteries, dry and wet
3331	Primary copper
3399	Primary metal products
3339	Primary nonferrous metals, nec
3672	Printed circuit boards
5111	Printing and writing paper
2893	Printing ink
3555	Printing trades machinery
3823	Process control instruments
3231	Products of purchased glass

SIC NO	PRODUCT
5049	Professional equipment, nec
8621	Professional organizations
2531	Public building and related furniture
7992	Public golf courses
8743	Public relations services
2611	Pulp mills
3561	Pumps and pumping equipment

R

SIC NO	PRODUCT
3663	Radio and t.v. communications equipment
7622	Radio and television repair
4832	Radio broadcasting stations
5731	Radio, television, and electronic stores
7313	Radio, television, publisher representatives
4812	Radiotelephone communication
3743	Railroad equipment
3273	Ready-mixed concrete
6531	Real estate agents and managers
6798	Real estate investment trusts
6519	Real property lessors, nec
2493	Reconstituted wood products
5735	Record and prerecorded tape stores
5561	Recreational vehicle dealers
4222	Refrigerated warehousing and storage
3585	Refrigeration and heating equipment
5078	Refrigeration equipment and supplies
7623	Refrigeration service and repair
4953	Refuse systems
9621	Regulation, administration of transportation
3625	Relays and industrial controls
8661	Religious organizations
4741	Rental of railroad cars
7699	Repair services, nec
8361	Residential care
1522	Residential construction, nec
3645	Residential lighting fixtures
5461	Retail bakeries
5261	Retail nurseries and garden stores
7641	Reupholstery and furniture repair
2095	Roasted coffee
2384	Robes and dressing gowns
3547	Rolling mill machinery
5033	Roofing, siding, and insulation
1761	Roofing, siding, and sheetmetal work
3021	Rubber and plastics footwear
3052	Rubber and plastics hose and beltings

S

SIC NO	PRODUCT
2068	Salted and roasted nuts and seeds
2656	Sanitary food containers
2676	Sanitary paper products
4959	Sanitary services, nec
2013	Sausages and other prepared meats
3425	Saw blades and handsaws
2421	Sawmills and planing mills, general
3596	Scales and balances, except laboratory
8299	Schools and educational services
5093	Scrap and waste materials
3451	Screw machine products
3812	Search and navigation equipment
3341	Secondary nonferrous metals
7338	Secretarial and court reporting
6211	Security brokers and dealers
7382	Security systems services
3674	Semiconductors and related devices
3263	Semivitreous table and kitchenware
5087	Service establishment equipment
3589	Service industry machinery, nec
7819	Services allied to motion pictures
8999	Services, nec
2652	Setup paperboard boxes
4952	Sewerage systems
3444	Sheet metalwork
3731	Shipbuilding and repairing
7251	Shoe repair and shoeshine parlors
5661	Shoe stores
6153	Short-term business credit
3993	Signs and advertising specialties
3914	Silverware and plated ware
1521	Single-family housing construction
8051	Skilled nursing care facilities
3484	Small arms

SIC NO	PRODUCT
3482	Small arms ammunition
2841	Soap and other detergents
8399	Social services, nec
2436	Softwood veneer and plywood
0711	Soil preparation services
2075	Soybean oil mills
0116	Soybeans
9661	Space research and technology
3769	Space vehicle equipment, nec
3544	Special dies, tools, jigs, and fixtures
3559	Special industry machinery, nec
2429	Special product sawmills, nec
1799	Special trade contractors, nec
4226	Special warehousing and storage, nec
8093	Specialty outpatient clinics, nec
3566	Speed changers, drives, and gears
3949	Sporting and athletic goods, nec
5091	Sporting and recreation goods
7032	Sporting and recreational camps
5941	Sporting goods and bicycle shops
5112	Stationery and office supplies
2678	Stationery products
5943	Stationery stores
3325	Steel foundries, nec
3324	Steel investment foundries
3317	Steel pipe and tubes
3493	Steel springs, except wire
3315	Steel wire and related products
3691	Storage batteries
3259	Structural clay products, nec
1791	Structural steel erection
2439	Structural wood members, nec
6552	Subdividers and developers, nec
2843	Surface active agents
3841	Surgical and medical instruments
3842	Surgical appliances and supplies
8713	Surveying services
3613	Switchgear and switchboard apparatus
2822	Synthetic rubber

T

SIC NO	PRODUCT
3795	Tanks and tank components
7291	Tax return preparation services
3661	Telephone and telegraph apparatus
4813	Telephone communication, except radio

SIC NO	PRODUCT
4833	Television broadcasting stations
1743	Terrazzo, tile, marble, mosaic work
8734	Testing laboratories
2393	Textile bags
2299	Textile goods, nec
3552	Textile machinery
7922	Theatrical producers and services
2282	Throwing and winding mills
0811	Timber tracts
2296	Tire cord and fabrics
7534	Tire retreading and repair shops
3011	Tires and inner tubes
5014	Tires and tubes
5194	Tobacco and tobacco products
5993	Tobacco stores and stands
2844	Toilet preparations
7532	Top and body repair and paint shops
4492	Towing and tugboat service
5092	Toys and hobby goods and supplies
3612	Transformers, except electric
5088	Transportation equipment and supplies
3799	Transportation equipment, nec
4789	Transportation services, nec
3792	Travel trailers and campers
3713	Truck and bus bodies
7513	Truck rental and leasing, without drivers
3715	Truck trailers
4231	Trucking terminal facilities
4213	Trucking, except local
3511	Turbines and turbine generator sets
0253	Turkeys and turkey eggs
2791	Typesetting

U

SIC NO	PRODUCT
3081	Unsupported plastics film and sheet
3082	Unsupported plastics profile shapes
2512	Upholstered household furniture
1094	Uranium-radium-vanadium ores
5521	Used car dealers
5932	Used merchandise stores
7519	Utility trailer rental

V

SIC NO	PRODUCT
3494	Valves and pipe fittings, nec
0161	Vegetables and melons

SIC NO	PRODUCT
3647	Vehicular lighting equipment
7841	Video tape rental
3262	Vitreous china table and kitchenware
3261	Vitreous plumbing fixtures
8249	Vocational schools, nec

W

SIC NO	PRODUCT
5075	Warm air heating and air conditioning
7631	Watch, clock, and jewelry repair
3873	Watches, clocks, watchcases, and parts
4941	Water supply
1781	Water well drilling
1623	Water, sewer, and utility lines
2385	Waterproof outerwear
3548	Welding apparatus
7692	Welding repair
2046	Wet corn milling
0111	Wheat
5182	Wine and distilled beverages
2084	Wines, brandy, and brandy spirits
3495	Wire springs
5632	Women's accessory and specialty stores
5137	Women's and children's clothing
2341	Women's and children's underwear
2331	Women's and misses' blouses and shirts
2339	Women's and misses' outerwear, nec
2337	Women's and misses' suits and coats
5621	Women's clothing stores
3144	Women's footwear, except athletic
3171	Women's handbags and purses
2335	Women's, junior's, and misses' dresses
2449	Wood containers, nec
2511	Wood household furniture
2434	Wood kitchen cabinets
2521	Wood office furniture
2448	Wood pallets and skids
2541	Wood partitions and fixtures
2491	Wood preserving
2499	Wood products, nec
2517	Wood television and radio cabinets
3553	Woodworking machinery
1795	Wrecking and demolition work

X

SIC NO	PRODUCT
3844	X-ray apparatus and tubes

SIC INDEX

Standard Industrial Classification Numerical Index

SIC NO	PRODUCT

01 agricultural production - crops

0111 Wheat
0115 Corn
0116 Soybeans
0119 Cash grains, nec
0139 Field crops, except cash grain
0161 Vegetables and melons
0171 Berry crops
0172 Grapes
0191 General farms, primarily crop

02 agricultural production - livestock and animal specialties

0211 Beef cattle feedlots
0213 Hogs
0241 Dairy farms
0252 Chicken eggs
0253 Turkeys and turkey eggs
0254 Poultry hatcheries
0279 Animal specialties, nec

07 agricultural services

0711 Soil preparation services
0721 Crop planting and protection
0723 Crop preparation services for market
0724 Cotton ginning
0751 Livestock services, except veterinary
0752 Animal specialty services
0781 Landscape counseling and planning
0782 Lawn and garden services
0783 Ornamental shrub and tree services

08 forestry

0811 Timber tracts

10 metal mining

1011 Iron ores
1031 Lead and zinc ores
1041 Gold ores
1061 Ferroalloy ores, except vanadium
1081 Metal mining services
1094 Uranium-radium-vanadium ores

12 coal mining

1221 Bituminous coal and lignite-surface mining
1222 Bituminous coal-underground mining
1231 Anthracite mining
1241 Coal mining services

13 oil and gas extraction

1311 Crude petroleum and natural gas
1321 Natural gas liquids
1381 Drilling oil and gas wells
1382 Oil and gas exploration services
1389 Oil and gas field services, nec

14 mining and quarrying of nonmetallic minerals, except fuels

1411 Dimension stone
1422 Crushed and broken limestone
1423 Crushed and broken granite
1429 Crushed and broken stone, nec
1442 Construction sand and gravel
1446 Industrial sand
1459 Clay and related minerals, nec
1479 Chemical and fertilizer mining
1481 Nonmetallic mineral services
1499 Miscellaneous nonmetallic mining

15 construction - general contractors & operative builders

1521 Single-family housing construction
1522 Residential construction, nec
1531 Operative builders
1541 Industrial buildings and warehouses

1542 Nonresidential construction, nec

16 heamy construction, except building construction, contractor

1611 Highway and street construction
1622 Bridge, tunnel, and elevated highway
1623 Water, sewer, and utility lines
1629 Heavy construction, nec

17 construction - special trade contractors

1711 Plumbing, heating, air-conditioning
1721 Painting and paper hanging
1731 Electrical work
1741 Masonry and other stonework
1742 Plastering, drywall, and insulation
1743 Terrazzo, tile, marble, mosaic work
1751 Carpentry work
1752 Floor laying and floor work, nec
1761 Roofing, siding, and sheetmetal work
1771 Concrete work
1781 Water well drilling
1791 Structural steel erection
1793 Glass and glazing work
1794 Excavation work
1795 Wrecking and demolition work
1796 Installing building equipment
1799 Special trade contractors, nec

20 food and kindred products

2011 Meat packing plants
2013 Sausages and other prepared meats
2015 Poultry slaughtering and processing
2021 Creamery butter
2022 Cheese; natural and processed
2023 Dry, condensed, evaporated products
2024 Ice cream and frozen deserts
2026 Fluid milk
2032 Canned specialties
2033 Canned fruits and specialties
2034 Dehydrated fruits, vegetables, soups
2035 Pickles, sauces, and salad dressings
2037 Frozen fruits and vegetables
2038 Frozen specialties, nec
2041 Flour and other grain mill products
2043 Cereal breakfast foods
2045 Prepared flour mixes and doughs
2046 Wet corn milling
2047 Dog and cat food
2048 Prepared feeds, nec
2051 Bread, cake, and related products
2052 Cookies and crackers
2053 Frozen bakery products, except bread
2063 Beet sugar
2064 Candy and other confectionery products
2066 Chocolate and cocoa products
2068 Salted and roasted nuts and seeds
2074 Cottonseed oil mills
2075 Soybean oil mills
2077 Animal and marine fats and oils
2079 Edible fats and oils
2082 Malt beverages
2083 Malt
2084 Wines, brandy, and brandy spirits
2085 Distilled and blended liquors
2086 Bottled and canned soft drinks
2087 Flavoring extracts and syrups, nec
2095 Roasted coffee
2096 Potato chips and similar snacks
2097 Manufactured ice
2098 Macaroni and spaghetti
2099 Food preparations, nec

21 tobacco products

2111 Cigarettes
2131 Chewing and smoking tobacco

22 textile mill products

2211 Broadwoven fabric mills, cotton
2221 Broadwoven fabric mills, manmade
2231 Broadwoven fabric mills, wool
2241 Narrow fabric mills
2252 Hosiery, nec
2253 Knit outerwear mills
2258 Lace and warp knit fabric mills
2259 Knitting mills, nec
2261 Finishing plants, cotton
2262 Finishing plants, manmade
2273 Carpets and rugs
2282 Throwing and winding mills
2295 Coated fabrics, not rubberized
2296 Tire cord and fabrics
2297 Nonwoven fabrics
2298 Cordage and twine
2299 Textile goods, nec

23 apparel, finished products from fabrics & similar materials

2311 Men's and boy's suits and coats
2321 Men's and boy's furnishings
2326 Men's and boy's work clothing
2329 Men's and boy's clothing, nec
2331 Women's and misses' blouses and shirts
2335 Women's, junior's, and misses' dresses
2337 Women's and misses' suits and coats
2339 Women's and misses' outerwear, nec
2341 Women's and children's underwear
2353 Hats, caps, and millinery
2361 Girl's and children's dresses, blouses
2371 Fur goods
2381 Fabric dress and work gloves
2384 Robes and dressing gowns
2385 Waterproof outerwear
2389 Apparel and accessories, nec
2391 Curtains and draperies
2392 Household furnishings, nec
2393 Textile bags
2394 Canvas and related products
2395 Pleating and stitching
2396 Automotive and apparel trimmings
2399 Fabricated textile products, nec

24 lumber and wood products, except furniture

2411 Logging
2421 Sawmills and planing mills, general
2426 Hardwood dimension and flooring mills
2429 Special product sawmills, nec
2431 Millwork
2434 Wood kitchen cabinets
2435 Hardwood veneer and plywood
2436 Softwood veneer and plywood
2439 Structural wood members, nec
2441 Nailed wood boxes and shook
2448 Wood pallets and skids
2449 Wood containers, nec
2451 Mobile homes
2452 Prefabricated wood buildings
2491 Wood preserving
2493 Reconstituted wood products
2499 Wood products, nec

25 furniture and fixtures

2511 Wood household furniture
2512 Upholstered household furniture
2514 Metal household furniture
2515 Mattresses and bedsprings
2517 Wood television and radio cabinets
2519 Household furniture, nec
2521 Wood office furniture
2522 Office furniture, except wood
2531 Public building and related furniture
2541 Wood partitions and fixtures

SIC NO PRODUCT	SIC NO PRODUCT	SIC NO PRODUCT

2542 Partitions and fixtures, except wood
2591 Drapery hardware and blinds and shades
2599 Furniture and fixtures, nec

26 paper and allied products

2611 Pulp mills
2621 Paper mills
2631 Paperboard mills
2652 Setup paperboard boxes
2653 Corrugated and solid fiber boxes
2655 Fiber cans, drums, and similar products
2656 Sanitary food containers
2657 Folding paperboard boxes
2671 Paper; coated and laminated packaging
2672 Paper; coated and laminated, nec
2673 Bags: plastic, laminated, and coated
2674 Bags: uncoated paper and multiwall
2675 Die-cut paper and board
2676 Sanitary paper products
2677 Envelopes
2678 Stationery products
2679 Converted paper products, nec

27 printing, publishing and allied industries

2711 Newspapers
2721 Periodicals
2731 Book publishing
2732 Book printing
2741 Miscellaneous publishing
2752 Commercial printing, lithographic
2754 Commercial printing, gravure
2759 Commercial printing, nec
2761 Manifold business forms
2771 Greeting cards
2782 Blankbooks and looseleaf binders
2789 Bookbinding and related work
2791 Typesetting
2796 Platemaking services

28 chemicals and allied products

2812 Alkalies and chlorine
2813 Industrial gases
2816 Inorganic pigments
2819 Industrial inorganic chemicals, nec
2821 Plastics materials and resins
2822 Synthetic rubber
2823 Cellulosic manmade fibers
2824 Organic fibers, noncellulosic
2833 Medicinals and botanicals
2834 Pharmaceutical preparations
2835 Diagnostic substances
2836 Biological products, except diagnostic
2841 Soap and other detergents
2842 Polishes and sanitation goods
2843 Surface active agents
2844 Toilet preparations
2851 Paints and allied products
2861 Gum and wood chemicals
2865 Cyclic crudes and intermediates
2869 Industrial organic chemicals, nec
2873 Nitrogenous fertilizers
2874 Phosphatic fertilizers
2875 Fertilizers, mixing only
2879 Agricultural chemicals, nec
2891 Adhesives and sealants
2892 Explosives
2893 Printing ink
2895 Carbon black
2899 Chemical preparations, nec

29 petroleum refining and related industries

2911 Petroleum refining
2951 Asphalt paving mixtures and blocks
2952 Asphalt felts and coatings
2992 Lubricating oils and greases
2999 Petroleum and coal products, nec

30 rubber and miscellaneous plastic products

3011 Tires and inner tubes
3021 Rubber and plastics footwear
3052 Rubber and plastics hose and beltings
3053 Gaskets; packing and sealing devices

3061 Mechanical rubber goods
3069 Fabricated rubber products, nec
3081 Unsupported plastics film and sheet
3082 Unsupported plastics profile shapes
3083 Laminated plastics plate and sheet
3084 Plastics pipe
3085 Plastics bottles
3086 Plastics foam products
3087 Custom compound purchased resins
3088 Plastics plumbing fixtures
3089 Plastics products, nec

31 leather and leather products

3111 Leather tanning and finishing
3131 Footwear cut stock
3142 House slippers
3143 Men's footwear, except athletic
3144 Women's footwear, except athletic
3151 Leather gloves and mittens
3161 Luggage
3171 Women's handbags and purses
3172 Personal leather goods, nec
3199 Leather goods, nec

32 stone, clay, glass, and concrete products

3211 Flat glass
3221 Glass containers
3229 Pressed and blown glass, nec
3231 Products of purchased glass
3241 Cement, hydraulic
3251 Brick and structural clay tile
3253 Ceramic wall and floor tile
3255 Clay refractories
3259 Structural clay products, nec
3261 Vitreous plumbing fixtures
3262 Vitreous china table and kitchenware
3263 Semivitreous table and kitchenware
3264 Porcelain electrical supplies
3269 Pottery products, nec
3271 Concrete block and brick
3272 Concrete products, nec
3273 Ready-mixed concrete
3274 Lime
3275 Gypsum products
3281 Cut stone and stone products
3291 Abrasive products
3292 Asbestos products
3295 Minerals, ground or treated
3296 Mineral wool
3297 Nonclay refractories
3299 Nonmetallic mineral products,

33 primary metal industries

3312 Blast furnaces and steel mills
3313 Electrometallurgical products
3315 Steel wire and related products
3316 Cold finishing of steel shapes
3317 Steel pipe and tubes
3321 Gray and ductile iron foundries
3322 Malleable iron foundries
3324 Steel investment foundries
3325 Steel foundries, nec
3331 Primary copper
3334 Primary aluminum
3339 Primary nonferrous metals, nec
3341 Secondary nonferrous metals
3351 Copper rolling and drawing
3353 Aluminum sheet, plate, and foil
3354 Aluminum extruded products
3355 Aluminum rolling and drawing, nec
3356 Nonferrous rolling and drawing, nec
3357 Nonferrous wiredrawing and insulating
3363 Aluminum die-castings
3364 Nonferrous die-castings except aluminum
3365 Aluminum foundries
3366 Copper foundries
3369 Nonferrous foundries, nec
3398 Metal heat treating
3399 Primary metal products

34 fabricated metal products

3411 Metal cans

3412 Metal barrels, drums, and pails
3421 Cutlery
3423 Hand and edge tools, nec
3425 Saw blades and handsaws
3429 Hardware, nec
3431 Metal sanitary ware
3432 Plumbing fixture fittings and trim
3433 Heating equipment, except electric
3441 Fabricated structural metal
3442 Metal doors, sash, and trim
3443 Fabricated plate work (boiler shop)
3444 Sheet metalwork
3446 Architectural metalwork
3448 Prefabricated metal buildings
3449 Miscellaneous metalwork
3451 Screw machine products
3452 Bolts, nuts, rivets, and washers
3462 Iron and steel forgings
3463 Nonferrous forgings
3465 Automotive stampings
3466 Crowns and closures
3469 Metal stampings, nec
3471 Plating and polishing
3479 Metal coating and allied services
3482 Small arms ammunition
3483 Ammunition, except for small arms, nec
3484 Small arms
3489 Ordnance and accessories, nec
3491 Industrial valves
3492 Fluid power valves and hose fittings
3493 Steel springs, except wire
3494 Valves and pipe fittings, nec
3495 Wire springs
3496 Miscellaneous fabricated wire products
3497 Metal foil and leaf
3498 Fabricated pipe and fittings
3499 Fabricated metal products, nec

35 industrial and commercial machinery and computer equipment

3511 Turbines and turbine generator sets
3519 Internal combustion engines, nec
3523 Farm machinery and equipment
3524 Lawn and garden equipment
3531 Construction machinery
3532 Mining machinery
3533 Oil and gas field machinery
3534 Elevators and moving stairways
3535 Conveyors and conveying equipment
3536 Hoists, cranes, and monorails
3537 Industrial trucks and tractors
3541 Machine tools, metal cutting type
3542 Machine tools, metal forming type
3543 Industrial patterns
3544 Special dies, tools, jigs, and fixtures
3545 Machine tool accessories
3546 Power-driven handtools
3547 Rolling mill machinery
3548 Welding apparatus
3549 Metalworking machinery, nec
3552 Textile machinery
3553 Woodworking machinery
3554 Paper industries machinery
3555 Printing trades machinery
3556 Food products machinery
3559 Special industry machinery, nec
3561 Pumps and pumping equipment
3562 Ball and roller bearings
3563 Air and gas compressors
3564 Blowers and fans
3565 Packaging machinery
3566 Speed changers, drives, and gears
3567 Industrial furnaces and ovens
3568 Power transmission equipment, nec
3569 General industrial machinery,
3571 Electronic computers
3572 Computer storage devices
3575 Computer terminals
3577 Computer peripheral equipment, nec
3578 Calculating and accounting equipment
3579 Office machines, nec
3581 Automatic vending machines

SIC NO	PRODUCT	SIC NO	PRODUCT	SIC NO	PRODUCT

3582 Commercial laundry equipment
3585 Refrigeration and heating equipment
3586 Measuring and dispensing pumps
3589 Service industry machinery, nec
3592 Carburetors, pistons, rings, valves
3593 Fluid power cylinders and actuators
3594 Fluid power pumps and motors
3596 Scales and balances, except laboratory
3599 Industrial machinery, nec

36 electronic & other electrical equipment & components

3612 Transformers, except electric
3613 Switchgear and switchboard apparatus
3621 Motors and generators
3624 Carbon and graphite products
3625 Relays and industrial controls
3629 Electrical industrial apparatus
3631 Household cooking equipment
3632 Household refrigerators and freezers
3633 Household laundry equipment
3634 Electric housewares and fans
3635 Household vacuum cleaners
3639 Household appliances, nec
3641 Electric lamps
3643 Current-carrying wiring devices
3644 Noncurrent-carrying wiring devices
3645 Residential lighting fixtures
3646 Commercial lighting fixtures
3647 Vehicular lighting equipment
3648 Lighting equipment, nec
3651 Household audio and video equipment
3652 Prerecorded records and tapes
3661 Telephone and telegraph apparatus
3663 Radio and t.v. communications equipment
3669 Communications equipment, nec
3672 Printed circuit boards
3674 Semiconductors and related devices
3675 Electronic capacitors
3676 Electronic resistors
3677 Electronic coils and transformers
3678 Electronic connectors
3679 Electronic components, nec
3691 Storage batteries
3692 Primary batteries, dry and wet
3694 Engine electrical equipment
3695 Magnetic and optical recording media
3699 Electrical equipment and supplies, nec

37 transportation equipment

3711 Motor vehicles and car bodies
3713 Truck and bus bodies
3714 Motor vehicle parts and accessories
3715 Truck trailers
3716 Motor homes
3721 Aircraft
3724 Aircraft engines and engine parts
3728 Aircraft parts and equipment, nec
3731 Shipbuilding and repairing
3732 Boatbuilding and repairing
3743 Railroad equipment
3751 Motorcycles, bicycles, and parts
3761 Guided missiles and space vehicles
3769 Space vehicle equipment, nec
3792 Travel trailers and campers
3795 Tanks and tank components
3799 Transportation equipment, nec

38 measuring, photographic, medical, & optical goods, & clocks

3812 Search and navigation equipment
3821 Laboratory apparatus and furniture
3822 Environmental controls
3823 Process control instruments
3824 Fluid meters and counting devices
3825 Instruments to measure electricity
3826 Analytical instruments
3827 Optical instruments and lenses
3829 Measuring and controlling devices, nec
3841 Surgical and medical instruments
3842 Surgical appliances and supplies
3843 Dental equipment and supplies
3844 X-ray apparatus and tubes

3845 Electromedical equipment
3851 Ophthalmic goods
3861 Photographic equipment and supplies
3873 Watches, clocks, watchcases, and parts

39 miscellaneous manufacturing industries

3911 Jewelry, precious metal
3914 Silverware and plated ware
3915 Jewelers' materials and lapidary work
3931 Musical instruments
3942 Dolls and stuffed toys
3944 Games, toys, and children's vehicles
3949 Sporting and athletic goods, nec
3952 Lead pencils and art goods
3953 Marking devices
3955 Carbon paper and inked ribbons
3961 Costume jewelry
3965 Fasteners, buttons, needles, and pins
3991 Brooms and brushes
3993 Signs and advertising specialties
3995 Burial caskets
3996 Hard surface floor coverings, nec
3999 Manufacturing industries, nec

42 motor freight transportation

4212 Local trucking, without storage
4213 Trucking, except local
4214 Local trucking with storage
4215 Courier services, except by air
4221 Farm product warehousing and storage
4222 Refrigerated warehousing and storage
4225 General warehousing and storage
4226 Special warehousing and storage, nec
4231 Trucking terminal facilities

44 water transportation

4424 Deep sea domestic transportation of freight
4491 Marine cargo handling
4492 Towing and tugboat service
4493 Marinas

45 transportation by air

4512 Air transportation, scheduled
4522 Air transportation, nonscheduled
4581 Airports, flying fields, and services

46 pipelines, except natural gas

4612 Crude petroleum pipelines

47 transportation services

4731 Freight transportation arrangement
4741 Rental of railroad cars
4783 Packing and crating
4789 Transportation services, nec

48 communications

4812 Radiotelephone communication
4813 Telephone communication, except radio
4832 Radio broadcasting stations
4833 Television broadcasting stations
4841 Cable and other pay television services
4899 Communication services, nec

49 electric, gas and sanitary services

4911 Electric services
4922 Natural gas transmission
4923 Gas transmission and distribution
4924 Natural gas distribution
4932 Gas and other services combined
4941 Water supply
4952 Sewerage systems
4953 Refuse systems
4959 Sanitary services, nec

50 wholesale trade - durable goods

5012 Automobiles and other motor vehicles
5013 Motor vehicle supplies and new parts
5014 Tires and tubes
5015 Motor vehicle parts, used
5021 Furniture
5023 Homefurnishings
5031 Lumber, plywood, and millwork

5032 Brick, stone, and related material
5033 Roofing, siding, and insulation
5039 Construction materials, nec
5043 Photographic equipment and supplies
5044 Office equipment
5045 Computers, peripherals, and software
5046 Commercial equipment, nec
5047 Medical and hospital equipment
5048 Ophthalmic goods
5049 Professional equipment, nec
5051 Metals service centers and offices
5052 Coal and other minerals and ores
5063 Electrical apparatus and equipment
5064 Electrical appliances, television and radio
5065 Electronic parts and equipment, nec
5072 Hardware
5074 Plumbing and hydronic heating supplies
5075 Warm air heating and air conditioning
5078 Refrigeration equipment and supplies
5082 Construction and mining machinery
5083 Farm and garden machinery
5084 Industrial machinery and equipment
5085 Industrial supplies
5087 Service establishment equipment
5088 Transportation equipment and supplies
5091 Sporting and recreation goods
5092 Toys and hobby goods and supplies
5093 Scrap and waste materials
5094 Jewelry and precious stones
5099 Durable goods, nec

51 wholesale trade - nondurable goods

5111 Printing and writing paper
5112 Stationery and office supplies
5113 Industrial and personal service paper
5122 Drugs, proprietaries, and sundries
5131 Piece goods and notions
5136 Men's and boy's clothing
5137 Women's and children's clothing
5139 Footwear
5141 Groceries, general line
5142 Packaged frozen goods
5143 Dairy products, except dried or canned
5144 Poultry and poultry products
5145 Confectionery
5146 Fish and seafoods
5147 Meats and meat products
5148 Fresh fruits and vegetables
5149 Groceries and related products, nec
5153 Grain and field beans
5154 Livestock
5159 Farm-product raw materials, nec
5162 Plastics materials and basic shapes
5169 Chemicals and allied products, nec
5171 Petroleum bulk stations and terminals
5172 Petroleum products, nec
5181 Beer and ale
5182 Wine and distilled beverages
5191 Farm supplies
5192 Books, periodicals, and newspapers
5193 Flowers and florists supplies
5194 Tobacco and tobacco products
5198 Paints, varnishes, and supplies
5199 Nondurable goods, nec

52 building materials, hardware, garden supplies & mobile homes

5211 Lumber and other building materials
5231 Paint, glass, and wallpaper stores
5251 Hardware stores
5261 Retail nurseries and garden stores

53 general merchandise stores

5311 Department stores
5399 Miscellaneous general merchandise

54 food stores

5411 Grocery stores
5421 Meat and fish markets
5431 Fruit and vegetable markets
5441 Candy, nut, and confectionery stores
5451 Dairy products stores

SIC

SIC NO	PRODUCT

5461 Retail bakeries
5499 Miscellaneous food stores

55 automotive dealers and gasoline service stations

5511 New and used car dealers
5521 Used car dealers
5531 Auto and home supply stores
5541 Gasoline service stations
5551 Boat dealers
5561 Recreational vehicle dealers
5571 Motorcycle dealers
5599 Automotive dealers, nec

56 apparel and accessory stores

5611 Men's and boys' clothing stores
5621 Women's clothing stores
5632 Women's accessory and specialty stores
5641 Children's and infants' wear stores
5651 Family clothing stores
5661 Shoe stores
5699 Miscellaneous apparel and accessories

57 home furniture, furnishings and equipment stores

5712 Furniture stores
5713 Floor covering stores
5714 Drapery and upholstery stores
5719 Miscellaneous homefurnishings
5722 Household appliance stores
5731 Radio, television, and electronic stores
5734 Computer and software stores
5735 Record and prerecorded tape stores
5736 Musical instrument stores

58 eating and drinking places

5812 Eating places
5813 Drinking places

59 miscellaneous retail

5912 Drug stores and proprietary stores
5921 Liquor stores
5932 Used merchandise stores
5941 Sporting goods and bicycle shops
5942 Book stores
5943 Stationery stores
5944 Jewelry stores
5945 Hobby, toy, and game shops
5947 Gift, novelty, and souvenir shop
5948 Luggage and leather goods stores
5961 Catalog and mail-order houses
5963 Direct selling establishments
5983 Fuel oil dealers
5984 Liquefied petroleum gas dealers
5992 Florists
5993 Tobacco stores and stands
5994 News dealers and newsstands
5995 Optical goods stores
5999 Miscellaneous retail stores, nec

61 nondepository credit institutions

6141 Personal credit institutions
6153 Short-term business credit
6159 Miscellaneous business credit

62 security & commodity brokers, dealers, exchanges & services

6211 Security brokers and dealers
6282 Investment advice

63 insurance carriers

6311 Life insurance

64 insurance agents, brokers and service

6411 Insurance agents, brokers, and service

65 real estate

6512 Nonresidential building operators
6515 Mobile home site operators
6519 Real property lessors, nec
6531 Real estate agents and managers
6552 Subdividers and developers, nec
6553 Cemetery subdividers and developers

67 holding and other investment offices

6719 Holding companies, nec
6726 Investment offices, nec
6794 Patent owners and lessors
6798 Real estate investment trusts
6799 Investors, nec

70 hotels, rooming houses, camps, and other lodging places

7011 Hotels and motels
7032 Sporting and recreational camps
7041 Membership-basis organization hotels

72 personal services

7212 Garment pressing and cleaners' agents
7213 Linen supply
7217 Carpet and upholstery cleaning
7218 Industrial launderers
7231 Beauty shops
7241 Barber shops
7251 Shoe repair and shoeshine parlors
7261 Funeral service and crematories
7291 Tax return preparation services
7299 Miscellaneous personal services

73 business services

7311 Advertising agencies
7312 Outdoor advertising services
7313 Radio, television, publisher representatives
7319 Advertising, nec
7322 Adjustment and collection services
7331 Direct mail advertising services
7334 Photocopying and duplicating services
7335 Commercial photography
7336 Commercial art and graphic design
7338 Secretarial and court reporting
7342 Disinfecting and pest control services
7349 Building maintenance services, nec
7352 Medical equipment rental
7353 Heavy construction equipment rental
7359 Equipment rental and leasing, nec
7363 Help supply services
7371 Custom computer programming services
7372 Prepackaged software
7373 Computer integrated systems design
7374 Data processing and preparation
7375 Information retrieval services
7376 Computer facilities management
7377 Computer rental and leasing
7378 Computer maintenance and repair
7379 Computer related services, nec
7382 Security systems services
7383 News syndicates
7384 Photofinish laboratories
7389 Business services, nec

75 automotive repair, services and parking

7513 Truck rental and leasing, without drivers
7514 Passenger car rental
7519 Utility trailer rental
7521 Automobile parking
7532 Top and body repair and paint shops
7533 Auto exhaust system repair shops
7534 Tire retreading and repair shops
7536 Automotive glass replacement shops
7537 Automotive transmission repair shops
7538 General automotive repair shops
7539 Automotive repair shops, nec
7549 Automotive services, nec

76 miscellaneous repair services

7622 Radio and television repair
7623 Refrigeration service and repair
7629 Electrical repair shops
7631 Watch, clock, and jewelry repair
7641 Reupholstery and furniture repair
7692 Welding repair
7694 Armature rewinding shops
7699 Repair services, nec

78 motion pictures

7812 Motion picture and video production

7819 Services allied to motion pictures
7822 Motion picture and tape distribution
7841 Video tape rental

79 amusement and recreation services

7922 Theatrical producers and services
7929 Entertainers and entertainment groups
7933 Bowling centers
7992 Public golf courses
7993 Coin-operated amusement devices
7997 Membership sports and recreation clubs
7999 Amusement and recreation, nec

80 health services

8011 Offices and clinics of medical doctors
8041 Offices and clinics of chiropractors
8049 Offices of health practitioner
8051 Skilled nursing care facilities
8052 Intermediate care facilities
8062 General medical and surgical hospitals
8071 Medical laboratories
8072 Dental laboratories
8093 Specialty outpatient clinics, nec
8099 Health and allied services, nec

81 legal services

8111 Legal services

82 educational services

8211 Elementary and secondary schools
8222 Junior colleges
8243 Data processing schools
8249 Vocational schools, nec
8299 Schools and educational services

83 social services

8322 Individual and family services
8331 Job training and related services
8351 Child day care services
8361 Residential care
8399 Social services, nec

84 museums, art galleries and botanical and zoological gardens

8412 Museums and art galleries

86 membership organizations

8611 Business associations
8621 Professional organizations
8641 Civic and social associations
8661 Religious organizations
8699 Membership organizations, nec

87 engineering, accounting, research, and management services

8711 Engineering services
8712 Architectural services
8713 Surveying services
8721 Accounting, auditing, and bookkeeping
8731 Commercial physical research
8732 Commercial nonphysical research
8733 Noncommercial research organizations
8734 Testing laboratories
8741 Management services
8742 Management consulting services
8743 Public relations services
8744 Facilities support services
8748 Business consulting, nec

89 services, not elsewhere classified

8999 Services, nec

91 executive, legislative & general government, except finance

9111 Executive offices
9199 General government, nec

92 justice, public order and safety

9221 Police protection

96 administration of economic programs

9621 Regulation, administration of transportation

SIC NO	PRODUCT	SIC NO	PRODUCT	SIC NO	PRODUCT
9661 Space research and technology		*97 national security and international affairs*		9711 National security	

SIC SECTION

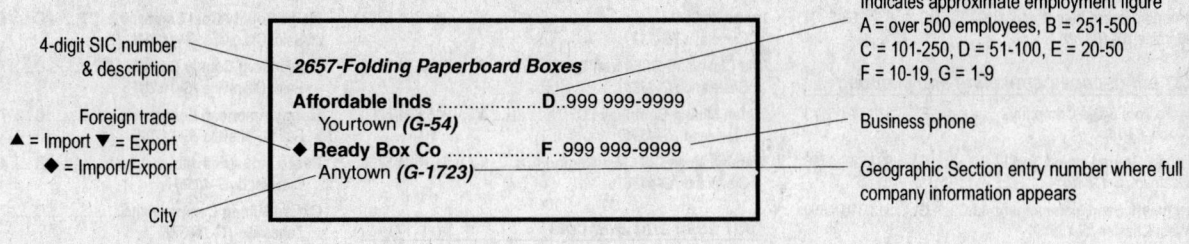

Indicates approximate employment figure
A = over 500 employees, B = 251-500
C = 101-250, D = 51-100, E = 20-50
F = 10-19, G = 1-9

2657-Folding Paperboard Boxes

4-digit SIC number & description

Affordable Inds ....**D**..999 999-9999
Yourtown *(G-54)*

Foreign trade
▲ = Import ▼ = Export
◆ = Import/Export

◆ **Ready Box Co** ....**F**..999 999-9999
Anytown *(G-1723)*

City

Business phone

Geographic Section entry number where full company information appears

See footnotes for symbols and codes identification.

- The SIC codes in this section are from the latest Standard Industrial Classification manual published by the U.S. Government's Office of Management and Budget. For more information regarding SICs, see the Explanatory Notes.
- Companies may be listed under multiple classifications.

01 AGRICULTURAL PRODUCTION - CROPS

0111 Wheat

Demmy Sand and Gravel LLC................ E
Springfield *(G-12301)*

Friesen Transfer Ltd................................ G..... 614 873-5672
Plain City *(G-11409)*

Schlessman Seed Co........................... E..... 419 499-2572
Milan *(G-9918)*

Wildcat Creek Farms Inc.................... G..... 419 263-2549
Payne *(G-11167)*

0115 Corn

Brinkman Turkey Farms Inc................ F..... 419 365-5127
Findlay *(G-6846)*

Demmy Sand and Gravel LLC................ E
Springfield *(G-12301)*

Friesen Transfer Ltd................................ G..... 614 873-5672
Plain City *(G-11409)*

Schlessman Seed Co........................... E..... 419 499-2572
Milan *(G-9918)*

Wildcat Creek Farms Inc.................... G..... 419 263-2549
Payne *(G-11167)*

0116 Soybeans

▲ **Advanced Biological Mktg Inc**.......... E..... 419 232-2461
Van Wert *(G-13525)*

Schlessman Seed Co........................... E..... 419 499-2572
Milan *(G-9918)*

Wildcat Creek Farms Inc.................... G..... 419 263-2549
Payne *(G-11167)*

0119 Cash grains, nec

Demmy Sand and Gravel LLC................ E
Springfield *(G-12301)*

Wildcat Creek Farms Inc.................... G..... 419 263-2549
Payne *(G-11167)*

0139 Field crops, except cash grain

Infinitaire Industries LLC.................. G..... 216 600-2051
Euclid *(G-6655)*

0161 Vegetables and melons

Chefs Garden Inc................................ C..... 419 433-4947
Sandusky *(G-11827)*

Russell L Garber................................ G..... 937 548-6224
Greenville *(G-7352)*

0171 Berry crops

◆ **Robert Rothschild Farm LLC**..........F 855 969-8050
West Chester *(G-14069)*

0172 Grapes

Ferrante Wine Farm Inc................... F 440 466-8466
Geneva *(G-7237)*

0191 General farms, primarily crop

Clovervale Farms LLC......................... D 440 960-0146
Amherst *(G-444)*

Green Field Farms Co-Op................. G 330 263-0246
Wooster *(G-14645)*

Hirzel Farms Inc................................ G 419 837-2710
Luckey *(G-8670)*

Humphrey Popcorn Company................ F 216 662-6629
Strongsville *(G-12565)*

Trevor Clatterbuck............................ G 330 359-2129
Wilmot *(G-14595)*

Wagner Farms Sawmill Ltd Lblty........... G 419 653-4126
Leipsic *(G-8315)*

02 AGRICULTURAL PRODUCTION - LIVESTOCK AND ANIMAL SPECIALTIES

0211 Beef cattle feedlots

Dairy Farmers America Inc................... G 330 670-7800
Medina *(G-9395)*

0213 Hogs

Winner Corporation............................ E 419 582-4321
Yorkshire *(G-14797)*

0241 Dairy farms

▲ **Miceli Dairy Products Co**................... D 216 791-6222
Cleveland *(G-4027)*

Youngs Jersey Dairy Inc.................... B 937 325-0629
Yellow Springs *(G-14794)*

0252 Chicken eggs

Cal-Maine Foods Inc........................... D 937 337-9576
Rossburg *(G-11655)*

Cal-Maine Foods Inc........................... F 937 968-4874
Union City *(G-13413)*

▲ **Daylay Egg Farm Inc**........................ C 937 355-6531
West Mansfield *(G-14178)*

Nature Pure LLC................................ E 937 358-2364
West Mansfield *(G-14180)*

Nature Pure LLC................................ F 937 358-2364
Raymond *(G-11553)*

▲ **Weaver Bros Inc**................................ D 937 526-3907
Versailles *(G-13605)*

0253 Turkeys and turkey eggs

Cooper Hatchery Inc........................... C 419 594-3325
Oakwood *(G-10897)*

V H Cooper & Co Inc........................... C 419 375-4116
Fort Recovery *(G-6973)*

0254 Poultry hatcheries

Cooper Hatchery Inc........................... C 419 594-3325
Oakwood *(G-10897)*

0279 Animal specialties, nec

Deer Creek Honey Farms Ltd................. G 740 852-0899
London *(G-8535)*

07 AGRICULTURAL SERVICES

0711 Soil preparation services

Garick LLC.. E 216 581-0100
Cleveland *(G-3755)*

Ream and Haager Laboratory Inc.......... F 330 343-3711
Dover *(G-6259)*

0721 Crop planting and protection

Ruhe Sales Inc................................... F 419 943-3357
Leipsic *(G-8314)*

0723 Crop preparation services for market

Andersons Inc................................... G 419 536-0460
Toledo *(G-12881)*

Andersons Inc................................... C 419 893-5050
Maumee *(G-9261)*

Ohigro Inc.. E 740 726-2429
Waldo *(G-13691)*

Schlessman Seed Co........................... E 419 499-2572
Milan *(G-9918)*

▼ **Verhoff Alfalfa Mills Inc**.................... G 419 523-4767
Ottawa *(G-11049)*

0724 Cotton ginning

▼ **Compass Systems & Sales LLC**....... D 330 733-2111
Barberton *(G-802)*

0751 Livestock services, except veterinary

Patrick M Davidson............................ G 513 897-2971
Waynesville *(G-13882)*

Winner Corporation............................ E 419 582-4321
Yorkshire *(G-14797)*

0752 Animal specialty services

Canine Creations Inc...................... G 937 667-8576
　Tipp City *(G-12817)*

◆ Heading4ward Investment Co............D 937 293-9994
　Moraine *(G-10169)*

0781 Landscape counseling and planning

▲ Acro Tool & Die Company.................. E 330 773-5173
　Akron *(G-16)*

All Ways Green Lawn & Turf LLC........ G 937 763-4766
　Seaman *(G-11889)*

Benchmark Land Management LLC...... G 513 310-7850
　West Chester *(G-13949)*

Green Impressions LLC..................... D 440 240-8508
　Sheffield Village *(G-11958)*

Hauser Services Llc........................... E 440 632-5126
　Middlefield *(G-9798)*

▲ Meridienne International Inc............. G 330 274-8317
　Aurora *(G-679)*

Morel Landscaping LLC..................... F 216 551-4395
　Broadview Heights *(G-1505)*

0782 Lawn and garden services

Benchmark Land Management LLC...... G 513 310-7850
　West Chester *(G-13949)*

Bismark Lawncare LLC....................... F 440 361-5561
　Austinburg *(G-696)*

▲ Brewer Company............................ G 800 394-0017
　Milford *(G-9926)*

Green Impressions LLC..................... D 440 240-8508
　Sheffield Village *(G-11958)*

Innovative Sport Surfacing LLC........... F 440 205-0875
　Mentor *(G-9532)*

Mapledale Farm Inc........................... F 440 286-3389
　Chardon *(G-2214)*

Mid-Wood Inc.................................... F 419 257-3331
　North Baltimore *(G-10614)*

Obersons Nurs & Landscapes LLC........ E 513 687-7379
　Hamilton *(G-7514)*

Richland Newhope Inds Inc................ C 419 774-4400
　Mansfield *(G-8848)*

Russell Hunt...................................... F 740 264-1196
　Steubenville *(G-12410)*

◆ Scotts Company LLC.......................C 937 644-0011
　Marysville *(G-9045)*

Smith & Thompson Entps LLC.............. F 330 386-9345
　East Liverpool *(G-6397)*

Spencer Feed & Supply LLC................ F 330 648-2111
　Spencer *(G-12235)*

Triple A Builders Inc.......................... G 216 249-0327
　Cleveland *(G-4428)*

0783 Ornamental shrub and tree services

Grand Archt Etrnl Eye 314 LLC.............. F 800 377-8147
　Cleveland *(G-3783)*

John P Ellis Clinic Podiatry................... G 440 460-0444
　Cleveland *(G-3890)*

Morel Landscaping LLC..................... F 216 551-4395
　Broadview Heights *(G-1505)*

Smith & Thompson Entps LLC.............. F 330 386-9345
　East Liverpool *(G-6397)*

08 FORESTRY

0811 Timber tracts

▲ Acro Tool & Die Company.................. E 330 773-5173
　Akron *(G-16)*

10 METAL MINING

1011 Iron ores

Cliffs & Associates Ltd........................ G 216 694-5700
　Cleveland *(G-3538)*

Cliffs Mining Company........................ F 216 694-5700
　Cleveland *(G-3539)*

Ironunits LLC.................................... E 216 694-5303
　Cleveland *(G-3871)*

The Cleveland-Cliffs Iron Co.................. C 216 694-5700
　Cleveland *(G-4380)*

Tilden Mining Company LC................... A 216 694-5700
　Cleveland *(G-4395)*

Wabush Mnes Clffs Min Mnging A........ F 216 694-5700
　Cleveland *(G-4486)*

1031 Lead and zinc ores

Abatement Lead Tstg Risk Assss........... G 330 785-6420
　Akron *(G-11)*

1041 Gold ores

Ivi Mining Group Ltd.......................... G 740 418-7745
　Vinton *(G-13623)*

1061 Ferroalloy ores, except vanadium

Renascent Prtction Sltions LLC............. D 678 910-0412
　Dublin *(G-6339)*

▲ Rhenium Alloys Inc.......................... E 440 365-7388
　North Ridgeville *(G-10747)*

1081 Metal mining services

Galt Alloys Enterprise......................... F 330 309-8194
　Canton *(G-1896)*

Omega Cementing Co......................... G 330 695-7147
　Apple Creek *(G-474)*

Western Kentucky Coal Co LLC............. D 740 338-3334
　Saint Clairsville *(G-11715)*

1094 Uranium-radium-vanadium ores

Centrus Energy Corp.......................... D 740 897-2217
　Piketon *(G-11306)*

12 COAL MINING

1221 Bituminous coal and lignite-surface mining

Anthony Mining Co Inc........................ G 740 282-5301
　Wintersville *(G-14610)*

B&N Coal Inc..................................... E 740 783-3575
　Dexter City *(G-6224)*

Buckingham Coal Company LLC............D
　Zanesville *(G-15002)*

Coal Resources Inc............................ E 216 765-1240
　Saint Clairsville *(G-11689)*

Coal Services Inc............................... B 740 795-5220
　Powhatan Point *(G-11497)*

Commercial Minerals Inc..................... G 330 549-2165
　North Lima *(G-10706)*

D & D Mining Co Inc........................... F 330 549-3127
　New Springfield *(G-10472)*

Franklin County Coal Company............. C 740 338-3100
　Saint Clairsville *(G-11692)*

Harrison County Coal Company............. F 740 338-3100
　Saint Clairsville *(G-11693)*

Holmes Limestone Co......................... G 330 893-2721
　Berlin *(G-1198)*

Ivi Mining Group Ltd.......................... G 740 418-7745
　Vinton *(G-13623)*

J & D Mining Inc................................ G 330 339-4935
　New Philadelphia *(G-10450)*

Kimble Company................................ C 330 343-1226
　Dover *(G-6250)*

L & M Mineral Co............................... G 330 852-3696
　Sugarcreek *(G-12640)*

Marietta Coal Co............................... E 740 695-2197
　Saint Clairsville *(G-11695)*

McElroy Coal Company....................... F 724 485-4000
　Saint Clairsville *(G-11699)*

Meigs County Coal Company................ C 740 338-3100
　Saint Clairsville *(G-11700)*

Muhlenberg County Coal Co LLC........... D 740 338-3100
　Saint Clairsville *(G-11701)*

Murray American Energy Inc................ C 740 338-3100
　Saint Clairsville *(G-11702)*

Nacco Industries Inc.......................... E 440 229-5151
　Cleveland *(G-4056)*

Oxford Mining Company Inc................. C 740 588-0190
　Zanesville *(G-15037)*

Oxford Mining Company Inc................. G 740 622-6302
　Coshocton *(G-5468)*

Oxford Mining Company LLC................ F 740 622-6302
　Coshocton *(G-5469)*

Oxford Mining Company - KY LLC.......... E 740 622-6302
　Coshocton *(G-5470)*

Rayle Coal Co.................................... F 740 695-2197
　Saint Clairsville *(G-11708)*

Rosebud Mining Company................... D 740 768-2275
　Bergholz *(G-1196)*

Thompson Bros Mining Co................... F 330 549-3979
　New Springfield *(G-10474)*

Valley Mining Inc............................... C 740 922-3942
　Dennison *(G-6220)*

Washington County Coal Company....... B 740 338-3100
　Saint Clairsville *(G-11714)*

Waterloo Coal Company Inc................. D 740 286-0004
　Jackson *(G-7955)*

Westmoreland Resources Gp LLC........ E 740 622-6302
　Coshocton *(G-5475)*

1222 Bituminous coal-underground mining

Coal Services Inc............................... B 740 795-5220
　Powhatan Point *(G-11497)*

Ivi Mining Group Ltd.......................... G 740 418-7745
　Vinton *(G-13623)*

Kenamerican Resources Inc................ C 740 338-3100
　Saint Clairsville *(G-11694)*

Murray Kentucky Energy Inc................ F 740 338-3100
　Saint Clairsville *(G-11703)*

Rosebud Mining Company................... D 740 768-2275
　Bergholz *(G-1196)*

Sterling Mining Corporation................. F 330 549-2165
　North Lima *(G-10714)*

Utahamerican Energy Inc.................... C 435 888-4000
　Powhatan Point *(G-11498)*

Western KY Coal Resources LLC........... E 740 338-3100
　Saint Clairsville *(G-11717)*

1231 Anthracite mining

◆ Carbon Enterprises Inc....................G 740 420-6472
　Circleville *(G-3249)*

Coal Services Inc............................... B 740 795-5220
　Powhatan Point *(G-11497)*

1241 Coal mining services

American Cnsld Ntral Rsrces In............. E 740 338-3100
　Saint Clairsville *(G-11685)*

American Coal Company..................... D 740 338-3334
　Saint Clairsville *(G-11686)*

Appalachian Fuels LLC....................... C 606 928-0460
　Dublin *(G-6276)*

Coal Services Inc............................... B 740 795-5220
　Powhatan Point *(G-11497)*

▼ Global Coal Sales Group LLC........... G 614 221-0101
　Dublin *(G-6298)*

Marshall Cnty Coal Rsources Inc.......... F 740 338-3100
　Saint Clairsville *(G-11698)*

Ohio Valley Coal Company.................. B 740 926-1351
　Saint Clairsville *(G-11706)*

Rosebud Mining Company .... D ... 740 658-4217
  Freeport **(G-7089)**

Strata Mine Services LLC .... F ... 740 695-0488
  Saint Clairsville **(G-11713)**

Suncoke Energy Inc .... E ... 513 727-5571
  Middletown **(G-9895)**

Terradyn Corporation .... F ... 614 805-0897
  Dublin **(G-6355)**

Western KY Cnsld Resources LLC .... G ... 740 338-3100
  Saint Clairsville **(G-11716)**

Western KY Resources Fing LLC .... G ... 740 338-3100
  Saint Clairsville **(G-11718)**

13 OIL AND GAS EXTRACTION

1311 Crude petroleum and natural gas

Andeavor Logistics LP .... F ... 419 421-2414
  Findlay **(G-6837)**

Apache Acquisitions LLC .... G ... 419 782-8003
  Defiance **(G-6096)**

Bakerwell Inc .... E ... 330 276-2161
  Killbuck **(G-8130)**

Bijoe Development Inc .... E ... 330 674-5981
  Millersburg **(G-9971)**

BP Products North America Inc .... F ... 419 698-6400
  Oregon **(G-10959)**

Brendel Producing Company .... G ... 330 854-4151
  Canton **(G-1844)**

Buckeye Energy Resources Inc .... G ... 740 452-9506
  Zanesville **(G-15001)**

Buckeye Oil Producing Co .... F ... 330 264-8847
  Wooster **(G-14629)**

Cameron Drilling Co Inc .... G ... 740 453-3300
  Zanesville **(G-15003)**

Cgas Exploration Inc .... F ... 614 436-4631
  Worthington **(G-14705)**

Cgas Inc .... G ... 614 975-4697
  Worthington **(G-14706)**

City of Lancaster .... E ... 740 687-6670
  Lancaster **(G-8188)**

D & L Energy Inc .... G ... 330 270-1201
  Canton **(G-1876)**

Derrick Petroleum Inc .... G ... 740 668-5711
  Bladensburg **(G-1232)**

Dome Drilling Company .... G ... 440 892-9434
  Westlake **(G-14299)**

Elkhead Gas & Oil Co .... G ... 740 763-3966
  Newark **(G-10500)**

Enrevo Pyro LLC .... G ... 203 517-5002
  Brookfield **(G-1514)**

Everflow Eastern Partners LP .... G ... 330 533-2692
  Canfield **(G-1809)**

Exco Resources (pa) LLC .... F ... 740 796-5231
  Adamsville **(G-7)**

Exco Resources LLC .... F ... 740 254-4061
  Tippecanoe **(G-12856)**

Franklin Gas & Oil Company LLC .... G ... 330 264-8739
  Wooster **(G-14638)**

G-R Contracting Inc .... F ... 740 567-3202
  Lewisville **(G-8366)**

General Electric Company .... G ... 330 425-3755
  Twinsburg **(G-13311)**

Green Energy Inc .... G ... 330 262-5112
  Wooster **(G-14644)**

Interstate Gas Supply LLC .... C ... 877 995-4447
  Dublin **(G-6311)**

JMB Energy Inc .... G ... 330 505-9610
  Mineral Ridge **(G-10029)**

John D Oil and Gas Company .... G ... 440 255-6325
  Mentor **(G-9543)**

Kenoil Inc .... G ... 330 262-1144
  Wooster **(G-14657)**

◆ Knight Material Tech LLC .... E ... 330 488-1651
  East Canton **(G-6378)**

Marietta Resources Corporation .... F ... 740 373-6305
  Marietta **(G-8927)**

Pin Oak Energy Partners LLC .... F ... 888 748-0763
  Akron **(G-258)**

R D Holder Oil Co Inc .... F ... 740 522-3136
  Heath **(G-7602)**

RCM Engineering Company .... G ... 330 666-0575
  Akron **(G-279)**

Sairam Oil Inc .... G ... 440 289-8232
  Parma **(G-11135)**

Sheridan One Stop Carryout Inc .... G ... 740 687-1300
  Lancaster **(G-8223)**

Stocker & Sitler Oil Company .... G ... 614 888-9588
  Columbus **(G-5294)**

Temple Oil and Gas LLC .... G ... 740 452-7878
  Crooksville **(G-5513)**

Ultra-Met Company .... F ... 937 653-7133
  Urbana **(G-13480)**

W H Patten Drilling Co Inc .... G ... 330 674-3046
  Millersburg **(G-10017)**

W P Brown Enterprises Inc .... G ... 740 685-2594
  Byesville **(G-1718)**

William S Miller Inc .... G ... 330 223-1794
  Kensington **(G-8011)**

Williams Partners LP .... D ... 330 414-6201
  North Canton **(G-10681)**

Xto Energy Inc .... G ... 740 671-9901
  Bellaire **(G-1090)**

1321 Natural gas liquids

Consolidated Gas Coop Inc .... G ... 419 946-6600
  Mount Gilead **(G-10209)**

Husky Marketing and Supply Co .... E ... 419 993-8000
  Lima **(G-8417)**

Markwest Energy Partners LP .... F ... 740 942-0463
  Cadiz **(G-1719)**

Markwest Energy Partners LP .... G ... 800 730-8388
  Jewett **(G-7989)**

Markwest Energy Partners LP .... F ... 740 838-1434
  Summerfield **(G-12660)**

RCM Engineering Company .... G ... 330 666-0575
  Akron **(G-279)**

1381 Drilling oil and gas wells

Artex Oil Company .... E ... 740 373-3313
  Marietta **(G-8902)**

Bakerwell Service Rigs Inc .... F ... 330 276-2161
  Killbuck **(G-8131)**

Brendel Producing Company .... G ... 330 854-4151
  Canton **(G-1844)**

Buckeye Oil Producing Co .... F ... 330 264-8847
  Wooster **(G-14629)**

Clearpath Utlity Solutions LLC .... F ... 740 661-4240
  Hebron **(G-7610)**

Decker Drilling Inc .... G ... 740 749-3939
  Vincent **(G-13620)**

Directional One Svcs Inc USA .... G ... 740 371-5031
  Marietta **(G-8913)**

Dugan Drilling Inc .... G ... 740 668-3811
  Walhonding **(G-13692)**

Eclipse Resources - Ohio LLC .... G ... 740 452-4503
  Zanesville **(G-15012)**

Fortis Energy Services Inc .... D ... 248 283-7100
  Saint Clairsville **(G-11691)**

Frank Csapo .... G ... 330 435-4458
  Creston **(G-5506)**

Groundhogs 2000 LLC .... G ... 440 653-1647
  Bedford **(G-1033)**

Hocking Hlls Enrgy Well Svcs L .... G ... 740 385-6690
  Logan **(G-8515)**

J D Drilling Company .... G ... 740 949-2512
  Racine **(G-11504)**

Jackson Wells Services .... F ... 419 886-2017
  Bellville **(G-1139)**

James R Smail Inc .... G ... 330 264-7500
  Wooster **(G-14654)**

Kilbarger Construction Inc .... C ... 740 385-6019
  Logan **(G-8518)**

Kirk Excavating & Construction .... E ... 614 444-4008
  Columbus **(G-5054)**

Mattmark Partners Inc .... F ... 740 439-3109
  Cambridge **(G-1748)**

Moore Well Services Inc .... F ... 330 650-4443
  Mogadore **(G-10080)**

Nomac Drilling LLC .... C ... 724 324-2205
  Saint Clairsville **(G-11704)**

Osair Inc .... G ... 440 974-6500
  Mentor **(G-9577)**

Petro Quest Inc .... G ... 740 593-3800
  Athens **(G-645)**

Temple Oil and Gas LLC .... G ... 740 452-7878
  Crooksville **(G-5513)**

Timco Inc .... G ... 740 685-2594
  Byesville **(G-1716)**

Viking Well Service Inc .... G ... 681 205-1999
  Lore City **(G-8589)**

Warren Drilling Co Inc .... G ... 740 783-2775
  Dexter City **(G-6225)**

Warthman Drilling Inc .... G ... 740 746-9950
  Sugar Grove **(G-12630)**

1382 Oil and gas exploration services

AB Resources LLC .... E ... 440 922-1098
  Brecksville **(G-1455)**

Antero Resources Corporation .... E ... 303 357-7310
  Caldwell **(G-1722)**

Antero Resources Corporation .... D ... 740 760-1000
  Marietta **(G-8901)**

BD Oil Gathering Corp .... E ... 740 374-9355
  Marietta **(G-8903)**

Beck Energy Corporation .... E ... 330 297-6891
  Ravenna **(G-11517)**

Blue Racer Midstream LLC .... F ... 740 630-7556
  Cambridge **(G-1737)**

Canton Oil Well Service Inc .... F ... 330 494-1221
  Canton **(G-1858)**

Cgas Exploration Inc .... F ... 614 436-4631
  Worthington **(C-14705)**

David R Hill Inc .... G ... 740 685-5168
  Byesville **(G-1708)**

Diversified Production LLC .... C ... 740 373-8771
  Marietta **(G-8914)**

Dlz Ohio Inc .... C ... 614 888-0040
  Columbus **(G-4887)**

Dome Drilling Company .... G ... 440 892-9434
  Westlake **(G-14299)**

Elkhead Gas & Oil Co .... G ... 740 763-3966
  Newark **(G-10500)**

Everflow Eastern Partners LP .... G ... 330 533-2692
  Canfield **(G-1809)**

G&O Resources Ltd .... G ... 330 253-2525
  Akron **(G-153)**

Gonzoil Inc .... G ... 330 497-5888
  Canton **(G-1903)**

Hocking Hlls Enrgy Well Svcs L .... G ... 740 385-6690
  Logan **(G-8515)**

John D Oil and Gas Company .... G ... 440 255-6325
  Mentor **(G-9543)**

K Petroleum Inc .... F ... 614 532-5420
  Gahanna **(G-7161)**

Knox Energy Inc .... F ... 740 927-6731
  Pataskala **(G-11143)**

S I C

Lake Region Oil Inc..................G 330 828-8420
Dalton *(G-5587)*

M3 Midstream LLC..................E 330 223-2220
Kensington *(G-8010)*

M3 Midstream LLC..................E 330 679-5580
Salineville *(G-11818)*

M3 Midstream LLC..................E 740 945-1170
Scio *(G-11888)*

MFC Drilling Inc..................F 740 622-5600
Coshocton *(G-5460)*

Mori Shuji..................G 614 459-1296
Columbus *(G-5111)*

New World Energy Resources..................F 740 344-4087
Newark *(G-10525)*

Ngo Development Corporation..................G 740 622-9560
Coshocton *(G-5464)*

Northwood Energy Corporation..................F 614 457-1024
Columbus *(G-5131)*

▲ Powder Alloy Corporation..................E 513 984-4016
Loveland *(G-8646)*

Precision Geophysical Inc..................E 330 674-2198
Millersburg *(G-10005)*

Prominence Energy Corporation..................G 513 818-8329
Cincinnati *(G-3008)*

Quantum Energy LLC..................F 440 285-7381
Chardon *(G-2219)*

Reserve Energy Exploration Co..................G 440 543-0770
Chagrin Falls *(G-2180)*

Silcor Oilfield Services Inc..................G 330 448-8500
Brookfield *(G-1518)*

Triad Energy Corporation..................G 740 374-2940
Marietta *(G-8956)*

True North Energy LLC..................E 440 442-0060
Mayfield Heights *(G-9343)*

Unlimited Energy Services LLC..................F 304 517-7097
Beverly *(G-1210)*

Utica East Ohio Midstream LLC..................C 740 431-4168
Dennison *(G-6219)*

Whitacre Enterprises Inc..................G 740 934-2331
Graysville *(G-7322)*

Zane Petroleum Inc..................F 740 454-8779
Columbus *(G-5379)*

1389 Oil and gas field services, nec

A1 Industrial Painting Inc..................E 330 750-9441
Youngstown *(G-14801)*

Acid Development LLC..................G 330 502-4164
Youngstown *(G-14805)*

Adapt Oil..................G 330 658-1482
Doylestown *(G-6269)*

Aim Services Company..................E 800 321-9038
Girard *(G-7263)*

Aj Enterprise LLC..................F 740 231-2205
Zanesville *(G-14984)*

All Trades Contractors LLC..................G 440 850-5693
Cleveland *(G-3328)*

Altier Brothers Inc..................G 740 347-4329
Corning *(G-5440)*

American Egle Prprty Prsrvtion..................G 855 440-6938
North Ridgeville *(G-10724)*

Appalachian Oilfield Svcs LLC..................F 337 216-0066
Sardis *(G-11887)*

Appalachian Well Surveys Inc..................G 740 255-7652
Cambridge *(G-1736)*

Artisan Constructors LLC..................E 216 800-7641
Cleveland *(G-3370)*

Bakerwell Inc..................E 330 276-2161
Killbuck *(G-8130)*

Barnes Services LLC..................G 440 319-2088
Maple Heights *(G-8877)*

Bijoe Development Inc..................E 330 674-5981
Millersburg *(G-9971)*

Bishop Well Services Corp..................G 330 264-2023
Wooster *(G-14626)*

Bismark Lawncare LLC..................F 440 361-5561
Austinburg *(G-696)*

Blue Fin Environmental LLC..................G 330 415-6010
Springboro *(G-12247)*

Brightstar Propane & Fuels..................G 614 891-8395
Westerville *(G-14204)*

Bunnell Hill Construction Inc..................F 513 932-6010
Lebanon *(G-8248)*

Care Industries..................G 614 584-6595
Grove City *(G-7376)*

Carper Well Service Inc..................F 740 374-2567
Marietta *(G-8907)*

CDK Perforating LLC..................D 817 862-9834
Marietta *(G-8908)*

Circleville Oil Co..................G 740 477-3341
Circleville *(G-3251)*

Commercial Cnstr Group LLC..................E 513 722-8952
Milford *(G-9930)*

Complete Energy Services Inc..................F 440 577-1070
Pierpont *(G-11304)*

Completeenergy Services..................F 440 576-6000
Pierpont *(G-11305)*

Concrete One Construction LLC..................F 740 595-9680
Delaware *(G-6140)*

Crescent Services LLC..................G 405 603-1200
Cambridge *(G-1740)*

Critical Ctrl Enrgy Svcs Inc..................F 330 539-4267
Girard *(G-7269)*

Diamond Oilfield Tech LLC..................G 234 806-4185
Warren *(G-13758)*

Dollars N Cent Inc..................F 971 381-0406
Cleveland *(G-3623)*

Dow Cameron Oil & Gas LLC..................G 740 452-1568
Zanesville *(G-15011)*

Eavan Corp..................F 216 401-8619
Olmsted Twp *(G-10945)*

Elite Property Group LLC..................F 216 356-7469
Elyria *(G-6527)*

Endless Home Improvements LLC..................G 614 599-1799
Columbus *(G-4901)*

EP Ferris & Associates Inc..................E 614 299-2999
Columbus *(G-4906)*

Everflow Eastern Partners LP..................G 330 537-3863
Salem *(G-11778)*

Express Energy Svcs Oper LP..................E 740 337-4530
Toronto *(G-13185)*

Facility Service Pros LLC..................G 419 577-6123
Collins *(G-4587)*

Formation Cementing Inc..................G 740 453-6926
Zanesville *(G-15015)*

Full Circle Oil Field Svcs Inc..................G 740 371-5422
Whipple *(G-14356)*

Gdn Welding LLC..................E 740 398-6109
Danville *(G-5599)*

Genco..................G 419 207-7648
Ashland *(G-536)*

Global Energy Partners LLC..................E 419 756-8027
Mansfield *(G-8792)*

Grand Archt Etrnl Eye 314 LLC..................F 800 377-8147
Cleveland *(G-3783)*

Gws Levi Up Home Solutions LLC..................E 419 667-6041
Toledo *(G-12979)*

Halliburton Energy Svcs Inc..................F 740 617-2917
Zanesville *(G-15018)*

Handshakers Construction LLC..................F 513 370-1371
Cincinnati *(G-2704)*

Holly Robakowski..................G 440 854-9317
Cleveland *(G-3834)*

Ingle-Barr Inc..................D 740 702-6117
Chillicothe *(G-2261)*

Inland Tarp & Liner LLC..................E 419 436-6001
Fostoria *(G-6984)*

Inline Undgrd Hrzntal Drctnal..................G 740 808-0316
Bremen *(G-1486)*

J-Well Service Inc..................G 330 824-2718
Warren *(G-13774)*

Jason Poffenberger..................G 937 369-1358
Dayton *(G-5827)*

JT Plus Well Service LLC..................F 740 347-0070
Corning *(G-5441)*

Kbc Services..................F 513 693-3743
Loveland *(G-8634)*

Kelchner Inc..................D 937 704-9890
Springboro *(G-12258)*

Killbuck Oil and Gas LLC..................G 330 447-8423
Akron *(G-195)*

Klx Energy Services LLC..................E 740 922-1155
Midvale *(G-9912)*

Kross Acquisition Company LLC..................E 513 554-0555
Loveland *(G-8636)*

L & S Home Improvement..................G 330 906-3199
Coventry Township *(G-5486)*

L Brown Loans & Investments..................G 216 308-1820
Cleveland *(G-3932)*

Leak Finder Inc..................G 440 735-0130
Hudson *(G-7849)*

Lubrisource Inc..................F 937 432-9292
Middletown *(G-9872)*

Mac Oil Field Service Inc..................G 330 674-7371
Millersburg *(G-9996)*

Markwest Energy Partners LP..................F 740 838-1434
Summerfield *(G-12660)*

MB Renovations & Designs LLC..................G 614 772-6139
Columbus *(G-5088)*

MGM Construction Inc..................G 440 234-7660
Berea *(G-1182)*

Oaktree Wireline LLC..................G 330 352-7250
New Philadelphia *(G-10461)*

Ohio Building Restoration Inc..................E 419 244-7372
Toledo *(G-13073)*

Omega Cementing Co..................G 330 695-7147
Apple Creek *(G-474)*

Omnipresence Cleaning LLC..................F 937 250-4749
Dayton *(G-5927)*

Ottawa Oil Co Inc..................F 419 425-3301
Findlay *(G-6905)*

Panhandle Olfld Svc Cmpnies In..................E 330 340-9525
Cambridge *(G-1754)*

Paragon Intgrted Svcs Group LL..................E 724 639-5126
Newcomerstown *(G-10574)*

Performance Technologies LLC..................D 330 875-1216
Louisville *(G-8613)*

Personnel Selection Services..................F 440 835-3255
Cleveland *(G-4153)*

Petrox Inc..................F 330 653-5526
Streetsboro *(G-12516)*

Primo Services LLC..................F 513 725-7888
Cincinnati *(G-2982)*

Producers Service Corporation..................D 740 454-6253
Zanesville *(G-15044)*

Prospect Rock LLC..................F 740 512-0542
Saint Clairsville *(G-11707)*

PSC Holdings Inc..................F 740 454-6253
Zanesville *(G-15045)*

R Anthony Enterprises LLC..................F 419 341-0961
Marion *(G-8991)*

Radon Eliminator LLC..................F 330 844-0703
North Canton *(G-10662)*

Ralph Robinson Inc..................G 740 385-2747
Logan *(G-8524)*

RDM Equipment Company Inc..................F 330 264-8808
Wooster *(G-14675)*

Ream and Haager Laboratory Inc.......... F 330 343-3711
Dover (G-6259)

Recon.. F 740 609-3050
Bridgeport (G-1495)

Ruscilli Real Estate Services................ F 614 923-6400
Dublin (G-6341)

Siler Excavation Services.................... E 513 400-8628
Milford (G-9953)

Stocker & Sitler Oil Company.............. G 614 888-9588
Columbus (G-5294)

Superior Energy Group Ltd................. E 216 282-4440
Willoughby Hills (G-14563)

Superior Property Restoration.............. F 513 509-6849
Cincinnati (G-3129)

Third Salvo Company........................ G 740 818-9669
Amesville (G-443)

TJ Oil & Gas Inc............................. G 740 623-0190
Fresno (G-7150)

Tk Gas Services Inc......................... E 740 826-0303
New Concord (G-10387)

Tkn Oilfield Services LLC.................... F 740 516-2583
Marietta (G-8955)

U S Weatherford L P......................... C 330 746-2502
Youngstown (G-14955)

United Chart Processors Inc................ G 740 373-5801
Marietta (G-8957)

Universal Well Services Inc................. D 814 333-2656
Millersburg (G-10016)

Vam Usa Llc................................. E 330 742-3130
Youngstown (G-14958)

Varco LP..................................... E 330 746-2922
Youngstown (G-14959)

Vigilante Love LLC........................... F 380 258-5983
Columbus (G-5349)

W Pole Contracting Inc...................... F 330 325-7177
Ravenna (G-11548)

Washita Valley Enterprises Inc............. F 330 510-1568
Louisville (G-8618)

◆ Westerman Inc............................C 800 338-8265
Bremen (G-1488)

Wooster Abruzzi Company................. E 330 345-3968
Wooster (G-14698)

Wrights Well Service LLC.................... G 740 380-9602
Logan (G-8528)

Wyoming Casing Service Inc............... D 330 479-8785
Canton (G-2049)

14 MINING AND QUARRYING OF NONMETALLIC MINERALS, EXCEPT FUELS

1411 Dimension stone

▲ Designer Stone Co........................ G 740 492-1300
Port Washington (G-11456)

Gregory Stone Co Inc....................... G 937 275-7455
Dayton (G-5805)

Helmart Company Inc....................... G 513 941-3095
Cincinnati (G-2715)

Irg Operating LLC........................... E 440 963-4008
Vermilion (G-13590)

National Lime and Stone Co................ E 419 562-0771
Bucyrus (G-1684)

North Hill Marble & Granite Co............. F 330 253-2179
Akron (G-249)

Ohio Beauty Cut Stone II Inc.............. G 330 644-2241
Akron (G-251)

Solid Surface Concepts Inc................ E 513 948-8677
Cincinnati (G-3099)

▲ Stone Statements Incorporated......... G 513 489-7866
Cincinnati (G-3120)

Stoneco Inc.................................. E 419 422-8854
Findlay (G-6923)

Waterloo Coal Company Inc................ D 740 286-0004
Jackson (G-7955)

Wyandot Dolomite Inc....................... E 419 396-7641
Carey (G-2064)

1422 Crushed and broken limestone

Acme Company.............................. D 330 758-2313
Poland (G-11434)

Allgeier & Son Inc........................... F 513 574-3735
Cincinnati (G-2351)

Ayers Limestone Quarry Inc................ F 740 633-2958
Martins Ferry (G-9009)

Beazer East Inc............................. E 937 364-2311
Hillsboro (G-7714)

Bluffton Stone Co........................... F 419 358-6941
Bluffton (G-1358)

Carmeuse Lime Inc.......................... D 419 986-5200
Bettsville (G-1207)

Carmeuse Lime Inc.......................... F 419 638-2511
Millersville (G-10027)

Carmeuse Lime Inc.......................... F 419 986-2000
Tiffin (G-12779)

Conag Inc................................... G 419 394-8870
Saint Marys (G-11736)

Cumberland Limestone LLC................. E 740 638-3942
Cumberland (G-5516)

Custar Stone Co............................. E 419 669-4327
Napoleon (G-10277)

Drummond Dolomite Inc.................... F 440 942-7000
Mentor (G-9511)

Duff Quarry Inc.............................. F 419 273-2518
Forest (G-6940)

Duff Quarry Inc.............................. F 937 686-2811
Huntsville (G-7863)

Feikert Sand & Gravel Co Inc.............. E 330 674-0038
Millersburg (G-9980)

Heidelberg Mtls Mdwest Agg Inc.......... E 419 983-2211
Bloomville (G-1240)

Heidelberg Mtls Mdwest Agg Inc.......... F 419 882-0123
Sylvania (G-12708)

Kellstone Inc................................ E 419 746-2396
Kelleys Island (G-8009)

▲ Lang Stone Company Inc................. E 614 235-4099
Columbus (G-5064)

Latham Limestone LLC...................... G 740 493-2677
Latham (G-8235)

Marietta Martin Materials Inc............... G 740 247-2211
Racine (G-11505)

Marietta Martin Materials Inc............... G 937 335-8313
Troy (G-13239)

Martin Marietta Materials Inc.............. F 513 701-1120
Mason (G-9124)

Martin Marietta Materials Inc.............. F 513 701-1140
West Chester (G-14026)

National Lime and Stone Co................ E 419 562-0771
Bucyrus (G-1684)

National Lime and Stone Co................ E 419 396-7671
Carey (G-2060)

National Lime and Stone Co................ E 740 548-4206
Delaware (G-6163)

National Lime and Stone Co................ E 419 423-3400
Findlay (G-6897)

National Lime and Stone Co................ F 419 228-3434
Lima (G-8435)

National Lime and Stone Co................ E 740 387-3485
Marion (G-8983)

National Lime and Stone Co................ E 330 966-4836
North Canton (G-10656)

National Lime and Stone Co................ G 419 657-6745
Wapakoneta (G-13726)

Oglebay Norton Mar Svcs Co LLC......... A 216 861-3300
Cleveland (G-4109)

Ohio Asphaltic Limestone Corp............ F 937 364-2191
Hillsboro (G-7721)

◆ Omya Industries Inc.......................D 513 387-4600
Mason (G-9133)

Oster Sand and Gravel Inc................. G 330 833-2649
Massillon (G-9229)

Piqua Materials Inc.......................... D 937 773-4824
Piqua (G-11377)

Piqua Materials Inc.......................... E 513 771-0820
Cincinnati (G-2964)

R W Sidley Incorporated.................... E 440 352-9343
Painesville (G-11108)

Ridge Township Stone Quarry.............. G 419 968-2222
Van Wert (G-13544)

Sharon Stone Inc............................ G 740 732-7100
Caldwell (G-1728)

Shelly Company.............................. G 216 688-0684
Cleveland (G-4291)

Shelly Materials Inc......................... E 740 666-5841
Ostrander (G-11029)

Shelly Materials Inc......................... E 740 246-6315
Toledo (G-13130)

Shelly Materials Inc......................... D 740 246-6315
Thornville (G-12770)

Sidwell Materials Inc........................ C 740 849-2422
Zanesville (G-15050)

Stoneco Inc.................................. E 419 893-7645
Maumee (G-9321)

Stoneco Inc.................................. E 419 393-2555
Oakwood (G-10900)

Stoneco Inc.................................. G 419 686-3311
Portage (G-11461)

The National Lime and Stone Company. E 419 422-4341
Findlay (G-6927)

Uniontown Stone............................. G 740 968-4313
Flushing (G-6937)

Wagner Quarries Company................. E 419 625-8141
Sandusky (G-11883)

Wyandot Dolomite Inc....................... E 419 396-7641
Carey (G-2064)

1423 Crushed and broken granite

Bradley Stone Industries LLC............... F 440 519-3277
Solon (G-12088)

Martin Marietta Materials Inc.............. F 513 701-1140
West Chester (G-14026)

The National Lime and Stone Company. E 419 422-4341
Findlay (G-6927)

1429 Crushed and broken stone, nec

Great Lakes Crushing Ltd.................... D 440 944-5500
Wickliffe (G-14376)

M & B Asphalt Company Inc................ F 419 992-4235
Tiffin (G-12787)

Medina Supply Company.................... D 330 364-4411
Medina (G-9425)

1442 Construction sand and gravel

Arden J Neer Sr............................. F 937 585-6733
Bellefontaine (G-1099)

Beck Sand & Gravel Inc.................... G 330 626-3863
Ravenna (G-11518)

Bonsal American Inc........................ E 513 398-7300
Cincinnati (G-2417)

Broadway Sand and Gravel LLC........... G 937 853-5555
Dayton (G-5686)

C F Poeppelman Inc........................ E 937 448-2191
Bradford (G-1451)

Canton Asphalt Co.......................... G 330 499-6888
Canton (G-1852)

SIC

Central Allied Enterprises Inc.............. E 330 477-6751
   Canton *(G-1862)*

Central Ready Mix LLC.......................... E 513 402-5001
   Cincinnati *(G-2451)*

Constrction Aggrgtes Corp Mich.......... E 616 842-7900
   Independence *(G-7893)*

▼ Covia Solutions LLC.......................... G 440 214-3200
   Independence *(G-7895)*

D H Bowman & Sons Inc...................... G 419 886-2711
   Bellville *(G-1137)*

Demilta Sand and Gravel Inc............... F 440 942-2015
   Willoughby *(G-14446)*

Demmy Sand and Gravel LLC.............. E
   Springfield *(G-12301)*

Feikert Sand & Gravel Co Inc.............. E 330 674-0038
   Millersburg *(G-9980)*

Fisher Sand & Gravel Inc..................... G 330 745-9239
   Norton *(G-10822)*

Fleming Construction Co....................... F 740 494-2177
   Prospect *(G-11501)*

FML Terminal Logistics LLC................ F 440 214-3200
   Independence *(G-7904)*

Foundry Sand Service LLC................... F 330 823-6152
   Sebring *(G-11894)*

Fouremans Sand & Gravel Inc............. G 937 547-1005
   Greenville *(G-7341)*

Hanson Aggregates East...................... G 513 353-1100
   Cleves *(G-4538)*

Hilltop Basic Resources Inc................. C 513 621-1500
   Cincinnati *(G-2723)*

Hilltop Basic Resources Inc................. G 937 859-3616
   Miamisburg *(G-9699)*

Hilltop Basic Resources Inc................. G 937 882-6357
   Springfield *(G-12322)*

Hocking Valley Concrete Inc................ F 740 385-2165
   Logan *(G-8516)*

Holmes Redimix Inc.............................. E 330 674-0865
   Holmesville *(G-7797)*

Holmes Supply Corp.............................. G 330 279-2634
   Holmesville *(G-7799)*

Hugo Sand Company.............................. G 216 570-1212
   Kent *(G-8036)*

James Bunnell Inc................................. F 513 353-1100
   Cleves *(G-4540)*

▲ John R Jurgensen Co........................ B 513 771-0820
   Cincinnati *(G-2768)*

Kenmore Construction Co Inc.............. D 330 832-8888
   Massillon *(G-9211)*

Kirby and Sons Inc............................... F 419 927-2260
   Upper Sandusky *(G-13445)*

Lakeside Sand & Gravel Inc................ E 330 274-2569
   Mantua *(G-8870)*

Martin Marietta Materials Inc.............. F 513 701-1140
   West Chester *(G-14026)*

Masons Sand and Gravel Co................ G 614 491-3611
   Obetz *(G-10924)*

Massillon Materials Inc........................ F 330 837-4767
   Dalton *(G-5589)*

McClelland Inc...................................... E 740 452-3036
   Zanesville *(G-15027)*

Mechanicsburg Sand & Gravel............ G 937 834-2606
   Mechanicsburg *(G-9367)*

Medina Supply Company....................... E 330 723-3681
   Medina *(G-9426)*

Morrow Gravel Company Inc................ F 513 899-2000
   Morrow *(G-10202)*

Morrow Gravel Company Inc................ E 513 771-0820
   Cincinnati *(G-2889)*

National Lime and Stone Co................ E 419 396-7671
   Carey *(G-2060)*

National Lime and Stone Co................ F 614 497-0083
   Lockbourne *(G-8491)*

Nelson Sand & Gravel Inc.................... F 440 224-0198
   Kingsville *(G-8139)*

Oscar Brugmann Sand & Gravel.......... E 330 274-8224
   Mantua *(G-8874)*

Oster Sand and Gravel Inc.................. G 330 874-3322
   Bolivar *(G-1387)*

Oster Sand and Gravel Inc.................. G 330 833-2649
   Massillon *(G-9229)*

Oster Sand and Gravel Inc.................. G 330 494-5472
   Canton *(G-1970)*

Phillips Companies................................ E 937 426-5461
   Beavercreek Township *(G-1003)*

Phoenix Asphalt Company Inc............. G 330 339-4935
   Magnolia *(G-8736)*

Portable Crushing LLC........................... G 330 618-5251
   New Franklin *(G-10393)*

Prairie Lane Corporation...................... G 330 262-3322
   Wooster *(G-14672)*

Putnam Aggregrates Co........................ G 419 523-6004
   Ottawa *(G-11043)*

R W Sidley Incorporated...................... E 440 564-2221
   Newbury *(G-10561)*

Rjw Trucking Company Ltd................... E 740 363-5343
   Delaware *(G-6169)*

Rupp Construction Inc........................... F 330 855-2781
   Marshallville *(G-9008)*

S & S Aggregates Inc........................... C 419 938-5604
   Perrysville *(G-11283)*

S & S Aggregates Inc........................... F 740 453-0721
   Zanesville *(G-15046)*

Seville Sand & Gravel Inc................... E 330 948-0168
   Strongsville *(G-12597)*

Shelly and Sands Inc............................ F 740 453-0721
   Zanesville *(G-15047)*

Shelly Materials Inc.............................. F 740 247-2311
   Racine *(G-11506)*

Shelly Materials Inc.............................. D 740 246-6315
   Thornville *(G-12770)*

Smith Concrete Co................................ E 740 373-7441
   Dover *(G-6262)*

Stafford Gravel Inc.............................. G 419 298-2440
   Edgerton *(G-6470)*

Stansley Mineral Resources Inc.......... E 419 843-2813
   Sylvania *(G-12724)*

Stocker Concrete Company................... F 740 254-4626
   Gnadenhutten *(G-7293)*

Stocker Sand & Gravel Co.................... F 740 254-4635
   Gnadenhutten *(G-7294)*

Streamside Materials Llc...................... G 419 423-1290
   Findlay *(G-6924)*

The National Lime and Stone Company. E 419 422-4341
   Findlay *(G-6927)*

The Olen Corporation............................ D 614 491-1515
   Columbus *(G-5321)*

Tiger Sand & Gravel LLC...................... F 330 833-6325
   Massillon *(G-9248)*

Tri County Concrete Inc........................ F 330 425-4464
   Twinsburg *(G-13386)*

Tuffco Sand and Gravel Inc.................. G 614 873-3977
   Plain City *(G-11422)*

W&W Rock Sand and Gravel................ G 513 266-3708
   Williamsburg *(G-14410)*

Ward Construction Co............................ F 419 943-2450
   Leipsic *(G-8316)*

Watson Gravel Inc................................. G 513 422-3781
   Middletown *(G-9902)*

Watson Gravel Inc................................. E 513 863-0070
   Hamilton *(G-7538)*

Wayne Concrete Company LLC............. F 937 545-9919
   Medway *(G-9466)*

Weber Sand & Gravel Inc..................... G 419 636-7920
   Bryan *(G-1666)*

Welch Holdings Inc............................... E 513 353-3220
   Cincinnati *(G-3216)*

Welch Sand & Gravel Inc..................... F 513 353-3220
   Cincinnati *(G-3217)*

Wysong Gravel Co Inc.......................... G 937 452-1523
   Camden *(G-1769)*

Wysong Gravel Co Inc.......................... G 937 839-5497
   West Alexandria *(G-13925)*

Wysong Gravel Co Inc.......................... F 937 456-4539
   West Alexandria *(G-13924)*

X L Sand and Gravel Co....................... G 330 426-9876
   Negley *(G-10316)*

Youngs Sand & Gravel Co Inc............. F 419 994-3040
   Loudonville *(G-8597)*

1446 Industrial sand

▼ CED Process Minerals Inc................ F 330 666-5500
   Akron *(G-94)*

◆ Covia Holdings LLC.......................... D 800 243-9004
   Independence *(G-7894)*

Farsight Management Inc...................... F 330 602-8338
   Dover *(G-6245)*

Wedron Silica LLC................................ D 815 433-2449
   Independence *(G-7924)*

1459 Clay and related minerals, nec

L & M Mineral Co.................................. G 330 852-3696
   Sugarcreek *(G-12640)*

Waterloo Coal Company Inc.................. D 740 286-0004
   Jackson *(G-7955)*

1479 Chemical and fertilizer mining

Glf International Inc............................... F 216 621-6901
   Cleveland *(G-3777)*

1481 Nonmetallic mineral services

Barr Engineering Incorporated............. E 614 714-0299
   Columbus *(G-4744)*

▲ M G Q Inc.. E 419 992-4236
   Tiffin *(G-12788)*

Robin Industries Inc............................. E 330 893-3501
   Berlin *(G-1199)*

Stoepfel Drilling Co.............................. G 419 532-3307
   Ottawa *(G-11048)*

Tresslers Plumbing LLC........................ G 419 784-2142
   Defiance *(G-6126)*

1499 Miscellaneous nonmetallic mining

Graftech Holdings Inc........................... D 216 676-2000
   Independence *(G-7905)*

Scots.. G 215 370-9498
   Shreve *(G-11987)*

The National Lime and Stone Company. E 419 422-4341
   Findlay *(G-6927)*

15 CONSTRUCTION - GENERAL CONTRACTORS & OPERATIVE BUILDERS

1521 Single-family housing construction

Acme Home Improvement Co Inc.......... F 614 252-2129
   Columbus *(G-4671)*

Al Yoder Construction Co..................... G 330 359-5726
   Millersburg *(G-9967)*

Artisan Constructors LLC...................... E 216 800-7641
   Cleveland *(G-3370)*

Building Concepts Inc........................... F 419 298-2371
   Edgerton *(G-6464)*

C-Link Enterprises LLC......................... F 937 222-2829
   Dayton *(G-5692)*

Cardinal Builders Inc............................G..... 614 237-1000
Columbus *(G-4801)*

Clearview Construction LLC.....................G..... 513 206-6415
Cincinnati *(G-2498)*

Custom Blind Corporation......................F..... 937 643-2907
Dayton *(G-5717)*

Fence One Inc.......................................F..... 216 441-2600
Cleveland *(G-3712)*

Gillard Construction Inc.........................F..... 740 376-9744
Marietta *(G-8919)*

Golden Angle Archtctral Group..............G..... 614 531-7932
Columbus *(G-4960)*

GUTTER TOPPER LTD............................G..... 513 797-5800
Batavia *(G-866)*

Gws Levi Up Home Solutions LLC.........E..... 419 667-6041
Toledo *(G-12979)*

Handshakers Construction LLC.............F..... 513 370-1371
Cincinnati *(G-2704)*

▲ Hoge Lumber Company......................E..... 419 753-2263
New Knoxville *(G-10398)*

Ingle-Barr Inc......................................D..... 740 702-6117
Chillicothe *(G-2261)*

JC Electric Llc.....................................F..... 330 760-2915
Garrettsville *(G-7221)*

Knapke Cabinets Inc............................E..... 937 335-8383
Troy *(G-13234)*

Manufactured Housing Entps Inc..........F..... 419 636-4511
Bryan *(G-1650)*

Patio Enclosures..................................F..... 513 733-4646
Cincinnati *(G-2944)*

Plumb Builders Inc...............................F..... 937 293-1111
Dayton *(G-5942)*

R L Waller Construction Inc...................G..... 740 772-6185
Chillicothe *(G-2278)*

RE Connors Construction Ltd................G..... 740 644-0261
Thornville *(G-12767)*

Superior Property Restoration...............F..... 513 509-6849
Cincinnati *(G-3129)*

The Galehouse Companies Inc..............E..... 330 658-2023
Doylestown *(G-6270)*

Third Salvo Company............................G..... 740 818-9669
Amesville *(G-443)*

Thomas J Weaver Inc...........................F..... 740 622-2040
Coshocton *(G-5474)*

Van Dyke Custom Iron Inc.....................G..... 614 860-9300
Pickerington *(G-11302)*

Volpe Millwork Inc................................G..... 216 581-0200
Cleveland *(G-4480)*

Waxco International Inc.........................F..... 937 746-4845
Miamisburg *(G-9752)*

1522 Residential construction, nec

American Egle Prprty Prsrvtion...............G..... 855 440-6938
North Ridgeville *(G-10724)*

Artisan Constructors LLC.......................E..... 216 800-7641
Cleveland *(G-3370)*

Bison Builders LLC................................F..... 614 636-0365
Columbus *(G-4756)*

Cardinal Builders Inc............................G..... 614 237-1000
Columbus *(G-4801)*

1531 Operative builders

Artisan Constructors LLC.......................E..... 216 800-7641
Cleveland *(G-3370)*

Commercial Cnstr Group LLC.................G..... 513 722-8952
Milford *(G-9930)*

Nova Structural Steel Inc.......................E..... 216 938-7476
Cleveland *(G-4100)*

▲ P R Machine Works Inc.......................D..... 419 529-5748
Ontario *(G-10952)*

The Galehouse Companies Inc..............E..... 330 658-2023
Doylestown *(G-6270)*

Universal Dsign Fbrication LLC..............F..... 419 202-5269
Sandusky *(G-11880)*

▲ Urban Industries of Ohio Inc..............E..... 419 468-3578
Galion *(G-7200)*

1541 Industrial buildings and warehouses

Agridry LLC...G..... 419 459-4399
Edon *(G-6472)*

Atlantic Welding LLC.............................F..... 937 570-5094
Piqua *(G-11335)*

Baker-Shindler Contracting Co..............E..... 419 782-5080
Defiance *(G-6100)*

◆ Enerfab LLC.....................................B..... 513 641-0500
Cincinnati *(G-2590)*

Falls Mtal Fbrctors Indus Svcs.............F..... 330 253-7181
Akron *(G-143)*

Fleming Construction Co.......................G..... 740 494-2177
Prospect *(G-11501)*

Ingle-Barr Inc......................................D..... 740 702-6117
Chillicothe *(G-2261)*

Jim Nier Construction Inc......................E..... 740 289-3925
Piketon *(G-11308)*

Milos Whole World Gourmet LLC...........G..... 740 589-6456
Nelsonville *(G-10319)*

Pawnee Maintenance Inc......................G..... 740 373-6861
Marietta *(G-8935)*

Precision Wldg Instllation LLC..............F..... 740 995-0613
Zanesville *(G-15043)*

R G Smith Company..............................D..... 330 456-3415
Canton *(G-1988)*

Stamm Contracting Company Inc..........F..... 330 274-8230
Mantua *(G-8875)*

Thomas J Weaver Inc...........................F..... 740 622-2040
Coshocton *(G-5474)*

▲ Universal Fabg Cnstr Svcs Inc...........F..... 614 274-1128
Columbus *(G-5338)*

1542 Nonresidential construction, nec

Aecom Energy & Cnstr Inc....................G..... 419 698-6277
Oregon *(G-10956)*

Baker-Shindler Contracting Co..............E..... 419 782-5080
Defiance *(G-6100)*

Beachy Barns Ltd.................................F..... 614 873-4193
Plain City *(G-11397)*

Brenmar Construction Inc......................D..... 740 286-2151
Jackson *(G-7941)*

Bud Corp..G..... 740 967-9992
Johnstown *(G-7994)*

Commercial Cnstr Group LLC.................G..... 513 722-8952
Milford *(G-9930)*

Facility Service Pros LLC.......................G..... 419 577-6123
Collins *(G-4587)*

Falls Mtal Fbrctors Indus Svcs.............F..... 330 253-7181
Akron *(G-143)*

Fleming Construction Co.......................G..... 740 494-2177
Prospect *(G-11501)*

Ingle-Barr Inc......................................D..... 740 702-6117
Chillicothe *(G-2261)*

Jim Nier Construction Inc......................E..... 740 289-3925
Piketon *(G-11308)*

Kel-Par Co Inc......................................F..... 740 344-2627
Newark *(G-10513)*

Kellys Wldg & Fabrication Ltd................G..... 440 593-6040
Conneaut *(G-5406)*

Ludy Greenhouse Mfg Corp...................D..... 800 255-5839
New Madison *(G-10422)*

MGM Construction Inc...........................G..... 440 234-7660
Berea *(G-1182)*

Precision Wldg Instllation LLC..............F..... 740 995-0613
Zanesville *(G-15043)*

Rebsco Inc...F..... 937 548-2246
Greenville *(G-7351)*

◆ Rough Brothers Mfg Inc.....................D..... 513 242-0310
Cincinnati *(G-3054)*

Scs Construction Services Inc...............E..... 513 929-0260
Cincinnati *(G-3071)*

Shelly and Sands Inc............................E..... 740 859-2104
Rayland *(G-11552)*

Stamm Contracting Company Inc..........F..... 330 274-8230
Mantua *(G-8875)*

The Galehouse Companies Inc..............E..... 330 658-2023
Doylestown *(G-6270)*

Third Salvo Company............................G..... 740 818-9669
Amesville *(G-443)*

Thomas Cabinet Shop Inc......................F..... 937 847-8239
Dayton *(G-6051)*

Thomas J Weaver Inc...........................F..... 740 622-2040
Coshocton *(G-5474)*

Youngstown Shade & Alum LLC.............G..... 330 782-2373
Youngstown *(G-14975)*

16 HEAMY CONSTRUCTION, EXCEPT BUILDING CONSTRUCTION, CONTRACTOR

1611 Highway and street construction

A & A Safety Inc...................................F..... 937 567-9781
Beavercreek *(G-987)*

A & A Safety Inc...................................E..... 513 943-6100
Amelia *(G-425)*

◆ Barrett Paving Materials Inc...............E..... 973 533-1001
Hamilton *(G-7468)*

Central Allied Enterprises Inc................E..... 330 477-6751
Canton *(G-1862)*

G-R Contracting Inc..............................F..... 740 567-3202
Lewisville *(G-8366)*

Gerken Materials Inc............................E..... 419 533-2421
Napoleon *(G-10281)*

Great Lakes Crushing Ltd......................D..... 440 944-5500
Wickliffe *(G-14376)*

Hull Ready Mix Concrete Inc..................E..... 419 625-8070
Sandusky *(G-11839)*

Image Pavement Maintenance...............G..... 937 833-9200
Brookville *(G-1571)*

▲ John R Jurgensen Co..........................B..... 513 771-0820
Cincinnati *(G-2768)*

Kenmore Construction Co Inc................D..... 330 832-8888
Massillon *(G-9211)*

Koski Construction Co............................G..... 440 997-5337
Ashtabula *(G-601)*

M & B Asphalt Company Inc...................F..... 419 992-4235
Tiffin *(G-12787)*

Morlock Asphalt Ltd..............................F..... 419 419-4772
Portage *(G-11459)*

Paul Peterson Company.........................F..... 614 486-4375
Columbus *(G-5178)*

Security Fence Group Inc......................E..... 513 681-3700
Cincinnati *(G-3074)*

Seneca Petroleum Co Inc......................F..... 419 691-3581
Toledo *(G-13127)*

Shelly Materials Inc..............................E..... 740 666-5841
Ostrander *(G-11029)*

Smalls Asphalt Paving Inc.....................G..... 740 427-4096
Gambier *(G-7214)*

▲ Terminal Ready-Mix Inc.......................E..... 440 288-0181
Lorain *(G-8583)*

Traffic Detectors & Signs Inc.................G..... 330 707-9060
Youngstown *(G-14949)*

Valley Asphalt Corporation.....................E..... 513 771-0820
Cincinnati *(G-3191)*

Ward Construction Co............................F..... 419 943-2450
Leipsic *(G-8316)*

S I C

Wilson Blacktop Corp............................ F 740 635-3566
Martins Ferry (G-9012)

Wyandot Dolomite Inc............................ E 419 396-7641
Carey (G-2064)

1622 Bridge, tunnel, and elevated highway

▼ Ohio Bridge Corporation...................... C 740 432-6334
Cambridge (G-1752)

1623 Water, sewer, and utility lines

Bi-Con Services Inc............................... B 740 685-2542
Derwent (G-6221)

Bob Lanes Welding Inc........................... G 740 373-3567
Marietta (G-8904)

Crazeweld LLC..................................... G 419 210-3668
Norwalk (G-10833)

Don Wartko Construction Inc................... D 330 673-5252
Kent (G-8026)

▼ Eastern Automated Piping..................... G 740 535-8184
Mingo Junction (G-10050)

Fishel Company..................................... C 614 850-4400
Columbus (G-4926)

Fleming Construction Co........................ G 740 494-2177
Prospect (G-11501)

Global Energy Partners LLC................... E 419 756-8027
Mansfield (G-8792)

Great Lakes Crushing Ltd....................... D 440 944-5500
Wickliffe (G-14376)

Great Lakes Telcom Ltd........................ E 330 629-8848
Youngstown (G-14870)

Groundhogs 2000 LLC........................... G 440 653-1647
Bedford (G-1033)

Mt Pleasant Blacktopping Inc.................. G 513 874-3777
Fairfield (G-6756)

Neptune Equipment Company.................. F 513 851-8008
Cincinnati (G-2898)

Parallel Technologies Inc....................... D 614 798-9700
Dublin (G-6328)

Preformed Line Products Co................... B 440 461-5200
Mayfield Village (G-9346)

Steelial Wldg Met Fbrction Inc................ E 740 669-5300
Vinton (G-13624)

Sterling Process Equipmen.................... E 614 868-5151
Columbus (G-5292)

◆ Terra Sonic International LLC............... E 740 374-6608
Marietta (G-8953)

1629 Heavy construction, nec

Advanced Indus Machining Inc................ F 614 596-4183
Powell (G-11481)

Artesian of Pioneer Inc.......................... F 419 737-2352
Pioneer (G-11318)

Atlantic Welding LLC............................. F 937 570-5094
Piqua (G-11335)

◆ Babcock & Wilcox Company................. A 330 753-4511
Akron (G-67)

Biedenbach Logging.............................. G 740 732-6477
Sarahsville (G-11884)

Breaker Technology Inc......................... F 440 248-7168
Solon (G-12090)

Dayton Waterjet LLC............................. G 937 428-0944
Miamisburg (G-9689)

◆ Enerfab LLC..................................... B 513 641-0500
Cincinnati (G-2590)

G-R Contracting Inc.............................. F 740 567-3202
Lewisville (G-8366)

Great Lakes Crushing Ltd....................... D 440 944-5500
Wickliffe (G-14376)

▼ Htec Systems Inc.............................. F 937 438-3010
Dayton (G-5816)

Image Pavement Maintenance................. G 937 833-9200
Brookville (G-1571)

Kars Ohio LLC..................................... G 614 655-1099
Pataskala (G-11142)

Miller Logging Inc................................. G 330 279-4721
Holmesville (G-7802)

Tri-America Contractors Inc.................... E 740 574-0148
Wheelersburg (G-14354)

Valley Mining Inc.................................. C 740 922-3942
Dennison (G-6220)

17 CONSTRUCTION - SPECIAL TRADE CONTRACTORS

1711 Plumbing, heating, air-conditioning

AAA Wastewater Services Inc................ F 937 746-6361
Franklin (G-7009)

Accurate Mechanical Inc....................... D 740 681-1332
Lancaster (G-8174)

Air-Tech Mechanical Inc........................ G 419 292-0074
Toledo (G-12867)

▲ Alan Manufacturing Inc...................... E 330 262-1555
Wooster (G-14621)

Approved Plumbing Co.......................... F 216 663-5063
Cleveland (G-3362)

Asidaco LLC.. G 800 204-1544
Dayton (G-5666)

◆ Babcock & Wilcox Company................. A 330 753-4511
Akron (G-67)

▲ Bear Mechanical LLC......................... G 937 288-2316
Hillsboro (G-7713)

Budde Sheet Metal Works Inc................ E 937 224-0868
Dayton (G-5689)

◆ Chick Master Incubator Company.......... D 330 722-5591
Medina (G-9387)

Cincinnati Air Conditioning Co................ D 513 721-5622
Cincinnati (G-2468)

Climate Pros LLC................................. D 216 881-5200
Cleveland (G-3541)

Climate Pros LLC................................. D 330 744-2732
Youngstown (G-14839)

Columbus Heating & Vent Co.................. C 614 274-1177
Columbus (G-4823)

Complete Mechanical Svcs LLC.............. D 513 489-3080
Cincinnati (G-2507)

Crazeweld LLC..................................... G 419 210-3668
Norwalk (G-10833)

Debra-Kuempel Inc............................... D 513 271-6500
Cincinnati (G-2543)

Dennis Constuction Sanitation................ G 419 332-8026
Fremont (G-7104)

E & M Liberty Welding Inc...................... G 330 866-2338
Waynesburg (G-13876)

▼ Eastern Automated Piping.................... G 740 535-8184
Mingo Junction (G-10050)

◆ Enerfab LLC..................................... B 513 641-0500
Cincinnati (G-2590)

Fellhauer Mechanical Systems............... E 419 734-3674
Port Clinton (G-11441)

Franck & Fric Incorporated.................... D 216 524-4451
Cleveland (G-3742)

Grid Industrial Heating Inc..................... G 330 332-9931
Salem (G-11783)

Gundlach Sheet Metal Works Inc............ E 419 626-4525
Sandusky (G-11837)

Hess Advanced Solutions Llc................. G 937 829-4794
Dayton (G-5809)

Holgate Metal Fab Inc........................... F 419 599-2000
Napoleon (G-10285)

Hvac Inc... F 330 343-5511
Dover (G-6247)

Industrial Power Systems Inc................. B 419 531-3121
Rossford (G-11659)

Integrated Development & Mfg................ F 440 247-5100
Chagrin Falls (G-2146)

Ioppolo Concrete Corporation................. G 440 439-6606
Bedford (G-1040)

Jacobs Mechanical Co.......................... C 513 681-6800
Cincinnati (G-2756)

JD Indoor Comfort Inc........................... F 440 949-8758
Sheffield Lake (G-11954)

Jfdb Ltd... C 513 870-0601
Cincinnati (G-2766)

Kel-Par Co Inc..................................... F 740 344-2627
Newark (G-10513)

◆ Kinetics Noise Control Inc................... C 614 889-0480
Dublin (G-6316)

Kirk Williams Company Inc..................... D 614 875-9023
Grove City (G-7393)

▲ Langdon Inc..................................... E 513 733-5955
Cincinnati (G-2811)

Lochard Inc... D 937 492-8811
Sidney (G-12031)

Lowry Furnace Co Inc........................... G 330 745-4822
Akron (G-211)

Mack Industries................................... F 419 353-7081
Bowling Green (G-1427)

Nbw Inc.. E 216 377-1700
Cleveland (G-4063)

Northeastern Rfrgn Corp....................... E 440 942-7676
Willoughby (G-14496)

PB Fbrction Mech Contrs Corp............... F 419 478-4869
Toledo (G-13091)

Personal Plumber Service Corp.............. F 440 324-4321
Elyria (G-6579)

▲ Pioneer Pipe Inc............................... A 740 376-2400
Marietta (G-8937)

Professional Supply Inc........................ F 419 332-7373
Fremont (G-7128)

Prout Boiler Htg & Wldg Inc................... E 330 744-0293
Youngstown (G-14921)

Schweizer Dipple Inc............................ D 440 786-8090
Cleveland (G-4277)

Sexton Industrial Inc............................ C 513 530-5555
West Chester (G-14144)

Temperature Controls Co Inc.................. F 330 773-6633
New Franklin (G-10395)

Terrasmart LLC.................................... E 239 362-0211
Columbus (G-5317)

The Hattenbach Company....................... D 216 881-5200
Cleveland (G-4384)

United Group Services Inc...................... C 800 633-9690
Cincinnati (G-3183)

V M Systems Inc.................................. D 419 535-1044
Toledo (G-13172)

Vector Mechanical LLC.......................... G 216 337-4042
Cleveland (G-4460)

Vintage Automotive Elc Inc.................... F 419 472-9349
Toledo (G-13175)

Weather King Heating & AC.................... G 330 908-0281
Northfield (G-10799)

Whempys Corp..................................... G 614 888-6670
Worthington (G-14729)

Young Regulator Company Inc................. E 440 232-9452
Bedford (G-1066)

1721 Painting and paper hanging

A & A Safety Inc.................................. F 937 567-9781
Beavercreek (G-987)

A & A Safety Inc.................................. E 513 943-6100
Amelia (G-425)

A1 Industrial Painting Inc...................... E 330 750-9441
Youngstown (G-14801)

All Ohio Companies Inc......................... G 216 420-9274
Cleveland (G-3325)

Banks Manufacturing Company............ F 440 458-8661
Grafton *(G-7299)*

Industrial Mill Maintenance................ F 330 746-1155
Youngstown *(G-14876)*

Js Fabrications Inc............................ G 419 333-0323
Fremont *(G-7118)*

Kars Ohio LLC................................. G 614 655-1099
Pataskala *(G-11142)*

Mes Painting & Graphics Ltd............ E 614 496-1696
Westerville *(G-14268)*

Mes Painting and Graphics.............. G 614 496-1696
Westerville *(G-14269)*

Napoleon Machine LLC..................... E 419 591-7010
Napoleon *(G-10293)*

Ohio Building Restoration Inc............ E 419 244-7372
Toledo *(G-13073)*

Procoat Painting Inc......................... G 513 735-2500
Batavia *(G-885)*

Semper Quality Industry Inc.............. G 440 352-8111
Mentor *(G-9613)*

1731 Electrical work

Akron Foundry Co............................. G 330 745-3101
Barberton *(G-791)*

Asg Division Jergens Inc.................. E 888 486-6163
Cleveland *(G-3377)*

Asidaco LLC.................................... G 800 204-1544
Dayton *(G-5666)*

Atlas Industrial Contrs LLC.............. B 614 841-4500
Columbus *(G-4732)*

Background Music & Sound Inc......... G 937 898-9871
Dayton *(G-5673)*

Controls Inc.................................... E 330 239-4345
Medina *(G-9390)*

Crase Communications Inc............... G 419 468-1173
Galion *(G-7186)*

D & J Electric Motor Repair Co......... F 330 336-4343
Wadsworth *(G-13634)*

◆ Df Supply Inc.................................E 330 650-9226
Twinsburg *(G-13294)*

DSI Management Holdings LLC......... F 800 645-7002
Kent *(G-8027)*

Dss Installations Ltd........................ G 513 761-7000
Cincinnati *(G-2563)*

Fishel Company............................... C 614 850-4400
Columbus *(G-4926)*

Franks Electric Inc........................... G 513 313-5883
Cincinnati *(G 2640)*

▲ Gatesair Inc................................ D 513 459-3400
Mason *(G-9102)*

Graham Electric............................... G 614 231-8500
Columbus *(G-4964)*

Grand Archt Etrnl Eye 314 LLC......... F 800 377-8147
Cleveland *(G-3783)*

Great Lakes Telcom Ltd.................... G 330 629-8848
Youngstown *(G-14870)*

Hess Advanced Solutions Llc........... G 937 829-4794
Dayton *(G-5809)*

Industrial Electronic Service.............. F 937 746-9750
Carlisle *(G-2066)*

Industrial Power Systems Inc............ B 419 531-3121
Rossford *(G-11659)*

▲ Instrmntation Ctrl Systems Inc........ E 513 662-2600
Cincinnati *(G-2747)*

JC Electric Llc................................. F 330 760-2915
Garrettsville *(G-7221)*

Jeff Bonham Electric Inc................... E 937 233-7662
Dayton *(G-5828)*

▲ Jobap Assembly Inc...................... G 440 632-5393
Middlefield *(G-9803)*

Legrand North America LLC............. B 937 224-0639
Dayton *(G-5843)*

Magnum Computers Inc.................... F 216 781-1757
Cleveland *(G-3981)*

Mikes Transm & Auto Svc LLC......... F 330 799-8266
Youngstown *(G-14901)*

Mirus Adapted Tech LLC................. E 614 402-4585
Dublin *(G-6320)*

▲ P S C Inc.................................... G 216 531-3375
Cleveland *(G-4130)*

Radon Eliminator LLC....................... F 330 844-0703
North Canton *(G-10662)*

Safe-Grain Inc................................. G 513 398-2500
Loveland *(G-8650)*

Security Fence Group Inc.................. G 513 681-3700
Cincinnati *(G-3074)*

Tcb Automation LLC......................... F 330 556-6444
Dover *(G-6265)*

Tekworx LLC.................................... F 513 533-4777
Cincinnati *(G-3142)*

The Wagner-Smith Company............ G 866 338-0398
Moraine *(G-10195)*

Town Cntry Technical Svcs Inc.......... F 614 866-7700
Reynoldsburg *(G-11582)*

Valley Electric Company................... G 419 332-6405
Fremont *(G-7142)*

Vertiv Group Corporation.................. G 440 460-3600
Cleveland *(G-4461)*

Village Controls LLC........................ F 614 600-8880
Powell *(G-11496)*

Waibel Electric Co Inc...................... F 740 964-2956
Etna *(G-6634)*

▲ Weidmann Electrical Tech Inc......... G 937 508-2112
Cleveland *(G-4497)*

1741 Masonry and other stonework

Albert Freytag Inc............................ E 419 628-2018
Minster *(G-10053)*

G L Pierce Inc.................................. G 513 772-7202
Cincinnati *(G-2647)*

North Central Con Designs Inc.......... G 419 606-1908
Wooster *(G-14669)*

▲ North Central Insulation Inc............ F 419 886-2030
Bellville *(G-1141)*

North Hill Marble & Granite Co.......... F 330 253-2179
Akron *(G-249)*

Ohio Building Restoration Inc............ E 419 244-7372
Toledo *(G-13073)*

Pioneer Cldding Glzing Systems........ E 216 816-4242
Cloveland *(G 1166)*

◆ Rmi Titanium Company LLC............ E 330 652-9952
Niles *(G-10604)*

Snyder Concrete Products Inc........... G 937 339-7577
Troy *(G-13257)*

▲ The Schaefer Group Inc................ E 937 253-3342
Beavercreek *(G-997)*

Third Salvo Company........................ G 740 818-9669
Amesville *(G-443)*

Whempys Corp................................. G 614 888-6670
Worthington *(G-14729)*

1742 Plastering, drywall, and insulation

Holland Assocts LLC DBA Archou....... F 513 891-0006
Cincinnati *(G-2727)*

▲ North Central Insulation Inc............ F 419 886-2030
Bellville *(G-1141)*

One Wish LLC.................................. F 800 505-6883
Bedford *(G-1052)*

1743 Terrazzo, tile, marble, mosaic work

◆ Cutting Edge Countertops Inc..........E 419 873-9500
Perrysburg *(G-11212)*

▲ Distinctive Marble & Gran Inc......... F 614 760-0003
Plain City *(G-11404)*

Prints & Paints Flr Cvg Co Inc........... E 419 462-5663
Galion *(G-7197)*

Stuart-Dean Co Inc.......................... G 412 765-2752
Cleveland *(G-4338)*

1751 Carpentry work

A & J Woodworking Inc..................... G 419 695-5655
Delphos *(G-6183)*

Accent Manufacturing Inc................. F 330 724-7704
Norton *(G-10816)*

Acme Home Improvement Co Inc........ F 614 252-2129
Columbus *(G-4671)*

AK Fabrication Inc............................ F 330 458-1037
Canton *(G-1827)*

Alside Inc....................................... E 419 865-0934
Maumee *(G-9258)*

American Platinum Door LLC............ G 440 497-6213
Solon *(G-12078)*

Architctral Mllwk Cbinetry Inc........... G 440 708-0086
Chagrin Falls *(G-2155)*

Artisan Constructors LLC................. E 216 800-7641
Cleveland *(G-3370)*

Cabinet Restylers Inc....................... D 419 281-8449
Ashland *(G-525)*

Case Crafters Inc............................. G 937 667-9473
Tipp City *(G-12819)*

Couch Business Development Inc........ G 937 253-1099
Dayton *(G-5711)*

Dgl Woodworking Inc........................ F 937 837-7091
Dayton *(G-5747)*

Display Dynamics Inc....................... F 937 832-2830
Englewood *(G-6612)*

Division Overhead Door Inc............... F 513 872-0888
Cincinnati *(G-2556)*

East Woodworking Company............. G 216 791-5950
Cleveland *(G-3649)*

Finelli Ornamental Iron Co................ E 440 248-0050
Cleveland *(G-3717)*

General Awning Company Inc............ G 216 749-0110
Cleveland *(G-3762)*

Golden Angle Archtctral Group.......... G 614 531-7932
Columbus *(G-4960)*

Hardwood Lumber Company Inc......... F 440 834-1891
Middlefield *(G-9797)*

Joseph Sabatino............................. G 330 332-5879
Salem *(G-11791)*

Midwest Curtainwalls Inc.................. D 216 641-7900
Cloveland *(G 1036)*

Millwood Wholesale Inc.................... F 330 359-6109
Dundee *(G-6369)*

Murray Display Fixtures Ltd............... F 614 875-1594
Grove City *(G-7403)*

Nagele Manufacturing Company......... E 216 433-1100
Beavercreek *(G-4057)*

▼ Nofziger Door Sales Inc................ C 419 337-9900
Wauseon *(G-13857)*

Overhead Door Corporation.............. F 440 593-5226
Conneaut *(G-5413)*

Overhead Door of Pike County.......... G 740 289-3925
Piketon *(G-11312)*

Premier Construction Company.......... G 513 874-2611
West Chester *(G-14053)*

Riverside Cnstr Svcs Inc.................. E 513 723-0900
Cincinnati *(G-3048)*

Seemray LLC.................................. E 440 536-8705
Cleveland *(G-4285)*

Sheridan Woodworks Inc.................. G 216 663-9333
Cleveland *(G-4292)*

Snows Wood Shop Inc...................... E 419 836-3805
Oregon *(G-10968)*

Thomas Cabinet Shop Inc................. F 937 847-8239
Dayton *(G-6051)*

Traichal Construction Company............ E 800 255-3667
Niles (G-10607)

Triple A Builders Inc................................ G 216 249-0327
Cleveland (G-4428)

Wades Woodworking Inc.......................... F 937 374-6470
Xenia (G-14784)

Yoder Window & Siding Ltd.................... F 330 695-6960
Fredericksburg (G-7072)

1752 Floor laying and floor work, nec

▲ Done-Rite Bowling Service Co.......... E 440 232-3280
Bedford (G-1028)

Hoover & Wells Inc.................................. C 419 691-9220
Toledo (G-12995)

◆ Tremco Incorporated............................ C 216 292-5000
Beachwood (G-956)

Triple A Builders Inc.............................. G 216 249-0327
Cleveland (G-4428)

X-Treme Finishes Inc.............................. F 330 474-0614
North Royalton (G-10790)

1761 Roofing, siding, and sheetmetal work

Acme Home Improvement Co Inc............ F 614 252-2129
Columbus (G-4671)

▲ Alan Manufacturing Inc...................... E 330 262-1555
Wooster (G-14621)

All-Type Welding & Fabrication............ E 440 439-3990
Cleveland (G-3329)

American Way Exteriors LLC.................. G 937 221-8860
Dayton (G-5656)

Ameridian Specialty Services................ E 513 769-0150
Cincinnati (G-2364)

Anchor Metal Processing Inc................ F 216 362-6463
Cleveland (G-3354)

Anchor Metal Processing Inc................ E 216 362-1850
Cleveland (G-3355)

Avon Lake Sheet Metal Co...................... E 440 933-3505
Avon Lake (G-750)

Batman Enterprises LLC........................ F 513 600-3079
Milford (G-9923)

Budde Sheet Metal Works Inc................ F 937 224-0868
Dayton (G-5689)

Cabinet Restylers Inc............................ D 419 281-8449
Ashland (G-525)

Cardinal Builders Inc............................ G 614 237-1000
Columbus (G-4801)

▲ Champion Opco LLC............................ B 513 327-7338
Cincinnati (G-2458)

Clearview Construction LLC.................. G 513 206-6415
Cincinnati (G-2498)

Cmt Machining & Fabg LLC.................... F 937 652-3740
Urbana (G-13459)

Defabco Inc.. D 614 231-2700
Columbus (G-4875)

Dimensional Metals Inc.......................... E 740 927-3633
Reynoldsburg (G-11565)

Ducts Inc.. G 216 391-2400
Cleveland (G-3637)

Everyday Technologies Inc.................... F 937 497-7774
Sidney (G-12018)

Federal Iron Works Company.................. G 330 482-5910
Columbiana (G-4617)

Franck and Fric Incorporated................ D 216 524-4451
Cleveland (G-3742)

General Awning Company Inc................ G 216 749-0110
Cleveland (G-3762)

Golden Angle Archtctral Group.............. G 614 531-7932
Columbus (G-4960)

Holgate Metal Fab Inc............................ F 419 599-2000
Napoleon (G-10285)

Jim Nier Construction Inc...................... E 740 289-3925
Piketon (G-11308)

◆ Kirk & Blum Manufacturing Co............ C 513 458-2600
Cincinnati (G-2797)

Martina Metal LLC.................................. E 614 291-9700
Columbus (G-5085)

MGM Construction Inc............................ G 440 234-7660
Berea (G-1182)

◆ Owens Corning Sales LLC.................. A 419 248-8000
Toledo (G-13088)

Precision Impacts LLC.......................... D 937 530-8254
Miamisburg (G-9728)

R G Smith Company................................ D 330 456-3415
Canton (G-1988)

RE Connors Construction Ltd................ G 740 644-0261
Thornville (G-12767)

Rmt Acquisition Inc................................ E 513 241-5566
Cincinnati (G-3050)

Roofing Annex LLC.................................. G 513 942-0555
West Chester (G-14141)

Scs Construction Services Inc.............. E 513 929-0260
Cincinnati (G-3071)

Seneca Sheet Metal Company................ F 419 447-8434
Tiffin (G-12800)

Simon Roofing and Shtmtl Corp............ C 330 629-7392
Youngstown (G-14932)

Tendon Manufacturing Inc...................... E 216 663-3200
Cleveland (G-4374)

◆ Tremco Incorporated............................ C 216 292-5000
Beachwood (G-956)

Triple A Builders Inc.............................. G 216 249-0327
Cleveland (G-4428)

Waxco International Inc.......................... F 937 746-4845
Miamisburg (G-9752)

Westlake Ryal Bldg Pdts USA In............ E 800 366-8472
Columbus (G-5365)

Yoder Window & Siding Ltd.................... F 330 695-6960
Fredericksburg (G-7072)

1771 Concrete work

Concrete One Construction LLC............ F 740 595-9680
Delaware (G-6140)

D H Bowman & Sons Inc.......................... G 419 886-2711
Bellville (G-1137)

Eldorado Stone LLC................................ E 330 698-3931
Apple Creek (G-467)

Ernst Enterprises Inc............................ E 513 829-8683
Fairfield (G-6733)

G Big Inc.. E 740 867-5758
Chesapeake (G-2229)

Gateway Con Forming Svcs Inc.............. D 513 353-2000
Miamitown (G-9758)

Gerdau Ameristeel US Inc...................... G 740 671-9410
Bellaire (G-1087)

Hilltop Basic Resources Inc.................. G 937 882-6357
Springfield (G-12322)

Image Pavement Maintenance................ G 937 833-9200
Brookville (G-1571)

Koski Construction Co............................ G 440 997-5337
Ashtabula (G-601)

M & B Asphalt Company Inc.................... F 419 992-4235
Tiffin (G-12787)

Morel Landscaping LLC.......................... F 216 551-4395
Broadview Heights (G-1505)

Morrow Gravel Company Inc.................. E 513 771-0820
Cincinnati (G-2889)

Mt Pleasant Blacktopping Inc................ G 513 874-3777
Fairfield (G-6756)

Protective Industrial Polymers.............. F 440 327-0015
North Ridgeville (G-10743)

▲ R W Sidley Incorporated.................... E 440 352-9343
Painesville (G-11109)

RE Connors Construction Ltd................ G 740 644-0261
Thornville (G-12767)

Smalls Asphalt Paving Inc...................... G 740 427-4096
Gambier (G-7214)

Stamm Contracting Company Inc.......... F 330 274-8230
Mantua (G-8875)

◆ Trewbric III Inc.................................... E 614 444-2184
Columbus (G-5330)

Triple A Builders Inc.............................. G 216 249-0327
Cleveland (G-4428)

W M Dauch Concrete Inc........................ G 419 562-6917
Bucyrus (G-1695)

Ward Construction Co............................ F 419 943-2450
Leipsic (G-8316)

Wilson Blacktop Corp............................ F 740 635-3566
Martins Ferry (G-9012)

1781 Water well drilling

Stoepfel Drilling Co................................ G 419 532-3307
Ottawa (G-11048)

Warthman Drilling Inc............................ G 740 746-9950
Sugar Grove (G-12630)

1791 Structural steel erection

Affiliated Metal Industries Inc.............. F 440 235-3345
Olmsted Falls (G-10936)

Atlantic Welding LLC.............................. F 937 570-5094
Piqua (G-11335)

Chagrin Vly Stl Erectors Inc.................. F 440 975-1556
Willoughby Hills (G-14557)

Chc Fabricating Corp.............................. D 513 821-7757
Cincinnati (G-2459)

◆ Columbiana Boiler Company LLC......E 330 482-3373
Columbiana (G-4611)

Concord Fabricators Inc........................ E 614 875-2500
Grove City (G-7377)

Crazeweld LLC.. G 419 210-3668
Norwalk (G-10833)

Evers Welding Co Inc.............................. G 513 385-7352
Cincinnati (G-2604)

Frederick Steel Company LLC................ D 513 821-6400
Cincinnati (G-2641)

G & P Construction LLC.......................... E 855 494-4830
North Royalton (G-10762)

GL Nause Co Inc...................................... E 513 722-9500
Loveland (G-8626)

Lake Building Products Inc.................... E 216 486-1500
Cleveland (G-3936)

Marysville Steel Inc.............................. E 937 642-5971
Marysville (G-9038)

Mound Technologies Inc........................ E 937 748-2937
Springboro (G-12260)

Parker Fabricating Co............................ E 330 379-0112
Akron (G-256)

Pro-Fab Inc.. G 330 644-0044
Akron (G-267)

Rex Welding Inc...................................... F 740 387-1650
Marion (G-8992)

Rittman Inc.. D 330 927-6855
Rittman (G-11627)

▼ Superior Walls of Ohio Inc................ D 330 393-4101
Warren (G-13799)

Upright Steel Inc.................................... E 216 923-0852
Cleveland (G-4449)

Wernke Wldg & Stl Erection Co.............. F 513 353-4173
North Bend (G-10622)

White Mule Company.............................. E 740 382-9008
Ontario (G-10954)

1793 Glass and glazing work

A Service Glass Inc................................ F 937 426-4920
Beavercreek (G-963)

▲ Afg Industries Inc.............................. D 614 322-4580
Grove City (G-7368)

All State GL Block Fctry Inc...................... G 440 205-8410
  Mentor (G-9476)

Kimmatt Corp.. G 937 228-3811
  West Alexandria (G-13920)

Niles Mirror & Glass Inc........................... E 330 652-6277
  Niles (G-10597)

Pentagon Protection Usa LLC.................. F 614 734-7240
  Dublin (G-6331)

Pioneer Cldding Glzing Systems............ E 216 816-4242
  Cleveland (G-4166)

Solon Glass Center Inc............................ F 440 248-5018
  Cleveland (G-4313)

1794 Excavation work

16363 Sca Inc.. G 330 448-0000
  Masury (G-9253)

Allgeier & Son Inc.................................... F 513 574-3735
  Cincinnati (G-2351)

◆ Barrett Paving Materials Inc................. E 973 533-1001
  Hamilton (G-7468)

Castalia Trenching & Ready Mix.............. F 419 684-5502
  Castalia (G-2095)

D H Bowman & Sons Inc.......................... G 419 886-2711
  Bellville (G-1137)

Dennis Constuction Sanitation................. G 419 332-8026
  Fremont (G-7104)

Don Wartko Construction Inc.................... D 330 673-5252
  Kent (G-8026)

Fleming Construction Co.......................... G 740 494-2177
  Prospect (G-11501)

Fouremans Sand & Gravel Inc................. G 937 547-1005
  Greenville (G-7341)

◆ Gayston Corporation............................. C 937 743-6050
  Miamisburg (G-9693)

Kelchner Inc.. D 937 704-9890
  Springboro (G-12258)

Koski Construction Co.............................. G 440 997-5337
  Ashtabula (G-601)

Paul R Lipp & Son Inc.............................. F 330 227-9614
  Rogers (G-11642)

Personal Plumber Service Corp............... F 440 324-4321
  Elyria (G-6579)

Phillips Companies................................... E 937 426-5461
  Beavercreek Township (G-1003)

Rbm Environmental & Cnstr Inc............... G 419 693-5840
  Oregon (G-10967)

Siler Excavation Services......................... E 513 400-8628
  Milford (G-9953)

1795 Wrecking and demolition work

Allgeier & Son Inc.................................... F 513 574-3735
  Cincinnati (G-2351)

Js Fabrications Inc................................... G 419 333-0323
  Fremont (G-7118)

Rnw Holdings Inc...................................... E 330 792-0600
  Youngstown (G-14925)

Sidwell Materials Inc................................ C 740 849-2422
  Zanesville (G-15050)

1796 Installing building equipment

Atlas Industrial Contrs LLC...................... B 614 841-4500
  Columbus (G-4732)

Chagrin Vly Stl Erectors Inc..................... F 440 975-1556
  Willoughby Hills (G-14557)

◆ Clopay Ames Inc................................... C 800 282-2260
  Mason (G-9087)

D & G Welding Inc.................................... G 419 445-5751
  Archbold (G-492)

Expert Crane Inc...................................... D 216 451-9900
  Wellington (G-13886)

Industrial Millwright Svcs LLC.................. E 419 523-9147
  Ottawa (G-11035)

Industrial Power Systems Inc................... B 419 531-3121
  Rossford (G-11659)

◆ Intertec Corporation............................. F 419 537-9711
  Toledo (G-13007)

K F T Inc.. D 513 241-5910
  Cincinnati (G-2776)

L Haberny Co Inc...................................... F 440 543-5999
  Chagrin Falls (G-2168)

Mainline Contracting LLC......................... F 513 202-1408
  Harrison (G-7559)

◆ McGill Airclean LLC.............................. D 614 829-1200
  Columbus (G-5089)

Nbw Inc... E 216 377-1700
  Cleveland (G-4063)

Northwest Installations Inc....................... E 419 423-5738
  Findlay (G-6900)

Otis Elevator Company............................ E 216 573-2333
  Cleveland (G-4127)

PMRservices LLC...................................... F 937 219-0062
  Spring Valley (G-12242)

▲ Spallinger Millwright Svc Co................ E 419 225-5830
  Lima (G-8452)

Stainless Crafts Inc.................................. G 513 353-4578
  Cincinnati (G-3110)

1799 Special trade contractors, nec

ABC Signs Inc... F 513 407-4367
  Cincinnati (G-2331)

Advantic Building Group LLC.................... E 513 290-4796
  Miamisburg (G-9661)

▲ Afg Industries Inc................................. D 614 322-4580
  Grove City (G-7368)

Akay Industries Inc................................... E 330 753-8458
  Barberton (G-790)

All Ohio Companies Inc............................ E 216 420-9274
  Cleveland (G-3325)

All Ohio Welding Inc................................. G 937 663-7116
  Saint Paris (G-11755)

All Signs of Chillicothe Inc....................... G 740 773-5016
  Chillicothe (G-2242)

American Way Exteriors LLC.................... G 937 221-8860
  Dayton (G-5656)

Archer Corporation................................... E 330 455-9995
  Canton (G-1831)

Banks Manufacturing Company.............. F 440 458-8661
  Grafton (G-7299)

Barr Engineering Incorporated................ E 614 714-0299
  Columbus (G-1744)

◆ Barrett Paving Materials Inc................. E 973 533-1001
  Hamilton (G-7468)

Beck Studios Inc....................................... E 513 831-6650
  Milford (G-9925)

Bob Lanes Welding Inc............................ G 740 373-3567
  Marietta (G-8904)

Bogie Industries Inc Ltd.......................... E 330 745-3105
  Akron (G-81)

Bowden Fence Co LLC.............................. G 614 272-8923
  Columbus (G-4771)

Brilliant Electric Sign Co Ltd.................... D 216 741-3800
  Brooklyn Heights (G-1529)

Burdens Machine & Welding Inc............. G 740 345-9246
  Newark (G-10496)

Cabinet Restylers Inc............................... D 419 281-8449
  Ashland (G-525)

Cardinal Builders Inc................................ G 614 237-1000
  Columbus (G-4801)

Carpe Diem Industries LLC...................... D 419 358-0129
  Bluffton (G-1359)

Carpe Diem Industries LLC...................... G 419 659-5639
  Columbus Grove (G-5382)

Classic Countertops LLC.......................... G 330 882-4220
  Akron (G-102)

▲ Cleveland Granite & Marble LLC.......... E 216 291-7637
  Cleveland (G-3512)

Connaughton Wldg & Fence LLC............. G 513 867-0230
  Hamilton (G-7480)

Corrpro Companies Inc............................ E 770 761-5400
  Medina (G-9392)

Crafted Surface and Stone LLC............... E 440 658-3799
  Chagrin Falls (G-2157)

Crazeweld LLC.. G 419 210-3668
  Norwalk (G-10833)

Cuyahoga Fence LLC................................ F 216 830-2200
  Cleveland (G-3591)

Danite Holdings Ltd.................................. E 614 444-3333
  Columbus (G-4870)

Double D D Mtls Instltion Inc................... G 937 898-2534
  Dayton (G-5750)

Dover Fabrication and Burn Inc............... G 330 339-1057
  Dover (G-6239)

Envirnmntal Cmpliance Tech LLC............ F 216 634-0400
  North Royalton (G-10760)

Euclid Welding Company Inc.................... F 216 289-0714
  Willoughby Hills (G-14559)

Extreme Microbial Tech LLC.................... E 844 885-0088
  Moraine (G-10162)

Fdi Cabinetry LLC..................................... G 513 353-4500
  Cleves (G-4537)

Fence One Inc... F 216 441-2600
  Cleveland (G-3712)

▲ Flow-Liner Systems Ltd........................ E 800 348-0020
  Zanesville (G-15014)

Gdn Welding LLC...................................... E 740 398-6109
  Danville (G-5599)

Gus Holthaus Signs Inc........................... G 513 861-0060
  Cincinnati (G-2697)

Handshakers Construction LLC................ F 513 370-1371
  Cincinnati (G-2704)

High-TEC Industrial Services................... D 937 667-1772
  Tipp City (G-12827)

Holdsworth Industrial Fabg LLC.............. G 330 874-3945
  Bolivar (G-1384)

Hy-Blast Inc.. F 513 424-0704
  Middletown (G-9864)

Identitek Systems Inc............................... D 330 832-9844
  Massillon (G-9206)

Image Pavement Maintenance................. G 937 833-9200
  Brookville (G-1571)

Imperial On-Pece Fibrgls Pools.............. F 740 747-2971
  Ashley (C 582)

Indoor Envmtl Specialists Inc.................. E 937 433-5202
  Dayton (G-5821)

Industrial Fiberglass Spc Inc................... E 937 222-9000
  Vandalia (G-13561)

Janson Industries..................................... D 330 455-7029
  Canton (G-1921)

Kcn Technologies LLC.............................. G 440 439-4219
  Bedford (G-1041)

Kellys Wldg & Fabrication Ltd.................. G 440 593-6040
  Conneaut (G-5406)

Knowlton Machine Inc.............................. G 419 281-6802
  Ashland (G-547)

Kross Acquisition Company LLC............. E 513 554-0555
  Loveland (G-8636)

L B Foster Company................................. F 330 652-1461
  Mineral Ridge (G-10030)

Laminate Shop.. F 740 749-3536
  Waterford (G-13827)

Leak Finder Inc... G 440 735-0130
  Hudson (G-7849)

▲ Lefeld Welding & Stl Sups Inc.............. E 419 678-2397
  Coldwater (G-4580)

Leon Newswanger...................................... F 419 896-3336
  Shiloh (G-11979)

S
I
C

M & M Certified Welding Inc...............F 330 467-1729
Macedonia *(G-8703)*

Macray Co LLC..................................G 937 325-1726
Springfield *(G-12345)*

Mae Fence LLC..................................F 614 929-3526
Fulton *(G-7151)*

Marsam Metalfab Inc..........................E 330 405-1520
Twinsburg *(G-13334)*

Massillon Machine & Die Inc.................G 330 833-8913
Massillon *(G-9219)*

◆ Master Builders LLC.........................E 800 228-3318
Beachwood *(G-928)*

Mel Wacker Signs Inc..........................G 330 832-1726
Massillon *(G-9222)*

▲ Meridienne International Inc...............G 330 274-8317
Aurora *(G-679)*

Mes Painting and Graphics...................G 614 496-1696
Westerville *(G-14269)*

▲ Mesocoat Inc..................................F 216 453-0866
Euclid *(G-6662)*

MGM Construction Inc.........................G 440 234-7660
Berea *(G-1182)*

MH & Son Machining & Wldg Co...........G 419 621-0690
Sandusky *(G-11859)*

▲ National Electro-Coatings Inc.............D 216 898-0080
Cleveland *(G-4059)*

▲ Nestaway LLC..................................D 216 587-1500
Cleveland *(G-4069)*

Ohio Building Restoration Inc................E 419 244-7372
Toledo *(G-13073)*

◆ Organized Living Inc.........................E 513 489-9300
Cincinnati *(G-2939)*

Parking & Traffic Control SEC...............F 440 243-7565
Cleveland *(G-4145)*

Paul Peterson Company.......................F 614 486-4375
Columbus *(G-5178)*

Paulo Products Company......................E 440 942-0153
Willoughby *(G-14505)*

Pietra Naturale Inc.............................F 937 438-8882
Dayton *(G-5940)*

PMRservices LLC................................F 937 219-0062
Spring Valley *(G-12242)*

▲ Ptmj Enterprises Inc.........................F 440 543-8000
Solon *(G-12170)*

Quality Fabricated Metals Inc................F
Salem *(G-11808)*

R W Sidley Incorporated......................C 440 298-3232
Thompson *(G-12763)*

Richtech Industries Inc........................G 440 937-4401
Avon *(G-738)*

Robs Welding Technologies Ltd..............G 937 890-4963
Dayton *(G-5987)*

Rusco Products Inc.............................G 330 758-0378
Youngstown *(G-14927)*

Security Fence Group Inc.....................E 513 681-3700
Cincinnati *(G-3074)*

Signature Sign Co Inc.........................G 216 426-1234
Cleveland *(G-4301)*

South Akron Awning Co.......................F 330 848-7611
Akron *(G-314)*

Spradlin Bros Welding Co.....................F 800 219-2182
Springfield *(G-12375)*

Steve Vore Welding and Steel...............F 419 375-4087
Fort Recovery *(G-6971)*

▲ Stone Statements Incorporated...........G 513 489-7866
Cincinnati *(G-3120)*

Stuart-Dean Co Inc.............................G 412 765-2752
Cleveland *(G-4338)*

▼ Stud Welding Associates Inc...............D 440 783-3160
Strongsville *(G-12607)*

Style-Line Incorporated........................E 614 291-0600
Columbus *(G-5295)*

Swingle Countertops...........................F 740 454-7368
Zanesville *(G-15052)*

United - Maier Signs Inc......................D 513 681-6600
Cincinnati *(G-3180)*

Universal Dsign Fbrication LLC..............F 419 202-5269
Sandusky *(G-11880)*

▲ Universal Fabg Cnstr Svcs Inc............F 614 274-1128
Columbus *(G-5338)*

Vector Mechanical LLC........................G 216 337-4042
Cleveland *(G-4460)*

Waco Scaffolding & Equipment Inc........A 216 749-8900
Cleveland *(G-4487)*

Weldments Inc...................................F 937 235-9261
Dayton *(G-6077)*

Witts Services LLC.............................G 740 543-8526
Bergholz *(G-1197)*

X-Treme Finishes Inc..........................F 330 474-0614
North Royalton *(G-10790)*

Youngstown Fence Incorporated...........G 330 788-8110
Youngstown *(G-14969)*

20 FOOD AND KINDRED PRODUCTS

2011 Meat packing plants

Acme Steak & Seafood Inc...................F 330 270-8000
Youngstown *(G-14806)*

Atlantic Veal & Lamb LLC.....................G 330 435-6400
Creston *(G-5505)*

Baltic Country Meats...........................G 330 897-7025
Baltic *(G-776)*

Bef Foods Inc...................................C 937 372-4493
Xenia *(G-14754)*

Bob Evans Farms Inc..........................A 740 245-5305
Bidwell *(G-1212)*

C J Kraft Enterprises Inc......................G 740 653-9606
Lancaster *(G-8184)*

Carl Rittberger Sr Inc.........................E 740 452-2767
Zanesville *(G-15004)*

Case Farms of Ohio Inc.......................C 330 359-7141
Winesburg *(G-14605)*

Comber Holdings Inc...........................E 216 961-8600
Cleveland *(G-3549)*

Curlys Custom Meats Inc.....................F 937 596-6518
Jackson Center *(G-7960)*

D & H Meats Inc................................G 419 387-7767
Vanlue *(G-13585)*

Dee-Jays Cstm Btchring Proc LL...........F 740 694-7492
Fredericktown *(G-7076)*

Empire Packing Company LLC...............A 901 948-4788
Mason *(G-9097)*

Empire Packing Company LP.................D 513 942-5400
West Chester *(G-14117)*

Farmerstown Meats.............................G 330 897-7972
Sugarcreek *(G-12638)*

Food Plant Engineering LLC..................F 513 618-3165
Blue Ash *(G-1275)*

Foris Extraordinary Meats LLC..............F 614 670-5726
Columbus *(G-4931)*

Fresh Mark Inc..................................A 330 455-5253
Canton *(G-1894)*

Fresh Mark Inc..................................A 330 332-8508
Salem *(G-11781)*

◆ Fresh Mark Inc................................B 330 832-7491
Massillon *(G-9192)*

Hartville Locker Service Ltd..................G 330 877-9547
Hartville *(G-7577)*

HK Cooperative Inc.............................G 419 626-2551
Sandusky *(G-11838)*

Hormel Foods Corp Svcs LLC................F 513 563-0211
Cincinnati *(G-2731)*

Horst Packing Inc..............................G 330 482-2997
Columbiana *(G-4618)*

J H Routh Packing Company..................B 419 626-2251
Sandusky *(G-11844)*

John Stehlin & Sons Co.......................G 513 385-6164
Cincinnati *(G-2769)*

Karn Meats Inc..................................E 614 252-3712
Columbus *(G-5046)*

King Kold Inc....................................E 937 836-2731
Englewood *(G-6617)*

Mannings Packing Co..........................G 937 446-3278
Sardinia *(G-11885)*

Marshallville Packing Co Inc.................G 330 855-2871
Marshallville *(G-9007)*

Mc Connells Market............................G 740 765-4300
Richmond *(G-11604)*

Medina Foods Inc...............................E 330 725-1390
Litchfield *(G-8481)*

National Beef Ohio LLC........................C 800 449-2333
North Baltimore *(G-10615)*

National Beef Packing Co LLC...............A 419 257-5500
North Baltimore *(G-10616)*

Ohio Beef USA LLC.............................G 419 257-5536
North Baltimore *(G-10617)*

Ohio Packing Company.........................C 614 445-0627
Columbus *(G-5151)*

Patrick M Davidson.............................G 513 897-2971
Waynesville *(G-13882)*

Phillips Meat Processing LLC.................F 740 453-3337
Zanesville *(G-15039)*

Pioneer Packing Co............................D 419 352-5283
Bowling Green *(G-1436)*

Presslers Meats Inc............................F 330 644-5636
Akron *(G-266)*

Roots Meat Market LLC........................E 419 332-0041
Fremont *(G-7129)*

Smithfield Direct LLC..........................D 419 422-2233
Findlay *(G-6920)*

◆ Smithfield Packaged Meats Corp.........C 513 782-3800
Cincinnati *(G-3097)*

Sugar Creek Packing Co.......................G 937 268-6601
Dayton *(G-6029)*

The Ellenbee-Leggett Company Inc........C 513 874-3200
Fairfield *(G-6782)*

Tr Boes Holdings Inc...........................F 419 595-2255
New Riegel *(G-10471)*

Troyers Trail Bologna Inc.....................G 330 893-2414
Dundee *(G-6370)*

Tyson Foods Inc.................................G 440 960-0146
Amherst *(G-453)*

V H Cooper & Co Inc...........................A 419 678-4853
Saint Henry *(G-11726)*

V H Cooper & Co Inc...........................A 419 678-4853
Saint Henry *(G-11727)*

V H Cooper & Co Inc...........................C 419 375-4116
Fort Recovery *(G-6973)*

Werling and Sons Inc..........................F 937 338-3281
Burkettsville *(G-1698)*

Winesburg Meats Inc...........................G 330 359-5092
Winesburg *(G-14609)*

Winner Corporation.............................E 419 582-4321
Yorkshire *(G-14797)*

Youngs Locker Service Inc...................F 740 599-6833
Danville *(G-5601)*

2013 Sausages and other prepared meats

A To Z Portion Ctrl Meats Inc...............E 419 358-2926
Bluffton *(G-1356)*

▲ Advancepierre Foods Inc...................B 513 874-8741
West Chester *(G-14097)*

Advancperre Foods Holdings Inc...........D 513 428-5699
West Chester *(G-14098)*

Amish Wedding Foods Inc...................... E 330 674-9199
Millersburg *(G-9969)*

B&G Foods Inc................................. D 513 482-8226
Cincinnati *(G-2397)*

Brinkman Turkey Farms Inc............... F 419 365-5127
Findlay *(G-6846)*

Carl Rittberger Sr Inc...................... E 740 452-2767
Zanesville *(G-15004)*

Duma Meats Inc............................ G 330 628-3438
Mogadore *(G-10074)*

Empire Packing Company LP............ D 513 942-5400
West Chester *(G-14117)*

Fink Meat Company Inc................... G 937 390-2750
Springfield *(G-12311)*

Foris Extraordinary Meats LLC......... F 614 670-5726
Columbus *(G-4931)*

Frank Brunckhorst Company LLC....... G 614 662-5300
Groveport *(G-7434)*

Fresh Mark Inc.............................. A 330 455-5253
Canton *(G-1894)*

Fresh Mark Inc.............................. A 330 332-8508
Salem *(G-11781)*

◆ Fresh Mark Inc........................... B 330 832-7491
Massillon *(G-9192)*

Hoffman Meat Processing................ G 419 864-3994
Cardington *(G-2054)*

Honeybaked Foods Inc.................... A 567 703-0002
Holland *(G-7767)*

Honeybaked Ham Company............. E 513 583-9700
Cincinnati *(G-2730)*

Iowa Quality Meats Ltd................... C 515 225-6868
Cincinnati *(G-2753)*

John Krusinski............................. F 216 441-0100
Cleveland *(G-3889)*

John Stehlin & Sons Co................... C 513 385-6164
Cincinnati *(G-2769)*

Karn Meats Inc............................. E 614 252-3712
Columbus *(G-5046)*

Keystone Foods LLC...................... C 419 257-2341
North Baltimore *(G-10613)*

King Kold Inc............................... E 937 836-2731
Englewood *(G-6617)*

Kraft Heinz Foods Company............. C 740 622-0523
Coshocton *(G-5458)*

Lee Williams Meats Inc................... E 419 729-3893
Toledo *(G-13031)*

Lipari Foods Operating Co LLC......... E 330 893-2479
Millersburg *(G-9992)*

Lipari Foods Operating Co LLC......... E 330 674-9199
Millersburg *(G-9993)*

Lous Sausage Ltd.......................... G 216 752-5060
Cleveland *(G-3968)*

Marshallville Packing Co Inc............. G 330 855-2871
Marshallville *(G-9007)*

Martin-Brower Company LLC............ C 513 773-2301
West Chester *(G-14027)*

Owens Foods Inc........................... B
New Albany *(G-10349)*

Patrick M Davidson........................ G 513 897-2971
Waynesville *(G-13882)*

Pettisville Meats Incorporated........... F 419 445-0921
Pettisville *(G-11286)*

Pierre Holding Corp....................... G 513 874-8741
West Chester *(G-14137)*

Queen City Sausage & Prov Inc......... E 513 541-5581
Cincinnati *(G-3025)*

Rays Sausage Inc.......................... G 216 921-8782
Cleveland *(G-4226)*

Simply Unique Snacks LLC............... E 513 223-7736
Cincinnati *(G-3092)*

Sugar Creek Packing Co.................. G 937 268-6601
Dayton *(G-6029)*

◆ Sugar Creek Packing Co................ B 513 551-5280
Cincinnati *(G-3122)*

Sunrise Foods Inc.......................... E 614 276-2880
Columbus *(G-5297)*

The Ellenbee-Leggett Company Inc...... C 513 874-3200
Fairfield *(G-6782)*

◆ White Castle System Inc................ B 614 228-5781
Columbus *(G-5367)*

Williams Pork Co Op....................... G 419 682-9022
Stryker *(G-12628)*

Winner Corporation........................ E 419 582-4321
Yorkshire *(G-14797)*

Youngs Locker Service Inc................ F 740 599-6833
Danville *(G-5601)*

◆ Zwanenberg Food Group (usa) Inc.... F 513 682-6000
Cincinnati *(G-3244)*

2015 Poultry slaughtering and processing

▲ Advancepierre Foods Inc............... B 513 874-8741
West Chester *(G-14097)*

▼ Ballas Egg Products Corp.............. D 614 453-0386
Zanesville *(G-14991)*

BE Products Inc............................ G 740 453-0386
Zanesville *(G-14994)*

Brinkman Turkey Farms Inc............. F 419 365-5127
Findlay *(G-6846)*

Cal-Maine Foods Inc....................... D 937 337-9576
Rossburg *(G-11655)*

Cal-Maine Foods Inc....................... F 937 968-4874
Union City *(G-13413)*

Case Farms LLC........................... D 330 832-0030
Massillon *(G-9178)*

Case Farms of Ohio Inc.................. C 330 359-7141
Winesburg *(G-14605)*

Case Farms Processing Inc.............. E 330 455-0241
Winesburg *(G-14606)*

Cooper Foods............................... E 419 232-2440
Van Wert *(G-13530)*

Cooper Hatchery Inc....................... C 419 238-4869
Van Wert *(G-13531)*

Cooper Hatchery Inc....................... C 419 594-3325
Oakwood *(G-10897)*

▲ Daylay Egg Farm Inc................... C 937 355-6531
West Mansfield *(G-14178)*

Fort Recovery Equity Inc................. E 419 375-4119
Fort Recovery *(G-6963)*

Gerber Farm Division LLC................ G 800 362-7381
Orrville *(G-10982)*

Gerber Poultry LLC........................ B 330 857-2731
Kidron *(G-8127)*

Imex Bz LLC................................ F 786 866-8798
Orrville *(G-10986)*

Just Natural Provision Company......... G 216 431-7922
Cleveland *(G-3899)*

Martin-Brower Company LLC............ C 513 773-2301
West Chester *(G-14027)*

Nature Pure LLC........................... E 937 358-2364
West Mansfield *(G-14180)*

▲ Ohio Fresh Eggs LLC................... G 740 893-7200
Croton *(G-5515)*

Pf Management Inc......................... G 513 874-8741
West Chester *(G-14136)*

Pierre Holding Corp....................... G 513 874-8741
West Chester *(G-14137)*

Rcf Kitchens Indiana LLC................ G 765 478-6600
Dayton *(G-5976)*

Roots Poultry Inc.......................... G 419 332-0041
Fremont *(G-7130)*

Sid-Mar Foods Inc......................... G 330 743-0112
Youngstown *(G-14931)*

The Ellenbee-Leggett Company Inc...... C 513 874-3200
Fairfield *(G-6782)*

V H Cooper & Co Inc...................... A 419 678-4853
Saint Henry *(G-11727)*

V H Cooper & Co Inc...................... C 419 375-4116
Fort Recovery *(G-6973)*

▲ Weaver Bros Inc........................ D 937 526-3907
Versailles *(G-13605)*

Whitewater Processing LLC............... D 513 367-4133
Harrison *(G-7572)*

2021 Creamery butter

Dairy Farmers America Inc.............. G 330 670-7800
Medina *(G-9395)*

Heavenly Creamery Inc................... G 440 593-6080
Conneaut *(G-5403)*

Minerva Dairy Inc......................... D 330 868-4196
Minerva *(G-10042)*

New Dairy Cincinnati LLC................ D 214 258-1200
Cincinnati *(G-2900)*

New Dairy Ohio LLC...................... D 214 258-1200
Cleveland *(G-4073)*

2022 Cheese; natural and processed

▲ 9444 Ohio Holding Co................. E 330 359-6291
Winesburg *(G-14604)*

A&M Cheese Co............................ D 419 476-8369
Toledo *(G-12860)*

Alpine Dairy LLC.......................... E 330 359-6291
Dundee *(G-6364)*

Amish Wedding Foods Inc............... E 330 674-9199
Millersburg *(G-9969)*

▼ Brewster Cheese Company........... C 330 767-3492
Brewster *(G-1490)*

Bunker Hill Cheese Co Inc.............. D 330 893-2131
Millersburg *(G-9973)*

Dairy Farmers America Inc.............. G 330 670-7800
Medina *(G-9395)*

◆ Great Lakes Cheese Co Inc........... B 440 834-2500
Hiram *(G-7739)*

Guggisberg Cheese Inc.................. E 330 893-2550
Millersburg *(G-9982)*

▲ Hans Rothenbuhler & Son Inc....... E 440 632-6000
Middlefield *(G-9796)*

▲ Holmes Cheese Co..................... E 330 674-6451
Millersburg *(G-9986)*

Inter American Products Inc............. D 800 645-2233
Cincinnati *(G-2748)*

Kathys Krafts and Kollectibles.......... G 423 787-3709
Medina *(G-9417)*

Kraft Heinz Foods Company............. E 513 339-0045
Mason *(G-9119)*

Krafts Exotika LLC........................ G 216 563-1178
Cleveland *(G-3928)*

▲ Lake Erie Frozen Foods Mfg Co...... D 419 289-9204
Ashland *(G-548)*

Lakeview Farms LLC...................... C 419 695-9925
Delphos *(G-6190)*

Land OLakes Inc........................... C 330 678-1578
Kent *(G-8045)*

Lipari Foods Operating Co LLC......... E 330 893-2479
Millersburg *(G-9992)*

Lipari Foods Operating Co LLC......... E 330 674-9199
Millersburg *(G-9993)*

▲ Miceli Dairy Products Co.............. D 216 791-6222
Cleveland *(G-4027)*

Middlebury Cheese Company LLC...... F 330 893-2500
Millersburg *(G-9997)*

Middlfeld Original Cheese Coop......... F 440 632-5567
Middlefield *(G-9812)*

Minerva Dairy Inc......................... D 330 868-4196
Minerva *(G-10042)*

Pearl Valley Cheese Inc.................. E 740 545-6002
Fresno *(G-7147)*

S
I
C

Rothenbuhler Cheese Chalet LLC.......... G 800 327-9477
Middlefield *(G-9824)*

Rothenbuhler Holding Company............ G 440 632-6000
Middlefield *(G-9825)*

Schindlers Broad Run Chshuse I............ F 330 343-4108
Dover *(G-6260)*

Tri State Dairy LLC................................ G 419 542-8788
Hicksville *(G-7653)*

Tri State Dairy LLC................................ G 330 897-5555
Baltic *(G-782)*

2023 Dry, condensed, evaporated products

Ai Life LLC... F 513 605-1079
Mason *(G-9058)*

All-In Nutritionals LLC........................... F 888 400-0333
Springfield *(G-12278)*

Eagle Family Foods Group LLC.............. E 330 382-3725
Cleveland *(G-3647)*

▲ Freedom Health LLC.......................... E 330 562-0888
Aurora *(G-670)*

▲ Hans Rothenbuhler & Son Inc.......... E 440 632-6000
Middlefield *(G-9796)*

▲ Infinit Nutrition LLC.......................... F 513 791-3500
Blue Ash *(G-1288)*

◆ Ingredia Inc.....................................E 419 738-4060
Wapakoneta *(G-13716)*

Innovated Health LLC........................... G 330 858-0651
Cuyahoga Falls *(G-5549)*

Instantwhip-Columbus Inc.................... E 614 871-9447
Grove City *(G-7391)*

Instantwhip-Dayton Inc........................ G 937 435-4371
Dayton *(G-5824)*

▲ Instantwhip-Dayton Inc.................... G 937 235-5930
Dayton *(G-5823)*

◆ J M Smucker Company.....................A 330 682-3000
Orrville *(G-10987)*

Minerva Dairy Inc................................ D 330 868-4196
Minerva *(G-10042)*

▲ Muscle Feast LLC............................. F 740 877-8808
Nashport *(G-10301)*

Nestle Usa Inc..................................... D 216 861-8350
Cleveland *(G-4070)*

Nestle Usa Inc..................................... B 440 349-5757
Solon *(G-12159)*

Nestle Usa Inc..................................... B 440 264-6600
Solon *(G-12160)*

New Dairy Ohio Transport LLC.............. D 214 258-1200
Cleveland *(G-4074)*

New Diry Cincinnati Trnspt LLC............. D 214 258-1200
Cincinnati *(G-2901)*

Nu Pet Company.................................. E 330 682-3000
Orrville *(G-10998)*

Rich Products Corporation.................... C 614 771-1117
Hilliard *(G-7699)*

▲ Stolle Milk Biologics Inc.................. G 513 489-7997
West Chester *(G-14150)*

Wileys Finest LLC................................ C 740 622-1072
Coshocton *(G-5478)*

▲ Yoders Fine Foods LLC.................... F 740 668-4961
Gambier *(G-7215)*

2024 Ice cream and frozen deserts

ABC Refreshments LLC......................... F 216 692-0697
Euclid *(G-6637)*

Cfgsc LLC.. G 513 772-5920
Cincinnati *(G-2454)*

Country Parlour Ice Cream Co............... G 440 237-4040
Cleveland *(G-3570)*

Crmd LLC.. G 440 225-7179
Columbus *(G-4861)*

Danone Us LLC.................................... E 513 229-0092
Mason *(G-9092)*

Danone Us LLC.................................... B 419 628-1295
Minster *(G-10055)*

Dietsch Brothers Incorporated.............. E 419 422-4474
Findlay *(G-6859)*

Fritzie Freeze Inc................................. G 419 727-0818
Toledo *(G-12969)*

Graeters Ice Cream Company................ D 513 721-3323
Cincinnati *(G-2687)*

Home City Ice Company........................ F 419 562-4953
Delaware *(G-6157)*

Honeybaked Ham Company................... E 513 583-9700
Cincinnati *(G-2730)*

International Brand Services.................. E 513 376-8209
Cincinnati *(G-2751)*

Jenis Splendid Ice Creams LLC............. E 614 488-3224
Columbus *(G-5036)*

Johnsons Real Ice Cream LLC............... D 614 231-0014
Columbus *(G-5042)*

▲ Malleys Candies LLC......................... D 216 362-8700
Cleveland *(G-3983)*

New Bltmore Ice Cream Pdts Inc.......... E 330 904-6687
Canton *(G-1956)*

Pierres Ice Cream Company Inc............. D 216 432-1144
Cleveland *(G-4164)*

Robert E McGrath Inc........................... F 440 572-7747
Strongsville *(G-12593)*

Smithfoods Inc.................................... E 330 683-8710
Orrville *(G-11008)*

Superior Dairy Inc................................ C 330 477-4515
Canton *(G-2021)*

Sweeties Olympia Treats LLC................ F 440 572-7747
Strongsville *(G-12608)*

Toft Dairy Inc...................................... D 419 625-4376
Sandusky *(G-11877)*

United Dairy Inc.................................. B 740 373-4121
Marietta *(G-8958)*

United Dairy Inc.................................. C 740 633-1451
Martins Ferry *(G-9011)*

United Dairy Farmers Inc...................... C 513 396-8700
Cincinnati *(G-3181)*

Velvet Ice Cream Company.................... D 740 892-3921
Utica *(G-13488)*

Weldon Ice Cream Company.................. G 740 467-2400
Millersport *(G-10026)*

Youngs Jersey Dairy Inc....................... B 937 325-0629
Yellow Springs *(G-14794)*

2026 Fluid milk

Arps Dairy Inc..................................... F 419 782-9116
Defiance *(G-6098)*

Borden Dairy Co Cincinnati LLC............ E 513 948-8811
Cleveland *(G-3428)*

Consun Food Industries Inc.................. E 440 322-6301
Elyria *(G-6514)*

Dairy Farmers America Inc.................... G 330 670-7800
Medina *(G-9395)*

Daisy Brand LLC.................................. F 330 202-4410
Wooster *(G-14633)*

Dfa Dairy Brands Ice Cream LLC........... B 419 473-9621
Toledo *(G-12943)*

Green Field Farms Co-Op...................... G 330 263-0246
Wooster *(G-14645)*

Instantwhip Connecticut Inc................. F 614 488-2536
Columbus *(G-5010)*

Instantwhip Foods Inc.......................... F 614 488-2536
Columbus *(G-5011)*

Instantwhip Products Co PA................. F 614 488-2536
Columbus *(G-5012)*

Instantwhip-Buffalo Inc........................ F 614 488-2536
Columbus *(G-5013)*

Instantwhip-Chicago Inc....................... F 614 488-2536
Columbus *(G-5014)*

Instantwhip-Columbus Inc.................... E 614 871-9447
Grove City *(G-7391)*

Instantwhip-Dayton Inc........................ G 937 435-4371
Dayton *(G-5824)*

▲ Instantwhip-Dayton Inc.................... G 937 235-5930
Dayton *(G-5823)*

Instantwhip-Syracuse Inc..................... F 614 488-2536
Columbus *(G-5015)*

Lakeview Farms LLC............................. C 419 695-9925
Delphos *(G-6190)*

Louis Instantwhip-St Inc....................... F 614 488-2536
Columbus *(G-5076)*

Peak Foods Llc.................................... D 937 440-0707
Troy *(G-13247)*

Philadelphia Instantwhip Inc................. F 614 488-2536
Columbus *(G-5191)*

Reiter Dairy LLC Dean Foods................ G 937 323-5777
Springfield *(G-12368)*

Reiter Dairy of Akron Inc...................... E 937 323-5777
Springfield *(G-12369)*

Smithfoods Inc.................................... E 330 683-8710
Orrville *(G-11008)*

Snowville Creamery LLC....................... E 740 698-2301
Pomeroy *(G-11438)*

Superior Dairy Inc................................ C 330 477-4515
Canton *(G-2021)*

Toft Dairy Inc...................................... D 419 625-4376
Sandusky *(G-11877)*

United Dairy Inc.................................. B 740 373-4121
Marietta *(G-8958)*

United Dairy Inc.................................. C 740 633-1451
Martins Ferry *(G-9011)*

United Dairy Farmers Inc...................... C 513 396-8700
Cincinnati *(G-3181)*

2032 Canned specialties

Abbott Laboratories............................. A 614 624-3191
Columbus *(G-4660)*

Ajinomoto Hlth Ntrtn N Amer In............ D 330 762-6652
Akron *(G-23)*

B&G Foods Inc.................................... D 513 482-8226
Cincinnati *(G-2397)*

Baxters North America Inc.................... E 513 552-7463
Blue Ash *(G-1247)*

Baxters North America Inc.................... C 513 552-7400
Blue Ash *(G-1248)*

Baxters North America Inc.................... E 513 552-7728
Blue Ash *(G-1249)*

◆ Baxters North America Inc.................D 513 552-7718
West Chester *(G-14106)*

▼ Baxters North America Inc................ E 513 552-7485
Cincinnati *(G-2404)*

Beckman & Gast Company.................... F 419 678-4195
Saint Henry *(G-11720)*

Bittersweet Inc.................................... D 419 875-6986
Whitehouse *(G-14358)*

Cheese Holdings Inc............................ E 330 893-2479
Millersburg *(G-9977)*

Clovervale Farms LLC........................... D 440 960-0146
Amherst *(G-444)*

Conagra Brands Inc............................. D 419 445-8015
Archbold *(G-491)*

Food Designs Inc................................. F 216 651-9221
Cleveland *(G-3733)*

▲ Hayden Valley Foods Inc.................. E 614 539-7233
Grove City *(G-7390)*

Heritage Cooperative Inc...................... F 740 828-2215
Nashport *(G-10300)*

JES Foods/Celina Inc........................... F 419 586-7446
Celina *(G-2112)*

John Zidian Company........................... F 330 965-8455
North Jackson *(G-10690)*

▲ John Zidian Company............. E 330 743-6050
Youngstown (G-14883)

Lonolife Inc................................. G 614 296-2250
Columbus (G-5074)

Magic Wok Inc............................ G 419 531-1818
Toledo (G-13044)

▲ More Than Gourmet Holdings Inc... E 330 762-6652
Akron (G-237)

▲ Oasis Mditerranean Cuisine Inc....... E 419 269-1459
Toledo (G-13067)

◆ Robert Rothschild Farm LLC..........F 855 969-8050
West Chester (G-14069)

▲ Skyline Cem Holdings LLC............... C 513 874-1188
Fairfield (G-6776)

Trevor Clatterbuck...................... G 330 359-2129
Wilmot (G-14595)

Wornick Holding Company Inc..... E 513 794-9800
Blue Ash (G-1354)

2033 Canned fruits and specialties

Agricool Veg & Fruits LLC.............. G 310 625-0024
South Euclid (G-12217)

Annarino Foods Ltd.................... E 937 274-3663
Dayton (G-5659)

B&G Foods Inc........................... D 513 482-8226
Cincinnati (G-2397)

Beckman & Gast Company......... F 419 678-4195
Saint Henry (G-11720)

Bellisio Foods Inc...................... C 740 286-5505
Jackson (G-7940)

Clovervale Farms LLC................ D 440 960-0146
Amherst (G-444)

Coopers Mill Inc......................... G 419 562-4215
Bucyrus (G-1676)

◆ Country Pure Foods Inc.............C 330 753-2293
Akron (G-108)

Dominion Liquid Tech LLC.......... E 513 272-2824
Cincinnati (G-2557)

Foster Canning Inc.................... E 419 841-6755
Toledo (G-12968)

Fremont Company....................... E 419 363-2924
Rockford (G-11630)

▼ Fremont Company.................... D 419 334-8995
Fremont (G-7108)

▼ Fry Foods Inc......................... E 419 448-0831
Tiffin (G-12784)

Gwj Liquidation Inc................... F 216 475-5770
Cleveland (G-3002)

Hirzel Canning Company............ G 419 523-3225
Ottawa (G-11034)

Hirzel Canning Company............ G 419 287-3288
Pemberville (G-11175)

▲ Hirzel Canning Company........... E 419 693-0531
Northwood (G-10803)

Inter American Products Inc........ D 800 645-2233
Cincinnati (G-2748)

◆ J M Smucker Company..............A 330 682-3000
Orrville (G-10987)

JES Foods Inc............................F 216 883-8987
Medina (G-9415)

JES Foods/Celina Inc................. F 419 586-7446
Celina (G-2112)

Knudsen & Sons Inc.................. G 330 682-3000
Orrville (G-10991)

Kraft Heinz Company.................. A 330 837-8331
Massillon (G-9213)

◆ Meiers Wine Cellars Inc........... E 513 891-2900
Cincinnati (G-2861)

Milos Whole World Gourmet LLC.... G 740 589-6456
Nelsonville (G-10319)

Nu Pet Company.......................... E 330 682-3000
Orrville (G-10998)

◆ Ohio Pure Foods Inc................. D 330 753-2293
Akron (G-254)

Pillsbury Company LLC.............. D 419 845-3751
Caledonia (G-1733)

Pillsbury Company LLC.............. D 740 286-2170
Wellston (G-13909)

▼ Portion Pac Inc....................... B 513 398-0400
Mason (G-9134)

RC Industries Inc...................... E 330 879-5486
Navarre (G-10313)

Refresco Us Inc......................... C 937 790-1400
Carlisle (G-2072)

◆ Robert Rothschild Farm LLC.......F 855 969-8050
West Chester (G-14069)

Rosebuds Ranch and Garden LLC........ F 937 214-1801
Covington (G-5499)

Smucker Foodservice Inc........... G 877 858-3855
Orrville (G-11009)

▼ Smucker International Inc......... F 330 682-3000
Orrville (G-11010)

Smucker Manufacturing Inc........ G 888 550-9555
Orrville (G-11011)

Smucker Retail Foods Inc.......... F 330 684-1500
Orrville (G-11013)

The Fremont Kraut Company....... F 419 332-6481
Fremont (G-7135)

Trevor Clatterbuck...................... G 330 359-2129
Wilmot (G-14595)

Two Grndmthers Gourmet Kit LLC........ G 614 746-0888
Reynoldsburg (G-11585)

Welch Foods Inc A Cooperative.... D 513 632-5610
Cincinnati (G-3215)

▲ Yoders Fine Foods LLC............. F 740 668-4961
Gambier (G-7215)

2034 Dehydrated fruits, vegetables, soups

Appalachia Freeze Dry Co LLC..... F 740 412-0169
Richmond Dale (G-11606)

Bosc & Brie................................. F 614 985-2215
Columbus (G-4769)

Frezerve Inc.............................. G 440 661-4037
Ashtabula (G-592)

Green Gourmet Foods LLC......... G 740 400-4212
Baltimore (G-786)

▲ Hayden Valley Foods Inc........... E 614 539-7233
Grove City (G-7390)

▲ Hirzel Canning Company........... E 419 693-0531
Northwood (G-10803)

Kanan Enterprises Inc............... D 440 248-8484
Solon (G-12135)

Kanan Enterprises Inc............... F 440 349-0719
Solon (G-12136)

◆ Kanan Enterprises Inc.............C 440 248-8484
Solon (G-12134)

Kettle Creations LLC................... E 567 940-9401
Lima (G-8423)

Peaceful Fruits LLC.................... F 330 356-8515
Barberton (G-832)

2035 Pickles, sauces, and salad dressings

Anderson Brothers Entps Inc................ E 440 269-3920
Willoughby (G-14420)

Annarino Foods Ltd.................... E 937 274-3663
Dayton (G-5659)

B&G Foods Inc........................... D 513 482-8226
Cincinnati (G-2397)

Belton Foods LLC...................... E 937 890-7768
Dayton (G-5676)

Consumer Guild Foods Inc.......... G 419 726-3406
Toledo (G-12931)

◆ Crowning Food Company...........D 937 323-4699
Springfield (G-12296)

Dave Krissinger.......................... G 440 669-9957
Chardon (G-2202)

Fremont Company....................... E 419 363-2924
Rockford (G-11630)

Hinkle Fine Foods Inc................. F 937 836-3665
Dayton (G-5810)

◆ J M Smucker Company..............A 330 682-3000
Orrville (G-10987)

JES Foods/Celina Inc................. F 419 586-7446
Celina (G-2112)

▲ Kaiser Foods Inc..................... E 513 621-2053
Cincinnati (G-2779)

Kaiser Pickles LLC...................... F 513 621-2053
Cincinnati (G-2781)

Kaiser Pickles LLC.................... G 513 621-2053
Cincinnati (G-2780)

Lancaster Colony Corporation...... F 614 792-9774
Dublin (G-6317)

◆ Lancaster Colony Corporation....E 614 224-7141
Westerville (G-14218)

Lancaster Glass Corporation....... C 614 224-7141
Westerville (G-14219)

Lariccias Italian Foods Inc......... F 330 729-0222
Youngstown (G-14887)

Lbzb Restaurants Inc.................. E 567 413-4700
Bowling Green (G-1424)

Lhpc Inc.................................... E 330 527-2696
Garrettsville (G-7224)

Mark Grzianis St Treats Ex Inc.............. F 330 414-6266
Kent (G-8049)

Michael Zakany LLC.................... G 740 221-3934
Zanesville (G-15028)

▲ National Foods Packaging Inc..... E 216 622-2740
Cleveland (G-4060)

Nu Pet Company.......................... E 330 682-3000
Orrville (G-10998)

▼ Portion Pac Inc....................... B 513 398-0400
Mason (G-9134)

Randys Pickles LLC.................... G 440 864-6611
Cleveland (G-4223)

RC Industries Inc...................... E 330 879-5486
Navarre (G-10313)

Ribs King Inc............................ G 513 791-1942
Cincinnati (G-3043)

◆ Robert Rothschild Farm LLC.......F 855 969-8050
West Chester (G-14069)

Sunrise Foods Inc..................... E 614 276-2880
Columbus (C 5207)

◆ Tmarzetti Company....................C 614 846-2232
Westerville (G-14237)

Tulkoff Food Products Ohio LLC........... G 410 864-0523
Cincinnati (G-3176)

◆ Woeber Mustard Mfg Co.............C 937 323-6281
Springfield (G-12394)

2037 Frozen fruits and vegetables

Beverages Holdings LLC............. A 513 483-3300
Blue Ash (G-1252)

Big Gus Onion Rings Inc............ G 216 883-9045
Cleveland (G-3418)

◆ Country Pure Foods Inc............C 330 753-2293
Akron (G-108)

Heinz Foreign Investment Co....... G 330 837-8331
Massillon (G-9200)

▲ HJ Heinz Company LP.............. D 330 837-8331
Massillon (G-9202)

▲ Lake Erie Frozen Foods Mfg Co.... D 419 289-9204
Ashland (G-548)

National Frt Vgtable Tech Corp.... F 740 400-4055
Columbus (G-5121)

Nestle Prepared Foods Company........... B 440 349-5757
Solon (G-12157)

▲ Nestle Prepared Foods Company..... A 440 248-3600
Solon *(G-12158)*

Ohios Best Juice Company LLC........... F 440 258-0834
Reynoldsburg *(G-11577)*

Simply Unique Snacks LLC.................. G 513 223-7736
Cincinnati *(G-3092)*

2038 Frozen specialties, nec

Athens Foods Inc................................... C 216 676-8500
Cleveland *(G-3384)*

Aunt Minnies Food Services Inc........... F 419 872-4396
Toledo *(G-12888)*

◆ Bellisio...F 740 286-5505
Jackson *(G-7939)*

Bellisio Foods Inc................................. C 740 286-5505
Jackson *(G-7940)*

Brilista Foods Company Inc................. G 614 299-4132
Columbus *(G-4780)*

Clovervale Farms LLC.......................... D 440 960-0146
Amherst *(G-444)*

Dioguardis Italian Foods Inc............... F 330 492-3777
Canton *(G-1883)*

▼ Frozen Specialties Inc..................... C 419 445-9015
Archbold *(G-494)*

▼ Fry Foods Inc.................................... E 419 448-0831
Tiffin *(G-12784)*

Jtm Provisions Company Inc............... B 513 367-4900
Harrison *(G-7557)*

Jtm Provisions Company Inc............... B 513 367-4900
Harrison *(G-7556)*

▲ Kahiki Foods Inc.............................. C 614 322-3180
Gahanna *(G-7162)*

King Kold Inc.. E 937 836-2731
Englewood *(G-6617)*

▲ Lake Erie Frozen Foods Mfg Co....... D 419 289-9204
Ashland *(G-548)*

◆ Lancaster Colony Corporation.........E 614 224-7141
Westerville *(G-14218)*

McDonalds.. F 513 753-6100
Amelia *(G-433)*

McDonalds.. F 513 752-2008
Cincinnati *(G-2313)*

McDonalds.. F 216 226-7754
Lakewood *(G-8169)*

McDonalds.. E 513 336-0820
Mason *(G-9127)*

McDonalds.. F 740 753-4018
Nelsonville *(G-10318)*

McDonalds.. F 419 935-1414
Willard *(G-14404)*

McDonalds.. F 330 792-0527
Youngstown *(G-14895)*

Nestle Prepared Foods Company........... B 440 349-5757
Solon *(G-12157)*

▲ Nestle Prepared Foods Company..... A 440 248-3600
Solon *(G-12158)*

Oats Overnight Inc............................... D 602 492-1751
West Chester *(G-14035)*

R & D Nestle Center Inc...................... C 440 349-5757
Solon *(G-12171)*

Rsw Distributors LLC........................... F 502 587-8877
Blue Ash *(G-1328)*

Schwans Mama Rosass LLC............... C 937 498-4511
Sidney *(G-12049)*

▲ Skyline Cem Holdings LLC.............. C 513 874-1188
Fairfield *(G-6776)*

Sonic Drive-In...................................... G 937 717-6917
Springfield *(G-12374)*

▲ Stouffer Corporation........................ C 440 349-5757
Solon *(G-12186)*

Sunrise Foods Inc............................... E 614 276-2880
Columbus *(G-5297)*

Superb Bakehouse Inc.......................... F 614 302-7242
Groveport *(G-7451)*

▲ Worthington Foods Inc...................... D 740 453-5501
Zanesville *(G-15055)*

2041 Flour and other grain mill products

1-2-3 Gluten Free Inc.......................... G 216 378-9233
Chagrin Falls *(G-2133)*

Archer-Daniels-Midland Company......... E 419 435-6633
Fostoria *(G-6975)*

Archer-Daniels-Midland Company......... G 419 705-3292
Toledo *(G-12884)*

Bunge North America East LLC............. G 419 483-5340
Bellevue *(G-1121)*

Cargill Incorporated............................. E 937 236-1971
Dayton *(G-5693)*

Countyline Co-Op Inc........................... F 419 287-3241
Pemberville *(G-11174)*

Crestar Crusts Inc................................ F 740 335-4813
Wshngtn Ct Hs *(G-14736)*

Dik Jaxon Products Co Inc................... F 937 890-7350
Dayton *(G-5748)*

H Nagel & Son Co.................................. F 513 665-4550
Cincinnati *(G-2700)*

Hansen-Mueller Co............................. G 419 729-5535
Toledo *(G-12986)*

I Dream of Cakes................................. G 937 533-6024
Eaton *(G-6455)*

Keynes Bros Inc................................... D 740 385-6824
Logan *(G-8517)*

Legacy Farmers Cooperative............... F 419 423-2611
Findlay *(G-6884)*

Mennel Milling Company...................... D 419 436-5130
Fostoria *(G-6989)*

Mennel Milling Company...................... F 419 435-8151
Fostoria *(G-6990)*

Mennel Milling Company...................... F 419 307-9657
Fostoria *(G-6991)*

Mennel Milling Company...................... E 740 385-6824
Logan *(G-8521)*

Mennel Milling Company...................... F 419 294-2337
Upper Sandusky *(G-13448)*

Mennel Milling Company...................... G 419 458-3041
Wharton *(G-14351)*

Minster Farmers Coop Exch................ D 419 628-4705
Minster *(G-10061)*

▼ Mullet Enterprises Inc..................... G 330 852-4681
Sugarcreek *(G-12643)*

Pettisville Grain Co.............................. E 419 446-2547
Pettisville *(G-11285)*

Pillsbury Company LLC........................ D 419 845-3751
Caledonia *(G-1733)*

Pillsbury Company LLC........................ D 740 286-2170
Wellston *(G-13909)*

Premier Feeds LLC.............................. G 937 584-2411
Sabina *(G-11683)*

Sunrise Cooperative Inc...................... G 419 628-4705
Minster *(G-10066)*

▲ The Mennel Milling Company........... E 419 435-8151
Fostoria *(G-7003)*

2043 Cereal breakfast foods

General Mills Inc.................................. D 513 771-8200
Cincinnati *(G-2663)*

General Mills Inc.................................. F 419 269-3100
Toledo *(G-12974)*

General Mills Inc.................................. D 740 286-2170
Wellston *(G-13907)*

Kellanova.. F 614 879-9659
West Jefferson *(G-14163)*

Kellanova.. C 740 453-5501
Zanesville *(G-15024)*

Kween and Co....................................... F 440 724-4342
Brooklyn Heights *(G-1534)*

Niese Farms... G 419 347-1204
Crestline *(G-5504)*

Olde Man Granola LLC......................... F 419 819-9576
Findlay *(G-6902)*

Treehouse Private Brands Inc.............. D 740 654-8880
Lancaster *(G-8231)*

Treehouse Private Brands Inc.............. E 740 654-8880
Lancaster *(G-8232)*

2045 Prepared flour mixes and doughs

◆ Abitec Corporation............................E 614 429-6464
Columbus *(G-4665)*

Athens Foods Inc................................. C 216 676-8500
Cleveland *(G-3384)*

Bakemark USA LLC.............................. F 440 323-5100
Elyria *(G-6501)*

Busken Bakery Inc............................... D 513 871-2114
Cincinnati *(G-2434)*

Cassanos Inc....................................... E 937 294-8400
Dayton *(G-5695)*

Fleetchem LLC..................................... F 513 539-1111
Monroe *(G-10105)*

Kween and Co....................................... Fy 440 724-4342
Brooklyn Heights *(G-1534)*

Mid American Ventures Inc.................. F 216 524-0974
Cleveland *(G-4031)*

▲ National Foods Packaging Inc........... E 216 622-2740
Cleveland *(G-4060)*

◆ Procter & Gamble Mfg Co................F 513 983-1100
Cincinnati *(G-3002)*

Rich Products Corporation................... C 614 771-1117
Hilliard *(G-7699)*

2046 Wet corn milling

Cargill Incorporated............................. E 937 236-1971
Dayton *(G-5693)*

Fluid Quip Ks LLC................................ D 937 324-0352
Springfield *(G-12313)*

Poet Biorefining Marion LLC................ E 740 383-4400
Marion *(G-8990)*

Primary Pdts Ingrdnts Amrcas L......... F 937 235-4074
Dayton *(G-5954)*

2047 Dog and cat food

Bil-Jac Foods Inc................................. E 330 722-7888
Medina *(G-9380)*

Bravo LLC.. F 866 922-9222
Moraine *(G-10151)*

Cargill Incorporated............................. G 419 394-3374
Saint Marys *(G-11735)*

Foster Canning Inc.............................. E 419 841-6755
Toledo *(G-12968)*

G & C Raw LLC.................................... G 937 827-0010
Versailles *(G-13595)*

Hartz Mountain Corporation................ D 513 877-2131
Pleasant Plain *(G-11432)*

JM Smucker LLC.................................. D 330 682-3000
Orrville *(G-10990)*

▼ Kelly Foods Corporation................... E 330 722-8855
Medina *(G-9418)*

Land OLakes Inc.................................. D 330 879-2158
Massillon *(G-9214)*

Mars Petcare Us Inc............................ E 614 878-7242
Columbus *(G-5083)*

Mars Petcare Us Inc............................ E 419 943-4280
Leipsic *(G-8307)*

Nestle Purina Petcare Company.......... C 740 454-8575
Zanesville *(G-15032)*

Ohio Blenders Inc................................ F 419 726-2655
Toledo *(G-13072)*

◆ Ohio Pet Foods Inc..............E 330 424-1431
Lisbon *(G-8477)*

◆ Pro-Pet LLC..............D 419 394-3374
Saint Marys *(G-11749)*

Purina Mills LLC..............G 330 682-1951
Orrville *(G-11002)*

▲ Vitakraft Sun Seed Inc..............D 419 832-1641
Weston *(G-14350)*

2048 Prepared feeds, nec

Alsatian Llc..............G 330 661-0600
Medina *(G-9374)*

Archer-Daniels-Midland Company..............G 330 852-3025
Sugarcreek *(G-12631)*

Archer-Daniels-Midland Company..............G 419 705-3292
Toledo *(G-12884)*

Brightpet Nutrition Group LLC..............E 330 424-1431
Lisbon *(G-8464)*

Cargill Incorporated..............D 330 745-0031
Akron *(G-90)*

Cargill Incorporated..............C 216 651-7200
Cleveland *(G-3470)*

Cargill Incorporated..............G 419 394-3374
Saint Marys *(G-11735)*

Cargill Incorporated..............F 937 497-4848
Sidney *(G-11999)*

Centerra Co-Op..............E 419 281-2153
Ashland *(G-526)*

Cooper Farms Inc..............D 419 594-3325
Oakwood *(G-10896)*

Cooper Hatchery Inc..............C 419 594-3325
Oakwood *(G-10897)*

D&D Ingredient Distrs Inc..............F 419 692-2667
Spencerville *(G-12237)*

Direct Action Co Inc..............F 330 364-3219
Dover *(G-6236)*

Four Natures Keepers Inc..............F 740 363-8007
Delaware *(G-6148)*

G A Wintzer and Son Company..............D 419 739-4913
Wapakoneta *(G-13712)*

G A Wintzer and Son Company..............F 419 739-4900
Wapakoneta *(G-13711)*

Gerber & Sons Inc..............E 330 897-6201
Baltic *(G-778)*

Ggc Feeds LLC..............E 419 445-2451
Archbold *(G-496)*

Granville Milling Co..............G 740 345-1305
Newark *(G-10505)*

▼ Hamlet Protein Inc..............E 567 525-5627
Findlay *(G-6876)*

Hanby Farms Inc..............E 740 763-3554
Nashport *(G-10299)*

Hartz Mountain Corporation..............D 513 877-2131
Pleasant Plain *(G-11432)*

▲ Kalmbach Feeds Inc..............E 419 294-3838
Upper Sandusky *(G-13443)*

▼ Kelly Foods Corporation..............E 330 722-8855
Medina *(G-9418)*

Land OLakes Inc..............D 330 879-2158
Massillon *(G-9214)*

Legacy Farmers Cooperative..............F 419 423-2611
Findlay *(G-6884)*

▲ Magnus International Group Inc..............G 216 592-8355
Painesville *(G-11097)*

Mars Horsecare Us Inc..............E 330 828-2251
Dalton *(G-5588)*

Mennel Milling Company..............G 419 458-3041
Wharton *(G-14351)*

Mid-Wood Inc..............G 419 257-3331
North Baltimore *(G-10614)*

Nature Pure LLC..............F 937 358-2364
Raymond *(G-11553)*

Natures Way Bird Products LLC..............E 440 554-6166
Chagrin Falls *(G-2172)*

Ohio Blenders Inc..............F 419 726-2655
Toledo *(G-13072)*

◆ Ohio Pet Foods Inc..............E 330 424-1431
Lisbon *(G-8477)*

Pettisville Grain Co..............E 419 446-2547
Pettisville *(G-11285)*

Premier Feeds LLC..............G 937 584-2411
Sabina *(G-11683)*

Premier Grain LLC..............G 937 584-6552
Bowersville *(G-1402)*

Premier Grain LLC..............G 937 584-6552
Sabina *(G-11684)*

◆ Pro-Pet LLC..............D 419 394-3374
Saint Marys *(G-11749)*

Provimi North America Inc..............E 937 770-2400
Lewisburg *(G-8363)*

Provimi North America Inc..............F 937 770-2400
Lewisburg *(G-8364)*

▲ Provimi North America Inc..............B 937 770-2400
Lewisburg *(G-8362)*

Quality Liquid Feeds Inc..............F 330 532-4635
Wellsville *(G-13913)*

Rek Associates LLC..............F 419 294-3838
Upper Sandusky *(G-13454)*

▼ Republic Mills Inc..............F 419 758-3511
Okolona *(G-10932)*

Ridley USA Inc..............F 800 837-8222
Botkins *(G-1398)*

Rowe Premix Inc..............G 937 678-9015
West Manchester *(G-14177)*

Spencer Feed & Supply LLC..............F 330 648-2111
Spencer *(G-12235)*

Stony Hill Mixing Ltd..............G 330 674-0814
Millersburg *(G-10011)*

The F L Emmert Co Inc..............F 513 721-5808
Cincinnati *(G-3147)*

▲ The Mennel Milling Company..............E 419 435-8151
Fostoria *(G-7003)*

Toledo Alfalfa Mills Inc..............G 419 836-3705
Oregon *(G-10969)*

▼ Verhoff Alfalfa Mills Inc..............G 419 523-4767
Ottawa *(G-11049)*

▲ Vitakraft Sun Seed Inc..............D 419 832-1641
Weston *(G-14350)*

Woodstock Products Inc..............G 216 641-3811
Cleveland *(G-1516)*

2051 Bread, cake, and related products

Alfred Nickles Bakery Inc..............E 740 453-6522
Zanesville *(G-14985)*

Amish Door Inc..............C 330 359-5464
Wilmot *(G-14592)*

Angelic Bakehouse LLC..............E 414 312-7300
Westerville *(G-14203)*

Arlington Valley Farms LLC..............E 216 426-5000
Hudson *(G-7833)*

B & J Baking Company..............F 513 541-2386
Cincinnati *(G-2394)*

Bimbo Qsr Us LLC..............G 740 562-4188
Zanesville *(G-14996)*

Blf Enterprises Inc..............F 937 642-6425
Westerville *(G-14246)*

Bread Kneads Inc..............G 419 422-3863
Findlay *(G-6845)*

Brooks Pastries Inc..............G 614 274-4880
Plain City *(G-11399)*

Buns of Delaware Inc..............F 740 363-2867
Delaware *(G-6135)*

Cake House Cleveland LLC..............F 216 870-4659
Cleveland *(G-3460)*

Cake In A Cup Inc..............G 419 491-1104
Toledo *(G-12909)*

Crispie Creme Chillicothe Inc..............G 740 774-3770
Chillicothe *(G-2249)*

Crumbs Inc..............F 740 592-3803
Athens *(G-637)*

Dandi Enterprises Inc..............G 419 516-9070
Solon *(G-12099)*

Evans Bakery Inc..............G 937 228-4151
Dayton *(G-5771)*

Fragapane Bakeries Inc..............F 440 779-6050
North Olmsted *(G-10721)*

Gardner Pie Company..............C 330 245-2030
Coventry Township *(G-5483)*

Garys Chesecakes Fine Desserts..............G 513 574-1700
Cincinnati *(G-2652)*

Gawa Traders LLC..............E 614 697-1440
Columbus *(G-4946)*

Graeters Ice Cream Company..............D 513 721-3323
Cincinnati *(G-2687)*

Hannibal Company Inc..............F 614 846-5060
Worthington *(G-14711)*

Harvest Commissary LLC..............E 513 706-1951
Granville *(G-7315)*

Heinens Inc..............C 330 562-5297
Aurora *(G-673)*

Home Bakery..............F 419 678-3018
Coldwater *(G-4578)*

Hostess Brands Inc..............D 816 701-4600
Orrville *(G-10984)*

Hostess Brands LLC..............D 816 701-4600
Orrville *(G-10985)*

◆ Interbake Foods LLC..............E 614 294-4931
Columbus *(G-5018)*

Investors United Inc..............G 419 473-8942
Toledo *(G-13008)*

▲ Jasmine Distributing Ltd..............E 216 251-9420
Cleveland *(G-3883)*

K & B Acquisitions Inc..............F 937 253-1163
Dayton *(G-5837)*

Kennedys Bakery Inc..............G 740 432-2301
Cambridge *(G-1746)*

Killer Brownie Ltd..............D 937 530-8600
Miamisburg *(G-9706)*

Killer Brownie Ltd..............E 937 535-5690
Miamisburg *(G-9705)*

Klosterman Baking Co LLC..............C 513 242-5667
Cincinnati *(G-2000)*

Klosterman Baking Co LLC..............F 513 398-2707
Mason *(G-9118)*

Krispy Kreme Doughnut Corp..............E 614 798-0812
Columbus *(G-5057)*

Krispy Kreme Doughnut Corp..............D 614 876-0058
Columbus *(G-5058)*

La Marquise Inc..............D 614 488-1911
Columbus *(G-5060)*

Main Street Gourmet LLC..............C 330 929-0000
Cuyahoga Falls *(G-5560)*

Mary Ann Donut Shoppe Inc..............G 330 478-1655
Canton *(G-1938)*

McHappys Dnuts Parkersburg Inc..............D 740 593-8744
Athens *(G-643)*

McL Inc..............E 614 861-6259
Columbus *(G-5092)*

Meeks Pastry Shop..............G 419 782-4871
Defiance *(G-6121)*

Morgan4140 LLC..............F 513 873-1426
Cincinnati *(G-2887)*

Mustard Seed Health Fd Mkt Inc..............E 440 519-3663
Solon *(G-12155)*

New Horizons Baking Co LLC..............C 419 668-8226
Norwalk *(G-10854)*

S
I
C

New York Frozen Foods Inc.................. E 626 338-3000
Westerville *(G-14223)*

New York Frozen Foods Inc.................. B 216 292-5655
Bedford *(G-1049)*

Norcia Bakery.................................. G 330 454-1077
Canton *(G-1959)*

▲ Orlando Baking Company.................. C 216 361-1872
Cleveland *(G-4124)*

Osmans Pies Inc.............................. E 330 607-9083
Stow *(G-12448)*

Papa Joes Pies Inc........................... F 440 960-7437
Amherst *(G-451)*

Pf Management Inc............................ G 513 874-8741
West Chester *(G-14136)*

Pierre Holding Corp........................... G 513 874-8741
West Chester *(G-14137)*

Quality Bakery Company Inc.............. C 614 224-1424
Columbus *(G-5218)*

Rich Products Corporation.................. C 614 771-1117
Hilliard *(G-7699)*

Riesbeck Food Markets Inc............... 740 695-3401
Saint Clairsville *(G-11709)*

Rudys Strudel Shop........................... G 440 886-4430
Cleveland *(G-4264)*

Scheiders Foods LLC........................ F 740 404-6641
Mount Perry *(G-10226)*

Schulers Bakery Inc.......................... E 937 323-4154
Springfield *(G-12371)*

Schwebel Baking Company................ F 216 481-1880
Euclid *(G-6678)*

Schwebel Baking Company................ E 330 783-2860
Hebron *(G-7635)*

Schwebel Baking Company................ F 330 926-9410
North Canton *(G-10667)*

Schwebel Baking Company................ C 440 248-1500
Solon *(G-12179)*

Schwebel Baking Company................ F 440 846-1921
Strongsville *(G-12595)*

Schwebel Baking Company................ E 330 783-2860
Youngstown *(G-14929)*

Schwebel Baking Company................ B 330 783-2860
Youngstown *(G-14928)*

Servatii Inc..................................... G 513 271-5040
Cincinnati *(G-3083)*

▲ Sister Schbrts Hmmade Rlls Inc........ C 334 335-2232
Westerville *(G-14233)*

Skyliner.. G 740 738-0874
Bridgeport *(G-1496)*

Studgionsgroup LLC.......................... E 216 804-1561
Cleveland *(G-4339)*

Suelos Sweetz LLC........................... G 440 478-1301
Willowick *(G-14568)*

Sweet Persuasions LLC.................... G 614 216-9052
Pickerington *(G-11301)*

Thurns Bakery & Deli........................ G 614 221-9246
Columbus *(G-5323)*

Toast With Cake LLC......................... G 937 554-5900
Miamisburg *(G-9748)*

Trumbull Mobile Meals...................... F 330 394-2538
Warren *(G-13803)*

Uncle Jays Cakes LLC....................... G 513 882-3433
Cincinnati *(G-3178)*

Uprising Food Inc............................. G 513 313-1087
Cincinnati *(G-3187)*

Wal-Bon of Ohio Inc.......................... E 740 423-8178
Belpre *(G-1156)*

Wal-Bon of Ohio Inc.......................... F 740 423-6351
Belpre *(G-1155)*

◆ White Castle System Inc................... B 614 228-5781
Columbus *(G-5367)*

2052 Cookies and crackers

Basic Grain Products Inc.................... D 419 678-2304
Coldwater *(G-4568)*

Blf Enterprises Inc........................... F 937 642-6425
Westerville *(G-14246)*

▲ Brand Castle LLC............................ E 216 292-7700
Bedford Heights *(G-1070)*

Cheryl & Co................................... F 614 776-1500
Obetz *(G-10923)*

Cookie Bouquets Inc........................ G 614 888-2171
Columbus *(G-4847)*

Ditsch Usa LLC............................... E 513 782-8888
Cincinnati *(G-2551)*

Ditsch Usa LLC............................... G 513 782-8888
Cincinnati *(G-2552)*

Hearthside Food Solutions LLC............ A 419 293-2911
Mc Comb *(G-9353)*

Imagine Baking Buyer LLC.................. F 419 502-9000
Sandusky *(G-11840)*

◆ Interbake Foods LLC......................... D 614 294-4931
Columbus *(G-5018)*

Keebler Company............................ C 513 271-3500
Cincinnati *(G-2790)*

Kennedys Bakery Inc........................ G 740 432-2301
Cambridge *(G-1746)*

La Marquise Inc............................... D 614 488-1911
Columbus *(G-5060)*

Main Street Gourmet LLC................... C 330 929-0000
Cuyahoga Falls *(G-5560)*

Mmelo Btq Confectioners LLC............. G 614 822-9530
Reynoldsburg *(G-11574)*

Norcia Bakery.................................. G 330 454-1077
Canton *(G-1959)*

◆ Norse Dairy Systems LP................... B 614 294-4931
Columbus *(G-5129)*

Osmans Pies Inc.............................. E 330 607-9083
Stow *(G-12448)*

Pepperidge Farm Incorporated............. G 419 933-2611
Willard *(G-14407)*

Rudys Strudel Shop........................... G 440 886-4430
Cleveland *(G-4264)*

Schulers Bakery Inc.......................... E 937 323-4154
Springfield *(G-12371)*

Yz Enterprises Inc............................ E 419 893-8777
Maumee *(G-9331)*

2053 Frozen bakery products, except bread

Gardner Pie Company....................... C 330 245-2030
Coventry Township *(G-5483)*

Keough and Associates LLC............... G 440 682-0514
Chardon *(G-2209)*

Main Street Gourmet LLC................... C 330 929-0000
Cuyahoga Falls *(G-5560)*

Pepperidge Farm Incorporated............. G 419 933-2611
Willard *(G-14407)*

2063 Beet sugar

Michigan Sugar Company................... F 419 332-9931
Fremont *(G-7123)*

2064 Candy and other confectionery products

▲ Amerisource Health Svcs LLC............ D 614 492-8177
Columbus *(G-4703)*

▲ Anthony-Thomas Candy Company....... C 614 274-8405
Columbus *(G-4719)*

Appalachia Freeze Dry Co LLC............. F 740 412-0169
Richmond Dale *(G-11606)*

Barfections LLC............................... G 330 759-3100
Hubbard *(G-7809)*

Barfections LLC............................... G 330 759-3100
Youngstown *(G-14818)*

Barfections LLC............................... F 330 759-3100
Girard *(G-7266)*

Bloomer Candy Co........................... C 740 452-7501
Zanesville *(G-14998)*

Bucks For Pups Confections LLC......... F 614 359-4672
Columbus *(G-4787)*

Chocolate Pig Inc............................ G 440 461-4511
Cleveland *(G-3496)*

Coblentz Family Brands Inc................ E 330 893-2995
Walnut Creek *(G-13693)*

▲ Crazy Monkey Baking Inc.................. G 419 903-0403
Ashland *(G-531)*

Dauphin Holdings Inc........................ G 330 733-4022
Akron *(G-116)*

Esther Price Candies Corporation......... E 937 253-2121
Dayton *(G-5769)*

Executive Sweets East Inc................. G 440 359-9866
Oakwood Village *(G-10905)*

Fawn Confectionery Inc..................... F 513 574-9612
Cincinnati *(G-2613)*

Giannios Candy Co Inc...................... E 330 755-7000
Struthers *(G-12618)*

Good Nutrition LLC.......................... F 216 534-6617
Oakwood Village *(G-10906)*

Graeters Ice Cream Company............. D 513 721-3323
Cincinnati *(G-2687)*

Great Lakes Popcorn Company........... G 419 732-3080
Port Clinton *(G-11443)*

▲ Hake Head LLC.............................. G 614 291-2244
Columbus *(G-4967)*

▲ Hayden Valley Foods Inc................... E 614 539-7233
Grove City *(G-7390)*

Humphrey Popcorn Company.............. F 216 662-6629
Strongsville *(G-12565)*

▼ International Confections.................. C 800 288-8002
Columbus *(G-5019)*

Island Delights Inc........................... G 866 887-4100
Seville *(G-11918)*

◆ Jml Holdings Inc............................. F 419 866-7500
Holland *(G-7770)*

Keho Fitness and Nutrition LLC............ G 740 587-1313
Hebron *(G-7621)*

Life Is Sweet LLC............................ F 330 342-0172
Cincinnati *(G-2821)*

Light Vision................................... G 513 351-9444
Cincinnati *(G-2822)*

▲ Malleys Candies LLC........................ D 216 362-8700
Cleveland *(G-3983)*

Maries Candies LLC.......................... G 937 465-3061
West Liberty *(G-14176)*

Marshas Buckeyes LLC..................... E 419 872-7666
Perrysburg *(G-11237)*

Milk Hney Cndy Soda Shoppe LLC........ G 330 492-5884
Canton *(G-1950)*

New Bloomer Candy Company LLC....... E 740 452-7501
Zanesville *(G-15033)*

Piqua Chocolate Company Inc............. G 937 773-1981
Piqua *(G-11374)*

Richards Maple Products Inc............... G 440 286-4160
Chardon *(G-2221)*

Robert A Malone.............................. F 740 947-2859
Waverly *(G-13873)*

▲ Spangler Candy Company.................. C 419 636-4221
Bryan *(G-1660)*

Superior Street Holding Inc................. F 419 626-5757
Sandusky *(G-11874)*

▲ Superior Street Holding Inc................. E 419 626-5757
Sandusky *(G-11873)*

Tiffin Paper Company........................ E 419 447-2121
Tiffin *(G-12804)*

2066 Chocolate and cocoa products

▲ Anthony-Thomas Candy Company... C 614 274-8405
Columbus (G-4719)

▲ Benjamin P Forbes Company........... F 440 838-4400
Broadview Heights (G-1499)

Brandts Candies Inc........................ G 440 942-1016
Willoughby (G-14433)

Brantley Partners IV LP.................... G 216 464-8400
Cleveland (G-3434)

Cheryl & Co...................................... F 614 776-1500
Obetz (G-10923)

Chocolate Pig Inc............................ G 440 461-4511
Cleveland (G-3496)

Coblentz Family Brands Inc............. E 330 893-2995
Walnut Creek (G-13693)

Dietsch Brothers Incorporated............. E .. 419 422-4474
Findlay (G-6859)

Executive Sweets East Inc.............. G 440 359-9866
Oakwood Village (G-10905)

Fannie May Confections Inc............. A 330 494-0833
North Canton (G-10638)

Fawn Confectionery Inc................... F 513 574-9612
Cincinnati (G-2613)

Giannios Candy Co Inc.................... E 330 755-7000
Struthers (G-12618)

Golden Turtle Chocolate Fctry........... G 513 932-1990
Lebanon (G-8264)

Gorant Chocolatier LLC................... C 330 726-8821
Boardman (G-1372)

Graeters Ice Cream Company........... D 513 721-3323
Cincinnati (G-2687)

▲ Harry London Candies Inc............... E 330 494-0833
North Canton (G-10645)

Hartville Chocolates Inc.................. G 330 877-1999
Hartville (G-7576)

▼ L C F Inc....................................... G 330 877-3322
Hartville (G-7579)

Linneas Candy Supplies Inc............. E 330 678-7112
Kent (G-8046)

▲ Malleys Candies LLC...................... D 216 362-8700
Cleveland (G-3983)

Milk Hney Cndy Soda Shoppe LLC........ G 330 492-5884
Canton (G-1950)

Mmelo Btq Confectioners LLC.......... G 614 822-9530
Reynoldsburg (G-11574)

Robert E McGrath Inc......................F 440 572-7747
Strongsville (G-12593)

Sweeties Olympia Treats LLC............. F 440 572-7747
Strongsville (G-12608)

2068 Salted and roasted nuts and seeds

▲ Anthony-Thomas Candy Company... C 614 274-8405
Columbus (G-4719)

CJ Dannemiller Co........................... E 330 825-7808
Norton (G-10819)

▲ Hayden Valley Foods Inc................ E 614 539-7233
Grove City (G-7390)

Kanan Enterprises Inc..................... D 440 248-8484
Solon (G-12135)

Kanan Enterprises Inc..................... F 440 349-0719
Solon (G-12136)

◆ Kanan Enterprises Inc....................C 440 248-8484
Solon (G-12134)

▲ Malleys Candies LLC...................... D 216 362-8700
Cleveland (G-3983)

Nuts Are Good Inc........................... F 586 619-2400
Columbus (G-5133)

Simply Unique Snacks LLC............... G 513 223-7736
Cincinnati (G-3092)

Trophy Nut Co................................. G 937 669-5513
Tipp City (G-12850)

◆ Trophy Nut Co................................E 937 667-8478
Tipp City (G-12849)

2074 Cottonseed oil mills

Hirzel Farms Inc.............................. G 419 837-2710
Luckey (G-8670)

2075 Soybean oil mills

Archer-Daniels-Midland Company.......... E 419 435-6633
Fostoria (G-6975)

Bunge North America East LLC............. G 419 483-5340
Bellevue (G-1121)

Cargill Incorporated......................... D 937 498-4555
Sidney (G-12000)

Schlessman Seed Co........................ E 419 499-2572
Milan (G-9918)

Solae LLC....................................... D 419 483-0400
Bellevue (G-1132)

2077 Animal and marine fats and oils

Archer-Daniels-Midland Company.......... E 419 435-6633
Fostoria (G-6975)

Cargill Incorporated......................... D 937 498-4555
Sidney (G-12000)

Darling Ingredients Inc..................... F 972 717-0300
Cincinnati (G-2541)

Darling Ingredients Inc..................... G 216 651-9300
Cleveland (G-3599)

Darling Ingredients Inc..................... G 216 351-3440
Cleveland (G-3600)

Fiske Brothers Refining Co................ D 419 691-2491
Toledo (G-12965)

Griffin Industries LLC....................... F 513 549-0041
Blue Ash (G-1279)

▲ Holmes By-Products Co Inc............. E 330 893-2322
Millersburg (G-9985)

Inland Products Inc.......................... F 740 245-5514
Rio Grande (G-11617)

Inland Products Inc.......................... F 614 443-3425
Columbus (G-5006)

◆ The Dupps Company........................D 937 855-6555
Germantown (G-7255)

▼ Werner G Smith Inc........................ F 216 861-3676
Cleveland (G-4501)

Wileys Finest LLC........................... C 740 622-1072
Coshocton (G-5478)

2079 Edible fats and oils

Cincinnati Biorefining Corp............... F 513 482-8800
Cincinnati (G-2471)

◆ Cincinnati Renewable Fuels LLC........D 513 482-8800
Cincinnati (G-2484)

Inter American Products Inc.............. D 800 645-2233
Cincinnati (G-2748)

◆ Liquid Manufacturing Solutions..........E 937 401-0821
Franklin (G-7031)

◆ Procter & Gamble Mfg Co...................F 513 983-1100
Cincinnati (G-3002)

Wileys Finest LLC........................... C 740 622-1072
Coshocton (G-5478)

2082 Malt beverages

Anheuser-Busch LLC........................ B 614 847-6213
Columbus (G-4718)

Artisan Ales LLC............................. G 216 544-8703
Cleveland (G-3369)

Bar 25 LLC..................................... E 216 373-3700
Cleveland (G-3404)

Bar 25 LLC..................................... G 216 621-4000
Cleveland (G-3403)

Branch & Bone Artisan Ales LLC........ F 937 723-7608
Dayton (G-5683)

Brew Kettle Inc............................... F 440 234-8788
Strongsville (G-12546)

Brew Kettle Strongsville LLC............. G 440 915-7074
Medina (G-9386)

Brewdog Brewing Company LLC.......... F 614 908-3051
Canal Winchester (G-1786)

Brewpub Restaurant Corporation........ F 614 228-2537
Columbus (G-4774)

Bummin Beaver Brewery LLC............ G 440 543-9900
Chagrin Falls (G-2156)

Cincinnati Beverage Company........... E 513 904-8910
Cincinnati (G-2470)

Columbus Kombucha Company LLC... G ... 614 262-0000
Columbus (G-4828)

Dayton Heidelberg Distrg Co............. C 440 989-1027
Lorain (G-8554)

▲ District Brewing Company Inc.......... E 614 224-3626
Columbus (G-4886)

Dswdwk LLC................................... G 513 853-5021
Cincinnati (G-2564)

Dvdbrew LLC.................................. F 513 677-2739
Loveland (G-8624)

Fifty West Brewing Company LLC......... E 740 775-2337
Chillicothe (G-2251)

Georgetown Vineyards Inc................. E 740 435-3222
Cambridge (G-1744)

Great Lakes Brewing Co................... E 216 771-4404
Cleveland (G-3788)

Great Lakes Brewing Co................... E 216 771-4404
Strongsville (G-12561)

◆ Great Lakes Brewing Co....................C 216 771-4404
Cleveland (G-3789)

Green Room Brewing LLC................. G 614 421-2337
Columbus (G-4966)

Lock 15 Brewing Company LLC.......... E 234 900-8277
Akron (G-208)

Lock 27 Brewing LLC....................... F 937 433-2739
Dayton (G-5853)

Mansfield Brew Works LLC................ F 419 631-3153
Mansfield (G-8818)

Maumee Bay Brewing Company.......... E 419 243-1253
Toledo (G-13047)

Miiler Brewing Company................... E 513 896-9200
Trenton (G-13193)

Molson Coors Bev Co USA LLC..........C 513 896-9200
Trenton (G-13194)

Nine Giant Brewing LLC................... G 510 220-5104
Cincinnati (G-2910)

Noble Beast Brewing LLC................. G 570 809-6405
Cleveland (G-1070)

Phunkenship - Platform Beer Co........ F 216 417-7743
Cleveland (G-4161)

Platform Beers LLC.......................... F 440 539-3245
Cleveland (G-4173)

Rhinegeist Holding Company Inc.......... G 513 381-1367
Cincinnati (G-3042)

Rocky River Brewing Co................... G 440 895-2739
Rocky River (G-11638)

Royal Docks Brewing Co LLC............ D 330 353-9103
Massillon (G-9239)

◆ Samuel Adams Brewery Company LtdD 513 412-3200
Cincinnati (G-3062)

Snyder Intl Brewing Group LLC.......... E 216 619-7424
Cleveland (G-4310)

South Side Drive Thru...................... G 937 295-2927
Fort Loramie (G-6957)

Wedco LLC..................................... G 513 309-0781
Mount Orab (G-10223)

Wild Ohio Brewing Company............. G 614 262-0000
Columbus (G-5368)

Willoughby Brewing Company LLC........ G 440 975-0202
Willoughby (G-14550)

2083 Malt

S
I
C

Ohio Crafted Malt House LLC................ G..... 614 961-7805
New Albany *(G-10347)*

2084 Wines, brandy, and brandy spirits

Amani Vines LLC............................... F..... 440 335-5432
Cleveland *(G-3338)*

Barrel Run Crssing Wnery Vnyrd.......... G..... 330 325-1075
Rootstown *(G-11647)*

Breitenbach Wine Cellars Inc.............. G..... 330 343-3603
Dover *(G-6232)*

Buckeye Lake Winery........................ F..... 614 439-7576
Thornville *(G-12765)*

Cask 307 LLC................................ F..... 440 307-9586
Madison *(G-8724)*

Chad M Marsh................................ G..... 419 994-0587
Loudonville *(G-8590)*

Chalet Debonne Vineyards Inc............. F..... 440 466-3485
Madison *(G-8725)*

Delaware City Vineyard..................... F..... 740 362-6383
Delaware *(G-6141)*

E & J Gallo Winery.......................... E..... 513 381-4050
Cincinnati *(G-2568)*

Ferrante Wine Farm Inc.................... F..... 440 466-8466
Geneva *(G-7237)*

Georgetown Vineyards Inc.................. E..... 740 435-3222
Cambridge *(G-1744)*

Gillig Custom Winery Inc.................... G..... 419 202-6057
Findlay *(G-6871)*

Glenn Ravens Winery........................ G..... 740 545-1000
West Lafayette *(G-14170)*

Hillside Winery.............................. G..... 419 456-3434
Gilboa *(G-7261)*

J E Nicolozakes Co.......................... G..... 740 310-1606
Cambridge *(G-1745)*

John Christ Winery Inc...................... G..... 440 933-9672
Avon Lake *(G-761)*

Kelleys Island Winery Inc................... G..... 419 746-2678
Kelleys Island *(G-8008)*

Klingshirn Winery Inc....................... G..... 440 933-6666
Avon Lake *(G-762)*

Laurentia Winery............................ F..... 440 296-9170
Madison *(G-8731)*

Lincoln Way Vineyards Inc.................. F..... 330 804-9463
Wooster *(G-14660)*

▲ Lonz Winery LLC.......................... E..... 419 625-5474
Sandusky *(G-11851)*

Losantiville Winery LLC..................... G..... 513 918-3015
Cincinnati *(G-2829)*

Marie Noble Wine Company................ E..... 216 633-0025
Euclid *(G-6659)*

Mastropietro Winery Inc.................... G..... 330 547-2151
Berlin Center *(G-1201)*

◆ Meiers Wine Cellars Inc................. E..... 513 891-2900
Cincinnati *(G-2861)*

Old Firehouse Winery Inc................... E..... 440 466-9300
Geneva *(G-7244)*

Old Mason Winery Inc....................... G..... 937 698-1122
West Milton *(G-14184)*

Olde Schlhuse Vnyrd Winery LLC......... F..... 937 472-9463
Eaton *(G-6461)*

▲ Paramount Distillers Inc................ B..... 216 671-6300
Cleveland *(G-4134)*

Perennial Vineyards LLC.................... F..... 330 832-3677
Navarre *(G-10310)*

Quinami LLC................................. G..... 419 797-4445
Port Clinton *(G-11450)*

R & T Estate LLC............................ F..... 216 862-0822
Cleveland *(G-4219)*

Sandra Weddington.......................... F..... 740 417-4286
Delaware *(G-6172)*

Sapphire Creek Wnery Grdns LLC........ F..... 440 543-7777
Chagrin Falls *(G-2182)*

Sarahs Vineyard Inc......................... G..... 330 929-8057
Cuyahoga Falls *(G-5571)*

Shawne Springs Winery...................... G..... 740 623-0744
Coshocton *(G-5472)*

Tramonte & Sons Inc........................ F..... 513 770-5501
Lebanon *(G-8290)*

Twenty One Barrels Ltd..................... G..... 937 467-4498
Bradford *(G-1453)*

Twisted Vine Family Vinyrd LLC........... G..... 740 256-1923
Patriot *(G-11152)*

Ugly Bunny Winery LLC...................... F..... 330 988-9057
Loudonville *(G-8596)*

Vineyards At Pine Lake Inc.................. E..... 330 549-0195
Columbiana *(G-4632)*

Vino Di Piccin LLC........................... F..... 740 738-0261
Lansing *(G-8234)*

Vinoklet Winery Inc.......................... E..... 513 385-9309
Cincinnati *(G-3206)*

Vintage Wine Distributor Inc............... F..... 513 443-4300
West Chester *(G-14090)*

Vpl LLC...................................... F..... 330 549-0195
Columbiana *(G-4634)*

Wine Mill.................................... G..... 234 571-2594
Peninsula *(G-11187)*

Winery At Wilcox Inc........................ G..... 937 526-3232
Versailles *(G-13606)*

Winery At Wolf Creek........................ F..... 330 666-9285
Barberton *(G-841)*

Wyandotte Winery LLC...................... F..... 614 357-7522
Columbus *(G-5376)*

2085 Distilled and blended liquors

Blue Collar M LLC........................... F..... 216 209-5666
Solon *(G-12086)*

Brain Brew Ventures 30 Inc................. F..... 513 310-6374
Newtown *(G-10583)*

Karrikin Spirits Company LLC.............. F..... 513 561-5000
Cincinnati *(G-2784)*

Luxco Inc.................................... G..... 216 671-6300
Cleveland *(G-3972)*

March First Manufacturing LLC............ G..... 513 266-3076
Cincinnati *(G-2845)*

▲ Paramount Distillers Inc................ B..... 216 671-6300
Cleveland *(G-4134)*

Simple Times LLC............................ G..... 614 504-3551
Columbus *(G-5270)*

Toledo Spirits Company LLC................ F..... 419 704-3705
Toledo *(G-13158)*

Veriano Fine Foods Spirits Ltd............. F..... 614 745-7705
New Albany *(G-10354)*

Watershed Distillery LLC.................... E..... 614 357-1936
Columbus *(G-5357)*

Western Reserve Distillers LLC............ G..... 330 780-9599
Lakewood *(G-8173)*

2086 Bottled and canned soft drinks

Abbott Laboratories........................ A..... 614 624-3191
Columbus *(G-4660)*

▲ Akron Coca-Cola Bottling Co........... A..... 330 784-2653
Akron *(G-27)*

American Bottling Company................. E..... 330 733-3830
Akron *(G-55)*

American Bottling Company................. D..... 513 381-4891
Cincinnati *(G-2356)*

American Bottling Company................. D..... 513 242-5151
Cincinnati *(G-2357)*

American Bottling Company................. D..... 614 237-4201
Columbus *(G-4692)*

American Bottling Company................. C..... 614 237-4201
Columbus *(G-4693)*

American Bottling Company................. C..... 937 236-0333
Dayton *(G-5650)*

American Bottling Company................. D..... 419 229-7777
Lima *(G-8387)*

American Bottling Company................. E..... 740 423-9230
Little Hocking *(G-8486)*

American Bottling Company................. E..... 740 922-5253
Midvale *(G-9906)*

American Bottling Company................. D..... 740 377-4371
South Point *(G-12222)*

American Bottling Company................. D..... 419 535-0777
Toledo *(G-12873)*

Belton Foods LLC............................ E..... 937 890-7768
Dayton *(G-5676)*

Beverages Holdings LLC..................... A..... 513 483-3300
Blue Ash *(G-1252)*

Borden Dairy Co Cincinnati LLC........... E..... 513 948-8811
Cleveland *(G-3428)*

Ccbcc Operations LLC....................... D..... 304 203-8647
Lockbourne *(G-8487)*

Central Coca-Cola Btlg Co Inc............. E..... 330 875-1487
Akron *(G-95)*

Central Coca-Cola Btlg Co Inc............. E..... 740 474-2180
Circleville *(G-3250)*

Central Coca-Cola Btlg Co Inc............. E..... 440 324-3335
Elyria *(G-6511)*

Central Coca-Cola Btlg Co Inc............. C..... 614 863-7200
Lockbourne *(G-8488)*

Central Coca-Cola Btlg Co Inc............. E..... 419 522-2653
Mansfield *(G-8773)*

Central Coca-Cola Btlg Co Inc............. C..... 419 476-6622
Toledo *(G-12913)*

Central Coca-Cola Btlg Co Inc............. C..... 330 425-4401
Twinsburg *(G-13285)*

Central Coca-Cola Btlg Co Inc............. E..... 440 269-1433
Willoughby *(G-14438)*

Central Coca-Cola Btlg Co Inc............. E..... 330 783-1982
Youngstown *(G-14833)*

Central Coca-Cola Btlg Co Inc............. E..... 740 452-3608
Zanesville *(G-15006)*

Central Investment LLC..................... F..... 513 563-4700
Cincinnati *(G-2450)*

Cincinnati Marlins Inc...................... G..... 513 761-3320
Cincinnati *(G-2480)*

Cleveland Coca-Cola Btlg Inc.............. C..... 216 690-2653
Bedford Heights *(G-1073)*

Coca-Cola Company.......................... E..... 614 491-6305
Columbus *(G-4815)*

Coca-Cola Consolidated Inc................ A..... 513 527-6600
Cincinnati *(G-2503)*

Coca-Cola Consolidated Inc................ A..... 937 878-5000
Dayton *(G-5704)*

Coca-Cola Consolidated Inc................ G..... 419 422-3743
Lima *(G-8395)*

Coca-Cola Consolidated Inc................ C..... 740 353-3133
Portsmouth *(G-11464)*

Consolidated Bottling Company............ C..... 419 227-3541
Lima *(G-8396)*

◆ Country Pure Foods Inc.................. C..... 330 753-2293
Akron *(G-108)*

Currier Richard & James.................... G..... 440 988-4132
Amherst *(G-445)*

Dr Pepper Bottlers Associates............. G..... 330 746-7651
Youngstown *(G-14849)*

Dr Pepper Snapple Group.................... G..... 419 223-0072
Lima *(G-8402)*

Dr Pepper/Seven Up Inc..................... F..... 513 875-2466
Fayetteville *(G-6827)*

Dr Pepper/Seven Up Inc..................... F..... 419 229-7777
Lima *(G-8403)*

Fbg Bottling Group LLC..................... G..... 614 580-7063
Columbus *(G-4920)*

G & J Pepsi-Cola Bottlers Inc.............. E..... 740 593-3366
Athens *(G-640)*

G & J Pepsi-Cola Bottlers Inc.............. E 740 774-2148
Chillicothe (G-2252)

G & J Pepsi-Cola Bottlers Inc.............. E 866 647-2734
Columbus (G-4942)

G & J Pepsi-Cola Bottlers Inc.............. A 614 253-8771
Columbus (G-4943)

G & J Pepsi-Cola Bottlers Inc.............. B 740 354-9191
Franklin Furnace (G-7058)

G & J Pepsi-Cola Bottlers Inc.............. D 513 896-3700
Hamilton (G-7492)

G & J Pepsi-Cola Bottlers Inc.............. E 740 354-9191
Zanesville (G-15017)

G & J Pepsi-Cola Bottlers Inc.............. F 513 785-6060
Cincinnati (G-2644)

Gehm & Sons Limited.......................... G 330 724-8423
Akron (G-158)

Gem Beverages Inc.............................. F 740 384-2411
Wellston (G-13906)

Gordon Brothers Btlg Group Inc........... G 330 337-8754
Salem (G-11782)

Hornell Brewing Co Inc........................ G 516 812-0384
Cincinnati (G-2732)

Keurig Dr Pepper Inc........................... D 614 237-4201
Columbus (G-5051)

Life Support Development Ltd............... G 614 221-1765
Columbus (G-5067)

◆ Meiers Wine Cellars Inc.................... E 513 891-2900
Cincinnati (G-2861)

National Beverage Corp....................... F 614 491-5415
Obetz (G-10925)

Ohio Beverage Systems Inc................. F 216 475-3900
Cleveland (G-4112)

Ohio Eagle Distributing LLC................ E 513 539-8483
West Chester (G-14037)

▲ Ohio Pure Foods Inc........................ D 330 753-2293
Akron (G-254)

On US LLC.. E 330 286-3436
Kent (G-8057)

P-Americas LLC................................... E 614 253-8771
Columbus (G-5167)

P-Americas LLC................................... F 440 323-5524
Elyria (G-6575)

P-Americas LLC................................... C 419 227-3541
Lima (G-8436)

P-Americas LLC................................... E 330 837-4224
Massillon (G-9230)

P-Americas LLC................................... E 740 266-6121
Steubenville (G-12409)

P-Americas LLC................................... E 330 746-7652
Youngstown (G-14910)

Pepsi-Cola Metro Btlg Co Inc.............. F 614 261-8193
Columbus (G-5185)

Pepsi-Cola Metro Btlg Co Inc.............. D 937 461-4664
Dayton (G-5936)

Pepsi-Cola Metro Btlg Co Inc.............. F 440 323-5524
Elyria (G-6577)

Pepsi-Cola Metro Btlg Co Inc.............. G 937 328-6750
Springfield (G-12361)

Pepsi-Cola Metro Btlg Co Inc.............. D 419 534-2186
Toledo (G-13093)

Pepsi-Cola Metro Btlg Co Inc.............. C 330 425-8236
Twinsburg (G-13353)

Pepsi-Cola Metro Btlg Co Inc.............. G 330 963-5300
Twinsburg (G-13354)

Shasta Beverages Inc......................... D 614 491-5415
Obetz (G-10926)

▼ Smucker International Inc................. F 330 682-3000
Orrville (G-11010)

Smucker Natural Foods Inc.................. A 330 682-3000
Orrville (G-11012)

2087 Flavoring extracts and syrups, nec

Abbott Laboratories............................. A 614 624-3191
Columbus (G-4660)

Agrana Fruit Us Inc............................. C 937 693-3821
Anna (G-459)

◆ Agrana Fruit Us Inc.......................... E 440 546-1199
Brecksville (G-1456)

Belton Foods LLC............................... E 937 890-7768
Dayton (G-5676)

◆ Berghausen Corporation.................... E 513 591-4491
Cincinnati (G-2406)

Cargill Incorporated............................ E 937 236-1971
Dayton (G-5693)

Central Coca-Cola Btlg Co Inc............. C 419 476-6622
Toledo (G-12913)

Dominion Liquid Tech LLC................... E 513 272-2824
Cincinnati (G-2557)

Flavor Producers LLC.......................... E 513 771-0777
Cincinnati (G-2625)

▲ Flavor Systems Intl Inc.................... E 513 870-4900
Cincinnati (G-2626)

◆ Frutarom USA Inc............................ C 513 870-4900
Cincinnati (G-2643)

Givaudan Flavors Corporation.............. G 513 948-8000
Cincinnati (G-2674)

◆ Givaudan Flavors Corporation........... C 513 948-8000
Cincinnati (G-2673)

Givaudan Fragrances Corp.................. D 513 948-3428
Cincinnati (G-2675)

Gwj Liquidation Inc............................. F 216 475-5770
Cleveland (G-3802)

Hen of Woods LLC.............................. G 513 954-8871
Cincinnati (G-2716)

Innovtive Cnfction Sltions LLC............. G 440 835-8001
Westlake (G-14311)

Inter American Products Inc................. D 800 645-2233
Cincinnati (G-2748)

◆ J M Smucker Company...................... A 330 682-3000
Orrville (G-10987)

▲ Joseph Adams Corp.......................... F 330 225-9125
Valley City (G-13500)

Mane Inc.. D 513 248-9876
Cincinnati (G-2843)

Mane Inc.. D 513 248-9876
Lebanon (G-8275)

◆ Mane Inc... D 513 248-9876
Lebanon (G-8276)

Mapledale Farm Inc............................ F 440 286-3389
Chardon (G-3314)

Nu Pet Company................................. E 330 682-3000
Orrville (G-10998)

Phillips Syrup LLC............................... F 440 835-8001
Westlake (G-14323)

Primary Pdts Ingrdnts Amrcas L.......... D 937 236-5906
Dayton (G-5955)

▲ Sensus LLC..................................... F 513 892-7100
Hamilton (G-7524)

▲ Slush Puppie................................... G 513 771-0940
West Chester (G-14147)

Third Wave Water LLC......................... F 855 590-4500
Xenia (G-14778)

▲ Wiley Companies............................. C 740 622-0755
Coshocton (G-5476)

2095 Roasted coffee

Altraserv LLC..................................... G 614 889-2500
Plain City (G-11393)

Beca House Coffee LLC....................... G 419 731-4961
Upper Sandusky (G-13435)

Boston Stoker Inc............................... F 937 890-6401
Vandalia (G-13551)

Crimson Cup Inc................................. F 614 252-3335
Columbus (G-4860)

Euclid Coffee Co Inc........................... G 216 481-3330
Cleveland (G-3689)

▲ Folger Coffee Company.................... F 800 937-9745
Orrville (G-10981)

Frezerve Inc....................................... G 440 661-4037
Ashtabula (G-592)

Generations Coffee Company LLC........ F 440 546-0901
Brecksville (G-1467)

Inter American Products Inc................. D 800 645-2233
Cincinnati (G-2748)

Kidd Properties LLC............................ G 513 779-6278
West Chester (G-14020)

Mc Concepts Llc................................. G 330 933-6402
Canton (G-1941)

▲ Millstone Coffee Inc......................... D 513 983-1100
Cincinnati (G-2881)

Ohio Coffee Collaborative Ltd.............. F 614 564-9852
Columbus (G-5139)

Rosebuds Ranch and Garden LLC........ F 937 214-1801
Covington (G-5499)

Shawadi LLC...................................... E 614 839-0698
Westerville (G-14275)

Spot On Main LLC.............................. F 740 285-0441
Jackson (G-7952)

Staufs Coffee Roasters Limited............ G 614 486-4479
Columbus (G-5290)

Wheeling Coffee & Spice Co............... F 304 232-0141
Saint Clairsville (G-11719)

2096 Potato chips and similar snacks

ABC Refreshments LLC........................ F 216 692-0697
Euclid (G-6637)

Advanced Green Tech Inc.................... G 614 397-8130
Plain City (G-11392)

Ballreich Bros Inc............................... C 419 447-1814
Tiffin (G-12777)

Basic Grain Products Inc..................... D 419 678-2304
Coldwater (G-4568)

Birds Eye Foods Inc............................ D 330 854-0818
Canal Fulton (G-1773)

Bsfc LLC.. D 419 447-1814
Tiffin (G-12778)

CJ Dannemiller Co.............................. E 330 825-7808
Norton (G-10819)

Conns Potato Chip Co Inc.................... E 614 252-2150
Columbus (G-4842)

Conns Potato Chip Co Inc.................... E 740 452-4615
Zanesville (G-15008)

Crack Corn Ltd................................... F 440 467-0108
Massillon (G-9182)

Evans Food Group Ltd......................... F 626 636-8110
Portsmouth (G-11465)

Evans Food Group Ltd......................... G 740 285-3078
Portsmouth (G-11466)

Frito-Lay North America Inc................. D 330 477-7009
Canton (G-1895)

Frito-Lay North America Inc................. D 972 334-7000
Wooster (G-14639)

Grippo Foods Inc................................ D 513 923-1900
Cincinnati (G-2693)

Grippo Potato Chip Co Inc................... F 513 923-1900
Cincinnati (G-2694)

Herr Foods Incorporated..................... D 740 773-8282
Chillicothe (G-2256)

Herr Foods Incorporated..................... F 800 344-3777
Chillicothe (G-2257)

Jones Potato Chip Co.......................... E 419 529-9424
Mansfield (G-8808)

Mike-Sells Potato Chip Co................... E 937 228-9400
Dayton (G-5884)

Mike-Sells Potato Chip Co................... D 937 228-9400
Sabina (G-11679)

Mike-Sells Potato Chip Co........................ E 937 228-9400
Dayton *(G-5885)*

Mike-Sells West Virginia Inc.................. D 937 228-9400
Dayton *(G-5886)*

Mumfords Potato Chips & Deli............. G 937 653-3491
Urbana *(G-13474)*

Robert E McGrath Inc........................... F 440 572-7747
Strongsville *(G-12593)*

◆ Rudolph Foods Company Inc............C 909 383-7463
Lima *(G-8446)*

Shearers Foods LLC............................. G 330 767-3426
Brewster *(G-1493)*

Shearers Foods LLC............................. D 330 767-7969
Massillon *(G-9242)*

◆ Shearers Foods LLC..........................A 800 428-6843
Massillon *(G-9241)*

◆ Snack Alliance Inc.............................B 330 767-3426
Massillon *(G-9245)*

Sweeties Olympia Treats LLC................. F 440 572-7747
Strongsville *(G-12608)*

White Feather Foods Inc......................... G 419 738-8975
Wapakoneta *(G-13730)*

2097 Manufactured ice

Haller Enterprises Inc........................... F 330 733-9693
Akron *(G-169)*

Home City Ice Company........................ G 440 439-5001
Bedford *(G-1036)*

Home City Ice Company........................ G 513 851-4040
Cincinnati *(G-2729)*

Home City Ice Company........................ G 937 461-6028
Dayton *(G-5812)*

Home City Ice Company........................ F 419 562-4953
Delaware *(G-6157)*

Home City Ice Company........................ F 614 836-2877
Groveport *(G-7438)*

Home City Ice Company........................ F 513 353-9346
Harrison *(G-7555)*

Lori Holding Co...................................... E 740 342-3230
New Lexington *(G-10403)*

Luc Ice Inc... G 419 734-2201
Huron *(G-7879)*

Millersburg Ice Company...................... E 330 674-3016
Millersburg *(G-10000)*

Velvet Ice Cream Company.................... E 419 562-2009
Bucyrus *(G-1693)*

Zygo Inc... G 513 281-0888
Cincinnati *(G-3245)*

2098 Macaroni and spaghetti

Fusion Noodle Company Inc................. G 740 589-5511
Athens *(G-639)*

▲ International Noodle Company.......... F 614 888-0665
Lewis Center *(G-8339)*

Lariccias Italian Foods Inc.................... F 330 729-0222
Youngstown *(G-14887)*

◆ Tmarzetti Company..............................C 614 846-2232
Westerville *(G-14237)*

YAR Corporation.................................... G 330 652-1222
Niles *(G-10611)*

2099 Food preparations, nec

Advancperre Foods Holdings Inc........... D 513 428-5699
West Chester *(G-14098)*

Agrana Fruit Us Inc...............................C 937 693-3821
Anna *(G-459)*

Alimento Ventures Inc........................... F 855 510-2866
Blue Ash *(G-1245)*

Amir Foods Inc...................................... G 440 646-9388
Cleveland *(G-3350)*

Amir International Foods Inc................. G 614 332-1742
Grove City *(G-7373)*

Amish Wedding Foods Inc..................... E 330 674-9199
Millersburg *(G-9969)*

▲ Andys Mdterranean Fd Pdts LLC...... G 513 281-9791
Cincinnati *(G-2370)*

Annarino Foods Ltd.............................. E 937 274-3663
Dayton *(G-5659)*

Apf Legacy Subs LLC........................... E 513 682-7173
West Chester *(G-14103)*

Ascot Valley Foods Ltd......................... E 330 376-9411
Cuyahoga Falls *(G-5527)*

B&G Foods Inc...................................... D 513 482-8226
Cincinnati *(G-2397)*

Ballreich Bros Inc.................................C 419 447-1814
Tiffin *(G-12777)*

Barkman Honey LLC............................. F 620 947-3173
Van Wert *(G-13527)*

Basic Grain Products Inc..................... D 419 678-2304
Coldwater *(G-4568)*

Beehex LLC.. F 512 633-5304
Columbus *(G-4749)*

Bfc Inc... E 330 364-6645
Dover *(G-6230)*

Big Gus Onion Rings Inc...................... G 216 883-9045
Cleveland *(G-3418)*

Brantley Partners IV LP........................ G 216 464-8400
Cleveland *(G-3434)*

Bread Kneads Inc.................................. G 419 422-3863
Findlay *(G-6845)*

Buckeye Valley Pizza Hut Ltd.............. E 419 586-5900
Celina *(G-2098)*

Caruso Foods LLC................................ D 513 860-9200
Cincinnati *(G-2440)*

Chefs Garden Inc..................................C 419 433-4947
Sandusky *(G-11827)*

Chieffos Frozen Foods Inc................... G 330 652-1222
Niles *(G-10585)*

CJ Dannemiller Co................................ E 330 825-7808
Norton *(G-10819)*

Conagra Brands Inc.............................. D 419 445-8015
Archbold *(G-491)*

Conagra Fods Pckaged Foods LLC....... E 937 440-2800
Troy *(G-13206)*

Country Parlour Ice Cream Co............. G 440 237-4040
Cleveland *(G-3570)*

Cuyahoga Vending Co Inc....................C 440 353-9595
North Ridgeville *(G-10728)*

Deer Creek Honey Farms Ltd.............. G 740 852-0899
London *(G-8535)*

Dismat Corporation.............................. F 419 531-8963
Toledo *(G-12944)*

Dno Inc... D 614 231-3601
Columbus *(G-4889)*

Dole Fresh Vegetables Inc...................C 937 525-4300
Springfield *(G-12303)*

Domino Foods Inc................................C 216 432-3222
Cleveland *(G-3625)*

Dure Foods Us LLC............................... F 614 409-9030
Columbus *(G-4891)*

Empanadas Aqui LLC............................ E 513 312-9566
Maineville *(G-8739)*

Essential Provisions LLC...................... G 937 271-0381
Wilmington *(G-14579)*

Firehouse Foods................................... G 614 592-8115
Columbus *(G-4925)*

Food 4 Your Soul................................... F 330 402-4073
Youngstown *(G-14856)*

Food Designs Inc.................................. F 216 651-9221
Cleveland *(G-3733)*

Foodies Vegan Ltd................................ F 513 487-3037
Cincinnati *(G-2632)*

Foris Extraordinary Meats LLC............ F 614 670-5726
Columbus *(G-4931)*

Frank L Harter & Son Inc..................... G 513 574-1330
Cincinnati *(G-2638)*

Fremont Company.................................. E 419 363-2924
Rockford *(G-11630)*

Freshly Preserved LLC......................... G 440 523-1099
North Royalton *(G-10761)*

Freshway Foods Company Inc.............. D 937 498-4664
Sidney *(G-12020)*

Frito-Lay North America Inc.................. D 330 477-7009
Canton *(G-1895)*

Frito-Lay North America Inc.................. D 972 334-7000
Wooster *(G-14639)*

Frog Ranch Foods Ltd.......................... F 740 767-3705
Glouster *(G-7290)*

Frutarom USA Inc.................................. G 513 870-4900
West Chester *(G-14122)*

◆ Frutarom USA Inc..............................C 513 870-4900
Cincinnati *(G-2643)*

General Mills Inc.................................. D 513 771-8200
Cincinnati *(G-2663)*

Generations Ace Inc............................G 440 835-4872
Bay Village *(G-902)*

Gold Star Chili Inc............................... D 513 631-1990
Cincinnati *(G-2682)*

Gold Star Chili Inc............................... E 513 231-4541
Cincinnati *(G-2681)*

Gomez Salsa LLC................................. F 513 314-1978
Cincinnati *(G-2683)*

Graffiti Foods Limited.......................... F 614 759-1921
Columbus *(G-4963)*

Grays Orange Barn Inc......................... G 419 568-2718
Wapakoneta *(G-13714)*

Great Lakes Popcorn Company............ G 419 732-3080
Port Clinton *(G-11443)*

Grippo Potato Chip Co Inc................... F 513 923-1900
Cincinnati *(G-2694)*

▲ Gsi of Ohio LLC................................ F 216 431-3344
Cleveland *(G-3799)*

Harry & David Operations Inc............. A 541 864-3710
Hebron *(G-7616)*

Harvest Commissary LLC...................... E 513 706-1951
Granville *(G-7315)*

Hen of Woods LLC................................ G 513 954-8871
Cincinnati *(G-2716)*

Heritage Cooperative Inc..................... F 740 828-2215
Nashport *(G-10300)*

Herold Salads Inc................................ F 216 991-7500
Cleveland *(G-3828)*

Hilltop Recreation Inc.......................... G 937 549-2904
Manchester *(G-8754)*

Holmes Made Foods LLC...................... G 216 618-5043
Cleveland *(G-3835)*

Honeybaked Ham Company.................. E 513 583-9700
Cincinnati *(G-2730)*

Hydrofresh Ltd...................................... G 567 765-1010
Delphos *(G-6187)*

Ingredient Innovations Intl Co.............. G 330 262-4440
Wooster *(G-14650)*

Inter American Products Inc................. D 800 645-2233
Cincinnati *(G-2748)*

◆ J M Smucker Company.......................A 330 682-3000
Orrville *(G-10987)*

John Krusinski...................................... F 216 441-0100
Cleveland *(G-3889)*

◆ Kantner Ingredients Inc....................G 614 766-3638
Columbus *(G-5045)*

Keho Fitness and Nutrition LLC............ G 740 587-1313
Hebron *(G-7621)*

Kerry Inc... E 440 229-5200
Wickliffe *(G-14379)*

Kraft Heinz Company............................ A 330 837-8331
Massillon *(G-9213)*

Kraft Heinz Foods Company.................. C 419 332-7357
Fremont *(G-7120)*

Krema Group Inc................................ F 614 889-4824
Plain City *(G-11413)*

La Perla Inc...................................... G 419 534-2074
Toledo *(G-13026)*

Lakeview Farms LLC.......................... C 419 695-9925
Delphos *(G-6190)*

Las Americas Inc............................... G 440 459-2030
Cleveland *(G-3943)*

Lasenor Usa LLC............................... F 800 754-1228
Salem *(G-11793)*

Lbzb Restaurants Inc.......................... F 567 413-4700
Bowling Green *(G-1424)*

Lipari Foods Operating Co LLC............. E 330 893-2479
Millersburg *(G-9992)*

Lipari Foods Operating Co LLC............. E 330 674-9199
Millersburg *(G-9993)*

Main Street Gourmet LLC..................... C 330 929-0000
Cuyahoga Falls *(G-5560)*

◆ Mane Inc.. D 513 248-9876
Lebanon *(G-8276)*

Miami Valley Meals Inc...................... F 937 938-7141
Dayton *(G-5878)*

Mid American Ventures Inc.................. E 216 524-0974
Cleveland *(G-4031)*

Momma Js Blazing Kitchen LLC............ G 216 551-8791
Cleveland Heights *(G-4530)*

▲ Mrs Mllers Hmmade Noodles Ltd....... F 330 694-5814
Fredericksburg *(G-7065)*

Nat2 Inc... G 614 270-2507
Lewis Center *(G-8345)*

Nates Nectar LLC............................... G 937 935-3289
De Graff *(G-6092)*

▲ National Foods Packaging Inc........... E 216 622-2740
Cleveland *(G-4060)*

Natures Health Food LLC..................... F 419 260-9265
Mount Victory *(G-10269)*

New Horizons Fd Solutions LLC............ E 614 861-3639
Columbus *(G-5126)*

Nu Pet Company................................. E 330 682-3000
Orrville *(G-10998)*

▲ Oasis Mditerranean Cuisine Inc........ E 419 269-1459
Toledo *(G-13067)*

Ohio Hckry Hrvest Brnd Pdts In............ E 330 644-6266
Akron *(G-253)*

Old Classic Delight Inc....................... D 419 394-7955
Saint Marys *(G-11744)*

Orval Kent Food Company LLC............. E 419 695-5015
Delphos *(G-6191)*

Pepperidge Farm Incorporated.............. G 419 933-2611
Willard *(G-14407)*

Pfizer Inc.. F 937 746-3603
Franklin *(G-7039)*

Pita Wrap LLC................................... G 330 886-8091
Boardman *(G-1375)*

Plant Plant Co.................................... E 303 809-9588
Heath *(G-7600)*

◆ Procter & Gamble Mfg Co................. F 513 983-1100
Cincinnati *(G-3002)*

Produce Packaging Inc....................... C 216 391-6129
Willoughby Hills *(G-14562)*

Pure Foods LLC................................. G 303 358-8375
Highland Heights *(G-7662)*

Purushealth LLC............................... F 800 601-0580
Shaker Heights *(G-11932)*

▲ R S Hanline and Co Inc.................... C 419 347-8077
Shelby *(G-11974)*

Rich Products Corporation.................... C 614 771-1117
Hilliard *(G-7699)*

Richelieu Foods Inc............................ E 740 335-4813
Wshngtn Ct Hs *(G-14744)*

Rosebuds Ranch and Garden LLC......... F 937 214-1801
Covington *(G-5499)*

Roy Retrac Incorporated...................... G 740 564-5552
Columbus *(G-5236)*

◆ Rudolph Foods Company Inc............ C 909 383-7463
Lima *(G-8446)*

Savor Seasonings LLC........................ F 513 732-2333
Batavia *(G-887)*

Savory Foods Inc.............................. D 740 354-6655
Portsmouth *(G-11476)*

◆ Sensoryffcts Powdr Systems Inc........ D 419 783-5518
Defiance *(G-6123)*

Smartsoda Holdings Inc...................... G 888 998-9668
Cleveland *(G-4307)*

▼ Smucker International Inc................ F 330 682-3000
Orrville *(G-11010)*

Solae LLC... F 419 483-5340
Bellevue *(G-1133)*

Sunrise Foods Inc............................. G 614 276-2880
Columbus *(G-5297)*

Tarrier Foods Corp............................. E 614 876-8594
Columbus *(G-5310)*

▼ Tortilleria La Bamba LLC................. G 216 515-1600
Cleveland *(G-4407)*

US Wellness LLC............................... G 216 772-3364
Cleveland *(G-4452)*

Wal-Bon of Ohio Inc.......................... E 740 423-8178
Belpre *(G-1156)*

Wannemacher Enterprises Inc.............. F 419 771-1101
Upper Sandusky *(G-13456)*

Weston Brands Inc.............................. F 800 814-4895
Independence *(G-7925)*

White Castle System Inc..................... D 513 563-2290
Cincinnati *(G-3223)*

White Feather Foods Inc...................... G 419 738-8975
Wapakoneta *(G-13730)*

Whitmore Productions Inc.................... G 216 752-3960
Warrensville Heights *(G-13819)*

Wildcat Creek Farms Inc.................... G 419 263-2549
Payne *(G-11167)*

Willys Inc... F 419 823-3200
Swanton *(G-12698)*

▼ Woeber Mustard Mfg Co................... C 937 342-9601
Springfield *(G-12395)*

◆ Woeber Mustard Mfg Co................... C 937 323-6281
Springfield *(G-12394)*

▼ Wyandot Usa LLC............................ C 740 383-4031
Marion *(G-9006)*

Zidian Management LLC...................... E 330 743-6050
Boardman *(G-1379)*

▲ Zidian Manufacturing LLC................ D 330 965-8455
Boardman *(G-1380)*

21 TOBACCO PRODUCTS

2111 Cigarettes

Discount Smokes & Gifts Xenia............ G 937 372-0259
Xenia *(G-14763)*

Memphis Smokehouse Inc.................... G 216 351-5321
Cleveland *(G-4020)*

2131 Chewing and smoking tobacco

◆ Scandinavian Tob Group Ln Ltd.......... C 770 934-4594
Akron *(G-306)*

Smoke-Rings Inc................................ G 419 420-9966
Findlay *(G-6921)*

22 TEXTILE MILL PRODUCTS

2211 Broadwoven fabric mills, cotton

Akron Cotton Products Inc.................. G 330 434-7171
Akron *(G-28)*

Canton Sterilized Wiping Cloth............. G 330 455-5179
Canton *(G-1860)*

▼ Ccp Industries Inc.......................... B 216 535-4227
Richmond Heights *(G-11609)*

Drapery Stitch - Cleveland Inc.............. G 216 252-3857
Cleveland *(G-3630)*

Heritage Hill LLC............................... G 513 237-0240
Blue Ash *(G-1285)*

▲ Inside Outfitters Inc....................... E 614 798-3500
Lewis Center *(G-8338)*

Linsalata Cpitl Prtners Fund I............... G 440 684-1400
Cleveland *(G-3962)*

Lumenomics Inc................................ E 614 798-3500
Lewis Center *(G-8342)*

▲ MGF Sourcing US LLC..................... D 614 904-3300
Columbus *(G-5097)*

▲ Mmi Textiles Inc............................. G 440 899-8050
Brooklyn *(G-1523)*

Noble Denim Workshop........................ G 513 560-5640
Cincinnati *(G-2913)*

R J Manray Inc.................................. G 330 559-6716
Canfield *(G-1814)*

Roach Studios LLC............................. F 614 725-1405
Columbus *(G-5233)*

▲ Sk Textile Inc................................ C 800 888-9112
Cincinnati *(G-3094)*

STI Liquidation Inc............................. E 614 733-0099
Plain City *(G-11418)*

Stitches Usa LLC.............................. F 330 852-0500
Walnut Creek *(G-13695)*

Struggle Grind Success LLC................. G 330 834-6738
Boardman *(G-1377)*

◆ Synthomer Inc................................ C 216 682-7000
Beachwood *(G-951)*

▲ Totes Isotoner Holdings LLC............. C 513 682-8200
Cincinnati *(G-3160)*

Tranzonic Companies.......................... C 440 446-0643
Cleveland *(G-4414)*

◆ Tz Acquisition Corp.......................... F 216 535-4300
Richmond Heights *(G-11613)*

Weiskopf Industries Corp..................... G 440 442-4400
Cleveland *(G-4498)*

Wonder-Shirts Inc.............................. G 917 679-2336
Dublin *(G-6361)*

2221 Broadwoven fabric mills, manmade

▲ Architectural Fiberglass Inc............ E 216 641-8300
Cleveland *(C-3364)*

Collins & Aikman Auto Mats LLC........... E 330 456-4543
Canton *(G-1869)*

Conform Automotive LLC.................... B 937 492-2708
Sidney *(G-12002)*

Drapery Stitch - Cleveland Inc.............. G 216 252-3857
Cleveland *(G-3630)*

▲ Inside Outfitters Inc....................... E 614 798-3500
Lewis Center *(G-8338)*

◆ King Bag and Manufacturing Co......... E 513 541-5440
Cincinnati *(G-2795)*

Lumenomics Inc................................ E 614 798-3500
Lewis Center *(G-8342)*

▲ Mmi Textiles Inc............................. G 440 899-8050
Brooklyn *(G-1523)*

PCR Restorations Inc........................ G 419 747-7957
Mansfield *(G-8844)*

Schmelzer Industries Inc.................... E 740 743-2866
Somerset *(G-12211)*

◆ Seaman Corporation......................... C 330 262-1111
Wooster *(G-14684)*

▲ Weaver Leather LLC......................... D 330 674-7548
Millersburg *(G-10019)*

2231 Broadwoven fabric mills, wool

S
I
C

Midwest Composites LLC...................F 419 738-2431
   Wapakoneta *(G-13721)*

R J Manray Inc.............................G 330 559-6716
   Canfield *(G-1814)*

2241 Narrow fabric mills

A & P Technology Inc.....................E 513 688-3200
   Cincinnati *(G-2290)*

A & P Technology Inc.....................E 513 688-3200
   Cincinnati *(G-2291)*

A & P Technology Inc.....................E 513 688-3200
   Cincinnati *(G-2292)*

A & P Technology Inc.....................E 513 688-3200
   Cincinnati *(G-2293)*

◆ A & P Technology Inc...................E 513 688-3200
   Cincinnati *(G-2294)*

Community Action Program Corp.........F 740 374-8501
   Marietta *(G-8911)*

Crane Consumables Inc....................E 513 539-9980
   Middletown *(G-9851)*

CT Specialty Polymers Ltd.............G 440 632-9311
   Middlefield *(G-9789)*

◆ Db Rediheat Inc........................E 216 361-0530
   Cleveland *(G-3604)*

◆ Denizen Inc.............................F 937 615-9561
   Piqua *(G-11344)*

▲ Grove Engineered Products...........G 419 659-5939
   Columbus Grove *(G-5383)*

◆ Keuchel & Associates Inc.............E 330 945-9455
   Cuyahoga Falls *(G-5554)*

◆ Mitchellace Inc.........................D 740 354-2813
   Portsmouth *(G-11471)*

Murrubber Technologies Inc.............E
   Stow *(G-12442)*

Northeast Tubular Inc....................G 330 567-2690
   Wooster *(G-14671)*

▲ Samsel Rope & Marine Supply Co.....E 216 241-0333
   Cleveland *(G-4272)*

◆ Shore To Shore Inc....................D 937 866-1908
   Dayton *(G-6004)*

▲ Sole Choice Inc........................E 740 354-2813
   Portsmouth *(G-11477)*

US Cotton LLC............................D 216 676-6400
   Cleveland *(G-4451)*

2252 Hosiery, nec

Hype Socks LLC...........................F 855 497-3769
   Columbus *(G-4994)*

Rock Em Sock Em Retro LLC..............G 419 575-9309
   Walbridge *(G-13688)*

Smithco Distributing......................E 419 367-7685
   Liberty Center *(G-8376)*

2253 Knit outerwear mills

Digitek Corp..............................F 513 794-3190
   Mason *(G-9094)*

E Retailing Associates LLC..............D 614 300-5785
   Columbus *(G-4894)*

Okm LLC..................................G 216 272-6375
   Cleveland *(G-4117)*

▲ Pjs Wholesale Inc......................G 614 402-9363
   Columbus *(G-5193)*

Spalding..................................F 440 286-5717
   Chardon *(G-2224)*

Tha Presidential Suite LLC..............G 216 338-7287
   Cleveland *(G-4376)*

Wonder-Shirts Inc........................G 917 679-2336
   Dublin *(G-6361)*

2258 Lace and warp knit fabric mills

Murray Fabrics Inc.......................F 216 881-4041
   Cleveland *(G-4053)*

2259 Knitting mills, nec

Ansell Healthcare Products LLC.........C 740 622-4369
   Coshocton *(G-5448)*

2261 Finishing plants, cotton

▲ Atlantis Sportswear Inc...............E 937 773-0680
   Piqua *(G-11336)*

▼ Duracote Corporation..................E 330 296-9600
   Ravenna *(G-11523)*

◆ Image Group Inc.......................E 419 866-3300
   Holland *(G-7769)*

Phantasm Dsgns Sprtsn More Ltd.......G 419 538-6737
   Ottawa *(G-11042)*

Precision Imprint.........................G 740 592-5916
   Athens *(G-646)*

Uptown Dog The Inc.....................G 740 592-4600
   Athens *(G-655)*

West-Camp Press Inc....................D 216 426-2660
   Cleveland *(G-4502)*

2262 Finishing plants, manmade

717 Inc...................................G 440 925-0402
   Lakewood *(G-8161)*

Cincinnati Advg Pdts LLC...............C 513 346-7310
   Cincinnati *(G-2467)*

Dwr Graphics Inc.........................E 614 863-6966
   Columbus *(G-4892)*

Flashions Sportswear Ltd...............G 937 323-5885
   Springfield *(G-12312)*

Kaylo Enterprises LLC...................G 330 535-1860
   Akron *(G-192)*

▲ Mmi Textiles Inc.......................G 440 899-8050
   Brooklyn *(G-1523)*

Phantasm Dsgns Sprtsn More Ltd........G 419 538-6737
   Ottawa *(G-11042)*

Sportsco Imprinting......................G 513 641-5111
   Cincinnati *(G-3106)*

Tranzonic Companies.....................C 440 446-0643
   Cleveland *(G-4414)*

◆ Tz Acquisition Corp....................F 216 535-4300
   Richmond Heights *(G-11613)*

2273 Carpets and rugs

3359 Kingston LLC.......................G 614 871-8989
   Grove City *(G-7365)*

4blar LLC.................................G 513 576-0441
   Milford *(G-9919)*

Alliance Carpet Cushion Co..............E 740 966-5001
   Johnstown *(G-7990)*

Angstrom Fiber Englewood LLC.........E 734 756-1164
   Englewood *(G-6607)*

◆ Boardman Molded Products Inc........D 330 788-2400
   Youngstown *(G-14822)*

▼ Ccp Industries Inc.....................B 216 535-4227
   Richmond Heights *(G-11609)*

Dribble Creek Inc........................F 440 439-8650
   Bedford *(G-1029)*

▲ Durable Corporation....................D 800 537-1603
   Norwalk *(G-10836)*

Johns Manville Corporation..............C 419 878-8111
   Waterville *(G-13835)*

Mat Basics Incorporated.................G 513 793-0313
   Blue Ash *(G-1302)*

Mohawk Industries Inc...................E 800 837-3812
   Grove City *(G-7402)*

Shaw Industries Inc......................A 513 942-3692
   Fairfield *(G-6775)*

Spacelinks Enterprises Inc..............E 330 788-2401
   Youngstown *(G-14935)*

Tranzonic Companies.....................C 440 446-0643
   Cleveland *(G-4414)*

2282 Throwing and winding mills

Alliance Carpet Cushion Co..............E 740 966-5001
   Johnstown *(G-7990)*

2295 Coated fabrics, not rubberized

Alron.....................................G 330 477-3405
   Strasburg *(G-12475)*

Bexley Fabrics Inc........................G 614 231-7272
   Columbus *(G-4753)*

▲ Biothane Coated Webbing Corp........E 440 327-0485
   North Ridgeville *(G-10727)*

▲ Buckeye Fabric Finishers Inc..........F 740 622-3251
   Coshocton *(G-5453)*

▲ Buschman Corporation.................F 216 431-6633
   Cleveland *(G-3453)*

Cemplex Group NC LLC.................F 513 671-3300
   Fairfield *(G-6718)*

◆ Diamond Polymers Incorporated.......D 330 773-2700
   Akron *(G-121)*

▼ Duracote Corporation..................E 330 296-9600
   Ravenna *(G-11523)*

Durez Corporation........................D 567 295-6400
   Kenton *(G-8097)*

Excello Fabric Finishers Inc.............G 740 622-7444
   Coshocton *(G-5454)*

Form Manufacturing Llc..................F 419 678-1400
   Coldwater *(G-4574)*

Hartco Inc................................E 513 771-4430
   Cincinnati *(G-2709)*

▲ Laurenco Systems of Ohio LLC........G
   Leavittsburg *(G-8240)*

Petfiber LLC..............................F 216 767-4535
   Cleveland *(G-4154)*

Prints & Paints Flr Cvg Co Inc..........E 419 462-5663
   Galion *(G-7197)*

◆ Schneller LLC...........................C 330 673-1400
   Kent *(G-8073)*

Shaheen Oriental Rug Co Inc............F 330 493-9000
   Canton *(G-2003)*

2296 Tire cord and fabrics

▲ ARC Abrasives Inc......................D 800 888-4885
   Troy *(G-13201)*

Cleveland Canvas Goods Mfg Co.........E 216 361-4567
   Cleveland *(G-3508)*

Mfh Partners Inc.........................B 440 461-4100
   Cleveland *(G-4025)*

Mpp Legacy Inc..........................F 440 237-9500
   North Royalton *(G-10775)*

2297 Nonwoven fabrics

▲ Amantea Nonwovens LLC...............G 513 842-6600
   Cincinnati *(G-2355)*

Autoneum North America Inc............B 419 693-0511
   Oregon *(G-10957)*

▼ Ccp Industries Inc.....................B 216 535-4227
   Richmond Heights *(G-11609)*

▲ Nikke Kureha America Co Ltd.........G 513 771-6788
   West Chester *(G-14033)*

2298 Cordage and twine

▲ Atwood Rope Manufacturing Inc.......E 614 920-0534
   Canal Winchester *(G-1784)*

Atwood Rope Manufacturing Inc.........F 614 920-0534
   Millersport *(G-10022)*

Automted Cmpnent Spcalists LLC........E 513 335-4285
   Cincinnati *(G-2391)*

◆ Core Optix Inc..........................F 855 267-3678
   Cincinnati *(G-2517)*

Infinitaire Industries LLC................G 216 600-2051
   Euclid *(G-6655)*

Katimex USA Inc.............................G 440 338-3500
Chagrin Falls *(G-2147)*

Radix Wire & Cable LLC........................D 216 731-9191
Solon *(G-12172)*

2299 Textile goods, nec

Big Productions Inc.............................G 440 775-0015
Oberlin *(G-10915)*

Dayton Bag & Burlap Co.....................F 937 253-1722
Dayton *(G-5721)*

J Rettenmaier USA LP.........................D 937 652-2101
Urbana *(G-13469)*

Meridian Industries Inc.......................E 330 359-5809
Beach City *(G-904)*

▲ NC Works Inc...................................F 937 514-7781
Franklin *(G-7037)*

▲ Ohio Table Pad Company..................F 419 872-6400
Perrysburg *(G-11246)*

▲ Ohio Table Pad of Indiana.................D 419 872-6400
Perrysburg *(G-11248)*

◆ Standard Textile Co Inc....................B 513 761-9255
Cincinnati *(G-3112)*

23 APPAREL, FINISHED PRODUCTS FROM FABRICS & SIMILAR MATERIALS

2311 Men's and boy's suits and coats

Bea-Ecc Apparels Inc.........................G 216 650-6336
Cleveland *(G-3411)*

Empirical Manufacturing Co Inc...........F 513 948-1616
Cincinnati *(G-2585)*

◆ Lion Apparel Inc.............................C 937 898-1949
Dayton *(G-5847)*

Lion Apparel Inc.................................D 937 898-1949
Dayton *(G-5848)*

Lion First Responder Ppe Inc..............D 937 898-1949
Dayton *(G-5849)*

Lion Group Inc...................................D 800 421-2926
Dayton *(G-5850)*

◆ The Fechheimer Brothers Co............C 513 793-5400
Blue Ash *(G-1342)*

Vgs Inc..C 216 431-7800
Cleveland *(G-4463)*

2321 Men's and boy's furnishings

Columbus Apparel Studio LLC.............F 614 706-7292
Columbus *(G-4817)*

J C L S Enterprises LLC......................G 740 472-0314
Woodsfield *(G-14613)*

2326 Men's and boy's work clothing

Barton-Carey Medical Pdts Inc............E 419 887-1285
Maumee *(G-9265)*

Cintas Corporation..............................D 513 631-5750
Cincinnati *(G-2494)*

◆ Cintas Corporation..........................A 513 459-1200
Mason *(G-9086)*

Cintas Corporation No 2.......................D 330 966-7800
Canton *(G-1865)*

Cintas Sales Corporation.....................B 513 459-1200
Cincinnati *(G-2495)*

Cleveland Canvas Goods Mfg Co.........E 216 361-4567
Cleveland *(G-3508)*

DCW Acquisition Inc............................G 216 451-0666
Cleveland *(G-3607)*

Epluno LLC...F 800 249-5275
Springboro *(G-12251)*

Geauga Group LLC.............................G 440 543-8797
Chagrin Falls *(G-2162)*

Kip-Craft Incorporated..........................D 216 898-5500
Cleveland *(G-3924)*

Leisure Time Pdts Design Corp............G 440 934-1032
Avon *(G-731)*

Linsalata Cpitl Prtners Fund I...............G 440 684-1400
Cleveland *(G-3962)*

Model Medical LLC..............................F 216 972-0573
Shaker Heights *(G-11931)*

▲ Morning Pride Mfg LLC....................A 937 264-2662
Dayton *(G-5894)*

▲ Rich Industries Inc..........................E 330 339-4113
New Philadelphia *(G-10465)*

Samson..G 614 504-8038
Columbus *(G-5247)*

School Uniforms and More Inc.............G 216 365-1957
Cleveland *(G-4275)*

Tranzonic Companies...........................C 440 446-0643
Cleveland *(G-4414)*

◆ Tz Acquisition Corp..........................F 216 535-4300
Richmond Heights *(G-11613)*

Vgs Inc...C 216 431-7800
Cleveland *(G-4463)*

2329 Men's and boy's clothing, nec

Adidas North America Inc.....................F 330 562-4689
Aurora *(G-659)*

Careismatic Brands LLC......................G 614 497-5289
Groveport *(G-7429)*

Carrera Holdings Inc............................G 216 687-1311
Cleveland *(G-3472)*

Columbus Apparel Studio LLC.............F 614 706-7292
Columbus *(G-4817)*

Fallon Pharaohs...................................G 216 990-2746
Cleveland *(G-3704)*

◆ Holloway Sportswear Inc..................D 937 497-7575
Sidney *(G-12023)*

▲ Kam Manufacturing Inc...................C 419 238-6037
Van Wert *(G-13538)*

◆ Neff Motivation Inc..........................C 937 548-3194
Greenville *(G-7348)*

Noxgear LLC.......................................G 937 317-0199
Worthington *(G-14722)*

Rocky Brands Inc................................C 740 753-1951
Nelsonville *(G-10320)*

▲ Universal Lettering Inc.....................F 419 238-9320
Van Wert *(G-13547)*

▲ Vesi Incorporated............................E 513 563-6002
Cincinnati *(G-3203)*

2331 Women's and misses' blouses and shirts

Columbus Apparel Studio LLC.............F 614 706-7292
Columbus *(G-4817)*

J C L S Enterprises LLC......................G 740 472-0314
Woodsfield *(G-14613)*

▲ Kam Manufacturing Inc...................C 419 238-6037
Van Wert *(G-13538)*

Love Laugh & Laundry..........................G 567 377-1951
Toledo *(G-13039)*

Rocky Brands Inc................................C 740 753-1951
Nelsonville *(G-10320)*

2335 Women's, junior's, and misses' dresses

Purple Orchid Boutique LLC.................G 614 554-7686
Columbus *(G-5214)*

Renee Grace LLC................................G 513 399-5616
Cincinnati *(G-3038)*

Shi Shi Events....................................G 440 623-3822
Bay Village *(G-903)*

Surili Couture LLC...............................F 440 600-1456
Westlake *(G-14338)*

2337 Women's and misses' suits and coats

Cintas Corporation..............................D 513 631-5750
Cincinnati *(G-2494)*

◆ Cintas Corporation..........................A 513 459-1200
Mason *(G-9086)*

Cintas Corporation No 2.......................D 330 966-7800
Canton *(G-1865)*

◆ The Fechheimer Brothers Co............C 513 793-5400
Blue Ash *(G-1342)*

2339 Women's and misses' outerwear, nec

▲ 5 BS Inc...C 740 454-8453
Zanesville *(G-14980)*

Barton-Carey Medical Pdts Inc............E 419 887-1285
Maumee *(G-9265)*

Blingflingforever LLC...........................G 216 215-6955
Mentor On The Lake *(G-9657)*

Bodied Beauties LLC...........................G 216 971-1155
Richmond Heights *(G-11608)*

Careismatic Brands LLC......................G 614 497-5289
Groveport *(G-7429)*

Carrera Holdings Inc............................G 216 687-1311
Cleveland *(G-3472)*

Columbus Apparel Studio LLC.............F 614 706-7292
Columbus *(G-4817)*

Fluff Boutique.....................................G 513 227-6614
Cincinnati *(G-2630)*

Geauga Group LLC.............................G 440 543-8797
Chagrin Falls *(G-2162)*

Hipsy LLC...G 513 403-5333
Fairfield *(G-6740)*

◆ Holloway Sportswear Inc..................D 937 497-7575
Sidney *(G-12023)*

Indra Holdings Corp.............................C 513 682-8200
Cincinnati *(G-2743)*

Kip-Craft Incorporated..........................D 216 898-5500
Cleveland *(G-3924)*

Rocky Brands Inc................................C 740 753-1951
Nelsonville *(G-10320)*

◆ The Fechheimer Brothers Co............C 513 793-5400
Blue Ash *(G-1342)*

▲ Universal Lettering Inc.....................F 419 238-9320
Van Wert *(G-13547)*

▲ Vesi Incorporated............................E 513 563-6002
Cincinnati *(G-3203)*

2341 Women's and children's underwear

Vs Service Company LLC.....................A 614 415-2348
Reynoldsburg *(G-11586)*

2353 Hats, caps, and millinery

▲ Barbs Graffiti Inc............................E 216 881-5550
Cleveland *(G-3405)*

Blonde Swan......................................F 419 307-8591
Fremont *(G-7095)*

Bows Barrettes & Baubles...................F 440 247-2697
Moreland Hills *(G-10198)*

◆ Pukka LLC......................................E 419 429-7808
Findlay *(G-6911)*

Thomas Creative Apparel Inc...............G 419 929-1506
New London *(G-10417)*

2361 Girl's and children's dresses, blouses

Justice...G 937 435-6928
Dayton *(G-5836)*

2371 Fur goods

Blonde Swan......................................F 419 307-8591
Fremont *(G-7095)*

2381 Fabric dress and work gloves

S I C

Admj Holdings LLC.................... E 216 588-0038
Cleveland **(G-3300)**

▲ Totes Isotoner Holdings LLC............ C 513 682-8200
Cincinnati **(G-3160)**

▲ Wcm Holdings Inc..................... C 513 705-2100
Cincinnati **(G-3213)**

▲ West Chester Holdings LLC............. C 513 705-2100
Cincinnati **(G-3220)**

2384 Robes and dressing gowns

Thomas Creative Apparel Inc................ G 419 929-1506
New London **(G-10417)**

2385 Waterproof outerwear

▲ Totes Isotoner Corporation............... D 513 682-8200
Cincinnati **(G-3159)**

2389 Apparel and accessories, nec

Akron Design & Costume LLC............ G 330 644-0425
Coventry Township **(G-5479)**

Careismatic Brands LLC................ G 614 497-5289
Groveport **(G-7429)**

Carters Inc........................... G 330 758-0390
Boardman **(G-1369)**

Costume Specialists Inc................ E 614 464-2115
Columbus **(G-4852)**

Direct Disposables LLC................ G 440 717-3335
Brecksville **(G-1463)**

▲ Fire-Dex LLC....................... D 330 723-0000
Medina **(G-9403)**

Indra Holdings Corp................... C 513 682-8200
Cincinnati **(G-2743)**

Ralphie Gianni Mfg & Co Ltd............ F 216 507-3873
Euclid **(G-6675)**

▲ Rich Industries Inc.................. E 330 339-4113
New Philadelphia **(G-10465)**

Rocky Brands Inc..................... C 740 753-1951
Nelsonville **(G-10320)**

Snaps Inc........................... G 419 477-5100
Mount Cory **(G-10205)**

▲ Status Mens Accessories.............. G 440 786-9394
Oakwood Village **(G-10909)**

Thomas Creative Apparel Inc............ G 419 929-1506
New London **(G-10417)**

Walter F Stephens Jr Inc............... E 937 746-0521
Franklin **(G-7055)**

2391 Curtains and draperies

Accent Drapery Co Inc................. E 614 488-0741
Columbus **(G-4667)**

Elden Draperies of Toledo Inc........... F 419 535-1909
Toledo **(G-12947)**

Electra Tarp Inc...................... F 330 477-7168
Canton **(G-1885)**

Ikiriska LLC......................... F 614 389-8994
Powell **(G-11489)**

Janson Industries.................... D 330 455-7029
Canton **(G-1921)**

▲ Sk Textile Inc...................... C 800 888-9112
Cincinnati **(G-3094)**

STI Liquidation Inc................... E 614 733-0099
Plain City **(G-11418)**

Style-Line Incorporated................ G 614 291-0600
Columbus **(G-5295)**

Tiffin Scenic Studios Inc............... E 800 445-1546
Tiffin **(G-12805)**

Vocational Services Inc................ F 216 431-8085
Cleveland **(G-4478)**

2392 Household furnishings, nec

A & W Table Pad Co................... F 800 541-0271
Cleveland **(G-3278)**

Brentwood Originals Inc................ D 330 793-2255
Youngstown **(G-14824)**

▲ Casco Mfg Solutions Inc.............. D 513 681-0003
Cincinnati **(G-2441)**

▼ Ccp Industries Inc................... B 216 535-4227
Richmond Heights **(G-11609)**

Columbus Canvas Products Inc.......... F 614 375-1397
Columbus **(G-4819)**

DCW Acquisition Inc.................. G 216 451-0666
Cleveland **(G-3607)**

Dorex LLC.......................... G 216 271-7064
Newburgh Heights **(G-10540)**

▲ Down-Lite International Inc............ C 513 229-3696
Mason **(G-9095)**

Downhome Inc....................... E 513 921-3373
Cincinnati **(G-2561)**

▲ Downhome Inc....................... E 513 921-3373
Cincinnati **(G-2562)**

◆ Easy Way Leisure Company LLC........ E 513 731-5640
Cincinnati **(G-2576)**

Fluvitex USA Inc..................... C 614 610-1199
Groveport **(G-7433)**

▲ Greendale Home Fashions LLC......... D 859 916-5475
Cincinnati **(G-2690)**

▲ Henty Usa LLC...................... F 513 984-5590
Cincinnati **(G-2718)**

◆ Holloway Sportswear Inc.............. D 937 497-7575
Sidney **(G-12023)**

◆ Impact Products LLC................. C 419 841-2891
Toledo **(G-13001)**

Integrant LLC........................ G 440 628-9550
North Royalton **(G-10767)**

◆ Master Mfg Co Inc................... E 216 641-0500
Cleveland **(G-3997)**

Nautical Needle LLC.................. G 419 732-2990
Port Clinton **(G-11446)**

▲ Nestaway LLC....................... D 216 587-1500
Cleveland **(G-4069)**

Ohio Table Pad Company............... G 419 872-6400
Perrysburg **(G-11247)**

▲ Ohio Table Pad Company............... F 419 872-6400
Perrysburg **(G-11246)**

◆ Saturday Knight Ltd.................. D 513 641-1400
Cincinnati **(G-3064)**

STI Liquidation Inc................... E 614 733-0099
Plain City **(G-11418)**

Tally Ho Slipcovers................... G 614 448-6170
Columbus **(G-5307)**

Twister Cleaning Tech Inc.............. G 865 521-3976
Toledo **(G-13167)**

2393 Textile bags

American Made Bags LLC............... F 330 475-1385
Akron **(G-56)**

▼ Baggallini Inc....................... F 800 448-8753
Pickerington **(G-11289)**

▲ Belaire Products Inc.................. E 330 253-3116
Akron **(G-75)**

Capital City Awning Co Inc............. E 614 221-5404
Columbus **(G-4796)**

Cleveland Canvas Goods Mfg Co......... E 216 361-4567
Cleveland **(G-3508)**

Columbus Canvas Products Inc.......... F 614 375-1397
Columbus **(G-4819)**

Dayton Bag & Burlap Co................ E 419 733-7108
Kettering **(G-8118)**

DCW Acquisition Inc.................. G 216 451-0666
Cleveland **(G-3607)**

▲ Global-Pak Inc...................... E 330 482-1993
Lisbon **(G-8467)**

▲ Hdt Expeditionary Systems Inc......... E 216 438-6111
Solon **(G-12121)**

◆ King Bag and Manufacturing Co........ E 513 541-5440
Cincinnati **(G-2795)**

Luxaire Cushion Co................... F 330 872-0995
Newton Falls **(G-10579)**

Queen City Carpets LLC............... F 513 823-8238
Cincinnati **(G-3021)**

R J Manray Inc....................... G 330 559-6716
Canfield **(G-1814)**

▲ Rich Industries Inc.................. E 330 339-4113
New Philadelphia **(G-10465)**

Sailors Tailor Inc.................... F 937 862-7781
Spring Valley **(G-12243)**

2394 Canvas and related products

ABC Signs Inc....................... F 513 407-4367
Cincinnati **(G-2331)**

▼ Advantage Tent Fittings Inc........... F 740 773-3015
Chillicothe **(G-2241)**

American Canvas Products Inc.......... G 419 382-8450
Toledo **(G-12874)**

Awning Fabri Caters Inc............... G 216 476-4888
Cleveland **(G-3397)**

Canvas Specialty Mfg Co............... G 216 881-0647
Cleveland **(G-3465)**

Capital City Awning Co Inc............. E 614 221-5404
Columbus **(G-4796)**

◆ Celina Tent Inc..................... D 419 586-3610
Celina **(G-2101)**

◆ Chalfant Sew Fabricators Inc........... E 216 521-7922
Cleveland **(G-3484)**

Cleveland Canvas Goods Mfg Co......... E 216 361-4567
Cleveland **(G-3508)**

Columbus Canvas Products Inc.......... F 614 375-1397
Columbus **(G-4819)**

Custom Canvas & Boat Repr Inc......... G 419 732-3314
Lakeside **(G-8157)**

Custom Tarpaulin Products Inc.......... F 330 758-1801
Youngstown **(G-14844)**

DCW Acquisition Inc.................. G 216 451-0666
Cleveland **(G-3607)**

Delphos Tent and Awning Inc........... G 419 692-5776
Delphos **(G-6186)**

Electra Tarp Inc...................... F 330 477-7168
Canton **(G-1885)**

Fabric Forms Inc..................... G 513 281-6300
Cincinnati **(G-2610)**

Forest City Companies Inc............. E 216 586-5279
Cleveland **(G-3735)**

Galion Canvas Products............... G 419 468-5333
Galion **(G-7191)**

Glawe Manufacturing Co Inc............ G 937 754-0064
Fairborn **(G-6694)**

Griffin Fisher Co Inc.................. G 513 961-2110
Cincinnati **(G-2692)**

▲ Hdt Expeditionary Systems Inc......... E 216 438-6111
Solon **(G-12121)**

Independent Awning & Canvas Co........ G 937 223-9661
Dayton **(G-5820)**

▲ Inside Outfitters Inc................. E 614 798-3500
Lewis Center **(G-8338)**

Lesch Boat Cover Canvas Co LLC........ G 419 668-6374
Norwalk **(G-10850)**

Lumenomics Inc...................... E 614 798-3500
Lewis Center **(G-8342)**

◆ Main Awning & Tent Inc............... G 513 621-6947
Cincinnati **(G-2842)**

National Bias Fabric Co................ G 216 361-0530
Cleveland **(G-4058)**

▲ Ohio Awning & Manufacturing Co....... E 216 861-2400
Cleveland **(G-4111)**

PCR Restorations Inc................. G 419 747-7957
Mansfield **(G-8844)**

Queen City Awning & Tent Co............ E 513 530-9660
Cincinnati *(G-3020)*

▲ Rainbow Industries Inc................ G 937 323-6493
Springfield *(G-12366)*

RFW Holdings Inc......................... G 440 331-8300
Cleveland *(G-4239)*

Sailors Tailor Inc........................ F 937 862-7781
Spring Valley *(G-12243)*

▲ Samsel Rope & Marine Supply Co... E 216 241-0333
Cleveland *(G-4272)*

Schaaf Co Inc............................ G 513 241-7044
Cincinnati *(G-3067)*

▲ Scherba Industries Inc................ D 330 273-3200
Brunswick *(G-1614)*

South Akron Awning Co................. F 330 848-7611
Akron *(G-314)*

Tarpco Inc............................... F 330 677-8277
Kent *(G-8086)*

Tarped Out Inc........................... G 330 325-7722
Ravenna *(G-11545)*

Toledo Tarp Service Inc................. E 419 837-5098
Perrysburg *(G-11276)*

Tri County Tarp LLC..................... E 419 288-3350
Gibsonburg *(G-7260)*

Wolf G T Awning & Tent Co.............. F 937 548-4161
Greenville *(G-7360)*

Youngstown Shade & Alum LLC......... G 330 782-2373
Youngstown *(G-14975)*

2395 Pleating and stitching

▲ 5 BS Inc............................... C 740 454-8453
Zanesville *(G-14980)*

Albany Screen Printing LLC............. F 614 585-3279
Reynoldsburg *(G-11555)*

Alley Cat Designs Inc.................... G 937 291-8803
Dayton *(G-5645)*

Appleheart Inc........................... G 937 384-0430
Miamisburg *(G-9666)*

▲ Atlantis Sportswear Inc............... E 937 773-0680
Piqua *(G-11336)*

Aubrey Rose Apparel LLC............... G 513 728-2681
Cincinnati *(G-2390)*

▲ Barbs Graffiti Inc..................... E 216 881-5550
Cleveland *(G-3405)*

Big Kahuna Graphics LLC................ G 330 455-2625
Canton *(G-1840)*

Cal Sales Embroidery.................... G 440 236-3820
Columbia Station *(G-4590)*

Campbell Signs & Apparel LLC.......... G 330 386-4768
East Liverpool *(G-6388)*

Carols Ultra Stitch & Variety............ G 419 935-8991
Willard *(G-14401)*

▲ Catania Medallic Specialty Inc........ E 440 933-9595
Avon Lake *(G-751)*

Chris Stepp.............................. G 513 248-0822
Milford *(G-9928)*

Color 3 Embroidery Inc.................. G 330 652-9495
Warren *(G-13753)*

Computer Stitch Designs Inc............ G 330 856-7826
Warren *(G-13754)*

Craco Embroidery Inc.................... G 513 563-6999
Cincinnati *(G-2522)*

Design Original Inc...................... F 937 596-5121
Jackson Center *(G-7961)*

Eastgate Custom Graphics Ltd.......... G 513 528-7922
Cincinnati *(G-2575)*

Embroidery Network Inc................. G 330 678-4887
Kent *(G-8030)*

Embroidme.............................. G 330 484-8484
Canton *(G-1887)*

Emroid ME............................... G 614 789-1898
Westerville *(G-14259)*

Fastpatch Ltd............................ F 513 367-1838
Harrison *(G-7550)*

Fineline Imprints Inc.................... G 740 453-1083
Zanesville *(G-15013)*

Finn Graphics Inc........................ E 513 941-6161
Cincinnati *(G-2624)*

Got Graphix Llc.......................... F 330 703-9047
Fairlawn *(G-6802)*

Graphic Stitch Inc....................... G 937 642-6707
Marysville *(G-9021)*

Ideal Drapery Company Inc.............. F 330 745-9873
Barberton *(G-813)*

Initial Designs Inc...................... G 419 475-3900
Toledo *(G-13004)*

K Ventures Inc.......................... F 419 678-2308
Coldwater *(G-4579)*

Kens His & Hers Shop Inc............... G 330 872-3190
Newton Falls *(G-10578)*

Kiwi Promotional AP & Prtg Co.......... G 330 487-5115
Twinsburg *(G-13325)*

Kts Cstm Lgs/Xclsvely You Inc.......... G 440 285-9803
Chardon *(G-2212)*

Kts Custom Logos....................... G 440 285-9803
Chardon *(G-2213)*

Kuhls Hot Sportspot.................... F 513 474-2282
Cincinnati *(G-2808)*

Logo This................................ G 419 445-1355
Archbold *(G-501)*

Markt LLC................................ G 740 397-5900
Mount Vernon *(G-10250)*

▲ McCc Sportswear Inc.................. G 513 583-9210
Milford *(G-9942)*

Mr Emblem Inc........................... G 419 697-1888
Oregon *(G-10964)*

◆ Neff Motivation Inc................... C 937 548-3194
Greenville *(G-7348)*

Novak J F Manufacturing Co LLC........ G 216 741-5112
Cleveland *(G-4102)*

Ohio Embroidery LLC.................... G 330 479-0029
Canton *(G-1965)*

Part 2 Screen Prtg Design Inc........... G 614 294-4429
Columbus *(G-5175)*

Phantasm Dsgns Sprtsn More Ltd....... G 419 538-6737
Ottawa *(G-11042)*

Precision Imprint........................ G 740 592-5916
Athens *(G-646)*

Qualitee Design Sportswear Co.......... F 740 333-8337
Wshngtn Ct Hs *(G-14742)*

Quality Rubber Stamp Inc............... G 614 235-2700
Lancaster *(G-8220)*

Queen City Spirit LLC................... F 513 533-2662
Cincinnati *(G-3026)*

R J Manray Inc.......................... G 330 559-6716
Canfield *(G-1814)*

Randy Gray.............................. G 513 533-3200
Cincinnati *(G-3032)*

Rnp Inc................................... G
Dellroy *(G-6182)*

Sew & Sew Embroidery Inc.............. F 330 676-1600
Kent *(G-8078)*

▲ Shamrock Companies Inc............. D 440 899-9510
Westlake *(G-14333)*

Sit Inc................................... E 330 758-8468
Youngstown *(G-14933)*

Sparta Embroidery Inc................... G 330 484-8484
Canton *(G-2009)*

Sportsco Imprinting..................... G 513 641-5111
Cincinnati *(G-3106)*

Sun Shine Awards....................... F 740 425-2504
Barnesville *(G-847)*

Superior Image Embroidery LLC......... G 513 991-7543
West Chester *(G-14151)*

T & L Custom Screening Inc............. G 937 237-3121
Dayton *(G-6036)*

▲ Thread Works Custom Embroidery... G 937 478-5231
Beavercreek *(G-986)*

Unisport Inc............................. F 419 529-4727
Ontario *(G-10953)*

United Sport Apparel.................... F 330 722-0818
Medina *(G-9460)*

Vasil Co Inc............................. G 419 562-2901
Bucyrus *(G-1692)*

Vector International Corp................ G 440 942-2002
Mentor *(G-9648)*

Wholesale Imprints Inc.................. E 440 224-3527
North Kingsville *(G-10700)*

▲ Zimmer Enterprises Inc............... E 937 428-1057
Dayton *(G-6090)*

2396 Automotive and apparel trimmings

A C Hadley - Printing Inc................ G 937 426-0952
Beavercreek *(G-962)*

Adcraft Decals Incorporated............ E 216 524-2934
Cleveland *(G-3297)*

Akron Felt Chenille Mfg Co Inc.......... F 330 733-7778
Akron *(G-30)*

All Streets Auto LLC.................... F 330 714-7717
Cleveland *(G-3327)*

American Imprssions Sportswear........ G 614 848-6677
Columbus *(G-4697)*

◆ Anomatic Corporation................. E 740 522-2203
New Albany *(G-10328)*

◆ Associated Premium Corporation..... E 513 679-4444
Cincinnati *(G-2381)*

▲ Atlantis Sportswear Inc............... E 937 773-0680
Piqua *(G-11336)*

Bates Metal Products Inc................ D 740 498-8371
Port Washington *(G-11455)*

Big Kahuna Graphics LLC................ G 330 455-2625
Canton *(G-1840)*

Brandon Screen Printing................ F 419 229-9837
Lima *(G-8391)*

Brass Bull 1 LLC........................ G 740 335-8030
Wshngtn Ct Hs *(G-14735)*

Brown Cnty Bd Mntal Rtardation........ G 937 378-4891
Georgetown *(G-7251)*

Cal Sales Embroidery.................... G 440 236-3820
Columbia Station *(G-4590)*

Charizma Corp.......................... G 216 621-2220
Cleveland *(C-3185)*

▲ City Apparel Inc...................... F 419 434-1155
Findlay *(G-6852)*

Conform Automotive LLC................ B 937 492-2708
Sidney *(G-12002)*

Design Original Inc...................... F 937 596-5121
Jackson Center *(G-7961)*

Discount Floral Supply Inc.............. G
Cleveland *(G-3617)*

Dupli-Systems Inc....................... C 440 234-9415
Strongsville *(G-12555)*

Eisenhauer Mfg Co LLC.................. D 419 238-0081
Van Wert *(G-13535)*

Erd Specialty Graphics Inc.............. G 419 242-9545
Toledo *(G-12955)*

Fineline Imprints Inc.................... G 740 453-1083
Zanesville *(G-15013)*

▲ Fortner Upholstering Inc.............. F 614 475-8282
Columbus *(G-4936)*

▲ General Theming Contrs LLC.......... C 614 252-6342
Columbus *(G-4948)*

▼ Greenfield Research Inc............... C 937 981-7763
Greenfield *(G-7330)*

Griffin Fisher Co Inc.................... G 513 961-2110
Cincinnati *(G-2692)*

SIC

Hall Company................................. E 937 652-1376
  Urbana *(G-13465)*

◆ Hfi LLC....................................... B 614 491-0700
  Canal Winchester *(G-1791)*

Hollywood Imprints LLC................. F 614 501-6040
  Gahanna *(G-7160)*

Indra Holdings Corp...................... C 513 682-8200
  Cincinnati *(G-2743)*

Jls Funeral Home.......................... F 614 625-1220
  Columbus *(G-5040)*

Kiwi Promotional AP & Prtg Co....... E 330 487-5115
  Twinsburg *(G-13325)*

Lesch Boat Cover Canvas Co LLC....... G 419 668-6374
  Norwalk *(G-10850)*

Lockfast LLC................................ G 800 543-7157
  Loveland *(G-8637)*

M&Ms Autosales LLC..................... F 234 334-7022
  Akron *(G-217)*

▲ Magna Visual Inc...................... E 314 843-9000
  Perrysburg *(G-11236)*

Michigan Silkscreen Inc................. G 419 885-1163
  Sylvania *(G-12715)*

Mr Emblem Inc............................. G 419 697-1888
  Oregon *(G-10964)*

National Bias Fabric Co.................. G 216 361-0530
  Cleveland *(G-4058)*

Northeastern Plastics Inc............... G 330 453-5925
  Canton *(G-1961)*

Ohio State Institute Fin Inc............ G 614 861-8811
  Reynoldsburg *(G-11576)*

Painted Hill Inv Group Inc.............. F 937 339-1756
  Troy *(G-13246)*

Personaliteez LLC......................... F 614 354-9108
  Columbus *(G-5189)*

Peska Inc.................................... F 440 998-4664
  Ashtabula *(G-611)*

Pieco Inc.................................... D 937 399-5100
  Springfield *(G-12363)*

Pieco Inc.................................... E 419 422-5335
  Findlay *(G-6908)*

▲ Plastic Card Inc........................ D 330 896-5555
  Uniontown *(G-13424)*

◆ Plus Mark LLC.......................... D 216 252-6770
  Cleveland *(G-4174)*

Promospark Inc............................ F 513 844-2211
  Fairfield *(G-6768)*

Quality Rubber Stamp Inc.............. G 614 235-2700
  Lancaster *(G-8220)*

R & A Sports Inc.......................... E 216 289-2254
  Euclid *(G-6674)*

Randy Gray.................................. G 513 533-3200
  Cincinnati *(G-3032)*

Roach Studios LLC........................ F 614 725-1405
  Columbus *(G-5233)*

Schilling Graphics Inc.................... E 419 468-1037
  Galion *(G-7198)*

Screen Works Inc.......................... E 937 264-9111
  Dayton *(G-6000)*

Silly Brandz Global LLC................. D 419 697-8324
  Toledo *(G-13132)*

Solar Arts Graphic Designs............ G 330 744-0535
  Youngstown *(G-14934)*

Spirit Avionics Ltd........................ F 614 237-4271
  Columbus *(G-5284)*

▲ Sroufe Healthcare Products LLC....... G 260 894-4171
  Wadsworth *(G-13672)*

Stakes Manufacturing LLC.............. D 216 245-4752
  Willowick *(G-14567)*

Sylvan Studios Inc........................ G 419 882-3423
  Sylvania *(G-12725)*

T & L Custom Screening Inc........... G 937 237-3121
  Dayton *(G-6036)*

Tee Creations.............................. G 937 878-2822
  Fairborn *(G-6702)*

Telempu N Hayashi Amer Corp......... G 513 932-9319
  Lebanon *(G-8288)*

Tendon Manufacturing Inc.............. E 216 663-3200
  Cleveland *(G-4374)*

Triage Ortho Group....................... G 937 653-6431
  Urbana *(G-13478)*

Trim Systems Operating Corp.......... B 740 772-5998
  Chillicothe *(G-2285)*

▲ TS Tech Americas Inc................. B 614 575-4100
  Reynoldsburg *(G-11583)*

▲ Universal Direct Fulfillment Corp....... F 330 650-5000
  Hudson *(G-7861)*

Vandava Inc................................. G 614 277-8003
  Grove City *(G-7421)*

Vasil Co Inc................................. G 419 562-2901
  Bucyrus *(G-1692)*

Vector International Corp................ G 440 942-2002
  Mentor *(G-9648)*

▲ Vgu Industries Inc..................... E 216 676-9093
  Cleveland *(G-4464)*

Visual Marking Systems Inc............ D 330 425-7100
  Twinsburg *(G-13393)*

▼ W J Egli Company Inc................. F 330 823-3666
  Alliance *(G-103)*

West & Barker Inc........................ F 330 652-9923
  Niles *(G-10609)*

Wholesale Imprints Inc.................. E 440 224-3527
  North Kingsville *(G-10700)*

Woodrow Manufacturing Co............ E 937 399-9333
  Springfield *(G-12396)*

Zide Sport Shop of Ohio Inc........... F 740 373-8199
  Marietta *(G-8963)*

2399 Fabricated textile products, nec

Akron Felt Chenille Mfg Co Inc......... F 330 733-7778
  Akron *(G-30)*

Annin & Co.................................. E 740 498-5008
  Newcomerstown *(G-10568)*

Annin & Co.................................. C 740 622-4447
  Coshocton *(G-5447)*

Besi Manufacturing Inc.................. G 513 874-1460
  West Chester *(G-13950)*

▲ Besi Manufacturing Inc.............. E 513 874-0232
  West Chester *(G-13951)*

▲ Coastal Pet Products Inc............ A 330 821-7363
  Alliance *(G-377)*

▲ Drifter Marine Inc..................... G 419 666-8144
  Perrysburg *(G-11217)*

Flag Lady Inc.............................. G 614 263-1776
  Columbus *(G-4927)*

Griffin Fisher Co Inc...................... G 513 961-2110
  Cincinnati *(G-2692)*

Markers Inc................................. G 440 933-5927
  Avon Lake *(G-764)*

Nationwide Belting Sls Svc LLC....... E 419 287-7092
  Pemberville *(G-11177)*

◆ Neff Motivation Inc.................... C 937 548-3194
  Greenville *(G-7348)*

▲ Party Animal Inc....................... F 440 471-1030
  Westlake *(G-14320)*

School Pride Limited..................... F 614 568-0697
  Columbus *(G-5254)*

Signme LLC................................. G 614 221-7803
  Columbus *(G-5269)*

TAC Industries Inc........................ B 937 328-5200
  Springfield *(G-12382)*

Watershed Mangement LLC............. F 740 852-5607
  Mount Sterling *(G-10230)*

24 LUMBER AND WOOD PRODUCTS, EXCEPT FURNITURE

2411 Logging

Beachs Trees Slctive Hrvstg LL......... G 513 289-5976
  Cincinnati *(G-2297)*

Biedenbach Logging...................... G 740 732-6477
  Sarahsville *(G-11884)*

Blair Logging.............................. G 740 934-2730
  Lower Salem *(G-8665)*

Blankenship Logging LLC................ G 740 372-3833
  Otway *(G-11058)*

Border Lumber & Logging Ltd.......... G 330 897-0177
  Fresno *(G-7145)*

Craig Saylor................................ G 740 352-8363
  Portland *(G-11462)*

Custom Material Hdlg Eqp LLC......... G 513 235-5336
  Cincinnati *(G-2531)*

Dale R Adkins.............................. G 740 682-7312
  Oak Hill *(G-10887)*

David Adkins Logging.................... G 740 533-0297
  Kitts Hill *(G-8147)*

▼ Facemyer Lumber Co Inc............ F 740 992-5965
  Pomeroy *(G-11437)*

Haessly Lumber Sales Co............... D 740 373-6681
  Marietta *(G-8922)*

HK Logging & Lumber Ltd............... G 440 632-1997
  Middlefield *(G-9801)*

Lee Saylor Logging LLC.................. G 740 682-0479
  Oak Hill *(G-10890)*

Miller Logging Inc........................ G 330 279-4721
  Holmesville *(G-7802)*

Oakbridge Timber Framing............. G 419 994-1052
  Loudonville *(G-8592)*

Ohio Timberland Products Inc......... F 419 682-6322
  Stryker *(G-12625)*

R & D Logging LLC........................ G 740 259-6127
  Lucasville *(G-8669)*

Stark Truss Company Inc............... E 419 298-3777
  Edgerton *(G-6471)*

2421 Sawmills and planing mills, general

Automated Bldg Components Inc......... E 419 257-2152
  North Baltimore *(G-10612)*

Baillie Lumber Co LP..................... E 419 462-2000
  Galion *(G-7179)*

Beach City Lumber Llc................... G 330 878-4097
  Strasburg *(G-12477)*

Beaver Wood Products................... G 740 226-6211
  Beaver *(G-960)*

Blaney Hardwoods Ohio Inc............ D 740 678-8288
  Vincent *(G-13619)*

▲ Bruewer Woodwork Mfg Co......... D 513 353-3505
  Cleves *(G-4532)*

Calvin W Lafferty......................... G 740 498-6566
  Kimbolton *(G-8136)*

Cherokee Hardwoods Inc............... G 440 632-0322
  Middlefield *(G-9787)*

Clarksville Stave & Lbr Co Ltd......... G 937 376-4618
  Xenia *(G-14759)*

◆ Clarksville Stave & Veneer Co......... F 740 947-4159
  Waverly *(G-13864)*

Coblentz Brothers Inc................... E 330 857-7211
  Apple Creek *(G-465)*

▲ Combs Manufacturing Inc........... D 330 784-3151
  Akron *(G-104)*

Conover Lumber Company Inc......... F 937 368-3010
  Conover *(G-5420)*

Contract Lumber Inc..................... F 614 751-1109
  Columbus *(G-4844)*

Crownover Lumber Company Inc.......... D 740 596-5229
  Mc Arthur (G-9349)

▼ Decorative Panels Intl Inc................... D 419 535-5921
  Toledo (G-12941)

Denoon Lumber Company LLC.......... D 740 768-2220
  Bergholz (G-1195)

▼ Facemyer Lumber Co Inc................... F 740 992-5965
  Pomeroy (G-11437)

Gardner Lumber Company Inc................. F 740 254-4664
  Tippecanoe (G-12857)

Gross Lumber Inc.................................. G 330 683-2055
  Apple Creek (G-469)

Haessly Lumber Sales Co....................... D 740 373-6681
  Marietta (G-8922)

▼ Hartzell Hardwoods Inc.................... D 937 773-7054
  Piqua (G-11351)

◆ Itl Corp... E 216 831-3140
  Cleveland (G-3874)

Kemps Ace Hardware Inc................... F 740 472-1651
  Woodsfield (G-14614)

Mac Lean J S Co.............................. G 614 878-5454
  Columbus (G-5078)

Marathon At Sawmill........................... F 614 734-0836
  Columbus (G-5080)

MB Manufacturing Corp....................... G 513 682-1461
  Fairfield (G-6753)

Miller Logging Inc............................. G 330 279-4721
  Holmesville (G-7802)

Miller Lumber Co Inc.......................... G 330 674-0273
  Millersburg (G-9998)

Millwood Lumber Inc........................... E 740 254-4681
  Gnadenhutten (G-7291)

Mohler Lumber Company...................... E 330 499-5461
  North Canton (G-10652)

Mowhawk Lumber Ltd.......................... E 330 698-5333
  Apple Creek (G-473)

Newberry Wood Enterprises Inc.......... G 440 238-6127
  Strongsville (G-12578)

No Name Lumber LLC.......................... G 740 289-3722
  Piketon (G-11309)

▼ Ohio Valley Veneer Inc.................... E 740 493-2901
  Piketon (G-11311)

R & D Hilltop Lumber Inc.................... E 740 342-3051
  New Lexington (G-10406)

Raber Lumber Co............................... G 330 893-2797
  Charm (G-2227)

Runkles Sawmill LLC........................ G 937 663-0115
  Saint Paris (G-11750)

S & J Lumber Company LLC................ F 740 245-5804
  Thurman (G-12771)

S Holley Lumber LLC........................ G 440 272-5315
  Windsor (G-14603)

S&R Lumber LLC............................. F 740 352-6135
  Piketon (G-11313)

Salt Creek Lumber Company Inc.......... G 330 695-3500
  Fredericksburg (G-7071)

Sawmill 9721 LLC............................. G 614 937-4400
  Powell (G-11494)

Sawmill Road Management Co LLC....... E 937 342-9071
  Columbus (G-5251)

Siefker Sawmill LLC.......................... G 419 339-8523
  Lima (G-8448)

Stark Truss Company Inc.................... D 330 756-3050
  Beach City (G-907)

▲ Stephen M Trudick........................... E 440 834-1891
  Burton (G-1704)

Sugarcreek Shavings LLC................... G 330 763-4239
  Sugarcreek (G-12651)

Superior Hardwoods Ohio Inc.............. E 740 439-2727
  Cambridge (G-1762)

Superior Hardwoods Ohio Inc.............. G 740 596-2561
  Mc Arthur (G-9350)

Superior Hardwoods Ohio Inc................ D 740 384-5677
  Wellston (G-13910)

T & D Thompson Inc......................... F 740 332-8515
  Laurelville (G-8238)

▼ Taylor Lumber Worldwide Inc............ C 740 259-6222
  Piketon (G-11315)

The F A Requarth Company................. E 937 224-1141
  Dayton (G-6048)

▲ The Mead Corporation....................... B 937 495-6323
  Dayton (G-6049)

▼ Trumbull County Hardwoods............. E 440 632-0555
  Middlefield (G-9833)

Tusco Hardwoods LLC....................... G 330 852-4281
  Sugarcreek (G-12655)

United Hardwoods Ltd....................... G 330 878-9510
  Strasburg (G-12483)

▲ Urban Industries of Ohio Inc............. E 419 468-3578
  Galion (G-7200)

Wagner Farms Sawmill Ltd Lblty.......... G 419 653-4126
  Leipsic (G-8315)

◆ Walnut Creek Planing Ltd................. D 330 893-3244
  Millersburg (G-10018)

Wappoo Wood Products Inc................ E 937 492-1166
  Sidney (G-12060)

Weaver Lumber Co............................. G 330 359-5091
  Wilmot (G-14596)

Whitewater Forest Products LLC........... F 513 724-0157
  Batavia (G-897)

Wilmington Forest Products................. G 937 382-7813
  Wilmington (G-14590)

Wooldridge Lumber Co....................... G 740 289-4912
  Piketon (G-11316)

Yoder Lumber Co Inc......................... G 330 674-1435
  Millersburg (G-10021)

Yoder Lumber Co Inc......................... E 330 893-3131
  Sugarcreek (G-12658)

▼ Yoder Lumber Co Inc........................ D 330 893-3121
  Millersburg (G-10020)

2426 Hardwood dimension and flooring mills

Armstrong Custom Moulding Inc.......... G 740 922-5931
  Uhrichsville (G-13401)

Baillie Lumber Co LP.......................... E 419 462-2000
  Galion (G-7179)

Beaver Wood Products......................... G 740 226-6211
  Beaver (G-960)

Canfield Manufacturing Co Inc............. G 330 533-3333
  North Jackson (G-10691)

Carter-Jones Lumber Company............. G 330 674-9060
  Millersburg (G-9975)

Cherokee Hardwoods Inc.................... G 440 632-0322
  Middlefield (G-9787)

Crownover Lumber Company Inc.......... G 740 596-5229
  Mc Arthur (G-9349)

Denoon Lumber Company LLC............. D 740 768-2220
  Bergholz (G-1195)

Furniture Concepts Inc....................... F 216 292-9100
  Cleveland (G-3745)

Gross Lumber Inc.............................. G 330 683-2055
  Apple Creek (G-469)

Haessly Lumber Sales Co................... D 740 373-6681
  Marietta (G-8922)

Halliday Holdings Inc......................... E 740 335-1430
  Washington Court Hou (G-13821)

▼ Hartzell Hardwoods Inc.................... D 937 773-7054
  Piqua (G-11351)

Holmes Lumber & Bldg Ctr Inc............. E 330 479-8314
  Canton (G-1912)

Holmes Lumber & Bldg Ctr Inc............. C 330 674-9060
  Millersburg (G-9989)

Itl LLC... G 216 831-3140
  Beachwood (G-923)

◆ Itl Corp... E 216 831-3140
  Cleveland (G-3874)

J McCoy Lumber Co Ltd..................... F 937 587-3423
  Peebles (G-11170)

Marsh Valley Forest Pdts Ltd............... G 440 632-1889
  Middlefield (G-9807)

Mid Ohio Wood Products Inc............... G 740 323-0427
  Newark (G-10520)

Mohler Lumber Company...................... E 330 499-5461
  North Canton (G-10652)

Ogonek Custom Hardwood Inc............. G 833 718-2531
  Barberton (G-827)

Ohio Valley Veneer Inc....................... F 740 289-4979
  Piketon (G-11310)

▼ Ohio Valley Veneer Inc.................... E 740 493-2901
  Piketon (G-11311)

Plank and Hide Co............................. E 888 462-6852
  Cincinnati (G-2968)

◆ Prestige Enterprise Intl Inc............... D 513 469-6044
  Blue Ash (G-1324)

◆ Regency Seating Inc......................... E 330 848-3700
  Akron (G-280)

◆ Robbins Sports Surfaces LLC............ E 513 871-8988
  Cincinnati (G-3051)

▲ Roppe Holding Company..................... B 419 435-8546
  Fostoria (G-6999)

Siefker Sawmill LLC.......................... G 419 339-8523
  Lima (G-8448)

Sportsmans Haven Inc....................... G 740 432-7243
  Cambridge (G-1761)

▲ Stephen M Trudick........................... E 440 834-1891
  Burton (G-1704)

Superior Hardwoods Ohio Inc.............. E 740 439-2727
  Cambridge (G-1762)

Superior Hardwoods Ohio Inc.............. G 740 596-2561
  Mc Arthur (G-9350)

Superior Hardwoods Ohio Inc.............. D 740 384-5677
  Wellston (G-13910)

T & D Thompson Inc......................... F 740 332-8515
  Laurelville (G-8238)

Timothy Whatman.............................. E 419 883-2443
  Bellville (G-1143)

▼ Trumbull County Hardwoods............. E 440 632-0555
  Middlefield (G-9833)

Urbn Timber LLC............................... G 614 981-3043
  Columbus (G-5341)

Wagner Farms Sawmill Ltd Lblty.......... G 419 653-4126
  Leipsic (G-8315)

◆ Walnut Creek Planing Ltd................. D 330 893-3244
  Millersburg (G-10018)

Wappoo Wood Products Inc................ E 937 492-1166
  Sidney (G-12060)

Woodcraft Industries Inc.................... E 440 632-9655
  Middlefield (G-9836)

Wooden Horse.................................. G 740 503-5243
  Baltimore (G-789)

Yoder Lumber Co Inc......................... E 330 893-3131
  Sugarcreek (G-12658)

▼ Yoder Lumber Co Inc........................ D 330 893-3121
  Millersburg (G-10020)

2429 Special product sawmills, nec

Brown-Forman Corporation.................. G 740 384-3027
  Wellston (G-13905)

▼ IVEX Protective Packaging LLC......... E 937 498-9298
  Sidney (G-12026)

2431 Millwork

1914 Mi Inc..................................... E 330 308-8667
  New Philadelphia (G-10428)

▲ 1914 Mi Inc..................................... D 800 426-4244
  New Philadelphia (G-10429)

SIC

A & J Woodworking Inc............................ G 419 695-5655
　Delphos *(G-6183)*

Aca Millworks Inc................................... F 419 339-7600
　Waynesfield *(G-13877)*

Ace Lumber Company............................. F 330 744-3167
　Youngstown *(G-14804)*

▲ Action Industries Ltd........................... G 216 252-7800
　Strongsville *(G-12531)*

▼ Advantage Tent Fittings Inc................ F 740 773-3015
　Chillicothe *(G-2241)*

Ailes Millwork Inc.................................. F 330 678-4300
　Kent *(G-8015)*

All Pro Ovrhd Door Systems LLC........... G 614 444-3667
　Columbus *(G-4684)*

Amcan Stair & Rail LLC......................... G 937 781-3084
　Springfield *(G-12279)*

American Plastech LLC.......................... G 330 538-0576
　North Jackson *(G-10682)*

Anderson Door Co.................................. F 216 475-5700
　Cleveland *(G-3358)*

Anthony Flottemesch & Son Inc........... F 513 561-1212
　Cincinnati *(G-2371)*

Armstrong Custom Moulding Inc.......... G 740 922-5931
　Uhrichsville *(G-13401)*

Art Woodworking & Mfg Co................... E 513 681-2986
　Cincinnati *(G-2379)*

Automated Bldg Components Inc.......... E 419 257-2152
　North Baltimore *(G-10612)*

Baird Brothers Sawmill Inc.................... C 330 533-3122
　Canfield *(G-1804)*

▲ Bautec N Technoform Amer Inc.......... E 330 487-6600
　Twinsburg *(G-13278)*

▲ Bruewer Woodwork Mfg Co................. D 513 353-3505
　Cleves *(G-4532)*

C & W Custom Wdwkg Co Inc................ G 513 891-6340
　Cincinnati *(G-2435)*

Cabintwrks Group Mddlfield LLC.......... C 440 437-8537
　Orwell *(G-11020)*

Carden Door Company LLC.................... G 513 459-2233
　Mason *(G-9076)*

▲ Carolina Stair Supply Inc.................... E 740 922-3333
　Uhrichsville *(G-13402)*

Carter-Jones Lumber Company.............. G 330 674-9060
　Millersburg *(G-9975)*

▲ Cascade Ohio Inc.............................. B 440 593-5800
　Conneaut *(G-5399)*

Cassady Woodworks Inc........................ F 937 256-7948
　Dayton *(G-5605)*

Cincinnati Stair & Handrail.................... F 513 722-3947
　Cincinnati *(G-2486)*

Cindoco Wood Products Co................... G 937 444-2504
　Mount Orab *(G-10216)*

Clark Wood Specialties Inc................... G 330 499-8711
　Clinton *(G-4553)*

◆ Clopay Ames Inc................................ C 800 282-2260
　Mason *(G-9087)*

◆ Clopay Corporation............................ E 513 770-4800
　Mason *(G-9088)*

Coolbreeze Technologies LLC............... G 440 748-1911
　Elyria *(G-6515)*

Courthouse Manufacturing LLC............. E 740 335-2727
　Washington Court Hou *(G-13820)*

Cox Interior Inc..................................... G 614 473-9169
　Columbus *(G-4855)*

Cox Interior Inc..................................... F 270 789-3129
　Norwood *(G-10867)*

Darby Creek Millwork LLC..................... G 614 873-3267
　Plain City *(G-11402)*

Decker Custom Wood Llc...................... G 419 332-3464
　Fremont *(G-7103)*

Dendratec Ltd....................................... G 330 473-4878
　Dalton *(G-5583)*

Denoon Lumber Company LLC.............. D 740 768-2220
　Bergholz *(G-1195)*

◆ Designer Doors Inc............................ G 330 772-6391
　Burghill *(G-1697)*

Display Dynamics Inc............................ F 937 832-2830
　Englewood *(G-6612)*

Division Overhead Door Inc................... F 513 872-0888
　Cincinnati *(G-2556)*

Dowel Yoder & Molding......................... G 330 231-2962
　Fredericksburg *(G-7063)*

Dublin Millwork Co Inc.......................... F 614 889-7776
　Dublin *(G-6294)*

Encompass Woodworking LLC............... G 513 569-2841
　Cincinnati *(G-2587)*

Fairfield Wood Works Ltd...................... G 740 689-1953
　Lancaster *(G-8201)*

Fdi Cabinetry LLC.................................. G 513 353-4500
　Cleves *(G-4537)*

Fifth Avenue Lumber Co........................ E 614 833-6655
　Canal Winchester *(G-1790)*

▼ Fixture Dimensions Inc...................... E 513 360-7512
　Liberty Twp *(G-8384)*

Forum Works LLC.................................. E 937 349-8685
　Milford Center *(G-9957)*

Fryburg Door Inc.................................... D 330 674-5252
　Millersburg *(G-9981)*

▼ Gateway Industrial Pdts Inc............... E 440 324-4112
　Elyria *(G-6539)*

Gerstenslager Construction................... G 330 832-3604
　Massillon *(G-9195)*

Great Lakes Stair & Mllwk Co................ G 330 225-2005
　Hinckley *(G-7731)*

Greenhart Rstoration Mllwk LLC............ G 330 502-6050
　Boardman *(G-1373)*

Gross & Sons Custom Millwork.............. G 419 227-0214
　Lima *(G-8411)*

Hardwood Lumber Company Inc............ F 440 834-1891
　Middlefield *(G-9797)*

Heartland Stairways Inc........................ G 330 279-2554
　Holmesville *(G-7796)*

Hinckley Wood Products Ltd.................. G 330 220-9999
　Hinckley *(G-7732)*

Hj Systems Inc...................................... F 614 351-9777
　Columbus *(G-4989)*

▲ Holmes Custom Moulding Ltd............ E 330 893-3598
　Millersburg *(G-9988)*

Holmes Lumber & Bldg Ctr Inc............. E 330 479-8314
　Canton *(G-1912)*

Holmes Lumber & Bldg Ctr Inc............. C 330 674-9060
　Millersburg *(G-9989)*

Hope Holdings Inc................................. G 330 674-7015
　Mount Hope *(G-10214)*

Hrh Door Corp....................................... E 513 674-9300
　Cincinnati *(G-2734)*

Hyde Park Lumber Company.................. E 513 271-1500
　Cincinnati *(G-2736)*

J McCoy Lumber Co Ltd........................ F 937 587-3423
　Peebles *(G-11170)*

Jeld-Wen Inc... C 740 964-1431
　Etna *(G-6635)*

Jeld-Wen Inc... C 740 397-1144
　Mount Vernon *(G-10246)*

Jeld-Wen Inc... G 740 397-3403
　Mount Vernon *(G-10247)*

Judy Mills Company Inc........................ E 513 271-4241
　Cincinnati *(G-2775)*

Khempco Bldg Sup Co Ltd Partnr.......... D 740 549-0465
　Delaware *(G-6159)*

L & L Ornamental Iron Co...................... F 513 353-1930
　Cleves *(G-4543)*

L and J Woodworking............................ F 330 359-3216
　Dundee *(G-6367)*

Laborie Enterprises LLC........................ G 419 686-6245
　Portage *(G-11458)*

▲ Lckbm Company................................ D 419 636-4555
　Bryan *(G-1648)*

Liechty Specialties Inc.......................... G 419 445-6696
　Archbold *(G-500)*

Lima Millwork Inc.................................. G 419 331-3303
　Elida *(G-6483)*

M H Woodworking LLC........................... G 330 893-3929
　Millersburg *(G-9995)*

M21 Industries LLC............................... G 937 781-1377
　Dayton *(G-5859)*

Mac Lean J S Co.................................... G 614 878-5454
　Columbus *(G-5078)*

▲ Mag Resources LLC........................... F 330 294-0494
　Barberton *(G-818)*

Masonite Corporation............................ C 937 454-9207
　Vandalia *(G-13569)*

McCoy Group Inc................................... G 330 753-1041
　Barberton *(G-821)*

Menard Inc.. F 513 250-4566
　Cincinnati *(G-2863)*

Menard Inc.. D 419 998-4348
　Lima *(G-8429)*

Menard Inc.. C 513 583-1444
　Loveland *(G-8642)*

Midwest Commercial Mllwk Inc............. F 419 224-5001
　Lima *(G-8433)*

Midwest Wood Trim Inc......................... E 419 592-3389
　Napoleon *(G-10291)*

▼ Miller Manufacturing Inc.................... G 330 852-0689
　Sugarcreek *(G-12642)*

Millwood Wholesale Inc........................ F 330 359-6109
　Dundee *(G-6369)*

Millwork Elements LLC.......................... G 614 905-8163
　Columbus *(G-5103)*

Nagele Manufacturing Company............ E 216 433-1100
　Cleveland *(G-4057)*

▲ National Door and Trim Inc............... E 419 238-9345
　Van Wert *(G-13543)*

▲ Novo Manufacturing LLC................... E 740 269-2221
　Bowerston *(G-1401)*

Oak Pointe Legacy LLC......................... E 740 498-9820
　Newcomerstown *(G-10573)*

Ogonek Custom Hardwood Inc.............. G 833 718-2531
　Barberton *(G-827)*

Ohio Custom Door LLC.......................... E 330 695-6301
　Fredericksburg *(G-7067)*

Ohio Woodworking Co Inc..................... G 513 631-0870
　Cincinnati *(G-2927)*

Overhead Door Corporation................... G 330 828-2291
　Dalton *(G-5590)*

Overhead Door Corporation................... D 740 383-6376
　Marion *(G-8987)*

Overhead Door Corporation................... F 419 294-3874
　Upper Sandusky *(G-13452)*

P & T Millwork Inc................................. F 440 543-2151
　Chagrin Falls *(G-2175)*

▲ Pease Enterprises Inc........................ F 513 871-8907
　Cincinnati *(G-2951)*

Pease Industies Inc.............................. G 513 870-3600
　Fairfield *(G-6764)*

Pickens Window Service Inc................. G 513 931-4432
　Cincinnati *(G-2962)*

Ply-Trim Inc.. E 330 799-7876
　Youngstown *(G-14917)*

Precise Custom Millwork Inc................. G 614 539-7855
　Grove City *(G-7408)*

Precision Wood Products Inc................. F 937 787-3523
　Camden *(G-1768)*

Profac Inc... D 440 942-0205
　Mentor *(G-9594)*

▲ Profac Inc................................. C 440 942-0205
    Mentor *(G-9593)*

Quality Woodproducts LLC................... G 330 279-2217
    Fredericksburg *(G-7069)*

R C Moore Lumber Co........................ F 740 732-4950
    Caldwell *(G-1727)*

Ramsey Stairs & Wdwkg LLC................. G 614 694-2101
    Columbus *(G-5223)*

Rebsco Inc.................................. F 937 548-2246
    Greenville *(G-7351)*

Renewal By Andersen LLC.................... G 614 781-9600
    Columbus *(G-4649)*

Reserve Millwork LLC....................... E 216 531-6982
    Bedford *(G-1056)*

Richardson Woodworking..................... G 614 893-8850
    Blacklick *(G-1229)*

▲ Rinos Woodworking Shop Inc............ F 440 946-1718
    Willoughby *(G-14518)*

Riverside Cnstr Svcs Inc................... E 513 723-0900
    Cincinnati *(G-3048)*

Robertson Cabinets Inc..................... G 937 698-3755
    West Milton *(G-14185)*

Robura Inc................................. G 330 857-7404
    Orrville *(G-11004)*

Rockwood Products Ltd...................... E 330 893-2392
    Millersburg *(G-10007)*

Roettger Hardwood Inc...................... G 937 693-6811
    Kettlersville *(G-8125)*

Round Mate Systems......................... G 419 675-3334
    Kenton *(G-8114)*

Rsl LLC.................................... E 330 392-8900
    Warren *(G-13795)*

Rush Fixture & Millwork Co................. F 216 241-9100
    Cleveland *(G-4265)*

S Holley Lumber LLC........................ G 440 272-5315
    Windsor *(G-14603)*

S R Door Inc............................... D 740 927-3558
    Hebron *(G-7634)*

Salem Mill & Cabinet Co.................... G 330 337-9568
    Salem *(G-11810)*

Saw Dust Ltd............................... G 740 862-0612
    Baltimore *(G-787)*

Seemray LLC................................ E 440 536-8705
    Cleveland *(G-4285)*

▲ Seneca Millwork Inc.................... E 419 435-6671
    Fostoria *(G-7001)*

Sheridan Woodworks Inc..................... G 216 663-9333
    Cleveland *(G-4292)*

Solid Surface Concepts Inc................. E 513 948-8677
    Cincinnati *(G-3099)*

Stein Inc.................................. F 419 747-2611
    Mansfield *(G-8854)*

▲ Stephen M Trudick...................... E 440 834-1891
    Burton *(G-1704)*

Stratton Creek Wood Works LLC.............. F 330 876-0005
    Kinsman *(G-8143)*

Stull Woodworks Inc........................ E 937 698-8181
    Troy *(G-13259)*

Summit Millwork LLC........................ G 330 920-4000
    Cuyahoga Falls *(G-5575)*

Swiss Woodcraft Inc........................ G 330 925-1807
    Rittman *(G-11628)*

T & D Thompson Inc......................... F 740 332-8515
    Laurelville *(G-8238)*

Ted Bolle Millwork Inc..................... F 937 325-8779
    Springfield *(G-12385)*

Teledoor LLC............................... G 419 227-3000
    Lima *(G-8455)*

The F A Requarth Company................... E 937 224-1141
    Dayton *(G-6048)*

The Galehouse Companies Inc................ E 330 658-2023
    Doylestown *(G-6270)*

Todco...................................... F 740 223-2542
    Marion *(G-9002)*

Trimco..................................... G 614 679-3931
    Westerville *(G-14238)*

Trimtec Systems Ltd........................ F 614 820-0340
    Grove City *(G-7419)*

Tuscarora Wood Midwest LLC................. G 937 603-8882
    Covington *(G-5500)*

Versailles Building Supply................. G 937 526-3238
    Versailles *(G-13603)*

Volpe Millwork Inc......................... G 216 581-0200
    Cleveland *(G-4480)*

Wedge Hardwood Products.................... G 330 525-7775
    Alliance *(G-415)*

Wengerd Wood Inc........................... F 330 359-4300
    Dundee *(G-6372)*

Westlake Ryal Bldg Pdts USA In............. E 800 366-8472
    Columbus *(G-5365)*

Whitmer Woodworks Inc...................... G 614 873-1196
    Plain City *(G-11427)*

▲ Wittrock Wdwkg & Mfg Co Inc........... D 513 891-5800
    Blue Ash *(G-1351)*

Wood Creations............................. G 419 692-2624
    Delphos *(G-6200)*

Woodcraft Industries Inc................... E 440 632-9655
    Middlefield *(G-9836)*

Woodworks Design........................... G 440 693-4414
    Middlefield *(G-9837)*

▼ Yoder Lumber Co Inc.................... D 330 893-3121
    Millersburg *(G-10020)*

Yoder Window & Siding Ltd.................. F 330 695-6960
    Fredericksburg *(G-7072)*

Youngstown Shade & Alum LLC................ G 330 782-2373
    Youngstown *(G-14975)*

▲ Yutzy Woodworking Ltd................. E 330 359-6166
    Dundee *(G-6374)*

2434 Wood kitchen cabinets

1914 Mi Inc................................ E 330 308-8667
    New Philadelphia *(G-10428)*

4-B Wood Specialties Inc................... G 330 769-2188
    Seville *(G-11908)*

A & J Woodworking Inc...................... G 419 695-5655
    Delphos *(G-6183)*

A-Display Service Corp..................... F 614 469-1230
    Columbus *(G-4657)*

Agean Marble Manufacturing Inc............. G 513 874-1475
    West Chester *(G-14099)*

Ailes Millwork Inc......................... F 330 678-4300
    Kent *(G-8015)*

Al-Co Products Inc......................... G 419 399-3867
    Latty *(G-8236)*

Anthony Flottemesch & Son Inc.............. F 513 561-1212
    Cincinnati *(G-2371)*

Apex Cabinetry Inc......................... E 513 832-7905
    Cincinnati *(G-2373)*

Approved Plumbing Co....................... F 216 663-5063
    Cleveland *(G-3362)*

As America Inc............................. D 419 522-4211
    Mansfield *(G-8763)*

Bear Cabinetry LLC......................... G 216 481-9282
    Euclid *(G-6643)*

Bestwood Cabinetry LLC..................... G 937 661-9621
    Xenia *(G-14755)*

Bison Builders LLC......................... F 614 636-0365
    Columbus *(G-4756)*

▲ Bruewer Woodwork Mfg Co............... D 513 353-3505
    Cleves *(G-4532)*

Cabinet and Granite Depot LLC.............. F 513 874-2100
    West Chester *(G-13953)*

Cabinet Concepts Inc....................... G 440 232-4644
    Oakwood Village *(G-10903)*

Cabinet Shop............................... G 614 885-9676
    Columbus *(G-4639)*

Cabinet Specialties Inc.................... G 330 695-3463
    Fredericksburg *(G-7061)*

Cabinetworks Group Mich LLC................ E 440 247-3091
    Chagrin Falls *(G-2137)*

Cabinetworks Group Mich LLC................ C 440 632-2547
    Middlefield *(G-9783)*

Cabintwrks Group Mddlfield LLC............. C 440 437-8537
    Orwell *(G-11020)*

◆ Cabintwrks Group Mddlfield LLC....... A 888 562-7744
    Middlefield *(G-9784)*

Carter-Jones Lumber Company................ G 330 674-9060
    Millersburg *(G-9975)*

Cedee Cedar Inc............................ F 740 363-3148
    Delaware *(G-6136)*

Century Components LLC..................... G 330 852-3610
    Sugarcreek *(G-12636)*

▲ Clark Son Actn Liquidation Inc........ G 330 866-9330
    East Sparta *(G-6411)*

Climate Pros LLC........................... D 216 881-5200
    Cleveland *(G-3541)*

Climate Pros LLC........................... D 330 744-2732
    Youngstown *(G-14839)*

Colby Woodworking Inc...................... E 937 224-7676
    Dayton *(G-5705)*

Counter-Advice Inc......................... G 937 291-1600
    Franklin *(G-7014)*

Creative Cabinets Ltd...................... F 740 689-0603
    Lancaster *(G-8190)*

Creative Edge Cbnets Wdwkg LLC............. G 419 453-3416
    Ottoville *(G-11053)*

Crowes Cabinets Inc........................ E 330 729-9911
    Youngstown *(G-14842)*

Custom Woodworking Inc..................... G 419 456-3330
    Ottawa *(G-11031)*

D Lewis Inc................................ G 740 695-2615
    Saint Clairsville *(G-11690)*

Dgl Woodworking Inc........................ F 937 837-7091
    Dayton *(G-5747)*

Distinctive Surfaces LLC................... F 614 431-0898
    Columbus *(G-4885)*

Dover Cabinet Industries Inc............... F 330 343-9074
    Dover *(G-6237)*

E J Skok Industries........................ E 216 292-7533
    Bedford *(G-1030)*

East Oberlin Cabinets LLC.................. G 440 775-1166
    Oberlin *(G 10016)*

Fairfield Wood Works Ltd................... G 740 689-1953
    Lancaster *(G-8201)*

Fdi Cabinetry LLC.......................... G 513 353-4500
    Cleves *(G-4537)*

Formware Inc............................... F 614 231-9387
    Columbus *(G-4932)*

Franklin Cabinet Company Inc............... E 937 743-9606
    Franklin *(G-7022)*

Gillard Construction Inc................... F 740 376-9744
    Marietta *(G-8919)*

Gross & Sons Custom Millwork............... G 419 227-0214
    Lima *(G-8411)*

Hampshire Co............................... F 937 773-3493
    Piqua *(G-11348)*

Holmes Lumber & Bldg Ctr Inc............... E 330 479-8314
    Canton *(G-1912)*

Holmes Lumber & Bldg Ctr Inc............... C 330 674-9060
    Millersburg *(G-9989)*

J & K Cabinetry Inc........................ G 513 860-3461
    West Chester *(G-14017)*

J L Custom Woodworking LLC................. G 419 704-5181
    Sullivan *(G-12659)*

Jacob & Levis Ltd.......................... G 330 852-7600
    Sugarcreek *(G-12639)*

Johannings Inc.............................. G 330 875-1706
Louisville (G-8607)

JP Cabinets LLC............................ G 440 232-9780
Cleveland (G-3896)

◆ Kellogg Cabinets Inc.................. G 614 833-9596
Canal Winchester (G-1792)

Kinnemyers Cornerstone Cab Inc........ G 513 353-3030
Cleves (G-4542)

Kinsella Manufacturing Co Inc............ F 513 561-5285
Cincinnati (G-2796)

Kitchen Designs Plus Inc................. G 419 536-6605
Toledo (G-13019)

▲ Kitchens By Rutenschroer Inc......... G 513 251-8333
Cincinnati (G-2799)

Knapke Cabinets Inc...................... E 937 335-8383
Troy (G-13234)

Knapke Custom Cabinetry Ltd........... G 937 459-8866
Versailles (G-13599)

Kreager Co LLC........................... G 740 345-1605
Newark (G-10515)

Laminated Concepts Inc.................. F 216 475-4141
Maple Heights (G-8885)

Leiden Cabinet Co........................ G 330 425-8555
Twinsburg (G-13329)

Lily Ann Cabinets......................... F 419 360-2455
Toledo (G-13036)

Lima Millwork Inc......................... G 419 331-3303
Elida (G-6483)

Mac Lean J S Co.......................... G 614 878-5454
Columbus (G-5078)

Mammana Custom Woodworking Inc.... E 216 581-9059
Maple Heights (G-8886)

Marzano Inc.............................. G 216 459-2051
Cleveland (G-3995)

Masterbrand Inc.......................... A 877 622-4782
Beachwood (G-929)

Miami Vly Counters & Spc Inc........... G 937 865-0562
Miamisburg (G-9714)

Miller Cabinet Ltd......................... F 614 873-4221
Plain City (G-11415)

Mills Pride Premier Inc.................... G 740 941-1300
Waverly (G-13867)

Mock Woodworking Company LLC....... E 740 452-2701
Zanesville (G-15029)

Modern Designs Inc....................... G 330 644-1771
Green (G-7323)

Mro Built LLC............................. D 330 526-0555
North Canton (G-10654)

Mullet Cabinets Inc....................... D 330 674-9646
Millersburg (G-10002)

Nagele Manufacturing Company.......... E 216 433-1100
Cleveland (G-4057)

North Star Building Pdts LLC.............. G 216 431-1000
Cleveland (G-4090)

Northeast Cabinet Co LLC................ G 614 759-0800
Columbus (G-5130)

Ohio River Valley Cabinet................. G 740 975-8846
Newark (G-10526)

Online Mega Sellers Corp................. G 888 384-6468
Toledo (G-13078)

Profiles In Design Inc..................... F 513 751-2212
Cincinnati (G-3006)

Reserve Millwork LLC..................... E 216 531-6982
Bedford (G-1056)

Rheaco Builders Inc....................... G 330 425-3090
Twinsburg (G-13366)

Riceland Cabinet Inc...................... D 330 601-1071
Wooster (G-14676)

Riceland Cabinet Corporation............ G 330 601-1071
Wooster (G-14677)

River East Custom Cabinets Inc.......... G 419 244-3226
Toledo (G-13113)

Riverside Cnstr Svcs Inc.................. E 513 723-0900
Cincinnati (G-3048)

Roettger Hardwood Inc.................... G 937 693-6811
Kettlersville (G-8125)

Royal Cabinet Design Co Inc.............. F 216 267-5330
Cleveland (G-4258)

S & G Manufacturing Group LLC......... D 614 529-0100
Hilliard (G-7700)

Salem Mill & Cabinet Co.................. G 330 337-9568
Salem (G-11810)

Signature Cabinetry Inc................... F 614 252-2227
Columbus (G-5266)

Snows Wood Shop Inc.................... E 419 836-3805
Oregon (G-10968)

Specified Structures Inc.................. G 330 753-0693
Barberton (G-839)

▲ Supply One Corporation............... F 937 297-1111
Bellbrook (G-1093)

TDS Custom Cabinets LLC................ G 614 850-7590
Columbus (G-5313)

The Hattenbach Company................. D 216 881-5200
Cleveland (G-4384)

Thomas Cabinet Shop Inc................. F 937 847-8239
Dayton (G-6051)

▼ Tiffin Metal Products Co............... D 419 447-8414
Tiffin (G-12803)

Troyers Cabinet Shop Ltd................. F 937 464-7702
Belle Center (G-1097)

Trutech Cabinetry LLC.................... G 614 338-0680
Columbus (G-5334)

Woodcraft Industries Inc.................. E 440 632-9655
Middlefield (G-9836)

Wurms Woodworking Company........... E 419 492-2184
New Washington (G-10484)

X44 Corp................................. F 330 657-2335
Peninsula (G-11188)

2435 Hardwood veneer and plywood

▲ American Veneer Edgebanding Co..... G 740 928-2700
Heath (G-7592)

Automated Bldg Components Inc.......... E 419 257-2152
North Baltimore (G-10612)

Beaver Wood Products.................... G 740 226-6211
Beaver (G-960)

▲ Bruewer Woodwork Mfg Co........... D 513 353-3505
Cleves (G-4532)

▲ Dimension Hardwood Veneers Inc..... E 419 272-2245
Edon (G-6473)

◆ Erath Veneer Corp Virginia............ G 540 483-5223
Granville (G-7314)

▼ Exhibit Concepts Inc.................. D 937 890-7000
Vandalia (G-13557)

Fifth Avenue Lumber Co.................. E 614 833-6655
Canal Winchester (G-1790)

Fryburg Door Inc......................... D 330 674-5252
Millersburg (G-9981)

Haessly Lumber Sales Co................. D 740 373-6681
Marietta (G-8922)

Hartzell Industries Inc.................... F 937 773-6295
Piqua (G-11352)

Mac Lean J S Co.......................... G 614 878-5454
Columbus (G-5078)

▼ Miller Manufacturing Inc.............. G 330 852-0689
Sugarcreek (G-12642)

Mohler Lumber Company................. E 330 499-5461
North Canton (G-10652)

▼ Ohio Valley Veneer Inc................ E 740 493-2901
Piketon (G-11311)

S & G Manufacturing Group LLC......... D 614 529-0100
Hilliard (G-7700)

▲ Sims-Lohman Inc...................... E 513 651-3510
Cincinnati (G-3093)

Universal Veneer Mill Corp................ C 740 522-1147
Newark (G-10538)

◆ Universal Veneer Sales Corp........... C 740 522-1147
Newark (G-10539)

Wappoo Wood Products Inc.............. E 937 492-1166
Sidney (G-12060)

Yoder Lumber Co Inc..................... E 330 893-3131
Sugarcreek (G-12658)

2436 Softwood veneer and plywood

▲ American Veneer Edgebanding Co..... G 740 928-2700
Heath (G-7592)

Beaver Wood Products.................... G 740 226-6211
Beaver (G-960)

◆ Clopay Corporation.................... E 513 770-4800
Mason (G-9088)

S & G Manufacturing Group LLC......... D 614 529-0100
Hilliard (G-7700)

◆ Universal Production Corp............. F 740 522-1147
Newark (G-10537)

Wappoo Wood Products Inc.............. E 937 492-1166
Sidney (G-12060)

2439 Structural wood members, nec

Automated Bldg Components Inc.......... E 419 257-2152
North Baltimore (G-10612)

Buckeye Components LLC................. E 330 482-5163
Columbiana (G-4607)

Building Concepts Inc.................... F 419 298-2371
Edgerton (G-6464)

Carter-Jones Lumber Company........... G 330 674-9060
Millersburg (G-9975)

Columbus Roof Trusses Inc.............. F 740 763-3000
Newark (G-10498)

Columbus Roof Trusses Inc.............. E 614 272-6464
Columbus (G-4832)

Contract Bldg Components Ltd............ E 937 644-0739
Marysville (G-9017)

Dutchcraft Truss Component Inc.......... G 330 862-2220
Minerva (G-10037)

Fifth Avenue Lumber Co.................. E 614 833-6655
Canal Winchester (G-1790)

Holmes Lumber & Bldg Ctr Inc........... E 330 479-8314
Canton (G-1912)

Holmes Lumber & Bldg Ctr Inc........... C 330 674-9060
Millersburg (G-9989)

Khempco Bldg Sup Co Ltd Partnr......... D 740 549-0465
Delaware (G-6159)

▲ Laminate Technologies Inc............ D 800 231-2523
Tiffin (G-12786)

Ohio Valley Truss Company............... E 937 393-3995
Hillsboro (G-7722)

R & L Truss Inc.......................... F 419 587-3440
Grover Hill (G-7459)

Richland Laminated Columns LLC........ F 419 895-0036
Greenwich (G-7364)

Schilling Truss Inc....................... F 740 984-2396
Beverly (G-1208)

Socar of Ohio Inc........................ D 419 596-3100
Continental (G-5423)

Stark Truss Company Inc................. D 330 756-3050
Beach City (G-907)

Stark Truss Company Inc................. D 330 478-2100
Canton (G-2015)

Stark Truss Company Inc................. G 330 478-6063
Canton (G-2016)

Stark Truss Company Inc................. E 419 298-3777
Edgerton (G-6471)

Stark Truss Company Inc................. D 740 335-4156
Washington Court Hou (G-13823)

Stark Truss Company Inc................. F 330 478-2100
Canton (G-2017)

▲ Thomas Do-It Center Inc.................. E 740 446-2002
  Gallipolis (G-7209)

Waynedale Truss and Panel Co............ E 330 698-7373
  Apple Creek (G-480)

2441 Nailed wood boxes and shook

Aerocase Incorporated........................... F 440 617-9294
  Westlake (G-14284)

Aslan Worldwide....................................... F 513 671-0671
  West Chester (G-13943)

Buckeye Diamond Logistics Inc........... C 937 462-8361
  South Charleston (G-12213)

Built-Rite Box & Crate Inc.................... E 330 263-0936
  Wooster (G-14630)

▲ Caravan Packaging Inc....................... G 440 243-4100
  Cleveland (G-3469)

Cassady Woodworks Inc......................... F 937 256-7948
  Dayton (G-5605)

Cedar Craft Products Inc....................... G 614 759-1600
  Blacklick (G-1222)

Clark Rm Inc... F 419 425-9889
  Findlay (G-6853)

Damar Products Inc................................. F 937 492-9023
  Sidney (G-12010)

Forest City Companies Inc..................... E 216 586-5279
  Cleveland (G-3735)

Global Packaging & Exports Inc............ G 513 454-2020
  Hamilton (G-7496)

▲ H Gerstner & Sons Inc....................... E 937 228-1662
  Dayton (G-5806)

Hann Manufacturing Inc......................... E 740 962-3752
  Mcconnelsville (G-9362)

▲ J & L Wood Products Inc.................... E 937 667-4064
  Tipp City (G-12829)

▲ Kennedy Group Incorporated............ D 440 951-7660
  Willoughby (G-14477)

Lalac One LLC... E 216 432-4422
  Cleveland (G-3937)

Lima Pallet Company Inc....................... E 419 229-5736
  Lima (G-8425)

Ohio Box & Crate Inc............................. G 440 526-3133
  Burton (G-1703)

Quadco Rehabilitation Ctr Inc.............. C 419 682-1011
  Stryker (G-12626)

Schaefer Box & Pallet Co....................... E 513 738-2500
  Hamilton (G-7523)

Sterling Industries Inc........................... F 419 523-3788
  Ottawa (G-11047)

Thomas J Weaver Inc.............................. F 740 622-2040
  Coshocton (G-5474)

Traveling Recycle WD Pdts Inc............. G 419 968-2649
  Middle Point (G-9764)

2448 Wood pallets and skids

A & D Wood Products Inc....................... G 419 331-8859
  Elida (G-6481)

A W Taylor Lumber Incorporated........... G 440 577-1889
  Pierpont (G-11303)

AAA Plastics & Pallets Inc..................... G 330 844-2556
  Mogadore (G-10068)

Able Pallet Mfg & Repr.......................... G 614 444-2115
  Columbus (G-4666)

Aero Pallets Inc....................................... E 330 260-7107
  Carrollton (G-2079)

Anderson Pallet & Packg Inc................. G 937 962-2614
  Lewisburg (G-8358)

B J Pallett.. G 419 447-9665
  Tiffin (G-12776)

Belco Works Inc....................................... D 740 695-0500
  Saint Clairsville (G-11688)

Boscowood Ventures Inc........................ F 800 526-1816
  Lorain (G-8548)

BR Pallet Inc.. E 419 427-2200
  Alvada (G-420)

Brookhill Center Inds Inc....................... C 419 876-3932
  Ottawa (G-11030)

Buckeye Diamond Logistics Inc........... C 937 462-8361
  South Charleston (G-12213)

Built-Rite Box & Crate Inc.................... E 330 263-0936
  Wooster (G-14630)

Cabot Lumber Inc................................... G 740 545-7109
  West Lafayette (G-14169)

Chep (usa) Inc... F 614 497-9448
  Columbus (G-4807)

Cima Inc... E 513 382-8976
  Hamilton (G-7477)

Clark Rm Inc.. F 419 425-9889
  Findlay (G-6853)

Coblentz Brothers Inc............................ E 330 857-7211
  Apple Creek (G-465)

Cox Wood Product Inc............................ F 740 372-4735
  Otway (G-11059)

Crosscreek Pallet Co............................. G 440 632-1940
  Middlefield (G-9788)

Custom Palet Manufacturing................. G 440 693-4603
  Middlefield (G-9790)

Damar Products Inc................................. F 937 492-9023
  Sidney (G-12010)

Dedicated Industries Inc....................... D 440 238-5200
  Strongsville (G-12553)

DM Pallet Service Inc............................. G 614 491-0881
  Columbus (G-4888)

▲ Emergency Products & RES Inc......... G 330 673-5003
  Kent (G-8031)

Findlay Pallet Inc................................... G 419 423-0511
  Findlay (G-6865)

Frankes Wood Products LLC................. E 937 642-0706
  Marysville (G-9020)

Franks Sawmill Inc................................. F 419 682-3831
  Stryker (G-12623)

Gardner Lumber Company Inc............... F 740 254-4664
  Tippecanoe (G-12857)

Global Packaging & Exports Inc............ G 513 454-2020
  Hamilton (G-7496)

GM Pallet LLC... G 859 408-1781
  Cincinnati (G-2678)

Grant Street Pallet Inc........................... G 330 424-0355
  Lisbon (G-8468)

Gross Lumber Inc................................... G 330 683-2055
  Apple Creek (G-469)

Guernsey Industries.............................. C 740 439-4452
  Byesville (G-1713)

Hacker Wood Products Inc..................... G 513 737-4462
  Hamilton (G-7499)

Haessly Lumber Sales Co....................... D 740 373-6681
  Marietta (G-8922)

Halliday Holdings Inc............................. G 740 335-1430
  Washington Court Hou (G-13821)

Hann Manufacturing Inc......................... E 740 962-3752
  Mcconnelsville (G-9362)

Hershberger Manufacturing................... E 440 272-5555
  Windsor (G-14601)

Hillside Pallet Ltd.................................. G 440 272-5425
  Windsor (G-14602)

Hope Timber & Marketing Group........... F 740 344-1788
  Newark (G-10507)

▼ Hope Timber Pallet Recycl LLC......... E 740 344-1788
  Newark (G-10509)

▲ Inca Presswood-Pallets Ltd.............. E 330 343-3361
  Dover (G-6248)

Inland Hardwood Corporation............... F 740 373-7187
  Marietta (G-8924)

Iron City Wood Products Inc................. E 330 755-2772
  Youngstown (G-14878)

J & K Pallet Inc....................................... G 937 526-5117
  Versailles (G-13597)

▲ J & L Wood Products Inc.................... E 937 667-4064
  Tipp City (G-12829)

J I T Pallets Inc....................................... G 330 424-0355
  Lisbon (G-8472)

Kamps Inc.. C 937 526-9333
  Versailles (G-13598)

Kamps Pallets... G 616 818-4323
  Columbus (G-5044)

Kmak Group LLC..................................... F 937 308-1023
  London (G-8538)

Knotty Pallet LLC................................... G 330 451-9838
  Canton (G-1928)

Lima Pallet Company Inc....................... E 419 229-5736
  Lima (G-8425)

◆ Litco International Inc......................... D 330 539-5433
  Vienna (G-13612)

▲ Litco Manufacturing LLC................... F 330 539-5433
  Warren (G-13777)

Lynk Packaging Inc................................. E 330 562-8080
  Aurora (G-677)

Makers Supply LLC................................. G 937 203-8245
  Piqua (G-11364)

Mid Ohio Wood Products Inc................. G 740 323-0427
  Newark (G-10520)

Mid Ohio Wood Recycling Inc............... G 419 673-8470
  Kenton (G-8107)

Middlefield Pallet Inc............................ E 440 632-0553
  Middlefield (G-9810)

Midtown Pallet & Recycling Inc............ G 419 241-1311
  Toledo (G-13054)

Milltree Lumber Holdings...................... G 740 226-2090
  Waverly (G-13868)

Millwood Inc.. C 330 857-3075
  Apple Creek (G-471)

Millwood Inc.. E 216 881-1414
  Cleveland (G-4042)

Millwood Inc.. D 330 359-5220
  Dundee (G-6368)

Millwood Inc.. D 440 914-0540
  Solon (G-12152)

Millwood Inc.. D 330 609-0220
  Vienna (G-13614)

Millwood Inc.. E 740 226-2090
  Waverly (G-13869)

Millwood Incorporated........................... F 330 704-6707
  Apple Creek (G-473)

Mjc Enterprise Inc.................................. G 330 669-3744
  Sterling (G-12398)

Montgomerys Pallet Service Inc............ G 330 297-6677
  Ravenna (G-11533)

◆ Morgan Wood Products Inc................. F 614 336-4000
  Powell (G-11492)

Mpi Logistics and Service Inc............... E 330 832-5309
  Massillon (G-9225)

Mt Eaton Pallet Ltd................................. E 330 893-2986
  Millersburg (G-10001)

National Pallet & Mulch LLC................. F 937 237-1643
  Dayton (G-5902)

Nelson Company..................................... G 614 444-1164
  Columbus (G-5123)

Nwp Manufacturing Inc.......................... F 419 894-6871
  Waldo (G-13690)

◆ Oak Chips Inc...................................... E 740 947-4159
  Waverly (G-13871)

Ohio Box & Crate Inc............................. G 440 526-3133
  Burton (G-1703)

Ohio State Pallet Corp........................... G 614 332-3961
  Homer (G-7804)

Olympic Forest Products Co................... E 216 421-2775
  Cleveland (G-4119)

Pallet Distributors Inc............................. E 330 852-3531
Sugarcreek *(G-12644)*

Pallet Specs Plus LLC............................. F 513 351-3200
Norwood *(G-10870)*

Pallet World Inc..................................... E 419 874-9333
Perrysburg *(G-11257)*

Pettits Pallets Inc.................................. G 614 351-4920
Galloway *(G-7210)*

Premier Pallet and Recycl Inc................. G 330 767-2221
Navarre *(G-10311)*

PRU Industries Inc................................. F 937 746-8702
Franklin *(G-7042)*

Quadco Rehabilitation Ctr Inc................. C 419 682-1011
Stryker *(G-12626)*

Queen City Pallets Inc........................... E 513 821-6700
Cincinnati *(G-3023)*

R W Long Lumber & Box Co Inc.............. F 513 932-5124
Lebanon *(G-8282)*

Raber Lumber Co.................................... G 330 893-2797
Charm *(G-2227)*

Rettig Family Pallets Inc........................ F 419 439-0776
Napoleon *(G-10297)*

Richland Newhope Inds Inc.................... C 419 774-4400
Mansfield *(G-8848)*

Riverview Indus WD Pdts Inc.................. G 330 669-8509
Smithville *(G-12068)*

Riverview Transport LLC......................... E 330 669-8509
Smithville *(G-12069)*

Russell L Garber.................................... G 937 548-6224
Greenville *(G-7352)*

S & W Express Inc................................. G 330 683-2747
Orrville *(G-11005)*

Satco Inc.. D 513 707-6150
Loveland *(G-8651)*

Schaefer Box & Pallet Co....................... E 513 738-2500
Hamilton *(G-7523)*

Schnider Pallet LLC............................... G 440 632-5346
Middlefield *(G-9826)*

Schrock John... G 937 544-8457
Peebles *(G-11172)*

Schutz Container Systems Inc................ D 419 872-2477
Perrysburg *(G-11261)*

▲ Sealco Inc... G 740 922-4122
Uhrichsville *(G-13405)*

Silvesco Inc... F 740 373-6661
Marietta *(G-8945)*

Southern Ohio Lumber LLC.................... G 614 436-4472
Peebles *(G-11173)*

Southwood Pallet LLC............................ D 330 682-3747
Orrville *(G-11014)*

Sterling Industries Inc.......................... F 419 523-3788
Ottawa *(G-11047)*

Stumptown Lbr Pallet Mills Ltd............... G 740 757-2275
Somerton *(G-12212)*

Swp Legacy Ltd.................................... D 330 340-9663
Sugarcreek *(G-12653)*

T & D Thompson Inc............................. F 740 332-8515
Laurelville *(G-8238)*

Terry Lumber and Supply Co.................. F 330 659-6800
Peninsula *(G-11184)*

Thomas J Weaver Inc............................ F 740 622-2040
Coshocton *(G-5474)*

Tolson Pallet Mfg Inc............................ F 937 787-3511
Gratis *(G-7321)*

Traveling Recycle WD Pdts Inc............... G 419 968-2649
Middle Point *(G-9764)*

Tri State Pallet Inc................................ E 937 746-8702
Franklin *(G-7053)*

Troymill Lumber Company....................... G 440 632-6353
Independence *(G-7923)*

Troymill Manufacturing Inc.................... F 440 632-5580
Middlefield *(G-9832)*

Tusco Hardwoods LLC............................ G 330 852-4281
Sugarcreek *(G-12655)*

Universal Pallets Inc.............................. E 614 444-1095
Columbus *(G-5339)*

Valley View Pallets LLC.......................... G 740 599-0010
Danville *(G-5600)*

Wellman Container Corporation.............. E 513 860-3040
Cincinnati *(G-3219)*

Wjf Enterprises LLC............................... G 513 871-7320
Cincinnati *(G-3228)*

Woodford Logistics................................ G 513 417-8453
South Charleston *(G-12214)*

Yoder Lumber Co Inc.............................. D 330 674-1435
Millersburg *(G-10021)*

▼ Yoder Lumber Co Inc......................... D 330 893-3121
Millersburg *(G-10020)*

Zanesville Pallet Co Inc......................... F 740 454-3700
Zanesville *(G-15058)*

2449 Wood containers, nec

Brimar Packaging Inc............................ E 440 934-3080
Avon *(G-717)*

Brown-Forman Corporation..................... G 740 384-3027
Wellston *(G-13905)*

Cassis Packaging Co.............................. F 937 223-8868
Dayton *(G-5696)*

▲ Cima Inc.. G 513 382-8976
Hamilton *(G-7476)*

Cima Inc.. E 513 382-8976
Hamilton *(G-7477)*

Clark Rm Inc... F 419 425-9889
Findlay *(G-6853)*

Custom Built Crates Inc......................... E
Milford *(G-9932)*

Dedicated Industries Inc........................ D 440 238-5200
Strongsville *(G-12553)*

Denoon Lumber Company LLC................ D 740 768-2220
Bergholz *(G-1195)*

Frankes Wood Products LLC................... E 937 642-0706
Marysville *(G-9020)*

Greif Inc.. E 740 657-6500
Delaware *(G-6150)*

◆ Greif Inc... E 740 549-6000
Delaware *(G-6149)*

Haessly Lumber Sales Co....................... D 740 373-6681
Marietta *(G-8922)*

▲ J & L Wood Products Inc................... E 937 667-4064
Tipp City *(G-12829)*

Overseas Packing LLC............................ G 440 232-2917
Bedford *(G-1053)*

Schaefer Box & Pallet Co....................... E 513 738-2500
Hamilton *(G-7523)*

Silvesco Inc... F 740 373-6661
Marietta *(G-8945)*

T & D Thompson Inc............................. F 740 332-8515
Laurelville *(G-8238)*

Terry Lumber and Supply Co.................. F 330 659-6800
Peninsula *(G-11184)*

Traveling Recycle WD Pdts Inc............... G 419 968-2649
Middle Point *(G-9764)*

Wellman Container Corporation.............. E 513 860-3040
Cincinnati *(G-3219)*

2451 Mobile homes

Clayton Homes...................................... F 937 592-3039
Bellefontaine *(G-1101)*

Manufactured Housing Entps Inc............ F 419 636-4511
Bryan *(G-1650)*

Mobile Conversions Inc.......................... F 513 797-1991
Amelia *(G-434)*

Muster Rdu Inc..................................... G 614 537-5440
Lancaster *(G-8212)*

Palm Harbor Homes Inc......................... G 937 725-9465
New Vienna *(G-10475)*

Skyline Corporation............................... C 330 852-2483
Sugarcreek *(G-12650)*

2452 Prefabricated wood buildings

Al Yoder Construction Co........................ G 330 359-5726
Millersburg *(G-9967)*

Beachy Barns Ltd.................................. F 614 873-4193
Plain City *(G-11397)*

Carter-Jones Lumber Company................ E 440 834-8164
Middlefield *(G-9785)*

Consoldted Anlytcal Systems In.............. F 513 542-1200
Cincinnati *(G-2510)*

Cooper Enterprises Inc........................... D 419 347-5232
Shelby *(G-11968)*

Everything In America............................ G 347 871-6872
Cleveland *(G-3695)*

Fifth Avenue Lumber Co........................ E 614 833-6655
Canal Winchester *(G-1790)*

Gillard Construction Inc......................... F 740 376-9744
Marietta *(G-8919)*

Hochstetler Milling LLC.......................... E 419 368-0004
Loudonville *(G-8591)*

J Aaron Weaver..................................... G 440 474-9185
Rome *(G-11644)*

Millers Storage Barns LLC...................... G 330 893-3293
Millersburg *(G-9999)*

Morton Buildings Inc............................. E 419 675-2311
Kenton *(G-8110)*

Nef Ltd.. G 419 445-6696
Archbold *(G-505)*

Patio Enclosures................................... F 513 733-4646
Cincinnati *(G-2944)*

Premier Construction Company............... G 513 874-2611
West Chester *(G-14053)*

Rona Enterprises Inc.............................. G 740 927-9971
Pataskala *(G-11148)*

Skyline Corporation............................... C 330 852-2483
Sugarcreek *(G-12650)*

Twin Oaks Barns LLC............................ F 330 893-3126
Dundee *(G-6371)*

Unibilt Industries Inc............................ E 937 890-7570
Vandalia *(G-13580)*

Vinyl Design Corporation........................ E 419 283-4009
Holland *(G-7790)*

Weaver Barns Ltd.................................. F 330 852-2103
Sugarcreek *(G-12656)*

2491 Wood preserving

Clark Rm Inc... F 419 425-9889
Findlay *(G-6853)*

Couch Business Development Inc............ G 937 253-1099
Dayton *(G-5711)*

Flagship Trading Corporation.................. E
Cleveland *(G-3722)*

ISK Americas Incorporated..................... F 440 357-4600
Concord Township *(G-5392)*

Joseph Sabatino................................... G 330 332-5879
Salem *(G-11791)*

Luxus Products LLC............................... G 937 444-6500
Mount Orab *(G-10218)*

The F A Requarth Company.................... E 937 224-1141
Dayton *(G-6048)*

Urbn Timber LLC................................... G 614 981-3043
Columbus *(G-5341)*

2493 Reconstituted wood products

▲ 1914 Mi Inc..................................... D 800 426-4244
New Philadelphia *(G-10429)*

Bmca Insulation Products Inc................. F 330 335-2501
Wadsworth *(G-13629)*

Frankes Wood Products LLC.............. E 937 642-0706
  Marysville (G-9020)

GMI Companies Inc............................ F 937 981-0244
  Greenfield (G-7327)

GMI Companies Inc............................ F 513 932-3445
  Lebanon (G-8263)

◆ GMI Companies Inc..........................C 513 932-3445
  Lebanon (G-8262)

◆ Michael Kaufman Companies Inc.......F 330 673-4881
  Kent (G-8053)

▼ Miller Manufacturing Inc.................. G 330 852-0689
  Sugarcreek (G-12642)

Rsp Industries Inc............................. G 440 823-4502
  Chagrin Falls (G-2150)

Solas Ltd.. E 650 501-0889
  Avon (G-739)

◆ Tectum Inc.....................................C 740 345-9691
  Newark (G-10535)

Tri-State Supply Co Inc..................... F 614 272-6767
  Columbus (G-5331)

2499 Wood products, nec

Acme Fence LLC................................ F 330 784-0456
  Akron (G-15)

Adroit Thinking Inc............................ F 419 542-9363
  Hicksville (G-7645)

Alfrebro LLC...................................... F 513 539-7373
  Monroe (G-10095)

American Wood Fibers Inc................. E 740 420-3233
  Circleville (G-3247)

Atkins Custom Framing Ltd............... G 740 816-1501
  Delaware (G-6132)

◆ Baker McMillen Co.........................D 330 923-8300
  Stow (G-12421)

Bc Investment Corporation............... C 330 262-3070
  Wooster (G-14625)

◆ Black Squirrel Holdings Inc.............E 513 577-7107
  Cincinnati (G-2412)

Blang Acquisition LLC........................ G 937 223-2155
  Dayton (G-5679)

Bonfoey Co....................................... F 216 621-0178
  Cleveland (G-3427)

Brown Wood Products Company.......... G 330 339-8000
  New Philadelphia (G-10433)

Bushworks Incorporated.................... G 937 767-1713
  Yellow Springs (G-14787)

Canfield Manufacturing Co Inc.......... G 330 533-3333
  North Jackson (G-10684)

Cass Frames Inc................................ G 419 468-2863
  Galion (G-7181)

◆ Cincinnati Dowel & WD Pdts Co........E 937 444-2502
  Mount Orab (G-10215)

▲ CM Paula Company......................... E 513 759-7473
  Mason (G-9090)

▲ Columbus Washboard Compan........ G 740 380-3828
  Logan (G-8512)

▲ Creative Plastic Concepts LLC......... F 419 927-9588
  Sycamore (G-12699)

Ely Road Reel Company Ltd............... E 330 683-1818
  Apple Creek (G-468)

Fenwick Gallery of Fine Arts............. E 419 475-1651
  Toledo (G-12962)

Frame Warehouse............................. G 614 861-4582
  Reynoldsburg (G-11570)

Garick LLC.. E 216 581-0100
  Cleveland (G-3755)

◆ Gayston Corporation.......................C 937 743-6050
  Miamisburg (G-9693)

▲ Grk Manufacturing Co..................... E 513 863-3131
  Hamilton (G-7497)

Growers Choice Ltd........................... G 330 262-8754
  Shreve (G-11981)

H Hafner & Sons Inc.......................... E 513 321-1895
  Cincinnati (G-2698)

Hardwood Store Inc.......................... G 937 864-2899
  Enon (G-6631)

Hauser Services Llc.......................... E 440 632-5126
  Middlefield (G-9798)

Hit Trophy Inc................................... G 419 445-5356
  Archbold (G-498)

Hollywood Dance Jams...................... G 419 234-0746
  Van Wert (G-13537)

▲ Holmes Wheel Shop Inc.................. E 330 279-2891
  Holmesville (G-7800)

Hope Timber & Marketing Group....... F 740 344-1788
  Newark (G-10507)

Hope Timber Mulch LLC.................... G 740 344-1788
  Newark (G-10508)

House of 10000 Picture Frames......... G 937 254-5541
  Dayton (G-5813)

Insta Plak Inc................................... G 419 537-1555
  Toledo (G-13006)

Intrism Inc.. G 614 787-4631
  Worthington (G-14716)

Irvine Wood Recovery Inc.................. E 513 831-0060
  Miamiville (G-9762)

J & D Wood Ltd.................................. G 937 778-9663
  Piqua (G-11359)

J R Custom Unlimited Inc.................. F 513 894-9800
  Hamilton (G-7507)

Jewett Supply.................................. G 419 738-9882
  Wapakoneta (G-13717)

Juno Enterprises LLC........................ G 419 448-9350
  New Riegel (G-10470)

Kalinich Fence Company Inc.............. F 440 238-6127
  Strongsville (G-12569)

Katch Kitchen LLC............................ E 513 537-8056
  Cincinnati (G-2785)

Lazars Art Gllery Crtive Frmng.......... G 330 477-8351
  Canton (G-1931)

▼ Miller Manufacturing Inc................ G 330 852-0689
  Sugarcreek (G-12642)

Mt Perry Foods Inc............................ D 740 743-3890
  Mount Perry (G-10225)

▲ Mulch Manufacturing Inc................ E 614 864-4004
  Reynoldsburg (G-11575)

Newbury Woodworks.......................... G 440 564-5273
  Newbury (G-10558)

Ohio Mulch Supply Inc...................... G 740 548-6242
  Lewis Center (G-8347)

▲ P & R Specialty Inc......................... E 937 773-0263
  Piqua (G-11370)

P & T Millwork Inc............................. F 440 543-2151
  Chagrin Falls (G-2175)

▲ P Graham Dunn Inc......................... B 330 828-2105
  Dalton (G-5798)

Peters Family Enterprises Inc............ G 419 339-0555
  Elida (G-6485)

Puttmann Industries Inc................... F 513 202-9444
  Harrison (G-7563)

Roe Transportation Entps Inc............ G 937 497-7161
  Sidney (G-12045)

Ryanworks Inc................................... G 937 438-1282
  Dayton (G-5990)

◆ Scotts Company LLC.......................C 937 644-0011
  Marysville (G-9045)

▲ Sealco Inc..................................... G 740 922-4122
  Uhrichsville (G-13405)

Signature Sign Co Inc....................... G 216 426-1234
  Cleveland (G-4301)

Singleton Reels Inc........................... E 330 274-2961
  Rootstown (G-11652)

Solas Ltd.. E 650 501-0889
  Avon (G-739)

▲ Solid Dimensions Inc...................... G 419 663-1134
  Norwalk (G-10862)

Sonoco Products Company................ E 614 759-8470
  Columbus (G-5276)

◆ Walnut Creek Planing Ltd...............D 330 893-3244
  Millersburg (G-10018)

Wurms Woodworking Company........... E 419 492-2184
  New Washington (G-10484)

▼ Yoder Lumber Co Inc...................... D 330 893-3121
  Millersburg (G-10020)

Youngstown Fence Incorporated........ G 330 788-8110
  Youngstown (G-14969)

Zaenkert Srvying Essntials Inc.......... G 513 738-2917
  Okeana (G-10931)

25 FURNITURE AND FIXTURES

2511 Wood household furniture

Andal Woodworking........................... F 330 897-8059
  Baltic (G-775)

Anthony Flottemesch & Son Inc.......... F 513 561-1212
  Cincinnati (G-2371)

◆ Archbold Furniture Co.................... E 567 444-4666
  Archbold (G-488)

Artistic Finishes Inc.......................... G 440 951-7850
  Willoughby (G-14427)

Basic Cases Inc................................ G 216 662-3900
  Cleveland (G-3409)

◆ Cabintwrks Group Mddlfield LLC........A 888 562-7744
  Middlefield (G-9784)

▼ Canal Dover Furniture LLC.............. D 330 359-5375
  Millersburg (G-9974)

Carlisle Oak..................................... G 330 852-8734
  Sugarcreek (G-12634)

Chris Haughey.................................. G 937 652-3338
  Urbana (G-13458)

Criswell Furniture LLC....................... F 330 695-2082
  Fredericksburg (G-7062)

Custom Surfaces Inc......................... G 440 439-2310
  Bedford (G-1024)

Diversified Products & Svcs............... F 740 393-6202
  Mount Vernon (G-10242)

Dje Management Consulting LLC......... G 330 760-2990
  Medina (G-9397)

Dorel Home Furnishings Inc.............. D 419 447-7448
  Tiffin (G-12782)

Dutch Legacy Company LLC.............. G 330 359-0270
  Apple Crook (C-166)

East Oberlin Cabinets LLC................. G 440 775-1166
  Oberlin (G-10916)

◆ Foundations Worldwide Inc.............E 330 722-5033
  Medina (G-9405)

▲ Furniture By Otmar Inc................... F 937 435-2039
  Dayton (G-5788)

Gasser Chair Co Inc.......................... D 330 759-2234
  Youngstown (G-14862)

Grabo Interiors Inc............................ G 216 391-6677
  Cleveland (G-3780)

◆ Greenway Home Products Inc...........F
  Perrysburg (G-11227)

▲ Grk Manufacturing Co..................... E 513 863-3131
  Hamilton (G-7497)

Guernsey Industries.......................... C 740 439-4452
  Byesville (G-1713)

Hardwood Lumber Company Inc.......... F 440 834-1891
  Middlefield (G-9797)

◆ Hen House Inc...............................G 419 663-3377
  Norwalk (G-10846)

Holmes Panel LLC............................. G 330 897-5040
  Baltic (G-779)

Installed Building Pdts LLC................ B 614 308-9900
  Columbus (G-5009)

James L Deckebach LLC...................... G 513 321-3733
Cincinnati *(G-2761)*

Jeffco Sheltered Workshop.................. G 740 264-4608
Steubenville *(G-12404)*

▲ Kitchens By Rutenschroer Inc........... G 513 251-8333
Cincinnati *(G-2799)*

Lauber Manufacturing Co..................... G 419 446-2450
Archbold *(G-499)*

Lima Millwork Inc............................... G 419 331-3303
Elida *(G-6483)*

Mamabees HM Gds Lifestyle LLC....... G 419 277-2914
Fostoria *(G-6987)*

Michaels Pre-Cast Con Pdts Inc............ F 513 683-1292
Loveland *(G-8643)*

Mielke Furniture Repair Inc................. G 419 625-4572
Sandusky *(G-11860)*

Miller Cabinet Ltd............................... F 614 873-4221
Plain City *(G-11415)*

Millwood Wholesale Inc...................... F 330 359-6109
Dundee *(G-6369)*

▲ Morris Furniture Co Inc..................... C 937 874-7100
Fairborn *(G-6697)*

N Wasserstrom & Sons Inc.................. F 614 737-5410
Columbus *(G-5119)*

Nagele Manufacturing Company............ E 216 433-1100
Cleveland *(G-4057)*

North Amercn Kit Solutions Inc........... F 800 854-3267
Elyria *(G-6570)*

Penwood Mfg....................................... G 330 359-5600
Fresno *(G-7148)*

◆ Progressive Furniture Inc.................. E 419 446-4500
Archbold *(G-508)*

◆ R A Hamed International Inc.............. G 330 247-0190
Twinsburg *(G-13363)*

Rnr Enterprises LLC............................ F 330 852-3022
Sugarcreek *(G-12647)*

Specialty Svcs Cabinetry Inc............... G 614 421-1599
Columbus *(G-5281)*

Stark Truss Company Inc..................... D 330 478-2100
Canton *(G-2015)*

Stark Truss Company Inc..................... E 419 298-3777
Edgerton *(G-6471)*

Tappan Chairs LLC.............................. G 800 840-9121
Blue Ash *(G-1340)*

Textiles Inc... G 614 529-8642
Hilliard *(G-7706)*

▲ Textiles Inc..................................... F 740 852-0782
London *(G-8542)*

Vocational Services Inc....................... F 216 431-8085
Cleveland *(G-4478)*

Waller Brothers Stone Company........... F 740 858-1948
Mc Dermott *(G-9356)*

Weaver Woodcraft L L C...................... G 330 695-2150
Apple Creek *(G-481)*

Western & Southern Lf Insur Co........... A 513 629-1800
Cincinnati *(G-3221)*

▼ Wine Cellar Innovations LLC............ C 513 321-3733
Cincinnati *(G-3227)*

Woodworking Shop LLC....................... F 513 330-9663
Miamisburg *(G-9753)*

2512 Upholstered household furniture

Buckeye Seating LLC........................... F 330 893-7700
Millersburg *(G-9972)*

Custom Craft Collection Inc................. F 440 998-3000
Ashtabula *(G-589)*

▲ Fortner Upholstering Inc.................. F 614 475-8282
Columbus *(G-4936)*

Franklin Cabinet Company Inc............. E 937 743-9606
Franklin *(G-7022)*

▲ Grk Manufacturing Co...................... E 513 863-3131
Hamilton *(G-7497)*

◆ H Goodman Inc................................ D 216 341-0200
Newburgh Heights *(G-10542)*

Hallmark Industries Inc....................... E 937 864-7378
Springfield *(G-12316)*

◆ Morris Furniture Co Inc..................... C 937 874-7100
Fairborn *(G-6697)*

Njm Furniture Outlet Inc...................... F 330 893-3514
Millersburg *(G-10004)*

Robert Mayo Industries........................ G 330 426-2587
East Palestine *(G-6406)*

◆ Sauder Woodworking Co................... A 419 446-2711
Archbold *(G-511)*

▲ Weavers Furniture Ltd...................... F 330 852-2701
Sugarcreek *(G-12657)*

2514 Metal household furniture

◆ Albion Industries Inc........................ E 440 238-1955
Strongsville *(G-12534)*

▲ Angels Landing Inc.......................... G 513 687-3681
Moraine *(G-10147)*

C-Link Enterprises LLC........................ F 937 222-2829
Dayton *(G-5692)*

Installed Building Pdts LLC................... B 614 308-9900
Columbus *(G-5009)*

Invacare Corporation........................... G 800 333-6900
Elyria *(G-6551)*

◆ Invacare Corporation....................... A 440 329-6000
Elyria *(G-6549)*

▲ Invacare Holdings Corporation........... B 440 329-6000
Elyria *(G-6554)*

◆ Medallion Lighting Corporation.......... E 440 255-8383
Mentor *(G-9561)*

Metal Fabricating Corporation.............. D 216 631-8121
Cleveland *(G-4023)*

◆ Rize Home LLC................................. D 800 333-8333
Glenwillow *(G-7288)*

▲ Sunnest Service LLC........................ E 740 283-2815
Steubenville *(G-12412)*

2515 Mattresses and bedsprings

Ahmf Inc... E 614 921-1223
Columbus *(G-4681)*

▲ Banner Mattress Co Inc.................... D 419 324-7181
Toledo *(G-12892)*

▲ Casco Mfg Solutions Inc.................. D 513 681-0003
Cincinnati *(G-2441)*

▲ Coconis Furniture Inc....................... E 740 452-1231
South Zanesville *(G-12232)*

▲ H Goodman Inc................................ D 216 341-0200
Newburgh Heights *(G-10542)*

Homecare Mattress Inc........................ F 937 746-2556
Franklin *(G-7027)*

HSP Bedding Solutions LLC................. E 440 437-4425
Orwell *(G-11021)*

Protective Industrial Polymers.............. F 440 327-0015
North Ridgeville *(G-10743)*

▲ Quilting Inc..................................... D 614 504-5971
Plain City *(G-11417)*

Sealy Mattress Mfg Co LLC................. E 800 697-3259
Medina *(G-9445)*

Select Mattress Co Inc........................ F 419 244-3645
Sylvania *(G-12722)*

◆ Solstice Sleep Products Inc.............. E 614 279-8850
Columbus *(G-5275)*

Tru Comfort Mattress.......................... G 614 595-8600
Dublin *(G-6357)*

V-I-S-c-e-r-o-t-o-n-i-c Inc.................... D 330 690-3355
Akron *(G-352)*

Walter F Stephens Jr Inc..................... E 937 746-0521
Franklin *(G-7055)*

2517 Wood television and radio cabinets

Innerwood & Company......................... F 513 677-2229
Loveland *(G-8631)*

Kraftmaid Trucking Inc........................ D 440 632-2531
Middlefield *(G-9805)*

◆ Progressive Furniture Inc.................. E 419 446-4500
Archbold *(G-508)*

2519 Household furniture, nec

Bulk Carrier Trnsp Eqp Co.................... G 330 339-3333
New Philadelphia *(G-10434)*

Evenflo Company Inc........................... D 937 773-3971
Troy *(G-13213)*

Hershy Way Ltd................................... G 330 893-2809
Millersburg *(G-9984)*

John Purdum.. G 513 897-9686
Waynesville *(G-13879)*

▲ Kitchens By Rutenschroer Inc........... G 513 251-8333
Cincinnati *(G-2799)*

Mar-Bal Pultrusion Inc........................ F 440 953-0456
Willoughby *(G-14485)*

Office Magic Inc.................................. F 510 782-6100
Medina *(G-9430)*

◆ Owens Corning................................. A 419 248-8000
Toledo *(G-13084)*

Sailors Tailor Inc................................ F 937 862-7781
Spring Valley *(G-12243)*

Sauder Woodworking Co....................... F 419 446-2711
Archbold *(G-510)*

◆ The Little Tikes Company.................. A 330 650-3000
Hudson *(G-7860)*

2521 Wood office furniture

August Incorporated............................ E 937 434-2520
Dayton *(G-5667)*

Basic Cases Inc.................................. G 216 662-3900
Cleveland *(G-3409)*

Buckeye Seating LLC........................... F 330 893-7700
Millersburg *(G-9972)*

▲ Buzz Seating Inc............................. G 877 263-5737
West Chester *(G-14109)*

Chagrin Valley Custom Furn LLC.......... G 440 591-5511
Warrensville Heights *(G-13816)*

Crow Works LLC.................................. E 888 811-2769
Killbuck *(G-8132)*

Custom Millcraft Corp......................... E 513 874-7080
West Chester *(G-13980)*

▼ Dvuv LLC.. E 216 741-5511
Cleveland *(G-3641)*

East Woodworking Company................. G 216 791-5950
Cleveland *(G-3649)*

Frontier Signs & Displays Inc.............. G 513 367-0813
Harrison *(G-7552)*

Gasser Chair Co Inc............................ D 330 759-2234
Youngstown *(G-14862)*

▲ Gasser Chair Co Inc........................ E 330 534-2234
Youngstown *(G-14861)*

Geograph Industries Inc....................... E 513 202-9200
Harrison *(G-7553)*

GMI Companies Inc............................. F 937 981-0244
Greenfield *(G-7327)*

GMI Companies Inc............................. E 513 932-3445
Lebanon *(G-8263)*

◆ GMI Companies Inc.......................... C 513 932-3445
Lebanon *(G-8262)*

Hardwood Lumber Company Inc............ F 440 834-1891
Middlefield *(G-9797)*

▲ Hoge Lumber Company...................... E 419 753-2263
New Knoxville *(G-10398)*

Innerwood & Company......................... F 513 677-2229
Loveland *(G-8631)*

Innovative Woodworking Inc................. G 513 531-1940
Cincinnati *(G-2746)*

Interior Products Co Inc.............................. G 216 641-1919
Cleveland *(G-3864)*

Lima Millwork Inc.................................... G 419 331-3303
Elida *(G-6483)*

Mel Heitkamp Builders Ltd....................... G 419 375-0405
Fort Recovery *(G-6969)*

Miller Cabinet Ltd.................................... F 614 873-4221
Plain City *(G-11415)*

Sauder Manufacturing Co......................... D 419 682-3061
Stryker *(G-12627)*

▲ Senator International Inc..................... E 419 887-5806
Maumee *(G-9316)*

Specialty Svcs Cabinetry Inc.................. G 614 421-1599
Columbus *(G-5281)*

Symatic Inc... G 330 225-1510
Medina *(G-9452)*

▼ Tiffin Metal Products Co..................... D 419 447-8414
Tiffin *(G-12803)*

▼ Workstream Inc.................................. D 513 870-4400
Fairfield *(G-6793)*

2522 Office furniture, except wood

1914 Mi Inc... E 330 308-8667
New Philadelphia *(G-10428)*

Americas Mdular Off Specialist............... G 614 277-0216
Grove City *(G-7372)*

Bavis Fabacraft Inc................................. E 513 677-0500
Maineville *(G-8738)*

▲ Biofit Engineered Product.................. E 419 823-1089
Bowling Green *(G-1411)*

▲ Casco Mfg Solutions Inc................... D 513 681-0003
Cincinnati *(G-2441)*

Custom Craft Collection Inc.................... F 440 998-3000
Ashtabula *(G-589)*

Custom Millcraft Corp............................ E 513 874-7080
West Chester *(G-13980)*

Dgl Woodworking Inc.............................. F 937 837-7091
Dayton *(G-5747)*

East Woodworking Company.................... G 216 791-5950
Cleveland *(G-3649)*

Edsal Sandusky Corporation.................... E 419 626-5465
Sandusky *(G-11829)*

▲ Ergo Desktop LLC............................. E 567 890-3746
Celina *(G-2105)*

Frontier Signs & Displays Inc.................. G 513 367-0813
Harrison *(G-7552)*

Gasser Chair Co Inc............................... D 330 759-2234
Youngstown *(G-14862)*

Geograph Industries Inc.......................... E 513 202-9200
Harrison *(G-7553)*

GMI Companies Inc................................. F 937 981-0244
Greenfield *(G-7327)*

GMI Companies Inc................................. F 513 932-3445
Lebanon *(G-8263)*

◆ GMI Companies Inc........................... F 513 932-3445
Lebanon *(G-8262)*

Hobart Cabinet Company......................... G 937 335-4666
Troy *(G-13224)*

▼ Infinium Wall Systems Inc.................. E 440 572-5000
Strongsville *(G-12567)*

Innovative Woodworking Inc.................... G 513 531-1940
Cincinnati *(G-2746)*

Jsc Employee Leasing Corp..................... D 330 773-8971
Akron *(G-189)*

Lakeside Cabins Ltd............................... G 419 896-2299
Shiloh *(G-11978)*

◆ M/W International Inc......................... F 440 526-6900
Lorain *(G-8566)*

Metal Fabricating Corporation................. D 216 631-8121
Cleveland *(G-4023)*

▲ National Electro-Coatings Inc............. D 216 898-0080
Cleveland *(G-4059)*

Office Magic Inc...................................... F 510 782-6100
Medina *(G-9430)*

Pucel Enterprises Inc.............................. D 216 881-4604
Cleveland *(G-4206)*

Recycled Systems Furniture Inc............... E 614 880-9110
Worthington *(G-14724)*

▲ Senator International Inc..................... E 419 887-5806
Maumee *(G-9316)*

Starr Fabricating Inc............................... D 330 394-9891
Vienna *(G-13618)*

▲ The Columbus Show Case Co............ C
Columbus *(G-5318)*

▼ Tiffin Metal Products Co..................... D 419 447-8414
Tiffin *(G-12803)*

Veterans Representative Co LLC.............. F 330 779-0768
Youngstown *(G-14960)*

▼ Workstream Inc.................................. D 513 870-4400
Fairfield *(G-6793)*

2531 Public building and related furniture

▲ 1914 Mi Inc....................................... D 800 426-4244
New Philadelphia *(G-10429)*

American Office Services Inc................... G 440 899-6888
Westlake *(G-14287)*

Bell Vault and Monu Works Inc................ F 937 866-2444
Miamisburg *(G-9668)*

▲ Biofit Engineered Product.................. E 419 823-1089
Bowling Green *(G-1411)*

Brocar Products Inc................................ E 513 922-2888
Cincinnati *(G-2428)*

▲ C E White Co.................................... E 419 492-2157
New Washington *(G-10477)*

Clarios LLC.. E 419 636-4211
Bryan *(G-1636)*

Clarios LLC.. E 440 205-7221
Mentor *(G-9499)*

Commercial Vehicle Group Inc................. B 614 289-5360
New Albany *(G-10336)*

◆ Evenflo Company Inc......................... A 937 415-3300
Miamisburg *(G-9692)*

Franklin Cabinet Company Inc................. F 937 743-9606
Franklin *(G-7022)*

Gasser Chair Co Inc............................... D 330 759-2234
Youngstown *(G-14862)*

▲ Gasser Chair Co Inc.......................... E 330 534-2234
Youngstown *(G-14861)*

General Motors LLC................................ A 216 265-5000
Cleveland *(G-3767)*

GMI Companies Inc................................. F 937 981-0244
Greenfield *(G-7327)*

GMI Companies Inc................................. F 513 932-3445
Lebanon *(G-8263)*

◆ GMI Companies Inc........................... C 513 932-3445
Lebanon *(G-8262)*

▲ Grand-Rock Company Inc................... E 440 639-2000
Painesville *(G-11089)*

Hann Manufacturing Inc.......................... E 740 962-3752
Mcconnelsville *(G-9362)*

▲ Jay Industries Inc.............................. A 419 747-4161
Mansfield *(G-8806)*

Johnson Controls Inc.............................. D 216 587-0100
Brecksville *(G-1474)*

Johnson Controls Inc.............................. D 513 489-0950
Cincinnati *(G-2771)*

Johnson Controls Inc.............................. F 513 671-6338
Cincinnati *(G-2772)*

Johnson Controls Inc.............................. D 614 895-6600
Westerville *(G-14267)*

Johnson Controls Inc.............................. E 330 270-4385
Youngstown *(G-14884)*

Magna Seating America Inc..................... C 330 824-3101
Sheffield Village *(G-11960)*

McGill Septic Tank Co............................. G 330 876-2171
Kinsman *(G-8141)*

Michaels Pre-Cast Con Pdts Inc.............. F 513 683-1292
Loveland *(G-8643)*

Mock Woodworking Company LLC............ E 740 452-2701
Zanesville *(G-15029)*

N Wasserstrom & Sons Inc...................... F 614 737-5410
Columbus *(G-5119)*

Oberfields LLC.. F 614 252-0955
Columbus *(G-5137)*

Sauder Manufacturing Co......................... D 419 682-3061
Stryker *(G-12627)*

◆ Sauder Manufacturing Co................... C 419 445-7670
Archbold *(G-509)*

▲ Setex Inc... B 419 394-7800
Saint Marys *(G-11752)*

▲ Shiffler Equipment Sales Inc............... E 440 285-9175
Chardon *(G-2222)*

Soft Touch Wood LLC.............................. E 330 545-4204
Girard *(G-7280)*

Summit County....................................... G 330 865-8065
Akron *(G-319)*

▼ Tiffin Metal Products Co..................... D 419 447-8414
Tiffin *(G-12803)*

Tri-State Supply Co Inc........................... F 614 272-6767
Columbus *(G-5331)*

Wurms Woodworking Company................ E 419 492-2184
New Washington *(G-10484)*

Yanfeng Intl Auto Tech US I LL................ E 419 662-4905
Northwood *(G-10815)*

2541 Wood partitions and fixtures

▲ 3jd Inc.. F 513 324-9655
Moraine *(G-10141)*

A & J Woodworking Inc........................... G 419 695-5655
Delphos *(G-6183)*

A G Industries Inc................................... G 216 252-7300
Cleveland *(G-3281)*

A J Construction Co................................ G 330 539-9544
Girard *(G-7262)*

Accent Manufacturing Inc........................ F 330 724-7704
Norton *(G-10816)*

American Countertops Inc........................ E 330 495-1915
Hartville *(G-7574)*

Amtekco Industries LLC.......................... D 614 228-6590
Columbus *(G-4708)*

Amtekco Industries Inc........................... E 614 228-6525
Columbus *(G-4709)*

▲ Archer Counter Design Inc................. G 513 396-7526
Cincinnati *(G-2374)*

Artistic Finishes Inc............................... G 440 951-7850
Willoughby *(G-14427)*

As America Inc.. D 419 522-4211
Mansfield *(G-8763)*

Automated Bldg Components Inc.............. E 419 257-2152
North Baltimore *(G-10612)*

Baker Store Equipment Company............. F
Shaker Heights *(G-11926)*

▲ Bruewer Woodwork Mfg Co................. D 513 353-3505
Cleves *(G-4532)*

Cabinet Restylers Inc.............................. D 419 281-8449
Ashland *(G-525)*

Cameo Countertops Inc........................... F 419 865-6371
Holland *(G-7748)*

◆ Cap & Associates Inc......................... C 614 863-3363
Columbus *(G-4794)*

Case Crafters Inc.................................... G 937 667-9473
Tipp City *(G-12819)*

Cassady Woodworks Inc.......................... F 937 256-7948
Dayton *(G-5605)*

◆ CIP International Inc........................... D 513 874-9925
West Chester *(G-13964)*

Climate Pros LLC.................................. D 216 881-5200
 Cleveland (G-3541)

Climate Pros LLC.................................. D 330 744-2732
 Youngstown (G-14839)

Couch Business Development Inc......... G 937 253-1099
 Dayton (G-5711)

Counter Concepts Inc........................... F 330 848-4848
 Wadsworth (G-13632)

Crafted Surface and Stone LLC............ E 440 658-3799
 Chagrin Falls (G-2157)

Creative Products Inc........................... G 419 866-5501
 Holland (G-7752)

Custom Design Cabinets & Tops........... G 440 639-9900
 Painesville (G-11075)

Customworks Inc.................................. G 614 262-1002
 Columbus (G-4866)

D Lewis Inc.. G 740 695-2615
 Saint Clairsville (G-11690)

Designer Cntemporary Laminates......... G 440 946-8207
 Painesville (G-11079)

Display Dynamics Inc........................... F 937 832-2830
 Englewood (G-6612)

Diversified Products & Svcs................. F 740 393-6202
 Mount Vernon (G-10242)

E J Skok Industries.............................. E 216 292-7533
 Bedford (G-1030)

▼ Fixture Dimensions Inc..................... E 513 360-7512
 Liberty Twp (G-8384)

▲ Formatech Inc.................................. E 330 273-2800
 Brunswick (G-1590)

◆ Formica Corporation........................ E 513 786-3400
 Cincinnati (G-2635)

Franklin Cabinet Company Inc.............. E 937 743-9606
 Franklin (G-7022)

▲ G & W Products LLC........................ C 513 860-4050
 Fairfield (G-6738)

◆ Gabriel Logan LLC........................... D 740 380-6809
 Groveport (G-7436)

Gary L Gast.. G 419 626-5915
 Sandusky (G-11835)

Geograph Industries Inc....................... G 513 202-9200
 Harrison (G-7553)

Global Retail Partners LLC................... E 614 409-9850
 Columbus (G-4958)

GMI Companies Inc.............................. F 937 981-0244
 Greenfield (G-7327)

GMI Companies Inc.............................. F 937 981-7724
 Greenfield (G-7328)

GMI Companies Inc.............................. F 513 932-3445
 Lebanon (G-8263)

◆ GMI Companies Inc......................... C 513 932-3445
 Lebanon (G-8262)

Gross & Sons Custom Millwork............ G 419 227-0214
 Lima (G-8411)

Hardwood Lumber Company Inc........... F 440 834-1891
 Middlefield (G-9797)

Helmart Company Inc........................... G 513 941-3095
 Cincinnati (G-2715)

Home Stor & Off Solutions Inc.............. E 216 362-4660
 Cleveland (G-3836)

▲ Idx Dayton LLC................................ C 937 401-3460
 Dayton (G-5818)

Ingle-Barr Inc...................................... D 740 702-6117
 Chillicothe (G-2261)

Kdm Signs Inc..................................... E 513 769-3900
 Cincinnati (G-2789)

◆ Kellogg Cabinets Inc....................... G 614 833-9596
 Canal Winchester (G-1792)

Kinsella Manufacturing Co Inc.............. F 513 561-5285
 Cincinnati (G-2796)

▲ Kitchens By Rutenschroer Inc.......... G 513 251-8333
 Cincinnati (G-2799)

Laminated Concepts Inc....................... F 216 475-4141
 Maple Heights (G-8885)

▲ Lckbm Company............................... D 419 636-4555
 Bryan (G-1648)

Leiden Cabinet Company LLC.............. G 330 425-8555
 Strasburg (G-12480)

Leiden Cabinet Company LLC.............. D 330 425-8555
 Twinsburg (G-13330)

Lima Millwork Inc................................ G 419 331-3303
 Elida (G-6483)

M21 Industries LLC............................. G 937 781-1377
 Dayton (G-5859)

Mac Lean J S Co.................................. G 614 878-5454
 Columbus (G-5078)

◆ Michael Kaufman Companies Inc...... F 330 673-4881
 Kent (G-8053)

Miller Cabinet Ltd................................ F 614 873-4221
 Plain City (G-11415)

Mock Woodworking Company LLC....... E 740 452-2701
 Zanesville (G-15029)

Murray Display Fixtures Ltd.................. F 614 875-1594
 Grove City (G-7403)

Nagele Manufacturing Company........... E 216 433-1100
 Cleveland (G-4057)

Norton Industries Inc........................... E 888 357-2345
 Lakewood (G-8171)

Ohio Woodworking Co Inc.................... G 513 631-0870
 Cincinnati (G-2927)

Partitions Plus Incorporated................. E 419 422-2600
 Findlay (G-6907)

Pfi Displays Inc.................................... E 330 925-9015
 Rittman (G-11626)

▲ Ptmj Enterprises Inc........................ F 440 543-8000
 Solon (G-12170)

R & R Fabrications Inc.......................... E 419 678-4831
 Saint Henry (G-11723)

Reserve Millwork LLC.......................... E 216 531-6982
 Bedford (G-1056)

Riceland Cabinet Inc............................ D 330 601-1071
 Wooster (G-14676)

▲ Rinos Woodworking Shop Inc........... F 440 946-1718
 Willoughby (G-14518)

Robertson Cabinets Inc........................ G 937 698-3755
 West Milton (G-14185)

Romline Express LLC........................... G 234 855-1905
 Youngstown (G-14926)

Rusco Products Inc.............................. G 330 758-0378
 Youngstown (G-14927)

▲ Scenic Solutions Ltd Lblty Co.......... F 937 866-5062
 Dayton (G-5996)

Shur-Fit Distributors Inc...................... F 937 746-0567
 Franklin (G-7049)

Solid Surface Concepts Inc.................. E 513 948-8677
 Cincinnati (G-3099)

Swingle Countertops............................ F 740 454-7368
 Zanesville (G-15052)

Symatic Inc.. G 330 225-1510
 Medina (G-9452)

▲ The Columbus Show Case Co........... C
 Columbus (G-5318)

The Hattenbach Company..................... D 216 881-5200
 Cleveland (G-4384)

Thomas Cabinet Shop Inc..................... F 937 847-8239
 Dayton (G-6051)

Trumbull Industries Inc........................ D 330 434-6174
 Akron (G-345)

Tusco Limited Partnership.................... C 740 254-4343
 Gnadenhutten (G-7295)

Ultrabuilt Play Systems Inc.................. F 419 652-2294
 Nova (G-10878)

Vances Department Store...................... G 937 549-3033
 Manchester (G-8756)

Vances Department Store...................... G 937 549-2188
 Manchester (G-8755)

Village Cabinet Shop Inc...................... G 704 966-0801
 Cincinnati (G-3205)

▼ W J Egli Company Inc...................... F 330 823-3666
 Alliance (G-414)

Wdi Group Inc...................................... D 216 251-5509
 Cleveland (G-4495)

Wilsonart LLC...................................... E 614 876-1515
 Columbus (G-5369)

▼ Wine Cellar Innovations LLC............ C 513 321-3733
 Cincinnati (G-3227)

Youngstown Curve Form Inc................. F 330 744-3028
 Youngstown (G-14968)

Zanesville Fabricators Inc.................... G 740 452-2439
 Zanesville (G-15057)

2542 Partitions and fixtures, except wood

3-D Technical Services Company.......... E 937 746-2901
 Franklin (G-7006)

▲ Accel Group Inc............................... D 330 336-0317
 Wadsworth (G-13625)

▲ B-R-O-T Incorporated....................... E 216 267-5335
 Cleveland (G-3401)

Bates Metal Products Inc...................... D 740 498-8371
 Port Washington (G-11455)

▼ Benko Products Inc.......................... E 440 934-2180
 Sheffield Village (G-11957)

Busch & Thiem Inc............................... E 419 625-7515
 Sandusky (G-11825)

◆ Cap & Associates Inc....................... C 614 863-3363
 Columbus (G-4794)

▲ Cdc Corporation............................... C 715 532-5548
 Maumee (G-9268)

Communication Exhibits Inc.................. D 330 854-4040
 Canal Fulton (G-1775)

Component Systems Inc........................ E 216 252-9292
 Cleveland (G-3556)

Control Electric Co.............................. E 216 671-8010
 Columbia Station (G-4592)

▲ Crescent Metal Products Inc............. C 440 350-1100
 Mentor (G-9507)

CSM Concepts LLC.............................. F 330 483-1320
 Valley City (G-13493)

Custom Millcraft Corp.......................... E 513 874-7080
 West Chester (G-13980)

D Lewis Inc.. G 740 695-2615
 Saint Clairsville (G-11690)

Danco Metal Products LLC................... D 440 871-2300
 Avon Lake (G-753)

Display Dynamics Inc........................... F 937 832-2830
 Englewood (G-6612)

Dwayne Bennett Industries................... G 440 466-5724
 Geneva (G-7235)

▲ E-B Display Company Inc.................. C 330 833-4101
 Massillon (G-9188)

▼ E2 Merchandising Inc....................... E 513 860-5444
 West Chester (G-14114)

◆ Esmet Inc.. E 330 452-9132
 Canton (G-1888)

▲ Formatech Inc.................................. E 330 273-2800
 Brunswick (G-1590)

G & P Construction LLC........................ E 855 494-4830
 North Royalton (G-10762)

◆ Heat Seal LLC.................................. C 216 341-2022
 Cleveland (G-3816)

HP Manufacturing Company Inc............ D 216 361-6500
 Cleveland (G-3841)

▲ Idx Dayton LLC................................ C 937 401-3460
 Dayton (G-5818)

Industrial Mfg Co Intl LLC.................... G 440 838-4555
 Upper Arlington (G-13431)

◆ Industrial Mfg Co LLC........................F 440 838-4700
Brecksville *(G-1472)*

◆ Kellogg Cabinets Inc........................G 614 833-9596
Canal Winchester *(G-1792)*

Mac Lean J S Co........................G 614 878-5454
Columbus *(G-5078)*

◆ Marlite Inc........................C .. 330 343-6621
Dover *(G-6252)*

Metal Fabricating Corporation................D .. 216 631-8121
Cleveland *(G-4023)*

◆ Mfs Supply LLC........................D .. 800 607-0541
Solon *(G-12149)*

Midmark Corporation........................G .. 937 526-3662
Versailles *(G-13600)*

◆ Midmark Corporation........................A .. 937 528-7500
Miamisburg *(G-9717)*

Midwest Retail Services Inc........... F 800 576-7577
Plain City *(G-11414)*

▲ Mills Partition Company LLC........... D .. 740 375-0770
Marion *(G-8979)*

▼ Modern Retail Solutions LLC........ E .. 330 527-4308
Garrettsville *(G-7227)*

Mro Built LLC........................D .. 330 526-0555
North Canton *(G-10654)*

Myers Industries Inc........................C .. 330 336-6621
Wadsworth *(G-13653)*

Nor-Fab Inc........................G .. 330 467-6580
Northfield *(G-10796)*

Ohio Displays Inc........................F 216 961-5600
Elyria *(G-6572)*

◆ Organized Living Inc........................E .. 513 489-9300
Cincinnati *(G-2939)*

Panacea Products Corporation........... E .. 614 429-6320
Columbus *(G-5170)*

◆ Panacea Products Corporation........E .. 614 850-7000
Columbus *(G-5171)*

Paul Yoder........................G .. 740 439-5811
Senecaville *(G-11906)*

▲ Pete Gaietto & Associates Inc........ D .. 513 771-0903
Cincinnati *(G-2956)*

Pfi Displays Inc........................E .. 330 925-9015
Rittman *(G-11626)*

Prestige Store Interiors Inc........... G .. 419 476-2106
Maumee *(G-9312)*

Pucel Enterprises Inc........................D .. 216 881-4604
Cleveland *(G-4206)*

Rack Processing Company Inc........... E .. 937 294-1911
Moraine *(G-10190)*

Rack Processing Company Inc........... G .. 937 294-1911
Moraine *(G-10189)*

Ray Communications Inc........................G .. 330 686-0226
Stow *(G-12453)*

Republic Storage Systems LLC........ B .. 330 438-5800
Canton *(G-1996)*

Rogers Display Inc........................E .. 440 951-9200
Mentor *(G-9609)*

Stein Holdings Inc........................E .. 440 526-9301
Independence *(G-7920)*

Stiber Fabricating Inc........................F 216 771-7210
Cleveland *(G-4332)*

◆ Ternion Inc........................E .. 216 642-6180
Cleveland *(G-4375)*

▼ Tiffin Metal Products Co........................D .. 419 447-8414
Tiffin *(G-12803)*

Tri County Tarp LLC........................E .. 419 288-3350
Gibsonburg *(G-7260)*

Tusco Limited Partnership........................C .. 740 254-4343
Gnadenhutten *(G-7295)*

Valley Plastics Company Inc........... E .. 419 666-2349
Toledo *(G-13173)*

W B Becherer Inc........................G .. 330 758-6616
Youngstown *(G-14965)*

▼ W J Egli Company Inc........................F 330 823-3666
Alliance *(G-414)*

2591 Drapery hardware and blinds and shades

11 92 Holdings LLC........................F 216 920-7790
Chagrin Falls *(G-2134)*

Cincinnati Window Shade Inc........... F 513 631-7200
Cincinnati *(G-2489)*

Custom Blind Corporation........................F 937 643-2907
Dayton *(G-5717)*

Designer Window Treatments Inc........... G .. 419 822-4967
Delta *(G-6204)*

Electra Tarp Inc........................F 330 477-7168
Canton *(G-1885)*

Golden Drapery Supply Inc........... E .. 216 351-3283
Cleveland *(G-3779)*

▲ Inside Outfitters Inc........................E .. 614 798-3500
Lewis Center *(G-8338)*

Lumenomics Inc........................E .. 614 798-3500
Lewis Center *(G-8342)*

▲ Mag Resources LLC........................F 330 294-0494
Barberton *(G-818)*

Youngstown Shade & Alum LLC........ G .. 330 782-2373
Youngstown *(G-14975)*

2599 Furniture and fixtures, nec

Appetzers R US St Eats 2 Go LL........... G .. 937 460-1470
Springfield *(G-12281)*

Aster Industries Inc........................E .. 330 762-7965
Akron *(G-62)*

Belmont Community Hospital........... E .. 740 671-1216
Bellaire *(G-1085)*

▲ Biofit Engineered Product........... E .. 419 823-1089
Bowling Green *(G-1411)*

Bolons Custom Kitchens Inc........... G .. 330 499-0092
Canton *(G-1842)*

Brodwill LLC........................G .. 513 258-2716
Cincinnati *(G-2429)*

Crow Works LLC........................E .. 888 811-2769
Killbuck *(G-8132)*

Darpro Storage Solutions LLC........ G .. 567 233-3190
Marengo *(G-8896)*

Epix Tube Co Inc........................F 937 529-4858
Dayton *(G-5766)*

Franklin Cabinet Company Inc........... E .. 937 743-9606
Franklin *(G-7022)*

Furniture Concepts Inc........................F 216 292-9100
Cleveland *(G-3745)*

GMI Companies Inc........................F 937 981-0244
Greenfield *(G-7327)*

GMI Companies Inc........................F 513 932-3445
Lebanon *(G-8263)*

◆ GMI Companies Inc........................C .. 513 932-3445
Lebanon *(G-8262)*

Grace Juice Company LLC........... F 614 398-6879
Westerville *(G-14261)*

Home Idea Center Inc........................G .. 419 375-4951
Fort Recovery *(G-6966)*

Howard B Claflin Co........................G .. 330 928-1704
Hudson *(G-7844)*

I 5S of Huron Inc........................G .. 419 433-9075
Huron *(G-7875)*

Justins Delight LLC........................G .. 567 234-3575
Toledo *(G-13014)*

Kinnemyers Cornerstone Cab Inc........... G .. 513 353-3030
Cleves *(G-4542)*

◆ Master Mfg Co Inc........................E .. 216 641-0500
Cleveland *(G-3997)*

Meccas Lounge LLC........................G .. 419 239-6918
Sandusky *(G-11857)*

◆ Michael Kaufman Companies Inc........F 330 673-4881
Kent *(G-8053)*

Modroto........................G .. 440 998-1202
Ashtabula *(G-606)*

Moorchild LLC........................F 513 649-8867
Middletown *(G-9880)*

Mro Built LLC........................D .. 330 526-0555
North Canton *(G-10654)*

Pride 821 LLC........................G .. 330 754-6320
Canton *(G-1981)*

Stainless Crafts Inc........................G .. 513 353-4578
Cincinnati *(G-3110)*

Sweets and Meats LLC........................F 513 888-4227
Cincinnati *(G-3133)*

Textiles Inc........................G .. 614 529-8642
Hilliard *(G-7706)*

▼ Tiffin Metal Products Co........................D .. 419 447-8414
Tiffin *(G-12803)*

Vivo Brothers LLC........................F 330 629-8686
Columbiana *(G-4633)*

Wades Woodworking Inc........................F 937 374-6470
Xenia *(G-14784)*

Woodworking Shop LLC........................F 513 330-9663
Miamisburg *(G-9753)*

26 PAPER AND ALLIED PRODUCTS

2611 Pulp mills

Advanced Green Tech Inc........................G .. 614 397-8130
Plain City *(G-11392)*

Billerud Americas Corporation........... D .. 901 369-4105
West Chester *(G-13952)*

◆ Billerud US Prod Holdg LLC........B .. 877 855-7243
Miamisburg *(G-9672)*

Caraustar Industries Inc........................D .. 740 862-4167
Baltimore *(G-784)*

Matthew Brun Enterprises Inc........... E .. 937 604-0057
Dayton *(G-5870)*

ND Paper Inc........................C .. 937 528-3822
Dayton *(G-5904)*

Polymer Tech & Svcs Inc........................F 740 929-5500
Heath *(G-7601)*

River Valley Paper Company LLC........F 330 535-1001
Akron *(G-286)*

Riverview Productions Inc........................G .. 740 441-1150
Gallipolis *(G-7208)*

Rumpke Transportation Co LLC........ B .. 513 242-4600
Cincinnati *(C-3057)*

▲ The Mead Corporation........................B .. 937 495-6323
Dayton *(G-6049)*

World Wide Recyclers Inc........................G .. 614 554-3296
Columbus *(G-5372)*

2621 Paper mills

◆ Action Specialty Packaging LLC........G
West Chester *(G-14096)*

▲ Ampac Plastics LLC........................B .. 513 671-1777
Cincinnati *(G-2367)*

Appvion Inc........................G .. 937 859-8262
West Carrollton *(G-13926)*

Associated Hygienic Pdts LLC........... A .. 770 497-9800
Delaware *(G-6131)*

Billerud Americas Corporation........... D .. 901 369-4105
West Chester *(G-13952)*

Billerud Americas Corporation........... E .. 877 855-7243
Miamisburg *(G-9669)*

Billerud Commercial LLC........................F 877 855-7243
Miamisburg *(G-9670)*

Billerud Escanaba LLC........................F 877 855-7243
Miamisburg *(G-9671)*

◆ Billerud US Prod Holdg LLC..............B 877 855-7243
Miamisburg *(G-9672)*

Blue Ridge Paper Products LLC..... E 440 235-7200
Olmsted Falls *(G-10938)*

Carlisle Prtg Walnut Creek Ltd.............. E 330 852-9922
Sugarcreek *(G-12635)*

Cheney Dynos Inc.............................. E 937 746-9991
Franklin *(G-7012)*

Corrchoice Cincinnati.............................. G 330 833-2884
Massillon *(G-9181)*

Domtar Corp................................. G 803 802-7500
Cincinnati *(G-2558)*

Domtar Corporation........................ E 937 859-8262
West Carrollton *(G-13927)*

Domtar Corporation........................ B 937 859-8261
West Carrollton *(G-13928)*

Domtar Paper Company LLC...... B 740 333-0003
Wshngtn Ct Hs *(G-14737)*

Eclipse 3d/Pi LLC........................ E 614 626-8536
Columbus *(G-4896)*

Essity Operations Wausau LLC...... E 513 217-3644
Middletown *(G-9858)*

Essity Prof Hygiene N Amer LLC...... F 513 217-3644
Middletown *(G-9859)*

Georgia-Pacific LLC........................ E 614 491-9100
Columbus *(G-4951)*

Georgia-Pacific LLC........................ E 330 794-4444
Mogadore *(G-10076)*

Georgia-Pacific LLC........................ E 513 942-4800
West Chester *(G-14010)*

Glatfelter Corporation.............. G 740 772-3893
Chillicothe *(G-2253)*

Glatfelter Corporation.............. F 740 775-6119
Chillicothe *(G-2254)*

Glatfelter Corporation.............. D 740 772-3111
Chillicothe *(G-2255)*

Glatfelter Corporation.............. G 740 289-5100
Piketon *(G-11307)*

Gr8 News Packaging LLC.............. F 314 739-1202
Lockbourne *(G-8489)*

Graphic Packaging Intl LLC.............. B 419 673-0711
Kenton *(G-8100)*

Graphic Paper Products Corp.............. D 937 325-5503
Springfield *(G-12315)*

Gvs Industries Inc.............. G 513 851-3606
Hamilton *(G-7498)*

Hanchett Paper Company.............. D 513 782-4440
Cincinnati *(G-2703)*

Honey Cell Inc Mid West.............. E 513 360-0280
Monroe *(G-10108)*

Honeycomb Midwest.............. E 513 360-0280
Monroe *(G-10109)*

International Paper Company.............. D 937 456-4131
Eaton *(G-6456)*

International Paper Company.............. C 513 248-6319
Loveland *(G-8633)*

International Paper Company.............. E 740 383-4061
Marion *(G-8974)*

International Paper Company.............. E 937 578-7718
Marysville *(G-9033)*

International Paper Company.............. D 800 473-0830
Middletown *(G-9866)*

International Paper Company.............. C 740 397-5215
Mount Vernon *(G-10245)*

Kaylo Enterprises LLC.............. G 330 535-1860
Akron *(G-192)*

▲ Kenag Inc.............. E 419 281-1204
Ashland *(G-546)*

Kn8designs LLC.............. G 859 380-5926
Cincinnati *(G-2801)*

New Page Corporation.............. D 877 855-7243
Miamisburg *(G-9721)*

Newpage Group Inc.............. A 937 242-9500
Miamisburg *(G-9722)*

▲ Novolyte Technologies Inc.............. B 216 867-1040
Cleveland *(G-4103)*

Ohio Pulp Mills Inc.............. E 513 631-7400
Cincinnati *(G-2925)*

Owens Corning Sales LLC.............. E 614 399-3915
Mount Vernon *(G-10255)*

Paper Service Inc.............. G 330 227-3546
Lisbon *(G-8478)*

Pixelle Spcialty Solutions LLC.............. A 740 772-3111
Chillicothe *(G-2272)*

Pixelle Spcialty Solutions LLC.............. B 419 333-6700
Fremont *(G-7126)*

◆ Plus Mark LLC.............. D 216 252-6770
Cleveland *(G-4174)*

◆ Polymer Packaging Inc.............. D 330 832-2000
North Canton *(G-10658)*

Pratt Industries Inc.............. F 937 583-4990
Lewisburg *(G-8361)*

Pratt Paper (oh) LLC.............. D 567 320-3353
Wapakoneta *(G-13727)*

Quest Solutions Group LLC.............. G 513 703-4520
Liberty Township *(G-8378)*

Rumford Paper Company.............. G 937 242-9230
Miamisburg *(G-9735)*

▲ SC Liquidation Company LLC.............. D 937 332-6500
Troy *(G-13252)*

▼ Solut Inc.............. E 740 549-3336
Lewis Center *(G-8354)*

◆ Special Pack Inc.............. E 330 458-3204
Canton *(G-2010)*

Spinnker Prssure Snstive Pdts.............. G 800 543-9452
Troy *(G-13258)*

▲ The Mead Corporation.............. B 937 495-6323
Dayton *(G-6049)*

Veritiv.............. F 614 323-3335
Columbus *(G-5347)*

Verso Paper Inc.............. E 901 369-4100
Miamisburg *(G-9751)*

Wausau Paper Corp.............. B 513 217-3623
Middletown *(G-9903)*

Welch Packaging Group Inc.............. C 614 870-2000
Columbus *(G-5359)*

◆ West Carrollton Converting Inc.............. F 937 859-3621
West Carrollton *(G-13932)*

2631 Paperboard mills

◆ Action Specialty Packaging LLC.............. G
West Chester *(G-14096)*

Ball Corporation.............. F 234 360-2141
Canton *(G-1836)*

Billerud Americas Corporation.............. D 901 369-4105
West Chester *(G-13952)*

▲ Buckeye Boxes Inc.............. D 614 274-8484
Columbus *(G-4783)*

Caraustar Industries Inc.............. D 740 862-4167
Baltimore *(G-784)*

Caraustar Industries Inc.............. E 513 871-7112
Cincinnati *(G-2438)*

Caraustar Industries Inc.............. F 216 939-3001
Cleveland *(G-3468)*

Caraustar Industries Inc.............. E 330 665-7700
Copley *(G-5432)*

Centor Inc.............. C 800 321-3391
Millersburg *(G-9976)*

Centor Inc.............. F 567 336-8094
Perrysburg *(G-11210)*

Churmac Industries Inc.............. G 740 773-5800
Chillicothe *(G-2248)*

Coburn Inc.............. D 419 368-4051
Hayesville *(G-7591)*

▲ Fibercorr Mills LLC.............. D 330 837-5151
Massillon *(G-9191)*

G S K Inc.............. G 937 547-1611
Greenville *(G-7342)*

Georgia-Pacific LLC.............. C 740 477-3347
Circleville *(G-3260)*

Graphic Packaging Intl LLC.............. C 513 424-4200
Middletown *(G-9863)*

Graphic Packaging Intl LLC.............. C 440 248-4370
Solon *(G-12118)*

▼ Loroco Industries Inc.............. D 513 891-9544
Cincinnati *(G-2828)*

Millcraft Purchasing Corp.............. G 216 441-5505
Cleveland *(G-4041)*

National Bias Fabric Co.............. G 216 361-0530
Cleveland *(G-4058)*

National Carton & Coating Company.............. D 937 347-1042
Xenia *(G-14772)*

Norse Dairy Systems Inc.............. C 614 294-4931
Columbus *(G-5128)*

▲ P & R Specialty Inc.............. E 937 773-0263
Piqua *(G-11370)*

Pactiv LLC.............. C 614 771-5400
Columbus *(G-5168)*

Safeway Packaging Inc.............. E 419 629-3200
New Bremen *(G-10366)*

Saica Pack US LLC.............. E 513 399-5602
Hamilton *(G-7522)*

Sonoco Products Company.............. E 614 759-8470
Columbus *(G-5276)*

Sonoco Products Company.............. E 330 688-8247
Munroe Falls *(G-10272)*

Summit Packaging Solutions LLC.............. F 719 481-8400
West Chester *(G-14079)*

▲ The Mead Corporation.............. B 937 495-6323
Dayton *(G-6049)*

Thorwald Holdings Inc.............. F 740 756-9271
Lancaster *(G-8229)*

▼ Valley Converting Co Inc.............. E 740 537-2152
Toronto *(G-13188)*

Wellman Container Corporation.............. E 513 860-3040
Cincinnati *(G-3219)*

Wrkco Inc.............. E 216 663-3344
Cleveland *(G-4518)*

2652 Setup paperboard boxes

A To Z Paper Box Company.............. G 330 325-8722
Rootstown *(G-11646)*

Boxit Corporation.............. E 216 416-9475
Cleveland *(G-3430)*

Boxit Corporation.............. F 216 631-6900
Cleveland *(G-3431)*

Brimar Packaging Inc.............. E 440 934-3080
Avon *(G-717)*

◆ Chilcote Company.............. C 216 781-6000
Cleveland *(G-3495)*

Clarke-Boxit Corporation.............. E 716 487-1950
Cleveland *(G-3502)*

Graphic Paper Products Corp.............. D 937 325-5503
Springfield *(G-12315)*

Sandusky Packaging Corporation.............. E 419 626-8520
Sandusky *(G-11870)*

▼ The Apex Paper Box Company.............. G 216 631-4000
Cleveland *(G-4377)*

2653 Corrugated and solid fiber boxes

A-Kobak Container Company Inc.............. F 330 225-7791
Hinckley *(G-7730)*

◆ Action Specialty Packaging LLC.............. G
West Chester *(G-14096)*

Adapt-A-Pak Inc.............. E 937 845-0386
Fairborn *(G-6684)*

▲ Akers Packaging Service Inc............ C 513 422-6312
Middletown *(G-9839)*

Akers Packaging Solutions Inc............. D 513 422-6312
Middletown *(G-9840)*

American Corrugated Products Inc........ C 614 870-2000
Columbus *(G-4696)*

American Made Crrgted Pckg Inc.......... G 937 981-2111
Greenfield *(G-7325)*

Archbold Container Corp..................... C 800 446-2520
Archbold *(G-487)*

B & B Box Company Inc..................... F 419 872-5600
Perrysburg *(G-11204)*

BBH Holdings Inc.............................. E 513 870-3000
Lebanon *(G-8246)*

Billerud Americas Corporation............. D 901 369-4105
West Chester *(G-13952)*

Brimar Packaging Inc......................... E 440 934-3080
Avon *(G-717)*

Bryan Packaging Inc.......................... F 419 636-2600
Bryan *(G-1633)*

▲ Buckeye Boxes Inc......................... D 614 274-8484
Columbus *(G-4783)*

Buckeye Corrugated Inc...................... D 330 264-6336
Wooster *(G-14628)*

Buckeye Corrugated Inc...................... D 330 576-0590
Fairlawn *(G-6797)*

Cambridge Packaging Inc.................... E 740 432-3351
Cambridge *(G-1738)*

▲ Cameron Packaging Inc................... G 419 222-9404
Lima *(G-8394)*

Chillicothe Packaging Corp.................. E 740 773-5800
Chillicothe *(G-2247)*

Clecorr Inc....................................... E 216 961-5500
Cleveland *(G-3505)*

◆ Cleveland Supplyone Inc.................. E 216 514-7000
Cleveland *(G-3527)*

Colepak LLC..................................... D 937 652-3910
Urbana *(G-13460)*

Combined Containerboard Inc.............. D 513 530-5700
Cincinnati *(G-2504)*

Corpad Company Inc.......................... D 419 522-7818
Mansfield *(G-8777)*

Creative Packaging LLC..................... E 740 452-8497
Zanesville *(G-15009)*

Digital Color Intl LLC......................... F
Akron *(G-123)*

Dixie Container Corporation................ D 513 860-1145
Fairfield *(G-6728)*

Family Packaging Inc.......................... G 937 325-4106
Springfield *(G-12310)*

Gatton Packaging Inc.......................... G 419 886-2577
Bellville *(G-1138)*

Georgia-Pacific LLC........................... D 740 477-3347
Circleville *(G-3260)*

Georgia-Pacific Pcpi Inc..................... D 513 932-9855
Lebanon *(G-8260)*

Graphic Paper Products Corp.............. D 937 325-5503
Springfield *(G-12315)*

Green Bay Packaging Inc.................... C 419 332-5593
Fremont *(G-7117)*

Green Bay Packaging Inc.................... D 513 489-8700
Lebanon *(G-8266)*

Greif Inc.. E 740 657-6500
Delaware *(G-6150)*

◆ Greif Inc....................................... E 740 549-6000
Delaware *(G-6149)*

Hinkle Manufacturing Inc.................... D 419 666-5550
Perrysburg *(G-11229)*

Honeymoon Paper Products Inc........... D 513 755-7200
Fairfield *(G-6741)*

International Paper Company................ C 740 369-7691
Delaware *(G-6158)*

International Paper Company................ C 740 522-3123
Newark *(G-10512)*

International Paper Company................ D 330 626-7300
Streetsboro *(G-12505)*

International Paper Company................ D 330 264-1322
Wooster *(G-14651)*

Jamestown Cont Cleveland Inc............ B 216 831-3700
Cleveland *(G-3882)*

Jeff Lori Jed Holdings Inc................... E 513 423-0319
Middletown *(G-9869)*

Jet Container Company....................... D 614 444-2133
Columbus *(G-5038)*

Jordon Auto Service & Tire Inc............ G 216 214-6528
Cleveland *(G-3891)*

Joseph T Snyder Industries Inc........... G 216 883-6900
Cleveland *(G-3892)*

Larsen Packaging Products Inc............ F 937 644-5511
Marysville *(G-9034)*

▲ Lewisburg Container Company.......... G 937 962-2681
Lewisburg *(G-8360)*

Litco Corner Protection LLC................ F 330 539-5433
Vienna *(G-13611)*

Lynk Packaging Inc............................ E 330 562-8080
Aurora *(G-677)*

▲ Marshalltown Packaging Inc............. G 641 753-5272
Columbus *(G-5084)*

Massillon Container Co....................... E 330 879-5653
Navarre *(G-10306)*

McElroy Contract Packaging Inc.......... F 330 682-2155
Orrville *(G-10994)*

McKinley Packaging Company............. F 216 663-3344
Maple Heights *(G-8887)*

Menasha Packaging Company LLC....... E 614 202-4084
West Jefferson *(G-14165)*

Metro Containers Inc.......................... D 513 351-6800
Cincinnati *(G-2872)*

▲ Miami Vly Packg Solutions Inc.......... F 937 224-1800
Dayton *(G-5879)*

Midwest Box Company........................ E 216 281-9021
Cleveland *(G-4035)*

▲ Midwest Filtration LLC.................... D 513 874-6510
Cincinnati *(G-2879)*

Mount Vernon Packaging Inc............... F 740 397-3221
Mount Vernon *(G-10253)*

Nebc Inc.. D 440 992-5500
Ashtabula *(G-610)*

▲ Omer J Smith Inc........................... E 513 921-4717
West Chester *(G-14038)*

Orbis Corporation.............................. D 262 560-5000
Perrysburg *(G-11251)*

Packaging Corporation America............ C 419 282-5809
Ashland *(G-559)*

Packaging Corporation America............ E 330 644-9542
Coventry Township *(G-5487)*

Packaging Corporation America............ D 513 424-3542
Middletown *(G-9883)*

Packaging Corporation America............ C 740 344-1126
Newark *(G-10528)*

▲ Piqua Paper Box Company................ E 937 773-0313
Piqua *(G-11378)*

Pjs Corrugated Inc............................. F 419 644-3383
Swanton *(G-12690)*

Pratt (jet Corr) Inc............................ A 937 390-7100
Springfield *(G-12364)*

Pratt (target Container) Inc................. E 513 770-0851
Mason *(G-9136)*

Pratt Industries Inc............................ F 513 262-6253
Dayton *(G-5943)*

Pratt Industries Inc............................ F 937 583-4990
Lewisburg *(G-8361)*

▲ Prestige Display and Packaging LLC F 513 285-1040
Fairfield *(G-6766)*

Pro-Pak Industries Inc........................ D 419 729-0751
Maumee *(G-9313)*

Protective Packg Solutions LLC............ E 513 769-5777
Cincinnati *(G-3010)*

Raymar Holdings Corporation............... E 614 497-3033
Columbus *(G-5225)*

Riverview Packaging Inc...................... E 937 743-9530
Franklin *(G-7045)*

Safeway Packaging Inc........................ E 419 629-3200
New Bremen *(G-10366)*

Schwarz Partners Packaging LLC.......... D 740 387-3700
Marion *(G-8996)*

Schwarz Partners Packaging LLC.......... F 317 290-1140
Sidney *(G-12050)*

Shelby Company................................ E 440 871-9901
Westlake *(G-14334)*

Skybox Packaging LLC........................ C 419 525-7209
Mansfield *(G-8853)*

Sobel Corrugated Containers Inc.......... C 216 475-2100
Cleveland *(G-4311)*

▼ Softbox Systems Inc........................ D 513 360-7189
Monroe *(G-10116)*

Solas Ltd... E 650 501-0889
Avon *(G-739)*

Sonoco Products Company................... E 614 759-8470
Columbus *(G-5276)*

Southern Champion Tray LP................. D 513 755-7200
Fairfield *(G-6777)*

Square One Solutions LLC................... E 419 425-5445
Findlay *(G-6922)*

Summit Container Corporation.............. F 719 481-8400
West Chester *(G-14078)*

Systems Pack Inc.............................. D 330 467-5729
Macedonia *(G-8719)*

Tavens Container Inc.......................... D 216 883-3333
Bedford *(G-1060)*

Tecumseh Packg Solutions Inc............. F 419 238-1122
Van Wert *(G-13545)*

Temple Inland................................... D 513 425-0830
Middletown *(G-9897)*

▲ The Mead Corporation...................... B 937 495-6323
Dayton *(G-6049)*

Trey Corrugated Inc........................... D 513 942-4800
West Chester *(G-14084)*

Tri-State Paper Inc............................. F 937 885-3365
Dayton *(G-6061)*

Unipac Inc.. E 740 929-2000
Hebron *(G-7643)*

Valley Containers Inc.......................... F 330 544-2244
Mineral Ridge *(G-10031)*

▲ Value Added Packaging Inc............... F 937 832-9595
Englewood *(G-6628)*

Viking Paper Company........................ E 419 729-4951
Toledo *(G-13174)*

Wellman Container Corporation............ C 513 860-3040
Cincinnati *(G-3219)*

Westrock Converting LLC.................... E 513 860-0225
West Chester *(G-14092)*

Westrock Rkt LLC.............................. E 330 296-5155
Ravenna *(G-11550)*

Westrock Rkt LLC.............................. C 513 860-5546
West Chester *(G-14093)*

Weyerhaeuser Company...................... G 740 335-4480
Wshngtn Ct Hs *(G-14751)*

2655 Fiber cans, drums, and similar products

Acme Sprlly Wound Ppr Pdts Inc.......... F 216 267-2950
Cleveland *(G-3291)*

Advanced Paper Tube Inc.................... G 216 281-5691
Cleveland *(G-3307)*

Caraustar Indus Cnsmr Pdts Gro.......... D 330 868-4111
Minerva *(G-10035)*

Caraustar Indus Cnsmr Pdts Gro........... D 419 690-0524
Oregon *(G-10960)*

Caraustar Industries Inc........................ E 330 665-7700
Copley *(G-5432)*

Caraustar Industries Inc........................ E 937 298-9969
Moraine *(G-10154)*

Custom Paper Tubes Inc........................ E 216 362-2964
Cleveland *(G-3586)*

Dayton Industrial Drum Inc.................... E 937 253-8933
Dayton *(G-5608)*

Erdie Industries Inc.............................. E 440 288-0166
Lorain *(G-8555)*

Greif Inc... E 740 657-6500
Delaware *(G-6150)*

Greif Inc... G 740 657-6500
Delaware *(G-6151)*

Greif Inc... D 330 879-2936
Massillon *(G-9197)*

Greif Inc... E 419 238-0565
Van Wert *(G-13536)*

◆ Greif Inc... E 740 549-6000
Delaware *(G-6149)*

Greif USA LLC..................................... D 740 549-6000
Delaware *(G-6153)*

Horwitz & Pintis Co.............................. F 419 666-2220
Toledo *(G-12996)*

Howard B Claflin Co............................. E 330 928-1704
Hudson *(G-7844)*

Hpc Holdings LLC................................ F 330 666-3751
Fairlawn *(G-6804)*

▲ Midwest Specialty Pdts Co Inc........... F 513 874-7070
Fairfield *(G-6755)*

Modroto.. G 440 998-1202
Ashtabula *(G-606)*

▲ North Coast Composites Inc.............. F 216 398-8550
Cleveland *(G-4082)*

Ohio Paper Tube Co............................. E 330 478-5171
Canton *(G-1967)*

Oldkor Inc... E 216 631-7800
Cleveland *(G-4118)*

Operational Support Svcs LLC............... F 419 425-0889
Findlay *(G-6904)*

Polystar Inc... F 330 963-5100
Stow *(G-12450)*

Sonoco Products Company.................... E 937 429-0040
Beavercreek Township *(G-1006)*

Sonoco Products Company.................... E 614 759-8470
Columbus *(G-5276)*

Sonoco Products Company.................... E 330 688-8247
Munroe Falls *(G-10272)*

Sonoco Products Company.................... E 513 870-3985
West Chester *(G-14148)*

2656 Sanitary food containers

◆ American Greetings Corporation........ A 216 252-7300
Cleveland *(G-3344)*

Billerud Americas Corporation.............. D 901 369-4105
West Chester *(G-13952)*

Clovernook Ctr For Blind Vslly.............. C 513 522-3860
Cincinnati *(G-2500)*

Graphic Packaging Intl LLC.................. B 419 673-0711
Kenton *(G-8100)*

Huhtamaki Inc..................................... D 513 201-1525
Batavia *(G-867)*

Huhtamaki Inc..................................... D 937 746-9700
Franklin *(G-7028)*

▲ Island Aseptics LLC.......................... C 740 685-2548
Byesville *(G-1714)*

Kerry Inc... E 760 685-2548
Byesville *(G-1715)*

Nelson Companies One LLC.................. E 330 239-4370
Wadsworth *(G-13654)*

◆ Norse Dairy Systems LP.................... B 614 294-4931
Columbus *(G-5129)*

Nuvo Packaging LLC............................ E 216 400-9676
Columbus *(G-5134)*

Ohio State Plastics............................... F 614 299-5618
Columbus *(G-5153)*

Premier Industries Inc.......................... E 513 271-2550
Cincinnati *(G-2979)*

Ricking Holding Co............................... F 513 825-3551
Cleveland *(G-4241)*

Solas Ltd.. E 650 501-0889
Avon *(G-739)*

▼ Solut Inc.. E 740 549-3336
Lewis Center *(G-8354)*

Sonoco Products Company.................... E 513 870-3985
West Chester *(G-14148)*

▲ Sunamericaconverting LLC................ D 330 821-6300
Alliance *(G-409)*

▲ The Mead Corporation....................... B 937 495-6323
Dayton *(G-6049)*

Washington Products Inc....................... F 330 837-5101
Massillon *(G-9252)*

2657 Folding paperboard boxes

American Corrugated Products Inc......... C 614 870-2000
Columbus *(G-4696)*

Boxit Corporation................................. E 216 416-9475
Cleveland *(G-3430)*

Boxit Corporation................................. F 216 631-6900
Cleveland *(G-3431)*

Brimar Packaging Inc........................... E 440 934-3080
Avon *(G-717)*

Cardpak Incorporated........................... C 440 542-3100
Solon *(G-12091)*

◆ Chilcote Company.............................. C 216 781-6000
Cleveland *(G-3495)*

Gpi Ohio LLC....................................... F 605 332-6721
Groveport *(G-7437)*

Graphic Packaging Intl LLC.................. C 513 424-4200
Middletown *(G-9863)*

Graphic Packaging Intl LLC.................. E 419 668-1006
Norwalk *(G-10844)*

Graphic Packaging Intl LLC.................. C 440 248-4370
Solon *(G-12118)*

Jefferson Smurfit Corporation............... G 440 248-4370
Solon *(G-12129)*

Oak Hills Carton Co............................. E 513 948-4200
Cincinnati *(G-2920)*

R R Donnelley & Sons Company............ E 513 870-4040
West Chester *(G-14062)*

Ranpak Holdings Corp.......................... D 440 354-4445
Concord Township *(G-5394)*

Roys Mueller Box Co............................ G 216 464-1191
Cleveland *(G-4260)*

Saica Pack US LLC............................... E 513 399-5602
Hamilton *(G-7522)*

Sandusky Packaging Corporation........... E 419 626-8520
Sandusky *(G-11870)*

Shelby Company.................................. E 440 871-9901
Westlake *(G-14334)*

▼ The Apex Paper Box Company........... G 216 631-4000
Cleveland *(G-4377)*

Unipac Inc... E 740 929-2000
Hebron *(G-7643)*

2671 Paper; coated and laminated packaging

Amatech Inc... E 614 252-2506
Columbus *(G-4691)*

American Corrugated Products Inc......... C 614 870-2000
Columbus *(G-4696)*

▲ Ampac Plastics LLC.......................... B 513 671-1777
Cincinnati *(G-2367)*

Austin Tape and Label Inc.................... D 330 928-7999
Stow *(G-12420)*

Bollin & Sons Inc................................. E 419 693-6573
Toledo *(G-12900)*

▲ Central Coated Products LLC............. D 330 821-9830
Alliance *(G-376)*

Central Ohio Paper & Packg Inc............ F 419 621-9239
Huron *(G-7870)*

Charter Next Generation Inc.................. C 740 369-2770
Delaware *(G-6138)*

Charter Next Generation Inc.................. C 419 884-8150
Lexington *(G-8367)*

Charter Next Generation Inc.................. C 419 884-8150
Lexington *(G-8368)*

Charter Next Generation Inc.................. C 419 884-8150
Lexington *(G-8369)*

Charter Next Generation Inc.................. C 419 884-8150
Lexington *(G-8370)*

Charter Next Generation Inc.................. C 419 884-8150
Lexington *(G-8371)*

Charter Next Generation Inc.................. C 330 830-6030
Massillon *(G-9179)*

Colepak LLC.. D 937 652-3910
Urbana *(G-13460)*

▲ Command Plastic Corporation............ F 800 321-8001
Bedford *(G-1022)*

Cpg - Ohio LLC................................... D 513 825-4800
Cincinnati *(G-2521)*

▼ Crayex Corporation............................ D 937 773-7000
Piqua *(G-11342)*

Creative Packaging LLC........................ E 740 452-8497
Zanesville *(G-15009)*

▲ Custom Products Corporation............. D 440 528-7100
Glenwillow *(G-7285)*

Diversipak Inc...................................... E 513 321-7884
Cincinnati *(G-2555)*

Dubose Strapping Inc........................... E 419 221-0626
Lima *(G-8404)*

▲ Engineered Films Division Inc............ D 419 884-8150
Lexington *(G-8373)*

Future Polytech Inc.............................. E 614 942-1209
Columbus *(G-4941)*

Georgia-Pacific LLC............................. C 740 477-3347
Circleville *(G-3260)*

Gt Industrial Supply Inc........................ F 513 771-7000
Cincinnati *(G-2695)*

Joseph T Snyder Industries Inc.............. G 216 883-6900
Cleveland *(G-3892)*

Kay Toledo Tag Inc............................... D 419 729-5479
Toledo *(G-13017)*

▲ Kroy LLC.. C 800 837-4323
Cleveland *(G-3929)*

Linneas Candy Supplies Inc.................. E 330 678-7112
Kent *(G-8046)*

Liqui-Box Corporation.......................... E 419 289-9696
Ashland *(G-549)*

▼ Loroco Industries Inc......................... D 513 891-9544
Cincinnati *(G-2828)*

Marlen Manufacturing & Dev Co............ F 216 292-7546
Bedford *(G-1047)*

National Glass Svc Group LLC............... F 614 652-3699
Dublin *(G-6323)*

◆ Nilpeter Usa Inc................................ C 513 489-4400
Cincinnati *(G-2909)*

Norse Dairy Systems Inc....................... C 614 294-4931
Columbus *(G-5128)*

North American Plas Chem Inc............... E 216 531-3400
Euclid *(G-6666)*

Novacel Inc... C 937 335-5611
Troy *(G-13243)*

Octal Extrusion Corp............................ D 513 881-6100
West Chester *(G-14135)*

Orflex Inc.. B
Cincinnati (G-2937)

▼ Pioneer Labels Inc........................... C 618 546-5418
West Chester (G-14048)

Plastic Works Inc.................................. F 440 331-5575
Cleveland (G-4171)

Plastipak Packaging Inc...................... B 937 596-6142
Jackson Center (G-7966)

◆ Polychem LLC.................................. C 440 357-1500
Mentor (G-9588)

Prime Industries Inc............................. F
Lorain (G-8574)

Proampac LLC..................................... A 513 671-1777
Cincinnati (G-2985)

Responsible Products Limited............. F 888 988-6627
West Chester (G-14065)

Retterbush Graphics Packg Corp......... G 513 779-4466
West Chester (G-14066)

Safeway Packaging Inc....................... E 419 629-3200
New Bremen (G-10366)

Schilling Graphics Inc........................ E 419 468-1037
Galion (G-7198)

Schwarz Partners Packaging LLC........ F 317 290-1140
Sidney (G-12050)

Signode Industrial Group LLC............. C 513 248-2990
Loveland (G-8653)

Sonoco Products Company.................. E 614 759-8470
Columbus (G-5276)

Springdot Inc...................................... D 513 542-4000
Cincinnati (G-3108)

Storopack Inc...................................... F 513 874-0314
West Chester (G-14077)

▲ Storopack Inc.................................. E 513 874-0314
Cincinnati (G-3121)

▲ Stretchtape Inc................................ E 216 486-9400
Cleveland (G-4333)

Sun America LLC................................ E 330 821-6300
Alliance (G-408)

Superior Label Systems Inc................ B 513 336-0825
Mason (G-9157)

▼ Tce International Ltd........................ F 800 962-2376
Perry (G-11199)

Tech/III Inc... E 513 482-7500
Fairfield (G-6781)

▲ The Hooven - Dayton Corp.............. C 937 233-4473
Miamisburg (G-9747)

Thomas Products Co Inc..................... E 513 756-9009
Cincinnati (G-3155)

Universal Packg Systems Inc.............. C 513 732-2000
Batavia (G-894)

Universal Packg Systems Inc.............. C 513 735-4777
Batavia (G-895)

Universal Packg Systems Inc.............. C 513 674-9400
Cincinnati (G-3186)

Valgroup North America Inc................. C 419 423-6500
Findlay (G-6929)

Versa-Pak Ltd..................................... E 419 586-5466
Celina (G-2127)

Visual Marking Systems Inc................ D 330 425-7100
Twinsburg (G-13393)

Zebco Industries Inc........................... F 740 654-4510
Lancaster (G-8233)

2672 Paper; coated and laminated, nec

3 Sigma LLC....................................... D 937 440-3400
Troy (G-13198)

3M Company.. D 330 725-1444
Medina (G-9369)

▲ Acpo Ltd... D 419 898-8273
Oak Harbor (G-10881)

Adcraft Decals Incorporated............... E 216 524-2934
Cleveland (G-3297)

Admiral Products Company Inc........... E 216 671-0600
Cleveland (G-3299)

Austin Tape and Label Inc.................. D 330 928-7999
Stow (G-12420)

Avery Dennison Corporation............... E 513 682-7500
Cincinnati (G-2393)

Avery Dennison Corporation............... G 216 267-8700
Cleveland (G-3391)

Avery Dennison Corporation............... B 440 358-4691
Concord Township (G-5385)

Avery Dennison Corporation............... F 440 534-6527
Mentor (G-9488)

Avery Dennison Corporation............... D 440 639-3900
Mentor (G-9490)

Avery Dennison Corporation............... D 440 358-2828
Mentor (G-9491)

Avery Dennison Corporation............... F 937 865-2439
Miamisburg (G-9667)

Avery Dennison Corporation............... F 419 898-8273
Oak Harbor (G-10882)

Avery Dennison Corporation............... C 440 358-3466
Painesville (G-11068)

Avery Dennison Corporation............... B 440 358-2564
Painesville (G-11069)

Avery Dennison Corporation............... B 440 878-7000
Strongsville (G-12543)

Avery Dennison Corporation............... A 440 534-6000
Mentor (G-9489)

Avery Dnnison G Holdings I LLC......... G 440 534-6000
Mentor (G-9492)

Beiersdorf Inc..................................... C 513 682-7300
West Chester (G-14107)

BMC Growth Fund LLC........................ C 937 291-4110
Miamisburg (G-9674)

Boehm Inc... E 614 875-9010
Grove City (G-7374)

Bollin & Sons Inc................................ E 419 693-6573
Toledo (G-12900)

CCL Label Inc..................................... E 216 676-2703
Cleveland (G-3480)

CCL Label Inc..................................... D 440 878-7000
Strongsville (G-12548)

▲ Central Coated Products LLC.......... D 330 821-9830
Alliance (G-376)

◆ Cortape Inc..................................... F 330 929-6700
Cuyahoga Falls (G-5535)

Deco Tools Inc.................................... E 419 476-9321
Toledo (G-12030)

Domtar Corporation............................. B 937 859-8261
West Carrollton (G-13928)

GBS Corp.. C 330 863-1828
Malvern (G-8750)

▲ GBS Corp.. C 330 494-5330
North Canton (G-10641)

Glatfelter Corporation......................... G 419 333-6700
Fremont (G-7115)

Hall Company...................................... E 937 652-1376
Urbana (G-13465)

▲ ID Images LLC................................ D 330 220-7300
Brunswick (G-1598)

◆ Kardol Quality Products LLC........... G 513 933-8206
Blue Ash (G-1293)

◆ Kent Adhesive Products Co............. D 330 678-1626
Kent (G-8039)

Label Technique Southeast LLC......... F 440 951-7660
Willoughby (G-14479)

Lam Pro Inc... F 216 426-0661
Cleveland (G-3938)

▲ Laminate Technologies Inc............. D 800 231-2523
Tiffin (G-12786)

Linneas Candy Supplies Inc............... E 330 678-7112
Kent (G-8046)

Lockfast LLC....................................... G 800 543-7157
Loveland (G-8637)

▼ Loroco Industries Inc...................... D 513 891-9544
Cincinnati (G-2828)

Magnum Tapes Films........................... G 877 460-8402
Caldwell (G-1726)

Marlen Manufacturing & Dev Co.......... F 216 292-7546
Bedford (G-1047)

Miller Products Inc.............................. C 330 938-2134
Sebring (G-11897)

▲ Miller Studio Inc............................. G 330 339-1100
New Philadelphia (G-10459)

◆ Morgan Adhesives Company LLC..... B 330 688-1111
Stow (G-12441)

▼ Mr Label Inc.................................... E 513 681-2088
Cincinnati (G-2891)

Multi-Color Corporation...................... C 513 381-1480
Batavia (G-878)

Multi-Color Corporation...................... G 513 459-3283
Mason (G-9130)

◆ Nilpeter Usa Inc.............................. C 513 489-4400
Cincinnati (G-2909)

◆ Novacel Prfmce Coatings Inc.......... D 937 552-4932
Troy (G-13244)

Novagard Solutions Inc....................... D 216 881-8111
Cleveland (G-4101)

▲ Novavision LLC............................... D 419 354-1427
Bowling Green (G-1430)

▲ Ohio Laminating & Binding Inc....... G 614 771-4868
Hilliard (G-7691)

Oliver Healthcare Packaging Co.......... C 513 860-6880
Hamilton (G-7516)

▼ Pioneer Labels Inc.......................... C 618 546-5418
West Chester (G-14048)

Progressive Supply LLC...................... G 570 688-9636
Willoughby (G-14510)

R R Donnelley & Sons Company.......... D 440 774-2101
Oberlin (G-10920)

Roemer Industries Inc......................... D 330 448-2000
Masury (G-9256)

▲ Sensical Inc.................................... D 216 641-1141
Solon (G-12180)

◆ SRC Liquidation LLC....................... A 937 221-1000
Dayton (G-6019)

▲ Stretchtape Inc............................... E 216 486-9400
Cleveland (G-4333)

Superior Label Systems Inc................ B 513 336-0825
Mason (G-9157)

◆ Technicote Inc................................ E 800 358-4448
Miamisburg (G-9745)

Tekni-Plex Inc..................................... E 419 491-2399
Holland (G-7786)

▲ The Hooven - Dayton Corp.............. C 937 233-4473
Miamisburg (G-9747)

Thomas Products Co Inc..................... E 513 756-9009
Cincinnati (G-3155)

▲ Waytek Corporation........................ E 937 743-6142
Franklin (G-7057)

2673 Bags: plastic, laminated, and coated

American Plastics LLC......................... C 419 423-1213
Findlay (G-6836)

◆ Ampac Holdings LLC........................ A 513 671-1777
Cincinnati (G-2365)

Automated Packg Systems Inc............ E 330 342-2000
Bedford (G-1013)

B K Plastics Inc.................................. G 937 473-2087
Covington (G-5490)

▲ Buckeye Boxes Inc.......................... D 614 274-8484
Columbus (G-4783)

Buckeye Packaging Co Inc.................. D 330 935-0301
Alliance (G-373)

Employee Codes: A=Over 500 employees, B=251-500   2025 Harris Ohio
C=101-250, D=51-100, E=20-50, F=10-19, G=1-9   Industrial Directory

                                                                                          737

Charter Nex Films - Delaware Oh Inc...... E 740 369-2770
Delaware **(G-6137)**

▲ Command Plastic Corporation.......... F 800 321-8001
Bedford **(G-1022)**

Cpg - Ohio LLC.............................. D ... 513 825-4800
Cincinnati **(G-2521)**

▼ Crayex Corporation....................... D 937 773-7000
Piqua **(G-11342)**

Custom Poly Bag LLC...................... D 330 935-2408
Alliance **(G-378)**

Dayton Industrial Drum Inc............... E 937 253-8933
Dayton **(G-5608)**

▲ Dazpak Flexible Packaging Corp....... C 614 252-2121
Columbus **(G-4872)**

▲ Engineered Films Division Inc.......... D 419 884-8150
Lexington **(G-8373)**

◆ Flavorseal LLC ....D 440 937-3900
Avon **(G-726)**

General Films Inc.......................... G 888 436-3456
Covington **(G-5493)**

Global Plastic Tech Inc................... G 440 879-6045
Lorain **(G-8556)**

Hood Packaging Corporation............ C 937 382-6681
Wilmington **(G-14584)**

▲ Kennedy Group Incorporated........... D 440 951-7660
Willoughby **(G-14477)**

Liqui-Box Corporation..................... E 419 289-9696
Ashland **(G-549)**

Noramco Inc................................. D 216 531-3400
Euclid **(G-6664)**

North American Plas Chem Inc........... E 216 531-3400
Euclid **(G-6666)**

▼ Packaging Materials Inc................. E 740 432-6337
Cambridge **(G-1753)**

Pexco Packaging Corp..................... E 419 470-5935
Toledo **(G-13096)**

Pitt Plastics Inc............................ D 614 868-8660
Columbus **(G-5192)**

Safeway Packaging Inc.................... E 419 629-3200
New Bremen **(G-10366)**

Signature Flexible Packg LLC........... F 614 252-2121
Columbus **(G-5267)**

2674 Bags: uncoated paper and multiwall

◆ Ampac Holdings LLC..................... A 513 671-1777
Cincinnati **(G-2365)**

▲ Brady Ruck Company..................... E 419 738-5126
Wapakoneta **(G-13708)**

Cleveland Canvas Goods Mfg Co........ E 216 361-4567
Cleveland **(G-3508)**

◆ Duro Bag Manufacturing Company....D 800 879-3876
Cincinnati **(G-2565)**

Ecopac LLC.................................. E 513 795-6002
Fairfield **(G-6730)**

Gateway Packaging Company LLC....... E 419 738-5126
Wapakoneta **(G-13713)**

Greif Inc..................................... E 740 657-6500
Delaware **(G-6150)**

◆ Greif Inc.................................... E 740 549-6000
Delaware **(G-6149)**

Hood Packaging Corporation............ C 937 382-6681
Wilmington **(G-14584)**

▲ Mid-America Packaging LLC........... A 330 963-4199
New Philadelphia **(G-10457)**

Pantrybag Inc............................... F 614 812-8073
Columbus **(G-5172)**

2675 Die-cut paper and board

▲ Art Guild Binders Inc.................... E 513 242-3000
Cincinnati **(G-2378)**

▲ Buckeye Boxes Inc....................... D 614 274-8484
Columbus **(G-4783)**

◆ Chilcote Company..........................C 216 781-6000
Cleveland **(G-3495)**

Commercial Cutng Graphics LLC.......... D 419 526-4800
Mansfield **(G-8776)**

Foldedpak Inc............................... G 740 527-1090
Hebron **(G-7614)**

Forest Converting Co Inc................. G 513 631-4190
Cincinnati **(G-2634)**

GBS Corp..................................... C 330 863-1828
Malvern **(G-8750)**

▲ GBS Corp.................................... C 330 494-5330
North Canton **(G-10641)**

Georgia-Pacific LLC........................ C 740 477-3347
Circleville **(G-3260)**

Harris Paper Crafts Inc.................... F 614 299-2141
Columbus **(G-4971)**

Honeymoon Paper Products Inc.......... D 513 755-7200
Fairfield **(G-6741)**

Keeler Enterprises Inc..................... G 330 336-7601
Wadsworth **(G-13646)**

◆ Kent Adhesive Products Co..............D 330 678-1626
Kent **(G-8039)**

▲ Keyah International Trdg LLC........... E 937 399-3140
Springfield **(G-12336)**

Lam Pro Inc.................................. F 216 426-0661
Cleveland **(G-3938)**

▼ Loroco Industries Inc.................... D 513 891-9544
Cincinnati **(G-2828)**

McElroy Contract Packaging Inc.......... F 330 682-2155
Orrville **(G-10994)**

Multi-Craft Litho Inc....................... E 859 581-2754
Blue Ash **(G-1312)**

Nordec Inc................................... D 330 940-3700
Stow **(G-12447)**

▲ P & R Specialty Inc....................... E 937 773-0263
Piqua **(G-11370)**

▲ Printers Bindery Services Inc.......... D 513 821-8039
Batavia **(G-884)**

▲ Rohrer Corporation....................... C 330 335-1541
Wadsworth **(G-13668)**

Smead Manufacturing Company.......... C 740 385-5601
Logan **(G-8527)**

Southern Champion Tray LP............... D 513 755-7200
Fairfield **(G-6777)**

Springdot Inc............................... D 513 542-4000
Cincinnati **(G-3108)**

Stat Industries Inc......................... G 740 779-6561
Chillicothe **(G-2283)**

Stat Industries Inc......................... G 513 860-4482
Hamilton **(G-7527)**

Stat Industries Inc......................... G 740 779-6561
Chillicothe **(G-2282)**

Vya Inc....................................... E 513 772-5400
Cincinnati **(G-3210)**

Williams Steel Rule Die Co............... G 216 431-3232
Cleveland **(G-4507)**

2676 Sanitary paper products

◆ Absorbent Products Company Inc......E 419 352-5353
Bowling Green **(G-1405)**

◆ Aci Industries Converting Ltd............F 740 368-4160
Delaware **(G-6129)**

Attends Healthcare Pdts Inc.............. G 740 368-7880
Delaware **(G-6133)**

▲ Eleeo Brands LLC.......................... G 513 572-8100
Cincinnati **(G-2582)**

▲ Giant Industries Inc....................... E 419 531-4600
Toledo **(G-12975)**

▲ Health Care Products Inc................. E 419 678-9620
Coldwater **(G-4577)**

Johnson & Johnson......................... E 513 786-7000
Blue Ash **(G-1290)**

Linsalata Cpitl Prtners Fund I............... G 440 684-1400
Cleveland **(G-3962)**

▲ Novex Products Inc....................... E 440 244-3330
Lorain **(G-8570)**

Playtex Manufacturing Inc................. E 937 498-4710
Sidney **(G-12039)**

▲ Principle Business Entps Inc............. C 419 352-1551
Bowling Green **(G-1437)**

Procter & Gamble Company............... E 513 983-1100
Cincinnati **(G-2987)**

Procter & Gamble Company............... E 513 266-4375
Cincinnati **(G-2988)**

Procter & Gamble Company............... F 513 871-7557
Cincinnati **(G-2989)**

Procter & Gamble Company............... F 513 482-6789
Cincinnati **(G-2991)**

Procter & Gamble Company............... C 513 983-3000
Cincinnati **(G-2993)**

Procter & Gamble Company............... D 513 627-7115
Cincinnati **(G-2994)**

Procter & Gamble Company............... E 513 945-0340
Cincinnati **(G-2997)**

Procter & Gamble Company............... C 513 622-1000
Mason **(G-9138)**

Procter & Gamble Company............... E 513 634-9600
West Chester **(G-14054)**

Procter & Gamble Company............... C 513 634-9110
West Chester **(G-14055)**

◆ Procter & Gamble Company...............A 513 983-1100
Cincinnati **(G-2999)**

Procter & Gamble Far East Inc........... C 513 983-1100
Cincinnati **(G-3000)**

Procter & Gamble Paper Pdts Co........ E 513 983-2222
Cincinnati **(G-3004)**

◆ Procter & Gamble Paper Pdts Co.......F 513 983-1100
Cincinnati **(G-3003)**

Sposie LLC................................... F 888 977-2229
Maumee **(G-9319)**

▲ Tambrands Sales Corp.................... C 513 983-1100
Cincinnati **(G-3137)**

This Is L Inc................................. G 415 630-5172
Cincinnati **(G-3154)**

Tranzonic Companies....................... C 440 446-0643
Cleveland **(G-4414)**

◆ Tz Acquisition Corp........................F 216 535-4300
Richmond Heights **(G-11613)**

2677 Envelopes

American Paper Group Inc................. B 330 758-4545
Youngstown **(G-14811)**

◆ Ampac Holdings LLC.......................A 513 671-1777
Cincinnati **(G-2365)**

Church-Budget Envelope Company....... E 800 446-9780
Salem **(G-11770)**

▲ E-1 (2012) Holdings Inc................... C 330 482-3900
Columbiana **(G-4615)**

▲ Envelope 1 Inc.............................. D 330 482-3900
Columbiana **(G-4616)**

Envelope Mart of Ohio Inc................. F 440 365-8177
Elyria **(G-6535)**

▲ Jbm Packaging Company................. C 513 933-8333
Lebanon **(G-8269)**

▲ Keene Building Products Co.............. E 440 605-1020
Cleveland **(G-3910)**

Ohio Envelope Manufacturing Co......... E 216 267-2920
Cleveland **(G-4114)**

Pac Worldwide Corporation............... E 800 535-0039
Monroe **(G-10114)**

Quality Envelope Inc....................... G 513 942-7578
West Chester **(G-14140)**

◆ SRC Liquidation LLC.......................A 937 221-1000
Dayton **(G-6019)**

United Envelope LLC.............................B 513 542-4700
Cincinnati (G-3182)

Western States Envelope Co................E 419 666-7480
Walbridge (G-13689)

2678 Stationery products

◆ American Greetings Corporation.......A 216 252-7300
Cleveland (G-3344)

Avery Dennison Corporation.................A 440 534-6000
Mentor (G-9489)

▼ Bookfactory LLC.................................E 937 226-7100
Dayton (G-5682)

CCL Label Inc.......................................E 216 676-2703
Cleveland (G-3480)

CCL Label Inc.......................................D 440 878-7000
Strongsville (G-12548)

▲ CM Paula Company..........................E 513 759-7473
Mason (G-9090)

Keeler Enterprises Inc.........................G 330 336-7601
Wadsworth (G-13646)

Selco Industries Inc.............................F 419 861-0336
Holland (G-7784)

◆ Steel City Corporation.....................E 330 792-7663
Ashland (G-575)

Westrock Mwv LLC..............................D 937 495-6323
Dayton (G-6079)

2679 Converted paper products, nec

4wallscom LLC.....................................F 216 432-1400
Cleveland (G-3277)

◆ American Greetings Corporation.......A 216 252-7300
Cleveland (G-3344)

Avery Dennison Corporation.................B 440 358-4691
Concord Township (G-5385)

Avery Dennison Corporation.................D 440 639-3900
Mentor (G-9490)

Btw LLC...G 419 382-4443
Toledo (G-12907)

▼ Buckeye Paper Co Inc......................E 330 477-5925
Canton (G-1847)

▲ Buschman Corporation......................F 216 431-6633
Cleveland (G-3453)

Caraustar Industries Inc......................E 330 665-7700
Copley (G-5432)

CCL Label Inc.......................................E 216 676-2703
Cleveland (G-3480)

▲ Cindus Corporation...........................D 513 948-9951
Cincinnati (G-2491)

E-Z Grader Company............................G 440 247-7511
Chagrin Falls (G-2141)

Eagles Nest Holdings LLC...................E 419 526-4123
Mansfield (G-8782)

▲ Fibercorr Mills LLC............................D 330 837-5151
Massillon (G-9191)

◆ Formica Corporation..........................E 513 786-3400
Cincinnati (G-2635)

Fremont Printing Inc.............................F 480 272-3443
Fremont (G-7112)

▲ Gemini Fiber Corporation..................F 330 874-4131
Bolivar (G-1383)

◆ General Data Company Inc...............B 513 752-7978
Cincinnati (G-2304)

Green Meadows Paper Company.........D 330 837-5151
Massillon (G-9196)

H Lee Philippi Co..................................F 513 321-5330
Cincinnati (G-2699)

Harris Paper Crafts Inc........................F 614 299-2141
Columbus (G-4971)

Kay Toledo Tag Inc..............................D 419 729-5479
Toledo (G-13017)

▲ Kennedy Group Incorporated............D 440 951-7660
Willoughby (G-14477)

◆ Kent Adhesive Products Co...............D 330 678-1626
Kent (G-8039)

L & F Products......................................G 937 498-4710
Sidney (G-12028)

▲ Label Aid Inc......................................E 419 433-2888
Huron (G-7876)

Label Technique Southeast LLC..........F 440 951-7660
Willoughby (G-14479)

▼ Mabis Shipping Solutions Inc...........G 330 650-1788
Hudson (G-7850)

▲ Millcraft Group LLC...........................D 216 441-5500
Independence (G-7911)

Multi-Color Corporation........................C 513 381-1480
Batavia (G-878)

Multi-Color Corporation........................G 513 459-3283
Mason (G-9130)

Oak Hills Carton Co..............................E 513 948-4200
Cincinnati (G-2920)

Orbytel Print and Packg Inc.................G 216 267-8734
Cleveland (G-4123)

Outhouse Paper Etc Inc.......................G 937 382-2800
Waynesville (G-13881)

Pressed Paperboard Tech LLC............C 419 423-4030
Findlay (G-6909)

Psix LLC...G 937 746-6841
Springboro (G-12264)

Roberds Converting Co Inc..................E 513 683-6667
Loveland (G-8648)

▼ Scratch-Off Systems Inc...................E 216 649-7800
Twinsburg (G-13376)

◆ Shore To Shore Inc...........................D 937 866-1908
Dayton (G-6004)

Signode Industrial Group LLC..............C 513 248-2990
Loveland (G-8653)

Stumps Converting Inc.........................F 419 492-2542
New Washington (G-10483)

T&T Graphics Inc.................................D 937 847-6000
Miamisburg (G-9742)

Tekni-Plex Inc......................................E 419 491-2399
Holland (G-7786)

◆ The Blonder Company........................C 216 431-3560
Cleveland (G-4379)

▲ The Hooven - Dayton Corp................C 937 233-4473
Miamisburg (G-9747)

Tri State Media LLC..............................F 513 933-0101
Wilmington (G-14588)

Verstrete In Mold Lbels USA In............F 513 943-0080
Batavia (G-896)

▲ Vista Industrial Packaging LLC..........E 800 454-6117
Columbus (G-5351)

Warren Printing & Off Pdts Inc.............F 419 523-3635
Ottawa (G-11050)

27 PRINTING, PUBLISHING AND ALLIED INDUSTRIES

2711 Newspapers

Akron Legal News Inc...........................F 330 296-7578
Akron (G-33)

Alliance Publishing Co Inc....................C 330 453-1304
Alliance (G-372)

American City Bus Journals Inc............D 513 337-9450
Cincinnati (G-2358)

American City Bus Journals Inc............C 937 528-4400
Dayton (G-5651)

American Community Newspapers........G 614 888-4567
Columbus (G-4695)

American Israelite Company Inc............G 513 621-3145
Cincinnati (G-2360)

▲ Amos Media Company........................C 937 498-2121
Sidney (G-11992)

Archbold Buckeye Inc...........................F 419 445-4466
Archbold (G-486)

Arens Corporation.................................G 937 473-2028
Covington (G-5489)

Arens Corporation.................................F 937 473-2028
Covington (G-5488)

Ashland Publishing Co..........................A 419 281-0581
Ashland (G-517)

Atrium At Anna Maria Inc.....................F 330 562-7777
Aurora (G-661)

Beacon Journal Publishing Co..............C 330 996-3600
Akron (G-74)

Belem Group LLC..................................G 614 604-6870
Columbus (G-4750)

Block Communications Inc....................F 419 724-6212
Toledo (G-12898)

Bluffton News Pubg & Prtg Co.............F 419 358-8010
Bluffton (G-1357)

Boardman News..................................G 330 758-6397
Boardman (G-1368)

Brown Publishing Co Inc.......................F 740 286-2187
Jackson (G-7942)

Brown Publishing Inc LLC....................G 513 794-5040
Blue Ash (G-1256)

Bryan Publishing Company...................D 419 636-1111
Bryan (G-1634)

Business Journal..................................E 330 744-5023
Youngstown (G-14830)

Cameco Communications LLC...............G 937 840-9490
Hillsboro (G-7715)

Carrollton Publishing Company.............G 330 627-5591
Carrollton (G-2081)

Catholic Diocese of Columbus..............G 614 224-5195
Columbus (G-4802)

Chagrin Valley Publishing Co................F 440 247-5335
Chagrin Falls (G-2139)

Choice Marketing..................................F 614 638-8404
Columbus (G-4808)

Cincinnati Enquirer...............................C 513 721-2700
Cincinnati (G-2474)

Cincinnati Ftn Sq News Inc...................F 513 421-4049
Mason (G-9084)

Cincinnati Site Solutions LLC...............G 513 373-5001
Cincinnati (G-2485)

Cleveland Jewish Publ Co.....................E 216 454-8300
Cleveland (G-3514)

Cleveland Jewish Publ Co Fdn..............F 216 454-8300
Beachwood (G-913)

Clevelandcom..G 216 862-7159
Cleveland (G-3534)

Columbus Messenger Company............E 614 272-5422
Columbus (G-4830)

Columbus-Sports Publications..............F 614 486-2202
Columbus (G-4838)

Comcorp Inc...C 718 981-1234
Cleveland (G-3550)

Copley Ohio Newspapers Inc................C 330 364-5577
New Philadelphia (G-10439)

Copley Ohio Newspapers Inc................E 585 598-0030
Canton (G-1871)

County Classifieds................................G 937 592-8847
Bellefontaine (G-1102)

Cox Newspapers LLC............................G
Franklin (G-7015)

Cox Newspapers LLC............................F 937 866-3331
Miamisburg (G-9684)

Cox Newspapers LLC............................G 513 523-4139
Oxford (G-11062)

Crain Communications Inc....................E 216 522-1383
Cleveland (G-3575)

Crain Communications Inc....................E 330 836-9180
Cuyahoga Falls (G-5536)

Daily Chief Union.................F..... 419 294-2331
Upper Sandusky (G-13438)

Daily Fantasy Circuit Inc.................G..... 614 989-8689
Columbus (G-4868)

Daily Growler Inc.................G..... 614 656-2337
Upper Arlington (G-13430)

Daily Reporter.................E..... 614 224-4835
Columbus (G-4869)

Dayton City Paper Group Llc.................F..... 937 222-8855
Dayton (G-5723)

Defiance Publishing Co Ltd.................B..... 419 784-5441
Defiance (G-6106)

Delaware Gazette Company.................F..... 740 363-1161
Delaware (G-6143)

Delphos Herald Inc.................G..... 419 399-4015
Paulding (G-11154)

Delphos Herald Inc.................D..... 419 695-0015
Delphos (G-6184)

Dispatch Consumer Services.................C..... 740 687-1893
Lancaster (G-8199)

Dispatch Printing Company.................F..... 614 461-5000
Columbus (G-4884)

Dispatch Printing Company.................F.... 740 548-5331
Lewis Center (G-8331)

Dispatch Printing Company.................A..... 614 220-5833
Columbus (G-4883)

Douthit Communications Inc.................D..... 419 855-7465
Millbury (G-9959)

Douthit Communications Inc.................D..... 419 625-5825
Sandusky (G-11828)

Dow Jones & Company Inc.................E..... 419 352-4696
Bowling Green (G-1417)

Euclid Media Group LLC.................F..... 216 241-7550
Cleveland (G-3690)

Fremont Discover Ltd.................G..... 419 332-8696
Fremont (G-7110)

Funny Times Inc.................G..... 216 371-8600
Cleveland (G-3744)

Gannett Stllite Info Ntwrk LLC.................F..... 513 768-8451
Cincinnati (G-2648)

Gannett Stllite Info Ntwrk LLC.................E..... 419 334-1012
Fremont (G-7113)

Gannett Stllite Info Ntwrk LLC.................E..... 304 485-1891
Marietta (G-8918)

Gate West Coast Ventures LLC.................F..... 513 891-1000
Blue Ash (G-1276)

Gazette Publishing Company.................D..... 419 335-2010
Napoleon (G-10280)

Gazette Publishing Company.................E..... 419 483-4190
Oberlin (G-10917)

Greenworld Enterprises Inc.................G..... 800 525-6999
West Chester (G-14123)

Hamilton Journal News Inc.................G..... 513 863-8200
Liberty Township (G-8377)

Hardin County Publishing Co.................E..... 419 674-4066
Kenton (G-8101)

Health Sense Inc.................G..... 440 354-8057
Painesville (G-11093)

Herald Reflector Inc.................E..... 419 668-3771
Norwalk (G-10847)

Hirt Publishing Co Inc.................E..... 419 946-3010
Mount Gilead (G-10210)

Holmes County Hub Inc.................G..... 330 674-1811
Millersburg (G-9987)

Horizon Ohio Publications Inc.................D..... 419 738-2128
Wapakoneta (G-13715)

Horizon Ohio Publications Inc.................F..... 419 394-7414
Saint Marys (G-11738)

Hubbard Publishing Co.................G..... 937 592-3060
Bellefontaine (G-1110)

Iheartcommunications Inc.................G..... 419 223-2060
Lima (G-8418)

Iiot World LLC.................G..... 440 715-0564
Westlake (G-14309)

Indian Lake Shoppers Edge.................G..... 937 843-6600
Russells Point (G-11669)

Isaac Foster Mack Co.................C..... 419 625-5500
Sandusky (G-11843)

Journal Register Company.................D..... 440 245-6901
Lorain (G-8560)

Journal Register Company.................B..... 440 951-0000
Willoughby (G-14473)

King Media Enterprises Inc.................F..... 216 588-6700
Cleveland (G-3921)

Kml Acquisitions Ltd.................G..... 614 732-9777
Plain City (G-11411)

Kroner Publications Inc.................E..... 330 544-5500
Niles (G-10594)

La Prensa Publications Inc.................G..... 419 870-6565
Toledo (G-13027)

Lake Community News.................G..... 440 946-2577
Willoughby (G-14480)

Leader Publications Inc.................G..... 330 665-9595
Fairlawn (G-6806)

Legal News Publishing Co.................E..... 216 696-3322
Cleveland (G-3949)

Marketing Essentials LLC.................E..... 419 629-0080
New Bremen (G-10362)

Marysville Newspaper Inc.................E..... 937 644-9111
Marysville (G-9037)

Medina Hntngton RE Group II LL.................E..... 330 591-2777
Medina (G-9424)

Messenger Publishing Company.................C..... 740 592-6612
Athens (G-644)

Mid American Publishing.................G..... 419 822-5662
Delta (G-6212)

Mirror Publishing Co Inc.................G..... 419 893-8135
Maumee (G-9310)

Morgan County Publishing Co.................G..... 740 962-3377
Mcconnelsville (G-9366)

News Watchman & Paper.................F..... 740 947-2149
Waverly (G-13870)

Newspaper Network Central OH.................G..... 419 524-3545
Mansfield (G-8839)

Nomis Publications Inc.................F..... 330 965-2380
Youngstown (G-14904)

O J C Publishing Co Inc.................G..... 614 337-2055
Columbus (G-5136)

Ocm LLC.................B..... 937 247-2700
Miamisburg (G-9723)

Ogden News Publishing Ohio Inc.................E..... 567 743-9843
Norwalk (G-10858)

Ogden News Publishing Ohio Inc.................E..... 419 625-5500
Sandusky (G-11861)

Ogden Newspapers Inc.................D..... 304 748-0606
Steubenville (G-12408)

Ogden Newspapers Ohio Inc.................F..... 419 448-3200
Tiffin (G-12794)

Ohio Irish American News.................G..... 216 647-1144
Cleveland (G-4115)

Ohio News Network.................G..... 614 460-3700
Columbus (G-5148)

Ohio Newspaper Services Inc.................G..... 614 486-6677
Columbus (G-5149)

Ohio Newspapers Inc.................C..... 937 335-3997
Troy (G-13245)

Ohio Newspapers Inc.................A..... 937 225-2000
Dayton (G-5926)

Ohio Newspapers Foundation.................G..... 614 486-6677
Columbus (G-5150)

Ohio Rights Group.................G..... 614 300-0529
Columbus (G-5152)

Pataskala Post.................F..... 740 964-6226
Pataskala (G-11145)

Peebles Messenger Newspaper.................G..... 937 587-1451
Peebles (G-11171)

Perry County Tribune.................F..... 740 342-4121
New Lexington (G-10405)

Premier Prtg Cntl Ohio Ltd.................E..... 937 642-0988
Marysville (G-9043)

Progressor Times.................G..... 419 396-7567
Carey (G-2062)

Progrssive Communications Corp.................F..... 740 397-5333
Mount Vernon (G-10261)

Record Herald Publishing Co.................E..... 717 762-2151
Cincinnati (G-3035)

Record Publishing Co.................D..... 330 688-0088
Stow (G-12454)

Reporter Newspaper Inc.................F..... 330 535-7061
Akron (G-281)

Richardson Publishing Company.................F..... 330 753-1068
Barberton (G-836)

Rural-Urban Record Inc.................G..... 440 236-8982
Columbia Station (G-4601)

Samuel L Peters LLC.................G..... 513 745-1500
Blue Ash (G-1329)

Schaffner Publication Inc.................G..... 419 732-2154
Port Clinton (G-11452)

Sdg News Group Inc.................F..... 419 929-3411
New London (G-10416)

Sesh Communications.................F..... 513 851-1693
Cincinnati (G-3084)

Smart Business Network Inc.................E..... 440 250-7000
Cleveland (G-4305)

Sojourners Truth Inc.................F..... 419 243-0007
Toledo (G-13133)

Southeast Publications Inc.................F..... 740 732-2341
Caldwell (G-1729)

Spectrum News Ohio.................F..... 614 384-2640
Columbus (G-5283)

Springfield Newspapers Inc.................F..... 937 323-5533
Springfield (G-12376)

Standard Printing Co Inc.................G..... 419 586-2371
Celina (G-2121)

Stark Cnty Fdrtion Cnsrvtion C.................E..... 330 268-1652
Canton (G-2013)

Streamline Media & Pubg LLC.................G..... 614 822-1817
Reynoldsburg (G-11581)

Sylvania Advantage.................G..... 419 725-2695
Sylvania (G-12726)

◆ Syracuse China LLC.................C..... 419 325-2100
Toledo (G-13138)

The Cleveland Jewish Publ Co.................E..... 216 454-8300
Beachwood (G-953)

The Gazette Printing Co Inc.................G..... 440 593-6030
Conneaut (G-5418)

The Gazette Printing Co Inc.................D..... 440 576-9125
Jefferson (G-7984)

The Vindicator Printing Company.................B..... 330 747-1471
Youngstown (G-14946)

Toledo Blade Company.................B..... 419 724-6000
Toledo (G-13148)

Travelers Vacation Guide.................G..... 440 582-4949
North Royalton (G-10786)

Tribune Printing Inc.................G..... 419 542-7764
Hicksville (G-7654)

Trogdon Publishing Inc.................E..... 330 721-7678
Medina (G-9458)

Upper Arlington Crew Inc.................G..... 614 485-0089
Columbus (G-5340)

Vindicator.................G..... 330 841-1600
Warren (G-13808)

Vindicator Printing Company.................E..... 330 744-8611
Youngstown (G-14962)

Welch Publishing Co.................G..... 419 666-5344
Rossford (G-11664)

Welch Publishing Co................................. E 419 874-2528
Perrysburg *(G-11279)*

Winkler Co Inc... G 937 294-2662
Dayton *(G-6082)*

Wooster Daily Record Inc LLC................. C 330 264-1125
Wooster *(G-14700)*

2721 Periodicals

400 SW 7th Street Partners Ltd.............. E 440 826-4700
Cincinnati *(G-2320)*

400 SW 7th Street Partners Ltd.............. E 772 781-2144
Cincinnati *(G-2321)*

614 Media Group LLC................................ F 614 488-4400
Columbus *(G-4654)*

Adams Street Publishing Co Inc............. E 419 244-9859
Toledo *(G-12864)*

Agri Communicators Inc........................... G 614 273-0465
Columbus *(G-4679)*

AGS Custom Graphics Inc....................... D 330 963-7770
Macedonia *(G-8676)*

▲ Alonovus Corp....................................... E 330 674-2300
Millersburg *(G-9968)*

American Ceramic Society....................... E 614 890-4700
Westerville *(G-14202)*

American Lawyers Co Inc......................... F 440 333-5190
Westlake *(G-14286)*

▲ Amos Media Company............................ C 937 498-2121
Sidney *(G-11992)*

Arens Corporation..................................... G 937 473-2028
Covington *(G-5489)*

Arens Corporation..................................... F 937 473-2028
Covington *(G-5488)*

▲ Asm International..................................... D 440 338-5151
Novelty *(G-10879)*

Atv Insider... G 740 282-7102
Steubenville *(G-12399)*

Babcox Media Inc..................................... D 330 670-1234
Akron *(G-70)*

Baker Media Group LLC.......................... F 330 253-0056
Akron *(G-71)*

Bbm Fairway Inc....................................... G 330 899-2200
Uniontown *(G-13417)*

▲ Benjamin Media Inc................................ E 330 467-7588
Brecksville *(G-1459)*

Bluffton News Pubg & Prtg Co................ F 419 358-8010
Bluffton *(G-1357)*

Breakwall Publishing LLC........................ F 813 575-2570
Medina *(G-9385)*

C & S Associates Inc............................... E 440 461-9661
Highland Heights *(G-7655)*

Carmel Publishing Inc.............................. G 330 478-9200
Canton *(G-1861)*

Cars and Parts Magazine......................... D 937 498-0803
Sidney *(G-12001)*

Center For Inquiry Inc.............................. G 330 671-7192
Peninsula *(G-11181)*

Cincinnati Family Magazine...................... G 513 842-0077
Blue Ash *(G-1262)*

Cincinnati Media LLC............................... G 513 562-2755
Cincinnati *(G-2481)*

City Visitor Inc.. G 216 661-6666
Hudson *(G-7837)*

Crain Communications Inc....................... E 216 522-1383
Cleveland *(G-3575)*

Crain Communications Inc....................... E 330 836-9180
Cuyahoga Falls *(G-5536)*

Cruisin Times Magazine........................... G 440 331-4615
Rocky River *(G-11633)*

Dominion Enterprises................................ F 216 472-1870
Cleveland *(G-3624)*

Ertel Publishing Inc.................................. G 937 767-1433
Yellow Springs *(G-14788)*

▲ F+w Media Inc.. A 513 531-2690
Blue Ash *(G-1274)*

Family Motor Coach Assn Inc.................. E 513 474-3622
Cincinnati *(G-2611)*

Family Motor Coaching Inc...................... D 513 474-3622
Cincinnati *(G-2612)*

Gardner Business Media Inc.................... F 513 527-8800
Cincinnati *(G-2650)*

Gardner Business Media Inc.................... C 513 527-8800
Cincinnati *(G-2651)*

Generals Books... G 614 870-1861
Columbus *(G-4949)*

Gie Media Inc... E 800 456-0707
Cleveland *(G-3775)*

Gongwer News Service Inc...................... F 614 221-1992
Columbus *(G-4962)*

Great Lakes Publishing Company........... D 216 771-2833
Cleveland *(G-3793)*

Greater Cincinnati Bowl Assn.................. E 513 761-7387
Cincinnati *(G-2689)*

▲ Highlights For Children Inc.................... C 614 486-0631
Columbus *(G-4983)*

Incorprted Trstees of The Gspl............... D 216 749-2100
Middleburg Heights *(G-9773)*

Informa Media Inc.................................... A 216 696-7000
Cleveland *(G-3859)*

Insights Sccess Media Tech LLC............ E 614 602-1754
Dublin *(G-6310)*

Kent Information Services Inc.................. G 330 672-2110
Kent *(G-8042)*

Kenyon Review.. G 740 427-5208
Gambier *(G-7211)*

Kyle Media Inc.. F 877 775-2538
Toledo *(G-13025)*

Legal News Publishing Co....................... E 216 696-3322
Cleveland *(G-3949)*

Lifestyle Media Group LLC...................... F 954 377-9470
Akron *(G-206)*

Lippincott and Peto Inc........................... G 330 864-2122
Akron *(G-207)*

Liturgical Publications Inc....................... D 216 325-6825
Cleveland *(G-3964)*

▲ Lorenz Corporation................................ D 937 228-6118
Dayton *(G-5855)*

Lyle Printing & Publishing Co.................. E 330 337-3419
Salem *(G-11796)*

Marketing Essentials LLC........................ F 419 629-0080
New Bremen *(G-10362)*

Matthew Bender & Company Inc............. C 518 487-3000
Miamisburg *(G-9710)*

Meister Media Worldwide Inc................... D 440 942-2000
Willoughby *(G-14486)*

Mid American Publishing.......................... G 419 822-5662
Delta *(G-6212)*

New Publishing Holdings LLC................. A 513 531-2690
Blue Ash *(G-1313)*

North Coast Minority Media LLC............. G 216 407-4327
Cleveland *(G-4088)*

Ohio Designer Craftsmen Entps............. F 614 486-7119
Columbus *(G-5141)*

Pardson Inc... F 740 373-5285
Marietta *(G-8934)*

Pearson Education Inc.............................. G 614 876-0371
Columbus *(G-5180)*

Pearson Education Inc.............................. E 614 841-3700
Columbus *(G-5181)*

Peninsula Publishing LLC........................ G 330 524-3359
Independence *(G-7914)*

Pjl Enterprise Inc..................................... F 937 293-1415
Moraine *(G-10183)*

Publishing Group Ltd................................ F 614 572-1240
Columbus *(G-5213)*

Rector Inc.. G 440 892-0444
Westlake *(G-14327)*

Relx Inc... G 937 865-6800
Miamisburg *(G-9730)*

Rubber World Magazine Inc..................... G 330 864-2122
Akron *(G-294)*

Schaeffers Investment Research Inc....... D 513 589-3800
Blue Ash *(G-1331)*

Sesh Communications............................... F 513 851-1693
Cincinnati *(G-3084)*

▲ St Media Group Intl Inc......................... D 513 421-2050
Blue Ash *(G-1332)*

▲ Standard Publishing LLC....................... C 513 931-4050
Cincinnati *(G-3111)*

Sterling Associates Inc............................ G 330 630-3500
Akron *(G-318)*

Suburban Communications Inc................ G 440 632-0130
Middlefield *(G-9829)*

Telex Communications Inc....................... F 419 865-0972
Toledo *(G-13140)*

Toastmasters International........................ F 937 429-2680
Dayton *(G-5624)*

Venue Lifestyle & Event Guide................ G 513 405-6822
Cincinnati *(G-3200)*

Welch Publishing Co................................. E 419 874-2528
Perrysburg *(G-11279)*

Youngs Publishing Inc............................. G 937 259-6575
Dayton *(G-5626)*

2731 Book publishing

American Legal Publishing Corp............. E 513 421-4248
Cincinnati *(G-2361)*

▲ Asm International..................................... D 440 338-5151
Novelty *(G-10879)*

Auguste Moone Enterprises Ltd.............. E 216 333-9248
Cleveland Heights *(G-4527)*

B & S Transport Inc................................. G 330 767-4319
Navarre *(G-10302)*

▼ Bearing Precious Seed Intl Inc............. G 513 575-1706
Milford *(G-9924)*

Benchmark Education Co LLC................. C 845 215-9808
Groveport *(G-7425)*

▲ Bendon Inc... D 419 207-3600
Ashland *(G-521)*

▼ Bookfactory LLC.................................... E 937 226-7100
Dayton *(G-5682)*

◆ Bookmasters Inc.................................... C 419 281-1802
Ashland *(G-533)*

Bright Star Books Inc.............................. G 330 888-2156
Akron *(G-84)*

Carmel Publishing Inc.............................. G 330 478-9200
Canton *(G-1861)*

Cengage Learning Inc.............................. C 513 234-5967
Mason *(G-9078)*

Cengage Learning Inc.............................. B 415 839-2300
Mason *(G-9080)*

◆ Cengage Learning Inc........................... D 617 289-7700
Mason *(G-9079)*

Cengage Lrng Holdings II Inc................. E 617 289-7700
Mason *(G-9081)*

Christian Missionary Alliance.................. C 380 208-6200
Reynoldsburg *(G-11562)*

Conway Greene Co Inc............................ G 440 230-2627
North Royalton *(G-10758)*

Cox Ohio Publishing................................. F 937 743-6700
Franklin *(G-7016)*

CSS Publishing Company......................... F 419 227-1818
Lima *(G-8398)*

Decent Hill Publishers LLC...................... G 216 548-1255
Hilliard *(G-7680)*

Dreamscape Media LLC............................ G 877 983-7326
Holland *(G-7757)*

Elloras Cave Publishing Inc.................. G..... 330 253-3521
Akron *(G-132)*

Equipping Ministries Intl Inc................ G..... 513 742-1100
Cincinnati *(G-2597)*

▲ F+w Media Inc.................................. A..... 513 531-2690
Blue Ash *(G-1274)*

Follett Hgher Edcatn Group Inc.......... C..... 419 281-5100
Ashland *(G-535)*

Gardner Business Media Inc............... F..... 513 527-8800
Cincinnati *(G-2650)*

Gardner Business Media Inc............... C..... 513 527-8800
Cincinnati *(G-2651)*

Gie Media Inc.................................... E..... 800 456-0707
Cleveland *(G-3775)*

▲ Golf Galaxy Golfworks Inc............... C..... 740 328-4193
Newark *(G-10504)*

Highlights Consumer Svcs Inc........... F..... 570 253-1164
Columbus *(G-4982)*

Horrorhound Ltd................................ F..... 513 239-7263
Cincinnati *(G-2733)*

Hubbard Company............................. E..... 419 784-4455
Defiance *(G-6111)*

J S C Publishing................................ G..... 614 424-6911
Columbus *(G-5027)*

Just Business Inc.............................. F..... 866 577-3303
Dayton *(G-5835)*

Kelley Communication Dev................. G..... 937 298-6132
Dayton *(G-5838)*

Kendall/Hunt Publishing Co............... C..... 877 275-4725
Cincinnati *(G-2792)*

Ketman Corporation........................... G..... 330 262-1688
Wooster *(G-14658)*

Lachina Creative Inc.......................... E..... 216 292-7959
Cleveland *(G-3934)*

Liturgical Publications Inc.................. D..... 216 325-6825
Cleveland *(G-3964)*

Marysville Newspaper Inc.................. E..... 937 644-9111
Marysville *(G-9037)*

▲ Master Communications Inc............. G..... 208 821-3473
Cincinnati *(G-2849)*

Matthew Bender & Company Inc......... C..... 518 487-3000
Miamisburg *(G-9710)*

McGraw-Hill Education Inc................. G..... 760 931-1290
Blacklick *(G-1225)*

McGraw-Hill Global Educatn LLC........ B..... 614 755-4151
Blacklick *(G-1226)*

McGraw-Hill Schl Edcatn Hldngs........ A..... 419 207-7400
Ashland *(G-551)*

McGraw-Hill Schl Edcatn Hldngs........ A..... 614 430-4000
Columbus *(G-4642)*

New Publishing Holdings LLC............ A..... 513 531-2690
Blue Ash *(G-1313)*

North Coast Media LLC..................... D..... 216 706-3700
Cleveland *(G-4087)*

Pardson Inc...................................... F..... 740 373-5285
Marietta *(G-8934)*

▲ Precision Metalforming Assn........... E..... 216 901-8800
Independence *(G-7916)*

Rebecca Benston.............................. F..... 937 360-0669
Springfield *(G-12367)*

Relx Inc... G..... 937 865-6800
Miamisburg *(G-9731)*

Reynolds Industries Group LLC......... E..... 614 363-9149
Blacklick *(G-1228)*

Scepter Publishers............................ G..... 212 354-0670
Strongsville *(G-12594)*

▲ St Media Group Intl Inc................... D..... 513 421-2050
Blue Ash *(G-1332)*

Swagg Productions2015llc................. F..... 614 601-7414
Worthington *(G-14726)*

▲ Teachers Publishing Group............. F..... 614 486-0631
Hilliard *(G-7705)*

Tgs International Inc.......................... F..... 330 893-4828
Berlin *(G-1200)*

Tomahawk Entrmt Group LLC............. F..... 216 505-0548
Euclid *(G-6680)*

University of Toledo........................... F..... 419 530-2311
Toledo *(G-13170)*

Wolters Kluwer Clinical D................... D..... 330 650-6506
Hudson *(G-7862)*

Woodburn Press Ltd.......................... G..... 937 293-9245
Dayton *(G-6085)*

World Book Company......................... A..... 440 892-3000
Westlake *(G-14346)*

World Harvest Church Inc.................. C..... 614 837-1990
Canal Winchester *(G-1800)*

▲ Zaner-Bloser Inc............................. C..... 614 486-0221
Columbus *(G-5380)*

2732 Book printing

American Printing & Lithog Co............ F..... 513 867-0602
Hamilton *(G-7463)*

Hf Group LLC.................................... C..... 440 729-9411
Newbury *(G-10554)*

Hf Group LLC.................................... F..... 440 729-2445
Aurora *(G-674)*

Hubbard Company............................. E..... 419 784-4455
Defiance *(G-6111)*

J & L Management Corporation........... G..... 440 205-1199
Mentor *(G-9537)*

Lsc Communications Inc.................... A..... 419 935-0111
Willard *(G-14403)*

Morse Enterprises Inc....................... G..... 513 229-3600
Mason *(G-9129)*

Multi-Craft Litho Inc.......................... E..... 859 581-2754
Blue Ash *(G-1312)*

Quebecor World Johnson Hardin........ G..... 614 326-0299
Cincinnati *(G-3019)*

Society of The Precious Blood........... E..... 419 925-4516
Celina *(G-2120)*

The Press of Ohio Inc....................... B..... 330 678-5868
Kent *(G-8090)*

2741 Miscellaneous publishing

▼ 48 Hr Books Inc............................. E..... 330 374-6917
Twinsburg *(G-13264)*

7octopus7 Inc................................... F..... 513 677-5044
Cincinnati *(G-2322)*

Action Express Inc............................ G..... 929 351-3620
Columbus *(G-4672)*

Ahalogy... E..... 314 974-5599
Cincinnati *(G-2344)*

Alscommunity................................... F..... 215 478-5095
Coventry Township *(G-5480)*

American City Bus Journals Inc.......... D..... 513 337-9450
Cincinnati *(G-2358)*

American Gild of English Hndbe......... G..... 937 438-0085
Cincinnati *(G-2359)*

American Legal Publishing Corp........ E..... 513 421-4248
Cincinnati *(G-2361)*

American Publishers LLC................... D..... 419 626-0623
Huron *(G-7867)*

Ameritech Publishing Inc................... A..... 614 895-6123
Columbus *(G-4704)*

Ameritech Publishing Inc................... A..... 330 896-6037
Uniontown *(G-13416)*

▲ Amos Media Company..................... C..... 937 498-2121
Sidney *(G-11992)*

Anadem Inc...................................... G..... 614 262-2539
Columbus *(G-4710)*

Archer Publishing LLC....................... G..... 440 338-5233
Bay Village *(G-899)*

Berry Company.................................. G..... 513 768-7800
Cincinnati *(G-2408)*

Bowmanmultimedia LLC..................... F..... 419 405-8648
Columbus *(G-4772)*

Cbus Inc.. F..... 614 327-6971
Pickerington *(G-11291)*

Cerkl Incorporated............................ D..... 513 813-8425
Blue Ash *(G-1261)*

Checkered Express Inc...................... F..... 330 530-8169
Girard *(G-7268)*

Christian Blue Pages......................... G..... 937 847-2583
Miamisburg *(G-9682)*

Clark Optimization LLC...................... E..... 330 417-2164
Canton *(G-1867)*

Cleveland Press................................ G..... 440 442-5101
Cleveland *(G-3519)*

Cleveland Press................................ G..... 440 289-3227
Cleveland *(G-3520)*

Computer Workshop Inc..................... G..... 216 901-0106
Cleveland *(G-3557)*

Computer Workshop Inc..................... E..... 614 798-9505
Dublin *(G-6291)*

County Classifieds............................ G..... 937 592-8847
Bellefontaine *(G-1102)*

Cox Publishing Hq............................ G..... 937 225-2000
Dayton *(G-5712)*

Deemsys Inc..................................... D..... 614 322-9928
Gahanna *(G-7155)*

▲ Depot Direct Inc............................. E..... 419 661-1233
Perrysburg *(G-11215)*

Diocesan Publications Inc.................. E..... 614 718-9500
Dublin *(G-6293)*

Discover Publications......................... G..... 877 872-3080
Columbus *(G-4882)*

Dotcentral LLC.................................. F..... 330 809-0112
Massillon *(G-9186)*

Douthit Communications Inc............... D..... 419 625-5825
Sandusky *(G-11828)*

Drawnear Inc.................................... G..... 567 215-5305
Ashland *(G-533)*

Ebsco Industries Inc......................... F..... 513 398-3695
Mason *(G-9096)*

▼ Educational Direction Inc................ G..... 330 836-8439
Fairlawn *(G-6799)*

Elloras Cave Publishing Inc............... G..... 330 253-3521
Akron *(G-132)*

Estr Publications............................... G..... 614 940-9996
Columbus *(G-4910)*

Evans Creative Group LLC................. G..... 614 657-9439
Columbus *(G-4914)*

Fleetmaster Express Inc..................... D..... 866 425-0666
Findlay *(G-6867)*

Franklin Covey Co............................. G..... 513 680-0975
Cincinnati *(G-2639)*

Fsqpronet LLC.................................. F..... 330 942-6014
Youngstown *(G-14859)*

Fullgospel Publishing........................ F..... 216 339-1973
Shaker Heights *(G-11930)*

Gardner Business Media Inc............... C..... 513 527-8800
Cincinnati *(G-2651)*

Gatekeeper Press LLC....................... F..... 866 535-0913
Grove City *(G-7388)*

Gb Liquidating Company Inc............... E..... 513 248-7600
Milford *(G-9935)*

Gordon Bernard Company LLC........... E..... 513 248-7600
Milford *(G-9936)*

Graphic Paper Products Corp............. D..... 937 325-5503
Springfield *(G-12315)*

Gray & Company Publishers............... G..... 216 431-2665
Cleveland *(G-3787)*

Haines Publishing Inc........................ F..... 330 494-9111
Canton *(G-1907)*

Identity Group LLC............................ G..... 614 337-6167
Westerville *(G-14213)*

Igloo Press LLC........................ G 614 787-5528
Worthington (G-14714)

Intelacomm Inc........................ G 888 610-9250
Newbury (G-10555)

IPA Ltd.................................... F 614 523-3974
Columbus (G-5024)

ITM Marketing Inc..................... C 740 295-3575
Coshocton (G-5457)

▲ Kaeden Publishing............... G 440 617-1400
Westlake (G-14312)

L J Publishing LLC................... G 888 749-5994
Hinckley (G-7734)

Lake Publishing Inc.................. G 440 299-8500
Mentor (G-9549)

Lanier & Associates Inc............ G 216 391-7735
Cleveland (G-3940)

▲ Lexisnexis Group.................. C 937 865-6800
Miamisburg (G-9709)

Liette L & S Express LLC.......... G 419 394-7077
Saint Marys (G-11741)

▲ Lorenz Corporation.............. D 937 228-6118
Dayton (G-5855)

Lsc Communications Inc........... A 419 935-0111
Willard (G-14403)

M R I Education Foundation....... E 513 281-3400
Cincinnati (G-2834)

Marketing Essentials LLC......... E 419 629-0080
New Bremen (G-10362)

Mid American Publishing........... G 419 822-5662
Delta (G-6212)

Midwest Menu Mate Inc............ F 740 323-2599
Newark (G-10521)

Miller Express Inc.................... G 330 714-6751
Copley (G-5435)

N2 Publishing......................... F 937 641-8277
West Carrollton (G-13930)

Nomis Publications Inc............. F 330 965-2380
Youngstown (G-14904)

Northstar Publishing Inc............ G 330 721-9126
Medina (G-9429)

Ogr Publishing Inc................... G 330 757-3020
Hilliard (G-7690)

Ohlinger Dev & Editorial Co....... D 614 261-5360
Columbus (G-5157)

Ohlinger Publishing Svcs Inc...... E 614 261-5360
Columbus (G-5158)

Omnipresence Cleaning LLC...... G 937 250-4749
Dayton (G-5927)

ONeil & Associates Inc............. C 937 865-0800
Miamisburg (G-9725)

Orange Frazer Press Inc............ G 937 382-3196
Wilmington (G-14585)

Organized Lightning LLC........... G 407 965-2730
Blue Ash (G-1315)

Peebles Creative Group Inc....... G 614 487-2011
Dublin (G-6329)

Pflaum Publishing Group........... G 937 293-1415
Moraine (G-10181)

Pjl Enterprise Inc.................... D 937 293-1415
Moraine (G-10182)

▲ Posterservice Incorporated.... G 513 577-7100
Cincinnati (G-2977)

Pressed Coffee Bar & Eatery...... G 330 746-8030
Youngstown (G-14920)

Printery Inc............................ G 513 574-1099
Cincinnati (G-2983)

Pro Press Inc.......................... F 216 631-8200
Cleveland (G-4197)

Promatch Solutions LLC........... F 877 299-0185
Moraine (G-10188)

Publishing Group Ltd................ F 614 572-1240
Columbus (G-5213)

▼ Quadriga Americas LLC......... G 614 890-6090
Westerville (G-14228)

Quality Solutions Inc................ E 440 933-9946
Cleveland (G-4216)

Questline Inc.......................... E 614 255-3166
Dublin (G-6338)

▼ Rcl Publishing Group LLC....... G 972 390-6400
Cincinnati (G-3033)

Ready Media LLC..................... G 614 441-8178
Columbus (G-4648)

Richland Source....................... E 419 610-2100
Mansfield (G-8850)

Road Apple Music..................... G 513 217-4444
Middletown (G-9891)

▲ S J T Enterprises Inc............. E 440 617-1100
Westlake (G-14329)

Samhain Publishing Ltd (llc)....... G 513 453-4688
Cincinnati (G-3061)

Schaeffers Investment Research Inc.. D 513 589-3800
Blue Ash (G-1331)

Scheel Publishing LLC.............. E 216 731-8616
Willoughby (G-14521)

Scriptype Publishing Inc............ F 330 659-0303
Richfield (G-11599)

See Ya There Inc..................... G 614 856-9037
Millersport (G-10025)

Senior Impact Publications LLC... F 513 791-8800
Cincinnati (G-3079)

Service Express LLC................. F 513 942-6170
West Chester (G-14143)

Severn River Publishing LLC....... G 703 819-4686
Kings Mills (G-8137)

Snook Advertising Al Publisher... G 614 866-3333
Reynoldsburg (G-11580)

Star Brite Express Car WA......... G 330 674-0062
Millersburg (G-10010)

Suburban Communications Inc.... G 440 632-0130
Middlefield (G-9829)

The419................................... F 855 451-1018
Lima (G-8456)

Tiny Lion Music Groups............. G 419 874-7353
Perrysburg (G-11271)

Trogdon Publishing Inc............. E 330 721-7678
Medina (G-9458)

▲ Universal Direct Fulfillment Corp..... F 330 650-5000
Hudson (G-7861)

Van-Griner LLC........................ G 419 733-7951
Cincinnati (G-3103)

Walter H Drane Co Inc.............. G 216 514-1022
Beachwood (G-957)

Willis Music Company............... F 513 671-3288
Cincinnati (G-3225)

Woodburn Press Ltd................. G 937 293-9245
Dayton (G-6085)

Works In Progress Inc............... F 802 658-3797
Cincinnati (G-3231)

World Book Company................ A 440 892-3000
Westlake (G-14346)

2752 Commercial printing, lithographic

1one Stop Printing Inc.............. F 614 216-1438
Columbus (G-4652)

7 7 Print Solutions LLC............. G 513 600-4597
Fairfield (G-6704)

A F Krainz Co.......................... G 216 431-4341
Cleveland (G-3280)

A Grade Notes Inc.................... G 614 299-9999
Dublin (G-6271)

A Z Printing Inc....................... G 513 733-3900
Cincinnati (G-2326)

A-A Blueprint Co Inc................. E 330 794-8803
Akron (G-10)

Academy Graphic Comm Inc...... F 216 661-2550
Cleveland (G-3289)

Acme Duplicating Co Inc........... G 216 241-1241
Westlake (G-14283)

▲ Activities Press Inc.............. E 440 953-1200
Mentor (G-9469)

Adcraft Decals Incorporated...... E 216 524-2934
Cleveland (G-3297)

Admark Printing Inc.................. G 937 833-5111
Brookville (G-1561)

Admiral Products Company Inc... E 216 671-0600
Cleveland (G-3299)

Advantage Print Solutions LLC... G 614 519-2392
Columbus (G-4677)

AGS Custom Graphics Inc.......... D 330 963-7770
Macedonia (G-8676)

Akland Printing....................... F 330 467-8292
Northfield (G-10791)

Akron Litho-Print Company Inc... F 330 434-3145
Akron (G-34)

Akron Thermography Inc............ F 330 896-9712
Akron (G-44)

Akron Thermography Inc............ G 330 896-9712
Akron (G-45)

▲ Alberts Screen Print Inc......... C 330 753-7559
Norton (G-10818)

All Points Printing Inc............... G 440 585-1125
Wickliffe (G-14365)

Allen Graphics Inc.................... G 440 349-4100
Solon (G-12075)

Alliance Publishing Co Inc......... C 330 453-1304
Alliance (G-372)

Allu Inc.................................. G 513 624-9333
Cincinnati (G-2352)

AlphaGraphics........................ G 513 204-6070
Mason (G-9059)

AlphaGraphics 507 Inc.............. G 440 878-9700
Strongsville (G-12535)

American Colorscans Inc........... E 614 895-0233
Columbus (G-4694)

American Printing Inc................ F 330 630-1121
Akron (G-58)

American Printing & Lithog Co.... F 513 867-0602
Hamilton (G-7463)

Amsvie OH LLC....................... D 937 885-8000
Miamisburg (G-9665)

Anderson Graphics Inc.............. E 330 745-2165
Barberton (C-703)

Andrin Enterprises Inc.............. F 937 276-7794
Moraine (G-10146)

Angel Prtg & Reproduction Co.... F 216 631-5225
Cleveland (G-3360)

Arens Corporation................... G 937 473-2028
Covington (G-5489)

Arens Corporation................... F 937 473-2028
Covington (G-5488)

Armstrong Stationery Co Corp.... G 513 891-0667
Cincinnati (G-2376)

Auld Corporation..................... G 614 454-1010
Columbus (G-4734)

Avon Lake Printing.................. G 440 933-2078
Avon Lake (G-749)

B & B Printing Graphics Inc........ F 419 893-7068
Maumee (G-9263)

B R Printers Inc....................... D 513 271-6035
Cincinnati (G-2396)

Baesman Group Inc.................. D 614 771-2300
Hilliard (G-7674)

Banbury Investments Inc........... G 513 677-4500
Cincinnati (G-2399)

Bansal Enterprises Inc.............. F 330 633-9355
Akron (G-72)

Barnhart Printing Corp............................ G..... 330 456-2279
  Canton *(G-1837)*
	CB Graphics LLC................................... G..... 216 749-5577
	  Cleveland *(G-3478)*
		DC Reprographics Co............................. F..... 614 297-1200
		  Columbus *(G-4873)*

Bates Printing Inc................................ F..... 330 833-5830
  Massillon *(G-9174)*
	Cbp Co Inc.. F..... 513 860-9053
	  Cincinnati *(G-2444)*
		Deerfield Ventures Inc........................... G..... 614 875-0688
		  Grove City *(G-7381)*

Bay Business Forms Inc......................... F..... 937 322-3000
  Springfield *(G-12285)*
	Century Graphics Inc............................. G..... 614 895-7698
	  Westerville *(G-14206)*
		Delaware Data Products Inc..................... G..... 740 369-5449
		  Delaware *(G-6142)*

BCT Alarm Services Inc......................... G..... 440 669-8153
  Lorain *(G-8546)*
	Cincinnati Convertors Inc....................... G..... 513 731-6600
	  Cincinnati *(G-2472)*
		Delphos Herald Inc.............................. D..... 419 695-0015
		  Delphos *(G-6184)*

Beckman Xmo...................................... G..... 614 864-2232
  Columbus *(G-4747)*
	Cincinnati Print Solutions LLC.................. G..... 513 943-9500
	  Milford *(G-9929)*
		Deshea Printing Company........................ G..... 330 336-7601
		  Wadsworth *(G-13635)*

Berea Printing Company......................... G..... 440 243-1080
  Berea *(G-1161)*
	City of Cleveland................................ E..... 216 664-3013
	  Cleveland *(G-3499)*
		Dewitt Group Inc................................. F..... 614 847-5919
		  Columbus *(G-4879)*

Best Graphics & Printing Inc................... G..... 513 535-3529
  Cincinnati *(G-2409)*
	City Printing Co Inc............................. F..... 330 747-5691
	  Youngstown *(G-14837)*
		Digital Color Intl LLC.......................... F
		  Akron *(G-123)*

Bethart Enterprises Inc......................... F..... 513 863-6161
  Hamilton *(G-7470)*
	Clints Printing Inc.............................. G..... 937 426-2771
	  Dayton *(G-5703)*
		Direct Digital Graphics Inc..................... G..... 330 405-3770
		  Twinsburg *(G-13295)*

Bindery & Spc Pressworks Inc.................. D..... 614 873-4623
  Plain City *(G-11398)*
	Color Bar Printing Centers Inc................. G..... 216 595-3939
	  Cleveland *(G-3546)*
		Directconnectgroup Ltd.......................... G..... 216 281-2866
		  Cleveland *(G-3616)*

Bis Printing...................................... G..... 440 951-2606
  Willoughby *(G-14431)*
	Color Process Inc............................... E..... 440 268-7100
	  Seville *(G-11915)*
		Distributor Graphics Inc........................ G..... 440 260-0024
		  Cleveland *(G-3620)*

Bizzy Bee Printing Inc.......................... G..... 614 771-1222
  Columbus *(G-4757)*
	Commercial Prtg Greenville Inc................. G..... 937 548-3835
	  Greenville *(G-7339)*
		Dla Document Services........................... F..... 937 257-6014
		  Dayton *(G-5610)*

Black River Group Inc.......................... E..... 419 524-6699
  Mansfield *(G-8765)*
	▲ Consolidated Graphics Group Inc........... C..... 216 881-9191
	  Cleveland *(G-3559)*
		Docmann Printing & Assoc Inc................... G..... 440 975-1775
		  Solon *(G-12101)*

Bloch Printing Company......................... G..... 330 576-6760
  Copley *(G-5431)*
	Consolidated Graphics Inc...................... C..... 740 654-2112
	  Lancaster *(G-8189)*
		Document Concepts Inc........................... F..... 330 575-5685
		  North Canton *(G-10636)*

Blooms Printing Inc............................. G..... 740 922-1765
  Dennison *(G-6216)*
	Copley Ohio Newspapers Inc.................... C..... 330 364-5577
	  New Philadelphia *(G-10439)*
		Doll Inc.. G..... 419 586-7880
		  Celina *(G-2103)*

Blt Inc.. F..... 513 631-5050
  Norwood *(G-10866)*
	Copy King Inc.................................... F..... 216 861-3377
	  Cleveland *(G-3567)*
		Donnelley Financial LLC......................... G..... 216 621-8384
		  Cleveland *(G-3626)*

Blue Crescent Enterprises Inc................. G..... 440 878-9700
  Strongsville *(G-12545)*
	Corporate Dcment Solutions Inc................ G..... 513 595-8200
	  Cincinnati *(G-2518)*
		▲ Dorn Color LLC............................... C..... 216 634-2252
		  Cleveland *(G-3627)*

Bodnar Printing Co Inc.......................... F..... 440 277-8295
  Lorain *(G-8547)*
	COS Blueprint Inc............................... E..... 330 376-0022
	  Akron *(G-107)*
		Dsk Imaging LLC................................. F..... 513 554-1797
		  Blue Ash *(G-1268)*

◆ Bookmasters Inc.............................. C..... 419 281-1802
  Ashland *(G-522)*
	County Classifieds.............................. G..... 937 592-8847
	  Bellefontaine *(G-1102)*
		Duck-T Printing LLC............................. F..... 216 312-0838
		  Cleveland *(G-3635)*

Bornhorst Printing Company Inc................ G..... 419 738-5901
  Wapakoneta *(G-13707)*
	Covap Inc... F..... 513 793-1855
	  Blue Ash *(G-1264)*
		Duke Graphics Inc............................... E..... 440 946-0606
		  Willoughby *(G-14450)*

BP 10 Inc... E..... 513 346-3900
  Hamilton *(G-7472)*
	Cox Printing Company............................ G..... 937 382-2312
	  Wilmington *(G-14576)*
		Duncan Press Corporation....................... E..... 330 477-4529
		  North Canton *(G-10637)*

Bramkamp Printing Company Inc................ G..... 513 241-1865
  Blue Ash *(G-1255)*
	Coyne Graphic Finishing Inc................... E..... 740 397-6232
	  Mount Vernon *(G-10241)*
		Dupli-Systems Inc............................... C..... 440 234-9415
		  Strongsville *(G-12555)*

Brandon Screen Printing........................ F..... 419 229-9837
  Lima *(G-8391)*
	Cpmm Services Group Inc........................ G..... 614 447-0165
	  Columbus *(G-4857)*
		◆ Dynamic Design & Systems Inc............. G..... 440 708-1010
		  Chagrin Falls *(G-2159)*

Brass Bull 1 LLC................................ G..... 740 335-8030
  Wshngtn Ct Hs *(G-14735)*
	Creative Impressions Inc....................... F..... 937 435-5296
	  Dayton *(G-5714)*
		E Bee Printing Inc.............................. G..... 614 224-0416
		  Columbus *(G-4893)*

Brentwood Printing & Sty....................... G..... 513 522-2679
  Cincinnati *(G-2421)*
	Crest Graphics Inc.............................. F..... 513 271-2200
	  Blue Ash *(G-1265)*
		Earl D Arnold Printing Company................. E..... 513 533-6900
		  Cincinnati *(G-2574)*

Brothers Printing Co Inc........................ G..... 216 621-6050
  Cleveland *(G-3444)*
	Crossbridge Mktg & Media Inc.................. G..... 330 682-5066
	  Orrville *(G-10979)*
		Eg Enterprise Services Inc...................... G..... 216 431-3300
		  Cleveland *(G-3658)*

Buckeye Business Forms Inc.................... G..... 614 882-1890
  Columbus *(G-4784)*
	Culaine Inc....................................... G..... 419 345-4984
	  Toledo *(G-12934)*
		Electronic Printing Pdts Inc.................... E..... 800 882-4050
		  Stow *(G-12428)*

Bucyrus Graphics Inc........................... F..... 419 562-2906
  Bucyrus *(G-1673)*
	Curless Printing Company...................... E..... 937 783-2403
	  Blanchester *(G-1235)*
		Empire Printing Inc............................. G..... 513 242-3900
		  Fairfield *(G-6732)*

Bush Inc... G..... 216 362-6700
  Cleveland *(G-3454)*
	Curv Imaging LLC................................ G..... 614 890-2878
	  Westerville *(G-14251)*
		Engler Printing Co.............................. G..... 419 332-2181
		  Fremont *(G-7106)*

C Massouh Printing Co Inc...................... F..... 330 408-7330
  Canal Fulton *(G-1774)*
	Custom Graphics Inc............................ D..... 330 963-7770
	  Macedonia *(G-8682)*
		Enlarging Arts Inc.............................. G..... 330 434-3433
		  Akron *(G-136)*

Capehart Enterprises LLC....................... F..... 614 769-7746
  Columbus *(G-4795)*
	Custom Imprint................................... F..... 440 238-4488
	  Strongsville *(G-12551)*
		Ennis Inc... E..... 800 537-8648
		  Toledo *(G-12954)*

Capitol Citicom Inc.............................. G..... 614 472-2679
  Columbus *(G-4799)*
	Cwh Graphics LLC................................ G..... 866 241-8515
	  Bedford Heights *(G-1075)*
		Enquirer Printing Co Inc........................ F..... 513 241-1956
		  Cincinnati *(G-2591)*

Capitol Square Printing Inc.................... G..... 614 221-2850
  Columbus *(G-4800)*
	D & J Printing Inc.............................. C..... 330 678-5868
	  Kent *(G-8024)*
		Envoi Design Inc................................ G..... 513 651-4229
		  Cincinnati *(G-2593)*

Carbon Web Print LLC............................ E..... 216 402-3504
  Willoughby Hills *(G-14556)*
	Daubenmires Printing Co LLC................... G..... 513 425-7223
	  Middletown *(G-9853)*
		▲ Etched Metal Company........................ E..... 440 248-0240
		  Solon *(G-12109)*

Carbonless On Demandcom LLC................ F..... 330 837-8611
  Massillon *(G-9177)*
	David A and Mary A Mathis...................... G..... 330 837-8611
	  (G-9185)
		Eugene Stewart.................................. G..... 937 898-1117
		  Dayton *(G-5770)*

Cardinal Printing Inc............................ G..... 330 773-7300
  Akron *(G-89)*
	◆ Davis Printing Company...................... E..... 330 745-3113
	  Barberton *(G-803)*
		▲ Eurostampa North America Inc.............. E..... 513 821-2275
		  Cincinnati *(G-2601)*

Cardpak Incorporated........................... C..... 440 542-3100
  Solon *(G-12091)*
	Dayton Legal Blank Inc......................... G..... 937 435-4405
	  Dayton *(G-5729)*
		Eveready Printing Inc........................... E..... 216 587-2389
		  Cleveland *(G-3693)*

Evolution Crtive Solutions Inc............. E 513 681-4450
Cincinnati *(G-2605)*

Excelsior Printing Co.......................... G 740 927-2934
Pataskala *(G-11138)*

Express Grphics Prtg Dsign Inc.......... G 513 728-3344
Cincinnati *(G-2609)*

Fair Publishing House Inc................... E 419 668-3746
Norwalk *(G-10841)*

Far Corner.. G 330 767-3734
Navarre *(G-10303)*

Feld Printing Co................................... G 513 271-6806
Cincinnati *(G-2619)*

Fgs-Wi LLC... E 630 375-8597
Newark *(G-10502)*

▲ Fine Line Graphics Corp.................. C 614 486-0276
Columbus *(G-4924)*

Finn Graphics Inc................................ E 513 941-6161
Cincinnati *(G-2624)*

Fleet Graphics Inc.............................. G 937 252-2552
Dayton *(G-5779)*

Fmh Enterprises LLC........................... F 937 478-2739
Dayton *(G-5781)*

Folks Creative Printers Inc............... G 740 383-6326
Marion *(G-8970)*

Follow Print Club On Facebook........... G 216 707-2579
Cleveland *(G-3732)*

Foote Printing Company Inc................ F 216 431-1757
Cleveland *(G-3734)*

Frame Warehouse.................................. G 614 861-4582
Reynoldsburg *(G-11570)*

Franklin Printing Company.................. F 740 452-6375
Zanesville *(G-15016)*

Freeport Press Inc.............................. C 330 308-3300
New Philadelphia *(G-10447)*

Fremont Printing Inc.......................... F 480 272-3443
Fremont *(G-7112)*

Friends Service Co Inc....................... F 800 427-1704
Dayton *(G-5785)*

Friends Service Co Inc....................... E 419 427-1704
Findlay *(G-6869)*

Frisby Printing Company..................... F 330 665-4565
Fairlawn *(G-6801)*

Fx Digital Media Inc........................... G 216 241-4040
Cleveland *(G-3747)*

▲ Galaxy Balloons Incorporated......... C 216 476-3360
Cleveland *(G-3753)*

Galley Printing Inc............................ G 330 220-5577
Brunswick *(G-1593)*

Gannett Stllite Info Ntwrk LLC.......... E 419 334-1012
Fremont *(G-7113)*

Gaspar Services LLC............................ G 330 467-8292
Macedonia *(G-8694)*

Gazette Publishing Company................ E 419 483-4190
Oberlin *(G-10917)*

Gb Liquidating Company Inc................ E 513 248-7600
Milford *(G-9935)*

GBS Corp... C 330 863-1828
Malvern *(G-8750)*

▲ GCI Digital Imaging Inc.................. F 513 521-7446
Cincinnati *(G-2653)*

Genie Repros Inc................................ G 216 696-6677
Cleveland *(G-3769)*

Gerald L Herrmann Company Inc........... F 513 661-1818
Cincinnati *(G-2669)*

Gergel-Kellem Company Inc.................. D 216 398-2000
Olmsted Falls *(G-10940)*

Gli Holdings Inc................................ D 440 892-7760
Stow *(G-12434)*

▲ Gli Holdings Inc........................... D 216 651-1500
Stow *(G-12433)*

Globus Printing & Packg Co Inc.......... D 419 628-2381
Minster *(G-10058)*

Golden Graphics Ltd............................ F 419 673-6260
Kenton *(G-8099)*

Gordon Bernard Company LLC.............. E 513 248-7600
Milford *(G-9936)*

Gordons Graphics Inc.......................... G 330 863-2322
Malvern *(G-8751)*

Graphic Info Systems Inc.................... F 513 948-1300
Mason *(G-9106)*

Graphic Paper Products Corp.............. D 937 325-5503
Springfield *(G-12315)*

Graphic Village LLC............................ C 513 241-1865
Blue Ash *(G-1278)*

Graphtech Communications Inc............ F 216 676-1020
Strongsville *(G-12560)*

Greg Blume... G 740 574-2308
Wheelersburg *(G-14353)*

Gregg Macmillan.................................. G 513 248-2121
Milford *(G-9937)*

Gtlp Holdings LLC................................ E 513 489-6700
Cincinnati *(G-2696)*

▲ Haman Enterprises Inc.................... F 614 888-7574
Columbus *(G-4968)*

Harper Engraving & Printing Co.......... D 614 276-0700
Columbus *(G-4970)*

Hartco Printing Company..................... G 614 761-1292
Dublin *(G-6301)*

Hawks & Associates Inc...................... E 513 752-4311
Cincinnati *(G-2305)*

Headlee Enterprises Ltd...................... G 614 785-1476
Columbus *(G-4641)*

Hecks Direct Mail & Prtg Svc.............. E 419 661-6028
Toledo *(G-12989)*

▲ Hecks Direct Mail Prtg Svc Inc....... F 419 697-3505
Toledo *(G-12990)*

Heeter Printing Company Inc............... G 440 946-0606
Eastlake *(G-6431)*

Heitkamp & Kremer Printing Inc.......... G 419 925-4121
Celina *(G-2109)*

Herald Inc... E 419 492-2133
New Washington *(G-10479)*

Heritage Press Inc.............................. E 419 289-9209
Ashland *(G-539)*

Heskamp Printing Co Inc..................... G 513 871-6770
Cincinnati *(G-2720)*

Hh Associates US Inc.......................... F 937 644-7492
Marysville *(G-9025)*

Hi-Point Graphics LLC.......................... G 937 407-6524
Bellefontaine *(G-1109)*

Highland Computer Forms Inc.............. D 937 393-4215
Hillsboro *(G-7718)*

Hilltop Printing................................. G 419 782-9898
Defiance *(G-6110)*

Hkm Drect Mkt Cmmnications Inc......... C 800 860-4456
Cleveland *(G-3832)*

Holmes W & Sons Printing................... G 937 325-1509
Springfield *(G-12323)*

Horizon Ohio Publications Inc............ D 419 738-2128
Wapakoneta *(G-13715)*

Hoster Graphics Company Inc.............. F 614 299-9770
Columbus *(G-4992)*

HOT Graphic Services Inc.................... E 419 242-7000
Northwood *(G-10804)*

Howland Printing Inc.......................... G 330 637-8255
Cortland *(G-5445)*

HP Industries Inc................................ E 419 478-0695
Toledo *(G-12997)*

Hubbard Company.................................. E 419 784-4455
Defiance *(G-6111)*

Hubbard Publishing Co......................... G 937 592-3060
Bellefontaine *(G-1110)*

▼ ICM Distributing Company Inc......... E 234 212-3030
Twinsburg *(G-13319)*

Identity Group LLC.............................. G 614 337-6167
Westerville *(G-14213)*

Image Concepts Inc.............................. F 216 524-9000
Cleveland *(G-3850)*

Image Print Inc................................... G 614 776-3985
Westerville *(G-14264)*

Imprint LLC... G 216 233-0066
Cleveland *(G-3856)*

Ink Inc... G 330 875-4789
Louisville *(G-8605)*

Innomark Communications LLC............ D 937 454-5555
Miamisburg *(G-9701)*

Innovative Graphics Ltd...................... F 877 406-3636
Columbus *(G-5007)*

Inskeep Brothers Inc.......................... G 614 898-6620
Columbus *(G-5008)*

Irwin Engraving & Printing Co.......... G 216 391-7300
Cleveland *(G-3872)*

Isaac Foster Mack Co.......................... C 419 625-5500
Sandusky *(G-11843)*

It XCEL Consulting LLC........................ F 513 847-8261
West Chester *(G-14016)*

J & L Management Corporation............ G 440 205-1199
Mentor *(G-9537)*

J & P Investments Inc.......................... F 513 821-2299
Cincinnati *(G-2755)*

J Solutions LLC................................... G 614 732-4857
Columbus *(G-5028)*

▲ Jack Walker Printing Co.................. F 440 352-4222
Mentor *(G-9540)*

Jakprints Inc..................................... C 877 246-3132
Cleveland *(G-3881)*

Jarman Printing LLC............................ G 330 823-8585
Alliance *(G-386)*

Jasper Printing Co LLC........................ G 937 294-5218
Kettering *(G-8121)*

Jay Tees LLC.. E 740 405-1579
Thornville *(G-12766)*

Jbnovember LLC................................... E 513 272-7000
Cincinnati *(G-2763)*

Jk Digital Publishing LLC.................. G 937 299-0185
Springboro *(G-12256)*

Joe The Printer Guy LLC...................... G 216 651-3880
Lakewood *(G-8168)*

Jos Berning Printing Co...................... F 513 721-0781
Cincinnati *(G-2773)*

Jt Premier Printing Corp.................... G 216 831-8785
Cleveland *(G-3908)*

Kahny Printing Inc.............................. E 513 251-2911
Cincinnati *(G-2778)*

Kay Toledo Tag Inc.............................. D 419 729-5479
Toledo *(G-13017)*

Keener Printing Inc............................ G 216 531-7595
Cleveland *(G-3911)*

▲ Kehl-Kolor Inc............................... E 419 281-3107
Ashland *(G-545)*

Kem Advertising and Prtg LLC............ G 330 818-5061
Barberton *(G-816)*

Kenwel Printers Inc............................ E 614 261-1011
Columbus *(G-5050)*

Kevin K Tidd....................................... G 419 885-5603
Sylvania *(G-12714)*

Kevin Noesner.................................... G 614 451-5459
Columbus *(G-5052)*

Key Maneuvers Inc.............................. G 440 285-0774
Chardon *(G-2210)*

Keystone Press Inc............................ G 419 243-7326
Toledo *(G-13018)*

Kimpton Printing & Spc Co.................. F 330 467-1640
Macedonia *(G-8702)*

Kinkos Inc... G 216 661-9950
Cleveland *(G-3922)*

SIC

Klingstedt Brothers Company	F	330 456-8319	
Canton (G-1926)			
KMS 2000 Inc	F	330 454-9444	
Canton (G-1927)			
▲ **Kramer Graphics Inc**	E	937 296-9600	
Moraine (G-10172)			
▼ **Krehbiel Holdings Inc**	D	513 271-6035	
Cincinnati (G-2807)			
L & T Collins Inc	G	740 345-4494	
Newark (G-10516)			
Lahlouh Inc	G	650 692-6600	
Monroe (G-10113)			
Lake Shore Graphic Inds Inc	G	419 626-8631	
Sandusky (G-11849)			
Larmax Inc	G	513 984-0783	
Blue Ash (G-1296)			
Laurenee Ltd	G	513 662-2225	
Cincinnati (G-2814)			
Lba Custom Printing	G	419 535-3151	
Toledo (G-13028)			
LBL Lithographers Inc	G	440 350-0106	
Painesville (G-11096)			
Lee Corporation	G	513 771-3602	
Cincinnati (G-2817)			
Legal News Publishing Co	E	216 696-3322	
Cleveland (G-3949)			
Legalcraft Inc	G	330 494-1261	
Canton (G-1932)			
Letterman Printing Inc	G	513 523-1111	
Oxford (G-11063)			
Liming Printing Inc	F	937 374-2646	
Xenia (G-14769)			
Litho-Print Ltd	F	937 222-4351	
Dayton (G-5852)			
Little Printing Company	G	937 773-4595	
Piqua (G-11363)			
Liturgical Publications Inc	D	216 325-6825	
Cleveland (G-3964)			
Loris Printing Inc	G	419 626-6648	
Sandusky (G-11852)			
Lsc Communications Inc	A	419 935-0111	
Willard (G-14403)			
Lyle Printing & Publishing Co	E	330 337-3419	
Salem (G-11796)			
M Rosenthal Company	F	513 563-0081	
Cincinnati (G-2835)			
Malik Media LLC	G	614 933-0328	
New Albany (G-10345)			
Marbee Inc	G	419 422-9441	
Findlay (G-6891)			
Mariotti Printing Co LLC	G	440 245-4120	
Lorain (G-8567)			
Mark Advertising Agency Inc	F	419 626-9000	
Sandusky (G-11856)			
◆ **Mass-Marketing Inc**	C	513 860-6200	
Fairfield (G-6750)			
Master Printing Group Inc	F	216 351-2246	
Berea (G-1180)			
Mbas Printing Inc	G	513 489-3000	
Blue Ash (G-1306)			
◆ **McNerney & Associates LLC**	E	513 241-9951	
West Chester (G-14132)			
Mercer Color Corporation	G	419 678-8273	
Coldwater (G-4582)			
Meridian Arts and Graphics	G	330 759-9099	
Youngstown (G-14898)			
Messenger Publishing Company	C	740 592-6612	
Athens (G-644)			
Metzgers	D	419 861-8611	
Toledo (G-13053)			
Meyers Printing & Design Inc	F	937 461-6000	
Dayton (G-5876)			

Miami Valley Publishing LLC	C	937 879-5678	
Fairborn (G-6696)			
Middaugh Enterprises Inc	G	330 852-2471	
Sugarcreek (G-12641)			
Middleton Printing Co Inc	G	614 294-7277	
Gahanna (G-7166)			
Milford Printers	E	513 831-6630	
Milford (G-9944)			
Millennium Printing LLC	G	513 489-3000	
Blue Ash (G-1311)			
Minuteman Press Inc	G	513 741-9056	
Cincinnati (G-2882)			
Mj Bornhorst Enterprises LLC	E	937 295-3469	
Fort Loramie (G-6951)			
Mmp Printing Inc	F	513 381-0990	
Cincinnati (G-2883)			
Mmp Toledo	G	419 472-0505	
Toledo (G-13057)			
Monks Copy Shop Inc	F	614 461-6438	
Columbus (G-5110)			
Morse Enterprises Inc	G	513 229-3600	
Mason (G-9129)			
Mound Printing Company Inc	E	937 866-2872	
Miamisburg (G-9720)			
Multi-Color Australia LLC	D	513 381-1480	
Batavia (G-877)			
Multi-Craft Litho Inc	E	859 581-2754	
Blue Ash (G-1312)			
Murr Corporation	G	330 264-2223	
Wooster (G-14668)			
Network Printing & Graphics	F	614 230-2084	
Columbus (G-5124)			
Nomis Publications Inc	G	330 965-2380	
Youngstown (G-14904)			
North Coast Litho Inc	E	216 881-1952	
Cleveland (G-4086)			
North Shore Printing LLC	G	740 876-9066	
Portsmouth (G-11472)			
North Toledo Graphics LLC	D	419 476-8808	
Toledo (G-13063)			
Northcoast Pmm LLC	F	419 540-8667	
Toledo (G-13064)			
Northeast Blueprint and Sup Co	G	216 261-7500	
Cleveland (G-4092)			
Northern Ohio Printing Inc	E	216 398-0000	
Cleveland (G-4094)			
◆ **Novelty Advertising Co Inc**	E	740 622-3113	
Coshocton (G-5465)			
Nta Graphics Inc	G	419 476-8808	
Toledo (G-13066)			
O Connor Office Pdts & Prtg	G	740 852-2209	
London (G-8540)			
▲ **Ohio Art Company**	D	419 636-3141	
Bryan (G-1655)			
Old Trail Printing Company	C	614 443-4852	
Columbus (G-5159)			
Oliver Printing & Packg Co LLC	D	330 425-7890	
Twinsburg (G-13346)			
Onetouchpoint East Corp	D	513 421-1600	
Cincinnati (G-2933)			
Optimum System Products Inc	E	614 885-4464	
Westerville (G-14273)			
Orange Blossom Press Inc	G	216 781-8655	
Willoughby (G-14502)			
Oregon Vlg Print Shoppe Inc	F	937 222-9418	
Dayton (G-5930)			
Orwell Printing	G	440 285-2233	
Chardon (G-2218)			
Ovp Inc	G	740 423-5171	
Belpre (G-1152)			
Page One Group	G	740 397-4240	
Mount Vernon (G-10257)			

Painesville Publishing Inc	G	440 354-4142	
Austinburg (G-701)			
Painted Hill Inv Group Inc	F	937 339-1756	
Troy (G-13246)			
▲ **Paragraphics Inc**	E	330 493-1074	
Canton (G-1971)			
Park Press Direct	G	419 626-4426	
Sandusky (G-11864)			
Patio Printing Inc	G	614 785-9553	
Columbus (G-5177)			
Patterson-Britton Printing Inc	G	216 781-7997	
Mentor (G-9583)			
PDQ Printing Service	F	216 241-5443	
Westlake (G-14321)			
Peerless Printing Company	F	513 721-4657	
Cincinnati (G-2952)			
Pen-Ann Corporation	G	740 373-2054	
Marietta (G-8936)			
Penguin Enterprises Inc	E	440 899-5112	
Westlake (G-14322)			
Perfection Printing	G	513 874-2173	
Fairfield (G-6765)			
Perrons Printing Company Inc	G	440 236-8870	
Columbia Station (G-4596)			
Persistence of Vision Inc	G	440 591-5443	
Chagrin Falls (G-2177)			
Phil Vedda & Sons Inc	G	216 671-2222	
Cleveland (G-4158)			
Phoenix Graphix Inc	G	513 751-4433	
Cincinnati (G-2961)			
Pinnacle Press Inc	G	330 453-7060	
Canton (G-1976)			
PM Graphics Inc	E	330 650-0861	
Streetsboro (G-12517)			
Porath Business Services Inc	F	216 626-0060	
Cleveland (G-4176)			
Post Business Properties Inc	D	419 628-2321	
Minster (G-10063)			
Preferred Printing	G	937 492-6961	
Sidney (G-12041)			
Preisser Inc	G	614 345-0199	
Columbus (G-5203)			
Premier Printing Corporation	F	216 478-9720	
Cleveland (G-4191)			
Premier Prtg Centl Ohio Ltd	E	937 642-0988	
Marysville (G-9043)			
Prime Printing Inc	E	937 438-3707	
Dayton (G-5956)			
Print All Inc	G	419 534-2880	
Toledo (G-13103)			
Print Centers of Ohio Inc	F	419 526-4139	
Mansfield (G-8846)			
▼ **Print Direct For Less 2 Inc**	F	440 236-8870	
Columbia Station (G-4598)			
Print Factory PII	G	330 549-9640	
North Lima (G-10711)			
Print Shop of Canton Inc	F	330 497-3212	
Canton (G-1983)			
Print Syndicate Inc	F	617 290-9550	
Columbus (G-5206)			
Print-Digital Incorporated	G	330 686-5945	
Stow (G-12451)			
Printed Image	F	614 221-1412	
Columbus (G-5207)			
Printers Devil Inc	F	330 650-1218	
Hudson (G-7854)			
▲ **Printers Edge Inc**	F	330 372-2232	
Warren (G-13791)			
Printex Incorporated	F	740 773-0088	
Chillicothe (G-2276)			
Printing Arts Press Inc	F	740 397-6106	
Mount Vernon (G-10260)			

Printing Dimensions Inc...................... F 937 256-0044
Dayton (G-5957)

Printing Express................................. G 937 276-7794
Moraine (G-10187)

Printing Service Company................... D 937 425-6100
Miamisburg (G-9729)

Printpoint Inc.................................... G 937 223-9041
Dayton (G-5958)

Pro-Decal Inc................................... G 330 484-0089
Canton (G-1984)

Professional Screen Printing............... G 740 687-0760
Lancaster (G-8219)

Profile Digital Printing LLC.................. E 937 866-4241
Dayton (G-5965)

Program Managers Inc....................... G 937 431-1982
Beavercreek (G-995)

Progressive Printers Inc..................... D 937 222-1267
Dayton (G-5967)

Progrssive Communications Corp........ F 740 397-5333
Mount Vernon (G-10261)

Promatch Solutions LLC..................... F 877 299-0185
Moraine (G-10188)

Quality Publishing Co......................... F 513 863-8210
Hamilton (G-7520)

Quebecor World Johnson Hardin......... G 614 326-0299
Cincinnati (G-3019)

Queen City Reprographics................... C 513 326-2300
Cincinnati (G-3024)

Quez Media Marketing Inc.................. G 216 910-0202
Independence (G-7918)

▼ Quick Tab II Inc............................. D 419 448-6622
Tiffin (G-12796)

Quick Tech Graphics Inc..................... F 937 743-5952
Springboro (G-12266)

R & J Bardon Inc.............................. G 614 457-5500
Columbus (G-5221)

R R Donnelley & Sons Company......... D 440 774-2101
Oberlin (G-10920)

R R Donnelley & Sons Company......... D 330 562-5250
Streetsboro (G-12518)

R&D Marketing Group Inc................... G 216 398-9100
Brooklyn Heights (G-1537)

Randd Assoc Prtg & Promotions.......... G 937 294-1874
Dayton (G-5975)

Rba Inc.. G 330 336-6700
Wadsworth (G-13667)

Record Herald Publishing Co............... E 717 762-2151
Cincinnati (G-3005)

▲ Repro Acquisition Company LLC...... G 216 738-3800
Cleveland (G-4235)

Resilient Holdings Inc........................ F 614 847-5600
Columbus (G-5227)

Reynolds and Reynolds Company........ F 419 584-7000
Celina (G-2117)

Rhoads Print Center Inc..................... G 330 678-2042
Tallmadge (G-12748)

▲ Richardson Printing Corp.............. D 800 848-9752
Marietta (G-8941)

Rl Smith Graphics LLC....................... G 330 629-8616
Youngstown (G-14924)

Robert Becker Impressions Inc........... F 419 385-5303
Toledo (G-13116)

Robin Enterprises Company............... C 614 891-0250
Westerville (G-14274)

Rotary Forms Press Inc..................... E 937 393-3426
Hillsboro (G-7724)

RPI Color Service Inc......................... D 513 471-4040
Cincinnati (G-3055)

Ryans Newark Leader Ex Prtg Co........ F 740 522-2149
Newark (G-10532)

S Beckman Print Grphic Sltons............ G 614 864-2232
Columbus (G-5240)

Schilling Graphics Inc........................ E 419 468-1037
Galion (G-7198)

Schlabach Printers LLC...................... E 330 852-4687
Sugarcreek (G-12649)

Schuerholz Inc.................................. G 937 294-5218
Dayton (G-5997)

Scorecards Unlimited LLC................... G 614 885-0796
Columbus (G-5257)

Scratch Off Works LLC....................... G 440 333-4302
Rocky River (G-11639)

▼ Scrip-Safe Security Products........... E 513 697-7789
Loveland (G-8652)

Sdg News Group Inc........................... F 419 929-3411
New London (G-10416)

Sdo Sports Ltd.................................. G 440 546-9998
Cleveland (G-4283)

Seemless Printing LLC....................... G 513 871-2366
Cincinnati (G-3075)

Sekuworks LLC.................................. E 513 202-1210
Harrison (G-7566)

Selby Service/Roxy Press Inc............. G 513 241-3445
Cincinnati (G-3078)

Seneca Enterprises Inc...................... G 814 432-7890
Batavia (G-888)

▲ Sensical Inc................................. D 216 641-1141
Solon (G-12180)

Sfc Graphics Cleveland Ltd................. F 419 255-1283
Toledo (G-13128)

Sharp Enterprises Inc........................ F 937 295-2965
Fort Loramie (G-6956)

▲ Shawnee Systems Inc.................... D 513 561-9932
Cincinnati (G-3087)

Shout Out Loud Prints........................ G 614 432-8990
Columbus (G-5264)

Sitler Printer Inc............................... G 330 482-4463
Columbiana (G-4628)

Skladany Enterprises Inc.................... G 614 823-6882
Westerville (G-14234)

Sky Wireless and Smoke Sp LLC........ E 513 488-5992
Cincinnati (G-3095)

Slimans Printery Inc.......................... G 330 454-9141
Canton (G-2007)

◆ SMI Holdings Inc............................ D 740 927-3464
Pataskala (G-11151)

Snow Printing Co Inc......................... F 419 229-7669
Lima (G-8451)

Soondook LLC................................... E 614 389-5757
Columbus (G-5277)

Source3media Inc............................. E 330 467-9003
Solon (G-12184)

Southeast Publications Inc................. F 740 732-2341
Caldwell (G-1729)

Southern Ohio Printing....................... G 513 241-5150
Cincinnati (G-3102)

SP Mount Printing Company............... G 216 881-3316
Cleveland (G-4318)

SPAOS Inc....................................... G 937 890-0783
Dayton (G-6014)

Specialty Lithographing Co................. F 513 621-0222
Cincinnati (G-3103)

Springdot Inc.................................... D 513 542-4000
Cincinnati (G-3108)

Sprint Print Inc................................. G 740 622-4429
Coshocton (G-5473)

SRC & Company................................ F 216 417-7477
Cleveland (G-4321)

Standard Printing Co of Canton........... D 330 453-8247
Canton (G-2012)

Star Calendar & Printing Inc................ G 216 741-3223
Cleveland (G-4328)

Star Printing Company Inc.................. G 330 376-0514
Akron (G-317)

Starr Services Inc............................. G 513 241-7708
Cincinnati (G-3114)

Stein-Palmer Printing Co.................... G 740 633-3894
Saint Clairsville (G-11711)

Stephen Andrews Inc......................... G 330 725-2672
Lodi (G-8507)

Stepping Stone Enterprises Inc........... F 419 472-0505
Maumee (G-9320)

Stevenson Color Inc.......................... C 513 321-7500
Cincinnati (G-3119)

Suburban Press Incorporated............. G 216 961-0766
Cleveland (G-4340)

Sun Art Decals Inc............................ G 440 234-9045
Berea (G-1189)

Superior Impressions Inc................... G 419 244-8676
Toledo (G-13136)

Swimmer Printing Inc......................... G 216 623-1005
Cleveland (G-4357)

T D Dynamics Inc.............................. F 216 881-0800
Cleveland (G-4362)

Taylor Communications Inc................. F 614 351-6868
Columbus (G-5312)

Taylor Communications Inc................. E 937 221-1000
Dayton (G-6039)

Taylor Quick Print.............................. G 740 439-2208
Cambridge (G-1763)

▼ Tce International Ltd....................... F 800 962-2376
Perry (G-11199)

Techniprint Inc.................................. F 614 899-1403
Westerville (G-14277)

Tecnocap LLC................................... C 330 392-7222
Warren (G-13800)

The Gazette Printing Co Inc................ G 440 593-6030
Conneaut (G-5418)

Theb Inc.. G 216 391-4800
Cleveland (G-4389)

Tj Metzgers Inc................................. D 419 861-8611
Toledo (G-13143)

Tkm Print Solutions Inc...................... F 330 237-4029
Uniontown (G-13427)

Tl Krieg Offset LLC............................ E 513 542-1522
Cincinnati (G-3158)

Toledo Ticket Company....................... E 419 476-5424
Toledo (G-13159)

Tope Printing Inc............................... G 330 674-4993
Millersburg (G-10014)

▲ Tpl Holdings LLC........................... F 800 475-4030
Mogadore (G-10090)

Tradewinds Prin Twear....................... G 740 214-5005
Roseville (G-11654)

◆ Transfer Express Inc..................... D 440 918-1900
Mentor (G-9642)

Traxium LLC..................................... E 330 572-8200
Stow (G-12466)

Traxler Printing................................. G 614 593-1270
Columbus (G-5329)

◆ Trebnick Systems LLC.................... E 937 743-1550
Springboro (G-12272)

Tri-State Publishing Company............. E 740 283-3686
Steubenville (G-12413)

Tribune Printing Inc........................... G 419 542-7764
Hicksville (G-7654)

Truax Printing Inc.............................. E 419 994-4166
Loudonville (G-8595)

True Dinero Records & Tech LLC......... G 513 428-4610
Cincinnati (G-3173)

Tucker Printers Inc............................ D 585 359-3030
West Chester (G-14086)

Ultimate Printing Inc.......................... G 330 847-2941
Warren (G-13804)

▼ United Trade Printers LLC............... E 614 326-4829
Dublin (G-6358)

USA Quickprint Inc..................... F 330 455-5119
Canton (G-2040)

V & C Enterprises Co..................... G 614 221-1412
Columbus (G-5343)

◆ Vectra Inc................................. C 614 351-6868
Columbus (G-5345)

Victory Direct LLC..................... G 614 626-0000
Gahanna (G-7172)

Vision Graphix Inc..................... G 440 835-6540
Westlake (G-14342)

Vision Press Inc......................... G 440 357-6362
Painesville (G-11122)

Visual Marking Systems Inc..................... D 330 425-7100
Twinsburg (G-13393)

Vpp Industries Inc..................... F 937 526-3775
Versailles (G-13604)

Vya Inc...................................... E 513 772-5400
Cincinnati (G-3210)

Warren Printing & Off Pdts Inc..................... F 419 523-3635
Ottawa (G-11050)

Watkins Printing Company..................... E 614 297-8270
Columbus (G-5358)

Welch Publishing Co..................... E 419 874-2528
Perrysburg (G-11279)

Wernet Inc................................. G 330 452-2200
Canton (G-2046)

West Bend Printing & Pubg Inc..................... G 419 258-2000
Antwerp (G-464)

West-Camp Press Inc..................... E 614 895-0233
Columbus (G-5362)

▲ West-Camp Press Inc..................... D 614 882-2378
Westerville (G-14281)

Westrock Commercial LLC..................... E 419 476-9101
Toledo (G-13178)

▲ Wfsr Holdings LLC..................... A 877 735-4966
Dayton (G-6081)

White Tiger Inc......................... F 740 852-4873
London (G-8543)

Wicked Premiums LLC..................... G 216 364-0322
Brecksville (G-1485)

William J Bergen & Co..................... G 440 248-6132
Solon (G-12208)

Willoughby Printing Co Inc..................... G 440 946-0800
Willoughby (G-14551)

Woodrow Manufacturing Co..................... E 937 399-9333
Springfield (G-12396)

◆ Workflowone LLC..................... A 877 735-4966
Dayton (G-6087)

Yespress Graphics LLC..................... G 614 899-1403
Westerville (G-14282)

Youngstown Letter Shop Inc..................... G 330 793-4935
Youngstown (G-14972)

Youngstown Pre-Press Inc..................... G 330 793-3690
Youngstown (G-14974)

Zippitycom Print LLC..................... F 216 438-0001
Cleveland (G-4525)

2754 Commercial printing, gravure

Admiral Products Company Inc..................... E 216 671-0600
Cleveland (G-3299)

Brook & Whittle Limited..................... E 513 860-2457
Hamilton (G-7474)

Cham Cor Industries Inc..................... G 740 967-9015
Johnstown (G-7995)

Commercial Cutng Graphics LLC..................... D 419 526-4800
Mansfield (G-8776)

Diversfied Lbling Slutions Inc..................... F 630 625-1225
Harrison (G-7549)

Dupli-Systems Inc..................... C 440 234-9415
Strongsville (G-12555)

Fx Digital Media Inc..................... F 216 241-4040
Cleveland (G-3746)

Graphic Paper Products Corp..................... D 937 325-5503
Springfield (G-12315)

Kenyetta Bagby Enterprise LLC..................... F 614 584-3426
Reynoldsburg (G-11573)

Klingstedt Brothers Company..................... F 330 456-8319
Canton (G-1926)

M PI Label Systems..................... G 330 938-2134
Sebring (G-11896)

Mpi Labels of Baltimore Inc..................... E 330 938-2134
Sebring (G-11899)

Multi-Color Australia LLC..................... D 513 381-1480
Batavia (G-877)

Ohio Envelope Manufacturing Co..................... E 216 267-2920
Cleveland (G-4114)

▲ Ohio Gravure Technologies Inc..................... F 937 439-1582
Miamisburg (G-9724)

▼ Pioneer Labels Inc..................... C 618 546-5418
West Chester (G-14048)

Retterbush Graphics Packg Corp..................... G 513 779-4466
West Chester (G-14066)

▼ Scratch-Off Systems Inc..................... E 216 649-7800
Twinsburg (G-13376)

Sekuworks LLC..................... E 513 202-1210
Harrison (G-7566)

▲ Shamrock Companies Inc..................... D 440 899-9510
Westlake (G-14333)

The Photo-Type Engraving Company.... D 513 281-0999
Cincinnati (G-3149)

Western Roto Engravers Inc..................... E 330 336-7636
Wadsworth (G-13677)

▲ Wfsr Holdings LLC..................... A 877 735-4966
Dayton (G-6081)

◆ Workflowone LLC..................... A 877 735-4966
Dayton (G-6087)

2759 Commercial printing, nec

4 Over LLC..................... E 937 610-0629
Dayton (G-5627)

A C Hadley - Printing Inc..................... G 937 426-0952
Beavercreek (G-962)

A E Wilson Holdings Inc..................... G 330 405-0316
Twinsburg (G-13265)

A To Z Paper Box Company..................... G 330 325-8722
Rootstown (G-11646)

A-A Blueprint Co Inc..................... E 330 794-8803
Akron (G-10)

Aardvark Screen Prtg & EMB LLC..................... F 419 354-6686
Bowling Green (G-1404)

Ableprint / Toucan Inc..................... F 419 522-9742
Mansfield (G-8758)

Absolute Impressions Inc..................... F 614 840-0599
Lewis Center (G-8319)

Ace Transfer Company..................... G 937 398-1103
Springfield (G-12276)

Ad-Sensations Inc..................... F 419 841-5395
Sylvania (G-12700)

Adcraft Decals Incorporated..................... E 216 524-2934
Cleveland (G-3297)

Admiral Products Company Inc..................... E 216 671-0600
Cleveland (G-3299)

Advanced Incentives Inc..................... F 419 471-9088
Toledo (G-12865)

Advertising Joe LLC Mean..................... G 440 247-8200
Chagrin Falls (G-2135)

▲ Aero Fulfillment Services Corp..................... D 800 225-7145
Mason (G-9056)

Agnone-Kelly Enterprises Inc..................... G 800 634-6503
Cincinnati (G-2343)

AGS Custom Graphics Inc..................... D 330 963-7770
Macedonia (G-8676)

◆ Airwaves LLC..................... C 740 548-1200
Lewis Center (G-8320)

Akron Litho-Print Company Inc..................... F 330 434-3145
Akron (G-34)

Albany Screen Printing LLC..................... F 614 585-3279
Reynoldsburg (G-11555)

▲ Alberts Screen Print Inc..................... C 330 753-7559
Norton (G-10818)

All Points Printing Inc..................... G 440 585-1125
Wickliffe (G-14365)

Allied Silk Screen Inc..................... G 937 223-4921
Dayton (G-5647)

American Business Forms Inc..................... E 513 312-2522
West Chester (G-14101)

American Imprssions Sportswear..................... G 614 848-6677
Columbus (G-4697)

American Printing & Lithog Co..................... F 513 867-0602
Hamilton (G-7463)

Anderson Graphics Inc..................... E 330 745-2165
Barberton (G-793)

Appleheart Inc..................... G 937 384-0430
Miamisburg (G-9666)

▲ Ares Sportswear Ltd..................... D 614 767-1950
Hilliard (G-7668)

Art Works..................... G 740 425-5765
Barnesville (G-843)

Ashton LLC..................... F 614 833-4165
Pickerington (G-11288)

Ashton LLC..................... F 336 447-4951
Pickerington (G-11287)

Assocted Vsual Cmmncations Inc..................... E 330 452-4449
Canton (G-1833)

Austin Tape and Label Inc..................... D 330 928-7999
Stow (G-12420)

Aztech Printing & Promotions..................... G 937 339-0100
Troy (G-13202)

Badlime Promo and Apparel LLC..................... F 330 425-7100
Twinsburg (G-13277)

Ball Jackets LLC..................... E 937 572-1114
Jamestown (G-7968)

Barnhart Printing Corp..................... G 330 456-2279
Canton (G-1837)

Bates Printing Inc..................... F 330 833-5830
Massillon (G-9174)

Bayard Inc..................... D 937 293-1415
Moraine (G-10149)

Berea Printing Company..................... G 440 243-1080
Berea (G-1161)

Better Living Concepts Inc..................... G 330 494-2213
Canton (G-1839)

Big Kahuna Graphics LLC..................... G 330 455-2625
Canton (G-1840)

Bindery & Spc Pressworks Inc..................... D 614 873-4623
Plain City (G-11398)

Bizall Inc..................... G 216 939-9580
Cleveland (G-3419)

Bluelogos Inc..................... F 614 898-9971
Westerville (G-14247)

Boehm Inc..................... E 614 875-9010
Grove City (G-7374)

Bollin & Sons Inc..................... E 419 693-6573
Toledo (G-12900)

▲ Bottomline Ink Corporation..................... E 419 897-8000
Perrysburg (G-11205)

Bramkamp Printing Company Inc..................... G 513 241-1865
Blue Ash (G-1255)

Brass Bull 1 LLC..................... G 740 335-8030
Wshngtn Ct Hs (G-14735)

Broadway Printing LLC..................... G 513 621-3429
Cincinnati (G-2427)

Brook & Whittle Limited..................... E 513 860-2457
Hamilton (G-7474)

Brothers Printing Co Inc..................... G 216 621-6050
Cleveland (G-3444)

BSN Sports	G	513 821-7575	
Cincinnati *(G-2431)*			
Buckeye Packaging Co Inc	D	330 935-0301	
Alliance *(G-373)*			
Campbell Signs & Apparel LLC	G	330 386-4768	
East Liverpool *(G-6388)*			
Carbonless Cut Sheet Forms Inc	F	740 826-1700	
New Concord *(G-10385)*			
Carey Color Inc	D	330 239-1835	
Sharon Center *(G-11938)*			
▲ Casad Company Inc	F	419 586-9457	
Coldwater *(G-4570)*			
CCL Label Inc	E	856 273-0700	
New Albany *(G-10334)*			
CCL Label Inc	B	440 878-7277	
Strongsville *(G-12549)*			
Century Graphics Inc	G	614 895-7698	
Westerville *(G-14206)*			
Century Marketing Corporation	C	419 354-2591	
Bowling Green *(G-1413)*			
Charles Huffman & Associates	G	216 295-0850	
Warrensville Heights *(G-13817)*			
Cincinnati Print Solutions LLC	G	513 943-9500	
Milford *(G-9929)*			
Clear Images LLC	G	419 241-9347	
Toledo *(G-12923)*			
▼ Cleveland Menu Printing Inc	E	216 241-5256	
Cleveland *(G-3516)*			
Cleveland Printwear Inc	G	216 521-5500	
Cleveland *(G-3521)*			
Club 513 LLC	G	800 530-2574	
Cincinnati *(G-2501)*			
▲ CMC Group Inc	D	419 354-2591	
Bowling Green *(G-1415)*			
Collotype Labels Usa Inc	D	513 381-1480	
Batavia *(G-858)*			
Columbus Custom Tees	F	614 573-5556	
Columbus *(G-4821)*			
Commercial Decal Ohio Inc	G	330 385-7178	
East Liverpool *(G-6390)*			
Concept 9 Inc	G	614 294-3743	
Columbus *(G-4840)*			
▲ Consoldated Graphics Group Inc	C	216 881-9191	
Cleveland *(G-3559)*			
Contemprary Image Labeling Inc	G	513 583-5699	
Lebanon *(G-8250)*			
Corporate Dcment Solutions Inc	G	513 595-8200	
Cincinnati *(G-2518)*			
Cox Printing Company	G	937 382-2312	
Wilmington *(G-14576)*			
Creative Dcument Solutions LLC	G	740 389-4252	
Marion *(G-8968)*			
Culaine Inc	G	419 345-4984	
Toledo *(G-12934)*			
Custom Apparel LLC	G	330 633-2626	
Akron *(G-111)*			
Custom Deco LLC	E	419 698-2900	
Toledo *(G-12935)*			
Custom Poly Bag LLC	D	330 935-2408	
Alliance *(G-378)*			
▲ Custom Products Corporation	D	440 528-7100	
Glenwillow *(G-7285)*			
Custom Sporstwear Imprints LLC	G	330 335-8326	
Wadsworth *(G-13633)*			
D&D Design Concepts Inc	F	513 752-2191	
Batavia *(G-860)*			
Dayton Legal Blank Inc	G	937 435-4405	
Dayton *(G-5729)*			
Dayton Mailing Services Inc	E	937 222-5056	
Dayton *(G-5731)*			
Dee Printing Inc	F	614 777-8700	
Columbus *(G-4874)*			

Dietrich Von Hldbrand Lgacy PR	G	703 496-7821	
Steubenville *(G-12402)*			
Diocesan Publications Inc	E	614 718-9500	
Dublin *(G-6293)*			
Dlh Enterprises LLC	G	330 253-6960	
Akron *(G-124)*			
▲ Donprint Inc	E	847 573-7777	
Strongsville *(G-12554)*			
Drycal Inc	G	440 974-1999	
Mentor *(G-9512)*			
DSC Supply Company LLC	G	614 891-1100	
Westerville *(G-14257)*			
Dupli-Systems Inc	C	440 234-9415	
Strongsville *(G-12555)*			
◆ Dynamic Design & Systems Inc	G	440 708-1010	
Chagrin Falls *(G-2159)*			
Earl D Arnold Printing Company	E	513 533-6900	
Cincinnati *(G-2574)*			
Ebel-Binder Printing Co Inc	G	513 471-1067	
Cincinnati *(G-2577)*			
Eci Macola/Max LLC	C	978 539-6186	
Dublin *(G-6296)*			
Electronic Imaging Svcs Inc	F	740 549-2487	
Lewis Center *(G-8332)*			
Empire Printing Inc	E	513 242-3900	
Fairfield *(G-6732)*			
Engineered Imaging LLC	F	419 255-1283	
Toledo *(G-12953)*			
Equip Business Solutions Co	G	614 854-9755	
Jackson *(G-7945)*			
Erd Specialty Graphics Inc	G	419 242-9545	
Toledo *(G-12955)*			
Everythings Image Inc	G	513 469-6727	
Blue Ash *(G-1273)*			
Fair Publishing House Inc	E	419 668-3746	
Norwalk *(G-10841)*			
Folks Creative Printers Inc	G	740 383-6326	
Marion *(G-8970)*			
Foote Printing Company Inc	F	216 431-1757	
Cleveland *(G-3734)*			
▲ Forward Movement	E	513 721-6659	
Cincinnati *(G-2636)*			
Four Ambition LLC	G	937 239-4479	
Dayton *(G-5783)*			
Fulton Sign & Decal Inc	G	440 951-1515	
Mentor *(G-9521)*			
Galactic Printing LLC	G		
Columbus *(G-4944)*			
Gb Liquidating Company Inc	E	513 248-7600	
Milford *(G-9935)*			
▲ GBS Corp	C	330 494-5330	
North Canton *(G-10641)*			
◆ General Data Company Inc	B	513 752-7978	
Cincinnati *(G-2304)*			
▲ General Theming Contrs LLC	G	614 252-6342	
Columbus *(G-4948)*			
Glavin Industries Inc	E	440 349-0049	
Solon *(G-12115)*			
Glen D Lala	G	937 274-7770	
Dayton *(G-5797)*			
Golden Graphics Ltd	F	419 673-6260	
Kenton *(G-8099)*			
Gordons Graphics Inc	G	330 863-2322	
Malvern *(G-8751)*			
Got Graphix Llc	F	330 703-9047	
Fairlawn *(G-6802)*			
Gq Business Products Inc	G	513 792-4750	
Loveland *(G-8627)*			
Grady McCauley Inc	D	330 494-9444	
Akron *(G-165)*			
▲ Grafisk Maskinfabrik Amer LLC	G	630 432-4370	
Lebanon *(G-8265)*			

Graphic Stitch Inc	G	937 642-6707	
Marysville *(G-9021)*			
Green Leaf Printing and Design	G	937 222-3634	
Dayton *(G-5803)*			
▲ Haman Enterprises Inc	F	614 888-7574	
Columbus *(G-4968)*			
Handcrafted Jewelry Inc	G	330 650-9011	
Hudson *(G-7843)*			
Harper Engraving & Printing Co	D	614 276-0700	
Columbus *(G-4970)*			
Hartman Distributing LLC	D	740 616-7764	
Heath *(G-7596)*			
Hawks & Associates Inc	E	513 752-4311	
Cincinnati *(G-2305)*			
Heartland Publications LLC	C	860 664-1075	
Miamisburg *(G-9698)*			
▲ Hecks Direct Mail Prtg Svc Inc	F	419 697-3505	
Toledo *(G-12990)*			
Heskamp Printing Co Inc	E	513 871-6770	
Cincinnati *(G-2720)*			
Hi Tech Printing Co Inc	E	513 874-5325	
Fairfield *(G-6739)*			
Hill Sign Company Inc	G	614 367-9221	
Columbus *(G-4988)*			
Hkm Drect Mkt Cmmnications Inc	F	440 934-3060	
Sheffield Village *(G-11959)*			
Hkm Drect Mkt Cmmnications Inc	D	330 395-9538	
Warren *(G-13771)*			
Hkm Drect Mkt Cmmnications Inc	C	800 860-4456	
Cleveland *(G-3832)*			
Horizon Ohio Publications Inc	D	419 738-2128	
Wapakoneta *(G-13715)*			
HP Industries Inc	E	419 478-0695	
Toledo *(G-12997)*			
Humtown Pattern Company	D	330 482-5555	
Columbiana *(G-4619)*			
Imagine This Renovations	G	330 833-6739	
Navarre *(G-10305)*			
Impact Printing and Design LLC	F	833 522-6200	
Columbus *(G-5003)*			
Industrial Screen Prcess Svc I	F	419 255-4900	
Toledo *(G-13003)*			
Innomark Communications LLC	D	513 285-1040	
Fairfield *(G-6744)*			
▲ Innovtive Lbling Solutions Inc	D	513 860-2457	
Hamilton *(G-7505)*			
Irwin Engraving & Printing Co	G	216 391-7300	
Cleveland *(G-3873)*			
▲ Jack Walker Printing Co	F	440 352-4222	
Mentor *(G-9540)*			
▼ Jamac Inc	E	419 625-9790	
Sandusky *(G-11845)*			
Jarman Printing LLC	G	330 823-8585	
Alliance *(G-386)*			
Jason Schirmer	G	937 433-3023	
Miamisburg *(G-9702)*			
Jupmode	E	419 318-2029	
Toledo *(G-13013)*			
Just Name It Inc	G	614 626-8662	
Ashland *(G-542)*			
◆ Kaufman Container Company	C	216 898-2000	
Cleveland *(G-3908)*			
Kay Toledo Tag Inc	D	419 729-5479	
Toledo *(G-13017)*			
Kdm Signs Inc	E	513 554-1393	
Cincinnati *(G-2788)*			
▲ Kdm Signs Inc	C	513 769-1932	
Cincinnati *(G-2787)*			
Kens His & Hers Shop Inc	G	330 872-3190	
Newton Falls *(G-10578)*			
Kenwel Printers Inc	E	614 261-1011	
Columbus *(G-5050)*			

Keystone Press Inc	G	419 243-7326	Toledo (G-13018)

Keystone Press Inc................... G 419 243-7326
Toledo (G-13018)

KMS 2000 Inc.......................... F 330 454-9444
Canton (G-1927)

Knight Line Signature AP Corp..... G 330 545-8108
Girard (G-7273)

Kopco Graphics Inc.................... E 513 874-7230
West Chester (G-14021)

▲ Label Aid Inc......................... E 419 433-2888
Huron (G-7876)

Label Technique Southeast LLC.... F 440 951-7660
Willoughby (G-14479)

Labeltek Inc............................. D 330 335-3110
Wadsworth (G-13648)

Lake Screen Printing Inc............. G 440 244-5707
Lorain (G-8563)

Laser Printing Solutions Inc......... G 216 351-4444
Cleveland (G-3944)

Lee Corporation....................... G 513 771-3602
Cincinnati (G-2817)

Letterman Printing Inc............... G 513 523-1111
Oxford (G-11063)

Liberty Sportswear LLC.............. G 513 755-8740
Hamilton (G-7510)

License Ad Plate Company........... F 216 265-4200
Cleveland (G-3954)

Lima Sporting Goods Inc............. E 419 222-1036
Lima (G-8427)

Liming Printing Inc.................... F 937 374-2646
Xenia (G-14769)

▲ Lorenz Corporation................. D 937 228-6118
Dayton (G-5855)

Loris Printing Inc...................... G 419 626-6648
Sandusky (G-11852)

Lsc Communications Inc.............. A 419 935-0111
Willard (G-14403)

Lyle Printing & Publishing Co....... E 330 337-3419
Salem (G-11796)

M & H Screen Printing................ G 740 522-1957
Newark (G-10517)

M PI Label Systems.................... G 330 938-2134
Sebring (G-11896)

M Rosenthal Company................ F 513 563-0081
Cincinnati (G-2835)

▼ Mabis Shipping Solutions Inc..... G 330 650-1788
Hudson (G-7850)

Marbee Inc............................. G 419 422-9441
Findlay (G-6891)

Marcus Uppe Inc...................... E 216 263-4000
Cleveland (G-3987)

Mariotti Printing Co LLC............. G 440 245-4120
Lorain (G-8567)

Markt LLC.............................. G 740 397-5900
Mount Vernon (G-10250)

▲ McC - Mason W&S.................. C 513 459-1100
Mason (G-9126)

McC-Norway LLC..................... G 513 381-1480
Batavia (G-871)

Meder Special-Tees Ltd.............. G 513 921-3800
Cincinnati (G-2855)

Melnor Graphics LLC................. E 419 476-8808
Toledo (G-13052)

Metro Flex Inc......................... G 937 299-5360
Moraine (G-10178)

Miami Graphics Services Inc........ F 937 698-4013
West Milton (G-14183)

▲ Microplex Printware Corp.......... F 440 374-2424
Solon (G-12151)

Mid-Ohio Screen Print Inc........... G 614 875-1774
Grove City (G-7400)

Middaugh Enterprises Inc............ G 330 852-2471
Sugarcreek (G-12641)

Middleton Printing Co Inc............ G 614 294-7277
Gahanna (G-7166)

Miller Products Inc.................... F 330 335-3110
Wadsworth (G-13651)

Miller Products Inc.................... D 330 335-3110
Wadsworth (G-13652)

ML Advertising & Design LLC....... G 419 447-6523
Tiffin (G-12791)

ML Erectors LLC...................... G 440 328-3227
Elyria (G-6565)

Mmp Printing Inc..................... F 513 381-0990
Cincinnati (G-2883)

Model GRAphics& Media Inc........ E 513 541-2355
West Chester (G-14031)

Morrison Sign Company Inc......... E 614 276-1181
Columbus (G-5112)

Mpi Labels of Baltimore Inc......... E 330 938-2134
Sebring (G-11899)

▼ Mr Label Inc........................ E 513 681-2088
Cincinnati (G-2891)

Multi-Color Australia LLC............ D 513 381-1480
Batavia (G-877)

Multi-Color Corporation.............. C 513 381-1480
Batavia (G-878)

Multi-Color Corporation.............. G 513 459-3283
Mason (G-9130)

Multi-Craft Litho Inc.................. E 859 581-2754
Blue Ash (G-1312)

◆ Murphy Dog LLC.................... E 614 755-4278
Blacklick (G-1227)

Mustang Printing...................... F 419 592-2746
Napoleon (G-10292)

Ncrformscom.......................... G 800 709-1938
Hudson (G-7853)

◆ Neff Motivation Inc................. C 937 548-3194
Greenville (G-7348)

Network Printing & Graphics........ F 614 230-2084
Columbus (G-5124)

New Dawn Distribution Inc........... G 330 759-3500
Girard (G-7277)

◆ Nilpeter Usa Inc.................... C 513 489-4400
Cincinnati (G-2909)

Nomis Publications Inc............... F 330 965-2380
Youngstown (G-14904)

Nordec Inc............................. D 330 940-3700
Stow (G-12447)

Northeastern Plastics Inc............ G 330 453-5925
Canton (G-1961)

Odyssey Spirits Inc................... F 330 562-1523
Chagrin Falls (G-2174)

▲ Off Contact Inc..................... F 419 255-5546
Toledo (G-13071)

Ohio Envelope Manufacturing Co... E 216 267-2920
Cleveland (G-4114)

Ohio Flexible Packaging Co.......... F 513 494-1800
South Lebanon (G-12220)

Ohio Label Inc........................ F 614 777-0180
Columbus (G-5146)

Old Trail Printing Company.......... C 614 443-4852
Columbus (G-5159)

Omni Systems LLC................... D 216 377-5160
Mayfield Village (G-9345)

Onetouchpoint East Corp............ D 513 421-1600
Cincinnati (G-2933)

P S Graphics Inc...................... G 440 356-9656
Rocky River (G-11636)

▼ Packaging Materials Inc........... E 740 432-6337
Cambridge (G-1753)

Painted Hill Inv Group Inc........... F 937 339-1756
Troy (G-13246)

Papel Couture.......................... G 614 848-5700
Columbus (G-5173)

Park PLC Prntg Cpyg & Dgtl IMG... G 330 799-1739
Youngstown (G-14913)

Part 2 Screen Prtg Design Inc....... G 614 294-4429
Columbus (G-5175)

Patio Printing Inc..................... G 614 785-9553
Columbus (G-5177)

Peebles Creative Group Inc.......... G 614 487-2011
Dublin (G-6329)

Penguin Enterprises Inc.............. E 440 899-5112
Westlake (G-14322)

▲ Performance Packaging Inc....... F 419 478-8805
Toledo (G-13094)

Pexco Packaging Corp................ E 419 470-5935
Toledo (G-13096)

PJ Bush Associates Inc............... F 216 362-6700
Cleveland (G-4168)

Pops Printed Apparel LLC........... G 614 372-5651
Columbus (G-5198)

Post Business Properties Inc........ D 419 628-2321
Minster (G-10063)

Precision Business Solutions........ F 419 661-8700
Perrysburg (G-11258)

Precision Imprint..................... G 740 592-5916
Athens (G-646)

◆ Premier Southern Ticket Co Inc... E 513 489-6700
Cincinnati (G-2980)

Press of Ohio Inc..................... F 330 678-5868
Kent (G-8062)

Primal Screen Inc..................... G 330 677-1766
Kent (G-8063)

Printex Incorporated................. F 740 773-0088
Chillicothe (G-2276)

Printing Dimensions Inc.............. F 937 256-0044
Dayton (G-5957)

▲ Prodigy Print Inc................... F
Dayton (G-5960)

Profile Digital Printing LLC.......... E 937 866-4241
Dayton (G-5965)

Proforma Systems Advantage....... G 419 224-8747
Lima (G-8440)

Progressive Printers Inc.............. D 937 222-1267
Dayton (G-5967)

Qualitee Design Sportswear Co..... F 740 333-8337
Wshngtn Ct Hs (G-14742)

Quebecor World Johnson Hardin.... G 614 326-0299
Cincinnati (G-3019)

Queen City Office Machine........... F 513 251-7200
Cincinnati (G-3022)

Queen City Spirit LLC................ F 513 533-2662
Cincinnati (G-3026)

Quest Service Labs Inc............... G 330 405-0316
Twinsburg (G-13362)

Quick Tech Business Forms Inc...... G 937 743-5952
Springboro (G-12265)

R R Donnelley & Sons Company..... B 740 928-6110
Hebron (G-7632)

R R Donnelley & Sons Company..... D 440 774-2101
Oberlin (G-10920)

R R Donnelley & Sons Company..... G 513 552-1512
West Chester (G-14061)

R&D Marketing Group Inc............ G 216 398-9100
Brooklyn Heights (G-1537)

Ray C Sprosty Bag Co Inc............ F 330 669-0045
Smithville (G-12067)

Repacorp Inc.......................... D 937 667-8496
Tipp City (G-12841)

Reynolds and Reynolds Company... F 419 584-7000
Celina (G-2117)

Richardson Supply Ltd............... G 614 539-3033
Grove City (G-7411)

Ryans Newark Leader Ex Prtg Co... F 740 522-2149
Newark (G-10532)

S F Mock & Associates LLC.............. F 937 438-0196
Dayton (G-5991)

Sams Graphic Industries.............. F 330 821-4710
Alliance (G-402)

Samuels Products Inc.............. E 513 891-4456
Blue Ash (G-1330)

Schilling Graphics Inc.............. E 419 468-1037
Galion (G-7198)

Schlabach Printers LLC.............. E 330 852-4687
Sugarcreek (G-12649)

▼ Scratch-Off Systems Inc.............. E 216 649-7800
Twinsburg (G-13376)

Sekuworks LLC.............. E 513 202-1210
Harrison (G-7566)

Selby Service/Roxy Press Inc.............. G 513 241-3445
Cincinnati (G-3078)

Seneca Label Inc.............. E 440 237-1600
Brunswick (G-1615)

▲ Sensical Inc.............. D 216 641-1141
Solon (G-12180)

Shops By Todd Inc.............. G 937 458-3192
Beavercreek (G-982)

Sit Inc.............. E 330 758-8468
Youngstown (G-14933)

Sitler Printer Inc.............. G 330 482-4463
Columbiana (G-4628)

Slimans Printery Inc.............. F 330 454-9141
Canton (G-2007)

Smartbill Ltd.............. F 740 928-6909
Hebron (G-7636)

Snow Printing Co Inc.............. F 419 229-7669
Lima (G-8451)

▲ Spear Inc.............. D 513 459-1100
Mason (G-9154)

Specialty Nameplate Corp.............. F 614 444-6876
Columbus (G-5279)

Specialty Printing and Proc.............. F 614 322-9035
Columbus (G-5280)

Springdot Inc.............. D 513 542-4000
Cincinnati (G-3108)

◆ SRC Liquidation LLC.............. A 937 221-1000
Dayton (G-6019)

▲ SRI Ohio Inc.............. E 740 653-5800
Lancaster (G-8226)

Standard Register Technologies.............. E 937 443-1000
Dayton (G-6023)

Standout Stickers Inc.............. G 877 449-7703
Brunswick (G-1010)

Star Calendar & Printing Inc.............. G 216 741-3223
Cleveland (G-4328)

Star Printing Company Inc.............. E 330 376-0514
Akron (G-317)

Starr Services Inc.............. G 513 241-7708
Cincinnati (G-3114)

Stephen Andrews Inc.............. G 330 725-2672
Lodi (G-8507)

Steves Sports Inc.............. G 440 735-0044
Northfield (G-10797)

Stolle Machinery Company LLC.............. C 937 497-5400
Sidney (G-12056)

▲ Studio Eleven Inc.............. F 937 295-2225
Fort Loramie (G-6958)

Suburban Press Incorporated.............. F 216 961-0766
Cleveland (G-4340)

Superior Label Systems Inc.............. B 513 336-0825
Mason (G-9157)

T & L Custom Screening Inc.............. G 937 237-3121
Dayton (G-6036)

T-Shirt Co.............. G 513 821-7100
Cincinnati (G-3135)

T&T Graphics Inc.............. D 937 847-6000
Miamisburg (G-9742)

Taylor Communications Inc.............. E 419 678-6000
Coldwater (G-4585)

Taylor Communications Inc.............. E 937 221-1000
Dayton (G-6039)

Taylor Communications Inc.............. E 614 277-7500
Urbancrest (G-13484)

Tech/III Inc.............. E 513 482-7500
Fairfield (G-6781)

▲ The Cyril-Scott Company.............. C 740 654-2112
Lancaster (G-8228)

▲ The D B Hess Company.............. E 330 678-5868
Kent (G-8089)

▲ The Hooven - Dayton Corp.............. C 937 233-4473
Miamisburg (G-9747)

The Label Team Inc.............. F 330 332-1067
Salem (G-11814)

Thomas Products Co Inc.............. E 513 756-9009
Cincinnati (G-3155)

Tj Metzgers Inc.............. D 419 861-8611
Toledo (G-13143)

Toledo Ticket Company.............. E 419 476-5424
Toledo (G-13159)

Tope Printing Inc.............. G 330 674-4993
Millersburg (G-10014)

Tpo Hess Holdings Inc.............. G 815 334-6140
Kent (G-8091)

◆ Transfer Express Inc.............. E 440 918-1900
Mentor (G-9642)

Traxium LLC.............. E 330 572-8200
Stow (G-12466)

◆ Trebnick Systems LLC.............. E 937 743-1550
Springboro (G-12272)

True Dinero Records & Tech LLC.............. G 513 428-4610
Cincinnati (G-3173)

▲ Underground Sports Shop Inc.............. F 513 751-1662
Cincinnati (G-3179)

Unisport Inc.............. F 419 529-4727
Ontario (G-10953)

United Sport Apparel.............. F 330 722-0818
Medina (G-9460)

Universal Ch Directories LLC.............. G 419 522-5011
Mansfield (G-8862)

Universal North Inc.............. F 440 230-1366
North Royalton (G-10787)

Uptown Dog The Inc.............. G 740 592-4600
Athens (G-655)

USA Label Express Inc.............. E 330 874-1001
Bolivar (G-1395)

Vagabond Creations Inc.............. G 937 298-1124
Moraine (G-10197)

Verstrete In Mold Lbels USA In.............. F 513 943-0080
Batavia (G-896)

▲ Vgu Industries Inc.............. E 216 676-9093
Cleveland (G-4464)

Victory Postcards Inc.............. G 614 764-8975
Dublin (G-6360)

Viewpoint Graphic Design.............. G 419 447-6073
Tiffin (G-12807)

Visual Marking Systems Inc.............. D 330 425-7100
Twinsburg (G-13393)

Vya Inc.............. E 513 772-5400
Cincinnati (G-3210)

W/S Packaging Group Inc.............. G 513 459-8800
Mason (G-9166)

Ward/Kraft Forms of Ohio Inc.............. E 740 694-0015
Fredericktown (G-7088)

Warren Printing & Off Pdts Inc.............. F 419 523-3635
Ottawa (G-11050)

Watson Haran & Company Inc.............. G 937 436-1414
Dayton (G-6076)

West Crrllton Prchment Cnvrtin.............. E 513 594-3341
West Carrollton (G-13933)

▲ West-Camp Press Inc.............. D 614 882-2378
Westerville (G-14281)

Western Roto Engravers Inc.............. E 330 336-7636
Wadsworth (G-13677)

▲ Wfsr Holdings LLC.............. A 877 735-4966
Dayton (G-6081)

William J Bergen & Co.............. G 440 248-6132
Solon (G-12208)

Williams Steel Rule Die Co.............. G 216 431-3232
Cleveland (G-4507)

◆ Workflowone LLC.............. A 877 735-4966
Dayton (G-6087)

Yockey Group Inc.............. G 513 860-9053
West Chester (G-14095)

2761 Manifold business forms

Anderson Graphics Inc.............. E 330 745-2165
Barberton (G-793)

▲ Custom Products Corporation.............. D 440 528-7100
Glenwillow (G-7285)

Dupli-Systems Inc.............. C 440 234-9415
Strongsville (G-12555)

▲ Eleet Cryogenics Inc.............. E 330 874-4009
Bolivar (G-1382)

GBS Corp.............. G 330 863-1828
Malvern (G-8750)

▲ GBS Corp.............. C 330 494-5330
North Canton (G-10641)

Glatfelter Corporation.............. G 419 333-6700
Fremont (G-7115)

▲ Kroy LLC.............. C 800 837-4323
Cleveland (G-3929)

Plastilene Inc.............. G 614 592-8699
Washington Court Hou (G-13822)

Print-Digital Incorporated.............. G 330 686-5945
Stow (G-12451)

Quick Tech Graphics Inc.............. F 937 743-5952
Springboro (G-12266)

R R Donnelley & Sons Company.............. D 440 774-2101
Oberlin (G-10920)

Reynolds and Reynolds Company.............. F 419 584-7000
Celina (G-2117)

Rotary Forms Press Inc.............. E 937 393-3426
Hillsboro (G-7724)

S F Mock & Associates LLC.............. F 937 438-0196
Dayton (G-5991)

▲ Shawnee Systems Inc.............. D 513 561-9932
Cincinnati (G-3087)

◆ SRC Liquidation LLC.............. A 937 221-1000
Dayton (G-6019)

Taylor Communications Inc.............. E 937 221-1000
Dayton (G-6039)

Taylor Communications Inc.............. F 732 356-0081
Dayton (G-6040)

Taylor Communications Inc.............. F 937 221-3347
Grove City (G-7415)

Taylor Communications Inc.............. F 216 265-1800
Richfield (G-11603)

Thomas Products Co Inc.............. E 513 756-9009
Cincinnati (G-3155)

Unit Sets Inc.............. E 937 840-6123
Hillsboro (G-7727)

▲ Wfsr Holdings LLC.............. A 877 735-4966
Dayton (G-6081)

2771 Greeting cards

◆ American Greetings Corporation.............. A 216 252-7300
Cleveland (G-3344)

▲ Papyrus-Recycled Greetings Inc.............. D 773 348-6410
Westlake (G-14319)

◆ Plus Mark LLC.............. D 216 252-6770
Cleveland (G-4174)

S
I
C

Schurman Fine Papers.............................. E 513 791-5554
Cincinnati (G-3068)

Those Chrcters From Clvland LL .... G 216 252-7300
Cleveland (G-4394)

Vagabond Creations Inc .... G 937 298-1124
Moraine (G-10197)

2782 Blankbooks and looseleaf binders

▲ Art Guild Binders Inc............................ E 513 242-3000
Cincinnati (G-2378)

Bell Binders LLC...................................... F 419 242-3201
Toledo (G-12895)

Deluxe Corporation................................. D 330 342-1500
Streetsboro (G-12497)

Dupli-Systems Inc................................... C 440 234-9415
Strongsville (G-12555)

Graphic Imaginations.............................. G 216 781-4880
Cleveland (G-3786)

Live Off Loyalty Inc................................. G 513 413-2401
Cincinnati (G-2825)

M & R Phillips Enterprises....................... F 740 323-0580
Newark (G-10518)

Mueller Art Cover & Binding Co............. E 440 238-3303
Strongsville (G-12577)

Quick Tech Graphics Inc......................... F 937 743-5952
Springboro (G-12266)

Tenacity Manufacturing Company.......... G 513 821-0201
West Chester (G-14081)

William Exline Inc.................................... G 216 941-0800
Cleveland (G-4506)

2789 Bookbinding and related work

A-A Blueprint Co Inc.............................. E 330 794-8803
Akron (G-10)

AAA Laminating and Bindery Inc............ G 513 860-2680
Fairfield (G-6705)

▲ Activities Press Inc.............................. E 440 953-1200
Mentor (G-9469)

AGS Custom Graphics Inc...................... D 330 963-7770
Macedonia (G-8676)

Allen Graphics Inc.................................. G 440 349-4100
Solon (G-12075)

American Printing & Lithog Co............... F 513 867-0602
Hamilton (G-7463)

Anderson Graphics Inc........................... E 330 745-2165
Barberton (G-793)

Andrin Enterprises Inc........................... F 937 276-7794
Moraine (G-10146)

▲ Art Guild Binders Inc............................ E 513 242-3000
Cincinnati (G-2378)

Baesman Group Inc................................ D 614 771-2300
Hilliard (G-7674)

Barnhart Printing Corp........................... G 330 456-2279
Canton (G-1837)

Bindery & Spc Pressworks Inc............... D 614 873-4623
Plain City (G-11398)

Bindtech LLC.. D 615 834-0404
Macedonia (G-8679)

Bindusa.. F 513 247-3000
Blue Ash (G-1253)

Black River Group Inc............................ E 419 524-6699
Mansfield (G-8765)

Blains Folding Service Inc...................... G 216 631-4700
Cleveland (G-3421)

▼ Bookfactory LLC.................................. E 937 226-7100
Dayton (G-5682)

Century Graphics Inc.............................. G 614 895-7698
Westerville (G-14206)

Classic Laminations Inc......................... E 440 735-1333
Oakwood Village (G-10904)

Clints Printing Inc.................................. G 937 426-2771
Dayton (G-5703)

▲ Consolidated Graphics Group Inc...... C 216 881-9191
Cleveland (G-3559)

Copley Ohio Newspapers Inc................. C 330 364-5577
New Philadelphia (G-10439)

COS Blueprint Inc................................... E 330 376-0022
Akron (G-107)

Cott Systems Inc.................................... D 614 847-4405
Columbus (G-4853)

Cox Printing Company............................ G 937 382-2312
Wilmington (G-14576)

Crossbridge Mktg & Media Inc............... G 330 682-5066
Orrville (G-10979)

Customformed Products Inc................... F 937 388-0480
Miamisburg (G-9685)

◆ Davis Printing Company....................... E 330 745-3113
Barberton (G-803)

Dayton Bindery Service Inc.................... E 937 235-3111
Dayton (G-5722)

Dayton Legal Blank Inc........................... G 937 435-4405
Dayton (G-5729)

Earl D Arnold Printing Company............. E 513 533-6900
Cincinnati (G-2574)

Eugene Stewart...................................... G 937 898-1117
Dayton (G-5770)

Folks Creative Printers Inc..................... G 740 383-6326
Marion (G-8970)

Franklin Printing Company...................... F 740 452-6375
Zanesville (G-15016)

G W Steffen Bookbinders Inc................. E 330 963-0300
Macedonia (G-8693)

▲ Gli Holdings Inc.................................... D 216 651-1500
Stow (G-12433)

Golden Graphics Ltd................................ F 419 673-6260
Kenton (G-8099)

Greg Blume... G 740 574-2308
Wheelersburg (G-14353)

Harris Paper Crafts Inc........................... F 614 299-2141
Columbus (G-4971)

▲ Hecks Direct Mail Prtg Svc Inc........... F 419 697-3505
Toledo (G-12990)

Hf Group LLC.. C 440 729-9411
Newbury (G-10553)

HP Industries Inc.................................... E 419 478-0695
Toledo (G-12997)

Innmark Communications LLC............... D 937 454-5555
Miamisburg (G-9701)

▲ Jack Walker Printing Co....................... F 440 352-4222
Mentor (G-9540)

▲ Kehl-Kolor Inc...................................... E 419 281-3107
Ashland (G-545)

Kenwel Printers Inc................................ E 614 261-1011
Columbus (G-5050)

Kevin K Tidd... G 419 885-5603
Sylvania (G-12714)

Keystone Press Inc................................. G 419 243-7326
Toledo (G-13018)

Laipplys Prtg Mktg Sltions Inc............... G 740 387-9282
Marion (G-8975)

Lam Pro Inc.. F 216 426-0661
Cleveland (G-3938)

Lee Corporation..................................... G 513 771-3602
Cincinnati (G-2817)

Legal News Publishing Co...................... E 216 696-3322
Cleveland (G-3949)

Liturgical Publications Inc...................... D 216 325-6825
Cleveland (G-3964)

Macke Brothers Inc................................ G 513 771-7500
Cincinnati (G-2838)

Mmp Printing Inc.................................... F 513 381-0990
Cincinnati (G-2883)

Multi-Craft Litho Inc............................... E 859 581-2754
Blue Ash (G-1312)

Network Printing & Graphics................... F 614 230-2084
Columbus (G-5124)

North End Press Incorporated............... G 740 653-6514
Lancaster (G-8215)

▲ Ohio Laminating & Binding Inc............ G 614 771-4868
Hilliard (G-7691)

Old Trail Printing Company..................... C 614 443-4852
Columbus (G-5159)

Onetouchpoint East Corp....................... D 513 421-1600
Cincinnati (G-2933)

Orange Blossom Press Inc...................... G 216 781-8655
Willoughby (G-14502)

Painesville Publishing Inc...................... G 440 354-4142
Austinburg (G-701)

Penguin Enterprises Inc......................... E 440 899-5112
Westlake (G-14322)

Prime Printing Inc.................................. E 937 438-3707
Dayton (G-5956)

Print-Digital Incorporated...................... G 330 686-5945
Stow (G-12451)

Printed Image... F 614 221-1412
Columbus (G-5207)

▲ Printers Bindery Services Inc............. D 513 821-8039
Batavia (G-884)

▲ Prodigy Print Inc.................................. F
Dayton (G-5960)

Promatch Solutions LLC......................... F 877 299-0185
Moraine (G-10188)

▼ Quick Tab II Inc................................... D 419 448-6622
Tiffin (G-12796)

▲ Repro Acquisition Company LLC.......... G 216 738-3800
Cleveland (G-4235)

Riverside Mfg Acquisition LLC............... G 585 458-2090
Cleveland (G-4244)

Rmt Holdings Inc.................................... F 419 221-1168
Lima (G-8445)

Robin Enterprises Company................... C 614 891-0250
Westerville (G-14274)

RT Industries Inc.................................... G 937 335-5784
Troy (G-13251)

Ryans Newark Leader Ex Prtg Co.......... F 740 522-2149
Newark (G-10532)

Spring Grove Manufacturing Inc............. G 513 542-6900
Cincinnati (G-3107)

Standard Printing Co of Canton............. D 330 453-8247
Canton (G-2012)

Star Printing Company Inc...................... E 330 376-0514
Akron (G-317)

Strong Bindery Inc.................................. G 216 231-0001
Cleveland (G-4337)

Suburban Press Incorporated................ F 216 961-0766
Cleveland (G-4340)

▲ The D B Hess Company........................ E 330 678-5868
Kent (G-8089)

Tj Metzgers Inc...................................... D 419 861-8611
Toledo (G-13143)

Tl Krieg Offset LLC................................. E 513 542-1522
Cincinnati (G-3158)

Traxium LLC... E 330 572-8200
Stow (G-12466)

Watkins Printing Company...................... E 614 297-8270
Columbus (G-5358)

▲ West-Camp Press Inc.......................... D 614 882-2378
Westerville (G-14281)

▲ Wfsr Holdings LLC............................... A 877 735-4966
Dayton (G-6081)

2791 Typesetting

A-A Blueprint Co Inc.............................. E 330 794-8803
Akron (G-10)

▲ Activities Press Inc.............................. E 440 953-1200
Mentor (G-9469)

AGS Custom Graphics Inc.................... D 330 963-7770
Macedonia *(G-8676)*

American Printing & Lithog Co............ F 513 867-0602
Hamilton *(G-7463)*

Anderson Graphics Inc....................... E 330 745-2165
Barberton *(G-793)*

Andrin Enterprises Inc....................... F 937 276-7794
Moraine *(G-10146)*

Asist Translation Services................. F 614 451-6744
Columbus *(G-4729)*

Baesman Group Inc............................ D 614 771-2300
Hilliard *(G-7674)*

Bindery & Spc Pressworks Inc............ D 614 873-4623
Plain City *(G-11398)*

Black River Group Inc........................ E 419 524-6699
Mansfield *(G-8765)*

Blt Inc.. F 513 631-5050
Norwood *(G-10866)*

◆ Bookmasters Inc............................. C 419 281-1802
Ashland *(G-522)*

Brass Bull 1 LLC................................ G 740 335-8030
Wshngtn Ct Hs *(G-14735)*

Carlisle Prtg Walnut Creek Ltd........... E 330 852-9922
Sugarcreek *(G-12635)*

Characters Inc................................... G 937 335-1976
Troy *(G-13204)*

Clints Printing Inc............................. G 937 426-2771
Dayton *(G-5703)*

Colortech Graphics & Printing............ F 614 766-2400
Columbus *(G-4816)*

▲ Consolidated Graphics Group Inc..... C 216 881-9191
Cleveland *(G-3559)*

Copley Ohio Newspapers Inc.............. C 330 364-5577
New Philadelphia *(G-10439)*

COS Blueprint Inc.............................. E 330 376-0022
Akron *(G-107)*

Crossbridge Mktg & Media Inc........... G 330 682-5066
Orrville *(G-10979)*

Daubenmires Printing Co LLC............. G 513 425-7223
Middletown *(G-9853)*

◆ Davis Printing Company.................. E 330 745-3113
Barberton *(G-803)*

Dayton Legal Blank Inc...................... G 937 435-4405
Dayton *(G-5729)*

Earl D Arnold Printing Company......... E 513 533-6900
Cincinnati *(G-2574)*

Eugene Stewart.................................. G 937 898-1117
Dayton *(G-5770)*

Franklin Printing Company................. F 740 452-6375
Zanesville *(G-15016)*

Gazette Publishing Company.............. E 419 483-4190
Oberlin *(G-10917)*

Greg Blume.. G 740 574-2308
Wheelersburg *(G-14353)*

Harlan Graphic Arts Svcs Inc............. E 513 251-5700
Cincinnati *(G-2706)*

▲ Hecks Direct Mail Prtg Svc Inc........ F 419 697-3505
Toledo *(G-12990)*

Heritage Press Inc............................. E 419 289-9209
Ashland *(G-539)*

Hkm Drect Mkt Cmmnications Inc....... C 800 860-4456
Cleveland *(G-3832)*

HOT Graphic Services Inc.................. E 419 242-7000
Northwood *(G-10804)*

HP Industries Inc.............................. E 419 478-0695
Toledo *(G-12997)*

Hubbard Publishing Co....................... G 937 592-3060
Bellefontaine *(G-1110)*

Imprints... F 330 650-0467
Hudson *(G-7846)*

▲ Jack Walker Printing Co.................. F 440 352-4222
Mentor *(G-9540)*

Keener Printing Inc............................ G 216 531-7595
Cleveland *(G-3911)*

▲ Kehl-Kolor Inc................................ E 419 281-3107
Ashland *(G-545)*

Kevin K Tidd...................................... G 419 885-5603
Sylvania *(G-12714)*

Keystone Press Inc............................ G 419 243-7326
Toledo *(G-13018)*

Laurenee Ltd..................................... G 513 662-2225
Cincinnati *(G-2814)*

Lee Corporation................................ G 513 771-3602
Cincinnati *(G-2817)*

Legal News Publishing Co.................. E 216 696-3322
Cleveland *(G-3949)*

Liming Printing Inc............................ F 937 374-2646
Xenia *(G-14769)*

Middleton Printing Co Inc.................. G 614 294-7277
Gahanna *(G-7166)*

Mmp Printing Inc............................... F 513 381-0990
Cincinnati *(G-2883)*

Multi-Craft Litho Inc.......................... E 859 581-2754
Blue Ash *(G-1312)*

Network Printing & Graphics.............. F 614 230-2084
Columbus *(G-5124)*

Old Trail Printing Company................ C 614 443-4852
Columbus *(G-5159)*

Onetouchpoint East Corp................... D 513 421-1600
Cincinnati *(G-2933)*

Orange Blossom Press Inc................. G 216 781-8655
Willoughby *(G-14502)*

Painesville Publishing Inc................. G 440 354-4142
Austinburg *(G-701)*

Penguin Enterprises Inc.................... E 440 899-5112
Westlake *(G-14322)*

Preisser Inc....................................... G 614 345-0199
Columbus *(G-5203)*

Prime Printing Inc............................. E 937 438-3707
Dayton *(G-5956)*

Printed Image..................................... F 614 221-1412
Columbus *(G-5207)*

Printery Inc....................................... G 513 574-1099
Cincinnati *(G-2983)*

Printing Arts Press Inc...................... F 740 397-6106
Mount Vernon *(G-10260)*

Progrssive Communications Corp....... F 740 397-5333
Mount Vernon *(G-10261)*

▼ Quick Tab II Inc............................. D 419 448-6622
Tiffin *(G-12796)*

Quick Tech Graphics Inc.................... F 937 743-5952
Springboro *(G-12266)*

Robin Enterprises Company............... C 614 891-0250
Westerville *(G-14274)*

▲ Royal Acme Corporation................. E 216 241-1477
Cleveland *(G-4256)*

RR Donnelley & Sons Company........... G 614 221-8385
Columbus *(G-5237)*

Ryans Newark Leader Ex Prtg Co........ F 740 522-2149
Newark *(G-10532)*

▲ St Media Group Intl Inc................... D 513 421-2050
Blue Ash *(G-1332)*

Standard Printing Co of Canton.......... G 330 453-8247
Canton *(G-2012)*

Suburban Press Incorporated............. F 216 961-0766
Cleveland *(G-4340)*

The Photo-Type Engraving Company.... D 513 281-0999
Cincinnati *(G-3149)*

Tj Metzgers Inc.................................. D 419 861-8611
Toledo *(G-13143)*

Watkins Printing Company................. E 614 297-8270
Columbus *(G-5358)*

▲ West-Camp Press Inc..................... D 614 882-2378
Westerville *(G-14281)*

Western Roto Engravers Inc............... E 330 336-7636
Wadsworth *(G-13677)*

▲ Wfsr Holdings LLC.......................... A 877 735-4966
Dayton *(G-6081)*

Winkler Co Inc................................... G 937 294-2662
Dayton *(G-6082)*

Wolters Kluwer Clinical D.................. D 330 650-6506
Hudson *(G-7862)*

◆ Workflowone LLC............................ A 877 735-4966
Dayton *(G-6087)*

2796 Platemaking services

▲ Amos Media Company...................... C 937 498-2121
Sidney *(G-11992)*

Anderson & Vreeland Inc................... D 419 636-5002
Bryan *(G-1629)*

Bomen Marking Products Inc.............. G 440 582-0053
Cleveland *(G-3426)*

Buckler Industries Inc........................ E 419 589-6134
Mansfield *(G-8769)*

Century Graphics Inc......................... G 614 895-7698
Westerville *(G-14206)*

Converters/Prepress Inc.................... F 937 743-0935
Carlisle *(G-2065)*

Csw Inc.. E 413 589-1311
Sylvania *(G-12703)*

Dynamic Dies Inc............................... E 419 865-0249
Holland *(G-7761)*

E C Shaw Company of Ohio................. E 513 721-6334
Cincinnati *(G-2569)*

Earl D Arnold Printing Company......... E 513 533-6900
Cincinnati *(G-2574)*

Gli Holdings Inc................................. D 440 892-7760
Stow *(G-12434)*

▲ Gli Holdings Inc............................. D 216 651-1500
Stow *(G-12433)*

Hadronics Inc.................................... D 513 321-9350
Cincinnati *(G-2702)*

Harris Paper Crafts Inc...................... F 614 299-2141
Columbus *(G-4971)*

▲ Kehl-Kolor Inc................................ E 419 281-3107
Ashland *(G-545)*

Keystone Press Inc............................ G 419 243-7326
Toledo *(G-13018)*

▲ Mark-All Enterprises LLC................ E 800 433-3615
Akron *(G-220)*

Penguin Enterprises Inc.................... E 440 899-5112
Westlake *(G-14322)*

Plate Engraving Corporation.............. G 330 239-2155
Medina *(G-9436)*

Precision Reflex Inc.......................... G 419 629-2603
New Bremen *(G-10365)*

Prime Printing Inc............................. E 937 438-3707
Dayton *(G-5956)*

Quality Rubber Stamp Inc.................. G 614 235-2700
Lancaster *(G-8220)*

R E May Inc....................................... G 216 771-6332
Cleveland *(G-4220)*

Roban Inc.. G 330 794-1059
Lakemore *(G-8156)*

Sams Graphic Industries.................... F 330 821-4710
Alliance *(G-402)*

Southern Graphic Systems LLC.......... E 513 648-4641
Cincinnati *(G-3101)*

Stevenson Color Inc.......................... C 513 321-7500
Cincinnati *(G-3119)*

The Photo-Type Engraving Company.... D 513 281-0999
Cincinnati *(G-3149)*

Universal Urethane Pdts Inc.............. D 419 693-7400
Toledo *(G-13169)*

▲ West-Camp Press Inc..................... D 614 882-2378
Westerville *(G-14281)*

SIC

Williams Steel Rule Die Co......................G 216 431-3232
Cleveland *(G-4507)*

◆ Wood Graphics Inc..................................E 513 771-6300
Cincinnati *(G-3230)*

28 CHEMICALS AND ALLIED PRODUCTS

2812 Alkalies and chlorine

Church & Dwight Co Inc........................G 740 852-3621
London *(G-8533)*

Church & Dwight Co Inc........................G 419 992-4244
Old Fort *(G-10933)*

Clorox Company......................................G 513 445-1840
Mason *(G-9089)*

Eltech Systems Corporation.....................G 440 285-0380
Concord Township *(G-5390)*

Geon Company...A 216 447-6000
Cleveland *(G-3771)*

◆ GFS Chemicals Inc...............................E 740 881-5501
Powell *(G-11488)*

▲ INEOS KOH INC....................................G 440 997-5221
Ashtabula *(G-596)*

Jci Jones Chemicals Inc..........................F 330 825-2531
Barberton *(G-814)*

▲ National Colloid Company....................E 740 282-1171
Steubenville *(G-12407)*

National Lime and Stone Co.....................E 419 396-7671
Carey *(G-2060)*

▲ Valvsys LLC..G 513 870-1234
Hamilton *(G-7536)*

2813 Industrial gases

Airgas Usa LLC..E 330 454-1330
Canton *(G-1826)*

Airgas Usa LLC..G 440 232-6397
Twinsburg *(G-13270)*

Atlantic Welding LLC................................F 937 570-5094
Piqua *(G-11335)*

▲ C A P Industries Inc.............................F 937 773-1824
Piqua *(G-11338)*

Cold Jet International LLC........................D 513 831-3211
Loveland *(G-8622)*

Delille Oxygen Company.........................G 937 325-9595
Springfield *(G-12300)*

Delille Oxygen Company.........................E 614 444-1177
Columbus *(G-4876)*

Eco Energy International LLC..................E 419 544-5000
Mansfield *(G-8783)*

Endurance Manufacturing Inc.................G 330 628-2600
Akron *(G-133)*

Eveready Products Corporation..............F 216 661-2755
Cleveland *(G-3694)*

Helium Seo...E 513 563-3065
Blue Ash *(G-1284)*

Invacare Corporation...............................G 800 333-6900
Elyria *(G-6551)*

◆ Invacare Corporation............................A 440 329-6000
Elyria *(G-6549)*

Linde Gas & Equipment Inc....................G 513 821-2192
Cincinnati *(G-2823)*

Linde Gas & Equipment Inc....................E 614 443-7687
Columbus *(G-5071)*

Linde Gas & Equipment Inc....................E 419 729-7732
Toledo *(G-13037)*

Linde Gas & Equipment Inc....................G 440 944-8844
Wickliffe *(G-14380)*

Linde Gas USA LLC.................................G 330 425-3989
Twinsburg *(G-13332)*

Linde Inc..F 440 994-1000
Ashtabula *(G-603)*

Linde Inc..G 330 825-4449
Barberton *(G-817)*

Linde Inc..F 440 237-8690
Cleveland *(G-3958)*

Linde Inc..G 419 698-8005
Oregon *(G-10962)*

Matheson Tri-Gas Inc..............................F 419 865-8881
Holland *(G-7772)*

Matheson Tri-Gas Inc..............................E 330 425-4407
Twinsburg *(G-13335)*

Messer LLC..E 216 533-7256
Cleveland *(G-4022)*

Messer LLC..G 419 822-3909
Delta *(G-6211)*

Messer LLC..G 614 539-2259
Grove City *(G-7399)*

Messer LLC..F 419 227-9585
Lima *(G-8430)*

Messer LLC..E 419 221-5043
Lima *(G-8431)*

Messer LLC..F 513 831-4742
Miamiville *(G-9763)*

Messer LLC..G 330 394-4541
Warren *(G-13782)*

National Gas & Oil Corporation...............E 740 344-2102
Newark *(G-10524)*

Neon..G 216 541-5600
Cleveland *(G-4065)*

Neon Health Services Inc.........................E 216 231-7700
Cleveland *(G-4066)*

Northeast Ohio Nghbrhood Hlth S...........E 216 751-3100
Cleveland *(G-4091)*

Ohio Nitrogen LLC...................................F 216 839-5485
Beachwood *(G-935)*

Osair Inc..G 440 974-6500
Mentor *(G-9577)*

◆ Plasti-Kote Co Inc.................................C 330 725-4511
Medina *(G-9435)*

Reliable Mfg Co LLC................................G 740 756-9373
Carroll *(G-2078)*

Welders Supply Inc..................................F 216 241-1696
Cleveland *(G-4500)*

Wellston Aerosol Mfg Co.........................G 740 384-2320
Wellston *(G-13911)*

◆ Western/Scott Fetzer Company..............E 440 892-3000
Westlake *(G-14343)*

Wright Brothers Inc..................................F 513 731-2222
Cincinnati *(G-3232)*

Wright Brothers Global Gas LLC.............F 513 731-2222
Cincinnati *(G-3233)*

▲ Zenex International................................G 440 232-4155
Bedford *(G-1067)*

2816 Inorganic pigments

◆ American Colors Inc..............................E 419 621-4000
Sandusky *(G-11821)*

Americhem Inc...E 330 926-3185
Cuyahoga Falls *(G-5524)*

◆ Americhem Inc......................................D 330 929-4213
Cuyahoga Falls *(G-5523)*

Ampacet Corporation...............................C 740 929-5521
Newark *(G-10490)*

Arconic..F 330 471-1844
Canton *(G-1832)*

Avient Corporation...................................D 419 668-4844
Norwalk *(G-10829)*

◆ Chromascape LLC.................................E 330 998-7574
Independence *(G-7892)*

◆ Colormatrix Corporation.......................C 216 622-0100
Berea *(G-1163)*

Colormatrix Group Inc..............................C 216 622-0100
Berea *(G-1164)*

Colormatrix Holdings Inc.........................F 440 930-3162
Berea *(G-1165)*

Day-Glo Color Corp.................................F 216 391-7070
Cleveland *(G-3603)*

Day-Glo Color Corp.................................F 216 391-7070
Twinsburg *(G-13291)*

▲ Day-Glo Color Corp.............................C 216 391-7070
Cleveland *(G-3602)*

▲ Degussa Incorporated.........................G 513 733-5111
Cincinnati *(G-2544)*

◆ Eckart America Corporation.................D 440 954-7600
Painesville *(G-11082)*

Enviri Corporation....................................F 330 372-1781
Warren *(G-13763)*

Ferro International Svcs Inc.....................G 216 875-5600
Mayfield Heights *(G-9333)*

General Color Investments Inc................D 330 868-4161
Minerva *(G-10038)*

▲ Gsdi Specialty Dispersions Inc...........E 330 848-9200
Massillon *(G-9198)*

Ironics Inc..G 330 652-0583
Niles *(G-10592)*

ISK Americas Incorporated......................F 440 357-4600
Concord Township *(G-5392)*

◆ Kish Company Inc.................................F 440 205-9970
Mentor *(G-9546)*

Lancer Dispersions Inc............................D
Akron *(G-202)*

Leonhardt Plating Company.....................G 513 242-1410
Cincinnati *(G-2819)*

Lyondllbsell Advnced Plymers I...............D 419 682-3311
Stryker *(G-12624)*

▲ Mason Color Works Inc........................F 330 385-4400
East Liverpool *(G-6395)*

McCann Color Inc....................................E 330 498-4840
Canton *(G-1942)*

Obron Atlantic Corporation......................D 440 954-7600
Painesville *(G-11100)*

PMC Specialties Group Inc......................F 513 242-3300
Cincinnati *(G-2972)*

◆ PMC Specialties Group Inc...................E 513 242-3300
Cincinnati *(G-2971)*

Revlis Corporation...................................F 330 535-2108
Barberton *(G-835)*

▲ Spectrum Dispersions Inc....................F 330 296-0600
Ravenna *(G-11542)*

Sun Chemical Corporation......................C 513 681-5950
Cincinnati *(G-3127)*

◆ The Shepherd Color Company..............C 513 874-0714
Cincinnati *(G-3151)*

◆ Thorworks Industries Inc......................C 419 626-4375
Sandusky *(G-11876)*

◆ Vibrantz Color Solutions Inc................C 440 997-5137
Ashtabula *(G-621)*

Vibrantz Corporation................................E 724 207-2152
Cleveland *(G-4465)*

Vibrantz Corporation................................D 732 287-4925
Cleveland *(G-4469)*

◆ Vibrantz Corporation............................D 216 875-5600
Mayfield Heights *(G-9344)*

Vwm-Republic Inc....................................G 216 641-2575
Cleveland *(G-4484)*

Whiterock Pigments Inc...........................F 216 391-7765
Cleveland *(G-4503)*

2819 Industrial inorganic chemicals, nec

Airgas Usa LLC..G 440 232-6397
Twinsburg *(G-13270)*

▲ Akron Dispersions Inc..........................E 330 666-0045
Copley *(G-5428)*

▲ Alchem Corporation.............................G 330 725-2436
Medina *(G-9373)*

Aldrich Chemical	D	937 859-1808	
Miamisburg (G-9663)			
Alfrebro LLC	F	513 539-7373	
Monroe (G-10095)			
Alpha Zeta Holdings Inc	G	216 271-1601	
Cleveland (G-3334)			
◆ Aluchem Inc	E	513 733-8519	
Cincinnati (G-2353)			
Aluchem of Jackson Inc	G	740 286-2455	
Jackson (G-7938)			
◆ Americhem Inc	D	330 929-4213	
Cuyahoga Falls (G-5523)			
Arboris LLC	E	740 522-9350	
Newark (G-10492)			
▲ Baerlocher Production Usa LLC	E	513 482-6300	
Cincinnati (G-2398)			
▲ Baerlocher Usa LLC	F	330 364-6000	
Dover (G-6229)			
▲ Barium & Chemicals Inc	E	740 282-9776	
Steubenville (G-12400)			
BASF Catalysts LLC	A	216 360-5005	
Cleveland (G-3408)			
BASF Catalysts LLC	A	440 322-3741	
Elyria (G-6502)			
BASF Corporation	D	614 662-5682	
Columbus (G-4745)			
Bio-Systems Corporation	G	608 365-9550	
Bowling Green (G-1410)			
BLaster Holdings LLC	E	216 901-5800	
Cleveland (G-3422)			
BLaster LLC	E	216 901-5800	
Cleveland (G-3423)			
Bleachtech LLC	E	216 921-1980	
Seville (G-11913)			
Bond Chemicals Inc	G	330 725-5935	
Medina (G-9382)			
◆ Borchers Americas Inc	D	440 899-2950	
Westlake (G-14295)			
Calgon Carbon Corporation	F	614 258-9501	
Columbus (G-4791)			
▲ Calvary Industries Inc	E	513 874-1113	
Fairfield (G-6716)			
▲ Capital Resin Corporation	D	614 445-7177	
Columbus (G-4798)			
Chem Technologies Ltd	D	440 632-9311	
Middlefield (G-9786)			
◆ Chemspec Usa Inc	D	330 669-8512	
Orrville (G-10977)			
Chemtrade Logistics Inc	F	216 566-8070	
Cleveland (G-3493)			
Chemtrade Refinery Svcs Inc	F	419 641-4151	
Cairo (G-1721)			
Christy Catalytics LLC	G	740 982-1302	
Crooksville (G-5509)			
▲ Cil Isotope Separations LLC	F	937 376-5413	
Xenia (G-14757)			
▲ Cirba Solutions Us Inc	E	740 653-6290	
Lancaster (G-8186)			
◆ Columbia Chemical Corporation	E	330 225-3200	
Brunswick (G-1584)			
◆ Current Lighting Solutions LLC	E	216 462-4700	
Cleveland (G-3581)			
Custom Metal Shearing Inc	F	937 233-6950	
Dayton (G-5718)			
◆ Detrex Corporation	F	216 749-2605	
Cleveland (G-3611)			
Diverseylever Inc	G	513 554-4200	
Cincinnati (G-2553)			
Diversified Brands	G	216 595-8777	
Bedford (G-1027)			
◆ Dover Chemical Corporation	C	330 343-7711	
Dover (G-6238)			

Drs Industrial LLC	G	419 861-0334	
Holland (G-7758)			
Drs Industries Inc	D	419 861-0334	
Holland (G-7759)			
Dupont Electronic Polymers LP	D	937 268-3411	
Dayton (G-5756)			
Eagle Chemicals Inc	F	513 868-9662	
Hamilton (G-7487)			
Elco Corporation	E	440 997-6131	
Ashtabula (G-590)			
◆ Eliokem Inc	D	330 734-1100	
Fairlawn (G-6800)			
Essential Elements Usa LLC	E	513 482-5700	
Cincinnati (G-2599)			
Evonik Corporation	E	513 554-8969	
Cincinnati (G-2606)			
Ferro Corporation	D	216 577-7144	
Bedford (G-1032)			
◆ Ferroglobe USA Mtlurgical Inc	C	740 984-2361	
Waterford (G-13826)			
Flexsys Inc	B	212 605-6000	
Akron (G-151)			
◆ Gayston Corporation	C	937 743-6050	
Miamisburg (G-9693)			
General Electric Company	G	216 268-3846	
Cleveland (G-3763)			
GFS Chemicals Inc	G	614 351-5347	
Columbus (G-4953)			
GFS Chemicals Inc	D	614 224-5345	
Columbus (G-4954)			
◆ GFS Chemicals Inc	E	740 881-5501	
Powell (G-11488)			
▲ Great River Re Inc	E	513 471-8770	
Cincinnati (G-2688)			
Helena Agri-Enterprises LLC	E	614 275-4200	
Columbus (G-4975)			
Helena Agri-Enterprises LLC	G	419 596-3806	
Continental (G-5422)			
▲ Heraeus Epurio LLC	E	937 264-1000	
Vandalia (G-13559)			
Hilltop Energy Inc	F	330 859-2108	
Mineral City (G-10028)			
Illinois Tool Works Inc	D	440 914-3100	
Solon (G-12126)			
Ineos Pigments Asu LLC	F	440 994-1999	
Ashtabula (G-597)			
Ineos Pigments USA Inc	C	440 994-1400	
Ashtabula (G-598)			
▲ J R M Chemical Inc	F	216 475-8488	
Cleveland (G-3878)			
◆ Jones-Hamilton Co	D	888 858-4425	
Maumee (G-9300)			
◆ Lithium Innovations Co LLC	G	419 725-3525	
Toledo (G-13038)			
Littlern Corporation	G	330 848-8847	
Fairlawn (G-6807)			
◆ Malco Products Inc	C	330 753-0361	
Barberton (G-819)			
Marsulex Inc	E	419 698-8181	
Oregon (G-10963)			
▲ Materion Advnced Mtls Tech Svc	D	216 486-4200	
Mayfield Heights (G-9335)			
McGean-Rohco Inc	G	216 441-4900	
Newburgh Heights (G-10545)			
◆ McGean-Rohco Inc	D	216 441-4900	
Cleveland (G-4009)			
▲ Nachurs Alpine Solutions LLC	E	740 382-5701	
Marion (G-8982)			
▲ National Colloid Company	E	740 282-1171	
Steubenville (G-12407)			
New Eezy-Gro Inc	F	419 927-6110	
Upper Sandusky (G-13449)			

Norlab Inc	F	440 282-5265	
Lorain (G-8569)			
Om Group Inc	F	216 781-0083	
Cleveland (G-4120)			
Omnova Wallcovering USA Inc	D	216 682-7000	
Beachwood (G-937)			
Omya Distribution LLC	F	513 387-4600	
Mason (G-9132)			
◆ Omya Inc	C	513 387-4600	
Cincinnati (G-2930)			
Pcs Phosphate Company Inc	C	513 738-1261	
Harrison (G-7560)			
◆ Perstorp Polyols Inc	C	419 729-5448	
Toledo (G-13095)			
PMC Specialties Group Inc	F	513 242-3300	
Cincinnati (G-2972)			
◆ PMC Specialties Group Inc	E	513 242-3300	
Cincinnati (G-2971)			
▲ Polymerics Inc	E	330 928-2210	
Cuyahoga Falls (G-5565)			
Primary Pdts Ingrdnts Amrcas L	D	937 236-5906	
Dayton (G-5955)			
Pureti Group LLC	G	513 708-3631	
Cincinnati (G-3012)			
PVS Chemical Solutions Inc	F	330 666-0888	
Copley (G-5439)			
Qc LLC	E	847 682-9072	
North Lima (G-10712)			
Quanta International LLC	F	513 354-3639	
Cincinnati (G-3018)			
Saint-Gobain Ceramics Plas Inc	C	440 564-8000	
Newbury (G-10564)			
Saint-Gobain Ceramics Plas Inc	D	330 673-5860	
Stow (G-12456)			
▲ Saint-Gobain Ceramics Plas Inc	A	610 893-6000	
Stow (G-12457)			
Shepherd Material Science Co	E	513 731-1110	
Norwood (G-10871)			
▲ Shepherd Widnes Ltd	D	513 731-1110	
Norwood (G-10872)			
Solvay Advanced Polymers LLC	E	740 373-9242	
Marietta (G-8947)			
Synthomer Inc	F	330 734-1237	
Akron (G-323)			
◆ Synthomer Inc	C	216 682-7000	
Beachwood (G-951)			
◆ The Shepherd Chemical Company	C	513 731-1110	
Norwood (G 10874)			
◆ United Initiators Inc	D	440 323-3112	
Elyria (G-6598)			
Univar Solutions USA LLC	E	513 714-5264	
West Chester (G-14157)			
Usalco Michigan City Plant LLC	D	440 992-7039	
Ashtabula (G-598)			
Usalco Michigan City Plant LLC	E	513 737-7100	
Fairfield (G-6787)			
Vibrantz Corporation	F	442 224-6100	
Cleveland (G-4466)			
▲ VWR Chemicals LLC	E	800 448-4442	
Solon (G-12204)			
WA Hammond Drierite Co Ltd	E	937 376-2927	
Xenia (G-14783)			
Wisconsin Indus Sand Co LLC	E	715 235-0942	
Independence (G-7926)			
◆ Zaclon LLC	E	216 271-1601	
Cleveland (G-4522)			

2821 Plastics materials and resins

A R E Logistics LLC	G	330 327-7315	
Massillon (G-9170)			
▼ Ada Solutions Inc	G	440 576-0423	
Jefferson (G-7971)			

Advanced Fiber LLC............E 419 562-1337	**Current Inc**............G 330 392-5151	**Hancor Inc**............E 419 424-8225
Bucyrus *(G-1671)*	Warren *(G-13756)*	Findlay *(G-6879)*
Aerosport Modeling Design LLC............F 614 834-5227	**Cuyahoga Molded Plastics Co (inc)**............E 216 261-2744	▲ **Hexa Americas Inc**............E 937 497-7900
Canal Winchester *(G-1783)*	Euclid *(G-6647)*	Sidney *(G-12022)*
Al-Co Products Inc............G 419 399-3867	**Ddp Specialty Electronic MA**............G 937 839-4612	**Hexion Inc**............C 888 443-9466
Latty *(G-8236)*	West Alexandria *(G-13918)*	Columbus *(G-4976)*
American Polymers Corporation............G 330 666-6048	**Deltech Polymers LLC**............G 937 339-3150	◆ **Hexion LLC**............D 614 225-4000
Akron *(G-57)*	Troy *(G-13210)*	Columbus *(G-4977)*
American Turf Recycling LLC............G 440 323-0306	**Dentsply Sirona Inc**............E 419 865-9497	▼ **Hexion Topco LLC**............D 614 225-4000
Elyria *(G-6496)*	Maumee *(G-9291)*	Columbus *(G-4978)*
Americas Styrenics LLC............D 740 302-8667	◆ **Diamond Polymers Incorporated**............D 330 773-2700	▼ **Hexion US Finance Corp**............F 614 225-4000
Ironton *(G-7930)*	Akron *(G-121)*	Columbus *(G-4979)*
Ampacet Corporation............E 513 247-5403	**Dow Chemical Company**............F 937 839-4612	▲ **Hexpol Compounding LLC**............E 440 834-4644
Mason *(G-9060)*	West Alexandria *(G-13919)*	Burton *(G-1700)*
Amros Industries Inc............F 216 433-0010	**Dupont Specialty Pdts USA LLC**............D 740 474-0635	**Hexpol Holding Inc**............F 440 834-4644
Cleveland *(G-3351)*	Circleville *(G-3254)*	Burton *(G-1701)*
Aptiv Services Us LLC............D 330 373-7614	**Dupont Specialty Pdts USA LLC**............E 740 474-0220	◆ **Hfi LLC**............B 614 491-0700
Warren *(G-13738)*	Circleville *(G-3255)*	Canal Winchester *(G-1791)*
Arclin USA LLC............F 419 726-5013	**Durez Corporation**............D 567 295-6400	**Hggc Citadel Plas Holdings Inc**............F 330 666-3751
Toledo *(G-12885)*	Kenton *(G-8097)*	Fairlawn *(G-6803)*
▲ **Aurora Plastics LLC**............E 330 422-0700	**E C Shaw Company of Ohio**............E 513 721-6334	**Hpc Holdings LLC**............F 330 666-3751
Streetsboro *(G-12488)*	Cincinnati *(G-2569)*	Fairlawn *(G-6804)*
Avient Corporation............E 440 930-3727	**E P S Specialists Ltd Inc**............G 513 489-3676	**Huntsman Advnced Mtls Amrcas L**............E 330 374-2424
Avon Lake *(G-747)*	Cincinnati *(G-2571)*	Akron *(G-177)*
Avient Corporation............F 440 930-1000	**Eagle Elastomer Inc**............E 330 923-7070	**Huntsman Advnced Mtls Amrcas L**............E 866 800-2436
Elyria *(G-6499)*	Peninsula *(G-11182)*	Akron *(G-178)*
Avient Corporation............E 800 727-4338	**Elyria Foundry Company LLC**............C 440 322-4657	**Huntsman Corporation**............D 330 374-2418
Greenville *(G-7335)*	Elyria *(G-6529)*	Akron *(G-179)*
Avient Corporation............E 330 834-3812	**Ep Bollinger LLC**............A 513 941-1101	▲ **ICP Adhesives and Sealants Inc**............E 330 753-4585
Massillon *(G-9173)*	Cincinnati *(G-2594)*	Norton *(G-10823)*
◆ **Avient Corporation**............D 440 930-1000	**Epsilyte Holdings LLC**............D 937 778-9500	▲ **Ier Fujikura Inc**............C 330 425-7121
Avon Lake *(G-748)*	Piqua *(G-11346)*	Macedonia *(G-8696)*
Aviles Construction Co Inc............G 216 939-1084	◆ **Etna Products Incorporated**............E 440 543-9845	**Illinois Tool Works Inc**............C 513 489-7600
Cleveland *(G-3392)*	Chagrin Falls *(G-2161)*	Blue Ash *(G-1286)*
Axiom International Inc............G 330 396-5942	◆ **Evans Adhesive Corporation Ltd**............E 614 451-2665	▲ **Incredible Solutions Inc**............F 330 898-3878
Akron *(G-66)*	Columbus *(G-4913)*	Warren *(G-13772)*
Bakelite Chemicals LLC............D 404 652-4000	**Evergreen Recycling LLC**............E 419 547-1400	**Industrial Thermoset Plas Inc**............F 440 975-0411
Columbus *(G-4741)*	Clyde *(G-4558)*	Mentor *(G-9531)*
BCi and V Investments Inc............G 330 538-0660	**Fibre Glast Dvlpments Corp LLC**............F 937 833-5200	▲ **Ineos LLC**............D 419 226-1200
North Jackson *(G-10683)*	Brookville *(G-1567)*	Lima *(G-8419)*
Benvic Trinity LLC............F 609 520-0000	**Flex Technologies Inc**............D 330 897-6311	◆ **Ineos ABS (usa) LLC**............C 513 467-2400
West Unity *(G-14192)*	Baltic *(G-777)*	Addyston *(G-8)*
Biobent Holdings LLC............G 513 658-5560	◆ **Flexsys America LP**............D 330 666-4111	**Ineos Joliet LLC**............F 815 314-4317
Columbus *(G-4755)*	Akron *(G-150)*	Dublin *(G-6307)*
▲ **Biothane Coated Webbing Corp**............E 440 327-0485	**Fortis Parent Inc**............D 614 790-9299	**Ineos Neal LLC**............E 610 790-3333
North Ridgeville *(G-10727)*	Columbus *(G-4935)*	Dublin *(G-6308)*
▼ **C4 Polymers Inc**............G 440 543-3866	◆ **Franklin International Inc**............B 614 443-0241	▲ **Ineos Nitriles USA LLC**............F 281 535-6600
Chagrin Falls *(G-2136)*	Columbus *(G-4938)*	Lima *(G-8420)*
Cameo Countertops Inc............F 419 865-6371	**Freeman Manufacturing & Sup Co**............E 440 934-1902	**Ineos Solvents Sales US Corp**............B 614 790-3333
Holland *(G-7748)*	Avon *(G-727)*	Dublin *(G-6309)*
▲ **Capital Resin Corporation**............D 614 445-7177	**Freudenberg-Nok General Partnr**............E 937 335-3306	**Integra Enclosures Limited**............D 440 269-4966
Columbus *(G-4798)*	Troy *(G-13216)*	Mentor *(G-9533)*
Carlisle Plastics Company............G 937 845-9411	◆ **Gabriel Phenoxies Inc**............E 704 499-9801	**Integrated Chem Concepts Inc**............G 440 838-5666
New Carlisle *(G-10369)*	Akron *(G-154)*	Brecksville *(G-1473)*
▲ **Chem-Materials Inc**............F 440 455-9465	**Genius Solutions Engrg Co**............E 419 794-9914	**Intergroup International Ltd**............D 216 965-0257
Westlake *(G-14297)*	Maumee *(G-9293)*	Akron *(G-183)*
▲ **Chemionics Corporation**............E 330 733-8834	▼ **Geo-Tech Polymers LLC**............F 614 797-2300	▲ **Interntnal Tchncal Plymr Syste**............E 330 505-1218
Tallmadge *(G-12731)*	Waverly *(G-13865)*	Niles *(G-10591)*
Chevron Phllips Chem Ltd Prtnr............E 740 374-2500	**Geon Company**............A 216 447-6000	**J P Industrial Products Inc**............F 330 627-1377
Marietta *(G-8909)*	Cleveland *(G-3771)*	Carrollton *(G-2086)*
Chroma Color Corporation............D 740 363-6622	**Geon Performance Solutions LLC**............D 440 930-1000	▲ **J P Industrial Products Inc**............G 330 424-1110
Delaware *(G-6139)*	Avon Lake *(G-757)*	Lisbon *(G-8473)*
Clyde Tool & Die Inc............F 419 547-9574	**Geon Performance Solutions LLC**............D 440 987-4553	◆ **Jain America Foods Inc**............G 614 850-9400
Clyde *(G-4557)*	Elyria *(G-6540)*	Columbus *(G-5030)*
◆ **Concrete Sealants Inc**............E 937 845-8776	▲ **Goldsmith & Eggleton Inc**............F 330 336-6616	**JB Polymers Inc**............G 216 941-7041
Tipp City *(G-12821)*	Wadsworth *(G-13640)*	Oberlin *(G-10919)*
Covestro LLC............C 740 929-2015	▲ **Goldsmith & Eggleton LLC**............F 203 855-6000	**Jeg Associates Inc**............G 614 882-1295
Hebron *(G-7611)*	Wadsworth *(G-13641)*	Westerville *(G-14266)*
Crane Blending Center............E 614 542-1199	**Gsh Industries Inc**............E 440 238-3009	**Jerico Plastic Industries Inc**............F 330 868-4600
Columbus *(G-4858)*	Cleveland *(G-3798)*	Minerva *(G-10039)*
▲ **Crown Plastics Co LLC**............D 513 367-0238	**Hamilton Polymers Company**............F 484 245-4557	**Jerico Plastic Industries Inc**............E 330 868-4600
Harrison *(G-7548)*	Leetonia *(G-8302)*	Wadsworth *(G-13645)*

▲ JMS Industries Inc................................ F 937 325-3502
Springfield *(G-12332)*

◆ Kardol Quality Products LLC...........G 513 933-8206
Blue Ash *(G-1293)*

Kathom Manufacturing Co Inc.............. E 513 868-8890
Middletown *(G-9871)*

◆ Key Resin Company............................F 513 943-4225
Batavia *(G-869)*

Kraton Corporation................................ E 740 423-7571
Belpre *(G-1148)*

Kraton Polymers US LLC....................... B 740 423-7571
Belpre *(G-1150)*

Lattice Composites LLC........................ F 440 759-2082
Solon *(G-12141)*

Louisville Molded Products Inc............. G 330 877-9740
Hartville *(G-7580)*

Lrbg Chemicals USA Inc........................ E 419 244-5856
Toledo *(G-13040)*

Lubrizol Global Management Inc............ E 440 933-0400
Avon Lake *(G-763)*

Lyondell Chemical Company................ C 440 352-9393
Fairport Harbor *(G-6818)*

Lyondllbsell Advnced Plymers I.......... C 330 773-2700
Akron *(G-213)*

Lyondllbsell Advnced Plymers I.......... C 330 630-0308
Akron *(G-214)*

Lyondllbsell Advnced Plymers I.......... D 330 630-3315
Akron *(G-215)*

Lyondllbsell Advnced Plymers I.......... D 440 224-7544
Geneva *(G-7243)*

Lyondllbsell Advnced Plymers I.......... D 419 872-1408
Perrysburg *(G-11235)*

Lyondllbsell Advnced Plymers I.......... D 419 682-3311
Stryker *(G-12624)*

▲ Maintenance Repair Supply Inc........ G 740 922-3006
Midvale *(G-9913)*

◆ Mar-Bal Inc.. D 440 543-7526
Chagrin Falls *(G-2170)*

Material Processing & Hdlg Co............. F 419 436-9562
Fostoria *(G-6988)*

Meggitt (erlanger) LLC......................... D 513 851-5550
Cincinnati *(G-2858)*

◆ Mexichem Specialty Resins Inc.........E 440 930-1435
Avon Lake *(G-765)*

Michael Day Enterprises LLC............... E 330 335-5100
Wadsworth *(G-13650)*

Mitsubishi Chemical Amer Inc.............. C 586 755-1660
Bellevue *(C 1127)*

Morbern USA.. F 937 298-2176
Dayton *(G-5893)*

◆ Multi-Plastics Inc...............................D 740 548-4894
Lewis Center *(G-8344)*

▲ Multibase Inc.................................... D 330 666-0505
Akron *(G-240)*

◆ Mum Industries Inc............................ D 440 269-4966
Mentor *(G-9569)*

Nanofiber Solutions LLC....................... F 614 319-3075
Dublin *(G-6322)*

▼ Nanosperse LLC................................ G 937 296-5030
Kettering *(G-8122)*

◆ Network Polymers Inc.........................E 330 773-2700
Akron *(G-244)*

◆ Next Specialty Resins Inc..................E 419 843-4600
Sylvania *(G-12719)*

North American Composites.................G 440 930-0602
Avon Lake *(G-767)*

Nu-Tech Polymers Co Inc.....................G 513 942-6003
Cincinnati *(G-2916)*

Oak View Enterprises Inc..................... E 513 860-4446
Bucyrus *(G-1685)*

Ohio Foam Corporation........................ F 419 492-2151
New Washington *(G-10482)*

Ohio Plastics & Belting Co LLC............. G 330 882-6764
New Franklin *(G-10391)*

Ohio Rotational Molding LLC................ G 419 608-5040
Findlay *(G-6901)*

OK Industries Inc.................................. E 419 435-2361
Fostoria *(G-6996)*

OPC Polymers LLC............................... D 614 253-8511
Columbus *(G-5161)*

▲ OSI Global Sourcing LLC................... G 614 471-4800
Columbus *(G-5164)*

▲ Ovation Plymr Tech Engnred Mtl........ E 330 723-5686
Medina *(G-9432)*

Owens Corning Sales LLC................... F 330 633-6735
Tallmadge *(G-12745)*

Pace Mold & Machine LLC.................... G 330 879-1777
Massillon *(G-9231)*

▲ Performnce Plymr Solutions Inc........ F 937 298-3713
Moraine *(G-10180)*

◆ Perstorp Polyols Inc...........................C 419 729-5448
Toledo *(G-13095)*

◆ Pet Processors LLc........................... D 440 354-4321
Painesville *(G-11105)*

Pilot Polymer Technologies................... G 412 735-4799
West Chester *(G-14047)*

Pitt Plastics Inc.................................... D 614 868-8660
Columbus *(G-5192)*

Plaskolite LLC...................................... D 614 294-3281
Columbus *(G-5195)*

Plaskolite LLC...................................... C 740 450-1109
Zanesville *(G-15040)*

◆ Plaskolite LLC....................................C 614 294-3281
Columbus *(G-5194)*

Plastic Compounders Inc...................... E 740 432-7371
Cambridge *(G-1755)*

Plastic Materials Inc............................. E 330 468-5706
Macedonia *(G-8705)*

Polimeros Usa LLC............................... G 216 591-0175
Warren *(G-13790)*

▲ Poly-Carb Inc..................................... F 440 248-1223
Macedonia *(G-8707)*

▼ Polymer Concepts Inc........................ G 440 953-9605
Mentor *(G-9589)*

◆ Polymer Packaging Inc........................D 330 832-2000
North Canton *(G-10658)*

Polymer Tech & Svcs Inc...................... F 740 929-5500
Heath *(G-7601)*

Polymerics Inc...................................... E 330 677-1131
Kent *(C 8060)*

▲ Polymerics Inc.................................... E 330 928-2210
Cuyahoga Falls *(G-5565)*

Polynew Inc.. G 330 897-3202
Baltic *(G-780)*

Polynt Composites USA Inc................... E 816 391-6000
Sandusky *(G-11866)*

Polyone Corporation............................ G 216 622-0100
Berea *(G-1185)*

Polyone Corporation............................ D 330 467-8108
Macedonia *(G-8708)*

Polyone LLC... F 440 930-1000
Avon Lake *(G-769)*

◆ Prime Conduit Inc...............................F 216 464-3400
Beachwood *(G-941)*

Prime Industries Inc.............................. F
Lorain *(G-8574)*

▲ Progressive Foam Tech Inc................. C 330 756-3200
Beach City *(G-906)*

Protech Pet LLC................................... F 419 552-4617
Gibsonburg *(G-7258)*

Quality Plastics LLC............................. F 330 695-5920
Fredericksburg *(G-7068)*

▼ Rauh Polymers Inc.............................. F 330 376-1120
Akron *(G-278)*

Ravago Americas LLC........................... D 330 825-2505
Medina *(G-9440)*

Ray Fogg Construction Inc.................... G 216 351-7976
Cleveland *(G-4225)*

▲ Renegade Materials Corporation........ D 937 350-5274
Miamisburg *(G-9732)*

◆ Resinoid Engineering Corp.................D 740 928-6115
Hebron *(G-7633)*

Return Polymers Inc............................. D 419 289-1998
Ashland *(G-570)*

◆ Roechling Indus Cleveland LP............C 216 486-0100
Cleveland *(G-4248)*

Rotopolymers.. G 216 645-0333
Warren *(G-13794)*

Saco Aei Polymers Inc.......................... F 330 995-1600
Aurora *(G-688)*

Saint-Gobain Prfmce Plas Corp............ C 614 889-2220
Dublin *(G-6342)*

Saint-Gobain Prfmce Plas Corp............ C 330 296-9948
Ravenna *(G-11538)*

▲ Scott Bader Inc.................................. G 330 920-4410
Stow *(G-12459)*

Scott Molders Incorporated.................. D 330 673-5777
Kent *(G-8074)*

Sherwood Rtm Corp.............................. G 330 875-7151
Louisville *(G-8616)*

▼ Soelter Corporation............................ F 800 838-8984
Brookville *(G-1576)*

Solvay Spclty Polymers USA LLC.......... F 740 373-9242
Marietta *(G-8948)*

Sorbothane Inc..................................... E 330 678-9444
Kent *(G-8081)*

Spartech Mexico Holding Co Two.......... F 440 930-3619
Avon Lake *(G-770)*

STC International Co Ltd........................ G 561 308-6002
Lebanon *(G-8287)*

◆ Tembec Btlsr Inc................................E 419 244-5856
Toledo *(G-13141)*

Thermocolor LLC.................................. E 419 626-5677
Sandusky *(G-11875)*

▲ Tlg Cochran Inc.................................. E 440 914-1122
Twinsburg *(G-13385)*

Transdigm Inc....................................... G 330 676-7147
Kent *(G-8092)*

◆ Tribotech Composites Inc...................G 216 901-1300
Cleveland *(G-4422)*

◆ Triple Arrow Industries Inc.................G 614 437-5588
Maryville *(C 0054)*

Uniloy Century LLC.............................. D 419 332-2693
Fremont *(G-7140)*

◆ Uniloy Milacron Inc.............................E 513 487-5000
Batavia *(G-893)*

Univar Solutions USA LLC.................... F 800 531-7106
Dublin *(G-6359)*

Urethane Polymers Intl.......................... F 216 430-3655
Cleveland *(G-4450)*

V & A Process Inc................................. F 440 288-8137
Lorain *(G-8584)*

Ventek Solutions LLC............................ F 419 420-0029
Findlay *(G-6930)*

Vinylmng LLC....................................... E 440 261-5799
Cleveland *(G-4475)*

Westlake Corporation........................... D 614 986-2497
Columbus *(G-5364)*

Wilsonart LLC....................................... E 614 876-1515
Columbus *(G-5369)*

Win Cd Inc.. F 330 929-1999
Cuyahoga Falls *(G-5582)*

Win Plastic Extrusions LLC................... G 330 929-1999
Cincinnati *(G-3226)*

Yoders Produce Inc.............................. F 330 695-5900
Fredericksburg *(G-7073)*

2822 Synthetic rubber

Allied Polymers............................ G 330 975-4200
Seville *(G-11909)*

Ansell Healthcare Products LLC............. C 740 622-4369
Coshocton *(G-5448)*

Blair Sales Inc............................ D 330 769-5586
Seville *(G-11912)*

Brain Child Products LLC.................. F 419 698-4020
Toledo *(G-12904)*

◆ Brp Manufacturing Company............ E 800 858-0482
Lima *(G-8393)*

Canton OH Rubber Speclty Prods.......... G 330 454-3847
Canton *(G-1857)*

▲ Cardinal Rubber Company............... E 330 745-2191
Barberton *(G-801)*

◆ Concrete Sealants Inc.................. E 937 845-8776
Tipp City *(G-12821)*

Covestro LLC.............................. C 740 929-2015
Hebron *(G-7611)*

Crushproof Tubing Co..................... E 419 293-2111
Mc Comb *(G-9352)*

◆ East West Copolymer LLC.............. D 225 267-3400
Cleveland *(G-3648)*

◆ Flexsys America LP.................... D 330 666-4111
Akron *(G-150)*

Gdc Inc.................................. F 574 533-3128
Wooster *(G-14642)*

Geon Performance Solutions LLC.......... F 800 438-4366
Westlake *(G-14304)*

Great Lakes Polymer Proc Inc............ F 313 655-4024
Akron *(G-166)*

▲ High Tech Elastomers Inc.............. E 937 236-6575
Vandalia *(G-13560)*

◆ Innoplast Inc..........................F 440 543-8660
Cleveland *(G-3861)*

◆ Key Resin Company.....................F 513 943-4225
Batavia *(G-869)*

Kraton Emplyees Recreation CLB.......... G 740 423-7571
Belpre *(G-1149)*

Kraton Polymers US LLC.................. B 740 423-7571
Belpre *(G-1150)*

Lyondell Chemical Company.............. C 513 530-4000
Cincinnati *(G-2833)*

Mantaline Corporation.................... C 330 274-2264
Mantua *(G-8872)*

Meggitt (erlanger) LLC................... D 513 851-5550
Cincinnati *(G-2858)*

◆ Mexichem Specialty Resins Inc.........E 440 930-1435
Avon Lake *(G-765)*

◆ Midwest Elastomers Inc...............D 419 738-8844
Wapakoneta *(G-13722)*

Mitsubishi Chemical Amer Inc............ C 586 755-1660
Bellevue *(G-1127)*

Mohican Industries Inc................... G 330 869-0500
Akron *(G-235)*

Mondo Polymer Technologies Inc.......... E 740 376-9396
Marietta *(G-8930)*

▲ North Coast Seal Incorporated.......... F 216 898-5000
Brookpark *(G-1556)*

Novagard Solutions Inc................... D 216 881-8111
Cleveland *(G-4101)*

Protective Industrial Polymers........... F 440 327-0015
North Ridgeville *(G-10743)*

S P E Inc................................ E 330 733-0101
Mogadore *(G-10084)*

◆ Shin-Etsu Silicones of America Inc....C 330 630-9460
Akron *(G-309)*

▲ Shincor Silicones Inc.................. E 330 630-9460
Akron *(G-310)*

T L Squire and Company Inc.............. G 330 668-2604
Akron *(G-326)*

Universal Urethane Pdts Inc.............. D 419 693-7400
Toledo *(G-13169)*

Wayne County Rubber Inc................. E 330 264-5553
Wooster *(G-14696)*

2823 Cellulosic manmade fibers

Advanced Fiber LLC...................... E 419 562-1337
Bucyrus *(G-1671)*

◆ Flexsys America LP....................D 330 666-4111
Akron *(G-150)*

J Rettenmaier USA LP.................... D 937 652-2101
Urbana *(G-13469)*

◆ Mfg Composite Systems Company.....B 440 997-5851
Ashtabula *(G-605)*

◆ Morgan Adhesives Company LLC.....B 330 688-1111
Stow *(G-12441)*

2824 Organic fibers, noncellulosic

Bridge Components Incorporated.......... G 614 873-0777
Columbus *(G-4775)*

Cast Nylons Co Ltd....................... D 440 269-2300
Willoughby *(G-14437)*

▲ Dowco LLC............................ E 330 773-6654
Akron *(G-125)*

Matrix Meats Inc........................ F 614 602-1846
Dublin *(G-6319)*

▲ Mytee Products Inc.................... D 888 705-8277
Solon *(G-12156)*

2833 Medicinals and botanicals

B & A Holistic Fd & Herbs LLC............ F 614 747-2200
Columbus *(G-4738)*

Clean Remedies LLC..................... F 440 670-2112
Avon *(G-719)*

Earthley Wellness....................... E 614 625-1064
Columbus *(G-4895)*

◆ Frutarom USA Inc......................C 513 870-4900
Cincinnati *(G-2643)*

Galapagos Inc........................... F 937 890-3068
Dayton *(G-5789)*

Graminex LLC........................... F 419 278-1023
Deshler *(G-6222)*

▲ Joseph Adams Corp.................... F 330 225-9125
Valley City *(G-13500)*

Natural Optons Armatherapy LLC.......... F 419 886-3736
Bellville *(G-1140)*

Neuronoff Inc........................... E 216 505-1818
Cleveland *(G-4072)*

Nufacturing Inc......................... E 330 814-5259
Brunswick *(G-1603)*

Nutritional Medicinals LLC............... F 937 433-4673
West Chester *(G-14034)*

Pfizer Inc.............................. F 937 746-3603
Franklin *(G-7039)*

Pharmacia Hepar LLC.................... G 937 746-3603
Franklin *(G-7040)*

▲ Polar Products Inc.................... E 330 253-9973
Stow *(G-12449)*

Range Impact Inc....................... G 216 304-6556
Cleveland *(G-4224)*

USB Corporation........................ F 216 765-5000
Cleveland *(G-4454)*

Valley Vitamins II Inc................... F 330 533-0051
Columbus *(G-5344)*

◆ Vitamin Shoppe Florida LLC.............F
Delaware *(G-6178)*

Vitamin Shoppe Industries LLC............ A
Delaware *(G-6179)*

▲ VWR Part of Avantor................... E 440 349-1199
Solon *(G-12205)*

2834 Pharmaceutical preparations

2 Retrievers LLC........................ G 216 200-9040
Cleveland *(G-3276)*

Abbott.................................. G 608 931-1057
Columbus *(G-4659)*

Abbott Laboratories..................... A 614 624-3191
Columbus *(G-4660)*

Abbott Laboratories..................... F 614 624-3192
Columbus *(G-4661)*

Abbott Laboratories..................... D 847 937-6100
Columbus *(G-4662)*

Abbott Laboratories..................... C 800 551-5838
Columbus *(G-4663)*

Abbott Laboratories..................... E 614 624-7677
Columbus *(G-4664)*

▲ Abbott Laboratories................... F 937 503-3405
Tipp City *(G-12812)*

Abeona Therapeutics Inc................. D 646 813-4701
Cleveland *(G-3287)*

◆ Abitec Corporation.....................E 614 429-6464
Columbus *(G-4665)*

▲ Adare Pharmaceuticals Inc............. C 937 898-9669
Vandalia *(G-13548)*

Aerpio Therapeutics LLC................. E 513 985-1920
Blue Ash *(G-1244)*

Alkermes Inc............................ E 937 382-5642
Wilmington *(G-14571)*

Allergan Sales LLC...................... C 513 271-6800
Cincinnati *(G-2349)*

Allergan Sales LLC...................... E 513 271-6800
Cincinnati *(G-2350)*

American Regent Inc..................... D 614 436-2222
Columbus *(G-4701)*

American Regent Inc..................... D 614 436-2222
Hilliard *(G-7667)*

American Regent Inc..................... D 614 436-2222
New Albany *(G-10326)*

Amgen Inc.............................. F 805 447-1000
New Albany *(G-10327)*

Amylin Ohio............................ E 512 592-8710
West Chester *(G-13938)*

Analiza Inc............................. G 216 432-9050
Cleveland *(G-3352)*

Andelyn Biosciences Inc................. C 614 332-0554
Dublin *(G-6275)*

Andelyn Biosciences Inc................. E 844 228-2366
Columbus *(G-4715)*

Aprecia Pharmaceuticals LLC............. F 513 984-5000
Mason *(G-9062)*

Astrazeneca Pharmaceuticals LP.......... D 513 645-2600
West Chester *(G-13944)*

Axalta................................. G 855 629-2582
Toledo *(G-12890)*

Barr Laboratories Inc.................... A 513 731-9900
Cincinnati *(G-2400)*

BASF Corporation....................... D 614 662-5682
Columbus *(G-4745)*

Bayer.................................. G 513 336-6600
Fairfield *(G-6712)*

▲ Ben Venue Laboratories Inc............. A 800 989-3320
Bedford *(G-1016)*

Berlin Industries Inc.................... F 330 549-2100
Youngstown *(G-14819)*

Bigmar Inc............................. E 740 966-5800
Johnstown *(G-7992)*

Biosortia Pharmaceuticals Inc............ F 614 636-4850
Dublin *(G-6281)*

Buderer Drug Company Inc............... E 419 627-2800
Sandusky *(G-11824)*

Camargo Phrm Svcs LLC................. F 513 561-3329
Cincinnati *(G-2436)*

Cardinal Health 110 LLC................. E 800 727-6331
Dublin *(G-6287)*

Cardinal Health 414 LLC.................... G 513 759-1900
West Chester *(G-13954)*

▲ Cardinal Health 414 LLC................. C 614 757-5000
Dublin *(G-6288)*

Chester Labs Inc............................. E 513 458-3871
Cincinnati *(G-2461)*

Clinical Specialties Inc.................... D 888 873-7888
Hudson *(G-7840)*

CMC Pharmaceuticals Inc................. G 216 600-9430
Solon *(G-12095)*

Diasome Pharmaceuticals Inc........... F 216 444-7110
Cleveland *(G-3614)*

Encapsulation Technologies LLC........ G 419 819-6319
Austinburg *(G-697)*

Eyescience Labs LLC...................... G 614 885-7100
Powell *(G-11487)*

▲ Flow Dry Technology Inc................ C 937 833-2161
Brookville *(G-1568)*

Ftd Investments LLC...................... A 937 833-2161
Brookville *(G-1569)*

Galenas LLC................................. F 330 208-9423
Akron *(G-155)*

Ganeden Biotech Inc...................... E 440 229-5200
Mayfield Heights *(G-9334)*

▲ Gebauer Company......................... E 216 581-3030
Cleveland *(G-3761)*

Girindus America Inc...................... E 513 679-3000
Cincinnati *(G-2671)*

Glaxosmithkline LLC....................... G 937 623-2680
Columbus *(G-4955)*

Glaxosmithkline LLC....................... G 614 570-5970
Columbus *(G-4956)*

Graminex LLC................................ F 419 278-1023
Deshler *(G-6222)*

Hikma Labs Inc............................. G 614 276-4000
Columbus *(G-4984)*

▲ Hikma Labs Inc............................ C 614 276-4000
Columbus *(G-4985)*

Hikma Pharmaceuticals USA Inc........ E 732 542-1191
Bedford *(G-1035)*

Hikma Pharmaceuticals USA Inc........ E 614 276-4000
Columbus *(G-4986)*

Hikma Pharmaceuticals USA Inc........ E 732 542-1191
Lockbourne *(G-8490)*

Hikma Specialty USA Inc................. F 856 489-2110
Columbus *(G-4987)*

▲ Imcd Us LLC................................. C 216 228-8900
Westlake *(G-14310)*

Invirsa Inc................................... G 614 344-1765
Columbus *(G-5023)*

Isp Chemicals LLC......................... D 614 876-3637
Columbus *(G-5026)*

Johnson & Johnson........................ E 513 786-7000
Blue Ash *(G-1290)*

Kdc US Holdings Inc....................... B 614 656-1130
New Albany *(G-10344)*

Kenvue Brands LLC......................... F 513 985-1540
Cincinnati *(G-2794)*

Lib Therapeutics Inc...................... F 859 240-7764
Cincinnati *(G-2820)*

◆ Lubrizol Global Management Inc........ F 216 447-5000
Cleveland *(G-3970)*

Masters Pharmaceutical Inc............. G 513 290-2969
Fairfield *(G-6752)*

Medpace Core Laboratories LLC......... F 513 579-9911
Cincinnati *(G-2856)*

Medpace Holdings Inc..................... C 513 579-9911
Cincinnati *(G-2857)*

Meridian Bioscience Inc.................. C 513 271-3700
Cincinnati *(G-2864)*

Mp Biomedicals LLC....................... C 440 337-1200
Solon *(G-12154)*

Mvp Pharmacy............................... G 614 449-8000
Columbus *(G-5117)*

N-Molecular Inc............................. F 440 439-5356
Oakwood Village *(G-10907)*

Nanofiber Solutions LLC.................. F 614 319-3075
Dublin *(G-6322)*

Navidea Biopharmaceuticals Inc........ G 614 793-7500
Dublin *(G-6324)*

Nnodum Pharmaceuticals Corp.......... F 513 861-2329
Cincinnati *(G-2912)*

Nostrum Laboratories Inc................. E 419 636-1168
Bryan *(G-1653)*

Oakwood Laboratories LLC............... D 440 505-2011
Solon *(G-12163)*

Oakwood Laboratories LLC............... E 440 359-0000
Oakwood Village *(G-10908)*

Optum Infusion Svcs 550 LLC........... D 866 442-4679
Cincinnati *(G-2936)*

Organon Inc.................................. F 440 729-2290
Chesterland *(G-2238)*

Patheon Pharmaceuticals Inc............ A 513 948-9111
Blue Ash *(G-1318)*

Patheon Pharmaceuticals Inc............ A 513 948-9111
Cincinnati *(G-2943)*

PBM Covington LLC........................ G 937 473-2050
Covington *(G-5497)*

Performanx Specialty Chem LLC........ G 614 300-7001
Waverly *(G-13872)*

Perrigo.. E 937 473-2050
Covington *(G-5498)*

Petnet Solutions Cleveland LLC......... F 865 218-2000
Cleveland *(G-4155)*

Pfizer Inc.................................... F 937 746-3603
Franklin *(G-7039)*

Pharmacia Hepar LLC..................... G 937 746-3603
Franklin *(G-7040)*

Pharmaforce Inc............................ C
Columbus *(G-5190)*

Piedmont Water Services LLC........... G 216 554-4747
Cleveland *(G-4162)*

Polynt Composites USA Inc............... E 816 391-6000
Sandusky *(G-11866)*

▲ Prasco LLC.................................. E 513 204-1100
Mason *(G-9135)*

Principled Dynamics Inc.................. G 419 351-6303
Holland *(G-7779)*

Pyros Pharmaceuticals Inc............... G 201 743-9468
Westerville *(G-14227)*

Quality Care Products LLC............... G 734 847-2704
Holland *(G-7780)*

Resilience Us Inc........................... B 513 645-2600
West Chester *(G-14064)*

River City Pharma.......................... G 513 870-1680
Fairfield *(G-6772)*

Safecor Health LLC........................ G 614 351-6117
Columbus *(G-5243)*

Safecor Health LLC........................ D 800 447-1006
Columbus *(G-5242)*

Sara Wood Pharmaceuticals LLC....... G 513 833-5502
Mason *(G-9148)*

Sarepta Therapeutics Inc................. D 380 324-3973
Columbus *(G-5249)*

Sermonix Pharmaceuticals Inc.......... F 614 864-4919
Columbus *(G-5262)*

Soleo Health Inc............................ E 844 467-8200
Dublin *(G-6348)*

Standard Wellness Company LLC....... C 330 931-1037
Gibsonburg *(G-7259)*

Staq Pharma of Ohio LLC................. F 833 397-0106
Columbus *(G-5288)*

Teva Pharmaceuticals Usa Inc.......... C 513 731-9900
Cincinnati *(G-3144)*

Teva Womens Health LLC................. C 513 731-9900
Cincinnati *(G-3145)*

Tri-Tech Laboratories Inc................. E 740 927-2817
Johnstown *(G-8000)*

USB Corporation............................ F 216 765-5000
Cleveland *(G-4454)*

◆ West-Ward Columbus Inc................ A 614 276-4000
Columbus *(G-5363)*

Wright Enrichment Incorporated......... F 337 783-3096
Plain City *(G-11429)*

Xellia Pharmaceuticals Inc............... G 847 947-0200
Beachwood *(G-958)*

Z M O Company............................. G 614 875-0230
Columbus *(G-5378)*

2835 Diagnostic substances

Cardinal Health 414 LLC.................. G 513 759-1900
West Chester *(G-13954)*

▲ Cardinal Health 414 LLC................. C 614 757-5000
Dublin *(G-6288)*

Cleveland AEC West LLC................. G 216 362-6000
Cleveland *(G-3506)*

Diagnostic Hybrids Inc................... C 740 593-1784
Athens *(G-638)*

GE Healthcare Inc......................... F 513 241-5955
Cincinnati *(G-2657)*

John P Ellis Clinic Podiatry............. G 440 460-0444
Cleveland *(G-3890)*

Meridian Bioscience Inc.................. C 513 271-3700
Cincinnati *(G-2864)*

Meridian Life Science Inc................ F 513 271-3700
Cincinnati *(G-2865)*

Nanofiber Solutions LLC.................. F 614 319-3075
Dublin *(G-6322)*

Navidea Biopharmaceuticals Inc........ G 614 793-7500
Dublin *(G-6324)*

Petnet Solutions Inc...................... G 865 218-2000
Cincinnati *(G-2959)*

Petnet Solutions Cleveland LLC......... F 865 218-2000
Cleveland *(G-4155)*

Quest Diagnostics Incorporated......... G 513 229-5500
Mason *(G-9140)*

Quidel Corporation......................... E 858 552-1100
Athens *(G-649)*

Quidel Corporation......................... G 740 589-3300
Athens *(G-650)*

Revvity Health Sciences Inc............. D 330 825-4525
Akron *(C 283)*

Thermo Fisher Scientific Inc............. E 800 871-8909
Oakwood Village *(G-10910)*

USB Corporation............................ F 216 765-5000
Cleveland *(G-4454)*

2836 Biological products, except diagnostic

ABI Inc....................................... F 800 847-8950
Cleveland *(G-3288)*

Algix LLC.................................... G 706 207-3425
Stow *(G-12417)*

Bio-Blood Components Inc................ D 614 294-3183
Columbus *(G-4754)*

Decaria Brothers Inc...................... G 330 385-0825
East Liverpool *(G-6391)*

EMD Millipore Corporation............... C 513 631-0445
Norwood *(G-10868)*

Envirozyme LLC............................. F 800 232-2847
Bowling Green *(G-1419)*

Ferro Corporation.......................... D 216 577-7144
Bedford *(G-1032)*

Forge Biologics Inc........................ G 216 401-7611
Grove City *(G-7387)*

General Envmtl Science Corp............ G 216 464-0680
Beachwood *(G-919)*

Jsh International LLC.................................G 330 734-0251
Akron *(G-190)*

No Rinse Laboratories LLC....................G 937 746-7357
Springboro *(G-12261)*

PEC Biofuels LLC.....................................G 419 542-8210
Hicksville *(G-7651)*

▲ Powder Alloy Corporation.................E 513 984-4016
Loveland *(G-8646)*

Protein Technologies Ltd........................G 513 769-0840
Cincinnati *(G-3011)*

Revvity Health Sciences Inc...................D 330 825-4525
Akron *(G-283)*

2841 Soap and other detergents

AIN Industries Inc....................................G 440 781-0950
Cleveland *(G-3315)*

Beiersdorf Inc...C 513 682-7300
West Chester *(G-14107)*

Chemstation International Inc.................E 937 294-8265
Dayton *(G-5701)*

◆ Chemtool Incorporated.....................C 815 957-4140
Wickliffe *(G-14369)*

Cincinnati - Vulcan Company.................D 513 242-5300
Cincinnati *(G-2465)*

Cleaning Lady Inc....................................G 419 589-5566
Mansfield *(G-8774)*

Cr Holding Inc..D 513 860-5039
West Chester *(G-13976)*

▼ Cresset Chemical Co Inc....................F 419 669-2041
Weston *(G-14347)*

◆ Damon Industries Inc.........................D 330 821-5310
Alliance *(G-379)*

▲ DSM Industries Inc.............................F 440 585-1100
Wickliffe *(G-14374)*

Edmar Chemical Company......................G 440 247-9560
Chagrin Falls *(G-2142)*

▲ Foam-Tex Solutions Corp...................G 216 889-2702
Cleveland *(G-3731)*

Henkel US Operations Corp....................C 740 363-1351
Delaware *(G-6156)*

Jtm Products Inc......................................E 440 287-2302
Solon *(G-12133)*

◆ KAO USA Inc...B 513 421-1400
Cincinnati *(G-2782)*

◆ Kardol Quality Products LLC..............G 513 933-8206
Blue Ash *(G-1293)*

Kutol Products Company Inc..................D 513 527-5500
Sharonville *(G-11947)*

▲ Kutol Products Company Inc...............D 513 527-5500
Sharonville *(G-11946)*

◆ Malco Products Inc..............................C 330 753-0361
Barberton *(G-819)*

Mix-Masters Inc.......................................F 513 228-2800
Lebanon *(G-8277)*

Natreeola Soap Company LLC................G 513 390-2247
Middletown *(G-9881)*

New Vulco Mfg & Sales Co LLC..............D 513 242-2672
Cincinnati *(G-2904)*

◆ Pilot Chemical Company Ohio.............E 513 326-0600
West Chester *(G-14045)*

Pilot Chemical Corp.................................C 513 424-9700
Middletown *(G-9886)*

◆ Pilot Chemical Corp............................C 513 326-0600
West Chester *(G-14046)*

▲ Pioneer Manufacturing Inc..................D 216 671-5500
Cleveland *(G-4167)*

Pneumatic Specialties Inc......................G 440 729-4400
Chesterland *(G-2239)*

▼ Polar Inc...F 937 297-0911
Moraine *(G-10185)*

Procter & Gamble Company....................E 513 983-1100
Cincinnati *(G-2987)*

Procter & Gamble Company....................E 513 266-4375
Cincinnati *(G-2988)*

Procter & Gamble Company....................F 513 871-7557
Cincinnati *(G-2989)*

Procter & Gamble Company....................F 513 482-6789
Cincinnati *(G-2991)*

Procter & Gamble Company....................C 513 983-3000
Cincinnati *(G-2993)*

Procter & Gamble Company....................D 513 627-7115
Cincinnati *(G-2994)*

Procter & Gamble Company....................E 513 945-0340
Cincinnati *(G-2997)*

Procter & Gamble Company....................C 513 622-1000
Mason *(G-9138)*

Procter & Gamble Company....................C 513 634-9600
West Chester *(G-14054)*

Procter & Gamble Company....................C 513 634-9110
West Chester *(G-14055)*

Procter & Gamble Distrg LLC.................C 937 387-5189
Union *(G-13411)*

◆ Procter & Gamble Mfg Co...................F 513 983-1100
Cincinnati *(G-3002)*

Renegade Brands LLC.............................G 216 342-4347
Cleveland *(G-4233)*

Royal Chemical Company Ltd..................F 330 467-1300
Twinsburg *(G-13369)*

Royal Chemical Company Ltd..................D 330 467-1300
Macedonia *(G-8711)*

State Industrial Products Corp...............D 740 929-6370
Hebron *(G-7637)*

◆ State Industrial Products Corp...........B 877 747-6986
Cleveland *(G-4329)*

US Industrial Lubricants Inc...................E 513 541-2225
Cincinnati *(G-3189)*

◆ Wallover Oil Company Inc...................E 440 238-9250
Strongsville *(G-12613)*

▼ Washing Systems LLC.........................C 800 272-1974
Loveland *(G-8656)*

2842 Polishes and sanitation goods

▲ Alco-Chem Inc......................................E 330 253-3535
Akron *(G-47)*

Aromair Fine Fragrance Company...........B 614 984-2900
New Albany *(G-10330)*

B&D Water Inc..E 330 771-3318
Quaker City *(G-11503)*

◆ Betco Corporation Ltd.........................C 419 241-2156
Bowling Green *(G-1409)*

BLaster Holdings LLC..............................E 216 901-5800
Cleveland *(G-3422)*

BLaster LLC..E 216 901-5800
Cleveland *(G-3423)*

◆ Canberra Corporation..........................C 419 724-4300
Toledo *(G-12910)*

Carbonklean Llc.......................................G 614 980-9515
Powell *(G-11483)*

Chemical Methods Incorporated.............E 216 476-8400
Brunswick *(G-1582)*

▲ Chempace Corporation........................F 419 535-0101
Toledo *(G-12919)*

Chemstation International Inc.................E 937 294-8265
Dayton *(G-5701)*

◆ Chemtool Incorporated.......................C 815 957-4140
Wickliffe *(G-14369)*

Cincinnati - Vulcan Company.................D 513 242-5300
Cincinnati *(G-2465)*

Clorox Company.......................................G 513 445-1840
Mason *(G-9089)*

Consolidated Coatings Corp...................A 216 514-7596
Cleveland *(G-3561)*

◆ D & J Distributing & Mfg....................F 419 865-2552
Holland *(G-7753)*

◆ Damon Industries Inc..........................D 330 821-5310
Alliance *(G-379)*

Ddp Specialty Electronic MA..................G 937 839-4612
West Alexandria *(G-13918)*

Ecolab Inc..G 513 932-0830
Lebanon *(G-8253)*

Edmar Chemical Company......................G 440 247-9560
Chagrin Falls *(G-2142)*

EMD Millipore Corporation.....................C 513 631-0445
Norwood *(G-10868)*

Emes Supply LLC.....................................G 216 400-8025
Willowick *(G-14566)*

Enginred Atmsphric Mtgtion LLC............G 740 385-6690
Logan *(G-8513)*

Environmental Chemical Corp.................F 330 453-5200
Uniontown *(G-13419)*

EZ Brite Brands Inc.................................F 440 871-7817
Cleveland *(G-3701)*

Ferro Corporation....................................D 216 577-7144
Bedford *(G-1032)*

Finale Products Inc.................................G 419 874-2662
Perrysburg *(G-11221)*

◆ Fresh Products LLC.............................D 419 531-9741
Perrysburg *(G-11224)*

Fuchs Lubricants Co................................F 330 963-0400
Twinsburg *(G-13306)*

Germ-Busters Solutions LLC...................G 330 610-0480
Youngstown *(G-14867)*

Glister Inc...E 614 252-6400
Columbus *(G-4957)*

Gojo Canada Inc......................................F 330 255-6000
Akron *(G-162)*

Gojo Industries Inc..................................F 330 255-6000
Cuyahoga Falls *(G-5545)*

▼ Gojo Industries Inc.............................F 330 255-6527
Cuyahoga Falls *(G-5546)*

Gojo Industries Inc..................................G 330 255-6000
Navarre *(G-10304)*

Gojo Industries Inc..................................G 330 255-6525
Stow *(G-12435)*

◆ Gojo Industries Inc.............................C 330 255-6000
Akron *(G-163)*

Henkel US Operations Corp....................C 216 475-3600
Cleveland *(G-3821)*

Henkel US Operations Corp....................C 740 363-1351
Delaware *(G-6156)*

James C Robinson....................................G 513 969-7482
Cincinnati *(G-2760)*

Jax Wax Inc...F 614 476-6769
Columbus *(G-5033)*

K-O-K Products Inc..................................F 740 548-0526
Galena *(G-7173)*

◆ Kardol Quality Products LLC..............G 513 933-8206
Blue Ash *(G-1293)*

Kcs Cleaning Service...............................F 740 418-5479
Oak Hill *(G-10889)*

Kinzua Environmental Inc........................E 216 881-4040
Cleveland *(G-3923)*

Kleen Test Products Corp........................B 330 878-5586
Strasburg *(G-12479)*

▲ Kona Blackbird Inc..............................E 440 285-3189
Chardon *(G-2211)*

Leonhardt Plating Company.....................G 513 242-1410
Cincinnati *(G-2819)*

◆ Malco Products Inc.............................C 330 753-0361
Barberton *(G-819)*

▲ McCrary Metal Polishing Co Inc.........F 937 492-1979
Port Jefferson *(G-11454)*

McGean-Rohco Inc...................................G 216 441-4900
Newburgh Heights *(G-10545)*

Metaltek Industries Inc...........................F 937 342-1750
Springfield *(G-12353)*

Milsek Furniture Polish Inc.................. G 330 542-2700
Salem *(G-11801)*

Mix-Masters Inc.................................. F 513 228-2800
Lebanon *(G-8277)*

Mold Masters Intl LLC......................... C 440 953-0220
Eastlake *(G-6438)*

▲ National Colloid Company................ E 740 282-1171
Steubenville *(G-12407)*

New Vulco Mfg & Sales Co LLC........... D 513 242-2672
Cincinnati *(G-2904)*

New Waste Concepts Inc.................... F 877 736-6924
Perrysburg *(G-11241)*

◆ Nilodor Inc...................................... E 800 443-4321
Bolivar *(G-1386)*

Nwp Manufacturing Inc...................... F 419 894-6871
Waldo *(G-13690)*

Ohio Auto Supply Company................ G 330 454-5105
Canton *(G-1964)*

Ohio Mills Corporation...................... G 216 431-3979
Cleveland *(G-4116)*

▲ Paro Services Co............................. F 330 467-1300
Twinsburg *(G-13350)*

Personal Plumber Service Corp............ F 440 324-4321
Elyria *(G-6579)*

Pilot Chemical Corp........................... C 513 424-9700
Middletown *(G-9886)*

▲ Pioneer Manufacturing Inc.............. D 216 671-5500
Cleveland *(G-4167)*

Pneumatic Specialties Inc.................. G 440 729-4400
Chesterland *(G-2239)*

Polynt Composites USA Inc................ E 816 391-6000
Sandusky *(G-11866)*

Procter & Gamble Company................ E 513 983-1100
Cincinnati *(G-2987)*

Procter & Gamble Company................ E 513 266-4375
Cincinnati *(G-2988)*

Procter & Gamble Company................ F 513 871-7557
Cincinnati *(G-2989)*

Procter & Gamble Company................ F 513 482-6789
Cincinnati *(G-2991)*

Procter & Gamble Company................ C 513 983-3000
Cincinnati *(G-2993)*

Procter & Gamble Company................ D 513 627-7115
Cincinnati *(G-2994)*

Procter & Gamble Company................ E 513 945-0340
Cincinnati *(G-2997)*

Procter & Gamble Company................ E 513 622-1000
Mason *(G-9138)*

Procter & Gamble Company................ C 513 634-9600
West Chester *(G-14054)*

Procter & Gamble Company................ C 513 634-9110
West Chester *(G-14055)*

◆ Procter & Gamble Company............. A 513 983-1100
Cincinnati *(G-2999)*

Procter & Gamble Far East Inc............. C 513 983-1100
Cincinnati *(G-3000)*

Products Chemical Company LLC........ F 216 218-1155
Cleveland *(G-4198)*

Reid Asset Management Company........ E 440 942-8488
Willoughby *(G-14516)*

◆ Republic Powdered Metals Inc.........D 330 225-3192
Medina *(G-9441)*

◆ RPM International Inc...................... D 330 273-5090
Medina *(G-9442)*

Saint Ctherines Metalworks Inc............ G 216 409-0576
Cleveland *(G-4269)*

Sherwin-Williams Company................. C 330 830-6000
Massillon *(G-9243)*

Skybryte Company Inc........................ G 216 771-1590
Cleveland *(G-4304)*

Smart Sonic Corporation..................... G 818 610-7900
Cleveland *(G-4306)*

◆ State Industrial Products Corp...........B 877 747-6986
Cleveland *(G-4329)*

◆ Tolco Corporation............................E 419 241-1113
Toledo *(G-13147)*

◆ Tranzonic Companies....................... C 440 446-0643
Cleveland *(G-4414)*

◆ Tremco Incorporated........................C 216 292-5000
Beachwood *(G-956)*

▲ Troy Chemical Industries Inc.......... F 440 834-4408
Burton *(G-1705)*

◆ Tz Acquisition Corp......................... F 216 535-4300
Richmond Heights *(G-11613)*

Univar Solutions USA LLC................... E 513 714-5264
West Chester *(G-14157)*

US Industrial Lubricants Inc................. E 513 541-2225
Cincinnati *(G-3189)*

▼ Ventco Inc...................................... F 440 834-8888
Chagrin Falls *(G-2190)*

Vitex Corporation.............................. F 216 883-0920
Cleveland *(G-4477)*

▲ Woodbine Products Company........... F 330 725-0165
Medina *(G-9465)*

2843 Surface active agents

BASF Corporation.............................. D 614 662-5682
Columbus *(G-4745)*

◆ Berghausen Corporation...................E 513 591-4491
Cincinnati *(G-2406)*

Howard Industries Inc........................ F 614 444-9900
Columbus *(G-4993)*

Peter Cremer N Amer Enrgy Inc........... E 513 557-3943
Cincinnati *(G-2957)*

◆ Pilot Chemical Company Ohio...........E 513 326-0600
West Chester *(G-14045)*

◆ Pilot Chemical Corp........................C 513 326-0600
West Chester *(G-14046)*

2844 Toilet preparations

AA Hand Sanitizer.............................. G 513 506-7575
Cincinnati *(G-2328)*

◆ Abitec Corporation..........................E 614 429-6464
Columbus *(G-4665)*

Aeroscena LLC.................................. G 800 671-1890
Cleveland *(G-3311)*

B & P Company Inc............................ G 937 298-0265
Centerville *(G-2130)*

▲ Barbasol LLC.................................. E 419 903-0738
Ashland *(G-520)*

◆ Bath & Body Works LLC..................B 614 856-6000
Reynoldsburg *(G-11557)*

◆ Beautyavenues LLC..........................F 614 856-6000
Reynoldsburg *(G-11558)*

Beiersdorf Inc................................... C 513 682-7300
West Chester *(G-14107)*

Bocchi Laboratories Ohio LLC............ B 614 741-7458
New Albany *(G-10332)*

Bonne Bell Inc.................................. C 440 835-2440
Westlake *(G-14293)*

◆ Bonne Bell LLC...............................G 440 835-2440
Westlake *(G-14294)*

Brand5 LLC...................................... F 614 920-9254
Pickerington *(G-11290)*

Bright Holdco LLC............................ C 614 741-7458
New Albany *(G-10333)*

◆ Cameo Inc.....................................G 419 661-9611
Perrysburg *(G-11208)*

Colgate-Palmolive Company............... C 212 310-2000
Cambridge *(G-1739)*

Dover Wipes Company........................ F 513 983-1100
Cincinnati *(G-2560)*

Edgewell Personal Care LLC............... C 937 492-1057
Sidney *(G-12015)*

French Transit LLC............................ G 650 431-3959
Mason *(G-9101)*

Gojo Industries Inc........................... G 330 255-6525
Stow *(G-12435)*

◆ Gojo Industries Inc.........................C 330 255-6000
Akron *(G-163)*

IMH LLC... F 513 800-9830
Columbus *(G-5001)*

IMH LLC... G 614 436-0991
Columbus *(G-5002)*

▼ Innove LLC..................................... D 440 836-0199
Macedonia *(G-8697)*

Interco Division 10 Ohio Inc................ G 614 875-2959
Grove City *(G-7392)*

John Frieda Prof Hair Care Inc............. E 800 521-3189
Cincinnati *(G-2767)*

KAO USA Inc..................................... F 513 629-5210
Cincinnati *(G-2783)*

KAO USA Inc..................................... E 513 341-2630
West Chester *(G-14018)*

◆ KAO USA Inc...................................B 513 421-1400
Cincinnati *(G-2782)*

Kdc One... G 614 984-2871
New Albany *(G-10343)*

Luminex HM Dcor Frgrnce Hldg C........ A 513 563-1113
Cincinnati *(G-2831)*

Meridian Industries Inc..................... E 330 359-5809
Beach City *(G-904)*

Merle Norman Cosmetics Inc.............. E 419 282-0630
Mansfield *(G-8824)*

Midwest Sea Salt Company Inc............. F 513 770-9177
West Chester *(G-14029)*

Monique Bath and Body Ltd................ G 513 440-7370
Canton *(G-1951)*

Montgomery Ellis LLC......................... C 614 226-7976
Westerville *(G-14271)*

Natural Beauty Products Inc............... F 513 420-9400
Middletown *(G-9882)*

Natural Essentials Inc........................ F 330 562-8022
Aurora *(G-680)*

◆ Natural Essentials Inc......................C 330 562-8022
Streetsboro *(G-12513)*

▲ Nehemiah Manufacturing Co LLC..... D 513 351-5700
Cincinnati *(G-2897)*

Oasis Consumer Healthcare LLC.......... G 216 394-0544
Cleveland *(G-4106)*

Pfizer Inc.. F 937 746-3603
Franklin *(G 7030)*

Primal Life Organics LLC................... E 800 260-4946
Copley *(G-5438)*

Procter & Gamble Company................ E 513 626-2500
Blue Ash *(G-1325)*

Procter & Gamble Company................ E 513 983-1100
Cincinnati *(G-2987)*

Procter & Gamble Company................ E 513 266-4375
Cincinnati *(G-2988)*

Procter & Gamble Company................ F 513 871-7557
Cincinnati *(G-2989)*

Procter & Gamble Company................ D 513 983-1100
Cincinnati *(G-2990)*

Procter & Gamble Company................ F 513 482-6789
Cincinnati *(G-2991)*

Procter & Gamble Company................ E 513 634-5069
Cincinnati *(G-2992)*

Procter & Gamble Company................ C 513 983-3000
Cincinnati *(G-2993)*

Procter & Gamble Company................ D 513 627-7115
Cincinnati *(G-2994)*

Procter & Gamble Company................ G 513 658-9853
Cincinnati *(G-2995)*

Procter & Gamble Company................ B 513 983-1100
Cincinnati *(G-2996)*

SIC

Procter & Gamble Company....................E 513 945-0340
Cincinnati *(G-2997)*

Procter & Gamble Company....................E 513 242-5752
Cincinnati *(G-2998)*

Procter & Gamble Company....................C 513 622-1000
Mason *(G-9138)*

Procter & Gamble Company....................C 513 634-9600
West Chester *(G-14054)*

Procter & Gamble Company....................C 513 634-9110
West Chester *(G-14055)*

◆ Procter & Gamble Company....................A 513 983-1100
Cincinnati *(G-2999)*

Procter & Gamble Far East Inc....................C 513 983-1100
Cincinnati *(G-3000)*

Procter & Gamble Hair Care LLC............E 513 983-4502
Cincinnati *(G-3001)*

Procter & Gamble Mfg Co....................C 419 226-5500
Lima *(G-8439)*

◆ Procter & Gamble Mfg Co....................F 513 983-1100
Cincinnati *(G-3002)*

▲ Proft & Gamble....................G 513 945-0340
Cincinnati *(G-3007)*

Redex Industries Inc....................F 330 332-9800
Salem *(G-11809)*

Scarlett Kitty LLC....................F 678 438-3796
Dayton *(G-5995)*

Shadow Holdings LLC....................B 614 741-7458
New Albany *(G-10350)*

Sysco Guest Supply LLC....................E 440 960-2515
Lorain *(G-8582)*

Universal Packg Systems Inc....................C 513 732-2000
Batavia *(G-894)*

Universal Packg Systems Inc....................C 513 735-4777
Batavia *(G-895)*

Universal Packg Systems Inc....................C 513 674-9400
Cincinnati *(G-3186)*

US Cotton LLC....................D 216 676-6400
Cleveland *(G-4451)*

Veepak OH LLC....................F 740 927-9002
New Albany *(G-10353)*

▲ Woodbine Products Company............F 330 725-0165
Medina *(G-9465)*

Zena Baby Soap Company....................G 216 317-6433
Bedford Heights *(G-1084)*

2851 Paints and allied products

◆ Aexcel Corporation....................E 440 974-3800
Mentor *(G-9472)*

◆ Akrochem Corporation....................D 330 535-2100
Akron *(G-24)*

◆ Akron Paint & Varnish Inc....................D 330 773-8911
Akron *(G-36)*

Akzo Nobel Coatings Inc....................C 614 294-3361
Columbus *(G-4683)*

Akzo Nobel Coatings Inc....................E 419 433-9143
Huron *(G-7866)*

Akzo Nobel Coatings Inc....................E 937 322-2671
Springfield *(G-12277)*

◆ Akzo Nobel Paints LLC....................A 440 297-8000
Strongsville *(G-12533)*

All Coatings Co Inc....................G 330 821-3806
Alliance *(G-367)*

◆ Americhem Inc....................D 330 929-4213
Cuyahoga Falls *(G-5523)*

▲ Aps-Materials Inc....................D 937 278-6547
Dayton *(G-5662)*

Avient Corporation....................D 419 668-4844
Norwalk *(G-10829)*

Axalt Powde Coati Syste Usa I....................G 614 921-8000
Hilliard *(G-7671)*

Axalt Powde Coati Syste Usa I....................G 614 600-4104
Hilliard *(G-7672)*

Basic Coatings LLC....................F 419 241-2156
Bowling Green *(G-1408)*

Bollin & Sons Inc....................E 419 693-6573
Toledo *(G-12900)*

Brinkman LLC....................F 419 204-5934
Lima *(G-8392)*

▲ Buckeye Fabric Finishers Inc....................F 740 622-3251
Coshocton *(G-5453)*

Cansto Coatings Ltd....................F 216 231-6115
Cleveland *(G-3463)*

Cansto Paint and Varnish Co....................G
Cleveland *(G-3464)*

Certon Technologies Inc....................F 440 786-7185
Bedford *(G-1021)*

◆ Chemmasters Inc....................E 440 428-2105
Madison *(G-8726)*

▼ Chemspec Usa LLC....................D 330 669-8512
Orrville *(G-10976)*

◆ Chemspec Usa Inc....................D 330 669-8512
Orrville *(G-10977)*

◆ Coloramics LLC....................E 614 876-1171
Hilliard *(G-7678)*

◆ Comex North America Inc....................D 303 307-2100
Cleveland *(G-3551)*

◆ Consolidated Coatings Corp....................A 216 514-7596
Cleveland *(G-3561)*

CPC Holding Inc....................E 216 383-3932
Cleveland *(G-3572)*

CPI Industrial Co....................E 614 445-0800
Mount Sterling *(G-10227)*

CTS National Corporation....................E 216 566-2000
Cleveland *(G-3578)*

Dap Products Inc....................D 937 667-4461
Tipp City *(G-12822)*

David E Easterday and Co Inc....................F 330 359-0700
Wilmot *(G-14594)*

Day-Glo Color Corp....................F 216 391-7070
Cleveland *(G-3603)*

▲ Day-Glo Color Corp....................C 216 391-7070
Cleveland *(G-3602)*

Epoxy Systems Blstg Cating Inc....................F 513 924-1800
Cleves *(G-4535)*

◆ Epsilon Management Corporation....................C 216 634-2500
Cleveland *(G-3681)*

EZ Concrete Supply LLC....................G 844 393-7699
Lima *(G-8407)*

Ferro Corporation....................D 216 577-7144
Bedford *(G-1032)*

Fuchs Lubricants Co....................F 330 963-0400
Twinsburg *(G-13306)*

General Electric Company....................G 216 268-3846
Cleveland *(G-3763)*

Grand Archt Etrnl Eye 314 LLC....................F 800 377-8147
Cleveland *(G-3783)*

◆ Harrison Paint Company....................E 330 455-5120
Canton *(G-1909)*

Henkel US Operations Corp....................C 216 475-3600
Cleveland *(G-3821)*

Hexpol Compounding LLC....................C 440 834-4644
Burton *(G-1699)*

Hoover & Wells Inc....................C 419 691-9220
Toledo *(G-12995)*

Hudson Hines Hill Company....................D 330 562-1970
Streetsboro *(G-12504)*

Ineos Neal LLC....................E 610 790-3333
Dublin *(G-6308)*

Ineos Solvents Sales US Corp....................B 614 790-3333
Dublin *(G-6309)*

◆ J C Whitlam Manufacturing Co....................E 330 334-2524
Wadsworth *(G-13644)*

▲ Kalcor Coatings Company....................E 440 946-4700
Willoughby *(G-14474)*

◆ Kardol Quality Products LLC....................G 513 933-8206
Blue Ash *(G-1293)*

Kars Ohio LLC....................G 614 655-1099
Pataskala *(G-11142)*

Karyall-Telday Inc....................G 216 281-4063
Cleveland *(G-3906)*

Leonhardt Plating Company....................G 513 242-1410
Cincinnati *(G-2819)*

Lyondllbsell Advnced Plymers I....................D 419 682-3311
Stryker *(G-12624)*

Mameco International Inc....................F 216 752-4400
Cleveland *(G-3984)*

Mansfield Paint Co Inc....................G 330 725-2436
Medina *(G-9422)*

◆ Master Builders LLC....................E 800 228-3318
Beachwood *(G-928)*

Matrix Sys Auto Finishes LLC....................B 248 668-8135
Massillon *(G-9221)*

McCann Color Inc....................E 330 498-4840
Canton *(G-1942)*

Meggitt (erlanger) LLC....................D 513 851-5550
Cincinnati *(G-2858)*

Mid-America Chemical Corp....................G 216 749-0100
Cleveland *(G-4032)*

▼ Nanosperse LLC....................G 937 296-5030
Kettering *(G-8122)*

Nippon Paint (usa) Inc....................C 216 651-5900
Cleveland *(G-4078)*

▲ North Shore Strapping Company....................E 216 661-5200
Brooklyn Heights *(G-1536)*

▲ Npa Coatings Inc....................C 216 651-5900
Cleveland *(G-4104)*

OPC Polymers LLC....................D 614 253-8511
Columbus *(G-5161)*

P3 Infrastructure Inc....................F 330 408-9504
Twinsburg *(G-13348)*

Parker Trutec Incorporated....................D 937 653-8500
Urbana *(G-13476)*

◆ Perstorp Polyols Inc....................C 419 729-5448
Toledo *(G-13095)*

Pittsburgh Paints Co....................E 740 774-7600
Chillicothe *(G-2271)*

Pittsburgh Paints Co....................F 513 242-3050
Cincinnati *(G-2965)*

Pittsburgh Paints Co....................F 513 563-0220
Cincinnati *(G-2966)*

Pittsburgh Paints Co....................C 419 433-5664
Huron *(G-7881)*

Pittsburgh Paints Co....................B 440 826-5100
Strongsville *(G-12586)*

◆ Plasti-Kote Co Inc....................C 330 725-4511
Medina *(G-9435)*

Pmbp Legacy Co Inc....................E 330 253-8148
Akron *(G-262)*

▲ Polymerics Inc....................E 330 928-2210
Cuyahoga Falls *(G-5565)*

Polynt Composites USA Inc....................E 816 391-6000
Sandusky *(G-11866)*

▲ Postle Industries Inc....................E 216 265-9000
Cleveland *(G-4177)*

▼ PPG Architectural Coatings LLC....................D 440 297-8000
Strongsville *(G-12587)*

PPG Industries Inc....................E 330 825-0831
Barberton *(G-834)*

PPG Industries Inc....................F 740 774-8734
Chillicothe *(G-2273)*

PPG Industries Inc....................E 740 774-7600
Chillicothe *(G-2274)*

PPG Industries Inc....................F 740 774-7600
Chillicothe *(G-2275)*

PPG Industries Inc....................D 740 474-3161
Circleville *(G-3262)*

PPG Industries Inc................................ G 216 671-7793
Cleveland (G-4179)

PPG Industries Inc................................ G 740 363-9610
Delaware (G-6166)

PPG Industries Inc................................ G 419 331-2011
Lima (G-8438)

PPG Industries Inc................................ F 513 576-0360
Milford (G-9948)

PPG Industries Inc................................ D 440 572-2800
Strongsville (G-12588)

PPG Industries Ohio Inc......................... C 412 434-3888
Cleveland (G-4181)

PPG Industries Ohio Inc......................... C 740 363-9610
Delaware (G-6167)

PPG Industries Ohio Inc......................... D 412 434-1542
Euclid (G-6672)

PPG Industries Ohio Inc......................... D 440 572-6777
Strongsville (G-12589)

◆ PPG Industries Ohio Inc...................... A 216 671-0050
Cleveland (G-4180)

Precisions Paint Systems LLC............... F 740 894-6224
South Point (G-12229)

Premier Ink Systems Inc....................... F 513 367-2300
Harrison (G-7562)

Priest Services Inc............................... G 440 333-1123
Mayfield Heights (G-9340)

Quality Durable Indus Floors................. F 937 696-2833
Farmersville (G-6823)

◆ Republic Powdered Metals Inc............ D 330 225-3192
Medina (G-9441)

◆ Rolled Alloys Inc.............................. D 800 521-0332
Maumee (G-9315)

◆ RPM International Inc......................... D 330 273-5090
Medina (G-9442)

Sheffield Bronze Paint Corp.................. E 216 481-8330
Cleveland (G-4290)

Sherwin-Williams Company................... G 330 528-0124
Hudson (G-7856)

Sherwin-Williams Company................... C 330 830-6000
Massillon (G-9243)

Sherwin-Williams Company................... F 440 846-4328
Strongsville (G-12600)

Sherwin-Williams Company................... A 216 566-2000
Cleveland (G-4293)

Sherwin-Williams Mfg Co....................... F 216 566-2000
Cleveland (G-4294)

◆ Sherwn-Wllams Auto Fnshes Corp..... E 216 332-8330
Cleveland (G-4295)

▲ Spectrum Dispersions Inc.................. F 330 296-0600
Ravenna (G-11542)

Strong-Coat LLC.................................. G 440 299-2068
Willoughby (G-14535)

Superior Printing Ink Co Inc.................. G 216 328-1720
Cleveland (G-4346)

▲ Teknol Inc.. D 937 264-0190
Dayton (G-6043)

The Garland Company Inc..................... D 216 641-7500
Cleveland (G-4382)

◆ Tremco Incorporated......................... C 216 292-5000
Beachwood (G-956)

Treved Exteriors.................................. G 513 771-3888
Cincinnati (G-3167)

Trexler Rubber Co Inc.......................... E 330 296-9677
Ravenna (G-11546)

Universal Urethane Pdts Inc.................. D 419 693-7400
Toledo (G-13169)

Urethane Polymers Intl.......................... F 216 430-3655
Cleveland (G-4450)

Vanguard Paints and Finishes Inc.......... E 740 373-5261
Marietta (G-8959)

Vibrantz Corporation............................ C 216 875-6213
Cleveland (G-4468)

Vibrantz Corporation............................ D 732 287-4925
Cleveland (G-4469)

◆ Vibrantz Corporation......................... D 216 875-5600
Mayfield Heights (G-9344)

▼ Waterlox Coatings Corporation.......... F 216 641-4877
Cleveland (G-4493)

▼ Wooster Products Inc........................ D 330 264-2844
Wooster (G-14701)

X-Treme Finishes Inc........................... F 330 474-0614
North Royalton (G-10790)

▲ Zircoa Inc.. C 440 248-0500
Cleveland (G-4526)

2861 Gum and wood chemicals

◆ Damon Industries Inc......................... D 330 821-5310
Alliance (G-379)

◆ Oak Chips Inc................................... E 740 947-4159
Waverly (G-13871)

▼ PPG Architectural Coatings LLC......... D 440 297-8000
Strongsville (G-12587)

2865 Cyclic crudes and intermediates

Altivia Petrochemicals LLC................... E 740 532-3420
Haverhill (G-7585)

Americhem Inc.................................... D 330 926-3185
Cuyahoga Falls (G-5524)

◆ Americhem Inc.................................. D 330 929-4213
Cuyahoga Falls (G-5523)

Avient Corporation............................... D 419 668-4844
Norwalk (G-10829)

◆ Berghausen Corporation.................... E 513 591-4491
Cincinnati (G-2406)

Color Products Inc.............................. G 513 860-2749
Hamilton (G-7479)

◆ Colormatrix Corporation..................... C 216 622-0100
Berea (G-1163)

Colormatrix Group Inc.......................... C 216 622-0100
Berea (G-1164)

Colormatrix Holdings Inc...................... F 440 930-3162
Berea (G-1165)

Ferro Corporation................................ E 330 682-8015
Orrville (G-10980)

Flint CPS Inks North Amer LLC............. E 513 619-2089
Cincinnati (G-2628)

Flint Group US LLC.............................. G 513 552-7232
West Chester (G-13999)

Hexpol Compounding LLC..................... C 440 834-4644
Burton (G-1699)

Lyondllbsell Advnced Plymers I............. D 419 682-3311
Stryker (G-12624)

◆ Marathon Petroleum Company LP....... F 419 422-2121
Findlay (G-6889)

Marion County Coal Company............... D 740 338-3100
Saint Clairsville (G-11697)

Neyra Interstate Inc............................ E 513 733-1000
Cincinnati (G-2908)

Pmbp Legacy Co Inc........................... F 330 253-8148
Akron (G-261)

▲ Polymerics Inc.................................. E 330 928-2210
Cuyahoga Falls (G-5565)

◆ Republic Powdered Metals Inc............ D 330 225-3192
Medina (G-9441)

▲ Revlis Corporation............................ E 330 535-2100
Akron (G-282)

◆ RPM International Inc......................... D 330 273-5090
Medina (G-9442)

▲ Spectrum Dispersions Inc.................. F 330 296-0600
Ravenna (G-11542)

Standridge Color Corporation................ F 770 464-3362
Defiance (G-6124)

Sun Chemical Corporation.................... D 513 753-9550
Amelia (G-439)

Sun Chemical Corporation.................... E 513 830-8667
Cincinnati (G-3126)

Sun Chemical Corporation.................... C 513 681-5950
Cincinnati (G-3127)

◆ Vibrantz Color Solutions Inc.............. C 440 997-5137
Ashtabula (G-621)

Vibrantz Corporation............................ C 216 875-6213
Cleveland (G-4468)

Vibrantz Corporation............................ D 732 287-4925
Cleveland (G-4469)

2869 Industrial organic chemicals, nec

A-Gas US Holdings Inc......................... F 419 867-8990
Bowling Green (G-1403)

◆ Abitec Corporation............................ E 614 429-6464
Columbus (G-4665)

ABS Materials Inc................................ D 330 234-7999
Wooster (G-14617)

Adr Fuel Inc....................................... G 419 872-2178
Perrysburg (G-11201)

▲ Alco-Chem Inc.................................. E 330 253-3535
Akron (G-47)

Aldrich Chemical................................. D 937 859-1808
Miamisburg (G-9663)

Alpha Zeta Holdings Inc....................... G 216 271-1601
Cleveland (G-3334)

Ampacet Corporation........................... C 740 929-5521
Newark (G-10490)

Andersons Mrathon Holdings LLC......... E 937 316-3700
Greenville (G-7334)

Barentz N Amer Intrmdate Hldng........... G 440 937-1000
Avon (G-715)

BASF Corp... G 513 681-9100
Cincinnati (G-2401)

BASF Corporation................................ C 513 482-3000
Cincinnati (G-2402)

BASF Corporation................................ D 614 662-5682
Columbus (G-4745)

BASF Corporation................................ D 440 329-2525
Elyria (G-6503)

BASF Corporation................................ C 419 877-5308
Whitehouse (G-14357)

▲ Biowish Technologies Inc.................. G 312 572-6700
Cincinnati (G-2410)

Biowish Technologies Inc...................... E 312 572-6700
Cincinnati (G-2411)

Blinged & Bronzed............................... F 330 631-1255
Akron (G-80)

◆ Borchers Americas Inc...................... D 440 899-2950
Westlake (G-14295)

Brightstar Propane & Fuels................... G 614 891-8395
Westerville (G-14204)

Buckman Ltd....................................... G 419 420-1687
Findlay (G-6848)

Canton OH Rubber Specity Prods.......... G 330 454-3847
Canton (G-1857)

◆ Carson-Saeks Inc............................. E 937 278-5311
Dayton (G-5694)

Catexel Nease LLC.............................. D 513 738-1255
Harrison (G-7544)

◆ Catexel Nease LLC........................... F 513 587-2800
West Chester (G-13955)

Champion Company............................. D 937 324-5681
Springfield (G-12291)

Chem-Sales Inc.................................. F
Toledo (G-12918)

Chemcore Inc..................................... F 937 228-6118
Dayton (G-5699)

▲ Chemionics Corporation.................... E 330 733-8834
Tallmadge (G-12731)

Coil Specialty Chemicals LLC............... G 740 236-2407
Marietta (G-8910)

Corrugated Chemicals Inc........................ G 513 561-7773
Cincinnati *(G-2519)*

Ddp Specialty Electronic MA.................. G 937 839-4612
West Alexandria *(G-13918)*

◆ Dover Chemical Corporation.............C 330 343-7711
Dover *(G-6238)*

East Side Fuel Plus Operations.............. G 419 563-0777
Bucyrus *(G-1680)*

Eco Fuel Solution LLC........................... G 440 282-8592
Amherst *(G-446)*

Ecochem Alternative Fuels LLC............. E 614 764-3835
Plain City *(G-11406)*

Elco Corporation................................... E 440 997-6131
Ashtabula *(G-590)*

◆ Elco Corporation................................E 800 321-0467
Cleveland *(G-3659)*

Eqm Technologies & Energy Inc............ E 513 825-7500
Cincinnati *(G-2596)*

Equistar Chemicals LP.......................... D 513 530-4000
Cincinnati *(G-2598)*

Evonik Corporation................................ E 330 668-2235
Akron *(G-140)*

Exp Fuels Inc.. G 419 382-7713
Toledo *(G-12960)*

Ferro Corporation.................................. D 216 577-7144
Bedford *(G-1032)*

Frutarom USA Holding Inc..................... G 201 861-9500
West Chester *(G-14121)*

Gdc Inc.. F 574 533-3128
Wooster *(G-14642)*

Geon Company...................................... A 216 447-6000
Cleveland *(G-3771)*

GFS Chemicals Inc............................... D 614 224-5345
Columbus *(G-4954)*

◆ GFS Chemicals Inc............................E 740 881-5501
Powell *(G-11488)*

Givaudan Flavors Corporation................ E 513 948-3428
Cincinnati *(G-2672)*

◆ Givaudan Flavors Corporation.............C 513 948-8000
Cincinnati *(G-2673)*

Givaudan Fragrances Corp.................... D 513 948-3428
Cincinnati *(G-2675)*

◆ Givaudan Fragrances Corp.................B 513 948-8000
Cincinnati *(G-2676)*

Guardian Lima LLC............................... E 567 940-9500
Lima *(G-8412)*

Gushen America Inc.............................. G 708 664-2852
Heath *(G-7595)*

H&G Legacy Co..................................... F 513 921-1075
Cincinnati *(G-2701)*

Ha-International LLC.............................. E 419 537-0096
Toledo *(G-12982)*

▲ Hardy Industrial Tech LLC.................. D 440 350-6300
Painesville *(G-11092)*

▲ Heraeus Epurio LLC........................... E 937 264-1000
Vandalia *(G-13559)*

▼ Hexion Topco LLC.............................. D 614 225-4000
Columbus *(G-4978)*

◆ Hunt Imaging LLC..............................E 440 826-0433
Berea *(G-1176)*

Ibidltd-Blue Green Energy...................... F 909 547-5160
Toledo *(G-12998)*

◆ Jatrodiesel Inc...................................F
Miamisburg *(G-9703)*

Lanxess Corporation............................. G 440 324-6060
Elyria *(G-6557)*

▲ Lipo Technologies Inc......................... E 937 264-1222
Englewood *(G-6618)*

Littlern Corporation............................... G 330 848-8847
Fairlawn *(G-6807)*

Lyondell Chemical Company.................. C 513 530-4000
Cincinnati *(G-2833)*

Lyondllbsell Advnced Plymers I............. D 440 224-7291
Conneaut *(G-5411)*

Mart Plus Fuel...................................... G 216 261-0420
Euclid *(G-6660)*

◆ Michelman Inc....................................C 513 793-7766
Cincinnati *(G-2875)*

Mid-America Chemical Corp................... G 216 749-0100
Cleveland *(G-4032)*

▲ Momentive Perf Mtrls Quartz.............. G 408 436-6221
Strongsville *(G-12574)*

Momentive Performance Mtls Inc........... A 614 986-2495
Columbus *(G-5109)*

Momentive Performance Mtls Inc........... B 740 928-7010
Hebron *(G-7624)*

Momentive Performance Mtls Inc........... C 440 878-5705
Richmond Heights *(G-11611)*

Momentive Performance Mtls Inc........... C 740 929-8732
Willoughby *(G-14491)*

◆ Momentive Prfmce Mtls Qrtz Inc.........E 440 878-5700
Strongsville *(G-12575)*

Mp Biomedicals LLC............................. C 440 337-1200
Solon *(G-12154)*

▲ Nachurs Alpine Solutions LLC........... E 740 382-5701
Marion *(G-8982)*

▲ National Colloid Company.................. E 740 282-1171
Steubenville *(G-12407)*

Nationwide Chemical Products............... G 419 714-7075
Perrysburg *(G-11240)*

North East Fuel Inc............................... G 330 264-4454
Wooster *(G-14670)*

Novagard Solutions Inc......................... D 216 881-8111
Cleveland *(G-4101)*

Novation Solutions LLC......................... F 330 620-6721
Barberton *(G-825)*

▼ Noveon Fcc Inc.................................. F 440 943-4200
Wickliffe *(G-14384)*

Ohio Biosystems Coop Inc..................... G 419 980-7663
Loudonville *(G-8593)*

OPC Polymers LLC................................ D 614 253-8511
Columbus *(G-5161)*

Orion Engineered Carbons LLC............. D 740 423-9571
Belpre *(G-1151)*

Oxyrase Inc.. F 419 589-8800
Ontario *(G-10951)*

Poet Biorefining - Leipsic LLC............... E 419 943-7447
Leipsic *(G-8309)*

Poet Biorefining Marion LLC.................. E 740 383-4400
Marion *(G-8990)*

Poet Borefining - Fostoria LLC.............. G 419 436-0954
Fostoria *(G-6997)*

Polychem Dispersions Inc...................... E 800 545-3530
Middlefield *(G-9822)*

Polymer Diagnostics Inc........................ E 440 930-1361
Avon Lake *(G-768)*

◆ Reclamation Technologies Inc.............E 800 372-1301
Bowling Green *(G-1438)*

▲ Research Organics LLC...................... D 216 883-8025
Cleveland *(G-4236)*

▲ Revlis Corporation.............................. E 330 535-2100
Akron *(G-282)*

Rex American Resources Corp............... C 937 276-3931
Dayton *(G-5982)*

Ronald T Dodge Co............................... F 937 439-4497
Dayton *(G-5988)*

Sdg Inc.. F 440 893-0771
Cleveland *(G-4282)*

Shepherd Material Science Co............... E 513 731-1110
Norwood *(G-10871)*

Shin-Etsu Silicones Amer Inc................ F 330 630-9860
Akron *(G-308)*

◆ Shin-Etsu Silicones of America Inc.....C 330 630-9460
Akron *(G-309)*

▲ Shincor Silicones Inc......................... E 330 630-9460
Akron *(G-310)*

Silicone Solutions Inc........................... F 330 920-3125
Cuyahoga Falls *(G-5572)*

Symrise Inc.. C 440 324-6060
Elyria *(G-6594)*

The Andersons Clymers Ethanol LLC.... E 574 722-2627
Maumee *(G-9324)*

◆ The Lubrizol Corporation....................A 440 943-4200
Wickliffe *(G-14395)*

◆ The Shepherd Chemical Company......C 513 731-1110
Norwood *(G-10874)*

Twin Rvers Tech - Pnsville LLC............. G 440 350-6300
Painesville *(G-11120)*

Ultimate Chem Solutions Inc................. F 440 998-6751
Ashtabula *(G-618)*

Union Carbide Corporation.................... F 216 529-3784
Cleveland *(G-4440)*

◆ United Initiators Inc............................D 440 323-3112
Elyria *(G-6598)*

Univar Solutions USA LLC..................... E 513 714-5264
West Chester *(G-14157)*

Vantage Spclty Ingredients Inc.............. E 937 264-1222
Englewood *(G-6629)*

Vibrantz Technologies Inc..................... G 330 765-4378
Orrville *(G-11017)*

Wacker Chemical Corporation............... C 330 899-0847
Canton *(G-2044)*

▼ Werner G Smith Inc............................ F 216 861-3676
Cleveland *(G-4501)*

Wiley Companies.................................. C 740 622-0755
Coshocton *(G-5477)*

▲ Wiley Companies............................... C 740 622-0755
Coshocton *(G-5476)*

2873 Nitrogenous fertilizers

Agrium Advanced Tech US Inc.............. G 614 276-5103
Columbus *(G-4680)*

Amsoil Inc.. G 614 274-9851
Urbancrest *(G-13482)*

Andersons Inc....................................... G 419 243-6800
Toledo *(G-12880)*

CF Industries Inc.................................. C 330 385-5424
East Liverpool *(G-6389)*

Hyponex Corporation............................ C 330 262-1300
Shreve *(G-11982)*

Hyponex Corporation............................ D 937 644-0011
Marysville *(G-9031)*

Inspirtec LLC.. G 614 571-7130
Versailles *(G-13596)*

Keystone Cooperative Inc...................... G 937 884-5526
Verona *(G-13591)*

Pcs Nitrogen Inc................................... F 419 226-1200
Lima *(G-8437)*

R & J AG Manufacturing Inc.................. F 419 962-4707
Ashland *(G-568)*

Royster-Clark Inc.................................. G 513 941-4100
North Bend *(G-10621)*

Scotts Company LLC............................. F 937 454-2782
Dayton *(G-5999)*

◆ Scotts Company LLC..........................C 937 644-0011
Marysville *(G-9045)*

Scotts Miracle-Gro Company................. E 937 578-5065
Marysville *(G-9047)*

Scotts Miracle-Gro Company................. G 330 684-0421
Orrville *(G-11007)*

▲ Scotts Miracle-Gro Company.............. B 937 644-0011
Marysville *(G-9046)*

Smgm LLC.. F 937 644-0011
Marysville *(G-9050)*

Summers Organization LLC................... E 740 286-1322
Jackson *(G-7954)*

Synagro Midwest Inc.............................F 937 384-0669
Miamisburg *(G-9741)*

Talus Renewables Inc............................F 650 248-5374
Cleveland Heights *(G-4531)*

▼ Turf Care Supply LLC.........................D 877 220-1014
Brunswick *(G-1620)*

2874 Phosphatic fertilizers

Andersons Inc.......................................G 419 536-0460
Toledo *(G-12881)*

Andersons Inc.......................................C 419 893-5050
Maumee *(G-9261)*

◆ Scotts Company LLC............................C 937 644-0011
Marysville *(G-9045)*

2875 Fertilizers, mixing only

All Ways Green Lawn & Turf LLC...........G 937 763-4766
Seaman *(G-11889)*

Countyline Co-Op Inc............................F 419 287-3241
Pemberville *(G-11174)*

Garick LLC..E 216 581-0100
Cleveland *(G-3755)*

Hyponex Corporation.............................C 330 262-1300
Shreve *(G-11982)*

Hyponex Corporation.............................D 937 644-0011
Marysville *(G-9031)*

Insta-Gro Manufacturing Inc.................G 419 845-3046
Caledonia *(G-1732)*

▲ Kurtz Bros Compost Services...........G 330 864-2621
Akron *(G-200)*

Legacy Farmers Cooperative.................F 419 423-2611
Findlay *(G-6884)*

Lesco Inc..F 740 633-6366
Martins Ferry *(G-9010)*

Midwest Compost Inc............................F 419 547-7979
Clyde *(G-4560)*

▲ Nachurs Alpine Solutions LLC..........E 740 382-5701
Marion *(G-8982)*

Nutrien AG Solutions Inc.......................G 614 873-4253
Milford Center *(G-9958)*

Ohigro Inc...E 740 726-2429
Waldo *(G-13691)*

Opal Diamond LLC.................................G 330 653-5876
Rocky River *(G-11635)*

Ottokee Group Inc.................................G 419 636-1932
Bryan *(G-1656)*

Price Farms Organics Ltd......................F 740 369-1000
Delaware *(G-0100)*

Rod McLellan Company..........................G 937 578-5284
Marysville *(G-9044)*

Roe Transportation Entps Inc................G 937 497-7161
Sidney *(G-12045)*

Tyler Grain & Fertilizer Co.....................F 330 669-2341
Smithville *(G-12070)*

United Industries Incorporated..............D 330 682-5010
Orrville *(G-11015)*

Van Tilburg Farms Inc...........................F 419 586-3077
Celina *(G-2126)*

Werlor Inc...F 419 784-4285
Defiance *(G-6127)*

2879 Agricultural chemicals, nec

A Best Trmt & Pest Ctrl Sups................G 330 434-5555
Akron *(G-9)*

Abbott Laboratories...............................D 847 937-6100
Columbus *(G-4662)*

▲ Advanced Biological Mktg Inc...........E 419 232-2461
Van Wert *(G-13525)*

BASF Corporation.................................G 614 662-5682
Columbus *(G-4745)*

Bird Control International.......................G 330 425-2377
Twinsburg *(G-13281)*

◆ Damon Industries Inc..........................D 330 821-5310
Alliance *(G-379)*

Dupont Wealth Solutions LLC...............F 614 384-5246
Dublin *(G-6295)*

▲ Hawthorne Hydroponics LLC.............F 888 478-6544
Marysville *(G-9024)*

Keystone Cooperative Inc......................G 937 884-5526
Verona *(G-13591)*

Meristem Crop Prfmce Group LLC.........E 833 637-4783
Powell *(G-11490)*

Monsanto Company................................F 937 548-7858
Greenville *(G-7347)*

▲ Quality Borate Co LLC........................F 216 896-1949
Cleveland *(G-4212)*

◆ Scotts Company LLC............................C 937 644-0011
Marysville *(G-9045)*

Scotts Miracle-Gro Company.................E 937 578-5065
Marysville *(G-9047)*

▲ Scotts Miracle-Gro Company.............B 937 644-0011
Marysville *(G-9046)*

▲ TLC Products Inc................................F 216 472-3030
Westlake *(G-14340)*

2891 Adhesives and sealants

▲ Adchem Adhesives Inc........................F 440 526-1976
Cleveland *(G-3296)*

◆ Akron Paint & Varnish Inc..................D 330 773-8911
Akron *(G-36)*

◆ Akzo Nobel Paints LLC........................A 440 297-8000
Strongsville *(G-12533)*

Alpha Coatings Inc................................C 419 435-5111
Fostoria *(G-6974)*

Arclin USA LLC.....................................F 419 726-5013
Toledo *(G-12885)*

Avery Dennison Corporation..................B 440 358-2564
Painesville *(G-11069)*

Bostik Inc...E 419 289-9588
Ashland *(G-524)*

Bostik Inc...E 614 232-8510
Columbus *(G-4770)*

Brewer Company...................................G 513 576-6300
Cincinnati *(G-2422)*

▲ Cardinal Rubber Company..................E 330 745-2191
Barberton *(G-801)*

Certon Technologies Inc.......................F 440 786-7185
Bedford *(G-1021)*

◆ Chemmasters Inc................................E 440 428-2105
Madison *(G-0770)*

Chemspec Ltd.......................................F 330 364-4422
New Philadelphia *(G-10437)*

◆ Chemspec Ltd.....................................E 330 896-0355
Canton *(G-1864)*

▲ Chemspec Usa Inc..............................D 330 669-8512
Orrville *(G-10977)*

Choice Brands Adhesives Ltd................E 800 330-5566
Cincinnati *(G-2462)*

CIC Old Corporation..............................E 330 457-2367
New Waterford *(G-10487)*

▲ Cincinnati Assn For The Blind............C 513 221-8558
Cincinnati *(G-2469)*

◆ Concrete Sealants Inc.........................E 937 845-8776
Tipp City *(G-12821)*

Consolidated Coatings Corp..................A 216 514-7596
Cleveland *(G-3561)*

▲ Conversion Tech Intl Inc.....................E 419 924-5566
West Unity *(G-14193)*

Dap Products Inc..................................D 937 667-4461
Tipp City *(G-12822)*

Ddp Specialty Electronic MA.................G 937 839-4612
West Alexandria *(G-13918)*

Durez Corporation.................................D 567 295-6400
Kenton *(G-8097)*

▲ Edge Adhesives Inc............................E 614 875-6343
Grove City *(G-7383)*

Egc Operating Company LLC.................D 440 285-5835
Chardon *(G-2204)*

Elmers Products Inc..............................C 614 225-4000
Columbus *(G-4900)*

Engineered Conductive Mtl LLC............G 740 362-4444
Delaware *(G-6146)*

Entrochem Inc.......................................F 614 946-7602
Columbus *(G-4904)*

Evans Adhesive Corporation.................E 614 451-2665
Columbus *(G-4912)*

◆ Evans Adhesive Corporation Ltd........E 614 451-2665
Columbus *(G-4913)*

▲ FedPro Inc..E 216 464-6440
Cleveland *(G-3711)*

Foam Seal Inc.......................................C 216 881-8111
Cleveland *(G-3730)*

◆ Franklin International Inc....................B 614 443-0241
Columbus *(G-4938)*

Gdc Inc...F 574 533-3128
Wooster *(G-14642)*

Glenrock Company................................G 513 489-6710
Blue Ash *(G-1277)*

Hartline Products Coinc........................G 216 851-7189
Cleveland *(G-3811)*

HB Fuller Company................................G 833 672-1482
Bellevue *(G-1124)*

HB Fuller Company................................D 513 719-3600
Blue Ash *(G-1282)*

HB Fuller Company................................F 513 719-3600
Blue Ash *(G-1283)*

HB Fuller Company................................F 440 708-1212
Chagrin Falls *(G-2164)*

Henkel US Operations Corp...................E 513 830-0260
Cincinnati *(G-2717)*

Henkel US Operations Corp...................C 216 475-3600
Cleveland *(G-3821)*

Henkel US Operations Corp...................C 440 255-8900
Mentor *(G-9528)*

Henkel US Operations Corp...................D 440 250-7700
Westlake *(G-14305)*

▼ Hexpol Cmpnding Amrcas Mfg LLC...C 440 632-0901
Middlefield *(G-9799)*

Hexpol Compounding LLC......................C 440 834-4644
Burton *(G-1699)*

Hoover & Wells Inc...............................C 419 691-9220
Toledo *(G-12006)*

Hydratech Engineered Pdts LLC...........F 513 827-9169
Cincinnati *(G-2737)*

▲ ICP Adhesives and Sealants Inc........E 330 753-4585
Norton *(G-10823)*

Illinois Tool Works Inc..........................C 513 489-7600
Blue Ash *(G-1286)*

Illinois Tool Works Inc..........................D 440 914-3100
Solon *(G-12126)*

Imperial Adhesives...............................G 513 351-1300
Cincinnati *(G-2741)*

◆ J C Whitlam Manufacturing Co...........E 330 334-2524
Wadsworth *(G-13644)*

Jetcoat LLC...E 800 394-0047
Columbus *(G-5039)*

Laird Technologies Inc.........................D 216 939-2300
Cleveland *(G-3935)*

▲ Laminate Technologies Inc................D 800 231-2523
Tiffin *(G-12786)*

▲ Laurenco Systems of Ohio LLC.........G
Leavittsburg *(G-8240)*

◆ Lubrizol Global Management Inc.........F 216 447-5000
Cleveland *(G-3970)*

M Argueso & Co Inc..............................C 216 252-4122
Cleveland *(G-3974)*

Mactac Americas LLC...................... D 800 762-2822
Stow *(G-12439)*

Mameco International Inc................... F 216 752-4400
Cleveland *(G-3984)*

Marlen Manufacturing & Dev Co........ F 216 292-7546
Bedford *(G-1047)*

▲ Merryweather Foam Inc................. E 330 753-0353
Barberton *(G-822)*

Millennium Adhesive Pdts LLC.......... F 440 708-1212
Chagrin Falls *(G-2149)*

Mitsubishi Chemical Amer Inc........... D 419 483-2931
Bellevue *(G-1126)*

◆ Morgan Adhesives Company LLC.....B 330 688-1111
Stow *(G-12441)*

▲ Nagase Chemtex America LLC........ E 740 362-4444
Delaware *(G-6162)*

▼ Nanosperse LLC........................... G 937 296-5030
Kettering *(G-8122)*

National Polymer Inc........................ F 440 708-1245
Chagrin Falls *(G-2171)*

Neyra Interstate Inc......................... E 513 733-1000
Cincinnati *(G-2908)*

P & T Products Inc.......................... E 419 621-1966
Sandusky *(G-11863)*

▲ Paramelt Argueso Kindt Inc........... G 216 252-4122
Cleveland *(G-4133)*

Pmbp Legacy Co Inc........................ E 330 253-8148
Akron *(G-262)*

▲ Polymerics Inc............................. E 330 928-2210
Cuyahoga Falls *(G-5565)*

▼ PPG Architectural Coatings LLC....... D 440 297-8000
Strongsville *(G-12587)*

▲ Premier Building Solutions LLC....... E 330 244-2907
Massillon *(G-9235)*

Priest Services Inc.......................... G 440 333-1123
Mayfield Heights *(G-9340)*

Quanex Ig Systems Inc.................... D 740 435-0444
Cambridge *(G-1756)*

Quest Solutions Group LLC............... G 513 703-4520
Liberty Township *(G-8378)*

▲ Renegade Materials Corporation...... D 937 350-5274
Miamisburg *(G-9732)*

◆ Republic Powdered Metals Inc.........D 330 225-3192
Medina *(G-9441)*

Royal Adhesives & Sealants LLC......... F 440 708-1212
Chagrin Falls *(G-2181)*

◆ RPM International Inc.....................D 330 273-5090
Medina *(G-9442)*

▼ Rubex Inc.................................... G 614 875-6343
Grove City *(G-7412)*

Ruscoe Company............................ E 330 253-8148
Akron *(G-295)*

Sem-Com Company Inc.................... F 419 537-8813
Toledo *(G-13125)*

Sherwin-Williams Company............... C 330 830-6000
Massillon *(G-9243)*

▲ Shincor Silicones Inc.................... E 330 630-9460
Akron *(G-310)*

Signature Flexible Packg LLC............. F 614 252-2121
Columbus *(G-5267)*

Silicone Solutions Inc...................... G 330 920-3125
Cuyahoga Falls *(G-5572)*

◆ Simona Boltaron Inc......................D 740 498-5900
Newcomerstown *(G-10575)*

▲ Sirrus Inc.................................... E 513 448-0308
Loveland *(G-8654)*

Sonoco Products Company................ E 937 429-0040
Beavercreek Township *(G-1006)*

Spectra Group Limited Inc................ G 419 837-9783
Millbury *(G-9965)*

Spectrum Adhesives Inc................... G 740 763-2886
Newark *(G-10533)*

Summitville Tiles Inc........................ D 330 868-6463
Minerva *(G-10048)*

▲ Sunstar Engrg Americas Inc........... E 937 746-8575
Springboro *(G-12268)*

Synthomer Adhesive Tech LLC........... F 216 682-7000
Beachwood *(G-950)*

◆ Synthomer USA LLC......................E 678 400-6655
Beachwood *(G-952)*

◆ Technical Rubber Company Inc.........C 740 967-9015
Johnstown *(G-7999)*

Technicote Inc................................ E 330 928-1476
Cuyahoga Falls *(G-5576)*

Techno Adhesives Co....................... G 513 771-1584
Cincinnati *(G-3141)*

▲ Teknol Inc................................... D 937 264-0190
Dayton *(G-6043)*

▲ Thermagon Inc............................. D 216 939-2300
Cleveland *(G-4390)*

◆ Thorworks Industries Inc.................C 419 626-4375
Sandusky *(G-11876)*

Three Bond International Inc.............. E 937 610-3000
Dayton *(G-6052)*

▲ Three Bond International Inc............ D 513 779-7300
West Chester *(G-14082)*

▲ Toagosei America Inc..................... D 614 718-3855
West Jefferson *(G-14168)*

Tremco Cpg Inc.............................. C 419 289-2050
Ashland *(G-580)*

Tremco Cpg Inc.............................. E 216 514-7783
Beachwood *(G-955)*

◆ Tremco Incorporated.....................C 216 292-5000
Beachwood *(G-956)*

◆ Truseal Technologies Inc.................E 216 910-1500
Akron *(G-346)*

▲ United McGill Corporation............... E 614 829-1200
Groveport *(G-7455)*

▲ Valco Cincinnati Inc....................... C 513 874-6550
Cincinnati *(G-3190)*

▲ Waytek Corporation....................... E 937 743-6142
Franklin *(G-7057)*

2892 Explosives

Austin Powder Company.................... G 419 299-3347
Findlay *(G-6838)*

Austin Powder Company.................... C 740 596-5286
Mc Arthur *(G-9348)*

Austin Powder Company.................... G 740 968-1555
Saint Clairsville *(G-11687)*

▲ Austin Powder Company................ D 216 464-2400
Cleveland *(G-3386)*

◆ Austin Powder Holdings Company....D 216 464-2400
Cleveland *(G-3387)*

Hilltop Energy Inc........................... F 330 859-2108
Mineral City *(G-10028)*

Sloat Inc....................................... G 440 951-9554
Willoughby *(G-14530)*

2893 Printing ink

American Inks and Coatings Co........... G 513 552-7200
Fairfield *(G-6710)*

◆ Eckart America Corporation............D 440 954-7600
Painesville *(G-11082)*

Flint CPS Inks North Amer LLC........... E 513 619-2089
Cincinnati *(G-2628)*

▲ Glass Coatings & Concepts LLC....... E 513 539-5300
Monroe *(G-10107)*

◆ Ink Technology Corporation.............E 216 486-6720
Cleveland *(G-3860)*

INX International Ink Co.................... F 440 239-1766
Cleveland *(G-3867)*

INX International Ink Co.................... F 707 693-2990
Lebanon *(G-8268)*

Joules Angstrom Uv Prtg Inks C......... E 740 964-9113
Pataskala *(G-11141)*

Kennedy Ink Company Inc................ F 513 871-2515
Cincinnati *(G-2793)*

Kohl & Madden Inc.......................... G 513 326-6900
Cincinnati *(G-2804)*

Magnum Magnetics Corporation......... E 740 516-6237
Caldwell *(G-1725)*

Magnum Magnetics Corporation......... E 513 360-0790
Middletown *(G-9876)*

Premier Ink Systems Inc.................. E 513 367-2300
Harrison *(G-7562)*

Printink Inc................................... G 513 943-0599
Amelia *(G-435)*

▲ Red Tie Group Inc........................ E
Cleveland *(G-4229)*

Sun Chemical Corporation................ D 513 753-9550
Amelia *(G-439)*

Sun Chemical Corporation................ D 513 671-0407
Cincinnati *(G-3123)*

Sun Chemical Corporation................ E 513 681-5950
Cincinnati *(G-3124)*

Sun Chemical Corporation................ E 513 681-5950
Cincinnati *(G-3125)*

Sun Chemical Corporation................ G 513 830-8667
Cincinnati *(G-3126)*

Sun Chemical Corporation................ D 419 891-3514
Maumee *(G-9322)*

Superior Printing Ink Co Inc............. G 216 328-1720
Cleveland *(G-4346)*

Vibrantz Corporation....................... C 216 875-6213
Cleveland *(G-4468)*

Wikoff Color Corporation.................. G 513 423-0727
Middletown *(G-9905)*

Zeres Inc...................................... E 419 354-5555
Bowling Green *(G-1450)*

2895 Carbon black

◆ Chromascape LLC.........................E 330 998-7574
Independence *(G-7892)*

◆ Jacobi Carbons Inc.......................D 215 546-3900
Columbus *(G-5029)*

Orion Engineered Carbons LLC........... E 985 312-7406
Marietta *(G-8933)*

2899 Chemical preparations, nec

▲ Akron Dispersions Inc................... E 330 666-0045
Copley *(G-5428)*

Aldrich Chemical............................ D 937 859-1808
Miamisburg *(G-9663)*

Alterra Energy LLC.......................... G 800 569-6061
Akron *(G-53)*

American Fireworks Inc.................... A 330 650-1776
Hudson *(G-7829)*

American Fireworks Company............ A 330 650-1776
Hudson *(G-7830)*

▼ AP Tech Group Inc........................ F 513 761-8111
West Chester *(G-13940)*

▲ Apex Advanced Technologies LLC.... G 216 898-1595
Cleveland *(G-3361)*

◆ Applied Specialties Innovations LLC.E 440 933-9442
Avon Lake *(G-746)*

▲ Aps-Materials Inc......................... D 937 278-6547
Dayton *(G-5662)*

Aqua Science Inc............................ E 614 252-5000
Columbus *(G-4723)*

Aquablue Incorporated.................... G 330 343-0220
New Philadelphia *(G-10430)*

Ashland Chemco Inc........................ F 216 961-4690
Cleveland *(G-3378)*

Ashland Chemco Inc........................ C 614 790-3333
Columbus *(G-4727)*

Ashland Spcalty Ingredients GP............C 614 529-3311
   Columbus *(G-4728)*

◆ ASK Chemicals LLC................................B 800 848-7485
   Dublin *(G-6277)*

◆ Asterion LLC..E 317 875-0051
   Cincinnati *(G-2382)*

Atotech Usa LLC...................................... F 216 398-0550
   Cleveland *(G-3385)*

BASF Corporation...................................... D 614 662-5682
   Columbus *(G-4745)*

▲ Bernard Laboratories Inc ....E 513 681-7373
   Cincinnati *(G-2407)*

Bird Control International.........................G 330 425-2377
   Twinsburg *(G-13281)*

Blackthorn LLC... F 937 836-9296
   Clayton *(G-3272)*

BLaster LLC...E 216 901-5800
   Cleveland *(G-3423)*

Bond Chemicals Inc.................................G 330 725-5935
   Medina *(G-9382)*

Bond Distributing LLC.............................G 440 461-7920
   Eastlake *(G-6420)*

◆ Borchers Americas Inc ....D 440 899-2950
   Westlake *(G-14295)*

Broco Products Inc..................................G 216 531-0880
   Cleveland *(G-3441)*

▲ Buckeye Fabric Finishers Inc .... F 740 622-3251
   Coshocton *(G-5453)*

◆ Buckingham Src Inc............................... F 216 941-6115
   Cleveland *(G-3448)*

Cargill Incorporated................................ C 216 651-7200
   Cleveland *(G-3470)*

Cfo Ntic... C 216 450-5700
   Beachwood *(G-911)*

Chem Technologies Ltd ....D 440 632-9311
   Middlefield *(G-9786)*

Chemical Methods Incorporated.............E 216 476-8400
   Brunswick *(G-1582)*

◆ Chemmasters Inc ....E 440 428-2105
   Madison *(G-8726)*

Chemstation International Inc ....E 937 294-8265
   Dayton *(G-5701)*

◆ Chemtool Incorporated...........................C 815 957-4140
   Wickliffe *(G-14369)*

Cinchempro Inc.. C 513 724-6111
   Batavia *(G-855)*

Cincinnati - Vulcan Company..................D 513 242-5300
   Cincinnati *(G-2465)*

City of Mount Vernon...............................G 740 393-9508
   Mount Vernon *(G-10240)*

CJ Salt World..G 440 343-5661
   Wickliffe *(G-14370)*

Color Resolutions International LLC......C 513 552-7200
   Fairfield *(G-6724)*

CP Chemicals Group LP.........................G 440 833-3000
   Wickliffe *(G-14372)*

Cresset Chemical Co Inc......................... F 419 669-2041
   Weston *(G-14348)*

▼ Cresset Chemical Co Inc...................... F 419 669-2041
   Weston *(G-14347)*

◆ Damon Industries Inc.............................D 330 821-5310
   Alliance *(G-379)*

◆ Dayton Superior Corporation.................C 937 866-0711
   Miamisburg *(G-9687)*

Dinol US Inc...E 740 548-1656
   Lewis Center *(G-8330)*

Distillata Company...................................D 216 771-2900
   Cleveland *(G-3619)*

◆ Dover Chemical Corporation.................330 343-7711
   Dover *(G-6238)*

Edgewater Capital Partners LP...............G 216 292-3838
   Independence *(G-7901)*

Elco Corporation......................................E 440 997-6131
   Ashtabula *(G-590)*

EMD Millipore Corporation......................C 513 631-0445
   Norwood *(G-10868)*

◆ Emery Oleochemicals LLC.....................E 513 762-2500
   Cincinnati *(G-2584)*

Ensign Product Company Inc..................G 216 341-5911
   Cleveland *(G-3676)*

Enviri Corporation.................................... F 330 372-1781
   Warren *(G-13763)*

Environmental Chemical Corp.................. F 330 453-5200
   Uniontown *(G-13419)*

ESP Akron Sub LLC.................................D 330 374-2242
   Akron *(G-139)*

Essential Elements Usa LLC..................E 513 482-5700
   Cincinnati *(G-2599)*

◆ Etna Products Incorporated...................E 440 543-9845
   Chagrin Falls *(G-2161)*

Euclid Chemical Company....................... F 216 292-5000
   Beachwood *(G-918)*

◆ Euclid Chemical Company.....................E 800 321-7628
   Cleveland *(G-3688)*

▲ Ferrum Industries Inc ....G 440 519-1768
   Twinsburg *(G-13303)*

Fire Containment Concepts LLC............. F 800 877-2204
   Hartville *(G-7575)*

◆ Flexsys America LP................................D 330 666-4111
   Akron *(G-150)*

Formlabs Ohio Inc....................................E 419 837-9783
   Millbury *(G-9961)*

Fuchs Lubricants Co................................ F 330 963-0400
   Twinsburg *(G-13306)*

◆ Fusion Ceramics Inc ....E 330 627-5821
   Carrollton *(G-2083)*

▲ Fusion Incorporated...............................D 440 946-3300
   Willoughby *(G-14460)*

Galapagos Inc.. F 937 890-3068
   Dayton *(G-5789)*

Gasflux Company.....................................G 440 365-1941
   Elyria *(G-6538)*

General Electric Company.......................G 216 268-3846
   Cleveland *(G-3763)*

GFS Chemicals Inc..................................D 614 224-5345
   Columbus *(G-4954)*

◆ GFS Chemicals Inc................................E 740 881-5501
   Powell *(G-11488)*

▲ Great River Re Inc.................................E 513 471-8770
   Cincinnati *(G-2688)*

▲ H B Chemical Corporation.....................G 330 920-8023
   Twinsburg *(G-13313)*

H&G Legacy Co....................................... F 513 921-1075
   Cincinnati *(G-2701)*

◆ Hexion LLC...D 614 225-4000
   Columbus *(G-4977)*

Hexpol Compounding LLC.......................C 440 834-4644
   Burton *(G-1699)*

Howard Industries Inc............................. F 614 444-9900
   Columbus *(G-4993)*

◆ Hunt Imaging LLC...................................E 440 826-0433
   Berea *(G-1176)*

Huntsman Corporation.............................D 330 374-2418
   Akron *(G-179)*

Illinois Tool Works Inc.............................D 440 914-3100
   Solon *(G-12126)*

Innovative Food Processors Inc.............G 507 334-2730
   Defiance *(G-6112)*

Intercontinental Chemical Corp...............E 513 541-7100
   Cincinnati *(G-2749)*

Italmatch Sc LLC..................................... F 216 749-2605
   Cleveland *(G-3873)*

◆ J C Whitlam Manufacturing Co.............E 330 334-2524
   Wadsworth *(G-13644)*

◆ J W Harris Co Inc...................................B 513 754-2000
   Mason *(G-9116)*

Koki Laboratories Inc.............................E 330 773-7669
   Akron *(G-198)*

▲ Kona Blackbird Inc ....E 440 285-3189
   Chardon *(G-2211)*

Kost Usa Inc...E 513 583-7070
   Cincinnati *(G-2806)*

Leonhardt Plating Company....................G 513 242-1410
   Cincinnati *(G-2819)*

Lfg Specialties LLC.................................E 419 424-4999
   Findlay *(G-6885)*

Lg Chem Ohio Petrochemical Inc........... F 470 792-5127
   Ravenna *(G-11530)*

Link To Success Inc................................G 888 959-4203
   Norwalk *(G-10851)*

▲ Liquid Development Company...............G 216 641-9366
   Independence *(G-7907)*

Lubrizol Advanced Mtls Inc.................... F 216 447-5000
   Brecksville *(G-1476)*

Lubrizol Global Management...................E 419 352-5565
   Bowling Green *(G-1426)*

Lubrizol Global Management Inc............E 440 933-0400
   Avon Lake *(G-763)*

◆ Lubrizol Global Management Inc............ F 216 447-5000
   Cleveland *(G-3970)*

Lubrizol Holdings LLC............................. F 440 943-4200
   Wickliffe *(G-14381)*

Luxfer Magtech Inc.................................. F 513 772-3066
   Cincinnati *(G-2832)*

◆ Malco Products Inc.................................C 330 753-0361
   Barberton *(G-819)*

◆ Mar-Flex Systems LLC...........................E 513 422-7285
   Carlisle *(G-2068)*

Master Bldrs Sltons Admxtres U............ C 216 839-7500
   Beachwood *(G-927)*

◆ Master Builders LLC..............................E 800 228-3318
   Beachwood *(G-928)*

◆ Master Chemical Corporation.................D 419 874-7902
   Perrysburg *(G-11238)*

McGean-Rohco Inc...................................G 216 441-4900
   Newburgh Heights *(G-10545)*

◆ McGean-Rohco Inc.................................D 216 441-4900
   Cleveland *(G-4009)*

Midwest Glycol Services LLC.................E 419 946-3326
   Marion *(G-8978)*

◆ Milacron LLC...E 513 487-5000
   Cincinnati *(G-2880)*

Morgan Advanced Ceramics Inc.............E 330 405-1033
   Twinsburg *(G-13344)*

Morton Salt Inc...G 513 941-1578
   Cincinnati *(G-2890)*

Morton Salt Inc...E 216 664-0728
   Cleveland *(G-4048)*

Morton Salt Inc...C 330 925-3015
   Rittman *(G-11625)*

Mxr Imaging Inc.......................................G 614 219-2011
   Hilliard *(G-7688)*

▲ National Colloid Company......................E 740 282-1171
   Steubenville *(G-12407)*

◆ Natural Essentials Inc............................C 330 562-8022
   Streetsboro *(G-12513)*

Natures Own Source LLC.......................G 440 838-5135
   Brecksville *(G-1477)*

▲ Net Braze LLC.. F 937 444-1444
   Mount Orab *(G-10220)*

New Vulco Mfg & Sales Co LLC.............D 513 242-2672
   Cincinnati *(G-2904)*

No Burn Inc..G 330 336-1500
   Wadsworth *(G-13655)*

◆ Noco Company..D 216 464-8131
   Glenwillow *(G-7286)*

SIC

▲ Nof Metal Coatings N Amer Inc......... E 440 285-2231
Chardon *(G-2215)*

▲ Northern Chem Blnding Corp Inc...... G 216 781-7799
Cleveland *(G-4093)*

▼ Noveon Fcc Inc............................. F 440 943-4200
Wickliffe *(G-14384)*

Obersons Nurs & Landscapes LLC....... E 513 687-7379
Hamilton *(G-7514)*

Ohio Aluminum Chemicals LLC.......... G 513 860-3842
West Chester *(G-14036)*

◆ Opw Fueling Components Inc...........D 800 422-2525
West Chester *(G-14040)*

Parker Trutec Incorporated..................... D 937 653-8500
Urbana *(G-13476)*

Pemro Corporation............................. F 800 440-5441
Cleveland *(G-4151)*

◆ Peter Cremer North America LP.........D 513 471-7200
Cincinnati *(G-2958)*

Phantom Fireworks Wstn Reg LLC...... G 330 746-1064
Youngstown *(G-14916)*

▼ Plating Process Systems Inc............. G
Mentor *(G-9587)*

Polymer Additives Holdings Inc............. C 216 875-7200
Independence *(G-7915)*

Polymerics Inc.................................... E 330 677-1131
Kent *(G-8060)*

▼ PPG Architectural Coatings LLC....... D 440 297-8000
Strongsville *(G-12587)*

Premier Ink Systems Inc..................... F 513 367-2300
Harrison *(G-7562)*

Primary Pdts Ingrdnts Amrcas L.......... D 937 236-5906
Dayton *(G-5955)*

Proklean Services LLC....................... E 330 273-0122
Brunswick *(G-1609)*

Pyro-Chem Corporation....................... F 740 377-2244
South Point *(G-12230)*

▲ Quaker Chemical Corporation......... E 513 422-9600
Middletown *(G-9888)*

▲ Ques Industries Inc........................ F 216 267-8989
Cleveland *(G-4218)*

Quikrete Companies LLC.................... D 614 885-4406
Columbus *(G-5220)*

Rambasek Realty Inc........................... F 937 228-1189
Dayton *(G-5974)*

Ravago Chemical Dist Inc.................... E 330 920-8023
Twinsburg *(G-13364)*

◆ Republic Powdered Metals Inc...........D 330 225-3192
Medina *(G-9441)*

▲ Research Organics LLC................... D 216 883-8025
Cleveland *(G-4236)*

▲ Rhenium Alloys Inc......................... E 440 365-7388
North Ridgeville *(G-10747)*

◆ Rolled Alloys Inc.............................D 800 521-0332
Maumee *(G-9315)*

Rossborough Automotive Corp............. F 216 941-6115
Cleveland *(G-4254)*

Rozzi Company Inc............................ F 513 683-0620
Martinsville *(G-9013)*

▲ Rozzi Company Inc......................... E 513 683-0620
Loveland *(G-8649)*

RP Hoskins Inc................................ G 216 631-1000
Cleveland *(G-4261)*

◆ RPM International Inc.......................D 330 273-5090
Medina *(G-9442)*

▲ SC Fire Protection Ltd.................... G 330 468-3300
Macedonia *(G-8712)*

Scioto Fleet Services LLC.................... G 614 749-2318
Columbus *(G-5256)*

Sigma-Aldrich Corporation................... D 216 206-5424
Cleveland *(G-4300)*

Signet Enterprises LLC....................... E 330 762-9102
Akron *(G-312)*

◆ SRC Worldwide Inc.......................... F 216 941-6115
Cleveland *(G-4322)*

◆ State Industrial Products Corp............B 877 747-6986
Cleveland *(G-4329)*

Stellar Group Inc................................ F 330 769-8484
Seville *(G-11921)*

Summitville Tiles Inc......................... D 330 868-6463
Minerva *(G-10048)*

Sun Chemical Corporation................. D 513 671-0407
Cincinnati *(G-3123)*

◆ Superior Flux & Mfg Co....................F 440 349-3000
Cleveland *(G-4343)*

▲ Teknol Inc...................................... D 937 264-0190
Dayton *(G-6043)*

The Lubrizol Corporation..................... G 216 447-6212
Akron *(G-331)*

The Lubrizol Corporation..................... C 440 357-7064
Painesville *(G-11117)*

◆ The Lubrizol Corporation..................A 440 943-4200
Wickliffe *(G-14395)*

◆ U S Chemical & Plastics...................G 330 830-6000
Massillon *(G-9250)*

▲ Unitrex Ltd.................................... D 216 831-1900
Bedford Heights *(G-1083)*

Univar Solutions USA LLC.................. E 513 714-5264
West Chester *(G-14157)*

Urethane Polymers Intl....................... F 216 430-3655
Cleveland *(G-4450)*

US Water Company LLC..................... G 740 453-0604
Zanesville *(G-15053)*

Usalco Fairfield Plant LLC.................. E 513 737-7100
Fairfield *(G-6786)*

Valtris Specialty Chemicals................. F 216 875-7200
Walton Hills *(G-13704)*

Vesuvius U S A Corporation............... G 440 593-1161
Conneaut *(G-5419)*

Vibrantz Corporation........................ E 216 875-5600
Cleveland *(G-4467)*

Vibrantz Corporation........................ C 216 875-6213
Cleveland *(G-4468)*

▲ Wild Berry Incense Inc..................... F 513 523-8583
Oxford *(G-11065)*

◆ Zinkan Enterprises Inc.....................F 330 487-1500
Twinsburg *(G-13400)*

29 PETROLEUM REFINING AND RELATED INDUSTRIES

2911 Petroleum refining

Aecom Energy & Cnstr Inc.................. G 419 698-6277
Oregon *(G-10956)*

Blaster Corporation........................... F 216 901-5800
Medina *(G-9381)*

BLaster Holdings LLC....................... E 216 901-5800
Cleveland *(G-3422)*

BLaster LLC..................................... E 216 901-5800
Cleveland *(G-3423)*

BP Products North America Inc............. E 419 537-9540
Toledo *(G-12901)*

Capital City Oil Inc............................ G 740 397-4483
Mount Vernon *(G-10238)*

Cyberutility LLC................................ G 216 291-8723
Cleveland *(G-3595)*

Eidp Inc.. F 440 934-6444
Avon *(G-725)*

Enrevo Pyro LLC............................... G 203 517-5002
Brookfield *(G-1514)*

Foam Seal Inc................................... C 216 881-8111
Cleveland *(G-3730)*

▼ Functional Products Inc..................... F 330 963-3060
Macedonia *(G-8692)*

Gfl Environmental Svcs USA Inc............. E 614 441-4001
Columbus *(G-4952)*

Gfl Environmental Svcs USA Inc............. E 281 486-4182
Norwalk *(G-10842)*

◆ Giant Industries Inc.........................D 419 421-2121
Findlay *(G-6870)*

Husky Lima Refinery.......................... E 419 226-2300
Lima *(G-8416)*

Hydrodec Inc................................... G 330 454-8202
Canton *(G-1914)*

▼ Hydrodec of North America LLC...... E 330 454-8202
Canton *(G-1915)*

Ineos Neal LLC................................ E 610 790-3333
Dublin *(G-6308)*

▲ Isp Lima LLC.................................. E 419 998-8700
Lima *(G-8421)*

Jet Fuel Strategies LLC...................... G 440 323-4220
Elyria *(G-6556)*

◆ Knight Material Tech LLC................. E 330 488-1651
East Canton *(G-6378)*

Marathon Intl Pdts Sup LLC................. G 419 422-2121
Findlay *(G-6887)*

Marathon Oil Company....................... E 419 422-2121
Findlay *(G-6888)*

▲ Marathon Petroleum Corporation...... A 419 422-2121
Findlay *(G-6890)*

Mkfour Inc....................................... G 620 629-1120
Granville *(G-7318)*

Mplx GP LLC................................... G 419 422-2121
Findlay *(G-6896)*

Ohio Refining Company LLC................. A 614 210-2300
Dublin *(G-6326)*

Pbf Holding Company LLC................. D 419 698-6600
Oregon *(G-10965)*

PEC Biofuels LLC............................. G 419 542-8210
Hicksville *(G-7651)*

PSC 272 TRC Pbf.............................. E 419 466-7129
Oregon *(G-10966)*

Seneca Petroleum Co Inc................... F 419 691-3581
Toledo *(G-13126)*

Seneca Petroleum Co Inc................... F 419 691-3581
Toledo *(G-13127)*

Stark Materials Inc............................ F 330 497-1648
Canton *(G-2014)*

Varouh Oil Inc.................................. F 440 482-8686
Elyria *(G-6599)*

2951 Asphalt paving mixtures and blocks

Advanced Fiber LLC.......................... E 419 562-1337
Bucyrus *(G-1671)*

All Coatings Co Inc............................ G 330 821-3806
Alliance *(G-367)*

Allied Corporation Inc........................ F 330 425-7861
Twinsburg *(G-13272)*

Asphalt Fabrics & Specialties............... E 440 786-1077
Solon *(G-12080)*

Atlas Roofing Corporation.................. C 937 746-9941
Franklin *(G-7010)*

◆ Barrett Paving Materials Inc...............E 973 533-1001
Hamilton *(G-7468)*

Bluffton Stone Co............................. F 419 358-6941
Bluffton *(G-1358)*

Bowerston Shale Company................. E 740 269-2921
Bowerston *(G-1399)*

▲ Brewer Company............................ G 800 394-0017
Milford *(G-9926)*

Central Allied Enterprises Inc................ E 330 477-6751
Canton *(G-1862)*

Central Oil Asphalt Corp..................... G 614 224-8111
Columbus *(G-4803)*

Crafco Inc....................................... F 330 270-3034
Youngstown *(G-14841)*

Extendit Company.....................G 330 743-4343
New Springfield (G-10473)

Gbr Property Maintenance LLC ..... F 937 879-0200
Fairborn (G-6693)

Gerken Materials Inc......................E 419 533-2421
Napoleon (G-10281)

Heidelberg Mtls Mdwest Agg Inc...........G 419 983-2211
Bloomville (G-1240)

Heidelberg Mtls Mdwest Agg Inc...........G 419 878-2006
Waterville (G-13834)

Heritage Group Inc........................A 330 875-5566
Louisville (G-8603)

Holmes Supply Corp....................G 330 279-2634
Holmesville (G-7799)

Hy-Grade Corporation....................E 216 341-7711
Cleveland (G-3846)

Image Pavement Maintenance...............G 937 833-9200
Brookville (G-1571)

Kokosing Materials Inc...................F 740 694-5872
Fredericktown (G-7081)

Kokosing Materials Inc...................F 419 522-2715
Mansfield (G-8811)

Kokosing Materials Inc...................F 740 745-3341
Saint Louisville (G-11729)

Kokosing Materials Inc...................G 614 491-1199
Columbus (G-5055)

Kokosing Materials Inc...................F 740 694-9585
Fredericktown (G-7082)

Koski Construction Co....................G 440 997-5337
Ashtabula (G-601)

LA Rose Paving Co........................G 440 632-0330
Middlefield (G-9806)

M & B Asphalt Company Inc...............E 419 992-4235
Tiffin (G-12787)

Mae Materials LLC........................E 740 778-2242
South Webster (G-12231)

◆ Maintenance + Inc.....................F 330 264-6262
Wooster (G-14663)

Mar-Zane Inc.............................F 740 453-0721
Zanesville (G-15026)

◆ Marathon Petroleum Company LP........F 419 422-2121
Findlay (G-6889)

Miller Bros Paving Inc...................F 419 445-1015
Archbold (G-503)

Morrow Gravel Company Inc...............E 513 771-0820
Cincinnati (G-2889)

Mplx Terminals LLC.......................F 330 479-5539
Canton (G-1952)

Mt Pleasant Blacktopping Inc.............G 513 874-3777
Fairfield (G-6756)

▲ Reading Rock Incorporated.............D 513 874-2345
Cincinnati (G-3034)

Russell Standard Corporation.............G 330 733-9400
Akron (G-299)

Rutland Township.........................G 740 742-2805
Bidwell (G-1214)

Seal Master Corporation..................E 330 673-8410
Kent (G-8075)

Seneca Petroleum Co Inc.................F 419 691-3581
Toledo (G-13126)

Shelly and Sands Inc.....................E 740 859-2104
Rayland (G-11552)

Shelly and Sands Inc.....................F 740 453-0721
Zanesville (G-15047)

Shelly Materials Inc......................F 419 622-2101
Convoy (G-5425)

Shelly Materials Inc......................E 740 666-5841
Ostrander (G-11029)

Shelly Materials Inc......................G 740 246-5009
Thornville (G-12769)

Shelly Materials Inc......................G 419 273-2510
Forest (G-6941)

Shelly Materials Inc......................D 740 246-6315
Thornville (G-12770)

Sidwell Materials Inc.....................C 740 849-2422
Zanesville (G-15050)

Smalls Asphalt Paving Inc................G 740 427-4096
Gambier (G-7214)

Smith & Thompson Entps LLC.............F 330 386-9345
East Liverpool (G-6397)

▼ Specialty Technology & Res............G 614 870-0744
Columbus (G-5282)

Stark Materials Inc.......................F 330 497-1648
Canton (G-2014)

Stoneco Inc..............................E 419 393-2555
Oakwood (G-10900)

Stoneco Inc..............................G 419 693-3933
Toledo (G-13134)

Stoneco Inc..............................E 419 422-8854
Findlay (G-6923)

◆ Thorworks Industries Inc..............C 419 626-4375
Sandusky (G-11876)

Valley Asphalt Corporation...............G 513 381-0652
Morrow (G-10203)

Valley Asphalt Corporation...............E 513 771-0820
Cincinnati (G-3191)

Wilson Blacktop Corp....................F 740 635-3566
Martins Ferry (G-9012)

Wyandot Dolomite Inc....................E 419 396-7641
Carey (G-2064)

2952 Asphalt felts and coatings

Atlas Roofing Corporation................C 937 746-9941
Franklin (G-7010)

Brewer Company.........................G 513 576-6300
Cincinnati (G-2422)

Brewer Company.........................G 440 944-3800
Wickliffe (G-14368)

▲ Brewer Company.......................G 800 394-0017
Milford (G-9926)

C Green & Sons Incorporated.............F 740 745-2998
Saint Louisville (G-11728)

Certainteed LLC..........................C 419 499-2581
Milan (G-9914)

◆ Chemspec Ltd.........................E 330 896-0355
Canton (G-1864)

CIC Old Corporation......................E 330 457-2367
New Waterford (G-10487)

Consolidated Coatings Corp..............A 216 514-7596
Cleveland (G-3561)

Fluid Applied Roofing LLC................F 855 860-2300
Beavercreek Township (G-998)

Garland Industries Inc....................G 216 641-7500
Cleveland (G-3757)

Garland/Dbs Inc.........................G 216 641-7500
Cleveland (G-3758)

Hy-Grade Corporation....................E 216 341-7711
Cleveland (G-3846)

▼ Hyload Inc.............................G 330 336-6604
Seville (G-11917)

Iko Production Inc........................E 937 746-4561
Franklin (G-7029)

◆ Isaiah Industries Inc..................E 937 773-9840
Piqua (G-11358)

Johns Manville Corporation...............D 419 499-1400
Milan (G-9916)

M & B Asphalt Company Inc...............F 419 992-4235
Tiffin (G-12787)

Metal Sales Manufacturing Corp...........E 440 319-3779
Jefferson (G-7978)

Mfm Building Products Corp...............E 740 622-2645
Coshocton (G-5461)

◆ Mfm Building Products Corp............E 740 622-2645
Coshocton (G-5462)

National Tool & Equipment Inc............F 330 629-8665
Youngstown (G-14903)

Neyra Interstate Inc......................E 513 733-1000
Cincinnati (G-2908)

◆ Owens Corning Sales LLC.............A 419 248-8000
Toledo (G-13088)

▲ Pioneer Manufacturing Inc.............D 216 671-5500
Cleveland (G-4167)

Roof Maxx Technologies LLC..............E 855 766-3629
Westerville (G-14231)

RP Hoskins Inc...........................G 216 631-1000
Cleveland (G-4261)

Simon Roofing and Shtmtl Corp...........C 330 629-7392
Youngstown (G-14932)

Sr Products..............................F 330 998-6500
Youngstown (G-14939)

◆ State Industrial Products Corp.........B 877 747-6986
Cleveland (G-4329)

Terry Asphalt Materials Inc...............E 513 874-6192
Hamilton (G-7529)

The Garland Company Inc.................D 216 641-7500
Cleveland (G-4382)

◆ Thorworks Industries Inc..............C 419 626-4375
Sandusky (G-11876)

Transtar Holding Company LLC............G 800 359-3339
Walton Hills (G-13703)

◆ Tremco Incorporated..................C 216 292-5000
Beachwood (G-956)

Westlake Ryal Bldg Pdts USA In...........E 800 366-8472
Columbus (G-5365)

2992 Lubricating oils and greases

AAA Wastewater Services Inc.............F 937 746-6361
Franklin (G-7009)

Advanced Fluids Inc......................G 216 692-3050
Cleveland (G-3305)

▲ Aerospace Lubricants LLC..............F 614 878-3600
Columbus (G-4678)

American Ultra Specialties Inc.............F 330 656-5000
Hudson (G-7831)

▲ Aml Industries Inc.....................G 330 399-5000
Warren (G-13737)

Amsoil Inc...............................G 614 274-9851
Urbancrest (G-13482)

▲ Bechem Lubrication Tech LLC..........F 440 543-9845
Beachwood (G-910)

BLaster LLC.............................E 216 901-5800
Cleveland (G-3423)

◆ Borchers Americas Inc.................D 440 899-2950
Westlake (G-14295)

Cambridge Mill Products Inc...............G 330 863-1121
Malvern (G-8747)

Chemical Methods Incorporated...........E 216 476-8400
Brunswick (G-1582)

▲ Chemical Solvents Inc.................E 216 741-9310
Cleveland (G-3492)

◆ Chemtool Incorporated................C 815 957-4140
Wickliffe (G-14369)

Cincinnati - Vulcan Company..............D 513 242-5300
Cincinnati (G-2465)

Cochem Inc..............................E 216 341-8914
Cleveland (G-3543)

Digilube Systems Inc.....................F 937 748-2209
Springboro (G-12250)

Emaxx Northeast Ohio LLC...............G 844 645-6299
Canton (G-1886)

Eni USA R&M Co Inc.....................F 330 723-6457
Medina (G-9399)

Ensign Product Company Inc..............G 216 341-5911
Cleveland (G-3676)

◆ Etna Products Incorporated............E 440 543-9845
Chagrin Falls (G-2161)

Fiske Brothers Refining Co................. D 419 691-2491
Toledo *(G-12965)*

Fuchs Lubricants Co............................. F 330 963-0400
Twinsburg *(G-13306)*

▲ Groeneveld-Beka Usa Inc .... G 330 225-4949
Sharon Center *(G-11941)*

Ha-International LLC .... E 419 537-0096
Toledo *(G-12982)*

Illinois Tool Works Inc .... D 440 914-3100
Solon *(G-12126)*

Interlube Corporation .... F 513 531-1777
Cincinnati *(G-2750)*

◆ J C Whitlam Manufacturing Co........ E 330 334-2524
Wadsworth *(G-13644)*

Jtm Products Inc .... E 440 287-2302
Solon *(G-12133)*

Kost Usa Inc .... E 513 583-7070
Cincinnati *(G-2806)*

Lubrication Specialties LLC .... E 800 341-6516
Mount Gilead *(G-10212)*

Lubriplate Lubricants Company .... G 419 691-2491
Toledo *(G-13041)*

▲ Magnus International Group Inc....... G 216 592-8355
Painesville *(G-11097)*

McO Inc .... E 216 341-8914
Cleveland *(G-4014)*

New Vulco Mfg & Sales Co LLC........... D 513 242-2672
Cincinnati *(G-2904)*

▲ North Shore Strapping Company...... E 216 661-5200
Brooklyn Heights *(G-1536)*

Perma-Fix of Dayton Inc .... F 937 268-6501
Dayton *(G-5938)*

Phymet Inc .... F 937 743-8061
Springboro *(G-12263)*

◆ Plasti-Kote Co Inc........................... C 330 725-4511
Medina *(G-9435)*

▲ Quaker Chemical Corporation.......... E 513 422-9600
Middletown *(G-9888)*

Quaker Houghton Pa Inc .... G 513 422-9600
Middletown *(G-9889)*

R and J Corporation .... E 440 871-6009
Westlake *(G-14326)*

◆ State Industrial Products Corp......... B 877 747-6986
Cleveland *(G-4329)*

The Lubrizol Corporation.................... C 440 357-7064
Painesville *(G-11117)*

Triad Energy Corporation .... G 740 374-2940
Marietta *(G-8956)*

Universal Oil Inc .... E 216 771-4300
Cleveland *(G-4447)*

US Industrial Lubricants Inc................ E 513 541-2225
Cincinnati *(G-3189)*

▼ Ventco Inc.. F 440 834-8888
Chagrin Falls *(G-2190)*

Wallover Enterprises Inc .... E 440 238-9250
Strongsville *(G-12612)*

◆ Wallover Oil Company Inc................ E 440 238-9250
Strongsville *(G-12613)*

Wallover Oil Hamilton Inc................... G 513 896-6692
Hamilton *(G-7537)*

2999 Petroleum and coal products, nec

Buckeye Terminals............................. G 330 453-4170
Canton *(G-1848)*

◆ The Kindt-Collins Company LLC........ D 216 252-4122
Cleveland *(G-4387)*

30 RUBBER AND MISCELLANEOUS PLASTIC PRODUCTS

3011 Tires and inner tubes

◆ 31 Inc... D 800 438-3302
Newcomerstown *(G-10566)*

Americana Development Inc................ D 330 633-3278
Tallmadge *(G-12730)*

B & S Transport Inc .... G 330 767-4319
Navarre *(G-10302)*

▲ Bkt USA Inc .... F 330 836-1090
Copley *(G-5430)*

Bridgstone Amrcas Tire Oprtons......... D 330 379-3714
Akron *(G-83)*

◆ Chemspec Ltd .... E 330 896-0355
Canton *(G-1864)*

◆ Cooper Tire & Rubber Co LLC...........A 419 423-1321
Findlay *(G-6856)*

▲ Cooper Tire Vhcl Test Ctr Inc............ F 419 423-1321
Findlay *(G-6857)*

▲ Denman Tire Corporation................. C 330 675-4242
Leavittsburg *(G-8239)*

Gluetread LLC .... F 800 238-9791
Hiram *(G-7738)*

◆ Goodyear Tire & Rubber Company.....A 330 796-2121
Akron *(G-164)*

▲ Grove Engineered Products.............. G 419 659-5939
Columbus Grove *(G-5383)*

H & H Industries Inc........................... D 740 682-7721
Oak Hill *(G-10888)*

Nice Body Automotive LLC................. G 440 752-5568
Elyria *(G-6569)*

North American Assemblies LLC.......... E 843 420-5354
Dublin *(G-6325)*

Oliver Rubber Co................................ F 419 420-6235
Findlay *(G-6903)*

◆ Technical Rubber Company Inc..........C 740 967-9015
Johnstown *(G-7999)*

Titan Tire Corporation........................ B 419 633-4221
Bryan *(G-1662)*

Titan Tire Corporation Bryan .... E 419 633-4224
Bryan *(G-1663)*

Troy Engnred Cmpnnts Assmblies........ G 937 335-8070
Dayton *(G-6065)*

Truflex Rubber Products Co................ G 740 967-9015
Johnstown *(G-8001)*

Umd Contractors Inc........................... F 740 694-8614
Fredericktown *(G-7087)*

◆ Yokohama Tws North America Inc......E 330 436-5168
Akron *(G-361)*

3021 Rubber and plastics footwear

Advantage Products Corporation.......... G 513 489-2283
Blue Ash *(G-1243)*

Cobblers Corner LLC.......................... G 330 482-4005
Columbiana *(G-4609)*

Georgia-Boot Inc................................ D 740 753-1951
Nelsonville *(G-10317)*

Mettler Footwear Inc.......................... G 330 703-0079
Hudson *(G-7852)*

Mulhern Belting Inc............................ E 201 337-5700
Fairfield *(G-6757)*

▲ Totes Isotoner Holdings LLC............ C 513 682-8200
Cincinnati *(G-3160)*

US Footwear Holdings LLC................. C 740 753-9100
Nelsonville *(G-10322)*

3052 Rubber and plastics hose and beltings

◆ Advanced Technology Products Inc....D 937 349-4055
Milford Center *(G-9956)*

Allied Fabricating & Wldg Co............... E 614 868-8680
Columbus *(G-4687)*

Cmt Machining & Fabg LLC .... F 937 652-3740
Urbana *(G-13459)*

Cooper-Standard Automotive Inc.......... D 419 352-3533
Bowling Green *(G-1416)*

Crushproof Tubing Co......................... E 419 293-2111
Mc Comb *(G-9352)*

Danfoss Power Solutions II LLC........... F 419 238-1190
Van Wert *(G-13533)*

Eaton Aeroquip LLC............................A 419 891-7775
Maumee *(G-9292)*

◆ Eaton Aeroquip LLC........................C 440 523-5000
Cleveland *(G-3650)*

Eaton Corporation .... E 330 274-0743
Aurora *(G-667)*

Eaton Corporation ....A 419 238-1190
Van Wert *(G-13534)*

▲ Engineered Plastics Corp................. G 330 376-7700
Akron *(G-135)*

▲ Fenner Dunlop (toledo) LLC............. F 419 531-5300
Toledo *(G-12961)*

◆ HBD Industries Inc........................... E 614 526-7000
Dublin *(G-6302)*

▼ Hbd/Thermoid Inc........................... C 800 543-8070
Bellefontaine *(G-1108)*

Kent Elastomer Products Inc............... E 800 331-4762
Mogadore *(G-10079)*

Kentak Products Company................... D 330 386-3700
East Liverpool *(G-6393)*

▲ Kentak Products Company................ E 330 382-2000
East Liverpool *(G-6394)*

Mm Outsourcing LLC........................... F 937 661-4300
Leesburg *(G-8300)*

Myers Industries Inc........................... C 330 336-6621
Wadsworth *(G-13653)*

Myers Industries Inc........................... E 330 253-5592
Akron *(G-243)*

Novex Operating Company LLC........... F 330 335-2371
Barberton *(G-826)*

Parker-Hannifin Corporation............... G 704 637-1190
Wickliffe *(G-14388)*

Polychem LLC..................................... D 419 547-1400
Clyde *(G-4561)*

Rust Belt Broncos LLC........................ E 330 533-0048
Canfield *(G-1815)*

▲ Salem-Republic Rubber Company..... E 877 425-5079
Sebring *(G-11901)*

◆ Sumiriko Ohio Inc............................D 419 358-2121
Bluffton *(G-1365)*

◆ Watteredge LLC...............................D 440 933-6110
Avon Lake *(G-773)*

3053 Gaskets; packing and sealing devices

◆ Accel Performance Group LLC...........C 216 658-6413
Independence *(G-7887)*

Air Heater Seal Company Inc............... E 740 984-2146
Waterford *(G-13825)*

▲ Akalina Associates Inc...................... C 440 992-2195
Ashtabula *(G-586)*

▲ Akron Gasket & Packg Entps Inc....... F 330 633-3742
Tallmadge *(G-12729)*

AMG Products LLC.............................. F 614 507-7749
Mount Vernon *(G-10234)*

AP Services LLC................................. D 216 267-3200
Middleburg Heights *(G-9766)*

Blackthorn LLC................................... F 937 836-9296
Clayton *(G-3272)*

◆ Cincinnati Gasket Pkg Mfg Inc.......... E 513 761-3458
Cincinnati *(G-2475)*

◆ Concrete Sealants Inc.......................E 937 845-8776
Tipp City *(G-12821)*

▲ Dana Limited.................................... B 419 887-3000
Maumee *(G-9282)*

Die-Cut Products Co............................ F 216 771-6994
Cleveland *(G-3615)*

▲ Durox Company................................ D 440 238-5350
Strongsville *(G-12556)*

Dynamic Hydraulic Svcs Co LLC .... E 330 447-8967
Dover *(G-6243)*

Eagleburgmann Industries LP .... F 513 563-7325
Cincinnati *(G-2573)*

Egc Operating Company LLC .... D 440 285-5835
Chardon *(G-2204)*

Emssons Faurecia Ctrl Systems .... B 937 743-0551
Franklin *(G-7018)*

Epg Inc .... D 330 995-5125
Aurora *(G-669)*

Epg Inc .... F 330 995-9725
Streetsboro *(G-12501)*

Espi Enterprises Inc .... G 440 543-8108
Chagrin Falls *(G-2160)*

▲ **Ferrotherm Corporation** .... C 216 883-9350
Cleveland *(G-3714)*

▲ **Fibercore LLC** .... F 216 249-2100
Cleveland *(G-3715)*

▲ **Flow Dry Technology Inc** .... C 937 833-2161
Brookville *(G-1568)*

Forest City Technologies Inc .... C 440 647-2115
Wellington *(G-13888)*

Forest City Technologies Inc .... C 440 647-2115
Wellington *(G-13889)*

Forest City Technologies Inc .... C 440 647-2115
Wellington *(G-13890)*

▲ **Forest City Technologies Inc** .... B 440 647-2115
Wellington *(G-13891)*

▲ **Fouty & Company Inc** .... E 419 693-0017
Oregon *(G-10961)*

Freudenberg-Nok General Partnr .... C 419 427-5221
Findlay *(G-6868)*

G-M-I Inc .... G 440 953-8811
Willoughby *(G-14461)*

Gasko Fabricated Products LLC .... E 330 239-1781
Medina *(G-9407)*

◆ **Grand River Rubber & Plas** .... C 440 998-2900
Ashtabula *(G-594)*

Green Technologies Ohio LLC .... G 330 630-3350
Tallmadge *(G-12735)*

▲ **Ier Fujikura Inc** .... C 330 425-7121
Macedonia *(G-8696)*

▲ **Industry Products Co** .... B 937 778-0585
Piqua *(G-11356)*

▲ **Ishikawa Gasket America Inc** .... F 419 353-7300
Maumee *(G-9299)*

▲ **James K Green Enterprises Inc** .... G 614 878-6041
Columbus *(G-6031)*

▲ **Jbc Technologies Inc** .... D 440 327-4522
North Ridgeville *(G-10737)*

Jet Rubber Company .... E 330 325-1821
Rootstown *(G-11648)*

Johnson Bros Rubber Co Inc .... E 419 752-4814
Greenwich *(G-7362)*

Jtm Products Inc .... E 440 287-2302
Solon *(G-12133)*

K Wm Beach Mfg Co Inc .... C 937 399-3838
Springfield *(G-12334)*

May Lin Silicone Products Inc .... G 330 825-9019
Barberton *(G-820)*

Mechanical Dynamics Analis LLC .... E 440 946-0082
Euclid *(G-6661)*

Mechanical Rubber Ohio LLC .... E 845 986-2271
Strongsville *(G-12573)*

Middlefield Plastics Inc .... E 440 834-4638
Middlefield *(G-9811)*

Miles Rubber & Packing Company .... E 330 425-3888
Twinsburg *(G-13341)*

Mvgg Inc .... F 937 228-0781
Dayton *(G-5899)*

Netherland Rubber Company .... F 513 733-0883
Cincinnati *(G-2899)*

Newman Diaphragms LLC .... E 513 932-7379
Lebanon *(G-8278)*

Newman Sanitary Gasket Company ...... E 513 932-7379
Lebanon *(G-8279)*

▲ **North Coast Seal Incorporated** .... F 216 898-5000
Brookpark *(G-1556)*

◆ **Ohio Gasket and Shim Co Inc** .... E 330 630-0626
Akron *(G-252)*

▲ **P & R Specialty Inc** .... E 937 773-0263
Piqua *(G-11370)*

P&E Sales Ltd .... G 330 829-0100
Alliance *(G-397)*

Paul J Tatulinski Ltd .... F 330 584-8251
North Benton *(G-10623)*

Phoenix Associates .... E 440 543-9701
Chagrin Falls *(G-2178)*

Quanex Ig Systems Inc .... E 740 439-2338
Cambridge *(G-1757)*

◆ **Quanex Ig Systems Inc** .... C 216 910-1500
Akron *(G-273)*

R and J Corporation .... E 440 871-6009
Westlake *(G-14326)*

▲ **Royal Acme Corporation** .... E 216 241-1477
Cleveland *(G-4256)*

Rubbertec Industrial Pdts Co .... G 740 657-3345
Lewis Center *(G-8352)*

Saint-Gobain Prfmce Plas Corp .... B 440 836-6900
Solon *(G-12178)*

Seal Master Corporation .... E 330 673-8410
Kent *(G-8076)*

SKF USA Inc .... E 800 589-5563
Cleveland *(G-4303)*

Superior Plastics Intl Inc .... F 419 424-3113
Findlay *(G-6925)*

◆ **Sur-Seal LLC** .... C 513 574-8500
Cincinnati *(G-3130)*

◆ **Thermoseal Inc** .... G 937 498-2222
Sidney *(G-12057)*

Treaty City Industries Inc .... F 937 548-9000
Greenville *(G-7358)*

◆ **Vertex Inc** .... E 330 628-6230
Mogadore *(G-10092)*

Youngstown Specialty Mtls Inc .... G 330 259-1110
Youngstown *(G-14976)*

3061 Mechanical rubber goods

▲ **Akalina Associates Inc** .... C 440 992-2195
Ashtabula *(G-686)*

Alloy Extrusion Company .... E 330 677-4946
Kent *(G-8016)*

ARC Rubber Inc .... F 440 466-4555
Geneva *(G-7233)*

◆ **Brp Manufacturing Company** .... E 800 858-0482
Lima *(G-8393)*

C & M Rubber Co Inc .... F 937 299-2782
Dayton *(G-5690)*

Canton OH Rubber Speclty Prods .... G 330 454-3847
Canton *(G-1857)*

▲ **Cardinal Rubber Company** .... E 330 745-2191
Barberton *(G-801)*

Chardon Custom Polymers LLC .... F 440 285-2161
Chardon *(G-2197)*

Clark Rubber & Plastic Company .... C 440 255-9793
Mentor *(G-9500)*

Colonial Rubber Company .... E 330 296-2831
Ravenna *(G-11522)*

▲ **Contitech North America Inc** .... F 330 664-7180
Fairlawn *(G-6798)*

◆ **Datwyler Sling Sltions USA Inc** .... D 937 387-2800
Vandalia *(G-13554)*

Dayton Molded Urethanes LLC .... E 937 279-1910
Dayton *(G-5733)*

Dybrook Products Inc .... E 330 392-7665
Warren *(G-13761)*

Epg Inc .... D 330 995-5125
Aurora *(G-669)*

Epg Inc .... F 330 995-9725
Streetsboro *(G-12501)*

Extruded Slcone Pdts Gskets In .... E 330 733-0101
Mogadore *(G-10075)*

Frankes Wood Products LLC .... E 937 642-0706
Marysville *(G-9020)*

Harwood Entp Holdings Inc .... F 330 923-3256
Cuyahoga Falls *(G-5548)*

Hygenic Acquisition Co .... C 330 633-8460
Akron *(G-180)*

◆ **Hygenic Company LLC** .... B 330 633-8460
Akron *(G-181)*

▲ **Ier Fujikura Inc** .... C 330 425-7121
Macedonia *(G-8696)*

Jakmar Incorporated .... G 513 631-4303
Cincinnati *(G-2758)*

◆ **Johnson Bros Rubber Co** .... D 419 853-4122
West Salem *(G-14188)*

Karman Rubber Company .... D 330 864-2161
Akron *(G-191)*

◆ **Koneta Inc** .... D 419 739-4200
Wapakoneta *(G-13720)*

Macdivitt Rubber Company LLC .... E 440 259-5937
Perry *(G-11195)*

Mantaline Corporation .... F 330 569-3147
Hiram *(G-7740)*

Mantaline Corporation .... F 330 274-2264
Mantua *(G-8871)*

Mantaline Corporation .... C 330 274-2264
Mantua *(G-8872)*

Martin Industries Inc .... G 419 862-2694
Elmore *(G-6490)*

Meridian Industries Inc .... D 330 673-1011
Kent *(G-8051)*

◆ **Midlands Millroom Supply Inc** .... E 330 453-9100
Canton *(G-1949)*

Mm Outsourcing LLC .... F 937 661-4300
Leesburg *(G-8300)*

◆ **Namoh Ohio Holdings Inc** .... G
Norwood *(G-10869)*

Performance Elastomers Corporation ... D 330 297-2255
Ravenna *(G-11535)*

Plabell Rubber Products Corp .... E 419 691-5878
Toledo *(G-13101)*

Prospira America Corporation .... D 419 294-6989
Upper Sandusky *(G-13453)*

▲ **Q Holding Company** .... B 440 903-1827
Twinsburg *(G-13361)*

Qualiform Inc .... E 330 336-6777
Wadsworth *(G-13663)*

Quanex Ig Systems Inc .... E 740 439-2338
Cambridge *(G-1757)*

◆ **Quanex Ig Systems Inc** .... C 216 910-1500
Akron *(G-273)*

Robin Industries Inc .... E 330 893-3501
Berlin *(G-1199)*

Robin Industries Inc .... D 330 695-9300
Fredericksburg *(G-7070)*

Robin Industries Inc .... D 330 359-5418
Winesburg *(G-14608)*

▲ **Robin Industries Inc** .... F 216 631-7000
North Canton *(G-10665)*

Rubber-Tech Inc .... F 937 274-1114
Dayton *(G-5989)*

Saint-Gobain Prfmce Plas Corp .... C 330 798-6981
Akron *(G-305)*

▲ **Shreiner Sole Company Inc** .... F 330 276-6135
Killbuck *(G-8133)*

Employee Codes: A=Over 500 employees, B=251-500
C=101-250, D=51-100, E=20-50, F=10-19, G=1-9   2025 Harris Ohio
Industrial Directory   771

Sperry & Rice LLC........................... F 330 276-2801
Killbuck *(G-8134)*

Sperry & Rice LLC........................... G 765 647-4141
Killbuck *(G-8135)*

▲ TAC Materials Inc........................... C 330 425-8472
Twinsburg *(G-13382)*

◆ The D S Brown Company.................C 419 257-3561
North Baltimore *(G-10619)*

▲ Tigerpoly Manufacturing Inc............. B 614 871-0045
Grove City *(G-7416)*

▲ United Feed Screws Ltd................... F 330 798-5532
Akron *(G-351)*

Universal Urethane Pdts Inc...................D 419 693-7400
Toledo *(G-13169)*

▲ V & M Star LP................................. F 330 742-6300
Youngstown *(G-14956)*

◆ Vertex Inc.......................................E 330 628-6230
Mogadore *(G-10092)*

Woodlawn Rubber Co........................ F 513 489-1718
Blue Ash *(G-1353)*

Yokohama Tire Corporation................. D 440 352-3321
Painesville *(G-11125)*

◆ Yokohama Tws North America Inc......E 330 436-5168
Akron *(G-361)*

3069 Fabricated rubber products, nec

Ace Products & Consulting LLC........... F 330 577-4088
Ravenna *(G-11512)*

Action Rubber Co Inc........................ F 937 866-5975
Dayton *(G-5633)*

▲ Akalina Associates Inc................... C 440 992-2195
Ashtabula *(G-586)*

American Ntrile Operations LLC........... G 614 425-5211
Grove City *(G-7371)*

American Rubber Pdts Co Inc............. G 440 461-0900
Solon *(G-12079)*

Ansell Healthcare Products LLC........... E 740 622-4311
Coshocton *(G-5449)*

ARC Rubber Inc................................ F 440 466-4555
Geneva *(G-7233)*

Archem America Inc.......................... F 419 294-6304
Upper Sandusky *(G-13433)*

◆ B D G Wrap-Tite Inc........................E 440 349-5400
Solon *(G-12081)*

Batman Enterprises LLC..................... F 513 600-3079
Milford *(G-9923)*

Bdu Holdings Inc............................. F 330 374-1810
Akron *(G-73)*

◆ Blair Rubber Company.....................D 330 769-5583
Seville *(G-11911)*

Boomerang Rubber Inc....................... E 937 693-4611
Botkins *(G-1396)*

◆ Brp Manufacturing Company.............E 800 858-0482
Lima *(G-8393)*

Canton OH Rubber Speclty Prods....... G 330 454-3847
Canton *(G-1857)*

▲ Cardinal Rubber Company............... E 330 745-2191
Barberton *(G-801)*

Censtar Coatings Inc........................ G 330 723-8000
West Salem *(G-14186)*

Cent-Roll Products Inc....................... E 513 829-5201
Fairfield *(G-6719)*

◆ Chalfant Sew Fabricators Inc............E 216 521-7922
Cleveland *(G-3484)*

Chardon Custom Polymers LLC........... F 440 285-2161
Chardon *(G-2197)*

▲ Chemionics Corporation.................. E 330 733-8834
Tallmadge *(G-12731)*

Clark Rubber & Plastic Company.......... C 440 255-9793
Mentor *(G-9500)*

Clearview Construction LLC................. G 513 206-6415
Cincinnati *(G-2498)*

Colonial Rubber Company................... E 330 296-2831
Ravenna *(G-11522)*

◆ Contitech Usa Llc...........................F 330 664-7000
Akron *(G-105)*

Cooper-Standard Holdings Inc............. G 800 683-0676
New Philadelphia *(G-10438)*

Curtis Hilbruner.............................. G 330 947-3527
Atwater *(G-658)*

◆ Custom Rubber Corporation..............D 216 391-2928
Cleveland *(G-3587)*

Dandy Products Inc.......................... G 513 625-3000
Goshen *(G-7296)*

◆ Datwyler Sling Sltions USA Inc..........D 937 387-2800
Vandalia *(G-13554)*

Delphos Rubber Company................... E 419 692-3000
Delphos *(G-6185)*

◆ Deruijter Intl USA Inc......................F 419 678-3909
Coldwater *(G-4572)*

Die-Cut Products Co.......................... F 216 771-6994
Cleveland *(G-3615)*

▲ Dnh Mixing Inc.............................. E 330 296-6327
Mogadore *(G-10073)*

▲ Durable Corporation........................ D 800 537-1603
Norwalk *(G-10836)*

◆ Duramax Marine LLC.......................D 440 834-5400
Hiram *(G-7737)*

Eagle Elastomer Inc.......................... E 330 923-7070
Peninsula *(G-11182)*

◆ Eaton Aeroquip LLC.........................C 440 523-5000
Cleveland *(G-3650)*

Elastostar Rubber Corp....................... E 614 841-4400
Plain City *(G-11407)*

Elbex Corporation............................. D 330 673-3233
Kent *(G-8029)*

Enduro Rubber Company..................... G 330 296-9603
Ravenna *(G-11524)*

Express Pharmacy & Dme LLC............. G 210 981-9690
Columbus *(G-4915)*

Finzer Roller Inc.............................. F 937 746-4069
Franklin *(G-7021)*

◆ Firestone Polymers LLC...................D 330 379-7000
Akron *(G-148)*

First Brnds Group Holdings LLC........... E 216 589-0198
Cleveland *(G-3719)*

First Brnds Group Intrmdate LL........... F 216 589-0198
Cleveland *(G-3720)*

Flexsys America LP........................... F 618 482-6371
Columbus *(G-4928)*

◆ Flexsys America LP.........................D 330 666-4111
Akron *(G-150)*

G Grafton Machine & Rubber............... F 330 297-1062
Ravenna *(G-11525)*

Garro Tread Corporation..................... G 330 376-3125
Akron *(G-156)*

Gdc Inc.. F 574 533-3128
Wooster *(G-14642)*

Gen-Rubber LLC.............................. G 440 655-3643
Galion *(G-7192)*

▲ Goldsmith & Eggleton Inc................. F 330 336-6616
Wadsworth *(G-13640)*

▲ Goldsmith & Eggleton LLC................ F 203 855-6000
Wadsworth *(G-13641)*

Goodlevel Enterprises LLC.................. G 419 668-8261
Norwalk *(G-10843)*

◆ Grand River Rubber & Plas...............C 440 998-2900
Ashtabula *(G-594)*

◆ Green Tokai Co Ltd.........................A 937 833-5444
Brookville *(G-1570)*

Grypmat Inc.................................... G 419 953-7607
Celina *(G-2107)*

▲ Guardian Manufacturing Co LLC........ E 419 933-2711
Willard *(G-14402)*

Hannecard Roller Coatings Inc............. E 330 753-8458
Barberton *(G-809)*

▼ Hexpol Cmpnding Amrcas Mfg LLC.. C 440 632-0901
Middlefield *(G-9799)*

Hexpol Compounding LLC................... C 440 682-4038
Akron *(G-175)*

▲ Hexpol Compounding Pc Inc............. C 330 798-4790
Barberton *(G-810)*

Hygenic Acquisition Co...................... C 330 633-8460
Akron *(G-180)*

◆ Hygenic Company LLC.....................B 330 633-8460
Akron *(G-181)*

▼ Hyload Inc.................................... G 330 336-6604
Seville *(G-11917)*

Hytech Silicone Products Inc............... G 330 297-1888
Ravenna *(G-11528)*

▲ Ier Fujikura Inc............................. C 330 425-7121
Macedonia *(G-8696)*

Innovative Sport Surfacing LLC............ F 440 205-0875
Mentor *(G-9532)*

International Automotive Compo............ F 330 279-6557
Holmesville *(G-7801)*

ISO Technologies Inc........................ F 740 928-0084
Hebron *(G-7620)*

▲ James K Green Enterprises Inc.......... G 614 878-6041
Columbus *(G-5031)*

Jet Rubber Company.......................... E 330 325-1821
Rootstown *(G-11648)*

▲ Johnsonite Inc............................... B 440 543-8916
Solon *(G-12131)*

Karman Rubber Company.................... D 330 864-2161
Akron *(G-191)*

Keener Rubber Company..................... F 330 821-1880
Alliance *(G-387)*

▲ Kent Elastomer Products Inc............. C 330 673-1011
Kent *(G-8041)*

Killian Latex Inc.............................. E 330 644-6746
Akron *(G-196)*

◆ Kn Rubber LLC..............................C 419 739-4200
Wapakoneta *(G-13719)*

Krupp Rubber Machinery..................... G 330 864-0800
Akron *(G-199)*

◆ Lauren International Ltd...................C 234 303-2400
New Philadelphia *(G-10454)*

Leisure Time Pdts Design Corp............. G 440 934-1032
Avon *(G-731)*

▲ Lexington Rubber Group Inc............. G 330 425-8472
Twinsburg *(G-13331)*

Lockfast LLC................................... G 800 543-7157
Loveland *(G-8637)*

◆ Ludlow Composites Corporation........C 419 332-5531
Fremont *(G-7122)*

M7 Hrp LLC.................................... F 330 923-3256
Akron *(G-218)*

Macdivitt Rubber Company LLC............ E 440 259-5937
Perry *(G-11195)*

Magnum Tapes Films......................... G 877 460-8402
Caldwell *(G-1726)*

Mameco International Inc..................... F 216 752-4400
Cleveland *(G-3984)*

Mantaline Corporation........................ C 330 274-2264
Mantua *(G-8872)*

Martin Industries Inc......................... G 419 862-2694
Elmore *(G-6490)*

◆ Master Mfg Co Inc..........................E 216 641-0500
Cleveland *(G-3997)*

May Lin Silicone Products Inc.............. G 330 825-9019
Barberton *(G-820)*

▲ MCR of Norwalk Inc........................ E 419 668-8261
Norwalk *(G-10852)*

Meridian Industries Inc...................... D 330 673-1011
Kent *(G-8051)*

Meridian Industries Inc.............................D 330 359-5447
Winesburg *(G-14607)*

▲ Merryweather Foam Inc ....E 330 753-0353
Barberton *(G-822)*

▲ Meteor Sealing Systems LLC..............C 330 343-9595
Dover *(G-6253)*

◆ Midwest Elastomers Inc......................D 419 738-8844
Wapakoneta *(G-13722)*

Miles Rubber & Packing Company.........E 330 425-3888
Twinsburg *(G-13341)*

Mitchell Plastics Inc 330 825-2461
Barberton *(G-823)*

Mullins Rubber Products Inc..................D 937 233-4211
Dayton *(G-5898)*

Murrubber Technologies Inc...................E
Stow *(G-12442)*

Myers Industries Inc..............................C 330 336-6621
Wadsworth *(G-13653)*

Myers Industries Inc..............................E 330 253-5592
Akron *(G-243)*

▲ Neff-Perkins Company ....D 440 632-1658
Middlefield *(G-9818)*

Nelson Companies One LLC ....E 330 239-4370
Wadsworth *(G-13654)*

Newact Inc..F 513 321-5177
Batavia *(G-879)*

Newell Brands Inc...................................F 330 733-1184
Kent *(G-8056)*

Niles Roll Service Inc ....F 330 544-0026
Niles *(G-10598)*

▲ North Coast Seal Incorporated...........F 216 898-5000
Brookpark *(G-1556)*

▲ Novatex North America Inc ....D 419 282-4264
Ashland *(G-555)*

Novex Operating Company LLC ....F 330 335-2371
Barberton *(G-826)*

Ohio Foam Corporation...........................G 614 252-4877
Columbus *(G-5145)*

Ohio Foam Corporation...........................F 419 492-2151
New Washington *(G-10482)*

Ohio Foam Corporation............................... 330 799-4553
Youngstown *(G-14906)*

▲ Okamoto Sandusky Mfg LLC ....D 419 626-1633
Sandusky *(G-11862)*

Ottawa Rubber Company.........................F 419 865-1378
Holland *(G-7775)*

◆ Park-Ohio Holdings Corp......................F 440 947-2000
Cleveland *(G-4136)*

Park-Ohio Industries Inc ....C 440 947-2000
Cleveland *(G-4137)*

▲ Park-Ohio Products Inc ....D 216 961-7200
Cleveland *(G-4138)*

Parkohio Worldwide LLC...............................440 947-2000
Cleveland *(G-4146)*

Perfect Products Company ....E
Malvern *(G-8752)*

◆ Pfp Holdings LLC...................................A 419 647-4191
Spencerville *(G-12239)*

Philpott Rubber LLC................................G 330 225-3344
Aurora *(G-685)*

▲ Philpott Rubber LLC ....E 330 225-3344
Brunswick *(G-1605)*

Pinnacle Roller Co...................................F 513 369-4830
Cincinnati *(G-2963)*

Pioneer National Latex Inc ....D 419 289-3300
Ashland *(G-562)*

Pioneer National Latex Inc ....E 419 289-3300
Ashland *(G-563)*

Plabell Rubber Products Corp.......................419 691-5878
Toledo *(G-13101)*

Plymouth Foam LLC.................................D 740 254-1188
Gnadenhutten *(G-7292)*

▲ Polymerics Inc.......................................E 330 928-2210
Cuyahoga Falls *(G-5565)*

Ppafco Inc...F 614 488-7259
Columbus *(G-5201)*

Prcc Holdings Inc ....C 330 798-4790
Copley *(G-5437)*

Precision Fab Products Inc ....G 937 526-5681
Versailles *(G-13602)*

Q Model Inc...F 330 733-6545
Akron *(G-271)*

Qualiform Inc..E 330 336-6777
Wadsworth *(G-13663)*

R C Musson Rubber Co............................E 330 773-7651
Akron *(G-276)*

Rainbow Master Mixing Inc.....................E 330 374-1810
Akron *(G-277)*

Raydar Inc of Ohio..................................G 330 334-6111
Wadsworth *(G-13666)*

▲ Remington Products Company..............D 330 335-1571
Upper Arlington *(G-13432)*

◆ Republic Powdered Metals Inc.............D 330 225-3192
Medina *(G-9441)*

◆ Rhein Chemie Corporation....................C 440 279-2367
Chardon *(G-2220)*

◆ Rjf International Corporation.................A 330 668-2069
Fairlawn *(G-6809)*

Robin Industries Inc...............................E 330 893-3501
Berlin *(G-1199)*

Robin Industries Inc...............................C 330 695-9300
Fredericksburg *(G-7070)*

Robin Industries Inc...............................D 330 359-5418
Winesburg *(G-14608)*

▲ Robin Industries Inc.............................F 216 631-7000
North Canton *(G-10665)*

Roller Source Inc....................................F 440 748-4033
Columbia Station *(G-4599)*

◆ Roppe Corporation.................................B 419 435-8546
Fostoria *(G-6998)*

Roppe Holding Company.........................G 419 435-6601
Fostoria *(G-7000)*

▲ Roppe Holding Company.......................B 419 435-8546
Fostoria *(G-6999)*

◆ RPM International Inc.............................D 330 273-5090
Medina *(G-9442)*

◆ Rubber Associates Inc...........................D 330 745-2186
New Franklin *(G-10394)*

◆ Rubber Grinding Inc...............................D 419 692-3000
Delphos *(G-6103)*

Rubber-Tech Inc......................................F 937 274-1114
Dayton *(G-5989)*

Rubicon Rubber LLC................................F 234 678-0078
Seville *(G-11920)*

S P E Inc..E 330 733-0101
Mogadore *(G-10084)*

▲ Safeguard Technology Inc.....................E 330 995-5200
Streetsboro *(G-12522)*

▲ Salem-Republic Rubber Company....E 877 425-5079
Sebring *(G-11901)*

▲ Scherba Industries Inc..........................D 330 273-3200
Brunswick *(G-1614)*

▲ Shreiner Sole Company Inc...................F 330 276-6135
Killbuck *(G-8133)*

Soprema USA Inc....................................E 330 334-0066
Wadsworth *(G-13671)*

Sorbothane Inc.......................................E 330 678-9444
Kent *(G-8081)*

▲ Sparton Enterprises LLC.......................E 877 772-7866
Barberton *(G-838)*

Spiralcool Company................................G 419 483-2510
Bellevue *(G-1134)*

◆ Sumiriko Ohio Inc...................................... 419 358-2121
Bluffton *(G-1365)*

◆ Sur-Seal LLC...C 513 574-8500
Cincinnati *(G-3130)*

▼ Survitec Group (usa) Inc........................G 330 239-4331
Sharon Center *(G-11943)*

◆ Synthomer Inc...C 216 682-7000
Beachwood *(G-951)*

T-Mac Machine Inc..................................G 330 673-0621
Kent *(G-8085)*

Tahoma Enterprises Inc..........................D 330 745-9016
Barberton *(G-840)*

◆ Tahoma Rubber & Plastics Inc..............D 330 745-9016
Ashland *(G-579)*

Tarkett Inc...E 440 543-8916
Chagrin Falls *(G-2187)*

Tarkett Inc...F 800 771-7476
Middlefield *(G-9830)*

Tarkett Inc...F 614 349-1565
West Jefferson *(G-14167)*

▲ Tarkett Inc..D 800 899-8916
Solon *(G-12192)*

Tb Backstop Inc......................................F 330 434-4442
Akron *(G-329)*

◆ The R C A Rubber Company...................D 330 784-1291
Akron *(G-333)*

Timco Rubber Products Inc.....................E 216 267-6242
Berea *(G-1191)*

▼ Tmi Inc...E 330 270-9780
Youngstown *(G-14948)*

▼ Topps Products Inc ....F 913 685-2500
Cleveland *(G-4404)*

Trades Restore LLC.................................F 440 614-0480
Blacklick *(G-1230)*

Trexler Rubber Co Inc.............................E 330 296-9677
Ravenna *(G-11546)*

◆ Trico Products Corporation....................C 800 388-7428
Cleveland *(G-4425)*

Tristan Rubber Molding Inc.....................F 330 499-4055
North Canton *(G-10678)*

Truflex Rubber Products Co....................C 740 967-9015
Johnstown *(G-8001)*

Ultimate Rb Inc.......................................F 419 692-3000
Delphos *(G-6195)*

◆ Ultimate Systems Ltd.............................E 419 692-3005
Delphos *(G-6196)*

United Roller Co LLC...............................F 440 564-9698
Newbury *(G-10565)*

Universal Polymer & Rubber Ltd.............F 330 633-1666
Tallmadge *(G-12737)*

▲ Universal Polymer & Rubber Ltd...........C 440 632-1691
Middlefield *(G-9834)*

Universal Urethane Pdts Inc...................D 419 693-7400
Toledo *(G-13169)*

▲ Vernay Manufacturing Inc.....................E 404 994-2000
Yellow Springs *(G-14791)*

◆ Vertex Inc...E 330 628-6230
Mogadore *(G-10092)*

Vulcan International Corp........................G 513 621-2850
Cincinnati *(G-3208)*

Wayne County Rubber Inc.......................E 330 264-5553
Wooster *(G-14696)*

West & Barker Inc...................................F 330 652-9923
Niles *(G-10609)*

▲ Westlake Dimex LLC..............................C 800 334-3776
Marietta *(G-8961)*

Woodbridge Group...................................C 419 334-3666
Fremont *(G-7144)*

Woodlawn Rubber Co..............................F 513 489-1718
Blue Ash *(G-1353)*

▲ Yokohama Inds Amricas Ohio Inc.....D 440 352-3321
Painesville *(G-11124)*

▼ Yusa Corporation...................................E 740 335-0335
Washington Court Hou *(G-13824)*

Employee Codes: A=Over 500 employees, B=251-500
C=101-250, D=51-100, E=20-50, F=10-19, G=1-9

SIC

3081 Unsupported plastics film and sheet

◆ Advanced Polymer Coatings Ltd........E 440 937-6218
　Avon *(G-712)*

American Insulation Tech LLC............... F 513 733-4248
　Milford *(G-9921)*

◆ Ampac Holdings LLC.........................A 513 671-1777
　Cincinnati *(G-2365)*

▲ Automated Packaging Systems LLC　C 330 528-2000
　Streetsboro *(G-12490)*

Automated Packg Systems Inc............ G 330 626-2313
　Streetsboro *(G-12491)*

Avery Dennison Corporation.................D 440 639-3900
　Mentor *(G-9490)*

Avery Dennison Corporation................. A 440 534-6000
　Mentor *(G-9489)*

◆ Avient Corporation..............................D 440 930-1000
　Avon Lake *(G-748)*

◆ Berry Film Products Co Inc.................D 800 225-6729
　Mason *(G-9071)*

Berry Global Inc................................... G 419 887-1602
　Maumee *(G-9266)*

Berry Global Inc....................................D 419 465-2291
　Monroeville *(G-10117)*

▲ Berry Plastics Filmco Inc................... F 330 562-6111
　Aurora *(G-664)*

Bprex Plastic Services Co Inc.............. G 419 247-5000
　Toledo *(G-12903)*

Brr Bear Ltd... F 419 666-1111
　Perrysburg *(G-11207)*

Buckeye Packaging Co Inc....................D 330 935-0301
　Alliance *(G-373)*

CCL Label Inc....................................... E 216 676-2703
　Cleveland *(G-3480)*

CCL Label Inc.......................................D 440 878-7000
　Strongsville *(G-12548)*

Charter Nex Films - Delaware Oh Inc..... E 740 369-2770
　Delaware *(G-6137)*

Clarkwestern Dietrich Building...............D 330 372-5564
　Warren *(G-13752)*

▼ Clarkwstern Dtrich Bldg System....... C 513 870-1100
　West Chester *(G-13966)*

◆ Clopay Ames Inc.................................C 800 282-2260
　Mason *(G-9087)*

▲ Command Plastic Corporation.......... F 800 321-8001
　Bedford *(G-1022)*

▼ Crayex Corporation.............................D 937 773-7000
　Piqua *(G-11342)*

▲ Crown Plastics Co LLC.......................D 513 367-0238
　Harrison *(G-7548)*

◆ DJM Plastics Ltd................................F 419 424-5250
　Findlay *(G-6860)*

Dupont Specialty Pdts USA LLC............ E 740 474-0220
　Circleville *(G-3255)*

▲ Entrotech Inc...................................... F 614 946-7602
　Columbus *(G-4905)*

◆ General Data Company Inc.................B 513 752-7978
　Cincinnati *(G-2304)*

General Films Inc..................................D 888 436-3456
　Covington *(G-5493)*

▲ Industry Products Co.......................... B 937 778-0585
　Piqua *(G-11356)*

Intertape Polymer Corp.......................... E 704 279-3011
　Springfield *(G-12330)*

◆ Jain America Foods Inc......................G 614 850-9400
　Columbus *(G-5030)*

Liqui-Box Corporation............................ E 419 289-9696
　Ashland *(G-549)*

◆ Ludlow Composites Corporation........C 419 332-5531
　Fremont *(G-7122)*

Magnum Tapes Films............................. G 877 460-8402
　Caldwell *(G-1726)*

▲ MAI-Weave LLC.................................. D 937 322-1698
　Springfield *(G-12347)*

◆ Mar-Bal Inc...D 440 543-7526
　Chagrin Falls *(G-2170)*

Mikron Industries Inc............................ D 713 961-4600
　Akron *(G-232)*

New Tech Plastics LLC.......................... D 937 473-3011
　Covington *(G-5496)*

▲ North Shore Strapping Company...... E 216 661-5200
　Brooklyn Heights *(G-1536)*

Orbis Rpm LLC..................................... G 419 307-8511
　Columbus *(G-5163)*

Orbis Rpm LLC..................................... F 419 355-8310
　Fremont *(G-7125)*

▼ Packaging Materials Inc..................... E 740 432-6337
　Cambridge *(G-1753)*

Pexco Packaging Corp.......................... E 419 470-5935
　Toledo *(G-13096)*

Profusion Industries LLC...................... D 740 374-6400
　Marietta *(G-8938)*

Profusion Industries LLC...................... G 800 938-2858
　Fairlawn *(G-6808)*

Putnam Plastics Inc.............................. G 937 866-6261
　Dayton *(G-5969)*

▲ Renegade Materials Corporation....... D 937 350-5274
　Miamisburg *(G-9732)*

◆ Rjf International Corporation...............A 330 668-2069
　Fairlawn *(G-6809)*

Rotary Products Inc.............................. F 740 747-2623
　Ashley *(G-583)*

Rotary Products Inc.............................. F 740 747-2623
　Ashley *(G-584)*

Sancap Liner Technology Inc................ D 330 821-1166
　Alliance *(G-403)*

▲ Scherba Industries Inc....................... D 330 273-3200
　Brunswick *(G-1614)*

◆ Simona Boltaron Inc............................D 740 498-5900
　Newcomerstown *(G-10575)*

Simona PMC LLC................................. D 419 429-0042
　Findlay *(G-6918)*

Spartech LLC.. C 937 548-1395
　Greenville *(G-7353)*

Spartech LLC.. D 419 399-4050
　Paulding *(G-11162)*

◆ Synthomer Inc.....................................C 216 682-7000
　Beachwood *(G-951)*

Toga-Pak Inc.. E 937 294-7311
　Dayton *(G-6056)*

Transcendia Inc.................................... C 740 929-5100
　Hebron *(G-7641)*

Transcendia Inc.................................... D 440 638-2000
　Strongsville *(G-12610)*

Tsp Inc... F 513 732-8900
　Batavia *(G-892)*

Valgroup LLC.. E 419 423-6500
　Findlay *(G-6928)*

▲ Walton Plastics Inc............................ E 440 786-7711
　Bedford *(G-1064)*

Western Reserve Sleeve Inc................. G 440 238-8850
　Strongsville *(G-12614)*

World Connections Corps...................... G 419 363-2681
　Rockford *(G-11631)*

3082 Unsupported plastics profile shapes

ABC Technologies Dlhb Inc................... E 330 488-0716
　East Canton *(G-6376)*

▲ Advanced Composites Inc.................. C 937 575-9800
　Sidney *(G-11990)*

▲ Akron Polymer Products Inc............. D 330 628-5551
　Akron *(G-38)*

Alkon Corporation................................. F 614 799-6650
　Dublin *(G-6274)*

▲ Alkon Corporation.............................. D 419 355-9111
　Fremont *(G-7090)*

Bobbart Industries Inc.......................... G 419 350-5477
　Sylvania *(G-12702)*

▲ Cosmo Plastics Company................... C 440 498-7500
　Cleveland *(G-3569)*

Dayton Technologies............................. G 513 539-5474
　Monroe *(G-10101)*

▲ Deceuninck North America LLC......... E 513 539-4444
　Monroe *(G-10102)*

▼ Duracote Corporation......................... E 330 296-9600
　Ravenna *(G-11523)*

HP Manufacturing Company Inc............ D 216 361-6500
　Cleveland *(G-3841)*

Kentak Products Company..................... D 330 386-3700
　East Liverpool *(G-6393)*

▲ Kentak Products Company................. E 330 382-2000
　East Liverpool *(G-6394)*

▲ Machining Technologies Inc.............. E 419 862-3110
　Elmore *(G-6489)*

Meridian Industries Inc......................... D 330 673-1011
　Kent *(G-8051)*

Normandy Products Co.......................... D 440 632-5050
　Middlefield *(G-9819)*

Pexco Packaging Corp.......................... E 419 470-5935
　Toledo *(G-13096)*

Precision Products Group Inc............... G 330 698-4711
　Apple Creek *(G-475)*

Roach Wood Products & Plas Inc......... G 740 532-4855
　Ironton *(G-7934)*

◆ Trico Products Corporation................C 800 388-7428
　Cleveland *(G-4425)*

Wurms Woodworking Company............. E 419 492-2184
　New Washington *(G-10484)*

3083 Laminated plastics plate and sheet

Advanced Drainage Systems Inc........... E 419 424-8324
　Findlay *(G-6835)*

Advanced Drainage Systems Inc........... E 419 599-9565
　Napoleon *(G-10274)*

Advanced Drainage Systems Inc........... E 330 264-4949
　Wooster *(G-14618)*

Applied Medical Technology Inc............ F 440 717-4000
　Brecksville *(G-1457)*

Arthur Corporation................................ D 419 433-7202
　Huron *(G-7868)*

▲ Biothane Coated Webbing Corp......... E 440 327-0485
　North Ridgeville *(G-10727)*

Blt Inc.. F 513 631-5050
　Norwood *(G-10866)*

Brr Bear Ltd... F 419 666-1111
　Perrysburg *(G-11207)*

▲ Bruewer Woodwork Mfg Co............... D 513 353-3505
　Cleves *(G-4532)*

Counter Concepts Inc........................... F 330 848-4848
　Wadsworth *(G-13632)*

Designed Images Inc............................ G 440 708-2526
　Chagrin Falls *(G-2158)*

Designer Cntemporary Laminates......... G 440 946-8207
　Painesville *(G-11079)*

▼ Duracote Corporation......................... E 330 296-9600
　Ravenna *(G-11523)*

Durivage Pattern and Mfg Inc............... E 419 836-8655
　Williston *(G-14411)*

◆ Elster Perfection Corporation.............D 440 428-1171
　Geneva *(G-7236)*

Fdi Cabinetry LLC................................. G 513 353-4500
　Cleves *(G-4537)*

▼ Flex Technologies Inc........................ E 740 922-5992
　Midvale *(G-9910)*

▲ Fowler Products Inc........................... G 419 683-4057
　Crestline *(G-5502)*

Franklin Cabinet Company Inc.............E 937 743-9606
Franklin (G-7022)

General Electric Company......................G 740 623-5379
Coshocton (G-5456)

◆ Hancor Inc...B 614 658-0050
Hilliard (G-7683)

Iko Production Inc..............................E 937 746-4561
Franklin (G-7029)

Laminate Shop......................................F 740 749-3536
Waterford (G-13827)

Lwhs Ltd...F 419 407-5454
Toledo (G-13042)

McHenry Industries Inc.....................E 330 799-8930
Youngstown (G-14896)

Meridian Industries Inc.....................D 330 673-1011
Kent (G-8051)

▲ Meridienne International Inc..........G 330 274-8317
Aurora (G-679)

Mkgs Corp...G 937 254-8181
Dayton (G-5890)

◆ Organized Living Inc.......................E 513 489-9300
Cincinnati (G-2939)

Overhead Door Corporation..............F 440 593-5226
Conneaut (G-5413)

Plaskolite LLC.....................................B 614 294-3281
Columbus (G-5195)

Plaskolite LLC.....................................C 740 450-1109
Zanesville (G-15040)

▲ Poly TEC East Inc...........................G 330 799-7876
Youngstown (G-14918)

◆ Production Tube Cutting Inc...........E 937 254-6138
Dayton (G-5963)

Quality Rubber Stamp Inc.................G 614 235-2700
Lancaster (G-8220)

Recto Molded Products Inc...............D 513 871-5544
Cincinnati (G-3036)

◆ Resinoid Engineering Corp............D 740 928-6115
Hebron (G-7633)

◆ Roechling Indus Cleveland LP........C 216 486-0100
Cleveland (G-4248)

◆ Rowmark LLC...................................D 419 425-8974
Findlay (G-6914)

Saint-Gobain Prfmce Plas Corp........C 330 798-6981
Akron (G-305)

▲ Snyder Manufacturing Inc.............D 330 343-4456
Dover (G-6263)

Southern Cabinetry Inc.....................E 740 245-5992
Bidwell (G-1215)

Spartech LLC.......................................D 419 399-4050
Paulding (G-11162)

Ti Inc..E 419 332-8484
Fremont (G-7138)

▲ TS Trim Industries Inc....................B 614 837-4114
Canal Winchester (G-1799)

Wurms Woodworking Company........E 419 492-2184
New Washington (G-10484)

3084 Plastics pipe

ADS...G 419 422-6521
Findlay (G-6832)

ADS International Inc..........................G 614 658-0050
Hilliard (G-7663)

Advanced Drainage of Ohio Inc........G 614 658-0050
Hilliard (G-7665)

Advanced Drainage Systems Inc.......G 419 424-8222
Findlay (G-6834)

Advanced Drainage Systems Inc.......E 419 424-8324
Findlay (G-6835)

Advanced Drainage Systems Inc.......G 513 863-1384
Hamilton (G-7462)

Advanced Drainage Systems Inc.......C 740 852-2980
London (G-8529)

Advanced Drainage Systems Inc.......E 419 599-9565
Napoleon (G-10274)

Advanced Drainage Systems Inc.......E 330 264-4949
Wooster (G-14618)

▼ Advanced Drainage Systems Inc....D 614 658-0050
Hilliard (G-7666)

Baughman Tile Company.....................D 800 837-3160
Paulding (G-11153)

Cantex Inc...D 330 995-3665
Aurora (G-665)

Contech Engnered Solutions Inc.......A 513 645-7000
West Chester (G-13971)

◆ Contech Engnered Solutions LLC....C 513 645-7000
West Chester (G-13972)

Drainage Products Inc........................G 419 622-6951
Haviland (G-7587)

Dura-Line Services LLC.....................D 440 322-1000
Elyria (G-6521)

Dura-Line Services LLC.....................D 440 322-1000
Elyria (G-6522)

◆ Elster Perfection Corporation.........D 440 428-1171
Geneva (G-7236)

▼ Flex Technologies Inc......................E 740 922-5992
Midvale (G-9910)

▲ Fowler Products Inc.........................G 419 683-4057
Crestline (G-5502)

Geon Performance Solutions LLC......F 800 438-4366
Westlake (G-14304)

Hancor Inc..G 419 424-8222
Findlay (G-6878)

Hancor Inc..E 419 424-8225
Findlay (G-6879)

◆ Hancor Inc...B 614 658-0050
Hilliard (G-7683)

Harrison Mch & Plastic Corp............E 330 527-5641
Garrettsville (G-7220)

▼ Heritage Plastics Liquidation Inc....D 330 627-8002
Carrollton (G-2085)

Ipex USA LLC......................................G 513 942-9910
Fairfield (G-6745)

Nupco Inc...G 419 629-2259
New Bremen (G-10364)

Plas-Tanks Industries Inc..................E 513 942-3800
Hamilton (G-7517)

Savko Plastic Pipe & Fittings............F 614 885-8420
Columbus (G-5250)

Tolloti Pipe Inc...................................D 330 364-6627
New Philadelphia (G-10467)

Tolloti Plastic Pipe Inc......................E 330 364-6627
New Philadelphia (G-10468)

3085 Plastics bottles

AI Root Company.................................E 330 725-6677
Medina (G-9372)

▲ AI Root Company............................C 330 723-4359
Medina (G-9371)

Alpha Packaging Holdings Inc..........B 216 252-5595
Cleveland (G-3332)

Eco-Groupe Inc...................................F 937 898-2603
Dayton (G-5759)

◆ Encon Inc..C 937 898-2603
Dayton (G-5765)

Graham Packaging Pet Tech Inc........G 419 334-4197
Fremont (G-7116)

Graham Packg Plastic Pdts Inc.........C 419 421-8037
Findlay (G-6873)

▲ Novatex North America Inc.............D 419 282-4264
Ashland (G-555)

▲ Phoenix Technologies Intl LLC.......E 419 353-7738
Bowling Green (G-1434)

Plastipak Packaging Inc.....................C 740 928-4435
Hebron (G-7630)

Plastipak Packaging Inc.....................B 937 596-6142
Jackson Center (G-7966)

Rexam PLC..F 330 893-2451
Millersburg (G-10006)

Ring Container Tech LLC....................F 937 492-0961
Sidney (G-12044)

Silly Brandz Global LLC.....................D 419 697-8324
Toledo (G-13132)

Southeastern Container Inc...............D 419 352-6300
Bowling Green (G-1440)

3086 Plastics foam products

20/20 Custom Molded Plas LLC........D 419 506-5788
Holiday City (G-7742)

▲ Acor Orthopaedic LLC.....................E 216 662-4500
Cleveland (G-3293)

ADS Worldwide Inc.............................G 614 658-0050
Hilliard (G-7664)

▼ Advanced Drainage Systems Inc....D 614 658-0050
Hilliard (G-7666)

All Foam Products Co.........................G 330 849-3636
Middlefield (G-9779)

Allied Shipping and Packa..................F 937 222-7422
Moraine (G-10144)

Amatech Inc...E 614 252-2506
Columbus (G-4691)

American Corrugated Products Inc....C 614 870-2000
Columbus (G-4696)

◆ Ampac Packaging LLC.....................C 513 671-1777
Cincinnati (G-2366)

Aqua Lily Products LLC......................G 951 322-0981
Willoughby (G-14425)

Archbold Container Corp....................C 800 446-2520
Archbold (G-487)

Arkay Industries Inc...........................E 513 360-0390
Monroe (G-10096)

Arlington Rack & Packaging Co.........G 419 476-7700
Toledo (G-12886)

▼ Armaly LLC..E 740 852-3621
London (G-8530)

Atlas Roofing Corporation.................C 937 746-9941
Franklin (G-7010)

B B Bradley Company Inc...................G 614 777-5600
Columbus (G-4740)

B B Bradley Company Inc...................E 440 354-2005
Concord Township (G-5386)

Creative Foam Dayton Mold...............F 937 279-9987
Dayton (C 5713)

Cryovac LLC..F 513 771-7770
West Chester (G-13979)

Custom Foam Products Inc................F 937 295-2700
Fort Loramie (G-6945)

Dayton Polymeric Products Inc.........D 937 279-9987
Dayton (G-5736)

Ddp Specialty Electronic MA.............G 937 839-4612
West Alexandria (G-13918)

Deufol Worldwide Packaging LLC......E 440 232-1100
Bedford (G-1026)

▲ Eps Specialties Ltd Inc...................F 513 489-3676
Cincinnati (G-2595)

Extol of Ohio Inc................................C 419 668-2072
Norwalk (G-10838)

Foam Concepts & Design Inc............F 513 860-5589
West Chester (G-14000)

Gdc Inc..F 574 533-3128
Wooster (G-14642)

▲ Greif Packaging LLC........................E 740 549-6000
Delaware (G-6152)

Hedstrom Plastics LLC.......................D 419 289-9310
Ashland (G-538)

◆ Hfi LLC..B 614 491-0700
Canal Winchester (G-1791)

SIC

Hinkle Manufacturing Inc............D 419 666-5550
Perrysburg *(G-11229)*

Hitti Enterprises Inc............F 440 243-4100
Cleveland *(G-3831)*

▲ ICP Adhesives and Sealants Inc........E 330 753-4585
Norton *(G-10823)*

ISO Technologies Inc............E 740 928-0084
Heath *(G-7597)*

▼ IVEX Protective Packaging LLC........E 937 498-9298
Sidney *(G-12026)*

J P Industrial Products Inc............E 330 424-3388
Lisbon *(G-8474)*

◆ Jain America Foods Inc............G 614 850-9400
Columbus *(G-5030)*

▲ Johnsonite Inc............B 440 632-3441
Middlefield *(G-9804)*

Kingspan Insulation LLC............D 800 433-5551
Newark *(G-10514)*

▲ Merryweather Foam Inc............E 330 753-0353
Barberton *(G-822)*

Mlb Molded Urethane Pdts LLC .... G 419 825-9140
Swanton *(G-12688)*

Myers Industries Inc............E 330 253-5592
Akron *(G-243)*

◆ Ohio Decorative Products LLC.........C 419 647-9033
Spencerville *(G-12238)*

Ohio Foam Corporation............G 614 252-4877
Columbus *(G-5145)*

Orbis Corporation............D 262 560-5000
Perrysburg *(G-11251)*

Owens Corning Sales LLC............C 330 634-0460
Tallmadge *(G-12744)*

Palpac Industries Inc............F 419 523-3230
Ottawa *(G-11041)*

Paratus Supply Inc............330 745-3600
Barberton *(G-830)*

Plastic Forming Company Inc............E 330 830-5167
Massillon *(G-9233)*

Plastic Works Inc............F 440 331-5575
Cleveland *(G-4171)*

Prime Industries Inc............F
Lorain *(G-8574)*

S & A Industries Corporation............E 330 733-6040
Akron *(G-300)*

▲ S & A Industries Corporation............D 330 733-6040
Akron *(G-301)*

▲ Scottdel Cushion Inc............E 419 825-0432
Swanton *(G-12691)*

Skybox Packaging LLC............C 419 525-7209
Mansfield *(G-8853)*

Smithers-Oasis Company............F 330 673-5831
Kent *(G-8079)*

◆ Smithers-Oasis Company............F 330 945-5100
Kent *(G-8080)*

Solo Products Inc............F 513 321-7884
Cincinnati *(G-3100)*

Special Design Products Inc............E 614 272-6700
Columbus *(G-5278)*

Storopack Inc............F 513 874-0314
West Chester *(G-14077)*

▲ Storopack Inc............E 513 874-0314
Cincinnati *(G-3121)*

▲ Team Wendy LLC............D 216 738-2518
Cleveland *(G-4367)*

◆ Technifab Inc............E 440 934-8324
Avon *(G-740)*

Temprecision Intl Corp............G 855 891-7732
Kent *(G-8088)*

Trans-Foam Inc............G 330 630-9444
Tallmadge *(G-12755)*

Truechoicepack Corp............F 937 630-3832
West Chester *(G-14085)*

Ventek Solutions LLC............F 419 420-0029
Findlay *(G-6930)*

Wellman Container Corporation............E 513 860-3040
Cincinnati *(G-3219)*

Zebco Industries Inc............F 740 654-4510
Lancaster *(G-8233)*

3087 Custom compound purchased resins

▲ Accel Corporation............D 440 934-7711
Avon *(G-711)*

▲ Advanced Composites Inc............C 937 575-9800
Sidney *(G-11990)*

Aurora Plastics LLC............E 330 422-0700
Streetsboro *(G-12488)*

Avient Corporation............D 419 668-4844
Norwalk *(G-10829)*

◆ Avient Corporation............D 440 930-1000
Avon Lake *(G-748)*

◆ Bay State Polymer Distribution Inc......F 440 892-8500
Westlake *(G-14291)*

▲ Chemionics Corporation............E 330 733-8834
Tallmadge *(G-12731)*

Deltech Polymers LLC............G 937 339-3150
Troy *(G-13210)*

Flex Technologies Inc............D 330 897-6311
Baltic *(G-777)*

▼ Flex Technologies Inc............E 740 922-5992
Midvale *(G-9910)*

Freeman Manufacturing & Sup Co......... E 440 934-1902
Avon *(G-727)*

General Color Investments Inc............D 330 868-4161
Minerva *(G-10038)*

Hexpol Compounding LLC............C 440 834-4644
Burton *(G-1699)*

Hexpol Compounding LLC............C 440 632-1962
Middlefield *(G-9800)*

▲ Hexpol Compounding LLC............E 440 834-4644
Burton *(G-1700)*

Hexpol Holding Inc............F 440 834-4644
Burton *(G-1701)*

Howard Industries Inc............F 614 444-9900
Columbus *(G-4993)*

Jpi Coastal LLC............G 330 424-1110
Lisbon *(G-8475)*

Killian Latex Inc............E 330 644-6746
Akron *(G-196)*

Lancer Dispersions Inc............D
Akron *(G-202)*

McCann Plastics LLC............D 330 499-1515
Canton *(G-1943)*

▼ Nanosperse LLC............G 937 296-5030
Kettering *(G-8122)*

Polymera Inc............G 740 527-2069
Hebron *(G-7631)*

Polyone Corporation............D 330 467-8108
Macedonia *(G-8708)*

◆ Radici Plastics Usa Inc............E 330 336-7611
Wadsworth *(G-13665)*

Sherwin-Williams Company............C 330 830-6000
Massillon *(G-9243)*

Thermafab Alloy Inc............G 216 861-0540
Olmsted Falls *(G-10941)*

Tymex Plastics Inc............E 216 429-8950
Cleveland *(G-4437)*

◆ Vibrantz Color Solutions Inc............C 440 997-5137
Ashtabula *(G-621)*

3088 Plastics plumbing fixtures

◆ Ad Industries Inc............A 303 744-1911
Dayton *(G-5634)*

Add-A-Trap LLC............G 330 750-0417
Struthers *(G-12615)*

American Platinum Door LLC............G 440 497-6213
Solon *(G-12078)*

Bobbart Industries Inc............G 419 350-5477
Sylvania *(G-12702)*

▲ Cincinnati Machines Inc............G 513 536-2432
Batavia *(G-856)*

◆ Crane Plumbing LLC............A 419 522-4211
Mansfield *(G-8778)*

Cultured Marble Inc............G 330 549-2282
Poland *(G-11435)*

◆ E L Mustee & Sons Inc............D 216 267-3100
Brookpark *(G-1549)*

◆ Hancor Inc............B 614 658-0050
Hilliard *(G-7683)*

◆ Lubrizol Global Management Inc.......F 216 447-5000
Cleveland *(G-3970)*

◆ Mansfield Plumbing Pdts LLC............A 419 938-5211
Perrysville *(G-11282)*

Marble Arch Products Inc............G 937 746-8388
Franklin *(G-7032)*

Meese Inc............F 440 998-1202
Ashtabula *(G-604)*

Pro-Kleen Industrial Svcs Inc............E 740 689-1886
Lancaster *(G-8218)*

Safeway Safety Step LLC............F 513 942-7837
West Chester *(G-14072)*

Tower Industries Ltd............E 330 837-2216
Massillon *(G-9249)*

3089 Plastics products, nec

20/20 Custom Molded Plas LLC............D 419 506-5788
Holiday City *(G-7742)*

A Aabaco Plastics Inc............F 216 663-9494
Cleveland *(G-3279)*

AB Plastics Inc............G 513 576-6333
Milford *(G-9920)*

ABC Plastics Inc............E 330 948-3322
Lodi *(G-8495)*

ABC Technologies Dlhb Inc............E 330 479-7595
Canton *(G-1820)*

ABC Technologies Dlhb Inc............E 330 488-0716
East Canton *(G-6376)*

▲ ABC Technologies Wmg Usa Inc............F 419 483-0653
Bellevue *(G-1117)*

Accutech Plastic Molding Inc............G 937 233-0017
Dayton *(G-5632)*

Acme Fence LLC............F 330 784-0456
Akron *(G-15)*

◆ Aco Inc............E 440 639-7230
Mentor *(G-9468)*

◆ Ad Industries Inc............A 303 744-1911
Dayton *(G-5634)*

Ada Extrusions Inc............G 440 285-7653
Akron *(G-19)*

Advanced Plastic Systems Inc............F 614 759-6550
Gahanna *(G-7153)*

Advanced Plastics Inc............F 330 336-6681
Wadsworth *(G-13626)*

Advantage Mold Inc............G 419 691-5676
Toledo *(G-12866)*

Aerocase Incorporated............F 440 617-9294
Westlake *(G-14284)*

▲ Akron Polymer Products Inc............D 330 628-5551
Akron *(G-38)*

▲ Akron Porcelain & Plastics Co............C 330 745-2159
Akron *(G-39)*

All About Plastics LLC............G 937 547-0098
Greenville *(G-7333)*

All Srvice Plastic Molding Inc............C 937 415-3674
Fairborn *(G-6686)*

▲ All Srvice Plastic Molding Inc............D 937 890-0322
Vandalia *(G-13549)*

▲ Alliance Equipment Company Inc..... F 330 821-2291
    Alliance (G-370)

Alliance-Mcalpin Ny LLC................ B 585 426-5310
    Clyde (G-4556)

◆ Allied Moulded Products Inc............C 419 636-4217
    Bryan (G-1626)

Alpha Packaging Holdings Inc.......... B 216 252-5595
    Cleveland (G-3332)

▲ Alpla Inc............................... F 419 991-9484
    Lima (G-8460)

Alside Inc................................ E 419 865-0934
    Maumee (G-9258)

Alumo Extrusions and Mfg Co............ E 330 779-3333
    Youngstown (G-14810)

Amclo Group Inc........................ F 216 791-8400
    North Royalton (G-10754)

Amcor Rigid Packaging Usa LLC........ G 419 483-4343
    Bellevue (G-1118)

▲ AMD Plastics Inc...................... F 216 289-4862
    Euclid (G-6640)

Ameri-Kart Corp........................ D 800 232-0847
    Akron (G-54)

American Molded Plastics Inc............ F 330 872-3838
    Newton Falls (G-10576)

American Molding Company Inc.......... F 330 620-6799
    Barberton (G-792)

▲ American Plastic Tech Inc............ C 440 632-5203
    Middlefield (G-9780)

American Plastics LLC.................. C 419 423-1213
    Findlay (G-6836)

▼ American Way Manufacturing Inc..... E 330 824-2353
    Warren (G-13736)

AMP Plastics of Ohio LLC.............. E
    Montpelier (G-10126)

Ampacet Corporation.................... F 513 247-5400
    Cincinnati (G-2368)

AMS Global Ltd..........................G 937 620-1036
    West Alexandria (G-13916)

◆ Anchor Hocking LLC..................A 740 687-2500
    Columbus (G-4711)

Anchor Hocking Holdings Inc........... A 740 687-2500
    Columbus (G-4713)

Apogee Plastics Corp.................... G 937 864-1966
    Fairborn (G-6687)

Apollo Plastics Inc...................... F 440 951-7774
    Mentor (G-9484)

Apsx LLC................................ F 513 716-5992
    Blue Ash (G-1246)

Arkay Industries Inc.................... E 513 360-0390
    Monroe (G-10096)

Arkay Plastics Alabama Inc............. F 513 360-0390
    Monroe (G-10097)

▼ Armaly LLC........................... E 740 852-3621
    London (G-8530)

Arthur Corporation...................... D 419 433-7202
    Huron (G-7868)

Aspec Inc................................ G 513 561-9922
    Cincinnati (G-2380)

▲ Associated Materials LLC............. C 330 929-1811
    Cuyahoga Falls (G-5528)

Associated Materials Group Inc.......... D 330 929-1811
    Cuyahoga Falls (G-5529)

▲ Associated Plastics Corp............. D 419 634-3910
    Ada (G-3)

▲ Astro Manufacturing & Design Inc..... C 888 215-1746
    Eastlake (G-6417)

Astro Model Development Corp............ G 440 946-8855
    Eastlake (G-6418)

▲ Atc Group Inc......................... D 440 293-4064
    Andover (G-455)

Automation Plastics Corp................ D 330 562-5148
    Aurora (G-662)

Axiom Engineered Systems LLC.......... F 416 435-7313
    Toledo (G-12891)

Axion International Holdings Inc.......... C 740 452-2500
    Zanesville (G-14988)

Axion International Inc.................. G 740 452-2500
    Zanesville (G-14989)

Axion Strl Innovations LLC.............. F 740 452-2500
    Zanesville (G-14990)

Axium Packaging LLC.................... A 614 706-5955
    New Albany (G-10331)

▲ B & B Molded Products Inc........... E 419 592-8700
    Defiance (G-6099)

Bakelite N Sumitomo Amer Inc........... E 419 675-1282
    Kenton (G-8096)

Baker Plastics Inc...................... G 330 743-3142
    Youngstown (G-14817)

Bay Corporation........................ E 440 835-2212
    Westlake (G-14290)

Bc Investment Corporation.............. C 330 262-3070
    Wooster (G-14625)

Bell Binders LLC........................ F 419 242-3201
    Toledo (G-12895)

Bena Inc................................ G 419 299-3313
    Van Buren (G-13524)

Berlekamp Plastics Inc.................. F 419 334-4481
    Fremont (G-7094)

▲ Berman Industries Inc................ F 513 874-7477
    Blue Ash (G-1251)

Bernard Engraving Corp.................. F 419 478-5610
    Toledo (G-12896)

Berry Global Inc........................ G 419 887-1602
    Maumee (G-9266)

Berry Global Inc........................ D 419 465-2291
    Monroeville (G-10117)

Berry Global Inc........................ F 330 896-6700
    Streetsboro (G-12492)

Blackthorn LLC.......................... F 937 836-9296
    Clayton (G-3272)

Bloom Industries Inc.................... G 330 898-3878
    Warren (G-13743)

▲ Bmf Devices Inc...................... F 937 866-3451
    Miamisburg (G-9675)

Boardman Molded Intl LLC.............. C 800 233-4575
    Youngstown (G-14821)

◆ Boardman Molded Products Inc........D 330 788-2400
    Youngstown (G-14822)

Borke Mold Specialist Inc.............. F 513 870-8000
    Hamilton (G-7471)

Bourbon Plastics Inc.................... B 574 342-0893
    Cuyahoga Falls (G-5533)

◆ Bprex Hlthcare Brookville Inc...........C 847 541-9700
    Perrysburg (G-11206)

Bprex Plastic Packaging Inc............. F 419 247-5000
    Toledo (G-12902)

Brake Parts Holdings Inc................ B 216 589-0198
    Cleveland (G-3432)

Brittany Stamping LLC.................. A 216 267-0850
    Cleveland (G-3440)

Brown Company of Findlay Ltd........... E 419 425-3002
    Findlay (G-6847)

Buckeye Design & Engr Svc LLC........ D 419 375-4241
    Fort Recovery (G-6961)

Buckeye Stamping Company.............. D 877 728-0776
    Columbus (G-4786)

Bugh Inc................................ G 330 305-0978
    Canton (G-1849)

Builder Tech Wholesale LLC.............. G 419 535-7606
    Toledo (G-12908)

▲ C A Joseph Co........................ G 330 385-6869
    East Liverpool (G-6387)

C-Mold Inc.............................. E
    Shaker Heights (G-11927)

Calorplast USA LLC...................... G 513 576-6333
    Milford (G-9927)

Cantex Inc.............................. D 330 995-3665
    Aurora (G-665)

Caraustar Industries Inc................ E 330 665-7700
    Copley (G-5432)

Carbon Polymers Company................ D 330 948-3007
    Lodi (G-8499)

Cardinal Products Inc.................. G 440 237-8280
    North Royalton (G-10756)

Carlisle Plastics Company.............. G 937 845-9411
    New Carlisle (G-10369)

▲ Carney Plastics Inc.................. G 330 746-8273
    Youngstown (G-14831)

Carson Industries LLC.................. G 419 592-2309
    Napoleon (G-10276)

Ccp Newco LLC.......................... B 419 448-1700
    Tiffin (G-12780)

CD Company LLC........................ D 419 332-2693
    Fremont (G-7097)

▲ Cell-O-Core Co....................... E 330 239-4370
    Sharon Center (G-11939)

Cell-O-Core Co.......................... G 800 239-4370
    Wadsworth (G-13630)

Centrex Plastics LLC.................... E 877 504-2768
    Findlay (G-6851)

Century Container LLC.................. E 330 457-2367
    Columbiana (G-4608)

Century Container LLC.................. F 330 457-2367
    New Waterford (G-10485)

▼ Century Container Corporation........ C 330 457-2367
    New Waterford (G-10486)

Century Mold Company Inc.............. G 513 539-9283
    Middletown (G-9843)

▲ Champion Opco LLC.................. B 513 327-7338
    Cincinnati (G-2458)

Chapin Customer Molding Inc............ G 440 458-6550
    Elyria (G-6512)

Chuck Meadors Plastics Co.............. F 440 813-4466
    Jefferson (G-7972)

Claflin Co.............................. G 330 650-0582
    Hudson (G-7838)

Clark Rubber & Plastic Company.......... C 440 255-9793
    Mentor (G-9500)

Classic Laminations Inc................ E 440 735-1333
    Oakwood Village (G-10904)

Claycor Inc............................ F 419 318-7290
    Toledo (G-12033)

Cleveland Reclaim Inds Inc.............. G 440 282-4917
    Lorain (G-8551)

Cleveland Specialty Pdts Inc............ E 216 281-8300
    Cleveland (G-3525)

▲ CM Paula Company.................... E 513 759-7473
    Mason (G-9090)

▲ Comdess Company Inc................ F 330 769-2094
    Seville (G-11916)

◆ Comfort Line Ltd......................D 419 729-8520
    Toledo (G-12928)

Composite Technologies Co LLC.......... D 937 228-2880
    Dayton (G-5709)

Core Composites Cincinnati LLC.......... E 513 724-6111
    Batavia (G-859)

▲ Core Molding Technologies Inc........ A 614 870-5000
    Columbus (G-4850)

Corvac Composites LLC.................. D 248 807-0969
    Greenfield (G-7326)

Cosmo Plastics Company................ D 330 359-5429
    Wilmot (G-14593)

▲ Cosmo Plastics Company.............. C 440 498-7500
    Cleveland (G-3569)

Cpg International LLC.................... B 937 655-8766
    Wilmington (G-14577)

Employee Codes: A=Over 500 employees, B=251-500
C=101-250, D=51-100, E=20-50, F=10-19, G=1-9
    2025 Harris Ohio
    Industrial Directory
    777

Cpp Group Holdings LLC.................... E 216 453-4800
Cleveland (G-3574)

Creative Liquid Coatings Inc.................. C 419 485-1110
Montpelier (G-10127)

Creative Millwork Ohio Inc................... D 440 992-3566
Ashtabula (G-588)

Creative Plastics Intl............................ F 937 596-6769
Jackson Center (G-7959)

Crown Cork & Seal Usa Inc.................. D 740 681-3000
Lancaster (G-8193)

Ctc Plastics.. E 937 228-9184
Dayton (G-5716)

▲ Custom Molded Products LLC........ D 937 382-1070
Wilmington (G-14578)

Custom Poly Bag LLC.......................... D 330 935-2408
Alliance (G-378)

Custom Pultrusions Inc....................... D 330 562-5201
Aurora (G-666)

Cuyahoga Molded Plastics Co............. E 216 261-2744
Mentor (G-9509)

Cuyahoga Molded Plastics Co (inc)...... E 216 261-2744
Euclid (G-6647)

D and D Plastics Inc............................ F 330 376-0668
Akron (G-114)

D K Manufacturing............................... F 740 654-5566
Lancaster (G-8194)

D M Tool & Plastics Inc....................... F 937 962-4140
Brookville (G-1565)

D M Tool & Plastics Inc....................... F 937 962-4140
Lewisburg (G-8359)

D Martone Industries Inc..................... E 440 632-5800
Middlefield (G-9791)

Dadco Inc... F 513 489-2244
Cincinnati (G-2539)

Dak Enterprises Inc............................. F 740 828-3291
Marysville (G-9018)

David Wolfe Design Inc........................ F 330 633-6124
Akron (G-117)

▲ Dawn Enterprises Inc...................... E 216 642-5506
Cleveland (G-3601)

Dayton Molded Urethanes LLC............. G 937 279-9987
Dayton (G-5732)

◆ Dayton Superior Corporation............C 937 866-0711
Miamisburg (G-9687)

▲ Deimling/Jeliho Plastics Inc............. D 513 752-6653
Amelia (G-429)

Denney Plastics Machining LLC............ E 330 308-5300
New Philadelphia (G-10442)

▲ Design Molded Plastics Inc............. C 330 963-4400
Macedonia (G-8683)

Design Molded Products LLC................ E 330 963-4400
Macedonia (G-8685)

Design Molded Products LLC................ F 330 963-4400
Macedonia (G-8684)

Dester Corporation.............................. F 419 362-8020
Lima (G-8401)

◆ Dester Corporation..........................F 419 362-8020
Lima (G-8400)

Die-Gem Co Inc.................................. F 330 784-7400
Akron (G-122)

Diemaster Tool & Mold Inc.................. G 330 467-4281
Macedonia (G-8686)

Dimco Gray.. G 937 291-4720
Dayton (G-5749)

▲ Dimcogray Corporation.................... D 937 433-7600
Centerville (G-2131)

Dinesol Building Products Ltd............... E 330 270-0212
Youngstown (G-14848)

▲ Dinesol Plastics Inc........................ C 330 544-7171
Niles (G-10587)

Diskin Enterprises LLC........................ E 330 527-4308
Garrettsville (G-7218)

Diversity-Vuteq LLC............................. G 614 490-5034
Gahanna (G-7156)

◆ DJM Plastics Ltd.............................F 419 424-5250
Findlay (G-6860)

DK Manfcturing Frazeysburg Inc........... F 740 828-3291
Frazeysburg (G-7059)

DK Manufacturing Lancaster Inc........... D 740 654-5566
Lancaster (G-8200)

▲ Dometic Sanitation Corporation........ E 330 439-5550
Big Prairie (G-1216)

Don-Ell Corporation............................. G 419 841-7114
Sylvania (G-12705)

Don-Ell Corporation............................. E 419 841-7114
Sylvania (G-12704)

Dover High Prfmce Plas Inc.................. E 330 343-3477
Dover (G-6240)

Doyle Manufacturing Inc...................... D 419 865-2548
Holland (G-7756)

▲ Dreco Inc.. C 440 327-6021
North Ridgeville (G-10729)

Drs Industrial LLC............................... G 419 861-0334
Holland (G-7758)

Drs Industries Inc............................... D 419 861-0334
Holland (G-7759)

Drummond Corporation........................ F 440 834-9660
Middlefield (G-9792)

Dublin Plastics Inc.............................. G 216 641-5904
Cleveland (G-3634)

Duo-Corp.. F 330 549-2149
North Lima (G-10707)

Dyna-Vac Plastics Inc......................... G 937 773-0092
Piqua (G-11345)

Dynamic Plastics Inc........................... G 937 437-7261
New Paris (G-10426)

▲ E P P Inc.. D 440 322-8577
Elyria (G-6526)

Eaton Corporation............................... E 330 274-0743
Aurora (G-667)

Ebco Inc.. E 330 562-8265
Streetsboro (G-12500)

▲ Edge Plastics Inc............................ C 419 522-6696
Mansfield (G-8784)

Electr-Gnral Plas Corp Clumbus........... G 614 871-2915
Grove City (G-7385)

Electro-Cap International Inc................. F 937 456-6099
Eaton (G-6453)

Eliason Corporation............................. E 800 828-3655
West Chester (G-14116)

Elkhart Plastics LLC............................ E 888 605-2068
Akron (G-130)

Elra Industries Inc.............................. G 513 868-6228
Hamilton (G-7488)

◆ Elster Perfection Corporation............D 440 428-1171
Geneva (G-7236)

◆ Encon Inc..C 937 898-2603
Dayton (G-5765)

Encore Industries Inc.......................... C 419 626-8000
Sandusky (G-11830)

▲ Encore Industries Inc...................... E 419 626-8000
Cambridge (G-1743)

Encore Plastics Southeast LLC............ F 419 626-8000
Sandusky (G-11831)

Engineered Profiles LLC....................... B 614 754-3700
Columbus (G-4903)

▼ Enpac LLC....................................... D 440 975-0070
Eastlake (G-6425)

▼ Enpress LLC.................................... E 440 510-0108
Eastlake (G-6426)

▲ Enterprise Plastics Inc..................... E 330 346-0496
Kent (G-8032)

Evans Industries Inc............................ F 330 453-1122
Canton (G-1889)

Exterior Portfolio LLC........................... C 614 754-3400
Columbus (G-4916)

Extrudex Limited Partnership................ E 440 352-7101
Painesville (G-11085)

Fabohio Inc.. E 740 922-4233
Uhrichsville (G-13403)

Fastformingcom LLC............................ F 330 927-3277
Rittman (G-11621)

Fci Inc... D 216 251-5200
Cleveland (G-3708)

Fdi Enterprises.................................... G 440 269-8282
Cleveland (G-3709)

Felicity Plastics Machinery.................... G 513 876-7003
Felicity (G-6829)

▲ Ferriot Inc....................................... C 330 786-3000
Akron (G-147)

▲ Few Atmtive GL Applcations Inc....... D 234 249-1880
Wooster (G-14637)

Fiber -Tech Industries Inc.................... D 740 335-9400
Wshngtn Ct Hs (G-14739)

Fiberglass Technology Inds Inc............. E 740 335-9400
Wshngtn Ct Hs (G-14740)

Fibertech Networks.............................. G 614 436-3565
Worthington (G-14710)

▲ Fibreboard Corporation.................... C 419 248-8000
Toledo (G-12963)

Fields Process Technology Inc.............. G 216 781-4787
Cleveland (G-3716)

▲ Findlay Machine & Tool LLC............. E 419 434-3100
Findlay (G-6864)

▲ First Choice Packaging Inc.............. C 419 333-4100
Fremont (G-7107)

Flambeau Corporation.......................... D 440 632-6131
Middlefield (G-9794)

Flex Technologies Inc.......................... D 330 359-5415
Mount Eaton (G-10207)

▼ Flex Technologies Inc....................... E 740 922-5992
Midvale (G-9910)

Florida Production Engrg Inc................. C 740 420-5252
Circleville (G-3258)

Formco Inc... G 330 966-2111
Canton (G-1892)

▲ Forrest Enterprises Inc.................... F 937 773-1714
Piqua (G-11347)

Fortis Plastics LLC.............................. G 937 382-0966
Wilmington (G-14581)

Fountain Specialists Inc....................... E 513 831-5717
Milford (G-9934)

▲ Fowler Products Inc......................... G 419 683-4057
Crestline (G-5502)

▼ Fox Lite Inc...................................... E 937 864-1966
Fairborn (G-6692)

Fpe Inc.. C 740 420-5252
Circleville (G-3259)

Frantz Medical Development Ltd............ G 440 255-1155
Mentor (G-9519)

Fremont Plastic Products Inc................ C 419 332-6407
Fremont (G-7111)

▲ Fukuvi Usa Inc................................ D 937 236-7288
Dayton (G-5787)

G & J Extrusions Inc........................... G 330 753-0162
New Franklin (G-10389)

G I Plastek Inc................................... G 440 230-1942
Westlake (G-14302)

◆ G M R Technology Inc......................E 440 992-6003
Ashtabula (G-593)

G S K Inc... G 937 547-1611
Greenville (G-7342)

G3 Packaging LLC............................... G 334 799-0015
Monroe (G-10106)

Gad-Jets Investments Inc.................... G 937 274-2111
Franklin (G-7023)

Gas Assist Injction Mlding Exp .... G 440 632-5203
Middlefield *(G-9795)*

▼ Gateway Industrial Pdts Inc .... E 440 324-4112
Elyria *(G-6539)*

Genesis Plastic Tech LLC .... D 440 542-0722
Concord Township *(G-5391)*

Genpak LLC .... E 614 276-5156
Columbus *(G-4950)*

▲ Gentek Building Products Inc .... F 800 548-4542
Cuyahoga Falls *(G-5544)*

◆ Ghp II LLC .... C 740 687-2500
Lancaster *(G-8204)*

Gorell Enterprises Inc .... B 724 465-1800
Streetsboro *(G-12502)*

Graham Packaging Pet Tech Inc .... G 419 334-4197
Fremont *(G-7116)*

Graham Packaging Pet Tech Inc .... G 513 398-5000
Mason *(G-9105)*

GRANGER PLASTICS CO THE .... E 513 424-1955
Middletown *(G-9862)*

◆ Graphic Art Systems Inc .... E 216 581-9050
Cleveland *(G-3785)*

Great Lakes Window Inc .... A 419 666-5555
Walbridge *(G-13684)*

Greenfield Precision Plas LLC .... F 937 803-0328
Greenfield *(G-7329)*

Greenlight Optics LLC .... E 513 247-9777
Loveland *(G-8628)*

Greenville Techniology Inc .... G 937 642-6744
Marysville *(G-9022)*

Greif Inc .... E 740 657-6500
Delaware *(G-6150)*

◆ Greif Inc .... E 740 549-6000
Delaware *(G-6149)*

Griffin Technology Inc .... C 585 924-7121
Hudson *(G-7842)*

H & H Engineered Molded Pdts .... C 440 415-1814
Geneva *(G-7238)*

H P Manufacturing Co .... G 216 361-6500
Cleveland *(G-3805)*

Hamilton Custom Molding Inc .... G 513 844-6643
Hamilton *(G-7501)*

Hancor Inc .... E 419 424-8225
Findlay *(G-6879)*

◆ Hancor Inc .... B 614 658-0050
Hilliard *(G-7683)*

Hanlon Industries Inc .... F 216 261-7056
Cleveland *(G-3810)*

Harbor Industrial Corp .... F 440 599-8366
Conneaut *(G-5402)*

▲ Harmony Systems and Svc Inc .... D 937 778-1082
Piqua *(G-11349)*

Harrison Mch & Plastic Corp .... E 330 527-5641
Garrettsville *(G-7220)*

Hathaway Stamp Co .... F 513 621-1052
Cincinnati *(G-2712)*

▼ Haviland Plastic Products Co .... E 419 622-3110
Haviland *(G-7590)*

▲ Hc Companies Inc .... E 440 632-3333
Twinsburg *(G-13315)*

Hendrickson International Corp .... D 740 929-5600
Hebron *(G-7617)*

Hexpol Compounding Pc Inc .... F 330 258-2016
Akron *(G-176)*

HI Lite Plastic Products .... G 614 235-9050
Columbus *(G-4980)*

Hi-Tech Extrusions Ltd .... E 440 286-4000
Chardon *(G-2207)*

◆ HP Enterprise Inc .... E 800 232-7950
Streetsboro *(G-12503)*

HP Liquidating Inc .... D 614 861-1791
Blacklick *(G-1223)*

HP Manufacturing Company Inc .... D 216 361-6500
Cleveland *(G-3841)*

Hudson Extrusions Inc .... E 330 653-6015
Hudson *(G-7845)*

ICO Products LLC .... F 419 867-3900
Holland *(G-7768)*

▲ Identification Systems Inc .... E 614 448-1741
Columbus *(G-4999)*

Ieg Plastics LLC .... E 937 565-4211
Bellefontaine *(G-1111)*

Illinois Tool Works Inc .... D 419 633-3236
Bryan *(G-1644)*

Illinois Tool Works Inc .... E 419 636-3161
Bryan *(G-1646)*

Illinois Tool Works Inc .... E 937 332-2839
Troy *(G-13227)*

Iml Containers Ohio Inc .... F 330 754-1066
Alliance *(G-385)*

◆ Impact Products LLC .... C 419 841-2891
Toledo *(G-13001)*

Imperial Family Inc .... D 330 927-5065
Rittman *(G-11622)*

Indelco Custom Products Inc .... G 216 797-7300
Euclid *(G-6654)*

Industrial Farm Tank Inc .... E 937 843-2972
Lewistown *(G-8365)*

Inhance Technologies LLC .... E 614 846-6400
Columbus *(G-5005)*

Innovation Plastics LLC .... E 513 818-1771
Fostoria *(G-6985)*

Innovations In Plastic Inc .... G 216 541-6060
Cleveland *(G-3862)*

Innovative Plastic Molders LLC .... E 937 898-3775
Vandalia *(G-13562)*

Integra Enclosures Inc .... G 440 269-4966
Willoughby *(G-14469)*

Interntnl Auto Cmpnnts Group .... A 419 433-5653
Wauseon *(G-13853)*

▼ Interpak Inc .... E 440 974-8999
Mentor *(G-9535)*

◆ IPL Dayton Inc .... C 937 969-7000
Urbana *(G-13468)*

Iten Industries Inc .... F 440 997-6134
Ashtabula *(G-600)*

◆ Iten Industries Inc .... C 440 997-6134
Ashtabula *(G-599)*

J & O Plastics Inc .... E 330 927-3169
Rittman *(G-11023)*

J K Plastics Co .... G 440 632-1482
Middlefield *(G-9802)*

J K Precast LLC .... G 740 335-2188
Wshngtn Ct Hs *(G-14741)*

Jaco Manufacturing Company .... E 440 234-4000
Berea *(G-1177)*

Jaco Manufacturing Company .... E 440 234-4000
Berea *(G-1178)*

▲ Janorpot LLC .... E 330 564-0232
Mogadore *(G-10078)*

▼ Japo Inc .... E 614 263-2850
Columbus *(G-5032)*

▲ Jay Industries Inc .... A 419 747-4161
Mansfield *(G-8806)*

▲ Jdh Holdings Inc .... C 330 963-4400
Macedonia *(G-8700)*

▲ Johnsonite Inc .... B 440 543-8916
Solon *(G-12131)*

Joneszylon Company LLC .... G 740 545-6341
West Lafayette *(G-14173)*

Jos-Tech Inc .... E 330 678-3260
Kent *(G-8038)*

▲ Joslyn Manufacturing Company .... E 330 467-8111
Macedonia *(G-8701)*

JPS Technologies Inc .... F 513 984-6400
Blue Ash *(G-1292)*

JPS Technologies Inc .... F 513 984-6400
Blue Ash *(G-1291)*

◆ Kamco Industries Inc .... B 419 924-5511
West Unity *(G-14196)*

Kar-Del Plastics Inc .... G 419 289-9739
Ashland *(G-543)*

Kasai North America Inc .... E 614 356-1494
Dublin *(G-6314)*

Kathom Manufacturing Co Inc .... E 513 868-8890
Middletown *(G-9871)*

▲ Kennedy Group Incorporated .... D 440 951-7660
Willoughby *(G-14477)*

Kirtland Plastics Inc .... D 440 951-4466
Kirtland *(G-8145)*

Kittyhawk Molding Company Inc .... E 937 746-3663
Carlisle *(G-2067)*

▲ Klw Plastics Inc .... G 513 539-2673
Monroe *(G-10112)*

Kmak Group LLC .... F 937 308-1023
London *(G-8538)*

Koebbe Products Inc .... D 513 735-1400
Batavia *(G-870)*

Kolhfab Cstm Plstic Fbrication .... G 937 237-2098
Dayton *(G-5839)*

Kuhns Mold & Tool Co Inc .... D 937 833-2178
Brookville *(G-1572)*

▲ Kurz-Kasch Inc .... E 740 498-8343
Newcomerstown *(G-10572)*

L C Liming & Sons Inc .... G 513 876-2555
Felicity *(G-6830)*

Lalac - Hanlon LLC .... E 216 261-7056
Euclid *(G-6658)*

Lam Pro Inc .... F 216 426-0661
Cleveland *(G-3938)*

◆ Lancaster Commercial Pdts LLC .... E 844 324-1444
Columbus *(G-5062)*

Lancer Dispersions Inc .... D
Akron *(G-202)*

◆ Landmark Plastic Corporation .... C 330 785-2200
Akron *(G-203)*

Larmco Windows Inc .... E 216 502-2832
Cleveland *(G-3942)*

▲ Laszeray Technology LLC .... D 440 582-8430
North Royalton *(G-10770)*

Lee Plastic Company LLC .... G 937 456-5720
Eaton *(G-0439)*

▲ Lenz Inc .... E 937 277-9364
Dayton *(G-5844)*

Lewart Plastics LLC .... F 216 281-2333
Cleveland *(G-3952)*

Linneas Candy Supplies Inc .... E 330 678-7112
Kent *(G-8046)*

Liqui-Box Corporation .... E 419 289-9696
Ashland *(G-549)*

Liqui-Box Corporation .... E 419 294-3884
Upper Sandusky *(G-13446)*

Lotus Pipes & Rockdrills USA .... F 516 209-6995
Cleveland *(G-3967)*

◆ M T M Molded Products Company .... D 937 890-7461
Dayton *(G-5858)*

M W Solutions LLC .... F 419 782-1611
Defiance *(G-6118)*

Mae Fence LLC .... F 614 929-3526
Fulton *(G-7151)*

▲ Mag-Nif Inc .... D 440 255-9366
Mentor *(G-9557)*

▲ Magna Visual Inc .... E 314 843-9000
Perrysburg *(G-11236)*

Magnum Molding Inc .... G 937 368-3040
Conover *(G-5421)*

S
I
C

Majestic Plastics Inc................................ D 937 593-9500
  Bellefontaine *(G-1112)*

◆ Malish Corporation................................D 440 951-5356
  Mentor *(G-9558)*

◆ Mar-Bal Inc...D 440 543-7526
  Chagrin Falls *(G-2170)*

Marne Plastics LLC.................................. F 614 732-4666
  Grove City *(G-7397)*

Marshall Plastics Inc............................... G 937 653-4740
  Urbana *(G-13473)*

Maverick Corporation............................... F 513 469-9919
  Blue Ash *(G-1304)*

McCann Tool & Die Inc........................... G 330 264-8820
  Wooster *(G-14664)*

McNeal Enterprises LLC.......................... G 740 703-7108
  Chillicothe *(G-2264)*

MCS Midwest LLC................................... G 513 217-0805
  Franklin *(G-7033)*

Mdi of Ohio Inc.. E 937 866-2345
  Miamisburg *(G-9711)*

Meese Inc... F 440 998-1202
  Ashtabula *(G-604)*

Mega Plastics Co..................................... E 330 527-2211
  Garrettsville *(G-7226)*

Meggitt (erlanger) LLC............................ D 513 851-5550
  Cincinnati *(G-2858)*

Mercury Plastics LLC.............................. C 440 632-5281
  Middlefield *(G-9808)*

▲ Merryweather Foam Inc...................... E 330 753-0353
  Barberton *(G-822)*

Meteor Creative Inc................................. E 800 273-1535
  Tipp City *(G-12830)*

Miami Specialties Inc.............................. G 937 778-1850
  Piqua *(G-11366)*

▲ Miami Valley Plastics Inc.................... E 937 273-3200
  Eldorado *(G-6480)*

Middlefield Plastics Inc.......................... E 440 834-4638
  Middlefield *(G-9811)*

Mikron Industries Inc.............................. C 859 623-2643
  Akron *(G-231)*

Mikron Industries Inc.............................. C 713 961-4600
  Akron *(G-232)*

Modern Builders Supply Inc................... E 419 526-0002
  Mansfield *(G-8831)*

Modern Builders Supply Inc................... C 419 241-3961
  Toledo *(G-13058)*

Modern Mold Corporation....................... G 440 236-9600
  Columbia Station *(G-4594)*

Mold-Rite Plastics LLC........................... C 330 405-7739
  Twinsburg *(G-13342)*

Mold-Rite Plastics LLC........................... C 330 405-7739
  Twinsburg *(G-13343)*

Molded Fiber Glass Companies.............. D 440 997-5851
  Ashtabula *(G-608)*

Molded Fiber Glass Companies.............. D 440 994-5100
  Ashtabula *(G-609)*

◆ Molded Fiber Glass Companies..........A 440 997-5851
  Ashtabula *(G-607)*

Molding Dynamics Inc............................ F 440 786-8100
  Bedford *(G-1048)*

Molding Technologies Ltd....................... F 740 929-2065
  Hebron *(G-7623)*

Moldmakers Inc....................................... F 419 673-0902
  Kenton *(G-8108)*

▲ Molten North America Corp................ C 419 425-2700
  Findlay *(G-6895)*

▲ Mon-Say Corp.................................... G 419 720-0163
  Toledo *(G-13059)*

Montville Plastics & Rbr LLC................. D 440 548-2005
  Parkman *(G-11127)*

Montville Plastics & Rubber Inc............. E 440 548-3211
  Parkman *(G-11128)*

▲ Moore Industries Inc.......................... D 419 485-5572
  Montpelier *(G-10130)*

◆ Moriroku Technology N Amer Inc......A 937 548-3217
  Marysville *(G-9039)*

▲ Motherson Ychiyo Auto Tech PDT.... D 614 876-3220
  Columbus *(G-5113)*

Mvp Plastics Inc...................................... F 440 834-1790
  Middlefield *(G-9815)*

Mvp Plastics Sa LLC.............................. F 440 834-1790
  Middlefield *(G-9816)*

Mye Automotive Inc................................ G 330 253-5592
  Akron *(G-241)*

Myers Industries Inc............................... E 330 253-5592
  Akron *(G-242)*

Myers Industries Inc............................... C 330 821-4700
  Alliance *(G-396)*

Myers Industries Inc............................... E 440 632-1006
  Middlefield *(G-9817)*

Myers Industries Inc............................... G 330 253-5592
  Akron *(G-243)*

National Access Design LLC.................. F 513 351-3400
  Cincinnati *(G-2893)*

National Fleet Svcs Ohio LLC................ F 440 930-5177
  Avon Lake *(G-766)*

National Molded Products Inc................. E 440 365-3400
  Elyria *(G-6567)*

▲ Neff-Perkins Company........................ D 440 632-1658
  Middlefield *(G-9818)*

Newell Brands Inc................................... F 330 733-7771
  Mogadore *(G-10081)*

◆ Nickolas Plastics LLC.........................C 419 423-1213
  Findlay *(G-6899)*

Nifco America Corporation...................... D 614 836-3808
  Canal Winchester *(G-1795)*

Nifco America Corporation...................... E 614 836-8691
  Groveport *(G-7446)*

▲ Nifco America Corporation.................. B 614 920-6800
  Canal Winchester *(G-1794)*

▲ Nissen Chemitec America Inc............. B 740 852-3200
  London *(G-8539)*

Nitrojection... G 440 729-2711
  Chesterland *(G-2237)*

North Coast Custom Molding Inc........... F 419 905-6447
  Dunkirk *(G-6375)*

▲ North Coast Seal Incorporated.......... F 216 898-5000
  Brookpark *(G-1556)*

Northshore Mold Inc............................... G 440 838-8212
  Cleveland *(G-4098)*

Northstar Plastics Inc............................ D 216 340-7109
  Glenwillow *(G-7287)*

Northwest Molded Plastics..................... G 419 459-4414
  Edon *(G-6477)*

Norwesco Inc.. F 740 654-6402
  Lancaster *(G-8216)*

▲ Novatex North America Inc................. D 419 282-4264
  Ashland *(G-555)*

Octsys Security Corp.............................. G 614 470-4510
  Columbus *(G-5138)*

▲ Ohio Precision Molding Inc................ E 330 745-9393
  Barberton *(G-828)*

Olan Plastics Inc.................................... E 614 834-6526
  Canal Winchester *(G-1797)*

Omega Polymer Technologies Inc........... G 330 562-5201
  Aurora *(G-683)*

Omega Pultrusions Incorporated........... C 330 562-5201
  Aurora *(G-684)*

Orbis Corporation................................... B 937 652-1361
  Urbana *(G-13475)*

Orbit Manufacturing Inc.......................... G 513 732-6097
  Batavia *(G-881)*

▲ Osburn Associates Inc....................... F 740 385-5732
  Logan *(G-8522)*

Overhead Door Corporation..................... F 440 593-5226
  Conneaut *(G-5413)*

◆ Owens Corning Sales LLC..................A 419 248-8000
  Toledo *(G-13088)*

▲ P T I Inc.. F 419 445-2800
  Archbold *(G-507)*

▲ Paarlo Plastics Inc............................ D 330 494-3798
  North Canton *(G-10657)*

Pace Mold & Machine LLC..................... G 330 879-1777
  Massillon *(G-9231)*

▲ Padco Industries LLC......................... E 440 564-7160
  Newbury *(G-10560)*

Palpac Industries Inc.............................. F 419 523-3230
  Ottawa *(G-11041)*

▲ Patrick Products Inc.......................... C 419 943-4137
  Leipsic *(G-8308)*

Pave Technology Co................................ E 937 890-1100
  Dayton *(G-5934)*

PCR Restorations Inc............................. F 419 747-7957
  Mansfield *(G-8844)*

Pease Industies Inc................................ G 513 870-3600
  Fairfield *(G-6764)*

Performance Plastics Ltd........................ D 513 321-8404
  Cincinnati *(G-2955)*

Pickens Plastics Inc............................... G 440 576-4001
  Jefferson *(G-7980)*

▲ Pinnacle Industrial Entps Inc............ C 419 352-8688
  Bowling Green *(G-1435)*

Pioneer Custom Molding Inc................... E 419 737-3252
  Pioneer *(G-11324)*

Pioneer Plastics Corporation.................. C 330 896-2356
  Akron *(G-259)*

Plas-Tanks Industries Inc....................... E 513 942-3800
  Hamilton *(G-7517)*

Plas-TEC Corp.. D 419 272-2731
  Edon *(G-6478)*

Plastic Enterprises Inc........................... G 440 366-0220
  Elyria *(G-6581)*

▲ Plastic Enterprises Inc....................... E 440 324-3240
  Elyria *(G-6580)*

▼ Plastic Extrusion Tech Ltd................. E 440 632-5611
  Middlefield *(G-9821)*

Plastic Forming Company Inc................. E 330 830-5167
  Massillon *(G-9233)*

▲ Plastic Moldings Company Llc.......... D 513 921-5040
  Blue Ash *(G-1319)*

Plasticards Inc.. E 330 896-5555
  Uniontown *(G-13425)*

Plasticraft Usa LLC................................ G 513 761-2999
  Cincinnati *(G-2969)*

Plastics -R- Unique Inc.......................... E 330 334-4820
  Wadsworth *(G-13660)*

Plastics Family Holdings Inc.................. G 440 891-1140
  Cleveland *(G-4172)*

Plastics Family Holdings Inc.................. F 614 272-0777
  Columbus *(G-5196)*

Plastikos Corporation............................. E 513 732-0961
  Batavia *(G-882)*

Plastipak Packaging Inc.......................... C 740 928-4435
  Hebron *(G-7630)*

Plate Engraving Corporation................... G 330 239-2155
  Medina *(G-9436)*

Pleasant Precision Inc............................ E 419 675-0556
  Kenton *(G-8111)*

PMC Smart Solutions LLC...................... D 513 921-5040
  Blue Ash *(G-1320)*

Podnar Plastics Inc................................ G 330 673-2255
  Kent *(G-8059)*

Podnar Plastics Inc................................ E .....
  Kent *(G-8058)*

▲ Polyfill LLC.. E 937 493-0041
  Sidney *(G-12040)*

Polyflex LLC...........................F 440 946-0758
Willoughby *(G-14508)*

▼ Polymer & Steel Tech Inc.................. E 440 510-0108
Eastlake *(G-6441)*

Polysource LLC...........................E 937 778-9500
Piqua *(G-11379)*

Ppafco Inc...........................F 614 488-7259
Columbus *(G-5201)*

Precision Engineered Plas Inc............. E 216 334-1105
Cleveland *(G-4184)*

Precision Foam Fabrication Inc............ G 330 270-2440
Austintown *(G-707)*

Precision Mfg & Assembly LLC............. D 937 252-3507
Dayton *(G-5949)*

▼ Precision Polymer Casting............. F 440 205-1900
Perry *(G-11198)*

Precision Polymers Inc.................... E 614 322-9951
Reynoldsburg *(G-11578)*

◆ Precision Thrmplstc Cmpnnts I..........D 419 227-4500
Lima *(G-8461)*

Preferred Solutions Inc................... F 216 642-1200
Independence *(G-7917)*

Preformed Line Products Co............... F 330 920-1718
Peninsula *(G-11183)*

Premiere Mold and Machine Co............. G 330 874-3000
Bolivar *(G-1389)*

◆ Premium Balloon ACC Inc............. G 330 239-4547
Wadsworth *(G-13661)*

Premix-Hadlock Composites LLC..........D 440 335-4301
Geneva *(G-7245)*

▲ Premix-Hadlock Composites LLC.... E 440 335-4301
Conneaut *(G-5414)*

Prime Engineered Plastics Corp..........F 330 452-5110
Canton *(G-1982)*

Pro-TEC Industries Inc................... G 440 937-4142
Avon *(G-736)*

Professional Plastics Corp............... G 614 336-2498
Dublin *(G-6336)*

Proficient Plastics Inc................... F 440 205-9700
Mentor *(G-9596)*

Profile Plastics Inc................... E 330 452-7000
Canton *(G-1985)*

Profusion Industries LLC................. G 800 938-2858
Fairlawn *(G-6808)*

Progressive Molding Tech................. G 330 220-7030
Medina *(G-9437)*

Progrssive Molding Bolivar Inc.......... G 330 874-3000
Bolivar *(G-1390)*

Promold Inc...........................F 330 633-3532
Tallmadge *(G-12747)*

▲ Proto Plastics Inc................... E 937 667-8416
Tipp City *(G-12839)*

Proto-Mold Products Co Inc............. E 937 778-1959
Piqua *(G-11380)*

▲ Ptc Enterprises Inc................... E 419 272-2524
Edon *(G-6479)*

▲ PVS Plastics Technology Corp........ E 937 233-4376
Huber Heights *(G-7824)*

Pyramid Plastics Inc................... G 216 641-5904
Cleveland *(G-4209)*

Quality Blow Molding Inc................. D 440 458-6550
Elyria *(G-6583)*

Qube Corporation...........................F 440 543-2393
Chagrin Falls *(G-2179)*

Queen City Polymers Inc................. E 513 779-0990
West Chester *(G-14059)*

R A M Plastics Co Inc................... G 330 549-3107
North Lima *(G-10713)*

R and S Technologies Inc................. F 419 483-3691
Bellevue *(G-1129)*

R L Industries Inc................... D 513 874-2800
West Chester *(G-14060)*

Radar Love Co...........................G 419 951-4750
Findlay *(G-6912)*

◆ Radici Plastics Usa Inc.................E 330 336-7611
Wadsworth *(G-13665)*

▲ Rage Corporation...........................D 614 771-4771
Hilliard *(G-7698)*

Raven Concealment Systems LLC........ E 440 508-9000
North Ridgeville *(G-10745)*

▲ Reactive Resin Products Co............. F 419 666-6119
Perrysburg *(G-11259)*

Recto Molded Products Inc............. D 513 871-5544
Cincinnati *(G-3036)*

Reebar Die Casting Inc................... F 419 878-7591
Waterville *(G-13840)*

Reinalt-Thomas Corporation............. G 330 863-1936
Carrollton *(G-2089)*

Remram Recovery LLC................... F 740 667-0092
Tuppers Plains *(G-13262)*

◆ Replex Mirror Company................E 740 397-5535
Mount Vernon *(G-10262)*

◆ Resinoid Engineering Corp............D 740 928-6115
Hebron *(G-7633)*

▼ Resource Mtl Hdlg & Recycl Inc....... E 440 834-0727
Middlefield *(G-9823)*

Retterbush Fiberglass Corp............. E 937 778-1936
Piqua *(G-11382)*

Revere Plas Systems Group LLC..........B 419 547-6918
Clyde *(G-4562)*

Revere Plastics Systems LLC............. C 573 785-0871
Clyde *(G-4563)*

Rexles Inc...........................G 419 732-8188
Port Clinton *(G-11451)*

◆ Rez-Tech Corporation...........................E 330 673-4009
Kent *(G-8068)*

◆ Rjf International Corporation..........A 330 668-2069
Fairlawn *(G-6809)*

RMC USA Incorporation................. D 440 992-4906
Jefferson *(G-7982)*

▲ Ro-MAI Industries Inc................... E 330 425-9090
Twinsburg *(G-13367)*

◆ Roechling Indus Cleveland LP..........C 216 486-0100
Cleveland *(G-4248)*

▲ Rohrer Corporation...........................C 330 335-1541
Wadsworth *(G-13668)*

Roppe Holding Company................. G 419 435-6601
Fostoria *(G-7000)*

Ross Special Products Inc............. F 937 335-8406
Troy *(G-13250)*

Roto Solutions Inc................... G 330 279-2424
Holmesville *(G-7803)*

Rotosolutions Inc................... F 419 903-0800
Ashland *(G-571)*

◆ Rowmark LLC...........................D 419 425-8974
Findlay *(G-6914)*

▲ Royal Plastics Inc................... C 440 352-1357
Mentor *(G-9610)*

Rsl LLC...........................E 330 392-8900
Warren *(G-13795)*

◆ RTS Companies (us) Inc..............E 440 275-3077
Austinburg *(G-702)*

Rubbermaid Home Products............. B 330 733-7771
Mogadore *(G-10082)*

Rubbermaid Incorporated................. A 330 733-7771
Mogadore *(G-10083)*

◆ S Toys Holdings LLC..............A 330 656-0440
Streetsboro *(G-12521)*

▲ S&V Industries Inc................... E 330 666-1986
Medina *(G-9443)*

Saint-Gobain Hycomp LLC..........C 440 234-2002
Cleveland *(G-4270)*

Saint-Gobain Prfmce Plas Corp..........B 440 836-6900
Solon *(G-12178)*

Samuel Son & Co (usa) Inc..........D 740 522-2500
Heath *(G-7604)*

Schmidt Progressive LLC................. G 513 934-2600
Lebanon *(G-8285)*

◆ Scientific Plastics Ltd..........F 305 557-3737
Ravenna *(G-11540)*

Scott Molders Incorporated..........D 330 673-5777
Kent *(G-8074)*

▲ Seagate Plastics Company LLC........ E 419 878-5010
Waterville *(G-13842)*

Shelves West LLC...........................F 928 692-1449
Findlay *(G-6917)*

Shiloh Industries Inc................... F 937 236-5100
Dayton *(G-6003)*

Shirley KS LLC...........................G 740 331-7934
Zanesville *(G-15048)*

Shirley KS Storage Trays LLC..........G 740 868-8140
Zanesville *(G-15049)*

◆ Silgan Dispensing Systems Corp..........D 330 425-4260
Macedonia *(G-8713)*

Silgan Plastics LLC................... C 419 523-3737
Ottawa *(G-11045)*

Silmarillion Partners Inc................. C 330 821-4700
Alliance *(G-404)*

Silver Line Building Pdts LLC..........A 740 382-5595
Marion *(G-8998)*

Solutions In Polycarbonate LLC..........G 330 572-2860
Medina *(G-9449)*

Sonoco Products Company................. E 614 759-8470
Columbus *(G-5276)*

Southeastern Container Inc............. D 419 352-6300
Bowling Green *(G-1440)*

Spartech LLC...........................C 937 548-1395
Greenville *(G-7353)*

Spartech LLC...........................D 419 399-4050
Paulding *(G-11162)*

▲ Spectrum Plastics Corporation........ G 330 926-9766
Cuyahoga Falls *(G-5573)*

SPI Liquidation Inc...........................D
Middlefield *(G-9828)*

Springfield Plastics Inc................. F 937 322-6071
Springfield *(G-12377)*

Springseal Inc...........................F 330 626-0673
Ravenna *(G-11543)*

Stanek E F and Assoc Inc............. C 216 341-7700
Macedonia *(G-8717)*

▲ Stanley Electric US Co Inc............. E 740 852-5200
London *(G-8511)*

Starks Plastics LLC................... F 513 541-4591
Cincinnati *(G-3113)*

Steere Enterprises Inc................... C 330 633-4926
Tallmadge *(G-12750)*

▲ Steere Enterprises Inc................... D 330 633-4926
Tallmadge *(G-12751)*

◆ Step2 Company LLC................B 866 429-5200
Streetsboro *(G-12525)*

Sterilite Corporation...........................C 330 830-2204
Massillon *(G-9246)*

▲ Stewart Acquisition LLC................. E 330 963-0322
Twinsburg *(G-13380)*

Stonyridge Inc...........................F 937 845-9482
New Carlisle *(G-10380)*

Stuchell Products LLC................... E 330 821-4299
Alliance *(G-407)*

Style Crest Enterprises Inc................. E 419 355-8586
Fremont *(G-7134)*

◆ Suburban Plastics Co................B 847 741-4900
Bolivar *(G-1392)*

Sun State Plastics Inc................... E 330 494-5220
Canton *(G-2020)*

Superior Fibers Inc................... B 740 394-2491
Shawnee *(G-11952)*

SIC

Superior Plastics Inc.............................. F 614 733-0307
  Plain City *(G-11420)*

◆ Superior Plastics Inc.......................... E 614 733-0307
  Plain City *(G-11419)*

▼ Swapil Inc... D
  Columbus *(G-5303)*

Synergy Manufacturing LLC.................. E 740 352-5933
  Piketon *(G-11314)*

Tahoma Enterprises Inc........................ D 330 745-9016
  Barberton *(G-840)*

◆ Tahoma Rubber & Plastics Inc.......... D 330 745-9016
  Ashland *(G-579)*

Tbk Holdings LLC................................... G 313 584-0400
  Perrysburg *(G-11265)*

Team Plastics Inc................................... F 216 251-8270
  Cleveland *(G-4366)*

Tech-Way Industries Inc....................... D 937 746-1004
  Franklin *(G-7052)*

Teijin Automotive Tech Inc................... B 419 396-1980
  Carey *(G-2063)*

Teijin Automotive Tech Inc................... C 440 945-4800
  Conneaut *(G-5417)*

Teijin Automotive Tech Inc................... B 419 257-2231
  North Baltimore *(G-10618)*

Teijin Automotive Tech Inc................... B 419 238-4628
  Van Wert *(G-13546)*

Tetra Mold & Tool Inc........................... E 937 845-1651
  New Carlisle *(G-10382)*

Th Plastics Inc....................................... D 419 352-2770
  Bowling Green *(G-1442)*

Th Plastics Inc....................................... D 419 425-5825
  Findlay *(G-6926)*

The Crane Group Companies Limited.... E 614 754-3000
  Columbus *(G-5319)*

▲ Thermoprene Inc................................. F 440 543-8660
  Cleveland *(G-4392)*

◆ Thogus Products Company.................. D 440 933-8850
  Avon Lake *(G-771)*

▲ Thomas Tool & Mold Company.......... F 614 890-4978
  Westerville *(G-14278)*

▲ Tigerpoly Manufacturing Inc............. B 614 871-0045
  Grove City *(G-7416)*

◆ Timbertech Limited............................. B 937 655-8766
  Wilmington *(G-14586)*

Tire Tread Development Inc................... E 330 628-5666
  Mogadore *(G-10089)*

Tjar Innovations LLC.............................. F 937 347-1999
  Xenia *(G-14780)*

Tmd Wek North LLC............................... C 440 576-6940
  Jefferson *(G-7985)*

Toledo Molding & Die LLC..................... C 419 354-6050
  Bowling Green *(G-1443)*

Toledo Molding & Die LLC..................... C 419 692-6022
  Delphos *(G-6194)*

Toledo Molding & Die LLC..................... C 419 443-9031
  Tiffin *(G-12806)*

Toledo Molding & Die LLC..................... C 419 476-0581
  Toledo *(G-13154)*

◆ Toledo Molding & Die LLC.................. D 419 470-3950
  Toledo *(G-13153)*

Toledo Pro Fiberglass Inc.................... G 419 241-9390
  Toledo *(G-13156)*

▲ Tom Smith Industries Inc.................. D 937 832-1555
  Englewood *(G-6626)*

Tooling Tech Holdings LLC................... E 937 295-3672
  Fort Loramie *(G-6959)*

Toth Mold & Die Inc.............................. F 440 232-8530
  Bedford *(G-1062)*

Treemen Industries Inc......................... E 330 965-3777
  Boardman *(G-1378)*

Trellborg Sling Prfiles US Inc.............. C 330 995-9725
  Aurora *(G-690)*

Tri-Craft Inc... E 440 826-1050
  Cleveland *(G-4418)*

▲ Trifecta Tool and Engrg LLC............. G 937 291-0933
  Dayton *(G-357)*

Trilogy Plastics Alliance Inc................. F 330 821-4700
  Alliance *(G-413)*

Trimold LLC.. B 740 474-7591
  Circleville *(G-3268)*

Trinity Specialty Compounding Inc....... F 419 924-9090
  West Unity *(G-14198)*

Truechoicepack Corp............................. F 937 630-3832
  West Chester *(G-14085)*

Trusscore USA Inc................................. E 888 418-4679
  Dayton *(G-6066)*

TS Tech Co Ltd....................................... G 740 420-5617
  Circleville *(G-3269)*

Tsp Inc.. F 513 732-8900
  Batavia *(G-892)*

U S Molding Machinery Co Inc............. E 440 918-1701
  Willoughby *(G-14547)*

Udecx LLC... G 877 698-3329
  Tipp City *(G-12851)*

▲ United Security Seals Inc.................. E 614 443-7633
  Columbus *(G-5337)*

United States Plastic Corp.................... D 419 228-2242
  Lima *(G-8457)*

◆ Universal Polymer & Rubber Ltd....... C 440 632-1691
  Middlefield *(G-9834)*

UPL International Inc.............................. F 330 433-2860
  North Canton *(G-10680)*

▲ US Coexcell Inc.................................. E 419 897-9110
  Maumee *(G-9328)*

US Development Corp............................. D 330 673-6900
  Kent *(G-8094)*

Valley Plastics Company Inc................. E 419 666-2349
  Toledo *(G-13173)*

Ventek Solutions LLC............................ F 419 420-0029
  Findlay *(G-6930)*

Venture Packaging Inc.......................... F 419 465-2534
  Monroeville *(G-10122)*

Venture Packaging Midwest Inc........... G 419 465-2534
  Monroeville *(G-10123)*

◆ Venture Plastics Inc........................... C 330 872-5774
  Newton Falls *(G-10582)*

Vicas Manufacturing Co Inc................. E 513 791-7741
  Cincinnati *(G-3204)*

Vinyl Design Corporation...................... E 419 283-4009
  Holland *(G-7790)*

Vinyl Profiles Acquisition LLC............. F 330 538-0660
  North Jackson *(G-10698)*

Vinylume Products Inc.......................... F 330 799-2000
  Youngstown *(G-14964)*

Vision Color LLC.................................... G 419 924-9450
  West Unity *(G-14199)*

Vts Co Ltd... G 419 273-4010
  Forest *(G-6943)*

▼ W T Inc... F 419 224-6942
  Lima *(G-8458)*

Walleye Investments Ltd....................... G 440 564-7210
  Solon *(G-12206)*

▼ Warwick Products Company............... E 216 334-1200
  Cleveland *(G-4491)*

Wasca LLC... E 937 723-9031
  Dayton *(G-6075)*

Wch Molding LLC................................... E 740 335-6320
  Wshngtn Ct Hs *(G-14749)*

◆ Weatherchem Corporation.................. D 330 425-4206
  Twinsburg *(G-13394)*

West & Barker Inc................................. F 330 652-9923
  Niles *(G-10609)*

Westar Plastics Llc............................... G 419 636-1333
  Bryan *(G-1667)*

▲ Westlake Dimex LLC........................... C 800 334-3776
  Marietta *(G-8961)*

Wl Inc... C 440 576-6940
  Akron *(G-357)*

Wisco Products Incorporated............... E 937 228-2101
  Dayton *(G-6084)*

Woodbridge Englewood Inc.................. E 937 540-9889
  Englewood *(G-6630)*

▲ World Class Plastics Inc................... D 937 843-3003
  Russells Point *(G-11671)*

▲ World Resource Solutons Corp......... G 614 733-3737
  Plain City *(G-11428)*

▲ Worthignton Products Inc.................. G 330 452-7400
  East Canton *(G-6381)*

Wyatt Industries LLC............................ G 330 954-1790
  Aurora *(G-694)*

◆ Xaloy LLC.. C 330 726-4000
  Austintown *(G-709)*

▲ Y City Recycling LLC.......................... G 740 452-2500
  Zanesville *(G-15056)*

Yanfeng Intl Auto Tech US I LL............ D 419 633-1873
  Bryan *(G-1668)*

Yanfeng Intl Auto Tech US II L............ G 419 636-4211
  Bryan *(G-1670)*

▼ Zehrco-Giancola Composites Inc...... C 440 994-6317
  Ashtabula *(G-623)*

31 LEATHER AND LEATHER PRODUCTS

3111 Leather tanning and finishing

Bernard Engraving Corp......................... F 419 478-5610
  Toledo *(G-12896)*

▲ Leather Resource of America Inc...... E 440 262-5761
  Conneaut *(G-5407)*

Premier Tanning & Nutrition................. G 419 342-6259
  Shelby *(G-11973)*

Sisters Tanning Inc.............................. G 740 636-0303
  Wshngtn Ct Hs *(G-14746)*

3131 Footwear cut stock

Classic Countertops LLC....................... G 330 882-4220
  Akron *(G-102)*

Hudson Leather Ltd............................... G 419 485-8531
  Pioneer *(G-11321)*

▲ Remington Products Company........... D 330 335-1571
  Upper Arlington *(G-13432)*

3142 House slippers

▲ Principle Business Entps Inc............ C 419 352-1551
  Bowling Green *(G-1437)*

R G Barry Corporation........................... F 212 244-3145
  Pickerington *(G-11298)*

3143 Men's footwear, except athletic

▲ Acor Orthopaedic LLC........................ E 216 662-4500
  Cleveland *(G-3293)*

Careismatic Brands LLC........................ G 561 843-8727
  Groveport *(G-7428)*

Careismatic Brands LLC........................ G 614 497-5289
  Groveport *(G-7429)*

Georgia-Boot Inc................................... D 740 753-1951
  Nelsonville *(G-10317)*

Rbr Enterprises LLC.............................. F 866 437-9327
  Brecksville *(G-1480)*

Rocky Brands Inc................................... C 740 753-1951
  Nelsonville *(G-10320)*

3144 Women's footwear, except athletic

▲ Acor Orthopaedic LLC........................ E 216 662-4500
  Cleveland *(G-3293)*

Careismatic Brands LLC........................G 561 843-8727
Groveport (G-7428)

Careismatic Brands LLC........................G 614 497-5289
Groveport (G-7429)

Georgia-Boot Inc.................................D 740 753-1951
Nelsonville (G-10317)

Rocky Brands Inc................................C 740 753-1951
Nelsonville (G-10320)

3151 Leather gloves and mittens

▲ Totes Isotoner Holdings LLC...........C 513 682-8200
Cincinnati (G-3160)

3161 Luggage

▲ Belaire Products Inc.........................E 330 253-3116
Akron (G-75)

Buckeye Stamping Company...............D 877 728-0776
Columbus (G-4786)

Cleveland Canvas Goods Mfg Co.......E 216 361-4567
Cleveland (G-3508)

▲ Clipper Products Inc.........................G 513 688-7300
Cincinnati (G-2299)

Eagle Creek Inc..................................D 513 385-4442
Cincinnati (G-2572)

▲ Kam Manufacturing Inc....................C 419 238-6037
Van Wert (G-13538)

L M Engineering Inc............................E 330 270-2400
Austintown (G-706)

Made Men Circle LLC..........................G 216 501-0414
Cleveland Heights (G-4529)

Northhhill T-Shirt Print Dsign...............G 330 208-0338
Akron (G-250)

Plastic Forming Company Inc..............E 330 830-5167
Massillon (G-9233)

Professional Case Inc.........................F 513 682-2520
West Chester (G-14139)

T & CS Repairs & Retail LLC................E 704 964-7325
Akron (G-325)

Travelers Custom Case Inc.................F 216 621-8447
Mentor (G-9643)

▲ UNI Corp..E 800 782-3296
Canton (G-2031)

▲ Weaver Leather LLC.........................D 330 674-7548
Millersburg (G-10019)

Whitman Corporation...........................G 513 541-3223
Okeana (G-10930)

3171 Women's handbags and purses

▲ Hugo Bosca Company Inc................F 937 323-5523
Springfield (G-12327)

Judith Leiber LLC................................E 614 449-4217
Columbus (G-5043)

Ravenworks Deer Skin.........................G 937 354-5151
Mount Victory (G-10270)

3172 Personal leather goods, nec

Bison Leather Co.................................G 419 517-1737
Toledo (G-12897)

Down Home..G 740 393-1186
Mount Vernon (G-10243)

▲ Hamilton Manufacturing Corp..........E 419 867-4858
Holland (G-7766)

▲ Hugo Bosca Company Inc................F 937 323-5523
Springfield (G-12327)

Ravenworks Deer Skin.........................G 937 354-5151
Mount Victory (G-10270)

Total Education Solutions Inc..............D 330 668-4041
Fairlawn (G-6815)

▲ Weaver Leather LLC.........................D 330 674-7548
Millersburg (G-10019)

Williams Leather Products Inc.............G 740 223-1604
Marion (G-9004)

3199 Leather goods, nec

▲ Coastal Pet Products Inc..................A 330 821-7363
Alliance (G-377)

Cornerstone Brands Inc......................G 866 668-5962
West Chester (G-13975)

Diy Holster LLC...................................G 419 921-2168
Elyria (G-6520)

▲ Holmes Wheel Shop Inc...................E 330 279-2891
Holmesville (G-7800)

▲ Leather Resource of America Inc......E 440 262-5761
Conneaut (G-5407)

LLC Bowman Leather............................G 330 893-1954
Millersburg (G-9994)

Rantek Products LLC...........................G 419 485-2421
Montpelier (G-10133)

Sustainment Actions LLC.....................F 330 805-3468
Columbus (G-5302)

◆ Tarahill Inc..G 706 864-0808
Columbus (G-5308)

▲ Weaver Leather LLC.........................D 330 674-7548
Millersburg (G-10019)

Whitman Corporation...........................G 513 541-3223
Okeana (G-10930)

32 STONE, CLAY, GLASS, AND CONCRETE PRODUCTS

3211 Flat glass

Cardinal CT Company...........................E 740 892-2324
Utica (G-13486)

Cardinal Glass Industries Inc..............E 740 892-2324
Utica (G-13487)

Clearvue Insulating Glass Co..............G 216 651-1140
Cleveland (G-3504)

▲ Continental GL Sls & Inv Group........G 614 679-1201
Powell (G-11485)

Custom Glass Solutions LLC...............E 248 340-1800
Upper Sandusky (G-13437)

◆ Glasstech Inc....................................E 419 661-9500
Perrysburg (G-11226)

Guardian Fabrication LLC.....................C 419 855-7706
Millbury (G-9962)

Imaging Sciences LLC.........................G 440 975-9640
Willoughby (G-14468)

Knight Industries Corp.........................F 419 478-8550
Toledo (G-13020)

Machined Glass Specialist Inc............O 937 748-0100
Springboro (G-12259)

◆ Newell Holdings Delaware Inc..........D 740 681-6461
Lancaster (G-8214)

Niles Mirror & Glass Inc......................E 330 652-6277
Niles (G-10597)

Nsg Glass North America Inc..............C 734 755-5816
Luckey (G-8671)

Nsg Glass North America Inc..............E 419 247-4800
Toledo (G-13065)

◆ Pilkington Holdings Inc.....................B
Toledo (G-13097)

Pilkington North America Inc...............C 800 547-9280
Northwood (G-10808)

Pilkington North America Inc...............B 419 247-3211
Rossford (G-11660)

Pilkington North America Inc...............C 419 247-3731
Urbancrest (G-13483)

◆ Pilkington North America Inc............D 419 247-3731
Toledo (G-13098)

Rsl LLC..E 330 392-8900
Warren (G-13795)

S R Door LLC.......................................D 740 927-3558
Hebron (G-7634)

Schodorf Truck Body & Eqp Co...........F 614 228-6793
Columbus (G-5253)

Sonalysts Inc.......................................E 937 429-9711
Beavercreek (G-984)

Taylor Products Inc..............................E 419 263-2313
Payne (G-11166)

Therm-All Inc.......................................E 440 779-9494
Westlake (G-14339)

Trulite GL Alum Solutions LLC.............D 740 929-2443
Hebron (G-7642)

Vinylume Products Inc.........................F 330 799-2000
Youngstown (G-14964)

Wt Acquisition Company Ltd.................E 513 577-7980
Cincinnati (G-3234)

3221 Glass containers

Anchor Glass Container Corp..............D 740 452-2743
Zanesville (G-14987)

◆ Anchor Hocking LLC.........................A 740 687-2500
Columbus (G-4711)

Bprex Plastic Packaging Inc................F 419 247-5000
Toledo (G-12902)

Chantilly Development Corp.................E 419 243-8109
Toledo (G-12916)

Dura Temp Corporation........................F 419 866-4348
Holland (G-7760)

▲ Envases Media Inc...........................E 419 636-5461
Bryan (G-1640)

◆ Ghp II LLC..C 740 687-2500
Lancaster (G-8204)

O-I Glass Inc.......................................C 567 336-5000
Perrysburg (G-11244)

Owens-Brockway Glass Cont Inc.........E 740 455-4516
Zanesville (G-15036)

◆ Owens-Brockway Glass Cont Inc.....C 567 336-8449
Perrysburg (G-11252)

▲ Owens-Illinois General Inc...............A 567 336-5000
Perrysburg (G-11253)

◆ Owens-Illinois Group Inc..................D 567 336-5000
Perrysburg (G-11254)

Owens-Illinois Inc...............................A 567 336-5000
Perrysburg (G-11255)

Paddock Enterprises LLC.....................E 567 336-5000
Perrysburg (G-11256)

Pyromatics Corp..................................F 440 352-3500
Mentor (G-9599)

Tiama Americas Inc.............................E 269 274-3107
Maumee (G-9336)

Waterco of The Central States............E 937 294-0375
Fairfield (G-6791)

3229 Pressed and blown glass, nec

All State GL Block Fctry Inc.................G 440 205-8410
Mentor (G-9476)

◆ American De Rosa Lamparts LLC......D
Cuyahoga Falls (G-5522)

◆ Anchor Hocking LLC.........................A 740 687-2500
Columbus (G-4711)

▼ Anchor Hocking Consmr GL Corp.....G 740 653-2527
Lancaster (G-8176)

Anchor Hocking Corporation................G 614 633-4247
Columbus (G-4712)

Anderson Glass Co Inc........................G 614 476-4877
Columbus (G-4717)

Blockamerica Corporation....................G 614 274-0700
Columbus (G-4765)

Brubaker Metalcrafts Inc.....................G 937 456-5834
Eaton (G-6449)

◆ Cincinnati Gasket Pkg Mfg Inc.........E 513 761-3458
Cincinnati (G-2475)

Current Elec & Enrgy Solutions...........G 513 575-4600
Loveland (G-8623)

SIC

Dal-Little Fabricating Inc...................... G 216 883-3323
Cleveland *(G-3598)*

Eickholt Glass Inc.................................. F 614 638-4903
Columbus *(G-4899)*

G L Pierce Inc....................................... G 513 772-7202
Cincinnati *(G-2647)*

General Electric Company...................... G 740 385-2114
Logan *(G-8514)*

General Electric Company...................... G 330 373-1400
Warren *(G-13767)*

◆ Ghp II LLC .... C 740 687-2500
Lancaster *(G-8204)*

Glass Block Headquarters Inc .... G 216 941-5470
Cleveland *(G-3776)*

◆ Glasstech Inc.....................................C 419 661-9500
Perrysburg *(G-11226)*

▲ Global Glass Block Inc...................... G 216 731-2333
Euclid *(G-6651)*

Industrial Fiberglass Spc Inc .... E 937 222-9000
Vandalia *(G-13561)*

Integris Composites Inc....................... D 740 928-0326
Hebron *(G-7619)*

Interntnal Auto Cmpnnts Group............ A 419 433-5653
Wauseon *(G-13853)*

Jack Pine Studio LLC............................ G 740 332-2223
Laurelville *(G-8237)*

▲ John Krizay Inc................................. F 330 332-5607
Salem *(G-11790)*

Johns Manville Corporation................... C 419 878-8111
Waterville *(G-13835)*

Knoble Glass & Metal Inc...................... G 513 753-1246
Cincinnati *(G-2802)*

Libbey Glass LLC.................................. D 419 727-2211
Toledo *(G-13034)*

◆ Libbey Glass LLC..............................C 419 325-2100
Toledo *(G-13033)*

▼ Libbey Inc... C 419 325-2100
Toledo *(G-13035)*

◆ Mfg Composite Systems Company....B 440 997-5851
Ashtabula *(G-605)*

Midwest Composites LLC .... E 419 738-2431
Wapakoneta *(G-13721)*

Modern China Company Inc .... E 330 938-6104
Sebring *(G-11898)*

▲ Mosser Glass Inc.............................. E 740 439-1827
Cambridge *(G-1751)*

Nextgen Fiber Optics LLC..................... G 513 549-4691
Cincinnati *(G-2906)*

Owens Corning Ht Inc .... G 419 248-8000
Toledo *(G-13086)*

◆ Owens Corning Sales LLC.................A 419 248-8000
Toledo *(G-13088)*

◆ Pittsburgh Corning LLC.....................B 724 327-6100
Toledo *(G-13100)*

Plasticraft Usa LLC .... C 513 761-2999
Cincinnati *(G-2969)*

Rocket Ventures LLC............................ F 419 530-6083
Toledo *(G-13117)*

Scottrods LLC...................................... G 419 499-2705
Monroeville *(G-10120)*

Sem-Com Company Inc......................... F 419 537-8813
Toledo *(G-13125)*

Srico Inc.. G 614 799-0664
Columbus *(G-5287)*

Techneglas Inc..................................... E 419 873-2000
Perrysburg *(G-11267)*

Technical Glass Products Inc .... F 425 396-8420
Perrysburg *(G-11269)*

▲ Technical Glass Products Inc........... F 440 639-6399
Painesville *(G-11113)*

Variety Glass Inc.................................. F 740 432-3643
Cambridge *(G-1765)*

Wilson Optical Labs Inc........................ E 440 357-7000
Mentor *(G-9652)*

3231 Products of purchased glass

A & B Iron & Metal Co Inc .... F 937 228-1561
Dayton *(G-5629)*

A Service Glass Inc.............................. F 937 426-4920
Beavercreek *(G-963)*

Aag Glass LLC..................................... E 513 286-8268
Batavia *(G-849)*

Adria Scientific GL Works Co................ G 440 474-6691
Geneva *(G-7231)*

▲ Afg Industries Inc............................. D 614 322-4580
Grove City *(G-7368)*

Americana Glass Co Inc....................... F 330 938-6135
Sebring *(G-11890)*

◆ Amerihua Intl Entps Inc.....................G 740 549-0300
Lewis Center *(G-8321)*

◆ Anchi Inc...A 740 653-2527
Lancaster *(G-8175)*

Anderson Glass Co Inc......................... G 614 476-4877
Columbus *(G-4717)*

▲ Atc Lighting & Plastics Inc............... C 440 466-7670
Andover *(G-456)*

◆ Auto Temp Inc...................................C 513 732-6969
Batavia *(G-851)*

◆ Basco Manufacturing Company..........C 513 573-1900
Mason *(G-9069)*

Beach Manufacturing Co....................... C 937 882-6372
Donnelsville *(G-6227)*

Bruening Glass Works Inc.................... G 440 333-4768
Cleveland *(G-3445)*

Cdh Liquidation Inc.............................. E 419 720-4096
Toledo *(G-12912)*

Champion Window Co of Toledo............ G 419 841-0154
Perrysburg *(G-11211)*

Chantilly Development Corp.................. E 419 243-8109
Toledo *(G-12916)*

Custom GL Sltons Upper Sndsky.......... B 419 294-4921
Upper Sandusky *(G-13436)*

▲ East Palestine China Dctg LLC......... F 330 426-9600
East Palestine *(G-6403)*

▲ Enclosure Suppliers LLC.................. E 513 782-3900
Cincinnati *(G-2586)*

▲ Franklin Art Glass Studios............... E 614 221-2972
Columbus *(G-4937)*

Fuyao Glass America Inc...................... B 937 496-5777
Moraine *(G-10164)*

General Electric Company...................... G 740 385-2114
Logan *(G-8514)*

Ghp II LLC... F 740 681-6825
Lancaster *(G-8203)*

Glass Surface Systems Inc................... D 330 745-8500
Barberton *(G-808)*

◆ Glasstech Inc.....................................C 419 661-9500
Perrysburg *(G-11226)*

Great Day Improvements LLC................ B 267 223-1289
Macedonia *(G-8695)*

Guardian Fabrication LLC...................... C 419 855-7706
Millbury *(G-9962)*

Installed Building Pdts LLC................... B 614 308-9900
Columbus *(G-5009)*

Intigral Inc... G 440 439-0980
Youngstown *(G-14877)*

▲ Intigral Inc.. C 440 439-0980
Walton Hills *(G-13698)*

Jafe Decorating Inc.............................. C 937 547-1888
Greenville *(G-7343)*

Kimmatt Corp....................................... G 937 228-3811
West Alexandria *(G-13920)*

◆ Libbey Glass LLC..............................C 419 325-2100
Toledo *(G-13033)*

Macpherson Engineering Inc................. G 440 243-6565
Warren *(G-13779)*

Middlefield Glass Incorporated.............. G 440 632-5699
Middlefield *(G-9809)*

Miller-Holzwarth Inc............................. D 330 342-7224
Salem *(G-11800)*

▲ North Central Insulation Inc.............. F 419 886-2030
Bellville *(G-1141)*

Ohio Mirror Technologies Inc................ F 419 399-5903
Paulding *(G-11160)*

Oldcastle Buildingenvelope Inc............. C 800 537-4064
Perrysburg *(G-11249)*

Paragon Tempered Glass LLC............... C 419 258-5531
Antwerp *(G-463)*

Patriot Armored Systems LLC.............. F 413 637-1060
West Chester *(G-14042)*

▲ Pei Liquidation Company................... C 330 467-4267
Macedonia *(G-8704)*

Pilkington North America Inc................ B 419 247-3211
Rossford *(G-11660)*

Potters Industries LLC......................... D 216 621-0840
Cleveland *(G-4178)*

Pyromatics Corp................................... F 440 352-3500
Mentor *(G-9599)*

Rumpke Transportation Co LLC............. B 513 242-4600
Cincinnati *(G-3057)*

◆ Safelite Group Inc.............................A 614 210-9000
Columbus *(G-5244)*

Scs Construction Services Inc.............. E 513 929-0260
Cincinnati *(G-3071)*

Sem-Com Company Inc......................... F 419 537-8813
Toledo *(G-13125)*

▲ Sims Bros Inc.................................... D 740 387-9041
Marion *(G-9000)*

Solon Glass Center Inc........................ F 440 248-5018
Cleveland *(G-4313)*

Strategic Materials Inc......................... G 740 349-9523
Newark *(G-10534)*

Studio Arts and Glass Inc.................... F 330 494-9779
Canton *(G-2019)*

Taylor Products Inc.............................. E 419 263-2313
Payne *(G-11165)*

Taylor Products Inc.............................. E 419 263-2313
Payne *(G-11166)*

Technicolor Usa Inc............................. A 614 474-8821
Circleville *(G-3265)*

Trulite GL Alum Solutions LLC............. D 740 929-2443
Hebron *(G-7642)*

Whitney Stained GL Studio Inc............. G 216 348-1616
Cleveland *(G-4504)*

XS Smith Inc.. E 252 940-5060
Cincinnati *(G-3239)*

3241 Cement, hydraulic

Fairborn Cement Company LLC.............. C 937 879-8393
Xenia *(G-14764)*

Hartline Products Coinc........................ G 216 851-7189
Cleveland *(G-3811)*

Holcim (us) Inc..................................... G 216 781-9330
Cleveland *(G-3833)*

Holcim (us) Inc..................................... C 419 399-4861
Paulding *(G-11156)*

Huron Cement Products Company.......... E 419 433-4161
Huron *(G-7874)*

Independence Cement LLC..................... E 216 264-1212
Brecksville *(G-1471)*

▲ Kona Blackbird Inc............................ E 440 285-3189
Chardon *(G-2211)*

Quikrete Companies LLC....................... D 614 885-4406
Columbus *(G-5220)*

Quikrete Companies LLC....................... E 330 296-6080
Ravenna *(G-11536)*

Quikrete Companies LLC...................... F 419 241-1148
Toledo *(G-13106)*

Redland Quarries NY Inc...................... E 216 566-0545
Cleveland *(G-4230)*

USA Precast Concrete Limited............... E 330 854-9600
Canal Fulton *(G-1781)*

Wallseye Concrete Corp...................... F 419 483-2738
Castalia *(G-2096)*

Wallseye Concrete Corp...................... F 440 235-1800
Cleveland *(G-4489)*

3251 Brick and structural clay tile

Armstrong World Industries Inc............ E 614 771-9307
Hilliard *(G-7669)*

Belden Brick Company LLC................... D 330 456-0031
Sugarcreek *(G-12632)*

Belden Brick Company LLC................... D 330 265-2030
Sugarcreek *(G-12633)*

Bowerston Shale Company................... C 740 763-3921
Newark *(G-10494)*

Bowerston Shale Company................... E 740 269-2921
Bowerston *(G-1399)*

Glen-Gery Corporation......................... D 419 845-3321
Caledonia *(G-1731)*

Glen-Gery Corporation......................... E 419 468-4890
Galion *(G-7194)*

Glen-Gery Corporation......................... E 419 468-5002
Iberia *(G-7883)*

Kepcor Inc... F 330 868-6434
Minerva *(G-10040)*

▲ Kona Blackbird Inc........................... E 440 285-3189
Chardon *(G-2211)*

LBC Clay Co LLC................................ G 330 674-0674
Millersburg *(G-9991)*

Minteq International Inc....................... E 330 343-8821
Dover *(G-6254)*

Nutro Inc... E 440 572-3800
Strongsville *(G-12581)*

Resco Products Inc............................. G 740 682-7794
Oak Hill *(G-10893)*

Stebbins Engineering & Mfg Co............ G 740 922-3012
Uhrichsville *(G-13407)*

◆ The Belden Brick Company LLC.......... E 330 456-0031
Canton *(G-2024)*

Whitacre Greer Company..................... E 330 823-1610
Alliance *(G-416)*

3253 Ceramic wall and floor tile

Dai Ceramics LLC............................... D 440 946-6964
Willoughby *(G-14445)*

Kepcor Inc... F 330 868-6434
Minerva *(G-10040)*

Mohawk Industries Inc........................ E 800 837-3812
Grove City *(G-7402)*

▲ Ohio Tile & Marble Co...................... E 513 541-4211
Cincinnati *(G-2926)*

PCC Ceramic Group 1.......................... G 440 516-3672
Wickliffe *(G-14390)*

Stebbins Engineering & Mfg Co............ G 740 922-3012
Uhrichsville *(G-13407)*

Summitville Tiles Inc........................... E 330 868-6771
Minerva *(G-10047)*

▲ Summitville Tiles Inc........................ E 330 223-1511
Summitville *(G-12661)*

Tarkett USA Inc.................................. B 440 543-8916
Chagrin Falls *(G-2188)*

Tarkett USA Inc.................................. C 877 827-5388
Solon *(G-12193)*

Wccv Floor Coverings LLC................... F 330 688-0114
Peninsula *(G-11185)*

3255 Clay refractories

Bowerston Shale Company................... E 740 269-2921
Bowerston *(G-1399)*

Ethima Inc.. D 419 626-4912
Sandusky *(G-11834)*

Glen-Gery Corporation......................... D 419 845-3321
Caledonia *(G-1731)*

Glen-Gery Corporation......................... E 419 468-5002
Iberia *(G-7883)*

I Cerco Inc... C 740 982-2050
Crooksville *(G-5510)*

◆ Industrial Ceramic Products Inc......... D 937 642-3897
Marysville *(G-9032)*

Lakeway Mfg Inc................................ E 419 433-3030
Huron *(G-7877)*

Magneco/Metrel Inc............................ C 330 426-9468
Negley *(G-10315)*

Minteq International Inc....................... E 330 343-8821
Dover *(G-6254)*

Nock and Son Company....................... F 740 682-7741
Oak Hill *(G-10891)*

Resco Products Inc............................. G 330 488-1226
East Canton *(G-6380)*

Resco Products Inc............................. G 740 682-7794
Oak Hill *(G-10893)*

▲ Selas Heat Technology Co LLC........... E 800 523-6500
Streetsboro *(G-12523)*

Seven Lakeway Refractories LLC.......... F 419 433-3030
Huron *(G-7882)*

Specialty Ceramics Inc........................ D 330 482-0800
Columbiana *(G-4629)*

Stebbins Engineering & Mfg Co............ G 740 922-3012
Uhrichsville *(G-13407)*

Summitville Tiles Inc........................... D 330 868-6463
Minerva *(G-10048)*

◆ United Refractories Inc..................... E 330 372-3716
Warren *(G-13807)*

Veitsch-Radex America LLC................. D 717 793-7122
Ashtabula *(G-620)*

◆ Wahl Refractory Solutions LLC.......... D 419 334-2658
Fremont *(G-7143)*

Whitacre Greer Company..................... E 330 823-1610
Alliance *(G-416)*

3259 Structural clay products, nec

Baughman Tile Company...................... D 800 837-3160
Paulding *(G-11153)*

Clay Logan Products Company.............. D 740 385-2184
Logan *(G-9511)*

Haviland Drainage Products Co............. F 800 860-6294
Haviland *(G-7589)*

◆ Superior Clay Corporation................. D 740 922-4122
Uhrichsville *(G-13408)*

Terreal North America LLC................... C 888 582-9052
New Lexington *(G-10409)*

3261 Vitreous plumbing fixtures

Accent Manufacturing Inc.................... F 330 724-7704
Norton *(G-10816)*

As America Inc.................................... D 419 522-4211
Mansfield *(G-8763)*

As America Inc.................................... F 330 332-9954
Salem *(G-11762)*

Bridgits Bath LLC............................... G 937 259-1960
Dayton *(G-5684)*

◆ Crane Plumbing LLC.......................... A 419 522-4211
Mansfield *(G-8778)*

East Woodworking Company................. G 216 791-5950
Cleveland *(G-3649)*

◆ Mansfield Plumbing Pdts LLC............. A 419 938-5211
Perrysville *(G-11282)*

Watersource LLC................................ G 419 747-9552
Mansfield *(G-8864)*

3262 Vitreous china table and kitchenware

Americana Glass Co Inc....................... F 330 938-6135
Sebring *(G-11890)*

Libbey Glass LLC................................ D 419 727-2211
Toledo *(G-13034)*

▼ Libbey Inc...................................... C 419 325-2100
Toledo *(G-13035)*

◆ The China Hall Company.................... C 330 385-2900
East Liverpool *(G-6398)*

▲ Warrior Imports Inc.......................... E 954 935-5536
Youngstown *(G-14966)*

3263 Semivitreous table and kitchenware

Modern China Company Inc.................. E 330 938-6104
Sebring *(G-11898)*

3264 Porcelain electrical supplies

▲ Akron Porcelain & Plastics Co........... C 330 745-2159
Akron *(G-39)*

CAM-Lem Inc...................................... G 216 391-7750
Cleveland *(G-3461)*

▲ Channel Products Inc........................ D 440 423-0113
Solon *(G-12093)*

▲ Electrodyne Company Inc.................. F 513 732-2822
Batavia *(G-862)*

Ethima Inc.. D 419 626-4912
Sandusky *(G-11834)*

Fram Group Operations LLC................. E 419 436-5827
Fostoria *(G-6983)*

▲ Materion Brush Inc........................... D 216 486-4200
Mayfield Heights *(G-9336)*

▲ Newell - Psn LLC............................. G 304 387-2700
Columbiana *(G-4623)*

Petro Ware Inc.................................... G 740 982-1302
Crooksville *(G-5512)*

Vibrantz Corporation........................... C 216 875-6213
Cleveland *(G-4468)*

Weldco Inc... E 513 744-9353
Cincinnati *(G-3218)*

3269 Pottery products, nec

All Fired Up Pnt Your Own Pot.............. G 330 865-5858
Copley *(G-5429)*

Beaumont Bros Stoneware Inc.............. E 740 982-0055
Crooksville *(G-5508)*

Benzle Porcelain Company................... G 614 876-2159
Hilliard *(G-7676)*

Bodycote Imt Inc................................ F 740 852-5000
London *(G-8531)*

Brittany Stamping LLC......................... A 216 267-0850
Cleveland *(G-3440)*

Carruth Studio Inc.............................. F 419 878-3060
Waterville *(G-13831)*

▲ Clay Burley Products Co................... E 740 452-3633
Roseville *(G-11653)*

◆ E R Advanced Ceramics Inc.............. E 330 426-9433
East Palestine *(G-6402)*

Javanation.. F 419 584-1705
Celina *(G-2111)*

▼ Orton Edward Jr Crmic Fndation........ E 614 895-2663
Westerville *(G-14226)*

Strictly Stitchery Inc.......................... F 440 543-7128
Cleveland *(G-4335)*

W C Bunting Co Inc............................. G 330 385-2050
East Liverpool *(G-6399)*

Yellow Springs Pottery LLC................. F 937 767-1666
Yellow Springs *(G-14793)*

3271 Concrete block and brick

American Concrete Products Inc............ G 937 224-1433
Dayton *(G-5652)*

S
I
C

Beazer East Inc.................................F 740 474-3169
Circleville (G-3248)

Belden Brick Company LLC...................D 330 456-0031
Sugarcreek (G-12632)

Belden Brick Company LLC...................D 330 265-2030
Sugarcreek (G-12633)

Benchmark Land Management LLC......G 513 310-7850
West Chester (G-13949)

Cantelli Block and Brick Inc..................E 419 433-0102
Sandusky (G-11826)

Cement Products Inc..........................G 419 524-4342
Mansfield (G-8772)

Charles Svec Inc...............................E 216 662-5200
Maple Heights (G-8879)

Dearth Resources Inc.........................G 937 663-4171
Springfield (G-12299)

Dearth Resources Inc.........................G 937 325-0651
Springfield (G-12298)

E C S Corp.......................................G 440 323-1707
Elyria (G-6524)

Green Impressions LLC.......................D 440 240-8508
Sheffield Village (G-11958)

Green Vision Materials Inc...................F 440 564-5500
Newbury (G-10552)

Hazelbaker Industries Ltd....................G
Columbus (G-4973)

ICC Safety Service Inc........................G 614 261-4557
Columbus (G-4998)

Koltcz Concrete Block Co.....................E 440 232-3630
Bedford (G-1042)

▲ Meridienne International Inc...............G 330 274-8317
Aurora (G-679)

Midwest Specialties Inc.......................D 800 837-2503
Wapakoneta (G-13725)

National Lime and Stone Co..................F 614 497-0083
Lockbourne (G-8491)

North Central Con Designs Inc..............G 419 606-1908
Wooster (G-14669)

Oberfields LLC...................................F 614 252-0955
Columbus (G-5137)

▲ Osborne Inc...................................E 440 942-7000
Mentor (G-9578)

Portsmouth Block Inc..........................F 740 353-4113
Portsmouth (G-11474)

Prairie Builders Supply Inc...................G 419 332-7546
Fremont (G-7127)

Quality Block & Supply Inc...................E 330 364-4411
Mount Eaton (G-10208)

R W Sidley Incorporated......................E 440 564-2221
Newbury (G-10561)

RE Connors Construction Ltd................G 740 644-0261
Thornville (G-12767)

▲ Reading Rock Incorporated...............D 513 874-2345
Cincinnati (G-3034)

Ready Field Solutions LLC....................E 330 562-0550
Streetsboro (G-12520)

S & S Aggregates Inc..........................F 740 453-0721
Zanesville (G-15046)

Snyder Concrete Products Inc..............G 937 224-1433
Dayton (G-6011)

Snyder Concrete Products Inc..............G 937 339-7577
Troy (G-13257)

▲ Snyder Concrete Products Inc...........E 937 885-5176
Moraine (G-10192)

St Henry Tile Co Inc...........................G 937 548-1101
Greenville (G-7355)

St Henry Tile Co Inc...........................E 419 678-4841
Saint Henry (G-11724)

Stiger Pre Cast Inc.............................G 740 482-2313
Nevada (G-10324)

Stocker Concrete Company..................F 740 254-4626
Gnadenhutten (G-7293)

Stocker Sand & Gravel Co....................F 740 254-4635
Gnadenhutten (G-7294)

Sunny Brook Prest Concrete Co.............G 330 673-7667
Kent (G-8084)

The Ideal Builders Supply....................F 216 741-1600
Cleveland (G-4386)

Tri-County Block and Brick Inc..............E 419 826-7060
Swanton (G-12696)

Triple A Builders Inc...........................G 216 249-0327
Cleveland (G-4428)

Trumbull Cement Products Co...............G 330 372-4342
Warren (G-13802)

Tyjen Inc..G 740 797-4064
The Plains (G-12760)

William Dauch Concrete Company.........F 419 668-4458
Norwalk (G-10863)

3272 Concrete products, nec

9/10 Castings Inc...............................G 216 406-8907
Chardon (G-2196)

A L D Precast Corp.............................G 614 449-3366
Columbus (G-4656)

◆ Aco Inc...E 440 639-7230
Mentor (G-9468)

Agean Marble Manufacturing Inc...........G 513 874-1475
West Chester (G-14099)

Akron Vault Company Inc.....................F 330 784-5475
Akron (G-46)

Alexander Wilbert Vault Co...................G 419 468-3477
Galion (G-7177)

Allen Enterprises Inc..........................E 740 532-5913
Ironton (G-7928)

▲ American Spring Wire Corp...............C 216 292-4620
Bedford Heights (G-1068)

Ash Sewer & Drain Service...................G 330 376-9714
Akron (G-61)

Babbert Real Estate Inv Co Ltd.............D 614 837-8444
Canal Winchester (G-1785)

▲ Baswa Acoustics North Amer LLC......F 216 475-7197
Bedford (G-1014)

Baxter Burial Vault Svc Inc...................F 513 641-1010
Cincinnati (G-2403)

Baxter Holdings Inc............................G 513 860-3593
Hamilton (G-7469)

Bell Vault and Monu Works Inc..............F 937 866-2444
Miamisburg (G-9668)

Bilco Company..................................E 740 455-9020
Zanesville (G-14995)

Carey Precast Concrete Company..........G 419 396-7142
Carey (G-2057)

Carruth Studio Inc.............................F 419 878-3060
Waterville (G-13831)

Cement Products Inc..........................E 419 524-4342
Mansfield (G-8772)

Charles Svec Inc...............................E 216 662-5200
Maple Heights (G-8879)

Clark Grave Vault Company...................C 614 294-3761
Columbus (G-4809)

Columbus Art Memorial Inc...................G 614 221-9333
Columbus (G-4818)

Complete Cylinder Service Inc...............G 513 772-1500
Cincinnati (G-2506)

Contech Bridge Solutions LLC...............F 937 878-2170
Dayton (G-5710)

DCA Construction Products LLC.............E 330 527-4308
Garrettsville (G-7217)

Dennis Constuction Sanitation...............G 419 332-8026
Fremont (G-7104)

Dm2018 LLC.....................................G 513 893-5483
Liberty Twp (G-8382)

E A Cox Inc.......................................G 740 858-4400
Lucasville (G-8666)

E C Babbert Inc.................................D 614 837-8444
Canal Winchester (G-1789)

E C S Corp.......................................G 440 323-1707
Elyria (G-6524)

E Pompili Sons Inc.............................G 216 581-8080
Cleveland (G-3645)

Eldorado Stone LLC............................E 330 698-3931
Apple Creek (G-467)

Encore Precast LLC............................D 513 726-5678
Seven Mile (G-11907)

◆ Euclid Chemical Company..................E 800 321-7628
Cleveland (G-3688)

Fabcon Companies LLC.......................D 614 875-8601
Grove City (G-7386)

▲ Fibreboard Corporation.....................C 419 248-8000
Toledo (G-12963)

◆ Fin Pan Inc....................................F 513 870-9200
Hamilton (G-7490)

Fort Stben Burial Estates Assn..............G 740 266-6101
Steubenville (G-12403)

Forterra Pipe & Precast LLC.................F 614 445-3830
Columbus (G-4933)

Forterra Pipe & Precast LLC.................E 330 467-7890
Macedonia (G-8691)

Fountain Specialists Inc.......................G 513 831-5717
Milford (G-9934)

Gdy Installations Inc...........................F 419 467-0036
Toledo (G-12973)

Growco Inc..G 419 886-4628
Mansfield (G-8799)

Haviland Culvert Company....................G 419 622-6951
Haviland (G-7588)

Hazelbaker Industries Ltd....................G
Columbus (G-4973)

High Concrete Group LLC.....................B 937 748-2412
Springboro (G-12255)

Hilltop Basic Resources Inc...................C 513 621-1500
Cincinnati (G-2723)

Huron Cement Products Company..........E 419 433-4161
Huron (G-7874)

J K Precast LLC.................................G 740 335-2188
Wshngtn Ct Hs (G-14741)

Jackson Monument Inc........................G 740 286-1590
Jackson (G-7946)

▲ Jet Stream International Inc...............D 330 505-9988
Hubbard (G-7813)

K-Mar Structures LLC..........................E 231 924-5777
Junction City (G-8002)

KSA Limited Partnership.......................G 740 776-3238
Portsmouth (G-11468)

Landon Vault Company........................F 614 443-5505
Columbus (G-5063)

▲ Lang Stone Company Inc..................E 614 235-4099
Columbus (G-5064)

▼ Lindsay Precast LLC........................E 800 837-7788
Canal Fulton (G-1777)

◆ Ludowici Roof Tile Inc......................D 740 342-1995
New Lexington (G-10404)

M B K Inc...F 330 889-3451
Bristolville (G-1498)

Mack Concrete Industries Inc................F 330 483-3111
Valley City (G-13503)

Mack Industries.................................F 419 353-7081
Bowling Green (G-1427)

Mack Industries Inc............................F 740 393-1121
Mount Vernon (G-10249)

Mack Industries PA Inc........................D 330 638-7680
Vienna (G-13613)

Mack Industries PA Inc........................D 330 483-3111
Valley City (G-13504)

McGill Septic Tank Co..........................G 330 876-2171
Kinsman (G-8141)

Michaels Pre-Cast Con Pdts Inc............ F 513 683-1292
   Loveland (G-8643)

Neher Burial Vault Company................... G 937 399-4494
   Springfield (G-12357)

Next Surface Inc..................................... D 440 576-0194
   Jefferson (G-7979)

North American Cast Stone Inc............. G 440 286-1999
   Chardon (G-2216)

Northern Concrete Pipe Inc.................... F 419 841-3361
   Sylvania (G-12720)

▲ Norwalk Concrete Inds Inc .... E 419 668-8167
   Norwalk (G-10856)

Oberfields LLC.. F 614 252-0955
   Columbus (G-5137)

Oberfields LLC.. G 937 885-3711
   Dayton (G-5920)

Oberfields LLC.. E 740 369-7644
   Sunbury (G-12670)

Oberfields LLC.. D 740 369-7644
   Delaware (G-6165)

Occv1 Inc... G 419 248-8000
   Toledo (G-13069)

OK Brugmann Jr & Sons Inc................. G 330 274-2106
   Mantua (G-8873)

Oldcastle Apg Midwest Inc .... E 440 949-1815
   Sheffield Village (G-11961)

Oldcastle Infrastructure Inc.................. E 419 592-2309
   Napoleon (G-10294)

Olde Wood Ltd... E 330 866-1441
   Magnolia (G-8735)

One Wish LLC... F 800 505-6883
   Bedford (G-1052)

Orrville Trucking & Grading Co............. G 330 682-4010
   Orrville (G-11000)

Parksite Inc.. G 330 455-3782
   Louisville (G-8612)

Pavestone LLC.. D 513 474-3783
   Cincinnati (G-2948)

Pawnee Maintenance Inc........................ G 740 373-6861
   Marietta (G-8935)

Premere Precast Products...................... G 740 533-3333
   Ironton (G-7933)

Premiere Con Solutions LLC.................. F 419 737-9808
   Pioneer (G-11326)

Prestress Services Inds LLC.................. C 859 299-0461
   Grove City (G-7409)

Quaker City Concrete Pdts LLC............ G 330 427-2239
   Leetonia (G-8305)

Quikrete Companies LLC......................... D 614 885-4406
   Columbus (G-5220)

Quikrete Companies LLC......................... E 513 367-6135
   Harrison (G-7564)

Quikrete Companies LLC......................... E 330 296-6080
   Ravenna (G-11536)

Quikrete Companies LLC......................... F 419 241-1148
   Toledo (G-13106)

R & C Monument Company LLC............ G 216 297-5444
   Maple Heights (G-8890)

R W Sidley Incorporated........................ E 440 564-2221
   Newbury (G-10561)

R W Sidley Incorporated........................ C 440 298-3232
   Thompson (G-12763)

Riley Creek Holdings Inc....................... E 419 358-6946
   Bluffton (G-1364)

Rock Decor Company............................. E 330 830-9760
   Apple Creek (G-477)

Rocla Concrete Tie Inc.......................... E 740 776-3238
   Portsmouth (G-11475)

Russell Cast Stone Inc.......................... D 856 753-4000
   West Chester (G-14142)

S & S Aggregates Inc............................ F 740 453-0721
   Zanesville (G-15046)

Seislove Vault & Septic Tanks.............. G 419 447-5473
   Tiffin (G-12798)

Septic Products Inc................................ G 419 282-5933
   Ashland (G-573)

Smith Concrete Co................................. E 740 373-7441
   Dover (G-6262)

Snyder Concrete Products Inc.............. G 937 339-7577
   Troy (G-13257)

▲ Snyder Concrete Products Inc.......... E 937 885-5176
   Moraine (G-10192)

Southern Ohio Vault Co Inc................... G 740 456-5898
   Portsmouth (G-11478)

Spoerr Precast Concrete Inc................. F 419 625-9132
   Sandusky (G-11872)

St Henry Tile Co Inc.............................. G 937 548-1101
   Greenville (G-7355)

Star Manufacturing LLC......................... C 330 740-8300
   Youngstown (G-14940)

Stiger Pre Cast Inc................................ G 740 482-2313
   Nevada (G-10324)

Stuart Burial Vault Co Inc...................... F 740 569-4158
   Bremen (G-1487)

▼ Superior Walls of Ohio Inc................ D 330 393-4101
   Warren (G-13799)

Tamarron Technology Inc....................... F 800 277-3207
   Cincinnati (G-3136)

Toli Vault... G 866 998-8654
   Westlake (G-14341)

Tri County Concrete Inc......................... F 330 425-4464
   Twinsburg (G-13386)

Turner Vault Co...................................... E 419 537-1133
   Northwood (G-10812)

Uniontown Septic Tanks Inc.................. F 330 699-3386
   Uniontown (G-13428)

United Precast Inc.................................. C 740 393-1121
   Mount Vernon (G-10267)

◆ United Refractories Inc...................... E 330 372-3716
   Warren (G-13807)

Wauseon Silo & Coal Company.............. F
   Wauseon (G-13861)

Whempys Corp.. G 614 888-6670
   Worthington (G-14729)

William Dauch Concrete Company........ F 419 668-4458
   Norwalk (G-10863)

Wyandot Dolomite Inc............................ E 419 396-7641
   Carey (G-2064)

Youngstown Burial Vault Co................... G 330 782-0015
   Girard (G-7282)

3273 Ready-mixed concrete

Ace Ready Mix Concrete Co Inc............ F 330 745-8125
   Norton (G-10817)

Adams Bros Concrete Pdts Ltd............. E 740 452-7566
   Zanesville (G-14982)

Adams Brothers Inc................................ G 740 819-0323
   Zanesville (G-14983)

Alexis Concrete Enterprise Inc............. G 440 366-0031
   Elyria (G-6494)

Allega Concrete Corp............................. E 216 447-0814
   Richfield (G-11587)

Anderson Concrete Corp........................ C 614 443-0123
   Columbus (G-4716)

Associated Associates Inc..................... E 330 626-3300
   Mantua (G-8867)

Baird Concrete Products Inc................. F 740 623-8600
   Coshocton (G-5451)

Baker-Shindler Contracting Co.............. E 419 782-5080
   Defiance (G-6100)

Barrett Paving Materials Inc.................. F 937 293-9033
   Moraine (G-10148)

Beazer East Inc...................................... F 740 474-3169
   Circleville (G-3248)

Beazer East Inc...................................... E 937 364-2311
   Hillsboro (G-7714)

Beazer East Inc...................................... F 740 947-4677
   Waverly (G-13863)

Bhi Transition Inc................................... E 937 663-4152
   Saint Paris (G-11756)

Brock Corporation.................................. G 440 235-1806
   Olmsted Falls (G-10939)

Buckeye Ready Mix Concrete................ G 330 798-5511
   Akron (G-85)

Buckeye Ready-Mix LLC........................ E 740 967-4801
   Johnstown (G-7993)

Buckeye Ready-Mix LLC........................ G 614 879-6316
   West Jefferson (G-14160)

Buckeye Ready-Mix LLC........................ E 740 654-4423
   Lancaster (G-8182)

Buckeye Ready-Mix LLC........................ F 937 642-2951
   Marysville (G-9015)

Buckeye Ready-Mix LLC........................ G 614 575-2132
   Reynoldsburg (G-11561)

C F Poeppelman Inc............................... E 937 448-2191
   Bradford (G-1451)

Caldwell Lumber & Supply Co.............. F 740 732-2306
   Caldwell (G-1724)

Camden Ready Mix Co........................... G 937 456-4539
   Camden (G-1767)

Carr Bros Inc.. E 440 232-3700
   Bedford (G-1020)

Carr Bros Bldrs Sup & Coal Co............ E 440 232-3700
   Cleveland (G-3471)

Castalia Trenching & Rdymx LLC.......... F 419 684-5502
   Castalia (G-2094)

Castalia Trenching & Ready Mix........... F 419 684-5502
   Castalia (G-2095)

Cemco Construction Corporation.......... G 440 567-7708
   Concord Township (G-5388)

Cement Products Inc.............................. E 419 524-4342
   Mansfield (G-8772)

Cemex Cement Inc.................................. C 937 873-9858
   Fairborn (G-6688)

Cemex Materials LLC............................. C 330 654-2501
   Diamond (G-6226)

Center Concrete Inc............................... G 419 782-2495
   Defiance (G-6102)

Center Concrete Inc............................... F 800 453-4224
   Edgerton (G-6465)

Central Ready Mix LLC.......................... E 513 402-5001
   Cincinnati (G-2461)

Central Ready-Mix of Ohio LLC............ G 614 252-3452
   Cincinnati (G-2452)

Chappell-Zimmerman Inc....................... F 330 337-8711
   Salem (G-11769)

Cioffi Holdings LLC................................ G 330 794-9448
   Akron (G-101)

City Concrete LLc................................... F 330 743-2825
   Youngstown (G-14835)

Citywide Materials Inc............................ E 513 533-1111
   Cincinnati (G-2496)

Collinwood Shale Brick Sup Co............ E 216 587-2700
   Cleveland (G-3545)

Consumeracq Inc.................................... E 440 277-9305
   Lorain (G-8552)

Consumers Builders Supply Co............ G 440 277-9306
   Lorain (G-8553)

D G M Inc... F 740 286-2131
   Jackson (G-7943)

D W Dickey and Son Inc....................... C 330 424-1441
   Lisbon (G-8466)

Dearth Resources Inc............................ G 937 663-4171
   Springfield (G-12299)

Dearth Resources Inc............................ G 937 325-0651
   Springfield (G-12298)

S
I
C

Diano Construction and Sup Co	F 330 456-7229	**IMI Real Estate LLC**	G 513 769-3666
Canton *(G-1881)*		Cincinnati *(G-2740)*	
Ellis Brothers Inc Upg	F 740 397-9191	**IMI Real Estate LLC**	F 513 844-8444
Mount Vernon *(G-10244)*		Hamilton *(G-7504)*	
Elyria Concrete Inc	F 440 322-2750	**Integrated Resources Inc**	E 419 885-7122
Elyria *(G-6528)*		Sylvania *(G-12713)*	
Ernst Enterprises Inc	E 937 848-6811	**Ioppolo Concrete Corporation**	G 440 439-6606
Bellbrook *(G-1091)*		Bedford *(G-1040)*	
Ernst Enterprises Inc	F 937 866-9441	**K & L Ready Mix Inc**	F 419 293-2937
Carrollton *(G-2082)*		Mc Comb *(G-9354)*	
Ernst Enterprises Inc	G 513 367-1939	**K & L Ready Mix Inc**	F 419 523-4376
Cleves *(G-4536)*		Ottawa *(G-11037)*	
Ernst Enterprises Inc	F 614 308-0063	**Kuhlman Corporation**	E 330 724-9900
Columbus *(G-4907)*		Coventry Township *(G-5485)*	
Ernst Enterprises Inc	F 614 308-0063	**Kuhlman Corporation**	F 419 321-1670
Columbus *(G-4908)*		Toledo *(G-13022)*	
Ernst Enterprises Inc	E 614 443-9456	▲ **Kuhlman Corporation**	E 419 897-6000
Columbus *(G-4909)*		Maumee *(G-9303)*	
Ernst Enterprises Inc	F 937 878-9378	**Lancaster W Side Coal Co Inc**	F 740 862-4713
Fairborn *(G-6690)*		Lancaster *(G-8207)*	
Ernst Enterprises Inc	E 513 829-8683	**Lexington Concrete & Sup Inc**	G 419 529-3232
Fairfield *(G-6733)*		Mansfield *(G-8813)*	
Ernst Enterprises Inc	E 513 874-8300	**M & B Asphalt Company Inc**	G 419 992-4236
Lebanon *(G-8254)*		Old Fort *(G-10934)*	
Ernst Enterprises Inc	F 513 422-3651	**M & R Redi Mix Inc**	E 419 445-7771
Middletown *(G-9857)*		Pettisville *(G-11284)*	
Ernst Enterprises Inc	F 937 339-6249	**M B K Inc**	F 330 889-3451
Troy *(G-13212)*		Bristolville *(G-1498)*	
Ernst Enterprises Inc	F 937 233-7777	**Mack Concrete Industries Inc**	E 330 784-7008
West Milton *(G-14182)*		Akron *(G-219)*	
Ernst Enterprises Inc	E 937 233-5555	**Market Ready**	G 513 289-9231
Vandalia *(G-13556)*		Maineville *(G-8741)*	
EZ Concrete Supply LLC	G 844 393-7699	**McClelland Inc**	E 740 452-3036
Lima *(G-8407)*		Zanesville *(G-15027)*	
Fairborn Cement Plant	G 937 879-8466	**McGovney Ready Mix Inc**	G 740 353-4111
Fairborn *(G-6691)*		Portsmouth *(G-11469)*	
Feikert Sand & Gravel Co Inc	E 330 674-0038	**Medina Supply Company**	G 440 234-1321
Millersburg *(G-9980)*		Berea *(G-1181)*	
G Big Inc	F 740 867-5758	**Medina Supply Company**	D 330 425-0752
Chesapeake *(G-2229)*		Twinsburg *(G-13338)*	
Geauga Concrete Inc	F 440 338-4915	**Medina Supply Company**	E 330 723-3681
Newbury *(G-10551)*		Medina *(G-9426)*	
Grafton Ready Mix Concret Inc	C 440 926-2911	**Moritz Concrete Inc**	E 419 529-3232
Grafton *(G-7303)*		Mansfield *(G-8832)*	
Heidelberg Materials Us Inc	E 937 587-2671	**Moritz Materials Inc**	E 419 281-0575
Peebles *(G-11169)*		Ashland *(G-553)*	
Heidelberg Materials Us Inc	F 937 442-6009	**Moritz Ready Mix Inc**	E 419 253-0001
Winchester *(G-14598)*		Marengo *(G-8898)*	
Heidelberg Mtls US Cem LLC	F 330 499-9100	**National Lime and Stone Co**	E 419 423-3400
Middlebranch *(G-9765)*		Findlay *(G-6897)*	
Heidelberg Mtls US Cem LLC	G 972 653-5500	**OK Brugmann Jr & Sons Inc**	G 330 274-2106
Sylvania *(G-12709)*		Mantua *(G-8873)*	
Hilltop Basic Resources Inc	F 937 795-2020	**Olen Corporation**	F 419 294-2611
Aberdeen *(G-1)*		Upper Sandusky *(G-13451)*	
Hilltop Basic Resources Inc	E 513 242-8400	**Orrville Trucking & Grading Co**	E 330 682-4010
Cincinnati *(G-2722)*		Orrville *(G-11000)*	
Hilltop Basic Resources Inc	C 513 621-1500	**Osborne Inc**	F 440 232-1440
Cincinnati *(G-2723)*		Cleveland *(G-4125)*	
Hilltop Big Bend Quarry LLC	F 513 651-5000	▲ **Osborne Inc**	E 440 942-7000
Cincinnati *(G-2724)*		Mentor *(G-9578)*	
Hocking Valley Concrete Inc	G 740 592-5335	**Osborne Co**	G 440 942-7000
Athens *(G-642)*		Mentor *(G-9579)*	
Hocking Valley Concrete Inc	G 740 342-1948	**Pahl Ready Mix Concrete Inc**	F 419 636-4238
New Lexington *(G-10402)*		Bryan *(G-1657)*	
Hocking Valley Concrete Inc	F 740 385-2165	**Palmer Bros Transit Mix Con**	F 419 686-2366
Logan *(G-8516)*		Portage *(G-11460)*	
Hull Ready Mix Concrete Inc	F 419 625-8070	**Palmer Bros Transit Mix Con**	F 419 352-4681
Sandusky *(G-11839)*		Bowling Green *(G-1433)*	
Huron Cement Products Company	E 419 433-4161	**Paul R Lipp & Son Inc**	F 330 227-9614
Huron *(G-7874)*		Rogers *(G-11642)*	
Huth Ready Mix & Supply Co	G 330 833-4191	**Placecrete Inc**	G 937 298-2121
Massillon *(G-9203)*		Moraine *(G-10184)*	

Pleasant Valley Ready Mix Inc	F 330 852-2613
Sugarcreek *(G-12645)*	
Quality Block & Supply Inc	E 330 364-4411
Mount Eaton *(G-10208)*	
Quality Ready Mix Inc	F 419 394-8870
Saint Marys *(G-11750)*	
Quikrete Companies LLC	E 513 367-6135
Harrison *(G-7564)*	
Quikrete Companies LLC	E 330 296-6080
Ravenna *(G-11536)*	
R W Sidley Inc	G 440 224-2664
Marietta *(G-8939)*	
R W Sidley Incorporated	E 330 499-5616
Canton *(G-1990)*	
R W Sidley Incorporated	E 440 564-2221
Newbury *(G-10561)*	
R W Sidley Incorporated	D 440 298-3232
Thompson *(G-12762)*	
R W Sidley Incorporated	E 330 392-2721
Warren *(G-13792)*	
R W Sidley Incorporated	E 330 793-7374
Youngstown *(G-14923)*	
Reliable Ready Mix Co	E 330 453-8266
Canton *(G-1993)*	
Rock Away Capital Inc	E 216 432-9465
Cleveland *(G-4246)*	
Ross-Co Redi-Mix Co Inc	F 740 775-4466
Chillicothe *(G-2280)*	
S J Roth Enterprises Inc	D 513 543-1140
Cincinnati *(G-3059)*	
Sakrete Inc	E 513 242-3644
Cincinnati *(G-3060)*	
Sardinia Concrete Company	E 513 248-0090
Milford *(G-9951)*	
Sardinia Ready Mix Inc	E 937 446-2523
Sardinia *(G-11886)*	
Schwab Industries Inc	F 330 364-4411
Dover *(G-6261)*	
Scioto Ready Mix LLC	D 740 924-9273
Pataskala *(G-11150)*	
Shamrock Materials Inc	F 513 988-0647
Cincinnati *(G-3086)*	
Shelly Materials Inc	E 740 775-4567
Chillicothe *(G-2281)*	
Shelly Materials Inc	E 614 871-6704
Grove City *(G-7413)*	
Shelly Materials Inc	F 330 723-3681
Medina *(G-9448)*	
Shelly Materials Inc	G 937 325-7386
Springfield *(G-12372)*	
Shelly Materials Inc	F 330 963-5180
Twinsburg *(G-13378)*	
Sidwell Materials Inc	F 740 968-4313
Saint Clairsville *(G-11710)*	
Small Sand & Gravel Inc	E 740 427-3130
Gambier *(G-7212)*	
Smalls Inc	F 740 427-3633
Gambier *(G-7213)*	
Smith Concrete	F 740 439-7714
Cambridge *(G-1759)*	
Smith Concrete Co	G 740 593-5633
Athens *(G-652)*	
Smith Concrete Co	E 740 373-7441
Dover *(G-6262)*	
Smyrna Ready Mix Concrete LLC	D 937 855-0410
Germantown *(G-7254)*	
Smyrna Ready Mix Concrete LLC	D 937 773-0841
Piqua *(G-11385)*	
Smyrna Ready Mix Concrete LLC	C 937 698-7229
Vandalia *(G-13578)*	
Spurlino Materials LLC	G 513 202-1111
Cleves *(G-4548)*	

Spurlino Materials LLC.................... E 513 705-0111
Middletown *(G-9894)*

St Henry Tile Co Inc.................... E 419 678-4841
Saint Henry *(G-11724)*

Stamm Contracting Company Inc.......... F 330 274-8230
Mantua *(G-8875)*

Stocker Concrete Company.............. F 740 254-4626
Gnadenhutten *(G-7293)*

T C Redi Mix Youngstown Inc............ E 330 755-2143
Youngstown *(G-14942)*

Tech Ready Mix Inc.................... E 216 361-5000
Cleveland *(G-4369)*

▲ Terminal Ready-Mix Inc.............. E 440 288-0181
Lorain *(G-8583)*

The National Lime and Stone Company. E 419 422-4341
Findlay *(G-6927)*

Tri County Concrete Inc................ F 330 425-4464
Cleveland *(G-4417)*

Tri County Concrete Inc................ F 330 425-4464
Twinsburg *(G-13386)*

Turner Concrete Products.............. G 419 662-9007
Northwood *(G-10811)*

Twin Cities Concrete Co............... B 330 627-2158
Carrollton *(G-2091)*

Twin Cities Concrete Co............... F 330 343-4491
Dover *(G-6266)*

United Ready Mix Inc.................. G 216 696-1600
Cleveland *(G-4444)*

W M Dauch Concrete Inc................ G 419 562-6917
Bucyrus *(G-1695)*

Walden Industries Inc................. E 740 633-5971
Tiltonsville *(G-12810)*

Warren Concrete and Supply Co......... G 330 393-1581
Warren *(G-13810)*

Weber Ready Mix Inc.................. E 419 394-9097
Saint Marys *(G-11754)*

Wells Group LLC...................... F 740 532-9240
Ironton *(G-7937)*

Westview Concrete Corp............... F 440 458-5800
Elyria *(G-6602)*

Westview Concrete Corp............... E 440 235-1800
Olmsted Falls *(G-10943)*

William Dauch Concrete Company........ F 419 562-6917
Bucyrus *(G-1696)*

William Dauch Concrete Company........ F 419 668-4458
Norwalk *(G-10863)*

Williams Concrete Inc................. E 419 893-3251
Maumee *(G-9330)*

Winters Products Inc................. F 740 286-4149
Jackson *(G-7956)*

3274 Lime

Ayers Limestone Quarry Inc............ F 740 633-2958
Martins Ferry *(G-9009)*

Bluffton Stone Co..................... F 419 358-6941
Bluffton *(G-1358)*

▼ Graymont Dolime (oh) Inc........... D 419 855-8682
Genoa *(G-7247)*

Mineral Processing Company........... G 419 396-3501
Carey *(G-2059)*

National Lime and Stone Co........... E 419 396-7671
Carey *(G-2060)*

Piqua Materials Inc................... D 937 773-4824
Piqua *(G-11377)*

Shelly Materials Inc.................. E 740 666-5841
Ostrander *(G-11029)*

Sugarcreek Lime Service.............. G 330 364-4460
Dover *(G-6264)*

3275 Gypsum products

Caraustar Industries Inc.............. E 330 665-7700
Copley *(G-5432)*

Ernst Enterprises Inc................. F 419 222-2015
Lima *(G-8406)*

Mineral Processing Company........... G 419 396-3501
Carey *(G-2059)*

Next Sales LLC....................... F 330 704-4126
Dover *(G-6255)*

Owens Corning Sales LLC.............. C 330 634-0460
Tallmadge *(G-12744)*

Priest Services Inc.................. G 440 333-1123
Mayfield Heights *(G-9340)*

United States Gypsum Company......... B 419 734-3161
Gypsum *(G-7460)*

Wall Technology Inc.................. G 715 532-5548
Toledo *(G-13176)*

3281 Cut stone and stone products

1914 Mi Inc.......................... E 330 308-8667
New Philadelphia *(G-10428)*

Accent Manufacturing Inc............. F 330 724-7704
Akron *(G-13)*

Accent Manufacturing Inc............. F 330 724-7704
Norton *(G-10816)*

Agean Marble Manufacturing Inc....... G 513 874-1475
West Chester *(G-14099)*

Al-Co Products Inc................... G 419 399-3867
Latty *(G-8236)*

As America Inc....................... D 419 522-4211
Mansfield *(G-8763)*

Beazer East Inc...................... E 937 364-2311
Hillsboro *(G-7714)*

Bell Vault and Monu Works Inc........ F 937 866-2444
Miamisburg *(G-9668)*

Blu Bird LLC......................... G 513 271-5646
Cincinnati *(G-2413)*

Blu Bird LLC......................... G 614 276-3585
Columbus *(G-4766)*

Briar Hill Stone Co Inc.............. D 216 377-5100
Glenmont *(G-7284)*

Cardinal Aggregate Inc............... F 419 872-4380
Perrysburg *(G-11209)*

▲ Castelli Marble LLC............... G 216 361-1222
Cleveland *(G-3477)*

Classic Stone Company Inc............ F 614 833-3946
Columbus *(G-4810)*

Creative Countertops Ohio Inc........ F 937 540-9450
Englewood *(G-6610)*

◆ Cutting Edge Countertops Inc...... E 419 873-9500
Perrysburg *(G-11212)*

▲ Distinctive Marble & Gran Inc..... F 614 760-0003
Plain City *(G-11404)*

▲ Dutch Quality Stone Inc........... D 877 359-7866
Mount Eaton *(G-10206)*

Engineered Marble Inc................ G 614 308-0041
Columbus *(G-4902)*

Jalco Industries Inc................. F 740 286-3808
Jackson *(G-7947)*

Kellstone Inc........................ E 419 746-2396
Kelleys Island *(G-8009)*

▲ Lang Stone Company Inc........... E 614 235-4099
Columbus *(G-5064)*

Lima Millwork Inc.................... G 419 331-3303
Elida *(G-6483)*

Maple Grove Materials Inc............ F 419 992-4235
Tiffin *(G-12790)*

Maumee Valley Memorials Inc.......... F 419 878-9030
Waterville *(G-13839)*

Medina Supply Company................ E 330 723-3681
Medina *(G-9426)*

Melvin Stone Co LLC.................. F 513 771-0820
Cincinnati *(G-2862)*

◆ Michael Kaufman Companies Inc..... F 330 673-4881
Kent *(G-8053)*

National Lime and Stone Co........... E 419 562-0771
Bucyrus *(G-1684)*

National Lime and Stone Co........... E 419 396-7671
Carey *(G-2060)*

National Lime and Stone Co........... G 419 657-6745
Wapakoneta *(G-13726)*

North Hill Marble & Granite Co....... F 330 253-2179
Akron *(G-249)*

Ohio Beauty Cut Stone II Inc......... G 330 644-2241
Akron *(G-251)*

▲ Ohio Tile & Marble Co............. E 513 541-4211
Cincinnati *(G-2926)*

Pavestone LLC........................ D 513 474-3783
Cincinnati *(G-2948)*

Pietra Naturale Inc.................. F 937 438-8882
Dayton *(G-5940)*

Piqua Granite & Marble Co Inc........ G 937 773-2000
Piqua *(G-11376)*

▲ Quarrymasters Inc................. G 330 612-0474
Akron *(G-274)*

Riceland Cabinet Inc................. D 330 601-1071
Wooster *(G-14676)*

Shelly Materials Inc................. G 937 358-2224
West Mansfield *(G-14181)*

Sims-Lohman Inc...................... D 440 799-8285
Brooklyn Heights *(G-1540)*

Solid Surface Concepts Inc........... E 513 948-8677
Cincinnati *(G-3099)*

▲ Take It For Granite LLC........... F 513 735-0555
Cincinnati *(G-2316)*

▲ Terra Surfaces LLC............... G 937 836-1900
Dayton *(G-6044)*

Toledo Cut Stone Inc................. F 419 531-1623
Toledo *(G-13150)*

Transtar Holding Company LLC......... G 800 359-3339
Walton Hills *(G-13703)*

Waller Brothers Stone Company........ F 740 858-1948
Mc Dermott *(G-9356)*

Western Ohio Cut Stone Ltd........... F 937 492-4722
Sidney *(G-12061)*

Zelaya Stoneworks LLC................ F 513 777-8030
Liberty Township *(G-8380)*

3291 Abrasive products

Abrasive Products.................... G 513 502-9150
Cincinnati *(G-2335)*

Abrasive Source Inc.................. F 937 526-9753
Russia *(C-11672)*

▲ Abrasive Supply Company Inc....... F 330 894-2818
Minerva *(G-10032)*

▲ Abrasive Technology LLC........... C 740 548-4100
Lewis Center *(G-8317)*

Abrasive Technology Lapidary......... G 740 548-4855
Lewis Center *(G-8318)*

Action Super Abrasive Pdts Inc....... E 330 673-7333
Kent *(G-8014)*

Alb Tyler Holdings Inc............... G 440 946-7171
Mentor *(G-9475)*

◆ Ali Industries LLC................ B 937 878-3946
Fairborn *(G-6685)*

▲ Alliance Abrasives LLC............ F 330 823-7957
Alliance *(G-368)*

▲ ARC Abrasives Inc................. D 800 888-4885
Troy *(G-13201)*

▲ B & P Polishing Inc............... F 330 753-4202
Barberton *(G-795)*

Belanger Inc......................... D 517 870-3206
West Chester *(G-13948)*

Buckeye Abrasive Inc................. F 330 753-1041
Barberton *(G-799)*

Buffalo Abrasives Inc................ E 614 891-6450
Westerville *(G-14248)*

▲ Carborundum Grinding Whee............ E 740 385-2171
Logan *(G-8510)*

▲ Cleveland Granite & Marble LLC....... E 216 291-7637
Cleveland *(G-3512)*

◆ Diamond Innovations Inc................B 614 438-2000
Columbus *(G-4880)*

Enterprise Machine Inc.................... G 513 681-4409
Cincinnati *(G-2592)*

Even Cut Abrasive Company................ F 216 881-9595
Cleveland *(G-3692)*

Everett Industries LLC.................... G 330 372-3700
Warren *(G-13764)*

▲ Golden Dynamic Inc.................... G 614 575-1222
Columbus *(G-4961)*

▲ Hec Investments Inc.................... C 937 278-9123
Dayton *(G-5808)*

Hones Harbor House Gifts................. G 216 334-9836
Ashtabula *(G-595)*

Innovation Sales LLC..................... G 330 239-0400
Medina *(G-9412)*

◆ Lawrence Industries Inc..............E 216 518-7000
Cleveland *(G-3946)*

Libra Guaymas LLC........................ C 440 974-7770
Mentor *(G-9552)*

▲ Mill-Rose Company..................... F 440 255-9171
Mentor *(G-9566)*

Nanolap Technologies LLC................. G 877 658-4949
Englewood *(G-6619)*

National Lime and Stone Co............... E 419 396-7671
Carey *(G-2060)*

Performance Superabrasives LLC.......... G 440 946-7171
Mentor *(G-9586)*

▲ Qibco Buffing Pads Inc................ G 937 743-0805
Carlisle *(G-2071)*

▼ Regal Diamond Products Corp......... F 440 944-7700
Wickliffe *(G-14393)*

Research Abrasive Products Inc........... E 440 944-3200
Wickliffe *(G-14394)*

Schumann Enterprises Inc................. E 216 267-6850
Cleveland *(G-4276)*

▲ Sure-Foot Industries Corp............. E 440 234-4446
Cleveland *(G-4352)*

Tomson Steel Company..................... E 513 420-8600
Middletown *(G-9900)*

▲ Unisand Incorporated.................. E 330 722-0222
Medina *(G-9459)*

◆ US Technology Corporation............E 330 455-1181
Canton *(G-2039)*

US Technology Media Inc.................. F 330 874-3094
Bolivar *(G-1394)*

Vibra Finish Co.......................... E 513 870-6300
Fairfield *(G-6788)*

3292 Asbestos products

American Way Exteriors LLC............... G 937 221-8860
Dayton *(G-5656)*

◆ Owens Corning.........................A 419 248-8000
Toledo *(G-13084)*

Owens Corning Corp Svcs LLC.............. F 419 248-8000
Toledo *(G-13085)*

Owens Crning Tchncal Fbrics LL........... G 419 248-5535
Toledo *(G-13089)*

▲ Texas Tile Manufacturing LLC.......... G 713 869-5811
Solon *(G-12197)*

3295 Minerals, ground or treated

Acme Company............................. D 330 758-2313
Poland *(G-11434)*

Aquablok Ltd............................. F 419 825-1325
Swanton *(G-12679)*

Cimbar Performance Mnrl WV LLC........... E 330 532-2034
Wellsville *(G-13912)*

◆ Continental Mineral Proce............E 513 771-7190
Cincinnati *(G-2513)*

▼ Covia Solutions LLC................... G 440 214-3200
Independence *(G-7895)*

Edw C Levy Co............................ G 330 484-6328
Canton *(G-1884)*

Edw C Levy Co............................ G 419 822-8286
Delta *(G-6205)*

EMD Millipore Corporation................ C 513 631-0445
Norwood *(G-10868)*

Enviri Corporation....................... G 740 367-7322
Cheshire *(G-2231)*

Ethima Inc............................... D 419 626-4912
Sandusky *(G-11834)*

GRB Holdings Inc......................... G 937 236-3250
Dayton *(G-5802)*

Harbison Walker Intl Mnrl Inc............ G 513 251-1010
Cincinnati *(G-2705)*

Howard Industries Inc.................... F 614 444-9900
Columbus *(G-4993)*

▲ Industrial Quartz Corporation......... F 440 942-0909
Mentor *(G-9530)*

Ironics Inc.............................. G 330 652-0583
Niles *(G-10592)*

◆ Kish Company Inc......................F 440 205-9970
Mentor *(G-9546)*

Martin Marietta Materials Inc............ F 513 701-1140
West Chester *(G-14026)*

▲ Metaullics Systems LP................. C 509 926-6212
Solon *(G-12148)*

Reed Minerals LLC........................ E 216 652-2002
Niles *(G-10601)*

▲ Seaforth Mineral & Ore Co Inc......... F 216 292-5820
Beachwood *(G-948)*

Trans Ash Inc............................ F 859 341-1528
Cincinnati *(G-3164)*

3296 Mineral wool

American Insulation Tech LLC............. F 513 733-4248
Milford *(G-9921)*

Autoneum North America Inc............... B 419 693-0511
Oregon *(G-10957)*

Blackthorn LLC........................... F 937 836-9296
Clayton *(G-3272)*

Essi Acoustical Products................. F 216 251-7888
Cleveland *(G-3686)*

◆ Extol of Ohio Inc.....................F 419 668-2072
Norwalk *(G-10837)*

▲ Fibreboard Corporation................ C 419 248-8000
Toledo *(G-12963)*

▲ ICP Adhesives and Sealants Inc........ E 330 753-4585
Norton *(G-10823)*

Johns Manville Corporation............... D 419 782-0180
Defiance *(G-6113)*

Johns Manville Corporation............... D 419 784-7000
Defiance *(G-6114)*

Johns Manville Corporation............... E 419 784-7000
Defiance *(G-6115)*

Johns Manville Corporation............... E 419 878-8111
Defiance *(G-6116)*

Johns Manville Corporation............... E 419 878-8111
Waterville *(G-13835)*

Johns Manville Corporation............... D 419 878-8112
Waterville *(G-13836)*

◆ Kinetics Noise Control Inc............C 614 889-0480
Dublin *(G-6316)*

Metal Building Intr Pdts Co.............. F 440 322-6500
Elyria *(G-6562)*

◆ Mid-Continent Minerals Corp..........F 216 283-5700
Cleveland *(G-4034)*

Owens Corning............................ G 614 754-4098
Columbus *(G-5166)*

Owens Corning............................ G 419 248-8000
Navarre *(G-10309)*

Owens Corning Roofg & Asp LLC............ E 877 858-3855
Toledo *(G-13087)*

Owens Corning Sales LLC.................. E 614 539-0830
Grove City *(G-7407)*

Owens Corning Sales LLC.................. E 740 928-6620
Hebron *(G-7628)*

Owens Corning Sales LLC.................. E 614 399-3915
Mount Vernon *(G-10255)*

Owens Corning Sales LLC.................. G 419 248-5751
Swanton *(G-12689)*

◆ Owens Corning Sales LLC...............A 419 248-8000
Toledo *(G-13088)*

Owens Crning Inslting Systm.............. A 740 328-2300
Newark *(G-10527)*

◆ Premier Manufacturing Corp............C 216 941-9700
Cleveland *(G-4190)*

▲ Refractory Specialties Inc............ E 330 938-2101
Sebring *(G-11900)*

Sorbothane Inc........................... E 330 678-9444
Kent *(G-8081)*

◆ Tectum Inc............................C 740 345-9691
Newark *(G-10535)*

◆ Thermafiber Inc.......................D 260 563-2111
Toledo *(G-13142)*

3297 Nonclay refractories

A & M Refractories Inc................... E 740 456-8020
New Boston *(G-10355)*

◆ Allied Mineral Products LLC...........B 614 876-0244
Columbus *(G-4688)*

Castruction Company Inc.................. F 330 332-9622
Salem *(G-11768)*

◆ Ccpi Inc..............................E 937 783-2476
Blanchester *(G-1234)*

▲ E I Ceramics LLC...................... D 513 772-7001
Cincinnati *(G-2570)*

Ethima Inc............................... D 419 626-4912
Sandusky *(G-11834)*

Ets Schaefer LLC......................... F 330 468-6600
Macedonia *(G-8689)*

Ets Schaefer LLC......................... E 330 468-6600
Beachwood *(G-917)*

I Cerco Inc.............................. C 740 982-2050
Crooksville *(G-5510)*

Impact Armor Technologies LLC............ F 216 706-2024
Cleveland *(G-3853)*

◆ Industrial Ceramic Products Inc.......D 937 642-3897
Marysville *(G-9032)*

Johns Manville Corporation............... C 419 878-8111
Waterville *(G-13835)*

Magneco/Metrel Inc....................... C 330 426-9468
Negley *(G-10315)*

Martin Marietta Materials Inc............ F 513 701-1140
West Chester *(G-14026)*

Minteq International Inc................. F 419 636-4561
Bryan *(G-1651)*

Minteq International Inc................. E 330 343-8821
Dover *(G-6254)*

◆ Momentive Prfmce Mtls Qrtz Inc........E 440 878-5700
Strongsville *(G-12575)*

Ohio Vly Stmpng-Assemblies Inc........... F 419 522-0983
Mansfield *(G-8842)*

▲ Ormet Primary Aluminum Corp.......... A 740 483-1381
Hannibal *(G-7541)*

Plibrico Company LLC..................... F 740 682-7755
Oak Hill *(G-10892)*

Pmbp Legacy Co Inc....................... E 330 253-8148
Akron *(G-262)*

Pyromatics Corp.......................... F 440 352-3500
Mentor *(G-9599)*

▲ Refractory Specialties Inc................. E 330 938-2101
Sebring (G-11900)

Resco Products Inc........................... G 740 682-7794
Oak Hill (G-10893)

Saint-Gobain Ceramics Plas Inc........... D 330 673-5860
Stow (G-12456)

▲ Saint-Gobain Ceramics Plas Inc........ A 610 893-6000
Stow (G-12457)

◆ US Refractory Products LLC............E 440 386-4580
North Ridgeville (G-10752)

▲ Vacuform Inc.............................. E 330 938-9674
Sebring (G-11905)

▲ Zircoa Inc................................. C 440 248-0500
Cleveland (G-4526)

3299 Nonmetallic mineral products,

Aquablok Ltd................................. G 419 402-4170
Swanton (G-12678)

Aquablok Ltd................................. F 419 825-1325
Swanton (G-12679)

Astro Met Inc................................ F 513 772-1242
Cincinnati (G-2383)

▲ Ceramsource Inc.......................... F 732 257-5002
East Palestine (G-6401)

Cleveland Mica Co.......................... F 216 226-1360
Lakewood (G-8165)

Cultured Marble Inc........................ G 330 549-2282
Poland (G-11435)

◆ Fireline Inc...............................C 330 743-1164
Youngstown (G-14855)

Holmes Supply Corp........................ G 330 279-2634
Holmesville (G-7799)

Imperial Stucco LLC........................ G 614 787-5888
Dublin (G-6306)

Maverick Corporation....................... F 513 469-9919
Blue Ash (G-1304)

Maxim Integrated Products LLC........... E 216 375-1057
Cleveland (G-4000)

Momq Holding Company.................... A 440 878-5700
Strongsville (G-12576)

Occv2 LLC................................... G 419 248-8000
Toledo (G-13070)

▲ R W Sidley Incorporated................. E 440 352-9343
Painesville (G-11109)

Refractory Coating Tech Inc............... E 800 807-7464
Lorain (G-8576)

Richtech Industries Inc..................... G 440 937-4401
Avon (G-738)

The Fischer & Jirouch Company........... G 216 361-3840
Cleveland (G-4381)

33 PRIMARY METAL INDUSTRIES

3312 Blast furnaces and steel mills

A-1 Welding & Fabrication................. F 440 233-8474
Lorain (G-8544)

Acme Surface Dynamics Inc............... F 330 821-3900
Alliance (G-366)

◆ Aco Inc...................................E 440 639-7230
Mentor (G-9468)

▲ Adams Elevator Equipment Co.......... D 847 581-2900
Holland (G-7743)

Alba Manufacturing Inc.................... D 513 874-0551
Fairfield (G-6708)

▲ All Ohio Threaded Rod Co Inc........... E 216 426-1800
Cleveland (G-3326)

Alro Steel Corporation...................... E 937 253-6121
Dayton (G-5648)

AM Warren LLC.............................. D 330 841-2800
Warren (G-13734)

American Hvy Plate Sltions LLC........... C 740 331-4620
Clarington (G-3270)

American Posts LLC......................... D 419 720-0652
Toledo (G-12877)

American Steel & Alloys LLC............... G 330 847-0487
Warren (G-13735)

Amthor Steel Inc............................ G 330 759-0200
Youngstown (G-14814)

ATI Flat Rlled Pdts Hldngs LLC........... F 330 875-2244
Louisville (G-8598)

B & G Tool Company........................ G 614 451-2538
Columbus (G-4739)

◆ Bd Laplace LLC............................B 985 652-4900
Cleveland (G-3410)

Brenmar Construction Inc.................. D 740 286-2151
Jackson (G-7941)

Bridge Components Inds Inc................ F 614 873-0777
Columbus (G-4776)

▲ Buschman Corporation................... F 216 431-6633
Cleveland (G-3453)

C & R Inc.................................... E 614 497-1130
Groveport (G-7427)

◆ Canton Drop Forge Inc...................B 330 477-4511
Canton (G-1854)

Charles C Lewis Company.................. F 440 439-3150
Cleveland (G-3486)

Charter Manufacturing Co Inc.............. D 216 883-3800
Cleveland (G-3490)

Churchill Steel Plate Ltd................... E 330 425-9000
Twinsburg (G-13286)

Cleveland-Cliffs Columbus LLC............ E 614 492-8287
Columbus (G-4812)

◆ Cleveland-Cliffs Inc......................C 216 694-5700
Cleveland (G-3532)

Cleveland-Cliffs Steel Corp................ B 419 755-3011
Mansfield (G-8775)

Cleveland-Cliffs Steel Corp................ F 513 425-3593
Middletown (G-9845)

Cleveland-Cliffs Steel Corp................ C 513 425-5000
Middletown (G-9846)

Cleveland-Cliffs Steel Corp................ B 513 425-3694
Middletown (G-9847)

◆ Cleveland-Cliffs Steel Corp.............D 216 694-5700
Cleveland (G-3533)

Clevelnd-Clffs Clvland Wrks LL............ E 216 429-6000
Cleveland (G-3536)

▲ Clevelnd-Clffs Clvland Wrks LL......... C 216 429-6000
Cleveland (G-3535)

◆ Clevelnd-Cliffs Stl Holdg Corp.......... B 216 694-5700
Cleveland (G-3537)

Cliffs Steel Inc.............................. E 216 694-5700
Cleveland (G-3540)

Cohen Brothers Inc......................... E 513 217-5200
Middletown (G-9849)

Cohen Brothers Inc......................... E 513 422-3696
Middletown (G-9848)

Columbiana Foundry Company............ C 330 482-3336
Columbiana (G-4612)

Contractors Steel Company................ D 330 425-3050
Twinsburg (G-13289)

CPM Tool Co LLC........................... G 937 258-1176
Dayton (G-5606)

Crest Bending Inc.......................... E 419 492-2108
New Washington (G-10478)

Custom Blast & Coat Inc................... G 419 225-6024
Lima (G-8399)

▼ Eastern Automated Piping............... G 740 535-8184
Mingo Junction (G-10050)

◆ Elster Perfection Corporation...........D 440 428-1171
Geneva (G-7236)

▲ Ernst Metal Technologies LLC........... E 937 434-3133
Dayton (G-5767)

Evolve Solutions LLC....................... E 440 357-8964
Painesville (G-11083)

FBC Chemical Corporation................. E 216 341-2000
Cleveland (G-3707)

Forge Products Corporation................ E 216 231-2600
Cleveland (G-3736)

▲ Franklin Iron & Metal Corp............... C 937 253-8184
Dayton (G-5784)

▲ Fulton County Processing Ltd........... C 419 822-9266
Delta (G-6206)

▲ Garden Street Iron & Metal Inc.......... E 513 721-4660
Cincinnati (G-2649)

Geauga Coatings LLC....................... G 440 221-7286
Chardon (G-2206)

George Manufacturing Inc.................. F 513 932-1067
Lebanon (G-8258)

Gerdau Ameristeel US Inc.................. G 740 671-9410
Bellaire (G-1087)

Gerdau Ameristeel US Inc.................. F 513 869-7660
Hamilton (G-7493)

GKN Sinter Metals LLC..................... C 740 441-3203
Gallipolis (G-7206)

▲ Global Metal Services Ltd................ G 440 591-1264
Chagrin Falls (G-2163)

◆ Gray America Corp........................E 937 293-9313
Moraine (G-10166)

Great Lakes Mfg Group Ltd................ G 440 391-8266
Rocky River (G-11634)

Gregory Roll Form Inc...................... D 330 477-4800
Canton (G-1906)

Grenga Machine & Welding................ F 330 743-1113
Youngstown (G-14871)

Hadronics Inc............................... D 513 321-9350
Cincinnati (G-2702)

Harvard Coil Processing Inc................ F 216 883-6366
Cleveland (G-3812)

▲ Heidtman Steel Products Inc............. E 419 691-4646
Toledo (G-12992)

◆ Hickman Williams & Company............F 513 621-1946
Cincinnati (G-2721)

Holgate Metal Fab Inc...................... F 419 599-2000
Napoleon (G-10285)

I Jalcite Inc................................. F 216 622-5000
Cleveland (G-3848)

JSW Steel USA Ohio Inc.................... B 740 535-8172
Mingo Junction (G-10052)

Kda Manufacturing LLC..................... F 330 590-7431
Norton (G-10825)

◆ Kirtland Capital Partners LP.............E 216 593-0100
Beachwood (C-024)

L T V Steel Company Inc................... A 216 622-5000
Cleveland (G-3933)

▲ L&H Threaded Rods Corp................. C 937 294-6666
Moraine (G-10173)

Lapham-Hickey Steel Corp................. D 614 443-4881
Columbus (G-5065)

◆ Latrobe Spcialty Mtls Dist Inc...........D 330 609-5137
Vienna (G-13610)

Latrobe Specialty Mtls Co LLC............ E 419 335-8010
Wauseon (G-13854)

Liberty Iron & Metal Inc.................... E 724 347-4534
Girard (G-7274)

▲ Lokring Technology LLC.................. C 440 942-0880
Willoughby (G-14483)

Long View Steel Corp....................... F 419 747-1108
Mansfield (G-8814)

Lukjan Metal Products Inc.................. C 440 599-8127
Conneaut (G-5410)

Major Metals Company...................... E 419 886-4600
Mansfield (G-8815)

Marion Cnty Coal Resources Inc........... G 740 338-3100
Saint Clairsville (G-11696)

Marion County Coal Company.............. D 740 338-3100
Saint Clairsville (G-11697)

Marion Dofasco Inc.................................. G 740 382-3979
Marion *(G-8976)*

◆ McDonald Steel Corporation.............D 330 530-9118
Mc Donald *(G-9360)*

▼ McIntosh Manufacturing LLC............ D 513 424-5307
Middletown *(G-9878)*

McWane Inc... B 740 622-6651
Coshocton *(G-5459)*

Mercer Tool Corporation...................... E 419 394-7277
Saint Marys *(G-11742)*

Metallus Inc... G 216 825-2533
Canton *(G-1945)*

Metallus Inc... F 800 967-1218
Canton *(G-1946)*

Metallus Inc... E 330 471-7000
Canton *(G-1947)*

◆ Metallus Inc... A 330 471-7000
Canton *(G-1944)*

▲ Miba Sinter USA LLC........................... F 740 962-4242
Mcconnelsville *(G-9365)*

Mid-America Steel Corp........................ E 800 282-3466
Cleveland *(G-4033)*

Minco Tool and Mold Inc...................... E 937 890-0322
Vandalia *(G-13572)*

Msls Group LLC....................................... E 330 723-4431
Medina *(G-9428)*

Nanogate North America LLC.............. B 419 747-1096
Mansfield *(G-8835)*

New Age Design & Tool Inc.................. G 440 355-5400
Lagrange *(G-8152)*

Nichidai America Corporation.............. G 419 423-7511
Findlay *(G-6898)*

▲ North Shore Strapping Company........ E 216 661-5200
Brooklyn Heights *(G-1536)*

◆ Northlake Steel Corporation................ D 330 220-7717
Valley City *(G-13513)*

Nova Structural Steel Inc..................... E 216 938-7476
Cleveland *(G-4100)*

Nucor Corporation................................. G 937 390-2300
Beavercreek *(G-979)*

Nucor Corporation................................. E 407 855-2990
Cincinnati *(G-2917)*

Nucor Corporation................................. F 901 275-3826
Cincinnati *(G-2918)*

Nucor Logistics LLC.............................. F 901 275-3826
Cincinnati *(G-2919)*

Nucor Steel Marion Inc......................... E 740 383-6068
Marion *(G-8984)*

◆ Nucor Steel Marion Inc......................... B 740 383-4011
Marion *(G-8985)*

◆ Ohio Gratings Inc.................................. B 800 321-9800
Canton *(G-1966)*

Ohio Steel Processing LLC.................. D 419 241-9601
Toledo *(G-13075)*

Ohio Steel Sheet and Plate Inc.......... E 800 827-2401
Hubbard *(G-7815)*

▲ Ohio Valley Alloy Services Inc........... E 740 373-1900
Marietta *(G-8931)*

▲ Opp Dissolution LLC............................ D 419 241-9601
Toledo *(G-13080)*

OReilly Precision Pdts Inc................... E 937 526-4677
Russia *(G-11676)*

Phillips Mfg and Tower Co................... D 419 347-1720
Shelby *(G-11972)*

Phillips Tube Group Inc........................ E 205 338-4771
Middletown *(G-9885)*

▲ Pioneer Pipe Inc.................................... A 740 376-2400
Marietta *(G-8937)*

Precision Cut Fabricating Inc.............. F 440 877-1260
North Royalton *(G-10780)*

Precision Strip Inc................................ D 937 667-6255
Tipp City *(G-12836)*

◆ Prime Conduit Inc................................. F 216 464-3400
Beachwood *(G-941)*

Quaker City Castings Inc..................... A 330 332-1566
Salem *(G-11806)*

▼ Qual-Fab Inc... E 440 327-5000
Avon *(G-737)*

Quality Bar Inc....................................... E 330 755-0000
Struthers *(G-12620)*

Quality Tool Company........................... E 419 476-8228
Toledo *(G-13105)*

R & D Machine Inc.................................. F 937 339-2545
Troy *(G-13248)*

Racelite Southcoast Inc....................... F 216 581-4600
Maple Heights *(G-8891)*

Radix Wire & Cable LLC....................... D 216 731-9191
Solon *(G-12172)*

Republic Engineered Products........... E 440 277-2000
Lorain *(G-8577)*

Republic Steel....................................... F 330 438-5533
Canton *(G-1994)*

Republic Steel....................................... E 440 277-2000
Lorain *(G-8578)*

◆ Republic Steel....................................... E 330 438-5435
Canton *(G-1995)*

Rmi Titanium Company LLC................. B 330 471-1844
Canton *(G-1997)*

Rmi Titanium Company LLC................. B 330 453-2118
Canton *(G-1998)*

Robs Welding Technologies Ltd.......... G 937 890-4963
Dayton *(G-5987)*

Royal Metal Products LLC.................... C 740 397-8842
Mount Vernon *(G-10264)*

▲ Rti Alloys.. G 330 652-9952
Niles *(G-10605)*

▲ S&V Industries Inc............................... E 330 666-1986
Medina *(G-9443)*

Seilkop Industries Inc.......................... F 513 353-3090
Miamitown *(G-9760)*

Seneca Railroad & Mining Co............. G 419 483-7764
Bellevue *(G-1131)*

Sertek LLC.. D 614 504-5828
Dublin *(G-6344)*

Shaq Inc.. D 770 427-0402
Beachwood *(G-949)*

Shear Service Inc.................................. G 216 341-2700
Cleveland *(G-4289)*

Sigma Tube Company............................ F 419 729-9756
Toledo *(G-13131)*

Stainless Specialties Inc..................... E 440 942-4242
Eastlake *(G-6443)*

Steel Technologies LLC........................ E 419 523-5199
Ottawa *(G-11046)*

Steel Technologies LLC........................ D 440 946-8666
Willoughby *(G-14532)*

Steve Vore Welding and Steel............ F 419 375-4087
Fort Recovery *(G-6971)*

Suburban Steel Supply Co .... D 614 737-5501
Gahanna *(G-7170)*

▲ Tencom Ltd... G 419 865-5877
Holland *(G-7787)*

The Florand Company............................ G 330 747-8986
Youngstown *(G-14945)*

▲ The Hamilton Caster & Mfg................. D 513 863-3300
Hamilton *(G-7530)*

Thrift Tool Inc.. G 937 275-3600
Dayton *(G-6053)*

Timken Receivables Corporation......... F 234 262-3000
North Canton *(G-10675)*

Tms International LLC........................... E 216 441-9702
Cleveland *(G-4397)*

Tms International LLC........................... F 513 425-6462
Middletown *(G-9898)*

Tms International LLC........................... E 513 422-4572
Middletown *(G-9899)*

Trenchless Rsrces Globl Hldngs.......... F 419 419-6498
Bowling Green *(G-1444)*

Trupoint Products LLC.......................... F 330 204-3302
Sugarcreek *(G-12654)*

▲ United Security Seals Inc................... E 614 443-7633
Columbus *(G-5337)*

Universal Metals Cutting Inc.............. G 330 580-5192
Canton *(G-2038)*

Universal Urethane Pdts Inc............... D 419 693-7400
Toledo *(G-13169)*

Unlimited Machine and Tool LLC........ F 419 269-1730
Toledo *(G-13171)*

Wheatland Tube LLC.............................. C 724 342-6851
Niles *(G-10610)*

Wheatland Tube LLC.............................. C 330 372-6611
Warren *(G-13814)*

▼ Witt Industries Inc............................... D 513 871-5700
Mason *(G-9167)*

Wodin Inc.. E 440 439-4222
Cleveland *(G-4513)*

◆ Worthington Steel Company................ B 800 944-2255
Worthington *(G-14732)*

Worthngton Smuel Coil Proc LLC........ E 330 963-3777
Twinsburg *(G-13398)*

◆ Xtek Inc.. B 513 733-7800
Cincinnati *(G-3240)*

Youngstown Tube Co............................. E 330 743-7414
Youngstown *(G-14978)*

Zekelman Industries Inc....................... C 740 432-2146
Cambridge *(G-1766)*

3313 Electrometallurgical products

◆ ERAMET MARIETTA INC.......................C 740 374-1000
Marietta *(G-8916)*

◆ Ferroglobe USA Mtlurgical Inc...........C 740 984-2361
Waterford *(G-13826)*

GE Aviation Systems LLC...................... E 620 218-5237
Springdale *(G-12273)*

GE Aviation Systems LLC...................... E 513 889-5150
West Chester *(G-14005)*

International Metal Supply LLC........... G 330 764-1004
Medina *(G-9414)*

Morris Technologies Inc....................... E 513 733-1611
Cincinnati *(G-2888)*

Newton Materion Inc.............................. B 216 692-3990
Euclid *(G-6663)*

Real Alloy Specialty Pdts LLC............ D 844 732-5087
Beachwood *(G-943)*

▲ Rhenium Alloys Inc............................... E 440 365-7388
North Ridgeville *(G-10747)*

Theken Port Park LLC............................ D 330 733-7600
Akron *(G-335)*

3315 Steel wire and related products

Acme Fence LLC..................................... F 330 784-0456
Akron *(G-15)*

Advance Industries Group LLC............ E 216 741-1800
Cleveland *(G-3301)*

AJD Holding Co....................................... D 330 405-4477
Twinsburg *(G-13271)*

◆ American Spring Wire Corp..................C 216 292-4620
Bedford Heights *(G-1068)*

▲ American Wire & Cable Company..... E 440 235-1140
Olmsted Twp *(G-10944)*

Armco Inc.. G 740 829-3000
Coshocton *(G-5450)*

Bayloff Stmped Pdts Knsman Inc.......... D 330 876-4511
Kinsman *(G-8140)*

Bekaert Corporation.............................. E 330 683-5060
Orrville *(G-10975)*

Cherokee Manufacturing LLC.............. G 800 777-5030
Perry *(G-11191)*

Contour Forming Inc........................... F 740 345-9777
Newark *(G-10499)*

Custom Cltch Jint Hydrlics Inc.............. F 216 431-1630
Cleveland *(G-3584)*

D C Controls LLC................................ G 513 225-0813
West Chester *(G-14113)*

◆ Dayton Superior Corporation.............. C 937 866-0711
Miamisburg *(G-9687)*

▲ Engineered Wire Products Inc............. C 419 294-3817
Upper Sandusky *(G-13440)*

Enterprise Machine Inc........................ G 513 681-4409
Cincinnati *(G-2592)*

Euclid Steel & Wire Inc....................... G 216 731-6744
Lakewood *(G-8166)*

▲ Fenix LLC... F 419 739-3400
Wapakoneta *(G-13710)*

◆ Flextur Corp..................................... D 877 435-3988
Dalton *(G-5585)*

G & S Bar and Wire LLC..................... E 260 747-4154
Wooster *(G-14640)*

Hawthorne Wire Ltd............................ G 216 712-4747
Lakewood *(G-8167)*

Heilind Electronics Inc........................ E 440 473-9600
Cleveland *(G-3818)*

▲ Injection Alloys Incorporated.............. F 513 422-8819
Middletown *(G-9865)*

▲ JR Manufacturing Inc........................ C 419 375-8021
Fort Recovery *(G-6968)*

Mae Fence LLC................................... F 614 929-3526
Fulton *(G-7151)*

▲ Marlin Thermocouple Wire Inc............ E 440 835-1950
Westlake *(G-14314)*

Master-Halco Inc................................ F 513 869-7600
Fairfield *(G-6751)*

McHenry Industries Inc....................... E 330 799-8930
Youngstown *(G-14896)*

▼ Midwestern Industries Inc.................. D 330 837-4203
Massillon *(G-9223)*

▲ Polymet Corporation......................... E 513 874-3586
West Chester *(G-14051)*

Radix Wire & Cable LLC..................... D 216 731-9191
Solon *(G-12172)*

Ram Sensors Inc................................ E 440 835-3540
Cleveland *(G-4222)*

▲ Reinforcement Systems of .... G 330 469-6958
Warron *(G 13703)*

▲ Republic Steel Wire Proc LLC............ E 440 996-0740
Solon *(G-12175)*

◆ Republic Wire Inc............................. D 513 860-1800
West Chester *(G-14063)*

◆ Richards Whl Fence Co Inc................ E 330 773-0423
Akron *(G-284)*

▲ Save Edge Inc.................................. E 937 376-8268
Xenia *(G-14774)*

▲ Scovil Hanna LLC............................. E 216 581-1500
Cleveland *(G-4281)*

Seneca Wire & Manufacturing Co Inc... F 419 435-9261
Fostoria *(G-7002)*

▲ Solon Specialty Wire Co.................... E 440 248-7600
Solon *(G-12183)*

▲ Stop Stick Ltd.................................. E 513 202-5500
Harrison *(G-7570)*

Summit Engineered Products Inc........... F 330 854-5388
Canal Fulton *(G-1779)*

▲ Torque 2020 CMA Acqisition LLC...... C 330 874-2900
Bolivar *(G-1393)*

Tru-Form Steel & Wire Inc.................. E 765 348-5001
Toledo *(G-13166)*

Unison Industries LLC........................ F 937 426-0621
Alpha *(G-419)*

Wire Products Company Inc.................. F 216 267-0777
Cleveland *(G-4509)*

3316 Cold finishing of steel shapes

▲ All Ohio Threaded Rod Co Inc............ E 216 426-1800
Cleveland *(G-3326)*

Alro Steel Corporation......................... E 937 253-6121
Dayton *(G-5648)*

◆ American Spring Wire Corp................ C 216 292-4620
Bedford Heights *(G-1068)*

ATI Flat Rlled Pdts Hldngs LLC............ F 330 875-2244
Louisville *(G-8598)*

Bar Processing Corporation.................. F 330 872-0914
Newton Falls *(G-10577)*

Bekaert Corporation............................ E 330 683-5060
Orrville *(G-10975)*

Clark Grave Vault Company.................. C 614 294-3761
Columbus *(G-4809)*

▲ Clouth Sprenger LLC......................... G 937 642-8390
Lebanon *(G-8249)*

Consolidated Metal Pdts Inc................. D 513 251-2624
Cincinnati *(G-2511)*

◆ Dms Inc.. C 440 951-9838
Willoughby *(G-14449)*

Geneva Liberty Steel Ltd..................... E 330 740-0103
Youngstown *(G-14865)*

▲ Heidtman Steel Products Inc.............. E 419 691-4646
Toledo *(G-12992)*

▲ Hynes Industries Inc......................... D 800 321-9257
Youngstown *(G-14874)*

Lakeway Mfg Inc................................ E 419 433-3030
Huron *(G-7877)*

Lapham-Hickey Steel Corp.................. D 419 399-4803
Paulding *(G-11158)*

LLC Ring Masters............................... F 330 832-1511
Massillon *(G-9215)*

Mid-America Steel Corp...................... E 800 282-3466
Cleveland *(G-4033)*

MSC Walbridge Coatings Inc................ C 419 666-6130
Walbridge *(G-13686)*

◆ Nucor Steel Marion Inc..................... B 740 383-4011
Marion *(G-8985)*

Sandvik Inc....................................... C 614 438-6579
Columbus *(G-5248)*

◆ Superior Forge & Steel Corp.............. D 419 222-4412
Lima *(G-8453)*

Telling Industries LLC......................... E 740 435-8900
Cambridge *(C 1761)*

◆ Telling Industries LLC........................ F 440 974-3370
Willoughby *(G-14538)*

Worthington Cylinder Corp................... C 440 576-5847
Jefferson *(G-7987)*

Worthington Steel Inc.......................... B 614 840-3462
Columbus *(G-5374)*

◆ Worthington Steel Company............... B 800 944-2255
Worthington *(G-14732)*

Worthngton Stl Mexico SA De Cv.......... G 800 944-2255
Worthington *(G-14733)*

3317 Steel pipe and tubes

Alro Steel Corporation......................... E 937 253-6121
Dayton *(G-5648)*

Arcelrmttal Tblar Pdts Shlby L.............. A 419 347-2424
Shelby *(G-11966)*

Arcelrmttal Tblar Pdts USA LLC........... A 419 347-2424
Shelby *(G-11967)*

Atlantic Welding LLC........................... F 937 570-5094
Piqua *(G-11335)*

Busch & Thiem Inc............................. E 419 625-7515
Sandusky *(G-11825)*

Caparo Bull Moose Inc....................... G 330 448-4878
Masury *(G-9254)*

Chart International Inc......................... D 440 753-1490
Cleveland *(G-3489)*

◆ Clevelnd-Cliffs Tblar Cmpnnts L.......... D 419 661-4150
Walbridge *(G-13683)*

▲ Commercial Honing LLC..................... D 330 343-8896
Dover *(G-6235)*

Conduit Pipe Products Company........... D 614 879-9114
West Jefferson *(G-14161)*

Contech Engnered Solutions Inc........... A 513 645-7000
West Chester *(G-13971)*

◆ Contech Engnered Solutions LLC........ C 513 645-7000
West Chester *(G-13972)*

Crest Bending Inc.............................. E 419 492-2108
New Washington *(G-10478)*

◆ Dom Tube Corp................................ A 412 299-2616
Alliance *(G-381)*

Fd Rolls Corp.................................... G 216 916-1922
Solon *(G-12110)*

Grae-Con Process Piping LLC.............. E 740 282-6830
Marietta *(G-8920)*

◆ H-P Products Inc.............................. C 330 875-5556
Louisville *(G-8602)*

▲ Jackson Tube Service Inc................... C 937 773-8550
Piqua *(G-11361)*

Kenco Products Co Inc....................... E 216 351-7610
Cleveland *(G-3913)*

◆ Kirtland Capital Partners LP............... E 216 593-0100
Beachwood *(G-924)*

Lock Joint Tube Ohio LLC.................... C 210 278-3757
Orwell *(G-11023)*

▲ Lsp Tubes Inc.................................. D 216 378-2092
Orwell *(G-11024)*

Major Metals Company........................ E 419 886-4600
Mansfield *(G-8815)*

Mattr US Inc..................................... E 513 683-7800
Loveland *(G-8641)*

Metallus Inc...................................... E 330 471-7000
Canton *(G-1948)*

Phillips Mfg and Tower Co................... D 419 347-1720
Shelby *(G-11972)*

▲ PMC Industries Corp......................... D 440 943-3300
Wickliffe *(G-14391)*

Ptc Alliance LLC................................ C 330 821-5700
Alliance *(G-401)*

▲ Reliacheck Manufacturing Inc............. E 440 933-6162
Brookpark *(G-1557)*

◆ Rolled Alloys Inc.............................. D 800 521-0332
Maumee *(C 9315)*

▲ Shelar Inc....................................... C 419 729-9756
Toledo *(G-13129)*

T & D Fabricating Inc......................... E 440 951-5646
Eastlake *(G-6445)*

Terrasmart LLC.................................. E 239 362-0211
Columbus *(G-5317)*

TI Group Auto Systems LLC................. E 740 929-2049
Hebron *(G-7640)*

Tubetech Inc..................................... E 330 426-9476
East Palestine *(G-6409)*

Unison Industries LLC......................... B 904 667-9904
Dayton *(G-5625)*

United Tube Corporation...................... D 330 725-4196
Medina *(G-9461)*

Vallourec Star LP............................... C 330 742-6227
Girard *(G-7281)*

▲ Vallourec Star LP.............................. C 330 742-6300
Youngstown *(G-14957)*

Wheatland Tube LLC........................... C 724 342-6851
Niles *(G-10610)*

Wheatland Tube LLC........................... C 330 372-6611
Warren *(G-13814)*

Woodsage LLC................................... C 419 866-8000
Holland *(G-7792)*

Zekelman Industries Inc.......................... E 216 910-3700
  Beachwood *(G-959)*

Zekelman Industries Inc.......................... C 740 432-2146
  Cambridge *(G-1766)*

3321 Gray and ductile iron foundries

A C Williams Co Inc.............................. E 330 296-6110
  Ravenna *(G-11511)*

Akron Gear & Engineering Inc.............. E 330 773-6608
  Akron *(G-32)*

Amsted Industries Incorporated............ D 614 836-2323
  Groveport *(G-7422)*

Anchor Glass Container Corp................ D 740 452-2743
  Zanesville *(G-14987)*

Arcelrmttal Tblar Pdts Shlby L.............. A 419 347-2424
  Shelby *(G-11966)*

Barberton Steel Industries Inc.............. E 330 745-6837
  Barberton *(G-798)*

Brittany Stamping LLC.......................... A 216 267-0850
  Cleveland *(G-3440)*

Cast-Fab Technologies Inc.................... C 513 758-1000
  Cincinnati *(G-2442)*

Casting Solutions LLC........................... C 740 452-9371
  Zanesville *(G-15005)*

Castings Usa Inc................................... G 330 339-3611
  New Philadelphia *(G-10436)*

Chris Erhart Foundry & Mch Co.......... F 513 421-6550
  Cincinnati *(G-2463)*

▲ Cmt Imports Inc................................ G 513 615-1851
  Cincinnati *(G-2502)*

Col-Pump Company Inc........................ D 330 482-1029
  Columbiana *(G-4610)*

Columbiana Foundry Company............ C 330 482-3336
  Columbiana *(G-4612)*

D Picking & Co...................................... G 419 562-6891
  Bucyrus *(G-1677)*

▲ Dd Foundry Inc................................ F 216 362-4100
  Brookpark *(G-1548)*

Ej Usa Inc... G 614 871-2436
  Grove City *(G-7384)*

Ej Usa Inc... F 216 692-3001
  South Euclid *(G-12219)*

Ej Usa Inc... F 330 782-3900
  Youngstown *(G-14852)*

◆ Ellwood Engineered Castings Co....... C 330 568-3000
  Hubbard *(G-7810)*

Elyria Foundry Company LLC............... C 440 322-4657
  Elyria *(G-6529)*

Engines Inc of Ohio.............................. E 740 377-9874
  South Point *(G-12223)*

Ford Motor Company............................ C 216 676-7918
  Brookpark *(G-1550)*

General Motors LLC.............................. A 419 782-7010
  Defiance *(G-6107)*

Hamilton Brass & Alum Castings.......... G
  Hamilton *(G-7500)*

Hobart LLC.. D 937 332-2797
  Piqua *(G-11355)*

Hobart LLC.. E 937 332-3000
  Troy *(G-13225)*

▲ Hobart LLC...................................... D 937 332-3000
  Troy *(G-13226)*

Howmet Aerospace Inc........................ A 216 641-3600
  Newburgh Heights *(G-10543)*

Kenton Iron Products Inc..................... E 419 674-4178
  Kenton *(G-8102)*

▲ Knappco Corporation....................... C 513 870-3100
  Hamilton *(G-7509)*

▲ Korff Holdings LLC.......................... C 330 332-1566
  Salem *(G-11792)*

▲ Liberty Casting Company LLC......... D 740 363-1941
  Delaware *(G-6160)*

McWane Inc... B 740 622-6651
  Coshocton *(G-5459)*

Miami-Cast Inc...................................... F 937 866-2951
  Miamisburg *(G-9715)*

Old Smo Inc.. G 419 394-3346
  Saint Marys *(G-11745)*

Old Smo Inc.. C 419 394-3346
  Saint Marys *(G-11746)*

▲ OS Kelly Corporation...................... E 937 322-4921
  Springfield *(G-12358)*

Osco Industries Inc.............................. D 740 286-5004
  Jackson *(G-7950)*

◆ Osco Industries Inc.......................... B 740 354-3183
  Portsmouth *(G-11473)*

Pioneer City Casting Company............ E 740 423-7533
  Belpre *(G-1153)*

Piqua Champion Foundry Inc............... G
  Piqua *(G-11373)*

Quaker City Castings Inc..................... A 330 332-1566
  Salem *(G-11806)*

Quality Castings Company................... B 330 682-6010
  Orrville *(G-11003)*

Sancast Inc... E 740 622-8660
  Coshocton *(G-5471)*

Skuld LLC.. E 330 423-7339
  Piqua *(G-11384)*

T & B Foundry Company...................... G 216 391-4200
  Cleveland *(G-4360)*

Tangent Air Inc..................................... E 740 474-1114
  Circleville *(G-3264)*

▲ Thyssnkrupp Rothe Erde USA Inc..... C 330 562-4000
  Aurora *(G-689)*

Tiffin Foundry & Machine Inc.............. E 419 447-3991
  Tiffin *(G-12802)*

Tri Cast Limited Partnership................ E 330 733-8718
  Akron *(G-342)*

Tri-Cast Inc... E 330 733-8718
  Akron *(G-343)*

Vanex Tube Corporation...................... D 330 544-9500
  Niles *(G-10608)*

▲ W E Lott Company.......................... F 419 563-9400
  Bucyrus *(G-1694)*

▲ Wallace Forge Company.................. D 330 488-1203
  Canton *(G-2045)*

Whemco-Ohio Foundry Inc.................. C 419 222-2111
  Lima *(G-8459)*

Yellow Creek Casting Co Inc............... G 330 532-4608
  Wellsville *(G-13915)*

3322 Malleable iron foundries

Cast-Fab Technologies Inc.................... C 513 758-1000
  Cincinnati *(G-2442)*

Ej Usa Inc... F 216 692-3001
  South Euclid *(G-12219)*

◆ Ellwood Engineered Castings Co....... C 330 568-3000
  Hubbard *(G-7810)*

General Motors LLC.............................. A 419 782-7010
  Defiance *(G-6107)*

Kenton Iron Products Inc..................... E 419 674-4178
  Kenton *(G-8102)*

Old Smo Inc.. C 419 394-3346
  Saint Marys *(G-11746)*

Osco Industries Inc.............................. D 740 286-5004
  Jackson *(G-7950)*

Pioneer City Casting Company............ E 740 423-7533
  Belpre *(G-1153)*

Sancast Inc... E 740 622-8660
  Coshocton *(G-5471)*

T & B Foundry Company...................... G 216 391-4200
  Cleveland *(G-4360)*

Tiffin Foundry & Machine Inc.............. E 419 447-3991
  Tiffin *(G-12802)*

Tooling Technology LLC....................... D 937 381-9211
  Fort Loramie *(G-6960)*

▲ W E Lott Company.......................... F 419 563-9400
  Bucyrus *(G-1694)*

Whemco-Ohio Foundry Inc.................. C 419 222-2111
  Lima *(G-8459)*

Yellow Creek Casting Co Inc............... G 330 532-4608
  Wellsville *(G-13915)*

3324 Steel investment foundries

Aeropact Manufacturing LLC................ F 419 373-1711
  Bowling Green *(G-1406)*

B W Grinding Co.................................... E 419 923-1376
  Lyons *(G-8673)*

▲ Bescast Inc...................................... C 440 946-5300
  Willoughby *(G-14430)*

Brost Foundry Company....................... E 216 641-1131
  Cleveland *(G-3443)*

▲ Castalloy Inc................................... D 216 961-7990
  Cleveland *(G-3476)*

▲ Cmt Imports Inc.............................. G 513 615-1851
  Cincinnati *(G-2502)*

▲ Consolidated Foundries Inc............ D 909 595-2252
  Cleveland *(G-3562)*

▲ Dd Foundry Inc............................... F 216 362-4100
  Brookpark *(G-1548)*

Harbor Castings Inc............................. E 330 499-7178
  Cuyahoga Falls *(G-5547)*

▲ Interntnal Prcsion Cast Sups I......... G 330 342-0407
  Hudson *(G-7847)*

◆ Kovatch Castings Inc....................... C 330 896-9944
  Uniontown *(G-13421)*

Mercury Machine Co............................. D 440 349-3222
  Solon *(G-12147)*

Mold Masters Intl LLC.......................... C 440 953-0220
  Eastlake *(G-6438)*

PCC Airfoils LLC................................... C 440 255-9770
  Mentor *(G-9584)*

PCC Airfoils LLC................................... C 330 868-6441
  Minerva *(G-10045)*

Precision Castparts Corp...................... F 440 350-6150
  Painesville *(G-11106)*

▲ Rimer Enterprises Inc..................... E 419 878-8156
  Waterville *(G-13841)*

▲ Steel Ceilings Inc............................ E 740 967-1063
  Johnstown *(G-7998)*

▲ W E Lott Company.......................... F 419 563-9400
  Bucyrus *(G-1694)*

▲ Xapc Co.. C 216 362-4100
  Cleveland *(G-4520)*

3325 Steel foundries, nec

▲ Alcon Industries Inc........................ D 216 961-1100
  Cleveland *(G-3321)*

Brost Foundry Company....................... E 216 641-1131
  Cleveland *(G-3443)*

Castings Usa Inc................................... G 330 339-3611
  New Philadelphia *(G-10436)*

Columbiana Foundry Company............ C 330 482-3336
  Columbiana *(G-4612)*

▲ Columbus Steel Castings Co.......... A 614 444-2121
  Columbus *(G-4834)*

Coronado Steel Co............................... E 330 744-1143
  Youngstown *(G-14840)*

▲ Dd Foundry Inc............................... F 216 362-4100
  Brookpark *(G-1548)*

Durivage Pattern and Mfg Inc.............. E 419 836-8655
  Williston *(G-14411)*

Elyria Foundry Company LLC............... C 440 322-4657
  Elyria *(G-6529)*

Engines Inc of Ohio.............................. E 740 377-9874
  South Point *(G-12223)*

▲ Evertz Technology Svc USA Inc........ F 513 422-8400
Middletown *(G-9860)*

Harbor Castings Inc................... E 330 499-7178
Cuyahoga Falls *(G-5547)*

▲ Jmac Inc................................ E 614 436-2418
Columbus *(G-5041)*

▲ Jrm 2 Company...................... D 513 554-1700
Cincinnati *(G-2774)*

▲ Korff Holdings LLC................. C 330 332-1566
Salem *(G-11792)*

▲ Kovatch Castings Inc..............C 330 896-9944
Uniontown *(G-13421)*

Lakeway Mfg Inc...................... E 419 433-3030
Huron *(G-7877)*

Premier Inv Cast Group LLC.......... E 937 299-7333
Moraine *(G-10186)*

Quaker City Castings Inc............ A 330 332-1566
Salem *(G-11806)*

Rampp Company........................ E 740 373-7886
Marietta *(G-8940)*

◆ Sandusky International Inc.......C 419 626-5340
Sandusky *(G-11868)*

Shl Liquidation Medina Inc.......... C
Valley City *(G-13519)*

Sjv Investment Inc.................... E 330 452-9711
Canton *(G-2006)*

Tiffin Foundry & Machine Inc......... E 419 447-3991
Tiffin *(G-12802)*

United Engineering & Fndry Co........ G 330 456-2761
Canton *(G-2034)*

▲ W E Lott Company.................. F 419 563-9400
Bucyrus *(G-1694)*

Whemco-Ohio Foundry Inc............. E 419 222-2111
Lima *(G-8459)*

◆ Worthington Enterprises Inc......C 614 438-3210
Worthington *(G-14731)*

Worthngton Stelpac Systems LLC....... C 614 438-3205
Columbus *(G-5375)*

3331 Primary copper

Hildreth Mfg LLC....................... E 740 375-5832
Marion *(G-8973)*

▲ Sam Dong Ohio Inc................ D 740 363-1985
Delaware *(G-6171)*

3334 Primary aluminum

◆ Alcan Primary Products Corp........C
Independence *(G-7889)*

Boggs Recycling Inc.................. G 800 837-8101
Newbury *(G-10547)*

Homan Metals LLC..................... G 513 721-5010
Cincinnati *(G-2728)*

Kaiser Aluminum Fab Pdts LLC........ C 740 522-1151
Heath *(G-7598)*

◆ Ormet Corporation................. A 740 483-1381
Hannibal *(G-7540)*

▲ Ormet Primary Aluminum Corp....... A 740 483-1381
Hannibal *(G-7541)*

P&The Mfg Acquisition LLC........... D 937 492-4134
Sidney *(G-12037)*

Real Alloy Specialty Pdts LLC........ D 844 732-5087
Beachwood *(G-943)*

3339 Primary nonferrous metals, nec

◆ Aci Industries Ltd.................E 740 368-4160
Delaware *(G-6128)*

▲ Advance Materials Products Inc........ G 330 650-4000
Hudson *(G-7827)*

Alexy Metals Ltd...................... F 216 410-8661
Willoughby *(G-14416)*

▲ American Friction Tech LLC......... D 216 823-0861
Cleveland *(G-3343)*

◆ American Spring Wire Corp............C 216 292-4620
Bedford Heights *(G-1068)*

◆ AMG Aluminum North America LLC..F 659 348-3620
Cambridge *(G-1735)*

Elemetal Refining LLC................ C 740 286-6457
Jackson *(G-7944)*

Elmet Euclid LLC...................... D 216 692-3990
Euclid *(G-6648)*

Elmet Technologies Inc............... F 216 692-3990
Cleveland *(G-3663)*

◆ Ferroglobe USA Mtlurgical Inc......C 740 984-2361
Waterford *(G-13826)*

Galt Alloys Inc Main Ofc............. G 330 453-4678
Canton *(G-1897)*

Gdc Industries LLC................... G 937 367-7229
Dayton *(G-5790)*

▲ Magnesium Refining Techno........ D 419 483-9199
Cleveland *(G-3980)*

Materion Brush Inc................... A 419 862-2745
Elmore *(G-6491)*

▲ Materion Brush Inc................. D 216 486-4200
Mayfield Heights *(G-9336)*

◆ Materion Corporation..............C 216 486-4200
Mayfield Heights *(G-9337)*

▲ Metallic Resources Inc............. E 330 425-3155
Twinsburg *(G-13340)*

Newton Materion Inc................. B 216 692-3990
Euclid *(G-6663)*

Ohio Valley Specialty Company........ F 740 373-2276
Marietta *(G-8932)*

◆ Quality Gold Inc................... B 513 942-7659
Fairfield *(G-6769)*

▲ Rhenium Alloys Inc................. E 440 365-7388
North Ridgeville *(G-10747)*

Silicon Processors Inc............... G 740 373-2252
Marietta *(G-8944)*

Swift Manufacturing Co Inc........... G 740 237-4405
Ironton *(G-7935)*

▲ Zircoa Inc.......................... C 440 248-0500
Cleveland *(G-4526)*

3341 Secondary nonferrous metals

A & B Iron & Metal Co Inc............ F 937 228-1561
Dayton *(G-5629)*

◆ Aci Industries Ltd.................E 740 368-4160
Delaware *(G-6128)*

Agmet LLC............................ F 216 663-8200
Cleveland *(G-3314)*

Applied Materials Finshg Ltd......... E 330 336-5645
Brooklyn Heights *(G-1527)*

Auris Noble LLC...................... E 330 321-6649
Akron *(G-64)*

Beck Aluminum Alloys Ltd............. D 216 861-4455
Mayfield Heights *(G-9332)*

▲ Cirba Solutions Us Inc............. E 740 653-6290
Lancaster *(G-8186)*

Circuit Board Mining LLC............. G 419 348-1057
Alvada *(G-421)*

Cohen Brothers Inc................... E 513 217-5200
Middletown *(G-9849)*

Cohen Brothers Inc................... E 513 422-3696
Middletown *(G-9848)*

Continental Metal Proc Co............ E 216 268-0000
Cleveland *(G-3564)*

Continental Metal Proc Co............ F 216 268-0000
Cleveland *(G-3563)*

Elemetal Refining LLC................ C 740 286-6457
Jackson *(G-7944)*

▼ Fex LLC............................. F 412 604-0400
Mingo Junction *(G-10051)*

◆ Fpt Cleveland LLC.................. C 216 441-3800
Cleveland *(G-3740)*

▲ Franklin Iron & Metal Corp......... C 937 253-8184
Dayton *(G-5784)*

◆ Fusion Incorporated................ D 440 946-3300
Willoughby *(G-14460)*

G A Avril Company.................... F 513 641-0566
Cincinnati *(G-2645)*

▲ Garden Street Iron & Metal Inc........ E 513 721-4660
Cincinnati *(G-2649)*

Gnw Aluminum Inc..................... E 330 821-7955
Alliance *(G-383)*

I H Schlezinger Inc.................. E 614 252-1188
Columbus *(G-4996)*

◆ I Schumann & Co LLC...............C 440 439-2300
Bedford *(G-1038)*

▲ Jrm 2 Company...................... D 513 554-1700
Cincinnati *(G-2774)*

▲ Materion Advnced Mtls Tech Svc.... D 216 486-4200
Mayfield Heights *(G-9335)*

Materion Brush Inc................... A 419 862-2745
Elmore *(G-6491)*

▲ Materion Brush Inc................. D 216 486-4200
Mayfield Heights *(G-9336)*

◆ Materion Corporation..............C 216 486-4200
Mayfield Heights *(G-9337)*

▼ Mek Van Wert Inc................... E 419 203-4902
Van Wert *(G-13542)*

Metal Shredders Inc.................. G 937 866-0777
Miamisburg *(G-9712)*

Metalico Akron Inc................... F 330 376-1400
Akron *(G-229)*

Mw Metals Group LLC.................. D 937 222-5992
Dayton *(G-5900)*

▲ National Bronze Mtls Ohio Inc...... E 440 277-1226
Lorain *(G-8568)*

▲ Novelis Alr Recycling Ohio LLC...... C 740 922-2373
Uhrichsville *(G-13404)*

Novelis Corporation.................. C 740 983-2571
Ashville *(G-628)*

◆ Oakwood Industries Inc.............D 440 232-8700
Bedford *(G-1051)*

Ohio Metal Processing LLC............ G 740 912-2057
Jackson *(G-7949)*

▲ Ohio Valley Alloy Services Inc...... E 740 373-1900
Marietta *(G-8931)*

Old Rar Inc.......................... A 216 545-7249
Beachwood *(G-936)*

▲ Polymet Corporation................ E 513 874-3586
West Chester *(C-11051)*

Precision Strip Inc.................. D 419 674-4186
Kenton *(G-8112)*

R L S Corporation.................... G 740 773-1440
Chillicothe *(G-2277)*

▲ Real Alloy Recycling LLC........... D 216 755-8900
Beachwood *(G-942)*

Real Alloy Specialty Pdts LLC........ D 844 732-5087
Beachwood *(G-943)*

Rm Advisory Group Inc................ E 513 242-2100
Cincinnati *(G-3049)*

Rmi Titanium Company LLC............. B 330 471-1844
Canton *(G-1997)*

Rmi Titanium Company LLC............. B 330 453-2118
Canton *(G-1998)*

Rnw Holdings Inc..................... E 330 792-0600
Youngstown *(G-14925)*

◆ Rolled Alloys Inc..................D 800 521-0332
Maumee *(G-9315)*

Rumpke Transportation Co LLC......... B 513 242-4600
Cincinnati *(G-3057)*

▲ Sims Bros Inc...................... D 740 387-9041
Marion *(G-9000)*

Thyssenkrupp Materials NA Inc........ D 216 883-8100
Independence *(G-7921)*

Employee Codes: A=Over 500 employees, B=251-500
C=101-250, D=51-100, E=20-50, F=10-19, G=1-9   2025 Harris Ohio
Industrial Directory   795

S I C

Victory White Metal Company............. F 216 271-1400
Cleveland *(G-4474)*

W R G Inc.. E 216 351-8494
Avon Lake *(G-772)*

▲ Wieland Metal Svcs Foils LLC........... D 330 823-1700
Alliance *(G-417)*

3351 Copper rolling and drawing

◆ Alcan Corporation...............................E
Cleveland *(G-3320)*

▲ American Wire & Cable Company..... E 440 235-1140
Olmsted Twp *(G-10944)*

Arem Co... G 440 974-6740
Willoughby *(G-14426)*

Avtron Aerospace Inc..................... C 216 750-5152
Cleveland *(G-3393)*

◆ Core Optix Inc...............................F 855 267-3678
Cincinnati *(G-2517)*

Federal Metal Company.................... F 440 232-8700
Bedford *(G-1031)*

Jj Seville LLC................................. E 330 769-2071
Seville *(G-11919)*

▲ Materion Brush Inc......................... D 216 486-4200
Mayfield Heights *(G-9336)*

◆ Materion Corporation.....................C 216 486-4200
Mayfield Heights *(G-9337)*

◆ Production Tube Cutting Inc.............E 937 254-6138
Dayton *(G-5963)*

◆ Republic Wire Inc..........................D 513 860-1800
West Chester *(G-14063)*

Stoutheart Corporation.................... E 800 556-6470
Chagrin Falls *(G-2185)*

T & D Fabricating Inc....................... E 440 951-5646
Eastlake *(G-6445)*

3353 Aluminum sheet, plate, and foil

B&B Distributors LLC....................... F 440 324-1293
Elyria *(G-6500)*

Holmes Manufacturing...................... G 330 231-6327
Millersburg *(G-9990)*

Howmet Aerospace Inc..................... C 330 848-4000
Barberton *(G-811)*

Howmet Aerospace Inc..................... E 330 544-7633
Niles *(G-10590)*

Howmet Aerospace Inc..................... D 330 222-1501
Salem *(G-11786)*

▲ Monarch Steel Company Inc........... E 216 587-8000
Cleveland *(G-4045)*

Novelis Alr Almnum-Alabama LLC..... E 256 353-1550
Beachwood *(G-932)*

Novelis Corporation......................... D 330 841-3456
Warren *(G-13784)*

PB Fbrction Mech Contrs Corp.......... F 419 478-4869
Toledo *(G-13091)*

Polytech America LLC...................... G 904 728-7458
Canton *(G-1978)*

Tdb Associates Inc.......................... F 937 459-5730
Greenville *(G-7357)*

▲ Wieland Metal Svcs Foils LLC........... D 330 823-1700
Alliance *(G-417)*

3354 Aluminum extruded products

Accu-Tek Tool & Die Inc.................. G 330 726-1946
Salem *(G-11760)*

◆ Alanod Westlake Metal Ind Inc..........E 440 327-8184
North Ridgeville *(G-10723)*

▲ Alufab Inc.................................... G 513 528-7281
Cincinnati *(G-2296)*

Aluminum Extruded Shapes Inc........ C 513 563-2205
Cincinnati *(G-2354)*

▲ American Aluminum Extrusions....... G 330 458-0300
Canton *(G-1830)*

◆ AMG Aluminum North America LLC...F 659 348-3620
Cambridge *(G-1735)*

Arem Co... G 440 974-6740
Willoughby *(G-14426)*

Astro Aluminum Enterprises Inc........ G 330 755-1414
Struthers *(G-12616)*

Astro-Coatings Inc.......................... G 330 755-1414
Struthers *(G-12617)*

Bidwell Family Corporation............... C 513 988-6351
Trenton *(G-13191)*

BRT Extrusions Inc.......................... C 330 544-0177
Niles *(G-10584)*

Central Aluminum Company LLC........ E 614 491-5700
Obetz *(G-10922)*

Da Investments Inc.......................... D 330 781-6100
Youngstown *(G-14845)*

▲ Extrudex Aluminum Inc................... C 330 538-4444
North Jackson *(G-10687)*

◆ Flexrack By Qcells LLC..................C 216 998-5988
Cleveland *(G-3725)*

◆ Fom USA Incorporated.................... G 234 248-4400
Medina *(G-9404)*

Gei of Columbiana Inc..................... E 330 783-0270
Youngstown *(G-14863)*

General Extrusions Intl LLC.............. C 330 783-0270
Youngstown *(G-14864)*

◆ H-P Products Inc............................C 330 875-5556
Louisville *(G-8602)*

Hydro Aluminum Fayetteville............ G 937 492-9194
Sidney *(G-12024)*

Industrial Mold Inc.......................... E 330 425-7374
Twinsburg *(G-13320)*

Isaiah Industries Inc....................... G 937 778-2246
Piqua *(G-11357)*

◆ Isaiah Industries Inc......................E 937 773-9840
Piqua *(G-11358)*

Knoble Glass & Metal Inc................. G 513 753-1246
Cincinnati *(G-2802)*

L & L Ornamental Iron Co................. F 513 353-1930
Cleves *(G-4543)*

M-D Building Products Inc................ F 513 539-2255
Middletown *(G-9874)*

▲ McKnight Industries Inc.................. F 937 592-9010
Bellefontaine *(G-1113)*

▲ National Metal Shapes Inc.............. E 740 363-9559
Delaware *(G-6164)*

Novelis Alr Aluminum LLC................ A 216 910-3400
Beachwood *(G-933)*

▲ Orrvilon Inc.................................. C 330 684-9400
Orrville *(G-11001)*

Owens Corning Sales LLC................ F 740 983-1300
Ashville *(G-629)*

Patton Aluminum Products Inc.......... F 937 845-9404
New Carlisle *(G-10378)*

Pennex Aluminum Company LLC........ C 330 427-6704
Leetonia *(G-8304)*

Star Extruded Shapes LLC................ B 330 533-9863
Canfield *(G-1816)*

Star Fab Inc................................... E 330 482-1601
Columbiana *(G-4630)*

▲ Star Fab LLC................................. C 330 533-9863
Canfield *(G-1817)*

Systems Kit LLC MB........................ E 330 945-4500
Akron *(G-324)*

T & D Fabricating Inc....................... E 440 951-5646
Eastlake *(G-6445)*

Tecnocap LLC................................. C 330 392-7222
Warren *(G-13800)*

Teh Investments Inc........................ D 330 782-1127
Youngstown *(G-14944)*

Tri County Tarp LLC......................... E 419 288-3350
Gibsonburg *(G-7260)*

▲ Trivium Alum Packg USA Corp.......... E 330 744-2267
Youngstown *(G-14952)*

▲ Urban Industries of Ohio Inc............ E 419 468-3578
Galion *(G-7200)*

▼ Vari-Wall Tube Specialists Inc.......... D 330 482-0000
Columbiana *(G-4631)*

Youngstown Tool & Die Company....... D 330 747-4464
Youngstown *(G-14977)*

Zarbana Alum Extrusions LLC........... E 330 482-5092
Columbiana *(G-4635)*

Zarbana Industries Inc..................... E 330 482-5092
Columbiana *(G-4636)*

3355 Aluminum rolling and drawing, nec

◆ Alcan Corporation...............................E
Cleveland *(G-3320)*

Aleris Rm Inc................................. B 216 910-3400
Beachwood *(G-909)*

◆ AMG Aluminum North America LLC...F 659 348-3620
Cambridge *(G-1735)*

Amh Holdings II Inc........................ B 330 929-1811
Cuyahoga Falls *(G-5525)*

Eastman Kodak Company................. E 937 259-3000
Dayton *(G-5758)*

Homan Metals LLC.......................... G 513 721-5010
Cincinnati *(G-2728)*

Howmet Aerospace Inc..................... E 330 544-7633
Niles *(G-10590)*

Kaiser Aluminum Fab Pdts LLC......... C 740 522-1151
Heath *(G-7598)*

Mac Its LLC................................... G 937 454-0722
Vandalia *(G-13565)*

Novelis Alr Aluminum LLC................ A 216 910-3400
Beachwood *(G-933)*

Novelis Alr Rolled Pdts LLC............. A 740 983-2571
Ashville *(G-627)*

▲ Novelis Alr Rolled Pdts LLC............. E 216 910-3400
Beachwood *(G-934)*

Novelis Corporation......................... D 330 841-3456
Warren *(G-13784)*

◆ Pandrol Inc...................................E 419 592-5050
Napoleon *(G-10295)*

Real Alloy Specialty Pdts LLC.......... E 440 322-0072
Elyria *(G-6584)*

Waxco International Inc.................... F 937 746-4845
Miamisburg *(G-9752)*

3356 Nonferrous rolling and drawing, nec

Air Craft Wheels LLC....................... G 440 937-7903
Ravenna *(G-11513)*

Alexy Metals Ltd............................. F 216 410-8661
Willoughby *(G-14416)*

Allied Mask and Tooling Inc............. G 419 470-2555
Toledo *(G-12870)*

BCi and V Investments Inc............... G 330 538-0660
North Jackson *(G-10683)*

Bunting Bearings LLC...................... E 419 522-3323
Mansfield *(G-8770)*

◆ Canton Drop Forge Inc...................B 330 477-4511
Canton *(G-1854)*

▲ Cleanlife Energy LLC...................... F 800 316-2532
Cleveland *(G-3503)*

Consolidated Metal Pdts Inc............ D 513 251-2624
Cincinnati *(G-2511)*

Contour Forming Inc........................ F 740 345-9777
Newark *(G-10499)*

Curtiss-Wright Flow Ctrl Corp.......... D 216 267-3200
Cleveland *(G-3583)*

Elemetal Refining LLC..................... C 740 286-6457
Jackson *(G-7944)*

ESAB Group Incorporated................ G 440 813-2506
Ashtabula *(G-591)*

▲ Fusion Incorporated.............................D 440 946-3300
Willoughby *(G-14460)*

◆ G & S Titanium Inc.............................E 330 263-0564
Wooster *(G-14641)*

G A Avril Company.................................F 513 731-5133
Cincinnati *(G-2646)*

G A Avril Company.................................F 513 641-0566
Cincinnati *(G-2645)*

Gem City Metal Tech LLC.......................E 937 252-8998
Dayton *(G-5793)*

◆ J W Harris Co Inc................................B 513 754-2000
Mason *(G-9116)*

Kilroy Company.....................................D 440 951-8700
Cleveland *(G-3920)*

Lite Metals Company..............................E 330 296-6110
Ravenna *(G-11532)*

▲ Materion Advnced Mtls Tech Svc......D 216 486-4200
Mayfield Heights *(G-9335)*

▲ Materion Brush Inc..............................D 216 486-4200
Mayfield Heights *(G-9336)*

◆ Materion Corporation...........................C 216 486-4200
Mayfield Heights *(G-9337)*

Mestek Inc..F 419 288-2703
Bradner *(G-1454)*

▲ Metallic Resources Inc........................D 330 425-3155
Twinsburg *(G-13340)*

Newton Materion Inc..............................B 216 692-3990
Euclid *(G-6663)*

▲ Nova Machine Products Inc.................C 216 267-3200
Middleburg Heights *(G-9775)*

Patriot Special Metals Inc.......................D 330 580-9600
Canton *(G-1973)*

▲ Rhenium Alloys Inc.............................F 440 365-7388
North Ridgeville *(G-10747)*

Rmi Titanium Company LLC....................G 330 652-9955
Niles *(G-10603)*

◆ Rmi Titanium Company LLC.................E 330 652-9952
Niles *(G-10604)*

◆ Rti International Metals Inc...................A
Niles *(G-10606)*

Tailwind Technologies Inc.......................A 937 778-4200
Piqua *(G-11386)*

Th Magnesium Inc.................................G 513 285-7568
Cincinnati *(G-3146)*

Tin Wizard Heating & Coolg Inc...............G 330 467-9826
Macedonia *(G-8720)*

Titanium Metals Corporation...................A 740 537-1571
Toronto *(G-13187)*

Victory White Metal Company..................F 216 641-2575
Cleveland *(G-4473)*

▲ Victory White Metal Company..............D 216 271-1400
Cleveland *(G-4472)*

▲ Water Star Inc....................................F 440 996-0800
Concord Township *(G-5397)*

3357 Nonferrous wiredrawing and insulating

◆ Alcan Corporation................................E
Cleveland *(G-3320)*

▲ American Wire & Cable Company.........E 440 235-1140
Olmsted Twp *(G-10944)*

◆ Arnco Corporation...............................F 800 847-7661
Elyria *(G-6498)*

Astro Industries Inc...............................E 937 429-5900
Beavercreek *(G-966)*

AT&T Enterprises LLC............................G 513 792-9300
Cincinnati *(G-2384)*

Calvert Wire & Cable Corp......................E 330 494-3248
North Canton *(G-10631)*

Cbst Acquisition LLC.............................D 513 361-9600
Cincinnati *(G-2445)*

▲ Connectors Unlimited Inc....................E 440 357-1161
Painesville *(G-11074)*

◆ Core Optix Inc.....................................F 855 267-3678
Cincinnati *(G-2517)*

Electrovations Inc..................................G 330 274-3558
Solon *(G-12103)*

▼ Flex Technologies Inc..........................E 740 922-5992
Midvale *(G-9910)*

Legrand North America LLC....................B 937 224-0639
Dayton *(G-5843)*

▲ Mueller Electric Company Inc..............D 216 771-5225
Akron *(G-239)*

Ohio Associated Entps LLC.....................F 440 354-3148
Painesville *(G-11101)*

Projects Unlimited Inc............................C 937 918-2200
Dayton *(G-5968)*

Radix Wire Co.......................................F 330 995-3677
Aurora *(G-686)*

Radix Wire Co.......................................F 216 731-9191
Solon *(G-12174)*

Radix Wire Co.......................................D 216 731-9191
Solon *(G-12173)*

▲ Rah Investment Holding Inc.................D 330 832-8124
Massillon *(G-9237)*

◆ Ribbon Technology Corporation............F 614 864-5444
Gahanna *(G-7168)*

Sam Dong America Inc...........................F 740 363-1985
Delaware *(G-6170)*

Schneider Electric Usa Inc......................B 513 523-4171
Oxford *(G-11064)*

Scott Fetzer Company.............................C 216 267-9000
Cleveland *(G-4278)*

Syscom Advanced Materials Inc..............E 614 487-3626
Columbus *(G-5304)*

Therm-O-Link Inc..................................G 330 393-7600
Warren *(G-13801)*

▲ Therm-O-Link Inc...............................D 330 527-2124
Garrettsville *(G-7228)*

Vulkor Incorporated...............................E 330 393-7600
Warren *(G-13809)*

Wiremax Ltd..F 419 531-9500
Toledo *(G-13179)*

Xponet Inc..G 440 354-6617
Painesville *(G-11123)*

3363 Aluminum die-castings

Accro-Cast Corporation..........................G 937 228-0497
Dayton *(G-5630)*

▲ Ahresty Wilmington Corporation..........B 937 382-6112
Wilmington *(G-14570)*

Akron Foundry Co..................................C 330 745-3101
Akron *(G-31)*

American Light Metals LLC......................C 330 908-3065
Macedonia *(G-8677)*

Apex Aluminum Die Cast Co Inc..............E 937 773-0432
Piqua *(G-11334)*

Cast Specialties Inc...............................E 216 292-7393
Cleveland *(G-3475)*

▲ Cmt Imports Inc..................................G 513 615-1851
Cincinnati *(G-2502)*

Destin Die Casting LLC...........................E 937 347-1111
Xenia *(G-14762)*

▼ Edc Liquidating Inc..............................C 330 467-0750
Macedonia *(G-8688)*

Enterprise Machine Inc...........................G 513 681-4409
Cincinnati *(G-2592)*

◆ Fort Recovery Industries Inc................C 419 375-4121
Fort Recovery *(G-6964)*

General Die Casters Inc..........................D 330 467-6700
Northfield *(G-10793)*

▲ General Die Casters Inc.......................E 330 678-2528
Twinsburg *(G-13310)*

Krengel Equipment LLC...........................C 440 946-3570
Eastlake *(G-6434)*

Matalco (us) Inc....................................E 234 806-0600
Warren *(G-13781)*

▲ Matalco (us) Inc..................................E 330 452-4760
Canton *(G-1939)*

Model Pattern & Foundry Co....................G 513 542-2322
Cincinnati *(G-2884)*

▲ Ohio Aluminum Industries Inc.............C 216 641-8865
Cleveland *(G-4110)*

◆ Ohio Decorative Products LLC.............C 419 647-9033
Spencerville *(G-12238)*

▲ Omni Die Casting Inc..........................D 330 830-5500
Massillon *(G-9227)*

Omni USA Inc.......................................G 330 830-5500
Massillon *(G-9228)*

◆ Park-Ohio Holdings Corp......................F 440 947-2000
Cleveland *(G-4136)*

Park-Ohio Industries Inc.........................C 440 947-2000
Cleveland *(G-4137)*

Plaster Process Castings Co....................E 216 663-1814
Cleveland *(G-4170)*

Ramco Electric Motors Inc......................D 937 548-2525
Greenville *(G-7350)*

Ravana Industries Inc.............................G 330 536-4015
Lowellville *(G-8664)*

Reliable Castings Corporation..................D 937 497-5217
Sidney *(G-12043)*

▲ Ross Casting & Innovation LLC............B 937 497-4500
Sidney *(G-12047)*

Seilkop Industries Inc.............................F 513 679-5680
Cincinnati *(G-3076)*

Seilkop Industries Inc.............................E 513 761-1035
Cincinnati *(G-3077)*

Seyekcub Inc..G 330 324-1394
Uhrichsville *(G-13406)*

SRS Die Casting Holdings LLC................E 330 467-0750
Macedonia *(G-8714)*

SRS Light Metals Inc.............................F 330 467-0750
Macedonia *(G-8715)*

The Basic Aluminum Castings Co............D 216 481-5606
Cleveland *(G-4378)*

◆ The Kindt-Collins Company LLC...........D 216 252-4122
Cleveland *(G-4387)*

▲ Thompson Aluminum Casting Co..........E 216 206-2781
Cleveland *(G-4393)*

Tooling Technology LLC..........................D 937 381-9211
Fort Loramie *(G-6960)*

United States Drill Head Co.....................F 513 941-0300
Cincinnati *(G-3185)*

▲ W E Lott Company...............................F 419 563-9400
Bucyrus *(G-1694)*

Yoder Industries Inc...............................C 937 278-5769
Dayton *(G-6089)*

3364 Nonferrous die-castings except aluminum

◆ American De Rosa Lamparts LLC.........D
Cuyahoga Falls *(G-5522)*

American Light Metals LLC......................C 330 908-3065
Macedonia *(G-8677)*

Cast Specialties Inc...............................E 216 292-7393
Cleveland *(G-3475)*

D Picking & Co......................................G 419 562-6891
Bucyrus *(G-1677)*

▲ Dd Foundry Inc...................................F 216 362-4100
Brookpark *(G-1548)*

▼ Edc Liquidating Inc..............................C 330 467-0750
Macedonia *(G-8688)*

Federal Metal Company..........................F 440 232-8700
Bedford *(G-1031)*

General Die Casters Inc..........................D 330 467-6700
Northfield *(G-10793)*

S
I
C

▲ General Die Casters Inc...................E 330 678-2528
Twinsburg *(G-13310)*

Hamilton Brass & Alum Castings...........G
Hamilton *(G-7500)*

M & M Dies Inc...................G 216 883-6628
Cleveland *(G-3973)*

Martina Metal LLC...................E 614 291-9700
Columbus *(G-5085)*

Model Pattern & Foundry Co...................G 513 542-2322
Cincinnati *(G-2884)*

◆ Oakwood Industries Inc...................D 440 232-8700
Bedford *(G-1051)*

Plaster Process Castings Co...................E 216 663-1814
Cleveland *(G-4170)*

Reebar Die Casting Inc...................F 419 878-7591
Waterville *(G-13840)*

SRS Die Casting Holdings LLC...................E 330 467-0750
Macedonia *(G-8714)*

SRS Light Metals Inc...................F 330 467-0750
Macedonia *(G-8715)*

Support Svc LLC...................G 419 617-0660
Lexington *(G-8375)*

◆ The Kindt-Collins Company LLC...................D 216 252-4122
Cleveland *(G-4387)*

▲ Thompson Aluminum Casting Co.....E 216 206-2781
Cleveland *(G-4393)*

Yoder Industries Inc...................C 937 278-5769
Dayton *(G-6089)*

3365 Aluminum foundries

◆ 889 Global Solutions Ltd...................F 614 235-8889
Columbus *(G-4655)*

Acuity Brands Lighting Inc...................D 740 349-4343
Newark *(G-10489)*

Air Craft Wheels LLC...................G 440 937-7903
Ravenna *(G-11513)*

Akron Foundry Co...................G 330 745-3101
Barberton *(G-791)*

Akron Foundry Co...................G 330 745-3101
Akron *(G-31)*

Albco Foundry Inc...................F 330 424-7716
Lisbon *(G-8463)*

◆ Aluminum Line Products Company....D 440 835-8880
Westlake *(G-14285)*

◆ AMG Aluminum North America LLC..F 659 348-3620
Cambridge *(G-1735)*

Aztec Manufacturing Inc...................E 330 783-9747
Youngstown *(G-14816)*

Brost Foundry Company...................E 216 641-1131
Cleveland *(G-3443)*

C M M S - Re LLC...................F 513 489-5111
Blue Ash *(G-1257)*

Cast Metals Technology Inc...................E 937 968-5460
Union City *(G-13414)*

Castek Inc...................E 440 365-2333
Elyria *(G-6510)*

▲ Dd Foundry Inc...................F 216 362-4100
Brookpark *(G-1548)*

Durivage Pattern and Mfg Inc...................E 419 836-8655
Williston *(G-14411)*

▲ Enprotech Industrial Tech LLC...................E 216 883-3220
Cleveland *(G-3675)*

Francis Manufacturing Company...........C 937 526-4551
Russia *(G-11673)*

General Aluminum Mfg Company...........E 330 297-1020
Ravenna *(G-11526)*

General Aluminum Mfg LLC...................B 440 593-6225
Conneaut *(G-5401)*

◆ General Aluminum Mfg LLC...................D 330 297-1225
Ravenna *(G-11527)*

▲ General Die Casters Inc...................E 330 678-2528
Twinsburg *(G-13310)*

General Motors LLC...................A 419 782-7010
Defiance *(G-6107)*

General Precision Corporation...................G 440 951-9380
Willoughby *(G-14463)*

Howmet Aluminum Casting Inc...................E 216 641-4340
Newburgh Heights *(G-10544)*

Htci Co...................F 937 845-1204
New Carlisle *(G-10372)*

Iabf Inc...................G 614 279-4498
Columbus *(G-4997)*

▲ Jrm 2 Corporation...................D 513 554-1700
Cincinnati *(G-2774)*

◆ Kovatch Castings Inc...................C 330 896-9944
Uniontown *(G-13421)*

Lite Metals Company...................E 330 296-6110
Ravenna *(G-11532)*

Mansfield Brass & Aluminu...................D 419 492-2154
New Washington *(G-10480)*

▲ Miba Bearings US LLC...................B 740 962-4242
Mcconnelsville *(G-9364)*

Miller Castings Inc...................E 330 482-2923
Columbiana *(G-4622)*

Model Pattern & Foundry Co...................G 513 542-2322
Cincinnati *(G-2884)*

Morris Bean & Company...................C 937 767-7301
Yellow Springs *(G-14790)*

Mpe Aeroengines Inc...................E 937 878-3800
Huber Heights *(G-7823)*

Multi Cast LLC...................E 419 335-0010
Wauseon *(G-13856)*

Nelson Aluminum Foundry Inc...................G 440 543-1941
Chagrin Falls *(G-2173)*

New Mansfield Brass & Alum Co...................G 419 492-2166
New Washington *(G-10481)*

Non-Ferrous Casting Company...................G 937 228-1162
Dayton *(G-5909)*

P C M Co...................E 330 336-8040
Wadsworth *(G-13656)*

Piqua Emery Cutter & Fndry Co...................D 937 773-4134
Piqua *(G-11375)*

▲ Pride Cast Metals Inc...................D 513 541-1295
Cincinnati *(G-2981)*

▲ Range Kleen Mfg Inc...................B 419 331-8000
Elida *(G-6487)*

Ransom & Randolph LLC...................G 419 865-9497
Maumee *(G-9314)*

Reliable Castings Corporation...................D 937 497-5217
Sidney *(G-12043)*

Reliable Castings Corporation...................D 513 541-2627
Cincinnati *(G-3037)*

▲ Ross Aluminum Castings LLC...................C 937 492-4134
Sidney *(G-12046)*

Rotocast Technologies Inc...................E 330 798-9091
Akron *(G-291)*

Seilkop Industries Inc...................F 513 679-5680
Cincinnati *(G-3076)*

Skuld LLC...................E 330 423-7339
Piqua *(G-11384)*

▼ Specialized Castings Ltd...................F 937 669-5620
Greenville *(G-7354)*

▲ Stripmatic Products Inc...................E 216 241-7143
Cleveland *(G-4336)*

T W Corporation...................G 440 461-3234
Akron *(G-327)*

Tessec LLC...................D 937 576-0010
Dayton *(G-6045)*

▲ Thompson Aluminum Casting Co.....E 216 206-2781
Cleveland *(G-4393)*

Tooling Technology LLC...................D 937 381-9211
Fort Loramie *(G-6960)*

Tri - Flex of Ohio Inc...................G 330 705-7084
North Canton *(G-10677)*

◆ US Metalcraft Inc...................F 419 692-4962
Delphos *(G-6197)*

Yoder Industries Inc...................C 937 278-5769
Dayton *(G-6089)*

Zephyr Industries Inc...................G 419 281-4485
Ashland *(G-581)*

3366 Copper foundries

Accurate Products Company...................G 740 498-7202
Newcomerstown *(G-10567)*

▲ Advance Bronze Inc...................F 330 948-1231
Lodi *(G-8496)*

Advance Bronzehubco Div...................E 304 232-4414
Lodi *(G-8497)*

Albco Foundry Inc...................F 330 424-7716
Lisbon *(G-8463)*

American Bronze Corporation...................E 216 341-7800
Cleveland *(G-3342)*

Brost Foundry Company...................E 419 522-1133
Mansfield *(G-8768)*

Brost Foundry Company...................E 216 641-1131
Cleveland *(G-3443)*

Buckeye Machining Inc...................G 216 731-9535
Euclid *(G-6645)*

Bunting Bearings LLC...................E 419 522-3323
Mansfield *(G-8770)*

▲ Bunting Bearings LLC...................D 419 866-7000
Holland *(G-7747)*

Calmego Specialized Pdts LLC...................F 937 669-5620
Greenville *(G-7337)*

▲ Climax Metal Products Company......D 440 943-8898
Mentor *(G-9502)*

D Picking & Co...................G 419 562-6891
Bucyrus *(G-1677)*

D4 Industries Inc...................G 419 523-9555
Ottawa *(G-11032)*

Dupont Specialty Pdts USA LLC...................C 216 901-3600
Cleveland *(G-3638)*

◆ Falcon Foundry Company...................D 330 536-6221
Lowellville *(G-8661)*

Foundry Artists Inc...................G 216 391-9030
Cleveland *(G-3739)*

Hadronics Inc...................D 513 321-9350
Cincinnati *(G-2702)*

High Tech Castings...................G 937 845-1204
New Carlisle *(G-10371)*

Johnson Metall Inc...................D 440 245-6826
Lorain *(G-8559)*

◆ Kovatch Castings Inc...................C 330 896-9944
Uniontown *(G-13421)*

M A Harrison Mfg Co Inc...................E 440 965-4306
Wakeman *(G-13682)*

Maass Midwest Mfg Inc...................E 419 894-6424
Arcadia *(G-482)*

▲ McNeil Industries Inc...................E 440 951-7756
Painesville *(G-11099)*

▲ Meierjohan-Wengler Inc...................E 513 771-6074
Cincinnati *(G-2860)*

Metaltek International Inc...................D 419 626-5340
Sandusky *(G-11858)*

Model Pattern & Foundry Co...................G 513 542-2322
Cincinnati *(G-2884)*

▲ National Bronze Mtls Ohio Inc...................E 440 277-1226
Lorain *(G-8568)*

Non-Ferrous Casting Company...................G 937 228-1162
Dayton *(G-5909)*

Oakes Foundry Inc...................E 330 372-4010
Warren *(G-13785)*

Orrville Bronze & Aluminum Co...................E 330 682-4015
Orrville *(G-10999)*

Piqua Emery Cutter & Fndry Co...................D 937 773-4134
Piqua *(G-11375)*

▲ Pride Cast Metals Inc .... D 513 541-1295
Cincinnati *(G-2981)*

Randall Bearings Inc .... F 419 678-2486
Coldwater *(G-4583)*

▲ Randall Bearings Inc .... D 419 223-1075
Lima *(G-8442)*

▲ Ryder-Heil Bronze Inc .... E 419 562-2841
Bucyrus *(G-1690)*

▲ S C Industries Inc .... E 216 732-9000
Euclid *(G-6677)*

▲ Santos Industrial Ltd .... E 937 299-7333
Dayton *(G-5994)*

▲ Semco Inc .... D 800 848-5764
Marion *(G-8997)*

▲ Stripmatic Products Inc .... E 216 241-7143
Cleveland *(G-4336)*

Whip Guide Co .... F 440 543-5151
Chagrin Falls *(G-2191)*

3369 Nonferrous foundries, nec

◆ 889 Global Solutions Ltd .... F 614 235-8889
Columbus *(G-4655)*

A C Williams Co Inc .... E 330 296-6110
Ravenna *(G-11511)*

Air Craft Wheels LLC .... G 440 937-7903
Ravenna *(G-11513)*

Akron Foundry Co .... C 330 745-3101
Akron *(G-31)*

Albco Foundry Inc .... F 330 424-7716
Lisbon *(G-8463)*

▲ Alcon Industries Inc .... D 216 961-1100
Cleveland *(G-3321)*

Apex Aluminum Die Cast Co Inc ..... E 937 773-0432
Piqua *(G-11334)*

Brost Foundry Company .... E 216 641-1131
Cleveland *(G-3443)*

Bunting Bearings LLC .... E 419 522-3323
Mansfield *(G-8770)*

▲ Catania Medallic Specialty Inc .... E 440 933-9595
Avon Lake *(G-751)*

Columbiana Foundry Company .... C 330 482-3336
Columbiana *(G-4612)*

Consoldted Precision Pdts Corp ..... C 440 953-0053
Eastlake *(G-6421)*

Cpp-Cleveland Inc .... C 440 953-0053
Eastlake *(G-6422)*

Cpp-Cleveland Inc .... D 216 453-4800
Euclid *(G-6646)*

Curtiss-Wright Flow Ctrl Corp .... D 216 267-3200
Cleveland *(G-3583)*

▲ Dd Foundry Inc .... F 216 362-4100
Brookpark *(G-1548)*

DMK Industries Inc .... F 513 727-4549
Middletown *(G-9854)*

Durivage Pattern and Mfg Inc .... E 419 836-8655
Williston *(G-14411)*

Ecm Industries LLC .... F 513 533-6242
Cincinnati *(G-2578)*

◆ Ellwood Engineered Castings Co ...... C 330 568-3000
Hubbard *(G-7810)*

Elyria Foundry Company LLC .... E 440 322-4657
Elyria *(G-6529)*

Esco Turbine Technologies .... C 440 953-0053
Eastlake *(G-6428)*

Francis Manufacturing Company ..... C 937 526-4551
Russia *(G-11673)*

◆ Frohn North America Inc .... G 770 819-0089
Bedford Heights *(G-1077)*

◆ Garfield Alloys Inc .... F 216 587-4843
Cleveland *(G-3754)*

General Aluminum Mfg Company ..... E 330 297-1020
Ravenna *(G-11526)*

General Aluminum Mfg LLC .... B 440 593-6225
Conneaut *(G-5401)*

◆ General Aluminum Mfg LLC .... D 330 297-1225
Ravenna *(G-11527)*

▲ General Die Casters Inc .... E 330 678-2528
Twinsburg *(G-13310)*

General Motors LLC .... A 419 782-7010
Defiance *(G-6107)*

Harbor Castings Inc .... E 330 499-7178
Cuyahoga Falls *(G-5547)*

Hydro-Aire Aerospace Corp .... C 440 323-3211
Elyria *(G-6544)*

Iabf Inc .... G 614 279-4498
Columbus *(G-4997)*

▲ Ilsco LLC .... C 513 533-6200
Blue Ash *(G-1287)*

▲ Jrm 2 Company .... D 513 554-1700
Cincinnati *(G-2774)*

◆ Kovatch Castings Inc .... C 330 896-9944
Uniontown *(G-13421)*

Kse Manufacturing .... G 937 409-9831
Sidney *(G-12027)*

Lite Magnesium Products Inc .... D 330 296-6110
Ravenna *(G-11531)*

Lite Metals Company .... E 330 296-6110
Ravenna *(G-11532)*

▲ Materion Advnced Mtls Tech Svc .... D 216 486-4200
Mayfield Heights *(G-9335)*

Materion Brush Inc .... A 419 862-2745
Elmore *(G-6491)*

McM Precision Castings Inc .... E 419 669-3226
Weston *(G-14349)*

Morris Bean & Company .... G 937 767-7301
Yellow Springs *(G-14790)*

Nelson Aluminum Foundry Inc .... G 440 543-1941
Chagrin Falls *(G-2173)*

▲ Nova Machine Products Inc .... C 216 267-3200
Middleburg Heights *(G-9775)*

◆ Ohio Decorative Products LLC ..... C 419 647-9033
Spencerville *(G-12238)*

Old Smo Inc .... C 419 394-3346
Saint Marys *(G-11746)*

PCC Airfoils LLC .... B 216 692-7900
Cleveland *(G-4148)*

PCC Airfoils LLC .... B 740 982-6025
Crooksville *(G-5511)*

PCC Airfoils LLC .... B 440 585-8247
Eastlake *(G-6110)*

PCC Airfoils LLC .... C 440 255-9770
Mentor *(G-9584)*

PCC Airfoils LLC .... C 330 868-6441
Minerva *(G-10045)*

PCC Airfoils LLC .... C 440 350-6150
Painesville *(G-11104)*

◆ PCC Airfoils LLC .... E 216 831-3590
Beachwood *(G-938)*

PCC Airfoils LLC .... D 216 766-6206
Beachwood *(G-939)*

Piqua Emery Cutter & Fndry Co ...... D 937 773-4134
Piqua *(G-11375)*

Precision Castparts Corp .... F 440 350-6150
Painesville *(G-11106)*

Reliable Castings Corporation .... D 937 497-5217
Sidney *(G-12043)*

◆ Rolled Alloys Inc .... D 800 521-0332
Maumee *(G-9315)*

▲ Ross Aluminum Castings LLC ...... E 937 492-4134
Sidney *(G-12046)*

Rossborough Supply Co .... G 216 941-6115
Cleveland *(G-4255)*

Sam Americas Inc .... E 330 628-1118
Mogadore *(G-10085)*

◆ Sandusky International Inc .... C 419 626-5340
Sandusky *(G-11868)*

Seaport Mold & Casting Company ..... G 419 243-1422
Toledo *(G-13123)*

Seilkop Industries Inc .... F 513 679-5680
Cincinnati *(G-3076)*

T & B Foundry Company .... G 216 391-4200
Cleveland *(G-4360)*

▲ Technology House Ltd .... G 440 248-3025
Streetsboro *(G-12527)*

Telcon LLC .... D 330 562-5566
Streetsboro *(G-12528)*

▲ Thompson Aluminum Casting Co ..... E 216 206-2781
Cleveland *(G-4393)*

◆ Voss Industries LLC .... C 216 771-7655
Cleveland *(G-4482)*

Warren Castings Inc .... G 216 883-2520
Cleveland *(G-4490)*

Yoder Industries Inc .... C 937 278-5769
Dayton *(G-6089)*

3398 Metal heat treating

Akron Steel Treating Co .... E 330 773-8211
Akron *(G-43)*

Al Fe Heat Treating-Ohio Inc .... E 330 336-0211
Wadsworth *(G-13628)*

Al-Fe Heat Treating LLC .... F 419 782-7200
Defiance *(G-6095)*

AM Castle & Co .... F 330 425-7000
Bedford *(G-1011)*

▲ Amac Enterprises Inc .... C 216 362-1880
Parma *(G-11129)*

▲ American Metal Treating Co .... E 216 431-4492
Cleveland *(G-3346)*

American Quality Stripping Inc .... E 419 625-6288
Sandusky *(G-11822)*

American Steel Treating Inc .... D 419 874-2044
Perrysburg *(G-11202)*

ATI Flat Rlled Pdts Hldngs LLC ...... F 330 875-2244
Louisville *(G-8598)*

Atmosphere Annealing LLC .... D 330 478-0314
Kenton *(G-8095)*

B&C Machine Co LLC .... F 330 745-4013
Barberton *(G-796)*

Bekaert Corporation .... E 330 683-5060
Orrville *(G-10975)*

Berkshire Road Holdings Inc .... F 216 883-4200
Cleveland *(G-3416)*

Bob Lanes Welding Inc .... G 740 373-3567
Marietta *(G-8904)*

Bodycote Imt Inc .... F 740 852-5000
London *(G-8531)*

Bodycote Srfc Tech Prperty LLC ..... C 513 770-4900
Mason *(G-9072)*

Bodycote Surfc Tech Mexico LLC ..... C 513 770-4900
Mason *(G-9075)*

Bodycote Thermal Proc Inc .... E 513 921-2300
Cincinnati *(G-2416)*

Bodycote Thermal Proc Inc .... E 440 473-2020
Cleveland *(G-3425)*

Bodycote Thermal Proc Inc .... C 740 852-4955
London *(G-8532)*

Bolttech Mannings LLC .... G 614 836-0021
Groveport *(G-7426)*

Bowdil Company .... F 800 356-8663
Canton *(G-1843)*

Carpe Diem Industries LLC .... D 419 358-0129
Bluffton *(G-1359)*

Carpe Diem Industries LLC .... D 419 659-5639
Columbus Grove *(G-5382)*

Certified Heat Treating Inc .... G 937 866-0245
Dayton *(G-5697)*

Employee Codes: A=Over 500 employees, B=251-500
C=101-250, D=51-100, E=20-50, F=10-19, G=1-9
     2025 Harris Ohio
Industrial Directory   799

S
I
C

Cincinnati Gearing Systems Inc............. D 513 527-8600
Cincinnati (G-2476)

Cincinnati Stl Treating Co LLC.............. E 513 271-3173
Cincinnati (G-2487)

▲ Cleveland-Cliffs Columbus LLC....... C 614 492-6800
Richfield (G-11589)

◆ Clifton Steel Company.....................D 216 662-6111
Maple Heights (G-8881)

Commercial Steel Treating Co.............. F 216 431-8204
Cleveland (G-3553)

Curtiss-Wright Surfc Tech LLC.............. F 330 425-1490
Twinsburg (G-13290)

Dayton Forging Heat Treating............. D 937 253-4126
Dayton (G-5726)

Derrick Company Inc......................... E 513 321-8122
Cincinnati (G-2546)

Detroit Flame Hardening Co................ F 513 942-1400
Fairfield (G-6727)

Dewitt Inc... G 216 662-0800
Maple Heights (G-8882)

▲ Die Co Inc.................................... E 440 942-8856
Eastlake (G-6423)

▲ Dowa Tht America Inc.................... E 419 354-4144
Bowling Green (G-1418)

Erie Steel Ltd.................................. E 419 478-3743
Toledo (G-12956)

Euclid Heat Treating Co.................... D 216 481-8444
Euclid (G-6650)

FB Acquisition LLC.......................... E 513 459-7782
Lebanon (G-8255)

Fbf Limited..................................... E 513 541-6300
Cincinnati (G-2615)

Flynn Inc... G 419 478-3743
Toledo (G-12966)

▲ Fusion Incorporated..................... D 440 946-3300
Willoughby (G-14460)

Gerdau McSteel Atmsphere Annli........ E 330 478-0314
Canton (G-1900)

Gt Technologies Inc.......................... E 419 782-8955
Defiance (G-6109)

H & M Metal Processing Co................ E 330 745-3075
Akron (G-168)

Heat Treating Inc............................. E 937 325-3121
Springfield (G-12319)

Heat Treating Equipment Inc.............. E 740 549-3700
Lewis Center (G-8335)

Heat Treating Inc............................. E 614 759-9963
Gahanna (G-7159)

Heat-Treating Technologies Inc........... E 419 224-8324
Lima (G-8413)

HI Tecmetal Group Inc....................... E 216 881-8100
Wickliffe (G-14378)

Hmt Inc... G 440 599-7005
Conneaut (G-5404)

Kando of Cincinnati Inc..................... E 513 459-7782
Lebanon (G-8271)

Kowalski Heat Treating Co................. F 216 631-4411
Cleveland (G-3927)

Lapham-Hickey Steel Corp................. D 614 443-4881
Columbus (G-5065)

Lapham-Hickey Steel Corp................. D 419 399-4803
Paulding (G-11158)

McDonald Steel Plate Inc................... E 216 883-4200
Cleveland (G-4008)

McOn Inds Inc.................................. E 937 294-2681
Moraine (G-10176)

Metal Improvement Company LLC........ D 513 489-6484
Blue Ash (G-1309)

Metal Improvement Company LLC........ E 330 425-1490
Twinsburg (G-13339)

Metallurgical Service Inc.................... F 937 294-2681
Moraine (G-10177)

Moore Mc Millen Holdings................... E 330 745-3075
Cuyahoga Falls (G-5561)

National Peening............................... G 216 342-9155
Bedford Heights (G-1080)

▲ Neturen America Corporation......... F 513 863-1900
Hamilton (G-7512)

◆ Northlake Steel Corporation...........D 330 220-7717
Valley City (G-13513)

Northwind Industries Inc.................... G 216 433-0666
Cleveland (G-4099)

Ohio Flame Hardening Company.......... E 513 336-6160
Cincinnati (G-2923)

Ohio Metallurgical Service Inc............. D 440 365-4104
Elyria (G-6573)

▲ Oliver Steel Plate Co.................... D 330 425-7000
Twinsburg (G-13347)

P & L Heat Trting Grinding Inc............. E 330 746-1339
Youngstown (G-14907)

P & L Precision Grinding Llc............... F 330 746-8081
Youngstown (G-14909)

▲ Parker Trutec Incorporated............ D 937 323-8833
Springfield (G-12359)

Precision Powder Coating Inc............. F 330 478-0741
Canton (G-1980)

Pressure Technology Ohio Inc............. E 215 628-1975
Concord Township (G-5393)

Pride Investments LLC....................... F 937 461-1121
Dayton (G-5953)

Pro-TEC Coating Company LLC.......... D 419 943-1100
Leipsic (G-8313)

Ridge Machine & Welding Co.............. G 740 537-2821
Toronto (G-13186)

Surface Enhancement Tech LLC.......... F 513 561-1520
Cincinnati (G-3131)

Team Inc.. F 614 263-1808
Columbus (G-5314)

Techniques Surfaces Usa Inc.............. G 937 323-2556
Springfield (G-12384)

Thermal Solutions Inc........................ E 614 263-1808
Columbus (G-5322)

Thermal Treatment Center Inc............. E 216 881-8100
Wickliffe (G-14396)

Universal Heat Treating Inc................. E 216 641-2000
Aurora (G-691)

USA Heat Treating Inc........................ E 216 587-4700
Cleveland (G-4453)

Vicon Fabricating Company Ltd........... E 440 205-6700
Mentor (G-9649)

Weiss Industries Inc.......................... E 419 526-2480
Mansfield (G-8865)

Winston Heat Treating Inc.................. E 937 226-0110
Dayton (G-6083)

Worthngton Smuel Coil Proc LLC......... E 330 963-3777
Twinsburg (G-13398)

◆ Xtek Inc....................................... B 513 733-7800
Cincinnati (G-3240)

Youngstown Heat Trting Ntrding........... G 330 788-3025
Youngstown (G-14971)

Zion Industries Inc............................ E 330 483-4650
Valley City (G-13523)

3399 Primary metal products

A-Gas US Holdings Inc....................... F 419 867-8990
Bowling Green (G-1403)

Additive Metal Alloys Ltd................... G 800 687-6110
Holland (G-7744)

Bogie Industries Inc Ltd.................... E 330 745-3105
Akron (G-81)

Contitech Usa LLC............................ C 937 644-8900
Marysville (G-9016)

◆ Destiny Manufacturing Inc............E 330 273-9000
Brunswick (G-1588)

Duffee Finishing Inc.......................... G 740 965-4848
Sunbury (G-12663)

▲ E-B Wire Works Inc...................... D 330 833-4101
Massillon (G-9189)

◆ Eckart America Corporation..........D 440 954-7600
Painesville (G-11082)

General Nano LLC............................. F 513 309-5947
Cincinnati (G-2664)

▲ Key Finishes LLC......................... G 614 351-8393
Columbus (G-5053)

▲ Midwest Motor Supply Co............. C 800 233-1294
Columbus (G-5100)

Obron Atlantic Corporation................ D 440 954-7600
Painesville (G-11100)

Ohio Valley Manufacturing Inc............ D 419 522-5818
Mansfield (G-8841)

Powdermet Inc.................................. E 216 404-0053
Euclid (G-6670)

Precision Pressed Powdered Met......... F 937 433-6802
Dayton (G-5951)

◆ Rmi Titanium Company LLC...........E 330 652-9952
Niles (G-10604)

Royal Powder Corporation.................. G 216 898-0074
Cleveland (G-4259)

Seaway Bolt And Specials Company..... D 440 236-5015
Columbia Station (G-4602)

◆ Shinagawa Inc..............................E 330 628-1118
Mogadore (G-10086)

Stein LLC.. D 216 883-7444
Cleveland (G-4331)

▲ Stein LLC.................................... F 440 526-9301
Independence (G-7919)

Third Millennium Materials LLC........... G 740 947-1023
Waverly (G-13874)

▼ Transmet Corporation................... G 614 276-5522
Columbus (G-5328)

◆ Truck Fax Inc...............................G 216 921-8866
Cleveland (G-4431)

Vital & Fhr North America LLC............. E 650 405-9975
Bowling Green (G-1446)

▲ Waterford Tank Fabrication Ltd........ D 740 984-4100
Beverly (G-1211)

34 FABRICATED METAL PRODUCTS

3411 Metal cans

◆ Anchor Hocking LLC......................A 740 687-2500
Columbus (G-4711)

Ball Arosol Specialty Cont Inc............. E 330 534-1903
Hubbard (G-7808)

Ball Corporation............................... D 614 771-9112
Columbus (G-4742)

Ball Corporation............................... E 419 423-3071
Findlay (G-6840)

Ball Corporation............................... F 330 244-2313
North Canton (G-10629)

Ball Metal Beverage Cont Corp............ C 419 423-3071
Findlay (G-6841)

Buckeye Stamping Company................ D 877 728-0776
Columbus (G-4786)

Cardinal Welding Inc......................... G 330 426-2404
East Palestine (G-6400)

Cleveland Steel Container Corp............ E 330 656-5600
Streetsboro (G-12493)

Crown Cork & Seal Usa Inc................. C 937 299-2027
Dayton (G-5715)

Crown Cork & Seal Usa Inc................. D 740 681-6593
Lancaster (G-8192)

Crown Cork & Seal Usa Inc................. D 740 681-3000
Lancaster (G-8193)

Crown Cork & Seal Usa Inc .... B 330 833-1011
Massillon *(G-9183)*

Crown Cork & Seal Usa Inc .... C 419 727-8201
Toledo *(G-12933)*

Drt Holdings LLC .... G 937 297-6676
West Chester *(G-13987)*

Eisenhauer Mfg Co LLC .... D 419 238-0081
Van Wert *(G-13535)*

Encore Industries Inc .... C 419 626-8000
Sandusky *(G-11830)*

▲ Envases Media Inc .... E 419 636-5461
Bryan *(G-1640)*

◆ G & S Metal Products Co Inc .... C 216 441-0700
Cleveland *(G-3748)*

G W Cobb Co .... F 216 341-0100
Cleveland *(G-3751)*

◆ Ghp II LLC .... C 740 687-2500
Lancaster *(G-8204)*

Independent Can Company .... F 440 593-5300
Conneaut *(G-5405)*

◆ Organized Living Inc .... E 513 489-9300
Cincinnati *(G-2939)*

◆ Packaging Specialties Inc .... E 330 723-6000
Medina *(G-9433)*

▲ SSP Industrial Group Inc .... G 330 665-2900
Fairlawn *(G-6814)*

Stolle Machinery Company LLC .... E 330 244-0555
Canton *(G-2018)*

▲ Trivium Alum Packg USA Corp .... E 330 744-2267
Youngstown *(G-14952)*

▲ Winzeler Stamping Co .... E 419 485-3147
Montpelier *(G-10138)*

▼ Witt Industries Inc .... D 513 871-5700
Mason *(G-9167)*

3412 Metal barrels, drums, and pails

Champion Company .... G 937 324-5681
Springfield *(G-12290)*

Champion Company .... D 937 324-5681
Springfield *(G-12291)*

Cleveland Steel Container Corp .... E 330 544-2271
Niles *(G-10586)*

Cleveland Steel Container Corp .... E 330 656-5600
Streetsboro *(G-12493)*

◆ Cleveland Steel Container .... E 440 349-8000
Hudson *(G-7839)*

Deufol Worldwide Packaging LLC .... E 440 232-1100
Bedford *(G-1026)*

Eisenhauer Mfg Co LLC .... D 419 238-0081
Van Wert *(G-13535)*

Georgia-Pacific LLC .... C 740 477-3347
Circleville *(G-3260)*

Green Bay Packaging Inc .... E 419 332-5593
Fremont *(G-7117)*

Green Bay Packaging Inc .... D 513 489-8700
Lebanon *(G-8266)*

Greif Inc .... E 740 657-6500
Delaware *(G-6150)*

◆ Greif Inc .... E 740 549-6000
Delaware *(G-6149)*

Horwitz & Pintis Co .... F 419 666-2220
Toledo *(G-12996)*

Mauser Usa LLC .... D 513 398-1300
Mason *(G-9125)*

Mauser Usa LLC .... D 740 397-1762
Mount Vernon *(G-10251)*

North Coast Container LLC .... E 216 441-6214
Cleveland *(G-4083)*

Overseas Packing LLC .... G 440 232-2917
Bedford *(G-1053)*

◆ Packaging Specialties Inc .... E 330 723-6000
Medina *(G-9433)*

▲ Sabco Industries Inc .... E 419 531-5347
Toledo *(G-13120)*

Schwarz Partners Packaging LLC .... F 317 290-1140
Sidney *(G-12050)*

▲ SSP Industrial Group Inc .... G 330 665-2900
Fairlawn *(G-6814)*

Strawser Steel Drum Ohio Ltd .... E 614 856-5982
Mount Vernon *(G-10266)*

Syme Inc .... E 330 723-6000
Medina *(G-9453)*

Tavens Container Inc .... D 216 883-3333
Bedford *(G-1060)*

▼ Werk-Brau Company .... C 419 422-2912
Findlay *(G-6933)*

▼ Witt Industries Inc .... D 513 871-5700
Mason *(G-9167)*

3421 Cutlery

Accu-Grind Inc .... G 330 677-2225
Kent *(G-8012)*

Advetech Inc .... E 330 533-2227
Canfield *(G-1801)*

American Punch Co .... E 216 731-4501
Euclid *(G-6642)*

American Quicksilver Company .... G 513 871-4517
Cincinnati *(G-2362)*

Busse Knife Co .... G 419 923-6471
Wauseon *(G-13846)*

▲ Crescent Manufacturing Company ...... D 419 332-6484
Fremont *(G-7099)*

E Warther & Sons Inc .... F 330 343-7513
Dover *(G-6244)*

Edgewell Per Care Brands LLC .... F 330 527-2191
Garrettsville *(G-7219)*

Edgewell Personal Care Company .... G 740 374-1905
Marietta *(G-8915)*

Energizer Global Auto Care .... G 937 742-4500
Vandalia *(G-13555)*

◆ G & S Metal Products Co Inc .... C 216 441-0700
Cleveland *(G-3748)*

General Cutlery Inc .... F 419 332-2316
Fremont *(G-7114)*

Gillette Company LLC .... D 513 983-1100
Cincinnati *(G-2670)*

▲ Heinemann Saw Company .... E 330 456-4721
Canton *(G-1910)*

Kabab-G Inc .... G 216 476-3335
Cleveland *(G-3904)*

Klenk Industries Inc .... G 330 453-7857
Canton *(G-1925)*

Libbey Glass LLC .... D 419 727-2211
Toledo *(G-13034)*

Lt Wright Handcrafted Knife Co .... F 740 317-1404
Steubenville *(G-12405)*

Madison Property Holdings Inc .... E 800 215-3210
Cincinnati *(G-2839)*

New York Frozen Foods Inc .... F 614 846-2232
Westerville *(G-14224)*

Northstar Plastics Inc .... D 216 340-7109
Glenwillow *(G-7287)*

◆ Npk Construction Equipment Inc .... D 440 232-7900
Bedford *(G-1050)*

Procter & Gamble Company .... D 513 983-1100
Cincinnati *(G-2987)*

Procter & Gamble Company .... E 513 266-4375
Cincinnati *(G-2988)*

Procter & Gamble Company .... F 513 871-7557
Cincinnati *(G-2989)*

Procter & Gamble Company .... F 513 482-6789
Cincinnati *(G-2991)*

Procter & Gamble Company .... C 513 983-3000
Cincinnati *(G-2993)*

Procter & Gamble Company .... D 513 627-7115
Cincinnati *(G-2994)*

Procter & Gamble Company .... E 513 945-0340
Cincinnati *(G-2997)*

Procter & Gamble Company .... C 513 622-1000
Mason *(G-9138)*

Procter & Gamble Company .... C 513 634-9600
West Chester *(G-14054)*

Procter & Gamble Company .... C 513 634-9110
West Chester *(G-14055)*

◆ Procter & Gamble Company .... A 513 983-1100
Cincinnati *(G-2999)*

R & F Franchise Group LLC .... G 440 942-7140
Willoughby *(G-14515)*

3423 Hand and edge tools, nec

▲ A JC Inc .... F 800 428-2438
Hudson *(G-7826)*

Acme Company .... D 330 758-2313
Poland *(G-11434)*

Advetech Inc .... E 330 533-2227
Canfield *(G-1802)*

Advetech Inc .... E 330 533-2227
Canfield *(G-1801)*

Allegion Access Tech LLC .... E 440 461-5500
Cleveland *(G-3330)*

▼ Amcraft Inc .... G 419 729-7900
Toledo *(G-12872)*

◆ American Agritech LLC .... E 480 777-2000
Marysville *(G-9014)*

◆ American Power Pull Corp .... G 419 335-7050
Archbold *(G-485)*

Ames Companies Inc .... E 740 783-2535
Dexter City *(G-6223)*

ASG .... F 216 486-6163
Cleveland *(G-3376)*

Asg Division Jergens Inc .... E 888 486-6163
Cleveland *(G-3377)*

Bully Tools Inc .... E 740 282-5834
Steubenville *(G-12401)*

C B Mfg & Sls Co Inc .... F 937 866-5986
Dayton *(G-5691)*

▲ C B Mfg & Sls Co Inc .... D 937 866-5986
Miamisburg *(G-9678)*

Cannon Salt & Supply Inc .... G 440 232-1700
Bedford *(G-1019)*

Chrisnik Inc .... G 513 738-2920
Okeana *(G-10027)*

Cornwell Quality Tools Company .... D 330 628-2627
Mogadore *(G-10071)*

D & M Saw & Tool Inc .... G 513 871-5433
Cincinnati *(G-2535)*

▲ E Z Grout Corporation .... E 740 749-3512
Malta *(G-8744)*

▲ Eaton Electric Holdings LLC .... B 440 523-5000
Cleveland *(G-3654)*

Edgerton Forge Inc .... D 419 298-2333
Edgerton *(G-6466)*

▲ Electric Eel Mfg Co Inc .... E 937 323-4644
Springfield *(G-12306)*

Empire Plow Company Inc .... E 216 641-2290
Berea *(G-1169)*

◆ Everhard Products Inc .... C 330 453-7786
Canton *(G-1890)*

Falcon Industries Inc .... E 330 723-0099
Medina *(G-9401)*

◆ Furukawa Rock Drill USA Co Ltd .... F 330 673-5826
Kent *(G-8034)*

▲ Hamilton Industrial Grinding Inc .... E 513 863-1221
Hamilton *(G-7502)*

Handy Twine Knife Co .... G 419 294-3424
Upper Sandusky *(G-13442)*

J & S Tool Corporation.............. G 216 676-8330
Lorain *(G-8558)*

Knight Ergonomics Inc................. F 440 746-0044
Brecksville *(G-1475)*

▲ Matco Tools Corporation........... B 330 929-4949
Stow *(G-12440)*

Michael Byrne Manufacturing Co Inc..... E 419 525-1214
Mansfield *(G-8825)*

Midwest Knife Grinding Inc........... F 330 854-1030
Canal Fulton *(G-1778)*

Myers Industries Inc.................. E 440 632-1006
Middlefield *(G-9817)*

National Skilled Trades Netwrk...... F 614 230-2852
Columbus *(G-5122)*

▲ Norbar Torque Tools Inc.............. F 440 953-1175
Willoughby *(G-14495)*

Panacea Products Corporation........ E 614 429-6320
Columbus *(G-5170)*

Randolph Tool Company Inc........... F 330 877-4923
Hartville *(G-7582)*

◆ Rex International USA Inc..............E 800 321-7950
Ashtabula *(G-615)*

◆ Ridge Tool Company................ A 440 323-5581
Elyria *(G-6586)*

Ridge Tool Manufacturing Co........ F 440 323-5581
Elyria *(G-6588)*

▲ S & H Industries Inc.................. E 216 831-0550
Cleveland *(G-4266)*

S & H Industries Inc................. F 216 831-0550
Bedford *(G-1058)*

▲ Save Edge Inc....................... E 937 376-8268
Xenia *(G-14774)*

Sewer Rodding Equipment Co.......... C 419 991-2065
Lima *(G-8447)*

Simon Ellis Superabrasives Inc....... G 937 226-0683
Dayton *(G-6009)*

▲ Stanley Industrial & Auto LLC...... D 614 755-7000
Dublin *(G-6349)*

◆ Step2 Company LLC................. B 866 429-5200
Streetsboro *(G-12525)*

Stride Tool LLC..................... C 440 247-4600
Glenwillow *(G-7289)*

Sumitomo Elc Carbide Mfg Inc....... F 440 354-0600
Grand River *(G-7312)*

▲ Superion Inc....................... E 937 374-0033
Xenia *(G-14776)*

◆ Superior Tool Corporation......... E 216 398-8600
Cleveland *(G-4348)*

▲ The Cornwell Quality Tool.......... D 330 336-3506
Wadsworth *(G-13674)*

White Industrial Tool Inc........... G 330 773-6889
Akron *(G-356)*

Wise Edge LLC....................... G 330 208-0889
Mogadore *(G-10094)*

▲ Wright Tool Company.............. C 330 848-0600
Barberton *(G-842)*

Your Carpenter Inc.................. G 216 621-2166
Cleveland *(G-4521)*

3425 Saw blades and handsaws

◆ Callahan Cutting Tools Inc.........G 614 294-1649
Columbus *(G-4792)*

Cammel Saw Company................ F 330 477-3764
Canton *(G-1851)*

▲ Crescent Manufacturing Company... D 419 332-6484
Fremont *(G-7099)*

Dynatech Systems Inc................ F 440 365-1774
Elyria *(G-6523)*

▲ Heinemann Saw Company.......... E 330 456-4721
Canton *(G-1910)*

J & S Tool Corporation............. G 216 676-8330
Lorain *(G-8558)*

◆ M K Morse Company.................B 330 453-8187
Canton *(G-1935)*

Martindale Electric Company......... E 216 521-8567
Cleveland *(G-3994)*

◆ Peerless Saw Company.............. E 614 836-5790
Groveport *(G-7448)*

▼ Regal Diamond Products Corp....... F 440 944-7700
Wickliffe *(G-14393)*

▲ Superion Inc....................... E 937 374-0033
Xenia *(G-14776)*

Uhrichsville Carbide Inc............. F 740 922-9197
Uhrichsville *(G-13409)*

Woodworking Shop LLC.............. F 513 330-9663
Miamisburg *(G-9753)*

3429 Hardware, nec

▲ A JC Inc........................... F 800 428-2438
Hudson *(G-7826)*

AB Bonded Locksmiths Inc...........G 513 531-7334
Cincinnati *(G-2330)*

Acorn Technology Corporation....... E 216 663-1244
Shaker Heights *(G-11925)*

▲ Action Coupling & Eqp Inc......... D 330 279-4242
Holmesville *(G-7793)*

Aluminum Bearing Co of America...... G 216 267-8560
Cleveland *(G-3336)*

Ampex Metal Products Company...... D 216 267-9242
Brookpark *(G-1544)*

Annin & Co Inc...................... C 740 622-4447
Coshocton *(G-5447)*

◆ Arnco Corporation..................F 800 847-7661
Elyria *(G-6498)*

Arrow Tru-Line Inc.................. G 419 636-7013
Bryan *(G-1630)*

▲ Bianchi Usa Inc.................... F 440 801-1083
North Olmsted *(G-10718)*

◆ Boardman Molded Products Inc......D 330 788-2400
Youngstown *(G-14822)*

Bowes Manufacturing Inc............ F 216 378-2110
Solon *(G-12087)*

▲ Case Maul Clamps Inc............. G 419 668-6563
Norwalk *(G-10832)*

Chantilly Development Corp......... E 419 243-8109
Toledo *(G-12916)*

◆ Clampco Products Inc..............C 330 336-8857
Wadsworth *(G-13631)*

Cleveland Steel Specialty Co........ E 216 464-9400
Bedford Heights *(G-1074)*

Conform Automotive LLC............ B 937 492-2708
Sidney *(G-12002)*

Curtiss-Wright Flow Ctrl Corp....... D 216 267-3200
Cleveland *(G-3583)*

Custom Metal Works Inc............. F 419 668-7831
Norwalk *(G-10834)*

Dayton Superior Corporation........ F 937 682-4015
Rushsylvania *(G-11665)*

Desco Corporation.................. G 614 888-8855
New Albany *(G-10339)*

▲ Die Co Inc......................... E 440 942-8856
Eastlake *(G-6423)*

Dudick Inc.......................... E 330 562-1970
Streetsboro *(G-12499)*

◆ Eaton Aeroquip LLC................C 440 523-5000
Cleveland *(G-3650)*

Eaton Corporation.................. E 330 274-0743
Aurora *(G-667)*

Eaton Corporation.................. A 419 238-1190
Van Wert *(G-13534)*

Edward W Daniel LLC................ F 440 647-1960
Wellington *(G-13885)*

◆ Elster Perfection Corporation......D 440 428-1171
Geneva *(G-7236)*

Endura Products LLC................. F 419 248-8911
Toledo *(G-12952)*

◆ Esmet Inc..........................E 330 452-9132
Canton *(G-1888)*

▼ Esterline Technologies Corp........ E 216 706-2960
Cleveland *(G-3687)*

Etl Performance Products Inc........ G 234 575-7226
Salem *(G-11777)*

Faull & Son LLC..................... F 330 652-4341
Niles *(G-10588)*

▲ Federal Equipment Company........ D 513 621-5260
Cincinnati *(G-2616)*

Feitl Manufacturing Co Inc.......... F 330 405-6600
Macedonia *(G-8690)*

First Francis Company Inc........... E 440 352-8927
Painesville *(G-11087)*

Flex-Strut Inc...................... D 330 372-9999
Warren *(G-13765)*

Florida Production Engrg Inc........ D 937 996-4361
New Madison *(G-10421)*

◆ Fort Recovery Industries Inc.......C 419 375-4121
Fort Recovery *(G-6964)*

▲ Fortner Upholstering Inc........... F 614 475-8282
Columbus *(G-4936)*

Gateway Con Forming Svcs Inc....... D 513 353-2000
Miamitown *(G-9758)*

◆ Group Industries Inc...............E 216 271-0702
Cleveland *(G-3796)*

▼ Hbd/Thermoid Inc.................. C 800 543-8070
Bellefontaine *(G-1108)*

Hdt Expeditionary Systems Inc....... F 513 943-1111
Cincinnati *(G-2306)*

Heller Machine Products Inc......... G 216 281-2951
Cleveland *(G-3820)*

▲ Hercules Industries Inc............ E 740 494-2620
Prospect *(G-11502)*

Herman Machine Inc................. F 330 633-3261
Tallmadge *(G-12736)*

◆ Hfi LLC............................B 614 491-0700
Canal Winchester *(G-1791)*

Hydromotive Engineering Co......... G 330 425-4266
Twinsburg *(G-13317)*

▲ Independence 2 LLC................ F 800 414-0545
Hubbard *(G-7811)*

Interntnal Auto Cmpnnts Group......... A 419 433-5653
Wauseon *(G-13853)*

J L R Products Inc.................. G 330 832-9557
Massillon *(G-9207)*

J W Goss Company................... F 330 395-0739
Warren *(G-13773)*

Kasai North America Inc............. E 614 356-1494
Dublin *(G-6314)*

▼ Kirk Key Interlock Company LLC...... E 330 833-8223
North Canton *(G-10648)*

L & W Inc........................... D 734 397-6300
Avon *(G-730)*

Langenau Manufacturing Company....... F 216 651-3400
Cleveland *(G-3939)*

Linear It Solutions LLC.............. F 614 306-0761
Marysville *(G-9035)*

▲ Marlboro Manufacturing Inc........ E 330 935-2221
Alliance *(G-392)*

◆ Master Mfg Co Inc.................E 216 641-0500
Cleveland *(G-3997)*

▲ Matdan Corporation................ E 513 794-0500
Blue Ash *(G-1303)*

Maumee Hose & Fitting Inc.......... G 419 893-7252
Maumee *(G-9308)*

▲ McGregor Mtal Yllow Sprng Wrks...... D 937 325-5561
Springfield *(G-12351)*

Meese Inc........................... F 440 998-1202
Ashtabula *(G-604)*

Midlake Products & Mfg Co.................. D 330 875-4202
Louisville *(G-8608)*

▲ Miller Studio Inc .... G 330 339-1100
New Philadelphia *(G-10459)*

◆ Napoleon Spring Works Inc.............. C 419 445-1010
Archbold *(G-504)*

Netherland Rubber Company .... F 513 733-0883
Cincinnati *(G-2899)*

▲ Nova Machine Products Inc .... C 216 267-3200
Middleburg Heights *(G-9775)*

Ohio Hydraulics Inc .... E 513 771-2590
Cincinnati *(G-2924)*

Ottawa Products Co .... E 419 836-5115
Curtice *(G-5517)*

Parker-Hannifin Corporation .... G 704 637-1190
Wickliffe *(G-14388)*

Peterson American Corporation........... E 419 867-8711
Holland *(G-7777)*

◆ Premier Farnell Holding Inc .... D 330 523-4273
Richfield *(G-11597)*

Qualitor Subsidiary H Inc .... E 419 562-7987
Bucyrus *(G-1686)*

▲ R & R Tool Inc .... E 937 783-8665
Blanchester *(G-1237)*

R H Industries Inc .... E 216 281-5210
Cleveland *(G-4221)*

Racelite Southcoast Inc .... F 216 581-4600
Maple Heights *(G-8891)*

S & K Products Company .... E 419 268-2244
Celina *(G-2118)*

S Lehman Central Warehouse.............. G 330 828-8828
Dalton *(G-5594)*

▲ Samsel Rope & Marine Supply Co ..... E 216 241-0333
Cleveland *(G-4272)*

▲ Sarasota Quality Products .... G 440 899-9820
Westlake *(G-14331)*

Sensible Products Inc .... G 330 659-4212
Richfield *(G-11600)*

Sheet Metal Products Co Inc .... E 440 392-9000
Mentor *(G-9615)*

◆ Specialty Hardware Inc .... G 216 291-1160
Cleveland *(G-4319)*

▲ Summers Acquisition Corp .... E 216 941-7700
Cleveland *(G-4341)*

◆ Superior Metal Products Inc .... E 419 228-1145
Lima *(G-8454)*

▲ Te-Co Manufacturing LLC .... D 937 836-0961
Englewood *(G-6625)*

▲ Technoform GL Insul N Amer Inc...... E 330 487-6600
Twinsburg *(G-13384)*

Tessec LLC .... D 937 576-0010
Dayton *(G-6045)*

Thermo-Rite Mfg Company .... E 330 633-8680
Akron *(G-336)*

▲ Trim Parts Inc .... E 513 934-0815
Lebanon *(G-8291)*

▲ Triton Global Products Inc .... F 440 248-5480
Solon *(G-12199)*

Twin Valley Metalcraft Asm LLC.......... G 937 787-4634
West Alexandria *(G-13922)*

United Die & Mfg Sales Co .... E 330 938-6141
Sebring *(G-11904)*

▲ Universal Industrial Pdts Inc .... F 419 737-9584
Pioneer *(G-11331)*

Verhoff Machine & Welding Inc........... C 419 596-3202
Continental *(G-5424)*

Voss Industries LLC .... D 216 771-7655
Berea *(G-1193)*

◆ Voss Industries LLC .... C 216 771-7655
Cleveland *(G-4482)*

Washington Products Inc .... F 330 837-5101
Massillon *(G-9252)*

Wecall Inc... G 440 437-8202
Chardon *(G-2226)*

◆ Whiteside Manufacturing Co.............. E 740 363-1179
Delaware *(G-6181)*

▲ Wilson Bohannan Company .... D 740 382-3639
Marion *(G-9005)*

◆ Winzeler Stamping Co........................ E 419 485-3147
Montpelier *(G-10138)*

◆ Worthignton Products Inc .... G 330 452-7400
East Canton *(G-6381)*

3431 Metal sanitary ware

Accent Manufacturing Inc.................... F 330 724-7704
Norton *(G-10816)*

Agean Marble Manufacturing Inc......... G 513 874-1475
West Chester *(G-14099)*

As America Inc .... D 419 522-4211
Mansfield *(G-8763)*

BJ Equipment Ltd.................................. F 614 497-1188
Columbus *(G-4758)*

◆ Crane Plumbing LLC...........................A 419 522-4211
Mansfield *(G-8778)*

Extrudex Limited Partnership............... E 440 352-7101
Painesville *(G-11085)*

◆ Lvd Acquisition LLC .... D 614 861-1350
Columbus *(G-5077)*

◆ Mansfield Plumbing Pdts LLC.............A 419 938-5211
Perrysville *(G-11282)*

Zurn Industries LLC.............................. F 814 455-0921
Hilliard *(G-7712)*

3432 Plumbing fixture fittings and trim

▲ American Brass Mfg Co .... G 216 431-6565
Cleveland *(G-3341)*

As America Inc .... F 330 332-9954
Salem *(G-11762)*

Atlantic Co .... F 440 944-8988
Willoughby Hills *(G-14555)*

Ferguson Enterprises LLC .... G 216 635-2493
Parma *(G-11131)*

◆ Field Stone Inc .... E 937 898-3236
Tipp City *(G-12825)*

Fort Recovery Industries Inc................ D 419 375-3005
Fort Recovery *(G-6965)*

◆ Fort Recovery Industries Inc..............C 419 375-4121
Fort Recovery *(G-6964)*

▼ Krendl Machine Company .... D 419 692-3060
Delphos *(G-6189)*

Langenau Manufacturing Company...... F 216 651-3400
Cleveland *(G-3939)*

Lsq Manufacturing Inc .... F 330 725-4905
Medina *(G-9421)*

Maass Midwest Mfg Inc....................... F 419 894-6424
Arcadia *(G-482)*

◆ Mansfield Plumbing Pdts LLC.............A 419 938-5211
Perrysville *(G-11282)*

◆ Merit Brass Co.................................... C 216 261-9800
Cleveland *(G-4021)*

◆ Moen Incorporated ....E 800 289-6636
North Olmsted *(G-10722)*

▲ Mssk Manufacturing Inc.................... F 330 393-6624
Warren *(G-13783)*

▲ Multi Fittings Corporation .... E 513 942-9910
West Chester *(G-14032)*

Next Gerenation Crimping.................... G 440 237-6300
North Royalton *(G-10776)*

Toolbold Corporation............................ F 440 543-1660
Cleveland *(G-4401)*

◆ Waxman Industries Inc ....C 440 439-1830
Bedford *(G-1065)*

Wolff Bros Supply Inc .... F 440 327-1650
North Ridgeville *(G-10753)*

Wsi Seller Inc....................................... F 330 379-0270
Akron *(G-359)*

Zekelman Industries Inc .... C 740 432-2146
Cambridge *(G-1766)*

3433 Heating equipment, except electric

Accent Manufacturing Inc.................... F 330 724-7704
Norton *(G-10816)*

Aitken Products Inc.............................. G 440 466-5711
Geneva *(G-7232)*

▲ Beckett Air Incorporated................... D 440 327-9999
North Ridgeville *(G-10725)*

▼ Beckett Gas Inc.................................. E 440 327-3141
North Ridgeville *(G-10726)*

Bessamaire Sales Intl LLC................... F 800 321-5992
Twinsburg *(G-13280)*

Data Cooling Technologies LLC............ E 330 954-3800
Cleveland Heights *(G-4528)*

◆ Dcm Manufacturing Inc......................E 216 265-8006
Cleveland *(G-3606)*

Dmi Manufacturing Inc......................... F 800 238-5384
Mentor *(G-9510)*

Dmi Manufacturing Inc......................... F 440 975-8645
Willoughby *(G-14448)*

◆ Ebner Furnaces Inc ....D 330 335-2311
Wadsworth *(G-13637)*

▲ Enerco Group Inc .... C 216 916-3000
Cleveland *(G-3671)*

▲ Enerco Technical Products Inc........... D 216 916-3000
Cleveland *(G-3672)*

Es Thermal Inc .... E 440 323-3291
Berea *(G-1170)*

Ets Schaefer LLC.................................. F 330 468-6600
Macedonia *(G-8689)*

Ets Schaefer LLC.................................. E 330 468-6600
Beachwood *(G-917)*

Famous Industries Inc.......................... F 740 685-2592
Byesville *(G-1711)*

First Solar Inc....................................... F 419 661-1478
Perrysburg *(G-11222)*

◆ Fives N Amercn Combustn Inc............C 216 271-6000
Cleveland *(G-3721)*

Glo-Quartz Electric Htr Co Inc............. E 440 255-9701
Mentor *(G-9524)*

Grid Industrial Heating Inc .... G 330 332-9931
Salem *(G-11783)*

◆ Hartzell Fan Inc..................................C 937 773-7411
Piqua *(G-11360)*

Hdt Ep Inc .... C 216 438-6111
Solon *(G-12120)*

Hdt Expeditionary Systems Inc............ F 440 466-6640
Geneva *(G-7239)*

▼ Hunter Defense Tech Inc.................... E 216 438-6111
Solon *(G-12124)*

Iosil Energy Corporation...................... F
Groveport *(G-7439)*

Lakeway Mfg Inc................................... E 419 433-3030
Huron *(G-7877)*

▲ Mr Heater Inc .... E 216 916-3000
Cleveland *(G-4051)*

▲ Mssk Manufacturing Inc.................... F 330 393-6624
Warren *(G-13783)*

▲ Onix Corporation................................ E 800 844-0076
Perrysburg *(G-11250)*

▼ Qual-Fab Inc....................................... E 440 327-5000
Avon *(G-737)*

▲ RW Beckett Corporation..................... C 440 327-1060
North Ridgeville *(G-10749)*

▲ Selas Heat Technology Co LLC........... E 800 523-6500
Streetsboro *(G-12523)*

Sgm Co Inc .... E 440 255-1190
Mentor *(G-9614)*

SIC

Solarflo Corporation............... F 440 439-1680
Cleveland (G-4312)

Specialty Ceramics Inc.................. D 330 482-0800
Columbiana (G-4629)

Stelter and Brinck Inc................. E 513 367-9300
Harrison (G-7569)

Sticker Corporation.................. F 440 946-2100
Willoughby (G-14534)

Swagelok Company.................. E 440 349-5836
Solon (G-12190)

T J F Inc................................ F 419 878-4400
Waterville (G-13843)

Thermo Systems Technology Inc......... G 216 292-8250
Cleveland (G-4391)

Weather King Heating & AC................. G 330 908-0281
Northfield (G-10799)

Ws Thermal Process Tech Inc............ G 440 385-6829
Lorain (G-8587)

▲ Xunlight Corporation...................... D 419 469-8600
Toledo (G-13181)

3441 Fabricated structural metal

277 Northfield Inc.................... G 440 439-1029
Bedford (G-1009)

3d Partners LLC....................... G 330 323-6453
Canton (G-1819)

▲ A & G Manufacturing Co Inc........... E 419 468-7433
Galion (G-7176)

A-1 Fabricators Finishers LLC............ D 513 724-0383
Batavia (G-848)

A+ Engineering Fabrication Inc........... F 419 832-0748
Grand Rapids (G-7307)

AC Green LLC........................ F 740 292-2604
Athens (G-631)

Accurate Fab LLC.................... G 330 562-3140
Streetsboro (G-12484)

Ace Boiler & Welding Co Inc............ G 330 745-4443
Copley (G-5427)

Acme Home Improvement Co Inc........ F 614 252-2129
Columbus (G-4671)

Acmi LLC............................ G 330 501-0728
Youngstown (G-14807)

Action Group Inc.................... E 614 868-8868
Blacklick (G-1219)

Advance Industrial Mfg Inc............ E 614 871-3333
Grove City (G-7367)

Advance Industries Group LLC........... E 216 741-1800
Cleveland (G-3301)

Advance Metal Products Inc............ G 216 741-1800
Cleveland (G-3303)

Air Heater Seal Company Inc........... E 740 984-2146
Waterford (G-13825)

▲ Akron Rebar Co.................... E 330 745-7100
Akron (G-40)

Albert Freytag Inc.................. E 419 628-2018
Minster (G-10053)

▲ Alcon Industries Inc............... D 216 961-1100
Cleveland (G-3321)

Allied Fabricating & Wldg Co............ E 614 868-8680
Columbus (G-4687)

Alloy Fabricators Inc................. F 330 948-3535
Lodi (G-8498)

Alloy Welding & Fabricating............ F 440 914-0650
Solon (G-12076)

Alpha Control LLC.................. E 740 377-3400
South Point (G-12221)

Alro Steel Corporation................ E 937 253-6121
Dayton (G-5648)

Ameco USA Met Fbrction Sltons........... F 440 899-9400
Cleveland (G-3339)

◆ American Ir Met Cleveland LLC......... E 216 266-0509
Cleveland (G-3345)

▲ American Manufacturing Inc............ F 419 531-9471
Toledo (G-12875)

American Metal Stamping Co LLC......... F 216 531-3100
Euclid (G-6641)

American Steel Assod Pdts Inc........... D 419 531-9471
Toledo (G-12878)

Ameridian Specialty Services........... E 513 769-0150
Cincinnati (G-2364)

▲ Ametco Manufacturing Corp............ E 440 951-4300
Willoughby (G-14418)

Amrod Bridge & Iron LLC............... E
Mc Donald (G-9357)

Amtech Tool & Machine Inc............ G 330 758-8215
Youngstown (G-14813)

Apex Bolt & Machine Company............ E 419 729-3741
Toledo (G-12882)

▲ Appian Manufacturing Corp............ E 614 445-2230
Columbus (G-4721)

Applied Energy Tech Inc............... G 419 537-9052
Maumee (G-9262)

Applied Engneered Surfaces Inc........... F 440 366-0440
Elyria (G-6497)

Arbenz Inc......................... F 614 274-6800
Columbus (G-4724)

Arctech Fabricating Inc.............. E 937 525-9353
Springfield (G-12282)

Armor Consolidated Inc............... A 513 923-5260
Mason (G-9064)

▲ Armor Metal Group Mason Inc........... C 513 769-0700
Mason (G-9066)

▲ Art Iron Inc...................... D 419 241-1261
Toledo (G-12887)

◆ Astro-TEC Mfg Inc.................. E 330 854-2209
Canal Fulton (G-1772)

Automated Laser Fabrication Co............ G 330 562-7200
Streetsboro (G-12489)

Avenue Fabricating Inc............... E 513 752-1911
Batavia (G-852)

Axis Corporation.................. F 937 592-1958
Bellefontaine (G-1100)

Banks Manufacturing Company........... F 440 458-8661
Grafton (G-7299)

Bauer Corporation.................. E 800 321-4760
Wooster (G-14624)

Beauty Cft Met Fabricators Inc............ F 440 439-0710
Bedford (G-1015)

Benchmark Precision Fab Inc............ E 419 647-2003
Wapakoneta (G-13706)

Berkshire Road Holdings Inc............ F 216 883-4200
Cleveland (G-3416)

Berran Industrial Group Inc............ E 330 253-5800
Akron (G-77)

Best Process Solutions Inc............ E 330 220-1440
Brunswick (G-1581)

Bethel Engineering and Eqp Inc........... E 419 568-1100
New Hampshire (G-10396)

Bickers Metal Products Inc............ E 513 353-4000
Miamitown (G-9756)

Bird Equipment LLC.................. E 330 549-1004
North Lima (G-10704)

Black Lion Products LLC............... E 234 232-3680
Youngstown (G-14820)

Blackburns Fabrication Inc............ E 614 875-0784
Columbus (G-4762)

Blevins Metal Fabrication Inc............ E 419 522-6082
Mansfield (G-8766)

Blue Chip Manufacturing & Sales Inc..... E 614 475-3853
Columbus (G-4767)

Blue Skies Operating Corp............. F 877 330-2354
Sidney (G-11998)

Boardman Steel Inc.................. D 330 758-0951
Columbiana (G-4606)

Breitinger Company.................. C 419 526-4255
Mansfield (G-8767)

▲ Brilex Industries Inc............... D 330 744-1114
Youngstown (G-14827)

◆ Buck Equipment Inc................. E 614 539-3039
Grove City (G-7375)

Buckeye Steel Inc................... F 740 425-2306
Barnesville (G-844)

Burghardt Manufacturing Inc............ G 330 253-7590
Akron (G-86)

Burghardt Metal Fabg Inc............. F 330 794-1830
Akron (G-87)

C A Joseph Co..................... F 330 532-4646
Irondale (G-7927)

C-N-D Industries Inc................. F 330 478-8811
Massillon (G-9176)

C&C Fabrication LLC................. E 419 592-1408
Napoleon (G-10275)

Camelot Manufacturing Inc............ G 419 678-2603
Coldwater (G-4569)

Cast-Fab Technologies Inc............. C 513 758-1000
Cincinnati (G-2442)

Ceco Environmental Corp............. D 513 874-8915
Cincinnati (G-2446)

Central Ohio Fabricators LLC............ F 740 393-3892
Mount Vernon (G-10239)

Chagrin Vly Stl Erectors Inc............ F 440 975-1556
Willoughby Hills (G-14557)

Champion Bridge Company............. E 937 382-2521
Wilmington (G-14575)

Charles Mfg Co.................... F 330 395-3490
Warren (G-13751)

Chc Fabricating Corp................ D 513 821-7757
Cincinnati (G-2459)

Chc Manufacturing Inc............... E 513 821-7757
Cincinnati (G-2460)

▲ Cincinnati Industrial McHy Inc........... C 513 923-5600
Mason (G-9085)

Cincinnati Laser Cutting LLC............ E 513 779-7200
Cincinnati (G-2479)

Cincy Glass Inc.................... G 513 241-0455
Cincinnati (G-2490)

Clarkwstern Dtrich Bldg System........... D 330 372-4014
Vienna (G-13608)

Clearvue Products LLC................ F 440 871-4209
Bay Village (G-900)

◆ Clermont Steel Fabricators LLC........... D 513 732-6033
Batavia (G-857)

Cleveland City Forge Inc............. E 440 647-5400
Wellington (G-13884)

Clifton Capital Holdings LLC............ F 330 562-9000
Maple Heights (G-8880)

◆ Clifton Steel Company............... D 216 662-6111
Maple Heights (G-8881)

Clipsons Metal Working Inc............ G 513 772-6393
Cincinnati (G-2499)

Cohen Brothers Inc................. E 513 422-3696
Middletown (G-9848)

Com-Fab Inc....................... E 740 857-1107
Plain City (G-11401)

Comm Steel Inc.................... E 216 881-4600
North Royalton (G-10757)

Commercial Mtal Fbricators Inc............ E 937 233-4911
Dayton (G-5707)

Concord Fabricators Inc............. E 614 875-2500
Grove City (G-7377)

Contech Engnered Solutions Inc........... A 513 645-7000
West Chester (G-13971)

◆ Contech Engnered Solutions LLC......... C 513 645-7000
West Chester (G-13972)

▲ Continental GL Sls & Inv Group........... G 614 679-1201
Powell (G-11485)

Cornerstone Wauseon Inc................... C 419 337-0940
  Wauseon (G-13847)

County of Lake.................................... F 440 269-2193
  Willoughby (G-14443)

Coventry Steel Services Inc................ G 216 883-4477
  Cleveland (G-3571)

Cramers Inc....................................... E 330 477-4571
  Canton (G-1873)

Creative Fab & Welding LLC............... E 937 780-5000
  Leesburg (G-8298)

Cw Liquidation Inc............................. D
  Cleveland (G-3593)

Dae Holdings LLC.............................. E 419 866-6301
  Swanton (G-12681)

Dal-Little Fabricating Inc.................... G 216 883-3323
  Cleveland (G-3598)

Davis Fabricators Inc......................... E 419 898-5297
  Oak Harbor (G-10885)

Dearing Compressor and Pu.............. E 330 783-2258
  Youngstown (G-14847)

Debra-Kuempel Inc............................ D 513 271-6500
  Cincinnati (G-2543)

Defabco Inc....................................... D 614 231-2700
  Columbus (G-4875)

Diamond Mfg Bluffton Ltd.................. D 419 358-0129
  Bluffton (G-1360)

Diamond Wipes Intl Inc...................... G 419 562-3575
  Bucyrus (G-1678)

▼ Dietrich Industries Inc.................... D 800 873-2604
  Worthington (G-14708)

DL Schwartz Co LLC.......................... G 260 692-1464
  Hicksville (G-7647)

Dover Conveyor Inc........................... E 740 922-9390
  Midvale (G-9908)

Dover Tank and Plate Company.......... E 330 343-4443
  Dover (G-6242)

◆ Dracool-Usa Inc............................. E 937 743-5899
  Franklin (G-7017)

▲ DS Techstar Inc.............................. G 419 424-0888
  Findlay (G-6861)

Dwayne Bennett Industries................ G 440 466-5724
  Geneva (G-7235)

Dwyer Companies Inc........................ D 513 777-0998
  West Chester (G-13988)

E B P Inc... E 216 241-2550
  Solon (G-12102)

▼ E-Pak Manufacturing LLC.............. E 330 264-0825
  Wooster (G-14636)

◆ Ebner Furnaces Inc......................... D 330 335-2311
  Wadsworth (G-13637)

◆ Emh Inc.. D 330 220-8600
  Valley City (G-13495)

Enterprise Welding Fbrctn.................. G 440 354-3868
  Mentor (G-9514)

EPI of Cleveland Inc.......................... G 330 468-2872
  Twinsburg (G-13299)

Erico International Corp...................... B 440 248-0100
  Solon (G-12107)

▲ Erico Products Inc.......................... B 440 248-0100
  Cleveland (G-3683)

Euclid Welding Company Inc.............. F 216 289-0714
  Willoughby Hills (G-14559)

Evers Welding Co Inc......................... G 513 385-7352
  Cincinnati (G-2604)

F M Machine Co................................. E 330 773-8237
  Akron (G-142)

▲ Fabco Inc.. D 419 422-4533
  Findlay (G-6862)

Fabx LLC... F 614 565-5835
  Columbus (G-4918)

Farasey Steel Fabricators Inc............. F 216 641-1853
  Cleveland (G-3706)

Fastfeed Corporation......................... G 330 948-7333
  Lodi (G-8501)

Fenix Fabrication Inc.......................... F 330 745-8731
  Akron (G-146)

Fiedeldey Stl Fabricators Inc.............. E 513 353-3300
  Cincinnati (G-2620)

Firelands Fabrication......................... F 419 929-0680
  New London (G-10411)

Flex-Strut Inc.................................... D 330 372-9999
  Warren (G-13765)

◆ Flextur Corp................................... D 877 435-3988
  Dalton (G-5585)

Fostoria MT&f Corp............................ E 419 435-7676
  Fostoria (G-6982)

Franck and Fric Incorporated............. D 216 524-4451
  Cleveland (G-3742)

Frederick Steel Company LLC............ D 513 821-6400
  Cincinnati (G-2641)

Fulton Equipment Co.......................... F 419 290-5393
  Toledo (G-12970)

◆ G & S Titanium Inc......................... E 330 263-0564
  Wooster (G-14641)

▲ G & W Products LLC....................... C 513 860-4050
  Fairfield (G-6738)

▲ Galion-Godwin Truck Bdy Co LLC... F 330 359-5495
  Dundee (G-6365)

Garland Welding Co Inc...................... F 330 536-6506
  Lowellville (G-8662)

Gb Fabrication Company..................... E 419 347-1835
  Shelby (G-11970)

General Machine & Saw Company....... D 740 382-1104
  Marion (G-8971)

George Steel Fabricating Inc.............. E 513 932-2887
  Lebanon (G-8259)

Gilson Machine & Tool Co Inc............ E 419 592-2911
  Napoleon (G-10282)

GL Nause Co Inc................................ E 513 722-9500
  Loveland (G-8626)

Glenwood Erectors Inc....................... G 330 652-9616
  Warren (G-13769)

Global Body & Equipment Co............. D 330 264-6640
  Wooster (G-14643)

▲ Gokoh Corporation......................... F 937 339-4977
  Troy (G-13218)

▲ Goyal Industries Inc....................... E 419 522-7099
  Mansfield (G-8796)

Greenpoint Metals Inc........................ E 937 743-4075
  Franklin (G-7026)

◆ Gregory Industries Inc.................... D 330 477-4800
  Canton (G-1905)

Grenga Machine & Welding................ F 330 743-1113
  Youngstown (G-14871)

Gunderson Rail Services LLC............. D 330 792-6521
  Youngstown (G-14872)

◆ Halvorsen Company......................... E 216 341-7500
  Cleveland (G-3809)

Hancock Structural Steel LLC............ E 419 424-1217
  Findlay (G-6877)

Harvey Brothers Inc........................... G 513 541-2622
  Cincinnati (G-2710)

Hays Fabricating & Welding Inc.......... E 937 325-0031
  Springfield (G-12317)

Herman Manufacturing LLC............... F 216 251-6400
  Cleveland (G-3827)

High Production Technology LLC........ F 419 591-7000
  Napoleon (G-10284)

Holgate Metal Fab Inc........................ F 419 599-2000
  Napoleon (G-10285)

Hoppel Fabrication Spc Inc................ F 330 823-5700
  Louisville (G-8604)

▲ Horizon Metals Inc.......................... E 440 235-3338
  Berea (G-1175)

Hr Machine llc.................................... G 937 222-7644
  Dayton (G-5815)

Hunkar Technologies Inc.................... C 513 272-1010
  Cincinnati (G-2735)

▲ Hynes Industries Inc....................... D 800 321-9257
  Youngstown (G-14874)

Ice Industries Columbus Inc.............. E 614 475-3853
  Sylvania (G-12711)

Indian Creek Fabricators Inc.............. E 937 667-7214
  Tipp City (G-12828)

Industrial Mill Maintenance............... F 330 746-1155
  Youngstown (G-14876)

Iron Gate Industries LLC.................... E 330 264-0626
  Wooster (G-14652)

Ironfab LLC....................................... F 614 443-3900
  Columbus (G-5025)

Ironhead Fabg & Contg Inc................. G 419 690-0000
  Toledo (G-13010)

Ivies Wholistic Dynamics................... G 216 469-3103
  Wooster (G-14653)

J & L Specialty Steel Inc.................... G 330 875-6200
  Louisville (G-8606)

J & M Fabrications LLC...................... G 330 860-4346
  Clinton (G-4554)

J A McMahon Incorporated................ E 330 652-2588
  Niles (G-10593)

J Horst Manufacturing Co.................. D 330 828-2216
  Dalton (G-5586)

Jh Industries Inc............................... E 330 963-4105
  Twinsburg (G-13321)

JJ&pl Services-Consulting LLC.......... E 330 923-5783
  Cuyahoga Falls (G-5552)

Joe Rees Welding.............................. G 937 652-4067
  Urbana (G-13471)

Johnson-Nash Metal Pdts Inc............ F 513 874-7022
  Fairfield (G-6748)

Jomac Ltd.. E 330 627-7727
  Carrollton (G-2087)

▲ JR Manufacturing Inc...................... C 419 375-8021
  Fort Recovery (G-6968)

Js Fabrications Inc............................ G 419 333-0323
  Fremont (G-7118)

Judo Steel Company Inc.................... F
  Dayton (G-5833)

Kebco Prcision Fabricators Inc.......... F 330 456-0808
  Canton (G-1924)

Kecoat LLC.. G 330 527-0215
  Garrettsville (G-7223)

Kel-Par Co Inc................................... F 740 344-2627
  Newark (G-10513)

Kellys Wldg & Fabrication Ltd............ G 440 593-6040
  Conneaut (G-5406)

Kenton Strl & Orn Ir Works................. D 419 674-4025
  Kenton (G-8103)

Kings Welding and Fabg Inc............... G 330 738-3592
  Mechanicstown (G-9368)

Kirwan Industries Inc........................ G 513 333-0766
  Cincinnati (G-2798)

▲ Kottler Metal Products Co Inc.......... E 440 946-7473
  Willoughby (G-14478)

Kramer Power Equipment Co.............. G 937 456-2232
  Eaton (G-6457)

L & W Inc.. D 734 397-6300
  Avon (G-730)

Lake Building Products Inc................. E 216 486-1500
  Cleveland (G-3936)

Lake Erie Ship Repr Fbrction L........... F 440 228-7110
  Jefferson (G-7977)

▲ Langdon Inc.................................... E 513 733-5955
  Cincinnati (G-2811)

Lapham-Hickey Steel Corp................. D 614 443-4881
  Columbus (G-5065)

S
I
C

Laserfab Technologies Inc	F	937 493-0800	
Sidney (G-12030)			
▲ Lefeld Welding & Stl Sups Inc	E	419 678-2397	
Coldwater (G-4580)			
Leitner Fabrication LLC	E	330 721-7374	
Medina (G-9420)			
Lilly Industries Inc	E	419 946-7908	
Mount Gilead (G-10211)			
Louis Arthur Steel Company	E	440 997-5545	
Geneva (G-7242)			
Louis Arthur Steel Company	G	440 997-5545	
Geneva (G-7241)			
Lyco Corporation	G	412 973-9176	
Lowellville (G-8663)			
M & H Fabricating Co Inc	F	937 325-8708	
Springfield (G-12344)			
M & M Fabrication Inc	F	740 779-3071	
Chillicothe (G-2263)			
M K Metals	G	330 482-3351	
Leetonia (G-8303)			
M R Trailer Sales Inc	G	330 339-7701	
New Philadelphia (G-10456)			
Machine Tool Design & Fab LLC	F	419 435-7676	
Tiffin (G-12789)			
Mad River Steel Ltd	G	937 845-4046	
New Carlisle (G-10375)			
Magnesium Products Group Inc	G	310 971-5799	
Maumee (G-9306)			
Magni-Power Company	D	330 264-3637	
Wooster (G-14662)			
Magnum Piering Inc	E	513 759-3348	
West Chester (G-14131)			
Manco Manufacturing Co	E	419 925-4152	
Maria Stein (G-8899)			
▼ Manifold & Phalor Inc	E	614 920-1200	
Canal Winchester (G-1793)			
Marsam Metalfab Inc	E	330 405-1520	
Twinsburg (G-13334)			
Martina Metal LLC	E	614 291-9700	
Columbus (G-5085)			
Martins Steel Fabrication Inc	E	330 882-4311	
New Franklin (G-10390)			
Marysville Steel Inc	E	937 642-5971	
Marysville (G-9038)			
Mason Structural Steel LLC	E	440 439-1040	
Walton Hills (G-13699)			
Masonite International Corp	F	937 454-9308	
Vandalia (G-13570)			
Maumee Valley Fabricators Inc	E	419 476-1411	
Toledo (G-13050)			
Mc Brown Industries Inc	F	419 963-2800	
Findlay (G-6892)			
Mc Elwain Industries Inc	F	419 532-3126	
Ottawa (G-11038)			
McDonald Steel Plate Inc	F	216 883-4200	
Cleveland (G-4008)			
McNeil Holdings LLC	G	614 298-0300	
Columbus (G-5094)			
McWane Inc	B	740 622-6651	
Coshocton (G-5459)			
Mercury Iron and Steel Co	F	440 349-1500	
Solon (G-12146)			
Metal Man Inc	G	614 830-0968	
Groveport (G-7445)			
Metal Sales Manufacturing Corp	E	440 319-3779	
Jefferson (G-7978)			
Metalfab Group	G	440 543-6234	
Streetsboro (G-12509)			
Miracle Welding Inc	G	937 746-9977	
Franklin (G-7034)			
Mk Metal Products Inc	F	330 669-2631	
Smithville (G-12066)			

Mk Metal Products Entps Inc	E	419 756-3644	
Mansfield (G-8830)			
Mound Technologies Inc	E	937 748-2937	
Springboro (G-12260)			
Mssi Group Inc	D	440 439-1040	
Walton Hills (G-13701)			
Nct Technologies Group Inc	F	937 882-6800	
New Carlisle (G-10376)			
Neidert Fabricating Inc	G	330 753-3331	
Barberton (G-824)			
New Wayne Inc	G	740 453-3454	
Zanesville (G-15034)			
Niles Building Products Company	F	330 544-0880	
Niles (G-10595)			
▲ Northern Manufacturing Co Inc	C	419 898-2821	
Oak Harbor (G-10886)			
Northwest Installations Inc	E	419 423-5738	
Findlay (G-6900)			
Northwind Industries Inc	G	216 433-0666	
Cleveland (G-4099)			
Nova Structural Steel Inc	E	216 938-7476	
Cleveland (G-4100)			
◆ Nucor Steel Marion Inc	B	740 383-4011	
Marion (G-8985)			
Ohio Fabricators Company	F	740 622-5922	
Coshocton (G-5467)			
◆ Ohio Gratings Inc	B	800 321-9800	
Canton (G-1966)			
▲ Ohio Metal Technologies Inc	D	740 928-8288	
Hebron (G-7627)			
Ohio Steel Industries Inc	D	740 927-9500	
Pataskala (G-11144)			
◆ Ohio Steel Industries Inc	D	614 471-4800	
Columbus (G-5154)			
Olson Sheet Metal Cnstr Co	G	330 745-8225	
Barberton (G-829)			
Omco Holdings Inc	E	440 944-2100	
Wickliffe (G-14386)			
Outotec Oyj	D	440 783-3336	
Strongsville (G-12583)			
Overhead Door Corporation	D	740 383-6376	
Marion (G-8987)			
▲ P & L Metalcrafts LLC	F	330 793-2178	
Youngstown (G-14908)			
Parker Fabricating Co	E	330 379-0112	
Akron (G-256)			
PB Fbrction Mech Contrs Corp	F	419 478-4869	
Toledo (G-13091)			
▲ PC Campana Inc	D	800 321-0151	
Lorain (G-8571)			
▲ PC Campana Inc	E	800 321-0151	
Lorain (G-8572)			
Penny Fab LLC	F	740 967-3669	
Columbus (G-5184)			
Perfection Fabricators Inc	F	440 365-5850	
Elyria (G-6578)			
Perry Welding Service Inc	F	330 425-2211	
Twinsburg (G-13355)			
Phoenix Metal Works Inc	G	937 274-5555	
Dayton (G-5939)			
Phoenix Mtal Sls Fbrcation LLC	F	330 562-0585	
Twinsburg (G-13356)			
Pioneer Machine Inc	G	330 948-6500	
Lodi (G-8505)			
▲ Pioneer Pipe Inc	A	740 376-2400	
Marietta (G-8937)			
Pittman Engineering Inc	F	330 821-4365	
Alliance (G-399)			
PJs Fabricating Inc	E	330 478-1120	
Canton (G-1977)			
Porters Welding Inc	G	740 452-4181	
Zanesville (G-15041)			

Precise Metal Form Inc	F	419 636-5221	
Bryan (G-1658)			
Precision Cutoff LLC	F	419 866-8000	
Holland (G-7778)			
Precision Fabg & Stamping Inc	G	740 453-7310	
Zanesville (G-15042)			
Precision International LLC	E	330 793-0900	
Brecksville (G-1479)			
Precision Laser & Forming Inc	F	419 943-4350	
Leipsic (G-8310)			
Precision Quincy Inds Inc	B	888 312-5442	
Mason (G-9137)			
Precision Welding Corporation	E	216 524-6110	
Cleveland (G-4187)			
Precision Wldg Instllation LLC	F	740 995-0613	
Zanesville (G-15043)			
Pro-Fab Inc	G	330 644-0044	
Akron (G-267)			
Production Support Inc	F	937 526-3897	
Russia (G-11677)			
Prototype Fabricators Co	F	216 252-0080	
Cleveland (G-4203)			
Pucel Enterprises Inc	D	216 881-4604	
Cleveland (G-4206)			
Puritas Metal Products Inc	G	440 353-1917	
North Ridgeville (G-10744)			
Q S I Fabrication Inc	G	419 832-1680	
Grand Rapids (G-7308)			
Quality Steel Fabrication	F	937 492-9503	
Sidney (G-12042)			
R G Smith Company	D	330 456-3415	
Canton (G-1988)			
R L Torbeck Industries Inc	G	513 367-0080	
Harrison (G-7565)			
R L Waller Construction Inc	G	740 772-6185	
Chillicothe (G-2278)			
Rads LLC	F	330 671-0464	
Berea (G-1187)			
Rance Industries Inc	F	330 482-1745	
Columbiana (G-4626)			
Rankin Mfg Inc	G	419 929-8338	
New London (G-10414)			
Rbm Environmental & Cnstr Inc	G	419 693-5840	
Oregon (G-10967)			
Republic Storage Systems LLC	B	330 438-5800	
Canton (G-1996)			
Response Metal Fabricators	F	937 222-9000	
Dayton (G-5981)			
Rex Welding Inc	F	740 387-1650	
Marion (G-8992)			
Richard Steel Company Inc	G	216 520-6390	
Cleveland (G-4240)			
Ripley Metalworks LLC	E	937 392-4992	
Ripley (G-11619)			
Rittman Inc	D	330 927-6855	
Rittman (G-11627)			
▼ Riverside Steel Inc	F	330 856-5299	
Vienna (G-13617)			
RLM Fabricating Inc	E	419 729-6130	
Toledo (G-13115)			
Rmi Titanium Company LLC	C	330 544-9470	
Niles (G-10602)			
Rmt Acquisition Inc	E	513 241-5566	
Cincinnati (G-3050)			
Robs Welding Technologies Ltd	G	937 890-4963	
Dayton (G-5987)			
Rock Hard Industries LLC	G	440 327-3077	
North Ridgeville (G-10748)			
▼ Rol- Fab Inc	E	216 662-2500	
Cleveland (G-4249)			
Romar Metal Fabricating Inc	G	740 682-7731	
Oak Hill (G-10894)			

Rose Metal Industries LLC.................... E 216 426-8615
Cleveland (G-4251)

Rose Metal Industries LLC.................... F 216 881-3355
Cleveland (G-4250)

Rose Properties Inc.............................G 216 881-6000
Cleveland (G-4252)

Rsv Wlding Fbrction McHning In .... F 419 592-0993
Napoleon (G-10298)

◆ Rti International Metals Inc.................A
Niles (G-10606)

S & G Manufacturing Group LLC.......... D 614 529-0100
Hilliard (G-7700)

Sabre Industries Inc............................ F 419 542-1420
Hicksville (G-7652)

▲ Sausser Steel Company Inc.............. G 419 422-9632
Findlay (G-6916)

Schoonover Industries Inc.................... F 419 289-8332
Ashland (G-572)

Schuck Mtal Fbrction Dsign Inc............ F 419 586-1054
Celina (G-2119)

Shaffer Metal Fab Inc........................ E 937 492-1384
Sidney (G-12052)

Sharon Manufacturing Inc.................... E 330 239-1561
Sharon Center (G-11942)

Sintered Metal Industries Inc................. E 330 650-4000
Hudson (G-7857)

Sirius Steel Services Inc..................... F 937 797-3975
Columbus (G-5273)

Socar of Ohio Inc............................D 419 596-3100
Continental (G-5423)

Somerville Manufacturing Inc.............. E 740 336-7847
Marietta (G-8949)

South Central Industrial LLC................. F 740 333-5401
Wshngtn Ct Hs (G-14747)

Spradlin Bros Welding Co..................... F 800 219-2182
Springfield (G-12375)

St Lawrence Holdings LLC................... E 330 562-9000
Maple Heights (G-8892)

◆ St Lawrence Steel Corporation........... E 330 562-9000
Maple Heights (G-8893)

Stainless Specialties Inc..................... E 440 942-4242
Eastlake (G-6443)

Standard Wldg & Stl Pdts Inc.............. F 330 273-2777
Medina (G-9450)

Starr Fabricating Inc.......................... D 330 394-9891
Vienna (G-13618)

Stays Lighting Inc............................. G 440 328-3254
Elyria (G-6693)

▼ Steel & Alloy Utility Pdts Inc.............. E 330 530-2220
Mc Donald (G-9361)

Steel City Contractors LLC................... F 330 519-8873
Campbell (G-1771)

▲ Steel Eqp Specialists Inc.................. D 330 823-8260
Alliance (G-406)

Steel It LLC.................................... E 513 253-3111
Cincinnati (G-3115)

Steel Quest Inc............................... G 513 772-5030
Cincinnati (G-3116)

Steelcon LLC.................................. E 330 457-4003
Rogers (G-11643)

Steelial Wlding Met Fbrction Inc.............. E 740 669-5300
Vinton (G-13624)

Steeltec Products LLC........................ F 216 681-1114
Cleveland (G-4330)

Steve Vore Welding and Steel.............. F 419 375-4087
Fort Recovery (G-6971)

Sticker Corporation........................... G 440 942-4700
Willoughby (G-14533)

Stock Mfg & Design Co Inc................. F 513 353-3600
Cleves (G-4549)

Stover International LLC..................... E 740 363-5251
Delaware (G-6175)

Straightaway Fabrications Ltd............... F 419 281-9440
Ashland (G-576)

Suburban Metal Products Inc................ F 740 474-4237
Circleville (G-3263)

Suburban Steel Supply Co .... D 614 737-5501
Gahanna (G-7170)

Suburban Stl Sup Co Ltd Partnr........... G 317 783-6555
Columbus (G-5296)

Sulecki Precision Products Inc.............. F 440 255-5454
Mentor (G-9630)

Superior Metal Worx LLC.................... F 614 879-9400
Columbus (G-5298)

Superior Soda Service LLC.................. G 937 657-9700
Beavercreek (G-996)

Superior Steel Service LLC................. F 513 724-7888
Batavia (G-890)

Surface Recovery Tech LLC................. F 937 879-5864
Fairborn (G-6700)

Tarrier Steel Company Inc................... E 614 444-4000
Columbus (G-5311)

Tech Dynamics Inc........................... F 419 666-1666
Perrysburg (G-11266)

Ted M Figgins................................. F 740 277-3750
Lancaster (G-8227)

Terrasmart LLC............................... F 239 362-0211
Columbus (G-5317)

▲ The Armor Group Inc...................... C 513 923-5260
Mason (G-9161)

◆ The D S Brown Company.................C 419 257-3561
North Baltimore (G-10619)

The Mansfield Strl & Erct Co................ F 419 522-5911
Mansfield (G-8859)

Thieman Quality Metal Fab Inc.............. D 419 629-2612
New Bremen (G-10367)

Thomas Steel Inc.............................. F 419 483-7540
Bellevue (G-1135)

TJ Clark International LLC.................... F 614 388-8869
Delaware (G-6176)

Transco Railway Products Inc.............. E 330 872-0934
Newton Falls (G-10581)

Tri-America Contractors Inc................. E 740 574-0148
Wheelersburg (G-14354)

Tri-Fab Inc.................................... E 330 337-3425
Salem (G-11815)

Tri-State Fabricators Inc.................... E 513 752-5005
Amelia (G-440)

Triad Capital Group LLC.................... G 440 236-6677
Cleveland (G-1110)

Triad Capital Group LLC.................... G 440 236-6677
Independence (G-7922)

Triangle Precision Inds Inc.................. D 937 299-6776
Dayton (G-6062)

Tristate Steel Contractors LLC.............. G 513 648-9000
Cincinnati (G-3169)

Tru-Fab Inc.................................... F 937 435-1733
Miamisburg (G-9750)

Tru-Form Steel & Wire Inc.................. E 765 348-5001
Toledo (G-13166)

▲ Truck Cab Manufacturers Inc............. E 513 922-1300
Cincinnati (G-3172)

Turn-Key Industrial Svcs LLC............... D 614 274-1128
Grove City (G-7420)

Umd Automated Systems Inc.............. D 740 694-8614
Fredericktown (G-7086)

Union Fabricating and Mch Co............. G 419 626-5963
Sandusky (G-11879)

Unique Fabrications Inc..................... F 419 355-1700
Fremont (G-7141)

United Metal Fabricators Inc............... E 216 662-2000
Maple Heights (G-8894)

Universal Dsign Fbrication LLC............. F 419 202-5269
Sandusky (G-11880)

▲ Universal Fabg Cnstr Svcs Inc........... F 614 274-1128
Columbus (G-5338)

Upright Steel LLC............................ E 216 923-0852
Cleveland (G-4449)

V & S Schuler Engineering Inc.............. D 330 452-5200
Middlefield (G-9835)

V & S Schuler Engineering Inc.............. E 330 452-5200
Canton (G-2041)

Valco Industries LLC........................ E 937 399-7400
Springfield (G-12391)

Vanscoyk Sheet Metal Corp................. G 937 845-0581
New Carlisle (G-10383)

Verhoff Machine & Welding Inc.............. C 419 596-3202
Continental (G-5424)

Vicon Fabricating Company Ltd............. E 440 205-6700
Mentor (G-9649)

Viking Fabricators Inc....................... G 740 374-5246
Marietta (G-8960)

Vscorp LLC.................................... F 937 305-3562
Tipp City (G-12853)

W & W Custom Fabrication Inc.............. G 513 353-4617
Cleves (G-4552)

Wanner Metal Worx Inc...................... E 740 369-4034
Delaware (G-6180)

Warmus and Associates Inc................. G 330 659-4440
Bath (G-898)

◆ Warren Fabricating Corporation.........D 330 534-5017
Hubbard (G-7818)

▲ Waterford Tank Fabrication Ltd........... D 740 984-4100
Beverly (G-1211)

Wecan Fabricators LLC..................... G 740 667-0731
Tuppers Plains (G-13263)

Welage Corporation.......................... F 513 681-2300
Cincinnati (G-3214)

Welding Improvement Company............ G 330 424-9666
Lisbon (G-8480)

Werks Kraft Engineering LLC............... E 330 721-7374
Medina (G-9464)

Wernke Wldg & Stl Erection Co............ F 513 353-4173
North Bend (G-10622)

Westwood Fbrction Shtmetal Inc............ E 937 837-0494
Dayton (G-6080)

▲ Whitacre Engineering Company........ E 330 455-8505
Canton (G-2048)

White Machine & Mfg Co..................... F 740 453-5451
Zanesville (G-15054)

◆ Whole Shop Inc............................. F 330 630-5305
Tallmadge (C 12750)

William Niccum............................... G 330 415-0154
East Sparta (G-6413)

Wiseman Bros Fabg & Stl Ltd............... F 740 988-5121
Beaver (G-961)

▼ Witt Industries Inc........................ D 513 871-5700
Mason (G-9167)

Wm Lang & Sons Company.................. F 513 541-3304
Cincinnati (G-3229)

▲ Wrayco Industries Inc...................... C 330 688-5617
Stow (G-12473)

Zimmerman Steel & Sup Co LLC........... F 330 828-1010
Dalton (G-5597)

3442 Metal doors, sash, and trim

All Pro Ovrhd Door Systems LLC.......... G 614 444-3667
Columbus (G-4684)

Aluminum Color Industries Inc.............. E 330 536-6295
Lowellville (G-8657)

Anderson Door Co............................ F 216 475-5700
Cleveland (G-3358)

Architctral Mllwk Cbinetry Inc............... G 440 708-0086
Chagrin Falls (G-2155)

◆ Assa Abloy Entrnce Systems HLA.......D 419 294-3373
Upper Sandusky (G-13434)

▲ Associated Materials LLC.............. C 330 929-1811
Cuyahoga Falls *(G-5528)*

Associated Materials Group Inc......... D .. 330 929-1811
Cuyahoga Falls *(G-5529)*

Associated Mtls Holdings LLC........... A .. 330 929-1811
Cuyahoga Falls *(G-5530)*

Atrium Centers Inc.......................... F 513 830-5014
Cincinnati *(G-2389)*

Automted Cmpnent Spcalists LLC....... E .. 513 335-4285
Cincinnati *(G-2391)*

Bilco Company............................. E 740 455-9020
Zanesville *(G-14995)*

Brainerd Industries Inc.................. E .. 937 228-0488
Miamisburg *(G-9676)*

Capitol Aluminum & Glass Corp......... D .. 800 331-8268
Bellevue *(G-1122)*

▲ Cascade Ohio Inc......................... B .. 440 593-5800
Conneaut *(G-5399)*

▲ Champion Opco LLC....................... B .. 513 327-7338
Cincinnati *(G-2458)*

◆ Champion Win Co Cleveland LLC....G .. 440 899-2562
Macedonia *(G-8681)*

Champion Window Co of Toledo........... G 419 841-0154
Perrysburg *(G-11211)*

Chase Industries Inc...................... E .. 513 603-2936
West Chester *(G-14110)*

◆ Clopay Ames Inc............................C .. 800 282-2260
Mason *(G-9087)*

Creative Millwork Ohio Inc............. D .. 440 992-3566
Ashtabula *(G-588)*

Custom Quality Products Inc............. E
Cincinnati *(G-2532)*

Dale Kestler................................. G .. 513 871-9000
Cincinnati *(G-2540)*

Desco Corporation.......................... G .. 614 888-8855
New Albany *(G-10339)*

Division Overhead Door Inc............. F 513 872-0888
Cincinnati *(G-2556)*

Duo-Corp...................................... F 330 549-2149
North Lima *(G-10707)*

Eliason Corporation....................... E .. 800 828-3655
West Chester *(G-14116)*

Euclid Jalousies Inc...................... G .. 440 953-1112
Chardon *(G-2205)*

Fostoria MT&f Corp......................... F 419 435-7676
Fostoria *(G-6982)*

Francis-Schulze Co......................... F 937 295-3941
Russia *(G-11674)*

Haas Door Company.......................... C .. 419 337-9900
Wauseon *(G-13850)*

Hope Holdings Inc........................... G .. 330 674-7015
Mount Hope *(G-10214)*

Hrh Door Corp............................... E .. 513 674-9300
Cincinnati *(G-2734)*

Installed Building Pdts LLC............. B .. 614 308-9900
Columbus *(G-5009)*

Kawneer Company Inc...................... C .. 216 252-3203
Cleveland *(G-3909)*

M-D Building Products Inc............... D .. 513 539-2255
Middletown *(G-9873)*

M-D Building Products Inc............... F 513 539-2255
Middletown *(G-9874)*

Masonite International Corp............. F 937 454-9308
Vandalia *(G-13570)*

Mestek Inc................................... D .. 419 288-2703
Bowling Green *(G-1429)*

Mestek Inc................................... F 419 288-2703
Bradner *(G-1454)*

Midwest Curtainwalls Inc................ D .. 216 641-7900
Cleveland *(G-4036)*

Modern Builders Supply Inc............. C .. 419 241-3961
Toledo *(G-13058)*

National Access Design LLC............. F 513 351-3400
Cincinnati *(G-2893)*

Niles Building Products Company........ F 330 544-0880
Niles *(G-10595)*

Nofziger Door Sales Inc................. F 419 445-2961
Archbold *(G-506)*

▼ Nofziger Door Sales Inc............... C .. 419 337-9900
Wauseon *(G-13857)*

▲ Orrvilon Inc............................. C .. 330 684-9400
Orrville *(G-11001)*

Overhead Door Corporation.............. G .. 330 828-2291
Dalton *(G-5590)*

Overhead Door Corporation.............. D .. 740 383-6376
Marion *(G-8987)*

Overhead Door Corporation.............. F 419 294-3874
Upper Sandusky *(G-13452)*

Overhead Door of Pike County............ G .. 740 289-3925
Piketon *(G-11312)*

Overhead Inc............................... G .. 419 476-0300
Toledo *(G-13083)*

Pease Industies Inc....................... G .. 513 870-3600
Fairfield *(G-6764)*

Phillips Manufacturing Co................ D .. 330 652-4335
Niles *(G-10600)*

Phoenix Door Systems Inc................ E .. 513 492-8213
West Chester *(G-14044)*

Prentke Romich Company.................. C .. 330 262-1984
Wooster *(G-14673)*

Provia Holdings Inc....................... C .. 330 852-4711
Sugarcreek *(G-12646)*

Renewal By Andersen LLC................ G .. 614 781-9600
Columbus *(G-4649)*

Rosatis Window Co LLC.................... D .. 614 777-4806
Columbus *(G-5235)*

Rsl LLC...................................... E .. 330 392-8900
Warren *(G-13795)*

S R Door Inc............................... D .. 740 927-3558
Hebron *(G-7634)*

Senneca Holdings Inc..................... E .. 800 543-4455
Cincinnati *(G-3080)*

▲ Stephen M Trudick....................... E .. 440 834-1891
Burton *(G-1704)*

Superior Weld and Fabg Co Inc.......... G 216 249-5122
Cleveland *(G-4349)*

Thomas J Weaver Inc...................... F 740 622-2040
Coshocton *(G-5474)*

Traichal Construction Company.......... E .. 800 255-3667
Niles *(G-10607)*

Vinylume Products Inc.................... F 330 799-2000
Youngstown *(G-14964)*

YKK AP America Inc........................ E .. 513 942-7200
West Chester *(G-14094)*

Youngstown Shade & Alum LLC.......... G 330 782-2373
Youngstown *(G-14975)*

3443 Fabricated plate work (boiler shop)

▲ A & G Manufacturing Co Inc........... E .. 419 468-7433
Galion *(G-7176)*

A H Marty Co Ltd........................... F 216 641-8950
Cleveland *(G-3282)*

A-1 Welding & Fabrication.............. F 440 233-8474
Lorain *(G-8544)*

Active Chemical Systems Inc............ F 440 543-7755
Chagrin Falls *(G-2154)*

Advance Industrial Mfg Inc............. E .. 614 871-3333
Grove City *(G-7367)*

Air-Tech Mechanical Inc................ G .. 419 292-0074
Toledo *(G-12867)*

▲ Allgaier Process Technology.......... G .. 513 402-2566
West Chester *(G-13937)*

▼ Alloy Engineering Company............. D .. 440 243-6800
Berea *(G-1158)*

▲ Allpass Corporation.................... F 440 998-6300
Madison *(G-8723)*

AM Castle & Co............................. F 330 425-7000
Bedford *(G-1011)*

▲ American Tank & Fabricating Co....... D .. 216 252-1500
Cleveland *(G-3348)*

AMF Burns.................................... G .. 330 650-6500
Hudson *(G-7832)*

▲ Amko Service Company.................. E .. 330 364-8857
Midvale *(G-9907)*

Apex Welding Incorporated.............. F 440 232-6770
Bedford *(G-1012)*

Ares Inc.................................... D .. 419 635-2175
Port Clinton *(G-11439)*

Armor Consolidated Inc.................. A .. 513 923-5260
Mason *(G-9064)*

▲ Armor Metal Group Mason Inc.......... C .. 513 769-0700
Mason *(G-9066)*

▲ AT&f Advanced Metals LLC.............. E .. 330 684-1122
Cleveland *(G-3383)*

Ayling and Reichert Co Consent........ G .. 419 898-2471
Oak Harbor *(G-10883)*

Babcock & Wilcox Company............... E .. 330 753-4511
Barberton *(G-797)*

◆ Babcock & Wilcox Company.............A .. 330 753-4511
Akron *(G-67)*

Bar Processing Corporation.............. F 440 943-0094
Wickliffe *(G-14367)*

Baxter Holdings Inc....................... G .. 513 860-3593
Hamilton *(G-7469)*

Bi-Con Services Inc...................... B .. 740 685-2542
Derwent *(G-6221)*

▲ Bico Akron Inc........................... G .. 330 794-1716
Mogadore *(G-10070)*

BJ Equipment Ltd.......................... F 614 497-1188
Columbus *(G-4758)*

Blackwood Sheet Metal Inc.............. G .. 614 291-3115
Columbus *(G-4764)*

Blevins Metal Fabrication Inc.......... E .. 419 522-6082
Mansfield *(G-8766)*

Breitinger Company........................ C .. 419 526-4255
Mansfield *(G-8767)*

▼ Buckeye Fabricating Company......... E .. 937 746-9822
Springboro *(G-12248)*

Buckeye Stamping Company................ D .. 877 728-0776
Columbus *(G-4786)*

Bwxt Nclear Oprtions Group Inc........ A .. 216 912-3000
Cleveland *(G-3455)*

C & R Inc.................................. E .. 614 497-1130
Groveport *(G-7427)*

C A Joseph Co.............................. F 330 532-4646
Irondale *(G-7927)*

▲ C A Litzler Co Inc...................... E .. 216 267-8020
Cleveland *(G-3457)*

Capital Tool Company..................... E .. 216 661-5750
Cleveland *(G-3467)*

▲ Cardinal Pumps Exchangers Inc....... F 330 332-8558
Salem *(G-11767)*

Ceco Environmental Corp................. D .. 513 874-8915
Cincinnati *(G-2446)*

Central Fabricators Inc.................. E .. 513 621-1240
Cincinnati *(G-2449)*

Chart Asia Inc............................. E .. 440 753-1490
Cleveland *(G-3487)*

Chart Industries Inc..................... C .. 440 753-1490
Cleveland *(G-3488)*

Chart International Inc.................. D .. 440 753-1490
Cleveland *(G-3489)*

▲ Che Holdings Inc........................ G .. 513 770-0777
Mason *(G-9082)*

Cheap Dumpsters Llc....................... G .. 614 285-5865
Columbus *(G-4806)*

Chromium Corporation.............................E 216 271-4910
Cleveland (G-3498)

Chute Source LLC.................................F 330 475-0377
Akron (G-99)

Cleveland Steel Specialty Co..................E 216 464-9400
Bedford Heights (G-1074)

Clifton Capital Holdings LLC...................F 330 562-9000
Maple Heights (G-8880)

◆ Clifton Steel Company.......................D 216 662-6111
Maple Heights (G-8881)

◆ Columbiana Boiler Company LLC......E 330 482-3373
Columbiana (G-4611)

◆ Commercial Mtal Fbricators Inc..........E 937 233-4911
Dayton (G-5707)

Compco Columbiana Company...............D 330 482-0200
Columbiana (G-4613)

Compco Youngstown Company..............D 330 482-6488
Columbiana (G-4614)

Complete Mechanical Svcs LLC.............D 513 489-3080
Cincinnati (G-2507)

Contech Bridge Solutions LLC..............F 513 645-7000
West Chester (G-13969)

Contech Cnstr Pdts Hldings Inc.............A 513 645-7000
West Chester (G-13970)

Contech Engnered Solutions Inc............A 513 645-7000
West Chester (G-13971)

◆ Contech Engnered Solutions LLC......C 513 645-7000
West Chester (G-13972)

Convault of Ohio Inc...........................G 614 252-8422
Columbus (G-4846)

Cooper-Standard Automotive Inc...........D 740 342-3523
New Lexington (G-10401)

Cramers Inc.......................................E 330 477-4571
Canton (G-1873)

Curtiss-Wright Flow Ctrl Corp...............D 513 528-7900
Cincinnati (G-2300)

Dabar Industries LLC.........................F 614 873-3949
Columbus (G-4867)

Danco Metal Products LLC...................D 440 871-2300
Avon Lake (G-753)

Debra-Kuempel Inc..............................D 513 271-6500
Cincinnati (G-2543)

Defabco Inc..D 614 231-2700
Columbus (G-4875)

▲ Defiance Metal Products Co..............B 419 784-5332
Defiance (G-6105)

Deibel Industries LLC..........................E 330 482-3351
Leetonia (G-8301)

Diller Metals Inc.................................G 419 943-3364
Leipsic (G-8306)

Dover Tank and Plate Company.............E 330 343-4443
Dover (G-6242)

Dynamat Inc.......................................F 513 860-5094
Hamilton (G-7485)

▲ Dynamic Control North Amer Inc........F 513 860-5094
Hamilton (G-7486)

▼ E-Pak Manufacturing LLC.................E 330 264-0825
Wooster (G-14636)

Eagle Welding & Fabg Inc....................E 440 946-0692
Willoughby (G-14453)

▲ Eaton Fabricating Company Inc.........E 440 926-3121
Grafton (G-7301)

◆ Ebner Furnaces Inc..........................D 330 335-2311
Wadsworth (G-13637)

▲ Eleet Cryogenics Inc........................E 330 874-4009
Bolivar (G-1382)

Elliott Machine Works Inc....................E 419 468-4709
Galion (G-7189)

En-Hanced Products Inc.......................G 614 882-7400
Sunbury (G-12664)

◆ Enerfab LLC....................................B 513 641-0500
Cincinnati (G-2590)

Energy Hbr Nclear Gnration LLC............G 888 254-6359
Akron (G-134)

Enviri Corporation...............................G 216 961-1570
Cleveland (G-3678)

▲ Exothermics....................................E 419 729-9726
Toledo (G-12959)

▲ Fabco Inc..D 419 422-4533
Findlay (G-6862)

Fabrication Shop Inc...........................F 419 435-7934
Fostoria (G-6978)

Fiba Technologies Inc..........................F 330 602-7300
Midvale (G-9909)

▲ Flow-Liner Systems Ltd....................E 800 348-0020
Zanesville (G-15014)

Fulton Equipment Co............................F 419 290-5393
Toledo (G-12970)

Gaspar Inc...D 330 477-2222
Canton (G-1898)

◆ Gayston Corporation.........................C 937 743-6050
Miamisburg (G-9693)

▲ General Technologies Inc..................E 419 747-1800
Mansfield (G-8791)

▲ General Tool Company.......................C 513 733-5500
Cincinnati (G-2666)

Giuseppes Concessions LLC.................F 614 554-2551
Marengo (G-8897)

GL Nause Co Inc................................E 513 722-9500
Loveland (G-8626)

Grenga Machine & Welding....................F 330 743-1113
Youngstown (G-14871)

H P E Inc...G 330 833-3161
Massillon (G-9199)

◆ Halvorsen Company...........................E 216 341-7500
Cleveland (G-3809)

Hamilton Tanks LLC.............................F 614 445-8446
Columbus (G-4969)

▲ Hammelmann Corporation..................F 937 859-8777
Miamisburg (G-9695)

Hason USA Corp.................................G 513 248-0287
Cincinnati (G-2711)

Heat Exchange Applied Tech Inc............D 330 682-4328
Orrville (G-10983)

Howden North America Inc....................F 330 721-7374
Medina (G-9409)

Howden North America Inc....................F 330 867-8540
Medina (G-9410)

Hutnik Company.................................G 330 336-9700
Wadsworth (G-13643)

Hydraulic Specialists Inc......................G 740 922-3343
Midvale (G-9911)

▼ Hydro-Thrift Corporation...................E 330 837-5141
Massillon (G-9205)

Indian Creek Fabricators Inc.................E 937 667-7214
Tipp City (G-12828)

Industrial Fabrication and Mch..............G 330 454-7644
Canton (G-1917)

Industrial Farm Tank Inc......................E 937 843-2972
Lewistown (G-8365)

Industrial Repair and Mfg.....................F 419 822-0314
Delta (G-6209)

▲ Industrial Repair and Mfg..................E 419 822-4232
Delta (G-6210)

Industrial Tank & Containment..............F 330 448-4876
Brookfield (G-1515)

Jacp Inc..G 513 353-3660
Miamitown (G-9759)

▲ Jergens Inc.....................................C 216 486-5540
Cleveland (G-3885)

Jh Industries Inc................................E 330 963-4105
Twinsburg (G-13321)

Jis Distribution LLC............................F 216 706-6552
Cleveland (G-3888)

JMw Welding and Mfg Inc.....................E 330 484-2428
Canton (G-1922)

Kard Welding Inc.................................E 419 628-2598
Minster (G-10059)

▲ Kendall Holdings Ltd........................E 614 486-4750
Columbus (G-5049)

Kenton Strl & Orn Ir Works...................D 419 674-4025
Kenton (G-8103)

◆ Kirk & Blum Manufacturing Co...........C 513 458-2600
Cincinnati (G-2797)

Krista Messer...................................G 734 459-1952
Sunbury (G-12668)

Laird Technologies Inc.........................E 234 806-0105
Warren (G-13776)

▲ Langdon Inc.....................................E 513 733-5955
Cincinnati (G-2811)

Lapham-Hickey Steel Corp....................D 614 443-4881
Columbus (G-5065)

Lincoln Electric Automtn Inc.................E 614 471-5926
Columbus (G-5070)

Lion Industries LLC.............................E 740 676-1100
Bellaire (G-1089)

Liquid Luggers LLC..............................E 330 426-2538
East Palestine (G-6404)

▲ Long-Stanton Mfg Company................E 513 874-8020
West Chester (G-14024)

Louis Arthur Steel Company..................G 440 997-5545
Geneva (G-7241)

◆ Loveman Steel Corporation................D 440 232-6200
Bedford (G-1044)

M & H Fabricating Co Inc......................G 937 325-8708
Springfield (G-12343)

Mack Iron Works Company.....................E 419 626-3712
Sandusky (G-11855)

Mahle Behr Dayton LLC.........................A 937 369-2000
Dayton (G-5862)

Mahle Behr USA Inc.............................G 937 369-2610
Xenia (G-14770)

▲ Mc Machine Llc................................E 216 398-3666
Cleveland (G-4007)

Mercury Iron and Steel Co.....................F 440 349-1500
Solon (G-12146)

Metal Fabricating Corporation...............D 216 631-8121
Cleveland (G-4023)

Metalfab Group...................................G 440 543-6234
Streetsboro (G-12509)

Micc Manufacturing Corporation.............G 567 331-0101
Perrysburg (G-11209)

▼ Midwestern Industries Inc.................D 330 837-4203
Massillon (G-9223)

Modern Welding Co Ohio Inc..................E 740 344-9425
Newark (G-10522)

Moore Mr Specialty Company.................G 330 332-1229
Salem (G-11803)

▼ Morrison Products Inc......................C 216 486-4000
Cleveland (G-4047)

Myers Industries Inc...........................E 330 253-5592
Akron (G-242)

Myers Industries Inc...........................C 330 336-6621
Wadsworth (G-13653)

Nbw Inc...E 216 377-1700
Cleveland (G-4063)

New Wayne Inc....................................G 740 453-3454
Zanesville (G-15034)

Northeast Fabricators LLC.....................E 330 747-3484
Youngstown (G-14905)

Northwest Installations Inc...................E 419 423-5738
Findlay (G-6900)

Novoco LLC..E 330 359-5315
Fredericksburg (G-7066)

Odom Industries Inc............................E 513 248-0287
Milford (G-9945)

S
I
C

Ohio Heat Transfer.................................. G 513 870-5323
Hamilton *(G-7515)*

▲ Ohio Heat Transfer Ltd......................... F 877 633-0391
Saint Clairsville *(G-11705)*

▲ Oliver Steel Plate Co............................ D 330 425-7000
Twinsburg *(G-13347)*

OSI Environmental LLC .... E 440 237-4600
North Royalton *(G-10779)*

Parker-Hannifin Corporation.................... G 330 336-3511
Wadsworth *(G-13658)*

PB Fbrction Mech Contrs Corp................ F 419 478-4869
Toledo *(G-13091)*

Phe Manufacturing Inc............................ G 937 790-1582
Franklin *(G-7041)*

▲ Pioneer Pipe Inc.................................. A 740 376-2400
Marietta *(G-8937)*

Process Dynamics Inc............................ G 330 686-2597
Stow *(G-12452)*

Prout Boiler Htg & Wldg Inc.................... E 330 744-0293
Youngstown *(G-14921)*

Pucel Enterprises Inc............................. D 216 881-4604
Cleveland *(G-4206)*

Quintus Technologies LLC...................... E 614 891-2732
Lewis Center *(G-8349)*

R G Smith Company................................ D 330 456-3415
Canton *(G-1988)*

Rampp Company..................................... E 740 373-7886
Marietta *(G-8940)*

RCE Heat Exchangers LLC..................... E 330 627-0300
Carrollton *(G-2088)*

Rcr Partnership...................................... G 419 340-1202
Genoa *(G-7249)*

Rebsco Inc... F 937 548-2246
Greenville *(G-7351)*

Rhodes Manufacturing Co Inc................. E 740 743-2614
Somerset *(G-12210)*

▲ Ridge Corporation................................ D 614 421-7434
Pataskala *(G-11147)*

▲ Rimrock Corporation............................. E 614 471-5926
Columbus *(G-5230)*

Rimrock Holdings Corporation................. C 614 471-5926
Columbus *(G-5231)*

Rmt Acquisition Inc................................ E 513 241-5566
Cincinnati *(G-3050)*

Rose Metal Industries LLC...................... F 216 881-3355
Cleveland *(G-4250)*

Ross Hx LLC.. E 513 217-1565
Middletown *(G-9892)*

S-P Company Inc.................................... D 330 782-5651
Columbiana *(G-4627)*

▲ Sausser Steel Company Inc................. G 419 422-9632
Findlay *(G-6916)*

Schaeffer Metal Products Inc.................. G 330 296-6226
Ravenna *(G-11539)*

Schweizer Dipple Inc.............................. D 440 786-8090
Cleveland *(G-4277)*

Seneca Environmental Products Inc......... E 419 447-1282
Tiffin *(G-12799)*

Sexton Industrial Inc.............................. C 513 530-5555
West Chester *(G-14144)*

▼ Sgl Carbon Technic LLC...................... E 440 572-3600
Strongsville *(G-12598)*

Sharon Manufacturing Inc....................... E 330 239-1561
Sharon Center *(G-11942)*

▲ Spirex Corporation............................... C 330 726-1166
Youngstown *(G-14938)*

Spradlin Bros Welding Co........................ F 800 219-2182
Springfield *(G-12375)*

St Lawrence Holdings LLC...................... E 330 562-9000
Maple Heights *(G-8892)*

◆ St Lawrence Steel Corporation.............. E 330 562-9000
Maple Heights *(G-8893)*

STA-Warm Electric Company................... F 330 296-6461
Ravenna *(G-11544)*

Stanwade Metal Products Inc.................. E 330 772-2421
Hartford *(G-7573)*

▼ Steel & Alloy Utility Pdts Inc................ E 330 530-2220
Mc Donald *(G-9361)*

Steel Valley Tank & Welding.................... F 740 598-4994
Brilliant *(G-1497)*

Steve Vore Welding and Steel.................. F 419 375-4087
Fort Recovery *(G-6971)*

Sticker Corporation................................ F 440 946-2100
Willoughby *(G-14534)*

◆ Strohecker Incorporated.......................E 330 426-9496
East Palestine *(G-6407)*

Swagelok Company................................. D 440 349-5934
Solon *(G-12191)*

Swanton Wldg Machining Co Inc............. D 419 826-4816
Swanton *(G-12694)*

▲ The Armor Group Inc............................ C 513 923-5260
Mason *(G-9161)*

▼ Toledo Metal Spinning Company............ E 419 535-5931
Toledo *(G-13152)*

Triangle Precision Inds Inc...................... D 937 299-6776
Dayton *(G-6062)*

Triumph Thermal Systems LLC............... D 419 273-2511
Forest *(G-6942)*

Universal Dsign Fbrication LLC............... F 419 202-5269
Sandusky *(G-11880)*

Universal Hydraulik USA Corp................. G 419 873-6340
Perrysburg *(G-11277)*

▲ Universal Rack & Eqp Co Inc................ G 330 963-6776
Twinsburg *(G-13390)*

▲ Val-Co Pax Inc.................................... D 717 354-4586
Coldwater *(G-4586)*

Verhoff Machine & Welding Inc................ C 419 596-3202
Continental *(G-5424)*

Viking Fabricators Inc............................ G 740 374-5246
Marietta *(G-8960)*

Vortec Corporation................................. E 513 891-7485
Blue Ash *(G-1348)*

Warren Fabricating Corporation...........D 330 534-5017
Hubbard *(G-7818)*

Washington Products Inc......................... F 330 837-5101
Massillon *(G-9252)*

Wcr Incorporated.................................... F 740 333-3448
Wshngtn Ct Hs *(G-14750)*

◆ Wcr Incorporated.................................E 937 223-0703
Fairborn *(G-6703)*

Will-Burt Company.................................. F 330 682-7015
Orrville *(G-11019)*

▲ Will-Burt Company................................ C 330 682-7015
Orrville *(G-11018)*

▲ Worthignton Products Inc...................... G 330 452-7400
East Canton *(G-6381)*

Worthington Cylinder Corp...................... C 740 569-4143
Bremen *(G-1489)*

Worthington Cylinder Corp...................... C 614 438-7900
Columbus *(G-5373)*

Worthington Cylinder Corp...................... C 614 840-3800
Westerville *(G-14242)*

Worthington Cylinder Corp...................... D 330 262-1762
Wooster *(G-14703)*

◆ Worthington Cylinder Corp....................C 614 840-3210
Worthington *(G-14730)*

3444 Sheet metalwork

A & C Welding Inc.................................. E 330 762-4777
Peninsula *(G-11179)*

▲ A & G Manufacturing Co Inc................. E 419 468-7433
Galion *(G-7176)*

Accufab Inc.. G 513 942-1929
West Chester *(G-13934)*

▲ Acro Tool & Die Company...................... E 330 773-5173
Akron *(G-16)*

▲ Active Metal and Molds Inc.................. F 419 281-9623
Ashland *(G-514)*

Affiliated Metal Industries Inc................. F 440 235-3345
Olmsted Falls *(G-10936)*

Ahner Fabricating & Shtmtl Inc.............. E 419 626-6641
Sandusky *(G-11820)*

Airsources Inc.. G 610 983-0102
North Canton *(G-10627)*

Akron Foundry Co.................................. G 330 745-3101
Barberton *(G-791)*

▲ Alan Manufacturing Inc........................ E 330 262-1555
Wooster *(G-14621)*

All Metal Fabricators Inc........................ F 216 267-0033
Cleveland *(G-3324)*

Allen County Fabrication Inc................... E 419 227-7447
Lima *(G-8386)*

Allfab Inc.. F 614 491-4944
Columbus *(G-4686)*

Allied Fabricating & Wldg Co.................. E 614 868-8680
Columbus *(G-4687)*

Allied Mask and Tooling Inc.................... G 419 470-2555
Toledo *(G-12870)*

Alro Steel Corporation............................ E 614 878-7271
Columbus *(G-4690)*

Alro Steel Corporation............................ D 419 720-5300
Toledo *(G-12871)*

Alumetal Manufacturing Company............ E 419 268-2311
Coldwater *(G-4567)*

Aluminum Color Industries Inc................. E 330 536-6295
Lowellville *(G-8657)*

Aluminum Extruded Shapes Inc.............. C 513 563-2205
Cincinnati *(G-2354)*

AM Castle & Co...................................... F 330 425-7000
Bedford *(G-1011)*

AMD Fabricators Inc.............................. F 440 946-8855
Willoughby *(G-14417)*

▲ American Frame Corporation................. E 419 893-5595
Maumee *(G-9259)*

▲ Ampp Incorporated.............................. C 419 666-4747
Perrysburg *(G-11203)*

Anchor Metal Processing Inc................... F 216 362-6463
Cleveland *(G-3354)*

Anchor Metal Processing Inc................... E 216 362-1850
Cleveland *(G-3355)*

Antique Auto Sheet Metal Inc................. F 937 833-4422
Brookville *(G-1562)*

Apex Welding Incorporated...................... F 440 232-6770
Bedford *(G-1012)*

Arbenz Inc... F 614 274-6800
Columbus *(G-4724)*

▲ Arku Inc.. F 513 985-0500
Cincinnati *(G-2375)*

Armor Metal Group Elkhart Inc................ F 800 672-6373
Mason *(G-9065)*

▲ Armor Metal Group Mason Inc.............. C 513 769-0700
Mason *(G-9066)*

Arsco Custom Metals LLC....................... D 513 385-0555
Cincinnati *(G-2377)*

▲ Astro Manufacturing & Design Inc......... C 888 215-1746
Eastlake *(G-6417)*

▼ Auburn Metal Processing LLC............... G 315 253-2565
Stow *(G-12419)*

Autoneum North America Inc................... B 419 693-0511
Oregon *(G-10957)*

Avon Lake Sheet Metal Co...................... E 440 933-3505
Avon Lake *(G-750)*

Aztec Manufacturing Inc........................ E 330 783-9747
Youngstown *(G-14816)*

▲ B-R-O-T Incorporated.......................... E 216 267-5335
Cleveland *(G-3401)*

Bainter Machining Company .... G 740 653-2422
     Lancaster *(G-8180)*

Bayloff Stmped Pdts Knsman Inc .... D 330 876-4511
     Kinsman *(G-8140)*

Beacon Metal Fabricators Inc .... G 216 391-7444
     Cleveland *(G-3412)*

Berran Industrial Group Inc .... E 330 253-5800
     Akron *(G-77)*

Bickers Metal Products Inc .... E 513 353-4000
     Miamitown *(G-9756)*

Billington Company Inc .... E 440 647-3039
     Wellington *(G-13883)*

▲ Biofit Engineered Product .... E 419 823-1089
     Bowling Green *(G-1411)*

BJ Equipment Ltd. .... F 614 497-1188
     Columbus *(G-4758)*

Blevins Metal Fabrication Inc .... E 419 522-6082
     Mansfield *(G-8766)*

Bob Lanes Welding Inc .... G 740 373-3567
     Marietta *(G-8904)*

Bogie Industries Inc Ltd .... E 330 745-3105
     Akron *(G-81)*

Breining Mech Systems Inc .... G 216 391-2400
     Cleveland *(G-3435)*

Breitinger Company .... C 419 526-4255
     Mansfield *(G-8767)*

Buckeye Metal Works Inc .... G 614 239-8000
     Columbus *(G-4785)*

Bud Corp .... G 740 967-9992
     Johnstown *(G-7994)*

Budde Sheet Metal Works Inc .... E 937 224-0868
     Dayton *(G-5689)*

Busch & Thiem Inc .... E 419 625-7515
     Sandusky *(G-11825)*

Byg Industries Inc .... E 216 961-5436
     Cleveland *(G-3456)*

C & R Inc .... E 614 497-1130
     Groveport *(G-7427)*

C A Joseph Co .... F 330 532-4646
     Irondale *(G-7927)*

C L W Inc .... G 740 374-8443
     Marietta *(G-8905)*

C-N-D Industries Inc .... F 330 478-8811
     Massillon *(G-9176)*

Cabletek Wiring Products Inc .... E 800 562-9378
     Elyria *(G-6508)*

Captive-Aire Systems Inc .... E 513 860-5555
     Cincinnati *(G-2437)*

Champion Window Co of Toledo .... G 419 841-0154
     Perrysburg *(G-11211)*

Chute Source LLC .... F 330 475-0377
     Akron *(G-99)*

Cinfab LLC .... C 513 396-6100
     Cincinnati *(G-2493)*

Clarkwestern Dietrich Building .... D 330 372-5564
     Warren *(G-13752)*

▼ Clarkwstern Dtrich Bldg System .... C 513 870-1100
     West Chester *(G-13966)*

Cleveland Steel Specialty Co .... E 216 464-9400
     Bedford Heights *(G-1074)*

Columbus Steelmasters Inc .... F 614 231-2141
     Columbus *(G-4835)*

Commercial Mtal Fbricators Inc .... E 937 233-4911
     Dayton *(G-5707)*

Compco Youngstown Company .... D 330 482-6488
     Columbiana *(G-4614)*

Contech Engnered Solutions Inc .... A 513 645-7000
     West Chester *(G-13971)*

◆ Contech Engnered Solutions LLC .... C 513 645-7000
     West Chester *(G-13972)*

Contour Forming Inc .... F 740 345-9777
     Newark *(G-10499)*

Controls and Sheet Metal Inc .... E 513 721-3610
     Cincinnati *(G-2515)*

COW Industries Inc .... E 614 443-6537
     Columbus *(G-4854)*

Cramers Inc .... E 330 477-4571
     Canton *(G-1873)*

Crest Products Inc .... F 440 942-5770
     Mentor *(G-9508)*

▲ Crown Electric Engrg & Mfg LLC .... E 513 539-7394
     Middletown *(G-9852)*

Custom Metal Products Inc .... F 614 855-2263
     New Albany *(G-10337)*

Custom Metal Shearing Inc .... F 937 233-6950
     Dayton *(G-5718)*

Da Investments Inc .... D 330 781-6100
     Youngstown *(G-14845)*

Dae Holdings LLC .... E 419 866-6301
     Swanton *(G-12681)*

Danco Metal Products LLC .... D 440 871-2300
     Avon Lake *(G-753)*

▲ DBs Stnless Stl Fbrctors Inc .... G 513 856-9600
     Hamilton *(G-7483)*

Defabco Inc .... D 614 231-2700
     Columbus *(G-4875)*

Delafoil Pennsylvania Inc .... G 610 327-9565
     Perrysburg *(G-11214)*

Delma Corp .... D 937 253-2142
     Dayton *(G-5745)*

Di Iorio Sheet Metal Inc .... F 216 961-3703
     Cleveland *(G-3612)*

Die-Cut Products Co .... F 216 771-6994
     Cleveland *(G-3615)*

Dimensional Metals Inc .... E 740 927-3633
     Reynoldsburg *(G-11565)*

Dover Tank and Plate Company .... E 330 343-4443
     Dover *(G-6242)*

Duct Fabricators Inc .... G 216 391-2400
     Cleveland *(G-3636)*

Ducts Inc .... G 216 391-2400
     Cleveland *(G-3637)*

Dynamic Weld Corporation .... E 419 582-2900
     Osgood *(G-11026)*

E & K Products Co Inc .... G 216 631-2510
     Cleveland *(G-3643)*

E B P Inc .... E 216 241-2550
     Solon *(G-12102)*

Eagle Welding & Fabg Inc .... E 440 946-0692
     Willoughby *(C-11463)*

▲ Eastern Sheet Metal Inc .... D 513 793-3440
     Blue Ash *(G-1270)*

▲ Eaton Fabricating Company Inc .... E 440 926-3121
     Grafton *(G-7301)*

◆ Ebner Furnaces Inc .... D 330 335-2311
     Wadsworth *(G-13637)*

Edwards Sheet Metal Works Inc .... F 740 694-0010
     Fredericktown *(G-7078)*

Enterprise Welding & Fabg Inc .... C 440 354-4128
     Mentor *(G-9513)*

Ethima Inc .... D 419 626-4912
     Sandusky *(G-11834)*

Everyday Technologies Inc .... F 937 497-7774
     Sidney *(G-12018)*

Everyday Technologies Inc .... F 419 739-6104
     Wapakoneta *(G-13709)*

Everyday Technologies Inc .... F 937 492-4171
     Sidney *(G-12019)*

▲ Fabco Inc .... D 419 422-4533
     Findlay *(G-6862)*

Fabcor Inc .... F 419 628-4428
     Minster *(G-10057)*

Fabricating Solutions Inc .... F 330 486-0998
     Twinsburg *(G-13301)*

Falcon Industries Inc .... E 330 723-0099
     Medina *(G-9401)*

Famous Industries Inc .... E 330 535-1811
     Akron *(G-145)*

Feather Lite Innovations Inc .... F 513 893-5483
     Liberty Twp *(G-8383)*

▲ Feather Lite Innovations Inc .... E 937 743-9008
     Springboro *(G-12252)*

Firestone Laser and Mfg LLC .... E 330 337-9551
     Salem *(G-11779)*

First Francis Company Inc .... E 440 352-8927
     Painesville *(G-11087)*

Flood Heliarc Inc .... F 614 835-3929
     Groveport *(G-7432)*

Franck and Fric Incorporated .... D 216 524-4451
     Cleveland *(G-3742)*

Freeman Enclosure Systems LLC .... C 877 441-8555
     Batavia *(G-865)*

Fulton Equipment Co .... F 419 290-5393
     Toledo *(G-12970)*

◆ G & S Titanium Inc .... E 330 263-0564
     Wooster *(G-14641)*

G T Metal Fabricators Inc .... F 440 237-8745
     Cleveland *(G-3750)*

G2 Materials LLC .... G 216 293-4211
     Cleveland *(G-3752)*

Galion LLC .... C 419 468-5214
     Galion *(G-7190)*

▲ Galion-Godwin Truck Bdy Co LLC ...... F 330 359-5495
     Dundee *(G-6365)*

Gaspar Inc .... D 330 477-2222
     Canton *(G-1898)*

Gem City Metal Tech LLC .... E 937 252-8998
     Dayton *(G-5793)*

General Awning Company Inc .... G 216 749-0110
     Cleveland *(G-3762)*

▲ General Technologies Inc .... E 419 747-1800
     Mansfield *(G-8791)*

▲ General Tool Company .... C 513 733-5500
     Cincinnati *(G-2666)*

▲ Gentek Building Products Inc .... F 800 548-4542
     Cuyahoga Falls *(G-5544)*

George Manufacturing Inc .... F 513 932-1067
     Lebanon *(G-8258)*

Gilson Screen Incorporated .... E 419 256-7711
     Malinta *(G-8742)*

GL Nause Co Inc .... E 513 722-9500
     Loveland *(O-0020)*

▲ Glunt Industries Inc .... C 330 399-7585
     Warren *(G-13770)*

Golden Angle Archtctral Group .... G 614 531-7932
     Columbus *(G-4960)*

Great Day Improvements LLC .... B 267 223-1289
     Macedonia *(G-8695)*

Gunderson Rail Services LLC .... D 330 792-6521
     Youngstown *(G-14872)*

Gundlach Sheet Metal Works Inc .... E 419 626-4525
     Sandusky *(G-11837)*

GUTTER TOPPER LTD. .... G 513 797-5800
     Batavia *(G-866)*

Hall Company .... E 937 652-1376
     Urbana *(G-13465)*

◆ Halvorsen Company .... E 216 341-7500
     Cleveland *(G-3809)*

Harray LLC .... G 888 568-8371
     Cincinnati *(G-2707)*

Harrison Mch & Plastic Corp .... E 330 527-5641
     Garrettsville *(G-7220)*

Hartzell Mfg Co LLC .... F 937 859-5955
     Miamisburg *(G-9696)*

HCC Holdings Inc .... G 800 203-1155
     Cleveland *(G-3813)*

Heim Sheet Metal Inc............................ G..... 330 424-7820
Lisbon *(G-8469)*

▲ Hidaka Usa Inc................................... E..... 614 889-8611
Dublin *(G-6303)*

Higgins Construction & Supply Co Inc.. F..... 937 364-2331
Hillsboro *(G-7717)*

Highway Safety Corp............................. F..... 740 387-6991
Marion *(G-8972)*

Holgate Metal Fab Inc........................... F..... 419 599-2000
Napoleon *(G-10285)*

Hvac Inc.. F..... 330 343-5511
Dover *(G-6247)*

I-M-A Enterprises Inc............................ F..... 330 948-3535
Lodi *(G-8502)*

Indian Creek Fabricators Inc.................. E..... 937 667-7214
Tipp City *(G-12828)*

Industrial Fabricators Inc...................... E..... 614 882-7423
Westerville *(G-14265)*

Industrial Mill Maintenance................... F..... 330 746-1155
Youngstown *(G-14876)*

Innovative Mech Systems LLC............... G..... 937 813-8713
Dayton *(G-5614)*

Interstate Contractors LLC.................... E..... 513 372-5393
Mason *(G-9115)*

◆ Isaiah Industries Inc............................ E..... 937 773-9840
Piqua *(G-11358)*

Jacobs Mechanical Co........................... C..... 513 681-6800
Cincinnati *(G-2756)*

Jh Industries Inc.................................... E..... 330 963-4105
Twinsburg *(G-13321)*

Jim Nier Construction Inc....................... E..... 740 289-3925
Piketon *(G-11308)*

Joining Metals Inc.................................. F..... 440 259-1790
Perry *(G-11193)*

Jones Metal Products Co LLC................ E..... 740 545-6381
West Lafayette *(G-14171)*

Joyce Manufacturing Co......................... D..... 440 239-9100
Berea *(G-1179)*

Kalron LLC.. E..... 440 647-3039
Wellington *(G-13893)*

Kalron LLC.. G..... 440 647-3039
Wellington *(G-13894)*

Kenton Strl & Orn Ir Works.................... D..... 419 674-4025
Kenton *(G-8103)*

Kerber Sheetmetal Works Inc................ F..... 937 339-6366
Troy *(G-13233)*

Kidron Inc.. B..... 330 857-3011
Kidron *(G-8129)*

Kilroy Company..................................... D..... 440 951-8700
Cleveland *(G-3920)*

◆ Kirk & Blum Manufacturing Co............. C..... 513 458-2600
Cincinnati *(G-2797)*

Kirk Williams Company Inc.................... D..... 614 875-9023
Grove City *(G-7393)*

Knight Manufacturing Co Inc................. G..... 740 676-5516
Shadyside *(G-11922)*

Korda Manufacturing LLC...................... F..... 330 262-1555
Wooster *(G-14659)*

Kramer Power Equipment Co................. G..... 937 456-2232
Eaton *(G-6457)*

Kuhlman Engineering Co........................ F..... 419 243-2196
Toledo *(G-13023)*

Kuhn Fabricating Inc.............................. G..... 440 277-4182
Lorain *(G-8562)*

▲ Kundel Industries Inc........................... D..... 330 469-6147
Vienna *(G-13609)*

L & W Investments Inc.......................... D..... 937 492-4171
Sidney *(G-12029)*

◆ Lake Shore Electric Corp..................... E..... 440 232-0200
Bedford *(G-1043)*

Lambert Sheet Metal Inc........................ F..... 614 237-0384
Columbus *(G-5061)*

▲ Langdon Inc... E..... 513 733-5955
Cincinnati *(G-2811)*

Lima Sheet Metal Mch & Mfg Inc........... F..... 419 229-1161
Lima *(G-8426)*

Lippert Components Inc......................... G..... 574 537-8900
Payne *(G-11164)*

▲ Long-Stanton Mfg Company................. E..... 513 874-8020
West Chester *(G-14024)*

Louis Arthur Steel Company.................. G..... 440 997-5545
Geneva *(G-7241)*

Lowry Furnace Co Inc............................ G..... 330 745-4822
Akron *(G-211)*

▲ Lt Enterprises of Ohio LLC.................... E..... 330 526-6908
North Canton *(G-10649)*

Lukjan Metal Pdts Holdg Co Inc............. G..... 440 599-8127
Conneaut *(G-5409)*

Lukjan Metal Products Inc..................... C..... 440 599-8127
Conneaut *(G-5410)*

Lund Equipment Company...................... E..... 330 659-4800
Akron *(G-212)*

M3 Technologies Inc............................. F..... 216 898-9936
Cleveland *(G-3977)*

Mack Iron Works Company.................... E..... 419 626-3712
Sandusky *(G-11855)*

Mantych Metalworking Inc..................... F..... 937 258-1373
Dayton *(G-5619)*

Marsam Metalfab Inc............................. E..... 330 405-1520
Twinsburg *(G-13334)*

Martina Metal LLC................................. E..... 614 291-9700
Columbus *(G-5085)*

Matern Metal Works Inc........................ F..... 419 529-3100
Mansfield *(G-8821)*

Matteo Aluminum Inc............................ E..... 440 585-5213
Wickliffe *(G-14382)*

May Industries of Ohio Inc.................... E..... 440 237-8012
North Royalton *(G-10773)*

May Tool & Die Co................................. G..... 440 237-8012
Cleveland *(G-4001)*

▲ Mc Machine Llc.................................... E..... 216 398-3666
Cleveland *(G-4007)*

McGill Airflow LLC................................. D..... 614 829-1200
Columbus *(G-5090)*

◆ McGill Corporation.............................. F..... 614 829-1200
Groveport *(G-7444)*

McWane Inc... B..... 740 622-6651
Coshocton *(G-5459)*

Medway Tool Corp................................. G..... 937 335-7717
Troy *(G-13240)*

Meese Inc... F..... 440 998-1202
Ashtabula *(G-604)*

Mestek Inc.. D..... 419 288-2703
Bowling Green *(G-1429)*

Mestek Inc.. F..... 419 288-2703
Bradner *(G-1454)*

Metal Coaters....................................... D..... 740 432-7351
Cambridge *(G-1749)*

Metal Fabricating Corporation.............. D..... 216 631-8121
Cleveland *(G-4023)*

Metal Panel Systems LLC..................... E..... 513 554-6120
Cincinnati *(G-2869)*

Metal Sales Manufacturing Corp........... E..... 440 319-3779
Jefferson *(G-7978)*

Metal Seal Precision Ltd....................... C..... 440 255-8888
Willoughby *(G-14488)*

▼ Metal Seal Precision Ltd....................... D..... 440 255-8888
Mentor *(G-9563)*

Metal-Max Inc....................................... G..... 330 673-9926
Kent *(G-8052)*

Metalfab Group..................................... G..... 440 543-6234
Streetsboro *(G-12509)*

▲ Mid-Ohio Products Inc......................... D..... 614 771-2795
Hilliard *(G-7686)*

Midwest Fabrications Inc....................... F..... 330 633-0191
Tallmadge *(G-12741)*

Midwest Metal Fabricators.................... F..... 419 739-7077
Wapakoneta *(G-13723)*

Midwest Metal Fabricators Ltd.............. F..... 419 739-7077
Wapakoneta *(G-13724)*

Midwest Metal Products LLC................. E..... 614 539-7322
Grove City *(G-7401)*

Mike Loppe... F..... 937 969-8102
Tremont City *(G-13189)*

◆ Modern Ice Equipment & Sup Co.......... E..... 513 367-2101
Cincinnati *(G-2885)*

Modern Sheet Metal Works Inc............. E..... 513 353-3666
Cleves *(G-4545)*

▲ MRS Industrial Inc............................... E..... 614 308-1070
Columbus *(G-5115)*

Mwgh LLC.. C..... 513 521-4114
Cincinnati *(G-2892)*

◆ N Wasserstrom & Sons Inc.................. C..... 614 228-5550
Columbus *(G-5118)*

National Indus Concepts Inc................. F..... 615 989-9101
Chillicothe *(G-2267)*

▼ National Sign Systems Inc................... D..... 614 850-2540
Hilliard *(G-7689)*

Niles Manufacturing & Finshg............... C..... 330 544-0402
Niles *(G-10596)*

▲ Nissin Precision N Amer Inc................. D..... 937 836-1910
Englewood *(G-6620)*

Northwest Installations Inc................... E..... 419 423-5738
Findlay *(G-6900)*

Northwind Industries Inc....................... G..... 216 433-0666
Cleveland *(G-4099)*

Novelis Corporation.............................. C..... 740 983-2571
Ashville *(G-628)*

Nvent Management Company................. A..... 440 248-0100
Solon *(G-12162)*

▲ Oatey Co.. B..... 800 203-1155
Cleveland *(G-4107)*

◆ Oatey Supply Chain Svcs Inc............... C..... 216 267-7100
Cleveland *(G-4108)*

Obr Cooling Towers LLC........................ E..... 419 243-3443
Northwood *(G-10807)*

Ohio Blow Pipe Company....................... E..... 216 681-7379
Cleveland *(G-4113)*

◆ Ohio Gratings Inc................................. B..... 800 321-9800
Canton *(G-1966)*

Ohio Steel Sheet and Plate Inc............. E..... 800 827-2401
Hubbard *(G-7815)*

Ohio Trailer Inc..................................... G..... 330 392-4444
Warren *(G-13787)*

▲ Oliver Steel Plate Co............................ D..... 330 425-7000
Twinsburg *(G-13347)*

◆ Options Plus Incorporated................... F..... 740 694-9811
Fredericktown *(G-7083)*

Owens Corning Sales LLC..................... F..... 740 983-1300
Ashville *(G-629)*

▲ P & L Metalcrafts LLC.......................... F..... 330 793-2178
Youngstown *(G-14908)*

Parker-Hannifin Corporation................. G..... 330 336-3511
Wadsworth *(G-13658)*

Paul Wilke & Son Inc............................ F..... 513 921-3163
Cincinnati *(G-2947)*

PB Fbrction Mech Contrs Corp.............. F..... 419 478-4869
Toledo *(G-13091)*

▲ Pei Liquidation Company...................... C..... 330 467-4267
Macedonia *(G-8704)*

Pennant Moldings Inc............................ C..... 937 584-5411
Sabina *(G-11682)*

Phillips Manufacturing Co...................... D..... 330 652-4335
Niles *(G-10600)*

Plas-Tanks Industries Inc..................... E..... 513 942-3800
Hamilton *(G-7517)*

▲ Porcelain Steel Buildings Company. D 614 228-5781
Columbus *(G-5199)*

Precision Duct Fabrication LLC............ F 614 580-9385
Columbus *(G-5202)*

Precision Metal Products Inc................ C 614 526-7000
Dublin *(G-6334)*

Precision Mtal Fabrication Inc.............. D 937 235-9261
Dayton *(G-5950)*

Precision Welding Corporation............. E 216 524-6110
Cleveland *(G-4187)*

Production Manufacturing Inc.............. E 513 892-2331
Hamilton *(G-7518)*

Quality Steel Fabrication..................... F 937 492-9503
Sidney *(G-12042)*

Quass Sheet Metal Inc....................... G 330 477-4841
Canton *(G-1986)*

R G Smith Company............................ D 330 456-3415
Canton *(G-1988)*

R L Torbeck Industries Inc................... G 513 367-0080
Harrison *(G-7565)*

Raka Corporation................................ D 419 476-6572
Toledo *(G-13110)*

Rapid Machine Inc.............................. F 419 737-2377
Pioneer *(G-11327)*

▲ Raymath Company.......................... C 937 335-1860
Troy *(G-13249)*

Regional Sheetmetal Mfg L................ G 937 425-6972
Dayton *(G-5622)*

Rex Welding Inc................................. F 740 387-1650
Marion *(G-8992)*

Rmt Acquisition Inc............................ E 513 241-5566
Cincinnati *(G-3050)*

▲ Robinson Fin Machines Inc.............. E 419 674-4152
Kenton *(G-8113)*

▲ Rockwell Metals Company LLC........ F 440 242-2420
Lorain *(G-8579)*

Romar Metal Fabricating Inc............... G 740 682-7731
Oak Hill *(G-10894)*

Roofing Annex LLC............................. G 513 942-0555
West Chester *(G-14141)*

Royal Metal Products LLC................... C 740 397-8842
Mount Vernon *(G-10264)*

Royalton Archtctral Fbrication............. F 440 582-0400
North Royalton *(G-10782)*

S & D Architectural Metals................. G 440 582-2560
North Royalton *(G-10784)*

S & G Manufacturing Group LLC......... D 614 529-0100
Hilliard *(G-7700)*

▼ S&B Metal Pdts Twinsburg LLC........ E 330 487-5790
Twinsburg *(G-13372)*

Sarka Shtmtl & Fabrication Inc............ E 419 447-4377
Tiffin *(G-12797)*

▲ Sausser Steel Company Inc............. G 419 422-9632
Findlay *(G-6916)*

Schoonover Industries Inc.................. F 419 289-8332
Ashland *(G-572)*

Schweizer Dipple Inc.......................... D 440 786-8090
Cleveland *(G-4277)*

Scott Fetzer Company......................... C 216 267-9000
Cleveland *(G-4278)*

Selmco Metal Fabricators Inc............. F 937 498-1331
Sidney *(G-12051)*

Seneca Sheet Metal Company............ F 419 447-8434
Tiffin *(G-12800)*

SFM Corp.. E 440 951-5500
Willoughby *(G-14523)*

Shaffer Metal Fab Inc......................... E 937 492-1384
Sidney *(G-12052)*

Shape Supply Inc............................... G 513 863-6695
Hamilton *(G-7525)*

Sheet Metal Products Co Inc............... E 440 392-9000
Mentor *(G-9615)*

Sheetmetal Crafters Inc...................... F 330 452-6700
Canton *(G-2005)*

▼ Sheffield Metals Cleveland LLC........ F 800 283-5262
Sheffield Village *(G-11964)*

▼ Sidney Manufacturing Company........ E 937 492-4154
Sidney *(G-12053)*

Skyline Material Sales LLC.................. G 937 981-5505
Greenfield *(G-7331)*

Skyline Steel LLC.............................. G 740 423-8544
Belpre *(G-1154)*

Smith Rn Sheet Metal Shop Inc........... F 740 653-5011
Lancaster *(G-8224)*

Somerville Manufacturing Inc............. E 740 336-7847
Marietta *(G-8949)*

Spradlin Bros Welding Co................... F 800 219-2182
Springfield *(G-12375)*

▲ Staber Industries Inc....................... E 614 836-5995
Groveport *(G-7450)*

Standard Technologies LLC................. D 419 332-6434
Fremont *(G-7133)*

Starr Fabricating Inc........................... D 330 394-9891
Vienna *(G-13618)*

▼ Steel & Alloy Utility Pdts Inc............. E 330 530-2220
Mc Donald *(G-9361)*

Steelial Wldg Met Fbrction Inc............ E 740 669-5300
Vinton *(G-13624)*

Steve Vore Welding and Steel............. F 419 375-4087
Fort Recovery *(G-6971)*

Suburban Metal Products Inc.............. F 740 474-4237
Circleville *(G-3263)*

Sulecki Precision Products Inc............ F 440 255-5454
Mentor *(G-9630)*

Swanton Wldg Machining Co Inc......... E 419 826-4816
Swanton *(G-12694)*

Systech Handling Inc......................... E 419 445-8226
Archbold *(G-512)*

Tallmadge Spinning & Metal Co........... F 330 794-2277
Akron *(G-328)*

Tangent Air Inc.................................. E 740 474-1114
Circleville *(G-3264)*

TDS-Bf/Ls Holdings Inc...................... E 440 327-5800
North Ridgeville *(G-10751)*

▲ Technibus Inc................................. D 330 479-4202
Canton *(G-2022)*

◆ Tectum Inc.................................... C 740 345-9691
Newark *(G-10535)*

Teh Investments Inc.......................... D 330 782-1127
Youngstown *(G-11011)*

Tendon Manufacturing Inc.................. E 216 663-3200
Cleveland *(G-4374)*

▲ The Armor Group Inc...................... C 513 923-5260
Mason *(G-9161)*

TL Industries Inc............................... C 419 666-8144
Perrysburg *(G-11272)*

TNT Solid Solutions LLC.................... F 419 262-6228
Toledo *(G-13146)*

Toledo Window & Awning Inc.............. F 419 474-3396
Toledo *(G-13162)*

Tool and Die Systems........................ G 440 327-5800
Elyria *(G-6596)*

Transtar Holding Company LLC........... G 800 359-3339
Walton Hills *(G-13703)*

Tri-Fab Inc.. E 330 337-3425
Salem *(G-11815)*

Tri-Mac Mfg & Svcs Co...................... F 513 896-4445
Hamilton *(G-7533)*

Tri-State Fabricators Inc..................... E 513 752-5005
Amelia *(G-440)*

Triangle Precision Inds Inc................. D 937 299-6776
Dayton *(G-6062)*

◆ Tricor Industrial Inc........................ D 330 264-3299
Wooster *(G-14692)*

Tru Form Metal Products Inc............... G 216 252-3700
Cleveland *(G-4430)*

▲ United McGill Corporation............... E 614 829-1200
Groveport *(G-7455)*

▲ Universal Steel Company................. D 216 883-4972
Cleveland *(G-4448)*

V & S Schuler Engineering Inc............ E 330 452-5200
Canton *(G-2041)*

V M Systems Inc................................ D 419 535-1044
Toledo *(G-13172)*

Valley Metal Works Inc....................... E 513 554-1022
Cincinnati *(G-3192)*

Varmland Inc..................................... F 216 741-1510
Cleveland *(G-4458)*

Venti-Now... F 513 334-3375
Montgomery *(G-10125)*

Verhoff Machine & Welding Inc........... C 419 596-3202
Continental *(G-5424)*

Vicart Prcsion Fabricators Inc............. E 614 771-0080
Hilliard *(G-7710)*

▼ W J Egli Company Inc..................... F 330 823-3666
Alliance *(G-414)*

Warner Fabricating Inc....................... F 330 848-3191
Wadsworth *(G-13676)*

◆ Warren Fabricating Corporation........ D 330 534-5017
Hubbard *(G-7818)*

Waterville Sheet Metal Co Inc............. G 419 878-5050
Waterville *(G-13844)*

Weld Tech LLC.................................. G 419 357-3214
Berlin Heights *(G-1206)*

Weybridge LLC.................................. E 440 951-5500
Willoughby *(G-14549)*

▲ Will-Burt Company......................... C 330 682-7015
Orrville *(G-11018)*

Wolf Metals Inc.................................. G 614 461-6361
Columbus *(G-5371)*

Wooster Abruzzi Company.................. E 330 345-3968
Wooster *(G-14698)*

Youngstown Shade & Alum LLC........... G 330 782-2373
Youngstown *(G-14975)*

Z Line Kitchen and Bath LLC............... G 614 777-5004
Marysville *(G-9055)*

3446 Architectural metalwork

▲ A & G Manufacturing Co Inc............ E 419 468-7433
Galion *(G-7176)*

Acme Fence LLC................................ F 330 784-0456
Akron *(C-15)*

▲ Agratronix LLC............................... E 330 562-2222
Streetsboro *(G-12485)*

Akron Products Company.................... D 330 576-1750
Wadsworth *(G-13627)*

All Ohio Companies Inc...................... G 216 420-9274
Cleveland *(G-3325)*

Annin & Co Inc.................................. C 740 622-4447
Coshocton *(G-5447)*

Armor Consolidated Inc...................... A 513 923-5260
Mason *(G-9064)*

▲ Armor Metal Group Mason Inc......... C 513 769-0700
Mason *(G-9066)*

▲ Art Iron Inc................................... D 419 241-1261
Toledo *(G-12887)*

AT&f Advanced Metals LLC................. F 330 684-1122
Orrville *(G-10973)*

▲ AT&f Advanced Metals LLC............. E 330 684-1122
Cleveland *(G-3383)*

Auld Corporation............................... G 614 454-1010
Columbus *(G-4734)*

Autogate Inc...................................... E 419 588-2796
Berlin Heights *(G-1203)*

Bauer Corporation.............................. E 800 321-4760
Wooster *(G-14624)*

S
I
C

Beacon Metal Fabricators Inc.............. G 216 391-7444
Cleveland *(G-3412)*

◆ Bil-Jax Inc..F 419 445-8915
Archbold *(G-490)*

Blevins Metal Fabrication Inc............. E 419 522-6082
Mansfield *(G-8766)*

Bowden Fence Co LLC....................... G 614 272-8923
Columbus *(G-4771)*

Chc Fabricating Corp.......................... D 513 821-7757
Cincinnati *(G-2459)*

Chc Manufacturing Inc........................ E 513 821-7757
Cincinnati *(G-2460)*

Cozmyk Enterprises Inc......................F 614 231-1370
Columbus *(G-4856)*

Cramers Inc... E 330 477-4571
Canton *(G-1873)*

Cuyahoga Fence LLC...........................F 216 830-2200
Cleveland *(G-3591)*

Debra-Kuempel Inc.............................. D 513 271-6500
Cincinnati *(G-2543)*

Dover Tank and Plate Company........... E 330 343-4443
Dover *(G-6242)*

E B P Inc.. E 216 241-2550
Solon *(G-12102)*

E C S Corp.. G 440 323-1707
Elyria *(G-6524)*

Enviri Corporation...............................F 740 387-1150
Marion *(G-8969)*

Federal Iron Works Company.............. G 330 482-5910
Columbiana *(G-4617)*

Finelli Ornamental Iron Co.................. E 440 248-0050
Cleveland *(G-3717)*

Fortin Welding & Mfg Inc..................... E 614 291-4342
Columbus *(G-4934)*

Gem City Metal Tech LLC.................... E 937 252-8998
Dayton *(G-5793)*

GL Nause Co Inc.................................. E 513 722-9500
Loveland *(G-8626)*

Glas Ornamental Metals Inc................ G 330 753-0215
Barberton *(G-807)*

Hansen Scaffolding LLC......................F 513 574-9000
West Chester *(G-14124)*

Hart & Cooley LLC.............................. D 937 832-7800
Englewood *(G-6614)*

Haulotte North America Mfg LLC........ G 419 445-8915
Archbold *(G-497)*

Hayes Bros Orna Ir Works Inc.............F 419 531-1491
Toledo *(G-12987)*

Indian Creek Fabricators Inc............... E 937 667-7214
Tipp City *(G-12828)*

Jerry Harolds Doors Unlimited............ G 740 635-4949
Bridgeport *(G-1494)*

Joyce Manufacturing Co...................... D 440 239-9100
Berea *(G-1179)*

Kenton Strl & Orn Ir Works.................. D 419 674-4025
Kenton *(G-8103)*

◆ Kinetics Noise Control Inc................C 614 889-0480
Dublin *(G-6316)*

L & L Ornamental Iron Co....................F 513 353-1930
Cleves *(G-4543)*

Lakeway Mfg Inc.................................. E 419 433-3030
Huron *(G-7877)*

▲ Langdon Inc..................................... E 513 733-5955
Cincinnati *(G-2811)*

M F Y Inc..F 330 747-1334
Youngstown *(G-14890)*

Mack Iron Works Company.................. E 419 626-3712
Sandusky *(G-11855)*

Metal Maintenance Inc.........................F 513 661-3300
Cleves *(G-4544)*

Michaels Pre-Cast Con Pdts Inc..........F 513 683-1292
Loveland *(G-8643)*

Modern Builders Supply Inc................C 419 241-3961
Toledo *(G-13058)*

◆ Momentive Prfmce Mtls Qrtz Inc......E 440 878-5700
Strongsville *(G-12575)*

Mound Technologies Inc...................... E 937 748-2937
Springboro *(G-12260)*

National Stair Corp.............................. G 937 325-1347
Springfield *(G-12356)*

Newman Brothers Inc.......................... G
Cincinnati *(G-2905)*

◆ Ohio Gratings Inc.............................B 800 321-9800
Canton *(G-1966)*

One Wish LLC......................................F 800 505-6883
Bedford *(G-1052)*

▲ P & L Metalcrafts LLC......................F 330 793-2178
Youngstown *(G-14908)*

Phase II Enterprises Inc...................... G 330 484-2113
Canton *(G-1975)*

Quality Architectural and Fabr.............F 937 743-2923
Franklin *(G-7043)*

Royalton Archtctral Fbrication.............F 440 582-0400
North Royalton *(G-10782)*

▲ Sausser Steel Company Inc............. G 419 422-9632
Findlay *(G-6916)*

Sewah Studios Inc...............................F 740 373-2087
Marietta *(G-8943)*

Sky Climber Wind Solutions LLC........ E 740 203-3900
Delaware *(G-6174)*

▲ Spallinger Millwright Svc Co............. E 419 225-5830
Lima *(G-8452)*

Stephens Pipe & Steel LLC.................C 740 869-2257
Mount Sterling *(G-10229)*

Swanton Wldg Machining Co Inc......... D 419 826-4816
Swanton *(G-12694)*

Tarrier Steel Company Inc................... E 614 444-4000
Columbus *(G-5311)*

▲ The Armor Group Inc.......................C 513 923-5260
Mason *(G-9161)*

The Sharon Companies Ltd.................C 614 438-3210
Worthington *(G-14727)*

Tim Calvin Access Controls................. G 740 494-4200
Radnor *(G-11507)*

◆ Trewbric III Inc.................................E 614 444-2184
Columbus *(G-5330)*

Triangle Precision Inds Inc.................. D 937 299-6776
Dayton *(G-6062)*

Upright Steel LLC................................. E 216 923-0852
Cleveland *(G-4449)*

▲ Urban Industries of Ohio Inc........... E 419 468-3578
Galion *(G-7200)*

Van Dyke Custom Iron Inc................... G 614 860-9300
Pickerington *(G-11302)*

Viking Fabricators Inc......................... G 740 374-5246
Marietta *(G-8960)*

Waco Scaffolding & Equipment Inc....... A 216 749-8900
Cleveland *(G-4487)*

Wall Technology Inc............................ G 715 532-5548
Toledo *(G-13176)*

Wooster Products Inc...........................F 330 264-2854
Wooster *(G-14702)*

▼ Wooster Products Inc...................... D 330 264-2844
Wooster *(G-14701)*

Worthington Mid-Rise Cnstr Inc.......... E 216 472-1511
Cleveland *(G-4517)*

Wright Brothers Inc..............................F 513 731-2222
Cincinnati *(G-3232)*

3448 Prefabricated metal buildings

Affordable Barn Co Ltd........................ G 330 674-3001
Millersburg *(G-9966)*

American Ramp Systems....................... G 440 336-4988
North Olmsted *(G-10716)*

▲ Benchmark Archtectural Systems.... E 614 444-0110
Columbus *(G-4751)*

▼ Benko Products Inc.......................... E 440 934-2180
Sheffield Village *(G-11957)*

C Green & Sons Incorporated..............F 740 745-2998
Saint Louisville *(G-11728)*

Cdc Fab Co...F 419 866-7705
Maumee *(G-9269)*

Commercial Dock & Door Inc.............. E 440 951-1210
Mentor *(G-9503)*

Connect Housing Blocks LLC.............. E 614 503-4344
Columbus *(G-4841)*

Consoldted Anlytcal Systems In..........F 513 542-1200
Cincinnati *(G-2510)*

Cornerstone Bldg Brands Inc..............C 937 584-3300
Middletown *(G-9850)*

◆ Cropking Incorporated.....................F 330 302-4203
Lodi *(G-8500)*

▲ Enclosure Suppliers LLC................. E 513 782-3900
Cincinnati *(G-2586)*

Fairborn USA Inc................................. E 419 294-4987
Upper Sandusky *(G-13441)*

Golden Giant Inc................................. E 419 674-4038
Kenton *(G-8098)*

Great Day Improvements LLC.............. B 267 223-1289
Macedonia *(G-8695)*

Haz-Safe LLC.......................................F 330 793-0900
Austintown *(G-705)*

▲ Hoge Lumber Company..................... E 419 753-2263
New Knoxville *(G-10398)*

Homecare Mattress Inc........................F 937 746-2556
Franklin *(G-7027)*

Iron Works Inc......................................F 937 420-2100
Fort Loramie *(G-6949)*

Jack Walters & Sons Corp.................. E 937 653-8986
Urbana *(G-13470)*

Jentgen Steel Services LLC.................F 614 268-6340
Columbus *(G-5037)*

▼ Jet Dock Systems Inc....................... E 216 750-2264
Cleveland *(G-3886)*

Jh Industries Inc.................................. E 330 963-4105
Twinsburg *(G-13321)*

Joyce Manufacturing Co...................... D 440 239-9100
Berea *(G-1179)*

Lab-Pro Inc... G 937 434-9600
Miamisburg *(G-9708)*

Ludy Greenhouse Mfg Corp................ D 800 255-5839
New Madison *(G-10422)*

Morton Buildings Inc........................... G 419 399-4549
Kenton *(G-8109)*

Morton Buildings Inc........................... E 419 675-2311
Kenton *(G-8110)*

Morton Buildings Inc........................... E 330 345-6188
Wooster *(G-14667)*

Overhead Door Corporation.................F 419 294-3874
Upper Sandusky *(G-13452)*

Patton Aluminum Products Inc.............F 937 845-9404
New Carlisle *(G-10378)*

▲ Pei Liquidation Company..................C 330 467-4267
Macedonia *(G-8704)*

Pioneer Cldding Glzing Systems......... E 216 816-4242
Cleveland *(G-4166)*

Prospiant Inc....................................... D 513 242-0310
Cincinnati *(G-3009)*

R L Torbeck Industries Inc.................. G 513 367-0080
Harrison *(G-7565)*

Rayhaven Group Inc............................ G 330 659-3183
Richfield *(G-11598)*

Rebsco Inc...F 937 548-2246
Greenville *(G-7351)*

Reliable Metal Buildings LLC.............. G 419 737-1300
Pioneer *(G-11329)*

◆ Rough Brothers Mfg Inc ....D 513 242-0310
   Cincinnati *(G-3054)*

Shrock Prefab LLC .... E 419 994-1900
   Loudonville *(G-8594)*

Skyline Corporation .... C 330 852-2483
   Sugarcreek *(G-12650)*

Wyse Industrial Carts Inc .... G 419 923-7353
   Wauseon *(G-13862)*

XS Smith Inc .... E 252 940-5060
   Cincinnati *(G-3239)*

3449 Miscellaneous metalwork

▲ Active Metal and Molds Inc .... F 419 281-9623
   Ashland *(G-514)*

Advance Industrial Mfg Inc .... E 614 871-3333
   Grove City *(G-7367)*

▲ Akron Rebar Co .... E 330 745-7100
   Akron *(G-40)*

▼ American Roll Formed Pdts Corp ..... C 440 352-0753
   Youngstown *(G-14812)*

Arrow Tru-Line Inc .... G 419 636-7013
   Bryan *(G-1630)*

◆ Barsplice Products Inc ....E 937 275-8700
   Dayton *(G-5674)*

Bridge Components Incorporated .... G 614 873-0777
   Columbus *(G-4775)*

Buckeye Stamping Company .... D 877 728-0776
   Columbus *(G-4786)*

Burghardt Metal Fabg Inc .... F 330 794-1830
   Akron *(G-87)*

Cdh Custom Roll Form LLC .... E 330 984-0555
   Warren *(G-13750)*

Custom Control Tech LLC .... E 419 342-5593
   Shelby *(G-11969)*

Ej Usa Inc .... F 330 782-3900
   Youngstown *(G-14852)*

Fc Industries Inc .... E 937 275-8700
   Dayton *(G-5774)*

Formasters Corporation .... G 440 639-9206
   Mentor *(G-9518)*

Fortin Welding & Mfg Inc .... E 614 291-4342
   Columbus *(G-4934)*

▲ Foundation Systems Anchors Inc ..... F 330 454-1700
   Canton *(G-1893)*

Gateway Con Forming Svcs Inc .... D 513 353-2000
   Miamitown *(G-9758)*

Hynes Holding Company .... G 330 799-3221
   Youngstown *(G-14873)*

▲ Hynes Industries Inc .... D 800 321-9257
   Youngstown *(G-14874)*

Industrial Millwright Svcs LLC .... E 419 523-9147
   Ottawa *(G-11035)*

Kenton Strl & Orn Ir Works .... D 419 674-4025
   Kenton *(G-8103)*

Lion Industries LLC .... E 740 676-1100
   Bellaire *(G-1089)*

▲ Markley Enterprises LLC .... E 513 771-1290
   Cincinnati *(G-2847)*

Matteo Aluminum Inc .... E 440 585-5213
   Wickliffe *(G-14382)*

Metal Sales Manufacturing Corp .... E 440 319-3779
   Jefferson *(G-7978)*

Metalfab Group .... G 440 543-6234
   Streetsboro *(G-12509)*

Midwest Curtainwalls Inc .... D 216 641-7900
   Cleveland *(G-4036)*

Ncf Cim Fabricators LLC .... E 863 425-1000
   Ontario *(G-10950)*

▲ Nmc Metals Inc .... E 330 652-2501
   Niles *(G-10599)*

▼ Ohio Bridge Corporation .... C 740 432-6334
   Cambridge *(G-1752)*

▲ Ohio Moulding Corporation .... E 440 944-2100
   Wickliffe *(G-14385)*

Precision Impacts LLC .... D 937 530-8254
   Miamisburg *(G-9728)*

Scs Construction Services Inc .... E 513 929-0260
   Cincinnati *(G-3071)*

Simcote Inc .... F 740 382-5000
   Marion *(G-8999)*

Sky Climber Fabricating LLC .... G 740 990-9430
   Delaware *(G-6173)*

T J F Inc .... F 419 878-4400
   Waterville *(G-13843)*

▲ Ver-Mac Industries Inc .... E 740 397-6511
   Mount Vernon *(G-10268)*

Veterans Steel Inc .... F 216 938-7476
   Cleveland *(G-4462)*

◆ Watteredge LLC ....D 440 933-6110
   Avon Lake *(G-773)*

Welser Profile North Amer LLC .... E 330 225-2500
   Valley City *(G-13522)*

Will-Burt Company .... F 330 682-7015
   Orrville *(G-11019)*

▲ Will-Burt Company .... C 330 682-7015
   Orrville *(G-11018)*

◆ Worthington Enterprises Inc ....C 614 438-3210
   Worthington *(G-14731)*

Wt Acquisition Company Ltd .... E 513 577-7980
   Cincinnati *(G-3234)*

YKK AP America Inc .... E 513 942-7200
   West Chester *(G-14094)*

3451 Screw machine products

Abco Bar & Tube Cutng Svc Inc .... E 513 697-9487
   Maineville *(G-8737)*

Abel Fbrction Prcsion Pdts Inc .... F 513 681-5000
   Cincinnati *(G-2332)*

Abel Manufacturing Company .... F 513 681-5000
   Cincinnati *(G-2333)*

▲ Acme Machine Automatics Inc .... E 419 453-0010
   Ottoville *(G-11051)*

Adams Automatic Inc .... F 440 235-4416
   Olmsted Falls *(G-10935)*

Alco Manufacturing Corp LLC .... E 440 458-5165
   Elyria *(G-6493)*

Amco Products Inc .... F 937 433-7982
   Dayton *(G-5603)*

Amerascrew Inc .... E 419 522-2232
   Mansfield *(G-8762)*

American Aero Components Llc .... G 937 367-5068
   Dayton *(G-5649)*

◆ American Micro Products Inc ....C 513 732-2674
   Batavia *(G-850)*

Amt Machine Systems Limited .... F 740 965-2693
   Columbus *(G-4707)*

▲ Ashley F Ward Inc .... C 513 398-1414
   Mason *(G-9067)*

Atlas Machine Products Co .... G 216 228-3688
   Oberlin *(G-10914)*

Ban Inc .... E 937 325-5539
   Springfield *(G-12284)*

Bront Machining Inc .... E 937 228-4551
   Moraine *(G-10152)*

Chardon Metal Products Co .... E 440 285-2147
   Chardon *(G-2198)*

Clear Creek Screw Machine Co .... G 740 969-2113
   Amanda *(G-423)*

Condo Incorporated .... D 330 609-6021
   Warren *(G-13755)*

Dunham Products Inc .... F 440 232-0885
   Walton Hills *(G-13697)*

Eastlake Machine Products LLC .... G 440 953-1014
   Willoughby *(G-14454)*

Ecm Industries LLC .... F 513 533-6242
   Cincinnati *(G-2578)*

▲ Elyria Manufacturing Corp .... E 440 365-4171
   Elyria *(G-6530)*

Enterprise Machine Inc .... G 513 681-4409
   Cincinnati *(G-2592)*

Eureka Screw Machine Pdts Co .... G 216 883-1715
   Cleveland *(G-3691)*

Fairfield Machined Pdts Inc .... G 740 756-4409
   Carroll *(G-2076)*

Falmer Screw Pdts & Mfg Inc .... F 330 758-0593
   Youngstown *(G-14854)*

Forrest Machine Pdts Co Ltd .... E 419 589-3774
   Mansfield *(G-8790)*

Gent Machine Company .... E 216 481-2334
   Cleveland *(G-3770)*

H & W Screw Products Inc .... G 937 866-2577
   Franklin *(G-7026)*

Helix Operating Company LLC .... G 855 435-4958
   Beachwood *(G-921)*

Heller Machine Products Inc .... G 216 281-2951
   Cleveland *(G-3820)*

Houston Machine Products Inc .... E 937 322-8022
   Springfield *(G-12326)*

▲ Hy-Production LLC .... C 330 273-2400
   Valley City *(G-13499)*

▲ Hyland Machine Company .... E 937 233-8600
   Dayton *(G-5817)*

▲ Ilsco LLC .... C 513 533-6200
   Blue Ash *(G-1287)*

Integrity Manufacturing Corp .... F 937 233-6792
   Dayton *(G-5825)*

JAD Machine Company Inc .... F 419 256-6332
   Malinta *(G-8743)*

Karma Metal Products Inc .... F 419 524-4371
   Mansfield *(G-8810)*

Ken Emerick Machine Products .... G 440 834-4501
   Burton *(G-1702)*

▲ Kernells Autmtc Machining Inc .... E 419 588-2164
   Berlin Heights *(G-1205)*

▲ Kerr Lakeside Inc .... D 216 261-2100
   Euclid *(G-6657)*

Krausher Machining Inc .... G 440 839-2828
   Wakeman *(G-13681)*

Kts Met-Bar Products Inc .... G 440 288-9308
   Lorain *(G-8561)*

Lehner Screw Machine LLC .... E 330 688-6616
   Akron *(C 204)*

Machine Tek Systems Inc .... E 330 527-4450
   Garrettsville *(G-7225)*

Magnetic Screw Machine Pdts .... G 937 348-2807
   Marysville *(G-9036)*

Maumee Machine & Tool Corp .... E 419 385-2501
   Toledo *(G-13048)*

McDaniel Products Inc .... F 419 524-5841
   Mansfield *(G-8823)*

McDaniel Products Inc .... G 419 524-5841
   Mansfield *(G-8822)*

McGregor Metal National Works LLC ..... E 937 882-6347
   Springfield *(G-12348)*

▲ McGregor Mtal Yllow Sprng Wrks ..... D 937 325-5561
   Springfield *(G-12351)*

Meistermatic Inc .... G 216 481-7773
   Chesterland *(G-2235)*

Metal Seal & Products Inc .... C 440 946-8500
   Mentor *(G-9562)*

Mettlr-Tledo Globl Hldings LLC .... E 614 438-4511
   Columbus *(G-4645)*

Midwest Precision LLC .... D 440 951-2333
   Eastlake *(G-6437)*

Mosher Machine & Tool Co Inc .... E 937 258-8070
   Beavercreek Township *(G-999)*

Murray Machine and Tool Inc.................. G 216 267-1126
Cleveland *(G-4054)*

Nolte Precise Manufacturing Inc............ D 513 923-3100
Cincinnati *(G-2914)*

▲ Nook Industries LLC........................... C 216 271-7900
Cleveland *(G-4080)*

◆ NSK Industries Inc............................. D 330 923-4112
Cuyahoga Falls *(G-5563)*

Obars Machine and Tool Company........ E 419 535-6307
Toledo *(G-13068)*

▲ Ohio Metal Products Company........... F 937 228-6101
Dayton *(G-5925)*

Ohio Screw Products Inc..................... D 440 322-6341
Elyria *(G-6574)*

▲ Pfi Precision Inc................................ E 937 845-3563
New Carlisle *(G-10379)*

Pohlman Precision LLC....................... E 636 537-1909
Massillon *(G-9234)*

Port Clinton Manufacturing LLC........... E 419 734-2141
Port Clinton *(G-11447)*

▲ Precision Fittings LLC........................ E 440 647-4143
Wellington *(G-13899)*

◆ Premier Farnell Corp.......................... D 330 659-0459
Richfield *(G-11596)*

Profile Grinding Inc............................. F 216 351-0600
Cleveland *(G-4199)*

Qcsm LLC.. G 216 650-8731
Cleveland *(G-4210)*

Qualitor Subsidiary H Inc.................... E 419 562-7987
Bucyrus *(G-1686)*

▲ Quality Machining and Mfg Inc........... F 419 899-2543
Sherwood *(G-11976)*

R T & T Machining Co Inc.................... F 440 974-8479
Mentor *(G-9605)*

R W Screw Products Inc...................... C 330 837-9211
Massillon *(G-9236)*

Rable Machine Inc............................... D 419 525-2255
Mansfield *(G-8847)*

Raka Corporation................................ D 419 476-6572
Toledo *(G-13110)*

Rely-On Manufacturing Inc.................. G 937 254-0118
Dayton *(G-5979)*

Richland Screw Mch Pdts Inc.............. E 419 524-1272
Mansfield *(G-8849)*

Rtsi LLC... G 440 542-3066
Solon *(G-12176)*

▲ Semtorq Inc...................................... F 330 487-0600
Twinsburg *(G-13377)*

Shanafelt Manufacturing Co................ E 330 455-0315
Canton *(G-2004)*

Soemhejee Inc.................................... E 419 298-2306
Edgerton *(G-6469)*

Stadco Inc.. E 937 878-0911
Fairborn *(G-6699)*

Superior Bar Products Inc................... E 419 784-2590
Defiance *(G-6125)*

Tri-K Enterprises Inc........................... G 330 832-7380
Canton *(G-2028)*

Triangle Machine Products Co.............. E 216 524-5872
Cleveland *(G-4420)*

Twin Valley Metalcraft Asm LLC........... G 937 787-4634
West Alexandria *(G-13922)*

Usm Precision Products Inc................. D 440 975-8600
Wickliffe *(G-14400)*

Valley Tool & Die Inc.......................... D 440 237-0160
North Royalton *(G-10788)*

Vanamatic Company............................ D 419 692-6085
Delphos *(G-6199)*

Vulcan Products Co Inc....................... G 419 468-1039
Galion *(G-7201)*

Watters Manufacturing Co Inc.............. G 216 281-8600
Cleveland *(G-4494)*

Whirlaway Corporation........................ D 440 647-4711
Wellington *(G-13902)*

Whirlaway Corporation........................ D 440 647-4711
Wellington *(G-13903)*

▲ Whirlaway Corporation...................... C 440 647-4711
Wellington *(G-13904)*

Wood-Sebring Corporation................... G 216 267-3191
Cleveland *(G-4514)*

3452 Bolts, nuts, rivets, and washers

Abco Bar & Tube Cutng Svc Inc........... E 513 697-9487
Maineville *(G-8737)*

◆ Agrati - Medina LLC........................... C 330 725-8853
Medina *(G-9370)*

Agrati - Tiffin LLC............................... D 419 447-2221
Tiffin *(G-12772)*

Airfasco Inc.. E 330 430-6190
Canton *(G-1824)*

Airfasco Inds Fstner Group LLC........... E 330 430-6190
Canton *(G-1825)*

▲ Akko Fastener Inc............................. F 513 489-8300
Middletown *(G-9841)*

▲ Altenloh Brinck & Co Inc................... C 419 636-6715
Bryan *(G-1627)*

▲ Altenloh Brinck & Co US Inc.............. E 419 737-2381
Pioneer *(G-11317)*

▲ Altenloh Brinck & Co US Inc.............. E 419 636-6715
Bryan *(G-1628)*

▲ Amanda Bent Bolt Company............... C 740 385-6893
Logan *(G-8508)*

◆ American Micro Products Inc.............. C 513 732-2674
Batavia *(G-850)*

Ampex Metal Products Company.......... D 216 267-9242
Brookpark *(G-1544)*

Andre Corporation............................... E 574 293-0207
Mason *(G-9061)*

▲ Atlas Bolt & Screw Company LLC....... C 419 289-6171
Ashland *(G-519)*

Auto Bolt Company............................. D 216 881-3913
Cleveland *(G-3388)*

Bowes Manufacturing Inc.................... F 216 378-2110
Solon *(G-12087)*

Brainard Rivet Company...................... E 330 545-4931
Girard *(G-7267)*

▲ Cold Headed Fas Assemblies Inc....... F 330 833-0800
Massillon *(G-9180)*

Component Solutions Group Inc........... F 937 434-8100
Dayton *(G-5708)*

Consolidated Metal Pdts Inc................ D 513 251-2624
Cincinnati *(G-2511)*

Core Manufacturing LLC...................... G 440 946-8002
Mentor *(G-9505)*

▲ Crawford Products Inc....................... E 614 890-1822
Columbus *(G-4859)*

Curtiss-Wright Flow Ctrl Corp.............. D 216 267-3200
Cleveland *(G-3583)*

◆ Dayton Superior Corporation.............. C 937 866-0711
Miamisburg *(G-9687)*

Die-Cut Products Co........................... F 216 771-6994
Cleveland *(G-3615)*

▲ Dimcogray Corporation...................... D 937 433-7600
Centerville *(G-2131)*

Edward W Daniel LLC.......................... F 440 647-1960
Wellington *(G-13885)*

◆ Facil North America Inc...................... C 330 487-2500
Twinsburg *(G-13302)*

Fastener Industries Inc........................ E 440 891-2031
Berea *(G-1172)*

◆ Fastener Industries Inc...................... G 440 243-0034
Berea *(G-1173)*

General Plastex Inc............................. E 330 745-7775
Barberton *(G-806)*

◆ Gray America Corp............................. E 937 293-9313
Moraine *(G-10166)*

▲ Great Lakes Fasteners Inc................. E 330 425-4488
Twinsburg *(G-13312)*

◆ Group Industries Inc.......................... E 216 271-0702
Cleveland *(G-3796)*

▲ Hexagon Industries Inc...................... E 216 249-0200
Cleveland *(G-3829)*

▲ Industrial Nut Corp............................ D 419 625-8543
Sandusky *(G-11842)*

Ivostud LLC.. G 440 925-4227
Brookpark *(G-1553)*

▲ Iwata Bolt USA Inc............................ F 513 942-5050
Fairfield *(G-6747)*

Jacodar Inc.. F 330 832-9557
Massillon *(G-9208)*

Jacodar Fsa LLC................................ E 330 454-1832
Canton *(G-1920)*

▲ Jergens Inc....................................... C 216 486-5540
Cleveland *(G-3885)*

Jerry Tools Inc.................................... F 513 242-3211
Cincinnati *(G-2765)*

Kelko Manufacturing LLC..................... E 419 626-2571
Sandusky *(G-11847)*

▲ Kerr Lakeside Inc.............................. D 216 261-2100
Euclid *(G-6657)*

◆ Keystone Bolt & Nut Company............ D 216 524-9626
Cleveland *(G-3916)*

Lear Mfg Co Inc.................................. F 440 324-1111
Elyria *(G-6558)*

Long-Lok Fasteners Corporation........... E 513 772-1880
Cincinnati *(G-2827)*

Magnus Engineered Eqp LLC............... E 440 942-8488
Willoughby *(G-14484)*

Master Products Company.................... D 216 341-1740
Cleveland *(G-3998)*

▲ Matdan Corporation........................... E 513 794-0500
Blue Ash *(G-1303)*

Mid-West Fabricating Co...................... E 740 277-7021
Lancaster *(G-8211)*

▲ Miller Studio Inc............................... G 330 339-1100
New Philadelphia *(G-10459)*

◆ Namoh Ohio Holdings Inc.................. G
Norwood *(G-10869)*

◆ Nelson Stud Welding Inc.................... D 440 329-0400
Elyria *(G-6568)*

North Coast Rivet Inc.......................... F 440 366-6829
Elyria *(G-6571)*

▲ Nova Machine Products Inc................ C 216 267-3200
Middleburg Heights *(G-9775)*

▲ Ohashi Technica USA Inc................... E 740 965-5115
Sunbury *(G-12671)*

▲ Paulin Industries Inc......................... E 216 433-7633
Parma *(G-11134)*

Peterson American Corporation............ E 419 867-8711
Holland *(G-7777)*

▲ Precision Fittings LLC........................ E 440 647-4143
Wellington *(G-13899)*

Qrp Inc.. D 910 371-0700
Berea *(G-1186)*

◆ Ramco Specialties Inc........................ D 330 653-5135
Hudson *(G-7855)*

▲ RB&w Manufacturing LLC.................. G 234 380-8540
Streetsboro *(G-12519)*

Rs Manufacturing Inc.......................... G 440 946-8002
Mentor *(G-9611)*

Saf-Holland Inc................................... G 513 874-7888
Fairfield *(G-6773)*

Simpson Strong-Tie Company Inc......... B 614 876-8060
Columbus *(G-5271)*

▲ Solon Manufacturing Company........... E 440 286-7149
Chardon *(G-2223)*

◆ **Stafast Products Inc**..............E 440 357-5546
Painesville *(G-11111)*

▲ **Stanley Industrial & Auto LLC**..... D 614 755-7000
Dublin *(G-6349)*

▲ **Steeramerica Inc**....................... F 330 563-4407
Uniontown *(G-13426)*

◆ **Stelfast LLC**..............................E..... 440 879-0077
Strongsville *(G-12606)*

Supply Technologies LLC............... E 614 759-9939
Columbus *(G-5301)*

Supply Technologies LLC............... G 937 898-5795
Dayton *(G-6032)*

◆ **Supply Technologies LLC**...........C..... 440 947-2100
Cleveland *(G-4351)*

Tessec Manufacturing Svcs LLC........... E 937 985-3552
Dayton *(G-6046)*

◆ **The Dyson Corporation**...............C..... 440 946-3500
Painesville *(G-11116)*

◆ **Tinnerman Palnut Engineered PR**......F 330 220-5100
Brunswick *(G-1619)*

Twin Ventures Inc.......................... F 330 405-3838
Twinsburg *(G-13388)*

▲ **United Titanium Inc**..................... C 330 264-2111
Wooster *(G-14694)*

Valley Tool & Die Inc...................... D 440 237-0160
North Royalton *(G-10788)*

▲ **Wallace Forge Company**................ D 330 488-1203
Canton *(G-2045)*

Wecall Inc................................... G 440 437-8202
Chardon *(G-2226)*

Wheel Group Holdings LLC............... G 614 253-6247
Columbus *(G-5366)*

Wodin Inc.................................... E 440 439-4222
Cleveland *(G-4513)*

3462 Iron and steel forgings

Accurate Gear Mfg Co Inc............... G 513 761-3220
Cincinnati *(G-2337)*

Advanced FME Products Inc.............. G 440 953-0700
Mentor *(G-9470)*

Aero Tech Tool & Mold Inc.............. G 440 942-3327
Mentor *(G-9471)*

Akron Gear & Engineering Inc........... E 330 773-6608
Akron *(G-32)*

Alliance Forging Group LLC............... G 330 680-4861
Akron *(G-52)*

Alta Mira Corporation..................... D 330 648-2461
Spencer *(G-12233)*

American Cold Forge LLC................. E 419 836-1062
Northwood *(G-10802)*

▲ **Anchor Flange Company**............... D 513 527-3512
Cincinnati *(G-2369)*

▲ **Anchor Industries Incorporated**....... E 440 473-1414
Cleveland *(G-3353)*

Brooker Bros Forging Co Inc............. E 419 668-2535
Norwalk *(G-10831)*

Bula Forge & Machine Inc............... F 216 252-7600
Cleveland *(G-3451)*

Cailin Development LLC................... F 216 408-6261
Cleveland *(G-3459)*

◆ **Canton Drop Forge Inc**.................B..... 330 477-4511
Canton *(G-1854)*

Carbo Forge Inc............................ E 419 334-9788
Fremont *(G-7096)*

Cincinnati Gearing Systems Inc........... E 513 527-8634
Cincinnati *(G-2477)*

Colfor Manufacturing Inc................ B 330 863-0404
Minerva *(G-10036)*

▲ **Colfor Manufacturing Inc**.............. B 330 623-7814
Malvern *(G-8748)*

Cordier Group Holdings Inc............... B 330 477-4511
Canton *(G-1872)*

Crum Manufacturing Inc.................. E 419 878-9779
Waterville *(G-13832)*

Dayton Forging Heat Treating.................. D 937 253-4126
Dayton *(G-5726)*

◆ **Dayton Superior Corporation**.........C..... 937 866-0711
Miamisburg *(G-9687)*

Edgerton Forge Inc........................ D 419 298-2333
Edgerton *(G-6466)*

Edward W Daniel LLC..................... F 440 647-1960
Wellington *(G-13885)*

▲ **Ferrotherm Corporation**................ C 216 883-9350
Cleveland *(G-3714)*

▲ **Firth Rixson Inc**.......................... D 860 760-1040
Newburgh Heights *(G-10541)*

For Call Inc.................................. G 330 863-0404
Malvern *(G-8749)*

Forge Products Corporation............... E 216 231-2600
Cleveland *(G-3736)*

Gear Company of America Inc............ D 216 671-5400
Cleveland *(G-3760)*

GKN PLC..................................... G 740 446-9211
Gallipolis *(G-7205)*

GKN Sinter Metals LLC................... C 740 441-3203
Gallipolis *(G-7206)*

◆ **HBD Industries Inc**......................E..... 614 526-7000
Dublin *(G-6302)*

Horseshoe Express Inc.................... G 330 692-1209
Canfield *(G-1810)*

▲ **J & H Manufacturing LLC**............... G 330 482-2636
Columbiana *(G-4620)*

Ken Forging Inc............................ C 440 993-8091
Jefferson *(G-7974)*

King Forge and Machine Company...... F 330 963-0600
Twinsburg *(G-13323)*

King-Indiana Forge Inc.................... G 330 425-4250
Twinsburg *(G-13324)*

Landerwood Industries Inc................ E 440 233-4234
Willoughby *(G-14481)*

Lange Precision Inc........................ F 513 530-9500
Lebanon *(G-8273)*

Lextech Industries Ltd..................... G 216 883-7900
Cleveland *(G-3953)*

Majestic Fireplace Distr................... G 440 439-1040
Bedford *(G-1045)*

Maxx Iron LLC.............................. G 614 753-9697
Worthington *(G-14718)*

Metal Forming & Coining LLC............ D 419 893-8748
Maumee *(G-9309)*

Mid-West Forge Corporation............. C 216 481-3030
Willoughby *(G-14489)*

▲ **Ohio Star Forge Co**...................... E 330 847-6360
Warren *(G-13786)*

◆ **Park-Ohio Holdings Corp**..............F..... 440 947-2000
Cleveland *(G-4136)*

Park-Ohio Industries Inc.................. C 440 947-2000
Cleveland *(G-4137)*

Penn Machine Company LLC............. D 814 288-1547
Twinsburg *(G-13351)*

Powers and Sons LLC..................... G 419 737-2373
Pioneer *(G-11325)*

Presrite Corporation....................... D 440 576-0015
Jefferson *(G-7981)*

Presrite Corporation....................... B 216 441-5990
Cleveland *(G-4193)*

Pumpco Concrete Pumping LLC......... F 740 809-1473
Johnstown *(G-7997)*

▲ **Queen City Forging Company**.......... F 513 321-2003
Cincinnati *(G-2315)*

R E H Inc.................................... B 330 876-2775
Kinsman *(G-8142)*

Rose Metal Industries LLC................ F 216 881-3355
Cleveland *(G-4250)*

Rudd Equipment Company Inc.............. E 513 321-7833
Cincinnati *(G-3056)*

▲ **Sakamura USA Inc**....................... F 740 223-7777
Marion *(G-8995)*

▲ **Schaefer Equipment Inc**................. D 330 372-4006
Warren *(G-13797)*

◆ **Sifco Industries Inc**......................D..... 216 881-8600
Cleveland *(G-4299)*

Solmet Technologies Inc................... E 330 915-4160
Canton *(G-2008)*

Stahl Gear & Machine Co................. G 216 431-2820
Cleveland *(G-4323)*

◆ **Superior Forge & Steel Corp**...........D..... 419 222-4412
Lima *(G-8453)*

T & W Forge Inc............................ D
Alliance *(G-410)*

▲ **Tekfor Inc**................................. B 330 202-7420
Wooster *(G-14690)*

▲ **Tfo Tech Co Ltd**.......................... C 740 426-6381
Jeffersonville *(G-7988)*

▲ **Thyssnkrupp Rothe Erde USA Inc**..... C 330 562-4000
Aurora *(G-689)*

TRM Manufacturing Inc................... F 330 769-2600
Cuyahoga Falls *(G-5578)*

TRM Manufacturing Inc................... F 330 769-2600
Cuyahoga Falls *(G-5577)*

Tymoca Partners LLC...................... F 440 946-4327
Eastlake *(G-6446)*

US Tsubaki Power Transm LLC........... C 419 626-4560
Sandusky *(G-11881)*

Viking Forge LLC........................... C 330 562-3366
Streetsboro *(G-12529)*

▲ **W E Lott Company**....................... F 419 563-9400
Bucyrus *(G-1694)*

▲ **Wallace Forge Company**................ D 330 488-1203
Canton *(G-2045)*

Wodin Inc.................................... E 440 439-4222
Cleveland *(G-4513)*

▲ **Wright Tool Company**................... C 330 848-0600
Barberton *(G-842)*

Wyman-Gordon Company................. E 216 341-0085
Cleveland *(G-4519)*

3463 Nonferrous forgings

American Cold Forge LLC................. E 419 836-1062
Northwood *(G-10802)*

◆ **Canton Drop Forge Inc**.................B..... 330 477-4511
Canton *(C 1854)*

Clarke Power Services Inc................. E 513 771-2200
Cincinnati *(G-2497)*

▲ **Colfor Manufacturing Inc**.............. B 330 623-7814
Malvern *(G-8748)*

Edward W Daniel LLC..................... F 440 647-1960
Wellington *(G-13885)*

Forge Products Corporation............... E 216 231-2600
Cleveland *(G-3736)*

▲ **Guarantee Specialties Inc**............... G 216 451-9744
Strongsville *(G-12562)*

Howmet Aerospace Inc.................... A 216 641-3600
Newburgh Heights *(G-10543)*

Howmet Aerospace Inc.................... E 330 544-7633
Niles *(G-10590)*

◆ **Mansfield Plumbing Pdts LLC**..........A..... 419 938-5211
Perrysville *(G-11282)*

Mp Technologies Inc....................... F 440 838-4466
Ashland *(G-554)*

Powers and Sons LLC..................... G 419 737-2373
Pioneer *(G-11325)*

▲ **Thyssnkrupp Rothe Erde USA Inc**..... C 330 562-4000
Aurora *(G-689)*

Turbine Eng Cmpnents Tech Corp....... B 216 692-5200
Cleveland *(G-4433)*

▲ Wallace Forge Company..................D 330 488-1203
Canton *(G-2045)*

Wodin Inc..................................E 440 439-4222
Cleveland *(G-4513)*

3465 Automotive stampings

American Trim LLC............................A 419 228-1145
Sidney *(G-11991)*

▲ Anchor Tool & Die Co......................B 216 362-1850
Cleveland *(G-3356)*

Antique Auto Sheet Metal Inc..............F 937 833-4422
Brookville *(G-1562)*

Aptiv Services Us LLC......................A 330 373-3568
Warren *(G-13739)*

◆ Artiflex Manufacturing Inc................B 330 262-2015
Wooster *(G-14623)*

Buyers Products Company....................B 440 974-8888
Mentor *(G-9497)*

Cleveland Metal Processing Inc............C 440 243-3404
Cleveland *(G-3517)*

Clevelnd-Clffs Tling Stmping H............F 519 969-4632
West Chester *(G-13967)*

Clevelnd-Clffs Toling Stamping............C 216 694-5700
West Chester *(G-13968)*

Cole Tool & Die Company...................D 419 522-1272
Ontario *(G-10948)*

Compco Quaker Mfg Inc.....................E 330 482-0200
Salem *(G-11772)*

Decoma Systems Integration Gro...........D 419 324-3387
Toledo *(G-12940)*

Exact-Tool & Die Inc.......................E 216 676-9140
Cleveland *(G-3696)*

Falls Stamping & Welding Co...............F 216 771-9635
Cleveland *(G-3705)*

Falls Stamping & Welding Co...............C 330 928-1191
Cuyahoga Falls *(G-5541)*

Falls Tool and Die Inc.....................G 330 633-4884
Akron *(G-144)*

▲ Feintool Cincinnati Inc...................C 513 247-0110
Cincinnati *(G-2617)*

▲ Feintool US Operations Inc...............C 513 247-0110
Cincinnati *(G-2618)*

◆ Findlay Products Corporation.............C 419 423-3324
Findlay *(G-6866)*

Florida Production Engrg Inc..............D 937 996-4361
New Madison *(G-10421)*

Fulton Industries Inc......................D 419 270-3937
Wauseon *(G-13849)*

General Motors LLC.........................A 216 265-5000
Cleveland *(G-3767)*

Grouper Acquisition Co LLC................D 248 299-7500
Valley City *(G-13498)*

Grouper Acquisition Co LLC................C 330 558-2600
Wellington *(G-13892)*

Gt Technologies Inc........................D 419 324-7300
Toledo *(G-12978)*

▲ Guarantee Specialties Inc................G 216 451-9744
Strongsville *(G-12562)*

Hayford Technologies Inc..................D 419 524-7627
Mansfield *(G-8800)*

Honda Dev & Mfg Amer LLC.................C 937 644-0724
Marysville *(G-9028)*

Hydro Extrusion Usa LLC...................C 888 935-5759
Sidney *(G-12025)*

Interntnal Cutng Solutions Inc............G 440 786-1700
Streetsboro *(G-12506)*

JA Acquisition Corp........................F 419 287-3223
Pemberville *(G-11176)*

Kasai North America Inc...................C 419 209-0399
Upper Sandusky *(G-13444)*

▲ Kirchhoff Auto Waverly Inc...............F 740 947-7763
Waverly *(G-13866)*

L & W Inc..................................D 734 397-6300
Avon *(G-730)*

Lakepark Industries Inc....................C 419 752-4471
Greenwich *(G-7363)*

Langenau Manufacturing Company.......F 216 651-3400
Cleveland *(G-3939)*

◆ Matsu Ohio Inc............................C 419 298-2394
Edgerton *(G-6467)*

Milark Industries Inc......................D 419 524-7627
Mansfield *(G-8827)*

Milark Industries Inc......................D 419 524-7627
Mansfield *(G-8828)*

▲ Motherson Ychiyo Auto Tech PDT....D 614 876-3220
Columbus *(G-5113)*

Muncy Corporation.........................D 937 346-0800
Springfield *(G-12355)*

▲ Murotech Ohio Corporation...............C 419 394-6529
Saint Marys *(G-11743)*

◆ Namoh Ohio Holdings Inc.................G
Norwood *(G-10869)*

Nasg Seating Paulding LLC.................F 419 399-4500
Paulding *(G-11159)*

Nn Metal Stampings LLC...................E 419 737-2311
Pioneer *(G-11322)*

Northern Stamping Co......................F 216 883-8888
Cleveland *(G-4095)*

Northern Stamping Co......................F 216 642-8081
Cleveland *(G-4097)*

◆ Northern Stamping Co.....................C 216 883-8888
Cleveland *(G-4096)*

Oerlikon Frction Systems US In............E 937 233-9191
Dayton *(G-5921)*

▲ P & A Industries Inc......................D 419 422-7070
Findlay *(G-6906)*

Pennant Companies.........................E 614 451-1782
Sabina *(G-11681)*

▲ Quaker Mfg Corp..........................C 330 332-4631
Salem *(G-11807)*

▲ R K Industries Inc........................D 419 523-5001
Ottawa *(G-11044)*

Regal Metal Products Co....................E 330 868-6343
Minerva *(G-10046)*

Shiloh Industries Inc.......................A 330 558-2000
Valley City *(G-13516)*

◆ Shl Liquidation Industries Inc............A 330 558-2600
Valley City *(G-13517)*

Shl Liquidation Mfg LLC....................E 330 558-2600
Valley City *(G-13520)*

▲ SSP Industrial Group Inc.................G 330 665-2900
Fairlawn *(G-6814)*

◆ Stamco Industries Inc.....................E 216 731-9333
Cleveland *(G-4325)*

▲ Stripmatic Products Inc...................E 216 241-7143
Cleveland *(G-4336)*

▲ T A Bacon Co.............................G 216 595-1310
Cleveland *(G-4361)*

▲ Taylor Metal Products Co.................C 419 522-3471
Mansfield *(G-8857)*

▲ Tfo Tech Co Ltd...........................C 740 426-6381
Jeffersonville *(G-7988)*

Tower Atmtive Oprtons USA I LL..........B 419 358-8966
Bluffton *(G-1366)*

Trellborg Sling Prfiles US Inc...............C 330 995-9725
Aurora *(G-690)*

Triton Duro Werks Inc......................F 216 267-1117
Cleveland *(G-4429)*

▲ Trucut Incorporated.......................D 330 938-9806
Sebring *(G-11903)*

▲ TS Trim Industries Inc....................B 614 837-4114
Canal Winchester *(G-1799)*

Twb Company LLC..........................E 330 558-2026
Valley City *(G-13521)*

Valco Industries LLC.......................E 937 399-7400
Springfield *(G-12391)*

Valley Tool & Die Inc.......................D 440 237-0160
North Royalton *(G-10788)*

◆ Vehtek Systems Inc.......................A 419 373-8741
Bowling Green *(G-1445)*

▲ Winzeler Stamping Co.....................E 419 485-3147
Montpelier *(G-10138)*

Yanfeng Intl Auto Tech US I LL............D 419 633-1873
Bryan *(G-1668)*

3466 Crowns and closures

◆ Boardman Molded Products Inc........D 330 788-2400
Youngstown *(G-14822)*

Crown Cork & Seal Usa Inc................D 740 681-3000
Lancaster *(G-8193)*

Eisenhauer Mfg Co LLC....................D 419 238-0081
Van Wert *(G-13535)*

Winzeler Couplings & Mtls LLC.............C 419 485-3147
Montpelier *(G-10136)*

3469 Metal stampings, nec

◆ A J Rose Mfg Co..........................C 216 631-4645
Avon *(G-710)*

▲ A-1 Resources Ltd........................F 330 695-9351
Fredericksburg *(G-7060)*

AAA Stamping Inc..........................E 216 749-4494
Cleveland *(G-3284)*

Abbott Tool Inc............................E 419 476-6742
Toledo *(G-12861)*

▲ Acro Tool & Die Company................E 330 773-5173
Akron *(G-16)*

◆ Advanced Technology Corp...............F 440 293-4064
Andover *(G-454)*

Afc Stamping & Production Inc.............C 937 275-8700
Dayton *(G-5639)*

Agb LLC...................................G 419 924-5216
West Unity *(G-14191)*

AJD Holding Co............................D 330 405-4477
Twinsburg *(G-13271)*

Allied Tool & Die Inc.......................F 216 941-6196
Cleveland *(G-3331)*

Amano USA Holdings Inc...................G 973 403-1900
Loveland *(G-8620)*

Amaroq Inc................................G 419 747-2110
Mansfield *(G-8760)*

Amclo Group Inc...........................F 216 791-8400
North Royalton *(G-10754)*

▼ Amcraft Inc...............................G 419 729-7900
Toledo *(G-12872)*

American Rugged Enclosures Inc..........F 513 942-3004
Hamilton *(G-7464)*

American Tool and Die Inc.................F 419 726-5394
Toledo *(G-12879)*

American Trim LLC.........................A 419 228-1145
Sidney *(G-11991)*

American Trim LLC.........................C 419 738-9664
Wapakoneta *(G-13705)*

◆ American Trim LLC........................E 419 228-1145
Lima *(G-8388)*

AMG Industries LLC........................D 740 397-4044
Mount Vernon *(G-10233)*

Ampex Metal Products Company..........D 216 267-9242
Brookpark *(G-1544)*

Amtekco Industries LLC....................D 614 228-6590
Columbus *(G-4708)*

Amtekco Industries Inc....................E 614 228-6525
Columbus *(G-4709)*

Anchor Fabricators Inc.....................E 937 836-5117
Clayton *(G-3271)*

Anchor Hocking Holdings Inc...............A 740 687-2500
Columbus *(G-4713)*

▲ Anchor Tool & Die Co........................ B 216 362-1850
Cleveland (G-3356)

Andre Corporation.............................. E 574 293-0207
Mason (G-9061)

◆ Anomatic Corporation........................E 740 522-2203
New Albany (G-10328)

Arbor Industries Inc........................... D 440 255-4720
Mentor (G-9485)

ARC Metal Stamping LLC.................. D 517 448-8954
Wauseon (G-13845)

▼ Armorsource LLC............................. E 740 928-0070
Hebron (G-7608)

Arrow Tru-Line Inc............................. G 419 636-7013
Bryan (G-1630)

◆ Arrow Tru-Line Inc............................C 419 446-2785
Archbold (G-489)

▲ Art Technologies LLC....................... D 513 942-8800
Hamilton (G-7466)

▲ Artiflex Manufacturing Inc................. B 330 262-2015
Wooster (G-14623)

Artisan Equipment Inc....................... F 740 756-9135
Carroll (G-2073)

▼ Artisan Tool & Die Corp.................... F 216 883-2769
Cleveland (G-3371)

Artistic Metal Spinning Inc................. G 216 961-3336
Cleveland (G-3372)

◆ Atlantic Tool & Die Company............C 440 238-6931
Strongsville (G-12539)

Atra Metal Spinning Inc..................... F 440 354-9525
Painesville (G-11067)

Automatic Stamp Products Inc........... G 216 781-7933
Cleveland (G-3390)

Ayling and Reichert Co Consent.......... G 419 898-2471
Oak Harbor (G-10883)

B&A Ison Steel Inc........................... F 216 663-4300
Cleveland (G-3400)

Banner Metals Group Inc................... E 614 291-3105
Columbus (G-4743)

Barbara A Lieurance.......................... G 937 382-2864
Wilmington (G-14573)

Barnes Group Inc.............................. G 440 526-5900
Brecksville (G-1458)

Bates Metal Products Inc................... D 740 498-8371
Port Washington (G-11455)

Bayloff Stmped Pdts Knsman Inc.......... D 330 876-4511
Kinsman (G-8140)

Bennett Machine & Stamping Co......... E 440 415-0401
Geneva (G-7234)

Beverly Dove Inc.............................. G 740 495-5200
New Holland (G-10397)

Boehm Pressed Steel Company........... E 330 220-8000
Valley City (G-13491)

Brainerd Industries Inc...................... E 937 228-0488
Miamisburg (G-9676)

Breitinger Company........................... C 419 526-4255
Mansfield (G-8767)

Brittany Stamping LLC....................... A 216 267-0850
Cleveland (G-3440)

Brw Tool Inc.................................... F 419 394-3371
Saint Marys (G-11734)

Buckeye Stamping Company............... D 877 728-0776
Columbus (G-4786)

Buckley Manufacturing Company......... F 513 821-4444
Cincinnati (G-2432)

Camelot Manufacturing Inc................ G 419 678-2603
Coldwater (G-4569)

▲ Catania Medallic Specialty Inc.......... E 440 933-9595
Avon Lake (G-751)

Central Ohio Met Stmping Fbrct........... E 614 861-3332
New Albany (G-10335)

Clemens License Agency................... G 614 288-8007
Pickerington (G-11292)

◆ Cleveland Die & Mfg Co....................C 440 243-3404
Middleburg Heights (G-9767)

Cleveland Metal Stamping Co.............. F 440 234-0010
Berea (G-1162)

Cole Tool & Die Company................... E 419 522-1272
Ontario (G-10948)

◆ Com-Corp Industries Inc..................D 216 431-6266
Cleveland (G-3548)

Compco Columbiana Company............ D 330 482-0200
Columbiana (G-4613)

Compco Quaker Mfg Inc..................... E 330 482-0200
Salem (G-11772)

Compco Youngstown Company........... D 330 482-6488
Columbiana (G-4614)

Connaughton Wldg & Fence LLC........... G 513 867-0230
Hamilton (G-7480)

Continental Business Entps Inc............ F 440 439-4400
Bedford (G-1023)

Contour Forming Inc.......................... F 740 345-9777
Newark (G-10499)

Cql Mfg LLC..................................... D 330 482-5846
Salem (G-11773)

Cqt Kennedy LLC............................. D 419 238-2442
Van Wert (G-13532)

Cubbison Company........................... D 330 793-2481
Youngstown (G-14843)

Customformed Products Inc............... F 937 388-0480
Miamisburg (G-9685)

D J Klingler Inc................................ G 513 891-2284
Montgomery (G-10124)

Danco Metal Products LLC.................. D 440 871-2300
Avon Lake (G-753)

Dayton Rogers of Ohio Inc.................. D 614 491-1477
Columbus (G-4871)

Deerfield Manufacturing Inc............... E 513 398-2010
Mason (G-9093)

▲ Defiance Stamping Co...................... D 419 782-5781
Napoleon (G-10278)

Delafoil Pennsylvania Inc................... G 610 327-9565
Perrysburg (G-11214)

Delta Tool & Die Stl Block Inc.............. E 419 822-5939
Delta (G-6203)

Dependable Stamping Company........... E 216 486-5522
Cleveland (G-3609)

◆ Destiny Manufacturing Inc................E 330 273-9000
Brunswick (G-1588)

◆ Diamond America Corporation............ F 330 762-9269
Akron (G-119)

▲ Die Co Inc..................................... E 440 942-8856
Eastlake (G-6423)

▲ Die-Matic Corporation...................... D 216 749-4656
Independence (G-7897)

▼ Die-Mension Corporation.................. F 330 273-5872
Brunswick (G-1589)

Dove Die and Stamping Company........ E 216 267-3720
Cleveland (G-3628)

Durivage Pattern and Mfg Inc.............. E 419 836-8655
Williston (G-14411)

Dyco Manufacturing Inc.................... F 419 485-5525
Montpelier (G-10128)

E C Shaw Company of Ohio................ E 513 721-6334
Cincinnati (G-2569)

Eagle Precision Products LLC............. G 440 582-9393
North Royalton (G-10759)

Ecm Industries LLC.......................... F 513 533-6242
Cincinnati (G-2578)

▲ Ecp Corporation............................. E 440 934-0444
Avon (G-724)

Eisenhauer Mfg Co LLC...................... D 419 238-0081
Van Wert (G-13535)

Elyria Metal Spinning Fabg Co............. G 440 323-8068
Elyria (G-6531)

Elyria Spring Spclty Holdg Inc.............. G 440 323-5502
Cleveland (G-3664)

Ernst Metal Technologies LLC.............. D 937 434-3133
Moraine (G-10161)

▲ Ernst Metal Technologies LLC........... E 937 434-3133
Dayton (G-5767)

Eurocase Archtctral Cbnets Mll............ F 330 674-0681
Millersburg (G-9979)

Exact-Tool & Die Inc........................ E 216 676-9140
Cleveland (G-3696)

F & G Tool and Die Co....................... G 937 746-3658
Franklin (G-7019)

F C Brengman and Assoc LLC............. E 740 756-4308
Carroll (G-2075)

▲ Fairfield Manufacturing Inc............... B 513 642-0081
Fairfield (G-6734)

Falls Stamping & Welding Co.............. C 330 928-1191
Cuyahoga Falls (G-5541)

Falls Tool and Die Inc...................... G 330 633-4884
Akron (G-144)

Famous Industries Inc...................... F 740 685-2592
Byesville (G-1711)

Faull & Son LLC............................... F 330 652-4341
Niles (G-10588)

Fc Industries Inc.............................. E 937 275-8700
Dayton (G-5774)

▲ Feintool US Operations Inc.............. C 513 247-0110
Cincinnati (G-2618)

Feitl Manufacturing Co Inc.................. F 330 405-6600
Macedonia (G-8690)

◆ Findlay Products Corporation............C 419 423-3324
Findlay (G-6866)

Five Handicap Inc............................ F 419 525-2511
Mansfield (G-8788)

Flood Heliarc Inc............................. F 614 835-3929
Groveport (G-7432)

Formasters Corporation...................... F 440 639-9206
Mentor (G-9518)

◆ Freeway Corporation........................C 216 524-9700
Cleveland (G-3743)

Fremont Plastic Products Inc............... C 419 332-6407
Fremont (G-7111)

Fulton Manufacturing Inds LLC............. E
Brecksville (G-1466)

◆ G & S Metal Products Co Inc..............C 216 441-0700
Cleveland (G-3748)

▲ G & W Products LLC....................... C 513 860-4050
Fairfield (G-6738)

Gb Fabrication Company..................... E 419 347-1835
Shelby (G-11970)

Gb Fabrication Company..................... D 419 896-3191
Shiloh (G-11977)

▲ Gb Manufacturing Company.............. D 419 822-5323
Delta (G-6207)

Gdn Welding LLC.............................. E 740 398-6109
Danville (G-5599)

Gem City Metal Tech LLC.................... E 937 252-8998
Dayton (G-5793)

▲ General Technologies Inc................. E 419 747-1800
Mansfield (G-8791)

Gentzler Tool & Die Corp.................... E 330 896-1941
Akron (G-161)

Greenfield Die & Mfg Corp.................. F 734 454-4000
Valley City (G-13497)

Grenada Stamping Assembly Inc........... E 419 842-3600
Sylvania (G-12707)

Gt Technologies Inc.......................... D 419 324-7300
Toledo (G-12978)

▲ Guarantee Specialties Inc................ G 216 451-9744
Strongsville (G-12562)

H&M Mtal Stamping Assembly Inc......... F 216 898-9030
Brook Park (G-1513)

S
I
C

▲ Hamlin Newco LLC.................................. D 330 753-7791
Akron *(G-170)*

Hamlin Steel Products LLC...................... F 330 753-7791
Akron *(G-171)*

Hashier & Hashier Mfg........................... G 440 933-4883
Avon Lake *(G-758)*

Hayford Technologies Inc...................... D 419 524-7627
Mansfield *(G-8800)*

Herd Manufacturing Inc........................ E 216 651-4221
Cleveland *(G-3826)*

▲ Hidaka Usa Inc.................................... E 614 889-8611
Dublin *(G-6303)*

▲ Hill Manufacturing Inc........................ E 419 335-5006
Wauseon *(G-13851)*

▲ Ice Industries Inc................................ E 419 842-3600
Sylvania *(G-12710)*

▲ Ilsco LLC.. C 513 533-6200
Blue Ash *(G-1287)*

Impact Industries Inc............................ F 440 327-2360
North Ridgeville *(G-10735)*

Imperial Die & Mfg Co........................... G 440 268-9080
Strongsville *(G-12566)*

Imperial Metal Spinning Co.................... G 216 524-5020
Cleveland *(G-3855)*

Independent Power Cons Inc.................. G 419 476-8383
Toledo *(G-13002)*

Independent Stamping Inc..................... F 216 251-3500
Cleveland *(G-3857)*

Interlake Stamping Ohio Inc................... E 440 942-0800
Willoughby *(G-14471)*

J B Stamping Inc.................................... E 216 631-0013
Cleveland *(G-3877)*

J Schrader Company.............................. G 216 961-2890
Cleveland *(G-3879)*

JA Acquisition Corp................................ F 419 287-3223
Pemberville *(G-11176)*

▲ Jet Stream International Inc................. D 330 505-9988
Hubbard *(G-7813)*

Jmac Inc... E 937 346-0800
Springfield *(G-12331)*

Jones Metal Products Co LLC................. E 740 545-6381
West Lafayette *(G-14171)*

◆ Kg63 LLC.. F 216 941-7766
Cleveland *(G-3917)*

▲ KMC Holdings LLC.............................. C 419 238-2442
Van Wert *(G-13539)*

Knight Manufacturing Co Inc.................. G 740 676-5516
Shadyside *(G-11922)*

Knight Manufacturing Co Inc.................. F 740 676-9532
Shadyside *(G-11923)*

Knowlton Manufacturing Co Inc............. F 513 631-7353
Cincinnati *(G-2803)*

Kreider Corp... D 937 325-8787
Springfield *(G-12341)*

L & W Inc... D 734 397-6300
Avon *(G-730)*

Lakepark Industries Inc......................... C 419 752-4471
Greenwich *(G-7363)*

Langenau Manufacturing Company......... F 216 651-3400
Cleveland *(G-3939)*

Lewark Metal Spinning Inc.................... G 937 275-3303
Dayton *(G-5845)*

Lextech Industries Ltd.......................... G 216 883-7900
Cleveland *(G-3953)*

Lippert Components Inc........................ G 574 537-8900
Payne *(G-11164)*

▲ Logan Machine Company...................... D 330 633-6163
Akron *(G-210)*

▲ Long-Stanton Mfg Company................. E 513 874-8020
West Chester *(G-14024)*

Mahoning Valley Mfg Inc........................ E 330 537-4492
Beloit *(G-1145)*

◆ Malin Co.. E 216 267-9080
Cleveland *(G-3982)*

Mallory Pattern Works Inc...................... G 419 726-8001
Toledo *(G-13046)*

Mansfield Industries Inc......................... F 419 524-1300
Mansfield *(G-8820)*

Manufacturers Service Inc..................... E 216 267-3771
Cleveland *(G-3985)*

▼ Marc V Concepts Inc.......................... F 419 782-6505
Defiance *(G-6119)*

Master Products Company...................... D 216 341-1740
Cleveland *(G-3998)*

▲ Matco Tools Corporation..................... B 330 929-4949
Stow *(G-12440)*

Maumee Assembly & Stamping LLC....... C 419 304-2887
Maumee *(G-9307)*

May Industries of Ohio Inc..................... E 440 237-8012
North Royalton *(G-10773)*

McAfee Tool & Die Inc.......................... E 330 896-9555
Uniontown *(G-13423)*

McGlennon Metal Products Inc.............. F 614 252-7114
Columbus *(G-5091)*

McGregor Mtal Innsfllen Wrks L............ C 937 322-3880
Springfield *(G-12349)*

▲ McGregor Mtal Yllow Sprng Wrks....... D 937 325-5561
Springfield *(G-12351)*

Metal & Wire Products Company............. F 330 332-1015
Salem *(G-11798)*

Metal & Wire Products Company............. E 330 332-9448
Salem *(G-11799)*

Metal Fabricating Corporation................. D 216 631-8121
Cleveland *(G-4023)*

Metal Products Company........................ E 330 652-2558
Powell *(G-11491)*

Metal Stampings Unlimited Inc............... F 937 328-0206
Springfield *(G-12352)*

Mic-Ray Metal Products Inc.................... F 216 791-2206
Cleveland *(G-4026)*

Mid-America Steel Corp.......................... E 800 282-3466
Cleveland *(G-4033)*

Middletown License Agency Inc............. G 513 422-7225
Middletown *(G-9879)*

Midway Products Group Inc................... F 419 422-7070
Findlay *(G-6893)*

Milark Industries Inc............................. D 419 524-7627
Mansfield *(G-8827)*

Milark Industries Inc.............................. D 419 524-7627
Mansfield *(G-8828)*

Modern Engineering Inc........................ G 440 593-5414
Conneaut *(G-5412)*

Mohawk Manufacturing Inc.................... G 860 632-2345
Mount Vernon *(G-10252)*

▼ Mohr Stamping Inc.............................. E 440 647-4316
Wellington *(G-13896)*

Monode Steel Stamp Inc........................ F 440 975-8802
Mentor *(G-9568)*

MSC Industries Inc................................ G 440 474-8788
Rome *(G-11645)*

◆ Mtd Holdings Inc................................. B 330 225-2600
Valley City *(G-13508)*

Nasg Auto-Seat Tec LLC........................ E 419 359-5954
Ridgeville Corners *(G-11615)*

Nasg Ohio LLC...................................... F 419 634-3125
Ada *(G-4)*

▲ Nasg Seating Bryan LLC..................... D 419 633-0662
Bryan *(G-1652)*

Nation Tool & Die Ltd............................ E 419 822-5939
Delta *(G-6213)*

New Bremen Machine & Tool Co............ E 419 629-3295
New Bremen *(G-10363)*

Neway Stamping & Mfg Inc.................... D 440 951-8500
Willoughby *(G-14494)*

Niles Manufacturing & Finshg................ C 330 544-0402
Niles *(G-10596)*

Nn Metal Stampings LLC........................ E 419 737-2311
Pioneer *(G-11322)*

Northern Stamping Co............................ F 216 883-8888
Cleveland *(G-4095)*

◆ Northern Stamping Co......................... C 216 883-8888
Cleveland *(G-4096)*

Northwind Industries Inc....................... G 216 433-0666
Cleveland *(G-4099)*

Northwood Industries Inc....................... F 419 666-2100
Perrysburg *(G-11243)*

Norwood Medical LLC............................. A 937 228-4101
Dayton *(G-5913)*

Norwood Tool Company.......................... G 937 228-4101
Dayton *(G-5914)*

Ohio Associated Entps LLC.................... F 440 354-3148
Painesville *(G-11101)*

◆ Ohio Gasket and Shim Co Inc........... E 330 630-0626
Akron *(G-252)*

Ohio Valley Manufacturing Inc............... D 419 522-5818
Mansfield *(G-8841)*

Omni Manufacturing Inc........................ F 419 394-7424
Saint Marys *(G-11748)*

▲ Omni Manufacturing Inc..................... D 419 394-7424
Saint Marys *(G-11747)*

Orick Stamping Inc................................ D 419 331-0600
Elida *(G-6484)*

Ottawa Products Co................................ E 419 836-5115
Curtice *(G-5517)*

▲ Pacific Manufacturing Ohio Inc........... B 513 860-3900
Fairfield *(G-6762)*

Parker-Hannifin Corporation................... G 330 336-3511
Wadsworth *(G-13658)*

Parma Heights License Bureau............... G 440 888-0388
Cleveland *(G-4147)*

▼ Pax Machine Works Inc...................... D 419 586-2337
Celina *(G-2114)*

▲ PE Usa LLC... F 513 771-7374
Cincinnati *(G-2950)*

Peerless Metal Products Inc.................. G 216 431-6905
Cleveland *(G-4149)*

Pennant Moldings Inc............................ C 937 584-5411
Sabina *(G-11682)*

◆ Pentaflex Inc....................................... C 937 325-5551
Springfield *(G-12360)*

Perry Welding Service Inc...................... F 330 425-2211
Twinsburg *(G-13355)*

Pettit W T & Sons Co Inc...................... G 330 539-6100
Girard *(G-7278)*

Phillips Mch & Stamping Corp................ G 330 882-6714
New Franklin *(G-10392)*

▲ Plating Technology Inc....................... D 937 268-6882
Dayton *(G-5941)*

Precision Metal Products Inc................. E 216 447-1900
Cleveland *(G-4185)*

Precision Metal Products Inc................. F 216 447-1900
Cleveland *(G-4186)*

◆ Production Products Inc...................... D 734 241-7242
Columbus Grove *(G-5384)*

Progress Tool & Stamping Inc............... E 419 628-2384
Minster *(G-10064)*

◆ Progressive Stamping Inc................... C 419 453-1111
Ottoville *(G-11057)*

Public Safety Ohio Department............. G 440 943-5545
Willoughby *(G-14511)*

Q Model Inc... F 330 733-6545
Akron *(G-271)*

Qfm Stamping Inc.................................. G 330 337-3311
Columbiana *(G-4625)*

▲ Quaker Mfg Corp................................. C 330 332-4631
Salem *(G-11807)*

Quality Fabricated Metals Inc.............F
Salem *(G-11808)*

Quality Stamping Products Co.............F 216 441-2700
Cleveland *(G-4217)*

Quality Tool Company.............E 419 476-8228
Toledo *(G-13105)*

R K Metals Ltd.............E 513 874-6055
Fairfield *(G-6771)*

R L Rush Tool & Pattern Inc.............G 419 562-9849
Bucyrus *(G-1687)*

Racelite Southcoast Inc.............F 216 581-4600
Maple Heights *(G-8891)*

▲ Range Kleen Mfg Inc.............B 419 331-8000
Elida *(G-6487)*

Rapid Machine Inc.............F 419 737-2377
Pioneer *(G-11327)*

Ratliff Metal Spinning Company.............E 937 836-3900
Englewood *(G-6622)*

▲ RB&w Manufacturing LLC.............G 234 380-8540
Streetsboro *(G-12519)*

Ridge Tool Manufacturing Co.............F 440 323-5581
Elyria *(G-6588)*

Rjm Stamping Co.............F 614 443-1191
Pickerington *(G-11300)*

Roemer Industries Inc.............D 330 448-2000
Masury *(G-9256)*

Ronfeldt Manufacturing LLC.............F 419 382-5641
Toledo *(G-13119)*

Ronlen Industries Inc.............E 330 273-6468
Brunswick *(G-1613)*

S & K Products Company.............E 419 268-2244
Celina *(G-2118)*

S-P Company Inc.............D 330 782-5651
Columbiana *(G-4627)*

Saco Lowell Parts LLC.............G 330 794-1535
Akron *(G-303)*

Sadler Corporation.............G 330 688-0009
Stow *(G-12455)*

Schott Metal Products Company.............G 330 773-7873
Akron *(G-307)*

Scott Fetzer Company.............C 216 267-9000
Cleveland *(G-4278)*

Seilkop Industries Inc.............E 513 761-1035
Cincinnati *(G-3077)*

Service Stampings Inc.............E 440 946-2330
Willoughby *(G-14522)*

Seven Ranges Mfg Corp.............G 330 627-7155
Carrollton *(C 2000)*

Shl Liquidation Industries Inc.............D 440 647-2100
Wellington *(G-13901)*

◆ Shl Liquidation Industries Inc.............A 330 558-2600
Valley City *(G-13517)*

Shl Liquidation Liverpool Inc.............E 330 558-2600
Valley City *(G-13518)*

Shl Liquidation Medina Inc.............C
Valley City *(G-13519)*

Smithville Mfg Co.............F 330 345-5818
Wooster *(G-14687)*

Soemhejee Inc.............E 419 298-2306
Edgerton *(G-6469)*

Spectrum Machine Inc.............F 330 626-3666
Streetsboro *(G-12524)*

Spirol Shim Corporation.............E 330 920-3655
Stow *(G-12462)*

Stamp & Flash Inc.............D 419 335-3015
Wauseon *(G-13859)*

Stamped Steel Products Inc.............F 330 538-3951
North Jackson *(G-10695)*

◆ Steel Forming Inc.............C 714 532-6321
Youngstown *(G-14941)*

Stolle Machinery Company LLC.............C 937 497-5400
Sidney *(G-12056)*

Stolle Properties Inc.............A 513 932-8664
Blue Ash *(G-1335)*

▲ Stripmatic Products Inc.............E 216 241-7143
Cleveland *(G-4336)*

Suburban Manufacturing Co.............D 440 953-2024
Eastlake *(G-6444)*

Suburbanite Inc.............G 419 756-4390
Mansfield *(G-8856)*

◆ Sunfield Inc.............D 740 928-0405
Hebron *(G-7638)*

◆ Superior Metal Products Inc.............E 419 228-1145
Lima *(G-8454)*

▲ Superior Production LLC.............C 614 444-2181
Columbus *(G-5299)*

Supply Technologies LLC.............G 937 898-5795
Dayton *(G-6032)*

◆ Supply Technologies LLC.............D 440 947-2100
Cleveland *(G-4351)*

T & D Fabricating Inc.............E 440 951-5646
Eastlake *(G-6445)*

▲ Takk Industries Inc.............F 513 353-4306
Cleves *(G-4550)*

Takumi Stamping Inc.............C 513 642-0081
Fairfield *(G-6780)*

▲ Talan Products Inc.............D 216 458-0170
Cleveland *(G-4363)*

▲ Talent Tool & Die Inc.............E 440 239-8777
Berea *(G-1190)*

▲ Taylor Metal Products Co.............C 419 522-3471
Mansfield *(G-8857)*

TDS-Bf/Ls Holdings Inc.............E 440 327-5800
North Ridgeville *(G-10751)*

Tech-Med Inc.............E 216 486-0900
Euclid *(G-6679)*

Tenacity Manufacturing Company.............G 513 821-0201
West Chester *(G-14081)*

Tfi Manufacturing LLC.............F 440 290-9411
Mentor *(G-9636)*

The Kordenbrock Tool and Die Co.............F 513 326-4390
Cincinnati *(G-3148)*

The Pioneer Tool and Die Co.............D 330 724-5572
Akron *(G-332)*

The Reliable Spring Wire Frms.............E 440 365-7400
Elyria *(G-6595)*

▲ Thk Manufacturing America Inc.............C 740 928-1415
Hebron *(G-7639)*

▼ Toledo Metal Spinning Company.............E 419 535-5931
Toledo *(C 13152)*

Toledo Tool and Die Co Inc.............F 419 476-4422
Toledo *(G-13160)*

▲ Toledo Tool and Die Co Inc.............C 419 476-4422
Toledo *(G-13161)*

Torrmetal LLC.............E 216 671-1616
Cleveland *(G-4405)*

Torrmetal Corporation.............E 216 671-1616
Cleveland *(G-4406)*

▲ Transue & Williams Stampg Corp.............E 330 821-5777
Austintown *(G-708)*

Treaty City Industries Inc.............F 937 548-9000
Greenville *(G-7358)*

Tri-Craft Inc.............E 440 826-1050
Cleveland *(G-4418)*

Triton Duro Werks Inc.............F 216 267-1117
Cleveland *(G-4429)*

▲ Trucut Incorporated.............D 330 938-9806
Sebring *(G-11903)*

Twist Inc.............G 937 675-9581
Jamestown *(G-7970)*

▲ Twist Inc.............C 937 675-9581
Jamestown *(G-7969)*

United Die & Mfg Sales Co.............E 330 938-6141
Sebring *(G-11904)*

Universal Metal Products Inc.............E 419 287-3223
Pemberville *(G-11178)*

▲ Universal Metal Products Inc.............C 440 943-3040
Wickliffe *(G-14399)*

Valley Tool & Die Inc.............D 440 237-0160
North Royalton *(G-10788)*

▼ Varbros LLC.............D 216 267-5200
Cleveland *(G-4457)*

Verhoff Machine & Welding Inc.............C 419 596-3202
Continental *(G-5424)*

Voisard Manufacturing Inc.............D 419 896-3191
Shiloh *(G-11980)*

◆ Voss Industries LLC.............C 216 771-7655
Cleveland *(G-4482)*

Washington Products Inc.............F 330 837-5101
Massillon *(G-9252)*

▲ Wedge Products Inc.............B 330 405-4477
Twinsburg *(G-13395)*

Weiss Industries Inc.............E 419 526-2480
Mansfield *(G-8865)*

Welage Corporation.............F 513 681-2300
Cincinnati *(G-3214)*

Western Ohio Technologies LLC.............G 937 947-8810
Russia *(G-11678)*

Westlake Tool & Die Mfg Co.............D 440 934-5305
Avon *(G-742)*

▲ Whirlaway Corporation.............C 440 647-4711
Wellington *(G-13904)*

▲ Winzeler Stamping Co.............E 419 485-3147
Montpelier *(G-10138)*

Wire Products Company Inc.............F 216 267-0777
Cleveland *(G-4509)*

Wisco Products Incorporated.............E 937 228-2101
Dayton *(G-6084)*

▼ Witt Industries Inc.............D 513 871-5700
Mason *(G-9167)*

▲ WLS Stamping Co.............D 216 271-5100
Cleveland *(G-4511)*

Wtd Real Estate Inc.............D 440 934-5305
Avon *(G-745)*

▲ Ysk Corporation.............B 740 774-7315
Chillicothe *(G-2288)*

3471 Plating and polishing

A & B Deburring Company.............F 513 723-0444
Cincinnati *(G-2323)*

Abel Metal Processing Inc.............F 216 881-4156
Cleveland *(O-3200)*

Acme Industrial Group Inc.............G 330 821-3900
Alliance *(G-365)*

Advanced Surface Technology.............G 216 476-8600
Cleveland *(G-3308)*

Aetna Plating Co.............F 216 341-9111
Cleveland *(G-3312)*

Akron Plating Co Inc.............F 330 773-6878
Akron *(G-37)*

Allen Aircraft Products Inc.............E 330 296-9621
Ravenna *(G-11514)*

Allen Aircraft Products Inc.............E 330 296-1531
Ravenna *(G-11515)*

▲ Allen Aircraft Products Inc.............D 330 296-9621
Ravenna *(G-11516)*

Aluminum Color Industries Inc.............E 330 536-6295
Lowellville *(G-8657)*

Aluminum Extruded Shapes Inc.............C 513 563-2205
Cincinnati *(G-2354)*

Amac Enterprises Inc.............F 216 362-1880
Cleveland *(G-3337)*

▲ Amac Enterprises Inc.............C 216 362-1880
Parma *(G-11129)*

American Indus Maintenance.............G 937 254-3400
Dayton *(G-5653)*

S
I
C

American Quality Stripping Inc............... E 419 625-6288
Sandusky *(G-11822)*

American Utility Proc LLC...................... E 330 535-3000
Akron *(G-59)*

Anchor Fabricators Inc......................... E 937 836-5117
Clayton *(G-3271)*

Anodizing Specialists Inc...................... E 440 951-0257
Mentor *(G-9482)*

Anomatic Corporation............................ B 740 522-2203
Newark *(G-10491)*

◆ Anomatic Corporation......................... E 740 522-2203
New Albany *(G-10328)*

Anotex Industries Inc.......................... G 513 860-1165
West Chester *(G-13939)*

Applied Metals Tech Ltd....................... E 216 741-3236
Brooklyn Heights *(G-1528)*

Arem Co.. G 440 974-6740
Willoughby *(G-14426)*

Areway Acquisition Inc......................... D 216 651-9022
Brooklyn *(G-1519)*

ATI Flat Rlled Pdts Hldngs LLC............... F 330 875-2244
Louisville *(G-8598)*

▲ Atom Blasting and Finshg Inc............. G 440 235-4765
Columbia Station *(G-4589)*

▲ Badboy Blasters Incorporated............ F 330 454-2699
Canton *(G-1835)*

Bar Processing Corporation................... F 330 872-0914
Newton Falls *(G-10577)*

▲ Barker Products Company................... E
Cleveland *(G-3406)*

Beringer Plating Inc............................ G 330 633-8409
Akron *(G-76)*

Boville Indus Coatings Inc.................... E 330 669-8558
Smithville *(G-12064)*

Bricker Plating Inc............................. G 419 636-1990
Bryan *(G-1632)*

Buffex Metal Finishing Inc.................... G 216 631-2202
Cleveland *(G-3450)*

Burton Metal Finishing Inc.................... E 614 252-9523
Columbus *(G-4788)*

Canton Plating Co Inc.......................... E 330 452-7808
Canton *(G-1859)*

Carlisle and Finch Company................... E 513 681-6080
Cincinnati *(G-2439)*

Carpe Diem Industries LLC.................... D 419 358-0129
Bluffton *(G-1359)*

Carpe Diem Industries LLC.................... D 419 659-5639
Columbus Grove *(G-5382)*

Chemical Methods Incorporated.............. E 216 476-8400
Brunswick *(G-1582)*

▲ Chemical Solvents Inc....................... E 216 741-9310
Cleveland *(G-3492)*

Chromatic Inc.................................... F 216 881-2228
Cleveland *(G-3497)*

Chrome Deposit Corporation.................. E 330 773-7800
Akron *(G-98)*

Chrome Deposit Corporation.................. E 513 539-8486
Monroe *(G-10098)*

Chromium Corporation.......................... E 216 271-4910
Cleveland *(G-3498)*

Cincinnati Abrasive Supply Co................ E 513 941-8866
Hamilton *(G-7478)*

Cincinnati Gearing Systems Inc.............. D 513 527-8600
Cincinnati *(G-2476)*

City Plating and Polishing LLC............... G 216 267-8158
Cleveland *(G-3501)*

Cleveland Black Oxide Inc..................... F 216 861-4431
Cleveland *(G-3507)*

Cleveland Plating LLC.......................... G 216 249-0300
Cleveland *(G-3518)*

▲ Cleveland-Cliffs Columbus LLC........... C 614 492-6800
Richfield *(G-11589)*

Commercial Anodizing Co...................... F 440 942-8384
Willoughby *(G-14440)*

▲ Commercial Honing LLC...................... D 330 343-8896
Dover *(G-6235)*

Commercial Steel Treating Co................ F 216 431-8204
Cleveland *(G-3553)*

Custom Nickel LLC.............................. G 937 222-1995
Dayton *(G-5719)*

Customchrome Plating Inc..................... F 440 926-3116
Grafton *(G-7300)*

Delta Plating Inc............................... E 330 452-2300
Canton *(G-1880)*

Derrick Company Inc........................... E 513 321-8122
Cincinnati *(G-2546)*

▲ Die Co Inc...................................... E 440 942-8856
Eastlake *(G-6423)*

Durable Plating Co............................. G 216 391-2132
Cleveland *(G-3639)*

Duray Plating Company Inc.................... E 216 941-5540
Cleveland *(G-3640)*

E L Stone Company.............................. E 330 825-4565
Norton *(G-10820)*

Electro Polish Company........................ E 937 222-3611
Dayton *(G-5761)*

Electro Prime Assembly Inc................... G 419 476-0100
Rossford *(G-11656)*

Electro-Metallics Co........................... G 513 423-8091
Middletown *(G-9856)*

Electrolizing Corp of Ohio.................... E 800 451-8655
Cleveland *(G-3661)*

Electrolizing Corporation Ohio.............. F 216 451-8653
Cleveland *(G-3662)*

Elyria Plating Corporation.................... E 440 365-8300
Elyria *(G-6533)*

◆ Epsilon Management Corporation.......... C 216 634-2500
Cleveland *(G-3681)*

Equinox Enterprises LLC....................... G 419 627-0022
Sandusky *(G-11833)*

Erieview Metal Treating Co.................... D 216 663-1780
Cleveland *(G-3685)*

▲ Etched Metal Company........................ E 440 248-0240
Solon *(G-12109)*

Flight Bright Ltd............................... F 216 663-6677
Cleveland *(G-3726)*

Future Finishes Inc............................ G 513 860-0020
Hamilton *(G-7491)*

Gei of Columbiana Inc.......................... E 330 783-0270
Youngstown *(G-14863)*

General Extrusions Intl LLC................... C 330 783-0270
Youngstown *(G-14864)*

GRB Holdings Inc................................ G 937 236-3250
Dayton *(G-5802)*

▲ Guaranteed Fnshg Unlimited Inc........... E 216 252-8200
Cleveland *(G-3800)*

H & R Metal Finishing Inc..................... G 440 942-6656
Eastlake *(G-6430)*

Hadronics Inc.................................... D 513 321-9350
Cincinnati *(G-2702)*

Hale Performance Coatings Inc............... E 419 244-6451
Toledo *(G-12984)*

Hall Company.................................... E 937 652-1376
Urbana *(G-13465)*

Hartzell Mfg Co LLC............................ E 937 859-5955
Miamisburg *(G-9696)*

Hearn Plating Co Ltd........................... F 419 473-9773
Toledo *(G-12988)*

Hy-Blast Inc..................................... F 513 424-0704
Middletown *(G-9864)*

Industrial Mill Maintenance.................. F 330 746-1155
Youngstown *(G-14876)*

Industrial Paint & Strip Inc.................. E 419 568-2222
Waynesfield *(G-13878)*

Ips Treatments Inc............................. G 419 241-5955
Toledo *(G-13009)*

J Horst Manufacturing Co...................... D 330 828-2216
Dalton *(G-5586)*

JM Hamilton Group Inc......................... F 419 229-4010
Lima *(G-8422)*

Jotco Inc.. G 513 721-4943
Mansfield *(G-8809)*

K-B Plating Inc.................................. F 216 341-1115
Cleveland *(G-3903)*

Kel-Mar Inc...................................... E 419 806-4600
Bowling Green *(G-1423)*

Kelly Plating Co................................ G 216 961-1080
Cleveland *(G-3912)*

Krendl Rack Co Inc.............................. G 419 667-4800
Venedocia *(G-13586)*

Lake City Plating LLC.......................... D 440 964-3555
Jefferson *(G-7976)*

Lake City Plating LLC.......................... D 440 964-3555
Ashtabula *(G-602)*

Lake County Plating Corp...................... F 440 255-8835
Mentor *(G-9548)*

Leonhardt Plating Company................... G 513 242-1410
Cincinnati *(G-2819)*

Luke Engineering & Mfg Corp.................. E 330 925-3344
Rittman *(G-11624)*

◆ Luke Engineering & Mfg Corp.............. E 330 335-1501
Wadsworth *(G-13649)*

Lustrous Metal Coatings Inc.................. E 330 478-4653
Canton *(G-1933)*

M I P Inc... F 330 744-0215
Youngstown *(G-14891)*

McGean-Rohco Inc............................... G 216 441-4900
Newburgh Heights *(G-10545)*

◆ McGean-Rohco Inc............................. D 216 441-4900
Cleveland *(G-4009)*

Mechanical Finishers Inc LLC................. E 513 641-5419
Cincinnati *(G-2853)*

Mechanical Finishing Inc...................... G 513 641-5419
Cincinnati *(G-2854)*

▲ Mechanical Galv-Plating Corp.............. E 937 492-3143
Sidney *(G-12033)*

Metal Seal & Products Inc..................... C 440 946-8500
Mentor *(G-9562)*

Metalbrite Polishing LLC...................... F 937 278-9739
Dayton *(G-5874)*

Miami Valley Polishing LLC.................... F 937 615-9353
Sidney *(G-12034)*

▲ Miba Bearings US LLC......................... B 740 962-4242
Mcconnelsville *(G-9364)*

Micro Metal Finishing LLC..................... D 513 541-3095
Cincinnati *(G-2876)*

Micro Products Co Inc.......................... E 440 943-0258
Willoughby Hills *(G-14560)*

Microfinish LLC................................. D 937 264-1598
Vandalia *(G-13571)*

Microsheen Corporation........................ F 216 481-5610
Cleveland *(G-4029)*

▲ Microtek Finishing LLC...................... E 513 766-5600
West Chester *(G-14133)*

Milestone Services Corp....................... G 330 374-9988
Akron *(G-233)*

Miller Plating LLC.............................. E 330 952-2550
Medina *(G-9427)*

Mmf Inc.. G 614 252-2522
Columbus *(G-5105)*

Monaco Plating Inc............................. F 216 206-2360
Cleveland *(G-4044)*

Moore Chrome Products Company.............. G 419 843-3510
Sylvania *(G-12717)*

MPC Plastics Inc................................ G 216 881-7220
Cleveland *(G-4049)*

▲ MPC Plating LLC.......................... D 216 881-7220
Cleveland *(G-4050)*

Mpc Plating Inc............................... G 216 881-7220
Brooklyn *(G-1524)*

National Aerospace Proc LLC.............. G 234 900-6497
Stow *(G-12443)*

National Plating Corporation............... E 216 341-6707
Cleveland *(G-4061)*

National Polishing Systems Inc............ E 330 659-6547
Broadview Heights *(G-1506)*

Newbury Sndblst & Pntg Inc................ G 440 564-7204
Newbury *(G-10557)*

Newsome & Work Metalizing Co............ G 330 376-7144
Akron *(G-246)*

Nicks Plating Co............................. F 937 773-3175
Piqua *(G-11367)*

Niles Manufacturing & Finshg............ C 330 544-0402
Niles *(G-10596)*

◆ Ohio Decorative Products LLC............ C 419 647-9033
Spencerville *(G-12238)*

Ohio Electro-Polishing Co Inc............ G 419 667-2281
Venedocia *(G-13587)*

▲ Ohio Metal Products Company............ F 937 228-6101
Dayton *(G-5925)*

Ohio Roll Grinding Inc..................... E 330 453-1884
Louisville *(G-8610)*

▼ P & J Industries Inc...................... C 419 726-2675
Toledo *(G-13090)*

P & L Heat Trting Grinding Inc............ E 330 746-1339
Youngstown *(G-14907)*

Parker Rst-Proof Cleveland Inc............ E 216 481-6680
Cleveland *(G-4142)*

Parker Trutec Incorporated................. D 937 653-8500
Urbana *(G-13476)*

Paxos Plating Inc........................... E 330 479-0022
Canton *(G-1974)*

Pki Inc...................................... F 513 832-8749
Cincinnati *(G-2967)*

Plasman AB LP.............................. C 216 252-2995
Cleveland *(G-4169)*

Plate-All Metal Company Inc............... G 330 633-6166
Akron *(G-260)*

Plating Perceptions Inc.................... G 330 425-4180
Twinsburg *(G-13357)*

▲ Plating Technology Inc................... D 937 268-6882
Dayton *(G-5941)*

Polymet Recovery LLC...................... G 330 630-9006
Akron *(G-263)*

Porter-Guertin Co Inc...................... G 513 241-7663
Cincinnati *(G-2975)*

Precision Finishing Systems.............. E 937 415-5794
Dayton *(G-5945)*

Precision Powder Coating Inc............. F 330 478-0741
Canton *(G-1980)*

Pro Line Collision and Pnt LLC............ G 937 223-7611
Dayton *(G-5959)*

▲ Quality Plating Co........................ G 216 361-0151
Cleveland *(G-4215)*

R A Heller Company......................... F 513 771-6100
Cincinnati *(G-3027)*

Rack Processing Company Inc............. E 937 294-1911
Moraine *(G-10190)*

Rack Processing Company Inc............. E 937 294-1911
Moraine *(G-10189)*

Raf Acquisition Co......................... E 440 572-5999
Valley City *(G-13514)*

REA Polishing Inc.......................... D 419 470-0216
Toledo *(G-13111)*

▲ Reifel Industries Inc.................... D 419 737-2138
Pioneer *(G-11328)*

Roberts Demand No 3 Corp................. G 216 641-0660
Cleveland *(G-4245)*

Russell Products Co Inc................... F 330 535-9246
Akron *(G-296)*

Russell Products Co Inc................... G 330 535-3391
Akron *(G-297)*

◆ Russell Products Co Inc.................. F 330 535-9246
Akron *(G-298)*

S & K Metal Polsg & Buffing............... G 513 732-6662
Batavia *(G-886)*

Sandwisch Enterprises Inc................. G 419 944-6446
Toledo *(G-13121)*

▲ Sawyer Technical Materials LLC.......... E 440 951-8770
Willoughby *(G-14520)*

Scot Industries Inc........................ C 330 262-7585
Wooster *(G-14683)*

Shalmet Corporation........................ E 440 236-8840
Elyria *(G-6589)*

Sifco Applied Srfc Cncepts LLC........... E 216 524-0099
Cleveland *(G-4298)*

◆ Sifco Industries Inc..................... D 216 881-8600
Cleveland *(G-4299)*

Smith Electro Chemical Co................. G 513 351-7227
Cincinnati *(G-3096)*

South Shore Finishers Inc................. G 216 664-1792
Cleveland *(G-4317)*

▼ Spectrum Metal Finishing Inc............ D 330 758-8358
Youngstown *(G-14937)*

Springco Metal Coatings Inc.............. C 216 941-0020
Cleveland *(G-4320)*

Stricker Refinishing Inc.................. G 216 696-2906
Cleveland *(G-4334)*

Stuart-Dean Co Inc......................... G 412 765-2752
Cleveland *(G-4338)*

Sun Polishing Corp......................... G 440 237-5525
Cleveland *(G-4342)*

Superfinishers Inc......................... G 330 467-2125
Macedonia *(G-8718)*

Tablox Inc.................................. G 440 953-1951
Willoughby *(G-14537)*

Tatham Schulz Incorporated................ E 216 861-4431
Cleveland *(G-4364)*

Techmetals Inc............................. D 937 253-5311
Dayton *(G-6042)*

Teikuro Corporation........................ E 937 327-3955
Springfield *(G-12386)*

Toledo Metal Finishing Inc................ G 419 661-1422
Northwood *(G-10809)*

Trans-Acc Inc.............................. E 513 793-6410
Cincinnati *(G-3165)*

Transport Buff Intl Inc................... G 419 332-5110
Fremont *(G-7139)*

Tri-State Fabricators Inc................. E 513 752-5005
Amelia *(G-440)*

Tri-State Plating & Polishing............. G 304 529-2579
Proctorville *(G-11500)*

Tubetech Inc............................... E 330 426-9476
East Palestine *(G-6409)*

▲ Twist Inc................................ C 937 675-9581
Jamestown *(G-7969)*

U S Chrome Corporation Ohio............... F 877 872-7716
Dayton *(G-6068)*

United Surface Finishing Inc.............. F 330 453-2786
Canton *(G-2037)*

Varland Metal Service Inc................. E 513 861-0555
Cincinnati *(G-3195)*

Vectron Inc................................ F 440 323-3369
Elyria *(G-6600)*

Westshore Metal Finishing LLC............ G 440 892-0774
Westlake *(G-14345)*

▲ Whitaker Finishing LLC................... E 419 666-7746
Northwood *(G-10814)*

▲ Wieland Metal Svcs Foils LLC............ D 330 823-1700
Alliance *(G-417)*

Witt Enterprises Inc....................... G 440 992-8333
Ashtabula *(G-622)*

Woodhill Plating Works Company........... E 216 883-1344
Cleveland *(G-4515)*

◆ Worthington Steel Company............... B 800 944-2255
Worthington *(G-14732)*

Worthngton Smuel Coil Proc LLC........... E 330 963-3777
Twinsburg *(G-13398)*

Yoder Industries Inc....................... C 937 278-5769
Dayton *(G-6089)*

Youngstown Hard Chrome Pltg Gr.......... E 330 758-9721
Youngstown *(G-14970)*

Yourway Coatings LLC....................... F 216 651-9022
Brooklyn *(G-1526)*

3479 Metal coating and allied services

A & E Powder Coating Ltd.................. G 937 525-3750
Springfield *(G-12274)*

A Plus Powder Coaters Inc................. E 330 482-4389
Columbiana *(G-4604)*

AAA Galvanizing - Joliet Inc.............. F 513 871-5700
Cincinnati *(G-2329)*

Advanced Technical Pdts Sup Co........... F 513 851-6858
West Chester *(G-13936)*

Advantage Powder Coating Inc............. D 419 782-2363
Defiance *(G-6094)*

Aesthetic Finishers Inc................... E 937 778-8777
Piqua *(G-11332)*

Akron Steel Treating Co.................... E 330 773-8211
Akron *(G-43)*

Alexander Pierce Corp...................... G 330 798-9840
Akron *(G-49)*

Allied Coating Corporation................ F 937 615-0391
Piqua *(G-11333)*

Alpha Coatings Inc......................... C 419 435-5111
Fostoria *(G-6974)*

American Metal Coatings Inc............... E 216 451-3131
Mentor *(G-9479)*

American Tchnical Coatings Inc............ G 440 401-2270
Westlake *(G-14288)*

▲ Anest Iwata Usa Inc...................... F 513 755-3100
West Chester *(G-14102)*

Aps-Materials Inc.......................... G 937 278-6547
Dayton *(G-5663)*

▲ Aps-Materials Inc........................ D 937 278-6547
Dayton *(G-5662)*

Architctral Indus Met Fnshg LL............ F 440 963-0410
Vermilion *(G-13688)*

Armoloy of Ohio Inc........................ F 937 323-8702
Springfield *(G-12283)*

Art Galvanizing Works Inc................. G 216 749-0020
Cleveland *(G-3368)*

Bekaert Corporation........................ E 330 683-5060
Orrville *(G-10975)*

Bodycote Surface Tech Inc................. F 513 770-4922
Mason *(G-9073)*

Bodycote Surfc Tech Group Inc............ F 513 770-4900
Mason *(G-9074)*

Boville Indus Coatings Inc................ E 330 669-8558
Smithville *(G-12064)*

BTA of Motorcars Inc....................... G 440 716-1000
North Olmsted *(G-10719)*

Canfield Coating LLC....................... E 330 533-3311
Canfield *(G-1806)*

Canfield Metal Coating Corp............... D 330 702-3876
Canfield *(G-1807)*

Canton Galvanizing LLC..................... E 330 685-9060
Canton *(G-1855)*

▲ Cardinal Rubber Company.................. E 330 745-2191
Barberton *(G-801)*

Carpe Diem Industries LLC................. D 419 358-0129
Bluffton *(G-1359)*

Carpe Diem Industries LLC.................. D 419 659-5639
Columbus Grove *(G-5382)*

◆ Ccpi Inc..................................E 937 783-2476
Blanchester *(G-1234)*

Central Aluminum Company LLC......... E 614 491-5700
Obetz *(G-10922)*

▲ Certified Tool & Grinding Inc............ G 937 865-5934
Miamisburg *(G-9680)*

Cincinnati Thermal Spray Inc.............. E 513 793-1037
Blue Ash *(G-1263)*

▲ Cincinnati Thermal Spray Inc.......... F 513 793-0670
Cincinnati *(G-2488)*

Classic Coatings............................ G 330 421-3703
North Olmsted *(G-10720)*

▲ Cleveland-Cliffs Columbus LLC....... C 614 492-6800
Richfield *(G-11589)*

CLS Finishing Inc........................... F 330 784-4134
Tallmadge *(G-12733)*

Coating Systems Inc....................... F 513 367-5600
Harrison *(G-7547)*

Columbus V&S Galvanizing LLC......... D 614 449-8281
Columbus *(G-4836)*

Corrotec Inc.................................. E 937 325-3585
Springfield *(G-12294)*

Crown Group Co.............................. E 586 575-9800
Lima *(G-8397)*

Cubbison Company........................... D 330 793-2481
Youngstown *(G-14843)*

Dayton Coating Tech LLC.................. G 937 278-2060
Dayton *(G-5725)*

De Vore Engraving Co....................... G 330 454-6820
Canton *(G-1878)*

Duffee Finishing Inc......................... G 740 965-4848
Sunbury *(G-12663)*

Duracoat Powder Finishing Inc.......... F 419 636-3111
Bryan *(G-1639)*

E L Stone Company.......................... E 330 825-4565
Norton *(G-10820)*

Enamelac Company.......................... F 216 481-8878
Cleveland *(G-3670)*

◆ Enerfab LLC................................ B 513 641-0500
Cincinnati *(G-2590)*

Epco Extrusion Painting Co............... E 330 781-6100
Youngstown *(G-14853)*

▲ Etched Metal Company................... E 440 248-0240
Solon *(G-12109)*

Euclid Refinishing Compnay Inc......... F 440 275-3356
Austinburg *(G-698)*

Finishing Department....................... F 419 737-3334
Pioneer *(G-11320)*

General Plastics North Corp.............. C 800 542-2466
Cincinnati *(G-2665)*

George Manufacturing Inc................. F 513 932-1067
Lebanon *(G-8258)*

▲ Glass Coatings & Concepts LLC....... E 513 539-5300
Monroe *(G-10107)*

▲ Godfrey & Wing Inc...................... E 330 562-1440
Aurora *(G-671)*

▲ Gramke Enterprises Ltd................. G 614 252-8711
Columbus *(G-4965)*

Great Lakes Etching Finshg Co........... G 440 439-3624
Cleveland *(G-3790)*

Greber Machine Tool Inc................... G 440 322-3685
Elyria *(G-6541)*

▲ Greenkote Usa Inc....................... G 440 243-2865
Brookpark *(G-1551)*

Hadronics Inc................................. D 513 321-9350
Cincinnati *(G-2702)*

Hardline International Inc................. F 419 924-9556
West Unity *(G-14195)*

Hartzell Mfg Co LLC......................... E 937 859-5955
Miamisburg *(G-9696)*

Harwood Entp Holdings Inc............... F 330 923-3256
Cuyahoga Falls *(G-5548)*

Hathaway Stamp Idntfction Cncn.......... G 513 621-1052
Cincinnati *(G-2713)*

▲ Hemmelrath Coatings Inc................ F
Lima *(G-8414)*

Herbert E Orr Company Inc............... C 419 399-4866
Paulding *(G-11155)*

▲ Heritage Industrial Finshg Inc......... D 330 798-9840
Akron *(G-174)*

▲ High Tech Elastomers Inc............... E 937 236-6575
Vandalia *(G-13560)*

Highway Safety Corp....................... F 740 387-6991
Marion *(G-8972)*

Hydro Extrusion Usa LLC.................. C 888 935-5759
Sidney *(G-12025)*

▲ I V Miller & Sons.......................... F 732 493-4040
Medina *(G-9411)*

Iconic Labs LLC.............................. F 216 759-4040
Westlake *(G-14308)*

Imperial Metal Solutions LLC............ F 216 781-4094
Cleveland *(G-3854)*

Industrial and Mar Eng Svc Co.......... F 740 694-0791
Fredericktown *(G-7080)*

Industrial Coating Tech Inc.............. F 513 376-9945
Cincinnati *(G-2744)*

Inter-Ion Inc.................................. E 330 928-9655
Cuyahoga Falls *(G-5550)*

Ion Vacuum Ivac Tech Corp.............. F 216 662-5158
Cleveland *(G-3868)*

Ionbond LLC................................... F 216 831-0880
Cleveland *(G-3869)*

JM Hamilton Group Inc..................... F 419 229-4010
Lima *(G-8422)*

Kars Ohio LLC................................. G 614 655-1099
Pataskala *(G-11142)*

Kecamm LLC.................................. G 330 527-2918
Garrettsville *(G-7222)*

Kyocera Hardcoating Tech Ltd........... G 330 686-2136
Cuyahoga Falls *(G-5556)*

Legacy Finishing Inc....................... E 937 743-7278
Franklin *(G-7030)*

Lisbon Powder Coating..................... G 234 567-1324
Lisbon *(G-8476)*

Logan Coatings LLC......................... F 740 380-0047
Logan *(G-8519)*

▼ Loroco Industries Inc.................... D 513 891-9544
Cincinnati *(G-2828)*

Material Sciences Corporation........... C 330 702-3882
Canfield *(G-1813)*

Material Sciences Corporation........... D 419 661-5905
Walbridge *(G-13685)*

▲ Mesocoat Inc............................... F 216 453-0866
Euclid *(G-6662)*

Metaltek Industries Inc.................... F 937 342-1750
Springfield *(G-12353)*

Metokote Corporation...................... G 937 233-1565
Dayton *(G-5875)*

▲ Metokote Corporation.................... B 419 996-7800
Lima *(G-8432)*

Miamisburg Coating......................... F 937 866-1323
Miamisburg *(G-9716)*

Michael W Newton........................... G 740 352-9334
Lucasville *(G-8668)*

Mmf Incorporated........................... F 614 252-0078
Columbus *(G-5106)*

Momentive Performance Mtls Inc........ B 740 928-7010
Hebron *(G-7624)*

Momentive Performance Mtls Inc........ C 440 878-5705
Richmond Heights *(G-11611)*

◆ Momentive Prfmce Mtls Qrtz Inc....... E 440 878-5700
Strongsville *(G-12575)*

MSC Walbridge Coatings Inc.............. C 419 666-6130
Walbridge *(G-13686)*

Nation Coating Systems Inc.............. F 937 746-7632
Franklin *(G-7036)*

National Power Coating Ohio............. G 330 405-5587
Twinsburg *(G-13345)*

Niles Manufacturing & Finshg........... C 330 544-0402
Niles *(G-10596)*

Northeast Coatings Inc.................... G 330 784-7773
Tallmadge *(G-12743)*

◆ NSK Industries Inc........................D 330 923-4112
Cuyahoga Falls *(G-5563)*

Oerlikon Blzers Cating USA Inc.......... G 330 343-9892
Dover *(G-6257)*

Office Magic Inc.............................. F 510 782-6100
Medina *(G-9430)*

Ohio Coatings Company.................... D 740 859-5500
Yorkville *(G-14798)*

Ohio Galvanizing LLC....................... E 740 387-6474
Marion *(G-8986)*

Ohio Industrial Coating Corp............. G 567 230-6719
Tiffin *(G-12795)*

Omni Manufacturing Inc................... F 419 394-7424
Saint Marys *(G-11748)*

▲ Omni Manufacturing Inc................. D 419 394-7424
Saint Marys *(G-11747)*

Parker Rst-Proof Cleveland Inc.......... E 216 481-6680
Cleveland *(G-4142)*

Parker Trutec Incorporated.............. D 937 653-8500
Urbana *(G-13476)*

▲ Parker Trutec Incorporated............ D 937 323-8833
Springfield *(G-12359)*

Pelletier Brothers Mfg Inc................ F 740 774-4704
Chillicothe *(G-2270)*

Perfection Finishers Inc................... E 419 337-8015
Wauseon *(G-13858)*

Pioneer Custom Coating LLC............. G 419 737-3152
Pioneer *(G-11323)*

Pki Inc... F 513 832-8749
Cincinnati *(G-2967)*

▲ Porcelain Steel Buildings Company. D 614 228-5781
Columbus *(G-5199)*

▲ Powder Alloy Corporation............... E 513 984-4016
Loveland *(G-8646)*

Precision Coatings Inc..................... G 216 441-0805
Cleveland *(G-4183)*

Precision Coatings Systems.............. F 937 642-4727
Marysville *(G-9042)*

▲ Prism Powder Coatings Ltd............. E 330 225-5626
Brunswick *(G-1608)*

▲ Pro-TEC Coating Company Inc......... C 419 943-1100
Leipsic *(G-8311)*

Pro-TEC Coating Company LLC.......... D 419 943-1100
Leipsic *(G-8312)*

Procoat Painting Inc....................... G 513 735-2500
Batavia *(G-885)*

Production Paint Finishers Inc........... D 937 448-2627
Bradford *(G-1452)*

Progressive Mfg Co Inc.................... G 330 784-4717
Akron *(G-269)*

Progressive Powder Coating Inc......... E 440 974-3478
Mentor *(G-9598)*

Protech Powder Coatings Inc............ G 216 244-2761
Cleveland *(G-4202)*

Rack Processing Company Inc........... E 937 294-1911
Moraine *(G-10190)*

Raf Acquisition Co.......................... E 440 572-5999
Valley City *(G-13514)*

▲ Reifel Industries Inc..................... D 419 737-2138
Pioneer *(G-11328)*

Roban Inc...................................... G 330 794-1059
Lakemore *(G-8156)*

Roemer Industries Inc...........................D 330 448-2000
   Masury (G-9256)

Russell Products Co Inc........................F 330 535-9246
   Akron (G-296)

◆ Russell Products Co Inc.....................F 330 535-9246
   Akron (G-298)

Russell T Bundy Associates Inc ....F 419 526-4454
   Mansfield (G-8851)

Russell T Bundy Associates Inc...........G 740 965-3008
   Sunbury (G-12675)

Ryder Engraving Inc............................G 740 927-7193
   Pataskala (G-11149)

Seacor Painting Corporation.................G 330 755-6361
   Campbell (G-1770)

Semper Quality Industry Inc.................G 440 352-8111
   Mentor (G-9613)

SH Bell Company.................................E 412 963-9910
   East Liverpool (G-6396)

▲ Signature Partners Inc.....................D 419 678-1400
   Coldwater (G-4584)

Simcote Inc...F 740 382-5000
   Marion (G-8999)

Springco Metal Coatings Inc.................C 216 941-0020
   Cleveland (G-4320)

▲ Star Fab LLC.....................................C 330 533-9863
   Canfield (G-1817)

Sterling Coating..................................G 513 942-4900
   West Chester (G-14076)

◆ Synthomer USA LLC.........................E 678 400-6655
   Beachwood (G-952)

▼ Tce International Ltd.........................F 800 962-2376
   Perry (G-11199)

TDS-Bf/Ls Holdings Inc.......................E 440 327-5800
   North Ridgeville (G-10751)

▲ Techneglas LLC................................F 419 873-2000
   Perrysburg (G-11268)

Tendon Manufacturing Inc....................E 216 663-3200
   Cleveland (G-4374)

Thornton Powder Coatings Inc..............G 419 522-7183
   Mansfield (G-8860)

Topkote Inc...G 440 428-0525
   Madison (G-8733)

Trans-Acc Inc......................................E 513 793-6410
   Cincinnati (G-3165)

Treemen Industries Inc.........................E 330 965-3777
   Boardman (G-1378)

Tri-State Fabricators Inc.......................E 513 752-5005
   Amelia (G-440)

Tsp Inc..F 513 732-8900
   Batavia (G-892)

▲ Universal Rack & Eqp Co Inc ....G 330 963-6776
   Twinsburg (G-13390)

▲ Vacono America LLC.........................E 216 938-7428
   Cleveland (G-4456)

Visimax Technologies Inc.....................E 330 405-8330
   Twinsburg (G-13392)

Visionmark Nameplate Co LLC..............E 419 977-3131
   New Bremen (G-10368)

▲ Voigt & Schweitzer LLC....................F 614 449-8281
   Columbus (G-5352)

▲ Water Star Inc..................................F 440 996-0800
   Concord Township (G-5397)

Westwood Finishing Company...............G 937 837-1488
   Xenia (G-14785)

▼ Witt Industries Inc...........................D 513 871-5700
   Mason (G-9167)

Woodrow Manufacturing Co..................E 937 399-9333
   Springfield (G-12396)

Worldclass Processing Corp..................E
   Twinsburg (G-13397)

X-Treme Finishes Inc...........................F 330 474-0614
   North Royalton (G-10790)

Yanfeng Intl Auto Tech US I LL.............D 419 633-1873
   Bryan (G-1668)

3482 Small arms ammunition

Ares Inc..D 419 635-2175
   Port Clinton (G-11439)

BTR Enterprises LLC............................G 740 975-2526
   Newark (G-10495)

Galion LLC..C 419 468-5214
   Galion (G-7190)

National Bullet Co...............................G 800 317-9506
   Eastlake (G-6439)

▲ Premier Shot Company.....................G 330 405-0583
   Twinsburg (G-13359)

R & S Monitions Inc.............................G 614 846-0597
   Columbus (G-5222)

3483 Ammunition, except for small arms, nec

◆ Faxon Machining LLC........................C 513 851-4644
   Cincinnati (G-2614)

L3harris Fzing Ord Systems Inc............A 513 943-2000
   Cincinnati (G-2311)

▲ Marine Jet Power Inc........................G 614 759-9000
   Blacklick (G-1224)

3484 Small arms

▲ Acme Machine Automatics Inc..........E 419 453-0010
   Ottoville (G-11051)

▲ American Apex Corporation...............F 614 652-2000
   Delaware (G-6130)

Ares Inc..D 419 635-2175
   Port Clinton (G-11439)

Highpoint Firearms..............................G 419 747-9444
   Mansfield (G-8803)

Kaeper Machine Inc.............................E 440 974-1010
   Mentor (G-9545)

Kelblys Rifle Range Inc........................G 330 683-4674
   North Lawrence (G-10701)

◆ Ohio Ordnance Works Inc.................E 440 285-3481
   Chardon (G-2217)

Stealth Arms LLC................................G 419 925-7005
   Celina (G-2122)

TS Sales LLC.......................................F 727 804-8060
   Akron (G-347)

3489 Ordnance and accessories, nec

▲ American Apex Corporation...............F 614 652-2000
   Delaware (G-6130)

Area 419 Firearms LLC.........................F 419 830-8353
   Delta (G-6201)

Ares Inc..D 419 635-2175
   Port Clinton (G-11439)

Teledyne Defense Elec LLC...................C 866 539-5916
   Miamisburg (G-9746)

3491 Industrial valves

4matic Valve Automtn Ohio LLC............F 614 806-1221
   Columbus (G-4653)

▼ Akron Steel Fabricators Co...............E 330 644-0616
   Akron (G-42)

Alkon Corporation...............................F 614 799-6650
   Dublin (G-6274)

▲ Alkon Corporation............................D 419 355-9111
   Fremont (G-7090)

Bosch Rexroth Corporation..................C 330 263-3300
   Wooster (G-14627)

◆ Clark-Reliance LLC...........................C 440 572-1500
   Strongsville (G-12550)

Curtiss-Wright Flow Ctrl Corp...............E 440 838-7690
   Brecksville (G-1461)

Flow Technology Inc.............................E 513 745-6000
   Cincinnati (G-2629)

▲ Hearth Products Controls Co.............F 937 436-9800
   Miamisburg (G-9697)

Honeywell International Inc...................A 937 484-2000
   Urbana (G-13466)

◆ Kaplan Industries Inc.......................D 856 779-8181
   Harrison (G-7558)

Maass Midwest Mfg Inc........................G 419 894-6424
   Arcadia (G-482)

Meador Supply Company Inc.................F 330 405-4403
   Walton Hills (G-13700)

Nupro Company...................................E 440 951-9729
   Willoughby (G-14498)

Parker-Hannifin Corporation.................D 419 542-6611
   Hicksville (G-7650)

Parker-Hannifin Corporation.................E 937 644-3915
   Marysville (G-9041)

Pima Valve LLC...................................D 330 337-9535
   Salem (G-11804)

▲ Richards Industrials Inc....................D 513 533-5600
   Cincinnati (G-3044)

◆ Rogers Industrial Products Inc..........E 330 535-3331
   Akron (G-290)

Ruthman Pump and Engineering............G 937 783-2411
   Blanchester (G-1238)

Seawin Inc..D 419 355-9111
   Fremont (G-7132)

Sherwood Valve LLC.............................E 216 264-5023
   Cleveland (G-4296)

▲ Superb Industries Inc.......................D 330 852-0500
   Sugarcreek (G-12652)

Swagelok Company..............................G 440 248-4600
   Solon (G-12187)

Swagelok Company..............................E 440 349-5652
   Solon (G-12189)

Swagelok Company..............................E 440 349-5836
   Solon (G-12190)

Swagelok Company..............................E 440 248-4600
   Willoughby Hills (G-14564)

◆ Swagelok Company...........................A 440 248-4600
   Solon (G-12188)

▲ Tylok International Inc......................D 216 261-7310
   Cleveland (G-4436)

Valv-Trol LLC.......................................F 330 686-2800
   Stow (G-12469)

Vickers International Inc........................G 419 867-2200
   Maumee (G-9329)

Watts Water...F 614 491-5143
   Groveport (G-7167)

◆ Waxman Industries Inc......................C 440 439-1830
   Bedford (G-1065)

◆ William Powell Company....................D 513 852-2000
   Cincinnati (G-3224)

Xomox Corporation..............................G 513 745-6000
   Blue Ash (G-1355)

Xomox Corporation..............................E 936 271-6500
   Cincinnati (G-3237)

Xomox Pft Corp....................................B 936 271-6500
   Cincinnati (G-3238)

3492 Fluid power valves and hose fittings

▲ Ace Manufacturing Company.............E 513 541-2490
   West Chester (G-13935)

Aerocontrolex Group Inc.......................D 216 291-6025
   South Euclid (G-12216)

▲ Alkon Corporation............................D 419 355-9111
   Fremont (G-7090)

▲ Amfm Inc..F 440 953-4545
   Willoughby (G-14419)

Cho Bedford Inc..................................D 330 343-8896
   Dover (G-6233)

Custom Cltch Jnt Hydrlics Inc...............F 216 431-1630
   Cleveland (G-3584)

▲ Dana Limited..................B 419 887-3000
Maumee *(G-9282)*

Danfoss Power Solutions II LLC.............F 419 238-1190
Van Wert *(G-13533)*

Dixon Valve & Coupling Co LLC.............F 330 425-3000
Twinsburg *(G-13296)*

DNC Hydraulics LLC.................F 419 963-2800
Rawson *(G-11551)*

▲ Dyna-Flex Inc...................F 440 946-9424
Painesville *(G-11081)*

Eaton Aeroquip LLC.................A 419 891-7775
Maumee *(G-9292)*

◆ Eaton Aeroquip LLC.................C 440 523-5000
Cleveland *(G-3650)*

◆ Eaton Corporation.................B 440 523-5000
Cleveland *(G-3652)*

Freudenberg-Nok General Partnr.........C 419 427-5221
Findlay *(G-6868)*

Hombre Capital Inc.................F 440 838-5335
Brecksville *(G-1470)*

▲ Hunt Valve Company Inc.............D 330 337-9535
Salem *(G-11788)*

▲ Hy-Production LLC.................C 330 273-2400
Valley City *(G-13499)*

▲ Hydac Technology Corp.............F 610 266-0100
Wooster *(G-14649)*

Hydraulic Manifolds USA LLC.........E 973 728-1214
Stow *(G-12436)*

Hydraulic Parts Store Inc.............G 330 364-6667
New Philadelphia *(G-10449)*

◆ Hydrotech Inc...................D 888 651-5712
West Chester *(G-14126)*

▲ Ic-Fluid Power Inc.................F 419 661-8811
Rossford *(G-11658)*

▼ Industrial Connections Inc.............G 330 274-2155
Mantua *(G-8869)*

◆ Kirtland Capital Partners LP.............E 216 593-0100
Beachwood *(G-924)*

Malabar.......................E 419 866-6301
Swanton *(G-12687)*

▲ Malone Specialty Inc.................F 440 255-4200
Mentor *(G-9559)*

Mid-State Sales Inc.................G 330 744-2158
Youngstown *(G-14900)*

▲ Mid-State Sales Inc.................D 614 864-1811
Columbus *(G-5099)*

National Aviation Products Inc.........G 330 688-6494
Stow *(G-12444)*

▲ National Machine Company.............C 330 688-6494
Stow *(G-12446)*

Netherland Rubber Company.........F 513 733-0883
Cincinnati *(G-2899)*

Ohio Hydraulics Inc.................E 513 771-2590
Cincinnati *(G-2924)*

Omega 1 Inc.....................F 216 663-8424
Willoughby *(G-14501)*

Parker-Hannifin Corporation.........C 937 456-5571
Eaton *(G-6462)*

Parker-Hannifin Corporation.........D 419 542-6611
Hicksville *(G-7650)*

Parker-Hannifin Corporation.........B 440 943-5700
Wickliffe *(G-14389)*

▲ Parker-Hannifin Corporation.............A 216 896-3000
Cleveland *(G-4143)*

Pima Valve LLC.................D 330 337-9535
Salem *(G-11804)*

Pioneer Solutions LLC.................E 216 383-3400
Euclid *(G-6669)*

◆ Pressure Connections Corp.............D 614 863-6930
Columbus *(G-5204)*

▲ Quality Machining and Mfg Inc.........F 419 899-2543
Sherwood *(G-11976)*

SMC Corporation of America.............F 330 659-2006
Richfield *(G-11601)*

▲ SSP Fittings Corp.................D 330 425-4250
Twinsburg *(G-13379)*

State Metal Hose Inc.................G 614 527-4700
Hilliard *(G-7703)*

Superior Holding LLC.................G 216 651-9400
Cleveland *(G-4344)*

Superior Products LLC.................D 216 651-9400
Cleveland *(G-4347)*

Swagelok Company.................E 440 349-5836
Solon *(G-12190)*

▲ Taiyo America Inc.................F 419 300-8811
Saint Marys *(G-11753)*

▲ The Sheffer Corporation.............D 513 489-9770
Cincinnati *(G-3150)*

◆ Thogus Products Company.............D 440 933-8850
Avon Lake *(G-771)*

Transdigm Inc.....................E 216 291-6025
Cleveland *(G-4411)*

▲ Tylok International Inc.................D 216 261-7310
Cleveland *(G-4436)*

Valv-Trol LLC.....................F 330 686-2800
Stow *(G-12469)*

Winzeler Manufacturing Company.........F 419 485-8147
Montpelier *(G-10137)*

Zaytran Inc.......................E 440 324-2814
Elyria *(G-6604)*

3493 Steel springs, except wire

▲ Dayton Progress Corporation.............A 937 859-5111
Dayton *(G-5737)*

Golden Spring Company Inc.............F 937 848-2513
Bellbrook *(G-1092)*

Hendrickson International Corp.............D 740 929-5600
Hebron *(G-7617)*

Jamestown Industries Inc.................D 330 779-0670
Youngstown *(G-14881)*

▲ Kern-Liebers Usa Inc.................D 419 865-2437
Holland *(G-7771)*

▲ Liteflex Disc LLC.................D 937 836-7025
Dayton *(G-5851)*

Marik Spring Inc.................E 330 564-0617
Tallmadge *(G-12740)*

Matthew Warren Inc.................E 614 418-0250
Columbus *(G-5087)*

◆ Napoleon Spring Works Inc.............C 419 445-1010
Archbold *(G-504)*

Peterson American Corporation.........E 419 867-8711
Holland *(G-7777)*

Service Spring Corp.................G 419 867-0212
Maumee *(G-9317)*

▼ Service Spring Corp.................D 419 838-6081
Maumee *(G-9318)*

▲ Solon Manufacturing Company.............E 440 286-7149
Chardon *(G-2223)*

Tadd Spring Co Inc.................G 440 572-1313
Strongsville *(G-12609)*

Zsi Manufacturing Inc.................F 440 266-0701
Concord Township *(G-5398)*

3494 Valves and pipe fittings, nec

16363 Sca Inc.....................G 330 448-0000
Masury *(G-9253)*

Adaptall America Inc.................F 330 425-4114
Twinsburg *(G-13269)*

◆ Alloy Precision Tech Inc.................D 440 266-7700
Mentor *(G-9477)*

▲ Anchor Flange Company.................D 513 527-3512
Cincinnati *(G-2369)*

Bay Corporation.....................E 440 835-2212
Westlake *(G-14290)*

Bosch Rexroth Corporation.............C 330 263-3300
Wooster *(G-14627)*

Bowden Manufacturing Corp.............E 440 946-1770
Willoughby *(G-14432)*

Bowes Manufacturing Inc.................F 216 378-2110
Solon *(G-12087)*

Calvin J Magsig.....................G 419 862-3311
Elmore *(G-6488)*

Crane Pumps & Systems Inc.............F 937 773-2442
Piqua *(G-11340)*

Cylinders and Valves Inc.................G 440 238-7343
Strongsville *(G-12552)*

Drainage Pipe & Fittings LLC.............G 419 538-6337
Ottawa *(G-11033)*

Eaton Corporation.....................E 330 274-0743
Aurora *(G-667)*

Edward W Daniel LLC.................F 440 647-1960
Wellington *(G-13885)*

▲ Fcx Performance Inc.................E 614 253-1996
Columbus *(G-4922)*

▲ General Plug and Mfg Co.............C 440 926-2411
Grafton *(G-7302)*

Greater Cleve Pipe Ftting Fund.............F 216 524-8334
Cleveland *(G-3795)*

H P E Inc.......................G 330 833-3161
Massillon *(G-9199)*

◆ H-P Products Inc.................C 330 875-5556
Louisville *(G-8602)*

Insulpro Inc.....................F 614 262-3768
Columbus *(G-5016)*

◆ Kirtland Capital Partners LP.............E 216 593-0100
Beachwood *(G-924)*

▲ Knappco Corporation.................C 513 870-3100
Hamilton *(G-7509)*

Lsq Manufacturing Inc.................F 330 725-4905
Medina *(G-9421)*

Mack Iron Works Company.............E 419 626-3712
Sandusky *(G-11855)*

▲ Mid-State Sales Inc.................D 614 864-1811
Columbus *(G-5099)*

Northcoast Valve and Gate Inc.............G 440 392-9910
Mentor *(G-9573)*

Nupro Company.....................E 440 951-9729
Willoughby *(G-14498)*

▲ Opw Engineered Systems Inc.............E 888 771-9438
West Chester *(G-14039)*

Parker-Hannifin Corporation.................C 614 279-7070
Columbus *(G-5174)*

Parker-Hannifin Corporation.................C 937 456-5571
Eaton *(G-6462)*

Pima Valve LLC.................D 330 337-9535
Salem *(G-11804)*

Precision McHning Cnnction LLC.............F 440 943-3300
Wickliffe *(G-14392)*

◆ Pressure Connections Corp.............D 614 863-6930
Columbus *(G-5204)*

▲ Richards Industrials Inc.................D 513 533-5600
Cincinnati *(G-3044)*

▲ Robeck Fluid Power Co.................D 330 562-1140
Aurora *(G-687)*

Ruthman Pump and Engineering.........G 937 783-2411
Blanchester *(G-1238)*

▲ Spirex Corporation.................C 330 726-1166
Youngstown *(G-14938)*

▲ SSP Fittings Corp.................D 330 425-4250
Twinsburg *(G-13379)*

Stelter and Brinck Inc.................E 513 367-9300
Harrison *(G-7569)*

Stephens Pipe & Steel LLC.................C 740 869-2257
Mount Sterling *(G-10229)*

Superior Holding LLC.................G 216 651-9400
Cleveland *(G-4344)*

Superior Products LLC....................D 216 651-9400
Cleveland (G-4347)

Swagelok Company...........................D 440 473-1050
Cleveland (G-4354)

Swagelok Company...........................F 440 442-6611
Cleveland (G-4355)

Swagelok Company...........................E 440 349-5652
Solon (G-12189)

Swagelok Company...........................E 440 349-5836
Solon (G-12190)

Swagelok Company...........................D 440 349-5934
Solon (G-12191)

◆ Swagelok Company.........................A 440 248-4600
Solon (G-12188)

▲ TCH Industries Incorporated...........F 330 487-5155
Twinsburg (G-13383)

▲ The Sheffer Corporation..................D 513 489-9770
Cincinnati (G-3150)

◆ Thogus Products Company...............D 440 933-8850
Avon Lake (G-771)

▲ Tylok International Inc.....................D 216 261-7310
Cleveland (G-4436)

US Fittings Inc................................F 234 212-9420
Twinsburg (G-13391)

◆ Waxman Industries Inc.....................C 440 439-1830
Bedford (G-1065)

Wells Inc..F 419 457-2611
Risingsun (G-11620)

◆ William Powell Company..................D 513 852-2000
Cincinnati (G-3224)

Xomox Corporation..........................E 936 271-6500
Cincinnati (G-3237)

Xomox Pft Corp...............................B 936 271-6500
Cincinnati (G-3238)

3495 Wire springs

Allied Shipping and Packa.................F 937 222-7422
Moraine (G-10144)

Aswpengg LLC................................F 216 292-4620
Bedford Heights (G-1069)

B & P Spring Prod Co Inc..................F 216 486-4260
Cleveland (G-3398)

Barnes Group Inc.............................G 440 526-5900
Brecksville (G-1458)

Barnes Group Inc.............................C 419 891-9292
Maumee (G-9264)

Betts Company................................E 330 533-0111
Canfield (G-1805)

▲ Bloomngburg Spring Wire Form I.....E 740 437-7614
Bloomingburg (G-1239)

▲ Dayton Progress Corporation...........A 937 859-5111
Dayton (G-5737)

Elyria Spring Spclty Holdg Inc............G 440 323-5502
Cleveland (G-3664)

Euclid Spring Co..............................E 440 943-3213
Wickliffe (G-14375)

▲ Kern-Liebers Usa Inc......................D 419 865-2437
Holland (G-7771)

Malabar..E 419 866-6301
Swanton (G-12687)

Matthew Warren Inc.........................E 614 418-0250
Columbus (G-5087)

Ohio Wire Form & Spring Co...............F 614 444-3676
Columbus (G-5156)

Six C Fabrication Inc........................B 330 296-5594
Ravenna (G-11541)

▲ Solon Manufacturing Company.........E 440 286-7149
Chardon (G-2223)

▼ Spring Team Inc.............................D 440 275-5981
Austinburg (G-703)

Spring Works Incorporated.................E 614 351-9345
Columbus (G-5286)

▲ Stalder Spring Works Inc.................G 937 322-6120
Springfield (G-12378)

▲ Supro Spring & Wire Forms Inc.........E 330 722-5628
Medina (G-9451)

Tadd Spring Co Inc...........................G 440 572-1313
Strongsville (G-12609)

The Reliable Spring Wire Frms............E 440 365-7400
Elyria (G-6595)

Timac Manufacturing Company............G 937 372-3305
Xenia (G-14779)

Trupoint Products LLC......................F 330 204-3302
Sugarcreek (G-12654)

Twist Inc..G 937 675-9581
Jamestown (G-7970)

▲ Twist Inc......................................C 937 675-9581
Jamestown (G-7969)

Wire Products Company Inc................F 216 267-0777
Cleveland (G-4509)

▼ Yost Superior Co............................E 937 323-7591
Springfield (G-12397)

3496 Miscellaneous fabricated wire products

A K Athletic Equipment Inc................E 614 920-3069
Canal Winchester (G-1782)

Adcura Mfg.....................................G 937 222-3800
Dayton (G-5635)

Advance Wire Forming Inc.................F 216 432-3250
Cleveland (G-3304)

Akron Belting & Supply Company........G 330 633-8212
Akron (G-25)

Alabama Sling Center Inc...................F 440 239-7000
Cleveland (G-3318)

◆ Alcan Corporation..........................E
Cleveland (G-3320)

▲ Amanda Bent Bolt Company.............C 740 385-6893
Logan (G-8508)

▲ Ametco Manufacturing Corp.............E 440 951-4300
Willoughby (G-14418)

Assembly Specialty Pdts Inc..............E 216 676-5600
Cleveland (G-3381)

Bekaert Corporation..........................F 330 683-5060
Orrville (G-10974)

▲ Bloomngburg Spring Wire Form I.....E 740 437-7614
Bloomingburg (G-1239)

▲ Brushes Inc...................................F 216 267-8084
Cleveland (G-3447)

Busch & Thiem Inc...........................E 419 625-7515
Sandusky (G-11825)

C & F Fabrications Inc.......................G 937 666-3234
East Liberty (G-6383)

▲ C C M Wire Inc..............................F 330 425-3421
Twinsburg (G-13283)

Canron Manufacturing Inc..................F 330 497-1131
Greentown (G-7332)

Clamps Inc......................................E 419 729-2141
Toledo (G-12921)

Cleveland Wire Cloth Mfg LLC............E 216 341-1832
Cleveland (G-3531)

Contitech Usa LLC...........................C 937 644-8900
Marysville (G-9016)

Dayton Wire Products Inc..................F 937 236-8000
Dayton (G-5741)

▲ Die Co Inc....................................E 440 942-8856
Eastlake (G-6423)

Dribble Creek Inc.............................F 440 439-8650
Bedford (G-1029)

Dysinger Incorporated......................E 937 297-7761
Dayton (G-5757)

Engineered Wire Products Inc.............E 330 469-6958
Warren (G-13762)

▲ Engineered Wire Products Inc...........C 419 294-3817
Upper Sandusky (G-13440)

▲ Ever Roll Specialties Co...................E 937 964-1302
Springfield (G-12309)

Fence One Inc..................................F 216 441-2600
Cleveland (G-3712)

◆ G & S Titanium Inc.........................E 330 263-0564
Wooster (G-14641)

Gateway Con Forming Svcs Inc...........D 513 353-2000
Miamitown (G-9758)

General Chain & Mfg Corp..................E 513 541-6005
Cincinnati (G-2659)

▼ Helical Line Products Co..................E 440 933-9263
Avon Lake (G-759)

Illinois Tool Works Inc.......................E 216 292-7161
Bedford (G-1039)

Interntnal Tchncal Catings Inc.............C 800 567-6592
Columbus (G-5021)

KEffs Inc..G 614 443-0586
Columbus (G-5047)

Kimmatt Corp..................................G 937 228-3811
West Alexandria (G-13920)

◆ Malin Co......................................E 216 267-9080
Cleveland (G-3982)

◆ Manufacturers Equipment Co............F 513 424-3573
Middletown (G-9877)

Marik Spring Inc...............................E 330 564-0617
Tallmadge (G-12740)

Mason Company LLC........................E 937 780-2321
Leesburg (G-8299)

▲ May Conveyor Inc...........................G 440 237-8012
North Royalton (G-10772)

Mazzella Jhh Company Inc.................D 440 239-7000
Cleveland (G-4004)

▲ Mazzella Lifting Tech Inc.................D 440 239-7000
Cleveland (G-4005)

McM Ind Co Inc................................F 216 641-6300
Cleveland (G-4013)

◆ McM Ind Co Inc.............................F 216 292-4506
Cleveland (G-4012)

Meese Inc.......................................E 440 998-1202
Ashtabula (G-604)

Merchants Metals LLC.......................E 513 942-0268
West Chester (G-14028)

Microplex Inc...................................E 330 498-0600
North Canton (G-10651)

◆ Mid-West Fabricating Co..................C 740 969-4411
Amanda (G-424)

▼ Midwestern Industries Inc................D 330 837-4203
Massillon (C-0220)

▲ Mueller Electric Company Inc............D 216 771-5225
Akron (G-239)

▲ Ofco Inc.......................................D 740 622-5922
Coshocton (G-5466)

Ohio Wire Form & Spring Co...............F 614 444-3676
Columbus (G-5156)

◆ Options Plus Incorporated................F 740 694-9811
Fredericktown (G-7083)

Panacea Products Corporation............E 614 429-6320
Columbus (G-5170)

◆ Panacea Products Corporation..........E 614 850-7000
Columbus (G-5171)

Parker-Hannifin Corporation...............D 330 336-3511
Wadsworth (G-13658)

Pennant Inc.....................................F 937 584-5411
Columbus (G-5183)

Peterson American Corporation...........E 419 867-8711
Holland (G-7777)

▲ Polymet Corporation.......................E 513 874-3586
West Chester (G-14051)

◆ Premier Manufacturing Corp.............C 216 941-9700
Cleveland (G-4190)

Production Plus Corp.........................F 740 983-5178
Ashville (G-630)

S
I
C

Providence REES Inc.............................. G 614 833-6231
Columbus (G-5212)

▲ Pwp Inc... E 216 251-2181
Ashland (G-567)

▲ Qualtek Electronics Corp.................. C 440 951-3300
Mentor (G-9603)

R G Smith Company............................ D 330 456-3415
Canton (G-1988)

◆ Rjs Corporation............................... E 330 896-2387
Akron (G-287)

Roy I Kaufman Inc.............................. G 740 382-0643
Marion (G-8994)

▲ Royal Wire Products Inc................... D 440 237-8787
North Royalton (G-10781)

▲ Saxon Products Inc.......................... G 419 241-6771
Toledo (G-13122)

Schweizer Dipple Inc......................... D 440 786-8090
Cleveland (G-4277)

▼ Sheffield Metals Intl Inc................... E 440 934-8500
Sheffield Village (G-11965)

▼ Spring Team Inc............................... D 440 275-5981
Austinburg (G-703)

Starr Fabricating Inc.......................... D 330 394-9891
Vienna (G-13618)

Stephens Pipe & Steel LLC................ C 740 869-2257
Mount Sterling (G-10229)

Stolle Machinery Company LLC.......... C 937 497-5400
Dayton (G-6027)

▼ Stud Welding Associates Inc............ D 440 783-3160
Strongsville (G-12607)

▼ T & R Welding Systems Inc.............. F 937 228-7517
Dayton (G-6037)

▲ Therm-O-Link Inc............................. D 330 527-2124
Garrettsville (G-7228)

Tom Thumb Clip Co Inc...................... F 440 953-9606
Willoughby (G-14542)

Top Knotch Products Inc.................... G 419 543-2266
Cleveland (G-4402)

▲ Tri-State Wire Rope Supply Inc......... D 513 871-8656
Cincinnati (G-3168)

▲ Tyler Haver Inc................................ E 440 974-1047
Mentor (G-9645)

Unified Scrning Crshing - OH I............ G 937 836-3201
Englewood (G-6627)

Utility Wire Products Inc.................... G 216 441-2180
Cleveland (G-4455)

▲ Ver-Mac Industries Inc..................... E 740 397-6511
Mount Vernon (G-10268)

▼ W J Egli Company Inc....................... F 330 823-3666
Alliance (G-414)

West Equipment Company Inc............ G 419 698-1601
Toledo (G-13177)

Wire Products Company LLC.............. D 216 267-0777
Cleveland (G-4510)

Wrwp LLC.. D 330 425-3421
Twinsburg (G-13399)

Yankee Wire Cloth Products Inc......... F 740 545-9129
West Lafayette (G-14174)

▼ Yost Superior Co.............................. E 937 323-7591
Springfield (G-12397)

3497 Metal foil and leaf

Avery Dennison Corporation............... D 440 639-3900
Mentor (G-9490)

Avery Dennison Corporation............... A 440 534-6000
Mentor (G-9489)

CCL Label Inc.................................... E 216 676-2703
Cleveland (G-3480)

CCL Label Inc.................................... D 440 878-7000
Strongsville (G-12548)

Compco Quaker Mfg Inc..................... E 330 482-0200
Salem (G-11772)

▲ Quaker Mfg Corp............................. C 330 332-4631
Salem (G-11807)

▲ Wieland Metal Svcs Foils LLC.......... D 330 823-1700
Alliance (G-417)

3498 Fabricated pipe and fittings

◆ Alloy Precision Tech Inc................... D 440 266-7700
Mentor (G-9477)

▼ American Roll Formed Pdts Corp...... C 440 352-0753
Youngstown (G-14812)

▲ Appian Manufacturing Corp.............. E 614 445-2230
Columbus (G-4721)

Arem Co.. G 440 974-6740
Willoughby (G-14426)

Atlas Industrial Contrs LLC................ B 614 841-4500
Columbus (G-4732)

B S F Inc... F 937 890-6121
Tipp City (G-12816)

B S F Inc... F 937 890-6121
Dayton (G-5672)

Bi-Con Services Inc............................ B 740 685-2542
Derwent (G-6221)

Chardon Metal Products Co................ E 440 285-2147
Chardon (G-2198)

Contractors Steel Company................ D 330 425-3050
Twinsburg (G-13289)

Crest Bending Inc.............................. E 419 492-2108
New Washington (G-10478)

De Kay Fabricators Inc....................... G 330 793-0826
Youngstown (G-14846)

▲ Duca Manufacturing & Cons............. E 330 758-0828
Youngstown (G-14850)

▲ Ebner Furnaces Inc.......................... D 330 335-2311
Wadsworth (G-13637)

Elliott Tool Technologies Ltd.............. D 937 253-6133
Dayton (G-5763)

◆ Elster Perfection Corporation............ D 440 428-1171
Geneva (G-7236)

Enterprise Machine Inc....................... G 513 681-4409
Cincinnati (G-2592)

Esterle Mold & Machine Co Inc........... E 330 686-1685
Stow (G-12429)

▲ Ever Roll Specialties Co................... E 937 964-1302
Springfield (G-12309)

Famous Industries Inc........................ F 740 685-2592
Byesville (G-1711)

Faull & Son LLC................................. F 330 652-4341
Niles (G-10588)

H-P Products Inc............................... C 330 875-7193
Louisville (G-8601)

◆ H-P Products Inc.............................. C 330 875-5556
Louisville (G-8602)

▼ Hollaender Manufacturing Co............ D 513 772-8800
Cincinnati (G-2726)

Honeywell Smart Energy..................... D 440 415-1606
Geneva (G-7240)

Hycom Inc... E 330 753-2330
Barberton (G-812)

▲ Hydro Tube Enterprises Inc.............. D 440 774-1022
Oberlin (G-10918)

Indelco Custom Products Inc.............. G 216 797-7300
Euclid (G-6654)

Industrial Power Systems Inc............. B 419 531-3121
Rossford (G-11659)

▲ Industrial Quartz Corporation........... F 440 942-0909
Mentor (G-9530)

Ipsco Tubulars Inc............................ D 330 448-6772
Brookfield (G-1516)

John H Hosking Co............................. G 513 422-9425
Middletown (G-9870)

Kenley Enterprises LLC...................... G 419 630-0921
Bryan (G-1647)

Kings Welding and Fabg Inc............... G 330 738-3592
Mechanicstown (G-9368)

◆ Kirtland Capital Partners LP.............. E 216 593-0100
Beachwood (G-924)

▲ Kottler Metal Products Co Inc........... E 440 946-7473
Willoughby (G-14478)

◆ Machine Dynamics & Engrg Inc......... D 330 868-5603
Minerva (G-10041)

Mitchell Piping LLC............................ E 330 245-0258
Hartville (G-7581)

Ms Murcko & Sons LLC...................... G 724 854-4907
Hubbard (G-7814)

Normandy Products Co....................... D 440 632-5050
Middlefield (G-9819)

Parker-Hannifin Corporation.............. C 937 456-5571
Eaton (G-6462)

Phillips Mfg and Tower Co.................. D 419 347-1720
Shelby (G-11972)

Phoenix Forge Group LLC................... B 800 848-6125
West Jefferson (G-14166)

▲ Pioneer Pipe Inc.............................. A 740 376-2400
Marietta (G-8937)

◆ Pipe Line Development Company........ D 440 871-5700
Strongsville (G-12585)

▲ Pipe Products Inc............................ C 513 587-7532
West Chester (G-14049)

Precision Bending Tech Inc................ F 440 974-2500
Mentor (G-9590)

▲ Precision Fittings LLC....................... E 440 647-4143
Wellington (G-13899)

◆ Pressure Connections Corp.............. D 614 863-6930
Columbus (G-5204)

◆ Production Tube Cutting Inc.............. E 937 254-6138
Dayton (G-5963)

▼ Qual-Fab Inc.................................... E 440 327-5000
Avon (G-737)

Quality Mechanicals Inc..................... E 513 559-0998
Cincinnati (G-3016)

▲ Rafter Equipment Company LLC........ E 440 572-3700
Strongsville (G-12592)

Rbm Environmental & Cnstr Inc.......... G 419 693-5840
Oregon (G-10967)

◆ Rexarc International Inc.................... E 937 839-4604
West Alexandria (G-13921)

▲ Rhenium Alloys Inc.......................... E 440 365-7388
North Ridgeville (G-10747)

▼ Riker Products Inc........................... D 419 729-1626
Toledo (G-13112)

Rocks General Maintenance LLC......... G 740 323-4711
Thornville (G-12768)

S-P Company Inc................................ D 330 782-5651
Columbiana (G-4627)

Scot Industries Inc............................ C 330 262-7585
Wooster (G-14683)

◆ Scott Process Systems Inc............... C 330 877-2350
Hartville (G-7584)

Seal Tite LLC.................................... D 937 393-4268
Hillsboro (G-7725)

Selling Precision Inc.......................... E 973 728-1214
Stow (G-12460)

▲ SSP Fittings Corp............................. D 330 425-4250
Twinsburg (G-13379)

▲ Stam Inc... E 440 974-2500
Mentor (G-9622)

▲ Stripmatic Products Inc.................... E 216 241-7143
Cleveland (G-4336)

Suburban Steel Supply Co.................. D 614 737-5501
Gahanna (G-7170)

Swagelok Company............................ E 440 349-5652
Solon (G-12189)

Swagelok Company............................ D 440 349-5934
Solon (G-12191)

T & D Fabricating Inc.............................. E 440 951-5646
  Eastlake (G-6445)

TI Group Auto Systems LLC.................. E 740 929-2049
  Hebron (G-7640)

Transit Sittings of NA........................... G 330 797-2516
  Youngstown (G-14951)

Tri-America Contractors Inc................... F 740 574-0148
  Wheelersburg (G-14355)

Tri-America Contractors Inc................... E 740 574-0148
  Wheelersburg (G-14354)

Tri-State Fabricators Inc........................ E 513 752-5005
  Amelia (G-440)

Unison Industries LLC........................... B 904 667-9904
  Dayton (G-5625)

United Group Services Inc...................... C 800 633-9690
  Cincinnati (G-3183)

Unity Tube Inc....................................... F 330 426-4282
  East Palestine (G-6410)

US Tubular Products Inc........................ D 330 832-1734
  North Lawrence (G-10703)

Vanex Tube Corporation........................ D 330 544-9500
  Niles (G-10608)

Vortec Corporation................................ E 513 891-7485
  Blue Ash (G-1348)

▼ W J Egli Company Inc........................ F 330 823-3666
  Alliance (G-414)

Zekelman Industries Inc........................ C 740 432-2146
  Cambridge (G-1766)

3499 Fabricated metal products, nec

Accurate Mechanical Inc....................... D 740 681-1332
  Lancaster (G-8174)

Ace Plastics Company........................... G 330 928-7720
  Stow (G-12414)

Addup Inc.. E 513 745-4510
  Blue Ash (G-1242)

Alacriant Inc.. E 330 562-7191
  Streetsboro (G-12487)

Alacriant Inc.. D 330 562-7191
  Streetsboro (G-12486)

All Ohio Welding Inc.............................. G 937 663-7116
  Saint Paris (G-11755)

Bauer Corporation................................. E 800 321-4760
  Wooster (G-14624)

Bc Investment Corporation..................... C 330 262-3070
  Wooster (G-14625)

◆ Black Squirrel Holdings Inc................ E 513 577-7107
  Cincinnati (G-2412)

Camaco LLC.. A 440 288-4444
  Lorain (G-8549)

Cast-Fab Technologies Inc..................... C 513 758-1000
  Cincinnati (G-2442)

Central Machinery Company LLC........... F 740 387-1289
  Marion (G-8966)

Champion Strapping Pdts Inc................. G 614 527-1454
  Columbus (G-4805)

COW Industries Inc............................... E 614 443-6537
  Columbus (G-4854)

Crest Craft Co....................................... F 513 271-4858
  Cincinnati (G-2525)

Custom Fabrication By Fisher................. G 513 738-4600
  Okeana (G-10928)

DA Precision Products Inc...................... F 513 459-1113
  West Chester (G-13981)

▲ Dern Trophies Corp.......................... G 614 895-3260
  Westerville (G-14207)

◆ Df Supply Inc................................... E 330 650-9226
  Twinsburg (G-13294)

Die-Cut Products Co............................. F 216 771-6994
  Cleveland (G-3615)

Diebold Nixdorf Incorporated................. C 740 928-1010
  Hebron (G-7612)

Diebold Nixdorf Incorporated................. A 330 490-4000
  North Canton (G-10635)

Donald E Didion II................................. E 419 483-2226
  Bellevue (G-1123)

Dubose Strapping Inc............................ E 419 221-0626
  Lima (G-8404)

▲ Dura Magnetics Inc.......................... F 419 882-0591
  Sylvania (G-12706)

▼ Eastern Automated Piping................. G 740 535-8184
  Mingo Junction (G-10050)

Exair LLC.. E 513 671-3322
  Cincinnati (G-2608)

EZ Grout Corporation Inc...................... E 740 962-2024
  Malta (G-8745)

Fabricating Solutions Inc....................... F 330 486-0998
  Twinsburg (G-13301)

◆ Flexmag Industries Inc...................... D 740 373-3492
  Marietta (G-8917)

Forgeo LLC... E 614 873-7030
  Plain City (G-11408)

Fountain Specialists Inc........................ G 513 831-5717
  Milford (G-9934)

Frame Warehouse.................................. G 614 861-4582
  Reynoldsburg (G-11570)

GCI Metals Inc...................................... F 937 835-7123
  Wilmington (G-14582)

General Metals Powder Co LLC.............. E 330 633-1226
  Akron (G-160)

Gerdau Ameristeel US Inc..................... G 740 671-9410
  Bellaire (G-1087)

▲ Hamilton Safe Co............................. F 513 874-3733
  Milford (G-9938)

▲ Hamilton Security Products Co........... E 513 874-3733
  Milford (G-9939)

Hit Trophy Inc....................................... G 419 445-5356
  Archbold (G-498)

IBI Brake Products Inc........................... G 440 543-7962
  Chagrin Falls (G-2166)

Infinite Energy Mfg LLC......................... F 440 759-5920
  Cleveland (G-3858)

◆ Jay Mid-South LLC............................ G 256 439-6600
  Mansfield (G-8807)

Jfdb Ltd... C 513 870-0601
  Cincinnati (G-2766)

Johnson Mfg Systems LLC..................... F 937 866-4744
  Miamisburg (G-9704)

Kard Welding Inc................................... E 419 628-2598
  Minster (G-10059)

Karyall-Telday Inc.................................. G 216 281-4063
  Cleveland (G-3906)

Ksm Metal Fabrication........................... F 937 339-6366
  Troy (G-13235)

Labcraft Inc.. E 419 878-4400
  Waterville (G-13838)

Lewark Metal Spinning Inc..................... E 937 275-3303
  Dayton (G-5845)

Linsalata Cpitl Prtners Fund I................. G 440 684-1400
  Cleveland (G-3962)

▼ Magnum Magnetics Corporation......... D 740 373-7770
  Marietta (G-8926)

MAK Fabricating Inc.............................. F 330 747-0040
  Youngstown (G-14894)

Mandrel Group LLC............................... F 330 881-1266
  Mc Donald (G-9359)

◆ Mansfield Engineered Comp.............. C 419 524-1300
  Mansfield (G-8819)

Mansfield Welding Service LLC.............. G 419 594-2738
  Oakwood (G-10898)

Mast Farm Service Ltd.......................... G 330 893-2972
  Walnut Creek (G-13694)

McIntosh Safe Corp.............................. F 937 222-7008
  Dayton (G-5871)

McNeil Group Inc.................................. E 614 298-0300
  Columbus (G-5093)

Midwest Strapping Products.................. G 614 527-1454
  Columbus (G-5101)

▲ North Shore Strapping Company......... E 216 661-5200
  Brooklyn Heights (G-1536)

▲ Nostalgic Images Inc........................ E 419 784-1728
  Defiance (G-6122)

◆ Ohio Gasket and Shim Co Inc............ E 330 630-0626
  Akron (G-252)

▲ Ohio Magnetics Inc.......................... E 216 662-8484
  Maple Heights (G-8888)

Organized Living................................... G 513 277-3700
  Cincinnati (G-2938)

Penny Fab LLC...................................... F 740 967-3669
  Columbus (G-5184)

◆ Peter Graham Dunn Inc..................... G 330 816-0035
  Dalton (G-5592)

Pfi USA... F 937 547-0413
  Greenville (G-7349)

▼ Projects Designed & Built.................. E 419 726-7400
  Toledo (G-13104)

PS Superior Inc.................................... G 216 587-1000
  Cleveland (G-4204)

Pucel Enterprises Inc............................ E 216 881-4604
  Cleveland (G-4206)

Pucel Enterprises Inc............................ G 800 336-4986
  Cleveland (G-4207)

Quest Technologies Inc......................... F 937 743-1200
  Franklin (G-7044)

R L Torbeck Industries Inc..................... G 513 367-0080
  Harrison (G-7565)

Rise Holdings LLC................................ F 440 946-9646
  Willoughby (G-14519)

Rmi Titanium Company LLC................... B 330 455-4010
  Canton (G-1999)

Seaway Bolt And Specials Company...... D 440 236-5015
  Columbia Station (G-4602)

Sharonco Inc.. G 419 882-3443
  Sylvania (G-12723)

Shim Shack... G 877 557-3930
  Harrison (G-7567)

▲ SK Wellman Corp.............................. C 440 528-4000
  Solon (G-12181)

Target Holdings Inc............................... E 513 474-4409
  Cincinnati (G-3138)

Tengam Pro Inc..................................... F 740 373-0909
  Marietta (G-8052)

Tribco Incorporated............................... E 216 486-2000
  Cleveland (G-4421)

Vortec Corporation................................ E 513 891-7485
  Blue Ash (G-1348)

◆ Voss Industries LLC.......................... C 216 771-7655
  Cleveland (G-4482)

Voyale Minority Enterprise LLC.............. E 216 271-3661
  Cleveland (G-4483)

◆ Walker National Inc........................... E 614 492-1614
  Columbus (G-5353)

◆ Wellman Products LLC....................... B 855 403-9083
  Medina (G-9463)

Williamson Safe Inc............................... G 937 393-9919
  Hillsboro (G-7729)

▲ Winkle Industries Inc........................ D 330 823-9730
  Alliance (G-418)

Wpc Successor Inc................................ F 937 233-6141
  Tipp City (G-12855)

Yarder Manufacturing Company............. E 419 476-3933
  Toledo (G-13182)

Zeda Inc... F 513 966-4633
  Cincinnati (G-3241)

35 INDUSTRIAL AND COMMERCIAL MACHINERY AND COMPUTER EQUIPMENT

3511 Turbines and turbine generator sets

Alin Machining Company Inc................. D 740 223-0200
Marion *(G-8964)*

Babcock & Wilcox Company.................. E 740 687-6500
Lancaster *(G-8178)*

Babcock & Wilcox Entps Inc.................. E 740 687-4370
Lancaster *(G-8179)*

Babcock & Wilcox Holdings LLC.......... A 330 453-4511
Akron *(G-69)*

Bwx Technologies Inc......................... D 740 687-4180
Lancaster *(G-8183)*

Canvus Inc.. E 216 340-7500
Rocky River *(G-11632)*

◆ Diamond Power Intl Inc....................D 740 687-6500
Lancaster *(G-8198)*

Eaton Leasing Corporation.................. B 216 382-2292
Beachwood *(G-916)*

Fluid System Service Inc..................... G 216 651-2450
Cleveland *(G-3728)*

Fluidpower Assembly Inc...................... G 419 394-7486
Saint Marys *(G-11737)*

Great Lakes Turbines Inc.................... G 419 705-0490
Holland *(G-7765)*

◆ Mendenhall Technical Services Inc.....E 513 860-1280
Fairfield *(G-6754)*

◆ Metalex Manufacturing Inc................C 513 489-0507
Blue Ash *(G-1310)*

▲ Miba Bearings US LLC...................... B 740 962-4242
Mcconnelsville *(G-9364)*

Muller Engine & Machine Co................ G 937 322-1861
Springfield *(G-12354)*

Onpower Inc...................................... E 513 228-2100
Lebanon *(G-8280)*

Pfpc Enterprises Inc........................... G 513 941-6200
Cincinnati *(G-2960)*

▲ Powder Alloy Corporation................. E 513 984-4016
Loveland *(G-8646)*

Precision Castparts Corp..................... F 440 350-6150
Painesville *(G-11106)*

R H Industries Inc............................. E 216 281-5210
Cleveland *(G-4221)*

◆ Rolls-Royce Energy Systems Inc........A 703 834-1700
Mount Vernon *(G-10263)*

Siemens Energy Inc........................... G 740 504-1947
Mount Vernon *(G-10265)*

Steam Trbine Altrntive Rsrces.............. E 740 387-5535
Marion *(G-9001)*

3519 Internal combustion engines, nec

▲ American Fine Sinter Co Ltd............ C 419 443-8880
Tiffin *(G-12774)*

B A Malcuit Racing Inc....................... G 330 878-7111
Strasburg *(G-12476)*

Bowden Manufacturing Corp................ E 440 946-1770
Willoughby *(G-14432)*

Brinkley Technology Group LLC.......... F 330 830-2498
Massillon *(G-9175)*

Chemequip Sales Inc......................... E 330 724-8300
Coventry Township *(G-5481)*

Clarke Fire Prtection Pdts Inc.............. F 513 771-2200
West Chester *(G-14111)*

Country Sales & Service LLC.............. F 330 683-2500
Orrville *(G-10978)*

Cummins - Allison Corp...................... G 513 469-2924
Blue Ash *(G-1266)*

Cummins - Allison Corp...................... G 440 824-5050
Cleveland *(G-3579)*

Cummins Inc..................................... F 614 604-6004
Grove City *(G-7379)*

Cummins Inc..................................... F 614 771-1000
Hilliard *(G-7679)*

◆ Detroit Desl Rmnfctrng-Ast Inc.........B 740 439-7701
Byesville *(G-1709)*

Detroit Desl Rmnufacturing LLC.......... C 740 439-7701
Cambridge *(G-1741)*

◆ Dmax Ltd..D 937 425-9700
Moraine *(G-10157)*

▲ DW Hercules LLC............................ G 330 830-2498
Massillon *(G-9187)*

Enjet Aero Dayton Inc........................ E 937 878-3800
Huber Heights *(G-7821)*

Ford Motor Company.......................... A 419 226-7000
Lima *(G-8408)*

GE Honda Aero Engines LLC.............. F 513 552-4322
West Chester *(G-14006)*

▲ General Engine Products LLC............ D 937 704-0160
Franklin *(G-7024)*

▲ Hy-Production LLC............................ C 330 273-2400
Valley City *(G-13499)*

Industrial Parts Depot LLC.................. G 440 237-9164
North Royalton *(G-10766)*

◆ Jatrodiesel Inc.................................F
Miamisburg *(G-9703)*

Kinstle Truck & Auto Svc Inc.............. G 419 738-7493
Wapakoneta *(G-13718)*

Maags Automotive & Mch Inc.............. G 419 626-1539
Sandusky *(G-11853)*

▲ Miba Bearings US LLC...................... B 740 962-4242
Mcconnelsville *(G-9364)*

▲ Miscor Group Ltd.............................. B 330 830-3500
Massillon *(G-9224)*

Performace Diesel Inc........................ F 740 392-3693
Mount Vernon *(G-10258)*

Performance Research Inc.................. G 614 475-8300
Columbus *(G-5187)*

Precision Castparts Corp..................... F 440 350-6150
Painesville *(G-11106)*

Western Branch Diesel LLC................. F 330 454-8800
Canton *(G-2047)*

3523 Farm machinery and equipment

Afs Technology LLC........................... F 937 545-0627
Dayton *(G-5641)*

American Baler Co............................. D 419 483-5790
Bellevue *(G-1119)*

Birds Eye Foods Inc.......................... D 330 854-0818
Canal Fulton *(G-1773)*

Cailin Development LLC...................... F 216 408-6261
Cleveland *(G-3459)*

◆ Chick Master Incubator Company.......D 330 722-5591
Medina *(G-9387)*

Country Manufacturing Inc.................. F 740 694-9926
Fredericktown *(G-7075)*

Creamer Metal Products Inc................ F 740 852-1752
London *(G-8534)*

Empire Plow Company Inc.................. E 216 641-2290
Berea *(G-1169)*

Fecon LLC.. E 513 696-4430
Lebanon *(G-8256)*

▲ Fecon LLC....................................... D 513 696-4430
Lebanon *(G-8257)*

Field Gymmy Inc............................... G 419 538-6511
Glandorf *(G-7283)*

◆ Finn Corporation..............................E 513 874-2818
West Chester *(G-13997)*

Flying Dutchman Inc.......................... G 330 669-2297
Smithville *(G-12065)*

◆ Fort Recovery Equipment Inc.............G 419 375-1006
Fort Recovery *(G-6962)*

Fremont Plastic Products Inc............... C 419 332-6407
Fremont *(G-7111)*

Gerald Grain Center Inc..................... F 419 445-2451
Archbold *(G-495)*

▲ Hawkline Nevada LLC....................... G 937 444-4295
Mount Orab *(G-10217)*

Heintz Farms Enterprise Partnr........... G 937 464-2535
Belle Center *(G-1095)*

Hershy Way Ltd................................. G 330 893-2809
Millersburg *(G-9984)*

Hog Slat Incorporated........................ E 937 968-3890
Union City *(G-13415)*

◆ Intertec Corporation.........................F 419 537-9711
Toledo *(G-13007)*

◆ J & M Manufacturing Co Inc..............C 419 375-2376
Fort Recovery *(G-6967)*

Kriss Kreations................................. G 330 405-6102
Twinsburg *(G-13326)*

Kts Equipment Inc............................. E 440 647-2015
Wellington *(G-13895)*

Ley Industries Inc.............................. G 419 238-6742
Van Wert *(G-13541)*

M & S AG Solutions LLC.................... F 419 598-8675
Napoleon *(G-10290)*

Norden Mfg LLC................................ E 440 693-4630
North Bloomfield *(G-10625)*

Ntech Industries Inc........................... G 707 467-3747
Dayton *(G-5917)*

◆ Ohio Machinery Co...........................C 440 526-6200
Broadview Heights *(G-1509)*

Precision Assemblies Inc.................... F 330 549-2630
North Lima *(G-10710)*

Randall Richard & Moore LLC............ E 330 455-8873
Canton *(G-1991)*

▲ Remlinger Manufacturing Co Inc........ E 419 532-3647
Kalida *(G-8005)*

▲ Rhinestahl Corporation..................... D 513 489-1317
Mason *(G-9144)*

Rld Transportation LLC....................... F 234 334-7777
North Canton *(G-10664)*

▲ S I Distributing Inc........................... F 419 647-4909
Spencerville *(G-12240)*

Safe-Grain Inc................................... G 513 398-2500
Dayton *(G-5992)*

Seppi M SPA.................................... G 513 443-6339
West Chester *(G-14075)*

Shearer Farm Inc.............................. C 330 345-9023
Wooster *(G-14685)*

Stein-Way Equipment......................... G 330 857-8700
Apple Creek *(G-478)*

Stephens Pipe & Steel LLC................. C 740 869-2257
Mount Sterling *(G-10229)*

◆ Sweet Manufacturing Company..........E 937 325-1511
Springfield *(G-12381)*

TD Landscape Inc.............................. F 740 694-0244
Fredericktown *(G-7085)*

◆ Unverferth Mfg Co Inc......................C 419 532-3121
Kalida *(G-8007)*

▲ Val-Co Pax Inc................................. D 717 354-4586
Coldwater *(G-4586)*

Yoder & Frey Inc............................... G 419 445-2070
Archbold *(G-513)*

3524 Lawn and garden equipment

◆ Arnold Corporation...........................C 330 225-2600
Valley City *(G-13489)*

Cannon Salt & Supply Inc................... G 440 232-1700
Bedford *(G-1019)*

Commercial Turf Products Ltd.............. F 330 995-7000
Streetsboro *(G-12494)*

▲ Cub Cadet Corporation Sales............ D 330 273-4550
Valley City *(G-13494)*

Dinsmore Inc................................ G 937 544-3332
West Union *(G-14190)*

▲ Elan Designs Inc.......................... G 614 985-5600
Westerville *(G-14258)*

Erosion Control Products Corp........... F 302 815-6500
West Chester *(G-13994)*

Extrudex Limited Partnership............. E 440 352-7101
Painesville *(G-11085)*

◆ Finn Corporation.......................... E 513 874-2818
West Chester *(G-13997)*

Franklin Equipment LLC.................. E 614 228-2014
Groveport *(G-7435)*

◆ Gardner Inc................................C 614 456-4000
Columbus *(G-4945)*

Hawthorne Gardening Company.......... E 360 883-8846
Marysville *(G-9023)*

Johnson & Johnson Services LLC........ F 513 289-4514
Cincinnati *(G-2770)*

Karl Kuemmerling Inc..................... F
Massillon *(G-9209)*

Koenig Equipment Inc.................... F 937 653-5281
Urbana *(G-13472)*

Mm Service................................. G 330 626-2520
Streetsboro *(G-12511)*

Mo-Trim Inc................................ G 740 439-2725
Cambridge *(G-1750)*

▼ Mtd Consumer Group Inc................ C 330 225-2600
Valley City *(G-13507)*

◆ Mtd Holdings Inc.........................B 330 225-2600
Valley City *(G-13508)*

Mtd International Operations............. G 330 225-2600
Valley City *(G-13509)*

Mtd Products Inc........................... C 419 342-6455
Shelby *(G-11971)*

Mtd Products Inc........................... C 330 225-1940
Valley City *(G-13511)*

Mtd Products Inc........................... C 330 225-9127
Valley City *(G-13512)*

Mtd Products Inc........................... G 419 951-9779
Willard *(G-14405)*

Mtd Products Inc........................... A 419 935-6611
Willard *(G-14406)*

◆ Mtd Products Inc.........................B 330 225-2600
Valley City *(G-13510)*

◆ Oase North America Inc................. G 800 365-3880
Aurora *(G-682)*

◆ Park-Ohio Holdings Corp...............F 440 947-2000
Cleveland *(G-4136)*

Park-Ohio Industries Inc.................. C 440 947-2000
Cleveland *(G-4137)*

▲ Power Distributors LLC.................. D 614 876-3533
Columbus *(G-5200)*

Rotoline USA LLC.......................... G 330 677-3223
Kent *(G-8071)*

Russell Hunt................................ F 740 264-1196
Steubenville *(G-12410)*

◆ Scotts Company LLC.....................C 937 644-0011
Marysville *(G-9045)*

Scotts Temecula Operations LLC......... G 800 221-1760
Marysville *(G-9048)*

Smg Growing Media Inc................... F 937 644-0011
Marysville *(G-9049)*

◆ Speed North America Inc................ E 330 202-7775
Wooster *(G-14688)*

Tierra-Derco International LLC............ G 419 929-2240
New London *(G-10418)*

▲ Venture Products Inc.................... G 330 683-0075
Orrville *(G-11016)*

3531 Construction machinery

1062 Technologies Inc.................... G 303 453-9251
Youngstown *(G-14799)*

2e Associates Inc......................... E 440 975-9955
Willoughby *(G-14412)*

▲ A JC Inc.................................. F 800 428-2438
Hudson *(G-7826)*

ACS Industries Inc........................ D 330 678-2511
Kent *(G-8013)*

▼ Aim Attachments......................... G 614 539-3030
Grove City *(G-7369)*

Allied Consolidated Inds Inc............. C 330 744-0808
Youngstown *(G-14808)*

Allied Industrial Dev Corp............... E 724 346-1984
Youngstown *(G-14809)*

Altec Industries........................... G 419 289-6066
Ashland *(G-515)*

Altec Industries Inc....................... F 205 408-2341
Cuyahoga Falls *(G-5521)*

▲ American Alloy Corporation............. E 216 642-9638
Cleveland *(G-3340)*

American Highway Products LLC.......... F 330 874-3270
Bolivar *(G-1381)*

◆ American Power Pull Corp...............G 419 335-7050
Archbold *(G-485)*

▲ Ballinger Industries Inc................. E 419 422-4533
Findlay *(G-6842)*

▲ Barbco Inc................................ E 330 488-9400
East Canton *(G-6377)*

Basetek LLC................................ F 877 712-2273
Middlefield *(G-9781)*

Brewpro Inc................................ G 513 577-7200
Cincinnati *(G-2423)*

Brian Hosher Backhoe Plum.............. G 740 503-4434
Baltimore *(G-783)*

◆ Buck Equipment Inc..................... G 614 539-3039
Grove City *(G-7375)*

◆ Bucyrus Blades Inc......................C 419 562-6015
Bucyrus *(G-1672)*

Caterpillar Industrial Inc................. G 440 247-8484
Chagrin Falls *(G-2138)*

◆ Chemineer Inc.............................C 937 454-3200
Dayton *(G-5700)*

Cityscapes International Inc.............. G 614 850-2540
Hilliard *(G-7677)*

Coe Manufacturing Company............. E 440 352-9381
Painesville *(G-11072)*

Concord Road Equipment Mfg Inc........ E 440 357-5344
Painesville *(G-11073)*

Concord Road Equipment Mfg LLC....... E 440 357-5344
Mentor *(G-9504)*

Crh US..................................... G 216 642-3920
Independence *(G-7896)*

Curtis Industires.......................... F 216 430-5759
Cleveland *(G-3582)*

CW Machine Worx Ltd..................... F 740 654-5304
Carroll *(G-2074)*

D & L Excavating Ltd..................... G 419 271-0635
Port Clinton *(G-11440)*

DA Precision Products Inc................ F 513 459-1113
West Chester *(G-13981)*

Desco Corporation........................ G 614 888-8855
New Albany *(G-10339)*

Dimensional Metals Inc................... E 740 927-3633
Reynoldsburg *(G-11565)*

Dragon Products LLC...................... E 330 345-3968
Wooster *(G-14635)*

▲ Drc Acquisition Inc...................... E 330 656-1600
Streetsboro *(G-12498)*

Driven Excavating LLC.................... E 567 224-1421
Crestline *(G-5501)*

Duplex Mill & Manufacturing Co.......... E 937 325-5555
Springfield *(G-12304)*

Dynamic Plastics Inc...................... G 937 437-7261
New Paris *(G-10426)*

◆ E R Advanced Ceramics Inc..............E 330 426-9433
East Palestine *(G-6402)*

▲ E Z Grout Corporation................... E 740 749-3512
Malta *(G-8744)*

Eagle Crusher Co Inc..................... D 419 562-1183
Bucyrus *(G-1679)*

◆ Eagle Crusher Co Inc....................D 419 468-2288
Galion *(G-7187)*

Enviri Corporation........................ F 740 387-1150
Marion *(G-8969)*

▲ Fabco Inc................................. D 419 422-4533
Findlay *(G-6862)*

▲ Fecon LLC................................ D 513 696-4430
Lebanon *(G-8257)*

Field Gymmy Inc.......................... G 419 538-6511
Glandorf *(G-7283)*

▲ Fives St Corp............................. E 234 217-9070
Wadsworth *(G-13638)*

◆ Forge Industries Inc..................... A 330 960-2468
Youngstown *(G-14857)*

G & T Manufacturing Co.................. F 440 639-7777
Mentor *(G-9522)*

Geauga Highway Co....................... F 440 834-4580
Windham *(G-14600)*

Gledhill Road Machinery Co.............. E 419 468-4400
Galion *(G-7193)*

◆ Global TBM Company.....................C 440 248-3303
Solon *(G-12117)*

▲ Gradall Industries LLC................... D 330 339-2211
New Philadelphia *(G-10448)*

Grand Archt Etrnl Eye 314 LLC........... F 800 377-8147
Cleveland *(G-3783)*

Grand Harbor Yacht Sales & Svc......... G 440 442-2919
Cleveland *(G-3784)*

▼ Grasan Equipment Company Inc........ D 419 526-4440
Mansfield *(G-8797)*

Hickmans Construction Co LLC........... F 866 271-2565
Euclid *(G-6653)*

▲ Hudco Manufacturing Inc................ G 440 951-4040
Willoughby *(G-14465)*

Ironhawk Industrial Dist LLC............. G 216 502-3700
Euclid *(G-6656)*

JB Pavers and Hardscapes LLC.......... G 937 454-1145
Vandalia *(G-13564)*

Jbw Systems Inc.......................... F 614 882-5008
Westerville *(G-14213)*

Jcl Equipment Co Inc..................... G 937 374-1010
Xenia *(G-14767)*

▲ Jennmar McSweeney LLC.................C 740 377-3354
South Point *(G-12224)*

Jlg Industries Inc......................... E 330 684-0132
Orrville *(G-10988)*

Jlg Industries Inc......................... D 330 684-0200
Orrville *(G-10989)*

Jordankelly LLC........................... F 216 855-8550
Akron *(G-187)*

▲ Jrb Attachments LLC..................... G 330 734-3000
Akron *(G-188)*

◆ Jrb Family Holdings Inc..................C
Wooster *(G-14656)*

Kaffenbarger Truck Eqp Co............... E 513 772-6800
Cincinnati *(G-2777)*

Kubota Tractor Corporation.............. E 614 835-3800
Groveport *(G-7442)*

▲ Kundel Industries Inc.................... D 330 469-6147
Vienna *(G-13609)*

Lake Township Trustees.................. E 419 836-1143
Millbury *(G-9963)*

Liverpool Township....................... G 330 483-4747
Valley City *(G-13502)*

Employee Codes: A=Over 500 employees, B=251-500
C=101-250, D=51-100, E=20-50, F=10-19, G=1-9   2025 Harris Ohio
Industrial Directory   831

Malta Dynamics LLC................................F 740 749-3512
   Waterford (G-13828)

▲ McSweeneys Inc..................................C 740 894-3353
   South Point (G-12228)

Mesa Industries Inc...............................F 513 999-9781
   Cincinnati (G-2867)

◆ Mesa Industries Inc............................E 513 321-2950
   Cincinnati (G-2866)

Meyer Products LLC...............................E 216 486-1313
   Cleveland (G-4024)

◆ Meyer Products LLC...........................D 216 486-1313
   Steubenville (G-12406)

Michael Byrne Manufacturing Co Inc.....E 419 525-1214
   Mansfield (G-8825)

▲ Minnich Manufacturing Co Inc...........E 419 903-0010
   Mansfield (G-8829)

Morbark LLC...C 330 264-8699
   Wooster (G-14666)

Murphy Tractor & Eqp Co Inc................G 330 220-4999
   Brunswick (G-1602)

Murphy Tractor & Eqp Co Inc................G 330 477-9304
   Canton (G-1954)

Murphy Tractor & Eqp Co Inc................G 614 876-1141
   Columbus (G-5116)

Murphy Tractor & Eqp Co Inc................G 419 221-3666
   Lima (G-8434)

Murphy Tractor & Eqp Co Inc................G 937 898-4198
   Vandalia (G-13573)

Nick Kostecki Excavating Inc.................E 330 242-0706
   Spencer (G-12234)

Norris Manufacturing LLC......................F 330 602-5005
   Dover (G-6256)

Nov Inc..D 937 454-3200
   Dayton (G-5915)

◆ Npk Construction Equipment Inc........D 440 232-7900
   Bedford (G-1050)

Otc Industrial Technologies....................F 800 837-6827
   Columbus (G-5165)

◆ Pace Consolidated Inc........................D 440 942-1234
   Willoughby (G-14503)

Pace Engineering Inc.............................C 440 942-1234
   Willoughby (G-14504)

Powerbilt Mtl Hdlg Sltions LLC..............D 937 592-5660
   Bellefontaine (G-1115)

◆ Pubco Corporation..............................D 216 881-5300
   Cleveland (G-4205)

Quikstir Inc..G 419 732-2601
   Port Clinton (G-11449)

Railroad Tools & Solutions Inc...............G 513 533-7070
   Cincinnati (G-3031)

Richland Township Bd Trustees..............F 419 358-4897
   Bluffton (G-1363)

▲ Rnm Holdings Inc................................E 937 704-9900
   Franklin (G-7046)

Roadsafe Traffic Systems Inc.................G 614 274-9782
   Columbus (G-5234)

Sandvik Rock Proc Sltons N AME..........F 216 431-2600
   Cleveland (G-4273)

◆ Sandvik Rock Proc Sltons N AME.......E 216 431-2600
   Cleveland (G-4274)

Sciath Aim Forge Inc.............................G 574 933-3479
   Cincinnati (G-3069)

Snow Dragon LLC..................................F 440 295-0238
   Cleveland (G-4309)

Splendid LLC..F 614 396-6481
   Columbus (G-5285)

Terex Utilities Inc...................................F 419 470-8408
   Perrysburg (G-11270)

▼ Tgs Industries Inc...............................E 330 339-2211
   New Philadelphia (G-10466)

The Wagner-Smith Company...................B 866 338-0398
   Moraine (G-10195)

◆ Thorworks Industries Inc.....................C 419 626-4375
   Sandusky (G-11876)

▲ Toku America Inc.................................F 440 954-9923
   Willoughby (G-14540)

Turn-Key Tunneling Inc..........................E 614 275-4832
   Columbus (G-5335)

▲ Uhrden Inc...E 330 456-0031
   Canton (G-2030)

Valence Industrial LLC...........................E 877 330-2354
   Sidney (G-12058)

Wellpoint...G 614 771-9600
   Worthington (G-14728)

Werk-Brau Company...............................C 419 422-2912
   Findlay (G-6934)

▲ Werk-Brau Company............................C 419 422-2912
   Findlay (G-6933)

◆ Winter Equipment Company ....E 440 946-8377
   Willoughby (G-14552)

Wonderly Trucking & Excvtg LLC...........F 419 837-6294
   Perrysburg (G-11281)

Y O H Inc...E 614 488-2861
   Columbus (G-5377)

3532 Mining machinery

▲ Belle Center Air Tool Co Inc...............G 937 464-7474
   Belle Center (G-1094)

Bowdil Company.....................................F 800 356-8663
   Canton (G-1843)

Breaker Technology Inc..........................F 440 248-7168
   Solon (G-12090)

▼ Brydet Development Corporation.........G 740 623-0455
   Coshocton (G-5452)

Cailin Development LLC..........................F 216 408-6261
   Cleveland (G-3459)

Carr Tool Company.................................F 513 825-2900
   Fairfield (G-6717)

Charles Machine Works Inc....................D 800 324-4930
   West Salem (G-14187)

Cleveland Vibrator Company...................G 800 221-3298
   Cleveland (G-3529)

Cool Machines Inc..................................F 419 232-4871
   Van Wert (G-13529)

▲ Davey Kent Inc....................................E 330 673-5400
   Kent (G-8025)

Dover Conveyor Inc................................E 740 922-9390
   Midvale (G-9908)

◆ Eagle Crusher Co Inc..........................D 419 468-2288
   Galion (G-7187)

Engines Inc of Ohio................................E 740 377-9874
   South Point (G-12223)

Epiroc USA LLC......................................F 717 552-8488
   Akron (G-137)

Epiroc USA LLC......................................F 844 437-4762
   Independence (G-7902)

▼ Grasan Equipment Company Inc........D 419 526-4440
   Mansfield (G-8797)

▲ Irock Crushers LLC.............................E 866 240-0201
   Cleveland (G-3870)

▲ Jennmar McSweeney LLC....................C 740 377-3354
   South Point (G-12224)

▲ Joy Global Underground Min LLC........C 440 248-7970
   Solon (G-12132)

Kaffenbarger Truck Eqp Co....................E 513 772-6800
   Cincinnati (G-2777)

Kennametal Inc.......................................C 440 349-5151
   Solon (G-12138)

Komatsu Mining Corp.............................C 216 503-5029
   Independence (G-7906)

Maag Automatik Inc................................E 330 677-2225
   Kent (G-8047)

▲ McSweeneys Inc..................................C 740 894-3353
   South Point (G-12228)

Nolan Company......................................G 740 269-1512
   Bowerston (G-1400)

Nolan Company......................................F 330 453-7922
   Canton (G-1958)

◆ Npk Construction Equipment Inc........D 440 232-7900
   Bedford (G-1050)

Penn Machine Company LLC...................D 814 288-1547
   Twinsburg (G-13351)

◆ Reduction Engineering Inc..................E 330 677-2225
   Kent (G-8067)

▲ Siebtechnik Tema Inc..........................E 513 489-7811
   Cincinnati (G-3088)

Strata Mine Services Inc........................G 740 695-6880
   Saint Clairsville (G-11712)

▲ Uhrden Inc...E 330 456-0031
   Canton (G-2030)

◆ Warren Fabricating Corporation..........D 330 534-5017
   Hubbard (G-7818)

Zen Industries Inc..................................E 216 432-3240
   Cleveland (G-4523)

3533 Oil and gas field machinery

Allied Machine Works Inc.......................G 740 454-2534
   Zanesville (G-14986)

Black Gold Capital LLC...........................E 614 348-7460
   Columbus (G-4761)

Buckeye Companies.................................E 740 452-3641
   Zanesville (G-15000)

Buckeye Oil Equipment Co.....................F 937 387-0671
   Dayton (G-5687)

Cameron International Corp.....................E 740 654-4260
   Lancaster (G-8185)

Edi Holding Company LLC......................G 740 401-4000
   Belpre (G-1146)

Electrnic Dsign For Indust Inc................E 740 401-4000
   Belpre (G-1147)

◆ Furukawa Rock Drill Usa Inc..............F 330 673-5826
   Kent (G-8033)

H P E Inc...G 330 833-3161
   Massillon (G-9199)

Jet Rubber Company...............................E 330 325-1821
   Rootstown (G-11648)

◆ Multi Products Company......................F 330 674-5981
   Millersburg (G-10003)

OSI Environmental LLC..........................E 440 237-4600
   North Royalton (G-10779)

Pride of The Hills Manufacturing Inc......D 330 567-3108
   Big Prairie (G-1217)

Rampp Company.....................................E 740 373-7886
   Marietta (G-8940)

▲ Reberland Equipment Inc....................F 330 698-5883
   Apple Creek (G-476)

◆ Rmi Titanium Company LLC................E 330 652-9952
   Niles (G-10604)

Robbins & Myers Inc..............................G 937 454-3200
   Dayton (G-5986)

◆ Saint-Gobain Norpro Corp..................C 330 673-5860
   Stow (G-12458)

◆ Terra Sonic International LLC..............E 740 374-6608
   Marietta (G-8953)

Tiger General LLC..................................F 330 239-4949
   Medina (G-9456)

Timco Inc...G 740 685-2594
   Byesville (G-1716)

3534 Elevators and moving stairways

▲ Adams Elevator Equipment Co...........D 847 581-2900
   Holland (G-7743)

Avt Beckett Elevators USA Inc...............G 844 360-0288
   Logan (G-8509)

▼ Benko Products Inc.............................E 440 934-2180
   Sheffield Village (G-11957)

◆ Canton Elevator Inc..................D 330 833-3600
North Canton *(G-10632)*

Dasher Lawless Automation LLC.......... E 855 755-7275
Warren *(G-13757)*

▲ Elevator Cncepts By Wurtec LLC...... F 734 246-4700
Toledo *(G-12950)*

▲ Federal Equipment Company............ D 513 621-5260
Cincinnati *(G-2616)*

Gray-Eering Ltd............................ G 740 498-8816
Tippecanoe *(G-12858)*

Heartland Stairways Inc.................... G 330 279-2554
Holmesville *(G-7795)*

Holmes Stair Parts Ltd.................... E 330 279-2797
Holmesville *(G-7798)*

Otis Elevator Company.................... E 216 573-2333
Cleveland *(G-4127)*

Schindler Elevator Corporation............. E 419 861-5900
Holland *(G-7783)*

Schindler Elevator Corporation............. C 937 492-3186
Sidney *(G-12048)*

◆ Sweet Manufacturing Company........ E 937 325-1511
Springfield *(G-12381)*

Versalift East Inc......................... C 610 866-1400
Canton *(G-2042)*

◆ Wittur Usa Inc...........................E 216 524-0100
Twinsburg *(G-13396)*

3535 Conveyors and conveying equipment

2e Associates Inc.......................... E 440 975-9955
Willoughby *(G-14412)*

◆ Ad Industries Inc.........................A 303 744-1911
Dayton *(G-5634)*

Advanced Equipment Systems LLC....... G 216 289-6505
Euclid *(G-6638)*

◆ Air Technical Industries Inc............E 440 951-5191
Mentor *(G-9474)*

Alan Bortree.............................. G 937 585-6962
De Graff *(G-6091)*

Alba Manufacturing Inc.....................D 513 874-0551
Fairfield *(G-6708)*

▲ Allgaier Process Technology........... G 513 402-2566
West Chester *(G-13937)*

Allied Consolidated Inds Inc............. C 330 744-0808
Youngstown *(G-14808)*

Allied Fabricating & Wldg Co............. E 614 868-8680
Columbus *(G-4687)*

Ambaflex Inc.............................. G 330 478-1858
Canton *(G-1829)*

▲ American Solving Inc.................... G 440 234-7373
Brookpark *(G-1543)*

Automation Systems Design Inc.......... E 937 387-0351
Dayton *(G-5669)*

▲ Barth Industries Co LLC................. E 216 267-1950
Cleveland *(G-3407)*

Bavis Fabacraft Inc....................... E 513 677-0500
Maineville *(G-8738)*

◆ Blair Rubber Company....................D 330 769-5583
Seville *(G-11911)*

Bobco Enterprises Inc.................... F 419 867-3560
Toledo *(G-12899)*

◆ Bry-Air Inc...............................E 740 965-2974
Sunbury *(G-12662)*

Bulk Handling Equipment Co.............. G 330 468-5703
Northfield *(G-10792)*

▲ C A Litzler Co Inc........................ E 216 267-8020
Cleveland *(G-3457)*

▲ Cincinnati Mine Machinery Co.......... E 513 522-7777
Cincinnati *(G-2482)*

Coating Systems Group Inc.............. F 440 816-9306
Middleburg Heights *(G-9768)*

Con-Belt Inc.............................. F 330 273-2003
Valley City *(G-13492)*

Conveyor Metal Works Inc................. E 740 477-8700
Frankfort *(G-7004)*

Conveyor Solutions LLC................... F 513 367-4845
Cleves *(G-4533)*

Conveyor Technologies Ltd................ G 513 248-0663
Milford *(G-9931)*

Coperion Process Solutions LLC.......... F 513 576-9200
Solon *(G-12098)*

▲ Daifuku America Corporation........... C 614 863-1888
Reynoldsburg *(G-11564)*

Decision Systems Inc..................... F 330 456-7600
Canton *(G-1879)*

Defabco Inc............................... D 614 231-2700
Columbus *(G-4875)*

Dematic Corp............................. D 440 526-2770
Brecksville *(G-1462)*

Dillin Engineered Systems Corp........... E 419 666-6789
Perrysburg *(G-11216)*

Dover Conveyor Inc....................... E 740 922-9390
Midvale *(G-9908)*

Duplex Mill & Manufacturing Co.......... E 937 325-5555
Springfield *(G-12304)*

◆ Eagle Crusher Co Inc....................D 419 468-2288
Galion *(G-7187)*

Enviri Corporation........................ F 740 387-1150
Marion *(G-8969)*

Esco Turbine Tech Cleveland............. F 440 953-0053
Eastlake *(G-6427)*

Fabacraft Inc............................. E 513 677-0500
Maineville *(G-8740)*

▲ Fabco Inc................................. D 419 422-4533
Findlay *(G-6862)*

Falcon Industries Inc..................... E 330 723-0099
Medina *(G-9401)*

▲ Federal Equipment Company............ D 513 621-5260
Cincinnati *(G-2616)*

Feedall Inc................................ F 440 942-8100
Willoughby *(G-14458)*

▲ Fenner Dunlop Port Clinton LLC....... C 419 635-2191
Port Clinton *(G-11442)*

◆ Fki Logistex Automation Inc............A 513 881-5251
West Chester *(G-14120)*

◆ Formtek Inc...............................D 216 292-4460
Cleveland *(G-3737)*

Fred D Pfening Company.................. E 614 294-5361
Columbus *(G-4939)*

◆ Glassline Corporation....................E 419 666-9712
Porrycburg *(G-11336)*

◆ Global TBM Company.....................C 440 248-3303
Solon *(G-12117)*

▼ Grasan Equipment Company Inc...... D 419 526-4440
Mansfield *(G-8797)*

Gray-Eering Ltd........................... G 740 498-8816
Tippecanoe *(G-12858)*

◆ Grob Systems Inc........................A 419 358-9015
Bluffton *(G-1361)*

Hoist Equipment Co Inc................... E 440 232-0300
Bedford Heights *(G-1078)*

Hostar International Inc................... F 440 564-5362
Solon *(G-12123)*

Imperial Conveying Systems LLC.......... F 330 491-3200
Canton *(G-1916)*

Innovative Controls Corp.................. F 419 691-6684
Maumee *(G-9298)*

Innovative Handling LLC.................. E 419 882-7480
Sylvania *(G-12712)*

Ins Robotics Inc........................... G 888 293-5325
Hilliard *(G-7684)*

Intelligrated.............................. A 513 874-0788
West Chester *(G-14127)*

▲ Intelligrated Inc.......................... E 866 936-7300
Mason *(G-9111)*

▲ Intelligrated Products LLC.............. E 740 490-0300
London *(G-8537)*

Intelligrated Sub Holdings Inc............ D 513 701-7300
Mason *(G-9112)*

▲ Intelligrated Systems Inc............... A 866 936-7300
Mason *(G-9113)*

▲ Intelligrated Systems LLC............... A 513 701-7300
West Chester *(G-14128)*

Intelligrated Systems Ohio LLC............ G 513 682-6600
West Chester *(G-14129)*

◆ Intelligrated Systems Ohio LLC.........A 513 701-7300
Mason *(G-9114)*

Joy Global Underground Min LLC......... E 440 248-7970
Cleveland *(G-3895)*

Jsj Sb Holdings Inc....................... G 216 398-7774
Cleveland *(G-3897)*

K F T Inc.................................. D 513 241-5910
Cincinnati *(G-2776)*

Kolinahr Systems Inc...................... F 513 745-9401
Blue Ash *(G-1294)*

Laser Automation Inc..................... G 440 543-9291
Chagrin Falls *(G-2169)*

◆ Lewco Inc................................C 419 625-4014
Sandusky *(G-11850)*

▲ Logitech Inc.............................. E 614 871-2822
Grove City *(G-7395)*

◆ Manufacturers Equipment Co............F 513 424-3573
Middletown *(G-9877)*

▲ Material Holdings Inc.................... E 513 583-5500
Loveland *(G-8640)*

▲ Mayfran International Inc................ C 440 461-4100
Cleveland *(G-4003)*

Met Fab Fabrication and Mch............. G 513 724-3715
Batavia *(G-872)*

Mfh Partners Inc.......................... B 440 461-4100
Cleveland *(G-4025)*

Midwest Conveyor Products Inc........... E 419 281-1235
Ashland *(G-552)*

Miller Products Inc....................... E 330 308-5934
New Philadelphia *(G-10458)*

◆ Modula Inc...............................D 207 440-5100
Franklin *(G-7035)*

Mulhern Belting Inc....................... E 201 337-5700
Fairfield *(G-6757)*

◆ Nesco Inc................................E 440 461-6000
Cleveland *(G-4068)*

◆ New Transcon LLC.......................G 440 255-7600
Mentor *(C-0570)*

▲ Ocs Intellitrak Inc....................... F 513 742-5600
Fairfield *(G-6760)*

▲ Ohio Magnetics Inc...................... E 216 662-8484
Maple Heights *(G-8888)*

▲ Opw Engineered Systems Inc........... E 888 771-9438
West Chester *(G-14039)*

Parker-Hannifin Corporation.............. G 330 336-3511
Wadsworth *(G-13658)*

PB Fbrction Mech Contrs Corp........... F 419 478-4869
Toledo *(G-13091)*

Pfpc Enterprises Inc...................... G 513 941-6200
Cincinnati *(G-2960)*

◆ Pneumatic Scale Corporation............C 330 923-0491
Cuyahoga Falls *(G-5564)*

Pomacon Inc.............................. F 330 273-1576
Brunswick *(G-1606)*

Precision Conveyor Technology............ F 440 352-6100
Perry *(G-11197)*

Pro Mach Inc............................. F 513 771-7374
Cincinnati *(G-2984)*

Quickdraft Inc............................ G 330 477-4574
Canton *(G-1987)*

Richmond Machine Co..................... E 419 485-5740
Montpelier *(G-10134)*

SIC

Rolcon Inc............................F 513 821-7259
Cincinnati *(G-3052)*

Sandusky Fabricating & Sls Inc.............E 419 626-4465
Sandusky *(G-11867)*

▲ Spirex Corporation.........................C 330 726-1166
Youngstown *(G-14938)*

◆ Stock Equipment Company Inc..........C 440 543-6000
Chagrin Falls *(G-2184)*

Stock Fairfield Corporation..................C 440 543-6000
Solon *(G-12185)*

◆ Sweet Manufacturing Company..........E 937 325-1511
Springfield *(G-12381)*

Tkf Conveyor Systems LLC..................C 513 621-5260
Cincinnati *(G-3157)*

▲ Transnorm System Inc.....................D 972 606-0303
Mason *(G-9163)*

▲ Uhrden Inc.................................E 330 456-0031
Canton *(G-2030)*

Ulterior Products LLC........................G 614 441-9465
Radnor *(G-11508)*

◆ Webster Industries Inc...................B 419 447-8232
Tiffin *(G-12808)*

Werks Kraft Engineering LLC................E 330 721-7374
Medina *(G-9464)*

3536 Hoists, cranes, and monorails

ACC Automation Co Inc.......................E 330 928-3821
Akron *(G-12)*

Acme Lifting Products Inc....................G 440 838-4430
Cleveland *(G-3290)*

◆ Air Technical Industries Inc.............E 440 951-5191
Mentor *(G-9474)*

Altec Industries Inc..........................F 205 408-2341
Cuyahoga Falls *(G-5521)*

◆ American Power Pull Corp................G 419 335-7050
Archbold *(G-485)*

ARI Phoenix Inc..............................E 513 229-3750
Sharonville *(G-11945)*

Bobco Enterprises Inc........................F 419 867-3560
Toledo *(G-12899)*

Cattron Holdings Inc.........................E 234 806-0018
Warren *(G-13748)*

Crane 1 Services Inc........................E 937 704-9900
West Chester *(G-13977)*

Crane Pro Services...........................G 937 525-5555
Springfield *(G-12295)*

Crane Training Usa Inc.......................G 513 755-2177
West Chester *(G-13978)*

◆ Demag Cranes & Components Corp...C 440 248-2400
Solon *(G-12100)*

▲ Drc Acquisition Inc.......................E 330 656-1600
Streetsboro *(G-12498)*

▲ Eaton Electric Holdings LLC.............B 440 523-5000
Cleveland *(G-3654)*

◆ Emh Inc....................................D 330 220-8600
Valley City *(G-13495)*

Enviri Corporation............................F 740 387-1150
Marion *(G-8969)*

Expert Crane Inc............................D 216 451-9900
Wellington *(G-13886)*

▲ Federal Equipment Company.............D 513 621-5260
Cincinnati *(G-2616)*

Flatiron Crane Oper Co LLC.................C 330 332-3300
Salem *(G-11780)*

Gray-Eering Ltd...............................G 740 498-8816
Tippecanoe *(G-12858)*

◆ Hiab USA Inc...............................D 419 482-6000
Perrysburg *(G-11228)*

Hoist Equipment Co Inc....................E 440 232-0300
Bedford Heights *(G-1078)*

IBI Brake Products Inc......................E 440 543-7962
Chagrin Falls *(G-2166)*

◆ Kci Holding USA Inc.......................C 937 525-5533
Springfield *(G-12335)*

Konecranes Inc.............................F 440 461-8400
Broadview Heights *(G-1504)*

Konecranes Inc.............................E 614 863-0150
Gahanna *(G-7163)*

Konecranes Inc.............................E 937 328-5100
Springfield *(G-12337)*

Konecranes Inc.............................F 419 382-7575
Toledo *(G-13021)*

Konecranes Inc.............................E 513 755-2800
West Chester *(G-14130)*

◆ Konecranes Inc...........................B 937 525-5533
Springfield *(G-12338)*

▲ Kundel Industries Inc.....................D 330 469-6147
Vienna *(G-13609)*

▲ Lift-Tech International Inc.................B 330 424-7248
Salem *(G-11794)*

Mainline Contracting LLC....................F 513 202-1408
Harrison *(G-7559)*

Morgan Engineering Systems Inc..........C 330 821-4721
Alliance *(G-393)*

▼ Morgan Engineering Systems Inc........E 330 823-6130
Alliance *(G-394)*

Radocy Inc...................................F 419 666-4400
Rossford *(G-11661)*

Rnm Holdings Inc...........................F 614 444-5556
Columbus *(G-5232)*

Rnm Holdings Inc...........................F 419 867-8712
Holland *(G-7782)*

Rp Manufacturing LLC......................G 419 468-5095
Iberia *(G-7884)*

Trane Technologies Company LLC.........E 419 633-6800
Bryan *(G-1665)*

▲ Uhrden Inc................................E 330 456-0031
Canton *(G-2030)*

3537 Industrial trucks and tractors

A-Star Transportation Company.............E 708 300-0067
Westerville *(G-14200)*

ADSr Ent LLC.................................F 773 280-2129
Columbus *(G-4674)*

Advance Trans Inc............................F 330 572-0390
Stow *(G-12415)*

AJD Holding Co...............................D 330 405-4477
Twinsburg *(G-13271)*

All Around Primo Logistics LLC.............G 513 725-7888
Cincinnati *(G-2347)*

Back In Black Co..............................E 419 425-5555
Findlay *(G-6839)*

Boltech Incorporated.........................G 330 746-6881
Youngstown *(G-14823)*

Bpr-Rico Equipment Inc......................D 330 723-4050
Medina *(G-9383)*

▲ Bpr-Rico Manufacturing Inc..............D 330 723-4050
Medina *(G-9384)*

Brattiegirlz LLC...............................G 513 607-4757
Columbus *(G-4773)*

◆ Canton Elevator Inc......................D 330 833-3600
North Canton *(G-10632)*

Cascade Corporation.........................E 937 327-0300
Springfield *(G-12287)*

City Machine Technologies Inc..............F 330 747-2639
Youngstown *(G-14836)*

▲ Crescent Metal Products Inc............C 440 350-1100
Mentor *(G-9507)*

Crown Credit Company.......................F 419 629-2311
New Bremen *(G-10357)*

Crown Equipment Corporation..............E 419 586-1100
Celina *(G-2102)*

Crown Equipment Corporation..............D 513 874-2600
Cincinnati *(G-2527)*

Crown Equipment Corporation..............D 937 295-4062
Fort Loramie *(G-6944)*

Crown Equipment Corporation..............D 614 274-7700
Grove City *(G-7378)*

Crown Equipment Corporation..............E 419 629-2311
New Bremen *(G-10359)*

Crown Equipment Corporation..............E 419 629-2311
New Bremen *(G-10360)*

Crown Equipment Corporation..............D 937 454-7545
Vandalia *(G-13552)*

◆ Crown Equipment Corporation...........A 419 629-2311
New Bremen *(G-10358)*

Dragon Products LLC........................E 330 345-3968
Wooster *(G-14635)*

◆ Eagle Industrial Truck Mfg LLC..........E 419 866-6301
Swanton *(G-12683)*

Elliott Machine Works Inc...................E 419 468-4709
Galion *(G-7189)*

Enviri Corporation............................F 740 387-1150
Marion *(G-8969)*

Express Ground Services Inc................G 216 870-9374
Cleveland *(G-3700)*

Forklift Solutions LLC.......................G 419 717-9496
Napoleon *(G-10279)*

Forte Industrial Equipmen...................E 513 398-2800
Mason *(G-9100)*

G & T Manufacturing Co......................F 440 639-7777
Mentor *(G-9522)*

G P Manufacturing Inc........................G 937 544-3190
Peebles *(G-11168)*

Gconsent LLC.................................F 614 886-2416
Dublin *(G-6297)*

General Electric Company....................E 513 977-1500
Cincinnati *(G-2662)*

Global Trucking LLC..........................F 614 598-6264
Columbus *(G-4959)*

▲ Gradall Industries LLC.....................D 330 339-2211
New Philadelphia *(G-10448)*

Grand Aire Inc................................E 419 861-6700
Swanton *(G-12684)*

Grand Harbor Yacht Sales & Svc...........G 440 442-2919
Cleveland *(G-3784)*

Heritage Truck Equipment Inc..............D 330 699-4491
Hartville *(G-7578)*

◆ Hobart Brothers LLC.......................A 937 332-5439
Troy *(G-13222)*

Hoist Equipment Co Inc....................E 440 232-0300
Bedford Heights *(G-1078)*

Hyster-Yale Inc..............................C 440 449-9600
Cleveland *(G-3847)*

◆ Intelligrated Systems Ohio LLC..........A 513 701-7300
Mason *(G-9114)*

Iron Works Inc...............................F 937 420-2100
Fort Loramie *(G-6949)*

▲ Jet Products Incorporated................G 937 866-7969
Dayton *(G-5829)*

Jh Industries Inc............................E 330 963-4105
Twinsburg *(G-13321)*

Lane Field Materials Inc....................G 330 526-8082
Canton *(G-1930)*

Lange Precision Inc.........................E 513 530-9500
Lebanon *(G-8273)*

Load32 LLC...................................F 614 984-6648
Columbus *(G-5072)*

▼ Macton Corporation........................D 330 259-8555
Youngstown *(G-14892)*

Marlow-2000 Inc............................F 216 362-8500
Cleveland *(G-3991)*

Martin Sheet Metal Inc......................E 216 377-8200
Cleveland *(G-3993)*

McCullough Industries Inc...................E 419 673-0767
Kenton *(G-8104)*

Mcl Inc... F 800 245-9490
Kenton *(G-8105)*

Mcl Inc... F 800 245-9490
Kenton *(G-8106)*

Medrano Usa Inc.............................. E 614 272-5856
Columbus *(G-5095)*

Miller Products Inc.......................... E 330 308-5934
New Philadelphia *(G-10458)*

Miners Tractor Sales Inc.................. F 330 325-9914
Rootstown *(G-11649)*

Mitchs Welding & Hitches................ G 419 893-3117
Maumee *(G-9311)*

Octopus Express Inc........................ E 614 412-1222
Westerville *(G-14225)*

Op Dawg Logistics LLC.................... E 937 844-3135
Dayton *(G-5928)*

Parobek Trucking Co........................ G 419 869-7500
West Salem *(G-14189)*

Perfecto Industries Inc.................... E 937 778-1900
Piqua *(G-11372)*

Pollock Research & Design Inc........ E 330 332-3300
Salem *(G-11805)*

Premier Container Inc...................... E 800 230-7132
Cleveland *(G-4189)*

Pucel Enterprises Inc....................... D 216 881-4604
Cleveland *(G-4206)*

Ready Rigs LLC................................. F 740 963-9203
Reynoldsburg *(G-11579)*

River City Body Company................. F 513 772-9317
Cincinnati *(G-3047)*

S&M Trucking LLC............................ F 661 310-2585
Mason *(G-9146)*

Saf-Holland Inc................................ E 513 874-7888
Fairfield *(G-6773)*

Sb Trans LLC.................................... F 407 477-2545
Cincinnati *(G-3066)*

Shanafelt Manufacturing Co............ E 330 455-0315
Canton *(G-2004)*

Shawn Fleming Ind Trckg LLC.......... G 937 707-8539
Dayton *(G-6002)*

Sher International Inc....................... E 800 895-9581
Middletown *(G-9893)*

Shousha Trucking LLC...................... F 937 270-4471
Dayton *(G-6005)*

Skylift Inc.. D 440 960-2100
Lorain *(G-8581)*

Stock Fairfield Corporation.............. C 440 543-6000
Solon *(G-12183)*

Surplus Freight Inc........................... G 614 235-7660
Gahanna *(G-7171)*

◆ Sweet Manufacturing Company........ E 937 325-1511
Springfield *(G-12381)*

Tarpco Inc.. F 330 677-8277
Kent *(G-8086)*

Tbt Hauling LLC................................ G 904 635-7631
Bowling Green *(G-1441)*

Tilt-Or-Lift Inc.................................. G 419 893-6944
Maumee *(G-9326)*

▲ Trailer Component Mfg Inc.............. E 440 255-2888
Mentor *(G-9640)*

Triumphant Enterprises Inc............. G 513 617-1668
Goshen *(G-7298)*

Truckcorp LLC.................................. D 234 666-5702
Canton *(G-2029)*

▲ Uhrden Inc...................................... E 330 456-0031
Canton *(G-2030)*

Venturo Manufacturing Inc.............. F 513 772-8448
Cincinnati *(G-3199)*

Volens LLC....................................... E 216 544-1200
Macedonia *(G-8721)*

◆ Waltco Lift Corp............................... C 330 633-9191
Streetsboro *(G-12530)*

▲ Whiteside Manufacturing Co............ E 740 363-1179
Delaware *(G-6181)*

Youngstown-Kenworth Inc................ F 330 534-9761
Hubbard *(G-7819)*

3541 Machine tools, metal cutting type

5 Axis Grinding Inc.......................... G 937 312-9797
Dayton *(G-5628)*

A & P Tool Inc.................................. E 419 542-6681
Hicksville *(G-7644)*

▲ Acro Tool & Die Company................ E 330 773-5173
Akron *(G-16)*

Advanced Innovative Mfg Inc........... D 330 562-2468
Aurora *(G-660)*

Advetech Inc.................................... E 330 533-2227
Canfield *(G-1801)*

▼ Alcon Tool Company....................... E 330 773-9171
Akron *(G-48)*

Ald Group LLC................................. G 440 942-9800
Willoughby *(G-14415)*

Applied Automation Entp Inc........... F 419 929-2428
New London *(G-10410)*

Apsx LLC... F 513 716-5992
Blue Ash *(G-1246)*

Arch Cutting Tls - Mentor LLC.......... F 440 350-9393
Mentor *(G-9486)*

▲ Areway LLC..................................... D 216 651-9022
Brooklyn *(G-1520)*

Aspra Industrial LLC........................ F 216 459-9200
Cleveland *(G-3380)*

B V Grinding Machining Inc.............. G 440 918-1884
Willoughby *(G-14429)*

▲ Barbco Inc....................................... G 330 488-9400
East Canton *(G-6377)*

▲ Bardons & Oliver Inc....................... C 440 498-5800
Solon *(G-12082)*

▲ Barth Industries Co LLC.................. E 216 267-1950
Cleveland *(G-3407)*

Beverly Dove Inc.............................. G 740 495-5200
New Holland *(G-10397)*

▼ Bor-It Mfg Co Inc............................ E 419 289-6639
Ashland *(G-523)*

Bortnick Tractor Sales Inc................ E 330 924-2555
Cortland *(G-5442)*

Bud May Inc..................................... F 216 676-8850
Cleveland *(G-3449)*

Butech Inc.. D 330 337-0000
Salem *(G-11764)*

Butech Inc.. D 330 337-0000
Salem *(G-11765)*

▲ Butech Inc....................................... D 330 337-0000
Salem *(G-11766)*

C M M S - Re LLC............................. F 513 489-5111
Blue Ash *(G-1257)*

◆ Callahan Cutting Tools Inc.............. G 614 294-1649
Columbus *(G-4792)*

▲ Cammann Inc.................................. F 440 965-4051
Wakeman *(G-13678)*

Cardinal Builders Inc....................... G 614 237-1000
Columbus *(G-4801)*

Carter Manufacturing Co Inc........... F 513 398-7303
Mason *(G-9077)*

▲ Channel Products Inc....................... D 440 423-0113
Solon *(G-12093)*

Chart-Tech Tool Inc......................... F 937 667-3543
Tipp City *(G-12820)*

▲ Cincinnati Gilbert Mch TI LLC........... G 513 541-4815
Cincinnati *(G-2478)*

▲ Cincinnati Mine Machinery Co......... E 513 522-7777
Cincinnati *(G-2482)*

▲ Cincinnati Radiator Inc................... F 513 874-5555
Fairfield *(G-6722)*

Columbus Design & Mfg LLC........... G 414 534-3273
Columbus *(G-4822)*

Commercial Grinding Svcs Inc......... E 330 273-5040
Medina *(G-9389)*

▲ Competetive Carbide Inc................. E 440 350-9393
Madison *(G-8727)*

Criterion Tool & Die Inc................... E 216 267-1733
Brookpark *(G-1545)*

▲ Cutting Systems Inc......................... F 216 928-0500
Cleveland *(G-3590)*

◆ Damon Industries Inc...................... D 330 821-5310
Alliance *(G-379)*

Dayton Machine Tool Company........ G 937 222-6444
Dayton *(G-5730)*

Dbcr Inc... E 330 920-1900
Cuyahoga Falls *(G-5537)*

Desmond-Stephan Mfgcompany....... E 937 653-7181
Urbana *(G-13461)*

Dixie Machinery Inc......................... F 513 360-0091
Monroe *(G-10103)*

Dmg Mori Usa Inc............................ F 440 546-7088
West Chester *(G-13984)*

◆ Drake Manufacturing Services Co.... D 330 847-7291
Warren *(G-13760)*

▲ Eagle Machinery & Supply Inc......... E 330 852-1300
Sugarcreek *(G-12637)*

Elliott Tool Technologies Ltd............ D 937 253-6133
Dayton *(G-5763)*

Esi-Extrusion Services Inc............... E 330 374-3388
Akron *(G-138)*

Falcon Industries Inc....................... E 330 723-0099
Medina *(G-9401)*

Falcon Tool & Machine Inc............... G 937 534-9999
Dayton *(G-5773)*

Fischer Special Tooling Corp........... G 440 951-8411
Mentor *(G-9516)*

Frazier Machine and Prod Inc.......... E 419 874-7321
Perrysburg *(G-11223)*

▼ Fredon Corporation.......................... D 440 951-5200
Mentor *(G-9520)*

General Electric Company................ C 513 341-0214
West Chester *(G-14008)*

▼ George A Mitchell Company............. E 330 758-5777
Youngstown *(G-14866)*

◆ Glassline Corporation...................... E 419 666-9712
Perrysburg *(G-11225)*

▲ Global Specialty Machines LLC....... F 513 701-0452
Mason *(G-9104)*

◆ Global TBM Company....................... C 440 248-3303
Solon *(G-12117)*

◆ Glt Inc... F 937 237-0055
Dayton *(G-5800)*

Grind-All Corporation....................... E 330 220-1600
Brunswick *(G-1596)*

▲ Grt Utilicorp Inc.............................. E 330 264-8444
Wooster *(G-14646)*

◆ Gzjb Holdings Inc............................ E 216 731-0500
Cleveland *(G-3803)*

▲ H & D Steel Service Inc.................... E 800 666-3390
North Royalton *(G-10764)*

Herco Inc... G 740 498-5181
Newcomerstown *(G-10571)*

Houston Machine Products Inc........ E 937 322-8022
Springfield *(G-12326)*

Industrial Paper Shredders Inc........ F 888 637-4733
North Lima *(G-10708)*

Innovtive McHning Slutions LLC....... F 419 925-2060
Celina *(G-2110)*

Interstate Tool Corporation.............. E 216 671-1077
Cleveland *(G-3866)*

J & S Tool Corporation..................... G 216 676-8330
Lorain *(G-8558)*

Jacp Inc..G 513 353-3660
Miamitown *(G-9759)*

Jilco LLC..G 330 270-9780
Youngstown *(G-14882)*

Kilroy Company.................................D 440 951-8700
Cleveland *(G-3920)*

KLm Manufacturing Co Inc..................G 740 666-5171
Ostrander *(G-11027)*

Lahm-Trosper Inc.............................F 937 252-8791
Dayton *(G-5841)*

Lawrence Industries Inc.....................C 216 518-1400
Cleveland *(G-3947)*

◆ Lawrence Industries Inc..................G 216 518-7000
Cleveland *(G-3946)*

Leland-Gifford Inc.............................G 330 785-9730
Akron *(G-205)*

Levan Enterprises Inc........................E 330 923-9797
Stow *(G-12438)*

Lincoln Electric Automtn Inc................E 614 471-5926
Columbus *(G-5070)*

◆ Makino Inc....................................B 513 573-7200
Mason *(G-9123)*

Martindale Electric Company...............E 216 521-8567
Cleveland *(G-3994)*

Masters Prcision Machining Inc............F 330 419-1933
Kent *(G-8050)*

Max - Pro Tools Inc...........................G 800 456-0931
Cleveland *(G-3999)*

Melin Tool Company Inc......................D 216 362-4200
Cleveland *(G-4019)*

Miami Ice Machine Inc........................G 513 863-6707
Overpeck *(G-11060)*

Michael Byrne Manufacturing Co Inc.....E 419 525-1214
Mansfield *(G-8825)*

Midwest Knife Grinding Inc..................F 330 854-1030
Canal Fulton *(G-1778)*

Midwest Specialties Inc......................D 800 837-2503
Wapakoneta *(G-13725)*

◆ Milacron Marketing Company LLC......E 513 536-2000
Batavia *(G-875)*

▲ Milan Tool Corp.............................E 216 661-1078
Cleveland *(G-4039)*

Monaghan & Associates Inc................F 937 253-7706
Dayton *(G-5892)*

More Manufacturing LLC....................F 937 233-3898
Tipp City *(G-12831)*

Morlock Asphalt Ltd...........................F 419 419-4772
Portage *(G-11459)*

National Machine Tool Company............G 513 541-6682
Cincinnati *(G-2894)*

◆ Nesco Inc.....................................E 440 461-6000
Cleveland *(G-4068)*

Nmgg Ctg LLC...................................C 419 447-5211
Tiffin *(G-12793)*

Northwood Industries Inc....................F 419 666-2100
Perrysburg *(G-11243)*

Obars Machine and Tool Company.........E 419 535-6307
Toledo *(G-13068)*

▼ Ohio Broach & Machine Company.......E 440 946-1040
Willoughby *(G-14499)*

Ohio Screw Products Inc....................D 440 322-6341
Elyria *(G-6574)*

Ohio Tool Work LLC...........................E 419 281-3700
Ashland *(G-557)*

OReilly Precision Pdts Inc...................E 937 526-4677
Russia *(G-11676)*

P M R Inc...G 440 937-6241
Avon *(G-733)*

▲ Peerless Saw Company..................E 614 836-5790
Groveport *(G-7448)*

Phillips Manufacturing Co...................D 330 652-4335
Niles *(G-10600)*

▲ Portage Machine Concepts Inc.........F 330 628-2343
Akron *(G-264)*

▲ Rafter Equipment Company LLC........E 440 572-3700
Strongsville *(G-12592)*

Rapid Machine Inc.............................F 419 737-2377
Pioneer *(G-11327)*

Ravana Industries Inc........................G 330 536-4015
Lowellville *(G-8664)*

Reliable Products Co..........................G 419 394-5854
Saint Marys *(G-11751)*

◆ Rex International USA Inc................E 800 321-7950
Ashtabula *(G-615)*

Ridge Tool Company..........................D 740 432-8782
Cambridge *(G-1758)*

Ridge Tool Company..........................C 440 329-4737
Elyria *(G-6587)*

◆ Ridge Tool Company......................A 440 323-5581
Elyria *(G-6586)*

Ridge Tool Manufacturing Co...............F 440 323-5581
Elyria *(G-6588)*

▲ Rimrock Corporation.......................E 614 471-5926
Columbus *(G-5230)*

Rimrock Holdings Corporation..............C 614 471-5926
Columbus *(G-5231)*

▼ Roll-In Saw Inc..............................F 216 459-9001
Brookpark *(G-1558)*

Sinico Mtm US Inc.............................F 216 264-8344
Middleburg Heights *(G-9777)*

Slater Road Mills Inc..........................E 330 332-9951
Salem *(G-11813)*

▲ Specialty Metals Proc Inc................E 330 656-2767
Hudson *(G-7858)*

Stadco Inc.......................................E 937 878-0911
Fairborn *(G-6699)*

STC International Co Ltd......................G 561 308-6002
Lebanon *(G-8287)*

Stevenson Mfg Co.............................G 330 532-1581
Wellsville *(G-13914)*

Sumitomo Elc Carbide Mfg Inc.............F 440 354-0600
Grand River *(G-7312)*

▲ Superion Inc.................................E 937 374-0033
Xenia *(G-14776)*

Superior Machining Inc.......................E 937 236-9619
Dayton *(G-6030)*

Tailored Systems Inc.........................G 937 299-3900
Moraine *(G-10194)*

Technidrill Systems Inc......................E 330 678-9980
Kent *(G-8087)*

The Ransohoff Company......................C 513 870-0100
West Chester *(G-14153)*

▲ The Vulcan Tool Company................G 937 253-6194
Dayton *(G-6050)*

Tooling Connection Inc.......................G 419 594-3339
Oakwood *(G-10901)*

Tykma Inc..D 740 779-9918
Chillicothe *(G-2286)*

U S Alloy Die Corp.............................F 216 749-9700
Cleveland *(G-4438)*

Updike Supply Company......................E 937 482-4000
Huber Heights *(G-7825)*

West Ohio Tool Co.............................F 937 842-6688
Russells Point *(G-11670)*

Wise Edge LLC..................................G 330 208-0889
Mogadore *(G-10094)*

Wonder Machine Services Inc...............E 440 937-7500
Avon *(G-743)*

3542 Machine tools, metal forming type

Accurate Manufacturing Company.........F 614 878-6510
Dublin *(G-6272)*

▲ Addition Manufacturing Te...............C 513 228-7000
Lebanon *(G-8241)*

Advanced Tech Utilization Co...............F 440 238-3770
Strongsville *(G-12532)*

Aida-America Corporation....................F 937 237-2382
Dayton *(G-5643)*

◆ Aida-America Corporation................D 937 237-2382
Dayton *(G-5644)*

Akay Holdings Inc..............................E 330 753-8458
Barberton *(G-790)*

Allied Mask and Tooling Inc.................G 419 470-2555
Toledo *(G-12870)*

American Fluid Power Inc....................G 877 223-8742
Elyria *(G-6495)*

Anderson & Vreeland Inc.....................D 419 636-5002
Bryan *(G-1629)*

Apeks LLC..E 740 809-1174
Johnstown *(G-7991)*

Barclay Machine Inc...........................F 330 337-9541
Salem *(G-11763)*

▲ Barth Industries Co LLC..................E 216 267-1950
Cleveland *(G-3407)*

Bendco Machine & Tool Inc..................F 419 628-3802
Minster *(G-10054)*

▲ Brilex Industries Inc.......................D 330 744-1114
Youngstown *(G-14827)*

Columbia Stamping Inc.......................G 440 236-6677
Columbia Station *(G-4591)*

▲ Columbus Jack Corporation..............E 614 443-7492
Swanton *(G-12680)*

Columbus Water Section Permit............G 614 645-8039
Columbus *(G-4837)*

▼ Compass Systems & Sales LLC........D 330 733-2111
Barberton *(G-802)*

D C Morrison Company Inc...................E 859 581-7511
Cincinnati *(G-2536)*

Danfoss Power Solutions II LLC............F 419 238-1190
Van Wert *(G-13533)*

Decked LLC......................................F 208 806-0251
Defiance *(G-6104)*

Diverse Mfg Solutions LLC...................F 740 363-3600
Delaware *(G-6144)*

▲ DRG Hydraulics Inc........................E 216 663-9747
Twinsburg *(G-13297)*

Eaton Corporation.............................C 216 281-2211
Cleveland *(G-3653)*

Ebog Legacy Inc...............................D 330 239-4933
Sharon Center *(G-11940)*

Elliott Tool Technologies Ltd.................D 937 253-6133
Dayton *(G-5763)*

Exito Manufacturing LLC.....................G 937 291-9871
Beavercreek *(G-991)*

F & G Tool and Die Co.........................G 937 746-3658
Franklin *(G-7019)*

Falls Mtal Fbrctors Indus Svcs.............F 330 253-7181
Akron *(G-143)*

First Tool Corp..................................E 937 254-6197
Dayton *(G-5777)*

Fluidpower Assembly Inc.....................G 419 394-7486
Saint Marys *(G-11737)*

Gad-Jets Investments Inc....................G 937 274-2111
Franklin *(G-7023)*

Gem City Metal Tech LLC....................E 937 252-8998
Dayton *(G-5793)*

▼ George A Mitchell Company.............E 330 758-5777
Youngstown *(G-14866)*

▲ GSE Production and Support LLC.....G 419 866-6301
Swanton *(G-12685)*

H&G Legacy Co.................................F 513 921-1075
Cincinnati *(G-2701)*

Henry & Wright Corporation.................F 216 851-3750
Cleveland *(G-3823)*

High Production Technology LLC...........G 419 599-1511
Napoleon *(G-10283)*

High Production Technology LLC......... F 419 591-7000
Napoleon (G-10284)

Hunter Hydraulics Inc..................... G 330 455-3983
Canton (G-1913)

Industrial Rlblity Spclsts Inc............. G 800 800-6345
Chillicothe (G-2259)

J & S Tool Corporation.................... G 216 676-8330
Lorain (G-8558)

Kiraly Tool and Die Inc.................... F 330 744-5773
Youngstown (G-14885)

Kotobuki-Reliable Die Casting Inc......... E 937 347-1111
Xenia (G-14768)

Levan Enterprises Inc..................... E 330 923-9797
Stow (G-12438)

Madison Property Holdings Inc............ E 800 215-3210
Cincinnati (G-2839)

◆ McNeil & Nrm Inc....................... D 330 761-1855
Akron (G-225)

Metal & Wire Products Company.......... E 330 332-9448
Salem (G-11799)

Monode Marking Products Inc............. F 419 929-0346
New London (G-10413)

Monode Marking Products Inc............. E 440 975-8802
Mentor (G-9567)

Monode Steel Stamp Inc.................. F 440 975-8802
Mentor (G-9568)

◆ NIDEC MINSTER CORPORATION....... C 419 628-2331
Minster (G-10062)

Phoenix Hydraulic Presses Inc............ F 614 850-8940
Hilliard (G-7696)

▲ Pines Manufacturing Inc................ E 440 835-5553
Westlake (G-14324)

Pioneer Solutions LLC.................... G 216 383-3400
Euclid (G-6669)

▲ Rafter Equipment Company LLC........ E 440 572-3700
Strongsville (G-12592)

Ram Products Inc......................... F 614 443-4634
Logan (G-8525)

▲ Ready Technology Inc.................. F 937 866-7200
Dayton (G-5978)

▼ Recycling Eqp Solutions Corp.......... G 330 920-1500
Cuyahoga Falls (G-5568)

Risk Industries LLC....................... D 440 835-5553
Westlake (G-14328)

Ritime Incorporated....................... G 330 273-3443
Cleveland (G-4242)

◆ Rogers Industrial Products Inc......... E 330 535-3331
Akron (G-290)

▲ Semtorq Inc........................... F 330 487-0600
Twinsburg (G-13377)

Spencer Manufacturing Company Inc.... D 330 648-2461
Spencer (G-12236)

Starkey Machinery Inc.................... E 419 468-2560
Galion (G-7199)

Stolle Machinery Company LLC.......... C 937 497-5400
Sidney (G-12056)

Stover International LLC.................. E 740 363-5251
Delaware (G-6175)

Stutzman Manufacturing Ltd.............. G 330 674-4359
Millersburg (G-10012)

◆ Taylor - Winfield Corporation.......... C 330 259-8500
Hubbard (G-7817)

▲ Technical Machine Products Inc........ F
Cleveland (G-4370)

Terminal Equipment Inds Inc............. G 330 468-0322
Northfield (G-10798)

Tfi Manufacturing LLC.................... F 440 290-9411
Mentor (G-9636)

The Basic Aluminum Castings Co......... D 216 481-5606
Cleveland (G-4378)

▲ The Vulcan Tool Company.............. G 937 253-6194
Dayton (G-6050)

▲ THT Presses Inc........................ E 937 898-2012
Dayton (G-6054)

Tri-K Enterprises Inc..................... G 330 832-7380
Canton (G-2028)

▲ Trucut Incorporated.................... D 330 938-9806
Sebring (G-11903)

Turner Machine Co....................... G 330 332-5821
Salem (G-11816)

Twist Inc................................. G 937 675-9581
Jamestown (G-7970)

▲ Twist Inc............................... G 937 675-9581
Jamestown (G-7969)

Uhrichsville Carbide Inc.................. F 740 922-9197
Uhrichsville (G-13409)

Valley Tool & Die Inc..................... D 440 237-0160
North Royalton (G-10788)

Vmaxx Inc................................ F 419 738-4044
Wapakoneta (G-13729)

▲ Yizumi-HPM Corporation............... G 740 382-5600
Iberia (G-7885)

3543 Industrial patterns

Accuform Manufacturing Inc.............. E 330 797-9291
Youngstown (G-14803)

Advantic Building Group LLC............. E 513 290-4796
Miamisburg (G-9661)

Air Power Dynamics LLC.................. C 440 701-2100
Mentor (G-9473)

Anchor Pattern Company.................. G 614 443-2221
Columbus (G-4714)

API Pattern Works Inc.................... F 440 269-1766
Willoughby (G-14421)

Cascade Pattern Company Inc............ E 440 323-4300
Elyria (G-6509)

Cincinnati Pattern Company Inc.......... G 513 241-9872
Cincinnati (G-2483)

Clinton Foundry Ltd...................... F 419 243-6885
Toledo (G-12924)

Clinton Pattern Works Inc................ G 419 243-0855
Toledo (G-12925)

▲ Colonial Patterns Inc.................. G 330 673-6475
Kent (G-8022)

Dayton Pattern Inc....................... G 937 277-0761
Dayton (G-5735)

Design Pattern Works Inc................. G 937 252-0797
Dayton (G-5746)

Elyria Pattern Co Inc..................... G 440 323-1526
Elyria (C 6532)

Founders Service & Mfg Inc.............. G 330 584-7759
Deerfield (G-6093)

Freeman Manufacturing & Sup Co........ E 440 934-1902
Avon (G-727)

H&M Machine & Tool LLC................ E 419 776-9220
Toledo (G-12980)

Humtown Pattern Company............... D 330 482-5555
Columbiana (G-4619)

Industrial Pattern & Mfg Co.............. F 614 252-0934
Columbus (G-5004)

Industrial Technologies Inc............... G 330 434-2033
Akron (G-182)

▲ J-Lenco Inc............................ F 740 499-2260
Morral (G-10199)

Ketco Inc................................. E 937 426-9331
Dayton (G-5615)

Liberty Pattern and Mold Inc............. G 330 788-9463
Youngstown (G-14888)

Lorain Modern Pattern Inc............... F 440 365-6780
Elyria (G-6559)

Maumee Pattern Company................ E 419 693-4968
Toledo (G-13049)

National Pattern Mfgco................... F 330 682-6871
Orrville (G-10997)

PCC Airfoils LLC......................... B 216 692-7900
Cleveland (G-4148)

Plas-Mac Corp............................ D 440 349-3222
Solon (G-12168)

R L Rush Tool & Pattern Inc.............. G 419 562-9849
Bucyrus (G-1687)

Reliable Castings Corporation............ D 513 541-2627
Cincinnati (G-3037)

Reliable Pattern Works Inc............... G 440 232-8820
Cleveland (G-4232)

▲ Ross Aluminum Castings LLC.......... C 937 492-4134
Sidney (G-12046)

Seaport Mold & Casting Company........ G 419 243-1422
Toledo (G-13123)

Seaway Pattern Mfg Inc.................. F 419 865-5724
Toledo (G-13124)

Seilkop Industries Inc.................... F 513 679-5680
Cincinnati (G-3076)

Sherwood Rtm Corp...................... G 330 875-7151
Louisville (G-8616)

Sinel Company Inc....................... F 937 433-4772
Dayton (G-6010)

Spectracam Ltd........................... G 937 223-3805
Dayton (G-6016)

Tempcraft Corporation.................... D 216 391-3885
Cleveland (G-4372)

Th Manufacturing Inc..................... G 330 893-3572
Millersburg (G-10013)

◆ Transducers Direct Llc................. F 513 247-0601
Cincinnati (G-3166)

TW Manufacturing Co..................... G 440 439-3243
Cleveland (G-4434)

United States Drill Head Co.............. F 513 941-0300
Cincinnati (G-3185)

3544 Special dies, tools, jigs, and fixtures

5me LLC.................................. E 513 719-1600
Cincinnati (G-2289)

A & B Tool & Manufacturing.............. G 419 382-0215
Toledo (G-12859)

A G Industries Inc........................ F 330 220-0050
Brunswick (G-1578)

Accu-Rite Tool & Die Co Corp............ G 330 497-9959
Canton (G-1822)

Accu-Tek Tool & Die Inc................. G 330 726-1946
Salem (G-11760)

Accu-Tool Inc............................ G 937 667-5878
Tipp City (G-12813)

Accuform Manufacturing Inc.............. E 330 797-9291
Youngstown (G-14803)

Ace American Wire Die Co................ F 330 425-7269
Twinsburg (G-13267)

▲ Acro Tool & Die Company.............. E 330 773-5173
Akron (G-16)

▲ Addition Manufacturing Te............. C 513 228-7000
Lebanon (G-8241)

Adept Manufacturing Corp................ F 937 222-7110
Dayton (G-5636)

▲ Advanced Engrg Solutions Inc......... D 937 743-6900
Springboro (G-12244)

▲ Advanced Intr Solutions Inc........... E 937 550-0065
Springboro (G-12245)

Aero Tech Tool & Mold Inc............... G 440 942-3327
Mentor (G-9471)

Afc Tool Co Inc.......................... E 937 275-8700
Dayton (G-5640)

Aims-CMI Technology LLC................ F 937 832-2000
Englewood (G-6605)

AJD Holding Co........................... D 330 405-4477
Twinsburg (G-13271)

Akron Centl Engrv Mold Mch Inc......... E 330 794-8704
Akron (G-26)

Allied Tool & Die Inc	F	216 941-6196	Cleveland (G-3331)

Allied Tool & Die Inc........................ F 216 941-6196
Cleveland (G-3331)

▲ Alpha Tool & Mold Inc....................... F 440 473-2343
Cleveland (G-3333)

Alpine Gage Inc............................... G 937 669-8665
Tipp City (G-12815)

Amaroq Inc.................................... G 419 747-2110
Mansfield (G-8760)

▼ Amcraft Inc................................. G 419 729-7900
Toledo (G-12872)

American Cube Mold Inc....................... G 330 558-0044
Brunswick (G-1580)

American Punch Co............................. E 216 731-4501
Euclid (G-6642)

American Tool and Die Inc..................... F 419 726-5394
Toledo (G-12879)

Amerimold Inc................................ G 800 950-8020
Mogadore (G-10069)

Amex Dies Inc................................ F 330 545-9766
Girard (G-7265)

Ampex Metal Products Company........... D 216 267-9242
Brookpark (G-1544)

Amtech Tool & Machine Inc.................... G 330 758-8215
Youngstown (G-14813)

Anchor Glass Container Corp................ D 740 452-2743
Zanesville (G-14987)

▲ Anchor Tool & Die Co...................... B 216 362-1850
Cleveland (G-3356)

Antwerp TI Die & Engrg Co Inc............. F 419 258-5271
Antwerp (G-461)

Apollo Plastics Inc.......................... F 440 951-7774
Mentor (G-9484)

Apollo Products Inc.......................... F 440 269-8551
Willoughby (G-14422)

Apr Tool Inc................................. F 440 946-0393
Willoughby (G-14424)

Arnett Tool Inc.............................. G 937 437-0361
New Paris (G-10425)

Artisan Equipment Inc........................ F 740 756-9135
Carroll (G-2073)

▼ Artisan Tool & Die Corp................... F 216 883-2769
Cleveland (G-3371)

Aspec Inc................................... G 513 561-9922
Cincinnati (G-2380)

Athens Mold and Machine Inc................ D 740 593-6613
Athens (G-633)

◆ Atlantic Tool & Die Company...............C 440 238-6931
Strongsville (G-12539)

Aukerman J F Steel Rule Die................ G 937 456-4498
Eaton (G-6448)

Automation Plastics Corp.................... D 330 562-5148
Aurora (G-662)

Automation Tool & Die Inc................... D 330 225-8336
Valley City (G-13490)

Autotec Corporation......................... E 419 885-2529
Toledo (G-12889)

B-K Tool & Design Inc....................... D 419 532-3890
Kalida (G-8003)

Balancing Company Inc....................... E 937 898-9111
Vandalia (G-13550)

Banner Metals Group Inc..................... E 614 291-3105
Columbus (G-4743)

▲ Basilius Inc............................... G 419 536-5810
Toledo (G-12893)

Bk Tool Company Inc......................... G 513 870-9622
Fairfield (G-6714)

Bloom Industries Inc......................... G 330 898-3878
Warren (G-13743)

Blue Ash Tool & Die Co Inc.................. F 513 793-4530
Blue Ash (G-1254)

Bollinger Tool & Die Inc..................... G 419 866-5180
Holland (G-7746)

Brake Parts Holdings Inc..................... B 216 589-0198
Cleveland (G-3432)

Brassgate Industries Inc..................... G..... 937 339-2192
Troy (G-13203)

▲ Brinkman Tool & Die Inc................... E 937 222-1161
Dayton (G-5685)

Brothers Tool and Mfg Ltd................... G 513 353-9700
Miamitown (G-9757)

Brw Tool Inc................................ F 419 394-3371
Saint Marys (G-11734)

Bryan Die-Cast Products Ltd................. G 419 252-6208
Toledo (G-12906)

Caliber Mold and Machine Inc................ E 330 633-8171
Akron (G-88)

CAM-Lem Inc................................ G 216 391-7750
Cleveland (G-3461)

▼ Camden Concrete Products LLC............ G 937 456-1229
Eaton (G-6451)

Capital Precision Machine & TI.............. G 937 258-1176
Dayton (G-5604)

Capital Tool Company........................ E 216 661-5750
Cleveland (G-3467)

Carter Manufacturing Co Inc................. F 513 398-7303
Mason (G-9077)

Catalysis Additive Tooling LLC.............. G 614 715-3674
Westerville (G-14249)

Centaur Tool & Die Inc...................... F 419 352-7704
Bowling Green (G-1412)

Chart-Tech Tool Inc......................... F 937 667-3543
Tipp City (G-12820)

Chippewa Tool and Mfg Co................... F 419 849-2790
Woodville (G-14616)

Clark Fixture Technologies Inc.............. E 419 354-1541
Bowling Green (G-1414)

◆ Cleveland Die & Mfg Co...................C 440 243-3404
Middleburg Heights (G-9767)

Cleveland Metal Processing Inc.............. C 440 243-3404
Cleveland (G-3517)

Cleveland Roll Forming Co................... G 216 281-0202
Cleveland (G-3524)

◆ Cleveland Steel Tool Company.............E 216 681-7400
Cleveland (G-3526)

Clyde Tool & Die Inc........................ F 419 547-9574
Clyde (G-4557)

CMI Technology Inc.......................... F 937 832-2000
Englewood (G-6609)

Cmt Machining & Fabg LLC................... F 937 652-3740
Urbana (G-13459)

Coach Tool & Die LLC........................ G 937 890-4716
Springboro (G-12249)

Coldwater Machine Company LLC.......... C 419 678-4877
Coldwater (G-4571)

Cole Tool & Die Company..................... E 419 522-1272
Ontario (G-10948)

Colonial Machine Company Inc............... D 330 673-5859
Kent (G-8021)

▲ Colonial Patterns Inc...................... G 330 673-6475
Kent (G-8022)

Columbia Stamping Inc....................... G 440 236-6677
Columbia Station (G-4591)

Compco Quaker Mfg Inc...................... E 330 482-0200
Salem (G-11772)

Condor Tool & Die Inc....................... E 216 671-6000
Cleveland (G-3558)

Conforming Matrix Corporation.............. E 419 729-3777
Toledo (G-12929)

Continental Business Entps Inc............. F 440 439-4400
Bedford (G-1023)

Contour Forming Inc......................... F 740 345-9777
Newark (G-10499)

Cornerstone Manufacturing Inc.............. G 937 456-5930
Eaton (G-6452)

Cornerstone Wauseon Inc.................... C 419 337-0940
Wauseon (G-13847)

Criterion Tool & Die Inc..................... E 216 267-1733
Brookpark (G-1545)

Crowe Manufacturing Services............... G 800 831-1893
Troy (G-13207)

Crum Manufacturing Inc...................... E 419 878-9779
Waterville (G-13832)

Csw Inc..................................... E 413 589-1311
Sylvania (G-12703)

Custom Machine Inc.......................... E 419 986-5122
Tiffin (G-12781)

Customformed Products Inc.................. F 937 388-0480
Miamisburg (G-9685)

D A Fitzgerald Co Inc........................ G 937 548-0511
Greenville (G-7340)

Darke Precision Inc......................... G 937 548-2232
Piqua (G-11343)

▲ Dayton Progress Corporation.............. A 937 859-5111
Dayton (G-5737)

Dayton Progress Intl Corp................... G 937 859-5111
Dayton (G-5738)

Dayton Stencil Works Company.............. F 937 223-3233
Dayton (G-5739)

▲ DC Legacy Corp........................... E 330 896-4220
Akron (G-118)

Dcd Technologies Inc........................ F 216 481-0056
Cleveland (G-3605)

Deca Mfg Co................................ F 419 884-0071
Mansfield (G-8780)

▲ Defiance Metal Products Co............... B 419 784-5332
Defiance (G-6105)

Delta Tool & Die Stl Block Inc.............. E 419 822-5939
Delta (G-6203)

Diamond America Corporation................ G 330 535-3330
Mogadore (G-10072)

▲ Diamond America Corporation............. F 330 762-9269
Akron (G-119)

Die Guys Inc................................ F 330 239-3437
Medina (G-9396)

▲ Die-Matic Corporation.................... D 216 749-4656
Independence (G-7897)

▼ Die-Mension Corporation................. F 330 273-5872
Brunswick (G-1589)

Direct Wire Service LLP...................... G 937 526-4447
Versailles (G-13594)

Diversified Mold Castings LLC.............. E 216 663-1814
Cleveland (G-3621)

DMG Tool & Die LLC.......................... G 937 407-0810
Bellefontaine (G-1106)

Dove Die and Stamping Company............. E 216 267-3720
Cleveland (G-3628)

Dover Machine Co............................ G 330 343-4123
Dover (G-6241)

Doyle Manufacturing Inc..................... D 419 865-2548
Holland (G-7756)

◆ Drt Mfg Co LLC...........................D 937 297-6670
Dayton (G-5754)

Duco Tool & Die Inc......................... F 419 628-2031
Minster (G-10056)

▲ Duncan Tool Inc........................... F 937 667-9364
Tipp City (G-12823)

Durivage Pattern and Mfg Inc............... F 419 836-8655
Williston (G-14411)

Dyco Manufacturing Inc...................... F 419 485-5525
Montpelier (G-10128)

Dynamic Dies Inc............................ E 513 705-9524
Middletown (G-9855)

Dynamic Dies Inc............................ E 419 865-0249
Holland (G-7761)

Dynamic Tool & Mold Inc..................... G 440 237-8665
Cleveland (G-3642)

Dysinger Incorporated .... E ..... 937 297-7761 Dayton *(G-5757)*	Gentzler Tool & Die Corp........................ E ..... 330 896-1941 Akron *(G-161)*	▲ Ishmael Precision Tool Corp............... E ..... 937 335-8070 Troy *(G-13230)*
E D M Fastar Inc .... G ..... 216 676-0100 Cleveland *(G-3644)*	Gilson Machine & Tool Co Inc .... E ..... 419 592-2911 Napoleon *(G-10282)*	J & J Tool & Die Inc .... G ..... 330 343-4721 Dover *(G-6249)*
Eagle Precision Products LLC .... G ..... 440 582-9393 North Royalton *(G-10759)*	▲ Gokoh Corporation .... F ..... 937 339-4977 Troy *(G-13218)*	J & M Industries Inc .... G ..... 440 951-1985 Mentor *(G-9538)*
Ecm Industries LLC .... F ..... 513 533-6242 Cincinnati *(G-2578)*	Gordon Tool Inc .... F ..... 419 263-3151 Payne *(G-11163)*	J & S Tool Corporation .... G ..... 216 676-8330 Lorain *(G-8558)*
Edfa LLC .... G ..... 937 222-1415 Dayton *(G-5760)*	Green Machine Tool Inc .... G ..... 937 253-0771 Dayton *(G-5612)*	J M Mold Inc .... G ..... 937 778-0077 Piqua *(G-11360)*
▲ EMI Corp .... D ..... 937 596-5511 Jackson Center *(G-7963)*	Greenfield Die & Mfg Corp...................... F ..... 734 454-4000 Valley City *(G-13497)*	J Tek Tool & Mold Inc .... F ..... 419 547-9476 Clyde *(G-4559)*
Engineered Mfg & Eqp Co .... G ..... 937 642-7776 Marysville *(G-9019)*	H G Schneider Company .... G ..... 614 882-6944 Westerville *(G-14262)*	J W Harwood Co.. F ..... 216 531-6230 Cleveland *(G-3880)*
Enterprise Tool & Die Company .... F ..... 216 351-1300 Cleveland *(G-3677)*	H&M Machine & Tool LLC .... E ..... 419 776-9220 Toledo *(G-12980)*	Jamen Tool & Die Co................................ E ..... 330 782-6731 Youngstown *(G-14880)*
Esi-Extrusion Services Inc .... E ..... 330 374-3388 Akron *(G-138)*	Hale Performance Coatings Inc .... E ..... 419 244-6451 Toledo *(G-12984)*	Jamen Tool & Die Co................................ F ..... 330 788-6521 Youngstown *(G-14879)*
Estee 2 Inc .... G ..... 937 224-7853 Dayton *(G-5768)*	Hamilton Custom Molding Inc .... G ..... 513 844-6643 Hamilton *(G-7501)*	JBI Corporation .... F ..... 419 855-3389 Genoa *(G-7248)*
Esterle Mold & Machine Co Inc.............. E ..... 330 686-1685 Stow *(G-12429)*	Hardin Creek Machine & Tl Inc............... F ..... 419 678-4913 Coldwater *(G-4576)*	Jena Tool Inc .... D ..... 937 296-1122 Moraine *(G-10171)*
Euclid Design and Mfg Inc .... F ..... 440 942-0066 Willoughby Hills *(G-14558)*	Hawthorne Tool LLC................................ F ..... 440 516-1891 Wickliffe *(G-14377)*	▲ Jergens Inc .... C ..... 216 486-5540 Cleveland *(G-3885)*
Exact-Tool & Die Inc .... E ..... 216 676-9140 Cleveland *(G-3696)*	Hedalloy Die Corporation .... G ..... 216 341-3768 Cleveland *(G-3817)*	Jet Di Inc .... G ..... 330 607-7913 Brunswick *(G-1600)*
◆ Exco Engineering USA Inc................... E ..... 419 726-1595 Toledo *(G-12958)*	Hedges Selective Tl & Prod Inc.............. F ..... 419 478-8670 Toledo *(G-12991)*	Johnston Mfg Co Inc................................ G ..... 440 269-1420 Mentor *(G-9544)*
Exito Manufacturing LLC......................... G ..... 937 291-9871 Beavercreek *(G-991)*	▲ Herbert Usa Inc .... D ..... 330 929-4297 Akron *(G-173)*	K B Machine & Tool Inc .... G ..... 937 773-1624 Piqua *(G-11362)*
F & G Tool and Die Co............................. E ..... 937 294-1405 Moraine *(G-10163)*	Herd Manufacturing Inc .... E ..... 216 651-4221 Cleveland *(G-3826)*	▲ Kalt Manufacturing Company............. D ..... 440 327-2102 North Ridgeville *(G-10738)*
Fabcor Inc .... F ..... 419 628-4428 Minster *(G-10057)*	Hess Industries Ltd .... F ..... 419 525-4000 Mansfield *(G-8802)*	Ken Forging Inc .... C ..... 440 993-8091 Jefferson *(G-7974)*
Fabrication Shop Inc .... F ..... 419 435-7934 Fostoria *(G-6978)*	Hi-Tech Wire Inc .... D ..... 419 678-8376 Saint Henry *(G-11721)*	Kent Mold and Manufacturing Co .... F ..... 330 673-3469 Kent *(G-8043)*
Faith Tool and Mfg Inc .... G ..... 440 951-5934 Willoughby *(G-14457)*	▲ Hi-Tek Manufacturing Inc .... C ..... 513 459-1094 Mason *(G-9108)*	Kiffer Industries Inc................................. E ..... 216 267-1818 Cleveland *(G-3919)*
Falls Stamping & Welding Co .... C ..... 330 928-1191 Cuyahoga Falls *(G-5541)*	High-Tech Mold & Machine Inc.............. F ..... 330 896-4466 Uniontown *(G-13420)*	Kilroy Company .... D ..... 440 951-8700 Cleveland *(G-3920)*
Falls Tool and Die Inc .... G ..... 330 633-4884 Akron *(G-144)*	Hocker Tool and Die Inc .... G ..... 937 274-3443 Dayton *(G-5811)*	Kiraly Tool and Die Inc .... F ..... 330 744-5773 Youngstown *(G-14885)*
Faull & Son LLC .... F ..... 330 652-4341 Niles *(G-10588)*	Hofacker Prcsion Machining LLC........... F ..... 937 832-7712 Clayton *(G-3273)*	Kirtland Plastics Inc................................. D ..... 440 951-4466 Kirtland *(G-8145)*
Fc Industries Inc .... E ..... 937 275-8700 Dayton *(G-5774)*	Holland Engraving Company .... G ..... 419 865-2765 Toledo *(G-12994)*	Knowlton Manufacturing Co Inc............. F ..... 513 631-7353 Cincinnati *(G-2803)*
Feitl Manufacturing Co Inc .... F ..... 330 405-6600 Macedonia *(G-8690)*	Homeworth Fabrication Mch Inc............. F ..... 330 525-5459 Homeworth *(C 7805)*	Koebbe Products Inc............................... D ..... 513 753-4200 Amelia *(G-430)*
Feller Tool Co.. F ..... 440 324-6277 Elyria *(G-6536)*	▲ Honda Engineering North A.............. B ..... 937 642-5000 Marysville *(G-9029)*	Kramer & Kiefer Inc................................. G ..... 330 336-8742 Wadsworth *(G-13647)*
▲ Ferriot Inc .... C ..... 330 786-3000 Akron *(G-147)*	Horizon Industries Corporation .... G ..... 937 323-0801 Springfield *(G-12324)*	Kreider Corp .... D ..... 937 325-8787 Springfield *(G-12341)*
First Machine & Tool Corp..................... G ..... 440 269-8644 Willoughby *(G-14459)*	Ibycorp... G ..... 330 425-8226 Twinsburg *(G-13318)*	Krengel Equipment LLC.......................... C ..... 440 946-3570 Eastlake *(G-6434)*
First Tool Corp .... F ..... 937 254-6197 Dayton *(G-5777)*	▲ Ilsco LLC .... C ..... 513 533-6200 Blue Ash *(G-1287)*	Krisdale Inc.. G ..... 330 225-2392 Valley City *(G-13501)*
Fischer Special Tooling Corp.................. G ..... 440 951-8411 Mentor *(G-9516)*	Impact Industries Inc .... F ..... 440 327-2360 North Ridgeville *(G-10735)*	Kuhns Mold & Tool Co Inc....................... D ..... 937 833-2178 Brookville *(G-1572)*
Founders Service & Mfg Inc................... G ..... 330 584-7759 Deerfield *(G-6093)*	Imperial Die & Mfg Co............................. G ..... 440 268-9080 Strongsville *(G-12566)*	Kurtz Tool & Die Co Inc.......................... G ..... 330 755-7723 Struthers *(G-12619)*
▼ Fremar Industries Inc .... E ..... 330 220-3700 Brunswick *(G-1592)*	Independent Stamping Inc .... F ..... 216 251-3500 Cleveland *(G-3857)*	Lahm-Trosper Inc .... F ..... 937 252-8791 Dayton *(G-5841)*
Fremont Cutting Dies Inc .... G ..... 419 334-5153 Fremont *(G-7109)*	Industrial Mold Inc .... E ..... 330 425-7374 Twinsburg *(G-13320)*	▲ Lako Tool & Manufacturing Inc.......... F ..... 419 662-5256 Perrysburg *(G-11234)*
Gasdorf Tool and Mch Co Inc................. E ..... 419 227-0103 Lima *(G-8409)*	▲ Industry Products Co........................... B ..... 937 778-0585 Piqua *(G-11356)*	Lange Precision Inc................................. F ..... 513 530-9500 Lebanon *(G-8273)*
Gem City Engineering Co .... C ..... 937 223-5544 Dayton *(G-5792)*	Innovative Plastic Molders LLC.............. E ..... 937 898-3775 Vandalia *(G-13562)*	Langenau Manufacturing Company .... F ..... 216 651-3400 Cleveland *(G-3939)*
▲ General Die Casters Inc .... E ..... 330 678-2528 Twinsburg *(G-13310)*	Innovative Tool & Die Inc....................... G ..... 419 599-0492 Napoleon *(G-10287)*	Lanko Industries Inc............................... G ..... 440 269-1641 Mentor *(G-9550)*
▲ General Tool Company .... C ..... 513 733-5500 Cincinnati *(G-2666)*	Intelitool Mfg Svcs Inc............................ G ..... 440 953-1071 Willoughby *(G-14470)*	Laspina Tool and Die Inc .... F ..... 330 923-9996 Stow *(G-12437)*

S
I
C

▲ Laszeray Technology LLC.............. D 440 582-8430
　North Royalton *(G-10770)*

Levan Enterprises Inc...................... E 330 923-9797
　Stow *(G-12438)*

Liberty Die Cast Molds Inc............... F 740 666-7492
　Ostrander *(G-11028)*

Lightning Mold & Machine Inc.............. F 440 593-6460
　Conneaut *(G-5408)*

Lincoln Electric Automtn Inc................ C 419 678-4877
　Coldwater *(G-4581)*

Lincoln Electric Automtn Inc................ B 937 295-2120
　Fort Loramie *(G-6950)*

Liqui-Box Corporation...................... E 419 294-3884
　Upper Sandusky *(G-13446)*

▲ Logan Machine Company................... D 330 633-6163
　Akron *(G-210)*

Lomar Enterprises Inc...................... F 614 409-9104
　Groveport *(G-7443)*

▲ Long-Stanton Mfg Company............. E 513 874-8020
　West Chester *(G-14024)*

Lorain Rled Die Pdts Indus Sup............. G 440 281-8607
　North Ridgeville *(G-10739)*

▼ Loroco Industries Inc..................... D 513 891-9544
　Cincinnati *(G-2828)*

Lowry Tool & Die Inc....................... F 330 332-1722
　Salem *(G-11795)*

Lrb Tool & Die Ltd......................... F 330 898-5783
　Warren *(G-13778)*

Lukens Inc................................. D 937 440-2500
　Troy *(G-13237)*

Lunar Tool & Mold Inc...................... E 440 237-2141
　North Royalton *(G-10771)*

M & M Dies Inc............................ G 216 883-6628
　Cleveland *(G-3973)*

Machine Tek Systems Inc................... E 330 527-4450
　Garrettsville *(G-7225)*

Machine Tool Design & Fab LLC........... F 419 435-7676
　Tiffin *(G-12789)*

Magnum Molding Inc....................... G 937 368-3040
　Conover *(G-5421)*

◆ Magnum Tool Corp......................... F 937 228-0900
　Dayton *(G-5861)*

Majestic Tool and Machine Inc............. G 440 248-5058
　Solon *(G-12144)*

Mallory Pattern Works Inc................. G 419 726-8001
　Toledo *(G-13046)*

Manufacturers Service Inc................. E 216 267-3771
　Cleveland *(G-3985)*

Mar-Con Tool Company..................... E 937 299-2244
　Moraine *(G-10175)*

Mar-Metal Mfg Inc......................... G 419 447-1102
　Upper Sandusky *(G-13447)*

Mar-Vel Tool Co........................... F 937 223-2137
　Dayton *(G-5868)*

Marsh Technologies Inc................... G 330 545-0085
　Girard *(G-7275)*

▼ Martin Pultrusion Group Inc............. G 440 439-9130
　Cleveland *(G-3992)*

Master Craft Products Inc................. F 216 281-5910
　Cleveland *(G-3996)*

Match Mold & Machine Inc................. G 330 830-5503
　Massillon *(G-9220)*

Maumee Pattern Company................... E 419 693-4968
　Toledo *(G-13049)*

May Industries of Ohio Inc................ E 440 237-8012
　North Royalton *(G-10773)*

McAfee Tool & Die Inc..................... E 330 896-9555
　Uniontown *(G-13423)*

▲ McGregor Mtal Yllow Sprng Wrks..... D 937 325-5561
　Springfield *(G-12351)*

McRon Finance Corp........................ C 513 487-5000
　Cincinnati *(G-2851)*

Mdf Tool Corporation...................... F 440 237-2277
　North Royalton *(G-10774)*

Medway Tool Corp.......................... G 937 335-7717
　Troy *(G-13240)*

Meese Inc................................. F 440 998-1202
　Ashtabula *(G-604)*

Meggitt (erlanger) LLC.................... D 513 851-5550
　Cincinnati *(G-2858)*

Mercury Machine Co........................ D 440 349-3222
　Solon *(G-12147)*

Metal & Wire Products Company............. E 330 332-9448
　Salem *(G-11799)*

◆ Metalex Manufacturing Inc.............. C 513 489-0507
　Blue Ash *(G-1310)*

▲ Mid-Ohio Products Inc................... D 614 771-2795
　Hilliard *(G-7686)*

▲ Midwest Mold & Texture Corp........... E 513 732-1300
　Batavia *(G-873)*

Midwest Tool & Engineering Co............. G
　Dayton *(G-5883)*

Milacron Holdings Corp.................... B 513 487-5000
　Batavia *(G-874)*

Milacron Plas Tech Group LLC............. A 937 444-2532
　Mount Orab *(G-10219)*

▲ Milacron Plas Tech Group LLC........... C 513 536-2000
　Batavia *(G-876)*

Minco Tool and Mold Inc................... D 937 890-7905
　Dayton *(G-5889)*

▼ Mohr Stamping Inc....................... E 440 647-4316
　Wellington *(G-13896)*

Mold Shop Inc............................. F 419 829-2041
　Sylvania *(G-12716)*

Mold Surface Textures Inc................. G 330 678-8590
　Kent *(G-8055)*

Moldmakers Inc............................ F 419 673-0902
　Kenton *(G-8108)*

Monarch Products Co....................... G 330 868-7717
　Minerva *(G-10044)*

Monitor Mold & Machine Co................. F 330 697-7800
　Rootstown *(G-11650)*

Mordies Inc............................... F 330 758-8050
　Youngstown *(G-14902)*

Mt Vernon Mold Works Inc................. E 618 242-6040
　Akron *(G-238)*

◆ Mtd Holdings Inc......................... B 330 225-2600
　Valley City *(G-13508)*

Mutual Tool LLC........................... F 937 667-5818
　Tipp City *(G-12832)*

Nation Tool & Die Ltd..................... E 419 822-5939
　Delta *(G-6213)*

National Pattern Mfgco.................... F 330 682-6871
　Orrville *(G-10997)*

National Roller Die Inc................... F 440 951-3850
　Willoughby *(G-14492)*

Nelson Tool Corporation................... F 740 965-1894
　Sunbury *(G-12669)*

◆ Nesco Inc................................ E 440 461-6000
　Cleveland *(G-4068)*

New Bremen Machine & Tool Co............. E 419 629-3295
　New Bremen *(G-10363)*

New Castings Inc.......................... E 330 645-6653
　Akron *(G-245)*

New Die Inc............................... E 419 726-7581
　Toledo *(G-13062)*

Neway Stamping & Mfg Inc................. D 440 951-8500
　Willoughby *(G-14494)*

Nichols Mold Inc.......................... G 330 297-9719
　Ravenna *(G-11534)*

Nn Metal Stampings LLC.................... E 419 737-2311
　Pioneer *(G-11322)*

Noble Tool Corp........................... E 937 461-4040
　Dayton *(G-5908)*

Northwestern Tools Inc.................... F 937 298-9994
　Dayton *(G-5911)*

Numerics Unlimited Inc.................... E 937 849-0100
　New Carlisle *(G-10377)*

▲ Oakley Die & Mold Co.................... E 513 754-8500
　Mason *(G-9131)*

Ohio Associated Entps LLC................. F 440 354-3148
　Painesville *(G-11101)*

Ohio Custom Dies LLC...................... F 330 538-3396
　North Jackson *(G-10691)*

Ohio Specialty Dies LLC................... F 330 538-3396
　North Jackson *(G-10692)*

Ohio Tool & Jig Grind Inc................. G 937 415-0692
　Springboro *(G-12262)*

Omni Manufacturing Inc.................... F 419 394-7424
　Saint Marys *(G-11748)*

▲ Omni Manufacturing Inc.................. D 419 394-7424
　Saint Marys *(G-11747)*

Orick Stamping Inc........................ D 419 331-0600
　Elida *(G-6484)*

P J Tool Company Inc...................... G 937 254-2817
　Dayton *(G-5933)*

P O McIntire Company...................... E 440 269-1848
　Wickliffe *(G-14387)*

PA MA Inc................................. G 440 846-3799
　Strongsville *(G-12584)*

Pace Mold & Machine LLC................... G 330 879-1777
　Massillon *(G-9231)*

Palisin & Associates Inc.................. E 216 252-3930
　Cleveland *(G-4132)*

Perry Welding Service Inc................. F 330 425-2211
　Twinsburg *(G-13355)*

Phillips Mch & Stamping Corp.............. G 330 882-6714
　New Franklin *(G-10392)*

Phoenix Tool Company...................... G 330 372-4627
　Warren *(G-13789)*

Pier Tool & Die Inc....................... F 440 236-3188
　Columbia Station *(G-4597)*

▲ Plastic Enterprises Inc................. E 440 324-3240
　Elyria *(G-6580)*

Plastic Mold Technology Inc............... G 330 848-4921
　Barberton *(G-833)*

Pleasant Precision Inc.................... E 419 675-0556
　Kenton *(G-8111)*

Plrs Legacy Inc........................... F 440 365-7333
　North Ridgeville *(G-10742)*

Porter Precision Products Co.............. D 513 385-1569
　Cincinnati *(G-2974)*

Precast Products LLC...................... E 419 668-1639
　Norwalk *(G-10859)*

Precision Details Inc..................... F 937 596-0068
　Jackson Center *(G-7967)*

Precision Die & Stamping Inc.............. G 513 942-8220
　West Chester *(G-14052)*

Premere Enterprises Inc................... G 330 874-3000
　Bolivar *(G-1388)*

Prime Industries Inc...................... F
　Lorain *(G-8574)*

Pro-Tech Manufacturing Inc................ F 937 444-6484
　Mount Orab *(G-10222)*

Progage Inc............................... F 440 951-4477
　Mentor *(G-9597)*

Progress Tool & Stamping Inc.............. E 419 628-2384
　Minster *(G-10064)*

Progrssive Molding Bolivar Inc............ G 330 874-3000
　Bolivar *(G-1390)*

Project Engineering Company............... G 937 743-9114
　Germantown *(G-7253)*

Promac Inc................................ G 937 864-1961
　Enon *(G-6632)*

▲ Prospect Mold & Die Company............ C 330 929-3311
　Cuyahoga Falls *(G-5566)*

▲ Proto Plastics Inc.............................. E 937 667-8416
Tipp City *(G-12839)*

▲ PSK Steel Corp.................................. E 330 759-1251
Hubbard *(G-7816)*

Pyramid Mold & Machine Co Inc............. G 330 673-5200
Kent *(G-8065)*

▲ Quaker Mfg Corp................................ C 330 332-4631
Salem *(G-11807)*

Qualiform Inc...................................... E 330 336-6777
Wadsworth *(G-13663)*

Quality Specialists Inc......................... G 440 946-9129
Willoughby *(G-14513)*

Quality Tooling Systems Inc.................. F 330 722-5025
Medina *(G-9439)*

Queen City Tool Works Inc................... G 513 874-0111
Fairfield *(G-6770)*

R M Tool & Die Inc.............................. F 440 238-6459
Strongsville *(G-12591)*

R T & T Machining Co Inc..................... F 440 974-8479
Mentor *(G-9605)*

▲ Rage Corporation............................... D 614 771-4771
Hilliard *(G-7698)*

Ram Tool Inc...................................... G 937 277-0717
Dayton *(G-5973)*

Rapid Machine Inc............................... F 419 737-2377
Pioneer *(G-11327)*

▲ Raymath Company.............................. C 937 335-1860
Troy *(G-13249)*

▲ Ready Technology Inc.......................... F 937 866-7200
Dayton *(G-5978)*

Regal Metal Products Co....................... E 330 868-6343
Minerva *(G-10046)*

Reuther Mold & Mfg Co Inc.................. D 330 923-5266
Cuyahoga Falls *(G-5569)*

▲ Reymond Products Intl Inc.................... E 330 339-3583
New Philadelphia *(G-10464)*

Rhinestahl Corporation........................ E 513 229-5300
Mason *(G-9143)*

Rmt Corporation................................. F 937 274-2121
Dayton *(G-5985)*

Rockstedt Tool & Die Inc...................... G 330 273-9000
Brunswick *(G-1612)*

Ron-Al Mold & Machine Inc................... F 330 673-7919
Kent *(G-8070)*

Ronlen Industries Inc........................... E 330 273-6468
Brunswick *(G-1613)*

Ross Special Products Inc...................... F 937 335-8406
Troy *(G-13250)*

Roto-Die Company Inc.......................... G 513 942-3500
West Chester *(G-14071)*

Rotocast Technologies Inc.................... E 330 798-9091
Akron *(G-291)*

RPM Carbide Die Inc............................ E 419 894-6426
Arcadia *(G-483)*

▲ Saehwa IMC Na Inc............................. D 330 645-6653
Akron *(G-304)*

Saint-Gobain Ceramics Plas Inc............. D 330 673-5860
Stow *(G-12456)*

▲ Saint-Gobain Ceramics Plas Inc........... A 610 893-6000
Stow *(G-12457)*

Schmitmeyer Inc................................. G 937 295-2091
Fort Loramie *(G-6954)*

Seaway Pattern Mfg Inc........................ F 419 865-5724
Toledo *(G-13124)*

Seilkop Industries Inc.......................... F 513 353-3090
Miamitown *(G-9760)*

Seilkop Industries Inc.......................... E 513 761-1035
Cincinnati *(G-3077)*

◆ Select Industries Corporation............... C 937 233-9191
Dayton *(G-6001)*

Select Machine Inc.............................. F 330 678-7676
Kent *(G-8077)*

Self Made Holdings LLC........................ E 330 477-1052
Canton *(G-2001)*

Shalix Inc.. F 216 941-3546
Cleveland *(G-4287)*

◆ Shl Liquidation Industries Inc.............. A 330 558-2600
Valley City *(G-13517)*

Short Run Machine Products Inc............. F 440 969-1313
Ashtabula *(G-616)*

Sk Mold & Tool Inc.............................. E 937 339-0299
Troy *(G-13255)*

Sk Mold & Tool Inc.............................. E 937 339-0299
Tipp City *(G-12844)*

Skrl Die Casting Inc............................ F 440 946-7200
Willoughby *(G-14528)*

Sluterbeck Tool & Die Co Inc................. F 937 836-5736
Clayton *(G-3275)*

Smithville Mfg Co................................ F 330 345-5818
Wooster *(G-14687)*

Spectracam Ltd.................................. F 937 223-3805
Dayton *(G-6016)*

Spintech Holdings Inc........................... E 937 912-3250
Miamisburg *(G-9738)*

Stan-Kell LLC..................................... F 440 998-1116
Ashtabula *(G-617)*

▲ Stanco Precision Mfg Inc..................... G 937 274-1785
Dayton *(G-6022)*

◆ Standard Engineering Group Inc........... G 330 494-4300
North Canton *(G-10669)*

Starkey Machinery Inc.......................... E 419 468-2560
Galion *(G-7199)*

Std Liquidation Inc.............................. C 937 492-6121
Sidney *(G-12055)*

Stolle Machinery Company LLC.............. C 937 497-5400
Dayton *(G-6027)*

Straight 72 Inc................................... D 740 943-5730
Marysville *(G-9051)*

Suburban Metal Products Inc................. F 740 474-4237
Circleville *(G-3263)*

Sulecki Precision Products Inc............... F 440 255-5454
Mentor *(G-9630)*

Sumitomo Elc Carbide Mfg Inc.............. F 440 354-0600
Grand River *(G-7312)*

▲ Summit Tool Company.......................... D 330 535-7177
Akron *(G-322)*

Superior Mold & Die Co........................ F 330 688-8251
Munroe Falls *(G-10273)*

▲ Superior Production LLC....................... C 614 444-2181
Columbus *(G-3299)*

Sure Tool & Manufacturing Co............... E 937 253-9111
Dayton *(G-6033)*

Sutterlin Machine & TI Co Inc................ F 440 357-0817
Mentor *(G-9632)*

Symbol Tool & Die Inc.......................... G 440 582-5989
North Royalton *(G-10785)*

Taft Tool & Production Co..................... F 419 385-2576
Toledo *(G-13139)*

▲ Talent Tool & Die Inc.......................... F 440 239-8777
Berea *(G-1190)*

Tangible Solutions Inc......................... E 937 912-4603
Fairborn *(G-6701)*

Taylor Tool & Die Inc........................... G 937 845-1491
New Carlisle *(G-10381)*

▲ Te-Co Manufacturing LLC..................... D 937 836-0961
Englewood *(G-6625)*

Tech Industries Inc.............................. F 216 861-7337
Cleveland *(G-4368)*

Tech Mold and Tool Co.......................... G 937 667-8851
Tipp City *(G-12847)*

Technical Tool & Gauge Inc................... F 330 273-1778
Brunswick *(G-1617)*

▲ Technology House Ltd.......................... F 440 248-3025
Streetsboro *(G-12527)*

Tempcraft Corporation......................... D 216 391-3885
Cleveland *(G-4372)*

Tessec Manufacturing Svcs LLC............. E 937 985-3552
Dayton *(G-6046)*

Tetra Mold & Tool Inc.......................... E 937 845-1651
New Carlisle *(G-10382)*

The Kordenbrock Tool and Die Co.......... F 513 326-4390
Cincinnati *(G-3148)*

▲ The Louis G Freeman Compa................. D 419 334-9709
Fremont *(G-7136)*

The Pioneer Tool and Die Co.................. D 330 724-5572
Akron *(G-332)*

▲ The Vulcan Tool Company..................... G 937 253-6194
Dayton *(G-6050)*

Tipco Punch Inc.................................. E 513 874-9140
Hamilton *(G-7532)*

Tipp Machine & Tool Inc....................... C 937 890-8428
Dayton *(G-6055)*

Tm Machine & Tool Inc......................... E 419 478-0310
Toledo *(G-13144)*

Tmd Inc.. C 419 476-4581
Toledo *(G-13145)*

Toledo Molding & Die LLC..................... C 419 476-0581
Toledo *(G-13154)*

◆ Toledo Molding & Die LLC.................... D 419 470-3950
Toledo *(G-13153)*

Toledo Tool and Die Co Inc................... F 419 476-9066
Pioneer *(G-11330)*

Toledo Tool and Die Co Inc................... F 419 476-4422
Toledo *(G-13160)*

▲ Toledo Tool and Die Co Inc.................. C 419 476-4422
Toledo *(G-13161)*

▲ Tom Smith Industries Inc..................... D 937 832-1555
Englewood *(G-6626)*

Tomahawk Tool Supply......................... G 419 485-8737
Montpelier *(G-10135)*

Tomco Tool Inc................................... G 937 322-5768
Springfield *(G-12388)*

Toney Tool Manufacturing Inc................ G 937 890-8535
Dayton *(G-6057)*

Tool Tech LLC..................................... E 614 893-5876
Springfield *(G-12389)*

Tool Technologies Van Dyke.................. F 937 349-4900
Marysville *(G-9053)*

Toolcraft Products Inc.......................... E 937 223-8271
Dayton *(G-6058)*

Tooling & Components Corp................... F 419 478-9122
Toledo *(G-13103)*

Tooling Connection Inc......................... G 419 594-3339
Oakwood *(G-10901)*

Tooling Technology LLC........................ D 937 381-9211
Fort Loramie *(G-6960)*

Tooling Zone Inc................................. E 937 550-4180
Springboro *(G-12271)*

Toolrite Manufacturing Inc.................... E 937 278-1962
Dayton *(G-6059)*

Top Tool & Die Inc.............................. G 216 267-5878
Cleveland *(G-4403)*

Torrmetal LLC..................................... E 216 671-1616
Cleveland *(G-4405)*

Torrmetal Corporation......................... E 216 671-1616
Cleveland *(G-4406)*

Tradye Machine & Tool Inc.................... E 740 625-7550
Centerburg *(G-2128)*

Trexler Rubber Co Inc.......................... E 330 296-9677
Ravenna *(G-11546)*

Tri-Craft Inc...................................... E 440 826-1050
Cleveland *(G-4418)*

▲ Trim Parts Inc.................................... E 513 934-0815
Lebanon *(G-8291)*

Trim Tool & Machine Inc....................... E 216 889-1916
Cleveland *(G-4426)*

S I C

Trimline Die Corporation............................ E 440 355-6900
Lagrange *(G-8154)*

Troy Precision Carbide Die Inc.............. G 440 834-4477
Burton *(G-1707)*

Tru-Tex International Corp...................... G 513 825-8844
Cincinnati *(G-3171)*

▲ Trucut Incorporated............................ D 330 938-9806
Sebring *(G-11903)*

True Industries Inc................................ E 330 296-4342
Ravenna *(G-11547)*

▲ Tuf-Tug Inc.. F 937 299-1213
Dayton *(G-6067)*

TW Manufacturing Co............................ G 440 439-3243
Cleveland *(G-4434)*

U S Alloy Die Corp............................... F 216 749-9700
Cleveland *(G-4438)*

United Extrusion Dies Inc..................... F 330 533-2915
Canfield *(G-1818)*

United Finshg & Die Cutng Inc.............. G 216 881-0239
Cleveland *(G-4442)*

Universal Tool Technology LLC.............. G 937 222-4608
Dayton *(G-6069)*

Unlimited Machine and Tool LLC........... F 419 269-1730
Toledo *(G-13171)*

Valley Tool & Die Inc........................... D 440 237-0160
North Royalton *(G-10788)*

Van Wert Machine Inc.......................... E 419 692-6836
Delphos *(G-6198)*

Velocity Concept Dev Group LLC.......... G 740 685-2637
Byesville *(G-1717)*

Village Plastics Co.............................. G 330 753-0100
Euclid *(G-6683)*

Vinyl Tool & Die Company.................... G 330 782-0254
Youngstown *(G-14963)*

Vinyltech Inc...................................... F 330 538-0369
North Jackson *(G-10699)*

▲ Vmi Americas Inc............................. E 330 929-6800
Stow *(G-12471)*

Walest Incorporated............................ G 216 362-8110
Brunswick *(G-1623)*

Walker Tool & Machine Company.......... F 419 661-8000
Perrysburg *(G-11278)*

Weiss Industries Inc............................ F 419 526-2480
Mansfield *(G-8865)*

Welage Corporation............................. F 513 681-2300
Cincinnati *(G-3214)*

▲ Wentworth Mold Inc Electra............... D 937 898-8460
Vandalia *(G-13583)*

Western Ohio Technologies LLC........... G 937 947-8810
Russia *(G-11678)*

White Machine Inc.............................. G 440 237-3282
North Royalton *(G-10789)*

Williams Steel Rule Die Co................... G 216 431-3232
Cleveland *(G-4507)*

Wilmington Prcsion McHning Inc........... E 937 382-3700
Wilmington *(G-14591)*

Windsor Tool Inc................................ F 216 671-1900
Cleveland *(G-4508)*

Wire Shop Inc.................................... E 440 354-6842
Mentor *(G-9653)*

▲ WLS Stamping Co............................ D 216 271-5100
Cleveland *(G-4511)*

▲ Wurtec Manufacturing Service........... E 419 726-1066
Toledo *(G-13180)*

XCEL Mold and Machine Inc................ F 330 499-8450
Canton *(G-2050)*

Youngstown Tool & Die Company.......... D 330 747-4464
Youngstown *(G-14977)*

3545 Machine tool accessories

Able Tool Corporation.......................... E 513 733-8989
Cincinnati *(G-2334)*

▲ Accretech SBS Inc............................ G 513 373-4844
Cincinnati *(G-2336)*

Advanced Holding Designs Inc............. G 330 928-4456
Cuyahoga Falls *(G-5520)*

Aeroll Engineering Corp...................... G 216 481-2266
Cleveland *(G-3310)*

Akron Gear & Engineering Inc............. E 330 773-6608
Akron *(G-32)*

◆ Alliance Knife Inc............................. E ... 513 367-9000
Harrison *(G-7542)*

▲ Allied Machine & Engrg Corp............ C 330 343-4283
Dover *(G-6228)*

Anchor Lamina America Inc................. F 330 952-1595
Medina *(G-9375)*

▲ Angstrom Precision Metals LLC......... F 440 255-6700
Mentor *(G-9481)*

Antwerp TI Die & Engrg Co Inc............ F 419 258-5271
Antwerp *(G-461)*

Apollo Products Inc............................ F 440 269-8551
Willoughby *(G-14422)*

Arch Cutng Tls Cincinnati LLC............. F 513 851-6363
West Chester *(G-14104)*

Arnold Gauge Co Inc.......................... F 877 942-4243
West Chester *(G-13942)*

Ata Tools Inc..................................... C 330 928-7744
Cuyahoga Falls *(G-5531)*

Atalys Ottoville LLC............................ E 419 453-3376
Ottoville *(G-11052)*

B & R Machine Co.............................. F 216 961-7370
Cleveland *(G-3399)*

BAP Manufacturing Inc....................... G 419 332-5041
Fremont *(G-7093)*

Bender Engineering Company.............. G 330 938-2355
Beloit *(G-1144)*

▲ Big Chief Manufacturing Ltd............. E 513 934-3888
Lebanon *(G-8247)*

Blue Ash Tool & Die Co Inc................. F 513 793-4530
Blue Ash *(G-1254)*

Capital Tool Company......................... E 216 661-5750
Cleveland *(G-3467)*

Carbide Probes Inc............................ E 937 429-9123
Beavercreek *(G-967)*

Certified Comparator Products............. G 937 426-9677
Miamisburg *(G-9679)*

Chardon Tool & Supply Co Inc............. E 440 286-6440
Chardon *(G-2200)*

Chart-Tech Tool Inc............................ F 937 667-3543
Tipp City *(G-12820)*

Chippewa Tool and Mfg Co................. F 419 849-2790
Woodville *(G-14616)*

Clapp & Haney Brazed TI Co Inc.......... G 740 922-3515
Dennison *(G-6217)*

Cleveland Spclty Insptn Svc In............. F 440 974-1818
Mentor *(G-9501)*

Coldwater Machine Company LLC......... C 419 678-4877
Coldwater *(G-4571)*

Commercial Grinding Svcs Inc............. E 330 273-5040
Medina *(G-9389)*

Container Graphics Corp...................... E 419 531-5133
Toledo *(G-12932)*

▲ Covert Manufacturing Inc................. C 419 468-1761
Galion *(G-7185)*

Cowles Industrial Tool Co LLC............. E 330 799-9100
Austintown *(G-704)*

D C Morrison Company Inc.................. E 859 581-7511
Cincinnati *(G-2536)*

DA Precision Products Inc.................... F 513 459-1113
West Chester *(G-13981)*

▲ Dayton Progress Corporation............ A 937 859-5111
Dayton *(G-5737)*

Diamond Products Limited................... G 440 323-4616
Elyria *(G-6516)*

Diamond Products Limited................... G 440 323-4616
Elyria *(G-6517)*

◆ Diamond Products Limited................ B 440 323-4616
Elyria *(G-6518)*

Diamond Reserve Inc.......................... F 440 892-7877
Westlake *(G-14298)*

▲ Diamonds Products LLC................... G 440 323-4616
Elyria *(G-6519)*

◆ Drt Mfg Co LLC............................... D ... 937 297-6670
Dayton *(G-5754)*

Dysinger Incorporated........................ E 937 297-7761
Dayton *(G-5757)*

E & J Demark Inc................................ E 419 337-5866
Wauseon *(G-13848)*

Eversharpe-Deburring Tool Co............. G 513 988-6240
Trenton *(G-13192)*

Feedall Inc.. F 440 942-8100
Willoughby *(G-14458)*

Fischer Special Tooling Corp................ G 440 951-8411
Mentor *(G-9516)*

Flex-E-On Inc.................................... F 330 928-4496
Cuyahoga Falls *(G-5542)*

Fox Tool Co Inc................................. G 330 928-3402
Cuyahoga Falls *(G-5543)*

▲ Frecon Technologies Inc.................. F 513 874-8981
West Chester *(G-14001)*

◆ Furukawa Rock Drill USA Co Ltd....... F 330 673-5826
Kent *(G-8034)*

George Whalley Company.................... F 216 453-0099
Fairport Harbor *(G-6816)*

◆ Glassline Corporation...................... E 419 666-9712
Perrysburg *(G-11225)*

◆ Gleason Metrology Systems Corp...... E 937 384-8901
Dayton *(G-5796)*

Greentec Precision Inc........................ G 937 431-1840
Beavercreek *(G-976)*

H & S Tool Inc................................... F 330 335-1536
Wadsworth *(G-13642)*

H3d Tool Corporation......................... E 740 498-5181
Newcomerstown *(G-10570)*

Hammill Manufacturing Co.................. G 419 476-0789
Maumee *(G-9295)*

◆ Hapco Inc...................................... F ... 330 678-9353
Kent *(G-8035)*

HI Carb Corp..................................... G 216 486-5000
Eastlake *(G-6432)*

▲ High Quality Tools Inc...................... F 440 975-9684
Eastlake *(G-6433)*

▲ Hudson Supply Company Inc............ G 216 518-3000
Cleveland *(G-3843)*

Imco Carbide Tool Inc......................... D 419 661-6313
Perrysburg *(G-11230)*

Interstate Tool Corporation.................. E 216 671-1077
Cleveland *(G-3866)*

Jbm Technologies of Ohio LLC............. G 216 264-1270
Willoughby *(G-14472)*

▲ Jergens Inc..................................... C 216 486-5540
Cleveland *(G-3885)*

Jerry Tools Inc................................... F 513 242-3211
Cincinnati *(G-2765)*

JM Performance Products Inc.............. F 440 357-1234
Fairport Harbor *(G-6817)*

Johnson Bros Rubber Co Inc............... E 419 752-4814
Greenwich *(G-7362)*

Kaeper Machine Inc............................ E 440 974-1010
Mentor *(G-9545)*

▲ Kalt Manufacturing Company............ D 440 327-2102
North Ridgeville *(G-10738)*

Karma Metal Products Inc................... F 419 524-4371
Mansfield *(G-8810)*

Keb Industries Inc.............................. G 440 953-4623
Willoughby *(G-14475)*

Kennametal Inc...................... D 440 437-5131
Orwell *(G-11022)*

Kennametal Inc...................... C 440 349-5151
Solon *(G-12138)*

Kiffer Industries Inc.............. E 216 267-1818
Cleveland *(G-3919)*

Kilroy Company..................... D 440 951-8700
Cleveland *(G-3920)*

▲ Knb Tools of America Inc............. F 614 733-0400
Plain City *(G-11412)*

Kongsberg Prcsion Ctng Systems........ F 937 800-2169
Miamisburg *(G-9707)*

Kyocera SGS Precision Tls Inc......... D 330 922-1953
Cuyahoga Falls *(G-5558)*

▲ Kyocera SGS Precision Tls Inc........ E 330 688-6667
Cuyahoga Falls *(G-5557)*

Lange Precision Inc................... F 513 530-9500
Lebanon *(G-8273)*

Levan Enterprises Inc................. E 330 923-9797
Stow *(G-12438)*

Lincoln Electric Automtn Inc.......... C 419 678-4877
Coldwater *(G-4581)*

Lord Corporation...................... C 937 278-9431
Dayton *(G-5854)*

LS Starrett Company................... D 440 835-0005
Westlake *(G-14313)*

Luther Machine Inc.................... G 440 259-5014
Perry *(G-11194)*

M & J Tooling Ltd..................... F 937 951-3527
Dayton *(G-5856)*

M A Harrison Mfg Co Inc............... E 440 965-4306
Wakeman *(G-13682)*

▲ Machining Technologies Inc........... F 419 862-3110
Elmore *(G-6489)*

Master Carbide Tools Company.......... F 440 352-1112
Perry *(G-11196)*

Matrix Tool & Machine Inc............. E 440 255-0300
Mentor *(G-9560)*

Mdf Tool Corporation.................. F 440 237-2277
North Royalton *(G-10774)*

Medway Tool Corp...................... G 937 335-7717
Troy *(G-13240)*

Melin Tool Company Inc................ D 216 362-4200
Cleveland *(G-4019)*

◆ Metalex Manufacturing Inc............ C 513 489-0507
Blue Ash *(G-1310)*

Midwest Tool & Engineering Co......... G
Dayton *(G-5893)*

Monaghan & Associates Inc............. F 937 253-7706
Dayton *(G-5892)*

MSC Industries Inc.................... G 440 474-8788
Rome *(G-11645)*

National Machine Co................... G 330 688-2584
Stow *(G-12445)*

▲ Oakley Die & Mold Co................. E 513 754-8500
Mason *(G-9131)*

Obars Machine and Tool Company........ E 419 535-6307
Toledo *(G-13068)*

▼ Ohio Broach & Machine Company........ E 440 946-1040
Willoughby *(G-14499)*

Ohio Drill & Tool Co.................. E 330 525-7717
Homeworth *(G-7806)*

Omwp Company.......................... E 330 453-8438
Canton *(G-1969)*

▲ Osg-Sterling Die Inc................. F 216 267-1300
Parma *(G-11133)*

P O McIntire Company.................. E 440 269-1848
Wickliffe *(G-14387)*

Pemco Inc............................. E 216 524-2990
Cleveland *(G-4150)*

Performance Superabrasives LLC........ G 440 946-7171
Mentor *(G-9586)*

Plrs Legacy Inc....................... F 440 365-7333
North Ridgeville *(G-10742)*

PMC Gage Inc.......................... E 440 953-1672
Willoughby *(G-14507)*

Positrol Inc.......................... E 513 272-0500
Cincinnati *(G-2976)*

Precise Tool & Mfg Corp............... F 216 524-1500
Cleveland *(G-4182)*

Precision Gage & Tool Company......... E 937 866-9666
Dayton *(G-5946)*

Preston............................... G 740 788-8208
Newark *(G-10529)*

Quality Cutter Grinding Co............ F 216 362-6444
Cleveland *(G-4213)*

R A Heller Company.................... F 513 771-6100
Cincinnati *(G-3027)*

R T & T Machining Co Inc.............. F 440 974-8479
Mentor *(G-9605)*

Red Head Brass Inc.................... F 330 567-2903
Shreve *(G-11985)*

▼ Regal Diamond Products Corp.......... F 440 944-7700
Wickliffe *(G-14393)*

Retention Knob Supply & Mfg Co........ F 937 686-6405
Huntsville *(G-7865)*

◆ Rex International USA Inc............. E 800 321-7950
Ashtabula *(G-615)*

Rhgs Company.......................... G 513 721-6299
Cincinnati *(G-3040)*

Ridge Tool Manufacturing Co........... F 440 323-5581
Elyria *(G-6588)*

Riten Industries Incorporated......... E 740 335-5353
Wshngtn Ct Hs *(G-14745)*

◆ Rol - Tech Inc....................... G 214 905-8050
Fort Loramie *(G-6953)*

Schumann Enterprises Inc.............. E 216 267-6850
Cleveland *(G-4276)*

Self Made Holdings LLC................ E 330 477-1052
Canton *(G-2001)*

Setco Industries Inc.................. D 513 941-5110
Cincinnati *(G-3085)*

Sharp Tool Service Inc................ E 330 273-4144
Cleveland *(G-4288)*

Shi Liquidation Medina Inc............ C
Valley City *(G-13519)*

Shook Manufactured Pdts Inc........... G 440 247-9130
Chagrin Falls *(G-2151)*

▲ Shook Manufactured Pdts Inc.......... G 330 848-9780
Akron *(C 311)*

Sjk Machine LLC....................... F 330 868-3072
North Lawrence *(G-10702)*

▲ Skidmore-Wilhelm Mfg Company......... G 216 481-4774
Solon *(G-12182)*

SL Endmills Inc....................... F 513 851-6363
West Chester *(G-1414v)*

Sorbothane Inc........................ E 330 678-9444
Kent *(G-8081)*

Sp3 Winco LLC......................... F 937 667-4476
Tipp City *(G-12846)*

Spectrum Machine Inc.................. F 330 626-3666
Streetsboro *(G-12524)*

Stanley Bittinger..................... G 740 942-4302
Cadiz *(G-1720)*

STC International Co Ltd............... G 561 308-6002
Lebanon *(G-8287)*

Sumitomo Elc Carbide Mfg Inc.......... F 440 354-0600
Grand River *(G-7312)*

▲ Superion Inc......................... E 937 374-0033
Xenia *(G-14776)*

Supplier Inspection Svcs Inc.......... F 877 263-7097
Dayton *(G-6031)*

Taft Tool & Production Co............. F 419 385-2576
Toledo *(G-13139)*

Te-Co Inc............................. F 937 836-0961
Union *(G-13412)*

▲ Te-Co Manufacturing LLC.............. D 937 836-0961
Englewood *(G-6625)*

Technidrill Systems Inc............... E 330 678-9980
Kent *(G-8087)*

Tessa Precision Product Inc........... E 440 392-3470
Painesville *(G-11115)*

▲ Thaler Machine Company LLC........... C 937 550-2400
Springboro *(G-12269)*

Thaler Machine Holdings LLC........... F 937 550-2400
Springboro *(G-12270)*

Tomco Tool Inc........................ G 937 322-5768
Springfield *(G-12388)*

Troyke Manufacturing Company.......... F 513 769-4242
Cincinnati *(G-3170)*

Uhrichsville Carbide Inc.............. F 740 922-9197
Uhrichsville *(G-13409)*

United States Drill Head Co........... F 513 941-0300
Cincinnati *(G-3185)*

Whip Guide Co......................... F 440 543-5151
Chagrin Falls *(G-2191)*

Wise Edge LLC......................... G 330 208-0889
Mogadore *(G-10094)*

Yoder Sharpening Ltd.................. F 330 359-0767
Dundee *(G-6373)*

3546 Power-driven handtools

▲ A JC Inc............................. F 800 428-2438
Hudson *(G-7826)*

▲ Aircraft Dynamics Corporation........ F 419 331-0371
Elida *(G-6482)*

Allegion Access Tech LLC.............. E 440 461-5500
Cleveland *(G-3330)*

Apex Tool Group LLC................... C 937 222-7871
Dayton *(G-5661)*

Black & Decker (us) Inc............... G 614 895-3112
Columbus *(G-4760)*

Black & Decker Corporation............ G 440 842-9100
Cleveland *(G-3420)*

◆ Ch Transition Company LLC............ C 800 543-6400
Cincinnati *(G-2457)*

Chicago Pneumatic Tool Co LLC......... F 704 883-3500
Broadview Heights *(G-1500)*

Corbett R Caudill Chipping Inc........ G 740 596-5984
Hamden *(G-7461)*

▲ ET&f Fastening Systems Inc........... G 800 248-2376
Solon *(G-12100)*

◆ Furukawa Rock Drill Usa Inc.......... F 330 673-5826
Kent *(G-8033)*

◆ Furukawa Rock Drill USA Co Ltd....... F 330 673-5826
Kent *(G-8034)*

◆ Gzjb Holdings Inc.................... E 216 731-0500
Cleveland *(G-3803)*

Hall-Toledo Inc....................... F 419 893-4334
Maumee *(G-9294)*

Huron Cement Products Company......... E 419 433-4161
Huron *(G-7874)*

▲ Kyocera Senco Indus Tls Inc.......... D 513 388-2000
Cincinnati *(G-2809)*

Madison Property Holdings Inc......... E 800 215-3210
Cincinnati *(G-2839)*

Michael Byrne Manufacturing Co Inc.... E 419 525-1214
Mansfield *(G-8825)*

◆ Npk Construction Equipment Inc....... D 440 232-7900
Bedford *(G-1050)*

Ohio Drill & Tool Co.................. E 330 525-7717
Homeworth *(G-7806)*

◆ Rex International USA Inc............. E 800 321-7950
Ashtabula *(G-615)*

◆ Ridge Tool Company................... A 440 323-5581
Elyria *(G-6586)*

Ridge Tool Manufacturing Co.............. F 440 323-5581
Elyria *(G-6588)*

◆ Rjs Corporation.............................E 330 896-2387
Akron *(G-287)*

Scepter Supply LLC............................ G 307 634-6074
Marietta *(G-8942)*

Sewer Rodding Equipment Co............ C 419 991-2065
Lima *(G-8447)*

Stanley Bittinger................................. G 740 942-4302
Cadiz *(G-1720)*

▲ Stanley Industrial & Auto LLC........ D 614 755-7000
Dublin *(G-6349)*

Suburban Manufacturing Co............... D 440 953-2024
Eastlake *(G-6444)*

Sumitomo Elc Carbide Mfg Inc......... F 440 354-0600
Grand River *(G-7312)*

T C Service Co..................................... E 440 954-7500
Willoughby *(G-14536)*

Technidrill Systems Inc...................... E 330 678-9980
Kent *(G-8087)*

Trane Technologies Company LLC....... E 419 633-6800
Bryan *(G-1665)*

Uhrichsville Carbide Inc..................... F 740 922-9197
Uhrichsville *(G-13409)*

Wolf Machine Company....................... E 513 791-5194
Blue Ash *(G-1352)*

3547 Rolling mill machinery

▲ Addition Manufacturing Te.............. C 513 228-7000
Lebanon *(G-8241)*

ADS Machinery Corp............................ D 330 399-3601
Warren *(G-13731)*

▲ Bardons & Oliver Inc..................... C 440 498-5800
Solon *(G-12082)*

Bendco Machine & Tool Inc .... F 419 628-3802
Minster *(G-10054)*

▲ Circle Machine Rolls Inc................ E 330 938-9010
Sebring *(G-11893)*

Cornerstone Wauseon Inc.................... C 419 337-0940
Wauseon *(G-13847)*

◆ E R Advanced Ceramics Inc............ E 330 426-9433
East Palestine *(G-6402)*

Element Machinery LLC...................... G 855 447-7648
Toledo *(G-12949)*

▲ Enprotech Industrial Tech LLC....... E 216 883-3220
Cleveland *(G-3675)*

◆ Fives Bronx Inc................................D 330 244-1960
North Canton *(G-10639)*

▲ Formtek Inc...................................... D 216 292-4460
Cleveland *(G-3737)*

Formtek Metal Forming Inc................ D 216 292-4460
Cleveland *(G-3738)*

▼ George A Mitchell Company............. E 330 758-5777
Youngstown *(G-14866)*

H P E Inc... G 330 833-3161
Massillon *(G-9199)*

Hydranamics Inc.................................. D 419 468-3530
Galion *(G-7195)*

J Horst Manufacturing Co................... D 330 828-2216
Dalton *(G-5586)*

▲ Kottler Metal Products Co Inc......... E 440 946-7473
Willoughby *(G-14478)*

Multi Galvanizing LLC......................... G 330 453-1441
Canton *(G-1953)*

◆ Park Corporation..............................B 216 267-4870
Medina *(G-9434)*

Perfecto Industries Inc....................... E 937 778-1900
Piqua *(G-11372)*

▲ Pines Manufacturing Inc................. E 440 835-5553
Westlake *(G-14324)*

▲ Rafter Equipment Company LLC...... E 440 572-3700
Strongsville *(G-12592)*

◆ Ridge Tool Company...........................A 440 323-5581
Elyria *(G-6586)*

Ridge Tool Manufacturing Co.............. F 440 323-5581
Elyria *(G-6588)*

Rki Inc... C 888 953-9400
Mentor *(G-9608)*

Sentek Corporation.............................. G 614 586-1123
Columbus *(G-5261)*

▲ Steel Eqp Specialists Inc................ D 330 823-8260
Alliance *(G-406)*

Sticker Corporation............................. F 440 946-2100
Willoughby *(G-14534)*

Turner Machine Co.............................. G 330 332-5821
Salem *(G-11816)*

◆ United Rolls Inc.................................D
Canton *(G-2036)*

◆ Warren Fabricating Corporation.......D 330 534-5017
Hubbard *(G-7818)*

◆ Xtek Inc..B 513 733-7800
Cincinnati *(G-3240)*

3548 Welding apparatus

Accurate Manufacturing Company....... F 614 878-6510
Dublin *(G-6272)*

Aerowave Inc....................................... G 440 731-8464
Elyria *(G-6492)*

AK Fabrication Inc............................... F 330 458-1037
Canton *(G-1827)*

◆ Ch Transition Company LLC.............C 800 543-6400
Cincinnati *(G-2457)*

▲ Fusion Incorporated........................ D 440 946-3300
Willoughby *(G-14460)*

Hobart Brothers LLC........................... C 937 332-5953
Piqua *(G-11354)*

Hobart Brothers LLC........................... C 937 332-5023
Troy *(G-13223)*

◆ Hobart Brothers LLC..........................A 937 332-5439
Troy *(G-13222)*

Imax Industries Inc............................. F 440 639-0242
Painesville *(G-11095)*

Ivostud LLC.. G 440 925-4227
Brookpark *(G-1553)*

◆ J W Harris Co Inc.............................B 513 754-2000
Mason *(G-9116)*

Kaliburn Inc... F 843 695-4073
Cleveland *(G-3905)*

◆ Lincoln Electric Company..................A 216 481-8100
Cleveland *(G-3955)*

Lincoln Electric Holdings Inc.............. B 216 481-8100
Cleveland *(G-3956)*

◆ Luvata Ohio Inc..................................D 740 363-1981
Delaware *(G-6161)*

Mansfield Welding Service LLC............ G 419 594-2738
Oakwood *(G-10898)*

◆ Miller Weldmaster Corporation.........D 330 833-6739
Navarre *(G-10307)*

◆ Nelson Stud Welding Inc...................D 440 329-0400
Elyria *(G-6568)*

O E Meyer Co....................................... E 614 428-5656
Columbus *(G-5135)*

O E Meyer Co....................................... G 419 332-6931
Fremont *(G-7124)*

Otto Konigslow Mfg Co....................... F 216 851-7900
Cleveland *(G-4128)*

Peco Holdings Corp............................. D 937 667-5705
Tipp City *(G-12835)*

▲ Polymet Corporation........................ E 513 874-3586
West Chester *(G-14051)*

▲ Postle Industries Inc....................... E 216 265-9000
Cleveland *(G-4177)*

◆ Process Equipment Co Tipp City...... E 937 667-5705
Tipp City *(G-12838)*

◆ Production Products Inc....................D 734 241-7242
Columbus Grove *(G-5384)*

Quality Components Inc....................... F 440 255-0606
Mentor *(G-9601)*

◆ Rexarc International Inc....................E 937 839-4604
West Alexandria *(G-13921)*

◆ Select-Arc Inc.....................................C 937 295-5215
Fort Loramie *(G-6955)*

▲ Semtorq Inc...................................... F 330 487-0600
Twinsburg *(G-13377)*

Sherbrooke Corporation....................... E 440 942-3520
Willoughby *(G-14525)*

Sherbrooke Metals............................... G 440 542-3066
Willoughby *(G-14526)*

▲ Spiegelberg Manufacturing Inc....... D 440 324-3042
Strongsville *(G-12604)*

Stryver Mfg Inc................................... E 937 854-3048
Dayton *(G-6028)*

Summit Machine Solutions LLC........... G 330 785-0781
Akron *(G-321)*

◆ Taylor - Winfield Corporation............C 330 259-8500
Hubbard *(G-7817)*

Taylor-Winfield Tech Inc...................... D 330 259-8500
Youngstown *(G-14943)*

Tech-Sonic Inc..................................... G 614 792-3117
Dublin *(G-6354)*

Weld-Action Company Inc................... G 330 372-1063
Warren *(G-13813)*

Worker Automation Inc........................ G 937 473-2111
Dayton *(G-6086)*

3549 Metalworking machinery, nec

Added Edge Assembly Inc.................... G 216 464-4305
Cleveland *(G-3298)*

▲ Addition Manufacturing Te.............. C 513 228-7000
Lebanon *(G-8241)*

ADS Machinery Corp............................ D 330 399-3601
Warren *(G-13731)*

Advance Manufacturing Corp.............. E 216 333-1684
Cleveland *(G-3302)*

▲ Arku Inc.. F 513 985-0500
Cincinnati *(G-2375)*

Armature Coil Equipment Inc............. F 216 267-6366
Strongsville *(G-12538)*

▲ Bardons & Oliver Inc....................... C 440 498-5800
Solon *(G-12082)*

▲ Barth Industries Co LLC.................. E 216 267-1950
Cleveland *(G-3407)*

Berran Industrial Group Inc............... E 330 253-5800
Akron *(G-77)*

▲ Brilex Industries Inc........................ D 330 744-1114
Youngstown *(G-14827)*

▲ C A Litzler Co Inc............................ E 216 267-8020
Cleveland *(G-3457)*

▲ Cammann Inc..................................... F 440 965-4051
Wakeman *(G-13678)*

Cincinnati Incorporated....................... C 513 367-7100
Harrison *(G-7545)*

Cline Machine and Automtn Inc........... E 740 474-4237
Circleville *(G-3252)*

Combined Tech Group Inc.................... E 937 274-4866
Dayton *(G-5706)*

Ctm Integration Incorporated.............. E 330 332-1800
Salem *(G-11774)*

Dayton Machine Tool Company............ G 937 222-6444
Dayton *(G-5730)*

Esi-Extrusion Services Inc.................. E 330 374-3388
Akron *(G-138)*

EZ Grout Corporation Inc.................... E 740 962-2024
Malta *(G-8745)*

Flexomation LLC.................................. G 513 825-0555
Cincinnati *(G-2627)*

▲ **Formtek Inc**.................................. D 216 292-4460
Cleveland *(G-3737)*

Forrest Machine Pdts Co Ltd.............. E 419 589-3774
Mansfield *(G-8790)*

Ged Holdings Inc.............................. G 330 963-5401
Twinsburg *(G-13309)*

Gem City Engineering Co.................... C 937 223-5544
Dayton *(G-5792)*

Generic Systems Inc.......................... F 419 841-8460
Holland *(G-7764)*

Gilson Machine & Tool Co Inc............ E 419 592-2911
Napoleon *(G-10282)*

▲ **Glunt Industries Inc**......................... C 330 399-7585
Warren *(G-13770)*

◆ **Guild International Inc**........................ E 440 232-5887
Bedford *(G-1034)*

Hahn Manufacturing Company............ E 216 391-9300
Cleveland *(G-3807)*

Heisler Tool Company........................ F 440 951-2424
Willoughby *(G-14464)*

Helix Linear Technologies Inc............ E 216 485-2263
Beachwood *(G-920)*

Helix Operating Company LLC............ G 855 435-4958
Beachwood *(G-921)*

Holdren Brothers Inc......................... F 937 465-7050
West Liberty *(G-14175)*

▼ **Hunter Defense Tech Inc**.................. E 216 438-6111
Solon *(G-12124)*

J Horst Manufacturing Co.................. D 330 828-2216
Dalton *(G-5586)*

Junker Inc... G 630 231-3770
Canton *(G-1923)*

▲ **Kalt Manufacturing Company**............ D 440 327-2102
North Ridgeville *(G-10738)*

Kenley Enterprises LLC...................... G 419 630-0921
Bryan *(G-1647)*

◆ **Kent Corporation**.............................. E 440 582-3400
North Royalton *(G-10768)*

Kilroy Company................................ D 440 951-8700
Cleveland *(G-3920)*

Midwest Laser Systems Inc.............. E 419 424-0062
Alvada *(G-422)*

◆ **Milacron LLC**................................... E 513 487-5000
Cincinnati *(G-2880)*

Peco Holdings Corp........................... D 937 667-5705
Tipp City *(G-12835)*

Perfecto Industries Inc...................... E 937 778-1900
Piqua *(G 11372)*

▲ **Pines Manufacturing Inc**.................. E 440 835-5553
Westlake *(G-14324)*

Precision Metal Products Inc.............. E 216 447-1900
Cleveland *(G-4185)*

▲ **Process Equipment Co Tipp City**........ E 937 667-5705
Tipp City *(G-12838)*

▲ **Rafter Equipment Company LLC**........ E 440 572-3700
Strongsville *(G-12592)*

Refurb-World LLC.............................. E 440 471-9030
North Ridgeville *(G-10746)*

Riverside Mch & Automtn Inc............ G 419 855-8308
Walbridge *(G-13687)*

Riverside Mch & Automtn Inc............ D 419 855-8308
Genoa *(G-7250)*

▲ **S A Oma-U Inc**................................ G 330 487-0602
Twinsburg *(G-13371)*

▲ **Semtorq Inc**.................................... F 330 487-0600
Twinsburg *(G-13377)*

Simon De Young Corporation............. G 440 834-3000
Middlefield *(G-9827)*

South Shore Controls Inc.................. E 440 259-2500
Mentor *(G-9618)*

Stainless Automation........................ G 216 961-4550
Cleveland *(G-4324)*

Stein LLC... D 216 883-7444
Cleveland *(G-4331)*

Sticker Corporation.......................... F 440 946-2100
Willoughby *(G-14534)*

Stover International LLC..................... E 740 363-5251
Delaware *(G-6175)*

Todd Industries Inc........................... E 440 439-2900
Cleveland *(G-4398)*

Tri-Mac Mfg & Svcs Co..................... F 513 896-4445
Hamilton *(G-7533)*

3552 Textile machinery

Alley Cat Designs Inc........................ G 937 291-8803
Dayton *(G-5645)*

American Precision Spindles.............. G 267 436-6000
Cleveland *(G-3347)*

◆ **Barudan America Inc**........................ F 440 248-8770
Solon *(G-12083)*

Bavis Fabacraft Inc........................... E 513 677-0500
Maineville *(G-8738)*

▲ **C A Litzler Co Inc**............................ E 216 267-8020
Cleveland *(G-3457)*

Karg Corporation.............................. F 330 633-4916
Tallmadge *(G-12738)*

Knitting Machinery Co Amer LLC........ F 937 548-2338
Greenville *(G-7346)*

Leesburg Looms Incorporated........... G 419 238-2738
Van Wert *(G-13540)*

Open Additive LLC............................ F 937 306-6140
Dayton *(G-5929)*

Painted Hill Inv Group Inc................. F 937 339-1756
Troy *(G-13246)*

Randy Gray...................................... G 513 533-3200
Cincinnati *(G-3032)*

▲ **Reed Gowdey Company**..................... G 401 723-6114
Granville *(G-7320)*

▲ **S A Oma-U Inc**................................ G 330 487-0602
Twinsburg *(G-13371)*

Schilling Graphics Inc....................... E 419 468-1037
Galion *(G-7198)*

Simon De Young Corporation............. G 440 834-3000
Middlefield *(G-9827)*

Slater Road Mills Inc........................ G 330 332-9951
Salem *(G-11813)*

Wise Edge LLC.................................. G 330 208-0889
Mogadore *(G-10094)*

Wolf Machine Company...................... F 513 791-5194
Blue Ash *(C 1352)*

3553 Woodworking machinery

Axiom Tool Group Inc....................... G 844 642-4902
Westerville *(G-14245)*

Coe Manufacturing Company.............. E 440 352-9381
Painesville *(G-11072)*

▲ **Dayton Hawker Corporation**.............. F 937 293-8147
Dayton *(G-5728)*

Diamond Machinery LLC.................... G 216 312-1235
Cleveland *(G-3613)*

General Intl Pwr Pdts LLC................. E 419 877-5234
Whitehouse *(G-14360)*

ITR Manufacturing LLC...................... F 419 763-1493
Saint Henry *(G-11722)*

Northcoast Woodcraft Inc.................. G 330 677-1189
Tallmadge *(G-12742)*

Seilkop Industries Inc........................ E 513 761-1035
Cincinnati *(G-3077)*

Springhill Dimensions....................... F 330 359-5972
Dalton *(G-5595)*

Trico Enterprises LLC........................ F 216 970-9984
Lakewood *(G-8172)*

3554 Paper industries machinery

Andritz Inc....................................... D 513 677-5620
Loveland *(G-8621)*

◆ **Baumfolder Corporation**.................... E 937 492-1281
Sidney *(G-11996)*

◆ **Chemineer Inc**.................................. C 937 454-3200
Dayton *(G-5700)*

Custom Threading Systems LLC......... G 937 846-1405
New Carlisle *(G-10370)*

Erd Specialty Graphics Inc................ G 419 242-9545
Toledo *(G-12955)*

◆ **Fq Sale Inc**...................................... E 937 324-0352
Springfield *(G-12314)*

G Fordyce Co.................................... G 937 393-3241
Hillsboro *(G-7716)*

▲ **J E Doyle Company**.......................... F 330 564-0743
Norton *(G-10824)*

◆ **Jen-Coat Inc**.................................... C 513 671-1777
Cincinnati *(G-2764)*

◆ **Kadant Black Clawson Inc**................. D 513 229-8100
Lebanon *(G-8270)*

◆ **Kohler Coating Inc**........................... E 330 499-1407
Canton *(G-1929)*

▼ **Magna Machine Co**........................... C 513 851-6900
Cincinnati *(G-2840)*

▲ **McIntosh Manufacturing LLC**............ D 513 424-5307
Middletown *(G-9878)*

▲ **Miami Machine Corporation**............... F 513 863-6707
Overpeck *(G-11061)*

National Oilwell Varco LP.................. C 937 454-4660
Dayton *(G-5901)*

◆ **Nilpeter Usa Inc**.............................. C 513 489-4400
Cincinnati *(G-2909)*

Pearce Inc.. F 216 252-0550
Hinckley *(G-7735)*

▲ **Press Technology & Mfg Inc**............. G 937 327-0755
Springfield *(G-12365)*

Rebiltco Inc..................................... G 513 424-2024
Middletown *(G-9890)*

Spectex LLC..................................... F 603 330-3334
Cincinnati *(G-3104)*

Tri-Mac Mfg & Svcs Co..................... F 513 896-4445
Hamilton *(G-7533)*

Vail Rubber Works Inc....................... F 513 705-2060
Middletown *(G-9901)*

3555 Printing trades machinery

Alchem Aluminum Europe Inc............ G 216 910-3400
Beachwood *(O-300)*

Anderson & Vreeland Inc.................. D 419 636-5002
Bryan *(G-1629)*

Armor.. G 614 459-1414
Columbus *(G-4726)*

Beehex Inc....................................... G 512 633-5304
Columbus *(G-4748)*

▼ **Boggs Graphics Equipment LLC**........ E 888 837-8101
Maple Heights *(G-8878)*

Container Graphics Corp.................... E 937 746-5666
Franklin *(G-7013)*

▲ **Desco Equipment Corp**...................... F 330 405-1581
Twinsburg *(G-13292)*

Dynamic Dies Inc............................. E 419 865-0249
Holland *(G-7761)*

E C Shaw Company of Ohio.............. E 513 721-6334
Cincinnati *(G-2569)*

Flexotech Graphics Inc...................... F 330 929-4743
Stow *(G-12432)*

Gedico International Inc..................... G 937 274-2167
West Chester *(G-14007)*

▲ **Gew Inc**... G 440 237-4439
Cleveland *(G-3774)*

Graphic Systems Services Inc............ E 937 746-0708
Springboro *(G-12254)*

Employee Codes: A=Over 500 employees, B=251-500
C=101-250, D=51-100, E=20-50, F=10-19, G=1-9   2025 Harris Ohio
Industrial Directory   845

SIC

Great Lakes Graphics Inc.............................. G 216 391-0077
  Cleveland *(G-3791)*

Hadronics Inc... D 513 321-9350
  Cincinnati *(G-2702)*

Hays Fabricating & Welding Inc................ E 937 325-0031
  Springfield *(G-12317)*

Imco Recycling of Indiana Inc.................. G 216 910-3400
  Beachwood *(G-922)*

◆ Kase Equipment Corporation.............. D 216 642-9040
  Cleveland *(G-3907)*

◆ Nilpeter Usa Inc...................................... C 513 489-4400
  Cincinnati *(G-2909)*

Pearce Inc.. F 216 252-0550
  Hinckley *(G-7735)*

▲ R & D Equipment Inc............................. F 419 668-8439
  Norwalk *(G-10860)*

Retain Loyalty LLC..................................... G 330 830-0839
  Massillon *(G-9238)*

Roessner Holdings Inc.............................. E 419 356-2123
  Fort Recovery *(G-6970)*

Schilling Graphics Inc.............................. E 419 468-1037
  Galion *(G-7198)*

Suspension Feeder Corporation.............. F 419 763-1377
  Fort Recovery *(G-6972)*

▲ Tinker Omega Sinto LLC....................... E 937 322-2272
  Springfield *(G-12387)*

Tykma Inc... D 740 779-9918
  Chillicothe *(G-2286)*

Wise Edge LLC... G 330 208-0889
  Mogadore *(G-10094)*

◆ Wood Graphics Inc................................. E 513 771-6300
  Cincinnati *(G-3230)*

3556 Food products machinery

Abj Equipfix LLC.. E 419 684-5236
  Castalia *(G-2093)*

Acreo Inc.. G 513 734-3327
  Amelia *(G-426)*

◆ American Pan Company.......................... C 937 652-3232
  Urbana *(G-13457)*

◆ Anderson International Corp................. D 216 641-1112
  Stow *(G-12418)*

Arbor Foods Inc.. E 419 698-4442
  Toledo *(G-12883)*

Binos Inc.. G 330 938-0888
  Sebring *(G-11892)*

Biro Manufacturing Company.................. F 419 798-4451
  North Canton *(G-10630)*

◆ Biro Manufacturing Company............. D 419 798-4451
  Marblehead *(G-8895)*

◆ Chemineer Inc... C 937 454-3200
  Dayton *(G-5700)*

Christy Machine Company......................... G 419 332-6451
  Fremont *(G-7098)*

▲ Cleveland Range LLC............................. E 216 481-4900
  Cleveland *(G-3522)*

CM Slicechief Co.. G 419 241-7647
  Toledo *(G-12926)*

Coperion Food Equipment LLC................ E 937 492-4158
  Sidney *(G-12009)*

▲ Crescent Metal Products Inc.............. C 440 350-1100
  Mentor *(G-9507)*

Drink Modern Technologies LLC............ G 216 577-1536
  Cleveland *(G-3633)*

Edge Exponential LLC............................... F 614 226-4421
  Columbus *(G-4898)*

Fred D Pfening Company........................... G 614 294-5361
  Columbus *(G-4940)*

Fred D Pfening Company........................... E 614 294-5361
  Columbus *(G-4939)*

Frost Engineering Inc................................ E 513 541-6330
  Cincinnati *(G-2642)*

◆ G & S Metal Products Co Inc................ C 216 441-0700
  Cleveland *(G-3748)*

G F Frank and Sons Inc............................. F 513 870-9075
  West Chester *(G-14002)*

◆ Garland Commercial Industries LLC.. G 800 338-2204
  Cleveland *(G-3756)*

◆ Gold Medal Products Co......................... B 513 769-7676
  Cincinnati *(G-2680)*

▲ Harry C Lobalzo & Sons Inc.............. E 330 666-6758
  Akron *(G-172)*

Heavenly Creamery Inc............................ G 440 593-6080
  Conneaut *(G-5403)*

Hobart LLC... D 937 332-2797
  Piqua *(G-11355)*

Hobart LLC... E 937 332-3000
  Troy *(G-13225)*

▲ Hobart LLC.. D 937 332-3000
  Troy *(G-13226)*

▼ Ingredient Masters Inc........................ G 513 231-7432
  Batavia *(G-868)*

Innovative Controls Corp.......................... F 419 691-6684
  Maumee *(G-9298)*

ITW Food Equipment Group LLC............ C 937 393-4271
  Hillsboro *(G-7719)*

◆ ITW Food Equipment Group LLC....... A 937 332-2396
  Troy *(G-13231)*

Jbt Marel Corporation................................ C 513 433-2500
  Middletown *(G-9868)*

Jbt Marel Corporation................................ B 419 626-0304
  Sandusky *(G-11846)*

◆ JE Grote Company Inc......................... D 614 868-8414
  Columbus *(G-5035)*

Kasel Engineering LLC............................. G 937 854-8875
  Trotwood *(G-13196)*

▲ Lem Products Holding LLC................. E 513 202-1188
  West Chester *(G-14023)*

Lima Sheet Metal Mch & Mfg Inc.......... F 419 229-1161
  Lima *(G-8426)*

▲ Lincoln Foodservice Products LLC.. B 260 459-8200
  Cleveland *(G-3957)*

Listermann Mfg Co Inc.............................. G 513 731-1130
  Cincinnati *(G-2824)*

▼ Magna Machine Co................................ C 513 851-6900
  Cincinnati *(G-2840)*

◆ Maverick Innvtive Slutions LLC......... D 419 281-7944
  Ashland *(G-550)*

◆ Meyer Company....................................... C 216 587-3400
  Chagrin Falls *(G-2148)*

Mojonnier Usa LLC.................................... E 844 665-6664
  Streetsboro *(G-12512)*

◆ N Wasserstrom & Sons Inc................ C 614 228-5550
  Columbus *(G-5118)*

National Oilwell Varco LP........................ C 937 454-4660
  Dayton *(G-5901)*

▼ Nemco Food Equipment Ltd.............. D 419 542-7751
  Hicksville *(G-7649)*

Nestle Usa Inc.. C 440 349-5757
  Solon *(G-12161)*

Norse Dairy Systems Inc......................... C 614 294-4931
  Columbus *(G-5128)*

◆ Norse Dairy Systems LP...................... B 614 294-4931
  Columbus *(G-5129)*

Omar Associates LLC................................. G 419 426-0610
  Attica *(G-657)*

◆ Peerless Foods Inc................................ D 937 492-4158
  Sidney *(G-12038)*

Peerless Stove & Mfg Co.......................... F 419 625-4514
  Sandusky *(G-11865)*

Premier Industries Inc.............................. E 513 271-2550
  Cincinnati *(G-2979)*

◆ Prime Equipment Group LLC.............. D 614 253-8590
  Columbus *(G-5205)*

Processall Inc... F 513 771-2266
  Cincinnati *(G-2986)*

R and J Corporation................................... E 440 871-6009
  Westlake *(G-14326)*

RS Industries Inc.. G 216 351-8200
  Brooklyn Heights *(G-1539)*

Sarka Bros Machining Inc....................... G 419 532-2393
  Kalida *(G-8006)*

▼ Sidney Manufacturing Company....... E 937 492-4154
  Sidney *(G-12053)*

▲ Siebtechnik Tema Inc.......................... E 513 489-7811
  Cincinnati *(G-3088)*

▲ Simmons Feed & Supply LLC............ E 800 754-1228
  Salem *(G-11812)*

Sir Steak Machinery Inc........................... E 419 526-9181
  Mansfield *(G-8852)*

Sterling Process Equipmen..................... E 614 868-5151
  Columbus *(G-5292)*

the Perfect Score Company...................... F 440 439-9320
  Bedford Heights *(G-1082)*

▲ Tomlinson Industries LLC................... C 216 587-3400
  Cleveland *(G-4399)*

Total Baking Solutions LLC..................... E
  Wilmington *(G-14587)*

Wolf Machine Company.............................. E 513 791-5194
  Blue Ash *(G-1352)*

3559 Special industry machinery, nec

A & B Foundry LLC..................................... F 937 412-1900
  Tipp City *(G-12811)*

Agmet Metals Inc.. E 440 439-7400
  Oakwood Village *(G-10902)*

Alstart Enterprises LLC............................ F 330 533-3222
  Canfield *(G-1803)*

Amano Cincinnati Incorporated.............. F 513 697-9000
  Loveland *(G-8619)*

American Manufacturing & Eqp.............. G 513 829-2248
  Fairfield *(G-6711)*

▲ American Plastic Tech Inc................... C 440 632-5203
  Middlefield *(G-9780)*

◆ Anderson International Corp............... D 216 641-1112
  Stow *(G-12418)*

Aot LLC.. F 937 323-9669
  Springfield *(G-12280)*

Aquila Pharmatech LLC............................ G 419 386-2527
  Waterville *(G-13830)*

ARS Recycling Systems LLC.................. F 330 536-8210
  Lowellville *(G-8658)*

Auto-Tap Inc.. G 216 671-1043
  Cleveland *(G-3389)*

Autotool Inc.. E 614 733-0222
  Plain City *(G-11395)*

Bethel Engineering and Eqp Inc............ E 419 568-1100
  New Hampshire *(G-10396)*

Broco Products Inc..................................... G 216 531-0880
  Cleveland *(G-3441)*

▲ Buddy Backyard Inc.............................. E 800 837-9353
  Warren *(G-13746)*

Budget Molders Supply Inc...................... F 216 367-7050
  Macedonia *(G-8680)*

CAM-Lem Inc.. G 216 391-7750
  Cleveland *(G-3461)*

▲ Cammann Inc.. F 440 965-4051
  Wakeman *(G-13678)*

Cantrell Rfinery Sls Trnsp Inc............... G 937 695-0318
  Winchester *(G-14597)*

Chart International Inc.............................. D 440 753-1490
  Cleveland *(G-3489)*

◆ Chemineer Inc... C 937 454-3200
  Dayton *(G-5700)*

City of Cleveland... E 216 664-2711
  Cleveland *(G-3500)*

Cohesant Inc.................................E 216 910-1700
Beachwood *(G-913)*

Conforming Matrix Corporation...........E 419 729-3777
Toledo *(G-12929)*

Conviber Inc..................................F 330 723-6006
Medina *(G-9391)*

Cornerstone Wauseon Inc.................C 419 337-0940
Wauseon *(G-13847)*

Corrotec Inc.................................E 937 325-3585
Springfield *(G-12294)*

Crowne Group LLC.........................F 216 589-0198
Cleveland *(G-3577)*

Decision Systems Inc.....................F 330 456-7600
Canton *(G-1879)*

▲ Dengensha America Corporation......F 440 439-8081
Bedford *(G-1025)*

Designetics Inc.............................D 419 866-0700
Holland *(G-7755)*

▲ DRG Hydraulics Inc......................E 216 663-9747
Twinsburg *(G-13297)*

Dura Temp Corporation...................F 419 866-4348
Holland *(G-7760)*

◆ Eaton Corporation.......................B 440 523-5000
Cleveland *(G-3652)*

▲ Eden Cryogenics LLC....................E 614 873-3949
Columbus *(G-4897)*

◆ Empire Systems Inc.....................G 440 653-9300
Avon Lake *(G-755)*

Encore Industries Inc.....................C 419 626-8000
Sandusky *(G-11830)*

Enerfab Inc...................................G 513 771-2300
Cincinnati *(G-2589)*

▲ Equipment Mfrs Intl Inc................E 216 651-6700
Cleveland *(G-3682)*

Ernest Industries Inc......................E 937 325-9851
Lowellville *(G-8660)*

Esi-Extrusion Services Inc................E 330 374-3388
Akron *(G-138)*

Exomet Inc...................................F 440 593-1161
Conneaut *(G-5400)*

Fawcett Co Inc.............................G 330 659-4187
Richfield *(G-11592)*

◆ Ganzcorp Investments Inc.............E 330 963-5400
Twinsburg *(G-13307)*

Ged Holdings Inc............................G 330 963-5401
Twinsburg *(G-13309)*

General Fabrications Corp................E 419 625-6055
Sandusky *(G-11836)*

Girard Machine Company Inc.............G 330 545-9731
Girard *(G-7272)*

▼ Glenn Hunter & Associates Inc.......D 419 533-0925
Delta *(G-6208)*

▲ Gokoh Corporation......................F 937 339-4977
Troy *(G-13218)*

▼ Grasan Equipment Company Inc......G 419 526-4440
Mansfield *(G-8797)*

Guild Associates Inc.......................G 843 573-0095
Dublin *(G-6299)*

▲ Guild Associates Inc....................D 614 798-8215
Dublin *(G-6300)*

▲ Haeco Inc...................................G 513 722-1030
Loveland *(G-8629)*

Heartland Group Holdings LLC...........D 614 441-4001
Columbus *(G-4974)*

▲ High Temperature Systems Inc.......F 440 543-8271
Chagrin Falls *(G-2165)*

Hydro Systems Company.................F 513 271-8800
West Chester *(G-14014)*

◆ Industrial Thermal Systems Inc.......F 513 561-2100
Cincinnati *(G-2745)*

▼ Ingredient Masters Inc..................G 513 231-7432
Batavia *(G-868)*

◆ Innoplast Inc...............................F 440 543-8660
Cleveland *(G-3861)*

Inpower LLC..................................F 740 548-0965
Lewis Center *(G-8337)*

Integrity Parking LLC......................F 440 543-4123
Aurora *(G-675)*

▲ Intelliworks Ht LLC.......................G 419 660-9050
Norwalk *(G-10848)*

◆ Intertec Corporation.....................F 419 537-9711
Toledo *(G-13007)*

J & S Industrial Mch Pdts Inc............E 419 691-1380
Toledo *(G-13012)*

Jaco Manufacturing Company............E 440 234-4000
Berea *(G-1177)*

Jbw Systems Inc...........................F 614 882-5008
Westerville *(G-14215)*

▲ JC Carter LLC..............................G 440 569-1818
Richmond Heights *(G-11610)*

JM Hamilton Group Inc....................F 419 229-4010
Lima *(G-8422)*

◆ Johndow Industries Inc.................E 330 753-6895
Barberton *(G-815)*

◆ Knight Material Tech LLC................E 330 488-1651
East Canton *(G-6378)*

◆ Kobelco Stewart Bolling Inc............D 330 655-3111
Hudson *(G-7848)*

Lifeformations Inc..........................E 419 352-2101
Bowling Green *(G-1425)*

Linden-Two Inc.............................E 330 928-4064
Cuyahoga Falls *(G-5559)*

▲ Liquid Development Company...........G 216 641-9366
Independence *(G-7907)*

◆ Luke Engineering & Mfg Corp...........E 330 335-1501
Wadsworth *(G-13649)*

M W Solutions LLC.........................F 419 782-1611
Defiance *(G-6118)*

▼ Manifold & Phalor Inc....................E 614 920-1200
Canal Winchester *(G-1793)*

Manufctring Bus Dev Sltons LLC........D 419 294-1313
Findlay *(G-6886)*

▲ Materion Advnced Mtls Tech Svc......D 216 486-4200
Mayfield Heights *(G-9335)*

▲ McFlusion Inc..............................G 800 341-8616
Twinsburg *(G-13337)*

◆ McNeil & Nrm Inc..........................D 330 761-1855
Akron *(G-225)*

McNeil & Nrm Intl Inc......................D 330 253-2525
Akron *(G-226)*

◆ Micro-Pise Msrment Systems LLC.....C 330 541-9100
Streetsboro *(G-12510)*

▼ Midwestern Industries Inc.............D 330 837-4203
Massillon *(G-9223)*

Mikes Transm & Auto Svc LLC...........F 330 799-8266
Youngstown *(G-14901)*

Mirion Technologies Ist Corp.............D 614 367-2050
Pickerington *(G-11296)*

Mjcj Holdings Inc...........................G 937 885-0800
Miamisburg *(G-9719)*

▲ Mm Industries Inc........................E 330 332-5947
Salem *(G-11802)*

Modular Assmbly Innvations LLC........E 614 389-4860
Dublin *(G-6321)*

Morgan Engineering Systems Inc........E 330 545-9731
Girard *(G-7276)*

Nutro Corporation..........................D 440 572-3800
Strongsville *(G-12580)*

Nutro Inc......................................E 440 572-3800
Strongsville *(G-12581)*

◆ Ohio Magnetics Inc.......................E 216 662-8484
Maple Heights *(G-8888)*

▲ Omco Usa LLC..............................G 740 588-1722
Zanesville *(G-15035)*

◆ Plastic Process Equipment Inc.........E 216 367-7000
Macedonia *(G-8706)*

Poly Products Inc..........................G 216 391-7659
Cleveland *(G-4175)*

Processall Inc...............................F 513 771-2266
Cincinnati *(G-2986)*

Production Design Services Inc..........D 937 866-3377
Dayton *(G-5962)*

◆ Production Tube Cutting Inc............E 937 254-6138
Dayton *(G-5963)*

Rite Track Equipment Services LLC.....D 513 881-7820
West Chester *(G-14068)*

◆ Rjs Corporation............................E 330 896-2387
Akron *(G-287)*

▲ RMS Equipment LLC.......................A 330 564-1360
Cuyahoga Falls *(G-5570)*

▲ Roberts Machine Products LLC.........F 937 682-4015
Rushsylvania *(G-11666)*

▼ RSI Company................................F 216 360-9800
Beachwood *(G-946)*

▲ Rubber City Machinery Corp............E 330 434-3500
Akron *(G-293)*

SDS National LLC...........................G 330 759-8066
Boardman *(G-1376)*

◆ Segna Inc....................................F 937 335-6700
Troy *(G-13253)*

Service Station Equipment Co...........G 216 431-6100
Cleveland *(G-4286)*

▼ Singleton Corporation....................F 216 651-7800
Cleveland *(G-4302)*

Skuld LLC.....................................E 330 423-7339
Piqua *(G-11384)*

Stainless Automation Inc.................G 216 961-4550
Cleveland *(G-4324)*

Starkey Machinery Inc.....................E 419 468-2560
Galion *(G-7199)*

▲ Steelastic Company LLC.................E 330 633-0505
Cuyahoga Falls *(G-5574)*

Steinert Industries Inc....................G 330 678-0028
Kent *(G-8083)*

Storetek Engineering Inc..................G 330 294-0678
Tallmadge *(G-12752)*

Stride Out Rnch N Rodeo Sp LLC........F 937 539-1537
Springfield *(G-12380)*

Summit Design and Tech Inc.............F 330 733-6662
Akron *(G-320)*

Taikisha Usa Inc............................D 614 444-5602
Columbus *(G-5300)*

▲ Technical Machine Products Inc.......F
Cleveland *(G-4370)*

Technology House Ltd.....................F 440 248-3025
Streetsboro *(G-12526)*

Tiba LLC.......................................E 614 328-2040
Columbus *(G-5324)*

◆ Toledo Engineering Co Inc..............D 419 537-9711
Toledo *(G-13151)*

▲ Tom Richards Inc..........................C 440 974-1300
Willoughby *(G-14541)*

Toney Tool Manufacturing Inc............G 937 890-8535
Dayton *(G-6057)*

Tooltex Inc...................................F 614 539-3222
Circleville *(G-3267)*

▲ Universal Rack & Eqp Co Inc............G 330 963-6776
Twinsburg *(G-13390)*

Velocys Inc..................................D 614 733-3300
Plain City *(G-11424)*

Vulcan Machinery Corporation...........F 330 376-6025
Akron *(G-355)*

▲ Wentworth Mold Inc Electra............D 937 898-8460
Vandalia *(G-13583)*

Wesco Machine Inc.........................F 330 688-6973
Ravenna *(G-11549)*

◆ Woodman Agitator Inc...............F 440 937-9865
Avon (G-744)

Youngstown Plastic Tooling...............F 330 782-7222
Youngstown (G-14973)

Zed Industries Inc...............D 937 667-8407
Vandalia (G-13584)

▲ Zook Enterprises LLC...............E 440 543-1010
Chagrin Falls (G-2195)

3561 Pumps and pumping equipment

A & F Machine Products Co...............E 440 826-0959
Berea (G-1157)

▼ Advanced Fuel Systems Inc...............G 614 252-8422
Columbus (G-4676)

▲ Ashland Water Group Inc...............G 877 326-3561
Ashland (G-518)

Ayling and Reichert Co Consent...............G 419 898-2471
Oak Harbor (G-10883)

Bergstrom Company Ltd Partnr...............F 440 232-2282
Cleveland (G-3415)

Bowden Manufacturing Corp...............E 440 946-1770
Willoughby (G-14432)

Certified Labs & Service Inc...............G 419 289-7462
Ashland (G-527)

Chaos Entertainment...............G 937 520-5260
Dayton (G-5698)

▲ Cima Inc...............G 513 382-8976
Hamilton (G-7476)

City of Newark...............E 740 349-6765
Newark (G-10497)

Columbia Industrial Pdts Inc...............F 216 431-6633
Cleveland (G-3547)

Crane Pumps & Systems Inc...............E 937 778-8947
Piqua (G-11339)

◆ Crane Pumps & Systems LLC...............E 937 773-2442
Piqua (G-11341)

Custom Cltch Jjnt Hydrlics Inc...............F 216 431-1630
Cleveland (G-3584)

◆ Dreison International Inc...............C 216 362-0755
Cleveland (G-3632)

◆ E R Advanced Ceramics Inc...............E 330 426-9433
East Palestine (G-6402)

Eaton Aeroquip LLC...............A 419 891-7775
Maumee (G-9292)

Fill-Rite Company...............E 419 755-1011
Mansfield (G-8787)

Flowserve Corporation...............D 937 226-4000
Dayton (G-5780)

Flowserve Corporation...............G 513 874-6990
Loveland (G-8625)

Fluid Automation Inc...............E 248 912-1970
North Canton (G-10640)

GE Vernova International LLC...............G 330 963-2066
Twinsburg (G-13308)

General Electric Company...............E 216 883-1000
Cleveland (G-3766)

Gerow Equipment Company Inc...............G 216 383-8800
Cleveland (G-3772)

▲ Giant Industries Inc...............E 419 531-4600
Toledo (G-12975)

Gorman-Rupp Company...............B 419 755-1011
Mansfield (G-8793)

Gorman-Rupp Company...............G 419 755-1245
Mansfield (G-8795)

Gorman-Rupp Company...............C 419 755-1011
Mansfield (G-8794)

▼ Hydromatic Pumps Inc...............G 419 289-1144
Ashland (G-541)

Idex Corporation...............G 419 526-7222
Mansfield (G-8805)

Indelco Custom Products Inc...............G 216 797-7300
Euclid (G-6654)

Interstate Pump Company Inc...............G 330 222-1006
Salem (G-11789)

▲ Keen Pump Company Inc...............E 419 207-9400
Ashland (G-544)

Lakecraft Inc...............G 419 734-2828
Port Clinton (G-11444)

Lubrisource Inc...............F 937 432-9292
Middletown (G-9872)

M T Systems Inc...............G 330 453-4646
Canton (G-1936)

Maag Reduction Inc...............E 704 716-9000
Kent (G-8048)

Magnum Piering Inc...............E 513 759-3348
West Chester (G-14131)

▲ Metaullics Systems LP...............C 509 926-6212
Solon (G-12148)

▲ Molten Mtal Eqp Innvations LLC...............E 440 632-9119
Middlefield (G-9813)

▲ Pckd Enterprises Inc...............G 440 632-9119
Middlefield (G-9820)

Pentair...............E 440 248-0100
Solon (G-12167)

Pentair Pump Group Inc...............F 419 281-9918
Ashland (G-560)

Process Dynamics Inc...............G 330 686-2597
Stow (G-12452)

Quikstir Inc...............G 419 732-2601
Port Clinton (G-11449)

Rolcon Inc...............F 513 821-7259
Cincinnati (G-3052)

Rumpke Transportation Co LLC...............F 513 851-0122
Cincinnati (G-3058)

◆ Seepex Inc...............C 937 864-7150
Enon (G-6633)

Stahl Gear & Machine Co...............G 216 431-2820
Cleveland (G-4323)

Suburban Manufacturing Co...............D 440 953-2024
Eastlake (G-6444)

Systecon LLC...............D 513 777-7722
West Chester (G-14080)

Tark Inc...............E 937 434-6766
Miamisburg (G-9743)

Teikoku USA Inc...............F 304 699-1156
Marietta (G-8951)

Thieman Tailgates Inc...............D 419 586-7727
Celina (G-2125)

TJ Clark International LLC...............F 614 388-8869
Delaware (G-6176)

◆ Tolco Corporation...............E 419 241-1113
Toledo (G-13147)

Trane Technologies Company LLC...............F 419 636-4242
Bryan (G-1664)

Trane Technologies Company LLC...............E 419 633-6800
Bryan (G-1665)

Trane Technologies Company LLC...............E 513 459-4580
Cincinnati (G-3162)

Transdigm Inc...............E 216 291-6025
Cleveland (G-4411)

Transdigm Inc...............E 440 352-6182
Painesville (G-11119)

▲ Uhrden Inc...............E 330 456-0031
Canton (G-2030)

▲ Valco Cincinnati Inc...............C 513 874-6550
Cincinnati (G-3190)

Vertiflo Pump Company...............F 513 530-0888
Cincinnati (G-3202)

Vickers International Inc...............G 419 867-2200
Maumee (G-9329)

◆ Warren Rupp Inc...............C 419 524-8388
Mansfield (G-8863)

▲ Wayne Water Systems Inc...............C 800 237-0987
Harrison (G-7571)

3562 Ball and roller bearings

Bearings Manufacturing Company...............F 440 846-5517
Strongsville (G-12544)

Extreme Caster Services Inc...............G 330 637-9030
Cortland (G-5444)

Gt Technologies Inc...............E 419 782-8955
Defiance (G-6109)

▲ HMS Industries LLC...............F 440 899-0001
Westlake (G-14306)

▲ Jay Dee Service Corporation...............G 330 425-1546
Macedonia (G-8699)

◆ Kaydon Corporation...............D 231 755-3741
Avon (G-729)

Miller Bearing Company Inc...............E 330 678-8844
Kent (G-8054)

Nn Inc...............E 440 647-4711
Wellington (G-13897)

Schaeffler Group USA Inc...............E 800 274-5001
Valley City (G-13515)

Schaeffler Group USA Inc...............E 330 202-6752
Wooster (G-14679)

Superior Caster Inc...............F 513 539-8980
Middletown (G-9896)

▲ The Hamilton Caster & Mfg...............D 513 863-3300
Hamilton (G-7530)

▲ Thyssnkrupp Rothe Erde USA Inc...............C 330 562-4000
Aurora (G-689)

Timken Company...............F 614 836-3337
Groveport (G-7453)

◆ Timken Company...............A 234 262-3000
North Canton (G-10673)

Timken Newco I LLC...............G 234 262-3000
North Canton (G-10674)

▲ Tsk America Co Ltd...............F 513 942-4002
West Chester (G-14156)

3563 Air and gas compressors

Aci Services Inc...............E 740 435-0240
Cambridge (G-1734)

◆ Airbase Industries LLC...............F 937 540-1140
Englewood (G-6606)

Airtx International Ltd...............F 513 631-0660
Cincinnati (G-2346)

Ariel Corporation...............D 330 896-2660
Akron (G-60)

Ariel Corporation...............F 740 397-0311
Mount Vernon (G-10235)

◆ Ariel Corporation...............C 740 397-0311
Mount Vernon (G-10236)

▲ Armour Spray Systems Inc...............F 216 398-3838
Cleveland (G-3366)

▼ Ats Ohio Inc...............C 614 888-2344
Lewis Center (G-8323)

Autobody Supply Company Inc...............D 614 228-4328
Columbus (G-4735)

◆ Ch Transition Company LLC...............C 800 543-6400
Cincinnati (G-2457)

Cohesant Inc...............E 216 910-1700
Beachwood (G-913)

Deco Tools Inc...............E 419 476-9321
Toledo (G-12939)

◆ Eaton Comprsr Fabrication Inc...............D 937 540-1140
Englewood (G-6613)

Ernest Industries Inc...............F 937 325-9851
Springfield (G-12307)

Field Gymmy Inc...............G 419 538-6511
Glandorf (G-7283)

▼ Finishing Brands Holdings Inc...............C 260 665-8800
Toledo (G-12964)

G Denver and Co LLC...............E 937 498-2555
Sidney (G-12021)

General Fabrications Corp................... E 419 625-6055
Sandusky *(G-11836)*

Glascraft Inc.. G 330 966-3000
North Canton *(G-10642)*

Keystone Automotive Inds Inc............... G 614 228-4328
Groveport *(G-7440)*

Kingsly Compression Inc..................... G 740 439-0772
Cambridge *(G-1747)*

Lincoln Electric Automtn Inc................. E 614 471-5926
Columbus *(G-5070)*

Lsq Manufacturing Inc........................... F 330 725-4905
Medina *(G-9421)*

National Compressor Svcs LLC.......... E 419 868-4980
Holland *(G-7773)*

Nordson Corporation............................. B 440 985-4496
Amherst *(G-448)*

Nordson Corporation............................. B 440 985-4458
Amherst *(G-449)*

Nordson Corporation............................. B 440 985-4000
Amherst *(G-450)*

Nordson Corporation............................. A 440 892-1580
Westlake *(G-14317)*

Nordson Medical Corporation............... D 440 892-1580
Westlake *(G-14318)*

Paratus Supply Inc................................ F 330 745-3600
Barberton *(G-830)*

Potemkin Industries Inc........................ F 740 397-4888
Mount Vernon *(G-10259)*

▲ Powerex-Iwata Air Tech Inc .... D 888 769-7979
Harrison *(G-7561)*

Quikstir Inc.. G 419 732-2601
Port Clinton *(G-11449)*

▲ Rimrock Corporation......................... E 614 471-5926
Columbus *(G-5230)*

Rimrock Holdings Corporation............. C 614 471-5926
Columbus *(G-5231)*

◆ Tolco Corporation.............................. E 419 241-1113
Toledo *(G-13147)*

Trail Sprayer & Service LLC................ F 330 720-2966
Canton *(G-2026)*

Transdigm Inc.. E 216 291-6025
Cleveland *(G-4411)*

Tri State Equipment Company.............. G 513 738-7227
Shandon *(G-11935)*

◆ United Air Specialists Inc................ C 513 891-0400
Blue Ash *(G-1345)*

▲ Wiwa LLC.. F 419 757-0141
Alger *(G-303)*

3564 Blowers and fans

◆ Ad Industries Inc............................... A 303 744-1911
Dayton *(G-5634)*

Air Enterprises Inc............................... A 330 794-9770
Akron *(G-22)*

▼ Air-Rite Inc... E 216 228-8200
Cleveland *(G-3316)*

▲ Airecon Manufacturing Corp........... E 513 561-5522
Cincinnati *(G-2345)*

Allied Separation Tech Inc................... G 704 736-0420
Twinsburg *(G-13273)*

◆ American Fan Company.................... C 513 874-2400
Fairfield *(G-6709)*

American Manufacturing & Eqp........... G 513 829-2248
Fairfield *(G-6711)*

Americraft Mfg Co Inc........................... F 513 489-1047
Cincinnati *(G-2363)*

ARI Phoenix Inc..................................... E 513 229-3750
Sharonville *(G-11945)*

Atmos360 Inc.. E 513 772-4777
West Chester *(G-14105)*

▲ Beckett Air Incorporated.................. D 440 327-9999
North Ridgeville *(G-10725)*

◆ Bry-Air Inc... E 740 965-2974
Sunbury *(G-12662)*

Buckeye BOP LLC................................. F 740 498-9898
Newcomerstown *(G-10569)*

Ceco Environmental Corp.................... F 513 458-2606
Blue Ash *(G-1259)*

Ceco Filters Inc..................................... G 513 458-2600
Cincinnati *(G-2447)*

Ceco Group Global Holdings LLC........ F 513 458-2600
Cincinnati *(G-2448)*

Cincinnati A Flter Sls Svc Inc.............. E 513 242-3400
Cincinnati *(G-2466)*

Cincinnati Fan & Ventilat....................... D 513 573-1000
Mason *(G-9083)*

Coperion Process Solutions LLC.......... F 513 576-9200
Solon *(G-12098)*

◆ Dreison International Inc...................C 216 362-0755
Cleveland *(G-3632)*

Effox-Flextor-Mader Inc........................ F 513 874-8915
West Chester *(G-14115)*

Envirofab Inc.. G 216 651-1767
Cleveland *(G-3679)*

Extreme Microbial Tech LLC................ E 844 885-0088
Moraine *(G-10162)*

Famous Industries Inc.......................... F 740 685-2592
Byesville *(G-1711)*

Flex Technologies Inc........................... D 330 359-5415
Mount Eaton *(G-10207)*

FM AF LLC.. C 866 771-6266
Fairfield *(G-6736)*

◆ Guardian Technologies LLC.............E 866 603-5900
Euclid *(G-6652)*

◆ H-P Products Inc................................ C 330 875-5556
Louisville *(G-8602)*

◆ Hartzell Fan Inc.................................C 937 773-7411
Piqua *(G-11350)*

Hdt Ep Inc.. C 216 438-6111
Solon *(G-12120)*

Hdt Expeditionary Systems Inc............ F 440 466-6640
Geneva *(G-7239)*

Herman Manufacturing LLC................. E 216 251-6400
Cleveland *(G-3827)*

▲ Howden North America Inc............... C 513 874-2400
Fairfield *(G-6742)*

▲ Howden USA Company...................... C 513 874-2400
Fairfield *(G-6743)*

Humongous Holdings Llc..................... F 216 663-8830
Cleveland *(G-3044)*

Hunter Environmental Corp.................. E 440 248-6111
Solon *(G-12125)*

Illinois Tool Works Inc.......................... E 262 248-8277
Bryan *(G-1645)*

Indoor Envmtl Specialists Inc.............. E 937 433-5202
Dayton *(G-5821)*

Jacp Inc... G 513 353-3660
Miamitown *(G-9759)*

Kirk Williams Company Inc................... D 614 875-9023
Grove City *(G-7393)*

▲ Langdon Inc... E 513 733-5955
Cincinnati *(G-2811)*

Lau Holdings LLC.................................. E 937 476-6500
Dayton *(G-5617)*

Lau Holdings LLC.................................. D 216 486-4000
Cleveland *(G-3945)*

▼ Lau Industries Inc.............................. A 937 476-6500
Dayton *(G-5618)*

◆ McGill Airclean LLC...........................D 614 829-1200
Columbus *(G-5089)*

◆ McGill Corporation.............................F 614 829-1200
Groveport *(G-7444)*

Mestek Inc.. F 419 288-2703
Bradner *(G-1454)*

Met-Pro Technologies LLC.................... F 513 458-2600
Cincinnati *(G-2868)*

▼ Midwestern Industries Inc................ D 330 837-4203
Massillon *(G-9223)*

▲ Multi-Wing America Inc...................... E 440 834-9400
Middlefield *(G-9814)*

Neundorfer Inc....................................... E 440 942-8990
Willoughby *(G-14493)*

Nupro Company..................................... E 440 951-9729
Willoughby *(G-14498)*

Ohio Blow Pipe Company...................... E 216 681-7379
Cleveland *(G-4113)*

OSI Environmental LLC......................... E 440 237-4600
North Royalton *(G-10779)*

Plas-Tanks Industries Inc.................... E 513 942-3800
Hamilton *(G-7517)*

▲ Qualtek Electronics Corp................... C 440 951-3300
Mentor *(G-9603)*

Quickdraft Inc.. E 330 477-4574
Canton *(G-1987)*

Rmt Acquisition Inc............................... E 513 241-5566
Cincinnati *(G-3050)*

▲ Selas Heat Technology Co LLC........ E 800 523-6500
Streetsboro *(G-12523)*

Seneca Environmental Products Inc....... E 419 447-1282
Tiffin *(G-12799)*

▲ Skuttle Mfg Co.................................... F 740 373-9169
Marietta *(G-8946)*

Sly Inc.. E 800 334-2957
Strongsville *(G-12601)*

Starr Fabricating Inc............................. D 330 394-9891
Vienna *(G-13618)*

Stelter and Brinck Inc........................... E 513 367-9300
Harrison *(G-7569)*

▲ Tisch Environmental Inc................... E 513 467-9000
Cleves *(G-4551)*

▲ Tlt-Babcock Inc.................................. D 330 867-8540
Akron *(G-339)*

▲ Tlt-Turbo Inc....................................... G 330 776-5115
Akron *(G-340)*

◆ Tosoh America Inc..............................B 614 539-8622
Grove City *(G-7417)*

Troy Filters Ltd...................................... E 614 777-8222
Columbus *(G-5333)*

◆ United Air Specialists Inc................C 513 891-0400
Blue Ash *(G-1345)*

◆ United McGill Corporation................ E 614 829-1200
Groveport *(G-7455)*

Vector Mechanical LLC......................... G 216 337-4042
Cleveland *(G-4460)*

▼ Verantis Corporation......................... E 440 243-0700
Middleburg Heights *(G-9778)*

Vortec and Paxton Products................. F 513 891-7474
Blue Ash *(G-1347)*

Weather King Heating & AC.................. G 330 908-0281
Northfield *(G-10799)*

3565 Packaging machinery

Able Tool Corporation........................... E 513 733-8989
Cincinnati *(G-2334)*

▲ Advanced Poly-Packaging Inc.......... C 330 785-4000
Akron *(G-21)*

Apackaging Group Ohio Inc................. F 419 785-8600
Defiance *(G-6097)*

▼ Atlas Vac Machine Co LLC............... G 513 407-3513
Cincinnati *(G-2386)*

Atmos360 Inc.. E 513 772-4777
West Chester *(G-14105)*

Audion Automation Ltd......................... E 216 267-1911
Berea *(G-1159)*

▲ Audion Automation Ltd..................... F 216 267-1911
Berea *(G-1160)*

S I C

▲ Automated Packaging Systems LLC C 330 528-2000
Streetsboro *(G-12490)*

Automated Packg Systems Inc............. E 330 342-2000
Bedford *(G-1013)*

Automated Packg Systems Inc............. G 330 626-2313
Streetsboro *(G-12491)*

B3 Fulfillment.................................. E 866 405-0910
Avon *(G-714)*

Barry-Wehmiller Companies Inc............. F 330 923-0491
Cuyahoga Falls *(G-5532)*

▼ Boggs Graphics Equipment LLC....... E 888 837-8101
Maple Heights *(G-8878)*

◆ Combi Packaging Systems Llc.......... D 330 456-9333
Canton *(G-1870)*

▲ Crown Closures Machinery............... E 740 681-6593
Lancaster *(G-8191)*

Ctm Integration Incorporated............. E 330 332-1800
Salem *(G-11774)*

Ctm Labeling Systems....................... E 330 332-1800
Salem *(G-11775)*

▲ Darifill Inc..................................... F 614 890-3274
Westerville *(G-14253)*

Exact Equipment Corporation............... F 215 295-2000
Columbus *(G-4640)*

Expo Packaging Inc......................... G 216 267-9700
Cleveland *(G-3699)*

Food Equipment Mfg Corp.................. E 216 672-5859
Bedford Heights *(G-1076)*

G and J Automatic Systems Inc............. E 216 741-6070
Cleveland *(G-3749)*

GL Industries Inc............................. E 513 874-1233
Hamilton *(G-7494)*

◆ Glassline Corporation..................... F 419 666-9712
Perrysburg *(G-11225)*

Gunnison Associates Llc.................... G 330 562-5230
Aurora *(G-672)*

H & G Equipment Inc........................ F 513 761-2060
Blue Ash *(G-1280)*

H&G Legacy Co................................ F 513 921-1075
Cincinnati *(G-2701)*

◆ Heat Seal LLC.............................. C 216 341-2022
Cleveland *(G-3816)*

Huhtamaki Inc................................. D 513 201-1525
Batavia *(G-867)*

Huhtamaki Inc................................. D 937 746-9700
Franklin *(G-7028)*

Hunkar Technologies Inc.................... E 513 272-1010
Cincinnati *(G-2735)*

Iconic Labs LLC.............................. F 216 759-4040
Westlake *(G-14308)*

Kaufman Engineered Systems Inc.......... D 419 878-9727
Waterville *(G-13837)*

▲ Kennedy Group Incorporated............ D 440 951-7660
Willoughby *(G-14477)*

Kolinahr Systems Inc......................... F 513 745-9401
Blue Ash *(G-1294)*

M PI Label Systems........................... G 330 938-2134
Sebring *(G-11896)*

◆ Miconvi Properties Inc..................... G 440 954-3500
Eastlake *(G-6435)*

Millwood Inc................................... E 513 860-4567
West Chester *(G-14030)*

Millwood Natural LLC........................ F 330 393-4400
Vienna *(G-13615)*

◆ Morgan Adhesives Company LLC..... B 330 688-1111
Stow *(G-12441)*

Mpi Labels of Baltimore Inc................ E 330 938-2134
Sebring *(G-11899)*

◆ Nilpeter Usa Inc............................ C 513 489-4400
Cincinnati *(G-2909)*

Norse Dairy Systems Inc.................... C 614 294-4931
Columbus *(G-5128)*

◆ OKL Can Line Inc............................E
Cincinnati *(G-2928)*

▲ Pack Line Corp............................. G 212 564-0664
Cleveland *(G-4131)*

Pak Master LLC.............................. E 330 523-5319
Richfield *(G-11595)*

▲ PE Usa LLC.................................. F 513 771-7374
Cincinnati *(G-2950)*

◆ Pneumatic Scale Corporation............C 330 923-0491
Cuyahoga Falls *(G-5564)*

Portage Packaging Systems Inc............ G 330 274-8295
Hiram *(G-7741)*

Precision Products Group Inc.............. G 330 698-4711
Apple Creek *(G-475)*

Precision Replacement LLC................ G 330 908-0410
Macedonia *(G-8709)*

◆ Quadrel Inc..................................E 440 602-4700
Mentor *(G-9600)*

▲ Reactive Resin Products Co.............. F 419 666-6119
Perrysburg *(G-11259)*

Recon Systems LLC......................... G 330 488-0368
East Canton *(G-6379)*

Rpmi Packaging Inc........................... F 513 398-4040
Lebanon *(G-8284)*

S A Langmack Company...................... G 216 541-0500
Cleveland *(G-4267)*

▲ Scanacon Incorporated................... G 330 877-7600
Hartville *(G-7583)*

Superior Label Systems Inc................. B 513 336-0825
Mason *(G-9157)*

Switchback Group Inc....................... E 216 290-6040
Cleveland *(G-4358)*

System Packaging of Glassline............. D 419 666-9712
Perrysburg *(G-11263)*

Titans Packaging LLC......................... F 513 449-0014
West Chester *(G-14155)*

Universal Packg Systems Inc............... C 513 732-2000
Batavia *(G-894)*

Universal Packg Systems Inc............... C 513 735-4777
Batavia *(G-895)*

Universal Packg Systems Inc............... C 513 674-9400
Cincinnati *(G-3186)*

Vistech Mfg Solutions LLC.................. F 513 933-9300
Lebanon *(G-8296)*

▲ Vmi Americas Inc........................... E 330 929-6800
Stow *(G-12471)*

3566 Speed changers, drives, and gears

Akron Gear & Engineering Inc............. E 330 773-6608
Akron *(G-32)*

Ametek Tchnical Indus Pdts Inc............ D 330 673-3451
Kent *(G-8017)*

Atc Legacy Inc................................. G 330 590-8105
Sharon Center *(G-11936)*

B & B Gear and Machine Co Inc............ E 937 687-1771
New Lebanon *(G-10399)*

▲ Bunting Bearings LLC...................... D 419 866-7000
Holland *(G-7747)*

Cage Gear & Machine LLC.................. E 330 452-1532
Canton *(G-1850)*

Canton Gear Mfg Designing Inc............. F 330 455-2771
Canton *(G-1856)*

▲ Cleveland Gear Company Inc............ D 216 641-9000
Cleveland *(G-3511)*

Dayton Gear and Tool Co.................... E 937 866-4327
Dayton *(G-5727)*

Eaton Leasing Corporation.................. B 216 382-2292
Beachwood *(G-916)*

Ebog Legacy Inc.............................. D 330 239-4933
Sharon Center *(G-11940)*

▲ Force Control Industries Inc............. E 513 868-0900
Fairfield *(G-6737)*

▲ Forge Industries Inc....................... A 330 960-2468
Youngstown *(G-14857)*

Gear Company of America Inc.............. D 216 671-5400
Cleveland *(G-3760)*

◆ Geartec Inc.................................. E 440 953-3900
Willoughby *(G-14462)*

▲ Great Lakes Power Products Inc......... D 440 951-5111
Madison *(G-8730)*

◆ HBD Industries Inc...........................E 614 526-7000
Dublin *(G-6302)*

▲ Hefty Hoist Inc.............................. E 740 467-2515
Millersport *(G-10023)*

◆ Horsburgh & Scott Co......................C 216 431-3900
Cleveland *(G-3839)*

◆ Industrial Mfg Co LLC.......................F 440 838-4700
Brecksville *(G-1472)*

▲ ITT Torque Systems Inc.................... C 216 524-8800
Cleveland *(G-3875)*

Jonmar Gear and Machine Inc.............. G 330 854-6500
Canal Fulton *(G-1776)*

▲ Joseph Industries Inc...................... D 330 528-0091
Streetsboro *(G-12507)*

▲ Julie Maynard Inc........................... F 937 443-0408
Dayton *(G-5834)*

Kenmore Gear & Machine Co Inc........... G 330 753-6671
Akron *(G-194)*

▲ Lhy Powertrain Corporation............... E 330 533-6801
Canfield *(G-1812)*

Little Mountain Precision LLC.............. E 440 290-2903
Mentor *(G-9555)*

◆ Luk Clutch Systems LLC...................E 330 264-4383
Wooster *(G-14661)*

▼ Matlock Electric Co Inc.................... E 513 731-9600
Cincinnati *(G-2850)*

Pentagear Products LLC.................... G 937 660-8182
Dayton *(G-5935)*

Petro Gear Corporation...................... F 216 431-2820
Cleveland *(G-4156)*

Precision Gear LLC............................ D 330 487-0888
Twinsburg *(G-13358)*

Radocy Inc.................................... F 419 666-4400
Rossford *(G-11661)*

Robertson Manufacturing Co................ F 216 531-8222
Concord Township *(G-5395)*

RTC Converters Inc.......................... F 937 743-2300
Franklin *(G-7047)*

Schaeffler Transm Systems LLC........... A 330 202-6212
Wooster *(G-14680)*

◆ Schaeffler Transm Systems LLC.........E 330 264-4383
Wooster *(G-14681)*

Sew-Eurodrive Inc........................... D 937 335-0036
Troy *(G-13254)*

▲ Skidmore-Wilhelm Mfg Company....... G 216 481-4774
Solon *(G-12182)*

Spang & Company............................. E 440 350-6108
Mentor *(G-9619)*

Stahl Gear & Machine Co.................... G 216 431-2820
Cleveland *(G-4323)*

Tgm Holdings Company...................... G 419 885-3769
Sylvania *(G-12728)*

Timken Newco I LLC......................... G 234 262-3000
North Canton *(G-10674)*

Titanium Metals Corporation................ A 740 537-1571
Toronto *(G-13187)*

◆ Wasserstrom Company......................B 614 228-6525
Columbus *(G-5356)*

Werks Kraft Engineering LLC................ E 330 721-7374
Medina *(G-9464)*

3567 Industrial furnaces and ovens

▲ A Jacks Manufacturing Co................. E 216 531-1010
Cleveland *(G-3283)*

◆ Abp Induction LLC ....F 262 878-6390
Massillon (G-9171)

Agridry LLC ....G 419 459-4399
Edon (G-6472)

◆ Ajax Tocco Magnethermic Corp ....C 800 547-1527
Warren (G-13732)

Armature Coil Equipment Inc ....F 216 267-6366
Strongsville (G-12538)

▼ Benko Products Inc ....E 440 934-2180
Sheffield Village (G-11957)

▲ C A Litzler Co Inc ....C 216 267-8020
Cleveland (G-3457)

▲ CA Litzler Holding Company ....D 216 267-8020
Cleveland (G-3458)

▲ CMI Industry Americas Inc ....D 330 332-4661
Salem (G-11771)

▲ Crescent Metal Products Inc ....C 440 350-1100
Mentor (G-9507)

▲ Duca Manufacturing & Cons ....E 330 758-0828
Youngstown (G-14850)

Duca Mfg & Consulting Inc ....G 330 726-7175
Youngstown (G-14851)

◆ Ebner Furnaces Inc ....D 330 335-2311
Wadsworth (G-13637)

▲ Facultatieve Tech Americas Inc ....E 330 723-6339
Medina (G-9400)

Furnace Technologies Inc ....G 419 878-2100
Waterville (G-13833)

◆ Garland Commercial Industries LLC ....G 800 338-2204
Cleveland (G-3756)

Glenro Inc ....G 606 564-4778
Ripley (G-11618)

Glo-Quartz Electric Htr Co Inc ....E 440 255-9701
Mentor (G-9524)

Hannon Company ....D 330 456-4728
Canton (G-1908)

◆ Harrop Industries Inc ....E 614 231-3621
Columbus (G-4972)

▲ Heat Sensor Technologie LLC ....D 513 228-0481
Lebanon (G-8267)

I Cerco Inc ....C 740 982-2050
Crooksville (G-5510)

◆ I Cerco Inc ....C 330 567-2145
Shreve (G-11983)

Induction Tooling Inc ....F 440 237-0711
North Royalton (G-10765)

Kaufman Engineered Systems Inc ....D 419 878-9727
Waterville (G-13837)

L Haberny Co Inc ....F 440 543-5999
Chagrin Falls (G-2168)

Lakeway Mfg Inc ....E 419 433-3030
Huron (G-7877)

Lanly Company ....E 216 731-1115
Cleveland (G-3941)

◆ Lewco Inc ....F 419 625-4014
Sandusky (G-11850)

Magneforce Inc ....F 330 856-9300
Warren (G-13780)

▲ Micropyretics Heaters Intl Inc ....F 513 772-0404
Cincinnati (G-2877)

Miller Core II Inc ....G 330 359-0500
Beach City (G-905)

Novagard Solutions Inc ....D 216 881-8111
Cleveland (G-4101)

▲ P S C Inc ....G 216 531-3375
Cleveland (G-4130)

◆ Park-Ohio Holdings Corp ....F 440 947-2000
Cleveland (G-4136)

Park-Ohio Industries Inc ....C 440 947-2000
Cleveland (G-4137)

Resilience Fund III LP ....F 216 292-0200
Cleveland (G-4237)

Robbins Industrial Frnc Co Inc ....F 440 949-2292
Sheffield Village (G-11963)

▲ Selas Heat Technology Co LLC ....E 800 523-6500
Streetsboro (G-12523)

▲ Sentro Tech Corporation ....G 440 260-0364
Strongsville (G-12596)

Star Engineering LLC ....E 740 342-3514
New Lexington (G-10408)

Stelter and Brinck Inc ....E 513 367-9300
Harrison (G-7569)

▲ Strohecker Incorporated ....D 330 426-9496
East Palestine (G-6407)

▲ Surface Combustion Inc ....D 419 891-7150
Maumee (G-9323)

T E Q HI Inc ....E 877 448-3701
Columbus (G-5305)

T J F Inc ....F 419 878-4400
Waterville (G-13843)

◆ Taylor - Winfield Corporation ....C 330 259-8500
Hubbard (G-7817)

▲ The Schaefer Group Inc ....E 937 253-3342
Beavercreek (G-997)

Thermo Systems Technology Inc ....G 216 292-8250
Cleveland (G-4391)

◆ United McGill Corporation ....E 614 829-1200
Groveport (G-7455)

◆ Warren Steel Holdings LLC ....B 330 847-0487
Warren (G-13812)

Williams Industrial Svc Inc ....E 419 353-2120
Bowling Green (G-1447)

3568 Power transmission equipment, nec

▲ Advance Bronze Inc ....F 330 948-1231
Lodi (G-8496)

Akron Gear & Engineering Inc ....C 330 773-6608
Akron (G-32)

B S F Inc ....F 937 890-6121
Tipp City (G-12816)

B S F Inc ....F 937 890-6121
Dayton (G-5672)

Bdi Inc ....C 330 498-4980
Canton (G-1838)

Bowes Manufacturing Inc ....F 216 378-2110
Solon (G-12087)

▲ Bucyrus Precision Tech Inc ....C 419 563-9950
Bucyrus (G-1674)

Bunting Bearings LLC ....E 419 522-3323
Mansfield (G-8770)

Cleveland Rebabbitting Svc Inc ....G 216 433-0123
Cleveland (G-3523)

▲ Climax Metal Products Company ....D 440 943-8898
Mentor (G-9502)

Custom Cltch Jint Hydrlics Inc ....F 216 431-1630
Cleveland (G-3584)

Danfoss Power Solutions II LLC ....F 419 238-1190
Van Wert (G-13533)

▲ Dayton Superior Pdts Co Inc ....G 937 332-1930
Troy (G-13209)

Dryden Shafts LLC ....E 937 365-7420
Moraine (G-10158)

Dupont Specialty Pdts USA LLC ....C 216 901-3600
Cleveland (G-3638)

Eaton Corporation ....C 216 281-2211
Cleveland (G-3653)

Ebog Legacy Inc ....D 330 239-4933
Sharon Center (G-11940)

Excel Loading Systems LLC ....G 513 504-1069
Hamilton (G-7489)

▲ Force Control Industries Inc ....E 513 868-0900
Fairfield (G-6737)

General Electric Company ....E 216 883-1000
Cleveland (G-3766)

General Metals Powder Co LLC ....E 330 633-1226
Akron (G-160)

GKN Sinter Metals LLC ....C 740 441-3203
Gallipolis (G-7206)

Hite Parts Exchange Inc ....G 614 272-5115
Chillicothe (G-2258)

J L R Products Inc ....G 330 832-9557
Massillon (G-9207)

Lextech Industries Ltd ....G 216 883-7900
Cleveland (G-3953)

▲ Logan Clutch Corporation ....E 440 808-4258
Cleveland (G-3966)

◆ Luk Clutch Systems LLC ....E 330 264-4383
Wooster (G-14661)

Master Products Company ....D 216 341-1740
Cleveland (G-3998)

▲ McGregor Mtal Yllow Sprng Wrks ....D 937 325-5561
Springfield (G-12351)

Mechanical Dynamics Analis LLC ....E 440 946-0082
Euclid (G-6661)

Mfh Partners Inc ....B 440 461-4100
Cleveland (G-4025)

◆ NIDEC MINSTER CORPORATION ....C 419 628-2331
Minster (G-10062)

▲ Opw Engineered Systems Inc ....E 888 771-9438
West Chester (G-14039)

Penn Machine Company LLC ....D 814 288-1547
Twinsburg (G-13351)

Poly Products Inc ....G 216 391-7659
Cleveland (G-4175)

Rail Bearing Service LLC ....B 234 262-3000
North Canton (G-10663)

Rampe Manufacturing Company ....F 440 352-8995
Fairport Harbor (G-6821)

Randall Bearings Inc ....F 419 678-2486
Coldwater (G-4583)

▲ Randall Bearings Inc ....D 419 223-1075
Lima (G-8442)

Robertson Manufacturing Co ....F 216 531-8222
Concord Township (G-5395)

Saf-Holland Inc ....C 513 874-7888
Fairfield (G-6773)

Sintered Metal Industries Inc ....F 330 650-4000
Hudson (G-7857)

Southeastern Shafting Mfg Inc ....F 740 342-4629
New Lexington (G-10407)

▲ Stripmatic Products Inc ....C 216 241-7143
Cleveland (G-4330)

◆ Taiho Corporation of America ....C 419 443-1645
Tiffin (G-12801)

Timken Newco I LLC ....G 234 262-3000
North Canton (G-10674)

▲ Torque 2020 CMA Acqisition LLC ....C 330 874-2900
Bolivar (G-1393)

▲ Tsk America Co Ltd ....F 513 942-4002
West Chester (G-14156)

US Tsubaki Power Transm LLC ....C 419 626-4560
Sandusky (G-11881)

Western Branch Diesel LLC ....F 330 454-8800
Canton (G-2047)

Wiholi Inc ....F 440 543-8233
Chagrin Falls (G-2192)

◆ Xtek Inc ....B 513 733-7800
Cincinnati (G-3240)

3569 General industrial machinery,

1200 Feet Limited ....G 419 827-6061
Lakeville (G-8159)

A-1 Sprinkler Company Inc ....D 937 859-6198
Miamisburg (G-9659)

▲ Abanaki Corporation ....F 440 543-7400
Chagrin Falls (G-2153)

▲ Action Coupling & Eqp Inc.................. D 330 279-4242
Holmesville *(G-7793)*

▲ Advanced Design Industries Inc.... F 440 277-4141
Sheffield Village *(G-11956)*

◆ Air Technical Industries Inc.........E 440 951-5191
Mentor *(G-9474)*

All-American Fire Eqp Inc................ F 800 972-6035
Wshngtn Ct Hs *(G-14734)*

▲ Allied Separation Tech Inc.............. E 704 732-8034
Twinsburg *(G-13274)*

Amatrol Inc..................................... 812 288-8285
Mansfield *(G-8761)*

American Baler Co........................... D 419 483-5790
Bellevue *(G-1119)*

◆ American Rescue Technology Inc......F 937 293-6240
Dayton *(G-5655)*

▲ Applied Marketing Services Inc.... E 440 716-9962
Westlake *(G-14289)*

Aquapro Systems LLC................... F 877 278-2797
Oakwood *(G-10895)*

Astro Manufacturing & Design Inc.... C 888 215-1746
Eastlake *(G-6417)*

▲ Ats Systems Oregon Inc................. F 541 738-0932
Lewis Center *(G-8324)*

Bellco Feeders LLC...................... F 440 728-5590
Concord Township *(G-5387)*

Cascade Corporation........................ E 419 425-3675
Findlay *(G-6850)*

Central Machinery Company LLC.......... G 740 387-1289
Marion *(G-8967)*

Chart International Inc..................... D 440 753-1490
Cleveland *(G-3489)*

Chromalloy Corporation................... F 937 890-3775
Dayton *(G-5702)*

▲ Cleveland Gear Company Inc .... D 216 641-9000
Cleveland *(G-3511)*

◆ Columbus Industries Inc..............D 740 983-2552
Ashville *(G-624)*

Columbus Industries One LLC............ F 740 983-2552
Ashville *(G-625)*

Computer Allied Technology Co.......... G 614 457-2292
Columbus *(G-4839)*

Cummins Filtration Inc.................... C
Findlay *(G-6858)*

Ddp Specialty Electronic MA............... G 937 839-4612
West Alexandria *(G-13918)*

Digilube Systems Inc...................... F 937 748-2209
Springboro *(G-12250)*

▲ Dosmatic USA Inc .... E 972 245-9765
Cincinnati *(G-2559)*

◆ E R Advanced Ceramics Inc............E 330 426-9433
East Palestine *(G-6402)*

Evoqua Water Technologies LLC........ G 614 861-5440
Pickerington *(G-11294)*

Falls Filtration Tech Inc.................. E 330 928-4100
Stow *(G-12430)*

Filter Technology Inc...................... G 614 921-9801
Baltimore *(G-785)*

Fire Fab Corp................................ G 330 759-9834
Girard *(G-7270)*

Fire Foe Corp................................ E 330 759-9834
Girard *(G-7271)*

Fluid Automation Inc....................... E 248 912-1970
North Canton *(G-10640)*

Gem City Engineering Co.................. C 937 223-5544
Dayton *(G-5792)*

◆ Globe Pipe Hanger Products Inc.........E 216 362-6300
Cleveland *(G-3778)*

Gould Fire Protection Inc.................. G 419 957-2416
Findlay *(G-6872)*

▲ Gvs Filtration Inc........................... B 419 423-9040
Findlay *(G-6875)*

H P E Inc.. G 330 833-3161
Massillon *(G-9199)*

▲ Hdt Tactical Systems Inc................ C 216 438-6111
Solon *(G-12122)*

▲ Hellan Strainer Company.................. G 216 206-4200
Cleveland *(G-3819)*

Hitachi Automation Ohio Inc............ F 937 753-1148
Covington *(G-5494)*

▼ Hunter Defense Tech Inc................ E 216 438-6111
Solon *(G-12124)*

Johnsons Fire Equipment Co........... F 740 357-4916
Wellston *(G-13908)*

Joyce/Dayton Corp........................... E 937 294-6261
Dayton *(G-5830)*

▲ Joyce/Dayton Corp........................... E 937 294-6261
Dayton *(G-5831)*

◆ Kc Robotics Inc............................. E 513 860-4442
West Chester *(G-14019)*

◆ Keltec Inc.....................................D 330 425-3100
Twinsburg *(G-13322)*

Koester Corporation........................ E 419 599-0291
Napoleon *(G-10289)*

La Mfg Inc..................................... G 513 577-7200
Cincinnati *(G-2810)*

▲ Lawrence Technologies Inc.............. G 937 274-7771
Dayton *(G-5842)*

Lincoln Electric Automtn Inc............ E 614 471-5926
Columbus *(G-5070)*

M4 Knick LLC................................ G 513 833-2500
Milford *(G-9941)*

▲ Metaullics Systems LP................... C 509 926-6212
Solon *(G-12148)*

▲ Midwest Filtration LLC................... C 513 874-6510
Cincinnati *(G-2879)*

Motionsource International LLC........ F 440 287-7037
Solon *(G-12153)*

Newco Industries............................ F 717 566-9560
Canton *(G-1957)*

Nmgg Ctg LLC................................ C 419 447-5211
Tiffin *(G-12793)*

Nov Inc.. D 937 454-3200
Dayton *(G-5915)*

Nupro Company.............................. E 440 951-9729
Willoughby *(G-14498)*

Nutro Corporation........................... D 440 572-3800
Strongsville *(G-12580)*

OSI Environmental LLC................... E 440 237-4600
North Royalton *(G-10779)*

Parker-Hannifin Corporation............. G 330 335-6740
Wadsworth *(G-13657)*

Pax Products Inc............................. F 419 586-2337
Celina *(G-2115)*

Petro Ware Inc................................ G 740 982-1302
Crooksville *(G-5512)*

Phoenix Safety Outfitters LLC........... G 614 361-0544
Springfield *(G-12362)*

◆ Pneumatic Scale Corporation..........C 330 923-0491
Cuyahoga Falls *(G-5564)*

Process Innovations Inc.................. G 330 856-5192
Vienna *(G-13616)*

Radco Fire Protection Inc................ G 419 476-0102
Toledo *(G-13108)*

Recognition Robotics Inc................ F 440 590-0499
Elyria *(G-6585)*

Red Head Brass Inc......................... F 330 567-2903
Shreve *(G-11985)*

▲ Reladyne Reliability Svcs Inc............ E 888 478-6996
Canton *(G-1992)*

Remtec Engineering......................... F 513 860-4299
Mason *(G-9142)*

Rennco Automation Systems Inc........ E 419 861-2340
Holland *(G-7781)*

◆ Rexarc International Inc.......................E 937 839-4604
West Alexandria *(G-13921)*

▲ Rhba Acquisitions LLC..................... D 330 567-2903
Shreve *(G-11986)*

▲ Rimrock Corporation....................... E 614 471-5926
Columbus *(G-5230)*

Rimrock Holdings Corporation.......... C 614 471-5926
Columbus *(G-5231)*

Rixan Associates Inc....................... E 937 438-3005
Dayton *(G-5984)*

◆ Rotex Global LLC...........................C 513 541-1236
Cincinnati *(G-3053)*

Rti Remmele Engineering Inc............ C 651 635-4179
Cleveland *(G-4263)*

S A Langmack Company..................... G 216 541-0500
Cleveland *(G-4267)*

Sensory Robotics Inc....................... G 513 545-9501
Cincinnati *(G-3082)*

Sentient Studios Ltd....................... E 330 204-8636
Fairlawn *(G-6811)*

▲ Siebtechnik Tema Inc...................... E 513 489-7811
Cincinnati *(G-3088)*

Siemens Industry Inc....................... F 513 576-2088
Milford *(G-9952)*

Stateline Power Corp....................... F 937 547-1006
Greenville *(G-7356)*

▼ Steel & Alloy Utility Pdts Inc............ E 330 530-2220
Mc Donald *(G-9361)*

Swift Filters Inc............................. E 877 887-9438
Bedford *(G-1059)*

Test Measurement Systems Inc............. G 888 867-4872
North Canton *(G-10671)*

The Ransohoff Company.................... C 513 870-0100
West Chester *(G-14153)*

◆ The Western States Machin..............D 513 863-4758
Fairfield *(G-6783)*

Two M Precision Co Inc................... E 440 946-2120
Willoughby *(G-14546)*

Tyco Fire Products LP...................... G 216 265-0505
Cleveland *(G-4435)*

Versatile Automation Tech Corp.......... G 330 220-2600
Brunswick *(G-1622)*

▲ Versatile Automation Tech Ltd.......... G 440 589-6700
Solon *(G-12202)*

Winston Oil Co Inc........................... G 740 373-9664
Marietta *(G-8962)*

Yaskawa America Inc....................... C 937 440-2600
Troy *(G-13261)*

Zephyr Industries Inc....................... G 419 281-4485
Ashland *(G-581)*

3571 Electronic computers

696 Ledgerock Cir............................. G 330 289-0996
Brunswick *(G-1577)*

Advance Products............................. F 419 882-8117
Sylvania *(G-12701)*

Ascendtech Inc............................... E 216 458-1101
Willoughby *(G-14428)*

AT&T Enterprises LLC...................... G 513 792-9300
Cincinnati *(G-2384)*

Coffman Media LLC......................... F 614 956-7015
Dublin *(G-6289)*

Dapsco.. F 937 294-5331
Moraine *(G-10155)*

Eaj Services LLC............................. F 513 792-3400
Blue Ash *(G-1269)*

◆ Eaton Corporation...........................B 440 523-5000
Cleveland *(G-3652)*

Fleet Graphics Inc........................... G 937 252-2552
Dayton *(G-5779)*

General Dynmics Mssion Systems........ G 937 723-2001
Dayton *(G-5794)*

Global Realms LLC................................ G 614 828-7284
Gahanna *(G-7158)*

Griffin Technology Inc........................... C 585 924-7121
Hudson *(G-7842)*

▲ Grimes Aerospace Company............ A 937 484-2000
Urbana *(G-13462)*

Inns Holdings Ltd................................. F 740 345-3700
Newark *(G-10511)*

Interntnal Pdts Srcing Group I............. B 614 334-1500
Columbus *(G-5020)*

Journey Systems LLC........................... F 513 831-6200
Milford *(G-9940)*

Magnum Computers Inc......................... F 216 781-1757
Cleveland *(G-3981)*

Oracle America Inc.............................. G 650 506-7000
Dublin *(G-6327)*

Park Place Technologies LLC............... C
Cleveland *(G-4135)*

Parker-Hannifin Corporation................ F 513 831-2340
Milford *(G-9947)*

Polycom Inc... G 937 245-1853
Englewood *(G-6621)*

▲ Powersonic Industries LLC............... E 513 429-2329
West Chester *(G-14138)*

Predicor LLC.. G 419 460-1831
Cleveland *(G-4188)*

▲ Systemax Manufacturing Inc............. G 937 368-2300
Dayton *(G-6035)*

Town Cntry Technical Svcs Inc............. F 614 866-7700
Reynoldsburg *(G-11582)*

Tracewell Systems Inc.......................... D 614 846-6175
Lewis Center *(G-8356)*

Vr Assets LLC...................................... G 440 600-2963
Solon *(G-12203)*

Walter North.. F 937 204-6050
Dayton *(G-6074)*

3572 Computer storage devices

Capsa Solutions LLC............................ D 800 437-6633
Canal Winchester *(G-1788)*

CHI Corporation................................... G 440 498-2300
Cleveland *(G-3494)*

Freedom Usa Inc.................................. E 216 503-6374
Twinsburg *(G-13305)*

Park Place Technologies LLC............... C
Cleveland *(G-4135)*

▲ Pinnacle Data Systems Inc.............. C 614 748-1150
Groveport *(G-7449)*

Quantum... F 740 328-2548
Newark *(G-10531)*

Quantum Solutions Group..................... G 614 442-0664
Columbus *(G-5219)*

▲ Sam Oht Services LLC..................... F 330 225-3117
Medina *(G-9444)*

Town Cntry Technical Svcs Inc............. F 614 866-7700
Reynoldsburg *(G-11582)*

Tracewell Systems Inc.......................... D 614 846-6175
Lewis Center *(G-8356)*

3575 Computer terminals

Copier Resources Inc........................... G 614 268-1100
Columbus *(G-4849)*

Freedom Usa Inc.................................. E 216 503-6374
Twinsburg *(G-13305)*

Parker-Hannifin Corporation................ F 513 831-2340
Milford *(G-9947)*

▲ Pinnacle Data Systems Inc.............. C 614 748-1150
Groveport *(G-7449)*

Td Synnex Corporation......................... E 614 669-6889
Groveport *(G-7452)*

3577 Computer peripheral equipment, nec

Abstract Displays Inc........................... F 513 985-9700
Blue Ash *(G-1241)*

AGE Graphics LLC............................... G 740 989-0006
Little Hocking *(G-8485)*

Airwave Communications Cons............. G 419 331-1526
Lima *(G-8385)*

Applied Vision Corporation................... D 330 926-2222
Cuyahoga Falls *(G-5526)*

AT&T Enterprises LLC.......................... G 513 792-9300
Cincinnati *(G-2384)*

Black Box Corporation.......................... F 800 676-8850
Brecksville *(G-1460)*

Black Box Corporation.......................... G 800 837-7777
Dublin *(G-6282)*

Black Box Corporation.......................... E 614 825-7400
Lewis Center *(G-8325)*

Black Box Corporation.......................... G 855 324-9909
Westlake *(G-14292)*

Brackish Media LLC............................. F 513 394-2871
Cincinnati *(G-2420)*

Cisco Systems Inc............................... G 330 523-2000
Richfield *(G-11588)*

Clarity Retail Services LLC.................. D 513 800-9369
West Chester *(G-13965)*

Contact Control Interfaces LLC............ G 609 333-3264
Cincinnati *(G-2512)*

▼ Data Processing Sciences................ G 513 791-7100
Cincinnati *(G-2542)*

Dataq Instruments Inc.......................... F 330 668-1444
Akron *(G-115)*

Dreamzone Media LLC.......................... F 216 532-3301
Cleveland *(G-3631)*

Eastman Kodak Company...................... E 937 259-3000
Dayton *(G-5758)*

Embedded Planet Inc........................... F 216 245-4180
Solon *(G-12104)*

Gameday Vision.................................... F 330 830-4550
Massillon *(G-9193)*

Gleason Metrology Systems Corp....... E 937 384-8901
Dayton *(G-5796)*

Government Acquisitions Inc................ E 513 721-8700
Cincinnati *(G-2685)*

▲ Grimes Aerospace Company............ A 937 484-2000
Urbana *(G-13462)*

Harris Mackessy & Brennan Inc............ C 614 221-6831
Westerville *(G-14212)*

Hunkar Technologies Inc...................... C 513 272-1010
Cincinnati *(G-2735)*

ID Images Inc...................................... E 330 220-7300
Brunswick *(G-1597)*

Interactive Products Corp..................... G 513 313-3397
Monroe *(G-10110)*

Kern Inc... C 440 930-7315
Cleveland *(G-3915)*

L3harris Electrodynamics Inc............... C 847 259-0740
Cincinnati *(G-2310)*

Loma Systems...................................... E 740 274-9047
Chillicothe *(G-2262)*

▲ Microcom Corporation...................... E 740 548-6262
Lewis Center *(G-8343)*

New Dawn Labs LLC............................. F 203 675-5644
Union *(G-13410)*

Parker-Hannifin Corporation................ F 513 831-2340
Milford *(G-9947)*

◆ Phase Array Company LLC................ G 513 785-0801
West Chester *(G-14043)*

▲ Qualtek Electronics Corp.................. C 440 951-3300
Mentor *(G-9603)*

Reflexis Systems Inc........................... C 614 948-1931
Westerville *(G-14229)*

▲ Scriptel Corporation......................... F 877 848-6824
Columbus *(G-5258)*

Sierra Nevada Corporation................... E 937 431-2800
Beavercreek *(G-983)*

Signature Technologies Inc.................. E 937 859-6323
Miamisburg *(G-9737)*

Stellar Systems Inc............................. G 513 921-8748
Cincinnati *(G-3118)*

Superior Label Systems Inc.................. B 513 336-0825
Mason *(G-9157)*

Sutter Llc... F 513 891-2261
Blue Ash *(G-1339)*

▲ Systemax Manufacturing Inc............. G 937 368-2300
Dayton *(G-6035)*

▲ Timekeeping Systems Inc................. F 216 595-0890
Solon *(G-12198)*

Treality Svs LLC.................................. E 937 372-7579
Xenia *(G-14781)*

Video Products Inc.............................. D 330 562-2622
Aurora *(G-693)*

Vyral LLC... F 937 993-7765
Dayton *(G-6073)*

Xponet Inc... G 440 354-6617
Painesville *(G-11123)*

Yonezawa Usa Inc............................... F 614 799-2210
Plain City *(G-11430)*

3578 Calculating and accounting equipment

Atm Nerds LLC.................................... F 614 983-3056
Columbus *(G-4733)*

Diebold Nixdorf Incorporated............... D 330 490-4000
Canton *(G-1882)*

Diebold Nixdorf Incorporated............... C 740 928-1010
Hebron *(G-7612)*

Diebold Nixdorf Incorporated............... D 740 928-0200
Hebron *(G-7613)*

Diebold Nixdorf Incorporated............... D 336 662-1115
North Canton *(G-10634)*

Diebold Nixdorf Incorporated............... G 330 899-1300
Uniontown *(G-13418)*

Diebold Nixdorf Incorporated............... A 330 490-4000
North Canton *(G-10635)*

Ganymede Technologies Corp.............. G 419 562-5522
Bucyrus *(G-1681)*

Ginko Voting Systems LLC.................... E 937 291-4060
Dayton *(G-5795)*

Glenn Michael Brick............................ F 740 391-5735
Flushing *(G-6936)*

NCR Technology Center........................ G 937 445-1936
Dayton *(C 5003)*

Testlink Usa Inc................................... E 513 272-1081
Cincinnati *(G-3143)*

Thyme Inc.. F 484 872-8430
Akron *(G-337)*

Total Touch LLC................................... F 800 726-2117
Cleveland *(G-4408)*

Verifone Inc... C 800 837-4366
Columbus *(G-5346)*

3579 Office machines, nec

◆ Baumfolder Corporation.................... E 937 492-1281
Sidney *(G-11996)*

Industrial Electronic Service................ F 937 746-9750
Carlisle *(G-2066)*

Kaylo Enterprises LLC.......................... G 330 535-1860
Akron *(G-192)*

Kern Inc... C 440 930-7315
Cleveland *(G-3915)*

▼ Mabis Shipping Solutions Inc........... G 330 650-1788
Hudson *(G-7850)*

RT Industries Inc................................. G 937 335-5784
Troy *(G-13251)*

Symatic Inc.. G 330 225-1510
Medina *(G-9452)*

S
I
C

3581 Automatic vending machines

Best Result Marketing Inc...................... G 234 212-1194
Bedford *(G-1017)*

Five Star Healthy Vending LLC............... F 330 549-6011
Akron *(G-149)*

▲ Giant Industries Inc.............................. E 419 531-4600
Toledo *(G-12975)*

◆ Gold Medal Products Co....................... B 513 769-7676
Cincinnati *(G-2680)*

Innovative Vend Solutions LLC............... F 866 931-9413
Dayton *(G-5822)*

Securastock LLC.................................... E 844 732-8727
Cleveland *(G-4284)*

▲ Ve Global Vending Inc.......................... G 216 785-2611
Cleveland *(G-4459)*

3582 Commercial laundry equipment

Ellis Laundry and Lin Sup Inc................. G 330 339-4941
New Philadelphia *(G-10444)*

Ha-International LLC............................... E 419 537-0096
Toledo *(G-12982)*

▲ Husqvarna US Holding Inc.................... D 216 898-1800
Cleveland *(G-3845)*

Whirlpool Corporation............................ C 419 547-7711
Clyde *(G-4565)*

3585 Refrigeration and heating equipment

Air Enterprises Inc................................. A 330 794-9770
Akron *(G-22)*

▼ Bard Manufacturing Company Inc...... D 419 636-1194
Bryan *(G-1631)*

▲ Beckett Air Incorporated.................... D 440 327-9999
North Ridgeville *(G-10725)*

Bessamaire Sales Inc............................ E 440 439-1200
Twinsburg *(G-13279)*

Bodor Vents Inc.................................... G 513 348-3853
Cincinnati *(G-2415)*

▲ Boston Beer Company........................ E 267 240-4429
Cincinnati *(G-2419)*

▲ Briskheat Corporation........................ C 614 294-3376
Columbus *(G-4781)*

◆ Bry-Air Inc... E 740 965-2974
Sunbury *(G-12662)*

◆ C Nelson Mfg Co................................ E 419 898-3305
Oak Harbor *(G-10884)*

Chilltex LLC.. F 937 710-3308
Anna *(G-460)*

Columbus Heating & Vent Co................. C 614 274-1177
Columbus *(G-4823)*

Copeland Corporation............................ F 937 498-3011
Sidney *(G-12004)*

Copeland LP... B 937 498-3011
Sidney *(G-12006)*

Copeland LP... B 937 498-3587
Sidney *(G-12007)*

◆ Copeland LP....................................... A 937 498-3011
Sidney *(G-12005)*

◆ Crawford Ae LLC................................ D 330 794-9770
Akron *(G-109)*

◆ Cryogenic Equipment & Svcs Inc....... F 513 761-4200
Hamilton *(G-7481)*

◆ Csafe LLC... G 513 360-7189
Monroe *(G-10100)*

Daikin Applied Americas Inc.................. G 614 351-9862
Westerville *(G-14252)*

▲ Dyoung Enterprise Inc........................ C 440 918-0505
Willoughby *(G-14452)*

◆ Eaton Aeroquip LLC............................ C 440 523-5000
Cleveland *(G-3650)*

◆ Ecu Corporation................................. F 513 898-9294
Cincinnati *(G-2579)*

Elitaire LLC.. D 513 475-3803
Blue Ash *(G-1271)*

Ellis & Watts Global Inds Inc................. E 513 752-9000
Batavia *(G-863)*

Emerson Network Power......................... G 614 841-8054
Ironton *(G-7931)*

▲ Energy Labs LLC................................. B 619 671-0100
Westerville *(G-14208)*

Famous Industries Inc........................... F 740 685-2592
Byesville *(G-1711)*

Famous Realty Cleveland Inc................. F 740 685-2533
Byesville *(G-1712)*

▲ Fire From Ice Ventures LLC................. F 419 944-6705
Solon *(G-12112)*

Forzza Corporation................................ E 440 998-6300
Madison *(G-8729)*

Fred D Pfening Company........................ E 614 294-5361
Columbus *(G-4939)*

◆ Guardian Technologies LLC................. E 866 603-5900
Euclid *(G-6652)*

Hanon Systems Usa LLC........................ C 313 920-0583
Carey *(G-2058)*

Hdt Ep Inc.. C 216 438-6111
Solon *(G-12120)*

Hdt Expeditionary Systems Inc.............. F 440 466-6640
Geneva *(G-7239)*

Hobart LLC... D 937 332-2797
Piqua *(G-11355)*

Hobart LLC... E 937 332-3000
Troy *(G-13225)*

▲ Hobart LLC... D 937 332-3000
Troy *(G-13226)*

▲ Hydro-Dyne Inc.................................. F 330 832-5076
Massillon *(G-9204)*

▼ Hydro-Thrift Corporation................... E 330 837-5141
Massillon *(G-9205)*

J&I Duct Fab Llc.................................... F 937 473-2121
Covington *(G-5495)*

▲ Jbar A/C Inc....................................... F 216 447-4294
Cleveland *(G-3884)*

JD Indoor Comfort Inc........................... F 440 949-8758
Sheffield Lake *(G-11954)*

Jnp Group LLC...................................... F 800 735-9645
Wooster *(G-14655)*

Lennox Industries Inc............................ G 216 739-1909
Cleveland *(G-3951)*

Lfg Specialties LLC............................... E 419 424-4999
Findlay *(G-6885)*

◆ Lintern Corporation............................ E 440 255-9333
Mentor *(G-9554)*

◆ Lvd Acquisition LLC........................... D 614 861-1350
Columbus *(G-5077)*

Mahle Behr Dayton LLC......................... A 937 369-2000
Dayton *(G-5862)*

Mahle Behr USA Inc............................... G 937 369-2610
Xenia *(G-14770)*

◆ Maverick Innvtive Slutions LLC........... D 419 281-7944
Ashland *(G-550)*

Northeastern Rfrgn Corp........................ E 440 942-7676
Willoughby *(G-14496)*

Nrc Inc... E 440 975-9449
Willoughby *(G-14497)*

Obhc Inc... G 440 236-5112
Columbia Station *(G-4595)*

Professional Supply Inc......................... F 419 332-7373
Fremont *(G-7128)*

Royal Metal Products LLC...................... C 740 397-8842
Mount Vernon *(G-10264)*

▼ RSI Company...................................... F 216 360-9800
Beachwood *(G-946)*

Rtx Corporation.................................... B 330 784-5477
North Canton *(G-10666)*

▲ Shoals Tubular Inc.............................. D 256 767-7171
Mason *(G-9150)*

Snap Rite Manufacturing Inc.................. E 910 897-4080
Cleveland *(G-4308)*

So-Low Environmental Eqp Co............... E 513 772-9410
Cincinnati *(G-3098)*

Sticker Corporation............................... F 440 946-2100
Willoughby *(G-14534)*

T J F Inc... F 419 878-4400
Waterville *(G-13843)*

◆ Taiho Corporation of America.............. C 419 443-1645
Tiffin *(G-12801)*

Taylor & Moore Co................................ F 513 733-5530
Cincinnati *(G-3139)*

◆ Tempest Inc.. E 216 883-6500
Cleveland *(G-4373)*

▲ The Columbus Show Case Co............. C
Columbus *(G-5318)*

Trane Inc.. E 440 946-7823
Cleveland *(G-4410)*

Trane US Inc... C 513 771-8884
Cincinnati *(G-3163)*

Trane US Inc... C 614 473-3131
Columbus *(G-5326)*

Trane US Inc... G 614 473-8701
Columbus *(G-5327)*

Trane US Inc... G 614 497-6300
Groveport *(G-7454)*

Trane US Inc... F 419 491-2278
Holland *(G-7788)*

Vertiv Corporation................................ C 614 841-6078
Delaware *(G-6177)*

Vertiv Corporation................................ G 614 491-9286
Groveport *(G-7456)*

◆ Vertiv Corporation.............................. A 614 888-0246
Westerville *(G-14239)*

Vertiv Group Corporation....................... A 614 888-0246
Westerville *(G-14240)*

Vertiv JV Holdings LLC.......................... A 614 888-0246
Columbus *(G-5348)*

Virginia Air Distributors Inc................... G 614 262-1129
Columbus *(G-5350)*

Vortec Corporation................................ E 513 891-7485
Blue Ash *(G-1348)*

Whirlpool Corporation............................ E 614 409-4340
Lockbourne *(G-8494)*

Yukon Industries Inc.............................. E 440 478-4174
Mentor *(G-9655)*

3586 Measuring and dispensing pumps

Bergstrom Company Ltd Partnr.............. F 440 232-2282
Cleveland *(G-3415)*

Cohesant Inc... E 216 910-1700
Beachwood *(G-913)*

Energy Manufacturing Ltd...................... G 419 355-9304
Fremont *(G-7105)*

◆ Field Stone Inc................................... G 937 898-3236
Tipp City *(G-12825)*

Gojo Industries Inc................................ G 330 255-6525
Stow *(G-12435)*

◆ Gojo Industries Inc............................. G 330 255-6000
Akron *(G-163)*

▲ Graco Ohio Inc................................... D 330 494-1313
North Canton *(G-10644)*

Lubrisource Inc..................................... F 937 432-9292
Middletown *(G-9872)*

Precision Conveyor Technology.............. F 440 352-6100
Perry *(G-11197)*

◆ Seepex Inc... C 937 864-7150
Enon *(G-6633)*

◆ Tolco Corporation............................... E 419 241-1113
Toledo *(G-13147)*

▲ Valco Cincinnati Inc............................ C 513 874-6550
Cincinnati *(G-3190)*

3589 Service industry machinery, nec

Accushred LLC.. F 419 244-7473
Toledo *(G-12863)*

Active Aeration Systems Inc................. G 614 873-3626
Plain City *(G-11390)*

Advanced Green Tech Inc...................... G 614 397-8130
Plain City *(G-11392)*

▲ Ameriwater LLC................................... E 937 461-8833
Dayton *(G-5657)*

Amsoil Inc.. G 614 274-9851
Urbancrest *(G-13482)*

Aqua Ohio Inc....................................... F 740 867-8700
Chesapeake *(G-2228)*

Aqua Pennsylvania Inc.......................... G 440 257-6190
Mentor On The Lake *(G-9656)*

Aquapro Systems LLC........................... F 877 278-2797
Oakwood *(G-10895)*

Artesian of Pioneer Inc......................... F 419 737-2352
Pioneer *(G-11318)*

As Clean As It Gets Off Brkroo.............. E 216 256-1143
South Euclid *(G-12218)*

Beckman Environmental Svcs Inc.......... F 513 752-3570
Batavia *(G-853)*

Belanger Inc.. D 517 870-3206
West Chester *(G-13948)*

Bell Industrial Services LLC.................. F 937 507-9193
Sidney *(G-11997)*

Best Equipment Co Inc.......................... E 440 237-3515
North Royalton *(G-10755)*

Chemtreat.. G 937 644-2525
East Liberty *(G-6384)*

City of Ashland...................................... G 419 289-8728
Ashland *(G-529)*

City of Athens....................................... F 740 592-3344
Athens *(G-636)*

City of Chardon..................................... E 440 286-2657
Chardon *(G-2201)*

City of Middletown................................ D 513 425-7781
Middletown *(G-9844)*

City of Ravenna..................................... G 330 296-5214
Ravenna *(G-11521)*

City of Troy... F 937 339-4826
Troy *(G-13205)*

City of Xenia... E 937 376-7269
Xenia *(C-14758)*

▲ Cleveland Range LLC........................... C 216 481-4900
Cleveland *(G-3522)*

Cold Jet International LLC...................... D 513 831-3211
Loveland *(G-8622)*

County of Lake....................................... G 440 428-1794
Madison *(G-8728)*

Crown Solutions Co LLC........................ C 937 890-4075
Vandalia *(G-13553)*

De Nora Holdings Us Inc....................... B 440 710-5300
Concord Township *(G-5389)*

▲ De Nora North America Inc.................. G 440 357-4000
Painesville *(G-11076)*

De Nora Tech Inc................................... G 440 285-0368
Painesville *(G-11077)*

◆ De Nora Tech LLC................................ D 440 710-5334
Painesville *(G-11078)*

◆ Detrex Corporation...............................F 216 749-2605
Cleveland *(G-3611)*

Diversey Taski Inc................................. E 419 531-2121
Toledo *(G-12945)*

◆ Eagle Crusher Co Inc............................D 419 468-2288
Galion *(G-7187)*

▲ Electric Eel Mfg Co Inc........................ E 937 323-4644
Springfield *(G-12306)*

◆ Enting Water Conditioning Inc........... E 937 294-5100
Moraine *(G-10160)*

Evers Enterprises Inc............................ G 513 541-7200
Cincinnati *(G-2603)*

Evoqua Water Technologies LLC........... F 614 491-5917
Groveport *(G-7431)*

◆ Garland Commercial Industries LLC...G 800 338-2204
Cleveland *(G-3756)*

▲ Giant Industries Inc............................ E 419 531-4600
Toledo *(G-12975)*

◆ Gold Medal Products Co........................B 513 769-7676
Cincinnati *(G-2680)*

Greene County....................................... G 937 429-0127
Dayton *(G-5613)*

▲ Hammersmith Bros Invstmnts Inc...... E 513 353-3000
North Bend *(G-10620)*

◆ Henny Penny Corporation....................A 937 456-8400
Eaton *(G-6454)*

◆ HI-Vac Corporation...............................C 740 374-2306
Marietta *(G-8923)*

High-TEC Industrial Services................. D 937 667-1772
Tipp City *(G-12827)*

Hobart LLC.. D 937 332-2797
Piqua *(G-11355)*

Hobart LLC.. E 937 332-3000
Troy *(G-13225)*

▲ Hobart LLC... D 937 332-3000
Troy *(G-13226)*

Holdren Brothers Inc............................ F 937 465-7050
West Liberty *(G-14175)*

Image By J & K LLC............................... F 888 667-6929
Maumee *(G-9297)*

Imet Corporation................................... G 440 799-3135
Cleveland *(G-3852)*

Industrial Fluid MGT Inc....................... F 419 748-7460
Mc Clure *(G-9351)*

◆ JE Grote Company Inc..........................D 614 868-8414
Columbus *(G-5035)*

◆ Jet Inc..E 440 461-2000
Cleveland *(G-3887)*

▲ Kaivac Inc.. D 513 887-4600
Hamilton *(G-7508)*

Kellermyer Bergensons Svcs LLC.......... D 419 867-4300
Maumee *(G-9301)*

◆ Kinetico Incorporated..........................B 440 564-9111
Newbury *(G-10556)*

Knight Manufacturing Co Inc................. G 740 676-5516
Chadyoido *(C-11032)*

L N Brut Manufacturing Co.................... G 330 833-9045
Shreve *(G-11984)*

Lima Sheet Metal Mch & Mfg Inc........... F 419 229-1161
Lima *(G-8426)*

Mack Industries PA Inc.......................... D 330 638-7680
Vienna *(G-13613)*

McNish Corporation............................... G 614 899-2282
Westerville *(G-14222)*

◆ MJB Toledo Inc.....................................D 419 531-2121
Toledo *(G-13056)*

Monarch Water Systems Inc.................. F 937 426-5773
Beavercreek *(G-978)*

MPW Industrial Svcs Group Inc............. B 740 927-8790
Hebron *(G-7625)*

N-Viro International Corp....................... F 419 535-6374
Toledo *(G-13061)*

National Pride Equipment Inc................ G 419 289-2886
Mansfield *(G-8837)*

New Aqua LLC....................................... F 614 265-9000
Columbus *(G-5125)*

◆ Norwalk Wastewater Eqp Co...............D 419 668-4471
Norwalk *(G-10857)*

Obic LLC.. F 419 633-3147
Bryan *(G-1654)*

Onesource Water LLC........................... F 866 917-7873
Toledo *(G-13077)*

▲ Or-Tec Inc.. G 216 475-5225
Maple Heights *(G-8889)*

Pelton Environmental Pdts Inc.............. G 440 838-1221
Lewis Center *(G-8348)*

Powerbuff Inc.. F 419 241-2156
Toledo *(G-13102)*

Proto-Vest Inc....................................... F 623 872-3495
Sheffield Village *(G-11962)*

R D Baker Enterprises Inc.................... G 937 461-5225
Dayton *(G-5971)*

Russ Jr Enterprises Inc......................... F 440 237-4642
North Royalton *(G-10783)*

Sammy S Auto Detail.............................. F 614 263-2728
Columbus *(G-5246)*

Samsco Corp... F 216 400-8207
Cleveland *(G-4271)*

▲ Siebtechnik Tema Inc........................... E 513 489-7811
Cincinnati *(G-3088)*

Smart Sonic Corporation....................... G 818 610-7900
Cleveland *(G-4306)*

Squeaky Clean Cincinnati Inc................ F 513 729-2712
Cincinnati *(G-3109)*

Tangent Company LLC............................ G 440 543-2775
Chagrin Falls *(G-2186)*

Tipton Environmental Intl Inc................. F 513 735-2777
Batavia *(G-891)*

Trinity Water Solutions LLC................... E 740 318-0585
Caldwell *(G-1730)*

Trionetics Inc.. F 216 812-3570
Brooklyn Heights *(G-1542)*

Trumbull Manufacturing Inc................... E 330 270-7888
Youngstown *(G-14953)*

Under Pressure Systems Inc.................. G 330 602-4466
New Philadelphia *(G-10469)*

United McGill Corporation...................... F 614 920-1267
Lithopolis *(G-8484)*

Veolia Wts Systems Usa Inc................. G 513 794-1010
Cincinnati *(G-3201)*

Veolia Wts Systems Usa Inc................. F 330 929-1639
Stow *(G-12470)*

Water & Waste Water Eqp Co................. G 440 542-0972
Solon *(G-12207)*

◆ William R Hague Inc.............................D 614 836-2115
Groveport *(G-7458)*

3592 Carburetors, pistons, rings, valves

Ad Piston Ring LLC................................ F 216 781-5200
Cleveland *(G-3294)*

Aswpengg LLC....................................... F 216 292-4620
Bedford Heights *(G-1069)*

Brooks Manufacturing............................ G 419 244-1777
Toledo *(G-12905)*

Buckeye BOP LLC.................................. F 740 498-9898
Newcomerstown *(G-10569)*

▲ Celina Alum Precision Tech Inc......... B 419 586-2278
Celina *(G-2099)*

◆ Group Industries Inc............................E 216 271-0702
Cleveland *(G-3796)*

Hite Parts Exchange Inc........................ G 614 272-5115
Chillicothe *(G-2258)*

Peterson American Corporation............. E 419 867-8711
Holland *(G-7777)*

Quaker City Castings Inc....................... A 330 332-1566
Salem *(G-11806)*

Race Winning Brands Inc....................... B 440 951-6600
Mentor *(G-9606)*

▲ Seabiscuit Motorsports Inc.................. B 440 951-6600
Mentor *(G-9612)*

Tiffin Foundry & Machine Inc................. E 419 447-3991
Tiffin *(G-12802)*

SIC

Valv-Trol LLC...................................... F 330 686-2800
Stow (G-12469)

3593 Fluid power cylinders and actuators

▲ American Hydraulic Svcs Inc............. E 606 739-8680
Ironton (G-7929)

B & H Machine Inc............................ E 330 868-6425
Minerva (G-10034)

Cascade Corporation............................ E 937 327-0300
Springfield (G-12287)

Cho Bedford Inc.................................. E 330 343-8896
Dover (G-6234)

▲ Control Line Equipment Inc............. F 216 433-7766
Cleveland (G-3565)

▲ Custom Hoists Inc........................... C 419 368-4721
Ashland (G-532)

Cylinders and Valves Inc...................... G 440 238-7343
Strongsville (G-12552)

▲ Dana Limited................................... B 419 887-3000
Maumee (G-9282)

Dynamic Hydraulic Svcs Co LLC........... E 330 447-8967
Dover (G-6243)

Eaton Aeroquip LLC........................... A 419 891-7775
Maumee (G-9292)

Eaton Leasing Corporation.................. B 216 382-2292
Beachwood (G-916)

Emerson Process Management.............. E 419 529-4311
Ontario (G-10949)

Emmco Inc.. G 216 429-2020
Euclid (G-6649)

▲ Hunger Hydraulics CC Ltd............... F 419 666-4510
Rossford (G-11657)

Hunt Valve Actuator LLC.................... D 330 337-9535
Salem (G-11787)

Hydranamics Inc................................ D 419 468-3530
Galion (G-7195)

Hydraulic Parts Store Inc.................... G 330 364-6667
New Philadelphia (G-10449)

▲ Hydraulic Products Inc.................... G 440 946-4575
Willoughby (G-14466)

Hydraulic Specialists Inc.................... G 740 922-3343
Midvale (G-9911)

▲ Ic-Fluid Power Inc........................... F 419 661-8811
Rossford (G-11658)

J D Hydraulic Inc............................... G 419 686-5234
Portage (G-11457)

Kyntronics Inc................................... F 440 220-5990
Solon (G-12140)

Moog Inc... E 330 682-0010
Orrville (G-10996)

North Coast Instruments Inc................ G 216 251-2353
Cleveland (G-4085)

Parker-Hannifin Corporation................ C 330 336-3511
Wadsworth (G-13659)

▲ Parker-Hannifin Corporation........... A 216 896-3000
Cleveland (G-4143)

Qcsm LLC... G 216 650-8731
Cleveland (G-4210)

R & J Cylinder & Machine Inc.............. D 330 364-8263
New Philadelphia (G-10463)

R & M Fluid Power Inc........................ E 330 758-2766
Youngstown (G-14922)

▲ Robeck Fluid Power Co.................... D 330 562-1140
Aurora (G-687)

Sebring Fluid Power Corp.................... G 330 938-9984
Sebring (G-11902)

▲ Skidmore-Wilhelm Mfg Company...... G 216 481-4774
Solon (G-12182)

▲ Steel Eqp Specialists Inc................. D 330 823-8260
Alliance (G-406)

Suburban Manufacturing Co................. D 440 953-2024
Eastlake (G-6444)

Swagelok Company............................. D 440 349-5934
Solon (G-12191)

▲ The Sheffer Corporation.................. D 513 489-9770
Cincinnati (G-3150)

United Hydraulics............................... G 440 585-0906
Wickliffe (G-14398)

◆ Waltco Lift Corp.............................. C 330 633-9191
Streetsboro (G-12530)

Worthington Cylinder Corp................... C 614 438-7900
Columbus (G-5373)

Xomox Corporation............................. E 936 271-6500
Cincinnati (G-3237)

Xomox Pft Corp.................................. B 936 271-6500
Cincinnati (G-3238)

Zaytran Inc.. E 440 324-2814
Elyria (G-6604)

3594 Fluid power pumps and motors

Aerocontrolex Group Inc..................... D 216 291-6025
South Euclid (G-12216)

Alkid Corporation............................... E 216 896-3000
Cleveland (G-3323)

▲ Anchor Flange Company.................. D 513 527-3512
Cincinnati (G-2369)

▲ Apph Wichita Inc............................ E 316 943-5752
Strongsville (G-12537)

Bergstrom Company Ltd Partnr............. F 440 232-2282
Cleveland (G-3415)

Bosch Rexroth Corporation.................. C 330 263-3300
Wooster (G-14627)

Custom Cltch Jint Hydrlics Inc.............. F 216 431-1630
Cleveland (G-3584)

Cylinders and Valves Inc...................... G 440 238-7343
Strongsville (G-12552)

Danfoss Power Solutions II LLC............ F 419 238-1190
Van Wert (G-13533)

Dynamic Hydraulic Svcs Co LLC........... E 330 447-8967
Dover (G-6243)

Eaton Aeroquip LLC........................... A 419 891-7775
Maumee (G-9292)

◆ Eaton Corporation........................... B 440 523-5000
Cleveland (G-3652)

Eaton Leasing Corporation.................. B 216 382-2292
Beachwood (G-916)

Emerson Process Management.............. E 419 529-4311
Ontario (G-10949)

Fluid Power Solutions LLC.................. G 614 777-8954
Hilliard (G-7682)

▲ Force Control Industries Inc............. E 513 868-0900
Fairfield (G-6737)

◆ Furukawa Rock Drill USA Co Ltd....... F 330 673-5826
Kent (G-8034)

▲ Giant Industries Inc........................ E 419 531-4600
Toledo (G-12975)

Gorman-Rupp Company....................... C 419 755-1011
Mansfield (G-8794)

Hite Parts Exchange Inc...................... G 614 272-5115
Chillicothe (G-2258)

▲ Hy-Production LLC........................... C 330 273-2400
Valley City (G-13499)

Hydraulic Parts Store Inc.................... G 330 364-6667
New Philadelphia (G-10449)

▲ Hydraulic Products Inc.................... G 440 946-4575
Willoughby (G-14466)

▲ Lhy Powertrain Corporation............. E 330 533-6801
Canfield (G-1812)

Midwest Tool & Engineering Co............. G
Dayton (G-5883)

◆ Oase North America Inc.................... G 800 365-3880
Aurora (G-682)

Parker Hannifin Partner B LLC.............. G 216 896-3000
Cleveland (G-4140)

Parker Royalty Partnership................... G 216 896-3000
Cleveland (G-4141)

Parker-Hannifin Corporation................ F 330 261-1618
Berlin Center (G-1202)

Parker-Hannifin Corporation................ E 937 644-3915
Marysville (G-9041)

Parker-Hannifin Corporation................ E 440 266-2300
Mentor (G-9582)

Parker-Hannifin Corporation................ C 419 644-4311
Metamora (G-9658)

Parker-Hannifin Corporation................ G 513 847-1758
West Chester (G-14041)

Parker-Hannifin Corporation................ G 330 740-8366
Youngstown (G-14914)

▲ Parker-Hannifin Corporation........... A 216 896-3000
Cleveland (G-4143)

▲ Permco Inc..................................... C 330 626-2801
Streetsboro (G-12515)

Pfpc Enterprises Inc........................... E 513 941-6200
Cincinnati (G-2960)

Quad Fluid Dynamics Inc..................... F 330 220-3005
Brunswick (G-1610)

Radocy Inc.. F 419 666-4400
Rossford (G-11661)

▲ Robeck Fluid Power Co.................... D 330 562-1140
Aurora (G-687)

▲ Semtorq Inc................................... F 330 487-0600
Twinsburg (G-13377)

Starkey Machinery Inc......................... E 419 468-2560
Galion (G-7199)

Suburban Manufacturing Co................. D 440 953-2024
Eastlake (G-6444)

Sunset Industries Inc.......................... E 440 306-8284
Mentor (G-9631)

Swagelok Company............................. E 440 349-5836
Solon (G-12190)

Toth Industries Inc............................. D 419 729-4669
Toledo (G-13164)

Trane Technologies Company LLC......... E 419 633-6800
Bryan (G-1665)

Vertiflo Pump Company....................... F 513 530-0888
Cincinnati (G-3202)

Vickers International Inc....................... G 419 867-2200
Maumee (G-9329)

Y O H Inc.. E 614 488-2861
Columbus (G-5377)

3596 Scales and balances, except laboratory

Cgmw Incorporated............................ G 614 236-8388
Columbus (G-4804)

▲ Etched Metal Company.................... E 440 248-0240
Solon (G-12109)

Exact Equipment Corporation.............. F 215 295-2000
Columbus (G-4640)

Hobart LLC....................................... D 937 332-2797
Piqua (G-11355)

Hobart LLC....................................... E 937 332-3000
Troy (G-13225)

▲ Hobart LLC..................................... D 937 332-3000
Troy (G-13226)

▲ Holtgreven Scale & Elec Corp.......... F 419 422-4779
Findlay (G-6881)

Interface Logic Systems Inc................. G 614 236-8388
Ashville (G-626)

K Davis Inc....................................... G 419 307-7051
Fremont (G-7119)

Mettler-Toledo LLC............................ C 614 841-7300
Columbus (G-5096)

Mettler-Toledo LLC............................ D 614 438-4511
Worthington (G-14719)

Mettler-Toledo LLC............................ C 614 438-4390
Worthington (G-14720)

◆ Mettler-Toledo Intl Inc..............A 614 438-4511
Columbus *(G-4643)*

◆ Mettler-Toledo LLC..................A 614 438-4511
Columbus *(G-4644)*

Rainin Instrument LLC................G 510 564-1600
Columbus *(G-4647)*

3599 Industrial machinery, nec

2-M Manufacturing Company Inc........ E 440 269-1270
Eastlake *(G-6414)*

3249 Inc................................. F 937 294-5692
Moraine *(G-10140)*

3d Sales & Consulting Inc............. E 513 422-1198
Middletown *(G-9838)*

5 S Inc.................................G 440 968-0212
Montville *(G-10139)*

A & B Foundry LLC...................... F 937 369-3007
Franklin *(G-7007)*

A & B Machine Inc..................... E 937 492-8662
Sidney *(G-11989)*

A & G Manufacturing Co Inc............ F 419 468-7433
Galion *(G-7175)*

▲ A & G Manufacturing Co Inc......... E 419 468-7433
Galion *(G-7176)*

A & R Machine Co Inc..................G 330 832-4631
Massillon *(G-9169)*

A and V Grinding Inc..................G 937 444-4141
Cincinnati *(G-2324)*

A&B Foundry & Machining LLC.......... E 937 746-3634
Franklin *(G-7008)*

A+ Engineering Fabrication Inc........ F 419 832-0748
Grand Rapids *(G-7307)*

AAM Mold and Machine Inc............. F 440 998-2040
Ashtabula *(G-585)*

Abco Bar & Tube Cutng Svc Inc........ E 513 697-9487
Maineville *(G-8737)*

Able Tool Corporation................. E 513 733-8989
Cincinnati *(G-2334)*

Accu-Grind & Mfg Co Inc.............. F 937 224-3303
Dayton *(G-5631)*

Accu-Tool Inc..........................G 937 667-5878
Tipp City *(G-12813)*

Accuform Manufacturing Inc............ E 330 797-9291
Youngstown *(G-14803)*

Accurate Manufacturing Company........ F 614 878-6510
Dublin *(G-6272)*

Accurate Metal Machining Inc........... C 440 350-8225
Painesville *(G-11066)*

Accurate Tech Inc.....................G 440 951-9153
Mentor *(G-9467)*

Ace Boiler & Welding Co Inc...........G 330 745-4443
Copley *(G-5427)*

Ace Grinding Co Inc...................G 440 951-6760
Willoughby *(G-14413)*

▲ Ace Manufacturing Company.......... E 513 541-2490
West Chester *(G-13935)*

▲ Ace Precision Industries Inc........ E 330 633-8523
Akron *(G-14)*

Action Machine & Mfg Inc..............G 513 899-3889
Morrow *(G-10201)*

▲ Active Metal and Molds Inc.......... F 419 281-9623
Ashland *(G-514)*

▲ Addition Manufacturing Te........... C 513 228-7000
Lebanon *(G-8241)*

ADI Machining Inc.....................G 440 277-4141
Sheffield Village *(G-11955)*

▲ Advance Apex Inc.................... E 614 539-3000
Grove City *(G-7366)*

Advance Manufacturing Corp............ E 216 333-1684
Cleveland *(G-3302)*

▲ Advanced Design Industries Inc...... F 440 277-4141
Sheffield Village *(G-11956)*

Advanced Engrg & Mfg Co Inc........... F 330 686-9911
Stow *(G-12416)*

Advanced Indus Machining Inc.......... F 614 596-4183
Powell *(G-11481)*

Advantage Machine Shop................G 330 337-8377
Salem *(G-11761)*

Advetech Inc.......................... E 330 533-2227
Canfield *(G-1801)*

Aeroserv Inc.......................... F 513 932-9227
Mason *(G-9057)*

Aerotech Enterprise................... F 440 729-2616
Chesterland *(G-2232)*

AGR Consulting Inc.................... F 440 974-4030
Eastlake *(G-6416)*

Aims-CMI Technology LLC............... F 937 832-2000
Englewood *(G-6605)*

Aircraft & Auto Fittings Co...........G 216 486-0047
Cleveland *(G-3317)*

Airgas Usa LLC........................G 740 353-5710
Portsmouth *(G-11463)*

Ajax-Ceco.............................G 440 295-0244
Euclid *(G-6639)*

Akay Holdings Inc..................... E 330 753-8458
Barberton *(G-790)*

Akro Tool Co Inc......................G 513 858-1555
Fairfield *(G-6707)*

▼ Akron Equipment Company............ D 330 645-3780
Akron *(G-29)*

Akron Gear & Engineering Inc.......... E 330 773-6608
Akron *(G-32)*

▼ Akron Special Machinery Inc......... E 330 753-1077
Akron *(G-41)*

Albion Machine & Tool Co Inc..........G 216 267-9627
Cleveland *(G-3319)*

◆ Alfons Haar Inc..................... E 937 560-2031
Springboro *(G-12246)*

Alfred Machine Co..................... D 440 248-4600
Cleveland *(G-3322)*

All Craft Manufacturing Co............ F 513 661-3383
Cincinnati *(G-2348)*

All-Tech Manufacturing Ltd............ E 330 633-1095
Akron *(G-50)*

All-Type Welding & Fabrication........ E 440 439-3990
Cleveland *(G-3329)*

Allen Randall Enterprises Inc......... F 330 374-9850
Akron *(G-51)*

▲ Alliance Automation LLC............. D 419 238-2520
Van Wert *(G-13636)*

Alliance Machine Company..............G 330 823-6120
Alliance *(G-371)*

Allied Machine Works Inc..............G 740 454-2534
Zanesville *(G-14986)*

Allied Mask and Tooling Inc........... F 419 470-2555
Toledo *(G-12870)*

Alloy Machining and Fabg Inc..........G 330 482-5543
Columbiana *(G-4605)*

◆ Alloy Precision Tech Inc............ D 440 266-7700
Mentor *(G-9477)*

Alternative Surface Grinding..........G 330 273-3443
Brunswick *(G-1579)*

American Aero Components Llc...........G 937 367-5068
Dayton *(G-5649)*

American Punch Co..................... E 216 731-4501
Euclid *(G-6642)*

American Tool Works Inc............... F 513 844-6363
Hamilton *(G-7465)*

Amerimold Inc.........................G 800 950-8020
Mogadore *(G-10069)*

Ampsco Division.......................G 614 444-2181
Columbus *(G-4706)*

Amtech Tool & Machine Inc.............G 330 758-8215
Youngstown *(G-14813)*

Anchor Fabricators Inc................ E 937 836-5117
Clayton *(G-3271)*

Anchor Metal Processing Inc........... F 216 362-6463
Cleveland *(G-3354)*

Anchor Metal Processing Inc........... E 216 362-1850
Cleveland *(G-3355)*

Andersons Inc......................... E 419 891-2930
Maumee *(G-9260)*

▲ Ansco Machine Company............... E 330 929-8181
Peninsula *(G-11180)*

Apex Specialty Co Inc.................G 330 725-6663
Medina *(G-9377)*

Apollo Manufacturing Co LLC........... E 440 951-9972
Mentor *(G-9483)*

Applied Experience LLC................G 614 943-2970
Plain City *(G-11394)*

Apr Tool Inc..........................G 440 946-0393
Willoughby *(G-14424)*

Aqua Precision LLC....................G 937 912-9582
Dayton *(G-5664)*

ARC Drilling Inc...................... E 216 525-0920
Cleveland *(G-3363)*

◆ ARM (usa) Inc....................... E 740 264-6599
Wintersville *(G-14611)*

Armor Aftermarket Inc................. F 513 923-5600
Mason *(G-9063)*

Arnold Machine Inc.................... F 419 443-1818
Tiffin *(G-12775)*

Artisan Equipment Inc................. F 740 756-9135
Carroll *(G-2073)*

Artisan Grinding Service Inc.......... F 937 667-7383
Dayton *(G-5665)*

Ashcraft Machine & Supply Inc......... F 740 349-8110
Newark *(G-10493)*

Ashland Precision Tooling LLC......... E 419 289-1736
Ashland *(G-516)*

Ashta Forge & Machine Inc............. F 216 252-7000
Cleveland *(G-3379)*

Aspen Machine and Plastics............G 937 526-4644
Versailles *(G-13592)*

Assembly Machining Wire Pdts..........G 614 443-1110
Columbus *(G-4730)*

Associated Press Repair Inc...........G 216 881-2288
Gates Mills *(G-7229)*

▲ Astro Manufacturing & Design Inc.... C 888 215-1746
Eastlake *(G-6417)*

Astro Technical Services Inc.......... E 330 394-4747
Warren *(C-13742)*

Athens Mold and Machine Inc........... D 740 593-6613
Athens *(G-633)*

◆ Atlas Industries Inc................A 419 355-1000
Fremont *(G-7091)*

Atlas Machine and Supply Inc.......... E 502 584-7262
Hamilton *(G-7467)*

Ats Machine & Tool Co................. F 440 255-1120
Eastlake *(G-6419)*

Auglaize Erie Machine Company......... E 419 629-2068
New Bremen *(G-10356)*

Austinburg Machine Inc................G 440 275-2001
Austinburg *(G-695)*

Automated Mfg Solutions Inc........... F 440 878-3711
Strongsville *(G-12541)*

Automatic Parts....................... E 419 524-5841
Mansfield *(G-8764)*

Automator Marking Systems Inc......... F 740 983-0157
Chillicothe *(G-2243)*

Autotec Corporation................... E 419 885-2529
Toledo *(G-12889)*

Axle Machine Services Ltd.............G 419 827-2000
Lakeville *(G-8160)*

B & B Gear and Machine Co Inc......... E 937 687-1771
New Lebanon *(G-10399)*

▲ B & C Research Inc............................ B 330 848-4000
Barberton (G-794)

B & D Machinists Inc............................ G 513 831-8588
Milford (G-9922)

B & F Manufacturing Co........................ F 216 518-0333
Warrensville Heights (G-13815)

B & G Tool Company............................. G 614 451-2538
Columbus (G-4739)

B & H Machine Inc............................... E 330 868-6425
Minerva (G-10034)

B & R Machine Co................................ F 216 961-7370
Cleveland (G-3399)

B & T Welding and Machine Co.............. G 740 687-1908
Lancaster (G-8177)

B B & H Tool Company......................... G 614 868-8634
Reynoldsburg (G-11556)

B S F Inc... F 937 890-6121
Tipp City (G-12816)

B&C Machine Co LLC........................... F 330 745-4013
Barberton (G-796)

Bainter Machining Company................. F 740 756-4598
Lancaster (G-8181)

Bainter Machining Company................. G 740 653-2422
Lancaster (G-8180)

Balancing Company Inc........................ E 937 898-9111
Vandalia (G-13550)

▲ Bardons & Oliver Inc......................... C 440 498-5800
Solon (G-12082)

Bc Machine Services Corp.................... G 513 428-0327
Trenton (G-13190)

Beacon Metal Fabricators Inc............... G 216 391-7444
Cleveland (G-3412)

▲ Bear Mechanical LLC........................ G 937 288-2316
Hillsboro (G-7713)

Beaverson Machine Inc........................ G 419 923-8064
Delta (G-6202)

Beckman Machine LLC.......................... E 513 242-2700
Cincinnati (G-2405)

Beemer Machine Company Inc.............. G 330 678-3822
Kent (G-8018)

Berran Industrial Group Inc.................. E 330 253-5800
Akron (G-77)

Best Inc... G 419 394-2745
Saint Marys (G-11732)

Best Mold & Manufacturing Inc............. E 330 896-9988
Akron (G-78)

Best Performance Inc.......................... G 419 394-2299
Saint Marys (G-11733)

Beta Industries Inc............................. F 937 299-7385
Dayton (G-5677)

Beverage Mch & Fabricators Inc........... F 216 252-5100
Cleveland (G-3417)

Bic Manufacturing Inc.......................... F 216 531-9393
Euclid (G-6644)

Blc Precision Machine Co Inc................ E 937 783-1406
Blanchester (G-1233)

Bishop Machine Tool & Die................... F 740 453-8818
Zanesville (G-14997)

Black Machining & Tech Inc.................. F 513 752-8625
Batavia (G-854)

Blacklick Machine Company.................. G 614 866-9300
Blacklick (G-1221)

Blairs Cnc Turning Inc......................... G 937 461-1100
Dayton (G-5678)

Blue Chip Tool Inc.............................. F 513 489-3561
Cincinnati (G-2414)

Bollari/Davis Inc................................. F 330 296-4445
Ravenna (G-11519)

Bomen Marking Products Inc................ G 440 582-0053
Cleveland (G-3426)

Bond Machine Company Inc.................. F 937 746-4941
Franklin (G-7011)

▼ Bonnot Company.............................. E 330 896-6544
Akron (G-82)

Borman Enterprises Inc........................ F 216 459-9292
Cleveland (G-3429)

Bowden Manufacturing Corp................. E 440 946-1770
Willoughby (G-14432)

Bowdil Company.................................. F 800 356-8663
Canton (G-1843)

Boyce Machine Inc.............................. G 330 678-3210
Kent (G-8019)

Brinkley Technology Group LLC............. F 330 830-2498
Massillon (G-9175)

Brocker Machine Inc........................... F 330 744-5858
Youngstown (G-14828)

Bronco Machine Inc............................ F 440 951-5015
Willoughby (G-14435)

Bront Machining Inc............................ E 937 228-4551
Moraine (G-10152)

Brooklyn Machine & Mfg Co Inc............ E 216 341-1846
Cleveland (G-3442)

Brown Cnc Machining Inc..................... F 937 865-9191
Miamisburg (G-9677)

Buckeye Mch Fabricators Inc................ E 419 273-2521
Forest (G-6939)

Buckeye State Wldg & Fabg Inc............ F 440 322-0319
Elyria (G-6506)

Buckys Machine and Fab Ltd................ G 419 981-5050
Mc Cutchenville (G-9355)

Budde Precision Machining Corp........... F 937 278-1962
Dayton (G-5688)

Bula Forge Machine............................ G 216 252-7600
Cleveland (G-3452)

▲ Bullen Ultrasonics Inc....................... D 937 456-7133
Eaton (G-6450)

Burdens Machine & Welding Inc............ G 740 345-9246
Newark (G-10496)

▲ Burke Products Inc........................... E 937 372-3516
Xenia (G-14756)

Burton Industries Inc.......................... D 440 974-1700
Mentor (G-9495)

Byg Industries Inc.............................. G 216 961-5436
Cleveland (G-3456)

C & H Enterprises Ltd......................... G 510 226-6083
Findlay (G-6849)

C & K Machine Co Inc......................... G 419 237-3203
Fayette (G-6824)

C A Joseph Inc.................................. F 330 532-4646
Irondale (G-7927)

▲ C A Joseph Co................................ G 330 385-6869
East Liverpool (G-6387)

C-N-D Industries Inc........................... F 330 478-8811
Massillon (G-9176)

C&W Swiss Inc................................... F 937 832-2889
Englewood (G-6608)

Cage Gear & Machine LLC................... E 330 452-1532
Canton (G-1850)

Calvin J Magsig................................. G 419 862-3311
Elmore (G-6488)

CAM Machine Inc............................... E 937 663-5000
Saint Paris (G-11757)

Cardinal Machine Company................... G 440 238-7050
Strongsville (G-12547)

Carnation Machine and Tool Inc............ G 330 823-5352
Alliance (G-375)

Cascade Unlimited LLC........................ G 440 352-7995
Painesville (G-11071)

▲ Case-Maul Manufacturing Co............. F 419 524-1061
Mansfield (G-8771)

Cave Tool & Mfg Inc........................... F 937 324-0662
Springfield (G-12288)

Cbn Westside Holdings Inc................... E 513 772-7000
West Chester (G-13956)

▲ Cbn Westside Technologies Inc.......... B 513 772-7000
West Chester (G-13957)

CBs Boring and Mch Co Inc.................. F 419 784-9500
Defiance (G-6101)

Celina Percision Machine..................... F 419 586-9222
Celina (G-2100)

Cen-Trol Machine Co........................... G 216 524-1932
Cleveland (G-3482)

Centerless Grinding Svc Inc................. G 216 251-4100
Cleveland (G-3483)

Central Machinery Company LLC........... F 740 387-1289
Marion (G-8966)

Central State Enterprises Inc................ E 419 468-8191
Galion (G-7182)

Century Tool & Stamping Co................. G 216 241-2032
Westlake (G-14296)

CF Tools LLC..................................... G 740 294-0419
Fresno (G-7146)

Chandler Machine Company.................. G 330 688-7615
Stow (G-12423)

Chandler Machine Company.................. E 330 688-5585
Stow (G-12424)

Chardon Metal Products Co.................. E 440 285-2147
Chardon (G-2198)

Charles Costa Inc............................... G 330 376-3636
Akron (G-97)

▼ Chickasaw Machine & TI Co Inc.......... F 419 925-4325
Chickasaw (G-2240)

Chips Manufacturing Inc...................... G 440 946-3666
Willowick (G-14565)

Christopher Tool & Mfg Co................... C 440 248-8080
Solon (G-12094)

▲ Cincinnati Babbitt Inc....................... F 513 942-5088
Fairfield (G-6720)

Cincinnati Grinding Technologies Inc...... G 866 983-1097
Fairfield (G-6721)

Cincinnati Precision McHy Inc............... G 513 860-4133
West Chester (G-13963)

▲ Cincinnati Radiator Inc..................... F 513 874-5555
Fairfield (G-6722)

Cinex Inc.. G 513 921-2825
Cincinnati (G-2492)

▲ Circle Machine Rolls Inc.................... E 330 938-9010
Sebring (G-11893)

Circle Mold Incorporated..................... F 330 633-7017
Tallmadge (G-12732)

City Machine Technologies Inc.............. F 330 747-2639
Youngstown (G-14836)

Clapp & Haney Brazed TI Co Inc........... G 740 922-3515
Dennison (G-6217)

Clear Creek Screw Machine Co............. G 740 969-2113
Amanda (G-423)

Cleary Machine Company Inc................ E 937 839-4278
West Alexandria (G-13917)

Cleveland Special Tool Inc................... F 440 944-1600
Wickliffe (G-14371)

◆ Cleveland Tool and Machine Inc.........F 216 267-6010
Cleveland (G-3528)

▲ Clinton Machine Co Inc..................... F 330 882-2060
New Franklin (G-10388)

Clipsons Metal Working Inc.................. G 513 772-6393
Cincinnati (G-2499)

CMI Technology Inc............................ F 937 832-2000
Englewood (G-6609)

Cmt Machining & Fabg LLC.................. F 937 652-3740
Urbana (G-13459)

Cnc Precision Machine Inc................... D 440 548-3880
Parkman (G-11126)

Coit Tool Company Inc........................ F 440 946-3377
Willoughby (G-14439)

▲ Cold Headed Fas Assemblies Inc....... F 330 833-0800
Massillon (G-9180)

Coleys Inc .... E 440 967-5630
Vermilion *(G-13589)*

▲ Colfor Manufacturing Inc .... B 330 623-7814
Malvern *(G-8748)*

Columbus Machine Works Inc .... F 614 409-0244
Columbus *(G-4829)*

▲ Combs Manufacturing Inc .... D 330 784-3151
Akron *(G-104)*

▲ Commercial Honing LLC .... D 330 343-8896
Dover *(G-6235)*

Compco Quaker Mfg Inc .... E 330 482-0200
Salem *(G-11772)*

Component Mfg & Design Inc .... G 330 225-8080
Brunswick *(G-1585)*

Comptons Precision Machine .... F 937 325-9139
Springfield *(G-12293)*

Concentric Corporation .... F 440 899-9090
Bay Village *(G-901)*

Concept Machine & Tool Inc .... F 937 473-3334
Covington *(G-5491)*

Conquest Industries Inc .... F 330 926-9236
Stow *(G-12425)*

Copen Machine Inc .... F 330 678-4598
Kent *(G-8023)*

Core-Tech Enterprises LLC .... G 440 946-8324
Mentor *(G-9506)*

Cornerstone Wauseon Inc .... C 419 337-0940
Wauseon *(G-13847)*

Covert Manufacturing Inc .... E 419 468-1761
Galion *(G-7184)*

Creative Mold and Machine Inc .... E 440 338-5146
Newbury *(G-10548)*

Creative Processing Inc .... G 440 834-4070
Mantua *(G-8868)*

Creative Tool & Die LLC .... G 614 836-0080
Groveport *(G-7430)*

Criterion Tool & Die Inc .... E 216 267-1733
Brookpark *(G-1545)*

Croft & Son Mfg Inc .... G 740 859-2200
Tiltonsville *(G-12809)*

Crowe Manufacturing Services .... G 800 831-1893
Troy *(G-13207)*

Crum Manufacturing Inc .... E 419 878-9779
Waterville *(G-13832)*

Ctek Tool & Machine Company .... G 513 742-0423
Cincinnati *(G-2529)*

Curtis Steel & Supply Inc .... F 330 376-7141
Akron *(G-110)*

Custom Fab By Fisher LLC .... G 513 738-4600
Hamilton *(G-7482)*

Custom Machine Inc .... E 419 986-5122
Tiffin *(G-12781)*

Custom Metal Works Inc .... F 419 668-7831
Norwalk *(G-10834)*

Custom Mfg Solutions Inc .... E 937 372-0777
Xenia *(G-14760)*

Custom Tooling Company .... F 513 733-5790
Cincinnati *(G-2533)*

Cutting Dynamics LLC .... D 440 249-4666
Avon *(G-722)*

Cutting Dynamics LLC .... D 440 930-2862
Avon Lake *(G-752)*

▲ Cutting Dynamics LLC .... E 440 249-4150
Avon *(G-723)*

Cutting Edge Manufacturing LLC .... E 419 355-0921
Fremont *(G-7102)*

Cuyahoga Machine Company LLC .... F 216 267-3560
Brookpark *(G-1547)*

D & B Industries Inc .... G 937 253-8658
Dayton *(G-5607)*

D & E Machine Co .... G 513 932-2184
Lebanon *(G-8251)*

D & J Machine Shop .... G 937 256-2730
Xenia *(G-14761)*

D & L Machine Co Inc .... E 330 785-0781
Akron *(G-113)*

D M Tool & Plastics Inc .... F 937 962-4140
Brookville *(G-1565)*

D M Tool & Plastics Inc .... F 937 962-4140
Lewisburg *(G-8359)*

D&D Quality Machining Co Inc .... G 440 942-2772
Willoughby *(G-14444)*

Dallas Design & Technology Inc .... G 419 884-9750
Mansfield *(G-8779)*

Dalton Stryker McHining Fcilty .... C 419 682-6328
Stryker *(G-12622)*

David Bixel .... F 440 474-4410
Rock Creek *(G-11629)*

Davis Machine Products Inc .... G 440 474-0247
Streetsboro *(G-12495)*

Day-TEC Tool & Mfg Inc .... F 937 847-0022
Miamisburg *(G-9686)*

Dayton One LLC .... G 937 265-0227
Dayton *(G-5734)*

Dayton Systems Group Inc .... F 937 885-5665
Miamisburg *(G-9688)*

Dayton Waterjet LLC .... G 937 428-0944
Miamisburg *(G-9689)*

Dearborn Inc .... E 440 234-1353
Berea *(G-1166)*

Deffren Machine Tool Svc Inc .... F 513 858-1555
Fairfield *(G-6726)*

▲ Deimling/Jeliho Plastics Inc .... D 513 752-6653
Amelia *(G-429)*

Delta Manufacturing Inc .... F 330 386-1270
East Liverpool *(G-6392)*

Deltec Incorporated .... E 513 732-0800
Batavia *(G-861)*

DES Machine Services Inc .... G 330 633-6897
Stow *(G-12426)*

Design and Fabrication Inc .... G 419 294-2414
Upper Sandusky *(G-13439)*

Design Technologies & Mfg Co .... F 937 335-0757
Troy *(G-13211)*

Detailed Machining Inc .... E 937 492-1264
Sidney *(G-12011)*

▲ Detroit Diesl Specialty TI Inc .... E 740 435-4452
Byesville *(G-1710)*

Deuce Machining LLC .... G 513 875-2291
Fayetteville *(G-6826)*

Devault Machine & Mould Co LLC .... G 740 654-5925
Lancaster *(G-8195)*

Dilco Industries Inc .... G 330 337-6732
Salem *(G-11776)*

Dillon Manufacturing Inc .... F 937 325-8482
Springfield *(G-12302)*

Dimension Industries Inc .... G 440 236-3265
Columbia Station *(G-4593)*

Dimension Machine Company Inc .... G 513 242-9996
Cincinnati *(G-2550)*

Diversified Mch Components LLC .... F 440 942-5701
Brook Park *(G-1512)*

DM Machine Co .... G 440 946-0771
Willoughby *(G-14447)*

DO Technologies Co .... F 330 725-4561
Medina *(G-9398)*

Douglas Industries LLC .... E 740 775-2400
Chillicothe *(G-2250)*

Dover Machine Co .... G 330 343-4123
Dover *(G-6241)*

Drabik Manufacturing Inc .... F 216 267-1616
Cleveland *(G-3629)*

Drake Manufacturing LLC .... E 330 847-7291
Warren *(G-13759)*

Drt Holdings LLC .... D 937 298-7391
Dayton *(G-5753)*

Drt Mfg Co LLC .... C 937 298-7391
Dayton *(G-5755)*

Drt Precision Mfg LLC .... E 937 507-4308
Sidney *(G-12014)*

▲ Duke Manufacturing Inc .... E 440 942-6537
Willoughby *(G-14451)*

▲ Duncan Tool Inc .... F 937 667-9364
Tipp City *(G-12823)*

Dunham Machine Inc .... G 216 398-4500
Independence *(G-7898)*

Dwd2 Inc .... F 513 563-0070
Cincinnati *(G-2566)*

Dynamic Industries Inc .... E 513 861-6767
Cincinnati *(G-2567)*

E & J Demark Inc .... E 419 337-5866
Wauseon *(G-13848)*

E & K Products Co Inc .... G 216 631-2510
Cleveland *(G-3643)*

E D M Star-One Inc .... F 440 647-0600
Wadsworth *(G-13636)*

E Systems Design & Automtn Inc .... G 419 443-0220
Tiffin *(G-12783)*

E Z Machine Inc .... G 330 784-3363
Tallmadge *(G-12734)*

Eaglehead Manufacturing Co .... F 440 951-0400
Eastlake *(G-6424)*

▲ East End Welding LLC .... C 330 677-6000
Kent *(G-8028)*

Eastlake Machine Products LLC .... G 440 953-1014
Willoughby *(G-14454)*

▲ Eaton Fabricating Company Inc .... E 440 926-3121
Grafton *(G-7301)*

Edward D Segen & Co LLC .... G 937 295-3672
Fort Loramie *(G-6946)*

Edwards Machine Service Inc .... F 937 295-2929
Fort Loramie *(G-6947)*

Efficient Machine Pdts Corp .... E 440 268-0205
Strongsville *(G-12557)*

Eitle Machine Tool Inc .... G 419 935-8753
Attica *(G-656)*

Eltool Corporation .... G 513 723-1772
Mansfield *(G-8785)*

Elyria Metal Spinning Fabg Co .... G 440 323-8068
Elyria *(G-6531)*

EMC Precision Machining II LLC .... F 440 365-4171
Elyria *(G-6634)*

▲ Enprotech Industrial Tech LLC .... E 216 883-3220
Cleveland *(G-3675)*

Enterprise Machine Inc .... G 513 681-4409
Cincinnati *(G-2592)*

Eos Technology Inc .... G 216 281-2999
Cleveland *(G-3680)*

Esterle Mold & Machine Co Inc .... E 330 686-1685
Stow *(G-12429)*

▲ Esterline & Sons Mfg Co LLC .... E 937 265-5278
Springfield *(G-12308)*

Eti Tech LLC .... F 937 832-4200
Kettering *(G-8120)*

Etko Machine Co .... G 330 745-4033
Norton *(G-10821)*

Euclid Precision Grinding Co .... G 440 946-8888
Eastlake *(G-6429)*

Euclid Welding Company Inc .... F 216 289-0714
Willoughby Hills *(G-14559)*

▲ Ewart-Ohlson Machine Company .... E 330 928-2171
Cuyahoga Falls *(G-5539)*

▲ Exact Cutting Service Inc .... G 440 546-1319
Brecksville *(G-1465)*

Excel Machine & Tool Inc .... F 419 678-3318
Coldwater *(G-4573)*

S
I
C

Excellent Tool & Die Inc.................... G 216 671-9222
Cleveland *(G-3697)*

F & G Tool and Die Co.................... E 937 294-1405
Moraine *(G-10163)*

F & S Hydraulics Inc.................... G 513 575-1600
Milford *(G-9933)*

F A Tech Corp.................... F 513 942-1920
West Chester *(G-13996)*

F M Machine Co.................... E 330 773-8237
Akron *(G-142)*

Fabricating Machine Tools Ltd.................... G 440 666-9187
Cleveland *(G-3702)*

Fabriweld Corporation.................... E 419 663-0279
Norwalk *(G-10840)*

▲ Fabriweld Corporation.................... E 419 668-3358
Norwalk *(G-10839)*

Falcon Innovations Inc.................... G 216 252-0676
Cleveland *(G-3703)*

Falcon Tool & Machine Inc.................... G 937 534-9999
Dayton *(G-5773)*

Falmer Screw Pdts & Mfg Inc.................... F 330 758-0593
Youngstown *(G-14854)*

Farr Automation Inc.................... G 419 289-1883
Ashland *(G-534)*

Fate Industries Inc.................... G 440 327-1770
North Ridgeville *(G-10730)*

▲ Faxon Machining LLC.................... C 513 851-4644
Cincinnati *(G-2614)*

Fdc Machine Repair Inc.................... E 216 362-1082
Parma *(G-11130)*

Federal Hose Manufacturing LLC.................... E 800 346-4673
Cleveland *(G-3710)*

Feilhauers Machine Shop Inc.................... F 513 202-0545
Harrison *(G-7551)*

Feller Tool Co.................... F 440 324-6277
Elyria *(G-6536)*

▲ Ferralloy Inc.................... G 440 250-1900
Cleveland *(G-3713)*

◆ Ferry Industries Inc.................... D 330 920-9200
Stow *(G-12431)*

Filmtec Fabrications LLC.................... E 419 435-1819
Fostoria *(G-6979)*

First Francis Company Inc.................... E 440 352-8927
Painesville *(G-11087)*

▲ Flash Industrial Tech Ltd.................... G 440 786-8979
Cleveland *(G-3723)*

Flohr Machine Company Inc.................... E 330 745-3030
Barberton *(G-804)*

◆ Floturn Inc.................... C 513 860-8040
Fairfield *(G-6735)*

Focus Manufacturing LLC.................... F 440 946-8766
Mentor *(G-9517)*

Foltz Machine LLC.................... E 330 453-9235
Canton *(G-1891)*

▲ Forge Industries Inc.................... A 330 960-2468
Youngstown *(G-14857)*

Fostoria MT&f Corp.................... F 419 435-7676
Fostoria *(G-6982)*

Fpc Holdings Inc.................... E 216 362-7888
Brunswick *(G-1591)*

Frantz Grinding Co.................... G 330 343-8689
New Philadelphia *(G-10446)*

Frazier Machine and Prod Inc.................... E 419 874-7321
Perrysburg *(G-11223)*

▼ Fredon Corporation.................... D 440 951-5200
Mentor *(G-9520)*

Fredrick Welding & Machining.................... G 614 866-9650
Reynoldsburg *(G-11571)*

Fries Machine & Tool Inc.................... G 937 898-6432
Dayton *(G-5786)*

◆ Furukawa Rock Drill Usa Inc.................... F 330 673-5826
Kent *(G-8033)*

G & L Machining Inc.................... G 513 724-2600
Williamsburg *(G-14409)*

G & M Precision Machining Inc.................... G 937 667-1443
Tipp City *(G-12826)*

G F Frank and Sons Inc.................... F 513 870-9075
West Chester *(G-14002)*

G Grafton Machine & Rubber.................... F 330 297-1062
Ravenna *(G-11525)*

G H Cutter Services Inc.................... G 419 476-0476
Toledo *(G-12971)*

Garvey Corporation.................... E 330 779-0700
Youngstown *(G-14860)*

Gasdorf Tool and Mch Co Inc.................... E 419 227-0103
Lima *(G-8409)*

Gedico International Inc.................... G 937 274-2167
West Chester *(G-14007)*

Gemco Machine & Tool Inc.................... F 740 344-3111
Newark *(G-10503)*

▲ General Plug and Mfg Co.................... C 440 926-2411
Grafton *(G-7302)*

General Sheave Company Inc.................... G 216 781-8120
Cleveland *(G-3768)*

▲ General Tool Company.................... C 513 733-5500
Cincinnati *(G-2666)*

George Steel Fabricating Inc.................... E 513 932-2887
Lebanon *(G-8259)*

Gilson Machine & Tool Co Inc.................... E 419 592-2911
Napoleon *(G-10282)*

Girard Machine Company Inc.................... G 330 545-9731
Girard *(G-7272)*

GL Heller Co Inc.................... F 419 877-5122
Whitehouse *(G-14361)*

▲ Glenridge Machine Co.................... E 440 975-1055
Solon *(G-12116)*

Global Laser Tek LLC.................... E 513 701-0452
Mason *(G-9103)*

▲ Global Srcing Support Svcs LLC.................... G 800 645-2986
Cincinnati *(G-2677)*

▲ Globe Products Inc.................... F 937 233-0233
Dayton *(G-5799)*

▲ Glunt Industries Inc.................... C 330 399-7585
Warren *(G-13770)*

▼ Gmd Industries LLC.................... E 937 252-3643
Dayton *(G-5801)*

▲ Goyal Industries Inc.................... E 419 522-7099
Mansfield *(G-8796)*

Grand Harbor Yacht Sales & Svc.................... G 440 442-2919
Cleveland *(G-3784)*

Graphel Corporation.................... C 513 779-6166
West Chester *(G-14012)*

Green Machine Tool Inc.................... G 937 253-0771
Dayton *(G-5612)*

Grenga Machine & Welding.................... F 330 743-1113
Youngstown *(G-14871)*

Grinding Equipment & McHy LLC.................... F 330 747-2313
North Jackson *(G-10688)*

Gt Technologies Inc.................... E 419 782-8955
Defiance *(G-6109)*

Guyer Precision Inc.................... F 440 354-8024
Painesville *(G-11091)*

H & H Machine Shop Akron Inc.................... E 330 773-3327
Akron *(G-167)*

H & H Quick Machine Inc.................... F 330 935-0944
Louisville *(G-8600)*

H & M Machine Shop Inc.................... F 419 453-3414
Ottoville *(G-11054)*

H K K Machining Co.................... E 419 924-5116
West Unity *(G-14194)*

Habco Tool and Dev Co Inc.................... E 440 946-5546
Mentor *(G-9525)*

Hafco-Case Inc.................... G 216 267-4644
Cleveland *(G-3806)*

Hahn Automation Group Us Inc.................... D 937 886-3232
Miamisburg *(G-9694)*

Hahn Manufacturing Company.................... E 216 391-9300
Cleveland *(G-3807)*

Haiss Fabripart LLC.................... E 330 821-2028
Alliance *(G-384)*

Hale Manufacturing LLC.................... F 937 382-2127
Wilmington *(G-14583)*

Hall Acquisition LLC.................... G 330 627-2119
Carrollton *(G-2084)*

Halo Metal Prep Inc.................... G 216 741-0506
Cleveland *(G-3808)*

Hamilton Machine Services Corp.................... G 513 895-7200
Hamilton *(G-7503)*

Hammill Manufacturing Co.................... E 419 476-9125
Toledo *(G-12985)*

Hannon Company.................... F 330 343-7758
Dover *(G-6246)*

Hard Surface Technology Inc.................... G 513 860-1156
West Chester *(G-14013)*

Hardin Creek Machine & Tl Inc.................... F 419 678-4913
Coldwater *(G-4576)*

Harding Machine Acquisition Co.................... D 937 666-3031
East Liberty *(G-6386)*

Harris Welding and Machine Co.................... F 419 281-8351
Ashland *(G-537)*

Haulette Manufacturing Inc.................... D 419 586-1717
Celina *(G-2108)*

Hawkins Machine Shop Inc.................... G 937 335-8737
Troy *(G-13221)*

▲ Hazenstab Machine Inc.................... G 330 337-1865
Salem *(G-11785)*

HBE Machine Incorporated.................... G 419 668-9426
Monroeville *(G-10119)*

Hearn Plating Co Ltd.................... F 419 473-9773
Toledo *(G-12988)*

Heisler Tool Company.................... F 440 951-2424
Willoughby *(G-14464)*

Hephaestus Technologies LLC.................... E 216 252-0430
Cleveland *(G-3825)*

Herd Manufacturing Inc.................... E 216 651-4221
Cleveland *(G-3826)*

Hergatt Machine Inc.................... G 419 589-2931
Mansfield *(G-8801)*

Herman Machine Inc.................... F 330 633-3261
Tallmadge *(G-12736)*

Heule Tool Corporation.................... E 513 860-9900
Loveland *(G-8630)*

▲ Hi-Tek Manufacturing Inc.................... C 513 459-1094
Mason *(G-9108)*

High Tech Metal Products LLC.................... G 419 227-9414
Lima *(G-8415)*

High-Tech Mold & Machine Inc.................... F 330 896-4466
Uniontown *(G-13420)*

Highland Products Corp.................... F 440 352-4777
Mentor *(G-9529)*

Hillman Precision Inc.................... F 419 289-1557
Ashland *(G-540)*

Hofacker Prcsion Machining LLC.................... F 937 832-7712
Clayton *(G-3273)*

Holdren Brothers Inc.................... F 937 465-7050
West Liberty *(G-14175)*

◆ Hose Master LLC.................... B 216 481-2020
Cleveland *(G-3840)*

Houston Machine Products Inc.................... E 937 322-8022
Springfield *(G-12326)*

Howland Machine Corp.................... E 330 544-4029
Niles *(G-10589)*

▼ Htec Systems Inc.................... F 937 438-3010
Dayton *(G-5816)*

Hubbell Machine Tooling Inc.................... F 216 524-1797
Cleveland *(G-3842)*

Hutnik Company............G ....330 336-9700 Wadsworth *(G-13643)*	**Jh Industries Inc**............E .....330 963-4105 Twinsburg *(G-13321)*	▲ **Kram Precision Machining Inc**..........G ....937 849-1301 New Carlisle *(G-10374)*
Hutter Racing Engines Ltd..................F ....440 285-2175 Chardon *(G-2208)*	**Jilco Precision Mold Mch Inc**................G .....330 633-9645 Akron *(G-186)*	**Kramer Power Equipment Co**............G ....937 456-2232 Eaton *(G-6457)*
▲ **Hy-Production LLC**...................C ....330 273-2400 Valley City *(G-13499)*	**Jj Sleeves Inc**............G .....440 205-1055 Mentor *(G-9542)*	▼ **Krendl Machine Company**...................D ....419 692-3060 Delphos *(G-6189)*
Hydro Supply Co............G ....740 454-3842 Zanesville *(G-15020)*	**Johnson Mfg Systems LLC**............F ....937 866-4744 Miamisburg *(G-9704)*	**Krenz Precision Machining Inc**............D ....440 237-1800 North Royalton *(G-10769)*
I G Brenner Inc............F ....740 345-8845 Newark *(G-10510)*	**Johnson Prcision Machining Inc**............G .....513 353-4252 Cleves *(G-4541)*	**Kuzma Industries LLC**............G ....419 701-7005 Fostoria *(G-6986)*
Imds Corporation............F ....330 219-4299 Youngstown *(G-14875)*	**Jonashtons LLC**............G .....419 488-2363 Cloverdale *(G-4555)*	**Kyron Tool & Machine Co Inc**............F ....614 231-6000 Columbus *(G-5059)*
Impac Hi-Performance Machining..........G ....419 726-7100 Toledo *(G-13000)*	**Jotco Inc**............G .....513 721-4943 Mansfield *(G-8809)*	**L & L Machine Inc**............F ....419 272-5000 Edon *(G-6474)*
Indelco Custom Products Inc............G ....216 797-7300 Euclid *(G-6654)*	**K & G Machine Company**............F .....216 732-7115 Cleveland *(G-3900)*	**L J Manufacturing Inc**............G ....440 352-1979 Mentor *(G-9547)*
Independent Machine & Wldg Inc..........G ....937 339-7330 Troy *(G-13228)*	**K & J Machine Inc**............G .....740 425-3282 Barnesville *(G-845)*	**Lab Quality Machining Inc**............G ....513 625-0219 Goshen *(G-7297)*
Industrial Machining Services............E ....937 295-2022 Fort Loramie *(G-6948)*	**K & K Precision Inc**............E .....513 336-0032 Mason *(G-9117)*	**Lake Park Tool & Machine LLC**............F ....330 788-2437 Youngstown *(G-14886)*
Innovative Tool & Die Inc............G ....419 599-0492 Napoleon *(G-10287)*	**K K Tool Co**............E .....937 325-1373 Springfield *(G-12333)*	**Lakecraft Inc**............G ....419 734-2828 Port Clinton *(G-11444)*
Inovent Engineering Inc............G ....330 468-0019 Macedonia *(G-8698)*	**K S Machine Inc**............G .....216 687-0459 Cleveland *(G-3901)*	**Lancaster Metal Products Inc**............F ....740 653-3421 Lancaster *(G-8206)*
Integrity Industrial Equipment............G ....937 335-5658 Troy *(G-13229)*	**K-M-S Industries Inc**............G .....440 243-6680 Brookpark *(G-1554)*	**Land Specialties LLC**............G ....330 663-6974 East Sparta *(G-6412)*
Integrity Manufacturing Corp............F ....937 233-6792 Dayton *(G-5825)*	▲ **Kalt Manufacturing Company**............D ....440 327-2102 North Ridgeville *(G-10738)*	**Langa Tool & Machine Inc**............G ....440 953-1138 Willoughby *(G-14482)*
International Bellows............F ....937 294-6261 Englewood *(G-6616)*	**Karon C Enold**............E .....740 269-3475 Sherrodsville *(G-11975)*	**Lange Grinding & Machining Inc**............E ....330 463-3500 Streetsboro *(G-12508)*
International Machining Inc............E ....330 225-1963 Brunswick *(G-1599)*	**Kaskell Manufacturing Inc**............F .....937 704-9700 Springboro *(G-12257)*	**Lange Precision Inc**............F ....513 530-9500 Lebanon *(G-8273)*
◆ **International Metal Hose Co**............D ....419 483-7690 Bellevue *(G-1125)*	**Kaws Inc**............E .....513 521-8292 Cincinnati *(G-2786)*	**Laspina Tool and Die Inc**............F ....330 923-9996 Stow *(G-12437)*
◆ **Interscope Manufacturing Inc**............E ....513 423-8866 Middletown *(G-9867)*	**Kda Manufacturing LLC**............F .....330 590-7431 Norton *(G-10825)*	**Last Arrow Manufacturing LLC**............D ....330 683-7777 Orrville *(G-10992)*
Intertek LLC............F ....440 323-3325 Elyria *(G-6545)*	**Keban Industries Inc**............G .....216 446-0159 Broadview Heights *(G-1503)*	**Latanick Equipment Inc**............E ....419 433-2200 Huron *(G-7878)*
J & C Industries Inc............G ....216 362-8867 Cleveland *(G-3876)*	▲ **Ken-Dal Corporation**............F .....330 644-7118 Coventry Township *(G-5484)*	**Lawrence Industries Inc**............C ....216 518-1400 Cleveland *(G-3947)*
J & D Steel Service Center LLC............G ....330 759-7430 Hubbard *(G-7812)*	**Kenmore Development & Mch Co**............F .....330 753-2274 Akron *(G-193)*	◆ **Lawrence Industries Inc**............E ....216 518-7000 Cleveland *(G-3946)*
J & P Products Inc............F ....440 974-2830 Mentor *(G-9539)*	**Kent Post Acquisition Inc**............F .....330 678-6343 Kent *(G-8044)*	**Leader Engnrng-Fabrication Inc**............G ....419 636-1731 Bryan *(G-1649)*
J B Manufacturing Inc............G ....330 676-9744 Kent *(G-8037)*	**Kerek Industries Ltd Lblty Co**............F Cleveland *(G-3914)*	**Lees Grinding Inc**............E ....440 572-4610 Strongsville *(G-12570)*
J Horst Manufacturing Co............G ....330 828-2216 Dalton *(G-5586)*	**Kiefer Tool & Mold Inc**............F .....216 251-0076 Cleveland *(G-3918)*	**Legacy Stwr LLC**............D ....937 440-2505 Troy *(G-13336)*
J&J Precision Fabricators Ltd............G ....330 482-4964 Columbiana *(G-4621)*	**Kiffer Industries Inc**............F .....216 267-1818 Cleveland *(G-3919)*	**Legend Metal and Rubber LLC**............F ....513 874-8020 West Chester *(G-14022)*
J&M Precision Die Casting LLC............F ....440 365-7388 Elyria *(G-6555)*	**Kiley Machine Company**............G .....513 875-3223 Fayetteville *(G-6828)*	**Lehner Screw Machine LLC**............E ....330 688-6616 Akron *(G-204)*
Jade Products Inc............F ....440 352-1700 Mentor *(G-9541)*	**Kimble Machines Inc**............G .....419 485-8449 Montpelier *(G-10129)*	**Lennox Machine Inc**............G ....419 525-1020 Mansfield *(G-8812)*
Jade Tool Company............G ....937 376-4740 Xenia *(G-14766)*	▲ **King Machine and Tool Co**............F .....330 833-7217 Massillon *(G-9212)*	**Leon Newswanger**............F ....419 896-3336 Shiloh *(G-11979)*
Jamar Precision Grinding Co............E ....330 220-0099 Hinckley *(G-7733)*	**Kings Welding and Fabg Inc**............G .....330 738-3592 Mechanicstown *(G-9368)*	**Lewis Unlimited Inc**............G ....216 514-8282 Beachwood *(G-925)*
Jay-Em Aerospace Corporation............E ....330 923-0333 Cuyahoga Falls *(G-5551)*	**Knape Industries Inc**............E .....614 885-3016 Worthington *(G-14717)*	**Libra Industries LLC**............C ....440 974-7770 Mentor *(G-9553)*
Jayna Inc............E ....937 335-8922 Troy *(G-13232)*	**Knight Manufacturing Co Inc**............F .....740 676-9532 Shadyside *(G-11923)*	**Lightning Mold & Machine Inc**............F ....440 593-6460 Conneaut *(G-5408)*
JB Industries Ltd............F ....330 856-4587 Warren *(G-13775)*	**Knowlton Machine Inc**............G .....419 281-6802 Ashland *(G-547)*	**Lima Sheet Metal Mch & Mfg Inc**............F ....419 229-1161 Lima *(G-8426)*
Jed Industries Inc............F ....440 639-9973 Grand River *(G-7310)*	**Knox Machine & Tool**............G .....740 392-3133 Mount Vernon *(G-10248)*	**Lincoln Electric Automtn Inc**............B ....937 295-2120 Fort Loramie *(G-6950)*
Jerl Machine Inc............D ....419 873-0270 Perrysburg *(G-11232)*	**Knutsen Machine Products Inc**............G .....216 751-6500 Cleveland *(G-3926)*	**Little Mountain Precision LLC**............E ....440 290-2903 Mentor *(G-9555)*
Jerpbak-Bayless Co............E ....440 248-5387 Solon *(G-12130)*	**Koester Machined Products Co**............G .....419 782-0291 Defiance *(G-6117)*	**Lmp Machine LLC**............G ....740 596-4559 Zaleski *(G-14979)*
JF Martt and Associates Inc............F ....330 938-4000 Sebring *(G-11895)*	**Krafft and Associates Inc**............G .....937 325-4671 Springfield *(G-12340)*	**Lochard Inc**............D ....937 492-8811 Sidney *(G-12031)*

Locher Inc.................................... G 740 654-8888
Lancaster (G-8208)

▲ Logan Machine Company................. D 330 633-6163
Akron (G-210)

▲ Lous Machine Company Inc.............. F 513 856-9199
Hamilton (G-7511)

▲ Lri Post-Acquisition Inc.................. E 419 227-2200
Lima (G-8428)

▲ M & J Machine Company.................. F 330 645-0042
Akron (G-216)

M A C Machine.............................. 410 944-6171
Canton (G-1934)

M S B Machine Inc.......................... G 330 686-7740
Munroe Falls (G-10271)

M&D Machine LLC.......................... G 419 214-0201
Toledo (G-13043)

▲ Machine Concepts Inc..................... E 419 628-3498
Minster (G-10060)

Machine Development Corp................ G 513 825-5885
Cincinnati (G-2836)

Machine Products Company............... F 937 890-6600
Dayton (G-5860)

Machine Tek Systems Inc................. E 330 527-4450
Garrettsville (G-7225)

▲ Machine-Pro Technologies Inc........... D 419 584-0086
Celina (G-2113)

▲ Machintek Co............................... D 513 551-1000
Fairfield (G-6749)

Macpro Inc.................................. F 513 575-3000
Loveland (G-8638)

Mader Automotive Center Inc.............. F 937 339-2681
Troy (G-13238)

▼ Magna Machine Co........................ C 513 851-6900
Cincinnati (G-2840)

Mainstream Waterjet LLC................. E 513 683-5426
Loveland (G-8639)

◆ Majestic Manufacturing Inc............... E 330 457-2447
New Waterford (G-10488)

Majestic Tool and Machine Inc........... G 440 248-5058
Solon (G-12144)

▼ Manifold & Phalor Inc..................... E 614 920-1200
Canal Winchester (G-1793)

Mantych Metalworking Inc................. F 937 258-1373
Dayton (G-5619)

Manufacturing Concepts................... G 330 784-9054
Tallmadge (G-12739)

Mar-Con Tool Company................... E 937 299-2244
Moraine (G-10175)

Margo Tool Technology Inc................ F 740 653-8115
Lancaster (G-8209)

Marich Machine and Tool Co.............. G 216 391-5502
Cleveland (G-3988)

Mark J Myers............................... E 513 753-7300
Amelia (G-432)

Markham Machine Company Inc.......... F 330 762-7676
Akron (G-222)

▲ Markley Enterprises LLC................. E 513 771-1290
Cincinnati (G-2847)

Marmax Machine Co....................... G 937 698-9900
Ludlow Falls (G-8672)

Massillon Machine & Die Inc.............. G 330 833-8913
Massillon (G-9219)

Master Swaging Inc........................ G 937 596-6171
Jackson Center (G-7965)

▲ Materials Science Intl Inc................ E 614 870-0400
Columbus (G-5086)

Matrix Tool & Machine Inc................ E 440 255-0300
Mentor (G-9560)

Mc Brown Industries Inc................... F 419 963-2800
Findlay (G-6892)

McCann Tool & Die Inc.................... G 330 264-8820
Wooster (G-14664)

▲ McCrary Metal Polishing Co Inc........ F 937 492-1979
Port Jefferson (G-11454)

McF Industries.............................. G 330 526-6337
North Canton (G-10650)

◆ McNeil & Nrm Inc.......................... D 330 761-1855
Akron (G-225)

McNeil & Nrm Intl Inc..................... D 330 253-2525
Akron (G-226)

◆ McSwain Manufacturing LLC............. C 513 619-1222
Cincinnati (G-2852)

Medway Tool Corp......................... G 937 335-7717
Troy (G-13240)

Meldrum Mechanical Services............ F 419 535-3500
Toledo (G-13051)

Melinz Industries Inc...................... F 440 946-3512
Willoughby (G-14487)

Mellott Bronze Inc......................... F 330 435-6304
Creston (G-5507)

Memac Industries Inc..................... G 740 653-4815
Lancaster (G-8210)

Met Fab Fabrication and Mch............. G 513 724-3715
Batavia (G-872)

Meta Manufacturing Corporation......... E 513 793-6382
Blue Ash (G-1308)

◆ Metalex Manufacturing Inc............... C 513 489-0507
Blue Ash (G-1310)

Metcut Research Associates Inc......... D 513 271-5100
Cincinnati (G-2871)

Metro Design Inc........................... F 440 458-4200
Elyria (G-6563)

Metro Design Inc........................... G 440 324-4700
Elyria (G-6564)

Metzger Machine Co....................... F 513 241-3360
Cincinnati (G-2873)

◆ Meyer Tool Inc.............................. A 513 681-7362
Cincinnati (G-2874)

MH & Son Machining & Wldg Co......... G 419 621-0690
Sandusky (G-11859)

Miami Valley Precision Inc................ F 937 866-1804
Miamisburg (G-9713)

Miami Vly Mfg & Assembly Inc........... F 937 254-6665
Dayton (G-5621)

Michael Byrne Manufacturing Co Inc.... E 419 525-1214
Mansfield (G-8825)

Michalek Manufacturing LLC............. G 740 763-0910
Newark (G-10519)

Micro Machine Ltd......................... G 330 438-7078
Brewster (G-1492)

Micro Machine Works Inc................. F 740 678-8471
Vincent (G-13622)

Micron Manufacturing Inc................. D 440 355-4200
Lagrange (G-8151)

Midstate Machine Ohio Facility........... G 513 619-1222
Cincinnati (G-2878)

Midway Machining Inc..................... F 740 373-8976
Marietta (G-8929)

Midwest Die Supply Company............ G 419 729-7141
Toledo (G-13055)

Midwest Laser Systems Inc.............. E 419 424-0062
Alvada (G-422)

Midwest Machine Service Inc............. F 216 631-8151
Cleveland (G-4037)

Midwest Precision......................... G 216 658-0058
Brooklyn Heights (G-1535)

Midwest Specialties Inc................... D 800 837-2503
Wapakoneta (G-13725)

Mike Loppe.................................. F 937 969-8102
Tremont City (G-13189)

▲ Mil-Mar Century Corporation............. F 937 275-4860
Miamisburg (G-9718)

Mill & Motion Inc........................... F 216 524-4000
Independence (G-7909)

▲ Millat Industries Corp..................... D 937 434-6666
Dayton (G-5888)

Millennium Machine Tech LLC............ G 440 269-8080
Willoughby (G-14490)

Miller Precision Manufact................. D 419 453-3251
Ottoville (G-11056)

Minerva Welding and Fabg Inc........... E 330 868-7731
Minerva (G-10043)

Miracle Welding Inc........................ G 937 746-9977
Franklin (G-7034)

▼ Mission Industrial Group LLC............ F 740 387-2287
Marion (G-8980)

Modern Engineering Inc................... G 440 593-5414
Conneaut (G-5412)

Modern Industries Inc..................... G 216 432-2855
Cleveland (G-4043)

Modern Machine Development............ F 937 253-4576
Dayton (G-5891)

Monroe Tool and Mfg Co.................. F 216 883-7360
Cleveland (G-4046)

Montgomery Mch Fabrication Inc......... E 740 286-2863
Jackson (G-7948)

▲ Monti Incorporated........................ D 513 761-7775
Cincinnati (G-2886)

Morgan Engineering Systems Inc........ E 330 545-9731
Girard (G-7276)

Morris Technologies Inc................... E 513 733-1611
Cincinnati (G-2888)

Mosher Machine & Tool Co Inc........... E 937 258-8070
Beavercreek Township (G-999)

Mossing Machine and Tool Inc........... G 419 476-5657
Toledo (G-13060)

Mound Manufacturing Center Inc........ F 937 236-8387
Dayton (G-5896)

Mt Vernon Machine & Tool Inc........... E 740 397-0311
Mount Vernon (G-10254)

Muller Engine & Machine Co.............. G 937 322-1861
Springfield (G-12354)

Munson Machine Company Inc........... G 740 967-6867
Johnstown (G-7996)

Murray Machine and Tool Inc............ G 216 267-1126
Cleveland (G-4054)

Muskingum Grinding and Mch Co........ F 740 622-4741
Coshocton (G-5463)

Mutual Tool LLC............................ F 937 667-5818
Tipp City (G-12832)

Myers Machining Inc....................... G 330 874-3005
Bolivar (G-1385)

Myers Precision Grinding Inc............. F 216 587-3737
Cleveland (G-4055)

Mysta Equipment Co....................... G 330 879-5353
Navarre (G-10308)

N & W Machining & Fabg Inc............. G 937 695-5582
Winchester (G-14599)

Napoleon Machine LLC.................... E 419 591-7010
Napoleon (G-10293)

Narrow Way Custom Tech Inc............ E 937 743-1611
Carlisle (G-2069)

▲ Nasg Sting Rdgvlle Corners LLC....... B 419 267-5240
Ridgeville Corners (G-11616)

National Aviation Products Inc............ G 330 688-6494
Stow (G-12444)

National Machine Co....................... G 330 688-2584
Stow (G-12445)

▲ National Machine Company............... C 330 688-6494
Stow (G-12446)

◆ National Machinery LLC................... B 419 447-5211
Tiffin (G-12792)

Neff Machinery and Supplies............. G 740 454-0128
Zanesville (G-15031)

Neidert Fabricating Inc.................... G 330 753-3331
Barberton (G-824)

Neil R Scholl Inc	F	740 653-6593	
Lancaster *(G-8213)*			
New Cut Tool and Mfg Corp	F	740 676-1666	
Shadyside *(G-11924)*			
New Pme Inc	F	513 671-1717	
Cincinnati *(G-2903)*			
▲ Next Wave Automation LLC	E	419 491-4520	
Perrysburg *(G-11242)*			
▲ Nfm/Welding Engineers Inc	C	330 837-3868	
Massillon *(G-9226)*			
Nichols Mold Inc	G	330 297-9719	
Ravenna *(G-11534)*			
Nippon Stl Intgrted Crnkshaft	F	419 435-0411	
Fostoria *(G-6994)*			
Nk Machine Inc	G	513 737-8035	
Hamilton *(G-7513)*			
Nn Autocam Precision Component	F	440 647-4711	
Wellington *(G-13898)*			
Norman Noble Inc	D	216 761-5387	
Cleveland *(G-4081)*			
North Ridge Enterprises Inc	F	440 965-5300	
Norwalk *(G-10855)*			
Northend Gear and Machine Inc	F	513 860-4334	
Fairfield *(G-6758)*			
Northern Precision Inc	F	513 860-4701	
Fairfield *(G-6759)*			
Northshore Mold Inc	G	440 838-8212	
Cleveland *(G-4098)*			
Northwind Industries Inc	G	216 433-0666	
Cleveland *(G-4099)*			
Nova Metal Products Inc	E	440 269-1741	
Mentor *(G-9574)*			
◆ Npk Construction Equipment Inc	D	440 232-7900	
Bedford *(G-1050)*			
Nu-Tool Industries Inc	F	440 237-9240	
North Royalton *(G-10777)*			
Oak Industrial Inc	G	440 263-2780	
North Royalton *(G-10778)*			
▲ Oakley Die & Mold Co	E	513 754-8500	
Mason *(G-9131)*			
Oaks Welding Inc	G	330 482-4216	
Columbiana *(G-4624)*			
▲ Odawara Automation Inc	E	937 667-8433	
Tipp City *(G-12833)*			
Odyssey Machine Company Ltd	G	419 455-6621	
Perrysburg *(G-11245)*			
▼ Ohio Broach & Machine Company	F	440 946-1040	
Willoughby *(C 14400)*			
◆ Ohio Gasket and Shim Co Inc	E	330 630-0626	
Akron *(G-252)*			
Ohio Hydraulics Inc	E	513 771-2590	
Cincinnati *(G-2924)*			
Ohio Metal Fabricating Inc	F	937 233-2400	
Dayton *(G-5924)*			
Ohio Precision Inc	G	330 453-9710	
Canton *(G-1968)*			
Ohio Roll Grinding Inc	E	330 453-1884	
Louisville *(G-8610)*			
Ohio Tool Works LLC	D		
Ashland *(G-558)*			
Ohio Transitional Mch & Tl Inc	G	419 476-0820	
Toledo *(G-13076)*			
Omega Machine & Tool Inc	F	440 946-6846	
Mentor *(G-9576)*			
Ometek LLC	D	614 861-6729	
Columbus *(G-5160)*			
Omni Technical Products Inc	F	216 433-1970	
Cleveland *(G-4121)*			
OReilly Precision Pdts Inc	E	937 526-4677	
Russia *(G-11676)*			
Outlook Tool Inc	G	937 235-6330	
Dayton *(G-5931)*			

Ovase Manufacturing LLC	G	937 275-0617	
Dayton *(G-5932)*			
P & L Heat Trting Grinding Inc	E	330 746-1339	
Youngstown *(G-14907)*			
P & P Machine Tool Inc	G	440 232-7404	
Cleveland *(G-4129)*			
P & P Mold & Die Inc	F	330 784-8333	
Tallmadge *(G-12746)*			
P J Tool Company Inc	G	937 254-2817	
Dayton *(G-5933)*			
▲ P R Machine Works Inc	D	419 529-5748	
Ontario *(G-10952)*			
▲ Padco Industries LLC	E	440 564-7160	
Newbury *(G-10560)*			
Palmer Products Inc	G	330 630-9397	
Akron *(G-255)*			
Parker Precision Inc	G	440 951-6501	
Mentor *(G-9581)*			
Parker-Hannifin Corporation	G	330 336-3511	
Wadsworth *(G-13658)*			
Parkn Manufacturing LLC	F	330 723-8172	
Litchfield *(G-8482)*			
Path Robotics Inc	C	330 808-2788	
Columbus *(G-5176)*			
Path Technologies Inc	G	440 358-1500	
Painesville *(G-11103)*			
Patriot Mfg Group Inc	D	937 746-2117	
Carlisle *(G-2070)*			
Pattons Trck & Hvy Eqp Svc Inc	F	740 385-4067	
Logan *(G-8523)*			
Paul Wilke & Son Inc	F	513 921-3163	
Cincinnati *(G-2947)*			
PDQ Technologies Inc	G	937 274-4958	
Tipp City *(G-12834)*			
Pearce Inc	F	216 252-0550	
Hinckley *(G-7735)*			
Peco Holdings Corp	D	937 667-5705	
Tipp City *(G-12835)*			
Pemco Inc	E	216 524-2990	
Cleveland *(G-4150)*			
Perfect Prcision Machining Ltd	G	330 475-0324	
Akron *(G-257)*			
Perfecto Industries Inc	E	937 778-1900	
Piqua *(G-11372)*			
Perry Welding Service Inc	F	330 425-2211	
Twinsburg *(G-13355)*			
PHI Werkes LLC	G	419 586-9222	
Celina *(G 2116)*			
Phil-Matic Screw Products Inc	F	440 942-7290	
Willoughby *(G-14506)*			
Phillips Mfg & Mch Corp	G	330 823-9178	
Alliance *(G-398)*			
Pierce-Wright Precision Inc	G	216 362-2870	
Cleveland *(G-4163)*			
▲ Pioneer Industrial Systems LLC	G	419 737-9506	
Montpelier *(G-10131)*			
Pioneer Machine Inc	G	330 948-6500	
Lodi *(G-8505)*			
Pittman Engineering Inc	F	330 821-4365	
Alliance *(G-399)*			
Plas-Mac Corp	D	440 349-3222	
Solon *(G-12168)*			
PME of Ohio Inc	E	513 671-1717	
Cincinnati *(G-2973)*			
Pohl Machining Inc	E	513 353-2929	
Cleves *(G-4546)*			
Polytech Component Corp	G	330 726-3235	
Youngstown *(G-14919)*			
▲ Positech Corp	F	513 942-7411	
Blue Ash *(G-1322)*			
Post Products Inc	G	330 678-0048	
Kent *(G-8061)*			

▲ Precise Tool & Die Company Inc	E	440 951-9173	
Willoughby *(G-14509)*			
Precision Arcft Components Inc	G	937 278-0265	
Dayton *(G-5944)*			
Precision Assemblies Inc	F	330 549-2630	
North Lima *(G-10710)*			
Precision Cnc	G	614 496-1048	
Pickerington *(G-11297)*			
Precision Cnc LLC	E	740 689-9009	
Lancaster *(G-8217)*			
Precision Component & Mch Inc	G	740 867-6366	
Chesapeake *(G-2230)*			
Precision Component Inds LLC	E	330 477-6287	
Canton *(G-1979)*			
Precision Hydrlic Cnnctors Inc	F	440 953-3778	
Euclid *(G-6673)*			
Precision Machine & Tool Co	G	419 334-8405	
Port Clinton *(G-11448)*			
Precision Machining Services	G	937 222-4608	
Dayton *(G-5947)*			
Precision McHning Srfacing Inc	G	440 439-9850	
Bedford *(G-1054)*			
Precision Metals Group LLC	G	440 255-8888	
Mentor *(G-9591)*			
▲ Precision Production LLC	E	216 252-0372	
Strongsville *(G-12590)*			
Precision Reflex Inc	G	419 629-2603	
New Bremen *(G-10365)*			
Precision Tool Grinding Inc	G	419 339-9959	
Elida *(G-6486)*			
Premier Aerospace Group LLC	E	937 233-8300	
Dayton *(G-5952)*			
▲ Pride Cast Metals Inc	D	513 541-1295	
Cincinnati *(G-2981)*			
▲ Princeton Tool Inc	C	440 290-8666	
Mentor *(G-9592)*			
Pro-Gram Engineering Corp	G	330 745-1004	
Akron *(G-268)*			
▲ Process Equipment Co Tipp City	E	937 667-5705	
Tipp City *(G-12838)*			
Production Design Services Inc	D	937 866-3377	
Dayton *(G-5962)*			
Proficient Machining Co	E	440 942-4942	
Mentor *(G-9595)*			
Profile Grinding Inc	F	216 351-0600	
Cleveland *(G-4199)*			
Progressive Mfg Co Inc	G	330 784-4717	
Akron *(C 260)*			
Prohos Inc	G	419 877-0153	
Whitehouse *(G-14363)*			
Prohos Manufacturing Co Inc	G	419 877-0153	
Whitehouse *(G-14364)*			
▼ Projects Designed & Built	E	419 726-7400	
Toledo *(G-13104)*			
Promac Inc	G	937 864-1961	
Enon *(G-6632)*			
Proto Machine & Mfg Inc	F	330 677-1700	
Kent *(G-8064)*			
Pumphrey Machine Corp	G	440 417-0481	
Madison *(G-8732)*			
Pvm Incorporated	G	614 871-0302	
Grove City *(G-7410)*			
Qcsm LLC	G	216 650-8731	
Cleveland *(G-4210)*			
▲ Quaker Mfg Corp	C	330 332-4631	
Salem *(G-11807)*			
Qualiturn Inc	E	513 868-3333	
West Chester *(G-14057)*			
Quality CNC Machining Inc	E	440 953-0723	
Willoughby *(G-14512)*			
Quality Design Machining Inc	G	440 352-7290	
Orwell *(G-11025)*			

S
I
C

Quality Industries Inc................ G 216 961-5566
Cleveland (G-4214)

Quality Machine Systems LLC............. G 440 223-2217
Mentor (G-9602)

▲ Quality Machining and Mfg Inc.......... F 419 899-2543
Sherwood (G-11976)

Quality Mfg Company Inc.................. G 513 921-4500
Cincinnati (G-3017)

Quality Specialists Inc................... G 440 946-9129
Willoughby (G-14513)

Queen City Tool Works Inc................ G 513 874-0111
Fairfield (G-6770)

Quest Technologies Inc................... F 937 743-1200
Franklin (G-7044)

Quick Service Welding & Mch Co..... F 330 673-3818
Kent (G-8066)

R & D Custom Machine & Tl Inc........ E 419 727-1700
Toledo (G-13107)

R & J Cylinder & Machine Inc............ D 330 364-8263
New Philadelphia (G-10463)

R & J Tool Inc........................... F 937 833-3200
Brookville (G-1575)

R A Heller Company..................... F 513 771-6100
Cincinnati (G-3027)

R and S Technologies Inc................ F 419 483-3691
Bellevue (G-1129)

R H Industries Inc....................... E 216 281-5210
Cleveland (G-4221)

R J K Enterprises Inc.................... F 440 257-6018
Mentor (G-9604)

▲ R R R Development Co.................. D 330 966-8855
North Canton (G-10661)

R T & T Machining Co Inc................ F 440 974-8479
Mentor (G-9605)

R Vandewalle Inc........................ G 513 921-2657
Cincinnati (G-3029)

▲ R W Machine & Tool Inc............... F 330 296-5211
Ravenna (G-11537)

◆ Radco Industries Inc..................F 419 531-4731
Toledo (G-13109)

Ram Innovative Tech LLC................. G 330 956-4056
Louisville (G-8614)

Ram Machining Inc....................... G 740 333-5522
Wshngtn Ct Hs (G-14743)

▲ Ram Precision Industries Inc.......... D 937 885-7700
Dayton (G-5972)

Randolph Tool Company Inc.............. F 330 877-4923
Hartville (G-7582)

Rankin Mfg Inc.......................... G 419 929-8338
New London (G-10414)

Ray-Tech Industries LLC................. G 419 923-0169
Lyons (G-8675)

Reese Machine Company Inc............. F 440 992-3942
Ashtabula (G-614)

Remington Engrg Machining Inc.......... G 513 965-8999
Milford (G-9950)

Repko Machine Inc....................... G 216 267-1144
Cleveland (G-4234)

Reuther Mold & Mfg Co Inc.............. D 330 923-5266
Cuyahoga Falls (G-5569)

Revolution Machine Works Inc........... F 706 505-6525
Cleveland (G-4238)

▲ Reymond Products Intl Inc............. E 330 339-3583
New Philadelphia (G-10464)

Reynolds Machinery Inc.................. F 937 847-8121
Dayton (G-5983)

RI Alto Mfg Inc......................... F 740 914-4230
Marion (G-8993)

Richmond Machine Co..................... E 419 485-5740
Montpelier (G-10134)

Ridge Machine & Welding Co............. G 740 537-2821
Toronto (G-13186)

Riffle Machine Works Inc................ G 740 775-2838
Chillicothe (G-2279)

Rimeco Products Inc..................... E 440 918-1220
Willoughby (G-14517)

Risher & Co............................. F 216 732-8351
Euclid (G-6676)

Ritime Incorporated..................... G 330 273-3443
Cleveland (G-4242)

Riverside Marine Inds Inc............... D 419 729-1621
Toledo (G-13114)

Riverside Mch & Automtn Inc............. D 419 855-8308
Genoa (G-7250)

RL Craig Inc............................ F 330 424-1525
Lisbon (G-8479)

Robert Long Manufacturing Co............ G 330 678-0911
Kent (G-8069)

Robert Smart Inc........................ G 330 454-8881
Canton (G-2000)

Roberts Machine Products LLC........... F 937 682-4015
Rushsylvania (G-11666)

▲ Roberts Manufacturing Co Inc......... E 419 594-2712
Oakwood (G-10899)

Rochester Manufacturing Inc............. F 440 647-2463
Wellington (G-13900)

Roerig Machine......................... G 440 647-4718
New London (G-10415)

Rogar International Inc................. F 419 476-5500
Toledo (G-13118)

Rolling Enterprises Inc................. E 937 866-4917
Moraine (G-10191)

Rotary Smer Spcalist Group LLC......... F 330 299-8210
Barberton (G-837)

Royalton Industries Inc................. F 440 748-9900
Columbia Station (G-4600)

Royalton Manufacturing Inc............. G 440 237-2233
Akron (G-292)

Rpg Industries Inc...................... G 937 698-9801
Tipp City (G-12842)

RTZ Manufacturing Co.................... G 614 848-8366
Heath (G-7603)

Rw Screw LLC........................... E 330 837-9211
Massillon (G-9240)

S & H Automation & Eqp Co Inc.......... F 419 636-0020
Bryan (G-1659)

S and S Tool Inc........................ G 440 593-4000
Conneaut (G-5415)

S R P M Inc............................. E 440 248-8440
Cleveland (G-4268)

S-P Company Inc......................... D 330 782-5651
Columbiana (G-4627)

Sadler Corporation..................... G 330 688-0009
Stow (G-12455)

Salco Machine Inc....................... F 330 456-8281
Louisville (G-8615)

Salem Manufacturing & Sls Inc........... G 614 572-4242
Columbus (G-5245)

Sample Machining Inc.................... E 937 258-3338
Dayton (G-5993)

Sandusky Machine & Tool Inc............. G 419 626-8359
Sandusky (G-11869)

▲ Sattler Companies Inc................. D 330 239-2552
Wadsworth (G-13670)

Schaffer Grinding Co Inc................ F 323 724-4476
Twinsburg (G-13374)

Schmidt Machine Company................ E 419 294-3814
Upper Sandusky (G-13455)

Schmitmeyer Inc......................... G 937 295-2091
Fort Loramie (G-6954)

Schwab Machine.......................... G 419 626-0245
Sandusky (G-11871)

Sebring Fluid Power Corp................ G 330 938-9984
Sebring (G-11902)

Seco Machine Inc........................ E 330 499-2150
North Canton (G-10668)

Secondary Machining Svcs Inc............ G 440 593-3040
Conneaut (G-5416)

Select Machine Inc...................... F 330 678-7676
Kent (G-8077)

Selecteon Corporation................... E 614 710-1132
Columbus (G-5260)

Self Made Holdings LLC.................. E 330 477-1052
Canton (G-2001)

▲ Semco Inc............................. D 800 848-5764
Marion (G-8997)

Sequa Can Machinery Inc................. E 330 493-0444
Canton (G-2002)

Shoreline Machine Products Co........... F 216 481-8033
Cleveland (G-4297)

Short Run Machine Products Inc.......... F 440 969-1313
Ashtabula (G-616)

▲ Siebtechnik Tema Inc.................. E 513 489-7811
Cincinnati (G-3088)

Sk Mold & Tool Inc...................... E 937 339-0299
Troy (G-13255)

Sk Mold & Tool Inc...................... E 937 339-0299
Tipp City (G-12844)

Skinner Machining Co.................... G 216 486-6636
Willoughby (G-14527)

Slabe.................................. G 440 298-3693
Thompson (G-12764)

▲ Slabe Machine Products LLC........... D 440 946-6555
Willoughby (G-14529)

Slimline Surgical Devices LLC........... G 937 335-0496
Troy (G-13256)

Sls Machining Group LLC................. F 330 428-2094
Akron (G-313)

Smith Machine Inc....................... G 330 821-9898
Alliance (G-405)

Sonoma Grinding Machining Inc........... G 440 918-7990
Mentor (G-9617)

Southeastern Shafting Mfg Inc........... F 740 342-4629
New Lexington (G-10407)

Southern Ohio Mfg Inc................... F 513 943-2555
Amelia (G-437)

Southstern McHning Feld Svc In.......... E 740 689-1147
Lancaster (G-8225)

Special Machined Components............. G 513 459-1113
Mason (G-9155)

Specialty Machines Inc.................. F 937 837-8852
Dayton (G-6015)

Spectrum Machine Inc.................... F 330 626-3666
Streetsboro (G-12524)

Spence Technologies Inc................. F 440 946-3035
Willoughby (G-14531)

▲ Spirex Corporation.................... C 330 726-1166
Youngstown (G-14938)

Sponseller Group Inc.................... G 937 492-9949
Sidney (G-12054)

Sponseller Group Inc.................... E 419 861-3000
Holland (G-7785)

Spz Machine Company Inc................. G 330 848-3286
Norton (G-10827)

SRS Manufacturing Corp.................. F 937 746-3086
Franklin (G-7050)

ST Tool & Design Inc.................... F 440 357-1250
Mentor (G-9621)

Stafford Gage & Tool Inc................ G 937 277-9944
Dayton (G-6021)

Stan-Kell LLC.......................... F 440 998-1116
Ashtabula (G-617)

▲ Stanco Precision Mfg Inc.............. G 937 274-1785
Dayton (G-6022)

Standard Aero Inc....................... D 937 840-1053
Hillsboro (G-7726)

Standard Jig Boring Svc LLC............D 330 644-5405
Akron *(G-316)*

▲ Standard Jig Boring Svc LLC...........E 330 896-9530
Akron *(G-315)*

Standard Machine Inc.............E 216 631-4440
Cleveland *(G-4326)*

◆ Standby Screw Machine Pdts Co......B 440 243-8200
Berea *(G-1188)*

▼ Stanley Industries Inc...........F 216 475-4000
Cleveland *(G-4327)*

Star Metal Products Co Inc..........C 440 899-7000
Westlake *(G-14336)*

▼ Stark Industrial LLC............E 330 966-8108
North Canton *(G-10670)*

Starr Machine Inc............E 740 753-0184
Nelsonville *(G-10321)*

Starwin Industries LLC............E 937 293-8568
Dayton *(G-6024)*

Staub Laser Cutting Inc............E 937 890-4486
Dayton *(G-6025)*

Std Liquidation Inc............C 937 492-6121
Sidney *(G-12055)*

▲ Steck Manufacturing Co LLC..........F 937 222-0062
Dayton *(G-6026)*

▲ Steel Eqp Specialists Inc............D 330 823-8260
Alliance *(G-406)*

Steel Products Corp Akron............E 330 688-6633
Stow *(G-12463)*

Stefra Inc............G 440 846-8240
Strongsville *(G-12605)*

Stegemeyer Machine Inc............G 513 321-5651
Cincinnati *(G-3117)*

Steinbarger Precision Cnc Inc..........G 937 376-0322
Xenia *(G-14775)*

Steinert Industries Inc............G 330 678-0028
Kent *(G-8083)*

Stevenson Mfg Co............G 330 532-1581
Wellsville *(G-13914)*

Strassells Machine Inc............F 419 747-1088
Mansfield *(G-8855)*

Stryver Mfg Inc............E 937 854-3048
Dayton *(G-6028)*

Suburban Manufacturing Co............D 440 953-2024
Eastlake *(G-6444)*

Suburban Metal Products Inc..........F 740 474-4237
Circleville *(G-3263)*

Sulecki Precision Products Inc..........F 440 255-5454
Mentor *(G-9630)*

▲ Summit Machine Ltd............F 330 628-2663
Mogadore *(G-10087)*

Summit Machining Co Ltd............F 330 628-2663
Mogadore *(G-10088)*

Sunset Industries Inc............E 440 306-8284
Mentor *(G-9631)*

Superalloy Mfg Solutions Corp..........F 513 605-8380
Blue Ash *(G-1336)*

Superfine Manufacturing Inc..........F 330 897-9024
Fresno *(G-7149)*

Superfinishers Inc............G 330 467-2125
Macedonia *(G-8718)*

Superior Machine Tool Inc............F 419 675-2363
Kenton *(G-8116)*

Superior Mold & Die Co............F 330 688-8251
Munroe Falls *(G-10273)*

Superior Precision Pdts Inc..........G 216 881-3696
Cleveland *(G-4345)*

Superior Welding Co............G 614 252-8539
Columbus *(G-5300)*

Swagelok Company............D 440 461-7714
Cleveland *(G-4353)*

Swagelok Company............E 440 349-5652
Solon *(G-12189)*

Swagelok Company............E 440 349-5836
Solon *(G-12190)*

Swagelok Company............E 440 248-4600
Willoughby Hills *(G-14564)*

◆ Swagelok Company............A 440 248-4600
Solon *(G-12188)*

Swanton Wldg Machining Co Inc..........D 419 826-4816
Swanton *(G-12694)*

Swihart Industries Inc............E 937 277-4796
Dayton *(G-6034)*

Systech Handling Inc............F 419 445-8226
Archbold *(G-512)*

T & S Machine Inc............G 419 453-2101
Wapakoneta *(G-13728)*

T-Mac Machine Inc............G 330 673-0621
Kent *(G-8085)*

T&T Machine Inc............F 440 354-0605
Painesville *(G-11112)*

Tahoma Engineered Solutions Inc..........E 330 345-6169
Ashland *(G-578)*

Tailored Systems Inc............G 937 299-3900
Moraine *(G-10194)*

Tarman Machine Company Inc..........F 614 834-4010
Canal Winchester *(G-1798)*

Tat Machine & Tool Ltd............E 419 836-7706
Curtice *(G-5518)*

▼ Tdl Tool Inc............F 937 374-0055
Xenia *(G-14777)*

TDS-Bf/Ls Holdings Inc............E 440 327-5800
North Ridgeville *(G-10751)*

▲ Te-Co Manufacturing LLC............D 937 836-0961
Englewood *(G-6625)*

Technology House Ltd............D 440 248-3025
Solon *(G-12194)*

Ted M Figgins............F 740 277-3750
Lancaster *(G-8227)*

Tegr Inc............E 419 678-4991
Saint Henry *(G-11725)*

Tek Gear & Machine Inc............G 330 455-3331
Canton *(G-2023)*

Tek Group International............G 330 706-0000
Canal Fulton *(G-1780)*

Tekraft Industries Inc............G 440 352-8321
Painesville *(G-11114)*

Telcon LLC............D 330 562-5566
Streetsboro *(G-12528)*

Ten Mfg LLC............F 440 487-1100
Mentor *(G-9636)*

Tendon Manufacturing Inc............E 216 663-3200
Cleveland *(G-4374)*

Terydon Inc............G 330 879-2448
Navarre *(G-10314)*

Tessa Precision Product Inc..........E 440 392-3470
Painesville *(G-11115)*

Tessec LLC............D 937 576-0010
Dayton *(G-6045)*

Tgm LLC............F 419 636-8567
Bryan *(G-1661)*

The Kordenbrock Tool and Die Co........F 513 326-4390
Cincinnati *(G-3148)*

The Q-P Manufacturing Co Inc..........F 440 946-2120
Chardon *(G-2225)*

Thees Machine & Tool Company..........G 419 586-4766
Celina *(G-2124)*

Ti Inc............E 419 332-8484
Fremont *(G-7138)*

Tiffin Foundry & Machine Inc..........E 419 447-3991
Tiffin *(G-12802)*

Timekap Inc............G 330 747-2122
Youngstown *(G-14947)*

▼ Timkensteel Material Svcs LLC..........C 281 449-0319
Canton *(G-2025)*

Tipp Machine & Tool Inc............C 937 890-8428
Dayton *(G-6055)*

Tm Machine & Tool Inc............G 419 478-0310
Toledo *(G-13144)*

Todd Industries Inc............E 440 439-2900
Cleveland *(G-4398)*

Tom Barbour Auto Parts Inc..........F 740 354-4654
Portsmouth *(G-11479)*

Tomco Machining Inc............E 937 264-1943
Miamisburg *(G-9749)*

Toolbold Corporation............E 216 676-9840
Cleveland *(G-4400)*

Tooling & Components Corp..........F 419 478-9122
Toledo *(G-13163)*

Total Manufacturing Co Inc..........E 440 205-9700
Mentor *(G-9638)*

Toth Industries Inc............D 419 729-4669
Toledo *(G-13164)*

Tq Manufacturing Company Inc..........G 440 255-9000
Mentor *(G-9639)*

Tracer Specialties Inc............G 216 696-2363
Cleveland *(G-4409)*

Tradye Machine & Tool Inc..........G 740 625-7550
Centerburg *(G-2128)*

▲ Trailer Component Mfg Inc..........E 440 255-2888
Mentor *(G-9640)*

Treadway Manufacturing LLC..........G 937 266-3423
Dayton *(G-6060)*

Trec Industries Inc............F 216 741-4114
Cleveland *(G-4415)*

Tri-R Tooling Inc............F 419 522-8665
Mansfield *(G-8861)*

Triangle Precision Inds Inc..........D 937 299-6776
Dayton *(G-6062)*

Trico Machine Products Corp..........F 216 662-4194
Cleveland *(G-4424)*

Trinel Inc............G 216 265-9190
Cleveland *(G-4427)*

Trotwood Corporation............G 937 854-3047
Trotwood *(G-13197)*

Troy Manufacturing Co............E 440 834-8262
Burton *(G-1706)*

Tru-Bore Machine Co Inc............G 330 928-6215
Cuyahoga Falls *(G-5579)*

Tru-Fab Technology Inc............F 440 954-9760
Willoughby *(G-14543)*

Trucast Inc............D 440 942-4923
Willoughby *(C-14544)*

True Step LLC............G 513 933-0933
Lebanon *(G-8292)*

Trulou Holdings Inc............E 513 347-0100
Cincinnati *(G-3174)*

Trust Manufacturing LLC............G 216 531-8787
Euclid *(G-6681)*

Trv LLC............E 440 951-7722
Willoughby *(G-14545)*

TSR Machinery Services Inc..........F 513 874-9697
Fairfield *(G-6785)*

TSS Acquisition Company............G 513 772-7000
Cincinnati *(G-3175)*

▲ Tsw Industries Inc............E 440 572-7200
Strongsville *(G-12611)*

Tubular Techniques Inc............G 614 529-4130
Hilliard *(G-7708)*

Turn-All Machine & Gear Co..........F 937 342-8710
Springfield *(G-12390)*

Turner Machine Co............G 330 332-5821
Salem *(G-11816)*

Twin Valley Metalcraft Asm LLC..........G 937 787-4634
West Alexandria *(G-13922)*

Two M Precision Co Inc............E 440 946-2120
Willoughby *(G-14546)*

S I C

U S Alloy Die Corp................................ F 216 749-9700
　Cleveland *(G-4438)*

Ultra Machine Inc............................... G 440 323-7632
　Elyria *(G-6597)*

▲ Ultra Tech Machinery Inc............... E 330 929-5544
　Cuyahoga Falls *(G-5580)*

◆ Ultra-Met Company...........................D 937 653-7133
　Urbana *(G-13481)*

▲ United Grinding and Machine Co...... E 330 453-7402
　Canton *(G-2035)*

United Machine and Tool Inc............ G 440 946-7677
　Eastlake *(G-6447)*

▲ United Precision Services Inc.......... G 513 851-6900
　Cincinnati *(G-3184)*

United Tool and Machine Inc............ F 937 843-5603
　Lakeview *(G-8158)*

▲ Universal Fabg Cnstr Svcs Inc......... F 614 274-1128
　Columbus *(G-5338)*

▼ Universal Grinding Corporation........ E 216 631-9410
　Cleveland *(G-4445)*

Universal J&Z Machine LLC............. E 216 486-2220
　Willoughby *(G-14548)*

Universal Tool Technology LLC........... G 937 222-4608
　Dayton *(G-6069)*

Valley Machine Tool Inc.................... E 513 899-2737
　Morrow *(G-10204)*

Valmac Industries Inc....................... E 937 890-5558
　Vandalia *(G-13581)*

Vectron Inc... F 440 323-3369
　Elyria *(G-6600)*

▲ Ver-Mac Industries Inc.................... E 740 397-6511
　Mount Vernon *(G-10268)*

Verhoff Machine & Welding Inc........ C 419 596-3202
　Continental *(G-5424)*

Versatile Machine............................. G 330 618-9895
　Tallmadge *(G-12758)*

Versi-Tech Incorporated..................... F 586 944-2230
　Apple Creek *(G-479)*

Vicas Manufacturing Co Inc............. E 513 791-7741
　Cincinnati *(G-3204)*

Vics Turning Coinc............................ G 216 531-5016
　Cleveland *(G-4470)*

Vision Manufacturing Inc................... G 937 332-1801
　Troy *(G-13260)*

Vision Projects Inc............................ G 937 667-8648
　Tipp City *(G-12852)*

Vrc Inc.. D 440 243-6666
　Berea *(G-1194)*

Vtd Systems Inc................................. E 440 323-4122
　Elyria *(G-6601)*

Wade Dynamics Inc........................... G 216 431-8484
　Cleveland *(G-4488)*

▲ Wagner Machine Inc....................... E 330 706-0700
　Norton *(G-10828)*

Walest Incorporated......................... G 216 362-8110
　Brunswick *(G-1623)*

◆ Warren Fabricating Corporation........D 330 534-5017
　Hubbard *(G-7818)*

Warren Screw Machine Inc.............. F 330 609-6020
　Warren *(G-13811)*

Wavy Ticket LLC............................... E 513 827-0886
　Okeana *(G-10929)*

Wedgeworks Mch Tl Boring Inc......... G 216 441-1200
　Cleveland *(G-4496)*

Wellex AMG...................................... G 513 734-1700
　Amelia *(G-441)*

Wellex Manufacturing Inc................. G 513 734-1700
　Amelia *(G-442)*

Wenrick Machine and Tool Corp........ F 937 667-7307
　Tipp City *(G-12854)*

Wesco Machine Inc........................... F 330 688-6973
　Ravenna *(G-11549)*

▲ Westbrook Mfg Inc......................... B 937 254-2004
　Dayton *(G-6078)*

White Machine Inc............................ G 440 237-3282
　North Royalton *(G-10789)*

White Machine & Mfg Co................... F 740 453-5451
　Zanesville *(G-15054)*

Whitt Machine Inc............................. F 513 423-7624
　Middletown *(G-9904)*

Will-Burt Company............................ F 330 682-7015
　Orrville *(G-11019)*

▲ Will-Burt Company.......................... C 330 682-7015
　Orrville *(G-11018)*

Willis Cnc... G 440 926-0434
　Grafton *(G-7306)*

Wipe Out Enterprises Inc................. G 937 497-9473
　Sidney *(G-12062)*

Wire Shop Inc.................................... E 440 354-6842
　Mentor *(G-9653)*

Wise Edge LLC................................. G 330 208-0889
　Mogadore *(G-10094)*

Wismar Prcsion Toling Prod Inc........ G 440 296-0487
　Mentor *(G-9654)*

Wm Plotz Machine and Forge Co........ F 216 861-0441
　Cleveland *(G-4512)*

Wodin Inc.. E 440 439-4222
　Cleveland *(G-4513)*

Wolfe Grinding Inc............................ G 330 929-6677
　Stow *(G-12472)*

Wolff Tool & Mfg Company Inc.......... F 440 933-7797
　Avon Lake *(G-774)*

Wonder Machine Services Inc.......... E 440 937-7500
　Avon *(G-743)*

Wray Precision Products Inc............. G 513 228-5000
　Lebanon *(G-8297)*

Wulco Inc.. D 513 679-2600
　Cincinnati *(G-3236)*

Wulco Inc.. D 513 379-6115
　Hamilton *(G-7539)*

▲ Wulco Inc....................................... D 513 679-2600
　Cincinnati *(G-3235)*

X-Mil Inc... E 937 444-1323
　Mount Orab *(G-10224)*

Xact Spec Industries LLC................. G 440 543-8157
　Chagrin Falls *(G-2193)*

Xact Spec Industries LLC................. E 440 543-8157
　Chagrin Falls *(G-2194)*

Youngstown Hard Chrome Pltg Gr........ E 330 758-9721
　Youngstown *(G-14970)*

Z & Z Manufacturing Inc................... F 440 953-2800
　Willoughby *(G-14553)*

Zeiger Industries Inc......................... E 330 484-4413
　Canton *(G-2051)*

Zephyr Industries Inc........................ G 419 281-4485
　Ashland *(G-581)*

36 ELECTRONIC & OTHER ELECTRICAL EQUIPMENT & COMPONENTS

3612 Transformers, except electric

ABB Inc... F 614 818-6300
　Westerville *(G-14201)*

Acuity Brands Lighting Inc................. D 740 349-4343
　Newark *(G-10489)*

▲ AES Beaver Valley LLC................... D
　Dayton *(G-5602)*

◆ Ajax Tocco Magnethermic Corp.........C 800 547-1527
　Warren *(G-13732)*

Arisdyne Systems Inc....................... F 216 458-1991
　Cleveland *(G-3365)*

Clark Substations LLC...................... G 330 452-5200
　Canton *(G-1868)*

Contact Industries Inc....................... E 419 884-9788
　Lexington *(G-8372)*

▲ Control Transformer Inc.................. E 330 637-6015
　Cortland *(G-5443)*

Darrah Electric Company................... F 216 631-0912
　Chesterland *(G-2233)*

Desco LLC.. F 513 860-4490
　Hamilton *(G-7484)*

Dongan Electric Mfg Co.................... G 419 737-2304
　Pioneer *(G-11319)*

E Technologies Inc............................ G 440 247-7000
　Chagrin Falls *(G-2140)*

▲ Eaton Electric Holdings LLC........... B 440 523-5000
　Cleveland *(G-3654)*

Eaton Leasing Corporation................. B 216 382-2292
　Beachwood *(G-916)*

Fishel Company................................. C 614 850-4400
　Columbus *(G-4926)*

◆ Foster Transformer Company...........E 513 681-2420
　Cincinnati *(G-2637)*

▲ Fostoria Bshngs Inslators Corp......... G 419 435-7514
　Fostoria *(G-6980)*

▲ Fostoria Bushings Inc..................... G 419 435-7514
　Fostoria *(G-6981)*

General Electric Company.................. E 216 883-1000
　Cleveland *(G-3766)*

Hannon Company.............................. D 330 456-4728
　Canton *(G-1908)*

Harrison Corporation......................... G 513 681-2420
　Cincinnati *(G-2708)*

◆ Lake Shore Electric Corp............... E 440 232-0200
　Bedford *(G-1043)*

▲ LTI Power Systems Inc................... E 440 327-5050
　Elyria *(G-6560)*

▼ Matlock Electric Co Inc.................. E 513 731-9600
　Cincinnati *(G-2850)*

▼ Morlan & Associates Inc................ E 614 889-6152
　Hilliard *(G-7687)*

▼ Norlake Manufacturing Company...... D 440 353-3200
　North Ridgeville *(G-10741)*

Npas Inc... F 614 595-6916
　Mansfield *(G-8840)*

◆ Ohio Semitronics Inc.....................D 614 777-1005
　Hilliard *(G-7692)*

▲ Otc Services Inc............................ D 330 871-2444
　Louisville *(G-8611)*

Peak Electric Inc............................... F 419 726-4848
　Toledo *(G-13092)*

Pmp Industries Inc............................ G 513 563-3028
　Blue Ash *(G-1321)*

▲ Qualtek Electronics Corp............... C 440 951-3300
　Mentor *(G-9603)*

Schneider Electric Usa Inc................. B 513 523-4171
　Oxford *(G-11064)*

Schneider Electric Usa Inc................. D 513 777-4445
　West Chester *(G-14073)*

◆ SGB Usa Inc..................................G 330 472-1187
　Tallmadge *(G-12749)*

Siemens Industry Inc......................... E 937 593-6010
　Bellefontaine *(G-1116)*

Spectre Sensors Inc.......................... G 440 250-0372
　Westlake *(G-14335)*

Staco Energy Products Co................. E 937 253-1191
　Dayton *(G-6020)*

◆ Staco Energy Products Co..............G 937 253-1191
　Miamisburg *(G-9739)*

Tesa Inc.. G 614 847-8200
　Lewis Center *(G-8355)*

Transformer Associates Limited........... G 330 430-0750
　Canton *(G-2027)*

3613 Switchgear and switchboard apparatus

ABB Inc...................................... F 614 818-6300
Westerville *(G-14201)*

Acorn Technology Corporation............. E 216 663-1244
Shaker Heights *(G-11925)*

Adgo Incorporated............................. E 513 752-6880
Cincinnati *(G-2295)*

All Pack Services LLC........................ G 614 935-0964
Grove City *(G-7370)*

▲ Altronic LLC................................. C 330 545-9768
Girard *(G-7264)*

▲ American Controls Inc.................... E 440 944-9735
Wickliffe *(G-14366)*

Asco Power Technologies LP.............. C 216 573-7600
Cleveland *(G-3374)*

Assembly Works Inc......................... G 419 433-5010
Huron *(G-7869)*

Avtron Loadbank Inc......................... C 216 573-7600
Cleveland *(G-3395)*

Bcs Technologies Ltd........................ F 513 829-4577
Fairfield *(G-6713)*

Bentronix Corp................................. G 440 632-0606
Middlefield *(G-9782)*

CDI Industries Inc............................ E 440 243-1100
Cleveland *(G-3481)*

Columbus Controls Inc...................... E 614 882-9029
Columbus *(G-4820)*

Control Craft LLC............................. F 513 674-0056
Cincinnati *(G-2514)*

▲ Control Interface Inc..................... G 513 874-2062
West Chester *(G-13974)*

Custom Craft Controls Inc.................. F 330 630-9599
Akron *(G-112)*

◆ Delta Systems Inc......................... B 330 626-2811
Streetsboro *(G-12496)*

Eaton Corporation............................. E 513 387-2000
West Chester *(G-13990)*

▲ Eaton Electric Holdings LLC........... B 440 523-5000
Cleveland *(G-3654)*

Electro Controls Inc.......................... E 866 497-1717
Sidney *(G-12016)*

Emerson Network Power..................... G 614 841-8054
Ironton *(G-7931)*

▲ Etched Metal Company................... E 440 248-0240
Solon *(G-12109)*

Flood Heliarc Inc............................. F 614 835-3929
Groveport *(G-7432)*

General Electric Company.................. E 216 883-1000
Cleveland *(G-3766)*

Hy-Tech Controls Inc........................ F 440 232-4040
Bedford *(G-1037)*

◆ Ideal Electric Power Co................. E 419 522-3611
Mansfield *(G-8804)*

Industrial and Mar Eng Svc Co........... F 740 694-0791
Fredericktown *(G-7080)*

Industrial Ctrl Dsign Mnt Inc.............. F 330 785-9840
Tallmadge *(G-12737)*

Industrial Solutions Inc..................... E 614 431-8118
Lewis Center *(G-8336)*

◆ Industrial Thermal Systems Inc........ F 513 561-2100
Cincinnati *(G-2745)*

Innovative Control Systems................. G 513 894-3712
Fairfield Township *(G-6796)*

Innovative Controls Corp.................... F 419 691-6684
Maumee *(G-9298)*

▲ Instrmntation Ctrl Systems Inc........ E 513 662-2600
Cincinnati *(G-2747)*

Jeff Bonham Electric Inc.................... E 937 233-7662
Dayton *(G-5828)*

▲ Joslyn Hi-Voltage Company LLC...... F 216 271-6600
Cleveland *(G-3893)*

Koester Corporation.......................... E 419 599-0291
Napoleon *(G-10289)*

◆ Lake Shore Electric Corp.............. E 440 232-0200
Bedford *(G-1043)*

Layerzero Power Systems Inc............. F 440 399-9000
Aurora *(G-676)*

Marathon Special Products Corp.......... C 419 352-8441
Bowling Green *(G-1428)*

Mercury Iron and Steel Co................. F 440 349-1500
Solon *(G-12146)*

Milathan Wholesalers........................ E 614 697-1458
Columbus *(G-5102)*

◆ Myers Power Products Inc............. C 330 834-3200
North Canton *(G-10655)*

Npas Inc.. F 614 595-6916
Mansfield *(G-8840)*

▲ Osborne Coinage Company LLC...... D 877 480-0456
Blue Ash *(G-1316)*

PA Technologies LLC........................ F 513 800-3541
Cincinnati *(G-2940)*

▲ Pacs Industries Inc...................... D 740 397-5021
Mount Vernon *(G-10256)*

Panel Master LLC............................ E 440 355-4442
Lagrange *(G-8153)*

Panel-Fab Inc................................. D ..... 513 771-14€2
Cincinnati *(G-2941)*

Panelmatic Inc................................ E 330 782-8007
Youngstown *(G-14911)*

Panelmatic Bldg Solutions Inc............ E 330 619-5235
Brookfield *(G-1517)*

▼ Panelmatic Youngstown Inc............ E 330 782-8007
Youngstown *(G-14912)*

Primex.. G 513 831-9959
Milford *(G-9949)*

Regal Beloit America Inc................... C 419 352-8441
Bowling Green *(G-1439)*

Roemer Industries Inc....................... D 330 448-2000
Masury *(G-9256)*

Schneider Electric Usa Inc................. D 513 777-4445
West Chester *(G-14073)*

Scott Fetzer Company........................ C 216 267-9000
Cleveland *(G-4278)*

Siemens Industry Inc........................ E 937 593-6010
Bellefontaine *(G-1116)*

Spang & Company............................ E 440 350-6108
Mentor *(G-9619)*

▲ Spectra-Tech Manufacturing Inc....... E 513 735-9300
Batavia *(G-889)*

Star Distribution and Mfg LLC............ E 513 860-3573
West Chester *(G-14149)*

Tcb Automation LLC......................... F 330 556-6444
Dover *(G-6265)*

Te Connectivity Corporation................ C 419 521-9500
Mansfield *(G-8858)*

Toledo Transducers Inc..................... E 419 724-4170
Maumee *(G-9327)*

▲ Trucut Incorporated...................... D 330 938-9806
Sebring *(G-11903)*

UCI Controls Inc............................. E 216 398-0330
Cleveland *(G-4439)*

◆ United Rolls Inc........................... D
Canton *(G-2036)*

Vacuum Electric Switch Co Inc........... F 330 374-5156
Mogadore *(G-10091)*

◆ Vertiv Corporation........................ A 614 888-0246
Westerville *(G-14239)*

▲ Westbrook Mfg Inc....................... B 937 254-2004
Dayton *(G-6078)*

3621 Motors and generators

Accurate Electronics Inc.................... F 330 682-7015
Orrville *(G-10972)*

Allied Motion At Dayton..................... E 937 228-3171
Dayton *(G-5646)*

American Armature Corporation........... G 419 448-1926
Tiffin *(G-12773)*

Ametek Inc..................................... G 302 636-5401
Columbus *(G-4705)*

Ametek Tchnical Indus Pdts Inc.......... D 330 673-3451
Kent *(G-8017)*

Ares Inc.. D 419 635-2175
Port Clinton *(G-11439)*

Babcock & Wilcox Entps Inc.............. C 330 753-4511
Akron *(G-68)*

Battle Motors Inc............................. C 888 328-5443
New Philadelphia *(G-10432)*

Brinkley Technology Group LLC........... F 330 830-2498
Massillon *(G-9175)*

Carter Carburetor LLC....................... A 216 314-2711
Cleveland *(G-3473)*

Charles Auto Electric Co Inc.............. G 330 535-6269
Akron *(G-96)*

Chemequip Sales Inc........................ E 330 724-8300
Coventry Township *(G-5481)*

City Machine Technologies Inc............ F 330 747-2639
Youngstown *(G-14836)*

Cleveland Wind Company LLC............. G 216 269-7667
Cleveland *(G-3530)*

Crescent & Sprague.......................... F 740 373-2331
Marietta *(G-8912)*

Cummins Inc................................... F 614 604-6004
Grove City *(G-7379)*

◆ Dayton-Phoenix Group Inc............. C 937 496-3900
Dayton *(G-5742)*

◆ Dcm Manufacturing Inc................. E 216 265-8006
Cleveland *(G-3606)*

◆ Dreison International Inc................ C 216 362-0755
Cleveland *(G-3632)*

Electric Service Co Inc..................... E 513 271-6387
Cincinnati *(G-2580)*

▲ Electrocraft Arkansas Inc............... G 501 268-4203
Gallipolis *(G-7203)*

Energy Technologies Inc.................... D 419 522-4444
Mansfield *(G-8786)*

General Electric Company.................. E 216 883-1000
Cleveland *(G-3766)*

◆ Gleason Metrology Systems Corp..... E 937 384-8901
Dayton *(G-5796)*

▲ Global Innovative Products LLC....... G 513 701-0441
Lebanon *(G-8261)*

▲ Globe Motors Inc......................... C 334 983-3542
Dayton *(C 5708)*

▲ Grand-Rock Company Inc............... E 440 639-2000
Painesville *(G-11089)*

Hannon Company.............................. D 330 456-4728
Canton *(G-1908)*

◆ HBD Industries Inc....................... E 614 526-7000
Dublin *(G-6302)*

◆ Ideal Electric Power Co................. E 419 522-3611
Mansfield *(G-8804)*

◆ Imperial Electric Company.............. B 330 734-3600
North Canton *(G-10647)*

Industrial and Mar Eng Svc Co........... F 740 694-0791
Fredericktown *(G-7080)*

JD Power Systems LLC..................... F 614 317-9394
Hilliard *(G-7685)*

Kirkwood Holding Inc........................ G 216 267-6200
Cleveland *(G-3925)*

◆ Lake Shore Electric Corp.............. E 440 232-0200
Bedford *(G-1043)*

▲ Lhy Powertrain Corporation............ E 330 533-6801
Canfield *(G-1812)*

Lite Magnesium Products Inc.............. D 330 296-6110
Ravenna *(G-11531)*

Martin Diesel Inc............................. E 419 782-9911
Defiance *(G-6120)*

S
I
C

▲ Ohio Magnetics Inc............................. E 216 662-8484
Maple Heights *(G-8888)*

◆ Ohio Semitronics Inc...........................D 614 777-1005
Hilliard *(G-7692)*

One Three Energy Inc.......................... F 513 996-6973
Cincinnati *(G-2932)*

Parker-Hannifin Corporation............... C 330 336-3511
Wadsworth *(G-13659)*

Peerless-Winsmith Inc......................... B 330 399-3651
Dublin *(G-6330)*

Precision Design Inc............................ G 419 289-1553
Ashland *(G-566)*

Qaf Technologies Inc........................... E 440 941-4348
Columbus *(G-5217)*

R E Smith Inc....................................... F 513 771-0645
Cincinnati *(G-3028)*

Ramco Electric Motors Inc................... D 937 548-2525
Greenville *(G-7350)*

Regal Beloit America Inc...................... E 608 364-8800
Lima *(G-8443)*

Regal Beloit America Inc...................... C 937 667-2431
Tipp City *(G-12840)*

Rv Mobile Power LLC............................ E 855 427-7978
Columbus *(G-5239)*

Safran Usa Inc..................................... C 513 247-7000
Sharonville *(G-11948)*

Siemens Industry Inc........................... C 513 841-3100
Norwood *(G-10873)*

Stateline Power Corp........................... F 937 547-1006
Greenville *(G-7356)*

▲ Swiger Coil Systems Ltd..................... C 216 362-7500
Cleveland *(G-4356)*

▲ Tigerpoly Manufacturing Inc............... B 614 871-0045
Grove City *(G-7416)*

Tremont Electric Incorporated............. G 888 214-3137
Cleveland *(G-4416)*

Triton Duro Werks Inc........................... G 407 497-9116
Akron *(G-344)*

Turtlecreek Township........................... F 513 932-4080
Lebanon *(G-8293)*

◆ Vanner Holdings Inc............................D 614 771-2718
Hilliard *(G-7709)*

Wabtec Corporation.............................. F 216 362-7500
Cleveland *(G-4485)*

Waibel Electric Co Inc.......................... F 740 964-2956
Etna *(G-6634)*

▲ Yamada North America Inc.................. B 937 462-7111
South Charleston *(G-12215)*

3624 Carbon and graphite products

Active Chemical Systems Inc................F 440 543-7755
Chagrin Falls *(G-2154)*

◆ American Spring Wire Corp.................C 216 292-4620
Bedford Heights *(G-1068)*

Applied Sciences Inc........................... E 937 766-2020
Cedarville *(G-2097)*

▲ Cammann Inc....................................... F 440 965-4051
Wakeman *(G-13678)*

◆ De Nora Tech LLC................................D 440 710-5334
Painesville *(G-11078)*

Ges AGM.. E 216 658-6528
Cleveland *(G-3773)*

◆ Ges Graphite Inc.................................E 216 658-6660
Parma *(G-11132)*

Graftech Holdings Inc........................... D 216 676-2000
Independence *(G-7905)*

Graftech International Ltd..................... D 216 676-2000
Brooklyn Heights *(G-1531)*

◆ Graftech Intl Holdings Inc...................C 216 676-2000
Brooklyn Heights *(G-1532)*

Graftech Intl Trdg Inc.......................... E 216 676-2000
Cleveland *(G-3782)*

Graphel Corporation............................ C 513 779-6166
West Chester *(G-14012)*

◆ Graphite Sales Inc..............................F 419 652-3388
Nova *(G-10877)*

▲ Metaullics Systems LP......................... C 509 926-6212
Solon *(G-12148)*

▲ Mill-Rose Company.............................. C 440 255-9171
Mentor *(G-9566)*

▼ Morgan Advanced Materials............... C 419 435-8182
Fostoria *(G-6992)*

Morgan AM&t.. G 419 435-8182
Fostoria *(G-6993)*

Neograf Solutions LLC.......................... C 216 529-3777
Lakewood *(G-8170)*

Ocsial LLC... F 415 906-5271
Gahanna *(G-7167)*

Ohio Carbon Blank Inc......................... E 440 953-9302
Willoughby *(G-14500)*

Ohio Carbon Industries Inc................. E 888 248-5029
Ashland *(G-556)*

Randall Bearings Inc............................ F 419 678-2486
Coldwater *(G-4583)*

▲ Randall Bearings Inc............................ D 419 223-1075
Lima *(G-8442)*

▲ Sangraf International Inc....................... G 216 543-3288
Westlake *(G-14330)*

Sentinel Management Inc..................... E 440 821-7372
Lorain *(G-8580)*

Sherbrooke Corporation....................... E 440 942-3520
Willoughby *(G-14525)*

▼ Wolf Composite Solutions.................... F 614 219-6990
Columbus *(G-5370)*

Xperion E & E USA LLC......................... E 740 788-9560
Heath *(G-7605)*

3625 Relays and industrial controls

Acon Inc... G 513 276-2111
Tipp City *(G-12814)*

▲ Altronic LLC... C 330 545-9768
Girard *(G-7264)*

Amano Cincinnati Incorporated............ F 513 697-9000
Loveland *(G-8619)*

Apex Control Systems Inc..................... D 330 938-2588
Sebring *(G-11891)*

Asco Power Technologies LP................ C 216 573-7600
Cleveland *(G-3374)*

Automation Technology Inc.................. E 937 233-6084
Dayton *(G-5670)*

Autoneum North America Inc............... B 419 693-0511
Oregon *(G-10957)*

Avtron Holdings LLC............................. E 216 642-1230
Cleveland *(G-3394)*

Avtron Loadbank Inc............................. C 216 573-7600
Cleveland *(G-3395)*

▼ Bay Controls LLC.................................. E 419 891-4390
Holland *(G-7745)*

▲ Bwi Eagle LLC...................................... E 724 283-4681
Warren *(G-13747)*

Cattron Holdings Inc............................. E 234 806-0018
Warren *(G-13748)*

◆ Cattron North America Inc...................F 234 806-0018
Warren *(G-13749)*

▲ Chandler Systems Incorporated.......... D 888 363-9434
Ashland *(G-528)*

▲ Channel Products Inc............................ D 440 423-0113
Solon *(G-12093)*

Cincinnati Ctrl Dynamics Inc................ G 513 242-7300
Cincinnati *(G-2473)*

Clark Substations LLC.......................... G 330 452-5200
Canton *(G-1868)*

Command Alkon Incorporated.............. E 614 799-0600
Dublin *(G-6290)*

Comtec Incorporated............................ F 330 425-8102
Twinsburg *(G-13288)*

Contact Industries Inc.......................... E 419 884-9788
Lexington *(G-8372)*

Control Electric Co............................... E 216 671-8010
Columbia Station *(G-4592)*

Controllix Corporation.......................... F 440 232-8757
Walton Hills *(G-13696)*

Controls Inc.. E 330 239-4345
Medina *(G-9390)*

Corrotec Inc.. E 937 325-3585
Springfield *(G-12294)*

Curtiss-Wright Ds Inc........................... E 937 252-5601
Fairborn *(G-6689)*

Dalton Corporation............................... E 419 682-6328
Stryker *(G-12621)*

Davis Technologies Inc......................... F 330 823-2544
Alliance *(G-380)*

◆ Delta Systems Inc................................B 330 626-2811
Streetsboro *(G-12496)*

▲ Dimcogray Corporation........................ D 937 433-7600
Centerville *(G-2131)*

Divelbiss Corporation........................... E 800 245-2327
Fredericktown *(G-7077)*

Eaton Corporation................................. C 440 826-1115
Cleveland *(G-3651)*

Eaton Corporation................................. C 216 281-2211
Cleveland *(G-3653)*

◆ Eaton Corporation................................B 440 523-5000
Cleveland *(G-3652)*

Eaton Electrical................................... F 787 257-4470
Cleveland *(G-3655)*

▲ Electrocraft Ohio Inc............................ E 740 441-6200
Gallipolis *(G-7204)*

Elite Industrial Controls Inc................. E 567 234-1057
Berlin Heights *(G-1204)*

Energy Technologies Inc...................... D 419 522-4444
Mansfield *(G-8786)*

◆ Filnor Inc...F 330 821-8731
Alliance *(G-382)*

Future Controls Corporation................. E 440 275-3191
Austinburg *(G-700)*

Gc Controls Inc..................................... G 440 779-4777
Westlake *(G-14303)*

Harris Instrument Corporation.............. G 740 369-3580
Delaware *(G-6155)*

Helm Instrument Company Inc............. E 419 893-4356
Maumee *(G-9296)*

Hite Parts Exchange Inc...................... G 614 272-5115
Chillicothe *(G-2258)*

◆ Ideal Electric Power Co........................E 419 522-3611
Mansfield *(G-8804)*

Ignio Systems LLC............................... G 419 708-0503
Toledo *(G-12399)*

Industrial and Mar Eng Svc Co............ F 740 694-0791
Fredericktown *(G-7080)*

Innovative Controls Corp..................... F 419 691-6684
Maumee *(G-9298)*

▲ ITT Torque Systems Inc........................ C 216 524-8800
Cleveland *(G-3875)*

▲ Keene Building Products Co................. E 440 605-1020
Cleveland *(G-3910)*

◆ Kinetics Noise Control Inc...................C 614 889-0480
Dublin *(G-6316)*

L3harris Electrodynamics Inc.............. C 847 259-0740
Cincinnati *(G-2310)*

◆ Lake Shore Electric Corp......................E 440 232-0200
Bedford *(G-1043)*

▲ Logisync Corporation............................ G 440 937-0388
Avon *(G-732)*

M Technologies Inc............................... F 330 477-9009
Canton *(G-1937)*

Maags Automotive & Mch Inc .... G 419 626-1539
 Sandusky (G-11853)

Machine Drive Company .... D ... 513 793-7077
 Cincinnati (G-2837)

Miami Control Systems Inc .... G 937 233-8146
 Dayton (G-5877)

Norgren LLC .... C ... 937 833-4033
 Brookville (G-1574)

Npas Inc .... F ... 614 595-6916
 Mansfield (G-8840)

▲ Ohio Magnetics Inc .... E ... 216 662-8484
 Maple Heights (G-8888)

◆ Ohio Semitronics Inc .... D ... 614 777-1005
 Hilliard (G-7692)

Omega Tek Inc .... G ... 419 756-9580
 Mansfield (G-8843)

▲ Opw Engineered Systems Inc .... E ... 888 771-9438
 West Chester (G-14039)

Otp Holding LLC .... E ... 614 733-0979
 Plain City (G-11416)

Panel Master LLC .... E ... 440 355-4442
 Lagrange (G-8153)

▲ Pepperl + Fuchs Inc .... C ... 330 425-3555
 Twinsburg (G-13352)

PMC Systems Limited .... E ... 330 538-2268
 North Jackson (G-10693)

Primex .... G ... 513 831-9959
 Milford (G-9949)

Projects Unlimited Inc .... C ... 937 918-2200
 Dayton (G-5968)

Quality Controls Inc .... F ... 513 272-3900
 Cincinnati (G-3015)

▲ R-K Electronics Inc .... F ... 513 204-6060
 Mason (G-9141)

Ramco Electric Motors Inc .... D ... 937 548-2525
 Greenville (G-7350)

Rbb Systems Inc .... C ... 330 263-4502
 Wooster (G-14674)

Regal Beloit America Inc .... C ... 608 364-8800
 Lima (G-8443)

Rockwell Automation Inc .... F ... 440 646-7900
 Cleveland (G-4247)

Rockwell Automation Inc .... D ... 440 646-5000
 Mayfield Heights (G-9341)

Rockwell Automation Inc .... B ... 330 425-3211
 Twinsburg (G-13368)

Rockwell Automation Inc .... E ... 513 942-9828
 West Chester (G-14070)

◆ Rogers Industrial Products Inc .... E ... 330 535-3331
 Akron (G-290)

Schneider Electric Usa Inc .... D ... 513 777-4445
 West Chester (G-14073)

Sdk Associates Inc .... G ... 330 745-3648
 Norton (G-10826)

Seneca Environmental Products Inc ...... E ... 419 447-1282
 Tiffin (G-12799)

Sieb & Meyer America Inc .... F ... 513 563-0860
 West Chester (G-14145)

SMC Corporation of America .... F ... 330 659-2006
 Richfield (G-11601)

Spang & Company .... E ... 440 350-6108
 Mentor (G-9619)

▲ SSC Controls Company .... E ... 440 205-1600
 Mentor (G-9620)

▲ Standex Electronics Inc .... D ... 513 871-3777
 Fairfield (G-6778)

Stock Fairfield Corporation .... C ... 440 543-6000
 Solon (G-12185)

▲ Superb Industries Inc .... D ... 330 852-0500
 Sugarcreek (G-12652)

Te Connectivity Corporation .... C ... 419 521-9500
 Mansfield (G-8858)

Tech Products Corporation .... F ... 937 438-1100
 Miamisburg (G-9744)

Tekworx LLC .... F ... 513 533-4777
 Cincinnati (G-3142)

Temple Israel .... G ... 330 762-8617
 Akron (G-330)

Thermotion Corp .... F ... 440 639-8325
 Mentor (G-9637)

Toledo Electromotive Inc .... G ... 419 874-7751
 Perrysburg (G-11274)

Toledo Transducers Inc .... E ... 419 724-4170
 Maumee (G-9327)

Transdigm Inc .... E ... 216 291-6025
 Cleveland (G-4411)

◆ TT Electronics Integrated .... B ... 440 352-8961
 Perry (G-11200)

Tvh Parts Co .... F ... 877 755-7311
 West Chester (G-14087)

Twinsource LLC .... F ... 440 248-6800
 Solon (G-12200)

Utility Relay Co Ltd .... E ... 440 708-1000
 Chagrin Falls (G-2189)

▲ Valve Related Controls Inc .... F ... 513 677-8724
 Loveland (G-8655)

▲ Venture Mfg Co .... G ... 937 233-8792
 Dayton (G-6071)

Village Controls LLC .... F ... 614 600-8880
 Powell (G-11496)

Vintage Automotive Elc Inc .... F ... 419 472-9349
 Toledo (G-13175)

Wes-Garde Components Group Inc .... G ... 614 885-0319
 Westerville (G-14280)

◆ Wrc Holdings Inc .... F ... 330 733-6662
 Akron (G-358)

3629 Electrical industrial apparatus

Asg Division Jergens Inc .... E ... 888 486-6163
 Cleveland (G-3377)

▲ Brookwood Group Inc .... F ... 513 791-3030
 Cincinnati (G-2430)

▲ Core Technology Inc .... F ... 440 934-9935
 Avon (G-721)

Crohm LLC .... G ... 513 921-9400
 Cincinnati (G-2526)

D C Systems Inc .... F ... 330 273-3030
 Brunswick (G-1587)

Dan-Mar Company Inc .... E ... 419 660-8830
 Norwalk (G-10035)

Energy Technologies Inc .... D ... 419 522-4444
 Mansfield (G-8786)

▲ Erico Products Inc .... B ... 440 248-0100
 Cleveland (G-3683)

Eti Tech LLC .... F ... 937 832-4200
 Kettering (G-8120)

Exide Technologies LLC .... G ... 614 863-3866
 Gahanna (G-7157)

Graftech Global Entps Inc .... G ... 216 676-2000
 Cleveland (G-3781)

▲ HDR Power Systems LLC .... F ... 614 308-5500
 Worthington (G-14712)

◆ Lubrizol Global Management Inc .... F ... 216 447-5000
 Cleveland (G-3970)

Myers Controlled Power LLC .... C ... 909 923-1800
 Canton (G-1955)

◆ Noco Company .... D ... 216 464-8131
 Glenwillow (G-7286)

Plug Power Inc .... G ... 518 605-5703
 West Carrollton (G-13931)

Power Source Service LLC .... C ... 513 607-4555
 Batavia (G-883)

Proteus Electronics Inc .... G ... 419 886-2296
 Bellville (G-1142)

Sarica Manufacturing Company .... E ... 937 484-4030
 Urbana (G-13477)

▲ Solidstate Controls LLC .... C ... 614 846-7500
 Columbus (G-5274)

Spirit Avionics Ltd .... F ... 614 237-4271
 Columbus (G-5284)

Superior Packaging .... F ... 419 380-3335
 Toledo (G-13137)

▲ Takk Industries Inc .... F ... 513 353-4306
 Cleves (G-4550)

▲ Tecmark Corporation .... D ... 440 205-7600
 Mentor (G-9634)

Thermo Fisher Scientific Inc .... F ... 513 948-6290
 Blue Ash (G-1343)

TL Industries Inc .... C ... 419 666-8144
 Perrysburg (G-11272)

◆ Vanner Holdings Inc .... D ... 614 771-2718
 Hilliard (G-7709)

3631 Household cooking equipment

◆ Garland Commercial Industries LLC ... G ... 800 338-2204
 Cleveland (G-3756)

Gosun Inc .... F ... 888 868-6154
 Cincinnati (G-2684)

3632 Household refrigerators and freezers

Dover Corporation .... D ... 513 870-3206
 West Chester (G-13985)

◆ Norcold LLC .... G ... 800 543-1219
 Sidney (G-12036)

Whirlpool Corporation .... C ... 419 547-7711
 Clyde (G-4565)

Whirlpool Corporation .... D ... 419 423-8123
 Findlay (G-6935)

Whirlpool Corporation .... E ... 614 409-4340
 Lockbourne (G-8494)

Whirlpool Corporation .... D ... 740 383-7122
 Marion (G-9003)

3633 Household laundry equipment

Kitchenaid Inc .... F ... 937 316-4782
 Greenville (G-7345)

▲ Staber Industries Inc .... E ... 614 836-5995
 Groveport (G-7450)

Whirlpool Corporation .... C ... 419 547-7711
 Clyde (G-4565)

Whirlpool Corporation .... E ... 419 547-2610
 Clyde (G-1666)

Whirlpool Corporation .... E ... 614 409-4340
 Lockbourne (G-8494)

Whirlpool Corporation .... D ... 740 383-7122
 Marion (G-9003)

3634 Electric housewares and fans

Acorn Technology Corporation .... E ... 216 663-1244
 Shaker Heights (G-11925)

◆ Ad Industries Inc .... A ... 303 744-1911
 Dayton (G-5634)

Aitken Products Inc .... G ... 440 466-5711
 Geneva (G-7232)

Ces Nationwide .... G ... 937 322-0771
 Springfield (G-12289)

▲ Cleveland Range LLC .... C ... 216 481-4900
 Cleveland (G-3522)

▲ Dyoung Enterprise Inc .... C ... 440 918-0505
 Willoughby (G-14452)

Glo-Quartz Electric Htr Co Inc .... E ... 440 255-9701
 Mentor (G-9524)

◆ Hinkley Lighting Inc .... E ... 440 653-5500
 Avon Lake (G-760)

◆ Hmi Industries Inc .... E ... 440 846-7800
 Brooklyn (G-1522)

Johnson Bros Rubber Co Inc...............E 419 752-4814
Greenwich (G-7362)

Nutone Inc................................A 888 336-3948
Blue Ash (G-1314)

ORourke Sales Company...............F 877 599-6548
Grove City (G-7406)

◆ Procter & Gamble Company...........A 513 983-1100
Cincinnati (G-2999)

▲ Qualtek Electronics Corp...............C 440 951-3300
Mentor (G-9603)

Revair LLC...............................F 440 462-6100
Macedonia (G-8710)

▲ Skuttle Mfg Co........................F 740 373-9169
Marietta (G-8946)

▲ The Kitchen Collection LLC.............A 740 773-9150
Chillicothe (G-2284)

Ventilation Systems Jsc...............F 513 348-3853
Cincinnati (G-3198)

◆ Vita-Mix Manufacturing Corporation..C 440 235-4840
Olmsted Falls (G-10942)

Whirlpool Corporation..................D 937 548-4126
Greenville (G-7359)

3635 Household vacuum cleaners

H-P Products Inc.......................C 330 875-7193
Louisville (G-8601)

J K Plastics Co.........................G 440 632-1482
Middlefield (G-9802)

Powerclean Equipment Company........F 513 202-0001
Cleves (G-4547)

Royal Appliance Intl Co..................F 440 996-2000
Cleveland (G-4257)

Scott Fetzer Company..................E 216 252-1190
Cleveland (G-4279)

▲ Stanley Steemer Intl Inc................C 614 764-2007
Dublin (G-6350)

Western/Scott Fetzer Company.........C 440 871-2160
Westlake (G-14344)

3639 Household appliances, nec

ABC Appliance Inc.....................E 419 693-4414
Oregon (G-10955)

▲ Anaheim Manufacturing Company.....E 800 767-6293
North Olmsted (G-10717)

◆ New Path International LLC.............F 614 410-3974
Powell (G-11493)

▲ RAD Technologies Incorporated.......F 513 641-0523
Cincinnati (G-3030)

◆ Robura LLC...........................D 800 438-5346
Dalton (G-5593)

Rv Mobile Power LLC..................E 855 427-7978
Columbus (G-5239)

Sandco Industries......................E 419 547-3273
Clyde (G-4564)

Whirlpool Corporation..................F 419 547-7711
Clyde (G-4565)

Whirlpool Corporation..................D 419 423-8123
Findlay (G-6935)

3641 Electric lamps

◆ Advanced Lighting Tech LLC...........D 888 440-2358
Solon (G-12073)

Carlisle and Finch Company.............E 513 681-6080
Cincinnati (G-2439)

Current Elec & Enrgy Solutions.........G 513 575-4600
Loveland (G-8623)

◆ Current Lighting Solutions LLC.........E 216 462-4700
Cleveland (G-3581)

General Electric Company...............E 419 563-1200
Bucyrus (G-1682)

General Electric Company...............F 216 391-8741
Cleveland (G-3764)

General Electric Company...............F 440 593-1156
Mc Donald (G-9358)

General Electric Company...............G 330 373-1400
Warren (G-13767)

◆ Kichler Lighting LLC...................B 216 573-1000
Solon (G-12139)

▲ Lumitex Inc...........................D 440 243-8401
Strongsville (G-12572)

◆ Medallion Lighting Corporation.........E 440 255-8383
Mentor (G-9561)

Osram Sylvania Inc....................D 800 463-9275
Independence (G-7913)

Savant Technologies LLC...............F 800 435-4448
East Cleveland (G-6382)

3643 Current-carrying wiring devices

Accurate Electronics Inc...............F 330 682-7015
Orrville (G-10972)

Alcon Inc..............................E 513 722-1037
Amelia (G-427)

Apex Control Systems Inc..............D 330 938-2588
Sebring (G-11891)

Astro Industries Inc....................E 937 429-5900
Beavercreek (G-966)

▲ Brumall Manufacturing Corp............E 440 974-2622
Mentor (G-9494)

▲ C C M Wire Inc.......................F 330 425-3421
Twinsburg (G-13283)

▼ Chalfant Manufacturing Company.......G 330 273-3510
Avon (G-718)

▲ Channel Products Inc..................D 440 423-0113
Solon (G-12093)

Connectronics Corp....................E 419 537-0020
Toledo (G-12930)

Cooper Wiring Devices Inc..............D 440 523-5000
Cleveland (G-3566)

▲ Crown Electric Engrg & Mfg LLC........E 513 539-7394
Middletown (G-9852)

De Nora Tech Inc......................C 440 285-0100
Chardon (G-2203)

Desco Corporation.....................G 614 888-8855
New Albany (G-10339)

◆ Dreison International Inc...............C 216 362-0755
Cleveland (G-3632)

▲ Dynalab Inc...........................D 614 866-9999
Reynoldsburg (G-11568)

Ecm Industries LLC....................F 513 533-6242
Cincinnati (G-2578)

◆ Electric Cord Sets Inc.................G 216 261-1000
Cleveland (G-3660)

▲ Erico Products Inc....................B 440 248-0100
Cleveland (G-3683)

◆ Ericson Manufacturing Co..............D 440 951-8000
Willoughby (G-14456)

▲ General Plug and Mfg Co...............C 440 926-2411
Grafton (G-7302)

Hermetic Seal Technology Inc...........F 513 851-4899
Cincinnati (G-2719)

▲ Ilsco LLC.............................C 513 533-6200
Blue Ash (G-1287)

Innovest Energy Group LLC.............G 440 644-1027
Chesterland (G-2234)

▲ International Hydraulics Inc.............E 440 951-7186
Mentor (G-9534)

Joslyn Sunbank Company LLC..........F 805 238-2840
Cleveland (G-3894)

Kathom Manufacturing Co Inc...........E 513 868-8890
Middletown (G-9871)

▲ Knappco Corporation..................C 513 870-3100
Hamilton (G-7509)

◆ Lake Shore Electric Corp..............E 440 232-0200
Bedford (G-1043)

Legrand AV Inc........................E 574 267-8101
Blue Ash (G-1297)

Legrand North America LLC.............B 937 224-0639
Dayton (G-5843)

Marathon Special Products Corp.........C 419 352-8441
Bowling Green (G-1428)

▲ Mueller Electric Company Inc...........D 216 771-5225
Akron (G-239)

Newact Inc............................F 513 321-5177
Batavia (G-879)

Ohio Associated Entps LLC.............E 440 354-3148
Painesville (G-11102)

Parker-Hannifin Corporation............C 330 336-3511
Wadsworth (G-13659)

Pave Technology Co....................E 937 890-1100
Dayton (G-5934)

Projects Unlimited Inc..................C 937 918-2200
Dayton (G-5968)

▲ Qualtek Electronics Corp...............C 440 951-3300
Mentor (G-9603)

Reliable Hermetic Seals LLC............F 888 747-3250
Beavercreek (G-981)

◆ Rogers Industrial Products Inc.........E 330 535-3331
Akron (G-290)

▲ Royal Plastics Inc.....................C 440 352-1357
Mentor (G-9610)

▲ Saia-Burgess Lcc.....................D 937 898-3621
Vandalia (G-13576)

Sanreed Management Group LLC.........A 513 722-1037
Amelia (G-436)

Schneider Electric Usa Inc..............D 513 777-4445
West Chester (G-14073)

Siemens Industry Inc...................E 937 593-6010
Bellefontaine (G-1116)

Simpson Strong-Tie Company Inc........B 614 876-8060
Columbus (G-5271)

▲ Solon Manufacturing Company.........E 440 286-7149
Chardon (G-2223)

▲ Tecmark Corporation..................D 440 205-7600
Mentor (G-9634)

▼ The National Telephone Su.............E 216 361-0221
Cleveland (G-4388)

▲ The Vulcan Tool Company..............G 937 253-6194
Dayton (G-6050)

Tip Products Inc.......................E 216 252-2535
New London (G-10419)

◆ Watteredge Inc.......................D 440 933-6110
Avon Lake (G-773)

▲ Wedge Products Inc...................B 330 405-4477
Twinsburg (G-13395)

Xponet Inc............................G 440 354-6617
Painesville (G-11123)

3644 Noncurrent-carrying wiring devices

Akron Foundry Co......................G 330 745-3101
Barberton (G-791)

Allied Tube & Conduit Corp.............F 740 928-1018
Hebron (G-7607)

◆ Arnco Corporation....................F 800 847-7661
Elyria (G-6498)

Barracuda Technologies Inc.............G 216 469-1566
Aurora (G-663)

Bourbon Plastics Inc...................E 574 342-0893
Cuyahoga Falls (G-5533)

Danco Metal Products LLC..............D 440 871-2300
Avon Lake (G-753)

▲ Eaton Electric Holdings LLC............B 440 523-5000
Cleveland (G-3654)

◆ Erico Inc.............................E 440 248-0100
Solon (G-12105)

▲ Erico Products Inc....................B 440 248-0100
Cleveland (G-3683)

Koebbe Products Inc.............................. D 513 753-4200
Amelia **(G-430)**

Lagonda Investments III Inc.................. F 937 325-7305
Springfield **(G-12342)**

▲ Madison Electric Products Inc............. E 216 391-7776
Solon **(G-12143)**

▲ Monti Incorporated.............................. D 513 761-7775
Cincinnati **(G-2886)**

▲ Mueller Electric Company Inc........... D 216 771-5225
Akron **(G-239)**

◆ Osborne Coinage Company LLC...... D 877 480-0456
Blue Ash **(G-1316)**

Power Shelf LLC.................................... G 419 775-6125
Plymouth **(G-11433)**

Preformed Line Products Co................. B 440 461-5200
Mayfield Village **(G-9346)**

Raceway Petroleum Inc......................... G 440 989-2660
Lorain **(G-8575)**

▲ Red Seal Electric Company.............. E 216 941-3900
Cleveland **(G-4228)**

Regal Beloit America Inc...................... C 419 352-8441
Bowling Green **(G-1439)**

◆ Roechling Indus Cleveland LP......... C 216 486-0100
Cleveland **(G-4248)**

Saylor Products Corporation................ F 419 832-2125
Grand Rapids **(G-7309)**

Standex International Corp.................... D 513 533-7171
Fairfield **(G-6779)**

Tri-Fab Inc.. E 330 337-3425
Salem **(G-11815)**

◆ Vertiv Energy Systems Inc.............. A 440 288-1122
Lorain **(G-8585)**

Vertiv Group Corporation..................... G 440 288-1122
Lorain **(G-8586)**

Von Roll Usa Inc.................................. D 216 433-7474
Cleveland **(G-4481)**

Zekelman Industries Inc....................... C 740 432-2146
Cambridge **(G-1766)**

3645 Residential lighting fixtures

Acuity Brands Lighting Inc................... D 740 349-4343
Newark **(G-10489)**

◆ Advanced Lighting Tech LLC........... D 888 440-2358
Solon **(G-12073)**

◆ Besa Lighting Co Inc...................... E 614 475-7046
Blacklick **(G-1220)**

EL Ostendorf Inc.................................. G 440 247-7631
Chagrin Falls **(G-2143)**

▲ Grimes Aerospace Company........... A 937 484-2000
Urbana **(G-13462)**

◆ Hinkley Lighting Inc........................ E 440 653-5500
Avon Lake **(G-760)**

J Schrader Company............................ G 216 961-2890
Cleveland **(G-3879)**

JB Machining Concepts LLC................ G 419 523-0096
Ottawa **(G-11036)**

◆ Kichler Lighting LLC....................... B 216 573-1000
Solon **(G-12139)**

▲ Led Lighting Center Inc.................. G 714 271-2633
Toledo **(G-13029)**

Led Lighting Center LLC...................... F 888 988-6533
Toledo **(G-13030)**

Lt Moses Willard Inc............................ E 513 248-5500
Amelia **(G-431)**

Manairco Inc.. G 419 524-2121
Mansfield **(G-8817)**

◆ Medallion Lighting Corporation....... E 440 255-8383
Mentor **(G-9561)**

▲ Microsun Lamps LLC...................... G 888 328-8701
Dayton **(G-5881)**

Morel Landscaping LLC........................ F 216 551-4395
Broadview Heights **(G-1505)**

3646 Commercial lighting fixtures

Acuity Brands Lighting Inc................... C 800 754-0463
Granville **(G-7313)**

Acuity Brands Lighting Inc................... D 740 349-4343
Newark **(G-10489)**

Acuity Brands Lighting Inc................... C 740 892-2011
Utica **(G-13485)**

◆ Advanced Lighting Tech LLC........... D 888 440-2358
Solon **(G-12073)**

◆ Besa Lighting Co Inc...................... E 614 475-7046
Blacklick **(G-1220)**

◆ Best Lighting Products Inc.............. D 740 964-1198
Pataskala **(G-11137)**

◆ Bock Company LLC.......................... G 216 912-7050
Twinsburg **(G-13282)**

Current Lighting Solutions LLC............ B 216 266-4416
Cleveland **(G-3580)**

◆ Current Lighting Solutions LLC........ G 216 462-4700
Cleveland **(G-3581)**

▲ Damak 1 LLC.................................. E 513 858-6004
Fairfield **(G-6725)**

◆ Eaton Electric Holdings LLC........... B 440 523-5000
Cleveland **(G-3654)**

Etherium Lighting LLC.......................... G 614 388-9893
Columbus **(G-4911)**

Evp International LLC............................ G 513 761-7614
Cincinnati **(G-2607)**

GE Lighting Inc.................................... D 216 266-2121
Cleveland **(G-3759)**

General Electric Company..................... F 330 458-3200
Canton **(G-1899)**

▲ Genesis Lamp Corp......................... F 440 354-0095
Painesville **(G-11088)**

▲ Grimes Aerospace Company........... A 937 484-2000
Urbana **(G-13462)**

Hercules Led LLC................................ E 844 437-2533
Boardman **(G-1374)**

◆ Hinkley Lighting Inc........................ E 440 653-5500
Avon Lake **(G-760)**

Holophane Corporation......................... F 740 349-4194
Newark **(G-10506)**

◆ Holophane Corporation.................... C 866 759-1577
Granville **(G-7316)**

J Schrader Company............................ G 216 961-2890
Cleveland **(G-3879)**

JB Machining Concepts LLC................ G 419 523-0096
Ottawa **(G-11036)**

▲ King Luminaire Company Inc.......... E 440 576-9073
Jefferson **(G-7975)**

▲ Led Lighting Center Inc.................. G 714 271-2633
Toledo **(G-13029)**

Led Lighting Center LLC...................... F 888 988-6533
Toledo **(G-13030)**

▲ Light Craft Manufacturing Inc......... F 419 332-0536
Fremont **(G-7121)**

LSI Industries Inc................................ C 913 281-1100
Blue Ash **(G-1299)**

▲ LSI Lightron Inc.............................. A 845 562-5500
Blue Ash **(G-1300)**

Lumenforce Led LLC............................ E 330 330-8962
Youngstown **(G-14889)**

▲ Lumitex Inc..................................... D 440 243-8401
Strongsville **(G-12572)**

M-Boss Inc.. E 216 441-6080
Cleveland **(G-3976)**

Magnum Asset Acquisition LLC........... E 330 915-2382
Hudson **(G-7851)**

▲ Nordic Light America Inc................ F 614 981-9497
Canal Winchester **(G-1796)**

Norton Industries Inc........................... E 888 357-2345
Lakewood **(G-8171)**

NRG Industrial Lighting Mfg Co........... G 419 354-8207
Bowling Green **(G-1431)**

Power Source Service LLC................... G 513 607-4555
Batavia **(G-883)**

SMS Technologies Inc.......................... F 419 465-4175
Monroeville **(G-10121)**

Stress-Crete Company.......................... E 440 576-9073
Jefferson **(G-7983)**

Treemen Industries Inc........................ E 330 965-3777
Boardman **(G-1378)**

3647 Vehicular lighting equipment

◆ Advanced Technology Corp............. F 440 293-4064
Andover **(G-454)**

Akron Brass Company.......................... E 614 529-7230
Columbus **(G-4682)**

Akron Brass Company.......................... E 800 228-1161
Wooster **(G-14619)**

◆ Akron Brass Company..................... B 330 264-5678
Wooster **(G-14620)**

▲ Atc Group Inc.................................. D 440 293-4064
Andover **(G-455)**

▲ Atc Lighting & Plastics Inc............. C 440 466-7670
Andover **(G-456)**

Grimes Aerospace Company................ D 937 484-2001
Urbana **(G-13464)**

▲ Grimes Aerospace Company........... A 937 484-2000
Urbana **(G-13462)**

▲ K-D Lamp Company......................... E 440 293-4064
Andover **(G-457)**

▲ Lighting Products Inc...................... F 440 293-4064
Andover **(G-458)**

Rvtronix Corporation............................ E 440 359-7200
Eastlake **(G-6442)**

▲ Stanley Electric US Co Inc.............. E 740 852-5200
London **(G-8541)**

Treemen Industries Inc........................ E 330 965-3777
Boardman **(G-1378)**

Washington Products Inc...................... F 330 837-5101
Massillon **(G-9252)**

3648 Lighting equipment, nec

Aat USA LLC....................................... G 614 388-8866
Columbus **(G-4658)**

Acuity Brands Lighting Inc................... D 740 349-4343
Newark **(G-10489)**

◆ ADB Safegate Americas LLC........... C 614 861-1304
Gahanna **(G-7152)**

◆ Advanced Lighting Tech LLC........... D 888 440-2358
Solon **(G-12073)**

Akron Brass Company.......................... E 614 529-7230
Columbus **(G-4682)**

Architectural Busstrut Corp.................. F 614 933-8695
New Albany **(G-10329)**

▲ Atc Lighting & Plastics Inc............. C 440 466-7670
Andover **(G-456)**

Avid Lighting LLC................................ G 614 502-2843
Hilliard **(G-7670)**

B2d Solutions Inc................................ G 855 484-1145
Cleveland **(G-3402)**

Brightguy Inc....................................... G 440 942-8318
Willoughby **(G-14434)**

Carlisle and Finch Company................ E 513 681-6080
Cincinnati **(G-2439)**

Cooper Lighting LLC............................ G 800 334-6871
Columbus **(G-4848)**

▲ Delta Power Supply Inc.................. F 513 771-3835
Cincinnati **(G-2545)**

◆ Ericson Manufacturing Co............... D 440 951-8000
Willoughby **(G-14456)**

Fulton Industries LLC........................... D 419 270-3937
Wauseon **(G-13849)**

S
I
C

General Electric Company.................G..... 330 373-1400
  Warren (G-13767)

▲ Genesis Lamp Corp.......................F..... 440 354-0095
  Painesville (G-11088)

▲ Global Lighting Tech Inc.................E..... 440 922-4584
  Brecksville (G-1468)

◆ Holophane Corporation..................C..... 866 759-1577
  Granville (G-7316)

Hughey & Phillips LLC......................E..... 937 652-3500
  Urbana (G-13467)

▼ Innove Inc......................................D..... 440 836-0199
  Macedonia (G-8697)

◆ Kichler Lighting LLC.......................B..... 216 573-1000
  Solon (G-12139)

◆ Lintern Corporation.........................E..... 440 255-9333
  Mentor (G-9554)

LSI Industries Inc.............................C..... 513 793-3200
  Cincinnati (G-2830)

▲ Lumitex Inc......................................D..... 440 243-8401
  Strongsville (G-12572)

Manairco Inc.....................................G..... 419 524-2121
  Mansfield (G-8817)

Miami Valley Lighting LLC................G..... 937 224-6000
  Dayton (G-5620)

Midmark Corporation........................G..... 937 526-3662
  Versailles (G-13600)

Midmark Corporation........................E..... 937 526-8387
  Versailles (G-13601)

◆ Midmark Corporation........................A..... 937 528-7500
  Miamisburg (G-9717)

▲ National Biological Corp..................E..... 216 831-0600
  Beachwood (G-931)

Stadium Grow Lighting Inc...............G..... 855 346-9403
  Warren (G-13798)

Stamp & Flash Inc...........................D..... 419 335-3015
  Wauseon (G-13859)

Starbright Lighting USA LLC.............G..... 330 650-2000
  Hudson (G-7859)

◆ Union Metal Corporation.................B..... 330 456-7653
  Canton (G-2032)

◆ Vanner Holdings Inc........................D..... 614 771-2718
  Hilliard (G-7709)

▲ Will-Burt Company..........................C..... 330 682-7015
  Orrville (G-11018)

3651 Household audio and video equipment

5 Core Inc.......................................F..... 951 386-6372
  Bellefontaine (G-1098)

Althar LLC.......................................F..... 216 408-9860
  Cleveland (G-3335)

Andersound PA Service.....................G..... 216 401-4631
  Cleveland (G-3359)

▲ Avtek International Inc.....................G..... 330 633-7500
  Silver Lake (G-12063)

Background Music & Sound Inc.........G..... 937 898-9871
  Dayton (G-5673)

Bose Corporation..............................G..... 513 891-4384
  Cincinnati (G-2418)

China Enterprises Inc.......................G..... 419 885-1485
  Toledo (G-12920)

▲ Cochran 6573 LLC...........................F..... 440 349-4900
  Solon (G-12097)

Dare Electronics Inc.........................E..... 937 335-0031
  Troy (G-13208)

Db Unlimited LLC.............................G..... 937 401-2602
  Dayton (G-5743)

Dr Z Amps Inc..................................F..... 216 475-1444
  Maple Heights (G-8883)

Eprad Inc...G..... 419 666-3266
  Perrysburg (G-11219)

Fellhauer Mechanical Systems..........E..... 419 734-3674
  Port Clinton (G-11441)

▲ Floyd Bell Inc..................................D..... 614 294-4000
  Columbus (G-4930)

◆ J & C Group Inc of Ohio..................G..... 440 205-9658
  Mentor (G-9536)

◆ Mitsubishi Elc Auto Amer Inc...........B..... 513 573-6614
  Mason (G-9128)

Ohio Hd Video..................................F..... 614 656-1162
  New Albany (G-10348)

◆ Phantom Sound...............................G..... 513 759-4477
  Loveland (G-8644)

◆ Pioneer Automotive Tech Inc...........C..... 937 746-2293
  Miamisburg (G-9727)

Pro Audio...G..... 513 752-7500
  Cincinnati (G-2314)

Tech Products Corporation................F..... 937 438-1100
  Miamisburg (G-9744)

Technical Artistry Inc.......................G..... 614 299-7777
  Columbus (G-5316)

Technicolor Usa Inc..........................A..... 614 474-8821
  Circleville (G-3265)

◆ Tls Corp...D..... 216 574-4759
  Cleveland (G-4396)

Tune Town Car Audio........................G..... 419 627-1100
  Sandusky (G-11878)

Tvone Ncsa.......................................G..... 859 282-7303
  Cincinnati (G-3177)

▲ UNI Corp...E..... 800 782-3296
  Canton (G-2031)

Universal Electronics Inc...................G..... 330 487-1110
  Twinsburg (G-13389)

3652 Prerecorded records and tapes

Cuttercroix LLC.................................E..... 330 289-6185
  Cleveland (G-3588)

Fluid Handling Dynamics Ltd.............F..... 419 633-0560
  Bryan (G-1642)

Jk Digital Publishing LLC..................G..... 937 299-0185
  Springboro (G-12256)

Qca Inc...E..... 513 681-8400
  Cincinnati (G-3014)

3661 Telephone and telegraph apparatus

7signal Inc.......................................E..... 216 777-2900
  Independence (G-7886)

◆ Arnco Corporation............................F..... 800 847-7661
  Elyria (G-6498)

AT&T Enterprises LLC.......................G..... 513 792-9300
  Cincinnati (G-2384)

Black Box Corporation......................E..... 614 825-7400
  Lewis Center (G-8325)

Black Box Corporation......................G..... 855 324-9909
  Westlake (G-14292)

Commercial Electric Pdts Corp..........E..... 216 241-2886
  Cleveland (G-3552)

Concentrix Cvg LLC..........................D..... 972 454-8000
  Cincinnati (G-2509)

Cotsworks Inc...................................D..... 440 446-8800
  Highland Heights (G-7656)

Crase Communications Inc................G..... 419 468-1173
  Galion (G-7186)

Cutting Edge Technologies Inc...........G..... 216 574-4759
  Cleveland (G-3589)

DSI Management Holdings LLC..........F..... 800 645-7002
  Kent (G-8027)

DTE Inc...E..... 419 522-3428
  Mansfield (G-8781)

▲ Dynalab Inc......................................D..... 614 866-9999
  Reynoldsburg (G-11568)

Em4 LLC...E..... 410 987-5600
  Cleveland (G-3666)

▲ Floyd Bell Inc..................................D..... 614 294-4000
  Columbus (G-4930)

Fremont Plastic Products Inc.............C..... 419 332-6407
  Fremont (G-7111)

▲ Kentrox Inc......................................D..... 614 798-2000
  Dublin (G-6335)

Preformed Line Products Co..............B..... 440 461-5200
  Mayfield Village (G-9346)

Pro Oncall Technologies LLC.............F..... 614 761-1400
  Dublin (G-6335)

Siemens AG......................................G..... 513 576-2451
  Mason (G-9151)

◆ Tls Corp...D..... 216 574-4759
  Cleveland (G-4396)

Total Call Center Solutions...............F..... 330 869-9844
  Akron (G-341)

◆ Vertiv Energy Systems Inc...............A..... 440 288-1122
  Lorain (G-8585)

Vertiv Group Corporation..................G..... 440 460-3600
  Cleveland (G-4461)

Vertiv Group Corporation..................G..... 440 288-1122
  Lorain (G-8586)

Wan Dynamics Inc............................F..... 877 400-9490
  Medina (G-9462)

3663 Radio and t.v. communications equipment

Accurate Electronics Inc...................F..... 330 682-7015
  Orrville (G-10972)

Barco Inc...E..... 937 372-7579
  Xenia (G-14753)

CDI Industries Inc.............................E..... 440 243-1100
  Cleveland (G-3481)

Central USA Wireless LLC.................G..... 513 469-1500
  Cincinnati (G-2453)

Circle Prime Manufacturing Inc..........E..... 330 923-0019
  Cuyahoga Falls (G-5534)

Control Industries Inc.......................G..... 937 653-7694
  Findlay (G-6855)

David Chojnacki................................E..... 303 905-1918
  Westerville (G-14254)

Diamond Electronics Inc....................G..... 740 652-9222
  Lancaster (G-8196)

Edl Displays Inc................................E..... 937 429-7423
  Beavercreek (G-974)

Eei Acquisition Corp.........................E..... 440 564-5484
  Middlefield (G-9793)

Electro-Magwave Inc.........................G..... 216 453-1160
  Twinsburg (G-13298)

Engineered Endeavors Inc.................E..... 440 564-5484
  Newbury (G-10550)

Estone Group LLC.............................E..... 888 653-2246
  Toledo (G-12957)

Garage Scenes Ltd...........................F..... 614 407-6094
  Westerville (G-14211)

▲ Gatesair Inc.....................................D..... 513 459-3400
  Mason (G-9102)

Great Lakes Telcom Ltd.....................E..... 330 629-8848
  Youngstown (G-14870)

Imagine Communications Corp...........G..... 513 459-3400
  Mason (G-9110)

L-3 Cmmncations Nova Engrg Inc.......F..... 877 282-1168
  Mason (G-9120)

L3 Technologies Inc..........................G..... 937 257-8501
  Dayton (G-5616)

Linear Acoustic Inc...........................G..... 717 735-3611
  Cleveland (G-3959)

Liquid Image Corp America................G..... 216 458-9800
  Cleveland (G-3963)

LSI Industries Inc.............................C..... 513 793-3200
  Cincinnati (G-2830)

▲ Nissin Precision N Amer Inc.............D..... 937 836-1910
  Englewood (G-6620)

◆ Ohio Semitronics Inc..........................D 614 777-1005
   Hilliard (G-7692)

Pole/Zero LLC.......................................C 513 870-9060
   West Chester (G-14050)

Punch Components Inc..........................E 419 224-1242
   Lima (G-8441)

Quasonix Inc..E 513 942-1287
   West Chester (G-14058)

Rev38 LLC...G 937 572-4000
   West Chester (G-14067)

Sagequest LLC......................................D 216 896-7243
   Solon (G-12177)

Starwin Industries LLC.........................E 937 293-8568
   Dayton (G-6024)

▲ Tencom Ltd..G 419 865-5877
   Holland (G-7787)

◆ Tls Corp...D 216 574-4759
   Cleveland (G-4396)

▲ Valco Melton Inc.................................E 513 874-6550
   West Chester (G-14158)

Watts Antenna Company.......................G 740 797-9380
   The Plains (G-12761)

Wireless Retail LLC..............................F 614 657-5182
   Blacklick (G-1231)

3669 Communications equipment, nec

A & A Safety Inc....................................F 937 567-9781
   Beavercreek (G-987)

▲ Athens Technical Specialists..............F 740 592-2874
   Athens (G-634)

Bender Communications Inc..................F 740 382-0000
   Marion (G-8965)

Bird Technologies Group Inc.................C 440 248-1200
   Solon (G-12085)

▲ Ceia Usa Ltd......................................D 330 310-4741
   Hudson (G-7836)

City Elyria Communication....................G 440 322-3329
   Elyria (G-6513)

City of Canton.......................................E 330 489-3370
   Canton (G-1866)

▼ Data Processing Sciences..................D 513 791-7100
   Cincinnati (G-2542)

▲ Findaway World LLC...........................E 440 893-0808
   Solon (G-12111)

▲ Floyd Bell Inc.....................................D 614 294-4000
   Columbus (G-4930)

General Dynmics Mssion Systems.........F 513 253-4770
   Beavercreek (G-975)

Honeywell International Inc...................A 937 484-2000
   Urbana (G-13466)

Intelligent Signal Tech Intl...................G 614 530-4784
   Loveland (G-8632)

Ohio Department Transportation...........E 614 351-2898
   Columbus (G-5140)

▲ Ohio Magnetics Inc............................E 216 662-8484
   Maple Heights (G-8888)

Paul Peterson Company........................F 614 486-4375
   Columbus (G-5178)

PM Power Products LLC........................G 614 652-6509
   Dublin (G-6332)

Quasonix Inc..E 513 942-1287
   West Chester (G-14058)

Resideo LLC..G 440 439-7002
   Bedford (G-1057)

Resideo LLC..F 513 772-1851
   Cincinnati (G-3039)

▲ Saltillo Corporation............................G 330 674-6722
   Millersburg (G-10008)

Security Fence Group Inc......................E 513 681-3700
   Cincinnati (G-3074)

Signature Technologies Inc...................E 937 859-6323
   Miamisburg (G-9737)

Sound Communications Inc...................E 614 875-8500
   Grove City (G-7414)

Status Solutions LLC............................D 434 296-1789
   Westerville (G-14235)

Total Life Safety LLC............................F 866 955-2318
   West Chester (G-14083)

Union Metal Industries Corp.................E 330 456-7653
   Canton (G-2033)

Voice Products Inc................................F 216 360-0433
   Cleveland (G-4479)

3672 Printed circuit boards

Accurate Electronics Inc.......................F 330 682-7015
   Orrville (G-10972)

Alektronics Inc.....................................F 937 429-2118
   Beavercreek (G-988)

Avcom Smt Inc......................................F 614 882-8176
   Westerville (G-14244)

Blue Creek Enterprises Inc...................F 937 222-9969
   Dayton (G-5680)

Blue Creek Enterprises Inc...................F 937 364-2920
   Manchester (G-8753)

C E Electronics Inc...............................D 419 636-6705
   Bryan (G-1635)

▼ Cartessa Corp....................................F 513 738-4477
   Shandon (G-11933)

Circle Prime Manufacturing Inc............G 330 923-0019
   Cuyahoga Falls (G-5534)

Cleveland Circuits Corp........................E 216 267-9020
   Cleveland (G-3509)

Cleveland Coretec Inc...........................G 314 727-2087
   North Jackson (G-10685)

Co-Ax Technology Inc...........................C 440 914-9200
   Solon (G-12096)

Ddi North Jackson Corp........................G 330 538-3900
   North Jackson (G-10686)

Deca Mfg Co..F 419 884-0071
   Mansfield (G-8780)

▲ Dynalab Inc..D 614 866-9999
   Reynoldsburg (G-11568)

Flex Fab LLC...G 330 757-8720
   Poland (G-11436)

Flextronics Intl USA Inc........................E 513 755-2500
   Middletown (G-9861)

▲ Interactive Engineering Corp..............E 330 239-6888
   Medina (G-9413)

Journey Electronics Corp......................G 513 539-9836
   Monroe (G-10111)

L3 Technologies Inc..............................E 513 943-2000
   Cincinnati (G-2309)

Levison Enterprises LLC.......................E 419 838-7365
   Millbury (G-9964)

Libra Industries LLC.............................C 440 974-7770
   Mentor (G-9553)

▲ Logisync Corporation.........................G 440 937-0388
   Avon (G-732)

▲ McGregor & Associates Inc...............C 937 629-4346
   Brookville (G-1573)

Metzenbaum Sheltered Inds Inc............E 440 729-1919
   Chesterland (G-2236)

Npas Inc..F 614 595-6916
   Mansfield (G-8840)

▲ Parlex USA LLC..................................F 937 898-3621
   Vandalia (G-13575)

Philway Products Inc............................C 419 281-7777
   Ashland (G-561)

Projects Unlimited Inc...........................C 937 918-2200
   Dayton (G-5968)

Proto Circuit Inc...................................G 330 572-3400
   Cuyahoga Falls (G-5567)

▲ Qualtech Technologies Inc..................E 440 946-8081
   Willoughby (G-14514)

Quarter Century Design LLC.................G 937 434-5127
   Dayton (G-5970)

▲ R-K Electronics Inc.............................F 513 204-6060
   Mason (G-9141)

Sinbon Ohio LLC...................................C 937 415-2070
   Vandalia (G-13577)

▲ Techtron Systems Inc.........................E 440 505-2990
   Solon (G-12195)

Tetrad Electronics Inc...........................D 440 946-6443
   Willoughby (G-14539)

Ttm Technologies Inc............................C 330 538-3900
   North Jackson (G-10696)

Ttm Technologies North America LLC... D 330 572-3400
   North Jackson (G-10697)

Valtronic Technology Inc.......................D 440 349-1239
   Solon (G-12201)

Versitec Manufacturing Inc...................F 440 354-4283
   Painesville (G-11121)

Vexos Inc...B 440 284-2500
   Lagrange (G-8155)

Wurth Electronics Ics Inc......................E 937 415-7700
   Miamisburg (G-9754)

3674 Semiconductors and related devices

AT&T Enterprises LLC...........................G 513 792-9300
   Cincinnati (G-2384)

Brocade Cmmnctions Systems LLC...... G 614 232-8015
   Columbus (G-4782)

▲ Burke Products Inc.............................E 937 372-3516
   Xenia (G-14756)

Ceso Inc..E 937 435-8584
   Miamisburg (G-9681)

▲ Cks Solution Incorporated..................E 513 947-1277
   Fairfield (G-6723)

Communication Concepts Inc................G 937 426-8600
   Beavercreek (G-968)

D F Electronics Inc...............................D 513 772-7792
   Cincinnati (G-2537)

Dan-Mar Company Inc...........................E 419 660-8830
   Norwalk (G-10835)

Darrah Electric Company......................F 216 631-0912
   Chesterland (G-2233)

Em4 LLC..E 608 240-4800
   Cleveland (G-3667)

Ezurio LLC...D 330 434-7929
   Akron (G-141)

First Solar Inc.......................................F 419 661-1478
   Perrysburg (G-11222)

Gen Digital Inc......................................G 330 252-1171
   Akron (G-159)

Gen Digital Inc......................................G 614 418-1700
   Columbus (G-4947)

Gopowerx Inc..E 440 707-6029
   Richfield (G-11594)

Greenfield Solar Corp...........................G 216 535-9200
   North Ridgeville (G-10732)

Harrison Corporation............................G 513 681-2420
   Cincinnati (G-2708)

▲ Hawthorne Hydroponics LLC..............F 888 478-6544
   Marysville (G-9024)

Heraeus Electro-Nite Co LLC................G 330 725-1419
   Medina (G-9408)

Honeywell International Inc...................E 302 327-8920
   Columbus (G-4990)

Hyper Tech Research Inc......................F 614 481-8050
   Columbus (G-4995)

Illuminate USA LLC..............................A 614 598-9742
   Pataskala (G-11140)

▲ Isofoton North America Inc.................F 419 591-4330
   Napoleon (G-10288)

Lam Research Corporation....................F 937 472-3311
   Eaton (G-6458)

Leidos Inc.................................D 937 656-8433
  Beavercreek *(G-977)*

Linear Asics Inc..........................G 330 474-3920
  Twinsburg *(G-13333)*

Linear Technology LLC...................G 440 239-0817
  Cleveland *(G-3960)*

▲ Materion Brush Inc....................D 216 486-4200
  Mayfield Heights *(G-9336)*

◆ Materion Corporation..................C 216 486-4200
  Mayfield Heights *(G-9337)*

Measurement Specialties Inc............C 937 427-1231
  Dayton *(G-5872)*

Micro Industries Corporation............D 740 548-7878
  Westerville *(G-14270)*

▲ Monti Incorporated....................D 513 761-7775
  Cincinnati *(G-2886)*

Niobium Microsystems Inc..............G 937 203-8117
  Dayton *(G-5907)*

◆ Ohio Semitronics Inc..................D 614 777-1005
  Hilliard *(G-7692)*

▲ Pepperl + Fuchs Inc..................C 330 425-3555
  Twinsburg *(G-13352)*

Plug Power Inc...........................G 518 605-5703
  West Carrollton *(G-13931)*

Redhawk Energy Systems LLC...........G 740 927-8244
  Pataskala *(G-11146)*

Refocus Holdings Inc....................E 216 751-8384
  Cleveland *(G-4231)*

◆ Rexon Components Inc................E 216 292-7373
  Beachwood *(G-945)*

Rv Mobile Power LLC....................E 855 427-7978
  Columbus *(G-5239)*

Saint-Gobain Ceramics Plas Inc........B 440 542-2712
  Newbury *(G-10563)*

Salient Systems Inc......................E 614 792-5800
  Dublin *(G-6343)*

SCI Engineered Materials Inc............E 614 486-0261
  Columbus *(G-5255)*

Signature Technologies Inc..............E 937 859-6323
  Miamisburg *(G-9737)*

Silfex Inc.................................B 937 324-2487
  Springfield *(G-12373)*

▲ Silfex Inc.............................E 937 472-3311
  Eaton *(G-6463)*

Smart Microsystems Ltd.................F 440 366-4257
  Elyria *(G-6590)*

Spang & Company........................E 440 350-6108
  Mentor *(G-9619)*

▲ Techneglas LLC.......................F 419 873-2000
  Perrysburg *(G-11268)*

Toledo Solar Inc..........................F 567 202-4145
  Perrysburg *(G-11275)*

▲ Tosoh SMD Inc........................D 614 875-7912
  Grove City *(G-7418)*

Tri-Tech Led Systems LLC...............G 614 593-2868
  Baltimore *(G-788)*

▲ Ustek Incorporated....................F 614 538-8000
  Columbus *(G-5342)*

Viavi Solutions Inc.......................F 316 522-4981
  Columbus *(G-4651)*

3675 Electronic capacitors

CPI Group Limited........................F 216 525-0046
  Cleveland *(G-3573)*

Oren Elliot Products LLC.................E 419 298-0015
  Edgerton *(G-6468)*

Soemhejee Inc...........................E 419 298-2306
  Edgerton *(G-6469)*

Standex International Corp...............D 513 533-7171
  Fairfield *(G-6779)*

3676 Electronic resistors

Apex Control Systems Inc................D 330 938-2588
  Sebring *(G-11891)*

Measurement Specialties Inc............C 937 427-1231
  Dayton *(G-5872)*

3677 Electronic coils and transformers

Barnes International LLC.................E 419 352-7501
  Bowling Green *(G-1407)*

Contech Strmwter Solutions LLC........G 513 645-7000
  West Chester *(G-13973)*

▲ Duca Manufacturing & Cons..........E 330 758-0828
  Youngstown *(G-14850)*

Electric Service Co Inc..................E 513 271-6387
  Cincinnati *(G-2580)*

Electromotive Inc.........................E 330 688-6494
  Stow *(G-12427)*

Fontaine Pieciak Engrg Inc..............G 413 592-2273
  Twinsburg *(G-13304)*

◆ Foster Transformer Company.........E 513 681-2420
  Cincinnati *(G-2637)*

Harrison Corporation.....................G 513 681-2420
  Cincinnati *(G-2708)*

Illinois Tool Works Inc...................E 262 248-8277
  Bryan *(G-1645)*

▲ Industrial Quartz Corporation.........F 440 942-0909
  Mentor *(G-9530)*

▲ Kurz-Kasch Inc........................E 740 498-8343
  Newcomerstown *(G-10572)*

◆ Micropure Filtration Inc...............G 952 472-2323
  Cleveland *(G-4028)*

▼ Norlake Manufacturing Company......D 440 353-3200
  North Ridgeville *(G-10741)*

Npas Inc..................................F 614 595-6916
  Mansfield *(G-8840)*

Nu Stream Filtration Inc.................F 937 949-3174
  Dayton *(G-5918)*

PCC Airfoils LLC.........................B 216 692-7900
  Cleveland *(G-4148)*

Rapid Mr International LLC...............G 614 486-6300
  Columbus *(G-5224)*

Schneider Electric Usa Inc...............B 513 523-4171
  Oxford *(G-11064)*

Staco Energy Products Co...............E 937 253-1191
  Dayton *(G-6020)*

◆ Staco Energy Products Co............G 937 253-1191
  Miamisburg *(G-9739)*

▲ Swiger Coil Systems Ltd..............C 216 362-7500
  Cleveland *(G-4356)*

▲ USA Instruments Inc..................C 330 562-1000
  Aurora *(G-692)*

Wabtec Corporation......................F 216 362-7500
  Cleveland *(G-4485)*

3678 Electronic connectors

◆ American Micro Products Inc..........C 513 732-2674
  Batavia *(G-850)*

Ankim Enterprises Incorporated.........G 937 599-1121
  Sidney *(G-11993)*

Astro Industries Inc......................E 937 429-5900
  Beavercreek *(G-966)*

▲ C C M Wire Inc........................F 330 425-3421
  Twinsburg *(G-13283)*

Canadus Power Systems LLC............F 216 831-6600
  Twinsburg *(G-13284)*

Connective Design Incorporated........F 937 746-8252
  Miamisburg *(G-9683)*

▲ Connectors Unlimited Inc.............E 440 357-1161
  Painesville *(G-11074)*

Connectronics Corp......................E 419 537-0020
  Toledo *(G-12930)*

▲ Custom Connector Corporation.......E 216 241-1679
  Cleveland *(G-3585)*

Dcm Soundex Inc.........................F 937 522-0371
  Dayton *(G-5744)*

▲ Dynalab Inc............................D 614 866-9999
  Reynoldsburg *(G-11568)*

Ecm Industries LLC......................F 513 533-6242
  Cincinnati *(G-2578)*

HCC/Sealtron.............................C 513 733-8400
  Cincinnati *(G-2714)*

▲ Ilsco LLC...............................C 513 533-6200
  Blue Ash *(G-1287)*

Joslyn Sunbank Company LLC...........F 805 238-2840
  Cleveland *(G-3894)*

▲ Lastar Inc..............................B 937 224-0639
  Moraine *(G-10174)*

Mueller Electric Company Inc...........G 614 888-8855
  New Albany *(G-10346)*

◆ Network Technologies Inc.............D 330 562-7070
  Aurora *(G-681)*

Ohio Associated Entps LLC..............F 440 354-3148
  Painesville *(G-11101)*

◆ Plcc2 LLC..............................G 614 279-1796
  Columbus *(G-5197)*

Powell Electrical Systems Inc............D 330 966-1750
  North Canton *(G-10660)*

Qnnect LLC...............................G 864 275-8970
  Painesville *(G-11107)*

Standex International Corp...............D 513 533-7171
  Fairfield *(G-6779)*

Xponet Inc................................G 440 354-6617
  Painesville *(G-11123)*

3679 Electronic components, nec

Accurate Electronics Inc.................F 330 682-7015
  Orrville *(G-10972)*

Advanced Cryogenic Entps Inc..........F 330 922-0750
  Akron *(G-20)*

Aeroseal LLC.............................E 937 428-9300
  Dayton *(G-5638)*

▲ Aeroseal LLC..........................E 937 428-9300
  Miamisburg *(G-9662)*

Alphabet Inc..............................D 330 856-3366
  Warren *(G-13733)*

American Advnced Assmblies LLC.......E 937 339-6267
  Troy *(G-13199)*

Ankim Enterprises Incorporated.........G 937 599-1121
  Sidney *(G-11993)*

Astro Industries Inc......................E 937 429-5900
  Beavercreek *(G-966)*

Bennett & Bennett Inc....................G 937 324-1100
  Yellow Springs *(G-14786)*

Berry Investments Inc....................G 937 293-0398
  Moraine *(G-10150)*

Black Box Corporation....................E 614 825-7400
  Lewis Center *(G-8325)*

Black Box Corporation....................G 855 324-9909
  Westlake *(G-14292)*

▲ C C M Wire Inc........................F 330 425-3421
  Twinsburg *(G-13283)*

C E Electronics Inc.......................D 419 636-6705
  Bryan *(G-1635)*

Captor Corporation.......................D 937 667-8484
  Tipp City *(G-12818)*

CEC Electronics Corp....................G 330 916-8100
  Akron *(G-92)*

▲ Channel Products Inc..................D 440 423-0113
  Solon *(G-12093)*

▲ Cks Solution Incorporated............E 513 947-1277
  Fairfield *(G-6723)*

▲ Cleanlife Energy LLC..................F 800 316-2532
  Cleveland *(G-3503)*

CMC Electronics Cincinn.................G 513 573-6316
  Mason *(G-9091)*

Co-Ax Technology Inc............................C 440 914-9200
Solon *(G-12096)*

Connective Design Incorporated...........F ... 937 746-8252
Miamisburg *(G-9683)*

Cutting Edge Technologies Inc..............G 216 574-4759
Cleveland *(G-3589)*

D H S LLC..F ... 937 599-2485
Bellefontaine *(G-1103)*

Dare Electronics Inc...............................E ... 937 335-0031
Troy *(G-13208)*

Darrah Electric Company.......................F ... 216 631-0912
Chesterland *(G-2233)*

Dcm Soundex Inc....................................F ... 937 522-0371
Dayton *(G-5744)*

Deca Mfg Co...F ... 419 884-0071
Mansfield *(G-8780)*

Dish One Up Satellite Inc.......................D ... 216 482-3875
Cleveland *(G-3618)*

Don-Ell Corporation.................................E ... 419 841-7114
Sylvania *(G-12704)*

Drivetrain USA Inc...................................F ... 614 733-0940
Plain City *(G-11405)*

▲ Dynalab Ems Inc...................................C ... 614 866-9999
Reynoldsburg *(G-11566)*

▲ Dynalab Ff Inc.......................................D ... 614 866-9999
Reynoldsburg *(G-11567)*

▲ Dynalab Inc..D ... 614 866-9999
Reynoldsburg *(G-11568)*

Electro-Line Inc.......................................F ... 937 461-5683
Dayton *(G-5762)*

Electromotive Inc....................................E ... 330 688-6494
Stow *(G-12427)*

◆ Electronauts LLC...................................F ... 859 261-3600
Cincinnati *(G-2581)*

Eti Tech LLC..F ... 937 832-4200
Kettering *(G-8120)*

Ewh Spectrum LLC.................................D ... 937 593-8010
Bellefontaine *(G-1107)*

Focus Manufacturing LLC......................F ... 440 946-8766
Mentor *(G-9517)*

Gem City Engineering Co.......................C ... 937 223-5544
Dayton *(G-5792)*

Gmelectric Inc...G ... 330 477-3392
Canton *(G-1902)*

▲ Great Lakes Glasswerks Inc...............G ... 440 358-0460
Painesville *(G-11090)*

Hall Company..E ... 937 652-1376
Urbana *(G-13465)*

Innocomp...G ... 440 248-5104
Solon *(G-12127)*

▲ Inservco Inc...D ... 847 855-9600
Lagrange *(G-8148)*

▲ Kent Displays Inc..................................D ... 330 673-8784
Kent *(G-8040)*

◆ Kontron America Incorporated............F ... 937 324-2420
Springfield *(G-12339)*

▲ L & J Cable Inc......................................E ... 937 526-9445
Russia *(G-11675)*

La Grange Elec Assemblies Co.............E ... 440 355-5388
Lagrange *(G-8149)*

Laird Technologies Inc...........................F ... 330 434-7929
Akron *(G-201)*

Lake Shore Cryotronics Inc...................D ... 614 891-2243
Westerville *(G-14217)*

Leidos Inc..D ... 937 656-8433
Beavercreek *(G-977)*

Lintech Electronics LLC.........................E ... 513 528-6190
Cincinnati *(G-2312)*

Malabar Properties LLC.........................F ... 419 884-0071
Mansfield *(G-8816)*

Mega Techway Inc..................................D ... 440 605-0700
Cleveland *(G-4018)*

Microplex Inc...E ... 330 498-0600
North Canton *(G-10651)*

▲ MJM Industries Inc...............................C ... 440 350-1230
Fairport Harbor *(G-6819)*

Mjo Industries Inc...................................D ... 800 590-4055
Huber Heights *(G-7822)*

Mueller Electric Company Inc................G ... 614 888-8855
New Albany *(G-10346)*

◆ Niktec Inc...G ... 513 282-3747
Franklin *(G-7038)*

▲ Nimers & Woody II Inc.........................C ... 937 454-0722
Vandalia *(G-13574)*

Ogc Industries Inc..................................F ... 330 456-1500
Canton *(G-1963)*

Ohio Power Systems LLC.......................F ... 419 396-4041
Carey *(G-2061)*

◆ Ohio Semitronics Inc............................D ... 614 777-1005
Hilliard *(G-7692)*

Ohio Wire Harness LLC..........................F ... 937 292-7355
Bellefontaine *(G-1114)*

Omega Engineering Inc..........................E ... 740 965-9340
Sunbury *(G-12673)*

Omegadyne Inc.......................................D ... 740 965-9340
Sunbury *(G-12674)*

Parker-Hannifin Corporation..................E ... 937 644-3915
Marysville *(G-9041)*

Per-Tech Inc..G ... 330 833-8824
Massillon *(G-9232)*

Performance Electronics Ltd...................G ... 513 777-5233
Cincinnati *(G-2954)*

Precision Manufacturing Co Inc.............D ... 937 236-2170
Dayton *(G-5948)*

Projects Unlimited Inc............................C ... 937 918-2200
Dayton *(G-5968)*

Qlog Corp..G ... 513 874-1211
Hamilton *(G-7519)*

◆ Quality Quartz Engineering Inc...........D ... 937 236-3250
Beavercreek Township *(G-1004)*

▲ Quality Quartz Engineering Inc...........E ... 510 791-1013
Beavercreek Township *(G-1005)*

Quality Switch Inc..................................E ... 330 872-5707
Newton Falls *(G-10580)*

Quartz Scientific Inc..............................E ... 360 574-6254
Fairport Harbor *(G-6820)*

Ra Consultants LLC................................E ... 513 469-6600
Blue Ash *(G-1326)*

Rct Industries Inc...................................F ... 937 602-1100
Dayton *(G-5977)*

Reliable Hermetic Seals LLC..................F ... 888 747-3250
Beavercreek *(G-981)*

RTD Electronics Inc................................G ... 330 487-0716
Twinsburg *(G-13370)*

Russell Group United LLC......................F ... 614 353-6853
Columbus *(G-5238)*

▲ S-Tek Inc..C ... 440 439-8232
Twinsburg *(G-13373)*

Saint-Gobain Ceramics Plas Inc............D ... 330 673-5860
Stow *(G-12456)*

▲ Saint-Gobain Ceramics Plas Inc.........A ... 610 893-6000
Stow *(G-12457)*

▲ Sawyer Technical Materials LLC..........E ... 440 951-8770
Willoughby *(G-14520)*

Sentrilock LLC...C ... 513 618-5800
West Chester *(G-14074)*

Shiloh Industries Inc..............................F ... 937 236-5100
Dayton *(G-6003)*

Sinbon Usa LLC......................................E ... 937 667-8999
Tipp City *(G-12843)*

Sovereign Circuits Inc............................G ... 330 538-3900
North Jackson *(G-10694)*

▲ Specialty Switch Company LLC............F ... 330 427-3000
Youngstown *(G-14936)*

Spectron Inc..G ... 937 461-5590
Dayton *(G-6017)*

◆ Thermtrol Corporation..........................A ... 330 497-4148
North Canton *(G-10672)*

Tinycircuits..G ... 330 329-5753
Akron *(G-338)*

TL Industries Inc....................................C ... 419 666-8144
Perrysburg *(G-11272)*

◆ Tls Corp...D ... 216 574-4759
Cleveland *(G-4396)*

▲ Twin Point Inc.......................................G ... 419 923-7525
Delta *(G-6214)*

US Lighting Group Inc...........................E ... 216 896-7000
Euclid *(G-6682)*

Valley Electric Company.........................G ... 419 332-6405
Fremont *(G-7142)*

Vertiv Group Corporation.......................A ... 614 888-0246
Westerville *(G-14240)*

Vertiv Holdings Co.................................C ... 614 888-0246
Westerville *(G-14241)*

Vertiv JV Holdings LLC...........................A ... 614 888-0246
Columbus *(G-5348)*

▲ Westbrook Mfg Inc................................B ... 937 254-2004
Dayton *(G-6078)*

Wetsu Group Inc....................................F ... 937 324-9353
Springfield *(G-12393)*

Wifi-Plus Inc...G ... 330 273-3665
Brunswick *(G-1624)*

▲ Workman Electronic Pdts Inc...............G ... 419 923-7525
Delta *(G-6215)*

3691 Storage batteries

Acculon Energy Inc.................................E ... 614 259-7792
Columbus *(G-4669)*

All Power Battery Inc..............................G ... 330 453-5236
Canton *(G-1828)*

Cirba Solutions Us Inc............................D ... 740 653-6290
Lancaster *(G-8187)*

Clarios LLC..A ... 419 865-0542
Holland *(G-7750)*

Crown Battery Manufacturing Co...........G ... 330 425-3308
Fremont *(G-7101)*

◆ Crown Battery Manufacturing Co.........B ... 419 334-7181
Fremont *(G-7100)*

Energizer Manufacturing Inc..................F
Westlake *(G-14301)*

Enersys...C ... 216 252-4242
Cleveland *(C-3673)*

Glx Power Systems Inc...........................G ... 440 338-6526
Chagrin Falls *(G-2145)*

Graywacke Inc..G ... 419 884-7014
Mansfield *(G-8798)*

Micropower Group US Inc.......................G ... 937 606-2793
Troy *(G-13241)*

Micropower LLC......................................G ... 937 606-2793
Troy *(G-13242)*

Millertech Energy Solutions...................F ... 855 629-5484
West Farmington *(G-14159)*

Reliant Worth Corp.................................G ... 440 232-1422
Bedford *(G-1055)*

Toxco Inc...E ... 740 653-6290
Lancaster *(G-8230)*

Transdigm Inc...E ... 216 291-6025
Cleveland *(G-4411)*

Xerion Advanced Battery Corp...............F ... 720 229-0697
Kettering *(G-8124)*

3692 Primary batteries, dry and wet

D C Systems Inc......................................F ... 330 273-3030
Brunswick *(G-1587)*

Glx Power Systems Inc...........................G ... 440 338-6526
Chagrin Falls *(G-2145)*

Employee Codes: A=Over 500 employees, B=251-500
C=101-250, D=51-100, E=20-50, F=10-19, G=1-9   2025 Harris Ohio
Industrial Directory   875

SIC

▲ Inventus Power (ohio) Inc.............. F 614 351-2191
Dublin *(G-6312)*

Ultium Cells Holdings LLC.............. C 313 818-6324
Warren *(G-13805)*

Ultium Cells LLC.............. C 313 818-6324
Warren *(G-13806)*

3694 Engine electrical equipment

▲ Altronic LLC.............. C 330 545-9768
Girard *(G-7264)*

Asidaco LLC.............. G 800 204-1544
Dayton *(G-5666)*

Brinkley Technology Group LLC.............. F 330 830-2498
Massillon *(G-9175)*

▲ C C M Wire Inc.............. F 330 425-3421
Twinsburg *(G-13283)*

Charles Auto Electric Co Inc.............. G 330 535-6269
Akron *(G-96)*

Commercial Vehicle Group Inc.............. B 614 289-5360
New Albany *(G-10336)*

Cummins Inc.............. F 614 604-6004
Grove City *(G-7379)*

Cuyahoga Rebuilders Inc.............. G 216 635-0659
Cleveland *(G-3592)*

Cycle Electric Inc.............. F 937 884-7300
Brookville *(G-1564)*

Egr Products Company Inc.............. F 330 833-6554
Dalton *(G-5584)*

Electra Sound Inc.............. D 216 433-9600
Avon Lake *(G-754)*

◆ Electripack LLC.............. E 937 433-2602
Moraine *(G-10159)*

Ewh Spectrum LLC.............. D 937 593-8010
Bellefontaine *(G-1107)*

Exact-Tool & Die Inc.............. E 216 676-9140
Cleveland *(G-3696)*

▲ Ferrotherm Corporation.............. C 216 883-9350
Cleveland *(G-3714)*

Flex Technologies Inc.............. D 330 359-5415
Mount Eaton *(G-10207)*

Gmelectric Inc.............. G 330 477-3392
Canton *(G-1902)*

▲ GSW Manufacturing Inc.............. C 419 423-7111
Findlay *(G-6874)*

Hitachi Astemo Americas Inc.............. C 937 783-4961
Blanchester *(G-1236)*

Hitachi Astemo Americas Inc.............. B 740 965-1133
Sunbury *(G-12666)*

Legacy Supplies Inc.............. F 330 405-4565
Twinsburg *(G-13328)*

M W Solutions LLC.............. F 419 782-1611
Defiance *(G-6118)*

Machine Products Company.............. F 937 890-6600
Dayton *(G-5860)*

▲ Mueller Electric Company Inc.............. D 216 771-5225
Akron *(G-239)*

Per-Tech Inc.............. E 330 833-8824
Massillon *(G-9232)*

Power Acquisition LLC.............. A 614 228-5000
Dublin *(G-6333)*

Rv Mobile Power LLC.............. E 855 427-7978
Columbus *(G-5239)*

▲ Sk Tech Inc.............. C 937 836-3535
Englewood *(G-6623)*

▲ Stanley Electric US Co Inc.............. E 740 852-5200
London *(G-8541)*

Sumitomo Elc Wirg Systems Inc.............. E 937 642-7579
Marysville *(G-9052)*

Thirion Brothers Eqp Co LLC.............. G 440 357-8004
Painesville *(G-11118)*

▲ Tri-W Group Inc.............. A 614 228-5000
Columbus *(G-5332)*

▲ United Ignition Wire Corp.............. G 216 898-1112
Cleveland *(G-4443)*

Vintage Automotive Elc Inc.............. F 419 472-9349
Toledo *(G-13175)*

Weldon Pump LLC.............. E 440 232-2282
Oakwood Village *(G-10913)*

WW Williams Company LLC.............. D 614 228-5000
Dublin *(G-6362)*

3695 Magnetic and optical recording media

CD Solutions Inc.............. G 937 676-2376
Pleasant Hill *(G-11431)*

Clockingme LLC.............. F 614 400-9727
Columbus *(G-4813)*

Folio Photonics Inc.............. F 440 420-4500
Solon *(G-12114)*

Ginko Voting Systems LLC.............. E 937 291-4060
Dayton *(G-5795)*

Paragon Robotics LLC.............. E 216 313-9299
Twinsburg *(G-13349)*

Signalysis Inc.............. F 513 528-6164
Cincinnati *(G-3090)*

3699 Electrical equipment and supplies, nec

A L Callahan Door Sales.............. G 419 884-3667
Mansfield *(G-8757)*

Aat USA LLC.............. G 614 388-8866
Columbus *(G-4658)*

▲ Action Industries Ltd.............. G 216 252-7800
Strongsville *(G-12531)*

▲ Agratronix LLC.............. E 330 562-2222
Streetsboro *(G-12485)*

Akron Brass Company.............. E 614 529-7230
Columbus *(G-4682)*

◆ Akron Brass Company.............. B 330 264-5678
Wooster *(G-14620)*

Akron Foundry Co.............. G 330 745-3101
Barberton *(G-791)*

Allen Fields Assoc Inc.............. E 513 228-1010
Lebanon *(G-8243)*

◆ Allied Moulded Products Inc.............. C 419 636-4217
Bryan *(G-1626)*

Ametek Inc.............. F 937 440-0800
Troy *(G-13200)*

Azz Inc.............. D 330 456-3241
Canton *(G-1834)*

▲ Barth Industries Co LLC.............. E 216 267-1950
Cleveland *(G-3407)*

Beta Industries Inc.............. F 937 299-7385
Dayton *(G-5677)*

▲ Cecil C Peck Co.............. F 330 785-0781
Akron *(G-93)*

Ces Nationwide.............. G 937 322-0771
Springfield *(G-12289)*

Checkpoint Systems Inc.............. C 330 456-7776
Canton *(G-1863)*

Ci Disposition Co.............. F 216 587-5200
Brooklyn Heights *(G-1530)*

Circle Prime Manufacturing Inc.............. E 330 923-0019
Cuyahoga Falls *(G-5534)*

Clark Substations LLC.............. G 330 452-5200
Canton *(G-1868)*

Commercial Electric Pdts Corp.............. E 216 241-2886
Cleveland *(G-3552)*

Corrpro Companies Inc.............. E 770 761-5400
Medina *(G-9392)*

Corrpro Companies Inc.............. E 330 725-6681
Medina *(G-9393)*

Corrpro Companies Intl Inc.............. F 330 723-5082
Medina *(G-9394)*

Diebold Nixdorf Incorporated.............. A 330 490-4000
North Canton *(G-10635)*

Double D D Mtls Instlltion Inc.............. G 937 898-2534
Dayton *(G-5750)*

E-Beam Services Inc.............. E 513 933-0031
Lebanon *(G-8252)*

Eagle Welding & Fabg Inc.............. E 440 946-0692
Willoughby *(G-14453)*

Electro Plasma Incorporated.............. C 419 838-7365
Millbury *(G-9960)*

▲ Emx Industries LLC.............. F 216 518-9888
Cleveland *(G-3669)*

Enespro Ppe.............. F 800 553-0672
Brooklyn *(G-1521)*

Engineered Mfg & Eqp Co.............. G 937 642-7776
Marysville *(G-9019)*

Erico Global Company.............. G 440 248-0100
Solon *(G-12106)*

Ever Secure SEC Systems Inc.............. F 937 369-8294
Dayton *(G-5772)*

Everon LLC.............. E 440 397-4428
Broadview Heights *(G-1502)*

Everon LLC.............. D 513 258-2409
Cincinnati *(G-2602)*

▲ Federal Equipment Company.............. D 513 621-5260
Cincinnati *(G-2616)*

▲ Fernandes Enterprises LLC.............. F 937 890-6444
Dayton *(G-5775)*

Fire-End & Croker Corp.............. E 513 870-0517
West Chester *(G-14119)*

▲ Flightsafety International Inc.............. C 614 324-3500
Columbus *(G-4929)*

FM Manufacturing Inc.............. G 419 445-0700
Archbold *(G-493)*

General Electric Company.............. F 714 668-0951
West Chester *(G-14009)*

Global Security Tech Inc.............. G 614 890-6400
Westerville *(G-14260)*

◆ GMI Holdings Inc.............. B 800 354-3643
Mount Hope *(G-10213)*

Graham Electric.............. G 614 231-8500
Columbus *(G-4964)*

Great Lakes Power Service Co.............. F 440 259-0025
Perry *(G-11192)*

◆ Halex Electric Company.............. E 800 749-3261
Harrison *(G-7554)*

Hannon Company.............. D 330 456-4728
Canton *(G-1908)*

Hanon Systems Usa LLC.............. C 313 920-0583
Carey *(G-2058)*

Hess Advanced Solutions Llc.............. G 937 829-4794
Dayton *(G-5809)*

Highcom Global Security Inc.............. G 727 592-9400
Columbus *(G-4981)*

Holland Assocts LLC DBA Archou.............. F 513 891-0006
Cincinnati *(G-2727)*

Honeywell International Inc.............. A 937 484-2000
Urbana *(G-13466)*

◆ I T Verdin Co.............. E 513 241-4010
Cincinnati *(G-2738)*

Innovar Systems Limited.............. E 330 538-3942
North Jackson *(G-10689)*

▲ Insource Technologies Inc.............. C 419 399-3600
Paulding *(G-11157)*

▼ Invue Security Products Inc.............. E 330 456-7776
Canton *(G-1919)*

JC Electric Llc.............. F 330 760-2915
Garrettsville *(G-7221)*

▲ Jobap Assembly Inc.............. G 440 632-5393
Middlefield *(G-9803)*

Kiemle-Hankins Company.............. E 419 661-2430
Perrysburg *(G-11233)*

Kraft Electrical Contg Inc.............. E 614 836-9300
Groveport *(G-7441)*

Laser Automation Inc .... G 440 543-9291
Chagrin Falls *(G-2169)*

▼ Lindsay Precast LLC........................ E 800 837-7788
Canal Fulton *(G-1777)*

Lucky Thirteen Inc............................. G 216 631-0013
Cleveland *(G-3971)*

Mac Tools Inc................................... E 614 755-7039
Westerville *(G-14221)*

◆ Mace Security Intl Inc...................... E 440 424-5325
Cleveland *(G-3979)*

▼ Matlock Electric Co Inc................... E 513 731-9600
Cincinnati *(G-2850)*

Midwest Security Services .... G 937 853-9000
Dayton *(G-5882)*

Mitsubishi Elc Automtn Inc................. E 937 492-3058
Sidney *(G-12035)*

Mixed Logic LLC............................... G 440 826-1676
Valley City *(G-13505)*

Momentum Fleet MGT Group Inc........ D 440 759-2219
Westlake *(G-14315)*

▲ Mueller Electric Company Inc......... D 216 771-5225
Akron *(G-239)*

Nabco Entrances Inc......................... F 419 842-0484
Sylvania *(G-12718)*

Niftech Inc....................................... F 440 257-6018
Mentor *(G-9572)*

▲ Nimers & Woody II Inc................... C 937 454-0722
Vandalia *(G-13574)*

▲ Overly Hautz Company.................. E 513 932-0025
Lebanon *(G-8281)*

Pacific Highway Products LLC............ G 740 914-5217
Marion *(G-8988)*

Peerless Laser Processors Inc........... F 614 836-5790
Groveport *(G-7447)*

Pentagon Protection Usa LLC............ F 614 734-7240
Dublin *(G-6331)*

◆ Philips Med Systems Clvland In........ B 440 483-3000
Cleveland *(G-4159)*

Powell Electrical Systems Inc............. D 330 966-1750
North Canton *(G-10660)*

Primex .... G 513 831-9959
Milford *(G-9949)*

Pt Metals LLC.................................. E 330 767-3003
Navarre *(G-10312)*

▲ Qualtech Technologies Inc............. E 440 946-8081
Willoughby *(G-14514)*

R F I .... G 740 654-4502
Lancaster *(G-0221)*

▲ Rah Investment Holding Inc............ D 330 832-8124
Massillon *(G-9237)*

Resonetics LLC................................ D 937 865-4070
Kettering *(G-8123)*

▼ Riverside Drives Inc...................... E 216 362-1211
Cleveland *(G-4243)*

Sage Integration Holdings LLC........... E 330 733-8183
Kent *(G-8072)*

▲ Say Security Group USA LLC.......... F 419 634-0004
Ada *(G-5)*

Schneider Automation Inc.................. C 612 426-0709
Fairfield *(G-6774)*

Schneider Electric Usa Inc................. B 513 523-4171
Oxford *(G-11064)*

Securcom Inc................................... E 419 628-1049
Minster *(G-10065)*

Sew-Eurodrive Inc............................ D 937 335-0036
Troy *(G-13254)*

Smart Sonic Corporation................... G 818 610-7900
Cleveland *(G-4306)*

Tech-Sonic Inc................................. E 614 792-3117
Dublin *(G-6354)*

Technlgy Install Partners LLC............. E 888 586-7040
Cleveland *(G-4371)*

Tip Products Inc................................ E 216 252-2535
New London *(G-10419)*

◆ Vanner Holdings Inc...................... D 614 771-2718
Hilliard *(G-7709)*

Vesco LLC....................................... E 330 374-5156
Mogadore *(G-10093)*

Vortec Corporation........................... E 513 891-7485
Blue Ash *(G-1348)*

Wesco Distribution Inc...................... F 419 666-1670
Northwood *(G-10813)*

37 TRANSPORTATION EQUIPMENT

3711 Motor vehicles and car bodies

Abranda Llc..................................... F 614 577-8080
Blacklick *(G-1218)*

Ackerman .... G 440 246-2034
Lorain *(G-8545)*

◆ Airstream Inc............................... B 937 596-6111
Jackson Center *(G-7958)*

Antique Auto Sheet Metal Inc............. F 937 833-4422
Brookville *(G-1562)*

Autowax Inc.................................... G 440 334-4417
Strongsville *(G-12542)*

◆ Bae Systems Survivability.............. A 513 881-9800
West Chester *(G-13945)*

Bobbart Industries Inc...................... G 419 350-5477
Sylvania *(G-12702)*

Braun Industries Inc......................... B 419 232-7020
Van Wert *(G-13528)*

Brookville Roadster Inc..................... G 937 833-4605
Brookville *(G-1563)*

Copley Fire & Rescue Assn................ F 330 666-6464
Copley *(G-5433)*

▲ Custom Chassis Inc...................... C 440 839-5574
Wakeman *(G-13679)*

D&D Clssic Auto Rstoration Inc.......... G 937 473-2229
Covington *(G-5492)*

Dakkota Integrated Systems LLC........ E 517 694-6500
Toledo *(G-12936)*

Eldorado National Kansas Inc............ C 937 596-6849
Jackson Center *(G-7962)*

▲ Electro Prime Group LLC............... E 419 476-0100
Toledo *(G-12948)*

Falls Stamping & Welding Co............. C 330 928-1191
Cuyahoga Falls *(G-5541)*

◆ Farber Specialty Vehicles Inc......... C 614 863-6470
Reynoldsburg *(G-11509)*

Federaleagle LLC............................. D 513 797-4100
West Chester *(G-14118)*

Ford Motor Company........................ C 440 933-1215
Avon Lake *(G-756)*

FOXCONN EV SYSTEM LLC.............. B 234 285-4001
Warren *(G-13766)*

▲ Galion-Godwin Truck Bdy Co LLC.... F 330 359-5495
Dundee *(G-6365)*

◆ Gerling and Associates Inc............. D 740 965-2888
Sunbury *(G-12665)*

Great Lakes Assemblies LLC............. D 937 645-3900
East Liberty *(G-6385)*

▼ Halcore Group Inc......................... C 614 539-8181
Grove City *(G-7389)*

Honda Dev & Mfg Amer LLC............. B 937 642-5000
Marysville *(G-9027)*

Honda Dev & Mfg Amer LLC............. C 937 644-0724
Marysville *(G-9028)*

◆ Honda Dev & Mfg Amer LLC........... A 937 642-5000
Marysville *(G-9026)*

Horizon Global Corporation............... E 734 656-3000
Cleveland *(G-3837)*

International Motors LLC.................... G 513 733-8500
Cincinnati *(G-2752)*

International Motors LLC.................... C 937 390-4776
Springfield *(G-12328)*

International Motors LLC.................... E 937 561-3315
Springfield *(G-12329)*

▲ Jefferson Industries Corp.............. C 614 879-5300
West Jefferson *(G-14162)*

La Boit Specialty Vehicles................. D 614 231-7640
Gahanna *(G-7164)*

Lawson Twing Auto Wrecking LLC...... F 216 883-9050
Cleveland *(G-3948)*

Lippert Components Inc.................... G 574 537-8900
Payne *(G-11164)*

Magic Dragon Machine Inc................ G 614 539-8004
Grove City *(G-7396)*

Mobile Solutions LLC........................ F 614 286-3944
Columbus *(G-5107)*

Monarch Plastic Inc.......................... G 330 683-0822
Orrville *(G-10995)*

▲ Obs Inc....................................... F 330 453-3725
Canton *(G-1962)*

◆ Ohio Module Manufacturing............ A 419 729-6700
Toledo *(G-13074)*

P C Workshop Inc............................ G 419 399-4805
Paulding *(G-11161)*

Paccar Inc...................................... D 740 774-5111
Chillicothe *(G-2269)*

▲ Reberland Equipment Inc............... F 330 698-5883
Apple Creek *(G-476)*

Scottrods LLC.................................. G 419 499-2705
Monroeville *(G-10120)*

Star Fab Inc.................................... E 330 482-1601
Columbiana *(G-4630)*

▼ Sutphen Corporation..................... C 800 726-7030
Dublin *(G-6353)*

Toledo Pro Fiberglass Inc.................. G 419 241-9390
Toledo *(G-13156)*

Tpam Inc... E 567 315-8694
Toledo *(G-13165)*

Transit Fittings N Amer Inc................ G 330 797-2516
Youngstown *(G-14950)*

▲ Tremcar USA Inc........................... D 330 878-7708
Strasburg *(G-12482)*

Village of Grafton............................ F 440 926-2075
Grafton *(G-7305)*

W&W Automotive & Towing Inc.......... F 937 429-1699
Beavercreek Township *(G-1007)*

Warfighter Fcsed Logistics Inc........... E 740 513-4692
West Chester *(G-14091)*

Workhorse Technologies Inc.............. E 888 646-5205
Sharonville *(G-11951)*

3713 Truck and bus bodies

Abutilon Company Inc....................... F 419 536-6123
Toledo *(G-12862)*

Ace Truck Equipment Co................... E 740 453-0551
Zanesville *(G-14981)*

◆ Airstream Inc............................... B 937 596-6111
Jackson Center *(G-7958)*

Altec Industries Inc.......................... F 205 408-2341
Cuyahoga Falls *(G-5521)*

ARE Inc.. A 330 830-7800
Massillon *(G-9172)*

▲ Atc Lighting & Plastics Inc.............. C 440 466-7670
Andover *(G-456)*

Bores Manufacturing Inc................... G 419 465-2606
Monroeville *(G-10118)*

▼ Bosserman Automotive Engrg LLC... G 419 722-2879
Findlay *(G-6844)*

▲ Brothers Body and Eqp LLC............ F 419 462-1975
Galion *(G-7180)*

SIC

Brown Industrial Inc.............................E 937 693-3838
　Botkins *(G-1397)*

Bush Specialty Vehicles Inc.................F 937 382-5502
　Wilmington *(G-14574)*

Cascade Corporation.............................G 937 327-0300
　Springfield *(G-12287)*

Cipted Corp...D 412 829-2120
　Monroe *(G-10099)*

▲ Cota International Inc.........................G 937 526-5520
　Versailles *(G-13593)*

Crane Carrier Company LLC.................C 918 286-2889
　New Philadelphia *(G-10440)*

Crane Carrier Holdings LLC.................C 918 286-2889
　New Philadelphia *(G-10441)*

Custom Truck One Source LP................D 330 409-7291
　Canton *(G-1874)*

Dan Patrick Enterprises Inc...................G 740 477-1006
　Circleville *(G-3253)*

Elliott Machine Works Inc.....................E 419 468-4709
　Galion *(G-7189)*

Field Gymmy Inc....................................G 419 538-6511
　Glandorf *(G-7283)*

Friesen Transfer Ltd..............................G 614 873-5672
　Plain City *(G-11409)*

▲ Galion-Godwin Truck Bdy Co LLC.....F 330 359-5495
　Dundee *(G-6365)*

H & H Truck Parts LLC..........................E 216 642-4540
　Cleveland *(G-3804)*

Hendrickson International Corp.............D 740 929-5600
　Hebron *(G-7617)*

▲ Joseph Industries Inc.......................D 330 528-0091
　Streetsboro *(G-12507)*

Kaffenbarger Truck Eqp Co...................E 513 772-6800
　Cincinnati *(G-2777)*

◆ Kaffenbarger Truck Eqp Co................C 937 845-3804
　New Carlisle *(G-10373)*

Kidron Inc...B 330 857-3011
　Kidron *(G-8129)*

▲ Kimble Custom Chassis Company.....D 877 546-2537
　New Philadelphia *(G-10452)*

▲ Kimble Mixer Company.....................D 330 308-6700
　New Philadelphia *(G-10453)*

▲ King Kutter II Inc.............................E 740 446-0351
　Gallipolis *(G-7207)*

Kruz Inc..E 330 878-5595
　Dover *(G-6251)*

Kuka Tledo Prdction Oprtons LL...........C 419 727-5500
　Toledo *(G-13024)*

La Boit Specialty Vehicles....................D 614 231-7640
　Gahanna *(G-7164)*

▼ Lifeline Mobile Inc...........................D 614 497-8300
　Columbus *(G-5068)*

Mancor Ohio Inc....................................C 937 228-6141
　Dayton *(G-5867)*

Mancor Ohio Inc....................................C 937 228-6141
　Dayton *(G-5866)*

Marengo Fabricated Steel Ltd................F 800 919-2652
　Cardington *(G-2055)*

Martin Sheet Metal Inc.........................E 216 377-8200
　Cleveland *(G-3993)*

McNeilus Truck and Mfg Inc..................G 614 868-0760
　Gahanna *(G-7165)*

Meritor Inc..C 740 348-3270
　Granville *(G-7317)*

Paccar Inc...D 740 774-5111
　Chillicothe *(G-2269)*

Proform Group Inc.................................F 614 332-9654
　Columbus *(G-5210)*

Q T Columbus LLC................................G 800 758-2410
　Columbus *(G-5216)*

▼ QT Equipment Company....................E 330 724-3055
　Akron *(G-272)*

Radar Love Co.......................................G 419 951-4750
　Findlay *(G-6912)*

▲ Reberland Equipment Inc..................F 330 698-5883
　Apple Creek *(G-476)*

Schodorf Truck Body & Eqp Co.............F 614 228-6793
　Columbus *(G-5253)*

Skymark Refuelers LLC.........................D 419 957-1709
　Findlay *(G-6919)*

Sutphen Towers Inc...............................D 614 876-1262
　Hilliard *(G-7704)*

▲ Tarpstop LLC...................................F 419 873-7867
　Perrysburg *(G-11264)*

▲ Truck Cab Manufacturers Inc............E 513 922-1300
　Cincinnati *(G-3172)*

Trucks & Parts of Tampa LLC.................E 937 437-0377
　New Paris *(G-10427)*

Unlimted Rcovery Solutions LLC............E 419 868-4888
　Wauseon *(G-13860)*

Valco Industries LLC.............................C 937 399-7400
　Springfield *(G-12391)*

▲ Venco Venturo Industries LLC...........E 513 772-8448
　Cincinnati *(G-3197)*

Vitatoe Industries Inc............................D 740 773-2425
　Chillicothe *(G-2287)*

▲ Wallace Forge Company....................D 330 488-1203
　Canton *(G-2045)*

Willard Machine & Welding Inc..............F 330 467-0642
　Macedonia *(G-8722)*

Youngstown-Kenworth Inc.....................F 330 534-9761
　Hubbard *(G-7819)*

Zie Bart Rhino Linings Toledo................G 419 841-2886
　Toledo *(G-13184)*

3714 Motor vehicle parts and accessories

◆ 31 Inc...D 800 438-3302
　Newcomerstown *(G-10566)*

A G Parts Inc..F 937 596-6448
　Jackson Center *(G-7957)*

A Good Mobile Detailing LLC.................G 513 316-3802
　Cincinnati *(G-2325)*

◆ ABC Technologies Dlhb Inc...............B 330 478-2503
　Canton *(G-1821)*

◆ Accel Performance Group LLC............C 216 658-6413
　Independence *(G-7887)*

Accuride Corporation.............................F 937 323-9669
　Springfield *(G-12275)*

◆ Ach LLC...G 419 621-5748
　Sandusky *(G-11819)*

◆ Ad Industries Inc...............................A 303 744-1911
　Dayton *(G-5634)*

▲ Ada Technologies Inc........................C 419 634-7000
　Ada *(G-2)*

◆ Adelmans Truck Parts Corp................E 330 456-0206
　Canton *(G-1823)*

Adient US LLC.......................................C 937 981-2176
　Greenfield *(G-7324)*

Adient US LLC.......................................C 419 662-4900
　Northwood *(G-10801)*

Adient US LLC.......................................E 419 394-7800
　Saint Marys *(G-11730)*

◆ Advics Manufacturing Ohio Inc..........A 513 932-7878
　Lebanon *(G-8242)*

◆ Airstream Inc.....................................B 937 596-6111
　Jackson Center *(G-7958)*

Airtex Industries LLC.............................F 330 899-0340
　Toledo *(G-12868)*

Albright Radiator Inc.............................G 330 264-8886
　Wooster *(G-14622)*

▲ Alegre Inc...F 937 885-6786
　Miamisburg *(G-9664)*

All Wright Enterprises LLC.....................G 440 259-5656
　Perry *(G-11190)*

Allied Separation Tech Inc.....................G 704 736-0420
　Twinsburg *(G-13273)*

Alta Mira Corporation............................D 330 648-2461
　Spencer *(G-12233)*

American Axle & Mfg Inc.......................G 330 863-7500
　Malvern *(G-8746)*

American Axle & Mfg Inc.......................D 330 868-5761
　Minerva *(G-10033)*

American Axle & Mfg Inc.......................C 330 486-3200
　Twinsburg *(G-13275)*

American Manufacturing & Eqp.............G 513 829-2248
　Fairfield *(G-6711)*

Americana Development Inc...................D 330 633-3278
　Tallmadge *(G-12730)*

Americlean 2 LLC..................................F 216 781-3720
　Cleveland *(G-3349)*

Amsoil Inc...G 614 274-9851
　Urbancrest *(G-13482)*

Amsted Industries Incorporated.............D 614 836-2323
　Groveport *(G-7422)*

Aptiv Services Us LLC............................C 330 367-6000
　Vienna *(G-13607)*

Aptiv Services Us LLC............................A 330 505-3150
　Warren *(G-13740)*

Aptiv Services Us LLC............................B 330 306-1000
　Warren *(G-13741)*

ARE Inc...A 330 830-7800
　Massillon *(G-9172)*

▲ Areway LLC.......................................D 216 651-9022
　Brooklyn *(G-1520)*

Arlington Rack & Packaging Co..............G 419 476-7700
　Toledo *(G-12886)*

◆ ASC Industries Inc............................D 800 253-6009
　North Canton *(G-10628)*

▲ Atc Lighting & Plastics Inc.................C 440 466-7670
　Andover *(G-456)*

Atwood Mobile Products LLC..................D 419 258-5531
　Antwerp *(G-462)*

Auria Fremont LLC................................B 419 332-1587
　Fremont *(G-7092)*

Auria Holmesville LLC...........................B 330 279-4505
　Holmesville *(G-7794)*

Auria Sidney LLC..................................B 937 492-1225
　Sidney *(G-11994)*

Autoneum North America Inc.................B 419 693-0511
　Oregon *(G-10957)*

Autoneum North America Inc.................D 419 690-8924
　Oregon *(G-10958)*

B A Malcuit Racing Inc...........................G 330 878-7111
　Strasburg *(G-12476)*

B&C Machine Co LLC.............................F 330 745-4013
　Barberton *(G-796)*

Beach Manufacturing Co........................C 937 882-6372
　Donnelsville *(G-6227)*

Beijing West Industries...........................G 937 455-5281
　Dayton *(G-5675)*

Bellevue Manufacturing Company..........D 419 483-3190
　Bellevue *(G-1120)*

◆ Bendix Coml Vhcl Systems LLC.........B 440 329-9000
　Avon *(G-716)*

Bergstrom Company Ltd Partnr...............F 440 232-2282
　Cleveland *(G-3415)*

◆ Better Brake Parts Inc.......................E 419 227-0685
　Lima *(G-8390)*

Bobbart Industries Inc............................G 419 350-5477
　Sylvania *(G-12702)*

Boler Company......................................C 330 445-6728
　Canton *(G-1841)*

Bores Manufacturing Inc........................G 419 465-2606
　Monroeville *(G-10118)*

Bowden Manufacturing Corp..................E 440 946-1770
　Willoughby *(G-14432)*

Brake Parts Inc China LLC.................. G 216 589-0198
Cleveland **(G-3433)**

Buckeye Brake Mfg Inc.......................... F 740 782-1379
Morristown **(G-10200)**

Buckley Manufacturing Company........... F 513 821-4444
Cincinnati **(G-2432)**

▲ Bucyrus Precision Tech Inc............... C 419 563-9950
Bucyrus **(G-1674)**

◆ Buyers Products Company.................C 440 974-8888
Mentor **(G-9496)**

Bwi Chassis Dynamics NA Inc............... F 937 455-5100
Kettering **(G-8117)**

▲ Bwi North America Inc...................... E 614 394-5983
Moraine **(G-10153)**

▲ Callies Performance Products Inc..... D 419 435-7448
Fostoria **(G-6977)**

Capco Automotive Products Corp.......... A 216 523-5000
Cleveland **(G-3466)**

▲ Cardington Yutaka Tech Inc.............. A 419 864-8777
Cardington **(G-2053)**

◆ Cequent Consumer Products Inc.......D 440 498-0001
Solon **(G-12092)**

Champion Laboratories Inc.................... G 330 899-0340
Toledo **(G-12914)**

▲ Champion Spark Plug Company....... D 419 535-2567
Toledo **(G-12915)**

Chantilly Development Corp................... E 419 243-8109
Toledo **(G-12916)**

Classic Reproductions.......................... G 937 548-9839
Greenville **(G-7338)**

▲ Cleveland Ignition Co Inc................ G 440 439-3688
Cleveland **(G-3513)**

◆ CMI Holding Company Crawford.......D 419 468-9122
Galion **(G-7183)**

▲ Cmt Imports Inc.............................. G 513 615-1851
Cincinnati **(G-2502)**

Comprehensive Logistics Co Inc............ E 440 934-3517
Avon **(G-720)**

Connective Design Incorporated............ F 937 746-8252
Miamisburg **(G-9683)**

Cooper-Standard Automotive Inc........... D 740 342-3523
New Lexington **(G-10401)**

Crown Div of Allen Gr........................... G 330 263-4919
Wooster **(G-14632)**

Cummins Filtration Inc.......................... C
Findlay **(G-6858)**

Cummins Inc.. F 614 604-6004
Grove City **(G-7379)**

▲ Custer Products Limited.................. F 330 490-3158
Massillon **(G-9184)**

Custom Cltch Jnt Hydrlics Inc............... F 216 431-1630
Cleveland **(G-3584)**

Custom Floaters LLC............................. G 216 536-8979
Brookpark **(G-1546)**

▲ Cvg National Seating Co LLC........... F 219 872-7295
New Albany **(G-10338)**

◆ Cwd LLC..E 310 218-1082
Cleveland **(G-3594)**

▲ D-Terra Solutions LLC.................... G 614 450-1040
Powell **(G-11486)**

D4 Industries Inc................................. F 419 523-9555
Ottawa **(G-11032)**

▲ Daido Metal Bellefontaine LLC........ F 937 592-5010
Bellefontaine **(G-1104)**

Dana.. E 419 887-3000
Toledo **(G-12937)**

◆ Dana Auto Systems Group LLC........E 419 887-3000
Maumee **(G-9270)**

Dana Automotive Mfg Inc..................... C 419 887-3000
Maumee **(G-9271)**

Dana Brazil Holdings I LLC................... E 419 887-3000
Maumee **(G-9272)**

◆ Dana Commercial Vhcl Pdts LLC........G 419 887-3000
Maumee **(G-9273)**

◆ Dana Driveshaft Products LLC.......... E 419 887-3000
Maumee **(G-9274)**

◆ Dana Global Products Inc................. G 419 887-3000
Maumee **(G-9275)**

◆ Dana Hvy Vhcl Systems Group LL.....E 419 887-3000
Maumee **(G-9276)**

Dana Incorporated............................... A 419 887-3000
Maumee **(G-9277)**

Dana Light Axle Mfg LLC...................... B 419 887-3000
Toledo **(G-12938)**

▲ Dana Light Axle Mfg LLC................. G 419 346-4528
Maumee **(G-9278)**

Dana Limited....................................... D 419 866-7253
Holland **(G-7754)**

Dana Limited....................................... E 419 887-3000
Maumee **(G-9279)**

Dana Limited....................................... D 419 887-3000
Maumee **(G-9280)**

Dana Limited....................................... D 419 482-2000
Maumee **(G-9281)**

▲ Dana Limited.................................. B 419 887-3000
Maumee **(G-9282)**

◆ Dana Off Highway Products LLC....... E 419 887-3000
Maumee **(G-9283)**

Dana Sac USA Inc................................ G 419 887-3550
Maumee **(G-9284)**

▲ Dana Sealing Manufacturing LLC...... F
Maumee **(G-9285)**

▲ Dana Sealing Products LLC............. F 419 887-3000
Maumee **(G-9286)**

Dana Structural Products LLC............... G 419 887-3000
Maumee **(G-9287)**

▲ Dana Thermal Products LLC............ F 419 887-3000
Maumee **(G-9288)**

Dana World Trade Corporation.............. F 419 887-3000
Maumee **(G-9289)**

Dayton Clutch & Joint Inc..................... F 937 236-9770
Dayton **(G-5724)**

▲ Dayton Wheel Concepts Inc............. F 937 438-0100
Dayton **(G-5740)**

◆ Dbw Fiber Corporation.....................D
Wooster **(G-14634)**

◆ Dcm Manufacturing Inc....................E 216 265-8006
Cleveland **(G-3606)**

Designed Harness Systems Inc.............. F 937 599-2485
Bellefontaine **(C 1105)**

Detroit Toledo Fiber LLC....................... F 248 647-0400
Toledo **(G-12942)**

Doran Mfg LLC.................................... D 866 816-7233
Blue Ash **(G-1267)**

Doug Marine Motors Inc....................... F 740 335-3700
Wshngtn Ct Hs **(G-14738)**

Driveline 1 Inc..................................... G 614 279-7734
Columbus **(G-4890)**

Eaton Corporation................................ B 440 523-5000
Beachwood **(G-915)**

Eaton Corporation................................ C 216 281-2211
Cleveland **(G-3653)**

Eaton Corporation................................ E 216 523-5000
Willoughby **(G-14455)**

◆ Eaton Corporation.......................... B 440 523-5000
Cleveland **(G-3652)**

Ebco Inc.. E 330 562-8265
Streetsboro **(G-12500)**

Ebog Legacy Inc.................................. D 330 239-4933
Sharon Center **(G-11940)**

Edgerton Forge Inc.............................. D 419 298-2333
Edgerton **(G-6466)**

Egr Products Company Inc.................... F 330 833-6554
Dalton **(G-5584)**

Emssons Faurecia Ctrl Systems............. B 937 743-0551
Franklin **(G-7018)**

▲ Emssons Faurecia Ctrl Systems....... C 812 341-2000
Toledo **(G-12951)**

Entratech Systems LLC......................... G 419 433-7683
Sandusky **(G-11832)**

Ernie Green Industries Inc.................... E 740 420-5252
Circleville **(G-3257)**

Ernie Green Industries Inc.................... E 614 219-1423
New Madison **(G-10420)**

Exito Manufacturing LLC....................... G 937 291-9871
Beavercreek **(G-991)**

▲ F&P America Mfg Inc...................... E 937 339-0212
Troy **(G-13214)**

Falls Stamping & Welding Co................ C 330 928-1191
Cuyahoga Falls **(G-5541)**

Farin Industries Inc.............................. G 440 275-2755
Austinburg **(G-699)**

FCA US LLC... B 419 661-3500
Perrysburg **(G-11220)**

First Brands Group LLC........................ E 888 565-9632
Cleveland **(G-3718)**

▲ Flaming River Industries Inc............ F 440 826-4488
Berea **(G-1174)**

Flex Technologies Inc........................... D 330 359-5415
Mount Eaton **(G-10207)**

Florence Alloys Inc.............................. G 330 745-9141
Barberton **(G-805)**

Florida Production Engrg Inc................. D 937 996-4361
New Madison **(G-10421)**

▲ Force Control Industries Inc............ E 513 868-0900
Fairfield **(G-6737)**

Ford Motor Company............................ C 216 676-7918
Brookpark **(G-1550)**

Forgeline Motorsports LLC.................... E 800 886-0093
Dayton **(G-5782)**

Fram Group.. G 479 271-7934
Cleveland **(G-3741)**

Fram Group Operations LLC.................. E 419 436-5827
Fostoria **(G-5983)**

Fremont Plastic Products Inc................. C 419 332-6407
Fremont **(G-7111)**

Freudenberg-Nok Sealing Tech.............. F 877 331-8427
Milan **(G-9915)**

◆ Friction Products Co.......................B 330 725-4941
Medina **(G-9406)**

Frontier Tank Center Inc....................... G 330 659-3888
Richfield **(G-11393)**

▲ Ft Precision Inc.............................. A 740 694-1500
Fredericktown **(G-7079)**

Ftd Investments LLC............................ A 937 833-2161
Brookville **(G-1569)**

▲ Ftech R&D North America Inc........... E 937 339-2777
Troy **(G-13217)**

◆ Fuserashi Intl Tech Inc....................E 330 273-0140
Valley City **(G-13496)**

Gear Company of America Inc............... D 216 671-5400
Cleveland **(G-3760)**

◆ Gear Star Amrcn Prfmce Trnsmss.....E 330 434-5216
Akron **(G-157)**

General Metals Powder Co LLC.............. E 330 633-1226
Akron **(G-160)**

General Motors LLC.............................. A 216 265-5000
Cleveland **(G-3767)**

General Motors LLC.............................. C 330 824-5840
Warren **(G-13768)**

GKN Driveline North Amer Inc............... D 419 354-3955
Bowling Green **(G-1422)**

Goodrich Corporation............................ A 937 339-3811
Troy **(G-13219)**

▲ Gra-Mag Truck Intr Systems LLC...... E 740 490-1000
London **(G-8536)**

▲ Grand-Rock Company Inc................ E 440 639-2000
　Painesville *(G-11089)*

Green Acquisition LLC...................... F 440 930-7600
　Avon *(G-728)*

Green Rdced Emssons Netwrk LLC....... G 330 340-0941
　Strasburg *(G-12478)*

Green Tokai Co Ltd........................... C 937 237-1630
　Dayton *(G-5804)*

◆ Green Tokai Co Ltd........................A 937 833-5444
　Brookville *(G-1570)*

▲ GSW Manufacturing Inc................. C 419 423-7111
　Findlay *(G-6874)*

Gt Technologies Inc......................... E 419 782-8955
　Defiance *(G-6109)*

Gt Technologies Inc......................... D 419 324-7300
　Toledo *(G-12978)*

Hall-Toledo Inc................................ F 419 893-4334
　Maumee *(G-9294)*

◆ Haltec Corporation........................C 330 222-1501
　Salem *(G-11784)*

Hanon Systems Usa LLC.................. C 313 920-0583
　Carey *(G-2058)*

Harco Manufacturing Group LLC.......... C 937 528-5000
　Moraine *(G-10168)*

▲ Harco Manufacturing Group LLC..... C 937 528-5000
　Moraine *(G-10167)*

▲ Hdt Tactical Systems Inc............... C 216 438-6111
　Solon *(G-12122)*

Hendrickson.................................... G 740 678-8033
　Vincent *(G-13621)*

Hendrickson International Corp............ D 740 929-5600
　Hebron *(G-7617)*

Hendrickson Usa LLC...................... C 330 456-7288
　Canton *(G-1911)*

Hendrickson Usa LLC...................... C 740 929-5600
　Hebron *(G-7618)*

Hendrickson Usa LLC...................... C 630 910-2800
　North Canton *(G-10646)*

◆ Hfi LLC.......................................B 614 491-0700
　Canal Winchester *(G-1791)*

▲ Hi-Tek Manufacturing Inc.............. C 513 459-1094
　Mason *(G-9108)*

Hitachi Astemo Americas Inc............. C 419 425-1259
　Findlay *(G-6880)*

Hite Parts Exchange Inc................... G 614 272-5115
　Chillicothe *(G-2258)*

Honda Dev & Mfg Amer LLC............. A 937 843-5555
　Russells Point *(G-11667)*

▲ Honda Transmission Manufa........... A 937 843-5555
　Russells Point *(G-11668)*

Horizon Global Corporation................ E 734 656-3000
　Cleveland *(G-3837)*

Hp2g LLC....................................... G 419 906-1525
　Napoleon *(G-10286)*

▲ Ig Watteeuw Usa LLC................... F 740 588-1722
　Zanesville *(G-15021)*

Igw USA... G 740 588-1722
　Zanesville *(G-15022)*

Illinois Tool Works Inc...................... C 513 489-7600
　Blue Ash *(G-1286)*

Illinois Tool Works Inc...................... E 262 248-8277
　Bryan *(G-1645)*

◆ Imasen Bucyrus Technology Inc........C 419 563-9590
　Bucyrus *(G-1683)*

▲ Industry Products Co.................... B 937 778-0585
　Piqua *(G-11356)*

Infinity Engineered Pdts LLC.............. E 234 466-7200
　Fairlawn *(G-6805)*

Interntnal Auto Cmpnnts Group........... D 419 335-1000
　Wauseon *(G-13852)*

Interntnal Auto Cmpnnts Group........... A 419 433-5653
　Wauseon *(G-13853)*

◆ Interstate Diesel Service Inc............C 216 881-0015
　Cleveland *(G-3865)*

Inteva Products LLC......................... C 937 280-8500
　Vandalia *(G-13563)*

Jae Tech Inc................................... D 330 698-2000
　Apple Creek *(G-470)*

Jake Sweeney Mazda Tri-County.......... G 513 782-1150
　Cincinnati *(G-2757)*

▲ Jbar A/C Inc............................... F 216 447-4294
　Cleveland *(G-3884)*

Johnson Controls Inc....................... G 414 524-1200
　Saint Marys *(G-11739)*

▲ Joseph Industries Inc................... D 330 528-0091
　Streetsboro *(G-12507)*

▲ Julie Maynard Inc........................ F 937 443-0408
　Dayton *(G-5834)*

K Wm Beach Mfg Co Inc................... C 937 399-3838
　Springfield *(G-12334)*

▲ Kalida Manufacturing Inc............... C 419 532-2026
　Kalida *(G-8004)*

Kasai North America Inc.................... E 614 356-1494
　Dublin *(G-6314)*

Kasai North America Inc.................... C 419 209-0399
　Upper Sandusky *(G-13444)*

Kenley Enterprises LLC..................... G 419 630-0921
　Bryan *(G-1647)*

Keystone Auto Glass Inc................... D 419 509-0497
　Maumee *(G-9302)*

KG Medina LLC................................ E 256 330-4273
　Medina *(G-9419)*

▲ Knippen Chrysler Ddge Jeep Inc...... F 419 695-4976
　Delphos *(G-6188)*

▲ Knott Brake Company................... E 800 566-8887
　Lodi *(G-8503)*

Kongsberg Actation Systems LLC........ E 440 639-8778
　Grand River *(G-7311)*

▲ Kosei St Marys Corporation........... A 419 394-7840
　Saint Marys *(G-11740)*

◆ Kth Parts Industries Inc..................A 937 663-5941
　Saint Paris *(G-11758)*

Ktri Holdings Inc.............................. B 216 400-9308
　Cleveland *(G-3931)*

Ktsdi LLC....................................... G 330 783-2000
　North Lima *(G-10709)*

KWD Automotive Inc......................... G 419 344-8232
　Whitehouse *(G-14362)*

▲ Kyklos Bearing International Llc....... A 419 627-7000
　Sandusky *(G-11848)*

▲ Lacal Equipment Inc..................... E 937 596-6106
　Jackson Center *(G-7964)*

▲ Lawrence Technologies Inc............. G 937 274-7771
　Dayton *(G-5842)*

▲ Leadec Corp................................ E 513 731-3590
　Cincinnati *(G-2815)*

Lear Corporation.............................. D 740 928-4358
　Hebron *(G-7622)*

Lear Corporation.............................. E 419 335-6010
　Wauseon *(G-13855)*

▲ Lhy Powertrain Corporation............ E 330 533-6801
　Canfield *(G-1812)*

Liberty Outdoors LLC........................ F 330 791-3149
　Uniontown *(G-13422)*

Linamar Strctures USA Mich Inc........... D 260 636-7030
　Edon *(G-6475)*

Linamar Strctures USA Mich Inc........... C 567 249-0838
　Edon *(G-6476)*

◆ Lintern Corporation.......................E 440 255-9333
　Mentor *(G-9554)*

Lippert Components Inc.................... G 574 537-8900
　Payne *(G-11164)*

Lorain County Auto Systems Inc........... A 248 442-6800
　Lorain *(G-8564)*

▲ Lorain County Auto Systems Inc...... E 440 960-7470
　Lorain *(G-8565)*

Lubriquip Inc................................... B 216 581-2000
　Cleveland *(G-3969)*

Lucas Sumitomo Brakes Inc.............. F 513 934-0024
　Lebanon *(G-8274)*

◆ Luk Clutch Systems LLC.................E 330 264-4383
　Wooster *(G-14661)*

Maags Automotive & Mch Inc............. G 419 626-1539
　Sandusky *(G-11853)*

▲ Magna Modular Systems LLC.......... D 419 324-3387
　Toledo *(G-13045)*

Magna Seating America Inc............... C 330 824-3101
　Sheffield Village *(G-11960)*

Magna Seating America Inc............... E 419 410-4780
　Swanton *(G-12686)*

Magnaco Industries Inc.................... E 216 961-3636
　Lodi *(G-8504)*

Mahle Behr Dayton LLC..................... A 937 369-2900
　Dayton *(G-5864)*

Mahle Behr Dayton LLC..................... B 937 356-2001
　Vandalia *(G-13566)*

◆ Mahle Behr Dayton LLC.................D 937 369-2900
　Dayton *(G-5863)*

Mahle Behr USA Inc......................... C 937 356-2001
　Vandalia *(G-13567)*

Mahle Eng Components USA Inc........... F 740 962-8004
　Mcconnelsville *(G-9363)*

Mahle Industries Incorporated............ E 937 890-2739
　Dayton *(G-5865)*

▲ Maradyne Corporation................... D 216 362-0755
　Cleveland *(G-3986)*

Marion Industries LLC....................... A 740 223-0075
　Marion *(G-8977)*

◆ Maval Industries LLC.....................C 330 405-1600
　Twinsburg *(G-13336)*

Maxion Wheels Sedalia LLC.............. A 330 794-2300
　Akron *(G-224)*

Merillat Racing LLC.......................... G 419 376-4833
　Archbold *(G-502)*

Meritor Inc...................................... C 740 348-3270
　Granville *(G-7317)*

Midwest Muffler Pros & More.............. G 937 293-2450
　Moraine *(G-10179)*

Milark Industries Inc......................... D 419 524-7627
　Mansfield *(G-8827)*

Milark Industries Inc......................... D 419 524-7627
　Mansfield *(G-8828)*

Millat Industries Corp....................... F 937 535-1500
　Dayton *(G-5887)*

▲ Millat Industries Corp................... D 937 434-6666
　Dayton *(G-5888)*

▲ Mitec Powertrain Inc..................... C 567 525-5606
　Findlay *(G-6894)*

◆ Mitsubishi Elc Auto Amer Inc...........B 513 573-6614
　Mason *(G-9128)*

▲ Modern Transmission Dev Co.......... C
　Valley City *(G-13506)*

Monarch Plastic Inc......................... F 330 683-0822
　Orrville *(G-10995)*

▲ Motherson Ychiyo Auto Tech PDT.... D 614 876-3220
　Columbus *(G-5113)*

Mrs Electronic Inc............................ F 937 660-6767
　Dayton *(G-5897)*

◆ Namoh Ohio Holdings Inc................G
　Norwood *(G-10869)*

Nanogate North America LLC.............. B 419 522-7745
　Mansfield *(G-8834)*

▲ Neaton Auto Products Mfg Inc......... E 937 456-7103
　Eaton *(G-6460)*

New Sabina Industries Inc................. G 937 584-2433
　Grove City *(G-7405)*

▲ New Sabina Industries Inc .... E 937 584-2433
Sabina *(G-11680)*

▲ Newman Technology Inc .... A 419 525-1856
Mansfield *(G-8838)*

Nippon Stl Intgrted Crnkshaft .... F 419 435-0411
Fostoria *(G-6994)*

Nitto Inc .... D 937 773-4820
Piqua *(G-11368)*

▲ Nitto Inc .... C 937 773-4820
Piqua *(G-11369)*

◆ Noco Company .... D 216 464-8131
Glenwillow *(G-7286)*

▼ Norlake Manufacturing Company ...... D 440 353-3200
North Ridgeville *(G-10741)*

◆ Norplas Industries Inc .... C 419 662-3200
Northwood *(G-10805)*

North Coast Exotics Inc .... G 216 651-5512
Cleveland *(G-4084)*

Northern Stamping Co .... F 216 642-8081
Cleveland *(G-4097)*

Norton Manufacturing Co Inc .... F 419 435-0411
Fostoria *(G-6995)*

Oakley Inds Sub Assmbly Div In .... E 419 661-8888
Northwood *(G-10806)*

Oe Exchange LLC .... G 440 266-1639
Mentor *(G-9575)*

Oerlikon Friction Systems .... E 937 449-4000
Dayton *(G-5922)*

◆ Oerlikon Friction Systems .... D 937 449-4000
Dayton *(G-5923)*

Ohio Auto Supply Company .... G 330 454-5105
Canton *(G-1964)*

▲ Ohta Press US Inc .... F 937 374-3382
Xenia *(G-14773)*

OReilly Equipment LLC .... G 440 564-1234
Newbury *(G-10559)*

◆ Pacific Industries USA Inc .... E 513 860-3900
Fairfield *(G-6761)*

▲ Pacific Manufacturing Ohio Inc .... B 513 860-3900
Fairfield *(G-6762)*

▲ Pako Inc .... C 440 946-8030
Mentor *(G-9580)*

Park-Ohio Industries Inc .... C 216 341-2300
Newburgh Heights *(G-10546)*

Parker-Hannifin Corporation .... B 440 943-5700
Wickliffe *(G-14389)*

▲ Pdi Ground Support Systems Inc .... D 216 271-7344
Solon *(G-12166)*

Performance Motorsports Inc .... F 440 951-6600
Mentor *(G-9585)*

◆ Pioneer Automotive Tech Inc .... C 937 746-2293
Miamisburg *(G-9727)*

Piston Automotive LLC .... D 313 541-8674
Avon *(G-735)*

Piston Automotive LLC .... A 740 223-0075
Marion *(G-8989)*

Piston Automotive LLC .... A 419 464-0250
Toledo *(G-13099)*

Powers and Sons LLC .... G 419 737-2373
Pioneer *(G-11325)*

▲ Powers and Sons LLC .... E 419 485-3151
Montpelier *(G-10132)*

Pt Tech LLC .... D 330 239-4933
Wadsworth *(G-13662)*

Pullman Company .... C 419 499-2541
Milan *(G-9917)*

Pullman Company .... C 419 592-2055
Napoleon *(G-10296)*

▲ Qualtor Inc .... D 248 204-8600
Cleveland *(G-4211)*

Qualitor Subsidiary H Inc .... E 419 562-7987
Bucyrus *(G-1686)*

Quality Reproductions Inc .... G 330 335-5000
Wadsworth *(G-13664)*

Race Winning Brands Inc .... B 440 951-6600
Mentor *(G-9606)*

Radar Love Co .... G 419 951-4750
Findlay *(G-6912)*

◆ Ramco Specialties Inc .... D 330 653-5135
Hudson *(G-7855)*

▲ Reactive Resin Products Co .... F 419 666-6119
Perrysburg *(G-11259)*

▲ Remington Steel Inc .... D 937 322-2414
Springfield *(G-12370)*

Restortion Parts Unlimited Inc .... F 513 934-0815
Lebanon *(G-8283)*

▼ Riker Products Inc .... D 419 729-1626
Toledo *(G-13112)*

Rochling Automotive USA LLP .... D 330 400-5785
Akron *(G-288)*

◆ Roki America Co Ltd .... B 419 424-9713
Findlay *(G-6913)*

RTC Converters Inc .... F 937 743-2300
Franklin *(G-7047)*

Rubber Duck 4x4 Inc .... G 513 889-1735
Hamilton *(G-7521)*

Saf-Holland Inc .... G 513 874-7888
Fairfield *(G-6773)*

▲ Saia-Burgess Lcc .... D 937 898-3621
Vandalia *(G-13576)*

▲ Sanoh America Inc .... D 419 425-2600
Findlay *(G-6915)*

Schaeffler Transm Systems LLC .... A 330 202-6212
Wooster *(G-14680)*

▲ Schaeffler Transm Systems LLC .... E 330 264-4383
Wooster *(G-14681)*

▲ Schaeffler Transmission Llc .... B 330 264-4383
Wooster *(G-14682)*

◆ Schafer Driveline LLC .... F 740 694-2055
Fredericktown *(G-7084)*

Schott Metal Products Company .... G 330 773-7873
Akron *(G-307)*

Scs Gearbox Inc .... F 419 483-7278
Bellevue *(G-1130)*

▲ Seabiscuit Motorsports Inc .... B 440 951-6600
Mentor *(G-9612)*

Sew-Eurodrive Inc .... D 937 335-0036
Troy *(G-13254)*

Sfs Group Usa Inc .... D 330 239-7100
Medina *(G-9446)*

Sfs Intec Inc .... E 330 239-7100
Medina *(G-9447)*

Soundwich Inc .... E 216 249-4900
Cleveland *(G-4315)*

Soundwich Inc .... D 216 486-2666
Cleveland *(G-4316)*

Spencer Manufacturing Company Inc .... D 330 648-2461
Spencer *(G-12236)*

▲ Steck Manufacturing Co LLC .... F 937 222-0062
Dayton *(G-6026)*

Steer & Gear Inc .... G 614 231-4064
Columbus *(G-5291)*

▲ Steere Enterprises Inc .... D 330 633-4926
Tallmadge *(G-12751)*

Stoneridge Inc .... A 419 884-1219
Lexington *(G-8374)*

◆ Sumiriko Ohio Inc .... D 419 358-2121
Bluffton *(G-1365)*

Sumitomo Elc Wirg Systems Inc .... E 937 642-7579
Marysville *(G-9052)*

▲ Superior Energy Systems LLC .... F 440 236-6009
Columbia Station *(G-4603)*

▲ Superior Production LLC .... C 614 444-2181
Columbus *(G-5299)*

▲ Supertrapp Industries Inc .... D 216 265-8400
Cleveland *(G-4350)*

◆ Taiho Corporation of America .... C 419 443-1645
Tiffin *(G-12801)*

Tdi Co .... G 937 898-9600
Dayton *(G-6041)*

Teijin Automotive Tech Inc .... B 419 396-1980
Carey *(G-2063)*

Teijin Automotive Tech Inc .... B 419 257-2231
North Baltimore *(G-10618)*

Teijin Automotive Tech Inc .... B 419 238-4628
Van Wert *(G-13546)*

Tetra Mold & Tool Inc .... E 937 845-1651
New Carlisle *(G-10382)*

▲ Tfo Tech Co Ltd .... C 740 426-6381
Jeffersonville *(G-7988)*

Thermal Solutions Mfg Inc .... G 800 776-4225
Brookpark *(G-1559)*

▲ Thyssenkrupp Bilstein Amer Inc .... C 513 881-7600
Hamilton *(G-7531)*

TI Group Auto Systems LLC .... E 740 929-2049
Hebron *(G-7640)*

▲ Tigerpoly Manufacturing Inc .... B 614 871-0045
Grove City *(G-7416)*

▲ Tmg Performance Products LLC .... D 440 891-0999
Berea *(G-1192)*

Toledo Molding & Die LLC .... C 419 692-6022
Delphos *(G-6193)*

Toledo Molding & Die LLC .... C 419 692-6022
Delphos *(G-6194)*

Toledo Pro Fiberglass Inc .... G 419 241-9390
Toledo *(G-13156)*

▲ Tom Smith Industries Inc .... D 937 832-1555
Englewood *(G-6626)*

▲ Torque 2020 CMA Acqisition LLC ...... C 330 874-2900
Bolivar *(G-1393)*

Torsion Control Products Inc .... F 248 537-1900
Wadsworth *(G-13675)*

Total Engine Airflow .... G 330 634-2155
Tallmadge *(G-12754)*

Tower Atmtive Oprtons USA I LL .... C 419 483-1500
Bellevue *(G-1136)*

▲ Trailer Component Mfg Inc .... E 440 255-2888
Mentor *(G-9640)*

Tri-Mac Mfg & Svcs Co .... F 513 896-4445
Hamilton *(G-7533)*

Trico Holding Corporation .... G 216 589-0198
Cleveland *(C-4420)*

◆ Trico Products Corporation .... C 800 388-7428
Cleveland *(G-4425)*

▲ Trim Parts Inc .... E 513 934-0815
Lebanon *(G-8291)*

▲ Trim Systems Operating Corp .... D 614 289-5360
New Albany *(G-10352)*

Trucks & Parts of Tampa LLC .... G 937 437-0377
New Paris *(G-10427)*

▼ Trulil Inc .... C 937 652-1242
Urbana *(G-13479)*

▲ TS Tech USA Corporation .... B 614 577-1088
Reynoldsburg *(G-11584)*

▲ TS Trim Industries Inc .... B 614 837-4114
Canal Winchester *(G-1799)*

Ucan Test Instruments LLC .... G 330 696-6624
Akron *(G-349)*

▲ UCI International LLC .... E 330 899-0340
North Canton *(G-10679)*

UGN Inc .... C 513 360-3500
Lebanon *(G-8294)*

Unison Industries LLC .... B 904 667-9904
Dayton *(G-5625)*

◆ United Components LLC .... E 330 899-0340
Toledo *(G-13168)*

▲ US Kondo Corporation...................... F 937 916-3045
Piqua *(G-11388)*

US Tsubaki Power Transm LLC................ C 419 626-4560
Sandusky *(G-11881)*

Usui International Corporation.............. C 513 448-0410
Sharonville *(G-11949)*

Usui International Corporation.............. D 734 354-3626
West Chester *(G-14089)*

▼ Varbros LLC.................................. D 216 267-5200
Cleveland *(G-4457)*

▲ Vari-Wall Tube Specialists Inc............. D 330 482-0000
Columbiana *(G-4631)*

Vehicle Systems Inc........................... G 330 854-0535
Massillon *(G-9251)*

▲ Venco Manufacturing Inc.................... F 513 772-8448
Cincinnati *(G-3196)*

▲ Venco Venturo Industries LLC.............. E 513 772-8448
Cincinnati *(G-3197)*

▲ Ventra Sandusky LLC........................ C 419 627-3600
Sandusky *(G-11882)*

Veoneer Brake Systems LLC.................. C 419 425-6725
Findlay *(G-6931)*

◆ Walor North America Inc....................B 614 445-6060
Columbus *(G-5354)*

Walther Engrg & Mfg Co Inc................. E 937 743-8125
Franklin *(G-7056)*

▲ Weastec Incorporated....................... C 937 393-6800
Hillsboro *(G-7728)*

West & Barker Inc.............................. F 330 652-9923
Niles *(G-10609)*

▲ Westbrook Mfg Inc........................... B 937 254-2004
Dayton *(G-6078)*

Western Branch Diesel LLC................... F 330 454-8800
Canton *(G-2047)*

Westfield Steel Inc............................. D 937 322-2414
Springfield *(G-12392)*

Wheel Group Holdings LLC.................. G 614 253-6247
Columbus *(G-5366)*

Whirlaway Corporation........................ D 440 647-4711
Wellington *(G-13902)*

Whirlaway Corporation........................ D 440 647-4711
Wellington *(G-13903)*

▲ Whirlaway Corporation...................... C 440 647-4711
Wellington *(G-13904)*

White Mule Company........................... E 740 382-9008
Ontario *(G-10954)*

▲ Winzeler Stamping Co....................... E 419 485-3147
Montpelier *(G-10138)*

Woodbridge Group.............................. C 419 334-3666
Fremont *(G-7144)*

Workhorse Group Inc........................... D 888 646-5205
Sharonville *(G-11950)*

Workhorse Technologies Inc.................. E 888 646-5205
Sharonville *(G-11951)*

▲ Yamada North America Inc.................. B 937 462-7111
South Charleston *(G-12215)*

Yanfeng Intl Auto Tech US I LL.............. D 419 633-1873
Bryan *(G-1668)*

Yanfeng Intl Auto Tech US I LL.............. D 616 834-9422
Bryan *(G-1669)*

ZF Active Safety & Elec US LLC............. D 216 750-2400
Cleveland *(G-4524)*

ZF Active Safety & Elec US LLC............. E 419 726-5599
Toledo *(G-13183)*

ZF Active Safety US Inc....................... F 419 237-2511
Fayette *(G-6825)*

3715 Truck trailers

4w Services....................................... F 614 554-5427
Hebron *(G-7606)*

▼ All A Cart Manufacturing Inc............... F 614 443-5544
Worthington *(G-14704)*

American Mnfctring Oprtons Inc............ G 419 269-1560
Toledo *(G-12876)*

Bell Logistics Co................................ E 740 702-9830
Chillicothe *(G-2245)*

Bruce-High Performance Tran................ G 440 357-8964
Painesville *(G-11070)*

Diamond Trailers Inc.......................... G 513 738-4500
Shandon *(G-11934)*

East Manufacturing Corporation............ C 330 325-9921
Randolph *(G-11509)*

▼ East Trailers LLC............................. E 330 325-9921
Randolph *(G-11510)*

Eastern Truck & Trailer LLC................. E 866 240-4422
Circleville *(G-3256)*

Engineered MBL Solutions Inc............... F 513 724-0247
Batavia *(G-864)*

H & H Equipment Inc.......................... G 330 264-5400
Wooster *(G-14647)*

Haulette Manufacturing Inc.................. D 419 586-1717
Celina *(G-2108)*

High Tech Prfmce Trlrs Inc................... E 440 357-8964
Painesville *(G-11094)*

J & L Body Inc................................... F 216 661-2323
Brooklyn Heights *(G-1533)*

Kenan Advantage Group Inc.................. G 614 878-4050
Columbus *(G-5048)*

Kidron Inc..B 330 857-3011
Kidron *(G-8129)*

Lyons.. G 440 224-0676
Kingsville *(G-8138)*

M & W Trailers Inc............................. F 419 453-3331
Ottoville *(G-11055)*

M R Trailer Sales Inc........................... G 330 339-7701
New Philadelphia *(G-10456)*

Mac Manufacturing Inc........................ C 330 829-1680
Salem *(G-11797)*

▲ Mac Manufacturing Inc...................... A 330 823-9900
Alliance *(G-388)*

Mac Steel Trailer Ltd.......................... G 330 823-9900
Alliance *(G-389)*

◆ Mac Trailer Manufacturing Inc............. A 800 795-8454
Alliance *(G-390)*

Mac Trailer Service Inc....................... E 330 823-9190
Alliance *(G-391)*

Martin Allen Trailer LLC...................... G 330 942-0217
Akron *(G-223)*

Moritz International Inc....................... E 419 526-5222
Mansfield *(G-8833)*

▼ Nelson Manufacturing Company........... D 419 523-5321
Ottawa *(G-11039)*

Paccar Inc.. D 740 774-5111
Chillicothe *(G-2269)*

▲ Pdi Ground Support Systems Inc.......... D 216 271-7344
Solon *(G-12166)*

◆ Quick Loadz Container Sys LLC............ E 888 304-3946
Athens *(G-648)*

Saf-Holland Inc................................. G 513 874-7888
Fairfield *(G-6773)*

Shilling Transport Inc......................... G 330 948-1105
Lodi *(G-8506)*

Stahl/Scott Fetzer Company.................. C 800 277-8245
Wooster *(G-14689)*

▼ Trailer One Inc............................... F 330 723-7474
Medina *(G-9457)*

Trailstar International Inc.................... E 330 823-9900
Alliance *(G-411)*

Trailstar International Inc.................... E 330 821-9900
Alliance *(G-412)*

Wabash National Corporation................ F 419 434-9409
Findlay *(G-6932)*

3716 Motor homes

Advanced Rv LLC................................ E 440 283-0405
Willoughby *(G-14414)*

◆ Airstream Inc..................................B 937 596-6111
Jackson Center *(G-7958)*

3721 Aircraft

Aerovation Tech Holdings LLC.............. G 567 208-5525
Forest *(G-6938)*

Avari Aero LLC.................................. G 513 828-0860
Cincinnati *(G-2392)*

Boeing Company................................ E 740 788-4000
Heath *(G-7594)*

▲ Consoldted Precision Pdts Corp.......... C 216 453-4800
Cleveland *(G-3560)*

Executive Wings Inc........................... G 440 254-1812
Painesville *(G-11084)*

Goodrich Corporation.......................... A 937 339-3811
Troy *(G-13219)*

Hii Mission Technologies Corp............... G 937 426-3421
Beavercreek *(G-992)*

K&M Aviation LLC.............................. D 216 261-9000
Cleveland *(G-3902)*

Nextant Aerospace LLC....................... E 216 898-4800
Cleveland *(G-4075)*

▲ Powder Alloy Corporation.................. E 513 984-4016
Loveland *(G-8646)*

Ruhe Sales Inc................................... F 419 943-3357
Leipsic *(G-8314)*

Snow Aviation Intl Inc......................... G 614 588-2452
Gahanna *(G-7169)*

Star Jet LLC...................................... G 614 338-4379
Columbus *(G-5289)*

Steel Aviation Aircraft Sales................. G 937 332-7587
Casstown *(G-2092)*

Technology House Ltd.......................... F 440 248-3025
Streetsboro *(G-12526)*

Tessec LLC....................................... D 937 576-0010
Dayton *(G-6045)*

Tessec Manufacturing Svcs LLC............ E 937 985-3552
Dayton *(G-6046)*

Theiss Uav Solutions LLC..................... G 330 584-2070
North Benton *(G-10624)*

Toledo Jet Center LLC......................... G 419 866-9050
Swanton *(G-12695)*

3724 Aircraft engines and engine parts

Advanced Ground Systems...................... F 513 402-7226
Cincinnati *(G-2338)*

Aero Jet Wash Llc............................... F 866 381-7955
Dayton *(G-5637)*

American Aero Components Llc.............. G 937 367-5068
Dayton *(G-5649)*

At Holdings Corporation....................... A 216 692-6000
Cleveland *(G-3382)*

Avidyne... G 800 284-3963
Dublin *(G-6280)*

Barnes Group Inc............................... F 513 779-6888
West Chester *(G-13946)*

CFM International Inc.......................... F 513 563-4180
Cincinnati *(G-2455)*

CFM International Inc.......................... F 513 563-4180
Cincinnati *(G-2456)*

CFM International Inc.......................... E 513 552-2787
West Chester *(G-13959)*

Defense Research Assoc Inc.................. E 937 431-1644
Dayton *(G-5609)*

◆ Dreison International Inc....................C 216 362-0755
Cleveland *(G-3632)*

Drt Aerospace LLC.............................. E 937 492-6121
Sidney *(G-12013)*

Eaton Industrial Corporation.................B 216 523-4205
Cleveland *(G-3656)*

Enjet Aero Dayton Inc.............................. E 937 878-3800
  Huber Heights *(G-7821)*

▲ Ferrotherm Corporation......................... C 216 883-9350
  Cleveland *(G-3714)*

General Electric Company........................ G 513 948-4170
  Cincinnati *(G-2660)*

Heico Aerospace Parts Corp.................... B 954 987-6101
  Highland Heights *(G-7659)*

▲ Henry Tools Inc.................................... G 216 291-1011
  Cleveland *(G-3824)*

▲ Hi-Tek Manufacturing Inc..................... C 513 459-1094
  Mason *(G-9108)*

Honeywell International I........................... F 513 282-5519
  Mason *(G-9109)*

Honeywell International Inc....................... F 216 459-6048
  Brookpark *(G-1552)*

Honeywell International Inc....................... E 440 329-9000
  Elyria *(G-6542)*

▲ Honeywell Lebow Products.................... C 614 850-5000
  Columbus *(G-4991)*

Lsp Technologies Inc.............................. E 614 718-3000
  Dublin *(G-6318)*

Magellan Arospc Middletown Inc............ D 513 422-2751
  Middletown *(G-9875)*

◆ Meyer Tool Inc.....................................A 513 681-7362
  Cincinnati *(G-2874)*

▲ Miba Bearings US LLC........................ B 740 962-4242
  Mcconnelsville *(G-9364)*

Optical Display Engrg Inc........................ F 440 995-6555
  Highland Heights *(G-7661)*

Otto Konigslow Mfg Co........................... F 216 851-7900
  Cleveland *(G-4128)*

▲ Pako Inc.. C 440 946-8030
  Mentor *(G-9580)*

Parker-Hannifin Corporation.................... C 440 284-6277
  Elyria *(G-6576)*

Pas Technologies Inc.............................. D 937 840-1053
  Hillsboro *(G-7723)*

PCC Airfoils LLC.................................... C 440 255-9770
  Mentor *(G-9584)*

Precision Castparts Corp......................... F 440 350-6150
  Painesville *(G-11106)*

◆ Sifco Industries Inc..............................D 216 881-8600
  Cleveland *(G-4299)*

Snow Aviation Intl Inc............................. G 614 588-2452
  Gahanna *(G-7169)*

Spirit Avionics Ltd.................................. F 614 237-4271
  Columbus *(G-5204)*

▲ Superalloy Mfg Solutions Corp............ C 513 489-9800
  Blue Ash *(G-1337)*

Tessec LLC.. D 937 576-0010
  Dayton *(G-6045)*

Turbine Eng Cmpnents Tech Corp.......... B 216 692-5200
  Cleveland *(G-4433)*

▲ Turbine Standard Ltd........................... G 419 865-0355
  Holland *(G-7789)*

Warfighter Fcsed Logistics Inc................ E 740 513-4692
  West Chester *(G-14091)*

▲ Welded Ring Products Co..................... D 216 961-3800
  Cleveland *(G-4499)*

3728 Aircraft parts and equipment, nec

Achilles Aerospace Pdts Inc................... E 330 425-8444
  Twinsburg *(G-13268)*

▼ Advanced Fuel Systems Inc................. G 614 252-8422
  Columbus *(G-4676)*

Aero Tech Tool & Mold Inc...................... G 440 942-3327
  Mentor *(G-9471)*

Aerospace LLC....................................... F 937 561-1104
  Moraine *(G-10143)*

▲ Aerospace Maint Solutions LLC........... E 440 729-7703
  Solon *(G-12074)*

Aim International..................................... G 513 831-2938
  Miamiville *(G-9761)*

Aircraft Wheel & Brake LLC.................... D 440 937-6211
  Avon *(G-713)*

Allen Aircraft Products Inc...................... E 330 296-9621
  Ravenna *(G-11514)*

▲ Allen Aircraft Products Inc.................. D 330 296-9621
  Ravenna *(G-11516)*

American Aero Components Llc.............. G 937 367-5068
  Dayton *(G-5649)*

Apph Wichita Inc.................................... E 316 943-5752
  Strongsville *(G-12537)*

Arctos Mission Solutions LLC................ E 813 609-5591
  Beavercreek *(G-965)*

At Holdings Corporation......................... A 216 692-6000
  Cleveland *(G-3382)*

Auto-Valve Inc....................................... E 937 854-3037
  Dayton *(G-5668)*

Aviation Cmpnent Solutions Inc............. F 440 295-6590
  Richmond Heights *(G-11607)*

Avtron Aerospace Inc............................. C 216 750-5152
  Cleveland *(G-3393)*

Aws Industries Inc.................................. E 513 932-7941
  Lebanon *(G-8245)*

Barnes Group Inc................................... G 513 779-6888
  West Chester *(G-13947)*

◆ Bosserman Aviation Equipment Inc....E 419 722-2879
  Carey *(G-2056)*

▲ Columbus Jack Corporation................. E 614 443-7492
  Swanton *(G-12680)*

Ctl-Aerospace Inc.................................. E 513 874-7900
  West Chester *(G-14112)*

Ctl-Aerospace Inc.................................. C 513 874-7900
  Cincinnati *(G-2530)*

Danfoss Power Solutions II LLC.............. F 419 238-1190
  Van Wert *(G-13533)*

Dircksen and Associates Inc.................. G 614 238-0413
  Columbus *(G-4881)*

Drone Express Inc.................................. F 513 577-5152
  Dayton *(G-5752)*

Drt Aerospace LLC................................. E 937 492-6121
  Sidney *(G-12013)*

Drt Holdings LLC.................................... D 937 298-7391
  Dayton *(G-5753)*

Dukes Aerospace Inc............................. D 818 998-9811
  Painesville *(G-11080)*

◆ Eaton Aeroquip LLC............................. C 440 523-5000
  Cleveland *(G-3050)*

Eaton Industrial Corporation................... C 216 692-5456
  Cleveland *(G-3657)*

Eaton Industrial Corporation................... B 216 523-4205
  Cleveland *(G-3656)*

Electronic Concepts Engrg Inc................ F 419 861-9000
  Holland *(G-7763)*

Enjet Aero LLC....................................... F 937 878-3800
  Huber Heights *(G-7820)*

Enjet Aero Dayton Inc............................ E 937 878-3800
  Huber Heights *(G-7821)*

▼ Esterline Technologies Corp............... E 216 706-2960
  Cleveland *(G-3687)*

Eti Tech LLC.. F 937 832-4200
  Kettering *(G-8120)*

Exito Manufacturing LLC......................... G 937 291-9871
  Beavercreek *(G-991)*

▲ Federal Equipment Company............... D 513 621-5260
  Cincinnati *(G-2616)*

Ferco Tech LLC...................................... C 937 746-6696
  Franklin *(G-7020)*

Field Aviation Inc................................... E 513 792-2282
  Cincinnati *(G-2622)*

Fluid Power Inc...................................... F 330 653-5107
  Hudson *(G-7841)*

◆ Friction Products Co............................ B 330 725-4941
  Medina *(G-9406)*

GE Aviation Systems LLC....................... B 937 898-5881
  Vandalia *(G-13558)*

GE Engine Services LLC......................... B 513 977-1500
  Cincinnati *(G-2656)*

GE Military Systems................................ G 513 243-2000
  Cincinnati *(G-2658)*

General Dynamics-Ots Inc....................... C 937 746-8500
  Springboro *(G-12253)*

General Electric Company....................... E 513 977-1500
  Cincinnati *(G-2662)*

Goodrich Corporation............................. G 440 262-1400
  Brecksville *(G-1469)*

Goodrich Corporation............................. G 330 374-2358
  North Canton *(G-10643)*

Goodrich Corporation............................. A 937 339-3811
  Troy *(G-13219)*

Goodrich Corporation............................. F 216 429-4378
  Troy *(G-13220)*

Grimes Aerospace Company................... D 937 484-2000
  Urbana *(G-13463)*

▲ Grimes Aerospace Company............... A 937 484-2000
  Urbana *(G-13462)*

▲ GSE Production and Support LLC........ G 419 866-6301
  Swanton *(G-12685)*

◆ Hartzell Propeller Inc...........................C 937 778-4200
  Piqua *(G-11353)*

Hdi Landing Gear USA Inc....................... E 937 325-1586
  Strongsville *(G-12563)*

Hdi Landing Gear USA Inc....................... D 937 325-1586
  Springfield *(G-12318)*

Heller Machine Products Inc................... G 216 281-2951
  Cleveland *(G-3820)*

Heroux-Devtek Inc.................................. F 937 325-1586
  Springfield *(G-12321)*

Hydro-Aire Inc....................................... C 440 323-3211
  Elyria *(G-6543)*

Hydro-Aire Aerospace Corp.................... C 440 323-3211
  Elyria *(G-6544)*

◆ Industrial Mfg Co LLC..........................F 440 838-4700
  Brecksville *(G-1472)*

Jay-Em Aerospace Corporation.............. E 330 923-0333
  Cuyahoga Falls *(G-5551)*

Kelly Arspc Thrmal Systems LLC............ E 440 951-4744
  Willoughby *(G-14476)*

▲ Lawrence Technologies Inc................. G 937 274-7771
  Dayton *(G-5042)*

Lincoln Electric Automtn Inc................... B 937 295-2120
  Fort Loramie *(G-6950)*

Lkd Aerospace Holdings Inc................... F 216 262-8481
  Cleveland *(G-3965)*

▲ Logan Machine Company..................... D 330 633-6163
  Akron *(G-210)*

Long-Lok LLC... E 336 343-7319
  Cincinnati *(G-2826)*

Magellan Arospc Middletown Inc............ D 513 422-2751
  Middletown *(G-9875)*

Malabar... E 419 866-6301
  Swanton *(G-12687)*

Mar-Con Tool Company........................... E 937 299-2244
  Moraine *(G-10175)*

Master Swaging Inc................................ G 937 596-6171
  Jackson Center *(G-7965)*

▲ Maverick Molding Co............................ F 513 387-6100
  Blue Ash *(G-1305)*

McKechnie Arospc Holdings Inc............. G 216 706-2960
  Cleveland *(G-4011)*

◆ Meggitt Arcft Brking Systems C........A 330 796-4400
  Akron *(G-228)*

Meggitt Polymers & Composites............. F 513 851-5550
  Cincinnati *(G-2859)*

Middleton Enterprises Inc.......................G..... 614 885-2514
Worthington *(G-14721)*

▼ Midwest Aircraft Products Co...........F..... 419 884-2164
Mansfield *(G-8826)*

▲ Milan Tool Corp.....................................E..... 216 661-1078
Cleveland *(G-4039)*

Pacific Piston Ring Co Inc....................E..... 513 387-6100
Blue Ash *(G-1317)*

▲ Pako Inc..C..... 440 946-8030
Mentor *(G-9580)*

Parker Meggitt..F..... 513 851-5550
Cincinnati *(G-2942)*

Parker-Hannifin Corporation..................C..... 440 937-6211
Avon *(G-734)*

Parker-Hannifin Corporation..................C..... 440 284-6277
Elyria *(G-6576)*

PCC Airfoils LLC...................................B..... 740 982-6025
Crooksville *(G-5511)*

▲ Skidmore-Wilhelm Mfg Company........G..... 216 481-4774
Solon *(G-12182)*

Snow Aviation Intl Inc...........................G..... 614 588-2452
Gahanna *(G-7169)*

Spectrum Textiles Inc............................F..... 513 933-8346
Lebanon *(G-8286)*

Starwin Industries LLC.........................937 293-8568
Dayton *(G-6024)*

Summit Avionics Inc..............................G..... 330 425-1440
Twinsburg *(G-13381)*

Taylor Manufacturing Co Inc.................F..... 937 322-8622
Springfield *(G-12383)*

Tessec Technology Services LLC..........E..... 513 240-5601
Dayton *(G-6047)*

Test-Fuchs Corporation.........................440 708-3505
Brecksville *(G-1483)*

Tracewell Systems Inc...........................D..... 614 846-6175
Lewis Center *(G-8356)*

Transdigm Group Incorporated..............B..... 216 706-2960
Cleveland *(G-4413)*

Triumph Thermal Systems LLC..............D..... 419 273-2511
Forest *(G-6942)*

◆ Tronair Inc..D..... 419 866-6301
Swanton *(G-12697)*

Truline Industries Inc............................D..... 440 729-0140
Wickliffe *(G-14397)*

Turbine Eng Cmpnents Tech Corp.........B..... 216 692-5200
Cleveland *(G-4433)*

Unison Industries LLC...........................B..... 904 667-9904
Dayton *(G-5625)*

US Aeroteam Inc....................................E..... 937 458-0344
Dayton *(G-6070)*

◆ US Technology Corporation..................E..... 330 455-1181
Canton *(G-2039)*

Weldon Pump LLC.................................E..... 440 232-2282
Oakwood Village *(G-10913)*

White Machine Inc..................................G..... 440 237-3282
North Royalton *(G-10789)*

3731 Shipbuilding and repairing

Dredger LLC...G..... 513 507-8774
West Chester *(G-13986)*

Great Lakes Group.................................C..... 216 621-4854
Cleveland *(G-3792)*

Ironhead Marine Inc...............................E..... 419 690-0000
Toledo *(G-13011)*

Lake Erie Ship Repr Fbrction L..............F..... 440 228-7110
Jefferson *(G-7977)*

McGinnis Inc...C..... 740 377-4391
South Point *(G-12226)*

McNational Inc.......................................D..... 740 377-4391
South Point *(G-12227)*

◆ Pinney Dock & Transport LLC...............F..... 440 964-7186
Ashtabula *(G-612)*

Professional Marine Repair LLC.............G..... 440 409-9957
Ashtabula *(G-613)*

Services Acquisition Co LLC..................G..... 330 479-9267
Dennison *(G-6218)*

Superior Marine Ways Inc......................C..... 740 894-6224
Proctorville *(G-11499)*

Tack-Anew Inc..G..... 419 734-4212
Port Clinton *(G-11453)*

The Great Lakes Towing Company..........D..... 216 621-4854
Cleveland *(G-4383)*

3732 Boatbuilding and repairing

Brewster Sugarcreek Twp Histo..............F..... 330 767-0045
Brewster *(G-1491)*

Checkmate Marine Inc............................G..... 419 562-3881
Bucyrus *(G-1675)*

Don Wartko Construction Inc..................D..... 330 673-5252
Kent *(G-8026)*

Dynamic Plastics Inc.............................G..... 937 437-7261
New Paris *(G-10426)*

Mariners Landing Inc.............................G..... 513 941-3625
Cincinnati *(G-2846)*

▲ Nauticus Inc..G..... 440 746-1290
Brecksville *(G-1478)*

Racelite Southcoast Inc.........................F..... 216 581-4600
Maple Heights *(G-8891)*

Tugz International LLC............................F..... 216 621-4854
Cleveland *(G-4432)*

W of Ohio Inc..G..... 614 873-4664
Plain City *(G-11426)*

3743 Railroad equipment

A Stucki Company..................................D..... 412 424-0560
North Canton *(G-10626)*

▲ Alliance Castings Company LLC............E..... 330 829-5600
Alliance *(G-369)*

Amsted Industries Incorporated.............D..... 614 836-2323
Groveport *(G-7422)*

B&C Machine Co LLC.............................F..... 330 745-4013
Barberton *(G-796)*

◆ Buck Equipment Inc.............................E..... 614 539-3039
Grove City *(G-7375)*

◆ Dayton-Phoenix Group Inc...................C..... 937 496-3900
Dayton *(G-5742)*

Engines Inc of Ohio...............................E..... 740 377-9874
South Point *(G-12223)*

Gunderson Rail Services LLC.................D..... 330 792-6521
Youngstown *(G-14872)*

▼ Jk-Co LLC...E..... 419 422-5240
Findlay *(G-6883)*

Johnson Bros Rubber Co Inc..................E..... 419 752-4814
Greenwich *(G-7362)*

K & G Machine Company........................F..... 216 732-7115
Cleveland *(G-3900)*

L B Foster Company...............................F..... 330 652-1461
Mineral Ridge *(G-10030)*

Midwest Rlwy Prsrvtion Soc Inc.............G..... 216 781-3629
Cleveland *(G-4038)*

Nolan Company......................................G..... 740 269-1512
Bowerston *(G-1400)*

Nolan Company......................................F..... 330 453-7922
Canton *(G-1958)*

Ohio Valley Trackwork Inc......................G..... 740 446-0181
Bidwell *(G-1213)*

Progress Rail Services Corp...................B..... 216 641-4000
Cleveland *(G-4200)*

Progress Rail Services Corp...................F..... 614 850-1730
Columbus *(G-5211)*

R H Little Co...G..... 330 477-3455
Canton *(G-1989)*

Ready 2 Ride Trnsp LLC.........................G..... 614 207-2683
Pickerington *(G-11299)*

Sperling Railway Services Inc................F..... 330 479-2004
Canton *(G-2011)*

Transco Railway Products Inc................E..... 330 872-0934
Newton Falls *(G-10581)*

Westinghouse A Brake Tech Corp..........G..... 419 526-5323
Mansfield *(G-8866)*

3751 Motorcycles, bicycles, and parts

B&D Truck Parts Sls & Svcs LLC...........G..... 419 701-7041
Fostoria *(G-6976)*

▲ Cmbf Products Inc................................C..... 855 403-9083
Medina *(G-9388)*

▲ Cobra Motorcycles Mfg.........................G..... 330 207-3844
North Lima *(G-10705)*

Colony Machine & Tool Inc.....................G..... 330 225-3410
Brunswick *(G-1583)*

Custom Assembly Inc.............................E..... 419 622-3040
Haviland *(G-7586)*

Custom Cycle ACC Mfg Dstrg Inc...........F..... 440 585-2200
Wickliffe *(G-14373)*

◆ Dco LLC...E..... 419 931-9086
Perrysburg *(G-11213)*

▲ Ktm North America Inc..........................D..... 855 215-6360
Amherst *(G-447)*

Milark Industries Inc..............................D..... 419 524-7627
Mansfield *(G-8827)*

Milark Industries Inc..............................D..... 419 524-7627
Mansfield *(G-8828)*

▲ Newman Technology Inc........................A..... 419 525-1856
Mansfield *(G-8838)*

Safe Haven Brands LLC.........................F..... 937 550-9407
Springboro *(G-12267)*

▲ Spiegler Brake Systems USA LLC.........G..... 937 291-1735
Dayton *(G-6018)*

Sunstar Engrg Americas Inc...................D..... 937 743-9049
Franklin *(G-7051)*

▲ Sunstar Engrg Americas Inc..................E..... 937 746-8575
Springboro *(G-12268)*

Thomas D Epperson.............................G..... 937 855-3300
Germantown *(G-7256)*

Ufo Bikes LLC..G..... 724 986-1417
Broadview Heights *(G-1510)*

▲ Vari-Wall Tube Specialists Inc...............D..... 330 482-0000
Columbiana *(G-4631)*

3761 Guided missiles and space vehicles

Space Exploration Tech Corp.................C..... 559 593-2731
Lockbourne *(G-8492)*

Starwin Industries LLC...........................E..... 937 293-8568
Dayton *(G-6024)*

Tessec Manufacturing Svcs LLC.............E..... 937 985-3552
Dayton *(G-6046)*

3769 Space vehicle equipment, nec

Curtiss-Wright Ds Inc.............................E..... 937 252-5601
Fairborn *(G-6689)*

Defense Co Inc.......................................G..... 413 998-1637
Cleveland *(G-3608)*

General Electric Company.......................E..... 513 977-1500
Cincinnati *(G-2662)*

◆ Gleason Metrology Systems Corp.........E..... 937 384-8901
Dayton *(G-5796)*

Grimes Aerospace Company...................D..... 937 484-2001
Urbana *(G-13464)*

▲ Industrial Quartz Corporation................F..... 440 942-0909
Mentor *(G-9530)*

L3harris Cincinnati Elec Corp.................A..... 513 573-6100
Mason *(G-9121)*

Lord Corporation....................................C..... 937 278-9431
Dayton *(G-5854)*

◆ Metalex Manufacturing Inc...................C..... 513 489-0507
Blue Ash *(G-1310)*

▲ Millat Industries Corp .... D 937 434-6666
Dayton (G-5888)

Morris Bean & Company .... C 937 767-7301
Yellow Springs (G-14790)

Sunpower Inc .... D 740 594-2221
Athens (G-654)

Te Connectivity Corporation .... C 419 521-9500
Mansfield (G-8858)

3792 Travel trailers and campers

◆ Airstream Inc ....B 937 596-6111
Jackson Center (G-7958)

ARE Inc .... A 330 830-7800
Massillon (G-9172)

Berlin Truck Caps & Tarps Ltd .... F 330 893-2811
Millersburg (G-9970)

Capitol City Trailers Inc .... D 614 491-2616
Obetz (G-10921)

Xtreme Outdoors LLC .... E 330 731-4137
Uniontown (G-13429)

3795 Tanks and tank components

▲ American Apex Corporation .... F 614 652-2000
Delaware (G-6130)

General Dynmics Land Systems I .... B 419 221-7000
Lima (G-8410)

Integris Composites Inc .... D 740 928-0326
Hebron (G-7619)

◆ Motherson Ychiyo US Auto Syste ... C 740 375-4687
Marion (G-8981)

Performance Tank Sales Inc .... G 330 602-8800
Dover (G-6258)

Tessec Manufacturing Svcs LLC .... E 937 985-3552
Dayton (G-6046)

Weldon Pump LLC .... E 440 232-2282
Oakwood Village (G-10913)

3799 Transportation equipment, nec

All Power Equipment LLC .... F 740 593-3279
Athens (G-632)

B & B Industries Inc .... G 614 871-3883
Orient (G-10970)

Bjs DEMo&hauling LLC .... G 216 904-8909
Garfield Heights (G-7216)

Bulk Carriers Service Inc .... G 330 339-3333
New Philadelphia (G-10435)

▲ Hawkline Nevada LLC .... G 937 444-4295
Mount Orab (G-10217)

Hitch-Hiker Mfg Inc .... F 330 542-3052
New Middletown (G-10424)

Interstate Truckway Inc .... F 614 771-1220
Columbus (G-5022)

Kmj Leasing Ltd .... G 614 871-3883
Orient (G-10971)

▲ Kolpin Outdoors Corporation .... E 330 328-0772
Cuyahoga Falls (G-5555)

◆ L & R Racing Inc .... E 330 220-3102
Brunswick (G-1601)

Loadmaster Trailer Company Ltd .... F 419 732-3434
Port Clinton (G-11445)

Malabar .... E 419 866-6301
Swanton (G-12687)

Midwest Motoplex LLC .... G 740 772-5300
Chillicothe (G-2266)

Otterbacher Trailers LLC .... F 419 462-1975
Galion (G-7196)

Performance Tank Sales Inc .... G 330 602-8800
Dover (G-6258)

Prostar LLC .... F 419 225-8806
Lima (G-8462)

Rankin Mfg Inc .... G 419 929-8338
New London (G-10414)

Rv Xpress Inc .... G 937 418-0127
Piqua (G-11383)

Siraj Recovery LLC .... G 614 893-3507
Columbus (G-5272)

◆ Wholecycle Inc .... E 330 929-8123
Peninsula (G-11186)

World Class Carriages LLC .... G 330 857-7811
Dalton (G-5596)

38 MEASURING, PHOTOGRAPHIC, MEDICAL, & OPTICAL GOODS, & CLOCKS

3812 Search and navigation equipment

Accurate Electronics Inc .... F 330 682-7015
Orrville (G-10972)

◆ ADB Safegate Americas LLC ....C 614 861-1304
Gahanna (G-7152)

Aero-Instruments Co LLC .... E 216 671-3133
Cleveland (G-3309)

Atk Space Systems LLC .... C 937 490-4121
Beavercreek (G-989)

Atk Systems .... G 937 429-8632
Beavercreek (G-990)

Atlantic Inertial Systems Inc .... C 740 788-3800
Heath (G-7593)

Boeing Company .... E 740 788-4000
Heath (G-7594)

Btc Inc .... F 740 549-2722
Lewis Center (G-8326)

Btc Technology Services Inc .... G 740 549-2722
Lewis Center (G-8327)

Cedar Elec Holdings Corp .... D 773 804-6288
West Chester (G-13958)

▲ Ceia Usa Ltd .... D 330 310-4741
Hudson (G-7836)

Circle Prime Manufacturing Inc .... E 330 923-0019
Cuyahoga Falls (G-5534)

▲ Consoldted Precision Pdts Corp ...... C 216 453-4800
Cleveland (G-3560)

Decibel Research Inc .... E 256 705-3341
Beavercreek (G-969)

Dedrone Defense Inc .... F 614 948-2002
Westerville (G-14255)

Dragoon Technologies Inc .... G 937 439-9223
Dayton (G-5751)

Drs Advanced Isr LLC .... C 937 429-7408
Beavercreek (G-970)

Drs Leonardo Inc .... E 937 429-7408
Beavercreek (G-971)

Drs Leonardo Inc .... E 513 943-1111
Cincinnati (G-2301)

▲ Editencom Ltd .... E 419 865-5877
Holland (G-7762)

Enjet Aero Dayton Inc .... E 937 878-3800
Huber Heights (G-7821)

▲ Escort Inc .... C 513 870-8500
West Chester (G-13995)

▼ Esterline Technologies Corp .... E 216 706-2960
Cleveland (G-3687)

Eti Tech LLC .... F 937 832-4200
Kettering (G-8120)

▲ Ferrotherm Corporation .... C 216 883-9350
Cleveland (G-3714)

GE Aviation Systems LLC .... E 513 470-2889
Cincinnati (G-2654)

GE Aviation Systems LLC .... D 937 898-9600
Dayton (G-5791)

GE Aviation Systems LLC .... F 513 786-4555
West Chester (G-14004)

▲ GE Aviation Systems LLC .... G 937 898-9600
Cincinnati (G-2655)

General Dynmics Mssion Systems .... F 513 253-4770
Beavercreek (G-975)

General Electric Company .... E 513 956-9051
Cincinnati (G-2661)

Genpact LLC .... E 513 763-7660
Cincinnati (G-2667)

Grimes Aerospace Company .... D 937 484-2001
Urbana (G-13464)

◆ HBD Industries Inc .... E 614 526-7000
Dublin (G-6302)

Heller Machine Products Inc .... G 216 281-2951
Cleveland (G-3820)

Honeywell International Inc .... A 937 484-2000
Urbana (G-13466)

Hunter Defense Tech Inc .... E 513 943-7880
Cincinnati (G-2307)

IEC Infrared Systems Inc .... E 440 234-8000
Middleburg Heights (G-9771)

IMT Defense Corp .... G 614 891-8812
Westerville (G-14214)

L3 Technologies Inc .... G 937 223-3285
Dayton (G-5840)

L3harris Cincinnati Elec Corp .... A 513 573-6100
Mason (G-9121)

L3harris Electrodynamics Inc .... E 847 259-0740
Cincinnati (G-2310)

Lake Shore Cryotronics Inc .... D 614 891-2243
Westerville (G-14217)

Landrum Brown Wrldwide Svcs LL .... G 513 530-5333
Blue Ash (G-1295)

Lite Magnesium Products Inc .... D 330 296-6110
Ravenna (G-11531)

Lockheed Mrtin Intgrted System .... C 330 796-2800
Akron (G-209)

Midwest Precision Holdings Inc .... F 440 497-4086
Eastlake (G-6436)

Mrl Materials Resources LLC .... E 937 531-6657
Xenia (G-14771)

Nhvs International Inc .... B 440 527-8610
Mentor (G-9571)

Northrop Grmman Innvtion Syste .... C 937 429-9261
Beavercreek (G-993)

Northrop Grmman Tchncal Svcs I .... C 937 320-3100
Beavercreek Township (G-1000)

Northrop Grumman Systems Corp .... C 937 490-4111
Beavercreek (G-994)

Northrop Grumman Systems Corp .... D 937 429-6450
Beavercreek Township (G-1001)

Northrop Grumman Systems Corp .... B 513 881-3296
West Chester (G-14134)

Oculii Corp .... E 937 912-9261
Beavercreek Township (G-1002)

Parker Aerospace .... G 216 225-2721
Cleveland (G-4139)

PCC Airfoils LLC .... B 216 692-7900
Cleveland (G-4148)

Personal Defense & Tactics LLC .... G 513 571-7163
Middletown (G-9884)

Quasonix Inc .... E 513 942-1287
West Chester (G-14058)

Raytheon Company .... F 937 429-5429
Beavercreek (G-980)

◆ Reuter-Stokes LLC .... B 330 425-3755
Twinsburg (G-13365)

Ryse Aero Holdco Inc .... E 513 318-9907
Mason (G-9145)

S&L Fleet Services Inc .... E 740 549-2722
Westerville (G-14232)

Skuld LLC .... E 330 423-7339
Piqua (G-11384)

SIC

▲ **Star Dynamics Corporation**.............. D 614 334-4510
Hilliard **(G-7702)**

Sunset Industries Inc.......................... E 440 306-8284
Mentor **(G-9631)**

Te Connectivity Corporation............... C 419 521-9500
Mansfield **(G-8858)**

▲ **Thermo Gamma-Metrics LLC**........... E 858 450-9811
Bedford **(G-1061)**

Transdigm Inc..................................... G 216 706-2960
Cleveland **(G-4412)**

Trimble Inc.. F 937 233-8921
Dayton **(G-6064)**

Trimble Inc.. F 937 233-8921
Tipp City **(G-12848)**

Valentine Research Inc....................... E 513 984-8900
Blue Ash **(G-1346)**

Vector Electromagnetics LLC.............. F 937 478-5904
Wilmington **(G-14589)**

Wall Colmonoy Corporation................ D 513 842-4200
Cincinnati **(G-3211)**

Watts Antenna Company..................... G 740 797-9380
The Plains **(G-12761)**

Yost Labs Inc...................................... F 740 876-4936
Portsmouth **(G-11480)**

3821 Laboratory apparatus and furniture

4r Enterprises Incorporated............... G 330 923-9799
Cuyahoga Falls **(G-5519)**

Accuscan Instruments Inc................... F 614 878-6644
Columbus **(G-4670)**

▲ **American Isostatic Presses Inc**....... F 614 497-3148
Columbus **(G-4698)**

▲ **American Sterilizer Company**........... E 440 392-8328
Mentor **(G-9480)**

▲ **Caron Products and Svcs Inc**.......... E 740 373-6809
Marietta **(G-8906)**

Cellular Technology Limited............... E 216 791-5084
Shaker Heights **(G-11928)**

Cheminstruments Inc.......................... G 513 860-1598
West Chester **(G-13960)**

Chemsultants International Inc............ G 513 860-1598
West Chester **(G-13962)**

Chemsultants International Inc............ G 440 974-3080
Mentor **(G-9498)**

Cortest Inc.. F 440 942-1235
Willoughby **(G-14442)**

Denton Atd Inc.................................... E 567 265-5200
Huron **(G-7871)**

Dentronix Inc...................................... D 330 916-7300
Cuyahoga Falls **(G-5538)**

◆ **E R Advanced Ceramics Inc**............ E 330 426-9433
East Palestine **(G-6402)**

Gdj Inc... G 440 975-0258
Mentor **(G-9523)**

▲ **Gilson Company Inc**......................... E 740 548-7298
Lewis Center **(G-8334)**

◆ **Global Cooling Inc**........................... C 740 274-7900
Athens **(G-641)**

Health Aid of Ohio Inc....................... E 216 252-3900
Cleveland **(G-3814)**

Ies Systems Inc.................................. E 330 533-6683
Canfield **(G-1811)**

Ignio Systems LLC............................. G 419 708-0503
Toledo **(G-12999)**

Malta Dynamics LLC.......................... F 740 749-3512
Waterford **(G-13828)**

◆ **Mettler-Toledo Intl Inc**..................... A 614 438-4511
Columbus **(G-4643)**

◆ **Mettler-Toledo LLC**.......................... A 614 438-4511
Columbus **(G-4644)**

◆ **Philips Med Systems Clvland In**........ B 440 483-3000
Cleveland **(G-4159)**

Powdermet Powder Prod Inc............... F 216 404-0053
Euclid **(G-6671)**

So-Low Environmental Eqp Co............ E 513 772-9410
Cincinnati **(G-3098)**

Strategic Technology Entp.................. G 440 354-2600
Mentor **(G-9628)**

Teledyne Instruments Inc.................... E 513 229-7000
Mason **(G-9158)**

Teledyne Tekmar Company.................. E 513 229-7000
Mason **(G-9160)**

Universal Scientific Inc....................... G 440 428-1777
Madison **(G-8734)**

Waller Brothers Stone Company........... F 740 858-1948
Mc Dermott **(G-9356)**

3822 Environmental controls

A & P Tool Inc.................................... E 419 542-6681
Hicksville **(G-7644)**

Action Air & Hydraulics Inc............... G 937 372-8614
Xenia **(G-14752)**

Acutemp Thermal Systems.................. F 937 312-0114
Moraine **(G-10142)**

Air Enterprises Inc............................. A 330 794-9770
Akron **(G-22)**

▲ **Alan Manufacturing Inc**.................... E 330 262-1555
Wooster **(G-14621)**

◆ **Babcock & Wilcox Company**............. A 330 753-4511
Akron **(G-67)**

◆ **Bry-Air Inc**....................................... E 740 965-2974
Sunbury **(G-12662)**

Building Ctrl Integrators LLC............. G 513 247-6154
Cincinnati **(G-2433)**

Building Ctrl Integrators LLC............. G 513 860-9600
West Chester **(G-14108)**

Building Ctrl Integrators LLC............. E 614 334-3300
Powell **(G-11482)**

Certified Labs & Service Inc............... G 419 289-7462
Ashland **(G-527)**

Cincinnati Air Conditioning Co............ D 513 721-5622
Cincinnati **(G-2468)**

Columbus Controls Inc....................... E 614 882-9029
Columbus **(G-4820)**

▲ **Conery Manufacturing Inc**................ F 419 289-1444
Ashland **(G-530)**

Doan/Pyramid Solutions LLC.............. E 216 587-9510
Cleveland **(G-3622)**

▲ **Dyoung Enterprise Inc**...................... C 440 918-0505
Willoughby **(G-14452)**

Ecopro Solutions LLC......................... E 216 232-4040
Independence **(G-7900)**

Energy & Ctrl Integrators Inc.............. G 419 222-0025
Lima **(G-8405)**

Envirnment Ctrl Sthwest Ohio I........... F 937 669-9900
Tipp City **(G-12824)**

▼ **Estabrook Assembly Svcs Inc**........... F 440 243-3350
Berea **(G-1171)**

Evokes LLC.. E 513 947-8433
Mason **(G-9099)**

Future Controls Corporation............... E 440 275-3191
Austinburg **(G-700)**

Honeywell International Inc.................. A 937 484-2000
Urbana **(G-13466)**

▼ **Hunter Defense Tech Inc**................... E 216 438-6111
Solon **(G-12124)**

Ignio Systems LLC............................. G 419 708-0503
Toledo **(G-12999)**

Integrated Development & Mfg.............. F 440 543-2423
Chagrin Falls **(G-2167)**

Integrated Development & Mfg.............. F 440 247-5100
Chagrin Falls **(G-2146)**

K Davis Inc... G 419 307-7051
Fremont **(G-7119)**

Karman Rubber Company..................... D 330 864-2161
Akron **(G-191)**

▲ **Logisync Corporation**....................... G 440 937-0388
Avon **(G-732)**

Mader Machine Co Inc......................... E 440 355-4505
Lagrange **(G-8150)**

Melink Corporation............................. D 513 685-0958
Milford **(G-9943)**

Mestek Inc.. D 419 288-2703
Bowling Green **(G-1429)**

Mestek Inc.. F 419 288-2703
Bradner **(G-1454)**

Parker-Hannifin Corporation.............. F 216 433-1795
Cleveland **(G-4144)**

▲ **Pepperl + Fuchs Inc**......................... C 330 425-3555
Twinsburg **(G-13352)**

▲ **Portage Electric Products Inc**............ C 330 499-2727
North Canton **(G-10659)**

Premier Enrgy Systems Ohio LLC......... F 304 252-1918
Athens **(G-647)**

Resideo LLC....................................... G 440 439-7002
Bedford **(G-1057)**

Resideo LLC....................................... F 513 772-1851
Cincinnati **(G-3039)**

Salus North America Inc..................... F 888 387-2587
Mason **(G-9147)**

▲ **Sasha Electronics Inc**....................... G 419 662-8100
Rossford **(G-11663)**

Sje Rhombus Controls......................... F 419 281-5767
Ashland **(G-574)**

▲ **Skuttle Mfg Co**................................. F 740 373-9169
Marietta **(G-8946)**

▲ **Therm-O-Disc Incorporated**.............. A 419 525-8500
Westerville **(G-14236)**

◆ **Thermtrol Corporation**...................... A 330 497-4148
North Canton **(G-10672)**

▲ **Tlt-Babcock Inc**................................ D 330 867-8540
Akron **(G-339)**

▲ **Ventra Sandusky LLC**........................ C 419 627-3600
Sandusky **(G-11882)**

Vib-Iso LLC.. F 800 735-9645
Wooster **(G-14695)**

Vortec Corporation............................. E 513 891-7485
Blue Ash **(G-1348)**

▲ **West 6th Products Company**.............. D 330 467-7446
Northfield **(G-10800)**

Young Regulator Company Inc.............. E 440 232-9452
Bedford **(G-1066)**

3823 Process control instruments

Adalet/Scott Fetzer Company.............. E 440 892-3074
Cleveland **(G-3295)**

▲ **Airmate Co Inc**................................. E 419 636-3184
Bryan **(G-1625)**

◆ **Alpha Technologies Svcs LLC**........... D 330 745-1641
Hudson **(G-7828)**

▲ **Altronic LLC**.................................... C 330 545-9768
Girard **(G-7264)**

American Water Services Inc............... G 440 243-9840
Strongsville **(G-12536)**

Aqua Technology Group LLC................ G 513 298-1183
West Chester **(G-13941)**

▼ **Arzel Technology Inc**........................ E 216 831-6068
Cleveland **(G-3373)**

Ascon Tecnologic N Amer LLC............. G 216 485-8350
Cleveland **(G-3375)**

Assetwatch Inc.................................. C 844 464-5652
Westerville **(G-14243)**

Automation and Ctrl Tech Inc............. E 614 495-1120
Dublin **(G-6279)**

Automation Technology Inc.................. E 937 233-6084
Dayton **(G-5670)**

Beaumont Machine LLC.................... F 513 701-0421
Mason (G-9070)

◆ Bry-Air Inc............................E 740 965-2974
Sunbury (G-12662)

Bwx Technologies Inc..................... C 330 860-1692
Barberton (G-800)

▲ Cammann Inc............................ F 440 965-4051
Wakeman (G-13678)

▲ Caron Products and Svcs Inc .... E 740 373-6809
Marietta (G-8906)

Catacel Corp............................... F
Ravenna (G-11520)

Cincinnati Test Systems Inc .... D 513 202-5100
Harrison (G-7546)

◆ Clark-Reliance LLC......................C 440 572-1500
Strongsville (G-12550)

Cleveland Controls Inc .... F 216 398-0330
Cleveland (G-3510)

Cleveland Electric Labs Co .... E 800 447-2207
Twinsburg (G-13287)

Command Alkon Incorporated........... E 614 799-0600
Dublin (G-6290)

Comtec Incorporated..................... F 330 425-8102
Twinsburg (G-13288)

Consoldted Anlytcal Systems In .... F 513 542-1200
Cincinnati (G-2510)

◆ Copeland Access + Inc.................F 937 498-3802
Sidney (G-12003)

▲ Copeland Scroll Compressors LP ..... G 937 498-3066
Sidney (G-12008)

Crawford United Corporation .... E 216 243-2614
Cleveland (G-3576)

De Nora Tech Inc .... C 440 285-0100
Chardon (G-2203)

Diamond Power Intl Inc .... F 740 687-4001
Lancaster (G-8197)

▲ Dixon Bayco USA........................ G 513 874-8499
Fairfield (G-6729)

▲ Doubleday Acquisitions LLC .... E 513 360-7189
Monroe (G-10104)

▲ Dyoung Enterprise Inc.................. C 440 918-0505
Willoughby (G-14452)

Emerson Commercial Reside............. E 937 493-2828
Sidney (G-12017)

Emerson Corp............................. G 614 841-5498
Delaware (G-6145)

Emerson Electric Co...................... C 513 731-2020
Cincinnati (G-2583)

Emerson Helix............................. F 937 710-5771
Dayton (G-5764)

Emerson Industrial Automation........... G 216 901-2400
Cleveland (G-3668)

Emerson Professional Tools LLC........ E 740 432-8782
Cambridge (G-1742)

Encompass Atmtn Engrg Tech LLC....... F 419 873-0000
Perrysburg (G-11218)

Ernst Flow Industries LLC................ F 732 938-5641
Strongsville (G-12558)

Facts Inc.................................. E 330 928-2332
Cuyahoga Falls (G-5540)

Fisher Controls Intl LLC.................. F 513 285-6000
West Chester (G-13998)

Five Star Technologies Ltd............... F 216 447-9422
Independence (G-7903)

Fluid Equipment Corporation............. G 419 636-0777
Bryan (G-1641)

Fluke Corporation........................ F 440 234-4809
Middleburg Heights (G-9770)

Future Controls Corporation............. E 440 275-3191
Austinburg (G-700)

Gem Instrument Company Inc .... G 330 273-6117
Brunswick (G-1594)

Gentherm Medical LLC.................... C 513 772-8810
Cincinnati (G-2668)

Geocorp Inc.............................. E 419 433-1101
Huron (G-7873)

◆ Gleason Metrology Systems Corp......E 937 384-8901
Dayton (G-5796)

Glo-Quartz Electric Htr Co Inc........... E 440 255-9701
Mentor (G-9524)

Godfrey & Wing Inc....................... F 419 980-4616
Defiance (G-6108)

Gooch & Housego (ohio) LLC............. D 216 486-6100
Highland Heights (G-7658)

H2flow Controls Inc...................... G 419 841-7774
Toledo (G-12981)

Harris Instrument Corporation .... G 740 369-3580
Delaware (G-6155)

Henry & Wright Corporation............. F 216 851-3750
Cleveland (G-3823)

Homeworth Fabrication Mch Inc......... F 330 525-5459
Homeworth (G-7805)

Honeywell International Inc.............. A 937 484-2000
Urbana (G-13466)

Hunkar Technologies Inc................. C 513 272-1010
Cincinnati (G-2735)

Innovative Controls Corp................ G 419 691-6684
Maumee (G-9298)

▲ ITT Torque Systems Inc................ C 216 524-8800
Cleveland (G-3875)

Jbt Marel Corporation.................... E 614 891-2732
Lewis Center (G-8340)

Journey Electronics Corp................. G 513 539-9836
Monroe (G-10111)

▲ Keithley Instruments LLC.............. D 440 248-0400
Solon (G-12137)

Koester Corporation..................... E 419 599-0291
Napoleon (G-10289)

Kuhlman Instrument Company........... G 419 668-9533
Norwalk (G-10849)

▲ L J Star Incorporated.................. E 330 405-3040
Twinsburg (G-13327)

L3harris Cincinnati Elec Corp............ A 513 573-6100
Mason (G-9121)

L3harris Electrodynamics Inc........... C 847 259-0740
Cincinnati (G-2310)

Lake Shore Cryotronics Inc............. D 614 891-2243
Westerville (G-14217)

Liebert Field Services Inc................ E 614 841-5763
Westerville (G-14220)

▲ Logisync Corporation................... G 440 937-0388
Avon (G-732)

LS Starrett Company..................... D 440 835-0005
Westlake (G-14313)

M T Systems Inc......................... G 330 453-4646
Canton (G-1936)

Machine Applications Corp.............. G 419 621-2322
Sandusky (G-11854)

◆ Marlin Manufacturing Corp..............D 216 676-1340
Cleveland (G-3990)

Measurement Computing Corp........... E 440 439-4091
Cleveland (G-4015)

▲ Meech Sttic Elminators USA Inc........ F 330 564-2000
Copley (G-5434)

Mercury Iron and Steel Co............... F 440 349-1500
Solon (G-12146)

◆ Mettler-Toledo Intl Inc..................A 614 438-4511
Columbus (G-4643)

◆ Mettler-Toledo LLC......................A 614 438-4511
Columbus (G-4644)

Nextech Materials Ltd.................... G 614 842-6606
Lewis Center (G-8346)

Nidec Avtron Automation Corporation... C 216 642-1230
Independence (G-7912)

Nidec Motor Corporation................. C 216 642-1230
Cleveland (G-4076)

Nidec Motor Corporation................. E 216 642-1230
Cleveland (G-4077)

▲ Noshok Inc.............................. E 440 243-0888
Berea (G-1184)

Nov Process & Flow Tech US Inc........ F 937 454-3300
Dayton (G-5916)

Overhoff Technology Corp............... F 513 248-2400
Milford (G-9946)

▲ Pacs Industries Inc..................... D 740 397-5021
Mount Vernon (G-10256)

Pg Square LLC........................... F 216 896-3000
Cleveland (G-4157)

▲ Prime Instruments Inc.................. D 216 651-0400
Cleveland (G-4195)

Primex.................................... G 513 831-9959
Milford (G-9949)

▼ Production Control Units Inc .... D 937 299-5594
Dayton (G-5961)

▲ Q-Lab Corporation...................... D 440 835-8700
Westlake (G-14325)

Ram Sensors Inc......................... E 440 835-3540
Cleveland (G-4222)

▲ Refractory Specialties Inc.............. G 330 938-2101
Sebring (G-11900)

◆ Reuter-Stokes LLC...................... B 330 425-3755
Twinsburg (G-13365)

◆ Rhi US Ltd...............................G 513 527-6160
Cincinnati (G-3041)

▲ Richards Industrials Inc................ D 513 533-5600
Cincinnati (G-3044)

Rickly Hydrological Co................... E 614 297-9877
Columbus (G-5229)

▲ Rsw Technologies LLC.................. F 419 662-8100
Rossford (G-11662)

Schneider Electric Usa Inc.............. D 513 777-4445
West Chester (G-14073)

Sealtron Inc.............................. E 513 733-8400
Cincinnati (G-3073)

Seekirk Inc............................... F 614 278-9200
Columbus (G-5259)

▲ Selas Heat Technology Co LLC......... E 800 523-6500
Streetsboro (G-12523)

Sherbrooke Corporation................. E 440 942-3520
Willoughby (G-14525)

Slone Gear International Inc............. E 507 401-4327
Tipp City (C 12045)

▲ Solon Manufacturing Company......... E 440 286-7149
Chardon (G-2223)

Stewart Manufacturing Corp............. F 937 390-3333
Springfield (G-12379)

Stock Fairfield Corporation.............. C 440 543-6000
Solon (G-12185)

Tecmark Corporation.................... E 440 205-9188
Mentor (G-9633)

▲ Tecmark Corporation................... D 440 205-7600
Mentor (G-9634)

▲ Therm-O-Disc Incorporated............. A 419 525-8500
Westerville (G-14236)

Thermo Fisher Scientific Inc............ E 513 948-6290
Blue Ash (G-1343)

▲ Thermo Gamma-Metrics LLC............ E 858 450-9811
Bedford (G-1061)

Thermo King Corporation................ F 567 280-9243
Fremont (G-7137)

▲ Thk Manufacturing America Inc........ C 740 928-1415
Hebron (G-7639)

◆ Tls Corp.................................D 216 574-4759
Cleveland (G-4396)

Toledo Controls......................... G 419 474-2537
Toledo (G-13149)

S
I
C

Toledo Transducers Inc.......................... E 419 724-4170
   Maumee *(G-9327)*

Tpf Inc.. G 513 761-9968
   Cincinnati *(G-3161)*

Trane Technologies Company LLC....... E 419 633-6800
   Bryan *(G-1665)*

▲ Unison UCI Inc.................................. G
   Cleveland *(G-4441)*

United Tool Supply Inc....................... G 513 752-6000
   Cincinnati *(G-2317)*

Valley List LLC.................................. G 740 760-6411
   Waterford *(G-13829)*

◆ Vanner Holdings Inc........................D 614 771-2718
   Hilliard *(G-7709)*

◆ Vega Americas Inc...........................C 513 272-0131
   Lebanon *(G-8295)*

Vertiv Corporation............................. C 740 547-5100
   Ironton *(G-7936)*

Visi-Trak Worldwide LLC.................... F 216 524-2363
   Cleveland *(G-4476)*

Vitec Inc... G 216 464-4670
   Bedford *(G-1063)*

WIKA Sensor Technlgy LP................. E 614 430-0683
   Lewis Center *(G-8357)*

Wild Fire Systems............................. G 440 442-8999
   Cleveland *(G-4505)*

Xylem Inc...D 937 767-7241
   Yellow Springs *(G-14792)*

◆ Ysi Incorporated.............................D 937 767-7241
   Yellow Springs *(G-14796)*

3824 Fluid meters and counting devices

Aclara Technologies LLC.................... F 440 528-7200
   Solon *(G-12072)*

Aqua Technology Group LLC.............. G 513 298-1183
   West Chester *(G-13941)*

Bif Co LLC.. F 330 564-0941
   Akron *(G-79)*

Brooks Manufacturing........................ G 419 244-1777
   Toledo *(G-12905)*

Commercial Electric Pdts Corp........... E 216 241-2886
   Cleveland *(G-3552)*

Eaton Corporation............................. B 440 523-5000
   Beachwood *(G-915)*

Ernst Flow Industries LLC.................. F 732 938-5641
   Strongsville *(G-12558)*

Exact Equipment Corporation............. F 215 295-2000
   Columbus *(G-4640)*

▲ Graco Ohio Inc...............................D 330 494-1313
   North Canton *(G-10644)*

L3harris Electrodynamics Inc.............. C 847 259-0740
   Cincinnati *(G-2310)*

Lake Shore Cryotronics Inc.................D 614 891-2243
   Westerville *(G-14217)*

Mill & Motion Properties Ltd............... F 216 524-4000
   Independence *(G-7910)*

Parking & Traffic Control SEC............. F 440 243-7565
   Cleveland *(G-4145)*

Reliable Manufacturing LLC................ E 740 756-9373
   Carroll *(G-2077)*

▲ Thermo Gamma-Metrics LLC............ E 858 450-9811
   Bedford *(G-1061)*

▲ Triplett Bluffton Corporation............. G 419 358-8750
   Bluffton *(G-1367)*

Westmont Inc..................................... G 330 862-3080
   Minerva *(G-10049)*

3825 Instruments to measure electricity

Aclara Technologies LLC.................... F 440 528-7200
   Solon *(G-12072)*

▲ Adams Elevator Equipment Co.........D 847 581-2900
   Holland *(G-7743)*

Advanced Integration LLC................... E 614 863-2433
   Reynoldsburg *(G-11554)*

Advanced Kiffer Systems Inc.............. E 216 267-8181
   Cleveland *(G-3306)*

Analytica Usa Inc.............................. G 513 348-2333
   Dayton *(G-5658)*

Andeen-Hagerling Inc........................ F 440 349-0370
   Cleveland *(G-3357)*

Aqua Technology Group LLC.............. G 513 298-1183
   West Chester *(G-13941)*

Automation Technology Inc................. E 937 233-6084
   Dayton *(G-5670)*

Avtron Holdings LLC.......................... E 216 642-1230
   Cleveland *(G-3394)*

Battery Unlimited............................... G 740 452-5030
   Zanesville *(G-14993)*

Bionix Safety Technologies Ltd........... E 419 727-0552
   Maumee *(G-9267)*

▲ Bird Electronic Corporation.............. C 440 248-1200
   Solon *(G-12084)*

Bird Technologies Group Inc.............. C 440 248-1200
   Solon *(G-12085)*

CDI Industries Inc.............................. E 440 243-1100
   Cleveland *(G-3481)*

Community Care Network Inc.............. E 216 671-0977
   Cleveland *(G-3554)*

Contact Industries Inc........................ E 419 884-9788
   Lexington *(G-8372)*

Desco Corporation............................. G 614 888-8855
   New Albany *(G-10339)*

Dewesoft LLC....................................D 855 339-3669
   Whitehouse *(G-14359)*

Drs Signal Technologies Inc............... G 937 429-7470
   Beavercreek *(G-972)*

Dss Installations Ltd.......................... G 513 761-7000
   Cincinnati *(G-2563)*

▲ Dynamp LLC................................... E 614 871-6900
   Grove City *(G-7382)*

Eazytrade Inc.................................... G 513 257-9189
   West Chester *(G-13992)*

Eazytrade Inc.................................... G 513 257-9189
   West Chester *(G-13991)*

F Squared Inc................................... G 419 752-7273
   Greenwich *(G-7361)*

Field Apparatus Service & Tstg.......... G 513 353-9399
   Cincinnati *(G-2621)*

Fluke Electronics Corporation............. G 800 850-4608
   Cleveland *(G-3729)*

GE Additive LLC................................ F 513 341-0597
   West Chester *(G-14003)*

▲ Hana Technologies Inc....................D 330 405-4600
   Twinsburg *(G-13314)*

Hannon Company...............................D 330 456-4728
   Canton *(G-1908)*

Hughes Corporation........................... E 440 238-2550
   Strongsville *(G-12564)*

▲ Keithley Instruments LLC.................D 440 248-0400
   Solon *(G-12137)*

Lake Shore Cryotronics Inc.................D 614 891-2243
   Westerville *(G-14217)*

Lomar Enterprises Inc........................ F 614 409-9104
   Groveport *(G-7443)*

Machine Products Company................ F 937 890-6600
   Dayton *(G-5860)*

Medina County.................................. E 330 723-3641
   Medina *(G-9423)*

Mueller Electric Company Inc............. G 614 888-8855
   New Albany *(G-10346)*

Nanotronics Imaging Inc.................... G 330 926-9809
   Cuyahoga Falls *(G-5562)*

Neptune Equipment Company............. F 513 851-8008
   Cincinnati *(G-2898)*

Nextech Materials Ltd.........................D 614 842-6606
   Lewis Center *(G-8346)*

Nu-Di Products Co Inc........................D 216 251-9070
   Cleveland *(G-4105)*

Omega Engineering Inc...................... E 740 965-9340
   Sunbury *(G-12673)*

Omegadyne Inc..................................D 740 965-9340
   Sunbury *(G-12674)*

▲ Opw Engineered Systems Inc.......... E 888 771-9438
   West Chester *(G-14039)*

▼ Orton Edward Jr Crmic Fndation...... E 614 895-2663
   Westerville *(G-14226)*

Palstar Inc.. F 937 773-6255
   Piqua *(G-11371)*

Paneltech LLC................................... G 440 516-1300
   Chagrin Falls *(G-2176)*

▲ Pile Dynamics Inc........................... E 216 831-6131
   Cleveland *(G-4165)*

▲ Pressco Technology Inc...................D 440 498-2600
   Cleveland *(G-4194)*

Resonant Sciences LLC...................... E 937 431-8180
   Dayton *(G-5980)*

Rubix LLC... G 330 577-8249
   Sugarcreek *(G-12648)*

▲ Skidmore-Wilhelm Mfg Company...... G 216 481-4774
   Solon *(G-12182)*

Tacoma Energy LLC........................... C 614 899-8990
   Westerville *(G-14276)*

Tektronix Inc..................................... G 440 248-0400
   Solon *(G-12196)*

Tektronix Inc..................................... F 248 305-5200
   West Chester *(G-14152)*

◆ Tmsi LLC..F 888 867-4872
   North Canton *(G-10676)*

Transcat Inc...................................... F 440 853-1907
   Mentor *(G-9641)*

▲ Triplett Bluffton Corporation............. G 419 358-8750
   Bluffton *(G-1367)*

Val-Con Inc....................................... G 440 357-1898
   Concord Township *(G-5396)*

◆ Westerman Inc................................C 800 338-8265
   Bremen *(G-1488)*

▲ Zts Inc... F 513 271-2557
   Cincinnati *(G-3243)*

3826 Analytical instruments

4r Enterprises Incorporated................ G 330 923-9799
   Cuyahoga Falls *(G-5519)*

Affymetrix Inc....................................D 800 321-9322
   Cleveland *(G-3313)*

Affymetrix Inc.................................... E 419 887-1233
   Maumee *(G-9257)*

▲ American Scientific LLC................... G 614 764-9002
   Columbus *(G-4702)*

Apera Instruments LLC...................... F 614 285-3080
   Columbus *(G-4720)*

Auto Technology Company.................. F 440 572-7800
   Strongsville *(G-12540)*

Bionix Safety Technologies Ltd........... E 419 727-0552
   Maumee *(G-9267)*

Bridge Analyzers Inc.......................... F 216 332-0592
   Bedford Heights *(G-1071)*

◆ Bry-Air Inc..................................... E 740 965-2974
   Sunbury *(G-12662)*

Columbus Instruments LLC................. E 614 276-0861
   Columbus *(G-4825)*

◆ Columbus Instruments Intl Corp....... E 614 276-0593
   Columbus *(G-4826)*

Compliant Healthcare Tech LLC.......... E 216 255-9607
   Cleveland *(G-3555)*

Consoldted Anlytcal Systems In.......... F 513 542-1200
   Cincinnati *(G-2510)*

Dentronix Inc............................D 330 916-7300
Cuyahoga Falls *(G-5538)*

Envirnmntal Cmpliance Tech LLC......... F 216 634-0400
North Royalton *(G-10760)*

Environmental Sample Technology Inc. E 513 642-0100
West Chester *(G-13993)*

▲ **HEF USA Corporation**......................G 937 323-2556
Springfield *(G-12320)*

IEC Infrared Systems LLC...................E 440 234-8000
Middleburg Heights *(G-9772)*

▲ **Laserlinc Inc**.................................E 937 318-2440
Fairborn *(G-6695)*

Metron Instruments Inc.....................G 216 332-0592
Bedford Heights *(G-1079)*

◆ **Mettler-Toledo Intl Inc**....................A 614 438-4511
Columbus *(G-4643)*

◆ **Mettler-Toledo LLC**.........................A 614 438-4511
Columbus *(G-4644)*

Mettlr-Tledo Globl Hldings LLC............E 614 438-4511
Columbus *(G-4645)*

Nanotronics Imaging Inc....................G 330 926-9809
Cuyahoga Falls *(G-5562)*

NDC Technologies Inc........................C 937 233-9935
Dayton *(G-5905)*

Northcoast Environmental Labs............G 330 342-3377
Streetsboro *(G-12514)*

Ohio Lumex Co Inc...........................E 440 264-2500
Solon *(G-12164)*

▼ **Orton Edward Jr Crmic Fndation**......E 614 895-2663
Westerville *(G-14226)*

PMC Gage Inc................................E 440 953-1672
Willoughby *(G-14507)*

Precision Anlytical Instrs Inc...............G 513 984-1600
Blue Ash *(G-1323)*

Prospira America Corporation..............F 419 423-9552
Findlay *(G-6910)*

Pts Prfssnal Technical Svc Inc............D 513 642-0111
West Chester *(G-14056)*

▲ **Q-Lab Corporation**.........................D 440 835-8700
Westlake *(G-14325)*

◆ **Reuter-Stokes LLC**.........................B 330 425-3755
Twinsburg *(G-13365)*

◆ **Rotex Global LLC**..........................C 513 541-1236
Cincinnati *(G-3053)*

▲ **S-Tek Inc**....................................G 440 439-8232
Twinsburg *(G-13373)*

Satelytics Inc.................................G 419 372-0160
Perrysburg *(G-11360)*

Targeted Cmpund Monitoring LLC........G 937 825-0842
Dayton *(G-6038)*

Tech4imaging LLC............................F 614 214-2655
Columbus *(G-5315)*

Teledyne Instruments Inc...................E 513 229-7000
Mason *(G-9158)*

Teledyne Instruments Inc...................D 603 886-8400
Mason *(G-9159)*

Teledyne Tekmar Company.................E 513 229-7000
Mason *(G-9160)*

Test-Fuchs Corporation.....................G 440 708-3505
Brecksville *(G-1483)*

Thermo Fisher Scientific Inc................F 513 948-6290
Blue Ash *(G-1343)*

Thermo Fisher Scientific Inc................G 800 955-6288
Cincinnati *(G-3152)*

Thermo Fisher Scientific Inc................F 513 659-7945
West Chester *(G-14154)*

Thermo Fsher Scntfic Ashvlle L............A 740 373-4763
Marietta *(G-8954)*

▲ **Thermo Gamma-Metrics LLC**.............E 858 450-9811
Bedford *(G-1061)*

Trek Diagnostics Inc.........................F 440 808-0000
Brooklyn Heights *(G-1541)*

Viavi Solutions Inc...........................F 316 522-4981
Columbus *(G-4651)*

▲ **Weidmann Electrical Tech Inc**...........G 937 508-2112
Cleveland *(G-4497)*

Xorb Corporation............................G 419 354-6021
Bowling Green *(G-1449)*

Ysi Environmental Inc.......................E 937 767-7241
Yellow Springs *(G-14795)*

◆ **Ysi Incorporated**...........................D 937 767-7241
Yellow Springs *(G-14796)*

3827 Optical instruments and lenses

Cincinnati Eye Inst - Estgate...............G 513 984-5133
Cincinnati *(G-2298)*

Genvac Aerospace Inc.......................F 440 646-9986
Highland Heights *(G-7657)*

Gooch & Housego (ohio) LLC..............D 216 486-6100
Highland Heights *(G-7658)*

Greenlight Optics LLC.......................G 513 247-9777
Loveland *(G-8628)*

▼ **Krendl Machine Company**.................D 419 692-3060
Delphos *(G-6189)*

Mercury Iron and Steel Co..................F 440 349-1500
Solon *(G-12146)*

Miller-Holzwarth Inc.........................D 330 342-7224
Salem *(G-11800)*

Optics Incorporated..........................E 800 362-1337
Brunswick *(G-1604)*

Point Source Inc..............................F 937 855-6020
Germantown *(G-7252)*

Punch Components Inc.......................E 419 224-1242
Lima *(G-8441)*

Sticktite Lenses LLC.........................F 571 276-9508
New Albany *(G-10351)*

▲ **Volk Optical Inc**.............................D 440 942-6161
Mentor *(G-9651)*

Vsp Lab Columbus...........................G 614 409-8900
Lockbourne *(G-8493)*

Wilson Optical Labs Inc.....................E 440 357-7000
Mentor *(G-9652)*

3829 Measuring and controlling devices, nec

1 A Lifesaver Inc.............................E 513 651-9560
Cincinnati *(G-2319)*

Aclara Technologies LLC....................F 440 528-7200
Solon *(G-12072)*

Advanced Gauging Tech LLC...............G 936 443-7129
Plain City *(G-11301)*

▲ **Advanced Indus Msrment Systems**.. F 937 320-4930
Miamisburg *(G-9660)*

Advanced Telemetrics Intl...................F 937 862-6948
Spring Valley *(G-12241)*

Amano Cincinnati Incorporated............F 513 697-9000
Loveland *(G-8619)*

American Cube Mold Inc.....................G 330 558-0044
Brunswick *(G-1580)*

American Thermal Instrs Inc................E 937 429-2114
Moraine *(G-10145)*

◆ **Arnco Corporation**.........................F 800 847-7661
Elyria *(G-6498)*

Automation and Ctrl Tech Inc..............E 614 495-1120
Dublin *(G-6279)*

Automation Technology Inc.................E 937 233-6084
Dayton *(G-5670)*

Babcock & Wilcox Entps Inc................C 330 753-4511
Akron *(G-68)*

Balmac Inc...................................G 614 876-1295
Hilliard *(G-7675)*

Bertec Corporation...........................E 614 543-8099
Columbus *(G-4752)*

▲ **Bilz Vibration Technology Inc**............F 330 468-2459
Macedonia *(G-8678)*

Bionix Safety Technologies Ltd..............E 419 727-0552
Maumee *(G-9267)*

Blaze Technical Services Inc................E 330 923-0409
Stow *(G-12422)*

Ccsi Inc.......................................G 800 742-8535
Akron *(G-91)*

▲ **Ceia Usa Ltd**.................................D 330 310-4741
Hudson *(G-7836)*

▲ **Cheminstruments Inc**......................G 513 860-1598
West Chester *(G-13961)*

Cincinnati Ctrl Dynamics Inc................E 513 242-7300
Cincinnati *(G-2473)*

Clark Fixture Technologies Inc..............E 419 354-1541
Bowling Green *(G-1414)*

▲ **Controlled Access Inc**.....................F 330 273-6185
Brunswick *(G-1586)*

▲ **Corporate Cnsulting Svc Instrs**.........F
Akron *(G-106)*

Crawford United Corporation................E 216 243-2614
Cleveland *(G-3576)*

Daytronic Corporation.......................G 937 866-3300
Miamisburg *(G-9690)*

Denton Atd Inc...............................E 567 265-5200
Huron *(G-7871)*

Eagle Composites LLC.......................E 513 330-6108
West Chester *(G-13989)*

Echo Therm LLC.............................F 937 322-5972
Springfield *(G-12305)*

Electric Speed Indicator Co.................F 216 251-2540
Aurora *(G-668)*

◆ **Ferry Industries Inc**........................D 330 920-9200
Stow *(G-12431)*

Fischer Engineering Co LLC.................G 937 754-1750
Dayton *(G-5778)*

▲ **Fluke Biomedical LLC**.....................C 440 248-9300
Solon *(G-12113)*

▲ **Fowler Products Inc**........................G 419 683-4057
Crestline *(G-5502)*

Gem Instrument Company Inc..............G 330 273-6117
Brunswick *(G-1594)*

▲ **Gilson Company Inc**.......................E 740 548-7298
Lewis Center *(G-8334)*

Gilson Screen Incorporated.................E 419 256-7711
Malinta *(G-8742)*

◆ **Gleason Metrology Systems Corp**......E 937 384-8901
Dayton *(G-5796)*

Global Gauge Corporation...................E 937 254-3500
Moraine *(G-10165)*

Halliday Technologies Inc....................G 614 504-4150
Delaware *(G-6154)*

Harris Instrument Corporation..............G 740 369-3580
Delaware *(G-6155)*

Helm Instrument Company Inc.............E 419 893-4356
Maumee *(G-9296)*

Henry & Wright Corporation................F 216 851-3750
Cleveland *(G-3823)*

Heraeus Electro-Nite Co LLC...............G 330 725-1419
Medina *(G-9408)*

Honeywell International Inc...................E 302 327-8920
Columbus *(G-4990)*

Instrumentors Inc............................G 440 238-3430
Strongsville *(G-12568)*

Karman Rubber Company....................D 330 864-2161
Akron *(G-191)*

◆ **Kinetics Noise Control Inc**................C 614 889-0480
Dublin *(G-6316)*

Krumor Inc....................................F 216 328-9802
Cleveland *(G-3930)*

Kw Acquisition Inc...........................G 740 548-7298
Lewis Center *(G-8341)*

Lake Shore Cryotronics Inc.................D 614 891-2243
Westerville *(G-14217)*

SIC

▲ LH Marshall Company...................... F 614 294-6433
Columbus (G-5066)

Lmg Holdings Inc................................ E 905 829-3541
Blue Ash (G-1298)

▲ Logisync Corporation...................... G 440 937-0388
Avon (G-732)

LS Starrett Company........................... D 440 835-0005
Westlake (G-14313)

▲ M&H Medical Holdings Inc................ E 419 727-8421
Maumee (G-9305)

M4 Knick LLC...................................... G 513 833-2500
Milford (G-9941)

Magna Three LLC................................ G 513 389-0776
Cincinnati (G-2841)

Magnetic Analysis Corporation............. G 330 758-1367
Youngstown (G-14893)

Malabar... E 419 866-6301
Swanton (G-12687)

Mapvision Inc...................................... G 513 400-1038
Blue Ash (G-1301)

Matrix Research Inc............................. D 937 427-8433
Dayton (G-5869)

▼ MB Dynamics Inc.............................. E 216 292-5850
Cleveland (G-4006)

Measurement Specialties Inc................ C 330 659-3312
Akron (G-227)

Micro Laboratories Inc........................ G 440 918-0001
Mentor (G-9564)

Multi Lapping Service Inc..................... G 440 944-7592
Wickliffe (G-14383)

◆ Multilink Inc....................................... C 440 366-6966
Elyria (G-6566)

National Pat Anlytical Systems............. E 419 526-6727
Mansfield (G-8836)

▲ NDC Technologies Inc........................ C 937 233-9935
Dayton (G-5906)

▲ Newall Electronics Inc........................ F 614 771-0213
Columbus (G-5127)

Nidec Avtron Automation Corporation... C 216 642-1230
Independence (G-7912)

Nidec Motor Corporation..................... E 216 642-1230
Cleveland (G-4077)

▲ Nucon International Inc....................... F 614 846-5710
Columbus (G-5132)

Omega Engineering Inc........................ E 740 965-9340
Sunbury (G-12673)

Omegadyne Inc................................... D 740 965-9340
Sunbury (G-12674)

Overhoff Technology Corp.................... F 513 248-2400
Milford (G-9946)

Performance Results Plus Inc.............. F 614 297-9877
Columbus (G-5188)

PMC Gage Inc..................................... E 440 953-1672
Willoughby (G-14507)

▲ Portage Electric Products Inc............ C 330 499-2727
North Canton (G-10659)

▲ Pressco Technology Inc..................... D 440 498-2600
Cleveland (G-4194)

▼ Production Control Units Inc.............. D 937 299-5594
Dayton (G-5961)

▲ Q-Lab Corporation.............................. D 440 835-8700
Westlake (G-14325)

Quality Controls Inc............................ F 513 272-3900
Cincinnati (G-3015)

Quidel Dhi... E 740 589-3300
Athens (G-651)

Ralston Instruments LLC...................... E 440 564-1430
Newbury (G-10562)

◆ Reuter-Stokes LLC............................. B 330 425-3755
Twinsburg (G-13365)

Safe-Grain Inc..................................... G 513 398-2500
Loveland (G-8650)

Science/Electronics Inc........................ G 937 224-4444
Dayton (G-5998)

Sensotec LLC...................................... G 614 481-8616
Hilliard (G-7701)

▲ Skidmore-Wilhelm Mfg Company...... G 216 481-4774
Solon (G-12182)

Smithers Group Inc.............................. D 330 833-8548
Massillon (G-9244)

◆ Struers Inc... D 440 871-0071
Westlake (G-14337)

◆ Sumiriko Ohio Inc.............................. D 419 358-2121
Bluffton (G-1365)

Super Systems Inc.............................. E 513 772-0060
Cincinnati (G-3128)

▲ Te-Co Manufacturing LLC.................. D 937 836-0961
Englewood (G-6625)

Tech Products Corporation.................. F 937 438-1100
Miamisburg (G-9744)

Tegam Inc... E 440 466-6100
Geneva (G-7246)

Teledyne Defense Elec LLC................. C 866 539-5916
Miamisburg (G-9746)

Teledyne Instruments Inc.................... E 513 229-7000
Mason (G-9158)

Teledyne Tekmar Company................. E 513 229-7000
Mason (G-9160)

Teradyne Inc....................................... F 937 427-1280
Beavercreek (G-985)

▼ Test Mark Industries Inc.................... F 330 426-2200
East Palestine (G-6408)

Test-Fuchs Corporation....................... G 440 708-3505
Brecksville (G-1483)

Toledo Transducers Inc....................... E 419 724-4170
Maumee (G-9327)

Tool Technologies Van Dyke................ F 937 349-4900
Marysville (G-9053)

◆ UPA Technology Inc........................... F 513 755-1380
West Chester (G-14088)

Waygate Technologies Usa LP............. D 866 243-2638
Cincinnati (G-3212)

Welding Consultants Inc...................... G 614 258-7018
Columbus (G-5360)

Xcite Systems Corporation.................. G 513 965-0300
Cincinnati (G-2318)

3841 Surgical and medical instruments

Abbott Laboratories............................ D 847 937-6100
Columbus (G-4662)

Applied Medical Technology Inc........... F 440 717-4000
Brecksville (G-1457)

▲ Atc Group Inc.................................... D 440 293-4064
Andover (G-455)

Atricure Inc... A 513 755-4100
Mason (G-9068)

Avalign - Integrated LLC..................... F 440 269-6984
Mentor (G-9487)

Aws Industries Inc.............................. E 513 932-7941
Lebanon (G-8245)

Axon Medical Llc................................ E 216 276-0262
Medina (G-9379)

Beam Technologies Inc........................ B 800 648-1179
Columbus (G-4746)

Becton Dickinson and Company.......... G 858 617-4272
Groveport (G-7424)

Bowden Manufacturing Corp............... E 440 946-1770
Willoughby (G-14432)

Buckeye Medical Tech LLC.................. G 330 719-9868
Warren (G-13745)

Butler Cnty Surgical Prpts LLC........... G 513 844-2200
Hamilton (G-7475)

Care Fusion....................................... G 216 521-1220
Lakewood (G-8164)

▲ Casco Mfg Solutions Inc.................... D 513 681-0003
Cincinnati (G-2441)

Cmd Medtech LLC.............................. F 614 364-4243
Columbus (G-4814)

◆ Codonics Inc...................................... C 800 444-1198
Cleveland (G-3544)

Coopersurgical Inc.............................. G 203 601-5200
Cincinnati (G-2516)

Covidien Holding Inc........................... C 513 948-7219
Cincinnati (G-2520)

Cqt Kennedy LLC................................ D 419 238-2442
Van Wert (G-13532)

▼ Daavlin Distributing Co...................... E 419 636-6304
Bryan (G-1637)

▲ Dayton Hawker Corporation............... F 937 293-8147
Dayton (G-5728)

Dentronix Inc...................................... D 330 916-7300
Cuyahoga Falls (G-5538)

Devicor Med Pdts Holdings Inc............ A 513 864-9000
Cincinnati (G-2548)

Diagnostic Hybrids Inc........................ C 740 593-1784
Athens (G-638)

Elite Biomedical Solutions LLC............ F 513 207-0602
Cincinnati (G-2302)

Encore Industries Inc.......................... E 419 626-8000
Sandusky (G-11830)

▼ Eoi Inc.. F 740 201-3300
Lewis Center (G-8333)

▲ Ethicon Endo-Surgery Inc.................. A 513 337-7000
Cincinnati (G-2600)

Eye Surgery Center Ohio Inc............... E 614 228-3937
Columbus (G-4917)

Findlay Amrcn Prsthtic Orthtic............. G 419 424-1622
Findlay (G-6863)

Frantz Medical Development Ltd........... G 440 255-1155
Mentor (G-9519)

◆ General Data Company Inc................. B 513 752-7978
Cincinnati (G-2304)

Gentherm Medical LLC........................ C 513 772-8810
Cincinnati (G-2668)

Grimm Scientific Inds Inc.................... F 740 374-3412
Marietta (G-8921)

Gyrus Acmi LP.................................... D 419 668-8201
Norwalk (G-10845)

◆ Haag-Streit Usa Inc........................... D 513 398-3937
Mason (G-9107)

Hdwt Holdings Inc.............................. D 440 269-6984
Mentor (G-9526)

◆ Hgi Holdings Inc................................ A 330 963-6996
Twinsburg (G-13316)

Hickok Waekon LLC............................ D 216 541-8060
Cleveland (G-3830)

Howmedica Osteonics Corp................. D 937 291-3900
Dayton (G-5814)

Icu Medical Inc................................... D 614 210-7300
Dublin (G-6305)

Inspyre Health Systems LLC............... G 440 412-7916
Grafton (G-7304)

Interntnal Cutng Solutions Inc............. G 440 786-1700
Streetsboro (G-12506)

▲ Invacare Holdings Corporation........... B 440 329-6000
Elyria (G-6554)

Johnson & Johnson............................. E 513 786-7000
Blue Ash (G-1290)

Kinetic Concepts Inc........................... F 440 234-8590
Middleburg Heights (G-9774)

Klarity Medical Products LLC.............. F 740 788-8107
Heath (G-7599)

▲ KMC Holdings LLC............................. C 419 238-2442
Van Wert (G-13539)

Leica Biosystems - TAS...................... E 513 864-9671
Cincinnati (G-2818)

Life Sciences - Vandalia LLC............C 937 387-0880
Dayton *(G-5846)*

▲ M&H Medical Holdings Inc............. E 419 727-8421
Maumee *(G-9305)*

Mark W Thruman............................. G 614 754-5500
Columbus *(G-5082)*

Markethtch Inc D/B/A Mh Eye CA...........F 330 376-6363
Akron *(G-221)*

Medical Quant USA Inc....................... F 440 542-0761
Solon *(G-12145)*

Mediview Xr Inc.............................. F 419 270-2774
Cleveland *(G-4016)*

Medtronic Inc............................... F 216 642-1977
Cleveland *(G-4017)*

Medtronic Inc............................... G 763 526-2566
Independence *(G-7908)*

▼ Megadyne Medical Products Inc....... C 801 576-9669
Blue Ash *(G-1307)*

Meridian LLC................................ G 330 995-0371
Aurora *(G-678)*

Micromd..................................... G 850 217-7412
Youngstown *(G-14899)*

Midmark Corporation......................... G 937 526-3662
Versailles *(G-13600)*

◆ Midmark Corporation....................... A 937 528-7500
Miamisburg *(G-9717)*

▲ Mill-Rose Company....................... C 440 255-9171
Mentor *(G-9566)*

Minimally Invasive Devices Inc........... G 614 484-5036
Columbus *(G-5104)*

Morris Technologies Inc.................... E 513 733-1611
Cincinnati *(G-2888)*

▲ National Biological Corp............... E 216 831-0600
Beachwood *(G-931)*

Nelson Labs Fairfield Inc................ E 973 227-6882
Broadview Heights *(G-1507)*

Nervive Inc............................... F 847 274-1790
Cleveland *(G-4067)*

Neurologix Technologies Inc.............. F 512 914-7941
Cleveland *(G-4071)*

Norman Noble Inc.......................... E 216 851-4007
Euclid *(G-6665)*

▲ Norman Noble Inc....................... B 216 761-5387
Highland Heights *(G-7660)*

Norwood Medical LLC....................... D 937 228-4101
Dayton *(G-5912)*

Nuevue Solutions Inc..................... G 440 836-4772
Rootstown *(G-11651)*

Ohiohealth Imaging Services.............. F 740 420-7925
Circleville *(G-3261)*

OMI Surgical Products..................... G 513 561-2241
Cincinnati *(G-2929)*

Optimum Surgical.......................... F 216 870-8526
Medina *(G-9431)*

Patriot Products Inc..................... F 419 865-9712
Holland *(G-7776)*

Pemco Inc................................. E 216 524-2990
Cleveland *(G-4150)*

Percuvision LLC........................... G 614 891-4800
Columbus *(G-5186)*

Peritec Biosciences Ltd.................. G 216 445-3756
Cleveland *(G-4152)*

Phoenix Quality Mfg LLC................... E 705 279-0538
Jackson *(G-7951)*

Pulse Worldwide Ltd...................... G 513 234-7829
Mason *(G-9139)*

Quality Electrodynamics LLC.............. C 440 638-5106
Mayfield Village *(G-9347)*

Resonetics LLC............................ D 937 865-4070
Kettering *(G-8123)*

Respironics Novametrix LLC................ A 800 345-6443
Columbus *(G-5228)*

Rhinosystems Inc......................... F 216 351-6262
Brooklyn *(G-1525)*

Rsb Spine LLC............................. G 216 241-2804
Cleveland *(G-4262)*

Rultract Inc.............................. G 330 856-9808
Warren *(G-13796)*

Scientific Molding Corp Ltd............... G 330 342-7800
Twinsburg *(G-13375)*

Scottcare Corporation..................... E 216 362-0550
Cleveland *(G-4280)*

Sense Diagnostics Inc..................... G 513 702-0376
Cincinnati *(G-3081)*

Smiths Medical Asd Inc.................... E 800 796-8701
Dublin *(G-6345)*

Smiths Medical Asd Inc................... C 614 889-2220
Dublin *(G-6346)*

Smiths Medical North America.............. G 614 210-7300
Dublin *(G-6347)*

Sonogage Inc............................. F 216 464-1119
Cleveland *(G-4314)*

Spartronics Strongsville Inc............. D 440 878-4630
Strongsville *(G-12603)*

Spring Hlthcare Dagnostics LLC............ D 866 201-9503
Jackson *(G-7953)*

SRI Healthcare LLC....................... G 513 398-6406
Mason *(G-9156)*

Standard Bariatrics Inc.................. E 513 620-7751
Blue Ash *(G-1334)*

Steris Corporation........................ D 440 354-2600
Mentor *(G-9623)*

◆ Steris Corporation...................... A 440 354-2600
Mentor *(G-9624)*

Steris Instrument MGT Svcs Inc............ C 800 783-9251
Stow *(G-12464)*

Stryker Orthopedic........................ G 614 766-2990
Dublin *(G-6352)*

Summit Online Products LLC................ G 800 326-1972
Powell *(G-11495)*

▼ Surgical Theater Inc................... E 216 452-2177
Pepper Pike *(G-11189)*

Surgrx Inc................................ F 650 482-2400
Blue Ash *(G-1338)*

Theken Companies LLC..................... F 330 733-7600
Akron *(G-334)*

Thermo Fisher Scientific Inc.............. E 800 871-8909
Oakwood Village *(G-10910)*

Torbot Group Inc.......................... F 419 724-1475
Northwood *(G-10810)*

Troy Innovative Instrs Inc................ E 440 834-9567
Middlefield *(G-9831)*

United Medical Supply Company............. F 866 678-8633
Brunswick *(G-1621)*

▲ United Sttes Endscopy Group In......... C 440 639-4494
Mentor *(G-9647)*

Valensil Technologies LLC................. E 440 937-8181
Avon *(G-741)*

Vesco Medical LLC........................ F 614 914-5991
Westerville *(G-14279)*

Ward Engineering Inc...................... G 614 442-8063
Columbus *(G-5355)*

◆ Ysi Incorporated........................ D 937 767-7241
Yellow Springs *(G-14796)*

3842 Surgical appliances and supplies

ABI Orthtc/Prosthetic Labs Ltd............ E 330 758-1143
Youngstown *(G-14802)*

Acor Orthopaedic Inc...................... F 440 532-0117
Cleveland *(G-3292)*

▲ Acor Orthopaedic LLC.................... E 216 662-4500
Cleveland *(G-3293)*

Akron Orthotic Solutions Inc.............. G 330 253-3002
Akron *(G-35)*

American Orthopedics Inc................. F 614 291-6454
Columbus *(G-4700)*

American Power LLC........................ F 937 235-0418
Dayton *(G-5654)*

Anatomical Concepts Inc................... F 330 757-3569
Youngstown *(G-14815)*

Ansell Healthcare Products LLC............ C 740 622-4369
Coshocton *(G-5448)*

Ansell Healthcare Products LLC............ E 740 622-4311
Coshocton *(G-5449)*

Axon Medical Llc......................... E 216 276-0262
Medina *(G-9379)*

Bahler Medical Inc........................ G 614 873-7600
Plain City *(G-11396)*

Barton-Carey Medical Pdts Inc............. E 419 887-1285
Maumee *(G-9265)*

▲ Beaufort Rfd Inc........................ F 330 239-4331
Sharon Center *(G-11937)*

Beiersdorf Inc........................... C 513 682-7300
West Chester *(G-14107)*

Capital Prsthtic Orthtic Ctr I............ F 614 451-0446
Columbus *(G-4797)*

Cardinal Health Inc...................... E 614 553-3830
Dublin *(G-6285)*

Cardinal Health Inc...................... G 614 757-2863
Lewis Center *(G-8328)*

◆ Cardinal Health Inc.................... A 614 757-5000
Dublin *(G-6286)*

Cleveland Medical Devices Inc............. E 216 619-5928
Cleveland *(G-3515)*

Cole Orthotics Prosthetic Ctr............. G 419 476-4248
Toledo *(G-12927)*

Columbus Prescr Rehabilitation............ G 614 294-1600
Westerville *(G-14250)*

Communications Aid Inc.................... F 513 475-8453
Cincinnati *(G-2505)*

Coopersurgical Inc........................ G 203 601-5200
Cincinnati *(G-2516)*

Cranial Technologies Inc.................. G 844 447-5894
Cincinnati *(G-2523)*

Dan Allen Surgical LLC.................... F 800 261-9953
Newbury *(G-10549)*

Deco Tools Inc............................ E 419 476-9321
Toledo *(G-12939)*

Dentronix Inc............................. D 330 916-7300
Cuyahoga Falls *(G-5538)*

Depuy Synthes Inc......................... G 614 472-8008
Columbus *(G-4870)*

Eleven 10 LLC............................. F 888 216-4049
Westlake *(G-14300)*

Enespro LLC.............................. G 630 332-2801
Cleveland *(G-3674)*

Ethicon Inc............................... C 513 786-7000
Blue Ash *(G-1272)*

▲ Faretec Inc............................ F 440 350-9510
Painesville *(G-11086)*

◆ Ferno-Washington Inc................... C 877 733-0911
Wilmington *(G-14580)*

Fidelity Orthopedic Inc.................. G 937 228-0682
Dayton *(G-5776)*

Findlay Amrcn Prsthtic Orthtic............ G 419 424-1622
Findlay *(G-6863)*

Florida Invacare Holdings LLC............. F 800 333-6900
Elyria *(G-6537)*

Forceone LLC.............................. G 513 939-1018
Hebron *(G-7615)*

Form5 Prosthetics Inc..................... F 614 226-1141
New Albany *(G-10341)*

Francisco Jaume........................... G 740 622-1200
Coshocton *(G-5455)*

▲ Frohock-Stewart Inc..................... E 440 329-6000
North Ridgeville *(G-10731)*

▲ Gelok International Corp................... G 419 352-1482
  Bowling Green *(G-1420)*

Gendron Inc.. E 419 636-0848
  Bryan *(G-1643)*

Gottfried Medical Inc......................... F 419 474-2973
  Toledo *(G-12976)*

▲ Greendale Home Fashions LLC....... D 859 916-5475
  Cincinnati *(G-2690)*

▲ Guardian Manufacturing Co LLC...... E 419 933-2711
  Willard *(G-14402)*

Hammill Manufacturing Co................. D 419 476-0789
  Maumee *(G-9295)*

Hdwt Holdings Inc............................. D 440 269-6984
  Mentor *(G-9526)*

Healthwares Manufacturing............... F 513 353-3691
  Cleves *(G-4539)*

Invacare Canadian Holdings Inc......... G 440 329-6000
  Elyria *(G-6546)*

Invacare Canadian Holdings LLC........ G 440 329-6000
  Elyria *(G-6547)*

Invacare Continuing Care Inc............. G 800 668-2337
  Elyria *(G-6548)*

Invacare Corporation......................... F 440 329-6000
  Elyria *(G-6550)*

Invacare Corporation......................... G 800 333-6900
  Elyria *(G-6551)*

Invacare Corporation......................... F 440 329-6000
  North Ridgeville *(G-10736)*

◆ Invacare Corporation........................A 440 329-6000
  Elyria *(G-6549)*

Invacare Hcs LLC.............................. F 330 634-9925
  Elyria *(G-6552)*

Invacare Holdings LLC....................... G 440 329-6000
  Elyria *(G-6553)*

▲ Invacare Holdings Corporation.........B 440 329-6000
  Elyria *(G-6554)*

Johnson & Johnson............................ E 513 786-7000
  Blue Ash *(G-1290)*

Jones Metal Products Co LLC............. E 740 545-6381
  West Lafayette *(G-14171)*

Jones Metal Products Company.......... E 740 545-6341
  West Lafayette *(G-14172)*

▲ Julius Zorn Inc.............................. D 330 923-4999
  Cuyahoga Falls *(G-5553)*

Kempf Surgical Appliances Inc............ G 513 984-5758
  Cincinnati *(G-2791)*

Leimkuehler Inc................................ E 440 899-7842
  Cleveland *(G-3950)*

Lion First Responder Ppe Inc............. D 937 898-1949
  Dayton *(G-5849)*

Luminaud Inc.................................... G 440 255-9082
  Mentor *(G-9556)*

Marlen Manufacturing & Dev Co......... F 216 292-7546
  Bedford *(G-1047)*

▲ Marlen Manufacturing & Dev Co....... G 216 292-7060
  Bedford *(G-1046)*

▲ Matplus Ltd.................................. G 440 352-7201
  Painesville *(G-11098)*

Medical Device Bus Svcs Inc.............. E 937 274-5850
  Dayton *(G-5873)*

Medline Industries LP........................ E 614 879-9728
  West Jefferson *(G-14164)*

Meridian Industries Inc...................... D 330 673-1011
  Kent *(G-8051)*

Midmark Corporation......................... G 937 526-3662
  Versailles *(G-13600)*

◆ Midmark Corporation........................A 937 528-7500
  Miamisburg *(G-9717)*

Morning Pride Mfg LLC...................... A 937 264-1726
  Dayton *(G-5895)*

▲ Morning Pride Mfg LLC.................... A 937 264-2662
  Dayton *(G-5894)*

Motion Mobility & Design Inc.............. F 330 244-9723
  North Canton *(G-10653)*

Mst Inc.. G 419 542-6645
  Hicksville *(G-7648)*

Myfootshopcom LLC.......................... G 740 522-5681
  Newark *(G-10523)*

◆ National Safety Apparel LLC...............D 800 553-0672
  Cleveland *(G-4062)*

Novagard Solutions Inc...................... D 216 881-8111
  Cleveland *(G-4101)*

Npl Homecare LLC............................ E 440 365-8581
  Strongsville *(G-12579)*

Opc Inc.. G 419 531-2222
  Toledo *(G-13079)*

Orthotic & Prosthetic Spc Inc............. E 216 531-2773
  Euclid *(G-6667)*

Orthotics Prsthtics Rhblttion.............. G 330 856-2553
  Warren *(G-13788)*

Osteonovus Inc................................. F 419 530-5940
  Toledo *(G-13081)*

Osteonovus Inc................................. G 419 530-5940
  Toledo *(G-13082)*

Osteosymbionics LLC........................ F 216 881-8500
  Cleveland *(G-4126)*

◆ Philips Med Systems Clvland In........B 440 483-3000
  Cleveland *(G-4159)*

Presque Isle Orthtics Prsthtic............. G 216 371-0660
  Cleveland *(G-4192)*

Reliable Wheelchair Trans.................. G 216 390-3999
  Beachwood *(G-944)*

Soundtrace Inc.................................. F 513 278-5288
  Mason *(G-9153)*

▼ Southpaw Enterprises Inc.................. E 937 252-7676
  Moraine *(G-10193)*

Spinal Balance Inc............................. G 419 530-5935
  Swanton *(G-12693)*

▲ Sroufe Healthcare Products LLC........ G 260 894-4171
  Wadsworth *(G-13672)*

Stable Step LLC................................ C 800 491-1571
  Wadsworth *(G-13673)*

Steris Corporation............................. D 330 696-9946
  Mentor *(G-9625)*

Steris Corporation............................. D 440 392-8079
  Mentor *(G-9626)*

Steris Corporation............................. C 440 354-2600
  Mentor *(G-9627)*

◆ Steris Corporation...........................A 440 354-2600
  Mentor *(G-9624)*

Steris-IMS....................................... G 330 686-4557
  Stow *(G-12465)*

▲ Surgical Appliance Inds Inc.............. C 513 271-4594
  Cincinnati *(G-3132)*

Surgical Recovery Systems LLC......... E 513 833-6868
  Hamilton *(G-7528)*

Theken Spine LLC............................. F 330 773-7677
  Medina *(G-9455)*

Thomas Products Co Inc.................... E 513 756-9009
  Cincinnati *(G-3155)*

▲ Tilt 15 Inc.................................... D 330 239-4192
  Sharon Center *(G-11944)*

Touch Bionics Inc............................. G 800 233-6263
  Dublin *(G-6356)*

▲ Vantage Orthopedics Inc.................. F 513 563-1690
  Cincinnati *(G-3194)*

▲ Wcm Holdings Inc........................... C 513 705-2100
  Cincinnati *(G-3213)*

▲ West Chester Holdings LLC.............. C 513 705-2100
  Cincinnati *(G-2516)*

◆ Willowwood Global LLC.....................C 740 869-3377
  Mount Sterling *(G-10231)*

Yanke Bionics Inc............................. E 330 762-6411
  Akron *(G-360)*

▲ Zimmer Surgical Inc........................ B 800 321-5533
  Dover *(G-6268)*

3843 Dental equipment and supplies

◆ Boxout LLC......................................C 833 462-7746
  Hudson *(G-7835)*

Dental Ceramics Inc.......................... E 330 523-5240
  Richfield *(G-11590)*

Dental Pure Water Inc....................... F 440 234-0890
  Berea *(G-1167)*

Dentronix Inc.................................... D 330 916-7300
  Cuyahoga Falls *(G-5538)*

Dentsply Sirona Inc........................... E 419 893-5672
  Maumee *(G-9290)*

Dentsply Sirona Inc........................... E 419 865-9497
  Maumee *(G-9291)*

Midmark Corporation......................... G 937 526-3662
  Versailles *(G-13600)*

◆ Midmark Corporation........................A 937 528-7500
  Miamisburg *(G-9717)*

Palm Plastics Ltd.............................. G 561 776-6700
  Bowling Green *(G-1432)*

Precision Swiss LLC.......................... G 513 716-7000
  Cincinnati *(G-2978)*

United Dental Laboratories................. E 330 253-1810
  Tallmadge *(G-12756)*

3844 X-ray apparatus and tubes

Control-X Inc.................................... G 614 777-9729
  Columbus *(G-4845)*

Dentsply Sirona Inc........................... E 419 865-9497
  Maumee *(G-9291)*

General Electric Company................... F 216 663-2110
  Cleveland *(G-3765)*

Leisure Time Pdts Design Corp........... G 440 934-1032
  Avon *(G-731)*

Metro Design Inc............................... F 440 458-4200
  Elyria *(G-6563)*

North Coast Medical Eqp Inc.............. F 440 243-6189
  Berea *(G-1183)*

Philips Med Systems Clvland In.......... C 617 245-5510
  Beachwood *(G-940)*

◆ Philips Med Systems Clvland In........B 440 483-3000
  Cleveland *(G-4159)*

Trionix Research Lab Inc.................... G 330 425-9055
  Twinsburg *(G-13387)*

Waygate Technologies Usa LP............ D 866 243-2638
  Cincinnati *(G-3212)*

3845 Electromedical equipment

▼ Alltech Med Systems Amer Inc.......... E 440 424-2240
  Solon *(G-12077)*

Avation Medical Inc........................... F 614 591-4201
  Columbus *(G-4736)*

Brainmaster Technologies Inc............. G 440 232-6000
  Bedford *(G-1018)*

Canary Health Technologies Inc.......... F 617 784-4021
  Cleveland *(G-3462)*

Cardiac Analytics LLC........................ F 614 314-1332
  Powell *(G-11484)*

Cardioinsight Technologies Inc........... G 216 274-2221
  Independence *(G-7890)*

Checkpoint Surgical Inc..................... D 216 378-9107
  Independence *(G-7891)*

Cleveland Medical Devices Inc............ E 216 619-5928
  Cleveland *(G-3515)*

Coopersurgical Inc............................ G 203 601-5200
  Cincinnati *(G-2516)*

Ctl Analyzers LLC............................. E 216 791-5084
  Shaker Heights *(G-11929)*

▼ Eoi Inc... F 740 201-3300
  Lewis Center *(G-8333)*

Furniss Corporation Ltd........................ F 614 871-1470
   Mount Sterling (G-10228)

Great Lkes Nrotechnologies Inc.......... E 855 456-3876
   Cleveland (G-3794)

Gyrus Acmi LP....................................D 419 668-8201
   Norwalk (G-10845)

Helm Instrument Company Inc............ E 419 893-4356
   Maumee (G-9296)

Imalux Corporation.............................. F 216 502-0755
   Cleveland (G-3851)

▲ Lumitex Inc.......................................D 440 243-8401
   Strongsville (G-12572)

Mrpicker.. G 440 354-6497
   Cleveland (G-4052)

◆ Ndi Medical LLC...............................E 216 378-9106
   Cleveland (G-4064)

Neuros Medical Inc............................G 440 951-2565
   Willoughby Hills (G-14561)

Nkh-Safety Inc.................................... F 513 771-3839
   Cincinnati (G-2911)

Norwood Medical LLC........................ G 937 228-4101
   Dayton (G-5912)

Pemco Inc... E 216 524-2990
   Cleveland (G-4150)

Rapiscan Systems High Enrgy In........ E 937 879-4200
   Fairborn (G-6698)

Respironics Novametrix LLC............... A 800 345-6443
   Columbus (G-5228)

Sonosite Inc....................................... G 425 951-1200
   Hamilton (G-7526)

◆ Steris Corporation............................A 440 354-2600
   Mentor (G-9624)

Thermo Fisher Scientific Inc.............. F 513 948-6290
   Blue Ash (G-1343)

Torax Medical Inc.............................. F 651 361-8900
   Blue Ash (G-1344)

Valued Relationships Inc.................... B 800 860-4230
   Franklin (G-7054)

Varian Medical Systems Inc.............. G 888 827-4265
   Liberty Township (G-8379)

▲ Viewray Inc......................................D 440 703-3210
   Oakwood Village (G-10911)

Viewray Technologies Inc................... F 440 703-3210
   Oakwood Village (G-10912)

3851 Ophthalmic goods

▲ Central-1-Optical LLC......................D 330 783-9660
   Youngstown (C-14834)

▲ Classic Optical Labs Inc..................C 330 759-8245
   Youngstown (G-14838)

Diversified Ophthalmics Inc............... E 803 783-3454
   Cincinnati (G-2554)

DMV Corporation............................... G 740 452-4787
   Zanesville (G-15010)

Essilor Laboratories Amer Inc........... G 330 425-3003
   Twinsburg (G-13300)

Essilor of America Inc....................... F 513 765-6000
   Mason (G-9098)

Glasses Guy LLC................................ E 970 624-9019
   Canton (G-1901)

Malta Dynamics LLC.......................... F 740 749-3512
   Waterford (G-13828)

Oakley Inc.. F 949 672-6560
   Dayton (G-5919)

Steiner Eoptics Inc............................D 937 426-2341
   Miamisburg (G-9740)

Sticktite Lenses LLC........................... F 571 276-9508
   New Albany (G-10351)

Toledo Optical Laboratory Inc............ G 419 248-3384
   Toledo (G-13155)

▲ Volk Optical Inc................................D 440 942-6161
   Mentor (G-9651)

Wilson Optical Labs Inc...................... E 440 357-7000
   Mentor (G-9652)

Zenni Usa Inc.....................................D 614 439-9850
   Columbus (G-5381)

3861 Photographic equipment and supplies

44toolscom... G 614 873-4800
   Plain City (G-11389)

AGFA Corporation.............................. E 513 829-6292
   Fairfield (G-6706)

▲ American Frame Corporation........... E 419 893-5595
   Maumee (G-9259)

Conquest Maps LLC........................... G 614 654-1627
   Columbus (G-4843)

Cree Logistics LLC............................. G 513 978-1112
   Cincinnati (G-2524)

Dupont Specialty Pdts USA LLC........ E 740 474-0220
   Circleville (G-3255)

Eastman Kodak Company................... G 937 259-3000
   Kettering (G-8119)

Eprad Inc... G 419 666-3266
   Perrysburg (G-11219)

Gvs Industries Inc.............................. G 513 851-3606
   Hamilton (G-7498)

◆ Horizons Incorporated......................C 216 475-0555
   Cleveland (G-3838)

Kay-Zee Inc....................................... G 330 339-1268
   New Philadelphia (G-10451)

◆ Kg63 LLC.. F 216 941-7766
   Cleveland (G-3917)

Legrand AV Inc.................................. E 574 267-8101
   Blue Ash (G-1297)

Mediajacked Sound Studio LLC.......... G 330 391-3123
   Youngstown (G-14897)

Miller-Holzwarth Inc..........................D 330 342-7224
   Salem (G-11800)

Ohio Hd Video.................................... F 614 656-1162
   New Albany (G-10348)

Ournashonisme Ent LLC..................... F 689 276-0367
   Euclid (G-6668)

Plastigraphics Inc.............................. F 513 771-8848
   Cincinnati (G-2970)

◆ Printer Components Inc....................G 585 924-5190
   Fairfield (G-6767)

▲ Pulsar Ecoproducts LLC.................. F 216 861-8800
   Cleveland (G-4208)

Rti Securex LLC................................. G 937 859-5290
   Miamisburg (C-0734)

Sound Laboratory LLC........................ F 330 968-4060
   Kent (G-8082)

Stewart Filmscreen Corp.................... E 513 753-0800
   Amelia (G-438)

▲ Stretchtape Inc................................ E 216 486-9400
   Cleveland (G-4333)

3873 Watches, clocks, watchcases, and parts

Amano Cincinnati Incorporated.......... F 513 697-9000
   Loveland (G-8619)

▲ Dimcogray Corporation....................D 937 433-7600
   Centerville (G-2131)

◆ I T Verdin Co................................... E 513 241-4010
   Cincinnati (G-2738)

Sgi Matrix LLC...................................D 937 438-9033
   Miamisburg (G-9736)

39 MISCELLANEOUS MANUFACTURING INDUSTRIES

3911 Jewelry, precious metal

◆ Associated Premium Corporation......E 513 679-4444
   Cincinnati (G-2381)

Bensan Jewelers Inc.......................... G 216 221-1434
   Lakewood (G-8163)

D & J Manufacturing Jeweler............ G 513 541-5200
   Cincinnati (G-2534)

Diamond Designs Inc......................... G 330 434-6776
   Akron (G-120)

Don Basch Jewelers Inc..................... F 330 467-2116
   Macedonia (G-8687)

Em Es Be Company LLC..................... G 216 761-9500
   Cleveland (G-3665)

Farah Jewelers Inc............................ G 614 438-6140
   Westerville (G-14210)

▲ Ginos Awards Inc............................ E 216 831-6565
   Warrensville Heights (G-13818)

Goyal Enterprises Inc........................ F 513 874-9303
   Cincinnati (G-2686)

Gustave Julian Jewelers Inc............. G 440 888-1100
   Cleveland (G-3801)

H P Nielsen Inc.................................. G 440 244-4255
   Lorain (G-8557)

Im Greenberg Inc............................... G 440 461-4464
   Cleveland (G-3849)

James C Free Inc............................... G 513 793-0133
   Cincinnati (G-2759)

▲ James C Free Inc............................ E 937 298-0171
   Dayton (G-5826)

Koop Diamond Cutters Inc................. F 513 621-2838
   Cincinnati (G-2805)

Lotus Love LLC................................... E 614 964-8477
   Columbus (G-5075)

M B Saxon Co Inc.............................. G 440 229-5006
   Cleveland (G-3975)

Marfo Company..................................D 614 276-3352
   Columbus (G-5081)

Markus Jewelers LLC......................... G 513 474-4950
   Cincinnati (G-2848)

Michael W Hyes Desgr Goldsmith...... G 440 519-0889
   Solon (G-12150)

▲ Prince & Izant LLC.......................... E 216 362-7000
   Cleveland (G-4196)

Rego Manufacturing Co Inc...............D 419 562-0466
   Bucyrus (G-1689)

Robert W Johnson Inc........................D 614 336-4545
   Dublin (G-6340)

Rosenfeld Jewelry Inc........................ G 440 446-0099
   Cleveland (G-4253)

Sheiban Jewelry Inc........................... F 440 238-0616
   Strongsville (G-12599)

Signet Group Inc................................ E 330 668-5000
   Fairlawn (G-6812)

Signet Group Services US Inc............ F 330 668-5000
   Fairlawn (G-6813)

Val Casting Inc.................................. G 419 562-2499
   Bucyrus (G-1691)

White Jewelers Inc............................ G 330 264-3324
   Wooster (G-14697)

▲ Whitehouse Bros Inc....................... G 513 621-2259
   Blue Ash (G-1350)

3914 Silverware and plated ware

Ahner Fabricating & Shtmtl Inc.......... E 419 626-6641
   Sandusky (G-11820)

Behrco Inc.. G 419 394-1612
   Saint Marys (G-11731)

▲ Ginos Awards Inc............................ E 216 831-6565
   Warrensville Heights (G-13818)

Hr Machine llc.................................... G 937 222-7644
   Dayton (G-5815)

▼ Online Engineering Corp................. G 513 561-8878
   Cincinnati (G-2934)

Professional Award Service................ G 513 389-3600
   Cincinnati (G-3005)

S
I
C

Tempo Manufacturing Company............ G..... 937 773-6613
Piqua *(G-11387)*

3915 Jewelers' materials and lapidary work

▲ Dayton Hawker Corporation............. F..... 937 293-8147
Dayton *(G-5728)*

Dentsply Sirona Inc.............................. E..... 419 865-9497
Maumee *(G-9291)*

Koop Diamond Cutters Inc.................... F..... 513 621-2838
Cincinnati *(G-2805)*

▲ Prince & Izant LLC............................. E..... 216 362-7000
Cleveland *(G-4196)*

Sunshine Products.............................. G..... 303 478-4913
Toledo *(G-13135)*

The-Fischer-Group.............................. G..... 513 285-1281
Fairfield *(G-6784)*

Zero-D Products Inc............................ G..... 440 942-5005
Willoughby *(G-14554)*

3931 Musical instruments

▲ A R Schopps Sons Inc...................... E..... 330 821-8406
Alliance *(G-364)*

Bbb Music LLC.................................. G..... 740 772-2262
Chillicothe *(G-2244)*

Belco Works Inc................................. D..... 740 695-0500
Saint Clairsville *(G-11688)*

Bell Industries................................... F..... 513 353-2355
Harrison *(G-7543)*

Brooks Manufacturing.......................... G..... 419 244-1777
Toledo *(G-12905)*

▼ Commercial Music Service Co............ G..... 740 746-8500
Sugar Grove *(G-12629)*

Conn-Selmer Inc................................ C..... 440 946-6100
Willoughby *(G-14441)*

D Picking & Co................................... G..... 419 562-6891
Bucyrus *(G-1677)*

▲ Earthquaker Devices LLC.................. E..... 330 252-9220
Akron *(G-129)*

▲ Grover Musical Products Inc.............. E..... 216 391-1188
Cleveland *(G-3797)*

◆ I T Verdin Co.................................... E..... 513 241-4010
Cincinnati *(G-2738)*

▲ Jatiga Inc....................................... D..... 859 817-7100
Cincinnati *(G-2762)*

Loft Violin Shop.................................. G..... 614 267-7221
Columbus *(G-5073)*

McHael D Goronok String Instrs........... G..... 216 421-4227
Cleveland *(G-4010)*

Muller Pipe Organ Co.......................... F..... 740 893-1700
Croton *(G-5514)*

Peebles - Herzog Inc........................... G..... 614 279-2211
Columbus *(G-5182)*

S I T Strings Co Inc............................ E..... 330 434-8010
Akron *(G-302)*

Schantz Organ Company...................... F..... 330 682-6065
Orrville *(G-11006)*

▲ Stewart-Macdonald Mfg Co............... E..... 740 592-3021
Athens *(G-653)*

The Holtkamp Organ Co....................... F..... 216 741-5180
Cleveland *(G-4385)*

Victor Organ Company......................... G..... 330 792-1321
Youngstown *(G-14961)*

3942 Dolls and stuffed toys

Love Yueh LLC................................... G..... 614 408-8677
Pickerington *(G-11295)*

Middleton Llyd Dolls Inc...................... G..... 740 989-2082
Coolville *(G-5426)*

3944 Games, toys, and children's vehicles

Advance Novelty Incorporated.............. G..... 419 424-0363
Findlay *(G-6833)*

▲ Ajj Enterprises LLC........................... F..... 513 755-9562
West Chester *(G-14100)*

▲ Anime Palace.................................. G..... 408 858-1918
Lewis Center *(G-8322)*

Aog Inc.. G..... 937 436-2412
Dayton *(G-5660)*

◆ Arrow International Inc....................... D..... 216 961-3500
Cleveland *(G-3367)*

▲ AW Faber-Castell Usa Inc................. D..... 216 643-4660
Cleveland *(G-3396)*

Container Graphics Corp...................... E..... 419 531-5133
Toledo *(G-12932)*

Cornhole Worldwide LLC...................... G..... 513 324-2777
Cleves *(G-4534)*

Evenflo Company Inc.......................... D..... 937 773-3971
Troy *(G-13213)*

◆ Foundations Worldwide Inc............... E..... 330 722-5033
Medina *(G-9405)*

Fremont Plastic Products Inc................ C..... 419 332-6407
Fremont *(G-7111)*

Hershberger Lawn Structures............... F..... 330 674-3900
Millersburg *(G-9983)*

▲ Late For Sky Production Co............... E..... 513 531-4400
Cincinnati *(G-2812)*

Lawbre Co... G..... 330 637-3363
Cortland *(G-5446)*

▲ Mag-Nif Inc.................................... D..... 440 255-9366
Mentor *(G-9557)*

Mahoning Valley Mfg Inc..................... E..... 330 537-4492
Beloit *(G-1145)*

▲ Mak Magic Inc................................ G..... 614 591-3551
Columbus *(G-5079)*

Ohio Model Products LLC.................... F..... 614 808-4488
Columbus *(G-5147)*

Pioneer National Latex Inc.................. E..... 419 289-3300
Ashland *(G-563)*

Plaid Hat Games................................ G..... 419 552-5490
Ashland *(G-564)*

Plaid Hat Games LLC.......................... G..... 419 552-5490
Ashland *(G-565)*

Rocky Hinge Inc................................. G..... 330 539-6296
Girard *(G-7279)*

◆ S Toys Holdings LLC........................ A..... 330 656-0440
Streetsboro *(G-12521)*

◆ Step2 Company LLC......................... B..... 866 429-5200
Streetsboro *(G-12525)*

The Guardtower Inc............................ F..... 614 488-4311
Hilliard *(G-7707)*

◆ The Little Tikes Company................. A..... 330 650-3000
Hudson *(G-7860)*

▲ Watch-Us Inc.................................. E..... 513 829-8870
Fairfield *(G-6790)*

Wells Manufacturing Llc...................... F..... 937 987-2481
New Vienna *(G-10476)*

3949 Sporting and athletic goods, nec

Adventurous Child Inc......................... G..... 513 531-7700
Cincinnati *(G-2339)*

Al-Co Products Inc.............................. G..... 419 399-3867
Latty *(G-8236)*

◆ American Heritage Billd LLC............. D..... 877 998-0908
Mentor *(G-9478)*

Arem Co... G..... 440 974-6740
Willoughby *(G-14426)*

▲ AWC Transition Corporation.............. F..... 614 846-2918
Columbus *(G-4737)*

Backyard Scoreboards LLC.................. G..... 513 702-6561
Middletown *(G-9842)*

▲ Belaire Products Inc......................... E..... 330 253-3116
Akron *(G-75)*

Black Wing Shooting Center LLC.......... G..... 740 363-7555
Delaware *(G-6134)*

◆ Blatchford Inc................................. D..... 937 291-3636
Miamisburg *(G-9673)*

Board of Park Commissioners.............. G..... 216 635-3200
Cleveland *(G-3424)*

Bradley Enterprises Inc....................... G..... 330 875-1444
Louisville *(G-8599)*

▲ Bullseye Dart Shoppe Inc................. G..... 440 951-9277
Willoughby *(G-14436)*

Columbus Canvas Products Inc............ F..... 614 375-1397
Columbus *(G-4819)*

Corner Alley LLC................................ G..... 216 298-4070
Cleveland *(G-3568)*

Country CLB Rtrment Ctr IV LLC........... G..... 740 676-2300
Bellaire *(G-1086)*

Creighton Sports Center Inc................. G..... 740 865-2521
New Matamoras *(G-10423)*

Darting Around LLC............................ G..... 330 639-3990
Canton *(G-1877)*

Dayton Stencil Works Company............ F..... 937 223-3233
Dayton *(G-5739)*

▲ Done-Rite Bowling Service Co........... E..... 440 232-3280
Bedford *(G-1028)*

Equipment Guys Inc........................... F..... 614 871-9220
Newark *(G-10501)*

▲ Forrest Enterprises Inc..................... G..... 937 773-1714
Piqua *(G-11347)*

Front Pocket Innovations LLC.............. G..... 330 441-2365
Wadsworth *(G-13639)*

Funtown Playgrounds Inc..................... G..... 513 871-8585
Cincinnati *(G-2303)*

▲ Galaxy Balloons Incorporated............ C..... 216 476-3360
Cleveland *(G-3753)*

▲ GL International LLC.......................... G..... 330 744-8812
Youngstown *(G-14868)*

Golf Car Company Inc......................... G..... 614 873-1055
Plain City *(G-11410)*

▲ Golf Galaxy Golfworks Inc................. C..... 740 328-4193
Newark *(G-10504)*

▲ H & S Distributing Inc...................... G..... 800 336-7784
North Ridgeville *(G-10733)*

Hofmanns Lures Inc............................ G..... 937 684-0338
Arcanum *(G-484)*

Hoistech LLC.................................... G..... 440 327-5379
North Ridgeville *(G-10734)*

House of Awards Inc........................... G..... 419 422-7877
Findlay *(G-6882)*

Huffy Sports Washington Inc................ G..... 937 865-2800
Miamisburg *(G-9700)*

▲ Hunters Manufacturing Co Inc........... E..... 330 628-9245
Mogadore *(G-10077)*

Imperial On-Pece Fibrgls Pools............ F..... 740 747-2971
Ashley *(G-582)*

Imperial Pools Inc.............................. G..... 513 771-1506
Cincinnati *(G-2742)*

▲ Kent Water Sports LLC..................... D..... 419 929-7021
New London *(G-10412)*

Leisure Time Pdts Design Corp............ G..... 440 934-1032
Avon *(G-731)*

▲ Lem Products Holding LLC................ E..... 513 202-1188
West Chester *(G-14023)*

Lifetime Products Inc.......................... G..... 614 272-1255
Columbus *(G-5069)*

Line Drive Sportz-Lcrc LLC.................. G..... 419 794-7150
Maumee *(G-9304)*

▲ Litehouse Products LLC.................... E..... 440 638-2350
Strongsville *(G-12571)*

Mc Alarney Pool Spas and Billd........... F..... 740 373-6698
Marietta *(G-8928)*

Meridian Industries Inc....................... D..... 330 359-5447
Winesburg *(G-14607)*

Meyer Design Inc............................... F..... 330 434-9176
Akron *(G-230)*

Mudbrook Golf Ctr At Thndrbird............ G 419 433-2945
  Huron *(G-7880)*

▲ Ohio Table Pad Company................ F 419 872-6400
  Perrysburg *(G-11246)*

◆ Rain Drop Products Llc.....................E 419 207-1229
  Ashland *(G-569)*

Raven Concealment Systems LLC......... E 440 508-9000
  North Ridgeville *(G-10745)*

Red Barakuda LLC............................. G 614 596-5432
  Columbus *(G-5226)*

Shoot-A-Way Inc................................. F 419 294-4654
  Nevada *(G-10323)*

◆ Sports Imports Incorporated..............F 614 771-0246
  Worthington *(G-14725)*

Steven A Esnbrown Lk Lure Qprt......... G 740 965-2200
  Galena *(G-7174)*

▲ Sunset Golf LLC............................ G 419 994-5563
  Tallmadge *(G-12753)*

Total Tennis Inc................................. F 614 488-5004
  Columbus *(G-5325)*

Total Tennis Inc................................. G 614 504-7446
  Plain City *(G-11421)*

Tuffy Pad Company............................ F 330 688-0043
  Stow *(G-12467)*

Ultrabuilt Play Systems Inc................ F 419 652-2294
  Nova *(G-10878)*

Uniwall Mfg Co................................... F 330 875-1444
  Louisville *(G-8617)*

Wholesale Bait Co Inc........................ G 513 863-2380
  Fairfield *(G-6792)*

Wilson Sporting Goods Co.................. C 419 634-9901
  Ada *(G-6)*

◆ Zebec of North America Inc.............G 513 829-5533
  Fairfield *(G-6794)*

3952 Lead pencils and art goods

▲ North Shore Strapping Company...... E 216 661-5200
  Brooklyn Heights *(G-1536)*

▲ Pulsar Ecoproducts LLC................ F 216 861-8800
  Cleveland *(G-4208)*

3953 Marking devices

◆ Akron Paint & Varnish Inc................D 330 773-8911
  Akron *(G-36)*

Bishop Machine Tool & Die................. F 740 453-8818
  Zanesville *(G-14997)*

Dayton Stencil Works Company........... F 937 223-3233
  Dayton *(G-5739)*

Desmond Engraving Co Inc................ G 216 265-8338
  Cleveland *(G-3610)*

E C Shaw Company of Ohio................ E 513 721-6334
  Cincinnati *(G-2569)*

Global Partners USA Co Inc............... G 513 276-4981
  West Chester *(G-14011)*

Greg G Wright & Sons LLC................. G 513 721-3310
  Cincinnati *(G-2691)*

Hathaway Stamp Co........................... F 513 621-1052
  Cincinnati *(G-2712)*

Hathaway Stamp Idntfction Cncn......... G 513 621-1052
  Cincinnati *(G-2713)*

Impact Printing and Design LLC.......... F 833 522-6200
  Columbus *(G-5003)*

▲ Infosight Corporation....................... D 740 642-3600
  Chillicothe *(G-2260)*

◆ Lectroetch Co...................................F 440 934-1249
  Mentor *(G-9551)*

▲ Magna Visual Inc........................... E 314 843-9000
  Perrysburg *(G-11236)*

▲ Mark-All Enterprises LLC................. E 800 433-3615
  Akron *(G-220)*

Marking Devices Inc........................... G 216 861-4498
  Cleveland *(G-3989)*

Metal Marker Manufacturing Co............ F 440 327-2300
  North Ridgeville *(G-10740)*

▲ Microcom Corporation....................... E 740 548-6262
  Lewis Center *(G-8343)*

Monode Marking Products Inc............. F 419 929-0346
  New London *(G-10413)*

Quality Rubber Stamp Inc.................. G 614 235-2700
  Lancaster *(G-8220)*

▲ REA Elektronik Inc.......................... F 440 232-0555
  Walton Hills *(G-13702)*

Rise Holdings LLC.............................. F 440 946-9646
  Willoughby *(G-14519)*

▲ Royal Acme Corporation.................... E 216 241-1477
  Cleveland *(G-4256)*

Sprinter Marking Inc........................... G 740 453-1000
  Zanesville *(G-15051)*

Stakes Manufacturing LLC................ D 216 245-4752
  Willowick *(G-14567)*

System Seals Inc.............................. E 216 220-1800
  Brecksville *(G-1481)*

▲ System Seals LLC.......................... E 440 735-0200
  Cleveland *(G-4359)*

▲ Telesis Technologies Inc................. C 740 477-5000
  Circleville *(G-3266)*

Visual Marking Systems Inc................ D 330 425-7100
  Twinsburg *(G-13393)*

Volk Corporation................................ G 513 621-1052
  Cincinnati *(G-3207)*

Williams Steel Rule Die Co................. G 216 431-3232
  Cleveland *(G-4507)*

3955 Carbon paper and inked ribbons

▲ All Write Ribbon Inc......................... F 513 753-8300
  Amelia *(G-428)*

▲ Kroy LLC.. C 800 837-4323
  Cleveland *(G-3929)*

◆ Printer Components Inc.....................G 585 924-5190
  Fairfield *(G-6767)*

Progressive Ribbon Inc...................... E 513 705-9319
  Middletown *(G-9887)*

◆ Pubco Corporation............................D 216 881-5300
  Cleveland *(G-4205)*

Wood County Ohio.............................. G 419 353-1227
  Bowling Green *(G-1448)*

3961 Costume jewelry

Bellas Jewels LLC.............................. G 216 551-9593
  Cleveland *(G-3414)*

Benzle Porcelain Company.................. G 614 876-2159
  Hilliard *(G-7676)*

Gardella Jewelry LLC.......................... G 440 877-9261
  North Royalton *(G-10763)*

Pughs Designer Jewelers Inc............. G 740 344-9259
  Newark *(G-10530)*

Silly Brandz Global LLC.................... D 419 697-8324
  Toledo *(G-13132)*

3965 Fasteners, buttons, needles, and pins

Bamal Corp.. G 937 492-9484
  Sidney *(G-11995)*

Beckett-Greenhill LLC....................... F 216 861-5730
  Cleveland *(G-3413)*

Cailin Development LLC..................... F 216 408-6261
  Cleveland *(G-3459)*

▲ Cardinal Fstener Specialty Inc........... E 216 831-3800
  Bedford Heights *(G-1072)*

▲ Catania Medallic Specialty Inc............ E 440 933-9595
  Avon Lake *(G-751)*

◆ Dimcogray Corporation.....................D 937 433-7600
  Centerville *(G-2131)*

Dubose Nat Enrgy Fas McHned PR..... E 216 362-1700
  Middleburg Heights *(G-9769)*

Efg Holdings LLC.............................. A 440 325-4337
  Berea *(G-1168)*

Erico International Corp....................... B 440 248-0100
  Solon *(G-12107)*

▲ ET&f Fastening Systems Inc............. G 800 248-2376
  Solon *(G-12108)*

Global Specialties Inc....................... G 800 338-0814
  Brunswick *(G-1595)*

Lockfast LLC...................................... G 800 543-7157
  Loveland *(G-8637)*

Master Bolt LLC................................. E 440 323-5529
  Elyria *(G-6561)*

▲ Midwest Motor Supply Co................. C 800 233-1294
  Columbus *(G-5100)*

▲ Ohashi Technica USA Mfg Inc........... F 740 965-9002
  Sunbury *(G-12672)*

Purebuttonscom LLC.......................... F 330 721-1600
  Medina *(G-9438)*

◆ Ramco Specialties Inc.....................D 330 653-5135
  Hudson *(G-7855)*

▲ Solution Industries LLC.................... F 440 816-9500
  Strongsville *(G-12602)*

Stanley Engineered Fasten................. G 440 657-3537
  Elyria *(G-6591)*

◆ Stelfast LLC.....................................E 440 879-0077
  Strongsville *(G-12606)*

◆ Tfp Corporation................................E 330 725-7741
  Medina *(G-9454)*

W W Cross Industries Inc.................. F 330 588-8400
  Canton *(G-2043)*

Wodin Inc... E 440 439-4222
  Cleveland *(G-4513)*

Youngstown Bolt & Supply Co............. G 330 799-3201
  Youngstown *(G-14967)*

3991 Brooms and brushes

Brushes Inc....................................... G 216 267-8084
  Cleveland *(G-3446)*

Deco Tools Inc................................... E 419 476-9321
  Toledo *(G-12939)*

Delaware Paint Company Ltd............... F 740 368-9981
  Plain City *(G-11403)*

Designetics Inc.................................. D 419 866-0700
  Holland *(G-7755)*

◆ Fimm USA Inc..................................F 614 568-4874
  Lancaster *(G-8202)*

◆ Malish Corporation...........................D 440 951-5356
  Mentor *(C 0550)*

▲ Mill Rose Laboratories Inc.............. E 440 974-6730
  Mentor *(G-9565)*

▲ Mill-Rose Company.......................... C 440 255-9171
  Mentor *(G-9566)*

Precision Brush Co............................. F 440 542-9600
  Solon *(G-12169)*

◆ Spiral Brushes Inc..........................E 330 686-2861
  Stow *(G-12461)*

▲ Stephen M Trudick........................... E 440 834-1891
  Burton *(G-1704)*

◆ The Wooster Brush Company.............C 330 264-4440
  Wooster *(G-14691)*

Tod Thin Brushes Inc........................ F 440 576-6859
  Jefferson *(G-7986)*

Trent Manufacturing Company............. G 216 391-1551
  Mentor *(G-9644)*

Unique Packaging & Printing............... F 440 785-6730
  Mentor *(G-9646)*

United Rotary Brush Inc...................... E 937 644-3515
  Plain City *(G-11423)*

Wooster Brush Company..................... G 440 322-8081
  Elyria *(G-6603)*

Wooster Brush Company..................... B 330 264-4440
  Wooster *(G-14699)*

S
I
C

3993 Signs and advertising specialties

1157 Designconcepts LLC.................. F 937 497-1157
Sidney (G-11988)

A & A Safety Inc.......................... F 937 567-9781
Beavercreek (G-987)

A & A Safety Inc.......................... E 513 943-6100
Amelia (G-425)

A Sign Above Inc.......................... F 330 425-7832
Twinsburg (G-13266)

A&E Signs and Lighting LLC.................. F 513 541-0024
Cincinnati (G-2327)

Abbott Image Solutions LLC.................. F 937 382-6677
Wilmington (G-14569)

ABC Signs Inc.......................... F 513 407-4367
Cincinnati (G-2331)

Accent Signage Systems Inc.................. E 612 377-9156
Findlay (G-6831)

Adcraft Decals Incorporated.................. E 216 524-2934
Cleveland (G-3297)

Advance Sign Group LLC.................. E 614 429-2111
Columbus (G-4675)

Affinity Disp Expositions Inc.................. F 513 771-2339
Cincinnati (G-2340)

Affinity Disp Expositions Inc.................. F 513 771-2339
Cincinnati (G-2342)

▲ Affinity Disp Expositions Inc.................. D 513 771-2339
Cincinnati (G-2341)

Agile Sign & Ltg Maint Inc.................. E 440 918-1311
Eastlake (G-6415)

▲ Alberts Screen Print Inc.................. C 330 753-7559
Norton (G-10818)

All Signs of Chillicothe Inc.................. G 740 773-5016
Chillicothe (G-2242)

All Star Sign Company.................. G 614 461-9052
Columbus (G-4685)

Allen Industries Inc.................. D 567 408-7538
Toledo (G-12869)

Allied Sign Co.................. G 614 443-9656
Columbus (G-4689)

▲ American Led-Gible Inc.................. F 614 851-1100
Columbus (G-4699)

Apex Signs Inc.................. G 330 952-2626
Medina (G-9376)

Archer Corporation.................. E 330 455-9995
Canton (G-1831)

Architctral Identification Inc.................. F 614 868-8400
Gahanna (G-7154)

Asi Visual Display Pdts Inc.................. E 330 308-8667
New Philadelphia (G-10431)

◆ Associated Premium Corporation.....E 513 679-4444
Cincinnati (G-2381)

Atchley Signs & Graphics LLC............. F 614 421-7446
Columbus (G-4731)

Atlantic Sign Company Inc.................. E 513 383-1504
Cincinnati (G-2385)

Auto Dealer Designs Inc.................. E 330 374-7666
Akron (G-65)

Avid Signs Plus LLC.................. G 513 932-7446
Lebanon (G-8244)

Baker Plastics Inc.................. G 330 743-3142
Youngstown (G-14817)

Barnes Advertising Corporation............. F 740 453-6836
Zanesville (G-14992)

Bates Metal Products Inc.................. D 740 498-8371
Port Washington (G-11455)

Becker Signs Inc.................. G 330 659-4504
Hudson (G-7834)

Beebe Worldwide Graphics Sign............ G 513 241-2726
Blue Ash (G-1250)

Behrco Inc.................. G 419 394-1612
Saint Marys (G-11731)

Belco Works Inc.................. D 740 695-0500
Saint Clairsville (G-11688)

Benchmark Craftsman Inc.................. E 866 313-4700
Seville (G-11910)

Blang Acquisition LLC.................. G 937 223-2155
Dayton (G-5679)

Brainerd Industries Inc.................. E 937 228-0488
Miamisburg (G-9676)

Brandon Screen Printing.................. F 419 229-9837
Lima (G-8391)

Brilliant Electric Sign Co Ltd.................. D 216 741-3800
Brooklyn Heights (G-1529)

Brown Cnty Bd Mntal Rtardation............ G 937 378-4891
Georgetown (G-7251)

▲ Buckeye Boxes Inc.................. D 614 274-8484
Columbus (G-4783)

Buds Sign Shop Inc.................. F 330 744-5555
Youngstown (G-14829)

Busch & Thiem Inc.................. E 419 625-7515
Sandusky (G-11825)

Business Idntfction Systems In.................. G 614 841-1255
Columbus (G-4789)

C JS Signs.................. G 330 821-7446
Alliance (G-374)

Campbell Signs & Apparel LLC............. G 330 386-4768
East Liverpool (G-6388)

▲ Casad Company Inc.................. F 419 586-9457
Coldwater (G-4570)

▲ Catalog Merchandiser Inc.................. F
Cincinnati (G-2443)

▲ Cgs Imaging Inc.................. F 419 897-3000
Holland (G-7749)

Chase Sign & Lighting Svc Inc.................. G 567 128-3444
Toledo (G-12917)

Cicogna Electric and Sign Co.................. D 440 998-2637
Ashtabula (G-587)

Classic Sign Company LLC.................. G 419 420-0058
Findlay (G-6854)

▲ Co-Pac Services Inc.................. F 216 688-1780
Cleveland (G-3542)

Columbus Graphics Inc.................. G 614 577-9360
Reynoldsburg (G-11563)

Columbus Sign Company.................. E 614 252-3133
Columbus (G-4833)

Communication Exhibits Inc.................. D 330 854-4040
Canal Fulton (G-1775)

CSP Group Inc.................. E 513 984-9500
Cincinnati (G-2528)

Cubbison Company.................. D 330 793-2481
Youngstown (G-14843)

Custom Retail Group LLC.................. G 614 409-9720
Columbus (G-4863)

Custom Sign Center.................. F 614 279-6035
Columbus (G-4864)

Custom Sign Center Inc.................. E 614 279-6700
Columbus (G-4865)

Danite Holdings Ltd.................. E 614 444-3333
Columbus (G-4870)

◆ Davis Printing Company.................. E 330 745-3113
Barberton (G-803)

Dayton Wire Products Inc.................. E 937 236-8000
Dayton (G-5741)

◆ Dee Sign Co.................. E 513 779-3333
West Chester (G-13982)

Dee Sign Usa LLC.................. F 513 779-3333
West Chester (G-13983)

▲ Dern Trophies Corp.................. G 614 895-3260
Westerville (G-14207)

Design Masters Inc.................. G 513 772-7175
Cincinnati (G-2547)

Digital Factory Tech Inc.................. E 513 560-4074
Cincinnati (G-2549)

Digital Sign Graphics Inc.................. G 937 492-9550
Sidney (G-12012)

Djmc Partners Inc.................. G 614 890-3821
Westerville (G-14256)

Doxie Inc.................. G 937 427-3431
Dayton (G-5611)

▲ Dualite Inc.................. C 513 724-7100
Williamsburg (G-14408)

E P Gerber & Sons Inc.................. D 330 857-2021
Kidron (G-8126)

▲ E-B Display Company Inc.................. C 330 833-4101
Massillon (G-9188)

Eaglestone Products LLC.................. G 440 463-8715
Brecksville (G-1464)

▲ Eighth Floor Promotions LLC.................. C 419 586-6433
Celina (G-2104)

Ellet Neon Sales & Service Inc.................. E 330 628-9907
Akron (G-131)

Engravers Gallery & Sign Co.................. G 330 830-1271
Massillon (G-9190)

Enlarging Arts Inc.................. G 330 434-3433
Akron (G-136)

▲ Etched Metal Company.................. E 440 248-0240
Solon (G-12109)

Fair Publishing House Inc.................. E 419 668-3746
Norwalk (G-10841)

Fast Signs.................. F 614 710-1312
Hilliard (G-7681)

Fastsigns.................. G 330 952-2626
Medina (G-9402)

Fastsigns.................. G 440 954-9191
Mentor (G-9515)

Fdi Cabinetry LLC.................. G 513 353-4500
Cleves (G-4537)

Federal Heath Sign Company LLC......... D 740 369-0999
Delaware (G-6147)

Fineline Imprints Inc.................. G 740 453-1083
Zanesville (G-15013)

Finn Graphics Inc.................. E 513 941-6161
Cincinnati (G-2624)

Folks Creative Printers Inc.................. G 740 383-6326
Marion (G-8970)

Forty Nine Degrees LLC.................. F 419 678-0100
Coldwater (G-4575)

Fourteen Ventures Group LLC............. G 937 866-2341
West Carrollton (G-13929)

Freds Sign Service Inc.................. G 937 335-1901
Troy (G-13215)

Frontier Signs & Displays Inc.................. G 513 367-0813
Harrison (G-7552)

▲ Galaxy Balloons Incorporated......... C 216 476-3360
Cleveland (G-3753)

Gardner Signs Inc.................. F 419 385-6669
Toledo (G-12972)

Gary Lawrence Enterprises Inc.................. G 330 833-7181
Massillon (G-9194)

Geograph Industries Inc.................. E 513 202-9200
Harrison (G-7553)

Gerber Wood Products Inc.................. D 330 857-9007
Kidron (G-8128)

▲ Ginos Awards Inc.................. E 216 831-6565
Warrensville Heights (G-13818)

Glavin Industries Inc.................. E 440 349-0049
Solon (G-12115)

▲ Global Lighting Tech Inc.................. E 440 922-4584
Brecksville (G-1468)

Grady McCauley Inc.................. D 330 494-9444
Akron (G-165)

Greg G Wright & Sons LLC.................. E 513 721-3310
Cincinnati (G-2691)

Gus Holthaus Signs Inc.................. E 513 861-0060
Cincinnati (G-2697)

Hall Company	E 937 652-1376	Megalift LLC	G 614 696-9086	Ricks Graphic Accents Inc	G 330 896-4700

Hall Company..............E 937 652-1376
Urbana *(G-13465)*

Ham Signs LLC DBA Fastsigns............F 937 890-6770
Dayton *(G-5807)*

Hendricks Vacuum Forming Inc.......F 330 837-2040
Massillon *(G-9201)*

Highrise Creative LLC...............F 614 890-3821
Westerville *(G-14263)*

Hill John...............F 419 727-8666
Toledo *(G-12993)*

Hill Sign Company Inc...............G 614 367-9227
Columbus *(G-4988)*

Hlsigns...............G 513 703-6363
Cincinnati *(G-2725)*

HP Manufacturing Company Inc.........D 216 361-6500
Cleveland *(G-3841)*

Hy-Ko Products Company LLC.........F 330 467-7446
Northfield *(G-10794)*

Identitek Systems Inc...............D 330 832-9844
Massillon *(G-9206)*

Ike Smart City...............E 614 294-4898
Columbus *(G-5000)*

Industrial and Mar Eng Svc Co.......F 740 694-0791
Fredericktown *(G-7080)*

Industrial Electronic Service..........F 937 746-9750
Carlisle *(G-2066)*

Innomark Group LLC...............G 419 720-8102
Toledo *(G-13005)*

Insignia Signs Inc...............G 937 866-2341
Moraine *(G-10170)*

Insta Plak Inc...............G 419 537-1555
Toledo *(G-13006)*

Interior Graphic Systems LLC..........G 330 244-0100
Canton *(G-1918)*

Interstate Sign Products Inc...........G 419 683-1962
Crestline *(G-5503)*

J Best Inc...............G 513 943-7000
Cincinnati *(G-2308)*

Kasper Enterprises Inc...............G 419 841-6656
Toledo *(G-13016)*

▲ **Kdm Signs Inc**...............C 513 769-1932
Cincinnati *(G-2787)*

Kessler Sign Company...............E 740 453-0668
Zanesville *(G-15025)*

Kinoly Signs...............G 740 451-7446
South Point *(G-12225)*

Kmgrafx Inc...............G 513 248-4100
Loveland *(G-8833)*

Krigbaum Inc...............E 614 478-6472
Columbus *(G-5056)*

Laad Sign & Lighting Inc...............F 330 379-2297
Ravenna *(G-11529)*

Lake Erie Graphics Inc...............E 216 575-1333
Brookpark *(G-1555)*

Lehner Signs Inc...............G 614 258-0500
Lithopolis *(G-8483)*

Lettergraphics Inc...............G 330 683-3903
Orrville *(G-10993)*

License Ad Plate Company...............F 216 265-4200
Cleveland *(G-3954)*

LSI Industries Inc...............G 513 793-3200
Cincinnati *(G-2830)*

Macray Co LLC...............G 937 325-1726
Springfield *(G-12345)*

▲ **Magna Visual Inc**...............E 314 843-9000
Perrysburg *(G-11236)*

Masterpiece Signs Graphics Inc.........F 419 358-0077
Bluffton *(G-1362)*

Mayfair Granite Co Inc...............G 216 382-8150
Cleveland *(G-4002)*

McRd Enterprises LLC...............F 740 775-2377
Chillicothe *(G-2265)*

Megalift LLC...............G 614 696-9086
Grove City *(G-7398)*

Mel Wacker Signs Inc...............G 330 832-1726
Massillon *(G-9222)*

Mes Painting & Graphics Ltd..........E 614 496-1696
Westerville *(G-14268)*

Mes Painting and Graphics...............E 614 496-1696
Westerville *(G-14269)*

Metalphoto of Cincinnati Inc..........E 513 772-8281
Cincinnati *(G-2870)*

Metromedia Technologies Inc.........D 330 264-2501
Wooster *(G-14665)*

Mitchell Plastics Inc...............E 330 825-2461
Barberton *(G-823)*

Morrison Sign Company Inc.........E 614 276-1181
Columbus *(G-5112)*

Myers and Lasch Inc...............G 440 235-2050
Westlake *(G-14316)*

National Illmination Sign Corp.........G 419 866-1666
Holland *(G-7774)*

National Scoreboards LLC...............G 513 791-5244
Cincinnati *(G-2895)*

▼ **National Sign Systems Inc**..........D 614 850-2540
Hilliard *(G-7689)*

North Coast Theatrical Inc...............G 330 762-1768
Akron *(G-248)*

North Hill Marble & Granite Co.........F 330 253-2179
Akron *(G-249)*

Norton Outdoor Advertising...............E 513 631-4864
Cincinnati *(G-2915)*

Nrka Corp...............G 440 817-0700
Broadview Heights *(G-1508)*

Obhc Inc...............G 440 236-5112
Columbia Station *(G-4595)*

▲ **Ohio Awning & Manufacturing Co**.......E 216 861-2400
Cleveland *(G-4111)*

Ohio Displays Inc...............F 216 961-5600
Elyria *(G-6572)*

Ohio Shelterall Inc...............F 614 882-1110
Westerville *(G-14272)*

Orange Barrel Media LLC...............D 614 294-4898
Columbus *(G-5162)*

Painted Hill Inv Group Inc...............F 937 339-1756
Troy *(G-13246)*

Patriot Signage Inc...............G 859 655-9009
Cincinnati *(G-2946)*

Paul Peterson Safety Div Inc.........E 614 486-4375
Columbus *(G-3179)*

Performance Wraps LLC...............G 937 535-2400
Miamisburg *(G-9726)*

Pfi Displays Inc...............E 330 925-9015
Rittman *(G-11626)*

Pierce Signs & Displays Inc.........G 408 292-3500
Sylvania *(G-12721)*

Plastigraphics Inc...............F 513 771-8848
Cincinnati *(G-2970)*

Power Media Inc...............G 330 475-0500
Copley *(G-5436)*

Pro A V of Ohio...............G 877 812-5350
New Philadelphia *(G-10462)*

Pro-Decal Inc...............G 330 484-0089
Canton *(G-1984)*

Quality Custom Signs LLC...............G 614 580-7233
Worthington *(G-14723)*

Queen Exhibits LLC...............G 937 615-6051
Piqua *(G-11381)*

▲ **Quikey Manufacturing Co Inc**.........C 330 633-8106
Akron *(G-275)*

Ray Meyer Sign Company Inc.........E 513 984-5446
Loveland *(G-8647)*

Retain Loyalty LLC...............G 330 830-0839
Massillon *(G-9238)*

Ricks Graphic Accents Inc...............G 330 896-4700
Akron *(G-285)*

▲ **Rocal Inc**...............D 740 998-2122
Frankfort *(G-7005)*

Roemer Industries Inc...............D 330 448-2000
Masury *(G-9256)*

Rogers Display Inc...............E 440 951-9200
Mentor *(G-9609)*

▲ **Royal Acme Corporation**...............E 216 241-1477
Cleveland *(G-4256)*

Ruff Neon & Lighting Maint Inc.........F 440 350-6267
Painesville *(G-11110)*

S&S Sign Service...............G 614 279-9722
Columbus *(G-5241)*

▲ **Sabco Industries Inc**...............E 419 531-5347
Toledo *(G-13120)*

Scioto Sign Co Inc...............E 419 673-1261
Kenton *(G-8115)*

Screen Works Inc...............E 937 264-9111
Dayton *(G-6000)*

Sdmk LLC...............G 330 965-0970
Youngstown *(G-14930)*

Select Signs...............E 937 262-7095
Dayton *(G-5623)*

▲ **Sensical Inc**...............D 216 641-1141
Solon *(G-12180)*

Sign America Incorporated...............G 740 765-5555
Richmond *(G-11605)*

Sign Connection Inc...............F 937 435-4070
Dayton *(G-6006)*

Sign Design Wooster Inc...............G 330 262-8838
Wooster *(G-14686)*

Sign Gypsies Cleveland LLC.........F 216 202-2093
Bedford Heights *(G-1081)*

Sign Source USA Inc...............D 419 224-1130
Lima *(G-8449)*

Sign Technologies LLC...............G 937 439-3970
Dayton *(G-6007)*

Signcom Incorporated...............F 614 228-9999
Columbus *(G-5268)*

Signs Limited LLC...............G 740 282-7715
Steubenville *(G-12411)*

Signs Ohio Inc...............G 419 228-7446
Lima *(G-8450)*

Signs Unlmted The Grphic Advnt....... G 614 836-7446
Logan *(G-8526)*

Signwire Worldwide Inc...............G 937 428-6189
Dayton *(G-0000)*

Speedpro Imaging...............G 513 771-4776
Cincinnati *(G-3105)*

Standard Signs Incorporated...............G 330 467-2030
Macedonia *(G-8716)*

Sterling Associates Inc...............G 330 630-3500
Akron *(G-318)*

▲ **Stratus Unlimited LLC**...............C 440 209-6200
Mentor *(G-9629)*

Superior Label Systems Inc...............B 513 336-0825
Mason *(G-9157)*

T&T Graphics Inc...............D 937 847-6000
Miamisburg *(G-9742)*

▼ **Tce International Ltd**...............F 800 962-2376
Perry *(G-11199)*

TCS Schindler & Co LLC...............G 937 836-9473
Englewood *(G-6624)*

◆ **Ternion Inc**...............E 216 642-6180
Cleveland *(G-4375)*

The Hartman Corp...............G 614 475-5035
Columbus *(G-5320)*

The Massillon-Cleveland-A...............C 330 833-3165
Massillon *(G-9247)*

Toledo Sign Company Inc...............E 419 244-4444
Toledo *(G-13157)*

Traffic Cntrl Sgnls Signs & MA.............. G 740 670-7763
  Newark *(G-10536)*

Traffic Detectors & Signs Inc................. G 330 707-9060
  Youngstown *(G-14949)*

Triangle Sign Co LLC.............................. G 513 266-1009
  Hamilton *(G-7534)*

Triumph Signs & Consulting Inc............. F 513 576-8090
  Milford *(G-9955)*

Troyer Signs Incorporated..................... G 330 263-1400
  Wooster *(G-14693)*

Tusco Limited Partnership...................... C 740 254-4343
  Gnadenhutten *(G-7295)*

United - Maier Signs Inc......................... D 513 681-6600
  Cincinnati *(G-3180)*

▲ **Vgu Industries Inc**................................ E 216 676-9093
  Cleveland *(G-4464)*

Vision Graphix Inc................................... G 440 835-6540
  Westlake *(G-14342)*

Vista Creations LLC................................ G 440 954-9191
  Mentor *(G-9650)*

Visual Marking Systems Inc.................... D 330 425-7100
  Twinsburg *(G-13393)*

▲ **Vmi Liquidating Inc**.............................. E 937 492-3100
  Sidney *(G-12059)*

W C Bunting Co Inc................................. G 330 385-2050
  East Liverpool *(G-6399)*

Wellman Container Corporation.............. E 513 860-3040
  Cincinnati *(G-3219)*

▲ **West 6th Products Company**................ D 330 467-7446
  Northfield *(G-10800)*

Wholesale Channel Letters..................... G 440 256-3200
  Kirtland *(G-8146)*

Williams Steel Rule Die Co..................... F 216 431-3232
  Cleveland *(G-4507)*

Wilson Sign Co Inc.................................. F 937 253-2246
  Germantown *(G-7257)*

▲ **Wurtec Manufacturing Service**............ E 419 726-1066
  Toledo *(G-13180)*

Zilla.. G 614 763-5311
  Dublin *(G-6363)*

3995 Burial caskets

American Steel Grave Vault Co................ F 419 468-6715
  Galion *(G-7178)*

Case Ohio Burial Co................................ F 440 779-1992
  Cleveland *(G-3474)*

3996 Hard surface floor coverings, nec

Armstrong World Industries Inc.............. E 614 771-9307
  Hilliard *(G-7669)*

▲ **Flowcrete North America Inc**............... E 936 539-6700
  Cleveland *(G-3727)*

Schlabach Woodworks Ltd...................... F 330 674-7488
  Millersburg *(G-10009)*

3999 Manufacturing industries, nec

3-D Technical Services Company........... E 937 746-2901
  Franklin *(G-7006)*

4S Company.. F 330 792-5518
  Youngstown *(G-14800)*

Aajaj Hair Company LLC.......................... F 216 309-0816
  Cleveland *(G-3285)*

Actual Industries LLC............................. G 614 379-2739
  Columbus *(G-4673)*

Advance Products.................................... F 419 882-8117
  Sylvania *(G-12701)*

Agile Manufacturing Tech LLC................ F 937 258-3338
  Dayton *(G-5642)*

Al Root Company..................................... E 330 725-6677
  Medina *(G-9372)*

▲ **Al Root Company**................................. C 330 723-4359
  Medina *(G-9371)*

AK Mansfield... F 419 755-3011
  Mansfield *(G-8759)*

Alene Candles Midwest LLC................... F 614 933-4005
  New Albany *(G-10325)*

◆ **Aluminum Line Products Company**.....D 440 835-8880
  Westlake *(G-14285)*

Ambrosia Inc... G 419 825-3896
  Swanton *(G-12676)*

Ambrosia Inc... G 734 529-5024
  Swanton *(G-12677)*

AMG Industries Inc................................. F 740 397-4044
  Mount Vernon *(G-10232)*

▲ **Anza Inc**... G 513 542-7337
  Cincinnati *(G-2372)*

◆ **Aquatic Technology**.............................F 440 236-8330
  Columbia Station *(G-4588)*

Ariezhair Collection LLC......................... F 614 964-5748
  Columbus *(G-4725)*

ARS Recycling Systems 2019 LLC......... E 330 536-8210
  Lowellville *(G-8659)*

Aster Industries Inc................................ E 330 762-7965
  Akron *(G-62)*

Atcpc of Ohio LLC.................................. E 330 670-9900
  Akron *(G-63)*

Automtve Rfnish Clor Sltons I............... E 330 461-6067
  Medina *(G-9378)*

Axalta Coating Systems USA LLC.......... D 614 777-7230
  Hilliard *(G-7673)*

B&M Underground LLC............................ G 740 505-3096
  Wilmington *(G-14572)*

Beaute Asylum LLC................................. F 419 377-9933
  Toledo *(G-12894)*

Beck Studios Inc..................................... E 513 831-6650
  Milford *(G-9925)*

Blackstar International Inc....................... G 917 510-5482
  Columbus *(G-4763)*

Candle Lab... G 614 488-2009
  Columbus *(G-4793)*

Candle-Lite Company LLC....................... D 937 780-2563
  Blue Ash *(G-1258)*

Canine Creations Inc.............................. G 937 667-8576
  Tipp City *(G-12817)*

Carapa Industries Inc............................. G 330 307-1890
  Masury *(G-9255)*

Carroll Hills Industries........................... G 330 627-5524
  Carrollton *(G-2080)*

Ccbdd.. F 330 424-0404
  Lisbon *(G-8465)*

Centerless Grinding Svc Inc................... G 216 251-4100
  Cleveland *(G-3483)*

Clarity Retail Services LLC..................... D 513 800-9369
  West Chester *(G-13965)*

▲ **Clearsonic Manufacturing Inc**............ G 828 772-9809
  Akron *(G-103)*

Cleveland Plant and Flower Co............... G 614 478-9900
  Columbus *(G-4811)*

▲ **CM Paula Company**............................. E 513 759-7473
  Mason *(G-9090)*

Colby Properties LLC.............................. G 937 390-0816
  Springfield *(G-12292)*

Connies Candles..................................... G 740 574-1224
  Wheelersburg *(G-14352)*

Country Lane Custom Buildings............. G 740 485-8481
  Danville *(G-5598)*

County of Holmes................................... G 330 674-2083
  Millersburg *(G-9978)*

◆ **Cropking Incorporated**........................F 330 302-4203
  Lodi *(G-8500)*

Crownme Coil Care LLC.......................... F 937 797-2070
  Trotwood *(G-13195)*

D Jacob Industries LLC........................... G 440 292-7277
  Cleveland *(G-3596)*

Dayton Armor LLC................................... G 937 723-8675
  Dayton *(G-5720)*

Denton Atd Inc.. E 567 265-5200
  Huron *(G-7871)*

Desco Machine Company LLC................. G 330 405-5181
  Twinsburg *(G-13293)*

Digimanufacturing Tech LLC.................. G 419 212-6414
  Bryan *(G-1638)*

DLAC Industries Inc................................ G 330 519-4789
  Canfield *(G-1808)*

◆ **Downing Enterprises Inc**.....................D 330 666-3888
  Akron *(G-126)*

Duraflow Industries Inc........................... G 440 965-5047
  Wakeman *(G-13680)*

Edi Custom Interiors Inc......................... F 513 829-3895
  Fairfield *(G-6731)*

Elaire Corporation................................... G 419 843-2192
  Toledo *(G-12946)*

Eleventh Candle Co................................. G 614 530-4853
  Worthington *(G-14709)*

Endurance Industries LLC....................... F 513 285-8503
  Cincinnati *(G-2588)*

Erie Street Thea Svcs Inc....................... G 216 426-0050
  Cleveland *(G-3684)*

Essentialware.. G 888 975-0405
  Kirtland *(G-8144)*

Everway LLC.. C 419 433-9800
  Huron *(G-7872)*

Excalibur Barber LLC.............................. F 330 729-9006
  Boardman *(G-1371)*

▲ **Faith Guiding Cafe LLC**....................... F 614 245-8451
  New Albany *(G-10340)*

Fallen Oak Candles Inc........................... G 419 204-8162
  Celina *(G-2106)*

FB Acquisition LLC.................................. E 513 459-7782
  Lebanon *(G-8255)*

Fcbdd... F 614 475-6440
  Columbus *(G-4921)*

Ferguson Fire Fabrication Inc................. E 614 299-2070
  Columbus *(G-4923)*

▲ **Fibercore LLC**...................................... F 216 249-2100
  Cleveland *(G-3715)*

Fire Safety Services Inc.......................... F 937 686-2000
  Huntsville *(G-7864)*

Five Star Fabrication LLC........................ F 440 666-0427
  Wellington *(G-13887)*

◆ **Foundation Industries Inc**....................E 330 564-1250
  Akron *(G-152)*

Front Pocket Innovations LLC................. G 330 441-2365
  Wadsworth *(G-13639)*

◆ **Gayston Corporation**............................C 937 743-6050
  Miamisburg *(G-9693)*

Gerber Wood Products Inc...................... D 330 857-9007
  Kidron *(G-8128)*

▲ **GKN Driveline Bowl Green Inc**............ E 419 373-7700
  Bowling Green *(G-1421)*

Gorant Chocolatier LLC.......................... C 330 726-8821
  Boardman *(G-1372)*

Gumbys LLC.. F 740 671-0818
  Bellaire *(G-1088)*

Hafners Hrdwood Connection LLC.......... G 419 726-4828
  Toledo *(G-12983)*

Hartz Mountain Corporation.................... D 513 877-2131
  Pleasant Plain *(G-11432)*

◆ **Heading4ward Investment Co**.............D 937 293-9994
  Moraine *(G-10169)*

Honda Transmission Manufacturi.......... F 937 843-5555
  Marysville *(G-9030)*

Housing & Emrgncy Lgstcs Plnnr......... E 209 201-7511
  Lisbon *(G-8470)*

▲ **Hunters Manufacturing Co Inc**............ E 330 628-9245
  Mogadore *(G-10077)*

▲ Ideal Image Inc.................... D 937 832-1660
Englewood *(G-6615)*

▲ Identiphoto Co Ltd.................... F 440 306-9000
Willoughby *(G-14467)*

Indispenser Ltd.................... E 419 625-5825
Sandusky *(G-11841)*

Inez Essentials LLC.................... F 216 701-8360
Maple Heights *(G-8884)*

Item NA.................... G 216 271-7241
Akron *(G-184)*

Janson Industries.................... D 330 455-7029
Canton *(G-1921)*

Jbs Industries Ltd.................... G 513 314-5599
Columbus *(G-5034)*

Jones Industries LLC.................... F 440 810-1251
Olmsted Twp *(G-10946)*

Jrb Industries LLC.................... E 567 825-7022
Greenville *(G-7344)*

Juba Industries Inc.................... G 440 655-9960
Jefferson *(G-7973)*

K K Tool Co.................... E 937 325-1373
Springfield *(G-12333)*

Kanya Industries LLC.................... G 330 722-5432
Medina *(G-9416)*

Kayden Industries.................... G 740 336-7801
Marietta *(G-8925)*

King Model Company.................... E 330 633-0491
Akron *(G-197)*

Kitto Katsu Inc.................... G 818 256-6997
Clayton *(G-3274)*

Lauren Manufacturing.................... D 330 339-3373
New Philadelphia *(G-10455)*

Lincoln Manufacturing Inc.................... F 330 878-7772
Strasburg *(G-12481)*

Little Busy Beez Erly Lrng Chl.................... G 216 477-1965
Northfield *(G-10795)*

▲ Lumi-Lite Candle Company.................... D 740 872-3248
Norwich *(G-10864)*

◆ Mace Personal Def & SEC Inc.................... E 440 424-5321
Cleveland *(G-3978)*

◆ Mace Security Intl Inc.................... E 440 424-5325
Cleveland *(G-3979)*

▲ Mak Magic Inc.................... G 614 591-3551
Columbus *(G-5079)*

▲ Makergear LLC.................... G 216 765-0030
Beachwood *(G-926)*

Mako Finished Products Inc.................... E 740 357-0839
Lucasville *(G-8007)*

Manufacturing Company LLC.................... F 414 708-7583
Cincinnati *(G-2844)*

Manufctred Assemblies Corp LLC.................... F 937 454-0722
Vandalia *(G-13568)*

▲ Mark-All Enterprises LLC.................... E 800 433-3615
Akron *(G-220)*

MCS Mfg LLC.................... G 419 923-0169
Lyons *(G-8674)*

Millers Aplus Cmpt Svcs LLC.................... F 330 620-5288
Akron *(G-234)*

MODE Industries Inc.................... G 614 504-8008
Columbus *(G-5108)*

Morgan Site Services Inc.................... E 330 823-6120
Alliance *(G-395)*

Morris Technologies Inc.................... E 513 733-1611
Cincinnati *(G-2888)*

MPS Manufacturing Company LLC.................... G 330 343-1435
New Philadelphia *(G-10460)*

My Splash Pad.................... G 330 705-1802
Louisville *(G-8609)*

Natural Beauty Hc Express.................... G 440 459-1776
Mayfield Heights *(G-9338)*

◆ Neff Motivation Inc.................... C 937 548-3194
Greenville *(G-7348)*

New Republic Industries LLC.................... G 614 580-9927
Marysville *(G-9040)*

Nfi Industries Inc.................... F 740 928-9522
Hebron *(G-7626)*

Njf Manufacturing LLC.................... G 419 294-0400
Upper Sandusky *(G-13450)*

Norkaam Industries LLC.................... G 330 873-9793
Akron *(G-247)*

Norris North Manufacturing.................... F 330 691-0449
Canton *(G-1960)*

Octsys Security Corp.................... G 614 470-4510
Columbus *(G-5138)*

Ohio Cbd Guy LLC.................... G 513 417-9806
Cincinnati *(G-2921)*

▲ Ohio Feather Company Inc.................... G 513 921-3373
Cincinnati *(G-2922)*

On Display Ltd.................... E 513 841-1600
Batavia *(G-880)*

On The Mantle LLC.................... G 740 702-1803
Chillicothe *(G-2268)*

Pacific Manufacturing Ohio Inc.................... G 513 860-3900
Fairfield *(G-6763)*

Palmer Donavin Manufacturing.................... F 740 527-1111
Hebron *(G-7629)*

◆ Partners In Recognition Inc.................... E 937 420-2150
Fort Loramie *(G-6952)*

Perma Edge Industries LLC.................... G 937 623-7819
Dayton *(G-5937)*

Platinum Industries LLC.................... F 740 285-2641
Ironton *(G-7932)*

Plumb Builders Inc.................... F 937 293-1111
Dayton *(G-5942)*

Power Media Inc.................... G 330 475-0500
Copley *(G-5436)*

Pragmatic Mfg LLC.................... G 330 222-6051
Brunswick *(G-1607)*

Precise Models Inc.................... G 440 365-5701
Elyria *(G-6582)*

▼ Premier Seals Mfg LLC.................... G 330 861-1060
Akron *(G-265)*

Production TI Co Cleveland Inc.................... F 330 425-4466
Twinsburg *(G-13360)*

Proto Prcsion Mfg Slutions LLC.................... F 614 771-0080
Hilliard *(G-7697)*

Pur Hair Extensions LLC.................... G 330 786-5772
Akron *(G-270)*

Pyramid Industries LLC.................... G 614 783-1543
Columbus *(G-5215)*

Quick Tech Business Forms Inc.................... G 937 743-5952
Springboro *(G-12265)*

Rable Machine Inc.................... E 740 689-9009
Lancaster *(G-8222)*

RB Sigma LLC.................... D 440 290-0577
Mentor *(G-9607)*

Rbs Manufacturing Inc.................... E 330 426-9486
East Palestine *(G-6405)*

Resource Recycling Inc.................... F 419 222-2702
Lima *(G-8444)*

▲ Rhc Inc.................... E 330 874-3750
Bolivar *(G-1391)*

Rowend Industries Inc.................... G 419 333-8300
Fremont *(G-7131)*

RS&b Industries LLC.................... E 330 255-6000
Wooster *(G-14678)*

Rubber City Industries Inc.................... G 330 990-9641
Wadsworth *(G-13669)*

Scarefactory Inc.................... F 614 565-3590
Columbus *(G-5252)*

Schell Scenic Studio Inc.................... G 614 444-9550
Millersport *(G-10024)*

Scott Models Inc.................... F 513 771-8005
Cincinnati *(G-3070)*

Sdi Industries.................... G 513 561-4032
Cincinnati *(G-3072)*

Serving Veterans Mobility Inc.................... G 937 746-4788
Franklin *(G-7048)*

Shafts Mfg.................... G 440 942-6012
Willoughby *(G-14524)*

Silly Brandz Global LLC.................... D 419 697-8324
Toledo *(G-13132)*

◆ Specialty Hardware Inc.................... G 216 291-1160
Cleveland *(G-4319)*

Spectre Industries LLC.................... G 440 665-2600
Chagrin Falls *(G-2183)*

Steves Vans ACC Unlimited LLC.................... G 740 374-3154
Marietta *(G-8950)*

Suppressor Co LLC.................... G 330 749-5234
Ashland *(G-577)*

T J Davies Company Inc.................... G 440 248-5510
Mantua *(G-8876)*

Tangent Company LLC.................... G 440 543-2775
Chagrin Falls *(G-2186)*

Tango Products Inc.................... G 440 353-2605
North Ridgeville *(G-10750)*

TI Marie Candle Company LLC.................... F 513 746-7798
Cincinnati *(G-3156)*

Tiffin Scenic Studios Inc.................... E 800 445-1546
Tiffin *(G-12805)*

Tiger Cat Furniture.................... G 330 220-7232
Brunswick *(G-1618)*

▲ TLC Products Inc.................... F 216 472-3030
Westlake *(G-14340)*

Tmt Inc.................... G 419 592-1041
Perrysburg *(G-11273)*

Trademark Designs Inc.................... E 419 628-3897
Minster *(G-10067)*

Travis Products Mfg Inc.................... G 234 759-3741
North Lima *(G-10715)*

Triboro Quilt Mfg Corp.................... F 937 222-2132
Vandalia *(G-13579)*

Trisource Exhibits.................... E 800 229-8600
Parma *(G-11136)*

Troyridge Mfg.................... G 330 893-7516
Millersburg *(G-10015)*

◆ Truck Fax Inc.................... G 216 921-8866
Cleveland *(G-4431)*

Tuffy Manufacturing.................... F 330 940-2356
Akron *(G-348)*

Twin Oaks Barns LLC.................... F 330 893-3126
Dundee *(G-0371)*

▲ Twin Sisters Productions LLC.................... E 330 631-0361
Stow *(G-12468)*

U S Hair Inc.................... G 614 235-5190
Columbus *(G-5336)*

United Candle Company LLC.................... G 740 872-3248
Norwich *(G-10865)*

Universal Manufacturing.................... G 816 396-0101
Cleveland *(G-4446)*

Vandalia Massage Therapy.................... G 937 890-8660
Vandalia *(G-13582)*

Velocity Concept Dev Group LLC.................... G 513 204-2100
Mason *(G-9164)*

Vic Maroscher.................... F 330 332-4958
Salem *(G-11817)*

Vistech Mfg Solutions LLC.................... F 513 860-1408
Fairfield *(G-6789)*

VT Industries LLC.................... G 614 804-6904
Hilliard *(G-7711)*

Waterloo Industries Inc.................... G 800 833-8851
Cleveland *(G-4492)*

Weaver Propack - Marc Drive.................... G 330 379-3660
Cuyahoga Falls *(G-5581)*

Woodsage Industries LLC.................... G 419 866-8000
Holland *(G-7791)*

Worldwide Brands Direct LLC.............. F 937 991-0999
Dayton *(G-6088)*

Wrayco Manufacturing In...................... F 330 688-5617
Stow *(G-12474)*

Yankee Candle Company Inc .... G 413 712-9416
Etna *(G-6636)*

Zorich Industries Inc...................... G 330 482-9803
Columbiana *(G-4637)*

42 MOTOR FREIGHT TRANSPORTATION

4212 Local trucking, without storage

Corbett R Caudill Chipping Inc............... G 740 596-5984
Hamden *(G-7461)*

Dale R Adkins .... G 740 682-7312
Oak Hill *(G-10887)*

Demilta Sand and Gravel Inc.................. F 440 942-2015
Willoughby *(G-14446)*

Edw C Levy Co............................. G 419 822-8286
Delta *(G-6205)*

Glenn Michael Brick........................ F 740 391-5735
Flushing *(G-6936)*

H Hafner & Sons Inc....................... E 513 321-1895
Cincinnati *(G-2698)*

Hershberger Manufacturing.................. E 440 272-5555
Windsor *(G-14601)*

Hull Ready Mix Concrete Inc.................. F 419 625-8070
Sandusky *(G-11839)*

Kirby and Sons Inc......................... F 419 927-2260
Upper Sandusky *(G-13445)*

M & R Redi Mix Inc......................... E 419 445-7771
Pettisville *(G-11284)*

Mac Oil Field Service Inc.................... G 330 674-7371
Millersburg *(G-9996)*

Mm Outsourcing LLC........................ F 937 661-4300
Leesburg *(G-8300)*

Move Ez Inc............................... D 844 466-8339
Columbus *(G-5114)*

Parobek Trucking Co........................ G 419 869-7500
West Salem *(G-14189)*

◆ Pro-Pet LLC............................. D 419 394-3374
Saint Marys *(G-11749)*

Rjw Trucking Company Ltd .... E 740 363-5343
Delaware *(G-6169)*

Roe Transportation Entps Inc................ G 937 497-7161
Sidney *(G-12045)*

S&M Trucking LLC.......................... F 661 310-2585
Mason *(G-9146)*

Shawn Fleming Ind Trckg LLC .... G 937 707-8539
Dayton *(G-6002)*

Smith & Thompson Entps LLC .... G 330 386-9345
East Liverpool *(G-6397)*

Tk Gas Services Inc........................ E 740 826-0303
New Concord *(G-10387)*

Ward Construction Co....................... F 419 943-2450
Leipsic *(G-8316)*

Werlor Inc................................ F 419 784-4285
Defiance *(G-6127)*

Wonderly Trucking & Excvtg LLC.......... F 419 837-6294
Perrysburg *(G-11281)*

Wooster Abruzzi Company.................. E 330 345-3968
Wooster *(G-14698)*

4213 Trucking, except local

Akron Centl Engrv Mold Mch Inc........... E 330 794-8704
Akron *(G-26)*

American Power LLC........................ F 937 235-0418
Dayton *(G-5654)*

◆ Barrett Paving Materials Inc.............. E 973 533-1001
Hamilton *(G-7468)*

Bc Investment Corporation.................. C 330 262-3070
Wooster *(G-14625)*

Buckeye Energy Resources Inc............. G 740 452-9506
Zanesville *(G-15001)*

Chagrin Vly Stl Erectors Inc............... F 440 975-1556
Willoughby Hills *(G-14557)*

Custom Built Crates Inc.................... E
Milford *(G-9932)*

◆ Euclid Chemical Company................. E 800 321-7628
Cleveland *(G-3688)*

Kmj Leasing Ltd........................... G 614 871-3883
Orient *(G-10971)*

Mpi Logistics and Service Inc.............. E 330 832-5309
Massillon *(G-9225)*

Parobek Trucking Co........................ G 419 869-7500
West Salem *(G-14189)*

Sandwisch Enterprises Inc.................. G 419 944-6446
Toledo *(G-13121)*

Shawn Fleming Ind Trckg LLC .... G 937 707-8539
Dayton *(G-6002)*

Tk Gas Services Inc........................ E 740 826-0303
New Concord *(G-10387)*

4214 Local trucking with storage

▲ M G Q Inc............................... E 419 992-4236
Tiffin *(G-12788)*

Resource Recycling Inc.................... F 419 222-2702
Lima *(G-8444)*

4215 Courier services, except by air

Akay Holdings Inc......................... E 330 753-8458
Barberton *(G-790)*

Grand Aire Inc............................ E 419 861-6700
Swanton *(G-12684)*

4221 Farm product warehousing and storage

▲ The Mennel Milling Company........... E 419 435-8151
Fostoria *(G-7003)*

4222 Refrigerated warehousing and storage

Pettisville Meats Incorporated.............. F 419 445-0921
Pettisville *(G-11286)*

Produce Packaging Inc..................... C 216 391-6129
Willoughby Hills *(G-14562)*

Youngs Locker Service Inc................. F 740 599-6833
Danville *(G-5601)*

4225 General warehousing and storage

▲ Aero Fulfillment Services Corp......... D 800 225-7145
Mason *(G-9056)*

▲ Alegre Inc.............................. F 937 885-6786
Miamisburg *(G-9664)*

Atotech Usa LLC........................... F 216 398-0550
Cleveland *(G-3385)*

▲ Cooper Tire Vhcl Test Ctr Inc........... F 419 423-1321
Findlay *(G-6857)*

Dayton Bag & Burlap Co.................... F 937 253-1722
Dayton *(G-5721)*

Fuchs Lubricants Co....................... F 330 963-0400
Twinsburg *(G-13306)*

John D Oil and Gas Company................ G 440 255-6325
Mentor *(G-9543)*

Klosterman Baking Co LLC.................. F 513 398-2707
Mason *(G-9118)*

▲ McCrary Metal Polishing Co Inc......... F 937 492-1979
Port Jefferson *(G-11454)*

▲ Ohio Valley Alloy Services Inc.......... E 740 373-1900
Marietta *(G-8931)*

P-Americas LLC............................ E 330 746-7652
Youngstown *(G-14910)*

▲ Performance Packaging Inc............. F 419 478-8805
Toledo *(G-13094)*

Precision Strip Inc........................ D 419 674-4186
Kenton *(G-8112)*

Precision Strip Inc........................ D 937 667-6255
Tipp City *(G-12836)*

SH Bell Company.......................... E 412 963-9910
East Liverpool *(G-6396)*

Taylor Communications Inc................. F 614 351-6868
Columbus *(G-5312)*

Trane Technologies Company LLC........ E 419 633-6800
Bryan *(G-1665)*

◆ Vectra Inc.............................. C 614 351-6868
Columbus *(G-5345)*

Victory White Metal Company.............. F 216 271-1400
Cleveland *(G-4474)*

◆ Workflowone LLC....................... A 877 735-4966
Dayton *(G-6087)*

4226 Special warehousing and storage, nec

Abbott Laboratories....................... D 847 937-6100
Columbus *(G-4662)*

Ballreich Bros Inc......................... C 419 447-1814
Tiffin *(G-12777)*

▲ Kuhlman Corporation.................... E 419 897-6000
Maumee *(G-9303)*

Lalac One LLC............................ E 216 432-4422
Cleveland *(G-3937)*

Littlern Corporation....................... G 330 848-8847
Fairlawn *(G-6807)*

▲ Multi Fittings Corporation.............. C 513 942-9910
West Chester *(G-14032)*

SH Bell Company.......................... E 412 963-9910
East Liverpool *(G-6396)*

▲ Vista Industrial Packaging LLC......... E 800 454-6117
Columbus *(G-5351)*

4231 Trucking terminal facilities

Jordankelly LLC........................... F 216 855-8550
Akron *(G-187)*

44 WATER TRANSPORTATION

4424 Deep sea domestic transportation of freight

S&M Trucking LLC.......................... F 661 310-2585
Mason *(G-9146)*

4491 Marine cargo handling

McGinnis Inc.............................. C 740 377-4391
South Point *(G-12226)*

McNational Inc............................ D 740 377-4391
South Point *(G-12227)*

◆ Pinney Dock & Transport LLC........... F 440 964-7186
Ashtabula *(G-612)*

Rayle Coal Co............................. F 740 695-2197
Saint Clairsville *(G-11708)*

4492 Towing and tugboat service

Great Lakes Group........................ C 216 621-4854
Cleveland *(G-3792)*

Shelly Materials Inc....................... F 740 247-2311
Racine *(G-11506)*

Shelly Materials Inc....................... D 740 246-6315
Thornville *(G-12770)*

The Great Lakes Towing Company........ D 216 621-4854
Cleveland *(G-4383)*

4493 Marinas

Mariners Landing Inc...................... G 513 941-3625
Cincinnati *(G-2846)*

Tack-Anew Inc............................ G 419 734-4212
Port Clinton *(G-11453)*

45 TRANSPORTATION BY AIR

4512 Air transportation, scheduled

Grand Aire Inc... E 419 861-6700
Swanton *(G-12684)*

Ruhe Sales Inc... F 419 943-3357
Leipsic *(G-8314)*

4522 Air transportation, nonscheduled

Grand Aire Inc... E 419 861-6700
Swanton *(G-12684)*

4581 Airports, flying fields, and services

Aero Jet Wash Llc....................................... F 866 381-7955
Dayton *(G-5637)*

Grand Aire Inc... E 419 861-6700
Swanton *(G-12684)*

Malta Dynamics LLC.................................... F 740 749-3512
Waterford *(G-13828)*

Ruhe Sales Inc... F 419 943-3357
Leipsic *(G-8314)*

Spirit Avionics Ltd...................................... F 614 237-4271
Columbus *(G-5284)*

Swagelok Company...................................... F 440 442-6611
Cleveland *(G-4355)*

Toledo Jet Center LLC................................ G 419 866-9050
Swanton *(G-12695)*

Unison Industries LLC................................ B 904 667-9904
Dayton *(G-5625)*

46 PIPELINES, EXCEPT NATURAL GAS

4612 Crude petroleum pipelines

Andeavor Logistics LP................................ F 419 421-2414
Findlay *(G-6837)*

47 TRANSPORTATION SERVICES

4731 Freight transportation arrangement

◆ Carbon Enterprises Inc..........................G 740 420-6472
Circleville *(G-3249)*

Millwood Natural LLC................................ F 330 393-4400
Vienna *(G-13615)*

Ogc Industries Inc...................................... F 330 456-1500
Canton *(G-1963)*

ODO National LLC...................................... G 330 759-8006
Boardman *(G-1376)*

◆ Workflowone LLC.................................. A 877 735-4966
Dayton *(G-6087)*

4741 Rental of railroad cars

Andersons Inc... G 419 536-0460
Toledo *(G-12881)*

Andersons Inc... C 419 893-5050
Maumee *(G-9261)*

4783 Packing and crating

▲ Amerisource Health Svcs LLC........... D 614 492-8177
Columbus *(G-4703)*

Bates Metal Products Inc......................... D 740 498-8371
Port Washington *(G-11455)*

▲ Caravan Packaging Inc........................ G 440 243-4100
Cleveland *(G-3469)*

Cassis Packaging Co.................................. F 937 223-8868
Dayton *(G-5696)*

Forest City Companies Inc....................... E 216 586-5279
Cleveland *(G-3735)*

▲ Forrest Enterprises Inc....................... F 937 773-1714
Piqua *(G-11347)*

Global Packaging & Exports Inc........... G 513 454-2020
Hamilton *(G-7496)*

Imex Bz LLC... F 786 866-8798
Orrville *(G-10986)*

Lalac One LLC... E 216 432-4422
Cleveland *(G-3937)*

McElroy Contract Packaging Inc............ F 330 682-2155
Orrville *(G-10994)*

◆ McNerney & Associates LLC............... E 513 241-9951
West Chester *(G-14132)*

Overseas Packing LLC............................... G 440 232-2917
Bedford *(G-1053)*

▲ Vista Industrial Packaging LLC......... E 800 454-6117
Columbus *(G-5351)*

4789 Transportation services, nec

Andersons Inc... G 419 536-0460
Toledo *(G-12881)*

Andersons Inc... C 419 893-5050
Maumee *(G-9261)*

Bulk Carriers Service Inc........................ G 330 339-3333
New Philadelphia *(G-10435)*

▼ Jk-Co LLC.. E 419 422-5240
Findlay *(G-6883)*

Simpson & Sons Inc.................................. G 513 367-0152
Harrison *(G-7568)*

Tmt Inc... G 419 592-1041
Perrysburg *(G-11273)*

48 COMMUNICATIONS

4812 Radiotelephone communication

911cellular LLC.. F 216 283-6100
Solon *(G-12071)*

Airwave Communications Cons............... G 419 331-1526
Lima *(G-8385)*

4813 Telephone communication, except radio

Airwave Communications Cons............... G 419 331-1526
Lima *(G-8385)*

AT&T Enterprises LLC............................... G 513 792-9300
Cincinnati *(G-2384)*

▼ Data Processing Sciences .... D 513 791-7100
Cincinnati *(G-2542)*

DSI Management Holdings LLC.............. F 800 645-7002
Kent *(G-8027)*

▲ F+w Media Inc....................................... A 513 531-2690
Blue Ash *(C-1274)*

Great Lakes Telcom Ltd........................... E 330 629-8848
Youngstown *(G-14870)*

Kraft Electrical Contg Inc....................... E 614 836-9300
Groveport *(G-7441)*

Kraftmaid Trucking Inc............................ D 440 632-2531
Middlefield *(G-9805)*

Revolution Group Inc................................ D 614 212-1111
Westerville *(G-14230)*

4832 Radio broadcasting stations

Iheartcommunications Inc....................... G 419 223-2060
Lima *(G-8418)*

Isaac Foster Mack Co............................... C 419 625-5500
Sandusky *(G-11843)*

Tomahawk Entrmt Group LLC................ F 216 505-0548
Euclid *(G-6680)*

4833 Television broadcasting stations

Block Communications Inc...................... F 419 724-6212
Toledo *(G-12898)*

Dispatch Printing Company...................... F 740 548-5331
Lewis Center *(G-8331)*

4841 Cable and other pay television services

Block Communications Inc...................... F 419 724-6212
Toledo *(G-12898)*

Ohio News Network.................................. G 614 460-3700
Columbus *(G-5148)*

4899 Communication services, nec

Brackish Media LLC................................... F 513 394-2871
Cincinnati *(G-2420)*

Springdot Inc.. D 513 542-4000
Cincinnati *(G-3108)*

49 ELECTRIC, GAS AND SANITARY SERVICES

4911 Electric services

Asidaco LLC... G 800 204-1544
Dayton *(G-5666)*

Hexion Inc.. C 888 443-9466
Columbus *(G-4976)*

National Gas & Oil Corporation.............. E 740 344-2102
Newark *(G-10524)*

▲ Powder Alloy Corporation................... E 513 984-4016
Loveland *(G-8646)*

Talus Renewables Inc.............................. F 650 248-5374
Cleveland Heights *(G-4531)*

4922 Natural gas transmission

◆ Knight Material Tech LLC.................... E 330 488-1651
East Canton *(G-6378)*

Markwest Energy Partners LP................ F 740 838-1434
Summerfield *(G-12660)*

National Gas & Oil Corporation.............. E 740 344-2102
Newark *(G-10524)*

4923 Gas transmission and distribution

Ngo Development Corporation................ G 740 622-9560
Coshocton *(G-5464)*

4924 Natural gas distribution

City of Lancaster...................................... E 740 687-6670
Lancaster *(G-8188)*

National Gas & Oil Corporation.............. E 740 344-2102
Newark *(G-10524)*

4932 Gas and other services combined

National Gas & Oil Corporation.............. E 740 344-2102
Newark *(G-10524)*

4941 Water supply

American Water Services Inc.................. G 440 243-9840
Strongsville *(G-12536)*

Aqua Pennsylvania Inc............................ G 440 257-6190
Mentor On The Lake *(G-9656)*

City of Athens... F 740 592-3344
Athens *(G-636)*

City of Middletown.................................... D 513 425-7781
Middletown *(G-9844)*

City of Troy.. F 937 339-4826
Troy *(G-13205)*

Greene County... G 937 429-0127
Dayton *(G-5613)*

Victory White Metal Company................ F 216 271-1400
Cleveland *(G-4474)*

4952 Sewerage systems

City of Ravenna... G 330 296-5214
Ravenna *(G-11521)*

4953 Refuse systems

A & B Iron & Metal Co Inc....................... F 937 228-1561
Dayton *(G-5629)*

S
I
C

A-Gas US Holdings Inc..........................F 419 867-8990
   Bowling Green *(G-1403)*

▼ Advanced Drainage Systems Inc...... D 614 658-0050
   Hilliard *(G-7666)*

Auris Noble LLC.................................E 330 321-6649
   Akron *(G-64)*

Capital City Oil Inc.............................G 740 397-4483
   Mount Vernon *(G-10238)*

▲ Cirba Solutions Us Inc.....................E 740 653-6290
   Lancaster *(G-8186)*

▲ Fpt Cleveland LLC...........................C 216 441-3800
   Cleveland *(G-3740)*

▲ Garden Street Iron & Metal Inc.........E 513 721-4660
   Cincinnati *(G-2649)*

▼ Grasan Equipment Company Inc...... D 419 526-4440
   Mansfield *(G-8797)*

Green Vision Materials Inc................. F 440 564-5500
   Newbury *(G-10552)*

H Hafner & Sons Inc..........................E 513 321-1895
   Cincinnati *(G-2698)*

Homan Metals LLC.............................E 513 721-5010
   Cincinnati *(G-2728)*

▼ Hope Timber Pallet Recycl LLC........E 740 344-1788
   Newark *(G-10509)*

Innovation Plastics LLC......................E 513 818-1771
   Fostoria *(G-6985)*

Koski Construction Co........................G 440 997-5337
   Ashtabula *(G-601)*

▲ Magnus International Group Inc........G 216 592-8355
   Painesville *(G-11097)*

Metalico Akron Inc............................. F 330 376-1400
   Akron *(G-229)*

Mondo Polymer Technologies Inc........E 740 376-9396
   Marietta *(G-8930)*

Montgomerys Pallet Service Inc...........G 330 297-6677
   Ravenna *(G-11533)*

▲ Novelis Alr Recycling Ohio LLC........C 740 922-2373
   Uhrichsville *(G-13404)*

Perma-Fix of Dayton Inc..................... F 937 268-6501
   Dayton *(G-5938)*

Polychem LLC................................... D 419 547-1400
   Clyde *(G-4561)*

Pratt Paper (oh) LLC......................... D 567 320-3353
   Wapakoneta *(G-13727)*

Resource Recycling Inc...................... F 419 222-2702
   Lima *(G-8444)*

Roe Transportation Entps Inc...............G 937 497-7161
   Sidney *(G-12045)*

Rumpke Transportation Co LLC........... B 513 242-4600
   Cincinnati *(G-3057)*

Rumpke Transportation Co LLC........... F 513 851-0122
   Cincinnati *(G-3058)*

Sidwell Materials Inc.........................C 740 849-2422
   Zanesville *(G-15050)*

Synagro Midwest Inc......................... F 937 384-0669
   Miamisburg *(G-9741)*

Unlimited Energy Services LLC........... F 304 517-7097
   Beverly *(G-1210)*

Werlor Inc.. F 419 784-4285
   Defiance *(G-6127)*

4959 Sanitary services, nec

Ash Sewer & Drain Service.................G 330 376-9714
   Akron *(G-61)*

Envirnmntal Cmpliance Tech LLC....... F 216 634-0400
   North Royalton *(G-10760)*

Green Impressions LLC...................... D 440 240-8508
   Sheffield Village *(G-11958)*

Image Pavement Maintenance.............G 937 833-9200
   Brookville *(G-1571)*

Ioppolo Concrete Corporation.............G 440 439-6606
   Bedford *(G-1040)*

Mapledale Farm Inc.......................... F 440 286-3389
   Chardon *(G-2214)*

N-Viro International Corp.................... F 419 535-6374
   Toledo *(G-13061)*

▲ Samsel Rope & Marine Supply Co..... E 216 241-0333
   Cleveland *(G-4272)*

Smith & Thompson Entps LLC............. F 330 386-9345
   East Liverpool *(G-6397)*

50 WHOLESALE TRADE - DURABLE GOODS

5012 Automobiles and other motor vehicles

Ace Truck Equipment Co....................E 740 453-0551
   Zanesville *(G-14981)*

Brown Industrial Inc..........................E 937 693-3838
   Botkins *(G-1397)*

Btw LLC...G 419 382-4443
   Toledo *(G-12907)*

Bulk Carrier Trnsp Eqp Co..................G 330 339-3333
   New Philadelphia *(G-10434)*

Cipted Corp..................................... D 412 829-2120
   Monroe *(G-10099)*

▲ Cvg National Seating Co LLC........... F 219 872-7295
   New Albany *(G-10338)*

Doug Marine Motors Inc..................... F 740 335-3700
   Wshngtn Ct Hs *(G-14738)*

Fire Safety Services Inc...................... F 937 686-2000
   Huntsville *(G-7864)*

Interstate Truckway Inc...................... F 614 771-1220
   Columbus *(G-5022)*

Kinstle Truck & Auto Svc Inc...............G 419 738-7493
   Wapakoneta *(G-13718)*

▲ Ktm North America Inc.................... D 855 215-6360
   Amherst *(G-447)*

◆ L & R Racing Inc.............................E 330 220-3102
   Brunswick *(G-1601)*

M & W Trailers Inc............................ F 419 453-3331
   Ottoville *(G-11055)*

M R Trailer Sales Inc.........................G 330 339-7701
   New Philadelphia *(G-10456)*

Mac Manufacturing Inc......................C 330 829-1680
   Salem *(G-11797)*

▲ Mac Manufacturing Inc................... A 330 823-9900
   Alliance *(G-388)*

◆ Mac Trailer Manufacturing Inc..........A 800 795-8454
   Alliance *(G-390)*

Midwest Motoplex LLC.......................G 740 772-5300
   Chillicothe *(G-2266)*

Schodorf Truck Body & Eqp Co............ F 614 228-6793
   Columbus *(G-5253)*

Tpam Inc..E 567 315-8694
   Toledo *(G-13165)*

▲ Venco Venturo Industries LLC.......... E 513 772-8448
   Cincinnati *(G-3197)*

Volens LLC.......................................G 216 544-1200
   Macedonia *(G-8721)*

◆ Wholecycle Inc...............................E 330 929-8123
   Peninsula *(G-11186)*

Youngstown-Kenworth Inc................... F 330 534-9761
   Hubbard *(G-7819)*

5013 Motor vehicle supplies and new parts

◆ Accel Performance Group LLC...........C 216 658-6413
   Independence *(G-7887)*

◆ Adelmans Truck Parts Corp..............E 330 456-0206
   Canton *(G-1823)*

▲ Alegre Inc..................................... F 937 885-6786
   Miamisburg *(G-9664)*

All Power Battery Inc.........................G 330 453-5236
   Canton *(G-1828)*

All Wright Enterprises LLC.................G 440 259-5656
   Perry *(G-11190)*

▲ Anest Iwata Usa Inc....................... F 513 755-3100
   West Chester *(G-14102)*

ARE Inc...A 330 830-7800
   Massillon *(G-9172)*

Autobody Supply Company Inc............ D 614 228-4328
   Columbus *(G-4735)*

◆ Bendix Coml Vhcl Systems LLC........B 440 329-9000
   Avon *(G-716)*

Black Gold Capital LLC......................E 614 348-7460
   Columbus *(G-4761)*

Brookville Roadster Inc......................G 937 833-4605
   Brookville *(G-1563)*

◆ Buyers Products Company................C 440 974-8888
   Mentor *(G-9496)*

Cedar Elec Holdings Corp.................. D 773 804-6288
   West Chester *(G-13958)*

▲ Chemspec Usa Inc......................... D 330 669-8512
   Orrville *(G-10977)*

Crane Carrier Company LLC................C 918 286-2889
   New Philadelphia *(G-10440)*

Crane Carrier Holdings LLC................C 918 286-2889
   New Philadelphia *(G-10441)*

▲ Custer Products Limited................... F 330 490-3158
   Massillon *(G-9184)*

D & J Electric Motor Repair Co............ F 330 336-4343
   Wadsworth *(G-13634)*

Dan Patrick Enterprises Inc................G 740 477-1006
   Circleville *(G-3253)*

Doran Mfg LLC................................. D 866 816-7233
   Blue Ash *(G-1267)*

◆ Dreison International Inc..................C 216 362-0755
   Cleveland *(G-3632)*

▲ Durable Corporation....................... D 800 537-1603
   Norwalk *(G-10836)*

▼ East Trailers LLC............................E 330 325-9921
   Randolph *(G-11510)*

▲ Emssons Faurecia Ctrl Systems....... C 812 341-2000
   Toledo *(G-12951)*

Exide Technologies LLC.....................G 614 863-3866
   Gahanna *(G-7157)*

Finale Products Inc...........................G 419 874-2662
   Perrysburg *(G-11221)*

Florence Alloys Inc...........................G 330 745-9141
   Barberton *(G-805)*

Frontier Tank Center Inc.....................G 330 659-3888
   Richfield *(G-11593)*

Fuyao Glass America Inc....................B 937 496-5777
   Moraine *(G-10164)*

◆ Gear Star Amrcn Prfmce Trnsmss.....E 330 434-5216
   Akron *(G-157)*

Gmelectric Inc..................................G 330 477-3392
   Canton *(G-1902)*

◆ Goodyear Tire & Rubber Company.....A 330 796-2121
   Akron *(G-164)*

Herbert E Orr Company Inc.................C 419 399-4866
   Paulding *(G-11155)*

Hite Parts Exchange Inc.....................G 614 272-5115
   Chillicothe *(G-2258)*

◆ Interstate Diesel Service Inc.............C 216 881-0015
   Cleveland *(G-3865)*

◆ Kaffenbarger Truck Eqp Co..............C 937 845-3804
   New Carlisle *(G-10373)*

Keystone Auto Glass Inc..................... D 419 509-0497
   Maumee *(G-9302)*

Keystone Automotive Inds Inc..............G 614 228-4328
   Groveport *(G-7440)*

◆ L & R Racing Inc.............................E 330 220-3102
   Brunswick *(G-1601)*

Legacy Supplies Inc.......................... F 330 405-4565
   Twinsburg *(G-13328)*

Lucas Sumitomo Brakes Inc.................. F 513 934-0024
Lebanon *(G-8274)*

◆ Mac Trailer Manufacturing Inc............A 800 795-8454
Alliance *(G-390)*

Mader Automotive Center Inc................ F 937 339-2681
Troy *(G-13238)*

▲ Malone Specialty Inc........................ F 440 255-4200
Mentor *(G-9559)*

Martin Diesel Inc................................. E 419 782-9911
Defiance *(G-6120)*

▲ Matco Tools Corporation................... B 330 929-4949
Stow *(G-12440)*

Motionsource International LLC.............. F 440 287-7037
Solon *(G-12153)*

Myers Industries Inc........................... E 330 253-5592
Akron *(G-243)*

▲ Mytee Products Inc.......................... D 888 705-8277
Solon *(G-12156)*

◆ Namoh Ohio Holdings Inc..................G
Norwood *(G-10869)*

Neff Machinery and Supplies............... G 740 454-0128
Zanesville *(G-15031)*

Nelson Companies One LLC................. E 330 239-4370
Wadsworth *(G-13654)*

Nu-Di Products Co Inc......................... D 216 251-9070
Cleveland *(G-4105)*

▲ Ohashi Technica USA Inc.................. E 740 965-5115
Sunbury *(G-12671)*

Ohio Auto Supply Company.................. G 330 454-5105
Canton *(G-1964)*

Ohio Trailer Supply Inc....................... G 614 471-9121
Columbus *(G-5155)*

OSI Environmental LLC....................... E 440 237-4600
North Royalton *(G-10779)*

Perkins Motor Service Ltd.................... F 440 277-1256
Lorain *(G-8573)*

◆ Pioneer Automotive Tech Inc.............C 937 746-2293
Miamisburg *(G-9727)*

▲ Qualitor Inc.................................... G 248 204-8600
Cleveland *(G-4211)*

Qualitor Subsidiary H Inc.................... E 419 562-7987
Bucyrus *(G-1686)*

▲ Sims Bros Inc................................. D 740 387-9041
Marion *(G-9000)*

▲ T A Bacon Co.................................. G 216 595-1310
Cleveland *(G-4361)*

▲ Thyssenkrupp Bilstein Amer Inc....... C 513 881-7600
Hamilton *(C-7531)*

◆ Tmsi LLC.. F 888 867-4872
North Canton *(G-10676)*

▲ TS Trim Industries Inc..................... B 614 837-4114
Canal Winchester *(G-1799)*

Tuffy Manufacturing............................ F 330 940-2356
Akron *(G-348)*

Ultra-Met Company............................. F 937 653-7133
Urbana *(G-13480)*

Vintage Automotive Elc Inc.................. F 419 472-9349
Toledo *(G-13175)*

Youngstown-Kenworth Inc................... F 330 534-9761
Hubbard *(G-7819)*

5014 Tires and tubes

Associates Tire and Svc Inc................. F 937 436-4692
Centerville *(G-2129)*

B & S Transport Inc............................ G 330 767-4319
Navarre *(G-10302)*

Bell Tire Co....................................... F 440 234-8022
Olmsted Falls *(G-10937)*

Best One Tire & Svc Lima Inc.............. G 419 425-3322
Findlay *(G-6843)*

▲ Best One Tire & Svc Lima Inc........... E 419 229-2380
Lima *(G-8389)*

Bob Sumerel Tire Co Inc..................... F 614 527-9700
Columbus *(G-4768)*

Bob Sumerel Tire Co Inc..................... G 740 432-5200
Lore City *(G-8588)*

Bob Sumerel Tire Company Inc............ G 740 927-2811
Reynoldsburg *(G-11559)*

Central Ohio Bandag LP...................... F 740 454-9728
Zanesville *(G-15007)*

Forklift Tire East Mich Inc................... F 586 771-1330
Toledo *(G-12967)*

▲ Grismer Tire Company...................... E 937 643-2526
Centerville *(G-2132)*

Gt Tire Service Inc............................. G 740 927-7226
Pataskala *(G-11139)*

Mark Knupp Muffler & Tire Inc.............. G 937 773-1334
Piqua *(G-11365)*

Myers Industries Inc........................... E 330 253-5592
Akron *(G-243)*

North Coast Tire Co Inc....................... G 216 447-1690
Cleveland *(G-4089)*

Pro Tire Inc....................................... F 614 864-8662
Columbus *(G-5208)*

◆ Technical Rubber Company Inc..........C 740 967-9015
Johnstown *(G-7999)*

Victor Bodie Tire Co........................... G 216 431-1700
Cleveland *(G-4471)*

Ziegler Tire and Supply Co.................. G 330 434-7126
Akron *(G-362)*

5015 Motor vehicle parts, used

Bob Sumerel Tire Co Inc..................... F 614 527-9700
Columbus *(G-4768)*

Cedar Elec Holdings Corp.................... D 773 804-6288
West Chester *(G-13958)*

Lucas Sumitomo Brakes Inc................. F 513 934-0024
Lebanon *(G-8274)*

◆ Mac Trailer Manufacturing Inc...........A 800 795-8454
Alliance *(G-390)*

5021 Furniture

Ahmf Inc... E 614 921-1223
Columbus *(G-4681)*

American Platinum Door LLC................ G 440 497-6213
Solon *(G-12078)*

▼ Eoi Inc... F 740 201-3300
Lewis Center *(G-8333)*

Fabcor Inc... F 419 628-4428
Minster *(C-10057)*

Friends Service Co Inc........................ F 800 427-1704
Dayton *(G-5785)*

Friends Service Co Inc........................ E 419 427-1704
Findlay *(G-6869)*

G & P Construction LLC...................... E 855 494-4830
North Royalton *(G-10762)*

Jsc Employee Leasing Corp................. D 330 773-8971
Akron *(G-189)*

▲ KMC Holdings LLC.......................... C 419 238-2442
Van Wert *(G-13539)*

Millwood Wholesale Inc....................... F 330 359-6109
Dundee *(G-6369)*

▲ National Electro-Coatings Inc............ D 216 898-0080
Cleveland *(G-4059)*

Partitions Plus Incorporated................. F 419 422-2600
Findlay *(G-6907)*

◆ Progressive Furniture Inc..................E 419 446-4500
Archbold *(G-508)*

◆ Rize Home LLC................................D 800 333-8333
Glenwillow *(G-7288)*

Sauder Woodworking Co...................... F 419 446-2711
Archbold *(G-510)*

◆ Sauder Woodworking Co...................A 419 446-2711
Archbold *(G-511)*

Urbn Timber LLC............................... G 614 981-3043
Columbus *(G-5341)*

◆ Wasserstrom Company......................B 614 228-6525
Columbus *(G-5356)*

5023 Homefurnishings

Accent Drapery Co Inc........................ E 614 488-0741
Columbus *(G-4667)*

▲ American Frame Corporation.............. E 419 893-5595
Maumee *(G-9259)*

Cincinnati Window Shade Inc............... F 513 631-7200
Cincinnati *(G-2489)*

Conquest Maps LLC........................... G 614 654-1627
Columbus *(G-4843)*

Creative Products Inc.......................... G 419 866-5501
Holland *(G-7752)*

Custom Blind Corporation.................... F 937 643-2907
Dayton *(G-5717)*

Dale Kestler...................................... G 513 871-9000
Cincinnati *(G-2540)*

◆ G & S Metal Products Co Inc.............C 216 441-0700
Cleveland *(G-3748)*

Ghp II LLC.. F 740 681-6825
Lancaster *(G-8203)*

Golden Drapery Supply Inc.................. E 216 351-3283
Cleveland *(G-3779)*

◆ Greenway Home Products Inc.............F
Perrysburg *(G-11227)*

▲ Inside Outfitters Inc......................... E 614 798-3500
Lewis Center *(G-8338)*

Lumenomics Inc................................. E 614 798-3500
Lewis Center *(G-8342)*

Luminex HM Dcor Frgrnce Hldg C........ A 513 563-1113
Cincinnati *(G-2831)*

▲ Mag Resources LLC......................... F 330 294-0494
Barberton *(G-818)*

Pfpc Enterprises Inc........................... G 513 941-6200
Cincinnati *(G-2960)*

▲ Rhc Inc.. E 330 874-3750
Bolivar *(G-1391)*

▲ S I Distributing Inc.......................... F 419 647-4909
Spencerville *(G-12240)*

◆ Standard Textile Co Inc....................B 513 761-9255
Cincinnati *(G-3112)*

Style-Line Incorporated....................... E 614 291-0600
Columbus *(G-5295)*

Walter F Stephens Jr Inc..................... E 937 746-0521
Franklin *(G-7035)*

Watershed Mangement LLC................. F 740 852-5607
Mount Sterling *(G-10230)*

▲ Weavers Furniture Ltd...................... F 330 852-2701
Sugarcreek *(G-12657)*

Yellow Springs Pottery LLC................. F 937 767-1666
Yellow Springs *(G-14793)*

5031 Lumber, plywood, and millwork

Alumo Extrusions and Mfg Co.............. E 330 779-3333
Youngstown *(G-14810)*

Architctral Mllwk Cbinetry Inc.............. G 440 708-0086
Chagrin Falls *(G-2155)*

▲ Associated Materials LLC.................. C 330 929-1811
Cuyahoga Falls *(G-5528)*

Associated Materials Group Inc............ D 330 929-1811
Cuyahoga Falls *(G-5529)*

Associated Mtls Holdings LLC.............. A 330 929-1811
Cuyahoga Falls *(G-5530)*

Baillie Lumber Co LP.......................... E 419 462-2000
Galion *(G-7179)*

Bison Builders LLC............................. F 614 636-0365
Columbus *(G-4756)*

Blockamerica Corporation.................... G 614 274-0700
Columbus *(G-4765)*

SIC

Buckeye Components LLC....................E 330 482-5163
Columbiana *(G-4607)*

Cabot Lumber Inc.....................G 740 545-7109
West Lafayette *(G-14169)*

Cameo Countertops Inc....................F 419 865-6371
Holland *(G-7748)*

Carter-Jones Lumber Company....................G 330 674-9060
Millersburg *(G-9975)*

◆ Champion Win Co Cleveland LLC....... G 440 899-2562
Macedonia *(G-8681)*

Clark Wood Specialties Inc....................G 330 499-8711
Clinton *(G-4553)*

Clarksville Stave & Lbr Co Ltd....................G 937 376-4618
Xenia *(G-14759)*

Component Solutions Group Inc.....F 937 434-8100
Dayton *(G-5708)*

Contract Lumber Inc....................F 614 751-1109
Columbus *(G-4844)*

Custom Design Cabinets & Tops..... G 440 639-9900
Painesville *(G-11075)*

◆ Df Supply Inc....................E 330 650-9226
Twinsburg *(G-13294)*

Double D D Mtls Instlltion Inc.................G 937 898-2534
Dayton *(G-5750)*

Dublin Millwork Co Inc....................F 614 889-7776
Dublin *(G-6294)*

▲ Enclosure Suppliers LLC.................E 513 782-3900
Cincinnati *(G-2586)*

Flagship Trading Corporation.................E
Cleveland *(G-3722)*

Francis-Schulze Co....................F 937 295-3941
Russia *(G-11674)*

Gorell Enterprises Inc....................B 724 465-1800
Streetsboro *(G-12502)*

Great Lakes Stair & Mllwk Co....................G 330 225-2005
Hinckley *(G-7731)*

Gross Lumber Inc....................G 330 683-2055
Apple Creek *(G-469)*

▼ Hartzell Hardwoods Inc....................D 937 773-7054
Piqua *(G-11351)*

Higgins Construction & Supply Co Inc.. F 937 364-2331
Hillsboro *(G-7717)*

Holmes Lumber & Bldg Ctr Inc.................E 330 479-8314
Canton *(G-1912)*

Holmes Lumber & Bldg Ctr Inc.............C 330 674-9060
Millersburg *(G-9989)*

Imex Bz LLC....................F 786 866-8798
Orrville *(G-10986)*

J McCoy Lumber Co Ltd....................F 937 587-3423
Peebles *(G-11170)*

Jerry Harolds Doors Unlimited.................G 740 635-4949
Bridgeport *(G-1494)*

Khempco Bldg Sup Co Ltd Partnr.....D 740 549-0465
Delaware *(G-6159)*

Kitchen Designs Plus Inc....................E 419 536-6605
Toledo *(G-13019)*

◆ Litco International Inc....................D..... 330 539-5433
Vienna *(G-13612)*

M-D Building Products Inc....................F 513 539-2255
Middletown *(G-9874)*

Mason Structural Steel LLC....................E 440 439-1040
Walton Hills *(G-13699)*

Modern Builders Supply Inc....................E 419 526-0002
Mansfield *(G-8831)*

Mssi Group Inc....................D 440 439-1040
Walton Hills *(G-13701)*

Orrville Trucking & Grading Co.............E 330 682-4010
Orrville *(G-11000)*

Overhead Door of Pike County.............G 740 289-3925
Piketon *(G-11312)*

Premier Construction Company.......... G 513 874-2611
West Chester *(G-14053)*

Provia Holdings Inc....................C 330 852-4711
Sugarcreek *(G-12646)*

R W Long Lumber & Box Co Inc............. F 513 932-5124
Lebanon *(G-8282)*

Rockwood Products Ltd....................E 330 893-2392
Millersburg *(G-10007)*

Roofing Annex LLC....................G 513 942-0555
West Chester *(G-14141)*

S R Door Inc....................D 740 927-3558
Hebron *(G-7634)*

Salt Creek Lumber Company Inc............ G 330 695-3500
Fredericksburg *(G-7071)*

Schwab Industries Inc....................F 330 364-4411
Dover *(G-6261)*

▲ Sims-Lohman Inc....................E 513 651-3510
Cincinnati *(G-3093)*

Stark Truss Company Inc....................F 330 478-2100
Canton *(G-2017)*

▲ Stephen M Trudick....................E 440 834-1891
Burton *(G-1704)*

The F A Requarth Company....................E 937 224-1141
Dayton *(G-6048)*

The Galehouse Companies Inc.................E 330 658-2023
Doylestown *(G-6270)*

Toledo Molding & Die LLC....................C 419 692-6022
Delphos *(G-6193)*

Toledo Window & Awning Inc....................F 419 474-3396
Toledo *(G-13162)*

Traichal Construction Company.........E 800 255-3667
Niles *(G-10607)*

Troymill Manufacturing Inc....................F 440 632-5580
Middlefield *(G-9832)*

Universal Pallets Inc....................E 614 444-1095
Columbus *(G-5339)*

Wappoo Wood Products Inc....................E 937 492-1166
Sidney *(G-12060)*

Youngstown Curve Form Inc.................F 330 744-3028
Youngstown *(G-14968)*

5032 Brick, stone, and related material

Acme Company....................D 330 758-2313
Poland *(G-11434)*

Allied Corporation Inc....................F 330 425-7861
Twinsburg *(G-13272)*

Basetek LLC....................F 877 712-2273
Middlefield *(G-9781)*

▲ Castelli Marble LLC....................G 216 361-1222
Cleveland *(G-3477)*

▲ Clay Burley Products Co....................E 740 452-3633
Roseville *(G-11653)*

Collinwood Shale Brick Sup Co.............E 216 587-2700
Cleveland *(G-3545)*

Encore Precast LLC....................D 513 726-5678
Seven Mile *(G-11907)*

Ernst Enterprises Inc....................F 937 233-7777
West Milton *(G-14182)*

▼ Exhibit Concepts Inc....................D 937 890-7000
Vandalia *(G-13557)*

Grafton Ready Mix Concret Inc.................C 440 926-2911
Grafton *(G-7303)*

Helmart Company Inc....................G 513 941-3095
Cincinnati *(G-2715)*

Hilltop Basic Resources Inc....................G 937 859-3616
Miamisburg *(G-9699)*

Huron Cement Products Company.........E 419 433-4161
Huron *(G-7874)*

Hy-Grade Corporation....................E 216 341-7711
Cleveland *(G-3846)*

Jalco Industries Inc....................F 740 286-3808
Jackson *(G-7947)*

Koltcz Concrete Block Co....................E 440 232-3630
Bedford *(G-1042)*

▲ Kuhlman Corporation....................E 419 897-6000
Maumee *(G-9303)*

Lancaster W Side Coal Co Inc.................F 740 862-4713
Lancaster *(G-8207)*

▲ Lang Stone Company Inc....................E 614 235-4099
Columbus *(G-5064)*

Mayfair Granite Co Inc....................G 216 382-8150
Cleveland *(G-4002)*

Michaels Pre-Cast Con Pdts Inc............. F 513 683-1292
Loveland *(G-8643)*

Modern Builders Supply Inc....................E 419 526-0002
Mansfield *(G-8831)*

Modern Builders Supply Inc....................C 419 241-3961
Toledo *(G-13058)*

Moritz Materials Inc....................E 419 281-0575
Ashland *(G-553)*

Ohio Beauty Cut Stone II Inc.................G 330 644-2241
Akron *(G-251)*

▲ Ohio Tile & Marble Co....................E 513 541-4211
Cincinnati *(G-2926)*

OK Brugmann Jr & Sons Inc....................G 330 274-2106
Mantua *(G-8873)*

Olen Corporation....................F 419 294-2611
Upper Sandusky *(G-13451)*

Palmer Bros Transit Mix Con.......... F 419 686-2366
Portage *(G-11460)*

Phoenix Asphalt Company Inc....................G 330 339-4935
Magnolia *(G-8736)*

◆ Pinney Dock & Transport LLC.........F 440 964-7186
Ashtabula *(G-612)*

Piqua Granite & Marble Co Inc.............G 937 773-2000
Piqua *(G-11376)*

Quality Block & Supply Inc....................E 330 364-4411
Mount Eaton *(G-10208)*

R W Sidley Incorporated....................C 440 298-3232
Thompson *(G-12763)*

R W Sidley Incorporated....................E 330 793-7374
Youngstown *(G-14923)*

Ridge Township Stone Quarry.............G 419 968-2222
Van Wert *(G-13544)*

Russell Standard Corporation.............G 330 733-9400
Akron *(G-299)*

Schwab Industries Inc....................F 330 364-4411
Dover *(G-6261)*

Sewer Rodding Equipment Co.............C 419 991-2065
Lima *(G-8447)*

Sidwell Materials Inc....................C 740 849-2422
Zanesville *(G-15050)*

Smyrna Ready Mix Concrete LLC......... D 937 855-0410
Germantown *(G-7254)*

Snyder Concrete Products Inc....................G 937 224-1433
Dayton *(G-6011)*

Snyder Concrete Products Inc....................G 937 339-7577
Troy *(G-13257)*

▲ Snyder Concrete Products Inc....................E 937 885-5176
Moraine *(G-10192)*

Stamm Contracting Company Inc......... F 330 274-8230
Mantua *(G-8875)*

Stocker Concrete Company....................F 740 254-4626
Gnadenhutten *(G-7293)*

Stoneco Inc....................E 419 893-7645
Maumee *(G-9321)*

Tamarron Technology Inc....................F 800 277-3207
Cincinnati *(G-3136)*

◆ The D S Brown Company....................C 419 257-3561
North Baltimore *(G-10619)*

The Ideal Builders Supply....................F 216 741-1600
Cleveland *(G-4386)*

Toledo Cut Stone Inc....................F 419 531-1623
Toledo *(G-13150)*

Trumbull Cement Products Co....................G 330 372-4342
Warren *(G-13802)*

Wallseye Concrete Corp.............................. F 419 483-2738
Castalia (G-2096)

Warren Concrete and Supply Co............ G 330 393-1581
Warren (G-13810)

William Dauch Concrete Company........ F 419 668-4458
Norwalk (G-10863)

5033 Roofing, siding, and insulation

Alside Inc... E 419 865-0934
Maumee (G-9258)

▲ Associated Materials LLC................. C 330 929-1811
Cuyahoga Falls (G-5528)

Associated Materials Group Inc............ D 330 929-1811
Cuyahoga Falls (G-5529)

Associated Mtls Holdings LLC............. A 330 929-1811
Cuyahoga Falls (G-5530)

◆ Denizen Inc.....................................F 937 615-9561
Piqua (G-11344)

GUTTER TOPPER LTD.......................... G 513 797-5800
Batavia (G-866)

Kingspan Insulation LLC..................... D 800 433-5551
Newark (G-10514)

Modern Builders Supply Inc................ E 419 526-0002
Mansfield (G-8831)

▲ Tlg Cochran Inc.............................. E 440 914-1122
Twinsburg (G-13385)

Vinyl Design Corporation.................... E 419 283-4009
Holland (G-7790)

5039 Construction materials, nec

A Service Glass Inc............................ F 937 426-4920
Beavercreek (G-963)

Active Aeration Systems Inc............. G 614 873-3626
Plain City (G-11390)

▲ Agratronix LLC.............................. E 330 562-2222
Streetsboro (G-12485)

Allen Enterprises Inc......................... E 740 532-5913
Ironton (G-7928)

Alumo Extrusions and Mfg Co............ E 330 779-3333
Youngstown (G-14810)

Anderson Glass Co Inc...................... G 614 476-4877
Columbus (G-4717)

Charles Mfg Co................................. F 330 395-3490
Warren (G-13751)

Clearvue Insulating Glass Co.............. G 216 651-1140
Cleveland (G-3504)

Dale Kestler..................................... G 513 871-9000
Cincinnati (G-2540)

▲ Global Glass Block Inc.................... G 216 731-2333
Euclid (G-6651)

Koebbe Products Inc......................... D 513 753-4200
Amelia (G-430)

Lab-Pro Inc...................................... G 937 434-9600
Miamisburg (G-9708)

Machined Glass Specialist Inc............. G 937 743-6166
Springboro (G-12259)

Marysville Steel Inc........................... E 937 642-5971
Marysville (G-9038)

Morton Buildings Inc.......................... E 419 675-2311
Kenton (G-8110)

Morton Buildings Inc.......................... E 330 345-6188
Wooster (G-14667)

Patio Enclosures............................... F 513 733-4646
Cincinnati (G-2944)

▲ Pease Enterprises Inc..................... F 513 871-8907
Cincinnati (G-2951)

▲ Richards Whl Fence Co Inc.............. E 330 773-0423
Akron (G-284)

Security Fence Group Inc................... E 513 681-3700
Cincinnati (G-3074)

Snyder Concrete Products Inc............. G 937 339-7577
Troy (G-13257)

Trulite GL Alum Solutions LLC.............. D 740 929-2443
Hebron (G-7642)

Will-Burt Company.............................. F 330 682-7015
Orrville (G-11019)

▲ Will-Burt Company.......................... C 330 682-7015
Orrville (G-11018)

5043 Photographic equipment and supplies

Eastman Kodak Company..................... E 937 259-3000
Dayton (G-5758)

▲ Identiphoto Co Ltd.......................... F 440 306-9000
Willoughby (G-14467)

5044 Office equipment

Copier Resources Inc......................... G 614 268-1100
Columbus (G-4849)

Cummins - Allison Corp...................... G 440 824-5050
Cleveland (G-3579)

Friends Service Co Inc....................... F 800 427-1704
Dayton (G-5785)

Friends Service Co Inc....................... E 419 427-1704
Findlay (G-6869)

McIntosh Safe Corp........................... F 937 222-7008
Dayton (G-5871)

Robert Becker Impressions Inc............. F 419 385-5303
Toledo (G-13116)

Symatic Inc...................................... G 330 225-1510
Medina (G-9452)

5045 Computers, peripherals, and software

▲ Accretech SBS Inc.......................... G 513 373-4844
Cincinnati (G-2336)

Application Link Incorporated.............. G 614 934-1735
Columbus (G-4722)

Arctos Mission Solutions LLC.............. G 813 609-5591
Beavercreek (G-965)

Ascendtech Inc................................. E 216 458-1101
Willoughby (G-14428)

B & S Transport Inc........................... G 330 767-4319
Navarre (G-10302)

Black Box Corporation........................ G 855 324-9909
Westlake (G-14292)

▼ Data Processing Sciences .... D 513 791-7100
Cincinnati (G-2542)

Eci Macola/Max LLC........................... C 978 539-6186
Dublin (G-6296)

Freedom Usa Inc............................... E 216 503-6374
Twinsburg (G-13306)

▲ Fscreations Corporation................... D 330 746-3015
Youngstown (G-14858)

▲ GBS Corp....................................... C 330 494-5330
North Canton (G-10641)

Government Acquisitions Inc................ E 513 721-8700
Cincinnati (G-2685)

▲ Identiphoto Co Ltd.......................... F 440 306-9000
Willoughby (G-14467)

Journey Systems LLC......................... F 513 831-6200
Milford (G-9940)

Legrand North America LLC................. B 937 224-0639
Dayton (G-5843)

Magnum Computers Inc....................... F 216 781-1757
Cleveland (G-3981)

Microplex Inc.................................... E 330 498-0600
North Canton (G-10651)

Miles Midprint Inc.............................. F 216 860-4770
Cleveland (G-4040)

Pemro Corporation............................. F 800 440-5441
Cleveland (G-4151)

◆ Printer Components Inc.................... G 585 924-5190
Fairfield (G-6767)

▲ Sam Oht Services LLC..................... F 330 225-3117
Medina (G-9444)

▲ Sarcom Inc.................................... A 614 854-1300
Lewis Center (G-8353)

Software Solutions Inc....................... E 513 932-6667
Dayton (G-6012)

▲ Systemax Manufacturing Inc............. G 937 368-2300
Dayton (G-6035)

Vr Assets LLC................................... G 440 600-2963
Solon (G-12203)

5046 Commercial equipment, nec

Abstract Displays Inc......................... F 513 985-9700
Blue Ash (G-1241)

Active Aeration Systems Inc............... G 614 873-3626
Plain City (G-11390)

Baker Plastics Inc.............................. G 330 743-3142
Youngstown (G-14817)

Behrco Inc....................................... G 419 394-1612
Saint Marys (G-11731)

Cgmw Incorporated........................... G 614 236-8388
Columbus (G-4804)

Cummins - Allison Corp...................... G 513 469-2924
Blue Ash (G-1266)

Cummins - Allison Corp...................... G 440 824-5050
Cleveland (G-3579)

G & P Construction LLC...................... E 855 494-4830
North Royalton (G-10762)

◆ General Data Company Inc................B 513 752-7978
Cincinnati (G-2304)

▲ Harry C Lobalzo & Sons Inc............. E 330 666-6758
Akron (G-172)

ITW Food Equipment Group LLC........... C 937 393-4271
Hillsboro (G-7719)

◆ ITW Food Equipment Group LLC........A 937 332-2396
Troy (G-13231)

Joneszylon Company LLC.................... G 740 545-6341
West Lafayette (G-14173)

Leiden Cabinet Company LLC.............. G 330 425-8555
Strasburg (G-12480)

◆ N Wasserstrom & Sons Inc...............C 614 228-5550
Columbus (G-5118)

National Pride Equipment Inc............... G 419 289-2886
Mansfield (G-8837)

Partitions Plus Incorporated................ E 419 422-2600
Findlay (G-6907)

Rayhaven Group Inc........................... G 330 659-3183
Richfield (G-11598)

RS Industries Inc............................... G 216 351-8200
Brooklyn Heights (G-1339)

Sign America Incorporated.................. G 740 765-5555
Richmond (G-11605)

Starks Plastics LLC............................ F 513 541-4591
Cincinnati (G-3113)

◆ Ternion Inc....................................E 216 642-6180
Cleveland (G-4375)

Tri-State Supply Co Inc...................... G 614 272-6767
Columbus (G-5331)

◆ Wasserstrom Company....................B 614 228-6525
Columbus (G-5356)

5047 Medical and hospital equipment

◆ 889 Global Solutions Ltd..................F 614 235-8889
Columbus (G-4655)

American Power LLC........................... F 937 235-0418
Dayton (G-5654)

Axon Medical Llc............................... E 216 276-0262
Medina (G-9379)

Berlin Industries Inc.......................... F 330 549-2100
Youngstown (G-14819)

◆ Blatchford Inc................................D 937 291-3636
Miamisburg (G-9673)

◆ Boxout LLC....................................C 833 462-7746
Hudson (G-7835)

Cardinal Health Inc.................... E 614 553-3830
Dublin (G-6285)

Cardinal Health Inc.................... G 614 757-2863
Lewis Center (G-8328)

◆ Cardinal Health Inc.................A 614 757-5000
Dublin (G-6286)

Cardinal Health 110 LLC........... E 800 727-6331
Dublin (G-6287)

Coopersurgical Inc................... G 203 601-5200
Cincinnati (G-2516)

Dentronix Inc............................ D 330 916-7300
Cuyahoga Falls (G-5538)

Electro-Cap International Inc...........F 937 456-6099
Eaton (G-6453)

▼ Eoi Inc................................... F 740 201-3300
Lewis Center (G-8333)

▲ Ethicon Endo-Surgery Inc........ A 513 337-7000
Cincinnati (G-2600)

▲ Faretec Inc............................. F 440 350-9510
Painesville (G-11086)

◆ Ferno-Washington Inc.............C 877 733-0911
Wilmington (G-14580)

Homecare Mattress Inc.............. F 937 746-2556
Franklin (G-7027)

Icu Medical Inc......................... D 614 210-7300
Dublin (G-6305)

Johnson & Johnson................... E 513 786-7000
Blue Ash (G-1290)

Jones Metal Products Company........... E 740 545-6341
West Lafayette (G-14172)

▲ Julius Zorn Inc........................ D 330 923-4999
Cuyahoga Falls (G-5553)

Kempf Surgical Appliances Inc......... G 513 984-5758
Cincinnati (G-2791)

Lion First Responder Ppe Inc........ D 937 898-1949
Dayton (G-5849)

Lion Group Inc.......................... D 800 421-2926
Dayton (G-5850)

Markethtch Inc D/B/A Mh Eye CA............F 330 376-6363
Akron (G-221)

▲ Mill Rose Laboratories Inc......... E 440 974-6730
Mentor (G-9565)

Optum Infusion Svcs 550 LLC...... D 866 442-4679
Cincinnati (G-2936)

◆ Philips Med Systems Clvland In........B 440 483-3000
Cleveland (G-4159)

RB Sigma LLC........................... D 440 290-0577
Mentor (G-9607)

Smiths Medical North America........... G 614 210-7300
Dublin (G-6347)

Stable Step LLC........................ C 800 491-1571
Wadsworth (G-13673)

Thermo Fisher Scientific Inc......... E 800 871-8909
Oakwood Village (G-10910)

◆ Tosoh America Inc....................B 614 539-8622
Grove City (G-7417)

Triage Ortho Group.................... G 937 653-6431
Urbana (G-13478)

Ultra-Met Company.................... F 937 653-7133
Urbana (G-13480)

United Medical Supply Company........... F 866 678-8633
Brunswick (G-1621)

▲ Viewray Inc............................. D 440 703-3210
Oakwood Village (G-10911)

5048 Ophthalmic goods

Diversified Ophthalmics Inc................... E 803 783-3454
Cincinnati (G-2554)

◆ Haag-Streit Usa Inc..................D 513 398-3937
Mason (G-9107)

Toledo Optical Laboratory Inc................... G 419 248-3384
Toledo (G-13155)

5049 Professional equipment, nec

Ahner Fabricating & Shtmtl Inc............. E 419 626-6641
Sandusky (G-11820)

Consoldted Anlytcal Systems In............. F 513 542-1200
Cincinnati (G-2510)

Diversified Ophthalmics Inc................... E 803 783-3454
Cincinnati (G-2554)

Erie Street Thea Svcs Inc................... G 216 426-0050
Cleveland (G-3684)

▲ Gilson Company Inc.................. E 740 548-7298
Lewis Center (G-8334)

◆ Hapco Inc...............................F 330 678-9353
Kent (G-8035)

▼ ICM Distributing Company Inc........ E 234 212-3030
Twinsburg (G-13319)

Laser Automation Inc.................. G 440 543-9291
Chagrin Falls (G-2169)

▲ Lorenz Corporation.................. D 937 228-6118
Dayton (G-5855)

◆ Mettler-Toledo LLC..................A 614 438-4511
Columbus (G-4644)

▲ Monarch Steel Company Inc....... E 216 587-8000
Cleveland (G-4045)

Novak J F Manufacturing Co LLC......... G 216 741-5112
Cleveland (G-4102)

Queen City Reprographics.......... C 513 326-2300
Cincinnati (G-3024)

Revvity Health Sciences Inc......... D 330 825-4525
Akron (G-283)

▲ S&V Industries Inc................... E 330 666-1986
Medina (G-9443)

Science/Electronics Inc.............. G 937 224-4444
Dayton (G-5998)

Tech4imaging LLC..................... F 614 214-2655
Columbus (G-5315)

Teledyne Instruments Inc........... E 513 229-7000
Mason (G-9158)

Teledyne Tekmar Company......... E 513 229-7000
Mason (G-9160)

▼ Test Mark Industries Inc........... F 330 426-2200
East Palestine (G-6408)

US Tsubaki Power Transm LLC............. C 419 626-4560
Sandusky (G-11881)

Zaenkert Srvying Essntials Inc........... G 513 738-2917
Okeana (G-10931)

▲ Zaner-Bloser Inc..................... C 614 486-0221
Columbus (G-5380)

5051 Metals service centers and offices

◆ Alanod Westlake Metal Ind Inc............E 440 327-8184
North Ridgeville (G-10723)

Alro Steel Corporation................ E 614 878-7271
Columbus (G-4690)

Alro Steel Corporation................ E 937 253-6121
Dayton (G-5648)

Alro Steel Corporation................ D 419 720-5300
Toledo (G-12871)

Aluminum Bearing Co of America......... G 216 267-8560
Cleveland (G-3336)

◆ Aluminum Line Products Company........D 440 835-8880
Westlake (G-14285)

AM Castle & Co........................ F 330 425-7000
Bedford (G-1011)

◆ American Ir Met Cleveland LLC............E 216 266-0509
Cleveland (G-3345)

American Posts LLC................... D 419 720-0652
Toledo (G-12877)

▲ American Tank & Fabricating Co........... D 216 252-1500
Cleveland (G-3348)

▲ Atlas Bolt & Screw Company LLC..... C 419 289-6171
Ashland (G-519)

B&A Ison Steel Inc.................... F 216 663-4300
Cleveland (G-3400)

Berkshire Road Holdings Inc........ F 216 883-4200
Cleveland (G-3416)

▲ Bico Akron Inc......................... D 330 794-1716
Mogadore (G-10070)

Blackburns Fabrication Inc.......... E 614 875-0784
Columbus (G-4762)

Canfield Coating LLC................. E 330 533-3311
Canfield (G-1806)

Canfield Metal Coating Corp........ D 330 702-3876
Canfield (G-1807)

Clifton Capital Holdings LLC.........F 330 562-9000
Maple Heights (G-8880)

◆ Clifton Steel Company...............D 216 662-6111
Maple Heights (G-8881)

▲ Cmt Imports Inc....................... G 513 615-1851
Cincinnati (G-2502)

Contractors Steel Company.......... D 330 425-3050
Twinsburg (G-13289)

Coventry Steel Services Inc......... G 216 883-4477
Cleveland (G-3571)

Curtis Steel & Supply Inc............ F 330 376-7141
Akron (G-110)

EPI of Cleveland Inc.................. G 330 468-2872
Twinsburg (G-13299)

▲ Ferralloy Inc........................... G 440 250-1900
Cleveland (G-3713)

▲ Fpt Cleveland LLC.................... C 216 441-3800
Cleveland (G-3740)

Grenga Machine & Welding.......... F 330 743-1113
Youngstown (G-14871)

▲ H & D Steel Service Inc............. E 800 666-3390
North Royalton (G-10764)

◆ Hickman Williams & Company............F 513 621-1946
Cincinnati (G-2721)

Howard Industries Inc................. F 614 444-9900
Columbus (G-4993)

JSW Steel USA Ohio Inc............. B 740 535-8172
Mingo Junction (G-10052)

◆ Kirtland Capital Partners LP.........E 216 593-0100
Beachwood (G-924)

Krendl Rack Co Inc.................... G 419 667-4800
Venedocia (G-13586)

Lake Building Products Inc.......... E 216 486-1500
Cleveland (G-3936)

Lapham-Hickey Steel Corp.......... D 614 443-4881
Columbus (G-5065)

◆ Latrobe Spcialty Mtls Dist Inc............D 330 609-5137
Vienna (G-13610)

Louis Arthur Steel Company......... G 440 997-5545
Geneva (G-7241)

◆ Loveman Steel Corporation..........D 440 232-6200
Bedford (G-1044)

M-D Building Products Inc........... F 513 539-2255
Middletown (G-9874)

Major Metals Company................ E 419 886-4600
Mansfield (G-8815)

Master-Halco Inc...................... F 513 869-7600
Fairfield (G-6751)

McDonald Steel Plate Inc............ F 216 883-4200
Cleveland (G-4008)

McOn Inds Inc.......................... E 937 294-2681
Moraine (G-10176)

McWane Inc............................. B 740 622-6651
Coshocton (G-5459)

▲ Merit Brass Co........................ C 216 261-9800
Cleveland (G-4021)

Mid-America Steel Corp.............. E 800 282-3466
Cleveland (G-4033)

Modern Welding Co Ohio Inc........ E 740 344-9425
Newark (G-10522)

▲ Monarch Steel Company Inc............ E 216 587-8000
Cleveland (G-4045)

▲ National Bronze Mtls Ohio Inc........ E 440 277-1226
Lorain (G-8568)

▲ Nimers & Woody II Inc.................. C 937 454-0722
Vandalia (G-13574)

Nucor Steel Marion Inc.................. E 740 383-6068
Marion (G-8984)

◆ Nucor Steel Marion Inc..................B 740 383-4011
Marion (G-8985)

Ohio Metal Processing LLC.............. G 740 912-2057
Jackson (G-7949)

Ohio Steel Sheet and Plate Inc......... E 800 827-2401
Hubbard (G-7815)

▲ Oliver Steel Plate Co.................... D 330 425-7000
Twinsburg (G-13347)

Omega 1 Inc............................... F 216 663-8424
Willoughby (G-14501)

◆ Panacea Products Corporation........E 614 850-7000
Columbus (G-5171)

▲ Pipe Products Inc....................... C 513 587-7532
West Chester (G-14049)

Radix Wire Co............................ D 216 731-9191
Solon (G-12173)

▲ Remington Steel Inc.................... E 937 322-2414
Springfield (G-12370)

Rex Welding Inc.......................... F 740 387-1650
Marion (G-8992)

▲ Rockwell Metals Company LLC........ F 440 242-2420
Lorain (G-8579)

◆ Rolled Alloys Inc........................D 800 521-0332
Maumee (G-9315)

▲ Samsel Rope & Marine Supply Co.... E 216 241-0333
Cleveland (G-4272)

Samuel Son & Co (usa) Inc............. D 740 522-2500
Heath (G-7604)

▲ Sausser Steel Company Inc........... G 419 422-9632
Findlay (G-6916)

Scot Industries Inc...................... C 330 262-7585
Wooster (G-14683)

Shaq Inc.................................. D 770 427-0402
Beachwood (G-949)

▲ Sims Bros Inc........................... D 740 387-9041
Marion (G-9000)

St Lawrence Holdings LLC............... E 330 562-9000
Maple Heights (G-8892)

◆ St Lawrence Steel Corporation........ E 330 562-9000
Maple Heights (O-0093)

Stamped Steel Products Inc............. F 330 538-3951
North Jackson (G-10695)

Stephens Pipe & Steel LLC.............. C 740 869-2257
Mount Sterling (G-10229)

Swagelok Company........................ D 440 349-5934
Solon (G-12191)

The Mansfield Strl & Erct Co............ F 419 522-5911
Mansfield (G-8859)

Thyssenkrupp Materials NA Inc......... D 216 883-8100
Independence (G-7921)

Tomson Steel Company................... E 513 420-8600
Middletown (G-9900)

▲ Tri-State Wire Rope Supply Inc........ G 513 871-8656
Cincinnati (G-3168)

◆ Tricor Industrial Inc....................D 330 264-3299
Wooster (G-14692)

▲ Tsk America Co Ltd..................... F 513 942-4002
West Chester (G-14156)

Tubular Techniques Inc.................. G 614 529-4130
Hilliard (G-7708)

▲ Universal Steel Company............... D 216 883-4972
Cleveland (G-4448)

Victory White Metal Company........... F 216 641-2575
Cleveland (G-4473)

◆ Watteredge LLC..........................D 440 933-6110
Avon Lake (G-773)

Westfield Steel Inc...................... D 937 322-2414
Springfield (G-12392)

Wheatland Tube LLC..................... C 724 342-6851
Niles (G-10610)

▲ Wieland Metal Svcs Foils LLC......... D 330 823-1700
Alliance (G-417)

Worthngton Smuel Coil Proc LLC....... E 330 963-3777
Twinsburg (G-13398)

Worthington Stelpac Systems LLC...... C 614 438-3205
Columbus (G-5375)

Youngstown Specialty Mtls Inc......... G 330 259-1110
Youngstown (G-14976)

5052 Coal and other minerals and ores

B & S Transport Inc..................... G 330 767-4319
Navarre (G-10302)

Graphel Corporation..................... C 513 779-6166
West Chester (G-14012)

◆ Hickman Williams & Company......... F 513 621-1946
Cincinnati (G-2721)

▲ Seaforth Mineral & Ore Co Inc........ F 216 292-5820
Beachwood (G-948)

◆ Tosoh America Inc......................B 614 539-8622
Grove City (G-7417)

5063 Electrical apparatus and equipment

Accurate Mechanical Inc................. D 740 681-1332
Lancaster (G-8174)

Acorn Technology Corporation.......... E 216 663-1244
Shaker Heights (G-11925)

Akron Foundry Co........................ C 330 745-3101
Akron (G-31)

Allen Fields Assoc Inc................... E 513 228-1010
Lebanon (G-8243)

Als High Tech Inc........................ F 440 232-7090
Bedford (G-1010)

◆ American De Rosa Lamparts LLC......D
Cuyahoga Falls (G-5522)

Ametek Inc................................ F 937 440-0800
Troy (G-13200)

Ametek Tchnical Indus Pdts Inc........ D 330 673-3451
Kent (G-8017)

Architectural Busstrut Corp............. F 614 933-8695
New Albany (G-10329)

Associated Mtls Holdings LLC.......... A 330 929-1811
Cuyahoga Falls (O-5530)

Astro Industries Inc..................... E 937 429-5900
Beavercreek (G-966)

B2d Solutions Inc........................ G 855 484-1145
Cleveland (G-3402)

Battery Unlimited........................ G 740 452-5030
Zanesville (G-14993)

Bennett Electric Inc..................... F 800 874-5405
Norwalk (G-10830)

◆ Best Lighting Products Inc.............D 740 964-1198
Pataskala (G-11137)

Big River Electric Inc.................... G 740 446-4360
Gallipolis (G-7202)

Black Box Corporation................... G 855 324-9909
Westlake (G-14292)

Bornhorst Motor Service Inc............ G 937 773-0426
Piqua (G-11337)

Cattron Holdings Inc..................... E 234 806-0018
Warren (G-13748)

Ces Nationwide........................... G 937 322-0771
Springfield (G-12289)

Clark-Fowler Enterprises Inc............ E 330 262-0906
Wooster (G-14631)

▲ Cleanlife Energy LLC.................... F 800 316-2532
Cleveland (G-3503)

Controllix Corporation................... F 440 232-8757
Walton Hills (G-13696)

Current Elec & Enrgy Solutions......... G 513 575-4600
Loveland (G-8623)

D C Systems Inc......................... F 330 273-3030
Brunswick (G-1587)

Fenton Bros Electric Co................. E 330 343-0093
New Philadelphia (G-10445)

◆ Filnor Inc...............................F 330 821-8731
Alliance (G-382)

Gt Industrial Supply Inc................. F 513 771-7000
Cincinnati (G-2695)

Hackworth Electric Motors Inc.......... G 330 345-6049
Wooster (G-14648)

Hannon Company......................... F 330 343-7758
Dover (G-6246)

Hannon Company......................... F 740 453-0527
Zanesville (G-15019)

Horner Industrial Services Inc.......... F 937 390-6667
Springfield (G-12325)

Hughes Corporation...................... E 440 238-2550
Strongsville (G-12564)

Ignio Systems LLC....................... G 419 708-0503
Toledo (G-12999)

Industrial Ctrl Dsign Mint Inc........... F 330 785-9840
Tallmadge (G-12737)

Industrial Power Systems Inc........... B 419 531-3121
Rossford (G-11659)

▼ Kirk Key Interlock Company LLC....... E 330 833-8223
North Canton (G-10648)

Legrand North America LLC............. B 937 224-0639
Dayton (G-5843)

Lima Armature Works Inc................ G 419 222-4010
Lima (G-8424)

LSI Industries Inc....................... C 913 281-1100
Blue Ash (G-1299)

▲ LSI Lightron Inc......................... A 845 562-5500
Blue Ash (G-1300)

M & R Electric Motor Svc Inc........... E 937 701-0475
Dayton (G-5857)

Machine Drive Company.................. D 513 793-7077
Cincinnati (G-2837)

Mader Elc Mtr Pwr Trnsmssons L....... G 937 325-5576
Springfield (G-12346)

Masteller Electric Motor Svc............ G 937 492-8500
Sidney (G-12032)

▼ Matlock Electric Co Inc................. F 513 731-9600
Cincinnati (G-2830)

Mid-Ohio Electric Co.................... E 614 274-8000
Columbus (G-5098)

Mjo Industries Inc....................... D 800 590-4055
Huber Heights (G-7822)

Moto-Electric Inc........................ G 419 668-7894
Norwalk (G-10853)

◆ Multilink Inc............................C 440 366-6966
Elyria (G-6566)

◆ Noco Company...........................D 216 464-8131
Glenwillow (G-7286)

Ohio Electric Motor Service Center Inc..F 614 444-1451
Columbus (G-5143)

One Wish LLC............................ F 800 505-6883
Bedford (G-1052)

▲ Osburn Associates Inc.................. F 740 385-5732
Logan (G-8522)

Peak Electric Inc........................ F 419 726-4848
Toledo (G-13092)

Phillips Electric Co..................... F 216 361-0014
Cleveland (G-4160)

Powell Electrical Systems Inc........... D 330 966-1750
North Canton (G-10660)

Powerbilt Mtl Hdlg Sltions LLC.......... D 937 592-5660
Bellefontaine (G-1115)

Resideo LLC...G..... 440 439-7002
Bedford *(G-1057)*

Resideo LLC...F..... 513 772-1851
Cincinnati *(G-3039)*

▼ Riverside Drives Inc.............................E..... 216 362-1211
Cleveland *(G-4243)*

Rv Mobile Power LLC.............................E..... 855 427-7978
Columbus *(G-5239)*

Schneider Electric Usa Inc....................B..... 513 523-4171
Oxford *(G-11064)*

Schneider Electric Usa Inc....................D..... 513 777-4445
West Chester *(G-14073)*

Scott Fetzer Company.............................C..... 216 267-9000
Cleveland *(G-4278)*

▲ Shoemaker Electric Company...........E..... 614 294-5626
Columbus *(G-5263)*

Sieb & Meyer America Inc.....................F..... 513 563-0860
West Chester *(G-14145)*

▲ Specialty Switch Company LLC........F..... 330 427-3000
Youngstown *(G-14936)*

Status Solutions LLC...............................D..... 434 296-1789
Westerville *(G-14235)*

Stock Fairfield Corporation....................C..... 440 543-6000
Solon *(G-12185)*

Sumitomo Elc Wirg Systems Inc...........E..... 937 642-7579
Marysville *(G-9052)*

Technical Artistry Inc.............................G..... 614 299-7777
Columbus *(G-5316)*

Tesa Inc...G..... 614 847-8200
Lewis Center *(G-8355)*

Total Life Safety LLC...............................F..... 866 955-2318
West Chester *(G-14083)*

Warmus and Associates Inc...................G..... 330 659-4440
Bath *(G-898)*

Wes-Garde Components Group Inc.......G..... 614 885-0319
Westerville *(G-14280)*

Western Branch Diesel LLC....................F..... 330 454-8800
Canton *(G-2047)*

Wheatley Electric Service Co.................G..... 513 531-4951
Cincinnati *(G-3222)*

Wifi-Plus Inc..G..... 330 273-3665
Brunswick *(G-1624)*

▲ Winkle Industries Inc.........................D..... 330 823-9730
Alliance *(G-418)*

5064 Electrical appliances, television and radio

◆ Associated Premium Corporation.......E..... 513 679-4444
Cincinnati *(G-2381)*

◆ GMI Holdings Inc................................B..... 800 354-3643
Mount Hope *(G-10213)*

Great Lakes Telcom Ltd..........................E..... 330 629-8848
Youngstown *(G-14870)*

Whirlpool Corporation.............................D..... 740 383-7122
Marion *(G-9003)*

World Wide Recyclers Inc.......................G..... 614 554-3296
Columbus *(G-5372)*

5065 Electronic parts and equipment, nec

ABC Appliance Inc...................................E..... 419 693-4414
Oregon *(G-10955)*

Background Music & Sound Inc...............G..... 937 898-9871
Dayton *(G-5673)*

Black Box Corporation.............................G..... 855 324-9909
Westlake *(G-14292)*

▼ Cartessa Corp....................................F..... 513 738-4477
Shandon *(G-11933)*

Cattron Holdings Inc...............................E..... 234 806-0018
Warren *(G-13748)*

Cbst Acquisition LLC...............................D..... 513 361-9600
Cincinnati *(G-2445)*

Certified Comparator Products..............G..... 937 426-9677
Miamisburg *(G-9679)*

▲ Cota International Inc.........................G..... 937 526-5520
Versailles *(G-13593)*

Db Unlimited LLC....................................G..... 937 401-2602
Dayton *(G-5743)*

Electra Sound Inc....................................D..... 216 433-9600
Avon Lake *(G-754)*

Electro-Line Inc.......................................F..... 937 461-5683
Dayton *(G-5762)*

Famous Industries Inc............................E..... 330 535-1811
Akron *(G-145)*

▲ Floyd Bell Inc.....................................D..... 614 294-4000
Columbus *(G-4930)*

H2flow Controls Inc.................................G..... 419 841-7774
Toledo *(G-12981)*

Heilind Electronics Inc............................E..... 440 473-9600
Cleveland *(G-3818)*

Holland Assocts LLC DBA Archou.........F..... 513 891-0006
Cincinnati *(G-2727)*

◆ J & C Group Inc of Ohio.....................G..... 440 205-9658
Mentor *(G-9536)*

Joslyn Sunbank Company LLC...............F..... 805 238-2840
Cleveland *(G-3894)*

◆ Kontron America Incorporated...........G..... 937 324-2420
Springfield *(G-12339)*

M4 Knick LLC..G..... 513 833-2500
Milford *(G-9941)*

◆ Mace Personal Def & SEC Inc............E..... 440 424-5321
Cleveland *(G-3978)*

Mjo Industries Inc...................................D..... 800 590-4055
Huber Heights *(G-7822)*

Pemro Corporation..................................F..... 800 440-5441
Cleveland *(G-4151)*

▲ Pepperl + Fuchs Inc..........................C..... 330 425-3555
Twinsburg *(G-13352)*

◆ Premier Farnell Holding Inc...............E..... 330 523-4273
Richfield *(G-11597)*

Pro Oncall Technologies LLC..................F..... 614 761-1400
Dublin *(G-6335)*

Projects Unlimited Inc.............................C..... 937 918-2200
Dayton *(G-5968)*

Quasonix Inc...E..... 513 942-1287
West Chester *(G-14058)*

Ray Communications Inc.........................G..... 330 686-0226
Stow *(G-12453)*

Rixan Associates Inc...............................E..... 937 438-3005
Dayton *(G-5984)*

▲ S-Tek Inc...G..... 440 439-8232
Twinsburg *(G-13373)*

Sage Integration Holdings LLC...............E..... 330 733-8183
Kent *(G-8072)*

Securcom Inc...E..... 419 628-1049
Minster *(G-10065)*

Smithco Distributing................................E..... 419 367-7685
Liberty Center *(G-8376)*

Spirit Avionics Ltd...................................F..... 614 237-4271
Columbus *(G-5284)*

▲ Standex Electronics Inc.....................D..... 513 871-3777
Fairfield *(G-6778)*

Wes-Garde Components Group Inc.......G..... 614 885-0319
Westerville *(G-14280)*

Wurth Electronics Ics Inc.......................G..... 937 415-7700
Miamisburg *(G-9754)*

5072 Hardware

▲ Akko Fastener Inc...............................F..... 513 489-8300
Middletown *(G-9841)*

▲ Atlas Bolt & Screw Company LLC.......C..... 419 289-6171
Ashland *(G-519)*

Barnes Group Inc.....................................C..... 419 891-9292
Maumee *(G-9264)*

Cammel Saw Company.............................F..... 330 477-3764
Canton *(G-1851)*

Chrisnik Inc...G..... 513 738-2920
Okeana *(G-10927)*

▲ Custer Products Limited.....................F..... 330 490-3158
Massillon *(G-9184)*

Diy Holster LLC..G..... 419 921-2168
Elyria *(G-6520)*

DL Schwartz Co LLC................................G..... 260 692-1464
Hicksville *(G-7647)*

Elliott Tool Technologies Ltd...................D..... 937 253-6133
Dayton *(G-5763)*

◆ Facil North America Inc......................C..... 330 487-2500
Twinsburg *(G-13302)*

◆ G & S Metal Products Co Inc..............C..... 216 441-0700
Cleveland *(G-3748)*

▲ Iwata Bolt USA Inc.............................F..... 513 942-5050
Fairfield *(G-6747)*

Khempco Bldg Sup Co Ltd Partnr...........D..... 740 549-0465
Delaware *(G-6159)*

▲ Lckbm Company..................................D..... 419 636-4555
Bryan *(G-1648)*

▲ Matco Tools Corporation.....................B..... 330 929-4949
Stow *(G-12440)*

Maumee Machine & Tool Corp.................E..... 419 385-2501
Toledo *(G-13048)*

National Tool & Equipment Inc................F..... 330 629-8665
Youngstown *(G-14903)*

◆ Noco Company......................................D..... 216 464-8131
Glenwillow *(G-7286)*

▲ Norbar Torque Tools Inc.....................F..... 440 953-1175
Willoughby *(G-14495)*

▲ Ohashi Technica USA Inc....................E..... 740 965-5115
Sunbury *(G-12671)*

▲ Paulin Industries Inc..........................E..... 216 433-7633
Parma *(G-11134)*

▲ Shook Manufactured Pdts Inc.............G..... 330 848-9780
Akron *(G-311)*

◆ Specialty Hardware Inc.......................G..... 216 291-1160
Cleveland *(G-4319)*

State Industrial Products Corp.................D..... 740 929-6370
Hebron *(G-7637)*

◆ State Industrial Products Corp............B..... 877 747-6986
Cleveland *(G-4329)*

Superior Caster Inc.................................F..... 513 539-8980
Middletown *(G-9896)*

Twin Cities Concrete Co..........................F..... 330 343-4491
Dover *(G-6266)*

Twin Ventures Inc...................................F..... 330 405-3838
Twinsburg *(G-13388)*

Uhrichsville Carbide Inc..........................F..... 740 922-9197
Uhrichsville *(G-13409)*

◆ Waxman Industries Inc.......................C..... 440 439-1830
Bedford *(G-1065)*

5074 Plumbing and hydronic heating supplies

Accurate Mechanical Inc.........................D..... 740 681-1332
Lancaster *(G-8174)*

Carter-Jones Lumber Company...............E..... 440 834-8164
Middlefield *(G-9785)*

▲ Chandler Systems Incorporated.........D..... 888 363-9434
Ashland *(G-528)*

Columbus Pipe and Equipment Co..........F..... 614 444-7871
Columbus *(G-4831)*

▲ Enting Water Conditioning Inc...........E..... 937 294-5100
Moraine *(G-10160)*

Famous Industries Inc............................E..... 330 535-1811
Akron *(G-145)*

Famous Realty Cleveland Inc..................F..... 740 685-2533
Byesville *(G-1712)*

Ferguson Enterprises LLC.................... G 216 635-2493
Parma (G-11131)

Ferguson Fire Fabrication Inc................. E 614 299-2070
Columbus (G-4923)

Hess Advanced Solutions Llc............... G 937 829-4794
Dayton (G-5809)

Hombre Capital Inc........................... F 440 838-5335
Brecksville (G-1470)

Indelco Custom Products Inc.............. G 216 797-7300
Euclid (G-6654)

◆ Kinetico Incorporated........................B 440 564-9111
Newbury (G-10556)

◆ Mansfield Plumbing Pdts LLC.............A 419 938-5211
Perrysville (G-11282)

Mason Structural Steel LLC.................. E 440 439-1040
Walton Hills (G-13699)

▲ Merit Brass Co.............................. C 216 261-9800
Cleveland (G-4021)

Mssi Group Inc.............................. D 440 439-1040
Walton Hills (G-13701)

▲ Mssk Manufacturing Inc.................. F 330 393-6624
Warren (G-13783)

◆ Oatey Supply Chain Svcs Inc............C 216 267-7100
Cleveland (G-4108)

Parker-Hannifin Corporation............... C 614 279-7070
Columbus (G-5174)

Parker-Hannifin Corporation............... C 937 456-5571
Eaton (G-6462)

Pelton Environmental Pdts Inc.............. G 440 838-1221
Lewis Center (G-8348)

Ppafco Inc.................................... F 614 488-7259
Columbus (G-5201)

R D Baker Enterprises Inc.................. G 937 461-5225
Dayton (G-5971)

Savko Plastic Pipe & Fittings................ F 614 885-8420
Columbus (G-5250)

Trumbull Industries Inc...................... D 330 434-6174
Akron (G-345)

US Water Company LLC..................... G 740 453-0604
Zanesville (G-15053)

◆ Waxman Industries Inc.....................C 440 439-1830
Bedford (G-1065)

▲ Wayne Water Systems Inc............... C 800 237-0987
Harrison (G-7571)

Wolff Bros Supply Inc....................... F 440 327-1650
North Ridgeville (G-10753)

Wsi Seller Inc................................ F 330 379-0270
Akron (G-359)

Zekelman Industries Inc..................... C 740 432-2146
Cambridge (G-1766)

Zurn Industries LLC.......................... F 814 455-0921
Hilliard (G-7712)

5075 Warm air heating and air conditioning

▼ Air-Rite Inc.................................. E 216 228-8200
Cleveland (G-3316)

Cincinnati A Flter Sls Svc Inc............... E 513 242-3400
Cincinnati (G-2466)

Controls and Sheet Metal Inc............... E 513 721-3610
Cincinnati (G-2515)

Daikin Applied Americas Inc............... G 614 351-9862
Westerville (G-14252)

◆ Glt Inc...................................... F 937 237-0055
Dayton (G-5800)

Rel Enterprises Inc.......................... E 216 741-1700
Brooklyn Heights (G-1538)

Shape Supply Inc............................ G 513 863-6695
Hamilton (G-7525)

Style Crest Enterprises Inc.................. E 419 355-8586
Fremont (G-7134)

Swift Filters Inc.............................. E 877 887-9438
Bedford (G-1059)

▼ Verantis Corporation........................ E 440 243-0700
Middleburg Heights (G-9778)

Weather King Heating & AC................. G 330 908-0281
Northfield (G-10799)

Yanfeng Intl Auto Tech US I LL............. E 419 662-4905
Northwood (G-10815)

5078 Refrigeration equipment and supplies

Climate Pros LLC............................ D 216 881-5200
Cleveland (G-3541)

Climate Pros LLC............................ D 330 744-2732
Youngstown (G-14839)

◆ Lvd Acquisition LLC.........................D 614 861-1350
Columbus (G-5077)

◆ Modern Ice Equipment & Sup Co........E 513 367-2101
Cincinnati (G-2885)

▲ Slush Puppie................................ G 513 771-0940
West Chester (G-14147)

The Hattenbach Company................... D 216 881-5200
Cleveland (G-4384)

5082 Construction and mining machinery

▲ Baswa Acoustics North Amer LLC.... F 216 475-7197
Bedford (G-1014)

Bauer Corporation........................... E 800 321-4760
Wooster (G-14624)

Brewpro Inc.................................. G 513 577-7200
Cincinnati (G-2423)

Columbus Pipe and Equipment Co........ F 614 444-7871
Columbus (G-4831)

EZ Grout Corporation Inc................... E 740 962-2024
Malta (G-8745)

Global Energy Partners LLC................ F 419 756-8027
Mansfield (G-8792)

Great Lakes Power Service Co............. F 440 259-0025
Perry (G-11192)

JD Power Systems LLC..................... F 614 317-9394
Hilliard (G-7685)

Koenig Equipment Inc....................... F 937 653-5281
Urbana (G-13472)

La Mfg Inc................................... G 513 577-7200
Cincinnati (G-2810)

McNeilus Truck and Mfg Inc................ G 614 868-0760
Gahanna (G-7165)

◆ Mesa Industries Inc.........................E 513 321-2950
Cincinnati (G-2866)

Murphy Tractor & Eqp Co Inc.............. G 330 220-4999
Brunswick (G-1602)

Murphy Tractor & Eqp Co Inc.............. G 330 477-9304
Canton (G-1954)

Murphy Tractor & Eqp Co Inc.............. G 614 876-1141
Columbus (G-5116)

Murphy Tractor & Eqp Co Inc.............. G 419 221-3666
Lima (G-8434)

Murphy Tractor & Eqp Co Inc.............. G 937 898-4198
Vandalia (G-13573)

◆ Npk Construction Equipment Inc........D 440 232-7900
Bedford (G-1050)

◆ Ohio Machinery Co...........................C 440 526-6200
Broadview Heights (G-1509)

Petrox Inc.................................... F 330 653-5526
Streetsboro (G-12516)

Shearer Farm Inc............................ C 330 345-9023
Wooster (G-14685)

Simpson Strong-Tie Company Inc......... B 614 876-8060
Columbus (G-5271)

Terry Asphalt Materials Inc.................. E 513 874-6192
Hamilton (G-7529)

The Wagner-Smith Company................ B 866 338-0398
Moraine (G-10195)

Thirion Brothers Eqp Co LLC............... G 440 357-8004
Painesville (G-11118)

Unified Scrning Crshing - OH I.............. G 937 836-3201
Englewood (G-6627)

Valence Industrial LLC....................... E 877 330-2354
Sidney (G-12058)

Waco Scaffolding & Equipment Inc........ A 216 749-8900
Cleveland (G-4487)

West Equipment Company Inc.............. G 419 698-1601
Toledo (G-13177)

◆ Winter Equipment Company ....E 440 946-8377
Willoughby (G-14552)

5083 Farm and garden machinery

All Power Equipment LLC.................... F 740 593-3279
Athens (G-632)

◆ Arnold Corporation..........................C 330 225-2600
Valley City (G-13489)

Bortnick Tractor Sales Inc.................. E 330 924-2555
Cortland (G-5442)

Buckeye Companies.......................... E 740 452-3641
Zanesville (G-15000)

◆ Fort Recovery Equipment Inc............G 419 375-1006
Fort Recovery (G-6962)

Franklin Equipment LLC..................... E 614 228-2014
Groveport (G-7435)

Hawthorne Gardening Company............ E 360 883-8846
Marysville (G-9023)

▲ Hawthorne Hydroponics LLC............. F 888 478-6544
Marysville (G-9024)

Karl Kuemmerling Inc....................... F
Massillon (G-9209)

▲ Reberland Equipment Inc................. F 330 698-5883
Apple Creek (G-476)

▲ S I Distributing Inc.......................... F 419 647-4909
Spencerville (G-12240)

Schmidt Machine Company.................. E 419 294-3814
Upper Sandusky (G-13455)

Smg Growing Media Inc..................... F 937 644-0011
Marysville (G-9049)

Yoder & Frey Inc............................. G 419 445-2070
Archbold (G-513)

5084 Industrial machinery and equipment

2e Associates Inc........................... E 440 975-9955
Willoughby (G-14412)

A & A Safety Inc............................. F 937 567-9781
Beavercreek (G-987)

A & A Safety Inc............................. E 513 943-6100
Amelia (G-425)

A & B Deburring Company................... F 513 723-0444
Cincinnati (G-2323)

▲ Adams Elevator Equipment Co........ D 847 581-2900
Holland (G-7743)

▲ Addition Manufacturing Te............... C 513 228-7000
Lebanon (G-8241)

Addup Inc.................................... E 513 745-4510
Blue Ash (G-1242)

Advanced Green Tech Inc................... G 614 397-8130
Plain City (G-11392)

Advanced Tech Utilization Co............... F 440 238-3770
Strongsville (G-12532)

Aerocontrolex Group Inc.................... D 216 291-6025
South Euclid (G-12216)

◆ Air Technical Industries Inc..............E 440 951-5191
Mentor (G-9474)

Airgas Usa LLC.............................. G 740 353-5710
Portsmouth (G-11463)

Airgas Usa LLC.............................. G 440 232-6397
Twinsburg (G-13270)

Alba Manufacturing Inc..................... D 513 874-0551
Fairfield (G-6708)

Aldrich Chemical............................. D 937 859-1808
Miamisburg (G-9663)

◆ Alfons Haar Inc.................................E 937 560-2031
Springboro *(G-12246)*

Alkon Corporation.............................F 614 799-6650
Dublin *(G-6274)*

▲ Alkon Corporation............................D 419 355-9111
Fremont *(G-7090)*

◆ American Rescue Technology Inc......F 937 293-6240
Dayton *(G-5655)*

▲ American Solving Inc........................G 440 234-7373
Brookpark *(G-1543)*

◆ Ampac Packaging LLC........................C 513 671-1777
Cincinnati *(G-2366)*

Anderson & Vreeland Inc..................D 419 636-5002
Bryan *(G-1629)*

ARC Solutions LLC............................E 419 542-9272
Hicksville *(G-7646)*

▲ Armour Spray Systems Inc................F 216 398-3838
Cleveland *(G-3366)*

Atlas Machine and Supply Inc............E 502 584-7262
Hamilton *(G-7467)*

▲ Ats Systems Oregon Inc....................F 541 738-0932
Lewis Center *(G-8324)*

Axion International Inc.......................G 740 452-2500
Zanesville *(G-14989)*

▲ Belle Center Air Tool Co Inc..............G 937 464-7474
Belle Center *(G-1094)*

▲ Bilz Vibration Technology Inc............F 330 468-2459
Macedonia *(G-8678)*

Bionix Safety Technologies Ltd..........E 419 727-0552
Maumee *(G-9267)*

Bobco Enterprises Inc.......................F 419 867-3560
Toledo *(G-12899)*

▼ Boggs Graphics Equipment LLC........E 888 837-8101
Maple Heights *(G-8878)*

Bollin & Sons Inc..............................E 419 693-6573
Toledo *(G-12900)*

Breaker Technology Inc.....................F 440 248-7168
Solon *(G-12090)*

Brown Industrial Inc..........................E 937 693-3838
Botkins *(G-1397)*

Bud Corp...G 740 967-9992
Johnstown *(G-7994)*

Bulk Carriers Service Inc...................G 330 339-3333
New Philadelphia *(G-10435)*

Cascade Corporation.........................E 419 425-3675
Findlay *(G-6850)*

◆ Chemineer Inc...................................C 937 454-3200
Dayton *(G-5700)*

Cintas Corporation............................D 513 631-5750
Cincinnati *(G-2494)*

◆ Cintas Corporation............................A 513 459-1200
Mason *(G-9086)*

Cintas Corporation No 2.....................D 330 966-7800
Canton *(G-1865)*

Combined Tech Group Inc..................E 937 274-4866
Dayton *(G-5706)*

Contitech Usa LLC.............................C 937 644-8900
Marysville *(G-9016)*

▲ Control Line Equipment Inc...............F 216 433-7766
Cleveland *(G-3565)*

Coperion Process Solutions LLC........F 513 576-9200
Solon *(G-12098)*

Cortest Inc..F 440 942-1235
Willoughby *(G-14442)*

Country Sales & Service LLC.............F 330 683-2500
Orrville *(G-10978)*

Ctm Integration Incorporated............E 330 332-1800
Salem *(G-11774)*

Cummins Inc......................................F 614 771-1000
Hilliard *(G-7679)*

Dearing Compressor and Pu..............G 330 783-2258
Youngstown *(G-14847)*

Delille Oxygen Company.....................G 937 325-9595
Springfield *(G-12300)*

▲ Dengensha America Corporation......F 440 439-8081
Bedford *(G-1025)*

▲ Depot Direct Inc................................E 419 661-1233
Perrysburg *(G-11215)*

Digilube Systems Inc.........................F 937 748-2209
Springboro *(G-12250)*

▲ Dura Magnetics Inc...........................F 419 882-0591
Sylvania *(G-12706)*

Eaton Corporation.............................F 216 523-5000
Willoughby *(G-14455)*

Edi Holding Company LLC..................G 740 401-4000
Belpre *(G-1146)*

Electrnic Dsign For Indust Inc...........E 740 401-4000
Belpre *(G-1147)*

Eltool Corporation.............................G 513 723-1772
Mansfield *(G-8785)*

◆ EMI Corp...D 937 596-5511
Jackson Center *(G-7963)*

Equipment Guys Inc...........................G 614 871-9220
Newark *(G-10501)*

▲ Equipment Mfrs Intl Inc.....................E 216 651-6700
Cleveland *(G-3682)*

◆ Esko-Graphics Inc.............................D 937 454-1721
Miamisburg *(G-9691)*

Exomet Inc..F 440 593-1161
Conneaut *(G-5400)*

Expert Crane Inc................................D 216 451-9900
Wellington *(G-13886)*

Fastener Industries Inc.......................E 440 891-2031
Berea *(G-1172)*

◆ Fastener Industries Inc.......................G 440 243-0034
Berea *(G-1173)*

▲ Fcx Performance Inc..........................E 614 253-1996
Columbus *(G-4922)*

Fluid Power Solutions LLC..................G 614 777-8954
Hilliard *(G-7682)*

Forte Industrial Equipmen..................E 513 398-2800
Mason *(G-9100)*

Freeman Manufacturing & Sup Co......E 440 934-1902
Avon *(G-727)*

G & P Construction LLC......................E 855 494-4830
North Royalton *(G-10762)*

G W Cobb Co......................................F 216 341-0100
Cleveland *(G-3751)*

GE Vernova International LLC..............G 330 963-2066
Twinsburg *(G-13308)*

Ged Holdings Inc...............................G 330 963-5401
Twinsburg *(G-13309)*

◆ General Data Company Inc................B 513 752-7978
Cincinnati *(G-2304)*

Gerow Equipment Company Inc..........G 216 383-8800
Cleveland *(G-3772)*

▲ Giant Industries Inc...........................E 419 531-4600
Toledo *(G-12975)*

Glavin Industries Inc..........................E 440 349-0049
Solon *(G-12115)*

▲ Gokoh Corporation............................F 937 339-4977
Troy *(G-13218)*

Gorman-Rupp Company......................G 419 755-1245
Mansfield *(G-8795)*

Grand Harbor Yacht Sales & Svc........G 440 442-2919
Cleveland *(G-3784)*

▲ Great Lakes Power Products Inc........D 440 951-5111
Madison *(G-8730)*

Grenga Machine & Welding.................F 330 743-1113
Youngstown *(G-14871)*

▲ Groeneveld-Beka Usa Inc..................G 330 225-4949
Sharon Center *(G-11941)*

▲ Grt Utilicorp Inc................................E 330 264-8444
Wooster *(G-14646)*

▲ Hammelmann Corporation.................F 937 859-8777
Miamisburg *(G-9695)*

Hannon Company................................D 330 456-4728
Canton *(G-1908)*

▲ Hawthorne Hydroponics LLC.............F 888 478-6544
Marysville *(G-9024)*

Hendrickson International Corp...........D 740 929-5600
Hebron *(G-7617)*

◆ Hiab USA Inc.....................................D 419 482-6000
Perrysburg *(G-11228)*

◆ Hickman Williams & Company............F 513 621-1946
Cincinnati *(G-2721)*

Hydraulic Manifolds USA LLC............E 973 728-1214
Stow *(G-12436)*

Hydraulic Parts Store Inc...................G 330 364-6667
New Philadelphia *(G-10449)*

Hydro Supply Co................................G 740 454-3842
Zanesville *(G-15020)*

◆ Hydrotech Inc....................................D 888 651-5712
West Chester *(G-14126)*

IBI Brake Products Inc.......................G 440 543-7962
Chagrin Falls *(G-2166)*

▲ Ic-Fluid Power Inc.............................F 419 661-8811
Rossford *(G-11658)*

Imco Carbide Tool Inc........................D 419 661-6313
Perrysburg *(G-11230)*

◆ Impact Products LLC..........................C 419 841-2891
Toledo *(G-13001)*

Industrial Parts Depot LLC.................G 440 237-9164
North Royalton *(G-10766)*

Innovative Handling LLC.....................E 419 882-7480
Sylvania *(G-12712)*

Instrumentors Inc..............................G 440 238-3430
Strongsville *(G-12568)*

Intelligrated Inc.................................A 513 874-0788
West Chester *(G-14127)*

▲ Intelligrated Systems Inc..................A 866 936-7300
Mason *(G-9113)*

Intelligrated Systems LLC..................A 513 701-7300
West Chester *(G-14128)*

◆ Intelligrated Systems Ohio LLC.........A 513 701-7300
Mason *(G-9114)*

Interstate Pump Company Inc............G 330 222-1006
Salem *(G-11789)*

Interstate Tool Corporation................E 216 671-1077
Cleveland *(G-3866)*

J & S Tool Corporation.......................G 216 676-8330
Lorain *(G-8558)*

▲ Jay Dee Service Corporation.............G 330 425-1546
Macedonia *(G-8699)*

Jcl Equipment Co Inc.........................G 937 374-1010
Xenia *(G-14767)*

Jed Industries Inc..............................F 440 639-9973
Grand River *(G-7310)*

▲ Jergens Inc.......................................C 216 486-5540
Cleveland *(G-3885)*

Jis Distribution LLC...........................F 216 706-6552
Cleveland *(G-3888)*

▲ Joseph Industries Inc........................D 330 528-0091
Streetsboro *(G-12507)*

JPS Technologies Inc.........................F 513 984-6400
Blue Ash *(G-1292)*

JPS Technologies Inc.........................F 513 984-6400
Blue Ash *(G-1291)*

Jsh International LLC..........................G 330 734-0251
Akron *(G-190)*

Kecamm LLC......................................G 330 527-2918
Garrettsville *(G-7222)*

◆ Kinetics Noise Control Inc.................C 614 889-0480
Dublin *(G-6316)*

Kingsly Compression Inc....................G 740 439-0772
Cambridge *(G-1747)*

Kolinahr Systems Inc .... F 513 745-9401
Blue Ash (G-1294)

Krupp Rubber Machinery .... G 330 864-0800
Akron (G-199)

▲ Kyocera SGS Precision Tls Inc .... E 330 688-6667
Cuyahoga Falls (G-5557)

◆ Lawrence Industries Inc .... E 216 518-7000
Cleveland (G-3946)

▲ Lefeld Welding & Stl Sups Inc .... E 419 678-2397
Coldwater (G-4580)

Linde Gas & Equipment Inc .... E 513 821-2192
Cincinnati (G-2823)

Linden-Two Inc .... E 330 928-4064
Cuyahoga Falls (G-5559)

▲ Logitech Inc .... E 614 871-2822
Grove City (G-7395)

Lubrisource Inc .... F 937 432-9292
Middletown (G-9872)

Maag Automatik Inc .... E 330 677-2225
Kent (G-8047)

▲ Maintenance Repair Supply Inc .... G 740 922-3006
Midvale (G-9913)

Marengo Fabricated Steel Ltd .... F 800 919-2652
Cardington (G-2055)

Martin Allen Trailer LLC .... G 330 942-0217
Akron (G-223)

Martin Diesel Inc .... E 419 782-9911
Defiance (G-6120)

Matheson Tri-Gas Inc .... F 419 865-8881
Holland (G-7772)

Matheson Tri-Gas Inc .... E 330 425-4407
Twinsburg (G-13335)

Mfh Partners Inc .... B 440 461-4100
Cleveland (G-4025)

▲ Mid-State Sales Inc .... D 614 864-1811
Columbus (G-5099)

◆ Midlands Millroom Supply Inc .... E 330 453-9100
Canton (G-1949)

Midwest Conveyor Products Inc .... E 419 281-1235
Ashland (G-552)

Millwood Inc .... E 513 860-4567
West Chester (G-14030)

Minerva Welding and Fabg Inc .... E 330 868-7731
Minerva (G-10043)

Mitsubishi Elc Automtn Inc .... E 937 492-3058
Sidney (G-12035)

Modern Machine Development .... F 937 253-4576
Dayton (C 5801)

Monaghan & Associates Inc .... F 937 253-7706
Dayton (G-5892)

Monode Marking Products Inc .... E 440 975-8802
Mentor (G-9567)

Motionsource International LLC .... F 440 287-7037
Solon (G-12153)

◆ Multi Products Company .... F 330 674-5981
Millersburg (G-10003)

National Tool & Equipment Inc .... F 330 629-8665
Youngstown (G-14903)

Neff Machinery and Supplies .... G 740 454-0128
Zanesville (G-15031)

Neil R Scholl Inc .... F 740 653-6593
Lancaster (G-8213)

Oak View Enterprises Inc .... E 513 860-4446
Bucyrus (G-1685)

▲ Off Contact Inc .... F 419 255-5546
Toledo (G-13071)

Ohio Hydraulics Inc .... E 513 771-2590
Cincinnati (G-2924)

Otis Elevator Company .... E 216 573-2333
Cleveland (G-4127)

◆ Park Corporation .... B 216 267-4870
Medina (G-9434)

Parker-Hannifin Corporation .... F 216 433-1795
Cleveland (G-4144)

Paul Peterson Company .... F 614 486-4375
Columbus (G-5178)

◆ PE Usa LLC .... F 513 771-7374
Cincinnati (G-2950)

Pfpc Enterprises Inc .... G 513 941-6200
Cincinnati (G-2960)

▲ Pines Manufacturing Inc .... E 440 835-5553
Westlake (G-14324)

◆ Plastic Process Equipment Inc .... E 216 367-7000
Macedonia (G-8706)

Pomacon Inc .... F 330 273-1576
Brunswick (G-1606)

▲ Power Distributors LLC .... D 614 876-3533
Columbus (G-5200)

Powerbilt Mtl Hdlg Sltions LLC .... D 937 592-5660
Bellefontaine (G-1115)

Powerclean Equipment Company .... E 513 202-0001
Cleves (G-4547)

▲ Princeton Tool Inc .... C 440 290-8666
Mentor (G-9592)

Process Dynamics Inc .... G 330 686-2597
Stow (G-12452)

Progressive Mfg Co Inc .... G 330 784-4717
Akron (G-269)

▲ Prospect Mold & Die Company .... C 330 929-3311
Cuyahoga Falls (G-5566)

R & M Fluid Power Inc .... E 330 758-2766
Youngstown (G-14922)

R and J Corporation .... E 440 871-6009
Westlake (G-14326)

Ralph Robinson Inc .... G 740 385-2747
Logan (G-8524)

Rayhaven Group Inc .... G 330 659-3183
Richfield (G-11598)

▲ Ready Technology Inc .... F 937 866-7200
Dayton (G-5978)

◆ Reduction Engineering Inc .... E 330 677-2225
Kent (G-8067)

Rel Enterprises Inc .... E 216 741-1700
Brooklyn Heights (G-1538)

Remtec Engineering .... F 513 860-4299
Mason (G-9142)

Rixan Associates Inc .... E 937 438-3005
Dayton (G-5984)

Rnm Holdings Inc .... F 614 444-5556
Columbus (C 5232)

Rnm Holdings Inc .... F 419 867-8712
Holland (G-7782)

▲ Robeck Fluid Power Co .... D 330 562-1140
Aurora (G-687)

◆ Rolls-Royce Energy Systems Inc .... A 703 834-1700
Mount Vernon (G-10263)

▲ Rubber City Machinery Corp .... G 330 434-3500
Akron (G-293)

Rumpke Transportation Co LLC .... F 513 851-0122
Cincinnati (G-3058)

Ryanworks Inc .... E 937 438-1282
Dayton (G-5990)

Salem Welding & Supply Company .... G 330 332-4517
Salem (G-11811)

Samsco Corp .... F 216 400-8207
Cleveland (G-4271)

Samuel Son & Co (usa) Inc .... D 740 522-2500
Heath (G-7604)

▲ Sausser Steel Company Inc .... G 419 422-9632
Findlay (G-6916)

Sequa Can Machinery Inc .... E 330 493-0444
Canton (G-2002)

▲ Siebtechnik Tema Inc .... E 513 489-7811
Cincinnati (G-3088)

South Shore Controls Inc .... E 440 259-2500
Mentor (G-9618)

Stanley Bittinger .... G 740 942-4302
Cadiz (G-1720)

▼ Stanley Industries Inc .... F 216 475-4000
Cleveland (G-4327)

Stanwade Metal Products Inc .... E 330 772-2421
Hartford (G-7573)

Starkey Machinery Inc .... E 419 468-2560
Galion (G-7199)

Super Systems Inc .... E 513 772-0060
Cincinnati (G-3128)

System Seals Inc .... E 216 220-1800
Brecksville (G-1481)

▲ System Seals LLC .... E 440 735-0200
Cleveland (G-4359)

T & D Fabricating Inc .... E 440 951-5646
Eastlake (G-6445)

▲ Taiyo America Inc .... F 419 300-8811
Saint Marys (G-11753)

Tech Products Corporation .... F 937 438-1100
Miamisburg (G-9744)

Tilt-Or-Lift Inc .... G 419 893-6944
Maumee (G-9326)

Toga-Pak Inc .... E 937 294-7311
Dayton (G-6056)

Tooltex Inc .... F 614 539-3222
Circleville (G-3267)

◆ Transducers Direct Llc .... F 513 247-0601
Cincinnati (G-3166)

▲ Transnorm System Inc .... D 972 606-0303
Mason (G-9163)

◆ Trewbric III Inc .... E 614 444-2184
Columbus (G-5330)

Tri State Equipment Company .... G 513 738-7227
Shandon (G-11935)

Tri-Mac Mfg & Svcs Co .... F 513 896-4445
Hamilton (G-7533)

United Hydraulics .... G 440 585-0906
Wickliffe (G-14398)

Valv-Trol LLC .... F 330 686-2800
Stow (G-12469)

▲ Valve Related Controls Inc .... F 513 677-8724
Loveland (G-8655)

▲ Venco Venturo Industries LLC .... E 513 772-8448
Cincinnati (G-3197)

Venturo Manufacturing Inc .... F 513 772-8448
Cincinnati (C 3100)

Versatile Automation Tech Corp .... G 330 220-2600
Brunswick (G-1622)

▲ Versatile Automation Tech Ltd .... G 440 589-6700
Solon (G-12202)

Weld-Action Company Inc .... G 330 372-1063
Warren (G-13813)

Weldco Inc .... E 513 744-9353
Cincinnati (G-3218)

Welders Supply Inc .... F 216 241-1696
Cleveland (G-4500)

Western Branch Diesel LLC .... F 330 454-8800
Canton (G-2047)

Wolf Machine Company .... E 513 791-5194
Blue Ash (G-1352)

Worker Automation Inc .... G 937 473-2111
Dayton (G-6086)

Wright Brothers Inc .... F 513 731-2222
Cincinnati (G-3232)

5085 Industrial supplies

Airgas Usa LLC .... G 440 232-6397
Twinsburg (G-13270)

Akron Belting & Supply Company .... G 330 633-8212
Akron (G-25)

Alb Tyler Holdings Inc.................... G 440 946-7171
Mentor *(G-9475)*

Alkon Corporation.......................... F 614 799-6650
Dublin *(G-6274)*

▲ Alkon Corporation........................ D 419 355-9111
Fremont *(G-7090)*

▲ All Ohio Threaded Rod Co Inc........ E 216 426-1800
Cleveland *(G-3326)*

◆ Alliance Knife Inc........................ E 513 367-9000
Harrison *(G-7542)*

Allied Shipping and Packa............. F 937 222-7422
Moraine *(G-10144)*

Alro Steel Corporation.................... E 614 878-7271
Columbus *(G-4690)*

Alro Steel Corporation.................... D 419 720-5300
Toledo *(G-12871)*

▲ Anchor Flange Company............... D 513 527-3512
Cincinnati *(G-2369)*

Andre Corporation.......................... E 574 293-0207
Mason *(G-9061)*

Aqua Technology Group LLC.......... G 513 298-1183
West Chester *(G-13941)*

▲ ARC Abrasives Inc...................... D 800 888-4885
Troy *(G-13201)*

▲ Atlas Bolt & Screw Company LLC... C 419 289-6171
Ashland *(G-519)*

▲ Atwood Rope Manufacturing Inc...... E 614 920-0534
Canal Winchester *(G-1784)*

B W Grinding Co............................. E 419 923-1376
Lyons *(G-8673)*

Bearings Manufacturing Company... F 440 846-5517
Strongsville *(G-12544)*

Brimar Packaging Inc..................... E 440 934-3080
Avon *(G-717)*

▲ C B Mfg & Sls Co Inc.................. D 937 866-5986
Miamisburg *(G-9678)*

◆ Carbon Enterprises Inc................ G 740 420-6472
Circleville *(G-3249)*

Chardon Tool & Supply Co Inc........ E 440 286-6440
Chardon *(G-2200)*

Ci Disposition Co........................... F 216 587-5200
Brooklyn Heights *(G-1530)*

Cincinnati Abrasive Supply Co........ G 513 941-8866
Hamilton *(G-7478)*

◆ Cleveland Supplyone Inc............. E 216 514-7000
Cleveland *(G-3527)*

Cmt Machining & Fabg LLC............. F 937 652-3740
Urbana *(G-13459)*

Commercial Electric Pdts Corp....... E 216 241-2886
Cleveland *(G-3552)*

Cornwell Quality Tools Company..... D 330 628-2627
Mogadore *(G-10071)*

Crane Pumps & Systems Inc........... F 937 773-2442
Piqua *(G-11340)*

▲ Crawford Products Inc................. E 614 890-1822
Columbus *(G-4859)*

▲ Creative Plastic Concepts LLC..... E 419 927-9588
Sycamore *(G-12699)*

Dadco Inc..................................... F 513 489-2244
Cincinnati *(G-2539)*

◆ Datwyler Sling Sltions USA Inc..... D 937 387-2800
Vandalia *(G-13554)*

Dayton Industrial Drum Inc............. E 937 253-8933
Dayton *(G-5608)*

Dayton Stencil Works Company....... F 937 223-3233
Dayton *(G-5739)*

Dearing Compressor and Pu.......... E 330 783-2258
Youngstown *(G-14847)*

Delille Oxygen Company................ E 614 444-1177
Columbus *(G-4876)*

Dixon Valve & Coupling Co LLC....... F 330 425-3000
Twinsburg *(G-13296)*

Dynatech Systems Inc.................... F 440 365-1774
Elyria *(G-6523)*

◆ Eagle Industrial Truck Mfg LLC..... E 419 866-6301
Swanton *(G-12683)*

Edward W Daniel LLC..................... F 440 647-1960
Wellington *(G-13885)*

Elyria Spring Spclty Holdg Inc......... G 440 323-5502
Cleveland *(G-3664)*

▲ ET&f Fastening Systems Inc........ G 800 248-2376
Solon *(G-12108)*

Evans Adhesive Corporation........... E 614 451-2665
Columbus *(G-4912)*

◆ Facil North America Inc............... C 330 487-2500
Twinsburg *(G-13302)*

▲ Fcx Performance Inc.................... E 614 253-1996
Columbus *(G-4922)*

First Francis Company Inc.............. E 440 352-8927
Painesville *(G-11087)*

◆ Forge Industries Inc.................... A 330 960-2468
Youngstown *(G-14857)*

▲ Fouty & Company Inc................... E 419 693-0017
Oregon *(G-10961)*

◆ Ges Graphite Inc........................ E 216 658-6660
Parma *(G-11132)*

▲ Gokoh Corporation...................... F 937 339-4977
Troy *(G-13218)*

▲ Great Lakes Fasteners Inc............ E 330 425-4488
Twinsburg *(G-13312)*

▲ Great Lakes Power Products Inc..... D 440 951-5111
Madison *(G-8730)*

▲ H & D Steel Service Inc............... E 800 666-3390
North Royalton *(G-10764)*

H3d Tool Corporation..................... E 740 498-5181
Newcomerstown *(G-10570)*

◆ Hickman Williams & Company....... F 513 621-1946
Cincinnati *(G-2721)*

▲ High Quality Tools Inc.................. F 440 975-9684
Eastlake *(G-6433)*

▲ HMS Industries LLC.................... F 440 899-0001
Westlake *(G-14306)*

Horwitz & Pintis Co........................ F 419 666-2220
Toledo *(G-12996)*

Hydraulic Manifolds USA LLC......... E 973 728-1214
Stow *(G-12436)*

▲ Ig Watteeuw Usa LLC.................. F 740 588-1722
Zanesville *(G-15021)*

Indelco Custom Products Inc.......... G 216 797-7300
Euclid *(G-6654)*

▼ Industrial Connections Inc........... G 330 274-2155
Mantua *(G-8869)*

Industrial Mold Inc......................... E 330 425-7374
Twinsburg *(G-13320)*

Interstate Pump Company Inc......... G 330 222-1006
Salem *(G-11789)*

Interstate Sign Products Inc........... G 419 683-1962
Crestline *(G-5503)*

▼ Japo Inc..................................... E 614 263-2850
Columbus *(G-5032)*

Jet Rubber Company...................... E 330 325-1821
Rootstown *(G-11648)*

◆ Kaufman Container Company........ C 216 898-2000
Cleveland *(G-3908)*

▲ Kenag Inc................................... E 419 281-1204
Ashland *(G-546)*

◆ Lancaster Commercial Pdts LLC... E 844 324-1444
Columbus *(G-5062)*

◆ Lawrence Industries Inc.............. E 216 518-7000
Cleveland *(G-3946)*

▲ Logan Clutch Corporation............ E 440 808-4258
Cleveland *(G-3966)*

Lynk Packaging Inc........................ E 330 562-8080
Aurora *(G-677)*

▲ Maintenance Repair Supply Inc..... G 740 922-3006
Midvale *(G-9913)*

Maumee Hose & Fitting Inc............. G 419 893-7252
Maumee *(G-9308)*

Mauser Usa LLC............................ D 740 397-1762
Mount Vernon *(G-10251)*

▲ McNeil Industries Inc................... E 440 951-7756
Painesville *(G-11099)*

McWane Inc................................... B 740 622-6651
Coshocton *(G-5459)*

◆ Mesa Industries Inc.................... E 513 321-2950
Cincinnati *(G-2866)*

Metzger Machine Co....................... F 513 241-3360
Cincinnati *(G-2873)*

▲ Miba Bearings US LLC................. B 740 962-4242
Mcconnelsville *(G-9364)*

Mid-State Sales Inc........................ G 330 744-2158
Youngstown *(G-14900)*

▲ Mill-Rose Company..................... C 440 255-9171
Mentor *(G-9566)*

Modroto.. G 440 998-1202
Ashtabula *(G-606)*

◆ Namoh Ohio Holdings Inc............ G
Norwood *(G-10869)*

Netherland Rubber Company.......... E 513 733-0883
Cincinnati *(G-2899)*

Newact Inc.................................... F 513 321-5177
Batavia *(G-879)*

▲ North Coast Seal Incorporated...... F 216 898-5000
Brookpark *(G-1556)*

◆ NSK Industries Inc..................... D 330 923-4112
Cuyahoga Falls *(G-5563)*

Ohio Drill & Tool Co....................... E 330 525-7717
Homeworth *(G-7806)*

Orbytel Print and Packg Inc............ G 216 267-8734
Cleveland *(G-4123)*

P&E Sales Ltd............................... G 330 829-0100
Alliance *(G-397)*

▲ Pipe Products Inc....................... E 513 587-7532
West Chester *(G-14049)*

◆ Plastic Process Equipment Inc..... E 216 367-7000
Macedonia *(G-8706)*

◆ Pressure Connections Corp.......... D 614 863-6930
Columbus *(G-5204)*

Quad Fluid Dynamics Inc................ F 330 220-3005
Brunswick *(G-1610)*

R C Musson Rubber Co.................. E 330 773-7651
Akron *(G-276)*

▲ RB&w Manufacturing LLC............ G 234 380-8540
Streetsboro *(G-12519)*

Ruthman Pump and Engineering...... G 937 783-2411
Blanchester *(G-1238)*

▲ Sabco Industries Inc.................... E 419 531-5347
Toledo *(G-13120)*

▲ Samsel Rope & Marine Supply Co... E 216 241-0333
Cleveland *(G-4272)*

Samuel Son & Co (usa) Inc............. D 740 522-2500
Heath *(G-7604)*

▲ Save Edge Inc............................ E 937 376-8268
Xenia *(G-14774)*

Service Spring Corp....................... E 419 867-0212
Maumee *(G-9317)*

Shaq Inc....................................... D 770 427-0402
Beachwood *(G-949)*

Sign Source USA Inc..................... D 419 224-1130
Lima *(G-8449)*

Smithco Distributing....................... E 419 367-7685
Liberty Center *(G-8376)*

Solo Products Inc.......................... F 513 321-7884
Cincinnati *(G-3100)*

▲ SSP Fittings Corp....................... D 330 425-4250
Twinsburg *(G-13379)*

◆ Stafast Products Inc................E 440 357-5546
Painesville *(G-11111)*

Steam Trbine Altrntive Rsrces...............E 740 387-5535
Marion *(G-9001)*

▼ Stud Welding Associates Inc........D 440 783-3160
Strongsville *(G-12607)*

▲ Summers Acquisition Corp..............E 216 941-7700
Cleveland *(G-4341)*

Superior Holding LLC......................G 216 651-9400
Cleveland *(G-4344)*

Superior Products LLC....................D 216 651-9400
Cleveland *(G-4347)*

Supply Technologies LLC.................G 937 898-5795
Dayton *(G-6032)*

◆ Supply Technologies LLC................C 440 947-2100
Cleveland *(G-4351)*

▲ TCH Industries Incorporated...........F 330 487-5155
Twinsburg *(G-13383)*

▲ The Cornwell Quality Tool...............D 330 336-3506
Wadsworth *(G-13674)*

◆ The Dyson Corporation...................C 440 946-3500
Painesville *(G-11116)*

◆ The Kindt-Collins Company LLC........D 216 252-4122
Cleveland *(G-4387)*

◆ Timken Company.........................A 234 262-3000
North Canton *(G-10673)*

▲ Tlg Cochran Inc..........................E 440 914-1122
Twinsburg *(G-13385)*

◆ Tolco Corporation........................E 419 241-1113
Toledo *(G-13147)*

Toledo Tarp Service Inc..................E 419 837-5098
Perrysburg *(G-11276)*

Trent Manufacturing Company...........G 216 391-1551
Mentor *(G-9644)*

◆ Tricor Industrial Inc.....................D 330 264-3299
Wooster *(G-14692)*

United Tool Supply Inc...................G 513 752-6000
Cincinnati *(G-2317)*

Valv-Trol LLC.............................F 330 686-2800
Stow *(G-12469)*

▲ Victory White Metal Company...........D 216 271-1400
Cleveland *(G-4472)*

◆ Watteredge LLC..........................D 440 933-6110
Avon Lake *(G-773)*

Wesco Distribution Inc...................F 419 666-1670
Northwood *(G-10813)*

Wulco Inc.................................D 513 379-6115
Hamilton *(G-7339)*

▲ Wulco Inc................................D 513 679-2600
Cincinnati *(G-3235)*

Youngstown Bolt & Supply Co............G 330 799-3201
Youngstown *(G-14967)*

5087 Service establishment equipment

A-1 Sprinkler Company Inc...............D 937 859-6198
Miamisburg *(G-9659)*

▲ Action Coupling & Eqp Inc..............D 330 279-4242
Holmesville *(G-7793)*

AIN Industries Inc.......................G 440 781-0950
Cleveland *(G-3315)*

▲ Alco-Chem Inc............................E 330 253-3535
Akron *(G-47)*

Allen Enterprises Inc.....................E 740 532-5913
Ironton *(G-7928)*

Baxter Burial Vault Svc Inc...............F 513 641-1010
Cincinnati *(G-2403)*

Beaute Asylum LLC.......................F 419 377-9933
Toledo *(G-12894)*

Case Ohio Burial Co......................F 440 779-1992
Cleveland *(G-3474)*

Chem-Sales Inc............................F
Toledo *(G-12918)*

Cooper Enterprises Inc...................D 419 347-5232
Shelby *(G-11968)*

Cummins - Allison Corp...................G 440 824-5050
Cleveland *(G-3579)*

Excalibur Barber LLC.....................F 330 729-9006
Boardman *(G-1371)*

Fire Safety Services Inc..................F 937 686-2000
Huntsville *(G-7864)*

Friends Service Co Inc...................F 800 427-1704
Dayton *(G-5785)*

Friends Service Co Inc...................F 419 427-1704
Findlay *(G-6869)*

Gt Industrial Supply Inc..................F 513 771-7000
Cincinnati *(G-2695)*

◆ Impact Products LLC.....................C 419 841-2891
Toledo *(G-13001)*

Jls Funeral Home.........................F 614 625-1220
Columbus *(G-5040)*

Johnsons Fire Equipment Co.............F 740 357-4916
Wellston *(G-13908)*

K-O-K Products Inc.......................F 740 548-0526
Galena *(G-7173)*

◆ Majestic Manufacturing Inc..............E 330 457-2447
New Waterford *(G-10488)*

Martin-Brower Company LLC..............C 513 773-2301
West Chester *(G-14027)*

National Pride Equipment Inc.............F 419 289-2886
Mansfield *(G-8837)*

▲ Pioneer Manufacturing Inc..............D 216 671-5500
Cleveland *(G-4167)*

Pneumatic Specialties Inc................G 440 729-4400
Chesterland *(G-2239)*

Service Station Equipment Co............G 216 431-6100
Cleveland *(G-4286)*

▼ Sutphen Corporation.....................C 800 726-7030
Dublin *(G-6353)*

◆ Wasserstrom Company...................B 614 228-6525
Columbus *(G-5356)*

5088 Transportation equipment and supplies

American Power LLC......................F 937 235-0418
Dayton *(G-5654)*

Amsted Industries Incorporated..........D 614 836-2323
Groveport *(G-7422)*

◆ Bendix Coml Vhcl Systems LLC.........B 440 329-9000
Avon *(G-716)*

◆ Buck Equipment Inc......................E 614 539-3039
Grove City *(G-7075)*

▲ Consoldted Precision Pdts Corp........C 216 453-4800
Cleveland *(G-3560)*

Dircksen and Associates Inc.............G 614 238-0413
Columbus *(G-4881)*

▲ Eleet Cryogenics Inc.....................E 330 874-4009
Bolivar *(G-1382)*

Grimes Aerospace Company..............D 937 484-2001
Urbana *(G-13464)*

Hydromotive Engineering Co..............G 330 425-4266
Twinsburg *(G-13317)*

Transdigm Group Incorporated...........B 216 706-2960
Cleveland *(G-4413)*

▼ Werner G Smith Inc......................F 216 861-3676
Cleveland *(G-4501)*

5091 Sporting and recreation goods

A K Athletic Equipment Inc...............E 614 920-3069
Canal Winchester *(G-1782)*

▼ Advantage Tent Fittings Inc..............F 740 773-3015
Chillicothe *(G-2241)*

Agean Marble Manufacturing Inc.........G 513 874-1475
West Chester *(G-14099)*

Akron Felt Chenille Mfg Co Inc...........F 330 733-7778
Akron *(G-30)*

▲ Atwood Rope Manufacturing Inc........E 614 920-0534
Canal Winchester *(G-1784)*

Berry Investments Inc....................G 937 293-0398
Moraine *(G-10150)*

Bradley Enterprises Inc...................G 330 875-1444
Louisville *(G-8599)*

▲ Done-Rite Bowling Service Co..........E 440 232-3280
Bedford *(G-1028)*

Electra Tarp Inc..........................F 330 477-7168
Canton *(G-1885)*

Garick LLC...............................E 216 581-0100
Cleveland *(G-3755)*

▲ Golf Galaxy Golfworks Inc...............C 740 328-4193
Newark *(G-10504)*

▲ H & S Distributing Inc....................G 800 336-7784
North Ridgeville *(G-10733)*

▲ Hammersmith Bros Invstmnts Inc.......E 513 353-3000
North Bend *(G-10620)*

Hershberger Lawn Structures............F 330 674-3900
Millersburg *(G-9983)*

House of Awards Inc.....................G 419 422-7877
Findlay *(G-6882)*

▲ Litehouse Products LLC..................E 440 638-2350
Strongsville *(G-12571)*

Mc Alarney Pool Spas and Blld...........F 740 373-6698
Marietta *(G-8928)*

R & A Sports Inc.........................E 216 289-2254
Euclid *(G-6674)*

Total Tennis Inc..........................F 614 488-5004
Columbus *(G-5325)*

◆ Zebec of North America Inc..............E 513 829-5533
Fairfield *(G-6794)*

5092 Toys and hobby goods and supplies

Advance Novelty Incorporated...........G 419 424-0363
Findlay *(G-6833)*

▲ AW Faber-Castell Usa Inc................D 216 643-4660
Cleveland *(G-3396)*

▲ Bendon Inc...............................D 419 207-3600
Ashland *(G-521)*

◆ Galaxy Balloons Incorporated...........C 216 476-3360
Cleveland *(G-3753)*

▼ ICM Distributing Company Inc...........E 234 212-3030
Twinsburg *(G-13319)*

Middleton Llyd Dolls Inc..................G 740 989-2082
Coolville *(G-5426)*

▲ Party Animal Inc..........................F 440 471-1030
Westlake *(G-14320)*

▲ Twin Sisters Productions LLC............E 330 631-0361
Stow *(G-12468)*

Wooden Horse...........................G 740 503-5243
Baltimore *(G-789)*

5093 Scrap and waste materials

A & B Iron & Metal Co Inc................F 937 228-1561
Dayton *(G-5629)*

◆ Aci Industries Ltd........................E 740 368-4160
Delaware *(G-6128)*

Agmet LLC...............................F 216 663-8200
Cleveland *(G-3314)*

Ascendtech Inc...........................E 216 458-1101
Willoughby *(G-14428)*

Auris Noble LLC..........................E 330 321-6649
Akron *(G-64)*

Cohen Brothers Inc.......................E 513 217-5200
Middletown *(G-9849)*

Cohen Brothers Inc.......................E 513 422-3696
Middletown *(G-9848)*

Edw C Levy Co...........................G 330 484-6328
Canton *(G-1884)*

▼ Fex LLC..................................F 412 604-0400
Mingo Junction *(G-10051)*

▲ Fpt Cleveland LLC.................................... C 216 441-3800
Cleveland *(G-3740)*

Frankes Wood Products LLC................... E 937 642-0706
Marysville *(G-9020)*

▲ Franklin Iron & Metal Corp..................... C 937 253-8184
Dayton *(G-5784)*

Garick LLC.. E 216 581-0100
Cleveland *(G-3755)*

Homan Metals LLC.................................... G 513 721-5010
Cincinnati *(G-2728)*

I H Schlezinger Inc................................... E 614 252-1188
Columbus *(G-4996)*

Lawson Twing Auto Wrecking LLC.......... F 216 883-9050
Cleveland *(G-3948)*

Makers Supply LLC................................... G 937 203-8245
Piqua *(G-11364)*

Metalico Akron Inc.................................... F 330 376-1400
Akron *(G-229)*

Mw Metals Group LLC............................. D 937 222-5992
Dayton *(G-5900)*

Nucor Steel Marion Inc............................ E 740 383-6068
Marion *(G-8984)*

R L S Corporation..................................... G 740 773-1440
Chillicothe *(G-2277)*

Rm Advisory Group Inc............................ E 513 242-2100
Cincinnati *(G-3049)*

Rnw Holdings Inc...................................... E 330 792-0600
Youngstown *(G-14925)*

▲ Sims Bros Inc... D 740 387-9041
Marion *(G-9000)*

◆ Triple Arrow Industries Inc...................... G 614 437-5588
Marysville *(G-9054)*

W R G Inc... E 216 351-8494
Avon Lake *(G-772)*

5094 Jewelry and precious stones

Behrco Inc... G 419 394-1612
Saint Marys *(G-11731)*

▲ Dern Trophies Corp.................................. G 614 895-3260
Westerville *(G-14207)*

Goyal Enterprises Inc............................... F 513 874-9303
Cincinnati *(G-2686)*

M B Saxon Co Inc..................................... G 440 229-5006
Cleveland *(G-3975)*

Marfo Company... D 614 276-3352
Columbus *(G-5081)*

Sharonco Inc... G 419 882-3443
Sylvania *(G-12723)*

Sheiban Jewelry Inc.................................. F 440 238-0616
Strongsville *(G-12599)*

5099 Durable goods, nec

A-Gas US Holdings Inc............................. F 419 867-8990
Bowling Green *(G-1403)*

All-American Fire Eqp Inc........................ F 800 972-6035
Wshngtn Ct Hs *(G-14734)*

Baker Plastics Inc..................................... G 330 743-3142
Youngstown *(G-14817)*

CD Solutions Inc....................................... G 937 676-2376
Pleasant Hill *(G-11431)*

Cindoco Wood Products Co...................... G 937 444-2504
Mount Orab *(G-10216)*

Club 513 LLC.. G 800 530-2574
Cincinnati *(G-2501)*

◆ Evenflo Company Inc.............................. A 937 415-3300
Miamisburg *(G-9692)*

Fire Safety Services Inc........................... F 937 686-2000
Huntsville *(G-7864)*

Gross Lumber Inc...................................... G 330 683-2055
Apple Creek *(G-469)*

Imex Bz LLC.. F 786 866-8798
Orrville *(G-10986)*

▼ Jatiga Inc... D 859 817-7100
Cincinnati *(G-2762)*

K Ventures Inc.. F 419 678-2308
Coldwater *(G-4579)*

▲ Klw Plastics Inc....................................... G 513 539-2673
Monroe *(G-10112)*

▼ Mabis Shipping Solutions Inc................. G 330 650-1788
Hudson *(G-7850)*

Macray Co LLC... G 937 325-1726
Springfield *(G-12345)*

McHael D Goronok String Instrs............. G 216 421-4227
Cleveland *(G-4010)*

Netherland Rubber Company.................... F 513 733-0883
Cincinnati *(G-2899)*

▼ Resource Mtl Hdlg & Recycl Inc............. E 440 834-0727
Middlefield *(G-9823)*

Smithco Distributing................................. E 419 367-7685
Liberty Center *(G-8376)*

Technical Artistry Inc............................... G 614 299-7777
Columbus *(G-5316)*

▲ TS Tech Americas Inc.............................. B 614 575-4100
Reynoldsburg *(G-11583)*

Victory Postcards Inc............................... G 614 764-8975
Dublin *(G-6360)*

▲ Wcm Holdings Inc.................................... C 513 705-2100
Cincinnati *(G-3213)*

▲ West Chester Holdings LLC..................... C 513 705-2100
Cincinnati *(G-3220)*

51 WHOLESALE TRADE - NONDURABLE GOODS

5111 Printing and writing paper

Gvs Industries Inc.................................... G 513 851-3606
Hamilton *(G-7498)*

▲ Microcom Corporation.............................. E 740 548-6262
Lewis Center *(G-8343)*

▲ Millcraft Group LLC.................................. D 216 441-5500
Independence *(G-7911)*

Phoenix Graphix Inc................................. G 513 751-4433
Cincinnati *(G-2961)*

5112 Stationery and office supplies

American Business Forms Inc.................. E 513 312-2522
West Chester *(G-14101)*

▲ AW Faber-Castell Usa Inc....................... D 216 643-4660
Cleveland *(G-3396)*

Bay Business Forms Inc........................... F 937 322-3000
Springfield *(G-12285)*

Bloch Printing Company............................ G 330 576-6760
Copley *(G-5431)*

Covap Inc.. F 513 793-1855
Blue Ash *(G-1264)*

Dewitt Group Inc....................................... F 614 847-5919
Columbus *(G-4879)*

Envelope Mart of Ohio Inc....................... F 440 365-8177
Elyria *(G-6535)*

Equip Business Solutions Co................... G 614 854-9755
Jackson *(G-7945)*

Friends Service Co Inc............................. F 800 427-1704
Dayton *(G-5785)*

Friends Service Co Inc............................. E 419 427-1704
Findlay *(G-6869)*

▲ GBS Corp.. C 330 494-5330
North Canton *(G-10641)*

Gq Business Products Inc........................ G 513 792-4750
Loveland *(G-8627)*

Gvs Industries Inc.................................... G 513 851-3606
Hamilton *(G-7498)*

Highland Computer Forms Inc.................. D 937 393-4215
Hillsboro *(G-7718)*

Identity Group LLC................................... G 614 337-6167
Westerville *(G-14213)*

▲ Jbm Packaging Company......................... C 513 933-8333
Lebanon *(G-8269)*

▲ Microcom Corporation.............................. E 740 548-6262
Lewis Center *(G-8343)*

Optimum System Products Inc................. E 614 885-4464
Westerville *(G-14273)*

Pac Worldwide Corporation...................... E 800 535-0039
Monroe *(G-10114)*

◆ Printer Components Inc............................ G 585 924-5190
Fairfield *(G-6767)*

▲ Pulsar Ecoproducts LLC........................... F 216 861-8800
Cleveland *(G-4208)*

Queen City Office Machine....................... F 513 251-7200
Cincinnati *(G-3022)*

▼ Quick Tab II Inc....................................... D 419 448-6622
Tiffin *(G-12796)*

▲ REA Elektronik Inc................................... F 440 232-0555
Walton Hills *(G-13702)*

▼ Scratch-Off Systems Inc.......................... E 216 649-7800
Twinsburg *(G-13376)*

▲ Shamrock Companies Inc......................... D 440 899-9510
Westlake *(G-14333)*

◆ Wasserstrom Company.............................. B 614 228-6525
Columbus *(G-5356)*

Western States Envelope Co.................... E 419 666-7480
Walbridge *(G-13689)*

Westrock Commercial LLC........................ E 419 476-9101
Toledo *(G-13178)*

William J Bergen & Co.............................. G 440 248-6132
Solon *(G-12208)*

5113 Industrial and personal service paper

A To Z Paper Box Company...................... G 330 325-8722
Rootstown *(G-11646)*

◆ Aci Industries Converting Ltd.................. F 740 368-4160
Delaware *(G-6129)*

Acme Steak & Seafood Inc....................... F 330 270-8000
Youngstown *(G-14806)*

Adapt-A-Pak Inc.. E 937 845-0386
Fairborn *(G-6684)*

American Made Crrgted Pckg Inc............. G 937 981-2111
Greenfield *(G-7325)*

▼ Buckeye Paper Co Inc.............................. E 330 477-5925
Canton *(G-1847)*

Canton Sterilized Wiping Cloth................. G 330 455-5179
Canton *(G-1860)*

CJ Dannemiller Co..................................... E 330 825-7808
Norton *(G-10819)*

◆ Cleveland Supplyone Inc.......................... E 216 514-7000
Cleveland *(G-3527)*

Dayton Industrial Drum Inc...................... E 937 253-8933
Dayton *(G-5608)*

▲ Dazpak Flexible Packaging Corp............. C 614 252-2121
Columbus *(G-4872)*

Deufol Worldwide Packaging LLC............. E 440 232-1100
Bedford *(G-1026)*

Gt Industrial Supply Inc........................... F 513 771-7000
Cincinnati *(G-2695)*

Gvs Industries Inc.................................... E 513 851-3606
Hamilton *(G-7498)*

Lynk Packaging Inc................................... E 330 562-8080
Aurora *(G-677)*

▲ Millcraft Group LLC.................................. D 216 441-5500
Independence *(G-7911)*

Ohio Paper Tube Co.................................. E 330 478-5171
Canton *(G-1967)*

◆ Polymer Packaging Inc............................. D 330 832-2000
North Canton *(G-10658)*

Precision Products Group Inc.................... G 330 698-4711
Apple Creek *(G-475)*

Putnam Plastics Inc .... G 937 866-6261
Dayton *(G-5969)*

Ray C Sprosty Bag Co Inc .... F 330 669-0045
Smithville *(G-12067)*

Responsible Products Limited .... F 888 988-6627
West Chester *(G-14065)*

Ricking Holding Co .... F 513 825-3551
Cleveland *(G-4241)*

Solas Ltd .... E 650 501-0889
Avon *(G-739)*

Sonoco Products Company .... E 937 429-0040
Beavercreek Township *(G-1006)*

Systems Pack Inc .... E 330 467-5729
Macedonia *(G-8719)*

Truechoicepack Corp .... F 937 630-3832
West Chester *(G-14085)*

Zebco Industries Inc .... F 740 654-4510
Lancaster *(G-8233)*

5122 Drugs, proprietaries, and sundries

American Regent Inc .... D 614 436-2222
Hilliard *(G-7667)*

◆ Beautyavenues LLC .... F 614 856-6000
Reynoldsburg *(G-11558)*

Beiersdorf Inc .... C 513 682-7300
West Chester *(G-14107)*

◆ Boxout LLC .... C 833 462-7746
Hudson *(G-7835)*

Buderer Drug Company Inc .... E 419 627-2800
Sandusky *(G-11824)*

Cardinal Health Inc .... C 614 553-3830
Dublin *(G-6285)*

Cardinal Health Inc .... G 614 757-2863
Lewis Center *(G-8328)*

◆ Cardinal Health Inc .... A 614 757-5000
Dublin *(G-6286)*

Direct Action Co Inc .... F 330 364-3219
Dover *(G-6236)*

▼ ICM Distributing Company Inc .... E 234 212-3030
Twinsburg *(G-13319)*

Midwest Sea Salt Company Inc .... F 513 770-9177
West Chester *(G-14029)*

Montgomery Ellis LLC .... C 614 226-7976
Westerville *(G-14271)*

▲ Nehemiah Manufacturing Co LLC ..... D 513 351-5700
Cincinnati *(G-2897)*

Optum Infusion Svcs 550 LLC .... D 866 442-4679
Cincinnati *(G-2936)*

River City Pharma .... G 513 870-1680
Fairfield *(G-6772)*

Samuels Products Inc .... E 513 891-4456
Blue Ash *(G-1330)*

Sysco Guest Supply LLC .... E 440 960-2515
Lorain *(G-8582)*

Teva Womens Health LLC .... C 513 731-9900
Cincinnati *(G-3145)*

Walter F Stephens Jr Inc .... E 937 746-0521
Franklin *(G-7055)*

Xellia Pharmaceuticals Inc .... G 847 947-0200
Beachwood *(G-958)*

5131 Piece goods and notions

▲ Custom Products Corporation .... D 440 528-7100
Glenwillow *(G-7285)*

◆ Db Rediheat Inc .... E 216 361-0530
Cleveland *(G-3604)*

Hill Sign Company Inc .... G 614 367-9227
Columbus *(G-4988)*

▲ Mmi Textiles Inc .... G 440 899-8050
Brooklyn *(G-1523)*

Purebuttonscom LLC .... F 330 721-1600
Medina *(G-9438)*

Style-Line Incorporated .... E 614 291-0600
Columbus *(G-5295)*

Sysco Guest Supply LLC .... E 440 960-2515
Lorain *(G-8582)*

▲ Tlg Cochran Inc .... E 440 914-1122
Twinsburg *(G-13385)*

5136 Men's and boy's clothing

▲ Barbs Graffiti Inc .... E 216 881-5550
Cleveland *(G-3405)*

Carters Inc .... G 330 758-0390
Boardman *(G-1369)*

Cintas Sales Corporation .... B 513 459-1200
Cincinnati *(G-2495)*

Design Original Inc .... F 937 596-5121
Jackson Center *(G-7961)*

Digitek Corp .... F 513 794-3190
Mason *(G-9094)*

Identity Group LLC .... G 614 337-6167
Westerville *(G-14213)*

▲ McCc Sportswear Inc .... G 513 583-9210
Milford *(G-9942)*

Precision Imprint .... G 740 592-5916
Athens *(G-646)*

R & A Sports Inc .... E 216 289-2254
Euclid *(G-6674)*

Rbr Enterprises LLC .... F 866 437-9327
Brecksville *(G-1480)*

Unisport Inc .... F 419 529-4727
Ontario *(G-10953)*

Walter F Stephens Jr Inc .... E 937 746-0521
Franklin *(G-7055)*

▲ West Chester Holdings LLC .... C 513 705-2100
Cincinnati *(G-3220)*

5137 Women's and children's clothing

▲ Barbs Graffiti Inc .... E 216 881-5550
Cleveland *(G-3405)*

Carters Inc .... G 330 758-0390
Boardman *(G-1369)*

Cintas Sales Corporation .... B 513 459-1200
Cincinnati *(G-2495)*

Design Original Inc .... F 937 596-5121
Jackson Center *(G-7961)*

Digitek Corp .... F 513 794-3190
Mason *(G-9094)*

Fluff Boutique .... G 513 227-6614
Cincinnati *(G-2630)*

K Ventures Inc .... F 419 678-2308
Coldwater *(G-4579)*

▲ McCc Sportswear Inc .... G 513 583-9210
Milford *(G-9942)*

◆ Philips Med Systems Clvland In .... B 440 483-3000
Cleveland *(G-4159)*

Precision Imprint .... G 740 592-5916
Athens *(G-646)*

R & A Sports Inc .... E 216 289-2254
Euclid *(G-6674)*

Rbr Enterprises LLC .... F 866 437-9327
Brecksville *(G-1480)*

Unisport Inc .... F 419 529-4727
Ontario *(G-10953)*

▲ West Chester Holdings LLC .... C 513 705-2100
Cincinnati *(G-3220)*

▲ Zimmer Enterprises Inc .... E 937 428-1057
Dayton *(G-6090)*

5139 Footwear

Careismatic Brands LLC .... E 561 843-8727
Groveport *(G-7428)*

Careismatic Brands LLC .... G 614 497-5289
Groveport *(G-7429)*

Georgia-Boot Inc .... D 740 753-1951
Nelsonville *(G-10317)*

Hudson Leather Ltd .... G 419 485-8531
Pioneer *(G-11321)*

Sysco Guest Supply LLC .... E 440 960-2515
Lorain *(G-8582)*

US Footwear Holdings LLC .... C 740 753-9100
Nelsonville *(G-10322)*

5141 Groceries, general line

Brantley Partners IV LP .... G 216 464-8400
Cleveland *(G-3434)*

Comber Holdings Inc .... E 216 961-8600
Cleveland *(G-3549)*

Imex Bz LLC .... F 786 866-8798
Orrville *(G-10986)*

La Perla Inc .... G 419 534-2074
Toledo *(G-13026)*

▲ R S Hanline and Co Inc .... C 419 347-8077
Shelby *(G-11974)*

Ricking Holding Co .... F 513 825-3551
Cleveland *(G-4241)*

The Ellenbee-Leggett Company Inc .... C 513 874-3200
Fairfield *(G-6782)*

◆ Zwanenberg Food Group (usa) Inc .... F 513 682-6000
Cincinnati *(G-3244)*

5142 Packaged frozen goods

A To Z Portion Ctrl Meats Inc .... E 419 358-2926
Bluffton *(G-1356)*

Dee-Jays Cstm Btchring Proc LL .... F 740 694-7492
Fredericktown *(G-7076)*

Foodies Vegan Ltd .... F 513 487-3037
Cincinnati *(G-2632)*

Frank Brunckhorst Company LLC .... G 614 662-5300
Groveport *(G-7434)*

King Kold Inc .... E 937 836-2731
Englewood *(G-6617)*

Lori Holding Co .... E 740 342-3230
New Lexington *(G-10403)*

The Ellenbee-Leggett Company Inc .... C 513 874-3200
Fairfield *(G-6782)*

◆ White Castle System Inc .... B 614 228-5781
Columbus *(G-5367)*

5143 Dairy products, except dried or canned

Acme Steak & Seafood Inc .... F 330 270-8000
Youngstown *(C-11806)*

Arps Dairy Inc .... F 419 782-9116
Defiance *(G-6098)*

Bfc Inc .... E 330 364-6645
Dover *(G-6230)*

Borden Dairy Co Cincinnati LLC .... E 513 948-8811
Cleveland *(G-3428)*

Cheese Holdings Inc .... E 330 893-2479
Millersburg *(G-9977)*

Country Parlour Ice Cream Co .... G 440 237-4040
Cleveland *(G-3570)*

Frank L Harter & Son Inc .... G 513 574-1330
Cincinnati *(G-2638)*

Grays Orange Barn Inc .... G 419 568-2718
Wapakoneta *(G-13714)*

◆ Great Lakes Cheese Co Inc .... B 440 834-2500
Hiram *(G-7739)*

▲ Hans Rothenbuhler & Son Inc .... E 440 632-6000
Middlefield *(G-9796)*

Instantwhip Connecticut Inc .... F 614 488-2536
Columbus *(G-5010)*

Instantwhip Foods Inc .... F 614 488-2536
Columbus *(G-5011)*

Instantwhip Products Co PA .... F 614 488-2536
Columbus *(G-5012)*

Instantwhip-Buffalo Inc.............................F 614 488-2536
Columbus *(G-5013)*

Instantwhip-Columbus Inc...................E 614 871-9447
Grove City *(G-7391)*

▲ Instantwhip-Dayton Inc............................G..... 937 235-5930
Dayton *(G-5823)*

Johnsons Real Ice Cream LLC............D 614 231-0014
Columbus *(G-5042)*

Lori Holding Co..E 740 342-3230
New Lexington *(G-10403)*

Louis Instantwhip-St Inc.........................F 614 488-2536
Columbus *(G-5076)*

Philadelphia Instantwhip Inc...................F 614 488-2536
Columbus *(G-5191)*

Snowville Creamery LLC.........................E 740 698-2301
Pomeroy *(G-11438)*

United Dairy Farmers Inc.........................C 513 396-8700
Cincinnati *(G-3181)*

Velvet Ice Cream Company.....................E 419 562-2009
Bucyrus *(G-1693)*

▲ Weaver Bros Inc....................................D 937 526-3907
Versailles *(G-13605)*

5144 Poultry and poultry products

▼ Ballas Egg Products Corp...................D 614 453-0386
Zanesville *(G-14991)*

Bfc Inc..E 330 364-6645
Dover *(G-6230)*

Borden Dairy Co Cincinnati LLC............E 513 948-8811
Cleveland *(G-3428)*

Frank L Harter & Son Inc.........................G 513 574-1330
Cincinnati *(G-2638)*

Just Natural Provision Company...........G 216 431-7922
Cleveland *(G-3899)*

▲ Ohio Fresh Eggs LLC............................G 740 893-7200
Croton *(G-5515)*

Roots Poultry Inc....................................G 419 332-0041
Fremont *(G-7130)*

5145 Confectionery

▲ Bendon Inc...D 419 207-3600
Ashland *(G-521)*

Bloomer Candy Co..................................C 740 452-7501
Zanesville *(G-14998)*

CJ Dannemiller Co...................................E 330 825-7808
Norton *(G-10819)*

Esther Price Candies Corporation.........E 937 253-2121
Dayton *(G-5769)*

Gehm & Sons Limited..............................G 330 724-8423
Akron *(G-158)*

◆ Gold Medal Products Co.......................B 513 769-7676
Cincinnati *(G-2680)*

Gorant Chocolatier LLC...........................C 330 726-8821
Boardman *(G-1372)*

▲ Hayden Valley Foods Inc......................E 614 539-7233
Grove City *(G-7390)*

Hen of Woods LLC...................................G 513 954-8871
Cincinnati *(G-2716)*

Humphrey Popcorn Company..................F 216 662-6629
Strongsville *(G-12565)*

◆ Jml Holdings Inc....................................F..... 419 866-7500
Holland *(G-7770)*

Jones Potato Chip Co..............................E 419 529-9424
Mansfield *(G-8808)*

Linneas Candy Supplies Inc....................E 330 678-7112
Kent *(G-8046)*

Mike-Sells Potato Chip Co......................E 937 228-9400
Dayton *(G-5885)*

Mike-Sells West Virginia Inc....................D 937 228-9400
Dayton *(G-5886)*

Nuts Are Good Inc...................................F 586 619-2400
Columbus *(G-5133)*

Ohio Hckry Hrvest Brnd Pdts In..............E 330 644-6266
Akron *(G-253)*

Robert E McGrath Inc..............................F 440 572-7747
Strongsville *(G-12593)*

◆ Shearers Foods LLC..............................A 800 428-6843
Massillon *(G-9241)*

Smithco Distributing...............................E 419 367-7685
Liberty Center *(G-8376)*

Sweeties Olympia Treats LLC..................F 440 572-7747
Strongsville *(G-12608)*

Tarrier Foods Corp..................................E 614 876-8594
Columbus *(G-5310)*

5146 Fish and seafoods

Acme Steak & Seafood Inc.....................F 330 270-8000
Youngstown *(G-14806)*

Alsatian Llc...G..... 330 661-0600
Medina *(G-9374)*

5147 Meats and meat products

Acme Steak & Seafood Inc.....................F 330 270-8000
Youngstown *(G-14806)*

Cheese Holdings Inc...............................E 330 893-2479
Millersburg *(G-9977)*

Empire Packing Company LP...................D 513 942-5400
West Chester *(G-14117)*

Fink Meat Company Inc...........................G 937 390-2750
Springfield *(G-12311)*

Foris Extraordinary Meats LLC................F 614 670-5726
Columbus *(G-4931)*

◆ Fresh Mark Inc......................................B 330 832-7491
Massillon *(G-9192)*

John Krusinski..F 216 441-0100
Cleveland *(G-3889)*

Lori Holding Co..E 740 342-3230
New Lexington *(G-10403)*

Marshallville Packing Co Inc....................G 330 855-2871
Marshallville *(G-9007)*

The Ellenbee-Leggett Company Inc.........C 513 874-3200
Fairfield *(G-6782)*

Winner Corporation.................................E 419 582-4321
Yorkshire *(G-14797)*

5148 Fresh fruits and vegetables

Bfc Inc..E 330 364-6645
Dover *(G-6230)*

Big Gus Onion Rings Inc..........................G 216 883-9045
Cleveland *(G-3418)*

C J Kraft Enterprises Inc.........................G 740 653-9606
Lancaster *(G-8184)*

Chefs Garden Inc....................................C 419 433-4947
Sandusky *(G-11827)*

Dno Inc...D 614 231-3601
Columbus *(G-4889)*

Dole Fresh Vegetables Inc......................C 937 525-4300
Springfield *(G-12303)*

Frank L Harter & Son Inc.........................G 513 574-1330
Cincinnati *(G-2638)*

Freshway Foods Company Inc.................D 937 498-4664
Sidney *(G-12020)*

Grays Orange Barn Inc............................G 419 568-2718
Wapakoneta *(G-13714)*

Produce Packaging Inc............................C 216 391-6129
Willoughby Hills *(G-14562)*

5149 Groceries and related products, nec

Acme Steak & Seafood Inc.....................F 330 270-8000
Youngstown *(G-14806)*

American Bottling Company....................C 614 237-4201
Columbus *(G-4693)*

◆ Amerihua Intl Entps Inc........................G..... 740 549-0300
Lewis Center *(G-8321)*

▲ Bendon Inc...D 419 207-3600
Ashland *(G-521)*

▲ Brand Castle LLC....................................E 216 292-7700
Bedford Heights *(G-1070)*

Bread Kneads Inc....................................G 419 422-3863
Findlay *(G-6845)*

Brew Kettle Inc..F 440 234-8788
Strongsville *(G-12546)*

Busken Bakery Inc...................................D 513 871-2114
Cincinnati *(G-2434)*

Cassanos Inc...E 937 294-8400
Dayton *(G-5695)*

Central Coca-Cola Btlg Co Inc.................C 419 476-6622
Toledo *(G-12913)*

Cheese Holdings Inc...............................E 330 893-2479
Millersburg *(G-9977)*

Coblentz Family Brands Inc.....................E 330 893-2995
Walnut Creek *(G-13693)*

Coopers Mill Inc......................................G 419 562-4215
Bucyrus *(G-1676)*

Distillata Company..................................D 216 771-2900
Cleveland *(G-3619)*

Ditsch Usa LLC..G 513 782-8888
Cincinnati *(G-2552)*

Food Plant Engineering LLC....................F 513 618-3165
Blue Ash *(G-1275)*

G & J Pepsi-Cola Bottlers Inc..................E 740 593-3366
Athens *(G-640)*

G & J Pepsi-Cola Bottlers Inc..................B 740 354-9191
Franklin Furnace *(G-7058)*

G & J Pepsi-Cola Bottlers Inc..................E 740 354-9191
Zanesville *(G-15017)*

Generations Coffee Company LLC............F 440 546-0901
Brecksville *(G-1467)*

Grace Juice Company LLC........................F 614 398-6879
Westerville *(G-14261)*

▲ Hayden Valley Foods Inc......................E 614 539-7233
Grove City *(G-7390)*

James C Robinson....................................G 513 969-7482
Cincinnati *(G-2760)*

JM Smucker LLC.......................................D 330 682-3000
Orrville *(G-10990)*

▲ Kaiser Foods Inc....................................E 513 621-2053
Cincinnati *(G-2779)*

Kerry Inc...E 760 685-2548
Byesville *(G-1715)*

Klosterman Baking Co LLC......................C 513 242-5667
Cincinnati *(G-2800)*

Luxfer Magtech Inc..................................F 513 772-3066
Cincinnati *(G-2832)*

Michael Zakany LLC................................G 740 221-3934
Zanesville *(G-15028)*

▲ More Than Gourmet Holdings Inc......E 330 762-6652
Akron *(G-237)*

Morton Salt Inc.......................................C 330 925-3015
Rittman *(G-11625)*

▲ Muscle Feast LLC...................................F 740 877-8808
Nashport *(G-10301)*

▲ National Foods Packaging Inc............E 216 622-2740
Cleveland *(G-4060)*

Natures Health Food LLC.........................F 419 260-9265
Mount Victory *(G-10269)*

Norcia Bakery...G 330 454-1077
Canton *(G-1959)*

Obhc Inc...G 440 236-5112
Columbia Station *(G-4595)*

Ohio Coffee Collaborative Ltd.................F 614 564-9852
Columbus *(G-5139)*

Ohio Hckry Hrvest Brnd Pdts In..............E 330 644-6266
Akron *(G-253)*

Osmans Pies Inc......................................E 330 607-9083
Stow *(G-12448)*

P-Americas LLC...............................C 419 227-3541
Lima (G-8436)

P-Americas LLC...............................E 330 746-7652
Youngstown (G-14910)

Pepsi-Cola Metro Btlg Co Inc............D 937 461-4664
Dayton (G-5936)

Pepsi-Cola Metro Btlg Co Inc............F 440 323-5524
Elyria (G-6577)

Pepsi-Cola Metro Btlg Co Inc............C 330 425-8236
Twinsburg (G-13353)

Rambasek Realty Inc.........................F 937 228-1189
Dayton (G-5974)

Richards Maple Products Inc............G 440 286-4160
Chardon (G-2221)

Schwebel Baking Company...............C 440 248-1500
Solon (G-12179)

▲ Skyline Cem Holdings LLC............C 513 874-1188
Fairfield (G-6776)

Stumps Converting Inc......................F 419 492-2542
New Washington (G-10483)

Tarrier Foods Corp............................E 614 876-8594
Columbus (G-5310)

Thurns Bakery & Deli.........................G 614 221-9246
Columbus (G-5323)

Tiffin Paper Company........................E 419 447-2121
Tiffin (G-12804)

US Wellness LLC................................G 216 772-3364
Cleveland (G-4452)

Wheeling Coffee & Spice Co..............F 304 232-0141
Saint Clairsville (G-11719)

5153 Grain and field beans

Andersons Inc....................................G 419 536-0460
Toledo (G-12881)

Andersons Inc....................................C 419 893-5050
Maumee (G-9261)

Cooper Hatchery Inc..........................C 419 594-3325
Oakwood (G-10897)

Countyline Co-Op Inc........................F 419 287-3241
Pemberville (G-11174)

Fort Recovery Equity Inc...................E 419 375-4119
Fort Recovery (G-6963)

Hanby Farms Inc................................E 740 763-3554
Nashport (G-10299)

Hansen-Mueller Co.............................G 419 729-5535
Toledo (G-12986)

Imex Bz LLC.......................................F 786 866-8798
Orrville (G-10986)

Keystone Cooperative Inc.................G 937 884-5526
Verona (G-13591)

Legacy Farmers Cooperative.............F 419 423-2611
Findlay (G-6884)

Mid-Wood Inc.....................................F 419 257-3331
North Baltimore (G-10614)

Minster Farmers Coop Exch..............D 419 628-4705
Minster (G-10061)

▼ Mullet Enterprises Inc.....................G 330 852-4681
Sugarcreek (G-12643)

Pettisville Grain Co............................E 419 446-2547
Pettisville (G-11285)

Premier Feeds LLC.............................G 937 584-2411
Sabina (G-11683)

▲ Simmons Feed & Supply LLC.........E 800 754-1228
Salem (G-11812)

Sunrise Cooperative Inc....................G 419 628-4705
Minster (G-10066)

Van Tilburg Farms Inc.......................F 419 586-3077
Celina (G-2126)

5154 Livestock

Gardner Lumber Company Inc............F 740 254-4664
Tippecanoe (G-12857)

Werling and Sons Inc.........................F 937 338-3281
Burkettsville (G-1698)

Winner Corporation............................E 419 582-4321
Yorkshire (G-14797)

5159 Farm-product raw materials, nec

G A Wintzer and Son Company...........F 419 739-4900
Wapakoneta (G-13711)

Griffin Industries LLC........................F 513 549-0041
Blue Ash (G-1279)

Inland Products Inc...........................E 614 443-3425
Columbus (G-5006)

5162 Plastics materials and basic shapes

Allied Shipping and Packa.................F 937 222-7422
Moraine (G-10144)

Alro Steel Corporation.......................E 614 878-7271
Columbus (G-4690)

Alro Steel Corporation.......................D 419 720-5300
Toledo (G-12871)

Ampacet Corporation........................F 513 247-5400
Cincinnati (G-2368)

◆ Avient Corporation.........................D 440 930-1000
Avon Lake (G-748)

◆ Bay State Polymer Distribution Inc..F 440 892-8500
Westlake (G-14291)

▲ Carney Plastics Inc........................G 330 746-8273
Youngstown (G-14831)

◆ Cleveland Supplyone Inc................E 216 514-7000
Cleveland (G-3527)

Epsilyte Holdings LLC.......................D 937 778-9500
Piqua (G-11346)

Hexpol Compounding LLC.................G 440 834-4644
Burton (G-1699)

HP Manufacturing Company Inc.........D 216 361-6500
Cleveland (G-3841)

Morbern USA.....................................F 937 298-2176
Dayton (G-5893)

◆ Network Polymers Inc....................E 330 773-2700
Akron (G-244)

Plastics -R- Unique Inc.....................E 330 334-4820
Wadsworth (G-13660)

Plastics Family Holdings Inc.............G 440 891-1140
Cleveland (G-4172)

Plastics Family Holdings Inc.............F 614 272-0777
Columbus (G-5196)

◆ Polymer Packaging Inc..................D 330 832-2000
North Canton (G-10658)

Queen City Polymers Inc..................E 513 779-0990
West Chester (G-14059)

Skybox Packaging LLC......................C 419 525-7209
Mansfield (G-8853)

Tahoma Enterprises Inc....................G 330 745-9016
Barberton (G-840)

◆ Tahoma Rubber & Plastics Inc.......D 330 745-9016
Ashland (G-579)

United States Plastic Corp................D 419 228-2242
Lima (G-8457)

Univar Solutions USA LLC.................F 800 531-7106
Dublin (G-6359)

UPL International Inc.........................G 330 433-2860
North Canton (G-10680)

5169 Chemicals and allied products, nec

AIN Industries Inc.............................G 440 781-0950
Cleveland (G-3315)

Airgas Usa LLC..................................G 440 232-6397
Twinsburg (G-13270)

◆ Akrochem Corporation....................D 330 535-2100
Akron (G-24)

Aquablue Incorporated......................G 330 343-0220
New Philadelphia (G-10430)

Ashland Chemco Inc..........................C 614 790-3333
Columbus (G-4727)

Barentz N Amer Intrmdate Hldng........G 440 937-1000
Avon (G-715)

Bleachtech LLC..................................E 216 921-1980
Seville (G-11913)

Brewpro Inc.......................................G 513 577-7200
Cincinnati (G-2423)

▲ Calvary Industries Inc....................E 513 874-1113
Fairfield (G-6716)

▼ Ccp Industries Inc..........................B 216 535-4227
Richmond Heights (G-11609)

Chem-Sales Inc..................................F
Toledo (G-12918)

Chemcore Inc.....................................F 937 228-6118
Dayton (G-5699)

▲ Chemical Solvents Inc....................E 216 741-9310
Cleveland (G-3492)

◆ Chemmasters Inc...........................E 440 428-2105
Madison (G-8726)

Chemstation International Inc............E 937 294-8265
Dayton (G-5701)

Cleaning Lady Inc..............................G 419 589-5566
Mansfield (G-8774)

Consolidated Coatings Corp..............A 216 514-7596
Cleveland (G-3561)

Corrugated Chemicals Inc.................G 513 561-7773
Cincinnati (G-2519)

D W Dickey and Son Inc.....................C 330 424-1441
Lisbon (G-8466)

◆ Dover Chemical Corporation...........C 330 343-7711
Dover (G-6238)

Environmental Chemical Corp............F 330 453-5200
Uniontown (G-13419)

Finale Products Inc............................G 419 874-2662
Perrysburg (G-11221)

Flex Technologies Inc........................D 330 897-6311
Baltic (G-777)

Formlabs Ohio Inc.............................E 419 837-9783
Millbury (G-9961)

Gehm & Sons Limited........................G 330 724-8423
Akron (G-158)

▲ Goldsmith & Eggleton Inc..............F 330 336-6616
Wadsworth (G-13640)

▲ Goldsmith & Eggleton LLC.............F 203 855-6000
Wadsworth (G-13641)

Hexion Inc...C 888 443-9466
Columbus (C-4070)

◆ Hickman Williams & Company.........F 513 621-1946
Cincinnati (G-2721)

▲ Imcd Us LLC....................................E 216 228-8900
Westlake (G-14310)

◆ Knight Material Tech LLC................E 330 488-1651
East Canton (G-6378)

Kraton Polymers US LLC....................B 740 423-7571
Belpre (G-1150)

Love Laugh & Laundry.......................G 567 377-1951
Toledo (G-13039)

Mantaline Corporation.......................F 330 274-2264
Mantua (G-8871)

◆ McGill Corporation..........................F 614 829-1200
Groveport (G-7444)

▲ Mesocoat Inc..................................F 216 453-0866
Euclid (G-6662)

▲ National Colloid Company...............E 740 282-1171
Steubenville (G-12407)

National Polymer Inc.........................F 440 708-1245
Chagrin Falls (G-2171)

Netherland Rubber Company..............F 513 733-0883
Cincinnati (G-2899)

Novagard Solutions Inc......................D 216 881-8111
Cleveland (G-4101)

▲ Phoenix Technologies Intl LLC.......... E 419 353-7738
Bowling Green *(G-1434)*

▼ Polar Inc................................. F 937 297-0911
Moraine *(G-10185)*

Polymer Additives Holdings Inc............ C 216 875-7200
Independence *(G-7915)*

PVS Chemical Solutions Inc................ F 330 666-0888
Copley *(G-5439)*

▲ Quality Borate Co LLC................... F 216 896-1949
Cleveland *(G-4212)*

◆ Rhein Chemie Corporation............... C 440 279-2367
Chardon *(G-2220)*

◆ Shin-Etsu Silicones of America Inc.....C 330 630-9460
Akron *(G-309)*

Sigma-Aldrich Corporation................. D 216 206-5424
Cleveland *(G-4300)*

▼ Singleton Corporation................... F 216 651-7800
Cleveland *(G-4302)*

◆ Tembec Btlsr Inc....................... E 419 244-5856
Toledo *(G-13141)*

▲ Toagosei America Inc................... D 614 718-3855
West Jefferson *(G-14168)*

◆ Tosoh America Inc.......................B 614 539-8622
Grove City *(G-7417)*

◆ Tricor Industrial Inc....................D 330 264-3299
Wooster *(G-14692)*

▲ United McGill Corporation............... E 614 829-1200
Groveport *(G-7455)*

Univar Solutions USA LLC................. F 800 531-7106
Dublin *(G-6359)*

Univar Solutions USA LLC................. E 513 714-5264
West Chester *(G-14157)*

▼ Washing Systems LLC................... C 800 272-1974
Loveland *(G-8656)*

5171 Petroleum bulk stations and terminals

Cincinnati - Vulcan Company.............. D 513 242-5300
Cincinnati *(G-2465)*

New Vulco Mfg & Sales Co LLC........... D 513 242-2672
Cincinnati *(G-2904)*

Universal Oil Inc......................... E 216 771-4300
Cleveland *(G-4447)*

5172 Petroleum products, nec

▲ Aerospace Lubricants LLC............... F 614 878-3600
Columbus *(G-4678)*

American Ultra Specialties Inc............ F 330 656-5000
Hudson *(G-7831)*

Centerra Co-Op........................... E 419 281-2153
Ashland *(G-526)*

D W Dickey and Son Inc.................. C 330 424-1441
Lisbon *(G-8466)*

Digilube Systems Inc..................... F 937 748-2209
Springboro *(G-12250)*

Eni USA R&M Co Inc...................... F 330 723-6457
Medina *(G-9399)*

▼ Functional Products Inc................. F 330 963-3060
Macedonia *(G-8692)*

Gfl Environmental Svcs USA Inc........... E 614 441-4001
Columbus *(G-4952)*

◆ Giant Industries Inc....................D 419 421-2121
Findlay *(G-6870)*

Grand Aire Inc........................... E 419 861-6700
Swanton *(G-12684)*

▲ Groeneveld-Beka Usa Inc............... G 330 225-4949
Sharon Center *(G-11941)*

◆ Knight Material Tech LLC................E 330 488-1651
East Canton *(G-6378)*

Lubriplate Lubricants Company............ G 419 691-2491
Toledo *(G-13041)*

◆ Marathon Petroleum Company LP........F 419 422-2121
Findlay *(G-6889)*

▲ Marathon Petroleum Corporation...... A 419 422-2121
Findlay *(G-6890)*

Minster Farmers Coop Exch.............. D 419 628-4705
Minster *(G-10061)*

Mplx Terminals LLC....................... F 330 479-5539
Canton *(G-1952)*

▼ Polar Inc................................. F 937 297-0911
Moraine *(G-10185)*

Sunrise Cooperative Inc................... G 419 628-4705
Minster *(G-10066)*

Varouh Oil Inc............................ F 440 482-8686
Elyria *(G-6599)*

5181 Beer and ale

Wild Ohio Brewing Company.............. G 614 262-0000
Columbus *(G-5368)*

5182 Wine and distilled beverages

Blue Collar M LLC......................... F 216 209-5666
Solon *(G-12086)*

Old Firehouse Winery Inc................. E 440 466-9300
Geneva *(G-7244)*

▲ Paramount Distillers Inc................. B 216 671-6300
Cleveland *(G-4134)*

Sandra Weddington....................... F 740 417-4286
Delaware *(G-6172)*

Veriano Fine Foods Spirits Ltd............ F 614 745-7705
New Albany *(G-10354)*

Watershed Distillery LLC.................. E 614 357-1936
Columbus *(G-5357)*

Wedco LLC................................ G 513 309-0781
Mount Orab *(G-10223)*

5191 Farm supplies

A Best Trmt & Pest Ctrl Sups.............. G 330 434-5555
Akron *(G-9)*

Andersons Inc............................ G 419 536-0460
Toledo *(G-12881)*

Andersons Inc............................ C 419 893-5050
Maumee *(G-9261)*

Cooper Farms Inc........................ D 419 594-3325
Oakwood *(G-10896)*

Countyline Co-Op Inc..................... F 419 287-3241
Pemberville *(G-11174)*

Darling Ingredients Inc................... G 216 651-9300
Cleveland *(G-3599)*

Gerald Grain Center Inc.................. F 419 445-2451
Archbold *(G-495)*

Granville Milling Co....................... G 740 345-1305
Newark *(G-10505)*

Green Field Farms Co-Op................. G 330 263-0246
Wooster *(G-14645)*

H Hafner & Sons Inc..................... E 513 321-1895
Cincinnati *(G-2698)*

Hanby Farms Inc......................... E 740 763-3554
Nashport *(G-10299)*

Helena Agri-Enterprises LLC.............. G 614 275-4200
Columbus *(G-4975)*

Helena Agri-Enterprises LLC.............. G 419 596-3806
Continental *(G-5422)*

▲ Imcd Us LLC............................. E 216 228-8900
Westlake *(G-14310)*

Keynes Bros Inc.......................... D 740 385-6824
Logan *(G-8517)*

Keystone Cooperative Inc................. G 937 884-5526
Verona *(G-13591)*

Land OLakes Inc.......................... D 330 879-2158
Massillon *(G-9214)*

Legacy Farmers Cooperative.............. F 419 423-2611
Findlay *(G-6884)*

Lesco Inc................................. F 740 633-6366
Martins Ferry *(G-9010)*

M B K Inc................................. F 330 889-3451
Bristolville *(G-1498)*

Matthew Brun Enterprises Inc............ E 937 604-0057
Dayton *(G-5870)*

Mennel Milling Company.................. E 740 385-6824
Logan *(G-8521)*

Minster Farmers Coop Exch.............. D 419 628-4705
Minster *(G-10061)*

Nutrien AG Solutions Inc.................. G 614 873-4253
Milford Center *(G-9958)*

Ohigro Inc................................ E 740 726-2429
Waldo *(G-13691)*

▲ Provimi North America Inc.............. B 937 770-2400
Lewisburg *(G-8362)*

▼ Republic Mills Inc....................... F 419 758-3511
Okolona *(G-10932)*

Ridley USA Inc............................ F 800 837-8222
Botkins *(G-1398)*

Schlessman Seed Co...................... E 419 499-2572
Milan *(G-9918)*

Stony Hill Mixing Ltd..................... G 330 674-0814
Millersburg *(G-10011)*

Sunrise Cooperative Inc................... G 419 628-4705
Minster *(G-10066)*

Tyler Grain & Fertilizer Co................ F 330 669-2341
Smithville *(G-12070)*

United Industries Incorporated............ D 330 682-5010
Orrville *(G-11015)*

XS Smith Inc.............................. E 252 940-5060
Cincinnati *(G-3239)*

5192 Books, periodicals, and newspapers

B & S Transport Inc...................... G 330 767-4319
Navarre *(G-10302)*

◆ Bookmasters Inc........................C 419 281-1802
Ashland *(G-522)*

CSS Publishing Company.................. F 419 227-1818
Lima *(G-8398)*

▲ Findaway World LLC..................... E 440 893-0808
Solon *(G-12111)*

Hecks Direct Mail & Prtg Svc............. E 419 661-6028
Toledo *(G-12989)*

Hubbard Company........................ E 419 784-4455
Defiance *(G-6111)*

McGraw-Hill Schl Edcatn Hldngs........... A 419 207-7400
Ashland *(G-551)*

▲ Zaner-Bloser Inc........................ C 614 486-0221
Columbus *(G-5380)*

5193 Flowers and florists supplies

Cleveland Plant and Flower Co............ G 614 478-9900
Columbus *(G-4811)*

5194 Tobacco and tobacco products

◆ Scandinavian Tob Group Ln Ltd........C 770 934-4594
Akron *(G-306)*

5198 Paints, varnishes, and supplies

Autobody Supply Company Inc............ D 614 228-4328
Columbus *(G-4735)*

▲ C A P Industries Inc.................... F 937 773-1824
Piqua *(G-11338)*

◆ Comex North America Inc...............D 303 307-2100
Cleveland *(G-3551)*

▲ Jmac Inc................................. E 614 436-2418
Columbus *(G-5041)*

Keystone Automotive Inds Inc............ G 614 228-4328
Groveport *(G-7440)*

Matrix Sys Auto Finishes LLC............. B 248 668-8135
Massillon *(G-9221)*

Sherwin-Williams Mfg Co.................. F 216 566-2000
Cleveland *(G-4294)*

▲ Teknol Inc.................................. D 937 264-0190
Dayton *(G-6043)*

◆ The Blonder Company.................C 216 431-3560
Cleveland *(G-4379)*

5199 Nondurable goods, nec

Ace Plastics Company........................... G 330 928-7720
Stow *(G-12414)*

▲ Acor Orthopaedic LLC .... E 216 662-4500
Cleveland *(G-3293)*

Ad-Sensations Inc.............................. F 419 841-5395
Sylvania *(G-12700)*

▲ Advanced Poly-Packaging Inc........... C 330 785-4000
Akron *(G-21)*

Allied Shipping and Packa........ F 937 222-7422
Moraine *(G-10144)*

American Business Forms Inc.......... E 513 312-2522
West Chester *(G-14101)*

◆ Aquatic Technology..................F 440 236-8330
Columbia Station *(G-4588)*

▼ Armaly LLC.............................. E 740 852-3621
London *(G-8530)*

◆ Associated Premium Corporation......E 513 679-4444
Cincinnati *(G-2381)*

Auto Dealer Designs Inc................... E 330 374-7666
Akron *(G-65)*

B B Bradley Company Inc................ G 614 777-5600
Columbus *(G-4740)*

◆ B D G Wrap-Tite Inc....................E 440 349-5400
Solon *(G-12081)*

▼ Baggallini Inc.......................... F 800 448-8753
Pickerington *(G-11289)*

Baker Plastics Inc........................... G 330 743-3142
Youngstown *(G-14817)*

Berlin Truck Caps & Tarps Ltd.............. F 330 893-2811
Millersburg *(G-9970)*

Blang Acquisition LLC..................... G 937 223-2155
Dayton *(G-5679)*

Bluelogos Inc.................................. G 614 898-9971
Westerville *(G-14247)*

▲ Bottomline Ink Corporation.......... E 419 897-8000
Perrysburg *(G-11205)*

BP 10 Inc....................................... E 513 346-3900
Hamilton *(G-7472)*

Bryan Packaging Inc....................... F 419 636-2600
Bryan *(G-1633)*

Cal Sales Embroidery....................... G 440 236-3820
Columbia Station *(G-4590)*

Cambridge Packaging Inc................ E 740 432-3351
Cambridge *(G-1738)*

Canton Sterilized Wiping Cloth........... G 330 455-5179
Canton *(G-1860)*

Capehart Enterprises LLC...........F 614 769-7746
Columbus *(G-4795)*

Charizma Corp................................ G 216 621-2220
Cleveland *(G-3485)*

▲ Custom Products Corporation.......... D 440 528-7100
Glenwillow *(G-7285)*

Custom Sportswear Imprints LLC.......... G 330 335-8326
Wadsworth *(G-13633)*

Diversified Products & Svcs.................. F 740 393-6202
Mount Vernon *(G-10242)*

Eleven 10 LLC................................. F 888 216-4049
Westlake *(G-14300)*

Flashions Sportswear Ltd.................. G 937 323-5885
Springfield *(G-12312)*

▲ Galaxy Balloons Incorporated.......... C 216 476-3360
Cleveland *(G-3753)*

Gary Lawrence Enterprises Inc............. G 330 833-7181
Massillon *(G-9194)*

▲ Global-Pak Inc.......................... E 330 482-1993
Lisbon *(G-8467)*

Gordon Bernard Company LLC........ E 513 248-7600
Milford *(G-9936)*

Gq Business Products Inc................ G 513 792-4750
Loveland *(G-8627)*

Gt Industrial Supply Inc.................. F 513 771-7000
Cincinnati *(G-2695)*

Home City Ice Company.................. F 614 836-2877
Groveport *(G-7438)*

▼ ICM Distributing Company Inc........ E 234 212-3030
Twinsburg *(G-13319)*

Identity Group LLC........................... G 614 337-6167
Westerville *(G-14213)*

Johnson Bros Rubber Co Inc............ E 419 752-4814
Greenwich *(G-7362)*

◆ Johnson Bros Rubber Co..................D 419 853-4122
West Salem *(G-14188)*

Kopco Graphics Inc......................... E 513 874-7230
West Chester *(G-14021)*

La Mfg Inc...................................... G 513 577-7200
Cincinnati *(G-2810)*

Lori Holding Co................................ E 740 342-3230
New Lexington *(G-10403)*

▲ Mosser Glass Inc........................ E 740 439-1827
Cambridge *(G-1751)*

Mr Emblem Inc................................ G 419 697-1888
Oregon *(G-10964)*

◆ Novelty Advertising Co Inc.............E 740 622-3113
Coshocton *(G-5465)*

▲ Nucon International Inc................ F 614 846-5710
Columbus *(G-5132)*

Ohio State Institute Fin Inc.............. G 614 861-8811
Reynoldsburg *(G-11576)*

▲ Papyrus-Recycled Greetings Inc....... D 773 348-6410
Westlake *(G-14319)*

▲ Peter Graham Dunn Inc.................G 330 816-0035
Dalton *(G-5592)*

◆ Pfp Holdings LLC.......................A 419 647-4191
Spencerville *(G-12239)*

◆ Posterservice Incorporated............. G 513 577-7100
Cincinnati *(G-2977)*

Protective Packg Solutions LLC........... E 513 769-5777
Cincinnati *(G-3010)*

PS Superior Inc............................... G 216 587-1000
Cleveland *(G-4204)*

Publishing Group Ltd....................... F 614 572-1240
Columbus *(G-5213)*

Putnam Plastics Inc........................ G 937 866-6261
Dayton *(G-5369)*

Randd Assoc Prtg & Promotions........... G 937 294-1874
Dayton *(G-5975)*

Samuel Son & Co (usa) Inc............. D 740 522-2500
Heath *(G-7604)*

Screen Works Inc........................... E 937 264-9111
Dayton *(G-6000)*

Sew & Sew Embroidery Inc............. F 330 676-1600
Kent *(G-8078)*

▲ Shamrock Companies Inc................ D 440 899-9510
Westlake *(G-14333)*

Skybox Packaging LLC.................... C 419 525-7209
Mansfield *(G-8853)*

Solar Arts Graphic Designs............. G 330 744-0535
Youngstown *(G-14934)*

Star Calendar & Printing Inc............. G 216 741-3223
Cleveland *(G-4328)*

Storopack Inc.................................. F 513 874-0314
West Chester *(G-14077)*

▲ Storopack Inc.......................... E 513 874-0314
Cincinnati *(G-3121)*

Systems Pack Inc........................... G 330 467-5729
Macedonia *(G-8719)*

T & L Custom Screening Inc........... G 937 237-3121
Dayton *(G-6036)*

Tahoma Enterprises Inc.................. D 330 745-9016
Barberton *(G-840)*

◆ Tahoma Rubber & Plastics Inc..........D 330 745-9016
Ashland *(G-579)*

Toga-Pak Inc.................................. E 937 294-7311
Dayton *(G-6056)*

Traichal Construction Company........... E 800 255-3667
Niles *(G-10607)*

Tri-State Paper Inc........................... F 937 885-3365
Dayton *(G-6061)*

▲ Underground Sports Shop Inc......... F 513 751-1662
Cincinnati *(G-3179)*

Versa-Pak Ltd................................. E 419 586-5466
Celina *(G-2127)*

▲ Weaver Leather LLC.................. D 330 674-7548
Millersburg *(G-10019)*

White Tiger Inc................................ F 740 852-4873
London *(G-8543)*

Wholesale Bait Co Inc..................... G 513 863-2380
Fairfield *(G-6792)*

52 BUILDING MATERIALS, HARDWARE, GARDEN SUPPLIES & MOBILE HOMES

5211 Lumber and other building materials

1914 Mi Inc.................................... E 330 308-8667
New Philadelphia *(G-10428)*

A L Callahan Door Sales................. G 419 884-3667
Mansfield *(G-8757)*

Ace Lumber Company....................... F 330 744-3167
Youngstown *(G-14804)*

Acme Fence LLC............................. F 330 784-0456
Akron *(G-15)*

Adams Brothers Inc......................... G 740 819-0323
Zanesville *(G-14983)*

Agean Marble Manufacturing Inc........... G 513 874-1475
West Chester *(G-14099)*

Alside Inc....................................... E 419 865-0934
Maumee *(G-9258)*

American Concrete Products Inc........... G 937 224-1433
Dayton *(G-5652)*

American Platinum Door LLC............... G 440 497-6213
Solon *(G-12078)*

Architctral Mllwk Cbinetry Inc................ G 440 708-0086
Chagrin Falls *(G-2155)*

Associated Associates Inc.................... E 330 626-3300
Mantua *(G-8867)*

Bugh Inc.. G 330 305-0978
Canton *(G-1849)*

Building Concepts Inc....................... F 419 298-2371
Edgerton *(G-6464)*

Cabinet Restylers Inc....................... D 419 281-8449
Ashland *(G-525)*

Carter-Jones Lumber Company............. E 440 834-8164
Middlefield *(G-9785)*

Carter-Jones Lumber Company............. G 330 674-9060
Millersburg *(G-9975)*

Champion Window Co of Toledo........... G 419 841-0154
Perrysburg *(G-11211)*

Clarksville Stave & Lbr Co Ltd............... G 937 376-4618
Xenia *(G-14759)*

Conover Lumber Company Inc........... F 937 368-3010
Conover *(G-5420)*

Consumeracq Inc............................. E 440 277-9305
Lorain *(G-8552)*

Consumers Builders Supply Co............. G 440 277-9306
Lorain *(G-8553)*

Contract Lumber Inc......................... F 614 751-1109
Columbus *(G-4844)*

Counter Concepts Inc............................. F 330 848-4848
Wadsworth *(G-13632)*

Cox Wood Product Inc............................. F 740 372-4735
Otway *(G-11059)*

Creative Products Inc............................. G 419 866-5501
Holland *(G-7752)*

Dale Kestler... G 513 871-9000
Cincinnati *(G-2540)*

Dearth Resources Inc............................ G 937 325-0651
Springfield *(G-12298)*

◆ Df Supply Inc....................................... E 330 650-9226
Twinsburg *(G-13294)*

Double D D Mtls Instlltion Inc............... G 937 898-2534
Dayton *(G-5750)*

Dowel Yoder & Molding.......................... G 330 231-2962
Fredericksburg *(G-7063)*

E P Gerber & Sons Inc........................... D 330 857-2021
Kidron *(G-8126)*

Encore Precast LLC............................... D 513 726-5678
Seven Mile *(G-11907)*

Ernst Enterprises Inc............................ E 614 443-9456
Columbus *(G-4909)*

Ernst Enterprises Inc............................ F 419 222-2015
Lima *(G-8406)*

Euclid Jalousies Inc.............................. G 440 953-1112
Chardon *(G-2205)*

Everything In America............................ G 347 871-6872
Cleveland *(G-3695)*

▲ Feather Lite Innovations Inc............... E 937 743-9008
Springboro *(G-12252)*

Gillard Construction Inc......................... F 740 376-9744
Marietta *(G-8919)*

Glen-Gery Corporation........................... D 419 845-3321
Caledonia *(G-1731)*

Gopowerx Inc... E 440 707-6029
Richfield *(G-11594)*

Grafton Ready Mix Concret Inc.............. C 440 926-2911
Grafton *(G-7303)*

Great Lakes Window Inc......................... A 419 666-5555
Walbridge *(G-13684)*

Gregory Stone Co Inc............................. G 937 275-7455
Dayton *(G-5805)*

Hardwood Store Inc................................ G 937 864-2899
Enon *(G-6631)*

Hazelbaker Industries Ltd...................... G
Columbus *(G-4973)*

Higgins Construction & Supply Co Inc.. F 937 364-2331
Hillsboro *(G-7717)*

Holmes Lumber & Bldg Ctr Inc.............. E 330 479-8314
Canton *(G-1912)*

Holmes Lumber & Bldg Ctr Inc.............. C 330 674-9060
Millersburg *(G-9989)*

Holmes Panel LLC................................. G 330 897-5040
Baltic *(G-779)*

Home Stor & Off Solutions Inc.............. G 216 362-4660
Cleveland *(G-3836)*

Huth Ready Mix & Supply Co................. G 330 833-4191
Massillon *(G-9203)*

Jerry Harolds Doors Unlimited.............. G 740 635-4949
Bridgeport *(G-1494)*

Judy Mills Company Inc......................... E 513 271-4241
Cincinnati *(G-2775)*

Khempco Bldg Sup Co Ltd Partnr.......... D 740 549-0465
Delaware *(G-6159)*

Kinsella Manufacturing Co Inc.............. F 513 561-5285
Cincinnati *(G-2796)*

Koltcz Concrete Block Co....................... E 440 232-3630
Bedford *(G-1042)*

Laborie Enterprises LLC........................ G 419 686-6245
Portage *(G-11458)*

Laminate Shop....................................... F 740 749-3536
Waterford *(G-13827)*

Lancaster W Side Coal Co Inc.............. F 740 862-4713
Lancaster *(G-8207)*

▲ Lang Stone Company Inc.................... E 614 235-4099
Columbus *(G-5064)*

M B K Inc... F 330 889-3451
Bristolville *(G-1498)*

Mack Industries..................................... F 419 353-7081
Bowling Green *(G-1427)*

Marble Arch Products Inc...................... G 937 746-8388
Franklin *(G-7032)*

Marsh Valley Forest Pdts Ltd................ G 440 632-1889
Middlefield *(G-9807)*

Medina Supply Company........................ E 330 723-3681
Medina *(G-9426)*

Menard Inc... C 513 583-1444
Loveland *(G-8642)*

Mohler Lumber Company........................ E 330 499-5461
North Canton *(G-10652)*

Nofziger Door Sales Inc......................... F 419 445-2961
Archbold *(G-506)*

▼ Nofziger Door Sales Inc..................... C 419 337-9900
Wauseon *(G-13857)*

North Star Building Pdts LLC................ G 216 431-1000
Cleveland *(G-4090)*

▲ Ohio Tile & Marble Co........................ E 513 541-4211
Cincinnati *(G-2926)*

OK Brugmann Jr & Sons Inc................. G 330 274-2106
Mantua *(G-8873)*

▲ Osborne Inc....................................... E 440 942-7000
Mentor *(G-9578)*

Overhead Inc.. G 419 476-0300
Toledo *(G-13083)*

P & T Millwork Inc................................ F 440 543-2151
Chagrin Falls *(G-2175)*

▲ Pease Enterprises Inc........................ F 513 871-8907
Cincinnati *(G-2951)*

Pickens Window Service Inc.................. G 513 931-4432
Cincinnati *(G-2962)*

Pleasant Valley Ready Mix Inc.............. F 330 852-2613
Sugarcreek *(G-12645)*

Portsmouth Block Inc............................ F 740 353-4113
Portsmouth *(G-11474)*

Prairie Builders Supply Inc................... G 419 332-7546
Fremont *(G-7127)*

Quikrete Companies LLC........................ E 330 296-6080
Ravenna *(G-11536)*

R C Moore Lumber Co............................ F 740 732-4950
Caldwell *(G-1727)*

Rockwood Products Ltd.......................... E 330 893-2392
Millersburg *(G-10007)*

Rosatis Window Co LLC.......................... D 614 777-4806
Columbus *(G-5235)*

◆ Saint-Gobain Norpro Corp.................. C 330 673-5860
Stow *(G-12458)*

Salem Mill & Cabinet Co........................ G 330 337-9568
Salem *(G-11810)*

Scioto Ready Mix LLC............................ D 740 924-9273
Pataskala *(G-11150)*

Seemray LLC.. E 440 536-8705
Cleveland *(G-4285)*

Smyrna Ready Mix Concrete LLC........... D 937 855-0410
Germantown *(G-7254)*

Snyder Concrete Products Inc.............. G 937 339-7577
Troy *(G-13257)*

St Henry Tile Co Inc.............................. G 937 548-1101
Greenville *(G-7355)*

St Henry Tile Co Inc.............................. E 419 678-4841
Saint Henry *(G-11724)*

Stamm Contracting Company Inc.......... F 330 274-8230
Mantua *(G-8875)*

Stiber Fabricating Inc........................... F 216 771-7210
Cleveland *(G-4332)*

Stocker Concrete Company.................... F 740 254-4626
Gnadenhutten *(G-7293)*

T C Redi Mix Youngstown Inc............... E 330 755-2143
Youngstown *(G-14942)*

Terry Lumber and Supply Co................. F 330 659-6800
Peninsula *(G-11184)*

The F A Requarth Company.................... E 937 224-1141
Dayton *(G-6048)*

The Galehouse Companies Inc.............. E 330 658-2023
Doylestown *(G-6270)*

The Ideal Builders Supply...................... F 216 741-1600
Cleveland *(G-4386)*

▲ Thomas Do-It Center Inc................... E 740 446-2002
Gallipolis *(G-7209)*

Toledo Window & Awning Inc................. F 419 474-3396
Toledo *(G-13162)*

Tri-County Block and Brick Inc.............. E 419 826-7060
Swanton *(G-12696)*

Trumbull Cement Products Co............... G 330 372-4342
Warren *(G-13802)*

Vances Department Store....................... G 937 549-3033
Manchester *(G-8756)*

Vances Department Store....................... G 937 549-2188
Manchester *(G-8755)*

◆ Walnut Creek Planing Ltd.................. D 330 893-3244
Millersburg *(G-10018)*

Warren Concrete and Supply Co........... G 330 393-1581
Warren *(G-13810)*

Waxco International Inc.......................... F 937 746-4845
Miamisburg *(G-9752)*

Westview Concrete Corp......................... F 440 458-5800
Elyria *(G-6602)*

Westview Concrete Corp......................... E 440 235-1800
Olmsted Falls *(G-10943)*

Yoder Lumber Co Inc............................. E 330 893-3131
Sugarcreek *(G-12658)*

Youngstown Fence Incorporated........... G 330 788-8110
Youngstown *(G-14969)*

Zaenkert Srvying Essntials Inc............. G 513 738-2917
Okeana *(G-10931)*

5231 Paint, glass, and wallpaper stores

A Service Glass Inc............................... F 937 426-4920
Beavercreek *(G-963)*

All State GL Block Fctry Inc.................. G 440 205-8410
Mentor *(G-9476)*

American Indus Maintanence................. G 937 254-3400
Dayton *(G-5653)*

Blockamerica Corporation...................... G 614 274-0700
Columbus *(G-4765)*

◆ Comex North America Inc.................. D 303 307-2100
Cleveland *(G-3551)*

Dale Kestler... G 513 871-9000
Cincinnati *(G-2540)*

▲ Franklin Art Glass Studios................ E 614 221-2972
Columbus *(G-4937)*

Middlefield Glass Incorporated.............. G 440 632-5699
Middlefield *(G-9809)*

Niles Mirror & Glass Inc........................ E 330 652-6277
Niles *(G-10597)*

Ohio Trailer Inc..................................... G 330 392-4444
Warren *(G-13787)*

Oldcastle Buildingenvelope Inc.............. C 800 537-4064
Perrysburg *(G-11249)*

Prints & Paints Flr Cvg Co Inc.............. E 419 462-5663
Galion *(G-7197)*

Sherwin-Williams Company.................... G 330 528-0124
Hudson *(G-7856)*

Sherwin-Williams Company.................... F 440 846-4328
Strongsville *(G-12600)*

Sherwin-Williams Company.................... A 216 566-2000
Cleveland *(G-4293)*

◆ Sherwn-Wllams Auto Fnshes Corp.....E 216 332-8330
Cleveland *(G-4295)*

5251 Hardware stores

Caldwell Lumber & Supply Co.................F 740 732-2306
Caldwell *(G-1724)*

Cammel Saw Company........................F 330 477-3764
Canton *(G-1851)*

D & M Saw & Tool Inc.......................G 513 871-5433
Cincinnati *(G-2535)*

E P Gerber & Sons Inc......................D 330 857-2021
Kidron *(G-8126)*

Fountain Specialists Inc....................G 513 831-5717
Milford *(G-9934)*

Gordon Tool Inc.............................F 419 263-3151
Payne *(G-11163)*

▲ Graco Ohio Inc............................D 330 494-1313
North Canton *(G-10644)*

Hyde Park Lumber Company...................E 513 271-1500
Cincinnati *(G-2736)*

Judy Mills Company Inc.....................E 513 271-4241
Cincinnati *(G-2775)*

Kemps Ace Hardware Inc.....................F 740 472-1651
Woodsfield *(G-14614)*

Lochard Inc................................D 937 492-8811
Sidney *(G-12031)*

Mapledale Farm Inc.........................F 440 286-3389
Chardon *(G-2214)*

▲ Matco Tools Corporation..................B 330 929-4949
Stow *(G-12440)*

Mid-Wood Inc...............................F 419 257-3331
North Baltimore *(G-10614)*

National Tool & Equipment Inc..............F 330 629-8665
Youngstown *(G-14903)*

◆ Oase North America Inc...................G 800 365-3880
Aurora *(G-682)*

Rocky Hinge Inc............................G 330 539-6296
Girard *(G-7279)*

S Lehman Central Warehouse.................G 330 828-8828
Dalton *(G-5594)*

Spencer Feed & Supply LLC..................F 330 648-2111
Spencer *(G-12235)*

▲ Stanley Industrial & Auto LLC...........D 614 755-7000
Dublin *(G-6349)*

Terry Lumber and Supply Co.................F 330 659-6800
Peninsula *(G-11184)*

▲ Thomas Do-It Center Inc.................E 740 446-2002
Gallipolis *(G-7209)*

Wauseon Silo & Coal Company..............F
Wauseon *(G-13861)*

5261 Retail nurseries and garden stores

All Power Equipment LLC....................F 740 593-3279
Athens *(G-632)*

Bortnick Tractor Sales Inc.................E 330 924-2555
Cortland *(G-5442)*

Centerra Co-Op.............................E 419 281-2153
Ashland *(G-526)*

Fountain Specialists Inc...................G 513 831-5717
Milford *(G-9934)*

▲ Hc Companies Inc.........................E 440 632-3333
Twinsburg *(G-13315)*

Insta-Gro Manufacturing Inc................G 419 845-3046
Caledonia *(G-1732)*

Karl Kuemmerling Inc.......................F
Massillon *(G-9209)*

Keystone Cooperative Inc...................G 937 884-5526
Verona *(G-13591)*

M B K Inc..................................F 330 889-3451
Bristolville *(G-1498)*

Markers Inc................................G 440 933-5927
Avon Lake *(G-764)*

Mid-Wood Inc...............................F 419 257-3331
North Baltimore *(G-10614)*

New Eezy-Gro Inc...........................F 419 927-6110
Upper Sandusky *(G-13449)*

Nutrien AG Solutions Inc...................G 614 873-4253
Milford Center *(G-9958)*

Ohigro Inc.................................E 740 726-2429
Waldo *(G-13691)*

Ohio Drill & Tool Co.......................E 330 525-7717
Homeworth *(G-7806)*

Ohio Mulch Supply Inc......................G 740 548-6242
Lewis Center *(G-8347)*

Premier Feeds LLC..........................G 937 584-2411
Sabina *(G-11683)*

Riverview Productions Inc..................G 740 441-1150
Gallipolis *(G-7208)*

53 GENERAL MERCHANDISE STORES

5311 Department stores

Siemens Industry Inc.......................F 513 576-2088
Milford *(G-9952)*

5399 Miscellaneous general merchandise

John Purdum................................G 513 897-9686
Waynesville *(G-13879)*

Raven Concealment Systems LLC..............E 440 508-9000
North Ridgeville *(G-10745)*

54 FOOD STORES

5411 Grocery stores

Baltic Country Meats.......................G 330 897-7025
Baltic *(G-776)*

Bread Kneads Inc...........................G 419 422-3863
Findlay *(G-6845)*

Brinkman Turkey Farms Inc..................F 419 365-5127
Findlay *(G-6846)*

C J Kraft Enterprises Inc..................G 740 653-9606
Lancaster *(G-8184)*

Dioguardis Italian Foods Inc...............F 330 492-3777
Canton *(G-1883)*

Fragapane Bakeries Inc.....................G 440 779-6050
North Olmsted *(G-10721)*

Heinens Inc................................C 330 562-5297
Aurora *(G-673)*

Investors United Inc.......................G 419 473-8942
Toledo *(G-13008)*

Lariccias Italian Foods Inc................F 330 729-0222
Youngstown *(G-14887)*

Mumfords Potato Chips & Deli...............G 937 653-3491
Urbana *(G-13474)*

Nestle Prepared Foods Company..............B 440 349-5757
Solon *(G-12157)*

▲ Nestle Prepared Foods Company...........A 440 248-3600
Solon *(G-12158)*

Riesbeck Food Markets Inc..................C 740 695-3401
Saint Clairsville *(G-11709)*

Tbone Sales LLC............................G 330 897-6131
Baltic *(G-781)*

Troyers Trail Bologna Inc..................G 330 893-2414
Dundee *(G-6370)*

United Dairy Farmers Inc...................C 513 396-8700
Cincinnati *(G-3181)*

Whitacre Enterprises Inc...................G 740 934-2331
Graysville *(G-7322)*

Zygo Inc...................................G 513 281-0888
Cincinnati *(G-3245)*

5421 Meat and fish markets

D & H Meats Inc............................G 419 387-7767
Vanlue *(G-13585)*

Dee-Jays Cstm Btchring Proc LL.............F 740 694-7492
Fredericktown *(G-7076)*

Duma Meats Inc.............................G 330 628-3438
Mogadore *(G-10074)*

Foris Extraordinary Meats LLC..............F 614 670-5726
Columbus *(G-4931)*

Hoffman Meat Processing....................G 419 864-3994
Cardington *(G-2054)*

Honeybaked Ham Company.....................E 513 583-9700
Cincinnati *(G-2730)*

John Krusinski.............................F 216 441-0100
Cleveland *(G-3889)*

John Stehlin & Sons Co.....................G 513 385-6164
Cincinnati *(G-2769)*

Lee Williams Meats Inc.....................E 419 729-3893
Toledo *(G-13031)*

Marshallville Packing Co Inc...............G 330 855-2871
Marshallville *(G-9007)*

Mc Connells Market.........................G 740 765-4300
Richmond *(G-11604)*

Pettisville Meats Incorporated.............F 419 445-0921
Pettisville *(G-11286)*

Queen City Sausage & Prov Inc..............C 513 541-5581
Cincinnati *(G-3025)*

Riesbeck Food Markets Inc..................C 740 695-3401
Saint Clairsville *(G-11709)*

Winesburg Meats Inc........................G 330 359-5092
Winesburg *(G-14609)*

5431 Fruit and vegetable markets

Coopers Mill Inc...........................G 419 562-4215
Bucyrus *(G-1676)*

Grays Orange Barn Inc......................G 419 568-2718
Wapakoneta *(G-13714)*

5441 Candy, nut, and confectionery stores

▲ Anthony-Thomas Candy Company.............C 614 274-8405
Columbus *(G-4719)*

Brandts Candies Inc........................G 440 942-1016
Willoughby *(G-14433)*

Chocolate Pig Inc..........................G 440 461-4511
Cleveland *(G-3496)*

Coblentz Family Brands Inc.................E 330 893-2995
Walnut Creek *(G-13693)*

Dietsch Brothers Incorporated..............E 419 422-4474
Findlay *(G-6059)*

Esther Price Candies Corporation...........E 937 253-2121
Dayton *(G-5769)*

Fannie May Confections Inc.................A 330 494-0833
North Canton *(G-10638)*

Fawn Confectionery Inc.....................F 513 574-9612
Cincinnati *(G-2613)*

Golden Turtle Chocolate Fctry..............G 513 932-1990
Lebanon *(G-8264)*

Gorant Chocolatier LLC.....................C 330 726-8821
Boardman *(G-1372)*

Great Lakes Popcorn Company................G 419 732-3080
Port Clinton *(G-11443)*

▲ Harry London Candies Inc.................E 330 494-0833
North Canton *(G-10645)*

Hartville Chocolates Inc...................G 330 877-1999
Hartville *(G-7576)*

Island Delights Inc........................G 866 887-4100
Seville *(G-11918)*

◆ Jml Holdings Inc.........................F 419 866-7500
Holland *(G-7770)*

Linneas Candy Supplies Inc.................E 330 678-7112
Kent *(G-8046)*

▲ Malleys Candies LLC......................D 216 362-8700
Cleveland *(G-3983)*

SIC

Maries Candies LLC	G	937 465-3061	
West Liberty *(G-14176)*			
New Dawn Distribution Inc	'G	330 759-3500	
Girard *(G-7277)*			
Piqua Chocolate Company Inc	G	937 773-1981	
Piqua *(G-11374)*			
Robert E McGrath Inc	F	440 572-7747	
Strongsville *(G-12593)*			
Sweeties Olympia Treats LLC	F	440 572-7747	
Strongsville *(G-12608)*			
◆ Trophy Nut Co	E	937 667-8478	
Tipp City *(G-12849)*			

5451 Dairy products stores

Bunker Hill Cheese Co Inc .... D 330 893-2131
Millersburg *(G-9973)*

Food Plant Engineering LLC .... F 513 618-3165
Blue Ash *(G-1275)*

Grays Orange Barn Inc .... G 419 568-2718
Wapakoneta *(G-13714)*

Guggisberg Cheese Inc .... E 330 893-2550
Millersburg *(G-9982)*

▲ Hans Rothenbuhler & Son Inc ..... E 440 632-6000
Middlefield *(G-9796)*

Jenis Splendid Ice Creams LLC .... E 614 488-3224
Columbus *(G-5036)*

▲ Malleys Candies LLC .... D 216 362-8700
Cleveland *(G-3983)*

Milk Hney Cndy Soda Shoppe LLC .... G 330 492-5884
Canton *(G-1950)*

Schindlers Broad Run Chshuse I ...... F 330 343-4108
Dover *(G-6260)*

United Dairy Inc .... B 740 373-4121
Marietta *(G-8958)*

United Dairy Farmers Inc .... E 513 396-8700
Cincinnati *(G-3181)*

Youngs Jersey Dairy Inc .... B 937 325-0629
Yellow Springs *(G-14794)*

5461 Retail bakeries

Alfred Nickles Bakery Inc .... E 740 453-6522
Zanesville *(G-14985)*

Angelic Bakehouse LLC .... E 414 312-7300
Westerville *(G-14203)*

Blf Enterprises Inc .... F 937 642-6425
Westerville *(G-14246)*

Brooks Pastries Inc .... G 614 274-4880
Plain City *(G-11399)*

Buns of Delaware Inc .... F 740 363-2867
Delaware *(G-6135)*

Busken Bakery Inc .... D 513 871-2114
Cincinnati *(G-2434)*

Cake In A Cup Inc .... G 419 491-1104
Toledo *(G-12909)*

Cookie Bouquets Inc .... G 614 888-2171
Columbus *(G-4847)*

Crispie Creme Chillicothe Inc .... G 740 774-3770
Chillicothe *(G-2249)*

Crumbs Inc .... F 740 592-3803
Athens *(G-637)*

Dandi Enterprises Inc .... G 419 516-9070
Solon *(G-12099)*

Evans Bakery Inc .... G 937 228-4151
Dayton *(G-5771)*

Fragapane Bakeries Inc .... G 440 779-6050
North Olmsted *(G-10721)*

Hostess Brands Inc .... D 816 701-4600
Orrville *(G-10984)*

I Dream of Cakes .... G 937 533-6024
Eaton *(G-6455)*

Investors United Inc .... F 419 473-8942
Toledo *(G-13008)*

K & B Acquisitions Inc	F	937 253-1163	
Dayton *(G-5837)*			
Kennedys Bakery Inc	G	740 432-2301	
Cambridge *(G-1746)*			
Krispy Kreme Doughnut Corp	E	614 798-0812	
Columbus *(G-5057)*			

Krispy Kreme Doughnut Corp .... D 614 876-0058
Columbus *(G-5058)*

La Marquise Inc .... D 614 488-1911
Columbus *(G-5060)*

Mary Ann Donut Shoppe Inc .... G 330 478-1655
Canton *(G-1938)*

McHappys Dnuts Parkersburg Inc ...... D 740 593-8744
Athens *(G-643)*

Meeks Pastry Shop .... G 419 782-4871
Defiance *(G-6121)*

Norcia Bakery .... G 330 454-1077
Canton *(G-1959)*

Osmans Pies Inc .... E 330 607-9083
Stow *(G-12448)*

Pepperidge Farm Incorporated .... G 419 933-2611
Willard *(G-14407)*

Schulers Bakery Inc .... E 937 323-4154
Springfield *(G-12371)*

Schwebel Baking Company .... E 330 783-2860
Hebron *(G-7635)*

Schwebel Baking Company .... C 440 248-1500
Solon *(G-12179)*

Thurns Bakery & Deli .... G 614 221-9246
Columbus *(G-5323)*

Wal-Bon of Ohio Inc .... E 740 423-8178
Belpre *(G-1156)*

5499 Miscellaneous food stores

Aqua Pennsylvania Inc .... G 440 257-6190
Mentor On The Lake *(G-9656)*

Boston Stoker Inc .... F 937 890-6401
Vandalia *(G-13551)*

Crimson Cup Inc .... F 614 252-3335
Columbus *(G-4860)*

Dental Pure Water Inc .... F 440 234-0890
Berea *(G-1167)*

Generations Coffee Company LLC .... F 440 546-0901
Brecksville *(G-1467)*

Gold Star Chili Inc .... E 513 231-4541
Cincinnati *(G-2681)*

McDonalds .... G 513 753-6100
Amelia *(G-433)*

McDonalds .... F 513 752-2008
Cincinnati *(G-2313)*

McDonalds .... F 216 226-7754
Lakewood *(G-8169)*

McDonalds .... E 513 336-0820
Mason *(G-9127)*

McDonalds .... F 740 753-4018
Nelsonville *(G-10318)*

McDonalds .... F 419 935-1414
Willard *(G-14404)*

McDonalds .... F 330 792-0527
Youngstown *(G-14895)*

Mustard Seed Health Fd Mkt Inc .... E 440 519-3663
Solon *(G-12155)*

Nestle Usa Inc .... D 216 861-8350
Cleveland *(G-4070)*

Ohio Coffee Collaborative Ltd .... F 614 564-9852
Columbus *(G-5139)*

Premier Tanning & Nutrition .... G 419 342-6259
Shelby *(G-11973)*

Roots Poultry Inc .... G 419 332-0041
Fremont *(G-7130)*

Vitamin Shoppe Industries LLC .... A
Delaware *(G-6179)*

Wileys Finest LLC .... C 740 622-1072
Coshocton *(G-5478)*

55 AUTOMOTIVE DEALERS AND GASOLINE SERVICE STATIONS

5511 New and used car dealers

Doug Marine Motors Inc .... F 740 335-3700
Wshngtn Ct Hs *(G-14738)*

Ford Motor Company .... C 440 933-1215
Avon Lake *(G-756)*

Ford Motor Company .... A 419 226-7000
Lima *(G-8408)*

Friess Welding Inc .... G 330 644-8160
Coventry Township *(G-5482)*

General Motors LLC .... A 216 265-5000
Cleveland *(G-3767)*

General Motors LLC .... C 330 824-5840
Warren *(G-13768)*

Honda Dev & Mfg Amer LLC .... C 937 644-0724
Marysville *(G-9028)*

▲ Jmac Inc .... E 614 436-2418
Columbus *(G-5041)*

Kinstle Truck & Auto Svc Inc .... G 419 738-7493
Wapakoneta *(G-13718)*

▲ Knippen Chrysler Ddge Jeep Inc ...... F 419 695-4976
Delphos *(G-6188)*

Mitsubishi Chemical Amer Inc .... D 419 483-2931
Bellevue *(G-1126)*

◆ Mitsubishi Elc Auto Amer Inc .... B 513 573-6614
Mason *(G-9128)*

Mitsubishi Elc Automtn Inc .... E 937 492-3058
Sidney *(G-12035)*

Steves Vans ACC Unlimited LLC .... G 740 374-3154
Marietta *(G-8950)*

Tbone Sales LLC .... G 330 897-6131
Baltic *(G-781)*

Tiger General LLC .... F 330 239-4949
Medina *(G-9456)*

▼ Trailer One Inc .... F 330 723-7474
Medina *(G-9457)*

5521 Used car dealers

Cars and Parts Magazine .... D 937 498-0803
Sidney *(G-12001)*

D&D Clssic Auto Rstoration Inc .... G 937 473-2229
Covington *(G-5492)*

▲ Dawn Enterprises Inc .... E 216 642-5506
Cleveland *(G-3601)*

▲ King Kutter II Inc .... E 740 446-0351
Gallipolis *(G-7207)*

▲ Knippen Chrysler Ddge Jeep Inc ...... F 419 695-4976
Delphos *(G-6188)*

Suburbanite Inc .... G 419 756-4390
Mansfield *(G-8856)*

Trucks & Parts of Tampa LLC .... E 937 437-0377
New Paris *(G-10427)*

Tuffy Manufacturing .... F 330 940-2356
Akron *(G-348)*

▲ United Ignition Wire Corp .... G 216 898-1112
Cleveland *(G-4443)*

5531 Auto and home supply stores

AB Tire & Repair .... G 440 543-2929
Chagrin Falls *(G-2152)*

Abutilon Company Inc .... F 419 536-6123
Toledo *(G-12862)*

Ace Truck Equipment Co .... E 740 453-0551
Zanesville *(G-14981)*

▲ Allen Aircraft Products Inc .... D 330 296-9621
Ravenna *(G-11516)*

American Cold Forge LLC...................... E 419 836-1062
Northwood (G-10802)

Associates Tire and Svc Inc................... F 937 436-4692
Centerville (G-2129)

Battery Unlimited.................................. G 740 452-5030
Zanesville (G-14993)

Bell Tire Co... F 440 234-8022
Olmsted Falls (G-10937)

Best One Tire & Svc Lima Inc................ G 419 425-3322
Findlay (G-6843)

▲ Best One Tire & Svc Lima Inc............ E 419 229-2380
Lima (G-8389)

▲ Bkt USA Inc...................................... F 330 836-1090
Copley (G-5430)

Bob Sumerel Tire Co Inc...................... G 937 235-0062
Dayton (G-5681)

Bob Sumerel Tire Co Inc...................... G 740 432-5200
Lore City (G-8588)

Bob Sumerel Tire Co Inc...................... F 330 769-9092
Seville (G-11914)

Bob Sumerel Tire Co Inc...................... G 740 454-9728
Zanesville (G-14999)

Bob Sumerel Tire Company Inc............ G 740 927-2811
Reynoldsburg (G-11559)

Bowman Tire Repr Ctr Bxley LLC......... G 740 928-7000
Hebron (G-7609)

Boy-Rad Inc.. G 614 766-1228
Dublin (G-6283)

Bridgestone Ret Operations LLC........... G 740 592-3075
Athens (G-635)

Bridgestone Ret Operations LLC........... G 614 834-3672
Canal Winchester (G-1787)

Bridgestone Ret Operations LLC........... G 330 454-9478
Canton (G-1845)

Bridgestone Ret Operations LLC........... G 513 793-4550
Cincinnati (G-2424)

Bridgestone Ret Operations LLC........... G 513 677-5200
Cincinnati (G-2425)

Bridgestone Ret Operations LLC........... G 513 681-7682
Cincinnati (G-2426)

Bridgestone Ret Operations LLC........... G 440 842-3200
Cleveland (G-3436)

Bridgestone Ret Operations LLC........... G 440 461-4747
Cleveland (G-3437)

Bridgestone Ret Operations LLC........... G 216 229-2550
Cleveland (G-3438)

Bridgestone Ret Operations LLC........... G 216 382-8970
Cleveland (G-3439)

Bridgestone Ret Operations LLC........... F 614 864-3350
Columbus (G-4777)

Bridgestone Ret Operations LLC........... F 614 491-8062
Columbus (G-4778)

Bridgestone Ret Operations LLC........... G 614 224-4221
Columbus (G-4779)

Bridgestone Ret Operations LLC........... G 440 324-3327
Elyria (G-6504)

Bridgestone Ret Operations LLC........... G 440 365-8308
Elyria (G-6505)

Bridgestone Ret Operations LLC........... G 937 548-1197
Greenville (G-7336)

Bridgestone Ret Operations LLC........... G 513 868-7399
Hamilton (G-7473)

Bridgestone Ret Operations LLC........... G 330 673-1700
Kent (G-8020)

Bridgestone Ret Operations LLC........... F 440 299-6126
Mentor (G-9493)

Bridgestone Ret Operations LLC........... F 740 397-5601
Mount Vernon (G-10237)

Bridgestone Ret Operations LLC........... G 614 861-7994
Reynoldsburg (G-11560)

Bridgestone Ret Operations LLC........... G 419 625-6571
Sandusky (G-11823)

Bridgestone Ret Operations LLC........... F 937 325-4638
Springfield (G-12286)

Bridgestone Ret Operations LLC........... G 724 346-2621
Warren (G-13744)

Bridgestone Ret Operations LLC........... G 330 758-0921
Youngstown (G-14825)

Bridgestone Ret Operations LLC........... G 330 759-3697
Youngstown (G-14826)

▲ Bucyrus Precision Tech Inc............... C 419 563-9950
Bucyrus (G-1674)

C & F Tire & Truck Repair...................... F 419 526-1412
Ontario (G-10947)

Canton Bandag Co................................ G 330 454-3025
Canton (G-1853)

Capital Tire Inc..................................... E 330 364-4731
Toledo (G-12911)

◆ Cequent Consumer Products Inc....... D 440 498-0001
Solon (G-12092)

◆ Crown Equipment Corporation........... A 419 629-2311
New Bremen (G-10358)

Custom Recapping Inc........................... G 937 324-4331
Springfield (G-12297)

Doug Marine Motors Inc....................... F 740 335-3700
Wshngtn Ct Hs (G-14738)

Epix Tube Co Inc.................................. F 937 529-4858
Dayton (G-5766)

Exit 11 Truck Tire Service Inc.............. G 330 659-6372
Richfield (G-11591)

Finale Products Inc............................... G 419 874-2662
Perrysburg (G-11221)

Front Pocket Innovations LLC............... G 330 441-2365
Wadsworth (G-13639)

▲ Galion-Godwin Truck Bdy Co LLC.... F 330 359-5495
Dundee (G-6365)

Garro Tread Corporation........................ G 330 376-3125
Akron (G-156)

Goodyear Tire & Rubber Company........ F 419 643-8273
Beaverdam (G-1008)

Goodyear Tire & Rubber Company........ G 330 966-1274
Canton (G-1904)

Goodyear Tire & Rubber Company........ G 330 759-9343
Youngstown (G-14869)

◆ Goodyear Tire & Rubber Company.... A 330 796-2121
Akron (G-164)

▲ Grismer Tire Company...................... E 937 643-2526
Centerville (G-2132)

H & H Truck Parts LLC........................ E 216 642-4540
Cleveland (C-3804)

Horizon Global Corporation.................. E 734 656-3000
Cleveland (G-3837)

J & J Tire & Alignment........................ G 330 424-5200
Lisbon (G-8471)

JTL Enterprises LLC............................ E 937 890-8189
Dayton (G-5832)

K-M-S Industries Inc........................... G 440 243-6680
Brookpark (G-1554)

Kaffenbarger Truck Eqp Co.................. E 513 772-6800
Cincinnati (G-2777)

Keystone Auto Glass Inc...................... D 419 509-0497
Maumee (G-9302)

▲ Knippen Chrysler Ddge Jeep Inc....... F 419 695-4976
Delphos (G-6188)

M Technologies Inc.............................. F 330 477-9009
Canton (G-1937)

Mader Automotive Center Inc............... F 937 339-2681
Troy (G-13238)

Mark Knupp Muffler & Tire Inc............. G 937 773-1334
Piqua (G-11365)

Marlow-2000 Inc.................................. F 216 362-8500
Cleveland (G-3991)

Martin Diesel Inc.................................. E 419 782-9911
Defiance (G-6120)

Mid America Tire of Hillsboro Inc........... E 937 393-3520
Hillsboro (G-7720)

Mid-Wood Inc....................................... F 419 257-3331
North Baltimore (G-10614)

Mitchell Bros Tire Rtread Svc................ G 740 353-1551
Portsmouth (G-11470)

Muskingum Tire Company Inc............... G 740 453-8473
Zanesville (G-15030)

Ohio Auto Supply Company.................. G 330 454-5105
Canton (G-1964)

Overhead Door of Pike County.............. G 740 289-3925
Piketon (G-11312)

Pattons Trck & Hvy Eqp Svc Inc........... F 740 385-4067
Logan (G-8523)

Paul Shovlin.. G 330 757-0032
Youngstown (G-14915)

Perkins Motor Service Ltd..................... F 440 277-1256
Lorain (G-8573)

Q T Columbus LLC.............................. G 800 758-2410
Columbus (G-5216)

▼ QT Equipment Company................... E 330 724-3055
Akron (G-272)

Randys Tire & Auto Repair Inc.............. G 419 562-2926
Bucyrus (G-1688)

River City Body Company...................... F 513 772-9317
Cincinnati (G-3047)

Rust Belt Broncos LLC......................... G 330 533-0048
Canfield (G-1815)

Shrader Tire & Oil Inc........................... G 419 420-8435
Perrysburg (G-11262)

Skaggs Trlr & Tire Repr Co Inc.............. F 440 986-7470
Amherst (G-452)

Skinner Firestone Inc........................... G 740 984-4247
Beverly (G-1209)

Snider Tire Inc..................................... F 740 439-2741
Cambridge (G-1760)

Steves Vans ACC Unlimited LLC.......... G 740 374-3154
Marietta (G-8950)

▲ Superior Production LLC................... C 614 444-2181
Columbus (G-5299)

Support Svc LLC.................................. G 419 617-0660
Lexington (G-8375)

Sycamore Tire & Auto Repair................ G 513 793-0726
Cincinnati (G-3134)

Tbc Retail Group Inc............................ E 216 267-8040
Cleveland (G-4365)

Tbone Sales LLC.................................. G 330 897-6131
Baltic (G-701)

Tom Barbour Auto Parts Inc.................. F 740 354-4654
Portsmouth (G-11479)

Trucks & Parts of Tampa LLC................ E 937 437-0377
New Paris (G-10427)

Urra Co Inc.. G 330 673-8473
Kent (G-8093)

Victor Bodie Tire Co............................. G 216 431-1700
Cleveland (G-4471)

Vintage Automotive Elc Inc................... F 419 472-9349
Toledo (G-13175)

Wayne A Whaley.................................. G 330 525-7779
Homeworth (G-7807)

Western Branch Diesel LLC.................. F 330 454-8800
Canton (G-2047)

X-Treme Finishes Inc........................... F 330 474-0614
North Royalton (G-10790)

Ziegler Tire and Supply Co................... G 330 434-7126
Akron (G-362)

Ziegler Tire and Supply Co................... G 330 477-3463
Canton (G-2052)

Ziegler Tire and Supply Co................... E 330 343-7739
Dover (G-6267)

5541 Gasoline service stations

SIC

◆ Giant Industries Inc.............................D 419 421-2121
Findlay *(G-6870)*

Plug Power Inc.....................................G 518 605-5703
West Carrollton *(G-13931)*

Shelly and Sands Inc..........................F 740 453-0721
Zanesville *(G-15047)*

Tbone Sales LLC..................................G 330 897-6131
Baltic *(G-781)*

True North Energy LLC........................E 440 442-0060
Mayfield Heights *(G-9343)*

United Dairy Farmers Inc.....................C 513 396-8700
Cincinnati *(G-3181)*

5551 Boat dealers

Dynamic Plastics Inc...........................G 937 437-7261
New Paris *(G-10426)*

Hydromotive Engineering Co................G 330 425-4266
Twinsburg *(G-13317)*

Mariners Landing Inc...........................G 513 941-3625
Cincinnati *(G-2846)*

Sailors Tailor Inc.................................F 937 862-7781
Spring Valley *(G-12243)*

5561 Recreational vehicle dealers

All Power Equipment LLC......................F 740 593-3279
Athens *(G-632)*

Mitchs Welding & Hitches ....G 419 893-3117
Maumee *(G-9311)*

Steves Vans ACC Unlimited LLC..........G 740 374-3154
Marietta *(G-8950)*

5571 Motorcycle dealers

Abranda Llc..F 614 577-8080
Blacklick *(G-1218)*

◆ Gear Star Amrcn Prfmce Trnsmss......E 330 434-5216
Akron *(G-157)*

▲ Spiegler Brake Systems USA LLC.....G 937 291-1735
Dayton *(G-6018)*

◆ Wholecycle Inc...............................E 330 929-8123
Peninsula *(G-11186)*

5599 Automotive dealers, nec

Golf Car Company Inc..........................G 614 873-1055
Plain City *(G-11410)*

Jake Sweeney Mazda Tri-County...........G 513 782-1150
Cincinnati *(G-2757)*

M R Trailer Sales Inc............................G 330 339-7701
New Philadelphia *(G-10456)*

OReilly Equipment LLC.........................G 440 564-1234
Newbury *(G-10559)*

56 APPAREL AND ACCESSORY STORES

5611 Men's and boys' clothing stores

▲ City Apparel Inc.............................F 419 434-1155
Findlay *(G-6852)*

Rnp Inc...G
Dellroy *(G-6182)*

S F Mock & Associates LLC...................F 937 438-0196
Dayton *(G-5991)*

5621 Women's clothing stores

▲ City Apparel Inc.............................F 419 434-1155
Findlay *(G-6852)*

Fluff Boutique....................................G 513 227-6614
Cincinnati *(G-2630)*

5632 Women's accessory and specialty stores

Indra Holdings Corp.............................C 513 682-8200
Cincinnati *(G-2743)*

5641 Children's and infants' wear stores

Carters Inc...G 330 758-0390
Boardman *(G-1369)*

Love Laugh & Laundry.........................G 567 377-1951
Toledo *(G-13039)*

5651 Family clothing stores

Chris Stepp..G 513 248-0822
Milford *(G-9928)*

Odyssey Spirits Inc.............................F 330 562-1523
Chagrin Falls *(G-2174)*

Ohio Mills Corporation.........................G 216 431-3979
Cleveland *(G-4116)*

Vances Department Store.....................G 937 549-3033
Manchester *(G-8756)*

Vances Department Store.....................G 937 549-2188
Manchester *(G-8755)*

5661 Shoe stores

Cobblers Corner LLC............................G 330 482-4005
Columbiana *(G-4609)*

Hudson Leather Ltd.............................G 419 485-8531
Pioneer *(G-11321)*

Rnp Inc...G
Dellroy *(G-6182)*

Vances Department Store.....................G 937 549-3033
Manchester *(G-8756)*

Vances Department Store.....................G 937 549-2188
Manchester *(G-8755)*

5699 Miscellaneous apparel and accessories

Appleheart Inc....................................G 937 384-0430
Miamisburg *(G-9666)*

Bluelogos Inc.....................................F 614 898-9971
Westerville *(G-14247)*

Carols Ultra Stitch & Variety.................G 419 935-8991
Willard *(G-14401)*

Impact Printing and Design LLC............F 833 522-6200
Columbus *(G-5003)*

Indra Holdings Corp.............................C 513 682-8200
Cincinnati *(G-2743)*

Jason Schirmer...................................G 937 433-3023
Miamisburg *(G-9702)*

K Ventures Inc....................................F 419 678-2308
Coldwater *(G-4579)*

Karl Kuemmerling Inc..........................F
Massillon *(G-9209)*

Kip-Craft Incorporated.........................D 216 898-5500
Cleveland *(G-3924)*

LLC Bowman Leather............................G 330 893-1954
Millersburg *(G-9994)*

Markt LLC...G 740 397-5900
Mount Vernon *(G-10250)*

New Dawn Distribution Inc...................G 330 759-3500
Girard *(G-7277)*

Odyssey Spirits Inc.............................F 330 562-1523
Chagrin Falls *(G-2174)*

Rbr Enterprises LLC.............................F 866 437-9327
Brecksville *(G-1480)*

Rnp Inc...G
Dellroy *(G-6182)*

Shoot-A-Way Inc.................................F 419 294-4654
Nevada *(G-10323)*

Tee Creations.....................................G 937 878-2822
Fairborn *(G-6702)*

◆ The Fechheimer Brothers Co.............C 513 793-5400
Blue Ash *(G-1342)*

▲ Totes Isotoner Corporation..............D 513 682-8200
Cincinnati *(G-3159)*

▲ Totes Isotoner Holdings LLC............C 513 682-8200
Cincinnati *(G-3160)*

Unisport Inc.......................................F 419 529-4727
Ontario *(G-10953)*

Uptown Dog The Inc............................G 740 592-4600
Athens *(G-655)*

57 HOME FURNITURE, FURNISHINGS AND EQUIPMENT STORES

5712 Furniture stores

Ahmf Inc..E 614 921-1223
Columbus *(G-4681)*

Americas Mdular Off Specialist.............G 614 277-0216
Grove City *(G-7372)*

◆ Archbold Furniture Co......................E 567 444-4666
Archbold *(G-488)*

▲ Banner Mattress Co Inc...................D 419 324-7181
Toledo *(G-12892)*

Bruening Glass Works Inc.....................G 440 333-4768
Cleveland *(G-3445)*

Chagrin Valley Custom Furn LLC...........G 440 591-5511
Warrensville Heights *(G-13816)*

▲ Coconis Furniture Inc......................E 740 452-1231
South Zanesville *(G-12232)*

COS Blueprint Inc................................E 330 376-0022
Akron *(G-107)*

▼ Eoi Inc..F 740 201-3300
Lewis Center *(G-8333)*

▲ Fortner Upholstering Inc..................F 614 475-8282
Columbus *(G-4936)*

▲ Furniture By Otmar Inc....................G 937 435-2039
Dayton *(G-5788)*

Great Day Improvements LLC................B 267 223-1289
Macedonia *(G-8695)*

Hallmark Industries Inc........................E 937 864-7378
Springfield *(G-12316)*

Home Stor & Off Solutions Inc..............E 216 362-4660
Cleveland *(G-3836)*

Homecare Mattress Inc........................F 937 746-2556
Franklin *(G-7027)*

▲ Litehouse Products LLC....................E 440 638-2350
Strongsville *(G-12571)*

Mel Heitkamp Builders Ltd...................G 419 375-0405
Fort Recovery *(G-6969)*

▲ Morris Furniture Co Inc....................G 937 874-7100
Fairborn *(G-6697)*

Newbury Woodworks............................G 440 564-5273
Newbury *(G-10558)*

▲ Ohio Table Pad Company..................F 419 872-6400
Perrysburg *(G-11246)*

▲ Pei Liquidation Company..................C 330 467-4267
Macedonia *(G-8704)*

Precision Fab Products Inc....................G 937 526-5681
Versailles *(G-13602)*

Queen City Awning & Tent Co................E 513 530-9660
Cincinnati *(G-3020)*

Recycled Systems Furniture Inc............E 614 880-9110
Worthington *(G-14724)*

River East Custom Cabinets Inc............G 419 244-3226
Toledo *(G-13113)*

Sailors Tailor Inc.................................F 937 862-7781
Spring Valley *(G-12243)*

▲ Senator International Inc..................E 419 887-5806
Maumee *(G-9316)*

Urbn Timber LLC..................................G 614 981-3043
Columbus *(G-5341)*

5713 Floor covering stores

Armstrong World Industries Inc............E 614 771-9307
Hilliard *(G-7669)*

Prints & Paints Flr Cvg Co Inc.............. E 419 462-5663
Galion *(G-7197)*

Shaheen Oriental Rug Co Inc............... F 330 493-9000
Canton *(G-2003)*

▲ Stanley Steemer Intl Inc.................... C 614 764-2007
Dublin *(G-6350)*

Wccv Floor Coverings LLC.................. F 330 688-0114
Peninsula *(G-11185)*

5714 Drapery and upholstery stores

Accent Drapery Co Inc......................... E 614 488-0741
Columbus *(G-4667)*

Elden Draperies of Toledo Inc............. F 419 535-1909
Toledo *(G-12947)*

5719 Miscellaneous homefurnishings

All Fired Up Pnt Your Own Pot............ G 330 865-5858
Copley *(G-5429)*

Bonfoey Co.. F 216 621-0178
Cleveland *(G-3427)*

Bruening Glass Works Inc.................... G 440 333-4768
Cleveland *(G-3445)*

Buckeye BOP LLC................................ F 740 498-9898
Newcomerstown *(G-10569)*

Cincinnati Window Shade Inc.............. F 513 631-7200
Cincinnati *(G-2489)*

Dale Kestler... G 513 871-9000
Cincinnati *(G-2540)*

▲ Down-Lite International Inc............... C 513 229-3696
Mason *(G-9095)*

Fountain Specialists Inc....................... G 513 831-5717
Milford *(G-9934)*

General Electric Company.................... F 440 593-1156
Mc Donald *(G-9358)*

Great Day Improvements LLC.............. B 267 223-1289
Macedonia *(G-8695)*

Handy Twine Knife Co.......................... G 419 294-3424
Upper Sandusky *(G-13442)*

House of 10000 Picture Frames........... G 937 254-5541
Dayton *(G-5813)*

▲ Microsun Lamps LLC........................ G 888 328-8701
Dayton *(G-5881)*

▲ Morris Furniture Co Inc.................... C 937 874-7100
Fairborn *(G-6697)*

▲ Mosser Glass Inc.............................. E 740 439-1827
Cambridge *(G-1751)*

Overhead Inc.. G 419 476-0300
Toledo *(G-13083)*

▲ Pei Liquidation Company.................. C 330 467-4267
Macedonia *(G-8704)*

Savko Plastic Pipe & Fittings.............. F 614 885-8420
Columbus *(G-5250)*

Scs Construction Services Inc............. E 513 929-0260
Cincinnati *(G-3071)*

◆ The Blonder Company........................ C 216 431-3560
Cleveland *(G-4379)*

▲ The Kitchen Collection LLC.............. A 740 773-9150
Chillicothe *(G-2284)*

◆ Wasserstrom Company...................... B 614 228-6525
Columbus *(G-5356)*

Whempys Corp...................................... G 614 888-6670
Worthington *(G-14729)*

5722 Household appliance stores

ABC Appliance Inc............................... E 419 693-4414
Oregon *(G-10955)*

Bolons Custom Kitchens Inc................ G 330 499-0092
Canton *(G-1842)*

C-Link Enterprises LLC........................ F 937 222-2829
Dayton *(G-5692)*

Carbonless Cut Sheet Forms Inc......... F 740 826-1700
New Concord *(G-10385)*

▲ Kitchens By Rutenschroer Inc........... G 513 251-8333
Cincinnati *(G-2799)*

Miller Cabinet Ltd................................ F 614 873-4221
Plain City *(G-11415)*

Wolff Bros Supply Inc.......................... F 440 327-1650
North Ridgeville *(G-10753)*

Wsi Seller Inc...................................... G 330 379-0270
Akron *(G-359)*

Z Line Kitchen and Bath LLC.............. G 614 777-5004
Marysville *(G-9055)*

5731 Radio, television, and electronic stores

4r Enterprises Incorporated................ G 330 923-9799
Cuyahoga Falls *(G-5519)*

ABC Appliance Inc............................... E 419 693-4414
Oregon *(G-10955)*

Bender Communications Inc................ F 740 382-0000
Marion *(G-8965)*

Bose Corporation................................. G 513 891-4384
Cincinnati *(G-2418)*

Dish One Up Satellite Inc.................... D 216 482-3875
Cleveland *(G-3618)*

Dss Installations Ltd........................... G 513 761-7000
Cincinnati *(G-2563)*

Electra Sound Inc................................ D 216 433-9600
Avon Lake *(G-754)*

◆ Phantom Sound................................ G 513 759-4477
Loveland *(G-8644)*

◆ TT Electronics Integrated................ B 440 352-8961
Perry *(G-11200)*

Tune Town Car Audio.......................... G 419 627-1100
Sandusky *(G-11878)*

5734 Computer and software stores

Aztech Printing & Promotions.............. G 937 339-0100
Troy *(G-13202)*

Bizall Inc.. G 216 939-9580
Cleveland *(G-3419)*

▲ Computer Products Corporation....... E 513 221-0600
Cincinnati *(G-2508)*

Copier Resources Inc........................... G 614 268-1100
Columbus *(G-4849)*

Gordons Graphics Inc.......................... G 330 863-2322
Malvern *(G-8751)*

Journey Systems LLC.......................... F 513 831-6200
Milford *(G-9940)*

Lantek Systems Inc............................. G 877 805-1028
Macon *(G-0122)*

RB Sigma LLC...................................... D 440 290-0577
Mentor *(G-9607)*

Retalix Inc... G 937 384-2277
Miamisburg *(G-9733)*

Thyme Inc.. F 484 872-8430
Akron *(G-337)*

5735 Record and prerecorded tape stores

True Dinero Records & Tech LLC.......... G 513 428-4610
Cincinnati *(G-3173)*

5736 Musical instrument stores

Bbb Music LLC..................................... G 740 772-2262
Chillicothe *(G-2244)*

Loft Violin Shop................................... G 614 267-7221
Columbus *(G-5073)*

S I T Strings Co Inc............................ E 330 434-8010
Akron *(G-302)*

▲ Stewart-Macdonald Mfg Co............. E 740 592-3021
Athens *(G-653)*

Willis Music Company.......................... F 513 671-3288
Cincinnati *(G-3225)*

---

58 EATING AND DRINKING PLACES

5812 Eating places

Amish Door Inc.................................... C 330 359-5464
Wilmot *(G-14592)*

Beca House Coffee LLC....................... G 419 731-4961
Upper Sandusky *(G-13435)*

Binos Inc.. G 330 938-0888
Sebring *(G-11892)*

Breitenbach Wine Cellars Inc.............. G 330 343-3603
Dover *(G-6232)*

Brewpub Restaurant Corporation......... F 614 228-2537
Columbus *(G-4774)*

Brinkman LLC....................................... F 419 204-5934
Lima *(G-8392)*

Buckeye Valley Pizza Hut Ltd.............. E 419 586-5900
Celina *(G-2098)*

Bucks For Pups Confections LLC......... F 614 359-4672
Columbus *(G-4787)*

Bunker Hill Cheese Co Inc.................. D 330 893-2131
Millersburg *(G-9973)*

Buns of Delaware Inc.......................... F 740 363-2867
Delaware *(G-6135)*

Cassanos Inc.. E 937 294-8400
Dayton *(G-5695)*

Circleville Oil Co.................................. G 740 477-3341
Circleville *(G-3251)*

Ferrante Wine Farm Inc....................... F 440 466-8466
Geneva *(G-7237)*

Georgetown Vineyards Inc................... E 740 435-3222
Cambridge *(G-1744)*

Glenn Ravens Winery........................... G 740 545-1000
West Lafayette *(G-14170)*

Gold Star Chili Inc.............................. D 513 631-1990
Cincinnati *(G-2682)*

Gold Star Chili Inc.............................. E 513 231-4541
Cincinnati *(G-2681)*

Grace Juice Company LLC................... F 614 398-6879
Westerville *(G-14261)*

◆ Great Lakes Brewing Co................... C 216 771-4404
Cleveland *(G-3789)*

Guggisberg Cheese Inc....................... E 330 893-2550
Millersburg *(G-9982)*

International Brand Services................ G 513 376-8209
Cincinnati *(G-2751)*

John Purdum.. G 513 897-9686
Waynesville *(G-13879)*

Johnsons Real Ice Cream LLC............. D 614 231-0014
Columbus *(G-5042)*

Karrikin Spirits Company LLC............. F 513 561-5000
Cincinnati *(G-2784)*

Kenyetta Bagby Enterprise LLC........... F 614 584-3426
Reynoldsburg *(G-11573)*

La Marquise Inc................................... D 614 488-1911
Columbus *(G-5060)*

Lbzb Restaurants Inc........................... F 567 413-4700
Bowling Green *(G-1424)*

Magic Wok Inc..................................... G 419 531-1818
Toledo *(G-13044)*

Mark Grzianis St Treats Ex Inc........... F 330 414-6266
Kent *(G-8049)*

Maumee Bay Brewing Company........... E 419 243-1253
Toledo *(G-13047)*

McDonalds... F 513 753-6100
Amelia *(G-433)*

McDonalds... F 513 752-2008
Cincinnati *(G-2313)*

McDonalds... F 216 226-7754
Lakewood *(G-8169)*

SIC

McDonalds................................E 513 336-0820
Mason *(G-9127)*

McDonalds................................F 740 753-4018
Nelsonville *(G-10318)*

McDonalds................................F 419 935-1414
Willard *(G-14404)*

McDonalds................................F 330 792-0527
Youngstown *(G-14895)*

Milk Hney Cndy Soda Shoppe LLC........G 330 492-5884
Canton *(G-1950)*

Mustard Seed Health Fd Mkt Inc........E 440 519-3663
Solon *(G-12155)*

Ohio Coffee Collaborative Ltd..........G 614 564-9852
Columbus *(G-5139)*

▲ Paramount Distillers Inc.............B 216 671-6300
Cleveland *(G-4134)*

R & T Estate LLC.......................F 216 862-0822
Cleveland *(G-4219)*

Rivals Sports Grille LLC...............G 216 267-0005
Middleburg Heights *(G-9776)*

Rocky River Brewing Co.................G 440 895-2739
Rocky River *(G-11638)*

Shawadi LLC............................E 614 839-0698
Westerville *(G-14275)*

▲ Skyline Cem Holdings LLC.............C 513 874-1188
Fairfield *(G-6776)*

Sonic Drive-In.........................G 937 717-6917
Springfield *(G-12374)*

Sweets and Meats LLC...................F 513 888-4227
Cincinnati *(G-3133)*

Tr Boes Holdings Inc...................F 419 595-2255
New Riegel *(G-10471)*

Velvet Ice Cream Company...............D 740 892-3921
Utica *(G-13488)*

Wal-Bon of Ohio Inc....................F 740 423-6351
Belpre *(G-1155)*

White Castle System Inc................D 513 563-2290
Cincinnati *(G-3223)*

◆ White Castle System Inc..............B 614 228-5781
Columbus *(G-5367)*

Willoughby Brewing Company LLC.........G 440 975-0202
Willoughby *(G-14550)*

Youngs Jersey Dairy Inc................B 937 325-0629
Yellow Springs *(G-14794)*

5813 Drinking places

Artisan Ales LLC.......................G 216 544-8703
Cleveland *(G-3369)*

Bar 25 LLC.............................G 216 621-4000
Cleveland *(G-3403)*

Brewdog Brewing Company LLC............F 614 908-3051
Canal Winchester *(G-1786)*

▲ District Brewing Company Inc.........E 614 224-3626
Columbus *(G-4886)*

◆ Great Lakes Brewing Co...............C 216 771-4404
Cleveland *(G-3789)*

Green Room Brewing LLC.................G 614 421-2337
Columbus *(G-4966)*

Lock 15 Brewing Company LLC............E 234 900-8277
Akron *(G-208)*

Lock 27 Brewing LLC....................F 937 433-2739
Dayton *(G-5853)*

Mansfield Brew Works LLC...............F 419 631-3153
Mansfield *(G-8818)*

McDonalds................................F 513 753-6100
Amelia *(G-433)*

McDonalds................................F 513 752-2008
Cincinnati *(G-2313)*

McDonalds................................F 216 226-7754
Lakewood *(G-8169)*

McDonalds................................E 513 336-0820
Mason *(G-9127)*

McDonalds................................F 740 753-4018
Nelsonville *(G-10318)*

McDonalds................................F 419 935-1414
Willard *(G-14404)*

McDonalds................................F 330 792-0527
Youngstown *(G-14895)*

Rocky River Brewing Co.................G 440 895-2739
Rocky River *(G-11638)*

59 MISCELLANEOUS RETAIL

5912 Drug stores and proprietary stores

Express Pharmacy & Dme LLC.............G 210 981-9690
Columbus *(G-4915)*

Riesbeck Food Markets Inc..............C 740 695-3401
Saint Clairsville *(G-11709)*

Soleo Health Inc.......................E 844 467-8200
Dublin *(G-6348)*

5921 Liquor stores

Currier Richard & James................G 440 988-4132
Amherst *(G-445)*

Kelleys Island Winery Inc..............G 419 746-2678
Kelleys Island *(G-8008)*

Millersburg Ice Company................E 330 674-3016
Millersburg *(G-10000)*

Ohio Eagle Distributing LLC............E 513 539-8483
West Chester *(G-14037)*

Old Firehouse Winery Inc...............E 440 466-9300
Geneva *(G-7244)*

Sandra Weddington......................F 740 417-4286
Delaware *(G-6172)*

Toledo Spirits Company LLC.............F 419 704-3705
Toledo *(G-13158)*

5932 Used merchandise stores

John Purdum............................G 513 897-9686
Waynesville *(G-13879)*

Westlake Ryal Bldg Pdts USA In.........E 800 366-8472
Columbus *(G-5365)*

5941 Sporting goods and bicycle shops

Area 419 Firearms LLC..................F 419 830-8353
Delta *(G-6201)*

▲ Golf Galaxy Golfworks Inc............C 740 328-4193
Newark *(G-10504)*

Hershberger Lawn Structures............F 330 674-3900
Millersburg *(G-9983)*

Highpoint Firearms.....................G 419 747-9444
Mansfield *(G-8803)*

Lima Sporting Goods Inc................E 419 222-1036
Lima *(G-8427)*

National Bullet Co.....................G 800 317-9506
Eastlake *(G-6439)*

Peska Inc..............................F 440 998-4664
Ashtabula *(G-611)*

R & S Monitions Inc....................G 614 846-0597
Columbus *(G-5222)*

◆ Rubber Grinding Inc..................D 419 692-3000
Delphos *(G-6192)*

Sportsmans Haven Inc...................G 740 432-7243
Cambridge *(G-1761)*

▲ Sunset Golf LLC......................G 419 994-5563
Tallmadge *(G-12753)*

Target Holdings Inc....................E 513 474-4409
Cincinnati *(G-3138)*

The Hartman Corp.......................G 614 475-5035
Columbus *(G-5320)*

TS Sales LLC...........................F 727 804-8060
Akron *(G-347)*

5942 Book stores

Auguste Moone Enterprises Ltd..........E 216 333-9248
Cleveland Heights *(G-4527)*

▼ Bookfactory LLC......................E 937 226-7100
Dayton *(G-5682)*

Christian Missionary Alliance..........C 380 208-6200
Reynoldsburg *(G-11562)*

Incorprted Trstees of The Gspl.........D 216 749-2100
Middleburg Heights *(G-9773)*

Ketman Corporation.....................G 330 262-1688
Wooster *(G-14658)*

5943 Stationery stores

1914 Mi Inc............................E 330 308-8667
New Philadelphia *(G-10428)*

Avon Lake Printing.....................G 440 933-2078
Avon Lake *(G-749)*

COS Blueprint Inc......................E 330 376-0022
Akron *(G-107)*

Gordons Graphics Inc...................G 330 863-2322
Malvern *(G-8751)*

Hathaway Stamp Co......................F 513 621-1052
Cincinnati *(G-2712)*

Hubbard Company........................E 419 784-4455
Defiance *(G-6111)*

Murr Corporation.......................G 330 264-2223
Wooster *(G-14668)*

O Connor Office Pdts & Prtg............G 740 852-2209
London *(G-8540)*

Quick Tech Graphics Inc................F 937 743-5952
Springboro *(G-12266)*

Warren Printing & Off Pdts Inc.........F 419 523-3635
Ottawa *(G-11050)*

5944 Jewelry stores

Bensan Jewelers Inc....................G 216 221-1434
Lakewood *(G-8163)*

D & J Manufacturing Jeweler............G 513 541-5200
Cincinnati *(G-2534)*

Em Es Be Company LLC...................G 216 761-9500
Cleveland *(G-3665)*

Farah Jewelers Inc.....................G 614 438-6140
Westerville *(G-14210)*

Goyal Enterprises Inc..................F 513 874-9303
Cincinnati *(G-2686)*

Gustave Julian Jewelers Inc............G 440 888-1100
Cleveland *(G-3801)*

H P Nielsen Inc........................G 440 244-4255
Lorain *(G-8557)*

Handcrafted Jewelry Inc................G 330 650-9011
Hudson *(G-7843)*

James C Free Inc.......................G 513 793-0133
Cincinnati *(G-2759)*

▲ James C Free Inc.....................E 937 298-0171
Dayton *(G-5826)*

M B Saxon Co Inc.......................G 440 229-5006
Cleveland *(G-3975)*

Markus Jewelers LLC....................G 513 474-4950
Cincinnati *(G-2848)*

Michael W Hyes Desgr Goldsmith.........G 440 519-0889
Solon *(G-12150)*

Pughs Designer Jewelers Inc............G 740 344-9259
Newark *(G-10530)*

◆ Quality Gold Inc.....................B 513 942-7659
Fairfield *(G-6769)*

Robert W Johnson Inc...................D 614 336-4545
Dublin *(G-6340)*

Rosenfeld Jewelry Inc..................G 440 446-0099
Cleveland *(G-4253)*

Sheiban Jewelry Inc....................F 440 238-0616
Strongsville *(G-12599)*

White Jewelers Inc.....................G 330 264-3324
Wooster *(G-14697)*

5945 Hobby, toy, and game shops

▲ Anime Palace........................... G 408 858-1918
Lewis Center (G-8322)

▲ Franklin Art Glass Studios............... E 614 221-2972
Columbus (G-4937)

Intrism Inc................................. G 614 787-4631
Worthington (G-14716)

Middleton Llyd Dolls Inc............... G 740 989-2082
Coolville (G-5426)

▲ Ohio Art Company..................... D 419 636-3141
Bryan (G-1655)

The Guardtower Inc...................... F 614 488-4311
Hilliard (G-7707)

5947 Gift, novelty, and souvenir shop

Amish Door Inc........................... C 330 359-5464
Wilmot (G-14592)

▲ City Apparel Inc...................... F 419 434-1155
Findlay (G-6852)

Cookie Bouquets Inc.................... G 614 888-2171
Columbus (G-4847)

Down Home................................. G 740 393-1186
Mount Vernon (G-10243)

E Warther & Sons Inc.................. F 330 343-7513
Dover (G-6244)

Golden Turtle Chocolate Fctry............. G 513 932-1990
Lebanon (G-8264)

Gorant Chocolatier LLC................. C 330 726-8821
Boardman (G-1372)

Handcrafted Jewelry Inc................ G 330 650-9011
Hudson (G-7843)

Modern China Company Inc............. E 330 938-6104
Sebring (G-11898)

Odyssey Spirits Inc..................... F 330 562-1523
Chagrin Falls (G-2174)

Ohio Designer Craftsmen Entps............. F 614 486-7119
Columbus (G-5141)

Piqua Chocolate Company Inc............. G 937 773-1981
Piqua (G-11374)

▲ Pulsar Ecoproducts LLC............... F 216 861-8800
Cleveland (G-4208)

R J Manray Inc........................... G 330 559-6716
Canfield (G-1814)

S-P Company Inc......................... D 330 782-5651
Columbiana (G-4627)

Schindlers Broad Run Chshuse I........... F 330 343-4108
Dover (G-6260)

Shops By Todd Inc....................... G 937 458-3192
Beavercreek (G-982)

The Hartman Corp........................ G 614 475-5035
Columbus (G-5320)

Velvet Ice Cream Company............. D 740 892-3921
Utica (G-13488)

▲ Wild Berry Incense Inc............... F 513 523-8583
Oxford (G-11065)

Wooden Horse............................. G 740 503-5243
Baltimore (G-789)

Youngs Jersey Dairy Inc............... B 937 325-0629
Yellow Springs (G-14794)

5948 Luggage and leather goods stores

▼ Baggallini Inc........................ F 800 448-8753
Pickerington (G-11289)

5961 Catalog and mail-order houses

▲ American Frame Corporation............ E 419 893-5595
Maumee (G-9259)

▲ Bendon Inc............................ D 419 207-3600
Ashland (G-521)

Communication Concepts Inc............. G 937 426-8600
Beavercreek (G-968)

Diy Holster LLC.......................... G 419 921-2168
Elyria (G-6520)

E Retailing Associates LLC............. D 614 300-5785
Columbus (G-4894)

E-Z Grader Company...................... G 440 247-7511
Chagrin Falls (G-2141)

EZ Concrete Supply LLC................. G 844 393-7699
Lima (G-8407)

Guggisberg Cheese Inc.................. E 330 893-2550
Millersburg (G-9982)

Hen of Woods LLC........................ G 513 954-8871
Cincinnati (G-2716)

Midwest Sea Salt Company Inc............. F 513 770-9177
West Chester (G-14029)

Pardson Inc.............................. F 740 373-5285
Marietta (G-8934)

Sailors Tailor Inc...................... F 937 862-7781
Spring Valley (G-12243)

▲ Systemax Manufacturing Inc............ G 937 368-2300
Dayton (G-6035)

Tech Solutions LLC...................... G 419 852-7190
Celina (G-2123)

▲ Twin Sisters Productions LLC.......... E 330 631-0361
Stow (G-12468)

▲ Universal Direct Fulfillment Corp...... F 330 650-5000
Hudson (G-7861)

Vitamin Shoppe Industries LLC............. A
Delaware (G-6179)

World Book Company...................... A 440 892-3000
Westlake (G-14346)

5963 Direct selling establishments

Conns Potato Chip Co Inc............... E 740 452-4615
Zanesville (G-15008)

Fluff Boutique.......................... G 513 227-6614
Cincinnati (G-2630)

Oats Overnight Inc...................... D 602 492-1751
West Chester (G-14035)

Pro-Kleen Industrial Svcs Inc........... E 740 689-1886
Lancaster (G-8218)

Rambasek Realty Inc..................... F 937 228-1189
Dayton (G-5974)

Smartsoda Holdings Inc.................. G 888 998-9668
Cleveland (G-4307)

5983 Fuel oil dealers

Centerra Co-Op........................... E 419 281-2153
Ashland (C-526)

Cincinnati - Vulcan Company............. D 513 242-5300
Cincinnati (G-2465)

New Vulco Mfg & Sales Co LLC............. D 513 242-2672
Cincinnati (G-2904)

5984 Liquefied petroleum gas dealers

Brightstar Propane & Fuels............. G 614 891-8395
Westerville (G-14204)

Jomac Ltd................................ E 330 627-7727
Carrollton (G-2087)

Legacy Farmers Cooperative............. F 419 423-2611
Findlay (G-6884)

Ngo Development Corporation............. G 740 622-9560
Coshocton (G-5464)

Welders Supply Inc...................... G 216 267-4470
Brookpark (G-1560)

5992 Florists

Cleveland Plant and Flower Co............. G 614 478-9900
Columbus (G-4811)

5993 Tobacco stores and stands

Boston Stoker Inc....................... F 937 890-6401
Vandalia (G-13551)

Smoke-Rings Inc.......................... G 419 420-9966
Findlay (G-6921)

5994 News dealers and newsstands

Cruisin Times Magazine.................. G 440 331-4615
Rocky River (G-11633)

Gazette Publishing Company............. D 419 335-2010
Napoleon (G-10280)

Journal Register Company............... D 440 245-6901
Lorain (G-8560)

5995 Optical goods stores

▲ Central-1-Optical LLC................. D 330 783-9660
Youngstown (G-14834)

Zenni Usa Inc............................ D 614 439-9850
Columbus (G-5381)

5999 Miscellaneous retail stores, nec

ABC Appliance Inc....................... E 419 693-4414
Oregon (G-10955)

Akron Cotton Products Inc.............. G 330 434-7171
Akron (G-28)

Akron Orthotic Solutions Inc........... G 330 253-3002
Akron (G-35)

American Armature Corporation............. G 419 448-1926
Tiffin (G-12773)

Annin & Co Inc........................... C 740 622-4447
Coshocton (G-5447)

◆ Aquatic Technology................... F 440 236-8330
Columbia Station (G-4588)

ARC Solutions LLC....................... E 419 542-9272
Hicksville (G-7646)

◆ Bath & Body Works LLC................ B 614 856-6000
Reynoldsburg (G-11557)

Battery Unlimited....................... G 740 452-5030
Zanesville (G-14993)

Battle Motors Inc....................... C 888 328-5443
New Philadelphia (G-10432)

◆ Beautyavenues LLC.................... F 614 856-6000
Reynoldsburg (G-11558)

Becker Signs Inc........................ G 330 659-4504
Hudson (G-7834)

Behrco Inc............................... G 419 394-1612
Saint Marys (G-11731)

Bell Vault and Monu Works Inc............. F 937 866-2444
Miamisburg (G-9668)

▲ Bendon Inc............................ D 419 207-3600
Ashland (C-521)

Big River Electric Inc................. G 740 446-4360
Gallipolis (G-7202)

◆ Black Squirrel Holdings Inc.......... E 513 577-7107
Cincinnati (G-2412)

Blang Acquisition LLC................... G 937 223-2155
Dayton (G-5679)

◆ Blatchford Inc....................... D 937 291-3636
Miamisburg (G-9673)

◆ Boxout LLC........................... C 833 462-7746
Hudson (G-7835)

Business Idntfction Systems In............. G 614 841-1255
Columbus (G-4789)

▲ Catania Medallic Specialty Inc........ E 440 933-9595
Avon Lake (G-751)

Centerra Co-Op........................... E 419 281-2153
Ashland (G-526)

Chappell-Zimmerman Inc.................. F 330 337-8711
Salem (G-11769)

Communications Aid Inc................. F 513 475-8453
Cincinnati (G-2505)

Copier Resources Inc................... G 614 268-1100
Columbus (G-4849)

COS Blueprint Inc....................... E 330 376-0022
Akron (G-107)

Country Sales & Service LLC.................. F 330 683-2500
Orrville *(G-10978)*

Dinsmore Inc.................................... G 937 544-3332
West Union *(G-14190)*

▲ DW Hercules LLC............................ G 330 830-2498
Massillon *(G-9187)*

E M Service Inc................................. F 440 323-3260
Elyria *(G-6525)*

Eastgate Custom Graphics Ltd............... G 513 528-7922
Cincinnati *(G-2575)*

▼ Educational Direction Inc................... G 330 836-8439
Fairlawn *(G-6799)*

▲ Enting Water Conditioning Inc............. E 937 294-5100
Moraine *(G-10160)*

Erosion Control Products Corp............... F 302 815-6500
West Chester *(G-13994)*

Fenwick Gallery of Fine Arts................. G 419 475-1651
Toledo *(G-12962)*

▲ Findaway World LLC......................... E 440 893-0808
Solon *(G-12111)*

Fineline Imprints Inc.......................... G 740 453-1083
Zanesville *(G-15013)*

Fischer Engineering Co LLC.................. G 937 754-1750
Dayton *(G-5778)*

Flag Lady Inc................................... G 614 263-1776
Columbus *(G-4927)*

◆ Foundations Worldwide Inc................. E 330 722-5033
Medina *(G-9405)*

Franks Electric Inc............................ G 513 313-5883
Cincinnati *(G-2640)*

Gerber & Sons Inc............................. E 330 897-6201
Baltic *(G-778)*

Greg Blume....................................... G 740 574-2308
Wheelersburg *(G-14353)*

Haller Enterprises Inc......................... F 330 733-9693
Akron *(G-169)*

Hartville Chocolates Inc...................... G 330 877-1999
Hartville *(G-7576)*

Hathaway Stamp Co............................ F 513 621-1052
Cincinnati *(G-2712)*

◆ Heading4ward Investment Co............... D 937 293-9994
Moraine *(G-10169)*

Health Aid of Ohio Inc........................ E 216 252-3900
Cleveland *(G-3814)*

Health Nuts Media LLC........................ G 818 802-5222
Cleveland *(G-3815)*

Hirt Publishing Co Inc......................... E 419 946-3010
Mount Gilead *(G-10210)*

Hit Trophy Inc................................... G 419 445-5356
Archbold *(G-498)*

Home City Ice Company........................ G 440 439-5001
Bedford *(G-1036)*

Home City Ice Company........................ G 937 461-6028
Dayton *(G-5812)*

Home City Ice Company........................ F 614 836-2877
Groveport *(G-7438)*

House of 10000 Picture Frames.............. G 937 254-5541
Dayton *(G-5813)*

Incorprted Trstees of The Gspl.............. D 216 749-2100
Middleburg Heights *(G-9773)*

Indoor Envmtl Specialists Inc................ E 937 433-5202
Dayton *(G-5821)*

Jackson Monument Inc......................... G 740 286-1590
Jackson *(G-7946)*

Johnson & Johnson.............................. E 513 786-7000
Blue Ash *(G-1290)*

Johnsons Fire Equipment Co.................. F 740 357-4916
Wellston *(G-13908)*

K-Mar Structures LLC.......................... F 231 924-5777
Junction City *(G-8002)*

Kempf Surgical Appliances Inc............... G 513 984-5758
Cincinnati *(G-2791)*

Kriss Kreations................................. G 330 405-6102
Twinsburg *(G-13326)*

Lazars Art Gllery Crtive Frmng.............. G 330 477-8351
Canton *(G-1931)*

Leimkuehler Inc................................. E 440 899-7842
Cleveland *(G-3950)*

Lemsco Inc.. G 419 242-4005
Toledo *(G-13032)*

Linde Gas & Equipment Inc................... G 513 821-2192
Cincinnati *(G-2823)*

▲ Litehouse Products LLC..................... E 440 638-2350
Strongsville *(G-12571)*

Love Laugh & Laundry.......................... G 567 377-1951
Toledo *(G-13039)*

M & S AG Solutions LLC....................... F 419 598-8675
Napoleon *(G-10290)*

Maumee Valley Memorials Inc................ F 419 878-9030
Waterville *(G-13839)*

Mayfair Granite Co Inc......................... G 216 382-8150
Cleveland *(G-4002)*

Mel Wacker Signs Inc.......................... G 330 832-1726
Massillon *(G-9222)*

Michaels Pre-Cast Con Pdts Inc............. F 513 683-1292
Loveland *(G-8643)*

Midwest Sea Salt Company Inc............... F 513 770-9177
West Chester *(G-14029)*

Miners Tractor Sales Inc...................... F 330 325-9914
Rootstown *(G-11649)*

Mixed Logic LLC................................. G 440 826-1676
Valley City *(G-13505)*

Montgomery Ellis LLC.......................... C 614 226-7976
Westerville *(G-14271)*

Mt Vernon Machine & Tool Inc................ E 740 397-0311
Mount Vernon *(G-10254)*

National Lime and Stone Co................... E 740 387-3485
Marion *(G-8983)*

Natural Beauty Products Inc.................. F 513 420-9400
Middletown *(G-9882)*

North Hill Marble & Granite Co............... F 330 253-2179
Akron *(G-249)*

One Wish LLC..................................... F 800 505-6883
Bedford *(G-1052)*

▲ Osborne Coinage Company LLC........... D 877 480-0456
Blue Ash *(G-1316)*

Paul Peterson Safety Div Inc................. E 614 486-4375
Columbus *(G-5179)*

PCR Restorations Inc.......................... G 419 747-7957
Mansfield *(G-8844)*

Pettisville Grain Co............................ E 419 446-2547
Pettisville *(G-11285)*

Piqua Granite & Marble Co Inc............... G 937 773-2000
Piqua *(G-11376)*

Plumb Builders Inc............................. F 937 293-1111
Dayton *(G-5942)*

Pneumatic Specialties Inc..................... G 440 729-4400
Chesterland *(G-2239)*

Pomacon Inc...................................... F 330 273-1576
Brunswick *(G-1606)*

Precision Replacement LLC................... G 330 908-0410
Macedonia *(G-8709)*

Presque Isle Orthtics Prsthtic............... G 216 371-0660
Cleveland *(G-4192)*

Primal Life Organics LLC...................... E 800 260-4946
Copley *(G-5438)*

◆ Printer Components Inc...................... G 585 924-5190
Fairfield *(G-6767)*

Qualitee Design Sportswear Co.............. F 740 333-8337
Wshngtn Ct Hs *(G-14742)*

R & J AG Manufacturing Inc................... F 419 962-4707
Ashland *(G-568)*

▲ Rainbow Industries Inc...................... G 937 323-6493
Springfield *(G-12366)*

Ray Communications Inc....................... G 330 686-0226
Stow *(G-12453)*

▲ Rhc Inc... E 330 874-3750
Bolivar *(G-1391)*

Schmelzer Industries Inc...................... E 740 743-2866
Somerset *(G-12211)*

Securcom Inc..................................... E 419 628-1049
Minster *(G-10065)*

Sky Wireless and Smoke Sp LLC............. E 513 488-5992
Cincinnati *(G-3095)*

Stable Step LLC................................. C 800 491-1571
Wadsworth *(G-13673)*

Steves Vans ACC Unlimited LLC.............. G 740 374-3154
Marietta *(G-8950)*

Strictly Stitchery Inc.......................... F 440 543-7128
Cleveland *(G-4335)*

Studgionsgroup LLC............................ E 216 804-1561
Cleveland *(G-4339)*

Sun Shine Awards............................... F 740 425-2504
Barnesville *(G-847)*

Tha Presidential Suite LLC.................... G 216 338-7287
Cleveland *(G-4376)*

The Hartman Corp............................... G 614 475-5035
Columbus *(G-5320)*

▲ Thomas Do-It Center Inc.................... E 740 446-2002
Gallipolis *(G-7209)*

Toledo Pro Fiberglass Inc..................... G 419 241-9390
Toledo *(G-13156)*

Town Cntry Technical Svcs Inc............... F 614 866-7700
Reynoldsburg *(G-11582)*

US Water Company LLC......................... G 740 453-0604
Zanesville *(G-15053)*

Vandava Inc....................................... G 614 277-8003
Grove City *(G-7421)*

Walter F Stephens Jr Inc...................... E 937 746-0521
Franklin *(G-7055)*

Welders Supply Inc............................. E 216 267-4470
Brookpark *(G-1560)*

Welders Supply Inc............................. F 216 241-1696
Cleveland *(G-4500)*

Wheatley Electric Service Co................. G 513 531-4951
Cincinnati *(G-3222)*

◆ William R Hague Inc.......................... D 614 836-2115
Groveport *(G-7458)*

Worldwide Brands Direct LLC................ F 937 991-0999
Dayton *(G-6088)*

61 NONDEPOSITORY CREDIT INSTITUTIONS

6141 Personal credit institutions

◆ Mtd Holdings Inc............................. B 330 225-2600
Valley City *(G-13508)*

6153 Short-term business credit

Global Retail Partners LLC.................... E 614 409-9850
Columbus *(G-4958)*

6159 Miscellaneous business credit

Momentum Fleet MGT Group Inc............. D 440 759-2219
Westlake *(G-14315)*

◆ Ohio Machinery Co............................ C 440 526-6200
Broadview Heights *(G-1509)*

62 SECURITY & COMMODITY BROKERS, DEALERS, EXCHANGES & SERVICES

6211 Security brokers and dealers

Western & Southern Lf Insur Co........... A 513 629-1800
Cincinnati *(G-3221)*

6282 Investment advice

Linsalata Cpitl Prtners Fund I................ G..... 440 684-1400
Cleveland *(G-3962)*

Schaeffers Investment Research Inc...... D .. 513 589-3800
Blue Ash *(G-1331)*

63 INSURANCE CARRIERS

6311 Life insurance

Western & Southern Lf Insur Co........... A 513 629-1800
Cincinnati *(G-3221)*

64 INSURANCE AGENTS, BROKERS AND SERVICE

6411 Insurance agents, brokers, and service

Acu-Serve Corp........................... C 330 923-5258
Akron *(G-17)*

Beam Technologies Inc.................... B 800 648-1179
Columbus *(G-4746)*

▲ Forge Industries Inc................... A 330 960-2468
Youngstown *(G-14857)*

Move Ez Inc................................ D 844 466-8339
Columbus *(G-5114)*

Mxr Imaging Inc........................... G 614 219-2011
Hilliard *(G-7688)*

◆ Safelite Group Inc...................... A 614 210-9000
Columbus *(G-5244)*

65 REAL ESTATE

6512 Nonresidential building operators

Anthony Mining Co Inc.................... G 740 282-5301
Wintersville *(G-14610)*

At Holdings Corporation.................. A 216 692-6000
Cleveland *(G-3382)*

▲ Caravan Packaging Inc................. G 440 243-4100
Cleveland *(G-3469)*

Garland Industries Inc.................... G 216 641-7500
Cleveland *(G-3757)*

Garland/Dbs Inc............................ G 216 641-7500
Cleveland *(G-3758)*

◆ Park Corporation......................... B 216 267-4870
Medina *(G-9434)*

Perry County Tribune..................... F 740 342-4121
New Lexington *(G-10405)*

◆ Pubco Corporation....................... D 216 881-5300
Cleveland *(G-4205)*

S-P Company Inc.......................... D 330 782-5651
Columbiana *(G-4627)*

US Development Corp..................... D 330 673-6900
Kent *(G-8094)*

6515 Mobile home site operators

L C Liming & Sons Inc.................... G 513 876-2555
Felicity *(G-6830)*

6519 Real property lessors, nec

L Brown Loans & Investments............ G 216 308-1820
Cleveland *(G-3932)*

Prairie Lane Corporation................. G 330 262-3322
Wooster *(G-14672)*

6531 Real estate agents and managers

EL Ostendorf Inc........................... G 440 247-7631
Chagrin Falls *(G-2143)*

Elite Property Group LLC................. F 216 356-7469
Elyria *(G-6527)*

Hitti Enterprises Inc...................... F 440 243-4100
Cleveland *(G-3831)*

Kenyetta Bagby Enterprise LLC........... F 614 584-3426
Reynoldsburg *(G-11573)*

▲ Lenz Inc.................................. E 937 277-9364
Dayton *(G-5844)*

◆ Nesco Inc................................ E 440 461-6000
Cleveland *(G-4068)*

Rona Enterprises Inc..................... G 740 927-9971
Pataskala *(G-11148)*

Ruscilli Real Estate Services............ F 614 923-6400
Dublin *(G-6341)*

Sawmill Road Management Co LLC....... E 937 342-9071
Columbus *(G-5251)*

Stonyridge Inc............................. F 937 845-9482
New Carlisle *(G-10380)*

Wedco LLC................................. G 513 309-0781
Mount Orab *(G-10223)*

6552 Subdividers and developers, nec

Phillips Companies........................ E 937 426-5461
Beavercreek Township *(G-1003)*

Stonyridge Inc............................. F 937 845-9482
New Carlisle *(G-10380)*

6553 Cemetery subdividers and developers

Fort Stben Burial Estates Assn.............. G 740 266-6101
Steubenville *(G-12403)*

67 HOLDING AND OTHER INVESTMENT OFFICES

6719 Holding companies, nec

◆ Ampac Holdings LLC....................A 513 671-1777
Cincinnati *(G-2365)*

Armor Consolidated Inc.................. A 513 923-5260
Mason *(G-9064)*

Brake Parts Holdings Inc................ B 216 589-0198
Cleveland *(G-3432)*

Cpp Group Holdings LLC................ E 216 453-4800
Cleveland *(G-3574)*

Crane Carrier Holdings LLC............. C 918 286-2889
New Philadelphia *(G-10441)*

Drt Holdings LLC......................... D 937 298-7391
Dayton *(G-5753)*

Elite Property Group LLC................ F 216 356-7469
Elyria *(G-6527)*

Hartzell Industries Inc................... F 937 773-6295
Piqua *(G-11352)*

▼ Hexion Topco LLC....................... D 614 225-4000
Columbus *(G-4978)*

Hexpol Holding Inc....................... F 440 834-4644
Burton *(G-1701)*

Indra Holdings Corp...................... C 513 682-8200
Cincinnati *(G-2743)*

Kenyetta Bagby Enterprise LLC........... F 614 584-3426
Reynoldsburg *(G-11573)*

Lion Group Inc............................. D 800 421-2926
Dayton *(G-5850)*

Norse Dairy Systems Inc................. C 614 294-4931
Columbus *(G-5128)*

Vertiv JV Holdings LLC.................. A 614 888-0246
Columbus *(G-5348)*

6726 Investment offices, nec

▲ Westlake Dimex LLC.................... C 800 334-3776
Marietta *(G-8961)*

6794 Patent owners and lessors

Cassanos Inc............................... E 937 294-8400
Dayton *(G-5695)*

Chemstation International Inc.............. E 937 294-8265
Dayton *(G-5701)*

Gold Star Chili Inc........................ E 513 231-4541
Cincinnati *(G-2681)*

Instantwhip Foods Inc.................... F 614 488-2536
Columbus *(G-5011)*

R&D Marketing Group Inc................ G 216 398-9100
Brooklyn Heights *(G-1537)*

Sakrete Inc................................. E 513 242-3644
Cincinnati *(G-3060)*

▲ Skyline Cem Holdings LLC............. C 513 874-1188
Fairfield *(G-6776)*

▲ Stanley Steemer Intl Inc............... C 614 764-2007
Dublin *(G-6350)*

▲ The Cornwell Quality Tool.............. D 330 336-3506
Wadsworth *(G-13674)*

Tomahawk Entrmt Group LLC............. F 216 505-0548
Euclid *(G-6680)*

6798 Real estate investment trusts

Infinitaire Industries LLC................ G 216 600-2051
Euclid *(G-6655)*

6799 Investors, nec

Alpha Zeta Holdings Inc.................. G 216 271-1601
Cleveland *(G-3334)*

Brain Brew Ventures 30 Inc.............. F 513 310-6374
Newtown *(G-10583)*

Brantley Partners IV LP.................. G 216 464-8400
Cleveland *(G-3434)*

Edgewater Capital Partners LP............. G 216 292-3838
Independence *(G-7901)*

◆ Kinetico Incorporated................... B 440 564-9111
Newbury *(G-10556)*

Linsalata Cpitl Prtners Fund I............ G 440 684-1400
Cleveland *(G-3962)*

Resilience Fund III LP.................... F 216 292-0200
Cleveland *(G-4237)*

70 HOTELS, ROOMING HOUSES, CAMPS, AND OTHER LODGING PLACES

7011 Hotels and motels

Amish Door Inc............................ C 330 359-5464
Wilmot *(G-14592)*

Breitenbach Wine Cellars Inc.............. G 330 343-3603
Dover *(G-6232)*

▲ Continental GL Sls & Inv Group........ G 614 679-1201
Powell *(G-11485)*

Inns Holdings Ltd......................... F 740 345-3700
Newark *(G-10511)*

John Purdum.............................. G 513 897-9686
Waynesville *(G-13879)*

7032 Sporting and recreational camps

Prairie Lane Corporation................. G 330 262-3322
Wooster *(G-14672)*

7041 Membership-basis organization hotels

American Gild of English Hndbe........... G 937 438-0085
Cincinnati *(G-2359)*

72 PERSONAL SERVICES

7212 Garment pressing and cleaners' agents

Love Laugh & Laundry..................... G 567 377-1951
Toledo *(G-13039)*

7213 Linen supply

SIC

Geauga Group LLC................................ G 440 543-8797
Chagrin Falls *(G-2162)*

7217 Carpet and upholstery cleaning

Image By J & K LLC............................... F 888 667-6929
Maumee *(G-9297)*

Shaheen Oriental Rug Co Inc................. F 330 493-9000
Canton *(G-2003)*

▲ Stanley Steemer Intl Inc.................... C 614 764-2007
Dublin *(G-6350)*

7218 Industrial launderers

Cintas Corporation................................ D 513 631-5750
Cincinnati *(G-2494)*

◆ Cintas Corporation............................ A 513 459-1200
Mason *(G-9086)*

Cintas Sales Corporation...................... B 513 459-1200
Cincinnati *(G-2495)*

Pneumatic Specialties Inc..................... G 440 729-4400
Chesterland *(G-2239)*

7231 Beauty shops

Beaute Asylum LLC.............................. F 419 377-9933
Toledo *(G-12894)*

James C Robinson................................ G 513 969-7482
Cincinnati *(G-2760)*

Pur Hair Extensions LLC....................... G 330 786-5772
Akron *(G-270)*

7241 Barber shops

Excalibur Barber LLC............................ F 330 729-9006
Boardman *(G-1371)*

7251 Shoe repair and shoeshine parlors

Cobblers Corner LLC............................ G 330 482-4005
Columbiana *(G-4609)*

7261 Funeral service and crematories

Bell Vault and Monu Works Inc.............. F 937 866-2444
Miamisburg *(G-9668)*

7291 Tax return preparation services

Michele Caldwell................................. G 937 505-7744
Dayton *(G-5880)*

Steward Edge Bus Solutions.................. F 614 826-5305
Columbus *(G-5293)*

7299 Miscellaneous personal services

Akron Design & Costume LLC................ G 330 644-0425
Coventry Township *(G-5479)*

American Egle Prprty Prsrvtion.............. G 855 440-6938
North Ridgeville *(G-10724)*

Artisan Constructors LLC...................... E 216 800-7641
Cleveland *(G-3370)*

Buns of Delaware Inc........................... F 740 363-2867
Delaware *(G-6135)*

Costume Specialists Inc....................... E 614 464-2115
Columbus *(G-4852)*

D J Klingler Inc.................................... G 513 891-2284
Montgomery *(G-10124)*

Handshakers Construction LLC.............. F 513 370-1371
Cincinnati *(G-2704)*

Holmes Manufacturing.......................... G 330 231-6327
Millersburg *(G-9990)*

Kross Acquisition Company LLC............ E 513 554-0555
Loveland *(G-8636)*

Loris Printing Inc................................. G 419 626-6648
Sandusky *(G-11852)*

Mustard Seed Health Fd Mkt Inc............ F 440 519-3663
Solon *(G-12155)*

Premier Tanning & Nutrition.................. G 419 342-6259
Shelby *(G-11973)*

Sisters Tanning Inc.............................. G 740 636-0303
Wshngtn Ct Hs *(G-14746)*

Skyliner... G 740 738-0874
Bridgeport *(G-1496)*

Vandalia Massage Therapy.................... G 937 890-8660
Vandalia *(G-13582)*

Vulcan Machinery Corporation............... F 330 376-6025
Akron *(G-355)*

73 BUSINESS SERVICES

7311 Advertising agencies

Aardvark Screen Prtg & EMB LLC.......... F 419 354-6686
Bowling Green *(G-1404)*

Advertising Joe LLC Mean.................... G 440 247-8200
Chagrin Falls *(G-2135)*

▲ Airmate Co Inc................................. D 419 636-3184
Bryan *(G-1625)*

Black River Group Inc.......................... E 419 524-6699
Mansfield *(G-8765)*

Buckeye Business Forms Inc................. G 614 882-1890
Columbus *(G-4784)*

Dee Printing Inc.................................. F 614 777-8700
Columbus *(G-4874)*

Just Business Inc................................ F 866 577-3303
Dayton *(G-5835)*

Kyle Media Inc.................................... F 877 775-2538
Toledo *(G-13025)*

Mark Advertising Agency Inc................. F 419 626-9000
Sandusky *(G-11856)*

Pro Press Inc...................................... F 216 631-8200
Cleveland *(G-4197)*

7312 Outdoor advertising services

Barnes Advertising Corporation............. F 740 453-6836
Zanesville *(G-14992)*

Ike Smart City.................................... E 614 294-4898
Columbus *(G-5000)*

Kessler Sign Company.......................... E 740 453-0668
Zanesville *(G-15025)*

Norton Outdoor Advertising.................. E 513 631-4864
Cincinnati *(G-2915)*

Ohio Shelterall Inc.............................. F 614 882-1110
Westerville *(G-14272)*

Orange Barrel Media LLC...................... D 614 294-4898
Columbus *(G-5162)*

7313 Radio, television, publisher representatives

Agri Communicators Inc....................... G 614 273-0465
Columbus *(G-4679)*

American City Bus Journals Inc............. C 937 528-4400
Dayton *(G-5651)*

Brackish Media LLC............................. F 513 394-2871
Cincinnati *(G-2420)*

Copley Ohio Newspapers Inc................. C 330 364-5577
New Philadelphia *(G-10439)*

Gazette Publishing Company................. D 419 335-2010
Napoleon *(G-10280)*

Kyle Media Inc.................................... F 877 775-2538
Toledo *(G-13025)*

News Watchman & Paper....................... F 740 947-2149
Waverly *(G-13870)*

Ohio Newspaper Services Inc................. G 614 486-6677
Columbus *(G-5149)*

Progressor Times................................ G 419 396-7567
Carey *(G-2062)*

Retain Loyalty LLC.............................. G 330 830-0839
Massillon *(G-9238)*

7319 Advertising, nec

A Sign Above Inc................................. F 330 425-7832
Twinsburg *(G-13266)*

Aztech Printing & Promotions................ G 937 339-0100
Troy *(G-13202)*

▲ Cgs Imaging Inc............................... F 419 897-3000
Holland *(G-7749)*

Design Masters Inc.............................. G 513 772-7175
Cincinnati *(G-2547)*

Digital Color Intl LLC........................... F
Akron *(G-123)*

Display Dynamics Inc........................... F 937 832-2830
Englewood *(G-6612)*

Hollywood Imprints LLC........................ F 614 501-6040
Gahanna *(G-7160)*

Kyle Media Inc.................................... F 877 775-2538
Toledo *(G-13025)*

Malik Media LLC.................................. G 614 933-0328
New Albany *(G-10345)*

▲ Performance Packaging Inc................ F 419 478-8805
Toledo *(G-13094)*

Sprint Print Inc................................... G 740 622-4429
Coshocton *(G-5473)*

7322 Adjustment and collection services

C & S Associates Inc........................... E 440 461-9661
Highland Heights *(G-7655)*

ITM Marketing Inc................................ C 740 295-3575
Coshocton *(G-5457)*

7331 Direct mail advertising services

▲ Aero Fulfillment Services Corp........... D 800 225-7145
Mason *(G-9056)*

American Paper Group Inc..................... B 330 758-4545
Youngstown *(G-14811)*

Amsive OH LLC................................... D 937 885-8000
Miamisburg *(G-9665)*

Baesman Group Inc.............................. D 614 771-2300
Hilliard *(G-7674)*

Bindery & Spc Pressworks Inc............... D 614 873-4623
Plain City *(G-11398)*

Buckeye Business Forms Inc................. G 614 882-1890
Columbus *(G-4784)*

▲ Consoldated Graphics Group Inc......... C 216 881-9191
Cleveland *(G-3559)*

Covap Inc... F 513 793-1855
Blue Ash *(G-1264)*

Cpmm Services Group Inc..................... G 614 447-0165
Columbus *(G-4857)*

Dayton Mailing Services Inc.................. E 937 222-5056
Dayton *(G-5731)*

Digital Color Intl LLC........................... F
Akron *(G-123)*

Directconnectgroup Ltd........................ G 216 281-2866
Cleveland *(G-3616)*

Eg Enterprise Services Inc.................... G 216 431-3300
Cleveland *(G-3658)*

▲ Fine Line Graphics Corp.................... C 614 486-0276
Columbus *(G-4924)*

Franklin Printing Company.................... F 740 452-6375
Zanesville *(G-15016)*

Gerald L Herrmann Company Inc............ F 513 661-1818
Cincinnati *(G-2669)*

Hecks Direct Mail & Prtg Svc................ E 419 661-6028
Toledo *(G-12989)*

▲ Hecks Direct Mail Prtg Svc Inc........... F 419 697-3505
Toledo *(G-12990)*

Hkm Drect Mkt Cmmnications Inc........... C 800 860-4456
Cleveland *(G-3832)*

Laipplys Prtg Mktg Sltions Inc.............. G 740 387-9282
Marion *(G-8975)*

Macke Brothers Inc.............................. G 513 771-7500
Cincinnati *(G-2838)*

Malik Media LLC.. G 614 933-0328
New Albany *(G-10345)*

Master Printing Group Inc............................. F 216 351-2246
Berea *(G-1180)*

Network Printing & Graphics........................ F 614 230-2084
Columbus *(G-5124)*

Northcoast Pmm LLC.................................... F 419 540-8667
Toledo *(G-13064)*

Porath Business Services Inc........................ F 216 626-0060
Cleveland *(G-4176)*

Print All Inc.. G 419 534-2880
Toledo *(G-13103)*

Quez Media Marketing Inc............................ G 216 910-0202
Independence *(G-7918)*

Retain Loyalty LLC.. G 330 830-0839
Massillon *(G-9238)*

Selby Service/Roxy Press Inc...................... E 513 241-3445
Cincinnati *(G-3078)*

Traxium LLC.. E 330 572-8200
Stow *(G-12466)*

Victory Direct LLC... G 614 626-0000
Gahanna *(G-7172)*

Youngstown Letter Shop Inc......................... G 330 793-4935
Youngstown *(G-14972)*

7334 Photocopying and duplicating services

A Grade Notes Inc.. G 614 299-9999
Dublin *(G-6271)*

A-A Blueprint Co Inc..................................... E 330 794-8803
Akron *(G-10)*

Aztech Printing & Promotions...................... G 937 339-0100
Troy *(G-13202)*

Bethart Enterprises Inc................................. F 513 863-6161
Hamilton *(G-7470)*

Capitol Citicom Inc....................................... E 614 472-2679
Columbus *(G-4799)*

Cincinnati Print Solutions LLC..................... G 513 943-9500
Milford *(G-9929)*

Colortech Graphics & Printing...................... G 614 766-2400
Columbus *(G-4816)*

Corporate Dcment Solutions Inc................. G 513 595-8200
Cincinnati *(G-2518)*

Eg Enterprise Services Inc........................... G 216 431-3300
Cleveland *(G-3658)*

Hoster Graphics Company Inc...................... F 614 299-9770
Columbus *(G-4992)*

J & J Tire & Alignment.................................. G 330 424-5200
Lisbon *(G-8471)*

Monks Copy Shop Inc.................................. F 614 461-6438
Columbus *(G-5110)*

Morse Enterprises Inc.................................. G 513 229-3600
Mason *(G-9129)*

Northeast Blueprint and Sup Co................. G 216 261-7500
Cleveland *(G-4092)*

Print-Digital Incorporated............................ G 330 686-5945
Stow *(G-12451)*

Printers Devil Inc.. F 330 650-1218
Hudson *(G-7854)*

Profile Digital Printing LLC.......................... E 937 866-4241
Dayton *(G-5965)*

Queen City Reprographics........................... C 513 326-2300
Cincinnati *(G-3024)*

Rhoads Print Center Inc............................... G 330 678-2042
Tallmadge *(G-12748)*

Robert Becker Impressions Inc.................... F 419 385-5303
Toledo *(G-13116)*

Techniprint Inc.. F 614 899-1403
Westerville *(G-14277)*

7335 Commercial photography

Eclipse 3d/Pi LLC.. E 614 626-8536
Columbus *(G-4896)*

Golden Graphics Ltd..................................... F 419 673-6260
Kenton *(G-8099)*

Queen City Reprographics........................... C 513 326-2300
Cincinnati *(G-3024)*

The Photo-Type Engraving Company.... D 513 281-0999
Cincinnati *(G-3149)*

Tj Metzgers Inc.. D 419 861-8611
Toledo *(G-13143)*

Universal Ch Directories LLC....................... G 419 522-5011
Mansfield *(G-8862)*

7336 Commercial art and graphic design

Abstract Displays Inc................................... F 513 985-9700
Blue Ash *(G-1241)*

Academy Graphic Comm Inc........................ F 216 661-2550
Cleveland *(G-3289)*

▲ Alonovus Corp.. E 330 674-2300
Millersburg *(G-9968)*

Amatech Inc... E 614 252-2506
Columbus *(G-4691)*

Clarity Retail Services LLC.......................... D 513 800-9369
West Chester *(G-13965)*

Container Graphics Corp.............................. E 419 531-5133
Toledo *(G-12932)*

Converters/Prepress Inc.............................. F 937 743-0935
Carlisle *(G-2065)*

Coyne Graphic Finishing Inc........................ E 740 397-6232
Mount Vernon *(G-10241)*

Digital Color Intl LLC.................................... F
Akron *(G-123)*

Eastgate Custom Graphics Ltd.................... G 513 528-7922
Cincinnati *(G-2575)*

Enlarging Arts Inc... G 330 434-3433
Akron *(G-136)*

Envoi Design Inc.. G 513 651-4229
Cincinnati *(G-2593)*

Eugene Stewart.. G 937 898-1117
Dayton *(G-5770)*

Fx Digital Media Inc..................................... F 216 241-4040
Cleveland *(G-3746)*

▲ Galaxy Balloons Incorporated.................. F 216 476-3360
Cleveland *(G-3753)*

▲ General Theming Contrs LLC................... C 614 252-6342
Columbus *(G-4948)*

Golden Graphics Ltd..................................... F 419 673-6260
Kenton *(G-8099)*

Great Lakes Graphics Inc............................ G 216 391-0077
Cleveland *(G-3791)*

Gregg Macmillan.. G 513 248-2121
Milford *(G-9937)*

Hollywood Imprints LLC............................... F 614 501-6040
Gahanna *(G-7160)*

Insignia Signs Inc.. G 937 866-2341
Moraine *(G-10170)*

Kimpton Printing & Spc Co.......................... F 330 467-1640
Macedonia *(G-8702)*

Laipplys Prtg Mktg Sltions Inc..................... G 740 387-9282
Marion *(G-8975)*

Liming Printing Inc.. F 937 374-2646
Xenia *(G-14769)*

Malik Media LLC.. G 614 933-0328
New Albany *(G-10345)*

Meridian Arts and Graphics......................... G 330 759-9099
Youngstown *(G-14898)*

Midwest Menu Mate Inc............................... F 740 323-2599
Newark *(G-10521)*

ML Advertising & Design LLC...................... G 419 447-6523
Tiffin *(G-12791)*

Morse Enterprises Inc.................................. G 513 229-3600
Mason *(G-9129)*

Mueller Art Cover & Binding Co.................. E 440 238-3303
Strongsville *(G-12577)*

ONeil & Associates Inc................................ C 937 865-0800
Miamisburg *(G-9725)*

Painted Hill Inv Group Inc............................ F 937 339-1756
Troy *(G-13246)*

Perrons Printing Company Inc...................... G 440 236-8870
Columbia Station *(G-4596)*

Phantasm Dsgns Sprtsn More Ltd............. G 419 538-6737
Ottawa *(G-11042)*

Professional Screen Printing........................ G 740 687-0760
Lancaster *(G-8219)*

Qualitee Design Sportswear Co.................. F 740 333-8337
Wshngtn Ct Hs *(G-14742)*

Quez Media Marketing Inc............................ G 216 910-0202
Independence *(G-7918)*

Rba Inc... G 330 336-6700
Wadsworth *(G-13667)*

Roban Inc... G 330 794-1059
Lakemore *(G-8156)*

Sanger Holdings LLC................................... F 513 784-9046
Cincinnati *(G-3063)*

Schuerholz Inc.. G 937 294-5218
Dayton *(G-5997)*

Screen Works Inc... E 937 264-9111
Dayton *(G-6000)*

▲ Shamrock Companies Inc......................... D 440 899-9510
Westlake *(G-14333)*

Sylvan Studios Inc.. G 419 882-3423
Sylvania *(G-12725)*

The Photo-Type Engraving Company.... D 513 281-0999
Cincinnati *(G-3149)*

True Dinero Records & Tech LLC................ G 513 428-4610
Cincinnati *(G-3173)*

White Tiger Inc.. F 740 852-4873
London *(G-8543)*

Woodrow Manufacturing Co........................ E 937 399-9333
Springfield *(G-12396)*

Youngstown Pre-Press Inc........................... G 330 793-3690
Youngstown *(G-14974)*

7338 Secretarial and court reporting

Ohio Shelterall Inc....................................... F 614 882-1110
Westerville *(G-14272)*

Sound Communications Inc.......................... E 614 875-8500
Grove City *(G-7414)*

7342 Disinfecting and pest control services

A Best Trmt & Pest Ctrl Sups...................... G 330 434-5555
Akron *(C 0)*

Hawthorne Gardening Company................... E 360 883-8846
Marysville *(G-9023)*

Image By J & K LLC..................................... F 888 667-6929
Maumee *(G-9297)*

▲ Scotts Miracle-Gro Company................... B 937 644-0011
Marysville *(G-9046)*

7349 Building maintenance services, nec

All Pack Services LLC.................................. G 614 935-0964
Grove City *(G-7370)*

American Egle Prprty Prsrvtion..................... G 855 440-6938
North Ridgeville *(G-10724)*

Bleachtech LLC.. E 216 921-1980
Seville *(G-11913)*

▲ Chemical Solvents Inc............................. E 216 741-9310
Cleveland *(G-3492)*

Cincinnati A Flter Sls Svc Inc...................... E 513 242-3400
Cincinnati *(G-2466)*

Cleaning Lady Inc... G 419 589-5566
Mansfield *(G-8774)*

Contract Lumber Inc..................................... F 614 751-1109
Columbus *(G-4844)*

Green Impressions LLC................................ D 440 240-8508
Sheffield Village *(G-11958)*

Hercules Led LLC.................................E 844 437-2533
Boardman (G-1374)

High-TEC Industrial Services...............D 937 667-1772
Tipp City (G-12827)

Image By J & K LLC..............................F 888 667-6929
Maumee (G-9297)

Indoor Envmtl Specialists Inc..............E 937 433-5202
Dayton (G-5821)

▲ Leadec Corp.....................................E 513 731-3590
Cincinnati (G-2815)

Lima Sheet Metal Mch & Mfg Inc..........F 419 229-1161
Lima (G-8426)

Link To Success Inc.............................G 888 959-4203
Norwalk (G-10851)

MPW Industrial Svcs Group Inc............B 740 927-8790
Hebron (G-7625)

Obersons Nurs & Landscapes LLC........E 513 687-7379
Hamilton (G-7514)

Omega Cementing Co............................G 330 695-7147
Apple Creek (G-474)

Omnipresence Cleaning LLC..................F 937 250-4749
Dayton (G-5927)

▲ Paro Services Co...............................F 330 467-1300
Twinsburg (G-13350)

Phase II Enterprises Inc.......................G 330 484-2113
Canton (G-1975)

Primo Services LLC..............................F 513 725-7888
Cincinnati (G-2982)

Richland Newhope Inds Inc...................C 419 774-4400
Mansfield (G-8848)

RT Industries Inc.................................G 937 335-5784
Troy (G-13251)

Whempys Corp......................................G 614 888-6670
Worthington (G-14729)

7352 Medical equipment rental

Columbus Prescr Rehabilitation............G 614 294-1600
Westerville (G-14250)

Health Aid of Ohio Inc.........................E 216 252-3900
Cleveland (G-3814)

Kempf Surgical Appliances Inc.............G 513 984-5758
Cincinnati (G-2791)

7353 Heavy construction equipment rental

Brewpro Inc...G 513 577-7200
Cincinnati (G-2423)

Dover Fabrication and Burn Inc.............G 330 339-1057
Dover (G-6239)

▲ Eleet Cryogenics Inc........................E 330 874-4009
Bolivar (G-1382)

Ioppolo Concrete Corporation...............G 440 439-6606
Bedford (G-1040)

▲ Lefeld Welding & Stl Sups Inc..........E 419 678-2397
Coldwater (G-4580)

◆ Ohio Machinery Co............................C 440 526-6200
Broadview Heights (G-1509)

Pollock Research & Design Inc.............E 330 332-3300
Salem (G-11805)

Rnm Holdings Inc.................................F 614 444-5556
Columbus (G-5232)

◆ Terra Sonic International LLC.............E 740 374-6608
Marietta (G-8953)

The Wagner-Smith Company..................B 866 338-0398
Moraine (G-10195)

7359 Equipment rental and leasing, nec

A & A Safety Inc.................................F 937 567-9781
Beavercreek (G-987)

A & A Safety Inc.................................E 513 943-6100
Amelia (G-425)

AAA Wastewater Services Inc..............F 937 746-6361
Franklin (G-7009)

ABC Signs Inc.....................................F 513 407-4367
Cincinnati (G-2331)

▲ Aircraft Dynamics Corporation..........F 419 331-0371
Elida (G-6482)

BJ Equipment Ltd.................................F 614 497-1188
Columbus (G-4758)

Brinkman LLC.......................................F 419 204-5934
Lima (G-8392)

Cattron Holdings Inc............................E 234 806-0018
Warren (G-13748)

Certon Technologies Inc.......................F 440 786-7185
Bedford (G-1021)

Copier Resources Inc...........................G 614 268-1100
Columbus (G-4849)

Cuyahoga Vending Co Inc.....................C 440 353-9595
North Ridgeville (G-10728)

◆ De Nora Tech LLC............................D 440 710-5334
Painesville (G-11078)

Dearing Compressor and Pu.................E 330 783-2258
Youngstown (G-14847)

Eaton Leasing Corporation....................B 216 382-2292
Beachwood (G-916)

Elliott Tool Technologies Ltd.................D 937 253-6133
Dayton (G-5763)

Galion Canvas Products.........................G 419 468-5333
Galion (G-7191)

Glawe Manufacturing Co Inc..................G 937 754-0064
Fairborn (G-6694)

Golf Car Company Inc...........................G 614 873-1055
Plain City (G-11410)

Great Lakes Crushing Ltd.....................D 440 944-5500
Wickliffe (G-14376)

Hansen Scaffolding LLC........................F 513 574-9000
West Chester (G-14124)

Higgins Construction & Supply Co Inc...F 937 364-2331
Hillsboro (G-7717)

Hull Ready Mix Concrete Inc..................F 419 625-8070
Sandusky (G-11839)

Loft Violin Shop...................................G 614 267-7221
Columbus (G-5073)

Paul Peterson Company.........................F 614 486-4375
Columbus (G-5178)

Paul Peterson Safety Div Inc.................E 614 486-4375
Columbus (G-5179)

Powerclean Equipment Company............F 513 202-0001
Cleves (G-4547)

Pro-Kleen Industrial Svcs Inc...............E 740 689-1886
Lancaster (G-8218)

▲ Rainbow Industries Inc.....................G 937 323-6493
Springfield (G-12366)

Rambasek Realty Inc............................F 937 228-1189
Dayton (G-5974)

South Akron Awning Co........................F 330 848-7611
Akron (G-314)

Tarpco Inc...G 330 677-8277
Kent (G-8086)

Technical Artistry Inc...........................G 614 299-7777
Columbus (G-5316)

▲ Thomas Do-It Center Inc..................E 740 446-2002
Gallipolis (G-7209)

▼ Trailer One Inc................................F 330 723-7474
Medina (G-9457)

Tri State Equipment Company................G 513 738-7227
Shandon (G-11935)

Waco Scaffolding & Equipment Inc........A 216 749-8900
Cleveland (G-4487)

West Equipment Company Inc................G 419 698-1601
Toledo (G-13177)

Wolf G T Awning & Tent Co..................F 937 548-4161
Greenville (G-7360)

7363 Help supply services

Aqua Technology Group LLC..................G 513 298-1183
West Chester (G-13941)

▲ Channel Products Inc........................D 440 423-0113
Solon (G-12093)

▲ Cima Inc...G 513 382-8976
Hamilton (G-7476)

Fluff Boutique.....................................G 513 227-6614
Cincinnati (G-2630)

Industrial Repair and Mfg.....................F 419 822-0314
Delta (G-6209)

▲ Industrial Repair and Mfg.................E 419 822-4232
Delta (G-6210)

Theiss Uav Solutions LLC.....................G 330 584-2070
North Benton (G-10624)

Upshift Work LLC.................................E 513 813-5695
Cincinnati (G-3188)

7371 Custom computer programming services

Aclara Technologies LLC.......................F 440 528-7200
Solon (G-12072)

Advanced Prgrm Resources Inc.............E 614 761-9994
Dublin (G-6273)

Airwave Communications Cons...............G 419 331-1526
Lima (G-8385)

American Power LLC.............................F 937 235-0418
Dayton (G-5654)

Analytica Usa Inc................................G 513 348-2333
Dayton (G-5658)

Application Link Incorporated................G 614 934-1735
Columbus (G-4722)

Associated Software Cons Inc...............F 440 826-1010
Lakewood (G-8162)

Atr Distributing Company......................G 513 353-1800
Cincinnati (G-2387)

Auto Des Sys Inc.................................F 614 488-8838
Dublin (G-6278)

Brainmaster Technologies Inc................G 440 232-6000
Bedford (G-1018)

Cerkl Incorporated...............................D 513 813-8425
Blue Ash (G-1261)

Cerner Corporation...............................D 740 826-7678
New Concord (G-10386)

Cimx LLC...E 513 248-7700
Cincinnati (G-2464)

▲ Cincinnati Assn For The Blind...........C 513 221-8558
Cincinnati (G-2469)

Command Alkon Incorporated................E 614 799-0600
Dublin (G-6290)

Computer Allied Technology Co.............G 614 457-2292
Columbus (G-4839)

Computer Workshop Inc........................G 216 901-0106
Cleveland (G-3557)

Computer Workshop Inc........................E 614 798-9505
Dublin (G-6291)

Corporate Elevator LLC.........................G 614 288-1847
Columbus (G-4851)

Cott Systems Inc.................................D 614 847-4405
Columbus (G-4853)

Datcomedia LLC...................................G 419 866-6301
Swanton (G-12682)

Deemsys Inc..D 614 322-9928
Gahanna (G-7155)

Drb Holdings LLC.................................B 330 645-3299
Akron (G-127)

Drb Systems LLC.................................C 330 645-3299
Akron (G-128)

Drs Signal Technologies Inc..................G 937 429-7470
Beavercreek (G-972)

Eci Macola/Max LLC.............................C 978 539-6186
Dublin (G-6296)

Electronic Concepts Engrg Inc	F	419 861-9000
Holland (G-7763)		
Embedded Planet Inc	F	216 245-4180
Solon (G-12104)		
Empyracom Inc	F	330 744-5570
Boardman (G-1370)		
Facts Inc	E	330 928-2332
Cuyahoga Falls (G-5540)		
Forcam Inc	F	513 878-2780
Cincinnati (G-2633)		
Foundation Software LLC	B	330 220-8383
Strongsville (G-12559)		
▲ Fscreations Corporation	D	330 746-3015
Youngstown (G-14858)		
Ganymede Technologies Corp	G	419 562-5522
Bucyrus (G-1681)		
Gb Liquidating Company Inc	E	513 248-7600
Milford (G-9935)		
Generic Systems Inc	F	419 841-8460
Holland (G-7764)		
Global Realms LLC	G	614 828-7284
Gahanna (G-7158)		
▼ Gracie Plum Investments Inc	E	740 355-9029
Portsmouth (G-11467)		
H Mack Charles & Associates Inc	E	513 791-4456
Blue Ash (G-1281)		
Hab Inc	G	608 785-7650
Solon (G-12119)		
Health Nuts Media LLC	G	818 802-5222
Cleveland (G-3815)		
Intelligrated Inc	A	513 874-0788
West Chester (G-14127)		
▲ Intelligrated Systems Inc	A	866 936-7300
Mason (G-9113)		
Intelligrated Systems LLC	A	513 701-7300
West Chester (G-14128)		
IPA Ltd	F	614 523-3974
Columbus (G-5024)		
Jasstek Inc	F	614 808-3600
Dublin (G-6313)		
▲ Keithley Instruments LLC	D	440 248-0400
Solon (G-12137)		
Lantek Systems Inc	G	877 805-1028
Mason (G-9122)		
Leidos Inc	D	937 656-8433
Beavercreek (G-977)		
Link Systems Inc	F	800 321-8770
Solon (G-12142)		
Malik Media LLC	G	614 933-0328
New Albany (G-10345)		
Miles Midprint Inc	F	216 860-4770
Cleveland (G-4040)		
Navistone Inc	D	844 677-3667
Cincinnati (G-2896)		
NCR Technology Center	G	937 445-1936
Dayton (G-5903)		
Online Mega Sellers Corp	G	888 384-6468
Toledo (G-13078)		
Parker-Hannifin Corporation	F	513 831-2340
Milford (G-9947)		
Pathfinder Cmpt Systems Inc	G	330 928-1961
Barberton (G-831)		
Proficient Info Tech Inc	G	937 470-1300
Dayton (G-5964)		
Profound Logic Software Inc	E	937 439-7925
Dayton (G-5966)		
Qc Software LLC	E	513 469-1424
Cincinnati (G-3013)		
Quez Media Marketing Inc	G	216 910-0202
Independence (G-7918)		
Qxsoft LLC	G	740 777-9609
Lewis Center (G-8350)		

Sanctuary Software Studio Inc	E	330 666-9690
Fairlawn (G-6810)		
▲ Sarcom Inc	A	614 854-1300
Lewis Center (G-8353)		
Seapine Software Inc	F	513 754-1655
Mason (G-9149)		
Sest Inc	F	440 777-9777
Westlake (G-14332)		
Sightgain Inc	F	202 494-9317
Mason (G-9152)		
Signalysis Inc	F	513 528-6164
Cincinnati (G-3090)		
Simplevms LLC	F	888 255-8918
Cincinnati (G-3091)		
Soaring Software Solutions Inc	F	419 442-7676
Swanton (G-12692)		
Stellar Systems Inc	Gb	513 921-8748
Cincinnati (G-3118)		
Steward Edge Bus Solutions	F	614 826-5305
Columbus (G-5293)		
Tata America Intl Corp	B	513 677-6500
Milford (G-9954)		
▲ Teachers Publishing Group	F	614 486-0631
Hilliard (G-7705)		
Tech Solutions LLC	G	419 852-7190
Celina (G-2123)		
Tech4imaging LLC	F	614 214-2655
Columbus (G-5315)		
Technosoft Inc	F	513 985-9877
Blue Ash (G-1341)		
Thinkware Incorporated	E	513 598-3300
Cincinnati (G-3153)		
Thyme Inc	F	484 872-8430
Akron (G-337)		
▲ Timekeeping Systems Inc	F	216 595-0890
Solon (G-12198)		
Triad Governmental Systems	F	937 376-5446
Xenia (G-14782)		
◆ Truck Fax Inc	F	216 921-8866
Cleveland (G-4431)		
Virtual Hold Tech Slutions LLC	E	330 670-2200
Akron (G-354)		
Wentworth Solutions	F	440 212-7696
Hinckley (G-7736)		

7372 Prepackaged software

3gtms LLC	E	877 722-3538
Columbus (G-4638)		
911cellular LLC	F	216 283-6100
Solon (G-12071)		
Acclaimd Inc	G	614 219-9519
Columbus (G-4668)		
Acu-Serve Corp	C	330 923-5258
Akron (G-17)		
Ad Company Holdings Inc	F	404 256-3544
Akron (G-18)		
Advanced Prgrm Resources Inc	E	614 761-9994
Dublin (G-6273)		
Advant-E Corporation	F	937 429-4288
Beavercreek (G-964)		
Agile Global Solutions Inc	F	916 655-7745
Independence (G-7888)		
Application Link Incorporated	G	614 934-1735
Columbus (G-4722)		
Associated Software Cons Inc	F	440 826-1010
Lakewood (G-8162)		
Atr Distributing Company	F	513 353-1800
Cincinnati (G-2388)		
Atr Distributing Company	F	513 353-1800
Cincinnati (G-2387)		
Auto Des Sys Inc	F	614 488-8838
Dublin (G-6278)		

Automation Software & Engrg	F	330 405-2990
Twinsburg (G-13276)		
Avt Technology Solutions LLC	F	727 539-7429
Groveport (G-7423)		
Azteca Systems Inc	D	801 523-2751
Dayton (G-5671)		
Bjond Inc	G	614 537-7246
Columbus (G-4759)		
Brightwave Enterprises Inc	F	812 331-2391
Canton (G-1846)		
Building Block Performance LLC	G	614 918-7476
Plain City (G-11400)		
Butler Tech	E	513 867-1028
Fairfield Township (G-6795)		
Bybe Inc	F	614 706-3050
Columbus (G-4790)		
Cake LLC	G	614 592-7681
Dublin (G-6284)		
Capitol Citicom Inc	E	614 472-2679
Columbus (G-4799)		
Cayosoft Inc	F	614 423-6718
Westerville (G-14205)		
Cbts Technology Solutions LLC	B	440 569-2300
Cleveland (G-3479)		
CCA Youngstown	G	615 263-3000
Youngstown (G-14832)		
Cequence Security Inc	F	650 437-6338
Blue Ash (G-1260)		
Cerkl Incorporated	D	513 813-8425
Blue Ash (G-1261)		
Cerner Corporation	D	740 826-7678
New Concord (G-10386)		
Check Point Software Tech Inc	E	440 748-0900
Cleveland (G-3491)		
Chettapartners LLC	G	614 368-7600
Worthington (G-14707)		
Cimx LLC	E	513 248-7700
Cincinnati (G-2464)		
Clinicl Otcms Mngmnt Syst LLC	D	330 650-9900
Broadview Heights (G-1501)		
Coffing Corporation	E	513 919-2813
Liberty Twp (G-8381)		
Colburn Patterson LLC	G	419 866-5544
Holland (G-7751)		
Columbus Incontact	G	801 245-8369
Columbus (G-4824)		
Columbus International Corp	F	614 917-2274
Lewis Center (G-8329)		
Columbus International Corp	G	614 323-1086
Columbus (G-4827)		
▲ Computer Products Corporation	E	513 221-0600
Cincinnati (G-2508)		
Corporate Elevator LLC	G	614 288-1847
Columbus (G-4851)		
Creative Microsystems Inc	D	937 836-4499
Englewood (G-6611)		
Crimson Gate Consulting Co	G	614 805-0897
Dublin (G-6292)		
Csg Software	G	614 986-2600
Columbus (G-4862)		
Custom Information Systems Inc	F	614 875-2245
Grove City (G-7380)		
D+h USA Corporation	C	513 381-9400
Cincinnati (G-2538)		
Dakota Software Corporation	D	216 765-7100
Cleveland (G-3597)		
Datatrak International Inc	E	440 443-0082
Beachwood (G-914)		
Datcomedia LLC	G	419 866-6301
Swanton (G-12682)		
Delphia Consulting LLC	E	614 421-2000
Columbus (G-4877)		

S
I
C

Delta Media Group Inc	D	330 493-0350	
North Canton (G-10633)			
Digisoft Systems Corporation	G	937 833-5016	
Brookville (G-1566)			
Drb Holdings LLC	B	330 645-3299	
Akron (G-127)			
Drb Systems LLC	C	330 645-3299	
Akron (G-128)			
E Ventus Corporation	G	216 643-6840	
Independence (G-7899)			
Echo Mobile Solutions LLC	G	614 282-3756	
Pickerington (G-11293)			
Eci Macola/Max LLC	C	978 539-6186	
Dublin (G-6296)			
Eclipse	G	419 564-7482	
Galion (G-7188)			
Edict Systems Inc	E	937 429-4288	
Beavercreek (G-973)			
Empyracom Inc	F	330 744-5570	
Boardman (G-1370)			
◆ Esko-Graphics Inc	D	937 454-1721	
Miamisburg (G-9691)			
Ewebschedule	G	614 882-0726	
Westerville (G-14209)			
Explorys Inc	E	216 767-4700	
Cleveland (G-3698)			
Facilities Management Ex LLC	D	614 519-2186	
Columbus (G-4919)			
Fifth Third Proc Solutions Inc	E	800 972-3030	
Cincinnati (G-2623)			
Flexnova Inc	F	216 288-6961	
Cleveland (G-3724)			
Flypaper Studio Inc	G	602 801-2208	
Cincinnati (G-2631)			
Fmx 2018 Inc	F	440 247-5602	
Chagrin Falls (G-2144)			
Forcam Inc	F	513 878-2780	
Cincinnati (G-2633)			
Foundation Software LLC	B	330 220-8383	
Strongsville (G-12559)			
▲ Fscreations Corporation	D	330 746-3015	
Youngstown (G-14858)			
Glance Software LLC	F	844 383-2500	
Hamilton (G-7495)			
▼ Gracie Plum Investments Inc	E	740 355-9029	
Portsmouth (G-11467)			
H Mack Charles & Associates Inc	E	513 791-4456	
Blue Ash (G-1281)			
Hab Inc	G	608 785-7650	
Solon (G-12119)			
Health Nuts Media LLC	G	818 802-5222	
Cleveland (G-3815)			
Hometown Ticketing Inc	C	866 488-4849	
Dublin (G-6304)			
Hyland Software Inc	A	440 788-5000	
Westlake (G-14307)			
ICC Systems Inc	G	614 524-0299	
Sunbury (G-12667)			
Ideal Integrations LLC	E	614 786-7100	
Worthington (G-14713)			
Idialogs LLC	G	937 372-2890	
Xenia (G-14765)			
Igel Technology America LLC	F	954 739-9990	
Cincinnati (G-2739)			
Ignyte Assurance Platform	E	833 446-9831	
Dayton (G-5819)			
Incessant Software Inc	G	614 206-2211	
Lancaster (G-8205)			
Inneractiv Inc	F	888 798-7792	
Worthington (G-14715)			
Innerapps LLC	G	419 467-3110	
Perrysburg (G-11231)			

Integrity Group Consulting Inc	F	614 759-9148	
Reynoldsburg (G-11572)			
Intelligent Mobile Support Inc	F	888 980-9119	
Solon (G-12128)			
Intellinetics Inc	D	614 388-8908	
Columbus (G-5017)			
Iot Diagnostics LLC	G	844 786-7631	
West Chester (G-14015)			
Ireportsource	F	888 294-9578	
Cincinnati (G-2754)			
Ivy Ventures LLC	G	513 259-3307	
Fairfield (G-6746)			
Janova LLC	G	614 638-6785	
New Albany (G-10342)			
Jasstek Inc	F	614 808-3600	
Dublin (G-6313)			
Jda Software Group Inc	F	480 308-3000	
Akron (G-185)			
Jenzabar Inc	G	513 563-4542	
Blue Ash (G-1289)			
Jst LLC	G	614 423-7815	
Westerville (G-14216)			
Kapios LLC	G	567 661-0772	
Toledo (G-13015)			
Lantek Systems Inc	G	877 805-1028	
Mason (G-9122)			
Launch Scout LLC	F	513 449-6940	
Cincinnati (G-2813)			
Learn21 A Flxble Lrng Cllbrtiv	F	513 402-2121	
Cincinnati (G-2816)			
Liminal Esports LLC	G	440 423-5856	
Gates Mills (G-7230)			
Linestream Technologies Inc	G	216 862-7874	
Cleveland (G-3961)			
Link Systems Inc	F	800 321-8770	
Solon (G-12142)			
Lost Technology LLP	G	513 685-0054	
West Chester (G-14025)			
Matrix Management Solutions	G	330 470-3700	
Canton (G-1940)			
Miami Valley Eductl Cmpt Assn	F	937 767-1468	
Yellow Springs (G-14789)			
Michele Caldwell	G	937 505-7744	
Dayton (G-5880)			
Microsoft Corporation	G	216 986-1440	
Cleveland (G-4030)			
Microsoft Corporation	G	614 719-5900	
Columbus (G-4646)			
Miles Midprint Inc	F	216 860-4770	
Cleveland (G-4040)			
Mim Software Inc	D	216 455-0600	
Beachwood (G-930)			
Mirus Adapted Tech LLC	E	614 402-4585	
Dublin (G-6320)			
Move Ez Inc	D	844 466-8339	
Columbus (G-5114)			
Navistone Inc	D	844 677-3667	
Cincinnati (G-2896)			
New Life Chapel	F	513 298-2980	
Cincinnati (G-2902)			
Nextmed Systems Inc	E	216 674-0511	
Cincinnati (G-2907)			
Northrop Grmmn Spce & Mssn Sys	D	937 259-4956	
Dayton (G-5910)			
Nuance Company	G	740 964-0367	
Granville (G-7319)			
▲ Ohio Cllbrtive Lrng Sltons Inc	E	216 595-5289	
Strongsville (G-12582)			
Ohio Distinctive Enterprises	G	614 459-0453	
Columbus (G-5142)			
One Cloud Services LLC	G	513 231-9500	
Cincinnati (G-2931)			

Onx Acquisition LLC	B	440 569-2300	
Mayfield Heights (G-9339)			
Onx Holdings LLC	E	866 587-2287	
Cincinnati (G-2935)			
Open Text Inc	E	614 658-3588	
Hilliard (G-7693)			
Oracle Corporation	F	216 706-1500	
Cleveland (G-4122)			
Osb Software Inc	G	440 542-9145	
Solon (G-12165)			
Pakra LLC	F	614 477-6965	
Columbus (G-5169)			
Pamee LLC	E	216 232-9255	
Rocky River (G-11637)			
Parallel Technologies Inc	D	614 798-9700	
Dublin (G-6328)			
Pathfinder Cmpt Systems Inc	G	330 928-1961	
Barberton (G-831)			
Patrick J Burke & Co	E	513 455-8200	
Cincinnati (G-2945)			
Patriot Software LLC	D	877 968-7147	
Canton (G-1972)			
Paycor Hcm Inc	F	800 381-0053	
Cincinnati (G-2949)			
Perdatum Inc	G	614 761-1578	
Hilliard (G-7694)			
Perfect Probate	G	513 791-4100	
Cincinnati (G-2953)			
Phantom Technology LLC	G	614 710-0074	
Hilliard (G-7695)			
Posm Software LLC	F	859 274-0041	
Mansfield (G-8845)			
Proficient Info Tech Inc	G	937 470-1300	
Dayton (G-5964)			
Profile Imaging Columbus LLC	F	614 301-3444	
Columbus (G-5209)			
Profound Logic Software Inc	E	937 439-7925	
Dayton (G-5966)			
Projitech Inc	E	216 999-6228	
Cleveland (G-4201)			
Qc Software LLC	E	513 469-1424	
Cincinnati (G-3013)			
Quest Software Inc	D	614 336-9223	
Dublin (G-6337)			
Qxsoft LLC	G	740 777-9609	
Lewis Center (G-8350)			
R & H Enterprises Llc	G	216 702-4449	
Richmond Heights (G-11612)			
R & L Software LLC	G	513 847-4942	
Monroe (G-10115)			
Realeflow LLC	G	855 545-2095	
Brunswick (G-1611)			
Rebiz LLC	E	844 467-3249	
Cleveland (G-4227)			
Retail Management Products Ltd	G	740 548-1725	
Lewis Center (G-8351)			
Retalix Inc	G	937 384-2277	
Miamisburg (G-9733)			
Revolution Group Inc	D	614 212-1111	
Westerville (G-14230)			
Rina Systems LLC	E	513 469-7462	
Cincinnati (G-3046)			
Rivals Sports Grille LLC	E	216 267-0005	
Middleburg Heights (G-9776)			
Ross Group Inc	G	937 427-3069	
Blue Ash (G-1327)			
Samegoal Inc	F	216 766-5713	
Beachwood (G-947)			
Sanctuary Software Studio Inc	E	330 666-9690	
Fairlawn (G-6810)			
Sanger Holdings LLC	F	513 784-9046	
Cincinnati (G-3063)			

▲ Sarcom Inc.......................................A 614 854-1300
Lewis Center *(G-8353)*

SC Strategic Solutions LLC.....................C 567 424-6054
Norwalk *(G-10861)*

Seapine Software Inc.............................F 513 754-1655
Mason *(G-9149)*

Sest Inc...F 440 777-9777
Westlake *(G-14332)*

Sightgain Inc.......................................F 202 494-9317
Mason *(G-9152)*

Sigmatek Systems LLC...........................D 513 674-0005
Cincinnati *(G-3089)*

Signal Interactive.................................F 614 360-3938
Columbus *(G-5265)*

Simplevms LLC.....................................F 888 255-8918
Cincinnati *(G-3091)*

Snap-On Business Solutions Inc...........B 330 659-1600
Richfield *(G-11602)*

Soaring Software Solutions Inc............F 419 442-7676
Swanton *(G-12692)*

Software Solutions Inc.........................E 513 932-6667
Dayton *(G-6012)*

Southwestern Ohio Instrctnal Te...........F 937 746-6333
Dayton *(G-6013)*

Stack Construction Tech Inc.................F 513 445-5122
Blue Ash *(G-1333)*

Starwin Industries LLC..........................E 937 293-8568
Dayton *(G-6024)*

Sterling Commerce LLC.........................A 614 798-2192
Dublin *(G-6351)*

Steward Edge Bus Solutions................F 614 826-5305
Columbus *(G-5293)*

Sylvania Mose Ldge No 1579 Lya..........F 419 885-4953
Sylvania *(G-12727)*

Syntec LLC..F 440 229-6262
Rocky River *(G-11640)*

Tarigma Corporation..............................F 614 436-3734
Columbus *(G-5309)*

Tata America Intl Corp..........................B 513 677-6500
Milford *(G-9954)*

Teamcentral Inc....................................G 513 382-1497
Cincinnati *(G-3140)*

Tech Solutions LLC...............................G 419 852-7190
Celina *(G-2123)*

Technosoft Inc......................................F 513 985-9877
Blue Ash *(G-1341)*

Telehealth Care Solutions LLC..............G 440 823-6023
Brecksville *(G-1482)*

Thinkware Incorporated........................E 513 598-3300
Cincinnati *(G-3153)*

▲ Timekeeping Systems Inc.................F 216 595-0890
Solon *(G-12198)*

To Scale Software LLC...........................E 513 253-0053
Mason *(G-9162)*

TOA Technologies Inc............................C 216 925-5950
Beachwood *(G-954)*

Tracker Management Systems...............G 800 445-2438
Brecksville *(G-1484)*

Triad Governmental Systems.................F 937 376-5446
Xenia *(G-14782)*

Trimble Trnsp Entp Sltions Inc.............C 216 831-6606
Mayfield Heights *(G-9342)*

True Dinero Records & Tech LLC...........G 513 428-4610
Cincinnati *(G-3173)*

◆ Turning Technologies LLC.................D 330 746-3015
Youngstown *(G-14954)*

Tyler Technologies Inc...........................F 800 800-2581
Moraine *(G-10196)*

Ultraedit Inc...G 216 464-7465
Hamilton *(G-7535)*

Uninterrupted LLC................................F 216 771-2323
Akron *(G-350)*

Upshift Work LLC..................................E 513 813-5695
Cincinnati *(G-3188)*

Varian Medical Systems Inc...................G 888 827-4265
Liberty Township *(G-8379)*

Veeam Government Solutions LLC..........E 614 339-8200
Columbus *(G-4650)*

Vertical Data LLC.................................F 330 289-0313
Akron *(G-353)*

Virtual Hold Tech Slutions LLC.............E 330 670-2200
Akron *(G-354)*

Vista Community Church........................F 614 718-2294
Plain City *(G-11425)*

Vitals Matter LLC..................................G 937 848-8871
Dayton *(G-6072)*

Vndly LLC...E 513 572-2500
Mason *(G-9165)*

Vurvey Labs Inc...................................F 513 379-3595
Cincinnati *(G-3209)*

Wentworth Solutions.............................F 440 212-7696
Hinckley *(G-7736)*

Whatifsportscom Inc.............................G 513 333-0313
Blue Ash *(G-1349)*

Xchanging..G 440 914-2000
Solon *(G-12209)*

Zipscene LLC.......................................D 513 201-5174
Cincinnati *(G-3242)*

Zullix LLC..E 440 536-9300
Rocky River *(G-11641)*

7373 Computer integrated systems design

Aclara Technologies LLC.......................F 440 528-7200
Solon *(G-12072)*

Advanced Prgrm Resources Inc............E 614 761-9994
Dublin *(G-6273)*

Applied Experience LLC.........................G 614 943-2970
Plain City *(G-11394)*

Bcs Technologies Ltd............................F 513 829-4577
Fairfield *(G-6713)*

CHI Corporation...................................G 440 498-2300
Cleveland *(G-3494)*

Cincinnati Ctrl Dynamics Inc.................G 513 242-7300
Cincinnati *(G-2473)*

Cott Systems Inc.................................D 614 847-4405
Columbus *(G-4853)*

Creative Microsystems Inc....................D 937 836-4499
Englewood *(G-6611)*

▼ Data Processing Sciences.................D 513 791-7100
Cincinnati *(G-2542)*

David Chojnacki...................................E 303 905-1918
Westerville *(G-14254)*

Deemsys Inc..D 614 322-9928
Gahanna *(G-7155)*

Dewesoft LLC.......................................D 855 339-3669
Whitehouse *(G-14359)*

Drb Holdings LLC.................................B 330 645-3299
Akron *(G-127)*

Drb Systems LLC..................................C 330 645-3299
Akron *(G-128)*

Eaj Services LLC...................................F 513 792-3400
Blue Ash *(G-1269)*

Electronic Concepts Engrg Inc..............F 419 861-9000
Holland *(G-7763)*

Freedom Usa Inc..................................F 216 503-6374
Twinsburg *(G-13305)*

Generic Systems Inc............................F 419 841-8460
Holland *(G-7764)*

Industrial Screen Prcess Svc I..............F 419 255-4900
Toledo *(G-13003)*

IPA Ltd...F 614 523-3974
Columbus *(G-5024)*

◆ Kc Robotics Inc...............................E 513 860-4442
West Chester *(G-14019)*

Lantek Systems Inc...............................G 877 805-1028
Mason *(G-9122)*

Leidos Inc...D 937 656-8433
Beavercreek *(G-977)*

▲ Logisync Corporation.......................G 440 937-0388
Avon *(G-732)*

M T Systems Inc...................................G 330 453-4646
Canton *(G-1936)*

Matrix Management Solutions................G 330 470-3700
Canton *(G-1940)*

Millers Aplus Cmpt Svcs LLC................F 330 620-5288
Akron *(G-234)*

Northrop Grmman Tchncal Svcs I..........C 937 320-3100
Beavercreek Township *(G-1000)*

Online Mega Sellers Corp......................G 888 384-6468
Toledo *(G-13078)*

▲ Pinnacle Data Systems Inc...............C 614 748-1150
Groveport *(G-7449)*

R & L Software LLC..............................G 513 847-4942
Monroe *(G-10115)*

▲ Sarcom Inc.....................................A 614 854-1300
Lewis Center *(G-8353)*

Sentient Studios Ltd.............................E 330 204-8636
Fairlawn *(G-6811)*

Sest Inc...F 440 777-9777
Westlake *(G-14332)*

Sgi Matrix LLC.....................................D 937 438-9033
Miamisburg *(G-9736)*

Sightgain Inc.......................................F 202 494-9317
Mason *(G-9152)*

Software Solutions Inc.........................E 513 932-6667
Dayton *(G-6012)*

Sutter Llc...F 513 891-2261
Blue Ash *(G-1339)*

Syntec LLC..F 440 229-6262
Rocky River *(G-11640)*

▲ Systemax Manufacturing Inc............G 937 368-2300
Dayton *(G-6035)*

Tata America Intl Corp..........................B 513 677-6500
Milford *(G-9954)*

Thyme Inc...F 484 872-8430
Akron *(G-337)*

Town Cntry Technical Svcs Inc..............F 614 866-7700
Reynoldsburg *(G-11582)*

Worker Automation Inc..........................G 937 473-2111
Dayton *(G-6086)*

7374 Data processing and preparation

▲ Aero Fulfillment Services Corp..........D 800 225-7145
Mason *(G-9056)*

Amsive OH LLC.....................................D 937 885-8000
Miamisburg *(G-9665)*

CD Solutions Inc...................................G 937 676-2376
Pleasant Hill *(G-11431)*

Cpmm Services Group Inc.....................G 614 447-0165
Columbus *(G-4857)*

Datatrak International Inc......................E 440 443-0082
Beachwood *(G-914)*

Delaware Data Products Inc...................G 740 369-5449
Delaware *(G-6142)*

▼ Gracie Plum Investments Inc.............E 740 355-9029
Portsmouth *(G-11467)*

Great Lakes Publishing Company...........D 216 771-2833
Cleveland *(G-3793)*

IPA Ltd...F 614 523-3974
Columbus *(G-5024)*

ITM Marketing Inc.................................C 740 295-3575
Coshocton *(G-5457)*

Miami Valley Eductl Cmpt Assn.............F 937 767-1468
Yellow Springs *(G-14789)*

NCR Technology Center.........................G 937 445-1936
Dayton *(G-5903)*

S
I
C

Northrop Grmmn Spce & Mssn Sys....... D 937 259-4956
Dayton *(G-5910)*

Quez Media Marketing Inc.................... G 216 910-0202
Independence *(G-7918)*

Rebiz LLC... E 844 467-3249
Cleveland *(G-4227)*

▲ Sarcom Inc..................................... A 614 854-1300
Lewis Center *(G-8353)*

SC Strategic Solutions LLC................... C 567 424-6054
Norwalk *(G-10861)*

Sightgain Inc...................................... F 202 494-9317
Mason *(G-9152)*

Thinkware Incorporated...................... E 513 598-3300
Cincinnati *(G-3153)*

Vndly LLC.. E 513 572-2500
Mason *(G-9165)*

7375 Information retrieval services

Advant-E Corporation.......................... F 937 429-4288
Beavercreek *(G-964)*

AGS Custom Graphics Inc.................... D 330 963-7770
Macedonia *(G-8676)*

Hkm Drect Mkt Cmmnications Inc......... C 800 860-4456
Cleveland *(G-3832)*

▲ Lexisnexis Group............................ C 937 865-6800
Miamisburg *(G-9709)*

Promatch Solutions LLC....................... F 877 299-0185
Moraine *(G-10188)*

▲ Repro Acquisition Company LLC...... G 216 738-3800
Cleveland *(G-4235)*

Sightgain Inc...................................... F 202 494-9317
Mason *(G-9152)*

Welch Publishing Co........................... E 419 874-2528
Perrysburg *(G-11279)*

7376 Computer facilities management

Park Place Technologies LLC............... C
Cleveland *(G-4135)*

7377 Computer rental and leasing

▼ Data Processing Sciences .... D 513 791-7100
Cincinnati *(G-2542)*

7378 Computer maintenance and repair

Ascendtech Inc................................... E 216 458-1101
Willoughby *(G-14428)*

Eaj Services LLC................................. F 513 792-3400
Blue Ash *(G-1269)*

Government Acquisitions Inc................ E 513 721-8700
Cincinnati *(G-2685)*

Magnum Computers Inc........................ F 216 781-1757
Cleveland *(G-3981)*

Park Place Technologies LLC............... C
Cleveland *(G-4135)*

▲ Pinnacle Data Systems Inc.............. C 614 748-1150
Groveport *(G-7449)*

Vr Assets LLC.................................... G 440 600-2963
Solon *(G-12203)*

7379 Computer related services, nec

Advanced Prgrm Resources Inc............ E 614 761-9994
Dublin *(G-6273)*

American Power LLC........................... F 937 235-0418
Dayton *(G-5654)*

Arctos Mission Solutions LLC............... E 813 609-5591
Beavercreek *(G-965)*

Ascendtech Inc................................... E 216 458-1101
Willoughby *(G-14428)*

Cbts Technology Solutions LLC............ B 440 569-2300
Cleveland *(G-3479)*

▲ Computer Products Corporation....... E 513 221-0600
Cincinnati *(G-2508)*

David Chojnacki................................. E 303 905-1918
Westerville *(G-14254)*

Empyracom Inc................................... F 330 744-5570
Boardman *(G-1370)*

Freedom Usa Inc................................ E 216 503-6374
Twinsburg *(G-13305)*

▲ Fscreations Corporation.................. D 330 746-3015
Youngstown *(G-14858)*

Glance Software LLC.......................... F 844 383-2500
Hamilton *(G-7495)*

It XCEL Consulting LLC....................... F 513 847-8261
West Chester *(G-14016)*

Jasstek Inc.. F 614 808-3600
Dublin *(G-6313)*

Link Systems Inc................................ F 800 321-8770
Solon *(G-12142)*

NCR Technology Center....................... G 937 445-1936
Dayton *(G-5903)*

Onx Acquisition LLC............................ B 440 569-2300
Mayfield Heights *(G-9339)*

Onx Holdings LLC............................... E 866 587-2287
Cincinnati *(G-2935)*

Park Place Technologies LLC............... C
Cleveland *(G-4135)*

◆ Phase Array Company LLC...............G 513 785-0801
West Chester *(G-14043)*

Proficient Info Tech Inc....................... G 937 470-1300
Dayton *(G-5964)*

Profound Logic Software Inc................ E 937 439-7925
Dayton *(G-5966)*

Revolution Group Inc.......................... D 614 212-1111
Westerville *(G-14230)*

▲ Sarcom Inc..................................... A 614 854-1300
Lewis Center *(G-8353)*

Syntec LLC.. F 440 229-6262
Rocky River *(G-11640)*

Valley List LLC.................................. G 740 760-6411
Waterford *(G-13829)*

Vr Assets LLC.................................... G 440 600-2963
Solon *(G-12203)*

Wild Fire Systems.............................. G 440 442-8999
Cleveland *(G-4505)*

Wolters Kluwer Clinical D.................... D 330 650-6506
Hudson *(G-7862)*

7382 Security systems services

Fellhauer Mechanical Systems............. E 419 734-3674
Port Clinton *(G-11441)*

IEC Infrared Systems LLC.................... E 440 234-8000
Middleburg Heights *(G-9772)*

Johnson Controls Inc........................... F 513 671-6338
Cincinnati *(G-2772)*

Sage Integration Holdings LLC............. E 330 733-8183
Kent *(G-8072)*

▲ Say Security Group USA LLC........... F 419 634-0004
Ada *(G-5)*

Securcom Inc..................................... E 419 628-1049
Minster *(G-10065)*

Sound Communications Inc.................. E 614 875-8500
Grove City *(G-7414)*

Total Life Safety LLC.......................... F 866 955-2318
West Chester *(G-14083)*

7383 News syndicates

Ohio News Network............................. G 614 460-3700
Columbus *(G-5148)*

7384 Photofinish laboratories

Enlarging Arts Inc.............................. G 330 434-3433
Akron *(G-136)*

7389 Business services, nec

3-D Technical Services Company........... E 937 746-2901
Franklin *(G-7006)*

4r Enterprises Incorporated................. G 330 923-9799
Cuyahoga Falls *(G-5519)*

◆ 889 Global Solutions Ltd.................F 614 235-8889
Columbus *(G-4655)*

A Good Mobile Detailing LLC............... G 513 316-3802
Cincinnati *(G-2325)*

Abstract Displays Inc.......................... F 513 985-9700
Blue Ash *(G-1241)*

Acreo Inc.. G 513 734-3327
Amelia *(G-426)*

ADSr Ent LLC.....................................F 773 280-2129
Columbus *(G-4674)*

Advanced Cryogenic Entps Inc............. F 330 922-0750
Akron *(G-20)*

Aerosport Modeling Design LLC........... F 614 834-5227
Canal Winchester *(G-1783)*

▲ Amos Media Company...................... C 937 498-2121
Sidney *(G-11992)*

Amros Industries Inc........................... F 216 433-0010
Cleveland *(G-3351)*

Appalachia Freeze Dry Co LLC............. F 740 412-0169
Richmond Dale *(G-11606)*

Appetzers R US St Eats 2 Go LL........... G 937 460-1470
Springfield *(G-12281)*

Applied Experience LLC....................... G 614 943-2970
Plain City *(G-11394)*

As Clean As It Gets Off Brkroo............. E 216 256-1143
South Euclid *(G-12218)*

Asist Translation Services................... F 614 451-6744
Columbus *(G-4729)*

▲ Asm International.......................... D 440 338-5151
Novelty *(G-10879)*

Atchley Signs & Graphics LLC............. F 614 421-7446
Columbus *(G-4731)*

Aubrey Rose Apparel LLC.................... G 513 728-2681
Cincinnati *(G-2390)*

Automted Cmpnent Spcalists LLC......... E 513 335-4285
Cincinnati *(G-2391)*

Bansal Enterprises Inc.........................F 330 633-9355
Akron *(G-72)*

◆ Baumfolder Corporation..................E 937 492-1281
Sidney *(G-11996)*

▲ Belaire Products Inc....................... E 330 253-3116
Akron *(G-75)*

Benchmark Craftsman Inc.................... E 866 313-4700
Seville *(G-11910)*

▲ Bernard Laboratories Inc................ E 513 681-7373
Cincinnati *(G-2407)*

Bjond Inc.. G 614 537-7246
Columbus *(G-4759)*

Bjs DEMo&hauling LLC........................ G 216 904-8909
Garfield Heights *(G-7216)*

Bollin & Sons Inc............................... E 419 693-6573
Toledo *(G-12900)*

◆ Bookmasters Inc............................C 419 281-1802
Ashland *(G-522)*

Bridgits Bath LLC............................... G 937 259-1960
Dayton *(G-5684)*

Brown Company of Findlay Ltd............. E 419 425-3002
Findlay *(G-6847)*

▲ C A P Industries Inc....................... F 937 773-1824
Piqua *(G-11338)*

Capitol Citicom Inc............................ E 614 472-2679
Columbus *(G-4799)*

◆ CIP International Inc.......................D 513 874-9925
West Chester *(G-13964)*

▲ City Apparel Inc............................ F 419 434-1155
Findlay *(G-6852)*

Clarity Retail Services LLC................. D 513 800-9369
West Chester *(G-13965)*

Cleveland Spclty Insptn Svc In	F	440 974-1818
Mentor *(G-9501)*		
Clovernook Ctr For Blind Vslly	C	513 522-3860
Cincinnati *(G-2500)*		
▲ CMC Group Inc	D	419 354-2591
Bowling Green *(G-1415)*		
Coffing Corporation	E	513 919-2813
Liberty Twp *(G-8381)*		
Columbus Design & Mfg LLC	G	414 534-3273
Columbus *(G-4822)*		
Compliant Healthcare Tech LLC	E	216 255-9607
Cleveland *(G-3555)*		
Controls Inc	E	330 239-4345
Medina *(G-9390)*		
▲ Conversion Tech Intl Inc	E	419 924-5566
West Unity *(G-14193)*		
Country Lane Custom Buildings	G	740 485-8481
Danville *(G-5598)*		
Crain Communications Inc	E	330 836-9180
Cuyahoga Falls *(G-5536)*		
Crane Consumables Inc	E	513 539-9980
Middletown *(G-9851)*		
Creative Fabrication Ltd	G	740 262-5789
Richwood *(G-11614)*		
Crest Products Inc	F	440 942-5770
Mentor *(G-9508)*		
Custom Built Crates Inc	E	
Milford *(G-9932)*		
Custom Information Systems Inc	F	614 875-2245
Grove City *(G-7380)*		
Custom Metal Shearing Inc	F	937 233-6950
Dayton *(G-5718)*		
▲ Custom Products Corporation	D	440 528-7100
Glenwillow *(G-7285)*		
Custom Sportswear Imprints LLC	G	330 335-8326
Wadsworth *(G-13633)*		
D&D Clssic Auto Rstoration Inc	G	937 473-2229
Covington *(G-5492)*		
Dale R Adkins	G	740 682-7312
Oak Hill *(G-10887)*		
Dasher Lawless Automation LLC	E	855 755-7275
Warren *(G-13757)*		
David Wolfe Design Inc	F	330 633-6124
Akron *(G-117)*		
◆ Db Rediheat Inc	E	216 361-0530
Cleveland *(G-3604)*		
Dbcr Inc	E	330 920-1900
Cuyahoga Falls *(G-5537)*		
DCW Acquisition Inc	G	216 451-0666
Cleveland *(G-3607)*		
Delaware Data Products Inc	G	740 369-5449
Delaware *(G-6142)*		
▲ Depot Direct Inc	E	419 661-1233
Perrysburg *(G-11215)*		
Display Dynamics Inc	F	937 832-2830
Englewood *(G-6612)*		
Domino Foods Inc	C	216 432-3222
Cleveland *(G-3625)*		
◆ Downing Enterprises Inc	D	330 666-3888
Akron *(G-126)*		
Eavan Corp	F	216 401-8619
Olmsted Twp *(G-10945)*		
Echo Mobile Solutions LLC	G	614 282-3756
Pickerington *(G-11293)*		
Electrovations Inc	G	330 274-3558
Solon *(G-12103)*		
Elite Biomedical Solutions LLC	F	513 207-0602
Cincinnati *(G-2302)*		
Elkhart Plastics LLC	E	888 605-2068
Akron *(G-130)*		
Endless Home Improvements LLC	G	614 599-1799
Columbus *(G-4901)*		

Engravers Gallery & Sign Co	G	330 830-1271
Massillon *(G-9190)*		
Erd Specialty Graphics Inc	G	419 242-9545
Toledo *(G-12955)*		
▲ Ergo Desktop LLC	E	567 890-3746
Celina *(G-2105)*		
Essential Provisions LLC	G	937 271-0381
Wilmington *(G-14579)*		
Everything In America	G	347 871-6872
Cleveland *(G-3695)*		
▼ Exact Cutting Service Inc	G	440 546-1319
Brecksville *(G-1465)*		
▼ Exhibit Concepts Inc	D	937 890-7000
Vandalia *(G-13557)*		
Expo Packaging Inc	G	216 267-9700
Cleveland *(G-3699)*		
Express Ground Services Inc	G	216 870-9374
Cleveland *(G-3700)*		
Fire Containment Concepts LLC	F	800 877-2204
Hartville *(G-7575)*		
Fire Safety Services Inc	F	937 686-2000
Huntsville *(G-7864)*		
▲ First Choice Packaging Inc	C	419 333-4100
Fremont *(G-7107)*		
Flexsys Inc	B	212 605-6000
Akron *(G-151)*		
Freds Sign Service Inc	G	937 335-1901
Troy *(G-13215)*		
Fsqpronet LLC	F	330 942-6014
Youngstown *(G-14859)*		
G and J Automatic Systems Inc	E	216 741-6070
Cleveland *(G-3749)*		
G H Cutter Services Inc	G	419 476-0476
Toledo *(G-12971)*		
G S K Inc	G	937 547-1611
Greenville *(G-7342)*		
Geauga Highway Co	F	440 834-4580
Windham *(G-14600)*		
▲ General Theming Contrs LLC	C	614 252-6342
Columbus *(G-13039)*		
Geneva Liberty Steel Ltd	G	330 740-0103
Youngstown *(G-14865)*		
Genius Solutions Engrg Co	E	419 794-9914
Maumee *(G-9293)*		
Gerdau McSteel Atmsphere Annli	E	330 478-0314
Canton *(G-1900)*		
GL Industries Inc	E	513 874-1233
Hamilton *(G-7404)*		
Groundhogs 2000 LLC	G	440 653-1647
Bedford *(G-1033)*		
Hafners Hrdwood Connection LLC	G	419 726-4828
Toledo *(G-12983)*		
Handshakers Construction LLC	F	513 370-1371
Cincinnati *(G-2704)*		
Health Nuts Media LLC	G	818 802-5222
Cleveland *(G-3815)*		
Herman Machine Inc	F	330 633-3261
Tallmadge *(G-12736)*		
Hochstetler Milling LLC	E	419 368-0004
Loudonville *(G-8591)*		
Holly Robakowski	G	440 854-9317
Cleveland *(G-3834)*		
Howard Industries Inc	F	614 444-9900
Columbus *(G-4993)*		
▼ Htec Systems Inc	F	937 438-3010
Dayton *(G-5816)*		
Hutnik Company	G	330 336-9700
Wadsworth *(G-13643)*		
IBI Brake Products Inc	F	440 543-7962
Chagrin Falls *(G-2166)*		
Ideal Drapery Company Inc	G	330 745-9873
Barberton *(G-813)*		

IEC Infrared Systems LLC	E	440 234-8000
Middleburg Heights *(G-9772)*		
Ies Systems Inc	E	330 533-6683
Canfield *(G-1811)*		
Impact Printing and Design LLC	F	833 522-6200
Columbus *(G-5003)*		
Industrial Power Systems Inc	B	419 531-3121
Rossford *(G-11659)*		
◆ Ineos ABS (usa) LLC	C	513 467-2400
Addyston *(G-8)*		
◆ Interscope Manufacturing Inc	E	513 423-8866
Middletown *(G-9867)*		
ITM Marketing Inc	C	740 295-3575
Coshocton *(G-5457)*		
Jason Poffenberger	G	937 369-1358
Dayton *(G-5827)*		
Jls Funeral Home	F	614 625-1220
Columbus *(G-5040)*		
Jnp Group LLC	F	800 735-9645
Wooster *(G-14655)*		
Joseph T Snyder Industries Inc	G	216 883-6900
Cleveland *(G-3892)*		
Kaylo Enterprises LLC	G	330 535-1860
Akron *(G-192)*		
◆ Kent Adhesive Products Co	D	330 678-1626
Kent *(G-8039)*		
Konecranes Inc	F	440 461-8400
Broadview Heights *(G-1504)*		
Kts Cstm Lgs/Xclsvely You Inc	G	440 285-9803
Chardon *(G-2212)*		
▲ Kyocera Senco Indus Tls Inc	D	513 388-2000
Cincinnati *(G-2809)*		
Leak Finder Inc	G	440 735-0130
Hudson *(G-7849)*		
Link Systems Inc	F	800 321-8770
Solon *(G-12142)*		
Link To Success Inc	G	888 959-4203
Norwalk *(G-10851)*		
Love Laugh & Laundry	G	567 377-1951
Toledo *(G-13039)*		
Love Yueh LLC	G	614 408-8677
Pickerington *(G-11295)*		
Magnaco Industries Inc	E	216 961-3636
Lodi *(G-8504)*		
Marie Noble Wine Company	E	216 633-0025
Euclid *(G-6659)*		
Mark Grzianis St Treats Ex Inc	F	330 414-6266
Kent *(O-0049)*		
Metal Shredders Inc	G	937 866-0777
Miamisburg *(G-9712)*		
Metzenbaum Sheltered Inds Inc	E	440 729-1919
Chesterland *(G-2236)*		
Michele Caldwell	G	937 505-7744
Dayton *(G-5880)*		
Micro Products Co Inc	F	440 943-0258
Willoughby Hills *(G-14560)*		
Millers Aplus Cmpt Svcs LLC	F	330 620-5288
Akron *(G-234)*		
Momma Js Blazing Kitchen LLC	G	216 551-8791
Cleveland Heights *(G-4530)*		
National Wldg Tanker Repr LLC	G	614 875-3399
Grove City *(G-7404)*		
Natures Health Food LLC	F	419 260-9265
Mount Victory *(G-10269)*		
Natures Way Bird Products LLC	E	440 554-6166
Chagrin Falls *(G-2172)*		
Neurologix Technologies Inc	F	512 914-7941
Cleveland *(G-4071)*		
◆ New Path International LLC	F	614 410-3974
Powell *(G-11493)*		
▲ Nordic Light America Inc	F	614 981-9497
Canal Winchester *(G-1796)*		

North Shore Printing LLC .... G 740 876-9066
Portsmouth (G-11472)

Ogonek Custom Hardwood Inc .... G 833 718-2531
Barberton (G-827)

◆ Ohio Gasket and Shim Co Inc .... E 330 630-0626
Akron (G-252)

▲ Ohio Laminating & Binding Inc .... G 614 771-4868
Hilliard (G-7691)

Ohio Shelterall Inc .... F 614 882-1110
Westerville (G-14272)

Olde Man Granola LLC .... F 419 819-9576
Findlay (G-6902)

Op Dawg Logistics LLC .... G 937 844-3135
Dayton (G-5928)

P & L Precision Grinding Llc .... F 330 746-8081
Youngstown (G-14909)

P C Workshop Inc .... G 419 399-4805
Paulding (G-11161)

Pactiv LLC .... G 614 771-5400
Columbus (G-5168)

Park Press Direct .... G 419 626-4426
Sandusky (G-11864)

Paul Shovlin .... G 330 757-0032
Youngstown (G-14915)

Pentagear Products LLC .... G 937 660-8182
Dayton (G-5935)

▲ Performance Packaging Inc .... F 419 478-8805
Toledo (G-13094)

Personaliteez LLC .... F 614 354-9108
Columbus (G-5189)

Pettit W T & Sons Co Inc .... G 330 539-6100
Girard (G-7278)

Pioneer Solutions LLC .... G 216 383-3400
Euclid (G-6669)

PMRservices LLC .... F 937 219-0062
Spring Valley (G-12242)

Pollock Research & Design Inc .... E 330 332-3300
Salem (G-11805)

Precision Cut Fabricating Inc .... F 440 877-1260
North Royalton (G-10780)

Precision Products Group Inc .... G 330 698-4711
Apple Creek (G-475)

◆ Pro-Pet LLC .... D 419 394-3374
Saint Marys (G-11749)

Production Support Inc .... F 937 526-3897
Russia (G-11677)

Professional Award Service .... G 513 389-3600
Cincinnati (G-3005)

Prospect Rock LLC .... F 740 512-0542
Saint Clairsville (G-11707)

PS Superior Inc .... G 216 587-1000
Cleveland (G-4204)

Publishing Group Ltd .... F 614 572-1240
Columbus (G-5213)

Pughs Designer Jewelers Inc .... G 740 344-9259
Newark (G-10530)

Quality Durable Indus Floors .... F 937 696-2833
Farmersville (G-6823)

Queen City Spirit LLC .... F 513 533-2662
Cincinnati (G-3026)

Quest Technologies Inc .... F 937 743-1200
Franklin (G-7044)

Quintus Technologies LLC .... E 614 891-2732
Lewis Center (G-8349)

R & H Enterprises Llc .... G 216 702-4449
Richmond Heights (G-11612)

R and J Corporation .... E 440 871-6009
Westlake (G-14326)

R J K Enterprises Inc .... F 440 257-6018
Mentor (G-9604)

R J Manray Inc .... G 330 559-6716
Canfield (G-1814)

RE Connors Construction Ltd .... G 740 644-0261
Thornville (G-12767)

Red Barakuda LLC .... G 614 596-5432
Columbus (G-5226)

Rex Welding Inc .... F 740 387-1650
Marion (G-8992)

▲ Richardson Printing Corp .... D 800 848-9752
Marietta (G-8941)

Richland Newhope Inds Inc .... C 419 774-4400
Mansfield (G-8848)

Ryder Engraving Inc .... G 740 927-7193
Pataskala (G-11149)

▲ S C Industries Inc .... E 216 732-9000
Euclid (G-6677)

Safecor Health LLC .... G 614 351-6117
Columbus (G-5243)

Sandwisch Enterprises Inc .... G 419 944-6446
Toledo (G-13121)

Scot Industries Inc .... C 330 262-7585
Wooster (G-14683)

Scottrods LLC .... G 419 499-2705
Monroeville (G-10120)

Screen Works Inc .... E 937 264-9111
Dayton (G-6000)

▼ Scrip-Safe Security Products .... E 513 697-7789
Loveland (G-8652)

Sew & Sew Embroidery Inc .... F 330 676-1600
Kent (G-8078)

▲ Shamrock Companies Inc .... D 440 899-9510
Westlake (G-14333)

Shear Service Inc .... G 216 341-2700
Cleveland (G-4289)

Shoot-A-Way Inc .... F 419 294-4654
Nevada (G-10323)

Shousha Trucking LLC .... F 937 270-4471
Dayton (G-6005)

Signalysis Inc .... F 513 528-6164
Cincinnati (G-3090)

Signs Unlmted The Grphic Advnt .... G 614 836-7446
Logan (G-8526)

Simply Unique Snacks LLC .... G 513 223-7736
Cincinnati (G-3092)

Siraj Recovery LLC .... G 614 893-3507
Columbus (G-5272)

Southwood Pallet LLC .... D 330 682-3747
Orrville (G-11014)

◆ Standard Textile Co Inc .... B 513 761-9255
Cincinnati (G-3112)

Standard Wellness Company LLC .... C 330 931-1037
Gibsonburg (G-7259)

STI Liquidation Inc .... E 614 733-0099
Plain City (G-11418)

Struggle Grind Success LLC .... G 330 834-6738
Boardman (G-1377)

Stutzman Manufacturing Ltd .... G 330 674-4359
Millersburg (G-10012)

Supplier Inspection Svcs Inc .... F 877 263-7097
Dayton (G-6031)

Swagg Productions2015llc .... F 614 601-7414
Worthington (G-14726)

Systems Pack Inc .... E 330 467-5729
Macedonia (G-8719)

Tekni-Plex Inc .... E 419 491-2399
Holland (G-7786)

Teva Womens Health LLC .... C 513 731-9900
Cincinnati (G-3145)

TI Marie Candle Company LLC .... F 513 746-7798
Cincinnati (G-3156)

Tiny Lion Music Groups .... G 419 874-7353
Perrysburg (G-11271)

Tipp Machine & Tool Inc .... G 937 890-8428
Dayton (G-6055)

Tomahawk Entrmt Group LLC .... F 216 505-0548
Euclid (G-6680)

Total Call Center Solutions .... F 330 869-9844
Akron (G-341)

Total Life Safety LLC .... F 866 955-2318
West Chester (G-14083)

Triangle Sign Co LLC .... G 513 266-1009
Hamilton (G-7534)

Tugz International LLC .... F 216 621-4854
Cleveland (G-4432)

▲ Twin Sisters Productions LLC .... E 330 631-0361
Stow (G-12468)

▲ Ultra Tech Machinery Inc .... E 330 929-5544
Cuyahoga Falls (G-5580)

▲ Underground Sports Shop Inc .... F 513 751-1662
Cincinnati (G-3179)

Unique Packaging & Printing .... F 440 785-6730
Mentor (G-9646)

Universal Dsign Fbrication LLC .... F 419 202-5269
Sandusky (G-11880)

Universal Packg Systems Inc .... C 513 732-2000
Batavia (G-894)

Universal Packg Systems Inc .... C 513 735-4777
Batavia (G-895)

Universal Packg Systems Inc .... C 513 674-9400
Cincinnati (G-3186)

▲ Urban Industries of Ohio Inc .... E 419 468-3578
Galion (G-7200)

US Water Company LLC .... G 740 453-0604
Zanesville (G-15053)

Valley List LLC .... G 740 760-6411
Waterford (G-13829)

Valley View Pallets LLC .... G 740 599-0010
Danville (G-5600)

▲ Vista Industrial Packaging LLC .... E 800 454-6117
Columbus (G-5351)

Vitals Matter LLC .... G 937 848-8871
Dayton (G-6072)

Walter North .... F 937 204-6050
Dayton (G-6074)

Welch Packaging Group Inc .... C 614 870-2000
Columbus (G-5359)

◆ Whole Shop Inc .... F 330 630-5305
Tallmadge (G-12759)

◆ William R Hague Inc .... D 614 836-2115
Groveport (G-7458)

Worthngton Smuel Coil Proc LLC .... E 330 963-3777
Twinsburg (G-13398)

75 AUTOMOTIVE REPAIR, SERVICES AND PARKING

7513 Truck rental and leasing, without drivers

▲ Knippen Chrysler Ddge Jeep Inc .... F 419 695-4976
Delphos (G-6188)

Marlow-2000 Inc .... F 216 362-8500
Cleveland (G-3991)

◆ Ohio Machinery Co .... C 440 526-6200
Broadview Heights (G-1509)

7514 Passenger car rental

Precision Coatings Systems .... F 937 642-4727
Marysville (G-9042)

7519 Utility trailer rental

Advanced Rv LLC .... E 440 283-0405
Willoughby (G-14414)

▲ Eleet Cryogenics Inc .... E 330 874-4009
Bolivar (G-1382)

7521 Automobile parking

Dasher Lawless Automation LLC......... E 855 755-7275
Warren *(G-13757)*

Integrity Parking LLC............................ F 440 543-4123
Aurora *(G-675)*

Youngstown Letter Shop Inc................. G 330 793-4935
Youngstown *(G-14972)*

7532 Top and body repair and paint shops

Advanced Rv LLC.................................. E 440 283-0405
Willoughby *(G-14414)*

Bobbart Industries Inc.......................... G 419 350-5477
Sylvania *(G-12702)*

Chardon Square Auto & Body Inc......... F 440 286-7600
Chardon *(G-2199)*

D&D Clssic Auto Rstoration Inc............ G 937 473-2229
Covington *(G-5492)*

Design Masters Inc............................... G 513 772-7175
Cincinnati *(G-2547)*

Ham Signs LLC DBA Fastsigns............. F 937 890-6770
Dayton *(G-5807)*

Michael W Newton................................ G 740 352-9334
Lucasville *(G-8668)*

Mobile Conversions Inc........................ F 513 797-1991
Amelia *(G-434)*

National Fleet Svcs Ohio LLC............... F 440 930-5177
Avon Lake *(G-766)*

Newbury Sndblst & Pntg Inc................. G 440 564-7204
Newbury *(G-10557)*

▲ Obs Inc... F 330 453-3725
Canton *(G-1962)*

Precision Coatings Systems................. F 937 642-4727
Marysville *(G-9042)*

Q T Columbus LLC............................... G 800 758-2410
Columbus *(G-5216)*

▼ QT Equipment Company.................... E 330 724-3055
Akron *(G-272)*

Steves Vans ACC Unlimited LLC........... G 740 374-3154
Marietta *(G-8950)*

W&W Automotive & Towing Inc............. F 937 429-1699
Beavercreek Township *(G-1007)*

Webers Body & Frame Inc.................... G 937 839-5946
West Alexandria *(G-13923)*

Willard Machine & Welding Inc............. F 330 467-0642
Macedonia *(G-8722)*

7533 Auto exhaust system repair shops

Mark Knupp Muffler & Tire Inc............. G 937 773-1334
Piqua *(G-11365)*

7534 Tire retreading and repair shops

AB Tire & Repair.................................. G 440 543-2929
Chagrin Falls *(G-2152)*

Associates Tire and Svc Inc................. F 937 436-4692
Centerville *(G-2129)*

Bell Tire Co... F 440 234-8022
Olmsted Falls *(G-10937)*

Best One Tire & Svc Lima Inc............... G 419 425-3322
Findlay *(G-6843)*

▲ Best One Tire & Svc Lima Inc........... E 419 229-2380
Lima *(G-8389)*

Bob Sumerel Tire Co Inc...................... F 614 527-9700
Columbus *(G-4768)*

Bob Sumerel Tire Co Inc...................... G 937 235-0062
Dayton *(G-5681)*

Bob Sumerel Tire Co Inc...................... G 330 602-1733
Dover *(G-6231)*

Bob Sumerel Tire Co Inc...................... G 740 432-5200
Lore City *(G-8588)*

Bob Sumerel Tire Co Inc...................... F 330 769-9092
Seville *(G-11914)*

Bob Sumerel Tire Co Inc...................... G 740 454-9728
Zanesville *(G-14999)*

Bob Sumerel Tire Company Inc............. G 740 927-2811
Reynoldsburg *(G-11559)*

Bowman Tire Repr Ctr Bxley LLC.......... G 740 928-7000
Hebron *(G-7609)*

Boy-Rad Inc... G 614 766-1228
Dublin *(G-6283)*

Bridgestone Ret Operations LLC........... G 740 592-3075
Athens *(G-635)*

Bridgestone Ret Operations LLC........... G 614 834-3672
Canal Winchester *(G-1787)*

Bridgestone Ret Operations LLC........... G 330 454-9478
Canton *(G-1845)*

Bridgestone Ret Operations LLC........... G 513 793-4550
Cincinnati *(G-2424)*

Bridgestone Ret Operations LLC........... G 513 677-5200
Cincinnati *(G-2425)*

Bridgestone Ret Operations LLC........... G 513 681-7682
Cincinnati *(G-2426)*

Bridgestone Ret Operations LLC........... G 440 842-3200
Cleveland *(G-3436)*

Bridgestone Ret Operations LLC........... G 440 461-4747
Cleveland *(G-3437)*

Bridgestone Ret Operations LLC........... G 216 229-2550
Cleveland *(G-3438)*

Bridgestone Ret Operations LLC........... G 216 382-8970
Cleveland *(G-3439)*

Bridgestone Ret Operations LLC........... F 614 864-3350
Columbus *(G-4777)*

Bridgestone Ret Operations LLC........... F 614 491-8062
Columbus *(G-4778)*

Bridgestone Ret Operations LLC........... G 614 224-4221
Columbus *(G-4779)*

Bridgestone Ret Operations LLC........... G 440 324-3327
Elyria *(G-6504)*

Bridgestone Ret Operations LLC........... G 440 365-8308
Elyria *(G-6505)*

Bridgestone Ret Operations LLC........... G 937 548-1197
Greenville *(G-7336)*

Bridgestone Ret Operations LLC........... G 513 868-7399
Hamilton *(G-7473)*

Bridgestone Ret Operations LLC........... G 330 673-1700
Kent *(G-8020)*

Bridgestone Ret Operations LLC........... F 440 299-6126
Mentor *(G-9493)*

Bridgestone Ret Operations LLC........... F 740 397-5601
Mount Vernon *(C 10237)*

Bridgestone Ret Operations LLC........... G 614 861-7994
Reynoldsburg *(G-11560)*

Bridgestone Ret Operations LLC........... G 419 625-6571
Sandusky *(G-11823)*

Bridgestone Ret Operations LLC........... F 937 325-4638
Springfield *(G-12286)*

Bridgestone Ret Operations LLC........... G 724 346-2621
Warren *(G-13744)*

Bridgestone Ret Operations LLC........... G 330 758-0921
Youngstown *(G-14825)*

Bridgestone Ret Operations LLC........... G 330 759-3697
Youngstown *(G-14826)*

C & F Tire & Truck Repair.................... G 419 526-1412
Ontario *(G-10947)*

Canton Bandag Co................................ G 330 454-3025
Canton *(G-1853)*

Capital Tire Inc.................................... E 330 364-4731
Toledo *(G-12911)*

Central Ohio Bandag LP........................ F 740 454-9728
Zanesville *(G-15007)*

Certified Auto & Trck Repr Inc.............. G 440 288-2029
Lorain *(G-8550)*

Chardon Square Auto & Body Inc......... F 440 286-7600
Chardon *(G-2199)*

Cims Incorporated............................... G 330 794-8102
Akron *(G-100)*

Custom Recapping Inc.......................... G 937 324-4331
Springfield *(G-12297)*

Exit 11 Truck Tire Service Inc............... G 330 659-6372
Richfield *(G-11591)*

Fleet Relief Company........................... G 419 525-2625
Mansfield *(G-8789)*

Forklift Tire East Mich Inc.................... F 586 771-1330
Toledo *(G-12967)*

Goodyear Tire & Rubber Company........ F 419 643-8273
Beaverdam *(G-1008)*

Goodyear Tire & Rubber Company........ G 330 966-1274
Canton *(G-1904)*

Goodyear Tire & Rubber Company........ G 330 759-9343
Youngstown *(G-14869)*

◆ Goodyear Tire & Rubber Company....A 330 796-2121
Akron *(G-164)*

▲ Grismer Tire Company...................... E 937 643-2526
Centerville *(G-2132)*

Gt Tire Service Inc............................... G 740 927-7226
Pataskala *(G-11139)*

Heartland Retreaders Inc..................... F 740 472-0558
Woodsfield *(G-14612)*

Heisley Tire & Brake Inc....................... G 440 357-9797
Mentor *(G-9527)*

J & J Tire & Alignment......................... G 330 424-5200
Lisbon *(G-8471)*

JTL Enterprises LLC............................. E 937 890-8189
Dayton *(G-5832)*

Liberty Tire Recycling LLC.................... E 614 871-8097
Grove City *(G-7394)*

Mark Knupp Muffler & Tire Inc............. G 937 773-1334
Piqua *(G-11365)*

Mid America Tire of Hillsboro Inc.......... E 937 393-3520
Hillsboro *(G-7720)*

Mitchell Bros Tire Rtread Svc............... G 740 353-1551
Portsmouth *(G-11470)*

Muskingum Tire Company Inc............... G 740 453-8473
Zanesville *(G-15030)*

North Coast Tire Co Inc........................ G 216 447-1690
Cleveland *(G-4089)*

Ohio Made Tires LLC............................ G 740 421-4934
Woodsfield *(G-14615)*

Paul Shovlin.. G 330 757-0032
Youngstown *(G-14915)*

Premier Bandag 8 Inc.......................... F 330 823-3822
Alliance *(O-400)*

Pro Tire Inc... F 614 864-8662
Columbus *(G-5208)*

Randys Tire & Auto Repair Inc.............. G 419 562-2926
Bucyrus *(G-1688)*

Shrader Tire & Oil Inc.......................... G 419 420-8435
Perrysburg *(G-11262)*

Skaggs Trlr & Tire Repr Co Inc............. F 440 986-7470
Amherst *(G-452)*

Skinner Firestone Inc........................... G 740 984-4247
Beverly *(G-1209)*

Snider Tire Inc..................................... F 740 439-2741
Cambridge *(G-1760)*

Sycamore Tire & Auto Repair................ G 513 793-0726
Cincinnati *(G-3134)*

Tbc Retail Group Inc............................ E 216 267-8040
Cleveland *(G-4365)*

Urra Co Inc.. G 330 673-8473
Kent *(G-8093)*

Victor Bodie Tire Co............................. G 216 431-1700
Cleveland *(G-4471)*

Wayne A Whaley................................... G 330 525-7779
Homeworth *(G-7807)*

Ziegler Tire and Supply Co................... G 330 434-7126
Akron *(G-362)*

Ziegler Tire and Supply Co...................... G..... 330 477-3463
Canton *(G-2052)*

Ziegler Tire and Supply Co...................... E..... 330 343-7739
Dover *(G-6267)*

7536 Automotive glass replacement shops

A Service Glass Inc............................ F..... 937 426-4920
Beavercreek *(G-963)*

J W Goss Company............................. F..... 330 395-0739
Warren *(G-13773)*

Keystone Auto Glass Inc...................... D..... 419 509-0497
Maumee *(G-9302)*

◆ Safelite Group Inc..........................A..... 614 210-9000
Columbus *(G-5244)*

Support Svc LLC............................... G..... 419 617-0660
Lexington *(G-8375)*

Webers Body & Frame Inc.................... G..... 937 839-5946
West Alexandria *(G-13923)*

7537 Automotive transmission repair shops

Bob Sumerel Tire Co Inc...................... F..... 330 769-9092
Seville *(G-11914)*

Mikes Transm & Auto Svc LLC............. F..... 330 799-8266
Youngstown *(G-14901)*

Power Acquisition LLC......................... A..... 614 228-5000
Dublin *(G-6333)*

Rumpke Transportation Co LLC............. F..... 513 851-0122
Cincinnati *(G-3058)*

▲ Tri-W Group Inc............................. A..... 614 228-5000
Columbus *(G-5332)*

WW Williams Company LLC................. D..... 614 228-5000
Dublin *(G-6362)*

7538 General automotive repair shops

AB Tire & Repair............................... G..... 440 543-2929
Chagrin Falls *(G-2152)*

Abutilon Company Inc......................... F..... 419 536-6123
Toledo *(G-12862)*

Automtve Rfnish Clor Sltons I............... E..... 330 461-6067
Medina *(G-9378)*

Bob Sumerel Tire Co Inc...................... F..... 330 769-9092
Seville *(G-11914)*

Bowman Tire Repr Ctr Bxley LLC........... G..... 740 928-7000
Hebron *(G-7609)*

Bridgestone Ret Operations LLC........... F..... 440 299-6126
Mentor *(G-9493)*

Bridgestone Ret Operations LLC........... G..... 419 625-6571
Sandusky *(G-11823)*

C & F Tire & Truck Repair.................... G..... 419 526-1412
Ontario *(G-10947)*

Certified Auto & Trck Repr Inc.............. G..... 440 288-2029
Lorain *(G-8550)*

Cummins Inc.................................... F..... 614 771-1000
Hilliard *(G-7679)*

Dan Patrick Enterprises Inc................. G..... 740 477-1006
Circleville *(G-3253)*

Doug Marine Motors Inc...................... F..... 740 335-3700
Wshngtn Ct Hs *(G-14738)*

◆ Goodyear Tire & Rubber Company.....A..... 330 796-2121
Akron *(G-164)*

▲ Grismer Tire Company..................... E..... 937 643-2526
Centerville *(G-2132)*

Heisley Tire & Brake Inc..................... G..... 440 357-9797
Mentor *(G-9527)*

Hutter Racing Engines Ltd................... F..... 440 285-2175
Chardon *(G-2208)*

J & J Tire & Alignment........................ G..... 330 424-5200
Lisbon *(G-8471)*

Kaffenbarger Truck Eqp Co.................. E..... 513 772-6800
Cincinnati *(G-2777)*

Kinstle Truck & Auto Svc Inc............... G..... 419 738-7493
Wapakoneta *(G-13718)*

Kirbys Auto and Truck Repr Inc............. G..... 513 934-3999
Lebanon *(G-8272)*

▲ Knippen Chrysler Ddge Jeep Inc........ F..... 419 695-4976
Delphos *(G-6188)*

M & W Trailers Inc............................. F..... 419 453-3331
Ottoville *(G-11055)*

Maags Automotive & Mch Inc............... G..... 419 626-1539
Sandusky *(G-11853)*

Nice Body Automotive LLC................... G..... 440 752-5568
Elyria *(G-6569)*

Ohio Trailer Inc................................ G..... 330 392-4444
Warren *(G-13787)*

Pattons Trck & Hvy Eqp Svc Inc............ F..... 740 385-4067
Logan *(G-8523)*

Power Acquisition LLC......................... A..... 614 228-5000
Dublin *(G-6333)*

Randys Tire & Auto Repair Inc.............. G..... 419 562-2926
Bucyrus *(G-1688)*

Sammy S Auto Detail.......................... F..... 614 263-2728
Columbus *(G-5246)*

Skaggs Trlr & Tire Repr Co Inc............. F..... 440 986-7470
Amherst *(G-452)*

Sutphen Towers Inc............................ D..... 614 876-1262
Hilliard *(G-7704)*

Sycamore Tire & Auto Repair............... G..... 513 793-0726
Cincinnati *(G-3134)*

▲ Tri-W Group Inc............................. A..... 614 228-5000
Columbus *(G-5332)*

WW Williams Company LLC................. D..... 614 228-5000
Dublin *(G-6362)*

Youngstown-Kenworth Inc................... F..... 330 534-9761
Hubbard *(G-7819)*

7539 Automotive repair shops, nec

AB Tire & Repair............................... G..... 440 543-2929
Chagrin Falls *(G-2152)*

Albright Radiator Inc.......................... G..... 330 264-8886
Wooster *(G-14622)*

Bob Sumerel Tire Co Inc...................... F..... 330 769-9092
Seville *(G-11914)*

Bowman Tire Repr Ctr Bxley LLC........... G..... 740 928-7000
Hebron *(G-7609)*

Bridgestone Ret Operations LLC........... F..... 614 491-8062
Columbus *(G-4778)*

Brock RAD Wldg Fabrication Inc........... G..... 740 773-2540
Chillicothe *(G-2246)*

C & F Tire & Truck Repair.................... G..... 419 526-1412
Ontario *(G-10947)*

Capitol City Trailers Inc...................... D..... 614 491-2616
Obetz *(G-10921)*

Certified Auto & Trck Repr Inc.............. G..... 440 288-2029
Lorain *(G-8550)*

Chardon Square Auto & Body Inc........... F..... 440 286-7600
Chardon *(G-2199)*

▲ Cincinnati Radiator Inc.................... F..... 513 874-5555
Fairfield *(G-6722)*

Circleville Oil Co.............................. G..... 740 477-3341
Circleville *(G-3251)*

▼ East Trailers LLC............................ E..... 330 325-9921
Randolph *(G-11510)*

Entratech Systems LLC...................... G..... 419 433-7683
Sandusky *(G-11832)*

Friess Welding Inc............................ G..... 330 644-8160
Coventry Township *(G-5482)*

◆ Goodyear Tire & Rubber Company.....A..... 330 796-2121
Akron *(G-164)*

Greggs Specialty Services................... F..... 419 478-0803
Toledo *(G-12977)*

Heisley Tire & Brake Inc..................... G..... 440 357-9797
Mentor *(G-9527)*

J & J Tire & Alignment........................ G..... 330 424-5200
Lisbon *(G-8471)*

J & L Body Inc.................................. F..... 216 661-2323
Brooklyn Heights *(G-1533)*

Jordon Auto Service & Tire Inc............. G..... 216 214-6528
Cleveland *(G-3891)*

Kirbys Auto and Truck Repr Inc............. G..... 513 934-3999
Lebanon *(G-8272)*

M & W Trailers Inc............................. F..... 419 453-3331
Ottoville *(G-11055)*

Maags Automotive & Mch Inc............... G..... 419 626-1539
Sandusky *(G-11853)*

◆ Mac Trailer Manufacturing Inc...........A..... 800 795-8454
Alliance *(G-390)*

Mark Knupp Muffler & Tire Inc.............. G..... 937 773-1334
Piqua *(G-11365)*

▲ Mc Machine Llc............................. E..... 216 398-3666
Cleveland *(G-4007)*

Midwest Muffler Pros & More............... G..... 937 293-2450
Moraine *(G-10179)*

Mikes Transm & Auto Svc LLC............. F..... 330 799-8266
Youngstown *(G-14901)*

▲ Miscor Group Ltd........................... B..... 330 830-3500
Massillon *(G-9224)*

▼ Nelson Manufacturing Company........ D..... 419 523-5321
Ottawa *(G-11039)*

Nice Body Automotive LLC................... G..... 440 752-5568
Elyria *(G-6569)*

Perkins Motor Service Ltd................... F..... 440 277-1256
Lorain *(G-8573)*

Randys Tire & Auto Repair Inc.............. G..... 419 562-2926
Bucyrus *(G-1688)*

Skaggs Trlr & Tire Repr Co Inc............. F..... 440 986-7470
Amherst *(G-452)*

Support Svc LLC............................... G..... 419 617-0660
Lexington *(G-8375)*

Sycamore Tire & Auto Repair............... G..... 513 793-0726
Cincinnati *(G-3134)*

▲ Tuf-Tug Inc.................................. F..... 937 299-1213
Dayton *(G-6067)*

Vintage Automotive Elc Inc................. F..... 419 472-9349
Toledo *(G-13175)*

7549 Automotive services, nec

▲ Afg Industries Inc.......................... D..... 614 322-4580
Grove City *(G-7368)*

J & L Body Inc.................................. F..... 216 661-2323
Brooklyn Heights *(G-1533)*

Johns Welding & Towing Inc................. G..... 419 447-8937
Tiffin *(G-12785)*

Lubrication Specialties LLC................. E..... 800 341-6516
Mount Gilead *(G-10212)*

Mikes Transm & Auto Svc LLC............. F..... 330 799-8266
Youngstown *(G-14901)*

Mpi Logistics and Service Inc.............. E..... 330 832-5309
Massillon *(G-9225)*

Precision Coatings Systems................. F..... 937 642-4727
Marysville *(G-9042)*

Tbone Sales LLC.............................. G..... 330 897-6131
Baltic *(G-781)*

X-Treme Finishes Inc......................... F..... 330 474-0614
North Royalton *(G-10790)*

76 MISCELLANEOUS REPAIR SERVICES

7622 Radio and television repair

Cattron Holdings Inc.......................... E..... 234 806-0018
Warren *(G-13748)*

Cbst Acquisition LLC.......................... D..... 513 361-9600
Cincinnati *(G-2445)*

Central USA Wireless LLC................... G..... 513 469-1500
Cincinnati *(G-2453)*

Dss Installations Ltd........................ G 513 761-7000
Cincinnati *(G-2563)*

Electra Sound Inc........................... D 216 433-9600
Avon Lake *(G-754)*

Industrial Electronic Service.............. F 937 746-9750
Carlisle *(G-2066)*

7623 Refrigeration service and repair

▼ Air-Rite Inc............................... E 216 228-8200
Cleveland *(G-3316)*

Bell Industrial Services LLC............... F 937 507-9193
Sidney *(G-11997)*

Northeastern Rfrgn Corp................... E 440 942-7676
Willoughby *(G-14496)*

Weather King Heating & AC................ G 330 908-0281
Northfield *(G-10799)*

Wsi Seller Inc............................. F 330 379-0270
Akron *(G-359)*

7629 Electrical repair shops

Allied Machine Works Inc.................. G 740 454-2534
Zanesville *(G-14986)*

▲ Amko Service Company................... E 330 364-8857
Midvale *(G-9907)*

Ascendtech Inc............................ E 216 458-1101
Willoughby *(G-14428)*

Bentronix Corp............................ G 440 632-0606
Middlefield *(G-9782)*

Cbst Acquisition LLC...................... D 513 361-9600
Cincinnati *(G-2445)*

◆ Ceramic Holdings Inc.................... C 216 362-3900
Brook Park *(G-1511)*

Copier Resources Inc...................... G 614 268-1100
Columbus *(G-4849)*

Cornerstone Wauseon Inc.................. C 419 337-0940
Wauseon *(G-13847)*

D & J Electric Motor Repair Co............ F 330 336-4343
Wadsworth *(G-13634)*

DTE Inc................................... E 419 522-3428
Mansfield *(G-8781)*

Electric Service Co Inc.................... E 513 271-6387
Cincinnati *(G-2580)*

Emerson Network Power.................... G 614 841-8054
Ironton *(G-7931)*

▲ Enprotech Industrial Tech LLC.......... E 216 883-3220
Cleveland *(G-3675)*

General Electric Company.................. E 513 977-1500
Cincinnati *(G-2552)*

General Electric Company.................. E 216 883-1000
Cleveland *(G-3766)*

Greggs Specialty Services................. F 419 478-0803
Toledo *(G-12977)*

Hannon Company........................... F 330 343-7758
Dover *(G-6246)*

▲ Instrmntation Ctrl Systems Inc......... E 513 662-2600
Cincinnati *(G-2747)*

Interface Logic Systems Inc............... G 614 236-8388
Ashville *(G-626)*

Karon C Enold............................. E 740 269-3475
Sherrodsville *(G-11975)*

Kcn Technologies LLC...................... G 440 439-4219
Bedford *(G-1041)*

Kiemle-Hankins Company................... E 419 661-2430
Perrysburg *(G-11233)*

Mid-Ohio Electric Co...................... E 614 274-8000
Columbus *(G-5098)*

▲ Miscor Group Ltd........................ B 330 830-3500
Massillon *(G-9224)*

Narrow Way Custom Tech Inc............... E 937 743-1611
Carlisle *(G-2069)*

◆ Niktec Inc.............................. G 513 282-3747
Franklin *(G-7038)*

Oaks Welding Inc.......................... G 330 482-4216
Columbiana *(G-4624)*

Precision Assemblies Inc.................. F 330 549-2630
North Lima *(G-10710)*

Queen City Office Machine................. F 513 251-7200
Cincinnati *(G-3022)*

▲ Rubber City Machinery Corp............. E 330 434-3500
Akron *(G-293)*

▲ Sasha Electronics Inc................... G 419 662-8100
Rossford *(G-11663)*

Spirit Avionics Ltd....................... F 614 237-4271
Columbus *(G-5284)*

▲ Steel Eqp Specialists Inc............... D 330 823-8260
Alliance *(G-406)*

▲ Stein LLC............................... F 440 526-9301
Independence *(G-7919)*

Tegam Inc................................. E 440 466-6100
Geneva *(G-7246)*

Town Cntry Technical Svcs Inc............. F 614 866-7700
Reynoldsburg *(G-11582)*

Vacuum Electric Switch Co Inc............. F 330 374-5156
Mogadore *(G-10091)*

◆ Vertiv Corporation...................... A 614 888-0246
Westerville *(G-14239)*

◆ Vertiv Energy Systems Inc............... A 440 288-1122
Lorain *(G-8585)*

◆ Vertiv Group Corporation................ G 440 288-1122
Lorain *(G-8586)*

Wilson Sign Co Inc........................ F 937 253-2246
Germantown *(G-7257)*

7631 Watch, clock, and jewelry repair

Bensan Jewelers Inc....................... G 216 221-1434
Lakewood *(G-8163)*

Don Basch Jewelers Inc.................... F 330 467-2116
Macedonia *(G-8687)*

Gustave Julian Jewelers Inc............... G 440 888-1100
Cleveland *(G-3801)*

H P Nielsen Inc........................... G 440 244-4255
Lorain *(G-8557)*

Im Greenberg Inc.......................... G 440 461-4464
Cleveland *(G-3849)*

Koop Diamond Cutters Inc.................. F 513 621-2838
Cincinnati *(G-2805)*

Michael W Hyes Desgr Goldsmith........... G 440 519-0889
Solon *(G-12150)*

Pughs Designer Jewelers Inc............... G 740 344-9259
Newark *(G-10530)*

Sheiban Jewelry Inc....................... F 440 238-0616
Strongsville *(G-12599)*

White Jewelers Inc........................ G 330 264-3324
Wooster *(G-14697)*

7641 Reupholstery and furniture repair

American Office Services Inc............... G 440 899-6888
Westlake *(G-14287)*

▲ Casco Mfg Solutions Inc................. D 513 681-0003
Cincinnati *(G-2441)*

Custom Craft Collection Inc............... F 440 998-3000
Ashtabula *(G-589)*

▲ Fortner Upholstering Inc................ G 614 475-8282
Columbus *(G-4936)*

Furniture Concepts Inc.................... G 216 292-9100
Cleveland *(G-3745)*

Mielke Furniture Repair Inc............... G 419 625-4572
Sandusky *(G-11860)*

▲ National Electro-Coatings Inc........... D 216 898-0080
Cleveland *(G-4059)*

Office Magic Inc.......................... F 510 782-6100
Medina *(G-9430)*

Recycled Systems Furniture Inc............ E 614 880-9110
Worthington *(G-14724)*

Robert Mayo Industries.................... G 330 426-2587
East Palestine *(G-6406)*

Soft Touch Wood LLC....................... E 330 545-4204
Girard *(G-7280)*

7692 Welding repair

3-B Welding Ltd........................... G 740 819-4329
New Concord *(G-10384)*

A & C Welding Inc......................... E 330 762-4777
Peninsula *(G-11179)*

▲ A & G Manufacturing Co Inc............. E 419 468-7433
Galion *(G-7176)*

Abbott Tool Inc........................... E 419 476-6742
Toledo *(G-12861)*

▲ Active Metal and Molds Inc............. F 419 281-9623
Ashland *(G-514)*

Advanced Wldg Fabrication Inc............. F 440 724-9165
Sheffield Lake *(G-11953)*

Albright Radiator Inc..................... G 330 264-8886
Wooster *(G-14622)*

Alexy Metals Ltd.......................... F 216 410-8661
Willoughby *(G-14416)*

All - Do Weld & Fab LLC................... G 740 477-2133
Circleville *(G-3246)*

All Ohio Welding Inc...................... G 937 663-7116
Saint Paris *(G-11755)*

All-Type Welding & Fabrication............ E 440 439-3990
Cleveland *(G-3329)*

Allied Fabricating & Wldg Co.............. E 614 868-8680
Columbus *(G-4687)*

Amptech Machining & Welding............... G 419 652-3444
Nova *(G-10875)*

Apollo Welding & Fabg Inc................. F 440 942-0227
Willoughby *(G-14423)*

ARC Solutions LLC......................... E 419 542-9272
Hicksville *(G-7646)*

Arctech Fabricating Inc................... E 937 525-9353
Springfield *(G-12282)*

Athens Mold and Machine Inc............... D 740 593-6613
Athens *(G-633)*

B & R Fabricators & Maint Inc............. F 513 641-2222
Cincinnati *(G-2395)*

Bamf Welding & Fabrication LLC............ G 440 862-8286
Novelty *(G-10880)*

Baughman Machine & Weld Sp Inc............ G 330 866-9243
Waynesburg *(G-13875)*

Bayloff Stmped Pdts Knsman Inc............ D 330 876-4511
Kinsman *(G-140)*

Bear Welding Services LLC................. F 740 630-7538
Caldwell *(G-1723)*

Blackwood Sheet Metal Inc................. G 614 291-3115
Columbus *(G-4764)*

Blevins Metal Fabrication Inc............. E 419 522-6082
Mansfield *(G-8766)*

Bob Lanes Welding Inc..................... G 740 373-3567
Marietta *(G-8904)*

▲ Braze Solutions LLC.................... F 440 349-5100
Solon *(G-12089)*

Breitinger Company........................ C 419 526-4255
Mansfield *(G-8767)*

Brock RAD Wldg Fabrication Inc............ G 740 773-2540
Chillicothe *(G-2246)*

Brown Industrial Inc...................... E 937 693-3838
Botkins *(G-1397)*

Buckeye State Wldg & Fabg Inc............. G 440 322-0344
Elyria *(G-6507)*

▲ Byron Products Inc..................... D 513 870-9111
Fairfield *(G-6715)*

C & R Inc................................. E 614 497-1130
Groveport *(G-7427)*

C-N-D Industries Inc...................... F 330 478-8811
Massillon *(G-9176)*

Camelot Manufacturing Inc.................... G..... 419 678-2603
   Coldwater *(G-4569)*

Cardinal Welding Inc............................. G..... 330 426-2404
   East Palestine *(G-6400)*

Carter Manufacturing Co Inc................. F..... 513 398-7303
   Mason *(G-9077)*

▲ Case-Maul Manufacturing Co........... F..... 419 524-1061
   Mansfield *(G-8771)*

◆ Ceramic Holdings Inc....................... C..... 216 362-3900
   Brook Park *(G-1511)*

City Machine Technologies Inc............. F..... 330 747-2639
   Youngstown *(G-14836)*

Clemens Mobile Welding LLC............... E..... 419 782-4220
   Defiance *(G-6103)*

Clipsons Metal Working Inc.................. G..... 513 772-6393
   Cincinnati *(G-2499)*

Cmt Machining & Fabg LLC................... F..... 937 652-3740
   Urbana *(G-13459)*

Columbus Pipe and Equipment Co........ F..... 614 444-7871
   Columbus *(G-4831)*

▲ Combs Manufacturing Inc................. D..... 330 784-3151
   Akron *(G-104)*

Complete Metal Services...................... G..... 740 694-0000
   Fredericktown *(G-7074)*

Comptons Precision Machine................ F..... 937 325-9139
   Springfield *(G-12293)*

Connaughton Wldg & Fence LLC........... G..... 513 867-0230
   Hamilton *(G-7480)*

Crazeweld LLC..................................... G..... 419 210-3668
   Norwalk *(G-10833)*

Creative Fab & Welding LLC.................. E..... 937 780-5000
   Leesburg *(G-8298)*

Creative Fabrication Ltd....................... G..... 740 262-5789
   Richwood *(G-11614)*

Creative Mold and Machine Inc............. E..... 440 338-5146
   Newbury *(G-10548)*

Crest Bending Inc................................ E..... 419 492-2108
   New Washington *(G-10478)*

Custom Machine Inc............................. E..... 419 986-5122
   Tiffin *(G-12781)*

Custom Weld & Machine Corp............... G..... 330 452-3935
   Canton *(G-1875)*

D & G Welding Inc............................... G..... 419 445-5751
   Archbold *(G-492)*

Dana White Machining Wldg Inc............ G..... 419 652-3444
   Nova *(G-10876)*

Dayton Brick Company Inc.................... F..... 937 293-4189
   Moraine *(G-10156)*

Dbcr Inc.. E..... 330 920-1900
   Cuyahoga Falls *(G-5537)*

Dover Fabrication and Burn Inc............. G..... 330 339-1057
   Dover *(G-6239)*

Dover Machine Co................................ G..... 330 343-4123
   Dover *(G-6241)*

Drabik Manufacturing Inc..................... F..... 216 267-1616
   Cleveland *(G-3629)*

Drj Welding Services LLC..................... G..... 740 229-7428
   New Philadelphia *(G-10443)*

Duco Tool & Die Inc............................. F..... 419 628-2031
   Minster *(G-10056)*

Dynamic Weld Corporation.................... E..... 419 582-2900
   Osgood *(G-11026)*

E & M Liberty Welding Inc.................... G..... 330 866-2338
   Waynesburg *(G-13876)*

Eagle Welding & Fabg Inc.................... E..... 440 946-0692
   Willoughby *(G-14453)*

▲ East End Welding LLC...................... C..... 330 677-6000
   Kent *(G-8028)*

Fabrication Shop Inc............................ F..... 419 435-7934
   Fostoria *(G-6978)*

Falls Stamping & Welding Co................ C..... 330 928-1191
   Cuyahoga Falls *(G-5541)*

Fredrick Welding & Machining............... G..... 614 866-9650
   Reynoldsburg *(G-11571)*

Friess Welding Inc............................... G..... 330 644-8160
   Coventry Township *(G-5482)*

Garland Welding Co Inc....................... F..... 330 536-6506
   Lowellville *(G-8662)*

Gaspar Inc... D..... 330 477-2222
   Canton *(G-1898)*

Gdn Welding LLC................................. E..... 740 398-6109
   Danville *(G-5599)*

▲ General Technologies Inc................. E..... 419 747-1800
   Mansfield *(G-8791)*

▲ General Tool Company...................... C..... 513 733-5500
   Cincinnati *(G-2666)*

George Steel Fabricating Inc................ E..... 513 932-2887
   Lebanon *(G-8259)*

Gilson Machine & Tool Co Inc............... E..... 419 592-2911
   Napoleon *(G-10282)*

▲ Glenridge Machine Co...................... G..... 440 975-1055
   Solon *(G-12116)*

Gmp Welding & Fabrication Inc............. G..... 513 825-7861
   Cincinnati *(G-2679)*

Greber Machine Tool Inc....................... G..... 440 322-3685
   Elyria *(G-6541)*

Greggs Specialty Services.................... F..... 419 478-0803
   Toledo *(G-12977)*

H & H Machine Shop Akron Inc............. E..... 330 773-3327
   Akron *(G-167)*

Habco Tool and Dev Co Inc.................. E..... 440 946-5546
   Mentor *(G-9525)*

Harris Welding and Machine Co............. F..... 419 281-8351
   Ashland *(G-537)*

HI Tecmetal Group Inc......................... E..... 216 881-8100
   Wickliffe *(G-14378)*

▲ Hi-Tek Manufacturing Inc................. C..... 513 459-1094
   Mason *(G-9108)*

Highs Welding Inc................................ G..... 937 464-3029
   Belle Center *(G-1096)*

Holdren Brothers Inc........................... F..... 937 465-7050
   West Liberty *(G-14175)*

Holdsworth Industrial Fabg LLC............ G..... 330 874-3945
   Bolivar *(G-1384)*

Holmview Welding LLC......................... F..... 330 359-5315
   Fredericksburg *(G-7064)*

Independent Machine & Wldg Inc.......... G..... 937 339-7330
   Troy *(G-13228)*

▲ Industry Products Co........................ B..... 937 778-0585
   Piqua *(G-11356)*

J & S Industrial Mch Pdts Inc............... E..... 419 691-1380
   Toledo *(G-13012)*

J A B Welding Service Inc.................... E..... 740 453-5868
   Zanesville *(G-15023)*

J&J Precision Fabricators Ltd............... F..... 330 482-4964
   Columbiana *(G-4621)*

Jerl Machine Inc.................................. D..... 419 873-0270
   Perrysburg *(G-11232)*

JMw Welding and Mfg Inc..................... E..... 330 484-2428
   Canton *(G-1922)*

Johns Welding & Towing Inc................. G..... 419 447-8937
   Tiffin *(G-12785)*

K & J Machine Inc............................... G..... 740 425-3282
   Barnesville *(G-845)*

K-M-S Industries Inc............................ G..... 440 243-6680
   Brookpark *(G-1554)*

Kann Custom Welding LLC.................... G..... 330 231-2719
   Dundee *(G-6366)*

Kda Manufacturing LLC........................ F..... 330 590-7431
   Norton *(G-10825)*

Kel-Par Co Inc.................................... F..... 740 344-2627
   Newark *(G-10513)*

Kellys Wldg & Fabrication Ltd............... G..... 440 593-6040
   Conneaut *(G-5406)*

Kendel Wldg & Fabrication Inc.............. G..... 330 834-2429
   Massillon *(G-9210)*

Kings Welding and Fabg Inc.................. G..... 330 738-3592
   Mechanicstown *(G-9368)*

Kinninger Prod Wldg Co Inc.................. D..... 419 629-3491
   New Bremen *(G-10361)*

Kirbys Auto and Truck Repr Inc............ G..... 513 934-3999
   Lebanon *(G-8272)*

▲ Kottler Metal Products Co Inc........... E..... 440 946-7473
   Willoughby *(G-14478)*

Kramer Power Equipment Co................. G..... 937 456-2232
   Eaton *(G-6457)*

Lakecraft Inc....................................... G..... 419 734-2828
   Port Clinton *(G-11444)*

Lima Sheet Metal Mch & Mfg Inc.......... F..... 419 229-1161
   Lima *(G-8426)*

Lincoln Electric Automtn Inc................. B..... 937 295-2120
   Fort Loramie *(G-6950)*

Logan Welding Inc............................... G..... 740 385-9651
   Logan *(G-8520)*

▲ Long-Stanton Mfg Company.............. E..... 513 874-8020
   West Chester *(G-14024)*

Lunar Tool & Mold Inc......................... E..... 440 237-2141
   North Royalton *(G-10771)*

M & M Certified Welding Inc................ F..... 330 467-1729
   Macedonia *(G-8703)*

M & M Concepts Inc............................ G..... 937 355-1115
   West Mansfield *(G-14179)*

Majestic Tool and Machine Inc.............. G..... 440 248-5058
   Solon *(G-12144)*

Marengo Fabricated Steel Ltd............... F..... 800 919-2652
   Cardington *(G-2055)*

Marsam Metalfab Inc............................ E..... 330 405-1520
   Twinsburg *(G-13334)*

Martin Welding LLC.............................. F..... 937 687-3602
   New Lebanon *(G-10400)*

Mc Elwain Industries Inc...................... F..... 419 532-3126
   Ottawa *(G-11038)*

▲ Mc Machine Llc................................ E..... 216 398-3666
   Cleveland *(G-4007)*

▲ McGregor Mtal Leffel Works LLC....... D..... 937 325-5561
   Springfield *(G-12350)*

Meta Manufacturing Corporation........... E..... 513 793-6382
   Blue Ash *(G-1308)*

Mike Loppe... F..... 937 969-8102
   Tremont City *(G-13189)*

Mk Welding & Fabrication Inc............... G..... 937 603-4430
   Waynesville *(G-13880)*

Modern Machine Development................ F..... 937 253-4576
   Dayton *(G-5891)*

Montgomery & Montgomery LLC............ G..... 330 858-9533
   Akron *(G-236)*

Ms Welding LLC.................................. G..... 419 925-4141
   Maria Stein *(G-8900)*

Mt Vernon Mold Works Inc................... E..... 618 242-6040
   Akron *(G-238)*

National Wldg Tanker Repr LLC............ G..... 614 875-3399
   Grove City *(G-7404)*

Northwind Industries Inc....................... G..... 216 433-0666
   Cleveland *(G-4099)*

Oaks Welding Inc................................ G..... 330 482-4216
   Columbiana *(G-4624)*

Ohio Hydraulics Inc............................. E..... 513 771-2590
   Cincinnati *(G-2924)*

Ohio Trailer Inc.................................. G..... 330 392-4444
   Warren *(G-13787)*

Ohio Trailer Supply Inc....................... G..... 614 471-9121
   Columbus *(G-5155)*

Ottawa Defense Logistics LLC.............. F..... 419 596-3202
   Ottawa *(G-11040)*

Patriot Stainless Welding..................... G..... 740 297-6040
   Zanesville *(G-15038)*

Paul Wilke & Son Inc .... F 513 921-3163
Cincinnati (G-2947)

Paulo Products Company .... E 440 942-0153
Willoughby (G-14505)

◆ Pentaflex Inc .... C 937 325-5551
Springfield (G-12360)

Perkins Motor Service Ltd .... F 440 277-1256
Lorain (G-8573)

Perry Welding Service Inc .... F 330 425-2211
Twinsburg (G-13355)

Phillips Mfg and Tower Co .... D 419 347-1720
Shelby (G-11972)

Phoenix Inds & Apparatus Inc .... F 513 722-1085
Loveland (G-8645)

PMRservices LLC .... F 937 219-0062
Spring Valley (G-12242)

Pr-Weld & Manufacturing Ltd .... G 419 633-9204
West Unity (G-14197)

Precision Assemblies Inc .... G 330 549-2630
North Lima (G-10710)

Precision Mtal Fabrication Inc .... D 937 235-9261
Dayton (G-5950)

Precision Reflex Inc .... G 419 629-2603
New Bremen (G-10365)

Precision Welding & Mfg Inc .... F 937 444-6925
Mount Orab (G-10221)

Precision Welding Corporation .... E 216 524-6110
Cleveland (G-4187)

▲ Prince & Izant LLC .... E 216 362-7000
Cleveland (G-4196)

Process Eqp Co Wldg Svcs LLC .... G 937 667-4451
Tipp City (G-12837)

Prout Boiler Htg & Wldg Inc .... G 330 744-0293
Youngstown (G-14921)

Quality Welding Inc .... E 419 483-6067
Bellevue (G-1128)

Quick Service Welding & Mch Co .... F 330 673-3818
Kent (G-8066)

▲ R K Industries Inc .... D 419 523-5001
Ottawa (G-11044)

Rbm Environmental & Cnstr Inc .... G 419 693-5840
Oregon (G-10967)

Rex Welding Inc .... F 740 387-1650
Marion (G-8992)

RI Alto Mfg Inc .... F 740 914-4230
Marion (G-8993)

Ridge Engineering Inc .... G 513 681-5500
Cincinnati (G-3045)

Ridge Machine & Welding Co .... G 740 537-2821
Toronto (G-13186)

Rodney Wells .... G 740 425-2266
Barnesville (G-846)

Roetmans Welding LLC .... G 216 385-5938
Akron (G-289)

Romar Metal Fabricating Inc .... G 740 682-7731
Oak Hill (G-10894)

Rose Metal Industries LLC .... F 216 881-3355
Cleveland (G-4250)

Rsv Wlding Fbrction McHning In .... F 419 592-0993
Napoleon (G-10298)

Salem Welding & Supply Company ...... G 330 332-4517
Salem (G-11811)

Sauerwein Welding .... G 513 563-2979
Cincinnati (G-3065)

Schmidt Machine Company .... E 419 294-3814
Upper Sandusky (G-13455)

▲ Semtorq Inc .... F 330 487-0600
Twinsburg (G-13377)

Simpson & Sons Inc .... G 513 367-0152
Harrison (G-7568)

Sky Climber Fabricating LLC .... G 740 990-9430
Delaware (G-6173)

Smp Welding LLC .... F 440 205-9353
Mentor (G-9616)

Somerville Manufacturing Inc .... E 740 336-7847
Marietta (G-8949)

Spradlin Bros Welding Co .... F 800 219-2182
Springfield (G-12375)

Stan-Kell LLC .... F 440 998-1116
Ashtabula (G-617)

State Metal Hose Inc .... G 614 527-4700
Hilliard (G-7703)

Steve Vore Welding and Steel .... F 419 375-4087
Fort Recovery (G-6971)

Stud Welding Associates .... F 216 392-7808
Elyria (G-6593)

Suburban Metal Products Inc .... F 740 474-4237
Circleville (G-3263)

Superior Weld and Fabg Co Inc .... G 216 249-5122
Cleveland (G-4349)

Systech Handling Inc .... F 419 445-8226
Archbold (G-512)

▼ T & R Welding Systems Inc .... F 937 228-7517
Dayton (G-6037)

Tbone Sales LLC .... G 330 897-6131
Baltic (G-781)

Temperature Controls Co Inc .... F 330 773-6633
New Franklin (G-10395)

Tendon Manufacturing Inc .... E 216 663-3200
Cleveland (G-4374)

Toney Tool Manufacturing Inc .... G 937 890-8535
Dayton (G-6057)

Tonys Wldg & Fabrication LLC .... F 740 333-4000
Wshngtn Ct Hs (G-14748)

Tri-State Plating & Polishing .... G 304 529-2579
Proctorville (G-11500)

Triangle Precision Inds Inc .... D 937 299-6776
Dayton (G-6062)

Tru-Fab Technology Inc .... F 440 954-9760
Willoughby (G-14543)

Turn-Key Industrial Svcs LLC .... D 614 274-1128
Grove City (G-7420)

Two M Precision Co Inc .... E 440 946-2120
Willoughby (G-14546)

US Welding Training LLC .... G 440 669-9380
Fairport Harbor (G-6822)

Valley Machine Tool Inc .... E 513 899-2737
Morrow (G-10204)

Viking Fabricators Inc .... G 740 374-5246
Marietta (G-8060)

Webers Body & Frame Inc .... G 937 839-5946
West Alexandria (G-13923)

Welders Supply Inc .... E 216 267-4470
Brookpark (G-1560)

Welding Consultants Inc .... G 614 258-7018
Columbus (G-5360)

Welding Consultants LLC .... G 614 258-7018
Columbus (G-5361)

Weldments Inc .... F 937 235-9261
Dayton (G-6077)

Wenrick Machine and Tool Corp .... F 937 667-7307
Tipp City (G-12854)

Whitt Machine Inc .... F 513 423-7624
Middletown (G-9904)

Witts Services LLC .... G 740 543-8526
Bergholz (G-1197)

Wpc Successor Inc .... F 937 233-6141
Tipp City (G-12855)

7694 Armature rewinding shops

▲ 3-D Service Ltd .... C 330 830-3500
Massillon (G-9168)

Als High Tech Inc .... F 440 232-7090
Bedford (G-1010)

American Armature Corporation .... G 419 448-1926
Tiffin (G-12773)

Bennett Electric Inc .... F 800 874-5405
Norwalk (G-10830)

Big River Electric Inc .... G 740 446-4360
Gallipolis (G-7202)

Bornhorst Motor Service Inc .... G 937 773-0426
Piqua (G-11337)

City Machine Technologies Inc .... F 330 747-2639
Youngstown (G-14836)

Clark-Fowler Enterprises Inc .... E 330 262-0906
Wooster (G-14631)

D & J Electric Motor Repair Co .... F 330 336-4343
Wadsworth (G-13634)

E M Service Inc .... F 440 323-3260
Elyria (G-6525)

E-Z Electric Motor Svc Corp .... G 216 581-8820
Cleveland (G-3646)

Fenton Bros Electric Co .... E 330 343-0093
New Philadelphia (G-10445)

Franks Electric Inc .... G 513 313-5883
Cincinnati (G-2640)

Hackworth Electric Motors Inc .... G 330 345-6049
Wooster (G-14648)

Hannon Company .... G 330 343-7758
Dover (G-6246)

Hannon Company .... F 740 453-0527
Zanesville (G-15019)

Hennings Quality Service Inc .... F 216 941-9120
Cleveland (G-3822)

Horner Industrial Services Inc .... F 937 390-6667
Springfield (G-12325)

Horner Industrial Services Inc .... G 513 874-8722
West Chester (G-14125)

Integrated Power Services LLC .... D 216 433-7808
Cleveland (G-3863)

Integrated Power Services LLC .... E 513 863-8816
Hamilton (G-7506)

Kcn Technologies LLC .... G 440 439-4219
Bedford (G-1041)

Kiemle-Hankins Company .... E 419 661-2430
Perrysburg (G-11233)

Lemsco Inc .... G 419 242-4005
Toledo (G-13032)

Lima Armature Works Inc .... G 419 222-4010
Lima (G-8424)

M & R Electric Motor Svc Inc .... E 937 701-0475
Dayton (G-5057)

Mader Elc Mtr Pwr Trnsmssons L ..... G 937 325-5576
Springfield (G-12346)

Magnetech Industrial Svcs Inc .... G 330 830-3500
Massillon (G-9216)

Magnetech Industrial Svcs Inc .... F 330 830-3500
Massillon (G-9218)

▲ Magnetech Industrial Svcs Inc .... D 330 830-3500
Massillon (G-9217)

Masteller Electric Motor Svc .... G 937 492-8500
Sidney (G-12032)

▼ Matlock Electric Co Inc .... E 513 731-9600
Cincinnati (G-2850)

Mid-Ohio Electric Co. .... E 614 274-8000
Columbus (G-5098)

Moto-Electric Inc .... G 419 668-7894
Norwalk (G-10853)

◆ National Electric Coil Inc .... B 614 488-1151
Columbus (G-5120)

Ohio Electric Motor Service Center Inc ... F 614 444-1451
Columbus (G-5143)

Ohio Electric Motor Svc LLC .... G 614 444-1451
Columbus (G-5144)

Phillips Electric Co .... F 216 361-0014
Cleveland (G-4160)

Rel Enterprises Inc.............................. E 216 741-1700
  Brooklyn Heights *(G-1538)*

▲ Shoemaker Electric Company........... E 614 294-5626
  Columbus *(G-5263)*

Total Maintenance MGT Inc.................... G 513 228-2345
  Lebanon *(G-8289)*

Wheatley Electric Service Co................. G 513 531-4951
  Cincinnati *(G-3222)*

Whelco Industrial Ltd........................... D 419 385-4627
  Perrysburg *(G-11280)*

Yaskawa America Inc............................ C 937 847-6200
  Miamisburg *(G-9755)*

7699 Repair services, nec

▲ 3-D Service Ltd.................................. C 330 830-3500
  Massillon *(G-9168)*

A L Callahan Door Sales...................... G 419 884-3667
  Mansfield *(G-8757)*

AAA Wastewater Services Inc.............. F 937 746-6361
  Franklin *(G-7009)*

AB Bonded Locksmiths Inc.................. G 513 531-7334
  Cincinnati *(G-2330)*

Abj Equipfix LLC................................ E 419 684-5236
  Castalia *(G-2093)*

Able Pallet Mfg & Repr....................... G 614 444-2115
  Columbus *(G-4666)*

Accu-Grind Inc.................................... G 330 677-2225
  Kent *(G-8012)*

Aerosport Modeling Design LLC........... F 614 834-5227
  Canal Winchester *(G-1783)*

▼ Air-Rite Inc....................................... E 216 228-8200
  Cleveland *(G-3316)*

◆ Ajax Tocco Magnethermic Corp.........C 800 547-1527
  Warren *(G-13732)*

All Power Battery Inc........................... G 330 453-5236
  Canton *(G-1828)*

▲ American Frame Corporation............. E 419 893-5595
  Maumee *(G-9259)*

▲ American Hydraulic Svcs Inc............. E 606 739-8680
  Ironton *(G-7929)*

▲ Amko Service Company.................... E 330 364-8857
  Midvale *(G-9907)*

▲ Apph Wichita Inc.............................. E 316 943-5752
  Strongsville *(G-12537)*

ARC Solutions LLC.............................. E 419 542-9272
  Hicksville *(G-7646)*

ARS Recycling Systems LLC................ F 330 536-8210
  Lowellville *(G-8658)*

◆ Babcock & Wilcox Company..............A 330 753-4511
  Akron *(G-67)*

Battery Unlimited................................. G 740 452-5030
  Zanesville *(G-14993)*

Beaumont Machine LLC....................... F 513 701-0421
  Mason *(G-9070)*

Beckman Environmental Svcs Inc........ F 513 752-3570
  Batavia *(G-853)*

Cammel Saw Company........................ F 330 477-3764
  Canton *(G-1851)*

Canvas Specialty Mfg Co.................... G 216 881-0647
  Cleveland *(G-3465)*

Certified Labs & Service Inc................ G 419 289-7462
  Ashland *(G-527)*

Certon Technologies Inc...................... F 440 786-7185
  Bedford *(G-1021)*

Cleveland Electric Labs Co.................. E 800 447-2207
  Twinsburg *(G-13287)*

Commercial Electric Pdts Corp............. E 216 241-2886
  Cleveland *(G-3552)*

Conviber Inc....................................... F 330 723-6006
  Medina *(G-9391)*

Corrotec Inc.. E 937 325-3585
  Springfield *(G-12294)*

Csg Software...................................... G 614 986-2600
  Columbus *(G-4862)*

Custom Metal Works Inc...................... F 419 668-7831
  Norwalk *(G-10834)*

Cuyahoga Machine Company LLC........ F 216 267-3560
  Brookpark *(G-1547)*

D & M Saw & Tool Inc........................ G 513 871-5433
  Cincinnati *(G-2535)*

D C Systems Inc................................. F 330 273-3030
  Brunswick *(G-1587)*

Dayton Industrial Drum Inc.................. E 937 253-8933
  Dayton *(G-5608)*

Dayton Machine Tool Company............ G 937 222-6444
  Dayton *(G-5730)*

Dearing Compressor and Pu................ E 330 783-2258
  Youngstown *(G-14847)*

Diamond Machinery LLC...................... G 216 312-1235
  Cleveland *(G-3613)*

Division Overhead Door Inc.................. F 513 872-0888
  Cincinnati *(G-2556)*

DNC Hydraulics LLC........................... F 419 963-2800
  Rawson *(G-11551)*

Dynamic Hydraulic Svcs Co LLC......... E 330 447-8967
  Dover *(G-6243)*

Eaton Industrial Corporation............... C 216 692-5456
  Cleveland *(G-3657)*

Electric Speed Indicator Co................. F 216 251-2540
  Aurora *(G-668)*

Elite Biomedical Solutions LLC............ F 513 207-0602
  Cincinnati *(G-2302)*

Eversharpe-Deburring Tool Co............. G 513 988-6240
  Trenton *(G-13192)*

Evoqua Water Technologies LLC.......... F 614 491-5917
  Groveport *(G-7431)*

Expert Crane Inc................................. D 216 451-9900
  Wellington *(G-13886)*

Fawcett Co Inc.................................... G 330 659-4187
  Richfield *(G-11592)*

Fire Foe Corp..................................... E 330 759-9834
  Girard *(G-7271)*

Fluid System Service Inc..................... G 216 651-2450
  Cleveland *(G-3728)*

▲ Forge Industries Inc.......................... A 330 960-2468
  Youngstown *(G-14857)*

Fox Tool Co Inc.................................. G 330 928-3402
  Cuyahoga Falls *(G-5543)*

Frontier Tank Center Inc...................... G 330 659-3888
  Richfield *(G-11593)*

General Plastex Inc............................. E 330 745-7775
  Barberton *(G-806)*

GL Nause Co Inc................................. E 513 722-9500
  Loveland *(G-8626)*

Glen D Lala.. G 937 274-7770
  Dayton *(G-5797)*

Glenn Michael Brick............................ F 740 391-5735
  Flushing *(G-6936)*

Graphic Systems Services Inc............. E 937 746-0708
  Springboro *(G-12254)*

Grimes Aerospace Company............... D 937 484-2001
  Urbana *(G-13464)*

◆ Grob Systems Inc..............................A 419 358-9015
  Bluffton *(G-1361)*

▲ Hamilton Industrial Grinding Inc........ E 513 863-1221
  Hamilton *(G-7502)*

Handcrafted Jewelry Inc...................... G 330 650-9011
  Hudson *(G-7843)*

Hannon Company................................ F 330 343-7758
  Dover *(G-6246)*

Hannon Company................................ F 740 453-0527
  Zanesville *(G-15019)*

▲ Harry C Lobalzo & Sons Inc.............. E 330 666-6758
  Akron *(G-172)*

▲ Hunger Hydraulics CC Ltd.................. F 419 666-4510
  Rossford *(G-11657)*

Hunter Hydraulics Inc.......................... G 330 455-3983
  Canton *(G-1913)*

Hy-Blast Inc....................................... F 513 424-0704
  Middletown *(G-9864)*

▲ Hydraulic Products Inc....................... G 440 946-4575
  Willoughby *(G-14466)*

Hydraulic Specialists Inc..................... G 740 922-3343
  Midvale *(G-9911)*

Hydro Supply Co................................. G 740 454-3842
  Zanesville *(G-15020)*

▲ Ic-Fluid Power Inc.............................. F 419 661-8811
  Rossford *(G-11658)*

Industrial Ctrl Dsign Mint Inc............... F 330 785-9840
  Tallmadge *(G-12737)*

▲ Industrial Repair and Mfg................... E 419 822-4232
  Delta *(G-6210)*

Instrumentors Inc................................ G 440 238-3430
  Strongsville *(G-12568)*

JF Martt and Associates Inc................ F 330 938-4000
  Sebring *(G-11895)*

JJ&pl Services-Consulting LLC............. E 330 923-5783
  Cuyahoga Falls *(G-5552)*

Jonmar Gear and Machine Inc............. G 330 854-6500
  Canal Fulton *(G-1776)*

K & J Machine Inc.............................. G 740 425-3282
  Barnesville *(G-845)*

Karon C Enold.................................... E 740 269-3475
  Sherrodsville *(G-11975)*

Kars Ohio LLC.................................... G 614 655-1099
  Pataskala *(G-11142)*

◆ Lawrence Industries Inc.....................E 216 518-7000
  Cleveland *(G-3946)*

Loadmaster Trailer Company Ltd.......... F 419 732-3434
  Port Clinton *(G-11445)*

Loft Violin Shop.................................. G 614 267-7221
  Columbus *(G-5073)*

Lubrisource Inc................................... F 937 432-9292
  Middletown *(G-9872)*

Lyco Corporation................................ G 412 973-9176
  Lowellville *(G-8663)*

Machine Tool Design & Fab LLC.......... F 419 435-7676
  Tiffin *(G-12789)*

Magnetech Industrial Svcs Inc............. F 330 830-3500
  Massillon *(G-9218)*

McNational Inc.................................... D 740 377-4391
  South Point *(G-12227)*

MCS Midwest LLC............................... G 513 217-0805
  Franklin *(G-7033)*

Mechanical Dynamics Analis LLC........ E 440 946-0082
  Euclid *(G-6661)*

▲ Mesocoat Inc..................................... F 216 453-0866
  Euclid *(G-6662)*

Metro Design Inc................................ F 440 458-4200
  Elyria *(G-6563)*

◆ Mettler-Toledo LLC.............................A 614 438-4511
  Columbus *(G-4644)*

Midwest Knife Grinding Inc.................. F 330 854-1030
  Canal Fulton *(G-1778)*

Midwest Rlwy Prsrvtion Soc Inc........... G 216 781-3629
  Cleveland *(G-4038)*

Mjcj Holdings Inc............................... G 937 885-0800
  Miamisburg *(G-9719)*

Mpi Logistics and Service Inc.............. E 330 832-5309
  Massillon *(G-9225)*

National Tool & Equipment Inc............. F 330 629-8665
  Youngstown *(G-14903)*

National Wldg Tanker Repr LLC............ G 614 875-3399
  Grove City *(G-7404)*

Nbw Inc.. E 216 377-1700
  Cleveland *(G-4063)*

Nice Body Automotive LLC.................... G 440 752-5568
Elyria **(G-6569)**

North Coast Exotics Inc......................... G 216 651-5512
Cleveland **(G-4084)**

Northwood Industries Inc...................... F 419 666-2100
Perrysburg **(G-11243)**

Obr Cooling Towers LLC....................... E 419 243-3443
Northwood **(G-10807)**

Odyssey Machine Company Ltd........... G 419 455-6621
Perrysburg **(G-11245)**

▼ Ohio Broach & Machine Company..... E 440 946-1040
Willoughby **(G-14499)**

Ohio Hydraulics Inc.............................. E 513 771-2590
Cincinnati **(G-2924)**

◆ Ohio Machinery Co............................C 440 526-6200
Broadview Heights **(G-1509)**

◆ OKL Can Line Inc...............................E
Cincinnati **(G-2928)**

Optimum Surgical................................. F 216 870-8526
Medina **(G-9431)**

P & L Precision Grinding Llc................. F 330 746-8081
Youngstown **(G-14909)**

Pas Technologies Inc........................... D 937 840-1053
Hillsboro **(G-7723)**

Peebles - Herzog Inc............................ G 614 279-2211
Columbus **(G-5182)**

Perkins Motor Service Ltd.................... F 440 277-1256
Lorain **(G-8573)**

Pickens Window Service Inc................. G 513 931-4432
Cincinnati **(G-2962)**

Precision Gage & Tool Company.......... E 937 866-9666
Dayton **(G-5946)**

Pro-Kleen Industrial Svcs Inc............... E 740 689-1886
Lancaster **(G-8218)**

Process Dynamics Inc........................... G 330 686-2597
Stow **(G-12452)**

Quad Fluid Dynamics Inc...................... F 330 220-3005
Brunswick **(G-1610)**

Quality Components Inc........................ F 440 255-0606
Mentor **(G-9601)**

Quality Cutter Grinding Co.................... F 216 362-6444
Cleveland **(G-4213)**

Quintus Technologies LLC.................... E 614 891-2732
Lewis Center **(G-8349)**

Rbm Environmental & Cnstr Inc........... G 419 693-5840
Oregon **(G-10967)**

▲ Reberland Equipment Inc................. F 330 698-5883
Apple Creek **(G-176)**

Rudd Equipment Company Inc.............. E 513 321-7833
Cincinnati **(G-3056)**

▲ Sabco Industries Inc......................... E 419 531-5347
Toledo **(G-13120)**

▲ Save Edge Inc.................................. E 937 376-8268
Xenia **(G-14774)**

Schaeffer Metal Products Inc............... G 330 296-6226
Ravenna **(G-11539)**

Schindler Elevator Corporation............ E 419 861-5900
Holland **(G-7783)**

Seilkop Industries Inc........................... E 513 761-1035
Cincinnati **(G-3077)**

Slater Road Mills Inc............................ E 330 332-9951
Salem **(G-11813)**

Sportsmans Haven Inc.......................... G 740 432-7243
Cambridge **(G-1761)**

▲ Steel Eqp Specialists Inc.................. D 330 823-8260
Alliance **(G-406)**

▲ Stein LLC.. F 440 526-9301
Independence **(G-7919)**

▲ Superior Marine Ways Inc................. C 740 894-6224
Proctorville **(G-11499)**

Superior Soda Service LLC................... G 937 657-9700
Beavercreek **(G-996)**

Taft Tool & Production Co..................... F 419 385-2576
Toledo **(G-13139)**

Tektronix Inc.. F 248 305-5200
West Chester **(G-14152)**

Thirion Brothers Eqp Co LLC................ G 440 357-8004
Painesville **(G-11118)**

Tpf Inc... G 513 761-9968
Cincinnati **(G-3161)**

Tri State Equipment Company............... G 513 738-7227
Shandon **(G-11935)**

U S Molding Machinery Co Inc.............. E 440 918-1701
Willoughby **(G-14547)**

Uhrichsville Carbide Inc....................... F 740 922-9197
Uhrichsville **(G-13409)**

Unified Scrning Crshing - OH I.............. G 937 836-3201
Englewood **(G-6627)**

Unison Industries LLC.......................... F 937 426-0621
Alpha **(G-419)**

◆ UPA Technology Inc......................... F 513 755-1380
West Chester **(G-14088)**

Victor Organ Company.......................... G 330 792-1321
Youngstown **(G-14961)**

◆ Walker National Inc..........................E 614 492-1614
Columbus **(G-5353)**

Weather King Heating & AC.................. G 330 908-0281
Northfield **(G-10799)**

West Equipment Company Inc.............. G 419 698-1601
Toledo **(G-13177)**

▲ Winkle Industries Inc....................... D 330 823-9730
Alliance **(G-418)**

Wm Plotz Machine and Forge Co.......... F 216 861-0441
Cleveland **(G-4512)**

◆ Wood Graphics Inc........................... G 513 771-6300
Cincinnati **(G-3230)**

Yoder Sharpening Ltd........................... F 330 359-0767
Dundee **(G-6373)**

78 MOTION PICTURES

7812 Motion picture and video production

▲ Master Communications Inc............. G 208 821-3473
Cincinnati **(G-2849)**

World Harvest Church Inc..................... C 614 837-1990
Canal Winchester **(G-1800)**

7819 Services allied to motion pictures

Ournashonisme Ent LLC....................... F 689 276-0367
Euclid **(G-6668)**

Swagg Productions2015llc.................... F 614 601-7414
Worthington **(G-14726)**

Trisource Exhibits................................ E 800 229-8600
Parma **(G-11136)**

7822 Motion picture and tape distribution

Allied Shipping and Packa.................... F 937 222-7422
Moraine **(G-10144)**

7841 Video tape rental

Ohio Hd Video...................................... F 614 656-1162
New Albany **(G-10348)**

79 AMUSEMENT AND RECREATION SERVICES

7922 Theatrical producers and services

North Coast Theatrical Inc.................... G 330 762-1768
Akron **(G-248)**

▲ Scenic Solutions Ltd Lblty Co........... F 937 866-5062
Dayton **(G-5996)**

Schell Scenic Studio Inc....................... G 614 444-9550
Millersport **(G-10024)**

7929 Entertainers and entertainment groups

American Gild of English Hndbe............ G 937 438-0085
Cincinnati **(G-2359)**

Club 513 LLC....................................... G 800 530-2574
Cincinnati **(G-2501)**

Kenyetta Bagby Enterprise LLC............ F 614 584-3426
Reynoldsburg **(G-11573)**

Ournashonisme Ent LLC....................... F 689 276-0367
Euclid **(G-6668)**

Swagg Productions2015llc.................... F 614 601-7414
Worthington **(G-14726)**

Technical Artistry Inc........................... G 614 299-7777
Columbus **(G-5316)**

Tomahawk Entrmt Group LLC............... F 216 505-0548
Euclid **(G-6680)**

7933 Bowling centers

Greater Cincinnati Bowl Assn............... E 513 761-7387
Cincinnati **(G-2689)**

7992 Public golf courses

McClelland Inc..................................... E 740 452-3036
Zanesville **(G-15027)**

7993 Coin-operated amusement devices

Glenn Michael Brick............................. F 740 391-5735
Flushing **(G-6936)**

7997 Membership sports and recreation clubs

Cincinnati Marlins Inc........................... G 513 761-3320
Cincinnati **(G-2480)**

Hilltop Recreation Inc........................... G 937 549-2904
Manchester **(G-8754)**

Lake Township Trustees........................ E 419 836-1143
Millbury **(G-9963)**

Target Holdings Inc.............................. E 513 474-4409
Cincinnati **(G-3138)**

7999 Amusement and recreation, nec

▲ Asm International............................. D 440 338-5151
Novelty **(G-10879)**

Black Wing Shooting Center LLC.......... G 740 363-7555
Delaware **(G-6134)**

Building Block Performance LLC........... G 614 918-7476
Plain City **(G-11400)**

Giuseppes Concessions LLC................ F 614 554-2551
Marengo **(G-8897)**

▲ Jmac Inc... E 614 436-2418
Columbus **(G-5041)**

Kelblys Rifle Range Inc........................ G 330 683-4674
North Lawrence **(G-10701)**

Melinz Industries Inc............................ F 440 946-3512
Willoughby **(G-14487)**

◆ Park Corporation.............................. B 216 267-4870
Medina **(G-9434)**

Youngs Jersey Dairy Inc....................... B 937 325-0629
Yellow Springs **(G-14794)**

80 HEALTH SERVICES

8011 Offices and clinics of medical doctors

Community Action Program Corp.......... F 740 374-8501
Marietta **(G-8911)**

Evokes LLC.. E 513 947-8433
Mason **(G-9099)**

Eye Surgery Center Ohio Inc................ E 614 228-3937
Columbus **(G-4917)**

Francisco Jaume................................... G 740 622-1200
Coshocton **(G-5455)**

SIC

Nutritional Medicinals LLC................... F 937 433-4673
West Chester *(G-14034)*

Orthotics Prsthtics Rhbltton................. G 330 856-2553
Warren *(G-13788)*

Presque Isle Orthtics Prsthtic............... G 216 371-0660
Cleveland *(G-4192)*

▲ Volk Optical Inc........................... D 440 942-6161
Mentor *(G-9651)*

8041 Offices and clinics of chiropractors

◆ Boxout LLC.................................C 833 462-7746
Hudson *(G-7835)*

▲ Polar Products Inc......................... E 330 253-9973
Stow *(G-12449)*

8049 Offices of health practitioner

◆ Boxout LLC.................................C 833 462-7746
Hudson *(G-7835)*

Cincinnati Eye Inst - Estgate............... G 513 984-5133
Cincinnati *(G-2298)*

8051 Skilled nursing care facilities

Optum Infusion Svcs 550 LLC............... D 866 442-4679
Cincinnati *(G-2936)*

8052 Intermediate care facilities

Bittersweet Inc............................... D 419 875-6986
Whitehouse *(G-14358)*

▲ Cardinal Health 414 LLC.................. C 614 757-5000
Dublin *(G-6288)*

8062 General medical and surgical hospitals

Dan Allen Surgical LLC...................... F 800 261-9953
Newbury *(G-10549)*

8071 Medical laboratories

Cellular Technology Limited................. E 216 791-5084
Shaker Heights *(G-11928)*

John P Ellis Clinic Podiatry................. G 440 460-0444
Cleveland *(G-3890)*

Mp Biomedicals LLC......................... C 440 337-1200
Solon *(G-12154)*

Personnel Selection Services............... F 440 835-3255
Cleveland *(G-4153)*

Quest Diagnostics Incorporated........... G 513 229-5500
Mason *(G-9140)*

Smithers Group Inc.......................... D 330 833-8548
Massillon *(G-9244)*

8072 Dental laboratories

Dental Ceramics Inc......................... E 330 523-5240
Richfield *(G-11590)*

United Dental Laboratories................. E 330 253-1810
Tallmadge *(G-12756)*

8093 Specialty outpatient clinics, nec

Community Action Program Corp.......... F 740 374-8501
Marietta *(G-8911)*

8099 Health and allied services, nec

Bio-Blood Components Inc................... D 614 294-3183
Columbus *(G-4754)*

Kapios LLC.................................... G 567 661-0772
Toledo *(G-13015)*

81 LEGAL SERVICES

8111 Legal services

Akron Legal News Inc........................ F 330 296-7578
Akron *(G-33)*

Bigmar Inc.................................... E 740 966-5800
Johnstown *(G-7992)*

Gongwer News Service Inc................... F 614 221-1992
Columbus *(G-4962)*

Perfect Probate.............................. G 513 791-4100
Cincinnati *(G-2953)*

Petro Quest Inc.............................. G 740 593-3800
Athens *(G-645)*

82 EDUCATIONAL SERVICES

8211 Elementary and secondary schools

Butler Tech................................... E 513 867-1028
Fairfield Township *(G-6795)*

Society of The Precious Blood............. E 419 925-4516
Celina *(G-2120)*

8222 Junior colleges

Borman Enterprises Inc...................... F 216 459-9292
Cleveland *(G-3429)*

8243 Data processing schools

Computer Workshop Inc...................... G 216 901-0106
Cleveland *(G-3557)*

Computer Workshop Inc...................... E 614 798-9505
Dublin *(G-6291)*

Corporate Elevator LLC...................... G 614 288-1847
Columbus *(G-4851)*

Millers Aplus Cmpt Svcs LLC............... F 330 620-5288
Akron *(G-234)*

8249 Vocational schools, nec

▲ Flightsafety International Inc............. C 614 324-3500
Columbus *(G-4929)*

M R I Education Foundation................. E 513 281-3400
Cincinnati *(G-2834)*

Pakra LLC.................................... F 614 477-6965
Columbus *(G-5169)*

▲ Zaner-Bloser Inc.......................... C 614 486-0221
Columbus *(G-5380)*

8299 Schools and educational services

Auguste Moone Enterprises Ltd............ E 216 333-9248
Cleveland Heights *(G-4527)*

Deemsys Inc.................................. D 614 322-9928
Gahanna *(G-7155)*

Dietrich Von Hldbrand Lgacy PR........... G 703 496-7821
Steubenville *(G-12402)*

Equipping Ministries Intl Inc............... G 513 742-1100
Cincinnati *(G-2597)*

Health Sense Inc............................. G 440 354-8057
Painesville *(G-11093)*

Studio Arts and Glass Inc................... F 330 494-9779
Canton *(G-2019)*

Tangible Solutions Inc...................... E 937 912-4603
Fairborn *(G-6701)*

Toastmasters International.................. F 937 429-2680
Dayton *(G-5624)*

Wooden Horse................................ G 740 503-5243
Baltimore *(G-789)*

83 SOCIAL SERVICES

8322 Individual and family services

▲ Cincinnati Assn For The Blind........... C 513 221-8558
Cincinnati *(G-2469)*

Clovernook Ctr For Blind Vslly............. C 513 522-3860
Cincinnati *(G-2500)*

County of Lake............................... F 440 269-2193
Willoughby *(G-14443)*

Jeffco Sheltered Workshop.................. G 740 264-4608
Steubenville *(G-12404)*

Omnipresence Cleaning LLC................. F 937 250-4749
Dayton *(G-5927)*

Trumbull Mobile Meals....................... F 330 394-2538
Warren *(G-13803)*

8331 Job training and related services

Belco Works Inc.............................. D 740 695-0500
Saint Clairsville *(G-11688)*

Brookhill Center Inds Inc.................... C 419 876-3932
Ottawa *(G-11030)*

Brown Cnty Bd Mntal Rtardation........... G 937 378-4891
Georgetown *(G-7251)*

Carroll Hills Industries..................... G 330 627-5524
Carrollton *(G-2080)*

▲ Cincinnati Assn For The Blind........... C 513 221-8558
Cincinnati *(G-2469)*

County of Lake............................... F 440 269-2193
Willoughby *(G-14443)*

▲ Findaway World LLC....................... E 440 893-0808
Solon *(G-12111)*

Guernsey Industries......................... C 740 439-4452
Byesville *(G-1713)*

▼ Hunter Defense Tech Inc.................. E 216 438-6111
Solon *(G-12124)*

Jeffco Sheltered Workshop.................. G 740 264-4608
Steubenville *(G-12404)*

Metzenbaum Sheltered Inds Inc............ E 440 729-1919
Chesterland *(G-2236)*

Pakra LLC.................................... F 614 477-6965
Columbus *(G-5169)*

Quadco Rehabilitation Ctr Inc.............. C 419 682-1011
Stryker *(G-12626)*

Richland Newhope Inds Inc.................. C 419 774-4400
Mansfield *(G-8848)*

RT Industries Inc............................ G 937 335-5784
Troy *(G-13251)*

Sandco Industries........................... E 419 547-3273
Clyde *(G-4564)*

TAC Industries Inc........................... B 937 328-5200
Springfield *(G-12382)*

Vgs Inc....................................... C 216 431-7800
Cleveland *(G-4463)*

Vocational Services Inc...................... F 216 431-8085
Cleveland *(G-4478)*

8351 Child day care services

Learn21 A Flxble Lrng Cllbrtiv.............. F 513 402-2121
Cincinnati *(G-2816)*

8361 Residential care

Bittersweet Inc............................... D 419 875-6986
Whitehouse *(G-14358)*

RT Industries Inc............................ G 937 335-5784
Troy *(G-13251)*

8399 Social services, nec

Alscommunity................................. F 215 478-5095
Coventry Township *(G-5480)*

Community Action Program Corp.......... F 740 374-8501
Marietta *(G-8911)*

84 MUSEUMS, ART GALLERIES AND BOTANICAL AND ZOOLOGICAL GARDENS

8412 Museums and art galleries

Brewster Sugarcreek Twp Histo............ F 330 767-0045
Brewster *(G-1491)*

Velvet Ice Cream Company.................. D 740 892-3921
Utica *(G-13488)*

86 MEMBERSHIP ORGANIZATIONS

8611 Business associations

Cox Newspapers LLC.............................. G
  Franklin *(G-7015)*

▲ Hirzel Canning Company.................. E 419 693-0531
  Northwood *(G-10803)*

Interstate Contractors LLC.................... E 513 372-5393
  Mason *(G-9115)*

▲ Precision Metalforming Assn............ E 216 901-8800
  Independence *(G-7916)*

◆ Superior Clay Corporation................D 740 922-4122
  Uhrichsville *(G-13408)*

8621 Professional organizations

American Ceramic Society..................... E 614 890-4700
  Westerville *(G-14202)*

8641 Civic and social associations

Family Motor Coach Assn Inc................ E 513 474-3622
  Cincinnati *(G-2611)*

Sylvania Mose Ldge No 1579 Lya........... F 419 885-4953
  Sylvania *(G-12727)*

8661 Religious organizations

Christian Missionary Alliance................ C 380 208-6200
  Reynoldsburg *(G-11562)*

Incorprted Trstees of The Gspl.............. D 216 749-2100
  Middleburg Heights *(G-9773)*

New Life Chapel..................................... F 513 298-2980
  Cincinnati *(G-2902)*

Saint Ctherines Metalworks Inc............ G 216 409-0576
  Cleveland *(G-4269)*

Society of The Precious Blood.............. E 419 925-4516
  Celina *(G-2120)*

Temple Israel.. G 330 762-8617
  Akron *(G-330)*

Vista Community Church........................ F 614 718-2294
  Plain City *(G-11425)*

8699 Membership organizations, nec

American Gild of English Hndbe............ G 937 438-0085
  Cincinnati *(G-2359)*

Conquest Maps LLC............................... G 614 654-1627
  Columbus *(G-4843)*

Greater Cincinnati Bowl Assn................ E 513 761-7387
  Cincinnati *(G-2689)*

87 ENGINEERING, ACCOUNTING, RESEARCH, AND MANAGEMENT SERVICES

8711 Engineering services

4r Enterprises Incorporated.................. G 330 923-9799
  Cuyahoga Falls *(G-5519)*

A+ Engineering Fabrication Inc............. F 419 832-0748
  Grand Rapids *(G-7307)*

ACC Automation Co Inc......................... E 330 928-3821
  Akron *(G-12)*

▲ Advanced Design Industries Inc...... F 440 277-4141
  Sheffield Village *(G-11956)*

▲ Advanced Engrg Solutions Inc........ D 937 743-6900
  Springboro *(G-12244)*

Aerovation Tech Holdings LLC.............. G 567 208-5525
  Forest *(G-6938)*

◆ Alfons Haar Inc................................E 937 560-2031
  Springboro *(G-12246)*

▲ American Controls Inc..................... E 440 944-9735
  Wickliffe *(G-14366)*

Applied Experience LLC......................... G 614 943-2970
  Plain City *(G-11394)*

Atmos360 Inc.. E 513 772-4777
  West Chester *(G-14105)*

Automted Cmpnent Spcalists LLC......... E 513 335-4285
  Cincinnati *(G-2391)*

Autotec Corporation............................... E 419 885-2529
  Toledo *(G-12889)*

B&N Coal Inc... E 740 783-3575
  Dexter City *(G-6224)*

Babcock & Wilcox Holdings LLC........... A 330 453-4511
  Akron *(G-69)*

Barr Engineering Incorporated............. E 614 714-0299
  Columbus *(G-4744)*

Bender Engineering Company............... G 330 938-2355
  Beloit *(G-1144)*

Beringer Plating Inc............................... G 330 633-8409
  Akron *(G-76)*

Bertec Corporation................................ E 614 543-8099
  Columbus *(G-4752)*

▲ Braze Solutions LLC......................... F 440 349-5100
  Solon *(G-12089)*

▲ Cbn Westside Technologies Inc....... B 513 772-7000
  West Chester *(G-13957)*

▲ Cecil C Peck Co................................ F 330 785-0781
  Akron *(G-93)*

Ceso Inc.. E 937 435-8584
  Miamisburg *(G-9681)*

Circle Prime Manufacturing Inc............ E 330 923-0019
  Cuyahoga Falls *(G-5534)*

Clarkwestern Dietrich Building............. D 330 372-5564
  Warren *(G-13752)*

▼ Clarkwstern Dtrich Bldg System....... C 513 870-1100
  West Chester *(G-13966)*

Coal Services Inc................................... B 740 795-5220
  Powhatan Point *(G-11497)*

Coating Systems Group Inc.................. F 440 816-9306
  Middleburg Heights *(G-9768)*

Comtec Incorporated............................ F 330 425-8102
  Twinsburg *(G-13288)*

Consoldted Anlytcal Systems In........... F 513 542-1200
  Cincinnati *(G-2510)*

Control Electric Co................................ E 216 671-8010
  Columbia Station *(G-4592)*

Corrpro Companies Inc......................... E 770 761-5400
  Medina *(G-9392)*

Corrpro Companies Inc......................... E 330 725-6681
  Medina *(G-9393)*

CPI Group Limited.................................. E 216 525-0046
  Cleveland *(G-3573)*

Crown Solutions Co LLC........................ C 937 890-4075
  Vandalia *(G-13553)*

Crowne Group LLC................................ F 216 589-0198
  Cleveland *(G-3577)*

Curtiss-Wright Ds Inc............................ E 937 252-5601
  Fairborn *(G-6689)*

Custom Craft Controls Inc.................... F 330 630-9599
  Akron *(G-112)*

DA Precision Products Inc..................... F 513 459-1113
  West Chester *(G-13981)*

David Chojnacki..................................... E 303 905-1918
  Westerville *(G-14254)*

Davis Technologies Inc......................... F 330 823-2544
  Alliance *(G-380)*

Decision Systems Inc............................ F 330 456-7600
  Canton *(G-1879)*

Dillin Engineered Systems Corp........... E 419 666-6789
  Perrysburg *(G-11216)*

Dlz Ohio Inc.. C 614 888-0040
  Columbus *(G-4887)*

◆ Dms Inc..C 440 951-9838
  Willoughby *(G-14449)*

Donald E Didion II.................................. E 419 483-2226
  Bellevue *(G-1123)*

Dynamic Hydraulic Svcs Co LLC............ E 330 447-8967
  Dover *(G-6243)*

Electrovations Inc.................................. G 330 274-3558
  Solon *(G-12103)*

◆ Empire Systems Inc..........................G 440 653-9300
  Avon Lake *(G-755)*

▲ Enprotech Industrial Tech LLC......... E 216 883-3220
  Cleveland *(G-3675)*

EP Ferris & Associates Inc.................... E 614 299-2999
  Columbus *(G-4906)*

Eti Tech LLC... F 937 832-4200
  Kettering *(G-8120)*

Ever Secure SEC Systems Inc.............. F 937 369-8294
  Dayton *(G-5772)*

Field Apparatus Service & Tstg............. G 513 353-9399
  Cincinnati *(G-2621)*

Fishel Company...................................... C 614 850-4400
  Columbus *(G-4926)*

Fluid Equipment Corporation................ E 419 636-0777
  Bryan *(G-1641)*

Forte Industrial Equipmen..................... E 513 398-2800
  Mason *(G-9100)*

Frost Engineering Inc............................ E 513 541-6330
  Cincinnati *(G-2642)*

General Precision Corporation.............. E 440 951-9380
  Willoughby *(G-14463)*

Genius Solutions Engrg Co.................... E 419 794-9914
  Maumee *(G-9293)*

Genpact LLC... E 513 763-7660
  Cincinnati *(G-2667)*

Hahn Automation Group Us Inc............ D 937 886-3232
  Miamisburg *(G-9694)*

Halliday Technologies Inc...................... G 614 504-4150
  Delaware *(G-6154)*

▲ Hamilton Manufacturing Corp........... E 419 867-4858
  Holland *(G-7766)*

Hess Advanced Solutions Llc................ G 937 829-4794
  Dayton *(G-5809)*

Hexion Inc... C 888 443-9466
  Columbus *(G-4976)*

Hii Mission Technologies Corp.............. G 937 426-3421
  Beavercreek *(G-992)*

▼ Htec Systems Inc.............................. F 937 438-3010
  Dayton *(G-5816)*

▼ Hunter Defense Tech Inc................. E 216 438-6111
  Solon *(G-12124)*

▲ Hydro-Dyne Inc................................ F 330 832-5076
  Massillon *(G-9204)*

Imax Industries Inc................................ F 440 639-0242
  Painesville *(G-11095)*

Imds Corporation................................... F 330 219-4299
  Youngstown *(G-14875)*

Innovative Controls Corp....................... F 419 691-6684
  Maumee *(G-9298)*

Innovtive McHning Slutions LLC........... F 419 925-2060
  Celina *(G-2110)*

Inovent Engineering Inc........................ G 330 468-0019
  Macedonia *(G-8698)*

Integris Composites Inc........................ D 740 928-0326
  Hebron *(G-7619)*

JB Industries Ltd................................... D 330 856-4587
  Warren *(G-13775)*

JBI Corporation..................................... F 419 855-3389
  Genoa *(G-7248)*

Jet Di Inc... G 330 607-7913
  Brunswick *(G-1600)*

Johnson Mfg Systems LLC.................... F 937 866-4744
  Miamisburg *(G-9704)*

Jotco Inc.. G 513 721-4943
  Mansfield *(G-8809)*

◆ Keuchel & Associates Inc................E 330 945-9455
  Cuyahoga Falls *(G-5554)*

L-3 Cmmncations Nova Engrg Inc.......... F 877 282-1168
  Mason (G-9120)

Latanick Equipment Inc........................... E 419 433-2200
  Huron (G-7878)

▲ Lawrence Technologies Inc............... G 937 274-7771
  Dayton (G-5842)

Lintech Electronics LLC........................ E 513 528-6190
  Cincinnati (G-2312)

▲ Markley Enterprises LLC.................. E 513 771-1290
  Cincinnati (G-2847)

Matrix Research Inc............................... D 937 427-8433
  Dayton (G-5869)

◆ Maval Industries LLC........................C 330 405-1600
  Twinsburg (G-13336)

Melink Corporation................................. D 513 685-0958
  Milford (G-9943)

◆ Mendenhall Technical Services Inc.....E 513 860-1280
  Fairfield (G-6754)

Mercury Iron and Steel Co...................... F 440 349-1500
  Solon (G-12146)

Micro Industries Corporation................. D 740 548-7878
  Westerville (G-14270)

Mid-Ohio Electric Co............................. E 614 274-8000
  Columbus (G-5098)

Mill & Motion Inc.................................... F 216 524-4000
  Independence (G-7909)

◆ Modula Inc...D 207 440-5100
  Franklin (G-7035)

Morris Technologies Inc........................ E 513 733-1611
  Cincinnati (G-2888)

Mound Manufacturing Center Inc........... F 937 236-8387
  Dayton (G-5896)

Mrl Materials Resources LLC.................. E 937 531-6657
  Xenia (G-14771)

◆ Nesco Inc.. F 440 461-6000
  Cleveland (G-4068)

Neundorfer Inc....................................... E 440 942-8990
  Willoughby (G-14493)

New Dawn Labs LLC............................... F 203 675-5644
  Union (G-13410)

◆ New Path International LLC................F 614 410-3974
  Powell (G-11493)

Northrop Grmman Tchncal Svcs I........ C 937 320-3100
  Beavercreek Township (G-1000)

Northwood Industries Inc....................... F 419 666-2100
  Perrysburg (G-11243)

▲ Nucon International Inc..................... F 614 846-5710
  Columbus (G-5132)

Ohio Blow Pipe Company....................... E 216 681-7379
  Cleveland (G-4113)

Onpower Inc... E 513 228-2100
  Lebanon (G-8280)

Owens Corning Sales LLC...................... F 330 633-6735
  Tallmadge (G-12745)

PA Technologies LLC.............................. F 513 800-3541
  Cincinnati (G-2940)

▲ Padco Industries LLC....................... E 440 564-7160
  Newbury (G-10560)

Panelmatic Inc....................................... E 330 782-8007
  Youngstown (G-14911)

Parking & Traffic Control SEC................ F 440 243-7565
  Cleveland (G-4145)

▲ Performnce Plymr Solutions Inc...... F 937 298-3713
  Moraine (G-10180)

Pioneer Solutions LLC........................... E 216 383-3400
  Euclid (G-6669)

Plate-All Metal Company Inc................... G 330 633-6166
  Akron (G-260)

◆ Plcc2 LLC.. F 614 279-1796
  Columbus (G-5197)

PMC Systems Limited............................ E 330 538-2268
  North Jackson (G-10693)

Pollock Research & Design Inc............... E 330 332-3300
  Salem (G-11805)

Process Innovations Inc......................... G 330 856-5192
  Vienna (G-13616)

▼ Projects Designed & Built................. E 419 726-7400
  Toledo (G-13104)

Providence REES Inc.............................. G 614 833-6231
  Columbus (G-5212)

Qcsm LLC... G 216 650-8731
  Cleveland (G-4210)

▲ Quality Plating Co........................... G 216 361-0151
  Cleveland (G-4215)

Ra Consultants LLC................................ E 513 469-6600
  Blue Ash (G-1326)

Resonant Sciences LLC.......................... E 937 431-8180
  Dayton (G-5980)

◆ Rolls-Royce Energy Systems Inc.......A 703 834-1700
  Mount Vernon (G-10263)

Sest Inc... F 440 777-9777
  Westlake (G-14332)

Sgi Matrix LLC....................................... D 937 438-9033
  Miamisburg (G-9736)

Signalysis Inc.. F 513 528-6164
  Cincinnati (G-3090)

Sponseller Group Inc............................. G 937 492-9949
  Sidney (G-12054)

Sponseller Group Inc............................. E 419 861-3000
  Holland (G-7785)

Star Distribution and Mfg LLC............... E 513 860-3573
  West Chester (G-14149)

Stock Fairfield Corporation.................... C 440 543-6000
  Solon (G-12185)

Storetek Engineering Inc........................ E 330 294-0678
  Tallmadge (G-12752)

Straight 72 Inc....................................... D 740 943-5730
  Marysville (G-9051)

Sunpower Inc... D 740 594-2221
  Athens (G-654)

Support Svc LLC..................................... G 419 617-0660
  Lexington (G-8375)

Systech Handling Inc.............................. F 419 445-8226
  Archbold (G-512)

Systems Kit LLC MB............................... E 330 945-4500
  Akron (G-324)

Tangent Company LLC............................ G 440 543-2775
  Chagrin Falls (G-2186)

Tangible Solutions Inc........................... E 937 912-4603
  Fairborn (G-6701)

Tech4imaging LLC................................... F 614 214-2655
  Columbus (G-5315)

▲ Technology House Ltd....................... G 440 248-3025
  Streetsboro (G-12527)

Tekworx LLC... F 513 533-4777
  Cincinnati (G-3142)

Tfi Manufacturing LLC............................ F 440 290-9411
  Mentor (G-9636)

Thermal Treatment Center Inc............... E 216 881-8100
  Wickliffe (G-14396)

▲ Timekeeping Systems Inc................. F 216 595-0890
  Solon (G-12198)

TL Industries Inc.................................... C 419 666-8144
  Perrysburg (G-11272)

Torsion Control Products Inc.................. F 248 537-1900
  Wadsworth (G-13675)

Trumbull Industries Inc.......................... D 330 434-6174
  Akron (G-345)

Ultra-Met Company................................. F 937 653-7133
  Urbana (G-13480)

Vector Electromagnetics LLC................. F 937 478-5904
  Wilmington (G-14589)

Warmus and Associates Inc................... G 330 659-4440
  Bath (G-898)

Welding Consultants Inc......................... G 614 258-7018
  Columbus (G-5360)

Werks Kraft Engineering LLC................. E 330 721-7374
  Medina (G-9464)

◆ Wrc Holdings Inc...............................F 330 733-6662
  Akron (G-358)

◆ Xaloy LLC..C 330 726-4000
  Austintown (G-709)

Xcite Systems Corporation..................... G 513 965-0300
  Cincinnati (G-2318)

Youngstown Plastic Tooling.................... F 330 782-7222
  Youngstown (G-14973)

8712 Architectural services

Ceso Inc... E 937 435-8584
  Miamisburg (G-9681)

Dlz Ohio Inc... C 614 888-0040
  Columbus (G-4887)

Garland Industries Inc........................... G 216 641-7500
  Cleveland (G-3757)

Garland/Dbs Inc..................................... C 216 641-7500
  Cleveland (G-3758)

Golden Angle Archtctral Group.............. G 614 531-7932
  Columbus (G-4960)

Russell Group United LLC...................... F 614 353-6853
  Columbus (G-5238)

8713 Surveying services

Barr Engineering Incorporated............... E 614 714-0299
  Columbus (G-4744)

Dlz Ohio Inc... C 614 888-0040
  Columbus (G-4887)

8721 Accounting, auditing, and bookkeeping

Colburn Patterson LLC........................... G 419 866-5544
  Holland (G-7751)

Kent Information Services Inc................. G 330 672-2110
  Kent (G-8042)

Lipari Foods Operating Co LLC............... E 330 893-2479
  Millersburg (G-9992)

Michele Caldwell.................................... G 937 505-7744
  Dayton (G-5880)

Patrick J Burke & Co.............................. E 513 455-8200
  Cincinnati (G-2945)

Steward Edge Bus Solutions................... F 614 826-5305
  Columbus (G-5293)

Watson Haran & Company Inc................. G 937 436-1414
  Dayton (G-6076)

8731 Commercial physical research

Applied Medical Technology Inc............. F 440 717-4000
  Brecksville (G-1457)

Applied Sciences Inc.............................. E 937 766-2020
  Cedarville (G-2097)

Barco Inc.. E 937 372-7579
  Xenia (G-14753)

BASF Catalysts LLC................................ A 216 360-5005
  Cleveland (G-3408)

◆ Borchers Americas Inc.....................D 440 899-2950
  Westlake (G-14295)

Circle Prime Manufacturing Inc............. E 330 923-0019
  Cuyahoga Falls (G-5534)

Curtiss-Wright Ds Inc............................ E 937 252-5601
  Fairborn (G-6689)

Defense Research Assoc Inc.................. E 937 431-1644
  Dayton (G-5609)

Electronic Concepts Engrg Inc.............. F 419 861-9000
  Holland (G-7763)

EMD Millipore Corporation..................... E 513 631-0445
  Norwood (G-10868)

◆ Flexsys America LP...........................D 330 666-4111
  Akron (G-150)

▲ Ftech R&D North America Inc............ E 937 339-2777
  Troy *(G-13217)*

Global Realms LLC.............................. G 614 828-7284
  Gahanna *(G-7158)*

Guild Associates Inc........................... G 843 573-0095
  Dublin *(G-6299)*

▲ Guild Associates Inc......................... D 614 798-8215
  Dublin *(G-6300)*

▲ Heraeus Epurio LLC......................... E 937 264-1000
  Vandalia *(G-13559)*

Iconic Labs LLC................................... F 216 759-4040
  Westlake *(G-14308)*

Ion Vacuum Ivac Tech Corp................. F 216 662-5158
  Cleveland *(G-3868)*

Leidos Inc... D 937 656-8433
  Beavercreek *(G-977)*

Lyondell Chemical Company................. C 513 530-4000
  Cincinnati *(G-2833)*

Medpace Holdings Inc......................... C 513 579-9911
  Cincinnati *(G-2857)*

Moog Inc... E 330 682-0010
  Orrville *(G-10996)*

Morris Technologies Inc...................... E 513 733-1611
  Cincinnati *(G-2888)*

Mp Biomedicals LLC............................ C 440 337-1200
  Solon *(G-12154)*

Northcoast Environmental Labs............ G 330 342-3377
  Streetsboro *(G-12514)*

Open Additive LLC.............................. F 937 306-6140
  Dayton *(G-5929)*

Owens Corning Sales LLC................... F 330 633-6735
  Tallmadge *(G-12745)*

▲ Performnce Plymr Solutions Inc....... F 937 298-3713
  Moraine *(G-10180)*

Point Source Inc................................. F 937 855-6020
  Germantown *(G-7252)*

Range Impact Inc................................ G 216 304-6556
  Cleveland *(G-4224)*

Ronald T Dodge Co............................. F 937 439-4497
  Dayton *(G-5988)*

Rubicon Rubber LLC........................... F 234 678-0078
  Seville *(G-11920)*

Sierra Nevada Corporation.................. E 937 431-2800
  Beavercreek *(G-983)*

▼ Specialty Technology & Res............. G 614 870-0744
  Columbus *(G-5282)*

Srico Inc... G 614 799-0664
  Columbus *(G-5287)*

Steiner Eoptics Inc............................. D 937 426-2341
  Miamisburg *(G-9740)*

Sunpower Inc...................................... D 740 594-2221
  Athens *(G-654)*

Tacoma Energy LLC............................ C 614 899-8990
  Westerville *(G-14276)*

◆ Trico Products Corporation............... C 800 388-7428
  Cleveland *(G-4425)*

Vehicle Systems Inc........................... G 330 854-0535
  Massillon *(G-9251)*

Velocys Inc... D 614 733-3300
  Plain City *(G-11424)*

▲ Wiley Companies............................. C 740 622-0755
  Coshocton *(G-5476)*

8732 Commercial nonphysical research

Liminal Esports LLC............................ G 440 423-5856
  Gates Mills *(G-7230)*

Quality Solutions Inc........................... E 440 933-9946
  Cleveland *(G-4216)*

Steward Edge Bus Solutions............... F 614 826-5305
  Columbus *(G-5293)*

8733 Noncommercial research organizations

Mp Biomedicals LLC............................ C 440 337-1200
  Solon *(G-12154)*

▲ Performnce Plymr Solutions Inc....... F 937 298-3713
  Moraine *(G-10180)*

Quasonix Inc....................................... E 513 942-1287
  West Chester *(G-14058)*

Sdg Inc... F 440 893-0771
  Cleveland *(G-4282)*

Sunpower Inc...................................... D 740 594-2221
  Athens *(G-654)*

Tangent Company LLC......................... G 440 543-2775
  Chagrin Falls *(G-2186)*

Valensil Technologies LLC................... E 440 937-8181
  Avon *(G-741)*

8734 Testing laboratories

Agrana Fruit Us Inc............................. C 937 693-3821
  Anna *(G-459)*

Balancing Company Inc....................... E 937 898-9111
  Vandalia *(G-13550)*

Barr Engineering Incorporated............ E 614 714-0299
  Columbus *(G-4744)*

Chemsultants International Inc............ G 440 974-3080
  Mentor *(G-9498)*

Curtiss-Wright Flow Ctrl Corp............. D 513 528-7900
  Cincinnati *(G-2300)*

Fischer Engineering Co LLC................ G 937 754-1750
  Dayton *(G-5778)*

▲ Godfrey & Wing Inc......................... E 330 562-1440
  Aurora *(G-671)*

JBI Corporation.................................. F 419 855-3389
  Genoa *(G-7248)*

Jci Jones Chemicals Inc...................... F 330 825-2531
  Barberton *(G-814)*

◆ Kaplan Industries Inc...................... D 856 779-8181
  Harrison *(G-7558)*

Metcut Research Associates Inc........... D 513 271-5100
  Cincinnati *(G-2871)*

Micro Laboratories Inc........................ G 440 918-0001
  Mentor *(G-9564)*

Mjcj Holdings LLC............................... G 937 885-0800
  Miamisburg *(G-9719)*

Mrl Materials Resources LLC............... E 937 531-6657
  Xenia *(G-14771)*

National Polymer Inc........................... F 440 708-1245
  Chagrin Falls *(G-2171)*

Nelson Labs Fairfield Inc..................... E 973 227-6882
  Broadview Heights *(C-1507)*

▲ Nucon International Inc..................... F 614 846-5710
  Columbus *(G-5132)*

Ohio Lumex Co Inc............................. E 440 264-2500
  Solon *(G-12164)*

Phymet Inc.. F 937 743-8061
  Springboro *(G-12263)*

R D Baker Enterprises Inc................... G 937 461-5225
  Dayton *(G-5971)*

Ream and Haager Laboratory Inc......... F 330 343-3711
  Dover *(G-6259)*

Sample Machining Inc......................... E 937 258-3338
  Dayton *(G-5993)*

Smithers Group Inc............................. D 330 833-8548
  Massillon *(G-9244)*

Tangent Company LLC......................... G 440 543-2775
  Chagrin Falls *(G-2186)*

◆ Trico Products Corporation............... C 800 388-7428
  Cleveland *(G-4425)*

US Tubular Products Inc...................... D 330 832-1734
  North Lawrence *(G-10703)*

Wallover Enterprises Inc...................... F 440 238-9250
  Strongsville *(G-12612)*

Welding Consultants Inc...................... G 614 258-7018
  Columbus *(G-5360)*

Yoder Industries Inc........................... C 937 278-5769
  Dayton *(G-6089)*

8741 Management services

Ameridian Specialty Services.............. E 513 769-0150
  Cincinnati *(G-2364)*

◆ Babcock & Wilcox Company.............. A 330 753-4511
  Akron *(G-67)*

Cardinal Health Inc............................. E 614 553-3830
  Dublin *(G-6285)*

Cardinal Health Inc............................. G 614 757-2863
  Lewis Center *(G-8328)*

◆ Cardinal Health Inc.......................... A 614 757-5000
  Dublin *(G-6286)*

Central Coca-Cola Btlg Co Inc............. E 330 875-1487
  Akron *(G-95)*

Central Coca-Cola Btlg Co Inc............. E 740 474-2180
  Circleville *(G-3250)*

Coal Services Inc................................ B 740 795-5220
  Powhatan Point *(G-11497)*

◆ Dco LLC.. E 419 931-9086
  Perrysburg *(G-11213)*

▲ Eleet Cryogenics Inc....................... E 330 874-4009
  Bolivar *(G-1382)*

Elite Property Group LLC.................... F 216 356-7469
  Elyria *(G-6527)*

Ingle-Barr Inc..................................... D 740 702-6117
  Chillicothe *(G-2261)*

Instantwhip Foods Inc......................... F 614 488-2536
  Columbus *(G-5011)*

Instantwhip-Columbus Inc................... E 614 871-9447
  Grove City *(G-7391)*

Integrated Resources Inc..................... E 419 885-7122
  Sylvania *(G-12713)*

Ironhawk Industrial Dist LLC............... G 216 502-3700
  Euclid *(G-6656)*

▲ Jmac Inc.. E 614 436-2418
  Columbus *(G-5041)*

Kenyetta Bagby Enterprise LLC........... F 614 584-3426
  Reynoldsburg *(G-11573)*

▲ Kurtz Bros Compost Services........... G 330 864-2621
  Akron *(G-200)*

▲ Leadec Corp.................................... E 513 731-3590
  Cincinnati *(G-2815)*

Mel Heitkamp Builders Ltd.................. G 419 375-0405
  Fort Recovery *(G-6969)*

Momentum Fleet MGT Group Inc......... D 440 759-2219
  Westlake *(G-14313)*

▲ Ohio Cllbrtive Lrng Sltons Inc.......... E 216 595-5289
  Strongsville *(G-12582)*

Ohio Designer Craftsmen Entps.......... F 614 486-7119
  Columbus *(G-5141)*

Pf Management Inc.............................. G 513 874-8741
  West Chester *(G-14136)*

Protective Industrial Polymers............ F 440 327-0015
  North Ridgeville *(G-10743)*

RB Sigma LLC..................................... D 440 290-0577
  Mentor *(G-9607)*

Renascent Prtction Sltions LLC........... D 678 910-0412
  Dublin *(G-6339)*

Revolution Group Inc........................... D 614 212-1111
  Westerville *(G-14230)*

Steward Edge Bus Solutions............... F 614 826-5305
  Columbus *(G-5293)*

TAC Industries Inc.............................. B 937 328-5200
  Springfield *(G-12382)*

8742 Management consulting services

4r Enterprises Incorporated................ G 330 923-9799
  Cuyahoga Falls *(G-5519)*

5me LLC.. E 513 719-1600
  Cincinnati *(G-2289)*

S I C

◆ 889 Global Solutions Ltd................F 614 235-8889
Columbus *(G-4655)*

Advanced Prgrm Resources Inc............E 614 761-9994
Dublin *(G-6273)*

Akron Centl Engrv Mold Mch Inc........E 330 794-8704
Akron *(G-26)*

Alloy Extrusion Company................E 330 677-4946
Kent *(G-8016)*

American Egle Prprty Prsrvtion............G 855 440-6938
North Ridgeville *(G-10724)*

◆ Amerihua Intl Entps Inc................G..... 740 549-0300
Lewis Center *(G-8321)*

▲ Applied Marketing Services Inc.......E 440 716-9962
Westlake *(G-14289)*

◆ Applied Specialties Innovations LLC.E 440 933-9442
Avon Lake *(G-746)*

Capehart Enterprises LLC................F 614 769-7746
Columbus *(G-4795)*

Chemsultants International Inc............G 440 974-3080
Mentor *(G-9498)*

Clarity Retail Services LLC............D 513 800-9369
West Chester *(G-13965)*

◆ Comex North America Inc................D..... 303 307-2100
Cleveland *(G-3551)*

Crimson Gate Consulting Co............G 614 805-0897
Dublin *(G-6292)*

Crohm LLC................................G 513 921-9400
Cincinnati *(G-2526)*

Delphia Consulting LLC................E 614 421-2000
Columbus *(G-4877)*

◆ Dms Inc................................C..... 440 951-9838
Willoughby *(G-14449)*

Electronic Imaging Svcs Inc............F 740 549-2487
Lewis Center *(G-8332)*

Elite Property Group LLC................E 216 356-7469
Elyria *(G-6527)*

Eltool Corporation......................G 513 723-1772
Mansfield *(G-8785)*

EP Ferris & Associates Inc............E 614 299-2999
Columbus *(G-4906)*

Equip Business Solutions Co............G 614 854-9755
Jackson *(G-7945)*

▲ Faith Guiding Cafe LLC................F 614 245-8451
New Albany *(G-10340)*

Frankes Wood Products LLC............E 937 642-0706
Marysville *(G-9020)*

Harris Mackessy & Brennan Inc........C 614 221-6831
Westerville *(G-14212)*

Health Sense Inc........................G 440 354-8057
Painesville *(G-11093)*

Honda Dev & Mfg Amer LLC............C 937 644-0724
Marysville *(G-9028)*

Infinitaire Industries LLC................G 216 600-2051
Euclid *(G-6655)*

Integrity Parking LLC................F 440 543-4123
Aurora *(G-675)*

ITM Marketing Inc......................C 740 295-3575
Coshocton *(G-5457)*

Just Business Inc......................F 866 577-3303
Dayton *(G-5835)*

Kbc Services............................F 513 693-3743
Loveland *(G-8634)*

Ketman Corporation....................G 330 262-1688
Wooster *(G-14658)*

Kitto Katsu Inc........................G 818 256-6997
Clayton *(G-3274)*

Leidos Inc................................D 937 656-8433
Beavercreek *(G-977)*

Link To Success Inc....................G 888 959-4203
Norwalk *(G-10851)*

▲ Mag Resources LLC....................F 330 294-0494
Barberton *(G-818)*

◆ Malco Products Inc......................C 330 753-0361
Barberton *(G-819)*

Malik Media LLC........................G 614 933-0328
New Albany *(G-10345)*

Michele Caldwell........................G 937 505-7744
Dayton *(G-5880)*

▲ Midwest Motor Supply Co................C 800 233-1294
Columbus *(G-5100)*

Millers Aplus Cmpt Svcs LLC............F 330 620-5288
Akron *(G-234)*

Neurologix Technologies Inc............F 512 914-7941
Cleveland *(G-4071)*

One Wish LLC............................F 800 505-6883
Bedford *(G-1052)*

Page One Group........................G 740 397-4240
Mount Vernon *(G-10257)*

Pakra LLC................................F 614 477-6965
Columbus *(G-5169)*

Paycor Hcm Inc........................F 800 381-0053
Cincinnati *(G-2949)*

Proficient Info Tech Inc................G 937 470-1300
Dayton *(G-5964)*

▼ Projects Designed & Built..............E 419 726-7400
Toledo *(G-13104)*

Quality Solutions Inc....................E 440 933-9946
Cleveland *(G-4216)*

▲ Quarrymasters Inc......................G 330 612-0474
Akron *(G-274)*

Quez Media Marketing Inc..............G 216 910-0202
Independence *(G-7918)*

Recognition Robotics Inc................F 440 590-0499
Elyria *(G-6585)*

Russell Group United LLC................F 614 353-6853
Columbus *(G-5238)*

Salient Systems Inc....................E 614 792-5800
Dublin *(G-6343)*

Sightgain Inc............................F 202 494-9317
Mason *(G-9152)*

Simplevms LLC..........................F 888 255-8918
Cincinnati *(G-3091)*

Smithco Distributing....................E 419 367-7685
Liberty Center *(G-8376)*

▲ SSP Industrial Group Inc................G 330 665-2900
Fairlawn *(G-6814)*

Star Distribution and Mfg LLC............E 513 860-3573
West Chester *(G-14149)*

Streamside Materials Llc................G 419 423-1290
Findlay *(G-6924)*

Tdb Associates Inc......................F 937 459-5730
Greenville *(G-7357)*

Telex Communications Inc..............F 419 865-0972
Toledo *(G-13140)*

Tha Presidential Suite LLC..............G 216 338-7287
Cleveland *(G-4376)*

Tomahawk Entrmt Group LLC............F 216 505-0548
Euclid *(G-6680)*

Tramonte & Sons LLC....................F 513 770-5501
Lebanon *(G-8290)*

Vehicle Systems Inc....................G 330 854-0535
Massillon *(G-9251)*

Welding Consultants Inc................G 614 258-7018
Columbus *(G-5360)*

8743 Public relations services

Marketing Essentials LLC................E 419 629-0080
New Bremen *(G-10362)*

8744 Facilities support services

Facility Service Pros LLC................G 419 577-6123
Collins *(G-4587)*

▼ Fex LLC................................F 412 604-0400
Mingo Junction *(G-10051)*

Indoor Envmtl Specialists Inc............E 937 433-5202
Dayton *(G-5821)*

MPW Industrial Svcs Group Inc..........B 740 927-8790
Hebron *(G-7625)*

Radon Eliminator LLC....................F 330 844-0703
North Canton *(G-10662)*

Taylor Communications Inc..............E 937 221-1000
Dayton *(G-6039)*

8748 Business consulting, nec

Aeroseal LLC............................E 937 428-9300
Dayton *(G-5638)*

▲ Aeroseal LLC............................E 937 428-9300
Miamisburg *(G-9662)*

◆ Alpha Technologies Svcs LLC............D 330 745-1641
Hudson *(G-7828)*

▲ American Apex Corporation..............F 614 652-2000
Delaware *(G-6130)*

Apex Control Systems Inc................D 330 938-2588
Sebring *(G-11891)*

Architctral Identification Inc............F 614 868-8400
Gahanna *(G-7154)*

▲ Athens Technical Specialists..........F 740 592-2874
Athens *(G-634)*

Deemsys Inc............................D 614 322-9928
Gahanna *(G-7155)*

Defense Research Assoc Inc............E 937 431-1644
Dayton *(G-5609)*

Dje Management Consulting LLC..........G 330 760-2990
Medina *(G-9397)*

E Retailing Associates LLC..............D 614 300-5785
Columbus *(G-4894)*

Estone Group LLC........................E 888 653-2246
Toledo *(G-12957)*

Fluid Equipment Corporation............G 419 636-0777
Bryan *(G-1641)*

Great Lakes Mfg Group Ltd..............G 440 391-8266
Rocky River *(G-11634)*

Infinitaire Industries LLC................G 216 600-2051
Euclid *(G-6655)*

▲ Interactive Engineering Corp............E 330 239-6888
Medina *(G-9413)*

Jasstek Inc............................F 614 808-3600
Dublin *(G-6313)*

Ktsdi LLC................................G 330 783-2000
North Lima *(G-10709)*

Lake Publishing Inc......................G 440 299-8500
Mentor *(G-9549)*

Magnum Computers Inc..................F 216 781-1757
Cleveland *(G-3981)*

Melink Corporation......................D 513 685-0958
Milford *(G-9943)*

Millers Aplus Cmpt Svcs LLC............F 330 620-5288
Akron *(G-234)*

Nkh-Safety Inc..........................F 513 771-3839
Cincinnati *(G-2911)*

Optum Infusion Svcs 550 LLC............D 866 442-4679
Cincinnati *(G-2936)*

▼ Orton Edward Jr Crmic Fndation......E 614 895-2663
Westerville *(G-14226)*

▲ Pease Enterprises Inc..................F 513 871-8907
Cincinnati *(G-2951)*

Qlog Corp................................G 513 874-1211
Hamilton *(G-7519)*

Radon Eliminator LLC....................F 330 844-0703
North Canton *(G-10662)*

Ream and Haager Laboratory Inc..........F 330 343-3711
Dover *(G-6259)*

Russell Group United LLC................F 614 353-6853
Columbus *(G-5238)*

Sentek Corporation......................G 614 586-1123
Columbus *(G-5261)*

Simplevms LLC.. F 888 255-8918
  Cincinnati *(G-3091)*

Sutter Llc.. F 513 891-2261
  Blue Ash *(G-1339)*

Tangible Solutions Inc........................... E 937 912-4603
  Fairborn *(G-6701)*

Tekworx LLC... F 513 533-4777
  Cincinnati *(G-3142)*

Telex Communications Inc..................... F 419 865-0972
  Toledo *(G-13140)*

Tyler Grain & Fertilizer Co...................... F 330 669-2341
  Smithville *(G-12070)*

89 SERVICES, NOT ELSEWHERE CLASSIFIED

8999 Services, nec

4w Services... F 614 554-5427
  Hebron *(G-7606)*

Advanced Green Tech Inc....................... G 614 397-8130
  Plain City *(G-11392)*

Auguste Moone Enterprises Ltd............. E 216 333-9248
  Cleveland Heights *(G-4527)*

B&D Truck Parts Sls & Svcs LLC........... G 419 701-7041
  Fostoria *(G-6976)*

Bonfoey Co.. F 216 621-0178
  Cleveland *(G-3427)*

Kyle Media Inc....................................... F 877 775-2538
  Toledo *(G-13025)*

Mrl Materials Resources LLC.................. E 937 531-6657
  Xenia *(G-14771)*

▲ Nucon International Inc...................... F 614 846-5710
  Columbus *(G-5132)*

ONeil & Associates Inc........................... C 937 865-0800
  Miamisburg *(G-9725)*

Ournashonisme Ent LLC......................... F 689 276-0367
  Euclid *(G-6668)*

Those Chrcters From Clvland LL............ G 216 252-7300
  Cleveland *(G-4394)*

Whitney Stained GL Studio Inc............... G 216 348-1616
  Cleveland *(G-4504)*

91 EXECUTIVE, LEGISLATIVE & GENERAL GOVERNMENT, EXCEPT FINANCE

9111 Executive offices

City of Canton.. E 330 489-3370
  Canton *(G-1866)*

County of Holmes................................... G 330 674-2083
  Millersburg *(G-9978)*

Lake Township Trustees......................... E 419 836-1143
  Millbury *(G-9963)*

Liverpool Township................................ G 330 483-4747
  Valley City *(G-13502)*

Summit County....................................... G 330 865-8065
  Akron *(G-319)*

9199 General government, nec

City of Cleveland.................................... E 216 664-3013
  Cleveland *(G-3499)*

Turtlecreek Township.............................. F 513 932-4080
  Lebanon *(G-8293)*

92 JUSTICE, PUBLIC ORDER AND SAFETY

9221 Police protection

Public Safety Ohio Department............... G 440 943-5545
  Willoughby *(G-14511)*

96 ADMINISTRATION OF ECONOMIC PROGRAMS

9621 Regulation, administration of transportation

National Wldg Tanker Repr LLC.............. G 614 875-3399
  Grove City *(G-7404)*

Ohio Department Transportation............. E 614 351-2898
  Columbus *(G-5140)*

9661 Space research and technology

Weldon Pump LLC.................................. E 440 232-2282
  Oakwood Village *(G-10913)*

97 NATIONAL SECURITY AND INTERNATIONAL AFFAIRS

9711 National security

Dla Document Services............................ F 937 257-6014
  Dayton *(G-5610)*

S
I
C

R & R Sealants (HQ)..999 999-9999
651 Tally Blvd, Yourtown (99999) *(G-458)*

Ready Box Co 999 999-9999
704 Lawrence Rd, Anytown (99999) *(G-1723)*

Rendall Mfg Inc, Anytown Also Called RMI *(G-1730)*

Designates this location as a headquarters

Business phone

Geographic Section entry number where full company information appears

Address, city & ZIP

See footnotes for symbols and codes identification.
- Companies listed alphabetically.
- Complete physical or mailing address.

(Mcgregor Metal Yellow Springs Works Llc, Springfield, OH), Springfield Also Called: McGregor Mtal Innsfllen Wrks L *(G-12349)*

1 & 1 Property Preservation, North Ridgeville Also Called: American Egle Prprty Prsrvtion *(G-10724)*

1 A Lifesafer Inc (PA)..513 651-9560
3630 Park 42 Dr Ste 140c Cincinnati (45241) *(G-2319)*

1-2-3 Gluten Free Inc...216 378-9233
125 Orange Tree Dr Chagrin Falls (44022) *(G-2133)*

1-800-Usa-home.com, Columbus Also Called: Owens Corning *(G-5166)*

1062 Technologies Inc..303 453-9251
1062 Ohio Works Dr Youngstown (44510) *(G-14799)*

11 92 Holdings LLC...216 920-7790
8 E Washington St Ste 200 Chagrin Falls (44022) *(G-2134)*

1157 Designconcepts LLC...937 497-1157
210 S Lester Ave Sidney (45365) *(G-11988)*

1200 Feet Limited...419 827-6061
41 County Road 2350 Lakeville (44638) *(G-8159)*

16363 Sca Inc...330 448-0000
7800 Addison Rd Masury (44438) *(G-9253)*

1914 Mi Inc...330 308-8667
1117 Bowers Ave Nw New Philadelphia (44663) *(G-10428)*

1914 Mi Inc (PA)...800 426-4244
2301 E High Ave New Philadelphia (44663) *(G-10429)*

1one Stop Printing Inc...614 216-1438
1509 Blatt Blvd Ste 8303 Columbus (43230) *(G-4652)*

1st Choice Contractor, Elyria Also Called: Elite Property Group LLC *(G-6527)*

2 Retrievers LLC...216 200-9040
2515 Jav Ave Cleveland (44113) *(G-3276)*

2-M Manufacturing Company Inc................................440 269-1270
34560 Lakeland Blvd Eastlake (44095) *(G-6414)*

20/20 Custom Molded Plas LLC (HQ).........................419 506-5788
14620 Selwyn Dr Holiday City (43543) *(G-7742)*

277 Northfield Inc...440 439-1029
277 Northfield Rd Bedford (44146) *(G-1009)*

2checkout, Columbus Also Called: Verifone Inc *(G-5346)*

2cravealloys, Dalton Also Called: J Horst Manufacturing Co *(G-5586)*

2e Associates Inc..440 975-9955
38363 Airport Pkwy Willoughby (44094) *(G-14412)*

3 Sigma LLC...937 440-3400
1985 W Stanfield Rd Troy (45373) *(G-13198)*

3-B Welding Ltd...740 819-4329
2580 Holmes Rd New Concord (43762) *(G-10384)*

3-D Service Ltd (PA)..330 830-3500
800 Nave Rd Se Massillon (44646) *(G-9168)*

3-D Technical Services Company...............................937 746-2901
255 Industrial Dr Franklin (45005) *(G-7006)*

3-Dmed, Franklin Also Called: 3-D Technical Services Company *(G-7006)*

31 Inc...800 438-3302
100 Enterprise Dr Newcomerstown (43832) *(G-10566)*

3249 Inc...937 294-5692
3249 Dryden Rd Moraine (45439) *(G-10140)*

3359 Kingston LLC..614 871-8989
1111 London Groveport Rd Grove City (43123) *(G-7365)*

360 Wrapz, Columbus Also Called: Atchley Signs & Graphics LLC *(G-4731)*

3d Partners LLC..330 323-6453
1817 20th St Ne Canton (44714) *(G-1819)*

3d Sales & Consulting Inc...513 422-1198
408 Vanderveer St Middletown (45044) *(G-9838)*

3d Systems, Euclid Also Called: Village Plastics Co *(G-6683)*

3gtms LLC (PA)...877 722-3538
8760 Orion Pl Ste 300 Columbus (43240) *(G-4638)*

3i Solutions, Wooster Also Called: Ingredient Innovations Intl Co *(G-14650)*

3jd Inc..513 324-9655
2823 Northlawn Ave Moraine (45439) *(G-10141)*

3M, Medina Also Called: 3M Company *(G-9369)*

3M Company...330 725-1444
1030 Lake Rd Medina (44256) *(G-9369)*

4 Over LLC...937 610-0629
7801 Technology Blvd Dayton (45424) *(G-5627)*

4-B Wood Custom Cabinets, Seville Also Called: 4-B Wood Specialties Inc *(G-11908)*

4-B Wood Specialties Inc..330 769-2188
255 W Greenwich Rd Seville (44273) *(G-11908)*

400 SW 7th Street Partners Ltd..................................440 826-4700
3825 Edwards Rd Ste 800 Cincinnati (45209) *(G-2320)*

400 SW 7th Street Partners Ltd (PA)..........................772 781-2144
3825 Edwards Rd Ste 800 Cincinnati (45209) *(G-2321)*

44toolscom..614 873-4800
7640 Commerce Pl Plain City (43064) *(G-11389)*

48 Hr Books Inc..330 374-6917
1909 Summit Commerce Park Twinsburg (44087) *(G-13264)*

4blar LLC...513 576-0441
5948 Shallow Creek Dr Milford (45150) *(G-9919)*

4matic Valve Automtn Ohio LLC................................614 806-1221
4993 Cleveland Ave Columbus (43231) *(G-4653)*

4r Enterprises Incorporated......................................330 923-9799
700 Portage Trl Cuyahoga Falls (44221) *(G-5519)*

4S Company...330 792-5518
3730 Mahoning Ave Youngstown (44515) *(G-14800)*

4w Services..614 554-5427
7901 Minecaster Rd Hebron (43025) *(G-7606)*

4wallscom LLC...216 432-1400
4700 Lakeside Ave E Unit 173a Cleveland (44114) *(G-3277)*

5 Axis Grinding Inc...937 312-9797
86 Westpark Rd Dayton (45459) *(G-5628)*

5 BS Inc (PA)..740 454-8453
1000 5 Bs Dr Zanesville (43701) *(G-14980)*

5 Core Inc...951 386-6372
1221 W Sandusky Ave Bellefontaine (43311) *(G-1098)*

5 S Inc...440 968-0212
9755 Plank Rd Montville (44064) *(G-10139)*

5-Acre Mill, Hicksville Also Called: Adroit Thinking Inc *(G-7645)*

5me LLC...513 719-1600
4270 Ivy Pointe Blvd Ste 100 Cincinnati (45245) *(G-2289)*

614 Magazine, Columbus Also Called: 614 Media Group LLC *(G-4654)*

---

614 Media Group LLC.................................... 614 488-4400
  458 E Main St Columbus (43215) *(G-4654)*

64 Metals, Saint Louisville *Also Called: C Green & Sons Incorporated (G-11728)*

696 Ledgerock Cir.. 330 289-0996
  2950 Westway Dr Brunswick (44212) *(G-1577)*

7 7 Print Solutions LLC................................... 513 600-4597
  6601 Dixie Hwy Ste C Fairfield (45014) *(G-6704)*

7 Up / R C/Canada Dry Btlg Co, Columbus *Also Called: American Bottling Company (G-4693)*

7 Up Bottling Co, Lima *Also Called: American Bottling Company (G-8387)*

7 Up Bottling Co, Midvale *Also Called: American Bottling Company (G-9906)*

7 Up/ Royal Crown, Cincinnati *Also Called: American Bottling Company (G-2357)*

717 Inc.. 440 925-0402
  13000 Athens Ave Ste 110 Lakewood (44107) *(G-8161)*

717 Ink, Lakewood *Also Called: 717 Inc (G-8161)*

7octopus7 Inc... 513 677-5044
  8790 Governors Hill Dr Ste 102 Cincinnati (45249) *(G-2322)*

7signal Inc (PA).. 216 777-2900
  6155 Rockside Rd Ste 110 Independence (44131) *(G-7886)*

889 Global Solutions Ltd................................ 614 235-8889
  1943 W 5th Ave Columbus (43212) *(G-4655)*

9/10 Castings Inc.. 216 406-8907
  313 Greenway Dr Chardon (44024) *(G-2196)*

911cellular LLC.. 216 283-6100
  6001 Cochran Rd Ste 200 Solon (44139) *(G-12071)*

9444 Ohio Holding Co..................................... 330 359-6291
  1658 Us Route 62 E Winesburg (44690) *(G-14604)*

A & A Safety Inc (PA)...................................... 513 943-6100
  1126 Ferris Rd Amelia (45102) *(G-425)*

A & A Safety Inc.. 937 567-9781
  4080 Industrial Ln Beavercreek (45430) *(G-987)*

A & B, Cincinnati *Also Called: A & B Deburring Company (G-2323)*

A & B Deburring Company............................... 513 723-0444
  525 Carr St Cincinnati (45203) *(G-2323)*

A & B Foundry LLC (PA).................................. 937 369-3007
  835 N Main St Franklin (45005) *(G-7007)*

A & B Foundry LLC.. 937 412-1900
  4754 Us Route 40 Tipp City (45371) *(G-12811)*

A & B Iron & Metal Co Inc.............................. 937 228-1561
  329 Washington St Dayton (45402) *(G-5629)*

A & B Machine Inc... 937 492-8662
  2040 Commerce Dr Sidney (45365) *(G-11989)*

A & B Printing, Fort Loramie *Also Called: Sharp Enterprises Inc (G-6956)*

A & B Tool & Manufacturing........................... 419 382-0215
  2921 South Ave Toledo (43609) *(G-12859)*

A & C Welding Inc.. 330 762-4777
  80 Cuyahoga Falls Industrial Pkwy Peninsula (44264) *(G-11179)*

A & D Wood Products Inc (PA)........................ 419 331-8859
  4220 Sherrick Rd Elida (45807) *(G-6481)*

A & E Powder Coating Ltd............................... 937 525-3750
  1511 Sheridan Ave Springfield (45505) *(G-12274)*

A & F Machine Products Co............................. 440 826-0959
  454 Geiger St Berea (44017) *(G-1157)*

A & G Manufacturing Co Inc........................... 419 468-7433
  165 Gelsanliter Rd Galion (44833) *(G-7175)*

A & G Manufacturing Co Inc (PA)................... 419 468-7433
  280 Gelsanliter Rd Galion (44833) *(G-7176)*

A & I Metal Finishing, Vermilion *Also Called: Architctral Indus Met Fnshg LL (G-13588)*

A & J Woodworking Inc................................... 419 695-5655
  808 Ohio St Delphos (45833) *(G-6183)*

A & L Metal Processing, Sandusky *Also Called: Equinox Enterprises LLC (G-11833)*

A & M Refractories Inc.................................... 740 456-8020
  202 West Ave New Boston (45662) *(G-10355)*

A & P Technology Inc...................................... 513 688-3200
  4622 E Tech Dr Cincinnati (45245) *(G-2290)*

A & P Technology Inc...................................... 513 688-3200
  4578 E Tech Dr Cincinnati (45245) *(G-2291)*

A & P Technology Inc...................................... 513 688-3200
  4624 E Tech Dr Cincinnati (45245) *(G-2292)*

A & P Technology Inc...................................... 513 688-3200
  4599 E Tech Dr Cincinnati (45245) *(G-2293)*

A & P Technology Inc (PA).............................. 513 688-3200
  4595 E Tech Dr Cincinnati (45245) *(G-2294)*

A & P Tool Inc.. 419 542-6681
  801 Industrial Dr Hicksville (43526) *(G-7644)*

A & R Machine Co Inc...................................... 330 832-4631
  13212 Vega St Sw Massillon (44647) *(G-9169)*

A & W Table Pad Co... 800 541-0271
  6520 Carnegie Ave Cleveland (44103) *(G-3278)*

A A E, Canton *Also Called: American Aluminum Extrusions (G-1830)*

A Aabaco Plastics Inc..................................... 216 663-9494
  9520 Midwest Ave Cleveland (44125) *(G-3279)*

A and V Grinding Inc....................................... 937 444-4141
  1115 Straight St 17 Cincinnati (45214) *(G-2324)*

A B B Electric Systems, Westerville *Also Called: ABB Inc (G-14201)*

A B P Induction, Massillon *Also Called: Abp Induction LLC (G-9171)*

A Best Trmt & Pest Ctrl Sups......................... 330 434-5555
  891 Gorge Blvd Akron (44310) *(G-9)*

A C F, Lima *Also Called: Allen County Fabrication Inc (G-8386)*

A C Hadley - Printing Inc................................ 937 426-0952
  1530 Marsetta Dr Beavercreek (45432) *(G-962)*

A C Williams Co Inc (PA)................................ 330 296-6110
  700 N Walnut St Ravenna (44266) *(G-11511)*

A Division of Jmci, Springfield *Also Called: Jmac Inc (G-12331)*

A E T, Maumee *Also Called: Applied Energy Tech Inc (G-9262)*

A E Wilson Holdings Inc.................................. 330 405-0316
  2307 E Aurora Rd Twinsburg (44087) *(G-13265)*

A F Krainz Co... 216 431-4341
  1364 E 47th St Cleveland (44103) *(G-3280)*

A G Industries Inc... 330 220-0050
  2963 Interstate Pkwy Brunswick (44212) *(G-1578)*

A G Industries Inc... 216 252-7300
  1 American Rd Cleveland (44144) *(G-3281)*

A G Mercury, Galion *Also Called: A & G Manufacturing Co Inc (G-7176)*

A G Parts Inc.. 937 596-6448
  500 N Linden St Jackson Center (45334) *(G-7957)*

A G S Ohio, Macedonia *Also Called: AGS Custom Graphics Inc (G-8676)*

A Good Mobile Detailing LLC.......................... 513 316-3802
  2464 8 Mile Rd Cincinnati (45244) *(G-2325)*

A Grade Notes Inc (PA)................................... 614 299-9999
  6385 Shier Rings Rd Ste 1 Dublin (43016) *(G-6271)*

A H Marty Co Ltd... 216 641-8950
  6900 Union Ave Cleveland (44105) *(G-3282)*

A I M Specialists, Toledo *Also Called: Print All Inc (G-13103)*

A I P, Columbus *Also Called: American Isostatic Presses Inc (G-4698)*

A J C Hatchet Co, Hudson *Also Called: A JC Inc (G-7826)*

A J Construction Co.. 330 539-9544
  870 Shannon Rd Girard (44420) *(G-7262)*

A J Rose Mfg Co (PA)...................................... 216 631-4645
  38000 Chester Rd Avon (44011) *(G-710)*

A Jacks Manufacturing Co.............................. 216 531-1010
  1441 Chardon Rd Cleveland (44117) *(G-3283)*

A JC Inc.. 800 428-2438
  5145 Hudson Dr Hudson (44236) *(G-7826)*

A K Athletic Equipment Inc............................. 614 920-3069
  8015 Howe Industrial Pkwy Canal Winchester (43110) *(G-1782)*

A L Callahan Door Sales................................. 419 884-3667
  35 Industrial Dr Mansfield (44904) *(G-8757)*

A L D Precast Corp (PA).................................. 614 449-3366
  400 Frank Rd Columbus (43207) *(G-4656)*

A M C P, Greenfield *Also Called: American Made Crrgted Pckg Inc (G-7325)*

A M I, Olmsted Falls *Also Called: Affiliated Metal Industries Inc (G-10936)*

A M W, Columbus *Also Called: Assembly Machining Wire Pdts (G-4730)*

A P S, Dayton *Also Called: Aps-Materials Inc (G-5662)*

A P T, Middlefield *Also Called: American Plastic Tech Inc (G-9780)*

A Park Ohio Company, Wickliffe *Also Called: PMC Industries Corp (G-14391)*

A Plus Machining & Tooling, New Carlisle *Also Called: Custom Threading Systems LLC (G-10370)*

A Plus Powder Coaters Inc............................. 330 482-4389
  1384 Kauffman Ave Columbiana (44408) *(G-4604)*

(G-0000) Company's Geographic Section entry number

A Quick Copy Center, Cleveland *Also Called: Theb Inc (G-4389)*

A R C, Troy *Also Called: ARC Abrasives Inc (G-13201)*

A R E Logistics LLC.. 330 327-7315
400 Nave Rd Se Massillon (44646) *(G-9170)*

A R Schopps Sons Inc... 330 821-8406
14536 Oyster Rd Alliance (44601) *(G-364)*

A S C, Lakewood *Also Called: Associated Software Cons Inc (G-8162)*

A S D, Dayton *Also Called: Automation Systems Design Inc (G-5669)*

A S I, New Philadelphia *Also Called: Asi Visual Display Pdts Inc (G-10431)*

A Schulman, Conneaut *Also Called: Lyondllbsell Advnced Plymers I (G-5411)*

A Schulman Compression, Geneva *Also Called: Lyondllbsell Advnced Plymers I (G-7243)*

A Service Glass Inc.. 937 426-4920
1363 N Fairfield Rd Beavercreek (45432) *(G-963)*

A Sign Above Inc... 330 425-7832
8982 Dutton Dr Twinsburg (44087) *(G-13266)*

A Simona Group Company, Newcomerstown *Also Called: Simona Boltaron Inc (G-10575)*

A Stucki Company.. 412 424-0560
5335 Mayfair Rd North Canton (44720) *(G-10626)*

A T & F Co, Cleveland *Also Called: American Tank & Fabricating Co (G-3348)*

A T C, Westlake *Also Called: American Tchnical Coatings Inc (G-14288)*

A T I, Spring Valley *Also Called: Advanced Telemetrics Intl (G-12241)*

A T P, Milford Center *Also Called: Advanced Technology Products Inc (G-9956)*

A To Z Paper Box Company.. 330 325-8722
4477 Tallmadge Rd Rootstown (44272) *(G-11646)*

A To Z Portion Ctrl Meats Inc.. 419 358-2926
201 N Main St Bluffton (45817) *(G-1356)*

A V C, Canton *Also Called: Assocted Vsual Cmmncations Inc (G-1833)*

A W Taylor Lumber Incorporated.. 440 577-1889
1114 State Route 7 S Pierpont (44082) *(G-11303)*

A Z Printing Inc (PA)... 513 733-3900
10122 Reading Rd Cincinnati (45241) *(G-2326)*

A-1 Fabricators Finishers LLC... 513 724-0383
4220 Curliss Ln Batavia (45103) *(G-848)*

A-1 Resources Ltd.. 330 695-9351
8241 Tr 601 Fredericksburg (44627) *(G-7060)*

A-1 Sprinkler Company Inc... 937 859-6198
2383 Northpointe Dr Miamisburg (45342) *(G-9659)*

A-1 Welding & Fabrication... 440 233-8474
4909 Oak Point Rd Lorain (44053) *(G-8544)*

A-A Blueprint Co Inc.. 330 794-8803
2757 Gilchrist Rd Akron (44305) *(G-10)*

A-Best Termite and Pest Ctrl, Akron *Also Called: A Best Trmt & Pest Ctrl Sups (G-9)*

A-Display Service Corp... 614 469-1230
541 Dana Ave Columbus (43223) *(G-4657)*

A-Gas Americas, Bowling Green *Also Called: A-Gas US Holdings Inc (G-1403)*

A-Gas US Holdings Inc (OH).. 419 867-8990
1100 Haskins Rd Bowling Green (43402) *(G-1403)*

A-Kobak Container Company Inc.. 330 225-7791
1701 W 130th St Hinckley (44233) *(G-7730)*

A-Star Transportation Company.. 708 300-0067
470 Olde Worthington Rd Ste 200 Westerville (43082) *(G-14200)*

A-Wall, Cleveland *Also Called: Component Systems Inc (G-3556)*

A-Z Discount Printing, Cincinnati *Also Called: A Z Printing Inc (G-2326)*

A.I.M., Aurora *Also Called: Advanced Innovative Mfg Inc (G-660)*

A.V.E.C., Heath *Also Called: American Veneer Edgebanding Co (G-7592)*

A&B Fndry McHning Fabrications, Tipp City *Also Called: A & B Foundry LLC (G-12811)*

A&B Foundry & Machining LLC... 937 746-3634
835 N Main St Franklin (45005) *(G-7008)*

A&E Signs and Lighting LLC.. 513 541-0024
1030 Straight St Cincinnati (45214) *(G-2327)*

A&M Cheese Co.. 419 476-8369
253 Waggoner Blvd Toledo (43612) *(G-12860)*

A+ Engineering Fabrication Inc.. 419 832-0748
17562 Beech St Grand Rapids (43522) *(G-7307)*

A1 Industrial Painting Inc.. 330 750-9441
894 Coitsville Hubbard Rd Youngstown (44505) *(G-14801)*

AA Hand Sanitizer... 513 506-7575
2230 Park Ave Ste 202 Cincinnati (45206) *(G-2328)*

AAA Galvanizing - Joliet Inc... 513 871-5700
4454 Steel Pl Cincinnati (45209) *(G-2329)*

AAA Laminating & Bindery, Fairfield *Also Called: AAA Laminating and Bindery Inc (G-6705)*

AAA Laminating and Bindery Inc.. 513 860-2680
7209 Dixie Hwy Fairfield (45014) *(G-6705)*

AAA Plastics & Pallets Inc... 330 844-2556
246 N Cleveland Ave Mogadore (44260) *(G-10068)*

AAA Stamping Inc.. 216 749-4494
4001 Pearl Rd Uppr Cleveland (44109) *(G-3284)*

AAA Wastewater, Franklin *Also Called: AAA Wastewater Services Inc (G-7009)*

AAA Wastewater Services Inc.. 937 746-6361
3677 Anthony Ln Franklin (45005) *(G-7009)*

Aag Glass LLC.. 513 286-8268
760 Kent Rd Batavia (45103) *(G-849)*

Aajaj Hair Company LLC... 216 309-0816
3905 W 18th St Cleveland (44109) *(G-3285)*

Aalberts Surface Technologies, Kenton *Also Called: Atmosphere Annealing LLC (G-8095)*

AAM Mold and Machine Inc.. 440 998-2040
1015 Westwood Dr Ashtabula (44004) *(G-585)*

AAM Mtal Frmng-Mlvern Opration, Malvern *Also Called: American Axle & Mfg Inc (G-8746)*

Aardvark Screen Prtg & EMB LLC.. 419 354-6686
123 S Main St Bowling Green (43402) *(G-1404)*

Aat USA LLC (PA)... 614 388-8866
1850 Denune Ave Columbus (43211) *(G-4658)*

AB Bonded Locksmiths Inc... 513 531-7334
4344 Montgomery Rd Cincinnati (45212) *(G-2330)*

AB Plastics Inc.. 513 576-6333
1287 Us Route 50 Milford (45150) *(G-9920)*

AB Resources LLC.. 440 922-1098
6802 W Snowville Rd Ste E Brecksville (44141) *(G-1455)*

AB Tire & Repair... 440 543-2929
9685 Washington St Chagrin Falls (44023) *(G-2152)*

Abanaki Corporation (PA).. 440 543-7400
17387 Munn Rd Chagrin Falls (44023) *(G-2153)*

Abatement Lead Tstg Risk Assss.. 330 785-6420
404 Abbyshire Rd Akron (44319) *(G-11)*

ABB Inc... 614 818-6300
579 Executive Campus Dr Frnt Westerville (43082) *(G-14201)*

Abbey Carpet, Canton *Also Called: Shaheen Oriental Rug Co Inc (G-2003)*

Abbott... 608 931-1057
923 Dennison Ave Columbus (43201) *(G-4659)*

Abbott Image Solutions LLC... 937 382-6677
185 Park Dr Ste A Wilmington (45177) *(G-14569)*

Abbott Laboratories.. 614 624-3191
585 Cleveland Ave Columbus (43215) *(G-4660)*

Abbott Laboratories.. 614 624-3192
350 N 5th St Columbus (43215) *(G-4661)*

Abbott Laboratories.. 847 937-6100
2900 Easton Square Pl Columbus (43219) *(G-4662)*

Abbott Laboratories.. 800 551-5838
625 Cleveland Ave Columbus (43215) *(G-4663)*

Abbott Laboratories.. 614 624-7677
3300 Stelzer Rd Columbus (43219) *(G-4664)*

Abbott Laboratories.. 937 503-3405
1 Abbott Park Way Tipp City (45371) *(G-12812)*

Abbott Nutrition, Columbus *Also Called: Abbott Laboratories (G-4660)*

Abbott Tool Inc.. 419 476-6742
405 Dura Ave Toledo (43612) *(G-12861)*

ABC, Oregon *Also Called: ABC Appliance Inc (G-10955)*

ABC Appliance Inc... 419 693-4414
3012 Navarre Ave Oregon (43616) *(G-10955)*

ABC Plastics Inc.. 330 948-3322
140 West Dr Lodi (44254) *(G-8495)*

ABC Refreshments LLC... 216 692-0697
19541 Roseland Ave Euclid (44117) *(G-6637)*

ABC Signs Inc... 513 407-4367
2336 Iowa Ave Cincinnati (45206) *(G-2331)*

ABC Technologies Dlhb Inc... 330 479-7595
2310 Leo Ave Sw Canton (44706) *(G-1820)*

ABC Technologies Dlhb Inc (DH).. 330 478-2503
2422 Leo Ave Sw Canton (44706) *(G-1821)*

ABC Technologies Dlhb Inc... 330 488-0716
336 Wood St S East Canton (44730) *(G-6376)*

A
L
P
H
A
B
E
T
I
C

ABC Technologies Wmg Usa Inc (DH)............419 483-0653
560 Goodrich Rd Bellevue (44811) *(G-1117)*

Abco Bar & Tube Cutng Svc Inc............513 697-9487
7685 S State Route 48 Ste 1 Maineville (45039) *(G-8737)*

Abco Services, Toledo *Also Called: Abutilon Company Inc (G-12862)*

Abel Fabrication & Precision, Cincinnati *Also Called: Abel Fbrction Prcsion Pdts Inc (G-2332)*

Abel Fbrction Prcsion Pdts Inc............513 681-5000
3474 Beekman St Cincinnati (45223) *(G-2332)*

Abel Manufacturing Company............513 681-5000
3474 Beekman St Cincinnati (45223) *(G-2333)*

Abel Metal Processing Inc............216 881-4156
2105 E 77th St Cleveland (44103) *(G-3286)*

Abeona, Cleveland *Also Called: Abeona Therapeutics Inc (G-3287)*

Abeona Therapeutics Inc (PA)............646 813-4701
6555 Carnegie Ave Fl 4 Cleveland (44103) *(G-3287)*

ABI, Cleveland *Also Called: ABI Inc (G-3288)*

ABI Inc............800 847-8950
5350 Transportation Blvd Ste 18b Cleveland (44125) *(G-3288)*

ABI Orthtc/Prosthetic Labs Ltd............330 758-1143
930 Trailwood Dr Youngstown (44512) *(G-14802)*

Abitec Corporation (HQ)............614 429-6464
501 W 1st Ave Columbus (43215) *(G-4665)*

Abj, Castalia *Also Called: Abj Equipfix LLC (G-2093)*

Abj Equipfix LLC............419 684-5236
202 Lucas St W Castalia (44824) *(G-2093)*

Able Applied Technologies, Columbus *Also Called: Aat USA LLC (G-4658)*

Able Pallet Mfg & Repr............614 444-2115
1271 Harmon Ave Columbus (43223) *(G-4666)*

Able Tool Corporation............513 733-8989
617 N Wayne Ave Cincinnati (45215) *(G-2334)*

Ableprint / Toucan Inc............419 522-9742
26 W 6th St Mansfield (44902) *(G-8758)*

Abp Induction LLC (PA)............262 878-6390
607 1st St Sw Massillon (44646) *(G-9171)*

Abranda Llc............614 577-8080
7175 Havens Rd Blacklick (43004) *(G-1218)*

Abrasive Leaders & Innovators, Fairborn *Also Called: Ali Industries LLC (G-6685)*

Abrasive Products............513 502-9150
1028 Rosetree Ln Cincinnati (45230) *(G-2335)*

Abrasive Source Inc............937 526-9753
211 W Main St Russia (45363) *(G-11672)*

Abrasive Supply Company Inc............330 894-2818
25240 State Route 172 Minerva (44657) *(G-10032)*

Abrasive Technology LLC (PA)............740 548-4100
8400 Green Meadows Dr N Lewis Center (43035) *(G-8317)*

Abrasive Technology Lapidary............740 548-4855
8400 Green Meadows Dr N Lewis Center (43035) *(G-8318)*

ABS Materials Inc............330 234-7999
1909 Old Mansfield Rd Ste C Wooster (44691) *(G-14617)*

Absolute Impressions Inc............614 840-0599
281 Enterprise Dr Lewis Center (43035) *(G-8319)*

Absorbent Products Company Inc............419 352-5353
455 W Woodland Cir Bowling Green (43402) *(G-1405)*

Abstract Displays Inc............513 985-9700
6465 Creek Rd Blue Ash (45242) *(G-1241)*

Abutilon Company Inc............419 536-6123
701 N Westwood Ave Toledo (43607) *(G-12862)*

AC Green LLC............740 292-2604
6648 Hudnell Rd Athens (45701) *(G-631)*

Aca Millworks Inc............419 339-7600
16330 Waynesfield Rd Waynesfield (45896) *(G-13877)*

Academy Graphic Comm Inc............216 661-2550
1000 Brookpark Rd Cleveland (44109) *(G-3289)*

ACC Automation Co Inc............330 928-3821
475 Wolf Ledges Pkwy Akron (44311) *(G-12)*

Accel Color, Avon *Also Called: Accel Corporation (G-711)*

Accel Corporation (HQ)............440 934-7711
38620 Chester Rd Avon (44011) *(G-711)*

Accel Group Inc (PA)............330 336-0317
325 Quadral Dr Wadsworth (44281) *(G-13625)*

Accel Performance Group LLC (DH)............216 658-6413
6100 Oak Tree Blvd Ste 200 Independence (44131) *(G-7887)*

Accent Drapery Co Inc............614 488-0741
1180 Goodale Blvd Columbus (43212) *(G-4667)*

Accent Drapery Supply Co, Columbus *Also Called: Accent Drapery Co Inc (G-4667)*

Accent Manufacturing Inc............330 724-7704
80 Cole Ave Akron (44301) *(G-13)*

Accent Manufacturing Inc (PA)............330 724-7704
1026 Gardner Blvd Norton (44203) *(G-10816)*

Accent Showroom & Design Ctr, Norton *Also Called: Accent Manufacturing Inc (G-10816)*

Accent Signage Systems Inc............612 377-9156
5409 Hamlet Dr Findlay (45840) *(G-6831)*

Acclaimd Inc............614 219-9519
1275 Kinnear Rd Columbus (43212) *(G-4668)*

Accretech SBS Inc (PA)............513 373-4844
8790 Governors Hill Dr Cincinnati (45249) *(G-2336)*

Accro-Cast Corporation............937 228-0497
4147 Gardendale Ave Dayton (45427) *(G-5630)*

Accu Grind, Kent *Also Called: Reduction Engineering Inc (G-8067)*

Accu-Grind & Mfg Co Inc............937 224-3303
272 Leo St Dayton (45404) *(G-5631)*

Accu-Grind Inc............330 677-2225
4430 Crystal Pkwy Kent (44240) *(G-8012)*

Accu-Rite Tool & Die Co Corp............330 497-9959
7295 Sunset Strip Ave Nw Canton (44720) *(G-1822)*

Accu-Tek Tool & Die Inc............330 726-1946
1390 Allen Rd Bldg 1 Salem (44460) *(G-11760)*

Accu-Tool Inc............937 667-5878
9765 Julie Ct Tipp City (45371) *(G-12813)*

Accufab Inc............513 942-1929
9059 Sutton Pl West Chester (45011) *(G-13934)*

Accuform Manufacturing Inc............330 797-9291
2750 Intertech Dr Youngstown (44509) *(G-14803)*

Acculon Energy Inc............614 259-7792
1275 Kinnear Rd Columbus (43212) *(G-4669)*

Accurate, Painesville *Also Called: Accurate Metal Machining Inc (G-11066)*

Accurate Electronics Inc............330 682-7015
169 S Main St Orrville (44667) *(G-10972)*

Accurate Fab LLC............330 562-3140
1400 Miller Pkwy Streetsboro (44241) *(G-12484)*

Accurate Gear Mfg Co Inc............513 761-3220
16 E 73rd St Cincinnati (45216) *(G-2337)*

Accurate Manufacturing Company............614 878-6510
5765 Richgrove Ln Dublin (43016) *(G-6272)*

Accurate Mechanical Inc............740 681-1332
566 Mill Park Dr Lancaster (43130) *(G-8174)*

Accurate Metal Machining Inc............440 350-8225
882 Callendar Blvd Painesville (44077) *(G-11066)*

Accurate Products Company............740 498-7202
98 Elizabeth St Newcomerstown (43832) *(G-10567)*

Accurate Tech, Mentor *Also Called: Accurate Tech Inc (G-9467)*

Accurate Tech Inc............440 951-9153
7230 Industrial Park Blvd Mentor (44060) *(G-9467)*

Accuride Corporation............937 323-9669
4800 Gateway Blvd Springfield (45502) *(G-12275)*

Accuscan Instruments Inc............614 878-6644
5098 Trabue Rd Columbus (43228) *(G-4670)*

Accushred LLC............419 244-7473
1114 W Central Ave Toledo (43610) *(G-12863)*

Accutech Plastic Molding Inc............937 233-0017
5015 Kitridge Rd Dayton (45424) *(G-5632)*

Ace American Wire Die Co............330 425-7269
9041 Dutton Dr Twinsburg (44087) *(G-13267)*

Ace Boiler & Welding Co Inc............330 745-4443
118 Brookrun Dr Copley (44321) *(G-5427)*

Ace Equipment Company, Strongsville *Also Called: Armature Coil Equipment Inc (G-12538)*

Ace Grinding Co Inc............440 951-6760
37518 N Industrial Pkwy Willoughby (44094) *(G-14413)*

Ace Hydraulics, Bedford *Also Called: Kcn Technologies LLC (G-1041)*

Ace Lumber Company............330 744-3167
1039 Poland Ave Youngstown (44502) *(G-14804)*

Ace Manufacturing Company............513 541-2490
5219 Muhlhauser Rd West Chester (45011) *(G-13935)*

(G-0000) Company's Geographic Section entry number

Ace Metal Stamping Company, Bedford *Also Called: Continental Business Entps Inc* **(G-1023)**

Ace Plastics Company.. 330 928-7720
122 E Tuscarawas Ave Stow (44224) **(G-12414)**

Ace Precision Industries Inc.. 330 633-8523
925 Moe Dr Akron (44310) **(G-14)**

Ace Products & Consulting LLC..................................... 330 577-4088
6800 N Chestnut St Ste 3 Ravenna (44266) **(G-11512)**

Ace Ready Mix Concrete Co Inc.................................... 330 745-8125
3826 Summit Rd Norton (44203) **(G-10817)**

Ace Rubber Products Division, Akron *Also Called: Garro Tread Corporation* **(G-156)**

Ace Sanitary, West Chester *Also Called: Ace Manufacturing Company* **(G-13935)**

Ace Transfer Company.. 937 398-1103
1020 Hometown St Springfield (45504) **(G-12276)**

Ace Truck Equipment Co.. 740 453-0551
1130 Newark Rd Zanesville (43701) **(G-14981)**

Acex, Columbus *Also Called: Action Express Inc* **(G-4672)**

Ach LLC... 419 621-5748
3020 Tiffin Ave Sandusky (44870) **(G-11819)**

Ach Sandusky Plastics, Sandusky *Also Called: Ach LLC* **(G-11819)**

Achilles Aerospace Pdts Inc... 330 425-8444
2100 Enterprise Pkwy Twinsburg (44087) **(G-13268)**

Achilles Aerospace Products, Twinsburg *Also Called: Achilles Aerospace Pdts Inc* **(G-13268)**

Aci Industries Ltd (PA)... 740 368-4160
970 Pittsburgh Dr Frnt Delaware (43015) **(G-6128)**

Aci Industries Converting Ltd (HQ)............................... 740 368-4160
970 Pittsburgh Dr Delaware (43015) **(G-6129)**

Aci Services Inc (HQ).. 740 435-0240
125 Steubenville Ave Cambridge (43725) **(G-1734)**

Acid Development LLC... 330 502-4164
5700 Patriot Blvd Youngstown (44515) **(G-14805)**

Ackerman.. 440 246-2034
1138 W 19th St Lorain (44052) **(G-8545)**

Aclara Technologies LLC... 440 528-7200
30400 Solon Rd Solon (44139) **(G-12072)**

Acm, Brunswick *Also Called: American Cube Mold Inc* **(G-1580)**

Acm Ohio, Waverly *Also Called: News Watchman & Paper* **(G-13870)**

Acme, Poland *Also Called: Acme Company* **(G-11434)**

Acme Company.. 330 758-2313
9495 Harvard Blvd Poland (44514) **(G-11434)**

Acme Duplicating Co Inc.. 216 241-1241
1565 Greenleaf Cir Westlake (44145) **(G-14283)**

Acme Fence LLC... 330 784-0456
1053 Bank St Akron (44305) **(G-15)**

Acme Fence & Lumber, Akron *Also Called: Acme Fence LLC* **(G-15)**

Acme Home Improvement Co Inc................................... 614 252-2129
2909 E 4th Ave Columbus (43219) **(G-4671)**

Acme Industrial Group Inc... 330 821-3900
540 N Freedom Ave Alliance (44601) **(G-365)**

Acme Lifting Products Inc.. 440 838-4430
6892 W Snowville Rd Ste 2 Cleveland (44141) **(G-3290)**

Acme Machine Automatics Inc....................................... 419 453-0010
111 Progressive Dr Ottoville (45876) **(G-11051)**

Acme Paper Tube, Cleveland *Also Called: Acme Sprlly Wound Ppr Pdts Inc* **(G-3291)**

Acme Printing, Westlake *Also Called: Acme Duplicating Co Inc* **(G-14283)**

Acme Sprlly Wound Ppr Pdts Inc.................................. 216 267-2950
4810 W 139th St Cleveland (44135) **(G-3291)**

Acme Steak & Seafood Inc.. 330 270-8000
31 Bissell Ave Youngstown (44505) **(G-14806)**

Acme Surface Dynamics Inc.. 330 821-3900
555 N Freedom Ave Alliance (44601) **(G-366)**

Acmi LLC... 330 501-0728
229 N Four Mile Run Rd Ste A Youngstown (44515) **(G-14807)**

Aco Inc (DH).. 440 639-7230
9470 Pinecone Dr Mentor (44060) **(G-9468)**

Acon Inc.. 513 276-2111
11408 Dogleg Rd Tipp City (45371) **(G-12814)**

Acor Orthopaedic Inc... 440 532-0117
18700 S Miles Rd Cleveland (44128) **(G-3292)**

Acor Orthopaedic LLC (PA)... 216 662-4500
18530 S Miles Rd Cleveland (44128) **(G-3293)**

Acorn Rubber, Atwater *Also Called: Curtis Hilbruner* **(G-658)**

Acorn Technology Corporation...................................... 216 663-1244
3176 Morley Rd Shaker Heights (44122) **(G-11925)**

Acpo, Oak Harbor *Also Called: Acpo Ltd* **(G-10881)**

Acpo Ltd.. 419 898-8273
8035 W Lake Winds Dr Oak Harbor (43449) **(G-10881)**

Acreo Inc... 513 734-3327
3209 Marshall Dr Amelia (45102) **(G-426)**

Acro Tool & Die Company.. 330 773-5173
325 Morgan Ave Akron (44311) **(G-16)**

Acromet Metal Fabricators, Cleveland *Also Called: G T Metal Fabricators Inc* **(G-3750)**

ACS Commercial Graphics, Columbus *Also Called: American Colorscans Inc* **(G-4694)**

ACS Industries Inc.. 330 678-2511
2151 Mogadore Rd Kent (44240) **(G-8013)**

Act, Dublin *Also Called: Automation and Ctrl Tech Inc* **(G-6279)**

Action, Strongsville *Also Called: Action Industries Ltd* **(G-12531)**

Action Air & Hydraulics Inc... 937 372-8614
1087 Bellbrook Ave Xenia (45385) **(G-14752)**

Action Coupling & Eqp Inc.. 330 279-4242
8248 County Road 245 Holmesville (44633) **(G-7793)**

Action Express Inc... 929 351-3620
100 E Campus View Blvd Ste 250 Columbus (43235) **(G-4672)**

Action Group Inc.. 614 868-8868
411 Reynoldsburg New Albany Rd Blacklick (43004) **(G-1219)**

Action Industries Ltd (PA)... 216 252-7800
13325 Darice Pkwy Strongsville (44149) **(G-12531)**

Action Machine & Mfg Inc... 513 899-3889
6788 E Us Highway 22 And 3 Morrow (45152) **(G-10201)**

Action Rubber Co Inc... 937 866-5975
601 Fame Rd Dayton (45449) **(G-5633)**

Action Specialty Packaging LLC (DH)   4758 Devitt Dr West Chester (45246) **(G-14096)**

Action Super Abrasive Pdts Inc.................................... 330 673-7333
945 Greenbriar Pkwy Kent (44240) **(G-8014)**

Active Aeration Systems Inc.. 614 873-3626
7245 Industrial Pkwy Plain City (43064) **(G-11390)**

Active Chemical Systems Inc... 440 543-7755
16755 Park Circle Dr Chagrin Falls (44023) **(G-2154)**

Active Metal and Molds Inc.. 419 281-9623
2219 Cottage St Ashland (44805) **(G-514)**

Activities Press Inc.. 440 953-1200
7181 Industrial Park Blvd Mentor (44060) **(G-9469)**

Actual Industries LLC... 614 379-2739
655 N James Rd Columbus (43219) **(G-4673)**

Acu-Serve Corp (PA).. 330 923-5258
121 S Main St Ste 102 Akron (44308) **(G-17)**

Acuity Brands Lighting Inc... 800 754-0463
3825 Columbus Rd Bldg A Granville (43023) **(G-7313)**

Acuity Brands Lighting Inc... 740 349-4343
214 Oakwood Ave Newark (43055) **(G-10489)**

Acuity Brands Lighting Inc... 740 892-2011
140 Carey St Utica (43080) **(G-13485)**

Acutemp, Monroe *Also Called: Doubleday Acquisitions LLC* **(G-10104)**

Acutemp Thermal Systems.. 937 312-0114
2900 Dryden Rd Moraine (45439) **(G-10142)**

Ad Company Holdings Inc.. 404 256-3544
3245 Pickle Rd Akron (44312) **(G-18)**

Ad Industries Inc.. 303 744-1911
6450 Poe Ave Ste 109 Dayton (45414) **(G-5634)**

Ad Piston Ring, Cleveland *Also Called: Ad Piston Ring LLC* **(G-3294)**

Ad Piston Ring LLC... 216 781-5200
3145 Superior Ave E Cleveland (44114) **(G-3294)**

Ad-Sensations Inc.. 419 841-5395
3315 Centennial Rd Ste A Sylvania (43560) **(G-12700)**

Ada Extrusions Inc... 440 285-7653
505 W Wilbeth Rd Akron (44314) **(G-19)**

Ada Solutions Inc... 440 576-0423
901 Footville Richmond Rd E Jefferson (44047) **(G-7971)**

Ada Technologies Inc (HQ).. 419 634-7000
805 E North Ave Ada (45810) **(G-2)**

Adalet/Scott Fetzer Company.. 440 892-3074
10920 Madison Ave Cleveland (44102) **(G-3295)**

A
L
P
H
A
B
E
T
I
C

Adams Automatic Inc.................................. 440 235-4416
26070 N Depot St Olmsted Falls (44138) *(G-10935)*

Adams Bros Concrete Pdts Ltd...................... 740 452-7566
3401 East Pike Zanesville (43701) *(G-14982)*

Adams Brothers Inc................................... 740 819-0323
1501 Woodlawn Ave Zanesville (43701) *(G-14983)*

Adams County Lumber, Manchester *Also Called: Vances Department Store (G-8756)*

Adams Elevator Equipment Co (DH).................847 581-2900
1530 Timber Wolf Dr Holland (43528) *(G-7743)*

Adams Signs, Massillon *Also Called: Identitek Systems Inc (G-9206)*

Adams Street Publishing Co Inc..................... 419 244-9859
1120 Adams St Toledo (43604) *(G-12864)*

Adapt Oil.. 330 658-1482
188 N Portage St Doylestown (44230) *(G-6269)*

Adapt-A-Pak Inc...................................... 937 845-0386
678 Yellow Springs Fairfield Rd Ste 100 Fairborn (45324) *(G-6684)*

Adaptall America Inc................................. 330 425-4114
9047 Dutton Dr Twinsburg (44087) *(G-13269)*

Adapted Tech, Dublin *Also Called: Mirus Adapted Tech LLC (G-6320)*

Adare Pharmaceuticals Inc (DH)..................... 937 898-9669
845 Center Dr Vandalia (45377) *(G-13548)*

ADB, Gahanna *Also Called: ADB Safegate Americas LLC (G-7152)*

ADB Safegate Americas LLC........................ 614 861-1304
700 Science Blvd Gahanna (43230) *(G-7152)*

Adchem Adhesives Inc............................... 440 526-1976
4111 E Royalton Rd Cleveland (44147) *(G-3296)*

Adcraft Decals Incorporated......................... 216 524-2934
7708 Commerce Park Oval Cleveland (44131) *(G-3297)*

Adcura Mfg.. 937 222-3800
1314 Farr Dr Dayton (45404) *(G-5635)*

Adcura Mfg, Dayton *Also Called: Rct Industries Inc (G-5977)*

Add-A-Trap LLC...................................... 330 750-0417
488 Como St Struthers (44471) *(G-12615)*

Added Edge Assembly Inc........................... 216 464-4305
26800 Fargo Ave Ste A Cleveland (44146) *(G-3298)*

Addisonmckee, Lebanon *Also Called: Addition Manufacturing Technologies LLC (G-8241)*

Addition Manufacturing Technologies LLC........... 513 228-7000
1637 Kingsview Dr Lebanon (45036) *(G-8241)*

Additive Metal Alloys Ltd............................ 800 687-6110
1421 Holloway Rd Ste B Holland (43528) *(G-7744)*

Addup Inc... 513 745-4510
5101 Creek Rd Blue Ash (45242) *(G-1242)*

Adelman's Truck Sales, Canton *Also Called: Adelmans Truck Parts Corp (G-1823)*

Adelmans Truck Parts Corp (PA).................... 330 456-0206
2000 Waynesburg Dr Se Canton (44707) *(G-1823)*

Adelphia, Wellington *Also Called: Forest City Technologies Inc (G-13890)*

Adept Manufacturing Corp........................... 937 222-7110
1710 E 1st St Dayton (45403) *(G-5636)*

Adex International, Cincinnati *Also Called: Affinity Disp Expositions Inc (G-2340)*

Adex International, Cincinnati *Also Called: Affinity Disp Expositions Inc (G-2341)*

Adex International, Cincinnati *Also Called: Affinity Disp Expositions Inc (G-2342)*

Adgo Incorporated................................... 513 752-6880
3988 Mcmann Rd Cincinnati (45245) *(G-2295)*

Adhesves Sealants Coatings Div, Blue Ash *Also Called: HB Fuller Company (G-1282)*

ADI, Sheffield Village *Also Called: Advanced Design Industries Inc (G-11956)*

ADI Global Distribution, Bedford *Also Called: Resideo LLC (G-1057)*

ADI Global Distribution, Cincinnati *Also Called: Resideo LLC (G-3039)*

ADI Machining Inc.................................... 440 277-4141
4686 French Creek Rd Sheffield Village (44054) *(G-11955)*

Adidas North America Inc............................ 330 562-4689
549 S Chillicothe Rd Aurora (44202) *(G-659)*

Adidas Outlet Store Aurora, Aurora *Also Called: Adidas North America Inc (G-659)*

Adient US LLC.. 937 981-2176
1147 N Washington St Greenfield (45123) *(G-7324)*

Adient US LLC.. 419 662-4900
7560 Arbor Dr Northwood (43619) *(G-10801)*

Adient US LLC.. 419 394-7800
1111 Mckinley Rd Saint Marys (45885) *(G-11730)*

Adkins, Dale Logging, Oak Hill *Also Called: Dale R Adkins (G-10887)*

Adler Team Sports, Euclid *Also Called: R & A Sports Inc (G-6674)*

ADM, Fostoria *Also Called: Archer-Daniels-Midland Company (G-6975)*

ADM, Sugarcreek *Also Called: Archer-Daniels-Midland Company (G-12631)*

ADM, Toledo *Also Called: Archer-Daniels-Midland Company (G-12884)*

Adma Products, Hudson *Also Called: Advance Materials Products Inc (G-7827)*

Admark Printing Inc.................................. 937 833-5111
310 Sycamore St Brookville (45309) *(G-1561)*

Admiral Products Company Inc...................... 216 671-0600
4101 W 150th St Cleveland (44135) *(G-3299)*

Admj Holdings LLC.................................. 216 588-0038
5260 Commerce Pkwy W Cleveland (44130) *(G-3300)*

Adohio, Columbus *Also Called: Ohio Newspaper Services Inc (G-5149)*

Adr Fuel Inc.. 419 872-2178
353 Elm St Perrysburg (43551) *(G-11201)*

Adria Scientific GL Works Co........................ 440 474-6691
2683 State Route 534 S Geneva (44041) *(G-7231)*

Adroit Thinking Inc................................... 419 542-9363
10860 State Route 2 Hicksville (43526) *(G-7645)*

ADS... 419 422-6521
401 Olive St Findlay (45840) *(G-6832)*

ADS, Hilliard *Also Called: Advanced Drainage Systems Inc (G-7666)*

ADS, London *Also Called: Advanced Drainage Systems Inc (G-8529)*

ADS International Inc................................. 614 658-0050
4640 Trueman Blvd Hilliard (43026) *(G-7663)*

ADS Machinery Corp................................. 330 399-3601
1201 Vine Ave Ne Ste 1 Warren (44483) *(G-13731)*

ADS Worldwide Inc (HQ).............................614 658-0050
4640 Trueman Blvd Hilliard (43026) *(G-7664)*

Adsetting Service, Cleveland *Also Called: Royal Acme Corporation (G-4256)*

ADSr Ent LLC.. 773 280-2129
1888 Noe Bixby Rd Columbus (43232) *(G-4674)*

Advance Apex Inc (PA)..............................614 539-3000
2375 Harrisburg Pike Grove City (43123) *(G-7366)*

Advance Bronze Inc (PA)............................ 330 948-1231
139 Ohio St Lodi (44254) *(G-8496)*

Advance Bronzehubco Div (HQ)......................304 232-4414
139 Ohio St Lodi (44254) *(G-8497)*

Advance Cnc Machining, Grove City *Also Called: Advance Apex Inc (G-7366)*

Advance Digital, Columbus *Also Called: Dwr Graphics Inc (G-4892)*

Advance Door Co., Cleveland *Also Called: Admj Holdings LLC (G-3300)*

Advance Graphics, Columbus *Also Called: Hoster Graphics Company Inc (G-4992)*

Advance Industrial Mfg Inc........................... 614 871-3333
1996 Longwood Ave Grove City (43123) *(G-7367)*

Advance Industries Group LLC....................... 216 741-1800
3636 W 58th St Cleveland (44102) *(G-3301)*

Advance Manufacturing Corp......................... 216 333-1684
6800 Madison Ave Cleveland (44102) *(G-3302)*

Advance Materials Products Inc...................... 330 650-4000
1890 Georgetown Rd Hudson (44236) *(G-7827)*

Advance Metal Products Inc.......................... 216 741-1800
3636 W 58th St Cleveland (44102) *(G-3303)*

Advance Novelty Incorporated........................ 419 424-0363
101 Stanford Pkwy Findlay (45840) *(G-6833)*

Advance Printing Company, Cincinnati *Also Called: J & P Investments Inc (G-2755)*

Advance Products..................................... 419 882-8117
6041 Angleview Dr Sylvania (43560) *(G-12701)*

Advance Sign Group LLC............................. 614 429-2111
5150 Walcutt Ct Columbus (43228) *(G-4675)*

Advance Trans Inc................................... 330 572-0390
4833 Darrow Rd Ste 105 Stow (44224) *(G-12415)*

Advance Wire Forming Inc........................... 216 432-3250
3636 W 58th St Cleveland (44102) *(G-3304)*

Advanced Bar Technology, Canton *Also Called: Gerdau McSteel Atmsphere Annli (G-1900)*

Advanced Biological Mktg Inc........................ 419 232-2461
375 Bonnewitz Ave Van Wert (45891) *(G-13525)*

Advanced Composites Inc (DH)...................... 937 575-9800
1062 S 4th Ave Sidney (45365) *(G-11990)*

Advanced Cryogenic Entps Inc....................... 330 922-0750
1034 Home Ave Akron (44310) *(G-20)*

Advanced Design Industries, Sheffield Village *Also Called: ADI Machining Inc (G-11955)*

(G-0000) Company's Geographic Section entry number

Advanced Design Industries Inc.................... 440 277-4141
  4686 French Creek Rd Sheffield Village (44054) *(G-11956)*

Advanced Drainage of Ohio Inc.................... 614 658-0050
  4640 Trueman Blvd Hilliard (43026) *(G-7665)*

Advanced Drainage Systems Inc.................... 419 424-8222
  12370 Hancock County Rd Findlay (45840) *(G-6834)*

Advanced Drainage Systems Inc.................... 419 424-8324
  401 Olive St Findlay (45840) *(G-6835)*

Advanced Drainage Systems Inc.................... 513 863-1384
  2650 Hamilton Eaton Rd Hamilton (45011) *(G-7462)*

Advanced Drainage Systems Inc (PA).................... 614 658-0050
  4640 Trueman Blvd Hilliard (43026) *(G-7666)*

Advanced Drainage Systems Inc.................... 740 852-2980
  400 E High St London (43140) *(G-8529)*

Advanced Drainage Systems Inc.................... 419 599-9565
  1075 Independence Dr Napoleon (43545) *(G-10274)*

Advanced Drainage Systems Inc.................... 330 264-4949
  3113 W Old Lincoln Way Wooster (44691) *(G-14618)*

Advanced Engrg & Mfg Co Inc.................... 330 686-9911
  5026 Hudson Dr Ste D Stow (44224) *(G-12416)*

Advanced Engrg Solutions Inc.................... 937 743-6900
  250 Advanced Dr Springboro (45066) *(G-12244)*

Advanced Equipment Systems LLC.................... 216 289-6505
  22800 Lakeland Blvd Euclid (44132) *(G-6638)*

Advanced Fiber LLC.................... 419 562-1337
  100 Crossroads Blvd Bucyrus (44820) *(G-1671)*

Advanced Fluids Inc.................... 216 692-3050
  18127 Roseland Rd Cleveland (44112) *(G-3305)*

Advanced FME Products Inc.................... 440 953-0700
  9413 Hamilton Dr Mentor (44060) *(G-9470)*

Advanced Fuel Systems Inc.................... 614 252-8422
  841 Alton Ave Columbus (43219) *(G-4676)*

Advanced Gauging Tech LLC.................... 936 443-7129
  8430 Estates Ct Plain City (43064) *(G-11391)*

Advanced Green Tech Inc.................... 614 397-8130
  8059 Corporate Blvd Ste A Plain City (43064) *(G-11392)*

Advanced Ground Systems.................... 513 402-7226
  1650 Magnolia Dr Cincinnati (45215) *(G-2338)*

Advanced Holding Designs Inc.................... 330 928-4456
  3332 Cavalier Trl Cuyahoga Falls (44224) *(G-5520)*

Advanced Incentives Inc.................... 419 471-9088
  1732 W Alexis Rd Toledo (43613) *(G-12865)*

Advanced Indus Machining Inc (PA).................... 614 596-4183
  3982 Powell Rd Ste 218 Powell (43065) *(G-11481)*

Advanced Indus Msrment Systems (PA).................... 937 320-4930
  2580 Kohnle Dr Miamisburg (45342) *(G-9660)*

Advanced Innovative Mfg Inc.................... 330 562-2468
  255 Campus Dr Aurora (44202) *(G-660)*

Advanced Integration LLC.................... 614 863-2433
  6880 Tussing Rd Reynoldsburg (43068) *(G-11554)*

Advanced Intr Solutions Inc.................... 937 550-0065
  250 Advanced Dr Springboro (45066) *(G-12245)*

Advanced Kiffer Systems Inc.................... 216 267-8181
  4905 Rocky River Dr Cleveland (44135) *(G-3306)*

Advanced Lighting Tech LLC (PA).................... 888 440-2358
  6675 Parkland Blvd Ste 100 Solon (44139) *(G-12073)*

Advanced Paper Tube Inc.................... 216 281-5691
  1951 W 90th St Cleveland (44102) *(G-3307)*

Advanced Plastic Systems Inc.................... 614 759-6550
  990 Gahanna Pkwy Gahanna (43230) *(G-7153)*

Advanced Plastics Inc.................... 330 336-6681
  590 Corporate Pkwy Wadsworth (44281) *(G-13626)*

Advanced Poly-Packaging Inc (PA).................... 330 785-4000
  1331 Emmitt Rd Akron (44306) *(G-21)*

Advanced Polymer Coatings Ltd.................... 440 937-6218
  951 Jaycox Rd Avon (44011) *(G-712)*

Advanced Prgrm Resources Inc (PA).................... 614 761-9994
  2715 Tuller Pkwy Dublin (43017) *(G-6273)*

Advanced Recycling Systems, Lowellville *Also Called: ARS Recycling Systems LLC*
(G-8658)

Advanced Rv LLC.................... 440 283-0405
  4590 Hamann Pkwy Willoughby (44094) *(G-14414)*

Advanced Surface Technology.................... 216 476-8600
  12211 Sobieski Ave Cleveland (44135) *(G-3308)*

Advanced Tech Utilization Co.................... 440 238-3770
  12005 Prospect Rd Unit 1 Strongsville (44149) *(G-12532)*

Advanced Technical Pdts Sup Co.................... 513 851-6858
  6186 Centre Park Dr West Chester (45069) *(G-13936)*

Advanced Technology, Strongsville *Also Called: Advanced Tech Utilization Co (G-12532)*

Advanced Technology Corp.................... 440 293-4064
  101 Parker Dr Andover (44003) *(G-454)*

Advanced Technology Products Inc (PA).................... 937 349-4055
  190 N Mill St Milford Center (43045) *(G-9956)*

Advanced Telemetrics Intl.................... 937 862-6948
  2361 Darnell Dr Spring Valley (45370) *(G-12241)*

Advanced Visual Solutions, Hilliard *Also Called: National Sign Systems Inc (G-7689)*

Advanced Wldg Fabrication Inc (PA).................... 440 724-9165
  821 Lafayette Blvd Sheffield Lake (44054) *(G-11953)*

Advancepierre, West Chester *Also Called: Advancpierre Foods Holdings Inc (G-14098)*

Advancepierre Foods Inc (DH).................... 513 874-8741
  9990 Princeton Glendale Rd West Chester (45246) *(G-14097)*

Advancperre Foods Holdings Inc (HQ).................... 513 428-5699
  9990 Princeton Glendale Rd West Chester (45246) *(G-14098)*

Advant-E Corporation (PA).................... 937 429-4288
  2434 Esquire Dr Beavercreek (45431) *(G-964)*

Advantage Machine Shop.................... 330 337-8377
  777 S Ellsworth Ave Salem (44460) *(G-11761)*

Advantage Mold Inc.................... 419 691-5676
  525 N Wheeling St Toledo (43605) *(G-12866)*

Advantage Powder Coating Inc (PA).................... 419 782-2363
  2090 E 2nd St Ste 102 Defiance (43512) *(G-6094)*

Advantage Print Solutions LLC.................... 614 519-2392
  79 Acton Rd Columbus (43214) *(G-4677)*

Advantage Products Corporation (PA).................... 513 489-2283
  11559 Grooms Rd Blue Ash (45242) *(G-1243)*

Advantage Tent Fittings Inc.................... 740 773-3015
  11661 Pleasant Valley Rd Chillicothe (45601) *(G-2241)*

Advantage Truck Trailers, Columbus *Also Called: Kenan Advantage Group Inc (G-5048)*

Advantic Building Group LLC.................... 513 290-4796
  511 Byers Rd Miamisburg (45342) *(G-9661)*

Advent Designs, Logan *Also Called: Signs Unlmted The Grphic Advnt (G-8526)*

Adventurous Child Inc.................... 513 531-7700
  4781 Duck Creek Rd Cincinnati (45227) *(G-2339)*

Advertiser-Tribune, The, Tiffin *Also Called: Ogden Newspapers Ohio Inc (G-12794)*

Advertising Joe LLC Mean.................... 440 247-8200
  33 River St Ste 7 Chagrin Falls (44022) *(G-2135)*

Advertising Specialty Co, East Liverpool *Also Called: W C Bunting Co Inc (G-6399)*

Advetech Inc (PA).................... 330 533-2227
  445 W Main St Canfield (44406) *(C 1801)*

Advetech Inc.................... 330 533-2227
  451 W Main St Canfield (44406) *(G-1802)*

Advics, Lebanon *Also Called: Advics Manufacturing Ohio Inc (G-8242)*

Advics Manufacturing Ohio Inc.................... 513 932-7878
  1650 Kingsview Dr Lebanon (45036) *(G-8242)*

Advint, Reynoldsburg *Also Called: Advanced Integration LLC (G-11554)*

Aecom Energy & Cnstr Inc.................... 419 698-6277
  4001 Cedar Point Rd Oregon (43616) *(G-10956)*

Aero Fluid Products, Painesville *Also Called: Dukes Aerospace Inc (G-11080)*

Aero Fulfillment Services Corp (PA).................... 800 225-7145
  3900 Aero Dr Mason (45040) *(G-9056)*

Aero Instruments, Cleveland *Also Called: Aero-Instruments Co LLC (G-3309)*

Aero Jet Wash Llc.................... 866 381-7955
  450 Gargrave Rd Dayton (45449) *(G-5637)*

Aero Pallets Inc.................... 330 260-7107
  348 Raley Ave Se Carrollton (44615) *(G-2079)*

Aero Tech Tool & Mold Inc.................... 440 942-3327
  7224 Industrial Park Blvd Mentor (44060) *(G-9471)*

Aero-Instruments Co LLC.................... 216 671-3133
  4223 Monticello Blvd Cleveland (44121) *(G-3309)*

Aerobarrier, Dayton *Also Called: Aeroseal LLC (G-5638)*

Aerocase Incorporated.................... 440 617-9294
  1061 Bradley Rd Westlake (44145) *(G-14284)*

Aerocontrolex, Cleveland *Also Called: Transdigm Inc (G-4411)*

Aerocontrolex, South Euclid *Also Called: Aerocontrolex Group Inc (G-12216)*

Aerocontrolex Group Inc.. 216 291-6025
4223 Monticello Blvd South Euclid (44121) *(G-12216)*

Aerodyne, Chagrin Falls *Also Called: Abanaki Corporation (G-2153)*

Aeroflex Powell, Hilliard *Also Called: Star Dynamics Corporation (G-7702)*

Aerolite, Youngstown *Also Called: Teh Investments Inc (G-14944)*

Aeroll Engineering Corp.. 216 481-2266
18511 Euclid Ave Rear Cleveland (44112) *(G-3310)*

Aerontics Systems Arspc Strctr, Beavercreek *Also Called: Northrop Grumman Systems Corp (G-994)*

Aeropact Manufacturing LLC.. 419 373-1711
435 W Woodland Cir Bowling Green (43402) *(G-1406)*

Aeroscena LLC.. 800 671-1890
10000 Cedar Ave Cleveland (44106) *(G-3311)*

Aeroseal LLC... 937 428-9300
1851 S Metro Pkwy Dayton (45459) *(G-5638)*

Aeroseal LLC (PA).. 937 428-9300
225 Byers Rd # 1 Miamisburg (45342) *(G-9662)*

Aeroserv Inc... 513 932-9227
201 Industrial Row Dr Mason (45040) *(G-9057)*

Aerospace LLC... 937 561-1104
3300 Encrete Ln Moraine (45439) *(G-10143)*

Aerospace Logistics, Moraine *Also Called: Aerospace LLC (G-10143)*

Aerospace Lubricants LLC... 614 878-3600
1600 Georgesville Rd Columbus (43228) *(G-4678)*

Aerospace Maint Solutions LLC..................................... 440 729-7703
29401 Ambina Dr Solon (44139) *(G-12074)*

Aerospace Simulations, Akron *Also Called: Lockheed Mrtin Intgrted System (G-209)*

Aerosport Additive, Canal Winchester *Also Called: Aerosport Modeling Design LLC (G-1783)*

Aerosport Modeling Design LLC..................................... 614 834-5227
8090 Howe Industrial Pkwy Canal Winchester (43110) *(G-1783)*

Aerotech Enterprise.. 440 729-2616
8511 Mulberry Rd Chesterland (44026) *(G-2232)*

Aerotorque Corporation, Sharon Center *Also Called: Atc Legacy Inc (G-11936)*

Aerovation Tech Holdings LLC.. 567 208-5525
11651 Township Rd 81 Forest (45843) *(G-6938)*

Aerowave Inc.. 440 731-8464
361 Windward Dr Elyria (44035) *(G-6492)*

Aerpio Therapeutics LLC.. 513 985-1920
9987 Carver Rd Ste 420 Blue Ash (45242) *(G-1244)*

AES, Cincinnati *Also Called: Aluminum Extruded Shapes Inc (G-2354)*

AES Beaver Valley LLC
1065 Woodman Dr Dayton (45432) *(G-5602)*

Aesi, Springboro *Also Called: Advanced Engrg Solutions Inc (G-12244)*

Aesthetic Finishers Inc.. 937 778-8777
1502 S Main St Piqua (45356) *(G-11332)*

Aetna Plating Co.. 216 341-9111
6511 Morgan Ave Cleveland (44127) *(G-3312)*

Aexcel Corporation (PA).. 440 974-3800
7373 Production Dr Mentor (44060) *(G-9472)*

Afc Stamping & Production Inc....................................... 937 275-8700
4900 Webster St Dayton (45414) *(G-5639)*

Afc Tool Co Inc... 937 275-8700
4900 Webster St Dayton (45414) *(G-5640)*

Affiliated Metal Industries Inc....................................... 440 235-3345
25600 Chapin St Olmsted Falls (44138) *(G-10936)*

Affinity Disp Expositions Inc.. 513 771-2339
1375 Spring Park Walk Cincinnati (45215) *(G-2340)*

Affinity Disp Expositions Inc (PA).................................. 513 771-2339
1301 Glendale Milford Rd Cincinnati (45215) *(G-2341)*

Affinity Disp Expositions Inc.. 513 771-2339
1375 Glendale Milford Rd Cincinnati (45215) *(G-2342)*

Affordable Barn Co Ltd... 330 674-3001
4260 Township Road 617 Millersburg (44654) *(G-9966)*

Affordable Tire, Canton *Also Called: Ziegler Tire and Supply Co (G-2052)*

Affymetrix Inc... 800 321-9322
26111 Miles Rd Cleveland (44128) *(G-3313)*

Affymetrix Inc... 419 887-1233
434 W Dussel Dr Maumee (43537) *(G-9257)*

Afg Industries Inc.. 614 322-4580
4000 Gantz Rd Ste A Grove City (43123) *(G-7368)*

Afs Technology LLC... 937 545-0627
6649 Deer Bluff Dr Dayton (45424) *(G-5641)*

Agb LLC... 419 924-5216
15188 Us Highway 127 West Unity (43570) *(G-14191)*

AGC Automotive Americas, Grove City *Also Called: Afg Industries Inc (G-7368)*

AGE Graphics LLC (PA).. 740 989-0006
678 Collins Rd Little Hocking (45742) *(G-8485)*

Agean Marble Manufacturing Inc................................... 513 874-1475
9756 Princeton Glendale Rd West Chester (45246) *(G-14099)*

Agents of Gaming, Dayton *Also Called: Aog Inc (G-5660)*

AGFA Corporation.. 513 829-6292
6104 Monastery Dr Fairfield (45014) *(G-6706)*

Agile Global Solutions Inc... 916 655-7745
5755 Granger Rd Ste 610 Independence (44131) *(G-7888)*

Agile Manufacturing Tech LLC....................................... 937 258-3338
220 N Jersey St Dayton (45403) *(G-5642)*

Agile Sign & Ltg Maint Inc... 440 918-1311
35280 Lakeland Blvd Eastlake (44095) *(G-6415)*

Agmet LLC... 216 663-8200
5533 Dunham Rd Cleveland (44137) *(G-3314)*

Agmet Metals Inc.. 440 439-7400
7800 Medusa Rd Oakwood Village (44146) *(G-10902)*

Agnone-Kelly Enterprises Inc.. 800 634-6503
11658 Baen Rd Cincinnati (45242) *(G-2343)*

AGR Consulting Inc... 440 974-4030
35400 Lakeland Blvd Eastlake (44095) *(G-6416)*

Agrana Fruit Us Inc... 937 693-3821
16197 County Road 25a Anna (45302) *(G-459)*

Agrana Fruit Us Inc (DH).. 440 546-1199
6850 Southpointe Pkwy Brecksville (44141) *(G-1456)*

Agrati - Medina LLC (DH)... 330 725-8853
941 Lake Rd 955 Medina (44256) *(G-9370)*

Agrati - Tiffin LLC.. 419 447-2221
1988 S County Road 593 Tiffin (44883) *(G-12772)*

Agratronix LLC.. 330 562-2222
1790 Miller Pkwy Streetsboro (44241) *(G-12485)*

Agrauxine By Lesaffre, Van Wert *Also Called: Advanced Biological Mktg Inc (G-13525)*

Agri Communicators Inc.. 614 273-0465
280 N High St Fl 6 Columbus (43215) *(G-4679)*

Agricool Veg & Fruits LLC.. 310 625-0024
310 S Green Rd South Euclid (44121) *(G-12217)*

Agridry LLC.. 419 459-4399
3460 Us Highway 20 Edon (43518) *(G-6472)*

Agrium Advanced Tech US Inc....................................... 614 276-5103
701 Kaderly Dr Columbus (43228) *(G-4680)*

AGS Custom Graphics, Macedonia *Also Called: Custom Graphics Inc (G-8682)*

AGS Custom Graphics Inc... 330 963-7770
8107 Bavaria Dr E Macedonia (44056) *(G-8676)*

Agse Tooling, Cincinnati *Also Called: Advanced Ground Systems (G-2338)*

Ahalogy... 314 974-5599
1140 Main St # 3 Cincinnati (45202) *(G-2344)*

Ahd, Cuyahoga Falls *Also Called: Advanced Holding Designs Inc (G-5520)*

Ahmf Inc (PA).. 614 921-1223
2245 Wilson Rd Columbus (43228) *(G-4681)*

Ahner Fabricating & Shtmtl Inc..................................... 419 626-6641
2001 E Perkins Ave Sandusky (44870) *(G-11820)*

Ahresty Wilmington Corporation.................................... 937 382-6112
2627 S South St Wilmington (45177) *(G-14570)*

Ai Life LLC.. 513 605-1079
4680 Parkway Dr Ste 300 Mason (45040) *(G-9058)*

AI Root Company (PA).. 330 723-4359
623 W Liberty St Medina (44256) *(G-9371)*

AI Root Company... 330 725-6677
234 S State Rd Medina (44256) *(G-9372)*

Ai Wellness, Mason *Also Called: Ai Life LLC (G-9058)*

Aida-America Corporation.. 937 237-2382
7600 Center Point 70 Blvd Dayton (45424) *(G-5643)*

Aida-America Corporation (HQ)...................................... 937 237-2382
7660 Center Point 70 Blvd Dayton (45424) *(G-5644)*

Ailes Millwork Inc.. 330 678-4300
1520 Enterprise Way Kent (44240) *(G-8015)*

Aim Attachments.. 614 539-3030
1720 Feddern Ave Grove City (43123) *(G-7369)*

Aim International.. 513 831-2938
264 Center St Miamiville (45147) *(G-9761)*

Aim Services Company.. 800 321-9038
1500 Trumbull Ave Girard (44420) *(G-7263)*

Aims-CMI Technology LLC.. 937 832-2000
65 Haas Dr Englewood (45322) *(G-6605)*

AIN Industries Inc... 440 781-0950
13901 Aspinwall Ave Cleveland (44110) *(G-3315)*

Air Craft Wheels LLC.. 440 937-7903
700 N Walnut St Ravenna (44266) *(G-11513)*

Air Enterprises Inc.. 330 794-9770
735 Glaser Pkwy Akron (44306) *(G-22)*

Air Heater Seal Company Inc...................................... 740 984-2146
93 Sunset Ln Waterford (45786) *(G-13825)*

Air Power Dynamics LLC... 440 701-2100
7350 Corporate Blvd Mentor (44060) *(G-9473)*

Air Rite Service Supply, Cleveland Also Called: Air-Rite Inc *(G-3316)*

Air Supply Co, Twinsburg Also Called: Allied Separation Tech Inc *(G-13274)*

Air Technical Industries Inc....................................... 440 951-5191
7501 Clover Ave Mentor (44060) *(G-9474)*

Air-Rite Inc.. 216 228-8200
1290 W 117th St Cleveland (44107) *(G-3316)*

Air-Tech Mechanical Inc... 419 292-0074
4444 Monroe St Toledo (43613) *(G-12867)*

Airbase Industries LLC.. 937 540-1140
1000 Cass Dr Englewood (45315) *(G-6606)*

Aircraft & Auto Fittings Co... 216 486-0047
17120 Saint Clair Ave Cleveland (44110) *(G-3317)*

Aircraft Dynamics, Elida Also Called: Aircraft Dynamics Corporation *(G-6482)*

Aircraft Dynamics Corporation................................... 419 331-0371
418 E Kiracofe Ave Elida (45807) *(G-6482)*

Aircraft Wheel & Brake LLC.. 440 937-6211
1160 Center Rd Avon (44011) *(G-713)*

Aircraft-Refuelers.com, Findlay Also Called: Bosserman Automotive Engrg LLC *(G-6844)*

Airecon Manufacturing Corp....................................... 513 561-5522
5271 Brotherton Rd Cincinnati (45227) *(G-2345)*

Airfasco Inc... 330 430-6190
2655 Harrison Ave Sw Canton (44706) *(G-1824)*

Airfasco Inds Fstner Group LLC.................................. 330 430-6190
2655 Harrison Ave Sw Canton (44706) *(G-1825)*

Airgas Usa LLC... 330 454-1330
2505 Shepler Ave Sw Canton (44706) *(G-1826)*

Airgas Usa LLC... 740 353-5710
1411 Robinson Ave Portsmouth (45662) *(G-11463)*

Airgas Usa LLC... 440 232-6397
9155 Dutton Dr Twinsburg (44087) *(G-13270)*

Airmate Co Inc.. 419 636-3184
16280 County Road D Bryan (43506) *(G-1625)*

Airplaco Equipment Company, Cincinnati Also Called: Mesa Industries Inc *(G-2866)*

Airsources Inc... 610 983-0102
950 Honeysuckle Cir Ne North Canton (44720) *(G-10627)*

Airstream Inc (HQ).. 937 596-6111
1001 W Pike St Jackson Center (45334) *(G-7958)*

Airtex Industries LLC.. 330 899-0340
6056 Deer Park Ct Toledo (43614) *(G-12868)*

Airtx International Ltd.. 513 631-0660
6320 Wiehe Rd Cincinnati (45237) *(G-2346)*

Airwave Communications Cons.................................. 419 331-1526
1209 Allentown Rd Lima (45805) *(G-8385)*

Airwaves LLC... 740 548-1200
7750 Green Meadows Dr Ste A Lewis Center (43035) *(G-8320)*

Aitken, Geneva Also Called: Aitken Products Inc *(G-7232)*

Aitken Products Inc... 440 466-5711
566 N Eagle St Geneva (44041) *(G-7232)*

Aj Enterprise LLC.. 740 231-2205
1915 Hoge Ave Zanesville (43701) *(G-14984)*

Ajax Tocco Magnethermic Corp (HQ)......................... 800 547-1527
1745 Overland Ave Ne Warren (44483) *(G-13732)*

Ajax-Ceco.. 440 295-0244
1500 E 219th St Euclid (44117) *(G-6639)*

AJD Holding Co (PA).. 330 405-4477
2181 Enterprise Pkwy Twinsburg (44087) *(G-13271)*

Ajinomoto Hlth Ntrtn N Amer In................................. 330 762-6652
929 Home Ave Akron (44310) *(G-23)*

Ajj Enterprises LLC... 513 755-9562
10073 Commerce Park Dr West Chester (45246) *(G-14100)*

AK Fabrication Inc... 330 458-1037
1500 Allen Ave Se Canton (44707) *(G-1827)*

AK Mansfield... 419 755-3011
913 Bowman St Mansfield (44903) *(G-8759)*

Akalina Associates Inc.. 440 992-2195
2751 West Ave Ashtabula (44004) *(G-586)*

Akay Holdings Inc.. 330 753-8458
1031 Lambert St Barberton (44203) *(G-790)*

Akers Packaging Service Inc (PA)............................... 513 422-6312
2820 Lefferson Rd Middletown (45044) *(G-9839)*

Akers Packaging Service Group, Middletown Also Called: Akers Packaging Service Inc
(G-9839)

Akers Packaging Service Group, Middletown Also Called: Akers Packaging Solutions Inc
(G-9840)

Akers Packaging Solutions Inc (PA)............................ 513 422-6312
2820 Lefferson Rd Middletown (45044) *(G-9840)*

Akko Fastener Inc (PA).. 513 489-8300
1225 Hook Dr Middletown (45042) *(G-9841)*

Akland Printing.. 330 467-8292
145 W Aurora Rd Northfield (44067) *(G-10791)*

Akland Printing, Macedonia Also Called: Gaspar Services LLC *(G-8694)*

Akro Tool Co Inc.. 513 858-1555
240 Donald Dr Fairfield (45014) *(G-6707)*

Akro Tool Company, Fairfield Also Called: Deffren Machine Tool Svc Inc *(G-6726)*

Akro-Plastics, Kent Also Called: US Development Corp *(G-8094)*

Akrochem Corporation (PA).. 330 535-2100
3770 Embassy Pkwy Akron (44333) *(G-24)*

Akron Anodizing & Coating Div, Akron Also Called: Russell Products Co Inc *(G-297)*

Akron Beacon Journal, Akron Also Called: Beacon Journal Publishing Co *(G-74)*

Akron Belting & Supply Company................................. 330 633-8212
1244 Home Ave Akron (44310) *(G-25)*

Akron Brass Company.. 614 529-7230
3656 Paragon Dr Columbus (43228) *(G-4682)*

Akron Brass Company.. 800 228-1161
1615 Old Mansfield Rd Wooster (44691) *(G-14619)*

Akron Brass Company (DH)... 330 264-5678
343 Venture Blvd Wooster (44691) *(G-14620)*

Akron Canton Waste Oil, Canton Also Called: Emaxx Northeast Ohio LLC *(G-1886)*

Akron Centl Engrv Mold Mch Inc................................. 330 794-0704
1625 Massillon Rd Akron (44312) *(G-26)*

Akron Coca-Cola Bottling Co....................................... 330 784-2653
1560 Triplett Blvd Akron (44306) *(G-27)*

Akron Cotton Products Inc.. 330 434-7171
437 W Cedar St Akron (44307) *(G-28)*

Akron Crematory, Akron Also Called: Akron Vault Company Inc *(G-46)*

Akron Design & Costume LLC...................................... 330 644-0425
888 Tippecanoe Dr Coventry Township (44319) *(G-5479)*

Akron Dispersions Inc... 330 666-0045
3291 Sawmill Rd Copley (44321) *(G-5428)*

Akron Electric, Barberton Also Called: Akron Foundry Co *(G-791)*

Akron Equipment Company.. 330 645-3780
3522 Manchester Rd Ste B Akron (44319) *(G-29)*

Akron Felt Chenille Mfg Co Inc.................................... 330 733-7778
1671 E Market St Akron (44305) *(G-30)*

Akron Foundry Co (PA).. 330 745-3101
2728 Wingate Ave Akron (44314) *(G-31)*

Akron Foundry Co.... 330 745-3101
1025 Eagon St Barberton (44203) *(G-791)*

Akron Gasket & Packg Entps Inc................................. 330 633-3742
445 Northeast Ave Tallmadge (44278) *(G-12729)*

Akron Gear & Engineering Inc..................................... 330 773-6608
501 Morgan Ave Akron (44311) *(G-32)*

Akron Jewelry Rubber, Willoughby Also Called: Zero-D Products Inc *(G-14554)*

Akron Legal News Inc.. 330 296-7578
  60 S Summit St Akron (44308) *(G-33)*

Akron Life, Akron *Also Called: Baker Media Group LLC (G-71)*

Akron Litho-Print Company Inc................................. 330 434-3145
  1026 S Main St Akron (44311) *(G-34)*

Akron Orthotic Solutions Inc................................... 330 253-3002
  582 W Market St Akron (44303) *(G-35)*

Akron Paint & Varnish Inc...................................... 330 773-8911
  1390 Firestone Pkwy Akron (44301) *(G-36)*

Akron Plating Co Inc... 330 773-6878
  1774 Hackberry St Akron (44301) *(G-37)*

Akron Polymer Products Inc (PA).............................. 330 628-5551
  1471 Exeter Rd Akron (44306) *(G-38)*

Akron Porcelain & Plastic Co, Akron *Also Called: Akron Porcelain & Plastics Co (G-39)*

Akron Porcelain & Plastics Co (PA)........................... 330 745-2159
  2739 Cory Ave Akron (44314) *(G-39)*

Akron Products Company.. 330 576-1750
  6600 Ridge Rd Wadsworth (44281) *(G-13627)*

Akron Rebar Co (PA)... 330 745-7100
  809 W Waterloo Rd Akron (44314) *(G-40)*

Akron Special Machinery Inc (PA)............................. 330 753-1077
  2740 Cory Ave Akron (44314) *(G-41)*

Akron Steel Fabricators Co...................................... 330 644-0616
  3291 Manchester Rd Akron (44319) *(G-42)*

Akron Steel Treating Co.. 330 773-8211
  336 Morgan Ave Akron (44311) *(G-43)*

Akron Thermography Inc.. 330 896-9712
  3406 Fortuna Dr Akron (44312) *(G-44)*

Akron Thermography Inc.. 330 896-9712
  3506 Fortuna Dr Akron (44312) *(G-45)*

Akron Tool and Die, Akron *Also Called: Diamond America Corporation (G-119)*

Akron Vault Company Inc... 330 784-5475
  2399 Gilchrist Rd Akron (44305) *(G-46)*

Akzo Nobel Coatings Inc... 614 294-3361
  1313 Windsor Ave Ste 1313 Columbus (43211) *(G-4683)*

Akzo Nobel Coatings Inc... 419 433-9143
  300 Sprowl Rd Huron (44839) *(G-7866)*

Akzo Nobel Coatings Inc... 937 322-2671
  1550 Progress Rd Springfield (45505) *(G-12277)*

Akzo Nobel Paints LLC.. 440 297-8000
  8381 Pearl Rd Strongsville (44136) *(G-12533)*

Al Fe Heat Treating-Ohio Inc.................................... 330 336-0211
  979 Seville Rd Wadsworth (44281) *(G-13628)*

Al Yoder Construction Co... 330 359-5726
  3375 County Road 160 Millersburg (44654) *(G-9967)*

Al-Co Products Inc... 419 399-3867
  485 2nd St Latty (45855) *(G-8236)*

Al-Fe Heat Treating LLC.. 419 782-7200
  2066 E 2nd St Defiance (43512) *(G-6095)*

Al's Electric Motor Service, Bedford *Also Called: Als High Tech Inc (G-1010)*

Alabama Sling Center Inc... 440 239-7000
  21000 Aerospace Pkwy Cleveland (44142) *(G-3318)*

Alacriant Inc (PA).. 330 562-7191
  1760 Miller Pkwy Streetsboro (44241) *(G-12486)*

Alacriant Inc.. 330 562-7191
  2500 Crane Centre Dr Streetsboro (44241) *(G-12487)*

Alan Bortree.. 937 585-6962
  8176 State Route 508 De Graff (43318) *(G-6091)*

Alan Manufacturing Inc... 330 262-1555
  3927 E Lincoln Way Wooster (44691) *(G-14621)*

Alanod Westlake Metal Ind Inc................................. 440 327-8184
  36696 Sugar Ridge Rd North Ridgeville (44039) *(G-10723)*

Alb Tyler Holdings Inc.. 440 946-7171
  7255 Industrial Park Blvd Ste A Mentor (44060) *(G-9475)*

Alba Manufacturing Inc... 513 874-0551
  8950 Seward Rd Fairfield (45011) *(G-6708)*

Albany Screen Printing LLC...................................... 614 585-3279
  7049 Trillium Ln Reynoldsburg (43068) *(G-11555)*

Albco Foundry Inc.. 330 424-7716
  230 Maple St Lisbon (44432) *(G-8463)*

Albeco, Cleveland *Also Called: Aluminum Bearing Co of America (G-3336)*

Albert Freytag Inc.. 419 628-2018
  306 Executive Dr Minster (45865) *(G-10053)*

Albert Screenprint, Norton *Also Called: Alberts Screen Print Inc (G-10818)*

Alberts Screen Print Inc... 330 753-7559
  3704 Summit Rd Norton (44203) *(G-10818)*

Albion Industries Inc... 440 238-1955
  20246 Progress Dr Strongsville (44149) *(G-12534)*

Albion Machine & Tool Co Inc................................... 216 267-9627
  13200 Enterprise Ave Cleveland (44135) *(G-3319)*

Albright Radiator, Wooster *Also Called: Albright Radiator Inc (G-14622)*

Albright Radiator Inc... 330 264-8886
  331 N Hillcrest Dr Wooster (44691) *(G-14622)*

Alcan Corporation (HQ) 6060 Parkland Blvd Cleveland (44124) *(G-3320)*

Alcan Primary Products Corp
  6055 Rockside Woods Blvd N Ste 180 Independence (44131) *(G-7889)*

Alchem Aluminum Europe Inc.................................... 216 910-3400
  25825 Science Park Dr Ste 400 Beachwood (44122) *(G-908)*

Alchem Corporation.. 330 725-2436
  525 W Liberty St Medina (44256) *(G-9373)*

Alco, Akron *Also Called: Alco-Chem Inc (G-47)*

Alco Manufacturing Corp LLC (PA)............................ 440 458-5165
  10584 Middle Ave Elyria (44035) *(G-6493)*

Alco-Chem Inc (PA).. 330 253-3535
  45 N Summit St Akron (44308) *(G-47)*

Alcoa Titanium Engineered Pdts, Niles *Also Called: Rti International Metals Inc (G-10606)*

Alcon, Akron *Also Called: Alcon Tool Company (G-48)*

Alcon Inc (HQ)... 513 722-1037
  1132 Ferris Rd Amelia (45102) *(G-427)*

Alcon Connectors, Amelia *Also Called: Sanreed Management Group LLC (G-436)*

Alcon Industries Inc.. 216 961-1100
  7990 Baker Ave Cleveland (44102) *(G-3321)*

Alcon Tool Company... 330 773-9171
  565 Lafollette St Akron (44311) *(G-48)*

Ald Group LLC.. 440 942-9800
  34201 Melinz Pkwy Unit A Willoughby (44095) *(G-14415)*

Aldrich Chemical... 937 859-1808
  3858 Benner Rd Miamisburg (45342) *(G-9663)*

Aldridge Folders, Wadsworth *Also Called: Deshea Printing Company (G-13635)*

Aldridge Folders, Wadsworth *Also Called: Keeler Enterprises Inc (G-13646)*

Alegre Inc... 937 885-6786
  3101 W Tech Blvd Miamisburg (45342) *(G-9664)*

Alegre Global Supply Solutions, Miamisburg *Also Called: Alegre Inc (G-9664)*

Alektronics Inc... 937 429-2118
  4095 Executive Dr Beavercreek (45430) *(G-988)*

Alene Candles Midwest LLC...................................... 614 933-4005
  8860 Smiths Mill Rd Ste 100 New Albany (43054) *(G-10325)*

Aleris Rm Inc... 216 910-3400
  25825 Science Park Dr Ste 400 Beachwood (44122) *(G-909)*

Alex Products, Inc., Ridgeville Corners *Also Called: Nasg Sting Rdgvlle Corners LLC (G-11616)*

Alexander Pierce Corp.. 330 798-9840
  1874 Englewood Ave Akron (44312) *(G-49)*

Alexander Wilbert Vault Co (PA)............................... 419 468-3477
  1263 State Hwy 598 Galion (44833) *(G-7177)*

Alexis Concrete Enterprise Inc................................. 440 366-0031
  672 Sugar Ln Elyria (44035) *(G-6494)*

Alexy Metals Ltd.. 216 410-8661
  4610 Hamann Pkwy Willoughby (44094) *(G-14416)*

Alfa Green Supreme, Ottawa *Also Called: Verhoff Alfalfa Mills Inc (G-11049)*

Alfagreen Supreme, Toledo *Also Called: Ohio Blenders Inc (G-13072)*

Alfons Haar Inc... 937 560-2031
  150 Advanced Dr Springboro (45066) *(G-12246)*

Alfrebro LLC.. 513 539-7373
  1055 Reed Dr Monroe (45050) *(G-10095)*

Alfred Machine Co (HQ).. 440 248-4600
  29500 Solon Rd Cleveland (44139) *(G-3322)*

Alfred Nickles Bakery Inc.. 740 453-6522
  1147 Newark Rd Zanesville (43701) *(G-14985)*

Algix LLC... 706 207-3425
  3916 Clock Pointe Trl Ste 103 Stow (44224) *(G-12417)*

2025 Harris Ohio
Industrial Directory

(G-0000) Company's Geographic Section entry number

Ali Industries LLC.. 937 878-3946
747 E Xenia Dr Fairborn (45324) *(G-6685)*

Alimento Ventures Inc...................................... 855 510-2866
10001 Alliance Rd Blue Ash (45242) *(G-1245)*

Alin Machining Company Inc............................ 740 223-0200
875 E Mark St Marion (43302) *(G-8964)*

ALIN MACHINING COMPANY, INC., Marion *Also Called: Alin Machining Company Inc*
(G-8964)

Alkermes Inc.. 937 382-5642
265 Olinger Cir Wilmington (45177) *(G-14571)*

Alkid Corporation.. 216 896-3000
6035 Parkland Blvd Cleveland (44124) *(G-3323)*

Alkon Corporation.. 614 799-6650
6750 Crosby Ct Dublin (43016) *(G-6274)*

Alkon Corporation (PA).................................... 419 355-9111
728 Graham Dr Fremont (43420) *(G-7090)*

All - Do Weld & Fab LLC.................................. 740 477-2133
28155 River Dr Circleville (43113) *(G-3246)*

All A Cart Manufacturing Inc............................ 614 443-5544
870 High St Ste 15 Worthington (43085) *(G-14704)*

All About Plastics LLC...................................... 937 547-0098
5339 State Route 571 Greenville (45331) *(G-7333)*

All American Fire Equiptment, Wshngtn Ct Hs *Also Called: All-American Fire Eqp Inc*
(G-14734)

All Around Primo Logistics LLC........................ 513 725-7888
6027 Magnolia Woods Way Cincinnati (45247) *(G-2347)*

All Coatings Co Inc.. 330 821-3806
510 W Ely St Alliance (44601) *(G-367)*

All Craft Manufacturing Co................................ 513 661-3383
6500 Glenway Ave Side 2 Cincinnati (45211) *(G-2348)*

All Cstom Fabricators Erectors, Cleveland *Also Called: Varmland Inc (G-4458)*

All Fired Up Pnt Your Own Pot.......................... 330 865-5858
30 Rothrock Loop Copley (44321) *(G-5429)*

All Foam Pdts Safety Foam Proc, Middlefield *Also Called: All Foam Products Co (G-9779)*

All Foam Products Co (PA)................................ 330 849-3636
15005 Enterprise Way Middlefield (44062) *(G-9779)*

All Metal Fabricators Inc.................................. 216 267-0033
15400 Commerce Park Dr Cleveland (44142) *(G-3324)*

All Ohio Companies Inc.................................... 216 420-9274
2735 Scranton Rd Cleveland (44113) *(G-3325)*

All Ohio Threaded Rod Co Inc.......................... 216 426-1800
5349 Saint Clair Ave Cleveland (44103) *(G-3326)*

All Ohio Welding Inc.. 937 663-7116
3833 State Route 235 N Saint Paris (43072) *(G-11755)*

All Pack Services LLC...................................... 614 935-0964
3442 Grant Ave Grove City (43123) *(G-7370)*

All Points Printing Inc...................................... 440 585-1125
1330 Lloyd Rd Wickliffe (44092) *(G-14365)*

All Power Battery Inc.. 330 453-5236
1387 Clarendon Ave Sw Ste 6 Canton (44710) *(G-1828)*

All Power Equipment LLC (PA)........................ 740 593-3279
8880 United Ln Athens (45701) *(G-632)*

All Pro Ovrhd Door Systems LLC...................... 614 444-3667
1985 Oakland Park Ave Columbus (43224) *(G-4684)*

All Signs, Chillicothe *Also Called: All Signs of Chillicothe Inc (G-2242)*

All Signs of Chillicothe Inc.............................. 740 773-5016
12035 Pleasant Valley Rd Chillicothe (45601) *(G-2242)*

All Srvice Plastic Molding Inc.......................... 937 415-3674
611 Yellow Springs Fairfield Rd Fairborn (45324) *(G-6686)*

All Srvice Plastic Molding Inc (PA).................. 937 890-0322
850 Falls Creek Dr Vandalia (45377) *(G-13549)*

All Star Sign Company...................................... 614 461-9052
112 S Glenwood Ave Columbus (43222) *(G-4685)*

All State GL Block Fctry Inc.............................. 440 205-8410
8781 East Ave Mentor (44060) *(G-9476)*

All Streets Auto LLC.. 330 714-7717
15317 Chatfield Ave Cleveland (44111) *(G-3327)*

All Trades Contractors LLC.............................. 440 850-5693
9920 Olivet Ave Cleveland (44108) *(G-3328)*

All Ways Green Lawn & Turf LLC...................... 937 763-4766
1856 Greenbrier Rd Seaman (45679) *(G-11889)*

All Wright Enterprises LLC................................ 440 259-5656
4285 Main St Perry (44081) *(G-11190)*

All Write Ribbon Inc.. 513 753-8300
3916 Bach Buxton Rd Amelia (45102) *(G-428)*

All-American Fire Eqp Inc................................ 800 972-6035
5101 Us Highway 22 Sw Wshngtn Ct Hs (43160) *(G-14734)*

All-Craft Wellman Products, Willoughby *Also Called: Rise Holdings LLC (G-14519)*

All-In Nutritionals LLC...................................... 888 400-0333
5060 S Charleston Pike Springfield (45502) *(G-12278)*

All-Line Truck Sales, Hubbard *Also Called: Youngstown-Kenworth Inc (G-7819)*

All-Plant Liquid Plant Food, Ashland *Also Called: R & J AG Manufacturing Inc (G-568)*

All-Tech Manufacturing Ltd.............................. 330 633-1095
1477 Industrial Pkwy Akron (44310) *(G-50)*

All-Type Welding & Fabrication........................ 440 439-3990
7690 Bond St Cleveland (44139) *(G-3329)*

Allega Concrete Corp.. 216 447-0814
5146 Allega Way Richfield (44286) *(G-11587)*

Allegiance Select, Dublin *Also Called: Renascent Prtction Sltions LLC (G-6339)*

Allegion Access Tech LLC................................ 440 461-5500
5335 Avion Park Dr Cleveland (44143) *(G-3330)*

Allegra Marketing Print Mail, Blue Ash *Also Called: Dsk Imaging LLC (G-1268)*

Allen Aircraft Products Inc................................ 330 296-9621
312 E Lake St Ravenna (44266) *(G-11514)*

Allen Aircraft Products Inc................................ 330 296-1531
4879 Newton Falls Rd Ravenna (44266) *(G-11515)*

Allen Aircraft Products Inc (PA)........................ 330 296-9621
6168 Woodbine Rd Ravenna (44266) *(G-11516)*

Allen County Fabrication Inc............................ 419 227-7447
999 Industry Ave Lima (45804) *(G-8386)*

Allen Enterprises Inc.. 740 532-5913
2900 S 9th St Ironton (45638) *(G-7928)*

Allen Fields Assoc Inc...................................... 513 228-1010
3525 Grant Ave Ste D Lebanon (45036) *(G-8243)*

Allen Graphics Inc.. 440 349-4100
27100 Richmond Rd Ste 6 Solon (44139) *(G-12075)*

Allen Industries Inc.. 567 408-7538
7844 W Central Ave Toledo (43617) *(G-12869)*

Allen Randall Enterprises Inc............................ 330 374-9850
70 E Miller Ave Akron (44301) *(G-51)*

Allergan, Cincinnati *Also Called: Allergan Sales LLC (G-2349)*

Allergan Sales LLC.. 513 271-6800
5000 Brotherton Rd Cincinnati (45209) *(G-2349)*

Allergan Sales LLC.. 513 271-6800
3941 Brotherton Rd Cincinnati (45209) *(G-2350)*

Allermuir, Maumee *Also Called: Senator International Inc (G-9316)*

Alley Cat Designs Inc.. 937 291-8803
919 Oenate Dr Dayton (45459) *(G-5045)*

Allfab Inc.. 614 491-4944
2273 Williams Rd Columbus (43207) *(G-4686)*

Allgaier Process Technology.............................. 513 402-2566
9780 Windisch Rd West Chester (45069) *(G-13937)*

Allgeier & Son Inc (PA).................................... 513 574-3735
6386 Bridgetown Rd Cincinnati (45248) *(G-2351)*

Alliance Abrasives LLC.................................... 330 823-7957
23649 State Route 62 Alliance (44601) *(G-368)*

Alliance Automation LLC.................................. 419 238-2520
1100 John Brown Rd Van Wert (45891) *(G-13526)*

Alliance Carpet Cushion Co.............................. 740 966-5001
143 Commerce Blvd Johnstown (43031) *(G-7990)*

Alliance Castings Company LLC........................ 330 829-5600
1001 E Broadway St Alliance (44601) *(G-369)*

Alliance Equipment Company Inc...................... 330 821-2291
1000 N Union Ave Alliance (44601) *(G-370)*

Alliance Forging Group LLC.............................. 330 680-4861
847 Pier Dr # 1000 Akron (44307) *(G-52)*

Alliance Knife Inc.. 513 367-9000
124 May Dr Harrison (45030) *(G-7542)*

Alliance Machine Company................................ 330 823-6120
1049 S Mahoning Ave Alliance (44601) *(G-371)*

Alliance Publishing Co Inc (HQ)........................ 330 453-1304
40 S Linden Ave Alliance (44601) *(G-372)*

A L P H A B E T I C

Alliance-Mcalpin Ny LLC................................585 426-5310
  401 Elm St Clyde (43410) *(G-4556)*

Alliance, The, Reynoldsburg *Also Called: Christian Missionary Alliance (G-11562)*

Allied Coating Corporation...............................937 615-0391
  220 Fox Dr Piqua (45356) *(G-11333)*

Allied Consolidated Inds Inc (PA)......................330 744-0808
  2100 Poland Ave Youngstown (44502) *(G-14808)*

Allied Corporation Inc.....................................330 425-7861
  8920 Canyon Falls Blvd Ste 120 Twinsburg (44087) *(G-13272)*

Allied Erecting & Dismantling, Youngstown *Also Called: Allied Industrial Dev Corp (G-14809)*

Allied Fabricating & Wldg Co.............................614 868-8680
  5699 Chantry Dr Columbus (43232) *(G-4687)*

Allied Industrial Dev Corp.................................724 346-1984
  2100 Poland Ave Youngstown (44502) *(G-14809)*

Allied Machine & Engrg Corp (PA).......................330 343-4283
  120 Deeds Dr Dover (44622) *(G-6228)*

Allied Machine Works Inc..................................740 454-2534
  120 Graham St Zanesville (43701) *(G-14986)*

Allied Mask and Tooling Inc...............................419 470-2555
  6051 Telegraph Rd Ste 6 Toledo (43612) *(G-12870)*

Allied Mineral Products LLC (PA).........................614 876-0244
  2700 Scioto Pkwy Columbus (43221) *(G-4688)*

Allied Motion At Dayton....................................937 228-3171
  2275 Stanley Ave Dayton (45404) *(G-5646)*

Allied Moulded Products Inc (PA)........................419 636-4217
  222 N Union St Bryan (43506) *(G-1626)*

Allied Nutrients, Brunswick *Also Called: Turf Care Supply LLC (G-1620)*

Allied Polymers...330 975-4200
  21 Mill St Seville (44273) *(G-11909)*

Allied Separation Tech Inc.................................704 736-0420
  2300 E Enterprise Pkwy Twinsburg (44087) *(G-13273)*

Allied Separation Tech Inc (PA)..........................704 732-8034
  2300 E Enterprise Pkwy Twinsburg (44087) *(G-13274)*

Allied Shipping and Packaging Supplies Inc...........937 222-7422
  3681 Vance Rd Moraine (45439) *(G-10144)*

Allied Sign Co...614 443-9656
  818 Marion Rd Columbus (43207) *(G-4689)*

Allied Silk Screen Inc.......................................937 223-4921
  2740 Thunderhawk Ct Dayton (45414) *(G-5647)*

Allied Supplied Company, Twinsburg *Also Called: Allied Separation Tech Inc (G-13273)*

Allied Tool & Die Inc..216 941-6196
  16146 Puritas Ave Cleveland (44135) *(G-3331)*

Allied Tube & Conduit Corp................................740 928-1018
  250 Capital Dr Hebron (43025) *(G-7607)*

Alloy Engineering Company (PA)..........................440 243-6800
  844 Thacker St Berea (44017) *(G-1158)*

Alloy Extrusion Company...................................330 677-4946
  4211 Karg Industrial Pkwy Kent (44240) *(G-8016)*

Alloy Fabricators Inc.......................................330 948-3535
  700 Wooster St Lodi (44254) *(G-8498)*

Alloy Machining and Fabg Inc.............................330 482-5543
  1028 Lower Elkton Rd Columbiana (44408) *(G-4605)*

Alloy Manufacturing, Greenfield *Also Called: Skyline Material Sales LLC (G-7331)*

Alloy Precision Tech Inc....................................440 266-7700
  6989 Lindsay Dr Mentor (44060) *(G-9477)*

Alloy Welding & Fabricating...............................440 914-0650
  30340 Solon Industrial Pkwy Ste B Solon (44139) *(G-12076)*

Allpass Corporation...440 998-6300
  222 N Lake St Madison (44057) *(G-8723)*

Alltech Med Systems Amer Inc............................440 424-2240
  28900 Fountain Pkwy Ste B Solon (44139) *(G-12077)*

Allu Inc...513 624-9333
  432 Bishopsbridge Dr Cincinnati (45255) *(G-2352)*

Almira Tire & Supply Div, Olmsted Falls *Also Called: Bell Tire Co (G-10937)*

Almo Process Technology, West Chester *Also Called: Allgaier Process Technology (G-13937)*

Almondina Brand Biscuits, Maumee *Also Called: Yz Enterprises Inc (G-9331)*

Alonovus Corp..330 674-2300
  7368 County Road 623 Millersburg (44654) *(G-9968)*

Alpco, Westlake *Also Called: Aluminum Line Products Company (G-14285)*

Alpha, Hudson *Also Called: Alpha Technologies Svcs LLC (G-7828)*

Alpha Coatings Inc..419 435-5111
  622 S Corporate Dr W Fostoria (44830) *(G-6974)*

Alpha Container, Marysville *Also Called: Larsen Packaging Products Inc (G-9034)*

Alpha Control LLC...740 377-3400
  1042 County Road 60 South Point (45680) *(G-12221)*

Alpha Control Fabg & Mfg, South Point *Also Called: Alpha Control LLC (G-12221)*

Alpha Packaging Holdings Inc.............................216 252-5595
  14801 Emery Ave Cleveland (44135) *(G-3332)*

Alpha Strike, Kent *Also Called: Primal Screen Inc (G-8063)*

Alpha Technologies Svcs LLC (DH)........................330 745-1641
  6279 Hudson Crossing Pkwy Ste 200 Hudson (44236) *(G-7828)*

Alpha Tool & Mold Inc......................................440 473-2343
  83 Alpha Park Cleveland (44143) *(G-3333)*

Alpha Water Conditioning Co, Dayton *Also Called: R D Baker Enterprises Inc (G-5971)*

Alpha Zeta Holdings Inc (PA)..............................216 271-1601
  2981 Independence Rd Cleveland (44115) *(G-3334)*

Alphabet Inc (HQ)..330 856-3366
  8640 E Market St Warren (44484) *(G-13733)*

AlphaGraphics...513 204-6070
  7288 Central Parke Blvd Mason (45040) *(G-9059)*

AlphaGraphics, Cincinnati *Also Called: Banbury Investments Inc (G-2399)*

AlphaGraphics, Cleveland *Also Called: Swimmer Printing Inc (G-4357)*

AlphaGraphics, Columbus *Also Called: Headlee Enterprises Ltd (G-4641)*

AlphaGraphics, Columbus *Also Called: DC Reprographics Co (G-4873)*

AlphaGraphics, Strongsville *Also Called: AlphaGraphics 507 Inc (G-12535)*

AlphaGraphics 507 Inc......................................440 878-9700
  14765 Pearl Rd Strongsville (44136) *(G-12535)*

AlphaGraphics Cincinnati, Mason *Also Called: Morse Enterprises Inc (G-9129)*

AlphaGraphics Strongsville, Strongsville *Also Called: Blue Crescent Enterprises Inc (G-12545)*

AlphaGraphics Valley View, Cleveland *Also Called: Image Concepts Inc (G-3850)*

AlphaGraphics Westlake, Westlake *Also Called: Vision Graphix Inc (G-14342)*

Alpine Dairy LLC...330 359-6291
  1658 Township Road 660 Dundee (44624) *(G-6364)*

Alpine Gage Inc..937 669-8665
  7677 Winding Way S Tipp City (45371) *(G-12815)*

Alpla Inc...419 991-9484
  3320 Fort Shawnee Industrial Dr Lima (45806) *(G-8460)*

Alro Steel Corporation......................................614 878-7271
  555 Hilliard Rome Rd Columbus (43228) *(G-4690)*

Alro Steel Corporation......................................937 253-6121
  821 Springfield St Dayton (45403) *(G-5648)*

Alro Steel Corporation......................................419 720-5300
  3003 Airport Hwy Toledo (43609) *(G-12871)*

Alron..330 477-3405
  805 Margo Dr Sw Strasburg (44680) *(G-12475)*

Als High Tech Inc (PA)......................................440 232-7090
  135 Northfield Rd Bedford (44146) *(G-1010)*

Alsatian Llc...330 661-0600
  985 Boardman Aly Medina (44256) *(G-9374)*

Alscommunity...215 478-5095
  665 Cove Blvd Coventry Township (44319) *(G-5480)*

Alside Inc..419 865-0934
  3510 Briarfield Blvd Maumee (43537) *(G-9258)*

Alside Supply Center, Cuyahoga Falls *Also Called: Associated Materials LLC (G-5528)*

Alstart Enterprises LLC.....................................330 533-3222
  451 W Main St Canfield (44406) *(G-1803)*

Alta Mira Corporation.......................................330 648-2461
  225 N Main St Spencer (44275) *(G-12233)*

Alta Performance Materials, Columbus *Also Called: Fortis Parent Inc (G-4935)*

Altec Industries..419 289-6066
  1236 Township Road 1175 Ashland (44805) *(G-515)*

Altec Industries Inc...205 408-2341
  307 Munroe Falls Ave Cuyahoga Falls (44221) *(G-5521)*

Altenloh Brinck & Co Inc...................................419 636-6715
  2105 County Road 12c Bryan (43506) *(G-1627)*

Altenloh Brinck & Co US Inc (DH)........................419 636-6715
  2105 County Road 12c Bryan (43506) *(G-1628)*

Altenloh Brinck & Co US Inc...............................419 737-2381
  302 Clark St Pioneer (43554) *(G-11317)*

2025 Harris Ohio
Industrial Directory

(G-0000) Company's Geographic Section entry number

Alternative Surface Grinding.................................... 330 273-3443
 1093 Industrial Pkwy N Brunswick (44212) *(G-1579)*

Alterntive Sltons Innvtion Dev, Dayton *Also Called: Asidaco LLC (G-5666)*

Alterra Energy LLC.. 800 569-6061
 1200 E Waterloo Rd Akron (44306) *(G-53)*

Althar LLC.. 216 408-9860
 5432 Broadway Ave Cleveland (44127) *(G-3335)*

Altier Brothers Inc.. 740 347-4329
 155 Walnut St Corning (43730) *(G-5440)*

Altivia Petrochemicals LLC.................................... 740 532-3420
 1019 Haverhill Ohio Furnance Rd Haverhill (45636) *(G-7585)*

Altivity Packaging, Middletown *Also Called: Graphic Packaging Intl LLC (G-9863)*

Altivity Packaging, Solon *Also Called: Graphic Packaging Intl LLC (G-12118)*

Altraserv LLC... 614 889-2500
 8495 Estates Ct Plain City (43064) *(G-11393)*

Altronic LLC (DH).. 330 545-9768
 712 Trumbull Ave Girard (44420) *(G-7264)*

Aluchem Inc (PA)... 513 733-8519
 1 Landy Ln Ste 1 Cincinnati (45215) *(G-2353)*

Aluchem of Jackson Inc.. 740 286-2455
 14782 Beaver Pike Jackson (45640) *(G-7938)*

Alufab, Cincinnati *Also Called: Alufab Inc (G-2296)*

Alufab Inc... 513 528-7281
 1018 Seabrook Way Cincinnati (45245) *(G-2296)*

Alumetal Manufacturing Company............................ 419 268-2311
 4555 Sr 127 Coldwater (45828) *(G-4567)*

Aluminum Bearing Co of America............................. 216 267-8560
 4775 W 139th St Cleveland (44135) *(G-3336)*

Aluminum Color Industries Inc (PA).......................... 330 536-6295
 369 W Wood St Lowellville (44436) *(G-8657)*

Aluminum Extruded Shapes Inc............................... 513 563-2205
 10549 Reading Rd Cincinnati (45241) *(G-2354)*

Aluminum Line Products Company (PA)...................... 440 835-8880
 24460 Sperry Cir Westlake (44145) *(G-14285)*

Alumo Extrusions and Mfg Co................................. 330 779-3333
 3749 Mahoning Ave Ste 2 Youngstown (44515) *(G-14810)*

AM Castle & Co.. 330 425-7000
 26800 Miles Rd Bedford (44146) *(G-1011)*

AM Warren LLC... 330 841-2800
 2234 Main Ave. S.W. Warren (44481) *(G-13734)*

Amac Enterprises Inc... 216 362-1880
 5925 W 130th St Cleveland (44130) *(G-3337)*

Amac Enterprises Inc (PA)..................................... 216 362-1880
 5909 W 130th St Parma (44130) *(G-11129)*

Amanda Bent Bolt Company................................... 740 385-6893
 1120 C I C Dr Logan (43138) *(G-8508)*

Amanda Manufacturing, Logan *Also Called: Amanda Bent Bolt Company (G-8508)*

Amani Vines LLC... 440 335-5432
 3100 E 45th St Ste 512 Cleveland (44127) *(G-3338)*

Amano Cincinnati Incorporated............................... 513 697-9000
 130 Commerce Dr Loveland (45140) *(G-8619)*

Amano USA Holdings Inc....................................... 973 403-1900
 130 Commerce Dr Loveland (45140) *(G-8620)*

Amantea Nonwovens LLC...................................... 513 842-6600
 6715 Steger Dr Cincinnati (45237) *(G-2355)*

Amaroq Inc.. 419 747-2110
 648 N Trimble Rd Mansfield (44906) *(G-8760)*

Amatech Inc... 614 252-2506
 1633 Woodland Ave Columbus (43219) *(G-4691)*

Amatrol Inc.. 812 288-8285
 150 Industrial Dr Mansfield (44904) *(G-8761)*

Ambaflex Inc.. 330 478-1858
 1530 Raff Rd Sw Canton (44710) *(G-1829)*

Ambrosia Inc.. 419 825-3896
 395 W Airport Hwy Swanton (43558) *(G-12676)*

Ambrosia Inc.. 734 529-5024
 1680 Us Highway 20a Swanton (43558) *(G-12677)*

AMC, Wooster *Also Called: ABS Materials Inc (G-14617)*

Amcan Stair & Rail LLC.. 937 781-3084
 20 Zischler St Springfield (45504) *(G-12279)*

Amclo, North Royalton *Also Called: Amclo Group Inc (G-10754)*

Amclo Group Inc... 216 791-8400
 9721 York Alpha Dr North Royalton (44133) *(G-10754)*

Amco Products Inc.. 937 433-7982
 500 N Smithville Rd Dayton (45431) *(G-5603)*

Amcor Rigid Packaging Usa LLC............................. 419 483-4343
 975 W Main St Bellevue (44811) *(G-1118)*

Amcraft Inc.. 419 729-7900
 5144 Enterprise Blvd Toledo (43612) *(G-12872)*

Amcraft Manufacturing, Toledo *Also Called: Amcraft Inc (G-12872)*

AMD Fabricators Inc.. 440 946-8855
 4580 Beidler Rd Willoughby (44094) *(G-14417)*

AMD Plastics Inc (PA).. 216 289-4862
 27600 Lakeland Blvd Euclid (44132) *(G-6640)*

AME Nutrition Ingredients, Columbus *Also Called: Kantner Ingredients Inc (G-5045)*

Ameco USA Met Fbrction Sltons............................. 440 899-9400
 4600 W 160th St Cleveland (44135) *(G-3339)*

Amerascrew Inc.. 419 522-2232
 653 Lida St Mansfield (44903) *(G-8762)*

Ameri-Kart Corp.. 800 232-0847
 1293 S Main St Akron (44301) *(G-54)*

American Advnced Assmblies LLC........................... 937 339-6267
 37 Harolds Way Troy (45373) *(G-13199)*

American Aero Components Llc............................... 937 367-5068
 2601 W Stroop Rd Ste 62 Dayton (45439) *(G-5649)*

American Agritech LLC... 480 777-2000
 14111 Scottslawn Rd Marysville (43040) *(G-9014)*

American Alloy Corporation.................................... 216 642-9638
 9501 Allen Dr Cleveland (44125) *(G-3340)*

American Aluminum Extrusions............................... 330 458-0300
 4416 Louisville St Ne Canton (44705) *(G-1830)*

American Apex Corporation.................................... 614 652-2000
 105 Innovation Ct Ste I Delaware (43015) *(G-6130)*

American Armature Corporation............................... 419 448-1926
 980 S Morgan Ave Tiffin (44883) *(G-12773)*

American Augers, West Salem *Also Called: Charles Machine Works Inc (G-14187)*

American Axle & Mfg Inc....................................... 330 863-7500
 3255 Alliance Rd Nw Malvern (44644) *(G-8746)*

American Axle & Mfg Inc....................................... 330 868-5761
 461 Knox Ct Minerva (44657) *(G-10033)*

American Axle & Mfg Inc....................................... 330 486-3200
 8001 Bavaria Rd Twinsburg (44087) *(G-13275)*

American Baler Co... 419 483-5790
 800 E Center St Bellevue (44811) *(G-1119)*

American Belleville, Concord Township *Also Called: Zsi Manufacturing Inc (G-5398)*

American Bottling Company.................................... 330 733-3830
 1259 George Washington Blvd Akron (44312) *(G-55)*

American Bottling Company.................................... 513 381-4891
 125 E Court St Ste 820 Cincinnati (45202) *(G-2356)*

American Bottling Company.................................... 513 242-5151
 5151 Fischer Ave Cincinnati (45217) *(G-2357)*

American Bottling Company.................................... 614 237-4201
 960 Stelzer Rd Columbus (43219) *(G-4692)*

American Bottling Company.................................... 614 237-4201
 950 Stelzer Rd Columbus (43219) *(G-4693)*

American Bottling Company.................................... 937 236-0333
 3131 Transportation Rd Dayton (45404) *(G-5650)*

American Bottling Company.................................... 419 229-7777
 2350 Central Point Pkwy Lima (45804) *(G-8387)*

American Bottling Company.................................... 740 423-9230
 871 State Route 618 Little Hocking (45742) *(G-8486)*

American Bottling Company.................................... 740 922-5253
 Old Rte #250 Midvale (44653) *(G-9906)*

American Bottling Company.................................... 740 377-4371
 2531 County Road 1 South Point (45680) *(G-12222)*

American Bottling Company.................................... 419 535-0777
 224 N Byrne Rd Toledo (43607) *(G-12873)*

American Brass Mfg Co... 216 431-6565
 5000 Superior Ave Cleveland (44103) *(G-3341)*

American Brick & Block, Dayton *Also Called: American Concrete Products Inc (G-5652)*

American Bronze Corporation.................................. 216 341-7800
 2941 Broadway Ave Cleveland (44115) *(G-3342)*

A L P H A B E T I C

American Brzing Div Paulo Pdts, Willoughby *Also Called: Paulo Products Company* *(G-14505)*

American Buffing, Carlisle *Also Called: Qibco Buffing Pads Inc (G-2071)*

American Business Forms Inc.................................. 513 312-2522
10000 International Blvd West Chester (45246) *(G-14101)*

American Canvas Products Inc.................................. 419 382-8450
2925 South Ave Toledo (43609) *(G-12874)*

American Centrifuge Plant, Piketon *Also Called: Centrus Energy Corp (G-11306)*

American Ceramic Society (PA).................................. 614 890-4700
470 Olde Worthington Rd Ste 200 Westerville (43082) *(G-14202)*

American City Bus Journals Inc.................................. 513 337-9450
120 E 4th St Ste 230 Cincinnati (45202) *(G-2358)*

American City Bus Journals Inc.................................. 937 528-4400
40 N Main St Ste 810 Dayton (45423) *(G-5651)*

American Cnsld Ntral Rsrces In (PA).................................. 740 338-3100
46226 National Rd Saint Clairsville (43950) *(G-11685)*

American Cnsld Ntral Rsrces In, Saint Clairsville *Also Called: Marshall Cnty Coal Rsurces Inc* *(G-11698)*

American Coal Company.................................. 740 338-3334
46226 National Rd Saint Clairsville (43950) *(G-11686)*

American Cold Forge LLC.................................. 419 836-1062
5650 Woodville Rd Northwood (43619) *(G-10802)*

American Colors Inc (PA).................................. 419 621-4000
4602 Timber Commons Dr Sandusky (44870) *(G-11821)*

American Colorscans, Columbus *Also Called: West-Camp Press Inc (G-5362)*

American Colorscans Inc.................................. 614 895-0233
5178 Sinclair Rd Columbus (43229) *(G-4694)*

American Community Newspapers.................................. 614 888-4567
5255 Sinclair Rd Columbus (43229) *(G-4695)*

American Concrete Products Inc.................................. 937 224-1433
1433 S Euclid Ave Dayton (45417) *(G-5652)*

American Controls Inc.................................. 440 944-9735
1340 Lloyd Rd Wickliffe (44092) *(G-14366)*

American Corrugated Products Inc.................................. 614 870-2000
4700 Alkire Rd Columbus (43228) *(G-4696)*

American Countertops Inc.................................. 330 495-1915
7291 Swamp St Ne Hartville (44632) *(G-7574)*

American Coupler Systems, Kent *Also Called: ACS Industries Inc (G-8013)*

American Cube Mold Inc.................................. 330 558-0044
1636 W 130th St Brunswick (44212) *(G-1580)*

American Custom Industries, Sylvania *Also Called: Bobbart Industries Inc (G-12702)*

American De Rosa Lamparts LLC (HQ) 370 Falls Commerce Pkwy Cuyahoga Falls (44224) *(G-5522)*

American Diesel, Cleveland *Also Called: Interstate Diesel Service Inc (G-3865)*

American Egle Prprty Prsrvtion.................................. 855 440-6938
39050 Center Ridge Rd North Ridgeville (44039) *(G-10724)*

American Energy Pdts Inc Ind, Mount Vernon *Also Called: Capital City Oil Inc (G-10238)*

American Fan, Fairfield *Also Called: FM AF LLC (G-6736)*

American Fan, Fairfield *Also Called: Howden USA Company (G-6743)*

American Fan Company.................................. 513 874-2400
2933 Symmes Rd Fairfield (45014) *(G-6709)*

American Fine Sinter Co Ltd.................................. 419 443-8880
957 N Maule Rd Tiffin (44883) *(G-12774)*

American Fireworks, Hudson *Also Called: American Fireworks Inc (G-7829)*

American Fireworks Inc.................................. 330 650-1776
7041 Darrow Rd Hudson (44236) *(G-7829)*

American Fireworks Company.................................. 330 650-1776
7041 Darrow Rd Hudson (44236) *(G-7830)*

American Fluid Power Inc.................................. 877 223-8742
144 Reaser Ct Elyria (44035) *(G-6495)*

American Frame Corporation (PA).................................. 419 893-5595
400 Tomahawk Dr Maumee (43537) *(G-9259)*

American Friction Tech LLC.................................. 216 823-0861
9300 Midwest Ave Cleveland (44125) *(G-3343)*

American Gild of English Hndbe.................................. 937 438-0085
201 E 5th St Cincinnati (45202) *(G-2359)*

American Greetings, Cleveland *Also Called: American Greetings Corporation (G-3344)*

American Greetings Corporation (HQ).................................. 216 252-7300
1 American Blvd Cleveland (44145) *(G-3344)*

American Health Packaging, Columbus *Also Called: Amerisource Health Svcs LLC (G-4703)*

American Heat Treating, Dayton *Also Called: Pride Investments LLC (G-5953)*

American Heritage Blld LLC.................................. 877 998-0908
9248 Headlands Rd Mentor (44060) *(G-9478)*

American Highway Products LLC.................................. 330 874-3270
11723 Strasburg Bolivar Rd Nw Bolivar (44612) *(G-1381)*

American Hvy Plate Sltions LLC.................................. 740 331-4620
42722 State Route 7 Ste 12 Clarington (43915) *(G-3270)*

American Hydraulic Svcs Inc.................................. 606 739-8680
1912 S 1st St Ironton (45638) *(G-7929)*

American Imprssions Sportswear.................................. 614 848-6677
5523 Mercer St Columbus (43235) *(G-4697)*

American Imprssions Sportswear, Columbus *Also Called: American Imprssions Sportswear* *(G-4697)*

American Indus Maintenance.................................. 937 254-3400
605 Springfield St Dayton (45403) *(G-5653)*

American Inks and Coatings Co.................................. 513 552-7200
575 Quality Blvd Fairfield (45014) *(G-6710)*

American Insulation Tech LLC.................................. 513 733-4248
6071 Branch Hill Guinea Pike Ste A Milford (45150) *(G-9921)*

American Ir Met Cleveland LLC.................................. 216 266-0509
1240 Marquette St Cleveland (44114) *(G-3345)*

American Isostatic Presses Inc.................................. 614 497-3148
1205 S Columbus Airport Rd Columbus (43207) *(G-4698)*

American Israelite Company Inc.................................. 513 621-3145
18 W 9th St Ste 2 Cincinnati (45202) *(G-2360)*

American Israelite Newspaper, Cincinnati *Also Called: American Israelite Company Inc* *(G-2360)*

American Lawyers Co Inc (PA).................................. 440 333-5190
853 Westpoint Pkwy Ste 710 Westlake (44145) *(G-14286)*

American Lawyers Quarterly, Westlake *Also Called: American Lawyers Co Inc (G-14286)*

American Led-Gible Inc.................................. 614 851-1100
4734 Funston Ct Columbus (43232) *(G-4699)*

American Legal Publishing Corp.................................. 513 421-4248
525 Vine St Ste 300 Cincinnati (45202) *(G-2361)*

American Light Metals LLC.................................. 330 908-3065
635 Highland Rd E Macedonia (44056) *(G-8677)*

American Made Bags LLC.................................. 330 475-1385
999 Sweitzer Ave Akron (44311) *(G-56)*

American Made Crrgted Pckg Inc.................................. 937 981-2111
1100 N 5th St Greenfield (45123) *(G-7325)*

American Manufacturing Inc (PA).................................. 419 531-9471
2375 Dorr St Ste F Toledo (43607) *(G-12875)*

American Manufacturing & Eqp.................................. 513 829-2248
4990 Factory Dr Fairfield (45014) *(G-6711)*

American Metal Coatings Inc (PA).................................. 216 451-3131
7700 Tyler Blvd Mentor (44060) *(G-9479)*

American Metal Fabricators, Dayton *Also Called: Innovative Mech Systems LLC (G-5614)*

American Metal Stamping Co LLC.................................. 216 531-3100
20900 Saint Clair Ave Euclid (44117) *(G-6641)*

American Metal Treating Co.................................. 216 431-4492
1043 E 62nd St Cleveland (44103) *(G-3346)*

American Micro Products Inc (PA).................................. 513 732-2674
4288 Armstrong Blvd Batavia (45103) *(G-850)*

American Mine Door, Cleveland *Also Called: Zen Industries Inc (G-4523)*

American Mnfctring Oprtons Inc.................................. 419 269-1560
1931 E Manhattan Blvd Toledo (43608) *(G-12876)*

American Molded Plastics Inc.................................. 330 872-3838
3876 Newton Falls Bailey Rd Newton Falls (44444) *(G-10576)*

American Molding Company Inc.................................. 330 620-6799
711 Wooster Rd W Barberton (44203) *(G-792)*

American Nitrile, Grove City *Also Called: American Ntrile Operations LLC (G-7371)*

American Ntrile Operations LLC.................................. 614 425-5211
3500 Southwest Blvd Grove City (43123) *(G-7371)*

American Office Services Inc.................................. 440 899-6888
30257 Clemens Rd Ste C Westlake (44145) *(G-14287)*

American Orthopedics Inc (PA).................................. 614 291-6454
1151 W 5th Ave Columbus (43212) *(G-4700)*

American Paint Recyclers, Lima *Also Called: Brinkman LLC (G-8392)*

American Pan Company (PA).................................. 937 652-3232
417 E Water St Urbana (43078) *(G-13457)*

American Pan Company, Sunbury *Also Called: Russell T Bundy Associates Inc (G-12675)*

American Paper Group Inc.................................... 330 758-4545
8401 Southern Blvd Youngstown (44512) *(G-14811)*

American Paper Products Co Div, Youngstown *Also Called: American Paper Group Inc*
(G-14811)

American Plastech LLC....................................... 330 538-0576
11635 Mahoning Ave North Jackson (44451) *(G-10682)*

American Plastic Tech Inc.................................... 440 632-5203
15229 S State Ave Middlefield (44062) *(G-9780)*

American Plastics LLC.. 419 423-1213
814 W Lima St Findlay (45840) *(G-6836)*

American Platinum Door LLC................................ 440 497-6213
30335 Solon Industrial Pkwy Solon (44139) *(G-12078)*

American Polymers Corporation (PA)...................... 330 666-6048
231 Springside Dr Ste 145 Akron (44333) *(G-57)*

American Posts LLC.. 419 720-0652
810 Chicago St Toledo (43611) *(G-12877)*

American Power LLC.. 937 235-0418
1819 Troy St Dayton (45404) *(G-5654)*

American Power Pull Corp.................................... 419 335-7050
2022 S Defiance St Archbold (43502) *(G-485)*

American Precision Spindles................................ 267 436-6000
670 Alpha Dr Cleveland (44143) *(G-3347)*

American Printing Inc.. 330 630-1121
1121 Tower Dr Akron (44305) *(G-58)*

American Printing & Lithog Co (PA)........................ 513 867-0602
528 S 7th St Hamilton (45011) *(G-7463)*

American Publishers, Huron *Also Called: American Publishers LLC (G-7867)*

American Publishers LLC..................................... 419 626-0623
2401 Sawmill Pkwy Huron (44839) *(G-7867)*

American Punch Co... 216 731-4501
1655 Century Corners Pkwy Euclid (44132) *(G-6642)*

American Quality Stripping Inc.............................. 419 625-6288
1750 5th St Sandusky (44870) *(G-11822)*

American Quicksilver Company.............................. 513 871-4517
646 Rushton Rd Cincinnati (45226) *(G-2362)*

American Ramp Systems..................................... 440 336-4988
4327 Coe Ave North Olmsted (44070) *(G-10716)*

American Regent Inc... 614 436-2222
960 Crupper Ave Columbus (43229) *(G-4701)*

American Regent Inc... 614 436-2222
4150 Lyman Dr Hilliard (43026) *(G-7667)*

American Regent Inc... 614 436-2222
6610 New Albany Rd E New Albany (43054) *(G-10326)*

American Rescue Technology Inc........................... 937 293-6240
2780 Culver Ave Dayton (45429) *(G-5655)*

American Road Machinery Co, Canton *Also Called: Truckcorp LLC (G-2029)*

American Roll Formed Pdts Corp (DH)......................440 352-0753
3805 Hendricks Rd Ste A Youngstown (44515) *(G-14812)*

American Rubber Pdts Co Inc................................ 440 461-0900
30775 Solon Industrial Pkwy Solon (44139) *(G-12079)*

American Rugged Enclosures Inc (PA)...................... 513 942-3004
4 Standen Dr Hamilton (45015) *(G-7464)*

American Sand & Gravel Div, Massillon *Also Called: Kenmore Construction Co Inc (G-9211)*

American Scientific LLC...................................... 614 764-9002
6420 Fiesta Dr Columbus (43235) *(G-4702)*

American Solutions For Bus, West Chester *Also Called: American Business Forms Inc*
(G-14101)

American Solving Inc... 440 234-7373
6519 Eastland Rd Ste 5 Brookpark (44142) *(G-1543)*

American Spring Wire Corp (PA).............................216 292-4620
26300 Miles Rd Bedford Heights (44146) *(G-1068)*

American Standard Brands, Mansfield *Also Called: As America Inc (G-8763)*

American Steel & Alloys LLC................................ 330 847-0487
4000 Mahoning Ave Nw Warren (44483) *(G-13735)*

American Steel Assod Pdts Inc.............................. 419 531-9471
2375 Dorr St Ste F Toledo (43607) *(G-12878)*

American Steel Grave Vault Co.............................. 419 468-6715
799 Newberry Dr Galion (44833) *(G-7178)*

American Steel Treating Inc................................. 419 874-2044
29200 Glenwood Rd Perrysburg (43551) *(G-11202)*

American Sterilizer Company (PA)........................... 440 392-8328
5960 Heisley Rd Mentor (44060) *(G-9480)*

American Stirrup, Holmesville *Also Called: Holmes Wheel Shop Inc (G-7800)*

American Tank & Fabricating Co (PA)....................... 216 252-1500
12314 Elmwood Ave Cleveland (44111) *(G-3348)*

American Tchnical Coatings Inc............................. 440 401-2270
28045 Ranney Pkwy Westlake (44145) *(G-14288)*

American Thermal Instrs Inc (PA)........................... 937 429-2114
2400 E River Rd Moraine (45439) *(G-10145)*

American Tool and Die Inc................................... 419 726-5394
2024 Champlain St Toledo (43611) *(G-12879)*

American Tool Works Inc..................................... 513 844-6363
160 Hancock Ave Hamilton (45011) *(G-7465)*

American Trim, Lima *Also Called: Superior Metal Products Inc (G-8454)*

American Trim LLC (HQ)...................................... 419 228-1145
1005 W Grand Ave Lima (45801) *(G-8388)*

American Trim LLC... 419 228-1145
1501 Michigan St Ste 1 Sidney (45365) *(G-11991)*

American Trim LLC... 419 738-9664
713 Maple St Wapakoneta (45895) *(G-13705)*

American Turf Recycling LLC................................ 440 323-0306
860 Taylor St Elyria (44035) *(G-6496)*

American Ultra Specialties Inc.............................. 330 656-5000
6855 Industrial Pkwy Hudson (44236) *(G-7831)*

American Utility Proc LLC.................................... 330 535-3000
1246 Princeton St Akron (44301) *(G-59)*

American Veneer Edgebanding Co........................... 740 928-2700
1700 James Pkwy Heath (43056) *(G-7592)*

American Water Services Inc................................ 440 243-9840
17449 W Sprague Rd Strongsville (44136) *(G-12536)*

American Way Exteriors LLC................................. 937 221-8860
900 E Franklin St Dayton (45459) *(G-5656)*

American Way Manufacturing Inc........................... 330 824-2353
1871 Henn Pkwy Sw Warren (44481) *(G-13736)*

American Wire & Cable Company (PA)...................... 440 235-1140
7951 Bronson Rd Olmsted Twp (44138) *(G-10944)*

American Wood Fibers Inc................................... 740 420-3233
2500 Owens Rd Circleville (43113) *(G-3247)*

AMERICAN WOOD FIBERS, INC., Circleville *Also Called: American Wood Fibers Inc (G-3247)*

Americana Development Inc................................. 330 633-3278
342 West Ave Tallmadge (44278) *(G-12730)*

Americana Glass Co Inc...................................... 330 938-6135
356 E Maryland Ave Sebring (44672) *(G-11890)*

Americas Components, Springfield *Also Called: Konecranes Inc (G-12337)*

Americas Mdular Off Specialist.............................. 614 277-0216
4423 Broadway Ste A Grove City (43123) *(G-7372)*

Americas Styrenics LLC...................................... 740 302-8667
925 County Road 1a Ironton (45638) *(G-7930)*

Americhem, Cuyahoga Falls *Also Called: Americhem Inc (G-5524)*

Americhem Inc (PA).. 330 929-4213
2000 Americhem Way Cuyahoga Falls (44221) *(G-5523)*

Americhem Inc... 330 926-3185
155 E Steels Corners Rd Cuyahoga Falls (44224) *(G-5524)*

Americlean 2 LLC.. 216 781-3720
2061 Gehring Ave Cleveland (44113) *(G-3349)*

Americraft Bronze Co, Waterville *Also Called: Maumee Valley Memorials Inc (G-13839)*

Americraft Mfg Co Inc....................................... 513 489-1047
7937 School Rd Cincinnati (45249) *(G-2363)*

Ameridian Specialty Services............................... 513 769-0150
11520 Rockfield Ct Cincinnati (45241) *(G-2364)*

Amerihua Intl Entps Inc...................................... 740 549-0300
707 Radio Dr Lewis Center (43035) *(G-8321)*

Amerimold Inc... 800 950-8020
595 Waterloo Rd Ste A Mogadore (44260) *(G-10069)*

Amerimulch, Independence *Also Called: Chromascape LLC (G-7892)*

Amerisource Health Svcs LLC............................... 614 492-8177
2550 John Glenn Ave Ste A Columbus (43217) *(G-4703)*

Ameritech Publishing Inc.................................... 614 895-6123
2550 Corporate Exchange Dr Ste 310 Columbus (43231) *(G-4704)*

Ameritech Publishing Inc.................................... 330 896-6037
1530 Corporate Woods Pkwy Ste 100 Uniontown (44685) *(G-13416)*

Ameriwater LLC.. 937 461-8833
3345 Stop 8 Rd Dayton (45414) *(G-5657)*

A
L
P
H
A
B
E
T
I
C

Ameriwood Industries, Tiffin *Also Called: Dorel Home Furnishings Inc (G-12782)*

Ames Companies Inc.. 740 783-2535
21460 Ames Ln Dexter City (45727) *(G-6223)*

Ametco Manufacturing Corp................................. 440 951-4300
4326 Hamann Pkwy Willoughby (44094) *(G-14418)*

Ametek Inc.. 302 636-5401
875 Dearborn Dr Columbus (43085) *(G-4705)*

Ametek Inc.. 937 440-0800
66 Industry Ct Ste F Troy (45373) *(G-13200)*

Ametek Aerospace & Defense, Columbus *Also Called: Ametek Inc (G-4705)*

Ametek Electromechanical Group, Kent *Also Called: Ametek Tchnical Indus Pdts Inc (G-8017)*

Ametek HDR Power Systems, Worthington *Also Called: HDR Power Systems LLC (G-14712)*

Ametek Micro-Poise Measurement, Streetsboro *Also Called: Micro-Pise Msrment Systems LLC (G-12510)*

Ametek Presto Light Power, Troy *Also Called: Ametek Inc (G-13200)*

Ametek Solidstate Controls, Columbus *Also Called: Solidstate Controls LLC (G-5274)*

Ametek Tchnical Indus Pdts Inc (HQ)........................ 330 673-3451
100 E Erie St Ste 130 Kent (44240) *(G-8017)*

Amex Dies Inc.. 330 545-9766
932 N State St Girard (44420) *(G-7265)*

AMF Burns.. 330 650-6500
1797 Georgetown Rd Hudson (44236) *(G-7832)*

Amfm Inc... 440 953-4545
38373 Pelton Rd Willoughby (44094) *(G-14419)*

AMG Aluminum, Cambridge *Also Called: AMG Aluminum North America LLC (G-1735)*

AMG Aluminum North America LLC (HQ)........................ 659 348-3620
60790 Southgate Rd Cambridge (43725) *(G-1735)*

AMG Industries Inc... 740 397-4044
300 Commerce Dr Mount Vernon (43050) *(G-10232)*

AMG Industries LLC... 740 397-4044
200 Commerce Dr Mount Vernon (43050) *(G-10233)*

AMG Products LLC.. 614 507-7749
1375 Newark Rd Mount Vernon (43050) *(G-10234)*

AMG Trailer and Equipment, Akron *Also Called: Martin Allen Trailer LLC (G-223)*

Amgen Inc.. 805 447-1000
4150 Ganton Pkwy New Albany (43054) *(G-10327)*

Amh Holdings II Inc.. 330 929-1811
3773 State Rd Cuyahoga Falls (44223) *(G-5525)*

Amherst Party Shop, Amherst *Also Called: Currier Richard & James (G-445)*

Amir Foods Inc... 440 646-9388
761 Beta Dr Ste A Cleveland (44143) *(G-3350)*

Amir International Foods Inc................................ 614 332-1742
3504 Broadway Grove City (43123) *(G-7373)*

Amish Door Inc (PA).. 330 359-5464
1210 Winesburg St Wilmot (44689) *(G-14592)*

Amish Door Restaurant, Wilmot *Also Called: Amish Door Inc (G-14592)*

Amish Heritg WD Floors & Furn, Middlefield *Also Called: Cherokee Hardwoods Inc (G-9787)*

Amish Wedding Foods Inc................................... 330 674-9199
316 S Mad Anthony St Millersburg (44654) *(G-9969)*

Amko Service Company (DH)................................. 330 364-8857
3211 Brightwood Rd Midvale (44653) *(G-9907)*

Amko Service Company, Midvale *Also Called: Fiba Technologies Inc (G-9909)*

Aml Industries Inc... 330 399-5000
520 Pine Ave Se Ste 1 Warren (44483) *(G-13737)*

Amos Media Company (PA)................................... 937 498-2121
1660 Campbell Rd Ste A Sidney (45365) *(G-11992)*

AMP Plastics of Ohio LLC
1815 Magda Dr Montpelier (43543) *(G-10126)*

Ampac, Cincinnati *Also Called: Ampac Packaging LLC (G-2366)*

Ampac, Cincinnati *Also Called: Ampac Plastics LLC (G-2367)*

Ampac Holdings LLC (HQ)................................... 513 671-1777
12025 Tricon Rd Cincinnati (45246) *(G-2365)*

Ampac Packaging LLC (HQ).................................. 513 671-1777
12025 Tricon Rd Cincinnati (45246) *(G-2366)*

Ampac Plastics LLC... 513 671-1777
12025 Tricon Rd Cincinnati (45246) *(G-2367)*

Ampacet Corporation....................................... 513 247-5400
4705 Duke Dr # 400 Cincinnati (45249) *(G-2368)*

Ampacet Corporation....................................... 513 247-5403
4705 Duke Dr Ste 400 Mason (45040) *(G-9060)*

Ampacet Corporation....................................... 740 929-5521
1855 James Pkwy Newark (43056) *(G-10490)*

Ampak, Cleveland *Also Called: Heat Seal LLC (G-3816)*

Ampex Metal Products Company (PA)......................... 216 267-9242
5581 W 164th St Brookpark (44142) *(G-1544)*

Ampp, Perrysburg *Also Called: Ampp Incorporated (G-11203)*

Ampp Incorporated... 419 666-4747
28271 Cedar Park Blvd Ste 5 Perrysburg (43551) *(G-11203)*

Ampsco Division... 614 444-2181
2301 Fairwood Ave Columbus (43207) *(G-4706)*

Amptech Machining & Welding.............................. 419 652-3444
910 County Road 40 Nova (44859) *(G-10875)*

Amresco, LLC, Solon *Also Called: VWR Part of Avantor (G-12205)*

Amrican Spring Wire, Bedford Heights *Also Called: Aswpengg LLC (G-1069)*

Amrod Bridge & Iron LLC
105 Ohio Ave Mc Donald (44437) *(G-9357)*

Amros Industries Inc....................................... 216 433-0010
14701 Industrial Pkwy Cleveland (44135) *(G-3351)*

AMS, Strongsville *Also Called: Automated Mfg Solutions Inc (G-12541)*

AMS Global Ltd.. 937 620-1036
119 E Dayton St West Alexandria (45381) *(G-13916)*

Amsive OH LLC... 937 885-8000
3303 W Tech Blvd Miamisburg (45342) *(G-9665)*

Amsoil Inc... 614 274-9851
3389 Urbancrest Industrial Dr Urbancrest (43123) *(G-13482)*

Amsted Industries Incorporated............................. 614 836-2323
3900 Bixby Rd Groveport (43125) *(G-7422)*

Amt, Brecksville *Also Called: Applied Medical Technology Inc (G-1457)*

Amt Machine Systems Limited............................... 740 965-2693
1760 Zollinger Rd Ste 2 Columbus (43221) *(G-4707)*

Amtech Tool & Machine Inc................................. 330 758-8215
100 Mcclurg Rd Youngstown (44512) *(G-14813)*

Amtekco, Columbus *Also Called: Amtekco Industries LLC (G-4708)*

Amtekco Industries LLC (HQ)............................... 614 228-6590
2300 Lockbourne Rd Columbus (43207) *(G-4708)*

Amtekco Industries Inc.................................... 614 228-6525
33 W Hinman Ave Columbus (43207) *(G-4709)*

AMTEKCO INDUSTRIES INC, Columbus *Also Called: Amtekco Industries Inc (G-4709)*

Amthor Steel Inc... 330 759-0200
5019 Belmont Ave Youngstown (44505) *(G-14814)*

Amylin Ohio... 512 592-8710
8814 Trade Port Dr West Chester (45011) *(G-13938)*

Anadem Inc.. 614 262-2539
3620 N High St Ste 201 Columbus (43214) *(G-4710)*

Anaheim Manufacturing Company............................ 800 767-6293
25300 Al Moen Dr North Olmsted (44070) *(G-10717)*

Analiza Inc (PA)... 216 432-9050
3615 Superior Ave E Ste 4407b Cleveland (44114) *(G-3352)*

Analytica Usa Inc (PA)..................................... 513 348-2333
711 E Monument Ave Ste 309 Dayton (45402) *(G-5658)*

Anatomical Concepts Inc................................... 330 757-3569
1399 E Western Reserve Rd Youngstown (44514) *(G-14815)*

Anchi Inc.. 740 653-2527
1115 W 5th Ave Lancaster (43130) *(G-8175)*

Anchor Die Technologies, Cleveland *Also Called: Condor Tool & Die Inc (G-3558)*

Anchor Fabricators Inc..................................... 937 836-5117
386 Talmadge Rd Clayton (45315) *(G-3271)*

Anchor Flange Company (PA)................................ 513 527-3512
5553 Murray Ave Cincinnati (45227) *(G-2369)*

Anchor Fluid Power, Cincinnati *Also Called: Anchor Flange Company (G-2369)*

Anchor Glass Container Corp................................ 740 452-2743
1206 Brandywine Blvd Ste C Zanesville (43701) *(G-14987)*

Anchor Hocking, Lancaster *Also Called: Anchi Inc (G-8175)*

Anchor Hocking LLC (HQ).................................. 740 687-2500
1600 Dublin Rd Ste 200 Columbus (43215) *(G-4711)*

Anchor Hocking Company, The, Columbus *Also Called: Anchor Hocking LLC (G-4711)*

Anchor Hocking Consmr GL Corp............................ 740 653-2527
1115 W 5th Ave Lancaster (43130) *(G-8176)*

Anchor Hocking Corporation................................ 614 633-4247
1600 Dublin Rd Columbus (43215) *(G-4712)*

2025 Harris Ohio
Industrial Directory

(G-0000) Company's Geographic Section entry number

Anchor Hocking Holdings Inc (PA)................................ 740 687-2500
1600 Dublin Rd Ste 200 Columbus (43215) *(G-4713)*

Anchor Hocking Indus GL Div, Lancaster Also Called: Ghp II LLC *(G-8204)*

Anchor Industries Incorporated.................................... 440 473-1414
30775 Solon Industrial Pkwy Cleveland (44139) *(G-3353)*

Anchor Lamina America Inc.. 330 952-1595
445 W Liberty St Medina (44256) *(G-9375)*

Anchor Manufacturing Group, Cleveland Also Called: Anchor Tool & Die Co *(G-3356)*

Anchor Metal Processing Inc.. 216 362-6463
12200 Brookpark Rd Cleveland (44130) *(G-3354)*

Anchor Metal Processing Inc (PA)................................... 216 362-1850
11830 Brookpark Rd Cleveland (44130) *(G-3355)*

Anchor Pattern Company.. 614 443-2221
748 Frebis Ave Columbus (43206) *(G-4714)*

Anchor Tool & Die Co... 216 362-1850
12200 Brookpark Rd Cleveland (44130) *(G-3356)*

Ancom Business Products, Medina Also Called: Symatic Inc *(G-9452)*

Andal Woodworking... 330 897-8059
1411 Township Road 151 Baltic (43804) *(G-775)*

Andeavor Logistics LP (DH)... 419 421-2414
200 E Hardin St Findlay (45840) *(G-6837)*

Andeen-Hagerling Inc... 440 349-0370
31200 Bainbridge Rd Ste 2 Cleveland (44139) *(G-3357)*

Andelyn Biosciences Inc (HQ).. 844 228-2366
1180 Arthur E Adams Dr Columbus (43221) *(G-4715)*

Andelyn Biosciences Inc.. 614 332-0554
5185 Blazer Pkwy Dublin (43017) *(G-6275)*

Andelyn Development Center, Dublin Also Called: Andelyn Biosciences Inc *(G-6275)*

Anderson & Vreeland Inc.. 419 636-5002
15348 Us Highway 127 Ew Bryan (43506) *(G-1629)*

Anderson Brothers Entps Inc... 440 269-3920
38180 Airport Pkwy Willoughby (44094) *(G-14420)*

Anderson Concrete Corp.. 614 443-0123
400 Frank Rd Columbus (43207) *(G-4716)*

Anderson Door Co... 216 475-5700
18090 Miles Rd Cleveland (44128) *(G-3358)*

Anderson Glass Co Inc... 614 476-4877
2816 Morse Rd Columbus (43231) *(G-4717)*

Anderson Graphics Inc... 330 745-2165
711 Wooster Rd W Barberton (44203) *(G-793)*

Anderson International Corp... 216 641-1112
4545 Boyce Pkwy Stow (44224) *(G-12418)*

Anderson Pallet & Packg Inc... 937 962-2614
210 Western Ave Lewisburg (45338) *(G-8358)*

Anderson Pallet Service, Lewisburg Also Called: Anderson Pallet & Packg Inc *(G-8358)*

Anderson Vreeland Midwest, Bryan Also Called: Anderson & Vreeland Inc *(G-1629)*

Andersons Inc... 419 891-2900
415 Illinois Ave Maumee (43537) *(G-9260)*

Andersons Inc (PA)... 419 893-5050
1947 Briarfield Blvd Maumee (43537) *(G-9261)*

Andersons Inc... 419 243-6800
125 Edwin Dr Toledo (43609) *(G-12880)*

Andersons Inc... 419 536-0460
801 S Reynolds Rd Toledo (43615) *(G-12881)*

Andersons Mrathon Holdings LLC................................... 937 316-3700
5728 Sebring Warner Rd N Greenville (45331) *(G-7334)*

Andersons, The, Maumee Also Called: Andersons Inc *(G-9261)*

Andersound PA Service... 216 401-4631
15911 Harvard Ave Cleveland (44128) *(G-3359)*

Andre Corporation.. 574 293-0207
4600 N Mason Montgomery Rd Mason (45040) *(G-9061)*

Andrin Enterprises Inc.. 937 276-7794
3350 Kettering Blvd Moraine (45439) *(G-10146)*

Andritz Inc.. 513 677-5620
6680 Miami Woods Dr Loveland (45140) *(G-8621)*

Andys Mdterranean Fd Pdts LLC..................................... 513 281-9791
906 Nassau St Cincinnati (45206) *(G-2370)*

Anest Iwata Usa Inc.. 513 755-3100
10148 Commerce Park Dr West Chester (45246) *(G-14102)*

Angel Prtg & Reproduction Co... 216 631-5225
1400 W 57th St Cleveland (44102) *(G-3360)*

Angelic Bakehouse LLC... 414 312-7300
380 Polaris Pkwy Ste 110 Westerville (43082) *(G-14203)*

Angelic Bakehouse, Inc., Westerville Also Called: Angelic Bakehouse LLC *(G-14203)*

Angels Landing Inc... 513 687-3681
3430 S Dixie Dr Ste 301 Moraine (45439) *(G-10147)*

Angleboard, Loveland Also Called: Signode Industrial Group LLC *(G-8653)*

Angstrom Fiber Englewood LLC (PA).............................. 734 756-1164
300 Lau Pkwy Englewood (45315) *(G-6607)*

Angstrom Precision Metals LLC....................................... 440 255-6700
8229 Tyler Blvd Mentor (44060) *(G-9481)*

Anheuser-Busch, Columbus Also Called: Anheuser-Busch LLC *(G-4718)*

Anheuser-Busch LLC.. 614 847-6213
700 Schrock Rd Columbus (43229) *(G-4718)*

Anime Palace.. 408 858-1918
8185 Green Meadows Dr N Ste M Lewis Center (43035) *(G-8322)*

Ankim Enterprises Incorporated...................................... 937 599-1121
2005 Campbell Rd Sidney (45365) *(G-11993)*

Annarino Foods Ltd.. 937 274-3663
2787 Armstrong Ln Dayton (45414) *(G-5659)*

Annin & Co.. 740 498-5008
100 State Route 258 Newcomerstown (43832) *(G-10568)*

Annin & Co Inc.. 740 622-4447
700 S 3rd St Coshocton (43812) *(G-5447)*

ANNIN & CO., Newcomerstown Also Called: Annin & Co *(G-10568)*

Anodizing Specialists Inc... 440 951-0257
7547 Tyler Blvd Mentor (44060) *(G-9482)*

Anomatic Corporation (DH).. 740 522-2203
8880 Innovation Campus Way New Albany (43054) *(G-10328)*

Anomatic Corporation... 740 522-2203
1650 Tamarack Rd Newark (43055) *(G-10491)*

Anomatic Opportunity, New Albany Also Called: Anomatic Corporation *(G-10328)*

Anotex Industries Inc.. 513 860-1165
4914 Rialto Rd West Chester (45069) *(G-13939)*

Ansco Machine Company.. 330 929-8181
60 Cuyahoga Falls Industrial Pkwy Peninsula (44264) *(G-11180)*

Ansell Edmont Div, Coshocton Also Called: Ansell Healthcare Products LLC *(G-5448)*

Ansell Healthcare Products LLC...................................... 740 622-4369
925 Chestnut St Coshocton (43812) *(G-5448)*

Ansell Healthcare Products LLC...................................... 740 622-4311
925 Chestnut St Coshocton (43812) *(G-5449)*

Antero Resources Corporation.. 303 357-7310
44510 Marietta Rd Caldwell (43724) *(G-1722)*

Antero Resources Corporation.. 740 760-1000
27841 State Route 7 Marietta (45750) *(G-8901)*

Anthony Flottemesch & Son Inc....................................... 513 561-1212
8201 Camargo Rd Ste 1 Cincinnati (45243) *(G-2371)*

Anthony Mining Co Inc... 740 282-3301
72 Airport Rd Wintersville (43953) *(G-14610)*

Anthony-Thomas Candy Company (PA)........................... 614 274-8405
1777 Arlingate Ln Columbus (43228) *(G-4719)*

Anthony-Thomas Candy Shoppes, Columbus Also Called: Anthony-Thomas Candy Company *(G-4719)*

Antique Auto Sheet Metal Inc.. 937 833-4422
718 Albert Rd Brookville (45309) *(G-1562)*

Antique Power, Yellow Springs Also Called: Ertel Publishing Inc *(G-14788)*

Antwerp TI Die & Engrg Co Inc.. 419 258-5271
3167 County Road 424 Antwerp (45813) *(G-461)*

Anza Inc.. 513 542-7337
3265 Colerain Ave Ste 2 Cincinnati (45225) *(G-2372)*

Aog Inc.. 937 436-2412
7672 Mcewen Rd Dayton (45459) *(G-5660)*

Aot LLC... 937 323-9669
4800 Gateway Blvd Springfield (45502) *(G-12280)*

Aot Inc., Springfield Also Called: Aot LLC *(G-12280)*

AP Direct, Mentor Also Called: Activities Press Inc *(G-9469)*

AP Services LLC... 216 267-3200
18001 Sheldon Rd Middleburg Heights (44130) *(G-9766)*

AP Tech Group Inc.. 513 761-8111
5130 Rialto Rd West Chester (45069) *(G-13940)*

Apache Acquisitions LLC... 419 782-8003
1008 Jackson Ave Defiance (43512) *(G-6096)*

A
L
P
H
A
B
E
T
I
C

Apackaging Group Ohio Inc.................................419 785-8600
25925 Commerce Dr Defiance (43512) *(G-6097)*

APD, Mentor *Also Called: Air Power Dynamics LLC (G-9473)*

Apeks LLC...740 809-1174
31 Greenscape Ct Johnstown (43031) *(G-7991)*

Apeks Supercritical, Johnstown *Also Called: Apeks LLC (G-7991)*

Apera Instruments LLC.....................................614 285-3080
6656 Busch Blvd Columbus (43229) *(G-4720)*

Apex Advanced Technologies LLC........................216 898-1595
4857 W 130th St A Cleveland (44135) *(G-3361)*

Apex Aluminum Die Cast Co Inc.........................937 773-0432
8877 Sherry Dr Piqua (45356) *(G-11334)*

Apex Bag Company, Wapakoneta *Also Called: Brady Ruck Company (G-13708)*

Apex Bag Company, Wapakoneta *Also Called: Gateway Packaging Company LLC (G-13713)*

Apex Bolt & Machine Company............................419 729-3741
5324 Enterprise Blvd Toledo (43612) *(G-12882)*

Apex Bulk Handlers, Bedford *Also Called: Apex Welding Incorporated (G-1012)*

Apex Cabinetry, Cincinnati *Also Called: Apex Cabinetry Inc (G-2373)*

Apex Cabinetry Inc...513 832-7905
4536 W Mitchell Ave Cincinnati (45232) *(G-2373)*

Apex Control Systems Inc..................................330 938-2588
751 N Johnson Rd Sebring (44672) *(G-11891)*

Apex Metal Fabricating & Mch, Toledo *Also Called: Apex Bolt & Machine Company (G-12882)*

Apex Metals, Cleveland *Also Called: Erieview Metal Treating Co (G-3685)*

Apex Signs Inc...330 952-2626
2755 Medina Rd Medina (44256) *(G-9376)*

Apex Specialty Co Inc......................................330 725-6663
620 E Smith Rd Ste E7 Medina (44256) *(G-9377)*

Apex Tool Group LLC.......................................937 222-7871
762 W Stewart St Dayton (45417) *(G-5661)*

Apex Welding Incorporated................................440 232-6770
1 Industry Dr Bedford (44146) *(G-1012)*

Apf Legacy Subs LLC (DH)................................513 682-7173
9990 Princeton Glendale Rd West Chester (45246) *(G-14103)*

API Pattern Works Inc......................................440 269-1766
4456 Hamann Pkwy Willoughby (44094) *(G-14421)*

Apogee Plastics Corp.......................................937 864-1966
8300 Dayton Springfield Rd Fairborn (45324) *(G-6687)*

Apollo GL Mirror Win Screen Co, Cincinnati *Also Called: Dale Kestler (G-2540)*

Apollo Manufacturing Co LLC.............................440 951-9972
7911 Enterprise Dr Mentor (44060) *(G-9483)*

Apollo Plastics Inc..440 951-7774
7555 Tyler Blvd Ste 11 Mentor (44060) *(G-9484)*

Apollo Products Inc...440 269-8551
4456 Hamann Pkwy Willoughby (44094) *(G-14422)*

Apollo Welding & Fabg Inc (PA)..........................440 942-0227
35600 Curtis Blvd Willoughby (44095) *(G-14423)*

Apowermedia, Dayton *Also Called: American Power LLC (G-5654)*

Appalachia Freeze Dry Co LLC...........................740 412-0169
659 Jackson St Richmond Dale (45673) *(G-11606)*

Appalachian Fuels LLC (PA)..............................606 928-0460
6375 Riverside Dr Ste 200 Dublin (43017) *(G-6276)*

Appalachian Oilfield Svcs LLC............................337 216-0066
34602 State Route 7 Sardis (43946) *(G-11887)*

Appalachian Well Surveys Inc............................740 255-7652
10291 Ohio Ave Cambridge (43725) *(G-1736)*

Appetzers R US St Eats 2 Go LL.........................937 460-1470
2019 Ontario Ave Springfield (45505) *(G-12281)*

Apph, Strongsville *Also Called: Apph Wichita Inc (G-12537)*

Apph Wichita Inc..316 943-5752
15900 Foltz Pkwy Strongsville (44149) *(G-12537)*

Appian Manufacturing Corp................................614 445-2230
2025 Camaro Ave Columbus (43207) *(G-4721)*

Appleheart, Miamisburg *Also Called: Appleheart Inc (G-9666)*

Appleheart Inc...937 384-0430
2240 E Central Ave Miamisburg (45342) *(G-9666)*

Application Link Incorporated.............................614 934-1735
4449 Easton Way Fl 2 Columbus (43219) *(G-4722)*

Applied Automation Entp Inc..............................419 929-2428
24 Cedar St New London (44851) *(G-10410)*

Applied Collegiate Systems Div, Hudson *Also Called: Griffin Technology Inc (G-7842)*

Applied Energy Tech Inc....................................419 537-9052
1720 Indian Wood Cir Ste E Maumee (43537) *(G-9262)*

Applied Engneered Surfaces Inc..........................440 366-0440
535 Ternes Ln Rear Elyria (44035) *(G-6497)*

Applied Experience Inc.....................................614 943-2970
7780 Corporate Blvd Ste 82 Plain City (43064) *(G-11394)*

Applied Marketing Services Inc (HQ).....................440 716-9962
28825 Ranney Pkwy Westlake (44145) *(G-14289)*

Applied Materials Finshg Ltd..............................330 336-5645
1040 Valley Belt Rd Brooklyn Heights (44131) *(G-1527)*

Applied Medical Technology Inc (PA).....................440 717-4000
8006 Katherine Blvd Brecksville (44141) *(G-1457)*

Applied Metals Tech Ltd....................................216 741-3236
1040 Valley Belt Rd Brooklyn Heights (44131) *(G-1528)*

Applied Sciences Inc.......................................937 766-2020
141 W Xenia Ave Cedarville (45314) *(G-2097)*

Applied Specialties Innovations LLC......................440 933-9442
33555 Pin Oak Pkwy Avon Lake (44012) *(G-746)*

Applied Vision Corporation (PA)..........................330 926-2222
2020 Vision Ln Cuyahoga Falls (44223) *(G-5526)*

Approved Plbg & Sewer Clg Co, Cleveland *Also Called: Approved Plumbing Co (G-3362)*

Approved Plumbing Co......................................216 663-5063
770 Ken Mar Industrial Pkwy Cleveland (44147) *(G-3362)*

Appvion Inc (PA)..937 859-8262
1030 W Alex Bell Rd West Carrollton (45449) *(G-13926)*

Apr Tool Inc..440 946-0393
4712 Beidler Rd Ste A Willoughby (44094) *(G-14424)*

Aprecia Pharmaceuticals LLC (HQ).......................513 984-5000
7200 Industrial Row Dr Ste 200 Mason (45040) *(G-9062)*

Aps-Materials Inc (PA)......................................937 278-6547
4011 Riverside Dr Dayton (45405) *(G-5662)*

Aps-Materials Inc...937 278-6547
314 Leo St Dayton (45404) *(G-5663)*

Apsx LLC...513 716-5992
11121 Kenwood Rd Blue Ash (45242) *(G-1246)*

APT Manufacturing Solutions, Hicksville *Also Called: A & P Tool Inc (G-7644)*

Aptiv Services Us LLC......................................330 367-6000
3400 Aero Park Dr Vienna (44473) *(G-13607)*

Aptiv Services Us LLC......................................330 373-7614
1265 N River Rd Ne Warren (44483) *(G-13738)*

Aptiv Services Us LLC......................................330 373-3568
1265 N River Rd Ne # Fr11 Warren (44483) *(G-13739)*

Aptiv Services Us LLC......................................330 505-3150
1265 N River Rd Ne Warren (44483) *(G-13740)*

Aptiv Services Us LLC......................................330 306-1000
4551 Research Pkwy Nw Warren (44483) *(G-13741)*

Aptyx, Miamisburg *Also Called: Mdi of Ohio Inc (G-9711)*

APV Engineered Coatings, Akron *Also Called: Akron Paint & Varnish Inc (G-36)*

Aqua Lily Products LLC.....................................951 322-0981
4505 Beidler Rd Willoughby (44094) *(G-14425)*

Aqua Marine Supply, Millersport *Also Called: Hefty Hoist Inc (G-10023)*

Aqua Ohio, Mentor On The Lake *Also Called: Aqua Pennsylvania Inc (G-9656)*

Aqua Ohio Inc...740 867-8700
32 Private Drive 11100 Chesapeake (45619) *(G-2228)*

Aqua Pennsylvania Inc......................................440 257-6190
7748 Twilight Dr Mentor On The Lake (44060) *(G-9656)*

Aqua Precision LLC...937 912-9582
165 Janney Rd Dayton (45404) *(G-5664)*

Aqua Science Inc..614 252-5000
1877 E 17th Ave Columbus (43219) *(G-4723)*

Aqua Technology Group LLC..............................513 298-1183
8104 Beckett Center Dr West Chester (45069) *(G-13941)*

Aquablok Ltd...419 402-4170
230 W Airport Hwy Swanton (43558) *(G-12678)*

Aquablok Ltd (PA)...419 825-1325
175 Woodland Ave Ste A Swanton (43558) *(G-12679)*

Aquablue Incorporated......................................330 343-0220
1776 Tech Park Dr Ne New Philadelphia (44663) *(G-10430)*

Aquapro Systems LLC.......................................877 278-2797
223 Telford Ave Oakwood (45419) *(G-10895)*

Aquatic Technology.................................... 440 236-8330
26966 Royalton Rd Columbia Station (44028) *(G-4588)*

Aquila Pharmatech LLC.............................. 419 386-2527
8225 Farnsworth Rd Ste A7 Waterville (43566) *(G-13830)*

Aracor, Fairborn *Also Called: Rapiscan Systems High Enrgy In (G-6698)*

Aramsco Inc Plsboro NJ Rdnor P, Lima *Also Called: EZ Concrete Supply LLC (G-8407)*

Arbenz Inc.. 614 274-6800
1777 Mckinley Ave Columbus (43222) *(G-4724)*

Arbor Foods Inc....................................... 419 698-4442
3332 Saint Lawrence Dr Bldg C Toledo (43605) *(G-12883)*

Arbor Industries Inc.................................. 440 255-4720
6830 Patterson Dr Mentor (44060) *(G-9485)*

Arboris LLC.. 740 522-9350
1780 Tamarack Rd Newark (43055) *(G-10492)*

Arbortech, Wooster *Also Called: Stahl/Scott Fetzer Company (G-14689)*

ARC Abrasives Inc.................................... 800 888-4885
2131 Corporate Dr Troy (45373) *(G-13201)*

ARC Drilling Inc (PA)................................ 216 525-0920
9551 Corporate Cir Cleveland (44125) *(G-3363)*

ARC Metal Stamping LLC............................ 517 448-8954
447 E Walnut St Wauseon (43567) *(G-13845)*

ARC Rubber Inc....................................... 440 466-4555
100 Water St Geneva (44041) *(G-7233)*

ARC Solutions, Hicksville *Also Called: ARC Solutions LLC (G-7646)*

ARC Solutions LLC................................... 419 542-9272
605 Industrial Dr Hicksville (43526) *(G-7646)*

Arcadian Ohio, Lima *Also Called: Pcs Nitrogen Inc (G-8437)*

Arcani Coil Care, Trotwood *Also Called: Crownme Coil Care LLC (G-13195)*

Arcelormittal Tubular Pdts USA, Shelby *Also Called: Arcelrmttal Tblar Pdts Shlby L (G-11966)*

Arcelormittal Warren, Warren *Also Called: AM Warren LLC (G-13734)*

Arcelrmttal Tblar Pdts Shlby L.................... 419 347-2424
132 W Main St Shelby (44875) *(G-11966)*

Arcelrmttal Tblar Pdts USA LLC................... 419 347-2424
132 W Main St Shelby (44875) *(G-11967)*

Arch Cutng Tls Cincinnati LLC..................... 513 851-6363
133 Circle Freeway Dr West Chester (45246) *(G-14104)*

Arch Cutting Tls - Mentor LLC..................... 440 350-9393
9332 Pinecone Dr Mentor (44060) *(G-9486)*

Arch Polymers, Marysville *Also Called: Triple Arrow Industries Inc (G-9054)*

Archbold Buckeye Inc................................ 419 445-4466
207 N Defiance St Archbold (43502) *(G-486)*

Archbold Container Corp............................ 800 446-2520
800 W Barre Rd Archbold (43502) *(G-487)*

Archbold Furniture Co............................... 567 444-4666
733 W Barre Rd Archbold (43502) *(G-488)*

Archem America Inc (DH)........................... 419 294-6304
245 Commerce Way Upper Sandusky (43351) *(G-13433)*

Archer Corporation................................... 330 455-9995
1917 Henry Ave Sw Canton (44706) *(G-1831)*

Archer Counter Design Inc.......................... 513 396-7526
4433 Verne Ave Cincinnati (45209) *(G-2374)*

Archer Publishing LLC.............................. 440 338-5233
27101 E Oviatt Rd Bay Village (44140) *(G-899)*

Archer Sign, Canton *Also Called: Archer Corporation (G-1831)*

Archer-Daniels-Midland Company................ 419 435-6633
608 Findlay St Fostoria (44830) *(G-6975)*

Archer-Daniels-Midland Company................ 330 852-3025
554 Pleasant Valley Rd Nw Sugarcreek (44681) *(G-12631)*

Archer-Daniels-Midland Company................ 419 705-3292
1308 Miami St Toledo (43605) *(G-12884)*

Architctral Identification Inc (PA)................ 614 868-8400
1170 Claycraft Rd Gahanna (43230) *(G-7154)*

Architctral Indus Met Fnshg LL.................... 440 963-0410
1091 Sunnyside Rd Vermilion (44089) *(G-13588)*

Architctral Mllwk Cbinetry Inc.................... 440 708-0086
16715 W Park Circle Dr Chagrin Falls (44023) *(G-2155)*

Architechual Etc, Cortland *Also Called: Lawbre Co (G-5446)*

Architectural Busstrut Corp........................ 614 933-8695
4311 Brompton Ct New Albany (43054) *(G-10329)*

Architectural Fiberglass Inc........................ 216 641-8300
8300 Bessemer Ave Cleveland (44127) *(G-3364)*

Architectural Metal Maint, Cleves *Also Called: Metal Maintenance Inc (G-4544)*

Archoustics Mid-America, Cincinnati *Also Called: Holland Assocts LLC DBA Archou (G-2727)*

Arclin USA LLC....................................... 419 726-5013
6175 American Rd Toledo (43612) *(G-12885)*

Arconic... 330 471-1844
1935 Warner Rd Se Canton (44707) *(G-1832)*

Arctech Fabricating Inc (PA)....................... 937 525-9353
1317 Lagonda Ave Springfield (45503) *(G-12282)*

Arctos Mission Solutions LLC..................... 813 609-5591
2601 Mission Point Blvd Beavercreek (45431) *(G-965)*

Arden J Neer Sr....................................... 937 585-6733
4859 Township Road 45 Bellefontaine (43311) *(G-1099)*

ARE Inc... 330 830-7800
400 Nave Rd Sw Massillon (44646) *(G-9172)*

Area 419, Delta *Also Called: Area 419 Firearms LLC (G-6201)*

Area 419 Firearms LLC.............................. 419 830-8353
4750 County Road 5 Delta (43515) *(G-6201)*

Arem Co.. 440 974-6740
34188 Euclid Ave Willoughby (44094) *(G-14426)*

Arena Eye Surgeons, Columbus *Also Called: Eye Surgery Center Ohio Inc (G-4917)*

Arens Corporation (PA).............................. 937 473-2028
395 S High St Covington (45318) *(G-5488)*

Arens Corporation................................... 937 473-2028
22 N High St Covington (45318) *(G-5489)*

Arens Publications & Printing, Covington *Also Called: Arens Corporation (G-5489)*

Ares Inc... 419 635-2175
818 Front St Lake Erie Business Park Port Clinton (43452) *(G-11439)*

Ares Sportswear Ltd................................. 614 767-1950
3700 Lacon Rd Ste A Hilliard (43026) *(G-7668)*

Areway, Cleveland *Also Called: Epsilon Management Corporation (G-3681)*

Areway Acquisition Inc.............................. 216 651-9022
8525 Clinton Rd Brooklyn (44144) *(G-1519)*

Areway LLC.. 216 651-9022
8525 Clinton Rd Brooklyn (44144) *(G-1520)*

Arf, Youngstown *Also Called: American Roll Formed Pdts Corp (G-14812)*

Argo Tech Fluid Elec Dist Div, Cleveland *Also Called: Eaton Industrial Corporation (G-3657)*

ARI Phoenix Inc (PA)................................ 513 229-3750
11163 Woodward Ln Sharonville (45241) *(G-11945)*

Ariel Corporation.................................... 330 896-2660
3360 Miller Park Rd Akron (44312) *(G-60)*

Ariel Corporation.................................... 740 397-0311
8405 Blackjack Rd Mount Vernon (43050) *(G-10235)*

Ariel Corporation (PA).............................. 740 397-0311
35 Blackjack Road Ext Mount Vernon (43050) *(G-10236)*

Ariezhair Collection LLC............................ 614 964-5748
1747 Olentangy River Rd Columbus (43212) *(G-4725)*

Arisdyne Systems Inc................................ 216 458-1991
17830 Englewood Dr Ste 11 Cleveland (44130) *(G-3365)*

Arizona Beverages, Cincinnati *Also Called: Hornell Brewing Co Inc (G-2732)*

Arkay Industries Inc (PA)........................... 513 360-0390
240 American Way Monroe (45050) *(G-10096)*

Arkay Plastics Alabama Inc (HQ).................. 513 360-0390
220 American Way Monroe (45050) *(G-10097)*

Arku Inc (HQ)... 513 985-0500
7251 E Kemper Rd Cincinnati (45249) *(G-2375)*

Arlington Rack & Packaging Co.................... 419 476-7700
6120 N Detroit Ave Toledo (43612) *(G-12886)*

Arlington Valley Farms LLC (PA).................. 216 426-5000
5369 Hudson Dr Hudson (44236) *(G-7833)*

Arlington-Blaine Lumber Co, Delaware *Also Called: Khempco Bldg Sup Co Ltd Partnr (G-6159)*

ARM (usa) Inc... 740 264-6599
1506 Fernwood Rd Wintersville (43953) *(G-14611)*

Arm & Hammer, London *Also Called: Church & Dwight Co Inc (G-8533)*

Armaly Brands, London *Also Called: Armaly LLC (G-8530)*

Armaly LLC.. 740 852-3621
110 W 1st St London (43140) *(G-8530)*

Armature Coil Equipment Inc....................... 216 267-6366
22269 Horseshoe Ln Strongsville (44149) *(G-12538)*

Armco Inc.. 740 829-3000
17400 State Route 16 Coshocton (43812) *(G-5450)*

Armoloy of Ohio Inc.. 937 323-8702
1950 E Leffel Ln Springfield (45505) *(G-12283)*

Armor... 614 459-1414
2218 Bristol Rd Columbus (43221) *(G-4726)*

Armor Aftermarket Inc.. 513 923-5600
4600 N Mason Montgomery Rd Oh Mason (45040) *(G-9063)*

Armor Consolidated Inc (PA)...................................... 513 923-5260
4600 N Mason Montgomery Rd Mason (45040) *(G-9064)*

Armor Contract Manufacturing, Mason Also Called: The Armor Group Inc *(G-9161)*

Armor Metal Group Elkhart Inc.................................... 800 672-6373
4600 N Mason Montgomery Rd Mason (45040) *(G-9065)*

Armor Metal Group Mason Inc (HQ).............................. 513 769-0700
4600 N Mason Montgomery Rd Mason (45040) *(G-9066)*

Armormetal, Mason Also Called: Armor Metal Group Mason Inc *(G-9066)*

Armorsource LLC.. 740 928-0070
3600 Hebron Rd Hebron (43025) *(G-7608)*

Armour Spray Systems Inc... 216 398-3838
210 Hayes Dr Ste I Cleveland (44131) *(G-3366)*

Armstrong Custom Moulding Inc................................... 740 922-5931
6408 State Route 800 Se Uhrichsville (44683) *(G-13401)*

Armstrong Stationery Co Corp..................................... 513 891-0667
10235 Spartan Dr Ste G Cincinnati (45215) *(G-2376)*

Armstrong World, Hilliard Also Called: Armstrong World Industries Inc *(G-7669)*

Armstrong World Industries Inc................................... 614 771-9307
4241 Leap Rd Bldg A Hilliard (43026) *(G-7669)*

Arnco Corporation.. 800 847-7661
860 Garden St Elyria (44035) *(G-6498)*

Arnett Tool Inc... 937 437-0361
217 W Main St New Paris (45347) *(G-10425)*

Arnold Company, Valley City Also Called: Arnold Corporation *(G-13489)*

Arnold Corporation.. 330 225-2600
5965 Grafton Rd Valley City (44280) *(G-13489)*

Arnold Gauge Co Inc (PA).. 877 942-4243
9823 Harwood Ct West Chester (45014) *(G-13942)*

Arnold Machine, Tiffin Also Called: Arnold Machine Inc *(G-12775)*

Arnold Machine Inc.. 419 443-1818
19 Heritage Dr Tiffin (44883) *(G-12775)*

Arnold Magnetic Technologies, Marietta Also Called: Flexmag Industries Inc *(G-8917)*

Arnold Printing Co, Cincinnati Also Called: Earl D Arnold Printing Company *(G-2574)*

Arnold's Candies, Akron Also Called: Dauphin Holdings Inc *(G-116)*

Aromair Fine Fragrance Company.................................. 614 984-2900
8860 Smiths Mill Rd Ste 500 New Albany (43054) *(G-10330)*

Arps Dairy Inc.. 419 782-9116
136 Fox Run Dr Defiance (43512) *(G-6098)*

Arrow International Inc (PA)....................................... 216 961-3500
9900 Clinton Rd Cleveland (44144) *(G-3367)*

Arrow Print & Copy, Sylvania Also Called: Kevin K Tidd *(G-12714)*

Arrow Tru-Line Inc (PA).. 419 446-2785
2211 S Defiance St Archbold (43502) *(G-489)*

Arrow Tru-Line Inc... 419 636-7013
720 E Perry St Bryan (43506) *(G-1630)*

Arrowhead Industries, Cleveland Also Called: Scovil Hanna LLC *(G-4281)*

ARS Recycling Systems LLC (PA).................................. 330 536-8210
4000 Mccartney Rd Lowellville (44436) *(G-8658)*

ARS Recycling Systems 2019 LLC................................. 330 536-8210
4000 Mccartney Rd Lowellville (44436) *(G-8659)*

Arsco Custom Metals LLC... 513 385-0555
3330 E Kemper Rd Cincinnati (45241) *(G-2377)*

Arsco Manufacturing Company, Cincinnati Also Called: Arsco Custom Metals LLC *(G-2377)*

Art Galvanizing Works Inc.. 216 749-0020
3935 Valley Rd Cleveland (44109) *(G-3368)*

Art Guild Binders Inc... 513 242-3000
1068 Meta Dr Cincinnati (45237) *(G-2378)*

Art Iron Inc... 419 241-1261
860 Curtis St Toledo (43609) *(G-12887)*

Art Metals Group, Hamilton Also Called: Art Technologies LLC *(G-7466)*

Art Tech, Chillicothe Also Called: McRd Enterprises LLC *(G-2265)*

Art Technologies LLC... 513 942-8800
3795 Symmes Rd Hamilton (45015) *(G-7466)*

Art Woodworking & Mfg Co.. 513 681-2986
4238 Dane Ave Cincinnati (45223) *(G-2379)*

Art Works.. 740 425-5765
119 E Pike St Barnesville (43713) *(G-843)*

Arte Limited, Cleveland Also Called: Lawrence Industries Inc *(G-3947)*

Artesian of Pioneer Inc (PA)...................................... 419 737-2352
50 Industrial Ave Pioneer (43554) *(G-11318)*

Artex Oil Company.. 740 373-3313
2337 State Route 821 Marietta (45750) *(G-8902)*

Arthur Corporation... 419 433-7202
1305 Huron Avery Rd Huron (44839) *(G-7868)*

Arthur Louis Steel Co, Geneva Also Called: Louis Arthur Steel Company *(G-7242)*

Artiflex Manufacturing Inc (HQ)................................... 330 262-2015
1425 E Bowman St Wooster (44691) *(G-14623)*

Artisan Ales LLC.. 216 544-8703
17448 Lorain Ave Cleveland (44111) *(G-3369)*

Artisan Constructors LLC... 216 800-7641
600 Superior Ave E Cleveland (44114) *(G-3370)*

Artisan Equipment Inc.. 740 756-9135
5770 Winchester Rd Carroll (43112) *(G-2073)*

Artisan Grinding Service Inc....................................... 937 667-7383
1300 Stanley Ave Dayton (45404) *(G-5665)*

Artisan Renovations, Cleveland Also Called: Artisan Constructors LLC *(G-3370)*

Artisan Tool & Die Corp.. 216 883-2769
4911 Grant Ave Cleveland (44125) *(G-3371)*

Artistic Finishes Inc... 440 951-7850
38357 Apollo Pkwy Willoughby (44094) *(G-14427)*

Artistic Metal Spinning Inc.. 216 961-3336
4700 Lorain Ave Cleveland (44102) *(G-3372)*

Arvinmrtor Commerical Vhcl Sys, Granville Also Called: Meritor Inc *(G-7317)*

Arzel Technology Inc... 216 831-6068
4801 Commerce Pkwy Cleveland (44128) *(G-3373)*

Arzel Zoning Technology, Cleveland Also Called: Arzel Technology Inc *(G-3373)*

As America Inc.. 419 522-4211
41 Cairns Rd Mansfield (44903) *(G-8763)*

As America Inc.. 330 332-9954
605 S Ellsworth Ave Salem (44460) *(G-11762)*

As Clean As It Gets Off Brkroo.................................... 216 256-1143
4099 Lowden Rd South Euclid (44121) *(G-12218)*

ASAP, Moraine Also Called: Allied Shipping and Packaging Supplies Inc *(G-10144)*

ASC, North Canton Also Called: ASC Industries Inc *(G-10628)*

ASC Industries Inc (DH).. 800 253-6009
2100 International Pkwy North Canton (44720) *(G-10628)*

Ascendtech Inc.. 216 458-1101
4772 E 355th St Willoughby (44094) *(G-14428)*

Ascents, Cleveland Also Called: Aeroscena LLC *(G-3311)*

Asco Power Technologies LP... 216 573-7600
6255 Halle Dr Cleveland (44125) *(G-3374)*

Ascon Tecnologic, Cleveland Also Called: Ascon Tecnologic N Amer LLC *(G-3375)*

Ascon Tecnologic N Amer LLC....................................... 216 485-8350
1111 Brookpark Rd Cleveland (44109) *(G-3375)*

Ascot Valley Foods Ltd... 330 376-9411
205 Ascot Pkwy Cuyahoga Falls (44223) *(G-5527)*

ASG... 216 486-6163
15700 S Waterloo Rd Cleveland (44110) *(G-3376)*

Asg Division Jergens Inc... 888 486-6163
15700 S Waterloo Rd Jergens Way Cleveland (44110) *(G-3377)*

Ash Sewer & Drain Service.. 330 376-9714
451 E North St Akron (44304) *(G-61)*

Ashcraft Machine & Supply Inc..................................... 740 349-8110
185 Wilson St Newark (43055) *(G-10493)*

Ashland Chemco Inc... 216 961-4690
2191 W 110th St Cleveland (44102) *(G-3378)*

Ashland Chemco Inc... 614 790-3333
1979 Atlas St Columbus (43228) *(G-4727)*

Ashland Conveyor Products, Ashland Also Called: Midwest Conveyor Products Inc *(G-552)*

Ashland Distribution, Columbus Also Called: Ashland Chemco Inc *(G-4727)*

Ashland Precision Tooling LLC...................................... 419 289-1736
1750 S Baney Rd Ashland (44805) *(G-516)*

Ashland Publishing Co... 419 281-0581
40 E 2nd St Ashland (44805) *(G-517)*

Ashland Spcalty Ingredients GP.................................... 614 529-3311
1979 Atlas St Columbus (43228) *(G-4728)*

Ashland Times Gazette, Ashland *Also Called: Ashland Publishing Co (G-517)*

Ashland Water Group Inc (PA)..............................877 326-3561
1191 Commerce Pkwy Ashland (44805) *(G-518)*

Ashley F Ward Inc (PA)..513 398-1414
7490 Easy St Mason (45040) *(G-9067)*

Ashta Forge & Machine Inc....................................216 252-7000
3001 W 121st St Cleveland (44111) *(G-3379)*

Ashton Custom Prtg & Gift Sp, Pickerington *Also Called: Ashton LLC (G-11288)*

Ashton LLC (PA)...336 447-4951
77 E Columbus St Pickerington (43147) *(G-11287)*

Ashton LLC...614 833-4165
77 E Columbus St Pickerington (43147) *(G-11288)*

Asi Chemical Company, Avon Lake *Also Called: Applied Specialties Innovations LLC (G-746)*

Asi Sign Systems, Loveland *Also Called: Kmgrafx Inc (G-8635)*

Asi Visual Display Pdts Inc....................................330 308-8667
2301 E High Ave New Philadelphia (44663) *(G-10431)*

Asia For Kids, Cincinnati *Also Called: Master Communications Inc (G-2849)*

Asidaco LLC (PA)..800 204-1544
400 Linden Ave Ste 95 Dayton (45403) *(G-5666)*

Asist Translation Services.....................................614 451-6744
4891 Sawmill Rd Ste 200 Columbus (43235) *(G-4729)*

Asist Translation Services, Columbus *Also Called: Asist Translation Services (G-4729)*

Ask Chemicals, Cleveland *Also Called: Ashland Chemco Inc (G-3378)*

ASK Chemicals LLC...800 848-7485
495 Metro Pl S Dublin (43017) *(G-6277)*

Aslan Worldwide...513 671-0671
8583 Rupp Farm Dr West Chester (45069) *(G-13943)*

Asm International..440 338-5151
9639 Kinsman Rd Novelty (44073) *(G-10879)*

Aspec Inc...513 561-9922
5810 Carothers St Cincinnati (45227) *(G-2380)*

Aspen Machine and Plastics..................................937 526-4644
257 Baker Rd Versailles (45380) *(G-13592)*

Asphalt, Cincinnati *Also Called: Valley Asphalt Corporation (G-3191)*

Asphalt Fabrics & Specialties................................440 786-1077
7710 Bond St Solon (44139) *(G-12080)*

Aspra Industrial LLC..216 459-9200
1311 Brookpark Rd Cleveland (44109) *(G-3380)*

Assa Abloy Entrnce Systems HLA..........................419 294-3373
295 Commerce Way Upper Sandusky (43351) *(G-13434)*

Assembleis Co, Mansfield *Also Called: Mansfield Engineered Components LLC (G-8819)*

Assembly Division, Walbridge *Also Called: Riverside Mch & Automtn Inc (G-13687)*

Assembly Machining Wire Pdts................................614 443-1110
2375 Refugee Park Columbus (43207) *(G-4730)*

Assembly Specialty Pdts Inc..................................216 676-5600
14700 Brookpark Rd Cleveland (44135) *(G-3381)*

Assembly Tool Specialists, Twinsburg *Also Called: Production Tl Co Cleveland Inc (G-13360)*

Assembly Works Inc...419 433-5010
1705 Sawmill Pkwy Huron (44839) *(G-7869)*

Assembly Works Matrix Automtn, Huron *Also Called: Assembly Works Inc (G-7869)*

Assetwatch Inc..844 464-5652
60 Collegeview Rd Westerville (43081) *(G-14243)*

Associated Associates Inc.....................................330 626-3300
9551 Elliman Rd Mantua (44255) *(G-8867)*

Associated Hygienic Pdts LLC...............................770 497-9800
2332 Us Highway 42 S Delaware (43015) *(G-6131)*

Associated Materials LLC (PA)..............................330 929-1811
3773 State Rd Cuyahoga Falls (44223) *(G-5528)*

Associated Materials Group Inc (PA)......................330 929-1811
3773 State Rd Cuyahoga Falls (44223) *(G-5529)*

Associated Mtls Holdings LLC...............................330 929-1811
3773 State Rd Cuyahoga Falls (44223) *(G-5530)*

Associated Plastics Corp.......................................419 634-3910
502 Eric Wolber Dr Ada (45810) *(G-3)*

Associated Premium Corporation...........................513 679-4444
1870 Summit Rd Cincinnati (45237) *(G-2381)*

Associated Press Repair Inc..................................216 881-2288
7547 Brigham Rd Gates Mills (44040) *(G-7229)*

Associated Ready Mix Concrete, Mantua *Also Called: Associated Associates Inc (G-8867)*

Associated Software Cons Inc................................440 826-1010
1101 Forest Rd Lakewood (44107) *(G-8162)*

Associated Technical Sales, Franklin *Also Called: Gad-Jets Investments Inc (G-7023)*

Associates Tire and Svc Inc..................................937 436-4692
1099 S Main St Centerville (45458) *(G-2129)*

Assocted Vsual Cmmncations Inc...........................330 452-4449
7000 Firestone Ave Ne Canton (44721) *(G-1833)*

Aster Industries Inc...330 762-7965
275 N Arlington St Ste B Akron (44305) *(G-62)*

Asterion LLC..317 875-0051
3630 E Kemper Rd Cincinnati (45241) *(G-2382)*

Astrazeneca Pharmaceuticals LP...........................513 645-2600
8814 Trade Port Dr West Chester (45011) *(G-13944)*

Astro Aluminum Enterprises Inc.............................330 755-1414
65 Main St Struthers (44471) *(G-12616)*

Astro Industries Inc...937 429-5900
4403 Dayton Xenia Rd Beavercreek (45432) *(G-966)*

Astro Manufacturing & Design, Eastlake *Also Called: Astro Manufacturing & Design Inc (G-6417)*

Astro Manufacturing & Design Inc (PA)...................888 215-1746
34459 Curtis Blvd Eastlake (44095) *(G-6417)*

Astro Met Inc (PA)...513 772-1242
9974 Springfield Pike Cincinnati (45215) *(G-2383)*

Astro Model Development Corp...............................440 946-8855
34459 Curtis Blvd Eastlake (44095) *(G-6418)*

Astro Technical Services Inc..................................330 394-4747
2401 Parkman Rd Nw Warren (44485) *(G-13742)*

Astro-Coatings Inc..330 755-1414
65 Main St Struthers (44471) *(G-12617)*

Astro-TEC Mfg Inc...330 854-2209
550 Elm Ridge Ave Canal Fulton (44614) *(G-1772)*

Asw, Bedford Heights *Also Called: American Spring Wire Corp (G-1068)*

Aswpengg LLC...216 292-4620
26300 Miles Rd Bedford Heights (44146) *(G-1069)*

At Holdings Corporation...216 692-6000
23555 Euclid Ave Cleveland (44117) *(G-3382)*

AT&f Advanced Metals LLC (PA)............................330 684-1122
12314 Elmwood Ave Cleveland (44111) *(G-3383)*

AT&f Advanced Metals LLC.....................................330 684-1122
95 N Swinehart Rd Orrville (44667) *(G-10973)*

AT&T, Cincinnati *Also Called: AT&T Enterprises LLC (G-2384)*

AT&T Enterprises LLC...513 792-9300
7875 Montgomery Rd Ofc Cincinnati (45236) *(G-2384)*

Ata Tools Inc...330 928-7744
7 Ascot Pkwy Cuyahoga Falls (44223) *(G-5531)*

Atalys Ottoville LLC (HQ)......................................419 453-3376
14223 Rd 24 Ottoville (45876) *(G-11052)*

Atc Group Inc (PA)...440 293-4064
101 Parker Dr Andover (44003) *(G-455)*

Atc Legacy Inc...330 590-8105
1441 Wolf Creek Trail Sharon Center (44274) *(G-11936)*

Atc Lighting & Plastics, Andover *Also Called: Atc Group Inc (G-455)*

Atc Lighting & Plastics Inc (HQ)............................440 466-7670
101 Parker Dr Andover (44003) *(G-456)*

Atchley Signs & Graphics LLC...............................614 421-7446
1616 Transamerica Ct Columbus (43228) *(G-4731)*

Atcpc of Ohio LLC...330 670-9900
1055 Home Ave Akron (44310) *(G-63)*

Atech Fire Services, West Chester *Also Called: Total Life Safety LLC (G-14083)*

Athens Foods Inc...216 676-8500
13600 Snow Rd Cleveland (44142) *(G-3384)*

Athens Messenger, The, Athens *Also Called: Messenger Publishing Company (G-644)*

Athens Mold and Machine Inc................................740 593-6613
180 Mill St Athens (45701) *(G-633)*

Athens Technical Specialists..................................740 592-2874
8157 Us Highway 50 Athens (45701) *(G-634)*

ATI, Batavia *Also Called: Auto Temp Inc (G-851)*

ATI, Toledo *Also Called: Abbott Tool Inc (G-12861)*

ATI Flat Rlled Pdts Hldngs LLC.............................330 875-2244
1500 W Main St Louisville (44641) *(G-8598)*

ATI Flat Rolled Products, Louisville *Also Called: ATI Flat Rlled Pdts Hldngs LLC (G-8598)*

Atk Space Systems LLC...937 490-4121
1365 Technology Ct Beavercreek (45430) *(G-989)*

Atk Systems................................937 429-8632
1365 Technology Ct Beavercreek (45430) *(G-990)*

Atkins Custom Framing Ltd....................740 816-1501
3116 Troy Rd Delaware (43015) *(G-6132)*

Atlantic and Prfmce Rigging, Tiffin Also Called: Tiffin Scenic Studios Inc *(G-12805)*

Atlantic Co..................................440 944-8988
26651 Curtiss Wright Pkwy Willoughby Hills (44092) *(G-14555)*

Atlantic Inertial Systems Inc.................740 788-3800
781 Irving Wick Dr W Ste 01 Heath (43056) *(G-7593)*

Atlantic Sign Company Inc....................513 383-1504
2328 Florence Ave Cincinnati (45206) *(G-2385)*

Atlantic Tool & Die Company (PA).............440 238-6931
19963 Progress Dr Strongsville (44149) *(G-12539)*

Atlantic Veal & Lamb LLC.....................330 435-6400
2416 E West Salem Rd Creston (44217) *(G-5505)*

Atlantic Water Gardens, Aurora Also Called: Meridienne International Inc *(G-679)*

Atlantic Welding LLC.........................937 570-5094
1708 Commerce Dr Piqua (45356) *(G-11335)*

Atlantis Sportswear Inc......................937 773-0680
344 Fox Dr Piqua (45356) *(G-11336)*

Atlas Bolt & Screw Company LLC (DH)..........419 289-6171
1628 Troy Rd Ashland (44805) *(G-519)*

Atlas Dowel & Wood Products Co, Harrison Also Called: Puttmann Industries Inc *(G-7563)*

Atlas Fasteners For Cnstr, Ashland Also Called: Atlas Bolt & Screw Company LLC *(G-519)*

Atlas Industrial Contractors, Columbus Also Called: Atlas Industrial Contrs LLC *(G-4732)*

Atlas Industrial Contrs LLC (HQ).............614 841-4500
5275 Sinclair Rd Columbus (43229) *(G-4732)*

Atlas Industries Inc.........................419 355-1000
1750 E State St Fremont (43420) *(G-7091)*

Atlas Machine and Supply Inc.................502 584-7262
8556 Trade Center Dr # 250 Hamilton (45011) *(G-7467)*

Atlas Machine Products Co....................216 228-3688
44800 Us Highway 20 Oberlin (44074) *(G-10914)*

Atlas Portable Space Solutions, Oberlin Also Called: Atlas Machine Products Co *(G-10914)*

Atlas Roofing Corporation....................937 746-9941
675 Oxford Rd Franklin (45005) *(G-7010)*

Atlas Vac, Cincinnati Also Called: Atlas Vac Machine Co LLC *(G-2386)*

Atlas Vac Machine Co LLC.....................513 407-3513
9150 Reading Rd Cincinnati (45215) *(G-2386)*

Atm Nerds LLC................................614 983-3056
175 S 3rd St Ste 200 Columbus (43215) *(G-4733)*

Atmos 360 A Systems Solutions, West Chester Also Called: Atmos360 Inc *(G-14105)*

Atmos360 Inc.................................513 772-4777
4690 Interstate Dr Ste A West Chester (45246) *(G-14105)*

Atmosphere Annealing LLC.....................330 478-0314
1501 Raff Rd Sw Kenton (43326) *(G-8095)*

Atom Blasting and Finshg Inc.................440 235-4765
24933 Sprague Rd Columbia Station (44028) *(G-4589)*

Atotech Usa LLC..............................216 398-0550
1000 Harvard Ave Cleveland (44109) *(G-3385)*

Atr Automation, Cincinnati Also Called: Atr Distributing Company *(G-2387)*

Atr Distributing Company (PA)................513 353-1800
11857 Kemper Springs Dr Cincinnati (45240) *(G-2387)*

Atr Distributing Company.....................513 353-1800
11857 Kemper Springs Dr Cincinnati (45240) *(G-2388)*

Atra Metal Spinning Inc......................440 354-9525
572 S Saint Clair St Painesville (44077) *(G-11067)*

ATRICURE, Mason Also Called: Atricure Inc *(G-9068)*

Atricure Inc (PA)............................513 755-4100
7555 Innovation Way Mason (45040) *(G-9068)*

Atrium At Anna Maria Inc.....................330 562-7777
849 N Aurora Rd Aurora (44202) *(G-661)*

Atrium Centers Inc...........................513 830-5014
1400 Mallard Cove Dr Cincinnati (45246) *(G-2389)*

Ats Machine & Tool Co........................440 255-1120
37033 Lake Shore Blvd Eastlake (44095) *(G-6419)*

Ats Ohio Inc.................................614 888-2344
7115 Green Meadows Dr Lewis Center (43035) *(G-8323)*

Ats Systems Oregon Inc.......................541 738-0932
425 Enterprise Dr Lewis Center (43035) *(G-8324)*

Atsi, Athens Also Called: Athens Technical Specialists *(G-634)*

Attends Healthcare Pdts Inc..................740 368-7880
2332 Us Highway 42 S Delaware (43015) *(G-6133)*

Attindas Hygiene Partners, Delaware Also Called: Attends Healthcare Pdts Inc *(G-6133)*

Atv Insider..................................740 282-7102
742 Sunshine Park Rd Steubenville (43953) *(G-12399)*

ATW, Hamilton Also Called: American Tool Works Inc *(G-7465)*

Atwood Mobile Products LLC...................419 258-5531
5406 County Road 424 Antwerp (45813) *(G-462)*

Atwood Rope Manufacturing Inc................614 920-0534
121 N Trine St Canal Winchester (43110) *(G-1784)*

Atwood Rope Manufacturing Inc................614 920-0534
2185 Refugee St Millersport (43046) *(G-10022)*

Aubrey Rose Apparel LLC......................513 728-2681
3862 Race Rd Cincinnati (45211) *(G-2390)*

Auburn Metal Processing LLC (PA).............315 253-2565
4550 Darrow Rd Stow (44224) *(G-12419)*

Audimute Sndprfing Mdic Bttrie, Bedford Also Called: One Wish LLC *(G-1052)*

Audion Automation Ltd........................216 267-1911
775 Berea Industrial Pkwy Berea (44017) *(G-1159)*

Audion Automation Ltd (PA)...................216 267-1911
775 Berea Industrial Pkwy Berea (44017) *(G-1160)*

Audit Forms, Cleveland Also Called: Foote Printing Company Inc *(G-3734)*

Auglaize Erie Machine Company................419 629-2068
07148 Quellhorst Rd New Bremen (45869) *(G-10356)*

August Incorporated..........................937 434-2520
2122 Pelwood Dr Dayton (45459) *(G-5667)*

Auguste Moone Enterprises Ltd................216 333-9248
3355 Tullamore Rd Cleveland Heights (44118) *(G-4527)*

Aukerman J F Steel Rule Die..................937 456-4498
5582 Ozias Rd Eaton (45320) *(G-6448)*

Auld Corporation.............................614 454-1010
1569 Westbelt Dr Columbus (43228) *(G-4734)*

Aunt Minnies Food Services Inc...............419 872-4396
702 Searles Rd Toledo (43607) *(G-12888)*

Auria Fremont LLC............................419 332-1587
400 S Stone St Fremont (43420) *(G-7092)*

Auria Holmesville LLC........................330 279-4505
8281 County Road 245 Holmesville (44633) *(G-7794)*

Auria Sidney LLC.............................937 492-1225
2000 Schlater Dr Sidney (45365) *(G-11994)*

Auria Solutions, Fremont Also Called: Auria Fremont LLC *(G-7092)*

Auris Noble LLC (PA).........................330 321-6649
160 E Voris St Akron (44311) *(G-64)*

Aurora Balloon Company, Malvern Also Called: Perfect Products Company *(G-8752)*

Aurora Material Solutions, Streetsboro Also Called: Aurora Plastics LLC *(G-12488)*

Aurora Plastics LLC (HQ).....................330 422-0700
9280 Jefferson St Streetsboro (44241) *(G-12488)*

Austin Powder, Findlay Also Called: Austin Powder Company *(G-6838)*

Austin Powder Company (DH)...................216 464-2400
25800 Science Park Dr Ste 300 Cleveland (44122) *(G-3386)*

Austin Powder Company........................419 299-3347
3518 Township Road 142 Findlay (45840) *(G-6838)*

Austin Powder Company........................740 596-5286
430 Powder Plant Rd Mc Arthur (45651) *(G-9348)*

Austin Powder Company........................740 968-1555
74200 Edwards Rd Saint Clairsville (43950) *(G-11687)*

Austin Powder Holdings Company (HQ)..........216 464-2400
25800 Science Park Dr Ste 300 Cleveland (44122) *(G-3387)*

Austin Tape and Label Inc....................330 928-7999
3350 Cavalier Trl Stow (44224) *(G-12420)*

Austinburg Machine Inc.......................440 275-2001
2899 Industrial Park Dr Austinburg (44010) *(G-695)*

Auto Bolt and Nut Company, The, Cleveland Also Called: Auto Bolt Company *(G-3388)*

Auto Bolt Company............................216 881-3913
4740 Manufacturing Ave Cleveland (44135) *(G-3388)*

Auto Data, Akron Also Called: Ad Company Holdings Inc *(G-18)*

Auto Dealer Designs Inc......................330 374-7666
303 W Bartges St Akron (44307) *(G-65)*

Auto Des Sys Inc.............................614 488-8838
4242 Tuller Rd Ste B1 Dublin (43017) *(G-6278)*

Auto Technology Company.................................... 440 572-7800
20026 Progress Dr Strongsville (44149) *(G-12540)*

Auto Temp Inc.. 513 732-6969
950 Kent Rd Batavia (45103) *(G-851)*

Auto-Tap Inc.. 216 671-1043
3317 W 140th St Cleveland (44111) *(G-3389)*

Auto-Valve Inc... 937 854-3037
1707 Guenther Rd Dayton (45417) *(G-5668)*

Autobody Supply Company, Groveport *Also Called: Keystone Automotive Inds Inc (G-7440)*

Autobody Supply Company Inc............................. 614 228-4328
212 N Grant Ave Columbus (43215) *(G-4735)*

Autogate Inc.. 419 588-2796
7306 Driver Rd Berlin Heights (44814) *(G-1203)*

Automated Bldg Components Inc (PA).................. 419 257-2152
2359 Grant Rd North Baltimore (45872) *(G-10612)*

Automated Laser Fabrication Co.......................... 330 562-7200
1 Singer Dr Streetsboro (44241) *(G-12489)*

Automated Mfg Solutions Inc.............................. 440 878-3711
19706 Progress Dr Strongsville (44149) *(G-12541)*

Automated Packaging Systems LLC (HQ)............. 330 528-2000
10175 Philipp Pkwy Streetsboro (44241) *(G-12490)*

AUTOMATED PACKAGING SYSTEMS, INC., Streetsboro *Also Called: Automated Packg Systems Inc (G-12491)*

Automated Packg Systems Inc............................. 330 342-2000
25900 Solon Rd Bedford (44146) *(G-1013)*

Automated Packg Systems Inc............................. 330 626-2313
600 Mondial Pkwy Streetsboro (44241) *(G-12491)*

Automated Systems Div, Painesville *Also Called: Coe Manufacturing Company (G-11072)*

Automatic Parts.. 419 524-5841
433 Springmill St Mansfield (44903) *(G-8764)*

Automatic Parts, Mansfield *Also Called: McDaniel Products Inc (G-8822)*

Automatic Parts, Mansfield *Also Called: McDaniel Products Inc (G-8823)*

Automatic Stamp Products Inc............................ 216 781-7933
6700 Thornapple Dr Cleveland (44143) *(G-3390)*

Automation and Ctrl Tech Inc............................. 614 495-1120
6141 Avery Rd Dublin (43016) *(G-6279)*

Automation Plastics Corp.................................... 330 562-5148
150 Lena Dr Aurora (44202) *(G-662)*

Automation Software & Engrg (PA)..................... 330 405-2990
9321 Ravenna Rd Ste A Twinsburg (44087) *(G-13276)*

Automation Systems Design Inc.......................... 937 387-0351
3540 Vance Rd Dayton (45439) *(G-5669)*

Automation Technology Inc................................. 937 233-6084
1900 Troy St Dayton (45404) *(G-5670)*

Automation Tool & Die Inc................................. 330 225-8336
5576 Innovation Dr Valley City (44280) *(G-13490)*

Automation Tooling Systems, Lewis Center *Also Called: Ats Ohio, Inc (G-8323)*

Automator Marking Systems Inc.......................... 740 983-0157
475 Douglas Ave Chillicothe (45601) *(G-2243)*

Automotive Industries Division, Wauseon *Also Called: Interntnal Auto Cmpnnts Group (G-13853)*

Automted Cmpnent Spcalists LLC....................... 513 335-4285
7740 Reinhold Dr Cincinnati (45237) *(G-2391)*

Automtive Rfnish Clor Sltons I........................... 330 461-6067
2771 Sunburst Dr Medina (44256) *(G-9378)*

Autoneum North America Inc.............................. 419 693-0511
645 N Lallendorf Rd Oregon (43616) *(G-10957)*

Autoneum North America Inc.............................. 419 690-8924
4131 Spartan Dr Oregon (43616) *(G-10958)*

Autotec Corporation... 419 885-2529
6155 Brent Dr Toledo (43611) *(G-12889)*

Autotec Systems, Toledo *Also Called: Autotec Corporation (G-12889)*

Autotool Inc... 614 733-0222
7875 Corporate Blvd Plain City (43064) *(G-11395)*

Autowax Inc... 440 334-4417
15015 Foltz Pkwy Strongsville (44149) *(G-12542)*

Avadirect.com, Twinsburg *Also Called: Freedom Usa Inc (G-13305)*

Avalign - Integrated LLC.................................... 440 269-6984
7124 Industrial Park Blvd Mentor (44060) *(G-9487)*

Avalon, Cleveland *Also Called: Xapc Co (G-4520)*

Avari Aero LLC... 513 828-0860
7711 Affinity Pl Cincinnati (45231) *(G-2392)*

Avari Aerospace, Cincinnati *Also Called: Avari Aero LLC (G-2392)*

Avation Medical Inc.. 614 591-4201
1375 Perry St Columbus (43201) *(G-4736)*

Avcom Smt Inc... 614 882-8176
213 E Broadway Ave Westerville (43081) *(G-14244)*

Avecia, Cincinnati *Also Called: Girindus America Inc (G-2671)*

Avenue Fabricating Inc....................................... 513 752-1911
1281 Clough Pike Batavia (45103) *(G-852)*

Avery Dennison, Mentor *Also Called: Avery Dennison Corporation (G-9489)*

Avery Dennison Corporation............................... 513 682-7500
11101 Mosteller Rd Ste 2 Cincinnati (45241) *(G-2393)*

Avery Dennison Corporation............................... 216 267-8700
15939 Industrial Pkwy Cleveland (44135) *(G-3391)*

Avery Dennison Corporation............................... 440 358-4691
7600 Auburn Rd Bldg 18 Concord Township (44077) *(G-5385)*

Avery Dennison Corporation............................... 440 534-6527
8100 Tyler Blvd Mentor (44060) *(G-9488)*

Avery Dennison Corporation (PA)....................... 440 534-6000
8080 Norton Pkwy Mentor (44060) *(G-9489)*

Avery Dennison Corporation............................... 440 639-3900
5750 Heisley Rd Mentor (44060) *(G-9490)*

Avery Dennison Corporation............................... 440 358-2828
7100 Lindsay Dr Mentor (44060) *(G-9491)*

Avery Dennison Corporation............................... 937 865-2439
200 Monarch Ln Miamisburg (45342) *(G-9667)*

Avery Dennison Corporation............................... 419 898-8273
8035 W Lake Winds Dr Oak Harbor (43449) *(G-10882)*

Avery Dennison Corporation............................... 440 358-3466
670 Hardy Rd Painesville (44077) *(G-11068)*

Avery Dennison Corporation............................... 440 358-2564
250 Chester St Bldg 3 Painesville (44077) *(G-11069)*

Avery Dennison Corporation............................... 440 878-7000
17700 Foltz Pkwy Strongsville (44149) *(G-12543)*

Avery Dnnison G Holdings I LLC......................... 440 534-6000
8080 Norton Pkwy Mentor (44060) *(G-9492)*

Aviation Cmpnent Solutions Inc.......................... 440 295-6590
26451 Curtiss Wright Pkwy Ste 106 Richmond Heights (44143) *(G-11607)*

Avid Lighting LLC.. 614 502-2843
3757 Parkway Ln Hilliard (43026) *(G-7670)*

Avid Signs Plus LLC.. 513 932-7446
495 Lakeside Dr Lebanon (45036) *(G-8244)*

Avidyne... 800 284-3963
5980 Wilcox Pl Ste I Dublin (43016) *(G-6280)*

Avient, Avon Lake *Also Called: Avient Corporation (G-748)*

Avient Corporation... 440 930-3727
33587 Walker Rd # Rdb-418 Avon Lake (44012) *(G-747)*

Avient Corporation (PA)..................................... 440 930-1000
33587 Walker Rd Avon Lake (44012) *(G-748)*

Avient Corporation... 440 930-1000
1404 Lowell St Elyria (44035) *(G-6499)*

Avient Corporation... 800 727-4338
1050 Landsdowne Ave Greenville (45331) *(G-7335)*

Avient Corporation... 330 834-3812
1675 Navarre Rd Se Massillon (44646) *(G-9173)*

Avient Corporation... 419 668-4844
80 N West St Norwalk (44857) *(G-10829)*

Aviles Construction Co Inc.................................. 216 939-1084
7011 Clark Ave Cleveland (44102) *(G-3392)*

Aviva Metals, Lorain *Also Called: National Bronze Mtls Ohio Inc (G-8568)*

Avon, Cleveland *Also Called: Wallseye Concrete Corp (G-4489)*

Avon Concrete, Elyria *Also Called: Westview Concrete Corp (G-6602)*

Avon Lake Printing... 440 933-2078
32908 Sorrento Ln Avon Lake (44012) *(G-749)*

Avon Lake Sheet Metal Co.................................. 440 933-3505
33574 Pin Oak Pkwy Avon Lake (44012) *(G-750)*

Avt Beckett Elevators USA Inc............................ 844 360-0288
30130 Industrial Park Dr Logan (43138) *(G-8509)*

Avt Technology Solutions LLC............................ 727 539-7429
5350 Centerpoint Pkwy Groveport (43125) *(G-7423)*

Avtek International Inc.. 330 633-7500
2867 Lakeland Pkwy Silver Lake (44224) *(G-12063)*

Avtron Aerospace Inc................................ 216 750-5152
7900 E Pleasant Valley Rd Cleveland (44131) *(G-3393)*

Avtron Holdings LLC................................. 216 642-1230
7900 E Pleasant Valley Rd Cleveland (44131) *(G-3394)*

Avtron Industrial Automation, Independence Also Called: Nidec Avtron Automation Corporation *(G-7912)*

Avtron Loadbank Inc.................................. 216 573-7600
6255 Halle Dr Cleveland (44125) *(G-3395)*

AW Faber-Castell Usa Inc........................... 216 643-4660
9000 Rio Nero Dr Cleveland (44125) *(G-3396)*

Awardcraft, Celina Also Called: Eighth Floor Promotions LLC *(G-2104)*

AWC Transition Corporation......................... 614 846-2918
6540 Huntley Rd Columbus (43229) *(G-4737)*

Awning Fabri Caters Inc............................. 216 476-4888
10237 Lorain Ave Cleveland (44111) *(G-3397)*

Aws Industries Inc.................................. 513 932-7941
2600 Henkle Dr Lebanon (45036) *(G-8245)*

Axalt Powde Coati Syste Usa I...................... 614 921-8000
4150 Lyman Dr Hilliard (43026) *(G-7671)*

Axalt Powde Coati Syste Usa I...................... 614 600-4104
4130 Lyman Dr Hilliard (43026) *(G-7672)*

Axalta... 855 629-2582
1930 Tremainsville Rd Toledo (43613) *(G-12890)*

Axalta Coating Systems USA LLC.................... 614 777-7230
4130 Lyman Dr Hilliard (43026) *(G-7673)*

Axiom Engineered Systems LLC (PA)................ 416 435-7313
1 Seagate Fl 27 Toledo (43604) *(G-12891)*

Axiom International Inc.............................. 330 396-5942
3517 Embassy Pkwy Ste 150 Akron (44333) *(G-66)*

Axiom Tool Group Inc............................... 844 642-4902
270 Broad St Westerville (43081) *(G-14245)*

Axion International Holdings Inc.................... 740 452-2500
4005 All American Way Zanesville (43701) *(G-14988)*

Axion International Inc.............................. 740 452-2500
4005 All American Way Zanesville (43701) *(G-14989)*

Axion Strl Innovations LLC (PA).................... 740 452-2500
1100 Brandywine Blvd Ste H Zanesville (43701) *(G-14990)*

Axis Corporation.................................... 937 592-1958
314 Water Ave Bellefontaine (43311) *(G-1100)*

Axium Packaging LLC (PA).......................... 614 706-5955
9005 Smiths Mill Rd New Albany (43054) *(G-10331)*

Axium Plastics, New Albany Also Called: Axium Packaging LLC *(G-10331)*

Axle Machine Services Ltd.......................... 419 827-2000
41 County Road 2350 Lakeville (44638) *(G-8160)*

Axon Medical Llc................................... 216 276-0262
1484 Medina Rd Ste 117 Medina (44256) *(G-9379)*

Ayers Limestone Quarry Inc......................... 740 633-2958
2002 Colerain Pike Martins Ferry (43935) *(G-9009)*

Ayling and Reichert Co Consent..................... 419 898-2471
411 S Railroad St Oak Harbor (43449) *(G-10883)*

Aztec Manufacturing Inc............................ 330 783-9747
4325 Simon Rd Youngstown (44512) *(G-14816)*

Azteca Systems Inc................................. 801 523-2751
5475 Kellenburger Rd Dayton (45424) *(G-5671)*

Aztech Printing & Promotions....................... 937 339-0100
402 E Main St Troy (45373) *(G-13202)*

Aztlan Communications, Toledo Also Called: La Prensa Publications Inc *(G-13027)*

Azz Galvanizing - Cincinnati, Cincinnati Also Called: AAA Galvanizing - Joliet Inc *(G-2329)*

Azz Inc.. 330 456-3241
1723 Cleveland Ave Sw Canton (44707) *(G-1834)*

B & A Holistic Fd & Herbs LLC...................... 614 747-2200
4550 Heaton Rd Ste B7 Columbus (43229) *(G-4738)*

B & B Box Company Inc............................. 419 872-5600
26490 Southpoint Rd Perrysburg (43551) *(G-11204)*

B & B Gear and Machine Co Inc..................... 937 687-1771
440 W Main St New Lebanon (45345) *(G-10399)*

B & B Industries, Orient Also Called: Kmj Leasing Ltd *(G-10971)*

B & B Industries Inc................................ 614 871-3883
7001 Harrisburg Pike Orient (43146) *(G-10970)*

B & B Molded Products Inc.......................... 419 592-8700
1250 Ottawa Ave Defiance (43512) *(G-6099)*

B & B Printing Graphics Inc......................... 419 893-7068
1689 Lance Pointe Rd Maumee (43537) *(G-9263)*

B & C Research, Barberton Also Called: B & C Research Inc *(G-794)*

B & C Research Inc................................. 330 848-4000
842 Norton Ave Barberton (44203) *(G-794)*

B & D Machinists Inc................................ 513 831-8588
1350 Us Route 50 Milford (45150) *(G-9922)*

B & F Manufacturing Co............................. 216 518-0333
19050 Cranwood Pkwy Warrensville Heights (44128) *(G-13815)*

B & G Tool Company................................ 614 451-2538
4832 Kenny Rd Columbus (43220) *(G-4739)*

B & H Machine Inc.................................. 330 868-6425
15001 Lincoln St Se Minerva (44657) *(G-10034)*

B & J Baking Company.............................. 513 541-2386
4056 Colerain Ave Cincinnati (45223) *(G-2394)*

B & P Company Inc................................. 937 298-0265
301 Miamisburg Centerville Rd Centerville (45459) *(G-2130)*

B & P Polishing Inc................................. 330 753-4202
123 9th St Nw Barberton (44203) *(G-795)*

B & P Spring Prod Co Inc........................... 216 486-4260
19520 Nottingham Rd Cleveland (44110) *(G-3398)*

B & R Fabricators & Maint Inc....................... 513 641-2222
4524 W Mitchell Ave Cincinnati (45232) *(G-2395)*

B & R Machine Co.................................. 216 961-7370
2216 W 65th St Cleveland (44102) *(G-3399)*

B & S Transport Inc (PA)........................... 330 767-4319
11325 Lawndell Rd Sw Navarre (44662) *(G-10302)*

B & T Welding and Machine Co....................... 740 687-1908
423 S Mount Pleasant Ave Lancaster (43130) *(G-8177)*

B A Malcuit Racing Inc.............................. 330 878-7111
707 S Wooster Ave Strasburg (44680) *(G-12476)*

B B & H Tool Company.............................. 614 868-8634
7719 Taylor Rd Sw Reynoldsburg (43068) *(G-11556)*

B B Bradley Company Inc........................... 614 777-5600
2699 Scioto Pkwy Columbus (43221) *(G-4740)*

B B Bradley Company Inc (PA)...................... 440 354-2005
7755 Crile Rd Concord Township (44077) *(G-5386)*

B C I, Fairlawn Also Called: Buckeye Corrugated Inc *(G-6797)*

B C I, Powell Also Called: Building Ctrl Integrators LLC *(G-11482)*

B C T, Akron Also Called: Akron Thermography Inc *(G-44)*

B C T, Akron Also Called: Akron Thermography Inc *(G-45)*

B D G Wrap-Tite Inc (PA)........................... 440 349-5400
6200 Cochran Rd Solon (44139) *(G-12081)*

B J Pallett... 419 447-9665
324 4th Ave Tiffin (44883) *(G-12776)*

B K Plastics Inc.................................... 937 473-2087
1400 Mote Dr Covington (45318) *(G-5490)*

B P T, Bucyrus Also Called: Bucyrus Precision Tech Inc *(G-1674)*

B R Printers Inc.................................... 513 271-6035
3962 Virginia Ave Cincinnati (45227) *(G-2396)*

B S F Inc (PA)..................................... 937 890-6121
8895 N Dixie Dr Dayton (45414) *(G-5672)*

B S F Inc... 937 890-6121
320b S 5th St Tipp City (45371) *(G-12816)*

B V Grinding Machining Inc.......................... 440 918-1884
1438 E 363rd St Willoughby (44095) *(G-14429)*

B W Grinding Co.................................... 419 923-1376
15048 County Rd 10-3 Lyons (43533) *(G-8673)*

B-K Tool & Design Inc.............................. 419 532-3890
480 W Main St Kalida (45853) *(G-8003)*

B-R-O-T Incorporated............................... 216 267-5335
4730 Briar Rd Cleveland (44135) *(G-3401)*

B-Wear Sportswear, Zanesville Also Called: 5 BS Inc *(G-14980)*

B&A Ison Steel Inc.................................. 216 663-4300
3238 E 82nd St Cleveland (44104) *(G-3400)*

B&B Distributors LLC............................... 440 324-1293
811 Taylor St Elyria (44035) *(G-6500)*

B&C Machine Co LLC................................ 330 745-4013
401 Newell St Barberton (44203) *(G-796)*

B&D Truck Parts Sls & Svcs LLC..................... 419 701-7041
1498 Perrysburg Rd Fostoria (44830) *(G-6976)*

B&D Water Inc..330 771-3318
69478 Fairground Rd Quaker City (43773) *(G-11503)*

B&G Contractors Supply, Coventry Township *Also Called: Kuhlman Corporation (G-5485)*

B&G Foods Inc..513 482-8226
5204 Spring Grove Ave Cincinnati (45217) *(G-2397)*

B&M Underground LLC..740 505-3096
1403 Gurneyville Rd Wilmington (45177) *(G-14572)*

B&N Coal Inc..740 783-3575
38455 Marietta Rd Dexter City (45727) *(G-6224)*

B2d Solutions Inc..855 484-1145
3558 Lee Rd Cleveland (44120) *(G-3402)*

B3, Avon *Also Called: B3 Fulfillment (G-714)*

B3 Fulfillment..866 405-0910
3450 Nagel Rd Avon (44011) *(G-714)*

Babbert Real Estate Inv Co Ltd (PA)......................614 837-8444
7415 Diley Rd Canal Winchester (43110) *(G-1785)*

Babcock & Wilcox Co, Lancaster *Also Called: Babcock & Wilcox Company (G-8178)*

Babcock & Wilcox Company (HQ)............................330 753-4511
1200 E Market St Ste 650 Akron (44305) *(G-67)*

Babcock & Wilcox Company..................................330 753-4511
91 Stirling Ave Barberton (44203) *(G-797)*

Babcock & Wilcox Company..................................740 687-6500
2600 E Main St Lancaster (43130) *(G-8178)*

Babcock & Wilcox Entps Inc (PA)............................330 753-4511
1200 E Market St Ste 650 Akron (44305) *(G-68)*

Babcock & Wilcox Entps Inc..................................740 687-4370
2560 E Main St Lancaster (43130) *(G-8179)*

Babcock & Wilcox Holdings LLC............................330 453-4511
1200 E Market St Ste 650 Akron (44305) *(G-69)*

Babcox Media Inc..330 670-1234
3550 Embassy Pkwy Akron (44333) *(G-70)*

Back In Black Co..419 425-5555
2100 Fostoria Ave Findlay (45840) *(G-6839)*

Background Music & Sound Inc..............................937 898-9871
8529 N Dixie Dr Ste 325 Dayton (45414) *(G-5673)*

Backyard Scoreboards LLC..................................513 702-6561
431 Kenridge Dr Middletown (45042) *(G-9842)*

Badboy Blasters Incorporated..............................330 454-2699
1720 Wallace Ave Ne Canton (44705) *(G-1835)*

Badlime Promo and Apparel LLC............................330 425-7100
2146 E Aurora Rd Twinsburg (44087) *(G-13277)*

Bae Systems Survivability Systems LLC....................513 881-9800
9113 Le Saint Dr West Chester (45014) *(G-13945)*

Baerlocher, Dover *Also Called: Baerlocher Usa LLC (G-6229)*

Baerlocher Production Usa LLC............................513 482-6300
5890 Highland Ridge Dr Cincinnati (45232) *(G-2398)*

Baerlocher Usa LLC (DH)..................................330 364-6000
3676 Davis Rd Nw Dover (44622) *(G-6229)*

Baesman Group Inc (PA)....................................614 771-2300
4477 Reynolds Dr Hilliard (43026) *(G-7674)*

Bag & Bottle Manufacturing, Ashland *Also Called: Liqui-Box Corporation (G-549)*

Bag, The, Lancaster *Also Called: Dispatch Consumer Services (G-8199)*

Baggallini Inc..800 448-8753
13405 Yarmouth Dr Pickerington (43147) *(G-11289)*

Bagpack, Hamilton *Also Called: BP 10 Inc (G-7472)*

Bahler Medical Inc..614 873-7600
8910 Warner Rd Plain City (43064) *(G-11396)*

Baillie Lumber Co LP..419 462-2000
3953 County Road 51 Galion (44833) *(G-7179)*

Bainter Machining Company (PA)............................740 653-2422
1230 Rainbow Dr Ne Lancaster (43130) *(G-8180)*

Bainter Machining Company..................................740 756-4598
842 N Columbus St Lancaster (43130) *(G-8181)*

Baird Brothers Sawmill Inc..................................330 533-3122
7060 Crory Rd Canfield (44406) *(G-1804)*

Baird Concrete Products Inc..................................740 623-8600
15 Locust St Coshocton (43812) *(G-5451)*

Bakelite Chemicals LLC......................................404 652-4000
1975 Watkins Rd Columbus (43207) *(G-4741)*

Bakelite N Sumitomo Amer Inc..............................419 675-1282
13717 Us Highway 68 Kenton (43326) *(G-8096)*

Bakemark USA LLC..440 323-5100
6325 Gateway Blvd S Elyria (44035) *(G-6501)*

Baker & Taylor Publisher Svcs, Ashland *Also Called: Bookmasters Inc (G-522)*

Baker & Taylor Publisher Svcs, Ashland *Also Called: Follett Hgher Edcatn Group Inc (G-535)*

Baker McMillen Co (PA)....................................330 923-8300
3688 Wyoga Lake Rd Stow (44224) *(G-12421)*

Baker Media Group LLC....................................330 253-0056
1653 Merriman Rd Ste 116 Akron (44313) *(G-71)*

Baker Plastics Inc..330 743-3142
900 Mahoning Ave Youngstown (44502) *(G-14817)*

Baker Store Equipment Company
23449 Laureldale Rd Shaker Heights (44122) *(G-11926)*

Baker-Shindler Builders Sup Co, Defiance *Also Called: Baker-Shindler Contracting Co (G-6100)*

Baker-Shindler Contracting Co (PA)........................419 782-5080
525 Cleveland Ave Defiance (43512) *(G-6100)*

Bakers Welding, Zanesville *Also Called: J A B Welding Service Inc (G-15023)*

Bakerwell Inc (PA)..330 276-2161
10420 County Road 620 Killbuck (44637) *(G-8130)*

Bakerwell Service Rigs Inc (HQ)............................330 276-2161
10420 County Road 620 Killbuck (44637) *(G-8131)*

Balancing Company Inc (PA)................................937 898-9111
898 Center Dr Vandalia (45377) *(G-13550)*

Baldwin, Hilliard *Also Called: Mxr Imaging Inc (G-7688)*

Baleco International, North Bend *Also Called: Hammersmith Bros Invstmnts Inc (G-10620)*

Ball Aerosol And Specialty Container Inc., Hubbard *Also Called: Ball Arosol Specialty Cont Inc (G-7808)*

Ball Arosol Specialty Cont Inc..............................330 534-1903
644 Myron St Hubbard (44425) *(G-7808)*

Ball Corporation..234 360-2141
2121 Warner Rd Se Canton (44707) *(G-1836)*

Ball Corporation..614 771-9112
2690 Charter St Columbus (43228) *(G-4742)*

Ball Corporation..419 423-3071
1800 Production Dr Findlay (45840) *(G-6840)*

Ball Corporation..330 244-2313
3075 Brookline Rd North Canton (44720) *(G-10629)*

Ball Jackets LLC..937 572-1114
5120 Waynesville Jamestown Rd Jamestown (45335) *(G-7968)*

Ball Metal Beverage Cont Corp..............................419 423-3071
12340 Township Rd 99 E Findlay (45840) *(G-6841)*

Ball Metal Beverage Cont Div, Findlay *Also Called: Ball Metal Beverage Cont Corp (G-6841)*

Ball Metal Food Container, Columbus *Also Called: Ball Corporation (G-4742)*

Ballas Egg Products, Zanesville *Also Called: BE Products Inc (G-14994)*

Ballas Egg Products Corp....................................614 453-0386
40 N 2nd St Zanesville (43701) *(G-14991)*

Ballastshop, Cleveland *Also Called: B2d Solutions Inc (G-3402)*

Ballinger Industries Inc (PA)................................419 422-4533
2500 Fostoria Ave Findlay (45840) *(G-6842)*

Ballreich Bros Inc..419 447-1814
186 Ohio Ave Tiffin (44883) *(G-12777)*

Ballreichs Potato Chips Snacks, Tiffin *Also Called: Ballreich Bros Inc (G-12777)*

Balmac Inc..614 876-1295
4010 Main St Hilliard (43026) *(G-7675)*

Baltic Country Meats..330 897-7025
3320 State Route 557 Baltic (43804) *(G-776)*

Baltic Meats, Baltic *Also Called: Baltic Country Meats (G-776)*

Bamal Corp..937 492-9484
2580 Ross St Sidney (45365) *(G-11995)*

Bamf Welding & Fabrication LLC............................440 862-8286
9988 Kinsman Rd Novelty (44072) *(G-10880)*

Ban Inc..937 325-5539
619 S Belmont Ave Springfield (45505) *(G-12284)*

Banbury Investments Inc....................................513 677-4500
9160 Union Cemetery Rd Cincinnati (45249) *(G-2399)*

Bandag, Dover *Also Called: Bob Sumerel Tire Co Inc (G-6231)*

Bandag, Lima *Also Called: Best One Tire & Svc Lima Inc (G-8389)*

Bandag, Zanesville *Also Called: Central Ohio Bandag LP (G-15007)*

Banks Manufacturing Company..............................440 458-8661
40259 Banks Rd Grafton (44044) *(G-7299)*

Banner Mattress & Furniture Co, Toledo *Also Called: Banner Mattress Co Inc (G-12892)*

Banner Mattress Co Inc.. 419 324-7181
2544 N Reynolds Rd Toledo (43615) *(G-12892)*

Banner Metals Group Inc.. 614 291-3105
1308 Holly Ave Columbus (43212) *(G-4743)*

Bansal Enterprises Inc.. 330 633-9355
1538 Home Ave Akron (44310) *(G-72)*

BAP Manufacturing Inc.. 419 332-5041
601 N Stone St Ste 1 Fremont (43420) *(G-7093)*

Bar 25 LLC (PA).. 216 621-4000
1939 W 25th St Cleveland (44113) *(G-3403)*

Bar 25 LLC.. 216 373-3700
1849 W 24th St Cleveland (44113) *(G-3404)*

Bar Processing Corporation.. 330 872-0914
1000 Windham Rd Newton Falls (44444) *(G-10577)*

Bar Processing Corporation.. 440 943-0094
1271 E 289th St Wickliffe (44092) *(G-14367)*

Barbara A Lieurance.. 937 382-2864
180 E Sugartree St Wilmington (45177) *(G-14573)*

Barbasol LLC... 419 903-0738
2011 Ford Dr Ashland (44805) *(G-520)*

Barbco, East Canton *Also Called: Barbco Inc (G-6377)*

Barbco Inc.. 330 488-9400
315 Pekin Dr Se East Canton (44730) *(G-6377)*

Barberton Facility, Barberton *Also Called: Babcock & Wilcox Company (G-797)*

Barberton Herald, Barberton *Also Called: Richardson Publishing Company (G-836)*

Barberton Steel Industries Inc.. 330 745-6837
240 E Huston St Barberton (44203) *(G-798)*

Barbour Auto Parts, Portsmouth *Also Called: Tom Barbour Auto Parts Inc (G-11479)*

Barbs Graffiti Inc (PA).. 216 881-5550
3111 Carnegie Ave Cleveland (44115) *(G-3405)*

Barclay Machine Inc.. 330 337-9541
650 S Bdwy Ave Salem (44460) *(G-11763)*

Barclay Rolls, Salem *Also Called: Barclay Machine Inc (G-11763)*

Barco Inc... 937 372-7579
600 Bellbrook Ave Xenia (45385) *(G-14753)*

Bard Manufacturing Company Inc (PA).................................. 419 636-1194
1914 Randolph Dr Bryan (43506) *(G-1631)*

Bardons & Oliver Inc (PA)... 440 498-5800
5800 Harper Rd Solon (44139) *(G-12082)*

Bardwell Winery, Mount Orab *Also Called: Wedco LLC (G-10223)*

Barentz N Amer Intrmdate Hldng...................................... 440 937-1000
1390 Jaycox Rd Avon (44011) *(G-715)*

Barfections LLC (PA)... 330 759-3100
1598 Motor Inn Dr Girard (44420) *(G-7266)*

Barfections LLC... 330 759-3100
6105 W Liberty St Hubbard (44425) *(G-7809)*

Barfections LLC... 330 759-3100
4718 Belmont Ave Youngstown (44505) *(G-14818)*

Bargain Hunter, Millersburg *Also Called: Alonovus Corp (G-9968)*

Bargmann Management, L.L.C., Elyria *Also Called: Invacare Hcs LLC (G-6552)*

Barium & Chemicals Inc.. 740 282-9776
515 Kingsdale Rd Steubenville (43952) *(G-12400)*

Barker Products Company
1028 E 134th St Cleveland (44110) *(G-3406)*

Barkman Honey LLC.. 620 947-3173
550 Bonnewitz Ave Van Wert (45891) *(G-13527)*

Barlamy Supply, Wapakoneta *Also Called: Jewett Supply (G-13717)*

Barley's Brewing Company, Columbus *Also Called: Brewpub Restaurant Corporation (G-4774)*

Barnes Advertising Corporation.. 740 453-6836
1580 Fairview Rd Zanesville (43701) *(G-14992)*

Barnes Group Inc... 440 526-5900
10367 Brecksville Rd Brecksville (44141) *(G-1458)*

Barnes Group Inc... 419 891-9292
370 W Dussel Dr Ste A Maumee (43537) *(G-9264)*

Barnes Group Inc... 513 779-6888
9826 Crescent Park Dr West Chester (45069) *(G-13946)*

Barnes Group Inc... 513 779-6888
9826 Crescent Park Dr West Chester (45069) *(G-13947)*

Barnes International LLC... 419 352-7501
555 Van Camp Rd Bowling Green (43402) *(G-1407)*

Barnes Services LLC... 440 319-2088
20677 Centuryway Rd Maple Heights (44137) *(G-8877)*

Barnhart Printing Corp.. 330 456-2279
1107 Melchoir Pl Sw Canton (44707) *(G-1837)*

Barnhart Publishing, Canton *Also Called: Barnhart Printing Corp (G-1837)*

Barr Engineering Incorporated (PA).................................... 614 714-0299
2800 Corporate Exchange Dr Ste 240 Columbus (43231) *(G-4744)*

Barr Laboratories Inc.. 513 731-9900
5040 Duramed Rd Cincinnati (45213) *(G-2400)*

BARR LABORATORIES, INC., Cincinnati *Also Called: Barr Laboratories Inc (G-2400)*

Barracuda Technologies Inc.. 216 469-1566
2900 State Route 82 Aurora (44202) *(G-663)*

Barrel Run Crssing Wnery Vnyrd...................................... 330 325-1075
3272 Industry Rd Rootstown (44272) *(G-11647)*

Barrett Paving Materials Inc (DH).....................................973 533-1001
8590 Bilstein Blvd Ste 100 Hamilton (45015) *(G-7468)*

Barrett Paving Materials Inc.. 937 293-9033
2701 W Dorothy Ln Moraine (45439) *(G-10148)*

Barry-Wehmiller Companies Inc.. 330 923-0491
4485 Allen Rd Cuyahoga Falls (44224) *(G-5532)*

Barsplice Products Inc... 937 275-8700
4900 Webster St Dayton (45414) *(G-5674)*

Barth Industries Co LLC (PA)... 216 267-1950
12650 Brookpark Rd Cleveland (44130) *(G-3407)*

Barton-Carey Medical Pdts Inc (PA)...................................419 887-1285
1331 Conant St Ste 102 Maumee (43537) *(G-9265)*

Barudan, Solon *Also Called: Barudan America Inc (G-12083)*

Barudan America Inc (HQ)..440 248-8770
30901 Carter St Frnt A Solon (44139) *(G-12083)*

Basco Manufacturing Company (HQ)..................................513 573-1900
7201 Snider Rd Mason (45040) *(G-9069)*

Basco Shower Enclosures, Mason *Also Called: Basco Manufacturing Company (G-9069)*

Basetek LLC (PA)...877 712-2273
14975 White Rd Middlefield (44062) *(G-9781)*

BASF, Cleveland *Also Called: BASF Catalysts LLC (G-3408)*

BASF Catalysts LLC.. 216 360-5005
23800 Mercantile Rd Cleveland (44122) *(G-3408)*

BASF Catalysts LLC.. 440 322-3741
120 Pine St Elyria (44035) *(G-6502)*

BASF Corp... 513 681-9100
3131 Spring Grove Ave Cincinnati (45225) *(G-2401)*

BASF Corporation.. 513 482-3000
4900 Este Ave Cincinnati (45232) *(G-2402)*

BASF Corporation.. 614 662-5682
9565 Logistics Ct Columbus (43217) *(G-4745)*

BASF Corporation.. 440 329-2525
120 Pine St Elyria (44035) *(G-6503)*

BASF Corporation.. 419 877-5308
6125 Industrial Pkwy Whitehouse (43571) *(G-14357)*

Basic Cases Inc... 216 662-3900
19561 Miles Rd Cleveland (44128) *(G-3409)*

Basic Coatings LLC.. 419 241-2156
400 Van Camp Rd Bowling Green (43402) *(G-1408)*

Basic Grain Products Inc.. 419 678-2304
300 E Vine St 310 Coldwater (45828) *(G-4568)*

Basilius Inc... 419 536-5810
4338 South Ave Toledo (43615) *(G-12893)*

Bassett Nut Company, Holland *Also Called: Jml Holdings Inc (G-7770)*

Baswa Acoustics North Amer LLC..................................... 216 475-7197
21863 Aurora Rd Bedford (44146) *(G-1014)*

Bata Plastics, Toledo *Also Called: Lwhs Ltd (G-13042)*

Bates Metal Products Inc... 740 498-8371
403 E Mn St Port Washington (43837) *(G-11455)*

Bates Printing Inc.. 330 833-5830
150 23rd St Se Massillon (44646) *(G-9174)*

Bath & Body Works, Reynoldsburg *Also Called: Bath & Body Works LLC (G-11557)*

Bath & Body Works LLC (HQ).. 614 856-6000
7 Limited Pkwy E Reynoldsburg (43068) *(G-11557)*

Bath & Brass Emporium The, Columbus *Also Called: Savko Plastic Pipe & Fittings (G-5250)*

Bath and Body Works, Reynoldsburg *Also Called: Beautyavenues LLC (G-11558)*

Batman Enterprises LLC 513 600-3079
931 Business 28 Milford (45150) *(G-9923)*

Battery Unlimited 740 452-5030
1080 Linden Ave Zanesville (43701) *(G-14993)*

Battle Motors Inc 888 328-5443
1951 Reiser Ave Se New Philadelphia (44663) *(G-10432)*

Bauer Corporation (PA) 800 321-4760
2540 Progress Dr Wooster (44691) *(G-14624)*

Bauer Ladder, Wooster *Also Called: Bauer Corporation (G-14624)*

Baughman Machine & Weld Sp Inc 330 866-9243
6498 June Rd Nw Waynesburg (44688) *(G-13875)*

Baughman Tile Company 800 837-3160
8516 Road 137 Paulding (45879) *(G-11153)*

Baumfolder Corporation (DH) 937 492-1281
1660 Campbell Rd Sidney (45365) *(G-11996)*

Bautec N Technoform Amer Inc 330 487-6600
1755 Enterprise Pkwy Ste 300 Twinsburg (44087) *(G-13278)*

Bavis Fabacraft Inc 513 677-0500
201 Grandin Rd Maineville (45039) *(G-8738)*

Baxter Burial Vault Svc Inc 513 641-1010
909 E Ross Ave Cincinnati (45217) *(G-2403)*

Baxter Holdings Inc 513 860-3593
3370 Port Union Rd Hamilton (45014) *(G-7469)*

Baxter-Wilbert Burial Vault, Cincinnati *Also Called: Baxter Burial Vault Svc Inc (G-2403)*

Baxters North America Inc 513 552-7463
4700 Creek Rd Blue Ash (45242) *(G-1247)*

Baxters North America Inc 513 552-7400
10825 Kenwood Rd Blue Ash (45242) *(G-1248)*

Baxters North America Inc 513 552-7728
4602 Ilmenau Way Blue Ash (45242) *(G-1249)*

Baxters North America Inc (DH) 513 552-7485
4700 Creek Rd Cincinnati (45242) *(G-2404)*

Baxters North America Inc 513 552-7718
9756 International Blvd West Chester (45246) *(G-14106)*

Bay Business Forms Inc 937 322-3000
1803 W Columbia St Springfield (45504) *(G-12285)*

Bay Controls LLC 419 891-4390
1044 Hamilton Dr Holland (43528) *(G-7745)*

Bay Corporation 440 835-2212
867 Canterbury Rd Westlake (44145) *(G-14290)*

Bay Packing, Lancaster *Also Called: C J Kraft Enterprises Inc (G-8184)*

Bay State Polymer, Westlake *Also Called: Bay State Polymer Distribution Inc (G-14291)*

Bay State Polymer Distribution Inc 440 892-8500
27540 Detroit Rd Ste 102 Westlake (44145) *(G-14291)*

Bayard Inc 937 293-1415
2621 Dryden Rd Ste 300 Moraine (45439) *(G-10149)*

Bayer 513 336-6600
700 Nilles Rd Fairfield (45014) *(G-6712)*

Bayloff Stmped Pdts Knsman Inc 330 876-4511
8091 State Route 5 Kinsman (44428) *(G-8140)*

Bayou Steel Group, Cleveland *Also Called: Bd Laplace LLC (G-3410)*

Bbb Music LLC 740 772-2262
643 Central Ctr Chillicothe (45601) *(G-2244)*

BBC Technology Solutions, Blue Ash *Also Called: Sutter Llc (G-1339)*

BBH Holdings Inc 513 870-3000
1899 Kingsview Dr Lebanon (45036) *(G-8246)*

Bbm Fairway Inc 330 899-2200
3515 Massillon Rd Ste 200 Uniontown (44685) *(G-13417)*

Bc Investment Corporation 330 262-3070
1505 E Bowman St Wooster (44691) *(G-14625)*

Bc Machine Services Corp 513 428-0327
3104 Wayne Madison Rd Trenton (45067) *(G-13190)*

BCI, Toledo *Also Called: Block Communications Inc (G-12898)*

BCi and V Investments Inc 330 538-0660
11675 Mahoning Ave North Jackson (44451) *(G-10683)*

Bcs Technologies Ltd 513 829-4577
1041 Tedia Way Fairfield (45014) *(G-6713)*

BCT Alarm Services Inc 440 669-8153
5064 Oberlin Ave Lorain (44053) *(G-8546)*

Bcte, New Philadelphia *Also Called: Bulk Carriers Service Inc (G-10435)*

Bd Laplace LLC (PA) 985 652-4900
28026 Gates Mills Blvd Cleveland (44124) *(G-3410)*

BD Oil Gathering Corp. 740 374-9355
649 Mitchells Ln Marietta (45750) *(G-8903)*

Bdi, Canton *Also Called: Bdi Inc (G-1838)*

Bdi Inc 330 498-4980
417 Applegrove St Nw Canton (44720) *(G-1838)*

Bdl Supply, South Charleston *Also Called: Buckeye Diamond Logistics Inc (G-12213)*

Bdu Holdings Inc 330 374-1810
467 Dan St Akron (44310) *(G-73)*

BE Products Inc 740 453-0386
40 N 2nd St Zanesville (43701) *(G-14994)*

Bea-Ecc Apparels Inc 216 650-6336
1287 W 76th St Cleveland (44102) *(G-3411)*

Beach City Lumber Llc 330 878-4097
5177 Austin Ln Nw Strasburg (44680) *(G-12477)*

Beach Manufacturing Co 937 882-6372
118 N Hampton Rd Donnelsville (45319) *(G-6227)*

Beachs Trees, Cincinnati *Also Called: Beachs Trees Slctive Hrvstg LL (G-2297)*

Beachs Trees Slctive Hrvstg LL 513 289-5976
915 Wilma Cir Cincinnati (45245) *(G-2297)*

Beachy Barns Ltd 614 873-4193
8720 Amish Pike Plain City (43064) *(G-11397)*

Beacon Journal Publishing Co 330 996-3600
44 E Exchange St Akron (44308) *(G-74)*

Beacon Metal Fabricators Inc 216 391-7444
5425 Hamilton Ave Ste D Cleveland (44114) *(G-3412)*

Beacon, The, Port Clinton *Also Called: Schaffner Publication Inc (G-11452)*

Beam Technologies Inc 800 648-1179
80 E Rich St Ste 400 Columbus (43215) *(G-4746)*

Bean Bag City, Spring Valley *Also Called: Sailors Tailor Inc (G-12243)*

Bear Cabinetry LLC 216 481-9282
23560 Lakeland Blvd Euclid (44132) *(G-6643)*

Bear Mechanical LLC 937 288-2316
2336 State Route 131 Hillsboro (45133) *(G-7713)*

Bear Welding Services LLC 740 630-7538
18210 Myrtle Ake Rd Caldwell (43724) *(G-1723)*

Bearing & Transm Sup Co Div, Macedonia *Also Called: Jay Dee Service Corporation (G-8699)*

Bearing Precious Seed Intl Inc (PA) 513 575-1706
1369 Woodville Pike Unit B Milford (45150) *(G-9924)*

Bearings Manufacturing Company (PA) 440 846-5517
15157 Foltz Pkwy Strongsville (44149) *(G-12544)*

Beaufort Rfd Inc 330 239-4331
1420 Wolf Creek Trl Sharon Center (44274) *(G-11937)*

Beaumont Bros Stoneware Inc 740 982-0055
410 Keystone St Crooksville (43731) *(G-5508)*

Beaumont Brothers Pottery, Crooksville *Also Called: Beaumont Bros Stoneware Inc (G-5508)*

Beaumont Machine, Mason *Also Called: Beaumont Machine LLC (G-9070)*

Beaumont Machine LLC 513 701-0421
7697 Innovation Way Ste 1100 Mason (45040) *(G-9070)*

Beaute Asylum LLC 419 377-9933
2011 Glendale Ave Toledo (43614) *(G-12894)*

Beauty Cft Met Fabricators Inc 440 439-0710
5439 Perkins Rd Bedford (44146) *(G-1015)*

Beautyavenues LLC (HQ) 614 856-6000
7 Limited Pkwy E Reynoldsburg (43068) *(G-11558)*

Beaver Wood Products 740 226-6211
190 Buck Hollow Rd Beaver (45613) *(G-960)*

Beaverson Machine Inc 419 923-8064
11600 County Road 10 2 Delta (43515) *(G-6202)*

Beazer East Inc 740 474-3169
200 E Corwin St Circleville (43113) *(G-3248)*

Beazer East Inc 937 364-2311
4281 Roush Rd Hillsboro (45133) *(G-7714)*

Beazer East Inc 740 947-4677
9978 State Route 220 Waverly (45690) *(G-13863)*

Beca House Coffee LLC 419 731-4961
965 E Wyandot Ave Upper Sandusky (43351) *(G-13435)*

Bechem Lubrication Tech LLC 440 543-9845
2000 Auburn Dr Ste 200-402 Beachwood (44122) *(G-910)*

Beck Aluminum Alloys Ltd 216 861-4455
6150 Parkland Blvd Ste 260 Mayfield Heights (44124) *(G-9332)*

A
L
P
H
A
B
E
T
I
C

Beck Energy Corporation..330 297-6891
160 N Chestnut St Ravenna (44266) *(G-11517)*

Beck Sand & Gravel Inc..330 626-3863
2820 Webb Rd Ravenna (44266) *(G-11518)*

Beck Studios Inc..513 831-6650
1001 Tech Dr Milford (45150) *(G-9925)*

Becker Signs Inc..330 659-4504
6381 Chittenden Rd Ste E9 Hudson (44236) *(G-7834)*

Beckett Air Incorporated (PA)..440 327-9999
37850 Taylor Pkwy North Ridgeville (44039) *(G-10725)*

Beckett Gas Inc (HQ)..440 327-3141
38000 Taylor Pkwy North Ridgeville (44039) *(G-10726)*

Beckett Thermal Solutions, North Ridgeville Also Called: Beckett Gas Inc *(G-10726)*

Beckett-Greenhill LLC..216 861-5730
1800 E 30th St Cleveland (44114) *(G-3413)*

Beckman & Gast Company (PA)..419 678-4195
282 W Kremer Hoying Rd Saint Henry (45883) *(G-11720)*

Beckman Environmental Svcs Inc..513 752-3570
4259 Armstrong Blvd Batavia (45103) *(G-853)*

Beckman Machine LLC..513 242-2700
4684 Paddock Rd Cincinnati (45229) *(G-2405)*

Beckman Xmo..614 864-2232
376 Morrison Rd Ste D Columbus (43213) *(G-4747)*

Beckman Xmo, Columbus Also Called: S Beckman Print Grphic Sltons *(G-5240)*

Becton Dickinson and Company..858 617-4272
2727 London Groveport Rd Groveport (43125) *(G-7424)*

Bedford Gear, Solon Also Called: Joy Global Underground Min LLC *(G-12132)*

Bedford Laboratories, Bedford Also Called: Ben Venue Laboratories Inc *(G-1016)*

Bee Valve, Elyria Also Called: Plastic Enterprises Inc *(G-6581)*

Beebe Worldwide Graphics Sign..513 241-2726
9933 Alliance Rd Ste 2 Blue Ash (45242) *(G-1250)*

Beech Engineering & Mfg, New Philadelphia Also Called: Miller Products Inc *(G-10458)*

Beehex Inc..512 633-5304
1130 Gahanna Pkwy Columbus (43230) *(G-4748)*

Beehex LLC..512 633-5304
1130 Gahanna Pkwy Columbus (43230) *(G-4749)*

Beemer Machine Company Inc..330 678-3822
1530 Enterprise Way Kent (44240) *(G-8018)*

Bef Foods Inc..937 372-4493
640 Birch Rd Xenia (45385) *(G-14754)*

Behrco Inc..419 394-1612
1865 Celina Rd Saint Marys (45885) *(G-11731)*

Beiersdorf Inc..513 682-7300
5232 E Provident Dr West Chester (45246) *(G-14107)*

Beijing West Industries..937 455-5281
3100 Research Blvd Ste 10 Dayton (45420) *(G-5675)*

Beitner Tire, Toledo Also Called: Capital Tire Inc *(G-12911)*

Bekaert Corporation..330 683-5060
510 Collins Blvd Orrville (44667) *(G-10974)*

Bekaert Corporation..330 683-5060
322 E Pine St Orrville (44667) *(G-10975)*

Bekaert Orrville, Orrville Also Called: Bekaert Corporation *(G-10974)*

Bel-Air Mattress Company, Columbus Also Called: Solstice Sleep Products Inc *(G-5275)*

Belaire Products Inc..330 253-3116
763 S Broadway St Akron (44311) *(G-75)*

Belanger Inc (DH)..517 870-3206
9393 Princeton Glendale Rd West Chester (45011) *(G-13948)*

BELCO WORKS, Saint Clairsville Also Called: Belco Works Inc *(G-11688)*

Belco Works Inc..740 695-0500
68425 Hammond Rd Saint Clairsville (43950) *(G-11688)*

Belden Brick Company LLC..330 456-0031
700 Edelweiss Dr Ne Sugarcreek (44681) *(G-12632)*

Belden Brick Company LLC..330 265-2030
690 Dover Rd Ne Sugarcreek (44681) *(G-12633)*

Belden Brick Plant 3, Sugarcreek Also Called: Belden Brick Company LLC *(G-12633)*

Belem Group LLC..614 604-6870
6012 E Main St Columbus (43213) *(G-4750)*

Bell Binders LLC..419 242-3201
320 21st St Toledo (43604) *(G-12895)*

Bell Industrial Services LLC..937 507-9193
1553 Target Dr Sidney (45365) *(G-11997)*

Bell Industries..513 353-2355
9843 New Haven Rd Harrison (45030) *(G-7543)*

Bell Logistics Co..740 702-9830
27311 Old Route 35 Chillicothe (45601) *(G-2245)*

Bell Optical, Twinsburg Also Called: Essilor Laboratories Amer Inc *(G-13300)*

Bell Tire Co (PA)..440 234-8022
27003 Oakwood Cir Apt 107 Olmsted Falls (44138) *(G-10937)*

Bell Vault and Monu Works Inc..937 866-2444
1019 S Main St Miamisburg (45342) *(G-9668)*

Bellas Jewels LLC..216 551-9593
975 Parkwood Dr Apt 10ste1 Cleveland (44108) *(G-3414)*

Bellco Feeders LLC..440 728-5590
7757 Auburn Rd Ste 23 Concord Township (44077) *(G-5387)*

Belle Center Air Tool Co Inc..937 464-7474
202 N Elizabeth St Belle Center (43310) *(G-1094)*

Bellevue Gazette, Oberlin Also Called: Gazette Publishing Company *(G-10917)*

Bellevue Manufacturing Company (PA)..419 483-3190
520 Goodrich Rd Bellevue (44811) *(G-1120)*

Bellisio..740 286-5505
100 E Broadway St Jackson (45640) *(G-7939)*

Bellisio Foods Inc..740 286-5505
100 E Bdwy Jackson (45640) *(G-7940)*

Belmont Community Health Ctr, Bellaire Also Called: Belmont Community Hospital *(G-1085)*

Belmont Community Hospital..740 671-1216
4697 Harrison St Bellaire (43906) *(G-1085)*

Belmont Stamping, Shadyside Also Called: Knight Manufacturing Co Inc *(G-11922)*

Belot Concrete Block, Tiltonsville Also Called: Walden Industries Inc *(G-12810)*

Belton Foods, Dayton Also Called: Belton Foods LLC *(G-5676)*

Belton Foods LLC..937 890-7768
2701 Thunderhawk Ct Dayton (45414) *(G-5676)*

Ben Venue Laboratories Inc..800 989-3320
300 Northfield Rd Bedford (44146) *(G-1016)*

Bena Inc..419 299-3313
1390 Township Road 229 Van Buren (45889) *(G-13524)*

Benchmark Archtectural Systems..614 444-0110
720 Marion Rd Columbus (43207) *(G-4751)*

Benchmark Craftsman Inc..866 313-4700
4700 Greenwich Rd Seville (44273) *(G-11910)*

Benchmark Craftsmen, Seville Also Called: Benchmark Craftsman Inc *(G-11910)*

Benchmark Education Co LLC..845 215-9808
6295 Commerce Center Dr Ste B Groveport (43125) *(G-7425)*

Benchmark Land Management LLC..513 310-7850
9431 Butler Warren Rd West Chester (45069) *(G-13949)*

Benchmark Prcision Fabrication, Wapakoneta Also Called: Benchmark Precision Fab Inc *(G-13706)*

Benchmark Precision Fab Inc..419 647-2003
18692 Moulton Fort Amanda Rd Wapakoneta (45895) *(G-13706)*

Bendco Machine & Tool Inc..419 628-3802
283 W 1st St Minster (45865) *(G-10054)*

Bender Communications Inc (PA)..740 382-0000
1541 Harding Hwy E Marion (43302) *(G-8965)*

Bender Engineering Company..330 938-2355
17934 Mill St Beloit (44609) *(G-1144)*

Bendix, Avon Also Called: Bendix Coml Vhcl Systems LLC *(G-716)*

Bendix Coml Vhcl Systems LLC (DH)..440 329-9000
35500 Chester Rd Avon (44011) *(G-716)*

Bendon Inc (PA)..419 207-3600
1840 S Baney Rd Ashland (44805) *(G-521)*

Bendon Publishing Intl, Ashland Also Called: Bendon Inc *(G-521)*

Benjamin Media Inc..330 467-7588
10050 Brecksville Rd Brecksville (44141) *(G-1459)*

Benjamin P Forbes Company..440 838-4400
800 Ken Mar Industrial Pkwy Broadview Heights (44147) *(G-1499)*

Benko Products Inc..440 934-2180
5350 Evergreen Pkwy Sheffield Village (44054) *(G-11957)*

Benmit Division, North Lawrence Also Called: US Tubular Products Inc *(G-10703)*

Bennett & Bennett Inc (PA)..937 324-1100
888 Dayton St Yellow Springs (45387) *(G-14786)*

Bennett Displays, Geneva Also Called: Dwayne Bennett Industries *(G-7235)*

Bennett Electric Inc..800 874-5405
211 Republic St Norwalk (44857) *(G-10830)*

Bennett Machine & Stamping Co................................ 440 415-0401
   150 D Termination Ave Geneva (44041) *(G-7234)*

Bensan Jewelers Inc.. 216 221-1434
   14410 Madison Ave Lakewood (44107) *(G-8163)*

Bentronix Corp... 440 632-0606
   14999 Madison Rd Middlefield (44062) *(G-9782)*

Benvic Trinity LLC (DH)..609 520-0000
   600 Oak St West Unity (43570) *(G-14192)*

Benzle Porcelain Company...................................... 614 876-2159
   6100 Hayden Run Rd Hilliard (43026) *(G-7676)*

Berea Printing Company... 440 243-1080
   95 Pelret Industrial Pkwy Berea (44017) *(G-1161)*

Bergen, W J & Co, Solon *Also Called: William J Bergen & Co (G-12208)*

Berghausen Corporation.. 513 591-4491
   4524 Este Ave Cincinnati (45232) *(G-2406)*

Bergholz 7, Bergholz *Also Called: Rosebud Mining Company (G-1196)*

Bergstrom Company Ltd Partnr................................. 440 232-2282
   640 Golden Oak Pkwy Cleveland (44146) *(G-3415)*

Beringer Plating Inc.. 330 633-8409
   1211 Devalera St Akron (44310) *(G-76)*

Berkshire Road Holdings Inc.................................... 216 883-4200
   3344 E 80th St Cleveland (44127) *(G-3416)*

Berlekamp Plastics Inc.. 419 334-4481
   2587 County Road 99 Fremont (43420) *(G-7094)*

Berlin Inds Protector Pdts, Youngstown *Also Called: Berlin Industries Inc (G-14819)*

Berlin Industries Inc... 330 549-2100
   1275 Boardman Poland Rd Ste 1 Youngstown (44514) *(G-14819)*

Berlin Parts, Millersburg *Also Called: Berlin Truck Caps & Tarps Ltd (G-9970)*

Berlin Truck Caps & Tarps Ltd................................ 330 893-2811
   4560 State Route 39 Millersburg (44654) *(G-9970)*

Berman Industries Inc.. 513 874-7477
   10999 Reed Hartman Hwy Ste 204 Blue Ash (45242) *(G-1251)*

Bernard Engraving Corp.. 419 478-5610
   414 N Erie St Ste 100 Toledo (43604) *(G-12896)*

Bernard Laboratories Inc.. 513 681-7373
   1738 Townsend St Cincinnati (45223) *(G-2407)*

Berran Industrial Group Inc..................................... 330 253-5800
   570 Wolf Ledges Pkwy Akron (44311) *(G-77)*

Berry Company.. 513 768-7800
   312 Plum St Ste 600 Cincinnati (45202) *(G-2408)*

Berry Film Products Co Inc (DH)..............................800 225-6729
   8585 Duke Blvd Mason (45040) *(G-9071)*

Berry Global Inc.. 419 887-1602
   1695 Indian Wood Cir Maumee (43537) *(G-9266)*

Berry Global Inc.. 419 465-2291
   311 Monroe St Monroeville (44847) *(G-10117)*

Berry Global Inc.. 330 896-6700
   1275 Ethan Ave Streetsboro (44241) *(G-12492)*

Berry Investments Inc.. 937 293-0398
   3055 Kettering Blvd Ste 418 Moraine (45439) *(G-10150)*

Berry Plastics, Monroeville *Also Called: Berry Global Inc (G-10117)*

Berry Plastics Filmco Inc....................................... 330 562-6111
   1450 S Chillicothe Rd Aurora (44202) *(G-664)*

Bertec Corporation.. 614 543-8099
   2500 Citygate Dr Columbus (43219) *(G-4752)*

Besa Lighting Co Inc... 614 475-7046
   6695 Taylor Rd Blacklick (43004) *(G-1220)*

Bescast Inc... 440 946-5300
   4600 E 355th St Willoughby (44094) *(G-14430)*

Besco, Batavia *Also Called: Beckman Environmental Svcs Inc (G-853)*

Besi Manufacturing Inc.. 513 874-1460
   9445 Sutton Pl West Chester (45011) *(G-13950)*

Besi Manufacturing Inc (PA).................................... 513 874-0232
   9087 Sutton Pl West Chester (45011) *(G-13951)*

Bessamaire Sales Inc.. 440 439-1200
   1869 E Aurora Rd Ste 700 Twinsburg (44087) *(G-13279)*

Bessamaire Sales Intl LLC...................................... 800 321-5992
   1869 E Aurora Rd Twinsburg (44087) *(G-13280)*

Best Controls Company, Ashland *Also Called: Chandler Systems Incorporated (G-528)*

Best Equipment Co Inc... 440 237-3515
   12620 York Delta Dr North Royalton (44133) *(G-10755)*

Best Fab Co., Elyria *Also Called: Stays Lighting Inc (G-6592)*

Best Glass, West Alexandria *Also Called: Kimmatt Corp (G-13920)*

Best Graphics & Printing Inc.................................... 513 535-3529
   11836 Stone Mill Rd Cincinnati (45251) *(G-2409)*

Best Inc.. 419 394-2745
   State Rte 116 Saint Marys (45885) *(G-11732)*

Best Lighting Products, Pataskala *Also Called: Best Lighting Products Inc (G-11137)*

Best Lighting Products Inc (HQ)................................ 740 964-1198
   1213 Etna Pkwy Pataskala (43062) *(G-11137)*

Best Mold & Manufacturing Inc................................. 330 896-9988
   1546 E Turkeyfoot Lake Rd Akron (44312) *(G-78)*

Best One Tire & Svc Lima Inc................................... 419 425-3322
   10456 W Us Route 224 Unit 1 Findlay (45840) *(G-6843)*

Best One Tire & Svc Lima Inc (PA)............................419 229-2380
   701 E Hanthorn Rd Lima (45804) *(G-8389)*

Best One Tire of Hillsboro, Hillsboro *Also Called: Mid America Tire of Hillsboro Inc (G-7720)*

Best Performance Inc... 419 394-2299
   14381 State Route 116 Saint Marys (45885) *(G-11733)*

Best Process Solutions Inc...................................... 330 220-1440
   1071 Industrial Pkwy N Brunswick (44212) *(G-1581)*

Best Result Marketing Inc....................................... 234 212-1194
   7730 First Pl Ste E Bedford (44146) *(G-1017)*

Bestwood Cabinetry LLC... 937 661-9621
   117 W Main St Xenia (45385) *(G-14755)*

Beta Industries Inc (PA)... 937 299-7385
   2860 Culver Ave Dayton (45429) *(G-5677)*

Betco Corporation Ltd (HQ)..................................... 419 241-2156
   400 Van Camp Rd Bowling Green (43402) *(G-1409)*

Bethart Enterprises Inc (PA).................................... 513 863-6161
   531 Main St Hamilton (45013) *(G-7470)*

Bethart Printing Services, Hamilton *Also Called: Bethart Enterprises Inc (G-7470)*

Bethel Engineering, New Hampshire *Also Called: Bethel Engineering and Eqp Inc (G-10396)*

Bethel Engineering and Eqp Inc................................ 419 568-1100
   13830 Mcbeth Rd New Hampshire (45870) *(G-10396)*

Better Banner Printing, New Philadelphia *Also Called: Pro A V of Ohio (G-10462)*

Better Brake Parts Inc... 419 227-0685
   915 Shawnee Rd Lima (45805) *(G-8390)*

Better Foam Insulation, South Point *Also Called: Pyro-Chem Corporation (G-12230)*

Better Living Concepts Inc...................................... 330 494-2213
   7233 Freedom Ave Nw Canton (44720) *(G-1839)*

Betts Company.. 330 533-0111
   430 W Main St Canfield (44406) *(G-1805)*

Betts Hd, Canfield *Also Called: Betts Company (G-1805)*

Bevcorp Properties, Eastlake *Also Called: Miconvi Properties Inc (G-6435)*

Beverage Mch & Fabricators Inc............................... 216 252-5100
   13301 Lakewood Heights Blvd Cleveland (44107) *(G-3417)*

Beverages Holdings LLC.. 513 483-3300
   10300 Alliance Rd Ste 500 Blue Ash (45242) *(G-1252)*

Beverly Dove Inc.. 740 495-5200
   43 E Front St New Holland (43145) *(G-10397)*

Bexley Fabrics Inc.. 614 231-7272
   2476 E Main St Columbus (43209) *(G-4753)*

Bfc Inc (PA).. 330 364-6645
   1213 E 3rd St Dover (44622) *(G-6230)*

Bfs Supply, Cincinnati *Also Called: Frederick Steel Company LLC (G-2641)*

Bharat Trading, Cincinnati *Also Called: Goyal Enterprises Inc (G-2686)*

Bhi Transition Inc... 937 663-4152
   8801 Us Highway 36 Saint Paris (43072) *(G-11756)*

Bi-Con Services Inc.. 740 685-2542
   10901 Clay Pike Rd Derwent (43733) *(G-6221)*

Bia Factory, The, Hebron *Also Called: Keho Fitness and Nutrition LLC (G-7621)*

Bianchi Usa Inc... 440 801-1083
   31336 Industrial Pkwy Ste 3 North Olmsted (44070) *(G-10718)*

Bic Manufacturing Inc... 216 531-9393
   26420 Century Corners Pkwy Euclid (44132) *(G-6644)*

Blc Precision Machine Co Inc................................... 937 783-1406
   3004 Cherry St Blanchester (45107) *(G-1233)*

Bickers Metal Products Inc...................................... 513 353-4000
   5825 State Rte128 Miamitown (45041) *(G-9756)*

Bico Akron Inc... 330 794-1716
   3100 Gilchrist Rd Mogadore (44260) *(G-10070)*

A
L
P
H
A
B
E
T
I
C

Bico Steel Service Centers, Mogadore Also Called: Bico Akron Inc (G-10070)

Bidwell Family Corporation (HQ).................513 988-6351
400 E State St Trenton (45067) **(G-13191)**

Biedenbach Logging.................740 732-6477
48443 Seneca Lake Rd Sarahsville (43779) **(G-11884)**

Bif Co LLC.................330 564-0941
1405 Home Ave Akron (44310) **(G-79)**

Bif, LLC, Akron Also Called: Bif Co LLC (G-79)

Big Chief Manufacturing Ltd.................513 934-3888
250 Harmon Ave Lebanon (45036) **(G-8247)**

Big Gus Onion Rings Inc.................216 883-9045
4500 Turney Rd Cleveland (44105) **(G-3418)**

Big Kahuna Graphics, Canton Also Called: Big Kahuna Graphics LLC (G-1840)

Big Kahuna Graphics LLC.................330 455-2625
1255 Prospect Ave Sw Canton (44706) **(G-1840)**

Big Productions Inc.................440 775-0015
45300b Us Highway 20 Oberlin (44074) **(G-10915)**

Big River Electric, Gallipolis Also Called: Big River Electric Inc (G-7202)

Big River Electric Inc.................740 446-4360
299 Upper River Rd Gallipolis (45631) **(G-7202)**

Bigmar Inc.................740 966-5800
9711 Sportsman Club Rd Johnstown (43031) **(G-7992)**

Bijoe Development Inc.................330 674-5981
7188 State Rte 62 & 39 Millersburg (44654) **(G-9971)**

Bil-Jac Foods, Medina Also Called: Kelly Foods Corporation (G-9418)

Bil-Jac Foods Inc (PA).................330 722-7888
3337 Medina Rd Medina (44256) **(G-9380)**

Bil-Jax Inc (DH).................419 445-8915
125 Taylor Pkwy Archbold (43502) **(G-490)**

Bilco Company.................740 455-9020
3400 Jim Granger Dr Zanesville (43701) **(G-14995)**

Biljax Scaffolding, Archbold Also Called: Bil-Jax Inc (G-490)

Bill's Counter Tops, Saint Clairsville Also Called: D Lewis Inc (G-11690)

Billerud Americas Corporation (HQ).................877 855-7243
10050 Innovation Dr Ste 200 Miamisburg (45342) **(G-9669)**

Billerud Americas Corporation.................901 369-4105
9025 Centre Pointe Dr West Chester (45069) **(G-13952)**

Billerud Commercial LLC.................877 855-7243
8540 Gander Creek Dr Miamisburg (45342) **(G-9670)**

Billerud Escanaba LLC.................877 855-7243
8540 Gander Creek Dr Miamisburg (45342) **(G-9671)**

Billerud US Prod Holdg LLC (DH).................877 855-7243
10050 Innovation Dr Ste 200 Miamisburg (45342) **(G-9672)**

Billington Company Inc.................440 647-3039
143 Erie St Wellington (44090) **(G-13883)**

Billock, John N Cpo, Warren Also Called: Orthotics Prsthtics Rhbltion (G-13788)

Bilz Vibration Technology Inc.................330 468-2459
895 Highland Rd E Ste F Macedonia (44056) **(G-8678)**

Bimac, Dayton Also Called: Santos Industrial Ltd (G-5994)

Bimbo Qsr Us LLC.................740 562-4188
750 Airport Rd Zanesville (43701) **(G-14996)**

Bindery & Spc Pressworks Inc.................614 873-4623
351 W Bigelow Ave Plain City (43064) **(G-11398)**

Bindtech LLC.................615 834-0404
8212 Bavaria Dr E Macedonia (44056) **(G-8679)**

Bindusa.................513 247-3000
6819 Ashfield Dr Blue Ash (45242) **(G-1253)**

Binkley, Geoffrey, Columbus Also Called: Signme LLC (G-5269)

Binos Inc.................330 938-0888
700 W Ohio Ave Sebring (44672) **(G-11892)**

Bio-Blood Components Inc.................614 294-3183
1393 N High St Columbus (43201) **(G-4754)**

Bio-Systems Corporation.................608 365-9550
400 Van Camp Rd Bowling Green (43402) **(G-1410)**

Biobent Holdings LLC.................513 658-5560
1275 Kinnear Rd Ste 239 Columbus (43212) **(G-4755)**

Biobent Polymers, Columbus Also Called: Biobent Holdings LLC (G-4755)

Biofit Engineered Products Limited Partnership (PA).................419 823-1089
15500 Bio Fit Way Bowling Green (43402) **(G-1411)**

Bionix Radiation Therapy, Maumee Also Called: M&H Medical Holdings Inc (G-9305)

Bionix Safety Technologies Ltd (HQ).................419 727-0552
1670 Indian Wood Cir Maumee (43537) **(G-9267)**

Biosortia Pharmaceuticals Inc.................614 636-4850
4266 Tuller Rd Dublin (43017) **(G-6281)**

Biothane Coated Webbing Corp.................440 327-0485
34655 Mills Rd North Ridgeville (44039) **(G-10727)**

Biowish, Cincinnati Also Called: Biowish Technologies Inc (G-2410)

Biowish Technologies Inc.................312 572-6700
2724 Erie Ave Ste B Cincinnati (45208) **(G-2410)**

Biowish Technologies Inc.................312 572-6700
2717 Erie Ave Cincinnati (45208) **(G-2411)**

Bird Control International.................330 425-2377
1393 Highland Rd Twinsburg (44087) **(G-13281)**

Bird Electronic Corporation.................440 248-1200
30303 Aurora Rd Solon (44139) **(G-12084)**

Bird Equipment LLC.................330 549-1004
11950 South Ave North Lima (44452) **(G-10704)**

Bird Technologies Group Inc (PA).................440 248-1200
30303 Aurora Rd Solon (44139) **(G-12085)**

Bird Watcher's Digest, Marietta Also Called: Pardson Inc (G-8934)

Birds Eye Foods Inc.................330 854-0818
611 Elm Ridge Ave Canal Fulton (44614) **(G-1773)**

Biro Manufacturing Company (PA).................419 798-4451
1114 W Main St Marblehead (43440) **(G-8895)**

Biro Manufacturing Company.................419 798-4451
6658 Promway Ave Nw North Canton (44720) **(G-10630)**

Biro Manufacturing Company, Marblehead Also Called: Biro Manufacturing Company (G-8895)

Bis Printing.................440 951-2606
35401 Euclid Ave Willoughby (44094) **(G-14431)**

Bishop Machine Shop, Zanesville Also Called: Bishop Machine Tool & Die (G-14997)

Bishop Machine Tool & Die.................740 453-8818
2304 Hoge Ave Zanesville (43701) **(G-14997)**

Bishop Well Services Corp.................330 264-2023
416 N Bauer Rd Wooster (44691) **(G-14626)**

Bismark Lawncare LLC.................440 361-5561
4057 State Route 307 Austinburg (44010) **(G-696)**

Bison Builders LLC.................614 636-0365
6999 Huntley Rd Ste M Columbus (43229) **(G-4756)**

Bison Leather Co.................419 517-1737
7409 W Central Ave Toledo (43617) **(G-12897)**

Bitec, Dayton Also Called: Sample Machining Inc (G-5993)

BITTERSWEET FARMS, Whitehouse Also Called: Bittersweet Inc (G-14358)

Bittersweet Inc (PA).................419 875-6986
12660 Archbold Whitehouse Rd Whitehouse (43571) **(G-14358)**

Bittinger Carbide, Cadiz Also Called: Stanley Bittinger (G-1720)

Bizall Inc.................216 939-9580
1935 W 96th St Ste H Cleveland (44102) **(G-3419)**

Bizzy Bee Printing Inc.................614 771-1222
1500 W 3rd Ave Ste 106 Columbus (43212) **(G-4757)**

BJ Equipment Ltd.................614 497-1188
4522 Lockbourne Rd Columbus (43207) **(G-4758)**

Bjond Inc.................614 537-7246
1463 Briarmeadow Dr Columbus (43235) **(G-4759)**

Bjs DEMO&hauling LLC.................216 904-8909
4937 E 88th St Garfield Heights (44125) **(G-7216)**

Bk Tool Company Inc.................513 870-9622
300 Security Dr Fairfield (45014) **(G-6714)**

Bkt, Copley Also Called: Bkt USA Inc (G-5430)

Bkt USA Inc.................330 836-1090
202 Montrose West Ave Ste 240 Copley (44321) **(G-5430)**

Black & Decker, Cleveland Also Called: Black & Decker Corporation (G-3420)

Black & Decker (us) Inc.................614 895-3112
1948 Schrock Rd Columbus (43229) **(G-4760)**

Black & Decker Corporation.................440 842-9100
12100 Snow Rd Ste 1 Cleveland (44130) **(G-3420)**

Black Box Corporation.................800 676-8850
6650 W Snowville Rd Ste R Brecksville (44141) **(G-1460)**

Black Box Corporation.................800 837-7777
5400 Frantz Rd Ste 240 Dublin (43016) **(G-6282)**

Black Box Corporation.................614 825-7400
255 Enterprise Dr Lewis Center (43035) **(G-8325)**

(G-0000) Company's Geographic Section entry number

Black Box Corporation.................................... 855 324-9909
26100 1st St Westlake (44145) *(G-14292)*

Black Box Network Services, Lewis Center Also Called: Black Box Corporation *(G-8325)*

Black Box Network Services, Westlake Also Called: Black Box Corporation *(G-14292)*

Black Gold Capital LLC.................................... 614 348-7460
2121 Bethel Rd Ste A Columbus (43220) *(G-4761)*

Black Lab Custom Products, Chardon Also Called: Kona Blackbird Inc *(G-2211)*

Black Lion Products LLC.................................... 234 232-3680
3710 Hendricks Rd Youngstown (44515) *(G-14820)*

Black Machining & Tech Inc.................................... 513 752-8625
4020 Bach Buxton Rd Batavia (45103) *(G-854)*

Black River Display Group, Mansfield Also Called: Black River Group Inc *(G-8765)*

Black River Group Inc (PA).................................... 419 524-6699
195 E 4th St Mansfield (44902) *(G-8765)*

Black Squirrel Holdings Inc.................................... 513 577-7107
225 Northland Blvd Cincinnati (45246) *(G-2412)*

Black Wing Shooting Center LLC.................................... 740 363-7555
3722 Marysville Rd Delaware (43015) *(G-6134)*

Blackburns Fabrication Inc.................................... 614 875-0784
2467 Jackson Pike Columbus (43223) *(G-4762)*

Blacklick Machine Company.................................... 614 866-9300
265 North St Blacklick (43004) *(G-1221)*

Blackstar International Inc.................................... 917 510-5482
361 Indian Mound Rd Columbus (43213) *(G-4763)*

Blackthorn LLC.................................... 937 836-9296
6113 Brookville Salem Rd Clayton (45315) *(G-3272)*

Blackwood Sheet Metal Inc.................................... 614 291-3115
844 Kerr St Columbus (43215) *(G-4764)*

Blade Manufacturing Co, The, Columbus Also Called: Callahan Cutting Tools Inc *(G-4792)*

Blains Folding Service Inc.................................... 216 631-4700
4103 Detroit Ave Cleveland (44113) *(G-3421)*

Blair Logging.................................... 740 934-2730
30530 Lebanon Rd Lower Salem (45745) *(G-8665)*

Blair Rubber, Seville Also Called: Blair Sales Inc *(G-11912)*

Blair Rubber Company.................................... 330 769-5583
5020 Enterprise Pkwy Seville (44273) *(G-11911)*

Blair Sales Inc.................................... 330 769-5586
5020 Enterprise Pkwy Seville (44273) *(G-11912)*

Blair's Cnc, Dayton Also Called: Blairs Cnc Turning Inc *(G-5678)*

Blairs Cnc Turning Inc.................................... 937 461-1100
245 Leo St Dayton (45404) *(G-5678)*

Blaney Hardwoods Ohio Inc.................................... 740 678-8288
425 Timberline Dr Vincent (45784) *(G-13619)*

Blang Acquisition LLC.................................... 937 223-2155
7464 Webster St Dayton (45414) *(G-5679)*

Blankenship Logging LLC.................................... 740 372-3833
133 Curtis Smith Rd Otway (45667) *(G-11058)*

Blaster Corporation.................................... 216 901-5800
775 W Smith Rd Medina (44256) *(G-9381)*

BLaster Holdings LLC (PA).................................... 216 901-5800
8500 Sweet Valley Dr Cleveland (44125) *(G-3422)*

BLaster LLC (PA).................................... 216 901-5800
8500 Sweet Valley Dr Cleveland (44125) *(G-3423)*

Blastwrap, Columbus Also Called: Highcom Global Security Inc *(G-4981)*

Blatchford Inc.................................... 937 291-3636
1031 Byers Rd Miamisburg (45342) *(G-9673)*

Blaze Technical Services Inc.................................... 330 923-0409
1445 Commerce Dr Stow (44224) *(G-12422)*

Bleachtech LLC.................................... 216 921-1980
320 Ryan Rd Seville (44273) *(G-11913)*

Blend of Seven Winery, Delaware Also Called: Sandra Weddington *(G-6172)*

Blevins Fabrication, Mansfield Also Called: Blevins Metal Fabrication Inc *(G-8766)*

Blevins Metal Fabrication Inc.................................... 419 522-6082
288 Illinois Ave S Mansfield (44905) *(G-8766)*

Blf Enterprises Inc.................................... 937 642-6425
445 S State St Westerville (43081) *(G-14246)*

Blinged & Bronzed.................................... 330 631-1255
2303 Manchester Rd Akron (44314) *(G-80)*

Blingflingforever LLC.................................... 216 215-6955
7383 Dahlia Dr Mentor On The Lake (44060) *(G-9657)*

Blink Marketing Logistics, Perrysburg Also Called: Bottomline Ink Corporation *(G-11205)*

Blink Print & Mail, Toledo Also Called: Northcoast Pmm LLC *(G-13064)*

Bloch Printing Company.................................... 330 576-6760
3569 Copley Rd Copley (44321) *(G-5431)*

Block Communications Inc (PA).................................... 419 724-6212
405 Madison Ave Ste 2100 Toledo (43604) *(G-12898)*

Blockamerica Corporation.................................... 614 274-0700
750 Kaderly Dr Columbus (43228) *(G-4765)*

Blonde Swan.................................... 419 307-8591
307 W State St Fremont (43420) *(G-7095)*

Blonder Home Accents, Cleveland Also Called: The Blonder Company *(G-4379)*

Bloom Industries Inc.................................... 330 898-3878
1052 Mahoney Ave Nw Warren (44483) *(G-13743)*

Bloomer Candy Co.................................... 740 452-7501
3610 National Rd Zanesville (43701) *(G-14998)*

Blooming Services, Dennison Also Called: Blooms Printing Inc *(G-6216)*

Bloomngburg Spring Wire Form I.................................... 740 437-7614
83 Main St Bloomingburg (43106) *(G-1239)*

Blooms Printing Inc.................................... 740 922-1765
4792 N 4th Street Ext Se Dennison (44621) *(G-6216)*

Blt Inc.................................... 513 631-5050
2834 Highland Ave Norwood (45212) *(G-10866)*

Blu Bird LLC.................................... 513 271-5646
4820 Stafford St Cincinnati (45227) *(G-2413)*

Blu Bird LLC (PA).................................... 614 276-3585
1736 Mckinley Ave Columbus (43222) *(G-4766)*

Blue Ash Tool & Die Co Inc.................................... 513 793-4530
4245 Creek Rd Blue Ash (45241) *(G-1254)*

Blue Chip Manufacturing & Sales Inc.................................... 614 475-3853
3155 Lamb Ave Columbus (43219) *(G-4767)*

Blue Chip Tool Inc.................................... 513 489-3561
11511 Goldcoast Dr Cincinnati (45249) *(G-2414)*

Blue Collar M LLC.................................... 216 209-5666
31005 Bainbridge Rd Ste 2 Solon (44139) *(G-12086)*

Blue Creek Enterprises Inc.................................... 937 222-9969
2153 Winners Cir Dayton (45404) *(G-5680)*

Blue Creek Enterprises Inc.................................... 937 364-2920
401 Starks Ave Ste A Manchester (45144) *(G-8753)*

Blue Crescent Enterprises Inc.................................... 440 878-9700
17295 Foltz Pkwy Ste B Strongsville (44149) *(G-12545)*

Blue Fin Environmental LLC.................................... 330 415-6010
8753 Sycamore Trails Dr Springboro (45066) *(G-12247)*

Blue Grass Cooperage - Jackson, Wellston Also Called: Brown-Forman Corporation *(G-13905)*

Blue Racer Midstream LLC.................................... 740 630-7556
11388 E Pike Rd Unit B Cambridge (43725) *(G-1737)*

Blue Ridge Paper Products LLC.................................... 440 235-7200
7920 Mapleway Dr Olmsted Falls (44138) *(G-10938)*

Blue Skies Operating Corp.................................... 877 330-2354
1661 Saint Marys Rd Sidney (45365) *(G-11998)*

Bluelogos Inc.................................... 614 898-9971
130 Graphic Way Westerville (43081) *(G-14247)*

Bluffton News Pubg & Prtg Co (PA).................................... 419 358-8010
101 S Main St Bluffton (45817) *(G-1357)*

Bluffton News, The, Bluffton Also Called: Bluffton News Pubg & Prtg Co *(G-1357)*

Bluffton Stone Co.................................... 419 358-6941
310 Quarry Dr Bluffton (45817) *(G-1358)*

BMC, Strongsville Also Called: Bearings Manufacturing Company *(G-12544)*

BMC Growth Fund LLC.................................... 937 291-4110
2991 Newmark Dr Miamisburg (45342) *(G-9674)*

Bmca Insulation Products Inc.................................... 330 335-2501
270 Main St Wadsworth (44281) *(G-13629)*

Bmf Devices Inc.................................... 937 866-3451
510 S Riverview Ave Miamisburg (45342) *(G-9675)*

Board of Park Commissioners.................................... 216 635-3200
4101 Fulton Pkwy Cleveland (44144) *(G-3424)*

Boardman Molded Intl LLC.................................... 800 233-4575
1110 Thalia Ave Youngstown (44512) *(G-14821)*

Boardman Molded Products Inc (PA).................................... 330 788-2400
1110 Thalia Ave Youngstown (44512) *(G-14822)*

Boardman News.................................... 330 758-6397
8302 Southern Blvd Ste 2 Boardman (44512) *(G-1368)*

A
L
P
H
A
B
E
T
I
C

Boardman Printing, Youngstown *Also Called: Nomis Publications Inc (G-14904)*

Boardman Steel Inc..330 758-0951
156 Nulf Dr Columbiana (44408) *(G-4606)*

Bob Evans, Bidwell *Also Called: Bob Evans Farms Inc (G-1212)*

Bob Evans, Xenia *Also Called: Bef Foods Inc (G-14754)*

Bob Evans Farms Inc..740 245-5305
791 Farmview Rd Bidwell (45614) *(G-1212)*

Bob Lanes Welding Inc.......................................740 373-3567
5151 Warren Chapel Rd Marietta (45750) *(G-8904)*

Bob Sumerel Tire Co Inc.....................................614 527-9700
2807 International St Columbus (43228) *(G-4768)*

Bob Sumerel Tire Co Inc.....................................937 235-0062
7711 Center Point 70 Blvd Dayton (45424) *(G-5681)*

Bob Sumerel Tire Co Inc.....................................330 602-1733
204 Deeds Dr Dover (44622) *(G-6231)*

Bob Sumerel Tire Co Inc.....................................740 432-5200
63303 Institute Rd Lore City (43755) *(G-8588)*

Bob Sumerel Tire Co Inc.....................................330 769-9092
8692 Lake Rd Seville (44273) *(G-11914)*

Bob Sumerel Tire Co Inc.....................................740 454-9728
1140 Newark Rd Zanesville (43701) *(G-14999)*

Bob Sumerel Tire Company Inc.............................740 927-2811
67 Klema Dr N Ste D Reynoldsburg (43068) *(G-11559)*

Bobbart Industries Inc.......................................419 350-5477
5035 Alexis Rd Ste 1 Sylvania (43560) *(G-12702)*

Bobco Enterprises Inc..419 867-3560
2910 Glanzman Rd Toledo (43614) *(G-12899)*

Bocchi Laboratories, New Albany *Also Called: Shadow Holdings LLC (G-10350)*

Bocchi Laboratories Ohio LLC.............................614 741-7458
9200 Smiths Mill Rd N New Albany (43054) *(G-10332)*

Bock Company LLC..216 912-7050
2476 Edison Blvd Twinsburg (44087) *(G-13282)*

Bock Lighting, Twinsburg *Also Called: Bock Company LLC (G-13282)*

Bodied Beauties LLC...216 971-1155
4820 Geraldine Rd Richmond Heights (44143) *(G-11608)*

Bodnar Printing Co Inc..440 277-8295
3480 Colorado Ave Lorain (44052) *(G-8547)*

Bodor Vents Inc...513 348-3853
400 Murray Rd Cincinnati (45217) *(G-2415)*

Bodycote Imt Inc...740 852-5000
443 E High St London (43140) *(G-8531)*

Bodycote Kolsterising, London *Also Called: Bodycote Thermal Proc Inc (G-8532)*

Bodycote Srfc Tech Prperty LLC...........................513 770-4900
8118 Corporate Way Ste 201 Mason (45040) *(G-9072)*

Bodycote Surface Tech Inc (DH)...........................513 770-4922
8118 Corporate Way Ste 201 Mason (45040) *(G-9073)*

Bodycote Surfc Tech Group Inc (HQ)......................513 770-4900
8118 Corporate Way Ste 201 Mason (45040) *(G-9074)*

Bodycote Surfc Tech Mexico LLC..........................513 770-4900
8118 Corporate Way Ste 201 Mason (45040) *(G-9075)*

Bodycote Thermal Proc Inc..................................513 921-2300
710 Burns St Cincinnati (45204) *(G-2416)*

Bodycote Thermal Proc Inc..................................440 473-2020
5475 Avion Park Dr Cleveland (44143) *(G-3425)*

Bodycote Thermal Proc Inc..................................740 852-4955
443 E High St London (43140) *(G-8532)*

Boehm Inc (PA)..614 875-9010
2050 Hardy Parkway St Grove City (43123) *(G-7374)*

Boehm Pressed Steel Company............................330 220-8000
5440 Wegman Dr Valley City (44280) *(G-13491)*

Boeing, Heath *Also Called: Boeing Company (G-7594)*

Boeing Company..740 788-4000
801 Irving Wick Dr W Heath (43056) *(G-7594)*

Boes, Wilbert J, New Riegel *Also Called: Tr Boes Holdings Inc (G-10471)*

Boggs Equipment, Maple Heights *Also Called: Boggs Graphics Equipment LLC (G-8878)*

Boggs Graphics Equipment LLC............................888 837-8101
14901 Broadway Ave Maple Heights (44137) *(G-8878)*

Boggs Recycling Inc...800 837-8101
12355 Kinsman Rd Unit J Newbury (44065) *(G-10547)*

Bogie Industries Inc Ltd.....................................330 745-3105
1100 Home Ave Akron (44310) *(G-81)*

Boler Company..330 445-6728
2070 Industrial Pl Se Canton (44707) *(G-1841)*

Bollari/Davis Inc..330 296-4445
5292 S Prospect St Ravenna (44266) *(G-11519)*

Bollin & Sons Inc..419 693-6573
6001 Brent Dr Toledo (43611) *(G-12900)*

Bollin Label Systems, Toledo *Also Called: Bollin & Sons Inc (G-12900)*

Bollinger Tool & Die Inc......................................419 866-5180
959 Hamilton Dr Holland (43528) *(G-7746)*

Bolons Custom Kitchens Inc................................330 499-0092
6287 Promler St Nw Canton (44720) *(G-1842)*

Boltech Incorporated..330 746-6881
1201 Crescent St Youngstown (44502) *(G-14823)*

Bolttech Mannings LLC.......................................614 836-0021
351 Lowery Ct Ste 3 Groveport (43125) *(G-7426)*

Bomen Marking Products Inc...............................440 582-0053
12905 York Delta Dr Ste A Cleveland (44133) *(G-3426)*

Bond Chemicals Inc...330 725-5935
1154 W Smith Rd Medina (44256) *(G-9382)*

Bond Distributing LLC...440 461-7920
35585 Curtis Blvd Unit D Eastlake (44095) *(G-6420)*

Bond Machine Company Inc.................................937 746-4941
921 N Main St Franklin (45005) *(G-7011)*

Bonfoey Co...216 621-0178
1710 Euclid Ave Cleveland (44115) *(G-3427)*

Bonne Bell Company, The, Westlake *Also Called: Bonne Bell Inc (G-14293)*

Bonne Bell Inc...440 835-2440
1006 Crocker Rd Westlake (44145) *(G-14293)*

Bonne Bell LLC (PA)...440 835-2440
1006 Crocker Rd Westlake (44145) *(G-14294)*

Bonnot Company (PA)..330 896-6544
1301 Home Ave Akron (44310) *(G-82)*

Bonsal American Inc..513 398-7300
5155 Fischer Ave Cincinnati (45217) *(G-2417)*

Boogie Wipes, Cincinnati *Also Called: Eleeo Brands LLC (G-2582)*

Bookfactory LLC..937 226-7100
2302 S Edwin C Moses Blvd Dayton (45417) *(G-5682)*

Bookmasters Inc (HQ).......................................419 281-1802
30 Amberwood Pkwy Ashland (44805) *(G-522)*

Boomerang Rubber Inc.......................................937 693-4611
105 Dinsmore St Botkins (45306) *(G-1396)*

Bor-It Mfg Co Inc..419 289-6639
1687 Cleveland Rd Ashland (44805) *(G-523)*

Borchers Americas Inc (HQ)................................440 899-2950
811 Sharon Dr Westlake (44145) *(G-14295)*

Borden Dairy Co Cincinnati LLC (DH)....................513 948-8811
3068 W 106th St Cleveland (44111) *(G-3428)*

Border Lumber & Logging Ltd...............................330 897-0177
31181 County Road 10 Fresno (43824) *(G-7145)*

Bores Manufacturing Inc....................................419 465-2606
300 Sandusky St Monroeville (44847) *(G-10118)*

Bores, J F Mfg, Monroeville *Also Called: Bores Manufacturing Inc (G-10118)*

Borke Mold Specialist Inc...................................513 870-8000
9541 Glades Dr Hamilton (45011) *(G-7471)*

Borman Enterprises Inc......................................216 459-9292
1311 Brookpark Rd Cleveland (44109) *(G-3429)*

Bornhorst Motor Service Inc................................937 773-0426
8270 N Dixie Dr Piqua (45356) *(G-11337)*

Bornhorst Printing Company Inc............................419 738-5901
10139 County Road 25a Wapakoneta (45895) *(G-13707)*

Bortnick Tractor Sales Inc..................................330 924-2555
6192 Warren Rd Cortland (44410) *(G-5442)*

Bosc & Brie..614 985-2215
7625 N High St Columbus (43235) *(G-4769)*

Bosca Accesories, Springfield *Also Called: Hugo Bosca Company Inc (G-12327)*

Bosch Rexroth Corporation..................................330 263-3300
290 E Milltown Rd Wooster (44691) *(G-14627)*

Boscowood Ventures Inc......................................800 526-1816
7425 Industrial Parkway Dr Lorain (44053) *(G-8548)*

Bose Corporation...513 891-4384
7875 Montgomery Rd Spc 2422 Cincinnati (45236) *(G-2418)*

Bose Showcase Store, Cincinnati *Also Called: Bose Corporation (G-2418)*

Bosserman Automotive Engrg LLC................................ 419 722-2879
  18919 Olympic Dr Findlay (45840) *(G-6844)*

Bosserman Aviation Equipment Inc............................. 419 722-2879
  2327 State Highway 568 Carey (43316) *(G-2056)*

Bostik Inc... 419 289-9588
  1745 Cottage St Ashland (44805) *(G-524)*

Bostik Inc... 614 232-8510
  802 Harmon Ave Columbus (43223) *(G-4770)*

Boston Beer Company... 267 240-4429
  1625 Central Pkwy Cincinnati (45214) *(G-2419)*

Boston Stoker, Vandalia *Also Called: Boston Stoker Inc (G-13551)*

Boston Stoker Inc (PA)... 937 890-6401
  10855 Engle Rd Vandalia (45377) *(G-13551)*

Botanicare, Marysville *Also Called: American Agritech LLC (G-9014)*

Bottomline Ink Corporation....................................... 419 897-8000
  7829 Ponderosa Rd Perrysburg (43551) *(G-11205)*

Bourbon Plastics Inc... 574 342-0893
  111 Stow Ave Ste 100 Cuyahoga Falls (44221) *(G-5533)*

Boville Indus Coatings Inc... 330 669-8558
  7459 Leichty Rd Smithville (44677) *(G-12064)*

Bowden Fence Co LLC... 614 272-8923
  1560 Harmon Ave Columbus (43223) *(G-4771)*

Bowden Manufacturing Corp....................................... 440 946-1770
  4590 Beidler Rd Willoughby (44094) *(G-14432)*

Bowdil Company.. 800 356-8663
  2030 Industrial Pl Se Canton (44707) *(G-1843)*

Bowerston Shale Company (PA)................................... 740 269-2921
  515 Main St Bowerston (44695) *(G-1399)*

Bowerston Shale Company... 740 763-3921
  1329 Seven Hills Rd Newark (43055) *(G-10494)*

Bowes Manufacturing Inc... 216 378-2110
  30340 Solon Industrial Pkwy Ste B Solon (44139) *(G-12087)*

Bowman Tire Repr Ctr Bxley LLC................................. 740 928-7000
  110 Burch St Hebron (43025) *(G-7609)*

Bowmanmultimedia LLC... 419 405-8648
  470 W Broad St Columbus (43215) *(G-4772)*

Bowne of Columbus, Columbus *Also Called: RR Donnelley & Sons Company (G-5237)*

Bows Barrettes & Baubles... 440 247-2697
  4180 Chagrin River Rd Moreland Hills (44022) *(G-10198)*

Boxit Corporation.. 216 416-9475
  3000 Quigley Rd B Cleveland (44113) *(G-3430)*

Boxit Corporation (HQ).. 216 631-6900
  5555 Walworth Ave Cleveland (44102) *(G-3431)*

Boxout LLC (PA).. 833 462-7746
  6333 Hudson Crossing Pkwy Hudson (44236) *(G-7835)*

Boy-Rad Inc.. 614 766-1228
  7742 Sawmill Rd Dublin (43016) *(G-6283)*

Boyce Machine Inc... 330 678-3210
  3609 Mogadore Rd Kent (44240) *(G-8019)*

Boye & Emmes Machine, Cincinnati *Also Called: Enterprise Machine Inc (G-2592)*

BP 10 Inc... 513 346-3900
  9486 Sutton Pl Hamilton (45011) *(G-7472)*

BP Products North America Inc................................... 419 698-6400
  4001 Cedar Point Rd Oregon (43616) *(G-10959)*

BP Products North America Inc................................... 419 537-9540
  2450 Hill Ave Toledo (43607) *(G-12901)*

Bpr-Rico Equipment Inc (PA)....................................... 330 723-4050
  691 W Liberty St Medina (44256) *(G-9383)*

Bpr-Rico Manufacturing Inc....................................... 330 723-4050
  691 W Liberty St Medina (44256) *(G-9384)*

Bpr/Rico, Medina *Also Called: Bpr-Rico Manufacturing Inc (G-9384)*

Bprex Hlthcare Brookville Inc (DH)............................... 847 541-9700
  1899 N Wilkinson Way Perrysburg (43551) *(G-11206)*

Bprex Plastic Packaging Inc (DH)................................. 419 247-5000
  1 Seagate Toledo (43604) *(G-12902)*

Bprex Plastic Services Co Inc..................................... 419 247-5000
  1 Seagate Toledo (43604) *(G-12903)*

BR Ohio, Cincinnati *Also Called: B R Printers Inc (G-2396)*

BR Pallet Inc.. 419 427-2200
  21395 County Road 7 Alvada (44802) *(G-420)*

Brackish Media LLC... 513 394-2871
  2662 Mckinley Ave Cincinnati (45211) *(G-2420)*

Braden-Sutphin Ink Company, Cleveland *Also Called: Red Tie Group Inc (G-4229)*

Bradley Enterprises Inc (PA)....................................... 330 875-1444
  3750 Beck Ave Louisville (44641) *(G-8599)*

Bradley Stone Industries LLC..................................... 440 519-3277
  30801 Carter St Solon (44139) *(G-12088)*

Brady Ruck Company... 419 738-5126
  253 Indl Dr Wapakoneta (45895) *(G-13708)*

Brain Brew Ventures 30 Inc.. 513 310-6374
  3849 Edwards Rd Newtown (45244) *(G-10583)*

Brain Child Products LLC... 419 698-4020
  146 Main St Toledo (43605) *(G-12904)*

Brainard Rivet Company... 330 545-4931
  222 Harry St Girard (44420) *(G-7267)*

Brainerd Industries Inc (PA)....................................... 937 228-0488
  680 Precision Ct Miamisburg (45342) *(G-9676)*

Brainmaster Technologies Inc..................................... 440 232-6000
  195 Willis St # 3 Bedford (44146) *(G-1018)*

Brake Parts Holdings Inc (DH)..................................... 216 589-0198
  127 Public Sq Ste 5110 Cleveland (44114) *(G-3432)*

Brake Parts Inc China LLC (DH)................................... 216 589-0198
  127 Public Sq Ste 5110 Cleveland (44114) *(G-3433)*

Brake Products, Chagrin Falls *Also Called: IBI Brake Products Inc (G-2166)*

Bramkamp Printing Company Inc................................. 513 241-1865
  9933 Alliance Rd Ste 2 Blue Ash (45242) *(G-1255)*

Branch & Bone Artisan Ales LLC................................. 937 723-7608
  905 Wayne Ave Dayton (45410) *(G-5683)*

Brand Castle LLC.. 216 292-7700
  5111 Richmond Rd Bedford Heights (44146) *(G-1070)*

Brand5 LLC.. 614 920-9254
  106 Cool Spring Ct Pickerington (43147) *(G-11290)*

Brandon Screen Printing.. 419 229-9837
  1755 Shawnee Rd Lima (45805) *(G-8391)*

Brands' Marina, Port Clinton *Also Called: Tack-Anew Inc (G-11453)*

Brandts Candies Inc... 440 942-1016
  1238 Lost Nation Rd Willoughby (44094) *(G-14433)*

Brantley Partners IV LP... 216 464-8400
  3550 Lander Rd Ste 160 Cleveland (44124) *(G-3434)*

BRASS & BRONZE INGOT DIVISION, Cincinnati *Also Called: G A Avril Company (G-2645)*

Brass Bull 1 LLC... 740 335-8030
  1020 Leesburg Ave Wshngtn Ct Hs (43160) *(G-14735)*

Brass Lantern Antiques, Waynesville *Also Called: John Purdum (G-13879)*

Brassgate Industries Inc.. 937 339-2192
  650 Olympic Dr Troy (45373) *(G-13203)*

Brat Printing, Cincinnati *Also Called: Randy Gray (G-3032)*

Brattiegirlz LLC.. 513 007-4757
  175 S 3rd St Ste 200 Columbus (43215) *(G-4773)*

Braun Industries Inc.. 419 232-7020
  1170 Production Dr Van Wert (45891) *(G-13528)*

Bravo LLC (HQ)... 866 922-9222
  2425 W Dorothy Ln Moraine (45439) *(G-10151)*

Bravo Pet Foods, Moraine *Also Called: Bravo LLC (G-10151)*

Braze Solutions LLC.. 440 349-5100
  6850 Cochran Rd Solon (44139) *(G-12089)*

Bread Kneads Inc.. 419 422-3863
  510 S Blanchard St Findlay (45840) *(G-6845)*

Breaker Technology Inc.. 440 248-7168
  30625 Solon Industrial Pkwy Solon (44139) *(G-12090)*

Breakthrough Media Ministries, Canal Winchester *Also Called: World Harvest Church Inc (G-1800)*

Breakwall Publishing LLC... 813 575-2570
  3593 Medina Rd # 117 Medina (44256) *(G-9385)*

Breckenridge Paper & Packaging, Huron *Also Called: Central Ohio Paper & Packg Inc (G-7870)*

Breining Mech Systems Inc (PA)................................. 216 391-2400
  883 Addison Rd Cleveland (44103) *(G-3435)*

Breitenbach Bed & Breakfast, Dover *Also Called: Breitenbach Wine Cellars Inc (G-6232)*

Breitenbach Wine Cellars Inc..................................... 330 343-3603
  5934 Old Route 39 Nw Dover (44622) *(G-6232)*

Breitinger Company... 419 526-4255
  595 Oakenwaldt St Mansfield (44905) *(G-8767)*

A
L
P
H
A
B
E
T
I
C

Brendel Producing Company.....................330 854-4151
8215 Arlington Ave Nw Canton (44720) *(G-1844)*

Brenmar Construction Inc..........................740 286-2151
900 Morton St Jackson (45640) *(G-7941)*

Brennan Inds Clvland Mfg Group, Euclid *Also Called: Bic Manufacturing Inc (G-6644)*

Brenner International, Newark *Also Called: I G Brenner Inc (G-10510)*

Brentwood Originals Inc...........................330 793-2255
1309 N Meridian Rd Youngstown (44509) *(G-14824)*

Brentwood Printing & Sty..........................513 522-2679
8630 Winton Rd Cincinnati (45231) *(G-2421)*

Brew Kettle Inc.......................................440 234-8788
8377 Pearl Rd Strongsville (44136) *(G-12546)*

Brew Kettle Strongsville LLC........................440 915-7074
3520 Longwood Dr Medina (44256) *(G-9386)*

Brewdog, Canal Winchester *Also Called: Brewdog Brewing Company LLC (G-1786)*

Brewdog Brewing Company LLC (PA)..............614 908-3051
96 Gender Rd Canal Winchester (43110) *(G-1786)*

Brewer Company.......................................513 576-6300
7300 Main St Cincinnati (45244) *(G-2422)*

Brewer Company (PA).................................800 394-0017
25 Whitney Dr Ste 104 Milford (45150) *(G-9926)*

Brewer Company.......................................440 944-3800
30060 Lakeland Blvd Wickliffe (44092) *(G-14368)*

Brewer Products, Cincinnati *Also Called: La Mfg Inc (G-2810)*

Brewer Products Co, Cincinnati *Also Called: Brewpro Inc (G-2423)*

Brewercote, Milford *Also Called: Brewer Company (G-9926)*

Brewpro Inc...513 577-7200
9483 Reading Rd Cincinnati (45215) *(G-2423)*

Brewpub Restaurant Corporation...................614 228-2537
467 N High St Columbus (43215) *(G-4774)*

Brewster Cheese, Brewster *Also Called: Brewster Cheese Company (G-1490)*

Brewster Cheese Company (PA)....................330 767-3492
800 Wabash Ave S Brewster (44613) *(G-1490)*

BREWSTER HISTORICAL SOCIETY, Brewster *Also Called: Brewster Sugarcreek Twp Histo* *(G-1491)*

Brewster Sugarcreek Twp Histo...................330 767-0045
45 Wabash Ave S Brewster (44613) *(G-1491)*

Brian Hosher Backhoe Plum..........................740 503-4434
1053 W Market St Baltimore (43105) *(G-783)*

Briar Hill Stone Co Inc..............................216 377-5100
12470 State Route 520 Glenmont (44628) *(G-7284)*

Bricker Plating Inc..................................419 636-1990
612 E Edgerton St Bryan (43506) *(G-1632)*

Bridge Analyzers Inc.................................216 332-0592
5198 Richmond Rd Bedford Heights (44146) *(G-1071)*

Bridge Components Incorporated...................614 873-0777
3476 Millikin Ct Columbus (43228) *(G-4775)*

Bridge Components Inds Inc........................614 873-0777
3476 Millikin Ct Columbus (43228) *(G-4776)*

Bridgestone Ret Operations LLC...................740 592-3075
820 E State St Athens (45701) *(G-635)*

Bridgestone Ret Operations LLC...................614 834-3672
6574 Winchester Blvd Canal Winchester (43110) *(G-1787)*

Bridgestone Ret Operations LLC...................330 454-9478
3032 Atlantic Blvd Ne Canton (44705) *(G-1845)*

Bridgestone Ret Operations LLC...................513 793-4550
7800 Montgomery Rd Unit 18 Cincinnati (45236) *(G-2424)*

Bridgestone Ret Operations LLC...................513 677-5200
9107 Fields Ertel Rd Cincinnati (45249) *(G-2425)*

Bridgestone Ret Operations LLC...................513 681-7682
272 W Mitchell Ave Cincinnati (45232) *(G-2426)*

Bridgestone Ret Operations LLC...................440 842-3200
6874 Pearl Rd Cleveland (44130) *(G-3436)*

Bridgestone Ret Operations LLC...................440 461-4747
5117 Wilson Mills Rd Cleveland (44143) *(G-3437)*

Bridgestone Ret Operations LLC...................216 229-2550
12420 Cedar Rd Cleveland (44106) *(G-3438)*

Bridgestone Ret Operations LLC...................216 382-8970
700 Richmond Rd Cleveland (44143) *(G-3439)*

Bridgestone Ret Operations LLC...................614 864-3350
4015 E Broad St Columbus (43213) *(G-4777)*

Bridgestone Ret Operations LLC...................614 491-8062
35 Great Southern Blvd Columbus (43207) *(G-4778)*

Bridgestone Ret Operations LLC...................614 224-4221
180 N 3rd St Columbus (43215) *(G-4779)*

Bridgestone Ret Operations LLC...................440 324-3327
1951 Midway Mall Elyria (44035) *(G-6504)*

Bridgestone Ret Operations LLC...................440 365-8308
520 Abbe Rd S Elyria (44035) *(G-6505)*

Bridgestone Ret Operations LLC...................937 548-1197
425 Walnut St Greenville (45331) *(G-7336)*

Bridgestone Ret Operations LLC...................513 868-7399
33 N Brookwood Ave Hamilton (45013) *(G-7473)*

Bridgestone Ret Operations LLC...................330 673-1700
202 E Main St Kent (44240) *(G-8020)*

Bridgestone Ret Operations LLC...................440 299-6126
7495 Mentor Ave Mentor (44060) *(G-9493)*

Bridgestone Ret Operations LLC...................740 397-5601
855 Coshocton Ave Ste 21 Mount Vernon (43050) *(G-10237)*

Bridgestone Ret Operations LLC...................614 861-7994
7085 E Main St Reynoldsburg (43068) *(G-11560)*

Bridgestone Ret Operations LLC...................419 625-6571
4320 Milan Rd Sandusky (44870) *(G-11823)*

Bridgestone Ret Operations LLC...................937 325-4638
1475 Upper Valley Pike Springfield (45504) *(G-12286)*

Bridgestone Ret Operations LLC...................724 346-2621
370 High St Ne Warren (44481) *(G-13744)*

Bridgestone Ret Operations LLC...................330 758-0921
7401 Market St Rear Youngstown (44512) *(G-14825)*

Bridgestone Ret Operations LLC...................330 759-3697
3335 Belmont Ave Youngstown (44505) *(G-14826)*

Bridgetek, Dayton *Also Called: Contech Bridge Solutions LLC (G-5710)*

Bridgetek, West Chester *Also Called: Contech Bridge Solutions LLC (G-13969)*

Bridgits Bath LLC....................................937 259-1960
1226 Pursell Ave Dayton (45420) *(G-5684)*

Bridgstone Amrcas Tire Oprtons...................330 379-3714
1670 Firestone Pkwy Akron (44301) *(G-83)*

Bright Holdco LLC (PA)............................614 741-7458
9002 Smiths Mill Rd New Albany (43054) *(G-10333)*

Bright Innovation Labs, New Albany *Also Called: Bright Holdco LLC (G-10333)*

Bright Star Books Inc..............................330 888-2156
1357 Home Ave Akron (44310) *(G-84)*

Brightguy Inc...440 942-8318
38205b Stevens Blvd Willoughby (44094) *(G-14434)*

Brighton Mills, Cincinnati *Also Called: H Nagel & Son Co (G-2700)*

Brightpet Nutrition Group LLC (PA)...............330 424-1431
38251 Industrial Park Rd Lisbon (44432) *(G-8464)*

Brightstar Propane & Fuels........................614 891-8395
6190 Frost Rd Westerville (43082) *(G-14204)*

Brightwave Enterprises Inc........................812 331-2391
545 Market Ave N Ste 100 Canton (44702) *(G-1846)*

Brilex Industries Inc (PA).........................330 744-1114
1201 Crescent St Youngstown (44502) *(G-14827)*

Brilex Tech Services, Youngstown *Also Called: Brilex Industries Inc (G-14827)*

Brilista Foods Company Inc (PA)..................614 299-4132
1000 Goodale Blvd Columbus (43212) *(G-4780)*

Brilliant Electric Sign Co Ltd.....................216 741-3800
4811 Van Epps Rd Brooklyn Heights (44131) *(G-1529)*

Brimar Packaging Inc...............................440 934-3080
37520 Colorado Ave Avon (44011) *(G-717)*

Brinkley Technology Group LLC....................330 830-2498
2770 Erie St S Massillon (44646) *(G-9175)*

Brinkman LLC..419 204-5934
1524 Adak Ave Lima (45805) *(G-8392)*

Brinkman Tool & Die Inc............................937 222-1161
325 Kiser St Dayton (45404) *(G-5685)*

Brinkman Turkey Farms Inc (PA)...................419 365-5127
16314 State Route 68 Findlay (45840) *(G-6846)*

Brinkman's Country Corner, Findlay *Also Called: Brinkman Turkey Farms Inc (G-6846)*

Brio Coffee Co, Plain City *Also Called: Altraserv LLC (G-11393)*

Brisker Products, Cincinnati *Also Called: Pease Enterprises Inc (G-2951)*

Briskheat Corporation (DH)........................614 294-3376
4800 Hilton Corporate Dr Columbus (43232) *(G-4781)*

(G-0000) Company's Geographic Section entry number

Brittany Stamping LLC.. 216 267-0850
50 Public Sq Ste 4000 Cleveland (44113) *(G-3440)*

Broad Run Cheese House, Dover Also Called: Schindlers Broad Run Chshuse I *(G-6260)*

Broadband Hospitality, Youngstown Also Called: Great Lakes Telcom Ltd *(G-14870)*

Broadview Journal, The, Richfield Also Called: Scriptype Publishing Inc *(G-11599)*

Broadway Printing LLC.. 513 621-3429
530 Reading Rd Cincinnati (45202) *(G-2427)*

Broadway Sand and Gravel LLC............................ 937 853-5555
130 W 2nd St Ste 2000 Dayton (45402) *(G-5686)*

Brocade Cmmnctions Systems LLC...................... 614 232-8015
4200 Regent St Ste 200 Columbus (43219) *(G-4782)*

Brocar Products Inc.. 513 922-2888
4335 River Rd Cincinnati (45204) *(G-2428)*

Brock Corporation (PA).. 440 235-1806
26000 Sprague Rd Olmsted Falls (44138) *(G-10939)*

Brock RAD Wldg Fabrication Inc.......................... 740 773-2540
370 Douglas Ave Chillicothe (45601) *(G-2246)*

Brocker Machine Inc.. 330 744-5858
1530 Poland Ave Youngstown (44502) *(G-14828)*

Brocks RAD Wldg Fabrication I, Chillicothe Also Called: Brock RAD Wldg Fabrication Inc *(G-2246)*

Broco Products Inc.. 216 531-0880
8510 Bessemer Ave Cleveland (44127) *(G-3441)*

Brodwill LLC.. 513 258-2716
3900 Rose Hill Ave Ste C Cincinnati (45229) *(G-2429)*

Broestl & Wallis Fine Jewelers, Lakewood Also Called: Bensan Jewelers Inc *(G-8163)*

Bronco Machine Inc.. 440 951-5015
38411 Apollo Pkwy Willoughby (44094) *(G-14435)*

Bront Machining Inc.. 937 228-4551
2601 W Dorothy Ln Moraine (45439) *(G-10152)*

Bronx Taylor Wilson, North Canton Also Called: Fives Bronx Inc *(G-10639)*

Brook & Whittle Limited.. 513 860-2457
4000 Hamilton Middletown Rd Hamilton (45011) *(G-7474)*

Brooker Bros Forging Co Inc................................ 419 668-2535
102 Jefferson St Norwalk (44857) *(G-10831)*

Brookhill Center Inds Inc...................................... 419 876-3932
7989 State Route 108 Ottawa (45875) *(G-11030)*

Brooklyn Machine & Mfg Co Inc............................ 216 341-1846
5180 Grant Ave Cleveland (44125) *(G-3442)*

Brooks Manufacturing.. 419 244-1777
1102 N Summit St Toledo (43604) *(G-12905)*

Brooks Pastries Inc.. 614 274-4880
8205 Estates Pkwy Ste F Plain City (43064) *(G-11399)*

Brookville Roadster Inc.. 937 833-4605
718 Albert Rd Brookville (45309) *(G-1563)*

Brookwood Group Inc.. 513 791-3030
3210 Wasson Rd Cincinnati (45209) *(G-2430)*

Broshco Fabricated Products, Mansfield Also Called: Jay Industries Inc *(G-8806)*

Brost Foundry Company (PA)................................ 216 641-1131
2934 E 55th St Cleveland (44127) *(G-3443)*

Brost Foundry Company.. 419 522-1133
198 Wayne St Mansfield (44902) *(G-8768)*

Brothers Body and Eqp LLC................................ 419 462-1975
352 South St Door 26 Galion (44833) *(G-7180)*

Brothers Printing Co Inc...................................... 216 621-6050
2000 Euclid Ave Cleveland (44115) *(G-3444)*

Brothers Tool and Mfg Ltd.................................... 513 353-9700
8300 Harrison Ave Miamitown (45041) *(G-9757)*

Brown Box Company, Findlay Also Called: Square One Solutions LLC *(G-6922)*

Brown Cnc Machining Inc.................................... 937 865-9191
433 E Maple Ave Miamisburg (45342) *(G-9677)*

Brown Cnty Bd Mntal Rtardation.......................... 937 378-4891
325 W State St Bldg A Georgetown (45121) *(G-7251)*

Brown Company of Findlay Ltd............................ 419 425-3002
225 Stanford Pkwy Findlay (45840) *(G-6847)*

Brown Fired Heater Div, Berea Also Called: Es Thermal Inc *(G-1170)*

Brown Industrial Inc.. 937 693-3838
311 W South St Botkins (45306) *(G-1397)*

Brown Publishing, Jackson Also Called: Brown Publishing Co Inc *(G-7942)*

Brown Publishing Co Inc (PA).............................. 740 286-2187
1 Acy Ave Ste D Jackson (45640) *(G-7942)*

Brown Publishing Inc LLC.................................... 513 794-5040
4229 Saint Andrews Pl Blue Ash (45236) *(G-1256)*

Brown Wood Products Company............................ 330 339-8000
7783 Crooked Run Rd Sw New Philadelphia (44663) *(G-10433)*

Brown-Forman Corporation.................................. 740 384-3027
468 Salem Church Rd Wellston (45692) *(G-13905)*

Brp Manufacturing Company................................ 800 858-0482
637 N Jackson St Lima (45801) *(G-8393)*

Brr Bear Ltd.. 419 666-1111
232 J St Perrysburg (43551) *(G-11207)*

BRT Extrusions Inc.. 330 544-0177
1818 N Main St Unit 1 Niles (44446) *(G-10584)*

Brubaker Metalcrafts Inc.................................... 937 456-5834
209 N Franklin St Eaton (45320) *(G-6449)*

Bruce High Performance Tran.............................. 440 357-8964
1 High Tech Ave Painesville (44077) *(G-11070)*

Bruening Glass Works Inc.................................. 440 333-4768
20157 Lake Rd Cleveland (44116) *(G-3445)*

Bruewer Woodwork Mfg Co.................................. 513 353-3505
10000 Cilley Rd Cleves (45002) *(G-4532)*

Brumall Manufacturing Corp................................ 440 974-2622
7850 Division Dr Mentor (44060) *(G-9494)*

Brushes Inc.. 216 267-8084
5400 Smith Rd Cleveland (44142) *(G-3446)*

Brushes Inc.. 216 267-8084
5400 Smith Rd Cleveland (44142) *(G-3447)*

Brw Tool Inc.. 419 394-3371
502 Scott St Saint Marys (45885) *(G-11734)*

Brx, Rootstown Also Called: Barrel Run Crssing Wnery Vnyrd *(G-11647)*

Bry-Air Inc.. 740 965-2974
10793 E State Route 37 Sunbury (43074) *(G-12662)*

Bryan Die-Cast Products Ltd................................ 419 252-6208
4 Seagate Ste 803 Toledo (43604) *(G-12906)*

Bryan Packaging Inc.. 419 636-2600
620 E Perry St Bryan (43506) *(G-1633)*

Bryan Publishing Company (PA).......................... 419 636-1111
211 W High St Ste A Bryan (43506) *(G-1634)*

Brydet Development Corporation.......................... 740 623-0455
16867 State Route 83 Coshocton (43812) *(G-5452)*

BSC Environmental, Bowling Green Also Called: Bio-Systems Corporation *(G-1410)*

Bsfc LLC (HQ).. 419 447-1814
186 Ohio Ave Tiffin (44883) *(G-12778)*

BSI Group, The, Derwent Also Called: Bi-Con Services Inc *(G-6221)*

BSN Sports.. 513 821-7575
11480 Enterprise Park Dr Cincinnati (45241) *(G-2431)*

BTA of Motorcars Inc.. 440 716-1000
27500 Lorain Rd North Olmsted (44070) *(G-10719)*

Btc Inc.. 740 549-2722
8842 Whitney Dr Lewis Center (43035) *(G-8326)*

Btc Technology Services Inc................................ 740 549-2722
617 Carle Ave Lewis Center (43035) *(G-8327)*

BTR Enterprises LLC.. 740 975-2526
7371 Stewart Rd Newark (43055) *(G-10495)*

Btw LLC.. 419 382-4443
2226 Greenlawn Dr Toledo (43614) *(G-12907)*

Buck Equipment Inc.. 614 539-3039
1720 Feddern Ave Grove City (43123) *(G-7375)*

Buckeye Abrasive Inc.. 330 753-1041
1020 Eagon St Barberton (44203) *(G-799)*

Buckeye Blow Out Preventer, Newcomerstown Also Called: Buckeye BOP LLC *(G-10569)*

Buckeye BOP LLC.. 740 498-9898
401 Enterprise Dr Newcomerstown (43832) *(G-10569)*

Buckeye Boxes Inc (PA)...................................... 614 274-8484
601 N Hague Ave Columbus (43204) *(G-4783)*

Buckeye Brake Mfg Inc.. 740 782-1379
40168 National Rd W Morristown (43759) *(G-10200)*

Buckeye Building Products, Reynoldsburg Also Called: Buckeye Ready-Mix LLC *(G-11561)*

Buckeye Business Forms Inc.............................. 614 882-1890
1695 Northam Rd Columbus (43221) *(G-4784)*

Buckeye Business Products, Cleveland Also Called: Kroy LLC *(G-3929)*

Buckeye Companies (PA).................................... 740 452-3641
999 Zane St Zanesville (43701) *(G-15000)*

A
L
P
H
A
B
E
T
I
C

Buckeye Components LLC......................330 482-5163
1340 State Route 14 Columbiana (44408) *(G-4607)*

Buckeye Container Division, Wooster Also Called: Buckeye Corrugated Inc *(G-14628)*

Buckeye Corrugated Inc (PA)...................330 576-0590
822 Kumho Dr Ste 400 Fairlawn (44333) *(G-6797)*

Buckeye Corrugated Inc.........................330 264-6336
3350 Long Rd Wooster (44691) *(G-14628)*

Buckeye Design & Engr Svc LLC...............419 375-4241
2600 Wabash Rd Fort Recovery (45846) *(G-6961)*

Buckeye Diamond Logistics Inc (PA)...........937 462-8361
15 Sprague Rd South Charleston (45368) *(G-12213)*

Buckeye Energy Resources Inc.................740 452-9506
999 Zane St Zanesville (43701) *(G-15001)*

Buckeye Fabric Finishers Inc..................740 622-3251
1260 E Main St Coshocton (43812) *(G-5453)*

Buckeye Fabric Finishing Co, Coshocton Also Called: Buckeye Fabric Finishers Inc *(G-5453)*

Buckeye Fabricating Company..................937 746-9822
245 S Pioneer Blvd Springboro (45066) *(G-12248)*

Buckeye Fasteners Company, Berea Also Called: Fastener Industries Inc *(G-1173)*

BUCKEYE FASTENERS COMPANY, Streetsboro Also Called: Joseph Industries Inc *(G-12507)*

Buckeye Lady, The, Columbus Also Called: Bucks For Pups Confections LLC *(G-4787)*

Buckeye Lake Winery...........................614 439-7576
13750 Rosewood Dr Ne Thornville (43076) *(G-12765)*

Buckeye Machining Inc.........................216 731-9535
25020 Lakeland Blvd Euclid (44132) *(G-6645)*

Buckeye Mch Fabricators Inc (PA)..............419 273-2521
610 E Lima St Forest (45843) *(G-6939)*

Buckeye Medical Tech LLC......................330 719-9868
405 Niles Cortland Rd Se Ste 202 Warren (44484) *(G-13745)*

Buckeye Metal Works Inc.......................614 239-8000
3240 Petzinger Rd Columbus (43232) *(G-4785)*

Buckeye Metals, Avon Lake Also Called: W R G Inc *(G-772)*

Buckeye Metals Industries, Cleveland Also Called: B&A Ison Steel Inc *(G-3400)*

Buckeye Oil Equipment Co......................937 387-0671
20 Innovation Ct Dayton (45414) *(G-5687)*

Buckeye Oil Producing Co......................330 264-8847
544 E Liberty St Wooster (44691) *(G-14629)*

Buckeye Packaging Co Inc......................330 935-0301
12223 Marlboro Ave Ne Alliance (44601) *(G-373)*

Buckeye Paper Co Inc..........................330 477-5925
5233 Southway St Sw Ste 523 Canton (44706) *(G-1847)*

Buckeye Ready Mix, Columbus Also Called: Anderson Concrete Corp *(G-4716)*

Buckeye Ready Mix Concrete....................330 798-5511
1562 Massillon Rd Akron (44312) *(G-85)*

Buckeye Ready-Mix LLC.........................740 967-4801
7720 Johnstown Alexandria Rd Johnstown (43031) *(G-7993)*

Buckeye Ready-Mix LLC.........................614 879-6316
6600 State Route 29 West Jefferson (43162) *(G-14160)*

Buckeye Ready-Mix LLC.........................740 654-4423
1750 Logan Lancaster Rd Se Lancaster (43130) *(G-8182)*

Buckeye Ready-Mix LLC.........................937 642-2951
838 N Main St Marysville (43040) *(G-9015)*

Buckeye Ready-Mix LLC (PA)....................614 575-2132
7657 Taylor Rd Sw Reynoldsburg (43068) *(G-11561)*

Buckeye Rocker, Millersburg Also Called: M H Woodworking LLC *(G-9995)*

Buckeye Rubber Products, Lima Also Called: Brp Manufacturing Company *(G-8393)*

Buckeye Seating LLC...........................330 893-7700
6945 County Road 672 Millersburg (44654) *(G-9972)*

Buckeye Shapeform, Columbus Also Called: Buckeye Stamping Company *(G-4786)*

Buckeye Sports Bulletin, Columbus Also Called: Columbus-Sports Publications *(G-4838)*

Buckeye Stamping Company......................877 728-0776
555 Marion Rd Columbus (43207) *(G-4786)*

Buckeye State Wldg & Fabg Inc (PA)............440 322-0319
131 Buckeye St Elyria (44035) *(G-6506)*

Buckeye State Wldg & Fabg Inc.................440 322-0344
175 Woodford Ave Elyria (44035) *(G-6507)*

Buckeye Steel Inc.............................740 425-2306
607 Watt Ave Barnesville (43713) *(G-844)*

Buckeye Terminals.............................330 453-4170
807 Hartford Ave Se Canton (44707) *(G-1848)*

Buckeye Valley Pizza Hut Ltd..................419 586-5900
1152 E Market St Celina (45822) *(G-2098)*

Buckingham Coal Company LLC...................740 452-9506
11 N 4th St Zanesville (43701) *(G-15002)*

Buckingham Src Inc............................216 941-6115
3425 Service Rd Cleveland (44111) *(G-3448)*

Buckler Industries Inc........................419 589-6134
861 Expressview Dr Mansfield (44905) *(G-8769)*

Buckley Manufacturing Company.................513 821-4444
148 Caldwell Dr Cincinnati (45216) *(G-2432)*

Buckman Ltd...................................419 420-1687
1413 Forest Park Findlay (45840) *(G-6848)*

Bucks For Pups Confections LLC................614 359-4672
4493 N High St Columbus (43214) *(G-4787)*

Buckys Machine and Fab Ltd....................419 981-5050
8376 S County Road 47 Mc Cutchenville (44844) *(G-9355)*

Bucyrus Blades Inc (DH).......................419 562-6015
260 E Beal Ave Bucyrus (44820) *(G-1672)*

Bucyrus Graphics Inc..........................419 562-2906
214 W Liberty St Bucyrus (44820) *(G-1673)*

Bucyrus Ice Company, Bucyrus Also Called: Velvet Ice Cream Company *(G-1693)*

Bucyrus Precision Tech Inc....................419 563-9950
200 Crossroads Blvd Bucyrus (44820) *(G-1674)*

Bud Corp......................................740 967-9992
158 Commerce Blvd Johnstown (43031) *(G-7994)*

Bud May Inc...................................216 676-8850
16850 Hummel Rd Cleveland (44142) *(G-3449)*

Budde Precision Machining Corp................937 278-1962
2608 Nordic Rd Dayton (45414) *(G-5688)*

Budde Sheet Metal Works Inc (PA)..............937 224-0868
305 Leo St Dayton (45404) *(G-5689)*

Buddy Backyard Inc............................800 837-9353
140 Dana St Ne Warren (44483) *(G-13746)*

Buddy RC, Columbus Also Called: Ohio Model Products LLC *(G-5147)*

Buderer Drug Company Inc (PA).................419 627-2800
633 Hancock St Sandusky (44870) *(G-11824)*

Budget Molders Supply Inc.....................216 367-7050
8303 Corporate Park Dr Macedonia (44056) *(G-8680)*

Buds Sign Shop Inc............................330 744-5555
892 Mahoning Ave Youngstown (44502) *(G-14829)*

Budzar Industries, Willoughby Also Called: Dyoung Enterprise Inc *(G-14452)*

Buffalo Abrasives Inc.........................614 891-6450
1093 Smoke Burr Dr Westerville (43081) *(G-14248)*

Buffalo Peanuts, Columbus Also Called: Nuts Are Good Inc *(G-5133)*

Buffex Metal Finishing Inc....................216 631-2202
1935 W 96th St Ste L Cleveland (44102) *(G-3450)*

Bugh Inc......................................330 305-0978
8933 Cleveland Ave Nw Canton (44720) *(G-1849)*

Builder Tech Wholesale LLC.....................419 535-7606
2931 South Ave Toledo (43609) *(G-12908)*

Builder Tech Windows, Toledo Also Called: Builder Tech Wholesale LLC *(G-12908)*

Builders Straight Edge, Elyria Also Called: B&B Distributors LLC *(G-6500)*

Building Block Performance LLC.................614 918-7476
7920 Corporate Blvd Ste C Plain City (43064) *(G-11400)*

Building Concepts Inc (PA).....................419 298-2371
444 N Michigan Ave Edgerton (43517) *(G-6464)*

Building Ctrl Integrators LLC..................513 247-6154
300 E Business Way Ste 200 Cincinnati (45241) *(G-2433)*

Building Ctrl Integrators LLC (PA).............614 334-3300
383 N Liberty St Powell (43065) *(G-11482)*

Building Ctrl Integrators LLC..................513 860-9600
10174 International Blvd West Chester (45246) *(G-14108)*

Building Rlationships Together, Niles Also Called: BRT Extrusions Inc *(G-10584)*

Built-Rite Box & Crate Inc....................330 263-0936
608 Freedlander Rd Wooster (44691) *(G-14630)*

Bula Defense Systems, Cleveland Also Called: Bula Forge & Machine Inc *(G-3451)*

Bula Forge & Machine Inc (PA).................216 252-7600
3001 W 121st St Cleveland (44111) *(G-3451)*

Bula Forge Machine............................216 252-7600
12117 Berea Rd Ste 1 Cleveland (44111) *(G-3452)*

Bulk Apothecary, Streetsboro Also Called: Natural Essentials Inc *(G-12513)*

Bulk Carrier Trnsp Eqp Co..330 339-3333
2743 Brightwood Rd Se New Philadelphia (44663) *(G-10434)*

Bulk Carriers Service Inc...330 339-3333
2743 Brightwood Rd Se New Philadelphia (44663) *(G-10435)*

Bulk Handling Equipment Co...330 468-5703
28 W Aurora Rd Northfield (44067) *(G-10792)*

Bullen, Eaton *Also Called: Bullen Ultrasonics Inc (G-6450)*

Bullen Ultrasonics Inc...937 456-7133
1301 Miller Williams Rd Eaton (45320) *(G-6450)*

Bullseye, Willoughby *Also Called: Bullseye Dart Shoppe Inc (G-14436)*

Bullseye Dart Shoppe Inc..440 951-9277
950c Erie Rd Willoughby (44095) *(G-14436)*

Bully Tools Inc...740 282-5834
14 Technology Way Steubenville (43952) *(G-12401)*

Bummin Beaver Brewery LLC...440 543-9900
11610 Washington St Chagrin Falls (44023) *(G-2156)*

Bunge North America East LLC......................................419 483-5340
605 Goodrich Rd Bellevue (44811) *(G-1121)*

Bunker Hill Cheese Co Inc...330 893-2131
6005 County Road 77 Millersburg (44654) *(G-9973)*

Bunnell Hill Construction Inc..513 932-6010
3000g Henkle Dr Lebanon (45036) *(G-8248)*

Buns of Delaware Inc...740 363-2867
14 W Winter St Delaware (43015) *(G-6135)*

Buns Restaurant & Bakery, Delaware *Also Called: Buns of Delaware Inc (G-6135)*

Bunting Bearings LLC (PA)..419 866-7000
1001 Holland Park Blvd Holland (43528) *(G-7747)*

Bunting Bearings LLC..419 522-3323
153 E 5th St Mansfield (44902) *(G-8770)*

Burdens Machine & Welding Inc.....................................740 345-9246
94 S 5th St Newark (43055) *(G-10496)*

Burghardt Manufacturing Inc..330 253-7590
1524 Massillon Rd Akron (44306) *(G-86)*

Burghardt Metal Fabg Inc..330 794-1830
1638 Mcchesney Rd Akron (44306) *(G-87)*

Burial Vaults By Neher, Springfield *Also Called: Neher Burial Vault Company (G-12357)*

Burke & Company, Cincinnati *Also Called: Patrick J Burke & Co (G-2945)*

Burke Products Inc..937 372-3516
1355 Enterprise Ln Xenia (45385) *(G-14756)*

Burkettsville Stockyard, Burkettsville *Also Called: Werling and Sons Inc (G-1698)*

Burton Industries Inc...440 974-1700
7875 Division Dr Mentor (44060) *(G-9495)*

Burton Metal Finishing Inc...614 252-9523
1711 Woodland Ave Columbus (43219) *(G-4788)*

Burton Mtal Fnshg Inc Pwdr Cti, Columbus *Also Called: Burton Metal Finishing Inc (G-4788)*

Burton Rubber Processing, Burton *Also Called: Hexpol Compounding LLC (G-1699)*

Busch & Thiem Inc...419 625-7515
1316 Cleveland Rd Sandusky (44870) *(G-11825)*

Buschman Corporation..216 431-6633
4100 Payne Ave Ste 1 Cleveland (44103) *(G-3453)*

Bush Inc..216 362-6700
15901 Industrial Pkwy Cleveland (44135) *(G-3454)*

Bush Integrated, Cleveland *Also Called: PJ Bush Associates Inc (G-4168)*

Bush Specialty Vehicles Inc..937 382-5502
80 Park Dr Wilmington (45177) *(G-14574)*

Bushong Auto Service, Troy *Also Called: Mader Automotive Center Inc (G-13238)*

Bushworks Incorporated...937 767-1713
1280 Grinnell Dr Unit 1 Yellow Springs (45387) *(G-14787)*

Business Idntfction Systems In.......................................614 841-1255
6185 Huntley Rd Ste M Columbus (43229) *(G-4789)*

Business Journal...330 744-5023
25 E Boardman St Ste 306 Youngstown (44503) *(G-14830)*

Busken Bakery Inc (PA)..513 871-2114
2675 Madison Rd Cincinnati (45208) *(G-2434)*

Busse Combat Knives, Wauseon *Also Called: Busse Knife Co (G-13846)*

Busse Knife Co...419 923-6471
11651 County Road 12 Wauseon (43567) *(G-13846)*

Butech Bliss, Salem *Also Called: Butech Inc (G-11765)*

Butech Bliss, Salem *Also Called: Butech Inc (G-11766)*

Butech Inc...330 337-0000
633 S Broadway Ave Salem (44460) *(G-11764)*

Butech Inc...330 337-0000
240 Pennsylvania Ave Salem (44460) *(G-11765)*

Butech Inc (PA)...330 337-0000
550 S Ellsworth Ave Salem (44460) *(G-11766)*

Butler Cnty Surgical Prpts LLC.......................................513 844-2200
213 Dayton St Hamilton (45011) *(G-7475)*

Butler Tech...513 867-1028
3611 Hamilton Middletown Rd Fairfield Township (45011) *(G-6795)*

Butt Hut, Findlay *Also Called: Smoke-Rings Inc (G-6921)*

Buyers Products Company (PA).......................................440 974-8888
9049 Tyler Blvd Mentor (44060) *(G-9496)*

Buyers Products Company..440 974-8888
8120 Tyler Blvd Mentor (44060) *(G-9497)*

Buzz Seating Inc (PA)...877 263-5737
4774 Interstate Dr West Chester (45246) *(G-14109)*

Bw Supply Co., Lyons *Also Called: B W Grinding Co (G-8673)*

Bwi Chassis Dynamics NA Inc..937 455-5100
3100 Research Blvd Kettering (45420) *(G-8117)*

Bwi Eagle LLC..724 283-4681
655 N River Rd Nw Warren (44483) *(G-13747)*

Bwi Group, Moraine *Also Called: Bwi North America Inc (G-10153)*

Bwi North America Inc (DH)..614 394-5983
2586 E River Rd Moraine (45439) *(G-10153)*

Bwx Technologies Inc...330 860-1692
91 Stirling Ave Barberton (44203) *(G-800)*

Bwx Technologies Inc...740 687-4180
2600 E Main St Lancaster (43130) *(G-8183)*

Bwxt Nclear Oprtions Group Inc......................................216 912-3000
24703 Euclid Ave Cleveland (44117) *(G-3455)*

Bybe Inc...614 706-3050
107 S High St Columbus (43215) *(G-4790)*

Byg Industries Inc..216 961-5436
8003 Clinton Rd Cleveland (44144) *(G-3456)*

Byron Products Inc...513 870-9111
3781 Port Union Rd Fairfield (45014) *(G-6715)*

C & C Industries, Vandalia *Also Called: Sinbon Ohio LLC (G-13577)*

C & C Metal Products, Wooster *Also Called: Global Body & Equipment Co (G-14643)*

C & F Fabrications Inc..937 666-3234
3100 State St East Liberty (43319) *(G-6383)*

C & F Tire & Truck Repair..419 526-1412
3646 Mary Lou Ln S Ontario (44906) *(G-10947)*

C & H Enterprises Ltd..510 226-6083
2121 Bright Rd Findlay (45840) *(G-6849)*

C & K Machine Co Inc..419 237-3203
604 N Park St Fayette (43521) *(G-6824)*

C & L Supply, Logan *Also Called: Kilbarger Construction Inc (G-8518)*

C & M Rubber Co Inc...907 299-2702
414 Littell Ave Dayton (45419) *(G-5690)*

C & R Inc (PA)...614 497-1130
5600 Clyde Moore Dr Groveport (43125) *(G-7427)*

C & S Associates Inc...440 461-9661
729 Miner Rd Highland Heights (44143) *(G-7655)*

C & W Custom Wdwkg Co Inc..513 891-6340
11949 Tramway Dr Cincinnati (45241) *(G-2435)*

C A Joseph Co (PA)..330 385-6869
13712 Old Fredericktown Rd East Liverpool (43920) *(G-6387)*

C A Joseph Co..330 532-4646
170 Broadway St Irondale (43932) *(G-7927)*

C A Litzler Co Inc..216 267-8020
4800 W 160th St Cleveland (44135) *(G-3457)*

C A P Industries Inc..937 773-1824
543 Staunton St Piqua (45356) *(G-11338)*

C B C, Marysville *Also Called: Contract Bldg Components Ltd (G-9017)*

C B Mfg & Sls Co Inc...937 866-5986
4475 Infirmary Rd Dayton (45449) *(G-5691)*

C B Mfg & Sls Co Inc (PA)...937 866-5986
4455 Infirmary Rd Miamisburg (45342) *(G-9678)*

C C M Wire Inc...330 425-3421
1920 Case Pkwy S Twinsburg (44087) *(G-13283)*

C D I, Miamisburg *Also Called: Connective Design Incorporated (G-9683)*

C E Electronics Inc...419 636-6705
2107 Industrial Dr Bryan (43506) *(G-1635)*

ALPHABETIC

C E I, Circleville Also Called: Carbon Enterprises Inc **(G-3249)**

C E White Co (HQ)..419 492-2157
417 N Kibler St New Washington (44854) **(G-10477)**

C F Poeppelman Inc (PA)...937 448-2191
4755 N State Route 721 Bradford (45308) **(G-1451)**

C G S, Cleveland Also Called: Centerless Grinding Svc Inc **(G-3483)**

C Green & Sons Incorporated...740 745-2998
9020 Mount Vernon Rd Saint Louisville (43071) **(G-11728)**

C H T, Cleveland Also Called: Compliant Healthcare Tech LLC **(G-3555)**

C I P, Canton Also Called: Sequa Can Machinery Inc **(G-2002)**

C J Kraft Enterprises Inc...740 653-9606
301 S Maple St Lancaster (43130) **(G-8184)**

C JS Signs...330 821-7446
1670 Charl Ann Dr Alliance (44601) **(G-374)**

C L W Inc..740 374-8443
1201 Gilman Ave Marietta (45750) **(G-8905)**

C M C, Cleveland Also Called: ITT Torque Systems Inc **(G-3875)**

C M M S - Re LLC...513 489-5111
6130 Interstate Cir Blue Ash (45242) **(G-1257)**

C Massouh Printing, Canal Fulton Also Called: C Massouh Printing Co Inc **(G-1774)**

C Massouh Printing Co Inc...330 408-7330
590 Elm Ridge Ave Canal Fulton (44614) **(G-1774)**

C Nelson Mfg Co...419 898-3305
265 N Lake Winds Pkwy Oak Harbor (43449) **(G-10884)**

C P P, Cleveland Also Called: Consolidated Foundries Inc **(G-3562)**

C S I, Harrison Also Called: Coating Systems Inc **(G-7547)**

C S I, Toledo Also Called: Chem-Sales Inc **(G-12918)**

C V G, New Albany Also Called: Cvg National Seating Co LLC **(G-10338)**

C W Ohio, Conneaut Also Called: Cascade Ohio Inc **(G-5399)**

C-Link Enterprises LLC..937 222-2829
1825 Webster St Dayton (45404) **(G-5692)**

C-Mold Inc
22251 Mccauley Rd Shaker Heights (44122) **(G-11927)**

C-N-D Industries Inc...330 478-8811
359 State Ave Nw Massillon (44647) **(G-9176)**

C-Tech Industries, West Chester Also Called: Tvh Parts Co **(G-14087)**

C.T.L. Steel Division, Columbus Also Called: Clark Grave Vault Company **(G-4809)**

C&C Fabrication LLC...419 592-1408
13226 County Road R Napoleon (43545) **(G-10275)**

C&F Truck & Tire Service, Ontario Also Called: C & F Tire & Truck Repair **(G-10947)**

C&W Swiss Inc..937 832-2889
100 Lau Pkwy Englewood (45315) **(G-6608)**

C2g, Dayton Also Called: Legrand North America LLC **(G-5843)**

C4 Group, The, Chagrin Falls Also Called: C4 Polymers Inc **(G-2136)**

C4 Polymers Inc (PA)...440 543-3866
33 River St Chagrin Falls (44022) **(G-2136)**

CA Litzler Holding Company (PA)......................................216 267-8020
4800 W 160th St Cleveland (44135) **(G-3458)**

Cabinet and Granite Depot LLC..513 874-2100
8730 N Pavillion West Chester (45069) **(G-13953)**

Cabinet Concepts Inc...440 232-4644
590 Golden Oak Pkwy Unit B Oakwood Village (44146) **(G-10903)**

Cabinet Guys, The, Columbus Also Called: Bison Builders LLC **(G-4756)**

Cabinet Restylers, Ashland Also Called: Cabinet Restylers Inc **(G-525)**

Cabinet Restylers Inc...419 281-8449
419 E 8th St Ashland (44805) **(G-525)**

Cabinet Shop..614 885-9676
9075 Antares Ave Columbus (43240) **(G-4639)**

Cabinet Specialties Inc...330 695-3463
10738 Criswell Rd Fredericksburg (44627) **(G-7061)**

Cabinetworks Group Mich LLC..440 247-3091
25 N Franklin St Chagrin Falls (44022) **(G-2137)**

Cabinetworks Group Mich LLC..440 632-2547
15535 S State Ave Middlefield (44062) **(G-9783)**

Cabintwrks Group Mddlfield LLC (HQ)...............................888 562-7744
15535 S State Ave Middlefield (44062) **(G-9784)**

Cabintwrks Group Mddlfield LLC.......................................440 437-8537
150 Grand Valley Ave Orwell (44076) **(G-11020)**

Cablecraft Motion Controls, Bolivar Also Called: Torque 2020 CMA Acqisition LLC **(G-1393)**

Cabletek Wiring Products Inc..800 562-9378
1150 Taylor St Elyria (44035) **(G-6508)**

Cabot Lumber Inc...740 545-7109
304 E Union Ave West Lafayette (43845) **(G-14169)**

Cadillac Papers, Hamilton Also Called: Gvs Industries Inc **(G-7498)**

Cafco Filter, Cincinnati Also Called: Cincinnati A Flter Sls Svc Inc **(G-2466)**

Cage Gear & Machine LLC...330 452-1532
1776 Gateway Blvd Se Canton (44707) **(G-1850)**

Cailin Development LLC..216 408-6261
896 E 70th St Cleveland (44103) **(G-3459)**

Cake House Cleveland LLC..216 870-4659
1536 Saint Clair Ave Ne Ste 65 Cleveland (44114) **(G-3460)**

Cake In A Cup Inc...419 491-1104
6801 W Central Ave Ste B Toledo (43617) **(G-12909)**

Cake LLC..614 592-7681
6724 Perimeter Loop Rd Unit 254 Dublin (43017) **(G-6284)**

Cal Sales Embroidery...440 236-3820
13975 Station Rd Columbia Station (44028) **(G-4590)**

Cal-Maine Foods Inc...937 337-9576
3078 Washington Rd Rossburg (45362) **(G-11655)**

Cal-Maine Foods Inc...937 968-4874
1039 Zumbrum Rd Union City (45390) **(G-13413)**

Caldwell Lumber & Supply Co...740 732-2306
17990 Woodsfield Rd Caldwell (43724) **(G-1724)**

Calgon Carbon Corporation..614 258-9501
835 N Cassady Ave Columbus (43219) **(G-4791)**

Caliber Mold and Machine Inc...330 633-8171
2200 Massillon Rd Akron (44312) **(G-88)**

Call & Post, Cleveland Also Called: King Media Enterprises Inc **(G-3921)**

Callahan AMS Machine Company, Cincinnati Also Called: Omya Inc **(G-2930)**

Callahan Cutting Tools Inc..614 294-1649
915 Distribution Dr Ste A Columbus (43228) **(G-4792)**

Callender Group, The, Mentor Also Called: Lake Publishing Inc **(G-9549)**

Callies Performance Products Inc......................................419 435-7448
901 S Union St Fostoria (44830) **(G-6977)**

Calmego Specialized Pdts LLC...937 669-5620
1569 Martindale Rd Greenville (45331) **(G-7337)**

Calorplast USA LLC..513 576-6333
1287 Us Route 50 Milford (45150) **(G-9927)**

Calvary Industries Inc (PA)..513 874-1113
9233 Seward Rd Fairfield (45014) **(G-6716)**

Calvert Wire & Cable Corp...330 494-3248
4276 Strausser Street, Applegrove Ext North Canton (44720) **(G-10631)**

Calvin J Magsig..419 862-3311
343 Clinton St Elmore (43416) **(G-6488)**

Calvin W Lafferty...740 498-6566
72628 Hopewell Rd Kimbolton (43749) **(G-8136)**

CAM Books, Berlin Also Called: Tgs International Inc **(G-1200)**

CAM Machine Inc..937 663-5000
513 S Springfield St Saint Paris (43072) **(G-11757)**

CAM-Lem Inc..216 391-7750
1768 E 25th St Cleveland (44114) **(G-3461)**

Camaco LLC...440 288-4444
3400 River Industrial Park Rd Lorain (44052) **(G-8549)**

Camaco Lorain, Lorain Also Called: Camaco LLC **(G-8549)**

Camargo Phrm Svcs LLC (DH)...513 561-3329
1 E 4th St Ste 1400 Cincinnati (45202) **(G-2436)**

Cambridge Box & Gift Shop, Cambridge Also Called: Cambridge Packaging Inc **(G-1738)**

Cambridge Mill Products Inc...330 863-1121
6005 Alliance Rd Nw Malvern (44644) **(G-8747)**

Cambridge Packaging Inc..740 432-3351
60794 Southgate Rd Cambridge (43725) **(G-1738)**

Camden Concrete Products LLC...937 456-1229
4952 State Route 732 W Eaton (45320) **(G-6451)**

Camden Ready Mix, West Alexandria Also Called: Wysong Gravel Co Inc **(G-13924)**

Camden Ready Mix Co (PA)...937 456-4539
478 Camden College Corner Rd Camden (45311) **(G-1767)**

Cameco Communications LLC...937 840-9490
128 S High St Hillsboro (45133) **(G-7715)**

Camelot Manufacturing Inc...419 678-2603
210 Butler St Coldwater (45828) **(G-4569)**

2025 Harris Ohio
Industrial Directory

(G-0000) Company's Geographic Section entry number

Camelot Printing, Lodi *Also Called: Stephen Andrews Inc (G-8507)*

Cameo Inc.. 419 661-9611
995 3rd St - Ampoint Perrysburg (43551) *(G-11208)*

Cameo Countertops Inc (PA).. 419 865-6371
7723 Airport Hwy Holland (43528) *(G-7748)*

Cameron Drilling Co Inc.. 740 453-3300
3636 Adamsville Rd Zanesville (43701) *(G-15003)*

Cameron International Corp... 740 654-4260
471 Quarry Rd Se Lancaster (43130) *(G-8185)*

Cameron Packaging Inc... 419 222-9404
250 E Hanthorn Rd Lima (45804) *(G-8394)*

Cameron Valve & Measurement, Lancaster *Also Called: Cameron International Corp (G-8185)*

Cammann Inc.. 440 965-4051
7105 State Route 60 Wakeman (44889) *(G-13678)*

Cammel Saw Company.. 330 477-3764
4898 Hills And Dales Rd Nw Canton (44708) *(G-1851)*

Campbell Group, Cincinnati *Also Called: Ch Transition Company LLC (G-2457)*

Campbell Signs & Apparel LLC.. 330 386-4768
47366 Y And O Rd East Liverpool (43920) *(G-6388)*

Canadus Power Systems LLC... 216 831-6600
9347 Ravenna Rd Ste A Twinsburg (44087) *(G-13284)*

Canal Dover Furniture LLC... 330 359-5375
8211 Township Road 652 Millersburg (44654) *(G-9974)*

Canal Winchester Facility, Canal Winchester *Also Called: Nifco America Corporation (G-1795)*

Canary Health Technologies Inc...................................... 617 784-4021
5005 Rockside Rd Ste 600 Cleveland (44131) *(G-3462)*

Canberra Corporation.. 419 724-4300
3610 N Holland Sylvania Rd Toledo (43615) *(G-12910)*

Candle Lab... 614 488-2009
1251 Grandview Ave Columbus (43212) *(G-4793)*

Candle-Lite, Blue Ash *Also Called: Candle-Lite Company LLC (G-1258)*

Candle-Lite Company LLC (HQ)....................................... 937 780-2563
10521 Millington Ct Ste B Blue Ash (45242) *(G-1258)*

Canfield Coating LLC... 330 533-3311
460 W Main St Canfield (44406) *(G-1806)*

Canfield Manufacturing Co Inc.. 330 533-3333
489 Rosemont Rd North Jackson (44451) *(G-10684)*

Canfield Metal Coating Corp.. 330 702-3876
460 W Main St Canfield (44406) *(G-1807)*

Canine Creations Inc... 937 667-8576
120b W Broadway St # A Tipp City (45371) *(G-12817)*

Cannon Salt & Supply Inc.. 440 232-1700
26041 Cannon Rd Bedford (44146) *(G-1019)*

Canron Manufacturing Inc.. 330 497-1131
3979 State Street N W Greentown (44630) *(G-7332)*

Cansto Coatings Ltd.. 216 231-6115
9320 Woodland Ave Cleveland (44104) *(G-3463)*

Cansto Paint and Varnish Co
9320 Woodland Ave Cleveland (44104) *(G-3464)*

Cantelli Block and Brick Inc.. 419 433-0102
1602 Milan Rd Sandusky (44870) *(G-11826)*

Cantex Inc.. 330 995-3665
11444 Chamberlain Rd # 1 Aurora (44202) *(G-665)*

Canton Asphalt Co.. 330 499-6888
5947 Whipple Ave Nw Canton (44720) *(G-1852)*

Canton Bandag Co.. 330 454-3025
922 Benskin Ave Sw Canton (44710) *(G-1853)*

Canton Drop Forge, Canton *Also Called: Canton Drop Forge Inc (G-1854)*

Canton Drop Forge Inc.. 330 477-4511
4575 Southway St Sw Canton (44706) *(G-1854)*

Canton Elevator Inc.. 330 833-3600
2575 Greensburg Rd North Canton (44720) *(G-10632)*

Canton Galvanizing LLC... 330 685-9060
1821 Moore Ave Se Canton (44707) *(G-1855)*

Canton Gear Mfg Designing Inc....................................... 330 455-2771
1600 Tuscarawas St E Canton (44707) *(G-1856)*

Canton Hot Rolled Plant, Canton *Also Called: Republic Steel (G-1994)*

Canton Manufacturing, Valley City *Also Called: Greenfield Die & Mfg Corp (G-13497)*

Canton OH Rubber Speclty Prods.................................... 330 454-3847
1387 Clarendon Ave Sw Bldg 13 Canton (44710) *(G-1857)*

Canton Oil Well Service Inc.. 330 494-1221
7793 Pittsburg Ave Nw Canton (44720) *(G-1858)*

Canton Plating Co Inc... 330 452-7808
903 9th St Ne Canton (44704) *(G-1859)*

Canton Sterilized Wiping Cloth.. 330 455-5179
1401 Waynesburg Dr Se Canton (44707) *(G-1860)*

Canton Tool, Canton *Also Called: Stolle Machinery Company LLC (G-2018)*

Cantrell Rfinery Sls Trnsp Inc.. 937 695-0318
18856 State Route 136 Winchester (45697) *(G-14597)*

Canvas Specialty Mfg Co.. 216 881-0647
4045 Saint Clair Ave Cleveland (44103) *(G-3465)*

Canvus Inc... 216 340-7500
18500 Lake Rd Rocky River (44116) *(G-11632)*

Canyon Run Engineering, Troy *Also Called: Slimline Surgical Devices LLC (G-13256)*

Cap & Associates Inc.. 614 863-3363
445 Mccormick Blvd Columbus (43213) *(G-4794)*

Cap Fixtures, Columbus *Also Called: Cap & Associates Inc (G-4794)*

Caparo Bull Moose Inc.. 330 448-4878
1433 Standard Ave Masury (44438) *(G-9254)*

Caparo Bull Moose, Inc., Masury *Also Called: Caparo Bull Moose Inc (G-9254)*

Capco Automotive Products Corp..................................... 216 523-5000
1111 Superior Ave Eaton Ctr Cleveland (44114) *(G-3466)*

Capehart Enterprises LLC.. 614 769-7746
1724 Northwest Blvd Ste B Columbus (43212) *(G-4795)*

Capital City Awning Co Inc... 614 221-5404
577 N 4th St Columbus (43215) *(G-4796)*

Capital City Oil Inc... 740 397-4483
375 Columbus Rd Mount Vernon (43050) *(G-10238)*

Capital Office Supply, Columbus *Also Called: Dewitt Group Inc (G-4879)*

Capital Precision Machine & Tl.. 937 258-1176
1865 Radio Rd Dayton (45431) *(G-5604)*

Capital Prsthtic Orthtic Ctr I (PA)................................... 614 451-0446
4678 Larwell Dr Columbus (43220) *(G-4797)*

Capital Resin Corporation.. 614 445-7177
324 Dering Ave Columbus (43207) *(G-4798)*

Capital Spring, Columbus *Also Called: Matthew Warren Inc (G-5087)*

Capital Tire Inc... 330 364-4731
516 E Hudson St Toledo (43608) *(G-12911)*

Capital Toe Grinding, Columbus *Also Called: HI Lite Plastic Products (G-4980)*

Capital Tool Company.. 216 661-5750
1110 Brookpark Rd Cleveland (44109) *(G-3467)*

Capitol Aluminum & Glass Corp...................................... 800 331-8268
1276 W Main St Bellevue (44811) *(G-1122)*

Capitol Citicom Inc... 614 472-2679
2225 Citygate Dr Ste A Columbus (43219) *(G-4799)*

Capitol City Trailers Inc... 614 491-2616
3960 Groveport Rd Obetz (43207) *(G-10921)*

Capitol Square Printing Inc... 614 221-2850
60 E Gay St Columbus (43215) *(G-4800)*

Capsa Solutions LLC... 800 437-6633
8170 Dove Pkwy Canal Winchester (43110) *(G-1788)*

Capt, Celina *Also Called: Celina Alum Precision Tech Inc (G-2099)*

Captive-Aire Systems Inc.. 513 860-5555
1329 E Kemper Rd Ste 4210 Cincinnati (45246) *(G-2437)*

Captor Corporation.. 937 667-8484
5040 S County Road 25a Tipp City (45371) *(G-12818)*

Car Brite, Perrysburg *Also Called: Finale Products Inc (G-11221)*

Carapa Industries Inc... 330 307-1890
1080 Bedford Rd Masury (44438) *(G-9255)*

Caraustar, Copley *Also Called: Caraustar Industries Inc (G-5432)*

Caraustar, Oregon *Also Called: Caraustar Indus Cnsmr Pdts Gro (G-10960)*

Caraustar Indus Cnsmr Pdts Gro..................................... 330 868-4111
460 Knox Ct Minerva (44657) *(G-10035)*

Caraustar Indus Cnsmr Pdts Gro..................................... 419 690-0524
4031 Spartan Dr Oregon (43616) *(G-10960)*

Caraustar Industries Inc.. 740 862-4167
310 W Water St Baltimore (43105) *(G-784)*

Caraustar Industries Inc.. 513 871-7112
5500 Wooster Pike Cincinnati (45226) *(G-2438)*

Caraustar Industries Inc.. 216 939-3001
7960 Lorain Ave Cleveland (44102) *(G-3468)*

Caraustar Industries Inc.. 330 665-7700
202 Montrose West Ave Ste 315 Copley (44321) *(G-5432)*

A
L
P
H
A
B
E
T
I
C

Caraustar Industries Inc...............................937 298-9969
2601 E River Rd Moraine (45439) *(G-10154)*

Caravan Packaging Inc (PA).............................440 243-4100
6427 Eastland Rd Cleveland (44142) *(G-3469)*

Carbide Probes Inc.......................................937 429-9123
1328 Research Park Dr Beavercreek (45432) *(G-967)*

Carbo Forge Inc...419 334-9788
150 State Route 523 Fremont (43420) *(G-7096)*

Carbon Enterprises Inc (PA).............................740 420-6472
28205 Scippo Creek Rd Circleville (43113) *(G-3249)*

Carbon Polymers Company................................330 948-3007
104 Lee St Lodi (44254) *(G-8499)*

Carbon Products, West Chester *Also Called: Graphel Corporation (G-14012)*

Carbon Web Print LLC.....................................216 402-3504
38033 Dodds Hill Dr Willoughby Hills (44094) *(G-14556)*

Carbonklean Llc...614 980-9515
24 Village Pointe Dr Powell (43065) *(G-11483)*

Carbonless Cut Sheet Forms Inc........................740 826-1700
1948 John Glenn Hwy New Concord (43762) *(G-10385)*

Carbonless On Demandcom LLC.........................330 837-8611
332 Erie St S Massillon (44646) *(G-9177)*

Carborundum, Logan *Also Called: Carborundum Grinding Wheel Company (G-8510)*

Carborundum Grinding Wheel Company.................740 385-2171
1011 E Front St Logan (43138) *(G-8510)*

Carden Door Company LLC................................513 459-2233
1224 Castle Dr Mason (45040) *(G-9076)*

Cardiac Analytics LLC....................................614 314-1332
5683 Liberty Rd N Powell (43065) *(G-11484)*

Cardinal Aggregate Inc...................................419 872-4380
8026 Fremont Pike Perrysburg (43551) *(G-11209)*

Cardinal Builders Inc.....................................614 237-1000
4409 E Main St Columbus (43213) *(G-4801)*

Cardinal CT Company......................................740 892-2324
140 Carey St Utica (43080) *(G-13486)*

Cardinal Fastener, Bedford Heights *Also Called: Cardinal Fstener Specialty Inc (G-1072)*

Cardinal Fstener Specialty Inc..........................216 831-3800
5185 Richmond Rd Bedford Heights (44146) *(G-1072)*

Cardinal Glass Industries Inc............................740 892-2324
140 Carey St Utica (43080) *(G-13487)*

Cardinal Health Inc..614 553-3830
7200 Cardinal Pl W Dublin (43017) *(G-6285)*

Cardinal Health Inc (PA).................................614 757-5000
7000 Cardinal Pl Dublin (43017) *(G-6286)*

Cardinal Health Inc..614 757-2863
850 Corduroy Rd Ste 100 Lewis Center (43035) *(G-8328)*

Cardinal Health 110 LLC.................................800 727-6331
7000 Cardinal Pl Dublin (43017) *(G-6287)*

Cardinal Health 414 LLC (HQ)...........................614 757-5000
7000 Cardinal Pl Dublin (43017) *(G-6288)*

Cardinal Health 414 LLC.................................513 759-1900
9866 Windisch Rd Bldg 3 West Chester (45069) *(G-13954)*

Cardinal Hlth Nclear Prcsion H, Lewis Center *Also Called: Cardinal Health Inc (G-8328)*

Cardinal Machine Company...............................440 238-7050
14459 Foltz Pkwy Strongsville (44149) *(G-12547)*

Cardinal Printing Inc......................................330 773-7300
112 W Wilbeth Rd Akron (44301) *(G-89)*

Cardinal Products Inc.....................................440 237-8280
11929 Abbey Rd Ste D North Royalton (44133) *(G-10756)*

Cardinal Pumps Exchangers Inc (DH)..................330 332-8558
1425 Quaker Ct Salem (44460) *(G-11767)*

Cardinal Rubber Company................................330 745-2191
939 Wooster Rd N Barberton (44203) *(G-801)*

Cardinal Truss & Components, Edgerton *Also Called: Building Concepts Inc (G-6464)*

Cardinal Welding Inc......................................330 426-2404
895 E Taggart St East Palestine (44413) *(G-6400)*

Cardinalhealth, Dublin *Also Called: Cardinal Health Inc (G-6286)*

Cardington Yutaka Tech Inc (DH).......................419 864-8777
575 W Main St Cardington (43315) *(G-2053)*

Cardioinsight Technologies Inc..........................216 274-2221
3 Summit Park Dr Ste 400 Independence (44131) *(G-7890)*

Cardpak Incorporated.....................................440 542-3100
29601 Solon Rd Solon (44139) *(G-12091)*

Care Fusion..216 521-1220
14414 Detroit Ave Ste 205 Lakewood (44107) *(G-8164)*

Care Industries...614 584-6595
6137 Enterprise Pkwy Grove City (43123) *(G-7376)*

Carefusion, Groveport *Also Called: Becton Dickinson and Company (G-7424)*

Careismatic Brands LLC..................................561 843-8727
6625 Port Rd Groveport (43125) *(G-7428)*

Careismatic Brands LLC..................................614 497-5289
6755 Port Rd Groveport (43125) *(G-7429)*

Carey Color Inc..330 239-1835
6835 Ridge Rd Sharon Center (44274) *(G-11938)*

Carey Precast Concrete Company........................419 396-7142
3420 Township Highway 98 Carey (43316) *(G-2057)*

Cargill, Akron *Also Called: Cargill Incorporated (G-90)*

Cargill, Cleveland *Also Called: Cargill Incorporated (G-3470)*

Cargill, Dayton *Also Called: Cargill Incorporated (G-5693)*

Cargill, Saint Marys *Also Called: Cargill Incorporated (G-11735)*

Cargill Incorporated......................................330 745-0031
2065 Manchester Rd Akron (44314) *(G-90)*

Cargill Incorporated......................................216 651-7200
2400 Ships Channel Cleveland (44113) *(G-3470)*

Cargill Incorporated......................................937 236-1971
3201 Needmore Rd Dayton (45414) *(G-5693)*

Cargill Incorporated......................................419 394-3374
1400 Mckinley Rd Saint Marys (45885) *(G-11735)*

Cargill Incorporated......................................937 497-4848
701 S Vandemark Rd Sidney (45365) *(G-11999)*

Cargill Incorporated......................................937 498-4555
2400 Industrial Dr Sidney (45365) *(G-12000)*

Cargill Premix and Nutrition, Lewisburg *Also Called: Provimi North America Inc (G-8362)*

Carl Rittberger Sr Inc....................................740 452-2767
1900 Lutz Ln Zanesville (43701) *(G-15004)*

Carlisle and Finch Company.............................513 681-6080
4562 W Mitchell Ave Cincinnati (45232) *(G-2439)*

Carlisle Oak..330 852-8734
3872 Township Road 162 Sugarcreek (44681) *(G-12634)*

Carlisle Plastics Company................................937 845-9411
320 Ohio Ave New Carlisle (45344) *(G-10369)*

Carlisle Prtg Walnut Creek Ltd..........................330 852-9922
2673 Township Road 421 Sugarcreek (44681) *(G-12635)*

Carmel Publishing Inc....................................330 478-9200
4501 Hills And Dales Rd Nw Canton (44708) *(G-1861)*

Carmeuse Lime Inc.......................................419 986-5200
1967 W County Rd 42 Bettsville (44815) *(G-1207)*

Carmeuse Lime Inc.......................................419 638-2511
3964 County Road 41 Millersville (43435) *(G-10027)*

Carmeuse Lime Inc.......................................419 986-2000
1967 W County Rd 42 Tiffin (44883) *(G-12779)*

Carmeuse Lime & Stone, Millersville *Also Called: Carmeuse Lime Inc (G-10027)*

Carmeuse Natural Chemicals, Bettsville *Also Called: Carmeuse Lime Inc (G-1207)*

Carnation Machine and Tool Inc.........................330 823-5352
14632 Oyster Rd Alliance (44601) *(G-375)*

Carney Plastics Inc.......................................330 746-8273
1010 W Rayen Ave Youngstown (44502) *(G-14831)*

Carolina Knife Services, Hamilton *Also Called: Hamilton Industrial Grinding Inc (G-7502)*

Carolina Stair Supply Inc (PA)..........................740 922-3333
316 Herrick St Uhrichsville (44683) *(G-13402)*

Carols Ultra Stitch & Variety...........................419 935-8991
122 S Myrtle Ave Willard (44890) *(G-14401)*

Caron Products and Svcs Inc............................740 373-6809
27640 State Route 7 Marietta (45750) *(G-8906)*

CARONDELET FOUNDRY, Sandusky *Also Called: Sandusky International Inc (G-11868)*

Carpe Diem Industries LLC..............................419 358-0129
505 E Jefferson St Bluffton (45817) *(G-1359)*

Carpe Diem Industries LLC (PA)........................419 659-5639
4599 Campbell Rd Columbus Grove (45830) *(G-5382)*

Carper Well Service Inc..................................740 374-2567
30745 State Route 7 Marietta (45750) *(G-8907)*

Carr Bros Inc..440 232-3700
7177 Northfield Rd Bedford (44146) *(G-1020)*

Carr Bros Bldrs Sup & Coal Co............................... 440 232-3700
  7177 Northfield Rd Cleveland (44146) *(G-3471)*

Carr Tool Company.. 513 825-2900
  575 Security Dr Fairfield (45014) *(G-6717)*

Carrera Holdings Inc... 216 687-1311
  101 W Prospect Ave Cleveland (44115) *(G-3472)*

Carroll Hills Industries... 330 627-5524
  540 High St Nw Carrollton (44615) *(G-2080)*

Carrollton Publishing Company............................. 330 627-5591
  43 E Main St Carrollton (44615) *(G-2081)*

Carruth Studio Inc (PA)... 419 878-3060
  1178 Farnsworth Rd Waterville (43566) *(G-13831)*

Cars and Parts Magazine..................................... 937 498-08J3
  911 S Vandemark Rd Sidney (45365) *(G-12001)*

Carson Industries LLC.. 419 592-2309
  1675 Industrial Dr Napoleon (43545) *(G-10276)*

Carson-Saeks Inc (PA).. 937 278-5311
  2601 Timber Ln Dayton (45414) *(G-5694)*

Carter Carburetor LLC... 216 314-2711
  127 Public Sq Ste 5300 Cleveland (44114) *(G-3473)*

Carter Lumber, Middlefield *Also Called: Carter-Jones Lumber Company (G-9785)*

Carter Manufacturing Co Inc.................................. 513 398-7303
  4220 State Route 42 Mason (45040) *(G-9077)*

Carter-Jones Lumber Company............................. 440 834-8164
  14601 Kinsman Rd Middlefield (44062) *(G-9785)*

Carter-Jones Lumber Company............................. 330 674-9060
  6139 State Route 39 Millersburg (44654) *(G-9975)*

Carters Inc... 330 758-0390
  389 Boardman Poland Rd Boardman (44512) *(G-1369)*

Cartessa Corp.. 513 738-4477
  4825 Cincinnati Brookville Rd Shandon (45063) *(G-11933)*

Caruso Foods LLC... 513 860-9200
  3465 Hauck Rd Cincinnati (45241) *(G-2440)*

Cas, Cincinnati *Also Called: Consoldted Anlytcal Systems In (G-2510)*

Casa Di Sassi, Apple Creek *Also Called: Rock Decor Company (G-477)*

Casad Company Inc... 419 586-9457
  450 S 2nd St Coldwater (45828) *(G-4570)*

Cascade Corporation... 419 425-3675
  2000 Production Dr Findlay (45840) *(G-6850)*

Cascade Corporation... 937 327-0300
  2501 Sheridan Ave Springfield (45505) *(G-12287)*

Cascade Ohio Inc... 440 593-5800
  1209 Maple Ave Conneaut (44030) *(G-5399)*

Cascade Pattern Company Inc.............................. 440 323-4300
  519 Ternes Ln Elyria (44035) *(G-6509)*

Cascade Unlimited LLC.. 440 352-7995
  2510 Hale Rd Painesville (44077) *(G-11071)*

Casco Mfg Solutions Inc....................................... 513 681-0003
  3107 Spring Grove Ave Cincinnati (45225) *(G-2441)*

Case Crafters Inc... 937 667-9473
  211 S 1st St Tipp City (45371) *(G-12819)*

Case Farms LLC... 330 832-0030
  4001 Millennium Blvd Se Massillon (44646) *(G-9178)*

Case Farms Chicken, Winesburg *Also Called: Case Farms of Ohio Inc (G-14605)*

Case Farms of Ohio Inc.. 330 359-7141
  1818 County Rd 160 Winesburg (44690) *(G-14605)*

Case Farms Processing Inc................................... 330 455-0241
  1818 County Rd 160 Winesburg (44690) *(G-14606)*

Case Maul Clamps Inc.. 419 668-6563
  69 N West St Norwalk (44857) *(G-10832)*

Case Ohio Burial Co (PA)....................................... 440 779-1992
  1720 Columbus Rd Cleveland (44113) *(G-3474)*

Case-Maul Manufacturing Co................................ 419 524-1061
  30 Harker St Mansfield (44903) *(G-8771)*

Cashman Kiosk, Bedford *Also Called: Best Result Marketing Inc (G-1017)*

Cask 307 LLC.. 440 307-9586
  7259 Warner Rd Madison (44057) *(G-8724)*

Cass Frames Inc... 419 468-2863
  6052 State Route 19 Galion (44833) *(G-7181)*

Cassady Woodworks Inc....................................... 937 256-7948
  446 N Smithville Rd Dayton (45431) *(G-5605)*

Cassano's Pizza & Subs, Dayton *Also Called: Cassanos Inc (G-5695)*

Cassanos Inc (PA)... 937 294-8400
  1700 E Stroop Rd Dayton (45429) *(G-5695)*

Cassis Packaging Co.. 937 223-8868
  1235 Mccook Ave Dayton (45404) *(G-5696)*

Cast Metals Technology Inc................................... 937 968-5460
  305 Se Deerfield Rd Union City (45390) *(G-13414)*

Cast Nylons, Willoughby *Also Called: Cast Nylons Co Ltd (G-14437)*

Cast Nylons Co Ltd (PA).. 440 269-2300
  4300 Hamann Pkwy Willoughby (44094) *(G-14437)*

Cast Specialties Inc.. 216 292-7393
  26711 Miles Rd Cleveland (44128) *(G-3475)*

Cast-Fab Technologies Inc (PA)............................. 513 758-1000
  3040 Forrer St Cincinnati (45209) *(G-2442)*

Castalia Trenching & Rdymx LLC............................ 419 684-5502
  4814 State Route 269 S Castalia (44824) *(G-2094)*

Castalia Trenching & Ready Mix............................. 419 684-5502
  4814 State Route 269 S Castalia (44824) *(G-2095)*

Castalloy Inc.. 216 961-7990
  7990 Baker Ave Cleveland (44102) *(G-3476)*

Casteel, Belpre *Also Called: Skyline Steel LLC (G-1154)*

Castek Inc... 440 365-2333
  527 Ternes Ln Elyria (44035) *(G-6510)*

Castelli Marble LLC (PA)....................................... 216 361-1222
  3958 Superior Ave E Cleveland (44114) *(G-3477)*

Casting Solutions LLC.. 740 452-9371
  2345 Licking Rd Zanesville (43701) *(G-15005)*

Castings Usa Inc... 330 339-3611
  2061 Brightwood Rd Se New Philadelphia (44663) *(G-10436)*

Castle Blinds and Draperies, Dayton *Also Called: Custom Blind Corporation (G-5717)*

Castruction Company Inc...................................... 330 332-9622
  1588 Salem Pkwy Salem (44460) *(G-11768)*

Cat-Wood Metalworks, Moraine *Also Called: Rolling Enterprises Inc (G-10191)*

Catacel Corp
  785 N Freedom St Ravenna (44266) *(G-11520)*

Catalog Merchandiser Inc
  10525 Chester Rd Ste A Cincinnati (45215) *(G-2443)*

Catalysis Additive Tooling LLC............................... 614 715-3674
  190 Heatherdown Dr Westerville (43081) *(G-14249)*

Catania Medallic Specialities, Avon Lake *Also Called: Catania Medallic Specialty Inc (G-751)*

Catania Medallic Specialty Inc.............................. 440 933-9595
  668 Moore Rd Avon Lake (44012) *(G-751)*

Caterpillar Authorized Dealer, Broadview Heights *Also Called: Ohio Machinery Co (G-1509)*

Caterpillar Industrial Inc...................................... 440 247-8484
  45 E Washington St Ste 203 Chagrin Falls (44022) *(G-2138)*

Catexel Nease LLC.. 513 738-1255
  10740 Paddyo Run Rd Harrison (45030) *(C-7544)*

Catexel Nease LLC (DH)....................................... 513 587-2800
  9774 Windisch Rd West Chester (45069) *(G-13955)*

Catholic Diocese of Columbus............................... 614 224-5195
  197 E Gay St Ste 4 Columbus (43215) *(G-4802)*

Catholic Times, Columbus *Also Called: Catholic Diocese of Columbus (G-4802)*

Catstrap, Whitehouse *Also Called: KWD Automotive Inc (G-14362)*

Cattron Holdings Inc (HQ)..................................... 234 806-0018
  655 N River Rd Nw Ste A Warren (44483) *(G-13748)*

Cattron North America Inc (DH).............................. 234 806-0018
  655 N River Rd Nw Ste A Warren (44483) *(G-13749)*

Cave Tool & Mfg Inc.. 937 324-0662
  20 Walnut St Springfield (45505) *(G-12288)*

Cayosoft Inc (PA).. 614 423-6718
  470 Olde Worthington Rd Ste 200 Westerville (43082) *(G-14205)*

CB Graphics LLC... 216 749-5577
  5725 Brookpark Rd Cleveland (44129) *(G-3478)*

Cbc Global, Columbiana *Also Called: Columbiana Boiler Company LLC (G-4611)*

Cbf, Medina *Also Called: Cmbf Products Inc (G-9388)*

Cbn Westside Holdings Inc.................................... 513 772-7000
  8800 Global Way West Chester (45069) *(G-13956)*

Cbn Westside Technologies Inc.............................. 513 772-7000
  8800 Global Way West Chester (45069) *(G-13957)*

Cbp Co Inc.. 513 860-9053
  6545 Wiehe Rd Cincinnati (45237) *(G-2444)*

A L P H A B E T I C

CBs Boring and Mch Co Inc................................. 419 784-9500
  2064 E 2nd St Defiance (43512) *(G-6101)*

Cbst Acquisition LLC... 513 361-9600
  6900 Steger Dr Cincinnati (45237) *(G-2445)*

Cbts Technology Solutions LLC............................ 440 569-2300
  5910 Landerbrook Dr Ste 250 Cleveland (44124) *(G-3479)*

Cbus Inc.. 614 327-6971
  13799 Nantucket Ave Pickerington (43147) *(G-11291)*

CCA Youngstown... 615 263-3000
  2240 Hubbard Rd Youngstown (44505) *(G-14832)*

Ccbcc Operations LLC... 304 203-8647
  6040 Collings Dr Lockbourne (43137) *(G-8487)*

Ccbdd.. 330 424-0404
  35947 State Route 172 Lisbon (44432) *(G-8465)*

CCL Design, Strongsville *Also Called: CCL Label Inc (G-12548)*

CCL Design Electronics, Strongsville *Also Called: CCL Label Inc (G-12549)*

CCL Label Inc.. 216 676-2703
  15939 Industrial Pkwy Cleveland (44135) *(G-3480)*

CCL Label Inc.. 856 273-0700
  8600 Innovation Campus Way W New Albany (43054) *(G-10334)*

CCL Label Inc.. 440 878-7000
  17890 Foltz Pkwy Strongsville (44149) *(G-12548)*

CCL Label Inc.. 440 878-7277
  17700 Foltz Pkwy Strongsville (44149) *(G-12549)*

Ccp Industries, Richmond Heights *Also Called: Ccp Industries Inc (G-11609)*

Ccp Industries Inc.. 216 535-4227
  26301 Curtiss Wright Pkwy Ste 200 Richmond Heights (44143) *(G-11609)*

Ccp Newco LLC.. 419 448-1700
  1780 S County Road 1 Tiffin (44883) *(G-12780)*

Ccpi Inc (PA).. 937 783-2476
  838 Cherry St Blanchester (45107) *(G-1234)*

CCS Instruments, Akron *Also Called: Corporate Cnsulting Svc Instrs (G-106)*

Ccsi Inc.. 800 742-8535
  1868 Akron Peninsula Rd Akron (44313) *(G-91)*

CCT, Shelby *Also Called: Custom Control Tech LLC (G-11969)*

CD / Dvd Distribution, Dayton *Also Called: Chaos Entertainment (G-5698)*

CD Company LLC.. 419 332-2693
  215 N Stone St Fremont (43420) *(G-7097)*

CD Solutions Inc.. 937 676-2376
  100 W Monument St Pleasant Hill (45359) *(G-11431)*

Cdc Corporation.. 715 532-5548
  1445 Holland Rd Maumee (43537) *(G-9268)*

Cdc Fab Co.. 419 866-7705
  1445 Holland Rd Maumee (43537) *(G-9269)*

Cdh Custom Roll Form LLC................................. 330 984-0555
  1300 Phoenix Rd Ne Warren (44483) *(G-13750)*

Cdh Liquidation Inc.. 419 720-4096
  1343 Miami St Toledo (43605) *(G-12912)*

CDI, Avon *Also Called: Cutting Dynamics LLC (G-723)*

CDI Industries Inc.. 440 243-1100
  6800 Lake Abrams Dr Cleveland (44130) *(G-3481)*

CDK Perforating LLC... 817 862-9834
  2167 State Route 821 Marietta (45750) *(G-8908)*

CEC Electronics Corp.. 330 916-8100
  1739 Akron Peninsula Rd Akron (44313) *(G-92)*

Cecil C Peck Co.. 330 785-0781
  1029 Arlington Cir Akron (44306) *(G-93)*

Cecil Peck Co, Akron *Also Called: Summit Machine Solutions LLC (G-321)*

Ceco Environmental Corp.................................... 513 458-2606
  6245 Creek Rd Blue Ash (45242) *(G-1259)*

Ceco Environmental Corp.................................... 513 874-8915
  9759 Inter Ocean Dr Cincinnati (45246) *(G-2446)*

Ceco Filters Inc... 513 458-2600
  4625 Red Bank Rd Ste 200 Cincinnati (45227) *(G-2447)*

Ceco Group Global Holdings LLC (HQ).................. 513 458-2600
  4625 Red Bank Rd Ste 200 Cincinnati (45227) *(G-2448)*

CED Process Minerals Inc (PA)............................ 330 666-5500
  863 N Cleveland Massillon Rd Akron (44333) *(G-94)*

Cedar Craft Products Inc.................................... 614 759-1600
  776 Reynoldsburg New Albany Rd Blacklick (43004) *(G-1222)*

Cedar Elec Holdings Corp.................................... 773 804-6288
  5440 W Chester Rd West Chester (45069) *(G-13958)*

Cedar Woodworking, Delaware *Also Called: Cedee Cedar Inc (G-6136)*

Cedee Cedar Inc (PA)... 740 363-3148
  3903 Us Highway 42 S Delaware (43015) *(G-6136)*

Ceia USA, Hudson *Also Called: Ceia Usa Ltd (G-7836)*

Ceia Usa Ltd.. 330 310-4741
  6336 Hudson Crossing Pkwy Hudson (44236) *(G-7836)*

Celina Alum Precision Tech Inc............................ 419 586-2278
  7059 Staeger Rd Celina (45822) *(G-2099)*

Celina Percision Machine..................................... 419 586-9222
  1201 Havemann Rd Celina (45822) *(G-2100)*

Celina Tent Inc (PA)... 419 586-3610
  5373 State Route 29 Celina (45822) *(G-2101)*

Cell 4less, Lima *Also Called: Airwave Communications Cons (G-8385)*

Cell-O-Core, Wadsworth *Also Called: Nelson Companies One LLC (G-13654)*

Cell-O-Core Co... 330 239-4370
  6935 Ridge Rd Sharon Center (44274) *(G-11939)*

Cell-O-Core Co... 800 239-4370
  276 College St Wadsworth (44281) *(G-13630)*

Cellular Technology Limited................................. 216 791-5084
  20521 Chagrin Blvd Ste 200 Shaker Heights (44122) *(G-11928)*

Cellular Technology Ltd, Shaker Heights *Also Called: Ctl Analyzers LLC (G-11929)*

Cemco Construction Corporation.......................... 440 567-7708
  10176 Page Dr Concord Township (44060) *(G-5388)*

Cement Products Inc.. 419 524-4342
  389 Park Ave E Mansfield (44905) *(G-8772)*

Cemex Cement Inc.. 937 873-9858
  4410 State Route 235 Fairborn (45324) *(G-6688)*

Cemex Materials LLC.. 330 654-2501
  4200 Universal Dr Diamond (44412) *(G-6226)*

Cemplex Group NC LLC....................................... 513 671-3300
  3195 Profit Dr Fairfield (45014) *(G-6718)*

Cen-Trol Machine Co.. 216 524-1932
  7601 Commerce Park Oval Cleveland (44131) *(G-3482)*

Cengage Learning, Mason *Also Called: Cengage Lrng Holdings II Inc (G-9081)*

Cengage Learning Inc... 513 234-5967
  770 Broadway Mason (45036) *(G-9078)*

Cengage Learning Inc (HQ).................................. 617 289-7700
  5191 Natorp Blvd Mason (45040) *(G-9079)*

Cengage Learning Inc... 415 839-2300
  5191 Natorp Blvd Lowr Mason (45040) *(G-9080)*

Cengage Lrng Holdings II Inc (PA)......................... 617 289-7700
  5191 Natorp Blvd Mason (45040) *(G-9081)*

Cenmac Metalworks, Marion *Also Called: Central Machinery Company LLC (G-8966)*

Censtar Coatings Inc... 330 723-8000
  11829 Jeffrey Rd West Salem (44287) *(G-14186)*

Cent-Roll Products Inc.. 513 829-5201
  4866 Factory Dr Fairfield (45014) *(G-6719)*

Centaur Tool & Die Inc....................................... 419 352-7704
  2019 Wood Bridge Blvd Bowling Green (43402) *(G-1412)*

Center Concrete Inc.. 419 782-2495
  24187 Jewell Rd Defiance (43512) *(G-6102)*

Center Concrete Inc (PA)..................................... 800 453-4224
  8790 Us Highway 6 Edgerton (43517) *(G-6465)*

Center For Inquiry Inc... 330 671-7192
  6413 Riverview Rd Peninsula (44264) *(G-11181)*

Center Street Technologies, Youngstown *Also Called: 1062 Technologies Inc (G-14799)*

Centerless Grinding Svc Inc................................. 216 251-4100
  19500 S Miles Rd Cleveland (44128) *(G-3483)*

Centerra Co-Op (PA)... 419 281-2153
  813 Clark Ave Ashland (44805) *(G-526)*

Centor Inc.. 800 321-3391
  5091 County Road 120 Millersburg (44654) *(G-9976)*

Centor Inc (HQ).. 567 336-8094
  1899 N Wilkinson Way Perrysburg (43551) *(G-11210)*

Central Allied Enterprises Inc (PA)........................ 330 477-6751
  1243 Raff Rd Sw Canton (44710) *(G-1862)*

Central Aluminum Company LLC........................... 614 491-5700
  2045 Broehm Rd Obetz (43207) *(G-10922)*

Central Coated Products LLC............................... 330 821-9830
  2025 Mccrea St Alliance (44601) *(G-376)*

Central Coca-Cola Btlg Co Inc.............................. 330 875-1487
  1560 Triplett Blvd Akron (44306) *(G-95)*

(G-0000) Company's Geographic Section entry number

Central Coca-Cola Btlg Co Inc................................ 740 474-2180
387 Walnut St Circleville (43113) *(G-3250)*

Central Coca-Cola Btlg Co Inc................................ 440 324-3335
1410 Lake Ave Elyria (44035) *(G-6511)*

Central Coca-Cola Btlg Co Inc................................ 614 863-7200
6040 Collings Dr Lockbourne (43137) *(G-8488)*

Central Coca-Cola Btlg Co Inc................................ 419 522-2653
100 Industrial Pkwy Mansfield (44903) *(G-8773)*

Central Coca-Cola Btlg Co Inc................................ 419 476-6622
3970 Catawba St Toledo (43612) *(G-12913)*

Central Coca-Cola Btlg Co Inc................................ 330 425-4401
1882 Highland Rd Twinsburg (44087) *(G-13285)*

Central Coca-Cola Btlg Co Inc................................ 440 269-1433
4800 E 355th St Willoughby (44094) *(G-14438)*

Central Coca-Cola Btlg Co Inc................................ 330 783-1982
531 E Indianola Ave Youngstown (44502) *(G-14833)*

Central Coca-Cola Btlg Co Inc................................ 740 452-3608
154 S 7th St Zanesville (43701) *(G-15006)*

Central Fabricators Inc... 513 621-1240
408 Poplar St Cincinnati (45214) *(G-2449)*

Central Investment LLC (PA).................................. 513 563-4700
7265 Kenwood Rd Ste 240 Cincinnati (45236) *(G-2450)*

Central Machinery Company LLC........................... 740 387-1289
1339 E Fairground Rd Marion (43302) *(G-8966)*

Central Machinery Company LLC........................... 740 387-1289
116 S Main St Marion (43302) *(G-8967)*

Central Market Specialty Meats, Columbus *Also Called: Karn Meats Inc (G-5046)*

Central Ohio Bandag LP... 740 454-9728
1600 S Point Dr Zanesville (43701) *(G-15007)*

Central Ohio Bldg Components, Newark *Also Called: Columbus Roof Trusses Inc (G-10498)*

Central Ohio Fabricators LLC................................ 740 393-3892
105 Progress Dr Mount Vernon (43050) *(G-10239)*

Central Ohio Met Stmping Fbrct............................ 614 861-3332
4361 Brompton Ct New Albany (43054) *(G-10335)*

Central Ohio Paper & Packg Inc (PA).....................419 621-9239
2350 University Dr E Huron (44839) *(G-7870)*

Central Ohio Welding, Columbus *Also Called: COW Industries Inc (G-4854)*

Central Oil Asphalt Corp (PA)............................... 614 224-8111
8 E Long St Ste 400 Columbus (43215) *(G-4803)*

Central Power Systems, Columbus *Also Called: Power Distributors LLC (G-5200)*

Central Ready Mix LLC (PA)................................... 513 402-5001
6310 E Kemper Rd Ste 125 Cincinnati (45241) *(G-2451)*

Central Ready-Mix of Ohio LLC............................. 614 252-3452
6310 E Kemper Rd Ste 125 Cincinnati (45241) *(G-2452)*

Central State Enterprises Inc............................... 419 468-8191
1331 Freese Works Pl (Galion Indl Pk) Galion (44833) *(G-7182)*

Central USA Wireless LLC..................................... 513 469-1500
11210 Montgomery Rd Cincinnati (45249) *(G-2453)*

Central-1-Optical LLC... 330 783-9660
6981 Southern Blvd Ste B Youngstown (44512) *(G-14834)*

Centrex Plastics, Findlay *Also Called: American Plastics LLC (G-6836)*

Centrex Plastics LLC.. 877 504-2768
814 W Lima St Findlay (45840) *(G-6851)*

Centria Coil Coating Services, Cambridge *Also Called: Metal Coaters (G-1749)*

Centric Parts, Cleveland *Also Called: Cwd LLC (G-3594)*

Centrus Energy Corp... 740 897-2217
3930 Us Highway 23 Anx Piketon (45661) *(G-11306)*

Century Components LLC....................................... 330 852-3610
1691 Sr-39 Sugarcreek (44681) *(G-12636)*

Century Container LLC.. 330 457-2367
32 W Railroad St Columbiana (44408) *(G-4608)*

Century Container LLC (HQ)..................................330 457-2367
5331 State Route 7 New Waterford (44445) *(G-10485)*

Century Container Corporation.............................. 330 457-2367
5331 State Route 7 New Waterford (44445) *(G-10486)*

Century Graphics Inc.. 614 895-7698
9101 Hawthorne Pt Westerville (43082) *(G-14206)*

Century Marketing Corporation.............................. 419 354-2591
1145 Fairview Ave Bowling Green (43402) *(G-1413)*

Century Mold Company Inc.................................... 513 539-9283
55 Wright Dr Middletown (45044) *(G-9843)*

Century Tool & Stamping Co.................................. 216 241-2032
24600 Center Ridge Rd Ste 140 Westlake (44145) *(G-14296)*

Cequence Security Inc.. 650 437-6338
10805 Indeco Dr Ste B Blue Ash (45241) *(G-1260)*

Cequent Consumer Products, Solon *Also Called: Cequent Consumer Products Inc (G-12092)*

Cequent Consumer Products Inc............................ 440 498-0001
29000 Aurora Rd Ste 2 Solon (44139) *(G-12092)*

Ceramic Holdings Inc (DH).................................... 216 362-3900
20600 Sheldon Rd Brook Park (44142) *(G-1511)*

Ceramsource Inc.. 732 257-5002
193 N James St East Palestine (44413) *(G-6401)*

Cerkl, Blue Ash *Also Called: Cerkl Incorporated (G-1261)*

Cerkl Incorporated... 513 813-8425
11126 Kenwood Rd Blue Ash (45242) *(G-1261)*

Cermet Technologies, Cleveland *Also Called: Postle Industries Inc (G-4177)*

Cerner Corporation... 740 826-7678
140 S Friendship Dr New Concord (43762) *(G-10386)*

Certainteed LLC... 419 499-2581
11519 Us Highway 250 N Milan (44846) *(G-9914)*

Certified Auto & Trck Repr Inc............................... 440 288-2029
1405 E 28th St Lorain (44055) *(G-8550)*

Certified Comparator Products.............................. 937 426-9677
2580 Kohnle Dr Miamisburg (45342) *(G-9679)*

Certified Heat Treating Inc (PA)............................. 937 866-0245
4475 Infirmary Rd Dayton (45449) *(G-5697)*

Certified Labs & Service Inc................................. 419 289-7462
535 E 7th St Ashland (44805) *(G-527)*

Certified Tool & Grinding Inc................................. 937 865-5934
4455 Infirmary Rd Miamisburg (45342) *(G-9680)*

Certon Technologies Inc (PA)................................ 440 786-7185
60 S Park St Bedford (44146) *(G-1021)*

Ces Nationwide.. 937 322-0771
567 E Leffel Ln Springfield (45505) *(G-12289)*

Cesgroup, Hamilton *Also Called: Cryogenic Equipment & Svcs Inc (G-7481)*

Ceso, Miamisburg *Also Called: Ceso Inc (G-9681)*

Ceso Inc (PA)...937 435-8584
3601 Rigby Rd Ste 300 Miamisburg (45342) *(G-9681)*

Cetek, Brook Park *Also Called: Ceramic Holdings Inc (G-1511)*

CF Industries Inc... 330 385-5424
425 River Rd East Liverpool (43920) *(G-6389)*

CF Tools LLC... 740 294-0419
52025 Township Road 509 Fresno (43824) *(G-7146)*

Cfgsc LLC... 513 772-5920
5927 Belmont Ave Cincinnati (45224) *(G-2454)*

CFM International Inc.. 513 563-4180
111 Merchant St Cincinnati (45246) *(G-2455)*

CFM International Inc.. 513 500-4100
1 Neumann Way Cincinnati (45215) *(G-2456)*

CFM International Inc (PA)..................................... 513 552-2787
6440 Aviation Way West Chester (45069) *(G-13959)*

Cfo Ntic.. 216 450-5700
23205 Mercantile Rd Beachwood (44122) *(G-911)*

Cft Systems, Fairport Harbor *Also Called: George Whalley Company (G-6816)*

Cg Industries, Fairfield *Also Called: Cincinnati Grinding Technologies Inc (G-6721)*

Cgas Exploration Inc (HQ).................................... 614 436-4631
110 E Wilson Bridge Rd Ste 250 Worthington (43085) *(G-14705)*

Cgas Inc (PA)..614 975-4697
110 E Wilson Bridge Rd Ste 250 Worthington (43085) *(G-14706)*

Cgmw Incorporated.. 614 236-8388
1020 Taylor Station Rd Ste F Columbus (43230) *(G-4804)*

Cgs, Medina *Also Called: Commercial Grinding Svcs Inc (G-9389)*

Cgs Imaging Inc... 419 897-3000
6950 Hall St Holland (43528) *(G-7749)*

Ch Enterprises, Toledo *Also Called: Greggs Specialty Services (G-12977)*

Ch Mack, Blue Ash *Also Called: H Mack Charles & Associates Inc (G-1281)*

Ch Transition Company LLC (DH)...........................800 543-6400
225 Pictoria Dr Ste 210 Cincinnati (45246) *(G-2457)*

Chad M Marsh.. 419 994-0587
16104 State Route 39 Loudonville (44842) *(G-8590)*

Chagrin Valley Custom Furn LLC............................ 440 591-5511
26309 Miles Rd Ste 6 Warrensville Heights (44128) *(G-13816)*

A
L
P
H
A
B
E
T
I
C

Chagrin Valley Publishing Co 440 247-5335
525 Washington St Chagrin Falls (44022) *(G-2139)*

Chagrin Valley Times, Chagrin Falls *Also Called: Chagrin Valley Publishing Co (G-2139)*

Chagrin Vly Stl Erectors Inc 440 975-1556
2278 River Rd Willoughby Hills (44094) *(G-14557)*

Chalet Debonne, Madison *Also Called: Chalet Debonne Vineyards Inc (G-8725)*

Chalet Debonne Vineyards Inc 440 466-3485
7840 Doty Rd Madison (44057) *(G-8725)*

Chalet In The Valley, Millersburg *Also Called: Guggisberg Cheese Inc (G-9982)*

Chalfant Loading Dock Eqp, Cleveland *Also Called: Chalfant Sew Fabricators Inc (G-3484)*

Chalfant Manufacturing Company (DH) 330 273-3510
1050 Jaycox Rd Avon (44011) *(G-718)*

Chalfant Sew Fabricators Inc 216 521-7922
11525 Madison Ave Cleveland (44102) *(G-3484)*

Cham Cor Industries Inc 740 967-9015
117 W Coshocton St Johnstown (43031) *(G-7995)*

Champion, Cincinnati *Also Called: Enclosure Suppliers LLC (G-2586)*

Champion, Springfield *Also Called: Champion Company (G-12290)*

Champion Bridge Company 937 382-2521
261 E Sugartree St Wilmington (45177) *(G-14575)*

Champion Companies, The, Springfield *Also Called: Champion Company (G-12291)*

Champion Company 937 324-5681
1100 Kenton St Springfield (45505) *(G-12290)*

Champion Company (PA) 937 324-5681
400 Harrison St Springfield (45505) *(G-12291)*

Champion Equipment, Dayton *Also Called: Matthew Brun Enterprises Inc (G-5870)*

CHAMPION INDUSTRIES DIV, Troy *Also Called: RT Industries Inc (G-13251)*

Champion Laboratories Inc 330 899-0340
6056 Deer Park Ct Toledo (43614) *(G-12914)*

Champion Opco LLC (DH) 513 327-7338
12121 Champion Way Cincinnati (45241) *(G-2458)*

Champion Spark Plug Company 419 535-2567
900 Upton Ave Toledo (43607) *(G-12915)*

Champion Strapping Pdts Inc 614 527-1454
1819 Walcutt Rd Ste 13 Columbus (43228) *(G-4805)*

Champion Win Co Cleveland LLC 440 899-2562
9011 Freeway Dr Ste 1 Macedonia (44056) *(G-8681)*

Champion Window, Cincinnati *Also Called: Champion Opco LLC (G-2458)*

Champion Window Co of Toledo 419 841-0154
7546 Ponderosa Rd Ste A Perrysburg (43551) *(G-11211)*

Chandler Machine Company 330 688-7615
4960 Hudson Dr Stow (44224) *(G-12423)*

Chandler Machine Company 330 688-5585
4960 Hudson Dr Stow (44224) *(G-12424)*

Chandler Mch & Prod Gear & Bro, Stow *Also Called: Chandler Machine Company (G-12423)*

Chandler Systems Incorporated 888 363-9434
710 Orange St Ashland (44805) *(G-528)*

Chang Audio, Toledo *Also Called: China Enterprises Inc (G-12920)*

Channel Products Inc (PA) 440 423-0113
30700 Solon Industrial Pkwy Solon (44139) *(G-12093)*

Chantilly Development Corp 419 243-8109
3101 Monroe St Toledo (43606) *(G-12916)*

Chaos Entertainment 937 520-5260
7570 Mount Whitney St Dayton (45424) *(G-5698)*

Chapin Customer Molding Inc 440 458-6550
635 Oberlin Elyria Rd Elyria (44035) *(G-6512)*

Chappell Door Company, Washington Court Hou *Also Called: Courthouse Manufacturing LLC (G-13820)*

Chappell-Zimmerman Inc 330 337-8711
641 Olive St Salem (44460) *(G-11769)*

Characters Inc 937 335-1976
190 Peters Ave Ste A Troy (45373) *(G-13204)*

Chardon Custom Polymers LLC 440 285-2161
373 Washington St Chardon (44024) *(G-2197)*

Chardon Metal Products Co 440 285-2147
206 5th Ave Chardon (44024) *(G-2198)*

Chardon Square Auto & Body Inc (PA) 440 286-7600
525 Water St Chardon (44024) *(G-2199)*

Chardon Tire and Brake, Chardon *Also Called: Chardon Square Auto & Body Inc (G-2199)*

Chardon Tool & Supply Co Inc 440 286-6440
115 Parker Ct Chardon (44024) *(G-2200)*

Charizma Corp 216 621-2220
1400 E 30th St Ste 201 Cleveland (44114) *(G-3485)*

Charles Auto Electric Co Inc 330 535-6269
600 Grant St Akron (44311) *(G-96)*

Charles C Lewis Company 440 439-3150
1 W Interstate St Ste 200 Cleveland (44146) *(G-3486)*

Charles Costa Inc 330 376-3636
924 Home Ave Akron (44310) *(G-97)*

Charles Huffman & Associates 216 295-0850
19214 Gladstone Rd Warrensville Heights (44122) *(G-13817)*

Charles Machine Works Inc 800 324-4930
135 State Route 42 West Salem (44287) *(G-14187)*

Charles Mfg Co 330 395-3490
3021 Sferra Ave Nw Warren (44483) *(G-13751)*

Charles Rewinding Div, Canton *Also Called: Hannon Company (G-1908)*

Charles Svec Inc 216 662-5200
5470 Dunham Rd Maple Heights (44137) *(G-8879)*

Charleston Ordnance Center, Medina *Also Called: Park Corporation (G-9434)*

Chart Asia Inc 440 753-1490
1 Infinity Corporate Centre Dr Cleveland (44125) *(G-3487)*

Chart Industries Inc 440 753-1490
5885 Landerbrook Dr Ste 150 Cleveland (44124) *(G-3488)*

Chart International Inc (HQ) 440 753-1490
1 Infinity Corporate Centre Dr Cleveland (44125) *(G-3489)*

Chart-Tech Tool Inc 937 667-3543
4060 Lisa Dr Tipp City (45371) *(G-12820)*

Charter Manufacturing Co Inc 216 883-3800
4300 E 49th St Cleveland (44125) *(G-3490)*

Charter Nex Films, Delaware *Also Called: Charter Nex Films - Delaware Oh Inc (G-6137)*

Charter Nex Films - Delaware Oh Inc 740 369-2770
1188 S Houk Rd Delaware (43015) *(G-6137)*

Charter Next Generation Inc 740 369-2770
1188 S Houk Rd Delaware (43015) *(G-6138)*

Charter Next Generation Inc 419 884-8150
165 Industrial Dr Lexington (44904) *(G-8367)*

Charter Next Generation Inc 419 884-8150
1450 State Route 97 Lexington (44904) *(G-8368)*

Charter Next Generation Inc 419 884-8150
235 Industrial Dr Lexington (44904) *(G-8369)*

Charter Next Generation Inc 419 884-8150
145 Frecka Dr Lexington (44904) *(G-8370)*

Charter Next Generation Inc 419 884-8150
215 Industrial Dr Lexington (44904) *(G-8371)*

Charter Next Generation Inc 330 830-6030
8333 Navarre Rd Se Massillon (44646) *(G-9179)*

Chase Industries Inc 513 603-2936
10021 Commerce Park Dr West Chester (45246) *(G-14110)*

Chase Sign & Lighting Svc Inc 567 128-3444
5924 American Rd E Toledo (43612) *(G-12917)*

Chc Fabricating Corp (PA) 513 821-7757
10270 Wayne Ave Cincinnati (45215) *(G-2459)*

Chc Manufacturing Inc (PA) 513 821-7757
10270 Wayne Ave Cincinnati (45215) *(G-2460)*

Che Holdings Inc 513 770-0777
6404 Thornberry Ct Ste 440 Mason (45040) *(G-9082)*

Cheap Dumpsters Llc 614 285-5865
5042 Astoria Ave Columbus (43207) *(G-4806)*

Check Point Software Tech Inc 440 748-0900
6100 Oak Tree Blvd Ste 200 Cleveland (44131) *(G-3491)*

Checkered Express Inc 330 530-8169
2501 W Liberty St Girard (44420) *(G-7268)*

Checkmate Marine Inc 419 562-3881
3691 State Route 4 Bucyrus (44820) *(G-1675)*

Checkpoint Surgical Inc 216 378-9107
6050 Oak Tree Blvd Ste 360 Independence (44131) *(G-7891)*

Checkpoint Surgical Instrs Inc, Independence *Also Called: Checkpoint Surgical Inc (G-7891)*

Checkpoint Systems Inc 330 456-7776
1510 4th St Se Canton (44707) *(G-1863)*

Cheese Holdings Inc 330 893-2479
6597 County Road 625 Millersburg (44654) *(G-9977)*

Chefs Garden Inc 419 433-4947
1104 Scheid Rd Sandusky (44870) *(G-11827)*

Chelsea House Fabrics, Columbus *Also Called: Style-Line Incorporated (G-5295)*

Chem Instruments, West Chester *Also Called: Chemsultants International Inc (G-13962)*

Chem Technologies Ltd..............440 632-9311
14875 Bonner Dr Middlefield (44062) *(G-9786)*

Chem-Materials Inc..............440 455-9465
24700 Center Ridge Rd Ste 280 Westlake (44145) *(G-14297)*

Chem-Materials Co, Westlake *Also Called: Chem-Materials Inc (G-14297)*

Chem-Sales Inc
3860 Dorr St Toledo (43607) *(G-12918)*

Chemcore Inc (PA)..............937 228-6118
20 Madison St Dayton (45402) *(G-5699)*

Chemequip Sales Inc..............330 724-8300
1004 Swartz Rd Coventry Township (44319) *(G-5481)*

Chemical Instruments, West Chester *Also Called: Cheminstruments Inc (G-13960)*

Chemical Methods Incorporated..............216 476-8400
2853 Westway Dr # A Brunswick (44212) *(G-1582)*

Chemical Solvents Inc (PA)..............216 741-9310
3751 Jennings Rd Cleveland (44109) *(G-3492)*

Chemical Technologies, Swanton *Also Called: Magna Seating America Inc (G-12686)*

Chemineer, Dayton *Also Called: National Oilwell Varco LP (G-5901)*

Chemineer, Dayton *Also Called: Nov Inc (G-5915)*

Chemineer Inc..............937 454-3200
5870 Poe Ave Dayton (45414) *(G-5700)*

Cheminstruments Inc..............513 860-1598
510 Commercial Dr West Chester (45014) *(G-13960)*

Cheminstruments Inc (PA)..............513 860-1598
510 Commercial Dr West Chester (45014) *(G-13961)*

Chemionics Corporation..............330 733-8834
390 Munroe Falls Rd Tallmadge (44278) *(G-12731)*

Chemmasters Inc..............440 428-2105
300 Edwards St Madison (44057) *(G-8726)*

Chempace Corporation..............419 535-0101
339 Arco Dr Toledo (43607) *(G-12919)*

Chemres Trinity, West Unity *Also Called: Benvic Trinity LLC (G-14192)*

Chemspec Ltd (DH)..............330 896-0355
4450 Belden Village St Nw Ste 507 Canton (44718) *(G-1864)*

Chemspec Ltd..............330 364-4422
419 Tuscarawas Ave Nw New Philadelphia (44663) *(G-10437)*

Chemspec Polymer Additives, Canton *Also Called: Chemspec Ltd (G-1864)*

Chemspec Usa LLC..............330 669-8512
9287 Smucker Rd Orrville (44667) *(G-10976)*

Chemspec Usa Inc..............330 669-8512
9287 Smucker Rd Orrville (44667) *(G-10977)*

Chemstation, Dayton *Also Called: Chemstation International Inc (G-5701)*

Chemstation International Inc (PA)..............937 294-8265
3400 Encrete Ln Dayton (45439) *(G-5701)*

Chemsultants International Inc (PA)..............440 974-3080
9079 Tyler Blvd Mentor (44060) *(G-9498)*

Chemsultants International Inc..............513 860-1598
510 Commercial Dr West Chester (45014) *(G-13962)*

Chemtool Incorporated (DH)..............815 957-4140
29400 Lakeland Blvd Wickliffe (44092) *(G-14369)*

Chemtrade Logistics Inc..............216 566-8070
2545 W 3rd St Cleveland (44113) *(G-3493)*

Chemtrade Refinery Svcs Inc..............419 641-4151
7680 Ottawa Rd Cairo (45820) *(G-1721)*

Chemtreat..............937 644-2525
11000 State Route 347 East Liberty (43319) *(G-6384)*

Cheney Dynos Inc..............937 746-9991
1000 Anderson St Franklin (45005) *(G-7012)*

Chep (usa) Inc..............614 497-9448
2130 New World Dr Columbus (43207) *(G-4807)*

Cherokee Hardwoods Inc (PA)..............440 632-0322
16741 Newcomb Rd Middlefield (44062) *(G-9787)*

Cherokee Manufacturing LLC..............800 777-5030
3891 Shepard Rd Perry (44081) *(G-11191)*

Cheryl & Co..............614 776-1500
4465 Industrial Center Dr Obetz (43207) *(G-10923)*

Chester Labs Inc..............513 458-3871
900 Section Rd Ste A Cincinnati (45237) *(G-2461)*

Chettapartners LLC..............614 368-7600
105 W Wilson Bridge Rd Ste 180 Worthington (43085) *(G-14707)*

CHEVRON PHILLIPS CHEMICAL COMPANY LIMITED PARTNERSHIP, Marietta *Also Called: Chevron Phllips Chem Ltd Prtnr (G-8909)*

Chevron Phllips Chem Ltd Prtnr..............740 374-2500
17401 State Route 7 Marietta (45750) *(G-8909)*

CHI Corporation (PA)..............440 498-2300
5265 Naiman Pkwy Ste H Cleveland (44139) *(G-3494)*

CHI Storage Solutions Corp, Cleveland *Also Called: CHI Corporation (G-3494)*

Chicago Pneumatic Tool Co LLC..............704 883-3500
9100 Market Pl Rear Broadview Heights (44147) *(G-1500)*

Chick Master Incubator Company (PA)..............330 722-5591
779 W Smith Rd Medina (44256) *(G-9387)*

Chickasaw Machine & TI Co Inc..............419 925-4325
3050 Chickasaw Rd Chickasaw (45826) *(G-2240)*

Chieffos Frozen Foods Inc..............330 652-1222
406 S Main St Niles (44446) *(G-10585)*

Chilcote Company..............216 781-6000
4600 Tiedeman Rd Cleveland (44144) *(G-3495)*

Chillicothe Facility, Chillicothe *Also Called: Glatfelter Corporation (G-2255)*

Chillicothe Packaging Corp..............740 773-5800
4168 State Route 159 Chillicothe (45601) *(G-2247)*

Chillicothe Packing, Chillicothe *Also Called: Churmac Industries Inc (G-2248)*

Chilltex LLC..............937 710-3308
7440 Hoying Rd Anna (45302) *(G-460)*

Chime Master Systems, Sugar Grove *Also Called: Commercial Music Service Co (G-12629)*

China Enterprises Inc..............419 885-1485
5151 Monroe St Toledo (43623) *(G-12920)*

Chippewa Tool and Mfg Co..............419 849-2790
1101 Oak St Woodville (43469) *(G-14616)*

Chips Manufacturing Inc..............440 946-3666
260 E 312th St Willowick (44095) *(G-14565)*

Cho Bedford Inc (PA)..............330 343-8896
2997 Progress St Dover (44622) *(G-6233)*

Cho Bedford Inc..............330 343-8896
2997 Progress St Dover (44622) *(G-6234)*

Chocolate Pig Inc (PA)..............440 461-4511
5338 Mayfield Rd Cleveland (44124) *(G-3496)*

Choice Adhesives, Cincinnati *Also Called: Choice Brands Adhesives Ltd (G-2462)*

Choice Brands Adhesives Ltd..............800 330-5566
666 Redna Ter Ste 500 Cincinnati (45215) *(G-2462)*

Choice Marketing..............614 638-8404
5130 Transamerica Dr Columbus (43228) *(G-4808)*

Chris Erhart Foundry & Mch Co..............513 421-6550
1240 Mehring Way Cincinnati (45203) *(G-2463)*

Chris Haughey..............937 652-3338
1463 S Us Highway 68 Urbana (43078) *(G-13458)*

Chris Stepp..............513 248-0822
927 Business 28 Unit B Milford (45150) *(G-9928)*

Chrisnik Inc..............513 738-2920
7461 Cincinnati Brookville Rd Okeana (45053) *(G-10927)*

Christian Blue Pages (PA)..............937 847-2583
521 Byers Rd Ste 102 Miamisburg (45342) *(G-9682)*

Christian Missionary Alliance (PA)..............380 208-6200
6421 E Main St Reynoldsburg (43068) *(G-11562)*

Christopher Tool & Mfg Co..............440 248-8080
30500 Carter St Frnt Solon (44139) *(G-12094)*

Christy Catalytics LLC..............740 982-1302
713 Keystone St Crooksville (43731) *(G-5509)*

Christy Machine Company..............419 332-6451
1110 Napoleon St Fremont (43420) *(G-7098)*

Chroma Color Corporation..............740 363-6622
100 Colomet Dr Delaware (43015) *(G-6139)*

Chromaflo, Ashtabula *Also Called: Vibrantz Color Solutions Inc (G-621)*

Chromalloy Corporation..............937 890-3775
7425 Webster St Dayton (45414) *(G-5702)*

Chromascape LLC (PA)..............330 998-7574
7555 E Pleasant Valley Rd Ste 100 Independence (44131) *(G-7892)*

Chromatic Inc..............216 881-2228
839 E 63rd St Cleveland (44103) *(G-3497)*

Chrome Deposit Corporation..............330 773-7800
1566 Firestone Pkwy Akron (44301) *(G-98)*

A
L
P
H
A
B
E
T
I
C

Chrome Deposit Corporation.................................513 539-8486
341 Lawton Ave Monroe (45050) *(G-10098)*

Chromium Corporation......................................216 271-4910
8701 Union Ave Cleveland (44105) *(G-3498)*

Chuck Meadors Plastics Co..............................440 813-4466
150 S Cucumber St Jefferson (44047) *(G-7972)*

Church & Dwight Co Inc....................................740 852-3621
110 W 1st St London (43140) *(G-8533)*

Church & Dwight Co Inc....................................419 992-4244
2501 E County Rd 34 Old Fort (44861) *(G-10933)*

Church-Budget Envelope Company...................800 446-9780
271 S Ellsworth Ave Salem (44460) *(G-11770)*

Churchill Steel Plate Ltd..................................330 425-9000
7851 Bavaria Rd Twinsburg (44087) *(G-13286)*

Churmac Industries, Chillicothe Also Called: Chillicothe Packaging Corp *(G-2247)*

Churmac Industries Inc....................................740 773-5800
4168 State Route 159 Chillicothe (45601) *(G-2248)*

Chute Source LLC..330 475-0377
525 Kennedy Rd Akron (44305) *(G-99)*

Ci Disposition Co...216 587-5200
1000 Valley Belt Rd Brooklyn Heights (44131) *(G-1530)*

CIC Old Corporation..330 457-2367
5331 State Route 7 New Waterford (44445) *(G-10487)*

Cicogna, Ashtabula Also Called: Cicogna Electric and Sign Co *(G-587)*

Cicogna Electric and Sign Co (PA)...................440 998-2637
4330 N Bend Rd Ashtabula (44004) *(G-587)*

Cil Isotope Separations LLC.............................937 376-5413
1689 Burnett Dr Xenia (45385) *(G-14757)*

Cima, Hamilton Also Called: Wulco Inc *(G-7539)*

Cima Inc..513 382-8976
1010 Eaton Ave Ste B Hamilton (45013) *(G-7476)*

Cima Inc..513 382-8976
1010 Eaton Ave Ste B Hamilton (45013) *(G-7477)*

Cima Plastics Group, Twinsburg Also Called: Stewart Acquisition LLC *(G-13380)*

Cimbar Performance Mnrl WV LLC....................330 532-2034
2400 Clark Ave Wellsville (43968) *(G-13912)*

Cims Incorporated...330 794-8102
2701 Gilchrist Rd Akron (44305) *(G-100)*

Cimx LLC...513 248-7700
2368 Victory Pkwy Ste 120 Cincinnati (45206) *(G-2464)*

Cimx Software, Cincinnati Also Called: Cimx LLC *(G-2464)*

Cinchempro Inc..513 724-6111
458 W Main St Batavia (45103) *(G-855)*

Cincinnati - Vulcan Company............................513 242-5300
5353 Spring Grove Ave Cincinnati (45217) *(G-2465)*

Cincinnati A Fltr Sls Svc Inc.............................513 242-3400
4815 Para Dr Cincinnati (45237) *(G-2466)*

Cincinnati Abrasive Supply Co..........................513 941-8866
9431 Sutton Pl Hamilton (45011) *(G-7478)*

Cincinnati Advg Pdts LLC.................................513 346-7310
12150 Northwest Blvd Cincinnati (45246) *(G-2467)*

Cincinnati Air Conditioning Co.........................513 721-5622
2080 Northwest Dr Cincinnati (45231) *(G-2468)*

Cincinnati Assn For The Blind..........................513 221-8558
2045 Gilbert Ave Cincinnati (45202) *(G-2469)*

CINCINNATI ASSOCIATION FOR THE, Cincinnati Also Called: Cincinnati Assn For The Blind *(G-2469)*

Cincinnati Babbitt Inc......................................513 942-5088
9217 Seward Rd Fairfield (45014) *(G-6720)*

Cincinnati Beverage Company..........................513 904-8910
242 W Mcmicken Ave Cincinnati (45214) *(G-2470)*

Cincinnati Biorefining Corp (HQ).....................513 482-8800
470 Este Ave Cincinnati (45232) *(G-2471)*

Cincinnati Business Courier, Cincinnati Also Called: American City Bus Journals Inc *(G-2358)*

Cincinnati Chemical Processing, Batavia Also Called: Cinchempro Inc *(G-855)*

Cincinnati Convertors Inc.................................513 731-6600
1730 Cleneay Ave Cincinnati (45212) *(G-2472)*

Cincinnati Ctrl Dynamics Inc............................513 242-7300
4924 Para Dr Cincinnati (45237) *(G-2473)*

Cincinnati Dowel & WD Pdts Co........................937 444-2502
135 Oak St Mount Orab (45154) *(G-10215)*

Cincinnati Enquirer..513 721-2700
312 Elm St Fl 18 Cincinnati (45202) *(G-2474)*

Cincinnati Eye Inst - Estgate...........................513 984-5133
601 Ivy Gtwy Ste 301 Cincinnati (45245) *(G-2298)*

Cincinnati Family Magazine..............................513 842-0077
10945 Reed Hartman Hwy Ste 221 Blue Ash (45242) *(G-1262)*

Cincinnati Fan, Mason Also Called: Cincinnati Fan & Ventilator Company Inc *(G-9083)*

Cincinnati Fan & Ventilator Company Inc (DH)....513 573-1000
7697 Snider Rd Mason (45040) *(G-9083)*

Cincinnati Fdsrvice A Slutions, Cincinnati Also Called: Captive-Aire Systems Inc *(G-2437)*

Cincinnati Flame Hardening Co, Fairfield Also Called: Detroit Flame Hardening Co *(G-6727)*

Cincinnati Ftn Sq News Inc...............................513 421-4049
8739 S Shore Pl Mason (45040) *(G-9084)*

Cincinnati Gasket & Indus GL, Cincinnati Also Called: Cincinnati Gasket Pkg Mfg Inc *(G-2475)*

Cincinnati Gasket Pkg Mfg Inc..........................513 761-3458
40 Illinois Ave Cincinnati (45215) *(G-2475)*

Cincinnati Gearing Systems Inc (PA)................513 527-8600
5757 Mariemont Ave Cincinnati (45227) *(G-2476)*

Cincinnati Gearing Systems Inc........................513 527-8634
301 Milford Pkwy Cincinnati (45227) *(G-2477)*

Cincinnati Gilbert Mch TI LLC...........................513 541-4815
3366 Beekman St Cincinnati (45223) *(G-2478)*

Cincinnati GL Blck Dyton GL BI, Cincinnati Also Called: G L Pierce Inc *(G-2647)*

Cincinnati Grinding Technologies Inc................866 983-1097
300 Distribution Cir Ste G Fairfield (45014) *(G-6721)*

Cincinnati Incorporated (PA)............................513 367-7100
7420 Kilby Rd Harrison (45030) *(G-7545)*

Cincinnati Industrial McHy Inc..........................513 923-5600
4600 N Mason Montgomery Rd Mason (45040) *(G-9085)*

Cincinnati Laser Cutting LLC............................513 779-7200
891 Redna Ter Cincinnati (45215) *(G-2479)*

Cincinnati Machines Inc....................................513 536-2432
4165 Half Acre Rd Batavia (45103) *(G-856)*

Cincinnati Magazine, Cincinnati Also Called: Cincinnati Media LLC *(G-2481)*

Cincinnati Marlins Inc......................................513 761-3320
616 W North Bend Rd Cincinnati (45224) *(G-2480)*

Cincinnati Mechanical Svcs LLC, Cincinnati Also Called: Complete Mechanical Svcs LLC *(G-2507)*

Cincinnati Media LLC..513 562-2755
1818 Race St Ste 301 Cincinnati (45202) *(G-2481)*

Cincinnati Metal Fabricating, Cincinnati Also Called: Cincinnati Laser Cutting LLC *(G-2479)*

Cincinnati Mine Machinery Co (PA)...................513 522-7777
2950 Jonrose Ave Cincinnati (45239) *(G-2482)*

Cincinnati Paperboard, Cincinnati Also Called: Caraustar Industries Inc *(G-2438)*

Cincinnati Pattern Company Inc........................513 241-9872
2405 Spring Grove Ave Cincinnati (45214) *(G-2483)*

Cincinnati Precision McHy Inc...........................513 860-4133
9083 Sutton Pl West Chester (45011) *(G-13963)*

Cincinnati Print Solutions LLC..........................513 943-9500
2002 Ford Cir Ste G Milford (45150) *(G-9929)*

Cincinnati Prof Door Sls Div, Cincinnati Also Called: Division Overhead Door Inc *(G-2556)*

Cincinnati Radiator Inc....................................513 874-5555
8551a Seward Rd Fairfield (45011) *(G-6722)*

Cincinnati Renewable Fuels LLC.......................513 482-8800
4700 Este Ave Cincinnati (45232) *(G-2484)*

Cincinnati Retread Systems, Fairfield Also Called: American Manufacturing & Eqp *(G-6711)*

Cincinnati Site Solutions LLC...........................513 373-5001
36 E 7th St Ste 1650 Cincinnati (45202) *(G-2485)*

Cincinnati Stair & Handrail...............................513 722-3947
1220 Hill Smith Dr Ste C Cincinnati (45215) *(G-2486)*

Cincinnati Stl Treating Co LLC..........................513 271-3173
5701 Mariemont Ave Cincinnati (45227) *(G-2487)*

Cincinnati Test Systems Inc (HQ).....................513 202-5100
10100 Progress Way Harrison (45030) *(G-7546)*

Cincinnati Thermal Spray Inc............................513 793-1037
5901 Creek Rd Blue Ash (45242) *(G-1263)*

Cincinnati Thermal Spray Inc (PA)....................513 793-0670
10904 Deerfield Rd Cincinnati (45242) *(G-2488)*

Cincinnati Transfer Station, Cincinnati Also Called: Darling Ingredients Inc *(G-2541)*

Cincinnati Window Decor, Cincinnati *Also Called: Cincinnati Window Shade Inc (G-2489)*

Cincinnati Window Shade Inc (PA)............... 513 631-7200
3004 Harris Ave Cincinnati (45212) *(G-2489)*

Cincinnatti Processing, West Chester *Also Called: Empire Packing Company LP (G-14117)*

Cincy Deli & Carryout, Cincinnati *Also Called: Zygo Inc (G-3245)*

Cincy Glass Inc............... 513 241-0455
3249 Fredonia Ave Cincinnati (45229) *(G-2490)*

Cindoco Wood Products Co............... 937 444-2504
410 Mount Clifton Dr Mount Orab (45154) *(G-10216)*

Cindus Corporation............... 513 948-9951
515 Station Ave Cincinnati (45215) *(G-2491)*

Cinex Inc............... 513 921-2825
2641 Cummins St Cincinnati (45225) *(G-2492)*

Cinfab, Cincinnati *Also Called: Cinfab LLC (G-2493)*

Cinfab LLC............... 513 396-6100
5240 Lester Rd Cincinnati (45213) *(G-2493)*

Cinncinati Bindery, Cincinnati *Also Called: Spring Grove Manufacturing Inc (G-3107)*

Cintas, Canton *Also Called: Cintas Corporation No 2 (G-1865)*

Cintas, Cincinnati *Also Called: Cintas Sales Corporation (G-2495)*

Cintas, Mason *Also Called: Cintas Corporation (G-9086)*

Cintas Corporation............... 513 631-5750
5570 Ridge Ave Cincinnati (45213) *(G-2494)*

Cintas Corporation (PA)............... 513 459-1200
6800 Cintas Blvd Mason (45040) *(G-9086)*

Cintas Corporation No 2............... 330 966-7800
3865 Highland Park Nw Canton (44720) *(G-1865)*

Cintas Sales Corporation (HQ)............... 513 459-1200
6800 Cintas Blvd Cincinnati (45262) *(G-2495)*

Cintas Uniforms AP Fcilty Svcs, Cincinnati *Also Called: Cintas Corporation (G-2494)*

Cioffi Holdings LLC............... 330 794-9448
1001 Eastwood Ave Akron (44305) *(G-101)*

CIP International Inc............... 513 874-9925
9575 Le Saint Dr West Chester (45014) *(G-13964)*

Cipted Corp............... 412 829-2120
301 Lawton Ave Monroe (45050) *(G-10099)*

Cirba Solutions Us Inc (PA)............... 740 653-6290
265 Quarry Rd Se Lancaster (43130) *(G-8186)*

Cirba Solutions Us Inc............... 740 653-6290
265 Quarry Rd Se Lancaster (43130) *(G-8187)*

Circle Machine Rolls Inc............... 330 938-9010
245 W Kentucky Ave Sebring (44672) *(G-11893)*

Circle Mold & Machine Co, Tallmadge *Also Called: Circle Mold Incorporated (G-12732)*

Circle Mold Incorporated............... 330 633-7017
85 S Thomas Rd Tallmadge (44278) *(G-12732)*

Circle Prime Manufacturing Inc............... 330 923-0019
2114 Front St Cuyahoga Falls (44221) *(G-5534)*

Circleville Glass Operations, Circleville *Also Called: Technicolor Usa Inc (G-3265)*

Circleville Oil Co............... 740 477-3341
224 Lancaster Pike Circleville (43113) *(G-3251)*

Circuit Board Mining LLC............... 419 348-1057
23546 Us Highway 224 Alvada (44802) *(G-421)*

Cisco Systems, Richfield *Also Called: Cisco Systems Inc (G-11588)*

Cisco Systems Inc............... 330 523-2000
4125 Highlander Pkwy Richfield (44286) *(G-11588)*

Citadel Plastics, Fairlawn *Also Called: Hggc Citadel Plas Holdings Inc (G-6803)*

Citicom, Columbus *Also Called: Capitol Citicom Inc (G-4799)*

City Apparel Inc............... 419 434-1155
116 E Main Cross St Findlay (45840) *(G-6852)*

City Concrete LLc............... 330 743-2825
151 Old Division St Youngstown (44510) *(G-14835)*

City Elyria Communication............... 440 322-3329
851 Garden St Elyria (44035) *(G-6513)*

City Machine Technologies Inc (PA)............... 330 747-2639
773 W Rayen Ave Youngstown (44502) *(G-14836)*

City of Ashland............... 419 289-8728
310 W 12th St Ashland (44805) *(G-529)*

City of Athens............... 740 592-3344
395 W State St Athens (45701) *(G-636)*

City of Canton............... 330 489-3370
2436 30th St Ne Canton (44705) *(G-1866)*

City of Chardon............... 440 286-2657
201 N Hambden St Chardon (44024) *(G-2201)*

City of Cleveland............... 216 664-3013
1735 Lakeside Ave E Cleveland (44114) *(G-3499)*

City of Cleveland............... 216 664-2711
500 Lakeside Ave E Cleveland (44114) *(G-3500)*

City of Lancaster............... 740 687-6670
1424 Campground Rd Lancaster (43130) *(G-8188)*

City of Middletown............... 513 425-7781
805 Columbia Ave Middletown (45042) *(G-9844)*

City of Mount Vernon............... 740 393-9508
1550 Old Delaware Rd Mount Vernon (43050) *(G-10240)*

City of Newark............... 740 349-6765
164 Waterworks Rd Newark (43055) *(G-10497)*

City of Newark, Newark *Also Called: Traffic Cntrl Sgnls Signs & MA (G-10536)*

City of Ravenna............... 330 296-5214
3722 Hommon Rd Ravenna (44266) *(G-11521)*

City of Troy............... 937 339-4826
300 E Staunton Rd Troy (45373) *(G-13205)*

City of Xenia............... 937 376-7269
1831 Us Route 68 N Xenia (45385) *(G-14758)*

City Plating, Cleveland *Also Called: City Plating and Polishing LLC (G-3501)*

City Plating and Polishing LLC............... 216 267-8158
4821 W 130th St Cleveland (44135) *(G-3501)*

City Printing Co Inc............... 330 747-5691
122 Oak Hill Ave Youngstown (44502) *(G-14837)*

City Visitor Inc............... 216 661-6666
2099 Edgeview Dr Hudson (44236) *(G-7837)*

City Visitor Publications, Hudson *Also Called: City Visitor Inc (G-7837)*

Cityscapes International Inc............... 614 850-2540
4200 Lyman Ct Hilliard (43026) *(G-7677)*

Citywide Materials Inc............... 513 533-1111
5263 Wooster Pike Cincinnati (45226) *(G-2496)*

Citywide Ready Mix, Cincinnati *Also Called: Citywide Materials Inc (G-2496)*

Civacon, Hamilton *Also Called: Knappco Corporation (G-7509)*

Civica CMI, Englewood *Also Called: Creative Microsystems Inc (G-6611)*

Civitas Media, Miamisburg *Also Called: Heartland Publications LLC (G-9698)*

CJ Dannemiller Co............... 330 825-7808
5300 S Hametown Rd Norton (44203) *(G-10819)*

CJ Salt World............... 440 343-5661
29149 Euclid Ave Wickliffe (44092) *(G-14370)*

CK Technologies, Montpelier *Also Called: Creative Liquid Coatings Inc (G-10127)*

Cks Solution Incorporated (PA)............... 513 947-1277
4293 Muhlhauser Rd Fairfield (45014) *(G-6723)*

Claflin Co............... 330 650-0582
5270 Hudson Dr Hudson (44236) *(G-7838)*

Claflin Co, Hudson *Also Called: Howard B Claflin Co (G-7844)*

Claflin Company, Hudson *Also Called: Claflin Co (G-7838)*

Clampco, Wadsworth *Also Called: Clampco Products Inc (G-13631)*

Clampco Products Inc (PA)............... 330 336-8857
1743 Wall Rd Wadsworth (44281) *(G-13631)*

Clamps Inc............... 419 729-2141
5960 American Rd E Toledo (43612) *(G-12921)*

Clapp & Haney Brazed Tl Co Inc............... 740 922-3515
901 Race St Dennison (44621) *(G-6217)*

Clarios LLC............... 419 636-4211
918 S Union St Bryan (43506) *(G-1636)*

Clarios LLC............... 419 865-0542
10300 Industrial St Holland (43528) *(G-7750)*

Clarios LLC............... 440 205-7221
7780 Metric Dr Mentor (44060) *(G-9499)*

Clarity Retail Services LLC............... 513 800-9369
5115 Excello Ct West Chester (45069) *(G-13965)*

Clark & Son, East Sparta *Also Called: Clark Son Actn Liquidation Inc (G-6411)*

Clark Dietrich Building, Warren *Also Called: Clarkwestern Dietrich Building (G-13752)*

Clark Fixture Technologies Inc............... 419 354-1541
410 N Dunbridge Rd Bowling Green (43402) *(G-1414)*

Clark Grave Vault Company (PA)............... 614 294-3761
375 E 5th Ave Columbus (43201) *(G-4809)*

Clark Oil & Chemical Division, Cleveland *Also Called: Cochem Inc (G-3543)*

A
L
P
H
A
B
E
T
I
C

Clark Optimization LLC.................................. 330 417-2164
  1222 Easton St Ne Canton (44721) *(G-1867)*

Clark Rm Inc.. 419 425-9889
  400 Crystal Ave Findlay (45840) *(G-6853)*

Clark Rubber & Plastic Company.................... 440 255-9793
  8888 East Ave Mentor (44060) *(G-9500)*

Clark Rubber & Plastics, Mentor *Also Called: Clark Rubber & Plastic Company (G-9500)*

Clark Son Actn Liquidation Inc....................... 330 866-9330
  10233 Sandyville Ave Se East Sparta (44626) *(G-6411)*

Clark Substations, Canton *Also Called: Clark Substations LLC (G-1868)*

Clark Substations LLC................................... 330 452-5200
  2240 Allen Ave Se Canton (44707) *(G-1868)*

Clark Wood Specialties Inc........................... 330 499-8711
  9235 Shadybrook St Nw Clinton (44216) *(G-4553)*

Clark-Fowler Elc Mtr & Sups, Wooster *Also Called: Clark-Fowler Enterprises Inc (G-14631)*

Clark-Fowler Enterprises Inc......................... 330 262-0906
  510 W Henry St Wooster (44691) *(G-14631)*

Clark-Reliance LLC (PA)................................440 572-1500
  16633 Foltz Pkwy Strongsville (44149) *(G-12550)*

Clarkdietrich, West Chester *Also Called: Clarkwstern Dtrich Bldg System (G-13966)*

Clarke Fire Protection Product, Cincinnati *Also Called: Clarke Power Services Inc (G-2497)*

Clarke Fire Prtection Pdts Inc........................ 513 771-2200
  133 Circle Freeway Dr West Chester (45246) *(G-14111)*

Clarke Power Services Inc............................ 513 771-2200
  3133 E Kemper Rd Cincinnati (45241) *(G-2497)*

Clarke-Boxit Corporation................................ 716 487-1950
  5601 Walworth Ave Cleveland (44102) *(G-3502)*

Clarksville Stave & Lbr Co Ltd........................ 937 376-4618
  2808 Jasper Rd Xenia (45385) *(G-14759)*

Clarksville Stave & Veneer Co........................ 740 947-4159
  9329 State Route 220 Ste A Waverly (45690) *(G-13864)*

Clarkwestern Dietrich Building........................ 330 372-5564
  1985 N River Rd Ne Warren (44483) *(G-13752)*

Clarkwstern Dtrich Bldg System..................... 330 372-4014
  1455 Ridge Rd Vienna (44473) *(G-13608)*

Clarkwstern Dtrich Bldg System (HQ)............. 513 870-1100
  9050 Centre Pointe Dr Ste 400 West Chester (45069) *(G-13966)*

Classic Coatings.. 330 421-3703
  6074 Pebblebrook Ln North Olmsted (44070) *(G-10720)*

Classic Countertops LLC................................ 330 882-4220
  1519 Kenmore Blvd Akron (44314) *(G-102)*

Classic Delight, Saint Marys *Also Called: Old Classic Delight Inc (G-11744)*

Classic Laminations Inc................................. 440 735-1333
  7703 First Pl Ste B Oakwood Village (44146) *(G-10904)*

Classic Metal Roofing Systems, Piqua *Also Called: Isaiah Industries Inc (G-11358)*

Classic Monuments, Piqua *Also Called: Piqua Granite & Marble Co Inc (G-11376)*

Classic Optical Labs Inc................................ 330 759-8245
  3710 Belmont Ave Youngstown (44505) *(G-14838)*

Classic Reproductions.................................. 937 548-9839
  5315 Meeker Rd Greenville (45331) *(G-7338)*

Classic Sign Company LLC............................. 419 420-0058
  3230 Township Road 232 Findlay (45840) *(G-6854)*

Classic Stone Company Inc........................... 614 833-3946
  4090 Janitrol Rd Columbus (43228) *(G-4810)*

Clay Burley Products Co (PA)......................... 740 452-3633
  455 Gordon St Roseville (43777) *(G-11653)*

Clay Logan Products Company........................ 740 385-2184
  201 S Walnut St Logan (43138) *(G-8511)*

Claycor Inc... 419 318-7290
  5924 American Rd E Toledo (43612) *(G-12922)*

Clayton Homes... 937 592-3039
  2720 Us Highway 68 S Bellefontaine (43311) *(G-1101)*

Clean Remedies LLC.................................... 440 670-2112
  1431 Lear Industrial Pkwy Ste A Avon (44011) *(G-719)*

Cleancut, West Chester *Also Called: Safeway Safety Step LLC (G-14072)*

Cleaning Lady Inc.. 419 589-5566
  190 Stewart Rd N Mansfield (44905) *(G-8774)*

Cleaning Technologies Grp, Tiffin *Also Called: Nmgg Ctg LLC (G-12793)*

Cleanlife Energy LLC..................................... 800 316-2532
  7620 Hub Pkwy Cleveland (44125) *(G-3503)*

Cleanlife Products, Springboro *Also Called: No Rinse Laboratories LLC (G-12261)*

Clear Channel, Lima *Also Called: Iheartcommunications Inc (G-8418)*

Clear Creek Screw Machine Co....................... 740 969-2113
  4900 Julian Rd Sw Amanda (43102) *(G-423)*

Clear Images LLC... 419 241-9347
  121 11th St Toledo (43604) *(G-12923)*

Clearpath Utlity Solutions LLC........................ 740 661-4240
  2925 National Rd Sw Hebron (43025) *(G-7610)*

Clearsonic Manufacturing Inc......................... 828 772-9809
  1025 Evans Ave Akron (44305) *(G-103)*

Clearview Construction LLC............................ 513 206-6415
  4520 Bridgetown Rd # 1 Cincinnati (45211) *(G-2498)*

Clearview Roof and Remodelling, Cincinnati *Also Called: Clearview Construction LLC (G-2498)*

Clearvue Insulating Glass Co.......................... 216 651-1140
  14735 Lorain Ave Ste 1 Cleveland (44111) *(G-3504)*

Clearvue Products LLC.................................. 440 871-4209
  24620 Wolf Rd Bay Village (44140) *(G-900)*

Cleary Machine Company Inc......................... 937 839-4278
  4858 Us Route 35 E West Alexandria (45381) *(G-13917)*

Clecorr Inc... 216 961-5500
  10610 Berea Rd Rear Cleveland (44102) *(G-3505)*

Clecorr Packaging, Cleveland *Also Called: Clecorr Inc (G-3505)*

Clemens License Agency................................ 614 288-8007
  12825 Wheaton Ave Pickerington (43147) *(G-11292)*

Clemens Mobile Welding LLC........................ 419 782-4220
  25239 Commerce Dr Defiance (43512) *(G-6103)*

Clermont Steel Fabricators LLC...................... 513 732-6033
  2565 Old State Route 32 Batavia (45103) *(G-857)*

Cleveland AEC West LLC.............................. 216 362-6000
  14000 Keystone Pkwy Cleveland (44135) *(G-3506)*

Cleveland Black Oxide, Cleveland *Also Called: Tatham Schulz Incorporated (G-4364)*

Cleveland Black Oxide Inc............................. 216 861-4431
  11400 Brookpark Rd Cleveland (44130) *(G-3507)*

Cleveland Black Pages, Cleveland *Also Called: Lanier & Associates Inc (G-3940)*

Cleveland Canvas Goods Mfg Co..................... 216 361-4567
  1960 E 57th St Cleveland (44103) *(G-3508)*

Cleveland Church Supply, Cleveland *Also Called: Novak J F Manufacturing Co LLC (G-4102)*

Cleveland Circuits Corp.................................. 216 267-9020
  15516 Industrial Pkwy Cleveland (44135) *(G-3509)*

Cleveland City Forge Inc............................... 440 647-5400
  46950 State Route 18 Wellington (44090) *(G-13884)*

Cleveland Coca-Cola Btlg Inc......................... 216 690-2653
  25000 Miles Rd Bedford Heights (44146) *(G-1073)*

Cleveland Controls, Cleveland *Also Called: UCI Controls Inc (G-4439)*

Cleveland Controls Inc................................. 216 398-0330
  1111 Brookpark Rd Cleveland (44109) *(G-3510)*

Cleveland Coretec Inc.................................... 314 727-2087
  12080 Debartolo Dr North Jackson (44451) *(G-10685)*

Cleveland Cstm Pallet & Crate, Cleveland *Also Called: Millwood Inc (G-4042)*

Cleveland Die & Mfg, Middleburg Heights *Also Called: Cleveland Die & Mfg Co (G-9767)*

Cleveland Die & Mfg Co (PA)........................... 440 243-3404
  20303 1st Ave Middleburg Heights (44130) *(G-9767)*

Cleveland Digital Imaging Svcs, Cleveland *Also Called: Caraustar Industries Inc (G-3468)*

Cleveland Electric Labs, Twinsburg *Also Called: Cleveland Electric Labs Co (G-13287)*

Cleveland Electric Labs Co (PA)...................... 800 447-2207
  1776 Enterprise Pkwy Twinsburg (44087) *(G-13287)*

Cleveland Gear Company Inc (DH)................... 216 641-9000
  3249 E 80th St Cleveland (44104) *(G-3511)*

Cleveland Granite & Marble LLC...................... 216 291-7637
  4121 Carnegie Ave Cleveland (44103) *(G-3512)*

Cleveland Ignition Co Inc................................ 440 439-3688
  600 Golden Oak Pkwy Cleveland (44146) *(G-3513)*

Cleveland Indus Training Ctr, Cleveland *Also Called: Borman Enterprises Inc (G-3429)*

Cleveland Jewish News, Cleveland *Also Called: Cleveland Jewish Publ Co (G-3514)*

Cleveland Jewish Publ Co............................... 216 454-8300
  23880 Commerce Park Ste 1 Cleveland (44122) *(G-3514)*

Cleveland Jewish Publ Co Fdn........................ 216 454-8300
  23800 Commerce Park Beachwood (44122) *(G-912)*

Cleveland Magazine, Cleveland *Also Called: Great Lakes Publishing Company (G-3793)*

(G-0000) Company's Geographic Section entry number

Cleveland Medical Devices Inc......................216 619-5928
4415 Euclid Ave Ste 400 Cleveland (44103) *(G-3515)*

Cleveland Menu Printing Inc.......................216 241-5256
1441 E 17th St Cleveland (44114) *(G-3516)*

Cleveland Metal Processing Inc (PA)............440 243-3404
20303 1st Ave Cleveland (44130) *(G-3517)*

Cleveland Metal Stamping Co....................440 234-0010
1231 W Bagley Rd Ste 1 Berea (44017) *(G-1162)*

Cleveland Mica Co...................................216 226-1360
1360 Hird Ave Lakewood (44107) *(G-8165)*

Cleveland Plant and Flower Co...................614 478-9900
2370 Marilyn Park Ln Columbus (43219) *(G-4811)*

Cleveland Plating LLC..............................216 249-0300
1028 E 134th St Cleveland (44110) *(G-3518)*

Cleveland Press.....................................440 442-5101
452 Bishop Rd Cleveland (44143) *(G-3519)*

Cleveland Press.....................................440 289-3227
30628 Detroit Rd Cleveland (44145) *(G-3520)*

Cleveland Printwear Inc............................216 521-5500
13300 Madison Ave Cleveland (44107) *(G-3521)*

Cleveland Prosthetic Center, Cleveland *Also Called: Acor Orthopaedic Inc (G-3292)*

Cleveland Punch and Die Co, Ravenna *Also Called: True Industries Inc (G-11547)*

Cleveland Quarries, Vermilion *Also Called: Irg Operating LLC (G-13590)*

Cleveland Range LLC (DH).........................216 481-4900
760 Beta Dr Ste G Cleveland (44143) *(G-3522)*

Cleveland Rebabbitting Svc Inc...................216 433-0123
15593 Brookpark Rd Cleveland (44142) *(G-3523)*

Cleveland Rebar, Akron *Also Called: Akron Rebar Co (G-40)*

Cleveland Reclaim Inds Inc (PA).................440 282-4917
7400 Industrial Parkway Dr Lorain (44053) *(G-8551)*

Cleveland Roll Forming Co.........................216 281-0202
3170 W 32nd St Cleveland (44109) *(G-3524)*

Cleveland Spclty Insptn Svc In...................440 974-1818
8562 East Ave Mentor (44060) *(G-9501)*

Cleveland Special Tool Inc........................440 944-1600
1351 E 286th St Wickliffe (44092) *(G-14371)*

Cleveland Specialty Pdts Inc.....................216 281-8300
2130 W 110th St Cleveland (44102) *(G-3525)*

Cleveland Steel Container Corp...................330 544-2271
412 Mason St Niles (44446) *(G-10586)*

Cleveland Steel Container Corp...................330 656-5600
10048 Aurora Hudson Rd Streetsboro (44241) *(G-12493)*

Cleveland Steel Container Corporation (PA)....440 349-8000
100 Executive Pkwy Hudson (44236) *(G-7839)*

Cleveland Steel Specialty Co.....................216 464-9400
26001 Richmond Rd Bedford Heights (44146) *(G-1074)*

Cleveland Steel Tool Company....................216 681-7400
474 E 105th St Cleveland (44108) *(G-3526)*

Cleveland Supplyone Inc (DH)....................216 514-7000
26801b Fargo Ave Cleveland (44146) *(G-3527)*

Cleveland Tool and Machine Inc..................216 267-6010
4717 Hinckley Industrial Pkwy Cleveland (44109) *(G-3528)*

Cleveland Track Material, Cleveland *Also Called: Progress Rail Services Corp (G-4200)*

Cleveland Vibrator Company.......................800 221-3298
4544 Hinckley Industrial Pkwy Cleveland (44109) *(G-3529)*

Cleveland Wind Company LLC.....................216 269-7667
4176 Hinsdale Rd Cleveland (44121) *(G-3530)*

Cleveland Wire Cloth Mfg LLC....................216 341-1832
3573 E 78th St Cleveland (44105) *(G-3531)*

Cleveland-Cliffs, Cleveland *Also Called: Cleveland-Cliffs Steel Corp (G-3533)*

Cleveland-Cliffs Columbus LLC...................614 492-8287
4300 Alum Creek Dr Columbus (43207) *(G-4812)*

Cleveland-Cliffs Columbus LLC (DH).............614 492-6800
4020 Kinross Lakes Pkwy Ste 101 Richfield (44286) *(G-11589)*

Cleveland-Cliffs Inc (PA)..........................216 694-5700
200 Public Sq Ste 3300 Cleveland (44114) *(G-3532)*

Cleveland-Cliffs Steel Corp (DH).................216 694-5700
200 Public Sq Ste 3300 Cleveland (44114) *(G-3533)*

Cleveland-Cliffs Steel Corp.......................419 755-3011
913 Bowman St Mansfield (44903) *(G-8775)*

Cleveland-Cliffs Steel Corp.......................513 425-3593
622 Box Middletown (45042) *(G-9845)*

Cleveland-Cliffs Steel Corp.......................513 425-5000
1801 Crawford St Middletown (45044) *(G-9846)*

Cleveland-Cliffs Steel Corp.......................513 425-3694
801 Crawford St Middletown (45044) *(G-9847)*

Clevelandcom.......................................216 862-7159
4800 Tiedeman Rd Cleveland (44144) *(G-3534)*

Clevelandcrystals, Highland Heights *Also Called: Gooch & Housego (ohio) LLC (G-7658)*

Clevelnd-Clffs Clvland Wrks LL (HQ)............216 429-6000
3060 Eggers Ave Cleveland (44105) *(G-3535)*

Clevelnd-Clffs Clvland Wrks LL...................216 429-6000
3100 E 4th St Cleveland (44127) *(G-3536)*

Clevelnd-Clffs Mddletown Works, Middletown *Also Called: Cleveland-Cliffs Steel Corp (G-9846)*

Clevelnd-Clffs Tblar Cmpnnts L (DH)...........419 661-4150
30400 E Broadway St Walbridge (43465) *(G-13683)*

Clevelnd-Clffs Tling Stmping H (DH)............519 969-4632
9227 Centre Pointe Dr West Chester (45069) *(G-13967)*

Clevelnd-Clffs Toling Stamping (DH)............216 694-5700
9227 Centre Pointe Dr West Chester (45069) *(G-13968)*

Clevelnd-Cliffs Stl Holdg Corp (DH)............216 694-5700
200 Public Sq Ste 3300 Cleveland (44114) *(G-3537)*

Clevemed, Cleveland *Also Called: Cleveland Medical Devices Inc (G-3515)*

Clicks Document Management, Cleveland *Also Called: Marcus Uppe Inc (G-3987)*

Clientrax Software, Grove City *Also Called: Custom Information Systems Inc (G-7380)*

Cliffs, Cleveland *Also Called: Cleveland-Cliffs Inc (G-3532)*

Cliffs & Associates Ltd............................216 694-5700
1100 Superior Ave E Ste 1500 Cleveland (44114) *(G-3538)*

Cliffs Mining Company.............................216 694-5700
200 Public Sq Ste 3300 Cleveland (44114) *(G-3539)*

Cliffs Steel Inc (HQ)...............................216 694-5700
200 Public Sq Ste 3300 Cleveland (44114) *(G-3540)*

Clifton Capital Holdings LLC (PA)...............330 562-9000
16500 Rockside Rd Maple Heights (44137) *(G-8880)*

Clifton Steel Company (HQ).......................216 662-6111
16500 Rockside Rd Maple Heights (44137) *(G-8881)*

Climate Pros LLC...................................216 881-5200
5309 Hamilton Ave Cleveland (44114) *(G-3541)*

Climate Pros LLC...................................330 744-2732
52 E Myrtle Ave Youngstown (44507) *(G-14839)*

Climax Metal Products Company..................440 943-8898
8141 Tyler Blvd Mentor (44060) *(G-9502)*

Climax Packaging Machinery, Hamilton *Also Called: GL Industries Inc (G-7494)*

Cline Machine and Automtn Inc...................740 474-4237
1050 Tarlton Rd Circleville (43113) *(G-3252)*

Clinical Specialties Inc (HQ).....................888 873-7888
6288 Hudson Crossing Pkwy Hudson (44236) *(G-7840)*

Cliniel Otcme Mngmnt Syst LLC..................330 650-9900
9200 S Hills Blvd Ste 200 Broadview Heights (44147) *(G-1501)*

Clint's Prntng, Dayton *Also Called: Clints Printing Inc (G-5703)*

Clinton Foundry Ltd................................419 243-6885
1202 W Bancroft St Toledo (43606) *(G-12924)*

Clinton Machine Co Inc............................330 882-2060
6270 Van Buren Rd New Franklin (44216) *(G-10388)*

Clinton Pattern Works Inc.........................419 243-0855
1215 W Bancroft St Toledo (43606) *(G-12925)*

Clints Printing Inc.................................937 426-2771
1176 Little Sugar Creek Rd Dayton (45440) *(G-5703)*

Clipper Products, Cincinnati *Also Called: Clipper Products Inc (G-2299)*

Clipper Products Inc...............................513 688-7300
675 Cincinnati Batavia Pike Cincinnati (45245) *(G-2299)*

Clipson S Metalworking, Cincinnati *Also Called: Clipsons Metal Working Inc (G-2499)*

Clipsons Metal Working Inc.......................513 772-6393
127 Novner Dr Cincinnati (45215) *(G-2499)*

Clockingme LLC.....................................614 400-9727
3280 Morse Rd Ste 211 Columbus (43231) *(G-4813)*

Clopay, Mason *Also Called: Berry Film Products Co Inc (G-9071)*

Clopay Ames Inc (HQ).............................800 282-2260
8585 Duke Blvd Mason (45040) *(G-9087)*

Clopay Building Pdts Co Inc, Mason *Also Called: Clopay Corporation (G-9088)*

Clopay Corporation (DH)..........................513 770-4800
8585 Duke Blvd Mason (45040) *(G-9088)*

Clorox, Mason *Also Called: Clorox Company (G-9089)*

Clorox Company.. 513 445-1840
4680 Parkway Dr Ste 130 Mason (45040) *(G-9089)*

Closet Factory, The, Cleveland *Also Called: Home Stor & Off Solutions Inc (G-3836)*

Clouth Sprenger LLC.. 937 642-8390
1425 Kingsview Dr Lebanon (45036) *(G-8249)*

Clovernook Ctr For Blind Vslly (PA)...................... 513 522-3860
7000 Hamilton Ave Cincinnati (45231) *(G-2500)*

Clovervale Farms LLC (DH).................................. 440 960-0146
8133 Cooper Foster Park Rd Amherst (44001) *(G-444)*

Clovervale Foods, Amherst *Also Called: Clovervale Farms LLC (G-444)*

CLS Finishing Inc... 330 784-4134
409 Munroe Falls Rd Tallmadge (44278) *(G-12733)*

Club 513 LLC.. 800 530-2574
201 E 5th St 19th Fl Cincinnati (45202) *(G-2501)*

Clyde Foam, Clyde *Also Called: Clyde Tool & Die Inc (G-4557)*

Clyde Tool & Die Inc.. 419 547-9574
524 S Church St Clyde (43410) *(G-4557)*

CM Paula Company (PA)...................................... 513 759-7473
6049 Hi Tek Ct Mason (45040) *(G-9090)*

CM Slicechief Co.. 419 241-7647
3333 Maple St Toledo (43608) *(G-12926)*

Cmbf Products Inc (DH)...................................... 855 403-9083
920 Lake Rd Medina (44256) *(G-9388)*

CMC Consulting, Solon *Also Called: CMC Pharmaceuticals Inc (G-12095)*

CMC Electronics Cincinn...................................... 513 573-6316
7500 Innovation Way Mason (45040) *(G-9091)*

CMC Group Inc (PA)... 419 354-2591
12836 S Dixie Hwy Bowling Green (43402) *(G-1415)*

CMC Pharmaceuticals Inc (PA).............................. 216 600-9430
30625 Solon Rd Ste G Solon (44139) *(G-12095)*

Cmd Medtech LLC.. 614 364-4243
3585 Interchange Rd Columbus (43204) *(G-4814)*

Cmg Company Plant 2, West Mansfield *Also Called: M & M Concepts Inc (G-14179)*

CMI, Galion *Also Called: CMI Holding Company Crawford (G-7183)*

CMI Holding Company Crawford............................ 419 468-9122
1310 Freese Works Pl Galion (44833) *(G-7183)*

CMI Industry Americas Inc (DH)............................ 330 332-4661
435 W Wilson St Salem (44460) *(G-11771)*

CMI Technology Inc.. 937 832-2000
65 Haas Dr Englewood (45322) *(G-6609)*

Cmt Imports Inc (PA).. 513 615-1851
2930 Glendale Milford Rd Ste 330 Cincinnati (45241) *(G-2502)*

Cmt Machining & Fabg LLC.................................. 937 652-3740
1411 Kennard Kingscreek Rd Urbana (43078) *(G-13459)*

Cnc Machine Shop, Brunswick *Also Called: Fpc Holdings Inc (G-1591)*

Cnc Machining, Vermilion *Also Called: Coleys Inc (G-13589)*

Cnc Precision Machine Inc.................................... 440 548-3880
18360 Industrial Cir Parkman (44080) *(G-11126)*

Cnd Machine, Massillon *Also Called: C-N-D Industries Inc (G-9176)*

CNG, Lexington *Also Called: Charter Next Generation Inc (G-8368)*

Co-Ax Technology Inc... 440 914-9200
30301 Emerald Valley Pkwy Solon (44139) *(G-12096)*

Co-Pac Services Inc... 216 688-1780
3113 W 110th St Cleveland (44111) *(G-3542)*

Coach Tool & Die LLC... 937 890-4716
235 S Pioneer Blvd Springboro (45066) *(G-12249)*

Coal Resources Inc (PA)...................................... 216 765-1240
46226 National Rd Saint Clairsville (43950) *(G-11689)*

Coal Services Inc... 740 795-5220
155 Highway 7 S Powhatan Point (43942) *(G-11497)*

Coal Services Group, Powhatan Point *Also Called: Coal Services Inc (G-11497)*

Coastal Diamond, Mentor *Also Called: Performance Superabrasives LLC (G-9586)*

Coastal Pet Products Inc...................................... 330 821-7363
911 Leadway Ave Alliance (44601) *(G-377)*

Coating Systems Inc... 513 367-5600
150 Sales Ave Harrison (45030) *(G-7547)*

Coating Systems Group Inc.................................. 440 816-9306
6909 Engle Rd Bldg C Middleburg Heights (44130) *(G-9768)*

Coatings & Colorants, Cincinnati *Also Called: Evonik Corporation (G-2606)*

Coaxial Dynamics, Cleveland *Also Called: CDI Industries Inc (G-3481)*

Cobblers Corner LLC.. 330 482-4005
1115 Village Plz Columbiana (44408) *(G-4609)*

Coblentz Brothers Inc... 330 857-7211
7101 S Kohler Rd Apple Creek (44606) *(G-465)*

Coblentz Chocolate Co, Walnut Creek *Also Called: Coblentz Family Brands Inc (G-13693)*

Coblentz Family Brands Inc (PA)........................... 330 893-2995
4917 State Rte 515 Walnut Creek (44687) *(G-13693)*

Cobra Motorcycles Mfg....................................... 330 207-3844
11511 Springfield Rd North Lima (44452) *(G-10705)*

Coburn Inc (PA)... 419 368-4051
636 Ashland County Rd 30 A Hayesville (44838) *(G-7591)*

Coca-Cola, Akron *Also Called: Akron Coca-Cola Bottling Co (G-27)*

Coca-Cola, Akron *Also Called: Central Coca-Cola Btlg Co Inc (G-95)*

Coca-Cola, Bedford Heights *Also Called: Cleveland Coca-Cola Btlg Inc (G-1073)*

Coca-Cola, Cincinnati *Also Called: Coca-Cola Consolidated Inc (G-2503)*

Coca-Cola, Circleville *Also Called: Central Coca-Cola Btlg Co Inc (G-3250)*

Coca-Cola, Columbus *Also Called: Coca-Cola Company (G-4815)*

Coca-Cola, Dayton *Also Called: Coca-Cola Consolidated Inc (G-5704)*

Coca-Cola, Elyria *Also Called: Central Coca-Cola Btlg Co Inc (G-6511)*

Coca-Cola, Lima *Also Called: Coca-Cola Consolidated Inc (G-8395)*

Coca-Cola, Lockbourne *Also Called: Central Coca-Cola Btlg Co Inc (G-8488)*

Coca-Cola, Mansfield *Also Called: Central Coca-Cola Btlg Co Inc (G-8773)*

Coca-Cola, Portsmouth *Also Called: Coca-Cola Consolidated Inc (G-11464)*

Coca-Cola, Toledo *Also Called: Central Coca-Cola Btlg Co Inc (G-12913)*

Coca-Cola, Twinsburg *Also Called: Central Coca-Cola Btlg Co Inc (G-13285)*

Coca-Cola, Willoughby *Also Called: Central Coca-Cola Btlg Co Inc (G-14438)*

Coca-Cola, Youngstown *Also Called: Central Coca-Cola Btlg Co Inc (G-14833)*

Coca-Cola, Zanesville *Also Called: Central Coca-Cola Btlg Co Inc (G-15006)*

Coca-Cola Company.. 614 491-6305
2455 Watkins Rd Columbus (43207) *(G-4815)*

Coca-Cola Consolidated Inc................................. 513 527-6600
5100 Duck Creek Rd Cincinnati (45227) *(G-2503)*

Coca-Cola Consolidated Inc................................. 937 878-5000
1000 Coca Cola Blvd Dayton (45424) *(G-5704)*

Coca-Cola Consolidated Inc................................. 419 422-3743
201 N Shore Dr Lima (45801) *(G-8395)*

Coca-Cola Consolidated Inc................................. 740 353-3133
5050 Old Scioto Trl Portsmouth (45662) *(G-11464)*

Cochem Inc... 216 341-8914
7555 Bessemer Ave Cleveland (44127) *(G-3543)*

Cochran 6573 LLC... 440 349-4900
6573 Cochran Rd Ste I Solon (44139) *(G-12097)*

Coconis Furniture Inc (PA).................................. 740 452-1231
4 S Maysville Ave South Zanesville (43701) *(G-12232)*

Codonics Inc (PA).. 800 444-1198
17991 Englewood Dr Ste B Cleveland (44130) *(G-3544)*

Coe Manufacturing Company (HQ)........................ 440 352-9381
70 W Erie St Ste 150 Painesville (44077) *(G-11072)*

Coen Grinding, Sherrodsville *Also Called: Karon C Enold (G-11975)*

Coffey and Associates, West Chester *Also Called: D C Controls LLC (G-14113)*

Coffing Corporation (PA)...................................... 513 919-2813
5336 Lesourdsville West Chester Rd Liberty Twp (45011) *(G-8381)*

Coffman Media LLC.. 614 956-7015
5995 Wilcox Pl Ste A Dublin (43016) *(G-6289)*

Cohen Brothers Inc (PA)...................................... 513 422-3696
1520 14th Ave Middletown (45044) *(G-9848)*

Cohen Brothers Inc.. 513 217-5200
1300 Lafayette Ave Middletown (45044) *(G-9849)*

Cohen Brothers Inc Lafayette, Middletown *Also Called: Cohen Brothers Inc (G-9849)*

Cohesant Inc (PA).. 216 910-1700
3601 Green Rd Ste 308 Beachwood (44122) *(G-913)*

Coil Specialty Chemicals LLC............................... 740 236-2407
2375 Glendale Rd Marietta (45750) *(G-8910)*

Coin World, Sidney *Also Called: Amos Media Company (G-11992)*

Coit Tool Company Inc... 440 946-3377
38134 Western Pkwy Ste 3 Willoughby (44094) *(G-14439)*

Col-Pump Company Inc....................................... 330 482-1029
131 E Railroad St Columbiana (44408) *(G-4610)*

Colbleu Vodka, Solon *Also Called: Blue Collar M LLC (G-12086)*

Colburn Patterson LLC (PA)..419 866-5544
1100 S Holland Sylvania Rd Holland (43528) *(G-7751)*

Colby Properties LLC..937 390-0816
2071 N Bechtle Ave Springfield (45504) *(G-12292)*

Colby Woodworking Inc...937 224-7676
1912 Lucille Dr Dayton (45404) *(G-5705)*

Cold Headed Fas Assemblies Inc................................330 833-0800
1875 Harsh Ave Se Ste 3 Massillon (44646) *(G-9180)*

Cold Jet, Loveland *Also Called: Cold Jet International LLC (G-8622)*

Cold Jet International LLC (PA)..................................513 831-3211
455 Wards Corner Rd Loveland (45140) *(G-8622)*

Coldwater Machine Company LLC...............................419 678-4877
911 N 2nd St Coldwater (45828) *(G-4571)*

Cole Orthotics Prosthetic Ctr....................................419 476-4248
723 Phillips Ave Bldg F Toledo (43612) *(G-12927)*

Cole Tool & Die Company..419 522-1272
466 State Rte 314 N Ontario (44903) *(G-10948)*

Colepak LLC...937 652-3910
1030 S Edgewood Ave Urbana (43078) *(G-13460)*

Coleys Inc...440 967-5630
1775 Liberty Ave Vermilion (44089) *(G-13589)*

Colfor Manufacturing Inc (DH)..................................330 623-7814
3255 Alliance Rd Nw Malvern (44644) *(G-8748)*

Colfor Manufacturing Inc..330 863-0404
461 Knox Ct Minerva (44657) *(G-10036)*

Colgate-Palmolive, Cambridge *Also Called: Colgate-Palmolive Company (G-1739)*

Colgate-Palmolive Company.....................................212 310-2000
8800 Guernsey Industrial Blvd Cambridge (43725) *(G-1739)*

College Issue, Piqua *Also Called: Atlantis Sportswear Inc (G-11336)*

Collins & Aikman Auto Mats LLC...............................330 456-4543
1212 7th St Nw Canton (44711) *(G-1869)*

Collins & Venco Venturo, Cincinnati *Also Called: Venco Manufacturing Inc (G-3196)*

Collins Aerospace, Troy *Also Called: Goodrich Corporation (G-13219)*

Collinwood Shale Brick Sup Co (PA)...........................216 587-2700
16219 Saranac Rd Cleveland (44110) *(G-3545)*

Collotype Labels Usa Inc...513 381-1480
4053 Clough Woods Dr Batavia (45103) *(G-858)*

Colonial Machine Company Inc..................................330 673-5859
1041 Mogadore Rd Kent (44240) *(G-8021)*

Colonial Patterns Inc...330 673-6475
920 Overholt Rd Kent (44240) *(G-8022)*

Colonial Rubber Company (PA)..................................330 296-2831
706 Oakwood St Ravenna (44266) *(G-11522)*

Colonial Surface Solutions, Columbus Grove *Also Called: Carpe Diem Industries LLC (G-5382)*

Colony Hardware, Cleveland *Also Called: Beckett-Greenhill LLC (G-3413)*

Colony Machine & Tool Inc.......................................330 225-3410
1300 Industrial Pkwy N Brunswick (44212) *(G-1583)*

Color 3 Embroidery Inc...330 652-9495
2927 Mahoning Ave Nw Warren (44483) *(G-13753)*

Color Bar Printing Centers Inc..................................216 595-3939
4576 Renaissance Pkwy Cleveland (44128) *(G-3546)*

Color Process Inc...440 268-7100
8760 Guilford Rd Seville (44273) *(G-11915)*

Color Products Inc..513 860-2749
36 Standen Dr Hamilton (45015) *(G-7479)*

Color Resolutions International LLC............................513 552-7200
575 Quality Blvd Fairfield (45014) *(G-6724)*

Coloramics LLC..614 876-1171
4077 Weaver Ct S Hilliard (43026) *(G-7678)*

Colormatrix Corporation (HQ)...................................216 622-0100
680 N Rocky River Dr Berea (44017) *(G-1163)*

Colormatrix Group Inc..216 622-0100
680 N Rocky River Dr Berea (44017) *(G-1164)*

Colormatrix Holdings Inc (HQ)..................................440 930-3162
680 N Rocky River Dr Berea (44017) *(G-1165)*

Colortech Graphics & Printing (PA)............................614 766-2400
4000 Business Park Dr Columbus (43204) *(G-4816)*

Columbia, Vandalia *Also Called: Datwyler Sling Sltions USA Inc (G-13554)*

Columbia Chemical Corporation.................................330 225-3200
1000 Western Dr Brunswick (44212) *(G-1584)*

Columbia Industrial Pdts Inc....................................216 431-6633
4100 Payne Ave Cleveland (44103) *(G-3547)*

Columbia Industries, Cleveland *Also Called: Qcsm LLC (G-4210)*

Columbia Industries, Solon *Also Called: Skidmore-Wilhelm Mfg Company (G-12182)*

Columbia Stamping Inc..440 236-6677
13676 Station Rd Columbia Station (44028) *(G-4591)*

Columbiana Boiler Company LLC................................330 482-3373
200 W Railroad St Columbiana (44408) *(G-4611)*

Columbiana Foundry Company....................................330 482-3336
501 Lisbon St Columbiana (44408) *(G-4612)*

Columbus Apparel Studio, Columbus *Also Called: Columbus Apparel Studio LLC (G-4817)*

Columbus Apparel Studio LLC...................................614 706-7292
757 Garden Rd Ste 110 Columbus (43214) *(G-4817)*

Columbus Art Memorial Inc......................................614 221-9333
606 W Broad St Columbus (43215) *(G-4818)*

Columbus Brewing Company, Columbus *Also Called: District Brewing Company Inc (G-4886)*

Columbus Canvas Products, Columbus *Also Called: Columbus Canvas Products Inc (G-4819)*

Columbus Canvas Products Inc..................................614 375-1397
577 N 4th St Columbus (43215) *(G-4819)*

Columbus Castings, Columbus *Also Called: Columbus Steel Castings Co (G-4834)*

Columbus Controls Inc..614 882-9029
3573 Johnny Appleseed Ct Columbus (43231) *(G-4820)*

Columbus Custom Tees..614 573-5556
6419 Nicholas Dr Columbus (43235) *(G-4821)*

Columbus Design & Mfg LLC.....................................414 534-3273
3303 E 11th Ave Columbus (43219) *(G-4822)*

Columbus Dispatch, Columbus *Also Called: Dispatch Printing Company (G-4884)*

Columbus Dispatch, Lewis Center *Also Called: Dispatch Printing Company (G-8331)*

Columbus Gasket & Supply, Columbus *Also Called: James K Green Enterprises Inc (G-5031)*

Columbus Graphics Inc...614 577-9360
7295 Rickly St Reynoldsburg (43068) *(G-11563)*

Columbus Heating & Vent Co....................................614 274-1177
182 N Yale Ave Columbus (43222) *(G-4823)*

Columbus Incontact...801 245-8369
555 S Front St Columbus (43215) *(G-4824)*

Columbus Industries Inc (HQ)...................................740 983-2552
2938 State Route 752 Ashville (43103) *(G-624)*

Columbus Industries One LLC...................................740 983-2552
2938 State Route 752 Ashville (43103) *(G-625)*

Columbus Instruments, Columbus *Also Called: Columbus Instruments Intl Corp (G-4826)*

Columbus Instruments LLC.......................................614 276-0861
950 N Hague Ave Columbus (43204) *(G-4825)*

Columbus Instruments Intl Corp................................614 276-0593
950 N Hague Ave Columbus (43204) *(G-4826)*

Columbus International Corp (PA)...............................614 323-1086
200 E Campus View Blvd Ste 200 Columbus (43235) *(G-4827)*

Columbus International Corp.....................................614 917-2274
8876 Whitney Dr Lewis Center (43035) *(G-8329)*

Columbus Jack Corporation......................................614 443-7492
1 Air Cargo Pkwy E Swanton (43558) *(G-12680)*

Columbus Jack Regent, Swanton *Also Called: Columbus Jack Corporation (G-12680)*

Columbus Kombucha Company LLC.............................614 262-0000
930 Freeway Dr N Columbus (43229) *(G-4828)*

Columbus Machine Works Inc....................................614 409-0244
2491 Fairwood Ave Columbus (43207) *(G-4829)*

Columbus Messenger Company (PA)............................614 272-5422
3500 Sullivant Ave Columbus (43204) *(G-4830)*

Columbus Pipe and Equipment Co..............................614 444-7871
763 E Markison Ave Columbus (43207) *(G-4831)*

Columbus Prescr Rehabilitation.................................614 294-1600
975 Eastwind Dr Ste 155 Westerville (43081) *(G-14250)*

Columbus Roof Trusses Inc (PA)...............................614 272-6464
2525 Fisher Rd Columbus (43204) *(G-4832)*

Columbus Roof Trusses Inc......................................740 763-3000
400 Marne Dr Newark (43055) *(G-10498)*

Columbus Sign Company..614 252-3133
1515 E 5th Ave Columbus (43219) *(G-4833)*

Columbus Steel Castings Co.....................................614 444-2121
2211 Parsons Ave Columbus (43207) *(G-4834)*

A L P H A B E T I C

Columbus Steelmasters Inc.. 614 231-2141
   660 Concrea Rd Columbus (43219) *(G-4835)*

Columbus Underground, Columbus Also Called: Evans Creative Group LLC *(G-4914)*

Columbus V&S Galvanizing LLC..................................... 614 449-8281
   987 Buckeye Park Rd Columbus (43207) *(G-4836)*

Columbus Washboard Company Ltd................................ 740 380-3828
   4 E Main St Logan (43138) *(G-8512)*

Columbus Water Section Permit...................................... 614 645-8039
   910 Dublin Rd Columbus (43215) *(G-4837)*

Columbus Winter Fair, Columbus Also Called: Ohio Designer Craftsmen Entps *(G-5141)*

Columbus-Sports Publications....................................... 614 486-2202
   1200 Chambers Rd Columbus (43212) *(G-4838)*

Com-Corp Industries Inc... 216 431-6266
   7601 Bittern Ave Cleveland (44103) *(G-3548)*

Com-Fab Inc... 740 857-1107
   4657 Price Hilliards Rd Plain City (43064) *(G-11401)*

Com-Net Software Specialists, Miamisburg Also Called: Signature Technologies Inc *(G-9737)*

Comber Holdings Inc... 216 961-8600
   3304 W 67th Pl Cleveland (44102) *(G-3549)*

Combi Packaging Systems Llc....................................... 330 456-9333
   6299 Dressler Rd Nw Canton (44720) *(G-1870)*

Combined Containerboard Inc.. 513 530-5700
   7741 School Rd Cincinnati (45249) *(G-2504)*

Combined Tech Group Inc.. 937 274-4866
   6061 Milo Rd Dayton (45414) *(G-5706)*

Combs Manufacturing Inc.. 330 784-3151
   380 Kennedy Rd Akron (44305) *(G-104)*

Comcorp Inc (HQ).. 718 981-1234
   1801 Superior Ave E Cleveland (44114) *(G-3550)*

Comdess Company Inc... 330 769-2094
   8733 Wooster Pike Rd Seville (44273) *(G-11916)*

Comex Group, Cleveland Also Called: Comex North America Inc *(G-3551)*

Comex North America Inc (HQ)...................................... 303 307-2100
   101 W Prospect Ave Ste 1020 Cleveland (44115) *(G-3551)*

Comfort Line Ltd.. 419 729-8520
   5500 Enterprise Blvd Toledo (43612) *(G-12928)*

Comm Steel Inc.. 216 881-4600
   8043 Corporate Cir Ste 2 North Royalton (44133) *(G-10757)*

Command Alkon Incorporated.. 614 799-0600
   6750 Crosby Ct Dublin (43016) *(G-6290)*

Command Plastic Corporation.. 800 321-8001
   22475 Aurora Rd Bedford (44146) *(G-1022)*

Commercial Anodizing Co.. 440 942-8384
   38387 Apollo Pkwy Willoughby (44094) *(G-14440)*

Commercial Cnstr Group LLC.. 513 722-8952
   5902 Montclair Blvd Milford (45150) *(G-9930)*

Commercial Cutng Graphics LLC................................... 419 526-4800
   208 Central Ave Mansfield (44905) *(G-8776)*

Commercial Cutting, Mansfield Also Called: Commercial Cutng Graphics LLC *(G-8776)*

Commercial Decal Ohio Inc.. 330 385-7178
   46686 Y And O Rd East Liverpool (43920) *(G-6390)*

Commercial Dock & Door Inc.. 440 951-1210
   7653 Saint Clair Ave Mentor (44060) *(G-9503)*

Commercial Electric Pdts Corp (PA).............................. 216 241-2886
   1821 E 40th St Cleveland (44103) *(G-3552)*

Commercial Fluid Power, Dover Also Called: Commercial Honing LLC *(G-6235)*

Commercial Grinding Svcs Inc...................................... 330 273-5040
   1155 Industrial Pkwy Unit 1 Medina (44258) *(G-9389)*

Commercial Honing LLC (DH).. 330 343-8896
   2997 Progress St Dover (44622) *(G-6235)*

Commercial Interior Products, West Chester Also Called: CIP International Inc *(G-13964)*

Commercial Metal Forming, Youngstown Also Called: Star Manufacturing LLC *(G-14940)*

Commercial Metal Forming, Youngstown Also Called: Steel Forming Inc *(G-14941)*

Commercial Minerals Inc... 330 549-2165
   10900 South Ave North Lima (44452) *(G-10706)*

Commercial Mtal Fbricators Inc..................................... 937 233-4911
   150 Commerce Park Dr Dayton (45404) *(G-5707)*

Commercial Music Service Co.. 740 746-8500
   6312 Goss Rd Sugar Grove (43155) *(G-12629)*

Commercial Press, Canton Also Called: Wernet Inc *(G-2046)*

Commercial Printing Co, Greenville Also Called: Commercial Prtg Greenville Inc *(G-7339)*

Commercial Prtg Greenville Inc..................................... 937 548-3835
   314 S Broadway St Greenville (45331) *(G-7339)*

Commercial Steel Treating Co.. 216 431-8204
   1394 E 39th St Cleveland (44114) *(G-3553)*

Commercial Turf Products Ltd....................................... 330 995-7000
   1777 Miller Pkwy Streetsboro (44241) *(G-12494)*

Commercial Vehicle Group Inc (PA)............................... 614 289-5360
   7800 Walton Pkwy New Albany (43054) *(G-10336)*

Commerical Roofing, Milford Also Called: Batman Enterprises LLC *(G-9923)*

Communication Concepts Inc.. 937 426-8600
   508 Mill Stone Dr Beavercreek (45434) *(G-968)*

Communication Exhibits Inc.. 330 854-4040
   1119 Milan St N Canal Fulton (44614) *(G-1775)*

Communications Aid Inc.. 513 475-8453
   222 Piedmont Ave Ste 5200 Cincinnati (45219) *(G-2505)*

Community Action Program Corp................................... 740 374-8501
   696 Wayne St Marietta (45750) *(G-8911)*

Community Action Wic Hlth Svc, Marietta Also Called: Community Action Program Corp
(G-8911)

Community Care Network Inc (PA)................................. 216 671-0977
   4614 Prospect Ave Ste 240 Cleveland (44103) *(G-3554)*

Compass, Moraine Also Called: Angels Landing Inc *(G-10147)*

Compass Electronics Solutions, Vandalia Also Called: Mac Its LLC *(G-13565)*

Compass S&S, Barberton Also Called: Compass Systems & Sales LLC *(G-802)*

Compass Systems & Sales LLC.................................... 330 733-2111
   5185 New Haven Cir Barberton (44203) *(G-802)*

Compco Columbiana Company (HQ).............................. 330 482-0200
   400 W Railroad St Columbiana (44408) *(G-4613)*

Compco Industries, Columbiana Also Called: Compco Columbiana Company *(G-4613)*

Compco Industries, Columbiana Also Called: Compco Youngstown Company *(G-4614)*

Compco Quaker Mfg Inc.. 330 482-0200
   187 Georgetown Rd Salem (44460) *(G-11772)*

Compco Youngstown Company..................................... 330 482-6488
   400 W Railroad St Columbiana (44408) *(G-4614)*

Competetive Carbide Inc... 440 350-9393
   5879 Shore Dr Madison (44057) *(G-8727)*

Competitive Carbide, Madison Also Called: Competetive Carbide Inc *(G-8727)*

Complements Lighting, Mentor Also Called: Medallion Lighting Corporation *(G-9561)*

Complete Cylinder Service Inc...................................... 513 772-1500
   1240 Glendale Milford Rd Cincinnati (45215) *(G-2506)*

Complete Energy Services Inc....................................... 440 577-1070
   7338 Us Route 6 Pierpont (44082) *(G-11304)*

Complete Mechanical Svcs LLC.................................... 513 489-3080
   11399 Grooms Rd Cincinnati (45242) *(G-2507)*

Complete Metal Services.. 740 694-0000
   18581 Divelbiss Rd Fredericktown (43019) *(G-7074)*

Completeenergy Services... 440 576-6000
   7338 Us Route 6 Pierpont (44082) *(G-11305)*

Compliant Healthcare Tech LLC (PA)............................ 216 255-9607
   7123 Pearl Rd Ste 305 Cleveland (44130) *(G-3555)*

Component Mfg & Design Inc... 330 225-8080
   3121 Interstate Pkwy Brunswick (44212) *(G-1585)*

Component Solutions Group Inc (HQ)............................ 937 434-8100
   7755 Paragon Rd Ste 104 Dayton (45459) *(G-5708)*

Component Systems Inc.. 216 252-9292
   5350 Tradex Pkwy Cleveland (44102) *(G-3556)*

Composite Group, The, Fairlawn Also Called: Hpc Holdings LLC *(G-6804)*

Composite Technologies Co LLC................................... 937 228-2880
   401 N Keowee St Dayton (45404) *(G-5709)*

Compounded Eps, Piqua Also Called: Epsilyte Holdings LLC *(G-11346)*

Comprehensive Logistics Co Inc................................... 440 934-3517
   1200a Chester Industrial Pkwy Avon (44011) *(G-720)*

Comptons Precision Machine... 937 325-9139
   224 Dayton Ave Springfield (45506) *(G-12293)*

Compu-Print, Canton Also Called: Better Living Concepts Inc *(G-1839)*

Computer Allied Technology Co..................................... 614 457-2292
   3385 Somerford Rd Columbus (43221) *(G-4839)*

Computer Products Corporation (PA)............................. 513 221-0600
   3950 Virginia Ave Cincinnati (45227) *(G-2508)*

(G-0000) Company's Geographic Section entry number

Computer Stitch Designs Inc............................	330 856-7826
1414 Henn Hyde Rd Ne Warren (44484) *(G-13754)*	
Computer Workshop Inc....................................	216 901-0106
6100 Rockside Woods Blvd N Ste 235 Cleveland (44131) *(G-3557)*	
Computer Workshop Inc (PA)..............................	614 798-9505
5200 Upper Metro Pl Ste 140 Dublin (43017) *(G-6291)*	
Coms Interactive, Broadview Heights *Also Called: Clinicl Otcms Mngmnt Syst LLC (G-1501)*	
Comtec Incorporated..	330 425-8102
1800 Enterprise Pkwy Twinsburg (44087) *(G-13288)*	
Con-AG, Saint Marys *Also Called: Conag Inc (G-11736)*	
Con-Belt Inc..	330 273-2003
5656 Innovation Dr Valley City (44280) *(G-13492)*	
Con-Cure, Pioneer *Also Called: Premiere Con Solutions LLC (G-11326)*	
Conag Inc..	419 394-8870
16672 County Road 66a Saint Marys (45885) *(G-11736)*	
Conagra Brands Inc..	419 445-8015
901 Stryker St Archbold (43502) *(G-491)*	
Conagra Fods Pckaged Foods LLC......................	937 440-2800
801 Dye Mill Rd Troy (45373) *(G-13206)*	
Concentric Corporation.....................................	440 899-9090
27101 E Oviatt Rd Ste 8 Bay Village (44140) *(G-901)*	
Concentrix Cvg LLC (DH)...................................	972 454-8000
201 E 4th St Cincinnati (45202) *(G-2509)*	
Concept 9 Inc..	614 294-3743
1604 Clara St Columbus (43211) *(G-4840)*	
Concept Machine & Tool Inc..............................	937 473-3334
2065 Industrial Ct Covington (45318) *(G-5491)*	
Concord Fabricators Inc....................................	614 875-2500
6511 Seeds Rd Grove City (43123) *(G-7377)*	
Concord Road Equipment Mfg Inc.......................	440 357-5344
348 Chester St Painesville (44077) *(G-11073)*	
Concord Road Equipment Mfg LLC......................	440 357-5344
8200 Tyler Blvd Ste H Mentor (44060) *(G-9504)*	
Concrete One Construction LLC.........................	740 595-9680
755 Us Highway 23 N Ste E Delaware (43015) *(G-6140)*	
Concrete Sealants Inc......................................	937 845-8776
9325 State Route 201 Tipp City (45371) *(G-12821)*	
Condo Incorporated...	330 609-6021
3869 Niles Rd Se Warren (44484) *(G-13755)*	
Condor Tool & Die Inc.......................................	216 671-6000
4541 Industrial Pkwy Cleveland (44135) *(G-3558)*	
Conduit Pipe Products Company.........................	614 879-9114
1501 W Main St West Jefferson (43162) *(G-14161)*	
Conery Manufacturing Inc.................................	419 289-1444
1380 Township Road 743 Ashland (44805) *(G-530)*	
Conform Automotive LLC...................................	937 492-2708
1630 Ferguson Ct Sidney (45365) *(G-12002)*	
Conforming Matrix Corporation..........................	419 729-3777
6255 Suder Ave Toledo (43611) *(G-12929)*	
Conn-Selmer Inc..	440 946-6100
34199 Curtis Blvd Willoughby (44095) *(G-14441)*	
Connaughton Welding & Fence, Hamilton *Also Called: Connaughton Wldg & Fence LLC (G-7480)*	
Connaughton Wldg & Fence LLC.........................	513 867-0230
440 Vine St Hamilton (45011) *(G-7480)*	
Connect Housing Blocks LLC.............................	614 503-4344
3251 Westerville Rd Columbus (43224) *(G-4841)*	
Connective Design Incorporated........................	937 746-8252
3010 S Tech Blvd Miamisburg (45342) *(G-9683)*	
Connectors Unlimited Inc (PA)...........................	440 357-1161
1359 W Jackson St Painesville (44077) *(G-11074)*	
Connectronics Corp (DH)..................................	419 537-0020
2745 Avondale Ave Toledo (43607) *(G-12930)*	
Connies Candles..	740 574-1224
9103 Ohio River Rd Wheelersburg (45694) *(G-14352)*	
Conns Potato Chip Co Inc.................................	614 252-2150
1271 Alum Creek Dr Columbus (43209) *(G-4842)*	
Conns Potato Chip Co Inc (PA)..........................	740 452-4615
1805 Kemper Ct Zanesville (43701) *(G-15008)*	
Conover Lumber Company Inc...........................	937 368-3010
7960 N Alcony Conover Rd Conover (45317) *(G-5420)*	

Conquest Industries Inc...................................	330 926-9236
4488 Allen Rd Stow (44224) *(G-12425)*	
Conquest Maps LLC (PA)...................................	614 654-1627
5696 Westbourne Ave Columbus (43213) *(G-4843)*	
Conseal, Tipp City *Also Called: Concrete Sealants Inc (G-12821)*	
Consolidated Graphics Group Inc.......................	216 881-9191
1614 E 40th St Cleveland (44103) *(G-3559)*	
Consoldted Anlytcal Systems In.........................	513 542-1200
2629 Spring Grove Ave Cincinnati (45214) *(G-2510)*	
Consoldted Precision Pdts Corp (PA)..................	216 453-4800
1621 Euclid Ave Ste 1850 Cleveland (44115) *(G-3560)*	
Consoldted Precision Pdts Corp.........................	440 953-0053
34000 Lakeland Blvd Eastlake (44095) *(G-6421)*	
Consolidated Biscuit Company, Mc Comb *Also Called: Hearthside Food Solutions LLC (G-9353)*	
Consolidated Bottling Company..........................	419 227-3541
1750 Greely Chapel Rd Lima (45804) *(G-8396)*	
Consolidated Ceramic Products, Blanchester *Also Called: Ccpi Inc (G-1234)*	
Consolidated Coatings Corp..............................	216 514-7596
3735 Green Rd Cleveland (44122) *(G-3561)*	
Consolidated Foundries Inc (HQ).......................	909 595-2252
1621 Euclid Ave Ste 1850 Cleveland (44115) *(G-3562)*	
Consolidated Gas Coop Inc...............................	419 946-6600
5255 State Route 95 Mount Gilead (43338) *(G-10209)*	
Consolidated Graphics Inc................................	740 654-2112
3950 Lancaster New Lexington Rd Se Lancaster (43130) *(G-8189)*	
Consolidated Metal Pdts Inc (PA).......................	513 251-2624
1028 Depot St Cincinnati (45204) *(G-2511)*	
Consolidated Precision Pdts, Eastlake *Also Called: Esco Turbine Technologies - Cleveland Inc (G-6428)*	
Consolidated Solutions, Cleveland *Also Called: Consoldated Graphics Group Inc (G-3559)*	
Consolidated Vehicle Converter, Dayton *Also Called: Julie Maynard Inc (G-5834)*	
Constar International, Hebron *Also Called: Plastipak Packaging Inc (G-7630)*	
Constrction Adhsves Slants Div, Columbus *Also Called: Franklin International Inc (G-4938)*	
Constrction Aggrgtes Corp Mich.........................	616 842-7900
3 Summit Park Dr Ste 700 Independence (44131) *(G-7893)*	
Construction, Solon *Also Called: American Platinum Door LLC (G-12078)*	
Construction Journal, Cincinnati *Also Called: 400 SW 7th Street Partners Ltd (G-2321)*	
Consulting, Aurora *Also Called: Integrity Parking LLC (G-675)*	
Consumer Guild Foods Inc.................................	419 726-3406
5035 Enterprise Blvd Toledo (43612) *(G-12931)*	
Consumeracq Inc (PA)......................................	440 277-9305
2509 N Ridge Rd E Lorain (44055) *(G-8552)*	
Consumers Builders Supply Co (PA)....................	440 277-9306
2509 N Ridge Rd E Lorain (44055) *(G-8553)*	
Consun Food Industries Inc..............................	440 322-6301
123 Gateway Blvd N Elyria (44035) *(G-6514)*	
Contact Control Interfaces LLC.........................	609 333-3264
231 W 12th St Ste 201c Cincinnati (45202) *(G-2512)*	
Contact Industries Inc.....................................	419 884-9788
25 Industrial Dr Lexington (44904) *(G-8372)*	
Container Graphics Corp...................................	937 746-5666
1 Miller St Franklin (45005) *(G-7013)*	
Container Graphics Corp...................................	419 531-5133
305 Ryder Rd Toledo (43607) *(G-12932)*	
Contech Bridge Solutions LLC...........................	937 878-2170
7941 New Carlisle Pike Dayton (45424) *(G-5710)*	
Contech Bridge Solutions LLC (DH).....................	513 645-7000
9025 Centre Pointe Dr Ste 400 West Chester (45069) *(G-13969)*	
Contech Cnstr Pdts Hldings Inc.........................	513 645-7000
9025 Centre Pointe Dr Ste 400 West Chester (45069) *(G-13970)*	
Contech Engnered Solutions Inc........................	513 645-7000
9025 Centre Pointe Dr Ste 400 West Chester (45069) *(G-13971)*	
Contech Engnered Solutions LLC (HQ).................	513 645-7000
9025 Centre Pointe Dr Ste 400 West Chester (45069) *(G-13972)*	
Contech Strmwter Solutions LLC........................	513 645-7000
9025 Centre Pointe Dr Ste 400 West Chester (45069) *(G-13973)*	
Contemprary Image Labeling Inc........................	513 583-5699
2034 Mckinley Blvd Lebanon (45036) *(G-8250)*	
Continental Business Entps Inc (PA)...................	440 439-4400
7311 Northfield Rd Bedford (44146) *(G-1023)*	

A
L
P
H
A
B
E
T
I
C

Continental Cast Stone East, West Chester *Also Called: Russell Cast Stone Inc (G-14142)*

Continental Contitech, Akron *Also Called: Contitech Usa Llc (G-105)*

Continental Contitech, Marysville *Also Called: Contitech Usa LLC (G-9016)*

Continental GL Sls & Inv Group...................................614 679-1201
315 Ashmoore Cir W Powell (43065) *(G-11485)*

Continental Group, Powell *Also Called: Continental GL Sls & Inv Group (G-11485)*

Continental Metal Proc Co (PA)....................................216 268-0000
18711 Cleveland Ave Cleveland (44110) *(G-3563)*

Continental Metal Proc Co...216 268-0000
14919 Saranac Rd Cleveland (44110) *(G-3564)*

Continental Mineral Processing Corporation..............513 771-7190
11817 Mosteller Rd Cincinnati (45241) *(G-2513)*

Contitech North America Inc (DH)...............................330 664-7180
703 S Cleveland Massillon Rd Fairlawn (44333) *(G-6798)*

Contitech Usa Llc (DH)..330 664-7000
703 S Cleveland Massillon Rd Akron (44333) *(G-105)*

Contitech Usa LLC...937 644-8900
13601 Industrial Pkwy Marysville (43040) *(G-9016)*

Contour Forming Inc..740 345-9777
215 Oakwood Ave Newark (43055) *(G-10499)*

Contours, Orrville *Also Called: Bekaert Corporation (G-10975)*

Contract Bldg Components Ltd....................................937 644-0739
14540 Industrial Pkwy Marysville (43040) *(G-9017)*

Contract Lumber Inc..614 751-1109
200 Schofield Dr Columbus (43213) *(G-4844)*

Contractors Steel Company...330 425-3050
8383 Boyle Pkwy Twinsburg (44087) *(G-13289)*

Control Craft LLC..513 674-0056
1123 Hickorywood Ct Cincinnati (45233) *(G-2514)*

Control Electric Co..216 671-8010
12130 Eaton Commerce Pkwy Columbia Station (44028) *(G-4592)*

Control Industries Inc...937 653-7694
614 Central Ave Findlay (45840) *(G-6855)*

Control Interface Inc...513 874-2062
517 Commercial Dr West Chester (45014) *(G-13974)*

Control Line Equipment Inc..216 433-7766
14750 Industrial Pkwy Cleveland (44135) *(G-3565)*

Control Transformer Inc..330 637-6015
3701 Warren Meadville Rd Cortland (44410) *(G-5443)*

Control-X Inc...614 777-9729
3546 Rosburg Dr Columbus (43228) *(G-4845)*

Controlled Access Inc...330 273-6185
1535 Industrial Pkwy Brunswick (44212) *(G-1586)*

Controllix Corporation..440 232-8757
21415 Alexander Rd Walton Hills (44146) *(G-13696)*

Controls and Sheet Metal Inc (PA)..............................513 721-3610
1051 Sargent St Cincinnati (45203) *(G-2515)*

Controls Inc..330 239-4345
5204 Portside Dr Medina (44256) *(G-9390)*

Convault of Ohio Inc...614 252-8422
841 Alton Ave Columbus (43219) *(G-4846)*

Conversion Tech Intl Inc...419 924-5566
700 Oak St West Unity (43570) *(G-14193)*

Convertapax, Midvale *Also Called: Maintenance Repair Supply Inc (G-9913)*

Converters/Prepress Inc...937 743-0935
301 Industry Dr Carlisle (45005) *(G-2065)*

Conveyor Metal Works Inc..740 477-8700
2717 Bush Mill Rd Frankfort (45628) *(G-7004)*

Conveyor Solutions LLC..513 367-4845
6705 Dry Fork Rd Cleves (45002) *(G-4533)*

Conveyor Technologies Ltd...513 248-0663
501 Techne Center Dr Ste B Milford (45150) *(G-9931)*

Conviber Inc...330 723-6006
1066 Industrial Pkwy Medina (44256) *(G-9391)*

Conway Greene Co Inc..440 230-2627
17325 Parkside Dr North Royalton (44133) *(G-10758)*

Cookie Bouquet, Columbus *Also Called: Cookie Bouquets Inc (G-4847)*

Cookie Bouquets Inc...614 888-2171
6665 Huntley Rd Ste F Columbus (43229) *(G-4847)*

Cookie Cupboard, Cleveland *Also Called: Mid American Ventures Inc (G-4031)*

Cool Machines Inc...419 232-4871
740 Fox Rd Van Wert (45891) *(G-13529)*

Coolant Control, Inc., Cincinnati *Also Called: Great River Re Inc (G-2688)*

Coolbreeze Technologies LLC......................................440 748-1911
827 Walnut St Elyria (44035) *(G-6515)*

Coolseal USA, Perrysburg *Also Called: Brr Bear Ltd (G-11207)*

Cooper, Bowling Green *Also Called: Cooper-Standard Automotive Inc (G-1416)*

Cooper, Findlay *Also Called: Cooper Tire & Rubber Co LLC (G-6856)*

Cooper, Findlay *Also Called: Cooper Tire Vhcl Test Ctr Inc (G-6857)*

Cooper Enterprises Inc...419 347-5232
89 Curtis Dr Shelby (44875) *(G-11968)*

Cooper Farms, Oakwood *Also Called: Cooper Hatchery Inc (G-10897)*

Cooper Farms, Saint Henry *Also Called: V H Cooper & Co Inc (G-11726)*

Cooper Farms Inc (PA)...419 594-3325
22348 Road 140 Oakwood (45873) *(G-10896)*

Cooper Farms Cooked Meat, Van Wert *Also Called: Cooper Foods (G-13530)*

Cooper Farms Cooked Meats, Van Wert *Also Called: Cooper Hatchery Inc (G-13531)*

Cooper Foods..419 232-2440
6893 Us Route 127 Van Wert (45891) *(G-13530)*

Cooper Foods, Fort Recovery *Also Called: V H Cooper & Co Inc (G-6973)*

Cooper Hatchery Inc (PA)..419 594-3325
22348 Road 140 Oakwood (45873) *(G-10897)*

Cooper Hatchery Inc...419 238-4869
6793 Us Route 127 Van Wert (45891) *(G-13531)*

Cooper Lighting LLC..800 334-6871
Columbus (43218) *(G-4848)*

Cooper Lighting Solutions, Columbus *Also Called: Cooper Lighting LLC (G-4848)*

Cooper Tire & Rubber Co LLC (HQ)..............................419 423-1321
701 Lima Ave Findlay (45840) *(G-6856)*

Cooper Tire Vhcl Test Ctr Inc (DH)...............................419 423-1321
701 Lima Ave Findlay (45840) *(G-6857)*

Cooper Wiring Devices Inc..440 523-5000
1000 Eaton Blvd Cleveland (44122) *(G-3566)*

Cooper-Standard Automotive Inc................................419 352-3533
1175 N Main St Bowling Green (43402) *(G-1416)*

Cooper-Standard Automotive Inc................................740 342-3523
2378 State Route 345 Ne New Lexington (43764) *(G-10401)*

Cooper-Standard Holdings Inc....................................800 683-0676
1776 Tech Park Dr Ne Ste 221 New Philadelphia (44663) *(G-10438)*

Coopers Mill Inc...419 562-4215
1414 N Sandusky Ave Bucyrus (44820) *(G-1676)*

Coopersurgical Inc..203 601-5200
Cincinnati (45271) *(G-2516)*

Copeland Access + Inc..937 498-3802
1675 Campbell Rd Sidney (45365) *(G-12003)*

Copeland Corporation...937 498-3011
1675 W Campbell Rd Sidney (45365) *(G-12004)*

Copeland LP (HQ)..937 498-3011
1675 W Campbell Rd Sidney (45365) *(G-12005)*

Copeland LP...937 498-3011
756 Brooklyn Ave Sidney (45365) *(G-12006)*

Copeland LP...937 498-3587
1351 N Vandemark Rd Sidney (45365) *(G-12007)*

Copeland Scroll Compressors LP (DH).........................937 498-3066
1675 Campbell Rd Sidney (45365) *(G-12008)*

Copen Machine Inc...330 678-4598
501 Dodge St Kent (44240) *(G-8023)*

Coperion Food Equipment LLC (DH)............................937 492-4158
500 S Vandemark Rd Sidney (45365) *(G-12009)*

Coperion Process Solutions LLC.................................513 576-9200
30825 Aurora Rd # 150 Solon (44139) *(G-12098)*

Copier Resources Inc...614 268-1100
4800 Evanswood Dr Columbus (43229) *(G-4849)*

Copley Fire & Rescue Assn..330 666-6464
1540 S Cleveland Massillon Rd Copley (44321) *(G-5433)*

Copley Ohio Newspapers Inc (HQ)..............................585 598-0030
500 Market Ave S Canton (44702) *(G-1871)*

Copley Ohio Newspapers Inc.......................................330 364-5577
629 Wabash Ave Nw New Philadelphia (44663) *(G-10439)*

Copley Township Fire Dept, Copley *Also Called: Copley Fire & Rescue Assn (G-5433)*

Copperloy, Twinsburg *Also Called: Jh Industries Inc (G-13321)*

Copy King Inc..216 861-3377
3333 Chester Ave Cleveland (44114) *(G-3567)*

(G-0000) Company's Geographic Section entry number

Copy Print, Tallmadge *Also Called: Rhoads Print Center Inc (G-12748)*

Corbett R Caudill Chipping Inc..................................... 740 596-5984
35887 State Route 324 Hamden (45634) *(G-7461)*

Cordier Group Holdings Inc.. 330 477-4511
4575 Southway St Sw Canton (44706) *(G-1872)*

Core Composites Cincinnati LLC.................................. 513 724-6111
4174 Half Acre Rd Batavia (45103) *(G-859)*

Core Manufacturing, Mentor *Also Called: Core Manufacturing LLC (G-9505)*

Core Manufacturing LLC.. 440 946-8002
8878 East Ave Mentor (44060) *(G-9505)*

Core Molding Technologies Inc (PA).............................614 870-5000
800 Manor Park Dr Columbus (43228) *(G-4850)*

Core Optix Inc... 855 267-3678
821 Melbourne St Cincinnati (45229) *(G-2517)*

Core Technology Inc.. 440 934-9935
1260 Moore Rd Ste E Avon (44011) *(G-721)*

Core-Tech Enterprises LLC... 440 946-8324
7850 Enterprise Dr Mentor (44060) *(G-9506)*

Corhart Refractories, Stow *Also Called: Saint-Gobain Ceramics Plas Inc (G-12457)*

Corner Alley LLC (PA).. 216 298-4070
402 Euclid Ave Cleveland (44114) *(G-3568)*

Cornerstone Bldg Brands Inc..................................... 937 584-3300
2400 Yankee Rd Middletown (45044) *(G-9850)*

Cornerstone Brands Inc.. 866 668-5962
5568 W Chester Rd West Chester (45069) *(G-13975)*

Cornerstone Manufacturing Inc................................... 937 456-5930
861 Us Route 35 Eaton (45320) *(G-6452)*

Cornerstone Wauseon Inc.. 419 337-0940
995 Enterprise Ave Wauseon (43567) *(G-13847)*

Cornhole Worldwide LLC.. 513 324-2777
5337 Hamilton Cleves Rd Cleves (45002) *(G-4534)*

Cornwell Quality Tools, Mogadore *Also Called: Cornwell Quality Tools Company (G-10071)*

CORNWELL QUALITY TOOLS, Van Wert *Also Called: Cqt Kennedy LLC (G-13532)*

Cornwell Quality Tools, Wadsworth *Also Called: The Cornwell Quality Tools Company (G-13674)*

Cornwell Quality Tools Company.................................. 330 628-2627
200 N Cleveland Ave Mogadore (44260) *(G-10071)*

Coronado Steel Co... 330 744-1143
2360 Funston Dr Youngstown (44510) *(G-14840)*

Corpad Company Inc.. 419 522-7818
555 Park Ave E Mansfield (44905) *(G-8777)*

Corporate Cnsulting Svc Instrs
1868 Akron Peninsula Rd Akron (44313) *(G-106)*

Corporate Dcment Solutions Inc (PA)............................513 595-8200
11120 Ashburn Rd Cincinnati (45240) *(G-2518)*

Corporate Elevator LLC... 614 288-1847
35 E Gav St Ste 218 Columbus (43215) *(G-4851)*

Corporate Raw Materials, Solon *Also Called: Swagelok Company (G-12187)*

Corrchoice, Delaware *Also Called: Greif Packaging LLC (G-6152)*

Corrchoice Cincinnati... 330 833-2884
777 3rd St Nw Massillon (44647) *(G-9181)*

Corrosion Cntrl/Cthdic Prtctio, Medina *Also Called: Corrpro Companies Inc (G-9392)*

Corrotec Inc.. 937 325-3585
1125 W North St Springfield (45504) *(G-12294)*

Corrpro Companies Inc... 770 761-5400
820 Lafayette Rd Medina (44256) *(G-9392)*

Corrpro Companies Inc... 330 725-6681
820 Lafayette Rd Medina (44256) *(G-9393)*

Corrpro Companies Intl Inc.. 330 723-5082
820 Lafayette Rd Medina (44256) *(G-9394)*

Corrpro Waterworks, Medina *Also Called: Corrpro Companies Inc (G-9393)*

Corrugated Chemicals, Cincinnati *Also Called: Corrugated Chemicals Inc (G-2519)*

Corrugated Chemicals Inc.. 513 561-7773
3865 Virginia Ave Cincinnati (45227) *(G-2519)*

Cors Products, Canton *Also Called: Canton OH Rubber Speclty Prods (G-1857)*

Cortape Inc... 330 929-6700
60 Marc Dr Cuyahoga Falls (44223) *(G-5535)*

Cortest, Willoughby *Also Called: Cortest Inc (G-14442)*

Cortest Inc (PA)... 440 942-1235
38322 Apollo Pkwy Willoughby (44094) *(G-14442)*

Cortina Leathers, Conneaut *Also Called: Leather Resource of America Inc (G-5407)*

Corvac Composites LLC.. 248 807-0969
1025 N Washington St Greenfield (45123) *(G-7326)*

COS Blueprint Inc... 330 376-0022
590 N Main St Akron (44310) *(G-107)*

Coshocton Orthopedic Center, Coshocton *Also Called: Francisco Jaume (G-5455)*

Coshocton Pallet & Door Co, Coshocton *Also Called: Thomas J Weaver Inc (G-5474)*

Cosmo, Cleveland *Also Called: Cosmo Plastics Company (G-3569)*

Cosmo Plastics Co, Wilmot *Also Called: Cosmo Plastics Company (G-14593)*

Cosmo Plastics Company (HQ).................................... 440 498-7500
30201 Aurora Rd Cleveland (44139) *(G-3569)*

Cosmo Plastics Company.. 330 359-5429
211 Winesburg St Wilmot (44689) *(G-14593)*

Costa Machine, Akron *Also Called: Charles Costa Inc (G-97)*

Costume Specialists Inc.. 614 464-2115
1801 Lone Eagle St Columbus (43228) *(G-4852)*

Cota International Inc... 937 526-5520
67 Industrial Pkwy Versailles (45380) *(G-13593)*

Cotsworks Inc (PA)... 440 446-8800
749 Miner Rd Highland Heights (44143) *(G-7656)*

Cott Systems Inc.. 614 847-4405
2800 Corporate Exchange Dr Ste 300 Columbus (43231) *(G-4853)*

Couch Business Development Inc................................. 937 253-1099
32 Bates St Dayton (45402) *(G-5711)*

Counter Concepts Inc.. 330 848-4848
124 Townes End Dr Wadsworth (44281) *(G-13632)*

Counter-Advice Inc... 937 291-1600
7002 State Route 123 Franklin (45005) *(G-7014)*

Countertops Helmart, Cincinnati *Also Called: Helmart Company Inc (G-2715)*

Country CLB Rtrment Ctr IV LLC................................. 740 676-2300
55801 Conno Mara Dr Bellaire (43906) *(G-1086)*

Country Lane Custom Buildings.................................. 740 485-8481
21318 Pealer Mill Rd Danville (43014) *(G-5598)*

Country Manufacturing Inc.. 740 694-9926
333 Salem Ave Ext Fredericktown (43019) *(G-7075)*

Country Parlour Ice Cream Co.................................... 440 237-4040
12905 York Delta Dr Ste C Cleveland (44133) *(G-3570)*

Country Pure Foods Inc (PA)..................................... 330 753-2293
222 S Main St Ste 401 Akron (44308) *(G-108)*

Country Sales & Service LLC..................................... 330 683-2500
255 Tracy Bridge Rd Orrville (44667) *(G-10978)*

Countryside Construction, Danville *Also Called: Country Lane Custom Buildings (G-5598)*

County Classifieds.. 937 592-8847
117 E Patterson Ave Bellefontaine (43311) *(G-1102)*

County Line, Bryan *Also Called: Bryan Publishing Company (G-1634)*

County of Holmes.. 330 674-2083
75 E Clinton St Ste 112 Millersburg (44654) *(G-9978)*

County of Lake.. 440 428-1794
7815 Cashen Rd Madison (44057) *(G-8728)*

County of Lake.. 440 269-2193
2100 Joseph Lloyd Pkwy Willoughby (44094) *(G-14443)*

Countyline Co-Op Inc (PA)....................................... 419 287-3241
425 E Front St Pemberville (43450) *(G-11174)*

Courier, The, Sandusky *Also Called: Ogden News Publishing Ohio Inc (G-11861)*

Course Technology, Mason *Also Called: Cengage Learning Inc (G-9079)*

Courthouse Manufacturing LLC................................... 740 335-2727
1730 Washington Avenue, Solar Lane Washington Court Hou (43160) *(G-13820)*

Covap Inc... 513 793-1855
10829 Millington Ct Ste 1 Blue Ash (45242) *(G-1264)*

Coventry Steel Services Inc....................................... 216 883-4477
4200 E 71st St Ste 1 Cleveland (44105) *(G-3571)*

Covert, Galion *Also Called: Covert Manufacturing Inc (G-7185)*

Covert Manufacturing Inc.. 419 468-1761
303 E Parson St Galion (44833) *(G-7184)*

Covert Manufacturing Inc (PA)................................... 419 468-1761
328 S East St Galion (44833) *(G-7185)*

Covestro LLC.. 740 929-2015
1111 O Neill Dr Hebron (43025) *(G-7611)*

Covia Holdings LLC (PA).. 800 243-9004
3 Summit Park Dr Ste 700 Independence (44131) *(G-7894)*

Covia Solutions LLC (HQ)..................................440 214-3200
  3 Summit Park Dr Ste 700 Independence (44131) *(G-7895)*

Covidien, Cincinnati *Also Called: Covidien Holding Inc (G-2520)*

Covidien Holding Inc..513 948-7219
  2111 E Galbraith Rd Cincinnati (45237) *(G-2520)*

COW Industries Inc (PA)....................................614 443-6537
  1875 Progress Ave Columbus (43207) *(G-4854)*

Cowles Industrial Tool, Austintown *Also Called: Cowles Industrial Tool Co LLC (G-704)*

Cowles Industrial Tool Co LLC............................330 799-9100
  185 N Four Mile Run Rd Austintown (44515) *(G-704)*

Cox Interior Inc...614 473-9169
  2220 Citygate Dr Columbus (43219) *(G-4855)*

Cox Interior Inc...270 789-3129
  4080 Webster Ave Norwood (45212) *(G-10867)*

Cox Media Group, Dayton *Also Called: Ohio Newspapers Inc (G-5926)*

Cox Newspapers LLC
  129 S Main St Franklin (45005) *(G-7015)*

Cox Newspapers LLC..937 866-3331
  230 S 2nd St Miamisburg (45342) *(G-9684)*

Cox Newspapers LLC..513 523-4139
  30 W Park Pl Uppr Uppr Oxford (45056) *(G-11062)*

Cox Ohio Publishing...937 743-6700
  5000 Commerce Center Dr Franklin (45005) *(G-7016)*

Cox Painting, Wilmington *Also Called: Cox Printing Company (G-14576)*

Cox Printing Company..937 382-2312
  1087 Wayne Rd Wilmington (45177) *(G-14576)*

Cox Publishing Hq...937 225-2000
  1611 S Main St Dayton (45409) *(G-5712)*

Cox Wood Product Inc.......................................740 372-4735
  5715 State Route 348 Otway (45657) *(G-11059)*

Cox's Interior Supply, Columbus *Also Called: Cox Interior Inc (G-4855)*

Coyne Finishing, Mount Vernon *Also Called: Coyne Graphic Finishing Inc (G-10241)*

Coyne Graphic Finishing Inc...............................740 397-6232
  1301 Newark Rd Mount Vernon (43050) *(G-10241)*

Cozmyk Enterprises Inc......................................614 231-1370
  3757 Courtright Ct Columbus (43227) *(G-4856)*

CP Chemicals Group LP.....................................440 833-3000
  28960 Lakeland Blvd Wickliffe (44092) *(G-14372)*

CP Trading Group, Wickliffe *Also Called: CP Chemicals Group LP (G-14372)*

CPC Holding Inc..216 383-3932
  2926 Chester Ave Cleveland (44114) *(G-3572)*

Cpg - Ohio LLC (HQ)..513 825-4800
  470 Northland Blvd Cincinnati (45240) *(G-2521)*

Cpg International LLC...937 655-8766
  894 Prairie Rd Wilmington (45177) *(G-14577)*

Cpg Printing & Graphics, Toledo *Also Called: Culaine Inc (G-12934)*

CPI, Holland *Also Called: Creative Products Inc (G-7752)*

CPI Group Limited...216 525-0046
  13858 Tinkers Creek Rd Cleveland (44125) *(G-3573)*

CPI Industrial Co...614 445-0800
  299 Yankeetown St Mount Sterling (43143) *(G-10227)*

CPM Tool Co LLC..937 258-1176
  1865 Radio Rd Dayton (45431) *(G-5606)*

Cpmm Services Group Inc..................................614 447-0165
  3785 Indianola Ave Columbus (43214) *(G-4857)*

Cpp, Cleveland *Also Called: Consoldted Precision Pdts Corp (G-3560)*

Cpp Cleveland, Eastlake *Also Called: Consoldted Precision Pdts Corp (G-6421)*

Cpp Group Holdings LLC (PA)............................216 453-4800
  1621 Euclid Ave Ste 1850 Cleveland (44115) *(G-3574)*

Cpp-Cleveland Inc...440 953-0053
  34000 Lakeland Blvd Eastlake (44095) *(G-6422)*

Cpp-Cleveland Inc (HQ)......................................216 453-4800
  26855 Bluestone Blvd Euclid (44132) *(G-6646)*

Cpp-Eastlake, Eastlake *Also Called: Cpp-Cleveland Inc (G-6422)*

Cpp-Euclid, Euclid *Also Called: Cpp-Cleveland Inc (G-6646)*

Cql Mfg LLC...330 482-5846
  187 Georgetown Rd Salem (44460) *(G-11773)*

Cqt Kennedy LLC..419 238-2442
  1260 Industrial Dr Van Wert (45891) *(G-13532)*

Cr Holding Inc...513 860-5039
  9100 Centre Pointe Dr Ste 200 West Chester (45069) *(G-13976)*

Crack Corn Ltd..440 467-0108
  7993 Hills And Dales Rd Ne Massillon (44646) *(G-9182)*

Craco Embroidery Inc...513 563-6999
  37 Techview Dr Cincinnati (45215) *(G-2522)*

Crafco Inc..330 270-3034
  912 Salt Springs Rd Youngstown (44509) *(G-14841)*

Crafted Surface and Stone LLC..........................440 658-3799
  16625 Wren Rd Chagrin Falls (44023) *(G-2157)*

Craftwood, Mount Orab *Also Called: Cindoco Wood Products Co (G-10216)*

Craig Saylor..740 352-8363
  53020 State Route 124 Portland (45770) *(G-11462)*

Crain Communications Inc..................................216 522-1383
  700 W Saint Clair Ave Ste 310 Cleveland (44113) *(G-3575)*

Crain Communications Inc..................................330 836-9180
  2291 Riverfront Pkwy Ste 1000 Cuyahoga Falls (44221) *(G-5536)*

Crain's Cleveland Business, Cleveland *Also Called: Crain Communications Inc (G-3575)*

Cramers Inc..330 477-4571
  4944 Southway St Sw Canton (44706) *(G-1873)*

Crane 1 Services Inc (HQ)..................................937 704-9900
  9075 Centre Pointe Dr Ste 130 West Chester (45069) *(G-13977)*

Crane Blending Center.......................................614 542-1199
  2141 Fairwood Ave Columbus (43207) *(G-4858)*

Crane Carrier Company LLC (HQ)........................918 286-2889
  1951 Reiser Ave Se New Philadelphia (44663) *(G-10440)*

Crane Carrier Holdings LLC................................918 286-2889
  1951 Reiser Ave Se New Philadelphia (44663) *(G-10441)*

Crane Chempharma & Energy, Cincinnati *Also Called: Xomox Corporation (G-3237)*

Crane Consumables Inc.....................................513 539-9980
  155 Wright Dr Middletown (45044) *(G-9851)*

Crane Plumbing LLC..419 522-4211
  41 Cairns Rd Mansfield (44903) *(G-8778)*

Crane Pro Services..937 525-5555
  4401 Gateway Blvd Springfield (45502) *(G-12295)*

Crane Pro Services, Broadview Heights *Also Called: Konecranes Inc (G-1504)*

Crane Pro Services, Toledo *Also Called: Konecranes Inc (G-13021)*

Crane Pro Services, West Chester *Also Called: Konecranes Inc (G-14130)*

Crane Pumps & Systems Inc...............................937 778-8947
  1950 Covington Ave Piqua (45356) *(G-11339)*

Crane Pumps & Systems Inc...............................937 773-2442
  420 3rd St Piqua (45356) *(G-11340)*

Crane Pumps & Systems LLC (HQ)......................937 773-2442
  420 3rd St Piqua (45356) *(G-11341)*

Crane Pumps & Systems, Inc., Piqua *Also Called: Crane Pumps & Systems Inc (G-11339)*

Crane Training Usa Inc.......................................513 755-2177
  7908 Cincinnati Dayton Rd Ste H West Chester (45069) *(G-13978)*

Crane Xomox, Blue Ash *Also Called: Xomox Corporation (G-1355)*

Cranial Technologies Inc.....................................844 447-5894
  4030 Smith Rd Ste 105 Cincinnati (45209) *(G-2523)*

Crase Communications Inc..................................419 468-1173
  120 Harding Way E Ste 104 Galion (44833) *(G-7186)*

Crawford Ae LLC...330 794-9770
  735 Glaser Pkwy Akron (44306) *(G-109)*

Crawford Computer Center, Solon *Also Called: Swagelok Company (G-12190)*

Crawford Products Inc..614 890-1822
  3637 Corporate Dr Columbus (43231) *(G-4859)*

Crawford United, Cleveland *Also Called: Crawford United Corporation (G-3576)*

Crawford United Corporation (PA)........................216 243-2614
  10514 Dupont Ave Ste 200 Cleveland (44108) *(G-3576)*

Crayex Corporation (PA)......................................937 773-7000
  1747 Commerce Dr Piqua (45356) *(G-11342)*

Crazeweld LLC...419 210-3668
  1563 Johnson Rd Norwalk (44857) *(G-10833)*

Crazy Monkey Baking Inc....................................419 903-0403
  1191 Commerce Pkwy Ashland (44805) *(G-531)*

Crazy Richards, Plain City *Also Called: Krema Group Inc (G-11413)*

Creamer Metal Products Inc (PA).........................740 852-1752
  77 S Madison Rd London (43140) *(G-8534)*

Creative Cabinets Ltd...740 689-0603
  1807 Snoke Rd Sw Lancaster (43130) *(G-8190)*

Creative Countertops, Englewood *Also Called: Creative Countertops Ohio Inc (G-6610)*

Creative Countertops Ohio Inc......................... 937 540-9450
477 E Wenger Rd Englewood (45322) *(G-6610)*

Creative Dcument Solutions LLC...................... 740 389-4252
1629 Marion Waldo Rd Marion (43302) *(G-8968)*

Creative Edge Cbnets Wdwkg LLC.................... 419 453-3416
188 Nw Canal St Ottoville (45876) *(G-11053)*

Creative Edge Group, Canton *Also Called: Superior Dairy Inc (G-2021)*

Creative Fab & Welding LLC............................. 937 780-5000
9691 Stafford Rd Leesburg (45135) *(G-8298)*

Creative Fabrication Ltd................................... 740 262-5789
20110 Predmore Rd Richwood (43344) *(G-11614)*

Creative Foam Dayton Mold.............................. 937 279-9987
3337 N Dixie Dr Dayton (45414) *(G-5713)*

Creative Impressions Inc................................. 937 435-5296
4611 Gateway Cir Dayton (45440) *(G-5714)*

Creative Liquid Coatings Inc............................ 419 485-1110
1701 Magda Dr Montpelier (43543) *(G-10127)*

Creative Microsystems Inc............................... 937 836-4499
52 Hillside Ct Englewood (45322) *(G-6611)*

Creative Millwork Ohio Inc............................... 440 992-3566
1801 W 47th St Ashtabula (44004) *(G-588)*

Creative Mold and Machine Inc......................... 440 338-5146
10385 Kinsman Rd Newbury (44065) *(G-10548)*

Creative Packaging LLC.................................. 740 452-8497
1781 Kemper Ct Zanesville (43701) *(G-15009)*

Creative Plastic Concepts LLC (HQ).................. 419 927-9588
206 S Griffith St Sycamore (44882) *(G-12699)*

Creative Plastics Intl...................................... 937 596-6769
18163 Snider Rd Jackson Center (45334) *(G-7959)*

Creative Processing Inc.................................. 440 834-4070
17540 Rapids Rd Mantua (44255) *(G-8868)*

Creative Products Inc..................................... 419 866-5501
1430 Kieswetter Rd Holland (43528) *(G-7752)*

Creative Tool & Die LLC.................................. 614 836-0080
244 Main St Groveport (43125) *(G-7430)*

Creativity For Kids, Cleveland *Also Called: AW Faber-Castell Usa Inc (G-3396)*

Cree Logistics LLC.. 513 978-1112
7439 Wooster Pike Cincinnati (45227) *(G-2524)*

Creighton Sports Center Inc (PA)......................740 865-2521
205 Broadway Ave New Matamoras (45767) *(G-10423)*

Cres Cor, Mentor *Also Called: Crescent Metal Products Inc (G-9507)*

Crescent & Sprague....................................... 740 373-2331
1100 Greene St Marietta (45750) *(G-8912)*

Crescent Blades, Fremont *Also Called: Crescent Manufacturing Company (G-7099)*

Crescent Manufacturing Company (PA)............... 419 332-6484
1310 Majestic Dr Fremont (43420) *(G-7099)*

Crescent Metal Products Inc (PA)..................... 440 350-1100
5925 Heisley Rd Mentor (44060) *(G-9507)*

Crescent Services LLC.................................... 405 603-1200
11137 E Pike Rd Cambridge (43725) *(G-1740)*

Cresset Chemical Co Inc (PA).......................... 419 669-2041
13255 Main St Weston (43569) *(G-14347)*

Cresset Chemical Co Inc................................. 419 669-2041
13490 Silver St Weston (43569) *(G-14348)*

Crest Aluminum Products, Mentor *Also Called: Crest Products Inc (G-9508)*

Crest Bending Inc.. 419 492-2108
108 John St New Washington (44854) *(G-10478)*

Crest Craft Co.. 513 271-4858
4460 Lake Forest Dr Ste 232 Cincinnati (45242) *(G-2525)*

Crest Graphics Inc... 513 271-2200
9933 Alliance Rd Ste 1 Blue Ash (45242) *(G-1265)*

Crest Products Inc... 440 942-5770
8287 Tyler Blvd Mentor (44060) *(G-9508)*

Crestar Crusts Inc... 740 335-4813
1104 Clinton Ave Wshngtn Ct Hs (43160) *(G-14736)*

Crestar Foods, Wshngtn Ct Hs *Also Called: Crestar Crusts Inc (G-14736)*

Crg Worldwide, Columbus *Also Called: Custom Retail Group LLC (G-4863)*

Crh US... 216 642-3920
6925 Granger Rd Independence (44131) *(G-7896)*

Cri, Fairfield *Also Called: Color Resolutions International LLC (G-6724)*

Cri Digital, Columbus *Also Called: Copier Resources Inc (G-4849)*

Cricket, Blacklick *Also Called: Wireless Retail LLC (G-1231)*

Crimson Cup Inc (PA)......................................614 252-3335
700 Alum Creek Dr Ste 400 Columbus (43205) *(G-4860)*

Crimson Cup Coffee Roasters, Columbus *Also Called: Crimson Cup Inc (G-4860)*

Crimson Gate Consulting Co (PA)...................... 614 805-0897
6457 Reflections Dr S200 Dublin (43017) *(G-6292)*

Crispie Creme Chillicothe Inc........................... 740 774-3770
47 N Bridge St Chillicothe (45601) *(G-2249)*

Criswell Furniture LLC.................................... 330 695-2082
8139 Criswell Rd Fredericksburg (44627) *(G-7062)*

Criterion Instrument, Brookpark *Also Called: Criterion Tool & Die Inc (G-1545)*

Criterion Tool & Die Inc.................................. 216 267-1733
5349 W 161st St Brookpark (44142) *(G-1545)*

Critical Ctrl Enrgy Svcs Inc.............................. 330 539-4267
1688 Shannon Rd Girard (44420) *(G-7269)*

Crmd LLC.. 440 225-7179
1190 N High St Columbus (43201) *(G-4861)*

Croft & Son Mfg Inc....................................... 740 859-2200
509 Highland Ave Tiltonsville (43963) *(G-12809)*

Crohm LLC.. 513 921-9400
1640 Lionel Ave Cincinnati (45214) *(G-2526)*

Crook Miller Company, Stow *Also Called: Baker McMillen Co (G-12421)*

Cropking Incorporated..................................... 330 302-4203
134 West Dr Lodi (44254) *(G-8500)*

Crossbridge Mktg & Media Inc.......................... 330 682-5066
1645 N Main St Orrville (44667) *(G-10979)*

Crosscreek Pallet Co...................................... 440 632-1940
14530 Madison Rd Middlefield (44062) *(G-9788)*

Crow Works LLC... 888 811-2769
9595 Us-62 Killbuck (44637) *(G-8132)*

Crowe Manufacturing Services.......................... 800 831-1893
2731 Walnut Ridge Dr Troy (45373) *(G-13207)*

Crowes Cabinets Inc...................................... 330 729-9911
590 E Western Reserve Rd Bldg 8 Youngstown (44514) *(G-14842)*

Crown Battery, Fremont *Also Called: Crown Battery Manufacturing Co (G-7100)*

Crown Battery Manufacturing Co (PA)................. 419 334-7181
1445 Majestic Dr Fremont (43420) *(G-7100)*

Crown Battery Manufacturing Co........................ 330 425-3308
4750 Oak Harbor Rd Fremont (43420) *(G-7101)*

Crown Closures Machinery................................ 740 681-6593
1765 W Fair Ave Lancaster (43130) *(G-8191)*

Crown Cork & Seal Usa Inc.............................. 937 299-2027
5005 Springboro Pike Dayton (45439) *(G-5715)*

Crown Cork & Seal Usa Inc.............................. 740 681-6593
1765 W Fair Ave Lancaster (43130) *(G-8192)*

Crown Cork & Seal Usa Inc.............................. 740 681-3000
940 Mill Park Dr Lancaster (43130) *(G-8193)*

Crown Cork & Seal Usa Inc.............................. 330 833-1011
700 16th St Se Massillon (44646) *(G-9183)*

Crown Cork & Seal Usa Inc.............................. 419 727-8201
5201 Enterprise Blvd Toledo (43612) *(G-12933)*

Crown Credit Company.................................... 419 629-2311
44 S Washington St New Bremen (45869) *(G-10357)*

Crown Div of Allen Gr..................................... 330 263-4919
1654 Old Mansfield Rd Wooster (44691) *(G-14632)*

Crown Electric Engrg & Mfg LLC....................... 513 539-7394
175 Edison Dr Middletown (45044) *(G-9852)*

Crown Equipment Corporation........................... 419 586-1100
410 Grand Lake Rd Celina (45822) *(G-2102)*

Crown Equipment Corporation........................... 513 874-2600
10685 Medallion Dr Cincinnati (45241) *(G-2527)*

Crown Equipment Corporation........................... 937 295-4062
300 Tower Dr Fort Loramie (45845) *(G-6944)*

Crown Equipment Corporation........................... 614 274-7700
2100 Southwest Blvd Grove City (43123) *(G-7378)*

Crown Equipment Corporation (PA).................... 419 629-2311
44 S Washington St New Bremen (45869) *(G-10358)*

Crown Equipment Corporation........................... 419 629-2311
624 W Monroe St New Bremen (45869) *(G-10359)*

Crown Equipment Corporation........................... 419 629-2311
510 W Monroe St New Bremen (45869) *(G-10360)*

Crown Equipment Corporation........................937 454-7545
　750 Center Dr Vandalia (45377) *(G-13552)*

Crown Group Co (HQ)...................................586 575-9800
　1340 Neubrecht Rd Lima (45801) *(G-8397)*

Crown Lift Trucks, Celina *Also Called: Crown Equipment Corporation (G-2102)*

Crown Lift Trucks, Cincinnati *Also Called: Crown Equipment Corporation (G-2527)*

Crown Lift Trucks, Fort Loramie *Also Called: Crown Equipment Corporation (G-6944)*

Crown Lift Trucks, Grove City *Also Called: Crown Equipment Corporation (G-7378)*

Crown Lift Trucks, New Bremen *Also Called: Crown Equipment Corporation (G-10358)*

Crown Lift Trucks, New Bremen *Also Called: Crown Equipment Corporation (G-10359)*

Crown Lift Trucks, New Bremen *Also Called: Crown Equipment Corporation (G-10360)*

Crown Lift Trucks, Vandalia *Also Called: Crown Equipment Corporation (G-13552)*

Crown Mats & Mating, Fremont *Also Called: Ludlow Composites Corporation (G-7122)*

Crown Plastics Co LLC.................................513 367-0238
　116 May Dr Harrison (45030) *(G-7548)*

Crown Solutions, Vandalia *Also Called: Crown Solutions Co LLC (G-13553)*

Crown Solutions Co LLC...............................937 890-4075
　913 Industrial Park Dr Vandalia (45377) *(G-13553)*

Crowne Group LLC (PA)................................216 589-0198
　127 Public Sq Ste 5110 Cleveland (44114) *(G-3577)*

Crowning Food Company...............................937 323-4699
　1966 Commerce Cir Springfield (45504) *(G-12296)*

Crownme Coil Care LLC................................937 797-2070
　4910 Denlinger Rd Trotwood (45426) *(G-13195)*

Crownover Lumber Company Inc (PA)...............740 596-5229
　501 Fairview Ave Mc Arthur (45651) *(G-9349)*

Cruisin Times Magazine................................440 331-4615
　20545 Center Ridge Rd Ste LI40 Rocky River (44116) *(G-11633)*

Crum Manufacturing Inc...............................419 878-9779
　1265 Waterville Monclova Rd Waterville (43566) *(G-13832)*

Crumbs Inc...740 592-3803
　94 Columbus Rd Athens (45701) *(G-637)*

Crumbs Bakery, Athens *Also Called: Crumbs Inc (G-637)*

Crushproof Tubing Co (PA)............................419 293-2111
　100 North St Mc Comb (45858) *(G-9352)*

Cryogenic Equipment & Svcs Inc....................513 761-4200
　4583 Brate Dr Hamilton (45011) *(G-7481)*

Cryogenic Technical Services, Plain City *Also Called: Drivetrain USA Inc (G-11405)*

Cryovac LLC...513 771-7770
　7410 Union Centre Blvd West Chester (45014) *(G-13979)*

Crystal Water Company, Dayton *Also Called: Rambasek Realty Inc (G-5974)*

Crystalite, Lewis Center *Also Called: Abrasive Technology Lapidary (G-8318)*

Csafe, Monroe *Also Called: Csafe LLC (G-10100)*

Csafe LLC..513 360-7189
　675 Gateway Blvd Monroe (45050) *(G-10100)*

Csafe Passive Solutions, Monroe *Also Called: Softbox Systems Inc (G-10116)*

CSC Worldwide, Columbus *Also Called: The Columbus Show Case Company (G-5318)*

Csg Software...614 986-2600
　700 Taylor Ave Columbus (43219) *(G-4862)*

Csi Infusion Services, Hudson *Also Called: Clinical Specialties Inc (G-7840)*

CSM Concepts LLC.....................................330 483-1320
　6450 Grafton Rd Valley City (44280) *(G-13493)*

CSP Carey, Carey *Also Called: Teijin Automotive Tech Inc (G-2063)*

CSP Group Inc...513 984-9500
　7141 E Kemper Rd Cincinnati (45249) *(G-2528)*

CSP North Baltimore, North Baltimore *Also Called: Teijin Automotive Tech Inc (G-10618)*

CSP Van Wert, Van Wert *Also Called: Teijin Automotive Tech Inc (G-13546)*

CSS Publishing Company..............................419 227-1818
　5450 N Dixie Hwy Lima (45807) *(G-8398)*

Csw Inc...413 589-1311
　3545 Silica Rd Unit E Sylvania (43560) *(G-12703)*

CT Specialty Polymers Ltd............................440 632-9311
　14875 Bonner Dr Middlefield (44062) *(G-9789)*

Ctc / Roach Studios, Columbus *Also Called: Roach Studios LLC (G-5233)*

Ctc Plastics (HQ).......................................937 228-9184
　401 N Keowee St Dayton (45404) *(G-5716)*

Ctek Tool & Machine Company.......................513 742-0423
　11310 Southland Rd Cincinnati (45240) *(G-2529)*

Ctg, Miamisburg *Also Called: Certified Tool & Grinding Inc (G-9680)*

Ctl Analyzers, Shaker Heights *Also Called: Cellular Technology Limited (G-11928)*

Ctl Analyzers LLC (PA).................................216 791-5084
　20521 Chagrin Blvd Ste 200 Shaker Heights (44122) *(G-11929)*

Ctl-Aerospace Inc (PA)................................513 874-7900
　5616 Spellmire Dr Cincinnati (45246) *(G-2530)*

Ctl-Aerospace Inc......................................513 874-7900
　9970 International Blvd West Chester (45246) *(G-14112)*

Ctm Integration Incorporated........................330 332-1800
　1318 Quaker Cir Salem (44460) *(G-11774)*

Ctm Labeling Systems.................................330 332-1800
　1318 Quaker Cir Salem (44460) *(G-11775)*

CTS, Cincinnati *Also Called: Cincinnati Thermal Spray Inc (G-2488)*

CTS National Corporation.............................216 566-2000
　101 W Prospect Ave Ste 1020 Cleveland (44115) *(G-3578)*

Cub Cadet Corporation Sales........................330 273-4550
　614 Liverpool Dr Valley City (44280) *(G-13494)*

Cubbison Company (PA)...............................330 793-2481
　380 Victoria Rd Youngstown (44515) *(G-14843)*

Culaine Inc...419 345-4984
　1036 W Laskey Rd Toledo (43612) *(G-12934)*

Culinary Standards, Blue Ash *Also Called: Rsw Distributors LLC (G-1328)*

Culligan, Fairfield *Also Called: Waterco of The Central States (G-6791)*

Culligan, Zanesville *Also Called: US Water Company LLC (G-15053)*

Cultured Marble Inc....................................330 549-2282
　213 N Main St Poland (44514) *(G-11435)*

Cumberland Limestone LLC...........................740 638-3942
　53681 Spencer Rd Cumberland (43732) *(G-5516)*

Cummins, Blue Ash *Also Called: Cummins - Allison Corp (G-1266)*

Cummins, Cleveland *Also Called: Cummins - Allison Corp (G-3579)*

Cummins - Allison Corp................................513 469-2924
　11256 Cornell Park Dr Blue Ash (45242) *(G-1266)*

Cummins - Allison Corp................................440 824-5050
　6777 Engle Rd Ste H Cleveland (44130) *(G-3579)*

Cummins Filtration Inc
　2150 Industrial Dr Findlay (45840) *(G-6858)*

Cummins Inc...614 604-6004
　2297 Southwest Blvd Ste K Grove City (43123) *(G-7379)*

Cummins Inc...614 771-1000
　4000 Lyman Dr Hilliard (43026) *(G-7679)*

Cupboard Distributing, Urbana *Also Called: Chris Haughey (G-13458)*

Curless Printing Company.............................937 783-2403
　202 E Main St Unit 1 Blanchester (45107) *(G-1235)*

Curlys Custom Meats Inc..............................937 596-6518
　315 East St Jackson Center (45334) *(G-7960)*

Current Inc...330 392-5151
　455 N River Rd Nw Warren (44483) *(G-13756)*

Current Elec & Enrgy Solutions......................513 575-4600
　1527 State Route 28 Loveland (45140) *(G-8623)*

Current Electrical & Lighting, Loveland *Also Called: Current Elec & Enrgy Solutions (G-8623)*

Current Lighting Solutions LLC.......................216 266-4416
　1099 Ivanhoe Rd Cleveland (44110) *(G-3580)*

Current Lighting Solutions LLC (PA).................216 462-4700
　6085 Parkland Blvd Cleveland (44124) *(G-3581)*

Currier Richard & James..............................440 988-4132
　540 Mcintosh Ln Amherst (44001) *(G-445)*

Curtis Hilbruner..330 947-3527
　1315 Bank St Atwater (44201) *(G-658)*

Curtis Industires.......................................216 430-5759
　1301 E 9th St Ste 700 Cleveland (44114) *(G-3582)*

Curtis Steel & Supply Inc.............................330 376-7141
　1210 Curtis St Akron (44301) *(G-110)*

Curtiss-Wrght C5isr Data Slton, Fairborn *Also Called: Curtiss-Wright Ds Inc (G-6689)*

Curtiss-Wright Ds Inc..................................937 252-5601
　2600 Paramount Pl Ste 200 Fairborn (45324) *(G-6689)*

Curtiss-Wright Flow Ctrl Corp.......................440 838-7690
　10195 Brecksville Rd Brecksville (44141) *(G-1461)*

Curtiss-Wright Flow Ctrl Corp.......................513 528-7900
　4600 E Tech Dr Cincinnati (45245) *(G-2300)*

Curtiss-Wright Flow Ctrl Corp.......................216 267-3200
　18001 Sheldon Rd Cleveland (44130) *(G-3583)*

2025 Harris Ohio
Industrial Directory

(G-0000) Company's Geographic Section entry number

Curtiss-Wright Surfc Tech LLC..................... 330 425-1490
  1652 Highland Rd Twinsburg (44087) *(G-13290)*

Curv Imaging, Westerville Also Called: Curv Imaging LLC *(G-14251)*

Curv Imaging LLC..................................... 614 890-2878
  841 Green Crest Dr Westerville (43081) *(G-14251)*

Cushman Foundry Div, Cincinnati Also Called: Jrm 2 Company *(G-2774)*

Custar Stone Co.. 419 669-4327
  9072 County Road 424 Napoleon (43545) *(G-10277)*

Custer Products Limited............................. 330 490-3158
  1320 Sanders Ave Sw Massillon (44647) *(G-9184)*

Custom Aerosol Packaging, Piqua Also Called: C A P Industries Inc *(G-11338)*

Custom Apparel LLC................................... 330 633-2626
  1180 Brittain Rd Akron (44305) *(G-111)*

Custom Assembly Inc................................. 419 622-3040
  2952 Road 107 Haviland (45851) *(G-7586)*

Custom Blast, Lima Also Called: Custom Blast & Coat Inc *(G-8399)*

Custom Blast & Coat Inc............................ 419 225-6024
  1511 S Dixie Hwy Lima (45804) *(G-8399)*

Custom Blind Corporation........................... 937 643-2907
  2895 Culver Ave Dayton (45429) *(G-5717)*

Custom Built Crates Inc
  1700 Victory Park Dr Milford (45150) *(G-9932)*

Custom Canvas & Boat Repr Inc................... 419 732-3314
  29 S Bridge Rd Lakeside (43440) *(G-8157)*

Custom Canvas & Upholstery, Lakeside Also Called: Custom Canvas & Boat Repr Inc *(G-8157)*

Custom Chassis Inc................................... 440 839-5574
  52826 State Route 303 Wakeman (44889) *(G-13679)*

Custom Chrome Plating, Grafton Also Called: Customchrome Plating Inc *(G-7300)*

Custom Cltch Jint Hydrlics Inc (PA)............... 216 431-1630
  3417 Saint Clair Ave Ne Cleveland (44114) *(G-3584)*

Custom Connector Corporation.................... 216 241-1679
  1821 E 40th St Cleveland (44103) *(G-3585)*

Custom Control Specialists, Norton Also Called: Sdk Associates Inc *(G-10826)*

Custom Control Tech LLC............................ 419 342-5593
  4469 Funk Rd Shelby (44875) *(G-11969)*

Custom Craft, Akron Also Called: Custom Craft Controls Inc *(G-112)*

Custom Craft Collection Inc........................ 440 998-3000
  5422 Main Ave Ashtabula (44004) *(G-589)*

Custom Craft Controls Inc.......................... 330 630-9599
  1620 Triplett Blvd Akron (44306) *(G-112)*

Custom Cycle ACC Mfg Dstrg Inc.................. 440 585-2200
  29110 Anderson Rd Wickliffe (44092) *(G-14373)*

Custom Deco, Toledo Also Called: Cdh Liquidation Inc *(G-12912)*

Custom Deco LLC...................................... 419 698-2900
  1345 Miami St Toledo (43605) *(G-12935)*

Custom Design Cabinets & Tops................... 440 639-9900
  379 Fountain Ave Painesville (44077) *(G-11075)*

Custom Design Kitchen & Bath, Painesville Also Called: Custom Design Cabinets & Tops *(G-11075)*

Custom Dsign Chakra Reiki Jwly, Columbus Also Called: Lotus Love LLC *(G-5075)*

Custom Fab By Fisher LLC.......................... 513 738-4600
  5009 Cincinnati Brookville Rd Hamilton (45013) *(G-7482)*

Custom Fabrication By Fisher...................... 513 738-4600
  100 Weaver Rd Okeana (45053) *(G-10928)*

Custom Floaters LLC.................................. 216 536-8979
  6519 Eastland Rd Ste 101 Brookpark (44142) *(G-1546)*

Custom Foam Products Inc (PA)................... 937 295-2700
  900 Tower Dr Fort Loramie (45845) *(G-6945)*

Custom Formed Products, Miamisburg Also Called: Customformed Products Inc *(G-9685)*

Custom GL Sltons Upper Sndsky.................. 419 294-4921
  12688 State Highway 67 Upper Sandusky (43351) *(G-13436)*

Custom Glass Solutions LLC (PA)................. 248 340-1800
  12688 State Highway 67 Upper Sandusky (43351) *(G-13437)*

Custom Graphics Inc................................. 330 963-7770
  8107 Bavaria Dr E Macedonia (44056) *(G-8682)*

Custom Hitch & Trailer, Piketon Also Called: Overhead Door of Pike County *(G-11312)*

Custom Hoists Inc (HQ)............................. 419 368-4721
  771 County Road 30a Ashland (44805) *(G-532)*

Custom Imprint.. 440 238-4488
  19573 Progress Dr Strongsville (44149) *(G-12551)*

Custom Information Systems Inc................... 614 875-2245
  3347 Mcdowell Rd Grove City (43123) *(G-7380)*

Custom Machine Inc.................................. 419 986-5122
  3315 W Township Road 158 Tiffin (44883) *(G-12781)*

Custom Material Hdlg Eqp LLC.................... 513 235-5336
  7868 Gapstow Brg Cincinnati (45231) *(G-2531)*

Custom Metal Products Inc......................... 614 855-2263
  5037 Babbitt Rd New Albany (43054) *(G-10337)*

Custom Metal Shearing Inc........................ 937 233-6950
  80 Commerce Park Dr Dayton (45404) *(G-5718)*

Custom Metal Works Inc (PA)...................... 419 668-7831
  193 Akron Rd Norwalk (44857) *(G-10834)*

Custom Mfg Solutions Inc (PA).................... 937 372-0777
  479 Bellbrook Ave Xenia (45385) *(G-14760)*

Custom Millcraft Corp............................... 513 874-7080
  9092 Le Saint Dr West Chester (45014) *(G-13980)*

Custom Millwork Designs, Oakwood Village Also Called: Cabinet Concepts Inc *(G-10903)*

Custom Molded Products LLC...................... 937 382-1070
  92 Grant St Wilmington (45177) *(G-14578)*

Custom Nickel LLC.................................... 937 222-1995
  45 N Clinton St Dayton (45402) *(G-5719)*

Custom Palet Manufacturing....................... 440 693-4603
  9291 N Girdle Rd Middlefield (44062) *(G-9790)*

Custom Paper Tubes Inc............................ 216 362-2964
  6030 Carey Dr Cleveland (44125) *(G-3586)*

Custom Poly Bag LLC................................. 330 935-2408
  9465 Edison St Ne Alliance (44601) *(G-378)*

Custom Powdr Coating By Greber, Elyria Also Called: Greber Machine Tool Inc *(G-6541)*

Custom Products Corporation (PA)............... 440 528-7100
  7100 Cochran Rd Glenwillow (44139) *(G-7285)*

Custom Pultrusions Inc (HQ)...................... 330 562-5201
  1331 S Chillicothe Rd Aurora (44202) *(G-666)*

Custom Quality Products Inc
  1645 Blue Rock St Cincinnati (45223) *(G-2532)*

Custom Recapping Inc............................... 937 324-4331
  126 Linden Ave Springfield (45505) *(G-12297)*

Custom Reptile Habitats, Dayton Also Called: Worldwide Brands Direct LLC *(G-6088)*

Custom Retail Group LLC........................... 614 409-9720
  6311 Busch Blvd Columbus (43229) *(G-4863)*

Custom Rubber Corporation........................ 216 391-2928
  1274 E 55th St Cleveland (44103) *(G-3587)*

Custom Sign Center.................................. 614 279-6035
  400 N Wilson Rd Columbus (43204) *(G-4864)*

Custom Sign Center Inc............................. 614 279-6700
  3200 Valleyview Dr Columbus (43204) *(G-4865)*

Custom Sporstwear Imprints LLC................. 330 335-8326
  238 High St Wadsworth (44281) *(G-13633)*

Custom Surfaces Inc................................. 440 439-2310
  26185 Broadway Ave Bedford (44146) *(G-1024)*

Custom Tarpaulin Products Inc.................... 330 758-1801
  8095 Southern Blvd Youngstown (44512) *(G-14844)*

Custom Threading Systems LLC................... 937 846-1405
  1833 N Dayton Lakeview Rd New Carlisle (45344) *(G-10370)*

Custom Tire, Springfield Also Called: Custom Recapping Inc *(G-12297)*

Custom Tooling Company............................ 513 733-5790
  603 Wayne Park Dr Cincinnati (45215) *(G-2533)*

Custom Truck One Source LP...................... 330 409-7291
  3522 Middlebranch Ave Ne Canton (44705) *(G-1874)*

Custom Weld & Machine Corp...................... 330 452-3935
  1500 Henry Ave Sw Canton (44706) *(G-1875)*

Custom Woodworking Inc........................... 419 456-3330
  214 S Main St Ottawa (45875) *(G-11031)*

Customchrome Plating Inc.......................... 440 926-3116
  963 Mechanic St Grafton (44044) *(G-7300)*

Customformed Products Inc........................ 937 388-0480
  645 Precision Ct Miamisburg (45342) *(G-9685)*

Customized Girl, Columbus Also Called: E Retailing Associates LLC *(G-4894)*

Customworks Inc...................................... 614 262-1002
  330 Lenappe Dr Columbus (43214) *(G-4866)*

Cutter Equipment Company, Canton Also Called: Randall Richard & Moore LLC *(G-1991)*

Cuttercroix LLC.. 330 289-6185
  7251 Engle Rd Ste 350 Cleveland (44130) *(G-3588)*

(PA)=Parent Co (HQ)=Headquarters (DH)=Div Headquarters

Cutting Dynamics LLC...440 249-4666
  35050 Avon Commerce Pkwy Avon (44011) *(G-722)*

Cutting Dynamics LLC (HQ)....................................440 249-4150
  980 Jaycox Rd Avon (44011) *(G-723)*

Cutting Dynamics LLC...440 930-2862
  33597 Pin Oak Pkwy Avon Lake (44012) *(G-752)*

Cutting Edge Countertops Inc (PA)..........................419 873-9500
  1300 Flagship Dr Perrysburg (43551) *(G-11212)*

Cutting Edge Manufacturing LLC..............................419 355-0921
  220 Sullivan Rd Fremont (43420) *(G-7102)*

Cutting Edge Nameplate Company, Perry *Also Called: Tce International Ltd (G-11199)*

Cutting Edge Roofing Products, Tallmadge *Also Called: Trans-Foam Inc (G-12755)*

Cutting Edge Technologies Inc.................................216 574-4759
  1241 Superior Ave E Cleveland (44114) *(G-3589)*

Cutting Systems Inc...216 928-0500
  15593 Brookpark Rd Cleveland (44142) *(G-3590)*

Cuyahoga Fence LLC...216 830-2200
  3100 E 45th St Ste 504 Cleveland (44127) *(G-3591)*

Cuyahoga Group, The, North Ridgeville *Also Called: Cuyahoga Vending Co Inc (G-10728)*

Cuyahoga Machine Company LLC..............................216 267-3560
  5250 W 137th St Brookpark (44142) *(G-1547)*

Cuyahoga Molded Plastics Co...................................216 261-2744
  9351 Mercantile Dr Mentor (44060) *(G-9509)*

Cuyahoga Molded Plastics Co (inc) (PA)..................216 261-2744
  1265 Babbitt Rd Euclid (44132) *(G-6647)*

Cuyahoga Plastics, Euclid *Also Called: Cuyahoga Molded Plastics Co (inc) (G-6647)*

Cuyahoga Rebuilders Inc..216 635-0659
  5111 Brookpark Rd Cleveland (44134) *(G-3592)*

Cuyahoga Vending Co Inc..440 353-9595
  39405 Taylor Pkwy North Ridgeville (44035) *(G-10728)*

Cvc Thermoset Specialties, Akron *Also Called: Huntsman Corporation (G-179)*

Cvg, New Albany *Also Called: Commercial Vehicle Group Inc (G-10336)*

Cvg National Seating Co LLC.....................................219 872-7295
  7800 Walton Pkwy New Albany (43054) *(G-10338)*

Cvg Trim Systems, New Albany *Also Called: Trim Systems Operating Corp (G-10352)*

Cw Liquidation Inc
  1801 E 9th St Ste 1100 Cleveland (44114) *(G-3593)*

CW Machine Worx Ltd...740 654-5304
  4805 Scooby Ln Carroll (43112) *(G-2074)*

Cwd LLC (DH)...310 218-1082
  127 Public Sq Ste 5110 Cleveland (44114) *(G-3594)*

Cwh Graphics LLC..866 241-8515
  23196 Miles Rd Ste A Bedford Heights (44128) *(G-1075)*

Cyberutility LLC...216 291-8723
  1599 Maywood Rd Cleveland (44121) *(G-3595)*

Cycle Cat, Blacklick *Also Called: Abranda Llc (G-1218)*

Cycle Electric Inc..937 884-7300
  8734 Dayton Greenville Pike Brookville (45309) *(G-1564)*

Cylinders and Valves Inc...440 238-7343
  20811 Westwood Dr Strongsville (44149) *(G-12552)*

Cypress Court, Reynoldsburg *Also Called: Mulch Manufacturing Inc (G-11575)*

Cypress Valley Log Homes, Marietta *Also Called: Gillard Construction Inc (G-8919)*

Cyril-Scott Company, The, Lancaster *Also Called: Consolidated Graphics Inc (G-8189)*

D & B Industries Inc..937 253-8658
  5031 Linden Ave Ste B Dayton (45432) *(G-5607)*

D & D Mining Co Inc..330 549-3127
  3379 E Garfield Rd New Springfield (44443) *(G-10472)*

D & E Machine Co..513 932-2184
  962 S Us Route 42 Lebanon (45036) *(G-8251)*

D & G Welding Inc..419 445-5751
  302 W Barre Rd Archbold (43502) *(G-492)*

D & H Meats Inc..419 387-7767
  400 Blanchard St Vanlue (45890) *(G-13585)*

D & J Distributing & Mfg...419 865-2552
  1302 Holloway Rd Holland (43528) *(G-7753)*

D & J Electric Motor Repair Co.................................330 336-4343
  1734 Wall Rd Office Wadsworth (44281) *(G-13634)*

D & J Machine Shop..937 256-2730
  1296 S Patton St Xenia (45385) *(G-14761)*

D & J Manufacturing Jeweler.....................................513 541-5200
  7793 Colerain Ave Ste B Cincinnati (45239) *(G-2534)*

D & J Printing Inc...330 678-5868
  3765 Sunnybrook Rd Kent (44240) *(G-8024)*

D & L Energy Inc..330 270-1201
  3930 Fulton Dr Nw Ste 200 Canton (44718) *(G-1876)*

D & L Excavating Ltd...419 271-0635
  969 N Rymers Rd Port Clinton (43452) *(G-11440)*

D & L Machine Co Inc..330 785-0781
  1029 Arlington Cir Akron (44306) *(G-113)*

D & M Printing, Massillon *Also Called: David A and Mary A Mathis (G-9185)*

D & M Saw & Tool Inc...513 871-5433
  2974 P G Graves Ln Cincinnati (45241) *(G-2535)*

D & M Welding, Moraine *Also Called: Dayton Brick Company Inc (G-10156)*

D A Fitzgerald Co Inc..937 548-0511
  1045 Sater St Greenville (45331) *(G-7340)*

D and D Plastics Inc..330 376-0668
  581 E Tallmadge Ave Akron (44310) *(G-114)*

D C, Cleveland *Also Called: Die-Cut Products Co (G-3615)*

D C Controls LLC...513 225-0813
  4836 Duff Dr Ste E West Chester (45246) *(G-14113)*

D C G, Cleveland *Also Called: Directconnectgroup Ltd (G-3616)*

D C I, Akron *Also Called: Digital Color Intl LLC (G-123)*

D C Morrison Company Inc..859 581-7511
  11959 Tramway Dr Cincinnati (45241) *(G-2536)*

D C Systems Inc...330 273-3030
  1251 Industrial Pkwy N Brunswick (44212) *(G-1587)*

D F Electronics Inc...513 772-7792
  200 Novner Dr Cincinnati (45215) *(G-2537)*

D G M Inc..740 286-2131
  1668 Kessinger School Rd Jackson (45640) *(G-7943)*

D H Bowman & Sons Inc...419 886-2711
  1201 Mill Rd Bellville (44813) *(G-1137)*

D H S LLC..937 599-2485
  220 Reynolds Ave Bellefontaine (43311) *(G-1103)*

D J Klingler Inc...513 891-2284
  9999 Montgomery Rd Montgomery (45242) *(G-10124)*

D Jacob Industries LLC..440 292-7277
  13995 Enterprise Ave Cleveland (44135) *(G-3596)*

D K Manufacturing...740 654-5566
  2118 Commerce St Lancaster (43130) *(G-8194)*

D L T, Cincinnati *Also Called: Dominion Liquid Tech LLC (G-2557)*

D Lewis Inc..740 695-2615
  52235 National Rd Saint Clairsville (43950) *(G-11690)*

D M I, Reynoldsburg *Also Called: Dimensional Metals Inc (G-11565)*

D M Tool & Plastics Inc...937 962-4140
  11150 Baltimore Phillipsburg Rd Brookville (45309) *(G-1565)*

D M Tool & Plastics Inc (PA)......................................937 962-4140
  4140 Us Route 40 E Lewisburg (45338) *(G-8359)*

D M U, Dayton *Also Called: Dayton Molded Urethanes LLC (G-5732)*

D Martone Industries Inc..440 632-5800
  15060 Madison Rd Middlefield (44062) *(G-9791)*

D P I, Toledo *Also Called: Decorative Panels Intl Inc (G-12941)*

D Picking & Co...419 562-6891
  119 S Walnut St Bucyrus (44820) *(G-1677)*

D W Dickey, Lisbon *Also Called: D W Dickey and Son Inc (G-8466)*

D W Dickey and Son Inc (PA).....................................330 424-1441
  7896 Dickey Dr Lisbon (44432) *(G-8466)*

D-Terra Solutions LLC..614 450-1040
  35 Clairedan Dr Powell (43065) *(G-11486)*

D. A. Surgical, Newbury *Also Called: Dan Allen Surgical LLC (G-10549)*

D&D Classic Restoration, Covington *Also Called: D&D Clssic Auto Rstoration Inc (G-5492)*

D&D Clssic Auto Rstoration Inc.................................937 473-2229
  2300 Mote Dr Covington (45318) *(G-5492)*

D&D Design Concepts Inc..513 752-2191
  4360 Winding Creek Blvd Batavia (45103) *(G-860)*

D&D Ingredient Distrs Inc..419 692-2667
  1610 S Acadia Rd Spencerville (45887) *(G-12237)*

D&D Ingredients LLC, Spencerville *Also Called: D&D Ingredient Distrs Inc (G-12237)*

D&D Quality Machining Co Inc....................................440 942-2772
  36495 Reading Ave Ste 1 Willoughby (44094) *(G-14444)*

D+h USA Corporation...513 381-9400
  312 Plum St Ste 500 Cincinnati (45202) *(G-2538)*

2025 Harris Ohio
Industrial Directory

(G-0000) Company's Geographic Section entry number

D4 Industries Inc.. 419 523-9555
685 Woodland Dr Ottawa (45875) *(G-11032)*

Da Investments Inc..................................... 330 781-6100
4605 Lake Park Rd Youngstown (44512) *(G-14845)*

DA Precision Products Inc......................... 513 459-1113
9052 Goldpark Dr West Chester (45011) *(G-13981)*

Daavlin, Bryan *Also Called: Daavlin Distributing Co (G-1637)*

Daavlin Distributing Co............................. 419 636-6304
205 W Bement St Bryan (43506) *(G-1637)*

Dabar Industries LLC................................. 614 873-3949
7630 Copper Glen St Columbus (43235) *(G-4867)*

Dac, Dover *Also Called: Direct Action Co Inc (G-6236)*

Dacraft, Miamisburg *Also Called: Waxco International Inc (G-9752)*

Dadco Inc.. 513 489-2244
10111 Evendale Commons Dr Cincinnati (45241) *(G-2539)*

Dae Holdings LLC....................................... 419 866-6301
1 Air Cargo Pkwy E Swanton (43558) *(G-12681)*

Dae Industries, Swanton *Also Called: Dae Holdings LLC (G-12681)*

Dai Ceramics LLC....................................... 440 946-6964
38240 Airport Pkwy Willoughby (44094) *(G-14445)*

Daido Metal Bellefontaine LLC.................. 937 592-5010
1215 S Greenwood St Bellefontaine (43311) *(G-1104)*

Daifuku America Corporation (DH)............. 614 863-1888
6700 Tussing Rd Reynoldsburg (43068) *(G-11564)*

Daikin Applied Americas Inc...................... 614 351-9862
192 Heatherdown Dr Westerville (43081) *(G-14252)*

Daily Chief Union....................................... 419 294-2331
111 W Wyandot Ave Upper Sandusky (43351) *(G-13438)*

Daily Fantasy Circuit Inc........................... 614 989-8689
5 E Long St Ste 603 Columbus (43215) *(G-4868)*

Daily Growler Inc.. 614 656-2337
2812 Fishinger Rd Upper Arlington (43221) *(G-13430)*

Daily Legal News, Cleveland *Also Called: Legal News Publishing Co (G-3949)*

Daily Record, The, Millersburg *Also Called: Holmes County Hub Inc (G-9987)*

Daily Reporter.. 614 224-4835
580 S High St Ste 316 Columbus (43215) *(G-4869)*

Daily Standard The, Celina *Also Called: Standard Printing Co Inc (G-2121)*

Dairy Farmers America Inc......................... 330 670-7800
1035 Medina Rd Ste 300 Medina (44256) *(G-9395)*

Dairy Pak Div, Olmsted Falls *Also Called: Blue Ridge Paper Products LLC (G-10938)*

Daisy Brand LLC... 330 202-4410
3049 Daisy Way Wooster (44691) *(G-14633)*

Dak Enterprises Inc (PA)........................... 740 828-3291
18062 Timber Trails Rd Marysville (43040) *(G-9018)*

Dakkota Integrated Systems LLC............... 517 694-6500
315 Matzinger Rd Unit G Toledo (43612) *(G-12936)*

Dakota Software Corporation (PA)............. 216 765-7100
1375 Euclid Ave Ste 500 Cleveland (44115) *(G-3597)*

Dal-Little Fabricating Inc........................... 216 883-3323
11707 Putnam Ave Cleveland (44105) *(G-3598)*

Dalaco, Liberty Twp *Also Called: Dm2018 LLC (G-8382)*

Dale Kestler... 513 871-9000
3475 Cardiff Ave Cincinnati (45209) *(G-2540)*

Dale R Adkins... 740 682-7312
106 Smith St Oak Hill (45656) *(G-10887)*

Dallas Design & Technology Inc................ 419 884-9750
184 Industrial Dr Mansfield (44904) *(G-8779)*

Dalton Corporation.................................... 419 682-6328
310 Ellis St Stryker (43557) *(G-12621)*

Dalton Stryker McHining Fcilty.................. 419 682-6328
310 Ellis St Stryker (43557) *(G-12622)*

Damak 1 LLC.. 513 858-6004
33 Donald Dr Fairfield (45014) *(G-6725)*

Damar Products Inc.................................... 937 492-9023
516 Park St Sidney (45365) *(G-12010)*

Damon Industries Inc (PA)........................ 330 821-5310
12435 Rockhill Ave Ne Alliance (44601) *(G-379)*

Dan Allen Surgical LLC............................. 800 261-9953
11110 Kinsman Rd Unit 10 Newbury (44065) *(G-10549)*

Dan Patrick Enterprises Inc...................... 740 477-1006
8564 Zane Trail Rd Circleville (43113) *(G-3253)*

Dan-Mar Company Inc................................ 419 660-8830
200 Bluegrass Dr E Norwalk (44857) *(G-10835)*

Dana... 419 887-3000
3044 Jeep Pkwy Toledo (43610) *(G-12937)*

Dana, Maumee *Also Called: Dana Commercial Vhcl Pdts LLC (G-9273)*

Dana, Maumee *Also Called: Dana Incorporated (G-9277)*

Dana, Maumee *Also Called: Dana Off Highway Products LLC (G-9283)*

Dana, Maumee *Also Called: Dana Sac USA Inc (G-9284)*

Dana Auto Systems Group LLC (DH).......... 419 887-3000
3939 Technology Dr Maumee (43537) *(G-9270)*

Dana Automotive Aftermarket,, Maumee *Also Called: Dana Automotive Mfg Inc (G-9271)*

Dana Automotive Mfg Inc (HQ).................. 419 887-3000
3939 Technology Dr Maumee (43537) *(G-9271)*

Dana Automotive Systems, Maumee *Also Called: Dana Limited (G-9280)*

Dana Brazil Holdings I LLC....................... 419 887-3000
3939 Technology Dr Maumee (43537) *(G-9272)*

Dana Commercial Vhcl Pdts LLC (DH)........ 419 887-3000
3939 Technology Dr Maumee (43537) *(G-9273)*

Dana Driveshaft Products, Maumee *Also Called: Dana Driveshaft Products LLC (G-9274)*

Dana Driveshaft Products LLC (DH).......... 419 887-3000
3939 Technology Dr Maumee (43537) *(G-9274)*

Dana Global Products Inc (DH)................. 419 887-3000
3939 Technology Dr Maumee (43537) *(G-9275)*

Dana Heavy Vhcl Systems Group, Maumee *Also Called: Dana Hvy Vhcl Systems Group LL (G-9276)*

Dana Hvy Vhcl Systems Group LL (DH)..... 419 887-3000
3939 Technology Dr Maumee (43537) *(G-9276)*

Dana Incorporated (PA)............................. 419 887-3000
3939 Technology Dr Maumee (43537) *(G-9277)*

Dana Information Technology, Maumee *Also Called: Dana Limited (G-9281)*

Dana Light Axle Mfg LLC (DH).................. 419 346-4528
3939 Technology Dr Maumee (43537) *(G-9278)*

Dana Light Axle Mfg LLC.......................... 419 887-3000
3044 Jeep Pkwy Toledo (43610) *(G-12938)*

Dana Light Axle Products, Maumee *Also Called: Dana Light Axle Mfg LLC (G-9278)*

Dana Limited.. 419 866-7253
6201 Trust Dr Holland (43528) *(G-7754)*

Dana Limited.. 419 887-3000
6515 Maumee Western Rd Maumee (43537) *(G-9279)*

Dana Limited.. 419 887-3000
6515 Maumee Western Rd Maumee (43537) *(G-9280)*

Dana Limited.. 419 482-2000
580 Longbow Dr Maumee (43537) *(G-9281)*

Dana Limited (HQ)..................................... 419 887-3000
3939 Technology Dr Maumee (43537) *(G-9282)*

Dana Off Highway Products LLC (DH)....... 419 887-3000
3939 Technology Dr Maumee (43537) *(G-9283)*

Dana Sac USA Inc...................................... 419 887-3550
3939 Technology Dr Maumee (43537) *(G-9284)*

Dana Sealing Manufacturing LLC (DH) 3939 Technology Dr Maumee (43537) *(G-9285)*

Dana Sealing Products LLC (DH).............. 419 887-3000
3939 Technology Dr Maumee (43537) *(G-9286)*

Dana Structural Products, Maumee *Also Called: Dana Structural Products LLC (G-9287)*

Dana Structural Products LLC (DH).......... 419 887-3000
3939 Technology Dr Maumee (43537) *(G-9287)*

Dana Supply Chain Mgmt, Holland *Also Called: Dana Limited (G-7754)*

Dana Thermal Products, Maumee *Also Called: Dana Thermal Products LLC (G-9288)*

Dana Thermal Products LLC (DH).............. 419 887-3000
3939 Technology Dr Maumee (43537) *(G-9288)*

Dana White Machining Wldg Inc................ 419 652-3444
910 County Road 40 Nova (44859) *(G-10876)*

Dana World Trade Corporation (DH).......... 419 887-3000
3939 Technology Dr Maumee (43537) *(G-9289)*

Danco Metal Products LLC........................ 440 871-2300
760 Moore Rd Avon Lake (44012) *(G-753)*

Dandi Enterprises Inc................................ 419 516-9070
6353 Som Center Rd Solon (44139) *(G-12099)*

Dandy Products Inc (PA)............................ 513 625-3000
3314 State Route 131 Goshen (45122) *(G-7296)*

Danfoss, Van Wert *Also Called: Danfoss Power Solutions II LLC (G-13533)*

Danfoss Power Solutions II LLC................... 419 238-1190
1225 W Main St Van Wert (45891) *(G-13533)*

Danite Holdings Ltd.................................. 614 444-3333
1640 Harmon Ave Columbus (43223) *(G-4870)*

Danite Sign Co, Columbus Also Called: Danite Holdings Ltd *(G-4870)*

Danmarco, Norwalk Also Called: Dan-Mar Company Inc *(G-10835)*

Danone Us LLC...................................... 513 229-0092
7577 Central Parke Blvd Mason (45040) *(G-9092)*

Danone Us LLC...................................... 419 628-1295
216 Southgate Minster (45865) *(G-10055)*

Dap Products Inc.................................... 937 667-4461
875 N 3rd St Tipp City (45371) *(G-12822)*

Dapsco.. 937 294-5331
3110 Kettering Blvd Moraine (45439) *(G-10155)*

Darby Creek Millwork LLC......................... 614 873-3267
10001 Plain City Georgesville Rd Ne Plain City (43064) *(G-11402)*

Dare Electronics Inc............................... 937 335-0031
3245 S County Road 25a Troy (45373) *(G-13208)*

Darifill Inc... 614 890-3274
750 Green Crest Dr Westerville (43081) *(G-14253)*

Darke Precision Inc................................ 937 548-2232
291 Fox Dr Piqua (45356) *(G-11343)*

Darling Ingredients Inc............................ 972 717-0300
3105 Spring Grove Ave Cincinnati (45225) *(G-2541)*

Darling Ingredients Inc............................ 216 651-9300
1002 Peltnine Ave Cleveland (44109) *(G-3599)*

Darling Ingredients Inc............................ 216 351-3440
1002 Belt Line Ave Cleveland (44109) *(G-3600)*

Darpro Storage Solutions LLC.................... 567 233-3190
1089 County Road 26 Marengo (43334) *(G-8896)*

Darrah Electric Company (PA)..................... 216 631-0912
8834 Mayfield Rd Ste A Chesterland (44026) *(G-2233)*

Darting Around LLC................................ 330 639-3990
3058 Cromer Ave Nw Canton (44709) *(G-1877)*

Darusta Woodlife Division, Tipp City Also Called: Dap Products Inc *(G-12822)*

Das Deutsch Cheese, Middlefield Also Called: Middlfeld Original Cheese Coop *(G-9812)*

Dasher Lawless Automation LLC.................. 855 755-7275
310 Dana St Ne Warren (44483) *(G-13757)*

Data Cooling Technologies LLC................... 330 954-3800
3092 Euclid Heights Blvd Cleveland Heights (44118) *(G-4528)*

Data Processing Sciences Corporation........... 513 791-7100
2 Camargo Cyn Cincinnati (45243) *(G-2542)*

Datamax Oneil Printer Supplies, West Chester Also Called: Pioneer Labels Inc *(G-14048)*

Dataq Instruments Inc............................. 330 668-1444
241 Springside Dr Akron (44333) *(G-115)*

Datatrak International Inc......................... 440 443-0082
3690 Orange Pl Ste 375 Beachwood (44122) *(G-914)*

Datcomedia LLC.................................... 419 866-6301
1 Air Cargo Pkwy E Swanton (43558) *(G-12682)*

Datono Products, Dayton Also Called: Dayton Stencil Works Company *(G-5739)*

Datwyler Sling Sltions USA Inc................... 937 387-2800
875 Center Dr Vandalia (45377) *(G-13554)*

Daubenmires Printing Co LLC..................... 513 425-7223
1527 Central Ave Middletown (45044) *(G-9853)*

Dauphin Holdings Inc.............................. 330 733-4022
931 High Grove Blvd Akron (44312) *(G-116)*

Dave Krissinger.................................... 440 669-9957
12335 Old State Rd Chardon (44024) *(G-2202)*

Davenport Rolling Mill, Beachwood Also Called: Novelis Alr Aluminum LLC *(G-933)*

Davey Drill, Kent Also Called: Davey Kent Inc *(G-8025)*

Davey Kent Inc...................................... 330 673-5400
200 W Williams St Kent (44240) *(G-8025)*

David A and Mary A Mathis......................... 330 837-8611
332 Erie St S Massillon (44646) *(G-9185)*

David Adkins Logging.............................. 740 533-0297
1260 Township Road 256 Kitts Hill (45645) *(G-8147)*

David Bixel.. 440 474-4410
2683 State Route 534 Rock Creek (44084) *(G-11629)*

David Chojnacki.................................... 303 905-1918
5471 Camlin Pl E Westerville (43081) *(G-14254)*

David E Easterday and Co Inc..................... 330 359-0700
1225 Us Route 62 Unit C Wilmot (44689) *(G-14594)*

David R Hill Inc..................................... 740 685-5168
132 S 2nd St Byesville (43723) *(G-1708)*

David Round Company, The, Streetsboro Also Called: Drc Acquisition Inc *(G-12498)*

David Wolfe Design Inc............................ 330 633-6124
829 Moe Dr Akron (44310) *(G-117)*

Davidson Meat Processing Plant, Waynesville Also Called: Patrick M Davidson *(G-13882)*

Davis Fabricators Inc.............................. 419 898-5297
15765 W State Route 2 Oak Harbor (43449) *(G-10885)*

Davis Graphic Comm Solutions, Barberton Also Called: Davis Printing Company *(G-803)*

Davis Machine Products Inc....................... 440 474-0247
74 Sapphire Ln Streetsboro (44241) *(G-12495)*

Davis Printing Company............................ 330 745-3113
101 Robinson Ave Barberton (44203) *(G-803)*

Davis Technologies Inc............................ 330 823-2544
837 W Main St Alliance (44601) *(G-380)*

Dawn Enterprises Inc (PA)........................ 216 642-5506
9155 Sweet Valley Dr Cleveland (44125) *(G-3601)*

Day-Glo Color Corp (DH).......................... 216 391-7070
4515 Saint Clair Ave Cleveland (44103) *(G-3602)*

Day-Glo Color Corp................................ 216 391-7070
4518 Hamilton Ave Cleveland (44114) *(G-3603)*

Day-Glo Color Corp................................ 216 391-7070
1570 Highland Rd Twinsburg (44087) *(G-13291)*

Day-TEC Tool & Mfg Inc........................... 937 847-0022
4900 Lyons Rd Unit A Miamisburg (45342) *(G-9686)*

Daylay Egg Farm Inc............................... 937 355-6531
11177 Township Road 133 West Mansfield (43358) *(G-14178)*

Dayton Armor LLC.................................. 937 723-8675
2360 W Dorothy Ln Ste 107 Dayton (45439) *(G-5720)*

Dayton Bag & Burlap Co........................... 937 253-1722
448 Huffman Ave Dayton (45403) *(G-5721)*

Dayton Bag & Burlap Co........................... 419 733-7108
4248 Display Ln Kettering (45429) *(G-8118)*

Dayton Bindery Service Inc........................ 937 235-3111
3757 Inpark Dr Dayton (45414) *(G-5722)*

Dayton Brewery & Pub, Dayton Also Called: Lock 27 Brewing LLC *(G-5853)*

Dayton Brick Company Inc......................... 937 293-4189
2300 Arbor Blvd Moraine (45439) *(G-10156)*

Dayton Business Journal, Dayton Also Called: American City Bus Journals Inc *(G-5651)*

Dayton City Paper Group Llc...................... 937 222-8855
126 N Main St Ste 240 Dayton (45402) *(G-5723)*

Dayton Clutch & Joint Inc (PA).................... 937 236-9770
2005 Troy St 1 Dayton (45404) *(G-5724)*

Dayton Coating Tech LLC.......................... 937 278-2060
1926 E Siebenthaler Ave Dayton (45414) *(G-5725)*

Dayton Daily News, Troy Also Called: Ohio Newspapers Inc *(G-13245)*

Dayton Forging Heat Treating..................... 937 253-4126
215 N Findlay St Dayton (45403) *(G-5726)*

Dayton Gear and Tool Co........................... 937 866-4327
500 Fame Rd Dayton (45449) *(G-5727)*

Dayton Hawker Corporation....................... 937 293-8147
2844 Culver Ave Dayton (45429) *(G-5728)*

Dayton Heidelberg Distrg Co....................... 440 989-1027
5901 Baumhart Rd Lorain (44053) *(G-8554)*

DAYTON HEIDELBERG DISTRIBUTING CO., Lorain Also Called: Dayton Heidelberg Distrg Co *(G-8554)*

Dayton Industrial Drum Inc........................ 937 253-8933
1880 Radio Rd Dayton (45431) *(G-5608)*

Dayton Legal Blank Inc............................ 937 435-4405
875 Congress Park Dr Dayton (45459) *(G-5729)*

Dayton Machine Tool Company.................... 937 222-6444
1314 Webster St Dayton (45404) *(G-5730)*

Dayton Mailing Services Inc....................... 937 222-5056
100 S Keowee St Dayton (45402) *(G-5731)*

Dayton Manufacturing Company, Dayton Also Called: Delma Corp *(G-5745)*

Dayton Molded Urethanes LLC.................... 937 279-9987
3337 N Dixie Dr Dayton (45414) *(G-5732)*

Dayton Molded Urethanes LLC.................... 937 279-1910
6400 Sand Lake Rd Dayton (45414) *(G-5733)*

Dayton One LLC.................................... 937 265-0227
212 Heid Ave Dayton (45404) *(G-5734)*

Dayton Pattern Inc.. 937 277-0761
5591 Wadsworth Rd Dayton (45414) *(G-5735)*

Dayton Polymeric Products Inc............................... 937 279-9987
3337 N Dixie Dr Dayton (45414) *(G-5736)*

Dayton Progress Corporation (DH)........................... 937 859-5111
500 Progress Rd Dayton (45449) *(G-5737)*

Dayton Progress Intl Corp...................................... 937 859-5111
500 Progress Rd Dayton (45449) *(G-5738)*

Dayton Rogers of Ohio Inc...................................... 614 491-1477
2309 Mcgaw Rd Columbus (43207) *(G-4871)*

Dayton Stencil Works Company............................... 937 223-3233
113 E 2nd St Dayton (45402) *(G-5739)*

Dayton Superior Corporation (DH)........................... 937 866-0711
1125 Byers Rd Miamisburg (45342) *(G-9687)*

Dayton Superior Corporation.................................. 937 682-4015
270 Rush St Rushsylvania (43347) *(G-11665)*

Dayton Superior Pdts Co Inc.................................. 937 332-1930
1370 Lytle Rd Troy (45373) *(G-13209)*

Dayton Systems Group Inc...................................... 937 885-5665
3003 S Tech Blvd Miamisburg (45342) *(G-9688)*

Dayton Technologies.. 513 539-5474
351 N Garver Rd Monroe (45050) *(G-10101)*

Dayton Waterjet LLC.. 937 428-0944
8641 Washington Church Rd Miamisburg (45342) *(G-9689)*

Dayton Wheel Concepts Inc.................................... 937 438-0100
115 Compark Rd Dayton (45459) *(G-5740)*

Dayton Wire Products Inc...................................... 937 236-8000
7 Dayton Wire Pkwy Dayton (45404) *(G-5741)*

Dayton Wire Wheel, Dayton *Also Called: Dayton Wheel Concepts Inc (G-5740)*

Dayton-Phoenix Group Inc (PA)............................. 937 496-3900
1619 Kuntz Rd Dayton (45404) *(G-5742)*

Daytronic, Miamisburg *Also Called: Daytronic Corporation (G-9690)*

Daytronic Corporation (HQ).................................... 937 866-3300
965 Capstone Cir Miamisburg (45342) *(G-9690)*

Dazpak Flexible Packaging Corp (PA)...................... 614 252-2121
2901 E 4th Ave Columbus (43219) *(G-4872)*

Db Products USA, Dayton *Also Called: Db Unlimited LLC (G-5743)*

Db Rediheat Inc.. 216 361-0530
4516 Saint Clair Ave Cleveland (44103) *(G-3604)*

Db Unlimited LLC.. 937 401-2602
61 Marco Ln Dayton (45458) *(G-5743)*

Dbcr Inc... 330 920-1900
3400 Cavalier Trl Cuyahoga Falls (44224) *(G-5537)*

DBs Stnless Stl Fbrctors Inc................................. 513 856-9600
21 Standen Dr Hamilton (45015) *(G-7483)*

Dbw Fiber Corporation
1720 Enterprise Corporation Wooster (44691) *(G-14634)*

DC Legacy Corp.. 330 896-4220
3300 Massillon Rd Akron (44312) *(G-118)*

DC Reprographics Co... 614 297-1200
1254 Courtland Ave Columbus (43201) *(G-4873)*

Dc- Digital, Carlisle *Also Called: Industrial Electronic Service (G-2066)*

DCA Construction Products LLC.............................. 330 527-4308
10421 Industrial Dr Garrettsville (44231) *(G-7217)*

Dcd Technologies Inc... 216 481-0056
17920 S Waterloo Rd Cleveland (44119) *(G-3605)*

Dcm Manufacturing Inc (HQ).................................. 216 265-8006
4540 W 160th St Cleveland (44135) *(G-3606)*

Dcm Soundex Inc.. 937 522-0371
1901 E 5th St Dayton (45403) *(G-5744)*

Dco LLC (DH).. 419 931-9086
900 E Boundary St Ste 8a Perrysburg (43551) *(G-11213)*

DCW Acquisition Inc... 216 451-0666
10646 Leuer Ave Cleveland (44108) *(G-3607)*

Dd Foundry Inc (PA).. 216 362-4100
15583 Brookpark Rd Brookpark (44142) *(G-1548)*

Ddi North Jackson Corp... 330 538-3900
12080 Debartolo Dr North Jackson (44451) *(G-10686)*

Ddp Mailing & Printing, Delaware *Also Called: Delaware Data Products Inc (G-6142)*

Ddp Specialty Electronic MA.................................. 937 839-4612
10 Electric St West Alexandria (45381) *(G-13918)*

De Bra - Kuempel, Cincinnati *Also Called: Debra-Kuempel Inc (G-2543)*

De Kay Fabricators Inc.. 330 793-0826
295 S Meridian Rd Youngstown (44509) *(G-14846)*

De Nora Holdings Us Inc.. 440 710-5300
7590 Discovery Ln Concord Township (44077) *(G-5389)*

De Nora North America Inc..................................... 440 357-4000
7590 Discovery Ln Painesville (44077) *(G-11076)*

De Nora Tech Inc.. 440 285-0100
464 Center St Chardon (44024) *(G-2203)*

De Nora Tech LLC... 440 285-0368
7661 Crile Rdunit 1 Bldg 2 Painesville (44077) *(G-11077)*

De Nora Tech LLC (DH).. 440 710-5334
7590 Discovery Ln Painesville (44077) *(G-11078)*

De Vore Engraving Co.. 330 454-6820
1017 Tuscarawas St E Canton (44707) *(G-1878)*

Dearborn Inc.. 440 234-1353
678 Front St Berea (44017) *(G-1166)*

Dearfoams Div, Pickerington *Also Called: R G Barry Corporation (G-11298)*

Dearing Compressor and Pump Company (PA).......... 330 783-2258
3974 Simon Rd Youngstown (44501) *(G-14847)*

Dearth Resources Inc (PA)....................................937 325-0651
2301 Sheridan Ave Springfield (45505) *(G-12298)*

Dearth Resources Inc.. 937 663-4171
8801 State Route 36 Springfield (45501) *(G-12299)*

Debra-Kuempel Inc (HQ).. 513 271-6500
3976 Southern Ave Cincinnati (45227) *(G-2543)*

Deca Manufacturing, Mansfield *Also Called: Malabar Properties LLC (G-8816)*

Deca Mfg Co.. 419 884-0071
300 S Mill St Mansfield (44904) *(G-8780)*

Decaplus, Middletown *Also Called: Natural Beauty Products Inc (G-9882)*

Decaria Brothers Inc... 330 385-0825
104 E 5th St East Liverpool (43920) *(G-6391)*

Decent Hill Press, Hilliard *Also Called: Decent Hill Publishers LLC (G-7680)*

Decent Hill Publishers LLC..................................... 216 548-1255
2825 Wynneleaf St Hilliard (43026) *(G-7680)*

Deceuninck North America LLC (HQ)........................ 513 539-4444
351 N Garver Rd Monroe (45050) *(G-10102)*

Decibel Research Inc... 256 705-3341
2661 Commons Blvd Ste 136 Beavercreek (45431) *(G-969)*

DECIBEL RESEARCH, INC, Beavercreek *Also Called: Decibel Research Inc (G-969)*

Decision Systems Inc.. 330 456-7600
2935 Woodcliff Dr Nw Canton (44718) *(G-1879)*

Decked LLC.. 208 806-0251
25401 Elliott Rd Defiance (43512) *(G-6104)*

Decker Custom Wood Llc.. 419 332-3464
505 W Mcgormley Rd Fremont (43420) *(G-7103)*

Decker Custom Wood Working, Fremont *Also Called: Decker Custom Wood Llc (G-7103)*

Decker Drilling Inc... 740 749-3939
11565 State Route 676 Vincent (45784) *(G-13620)*

Deco Tools Inc.. 419 476-9321
1541 Coining Dr Toledo (43612) *(G-12939)*

Decoma Systems Integration Gro........................... 419 324-3387
1800 Nathan Dr Toledo (43611) *(G-12940)*

Decorative Panels Intl Inc (DH)..............................419 535-5921
2900 Hill Ave Toledo (43607) *(G-12941)*

Dedicated Industries Inc (PA)................................ 440 238-5200
13550 Falling Water Rd Ste 105 Strongsville (44136) *(G-12553)*

Dedrone Defense Inc... 614 948-2002
525 W Schrock Rd Westerville (43081) *(G-14255)*

Dee Printing Inc... 614 777-8700
4999 Transamerica Dr Columbus (43228) *(G-4874)*

Dee Sign Co (PA).. 513 779-3333
6163 Allen Rd West Chester (45069) *(G-13982)*

Dee Sign Usa LLC... 513 779-3333
6163 Allen Rd West Chester (45069) *(G-13983)*

Dee-Jays Cstm Btchring Proc LL............................. 740 694-7492
17460 Ankneytown Rd Fredericktown (43019) *(G-7076)*

Deemsys Inc (PA)..614 322-9928
800 Cross Pointe Rd Ste A Gahanna (43230) *(G-7155)*

Deer Creek Honey Farms Ltd.................................. 740 852-0899
551 E High St London (43140) *(G-8535)*

Deerfield Digital, Cincinnati *Also Called: Laurenee Ltd (G-2814)*

Deerfield Manufacturing Inc.. 513 398-2010
320 N Mason Montgomery Rd Mason (45040) *(G-9093)*

Deerfield Ventures Inc... 614 875-0688
2224 Stringtown Rd Grove City (43123) *(G-7381)*

Defabco Inc.. 614 231-2700
3765 E Livingston Ave Columbus (43227) *(G-4875)*

Defense Co Inc.. 413 998-1637
600 Superior Ave E Cleveland (44114) *(G-3608)*

Defense Research Assoc Inc....................................... 937 431-1644
3915 Germany Ln Ste 102 Dayton (45431) *(G-5609)*

Deffren Machine Tool Svc Inc..................................... 513 858-1555
240 Donald Dr Fairfield (45014) *(G-6726)*

Defiance Crescent News, The, Defiance *Also Called: Defiance Publishing Co Ltd (G-6106)*

Defiance Metal Products Co (HQ)................................ 419 784-5332
21 Seneca St Defiance (43512) *(G-6105)*

Defiance Operations, Defiance *Also Called: Gt Technologies Inc (G-6109)*

Defiance Publishing Co Ltd.. 419 784-5441
624 W 2nd St Defiance (43512) *(G-6106)*

Defiance Stamping Co.. 419 782-5781
800 Independence Dr Napoleon (43545) *(G-10278)*

Degussa, Akron *Also Called: Evonik Corporation (G-140)*

Degussa Construction, Beachwood *Also Called: Master Builders LLC (G-928)*

Degussa Incorporated... 513 733-5111
620 Shepherd Dr Cincinnati (45215) *(G-2544)*

Dei Fratelli, Northwood *Also Called: Hirzel Canning Company (G-10803)*

Deibel Industries LLC.. 330 482-3351
41659 Esterly Dr Leetonia (44431) *(G-8301)*

Deibel Manufacturing, Leetonia *Also Called: Deibel Industries LLC (G-8301)*

Deimling/Jeliho Plastics Inc....................................... 513 752-6653
4010 Bach Buxton Rd Amelia (45102) *(G-429)*

Delafoil, Perrysburg *Also Called: Delafoil Pennsylvania Inc (G-11214)*

Delafoil Pennsylvania Inc.. 610 327-9565
1775 Progress Dr Perrysburg (43551) *(G-11214)*

Delaware City Vineyard... 740 362-6383
32 Troy Rd Delaware (43015) *(G-6141)*

Delaware Company, Cleveland *Also Called: Tremont Electric Incorporated (G-4416)*

Delaware Data Products Inc....................................... 740 369-5449
439 Dunlap St Delaware (43015) *(G-6142)*

Delaware Gazette Company.. 740 363-1161
40 N Sandusky St Ste 202 Delaware (43015) *(G-6143)*

Delaware Paint Company Ltd...................................... 740 368-9981
8455 Rausch Dr Plain City (43064) *(G-11403)*

Delhi Welding Co, Cincinnati *Also Called: Ridge Engineering Inc (G-3045)*

Delille Oxygen Company (PA).................................... 614 444-1177
772 Marion Rd Columbus (43207) *(G-4876)*

Delille Oxygen Company... 937 325-9595
1101 W Columbia St Springfield (45504) *(G-12300)*

Delma Corp.. 937 253-2142
3327 Elkton Ave Dayton (45403) *(G-5745)*

Delphi, Vandalia *Also Called: Mahle Behr USA Inc (G-13567)*

Delphi, Vienna *Also Called: Aptiv Services Us LLC (G-13607)*

Delphi, Warren *Also Called: Aptiv Services Us LLC (G-13740)*

Delphi, Warren *Also Called: Aptiv Services Us LLC (G-13741)*

Delphi Pckard Eea - Wrren Plan, Warren *Also Called: Aptiv Services Us LLC (G-13738)*

Delphi-T - Vandalia Ptc, Dayton *Also Called: Mahle Industries Incorporated (G-5865)*

Delphia Consulting LLC... 614 421-2000
1550 Old Henderson Rd Columbus (43220) *(G-4877)*

Delphos Herald Inc (PA).. 419 695-0015
405 N Main St Delphos (45833) *(G-6184)*

Delphos Herald Inc... 419 399-4015
113 S Williams St Paulding (45879) *(G-11154)*

Delphos Plant 2, Delphos *Also Called: Toledo Molding & Die LLC (G-6193)*

Delphos Rubber Company.. 419 692-3000
1450 N Main St Delphos (45833) *(G-6185)*

Delphos Tent and Awning Inc..................................... 419 692-5776
1454 N Main St Delphos (45833) *(G-6186)*

Delta Manufacturing Inc.. 330 386-1270
49207 Calcutta Smithferry Rd East Liverpool (43920) *(G-6392)*

Delta Media Group Inc... 330 493-0350
7015 Sunset Strip Ave Nw North Canton (44720) *(G-10633)*

Delta Plating Inc... 330 452-2300
2125 Harrison Ave Sw Canton (44706) *(G-1880)*

Delta Power Supply Inc... 513 771-3835
10330 Chester Rd Cincinnati (45215) *(G-2545)*

Delta Systems Inc.. 330 626-2811
1734 Frost Rd Streetsboro (44241) *(G-12496)*

Delta Tool & Die, Delta *Also Called: Delta Tool & Die Stl Block Inc (G-6203)*

Delta Tool & Die Stl Block Inc.................................... 419 822-5939
5226 County Road 6 Delta (43515) *(G-6203)*

Deltacraft, Independence *Also Called: Millcraft Group LLC (G-7911)*

Deltec Incorporated.. 513 732-0800
4230 Grissom Dr Batavia (45103) *(G-861)*

Deltech Polymers LLC... 937 339-3150
1250 Union St Troy (45373) *(G-13210)*

Deluxe Business Systems, Streetsboro *Also Called: Deluxe Corporation (G-12497)*

Deluxe Corporation... 330 342-1500
10030 Philipp Pkwy Streetsboro (44241) *(G-12497)*

Dem Manufacturing, Newbury *Also Called: Padco Industries LLC (G-10560)*

Demag Cranes & Components Corp (DH)..................... 440 248-2400
6675 Parkland Blvd Ste 200 Solon (44139) *(G-12100)*

Demark, Wauseon *Also Called: E & J Demark Inc (G-13848)*

Dematic Corp... 440 526-2770
6930 Treeline Dr Brecksville (44141) *(G-1462)*

Demilta Sand and Gravel Inc...................................... 440 942-2015
921 Erie Rd Willoughby (44095) *(G-14446)*

Demmy Sand and Gravel LLC
4324 Fairfield Pike Springfield (45502) *(G-12301)*

Denbro Plastics Company, Toledo *Also Called: Claycor Inc (G-12922)*

Dendratec Ltd.. 330 473-4878
1417 Zuercher Rd Dalton (44618) *(G-5583)*

Dengensha America, Bedford *Also Called: Dengensha America Corporation (G-1025)*

Dengensha America Corporation................................. 440 439-8081
7647 First Pl Bedford (44146) *(G-1025)*

Denizen Inc.. 937 615-9561
130 Fox Dr Piqua (45356) *(G-11344)*

Denman Tire Corporation... 330 675-4242
400 Diehl South Rd Leavittsburg (44430) *(G-8239)*

Denney Plastics Machining LLC.................................. 330 308-5300
149 Stonecreek Rd Nw New Philadelphia (44663) *(G-10442)*

Dennis Constuction Sanitation.................................... 419 332-8026
1201 Siler St Fremont (43420) *(G-7104)*

Denoon Lumber Company LLC (PA)............................. 740 768-2220
571 County Road 52 Bergholz (43908) *(G-1195)*

Dental Ceramics Inc... 330 523-5240
3404 Brecksville Rd Richfield (44286) *(G-11590)*

Dental Pure Water Inc... 440 234-0890
336 Daisy Ave Ste 102b Berea (44017) *(G-1167)*

Denton & Anderson Mktg Div, Hubbard *Also Called: Taylor - Winfield Corporation (G-7817)*

Denton Atd Inc (PA)... 567 265-5200
900 Denton Dr Huron (44839) *(G-7871)*

Dentronix Inc... 330 916-7300
235 Ascot Pkwy Cuyahoga Falls (44223) *(G-5538)*

Dentsply Sirona Inc... 419 893-5672
520 Illinois Ave Maumee (43537) *(G-9290)*

Dentsply Sirona Inc... 419 865-9497
3535 Briarfield Blvd Maumee (43537) *(G-9291)*

Dependable Stamping Company.................................. 216 486-5522
1160 E 222nd St Cleveland (44117) *(G-3609)*

Depot Direct Inc... 419 661-1233
487 J St Perrysburg (43551) *(G-11215)*

Depuy Synthes Inc.. 614 472-8008
374 W Spring St Columbus (43215) *(G-4878)*

Dern Trophies Corp... 614 895-3260
6225 Frost Rd Westerville (43082) *(G-14207)*

Dern Trophy Mfg, Westerville *Also Called: Dern Trophies Corp (G-14207)*

Derrick Company Inc... 513 321-8122
4560 Kellogg Ave Cincinnati (45226) *(G-2546)*

Derrick Petroleum Inc... 740 668-5711
Market Street Bladensburg (43005) *(G-1232)*

(G-0000) Company's Geographic Section entry number

Deruijter Intl USA Inc....................................... 419 678-3909
120 Harvest Dr Coldwater (45828) *(G-4572)*

DES Machine Services Inc................................. 330 633-6897
4115 Baird Rd Stow (44224) *(G-12426)*

Des Tech, Troy *Also Called: Design Technologies & Mfg Co (G-13211)*

Desco LLC.. 513 860-4490
903 Belle Ave Hamilton (45015) *(G-7484)*

Desco Corporation (PA)..................................... 614 888-8855
7795 Walton Pkwy Ste 175 New Albany (43054) *(G-10339)*

Desco Equipment Corp...................................... 330 405-1581
1903 Case Pkwy Twinsburg (44087) *(G-13292)*

Desco Machine Company LLC............................. 330 405-5181
1903 Case Pkwy Twinsburg (44087) *(G-13293)*

Deshea Printing Company................................... 330 336-7601
924 Seville Rd Wadsworth (44281) *(G-13635)*

Design and Fabrication Inc................................ 419 294-2414
400 Malabar Dr Upper Sandusky (43351) *(G-13439)*

Design Concrete Surfaces, Kent *Also Called: Don Wartko Construction Inc (G-8026)*

Design Masters Inc.. 513 772-7175
800 Redna Ter Cincinnati (45215) *(G-2547)*

Design Molded Plastics Inc................................ 330 963-4400
8220 Bavaria Dr E Macedonia (44056) *(G-8683)*

Design Molded Products LLC (PA)....................... 330 963-4400
8220 Bavaria Dr E Macedonia (44056) *(G-8684)*

Design Molded Products LLC.............................. 330 963-4400
8272 Bavaria Dr E Macedonia (44056) *(G-8685)*

Design Original Inc.. 937 596-5121
402 Jackson St Jackson Center (45334) *(G-7961)*

Design Pattern Works Inc.................................. 937 252-0797
2312 E 3rd St Dayton (45403) *(G-5746)*

Design Technologies & Mfg Co........................... 937 335-0757
2000 Corporate Dr Troy (45373) *(G-13211)*

Design Wheel and Hub, Akron *Also Called: Schott Metal Products Company (G-307)*

Designed Harness Systems Inc.......................... 937 599-2485
227 Water Ave Bellefontaine (43311) *(G-1105)*

Designed Images Inc... 440 708-2526
10121 Stafford Rd Ste C Chagrin Falls (44023) *(G-2158)*

Designer Cntemporary Laminates....................... 440 946-8207
1700 Sheffield Ter Painesville (44077) *(G-11079)*

Designer Doors Inc... 330 772-6391
4810 State Route 7 Burghill (44404) *(G-1697)*

Designer Stone Co.. 740 492-1300
303 E Main St Port Washington (43837) *(G-11456)*

Designer Window Treatments Inc........................ 419 822-4967
302 Superior St Delta (43515) *(G-6204)*

Designetics Inc (PA).. 419 866-0700
1624 Eber Rd Holland (43528) *(G-7755)*

Desmond Engraving Co Inc................................ 216 265-8338
3264 W 105th St Cleveland (44111) *(G-3610)*

Desmond-Stephan Mfgcompany......................... 937 653-7181
121 W Water St Urbana (43078) *(G-13461)*

Dester Corporation (DH).................................... 419 362-8020
1200 E Kibby St Bldg 32 Lima (45804) *(G-8400)*

Dester Corporation... 419 362-8020
1200 E Kibby St Bldg 6 Lima (45804) *(G-8401)*

Destin Die Casting LLC...................................... 937 347-1111
851 Bellbrook Ave Xenia (45385) *(G-14762)*

Destiny Manufacturing Inc................................. 330 273-9000
2974 Interstate Pkwy Brunswick (44212) *(G-1588)*

Detailed Machining Inc...................................... 937 492-1264
2490 Ross St Sidney (45365) *(G-12011)*

Detrex Corporation (DH).................................... 216 749-2605
1000 Belt Line Ave Cleveland (44109) *(G-3611)*

Detroit Desl Rmnfctrng-Ast Inc......................... 740 439-7701
60703 Country Club Rd Byesville (43723) *(G-1709)*

Detroit Desl Rmnufacturing LLC......................... 740 439-7701
8475 Reitler Rd Cambridge (43725) *(G-1741)*

Detroit Diesl Specialty TI Inc............................. 740 435-4452
60703 Country Club Rd Byesville (43723) *(G-1710)*

Detroit Flame Hardening Co............................... 513 942-1400
375 Security Dr Fairfield (45014) *(G-6727)*

Detroit Toledo Fiber LLC................................... 248 647-0400
1245 E Manhattan Blvd Toledo (43608) *(G-12942)*

Deuce Machining LLC.. 513 875-2291
3088 Us Highway 50 Fayetteville (45118) *(G-6826)*

Deuce Shirt Customs & More, Miamisburg *Also Called: Jason Schirmer (G-9702)*

Deufol Worldwide Packaging LLC....................... 440 232-1100
19800 Alexander Rd Bedford (44146) *(G-1026)*

Devault Machine & Mould Co LLC....................... 740 654-5925
2294 Commerce St Lancaster (43130) *(G-8195)*

Devicor Med Pdts Holdings Inc.......................... 513 864-9000
300 E Business Way Fl 5 Cincinnati (45241) *(G-2548)*

Dewesoft, Whitehouse *Also Called: Dewesoft LLC (G-14359)*

Dewesoft LLC... 855 339-3669
10730 Logan St Whitehouse (43571) *(G-14359)*

Dewitt Inc.. 216 662-0800
14450 Industrial Ave N Maple Heights (44137) *(G-8882)*

Dewitt Group Inc.. 614 847-5919
777 Dearborn Park Ln Ste E Columbus (43085) *(G-4879)*

Df Supply, Twinsburg *Also Called: Df Supply Inc (G-13294)*

Df Supply Inc... 330 650-9226
8500 Hadden Rd Twinsburg (44087) *(G-13294)*

Dfa Dairy Brands Ice Cream LLC........................ 419 473-9621
4117 Fitch Rd Toledo (43613) *(G-12943)*

Dgl Woodworking Inc.. 937 837-7091
5931 Wolf Creek Pike Dayton (45426) *(G-5747)*

DH, Cincinnati *Also Called: D+h USA Corporation (G-2538)*

Dhpp, Dover *Also Called: Dover High Prfmce Plas Inc (G-6240)*

Dhs Innovations, Bellefontaine *Also Called: Designed Harness Systems Inc (G-1105)*

Di Iorio Sheet Metal Inc.................................... 216 961-3703
5002 Clark Ave Cleveland (44102) *(G-3612)*

Diagnostic Hybrids Inc...................................... 740 593-1784
2005 E State St Ste 100 Athens (45701) *(G-638)*

Diamond Aluminum Co, Middletown *Also Called: John H Hosking Co (G-9870)*

Diamond America Corporation (PA)..................... 330 762-9269
96 E Miller Ave Akron (44301) *(G-119)*

Diamond America Corporation............................ 330 535-3330
1436 Martin Rd Mogadore (44260) *(G-10072)*

Diamond Cellar, The, Dublin *Also Called: Robert W Johnson Inc (G-6340)*

Diamond Designs Inc.. 330 434-6776
231 Springside Dr Ste 145 Akron (44333) *(G-120)*

Diamond Door Limited, Fredericksburg *Also Called: Ohio Custom Door LLC (G-7067)*

Diamond Electronics, Lancaster *Also Called: Diamond Power Intl Inc (G-8197)*

Diamond Electronics Inc.................................... 740 652-9222
1858 Cedar Hill Rd Lancaster (43130) *(G-8196)*

Diamond Heavy Haul, Shandon *Also Called: Diamond Trailers Inc (G-11934)*

Diamond Innovations Inc (PA)............................ 614 438-2000
6325 Huntley Rd Columbus (43229) *(G-4880)*

Diamond Machine and Mfg, Bluffton *Also Called: Carpe Diem Industries LLC (G-1359)*

Diamond Machinery Company, Cleveland *Also Called: Diamond Machinery LLC (G-3613)*

Diamond Machinery LLC..................................... 216 312-1235
19525 Hilliard Blvd Unit 16729 Cleveland (44116) *(G-3613)*

Diamond Mfg Bluffton Ltd.................................. 419 358-0129
505 E Jefferson St Bluffton (45817) *(G-1360)*

Diamond Oilfield Tech LLC................................. 234 806-4185
106 E Market St Fl 2 Warren (44481) *(G-13758)*

Diamond Polymers Incorporated......................... 330 773-2700
1353 Exeter Rd Akron (44306) *(G-121)*

Diamond Power Intl Inc...................................... 740 687-4001
2530 E Main St Lancaster (43130) *(G-8197)*

Diamond Power Intl Inc (DH).............................. 740 687-6500
2600 E Main St Lancaster (43130) *(G-8198)*

Diamond Power Specialty, Lancaster *Also Called: Diamond Power Intl Inc (G-8198)*

Diamond Products Limited.................................. 440 323-4616
1201 Taylor St Elyria (44035) *(G-6516)*

Diamond Products Limited.................................. 440 323-4616
1111 Taylor St Elyria (44035) *(G-6517)*

Diamond Products Limited (DH).......................... 440 323-4616
333 Prospect St Elyria (44035) *(G-6518)*

Diamond Reserve Inc... 440 892-7877
801 Sharon Dr Westlake (44145) *(G-14298)*

A
L
P
H
A
B
E
T
I
C

Diamond Systems, Franklin *Also Called: Modula Inc (G-7035)*

Diamond Trailers Inc... 513 738-4500
  5045 Cincinnati-Brookville Rd Shandon (45063) *(G-11934)*

Diamond Wipes Intl Inc... 419 562-3575
  1375 Isaac Beal Rd Bucyrus (44820) *(G-1678)*

Diamonds Products LLC... 440 323-4616
  1250 E Broad St Elyria (44035) *(G-6519)*

Diamonite Plant, Shreve *Also Called: I Cerco Inc (G-11983)*

Diana Food, Elyria *Also Called: Symrise Inc (G-6594)*

Diano Construction and Sup Co............................. 330 456-7229
  1000 Warner Rd Se Canton (44707) *(G-1881)*

Diano Supply Co, Canton *Also Called: Diano Construction and Sup Co (G-1881)*

Diasome Pharmaceuticals Inc................................ 216 444-7110
  10000 Cedar Ave Ste 6 Cleveland (44106) *(G-3614)*

Dickens Foundry, Arcadia *Also Called: Maass Midwest Mfg Inc (G-482)*

Didion's Mechanical, Bellevue *Also Called: Donald E Didion II (G-1123)*

Die Co Inc.. 440 942-8856
  1889 E 337th St Eastlake (44095) *(G-6423)*

Die Craft Division, Cincinnati *Also Called: Markley Enterprises LLC (G-2847)*

Die Guys Inc.. 330 239-3437
  5238 Portside Dr Medina (44256) *(G-9396)*

Die-Cut Products Co.. 216 771-6994
  1801 E 30th St Cleveland (44114) *(G-3615)*

Die-Gem Co Inc... 330 784-7400
  394 Greenwood Ave Akron (44320) *(G-122)*

Die-Matic Corporation... 216 749-4656
  201 Eastview Dr Independence (44131) *(G-7897)*

Die-Mension Corporation....................................... 330 273-5872
  3020 Nationwide Pkwy Brunswick (44212) *(G-1589)*

Diebold, North Canton *Also Called: Diebold Nixdorf Incorporated (G-10634)*

Diebold Nixdorf, North Canton *Also Called: Diebold Nixdorf Incorporated (G-10635)*

Diebold Nixdorf Incorporated................................ 330 490-4000
  818 Mulberry Rd Se Canton (44707) *(G-1882)*

Diebold Nixdorf Incorporated................................ 740 928-1010
  511 Milliken Dr Hebron (43025) *(G-7612)*

Diebold Nixdorf Incorporated................................ 740 928-0200
  1050 O Neill Dr Hebron (43025) *(G-7613)*

Diebold Nixdorf Incorporated................................ 336 662-1115
  334 Orchard Ave Ne North Canton (44720) *(G-10634)*

Diebold Nixdorf Incorporated (PA)........................ 330 490-4000
  350 Orchard Ave Ne North Canton (44720) *(G-10635)*

Diebold Nixdorf Incorporated................................ 330 899-1300
  3792 Boettler Oaks Dr Ste A Uniontown (44685) *(G-13418)*

Diemaster Tool & Mold Inc................................... 330 467-4281
  895 Highland Rd E # 5 Macedonia (44056) *(G-8686)*

Dietrich Industries Inc (HQ)................................. 800 873-2604
  200 W Old Wilson Bridge Rd Worthington (43085) *(G-14708)*

Dietrich Von Hldbrand Lgacy PR.......................... 703 496-7821
  1235 University Blvd Steubenville (43952) *(G-12402)*

Dietsch Brothers Incorporated (PA)...................... 419 422-4474
  400 W Main Cross St Findlay (45840) *(G-6859)*

Digilube Systems Inc.. 937 748-2209
  216 E Mill St Springboro (45066) *(G-12250)*

Digimanufacturing Tech LLC................................. 419 212-6414
  207 Brown Dr Bryan (43506) *(G-1638)*

Digisoft Systems Corporation............................... 937 833-5016
  4520 Clayton Rd Brookville (45309) *(G-1566)*

Digital & Analog Design, Dublin *Also Called: Pro Oncall Technologies LLC (G-6335)*

Digital Color Intl LLC
  1653 Merriman Rd Ste 211 Akron (44313) *(G-123)*

Digital Factory, Cincinnati *Also Called: Digital Factory Tech Inc (G-2549)*

Digital Factory Tech Inc....................................... 513 560-4074
  407 Race St Cincinnati (45202) *(G-2549)*

Digital Sign Graphics Inc..................................... 937 492-9550
  837 Saint Marys Ave Sidney (45365) *(G-12012)*

Digital Technologies, Rossford *Also Called: Sasha Electronics Inc (G-11663)*

Digitek Corp.. 513 794-3190
  3785 Marble Ridge Ln Mason (45040) *(G-9094)*

Dik Jaxon Products Co Inc.................................... 937 890-7350
  6195 Webster St Dayton (45414) *(G-5748)*

Dilco Industries Inc... 330 337-6732
  300 Benton Rd Salem (44460) *(G-11776)*

Dillen Products, Middlefield *Also Called: Myers Industries Inc (G-9817)*

Diller Metals Inc.. 419 943-3364
  507 S Eastom St Leipsic (45856) *(G-8306)*

Dillin Engineered Systems Corp............................ 419 666-6789
  8030 Broadstone Rd Perrysburg (43551) *(G-11216)*

Dillon Manufacturing Inc...................................... 937 325-8482
  2115 Progress Rd Springfield (45505) *(G-12302)*

Dimco Gray.. 937 291-4720
  8200 S Suburban Dr Dayton (45458) *(G-5749)*

Dimco-Gray Company, Centerville *Also Called: Dimcogray Corporation (G-2131)*

Dimcogray Corporation (PA).................................. 937 433-7600
  900 Dimco Way Centerville (45458) *(G-2131)*

Dimension Hardwood Veneers Inc......................... 419 272-2245
  509 Woodville St Edon (43518) *(G-6473)*

Dimension Industries Inc...................................... 440 236-3265
  27335 Royalton Rd Columbia Station (44028) *(G-4593)*

Dimension Machine Company Inc.......................... 513 242-9996
  6614 Lebanon St Cincinnati (45216) *(G-2550)*

Dimensional Metals Inc (PA)................................. 740 927-3633
  58 Klema Dr N Reynoldsburg (43068) *(G-11565)*

Dinesol Building Products Ltd............................... 330 270-0212
  168 N Meridian Rd Youngstown (44509) *(G-14848)*

Dinesol Plastics, Niles *Also Called: Dinesol Plastics Inc (G-10587)*

Dinesol Plastics Inc.. 330 544-7171
  195 E Park Ave Niles (44446) *(G-10587)*

Dinol US Inc.. 740 548-1656
  8500 Cotter St Lewis Center (43035) *(G-8330)*

Dinsmore Inc... 937 544-3332
  11780 State Route 41 West Union (45693) *(G-14190)*

Diocesan Publications Inc (PA)............................. 614 718-9500
  6161 Wilcox Rd Dublin (43016) *(G-6293)*

Dioguardis Italian Foods Inc................................. 330 492-3777
  3116 Market Ave N Canton (44714) *(G-1883)*

Diplomat Spclty Infusion Group, Cincinnati *Also Called: Optum Infusion Svcs 550 LLC (G-2936)*

Dircksen and Associates Inc................................. 614 238-0413
  743 S Front St Columbus (43206) *(G-4881)*

Direct Action Co Inc... 330 364-3219
  6668 Old Route 39 Nw Dover (44622) *(G-6236)*

Direct Digital Graphics Inc................................... 330 405-3770
  1716 Enterprise Pkwy Twinsburg (44087) *(G-13295)*

Direct Disposables LLC... 440 717-3335
  10605 Snowville Rd Brecksville (44141) *(G-1463)*

Direct Wire Service LLP.. 937 526-4447
  100 Subler Dr Versailles (45380) *(G-13594)*

Directconnectgroup Ltd... 216 281-2866
  5501 Cass Ave Cleveland (44102) *(G-3616)*

Directional One Svcs Inc USA............................... 740 371-5031
  2163a-1 Gwb Complex 2 Bldg 6 State Route 821 Marietta (45750) *(G-8913)*

Discount Floral Supply Inc
  1734 Ivanhoe Rd Cleveland (44112) *(G-3617)*

Discount Smokes & Gifts Xenia............................ 937 372-0259
  37 E Main St Xenia (45385) *(G-14763)*

Discover Publications.. 877 872-3080
  6425 Busch Blvd Columbus (43229) *(G-4882)*

Dish One Up Satellite Inc..................................... 216 482-3875
  3634 Euclid Ave Ste 100 Cleveland (44115) *(G-3618)*

Diskin Enterprises LLC.. 330 527-4308
  10421 Industrial Dr Garrettsville (44231) *(G-7218)*

Dismat Corporation... 419 531-8963
  336 N Westwood Ave Toledo (43607) *(G-12944)*

Dispatch Consumer Services................................. 740 687-1893
  3160 W Fair Ave Lancaster (43130) *(G-8199)*

Dispatch Printing Company (PA)........................... 614 220-5833
  62 E Broad St Columbus (43215) *(G-4883)*

Dispatch Printing Company................................... 614 461-5000
  34 S 3rd St Columbus (43215) *(G-4884)*

Dispatch Printing Company................................... 740 548-5331
  7801 N Central Dr Lewis Center (43035) *(G-8331)*

Display Dynamics Inc 937 832-2830
1 Display Point Dr Englewood (45315) *(G-6612)*

Distillata Company (PA) 216 771-2900
1608 E 24th St Cleveland (44114) *(G-3619)*

Distinct Advantage Cabinetry, Toledo Also Called: Online Mega Sellers Corp *(G-13078)*

Distinctive Marble & Gran Inc 614 760-0003
7635 Commerce Pl Plain City (43064) *(G-11404)*

Distinctive Surfaces LLC 614 431-0898
4600 Bridgeway Ave Columbus (43219) *(G-4885)*

Distribution Center, West Chester Also Called: Martin-Brower Company LLC *(G-14027)*

Distributor Graphics Inc 440 260-0024
6909 Engle Rd Ste 13 Cleveland (44130) *(G-3620)*

District Brewing Company Inc 614 224-3626
2555 Harrison Rd Columbus (43204) *(G-4886)*

Distrubutors, Fairfield Also Called: Ecopac LLC *(G-6730)*

Ditsch Usa LLC 513 782-8888
1100 E Kemper Rd Cincinnati (45246) *(G-2551)*

Ditsch Usa LLC (DH) 513 782-8888
311 Northland Blvd Cincinnati (45246) *(G-2552)*

Ditz Designs, Norwalk Also Called: Hen House Inc *(G-10846)*

Divelbiss Corporation 800 245-2327
9778 Mount Gilead Rd Fredericktown (43019) *(G-7077)*

Diverse Mfg Solutions LLC 740 363-3600
970 Pittsburgh Dr Ste 22 Delaware (43015) *(G-6144)*

Diversey Taski Inc (PA) 419 531-2121
3115 Frenchmens Rd Toledo (43607) *(G-12945)*

Diverseylever Inc 513 554-4200
3630 E Kemper Rd Cincinnati (45241) *(G-2553)*

Diversfied Lbling Slutions Inc 630 625-1225
9487 Dry Fork Rd Harrison (45030) *(G-7549)*

Diversfied Mch Pdts Gnsvlle GA, Columbus Also Called: Prime Equipment Group LLC *(G-5205)*

Diversified Air Systems, Brooklyn Heights Also Called: Rel Enterprises Inc *(G-1538)*

Diversified Brands 216 595-8777
26300 Fargo Ave Bedford (44146) *(G-1027)*

Diversified Mch Components LLC 440 942-5701
6346 Eastland Rd Brook Park (44142) *(G-1512)*

Diversified Mold & Castings Co, Cleveland Also Called: Diversified Mold Castings LLC *(G-3621)*

Diversified Mold and Castings, Cleveland Also Called: Plaster Process Castings Co *(G-4170)*

Diversified Mold Castings LLC 216 663-1814
19800 Miles Rd Cleveland (44128) *(G-3621)*

Diversified Ophthalmics Inc 803 783-3454
250 Mccullough St Cincinnati (45226) *(G-2554)*

Diversified Production LLC 740 373-8771
111 Industry Rd Unit 206 Marietta (45750) *(G-8914)*

Diversified Products & Svcs 740 393-0202
1250 Vernonview Dr Mount Vernon (43050) *(G-10242)*

Diversified SE Division, Cincinnati Also Called: Diversified Ophthalmics Inc *(G-2554)*

Diversified Sign, West Chester Also Called: Dee Sign Co *(G-13982)*

Diversipak Inc 513 321-7884
838 Reedy St Cincinnati (45202) *(G-2555)*

Diversity-Vuteq LLC 614 490-5034
1015 Taylor Rd Gahanna (43230) *(G-7156)*

Division of Selling Materials, Dover Also Called: Smith Concrete Co *(G-6262)*

Division Overhead Door Inc (PA) 513 872-0888
861 Dellway St Cincinnati (45229) *(G-2556)*

Dixie Container Corporation 513 860-1145
3840 Port Union Rd Fairfield (45014) *(G-6728)*

Dixie Machinery Inc 513 360-0091
845 Todhunter Rd Monroe (45050) *(G-10103)*

Dixitech Cnc, Monroe Also Called: Dixie Machinery Inc *(G-10103)*

Dixon Bayco USA 513 874-8499
7280 Union Centre Blvd Fairfield (45014) *(G-6729)*

Dixon Valve & Coupling Co LLC 330 425-3000
1900 Enterprise Pkwy Twinsburg (44087) *(G-13296)*

Diy Holster, Elyria Also Called: Diy Holster LLC *(G-6520)*

Diy Holster LLC 419 921-2168
781 Finwood Ct Elyria (44035) *(G-6520)*

Dje Management Consulting LLC 330 760-2990
5590 Champion Creek Blvd Medina (44256) *(G-9397)*

DJM Plastics Ltd 419 424-5250
1530 Harvard Ave Findlay (45840) *(G-6860)*

Djmc Partners Inc 614 890-3821
654 Brooksedge Blvd Ste A Westerville (43081) *(G-14256)*

DK Bicycles, Springboro Also Called: Safe Haven Brands LLC *(G-12267)*

DK Manfcturing Frazeysburg Inc (HQ) 740 828-3291
119 W 2nd St Frazeysburg (43822) *(G-7059)*

DK Manufacturing, Frazeysburg Also Called: DK Manfcturing Frazeysburg Inc *(G-7059)*

DK Manufacturing Lancaster Inc 740 654-5566
2118 Commerce St Lancaster (43130) *(G-8200)*

DL Schwartz Co LLC 260 692-1464
9737 State Route 49 Hicksville (43526) *(G-7647)*

Dla Document Services 937 257-6014
4165 Communications Blvd Ste 2 Dayton (45433) *(G-5610)*

DLAC Industries Inc 330 519-4789
3755 Sugarbush Dr Canfield (44406) *(G-1808)*

Dlh Enterprises LLC 330 253-6960
2086 Romig Rd Ste 2 Akron (44320) *(G-124)*

DLM Plastics, Findlay Also Called: DJM Plastics Ltd *(G-6860)*

Dlz Ohio Inc (HQ) 614 888-0040
6121 Huntley Rd Columbus (43229) *(G-4887)*

DM Machine Co 440 946-0771
38338 Apollo Pkwy Ste 1a Willoughby (44094) *(G-14447)*

DM Pallet Service Inc 614 491-0881
2019 Rathmell Rd Columbus (43207) *(G-4888)*

Dm2018 LLC 513 893-5483
4805 Hamilton Middletown Rd Ste A Liberty Twp (45011) *(G-8382)*

Dmax, Moraine Also Called: Dmax Ltd *(G-10157)*

Dmax Ltd (DH) 937 425-9700
3100 Dryden Rd Moraine (45439) *(G-10157)*

Dmg Mori Usa Inc 440 546-7088
9415 Meridian Way West Chester (45069) *(G-13984)*

DMG Tool & Die LLC 937 407-0810
1215 S Greenwood St Bellefontaine (43311) *(G-1106)*

Dmi Manufacturing Inc 800 238-5384
7177 Industrial Park Blvd Mentor (44060) *(G-9510)*

Dmi Manufacturing Inc 440 975-8645
4780 Beidler Rd Willoughby (44094) *(G-14448)*

DMK Industries Inc 513 727-4549
1801 Made Dr Middletown (45044) *(G-9854)*

Dms Inc 440 951-9838
37121 Euclid Ave Ste 1 Willoughby (44094) *(G-14449)*

DMV Corporation 740 452-4787
1024 Military Rd Zanesville (43701) *(G-15010)*

DNC Hydraulics LLC 419 963-2800
5219 County Road 313 Rawson (45881) *(G-11551)*

Dnb Mixing Inc 330 296-6327
3939a Mogadore Industrial Pkwy Mogadore (44260) *(G-10073)*

Dno Inc 614 231-3601
3650 E 5th Ave Columbus (43219) *(G-4889)*

Do 210, Cleveland Also Called: Euclid Media Group LLC *(G-3690)*

Do All Sheet Metal, New Albany Also Called: Custom Metal Products Inc *(G-10337)*

Do Duds, Kent Also Called: Embroidery Network Inc *(G-8030)*

Do It Best, Caldwell Also Called: Caldwell Lumber & Supply Co *(G-1724)*

Do It Best, Cincinnati Also Called: Hyde Park Lumber Company *(G-2736)*

Do It Best, Sidney Also Called: Lochard Inc *(G-12031)*

DO Technologies Co 330 725-4561
667 Lafayette Rd Medina (44256) *(G-9398)*

Doan/Pyramid Solutions LLC 216 587-9510
5069 Corbin Dr Cleveland (44128) *(G-3622)*

Docmann Printing & Assoc Inc 440 975-1775
5275 Naiman Pkwy Ste E Solon (44139) *(G-12101)*

Document Concepts Inc 330 575-5685
607 S Main St # A North Canton (44720) *(G-10636)*

Docustar, Cincinnati Also Called: Vya Inc *(G-3210)*

Dodge Company, Dayton Also Called: Ronald T Dodge Co *(G-5988)*

Dole, Springfield Also Called: Dole Fresh Vegetables Inc *(G-12303)*

Dole Fresh Vegetables Inc 937 525-4300
600 Benjamin Dr Springfield (45502) *(G-12303)*

Doll Inc 419 586-7880
1901 Havemann Rd Celina (45822) *(G-2103)*

Doll Printing, Celina *Also Called: Doll Inc (G-2103)*

Dollars N Cent Inc..971 381-0406
1057 S Belvoir Blvd Cleveland (44121) *(G-3623)*

Dom Tube Corp..412 299-2616
640 Keystone St Alliance (44601) *(G-381)*

Dome Drilling Company (PA)...............................440 892-9434
2001 Crocker Rd Ste 420 Westlake (44145) *(G-14299)*

Dome Resources, Westlake *Also Called: Dome Drilling Company (G-14299)*

Domestic Nut, Painesville *Also Called: The Dyson Corporation (G-11116)*

Dometic Sanitation, Big Prairie *Also Called: Dometic Sanitation Corporation (G-1216)*

Dometic Sanitation Corporation..........................330 439-5550
13128 State Route 226 Big Prairie (44611) *(G-1216)*

Dominion Enterprises..216 472-1870
26301 Curtiss Wright Pkwy Cleveland (44143) *(G-3624)*

Dominion Liquid Tech LLC....................................513 272-2824
3965 Virginia Ave Cincinnati (45227) *(G-2557)*

Domino Foods Inc...216 432-3222
2075 E 65th St Cleveland (44103) *(G-3625)*

Domino Sugar, Cleveland *Also Called: Domino Foods Inc (G-3625)*

Domtar Corp...803 802-7500
9435 Waterstone Blvd Ste 360 Cincinnati (45249) *(G-2558)*

Domtar Corporation..937 859-8262
820 S Alex Rd West Carrollton (45449) *(G-13927)*

Domtar Corporation..937 859-8261
1030 W Alex Bell Rd West Carrollton (45449) *(G-13928)*

Domtar Paper Company LLC.................................740 333-0003
1803 Lowes Blvd Wshngtn Ct Hs (43160) *(G-14737)*

Don Basch Jewelers Inc.......................................330 467-2116
8210 Macedonia Commons Blvd Unit 36 Macedonia (44056) *(G-8687)*

Don Wartko Construction Inc...............................330 673-5252
975 Tallmadge Rd Kent (44240) *(G-8026)*

Don-Ell Corporation (PA).....................................419 841-7114
8450 Central Ave Sylvania (43560) *(G-12704)*

Don-Ell Corporation...419 841-7114
8456 Central Ave Sylvania (43560) *(G-12705)*

Donald E Didion II..419 483-2226
1027b County Road 308 Bellevue (44811) *(G-1123)*

Done-Rite Bowling Service Co (PA).....................440 232-3280
20434 Krick Rd Bedford (44146) *(G-1028)*

Dongan Electric Mfg Co.......................................419 737-2304
500 Cedar St Pioneer (43554) *(G-11319)*

Donnelley Financial LLC......................................216 621-8384
1300 E 9th St Ste 1200 Cleveland (44114) *(G-3626)*

Donprint Inc..847 573-7777
17700 Foltz Pkwy Strongsville (44149) *(G-12554)*

Door Engineering and Mfg, Cincinnati *Also Called: Senneca Holdings Inc (G-3080)*

Doors Unlimited, Bridgeport *Also Called: Jerry Harolds Doors Unlimited (G-1494)*

Doran Manufacturing Co., Blue Ash *Also Called: Osborne Coinage Company LLC (G-1316)*

Doran Mfg LLC...866 816-7233
4362 Glendale Milford Rd Blue Ash (45242) *(G-1267)*

Dorel Home Furnishings Inc................................419 447-7448
458 2nd Ave Tiffin (44883) *(G-12782)*

Dorex LLC..216 271-7064
4420 Gamma Ave Newburgh Heights (44105) *(G-10540)*

Dorn Color LLC...216 634-2252
11555 Berea Rd Cleveland (44102) *(G-3627)*

Dosmatic USA Inc...972 245-9765
3798 Round Bottom Rd Cincinnati (45244) *(G-2559)*

Dotcentral LLC..330 809-0112
1650 Deerford Ave Sw Massillon (44647) *(G-9186)*

Double D D Mtls Instllation In, Dayton *Also Called: Double D D Mtls Instlltion Inc (G-5750)*

Double D D Mtls Instlltion Inc.............................937 898-2534
7733 N Main St Dayton (45415) *(G-5750)*

Double Eagle Golf, Lima *Also Called: Lima Armature Works Inc (G-8424)*

Doubleday Acquisitions LLC (PA).......................513 360-7189
675 Gateway Blvd Monroe (45050) *(G-10104)*

Doug Marine Motors Inc......................................740 335-3700
1120 Clinton Ave Wshngtn Ct Hs (43160) *(G-14738)*

Douglas Industries LLC.......................................740 775-2400
379 Douglas Ave Chillicothe (45601) *(G-2250)*

Douthit Communications Inc................................419 855-7465
1550 Woodville Rd Millbury (43447) *(G-9959)*

Douthit Communications Inc (PA).......................419 625-5825
520 Warren St Sandusky (44870) *(G-11828)*

Dove Die and Stamping Company........................216 267-3720
15665 Brookpark Rd Cleveland (44142) *(G-3628)*

Dover Cabinet Industries Inc..............................330 343-9074
1568 State Route 39 Nw Dover (44622) *(G-6237)*

Dover Chemical Corporation (HQ).......................330 343-7711
3676 Davis Rd Nw Dover (44622) *(G-6238)*

Dover Conveyor Inc...740 922-9390
3323 Brightwood Rd Midvale (44653) *(G-9908)*

Dover Corporation...513 870-3206
9393 Princeton Glendale Rd West Chester (45011) *(G-13985)*

Dover Cryogenics, Midvale *Also Called: Amko Service Company (G-9907)*

Dover Fabrication and Burn Inc (HQ)..................330 339-1057
2996 Progress St Dover (44622) *(G-6239)*

Dover High Prfmce Plas Inc................................330 343-3477
140 Williams Dr Nw Dover (44622) *(G-6240)*

Dover Machine Co..330 343-4123
2208 State Route 516 Nw Dover (44622) *(G-6241)*

Dover Phila Heating & Cooling, Dover *Also Called: Hvac Inc (G-6247)*

Dover Roller Shutters, Upper Sandusky *Also Called: Assa Abloy Entrnce Systems HLA (G-13434)*

Dover Tank and Plate Company...........................330 343-4443
5725 Crown Rd Nw Dover (44622) *(G-6242)*

Dover Wipes Company...513 983-1100
1 Procter And Gamble Plz Cincinnati (45202) *(G-2560)*

Dow Cameron Oil & Gas LLC..............................740 452-1568
5555 Eden Park Dr Zanesville (43701) *(G-15011)*

Dow Chemical, Hebron *Also Called: Transcendia Inc (G-7641)*

Dow Chemical, West Alexandria *Also Called: Dow Chemical Company (G-13919)*

Dow Chemical Company.......................................937 839-4612
10 Electric St West Alexandria (45381) *(G-13919)*

Dow Jones, Bowling Green *Also Called: Dow Jones & Company Inc (G-1417)*

Dow Jones & Company Inc...................................419 352-4696
1100 Brim Rd Bowling Green (43402) *(G-1417)*

Dowa Tht America Inc..419 354-4144
2130 S Woodland Cir Bowling Green (43402) *(G-1418)*

Dowco LLC...330 773-6654
1374 Markle St Akron (44306) *(G-125)*

Dowel Yoder & Molding.......................................330 231-2962
4754 Township Road 613 Fredericksburg (44627) *(G-7063)*

Down Decor, Cincinnati *Also Called: Downhome Inc (G-2562)*

Down Decor Ohio Feather, Cincinnati *Also Called: Downhome Inc (G-2561)*

Down Home..740 393-1186
9 N Main St Mount Vernon (43050) *(G-10243)*

Down Home Leather, Mount Vernon *Also Called: Down Home (G-10243)*

Down-Lite International Inc (PA).........................513 229-3696
8153 Duke Blvd Mason (45040) *(G-9095)*

Downhome Inc...513 921-3373
1910 South St Cincinnati (45204) *(G-2561)*

Downhome Inc (PA)..513 921-3373
1 Kovach Dr Cincinnati (45215) *(G-2562)*

Downing Enterprises Inc.....................................330 666-3888
1287 Centerview Cir Akron (44321) *(G-126)*

Downing Exhibits, Akron *Also Called: Downing Enterprises Inc (G-126)*

Downlite, Mason *Also Called: Down-Lite International Inc (G-9095)*

Doxie Inc...937 427-3431
3197 Beaver Vu Dr Dayton (45434) *(G-5611)*

Doyle Manufacturing Inc.....................................419 865-2548
1440 Holloway Rd Holland (43528) *(G-7756)*

Doyle Systems, Norton *Also Called: J E Doyle Company (G-10824)*

Dpsciences, Cincinnati *Also Called: Data Processing Sciences Corporation (G-2542)*

Dr Pepper, Lima *Also Called: Dr Pepper Snapple Group (G-8402)*

Dr Pepper, Youngstown *Also Called: Dr Pepper Bottlers Associates (G-14849)*

Dr Pepper Bottlers Associates............................330 746-7651
500 Pepsi Pl Youngstown (44502) *(G-14849)*

Dr Pepper Snapple Group...................................419 223-0072
2480 Saint Johns Rd Lima (45804) *(G-8402)*

Dr Pepper/Seven Up Inc.................................. 513 875-2466
3943 Us Highway 50 Fayetteville (45118) *(G-6827)*

Dr Pepper/Seven Up Inc.................................. 419 229-7777
2350 Central Point Pkwy Lima (45804) *(G-8403)*

Dr Z Amplification, Maple Heights *Also Called: Dr Z Amps Inc (G-8883)*

Dr Z Amps Inc... 216 475-1444
17011 Broadway Ave Maple Heights (44137) *(G-8883)*

Dr. Pepper 7 Up Columbus, Columbus *Also Called: American Bottling Company (G-4692)*

Drabik Manufacturing Inc.............................. 216 267-1616
15601 Commerce Park Dr Cleveland (44142) *(G-3629)*

Dracool, Franklin *Also Called: Dracool-Usa Inc (G-7017)*

Dracool-Usa Inc (PA).................................... 937 743-5899
331 Industrial Dr Franklin (45005) *(G-7017)*

Dragon Products LLC..................................... 330 345-3968
3310 Columbus Rd Wooster (44691) *(G-14635)*

Dragoon Technologies Inc (PA)...................... 937 439-9223
900 Senate Dr Dayton (45459) *(G-5751)*

Dragoonitcn, Dayton *Also Called: Dragoon Technologies Inc (G-5751)*

Drainage Pipe & Fittings LLC......................... 419 538-6337
450 Tile Company St Ottawa (45875) *(G-11033)*

Drainage Products Inc................................... 419 622-6951
100 Main St Haviland (45851) *(G-7587)*

Drake Manufacturing, Warren *Also Called: Drake Manufacturing LLC (G-13759)*

Drake Manufacturing LLC (PA)........................ 330 847-7291
4371 N Leavitt Rd Nw Warren (44485) *(G-13759)*

Drake Manufacturing Services Co.................... 330 847-7291
4371 N Leavitt Rd Nw Warren (44485) *(G-13760)*

Drapery Stitch, Cleveland *Also Called: Drapery Stitch - Cleveland Inc (G-3630)*

Drapery Stitch - Cleveland Inc........................ 216 252-3857
12890 Berea Rd Cleveland (44111) *(G-3630)*

Drawnear Inc.. 567 215-5305
228 N Countryside Dr Ashland (44805) *(G-533)*

Drb Holdings LLC... 330 645-3299
3245 Pickle Rd Akron (44312) *(G-127)*

Drb Systems LLC (HQ).................................. 330 645-3299
3245 Pickle Rd Akron (44312) *(G-128)*

Drb Tunnel Solutions, Akron *Also Called: Drb Systems LLC (G-128)*

Drc Acquisition Inc...................................... 330 656-1600
10200 Wellman Rd Streetsboro (44241) *(G-12498)*

Dreamscape Media, Holland *Also Called: Dreamscape Media LLC (G-7757)*

Dreamscape Media LLC.................................. 877 983-7326
1417 Timber Wolf Dr Holland (43528) *(G-7757)*

Dreamzone Media LLC................................... 216 532-3301
850 Euclid Ave Ste 819 Cleveland (44114) *(G-3631)*

Dreco Inc.. 440 327-6021
7887 Root Rd North Ridgeville (44039) *(G-10729)*

Dredger LLC... 513 507-8774
5698 Sage Meadow Ct West Chester (45069) *(G-13986)*

Dreison International Inc (PA)........................ 216 362-0755
4540 W 160th St Cleveland (44135) *(G-3632)*

DRG Hydraulics Inc...................................... 216 663-9747
1900 Case Pkwy S Twinsburg (44087) *(G-13297)*

Dri Rubber, Coldwater *Also Called: Deruijter Intl USA Inc (G-4572)*

Dribble Creek Inc.. 440 439-8650
7160 Krick Rd Ste A Bedford (44146) *(G-1029)*

Drifter Marine Inc....................................... 419 666-8144
28271 Cedar Park Blvd Ste 6 Perrysburg (43551) *(G-11217)*

Drink Modern Technologies LLC...................... 216 577-1536
4125 Lorain Ave 2nd Fl Cleveland (44113) *(G-3633)*

Driveline 1 Inc... 614 279-7734
1369 Frank Rd Columbus (43223) *(G-4890)*

Driven Excavating LLC.................................. 567 224-1421
121 S Washington Ave Crestline (44827) *(G-5501)*

Drivetrain USA Inc....................................... 614 733-0940
8445 Rausch Dr Plain City (43064) *(G-11405)*

Drj Welding Services LLC.............................. 740 229-7428
936 Front Ave Sw New Philadelphia (44663) *(G-10443)*

Drone Express Inc (PA)................................. 513 577-5152
123 Webster St Dayton (45402) *(G-5752)*

Drr USA, Brunswick *Also Called: L & R Racing Inc (G-1601)*

Drs Advanced Isr LLC (DH)............................ 937 429-7408
2601 Mission Point Blvd Ste 250 Beavercreek (45431) *(G-970)*

Drs Industrial LLC....................................... 419 861-0334
1067 Hamilton Dr Holland (43528) *(G-7758)*

Drs Industries Inc....................................... 419 861-0334
1067 Hamilton Dr Holland (43528) *(G-7759)*

Drs Leonardo Inc.. 937 429-7408
2601 Mission Point Blvd Ste 250 Beavercreek (45431) *(G-971)*

Drs Leonardo Inc.. 513 943-1111
4043 Mcmann Rd Cincinnati (45245) *(G-2301)*

Drs Signal Technologies Inc........................... 937 429-7470
4393 Dayton Xenia Rd Beavercreek (45432) *(G-972)*

Drt, Dayton *Also Called: Drt Mfg Co LLC (G-5754)*

Drt Aerospace LLC (HQ)................................ 937 492-6121
1950 Campbell Rd Sidney (45365) *(G-12013)*

Drt Holdings LLC (PA).................................. 937 298-7391
618 Greenmount Blvd Dayton (45419) *(G-5753)*

Drt Holdings LLC... 937 297-6676
9025 Centre Pointe Dr Ste 120 West Chester (45069) *(G-13987)*

Drt Mfg Co LLC (HQ).................................... 937 297-6670
4201 Little York Rd Dayton (45414) *(G-5754)*

Drt Mfg Co LLC... 937 298-7391
618 Greenmount Blvd Dayton (45419) *(G-5755)*

Drt Precision Mfg LLC (HQ)............................ 937 507-4308
1985 Campbell Rd Sidney (45365) *(G-12014)*

Drum Parts, Cleveland *Also Called: Group Industries Inc (G-3796)*

Drum Runner, Marion *Also Called: Mission Industrial Group LLC (G-8980)*

Drummond Corporation................................. 440 834-9660
14990 Berkshire Industrial Pkwy Middlefield (44062) *(G-9792)*

Drummond Dolomite Inc................................ 440 942-7000
7954 Reynolds Rd Mentor (44060) *(G-9511)*

Drummond Dolomite Quarry, Mentor *Also Called: Drummond Dolomite Inc (G-9511)*

Drycal Inc.. 440 974-1999
7355 Production Dr Mentor (44060) *(G-9512)*

Dryden Shafts LLC....................................... 937 365-7420
3249 Dryden Rd Moraine (45439) *(G-10158)*

DS Techstar Inc.. 419 424-0888
1219 W Main Cross St Ste 204 Findlay (45840) *(G-6861)*

DSC Supply Company LLC.............................. 614 891-1100
237 E Broadway Ave Ste A Westerville (43081) *(G-14257)*

Dsg-Canusa, Loveland *Also Called: Mattr US Inc (G-8641)*

DSI Management Holdings LLC........................ 800 645-7002
1597 S Water St Kent (44240) *(G-8027)*

Dsk Imaging Inc.. 513 554-1797
6839 Ashfield Dr Blue Ash (45242) *(G-1268)*

DSM Industries Inc...................................... 440 585-1100
1340 E 289th St Wickliffe (44092) *(G-14374)*

Dss Installations Ltd.................................... 513 761-7000
6721 Montgomery Rd Ste 1 Cincinnati (45236) *(G-2563)*

Dss/Drect Tv/Rfs/Ms/rmediation, Cincinnati *Also Called: Dss Installations Ltd (G-2563)*

Dswdwk LLC... 513 853-5021
4831 Spring Grove Ave Cincinnati (45232) *(G-2564)*

DTE Inc... 419 522-3428
110 Baird Pkwy Mansfield (44903) *(G-8781)*

Dti, Alliance *Also Called: Davis Technologies Inc (G-380)*

Dualift Hoist, Iberia *Also Called: Rp Manufacturing LLC (G-7884)*

Dualite Inc (PA).. 513 724-7100
1 Dualite Ln Williamsburg (45176) *(G-14408)*

Dublin Millwork Co Inc................................. 614 889-7776
7575 Fishel Dr S Dublin (43016) *(G-6294)*

Dublin Plastics Inc...................................... 216 641-5904
9202 Reno Ave Cleveland (44105) *(G-3634)*

Dubose Nat Enrgy Fas McHned PR................... 216 362-1700
18737 Sheldon Rd Middleburg Heights (44130) *(G-9769)*

Dubose Strapping Inc................................... 419 221-0626
1221 Stewart Rd Lima (45801) *(G-8404)*

Duca Manufacturing & Consulting Inc (PA)....... 330 758-0828
761 Mcclurg Rd Youngstown (44512) *(G-14850)*

Duca Mfg & Consulting Inc............................ 330 726-7175
697 Mcclurg Rd Youngstown (44512) *(G-14851)*

Duck-T Printing, Cleveland *Also Called: Duck-T Printing LLC (G-3635)*

Duck-T Printing LLC............................... 216 312-0838
1544 E 86th St Cleveland (44106) *(G-3635)*

Duco Tool & Die Inc............................... 419 628-2031
19 S Main St Minster (45865) *(G-10056)*

Duct Fabricators Inc............................. 216 391-2400
883 Addison Rd Cleveland (44103) *(G-3636)*

Ducts Inc.. 216 391-2400
883 Addison Rd Cleveland (44103) *(G-3637)*

Dudick Inc....................................... 330 562-1970
1818 Miller Pkwy Streetsboro (44241) *(G-12499)*

Duff Quarry, Huntsville *Also Called: Duff Quarry Inc (G-7863)*

Duff Quarry Inc.................................. 419 273-2518
3798 State Route 53 Forest (45843) *(G-6940)*

Duff Quarry Inc (PA)............................. 937 686-2811
9042 State Route 117 Huntsville (43324) *(G-7863)*

Duffee Finishing Inc............................ 740 965-4848
4860 N County Line Rd Sunbury (43074) *(G-12663)*

Dugan Drilling Inc.............................. 740 668-3811
27238 New Guilford Rd Walhonding (43843) *(G-13692)*

Duke Graphics Inc............................... 440 946-0606
33212 Lakeland Blvd Willoughby (44095) *(G-14450)*

Duke Manufacturing Inc......................... 440 942-6537
38205 Western Pkwy Willoughby (44094) *(G-14451)*

Duke Printing, Willoughby *Also Called: Duke Graphics Inc (G-14450)*

Dukes Aerospace Inc............................ 818 998-9811
313 Gillett St Painesville (44077) *(G-11080)*

Duma Meats Inc................................. 330 628-3438
857 Randolph Rd Mogadore (44260) *(G-10074)*

Duncan Press Corporation....................... 330 477-4529
5122 Strausser St Nw North Canton (44720) *(G-10637)*

Duncan Tool Inc................................ 937 667-9364
9790 Julie Ct Tipp City (45371) *(G-12823)*

Dunham Machine Inc............................. 216 398-4500
1311 E Schaaf Rd Bldg A Independence (44131) *(G-7898)*

Dunham Products Inc............................ 440 232-0885
7400 Northfield Rd Walton Hills (44146) *(G-13697)*

Dunkin' Donuts, Solon *Also Called: Dandi Enterprises Inc (G-12099)*

Duo-Corp...................................... 330 549-2149
280 Miley Rd North Lima (44452) *(G-10707)*

Duplex Mill & Manufacturing Co................. 937 325-5555
415 Sigler St Springfield (45506) *(G-12304)*

Dupli-Systems Inc............................. 440 234-9415
8260 Dow Cir Strongsville (44136) *(G-12555)*

Dupont, Avon *Also Called: Eidp Inc (G-725)*

Dupont, Circleville *Also Called: Dupont Specialty Pdts USA LLC (G-3255)*

Dupont Electronic Polymers LP................. 937 268-3411
1515 Nicholas Rd Dayton (45417) *(G-5756)*

Dupont Specialty Pdts USA LLC................. 740 474-0635
800 Dupont Rd Circleville (43113) *(G-3254)*

Dupont Specialty Pdts USA LLC................. 740 474-0220
Rt 23 S Dupont Rd Circleville (43113) *(G-3255)*

Dupont Specialty Pdts USA LLC................. 216 901-3600
6200 Hillcrest Dr Cleveland (44125) *(G-3638)*

Dupont Vespel Parts and Shapes, Circleville *Also Called: Dupont Specialty Pdts USA LLC (G-3254)*

Dupont Vespel Parts and Shapes, Cleveland *Also Called: Dupont Specialty Pdts USA LLC (G-3638)*

Dupont Wealth Solutions LLC................... 614 384-5246
655 Metro Pl S Ste 600 Dublin (43017) *(G-6295)*

Dupps, Germantown *Also Called: The Dupps Company (G-7255)*

Dura Magnetics Inc............................ 419 882-0591
5500 Schultz Dr Sylvania (43560) *(G-12706)*

Dura Temp Corporation......................... 419 866-4348
949 S Mccord Rd Holland (43528) *(G-7760)*

Dura-Line Services LLC........................ 440 322-1000
860 Garden St Elyria (44035) *(G-6521)*

Dura-Line Services LLC........................ 440 322-1000
669 Sugar Ln Elyria (44035) *(G-6522)*

Durable Corporation........................... 800 537-1603
75 N Pleasant St Norwalk (44857) *(G-10836)*

Durable Plating Co............................ 216 391-2132
4404 Saint Clair Ave Cleveland (44103) *(G-3639)*

Duracoat Powder Finishing Inc (PA)............ 419 636-3111
1012 E Wilson St Bryan (43506) *(G-1639)*

Duracote Corporation.......................... 330 296-9600
350 N Diamond St Ravenna (44266) *(G-11523)*

Duraflow Industries Inc....................... 440 965-5047
15706 Garfield Rd Wakeman (44889) *(G-13680)*

Duramax Marine LLC............................ 440 834-5400
17990 Great Lakes Pkwy Hiram (44234) *(G-7737)*

Durango Boot, Nelsonville *Also Called: Georgia-Boot Inc (G-10317)*

Durashield, Urbana *Also Called: American Pan Company (G-13457)*

Duray Plating Company Inc..................... 216 941-5540
13701 Triskett Rd Cleveland (44111) *(G-3640)*

Dure Foods Us LLC............................. 614 409-9030
6967 Alum Creek Dr Columbus (43217) *(G-4891)*

Durez, Kenton *Also Called: Durez Corporation (G-8097)*

Durez Corporation............................. 567 295-6400
13717 Us Highway 68 Kenton (43326) *(G-8097)*

Durivage Pattern and Mfg Inc.................. 419 836-8655
20522 State Route 579 W Williston (43468) *(G-14411)*

Duro Bag Manufacturing Company (PA)........... 800 879-3876
441 Vine St Ste 200 Cincinnati (45202) *(G-2565)*

Duro Standard Products Company, Cincinnati *Also Called: Duro Bag Manufacturing Company (G-2565)*

Durox Company................................. 440 238-5350
12312 Alameda Dr Strongsville (44149) *(G-12556)*

Dutch Legacy Company LLC...................... 330 359-0270
9821 Harrison Rd Apple Creek (44606) *(G-466)*

Dutch Quality Stone Inc....................... 877 359-7866
18012 Dover Rd Mount Eaton (44659) *(G-10206)*

Dutchcraft Truss Component Inc................ 330 862-2220
2212 Fox Ave Se Minerva (44657) *(G-10037)*

Dvdbrew LLC................................... 513 677-2739
1555 Loveland Madeira Rd Loveland (45140) *(G-8624)*

Dvuv LLC...................................... 216 741-5511
4641 Hinckley Industrial Pkwy Cleveland (44109) *(G-3641)*

DW Hercules LLC............................... 330 830-2498
2770 Erie St S Massillon (44646) *(G-9187)*

Dwayne Bennett Industries..................... 440 466-5724
6708 N Ridge Rd W Geneva (44041) *(G-7235)*

Dwd2 Inc...................................... 513 563-0070
10200 Wayne Ave Cincinnati (45215) *(G-2566)*

Dwr Graphics Inc.............................. 614 863-6966
850 Science Blvd Columbus (43230) *(G-4892)*

Dwyer Companies Inc (PA)...................... 513 777-0998
6083 Schumacher Park Dr West Chester (45069) *(G-13988)*

Dwyer Concrete Lifting, West Chester *Also Called: Dwyer Companies Inc (G-13988)*

Dybrook Products Inc.......................... 330 392-7665
5232 Tod Ave Sw Ste 23 Warren (44481) *(G-13761)*

Dyco Manufacturing Inc........................ 419 485-5525
12708 State Route 576 Montpelier (43543) *(G-10128)*

Dyna-Flex Inc................................. 440 946-9424
1000 Bacon Rd Painesville (44077) *(G-11081)*

Dyna-Vac Plastics Inc......................... 937 773-0092
921 S Downing St Piqua (45356) *(G-11345)*

Dynalab Ems Inc............................... 614 866-9999
555 Lancaster Ave Reynoldsburg (43068) *(G-11566)*

Dynalab Ff Inc................................ 614 866-9999
555 Lancaster Ave Reynoldsburg (43068) *(G-11567)*

Dynalab Inc (PA).............................. 614 866-9999
555 Lancaster Ave Reynoldsburg (43068) *(G-11568)*

Dynamat, Hamilton *Also Called: Dynamat Inc (G-7485)*

Dynamat Inc (PA).............................. 513 860-5094
3042 Symmes Rd Hamilton (45015) *(G-7485)*

Dynamic Control, Hamilton *Also Called: Dynamic Control North Amer Inc (G-7486)*

Dynamic Control North Amer Inc (PA)........... 513 860-5094
3042 Symmes Rd Hamilton (45015) *(G-7486)*

Dynamic Design & Systems Inc.................. 440 708-1010
7639 Washington St Chagrin Falls (44023) *(G-2159)*

Dynamic Dies Inc.............................. 513 705-9524
1310 Hook Dr Middletown (45042) *(G-9855)*

Dynamic Dies Inc (PA)......................... 419 865-0249
1705 Commerce Rd Holland (43528) *(G-7761)*

(G-0000) Company's Geographic Section entry number

Dynamic Hydraulic Svcs Co LLC............................330 447-8967
205 Deeds Dr Dover (44622) *(G-6243)*

Dynamic Industries Inc.......................................513 861-6767
3611 Woodburn Ave Cincinnati (45207) *(G-2567)*

Dynamic Plastics Inc...937 437-7261
8207 H W Rd New Paris (45347) *(G-10426)*

Dynamic Tool & Mold Inc....................................440 237-8665
12126 York Rd Unit N Cleveland (44133) *(G-3642)*

Dynamic Weld, Osgood *Also Called: Dynamic Weld Corporation (G-11026)*

Dynamic Weld Corporation...................................419 582-2900
242 North St Osgood (45351) *(G-11026)*

Dynamp, Grove City *Also Called: Dynamp LLC (G-7382)*

Dynamp LLC..614 871-6900
3735 Gantz Rd Ste D Grove City (43123) *(G-7382)*

Dynatech Systems Inc...440 365-1774
161 Reaser Ct Elyria (44035) *(G-6523)*

Dynus Technologies, Cincinnati *Also Called: Cbst Acquisition LLC (G-2445)*

Dyoung Enterprise Inc..440 918-0505
38241 Willoughby Pkwy Willoughby (44094) *(G-14452)*

Dysinger Incorporated (PA)..................................937 297-7761
4316 Webster St Dayton (45414) *(G-5757)*

E & E Parts Machining, Strongsville *Also Called: Stefra Inc (G-12605)*

E & I, Westerville *Also Called: McNish Corporation (G-14222)*

E & J Demark Inc..419 337-5866
1115 N Ottokee St Wauseon (43567) *(G-13848)*

E & J Gallo Winery..513 381-4050
125 E Court St Cincinnati (45202) *(G-2568)*

E & K Products Co Inc...216 631-2510
3520 Cesko Ave Cleveland (44109) *(G-3643)*

E & M Liberty Welding Inc....................................330 866-2338
141 James St Waynesburg (44688) *(G-13876)*

E A Cox Inc..740 858-4400
11201 State Route 104 Lucasville (45648) *(G-8666)*

E B P Inc..216 241-2550
29125 Hall St Solon (44139) *(G-12102)*

E Bee Printing Inc..614 224-0416
70 S 4th St Columbus (43215) *(G-4893)*

E C Babbert Inc..614 837-8444
7415 Diley Rd Canal Winchester (43110) *(G-1789)*

E C E, Holland *Also Called: Electronic Concepts Engrg Inc (G-7763)*

E C S Corp..440 323-1707
8015 Murray Ridge Rd Elyria (44035) *(G-6524)*

E C Shaw Company of Ohio..................................513 721-6334
1242 Mehring Way Cincinnati (45203) *(G-2569)*

E D I, Belpre *Also Called: Electrnic Dsign For Indust Inc (G-1147)*

E D M Fastar Inc..216 676-0100
13410 Enterprise Ave Cleveland (44135) *(O-3044)*

E D M Star-One Inc...440 647-0600
6831 Ridge Rd Wadsworth (44281) *(G-13636)*

E H T Company, Euclid *Also Called: Euclid Heat Treating Co (G-6650)*

E I Ceramics LLC...513 772-7001
2600 Commerce Blvd Cincinnati (45241) *(G-2570)*

E J Skok Industries (PA).....................................216 292-7533
26901 Richmond Rd Bedford (44146) *(G-1030)*

E L I, Westerville *Also Called: Energy Labs LLC (G-14208)*

E L Mustee & Sons Inc (PA)...............................216 267-3100
5431 W 164th St Brookpark (44142) *(G-1549)*

E L Stone Company...330 825-4565
2998 Eastern Rd Norton (44203) *(G-10820)*

E M E C, Marysville *Also Called: Engineered Mfg & Eqp Co (G-9019)*

E M I, Cleveland *Also Called: Equipment Mfrs Intl Inc (G-3682)*

E M I Plastic Equipment, Jackson Center *Also Called: EMI Corp (G-7963)*

E M S, Batavia *Also Called: Engineered MBL Solutions Inc (G-864)*

E M Service Inc..440 323-3260
600 Lowell St Elyria (44035) *(G-6525)*

E M Wave, Twinsburg *Also Called: Electro-Magwave Inc (G-13298)*

E P Gerber & Sons Inc...330 857-2021
4918 Kidron Rd Kidron (44636) *(G-8126)*

E P P Inc..440 322-8577
710 Taylor St Elyria (44035) *(G-6526)*

E P S Specialists Ltd Inc......................................513 489-3676
7875 School Rd Cincinnati (45249) *(G-2571)*

E Pompili Sons Inc...216 581-8080
12307 Broadway Ave Cleveland (44125) *(G-3645)*

E R Advanced Ceramics Inc................................330 426-9433
600 E Clark St East Palestine (44413) *(G-6402)*

E Retailing Associates LLC..................................614 300-5785
2282 Westbrooke Dr Columbus (43228) *(G-4894)*

E S C, Akron *Also Called: Ellet Neon Sales & Service Inc (G-131)*

E Systems Design & Automtn Inc.........................419 443-0220
226 Heritage Dr Tiffin (44883) *(G-12783)*

E T I, Mansfield *Also Called: Energy Technologies Inc (G-8786)*

E Technologies Inc...440 247-7000
300 Industrial Pkwy Ste A Chagrin Falls (44022) *(G-2140)*

E Ventus Corporation..216 643-6840
5005 Rockside Rd Independence (44131) *(G-7899)*

E Warther & Sons Inc...330 343-7513
924 N Tuscarawas Ave Dover (44622) *(G-6244)*

E Z Grout Corporation...740 749-3512
1833 N Riverview Rd Malta (43758) *(G-8744)*

E Z Machine Inc..330 784-3363
298 Northeast Ave Tallmadge (44278) *(G-12734)*

E-1 (2012) Holdings Inc.......................................330 482-3900
41969 State Route 344 Columbiana (44408) *(G-4615)*

E-B Display Company Inc.....................................330 833-4101
1369 Sanders Ave Sw Massillon (44647) *(G-9188)*

E-B Wire Works Inc..330 833-4101
1350 Sanders Ave Sw Massillon (44647) *(G-9189)*

E-Beam Services Inc..513 933-0031
2775 Henkle Dr Unit B Lebanon (45036) *(G-8252)*

E-Pak Manufacturing LLC (PA)...........................330 264-0825
1109 Pittsburgh Ave Wooster (44691) *(G-14636)*

E-Z Electric Motor Svc Corp................................216 581-8820
8510 Bessemer Ave Cleveland (44127) *(G-3646)*

E-Z Grader Company...440 247-7511
300 Industrial Pkwy Ste A Chagrin Falls (44022) *(G-2141)*

E.C. Kitzel & Sons, Cleveland *Also Called: Schumann Enterprises Inc (G-4276)*

E2 Merchandising Inc...513 860-5444
9706 Inter Ocean Dr West Chester (45246) *(G-14114)*

Eagle Chemicals Inc..513 868-9662
2550 Bobmeyer Rd Hamilton (45015) *(G-7487)*

Eagle Coach Company, West Chester *Also Called: Federaleagle LLC (G-14118)*

Eagle Composites LLC...513 330-6108
8494 Firebird Dr West Chester (45014) *(G-13989)*

Eagle Creek Inc..513 385-4442
9799 Prechtel Rd Cincinnati (45252) *(G-2572)*

EAGLE CREEK, INC, Cincinnati *Also Called: Eagle Creek Inc (G-2572)*

Eagle Crusher Co Inc...419 562-1183
521 E Southern Ave Bucyrus (44820) *(G-1679)*

Eagle Crusher Co Inc (PA)...................................419 468-2288
525 S Market St Galion (44833) *(G-7187)*

Eagle Elastomer Inc...330 923-7070
70 Cuyahoga Falls Industrial Pkwy Peninsula (44264) *(G-11182)*

Eagle Family Foods Group LLC (PA).....................330 382-3725
1975 E 61st St Cleveland (44103) *(G-3647)*

Eagle Hardwoods, Windsor *Also Called: Hershberger Manufacturing (G-14601)*

Eagle Industrial Truck Mfg LLC............................419 866-6301
1 Air Cargo Pkwy E Swanton (43558) *(G-12683)*

Eagle Machinery & Supply Inc............................330 852-1300
422 Dutch Valley Dr Ne Sugarcreek (44681) *(G-12637)*

Eagle Precision Products LLC.............................440 582-9393
13800 Progress Pkwy Ste J North Royalton (44133) *(G-10759)*

Eagle Print, Delphos *Also Called: Delphos Herald Inc (G-6184)*

Eagle Tugs, Swanton *Also Called: Eagle Industrial Truck Mfg LLC (G-12683)*

Eagle Welding, Willoughby *Also Called: Eagle Welding & Fabg Inc (G-14453)*

Eagle Welding & Fabg Inc....................................440 946-0692
1766 Joseph Lloyd Pkwy Willoughby (44094) *(G-14453)*

Eagleburgmann Industries LP..............................513 563-7325
3478 Hauck Rd Ste A Cincinnati (45241) *(G-2573)*

Eaglehead Manufacturing Co...............................440 951-0400
35280 Lakeland Blvd Ste K Eastlake (44095) *(G-6424)*

Eagles Nest Holdings LLC..419 526-4123
1111 N Main St Mansfield (44903) *(G-8782)*

Eaglestone Products LLC...440 463-8715
8057 Amber Ln Brecksville (44141) *(G-1464)*

Eaj Services LLC..513 792-3400
4350 Glendale Milford Rd Ste 170 Blue Ash (45242) *(G-1269)*

Earl D Arnold Printing Company....................................513 533-6900
630 Lunken Park Dr Cincinnati (45226) *(G-2574)*

Earnie Green Industries, Circleville Also Called: Ernie Green Industries Inc *(G-3257)*

Earth and Atmospheric Sciences, Dayton Also Called: Science/Electronics Inc *(G-5998)*

Earth Dreams Jewelry, North Royalton Also Called: Gardella Jewelry LLC *(G-10763)*

Earthley Wellness..614 625-1064
320 Outerbelt St Ste J Columbus (43213) *(G-4895)*

Earthquaker Devices, Akron Also Called: Earthquaker Devices LLC *(G-129)*

Earthquaker Devices LLC...330 252-9220
350 W Bowery St Akron (44307) *(G-129)*

Easi, Berea Also Called: Estabrook Assembly Svcs Inc *(G-1171)*

East Chemical Plant, Marysville Also Called: Scotts Miracle-Gro Company *(G-9047)*

East End Welding, Kent Also Called: East End Welding LLC *(G-8028)*

East End Welding LLC...330 677-6000
357 Tallmadge Rd Kent (44240) *(G-8028)*

East Manufacturing Corporation....................................330 325-9921
3865 Waterloo Rd Randolph (44265) *(G-11509)*

EAST MANUFACTURING CORPORATION, Randolph Also Called: East Manufacturing Corporation *(G-11509)*

East Oberlin Cabinets LLC...440 775-1166
13184 Hale Rd Oberlin (44074) *(G-10916)*

East Palestine China Dctg LLC......................................330 426-9600
870 W Main St East Palestine (44413) *(G-6403)*

East Side Fuel Plus Operations.....................................419 563-0777
1505 N Sandusky Ave Bucyrus (44820) *(G-1680)*

East Trailers LLC (DH)..330 325-9921
1871 State Rt 44 Randolph (44265) *(G-11510)*

East West Copolymer, Cleveland Also Called: East West Copolymer LLC *(G-3648)*

East West Copolymer LLC (PA)......................................225 267-3400
28026 Gates Mills Blvd Cleveland (44124) *(G-3648)*

East Woodworking Company..216 791-5950
2044 Random Rd Cleveland (44106) *(G-3649)*

Easterday & Co, Wilmot Also Called: David E Easterday and Co Inc *(G-14594)*

Eastern Automated Piping...740 535-8184
424 State St Mingo Junction (43938) *(G-10050)*

Eastern Enterprise, Springfield Also Called: Comptons Precision Machine *(G-12293)*

Eastern Sheet Metal Inc (DH)..513 793-3440
8959 Blue Ash Rd Blue Ash (45242) *(G-1270)*

Eastern Truck & Trailer LLC...866 240-4422
177 Neville St Circleville (43113) *(G-3256)*

Eastgate Custom Graphics Ltd......................................513 528-7922
4459 Mount Carmel Tobasco Rd Cincinnati (45244) *(G-2575)*

Eastlake Machine Products LLC.....................................440 953-1014
1956 Joseph Lloyd Pkwy Willoughby (44094) *(G-14454)*

Eastlake Mfg Facility, Willoughby Also Called: Conn-Selmer Inc *(G-14441)*

Eastman Kodak Company...937 259-3000
3000 Research Blvd Dayton (45420) *(G-5758)*

Eastman Kodak Company...937 259-3000
3100 Research Blvd Ste 250 Kettering (45420) *(G-8119)*

Easy Way Leisure Company LLC (PA)............................513 731-5640
8950 Rossash Rd Cincinnati (45236) *(G-2576)*

Easy Way Products, Cincinnati Also Called: Easy Way Leisure Company LLC *(G-2576)*

Eaton, Cleveland Also Called: Eaton Corporation *(G-3652)*

Eaton Aeroquip LLC (HQ)..440 523-5000
1000 Eaton Blvd Cleveland (44122) *(G-3650)*

Eaton Aeroquip LLC...419 891-7775
1660 Indian Wood Cir Maumee (43537) *(G-9292)*

Eaton Compressor & Fabrication, Englewood Also Called: Airbase Industries LLC *(G-6606)*

Eaton Comprsr Fabrication Inc......................................937 540-1140
1000 Cass Dr Englewood (45315) *(G-6613)*

Eaton Corporation..330 274-0743
115 Lena Dr Aurora (44202) *(G-667)*

Eaton Corporation..440 523-5000
1000 Eaton Blvd Beachwood (44122) *(G-915)*

Eaton Corporation..440 826-1115
6055 Rockside Woods Blvd N Cleveland (44131) *(G-3651)*

Eaton Corporation (HQ)...440 523-5000
1000 Eaton Blvd Cleveland (44122) *(G-3652)*

Eaton Corporation..216 281-2211
9919 Clinton Rd Cleveland (44144) *(G-3653)*

Eaton Corporation..419 238-1190
1225 W Main St Van Wert (45891) *(G-13534)*

Eaton Corporation..513 387-2000
9902 Windisch Rd West Chester (45069) *(G-13990)*

Eaton Corporation..216 523-5000
34899 Curtis Blvd Willoughby (44095) *(G-14455)*

Eaton Electric Holdings LLC (HQ).................................440 523-5000
1000 Eaton Blvd Cleveland (44122) *(G-3654)*

Eaton Electrical...787 257-4470
23555 Euclid Ave Cleveland (44117) *(G-3655)*

Eaton Fabricating Company Inc.....................................440 926-3121
1009 Mcalpin Ct Grafton (44044) *(G-7301)*

Eaton Global Hose, Cleveland Also Called: Eaton Aeroquip LLC *(G-3650)*

Eaton Industrial Corporation (HQ)................................216 523-4205
23555 Euclid Ave Cleveland (44117) *(G-3656)*

Eaton Industrial Corporation...216 692-5456
1000 Eaton Blvd Cleveland (44122) *(G-3657)*

Eaton Leasing Corporation..216 382-2292
1000 Eaton Blvd Beachwood (44122) *(G-916)*

Eavan Corp...216 401-8619
8580 Evergreen Trl Apt 207 Olmsted Twp (44138) *(G-10945)*

Eazytrade, West Chester Also Called: Eazytrade Inc *(G-13991)*

Eazytrade Inc (PA)...513 257-9189
9743 Crescent Park Dr West Chester (45069) *(G-13991)*

Eazytrade Inc...513 257-9189
7503 Overglen Dr West Chester (45069) *(G-13992)*

Ebco Inc...330 562-8265
3500 Crane Centre Dr Streetsboro (44241) *(G-12500)*

Ebel Tape & Label, Cincinnati Also Called: Ebel-Binder Printing Co Inc *(G-2577)*

Ebel-Binder Printing Co Inc...513 471-1067
1630 Dalton Ave # 1 Cincinnati (45214) *(G-2577)*

Ebner Furnaces Inc..330 335-2311
224 Quadral Dr Wadsworth (44281) *(G-13637)*

Ebnerfab, Wadsworth Also Called: Ebner Furnaces Inc *(G-13637)*

Ebo Group, Inc., Sharon Center Also Called: Ebog Legacy Inc *(G-11940)*

Ebog Legacy Inc (HQ)..330 239-4933
1441 Wolf Creek Trail Sharon Center (44274) *(G-11940)*

Ebsco Industries Inc..513 398-3695
4680 Parkway Dr Ste 200 Mason (45040) *(G-9096)*

Ecc Company, Groveport Also Called: Lomar Enterprises Inc *(G-7443)*

Eccles Saw & Tool, Cincinnati Also Called: D & M Saw & Tool Inc *(G-2535)*

Echo Mobile Solutions LLC..614 282-3756
108 Leasure Dr Pickerington (43147) *(G-11293)*

Echo Therm LLC...937 322-5972
2755 Columbus Rd Springfield (45503) *(G-12305)*

Eci Macola/Max LLC (DH)..978 539-6186
5455 Rings Rd Ste 100 Dublin (43017) *(G-6296)*

Ecil Met TEC, Brookpark Also Called: Reliacheck Manufacturing Inc *(G-1557)*

Eckart Aluminum, Painesville Also Called: Eckart America Corporation *(G-11082)*

Eckart America, Painesville Also Called: Obron Atlantic Corporation *(G-11100)*

Eckart America Corporation (DH)...................................440 954-7600
830 E Erie St Painesville (44077) *(G-11082)*

Eclipse..419 564-7482
126 N Union St Galion (44833) *(G-7188)*

Eclipse 3d/Pi LLC..614 626-8536
825 Taylor Rd Columbus (43230) *(G-4896)*

Eclipse Resources - Ohio LLC.......................................740 452-4503
4900 Boggs Rd Zanesville (43701) *(G-15012)*

Ecm Industries LLC...513 533-6242
3898 Duck Creek Rd Cincinnati (45227) *(G-2578)*

Ecm Industries, Llc, Cincinnati Also Called: Ecm Industries LLC *(G-2578)*

Eco Energy International LLC...419 544-5000
233 Park Ave E Mansfield (44902) *(G-8783)*

Eco Fuel Solution LLC..440 282-8592
779 Sunrise Dr Amherst (44001) *(G-446)*

(G-0000) Company's Geographic Section entry number

Eco-Groupe Inc (PA)..937 898-2603
6161 Ventnor Ave Dayton (45414) *(G-5759)*

Ecochem Alternative Fuels LLC................................614 764-3835
7304 Town St Plain City (43064) *(G-11406)*

Ecolab Inc...513 932-0830
726 E Main St Ste F Lebanon (45036) *(G-8253)*

Ecopac LLC...513 795-6002
258 Donald Dr Fairfield (45014) *(G-6730)*

Ecopro Solutions LLC..216 232-4040
5617 E Schaaf Rd Independence (44131) *(G-7900)*

Ecp Corporation..440 934-0444
1305 Chester Industrial Pkwy Avon (44011) *(G-724)*

Ect, North Royalton Also Called: Envirnmntal Cmpliance Tech LLC *(G-10760)*

Ecu Corporation (PA)..513 898-9294
11500 Goldcoast Dr Cincinnati (45249) *(G-2579)*

Edac Composites, Cincinnati Also Called: Meggitt (erlanger) LLC *(G-2858)*

Edc Liquidating Inc..330 467-0750
635 Highland Rd E Macedonia (44056) *(G-8688)*

Edco Tool & Die, Toledo Also Called: Exco Engineering USA Inc *(G-12958)*

Eden Cryogenics LLC..614 873-3949
7630 Copper Glen St Columbus (43235) *(G-4897)*

Edfa LLC..937 222-1415
90 Vermont Ave Dayton (45404) *(G-5760)*

Edge Adhesives Inc...614 875-6343
3709 Grove City Rd Grove City (43123) *(G-7383)*

Edge Adhesives-Oh, Grove City Also Called: Rubex Inc *(G-7412)*

Edge Exponential LLC...614 226-4421
1140 Gahanna Pkwy Columbus (43230) *(G-4898)*

Edge Plastics Inc (PA)...419 522-6696
449 Newman St Mansfield (44902) *(G-8784)*

Edgeenergy, Cincinnati Also Called: One Three Energy Inc *(G-2932)*

Edgepark Medical Supplies, Twinsburg Also Called: Hgi Holdings Inc *(G-13316)*

Edgerton Forge Inc (HQ).......................................419 298-2333
257 E Morrison St Edgerton (43517) *(G-6466)*

Edgewater Capital Partners LP (PA)..........................216 292-3838
5005 Rockside Rd Ste 1300 Independence (44131) *(G-7901)*

Edgewell Per Care Brands LLC................................330 527-2191
10545 Freedom St Garrettsville (44231) *(G-7219)*

Edgewell Personal Care LLC..................................937 492-1057
1810 Progress Way Sidney (45365) *(G-12015)*

Edgewell Personal Care Company.............................740 374-1905
Marietta (45750) *(G-8915)*

Edi Custom Interiors Inc.......................................513 829-3895
5648 Lindenwood Ln Fairfield (45014) *(G-6731)*

Edi Holding Company LLC (PA)................................740 401-4000
100 Ayers Blvd Belpre (45714) *(G-1146)*

Edible Arrangement, Twinsburg Also Called: Kriss Kreations *(G-13326)*

Edict Systems Inc...937 429-4288
2434 Esquire Dr Beavercreek (45431) *(G-973)*

Editencom Ltd...419 865-5877
7134 Railroad St Holland (43528) *(G-7762)*

Edl Displays Inc...937 429-7423
1304 Research Park Dr Beavercreek (45432) *(G-974)*

Edmar Chemical Company......................................440 247-9560
539 Washington St Chagrin Falls (44022) *(G-2142)*

Edsal Sandusky Corporation...................................419 626-5465
117 E Washington Row Sandusky (44870) *(G-11829)*

EDSAL SANDUSKY CORPORATION, Sandusky Also Called: Edsal Sandusky Corporation *(G-11829)*

Educational Direction Inc.......................................330 836-8439
150 N Miller Rd Ste 200 Fairlawn (44333) *(G-6799)*

Educational Equipment, Kent Also Called: Michael Kaufman Companies Inc *(G-8053)*

Edw C Levy Co...330 484-6328
3715 Whipple Ave Sw Canton (44706) *(G-1884)*

Edw C Levy Co...419 822-8286
6565 County Road 9 Delta (43515) *(G-6205)*

Edward D Segen & Co LLC.....................................937 295-3672
100 Enterprise Dr Fort Loramie (45845) *(G-6946)*

Edward W Daniel LLC...440 647-1960
46950 State Route 18 Ste B Wellington (44090) *(G-13885)*

Edwards Culvert Co, Fredericktown Also Called: Edwards Sheet Metal Works Inc *(G-7078)*

Edwards Machine Service Inc.................................937 295-2929
8800 State Route 66 Fort Loramie (45845) *(G-6947)*

Edwards Sheet Metal Works Inc...............................740 694-0010
10439 Sparta Rd Fredericktown (43019) *(G-7078)*

Edwards Steel, Columbus Also Called: Arbenz Inc *(G-4724)*

Eei Acquisition Corp...440 564-5484
15175 Kinsman Rd Middlefield (44062) *(G-9793)*

Efficient Machine Pdts Corp...................................440 268-0205
12133 Alameda Dr Strongsville (44149) *(G-12557)*

Effox-Flextor-Mader Inc (HQ)..................................513 874-8915
9759 Inter Ocean Dr West Chester (45246) *(G-14115)*

Efg Holdings LLC..440 325-4337
777 W Bagley Rd Berea (44017) *(G-1168)*

Eg Enterprise Services Inc.....................................216 431-3300
5000 Euclid Ave Ste 100 Cleveland (44103) *(G-3658)*

Eg Industries, Circleville Also Called: Florida Production Engrg Inc *(G-3258)*

Eg Industries, New Madison Also Called: Ernie Green Industries Inc *(G-10420)*

Egc Enterprises, Chardon Also Called: Egc Operating Company LLC *(G-2204)*

Egc Operating Company LLC (PA)...........................440 285-5835
140 Parker Ct Chardon (44024) *(G-2204)*

Egr Products Company Inc (PA)...............................330 833-6554
55 Eckard Rd Dalton (44618) *(G-5584)*

Eia, Cleveland Also Called: Everything In America *(G-3695)*

Eickholt Glass Inc..614 638-4903
401 W Town St Fl 2 Columbus (43215) *(G-4899)*

Eidp Inc..440 934-6444
38620 Chester Rd Avon (44011) *(G-725)*

Eighth Floor Promotions LLC..................................419 586-6433
1 Visions Pkwy Celina (45822) *(G-2104)*

Einstruction Corporation, Youngstown Also Called: Fscreations Corporation *(G-14858)*

Eisenhauer Mfg Co LLC..419 238-0081
409 Center St Van Wert (45891) *(G-13535)*

Eitle Machine Tool Inc...419 935-8753
6036 Coder Rd Attica (44807) *(G-656)*

Ej Usa Inc...614 871-2436
1855 Feddern Ave Grove City (43123) *(G-7384)*

Ej Usa Inc...216 692-3001
4160 Glenridge Rd South Euclid (44121) *(G-12219)*

Ej Usa Inc...330 782-3900
4150 Simon Rd Youngstown (44512) *(G-14852)*

EL Ostendorf Inc..440 247-7631
3425 Roundwood Rd Chagrin Falls (44022) *(G-2143)*

Elaire Corporation...419 843-2192
7944 W Central Ave Ste 10 Toledo (43617) *(G-12946)*

Elan Designs Inc..614 985-5600
10 E Schrock Rd # 110 Westerville (43081) *(G-14258)*

Elastostar Rubber Corp...614 841-4400
8475 Rausch Dr Plain City (43064) *(G-11407)*

Elastotec Div, North Canton Also Called: Robin Industries Inc *(G-10665)*

Elbex, Kent Also Called: Elbex Corporation *(G-8029)*

Elbex Corporation...330 673-3233
300 Martinel Dr Kent (44240) *(G-8029)*

Elco, Cleveland Also Called: Elco Corporation *(G-3659)*

Elco Corporation...440 997-6131
1100 State Rd Ashtabula (44004) *(G-590)*

Elco Corporation (DH)..800 321-0467
1000 Belt Line Ave Cleveland (44109) *(G-3659)*

Elco Corporation, Ashtabula Also Called: Elco Corporation *(G-590)*

Elden Draperies of Toledo Inc.................................419 535-1909
1845 N Reynolds Rd Toledo (43615) *(G-12947)*

Eldorado National Kansas Inc.................................937 596-6849
419 W Pike St Jackson Center (45334) *(G-7962)*

Eldorado Stone LLC...330 698-3931
167 Maple St Apple Creek (44606) *(G-467)*

Electr-Gnral Plas Corp Clumbus..............................614 871-2915
6200 Enterprise Pkwy Grove City (43123) *(G-7385)*

Electra - Cord, Inc., Massillon Also Called: Rah Investment Holding Inc *(G-9237)*

Electra Sound Inc (PA)..216 433-9600
32483 English Turn Avon Lake (44012) *(G-754)*

Electra Tarp Inc...330 477-7168
2900 Perry Dr Sw Canton (44706) *(G-1885)*

A
L
P
H
A
B
E
T
I
C

Electraform Industries Div, Vandalia *Also Called: Wentworth Mold Inc Electra* **(G-13583)**

Electrasound TV & Appl Svc, Avon Lake *Also Called: Electra Sound Inc* **(G-754)**

Electric Cord Sets Inc (PA) 216 261-1000
4700 Manufacturing Ave Cleveland (44135) **(G-3660)**

Electric Eel Mfg Co Inc 937 323-4644
501 W Leffel Ln Springfield (45506) **(G-12306)**

Electric Motor Service, Piqua *Also Called: Bornhorst Motor Service Inc* **(G-11337)**

Electric Service Co Inc 513 271-6387
5331 Hetzell St Cincinnati (45227) **(G-2580)**

Electric Speed Indicator Co 216 251-2540
650 Cedar Bark Dr Aurora (44202) **(G-668)**

Electrical Insulation Company, Delta *Also Called: Workman Electronic Pdts Inc* **(G-6215)**

Electripack LLC 937 433-2602
2985 Springboro W Moraine (45439) **(G-10159)**

Electrnic Dsign For Indust Inc 740 401-4000
100 Ayers Blvd Belpre (45714) **(G-1147)**

Electro Controls Inc 866 497-1717
1625 Ferguson Ct Sidney (45365) **(G-12016)**

Electro Plasma Incorporated 419 838-7365
4400 Moline Martin Rd Millbury (43447) **(G-9960)**

Electro Polish Company 937 222-3611
332 Vermont Ave Dayton (45404) **(G-5761)**

Electro Prime, Toledo *Also Called: Electro Prime Group LLC* **(G-12948)**

Electro Prime Assembly Inc 419 476-0100
63 Dixie Hwy Ste 7 Rossford (43460) **(G-11656)**

Electro Prime Group LLC 419 476-0100
4510 Lint Ave Ste B Toledo (43612) **(G-12948)**

Electro-Cap International Inc 937 456-6099
1011 W Lexington Rd Eaton (45320) **(G-6453)**

Electro-Line Inc 937 461-5683
118 S Terry St Dayton (45403) **(G-5762)**

Electro-Magwave Inc 216 453-1160
2241 Pinnacle Pkwy Twinsburg (44087) **(G-13298)**

Electro-Metallics Co 513 423-8091
3004 Lefferson Rd Middletown (45044) **(G-9856)**

Electro-Plating & Fabricating, Cleveland *Also Called: Roberts Demand No 3 Corp* **(G-4245)**

Electroburr, Wellington *Also Called: Rochester Manufacturing Inc* **(G-13900)**

Electrocoat, Medina *Also Called: Office Magic Inc* **(G-9430)**

Electrocraft Arkansas Inc 501 268-4203
250 Mccormick Rd Gallipolis (45631) **(G-7203)**

Electrocraft Ohio Inc 740 441-6200
250 Mccormick Rd Gallipolis (45631) **(G-7204)**

Electrodyne Company Inc 513 732-2822
4188 Taylor Rd Batavia (45103) **(G-862)**

Electrolizing Corp of Ohio (PA) 800 451-8655
1325 E 152nd St Cleveland (44112) **(G-3661)**

ELECTROLIZING CORPORATION OF OHIO, Cleveland *Also Called: Electrolizing Corporation Ohio* **(G-3662)**

Electrolizing Corporation Ohio 216 451-8653
1655 Collamer Ave Cleveland (44110) **(G-3662)**

Electromechanical North Amer, Milford *Also Called: Parker-Hannifin Corporation* **(G-9947)**

Electromechanical North Amer, Wadsworth *Also Called: Parker-Hannifin Corporation* **(G-13658)**

Electromotive Inc (PA) 330 688-6494
4880 Hudson Dr Stow (44224) **(G-12427)**

Electronauts LLC 859 261-3600
621 Wilmer Ave Cincinnati (45226) **(G-2581)**

Electronic Concepts Engrg Inc 419 861-9000
1465 Timber Wolf Dr Holland (43528) **(G-7763)**

Electronic Imaging Svcs Inc 740 549-2487
8273 Green Meadows Dr N Ste 400 Lewis Center (43035) **(G-8332)**

Electronic Printing Pdts Inc 800 882-4050
4560 Darrow Rd Stow (44224) **(G-12428)**

Electronics & Communications, Dayton *Also Called: General Dynmcs Mssion Systems* **(G-5794)**

Electrovations Inc 330 274-3558
30333 Emerald Valley Pkwy Solon (44139) **(G-12103)**

Eleeo Brands LLC 513 572-8100
2150 Winchell Ave Cincinnati (45214) **(G-2582)**

Eleet Cryogenics Inc (PA) 330 874-4009
11132 Industrial Pkwy Nw Bolivar (44612) **(G-1382)**

Element Machinery LLC 855 447-7648
4801 Bennett Rd Toledo (43612) **(G-12949)**

Elemetal Refining LLC 740 286-6457
16064 Beaver Pike Jackson (45640) **(G-7944)**

Elevator Cncepts By Wurtec LLC 734 246-4700
6200 Brent Dr Toledo (43611) **(G-12950)**

Eleven 10 LLC 888 216-4049
975 Bassett Rd Ste B Westlake (44145) **(G-14300)**

Eleventh Candle Co 614 530-4853
559 High St Worthington (43085) **(G-14709)**

Eliason Corporation 800 828-3655
10021 Commerce Park Dr West Chester (45246) **(G-14116)**

Eliokem Inc (DH) 330 734-1100
175 Ghent Rd Fairlawn (44333) **(G-6800)**

Elitaire LLC 513 475-3803
4280 Glendale Milford Rd Blue Ash (45242) **(G-1271)**

Elite Biomedical Solutions LLC 513 207-0602
756 Cincinnati Batavia Pike Ste C Cincinnati (45245) **(G-2302)**

Elite Industrial Controls Inc 567 234-1057
7308 Driver Rd Berlin Heights (44814) **(G-1204)**

Elite Property Group LLC 216 356-7469
1036 N Pasadena Ave Elyria (44035) **(G-6527)**

Elkhart Plastics LLC (HQ) 888 605-2068
1293 S Main St Akron (44301) **(G-130)**

Elkhead Gas & Oil Co 740 763-3966
12163 Marne Rd Newark (43055) **(G-10500)**

Ellet Neon Sales & Service Inc 330 628-9907
3041 E Waterloo Rd Akron (44312) **(G-131)**

Elliott, Dayton *Also Called: Elliott Tool Technologies Ltd* **(G-5763)**

Elliott Machine Works Inc 419 468-4709
1351 Freese Works Pl Galion (44833) **(G-7189)**

Elliott Tool Technologies Ltd (PA) 937 253-6133
1760 Tuttle Ave Dayton (45403) **(G-5763)**

Ellis & Watts Global Inds Inc 513 752-9000
4400 Glen Willow Lake Ln Batavia (45103) **(G-863)**

Ellis Brothers Inc Upg 740 397-9191
14220 Parrott Ext Mount Vernon (43050) **(G-10244)**

Ellis Laundry and Lin Sup Inc 330 339-4941
213 8th Street Ext Sw New Philadelphia (44663) **(G-10444)**

Ellison Surface Technologies, Mason *Also Called: Bodycote Surface Tech Inc* **(G-9073)**

Elloras Cave Publishing Inc 330 253-3521
1056 Home Ave Akron (44310) **(G-132)**

Ellwood Engineered Castings Co 330 568-3000
7158 Hubbard Masury Rd Hubbard (44425) **(G-7810)**

Elmers Products Inc 614 225-4000
180 E Broad St Fl 4 Columbus (43215) **(G-4900)**

Elmet Euclid LLC 216 692-3990
21801 Tungsten Rd Euclid (44117) **(G-6648)**

Elmet Technologies Inc 216 692-3990
21801 Tungsten Rd Cleveland (44117) **(G-3663)**

Elmore Mfg Co, Elmore *Also Called: Calvin J Magsig* **(G-6488)**

Elra Industries Inc 513 868-6228
550 S Erie Hwy Hamilton (45011) **(G-7488)**

Elster Perfection, Geneva *Also Called: Honeywell Smart Energy* **(G-7240)**

Elster Perfection Corporation (DH) 440 428-1171
436 N Eagle St Geneva (44041) **(G-7236)**

Eltech Systems Corporation (PA) 440 285-0380
7590 Discovery Ln Concord Township (44077) **(G-5390)**

Eltool Corporation 513 723-1772
1400 Park Ave E Mansfield (44905) **(G-8785)**

Elugen Pharmaceuticals, Cleveland *Also Called: 2 Retrievers LLC* **(G-3276)**

Ely Road Reel Company Ltd 330 683-1818
9081 Ely Rd Apple Creek (44606) **(G-468)**

Elyria Concrete Inc 440 322-2750
400 Lowell St Elyria (44035) **(G-6528)**

Elyria Concrete Step Company, Elyria *Also Called: E C S Corp* **(G-6524)**

Elyria Foundry Company LLC (PA) 440 322-4657
120 Filbert St Elyria (44035) **(G-6529)**

Elyria Manufacturing Corp (PA) 440 365-4171
145 Northrup St Elyria (44035) **(G-6530)**

Elyria Metal Spinning Fabg Co 440 323-8068
7511 W River Rd S Elyria (44035) **(G-6531)**

Elyria Pattern Co Inc...440 323-1526
6785 W River Rd S Elyria (44035) *(G-6532)*

Elyria Plastic Products, Elyria Also Called: E P P Inc *(G-6526)*

Elyria Plating Corporation..440 365-8300
118 Olive St Elyria (44035) *(G-6533)*

Elyria Spring Spclty Holdg Inc (PA)............................440 323-5502
14577 Lorain Ave Cleveland (44111) *(G-3664)*

Em Es Be Company LLC...216 761-9500
18210 Saint Clair Ave Cleveland (44110) *(G-3665)*

Em4 LLC...410 987-5600
676 Alpha Dr Cleveland (44143) *(G-3666)*

Em4 LLC...608 240-4800
676 Alpha Dr Cleveland (44143) *(G-3667)*

Emaxx Northeast Ohio LLC..844 645-6299
1701 Sherrick Rd Se Canton (44707) *(G-1886)*

EMB Designs, Coldwater Also Called: K Ventures Inc *(G-4579)*

Embedded Planet Inc..216 245-4180
31225 Bainbridge Rd Ste N Solon (44139) *(G-12104)*

Embroidery Network Inc..330 678-4887
4693 Kent Rd Kent (44240) *(G-8030)*

Embroidme..330 484-8484
3611 Cleveland Ave S Canton (44707) *(G-1887)*

EMC Precision Machining, Elyria Also Called: Elyria Manufacturing Corp *(G-6530)*

EMC Precision Machining II LLC (PA)............................440 365-4171
145 Northrup St Elyria (44035) *(G-6534)*

EMD Millipore Corporation..513 631-0445
2909 Highland Ave Norwood (45212) *(G-10868)*

Emergency Products & RES Inc....................................330 673-5003
890 W Main St Kent (44240) *(G-8031)*

Emergency Training Inst Div, Fairlawn Also Called: Educational Direction Inc *(G-6799)*

Emerson, Cincinnati Also Called: Emerson Electric Co *(G-2583)*

Emerson Commercial Reside...937 493-2828
1675 Campbell Rd Sidney (45365) *(G-12017)*

Emerson Corp...614 841-5498
975 Pittsburgh Dr Delaware (43015) *(G-6145)*

Emerson Electric Co..513 731-2020
6000 Fernview Ave Cincinnati (45212) *(G-2583)*

Emerson Helix...937 710-5771
40 W Stewart St Dayton (45409) *(G-5764)*

Emerson Industrial Automation.....................................216 901-2400
7800 Hub Pkwy Cleveland (44125) *(G-3668)*

Emerson Network Power..614 841-8054
3040 S 9th St Ironton (45638) *(G-7931)*

Emerson Network Power System, Westerville Also Called: Liebert Field Services Inc *(G-14220)*

Emerson Process Management......................................419 529-4311
2500 Park Ave W Ontario (44906) *(G-10949)*

Emerson Professional Tools LLC...................................740 432-8782
9877 Brick Church Rd Cambridge (43725) *(G-1742)*

Emery, Cincinnati Also Called: Emery Oleochemicals LLC *(G-2584)*

Emery Oleochemicals LLC (HQ)...................................513 762-2500
4900 Este Ave Cincinnati (45232) *(G-2584)*

Emes Supply LLC...216 400-8025
35622 Vine St Willowick (44095) *(G-14566)*

Emh Inc (PA)..330 220-8600
550 Crane Dr Valley City (44280) *(G-13495)*

EMI Corp (PA)..937 596-5511
801 W Pike St Jackson Center (45334) *(G-7963)*

Eminent Transport, Cleveland Also Called: Express Ground Services Inc *(G-3700)*

Emmco Inc..216 429-2020
19199 Saint Clair Ave Euclid (44117) *(G-6649)*

Emmert Grains, Cincinnati Also Called: The F L Emmert Co Inc *(G-3147)*

Empanadas Aqui LLC..513 312-9566
8749 Surrey Pl Maineville (45039) *(G-8739)*

Empire Die Casting Co, Macedonia Also Called: Edc Liquidating Inc *(G-8688)*

Empire Die Casting Company, Macedonia Also Called: American Light Metals LLC *(G-8677)*

Empire Diecasting, Macedonia Also Called: SRS Die Casting Holdings LLC *(G-8714)*

Empire Packing Company LLC.......................................901 948-4788
4780 Alliance Dr Mason (45040) *(G-9097)*

Empire Packing Company LP..513 942-5400
113 Circle Freeway Dr West Chester (45246) *(G-14117)*

Empire Plow Company Inc (DH)....................................216 641-2290
343 W Bagley Rd Ste 214 Berea (44017) *(G-1169)*

Empire Printing Inc..513 242-3900
9560 Le Saint Dr Fairfield (45014) *(G-6732)*

Empire Systems Inc..440 653-9300
33683 Walker Rd Avon Lake (44012) *(G-755)*

Empirical Manufacturing Co Inc....................................513 948-1616
7616 Reinhold Dr Cincinnati (45237) *(G-2585)*

Empyracom Inc (PA)...330 744-5570
7510 Market St Ste 8 Boardman (44512) *(G-1370)*

Emroid ME...614 789-1898
6065 Shreven Dr Westerville (43081) *(G-14259)*

Emssons Faurecia Ctrl Systems.....................................937 743-0551
2301 Commerce Center Dr Franklin (45005) *(G-7018)*

Emssons Faurecia Ctrl Systems (DH).............................812 341-2000
543 Matzinger Rd Toledo (43612) *(G-12951)*

Emx Industries LLC (HQ)..216 518-9888
5660 Transportation Blvd Cleveland (44125) *(G-3669)*

Emx Industries, Inc., Cleveland Also Called: Emx Industries LLC *(G-3669)*

En-Hanced Products Inc...614 882-7400
14111 Chambers Rd Sunbury (43074) *(G-12664)*

Enamelac Company...216 481-8878
18103 Roseland Rd Cleveland (44112) *(G-3670)*

Encapsulation Technologies LLC...................................419 819-6319
2937 Industrial Park Dr Austinburg (44010) *(G-697)*

Enclosure Suppliers LLC...513 782-3900
12119 Champion Way Cincinnati (45241) *(G-2586)*

Encompass Atmtn Engrg Tech LLC................................419 873-0000
622 Eckel Rd Perrysburg (43551) *(G-11218)*

Encompass Woodworking LLC.......................................513 569-2841
1303 Monmouth St Cincinnati (45225) *(G-2587)*

Encon, Dayton Also Called: Encon Inc *(G-5765)*

Encon Inc...937 898-2603
6161 Ventnor Ave Dayton (45414) *(G-5765)*

Encore Industries Inc..419 626-8000
319 Howard Dr Sandusky (44870) *(G-11830)*

Encore Industries Inc (DH)..419 626-8000
725 Water St Cambridge (43725) *(G-1743)*

Encore Plastics, Cambridge Also Called: Encore Industries Inc *(G-1743)*

Encore Plastics Southeast LLC.....................................419 626-8000
319 Howard Dr Sandusky (44870) *(G-11831)*

Encore Precast LLC..513 726-5678
416 W Ritter Seven Mile (45062) *(G-11907)*

Endless Home Improvements LLC..................................614 599-1799
3897 Fergus Rd Columbus (43207) *(G-4901)*

Endolite, Miamisburg Also Called: Blatchford Inc *(G-9673)*

Endura Products LLC..419 248-8911
1 Owens Corning Pkwy Toledo (43659) *(G-12952)*

Endurance Industries LLC..513 285-8503
5055 Madison Rd Cincinnati (45227) *(G-2588)*

Endurance Manufacturing Inc.......................................330 628-2600
1615 E Market St Akron (44305) *(G-133)*

Enduro Rubber Company...330 296-9603
685 S Chestnut St Ravenna (44266) *(G-11524)*

Enerco Group Inc (PA)...216 916-3000
4560 W 160th St Cleveland (44135) *(G-3671)*

Enerco Technical Products Inc......................................216 916-3000
4560 W 160th St Cleveland (44135) *(G-3672)*

Enerfab Inc..513 771-2300
11861 Mosteller Rd Cincinnati (45241) *(G-2589)*

Enerfab LLC (PA)..513 641-0500
4430 Chickering Ave Cincinnati (45232) *(G-2590)*

Energizer Global Auto Care..937 742-4500
2800 Concorde Dr Vandalia (45377) *(G-13555)*

Energizer Manufacturing Inc
25225 Detroit Rd Westlake (44145) *(G-14301)*

Energy & Ctrl Integrators Inc (PA)................................419 222-0025
1130 E Albert St Lima (45804) *(G-8405)*

Energy Corportive, Coshocton Also Called: Ngo Development Corporation *(G-5464)*

Energy Hbr Nclear Gnration LLC...................................888 254-6359
168 E Market St Akron (44308) *(G-134)*

A
L
P
H
A
B
E
T
I
C

Energy Labs LLC (DH)................................619 671-0100
505 N Cleveland Ave Westerville (43082) *(G-14208)*

Energy Manufacturing Ltd................................419 355-9304
1830 Oak Harbor Rd Fremont (43420) *(G-7105)*

Energy Technologies Inc................................419 522-4444
219 Park Ave E Mansfield (44902) *(G-8786)*

Energy Transfer, Minerva *Also Called: Machine Dynamics & Engrg Inc (G-10041)*

Enersys................................216 252-4242
12690 Elmwood Ave Cleveland (44111) *(G-3673)*

Enespro LLC................................630 332-2801
15825 Industrial Pkwy Cleveland (44135) *(G-3674)*

Enespro Ppe................................800 553-0672
10601 Memphis Ave Brooklyn (44144) *(G-1521)*

Engineered Conductive Mtl LLC................................740 362-4444
132 Johnson Dr Delaware (43015) *(G-6146)*

Engineered Endeavors, Middlefield *Also Called: Eei Acquisition Corp (G-9793)*

Engineered Endeavors Inc................................440 564-5484
10975 Kinsman Rd Newbury (44065) *(G-10550)*

Engineered Films Division Inc................................419 884-8150
230 Industrial Dr Lexington (44904) *(G-8373)*

Engineered Imaging LLC................................419 255-1283
110 E Woodruff Ave Toledo (43604) *(G-12953)*

Engineered Marble Inc................................614 308-0041
4064 Fisher Rd Columbus (43228) *(G-4902)*

Engineered Material Handling, Valley City *Also Called: Emh Inc (G-13495)*

Engineered MBL Solutions Inc................................513 724-0247
4155 Taylor Rd Batavia (45103) *(G-864)*

Engineered Mfg & Eqp Co................................937 642-7776
11611 Industrial Pkwy Marysville (43040) *(G-9019)*

Engineered Plastics Corp................................330 376-7700
420 Kenmore Blvd Akron (44301) *(G-135)*

Engineered Products, Twinsburg *Also Called: EPI of Cleveland Inc (G-13299)*

Engineered Profiles LLC................................614 754-3700
2141 Fairwood Ave Columbus (43207) *(G-4903)*

Engineered Wire Products Inc (DH)................................419 294-3817
1200 N Warpole St Upper Sandusky (43351) *(G-13440)*

Engineered Wire Products Inc................................330 469-6958
3121 W Market St Warren (44485) *(G-13762)*

Engineering Chain Div, Sandusky *Also Called: US Tsubaki Power Transm LLC (G-11881)*

Engineering Dept, Troy *Also Called: Hobart LLC (G-13225)*

Engines Inc of Ohio................................740 377-9874
101 Commerce Dr South Point (45680) *(G-12223)*

Enginetics, Huber Heights *Also Called: Mpe Aeroengines Inc (G-7823)*

Enginetics Aero Space, Huber Heights *Also Called: Enjet Aero Dayton Inc (G-7821)*

Enginred Atmsphric Mtgtion LLC................................740 385-6690
32919 Logan Horns Mill Rd Logan (43138) *(G-8513)*

Engler Printing Co................................419 332-2181
808 W State St Fremont (43420) *(G-7106)*

Engravers Gallery & Sign Co................................330 830-1271
10 Lincoln Way E Massillon (44646) *(G-9190)*

Eni USA R&M Co Inc................................330 723-6457
740 S Progress Dr Medina (44256) *(G-9399)*

Enjet Aero LLC................................937 878-3800
7700 New Carlisle Pike Huber Heights (45424) *(G-7820)*

Enjet Aero Dayton, Huber Heights *Also Called: Enjet Aero LLC (G-7820)*

Enjet Aero Dayton Inc (DH)................................937 878-3800
7700 New Carlisle Pike Huber Heights (45424) *(G-7821)*

Enlarging Arts Inc................................330 434-3433
161 Tarbell St Akron (44303) *(G-136)*

Ennis Inc................................800 537-8648
4444 N Detroit Ave Toledo (43612) *(G-12954)*

Enpac LLC................................440 975-0070
34355 Melinz Pkwy Eastlake (44095) *(G-6425)*

Enpress LLC................................440 510-0108
34899 Curtis Blvd Eastlake (44095) *(G-6426)*

Enpro, West Chester *Also Called: Hydrotech Inc (G-14126)*

Enprotech Industrial Tech LLC (DH)................................216 883-3220
4259 E 49th St Cleveland (44125) *(G-3675)*

Enprotech Mechanical Services, Cleveland *Also Called: Enprotech Industrial Tech LLC (G-3675)*

Enquirer Printing Co Inc................................513 241-1956
7188 Main St Cincinnati (45244) *(G-2591)*

Enrevo Pyro LLC................................203 517-5002
6874 Strimbu Dr Brookfield (44403) *(G-1514)*

Ensign Product Company Inc................................216 341-5911
3528 E 76th St Cleveland (44105) *(G-3676)*

Enterprise Machine Inc................................513 681-4409
3640 Llewellyn Ave Cincinnati (45223) *(G-2592)*

Enterprise Plastics Inc................................330 346-0496
838 Overholt Rd Kent (44240) *(G-8032)*

Enterprise Tool & Die Company................................216 351-1300
4940 Schaaf Ln Cleveland (44131) *(G-3677)*

Enterprise Welding & Fabg Inc................................440 354-4128
6257 Heisley Rd Mentor (44060) *(G-9513)*

Enterprise Welding Fbrctn................................440 354-3868
9280 Pineneedle Dr Mentor (44060) *(G-9514)*

Enting Water Conditioning Inc (PA)................................937 294-5100
3211 Dryden Rd Frnt Moraine (45439) *(G-10160)*

Entratech Systems, Sandusky *Also Called: Entratech Systems LLC (G-11832)*

Entratech Systems LLC (PA)................................419 433-7683
202 Fox Rd Sandusky (44870) *(G-11832)*

Entrochem Inc................................614 946-7602
1245 Kinnear Rd Columbus (43212) *(G-4904)*

Entrotech Inc................................614 946-7602
1245 Kinnear Rd Columbus (43212) *(G-4905)*

Envases Media Inc................................419 636-5461
1 Toy St Bryan (43506) *(G-1640)*

Envelope 1, Columbiana *Also Called: E-1 (2012) Holdings Inc (G-4615)*

Envelope 1 Inc (PA)................................330 482-3900
41969 State Route 344 Columbiana (44408) *(G-4616)*

Envelope Mart of Ohio Inc................................440 365-8177
1540 Lowell St Elyria (44035) *(G-6535)*

Enviri Corporation................................740 367-7322
5486 State Route 7 N Cheshire (45620) *(G-2231)*

Enviri Corporation................................216 961-1570
7900 Hub Pkwy Cleveland (44125) *(G-3678)*

Enviri Corporation................................740 387-1150
3477 Harding Hwy E Marion (43302) *(G-8969)*

Enviri Corporation................................330 372-1781
101 Tidewater St Ne Warren (44483) *(G-13763)*

Envirnment Ctrl Sthwest Ohio I................................937 669-9900
7939 S County Road 25a Tipp City (45371) *(G-12824)*

Envirnmntal Cmpliance Tech LLC................................216 634-0400
13953 Progress Pkwy North Royalton (44133) *(G-10760)*

Envirofab Inc................................216 651-1767
7914 Lake Ave Cleveland (44102) *(G-3679)*

Environmental Chemical Corp................................330 453-5200
2167 Prestwick Dr Uniontown (44685) *(G-13419)*

Environmental Doctor, Dayton *Also Called: Indoor Envmtl Specialists Inc (G-5821)*

Environmental Growth Chambers, Chagrin Falls *Also Called: Integrated Development & Mfg (G-2146)*

Environmental Products Div, Sheffield Village *Also Called: Benko Products Inc (G-11957)*

Environmental Sample Technology Inc................................513 642-0100
503 Commercial Dr West Chester (45014) *(G-13993)*

Envirozyme, Bowling Green *Also Called: Envirozyme LLC (G-1419)*

Envirozyme LLC................................800 232-2847
400 Van Camp Rd Bowling Green (43402) *(G-1419)*

Envoi Design Inc................................513 651-4229
1332 Main St Frnt Cincinnati (45202) *(G-2593)*

Eoi Inc................................740 201-3300
8377 Green Meadows Dr N Ste C Lewis Center (43035) *(G-8333)*

Eos Technology Inc................................216 281-2999
8525 Clinton Rd Cleveland (44144) *(G-3680)*

Ep Bollinger LLC................................513 941-1101
2664 Saint Georges Ct Cincinnati (45233) *(G-2594)*

EP Ferris & Associates Inc................................614 299-2999
2130 Quarry Trails Dr # 2 Columbus (43228) *(G-4906)*

Epco, Germantown *Also Called: Thomas D Epperson (G-7256)*

Epco Extrusion Painting Co................................330 781-6100
4605 Lake Park Rd Youngstown (44512) *(G-14853)*

Epcor Foundries, Cincinnati *Also Called: Seilkop Industries Inc (G-3077)*

Epg Inc..330 995-5125
500 Lena Dr Aurora (44202) *(G-669)*

Epg Inc (DH)..330 995-9725
1780 Miller Pkwy Streetsboro (44241) *(G-12501)*

Epi Global, Millbury *Also Called: Electro Plasma Incorporated (G-9960)*

Epi Global, Millbury *Also Called: Levison Enterprises LLC (G-9964)*

EPI of Cleveland Inc.................................330 468-2872
2224 E Enterprise Pkwy Twinsburg (44087) *(G-13299)*

Epic Steel, Solon *Also Called: E B P Inc (G-12102)*

Epiroc USA LLC......................................717 552-8488
820 Glaser Pkwy Akron (44306) *(G-137)*

Epiroc USA LLC......................................844 437-4762
7171 E Pleasant Valley Rd Independence (44131) *(G-7902)*

Epix Tube Co Inc (PA)..............................937 529-4858
5800 Wolf Creek Pike Dayton (45426) *(G-5766)*

Epluno LLC...800 249-5275
420 Heatherwoode Cir Springboro (45066) *(G-12251)*

Epoxy Systems Blstg Cating Inc..................513 924-1800
5640 Morgan Rd Cleves (45002) *(G-4535)*

Epr, Kent *Also Called: Emergency Products & RES Inc (G-8031)*

Eprad, Perrysburg *Also Called: Eprad Inc (G-11219)*

Eprad Inc..419 666-3266
28271 Cedar Park Blvd Ste 1 Perrysburg (43551) *(G-11219)*

Eps Specialties Ltd Inc...........................513 489-3676
7875 School Rd # 77 Cincinnati (45249) *(G-2595)*

Epsilon Management Corporation..................216 634-2500
8525 Clinton Rd Cleveland (44144) *(G-3681)*

Epsilyte, Piqua *Also Called: Polysource LLC (G-11379)*

Epsilyte Holdings LLC.............................937 778-9500
555 E Statler Rd Piqua (45356) *(G-11346)*

Eqm Technologies & Energy Inc (PA)............513 825-7500
1800 Carillion Blvd Cincinnati (45240) *(G-2596)*

Equinox Enterprises LLC.........................419 627-0022
1920 George St Sandusky (44870) *(G-11833)*

Equip Business Solutions Co (PA)................614 854-9755
120 Twin Oaks Dr Jackson (45640) *(G-7945)*

Equipment Guys Inc...............................614 871-9220
185 Westgate Dr Newark (43055) *(G-10501)*

Equipment Mfrs Intl Inc..........................216 651-6700
16151 Puritas Ave Cleveland (44135) *(G-3682)*

Equipping Ministries Intl Inc.....................513 742-1100
3908 Plainville Rd # 200 Cincinnati (45227) *(G-2597)*

Equistar, Fairport Harbor *Also Called: Lyondell Chemical Company (G-6818)*

Equistar Chemicals LP............................513 530-4000
11530 Northlake Dr Cincinnati (45249) *(G-2598)*

ERAMET MARIETTA INC...........................740 374-1000
16706 State Route 7 Marietta (45750) *(C-8016)*

Erath Veneer, Granville *Also Called: Erath Veneer Corp Virginia (G-7314)*

Erath Veneer Corp Virginia.......................540 483-5223
2825 Hallie Ln # B Granville (43023) *(G-7314)*

Erd Specialty Graphics Inc.......................419 242-9545
3250 Monroe St Toledo (43606) *(G-12955)*

Erdie Industries Inc...............................440 288-0166
1205 Colorado Ave Lorain (44052) *(G-8555)*

Ergo Desktop LLC..................................567 890-3746
457 Grand Lake Rd Celina (45822) *(G-2105)*

Ergocan, Toledo *Also Called: Mon-Say Corp (G-13059)*

Erhart Foundry, Cincinnati *Also Called: Chris Erhart Foundry & Mch Co (G-2463)*

Erico, Cleveland *Also Called: Erico Products Inc (G-3683)*

Erico Inc...440 248-0100
34600 Solon Rd Solon (44139) *(G-12105)*

Erico Global Company.............................440 248-0100
31700 Solon Rd Solon (44139) *(G-12106)*

Erico International Corp...........................440 248-0100
34600 Solon Rd Solon (44139) *(G-12107)*

Erico Products Inc.................................440 248-0100
34600 Solon Rd Cleveland (44139) *(G-3683)*

Ericson Manufacturing Co.........................440 951-8000
4323 Hamann Pkwy Willoughby (44094) *(G-14456)*

Erie Steel Ltd......................................419 478-3743
5540 Jackman Rd Toledo (43613) *(G-12956)*

Erie Street Thea Svcs Inc.........................216 426-0050
1621 E 41st St Cleveland (44103) *(G-3684)*

Erieview Metal Treating Co........................216 663-1780
4465 Johnston Pkwy Cleveland (44128) *(G-3685)*

Ernest Industries Inc..............................937 325-9851
4000 Mccartney Rd Lowellville (44436) *(G-8660)*

Ernest Industries Inc..............................937 325-9851
1221 Groop Rd Springfield (45504) *(G-12307)*

Ernie Green Industries Inc........................740 420-5252
30627 Orr Rd Circleville (43113) *(G-3257)*

Ernie Green Industries Inc........................614 219-1423
1855 State Rd Ste 121n New Madison (45346) *(G-10420)*

Ernst Concrete, Cleves *Also Called: Ernst Enterprises Inc (G-4536)*

Ernst Concrete, Vandalia *Also Called: Ernst Enterprises Inc (G-13556)*

Ernst Concrete, West Milton *Also Called: Ernst Enterprises Inc (G-14182)*

Ernst Enterprises Inc..............................937 848-6811
2181 Ferry Rd Bellbrook (45305) *(G-1091)*

Ernst Enterprises Inc..............................937 866-9441
4710 Soldiers Home Rd Carrollton (44615) *(G-2082)*

Ernst Enterprises Inc..............................513 367-1939
7340 Dry Fork Rd Cleves (45002) *(G-4536)*

Ernst Enterprises Inc..............................614 308-0063
4252 Truro Station Service Rd Columbus (43232) *(G-4907)*

Ernst Enterprises Inc..............................614 308-0063
569 N Wilson Rd Columbus (43204) *(G-4908)*

Ernst Enterprises Inc..............................614 443-9456
711 Stimmel Rd Columbus (43223) *(G-4909)*

Ernst Enterprises Inc..............................937 878-9378
5325 Medway Rd Fairborn (45324) *(G-6690)*

Ernst Enterprises Inc..............................513 829-8683
107 River Cir Bldg 1 Fairfield (45014) *(G-6733)*

Ernst Enterprises Inc..............................513 874-8300
4250 Columbia Rd Lebanon (45036) *(G-8254)*

Ernst Enterprises Inc..............................419 222-2015
377 S Central Ave Lima (45804) *(G-8406)*

Ernst Enterprises Inc..............................513 422-3651
2504 S Main St Middletown (45042) *(G-9857)*

Ernst Enterprises Inc..............................937 339-6249
805 Union St Troy (45373) *(G-13212)*

Ernst Enterprises Inc (PA).........................937 233-5555
993 Falls Creek Dr Vandalia (45377) *(G-13556)*

Ernst Enterprises Inc..............................937 233-7777
7850 S Karns Rd West Milton (45383) *(G-14182)*

Ernst Flow Industries LLC........................732 938-5641
16633 Foltz Pkwy Strongsville (44149) *(G-12558)*

Ernst Metal Technologies LLC (DH)...............937 434-3133
2920 Kreitzer Rd Dayton (45439) *(G-5767)*

Ernst Metal Technologies LLC.....................937 434-3133
3031 Dryden Rd Moraine (45439) *(G-10161)*

Ernst Ready Mix Division, Lima *Also Called: Ernst Enterprises Inc (G-8406)*

Erosion Control Products Corp.....................302 815-6500
9281 Le Saint Dr West Chester (45014) *(G-13994)*

Ertel Publishing Inc...............................937 767-1433
506 S High St Yellow Springs (45387) *(G-14788)*

Es Steiner Dairy, Baltic *Also Called: Tri State Dairy LLC (G-782)*

Es Thermal Inc.....................................440 323-3291
388 Cranston Dr Berea (44017) *(G-1170)*

ES&w, Lakewood *Also Called: Euclid Steel & Wire Inc (G-8166)*

ESAB Group Incorporated.........................440 813-2506
3325 Middle Rd Ashtabula (44004) *(G-591)*

Escher Division, Toledo *Also Called: Maumee Valley Fabricators Inc (G-13050)*

Esco Turbine Tech Cleveland.....................440 953-0053
34000 Lakeland Blvd Eastlake (44095) *(G-6427)*

Esco Turbine Technologies - Cleveland Inc........440 953-0053
34000 Lakeland Blvd Eastlake (44095) *(G-6428)*

Escort Inc...513 870-8500
5440 W Chester Rd West Chester (45069) *(G-13995)*

Esi-Extrusion Services Inc........................330 374-3388
305 W North St Akron (44303) *(G-138)*

Esko-Graphics Inc (HQ).............................937 454-1721
8535 Gander Creek Dr Miamisburg (45342) *(G-9691)*

**A
L
P
H
A
B
E
T
I
C**

Eskoartwork, Miamisburg *Also Called: Esko-Graphics Inc (G-9691)*

Esmet Inc.. 330 452-9132
1406 5th St Sw Canton (44702) *(G-1888)*

ESP Akron Sub LLC.................................... 330 374-2242
240 W Emerling Ave Akron (44301) *(G-139)*

Espi Enterprises Inc (PA)........................... 440 543-8108
10145 Queens Way Chagrin Falls (44023) *(G-2160)*

Ess, Dayton *Also Called: Ever Secure SEC Systems Inc (G-5772)*

Essential Elements Usa LLC...................... 513 482-5700
4775 Paddock Rd Cincinnati (45229) *(G-2599)*

Essential Learning Products, Hilliard *Also Called: Teachers Publishing Group (G-7705)*

Essential Provisions LLC........................... 937 271-0381
292 Inwood Rd Wilmington (45177) *(G-14579)*

Essential Sealing Products, Chagrin Falls *Also Called: Espi Enterprises Inc (G-2160)*

Essentialware... 888 975-0405
7637 Euclid Chardon Rd Kirtland (44094) *(G-8144)*

Essi Acoustical Products........................... 216 251-7888
11750 Berea Rd Ste 1 Cleveland (44111) *(G-3686)*

Essilor Laboratories Amer Inc.................... 330 425-3003
9221 Ravenna Rd # 3 Twinsburg (44087) *(G-13300)*

Essilor of America Inc................................ 513 765-6000
4000 Luxottica Pl Mason (45040) *(G-9098)*

Essity Operations Wausau LLC................... 513 217-3644
700 Columbia Ave Middletown (45042) *(G-9858)*

Essity Prof Hygiene N Amer LLC................. 513 217-3644
700 Columbia Ave Middletown (45042) *(G-9859)*

ESSITY PROFESSIONAL HYGIENE NORTH AMERICA LLC, Middletown *Also Called: Essity Prof Hygiene N Amer LLC (G-9859)*

Est, Walton Hills *Also Called: Intigral Inc (G-13698)*

Est Analytical, West Chester *Also Called: Pts Prfssnal Technical Svc Inc (G-14056)*

Estabrook Assembly Svcs Inc.................... 440 243-3350
700 W Bagley Rd Berea (44017) *(G-1171)*

Estee 2 Inc... 937 224-7853
612 Linden Ave Dayton (45403) *(G-5768)*

Esterle Mold & Machine Co Inc (PA)........... 330 686-1685
1539 Commerce Dr Stow (44224) *(G-12429)*

Esterline, Cleveland *Also Called: Esterline Technologies Corp (G-3687)*

Esterline & Sons Mfg Co LLC...................... 937 265-5278
6508 Old Clifton Rd Springfield (45502) *(G-12308)*

Esterline Technologies Corp (HQ).............. 216 706-2960
1350 Euclid Ave Ste 1600 Cleveland (44114) *(G-3687)*

Esther Price Candies & Gifts, Dayton *Also Called: Esther Price Candies Corporation (G-5769)*

Esther Price Candies Corporation (PA)....... 937 253-2121
1709 Wayne Ave Dayton (45410) *(G-5769)*

Estone Group LLC...................................... 888 653-2246
2900 Carskaddon Ave # 200 Toledo (43606) *(G-12957)*

Estr Publications....................................... 614 940-9996
7464 Mapleleaf Ct Columbus (43235) *(G-4910)*

ET&f Fastening Systems Inc....................... 800 248-2376
29019 Solon Rd Solon (44139) *(G-12108)*

Etc Lighthing and Plastic, Andover *Also Called: K-D Lamp Company (G-457)*

Etched Metal Company............................... 440 248-0240
30200 Solon Industrial Pkwy Solon (44139) *(G-12109)*

Etherium Lighting LLC................................ 614 388-9893
6969 Alum Creek Dr Ste 4 Columbus (43217) *(G-4911)*

Ethicon Endo - Surgery, Blue Ash *Also Called: Ethicon Inc (G-1272)*

Ethicon Endo-Surgery Inc (HQ).................. 513 337-7000
4545 Creek Rd Cincinnati (45242) *(G-2600)*

Ethicon Inc.. 513 786-7000
10123 Alliance Rd Blue Ash (45242) *(G-1272)*

Ethima Inc... 419 626-4912
1528 First St Sandusky (44870) *(G-11834)*

Eti Tech LLC.. 937 832-4200
3387 Woodman Dr Kettering (45429) *(G-8120)*

Etko Machine Inc....................................... 330 745-4033
2796 Barber Rd Norton (44203) *(G-10821)*

Etl Performance Products Inc..................... 234 575-7226
1717 Pennsylvania Ave Salem (44460) *(G-11777)*

Etna Products Incorporated....................... 440 543-9845
16824 Park Circle Dr Chagrin Falls (44023) *(G-2161)*

Ets Schaefer LLC (DH)................................ 330 468-6600
3700 Park East Dr Ste 300 Beachwood (44122) *(G-917)*

Ets Schaefer LLC....................................... 330 468-6600
8050 Highland Pointe Pkwy Macedonia (44056) *(G-8689)*

Euclid Chemical Company.......................... 216 292-5000
3735 Green Rd Beachwood (44122) *(G-918)*

Euclid Chemical Company (DH).................. 800 321-7628
19215 Redwood Rd Cleveland (44110) *(G-3688)*

Euclid Coffee Co Inc.................................. 216 481-3330
17230 S Waterloo Rd Cleveland (44110) *(G-3689)*

Euclid Design and Mfg Inc......................... 440 942-0066
2895 Millgate Dr Willoughby Hills (44094) *(G-14558)*

Euclid Heat Treating Co............................. 216 481-8444
1408 E 222nd St Euclid (44117) *(G-6650)*

Euclid Jalousies Inc.................................. 440 953-1112
11668 Fowlers Mill Rd Chardon (44024) *(G-2205)*

Euclid Media Group LLC (PA)..................... 216 241-7550
737 Bolivar Rd Cleveland (44115) *(G-3690)*

Euclid Precision Grinding Co..................... 440 946-8888
35400 Lakeland Blvd Eastlake (44095) *(G-6429)*

Euclid Refinishing Compnay Inc................ 440 275-3356
2937 Industrial Park Dr Austinburg (44010) *(G-698)*

Euclid Spring Co....................................... 440 943-3213
30006 Lakeland Blvd Wickliffe (44092) *(G-14375)*

Euclid Steel & Wire Inc.............................. 216 731-6744
13000 Athens Ave Ste 101 Lakewood (44107) *(G-8166)*

Euclid Welding Company Inc..................... 216 289-0714
29956 White Rd Willoughby Hills (44092) *(G-14559)*

Eugene Stewart... 937 898-1117
5671 Webster St Dayton (45414) *(G-5770)*

Eureka Screw Machine Co, Cleveland *Also Called: Eureka Screw Machine Pdts Co (G-3691)*

Eureka Screw Machine Pdts Co.................. 216 883-1715
3960 E 91st St Cleveland (44105) *(G-3691)*

Eurocase Archtctral Cbnets Mll................. 330 674-0681
6086 State Route 241 Millersburg (44654) *(G-9979)*

Eurostampa North America Inc................... 513 821-2275
1440 Seymour Ave Cincinnati (45237) *(G-2601)*

Eurotherm, Westlake *Also Called: Gc Controls Inc (G-14303)*

Evans Adhesive Corporation (HQ).............. 614 451-2665
925 Old Henderson Rd Columbus (43220) *(G-4912)*

Evans Adhesive Corporation Ltd................ 614 451-2665
925 Old Henderson Rd Columbus (43220) *(G-4913)*

Evans Bakery Inc....................................... 937 228-4151
700 Troy St Dayton (45404) *(G-5771)*

Evans Creative Group LLC.......................... 614 657-9439
11 E Gay St Columbus (43215) *(G-4914)*

Evans Food Group Ltd................................ 626 636-8110
406 Barklow Extension Rd Portsmouth (45662) *(G-11465)*

Evans Food Group Ltd................................ 740 285-3078
2310 8th St Portsmouth (45662) *(G-11466)*

Evans Industries Inc................................. 330 453-1122
606 Walnut Ave Ne Canton (44702) *(G-1889)*

Even Cut Abrasive Company....................... 216 881-9595
850 E 72nd St Cleveland (44103) *(G-3692)*

Evenflo, Miamisburg *Also Called: Evenflo Company Inc (G-9692)*

Evenflo Company Inc (DH).......................... 937 415-3300
3131 Newmark Dr Ste 300 Miamisburg (45342) *(G-9692)*

Evenflo Company Inc................................. 937 773-3971
1801 W Main St Troy (45373) *(G-13213)*

Evening Leader, The, Saint Marys *Also Called: Horizon Ohio Publications Inc (G-11738)*

Ever Roll Specialties Co............................ 937 964-1302
3988 Lawrenceville Dr Springfield (45504) *(G-12309)*

Ever Secure SEC Systems Inc.................... 937 369-8294
5523 Salem Ave Ste 134 Dayton (45426) *(G-5772)*

Eveready Printing Inc................................. 216 587-2389
20700 Miles Pkwy Cleveland (44128) *(G-3693)*

Eveready Products Corporation.................. 216 661-2755
1101 Belt Line Ave Cleveland (44109) *(G-3694)*

Everett Industries LLC............................... 330 372-3700
3601 Larchmont Ave Ne Warren (44483) *(G-13764)*

Everflow Eastern Partners LP (PA)............. 330 533-2692
585 W Main St Canfield (44406) *(G-1809)*

Everflow Eastern Partners LP..................................... 330 537-3863
  29093 Salem Alliance Rd Salem (44460) *(G-11778)*

Evergreen Midwest, Clyde *Also Called: Evergreen Recycling LLC (G-4558)*

Evergreen Plastics, Clyde *Also Called: Polychem LLC (G-4561)*

Evergreen Recycling LLC (DH).................................... 419 547-1400
  202 Watertower Dr Clyde (43410) *(G-4558)*

Everhard, Canton *Also Called: Everhard Products Inc (G-1890)*

Everhard Products Inc (PA).. 330 453-7786
  1016 9th St Sw Canton (44707) *(G-1890)*

Everon LLC.. 440 397-4428
  9200 Market Pl Broadview Heights (44147) *(G-1502)*

Everon LLC.. 513 258-2409
  2300 Wall St Ste H Cincinnati (45212) *(G-2602)*

Evers Enterprises Inc... 513 541-7200
  1210 Ellis St Cincinnati (45223) *(G-2603)*

Evers Welding Co Inc... 513 385-7352
  4849 Blue Rock Rd Cincinnati (45247) *(G-2604)*

Eversharpe-Deburring Tool Co.................................... 513 988-6240
  10 Baltimore Ave Trenton (45067) *(G-13192)*

Evertz Technology Svc USA Inc.................................. 513 422-8400
  2601 S Verity Pkwy Bldg 102 Middletown (45044) *(G-9860)*

Everway LLC.. 419 433-9800
  2401 Sawmill Pkwy Ste 10-11 Huron (44839) *(G-7872)*

Everyday Technologies Inc.. 937 497-7774
  324 Adams St Bldg 1 Sidney (45365) *(G-12018)*

Everyday Technologies Inc.. 419 739-6104
  751 Industrial Dr Wapakoneta (45895) *(G-13709)*

Everyday Technologies Inc (PA).................................. 937 492-4171
  2005 Campbell Rd Sidney (45365) *(G-12019)*

Everything In America.. 347 871-6872
  4141 Stilmore Rd Cleveland (44121) *(G-3695)*

Everythings Image Inc... 513 469-6727
  9933 Alliance Rd Ste 2 Blue Ash (45242) *(G-1273)*

Evokes LLC... 513 947-8433
  8118 Corporate Way Ste 212 Mason (45040) *(G-9099)*

Evolution Crtive Solutions Inc.................................... 513 681-4450
  7107 Shona Dr Cincinnati (45237) *(G-2605)*

Evolve Solutions LLC... 440 357-8964
  1 High Tech Ave Painesville (44077) *(G-11083)*

Evonik Corporation.. 330 668-2235
  3500 Embassy Pkwy Ste 100 Akron (44333) *(G-140)*

Evonik Corporation.. 513 554-8969
  620 Shepherd Dr Cincinnati (45215) *(G-2606)*

Evoqua Water Technologies LLC................................. 614 491-5917
  6300 Commerce Center Dr Groveport (43125) *(G-7431)*

Evoqua Water Technologies LLC................................. 614 861-5440
  1154 Hill Rd N Pickerington (43147) *(G-11294)*

Evp International LLC... 513 761-7614
  2701 Short Vine St # 200 Cincinnati (45219) *(G-2607)*

Ewart-Ohlson Machine Company................................. 330 928-2171
  1435 Main St Cuyahoga Falls (44221) *(G-5539)*

Ewebschedule.. 614 882-0726
  180 Commerce Park Dr Westerville (43082) *(G-14209)*

Ewh Spectrum LLC.. 937 593-8010
  221 W Chillicothe Ave Bellefontaine (43311) *(G-1107)*

Exact Cutting Service Inc.. 440 546-1319
  6892 W Snowville Rd Ste 108 Brecksville (44141) *(G-1465)*

Exact Equipment Corporation (HQ).............................. 215 295-2000
  1900 Polaris Pkwy Columbus (43240) *(G-4640)*

Exact-Tool & Die Inc.. 216 676-9140
  5425 W 140th St Cleveland (44142) *(G-3696)*

Exair LLC.. 513 671-3322
  11510 Goldcoast Dr Cincinnati (45249) *(G-2608)*

Excalibur Barber LLC... 330 729-9006
  7401 Market St Boardman (44512) *(G-1371)*

Excel Loading Systems LLC....................................... 513 504-1069
  1051 Belle Ave Hamilton (45015) *(G-7489)*

Excel Machine & Tool Inc.. 419 678-3318
  212 Butler St Coldwater (45828) *(G-4573)*

Excellent Tool & Die Inc... 216 671-9222
  10921 Briggs Rd Cleveland (44111) *(G-3697)*

Excello Fabric Finishers Inc....................................... 740 622-7444
  802 S 2nd St Coshocton (43812) *(G-5454)*

Excelsior Marking, Akron *Also Called: Mark-All Enterprises LLC (G-220)*

Excelsior Printing Co... 740 927-2934
  1014 Putnam Rd Sw Pataskala (43062) *(G-11138)*

Exco Engineering USA Inc (HQ).................................. 419 726-1595
  5244 Enterprise Blvd Toledo (43612) *(G-12958)*

Exco Resources (pa) LLC.. 740 796-5231
  4100 Valley Rd Adamsville (43802) *(G-7)*

Exco Resources LLC.. 740 254-4061
  3618 Fallen Timber Rd Se Tippecanoe (44699) *(G-12856)*

Executive Sweets East Inc.. 440 359-9866
  7603 First Pl Oakwood Village (44146) *(G-10905)*

Executive Wings Inc.. 440 254-1812
  13550 Carter Rd Painesville (44077) *(G-11084)*

Exhibit Concepts Inc (PA)... 937 890-7000
  700 Crossroads Ct Vandalia (45377) *(G-13557)*

Exhibit Design International, Fairfield *Also Called: Edi Custom Interiors Inc (G-6731)*

Exide Technologies LLC.. 614 863-3866
  861 Taylor Rd Unit G Gahanna (43230) *(G-7157)*

Exit 11 Truck Tire Service Inc.................................... 330 659-6372
  5219 Brecksville Rd Ste B Richfield (44286) *(G-11591)*

Exito Manufacturing LLC... 937 291-9871
  4120 Industrial Ln Ste B Beavercreek (45430) *(G-991)*

Exomet Inc.. 440 593-1161
  1100 Maple Ave Conneaut (44030) *(G-5400)*

Exothermics.. 419 729-9726
  5040 Enterprise Blvd Toledo (43612) *(G-12959)*

Exotica Fresheners Co, Holland *Also Called: D & J Distributing & Mfg (G-7753)*

Exp Fuels Inc... 419 382-7713
  3070 Airport Hwy Toledo (43609) *(G-12960)*

Experimental Machine, Brecksville *Also Called: Exact Cutting Service Inc (G-1465)*

Expert Crane, Wellington *Also Called: Expert Crane Inc (G-13886)*

Expert Crane Inc.. 216 451-9900
  720 Shiloh Ave Wellington (44090) *(G-13886)*

Explorys Inc.. 216 767-4700
  1111 Superior Ave E Cleveland (44114) *(G-3698)*

Expo Machinery, Cleveland *Also Called: Expo Packaging Inc (G-3699)*

Expo Packaging Inc... 216 267-9700
  4832 Ridge Rd Cleveland (44144) *(G-3699)*

Express Energy Svcs Oper LP..................................... 740 337-4530
  1515 Franklin St Toronto (43964) *(G-13185)*

Express Ground Services Inc...................................... 216 870-9374
  1241 E 172nd St Cleveland (44119) *(G-3700)*

Express Grphics Prtg Dsign Inc.................................. 513 728-3344
  9695 Hamilton Ave Cincinnati (45231) *(G-2609)*

Express Pharmacy & Dme LLC..................................... 210 901-9090
  2750 S Hamilton Rd Ste 19 Columbus (43232) *(G-4915)*

Extendit Company... 330 743-4343
  14150 Beaver Springfield Rd New Springfield (44443) *(G-10473)*

Exterior Portfolio LLC.. 614 754-3400
  1441 Universal Rd Columbus (43207) *(G-4916)*

Extol of Ohio Inc (PA).. 419 668-2072
  208 Republic St Norwalk (44857) *(G-10837)*

Extol of Ohio Inc.. 419 668-2072
  208 Republic St Norwalk (44857) *(G-10838)*

Extra Seal, Newcomerstown *Also Called: 31 Inc (G-10566)*

Extreme Caster Services Inc...................................... 330 637-9030
  3333 Niles Cortland Rd Ne Cortland (44410) *(G-5444)*

Extreme Microbial Tech LLC....................................... 844 885-0088
  2800 E River Rd Moraine (45439) *(G-10162)*

Extreme Microbial Technologies, Moraine *Also Called: Extreme Microbial Tech LLC (G-10162)*

Extruded Silicone Products, Mogadore *Also Called: S P E Inc (G-10084)*

Extruded Slcone Pdts Gskets In.................................. 330 733-0101
  3300 Gilchrist Rd Mogadore (44260) *(G-10075)*

Extrudex, Painesville *Also Called: Extrudex Limited Partnership (G-11085)*

Extrudex Aluminum Inc.. 330 538-4444
  12051 Mahoning Ave North Jackson (44451) *(G-10687)*

Extrudex Limited Partnership (PA)............................... 440 352-7101
  310 Figgie Dr Painesville (44077) *(G-11085)*

Eye Surgery Center Ohio Inc (PA)................614 228-3937
  262 Neil Ave Ste 320 Columbus (43215) *(G-4917)*

Eyescience, Powell *Also Called: Eyescience Labs LLC (G-11487)*

Eyescience Labs LLC................614 885-7100
  493 Village Park Dr Powell (43065) *(G-11487)*

EZ Brite Brands Inc................440 871-7817
  806 Sharon Dr Ste C Cleveland (44145) *(G-3701)*

EZ Concrete Supply LLC (DH)................844 393-7699
  600 S Roberts Ave Lima (45804) *(G-8407)*

EZ Grout Corporation Inc................740 962-2024
  1833 N Riverview Rd Malta (43758) *(G-8745)*

Ezg Manufacturing, Malta *Also Called: E Z Grout Corporation (G-8744)*

Ezg Manufacturing, Malta *Also Called: EZ Grout Corporation Inc (G-8745)*

Ezurio LLC (PA)................330 434-7929
  50 S Main St Ste 1100 Akron (44308) *(G-141)*

F & G Tool and Die Co................937 746-3658
  130 Industrial Dr Franklin (45005) *(G-7019)*

F & G Tool and Die Co (PA)................937 294-1405
  3024 Dryden Rd Moraine (45439) *(G-10163)*

F & S Hydraulics Inc................513 575-1600
  6071 Branch Hill Guinea Pike Ste B Milford (45150) *(G-9933)*

F A S T, Cincinnati *Also Called: Field Apparatus Service & Tstg (G-2621)*

F A Tech Corp................513 942-1920
  9065 Sutton Pl West Chester (45011) *(G-13996)*

F C Brengman and Assoc LLC................740 756-4308
  86 High St Carroll (43112) *(G-2075)*

F I C, Akron *Also Called: Foundation Industries Inc (G-152)*

F I T, Valley City *Also Called: Fuserashi Intl Tech Inc (G-13496)*

F M Machine Co................330 773-8237
  1114 Triplett Blvd Akron (44306) *(G-142)*

F S A, Canton *Also Called: Foundation Systems Anchors Inc (G-1893)*

F Squared Inc................419 752-7273
  9 Sunset Dr Greenwich (44837) *(G-7361)*

F&P America Mfg Inc (HQ)................937 339-0212
  2101 Corporate Dr Troy (45373) *(G-13214)*

F+w Media Inc................513 531-2690
  9912 Carver Rd Ste 100 Blue Ash (45242) *(G-1274)*

FA Sibrling Ntrelm Mtro Pk Smm, Akron *Also Called: Summit County (G-319)*

Fab3 Group, Cleveland *Also Called: Duct Fabricators Inc (G-3636)*

Fabacraft Inc................513 677-0500
  201 Grandin Rd Maineville (45039) *(G-8740)*

Fabacraft Co, Maineville *Also Called: Fabacraft Inc (G-8740)*

Fabco Inc................419 422-4533
  2800 Fostoria Ave Findlay (45840) *(G-6862)*

Fabcon Companies LLC................614 875-8601
  3400 Jackson Pike Grove City (43123) *(G-7386)*

Fabcor Inc................419 628-4428
  350 S Ohio St Minster (45865) *(G-10057)*

Fabohio Inc................740 922-4233
  521 E 7th St Uhrichsville (44683) *(G-13403)*

Fabric Forms Inc................513 281-6300
  1320 Bates Ave Cincinnati (45225) *(G-2610)*

Fabricating Machine Tools Ltd................440 666-9187
  12360 Plaza Dr Cleveland (44130) *(G-3702)*

Fabricating Solutions Inc................330 486-0998
  7920 Bavaria Rd Twinsburg (44087) *(G-13301)*

Fabrication and Welding, Sandusky *Also Called: Universal Dsign Fbrication LLC (G-11880)*

Fabrication Division, Maumee *Also Called: Andersons Inc (G-9260)*

Fabrication Shop Inc................419 435-7934
  1395 Buckley St Fostoria (44830) *(G-6978)*

Fabriweld Corporation (PA)................419 668-3358
  405 Industrial Pkwy Norwalk (44857) *(G-10839)*

Fabriweld Corporation................419 663-0279
  360 Eastpark Dr Norwalk (44857) *(G-10840)*

Fabx LLC................614 565-5835
  1819 Walcutt Rd Ste 100 Columbus (43228) *(G-4918)*

Facemyer Lumber Co Inc (PA)................740 992-5965
  31940 Bailey Run Rd Pomeroy (45769) *(G-11437)*

Facil North America Inc (HQ)................330 487-2500
  2242 Pinnacle Pkwy Ste 100 Twinsburg (44087) *(G-13302)*

Facilities Management Ex LLC................614 519-2186
  800 Yard St Ste 115 Columbus (43212) *(G-4919)*

Facility Service Pros LLC................419 577-6123
  3206 Townsend Angling Rd Collins (44826) *(G-4587)*

Facts Inc................330 928-2332
  2737 Front St Cuyahoga Falls (44221) *(G-5540)*

Facultatieve Tech Americas Inc................330 723-6339
  940 Lake Rd Medina (44256) *(G-9400)*

Fair Publishing House Inc................419 668-3746
  15 Schauss Ave Norwalk (44857) *(G-10841)*

Fairborn Cement Company LLC................937 879-8393
  3250 Linebaugh Rd Xenia (45385) *(G-14764)*

Fairborn Cement Plant................937 879-8466
  3250 Linebaugh Rd Fairborn (45324) *(G-6691)*

Fairborn USA Inc (PA)................419 294-4987
  205 Broadview St Upper Sandusky (43351) *(G-13441)*

Fairfield Machined Pdts Inc................740 756-4409
  6215 Columbus Lancaster Rd Nw Carroll (43112) *(G-2076)*

Fairfield Manufacturing Inc................513 642-0081
  8585 Seward Rd Fairfield (45011) *(G-6734)*

Fairfield Wood Works Ltd................740 689-1953
  1612 E Main St Lancaster (43130) *(G-8201)*

Fairview Log Homes, Millersburg *Also Called: Al Yoder Construction Co (G-9967)*

Faith Guiding Cafe LLC................614 245-8451
  5195 Hampsted Village Center Way New Albany (43054) *(G-10340)*

Faith Tool and Mfg Inc................440 951-5934
  36575 Reading Ave Willoughby (44094) *(G-14457)*

Falcon, Medina *Also Called: Falcon Industries Inc (G-9401)*

Falcon Foundry Company................330 536-6221
  96 6th St Lowellville (44436) *(G-8661)*

Falcon Industries Inc (PA)................330 723-0099
  180 Commerce Dr Medina (44256) *(G-9401)*

Falcon Innovations Inc................216 252-0676
  3316 W 118th St Cleveland (44111) *(G-3703)*

Falcon Tool & Machine Inc................937 534-9999
  2795 Lance Dr Dayton (45409) *(G-5773)*

Falholt Division, Akron *Also Called: Russell Products Co Inc (G-298)*

Fallen Oak Candles Inc................419 204-8162
  917 Lilac St Celina (45822) *(G-2106)*

Fallon Pharaohs................216 990-2746
  3911 Grosvenor Rd Cleveland (44118) *(G-3704)*

Falls Filtration Tech Inc................330 928-4100
  115 E Steels Corners Rd Stow (44224) *(G-12430)*

Falls Mtal Fbrctors Indus Svcs................330 253-7181
  380 Kennedy Rd Akron (44305) *(G-143)*

Falls Stamping & Welding Co................216 771-9635
  1720 Fall St Cleveland (44113) *(G-3705)*

Falls Stamping & Welding Co (PA)................330 928-1191
  2900 Vincent St Cuyahoga Falls (44221) *(G-5541)*

Falls Tool and Die Inc................330 633-4884
  1416 Piedmont Ave Akron (44310) *(G-144)*

Falmer Screw Pdts & Mfg Inc................330 758-0593
  690 Mcclurg Rd Youngstown (44512) *(G-14854)*

Family Fun, Louisville *Also Called: Bradley Enterprises Inc (G-8599)*

Family Motor Coach Assn Inc (PA)................513 474-3622
  8291 Clough Pike Cincinnati (45244) *(G-2611)*

Family Motor Coaching, Cincinnati *Also Called: Family Motor Coaching Inc (G-2612)*

Family Motor Coaching Inc................513 474-3622
  8291 Clough Pike Cincinnati (45244) *(G-2612)*

Family Packaging Inc (PA)................937 325-4106
  504 W Euclid Ave Springfield (45506) *(G-12310)*

Famous Industries Inc (DH)................330 535-1811
  2620 Ridgewood Rd Ste 200 Akron (44313) *(G-145)*

Famous Industries Inc................740 685-2592
  356 Main St Byesville (43723) *(G-1711)*

Famous Realty Cleveland Inc................740 685-2533
  354 Main St Byesville (43723) *(G-1712)*

Famous Supply, Byesville *Also Called: Famous Realty Cleveland Inc (G-1712)*

Fanci Forms, Upper Sandusky *Also Called: Mar-Metal Mfg Inc (G-13447)*

Fannie May Confections Inc................330 494-0833
  5353 Lauby Rd North Canton (44720) *(G-10638)*

Fantasy Candies, Cleveland *Also Called: Chocolate Pig Inc (G-3496)*

Far Corner... 330 767-3734
13189 Mount Eaton St Sw Navarre (44662) *(G-10303)*

Farah Jewelers Inc... 614 438-6140
5965 Medallion Dr E Westerville (43082) *(G-14210)*

Farasey Steel Fabricators Inc... 216 641-1853
4000 Iron Ct Cleveland (44115) *(G-3706)*

Farber Specialty Vehicles Inc... 614 863-6470
7052 Americana Pkwy Reynoldsburg (43068) *(G-11569)*

Faretec Inc... 440 350-9510
1610 W Jackson St Unit 6 Painesville (44077) *(G-11086)*

Farin Industries Inc... 440 275-2755
2844 Industrial Park Dr Austinburg (44010) *(G-699)*

Farm & Dairy, Salem *Also Called: Lyle Printing & Publishing Co (G-11796)*

Farm Elevator, Upper Sandusky *Also Called: Mennel Milling Company (G-13448)*

Farm Products Division, Dayton *Also Called: Putnam Plastics Inc (G-5969)*

Farmer Hub, Wooster *Also Called: Wooster Daily Record Inc LLC (G-14700)*

Farmer Smiths Market, Dover *Also Called: Bfc Inc (G-6230)*

Farmerstown Meats.. 330 897-7972
2933 Township Road 163 Sugarcreek (44681) *(G-12638)*

Farr Automation Inc... 419 289-1883
58 Sugarbush Ct Ashland (44805) *(G-534)*

Farsight Management Inc... 330 602-8338
6790 Middle Run Rd Nw Dover (44622) *(G-6245)*

Fast Signs.. 614 710-1312
4440 Reynolds Dr Hilliard (43026) *(G-7681)*

Fastener Industries Inc.. 440 891-2031
33 Lou Groza Blvd Berea (44017) *(G-1172)*

Fastener Industries Inc (PA)... 440 243-0034
1 Berea Cmns Ste 209 Berea (44017) *(G-1173)*

Fastfeed Corporation... 330 948-7333
124 S Academy St Lodi (44254) *(G-8501)*

Fastformingcom LLC.. 330 927-3277
300 Morning Star Dr Rittman (44270) *(G-11621)*

Fastpatch Ltd.. 513 367-1838
10774 Carolina Trace Rd Harrison (45030) *(G-7550)*

Fastsigns... 330 952-2626
2736 Medina Rd Ste 109 Medina (44256) *(G-9402)*

Fastsigns... 440 954-9191
7538 Mentor Ave Mentor (44060) *(G-9515)*

Fastsigns, Akron *Also Called: Sterling Associates Inc (G-318)*

Fastsigns, Broadview Heights *Also Called: Nrka Corp (G-1508)*

Fastsigns, Cincinnati *Also Called: J Best Inc (G-2308)*

Fastsigns, Hilliard *Also Called: Fast Signs (G-7681)*

Fastsigns, Medina *Also Called: Apex Signs Inc (G-9376)*

Fastsigns, Medina *Also Called: Fastsigns (G-9402)*

Fastsigns, Mentor *Also Called: Vista Creations LLC (G-9650)*

Fastsigns, Westerville *Also Called: Djmc Partners Inc (G-14256)*

Fastsigns, Westerville *Also Called: Highrise Creative LLC (G-14263)*

Fastsigns, Youngstown *Also Called: Sdmk LLC (G-14930)*

Fate Industries Inc.. 440 327-1770
36682 Sugar Ridge Rd North Ridgeville (44039) *(G-10730)*

Faull & Son LLC... 330 652-4341
515 Holford Ave Niles (44446) *(G-10588)*

Fawcett Co Inc... 330 659-4187
3863 Congress Pkwy Richfield (44286) *(G-11592)*

Fawn Confectionery Inc (PA).. 513 574-9612
4271 Harrison Ave Cincinnati (45211) *(G-2613)*

Faxon Machining LLC... 513 851-4644
11101 Adwood Dr Cincinnati (45240) *(G-2614)*

FB Acquisition LLC... 513 459-7782
2025 Mckinley Blvd Lebanon (45036) *(G-8255)*

FB Ins, Fostoria *Also Called: Fostoria Bushings Inc (G-6981)*

FBC Chemical Corporation.. 216 341-2000
7301 Bessemer Ave Cleveland (44127) *(G-3707)*

Fbf Limited... 513 541-6300
2980 Spring Grove Ave Cincinnati (45225) *(G-2615)*

Fbg Bottling Group LLC... 614 580-7063
818 S Yearling Rd Columbus (43213) *(G-4920)*

Fc Industries Inc (PA).. 937 275-8700
4900 Webster St Dayton (45414) *(G-5774)*

FCA US LLC.. 419 661-3500
8000 Chrysler Dr Perrysburg (43551) *(G-11220)*

Fcbdd.. 614 475-6440
2879 Johnstown Rd Columbus (43219) *(G-4921)*

Fci Inc.. 216 251-5200
4801 W 160th St Cleveland (44135) *(G-3708)*

Fcx Performance Inc (HQ)... 614 253-1996
3000 E 14th Ave Columbus (43219) *(G-4922)*

Fd Machinery, Solon *Also Called: Fd Rolls Corp (G-12110)*

Fd Rolls Corp... 216 916-1922
30400 Solon Industrial Pkwy Solon (44139) *(G-12110)*

Fdc Machine Repair Inc... 216 362-1082
5585 Venture Dr Parma (44130) *(G-11130)*

Fdi, Cleves *Also Called: Fdi Cabinetry LLC (G-4537)*

Fdi Cabinetry LLC.. 513 353-4500
5555 Dry Fork Rd Cleves (45002) *(G-4537)*

Fdi Enterprises.. 440 269-8282
17700 Saint Clair Ave Cleveland (44110) *(G-3709)*

Feather Lite Innovations Inc... 513 893-5483
4805 Hamilton Middletown Rd Liberty Twp (45011) *(G-8383)*

Feather Lite Innovations Inc (PA)..................................... 937 743-9008
650 Pleasant Valley Dr Springboro (45066) *(G-12252)*

Fecon LLC.. 513 696-4430
1087b Mane Way Lebanon (45036) *(G-8256)*

Fecon LLC (PA).. 513 696-4430
3460 Grant Ave Lebanon (45036) *(G-8257)*

Federal Equipment Company (DH)..................................... 513 621-5260
5298 River Rd Cincinnati (45233) *(G-2616)*

Federal Gear, Eastlake *Also Called: Tymoca Partners LLC (G-6446)*

Federal Heath Sign Company LLC..................................... 740 369-0999
1020 Pittsburgh Dr Ste A Delaware (43015) *(G-6147)*

Federal Hose Manufacturing, Painesville *Also Called: First Francis Company Inc (G-11087)*

Federal Hose Manufacturing LLC...................................... 800 346-4673
10514 Dupont Ave Cleveland (44108) *(G-3710)*

Federal Iron Works Company.. 330 482-5910
42082 State Route 344 Columbiana (44408) *(G-4617)*

Federal Metal Co, Bedford *Also Called: Oakwood Industries Inc (G-1051)*

Federal Metal Company (HQ).. 440 232-8700
7250 Division St Bedford (44146) *(G-1031)*

Federaleagle LLC... 513 797-4100
64 Circle Freeway Dr West Chester (45246) *(G-14118)*

FedPro Inc (HQ).. 216 464-6440
4520 Richmond Rd Cleveland (44128) *(G-3711)*

Feedall Inc... 440 942-8100
38379 Pelton Rd Willoughby (44094) *(G-14458)*

Feikert Concrete, Millersburg *Also Called: Feikert Sand & Gravel Co Inc (G-9980)*

Feikert Sand & Gravel Co Inc... 330 674-0038
6971 County Road 189 Millersburg (44654) *(G-9980)*

Feilhauers Machine Shop Inc.. 513 202-0545
421 Industrial Dr Harrison (45030) *(G-7551)*

Feintool Cincinnati Inc (DH)... 513 247-0110
11280 Cornell Park Dr Cincinnati (45242) *(G-2617)*

Feintool US Operations Inc (DH)...................................... 513 247-0110
11280 Cornell Park Dr Cincinnati (45242) *(G-2618)*

Feitl Manufacturing Co Inc... 330 405-6600
8406 Bavaria Dr E Macedonia (44056) *(G-8690)*

Feld Printing Co... 513 271-6806
6806 Main St Cincinnati (45244) *(G-2619)*

Felicity Plastics Machinery.. 513 876-7003
892 Neville Penn Schoolhouse Rd Felicity (45120) *(G-6829)*

Feller Tool Co.. 440 324-6277
6285 Lake Ave Elyria (44035) *(G-6536)*

Fellhauer In-Focus, Port Clinton *Also Called: Fellhauer Mechanical Systems (G-11441)*

Fellhauer Mechanical Systems... 419 734-3674
2435 E Gill Rd Port Clinton (43452) *(G-11441)*

Femc, Bedford Heights *Also Called: Food Equipment Mfg Corp (G-1076)*

Fence One Inc.. 216 441-2600
11111 Broadway Ave Cleveland (44125) *(G-3712)*

Fenix LLC (HQ).. 419 739-3400
820 Willipie St Wapakoneta (45895) *(G-13710)*

A
L
P
H
A
B
E
T
I
C

Fenix Fabrication Inc... 330 745-8731
 2689 Wingate Ave Akron (44314) *(G-146)*

Fenner Dnlop Engnred Cnvyor Sl, Port Clinton *Also Called: Fenner Dunlop Port Clinton LLC*
(G-11442)

Fenner Dunlop (toledo) LLC.................................. 419 531-5300
 146 S Westwood Ave Toledo (43607) *(G-12961)*

Fenner Dunlop Port Clinton LLC........................... 419 635-2191
 5225 W Lakeshore Dr Ste 320 Port Clinton (43452) *(G-11442)*

Fenton Bros Electric Co... 330 343-0093
 235 Ray Ave Ne New Philadelphia (44663) *(G-10445)*

Fenton's Festival of Lights, New Philadelphia *Also Called: Fenton Bros Electric Co (G-10445)*

Fenwick Frame Shppe Art Gllery, Toledo *Also Called: Fenwick Gallery of Fine Arts (G-12962)*

Fenwick Gallery of Fine Arts (PA).......................... 419 475-1651
 3433 W Alexis Rd Frnt Toledo (43623) *(G-12962)*

Ferco Tech LLC.. 937 746-6696
 291 Conover Dr Franklin (45005) *(G-7020)*

Ferguson Enterprises LLC...................................... 216 635-2493
 2415 Brookpark Rd Parma (44134) *(G-11131)*

Ferguson Fire Fabrication Inc................................. 614 299-2070
 1640 Clara St Columbus (43211) *(G-4923)*

Fernandes Enterprises LLC (PA).............................937 890-6444
 2801 Ontario Ave Dayton (45414) *(G-5775)*

Ferno, Wilmington *Also Called: Ferno-Washington Inc (G-14580)*

Ferno-Washington Inc (PA)..................................... 877 733-0911
 70 Weil Way Wilmington (45177) *(G-14580)*

Ferralloy Inc... 440 250-1900
 28001 Ranney Pkwy Cleveland (44145) *(G-3713)*

Ferrante Wine Farm Inc... 440 466-8466
 5585 State Route 307 Geneva (44041) *(G-7237)*

Ferriot Inc... 330 786-3000
 1000 Arlington Cir Akron (44306) *(G-147)*

Ferro, Mayfield Heights *Also Called: Vibrantz Corporation (G-9344)*

Ferro Corporation.. 216 577-7144
 7050 Krick Rd Bedford (44146) *(G-1032)*

Ferro Corporation.. 330 682-8015
 1560 N Main St Orrville (44667) *(G-10980)*

Ferro International Svcs Inc (DH)............................216 875-5600
 6060 Parkland Blvd Ste 250 Mayfield Heights (44124) *(G-9333)*

Ferroglobe USA Mtllurgical Inc (DH).......................740 984-2361
 1595 Sparling Rd Waterford (45786) *(G-13826)*

Ferrotherm Corporation.. 216 883-9350
 4758 Warner Rd Cleveland (44125) *(G-3714)*

Ferrous Processing and Trading, Cleveland *Also Called: Fpt Cleveland LLC (G-3740)*

Ferrum Industries Inc (HQ)..................................... 440 519-1768
 1831 Highland Rd Twinsburg (44087) *(G-13303)*

Ferry & Quintax, Stow *Also Called: Ferry Industries Inc (G-12431)*

Ferry Industries Inc... 330 920-9200
 4445 Allen Rd Ste A Stow (44224) *(G-12431)*

Few Atmtive GL Applcations Inc.............................. 234 249-1880
 1720 Enterprise Pkwy Wooster (44691) *(G-14637)*

Fex LLC (PA).. 412 604-0400
 1058 Commercial St Mingo Junction (43938) *(G-10051)*

Fex Group, Mingo Junction *Also Called: Fex LLC (G-10051)*

Fgs-Wi LLC.. 630 375-8597
 37 S Park Pl Newark (43055) *(G-10502)*

Fiba Technologies Inc... 330 602-7300
 3211 Brightwood Road Midvale (44653) *(G-9909)*

Fiber -Tech Industries Inc....................................... 740 335-9400
 2000 Kenskill Ave Wshngtn Ct Hs (43160) *(G-14739)*

Fiber Frame, Toledo *Also Called: Comfort Line Ltd (G-12928)*

Fiber Systems, Vandalia *Also Called: Industrial Fiberglass Spc Inc (G-13561)*

Fibercore LLC.. 216 249-2100
 15625 Saranac Rd Cleveland (44110) *(G-3715)*

Fibercorr Mills LLC.. 330 837-5151
 670 17th St Nw Massillon (44647) *(G-9191)*

Fiberglass Engineering Co, Cleveland *Also Called: Hanlon Industries Inc (G-3810)*

Fiberglass Technology Inds Inc.............................. 740 335-9400
 2000 Kenskill Ave Wshngtn Ct Hs (43160) *(G-14740)*

Fibertech Networks... 614 436-3565
 720 Lakeview Plaza Blvd Worthington (43085) *(G-14710)*

Fiberworx, Cleveland *Also Called: Petfiber LLC (G-4154)*

Fibre Glast Dvlpments Corp LLC............................ 937 833-5200
 385 Carr Dr Brookville (45309) *(G-1567)*

Fibreboard Corporation (DH)...................................419 248-8000
 1 Owens Corning Pkwy Toledo (43659) *(G-12963)*

Fidelity Orthopedic Inc.. 937 228-0682
 8514 N Main St Dayton (45415) *(G-5776)*

Fiedeldey Stl Fabricators Inc.................................. 513 353-3300
 8487 E Miami River Rd Cincinnati (45247) *(G-2620)*

Field Apparatus Service & Tstg.............................. 513 353-9399
 4040 Rev Dr Cincinnati (45232) *(G-2621)*

Field Aviation Inc (PA).. 513 792-2282
 8044 Montgomery Rd Ste 530 Cincinnati (45236) *(G-2622)*

Field Gymmy Inc.. 419 538-6511
 138-143 S Main St Glandorf (45848) *(G-7283)*

Field Stone Inc... 937 898-3236
 2750 Us Route 40 Tipp City (45371) *(G-12825)*

Fields Process Technology Inc................................ 216 781-4787
 1849 W 24th St Cleveland (44113) *(G-3716)*

Fifth Avenue Lumber Co.. 614 833-6655
 5200 Winchester Pike Canal Winchester (43110) *(G-1790)*

Fifth Third Proc Solutions Inc................................. 800 972-3030
 38 Fountain Square Plz Cincinnati (45202) *(G-2623)*

Fifty West Brewing Company LLC............................ 740 775-2337
 1 N Paint St Chillicothe (45601) *(G-2251)*

Figley Stamping Company, Defiance *Also Called: Marc V Concepts Inc (G-6119)*

Fill-Rite Company (HQ)..419 755-1011
 600 S Airport Rd Mansfield (44903) *(G-8787)*

Filmtec Fabrications LLC... 419 435-1819
 1120 Sandusky St Fostoria (44830) *(G-6979)*

Filnor Inc (PA)... 330 821-8731
 227 N Freedom Ave Alliance (44601) *(G-382)*

Filter Technology Inc... 614 921-9801
 11885 Paddock View Ct Nw Baltimore (43105) *(G-785)*

Fimm USA Inc... 614 568-4874
 4155 Brook Rd Nw Lancaster (43130) *(G-8202)*

Fin Pan Inc (PA)... 513 870-9200
 3255 Symmes Rd Hamilton (45015) *(G-7490)*

Finale Products Inc.. 419 874-2662
 301 Walnut St Perrysburg (43551) *(G-11221)*

Findaway World LLC (PA).. 440 893-0808
 31999 Aurora Rd Solon (44139) *(G-12111)*

Findlay Amrcn Prsthtic Orthtic............................... 419 424-1622
 12474 County Road 99 Findlay (45840) *(G-6863)*

Findlay Machine & Tool LLC.................................... 419 434-3100
 2000 Industrial Dr Findlay (45840) *(G-6864)*

Findlay Pallet Inc... 419 423-0511
 300 Bell Ave Findlay (45840) *(G-6865)*

Findlay Party Mart, Findlay *Also Called: Ottawa Oil Co Inc (G-6905)*

Findlay Products Corporation................................. 419 423-3324
 2045 Industrial Dr Findlay (45840) *(G-6866)*

Fine Line Graphics, Columbus *Also Called: Fine Line Graphics Corp (G-4924)*

Fine Line Graphics Corp.. 614 486-0276
 2364 Featherwood Dr Columbus (43228) *(G-4924)*

Fine Lines, Wadsworth *Also Called: Quality Reproductions Inc (G-13664)*

Fineline Imprints Inc... 740 453-1083
 516 State St Zanesville (43701) *(G-15013)*

Finelli Architectural Iron Co, Cleveland *Also Called: Finelli Ornamental Iron Co (G-3717)*

Finelli Ornamental Iron Co...................................... 440 248-0050
 30815 Solon Rd Cleveland (44139) *(G-3717)*

Finish Line Binderies, Macedonia *Also Called: Bindtech LLC (G-8679)*

Finishing Brands, Toledo *Also Called: Finishing Brands Holdings Inc (G-12964)*

Finishing Brands Holdings Inc................................ 260 665-8800
 320 Phillips Ave Toledo (43612) *(G-12964)*

Finishing Department.. 419 737-3334
 201 Ohio St Pioneer (43554) *(G-11320)*

Finite Fibers, Akron *Also Called: Dowco LLC (G-125)*

Fink Meat Company Inc.. 937 390-2750
 2475 Troy Rd Springfield (45504) *(G-12311)*

Finn Corporation (HQ)...513 874-2818
 9281 Le Saint Dr West Chester (45014) *(G-13997)*

Finn Graphics Inc 513 941-6161
220 Stille Dr Cincinnati (45233) *(G-2624)*

Finzer Roller Inc 937 746-4069
315 Industrial Dr Franklin (45005) *(G-7021)*

Fire Containment Concepts LLC 800 877-2204
13155 Market Ave N Hartville (44632) *(G-7575)*

Fire Department, Grafton *Also Called: Village of Grafton (G-7305)*

Fire Fab Corp 330 759-9834
999 Trumbull Ave Girard (44420) *(G-7270)*

Fire Foe Corp 330 759-9834
999 Trumbull Ave Girard (44420) *(G-7271)*

Fire From Ice Ventures LLC 419 944-6705
30333 Emerald Valley Pkwy Solon (44139) *(G-12112)*

Fire Safety Services Inc 937 686-2000
6228 Township Road 95 Huntsville (43324) *(G-7864)*

Fire-Dex LLC (PA) 330 723-0000
780 S Progress Dr Medina (44256) *(G-9403)*

Fire-End & Croker Corp 513 870-0517
4690 Interstate Dr Ste P West Chester (45246) *(G-14119)*

FIRE-END & CROKER CORP., West Chester *Also Called: Fire-End & Croker Corp (G-14119)*

Firehouse Foods 614 592-8115
917 E Whittier St Columbus (43206) *(G-4925)*

Firelands Fabrication 419 929-0680
201 N Main St New London (44851) *(G-10411)*

Firelands Farmer, The, New London *Also Called: Sdg News Group Inc (G-10416)*

Fireline Inc (PA) 330 743-1164
300 Andrews Ave Youngstown (44505) *(G-14855)*

Fireline Tcon, Youngstown *Also Called: Fireline Inc (G-14855)*

Firestone, Athens *Also Called: Bridgestone Ret Operations LLC (G-635)*

Firestone, Beverly *Also Called: Skinner Firestone Inc (G-1209)*

Firestone, Canal Winchester *Also Called: Bridgestone Ret Operations LLC (G-1787)*

Firestone, Canton *Also Called: Bridgestone Ret Operations LLC (G-1845)*

Firestone, Cincinnati *Also Called: Bridgestone Ret Operations LLC (G-2424)*

Firestone, Cincinnati *Also Called: Bridgestone Ret Operations LLC (G-2425)*

Firestone, Cleveland *Also Called: Bridgestone Ret Operations LLC (G-3436)*

Firestone, Cleveland *Also Called: Bridgestone Ret Operations LLC (G-3437)*

Firestone, Cleveland *Also Called: Bridgestone Ret Operations LLC (G-3438)*

Firestone, Cleveland *Also Called: Bridgestone Ret Operations LLC (G-3439)*

Firestone, Columbus *Also Called: Bridgestone Ret Operations LLC (G-4777)*

Firestone, Columbus *Also Called: Bridgestone Ret Operations LLC (G-4778)*

Firestone, Columbus *Also Called: Bridgestone Ret Operations LLC (G-4779)*

Firestone, Elyria *Also Called: Bridgestone Ret Operations LLC (G-6504)*

Firestone, Elyria *Also Called: Bridgestone Ret Operations LLC (G-6505)*

Firestone, Greenville *Also Called: Bridgestone Ret Operations LLC (G-7336)*

Firestone, Hamilton *Also Called: Bridgestone Ret Operations LLC (G-7473)*

Firestone, Kent *Also Called: Bridgestone Ret Operations LLC (G-8020)*

Firestone, Mentor *Also Called: Bridgestone Ret Operations LLC (G-9493)*

Firestone, Mount Vernon *Also Called: Bridgestone Ret Operations LLC (G-10237)*

Firestone, Reynoldsburg *Also Called: Bridgestone Ret Operations LLC (G-11560)*

Firestone, Sandusky *Also Called: Bridgestone Ret Operations LLC (G-11823)*

Firestone, Springfield *Also Called: Bridgestone Ret Operations LLC (G-12286)*

Firestone, Warren *Also Called: Bridgestone Ret Operations LLC (G-13744)*

Firestone, Youngstown *Also Called: Bridgestone Ret Operations LLC (G-14825)*

Firestone, Youngstown *Also Called: Bridgestone Ret Operations LLC (G-14826)*

Firestone Laser and Mfg LLC 330 337-9551
14000 W Middletown Rd Salem (44460) *(G-11779)*

Firestone Machine, North Lima *Also Called: Precision Assemblies Inc (G-10710)*

Firestone Polymers LLC (DH) 330 379-7000
381 W Wilbeth Rd Akron (44301) *(G-148)*

Firovac, Apple Creek *Also Called: Reberland Equipment Inc (G-476)*

First Brands Group LLC (DH) 888 565-9632
127 Public Sq Ste 5300 Cleveland (44114) *(G-3718)*

First Brnds Group Holdings LLC (PA) 216 589-0198
127 Public Sq Ste 5300 Cleveland (44114) *(G-3719)*

First Brnds Group Intrmdate LL (HQ) 216 589-0198
127 Public Sq Ste 5110 Cleveland (44114) *(G-3720)*

First Choice Packaging Inc (PA) 419 333-4100
1501 W State St Fremont (43420) *(G-7107)*

First Choice Packg Solutions, Fremont *Also Called: First Choice Packaging Inc (G-7107)*

First Francis Company Inc (HQ) 440 352-8927
25 Florence Ave Painesville (44077) *(G-11087)*

First Machine & Tool Corp 440 269-8644
38181 Airport Pkwy Willoughby (44094) *(G-14459)*

First Solar Inc 419 661-1478
28101 Cedar Park Blvd Perrysburg (43551) *(G-11222)*

First Solar Electric, Perrysburg *Also Called: First Solar Inc (G-11222)*

First Tool Corp (PA) 937 254-6197
612 Linden Ave Dayton (45403) *(G-5777)*

Firth Rixson Inc 860 760-1040
1616 Harvard Ave Ste 53 Newburgh Heights (44105) *(G-10541)*

Fischer Engineering Co LLC 937 754-1750
8220 Expansion Way Dayton (45424) *(G-5778)*

Fischer Special Tooling Corp 440 951-8411
7219 Commerce Dr Mentor (44060) *(G-9516)*

Fishel Company 614 850-4400
1600 Walcutt Rd Columbus (43228) *(G-4926)*

Fisher Controls Intl LLC 513 285-6000
5453 W Chester Rd West Chester (45069) *(G-13998)*

Fisher Sand & Gravel Inc 330 745-9239
3322 Clark Mill Rd Norton (44203) *(G-10822)*

Fiske Brothers Refining Co 419 691-2491
1500 Oakdale Ave Toledo (43605) *(G-12965)*

Five Handicap Inc (PA) 419 525-2511
127 N Walnut St Mansfield (44902) *(G-8788)*

Five Star Fabrication LLC 440 666-0427
18308 Quarry Rd Wellington (44090) *(G-13887)*

Five Star Foodies, Cincinnati *Also Called: Foodies Vegan Ltd (G-2632)*

Five Star Healthy Vending LLC 330 549-6011
388 S Main St Ste 440 Akron (44311) *(G-149)*

Five Star Technologies Ltd 216 447-9422
6801 Brecksville Rd Ste 200 Independence (44131) *(G-7903)*

Fives Bronx Inc 330 244-1960
8817 Pleasantwood Ave Nw North Canton (44720) *(G-10639)*

Fives N Amercn Combustn Inc (DH) 216 271-6000
4455 E 71st St Cleveland (44105) *(G-3721)*

Fives St Corp 234 217-9070
1 Park Centre Dr Ste 210 Wadsworth (44281) *(G-13638)*

Fixture Dimensions Inc 513 360-7512
5660 Liberty Woods Dr Liberty Twp (45011) *(G-8384)*

Fki Logistex, West Chester *Also Called: Intelligrated Systems Ohio LLC (G-14129)*

Fki Logistex Automation Inc 513 881-5251
10045 International Blvd West Chester (45246) *(G-14120)*

Flag Lady Inc 614 263-1776
4567 N High St Columbus (43214) *(G-4927)*

Flag Lady's Flag Store, The, Columbus *Also Called: Flag Lady Inc (G-4927)*

Flagship Trading Corporation
734 Alpha Dr Ste J Cleveland (44143) *(G-3722)*

Flambeau Inc 440 632-6131
15981 Valplast St Middlefield (44062) *(G-9794)*

Flaming River Industries Inc 440 826-4488
800 Poertner Dr Berea (44017) *(G-1174)*

Flash Industrial Tech Ltd 440 786-8979
30 Industry Dr Cleveland (44146) *(G-3723)*

Flashions Sportswear Ltd 937 323-5885
1002 N Bechtle Ave Springfield (45504) *(G-12312)*

Flatiron Crane Oper Co LLC 330 332-3300
1134 Salem Pkwy Salem (44460) *(G-11780)*

Flavor Producers LLC 513 771-0777
2429 E Kemper Rd Cincinnati (45241) *(G-2625)*

Flavor Systems Intl Inc (HQ) 513 870-4900
5404 Duff Dr Cincinnati (45246) *(G-2626)*

Flavorseal LLC 440 937-3900
35179 Avon Commerce Pkwy Avon (44011) *(G-726)*

Fleet Graphics Inc 937 252-2552
1701 Thomas Paine Pkwy Dayton (45459) *(G-5779)*

Fleet Relief Company 419 525-2625
550 N Main St Mansfield (44902) *(G-8789)*

Fleetchem LLC 513 539-1111
651 N Garver Rd Monroe (45050) *(G-10105)*

Fleetmaster Express Inc 866 425-0666
5250 Distribution Dr Findlay (45840) *(G-6867)*

Fleming Construction Co 740 494-2177
5298 Marion Marysville Rd Prospect (43342) *(G-11501)*

Flesher Sand & Gravel, Norton *Also Called: Fisher Sand & Gravel Inc (G-10822)*

Flex Fab LLC 330 757-8720
3267 Olde Winter Trl Poland (44514) *(G-11436)*

Flex Technologies Inc 330 897-6311
3430 State Route 93 Baltic (43804) *(G-777)*

Flex Technologies Inc 330 359-5415
16183 East Main St Mount Eaton (44659) *(G-10207)*

Flex Technologies Inc (PA) 740 922-5992
5479 Gundy Dr Midvale (44653) *(G-9910)*

Flex-Core Division, Hilliard *Also Called: Morlan & Associates Inc (G-7687)*

Flex-E-On Inc 330 928-4496
3332 Cavalier Trl Cuyahoga Falls (44224) *(G-5542)*

Flex-Strut Inc 330 372-9999
2900 Commonwealth Ave Ne Warren (44483) *(G-13765)*

Flexarm, Wapakoneta *Also Called: Midwest Specialties Inc (G-13725)*

Flexmag Industries Inc (DH) 740 373-3492
107 Industry Rd Marietta (45750) *(G-8917)*

Flexnova Inc (PA) 216 288-6961
6100 Oak Tree Blvd Ste 200 Cleveland (44131) *(G-3724)*

Flexomation LLC 513 825-0555
11701 Chesterdale Rd Cincinnati (45246) *(G-2627)*

Flexotech Graphics Inc (PA) 330 929-4743
4830 Hudson Dr Stow (44224) *(G-12432)*

Flexrack By Qcells LLC (PA) 216 998-5988
23000 Harvard Rd Ste B Cleveland (44122) *(G-3725)*

Flexsys America, Akron *Also Called: Flexsys America LP (G-150)*

Flexsys America LP (HQ) 330 666-4111
260 Springside Dr Akron (44333) *(G-150)*

Flexsys America LP 618 482-6371
1658 Williams Rd Columbus (43207) *(G-4928)*

Flexsys Inc 212 605-6000
260 Springside Dr Akron (44333) *(G-151)*

Flextronics Intl USA Inc 513 755-2500
6224 Windham Ct Middletown (45044) *(G-9861)*

Flextur Corp 877 435-3988
16875 Jericho Rd Dalton (44618) *(G-5585)*

Flight Bright Ltd 216 663-6677
23100 Miles Rd Cleveland (44128) *(G-3726)*

Flight Operations, Cleveland *Also Called: Parker-Hannifin Corporation (G-4144)*

Flight Operations, Cleveland *Also Called: Swagelok Company (G-4355)*

Flight Specialties Components, Highland Heights *Also Called: Heico Aerospace Parts Corp (G-7659)*

Flightsafety International Inc (HQ) 614 324-3500
3100 Easton Square Pl Ste 100 Columbus (43219) *(G-4929)*

Flint CPS Inks North Amer LLC 513 619-2089
410 Glendale Milford Rd Cincinnati (45215) *(G-2628)*

Flint Group US LLC 513 552-7232
8660 Jacquemin Dr West Chester (45069) *(G-13999)*

Flohr Machine Company Inc 330 745-3030
1028 Coventry Rd Barberton (44203) *(G-804)*

Flohrmachine.com, Barberton *Also Called: Flohr Machine Company Inc (G-804)*

Flood Heliarc, Groveport *Also Called: Flood Heliarc Inc (G-7432)*

Flood Heliarc Inc 614 835-3929
4181 Venture Pl Groveport (43125) *(G-7432)*

Florence Alloys Inc 330 745-9141
121 Snyder Ave Barberton (44203) *(G-805)*

Florida Invacare Holdings LLC 800 333-6900
1 Invacare Way Elyria (44035) *(G-6537)*

Florida Production Engrg Inc 740 420-5252
30627 Orr Rd Circleville (43113) *(G-3258)*

Florida Production Engrg Inc 937 996-4361
1855 State Route 121 N New Madison (45346) *(G-10421)*

Floturn Inc (PA) 513 860-8040
4236 Thunderbird Ln Fairfield (45014) *(G-6735)*

Flow Dry Technology Inc (HQ) 937 833-2161
379 Albert Rd Brookville (45309) *(G-1568)*

Flow Technology Inc 513 745-6000
4444 Cooper Rd Cincinnati (45242) *(G-2629)*

Flow-Liner Systems Ltd 800 348-0020
4830 Northpointe Dr Zanesville (43701) *(G-15014)*

Flowcrete North America Inc 936 539-6700
19218 Redwood Rd Cleveland (44110) *(G-3727)*

Flowserve Corporation 937 226-4000
2200 E Monument Ave Dayton (45402) *(G-5780)*

Flowserve Corporation 513 874-6990
422 Wards Corner Rd Unit F Loveland (45140) *(G-8625)*

Floyd Bell Inc (PA) 614 294-4000
720 Dearborn Park Ln Columbus (43085) *(G-4930)*

Fluff Boutique 513 227-6614
6539 Harrison Ave Cincinnati (45247) *(G-2630)*

Fluid Applied Roofing LLC 855 860-2300
830 Space Dr Beavercreek Township (45434) *(G-998)*

Fluid Automation Inc 248 912-1970
8400 Port Jackson Ave Nw North Canton (44720) *(G-10640)*

Fluid Equipment Corporation 419 636-0777
7671 County Rd 7 G Bryan (43506) *(G-1641)*

Fluid Handling Dynamics Ltd 419 633-0560
815 Navarre Ave Bryan (43506) *(G-1642)*

Fluid Power Inc 330 653-5107
1300 Hudson Gate Dr Hudson (44236) *(G-7841)*

Fluid Power Plant, Beachwood *Also Called: Eaton Corporation (G-915)*

Fluid Power Solutions LLC (PA) 614 777-8954
4400 Edgewyn Ave Hilliard (43026) *(G-7682)*

Fluid Quip Ks LLC 937 324-0352
1940 S Yellow Springs St Ste 2 Springfield (45506) *(G-12313)*

Fluid System Service Inc 216 651-2450
13825 Triskett Rd Cleveland (44111) *(G-3728)*

Fluidpower Assembly Inc 419 394-7486
313 S Park Dr Saint Marys (45885) *(G-11737)*

Fluke Biomedical LLC (DH) 440 248-9300
28775 Aurora Rd Solon (44139) *(G-12113)*

Fluke Corporation 440 234-4809
17830 Englewood Dr Ste 17 Middleburg Heights (44130) *(G-9770)*

Fluke Electronics Corporation 800 850-4608
28775 Aurora Rd Cleveland (44139) *(G-3729)*

Fluvitex USA Inc 614 610-1199
6510 Pontius Rd Groveport (43125) *(G-7433)*

Flying Dutchman Inc 330 669-2297
6631 Egypt Rd Smithville (44677) *(G-12065)*

Flynn Inc 419 478-3743
5540 Jackman Rd Toledo (43613) *(G-12966)*

Flynn's Tire Co, Kent *Also Called: Urra Co Inc (G-8093)*

Flypaper Studio Inc 602 801-2208
311 Elm St Ste 200 Cincinnati (45202) *(G-2631)*

FM, Bedford *Also Called: Federal Metal Company (G-1031)*

FM AF LLC 866 771-6266
2933 Symmes Rd Fairfield (45014) *(G-6736)*

FM Manufacturing Inc 419 445-0700
300 E Mechanic St Archbold (43502) *(G-493)*

Fmh Enterprises LLC 937 478-2739
4220 Interpoint Blvd Dayton (45424) *(G-5781)*

FML Terminal Logistics LLC (DH) 440 214-3200
3 Summit Park Dr Ste 700 Independence (44131) *(G-7904)*

Fmt, Findlay *Also Called: Findlay Machine & Tool LLC (G-6864)*

Fmx 2018 Inc 440 247-5602
547 Washington St Ste 11 Chagrin Falls (44022) *(G-2144)*

Foam Concepts & Design Inc 513 860-5589
4602 Mulhauser Rd W Chester Township West Chester (45011) *(G-14000)*

Foam Pac Materials Company, Cincinnati *Also Called: Storopack Inc (G-3121)*

Foam Seal, Cleveland *Also Called: Novagard Solutions Inc (G-4101)*

Foam Seal Inc 216 881-8111
5109 Hamilton Ave Cleveland (44114) *(G-3730)*

Foam-Tex Solutions Corp 216 889-2702
13981 W Parkway Rd Cleveland (44135) *(G-3731)*

Focal Point Communications, West Chester *Also Called: Greenworld Enterprises Inc (G-14123)*

Focke Rubber Products Div, Dayton *Also Called: Mvgg Inc (G-5899)*

Focus Manufacturing LLC 440 946-8766
7770 Division Dr Mentor (44060) *(G-9517)*

Foldedpak Inc............740 527-1090
263 Milliken Dr Hebron (43025) *(G-7614)*

Folger Coffee Company (HQ)............800 937-9745
1 Strawberry Ln Orrville (44667) *(G-10981)*

Folgers, Orrville Also Called: Folger Coffee Company *(G-10981)*

Folio Photonics Inc............440 420-4500
6864 Cochran Rd Solon (44139) *(G-12114)*

Folks Creative Printers Inc............740 383-6326
101 E George St Marion (43302) *(G-8970)*

Follett Hgher Edcatn Group Inc............419 281-5100
30 Amberwood Pkwy Ashland (44805) *(G-535)*

Follow Print Club On Facebook............216 707-2579
11150 East Blvd Cleveland (44106) *(G-3732)*

Foltz Machine LLC............330 453-9235
2030 Allen Ave Se Canton (44707) *(G-1891)*

Fom USA Incorporated............234 248-4400
1065 Medina Rd Ste 800 Medina (44256) *(G-9404)*

Fontaine Pieciak Engrg Inc............413 592-2273
2300 E Enterprise Pkwy Twinsburg (44087) *(G-13304)*

Food 4 Your Soul............330 402-4073
3957 S Schenley Ave Youngstown (44511) *(G-14856)*

Food Designs Inc............216 651-9221
5299 Crayton Ave Cleveland (44104) *(G-3733)*

Food Equipment Mfg Corp............216 672-5859
22201 Aurora Rd Bedford Heights (44146) *(G-1076)*

Food Furniture, Lebanon Also Called: Schmidt Progressive LLC *(G-8285)*

Food Plant Engineering LLC............513 618-3165
10816 Millington Ct Ste 110 Blue Ash (45242) *(G-1275)*

Foodies Vegan Ltd............513 487-3037
4524 Este Ave Cincinnati (45232) *(G-2632)*

Foote Printing Company Inc............216 431-1757
2800 E 55th St Cleveland (44104) *(G-3734)*

For Call Inc............330 863-0404
3255 Alliance Rd Nw Malvern (44644) *(G-8749)*

Forbes Chocolate, Broadview Heights Also Called: Benjamin P Forbes Company *(G-1499)*

Forcam Inc............513 878-2780
3825 Edwards Rd Ste 103 Cincinnati (45209) *(G-2633)*

Force Control Industries Inc............513 868-0900
3660 Dixie Hwy Fairfield (45014) *(G-6737)*

Forceone LLC............513 939-1018
3600 Hebron Rd Hebron (43025) *(G-7615)*

Ford, Avon Lake Also Called: Ford Motor Company *(G-756)*

Ford, Brookpark Also Called: Ford Motor Company *(G-1550)*

Ford, Lima Also Called: Ford Motor Company *(G-8408)*

Ford, Wellington Also Called: Kts Equipment Inc *(G-13895)*

Ford Motor Company............440 933-1215
660 Miller Rd Avon Lake (44012) *(G-756)*

Ford Motor Company............216 676-7918
17601 Brookpark Rd Brookpark (44142) *(G-1550)*

Ford Motor Company............419 226-7000
1155 Bible Rd Lima (45801) *(G-8408)*

Fordyce Custom Finishing, Dayton Also Called: Couch Business Development Inc *(G-5711)*

Forest City Companies Inc............216 586-5279
3607 W 56th St Cleveland (44102) *(G-3735)*

Forest City Packaging, Cleveland Also Called: Forest City Companies Inc *(G-3735)*

Forest City Tech Plant 4, Wellington Also Called: Forest City Technologies Inc *(G-13889)*

Forest City Technologies, Wellington Also Called: Forest City Technologies Inc *(G-13888)*

Forest City Technologies Inc............440 647-2115
232 Maple St Wellington (44090) *(G-13888)*

Forest City Technologies Inc............440 647-2115
401 Magyar St Wellington (44090) *(G-13889)*

Forest City Technologies Inc............440 647-2115
299 Clay St Wellington (44090) *(G-13890)*

Forest City Technologies Inc (PA)............440 647-2115
299 Clay St Wellington (44090) *(G-13891)*

Forest Converting Co Inc............513 631-4190
4701 Forest Ave Cincinnati (45212) *(G-2634)*

Forge Biologics Inc............216 401-7611
3900 Gantz Rd Grove City (43123) *(G-7387)*

Forge Industries Inc (PA)............330 960-2468
4450 Market St Youngstown (44512) *(G-14857)*

Forge Products Corporation............216 231-2600
9503 Woodland Ave Cleveland (44104) *(G-3736)*

Forged Products, Cleveland Also Called: Forge Products Corporation *(G-3736)*

Forgeline Motorsports, Dayton Also Called: Forgeline Motorsports LLC *(G-5782)*

Forgeline Motorsports LLC............800 886-0093
3522 Kettering Blvd Dayton (45439) *(G-5782)*

Forgeo LLC............614 873-7030
8260 Estates Pkwy Plain City (43064) *(G-11408)*

Foris Extraordinary Meats LLC............614 670-5726
1145 Chesapeake Ave Ste E Columbus (43212) *(G-4931)*

Forklift Solutions LLC............419 717-9496
425 Oxford St Napoleon (43545) *(G-10279)*

Forklift Tire East Mich Inc............586 771-1330
4934 Lewis Ave Toledo (43612) *(G-12967)*

Form Manufacturing Llc............419 678-1400
149 Harvest Dr Coldwater (45828) *(G-4574)*

Form5 Prosthetics Inc............614 226-1141
6560 New Albany Condit Rd New Albany (43054) *(G-10341)*

Formasters Corporation............440 639-9206
5959 Pinecone Dr Mentor (44060) *(G-9518)*

Formatech Inc............330 273-2800
3024 Interstate Pkwy Brunswick (44212) *(G-1590)*

Formation Cementing Inc............740 453-6926
1800 Timber Port Dr Zanesville (43701) *(G-15015)*

Formco Inc............330 966-2111
5175 Stoneham Rd Canton (44720) *(G-1892)*

Formica Corporation (DH)............513 786-3400
10155 Reading Rd Cincinnati (45241) *(G-2635)*

Formlabs Ohio Inc............419 837-9783
27800 Lemoyne Rd Ste J Millbury (43447) *(G-9961)*

Formtek Inc (DH)............216 292-4460
4899 Commerce Pkwy Cleveland (44128) *(G-3737)*

Formtek International, Cleveland Also Called: Formtek Inc *(G-3737)*

Formtek Metal Forming Inc............216 292-4460
4899 Commerce Pkwy Cleveland (44128) *(G-3738)*

Formware Inc............614 231-9387
3441 Winchester Pike Columbus (43232) *(G-4932)*

Forre Sports Accessories, Piqua Also Called: Forrest Enterprises Inc *(G-11347)*

Forrest Enterprises Inc............937 773-1714
510 W Statler Rd Piqua (45356) *(G-11347)*

Forrest Machine Pdts Co Ltd............419 589-3774
145 Industrial Dr Mansfield (44904) *(G-8790)*

Forrest Scrw Machine, Mansfield Also Called: Forrest Machine Pdts Co Ltd *(G-8790)*

Fort Recovery Equipment Inc............419 375-1006
1201 Industrial Dr Fort Recovery (45846) *(G-6962)*

Fort Recovery Equity Inc (PA)............419 375-4119
2351 Wabash Rd Fort Recovery (45846) *(G-6963)*

Fort Recovery Industries Inc (PA)............419 375-4121
2440 State Route 49 Fort Recovery (45846) *(G-6964)*

Fort Recovery Industries Inc............419 375-3005
1200 Industrial Park Dr Fort Recovery (45846) *(G-6965)*

Fort Stben Burial Estates Assn............740 266-6101
801 Canton Rd Steubenville (43953) *(G-12403)*

Forte Industrial Equipment Systems Inc............513 398-2800
6037 Commerce Ct Mason (45040) *(G-9100)*

Forte Industries, Mason Also Called: Forte Industrial Equipment Systems Inc *(G-9100)*

Forterra Pipe & Precast LLC............614 445-3830
1500 Haul Rd Columbus (43207) *(G-4933)*

Forterra Pipe & Precast LLC............330 467-7890
7925 Empire Pkwy Macedonia (44056) *(G-8691)*

Fortin Ironworks, Columbus Also Called: Fortin Welding & Mfg Inc *(G-4934)*

Fortin Welding & Mfg Inc............614 291-4342
944 W 5th Ave Columbus (43212) *(G-4934)*

Fortis Energy Services Inc............248 283-7100
66999 Executive Dr Saint Clairsville (43950) *(G-11691)*

Fortis Parent Inc (HQ)............614 790-9299
955 Yard St Columbus (43212) *(G-4935)*

Fortis Plastics LLC............937 382-0966
185 Park Dr Wilmington (45177) *(G-14581)*

Fortner Upholstering Inc............614 475-8282
2050 S High St Columbus (43207) *(G-4936)*

A L P H A B E T I C

Forty Nine Degrees LLC.................................... 419 678-0100
149 Harvest Dr Coldwater (45828) *(G-4575)*

Forum Works LLC... 937 349-8685
77 Brown St Milford Center (43045) *(G-9957)*

Forward Day By Day, Cincinnati *Also Called: Forward Movement (G-2636)*

Forward Movement... 513 721-6659
412 Sycamore St Cincinnati (45202) *(G-2636)*

Forward Technologies, Blue Ash *Also Called: C M M S - Re LLC (G-1257)*

Forzza Corporation (PA)...................................440 998-6300
222 N Lake St Madison (44057) *(G-8729)*

Foseco Metallurgical, Conneaut *Also Called: Vesuvius U S A Corporation (G-5419)*

Foster Canning Inc....................................... 419 841-6755
6725 W Central Ave Ste T Toledo (43617) *(G-12968)*

Foster Transformer Company................................ 513 681-2420
3820 Colerain Ave Cincinnati (45223) *(G-2637)*

Fostoria Bshngs Inslators Corp............................ 419 435-7514
602 S Corporate Dr W Ste D Fostoria (44830) *(G-6980)*

Fostoria Bushings Inc.................................... 419 435-7514
602 S Corporate Dr W Fostoria (44830) *(G-6981)*

Fostoria Concrete, Bowling Green *Also Called: Palmer Bros Transit Mix Con (G-1433)*

Fostoria MT&f Corp.. 419 435-7676
1401 Sandusky St Fostoria (44830) *(G-6982)*

Foundation Industries Inc (PA)...........................330 564-1250
880 W Waterloo Rd Ste B Akron (44314) *(G-152)*

Foundation Software LLC (PA)............................. 330 220-8383
17999 Foltz Pkwy Strongsville (44149) *(G-12559)*

Foundation Systems Anchors Inc (PA)....................... 330 454-1700
2300 Allen Ave Se Canton (44707) *(G-1893)*

Foundation Wellness, Upper Arlington *Also Called: Remington Products Company (G-13432)*

Foundations, Medina *Also Called: Foundations Worldwide Inc (G-9405)*

Foundations Worldwide Inc (PA).......................... 330 722-5033
5216 Portside Dr Medina (44256) *(G-9405)*

Founder's Service Co, Deerfield *Also Called: Founders Service & Mfg Inc (G-6093)*

Founders Service & Mfg Inc (PA).......................... 330 584-7759
879 State Route 14 Deerfield (44411) *(G-6093)*

Foundry Artists Inc..................................... 216 391-9030
4404 Perkins Ave Cleveland (44103) *(G-3739)*

Foundry Sand Service LLC................................ 330 823-6152
20455 Lake Park Blvd Sebring (44672) *(G-11894)*

Fountain News, Mason *Also Called: Cincinnati Ftn Sq News Inc (G-9084)*

Fountain Specialists Inc................................ 513 831-5717
226 Main St Milford (45150) *(G-9934)*

Four Ambition LLC.. 937 239-4479
2821 Kenmore Ave Dayton (45420) *(G-5783)*

Four Natures Keepers Inc................................ 740 363-8007
4651 Marysville Rd Delaware (43015) *(G-6148)*

Four Seasons Manufacturing, Garrettsville *Also Called: Diskin Enterprises LLC (G-7218)*

Fouremans Sand & Gravel Inc.............................. 937 547-1005
2791 Wildcat Rd Greenville (45331) *(G-7341)*

Fourjay Industries, Dayton *Also Called: Fernandes Enterprises LLC (G-5775)*

Fourteen Ventures Group LLC.............................. 937 866-2341
3131 W Alex Bell Rd West Carrollton (45449) *(G-13929)*

Fouty & Company Inc..................................... 419 693-0017
5003 Bayshore Rd Oregon (43616) *(G-10961)*

Fowler Products Inc..................................... 419 683-4057
810 Colby Rd Crestline (44827) *(G-5502)*

Fox Lite Inc.. 937 864-1966
8300 Dayton Springfield Rd Fairborn (45324) *(G-6692)*

Fox Tool Co Inc... 330 928-3402
1471 Main St Cuyahoga Falls (44221) *(G-5543)*

FOXCONN EV SYSTEM LLC.................................... 234 285-4001
2300 Hallock Young Rd Sw Warren (44481) *(G-13766)*

Fpc Holdings Inc.. 216 362-7888
2867 Nationwide Pkwy Brunswick (44212) *(G-1591)*

Fpe Inc.. 740 420-5252
30627 Orr Rd Circleville (43113) *(G-3259)*

Fpt Cleveland LLC (DH)..................................216 441-3800
8550 Aetna Rd Cleveland (44105) *(G-3740)*

Fq Sale Inc (PA)...937 324-0352
1940 S Yellow Springs St Springfield (45506) *(G-12314)*

Fragapane Bakeries Inc (PA)............................. 440 779-6050
28625 Lorain Rd North Olmsted (44070) *(G-10721)*

Fragapane Bakery & Deli, North Olmsted *Also Called: Fragapane Bakeries Inc (G-10721)*

Fram Group... 479 271-7934
127 Public Sq Ste 5110 Cleveland (44114) *(G-3741)*

Fram Group Operations LLC................................ 419 436-5827
1600 N Union St Fostoria (44830) *(G-6983)*

Frame Usa, Inc., Cincinnati *Also Called: Black Squirrel Holdings Inc (G-2412)*

Frame Warehouse.. 614 861-4582
7502 E Main St Reynoldsburg (43068) *(G-11570)*

Francis Manufacturing Company............................ 937 526-4551
500 E Mn St Russia (45363) *(G-11673)*

Francis-Schulze Co....................................... 937 295-3941
3880 Rangeline Rd Russia (45363) *(G-11674)*

Francisco Jaume.. 740 622-1200
311 S 15th St Ste 206 Coshocton (43812) *(G-5455)*

Franck and Fric Incorporated............................ 216 524-4451
7919 Old Rockside Rd Cleveland (44131) *(G-3742)*

Frank Brunckhorst Company LLC............................ 614 662-5300
2225 Spiegel Dr Groveport (43125) *(G-7434)*

Frank Csapo.. 330 435-4458
157 Myers St Creston (44217) *(G-5506)*

Frank Csapo Oil & Gas Producer, Creston *Also Called: Frank Csapo (G-5506)*

Frank L Harter & Son Inc................................. 513 574-1330
3778 Frondorf Ave Cincinnati (45211) *(G-2638)*

Frankes Wood Products LLC............................... 937 642-0706
825 Collins Ave Marysville (43040) *(G-9020)*

Franklin Art Glass Studios............................... 614 221-2972
222 E Sycamore St Columbus (43206) *(G-4937)*

Franklin Brazing Met Treating, Lebanon *Also Called: Kando of Cincinnati Inc (G-8271)*

Franklin Cabinet Company Inc............................. 937 743-9606
2500 Commerce Center Dr Franklin (45005) *(G-7022)*

Franklin Chronicle, Franklin *Also Called: Cox Newspapers LLC (G-7015)*

Franklin County Coal Company............................. 740 338-3100
46226 National Rd Saint Clairsville (43950) *(G-11692)*

Franklin Covey Co.. 513 680-0975
7875 Montgomery Rd Spc 1202 Cincinnati (45236) *(G-2639)*

Franklin Equipment LLC (HQ)............................. 614 228-2014
4141 Hamilton Square Blvd Groveport (43125) *(G-7435)*

Franklin Gas & Oil Company LLC........................... 330 264-8739
1615 W Old Lincoln Way Wooster (44691) *(G-14638)*

Franklin International Inc (PA)...........................614 443-0241
2020 Bruck St Columbus (43207) *(G-4938)*

Franklin Iron & Metal Corp............................... 937 253-8184
1939 E 1st St Dayton (45403) *(G-5784)*

Franklin Mfg Div, Franklin *Also Called: Emssons Faurecia Ctrl Systems (G-7018)*

Franklin Printing Company................................ 740 452-6375
984 Beverly Ave Zanesville (43701) *(G-15016)*

Franklin's Printing, Cincinnati *Also Called: Allu Inc (G-2352)*

Franklin's Printing, Zanesville *Also Called: Franklin Printing Company (G-15016)*

Franks Electric Inc..................................... 513 313-5883
2640 Colerain Ave Cincinnati (45214) *(G-2640)*

Franks Electric Motor Repair, Cincinnati *Also Called: Franks Electric Inc (G-2640)*

Franks Sawmill Inc...................................... 419 682-3831
Rd 1950 Stryker (43557) *(G-12623)*

Frantz Grinding Co....................................... 330 343-8689
1879 E High Ave New Philadelphia (44663) *(G-10446)*

Frantz Medical Development Ltd (PA)......................440 255-1155
7740 Metric Dr Mentor (44060) *(G-9519)*

Frazier Machine and Prod Inc............................. 419 874-7321
26489 Southpoint Rd Perrysburg (43551) *(G-11223)*

Frd, Kent *Also Called: Furukawa Rock Drill USA Co Ltd (G-8034)*

Frecon Technologies Inc................................. 513 874-8981
9319 Princeton Glendale Rd West Chester (45011) *(G-14001)*

Fred D Pfening Company (PA)..............................614 294-5361
1075 W 5th Ave Columbus (43212) *(G-4939)*

Fred D Pfening Company................................... 614 294-5361
1075 W 5th Ave Columbus (43212) *(G-4940)*

Frederick Steel Company LLC............................. 513 821-6400
630 Glendale Milford Rd Cincinnati (45215) *(G-2641)*

Fredericksburg Facility, Fredericksburg Also Called: Robin Industries Inc (G-7070)

Fredon Corporation.. 440 951-5200
8990 Tyler Blvd Mentor (44060) (G-9520)

Fredrick Ramond, Avon Lake Also Called: Hinkley Lighting Inc (G-760)

Fredrick Welding & Machining................................. 614 866-9650
6840 Americana Pkwy Reynoldsburg (43068) (G-11571)

Freds Sign Service Inc... 937 335-1901
3055 S County Road 25a Troy (45373) (G-13215)

Free Press Standard, Carrollton Also Called: Carrollton Publishing Company (G-2081)

Freedom Health LLC.. 330 562-0888
65 Aurora Industrial Pkwy Aurora (44202) (G-670)

Freedom Usa Inc.. 216 503-6374
2045 Midway Dr Twinsburg (44087) (G-13305)

Freeman, Fremont Also Called: The Louis G Freeman Company LLC (G-7136)

Freeman Enclosure Systems LLC............................. 877 441-8555
4160 Half Acre Rd Batavia (45103) (G-865)

Freeman Manufacturing & Sup Co (PA)...................... 440 934-1902
1101 Moore Rd Avon (44011) (G-727)

Freeport Press Inc (PA).. 330 308-3300
2127 Reiser Ave Se New Philadelphia (44663) (G-10447)

Freeway Corporation (PA)....................................... 216 524-9700
9301 Allen Dr Cleveland (44125) (G-3743)

Fremar Industries Inc... 330 220-3700
2808 Westway Dr Brunswick (44212) (G-1592)

Fremont, Fremont Also Called: Fremont Company (G-7108)

Fremont, Rockford Also Called: Fremont Company (G-11630)

Fremont Company (PA)... 419 334-8995
802 N Front St Fremont (43420) (G-7108)

Fremont Company.. 419 363-2924
150 Hickory St Rockford (45882) (G-11630)

Fremont Cutting Dies Inc....................................... 419 334-5153
3179 Us 20 E Fremont (43420) (G-7109)

Fremont Discover Ltd.. 419 332-8696
315 Garrison St Fremont (43420) (G-7110)

Fremont Plastic Products Inc.................................. 419 332-6407
2101 Cedar St Fremont (43420) (G-7111)

Fremont Printing Inc... 480 272-3443
1208 Dickinson St Fremont (43420) (G-7112)

French Transit LLC.. 650 431-3959
7588 Central Parke Blvd Ste 220 Mason (45040) (G-9101)

Fresh and Limited, Sidney Also Called: Freshway Foods Company Inc (G-12020)

Fresh Mark Inc.. 330 455-5253
1600 Harmont Ave Ne Canton (44705) (G-1894)

Fresh Mark Inc (PA)... 330 832-7491
1888 Southway St Sw Massillon (44646) (G-9192)

Fresh Mark Inc.. 330 332-8508
1735 S Lincoln Ave Salem (44460) (G-11781)

Fresh Products LLC.. 419 531-9741
30600 Oregon Rd Perrysburg (43551) (G-11224)

Fresh Vegetable Technology, Columbus Also Called: National Frt Vgtable Tech Corp (G-5121)

Freshly Preserved LLC.. 440 523-1099
11798 York Rd North Royalton (44133) (G-10761)

Freshway Foods Company Inc (DH)........................... 937 498-4664
601 Stolle Ave Sidney (45365) (G-12020)

Freudenberg-Nok Findlay, Findlay Also Called: Freudenberg-Nok General Partnr (G-6868)

Freudenberg-Nok General Partnr............................. 419 427-5221
555 Marathon Blvd Findlay (45840) (G-6868)

Freudenberg-Nok General Partnr............................. 937 335-3306
1275 Archer Dr Troy (45373) (G-13216)

Freudenberg-Nok Sealing Tech................................ 877 331-8427
11617 State Route 13 Milan (44846) (G-9915)

Freudenberg-Nok Sealing Tech, Troy Also Called: Freudenberg-Nok General Partnr (G-13216)

Frezerve Inc.. 440 661-4037
1218 Lake Ave Ashtabula (44004) (G-592)

Friction Products Co.. 330 725-4941
920 Lake Rd Medina (44256) (G-9406)

Friends Business Source, Findlay Also Called: Friends Service Co Inc (G-6869)

Friends Service Co Inc.. 800 427-1704
4604 Salem Ave Dayton (45416) (G-5785)

Friends Service Co Inc (PA).................................... 419 427-1704
2300 Bright Rd Findlay (45840) (G-6869)

Fries Machine & Tool Inc.. 937 898-6432
5729 Webster St Dayton (45414) (G-5786)

Friesen Transfer Ltd.. 614 873-5672
9280 Iams Rd Plain City (43064) (G-11409)

Friess Welding Inc... 330 644-8160
3342 S Main St Coventry Township (44319) (G-5482)

Frisby Printing Company... 330 665-4565
3571 Brookwall Dr Unit C Fairlawn (44333) (G-6801)

Frito-Lay, Canton Also Called: Frito-Lay North America Inc (G-1895)

Frito-Lay, Wooster Also Called: Frito-Lay North America Inc (G-14639)

Frito-Lay North America Inc.................................... 330 477-7009
4030 16th St Sw Canton (44710) (G-1895)

Frito-Lay North America Inc.................................... 972 334-7000
1626 Old Mansfield Rd Wooster (44691) (G-14639)

Fritzie Freeze Inc.. 419 727-0818
5137 N Summit St Unit 1 Toledo (43611) (G-12969)

Frog Ranch Foods Ltd... 740 767-3705
5 S High St Glouster (45732) (G-7290)

Frohn North America Inc.. 770 819-0089
23800 Corbin Dr Ste B Bedford Heights (44128) (G-1077)

Frohock-Stewart Inc... 440 329-6000
39400 Taylor Pkwy North Ridgeville (44035) (G-10731)

Front Pocket Innovations LLC.................................. 330 441-2365
471 E Bergey St Ste C Wadsworth (44281) (G-13639)

Frontier Signs & Displays Inc.................................. 513 367-0813
525 New Biddinger Rd Harrison (45030) (G-7552)

Frontier Tank Center Inc.. 330 659-3888
3800 Congress Pkwy Richfield (44286) (G-11593)

Frost Engineering Inc.. 513 541-6330
3408 Beekman St Cincinnati (45223) (G-2642)

Frostop, Columbus Also Called: Fbg Bottling Group LLC (G-4920)

Frozen Specialties Inc.. 419 445-9015
720 W Barre Rd Archbold (43502) (G-494)

Frutarom, Cincinnati Also Called: Frutarom USA Inc (G-2643)

Frutarom USA Holding Inc...................................... 201 861-9500
5404 Duff Dr West Chester (45246) (G-14121)

Frutarom USA Inc (HQ)... 513 870-4900
5404 Duff Dr Cincinnati (45246) (G-2643)

Frutarom USA Inc.. 513 870-4900
9930 Commerce Park Dr West Chester (45246) (G-14122)

Fry Foods Inc... 419 448-0831
99 Maule Rd Tiffin (44883) (G-12784)

Fryburg Door Inc... 330 674-5252
6086 State Route 241 Millersburg (44654) (G-9981)

Fscreations Corporation (HQ).................................. 330 746-3015
255 W Federal St Youngstown (44503) (G-14858)

FSI, Archbold Also Called: Frozen Specialties Inc (G-494)

Fsqpronet LLC.. 330 942-6014
1152 Verona Ave Youngstown (44506) (G-14859)

Ft Precision Inc.. 740 694-1500
9731 Mount Gilead Rd Fredericktown (43019) (G-7079)

Ftd Investments LLC.. 937 833-2161
379 Albert Rd Brookville (45309) (G-1569)

Ftech R&D North America Inc (HQ)........................... 937 339-2777
1191 Horizon West Ct Troy (45373) (G-13217)

Ftp, Fredericktown Also Called: Ft Precision Inc (G-7079)

Fuchs Franklin Div, Twinsburg Also Called: Fuchs Lubricants Co (G-13306)

Fuchs Lubricants Co... 330 963-0400
8036 Bavaria Rd Twinsburg (44087) (G-13306)

Fukuvi Usa Inc.. 937 236-7288
7631 Progress Ct Dayton (45424) (G-5787)

Full Circle Oil Field Svcs Inc.................................. 740 371-5422
7585 State Route 821 Whipple (45788) (G-14356)

Fullgospel Publishing.. 216 339-1973
16781 Chagrin Blvd Ste 134 Shaker Heights (44120) (G-11930)

Fullton Mill Services, Delta Also Called: Edw C Levy Co (G-6205)

Fulton, Wauseon Also Called: Stamp & Flash Inc (G-13859)

Fulton County Expositor, Napoleon Also Called: Gazette Publishing Company (G-10280)

Fulton County Processing Ltd................................. 419 822-9266
7800 State Route 109 Delta (43515) (G-6206)

Fulton Equipment Co (PA)..419 290-5393
  823 Hamilton St Toledo (43607) *(G-12970)*

Fulton Industries, Wauseon *Also Called: Fulton Industries LLC (G-13849)*

Fulton Industries LLC..419 270-3937
  135 E Linfoot St Wauseon (43567) *(G-13849)*

Fulton Manufacturing Inds LLC
  6600 W Snowville Rd # 6500 Brecksville (44141) *(G-1466)*

Fulton Sign & Decal Inc...440 951-1515
  7144 Industrial Park Blvd Mentor (44060) *(G-9521)*

Functional Formularies, West Chester *Also Called: Nutritional Medicinals LLC (G-14034)*

Functional Products Inc...330 963-3060
  8282 Bavaria Dr E Macedonia (44056) *(G-8692)*

Funny Times Inc...216 371-8600
  2176 Lee Rd Cleveland (44118) *(G-3744)*

Funtown Playgrounds Inc...513 871-8585
  839 Cypresspoint Ct Cincinnati (45245) *(G-2303)*

Furn Tech, Waterville *Also Called: Furnace Technologies Inc (G-13833)*

Furnace Technologies Inc..419 878-2100
  1070 Disher Dr Waterville (43566) *(G-13833)*

Furniss Corporation Ltd..614 871-1470
  15812 State Route 56 W Mount Sterling (43143) *(G-10228)*

Furniture By Otmar Inc (PA).......................................937 435-2039
  301 Miamisburg Centerville Rd Dayton (45459) *(G-5788)*

Furniture Concepts Inc...216 292-9100
  4925 Galaxy Pkwy Ste G Cleveland (44128) *(G-3745)*

Furntech, Waterville *Also Called: Labcraft Inc (G-13838)*

Furukawa Rock Drill, Kent *Also Called: Furukawa Rock Drill Usa Inc (G-8033)*

Furukawa Rock Drill Usa Inc (HQ)...............................330 673-5826
  805 Lake St Kent (44240) *(G-8033)*

Furukawa Rock Drill USA Co Ltd (PA)............................330 673-5826
  711 Lake St Kent (44240) *(G-8034)*

Fuserashi Intl Tech Inc..330 273-0140
  5401 Innovation Dr Valley City (44280) *(G-13496)*

Fusion Ceramics Inc (PA)..330 627-5821
  160 Scio Rd Se Carrollton (44615) *(G-2083)*

Fusion Incorporated (PA)...440 946-3300
  4658 E 355th St Willoughby (44094) *(G-14460)*

Fusion Noodle Company Inc..740 589-5511
  30 E Union St Athens (45701) *(G-639)*

Future Controls Corporation..440 275-3191
  1419 State Route 45 Austinburg (44010) *(G-700)*

Future Finishes Inc..513 860-0020
  40 Standen Dr Hamilton (45015) *(G-7491)*

Future Polytech Inc (PA)..614 942-1209
  2215 Citygate Dr Ste D Columbus (43219) *(G-4941)*

Fuyao Glass America Inc (HQ)......................................937 496-5777
  800 Fuyao Ave Moraine (45439) *(G-10164)*

Fx Digital Media Inc (PA)...216 241-4040
  1600 E 23rd St Cleveland (44114) *(G-3746)*

Fx Digital Media Inc..216 241-4040
  2400 Superior Ave E Ste 100 Cleveland (44114) *(G-3747)*

G & C Raw LLC...937 827-0010
  225 N West St Versailles (45380) *(G-13595)*

G & C Raw Dog Food, Versailles *Also Called: G & C Raw LLC (G-13595)*

G & J Extrusions Inc...330 753-0162
  1580 Turkeyfoot Lake Rd New Franklin (44203) *(G-10389)*

G & J Packaging, Cleveland *Also Called: G and J Automatic Systems Inc (G-3749)*

G & J Pepsi-Cola Bottlers Inc.....................................740 593-3366
  2001 E State St Athens (45701) *(G-640)*

G & J Pepsi-Cola Bottlers Inc.....................................740 774-2148
  400 E 7th St Chillicothe (45601) *(G-2252)*

G & J Pepsi-Cola Bottlers Inc (PA)...............................513 785-6060
  9435 Waterstone Blvd Ste 390 Cincinnati (45249) *(G-2644)*

G & J Pepsi-Cola Bottlers Inc.....................................866 647-2734
  870 N 22nd St Columbus (43219) *(G-4942)*

G & J Pepsi-Cola Bottlers Inc.....................................614 253-8771
  1241 Gibbard Ave Columbus (43219) *(G-4943)*

G & J Pepsi-Cola Bottlers Inc.....................................740 354-9191
  4587 Gallia Pike Franklin Furnace (45629) *(G-7058)*

G & J Pepsi-Cola Bottlers Inc.....................................513 896-3700
  2580 Bobmeyer Rd Hamilton (45015) *(G-7492)*

G & J Pepsi-Cola Bottlers Inc.....................................740 354-9191
  336 N Sixth St Zanesville (43701) *(G-15017)*

G & L Machining Inc...513 724-2600
  299 N 3rd St Williamsburg (45176) *(G-14409)*

G & M Precision Machining Inc....................................937 667-1443
  9785 Wildcat Rd Tipp City (45371) *(G-12826)*

G & P Construction LLC...855 494-4830
  10139 Royalton Rd Ste D North Royalton (44133) *(G-10762)*

G & S Bar and Wire LLC...260 747-4154
  4000 E Lincoln Way Wooster (44691) *(G-14640)*

G & S Metal Products Co Inc (PA).................................216 441-0700
  3330 E 79th St Cleveland (44127) *(G-3748)*

G & S Titanium Inc..330 263-0564
  4000 E Lincoln Way Wooster (44691) *(G-14641)*

G & T Manufacturing Co...440 639-7777
  6085 Pinecone Dr Mentor (44060) *(G-9522)*

G & W Products LLC...513 860-4050
  8675 Seward Rd Fairfield (45011) *(G-6738)*

G A Avril Company (PA)..513 641-0566
  2108 Eagle Ct Cincinnati (45237) *(G-2645)*

G A Avril Company...513 731-5133
  2108 Eagle Ct Cincinnati (45237) *(G-2646)*

G A Wintzer and Son Company (PA)..............................419 739-4900
  204 W Auglaize St Wapakoneta (45895) *(G-13711)*

G A Wintzer and Son Company....................................419 739-4913
  12279 S Dixey Hwy Wapakoneta (45895) *(G-13712)*

G and J Automatic Systems Inc...................................216 741-6070
  14701 Industrial Pkwy Cleveland (44135) *(G-3749)*

G Big Inc (PA)..740 867-5758
  441 Rockwood Ave Chesapeake (45619) *(G-2229)*

G Denver and Co LLC..937 498-2555
  211 E Russell Rd Sidney (45365) *(G-12021)*

G E S, Parma *Also Called: Ges Graphite Inc (G-11132)*

G F Frank and Sons Inc...513 870-9075
  9075 Le Saint Dr West Chester (45014) *(G-14002)*

G Fordyce Co..937 393-3241
  210 Hobart Dr Hillsboro (45133) *(G-7716)*

G Grafton Machine & Rubber......................................330 297-1062
  640 Cleveland Rd Ravenna (44266) *(G-11525)*

G H Cutter Services Inc...419 476-0476
  6203 N Detroit Ave Toledo (43612) *(G-12971)*

G I Plastek Inc...440 230-1942
  24700 Center Ridge Rd Ste 8 Westlake (44145) *(G-14302)*

G L Pierce Inc...513 772-7202
  12100 Mosteller Rd Ste 500 Cincinnati (45241) *(G-2647)*

G M R Technology Inc...440 992-6003
  2131 Aetna Rd Ashtabula (44004) *(G-593)*

G P Manufacturing Inc...937 544-3190
  376 Buckeye St Peebles (45660) *(G-11168)*

G S K Inc..937 547-1611
  915 Front St Greenville (45331) *(G-7342)*

G S S, Barberton *Also Called: Glass Surface Systems Inc (G-808)*

G S S, Springboro *Also Called: Graphic Systems Services Inc (G-12254)*

G T Automotive Service Center, Pataskala *Also Called: Gt Tire Service Inc (G-11139)*

G T Metal Fabricators Inc...440 237-8745
  12126 York Rd Unit E Cleveland (44133) *(G-3750)*

G W Cobb Co..216 341-0100
  3914 Broadway Ave 16 Cleveland (44115) *(G-3751)*

G W Steffen Bookbinders Inc......................................330 963-0300
  8212 Bavaria Dr E Macedonia (44056) *(G-8693)*

G W Tool & Die Co, Fort Loramie *Also Called: Schmitmeyer Inc (G-6954)*

G-M-I Inc...440 953-8811
  4822 E 355th St Willoughby (44094) *(G-14461)*

G-R Contracting Inc..740 567-3202
  35479 State Route 78 Lewisville (43754) *(G-8366)*

G.M. Pallet Co., Cincinnati *Also Called: GM Pallet LLC (G-2678)*

G.S. Steel Company, Cuyahoga Falls *Also Called: Dbcr Inc (G-5537)*

G&H Baltimore, Cleveland *Also Called: Em4 LLC (G-3666)*

G&O Resources Ltd..330 253-2525
  677 Kling St Akron (44311) *(G-153)*

G2 Materials LLC...216 293-4211
  17325 Euclid Ave Ste 3038 Cleveland (44112) *(G-3752)*

2025 Harris Ohio
Industrial Directory

(G-0000) Company's Geographic Section entry number

G3 Packaging LLC..334 799-0015
4273 Salzman Rd Monroe (45044) *(G-10106)*

Gabriel Logan LLC (PA)...740 380-6809
4141 Hamilton Square Blvd Groveport (43125) *(G-7436)*

Gabriel Performance Products, Akron *Also Called: Huntsman Advnced Mtls Amrcas L (G-178)*

Gabriel Phenoxies Inc (PA).......................................704 499-9801
240 W Emerling Ave Akron (44301) *(G-154)*

Gad-Jets Investments Inc..937 274-2111
323 Industrial Dr Franklin (45005) *(G-7023)*

Galactic Printing LLC
3923 E Main St Columbus (43213) *(G-4944)*

Galapagos Inc (PA)...937 890-3068
3345 Old Salem Rd Dayton (45415) *(G-5789)*

Galaxy Balloons Incorporated.................................216 476-3360
11750 Berea Rd Ste 3 Cleveland (44111) *(G-3753)*

Galaxy Outdoor, Miamisburg *Also Called: Hearth Products Controls Co (G-9697)*

Galehouse Lumber, Doylestown *Also Called: The Galehouse Companies Inc (G-6270)*

Galenas LLC...330 208-9423
1956 S Main St Akron (44301) *(G-155)*

Galion LLC...419 468-5214
515 N East St Galion (44833) *(G-7190)*

Galion Canvas Products (PA)....................................419 468-5333
385 S Market St Galion (44833) *(G-7191)*

Galion Dump Bodies, Dundee *Also Called: Galion-Godwin Truck Bdy Co LLC (G-6365)*

Galion-Godwin Truck Bdy Co LLC.............................330 359-5495
7415 Township Road 666 Dundee (44624) *(G-6365)*

Galipols Reduction Co, Rio Grande *Also Called: Inland Products Inc (G-11617)*

Galley Printing Inc...330 220-5577
2892 Westway Dr Brunswick (44212) *(G-1593)*

Galley Printing Company, Brunswick *Also Called: Galley Printing Inc (G-1593)*

Galt Alloys, Canton *Also Called: Rmi Titanium Company LLC (G-1997)*

Galt Alloys Enterprise..330 309-8194
1550 Marietta Ave Se Canton (44707) *(G-1896)*

Galt Alloys Inc Main Ofc...330 453-4678
122 Central Plz N Canton (44702) *(G-1897)*

Gamco, Ravenna *Also Called: General Aluminum Mfg LLC (G-11527)*

Gameday Vision...330 830-4550
1147 Oberlin Ave Sw Massillon (44647) *(G-9193)*

Ganeden, Mayfield Heights *Also Called: Ganeden Biotech Inc (G-9334)*

Ganeden Biotech Inc..440 229-5200
5800 Landerbrook Dr Ste 300 Mayfield Heights (44124) *(G-9334)*

Gannett Stllite Info Ntwrk LLC.................................513 768-8451
6223 Lakewood Dr Cincinnati (45201) *(G-2648)*

Gannett Stllite Info Ntwrk LLC.................................419 334-1012
1800 E State St Ste B Fremont (43420) *(G-7113)*

Gannett Stllite Info Ntwrk LLC.................................304 485-1891
700 Channel Ln Marietta (45750) *(G-8918)*

Ganymede Technologies Corp..................................419 562-5522
1685 Marion Rd Bucyrus (44820) *(G-1681)*

Ganzcorp Investments Inc..330 963-5400
2300 Pinnacle Pkwy Twinsburg (44087) *(G-13307)*

Garage Scenes Ltd..614 407-6094
7385 State Route 3 Unit 112 Westerville (43082) *(G-14211)*

Garber Farms, Greenville *Also Called: Russell L Garber (G-7352)*

Gardella Jewelry LLC...440 877-9261
7432 Julia Dr North Royalton (44133) *(G-10763)*

Garden Street Iron & Metal Inc (PA)........................513 721-4660
2885 Spring Grove Ave Cincinnati (45225) *(G-2649)*

Gardner Inc (PA)..614 456-4000
3641 Interchange Rd Columbus (43204) *(G-4945)*

Gardner Business Media Inc.....................................513 527-8800
6925 Valley Ln Cincinnati (45244) *(G-2650)*

Gardner Business Media Inc (PA).............................513 527-8800
6915 Valley Ln Cincinnati (45244) *(G-2651)*

Gardner Lumber Company Inc..................................740 254-4664
5805 Laurel Creek Rd Se Tippecanoe (44699) *(G-12857)*

Gardner Pie Company...330 245-2030
191 Logan Pkwy Coventry Township (44319) *(G-5483)*

Gardner Signs Inc (PA)..419 385-6669
3800 Airport Hwy Toledo (43615) *(G-12972)*

Garfield Alloys Inc (PA)...216 587-4843
4878 Chaincraft Rd Cleveland (44125) *(G-3754)*

Garick LLC (HQ)..216 581-0100
8400 Sweet Valley Dr Ste 408 Cleveland (44125) *(G-3755)*

Garland Commercial Industries LLC........................800 338-2204
1333 E 179th St Cleveland (44110) *(G-3756)*

Garland Industries Inc (PA).....................................216 641-7500
3800 E 91st St Cleveland (44105) *(G-3757)*

Garland Welding Co Inc...330 536-6506
804 E Liberty St Lowellville (44436) *(G-8662)*

Garland/Dbs Inc..216 641-7500
3800 E 91st St Cleveland (44105) *(G-3758)*

Garro Tread Corporation (PA)...................................330 376-3125
100 Beech St Akron (44308) *(G-156)*

Garvey Corporation..330 779-0700
1019 Ohio Works Dr Youngstown (44510) *(G-14860)*

Garvin Industries Div, Strongsville *Also Called: Guarantee Specialties Inc (G-12562)*

Gary L Gast...419 626-5915
2024 Campbell St Sandusky (44870) *(G-11835)*

Gary Lawrence Enterprises Inc.................................330 833-7181
21 Charles Ave Sw Massillon (44646) *(G-9194)*

Garys Chesecakes Fine Desserts..............................513 574-1700
1875 Jonte St Cincinnati (45214) *(G-2652)*

Gas Assist Injction Mlding Exp.................................440 632-5203
15285 S State Ave Middlefield (44062) *(G-9795)*

Gas Products, Cambridge *Also Called: Aci Services Inc (G-1734)*

Gas Turbine Fuel Systems, Mentor *Also Called: Parker-Hannifin Corporation (G-9582)*

Gasdorf Tool and Mch Co Inc....................................419 227-0103
445 N Mcdonel St Lima (45801) *(G-8409)*

Gasflux Company...440 365-1941
32 Hawthorne St Elyria (44035) *(G-6538)*

Gasgas North America, Amherst *Also Called: Ktm North America Inc (G-447)*

Gasko Fabricated Products LLC (HQ).......................330 239-1781
4049 Ridge Rd Medina (44256) *(G-9407)*

Gaslight, Cincinnati *Also Called: Launch Scout LLC (G-2813)*

Gasoila Thred-Taper, Cleveland *Also Called: FedPro Inc (G-3711)*

Gaspar, Canton *Also Called: Gaspar Inc (G-1898)*

Gaspar Inc...330 477-2222
1545 Whipple Ave Sw Canton (44710) *(G-1898)*

Gaspar Services LLC..330 467-8292
7791 Capital Blvd Ste 2 Macedonia (44056) *(G-8694)*

Gasser Chair Co Inc (PA)...330 534-2234
4136 Logan Way Youngstown (44505) *(G-14861)*

Gasser Chair Co Inc...330 759-2234
2457 Logan Ave Youngstown (44505) *(G-14862)*

Gate West Coast Ventures LLC.................................513 891-1000
1001 Hunt Rd Ste 200 Blue Ash (45242) *(G-1270)*

Gatekeeper Press LLC...866 535-0913
2167 Stringtown Rd Ste 109 Grove City (43123) *(G-7388)*

Gatesair Inc (HQ)..513 459-3400
5300 Kings Island Dr Ste 101 Mason (45040) *(G-9102)*

Gateway Con Forming Svcs Inc................................513 353-2000
5938 Hamilton-Cleves Rd Miamitown (45041) *(G-9758)*

Gateway Industrial Pdts Inc.....................................440 324-4112
160 Freedom Ct Elyria (44035) *(G-6539)*

Gateway Packaging Company LLC............................419 738-5126
253 Indl Dr Wapakoneta (45895) *(G-13713)*

Gateway Printing, Wadsworth *Also Called: Rohrer Corporation (G-13668)*

Gatton Packaging Inc...419 886-2577
99 East St Bellville (44813) *(G-1138)*

Gawa Traders LLC..614 697-1440
250 West St Columbus (43215) *(G-4946)*

Gayston Corporation..937 743-6050
721 Richard St Miamisburg (45342) *(G-9693)*

Gazette Publishing, Conneaut *Also Called: The Gazette Printing Co Inc (G-5418)*

Gazette Publishing Company....................................419 335-2010
595 E Riverview Ave Napoleon (43545) *(G-10280)*

Gazette Publishing Company (PA)............................419 483-4190
42 S Main St Oberlin (44074) *(G-10917)*

Gb, Delta *Also Called: Gb Manufacturing Company (G-6207)*

Gb Fabrication Company.................................... 419 347-1835
   2510 Taylortown Rd Shelby (44875) *(G-11970)*

Gb Fabrication Company (HQ)........................ 419 896-3191
   60 Scott St Shiloh (44878) *(G-11977)*

Gb Liquidating Company Inc............................. 513 248-7600
   22 Whitney Dr Milford (45150) *(G-9935)*

Gb Manufacturing Company (PA)..................... 419 822-5323
   1120 E Main St Delta (43515) *(G-6207)*

Gbr Property Maintenance LLC........................ 937 879-0200
   1260 Spangler Rd Bldg 1 Fairborn (45324) *(G-6693)*

GBS Corp... 330 863-1828
   224 Morges Rd Malvern (44644) *(G-8750)*

GBS Corp (PA)... 330 494-5330
   7233 Freedom Ave Nw North Canton (44720) *(G-10641)*

GBS Filing Solutions, Malvern *Also Called: GBS Corp (G-8750)*

GBS Filing Solutions, North Canton *Also Called: GBS Corp (G-10641)*

Gc Controls Inc.. 440 779-4777
   30311 Clemens Rd Westlake (44145) *(G-14303)*

Gcc, Monroe *Also Called: Glass Coatings & Concepts LLC (G-10107)*

GCI Digital Imaging Inc.................................... 513 521-7446
   5031 Winton Rd Cincinnati (45232) *(G-2653)*

GCI Metals Inc... 937 835-7123
   259 Olinger Cir Wilmington (45177) *(G-14582)*

Gconsent LLC.. 614 886-2416
   5412 Talladega Dr Dublin (43016) *(G-6297)*

Gconsent Logistics, Dublin *Also Called: Gconsent LLC (G-6297)*

Gdc Inc... 574 533-3128
   1700 Old Mansfield Rd Wooster (44691) *(G-14642)*

Gdc Industries LLC.. 937 367-7229
   170 Gracewood Dr Dayton (45458) *(G-5790)*

Gdj Inc... 440 975-0258
   7585 Tyler Blvd Mentor (44060) *(G-9523)*

Gdn Welding LLC... 740 398-6109
   26697 Danville Amity Rd Danville (43014) *(G-5599)*

Gdy Installations Inc...................................... 419 467-0036
   302 Arco Dr Toledo (43607) *(G-12973)*

GDY INSTALLATIONS INC, Toledo *Also Called: Gdy Installations Inc (G-12973)*

GE, Aurora *Also Called: USA Instruments Inc (G-692)*

GE, Bucyrus *Also Called: General Electric Company (G-1682)*

GE, Canton *Also Called: General Electric Company (G-1899)*

GE, Cincinnati *Also Called: GE Engine Services LLC (G-2656)*

GE, Cincinnati *Also Called: General Electric Company (G-2660)*

GE, Cincinnati *Also Called: General Electric Company (G-2662)*

GE, Cleveland *Also Called: GE Lighting Inc (G-3759)*

GE, Cleveland *Also Called: General Electric Company (G-3763)*

GE, Cleveland *Also Called: General Electric Company (G-3764)*

GE, Cleveland *Also Called: General Electric Company (G-3765)*

GE, Cleveland *Also Called: General Electric Company (G-3766)*

GE, Coshocton *Also Called: General Electric Company (G-5456)*

GE, Logan *Also Called: General Electric Company (G-8514)*

GE, Mc Donald *Also Called: General Electric Company (G-9358)*

GE, Twinsburg *Also Called: GE Vernova International LLC (G-13308)*

GE, Twinsburg *Also Called: General Electric Company (G-13311)*

GE, Warren *Also Called: General Electric Company (G-13767)*

GE, West Chester *Also Called: General Electric Company (G-14009)*

GE Additive, West Chester *Also Called: General Electric Company (G-14008)*

GE Additive LLC... 513 341-0597
   5115 Excello Ct West Chester (45069) *(G-14003)*

GE Aviation, Cincinnati *Also Called: GE Aviation Systems LLC (G-2654)*

GE Aviation, Cincinnati *Also Called: GE Aviation Systems LLC (G-2655)*

GE Aviation, Springdale *Also Called: GE Aviation Systems LLC (G-12273)*

GE Aviation, West Chester *Also Called: GE Aviation Systems LLC (G-14004)*

GE Aviation Systems LLC................................ 513 470-2889
   10270 Saint Rita Ln Cincinnati (45215) *(G-2654)*

GE Aviation Systems LLC (HQ)........................ 937 898-9600
   1 Neumann Way Cincinnati (45215) *(G-2655)*

GE Aviation Systems LLC................................ 937 898-9600
   6800 Poe Ave Dayton (45414) *(G-5791)*

GE Aviation Systems LLC................................ 620 218-5237
   183 Progress Pl Springdale (45246) *(G-12273)*

GE Aviation Systems LLC................................ 937 898-5881
   740 E National Rd Vandalia (45377) *(G-13558)*

GE Aviation Systems LLC................................ 513 786-4555
   7831 Ashford Glen Ct West Chester (45069) *(G-14004)*

GE Aviation Systems LLC................................ 513 889-5150
   5223 Muhlhauser Rd West Chester (45011) *(G-14005)*

GE Current, Cleveland *Also Called: Current Lighting Solutions LLC (G-3580)*

GE Current, A Daintree Company, Cleveland *Also Called: Current Lighting Solutions LLC (G-3581)*

GE Engine Services LLC.................................. 513 977-1500
   201 W Crescentville Rd Cincinnati (45246) *(G-2656)*

GE Healthcare Inc.. 513 241-5955
   346 Gest St Cincinnati (45203) *(G-2657)*

GE Honda Aero Engines LLC........................... 513 552-4322
   9050 Centre Pointe Dr Ste 200 West Chester (45069) *(G-14006)*

GE Lighting Inc.. 216 266-2121
   1975 Noble Rd Cleveland (44112) *(G-3759)*

GE Lighting, A Savant Company, East Cleveland *Also Called: Savant Technologies LLC (G-6382)*

GE Military Systems.. 513 243-2000
   1 Neumann Way Cincinnati (45215) *(G-2658)*

GE Vernova International LLC.......................... 330 963-2066
   8941 Dutton Dr Twinsburg (44087) *(G-13308)*

Gear Company of America Inc......................... 216 671-5400
   14300 Lorain Ave Cleveland (44111) *(G-3760)*

Gear Star, Akron *Also Called: Gear Star Amrcn Prfmce Trnsmss (G-157)*

Gear Star Amrcn Prfmce Trnsmss.................. 330 434-5216
   132 N Howard St Akron (44308) *(G-157)*

Gear Wash, Medina *Also Called: Fire-Dex LLC (G-9403)*

Geartec Inc... 440 953-3900
   4245 Hamann Pkwy Willoughby (44094) *(G-14462)*

Geauga Coatings LLC..................................... 440 221-7286
   15120 Sisson Rd Chardon (44024) *(G-2206)*

Geauga Concrete LLC..................................... 440 338-4915
   10509 Kinsman Rd Newbury (44065) *(G-10551)*

Geauga Group LLC.. 440 543-8797
   11024 Wingate Dr Chagrin Falls (44023) *(G-2162)*

Geauga Highway Co....................................... 440 834-4580
   9215 State Route 303 Windham (44288) *(G-14600)*

Gebauer Company.. 216 581-3030
   4444 E 153rd St Cleveland (44128) *(G-3761)*

Ged Holdings Inc... 330 963-5401
   9280 Dutton Dr Twinsburg (44087) *(G-13309)*

Gedico International Inc.................................. 937 274-2167
   5337 Crossbridge Dr West Chester (45069) *(G-14007)*

Gehm & Sons Limited..................................... 330 724-8423
   825 S Arlington St Akron (44306) *(G-158)*

Gei of Columbiana Inc.................................... 330 783-0270
   4040 Lake Park Rd Youngstown (44512) *(G-14863)*

Geist, Westerville *Also Called: Vertiv Corporation (G-14239)*

Gelok International Corp.................................. 419 352-1482
   20189 Pine Lake Rd Bowling Green (43402) *(G-1420)*

Gem Attachments, Cuyahoga Falls *Also Called: TRM Manufacturing Inc (G-5577)*

Gem Beverages Inc.. 740 384-2411
   106 E 11th St Wellston (45692) *(G-13906)*

Gem City, Dayton *Also Called: Gem City Metal Tech LLC (G-5793)*

Gem City Engineering Co (DH)........................ 937 223-5544
   401 Leo St Dayton (45404) *(G-5792)*

Gem City Metal Tech LLC................................ 937 252-8998
   1825 E 1st St Dayton (45403) *(G-5793)*

Gem Instrument Company Inc......................... 330 273-6117
   2832 Nationwide Pkwy Brunswick (44212) *(G-1594)*

Gemco Machine & Tool Inc............................. 740 344-3111
   88 Decrow Ave Newark (43055) *(G-10503)*

Gemini Fiber Corporation............................... 330 874-4131
   11145 Industrial Pkwy Nw Bolivar (44612) *(G-1383)*

Gemini Products, Brecksville *Also Called: Knight Ergonomics Inc (G-1475)*

Gempco, Akron *Also Called: General Metals Powder Co LLC (G-160)*

Gen Digital Inc.. 330 252-1171
   159 S Main St Akron (44308) *(G-159)*

(G-0000) Company's Geographic Section entry number

Gen Digital Inc.. 614 418-1700
2720 Airport Dr Ste 100 Columbus (43219) *(G-4947)*

Gen X Sports, Miamisburg *Also Called: Huffy Sports Washington Inc (G-9700)*

Gen-Rubber LLC... 440 655-3643
352 South St Galion (44833) *(G-7192)*

Genco... 419 207-7648
1250 George Rd Ashland (44805) *(G-536)*

Gendron Inc.. 419 636-0848
520 W Mulberry St Ste 100 Bryan (43506) *(G-1643)*

General Aluminum Mfg Company................... 330 297-1020
5159 S Prospect St Ravenna (44266) *(G-11526)*

General Aluminum Mfg LLC............................ 440 593-6225
1370 Chamberlain Blvd Conneaut (44030) *(G-5401)*

General Aluminum Mfg LLC (HQ)...................330 297-1225
5159 S Prospect St Ravenna (44266) *(G-11527)*

General Awning Company Inc......................... 216 749-0110
1350 E Granger Rd Cleveland (44131) *(G-3762)*

General Book Binding, Newbury *Also Called: Hf Group LLC (G-10553)*

General Chain & Mfg Corp.............................. 513 541-6005
3274 Beekman St Cincinnati (45223) *(G-2659)*

General Color Investments Inc...................... 330 868-4161
250 Bridge St Minerva (44657) *(G-10038)*

General Contractor, Columbus *Also Called: Golden Angle Archtctral Group (G-4960)*

General Contractor, Milford *Also Called: Commercial Cnstr Group LLC (G-9930)*

General Cutlery Inc (PA)................................. 419 332-2316
1918 N County Road 232 Fremont (43420) *(G-7114)*

General Data Company Inc (PA).....................513 752-7978
4354 Ferguson Dr Cincinnati (45245) *(G-2304)*

General Die Casters Inc.................................. 330 467-6700
6212 Akron Peninsula Rd Northfield (44067) *(G-10793)*

General Die Casters Inc (HQ).........................330 678-2528
2150 Highland Rd Twinsburg (44087) *(G-13310)*

General Dynamics, Springboro *Also Called: General Dynamics-Ots Inc (G-12253)*

General Dynamics-Ots Inc.............................. 937 746-8500
200 S Pioneer Blvd Springboro (45066) *(G-12253)*

General Dynmics Land Systems I.................. 419 221-7000
1161 Buckeye Rd Lima (45804) *(G-8410)*

General Dynmics Lima Army Tank, Lima *Also Called: General Dynmics Land Systems I (G-8410)*

General Dynmics Mssion Systems.................. 513 253-4770
2673 Commons Blvd Ste 200 Beavercreek (45431) *(G-975)*

General Dynmics Mssion Systems.................. 937 723-2001
1900 Founders Dr Ste 106 Dayton (45420) *(G-5794)*

General Electric Company............................... 419 563-1200
1250 S Walnut St Bucyrus (44820) *(G-1682)*

General Electric Company............................... 330 458-3200
5555 Massillon Rd Bldg D Canton (44720) *(G-1899)*

General Electric Company............................... 513 948-4170
445 S Cooper Ave Cincinnati (45215) *(G-2660)*

General Electric Company............................... 513 956-9051
1 Neumann Way Cincinnati (45215) *(G-2661)*

General Electric Company............................... 513 977-1500
201 W Crescentville Rd Cincinnati (45246) *(G-2662)*

General Electric Company............................... 216 268-3846
1099 Ivanhoe Rd Cleveland (44110) *(G-3763)*

General Electric Company............................... 216 391-8741
1814 E 45th St Cleveland (44103) *(G-3764)*

General Electric Company............................... 216 663-2110
18683 S Miles Rd Cleveland (44128) *(G-3765)*

General Electric Company............................... 216 883-1000
4477 E 49th St Cleveland (44125) *(G-3766)*

General Electric Company............................... 740 623-5379
1350 S 2nd St Coshocton (43812) *(G-5456)*

General Electric Company............................... 740 385-2114
State Route 93 N Logan (43138) *(G-8514)*

General Electric Company............................... 440 593-1156
3159 Wildwood Dr Mc Donald (44437) *(G-9358)*

General Electric Company............................... 330 425-3755
8499 Darrow Rd Twinsburg (44087) *(G-13311)*

General Electric Company............................... 330 373-1400
1210 Park Warren (44483) *(G-13767)*

General Electric Company............................... 513 341-0214
8556 Trade Center Dr Ste 100 West Chester (45011) *(G-14008)*

General Electric Company............................... 714 668-0951
9701 Windisch Rd West Chester (45069) *(G-14009)*

General Engine Products LLC......................... 937 704-0160
2000 Watkins Glen Dr Franklin (45005) *(G-7024)*

General Envmtl Science Corp......................... 216 464-0680
3659 Green Rd Ste 306 Beachwood (44122) *(G-919)*

General Extrusions Intl LLC........................... 330 783-0270
4040 Lake Park Rd Youngstown (44512) *(G-14864)*

General Fabrications Corp.............................. 419 625-6055
7777 Milan Rd Sandusky (44870) *(G-11836)*

General Films Inc.. 888 436-3456
645 S High St Covington (45318) *(G-5493)*

General Intl Pwr Pdts LLC.............................. 419 877-5234
6243 Industrial Pkwy Whitehouse (43571) *(G-14360)*

General Ionics, Cincinnati *Also Called: Veolia Wts Systems Usa Inc (G-3201)*

General Ionics, Stow *Also Called: Veolia Wts Systems Usa Inc (G-12470)*

General Machine & Saw Company................... 740 382-1104
305 Davids St Marion (43302) *(G-8971)*

General Machine and Mould Co, Lancaster *Also Called: Devault Machine & Mould Co LLC (G-8195)*

General Metals Powder Co LLC (PA).............. 330 633-1226
1195 Home Ave Akron (44310) *(G-160)*

General Mills, Toledo *Also Called: General Mills Inc (G-12974)*

General Mills, Wellston *Also Called: General Mills Inc (G-13907)*

General Mills Inc... 513 771-8200
11301 Mosteller Rd Cincinnati (45241) *(G-2663)*

General Mills Inc... 419 269-3100
1250 W Laskey Rd Toledo (43612) *(G-12974)*

General Mills Inc... 740 286-2170
2403 S Pennsylvania Ave Wellston (45692) *(G-13907)*

General Motors, Defiance *Also Called: General Motors LLC (G-6107)*

General Motors, Warren *Also Called: General Motors LLC (G-13768)*

General Motors LLC.. 216 265-5000
5400 Chevrolet Blvd Cleveland (44130) *(G-3767)*

General Motors LLC.. 419 782-7010
26427 State Route 281 Defiance (43512) *(G-6107)*

General Motors LLC.. 330 824-5840
2369 Ellsworth Bailey Rd Sw Warren (44481) *(G-13768)*

General Nano LLC... 513 309-5947
10340 Julian Dr Cincinnati (45215) *(G-2664)*

General Plastex Inc... 330 745-7775
35 Stuver Pl Barberton (44203) *(G-806)*

General Plastics North Corp........................... 800 542-2466
5220 Vine St Cincinnati (45217) *(G-2665)*

General Plug and Mfg Co (PA)........................ 440 920-2411
455 Main St Grafton (44044) *(G-7302)*

General Precision Corporation....................... 440 951-9380
4553 Beidler Rd Willoughby (44094) *(G-14463)*

General Sheave Company Inc.......................... 216 781-8120
1335 Main Ave Cleveland (44113) *(G-3768)*

General Steel Corporation, Cleveland *Also Called: McDonald Steel Plate Inc (G-4008)*

General Technologies Inc............................... 419 747-1800
855 W Longview Ave Mansfield (44906) *(G-8791)*

General Theming Contrs LLC.......................... 614 252-6342
3750 Courtright Ct Columbus (43227) *(G-4948)*

General Tool Company (PA)............................513 733-5500
101 Landy Ln Cincinnati (45215) *(G-2666)*

Generals Books.. 614 870-1861
522 Norton Rd Columbus (43228) *(G-4949)*

Generations Ace Inc....................................... 440 835-4872
29121 Inverness Dr Bay Village (44140) *(G-902)*

Generations Coffee Company LLC (HQ)......... 440 546-0901
60100 West Snowell Brecksville (44141) *(G-1467)*

Generic Systems Inc....................................... 419 841-8460
10560 Geiser Rd Holland (43528) *(G-7764)*

Genesis Lamp Corp... 440 354-0095
375 N Saint Clair St Painesville (44077) *(G-11088)*

Genesis Plastic Tech LLC............................... 440 542-0722
7540 W Pond Ct Concord Township (44077) *(G-5391)*

Geneva Liberty Steel Ltd (PA)............................330 740-0103
947 Martin Luther King Jr Blvd Youngstown (44502) *(G-14865)*

Geneva Rubber Company, Cortland *Also Called: Control Transformer Inc (G-5443)*

Genex Mold, Canton *Also Called: ABC Technologies Dlhb Inc (G-1821)*

Genie Company, The, Mount Hope *Also Called: GMI Holdings Inc (G-10213)*

Genie Repros Inc...216 696-6677
2211 Hamilton Ave Cleveland (44114) *(G-3769)*

Genius Solutions Engrg Co (HQ)........................419 794-9914
6421 Monclova Rd Maumee (43537) *(G-9293)*

Genmak Geneva Liberty, Youngstown *Also Called: Geneva Liberty Steel Ltd (G-14865)*

Genpact LLC...513 763-7660
100 Tri County Pkwy Ste 200 Cincinnati (45246) *(G-2667)*

Genpak LLC..614 276-5156
845 Kaderly Dr Columbus (43228) *(G-4950)*

Gent Machine Company......................................216 481-2334
12315 Kirby Ave Cleveland (44108) *(G-3770)*

Gentek Building Products Inc (HQ)....................800 548-4542
3773 State Rd Cuyahoga Falls (44223) *(G-5544)*

Gentherm Medical LLC (HQ)..............................513 772-8810
12011 Mosteller Rd Cincinnati (45241) *(G-2668)*

Gentzler Tool & Die Corp (PA)...........................330 896-1941
3903 Massillon Rd Akron (44312) *(G-161)*

Genvac Aerospace Inc......................................440 646-9986
110 Alpha Park Highland Heights (44143) *(G-7657)*

Geo-Tech Polymers LLC...................................614 797-2300
479 Industrial Park Dr Waverly (45690) *(G-13865)*

Geocentral, Mason *Also Called: CM Paula Company (G-9090)*

Geocorp Inc...419 433-1101
9010 River Rd Huron (44839) *(G-7873)*

Geodyne One, Columbus *Also Called: Mori Shuji (G-5111)*

Geograph Industries Inc...................................513 202-9200
475 Industrial Dr Harrison (45030) *(G-7553)*

Geon Company...216 447-6000
6100 Oak Tree Blvd Cleveland (44131) *(G-3771)*

Geon Performance Solutions LLC.......................440 930-1000
556 Moore Rd Avon Lake (44012) *(G-757)*

Geon Performance Solutions LLC.......................440 987-4553
835 Leo Bullocks Pkwy Elyria (44035) *(G-6540)*

Geon Performance Solutions LLC (HQ)...............800 438-4366
25777 Detroit Rd Ste 200 Westlake (44145) *(G-14304)*

George A Mitchell Company...............................330 758-5777
557 Mcclurg Rd Youngstown (44512) *(G-14866)*

George Manufacturing Inc.................................513 932-1067
160 Harmon Ave Lebanon (45036) *(G-8258)*

George Steel Fabricating Inc.............................513 932-2887
1207 S Us Route 42 Lebanon (45036) *(G-8259)*

George Whalley Company...................................216 453-0099
1180 High St Ste 1 Fairport Harbor (44077) *(G-6816)*

Georgetown Vineyards, Cambridge *Also Called: Georgetown Vineyards Inc (G-1744)*

Georgetown Vineyards Inc.................................740 435-3222
62920 Georgetown Rd Cambridge (43725) *(G-1744)*

Georgia-Boot Inc..740 753-1951
39 E Canal St Nelsonville (45764) *(G-10317)*

Georgia-Pacific, Circleville *Also Called: Georgia-Pacific LLC (G-3260)*

Georgia-Pacific, Columbus *Also Called: Georgia-Pacific LLC (G-4951)*

Georgia-Pacific, Mogadore *Also Called: Georgia-Pacific LLC (G-10076)*

Georgia-Pacific, West Chester *Also Called: Georgia-Pacific LLC (G-14010)*

Georgia-Pacific LLC...740 477-3347
2850 Owens Rd Circleville (43113) *(G-3260)*

Georgia-Pacific LLC...614 491-9100
1975 Watkins Rd Columbus (43207) *(G-4951)*

Georgia-Pacific LLC...330 794-4444
3265 Gilchrist Rd Mogadore (44260) *(G-10076)*

Georgia-Pacific LLC...513 942-4800
9048 Port Union Rialto Rd West Chester (45069) *(G-14010)*

Georgia-Pacific Pcpi Inc..................................513 932-9855
1899 Kingsview Dr Lebanon (45036) *(G-8260)*

Gerald Grain Center Inc...................................419 445-2451
3265 County Road 24 Archbold (43502) *(G-495)*

Gerald L Herrmann Company Inc.........................513 661-1818
3325 Harrison Ave Cincinnati (45211) *(G-2669)*

Gerber & Sons, Baltic *Also Called: Gerber & Sons Inc (G-778)*

Gerber & Sons Inc (PA)...................................330 897-6201
201 E Main St Baltic (43804) *(G-778)*

Gerber Farm Division LLC................................800 362-7381
133 Collins Blvd Orrville (44667) *(G-10982)*

Gerber Lumber & Hardware, Kidron *Also Called: E P Gerber & Sons Inc (G-8126)*

Gerber Poultry LLC..330 857-2731
5889 Kidron Rd Kidron (44636) *(G-8127)*

Gerber Wood Products Inc................................330 857-9007
6075 Kidron Rd Kidron (44636) *(G-8128)*

Gerdau Ameristeel US Inc..................................740 671-9410
5310 Guernsey St Bellaire (43906) *(G-1087)*

Gerdau Ameristeel US Inc..................................513 869-7660
2175 Schlichter Dr Hamilton (45015) *(G-7493)*

Gerdau McSteel Atmsphere Annli.......................330 478-0314
1501 Raff Rd Sw Canton (44710) *(G-1900)*

Gergel-Kellem Company Inc..............................216 398-2000
8707 Forest View Dr Olmsted Falls (44138) *(G-10940)*

Gerken Materials Inc (PA).................................419 533-2421
9072 County Road 424 Napoleon (43545) *(G-10281)*

Gerling and Associates Inc...............................740 965-2888
200 Kintner Pkwy Sunbury (43074) *(G-12665)*

Germ Guardian, Euclid *Also Called: Guardian Technologies LLC (G-6652)*

Germ-Busters Solutions LLC.............................330 610-0480
3649 Northwood Ave Youngstown (44511) *(G-14867)*

Gerow Equipment Company Inc..........................216 383-8800
706 E 163rd St Cleveland (44110) *(G-3772)*

Gerstco Division, Wooster *Also Called: Artiflex Manufacturing Inc (G-14623)*

Gerstenslager Construction...............................330 832-3604
343 16th St Se Massillon (44646) *(G-9195)*

Gerstenslager Hardwood Pdts, Massillon *Also Called: Gerstenslager Construction (G-9195)*

Gerstner International, Dayton *Also Called: H Gerstner & Sons Inc (G-5806)*

Ges AGM...216 658-6528
12300 Snow Rd Cleveland (44130) *(G-3773)*

Ges Graphite Inc (PA)......................................216 658-6660
12300 Snow Rd Parma (44130) *(G-11132)*

Gew Inc...440 237-4439
11941 Abbey Rd Ste X Cleveland (44133) *(G-3774)*

Gfl Environmental Svcs USA Inc.........................614 441-4001
4001 E 5th Ave Columbus (43219) *(G-4952)*

Gfl Environmental Svcs USA Inc.........................281 486-4182
4376 State Route 601 Norwalk (44857) *(G-10842)*

GFS Chemicals, Powell *Also Called: GFS Chemicals Inc (G-11488)*

GFS Chemicals Inc..614 351-5347
800 Kaderly Dr Columbus (43228) *(G-4953)*

GFS Chemicals Inc..614 224-5345
851 Mckinley Ave Columbus (43222) *(G-4954)*

GFS Chemicals Inc (PA)...................................740 881-5501
155 Hidden Ravines Dr Powell (43065) *(G-11488)*

Ggc Feeds LLC..419 445-2451
3265 County Road 24 Archbold (43502) *(G-496)*

Ghent Manufacturing, Lebanon *Also Called: GMI Companies Inc (G-8262)*

Ghp II LLC..740 681-6825
2893 W Fair Ave Lancaster (43130) *(G-8203)*

Ghp II LLC (DH)...740 687-2500
1115 W 5th Ave Lancaster (43130) *(G-8204)*

Giannios Candy Co Inc (PA)...............................330 755-7000
430 Youngstown Poland Rd Struthers (44471) *(G-12618)*

Giant Industries Inc..419 531-4600
900 N Westwood Ave Toledo (43607) *(G-12975)*

Giant Industries Inc (DH)..................................419 421-2121
539 S Main St Findlay (45840) *(G-6870)*

Gibbco, Cincinnati *Also Called: Trans Ash Inc (G-3164)*

Gideon Owen Wine, Port Clinton *Also Called: Quinami LLC (G-11450)*

Gie Media Inc (PA)..800 456-0707
5811 Canal Rd Cleveland (44125) *(G-3775)*

Gillard Construction Inc....................................740 376-9744
1308 Greene St Marietta (45750) *(G-8919)*

Gillette, Cincinnati *Also Called: Gillette Company LLC (G-2670)*

Gillette Company LLC.......................................513 983-1100
1 Procter And Gamble Plz Cincinnati (45202) *(G-2670)*

Gillig Custom Winery Inc.................... 419 202-6057
1720 Northridge Rd Findlay (45840) *(G-6871)*

Gilson Company Inc (PA)...................740 548-7298
7975 N Central Dr Lewis Center (43035) *(G-8334)*

Gilson Machine & Tool Co Inc............... 419 592-2911
529 Freedom Dr Napoleon (43545) *(G-10282)*

Gilson Screen Incorporated.................. 419 256-7711
8-810 K-2 Rd Malinta (43535) *(G-8742)*

Ginko Systems, Dayton *Also Called: Ginko Voting Systems LLC (G-5795)*

Ginko Voting Systems LLC................... 937 291-4060
600 Progress Rd Dayton (45449) *(G-5795)*

Gino's Jewelers & Trophy Mfrs, Warrensville Heights *Also Called: Ginos Awards Inc (G-13818)*

Ginos Awards Inc........................... 216 831-6565
4701 Richmond Rd Ste 200 Warrensville Heights (44128) *(G-13818)*

Girard Machine Company Inc................. 330 545-9731
700 Dot St Girard (44420) *(G-7272)*

Girindus America Inc....................... 513 679-3000
10608 Deercreek Ln Cincinnati (45249) *(G-2671)*

Giuseppes Concessions LLC.................. 614 554-2551
5383 Township Road 187 Marengo (43334) *(G-8897)*

Givaudan, Cincinnati *Also Called: Givaudan Flavors Corporation (G-2673)*

Givaudan Flavors Corporation............... 513 948-3428
100 E 69th St Cincinnati (45216) *(G-2672)*

Givaudan Flavors Corporation (DH).......... 513 948-8000
1199 Edison Dr 1-2 Cincinnati (45216) *(G-2673)*

Givaudan Flavors Corporation............... 513 948-8000
110 E 70th St Cincinnati (45216) *(G-2674)*

Givaudan Fragrances Corp................... 513 948-3428
100 E 69th St Cincinnati (45216) *(G-2675)*

Givaudan Fragrances Corp (DH).............. 513 948-8000
1199 Edison Dr Ste 1-2 Cincinnati (45216) *(G-2676)*

Gizmo, Chagrin Falls *Also Called: Whip Guide Co (G-2191)*

GKN Driveline Bowl Green Inc (DH).......... 419 373-7700
2223 Wood Bridge Blvd Bowling Green (43402) *(G-1421)*

GKN Driveline Bowling Green, Bowling Green *Also Called: GKN Driveline North Amer Inc (G-1422)*

GKN Driveline North Amer Inc............... 419 354-3955
2223 Wood Bridge Blvd Bowling Green (43402) *(G-1422)*

GKN PLC................................... 740 446-9211
2160 Eastern Ave Gallipolis (45631) *(G-7205)*

GKN Sinter Metals, Gallipolis *Also Called: GKN PLC (G-7205)*

GKN Sinter Metals LLC...................... 740 441-3203
2160 Eastern Ave Gallipolis (45631) *(G-7206)*

GL Heller Co Inc........................... 419 877-5122
6246 Industrial Pkwy Whitehouse (43571) *(G-14361)*

GL Industries Inc.......................... 513 874-1233
25 Standen Dr Hamilton (45015) *(G-7494)*

GL International LLC........................ 330 744-8812
215 Sinter Ct Youngstown (44510) *(G-14868)*

GL Nause Co Inc............................ 513 722-9500
1971 Phoenix Dr Loveland (45140) *(G-8626)*

Glance Software LLC........................ 844 383-2500
1340 Missy Ct Hamilton (45013) *(G-7495)*

Glas Ornamental Metals Inc................. 330 753-0215
1559 Waterloo Rd Barberton (44203) *(G-807)*

Glascraft Inc.............................. 330 966-3000
8400 Port Jackson Ave Nw North Canton (44720) *(G-10642)*

Glass Block Headquarters Inc............... 216 941-5470
15501 Munn Rd Cleveland (44111) *(G-3776)*

Glass Block Warehouse, The, Columbus *Also Called: Blockamerica Corporation (G-4765)*

Glass City Machining and Fab, Lancaster *Also Called: Ted M Figgins (G-8227)*

Glass Coatings & Concepts LLC.............. 513 539-5300
300 Lawton Ave Monroe (45050) *(G-10107)*

Glass Surface Systems Inc.................. 330 745-8500
24 Brown St Barberton (44203) *(G-808)*

Glasses Guy LLC............................ 970 624-9019
5151 Tuscarawas St W Canton (44708) *(G-1901)*

Glassline Corporation (PA)................. 419 666-9712
28905 Glenwood Rd Perrysburg (43551) *(G-11225)*

Glasstech Inc (PA)......................... 419 661-9500
995 4th St Perrysburg (43551) *(G-11226)*

Glatfelter Corporation..................... 740 772-3893
353 S Paint St Chillicothe (45601) *(G-2253)*

Glatfelter Corporation..................... 740 775-6119
311 Caldwell St Chillicothe (45601) *(G-2254)*

Glatfelter Corporation..................... 740 772-3111
232 E 8th St Chillicothe (45601) *(G-2255)*

Glatfelter Corporation..................... 419 333-6700
2275 Commerce Dr Fremont (43420) *(G-7115)*

Glatfelter Corporation..................... 740 289-5100
200 Schuster Rd Piketon (45661) *(G-11307)*

Glatfelter Corporation, Chillicothe *Also Called: Glatfelter Corporation (G-2253)*

Glatfelter Corporation, Chillicothe *Also Called: Glatfelter Corporation (G-2254)*

GLATFELTER CORPORATION, Piketon *Also Called: Glatfelter Corporation (G-11307)*

Glavin Industries Inc...................... 440 349-0049
6835 Cochran Rd Ste A Solon (44139) *(G-12115)*

Glavin Specialty Co, Solon *Also Called: Glavin Industries Inc (G-12115)*

Glawe Awnings, Fairborn *Also Called: Glawe Manufacturing Co Inc (G-6694)*

Glawe Manufacturing Co Inc................. 937 754-0064
851 Zapata Dr Fairborn (45324) *(G-6694)*

Glaxosmithkline LLC........................ 937 623-2680
741 Chaffin Rdg Columbus (43214) *(G-4955)*

Glaxosmithkline LLC........................ 614 570-5970
359 Garden Rd Columbus (43214) *(G-4956)*

Gleason M & M Precision, Dayton *Also Called: Gleason Metrology Systems Corp (G-5796)*

Gleason Metrology Systems Corp (HQ)........ 937 384-8901
300 Progress Rd Dayton (45449) *(G-5796)*

Gledhill Road Machinery Co................. 419 468-4400
765 Portland Way S Galion (44833) *(G-7193)*

Glen D Lala................................ 937 274-7770
2610 Willowburn Ave Dayton (45417) *(G-5797)*

Glen-Gery Caledonia Plant, Caledonia *Also Called: Glen-Gery Corporation (G-1731)*

Glen-Gery Corporation...................... 419 845-3321
5692 Rinker Rd Caledonia (43314) *(G-1731)*

Glen-Gery Corporation...................... 419 468-4890
3785 Cardington Iberia Rd Galion (44833) *(G-7194)*

Glen-Gery Corporation...................... 419 468-5002
County Rd 9 Iberia (43325) *(G-7883)*

Glenn Hunter & Associates Inc.............. 419 533-0925
1222 County Road 6 Delta (43515) *(G-6208)*

Glenn Michael Brick........................ 740 391-5735
108 Wood St Flushing (43977) *(G-6936)*

Glenn Ravens Winery........................ 740 545-1000
56183 County Road 143 West Lafayette (43845) *(G-14170)*

Glenridge Machine Co....................... 440 975-1055
37435 Fawn Path Dr Solon (44139) *(G-12116)*

Glenro Inc................................. 606 564-4778
100 N 3rd St Ripley (45107) *(G-11018)*

Glenrock Company........................... 513 489-6710
10852 Millington Ct Blue Ash (45242) *(G-1277)*

Glenwood Erectors Inc...................... 330 652-9616
251 Durst Dr Nw Warren (44483) *(G-13769)*

Glf International Inc (PA).................. 216 621-6901
3690 Orange Pl Ste 495 Cleveland (44122) *(G-3777)*

Gli, Stow *Also Called: Gli Holdings Inc (G-12433)*

Gli Holdings Inc (PA)...................... 216 651-1500
4246 Hudson Dr Stow (44224) *(G-12433)*

Gli Holdings Inc........................... 440 892-7760
4484 Allen Rd Stow (44224) *(G-12434)*

Gli Pool Products, Youngstown *Also Called: GL International LLC (G-14868)*

Glidden Professional Paint Ctr, Strongsville *Also Called: Akzo Nobel Paints LLC (G-12533)*

Glister Inc................................ 614 252-6400
830 Harmon Ave Columbus (43223) *(G-4957)*

Glo-Quartz Electric Htr Co Inc............. 440 255-9701
7084 Maple St Mentor (44060) *(G-9524)*

Global Body & Equipment Co................. 330 264-6640
2061 Sylvan Rd Wooster (44691) *(G-14643)*

Global Coal Sales Group LLC................ 614 221-0101
6641 Dublin Center Dr Dublin (43017) *(G-6298)*

Global Cooling Inc......................... 740 274-7900
6000 Poston Rd Athens (45701) *(G-641)*

A
L
P
H
A
B
E
T
I
C

Global Energy Partners LLC.................................. 419 756-8027
   3401 State Route 13 Mansfield (44904) *(G-8792)*

Global Gauge Corporation.................................... 937 254-3500
   3200 Kettering Blvd Moraine (45439) *(G-10165)*

Global Glass Block Inc....................................... 216 731-2333
   23570 Lakeland Blvd Euclid (44132) *(G-6651)*

Global Innovative Products LLC............................. 513 701-0441
   235 Harmon Ave Lebanon (45036) *(G-8261)*

Global Laser Tek LLC.. 513 701-0452
   7697 Innovation Way Ste 700 Mason (45040) *(G-9103)*

Global Lighting Tech Inc...................................... 440 922-4584
   55 Andrews Cir Ste 1 Brecksville (44141) *(G-1468)*

Global Metal Services Ltd................................... 440 591-1264
   8401 Chagrin Rd Ste 14a Chagrin Falls (44023) *(G-2163)*

Global Packaging & Exports Inc (PA)..................... 513 454-2020
   9166 Sutton Pl Hamilton (45011) *(G-7496)*

Global Partners USA Co Inc.................................. 513 276-4981
   7544 Bermuda Trce West Chester (45069) *(G-14011)*

Global Plastic Tech Inc.. 440 879-6045
   1657 Bdwy Ave Lorain (44052) *(G-8556)*

Global Precision Parts, East Liberty Also Called: Harding Machine Acquisition Co *(G-6386)*

Global Precision Parts, Ottoville Also Called: Acme Machine Automatics Inc *(G-11051)*

Global Principals, Kirtland Also Called: Essentialware *(G-8144)*

Global Realms LLC... 614 828-7284
   81 Mill St Ste 300 Gahanna (43230) *(G-7158)*

Global Retail Partners LLC.................................. 614 409-9850
   2195 Broehm Rd Columbus (43207) *(G-4958)*

Global Security Tech Inc...................................... 614 890-6400
   132 Dorchester Sq S Ste 200 Westerville (43081) *(G-14260)*

Global Specialties Inc.. 800 338-0814
   2950 Westway Dr Ste 110 Brunswick (44212) *(G-1595)*

Global Specialty Machines LLC (PA)...................... 513 701-0452
   7697 Innovation Way Ste 700 Mason (45040) *(G-9104)*

Global Srcing Support Svcs LLC............................ 800 645-2986
   260 E University Ave Cincinnati (45219) *(G-2677)*

Global TBM Company (HQ)....................................440 248-3303
   29100 Hall St Solon (44139) *(G-12117)*

Global Technology Center, Holland Also Called: Tekni-Plex Inc *(G-7786)*

Global Tool, Dayton Also Called: Ovase Manufacturing LLC *(G-5932)*

Global Trucking LLC... 614 598-6264
   3723 Ellerdale Dr Columbus (43230) *(G-4959)*

Global-Pak Inc (PA)...330 482-1993
   9636 Elkton Rd Lisbon (44432) *(G-8467)*

Globe Motors, Dayton Also Called: Globe Motors Inc *(G-5798)*

Globe Motors Inc (HQ)..334 983-3542
   2275 Stanley Ave Dayton (45404) *(G-5798)*

Globe Pipe Hanger Products Inc............................ 216 362-6300
   14601 Industrial Pkwy Cleveland (44135) *(G-3778)*

Globe Products Inc (PA).......................................937 233-0233
   5051 Kitridge Rd Dayton (45424) *(G-5799)*

Globe Specialty Metals, Waterford Also Called: Ferroglobe USA Mtllurgical Inc *(G-13826)*

Globus Printing & Packg Co Inc (PA)...................... 419 628-2381
   1 Exec Pkwy Minster (45865) *(G-10058)*

Glt Inc (PA)... 937 237-0055
   3341 Successful Way Dayton (45414) *(G-5800)*

Gluetread LLC... 800 238-9791
   11684 Hayden Ave Hiram (44234) *(G-7738)*

Glunt Industries Inc... 330 399-7585
   319 N River Rd Nw Warren (44483) *(G-13770)*

Glx Power Systems Inc....................................... 440 338-6526
   46 Chagrin Plz Ste 201 Chagrin Falls (44022) *(G-2145)*

GM Pallet LLC... 859 408-1781
   121 Citycentre Dr Cincinnati (45216) *(G-2678)*

Gmd Industries LLC.. 937 252-3643
   1414 E 2nd St Dayton (45403) *(G-5801)*

Gmelectric Inc.. 330 477-3392
   4606 Southway St Sw Canton (44706) *(G-1902)*

Gmerecords, Worthington Also Called: Swagg Productions2015llc *(G-14726)*

GMI Companies Inc.. 937 981-0244
   512 S Washington St Greenfield (45123) *(G-7327)*

GMI Companies Inc.. 937 981-7724
   512 S Washington St Greenfield (45123) *(G-7328)*

GMI Companies Inc (PA)...................................... 513 932-3445
   2999 Henkle Dr Lebanon (45036) *(G-8262)*

GMI Companies Inc.. 513 932-3445
   2999 Henkle Dr Lebanon (45036) *(G-8263)*

GMI Holdings Inc (DH)..800 354-3643
   1 Door Dr Mount Hope (44660) *(G-10213)*

Gmp Welding & Fabrication Inc.............................. 513 825-7861
   11175 Adwood Dr Cincinnati (45240) *(G-2679)*

Gnw Aluminum Inc... 330 821-7955
   1356 Beeson St Ne Alliance (44601) *(G-383)*

Go For Broke Amusement, Flushing Also Called: Glenn Michael Brick *(G-6936)*

Goddess Maintenance Company, Westerville Also Called: Montgomery Ellis LLC *(G-14271)*

Godfrey & Wing Inc (PA)...................................... 330 562-1440
   220 Campus Dr Aurora (44202) *(G-671)*

Godfrey & Wing Inc.. 419 980-4616
   2066 E 2nd St Defiance (43512) *(G-6108)*

Gofs, Mansfield Also Called: Global Energy Partners LLC *(G-8792)*

Gojo, Akron Also Called: Gojo Industries Inc *(G-163)*

Gojo Canada Inc.. 330 255-6000
   1 Gojo Plz Ste 500 Akron (44311) *(G-162)*

Gojo Industries Inc (PA)..................................... 330 255-6000
   1 Gojo Plz Ste 500 Akron (44311) *(G-163)*

Gojo Industries Inc... 330 255-6000
   3783 State Rd Cuyahoga Falls (44223) *(G-5545)*

Gojo Industries Inc... 330 255-6527
   3783 State Rd Cuyahoga Falls (44223) *(G-5546)*

Gojo Industries Inc... 330 255-6000
   4676 Erie Ave Sw Navarre (44662) *(G-10304)*

Gojo Industries Inc... 330 255-6525
   1366 Commerce Dr Stow (44224) *(G-12435)*

Gokoh Corporation (HQ)......................................937 339-4977
   1280 Archer Dr Troy (45373) *(G-13218)*

Gold Medal Products Co (PA)................................513 769-7676
   10700 Medallion Dr Cincinnati (45241) *(G-2680)*

Gold Medal-Carolina, Cincinnati Also Called: Gold Medal Products Co *(G-2680)*

Gold Rush Jerky, Litchfield Also Called: Medina Foods Inc *(G-8481)*

Gold Star Chili, Cincinnati Also Called: Gold Star Chili Inc *(G-2681)*

Gold Star Chili, Cincinnati Also Called: Gold Star Chili Inc *(G-2682)*

Gold Star Chili Inc (PA)...................................... 513 231-4541
   650 Lunken Park Dr Cincinnati (45226) *(G-2681)*

Gold Star Chili Inc.. 513 631-1990
   5420 Ridge Ave Cincinnati (45213) *(G-2682)*

Golden Angle Archtctral Group.............................. 614 531-7932
   4207 E Broad St Ste C Columbus (43213) *(G-4960)*

Golden Drapery Supply Inc................................... 216 351-3283
   2500 Brookpark Rd Unit 3 Cleveland (44134) *(G-3779)*

Golden Dynamic Inc... 614 575-1222
   676 Brook Holw Ste 104 Columbus (43230) *(G-4961)*

Golden Eagle, Upper Sandusky Also Called: New Eezy-Gro Inc *(G-13449)*

Golden Giant Inc.. 419 674-4038
   13300 S Vision Dr Kenton (43326) *(G-8098)*

Golden Giants Building System, Kenton Also Called: Golden Giant Inc *(G-8098)*

Golden Graphics, Kenton Also Called: Golden Graphics Ltd *(G-8099)*

Golden Graphics Ltd... 419 673-6260
   314 W Franklin St Kenton (43326) *(G-8099)*

Golden Jersey Inn, Yellow Springs Also Called: Youngs Jersey Dairy Inc *(G-14794)*

Golden Spring Company Inc................................. 937 848-2513
   2143 Ferry Rd Bellbrook (45305) *(G-1092)*

Golden Turtle Chocolate Fctry.............................. 513 932-1990
   120 S Broadway St Ste 1 Lebanon (45036) *(G-8264)*

Golden Window Fashions, Cleveland Also Called: Golden Drapery Supply Inc *(G-3779)*

Goldsmith & Eggleton Inc.................................... 330 336-6616
   300 1st St Wadsworth (44281) *(G-13640)*

Goldsmith & Eggleton LLC................................... 203 855-6000
   300 1st St Wadsworth (44281) *(G-13641)*

Golf Car Company Inc... 614 873-1055
   8899 Memorial Dr Plain City (43064) *(G-11410)*

Golf Dsign Screcards Unlimited, Columbus Also Called: Scorecards Unlimited LLC *(G-5257)*

Golf Galaxy Golfworks Inc.................................. 740 328-4193
   4820 Jacksontown Rd Newark (43056) *(G-10504)*

Golfworks, The, Newark *Also Called: Golf Galaxy Golfworks Inc (G-10504)*

Gomez Salsa LLC.. 513 314-1978
8575 Coolwood Ct Cincinnati (45236) *(G-2683)*

Gongwer News Service Inc (PA)....................................614 221-1992
175 S 3rd St Columbus (43215) *(G-4962)*

Gonzoil Inc.. 330 497-5888
5260 Fulton Dr Nw Canton (44718) *(G-1903)*

Gooch & Housego (ohio) LLC.. 216 486-6100
676 Alpha Dr Highland Heights (44143) *(G-7658)*

Good Greens, Oakwood Village *Also Called: Good Nutrition LLC (G-10906)*

Good News, Middlefield *Also Called: Suburban Communications Inc (G-9829)*

Good Nutrition LLC.. 216 534-6617
7710 First Pl Oakwood Village (44146) *(G-10906)*

Goodlevel Enterprises LLC (PA)...................................... 419 668-8261
55 Newton St Norwalk (44857) *(G-10843)*

Goodrich Corporation.. 440 262-1400
9921 Brecksville Rd Brecksville (44141) *(G-1469)*

Goodrich Corporation.. 330 374-2358
6051 N Airport Dr North Canton (44720) *(G-10643)*

Goodrich Corporation.. 937 339-3811
101 Waco St Troy (45373) *(G-13219)*

Goodrich Corporation.. 216 429-4378
101 Walton St Troy (45373) *(G-13220)*

Goodyear, Akron *Also Called: Goodyear Tire & Rubber Company (G-164)*

Goodyear, Beaverdam *Also Called: Goodyear Tire & Rubber Company (G-1008)*

Goodyear, Canton *Also Called: Goodyear Tire & Rubber Company (G-1904)*

Goodyear, Dublin *Also Called: Boy-Rad Inc (G-6283)*

Goodyear, Youngstown *Also Called: Goodyear Tire & Rubber Company (G-14869)*

Goodyear Tire & Rubber Company (PA).......................330 796-2121
200 E Innovation Way Akron (44316) *(G-164)*

Goodyear Tire & Rubber Company.................................. 419 643-8273
415 E Main St Beaverdam (45808) *(G-1008)*

Goodyear Tire & Rubber Company.................................. 330 966-1274
6850 Frank Ave Nw Canton (44720) *(G-1904)*

Goodyear Tire & Rubber Company.................................. 330 759-9343
3651 Belmont Ave Youngstown (44505) *(G-14869)*

Gopowerx Inc.. 440 707-6029
3850 Sawbridge Dr Unit 24 Richfield (44286) *(G-11594)*

Gorant Chocolatier LLC (PA).. 330 726-8821
8301 Market St Boardman (44512) *(G-1372)*

Gorant's Yum Yum Tree, Boardman *Also Called: Gorant Chocolatier LLC (G-1372)*

Gordon Bernard Company LLC.. 513 248-7600
22 Whitney Dr Milford (45150) *(G-9936)*

Gordon Brothers Btlg Group Inc...................................... 330 337-8754
776 N Ellsworth Ave Salem (44460) *(G-11782)*

Gordon Tool Inc... 419 263-3151
1301 State Route 49 Payne (45000) *(G-11103)*

Gordons Graphics Inc... 330 863-2322
123 S Reed Ave Malvern (44644) *(G-8751)*

Gore-Tex, Nelsonville *Also Called: Rocky Brands Inc (G-10320)*

Gorell Enterprises Inc (DH)..724 465-1800
10250 Philipp Pkwy Streetsboro (44241) *(G-12502)*

Gorell Windows & Doors, Streetsboro *Also Called: Gorell Enterprises Inc (G-12502)*

Gorman-Rupp Company... 419 755-1011
305 Bowman St Mansfield (44903) *(G-8793)*

Gorman-Rupp Company (PA)... 419 755-1011
600 S Airport Rd Mansfield (44903) *(G-8794)*

Gorman-Rupp Company... 419 755-1245
100 Rupp Rd Mansfield (44903) *(G-8795)*

GORMAN-RUPP COMPANY, Mansfield *Also Called: Gorman-Rupp Company (G-8794)*

Gosun Inc.. 888 868-6154
5151 Fischer Ave Cincinnati (45217) *(G-2684)*

Got Graphix Llc.. 330 703-9047
3265 W Market St Fairlawn (44333) *(G-6802)*

Gottfried Medical Inc.. 419 474-2973
2920 Centennial Rd Toledo (43617) *(G-12976)*

Gould Fire Protection Inc... 419 957-2416
633 Bristol Dr Findlay (45840) *(G-6872)*

Government Acquisitions Inc.. 513 721-8700
2060 Reading Rd Fl 4 Cincinnati (45202) *(G-2685)*

Gowdey Reed, Granville *Also Called: Reed Gowdey Company (G-7320)*

Goyal Enterprises Inc... 513 874-9303
4836 Business Center Way Cincinnati (45246) *(G-2686)*

Goyal Industries Inc.. 419 522-7099
382 Park Ave E Mansfield (44905) *(G-8796)*

Gpi Ohio LLC.. 605 332-6721
6300 Commerce Center Dr Ste 100 Groveport (43125) *(G-7437)*

GPM, Franklin *Also Called: Greenpoint Metals Inc (G-7025)*

Gq Business Products Inc.. 513 792-4750
142 Commerce Dr Loveland (45140) *(G-8627)*

Gr Golf, New Washington *Also Called: Wurms Woodworking Company (G-10484)*

Gr8 News Packaging LLC.. 314 739-1202
3657 Tradeport Ct Lockbourne (43137) *(G-8489)*

Gra-Mag Truck Intr Systems LLC (DH).........................740 490-1000
470 E High St London (43140) *(G-8536)*

Grabo Interiors Inc.. 216 391-6677
3605 Perkins Ave Cleveland (44114) *(G-3780)*

Grace Juice Company LLC.. 614 398-6879
6318 E Dublin Granville Rd Westerville (43081) *(G-14261)*

Gracie Plum Investments, Portsmouth *Also Called: Gracie Plum Investments Inc (G-11467)*

Gracie Plum Investments Inc.. 740 355-9029
609 2nd St Unit 2 Portsmouth (45662) *(G-11467)*

Graco Ohio Inc (HQ)... 330 494-1313
8400 Port Jackson Ave Nw North Canton (44720) *(G-10644)*

Gradall, New Philadelphia *Also Called: Gradall Industries LLC (G-10448)*

Gradall Industries LLC (DH)..330 339-2211
406 Mill Ave Sw New Philadelphia (44663) *(G-10448)*

Grady McCauley Inc.. 330 494-9444
5127 Boyer Pkwy Akron (44312) *(G-165)*

Grae-Con Process Piping LLC.. 740 282-6830
300 Commerce Dr Marietta (45750) *(G-8920)*

Graeter's Ice Cream, Cincinnati *Also Called: International Brand Services (G-2751)*

Graeters Ice Cream Company (PA).................................. 513 721-3323
1175 Regina Graeter Way Cincinnati (45216) *(G-2687)*

Graffiti Co, Cleveland *Also Called: Barbs Graffiti Inc (G-3405)*

Graffiti Foods Limited... 614 759-1921
333 Outerbelt St Columbus (43213) *(G-4963)*

Grafisk Maskinfabrik Amer LLC....................................... 630 432-4370
603 Norgal Dr Ste F Lebanon (45036) *(G-8265)*

Grafisk Msknfabrik-America LLC, Lebanon *Also Called: Grafisk Maskinfabrik Amer LLC (G-8265)*

Grafix, Cleveland *Also Called: Graphic Art Systems Inc (G-3785)*

Graftech Global Entps Inc.. 216 676-2000
12900 Snow Rd Cleveland (44130) *(G-3781)*

Graftech Holdings Inc... 216 676-2000
6100 Oak Tree Blvd Ste 300 Independence (44131) *(G-7905)*

GRAFTECH INTERNATIONAL, Brooklyn Heights *Also Called: Graftech International Ltd (G-1531)*

Graftech International Ltd (PA)..216 676-2000
982 Keynote Cir Ste 6 Brooklyn Heights (44131) *(G-1531)*

Graftech Intl Holdings Inc (HQ)..216 676-2000
982 Keynote Cir Ste 6 Brooklyn Heights (44131) *(G-1532)*

Graftech Intl Trdg Inc... 216 676-2000
12900 Snow Rd Cleveland (44130) *(G-3782)*

Grafton Ready Mix Concret Inc... 440 926-2911
1155 Elm St Grafton (44044) *(G-7303)*

Graham Electric.. 614 231-8500
2855 Banwick Rd Columbus (43232) *(G-4964)*

Graham Packaging Pet Tech Inc....................................... 419 334-4197
725 Industrial Dr Fremont (43420) *(G-7116)*

Graham Packaging Pet Tech Inc....................................... 513 398-5000
1225 Castle Dr Mason (45040) *(G-9105)*

Graham Packg Plastic Pdts Inc.. 419 421-8037
170 Stanford Pkwy 7 Findlay (45840) *(G-6873)*

Graminex LLC... 419 278-1023
2300 County Road C Deshler (43516) *(G-6222)*

Gramke Enterprises Ltd.. 614 252-8711
3021 E 4th Ave Ste B Columbus (43219) *(G-4965)*

Grand Aire Inc (PA)... 419 861-6700
11777 W Airport Service Rd Swanton (43558) *(G-12684)*

Grand Architect, Cleveland *Also Called: Grand Archt Etrnl Eye 314 LLC (G-3783)*

Grand Archt Etrnl Eye 314 LLC.................................. 800 377-8147
  10413 Nelson Ave Cleveland (44105) *(G-3783)*

Grand Harbor Yacht Sales & Svc............................ 440 442-2919
  706 Alpha Dr Cleveland (44143) *(G-3784)*

Grand River Rubber & Plastics Company............... 440 998-2900
  2029 Aetna Rd Ashtabula (44004) *(G-594)*

Grand-Rock Company Inc.. 440 639-2000
  395 Fountain Ave Painesville (44077) *(G-11089)*

Grandinroad Catalog, West Chester Also Called: Cornerstone Brands Inc *(G-13975)*

Grandpa Jack's, Chillicothe Also Called: Crispie Creme Chillicothe Inc *(G-2249)*

GRANGER PLASTICS CO THE.................................. 513 424-1955
  1600 Made Dr Middletown (45044) *(G-9862)*

Grant Street Pallet Inc.. 330 424-0355
  39196 Grant St Lisbon (44432) *(G-8468)*

Granville Milling Co... 740 345-1305
  145 N Cedar St Newark (43055) *(G-10505)*

Granville Milling Drive-Thru, Newark Also Called: Granville Milling Co *(G-10505)*

Graphel Corporation.. 513 779-6166
  6115 Centre Park Dr West Chester (45069) *(G-14012)*

Graphic Art Systems Inc.. 216 581-9050
  5800 Pennsylvania Ave Cleveland (44137) *(G-3785)*

Graphic Imaginations... 216 781-4880
  2160 Superior Ave E Cleveland (44114) *(G-3786)*

Graphic Industries, Alliance Also Called: Sams Graphic Industries *(G-402)*

Graphic Info Systems Inc....................................... 513 948-1300
  7177 Central Parke Blvd Mason (45040) *(G-9106)*

Graphic Packaging Intl LLC.................................... 419 673-0711
  1300 S Main St Kenton (43326) *(G-8100)*

Graphic Packaging Intl LLC.................................... 513 424-4200
  407 Charles St Middletown (45042) *(G-9863)*

Graphic Packaging Intl LLC.................................... 419 668-1006
  209 Republic St Norwalk (44857) *(G-10844)*

Graphic Packaging Intl LLC.................................... 440 248-4370
  6385 Cochran Rd Solon (44139) *(G-12118)*

Graphic Paper Products Corp (HQ)........................ 937 325-5503
  6069 Yeazell Rd Springfield (45502) *(G-12315)*

Graphic Stitch Inc... 937 642-6707
  169 Grove St Rm A Marysville (43040) *(G-9021)*

Graphic Systems Services Inc................................ 937 746-0708
  400 S Pioneer Blvd Springboro (45066) *(G-12254)*

Graphic Village LLC... 513 241-1865
  4440 Creek Rd Blue Ash (45242) *(G-1278)*

Graphite Sales Inc (PA).. 419 652-3388
  220 Township Road 791 Nova (44859) *(G-10877)*

Graphtech Communications Inc.............................. 216 676-1020
  19001 Bennington Dr Strongsville (44136) *(G-12560)*

Grasan Equipment Co, Mansfield Also Called: Grasan Equipment Company Inc *(G-8797)*

Grasan Equipment Company Inc............................. 419 526-4440
  440 S Illinois Ave Mansfield (44907) *(G-8797)*

Gray & Company Publishers.................................. 216 431-2665
  1588 E 40th St Ste 1b Cleveland (44103) *(G-3787)*

Gray America Corp (PA)... 937 293-9313
  3050 Dryden Rd Moraine (45439) *(G-10166)*

Gray Area Bistro Ultra Lounge, Cleveland Also Called: R & T Estate LLC *(G-4219)*

Gray Tech International, Cleveland Also Called: Hephaestus Technologies LLC *(G-3825)*

Gray-Eering Ltd... 740 498-8816
  3158 Sandy Ridge Rd Se Tippecanoe (44699) *(G-12858)*

Graymont Dolime (oh) Inc..................................... 419 855-8682
  21880 State Route 163 Genoa (43430) *(G-7247)*

Grays Orange Barn Inc.. 419 568-2718
  14286 State Route 196 Wapakoneta (45895) *(G-13714)*

Graywacke Inc... 419 884-7014
  300 S Mill St Mansfield (44904) *(G-8798)*

GRB Holdings Inc.. 937 236-3250
  131 Janney Rd Dayton (45404) *(G-5802)*

Gre'n Disc, Strasburg Also Called: Green Rdced Emssons Netwrk LLC *(G-12478)*

Great Day Improvements LLC (HQ)........................ 267 223-1289
  700 Highland Rd E Macedonia (44056) *(G-8695)*

Great Harvest Bread, Westerville Also Called: Blf Enterprises Inc *(G-14246)*

Great Lake Fence, Cleveland Also Called: Fence One Inc *(G-3712)*

Great Lakes Assemblies LLC................................. 937 645-3900
  11590 Township Road 298 East Liberty (43319) *(G-6385)*

Great Lakes Brewing Co... 216 771-4404
  1947 W 28th St Cleveland (44113) *(G-3788)*

Great Lakes Brewing Co (PA).................................. 216 771-4404
  2516 Market Ave Cleveland (44113) *(G-3789)*

Great Lakes Brewing Co... 216 771-4404
  13675 Darice Pkwy Strongsville (44149) *(G-12561)*

Great Lakes Cheese Co Inc (PA)............................ 440 834-2500
  17825 Great Lakes Pkwy Hiram (44234) *(G-7739)*

Great Lakes Crushing Ltd...................................... 440 944-5500
  30831 Euclid Ave Wickliffe (44092) *(G-14376)*

Great Lakes Etching Finshg Co.............................. 440 439-3624
  7010 Krick Rd Cleveland (44146) *(G-3790)*

Great Lakes Fasteners Inc (PA).............................. 330 425-4488
  2204 E Enterprise Pkwy Twinsburg (44087) *(G-13312)*

Great Lakes Fasteners & Sup Co, Twinsburg Also Called: Great Lakes Fasteners Inc *(G-13312)*

Great Lakes Glasswerks Inc.................................. 440 358-0460
  360 W Prospect St Painesville (44077) *(G-11090)*

Great Lakes Graphics Inc...................................... 216 391-0077
  3354 Superior Ave E Cleveland (44114) *(G-3791)*

Great Lakes Group.. 216 621-4854
  4500 Division Ave Cleveland (44102) *(G-3792)*

Great Lakes Mfg Group Ltd................................... 440 391-8266
  19035 Old Detroit Rd Rocky River (44116) *(G-11634)*

Great Lakes Polymer Proc Inc (PA)........................ 313 655-4024
  1210 Massillon Rd Akron (44306) *(G-166)*

Great Lakes Popcorn Company.............................. 419 732-3080
  60 Madison St Port Clinton (43452) *(G-11443)*

Great Lakes Power Products Inc (PA)..................... 440 951-5111
  1973 Great Lakes Way Madison (44057) *(G-8730)*

Great Lakes Power Service Co.............................. 440 259-0025
  3691 Shepard Rd Perry (44081) *(G-11192)*

Great Lakes Publishing Company (PA).................... 216 771-2833
  1422 Euclid Ave Ste 730 Cleveland (44115) *(G-3793)*

Great Lakes Scuttlebutt, Toledo Also Called: Kyle Media Inc *(G-13025)*

Great Lakes Shipyard, Cleveland Also Called: The Great Lakes Towing Company *(G-4383)*

Great Lakes Stair & Mllwk Co............................... 330 225-2005
  1545 W 130th St Ste A1 Hinckley (44233) *(G-7731)*

Great Lakes Telcom Ltd (PA)................................. 330 629-8848
  590 E Western Reserve Rd Bldg 9c Youngstown (44514) *(G-14870)*

Great Lakes Towing, Cleveland Also Called: Great Lakes Group *(G-3792)*

Great Lakes Turbines Inc...................................... 419 705-0490
  1740 Eber Rd Ste N Holland (43528) *(G-7765)*

Great Lakes Window Inc.. 419 666-5555
  30499 Tracy Rd Walbridge (43465) *(G-13684)*

Great Lkes Nrotechnologies Inc............................ 855 456-3876
  6100 Rockside Woods Blvd N Ste 415 Cleveland (44131) *(G-3794)*

Great River Re Inc (HQ).. 513 471-8770
  5353 Spring Grove Ave Cincinnati (45217) *(G-2688)*

Greater Cincinnati Bowl Assn............................... 513 761-7387
  611 Mercury Dr Cincinnati (45215) *(G-2689)*

Greater Cleve Pipe Ftting Fund............................. 216 524-8334
  6305 Halle Dr Cleveland (44125) *(G-3795)*

Greber Machine Tool Inc....................................... 440 322-3685
  313 Clark St Elyria (44035) *(G-6541)*

Green Acquisition LLC... 440 930-7600
  1141 Jaycox Rd Avon (44011) *(G-728)*

Green Bay Packaging Inc....................................... 419 332-5593
  2323 Commerce Dr Fremont (43420) *(G-7117)*

Green Bay Packaging Inc....................................... 513 489-8700
  760 Kingsview Dr Lebanon (45036) *(G-8266)*

Green Bearing Co, Avon Also Called: Green Acquisition LLC *(G-728)*

Green County Wtr Sup & Trtmnt, Dayton Also Called: Greene County *(G-5613)*

Green Energy Inc.. 330 262-5112
  4489 E Lincoln Way Wooster (44691) *(G-14644)*

Green Field Farms Co-Op (PA)............................... 330 263-0246
  6464 Fredericksburg Rd Wooster (44691) *(G-14645)*

Green Gourmet Foods LLC.................................... 740 400-4212
  515 N Main St Baltimore (43105) *(G-786)*

(G-0000) Company's Geographic Section entry number

Green Impressions LLC.. 440 240-8508
  842 Abbe Rd Sheffield Village (44054) *(G-11958)*

Green Leaf Printing and Design............................... 937 222-3634
  1001 E 2nd St Ste 2485 Dayton (45402) *(G-5803)*

Green Machine Tool Inc.. 937 253-0771
  1865 Radio Rd Dayton (45431) *(G-5612)*

Green Meadows Paper Company................................ 330 837-5151
  670 17th St Nw Massillon (44647) *(G-9196)*

Green Rdced Emssons Netwrk LLC........................... 330 340-0941
  5029 Hilltop Dr Nw Strasburg (44680) *(G-12478)*

Green Room Brewing LLC... 614 421-2337
  1101 N 4th St Columbus (43201) *(G-4966)*

Green Technologies Ohio LLC.................................... 330 630-3350
  460 Tacoma Ave Ste B Tallmadge (44278) *(G-12735)*

Green Tokai Co Ltd (DH)... 937 833-5444
  55 Robert Wright Dr Brookville (45309) *(G-1570)*

Green Tokai Co Ltd... 937 237-1630
  3700 Inpark Dr Dayton (45414) *(G-5804)*

Green Vision Materials Inc... 440 564-5500
  11220 Kinsman Rd Newbury (44065) *(G-10552)*

Greenbridge, Mentor *Also Called: Polychem LLC (G-9588)*

Greenbrier Rail Services, Youngstown *Also Called: Gunderson Rail Services LLC (G-14872)*

Greendale Home Fashions LLC.................................. 859 916-5475
  5500 Muddy Creek Rd Cincinnati (45238) *(G-2690)*

Greene County.. 937 429-0127
  1122 Beaver Valley Rd Dayton (45434) *(G-5613)*

Greenfield Die & Mfg Corp (HQ)................................ 734 454-4000
  880 Steel Dr Valley City (44280) *(G-13497)*

Greenfield Precision Plas LLC.................................... 937 803-0328
  175 Industrial Park Dr Greenfield (45123) *(G-7329)*

Greenfield Research Inc (PA).................................... 937 981-7763
  347 Edgewood Ave Greenfield (45123) *(G-7330)*

Greenfield Solar Corp... 216 535-9200
  7881 Root Rd North Ridgeville (44039) *(G-10732)*

Greenhart Rstoration Mllwk LLC................................ 330 502-6050
  6001 Southern Blvd Ste 105 Boardman (44512) *(G-1373)*

Greenkote Usa Inc... 440 243-2865
  6435 Eastland Rd Brookpark (44142) *(G-1551)*

Greenlight Optics LLC... 513 247-9777
  8940 Glendale Milford Rd Loveland (45140) *(G-8628)*

Greenpoint Metals Inc... 937 743-4075
  301 Shotwell Dr Franklin (45005) *(G-7025)*

Greentec Precision Inc.. 937 431-1840
  2280 Grange Hall Rd Beavercreek (45431) *(G-976)*

Greenville Techniology Inc... 937 642-6744
  15000 Industrial Pkwy Marysville (43040) *(G-9022)*

Greenway Home Products Inc
  1270 Flagship Dr Perrysburg (43551) *(G-11227)*

Greenworld Enterprises Inc...................................... 800 525-6999
  61 Circle Freeway Dr West Chester (45246) *(G-14123)*

Greg Blume... 740 574-2308
  7459 Ohio River Rd Wheelersburg (45694) *(G-14353)*

Greg G Wright & Sons LLC... 513 721-3310
  10200 Springfield Pike Cincinnati (45215) *(G-2691)*

Gregg Macmillan.. 513 248-2121
  2002 Ford Cir Ste A Milford (45150) *(G-9937)*

Greggs Specialty Services... 419 478-0803
  306 Dura Ave Toledo (43612) *(G-12977)*

Gregory Industries Inc (PA)..................................... 330 477-4800
  4100 13th St Sw Canton (44710) *(G-1905)*

Gregory Roll Form Inc.. 330 477-4800
  4100 13th St Sw Canton (44710) *(G-1906)*

Gregory Stone Co Inc... 937 275-7455
  1860 N Gettysburg Ave Dayton (45417) *(G-5805)*

Greif, Delaware *Also Called: Greif Inc (G-6149)*

Greif Inc (PA)... 740 549-6000
  425 Winter Rd Delaware (43015) *(G-6149)*

Greif Inc... 740 657-6500
  366 Greif Pkwy Delaware (43015) *(G-6150)*

Greif Inc... 740 657-6500
  366 Greif Pkwy Delaware (43015) *(G-6151)*

Greif Inc... 330 879-2936
  787 Warmington Rd Se Massillon (44646) *(G-9197)*

Greif Inc... 419 238-0565
  975 Glenn St Van Wert (45891) *(G-13536)*

Greif Packaging LLC (HQ)...740 549-6000
  366 Greif Pkwy Delaware (43015) *(G-6152)*

Greif USA LLC (DH)...740 549-6000
  366 Greif Pkwy Delaware (43015) *(G-6153)*

Grenada Stamping Assembly Inc (HQ)........................419 842-3600
  3810 Herr Rd Sylvania (43560) *(G-12707)*

Grenga Machine & Welding.. 330 743-1113
  56 Wayne Ave Youngstown (44502) *(G-14871)*

Greyden Press, Springboro *Also Called: Jk Digital Publishing LLC (G-12256)*

Grid Industrial Heating Inc....................................... 330 332-9931
  1108 Salem Pkwy Salem (44460) *(G-11783)*

Grief Brothers, Delaware *Also Called: Greif Inc (G-6150)*

Griffin Fisher Co Inc... 513 961-2110
  1126 William Howard Taft Rd Cincinnati (45206) *(G-2692)*

Griffin Industries LLC... 513 549-0041
  11315 Reed Hartman Hwy Blue Ash (45241) *(G-1279)*

Griffin Technology Inc.. 585 924-7121
  50 Executive Pkwy Hudson (44236) *(G-7842)*

Grimes Aerospace Company (HQ)...............................937 484-2000
  550 State Route 55 Urbana (43078) *(G-13462)*

Grimes Aerospace Company...................................... 937 484-2000
  515 N Russell St Urbana (43078) *(G-13463)*

Grimes Aerospace Company...................................... 937 484-2001
  550 State Route 55 Urbana (43078) *(G-13464)*

Grimm Scientific Inds Inc... 740 374-3412
  1403 Pike St Marietta (45750) *(G-8921)*

Grind-All Corporation... 330 220-1600
  1113 Industrial Pkwy N Brunswick (44212) *(G-1596)*

Grinding Equipment & McHy LLC................................ 330 747-2313
  5417 S Salem Warren Rd North Jackson (44451) *(G-10688)*

Grippo Foods Inc (PA).. 513 923-1900
  6750 Colerain Ave Cincinnati (45239) *(G-2693)*

Grippo Potato Chip Co Inc... 513 923-1900
  6750 Colerain Ave Cincinnati (45239) *(G-2694)*

Grismer Tire, Centerville *Also Called: Associates Tire and Svc Inc (G-2129)*

Grismer Tire Company (PA).. 937 643-2526
  1099 S Main St Centerville (45458) *(G-2132)*

Grk Manufacturing Co... 513 863-3131
  1200 Dayton St Hamilton (45011) *(G-7497)*

Grob Systems Inc.. 419 358-9015
  1070 Navajo Dr Bluffton (45817) *(G-1361)*

Groeneveld-Beka Usa Inc (HQ)..................................330 225-4949
  1441 Wolf Creek Trl Sharon Center (44274) *(G-11941)*

Groenveld Lbrction Sltions Inc, Sharon Center *Also Called: Groeneveld-Beka Usa Inc (G-11941)*

Groovemaster Music, Perrysburg *Also Called: Tiny Lion Music Groups (G-11271)*

Gross & Sons Custom Millwork................................... 419 227-0214
  1219 Grant St Lima (45801) *(G-8411)*

Gross Lumber Inc.. 330 683-2055
  8848 Ely Rd Apple Creek (44606) *(G-469)*

Grote, Columbus *Also Called: JE Grote Company Inc (G-5035)*

Groundhogs 2000 LLC.. 440 653-1647
  33 Industry Dr Bedford (44146) *(G-1033)*

Group Industries Inc (PA).. 216 271-0702
  7580 Garfield Blvd Cleveland (44125) *(G-3796)*

Grouper Acquisition Co LLC....................................... 248 299-7500
  880 Steel Dr Valley City (44280) *(G-13498)*

Grouper Acquisition Co LLC....................................... 330 558-2600
  350 Maple St Wellington (44090) *(G-13892)*

Grove Engineered Products.. 419 659-5939
  201 E Cross St Columbus Grove (45830) *(G-5383)*

Grover Musical Products Inc (PA)............................. 216 391-1188
  9287 Midwest Ave Cleveland (44125) *(G-3797)*

Grover Trophy Musical Products, Cleveland *Also Called: Grover Musical Products Inc (G-3797)*

Growco Inc... 419 886-4628
  844 Kochheiser Rd Mansfield (44904) *(G-8799)*

Growers Choice Ltd.. 330 262-8754
  5505 S Elyria Rd Shreve (44676) *(G-11981)*

Grt Utilicorp Inc.. 330 264-8444
  9268 Ashland Rd Wooster (44691) *(G-14646)*

Grypmat Inc... 419 953-7607
  6886 Nancy Ave Celina (45822) *(G-2107)*

Gs Engineering, Maumee *Also Called: Genius Solutions Engrg Co (G-9293)*

Gsdi, Massillon *Also Called: Gsdi Specialty Dispersions Inc (G-9198)*

Gsdi Specialty Dispersions Inc................................. 330 848-9200
  1675 Navarre Rd Se Massillon (44646) *(G-9198)*

GSE Production and Support LLC (DH)........................ 419 866-6301
  1 Air Cargo Pkwy E Swanton (43558) *(G-12685)*

GSE Spares, Swanton *Also Called: GSE Production and Support LLC (G-12685)*

Gsh Industries Inc... 440 238-3009
  15242 Foltz Pkwy Cleveland (44149) *(G-3798)*

Gsi of Ohio LLC.. 216 431-3344
  3820 Lakeside Ave E Cleveland (44114) *(G-3799)*

GSW Manufacturing Inc (DH).................................. 419 423-7111
  1801 Production Dr Findlay (45840) *(G-6874)*

Gt Industrial Supply, Cincinnati *Also Called: Gt Industrial Supply Inc (G-2695)*

Gt Industrial Supply Inc.. 513 771-7000
  7775 E Kemper Rd Cincinnati (45249) *(G-2695)*

Gt Technlgies Tledo Operations, Toledo *Also Called: Gt Technologies Inc (G-12978)*

Gt Technologies Inc.. 419 782-8955
  1125 Precision Way Defiance (43512) *(G-6109)*

Gt Technologies Inc.. 419 324-7300
  99 N Fearing Blvd Toledo (43607) *(G-12978)*

Gt Tire Service Inc.. 740 927-7226
  15 W Broad St Pataskala (43062) *(G-11139)*

GTC, Brookville *Also Called: Green Tokai Co Ltd (G-1570)*

GTC Artist With Machines, Columbus *Also Called: General Theming Contrs LLC (G-4948)*

Gtlp Holdings LLC (PA).. 513 489-6700
  7911 School Rd Cincinnati (45249) *(G-2696)*

Guarantee Specialties Inc...................................... 216 451-9744
  21693 Drake Rd Strongsville (44149) *(G-12562)*

Guaranteed Fnshg Unlimited Inc............................... 216 252-8200
  3200 W 121st St Cleveland (44111) *(G-3800)*

Guardian Fabrication LLC....................................... 419 855-7706
  24145 W Moline Martin Rd Millbury (43447) *(G-9962)*

Guardian Gloves, Willard *Also Called: Guardian Manufacturing Co LLC (G-14402)*

Guardian Lima LLC.. 567 940-9500
  2485 Houx Pkwy Lima (45804) *(G-8412)*

Guardian Manufacturing Co LLC................................ 419 933-2711
  302 S Conwell Ave Willard (44890) *(G-14402)*

Guardian Mfg., Hudson *Also Called: Fluid Power Inc (G-7841)*

Guardian Millbury, Millbury *Also Called: Guardian Fabrication LLC (G-9962)*

Guardian Technologies LLC...................................... 866 603-5900
  26251 Bluestone Blvd Ste 7 Euclid (44132) *(G-6652)*

Guerin-Zimmerman Co, Cleveland *Also Called: Byg Industries Inc (G-3456)*

Guernsey Industries.. 740 439-4452
  60772 Southgate Rd Byesville (43723) *(G-1713)*

Guetle Die & Stamping, Mansfield *Also Called: Amaroq Inc (G-8760)*

Guggisberg Cheese Inc (PA).................................... 330 893-2550
  5060 State Route 557 Millersburg (44654) *(G-9982)*

Guild Associates Inc.. 843 573-0095
  4412 Tuller Rd Dublin (43017) *(G-6299)*

Guild Associates Inc (PA)....................................... 614 798-8215
  5750 Shier Rings Rd Dublin (43016) *(G-6300)*

Guild Biosciences, Dublin *Also Called: Guild Associates Inc (G-6299)*

Guild International, Bedford *Also Called: Guild International Inc (G-1034)*

Guild International Inc... 440 232-5887
  7273 Division St Bedford (44146) *(G-1034)*

Gumbys LLC.. 740 671-0818
  2300 Belmont St Bellaire (43906) *(G-1088)*

Gunderson Rail Services LLC..................................... 330 792-6521
  3710 Hendricks Rd Bldg 2a Youngstown (44515) *(G-14872)*

Gundlach, Cincinnati *Also Called: Rotex Global LLC (G-3053)*

Gundlach Sheet Metal Works Inc (PA).......................... 419 626-4525
  910 Columbus Ave Sandusky (44870) *(G-11837)*

Gunk, Cleveland *Also Called: BLaster Holdings LLC (G-3422)*

Gunnison Associates Llc... 330 562-5230
  114 Barrington Town Square Dr # 11 Aurora (44202) *(G-672)*

Gus Holthaus Signs Inc.. 513 861-0060
  817 Ridgeway Ave Cincinnati (45229) *(G-2697)*

Gushen America Inc.. 708 664-2852
  701 International Dr Heath (43056) *(G-7595)*

Gustave Julian Jewelers Inc...................................... 440 888-1100
  7432 State Rd Cleveland (44134) *(G-3801)*

GUTTER TOPPER LTD.. 513 797-5800
  4111 Founders Blvd Batavia (45103) *(G-866)*

Guttman Oil, Westerville *Also Called: Brightstar Propane & Fuels (G-14204)*

Guyer Precision Inc.. 440 354-8024
  280 W Prospect St Painesville (44077) *(G-11091)*

Gvs Filtration Inc (DH)... 419 423-9040
  2150 Industrial Dr Findlay (45840) *(G-6875)*

Gvs Industries Inc... 513 851-3606
  1030 Beissinger Rd Hamilton (45013) *(G-7498)*

Gwj Liquidation Inc.. 216 475-5770
  16153 Libby Rd Cleveland (44137) *(G-3802)*

Gws Levi Up Home Solutions LLC................................ 419 667-6041
  6020 W Bancroft St Unit 350061 Toledo (43615) *(G-12979)*

Gyrus Acmi LP.. 419 668-8201
  93 N Pleasant St Norwalk (44857) *(G-10845)*

Gzjb Holdings Inc.. 216 731-0500
  24000 Lakeland Blvd Cleveland (44132) *(G-3803)*

H & C Building Supplies, Huron *Also Called: Huron Cement Products Company (G-7874)*

H & D Steel Service Inc.. 800 666-3390
  9960 York Alpha Dr North Royalton (44133) *(G-10764)*

H & D Steel Service Center, North Royalton *Also Called: H & D Steel Service Inc (G-10764)*

H & G Equipment Inc (PA)....................................... 513 761-2060
  10837 Millington Ct Blue Ash (45242) *(G-1280)*

H & H Engineered Molded Pdts................................... 440 415-1814
  436 N Eagle St Geneva (44041) *(G-7238)*

H & H Equipment Inc... 330 264-5400
  6247 Ashland Rd Wooster (44691) *(G-14647)*

H & H Industries Inc... 740 682-7721
  5400 State Route 93 Oak Hill (45656) *(G-10888)*

H & H Machine Shop Akron Inc................................. 330 773-3327
  955 Grant St·Akron (44311) *(G-167)*

H & H Quick Machine Inc.. 330 935-0944
  7816 Edison St Ne Louisville (44641) *(G-8600)*

H & H Sailcraft, New Paris *Also Called: Dynamic Plastics Inc (G-10426)*

H & H Truck Parts LLC... 216 642-4540
  5500s Cloverleaf Pkwy Cleveland (44125) *(G-3804)*

H & M Machine Shop Inc... 419 453-3414
  290 State Route 189 Ottoville (45876) *(G-11054)*

H & M Metal Processing Co (HQ)................................. 330 745-3075
  1414 Kenmore Blvd Akron (44314) *(G-168)*

H & R Metal Finishing Inc.. 440 942-6656
  1052 E 347th St Eastlake (44095) *(G-6430)*

H & S Distributing Inc... 800 336-7784
  35478 Lorain Rd North Ridgeville (44039) *(G-10733)*

H & S Tool Inc... 330 335-1536
  715 Weber Dr Wadsworth (44281) *(G-13642)*

H & W Screw Products Inc....................................... 937 866-2577
  335 Industrial Dr Franklin (45005) *(G-7026)*

H B Chemical, Twinsburg *Also Called: Ravago Chemical Dist Inc (G-13364)*

H B Chemical Corporation (DH)................................... 330 920-8023
  1665 Enterprise Pkwy Twinsburg (44087) *(G-13313)*

H D C, Miamisburg *Also Called: The Hooven - Dayton Corp (G-9747)*

H G Schneider Company.. 614 882-6944
  291 Broad St Westerville (43081) *(G-14262)*

H Gerstner & Sons Inc... 937 228-1662
  20 Gerstner Way Dayton (45402) *(G-5806)*

H Goodman Inc.. 216 341-0200
  3201 Harvard Ave Newburgh Heights (44105) *(G-10542)*

H Hafner & Sons Inc.. 513 321-1895
  5445 Wooster Pike Cincinnati (45226) *(G-2698)*

H Hansen Industries, Toledo *Also Called: Riverside Marine Inds Inc (G-13114)*

H I T, Painesville *Also Called: Hardy Industrial Tech LLC (G-11092)*

H K K Machining Co.. 419 924-5116
  1201 Oak St West Unity (43570) *(G-14194)*

(G-0000) Company's Geographic Section entry number

H K M, Cleveland *Also Called: Hkm Drect Mkt Cmmnications Inc (G-3832)*

H K M Drect Mktg Cmmunications, Sheffield Village *Also Called: Hkm Drect Mkt Cmmnications Inc (G-11959)*

H Lee Philippi Co..513 321-5330
3660 Hyde Park Ave Cincinnati (45208) *(G-2699)*

H Mack Charles & Associates Inc.....................513 791-4456
10101 Alliance Rd Ste 10 Blue Ash (45242) *(G-1281)*

H Nagel & Son Co...513 665-4550
2641 Spring Grove Ave Cincinnati (45214) *(G-2700)*

H P E Inc (PA)...330 833-3161
2025 Harsh Ave Se Massillon (44646) *(G-9199)*

H P Manufacturing Co...216 361-6500
3740 Prospect Ave E Cleveland (44115) *(G-3805)*

H P Nielsen Inc..440 244-4255
753 Broadway Lorain (44052) *(G-8557)*

H-P Products Inc...330 875-7193
2000 W Main St Louisville (44641) *(G-8601)*

H-P Products Inc (PA)...330 875-5556
512 W Gorgas St Louisville (44641) *(G-8602)*

H. Meyer Dairy, Cleveland *Also Called: Borden Dairy Co Cincinnati LLC (G-3428)*

H.O.t, Northwood *Also Called: HOT Graphic Services Inc (G-10804)*

H&G Legacy Co (PA)..513 921-1075
1085 Summer St Cincinnati (45204) *(G-2701)*

H&M Machine & Tool LLC....................................419 776-9220
3823 Seiss Ave Toledo (43612) *(G-12980)*

H&M Mtal Stamping Assembly Inc.....................216 898-9030
5325 W 140th St Brook Park (44142) *(G-1513)*

H2flow Controls Inc..419 841-7774
7629 New West Rd Toledo (43617) *(G-12981)*

H3d Tool Corporation...740 498-5181
295 Enterprise Dr Newcomerstown (43832) *(G-10570)*

Ha-International LLC...419 537-0096
4243 South Ave Toledo (43615) *(G-12982)*

Haag-Streit Usa Inc (DH).....................................513 398-3937
3535 Kings Mills Rd Mason (45040) *(G-9107)*

Haas Door Company..419 337-9900
320 Sycamore St Wauseon (43567) *(G-13850)*

Haas Doors, Wauseon *Also Called: Nofziger Door Sales Inc (G-13857)*

Hab Computer Services, Solon *Also Called: Hab Inc (G-12119)*

Hab Inc...608 785-7650
28925 Fountain Pkwy Solon (44139) *(G-12119)*

Habco Tool and Dev Co Inc.................................440 946-5546
7725 Metric Dr Mentor (44060) *(G-9525)*

Hacker Wood Products Inc..................................513 737-4462
2144 Jackson Rd Hamilton (45011) *(G-7499)*

Hackworth Electric Motors Inc............................330 345-6049
500 E Henry St Wooster (44691) *(G-14648)*

Hadley Printing, Beavercreek *Also Called: A C Hadley - Printing Inc (G-962)*

Hadronics Inc..513 321-9350
4570 Steel Pl Cincinnati (45209) *(G-2702)*

Haeco Inc (PA)...513 722-1030
6504 Charles Snider Rd Loveland (45140) *(G-8629)*

Haessly Lumber Sales Co (PA)...........................740 373-6681
25 Sheets Run Rd Marietta (45750) *(G-8922)*

Hafco-Case Inc...216 267-4644
12212 Sprecher Ave Cleveland (44135) *(G-3806)*

Hafners Hrdwood Connection LLC......................419 726-4828
2845 111th St Toledo (43611) *(G-12983)*

Hague Quality Water Intl, Groveport *Also Called: William R Hague Inc (G-7458)*

Hahn Automation Group Us Inc..........................937 886-3232
10909 Industry Ln Miamisburg (45342) *(G-9694)*

Hahn Manufacturing Company...........................216 391-9300
5332 Hamilton Ave Cleveland (44114) *(G-3807)*

Haines Publishing Inc...330 494-9111
8050 Freedom Ave Nw Canton (44720) *(G-1907)*

Haiss Fabripart LLC..330 821-2028
22421 Lake Park Blvd Alliance (44601) *(G-384)*

Hake Head LLC..614 291-2244
1855 E 17th Ave Columbus (43219) *(G-4967)*

Halcore Group Inc (HQ).......................................614 539-8181
3800 Mcdowell Rd Grove City (43123) *(G-7389)*

Hale Manufacturing LLC......................................937 382-2127
1065 Wayne Rd Wilmington (45177) *(G-14583)*

Hale Performance Coatings Inc..........................419 244-6451
2282 Albion St Toledo (43606) *(G-12984)*

Halex Electric Company (HQ)..............................800 749-3261
101 Production Dr Harrison (45030) *(G-7554)*

Halex/Scott Fetzer Company, Harrison *Also Called: Halex Electric Company (G-7554)*

Hall Acquisition LLC...330 627-2119
1209 N Lisbon St Carrollton (44615) *(G-2084)*

Hall Closet, East Liverpool *Also Called: The China Hall Company (G-6398)*

Hall Company...937 652-1376
420 E Water St Urbana (43078) *(G-13465)*

Hall-Toledo Inc..419 893-4334
525 W Sophia St Maumee (43537) *(G-9294)*

Haller Enterprises Inc...330 733-9693
1621 E Market St Akron (44305) *(G-169)*

Halliburton Energy Svcs Inc...............................740 617-2917
4999 E Pointe Dr Zanesville (43701) *(G-15018)*

Halliday Holdings Inc..740 335-1430
1544 Old Us 35 Se Washington Court Hou (43160) *(G-13821)*

Halliday Technologies Inc...................................614 504-4150
105 Innovation Ct Ste F Delaware (43015) *(G-6154)*

Hallmark Industries Inc (PA)...............................937 864-7378
2233 N Limestone St Springfield (45503) *(G-12316)*

Halo Metal Prep Inc..216 741-0506
5712 Brookpark Rd Unit C Cleveland (44129) *(G-3808)*

Haltec Corporation..330 222-1501
32585 N Price Rd Salem (44460) *(G-11784)*

Halvorsen Company...216 341-7500
7500 Grand Division Ave Ste 1 Cleveland (44125) *(G-3809)*

Ham Signs LLC DBA Fastsigns...........................937 890-6770
6020 N Dixie Dr Dayton (45414) *(G-5807)*

Haman Enterprises Inc..614 888-7574
75 W Southington Ave Columbus (43085) *(G-4968)*

Haman Midwest, Columbus *Also Called: Haman Enterprises Inc (G-4968)*

Hamilton Brass & Alum Castings
706 S 8th St Hamilton (45011) *(G-7500)*

Hamilton Casework Solutions, Fairfield *Also Called: Workstream Inc (G-6793)*

Hamilton Custom Molding Inc..............................513 844-6643
1365 Shuler Ave Hamilton (45011) *(G-7501)*

Hamilton Industrial Grinding Inc (PA).................513 863-1221
240 N B St Hamilton (45013) *(G-7502)*

Hamilton Journal News Inc.................................513 863-8200
7320 Yankee Rd Liberty Township (45044) *(G-8377)*

Hamilton Machine Services Corp........................513 895-7200
2380 Hamilton Eaton Rd Hamilton (45011) *(G-7503)*

Hamilton Manufacturing Corp............................419 867-4858
1026 Hamilton Dr Holland (43528) *(G-7766)*

Hamilton Polymers Company..............................484 245-4557
446 Center St Leetonia (44431) *(G-8302)*

Hamilton Safe, Milford *Also Called: Hamilton Security Products Co (G-9939)*

Hamilton Safe Co (DH)..513 874-3733
1030 Round Bottom Rd Milford (45150) *(G-9938)*

Hamilton Safe Company, Milford *Also Called: Hamilton Safe Co (G-9938)*

Hamilton Security Products Co...........................513 874-3733
1030 Round Bottom Rd Milford (45150) *(G-9939)*

Hamilton Tanks LLC..614 445-8446
2200 Refugee Rd Columbus (43207) *(G-4969)*

Hamlet Protein Inc..567 525-5627
5289 Hamlet Dr Findlay (45840) *(G-6876)*

Hamlin Newco LLC..330 753-7791
2741 Wingate Ave Akron (44314) *(G-170)*

Hamlin Steel Products LLC..................................330 753-7791
2741 Wingate Ave Akron (44314) *(G-171)*

Hammelmann Corporation (HQ)..........................937 859-8777
436 Southpointe Dr Miamisburg (45342) *(G-9695)*

Hammersmith Bros Invstmnts Inc.......................513 353-3000
3200 State Line Rd North Bend (45052) *(G-10620)*

Hammill Manufacturing Co (PA)..........................419 476-0789
360 Tomahawk Dr Maumee (43537) *(G-9295)*

Hammill Manufacturing Co..................................419 476-9125
1517 Coining Dr Toledo (43612) *(G-12985)*

Hammond Kinetics, Dublin *Also Called: Kinetics Noise Control Inc (G-6316)*

Hampshire Co.. 937 773-3493
9225 State Route 66 Piqua (45356) *(G-11348)*

Hana Technologies Inc................................... 330 405-4600
2061 Case Pkwy S Twinsburg (44087) *(G-13314)*

Hanby Farms Inc... 740 763-3554
10790 Newark Rd Nashport (43830) *(G-10299)*

Hanchett Paper Company............................... 513 782-4440
12121 Best Pl Cincinnati (45241) *(G-2703)*

Hancock Structural Steel LLC........................ 419 424-1217
813 E Bigelow Ave Findlay (45840) *(G-6877)*

Hancor Inc... 419 424-8222
12370 Jackson Township Rd Findlay (45839) *(G-6878)*

Hancor Inc... 419 424-8225
433 Olive St Findlay (45840) *(G-6879)*

Hancor Inc (HQ).. 614 658-0050
4640 Trueman Blvd Hilliard (43026) *(G-7683)*

Handcrafted Jewelry Inc................................. 330 650-9011
116 N Main St Hudson (44236) *(G-7843)*

Handshakers Construction LLC...................... 513 370-1371
213 Assisiknoll Ct Cincinnati (45238) *(G-2704)*

Handy Twine Knife Co...................................... 419 294-3424
5676 County Highway 330 Upper Sandusky (43351) *(G-13442)*

Hanline Fresh, Shelby *Also Called: R S Hanline and Co Inc (G-11974)*

Hanlon Industries Inc...................................... 216 261-7056
1280 E 286th St Cleveland (44132) *(G-3810)*

Hann Manufacturing Inc.................................. 740 962-3752
4678 N State Route 60 Nw Mcconnelsville (43756) *(G-9362)*

Hannecard Roller Coatings Inc....................... 330 753-8458
1031 Lambert St Barberton (44203) *(G-809)*

Hannibal Company Inc..................................... 614 846-5060
6536 Proprietors Rd Worthington (43085) *(G-14711)*

Hannon Company (PA)...................................... 330 456-4728
1605 Waynesburg Dr Se Canton (44707) *(G-1908)*

Hannon Company... 330 343-7758
801 Commercial Pkwy Dover (44622) *(G-6246)*

Hannon Company... 740 453-0527
218 Adams St Zanesville (43701) *(G-15019)*

Hanon Systems Usa LLC................................. 313 920-0583
581 Arrowhead Dr Carey (43316) *(G-2058)*

Hans Rothenbuhler & Son Inc......................... 440 632-6000
15815 Nauvoo Rd Middlefield (44062) *(G-9796)*

Hansen Scaffolding LLC (PA).......................... 513 574-9000
193 Circle Freeway Dr West Chester (45246) *(G-14124)*

Hansen-Mueller Co.. 419 729-5535
1800 N Water St Toledo (43611) *(G-12986)*

Hanser Music Group, Cincinnati *Also Called: Jatiga Inc (G-2762)*

Hanson Aggregates, Sandusky *Also Called: Wagner Quarries Company (G-11883)*

Hanson Aggregates Eagle Quarry, Winchester *Also Called: Heidelberg Materials Us Inc (G-14598)*

Hanson Aggregates East................................. 513 353-1100
7000 Dry Fork Rd Cleves (45002) *(G-4538)*

Hanson Aggrgates Plum Run Quar, Peebles *Also Called: Heidelberg Materials Us Inc (G-11169)*

Hantech, Findlay *Also Called: Hancor Inc (G-6879)*

Hapco Inc.. 330 678-9353
390 Portage Blvd Kent (44240) *(G-8035)*

Happy Booker, Cincinnati *Also Called: Art Guild Binders Inc (G-2378)*

Happy Trails Rv, Cleveland *Also Called: Electric Cord Sets Inc (G-3660)*

Har Adhesive Technologies, Bedford *Also Called: Certon Technologies Inc (G-1021)*

Harbison Walker Intl Mnrl Inc.......................... 513 251-1010
1085 Summer St Cincinnati (45204) *(G-2705)*

Harbor Castings Inc (PA)................................. 330 499-7178
2508 Bailey Rd Cuyahoga Falls (44221) *(G-5547)*

Harbor Industrial Corp..................................... 440 599-8366
859 W Jackson St Conneaut (44030) *(G-5402)*

Harco Manufacturing Group LLC (PA).............. 937 528-5000
3535 Kettering Blvd Moraine (45439) *(G-10167)*

Harco Manufacturing Group LLC..................... 937 528-5000
3535 Kettering Blvd # 200 Moraine (45439) *(G-10168)*

Hard Drive Co, Barberton *Also Called: Florence Alloys Inc (G-805)*

Hard Surface Technology Inc........................... 513 860-1156
9461 Le Saint Dr West Chester (45014) *(G-14013)*

Hardcore Offroad Tires, Youngstown *Also Called: Warrior Imports Inc (G-14966)*

Hardin County Publishing Co (HQ)................... 419 674-4066
201 E Columbus St Kenton (43326) *(G-8101)*

Hardin Creek Machine & TI Inc......................... 419 678-4913
200 Hardin St Coldwater (45828) *(G-4576)*

Harding Machine Acquisition Co..................... 937 666-3031
13060 State Route 287 East Liberty (43319) *(G-6386)*

Hardline International Inc................................. 419 924-9556
1107 Oak St West Unity (43570) *(G-14195)*

Hardwood Connection, The, Toledo *Also Called: Hafners Hrdwood Connection LLC (G-12983)*

Hardwood Lumber Co, Burton *Also Called: Stephen M Trudick (G-1704)*

Hardwood Lumber Company Inc...................... 440 834-1891
13813 Station Rd Middlefield (44062) *(G-9797)*

Hardwood Store Inc... 937 864-2899
350 Enon Rd Enon (45323) *(G-6631)*

Hardy Industrial Tech LLC............................... 440 350-6300
679 Hardy Rd Painesville (44077) *(G-11092)*

Harknesservices, Norwalk *Also Called: Link To Success Inc (G-10851)*

Harlan Graphic Arts Svcs Inc.......................... 513 251-5700
4752 River Rd Cincinnati (45233) *(G-2706)*

Harmon Sign Company, Toledo *Also Called: Kasper Enterprises Inc (G-13016)*

Harmony Systems and Svc Inc........................ 937 778-1082
1711 Commerce Dr Piqua (45356) *(G-11349)*

Harper Engraving & Printing Co (PA)............... 614 276-0700
2626 Fisher Rd Columbus (43204) *(G-4970)*

Harray LLC... 888 568-8371
266 W Mitchell Ave Cincinnati (45232) *(G-2707)*

Harris Broadcast, Mason *Also Called: Imagine Communications Corp (G-9110)*

Harris Instrument Corporation........................ 740 369-3580
155 Johnson Dr Delaware (43015) *(G-6155)*

Harris Mackessy & Brennan Inc...................... 614 221-6831
570 Polaris Pkwy Ste 200 Westerville (43082) *(G-14212)*

Harris Paper Crafts Inc.................................... 614 299-2141
266 E 5th Ave Columbus (43201) *(G-4971)*

Harris Products Group, The, Mason *Also Called: J W Harris Co Inc (G-9116)*

Harris Welding and Machine Co....................... 419 281-8351
2219 Cottage St Ashland (44805) *(G-537)*

Harrison Corporation (PA)................................ 513 681-2420
3820 Colerain Ave Cincinnati (45223) *(G-2708)*

Harrison County Coal Company (HQ)............... 740 338-3100
46226 National Rd Saint Clairsville (43950) *(G-11693)*

Harrison Hub, Scio *Also Called: M3 Midstream LLC (G-11888)*

Harrison Mch & Plastic Corp (PA).................... 330 527-5641
11614 State Route 88 Garrettsville (44231) *(G-7220)*

Harrison Paint, Canton *Also Called: Harrison Paint Company (G-1909)*

Harrison Paint Company (PA).......................... 330 455-5120
1329 Harrison Ave Sw Canton (44706) *(G-1909)*

Harrison Plant, Canton *Also Called: Metallus Inc (G-1947)*

Harrop Industries Inc...................................... 614 231-3621
3470 E 5th Ave Columbus (43219) *(G-4972)*

Harry & David, Hebron *Also Called: Harry & David Operations Inc (G-7616)*

Harry & David Operations Inc.......................... 541 864-3710
111 Enterprise Dr Hebron (43025) *(G-7616)*

Harry C Lobalzo & Sons Inc............................. 330 666-6758
61 N Cleveland Massillon Rd Unit A Akron (44333) *(G-172)*

Harry London Candies Inc (DH)....................... 330 494-0833
5353 Lauby Rd North Canton (44720) *(G-10645)*

Harry London Chocolates, North Canton *Also Called: Harry London Candies Inc (G-10645)*

Hart & Cooley LLC... 937 832-7800
1 Lau Pkwy Englewood (45315) *(G-6614)*

Hartco Inc.. 513 771-4430
1280 Glendale Milford Rd Cincinnati (45215) *(G-2709)*

Hartco Printing Company (PA)......................... 614 761-1292
4106 Delancy Park Dr Dublin (43016) *(G-6301)*

Hartco Products, The, Dublin *Also Called: Hartco Printing Company (G-6301)*

Hartline Products Coinc................................... 216 851-7189
15035 Woodworth Rd Ste 3 Cleveland (44110) *(G-3811)*

Hartman Distributing LLC................................ 740 616-7764
1262 Bluejack Ln Heath (43056) *(G-7596)*

2025 Harris Ohio
Industrial Directory

(G-0000) Company's Geographic Section entry number

Hartman Trophies, Columbus *Also Called: The Hartman Corp (G-5320)*

Hartmann Electronic, Springfield *Also Called: Kontron America Incorporated (G-12339)*

Hartsgrove Machine, Rock Creek *Also Called: David Bixel (G-11629)*

Hartville Chocolate Factory, Hartville *Also Called: Hartville Chocolates Inc (G-7576)*

Hartville Chocolates Inc.. 330 877-1999
114 S Prospect Ave Hartville (44632) *(G-7576)*

Hartville Locker Service Ltd... 330 877-9547
119 Sunnyside St Sw Hartville (44632) *(G-7577)*

Hartz Mountain Corporation... 513 877-2131
5374 Long Spurling Rd Pleasant Plain (45162) *(G-11432)*

Hartzell Fan Inc (PA).. 937 773-7411
910 S Downing St Piqua (45356) *(G-11350)*

Hartzell Hardwoods Inc (PA).. 937 773-7054
1025 S Roosevelt Ave Piqua (45356) *(G-11351)*

Hartzell Industries Inc (PA)... 937 773-6295
1025 S Roosevelt Ave Piqua (45356) *(G-11352)*

Hartzell Mfg Co LLC... 937 859-5955
2533 Technical Dr Miamisburg (45342) *(G-9696)*

Hartzell Propeller Inc (HQ).. 937 778-4200
1 Propeller Pl Piqua (45356) *(G-11353)*

Harvard Coil Processing Inc.. 216 883-6366
5400 Harvard Ave Cleveland (44105) *(G-3812)*

Harvest Commissary LLC.. 513 706-1951
3825 Columbus Rd Bldg J Granville (43023) *(G-7315)*

Harvey Brothers Inc (PA).. 513 541-2622
3492 Spring Grove Ave Cincinnati (45223) *(G-2710)*

Harwood Entp Holdings Inc.. 330 923-3256
1365 Orlen Ave Cuyahoga Falls (44221) *(G-5548)*

Harwood Rubber Products, Akron *Also Called: M7 Hrp LLC (G-218)*

Harwood Screw Products, Springfield *Also Called: Ban Inc (G-12284)*

Hashier & Hashier Mfg.. 440 933-4883
644 Moore Rd Avon Lake (44012) *(G-758)*

Hason USA Corp... 513 248-0287
1080 Nimitzview Dr Ste 402 Cincinnati (45230) *(G-2711)*

Hathaway, Cincinnati *Also Called: Volk Corporation (G-3207)*

Hathaway Stamp, Cincinnati *Also Called: Hathaway Stamp Co (G-2712)*

Hathaway Stamp Co... 513 621-1052
304 E 8th St Cincinnati (45202) *(G-2712)*

Hathaway Stamp Identification, Cincinnati *Also Called: Hathaway Stamp Idntfction Cncn (G-2713)*

Hathaway Stamp Idntfction Cncn..................................... 513 621-1052
304 E 8th St Cincinnati (45202) *(G-2713)*

Hattenbach, Cleveland *Also Called: The Hattenbach Company (G-4384)*

Haulette Manufacturing Inc... 419 586-1717
8271 Us Route 127 Celina (45822) *(G-2108)*

Haulotte North America Mfg LLC..................................... 419 445-8915
125 Taylor Pkwy Archbold (43502) *(G-497)*

Hauser Landscaping, Middlefield *Also Called: Hauser Services Llc (G-9798)*

Hauser Services Llc... 440 632-5126
15668 Old State Rd Middlefield (44062) *(G-9798)*

Haviland Culvert Company.. 419 622-6951
100 Main St Haviland (45851) *(G-7588)*

Haviland Drainage Products Co (PA)................................ 800 860-6294
100 Main St Haviland (45851) *(G-7589)*

Haviland Plastic Products Co... 419 622-3110
119 Main St Haviland (45851) *(G-7590)*

Hawk Performance, Medina *Also Called: Friction Products Co (G-9406)*

Hawkins Machine Shop Inc.. 937 335-8737
1112 Race Dr Troy (45373) *(G-13221)*

Hawkline Nevada LLC... 937 444-4295
200 Front St Mount Orab (45154) *(G-10217)*

Hawks & Associates Inc... 513 752-4311
1029 Seabrook Way Cincinnati (45245) *(G-2305)*

Hawks Tag, Cincinnati *Also Called: Hawks & Associates Inc (G-2305)*

Hawthorne Gardening Co., Marysville *Also Called: Hawthorne Gardening Company (G-9023)*

Hawthorne Gardening Company (HQ)............................... 360 883-8846
14111 Scottslawn Rd Marysville (43040) *(G-9023)*

Hawthorne Hydrophonics Botanic, Marysville *Also Called: Hawthorne Hydroponics LLC (G-9024)*

Hawthorne Hydroponics LLC (DH).................................... 888 478-6544
14111 Scottslawn Rd Marysville (43040) *(G-9024)*

Hawthorne Tool LLC.. 440 516-1891
1340 Lloyd Rd Ste C Wickliffe (44092) *(G-14377)*

Hawthorne Wire Ltd... 216 712-4747
13000 Athens Ave Ste 101 Lakewood (44107) *(G-8167)*

Hayden Valley Foods Inc (PA).. 614 539-7233
3150 Urbancrest Industrial Dr Grove City (43123) *(G-7390)*

Hayes Bros Orna Ir Works Inc.. 419 531-1491
1830 N Reynolds Rd Toledo (43615) *(G-12987)*

Hayes, Michael Designer, Solon *Also Called: Michael W Hyes Desgr Goldsmith (G-12150)*

Hayford Technologies Inc.. 419 524-7627
500 S Airport Rd Mansfield (44903) *(G-8800)*

Haynes Manufacturing Company, Westlake *Also Called: R and J Corporation (G-14326)*

Hays Cleveland, Cleveland *Also Called: Unison UCI Inc (G-4441)*

Hays Fabricating & Welding Inc....................................... 937 325-0031
633 E Leffel Ln Springfield (45505) *(G-12317)*

Haz-Safe LLC... 330 793-0900
3850 Hendricks Rd Austintown (44515) *(G-705)*

Hazelbaker Industries Ltd
1661 Old Henderson Rd Columbus (43220) *(G-4973)*

Hazenstab Machine Inc... 330 337-1865
1575 Salem Pkwy Salem (44460) *(G-11785)*

HB Fuller Company... 833 672-1482
400 N Buckeye St Bellevue (44811) *(G-1124)*

HB Fuller Company... 513 719-3600
4450 Malsbary Rd Blue Ash (45242) *(G-1282)*

HB Fuller Company... 513 719-3600
4440 Malsbary Rd Blue Ash (45242) *(G-1283)*

HB Fuller Company... 440 708-1212
17340 Munn Rd Chagrin Falls (44023) *(G-2164)*

HBD Industries Inc (PA).. 614 526-7000
565 Metro Pl S Ste 250 Dublin (43017) *(G-6302)*

Hbd/Thermoid Inc... 800 543-8070
1301 W Sandusky Ave Bellefontaine (43311) *(G-1108)*

HBE Machine Incorporated... 419 668-9426
1100 State Route 61 N Monroeville (44847) *(G-10119)*

Hc Companies Inc (HQ)... 440 632-3333
2450 Edison Blvd Ste 3 Twinsburg (44087) *(G-13315)*

HCC Holdings Inc... 800 203-1155
4700 W 160th St Cleveland (44135) *(G-3813)*

HCC/Sealtron (DH).. 513 733-8400
9705 Reading Rd Cincinnati (45215) *(G-2714)*

Hdi Landing Gear USA Inc (DH)....................................... 937 325-1586
663 Montgomery Ave Springfield (45506) *(G-12318)*

Hdi Landing Gear USA Inc.. 937 325-1586
663 Montgomery Ave Strongsville (44149) *(G-12563)*

HDR Power Systems LLC.. 614 308-5500
530 Lakeview Plaza Blvd Ste C Worthington (43085) *(G-14712)*

Hdt Ep Inc.. 216 438-6111
30500 Aurora Rd Ste 100 Solon (44139) *(G-12120)*

Hdt Expeditionary Systems Inc.. 513 943-1111
1032 Seabrook Way Cincinnati (45245) *(G-2306)*

Hdt Expeditionary Systems Inc.. 440 466-6640
5455 Route 307 West Geneva (44041) *(G-7239)*

Hdt Expeditionary Systems Inc (HQ)................................ 216 438-6111
30500 Aurora Rd Ste 100 Solon (44139) *(G-12121)*

Hdt Global, Solon *Also Called: Hunter Defense Tech Inc (G-12124)*

Hdt Tactical Systems Inc.. 216 438-6111
30525 Aurora Rd Solon (44139) *(G-12122)*

Hdwt Holdings Inc... 440 269-6984
7124 Industrial Park Blvd Mentor (44060) *(G-9526)*

Heading4ward Investment Co (PA)................................... 937 293-9994
2425 W Dorothy Ln Moraine (45439) *(G-10169)*

Headlee Enterprises Ltd... 614 785-1476
9015 Antares Ave Columbus (43240) *(G-4641)*

Health Aid of Ohio Inc (PA).. 216 252-3900
6940 Engle Rd Ste A Cleveland (44130) *(G-3814)*

Health Care Products Inc.. 419 678-9620
410 Nisco St Coldwater (45828) *(G-4577)*

Health Nuts Media LLC.. 818 802-5222
4225 W 229th St Cleveland (44126) *(G-3815)*

Health Sense Inc.. 440 354-8057
433 S State St Painesville (44077) *(G-11093)*

Health-Mor, Brooklyn *Also Called: Hmi Industries Inc (G-1522)*

Healthsense, Painesville *Also Called: Health Sense Inc (G-11093)*

Healthwares Manufacturing..513 353-3691
5838b Hamilton Cleves Rd Cleves (45002) *(G-4539)*

Hearn Plating Co Ltd...419 473-9773
3184 Bellevue Rd Toledo (43606) *(G-12988)*

Hearth Products Controls Co..937 436-9800
2225 Lyons Rd Miamisburg (45342) *(G-9697)*

Hearthside Food Solutions LLC..419 293-2911
312 Rader Rd Mc Comb (45858) *(G-9353)*

Heartland Bread & Roll, Worthington *Also Called: Hannibal Company Inc (G-14711)*

Heartland Communications Div, Pataskala *Also Called: Pataskala Post (G-11145)*

Heartland Group Holdings LLC...614 441-4001
4001 E 5th Ave Columbus (43219) *(G-4974)*

Heartland Petroleum, Columbus *Also Called: Gfl Environmental Svcs USA Inc (G-4952)*

Heartland Publications LLC...860 664-1075
4500 Lyons Rd Miamisburg (45342) *(G-9698)*

Heartland Retreaders Inc..740 472-0558
103 N Sycamore St Woodsfield (43793) *(G-14612)*

Heartland Stairways Inc (PA)..330 279-2554
8230 County Road 245 Holmesville (44633) *(G-7795)*

Heartland Stairways Inc..330 279-2554
7964 Township Road 565 Holmesville (44633) *(G-7796)*

Heat & Sensor, Lebanon *Also Called: Heat Sensor Technologie LLC (G-8267)*

Heat Exchange Applied Tech Inc...330 682-4328
150b Allen Ave Orrville (44667) *(G-10983)*

Heat Seal LLC...216 341-1022
4922 E 49th St Ste 100 Cleveland (44125) *(G-3816)*

Heat Sensor Technologie LLC...513 228-0481
627 Norgal Dr Lebanon (45036) *(G-8267)*

Heat Treating Inc (PA)...937 325-3121
1762 W Pleasant St Springfield (45506) *(G-12319)*

Heat Treating Equipment Inc...740 549-3700
8185 Green Meadows Dr N Lewis Center (43035) *(G-8335)*

Heat Treating Inc...614 759-9963
675 Cross Pointe Rd Gahanna (43230) *(G-7159)*

Heat-Treating Technologies Inc...419 224-8324
1799 E 4th St Lima (45804) *(G-8413)*

Heatermeals, Cincinnati *Also Called: Luxfer Magtech Inc (G-2832)*

Heating & Cooling Products, Mount Vernon *Also Called: Royal Metal Products LLC (G-10264)*

Heatmax Heaters, Mentor *Also Called: Glo-Quartz Electric Htr Co Inc (G-9524)*

Heatstar, Cleveland *Also Called: Mr Heater Inc (G-4051)*

Heavenly Creamery Inc...440 593-6080
264 Sandusky St Conneaut (44030) *(G-5403)*

Hec Investments Inc...937 278-9123
4800 Wadsworth Rd Dayton (45414) *(G-5808)*

Heck's Diamond Printing, Toledo *Also Called: Hecks Direct Mail & Prtg Svc (G-12989)*

Hecks Direct Mail & Prtg Svc..419 661-6028
202 W Florence Ave Toledo (43605) *(G-12989)*

Hecks Direct Mail Prtg Svc Inc (PA)...419 697-3505
417 Main St Toledo (43605) *(G-12990)*

Hedalloy Die Corporation..216 341-3768
3266 E 49th St Cleveland (44127) *(G-3817)*

Hedges Selective TI & Prod Inc...419 478-8670
702 W Laskey Rd Toledo (43612) *(G-12991)*

Hedstrom Plastics LLC...419 289-9310
100 Hedstrom Dr Ashland (44805) *(G-538)*

Heeter Printing Company Inc...440 946-0606
33212 Lakeland Blvd Eastlake (44095) *(G-6431)*

HEF USA Corporation (PA)...937 323-2556
2015 Progress Rd Springfield (45505) *(G-12320)*

Hefty Hoist Inc..740 467-2515
2397a Refugee St Millersport (43046) *(G-10023)*

Heico Aerospace Parts Corp (DH)...954 987-6101
375 Alpha Park Highland Heights (44143) *(G-7659)*

Heidelberg Materials Us Inc..937 587-2671
848 Plum Run Rd Peebles (45660) *(G-11169)*

Heidelberg Materials Us Inc..937 442-6009
13526 Overstake Rd Winchester (45697) *(G-14598)*

Heidelberg Mtls Mdwest Agg Inc...419 983-2211
4575 S County Road 49 Bloomville (44818) *(G-1240)*

Heidelberg Mtls Mdwest Agg Inc...419 882-0123
8130 Brint Rd Sylvania (43560) *(G-12708)*

Heidelberg Mtls Mdwest Agg Inc...419 878-2006
600 S River Rd Waterville (43566) *(G-13834)*

Heidelberg Mtls US Cem LLC..330 499-9100
8282 Middlebranch Ave Ne Middlebranch (44652) *(G-9765)*

Heidelberg Mtls US Cem LLC..972 653-5500
8130 Brint Rd Sylvania (43560) *(G-12709)*

Heidtman Steel, Toledo *Also Called: Heidtman Steel Products Inc (G-12992)*

Heidtman Steel Products Inc (HQ)..419 691-4646
2401 Front St Toledo (43605) *(G-12992)*

Heilind Electronics Inc...440 473-9600
5300 Avion Park Dr Cleveland (44143) *(G-3818)*

Heim Sheet Metal Inc...330 424-7820
905 N Market St Lisbon (44432) *(G-8469)*

Heinemann Saw Company...330 456-4721
2017 Navarre Rd Sw Canton (44706) *(G-1910)*

Heinen's 8, Aurora *Also Called: Heinens Inc (G-673)*

Heinens Inc...330 562-5297
115 N Chillicothe Rd Aurora (44202) *(G-673)*

Heinis Cheese Chalet, Millersburg *Also Called: Bunker Hill Cheese Co Inc (G-9973)*

Heintz Conveying Belt Service, Medina *Also Called: Conviber Inc (G-9391)*

Heintz Farms Enterprise Partnr...937 464-2535
4367 State Route 273 W Belle Center (43310) *(G-1095)*

Heinz, Coshocton *Also Called: Kraft Heinz Foods Company (G-5458)*

Heinz Foreign Investment Co...330 837-8331
1301 Oberlin Ave Sw Massillon (44647) *(G-9200)*

Heinz Frozen Foods, Massillon *Also Called: HJ Heinz Company LP (G-9202)*

Heisler Tool Company..440 951-2424
38228 Western Pkwy Willoughby (44094) *(G-14464)*

Heisley Tire & Brake Inc...440 357-9797
5893 Heisley Rd Mentor (44060) *(G-9527)*

Heitkamp & Kremer Printing Inc..419 925-4121
6184 State Route 274 Celina (45822) *(G-2109)*

Helena Agri-Enterprises LLC...614 275-4200
800 Distribution Dr Columbus (43228) *(G-4975)*

Helena Agri-Enterprises LLC...419 596-3806
200 N Main St Continental (45831) *(G-5422)*

Helical Line Products Co...440 933-9263
659 Miller Rd Avon Lake (44012) *(G-759)*

Helium Seo..513 563-3065
11311 Cornell Park Dr Blue Ash (45242) *(G-1284)*

Helix Linear Technologies Inc..216 485-2263
23200 Commerce Park Beachwood (44122) *(G-920)*

Helix Operating Company LLC...855 435-4958
23200 Commerce Park Beachwood (44122) *(G-921)*

Hellan Strainer Company..216 206-4200
3249 E 80th St Cleveland (44104) *(G-3819)*

Heller Machine Products Inc..216 281-2951
1971 W 90th St Cleveland (44102) *(G-3820)*

Helm Instrument Company Inc...419 893-4356
361 W Dussel Dr Maumee (43537) *(G-9296)*

Helmart Company Inc...513 941-3095
4960 Hillside Ave Cincinnati (45233) *(G-2715)*

Hematite, Englewood *Also Called: Woodbridge Englewood Inc (G-6630)*

Hemmelrath, Lima *Also Called: Hemmelrath Coatings Inc (G-8414)*

Hemmelrath Coatings Inc
1340 Neubrecht Rd Lima (45801) *(G-8414)*

Hen House Inc...419 663-3377
100 N West St Norwalk (44857) *(G-10846)*

Hen of Woods LLC...513 954-8871
2116 Colerain Ave Cincinnati (45214) *(G-2716)*

Henderson Trucking, Delaware *Also Called: Rjw Trucking Company Ltd (G-6169)*

Hendrckson Trlr Coml Vhcl Syst, Canton *Also Called: Hendrickson Usa LLC (G-1911)*

Hendricks Vacuum Forming Inc...330 837-2040
3500 17th St Sw Massillon (44647) *(G-9201)*

Hendrickson..740 678-8033
1051 Windy Ridge Rd Vincent (45784) *(G-13621)*

2025 Harris Ohio
Industrial Directory

(G-0000) Company's Geographic Section entry number

Hendrickson Auxiliary Axles, Hebron *Also Called: Hendrickson International Corp (G-7617)*

Hendrickson International Corp............................ 740 929-5600
277 N High St Hebron (43025) *(G-7617)*

Hendrickson Usa LLC.. 330 456-7288
2070 Industrial Pl Se Canton (44707) *(G-1911)*

Hendrickson Usa LLC.. 740 929-5600
277 N High St Hebron (43025) *(G-7618)*

Hendrickson Usa LLC.. 630 910-2800
9260 Pleasantwood Ave Nw North Canton (44720) *(G-10646)*

Henkel Surface Technologies, Delaware *Also Called: Henkel US Operations Corp (G-6156)*

Henkel US Operations Corp................................. 513 830-0260
9435 Waterstone Blvd Cincinnati (45249) *(G-2717)*

Henkel US Operations Corp................................. 216 475-3600
18731 Cranwood Pkwy Cleveland (44128) *(G-3821)*

Henkel US Operations Corp................................. 740 363-1351
421 London Rd Delaware (43015) *(G-6156)*

Henkel US Operations Corp................................. 440 255-8900
7405 Production Dr Mentor (44060) *(G-9528)*

Henkel US Operations Corp................................. 440 250-7700
26235 1st St Westlake (44145) *(G-14305)*

Hennings Quality Service Inc.............................. 216 941-9120
3115 Berea Rd Cleveland (44111) *(G-3822)*

Henny Penny Corporation (PA)............................. 937 456-8400
1219 U S 35 W Eaton (45320) *(G-6454)*

Henry & Wright Corporation................................ 216 851-3750
1387 E 168th St Cleveland (44110) *(G-3823)*

Henry Filters, Bowling Green *Also Called: Barnes International LLC (G-1407)*

Henry Tools Inc.. 216 291-1011
498 S Belvoir Blvd Cleveland (44121) *(G-3824)*

Henty Usa LLC.. 513 984-5590
7260 Edington Dr Cincinnati (45249) *(G-2718)*

Hephaestus Technologies LLC............................. 216 252-0430
3811 W 150th St Cleveland (44111) *(G-3825)*

Heraeus Electro-Nite Co LLC.............................. 330 725-1419
6469 Fenn Rd Medina (44256) *(G-9408)*

Heraeus Epurio LLC.. 937 264-1000
970 Industrial Park Dr Vandalia (45377) *(G-13559)*

Herald Inc.. 419 492-2133
625 S Kibler St New Washington (44854) *(G-10479)*

Herald Reflector Inc (PA)................................. 419 668-3771
61 E Monroe St Norwalk (44857) *(G-10847)*

Herbert E Orr Company Inc................................ 419 399-4866
335 W Wall St Paulding (45879) *(G-11155)*

Herbert Usa Inc.. 330 929-4297
1480 Industrial Pkwy Akron (44310) *(G-173)*

Herco Inc.. 740 498-5181
295 Enterprise Dr Newcomerstown (43832) *(G-10571)*

Hercules, Wickliffe *Also Called: Universal Metal Products Inc (G-14399)*

Hercules Engine, Massillon *Also Called: Brinkley Technology Group LLC (G-9175)*

Hercules Engine Components, Massillon *Also Called: DW Hercules LLC (G-9187)*

Hercules Industries Inc.................................... 740 494-2620
7194 Prospect Delaware Rd Prospect (43342) *(G-11502)*

Hercules Led LLC.. 844 437-2533
5411 Market St Boardman (44512) *(G-1374)*

Hercules Stamping Co, Pemberville *Also Called: JA Acquisition Corp (G-11176)*

Herd, Cleveland *Also Called: Herd Manufacturing Inc (G-3826)*

Herd Manufacturing Inc.................................... 216 651-4221
9227 Clinton Rd Cleveland (44144) *(G-3826)*

Hergatt Machine Inc....................................... 419 589-2931
2530 Pavonia Rd Mansfield (44903) *(G-8801)*

Heritage Cooperative Inc.................................. 740 828-2215
10790 Newark Rd Nashport (43830) *(G-10300)*

Heritage Group Inc.. 330 875-5566
303 S Chapel St Louisville (44641) *(G-8603)*

Heritage Hill LLC.. 513 237-0240
11563 Grooms Rd Blue Ash (45242) *(G-1285)*

Heritage Industrial Finshg Inc............................ 330 798-9840
1874 Englewood Ave Akron (44312) *(G-174)*

Heritage Plastics, Carrollton *Also Called: Heritage Plastics Liquidation Inc (G-2085)*

Heritage Plastics Liquidation Inc.......................... 330 627-8002
861 N Lisbon St Carrollton (44615) *(G-2085)*

Heritage Press Inc... 419 289-9209
651 Sandusky St Ashland (44805) *(G-539)*

Heritage Tool & Manufacturing, Amelia *Also Called: Mark J Myers (G-432)*

Heritage Truck Equipment Inc............................. 330 699-4491
661 Powell Ave Hartville (44632) *(G-7578)*

Herman Machine Inc....................................... 330 633-3261
298 Northeast Ave Tallmadge (44278) *(G-12736)*

Herman Manufacturing LLC................................ 216 251-6400
13825 Triskett Rd Cleveland (44111) *(G-3827)*

Hermetic Seal Technology Inc............................. 513 851-4899
2150 Schappelle Ln Cincinnati (45240) *(G-2719)*

Herold Salads Inc.. 216 991-7500
17512 Miles Ave Cleveland (44128) *(G-3828)*

Heroux Devtek Landing Gear Div, Strongsville *Also Called: Hdi Landing Gear USA Inc (G-12563)*

Heroux-Devtek Inc... 937 325-1586
663 Montgomery Ave Springfield (45506) *(G-12321)*

Heroux-Devtek Springfield, Springfield *Also Called: Heroux-Devtek Inc (G-12321)*

Herr Foods Incorporated................................... 740 773-8282
476 E 7th St Chillicothe (45601) *(G-2256)*

Herr Foods Incorporated................................... 800 344-3777
104 S Mcarthur St Chillicothe (45601) *(G-2257)*

Hershberger Lawn Structures.............................. 330 674-3900
8990 State Route 39 Millersburg (44654) *(G-9983)*

Hershberger Manufacturing................................ 440 272-5555
7584 Rockwood Rd Windsor (44099) *(G-14601)*

Hershy Way Ltd.. 330 893-2809
5918 County Road 201 Millersburg (44654) *(G-9984)*

Heskamp Printing Co Inc.................................. 513 871-6770
5514 Fair Ln Cincinnati (45227) *(G-2720)*

Hess Advanced Solutions Llc............................. 937 829-4794
7415 Chambersburg Rd Dayton (45424) *(G-5809)*

Hess Industries Ltd.. 419 525-4000
108 Sawyer Pkwy Mansfield (44903) *(G-8802)*

Hess Print Solutions, Kent *Also Called: D & J Printing Inc (G-8024)*

Hess Print Solutions, Kent *Also Called: Press of Ohio Inc (G-8062)*

Hess Print Solutions, Kent *Also Called: The D B Hess Company (G-8089)*

Hess Print Solutions, Kent *Also Called: Tpo Hess Holdings Inc (G-8091)*

Hess Print Solutions - OH, Kent *Also Called: The Press of Ohio Inc (G-8090)*

Heule Tool Corporation.................................... 513 860-9900
131 Commerce Dr Loveland (45140) *(G-8630)*

Hexa Americas Inc.. 937 497-7900
1150 S Vandemark Rd Sidney (45365) *(G-12022)*

Hexagon Industries Inc.................................... 216 249-0200
1135 Ivanhoe Rd Cleveland (44110) *(G-3829)*

Hexion, Columbus *Also Called: Hexion Inc (G-4976)*

Hexion Inc (PA).. 888 443-9466
180 E Broad St Columbus (43215) *(G-4976)*

Hexion LLC (HQ)... 614 225-4000
180 E Broad St Fl 26 Columbus (43215) *(G-4977)*

Hexion Topco LLC (PA).................................... 614 225-4000
180 E Broad St Columbus (43215) *(G-4978)*

Hexion US Finance Corp................................... 614 225-4000
180 E Broad St Columbus (43215) *(G-4979)*

Hexpol Cmpnding Amrcas Mfg LLC........................ 440 632-0901
14910 Madison Rd Middlefield (44062) *(G-9799)*

Hexpol Compounding LLC.................................. 440 682-4038
1497 Exeter Rd Akron (44306) *(G-175)*

Hexpol Compounding LLC.................................. 440 834-4644
14330 Kinsman Rd Burton (44021) *(G-1699)*

Hexpol Compounding LLC (DH)............................ 440 834-4644
14330 Kinsman Rd Burton (44021) *(G-1700)*

Hexpol Compounding LLC.................................. 440 632-1962
14910 Madison Rd Middlefield (44062) *(G-9800)*

Hexpol Compounding Pc Inc............................... 330 258-2016
115 W Bartges St Akron (44311) *(G-176)*

Hexpol Compounding Pc Inc (HQ)......................... 330 798-4790
1020 Lambert St Barberton (44203) *(G-810)*

Hexpol Holding Inc (HQ)................................... 440 834-4644
14330 Kinsman Rd Burton (44021) *(G-1701)*

Hexpol Middlefield, Middlefield *Also Called: Hexpol Cmpnding Amrcas Mfg LLC (G-9799)*

A
L
P
H
A
B
E
T
I
C

Hexpol Polymers, Burton *Also Called: Hexpol Compounding LLC (G-1700)*

Hexpol Silicone, Akron *Also Called: Hexpol Compounding LLC (G-175)*

Hf Group LLC (PA)..440 729-2445
400 Aurora Commons Cir Unit 74 Aurora (44202) *(G-674)*

Hf Group LLC...440 729-9411
12375 Kinsman Rd Newbury (44065) *(G-10553)*

Hf Group LLC...440 729-9411
12375 Kinsman Rd Newbury (44065) *(G-10554)*

Hfi LLC (PA)..614 491-0700
59 Gender Rd Canal Winchester (43110) *(G-1791)*

Hggc Citadel Plas Holdings Inc.........................330 666-3751
3637 Ridgewood Rd Fairlawn (44333) *(G-6803)*

Hgi Holdings Inc..330 963-6996
1810 Summit Commerce Park Twinsburg (44087) *(G-13316)*

Hh Associates US Inc...937 644-7492
14111 Scottslawn Rd Marysville (43040) *(G-9025)*

Hhi, Canton *Also Called: Hunter Hydraulics Inc (G-1913)*

HI Carb Corp..216 486-5000
1857 E 337th St # A Eastlake (44095) *(G-6432)*

HI Lite Plastic Products...614 235-9050
3760 E 5th Ave Columbus (43219) *(G-4980)*

HI Standard Machine Co, De Graff *Also Called: Alan Bortree (G-6091)*

HI Tech Printing Co Inc...513 874-5325
3741 Port Union Rd Fairfield (45014) *(G-6739)*

HI Tecmetal Group Inc (PA)................................216 881-8100
28910 Lakeland Blvd Wickliffe (44092) *(G-14378)*

Hi-Point Firearms, Mansfield *Also Called: Highpoint Firearms (G-8803)*

Hi-Point Graphics LLC..937 407-6524
127 E Chillicothe Ave Bellefontaine (43311) *(G-1109)*

Hi-Stat A Stoneridge Co, Lexington *Also Called: Stoneridge Inc (G-8374)*

Hi-Tech Extrusions Ltd...440 286-4000
12621 Chardon Windsor Rd Chardon (44024) *(G-2207)*

Hi-Tech Wire Inc..419 678-8376
631 E Washington St Saint Henry (45883) *(G-11721)*

Hi-Tech Wire & Manufacturing, Saint Henry *Also Called: Hi-Tech Wire Inc (G-11721)*

Hi-Tek Manufacturing Inc....................................513 459-1094
6050 Hi Tek Ct Mason (45040) *(G-9108)*

HI-Vac Corporation (PA)..740 374-2306
117 Industry Rd Marietta (45750) *(G-8923)*

Hiab USA Inc (HQ)..419 482-6000
12233 Williams Rd Perrysburg (43551) *(G-11228)*

Hickman Williams & Company (PA).....................513 621-1946
250 E 5th St Ste 300 Cincinnati (45202) *(G-2721)*

Hickmans Construction Co LLC...........................866 271-2565
21150 Morris Ave Euclid (44123) *(G-6653)*

Hickok Ae LLC, Akron *Also Called: Crawford Ae LLC (G-109)*

Hickok Waekon LLC..216 541-8060
10514 Dupont Ave Cleveland (44108) *(G-3830)*

Hickory Harvest Foods, Akron *Also Called: Ohio Hckry Hrvest Brnd Pdts In (G-253)*

Hidaka Usa Inc...614 889-8611
5761 Shier Rings Rd Dublin (43016) *(G-6303)*

Higgins Construction & Supply Co Inc...............937 364-2331
3801 Us Highway 50 Hillsboro (45133) *(G-7717)*

Higgins Tool Rental, Hillsboro *Also Called: Higgins Construction & Supply Co Inc (G-7717)*

High Concrete Group LLC.....................................937 748-2412
95 Mound Park Dr Springboro (45066) *(G-12255)*

High Definition Tooling, Newcomerstown *Also Called: H3d Tool Corporation (G-10570)*

High Production Technology LLC.........................419 599-1511
13068 County Road R Napoleon (43545) *(G-10283)*

High Production Technology LLC (DH).................419 591-7000
476 E Riverview Ave Napoleon (43545) *(G-10284)*

High Quality Tools, Eastlake *Also Called: High Quality Tools Inc (G-6433)*

High Quality Tools Inc (PA)................................440 975-9684
34940 Lakeland Blvd Eastlake (44095) *(G-6433)*

High Tech Castings..937 845-1204
12170 Milton Carlisle Rd New Carlisle (45344) *(G-10371)*

High Tech Elastomers Inc (PA)...........................937 236-6575
885 Scholz Dr Vandalia (45377) *(G-13560)*

High Tech Metal Products LLC............................419 227-9414
1900 Garland Ave Lima (45804) *(G-8415)*

High Tech Prfmce Trlrs Inc...................................440 357-8964
1 High Tech Ave Painesville (44077) *(G-11094)*

High Temperature Systems Inc...........................440 543-8271
16755 Park Circle Dr Chagrin Falls (44023) *(G-2165)*

High-TEC Industrial Services................................937 667-1772
15 Industry Park Ct Tipp City (45371) *(G-12827)*

High-Tech Mold & Machine Inc...........................330 896-4466
3771 Tabs Dr Uniontown (44685) *(G-13420)*

Highcom Global Security Inc (HQ)......................727 592-9400
2901 E 4th Ave Unit J Columbus (43219) *(G-4981)*

Higher Ground Ministries, Springfield *Also Called: Rebecca Benston (G-12367)*

Highland Computer Forms Inc (PA)....................937 393-4215
1025 W Main St Hillsboro (45133) *(G-7718)*

Highland County Press, Hillsboro *Also Called: Cameco Communications LLC (G-7715)*

Highland Products Corp...440 352-4777
9331 Mercantile Dr Mentor (44060) *(G-9529)*

Highlights Consumer Svcs Inc.............................570 253-1164
1800 Watermark Dr Columbus (43216) *(G-4982)*

Highlights For Children Inc (PA)..........................614 486-0631
1800 Watermark Dr Columbus (43215) *(G-4983)*

Highlights For Children Publr, Columbus *Also Called: Highlights For Children Inc (G-4983)*

Highpoint Firearms..419 747-9444
1015 Springmill St Mansfield (44906) *(G-8803)*

Highrise Creative LLC...614 890-3821
654 Brooksedge Blvd Ste A Westerville (43081) *(G-14263)*

Highs Welding Inc...937 464-3029
3065 County Road 150 Belle Center (43310) *(G-1096)*

Highway Safety Corp..740 387-6991
473 W Fairground St Marion (43302) *(G-8972)*

HIGHWAY SAFETY CORP., Marion *Also Called: Highway Safety Corp (G-8972)*

Hii Mission Technologies Corp.............................937 426-3421
1430 Oak Ct Beavercreek (45430) *(G-992)*

Hikma Labs Inc...614 276-4000
1900 Arlingate Ln Columbus (43228) *(G-4984)*

Hikma Labs Inc (DH)..614 276-4000
1809 Wilson Rd Columbus (43216) *(G-4985)*

Hikma Pharmaceuticals, Columbus *Also Called: West-Ward Columbus Inc (G-5363)*

Hikma Pharmaceuticals USA Inc.........................732 542-1191
300 Northfield Rd Bedford (44146) *(G-1035)*

Hikma Pharmaceuticals USA Inc.........................614 276-4000
1809 Wilson Rd Columbus (43228) *(G-4986)*

Hikma Pharmaceuticals USA Inc.........................732 542-1191
2130 Rohr Rd Lockbourne (43137) *(G-8490)*

Hikma Specialty USA Inc......................................856 489-2110
1900 Arlingate Ln Columbus (43228) *(G-4987)*

Hildreth Mfg LLC...740 375-5832
1657 Cascade Dr Marion (43302) *(G-8973)*

Hill and Griffith Co, Cincinnati *Also Called: H&G Legacy Co (G-2701)*

Hill Bryce Concrete, Springfield *Also Called: Dearth Resources Inc (G-12298)*

Hill John...419 727-8666
3019 E Manhattan Blvd Toledo (43611) *(G-12993)*

Hill Manufacturing Inc..419 335-5006
318 W Chestnut St Wauseon (43567) *(G-13851)*

Hill Sign Company Inc...614 367-9227
4555 Groves Rd Ste 1 Columbus (43232) *(G-4988)*

Hillman Precision Inc..419 289-1557
462 E 9th St Ste 1 Ashland (44805) *(G-540)*

Hillside Pallet Ltd..440 272-5425
8552 Cox Rd Windsor (44099) *(G-14602)*

Hillside Winery...419 456-3434
221 Main St Gilboa (45875) *(G-7261)*

Hilltop Basic Resources Inc................................937 795-2020
8030 Rte 52 Us Aberdeen (45101) *(G-1)*

Hilltop Basic Resources Inc................................513 242-8400
900 Kieley Pl Cincinnati (45217) *(G-2722)*

Hilltop Basic Resources Inc................................513 621-1500
511 W Water St Cincinnati (45202) *(G-2723)*

Hilltop Basic Resources Inc................................937 859-3616
4710 Soldiers Home W Carrollton Rd Miamisburg (45342) *(G-9699)*

Hilltop Basic Resources Inc................................937 882-6357
1665 Enon Rd Springfield (45502) *(G-12322)*

2025 Harris Ohio
Industrial Directory

(G-0000) Company's Geographic Section entry number

Hilltop Big Bend Quarry LLC..513 651-5000
1 W 4th St Ste 1100 Cincinnati (45202) *(G-2724)*

Hilltop Cmpnies St Brnard Rdym, Cincinnati *Also Called: Hilltop Basic Resources Inc*
(G-2722)

Hilltop Concrete, Cincinnati *Also Called: Hilltop Basic Resources Inc (G-2723)*

Hilltop Energy Inc...330 859-2108
6978 Lindentree Rd Ne Mineral City (44656) *(G-10028)*

Hilltop Golf Course, Manchester *Also Called: Hilltop Recreation Inc (G-8754)*

Hilltop Printing..419 782-9898
1815 Baltimore St Defiance (43512) *(G-6110)*

Hilltop Recreation Inc...937 549-2904
1649 Brown Hill Rd Manchester (45144) *(G-8754)*

Hinchcliff Products, Strongsville *Also Called: Dedicated Industries Inc (G-12553)*

Hinckley Wood Products Ltd...330 220-9999
1545 W 130th St Hinckley (44233) *(G-7732)*

Hine Racing Equipment, Kinsman *Also Called: R E H Inc (G-8142)*

Hines Specialty Vehicle Group, New Philadelphia *Also Called: Kimble Mixer Company*
(G-10453)

Hinkle Fine Foods Inc...937 836-3665
4800 Wadsworth Rd Dayton (45414) *(G-5810)*

Hinkle Manufacturing, Perrysburg *Also Called: Orbis Corporation (G-11251)*

Hinkle Manufacturing Inc...419 666-5550
348 5th St Perrysburg (43551) *(G-11229)*

Hinkley Lighting Inc (PA)...440 653-5500
33000 Pin Oak Pkwy Avon Lake (44012) *(G-760)*

Hipsy LLC..513 403-5333
4951 Dixie Hwy Fairfield (45014) *(G-6740)*

Hirt Publishing Co Inc...419 946-3010
245 Neal Ave Ste A Mount Gilead (43338) *(G-10210)*

Hirzel Canning Company (PA)...419 693-0531
411 Lemoyne Rd Northwood (43619) *(G-10803)*

Hirzel Canning Company...419 523-3225
325 E Williamstown Rd Ottawa (45875) *(G-11034)*

Hirzel Canning Company...419 287-3288
115 Columbus St Pemberville (43450) *(G-11175)*

Hirzel Farms Inc...419 837-2710
20790 Bradner Rd Luckey (43443) *(G-8670)*

Hit Trophy Inc..419 445-5356
4989 State Route 66 Archbold (43502) *(G-498)*

Hitachi Astemo Americas Inc..937 783-4961
960 Cherry St Blanchester (45107) *(G-1236)*

Hitachi Astemo Americas Inc..419 425-1259
1901 Industrial Dr Findlay (45840) *(G-6880)*

Hitachi Astemo Americas Inc..740 965-1133
707 W Cherry St Sunbury (43074) *(G-12666)*

Hitachi Automation Ohio Inc...937 753-1148
2000 Industrial Ct Covington (45318) *(G-5494)*

Hitch-Hiker Mfg Inc..330 542-3052
10065 Rapp Rd New Middletown (44442) *(G-10424)*

Hite Parts Exchange Inc...614 272-5115
933 E Main St Chillicothe (45601) *(G-2258)*

Hitech Shapes & Designs, Cincinnati *Also Called: Seilkop Industries Inc (G-3076)*

Hitti Enterprises Inc...440 243-4100
6427 Eastland Rd Cleveland (44142) *(G-3831)*

HJ Heinz Company LP (DH)..330 837-8331
1301 Oberlin Ave Sw Massillon (44647) *(G-9202)*

Hj Systems Inc...614 351-9777
230 N Central Ave Columbus (43222) *(G-4989)*

HK Cooperative Inc...419 626-2551
4413 W Bogart Rd Sandusky (44870) *(G-11838)*

HK Coprative Inc/J H Routh Pkg, Sandusky *Also Called: HK Cooperative Inc (G-11838)*

HK Logging & Lumber Ltd..440 632-1997
16465 Farley Rd Middlefield (44062) *(G-9801)*

Hkm Drect Mkt Cmmnications Inc (PA).............................800 860-4456
5501 Cass Ave Cleveland (44102) *(G-3832)*

Hkm Drect Mkt Cmmnications Inc...................................440 934-3060
2931 Abbe Rd Sheffield Village (44054) *(G-11959)*

Hkm Drect Mkt Cmmnications Inc...................................330 395-9538
387 Chestnut Ave Ne Warren (44483) *(G-13771)*

Hlsigns...513 703-6363
817 Ridgeway Ave Cincinnati (45229) *(G-2725)*

Hmb Information Sys Developers, Westerville *Also Called: Harris Mackessy & Brennan Inc*
(G-14212)

Hmi Industries Inc (PA)..440 846-7800
1 American Rd Ste 1250 Brooklyn (44144) *(G-1522)*

HMS Industries, Westlake *Also Called: HMS Industries LLC (G-14306)*

HMS Industries LLC..440 899-0001
27995 Ranney Pkwy Westlake (44145) *(G-14306)*

Hmt Inc...440 599-7005
360 Commerce St Conneaut (44030) *(G-5404)*

Hobart, Hillsboro *Also Called: ITW Food Equipment Group LLC (G-7719)*

Hobart, Troy *Also Called: Hobart LLC (G-13226)*

Hobart, Troy *Also Called: ITW Food Equipment Group LLC (G-13231)*

Hobart Brothers LLC...937 332-5953
8585 Industry Park Dr Piqua (45356) *(G-11354)*

Hobart Brothers LLC (HQ)...937 332-5439
101 Trade Sq E Troy (45373) *(G-13222)*

Hobart Brothers LLC...937 332-5023
1260 Brukner Dr Troy (45373) *(G-13223)*

Hobart Cabinet Company...937 335-4666
1100 Wayne St Ste 1 Troy (45373) *(G-13224)*

Hobart LLC..937 332-2797
8515 Industry Park Dr Piqua (45356) *(G-11355)*

Hobart LLC..937 332-3000
401 S Market St Troy (45373) *(G-13225)*

Hobart LLC (DH)..937 332-3000
701 S Ridge Ave Troy (45373) *(G-13226)*

Hobart Sales & Service, Akron *Also Called: Harry C Lobalzo & Sons Inc (G-172)*

Hochstetler Milling LLC...419 368-0004
552 State Route 95 Loudonville (44842) *(G-8591)*

Hocker Tool and Die Inc...937 274-3443
5161 Webster St Dayton (45414) *(G-5811)*

Hocking Hills Hardwoods, Laurelville *Also Called: T & D Thompson Inc (G-8238)*

Hocking Hlls Enrgy Well Svcs L......................................740 385-6690
32919 Logan Horns Mill Rd Logan (43138) *(G-8515)*

Hocking Valley Concrete Inc...740 592-5335
748 W Union St Athens (45701) *(G-642)*

Hocking Valley Concrete Inc (PA)....................................740 385-2165
35255 Hocking Dr Logan (43138) *(G-8516)*

Hocking Valley Concrete Inc...740 342-1948
1500 Commerce Dr New Lexington (43764) *(G-10402)*

Hofacker Prcsion Machining LLC......................................937 832-7712
7560 Jacks Ln Clayton (45315) *(G-3273)*

Hoffman Meat Processing...419 864-3994
157 S 4th St Cardington (43315) *(G-2054)*

Hofmanns Lures Inc..937 684-0338
3937 Kilbourn Rd Arcanum (45304) *(G-484)*

Hog Slat Incorporated...937 968-3090
200 N Grandview St Union City (45390) *(G-13415)*

Hoge Brush, New Knoxville *Also Called: Hoge Lumber Company (G-10398)*

Hoge Lumber Company (PA)...419 753-2263
701 S Main St State New Knoxville (45871) *(G-10398)*

Hoist Equipment Co Inc (PA)..440 232-0300
26161 Cannon Rd Bedford Heights (44146) *(G-1078)*

Hoistech LLC...440 327-5379
32960 Fern Tree Ln North Ridgeville (44039) *(G-10734)*

Holcim (us) Inc...216 781-9330
2500 Elm St Cleveland (44113) *(G-3833)*

Holcim (us) Inc...419 399-4861
11435 Road 176 Paulding (45879) *(G-11156)*

Holding Company, Olmsted Twp *Also Called: Jones Industries LLC (G-10946)*

Holdren Brothers Inc...937 465-7050
301 Runkle St West Liberty (43357) *(G-14175)*

Holdsworth Industrial Fabg LLC......................................330 874-3945
10407 Welton Rd Ne Bolivar (44612) *(G-1384)*

Holgate Metal Fab Inc...419 599-2000
555 Independence Dr Napoleon (43545) *(G-10285)*

Holistic Botanicals, Bellville *Also Called: Natural Optons Armatherapy LLC (G-1140)*

Holistic Foods Herbs and Books, Columbus *Also Called: B & A Holistic Fd & Herbs LLC*
(G-4738)

Hollaender Manufacturing Co..513 772-8800
10285 Wayne Ave Cincinnati (45215) *(G-2726)*

A
L
P
H
A
B
E
T
I
C

Holland Assocts LLC DBA Archou................... 513 891-0006
316 W 4th St Ste 201 Cincinnati (45202) *(G-2727)*

Holland Engineering Co, Toledo *Also Called: Holland Engraving Company (G-12994)*

Holland Engraving Company........................ 419 865-2765
7340 Dorr St Toledo (43615) *(G-12994)*

Holland Grills Distributing, Spencerville *Also Called: S I Distributing Inc (G-12240)*

Holloway Sportswear Inc (DH).....................937 497-7575
2633 Campbell Rd Sidney (45365) *(G-12023)*

Holly Robakowski.................................. 440 854-9317
641 E 185th St Cleveland (44119) *(G-3834)*

Hollywood Dance Jams............................. 419 234-0746
8402 Hoaglin Center Rd Van Wert (45891) *(G-13537)*

Hollywood Imprints LLC........................... 614 501-6040
1000 Morrison Rd Ste D Gahanna (43230) *(G-7160)*

Holmco Division, Winesburg *Also Called: Robin Industries Inc (G-14608)*

Holmes By-Products Co Inc........................ 330 893-2322
3175 Township Road 411 Millersburg (44654) *(G-9985)*

Holmes Cheese Co................................. 330 674-6451
9444 State Route 39 Millersburg (44654) *(G-9986)*

Holmes County Gis, Millersburg *Also Called: County of Holmes (G-9978)*

Holmes County Hub Inc............................ 330 674-1811
6 W Jackson St Ste C Millersburg (44654) *(G-9987)*

Holmes Custom Moulding Ltd...................... 330 893-3598
5039 County Road 120 Millersburg (44654) *(G-9988)*

Holmes Limestone Co (PA).........................330 893-2721
4255 State Rte 39 Berlin (44610) *(G-1198)*

Holmes Lumber & Bldg Ctr Inc.................... 330 479-8314
1532 Perry Dr Sw Canton (44710) *(G-1912)*

Holmes Lumber & Bldg Ctr Inc (PA).............. 330 674-9060
6139 S R 39 Millersburg (44654) *(G-9989)*

Holmes Lumber & Supply, Millersburg *Also Called: Holmes Lumber & Bldg Ctr Inc (G-9989)*

Holmes Made Foods LLC............................ 216 618-5043
21315 Fairmount Blvd Cleveland (44118) *(G-3835)*

Holmes Manufacturing............................. 330 231-6327
6775 County Road 624 Millersburg (44654) *(G-9990)*

Holmes Panel LLC................................. 330 897-5040
3052 State Route 557 Baltic (43804) *(G-779)*

Holmes Printing, Springfield *Also Called: Holmes W & Sons Printing (G-12323)*

Holmes Redimix Inc............................... 330 674-0865
7571 State Route 83 Holmesville (44633) *(G-7797)*

Holmes Stair Parts Ltd........................... 330 279-2797
8614 Township Road 561 Holmesville (44633) *(G-7798)*

Holmes Supply Corp............................... 330 279-2634
7571 State Route 83 Holmesville (44633) *(G-7799)*

Holmes W & Sons Printing......................... 937 325-1509
401 E Columbia St Springfield (45503) *(G-12323)*

Holmes Wheel Shop Inc............................ 330 279-2891
7969 County Road 189 Holmesville (44633) *(G-7800)*

Holmview Welding LLC............................. 330 359-5315
4041 Township Road 606 Fredericksburg (44627) *(G-7064)*

Holophane, Granville *Also Called: Holophane Corporation (G-7316)*

Holophane Corporation (HQ).......................866 759-1577
3825 Columbus Rd Bldg A Granville (43023) *(G-7316)*

Holophane Corporation............................ 740 349-4194
515 Mckinley Ave Newark (43055) *(G-10506)*

Holtgreven Scale & Elec Corp..................... 419 422-4779
420 E Lincoln St Findlay (45840) *(G-6881)*

Holthaus Lackner Signs, Cincinnati *Also Called: Gus Holthaus Signs Inc (G-2697)*

Homan Metals LLC................................. 513 721-5010
1253 Knowlton St Cincinnati (45223) *(G-2728)*

Hombre Capital Inc............................... 440 838-5335
5945 W Snowville Rd Brecksville (44141) *(G-1470)*

Home Bakery...................................... 419 678-3018
109 W Main St Coldwater (45828) *(G-4578)*

Home City Ice Company............................ 440 439-5001
20282 Hannan Pkwy Bedford (44146) *(G-1036)*

Home City Ice Company............................ 513 851-4040
11920 Kemper Springs Dr Cincinnati (45240) *(G-2729)*

Home City Ice Company............................ 937 461-6028
1020 Gateway Dr Dayton (45404) *(G-5812)*

Home City Ice Company............................ 419 562-4953
150 Johnson Dr Delaware (43015) *(G-6157)*

Home City Ice Company............................ 614 836-2877
4505 S Hamilton Rd Groveport (43125) *(G-7438)*

Home City Ice Company............................ 513 353-9346
5709 State Rte 128 Harrison (45030) *(G-7555)*

Home Idea Center Inc............................. 419 375-4951
1100 Commerce St Fort Recovery (45846) *(G-6966)*

Home Stor & Off Solutions Inc.................... 216 362-4660
5305 Commerce Pkwy W Cleveland (44130) *(G-3836)*

Homecare Mattress Inc............................ 937 746-2556
303 Conover Dr Franklin (45005) *(G-7027)*

Hometown Ticketing Inc........................... 866 488-4849
4305 W Dublin Granville Rd Dublin (43017) *(G-6304)*

Homeworth Fabrication Mch Inc.................... 330 525-5459
23094 Georgetown Rd Homeworth (44634) *(G-7805)*

Homeworth Sales Service Div, Homeworth *Also Called: Ohio Drill & Tool Co (G-7806)*

Honda Dev & Mfg Amer LLC (DH)....................937 642-5000
24000 Honda Pkwy Marysville (43040) *(G-9026)*

Honda Dev & Mfg Amer LLC......................... 937 642-5000
25000 Honda Pkwy Marysville (43040) *(G-9027)*

Honda Dev & Mfg Amer LLC......................... 937 644-0724
19900 State Route 739 Marysville (43040) *(G-9028)*

Honda Dev & Mfg Amer LLC......................... 937 843-5555
6964 State Route 235 N Russells Point (43348) *(G-11667)*

Honda Engineering N Amer Inc, Marysville *Also Called: Honda Engineering North America LLC (G-9029)*

Honda Engineering North America LLC.............. 937 642-5000
24000 Honda Pkwy Marysville (43040) *(G-9029)*

Honda Support Office, Marysville *Also Called: Honda Dev & Mfg Amer LLC (G-9028)*

Honda Transmission Manufacturi.................. 937 843-5555
25000 Honda Pkwy Marysville (43040) *(G-9030)*

Honda Transmission Manufacturing of America Inc....... 937 843-5555
6964 State Route 235 N Russells Point (43348) *(G-11668)*

Hones Harbor House Gifts......................... 216 334-9836
720 E 6th St Ashtabula (44004) *(G-595)*

Honey Cell Inc Mid West.......................... 513 360-0280
6480 Hamilton Lebanon Rd Monroe (45044) *(G-10108)*

Honeybaked, Holland *Also Called: Honeybaked Foods Inc (G-7767)*

Honeybaked Foods Inc............................. 567 703-0002
6145 Merger Dr Holland (43528) *(G-7767)*

Honeybaked Ham Company (PA)......................513 583-9700
11935 Mason Montgomery Rd Ste 200 Cincinnati (45249) *(G-2730)*

Honeycomb Midwest................................ 513 360-0280
6480 Hamilton Lebanon Rd Monroe (45044) *(G-10109)*

Honeymoon Paper Products Inc..................... 513 755-7200
7100 Dixie Hwy Fairfield (45014) *(G-6741)*

Honeywell, Brookpark *Also Called: Honeywell International Inc (G-1552)*

Honeywell, Columbus *Also Called: Honeywell International Inc (G-4990)*

Honeywell, Elyria *Also Called: Honeywell International Inc (G-6542)*

Honeywell, Lancaster *Also Called: Diamond Electronics Inc (G-8196)*

Honeywell, Urbana *Also Called: Grimes Aerospace Company (G-13462)*

Honeywell, Urbana *Also Called: Grimes Aerospace Company (G-13464)*

Honeywell Authorized Dealer, Anna *Also Called: Chilltex LLC (G-460)*

Honeywell Authorized Dealer, Cincinnati *Also Called: Cincinnati Air Conditioning Co (G-2468)*

Honeywell Authorized Dealer, Cincinnati *Also Called: Wine Cellar Innovations LLC (G-3227)*

Honeywell Authorized Dealer, Sandusky *Also Called: Gundlach Sheet Metal Works Inc (G-11837)*

Honeywell First Responder Pdts, Dayton *Also Called: Morning Pride Mfg LLC (G-5894)*

Honeywell Intelligrated, Mason *Also Called: Intelligrated Systems Inc (G-9113)*

Honeywell International I......................... 513 282-5519
7901 Innovation Way Mason (45040) *(G-9109)*

Honeywell International Inc....................... 216 459-6048
2100 Apollo Dr Brookpark (44142) *(G-1552)*

Honeywell International Inc....................... 302 327-8920
2080 Arlingate Ln Columbus (43228) *(G-4990)*

Honeywell International Inc....................... 440 329-9000
Elyria (44036) *(G-6542)*

Honeywell International Inc....................... 937 484-2000
550 State Route 55 Urbana (43078) *(G-13466)*

Honeywell Lebow Products......................... 614 850-5000
2080 Arlingate Ln Columbus (43228) *(G-4991)*

(G-0000) Company's Geographic Section entry number

Honeywell Lightning & Elec, Urbana *Also Called: Grimes Aerospace Company (G-13463)*

Honeywell Senfopec, Columbus *Also Called: Honeywell Lebow Products (G-4991)*

Honeywell Smart Energy..440 415-1606
436 N Eagle St Geneva (44041) *(G-7240)*

Honeywell Smart Energy, Geneva *Also Called: Elster Perfection Corporation (G-7236)*

Hood Packaging Corporation.................................937 382-6681
1961 Rombach Ave Wilmington (45177) *(G-14584)*

Hoover & Wells Inc...419 691-9220
2011 Seaman St Toledo (43605) *(G-12995)*

Hop Munitions, Ashland *Also Called: Suppressor Co LLC (G-577)*

Hope Holdings Inc...330 674-7015
1 Door Dr Mount Hope (44660) *(G-10214)*

Hope Timber, Newark *Also Called: Hope Timber Pallet Recycl LLC (G-10509)*

Hope Timber & Marketing Group (PA).....................740 344-1788
141 Union St Newark (43055) *(G-10507)*

Hope Timber Mulch LLC......................................740 344-1788
141 Union St Newark (43055) *(G-10508)*

Hope Timber Pallet Recycl LLC............................740 344-1788
141 Union St Newark (43055) *(G-10509)*

Hopedale Fractionation Fcilty, Jewett *Also Called: Markwest Energy Partners LP (G-7989)*

Hopewell Oil and Gas, Columbus *Also Called: Zane Petroleum Inc (G-5379)*

Hoppel Fabrication Spc Inc.................................330 823-5700
9481 Columbus Rd Ne Ste 1 Louisville (44641) *(G-8604)*

Horizon Global Corporation (DH)..........................734 656-3000
127 Public Sq Ste 5300 Cleveland (44114) *(G-3837)*

Horizon Industries Corporation.............................937 323-0801
1801 W Columbia St Springfield (45504) *(G-12324)*

Horizon Metals Inc..440 235-3338
8059 Lewis Rd Ste 102 Berea (44017) *(G-1175)*

Horizon Ohio Publications Inc (HQ).......................419 394-7414
102 E Spring St Saint Marys (45885) *(G-11738)*

Horizon Ohio Publications Inc..............................419 738-2128
520 Industrial Dr Wapakoneta (45895) *(G-13715)*

Horizons Incorporated (PA).................................216 475-0555
18531 S Miles Rd Cleveland (44128) *(G-3838)*

Hormel, Cincinnati *Also Called: Hormel Foods Corp Svcs LLC (G-2731)*

Hormel Foods Corp Svcs LLC...............................513 563-0211
4055 Executive Park Dr Ste 300 Cincinnati (45241) *(G-2731)*

Hornell Brewing Co Inc.......................................516 812-0384
635 W 7th St Cincinnati (45203) *(G-2732)*

Horner Industrial Services Inc..............................937 390-6667
5330 Prosperity Dr Springfield (45502) *(G-12325)*

Horner Industrial Services Inc..............................513 874-8722
4721 Interstate Dr West Chester (45246) *(G-14125)*

Horrorhound Ltd..513 239-7263
1706 Republic St Cincinnati (45202) *(G-2733)*

Horsburgh & Scott Co (PA).................................216 431-3900
5114 Hamilton Ave Cleveland (44114) *(G-3839)*

Horseshoe Express Inc.......................................330 692-1209
8045 Camden Way Canfield (44406) *(G-1810)*

Horst Packing Inc...330 482-2997
3535 Renkenberger Rd Columbiana (44408) *(G-4618)*

Horton Emergency Vehicles, Grove City *Also Called: Halcore Group Inc (G-7389)*

Horwitz & Pintis Co...419 666-2220
1604 Tracy St Toledo (43605) *(G-12996)*

Hose Master LLC (PA).......................................216 481-2020
1233 E 222nd St Cleveland (44117) *(G-3840)*

Hostar International Inc (PA)................................440 564-5362
31005 Solon Rd Solon (44139) *(G-12123)*

Hoster Graphics Company Inc..............................614 299-9770
2580 Westbelt Dr Columbus (43228) *(G-4992)*

Hostess, Orrville *Also Called: Hostess Brands Inc (G-10984)*

Hostess Brands Inc (HQ)....................................816 701-4600
1 Strawberry Ln Orrville (44667) *(G-10984)*

Hostess Brands LLC (DH)...................................816 701-4600
1 Strawberry Ln Orrville (44667) *(G-10985)*

Hot Cards.com, Cleveland *Also Called: Fx Digital Media Inc (G-3747)*

HOT Graphic Services Inc...................................419 242-7000
2595 Tracy Rd Northwood (43619) *(G-10804)*

Hotcards of Akron, Akron *Also Called: Dlh Enterprises LLC (G-124)*

House of 10000 Picture Frames............................937 254-5541
2210 Wilmington Pike Dayton (45420) *(G-5813)*

House of Awards Inc..419 422-7877
419 N Main St Findlay (45840) *(G-6882)*

House of Plastics, Cleveland *Also Called: HP Manufacturing Company Inc (G-3841)*

Housing & Emrgncy Lgstcs Plnnr...........................209 201-7511
36905 State Route 30 Lisbon (44432) *(G-8470)*

Houston Machine Products Inc.............................937 322-8022
1065 W Leffel Ln Springfield (45506) *(G-12326)*

Howard B Claflin Co..330 928-1704
5270 Hudson Dr Hudson (44236) *(G-7844)*

Howard Industries Inc..614 444-9900
1840 Progress Ave Columbus (43207) *(G-4993)*

Howden North America, Fairfield *Also Called: Howden North America Inc (G-6742)*

Howden North America Inc..................................513 874-2400
2933 Symmes Rd Fairfield (45014) *(G-6742)*

Howden North America Inc..................................330 721-7374
935 Heritage Dr Medina (44256) *(G-9409)*

Howden North America Inc..................................330 867-8540
411 Independence Dr Medina (44256) *(G-9410)*

Howden USA Company..513 874-2400
2933 Symmes Rd Fairfield (45014) *(G-6743)*

Howland Machine Corp.......................................330 544-4029
947 Summit Ave Niles (44446) *(G-10589)*

Howland Printing Inc..330 637-8255
3117 Niles Cortland Rd Ne Cortland (44410) *(G-5445)*

Howmedica Osteonics Corp.................................937 291-3900
474 Windsor Park Dr Dayton (45459) *(G-5814)*

Howmet Aerospace Inc.......................................330 848-4000
842 Norton Ave Barberton (44203) *(G-811)*

Howmet Aerospace Inc.......................................216 641-3600
1600 Harvard Ave Newburgh Heights (44105) *(G-10543)*

Howmet Aerospace Inc.......................................330 544-7633
1000 Warren Ave Niles (44446) *(G-10590)*

Howmet Aerospace Inc.......................................330 222-1501
32585 N Price Rd Salem (44460) *(G-11786)*

HOWMET AEROSPACE INC, Barberton *Also Called: Howmet Aerospace Inc (G-811)*

HOWMET AEROSPACE INC, Newburgh Heights *Also Called: Howmet Aerospace Inc (G-10543)*

Howmet Aerospace Inc, Salem *Also Called: Howmet Aerospace Inc (G-11786)*

Howmet Aluminum Casting Inc (HQ).......................216 641-4340
1600 Harvard Ave Newburgh Heights (44105) *(G-10544)*

HP Enterprise Inc...800 232-7950
10008 State Route 43 Streetsboro (44241) *(G-12503)*

HP Industries Inc...419 478-0695
400 E State Line Rd Toledo (43612) *(G-12997)*

HP Liquidating Inc..614 861-1791
725 Reynoldsburg New Albany Rd Blacklick (43004) *(G-1223)*

HP Manufacturing Company Inc (PA).......................216 361-6500
3705 Carnegie Ave Cleveland (44115) *(G-3841)*

Hp2g LLC..419 906-1525
403 N Hill St Napoleon (43545) *(G-10286)*

Hpc Holdings LLC (HQ)......................................330 666-3751
3637 Ridgewood Rd Fairlawn (44333) *(G-6804)*

HPM North America Corp, Iberia *Also Called: Yizumi-HPM Corporation (G-7885)*

Hr Machine llc..937 222-7644
1300 Stanley Ave Dayton (45404) *(G-5815)*

Hrh Door Corp...513 674-9300
2136 Stapleton Ct Cincinnati (45240) *(G-2734)*

Hs Services, Westlake *Also Called: Imcd Us LLC (G-14310)*

HSP Bedding Solutions LLC.................................440 437-4425
243 Staley Rd Orwell (44076) *(G-11021)*

Hst, Cincinnati *Also Called: Hermetic Seal Technology Inc (G-2719)*

Htci Co..937 845-1204
12170 Milton Carlisle Rd New Carlisle (45344) *(G-10372)*

Htec Systems Inc...937 438-3010
561 Congress Park Dr Dayton (45459) *(G-5816)*

Hubbard Company...419 784-4455
612 Clinton St Defiance (43512) *(G-6111)*

Hubbard Feeds, Botkins *Also Called: Ridley USA Inc (G-1398)*

Hubbard Publishing Co..937 592-3060
127 E Chillicothe Ave Bellefontaine (43311) *(G-1110)*

Hubbell Machine Tooling Inc.............................. 216 524-1797
7507 Exchange St Cleveland (44125) *(G-3842)*

Hudco Manufacturing Inc................................... 440 951-4040
38250 Western Pkwy Willoughby (44094) *(G-14465)*

Hudson Extrusions Inc...................................... 330 653-6015
1255 Norton Rd Hudson (44236) *(G-7845)*

Hudson Feeds, Okolona *Also Called: Republic Mills Inc (G-10932)*

Hudson Hines Hill Company............................... 330 562-1970
1818 Miller Pkwy Streetsboro (44241) *(G-12504)*

Hudson Leather Ltd... 419 485-8531
14700 State Route 15 Pioneer (43554) *(G-11321)*

Hudson Leather Co, Pioneer *Also Called: Hudson Leather Ltd (G-11321)*

Hudson Supply Company Inc............................. 216 518-3000
4500 Lee Rd Ste 120 Cleveland (44128) *(G-3843)*

Hudson Workwear, Brecksville *Also Called: Rbr Enterprises LLC (G-1480)*

Huffy Sports Washington Inc.............................. 937 865-2800
225 Byers Rd Miamisburg (45342) *(G-9700)*

Hughes Corporation (PA)................................... 440 238-2550
16900 Foltz Pkwy Strongsville (44149) *(G-12564)*

Hughes-Peters, Huber Heights *Also Called: Mjo Industries Inc (G-7822)*

Hughey & Phillips LLC...................................... 937 652-3500
240 W Twain Ave Urbana (43078) *(G-13467)*

Hugo Bosca Company Inc (PA).......................... 937 323-5523
1905 W Jefferson St Springfield (45506) *(G-12327)*

Hugo Sand Company.. 216 570-1212
7055 State Route 43 Kent (44240) *(G-8036)*

Huhtamaki Inc... 513 201-1525
1985 James E Sauls Sr Dr Batavia (45103) *(G-867)*

Huhtamaki Inc... 937 746-9700
4000 Commerce Center Dr Franklin (45005) *(G-7028)*

Hull Builders Supply, Sandusky *Also Called: Hull Ready Mix Concrete Inc (G-11839)*

Hull Ready Mix Concrete Inc.............................. 419 625-8070
4419 Tiffin Ave Sandusky (44870) *(G-11839)*

Humongous Fan, Cleveland *Also Called: Humongous Holdings Llc (G-3844)*

Humongous Holdings Llc.................................. 216 663-8830
23103 Miles Rd Cleveland (44128) *(G-3844)*

Humphrey Popcorn Company (PA)...................... 216 662-6629
11606 Pearl Rd Strongsville (44136) *(G-12565)*

Humtown Pattern Company................................ 330 482-5555
44708 Columbiana Waterford Rd Columbiana (44408) *(G-4619)*

Humtown Products, Columbiana *Also Called: Humtown Pattern Company (G-4619)*

Hunger Hydraulics CC Ltd................................. 419 666-4510
63 Dixie Hwy Ste 1 Rossford (43460) *(G-11657)*

Hunger Industrial Complex, Rossford *Also Called: Hunger Hydraulics CC Ltd (G-11657)*

Hunkar Technologies Inc (PA)........................... 513 272-1010
2368 Victory Pkwy Ste 210 Cincinnati (45206) *(G-2735)*

Hunt Imaging LLC (PA)..................................... 440 826-0433
210 Sheldon Rd Berea (44017) *(G-1176)*

Hunt Valve Actuator LLC.................................. 330 337-9535
1913 E State St Salem (44460) *(G-11787)*

Hunt Valve Company Inc (DH)............................ 330 337-9535
1913 E State St Salem (44460) *(G-11788)*

Hunter Defense Tech Inc................................... 513 943-7880
1032 Seabrook Way Cincinnati (45245) *(G-2307)*

Hunter Defense Tech Inc (PA)............................ 216 438-6111
30500 Aurora Rd Ste 100 Solon (44139) *(G-12124)*

Hunter Environmental Corp................................ 440 248-6111
30525 Aurora Rd Solon (44139) *(G-12125)*

Hunter Hydraulics Inc....................................... 330 455-3983
2512 Columbus Rd Ne Canton (44705) *(G-1913)*

Hunter Manufacturing Company, Solon *Also Called: Hunter Environmental Corp (G-12125)*

Hunters Manufacturing Co Inc (PA)..................... 330 628-9245
1325 Waterloo Rd Mogadore (44260) *(G-10077)*

Huntsman Advnced Mtls Amrcas L...................... 330 374-2424
240 W Emerling Ave Akron (44301) *(G-177)*

Huntsman Advnced Mtls Amrcas L...................... 866 800-2436
240 W Emerling Ave Akron (44301) *(G-178)*

Huntsman Corporation....................................... 330 374-2418
240 W Emerling Ave Akron (44301) *(G-179)*

Huron Cement Products Company (PA).................. 419 433-4161
617 Main St Huron (44839) *(G-7874)*

Husky Lima Refinery... 419 226-2300
1150 S Metcalf St Lima (45804) *(G-8416)*

Husky Marketing and Supply Co.......................... 419 993-8000
1150 S Metcalf St Lima (45804) *(G-8417)*

Husqvarna Construction Pdts, Cleveland *Also Called: Husqvarna US Holding Inc (G-3845)*

Husqvarna US Holding Inc (HQ)........................ 216 898-1800
20445 Emerald Pkwy Ste 205 Cleveland (44135) *(G-3845)*

Huth Ready Mix & Supply Co.............................. 330 833-4191
501 5th St Nw Massillon (44647) *(G-9203)*

Huth Ready-Mix & Supply Co, Massillon *Also Called: Huth Ready Mix & Supply Co (G-9203)*

Hutnik Company.. 330 336-9700
350 State St Ste 5 Wadsworth (44281) *(G-13643)*

Hutter Racing Engines Ltd................................. 440 285-2175
12550 Gar Hwy Chardon (44024) *(G-2208)*

Hvac, Akron *Also Called: Lowry Furnace Co Inc (G-211)*

Hvac Inc.. 330 343-5511
133 W 3rd St Dover (44622) *(G-6247)*

Hvac Mech Cntrcto Plbg Ppfttin, Cincinnati *Also Called: Jfdb Ltd (G-2766)*

Hvfi, Massillon *Also Called: Hendricks Vacuum Forming Inc (G-9201)*

Hy-Blast Inc... 513 424-0704
70 Enterprise Dr Middletown (45044) *(G-9864)*

Hy-Grade Corporation (PA)................................ 216 341-7711
3993 E 93rd St Cleveland (44105) *(G-3846)*

Hy-Ko Products Company LLC............................ 330 467-7446
60 Meadow Ln Northfield (44067) *(G-10794)*

Hy-Production LLC.. 330 273-2400
6000 Grafton Rd Valley City (44280) *(G-13499)*

Hy-Tech Controls Inc.. 440 232-4040
7411 First Pl Bedford (44146) *(G-1037)*

Hycom Inc... 330 753-2330
374 5th St Nw Barberton (44203) *(G-812)*

Hydac Technology Corp..................................... 610 266-0100
4265 E Lincoln Way Unit C Wooster (44691) *(G-14649)*

Hyde Brothers Printing Co, Marietta *Also Called: Pen-Ann Corporation (G-8936)*

Hyde Park Lumber Company............................... 513 271-1500
3360 Red Bank Rd Cincinnati (45227) *(G-2736)*

Hydranamics Inc.. 419 468-3530
820 Edward St Galion (44833) *(G-7195)*

Hydranamics Div Carter Mch Co, Galion *Also Called: Hydranamics Inc (G-7195)*

Hydratech Engineered Pdts LLC.......................... 513 827-9169
10448 Chester Rd Cincinnati (45215) *(G-2737)*

Hydraulic Manifolds USA LLC............................ 973 728-1214
4540 Boyce Pkwy Stow (44224) *(G-12436)*

Hydraulic Parts Store Inc.................................. 330 364-6667
145 1st Dr Ne New Philadelphia (44663) *(G-10449)*

Hydraulic Products Inc...................................... 440 946-4575
4540 Beidler Rd Willoughby (44094) *(G-14466)*

Hydraulic Specialists Inc.................................. 740 922-3343
5655 Gundy Dr Midvale (44653) *(G-9911)*

Hydro Aluminum Fayetteville.............................. 937 492-9194
401 N Stolle Ave Sidney (45365) *(G-12024)*

Hydro Extrusion Usa LLC................................. 888 935-5759
401 N Stolle Ave Sidney (45365) *(G-12025)*

Hydro Supply Co.. 740 454-3842
3112 East Pike Zanesville (43701) *(G-15020)*

Hydro Systems Company................................... 513 271-8800
9393 Princeton Glendale Rd West Chester (45011) *(G-14014)*

Hydro Tube Enterprises Inc (PA)....................... 440 774-1022
137 Artino St Oberlin (44074) *(G-10918)*

Hydro-Aire Inc... 440 323-3211
241 Abbe Rd S Elyria (44035) *(G-6543)*

Hydro-Aire Aerospace Corp (HQ)........................ 440 323-3211
249 Abbe Rd S Elyria (44035) *(G-6544)*

Hydro-Dyne Inc.. 330 832-5076
225 Wetmore Ave Se Massillon (44646) *(G-9204)*

Hydro-Thrift Corporation.................................... 330 837-5141
1301 Sanders Ave Sw Massillon (44647) *(G-9205)*

Hydro-Vac, Wickliffe *Also Called: HI Tecmetal Group Inc (G-14378)*

Hydrodec Inc (PA)... 330 454-8202
2021 Steinway Blvd Se Canton (44707) *(G-1914)*

Hydrodec of North America LLC.......................... 330 454-8202
2021 Steinway Blvd Se Canton (44707) *(G-1915)*

Hydrofresh Ltd..567 765-1010
1571 Gressel Dr Delphos (45833) *(G-6187)*

Hydrofresh Hpp, Delphos Also Called: Hydrofresh Ltd *(G-6187)*

Hydromatic Pumps Inc.....................................419 289-1144
1101 Myers Pkwy Ashland (44805) *(G-541)*

Hydromotive Engineering Co..............................330 425-4266
9261 Ravenna Rd Bldg B1 Twinsburg (44087) *(G-13317)*

Hydrotech Inc (PA)..888 651-5712
10052 Commerce Park Dr West Chester (45246) *(G-14126)*

Hydrothrift, Massillon Also Called: Hydro-Thrift Corporation *(G-9205)*

Hygenic Acquisition Co...................................330 633-8460
1245 Home Ave Akron (44310) *(G-180)*

Hygenic Company LLC.....................................330 633-8460
1245 Home Ave Akron (44310) *(G-181)*

Hyland Machine Company.................................937 233-8600
1900 Kuntz Rd Dayton (45404) *(G-5817)*

Hyland Screw Machine Products, Dayton Also Called: Hyland Machine Company *(G-5817)*

Hyland Software Inc (HQ)................................440 788-5000
28105 Clemens Rd Westlake (44145) *(G-14307)*

Hyload Inc (DH)...330 336-6604
5020 Enterprise Pkwy Seville (44273) *(G-11917)*

Hynes Holding Company (HQ)...........................330 799-3221
3805 Hendricks Rd Youngstown (44515) *(G-14873)*

Hynes Industries, Youngstown Also Called: Hynes Holding Company *(G-14873)*

Hynes Industries Inc (PA)...............................800 321-9257
3805 Hendricks Rd Youngstown (44515) *(G-14874)*

Hype Socks LLC..855 497-3769
204 S Front St Apt 400 Columbus (43215) *(G-4994)*

Hyper Tech Research Inc.................................614 481-8050
539 Industrial Mile Rd Columbus (43228) *(G-4995)*

Hyperion, Columbus Also Called: Diamond Innovations Inc *(G-4880)*

Hyponex Corporation (DH)...............................937 644-0011
14111 Scottslawn Rd Marysville (43040) *(G-9031)*

Hyponex Corporation.....................................330 262-1300
3875 S Elyria Rd Shreve (44676) *(G-11982)*

Hyson Products, Brecksville Also Called: Barnes Group Inc *(G-1458)*

HYSTER, Cleveland Also Called: Hyster-Yale Inc *(G-3847)*

Hyster-Yale Inc (PA)......................................440 449-9600
5875 Landerbrook Dr Ste 300 Cleveland (44124) *(G-3847)*

Hytech Silicone Products Inc...........................330 297-1888
6112 Knapp Rd Ravenna (44266) *(G-11528)*

I 5S of Huron Inc...419 433-9075
356 Main St Huron (44839) *(G-7875)*

I B-Tech, Bucyrus Also Called: Imasen Bucyrus Technology Inc *(G-1683)*

I C S, Streetsboro Also Called: Interntnal Cutng Solutions Inc *(G-12506)*

I Cerco Inc..740 982-2050
410 Maple Ave Crooksville (43731) *(G-3310)*

I Cerco Inc (PA)..330 567-2145
453 W Mcconkey St Shreve (44676) *(G-11983)*

I D I, Wapakoneta Also Called: Ingredia Inc *(G-13716)*

I Dream of Cakes...937 533-6024
995 Camden Rd Eaton (45320) *(G-6455)*

I E R Industries, Macedonia Also Called: Ier Fujikura Inc *(G-8696)*

I G Brenner Inc...740 345-8845
1806 Stonewall Dr Newark (43055) *(G-10510)*

I H Schlezinger Inc.......................................614 252-1188
1041 Joyce Ave Columbus (43219) *(G-4996)*

I Jalcite Inc..216 622-5000
25 W Prospect Ave Cleveland (44115) *(G-3848)*

I L S, Cleveland Also Called: Supply Technologies LLC *(G-4351)*

I L S, Hamilton Also Called: Innovtive Lbling Solutions Inc *(G-7505)*

I P D, North Royalton Also Called: Industrial Parts Depot LLC *(G-10766)*

I P S, Rossford Also Called: Industrial Power Systems Inc *(G-11659)*

I S I, Lewis Center Also Called: Industrial Solutions Inc *(G-8336)*

I Schumann & Co, Bedford Also Called: I Schumann & Co LLC *(G-1038)*

I Schumann & Co LLC....................................440 439-2300
22500 Alexander Rd Bedford (44146) *(G-1038)*

I T Verdin Co (PA)..513 241-4010
444 Reading Rd Cincinnati (45202) *(G-2738)*

I V Miller & Sons..732 493-4040
940 Lafayette Rd Medina (44256) *(G-9411)*

I-M-A Enterprises Inc....................................330 948-3535
700 Wooster St Lodi (44254) *(G-8502)*

I.T. Plastics, Mentor Also Called: Industrial Thermoset Plas Inc *(G-9531)*

I2, Hubbard Also Called: Independence 2 LLC *(G-7811)*

Iabf Inc...614 279-4498
1890 Mckinley Ave Columbus (43222) *(G-4997)*

Ibi, Chillicothe Also Called: Ingle-Barr Inc *(G-2261)*

IBI Brake Products Inc...................................440 543-7962
16751 Hilltop Park Pl Chagrin Falls (44023) *(G-2166)*

Ibidltd-Blue Green Energy...............................909 547-5160
1456 N Summit St Toledo (43604) *(G-12998)*

Ibycorp...330 425-8226
8968 Dutton Dr Twinsburg (44087) *(G-13318)*

Ibycorp Tool & Die, Twinsburg Also Called: Ibycorp *(G-13318)*

Ic Roofing, Mason Also Called: Interstate Contractors LLC *(G-9115)*

Ic Scientific Solutions, Westlake Also Called: Iconic Labs LLC *(G-14308)*

Ic-Fluid Power Inc.......................................419 661-8811
63 Dixie Hwy Rossford (43460) *(G-11658)*

ICC, Brecksville Also Called: Integrated Chem Concepts Inc *(G-1473)*

ICC Safety Service Inc...................................614 261-4557
1070 Leona Ave Columbus (43201) *(G-4998)*

ICC Systems Inc..614 524-0299
5665 Blue Church Rd Ste 202 Sunbury (43074) *(G-12667)*

Iccnexergy, Dublin Also Called: Inventus Power (ohio) Inc *(G-6312)*

Ice Industries Inc (PA)..................................419 842-3600
3810 Herr Rd Sylvania (43560) *(G-12710)*

Ice Industries Columbus Inc...........................614 475-3853
3810 Herr Rd Sylvania (43560) *(G-12711)*

Ice Industries Deerfield, Mason Also Called: Deerfield Manufacturing Inc *(G-9093)*

Ice Industries Grenada, Sylvania Also Called: Grenada Stamping Assembly Inc *(G-12707)*

Ice Industries Ronfeldt, Toledo Also Called: Ronfeldt Manufacturing LLC *(G-13119)*

ICM Distributing Company Inc..........................234 212-3030
1755 Enterprise Pkwy Ste 200 Twinsburg (44087) *(G-13319)*

ICO Products LLC...419 867-3900
6415 Angola Rd Holland (43528) *(G-7768)*

Icomold By Fathom, Holland Also Called: ICO Products LLC *(G-7768)*

Iconic Labs LLC..216 759-4040
909 Canterbury Rd Ste G Westlake (44145) *(G-14308)*

ICP Adhesives and Sealants Inc (HQ).................330 753-4585
2775 Barber Rd Norton (44203) *(G-10823)*

Ics Electrical Services, Cincinnati Also Called: Instrmntation Ctrl Systems Inc *(G-2747)*

Ict Sales, Cincinnati Also Called: Industrial Coating Tech Inc *(G-2744)*

Icu Medical Inc...614 210-7300
5200 Upper Metro Pl Ste 200 Dublin (43017) *(G-6306)*

ID Images Inc...330 220-7300
1120 W 130th St Brunswick (44212) *(G-1597)*

ID Images LLC (PA)......................................330 220-7300
1120 W 130th St Brunswick (44212) *(G-1598)*

ID Plastech Engraving, Cincinnati Also Called: Professional Award Service *(G-3005)*

Idea Works, Sugarcreek Also Called: Middaugh Enterprises Inc *(G-12641)*

Ideal Branding, Englewood Also Called: Ideal Image Inc *(G-6615)*

Ideal Drapery Company Inc.............................330 745-9873
1024 Wooster Rd N Barberton (44203) *(G-813)*

Ideal Electric, Mansfield Also Called: Ideal Electric Power Co *(G-8804)*

Ideal Electric Power Co.................................419 522-3611
330 E 1st St Mansfield (44902) *(G-8804)*

Ideal Image Inc...937 832-1660
115 Haas Dr Englewood (45322) *(G-6615)*

Ideal Integrations LLC..................................614 786-7100
7420 Worthington Galena Rd Worthington (43085) *(G-14713)*

Identification Systems Inc.............................614 448-1741
1324 Stimmel Rd Columbus (43223) *(G-4999)*

Identiphoto Co Ltd.......................................440 306-9000
1810 Joseph Lloyd Pkwy Willoughby (44094) *(G-14467)*

Identitek Systems Inc...................................330 832-9844
1100 Industrial Ave Sw Massillon (44647) *(G-9206)*

Identity Group LLC.......................................614 337-6167
6111c Maxtown Rd Westerville (43082) *(G-14213)*

A
L
P
H
A
B
E
T
I
C

Identity Syncronizer, Perrysburg Also Called: Innerapps LLC (G-11231)

Identity Systems, Columbus Also Called: Identification Systems Inc (G-4999)

Idex Corporation.. 419 526-7222
800 N Main St Mansfield (44902) **(G-8805)**

Idialogs LLC... 937 372-2890
121 Pawleys Plantation Ct Xenia (45385) **(G-14765)**

IDM Computer Solutions, Hamilton Also Called: Ultraedit Inc (G-7535)

Idx Dayton LLC.. 937 401-3460
2875 Needmore Rd Dayton (45414) **(G-5818)**

IEC, Middleburg Heights Also Called: IEC Infrared Systems Inc (G-9771)

IEC, Middleburg Heights Also Called: IEC Infrared Systems LLC (G-9772)

IEC Infrared Systems Inc...................................... 440 234-8000
7803 Freeway Cir Middleburg Heights (44130) **(G-9771)**

IEC Infrared Systems LLC..................................... 440 234-8000
7803 Freeway Cir Middleburg Heights (44130) **(G-9772)**

Ieg Plastics LLC... 937 565-4211
223 Lock And Load Rd Bellefontaine (43311) **(G-1111)**

Ier Fujikura Inc (PA)... 330 425-7121
8271 Bavaria Dr E Macedonia (44056) **(G-8696)**

Ies Systems Inc.. 330 533-6683
464 Lisbon St Canfield (44406) **(G-1811)**

Ig Watteeuw Usa LLC.. 740 588-1722
1000 Linden Ave Zanesville (43701) **(G-15021)**

Igc Software, Reynoldsburg Also Called: Integrity Group Consulting Inc (G-11572)

Igel Technology America LLC................................. 954 739-9990
2106 Florence Ave Cincinnati (45206) **(G-2739)**

Igloo Press LLC.. 614 787-5528
39 W New England Ave Worthington (43085) **(G-14714)**

Ignio Systems LLC.. 419 708-0503
444 W Laskey Rd Ste V Toledo (43612) **(G-12999)**

Ignition Interlock, Cincinnati Also Called: 1 A Lifesafer Inc (G-2319)

Ignyte Assurance Platform.................................... 833 446-9831
714 E Monument Ave Dayton (45402) **(G-5819)**

Igw USA.. 740 588-1722
1000 Linden Ave Zanesville (43701) **(G-15022)**

Iheartcommunications Inc..................................... 419 223-2060
667 W Market St Lima (45801) **(G-8418)**

Ihi Connectors R, Mentor Also Called: International Hydraulics Inc (G-9534)

Iiot World LLC... 440 715-0564
25985 Rustic Ln Westlake (44145) **(G-14309)**

Ike Smart City.. 614 294-4898
250 N Hartford Ave Columbus (43222) **(G-5000)**

Ikiriska LLC... 614 389-8994
16 Village Pointe Dr Powell (43065) **(G-11489)**

Iko, Franklin Also Called: Iko Production Inc (G-7029)

Iko Production Inc.. 937 746-4561
1200 S Main St Franklin (45005) **(G-7029)**

Illinois Tool Works Inc.. 216 292-7161
26101 Fargo Ave Bedford (44146) **(G-1039)**

Illinois Tool Works Inc.. 513 489-7600
6600 Cornell Rd Blue Ash (45242) **(G-1286)**

Illinois Tool Works Inc.. 419 633-3236
730 E South St Bryan (43506) **(G-1644)**

Illinois Tool Works Inc.. 262 248-8277
730 E South St Bryan (43506) **(G-1645)**

Illinois Tool Works Inc.. 419 636-3161
730 E South St Bryan (43506) **(G-1646)**

Illinois Tool Works Inc.. 440 914-3100
6875 Parkland Blvd Solon (44139) **(G-12126)**

Illinois Tool Works Inc.. 937 332-2839
750 Lincoln Ave Troy (45373) **(G-13227)**

Illuminate USA LLC.. 614 598-9742
3600 Etna Pkwy Pataskala (43062) **(G-11140)**

Ilsco LLC (DH)... 513 533-6200
4701 Creek Rd Ste 110 Blue Ash (45242) **(G-1287)**

Im Greenberg Inc... 440 461-4464
5470 Mayfield Rd Cleveland (44124) **(G-3849)**

Image, Maumee Also Called: Image By J & K LLC (G-9297)

Image By J & K LLC.. 888 667-6929
1575 Henthorne Dr Maumee (43537) **(G-9297)**

Image Concepts Inc... 216 524-9000
8200 Sweet Valley Dr Ste 107 Cleveland (44125) **(G-3850)**

Image Graphics, Columbia Station Also Called: Perrons Printing Company Inc (G-4596)

Image Group Inc... 419 866-3300
1255 Corporate Dr Holland (43528) **(G-7769)**

Image Pavement Maintenance................................ 937 833-9200
425 Carr Dr Brookville (45309) **(G-1571)**

Image Print Inc.. 614 776-3985
6019 Jamesport Dr Westerville (43081) **(G-14264)**

Imagen Brands, Mason Also Called: Ebsco Industries Inc (G-9096)

Imagine Baking Buyer LLC.................................... 419 502-9000
1034 Hancock St Sandusky (44870) **(G-11840)**

Imagine Communications Corp............................... 513 459-3400
5300 Kings Island Dr Ste 101 Mason (45040) **(G-9110)**

Imagine This Renovations..................................... 330 833-6739
4220 Alabama Ave Sw Navarre (44662) **(G-10305)**

Imaging Sciences LLC.. 440 975-9640
38174 Willoughby Pkwy Willoughby (44094) **(G-14468)**

Imalux Corporation... 216 502-0755
11000 Cedar Ave Ste 250 Cleveland (44106) **(G-3851)**

Imasen Bucyrus Technology Inc............................. 419 563-9590
260 Crossroads Blvd Bucyrus (44820) **(G-1683)**

Imax Industries Inc.. 440 639-0242
117 W Walnut Ave Painesville (44077) **(G-11095)**

Imcd Us LLC (HQ).. 216 228-8900
2 Equity Way Ste 210 Westlake (44145) **(G-14310)**

Imco Carbide Tool Inc... 419 661-6313
28170 Cedar Park Blvd Perrysburg (43551) **(G-11230)**

Imco Recycling, Uhrichsville Also Called: Novelis Alr Recycling Ohio LLC (G-13404)

Imco Recycling of Indiana Inc............................... 216 910-3400
25825 Science Park Dr Ste 400 Beachwood (44122) **(G-922)**

Imds Corporate, Youngstown Also Called: Imds Corporation (G-14875)

Imds Corporation... 330 219-4299
935 Augusta Dr Youngstown (44512) **(G-14875)**

Imesco, Fredericktown Also Called: Industrial and Mar Eng Svc Co (G-7080)

Imet Corporation... 440 799-3135
13400 Glenside Rd Cleveland (44110) **(G-3852)**

Imex Bz LLC.. 786 866-8798
142 N Linden Ave Apt 502 Orrville (44667) **(G-10986)**

IMG, Cleveland Also Called: Im Greenberg Inc (G-3849)

IMH LLC... 513 800-9830
160 Easton Town Ctr Columbus (43219) **(G-5001)**

IMH LLC (PA)... 614 436-0991
7020 Huntley Rd Ste C Columbus (43229) **(G-5002)**

IMI Precision, Brookville Also Called: Norgren LLC (G-1574)

IMI Real Estate LLC.. 513 769-3666
2792 Glendale Milford Rd Cincinnati (45241) **(G-2740)**

IMI Real Estate LLC.. 513 844-8444
600 Augspurger Rd Hamilton (45011) **(G-7504)**

Iml Containers Ohio Inc....................................... 330 754-1066
2455 W Main St Alliance (44601) **(G-385)**

Impac Hi-Performance Machining........................... 419 726-7100
5515 Enterprise Blvd Toledo (43612) **(G-13000)**

Impact Armor Technologies LLC............................. 216 706-2024
17000 Saint Clair Ave Ste 106 Cleveland (44110) **(G-3853)**

Impact Cutoff Div, Maumee Also Called: Hammill Manufacturing Co (G-9295)

Impact Industries Inc.. 440 327-2360
5120 Mills Industrial Pkwy North Ridgeville (44039) **(G-10735)**

Impact Printing and Design LLC............................. 833 522-6200
4670 Groves Rd Columbus (43232) **(G-5003)**

Impact Products LLC... 419 841-2891
2840 Centennial Rd Toledo (43617) **(G-13001)**

Impact Weekly, Dayton Also Called: Dayton City Paper Group Llc (G-5723)

Imperial Adhesives... 513 351-1300
6315 Wiehe Rd Cincinnati (45237) **(G-2741)**

Imperial Conveying Systems LLC............................ 330 491-3200
4155 Martindale Rd Ne Canton (44705) **(G-1916)**

Imperial Die & Mfg Co.. 440 268-9080
22930 Royalton Rd Strongsville (44149) **(G-12566)**

Imperial Electric Company.................................... 330 734-3600
2575 Greensburg Rd North Canton (44720) **(G-10647)**

2025 Harris Ohio
Industrial Directory

(G-0000) Company's Geographic Section entry number

Imperial Family Inc... 330 927-5065
  80 Industrial St Rittman (44270) *(G-11622)*

Imperial Metal Solutions LLC............................. 216 781-4094
  2284 Scranton Rd Cleveland (44113) *(G-3854)*

Imperial Metal Spinning Co................................ 216 524-5020
  7600 Exchange St Cleveland (44125) *(G-3855)*

Imperial On-Pece Fibrgls Pools......................... 740 747-2971
  255 S Franklin St Ashley (43003) *(G-582)*

Imperial Orthodontics, Urbana *Also Called: Triage Ortho Group (G-13478)*

Imperial Pools Inc.. 513 771-1506
  12090 Best Pl Cincinnati (45241) *(G-2742)*

Imperial Stucco LLC... 614 787-5888
  Dublin (43017) *(G-6306)*

Imprint LLC... 216 233-0066
  3654 W 104th St Cleveland (44111) *(G-3856)*

Imprints.. 330 650-0467
  77 Maple Dr Hudson (44236) *(G-7846)*

Improv Electronics, Kent *Also Called: Kent Displays Inc (G-8040)*

IMT Defense, Westerville *Also Called: IMT Defense Corp (G-14214)*

IMT Defense Corp... 614 891-8812
  5386 Club Dr Westerville (43082) *(G-14214)*

In Sttches Ctr For Ltrgcal Art, Cleveland *Also Called: Strictly Stitchery Inc (G-4335)*

Inc., K.I.W.I., Twinsburg *Also Called: Kiwi Promotional AP & Prtg Co (G-13325)*

Inca Presswood-Pallets Ltd (PA)........................ 330 343-3361
  3005 Progress St Dover (44622) *(G-6248)*

Incessant Software Inc....................................... 614 206-2211
  8577 Ohio Wesleyan Ct Nw Lancaster (43130) *(G-8205)*

Incinerator Specialists, Medina *Also Called: Facultatieve Tech Americas Inc (G-9400)*

Incorprted Trstees of The Gspl........................... 216 749-2100
  19695 Commerce Pkwy Middleburg Heights (44130) *(G-9773)*

Incredible Plastics, Warren *Also Called: Bloom Industries Inc (G-13743)*

Incredible Solutions Inc..................................... 330 898-3878
  1052 Mahoning Ave Nw Warren (44483) *(G-13772)*

Indelco Custom Products Inc.............................. 216 797-7300
  25861 Tungsten Rd Euclid (44132) *(G-6654)*

Independence 2 LLC... 800 414-0545
  623 W Liberty St Hubbard (44425) *(G-7811)*

Independence Cement LLC................................. 216 264-1212
  9240 Noble Park Dr Brecksville (44141) *(G-1471)*

Independent Awning & Canvas Co...................... 937 223-9661
  791 Ashton Cir Apt 102 Dayton (45429) *(G-5820)*

Independent Can Company.................................. 440 593-5300
  1049 Chamberlain Blvd Conneaut (44030) *(G-5405)*

Independent Container, Delaware *Also Called: Greif Inc (G-6151)*

Independent Machine & Wldg Inc........................ 937 339-7330
  710 Boone Dr Troy (45373) *(G-13228)*

Independent Power Cone Inc............................... 419 470-0303
  6051 Telegraph Rd Ste 19 Toledo (43612) *(G-13002)*

Independent Stamping Inc.................................. 216 251-3500
  12025 Zelis Rd Cleveland (44135) *(G-3857)*

Indian Creek Fabricators Inc.............................. 937 667-7214
  1350 Commerce Park Dr Tipp City (45371) *(G-12828)*

Indian Creek Structures, Rome *Also Called: J Aaron Weaver (G-11644)*

Indian Lake Shoppers Edge................................ 937 843-6600
  204 1/2 Lincoln Blvd Russells Point (43348) *(G-11669)*

Indispenser Ltd.. 419 625-5825
  520 Warren St Sandusky (44870) *(G-11841)*

Indoor Envmtl Specialists Inc............................ 937 433-5202
  438 Windsor Park Dr Dayton (45459) *(G-5821)*

Indra Holdings Corp (PA).................................... 513 682-8200
  9655 International Blvd Cincinnati (45246) *(G-2743)*

Induction Tooling Inc... 440 237-0711
  12510 York Delta Dr North Royalton (44133) *(G-10765)*

Industrial Aluminum Foundry, Columbus *Also Called: Iabf Inc (G-4997)*

Industrial and Mar Eng Svc Co........................... 740 694-0791
  13843 Armentrout Rd Fredericktown (43019) *(G-7080)*

Industrial Ceramic Products Inc......................... 937 642-3897
  14401 Suntra Way Marysville (43040) *(G-9032)*

Industrial Coating Tech Inc................................ 513 376-9945
  1011 Sunset Ave Cincinnati (45205) *(G-2744)*

Industrial Connections Inc................................. 330 274-2155
  11730 Timber Point Trl Mantua (44255) *(G-8869)*

Industrial Ctrl Design & Maint, Tallmadge *Also Called: Industrial Ctrl Dsign Mint Inc (G-12737)*

Industrial Ctrl Dsign Mint Inc............................ 330 785-9840
  311 Geneva Ave Tallmadge (44278) *(G-12737)*

Industrial Electronic Service.............................. 937 746-9750
  325 Industry Dr Carlisle (45005) *(G-2066)*

Industrial Fabrication and Mch........................... 330 454-7644
  3216 Kuemerle Ct Ne Canton (44705) *(G-1917)*

Industrial Fabricators Inc.................................. 614 882-7423
  265 E Broadway Ave Westerville (43081) *(G-14265)*

Industrial Farm Tank Inc.................................... 937 843-2972
  10676 Township Road 80 Lewistown (43333) *(G-8365)*

Industrial Fiberglass Spc Inc............................. 937 222-9000
  896 Foxfire Trl Vandalia (45377) *(G-13561)*

Industrial Fluid MGT Inc.................................... 419 748-7460
  2926 Us Highway 6 Mc Clure (43534) *(G-9351)*

Industrial Machining Services............................ 937 295-2022
  700 Tower Dr Fort Loramie (45845) *(G-6948)*

Industrial Mfg Co Intl LLC.................................. 440 838-4555
  3366 Riverside Dr Ste 103 Upper Arlington (43221) *(G-13431)*

Industrial Mfg Co LLC (HQ)................................ 440 838-4700
  8223 Brecksville Rd Ste 100 Brecksville (44141) *(G-1472)*

Industrial Mill Maintenance............................... 330 746-1155
  1609 Wilson Ave Ste 2 Youngstown (44506) *(G-14876)*

Industrial Millwright Svcs LLC........................... 419 523-9147
  1024 Heritage Trl Ottawa (45875) *(G-11035)*

Industrial Mold Inc.. 330 425-7374
  2057 E Aurora Rd Twinsburg (44087) *(G-13320)*

Industrial Nut Corp.. 419 625-8543
  1425 Tiffin Ave Sandusky (44870) *(G-11842)*

Industrial Paint & Strip Inc................................ 419 568-2222
  1000 Commerce Ct Waynesfield (45896) *(G-13878)*

Industrial Paper Shredders Inc........................... 888 637-4733
  12037 South Ave North Lima (44452) *(G-10708)*

Industrial Parts Depot LLC................................. 440 237-9164
  11266 Royalton Rd North Royalton (44133) *(G-10766)*

Industrial Pattern & Mfg Co............................... 614 252-0934
  899 N 20th St Columbus (43219) *(G-5004)*

Industrial Power Systems Inc............................. 419 531-3121
  146 Dixie Hwy Rossford (43460) *(G-11659)*

Industrial Prfctn Mold & Mch, Twinsburg *Also Called: Industrial Mold Inc (G-13320)*

Industrial Profile Systems, Akron *Also Called: Systems Kit LLC MB (G-324)*

Industrial Quartz Corporation............................ 440 942-0909
  7552 Saint Clair Ave Ste D Mentor (44060) *(G-9530)*

Industrial Repair and Mfg.................................. 419 822-0314
  265 Rogers Rd Delta (43515) *(G-6209)*

Industrial Repair and Mfg (PA)........................... 419 822-4232
  1140 E Main St Delta (43515) *(G-6210)*

Industrial Rlblty Spclsts Inc (PA)...................... 800 800-6345
  370 Douglas Ave Chillicothe (45601) *(G-2259)*

Industrial Screen Prcess Svc I (PA)................... 419 255-4900
  17 17th St Toledo (43604) *(G-13003)*

Industrial Solutions Inc..................................... 614 431-8118
  8333 Green Meadows Dr N Ste A Lewis Center (43035) *(G-8336)*

Industrial Tank & Containment............................ 330 448-4876
  411 State Route 7 Se Ste 3 Brookfield (44403) *(G-1515)*

Industrial Technologies Inc................................ 330 434-2033
  1643 Massillon Rd Akron (44312) *(G-182)*

Industrial Thermal Systems Inc.......................... 513 561-2100
  3914 Virginia Ave Cincinnati (45227) *(G-2745)*

Industrial Thermoset Plas Inc............................ 440 975-0411
  7675 Jenther Dr Mentor (44060) *(G-9531)*

Industrial Timber & Lumber Co, Cleveland *Also Called: Itl Corp (G-3874)*

Industrial Timber and Lumber, Beachwood *Also Called: Itl LLC (G-923)*

Industrial WD Prts Fabrication, Archbold *Also Called: Liechty Specialties Inc (G-500)*

Industry Products Co (PA).................................. 937 778-0585
  500 W Statler Rd Piqua (45356) *(G-11356)*

Ineos, Addyston *Also Called: Ineos ABS (usa) LLC (G-8)*

Ineos LLC (PA)... 419 226-1200
  1900 Fort Amanda Rd Lima (45804) *(G-8419)*

Ineos ABS (usa) LLC... 513 467-2400
  356 Three Rivers Pkwy Addyston (45001) *(G-8)*

Ineos Joliet LLC.. 815 314-4317
  5220 Blazer Pkwy Dublin (43017) *(G-6307)*

INEOS KOH INC.. 440 997-5221
  3509 Middle Rd Ashtabula (44004) *(G-596)*

Ineos Neal LLC... 610 790-3333
  5220 Blazer Pkwy Dublin (43017) *(G-6308)*

Ineos Nitriles USA LLC (DH)..................................... 281 535-6600
  1900 Fort Amanda Rd Lima (45804) *(G-8420)*

Ineos Pigments Asu LLC... 440 994-1999
  2501 Middle Rd Ashtabula (44004) *(G-597)*

Ineos Pigments USA Inc.. 440 994-1400
  2900 Middle Rd Ashtabula (44004) *(G-598)*

Ineos Solvents Sales US Corp.................................. 614 790-3333
  5220 Blazer Pkwy Dublin (43017) *(G-6309)*

Inez Essentials LLC... 216 701-8360
  5333 Cato St Maple Heights (44137) *(G-8884)*

Infinit Nutrition LLC.. 513 791-3500
  11240 Cornell Park Dr Ste 110 Blue Ash (45242) *(G-1288)*

Infinitaire Industries, Euclid *Also Called: Infinitaire Industries LLC (G-6655)*

Infinitaire Industries LLC... 216 600-2051
  24370 Hartland Dr Euclid (44123) *(G-6655)*

Infinite Energy Mfg LLC... 440 759-5920
  4517 Industrial Pkwy Cleveland (44135) *(G-3858)*

Infinity Engineered Pdts LLC................................... 234 466-7200
  3524 Southwestern Blvd Fairlawn (44333) *(G-6805)*

Infinity Engineered Products, Fairlawn *Also Called: Infinity Engineered Pdts LLC (G-6805)*

Infinium Wall Systems Inc.. 440 572-5000
  21000 Infinium Way Strongsville (44149) *(G-12567)*

Inflatable Images, Brunswick *Also Called: Scherba Industries Inc (G-1614)*

Informa Media Inc.. 216 696-7000
  1300 E 9th St Cleveland (44114) *(G-3859)*

INFORMA MEDIA, INC., Cleveland *Also Called: Informa Media Inc (G-3859)*

Infosight Corporation... 740 642-3600
  20700 Us Highway 23 Chillicothe (45601) *(G-2260)*

Ingersoll Rand, Holland *Also Called: Trane US Inc (G-7788)*

Ingersoll-Rand, Bryan *Also Called: Trane Technologies Company LLC (G-1665)*

Ingersoll-Rand, Cincinnati *Also Called: Trane Technologies Company LLC (G-3162)*

Ingle-Barr Inc (PA)... 740 702-6117
  20 Plyleys Ln Chillicothe (45601) *(G-2261)*

Ingredia Inc... 419 738-4060
  625 Commerce Rd Wapakoneta (45895) *(G-13716)*

Ingredient Innovations Intl Co.................................. 330 262-4440
  146 S Bever St Wooster (44691) *(G-14650)*

Ingredient Masters Inc... 513 231-7432
  4001 Borman Dr Batavia (45103) *(G-868)*

Ingredient Technology Division, Elyria *Also Called: Lanxess Corporation (G-6557)*

Inhance Technologies LLC.. 614 846-6400
  6575 Huntley Rd Ste D Columbus (43229) *(G-5005)*

Initial Designs Inc... 419 475-3900
  2453 Tremainsville Rd Unit 2 Toledo (43613) *(G-13004)*

Injection Alloys Incorporated................................... 513 422-8819
  2601 S Verity Pkwy Bldg 1 Middletown (45044) *(G-9865)*

Ink Inc.. 330 875-4789
  200 S Bauman Ct Louisville (44641) *(G-8605)*

Ink Technology Corporation..................................... 216 486-6720
  18320 Lanken Ave Cleveland (44119) *(G-3860)*

Ink Well, Akron *Also Called: Bansal Enterprises Inc (G-72)*

Ink Well, Bedford Heights *Also Called: Cwh Graphics LLC (G-1075)*

Ink Well, Grove City *Also Called: Deerfield Ventures Inc (G-7381)*

Inkwell, The, Westerville *Also Called: Techniprint Inc (G-14277)*

Inland Hardwood Corporation.................................. 740 373-7187
  25 Sheets Run Rd Marietta (45750) *(G-8924)*

Inland Products Inc (PA).. 614 443-3425
  599 Frank Rd Columbus (43223) *(G-5006)*

Inland Products Inc... 740 245-5514
  Rio Grande (45674) *(G-11617)*

Inland Tarp & Liner LLC... 419 436-6001
  1600 N Main St Fostoria (44830) *(G-6984)*

Inland Wood Products, Marietta *Also Called: Inland Hardwood Corporation (G-8924)*

Inline Underground Hdd, Bremen *Also Called: Inline Undgrd Hrzntal Drctnal (G-1486)*

Inline Undgrd Hrzntal Drctnal................................... 740 808-0316
  5440 Marietta Rd Sw Bremen (43107) *(G-1486)*

Inn Maid Products, Westerville *Also Called: Tmarzetti Company (G-14237)*

Inneractiv, Worthington *Also Called: Inneractiv Inc (G-14715)*

Inneractiv Inc.. 888 798-7792
  7000 N High St Worthington (43085) *(G-14715)*

Innerapps LLC... 419 467-3110
  28350 Kensington Ln Ste 200 Perrysburg (43551) *(G-11231)*

Innerwood & Company.. 513 677-2229
  688 Elizabeth Ln Loveland (45140) *(G-8631)*

Innocomp... 440 248-5104
  33195 Wagon Wheel Dr Solon (44139) *(G-12127)*

Innomark Communications LLC................................ 513 285-1040
  375 Northpointe Dr Fairfield (45014) *(G-6744)*

Innomark Communications LLC................................ 937 454-5555
  3233 S Tech Blvd Miamisburg (45342) *(G-9701)*

Innomark Group LLC.. 419 720-8102
  1218 Madison Ave Toledo (43604) *(G-13005)*

Innoplast Inc (PA)... 440 543-8660
  5718 Transportation Blvd Cleveland (44125) *(G-3861)*

Innovar Systems Limited.. 330 538-3942
  12155 Commissioner Dr North Jackson (44451) *(G-10689)*

Innovated Health LLC.. 330 858-0651
  2241 Front St 1st Fl Cuyahoga Falls (44221) *(G-5549)*

Innovation Plastics LLC... 513 818-1771
  1150 State St Fostoria (44830) *(G-6985)*

Innovation Sales LLC... 330 239-0400
  803 E Washington St Ste 210 Medina (44256) *(G-9412)*

Innovations In Plastic Inc.. 216 541-6060
  1643 Eddy Rd Cleveland (44112) *(G-3862)*

Innovative Computer Forms, Columbus *Also Called: Bizzy Bee Printing Inc (G-4757)*

Innovative Control Systems....................................... 513 894-3712
  5870 Fairham Rd Fairfield Township (45011) *(G-6796)*

Innovative Controls Corp.. 419 691-6684
  6528 Weatherfield Ct Maumee (43537) *(G-9298)*

Innovative Creations, Dayton *Also Called: Glen D Lala (G-5797)*

Innovative Food Processors Inc................................ 507 334-2730
  136 Fox Run Dr Defiance (43512) *(G-6112)*

Innovative Graphics Ltd... 877 406-3636
  2580 Westbelt Dr Columbus (43228) *(G-5007)*

Innovative Handling LLC... 419 882-7480
  7755 Sylvania Ave Sylvania (43560) *(G-12712)*

Innovative Mech Systems LLC.................................. 937 813-8713
  3100 Plainfield Rd Ste A Dayton (45432) *(G-5614)*

Innovative Plastic Molders LLC................................ 937 898-3775
  10451 Dog Leg Rd Ste 200 Vandalia (45377) *(G-13562)*

Innovative Sport Surfacing LLC................................ 440 205-0875
  8425 Station St Mentor (44060) *(G-9532)*

Innovative Tool & Die Inc... 419 599-0492
  1700 Industrial Dr Napoleon (43545) *(G-10287)*

Innovative Vend Solutions LLC................................. 866 931-9413
  740 Royal Ridge Dr Dayton (45449) *(G-5822)*

Innovative Woodworking Inc..................................... 513 531-1940
  1901 Ross Ave Cincinnati (45212) *(G-2746)*

Innove Inc (PA).. 440 836-0199
  8909 Freeway Dr Macedonia (44056) *(G-8697)*

Innovest Energy Group LLC...................................... 440 644-1027
  8834 Mayfield Rd Ste A Chesterland (44026) *(G-2234)*

Innovtive Cnfction Sltions LLC................................. 440 835-8001
  28025 Ranney Pkwy Westlake (44145) *(G-14311)*

Innovtive Lbling Solutions Inc.................................. 513 860-2457
  4000 Hamilton Middletown Rd Hamilton (45011) *(G-7505)*

Innovtive McHning Slutions LLC............................... 419 925-2060
  6190 Franklin St Celina (45822) *(G-2110)*

Inns Holdings Ltd.. 740 345-3700
  29 W Locust St Newark (43055) *(G-10511)*

Inovent Engineering LLC.. 330 468-0019
  8877 Freeway Dr Macedonia (44056) *(G-8698)*

Inpower LLC.. 740 548-0965
  8311 Green Meadows Dr N Lewis Center (43035) *(G-8337)*

Ins Robotics Inc... 888 293-5325
   3600 Parkway Ln Hilliard (43026) *(G-7684)*

Inservco Inc (DH)... 847 855-9600
   110 Commerce Dr Lagrange (44050) *(G-8148)*

Inside Outfitters, Lewis Center *Also Called: Lumenomics Inc (G-8342)*

Inside Outfitters Inc... 614 798-3500
   8333 Green Meadows Dr N Ste B Lewis Center (43035) *(G-8338)*

Insights Sccess Media Tech LLC........................ 614 602-1754
   555 Metro Pl N Ste 100 Dublin (43017) *(G-6310)*

Insignia Signs Inc.. 937 866-2341
   2265 Dryden Rd Moraine (45439) *(G-10170)*

Inskeep Brothers Inc.. 614 898-6620
   3193 E Dublin Granville Rd Columbus (43231) *(G-5008)*

Inskeep Brothers Printers, Columbus *Also Called: Inskeep Brothers Inc (G-5008)*

Insource Technologies Inc................................ 419 399-3600
   12124 Road 111 Paulding (45879) *(G-11157)*

Inspirtec LLC.. 614 571-7130
   10203 Christian Rd Versailles (45380) *(G-13596)*

Inspyre Health Systems LLC............................ 440 412-7916
   1004 Commerce Dr Grafton (44044) *(G-7304)*

Insta Plak Inc (PA)... 419 537-1555
   5025 Dorr St Toledo (43615) *(G-13006)*

Insta-Gro Manufacturing Inc........................... 419 845-3046
   8217 Linn Hipsher Rd Caledonia (43314) *(G-1732)*

Insta-Plak, Toledo *Also Called: Insta Plak Inc (G-13006)*

Installed Building Pdts LLC.............................. 614 308-9900
   1320 Mckinley Ave Ste A Columbus (43222) *(G-5009)*

Instantorder, Celina *Also Called: Tech Solutions LLC (G-2123)*

Instantwhip Connecticut Inc (PA)...................... 614 488-2536
   2200 Cardigan Ave Columbus (43215) *(G-5010)*

Instantwhip Foods Inc (PA)............................... 614 488-2536
   2200 Cardigan Ave Columbus (43215) *(G-5011)*

Instantwhip of Pennsylvania, Columbus *Also Called: Instantwhip Products Co PA (G-5012)*

Instantwhip Products Co PA (HQ)....................... 614 488-2536
   2200 Cardigan Ave Columbus (43215) *(G-5012)*

Instantwhip-Buffalo Inc (HQ)........................... 614 488-2536
   2200 Cardigan Ave Columbus (43215) *(G-5013)*

Instantwhip-Chicago Inc (PA)........................... 614 488-2536
   2200 Cardigan Ave Columbus (43215) *(G-5014)*

Instantwhip-Columbus Inc (HQ)....................... 614 871-9447
   3855 Marlane Dr Grove City (43123) *(G-7391)*

Instantwhip-Dayton Inc (PA)............................ 937 235-5930
   5820 Executive Blvd Dayton (45424) *(G-5823)*

Instantwhip-Dayton Inc..................................... 937 435-4371
   967 Senate Dr Dayton (45459) *(G-5824)*

Instantwhip-Syracuse Inc (PA)......................... 614 488-2536
   2200 Cardigan Ave Columbus (43215) *(G-5015)*

Instrmntation Ctrl Systems Inc......................... 513 662-2600
   11355 Sebring Dr Cincinnati (45240) *(G-2747)*

Instrumatics, Cleveland *Also Called: Cleveland Circuits Corp (G-3509)*

Instrumentors Inc... 440 238-3430
   22077 Drake Rd Strongsville (44149) *(G-12568)*

Insulpro Inc.. 614 262-3768
   4650 Indianola Ave Columbus (43214) *(G-5016)*

Integra, Willoughby *Also Called: Integra Enclosures Inc (G-14469)*

Integra Enclosures Inc (PA).............................. 440 269-4966
   7750 Pyler Blvd Willoughby (44094) *(G-14469)*

Integra Enclosures Limited............................... 440 269-4966
   8989 Tyler Blvd Mentor (44060) *(G-9533)*

Integrant LLC... 440 628-9550
   12315 York Delta Dr North Royalton (44133) *(G-10767)*

Integrated Chem Concepts Inc......................... 440 838-5666
   6650 W Snowville Rd Ste F Brecksville (44141) *(G-1473)*

Integrated Development & Mfg (PA)................... 440 247-5100
   510 Washington St Chagrin Falls (44022) *(G-2146)*

Integrated Development & Mfg.......................... 440 543-2423
   8401 Washington St Chagrin Falls (44023) *(G-2167)*

Integrated Power Services LLC......................... 216 433-7808
   5325 W 130th St Cleveland (44130) *(G-3863)*

Integrated Power Services LLC......................... 513 863-8816
   2175a Schlichter Dr Hamilton (45015) *(G-7506)*

Integrated Resources Inc.................................. 419 885-7122
   7901 Sylvania Ave Sylvania (43560) *(G-12713)*

Integris Composites Inc.................................... 740 928-0326
   1051 O Neill Dr Hebron (43025) *(G-7619)*

Integrity Group Consulting Inc.......................... 614 759-9148
   6432 E Main St Ste 201 Reynoldsburg (43068) *(G-11572)*

Integrity Industrial Equipment......................... 937 335-5658
   18 E Water St Troy (45373) *(G-13229)*

Integrity Manufacturing Corp........................... 937 233-6792
   3723 Inpark Dr Dayton (45414) *(G-5825)*

Integrity Parking LLC.. 440 543-4123
   400 Aurora Commons Cir Unit 438 Aurora (44202) *(G-675)*

Intelacomm Inc.. 888 610-9250
   12375 Kinsman Rd Newbury (44065) *(G-10555)*

Intelitool Mfg Svcs Inc..................................... 440 953-1071
   36335 Reading Ave Ste 4 Willoughby (44094) *(G-14470)*

Intelligent Mobile Support Inc.......................... 888 980-9119
   28420 Blue Pond Trl Solon (44139) *(G-12128)*

Intelligent Signal Tech Intl............................... 614 530-4784
   6318 Dustywind Ln Loveland (45140) *(G-8632)*

Intelligrated Inc (HQ)....................................... 866 936-7300
   7901 Innovation Way Mason (45040) *(G-9111)*

Intelligrated Inc.. 513 874-0788
   10045 International Blvd West Chester (45246) *(G-14127)*

Intelligrated Products LLC............................... 740 490-0300
   475 E High St London (43140) *(G-8537)*

Intelligrated Sub Holdings Inc (PA)................... 513 701-7300
   7901 Innovation Way Mason (45040) *(G-9112)*

Intelligrated Systems Inc (HQ)......................... 866 936-7300
   7901 Innovation Way Mason (45040) *(G-9113)*

Intelligrated Systems LLC................................ 513 701-7300
   9842 International Blvd West Chester (45246) *(G-14128)*

Intelligrated Systems Ohio LLC (DH)................. 513 701-7300
   7901 Innovation Way Mason (45040) *(G-9114)*

Intelligrated Systems Ohio LLC......................... 513 682-6600
   10045 International Blvd West Chester (45246) *(G-14129)*

Intellinetics Inc (PA).. 614 388-8908
   2190 Dividend Dr Columbus (43228) *(G-5017)*

Intellitarget Marketing Svcs, Coshocton *Also Called: ITM Marketing Inc (G-5457)*

Intelliworks Ht LLC.. 419 660-9050
   61 Saint Marys St Norwalk (44857) *(G-10848)*

Intense Enterprises, Plain City *Also Called: Advanced Gauging Tech LLC (G-11391)*

Inter American Products Inc (HQ)...................... 800 645-2233
   1240 State Ave Cincinnati (45204) *(G-2748)*

Inter-Ion Inc.. 330 928-9655
   157 Ascot Pkwy Cuyahoga Falls (44223) *(G-5550)*

Interactive Engineering Corp........................... 330 239-6888
   884 Medina Rd Medina (44256) *(G-9413)*

Interactive Products Corp................................ 513 313-3397
   5346 Roden Park Dr Monroe (45050) *(G-10110)*

Interbake Foods LLC (HQ)................................. 614 294-4931
   1740 Joyce Ave Columbus (43219) *(G-5018)*

Interco Division 10 Ohio Inc.............................. 614 875-2959
   3600 Brookham Dr Ste D Grove City (43123) *(G-7392)*

Intercontinental Chemical Corp (PA)................. 513 541-7100
   4660 Spring Grove Ave Cincinnati (45232) *(G-2749)*

Interface Logic Systems, Columbus *Also Called: Cgmw Incorporated (G-4804)*

Interface Logic Systems Inc............................ 614 236-8388
   3368 State Route 752 Ste A Ashville (43103) *(G-626)*

Interfit, Akron *Also Called: Yokohama Tws North America Inc (G-361)*

Intergroup International Ltd.............................. 216 965-0257
   1653 Merriman Rd Ste 211 Akron (44313) *(G-183)*

Interior Graphic Systems LLC.......................... 330 244-0100
   4550 Aultman Rd Canton (44720) *(G-1918)*

Interior Products Co Inc................................... 216 641-1919
   3615 Superior Ave E Ste 3104f Cleveland (44114) *(G-3864)*

Interlake Stamping Ohio Inc............................. 440 942-0800
   4732 E 355th St Willoughby (44094) *(G-14471)*

Interlube Corporation...................................... 513 531-1777
   4646 Baker St Cincinnati (45212) *(G-2750)*

International Automotive Compo......................... 330 279-6557
   8281 County Road 245 Holmesville (44633) *(G-7801)*

International Bellows 937 294-6261
   2 Ferrari Ct Englewood (45315) *(G-6616)*

International Brand Services 513 376-8209
   3397 Erie Ave Apt 215 Cincinnati (45208) *(G-2751)*

International Confections Company LLC 800 288-8002
   1855 E 17th Ave Columbus (43219) *(G-5019)*

International Hydraulics Inc 440 951-7186
   7700 Saint Clair Ave Mentor (44060) *(G-9534)*

International Machining Inc 330 225-1963
   2885 Nationwide Pkwy Brunswick (44212) *(G-1599)*

International Metal Hose Co 419 483-7690
   520 Goodrich Rd Bellevue (44811) *(G-1125)*

International Metal Supply LLC 330 764-1004
   3995 Medina Rd Ste 200 Medina (44256) *(G-9414)*

International Motors LLC 513 733-8500
   11775 Highway Dr Cincinnati (45241) *(G-2752)*

International Motors LLC 937 390-4776
   6125 Urbana Rd Springfield (45502) *(G-12328)*

International Motors LLC 937 561-3315
   811 N Murray St Springfield (45503) *(G-12329)*

International Noodle Company 614 888-0665
   341 Enterprise Dr Lewis Center (43035) *(G-8339)*

International Paper, Eaton *Also Called: International Paper Company (G-6456)*

International Paper, Kenton *Also Called: Graphic Packaging Intl LLC (G-8100)*

International Paper, Loveland *Also Called: International Paper Company (G-8633)*

International Paper, Marion *Also Called: International Paper Company (G-8974)*

International Paper, Marysville *Also Called: International Paper Company (G-9033)*

International Paper, Middletown *Also Called: International Paper Company (G-9866)*

International Paper, Newark *Also Called: International Paper Company (G-10512)*

International Paper, Streetsboro *Also Called: International Paper Company (G-12505)*

International Paper Company 740 369-7691
   875 Pittsburgh Dr Delaware (43015) *(G-6158)*

International Paper Company 937 456-4131
   900 Us Route 35 Eaton (45320) *(G-6456)*

International Paper Company 513 248-6319
   6283 Tri Ridge Blvd Loveland (45140) *(G-8633)*

International Paper Company 740 383-4061
   1600 Cascade Dr Marion (43302) *(G-8974)*

International Paper Company 937 578-7718
   13307 Industrial Pkwy Marysville (43040) *(G-9033)*

International Paper Company 800 473-0830
   912 Nelbar St Middletown (45042) *(G-9866)*

International Paper Company 740 397-5215
   8800 Granville Rd Mount Vernon (43050) *(G-10245)*

International Paper Company 740 522-3123
   1851 Tamarack Rd Newark (43055) *(G-10512)*

International Paper Company 330 626-7300
   700 Mondial Pkwy Streetsboro (44241) *(G-12505)*

International Paper Company 330 264-1322
   689 Palmer St Wooster (44691) *(G-14651)*

Interntnal Auto Cmpnnts Group 419 335-1000
   555 W Linfoot St Wauseon (43567) *(G-13852)*

Interntnal Auto Cmpnnts Group 419 433-5653
   555 W Linfoot St Wauseon (43567) *(G-13853)*

Interntnal Cutng Solutions Inc 440 786-1700
   1790 Hannum Dr Streetsboro (44241) *(G-12506)*

Interntnal Pckg Pallets Crates, Sidney *Also Called: Wappoo Wood Products Inc (G-12060)*

Interntnal Pdts Srcing Group I 614 334-1500
   2701 Charter St Ste A Columbus (43228) *(G-5020)*

Interntnal Prcsion Cast Sups I 330 342-0407
   1570 Terex Rd Hudson (44236) *(G-7847)*

Interntnal Tchncal Catings Inc 800 567-6592
   845 E Markison Ave Columbus (43207) *(G-5021)*

Interntnal Tchncal Plymr Syste 330 505-1218
   852 Ann Ave Niles (44446) *(G-10591)*

Interpak Inc 440 974-8999
   7278 Justin Way Mentor (44060) *(G-9535)*

Interscope Manufacturing Inc 513 423-8866
   2901 Carmody Blvd Middletown (45042) *(G-9867)*

Intersource USA, East Palestine *Also Called: Ceramsource Inc (G-6401)*

Interstate Contractors LLC 513 372-5393
   762 Reading Rd # G Mason (45040) *(G-9115)*

Interstate Diesel Service Inc (PA) 216 881-0015
   5300 Lakeside Ave E Cleveland (44114) *(G-3865)*

Interstate Gas Supply, Dublin *Also Called: Interstate Gas Supply LLC (G-6311)*

Interstate Gas Supply LLC (PA) 877 995-4447
   6100 Emerald Pkwy Dublin (43016) *(G-6311)*

Interstate Pump Company Inc (PA) 330 222-1006
   33370 Winona Rd Salem (44460) *(G-11789)*

Interstate Sign Products Inc 419 683-1962
   432 E Main St Crestline (44827) *(G-5503)*

Interstate Tool Corporation 216 671-1077
   4538 W 130th St Cleveland (44135) *(G-3866)*

Interstate Truckway Inc 614 771-1220
   5440 Renner Rd Columbus (43228) *(G-5022)*

Intertape Polymer Corp 704 279-3011
   1800 E Pleasant St Springfield (45505) *(G-12330)*

Intertec Corporation (PA) 419 537-9711
   3400 Exec Pkwy Toledo (43606) *(G-13007)*

Intertek LLC 440 323-3325
   6805 W River Rd S Elyria (44035) *(G-6545)*

Inteva Products LLC 937 280-8500
   707 Crossroads Ct Vandalia (45377) *(G-13563)*

Intier Sting Systems-Lordstown, Sheffield Village *Also Called: Magna Seating America Inc (G-11960)*

Intigral Inc (PA) 440 439-0980
   7850 Northfield Rd Walton Hills (44146) *(G-13698)*

Intigral Inc 440 439-0980
   45 Karago Ave Youngstown (44512) *(G-14877)*

Intrism Inc 614 787-4631
   6969 Worthington Galena Rd Ste J Worthington (43085) *(G-14716)*

Invacare America, Elyria *Also Called: Invacare Corporation (G-6549)*

Invacare Canadian Holdings Inc 440 329-6000
   1 Invacare Way Elyria (44035) *(G-6546)*

Invacare Canadian Holdings LLC 440 329-6000
   1 Invacare Way Elyria (44035) *(G-6547)*

Invacare Continuing Care Inc 800 668-2337
   1 Invacare Way Elyria (44035) *(G-6548)*

Invacare Corporation (PA) 440 329-6000
   1 Invacare Way Elyria (44035) *(G-6549)*

Invacare Corporation 440 329-6000
   1200 Taylor St Elyria (44035) *(G-6550)*

Invacare Corporation 800 333-6900
   1320 Taylor St Elyria (44035) *(G-6551)*

Invacare Corporation 440 329-6000
   38683 Taylor Pkwy North Ridgeville (44035) *(G-10736)*

Invacare Hcs LLC 330 634-9925
   1 Invacare Way Elyria (44035) *(G-6552)*

Invacare Hme, North Ridgeville *Also Called: Invacare Corporation (G-10736)*

Invacare Holdings LLC 440 329-6000
   1 Invacare Way Elyria (44035) *(G-6553)*

Invacare Holdings Corporation 440 329-6000
   1 Invacare Way Elyria (44036) *(G-6554)*

Invacare It & Financial Svcs, Elyria *Also Called: Invacare Corporation (G-6551)*

Inventory Controlled Mdsg, Twinsburg *Also Called: ICM Distributing Company Inc (G-13319)*

Inventus Power (ohio) Inc (DH) 614 351-2191
   5115 Parkcenter Ave Ste 275 Dublin (43017) *(G-6312)*

Investors United Inc (PA) 419 473-8942
   4215 Monroe St Toledo (43606) *(G-13008)*

Invirsa Inc 614 344-1765
   1275 Kinnear Rd Ste 217 Columbus (43212) *(G-5023)*

Invue Security Products Inc 330 456-7776
   1510 4th St Se Canton (44707) *(G-1919)*

INX International Ink Co 440 239-1766
   18001 Englewood Dr Unit P Cleveland (44130) *(G-3867)*

INX International Ink Co 707 693-2990
   350 Homan Rd Lebanon (45036) *(G-8268)*

INX INTERNATIONAL INK CO, Lebanon *Also Called: INX International Ink Co (G-8268)*

Ion Vacuum Ivac Tech Corp 216 662-5158
   18678 Cranwood Pkwy Cleveland (44128) *(G-3868)*

Ion Vacuum Technologies, Cleveland *Also Called: Ion Vacuum Ivac Tech Corp (G-3868)*

Ionbond LLC..216 831-0880
24700 Highpoint Rd Cleveland (44122) *(G-3869)*

Ioppolo Concrete Corporation......................440 439-6606
10 Industry Dr Bedford (44146) *(G-1040)*

Iosil Energy Corporation
5700 Green Pointe Dr N Ste A Groveport (43125) *(G-7439)*

Iot Diagnostics LLC......................................844 786-7631
9361 Allen Rd West Chester (45069) *(G-14015)*

Iotech, Cleveland *Also Called: Measurement Computing Corp (G-4015)*

Iowa Quality Meats Ltd................................515 225-6868
805 E Kemper Rd Cincinnati (45246) *(G-2753)*

IPA Ltd..614 523-3974
199 Mckenna Creek Dr Columbus (43230) *(G-5024)*

Ipex USA LLC..513 942-9910
4507 Le Saint Ct Fairfield (45014) *(G-6745)*

IPL Dayton Inc..937 969-7000
1765 W County Line Rd Urbana (43078) *(G-13468)*

Ips, Wadsworth *Also Called: Parker-Hannifin Corporation (G-13657)*

Ips Treatments Inc......................................419 241-5955
3254 Hill Ave Toledo (43607) *(G-13009)*

Ipsco Tubulars Inc......................................330 448-6772
6880 Parkway Dr Brookfield (44403) *(G-1516)*

IPSCO TUBULARS, INC., Brookfield *Also Called: Ipsco Tubulars Inc (G-1516)*

Ipsg, Columbus *Also Called: Interntnal Pdts Srcing Group I (G-5020)*

Iptc, Troy *Also Called: Ishmael Precision Tool Corp (G-13230)*

Ireportsource..888 294-9578
7864 Camargo Rd Cincinnati (45243) *(G-2754)*

Irg Operating LLC..440 963-4008
850 W River Rd Vermilion (44089) *(G-13590)*

Irock Crushers, Cleveland *Also Called: Irock Crushers LLC (G-3870)*

Irock Crushers LLC......................................866 240-0201
5531 Canal Rd Cleveland (44125) *(G-3870)*

Iron City Wood Products Inc........................330 755-2772
900 Albert St Youngstown (44505) *(G-14878)*

Iron Gate Industries LLC..............................330 264-0626
1435 S Honeytown Rd Wooster (44691) *(G-14652)*

Iron Horse Engineering, Parkman *Also Called: Montville Plastics & Rbr LLC (G-11127)*

Iron Works Inc..937 420-2100
62 Elm St Ste A Fort Loramie (45845) *(G-6949)*

Ironfab LLC..614 443-3900
1771 Progress Ave Columbus (43207) *(G-5025)*

Ironhawk Industrial, Euclid *Also Called: Ironhawk Industrial Dist LLC (G-6656)*

Ironhawk Industrial Dist LLC........................216 502-3700
1261 Babbitt Rd Ste B Euclid (44132) *(G-6656)*

Ironhead Fabg & Contg Inc..........................419 690-0000
2245 Front St Toledo (43605) *(G-13010)*

Ironhead Marine Inc....................................419 690-0000
2245 Front St Toledo (43605) *(G-13011)*

Ironics Inc..330 652-0583
750 S Main St Niles (44446) *(G-10592)*

Ironunits LLC..216 694-5303
200 Public Sq Ste 3300 Cleveland (44114) *(G-3871)*

Irr, Chillicothe *Also Called: Industrial Rlblity Spclsts Inc (G-2259)*

Irvine Wood Recovery Inc (PA).....................513 831-0060
110 Glendale Milford Rd Miamiville (45147) *(G-9762)*

Irwin Engraving & Printing Co......................216 391-7300
5318 Saint Clair Ave Ste 1 Cleveland (44103) *(G-3872)*

Isaac Foster Mack Co (PA)...........................419 625-5500
314 W Market St Sandusky (44870) *(G-11843)*

Isaiah Industries Inc....................................937 778-2246
9234 Country Club Rd Piqua (45356) *(G-11357)*

Isaiah Industries Inc (PA).............................937 773-9840
8510 Industry Park Dr Piqua (45356) *(G-11358)*

Ishikawa Gasket America Inc........................419 353-7300
1745 Indian Wood Cir Ste 125 Maumee (43537) *(G-9299)*

Ishmael Precision Tool Corp........................937 335-8070
55 Industry Ct Troy (45373) *(G-13230)*

ISK Americas Incorporated (HQ)...................440 357-4600
7474 Auburn Rd Concord Township (44077) *(G-5392)*

Island Aseptics LLC....................................740 685-2548
100 Hope Ave Byesville (43723) *(G-1714)*

Island Delights Inc......................................866 887-4100
240 W Greenwich Rd Seville (44273) *(G-11918)*

ISO Technologies Inc....................................740 928-0084
1870 James Pkwy Heath (43056) *(G-7597)*

ISO Technologies Inc (PA).............................740 928-0084
200 Milliken Dr Hebron (43025) *(G-7620)*

Isofoton North America Inc..........................419 591-4330
800 Independence Dr Napoleon (43545) *(G-10288)*

Isotoner, Cincinnati *Also Called: Totes Isotoner Corporation (G-3159)*

Isp Chemicals LLC......................................614 876-3637
1979 Atlas St Columbus (43228) *(G-5026)*

Isp Lima LLC..419 998-8700
12220 S Metcalf St Lima (45804) *(G-8421)*

Isps, Toledo *Also Called: Industrial Screen Prcess Svc I (G-13003)*

Ist International, Loveland *Also Called: Intelligent Signal Tech Intl (G-8632)*

It XCEL Consulting LLC................................513 847-8261
7112 Office Park Dr West Chester (45069) *(G-14016)*

Italmatch Sc LLC..216 749-2605
1000 Belt Line Ave Cleveland (44109) *(G-3873)*

Itc Manufacturing, Columbus *Also Called: Interntnal Tchncal Catings Inc (G-5021)*

Item NA..216 271-7241
925 Glaser Pkwy Akron (44306) *(G-184)*

Iten Industries Inc (PA)................................440 997-6134
4602 Benefit Ave Ashtabula (44004) *(G-599)*

Iten Industries Inc......................................440 997-6134
3500 N Ridge Rd W Ashtabula (44004) *(G-600)*

Itl LLC..216 831-3140
23925 Commerce Park Rd Beachwood (44122) *(G-923)*

Itl Corp (HQ)..216 831-3140
23925 Commerce Park Cleveland (44122) *(G-3874)*

ITM Marketing Inc......................................740 295-3575
331 Main St Coshocton (43812) *(G-5457)*

Itps, Niles *Also Called: Interntnal Tchncal Plymr Syste (G-10591)*

ITR Manufacturing LLC................................419 763-1493
811 Ash St Saint Henry (45883) *(G-11722)*

ITT Torque Systems Inc................................216 524-8800
7550 Hub Pkwy Cleveland (44125) *(G-3875)*

ITW Evercoat, Blue Ash *Also Called: Illinois Tool Works Inc (G-1286)*

ITW Filtration Products, Bryan *Also Called: Illinois Tool Works Inc (G-1645)*

ITW Food Equipment Group LLC....................937 393-4271
1495 N High St Hillsboro (45133) *(G-7719)*

ITW Food Equipment Group LLC (HQ).............937 332-2396
701 S Ridge Ave Troy (45374) *(G-13231)*

ITW Hobart, Troy *Also Called: Illinois Tool Works Inc (G-13227)*

ITW Hobart Brothers, Troy *Also Called: Hobart Brothers LLC (G-13222)*

ITW Powertrain Components, Bryan *Also Called: Illinois Tool Works Inc (G-1644)*

IVEX Protective Packaging LLC (PA)...............937 498-9298
456 Stolle Ave Sidney (45365) *(G-12026)*

Ivi Mining Group Ltd....................................740 418-7745
72116 Grey Rd Vinton (45686) *(G-13623)*

Ivies Wholistic Dynamics.............................216 469-3103
2390 Cardinal Ct Apt D Wooster (44691) *(G-14653)*

Ivostud LLC..440 925-4227
6430 Eastland Rd Ste C Brookpark (44142) *(G-1553)*

Ivy Ventures LLC..513 259-3307
39 Citadel Dr Apt 2 Fairfield (45014) *(G-6746)*

Iwata Bolt, Fairfield *Also Called: Iwata Bolt USA Inc (G-6747)*

Iwata Bolt USA Inc (PA)...............................513 942-5050
102 Iwata Dr Fairfield (45014) *(G-6747)*

J & C Group Inc of Ohio..............................440 205-9658
6781 Hopkins Rd Mentor (44060) *(G-9536)*

J & C Industries Inc....................................216 362-8867
4808 W 130th St Cleveland (44135) *(G-3876)*

J & D Mining Inc..330 339-4935
3497 University Dr Ne New Philadelphia (44663) *(G-10450)*

J & D Steel Service Center LLC.....................330 759-7430
3030 Gale Dr Hubbard (44425) *(G-7812)*

J & D Wood Ltd..937 778-9663
401 S College St Piqua (45356) *(G-11359)*

J & H Manufacturing LLC.............................330 482-2636
1652 Columbiana Lisbon Rd Columbiana (44408) *(G-4620)*

ALPHABETIC

J & H Mfg, Columbiana Also Called: J & H Manufacturing LLC (G-4620)

J & J Tire & Alignment..330 424-5200
12649 State Route 45 Lisbon (44432) *(G-8471)*

J & J Tool & Die Inc..330 343-4721
203 W 4th St Dover (44622) *(G-6249)*

J & K Cabinetry Inc..513 860-3461
8800 Global Way # 200 West Chester (45069) *(G-14017)*

J & K Pallet Inc..937 526-5117
30 Subler Dr Versailles (45380) *(G-13597)*

J & L Body Inc..216 661-2323
4848 Van Epps Rd Brooklyn Heights (44131) *(G-1533)*

J & L Management Corporation..................................440 205-1199
8634 Station St Mentor (44060) *(G-9537)*

J & L Specialty Steel Inc..330 875-6200
1500 W Main St Louisville (44641) *(G-8606)*

J & L Wood Products Inc (PA)....................................937 667-4064
155 Lightner Rd Tipp City (45371) *(G-12829)*

J & M Fabrications LLC..330 860-4346
3000 S 1st St Clinton (44216) *(G-4554)*

J & M Industries Inc..440 951-1985
7775 Division Dr Mentor (44060) *(G-9538)*

J & M Machine, Fairport Harbor Also Called: JM Performance Products Inc (G-6817)

J & M Manufacturing Co Inc......................................419 375-2376
284 Railroad St Fort Recovery (45846) *(G-6967)*

J & M Precision Die Cast Inc, Elyria Also Called: J&M Precision Die Casting LLC (G-6555)

J & O Plastics Inc..330 927-3169
12475 Sheets Rd Rittman (44270) *(G-11623)*

J & P Investments Inc..513 821-2299
6006 Squirrelwood Ct Cincinnati (45247) *(G-2755)*

J & P Products Inc..440 974-2830
8865 East Ave Mentor (44060) *(G-9539)*

J & S Industrial Mch Pdts Inc....................................419 691-1380
123 Oakdale Ave Toledo (43605) *(G-13012)*

J & S Tool Corporation..216 676-8330
1606 W 12th St Lorain (44052) *(G-8558)*

J A B Welding Service Inc..740 453-5868
2820 S River Rd Zanesville (43701) *(G-15023)*

J A McMahon Incorporated..330 652-2588
6 E Park Ave Niles (44446) *(G-10593)*

J Aaron Weaver..440 474-9185
5759 Us Highway 6 Rome (44085) *(G-11644)*

J and J Sales, Delaware Also Called: Aci Industries Converting Ltd (G-6129)

J B Manufacturing Inc..330 676-9744
4465 Crystal Pkwy Kent (44240) *(G-8037)*

J B Stamping Inc..216 631-0013
7413 Associate Ave Cleveland (44144) *(G-3877)*

J Best Inc..513 943-7000
4476 Glen Este Withamsville Rd Cincinnati (45245) *(G-2308)*

J C L S Enterprises LLC..740 472-0314
742 Lewisville Rd Woodsfield (43793) *(G-14613)*

J C Robinson Products, Cincinnati Also Called: James C Robinson (G-2760)

J C Whitlam Manufacturing Co..................................330 334-2524
200 W Walnut St Wadsworth (44281) *(G-13644)*

J D Drilling Company..740 949-2512
107 S 3rd St Racine (45771) *(G-11504)*

J D Hydraulic Inc..419 686-5234
Rte 25 Portage (43451) *(G-11457)*

J D Indoor Comfort Duct Clg, Sheffield Lake Also Called: JD Indoor Comfort Inc (G-11954)

J D'S Pre Cast, Fremont Also Called: Dennis Constuction Sanitation (G-7104)

J E Doyle Company..330 564-0743
5186 New Haven Cir Norton (44203) *(G-10824)*

J E Nicolozakes Co..740 310-1606
62920 Georgetown Rd Cambridge (43725) *(G-1745)*

J G Pads, Akron Also Called: Markethtch Inc D/B/A Mh Eye CA (G-221)

J H Routh Packing Company......................................419 626-2251
4413 W Bogart Rd Sandusky (44870) *(G-11844)*

J Henry Holland, Cleveland Also Called: Mazzella Jhh Company Inc (G-4004)

J Horst Manufacturing Co..330 828-2216
279 E Main St Dalton (44618) *(G-5586)*

J I C, West Jefferson Also Called: Jefferson Industries Corp (G-14162)

J I T Pallets Inc..330 424-0355
39196 Grant St Lisbon (44432) *(G-8472)*

J K Plastics Co..440 632-1482
14135 Madison Rd Middlefield (44062) *(G-9802)*

J K Precast LLC..740 335-2188
1001 Armbrust Ave Wshngtn Ct Hs (43160) *(G-14741)*

J L Custom Woodworking LLC..................................419 704-5181
587 Us-224 Sullivan (44880) *(G-12659)*

J L R Products Inc..330 832-9557
1212 Oberlin Ave Sw Massillon (44647) *(G-9207)*

J M C Rollmasters, Mentor Also Called: Johnston Mfg Co Inc (G-9544)

J M Mold Inc..937 778-0077
1707 Commerce Dr Piqua (45356) *(G-11360)*

J M Smucker Company (PA)......................................330 682-3000
1 Strawberry Ln Orrville (44667) *(G-10987)*

J McCoy Lumber Co Ltd (PA)....................................937 587-3423
6 N Main St Peebles (45660) *(G-11170)*

J P Industrial Products Inc..330 627-1377
755 N Lisbon St Carrollton (44615) *(G-2086)*

J P Industrial Products Inc (PA)................................330 424-1110
11988 State Route 45 Lisbon (44432) *(G-8473)*

J P Industrial Products Inc..330 424-3388
State Rte 518 Lisbon (44432) *(G-8474)*

J R Custom Unlimited Inc..513 894-9800
2620 Bobmeyer Rd Hamilton (45015) *(G-7507)*

J R M Chemical Inc..216 475-8488
4881 Neo Pkwy Cleveland (44128) *(G-3878)*

J R Tool & Die, Wooster Also Called: McCann Tool & Die Inc (G-14664)

J Rettenmaier USA LP..937 652-2101
1228 Muzzy Rd Urbana (43078) *(G-13469)*

J S C Publishing..614 424-6911
958 King Ave Columbus (43212) *(G-5027)*

J Schrader Company..216 961-2890
4603 Fenwick Ave Cleveland (44102) *(G-3879)*

J Solutions LLC..614 732-4857
216 E Hinman Ave Columbus (43207) *(G-5028)*

J T M, Solon Also Called: Jtm Products Inc (G-12133)

J Tek Tool & Mold Inc..419 547-9476
304 Elm St Clyde (43410) *(G-4559)*

J W Goss Company (PA)..330 395-0739
410 South St Sw Warren (44483) *(G-13773)*

J W Harris Co Inc (HQ)..513 754-2000
4501 Quality Pl Mason (45040) *(G-9116)*

J W Harwood Co (PA)..216 531-6230
18001 Roseland Rd Cleveland (44112) *(G-3880)*

J W P, Urbana Also Called: Trulil Inc (G-13479)

J-Lenco Inc..740 499-2260
664 N High St Morral (43337) *(G-10199)*

J-Mak Industries, Columbus Also Called: Panacea Products Corporation (G-5171)

J-Well Service Inc..330 824-2718
6345 Tod Ave Sw Warren (44481) *(G-13774)*

J&D Wood Enterprises, Piqua Also Called: J & D Wood Ltd (G-11359)

J&I Duct Fab Llc..937 473-2121
7502 W State Route 41 Covington (45318) *(G-5495)*

J&J Precision Fabrication, Columbiana Also Called: J&J Precision Fabricators Ltd (G-4621)

J&J Precision Fabricators Ltd....................................330 482-4964
1341 Heck Rd Columbiana (44408) *(G-4621)*

J&M Precision Die Casting LLC..................................440 365-7388
1329 Taylor St Elyria (44035) *(G-6555)*

J3 Point-Of-Sale, Bucyrus Also Called: Ganymede Technologies Corp (G-1681)

JA Acquisition Corp..419 287-3223
850 W Front St Pemberville (43450) *(G-11176)*

Jack Pine Studio LLC..740 332-2223
21397 State Route 180 Laurelville (43135) *(G-8237)*

Jack Walker Printing Co..440 352-4222
9517 Jackson St Mentor (44060) *(G-9540)*

Jack Walters & Sons Corp..937 653-8986
5045 N Us Highway 68 Urbana (43078) *(G-13470)*

Jackson Monument Inc..740 286-1590
14 Fairmount St Jackson (45640) *(G-7946)*

Jackson Tube Service Inc (PA)..................................937 773-8550
8210 Industry Park Dr Piqua (45356) *(G-11361)*

Jackson Wells Services.. 419 886-2017	**Janna Access, Elyria** *Also Called: Coolbreeze Technologies LLC (G-6515)*
1201 Mill Rd Bellville (44813) *(G-1139)*	**Janorpot LLC**.. 330 564-0232
Jaco Manufacturing Company................................ 440 234-4000	3175 Gilchrist Rd Mogadore (44260) *(G-10078)*
90 Karl St Berea (44017) *(G-1177)*	**Janova LLC**.. 614 638-6785
Jaco Manufacturing Company (PA)........................ 440 234-4000	7570 N Goodrich Sq New Albany (43054) *(G-10342)*
468 Geiger St Berea (44017) *(G-1178)*	**Janson Industries**... 330 455-7029
Jaco Products, Middlefield *Also Called: D Martone Industries Inc (G-9791)*	1200 Garfield Ave Sw Canton (44706) *(G-1921)*
Jacob & Levis Ltd... 330 852-7600	**Japo Inc**.. 614 263-2850
1689 State Route 39 Sugarcreek (44681) *(G-12639)*	3902 Indianola Ave Columbus (43214) *(G-5032)*
Jacobi Carbons Inc.. 215 546-3900	**Jarman Printing LLC**.. 330 823-8585
432 Mccormick Blvd Columbus (43215) *(G-5029)*	350 S Union Ave Alliance (44601) *(G-386)*
Jacobs, Cincinnati *Also Called: Jacobs Mechanical Co (G-2756)*	**Jasa Asphalt Russell Standard, Akron** *Also Called: Russell Standard Corporation (G-299)*
Jacobs Mechanical Co.. 513 681-6800	**Jasmine Distributing Ltd**...................................... 216 251-9420
4500 W Mitchell Ave Cincinnati (45232) *(G-2756)*	12117 Berea Rd Cleveland (44111) *(G-3883)*
Jacodar Inc.. 330 832-9557	**Jason Poffenberger**.. 937 369-1358
1212 Oberlin Ave Sw Massillon (44647) *(G-9208)*	122 Willowwood Dr Dayton (45405) *(G-5827)*
Jacodar Fsa LLC.. 330 454-1832	**Jason Schirmer**.. 937 433-3023
2300 Allen Ave Se Canton (44707) *(G-1920)*	3020 S Tech Blvd Miamisburg (45342) *(G-9702)*
Jacp Inc (PA)... 513 353-3660	**Jasper Printing Co LLC**.. 937 294-5218
5928 Hamilton Cleves Rd Miamitown (45041) *(G-9759)*	3540 Marshall Rd Kettering (45429) *(G-8121)*
JAD Machine Company Inc................................... 419 256-6332	**Jasstek Inc**.. 614 808-3600
10620 County Road J Malinta (43535) *(G-8743)*	555 Metro Pl N Ste 100 Dublin (43017) *(G-6313)*
Jade Products Inc.. 440 352-1700	**Jatiga Inc (PA)**... 859 817-7100
9309 Mercantile Dr Mentor (44060) *(G-9541)*	5823 Ravens Ridge Ln Cincinnati (45247) *(G-2762)*
Jade Tool Company.. 937 376-4740	**Jatrodiesel, Miamisburg** *Also Called: Jatrodiesel Inc (G-9703)*
1280 Burnett Dr Xenia (45385) *(G-14766)*	**Jatrodiesel Inc**
Jae Tech Inc.. 330 698-2000	845 N Main St Miamisburg (45342) *(G-9703)*
32 Hunter St Apple Creek (44606) *(G-470)*	**Javanation**... 419 584-1705
Jafe Decorating Inc.. 937 547-1888	108 S Main St Celina (45822) *(G-2111)*
1250 Martin St Greenville (45331) *(G-7343)*	**Jax Wax Inc**... 614 476-6769
Jails Correctional Products, Minster *Also Called: Fabcor Inc (G-10057)*	3145 E 17th Ave Columbus (43219) *(G-5033)*
Jain America Foods Inc (HQ)................................614 850-9400	**Jaxon's, Dayton** *Also Called: Dik Jaxon Products Co Inc (G-5748)*
1819 Walcutt Rd Ste I Columbus (43228) *(G-5030)*	**Jay Dee Service Corporation**................................ 330 425-1546
Jain Americas, Columbus *Also Called: Jain America Foods Inc (G-5030)*	1320 Highland Rd E Macedonia (44056) *(G-8699)*
Jake Sweeney Mazda Tri-County........................... 513 782-1150	**Jay Industries Inc**.. 419 747-4161
135 Northland Blvd Cincinnati (45246) *(G-2757)*	1595 W Longview Ave Mansfield (44906) *(G-8806)*
Jakmar Incorporated... 513 631-4303	**Jay Mid-South LLC**.. 256 439-6600
3280 Hageman Ave Cincinnati (45241) *(G-2758)*	150 Longview Ave E Mansfield (44903) *(G-8807)*
Jakprints Inc... 877 246-3132	**Jay Tees LLC**... 740 405-1579
3133 Chester Ave Cleveland (44114) *(G-3881)*	8941 Somerset Rd Thornville (43076) *(G-12766)*
Jalco Industries Inc.. 740 286-3808	**Jay-Em Aerospace Corporation**............................. 330 923-0333
330 Athens St Jackson (45640) *(G-7947)*	75 Marc Dr Cuyahoga Falls (44223) *(G-5551)*
Jamac Inc.. 419 625-9790	**Jayna Inc (PA)**... 937 335-8922
422 Buchanan St Sandusky (44870) *(G-11845)*	15 Marybill Dr S Troy (45373) *(G-13232)*
Jamar Precision Grinding Co................................ 330 220-0099	**Jaytee Division, Willoughby** *Also Called: Arem Co (G-14426)*
2661 Center Rd Hinckley (44233) *(G-7733)*	**JB Industries Ltd (PA)**... 330 856-4587
Jamen Tool & Die Co (PA).................................... 330 788-6521	160 Clifton Dr Ne Ste 4 Warren (44484) *(G-13775)*
4450 Lake Park Rd Youngstown (44512) *(G-14879)*	**JB Machining Concepts LLC**................................. 419 523-0096
Jamen Tool & Die Co... 330 782-6731	995 Sugar Mill Dr Ottawa (45875) *(G-11036)*
914 E Indianola Ave Youngstown (44502) *(G-14880)*	**JB Pavers and Hardscapes LLC**............................ 937 454-1145
James Bunnell Inc.. 513 353-1100	812 E National Rd Vandalia (45377) *(G-13564)*
7000 Dry Fork Rd Cleves (45002) *(G-4540)*	**JB Polymers Inc**... 216 941-7041
James C Free Inc... 513 793-0133	55 S Main St Pmb 204 Oberlin (44074) *(G-10919)*
9555 Main St Ste 1 Cincinnati (45242) *(G-2759)*	**Jbar, Cleveland** *Also Called: Jbar A/C Inc (G-3884)*
James C Free Inc (PA)... 937 298-0171	**Jbar A/C Inc**.. 216 447-4294
3100 Far Hills Ave Dayton (45429) *(G-5826)*	15501 Chatfield Ave Cleveland (44111) *(G-3884)*
James C Robinson.. 513 969-7482	**Jbc Technologies Inc (PA)**.................................... 440 327-4522
442 Chestnut St Apt 1 Cincinnati (45203) *(G-2760)*	7887 Bliss Pkwy North Ridgeville (44039) *(G-10737)*
James Free Jewelers, Dayton *Also Called: James C Free Inc (G-5826)*	**JBI Corporation**... 419 855-3389
James Free Jewellers, Cincinnati *Also Called: James C Free Inc (G-2759)*	22325 State Route 51 W Genoa (43430) *(G-7248)*
James K Green Enterprises Inc............................. 614 878-6041	**Jbk Manufacturing & Dev Co, Dayton** *Also Called: Premier Aerospace Group LLC (G-5952)*
1875 Lone Eagle St Columbus (43228) *(G-5031)*	**Jbm Packaging, Lebanon** *Also Called: Jbm Packaging Company (G-8269)*
James L Deckebach LLC....................................... 513 321-3733	**Jbm Packaging Company**...................................... 513 933-8333
4575 Eastern Ave Cincinnati (45226) *(G-2761)*	2850 Henkle Dr Lebanon (45036) *(G-8269)*
James R Smail Inc.. 330 264-7500	**Jbm Technologies of Ohio LLC**............................. 216 264-1270
2285 Eagle Pass Ste B Wooster (44691) *(G-14654)*	4515 Glenbrook Rd Willoughby (44094) *(G-14472)*
Jamestown Cont Cleveland Inc............................. 216 831-3700	**Jbnovember LLC**... 513 272-7000
4500 Renaissance Pkwy Cleveland (44128) *(G-3882)*	3950 Virginia Ave Cincinnati (45227) *(G-2763)*
Jamestown Industries Inc.................................... 330 779-0670	**Jbs Industries, Lebanon** *Also Called: Mix-Masters Inc (G-8277)*
650 N Meridian Rd Ste 3 Youngstown (44509) *(G-14881)*	**Jbs Industries Ltd**.. 513 314-5599
Jamesway Chick Mstr Incubator, Medina *Also Called: Chick Master Incubator Company (G-9387)*	1001 Atlantic Ave Apt 783 Columbus (43229) *(G-5034)*

Jbt Foodtech, Sandusky *Also Called: Jbt Marel Corporation (G-11846)*

Jbt Marel Corporation.. 614 891-2732
8270 Green Meadows Dr N Lewis Center (43035) *(G-8340)*

Jbt Marel Corporation.. 513 433-2500
2601 S Verity Pkwy Bldg 13 Middletown (45044) *(G-9868)*

Jbt Marel Corporation.. 419 626-0304
1622 First St Sandusky (44870) *(G-11846)*

Jbw Systems Inc... 614 882-5008
5840 Chandler Ct Westerville (43082) *(G-14215)*

JC Carter LLC (DH)... 440 569-1818
26451 Curtiss Wright Pkwy Ste 106 Richmond Heights (44143) *(G-11610)*

JC Carter Nozzles, Richmond Heights *Also Called: JC Carter LLC (G-11610)*

JC Electric Llc... 330 760-2915
9717 State Route 88 Garrettsville (44231) *(G-7221)*

Jci Jones Chemicals Inc.. 330 825-2531
2500 Vanderhoof Rd Barberton (44203) *(G-814)*

Jcl Equipment Co Inc.. 937 374-1010
915 Trumbull St Xenia (45385) *(G-14767)*

JD Indoor Comfort Inc... 440 949-8758
4040 Colorado Ave Sheffield Lake (44054) *(G-11954)*

JD Power Systems LLC.. 614 317-9394
3979 Parkway Ln Hilliard (43026) *(G-7685)*

Jda Software Group Inc... 480 308-3000
308 N Cleveland Massillon Rd Akron (44333) *(G-185)*

JDA SOFTWARE GROUP, INC., Akron *Also Called: Jda Software Group Inc (G-185)*

Jdh Holdings Inc.. 330 963-4400
8220 Bavaria Dr E Macedonia (44056) *(G-8700)*

JE Grote Company Inc (PA).. 614 868-8414
1160 Gahanna Pkwy Columbus (43230) *(G-5035)*

Jed Industries Inc... 440 639-9973
320 River St Grand River (44045) *(G-7310)*

Jeff Bonham Electric Inc.. 937 233-7662
3647 Wright Way Rd Dayton (45424) *(G-5828)*

Jeff Lori Jed Holdings Inc.. 513 423-0319
1500 S University Blvd Middletown (45044) *(G-9869)*

Jeffco Sheltered Workshop... 740 264-4608
256 John Scott Hwy Steubenville (43952) *(G-12404)*

Jefferson Industries Corp (HQ)...................................... 614 879-5300
6670 State Route 29 West Jefferson (43162) *(G-14162)*

Jefferson Smurfit Corporation....................................... 440 248-4370
6385 Cochran Rd Solon (44139) *(G-12129)*

Jeg Associates, Westerville *Also Called: Jeg Associates Inc (G-14266)*

Jeg Associates Inc... 614 882-1295
509 S Otterbein Ave Ste 7 Westerville (43081) *(G-14266)*

Jeld-Wen Inc... 740 964-1431
91 Heritage Dr Etna (43062) *(G-6635)*

Jeld-Wen Inc... 740 397-1144
1201 Newark Rd Mount Vernon (43050) *(G-10246)*

Jeld-Wen Inc... 740 397-3403
335 Commerce Dr Mount Vernon (43050) *(G-10247)*

Jeld-Wen Millwork Masters, Etna *Also Called: Jeld-Wen Inc (G-6635)*

Jeld-Wen Windows, Mount Vernon *Also Called: Jeld-Wen Inc (G-10246)*

Jen-Coat Inc (DH)... 513 671-1777
12025 Tricon Rd Cincinnati (45246) *(G-2764)*

Jena Tool Inc... 937 296-1122
5219 Springboro Pike Moraine (45439) *(G-10171)*

Jenis Splendid Ice Creams LLC (PA)............................. 614 488-3224
401 N Front St Ste 300 Columbus (43215) *(G-5036)*

Jennmar McSweeney... 740 377-3354
235 Commerce Dr South Point (45680) *(G-12224)*

Jentgen Steel Services LLC.. 614 268-6340
611 E Weber Rd Ste 201 Columbus (43211) *(G-5037)*

Jenzabar Inc... 513 563-4542
10260 Alliance Rd Blue Ash (45242) *(G-1289)*

Jergens Inc (PA).. 216 486-5540
15700 S Waterloo Rd Cleveland (44110) *(G-3885)*

Jerguson, Strongsville *Also Called: Clark-Reliance LLC (G-12550)*

Jerico Industries, Wadsworth *Also Called: Jerico Plastic Industries Inc (G-13645)*

Jerico Plastic Industries Inc... 330 868-4600
250 Bridge St Minerva (44657) *(G-10039)*

Jerico Plastic Industries Inc (PA).................................. 330 868-4600
7970 Boneta Rd Wadsworth (44281) *(G-13645)*

Jerl Machine Inc.. 419 873-0270
11140 Avenue Rd Perrysburg (43551) *(G-11232)*

Jerpbak-Bayless Co.. 440 248-5387
34150 Solon Rd Solon (44139) *(G-12130)*

Jerry Harolds Doors Unlimited...................................... 740 635-4949
415 Hall St Bridgeport (43912) *(G-1494)*

Jerry Tools Inc.. 513 242-3211
6200 Vine St Cincinnati (45216) *(G-2765)*

JES Foods Inc (PA).. 216 883-8987
865 W Liberty St Ste 200 Medina (44256) *(G-9415)*

JES Foods/Celina Inc.. 419 586-7446
1800 Industrial Dr Celina (45822) *(G-2112)*

Jet Container Company.. 614 444-2133
1033 Brentnell Ave Ste 100 Columbus (43219) *(G-5038)*

Jet Di Inc... 330 607-7913
1736 W 130th St Ste 200 Brunswick (44212) *(G-1600)*

Jet Dock Systems Inc... 216 750-2264
9601 Corporate Cir Cleveland (44125) *(G-3886)*

Jet Fuel Strategies LLC... 440 323-4220
44050 Russia Rd Elyria (44035) *(G-6556)*

Jet Inc.. 440 461-2000
750 Alpha Dr Cleveland (44143) *(G-3887)*

Jet Machine, Cincinnati *Also Called: Wulco Inc (G-3236)*

Jet Machine & Manufacturing, Cincinnati *Also Called: Wulco Inc (G-3235)*

Jet Products Incorporated.. 937 866-7969
535 E Dixie Dr Dayton (45449) *(G-5829)*

Jet Rubber Company... 330 325-1821
4457 Tallmadge Rd Rootstown (44272) *(G-11648)*

Jet Stream International Inc.. 330 505-9988
644 Myron St Hubbard (44425) *(G-7813)*

Jetcoat, Columbus *Also Called: Jetcoat LLC (G-5039)*

Jetcoat LLC.. 800 394-0047
472 Brehl Ave Columbus (43223) *(G-5039)*

Jewelry Art, Hudson *Also Called: Handcrafted Jewelry Inc (G-7843)*

Jewett Supply.. 419 738-9882
607 N Water St Wapakoneta (45895) *(G-13717)*

Jewish Synagogue, Akron *Also Called: Temple Israel (G-330)*

JF Martt and Associates Inc... 330 938-4000
501 N Johnson Rd Sebring (44672) *(G-11895)*

Jfdb Ltd.. 513 870-0601
10036 Springfield Pike Cincinnati (45215) *(G-2766)*

Jh Industries Inc... 330 963-4105
1981 E Aurora Rd Twinsburg (44087) *(G-13321)*

Jh Instruments, Columbus *Also Called: Fcx Performance Inc (G-4922)*

Jilco, Akron *Also Called: Jilco Precision Mold Mch Inc (G-186)*

Jilco LLC... 330 270-9780
Youngstown (44515) *(G-14882)*

Jilco Precision Mold Mch Inc.. 330 633-9645
1245 Devalera St Akron (44310) *(G-186)*

Jim Nier Construction Inc (PA)...................................... 740 289-3925
340 Bailey Chapel Rd Piketon (45661) *(G-11308)*

Jis Distribution LLC (HQ).. 216 706-6552
15700 S Waterloo Rd Cleveland (44110) *(G-3888)*

Jit Milrob, Aurora *Also Called: Lynk Packaging Inc (G-677)*

Jj Seville LLC... 330 769-2071
22 Milton St Seville (44273) *(G-11919)*

Jj Sleeves Inc... 440 205-1055
6850 Patterson Dr Mentor (44060) *(G-9542)*

JJ&pl Services-Consulting LLC...................................... 330 923-5783
1474 Main St Cuyahoga Falls (44221) *(G-5552)*

Jk Digital Publishing LLC.. 937 299-0185
20 Heatherwoode Cir Springboro (45066) *(G-12256)*

Jk-Co LLC... 419 422-5240
16960 E State Route 12 Findlay (45840) *(G-6883)*

Jkrg Construction Services, West Chester *Also Called: Clarity Retail Services LLC (G-13965)*

Jlg Industries Inc.. 330 684-0132
2927 E Paradise Street Ext Orrville (44667) *(G-10988)*

Jlg Industries Inc.. 330 684-0200
600 E Chestnut St Orrville (44667) *(G-10989)*

Jls Funeral Home... 614 625-1220
2322 Randy Ct Columbus (43232) *(G-5040)*

(G-0000) Company's Geographic Section entry number

JM Hamilton Group Inc...................................... 419 229-4010
1700 Elida Rd Lima (45805) *(G-8422)*

JM Performance Products Inc.............................. 440 357-1234
1234 High St Fairport Harbor (44077) *(G-6817)*

JM Smucker LLC (HQ)....................................... 330 682-3000
1 Strawberry Ln Orrville (44667) *(G-10990)*

Jmac Inc (PA)... 614 436-2418
200 W Nationwide Blvd Unit 1 Columbus (43215) *(G-5041)*

Jmac Inc.. 937 346-0800
2020 Progress Rd Springfield (45505) *(G-12331)*

JMB Energy Inc.. 330 505-9610
3729 Union St Mineral Ridge (44440) *(G-10029)*

Jml Holdings Inc... 419 866-7500
6210 Merger Dr Holland (43528) *(G-7770)*

JMS Composites, Springfield *Also Called: JMS Industries Inc (G-12332)*

JMS Industries Inc.. 937 325-3502
3240 E National Rd Springfield (45505) *(G-12332)*

JMw Welding and Mfg Inc.................................. 330 484-2428
512 45th St Sw Canton (44706) *(G-1922)*

Jnc,, Piketon *Also Called: Jim Nier Construction Inc (G-11308)*

Jnp Group LLC... 800 735-9645
449 Freedlander Rd Wooster (44691) *(G-14655)*

Jobap Assembly Inc.. 440 632-5393
16090 Industrial Pkwy Unit 9 Middlefield (44062) *(G-9803)*

Jobskin Division, Northwood *Also Called: Torbot Group Inc (G-10810)*

Joe Rees Welding.. 937 652-4067
326 W Twain Ave Urbana (43078) *(G-13471)*

Joe The Printer Guy LLC.................................. 216 651-3880
1590 Parkwood Rd Lakewood (44107) *(G-8168)*

Johannings Inc.. 330 875-1706
3244 S Nickelplate St Louisville (44641) *(G-8607)*

John C Meier Grape Juice Co, Cincinnati *Also Called: Meiers Wine Cellars Inc (G-2861)*

John Christ Winery Inc..................................... 440 933-9672
32421 Walker Rd Avon Lake (44012) *(G-761)*

John D Oil and Gas Company.............................. 440 255-6325
7001 Center St Mentor (44060) *(G-9543)*

John Deere Authorized Dealer, Brunswick *Also Called: Murphy Tractor & Eqp Co Inc (G-1602)*

John Deere Authorized Dealer, Canton *Also Called: Murphy Tractor & Eqp Co Inc (G-1954)*

John Deere Authorized Dealer, Canton *Also Called: Western Branch Diesel LLC (G-2047)*

John Deere Authorized Dealer, Columbus *Also Called: Murphy Tractor & Eqp Co Inc (G-5116)*

John Deere Authorized Dealer, Hilliard *Also Called: JD Power Systems LLC (G-7685)*

John Deere Authorized Dealer, Lima *Also Called: Murphy Tractor & Eqp Co Inc (G-8434)*

John Deere Authorized Dealer, Madison *Also Called: Great Lakes Power Products Inc (G-8730)*

John Deere Authorized Dealer, Perry *Also Called: Great Lakes Power Service Co (G-11192)*

John Deere Authorized Dealer, Urbana *Also Called: Koenig Equipment Inc (G-13472)*

John Deere Authorized Dealer, Vandalia *Also Called: Murphy Tractor & Eqp Co Inc (G-13573)*

John Deere Authorized Dealer, Wooster *Also Called: Shearer Farm Inc (G-14685)*

John Frieda Prof Hair Care Inc (DH)..................... 800 521-3189
2535 Spring Grove Ave Cincinnati (45214) *(G-2767)*

John H Hosking Co.. 513 422-9425
4665 Emerald Way Middletown (45044) *(G-9870)*

John Krizay Inc... 330 332-5607
1777 Pennsylvania Ave Salem (44460) *(G-11790)*

John Krusinski.. 216 441-0100
6300 Heisley Ave Cleveland (44105) *(G-3889)*

John P Ellis Clinic Podiatry.............................. 440 460-0444
730 Som Center Rd Ste 350 Cleveland (44143) *(G-3890)*

John Purdum.. 513 897-9686
100 S Main St Waynesville (45068) *(G-13879)*

John R Jurgensen Co (PA)................................. 513 771-0820
11641 Mosteller Rd Cincinnati (45241) *(G-2768)*

John Stehlin & Sons Co.................................... 513 385-6164
10134 Colerain Ave Cincinnati (45251) *(G-2769)*

John Zidian Company....................................... 330 965-8455
382 Rosemont Rd North Jackson (44451) *(G-10690)*

John Zidian Company (PA)................................. 330 743-6050
574 Mcclurg Rd Youngstown (44512) *(G-14883)*

Johndow Industries Inc................................... 330 753-6895
151 Snyder Ave Barberton (44203) *(G-815)*

Johnny Johnson Sports, Ontario *Also Called: Unisport Inc (G-10953)*

Johns Manville Corporation............................... 419 782-0180
1410 Columbus Ave Defiance (43512) *(G-6113)*

Johns Manville Corporation............................... 419 784-7000
925 Carpenter Rd Defiance (43512) *(G-6114)*

Johns Manville Corporation............................... 419 784-7000
3rd And Perry Defiance (43512) *(G-6115)*

Johns Manville Corporation............................... 419 878-8111
408 Perry St Defiance (43512) *(G-6116)*

Johns Manville Corporation............................... 419 499-1400
49 Lockwood Rd Milan (44846) *(G-9916)*

Johns Manville Corporation............................... 419 878-8111
7500 Dutch Rd Waterville (43566) *(G-13835)*

Johns Manville Corporation............................... 419 878-8112
6050 N River Rd Waterville (43566) *(G-13836)*

Johns Welding & Towing Inc.............................. 419 447-8937
850 N County Road 11 Tiffin (44883) *(G-12785)*

Johnson & Johnson... 513 786-7000
4545 Creek Rd Blue Ash (45242) *(G-1290)*

Johnson & Johnson Services LLC......................... 513 289-4514
273 Mccormick Pl Cincinnati (45219) *(G-2770)*

Johnson Bros Greenwich, Greenwich *Also Called: Johnson Bros Rubber Co Inc (G-7362)*

Johnson Bros Rubber Co (PA)............................. 419 853-4122
42 W Buckeye St West Salem (44287) *(G-14188)*

Johnson Bros Rubber Co Inc.............................. 419 752-4814
41 Center St Greenwich (44837) *(G-7362)*

Johnson Contrls Authorized Dlr, Akron *Also Called: Famous Industries Inc (G-145)*

Johnson Contrls Authorized Dlr, Dayton *Also Called: Glt Inc (G-5800)*

Johnson Contrls Authorized Dlr, Northwood *Also Called: Yanfeng Intl Auto Tech US I LL (G-10815)*

Johnson Controls, Brecksville *Also Called: Johnson Controls Inc (G-1474)*

Johnson Controls, Bryan *Also Called: Clarios LLC (G-1636)*

Johnson Controls, Cincinnati *Also Called: Johnson Controls Inc (G-2771)*

Johnson Controls, Cincinnati *Also Called: Johnson Controls Inc (G-2772)*

Johnson Controls, Holland *Also Called: Clarios LLC (G-7750)*

Johnson Controls, Mentor *Also Called: Clarios LLC (G-9499)*

Johnson Controls, Saint Marys *Also Called: Johnson Controls Inc (G-11739)*

Johnson Controls, Westerville *Also Called: Johnson Controls Inc (G-14267)*

Johnson Controls, Youngstown *Also Called: Johnson Controls Inc (G-14884)*

Johnson Controls Inc....................................... 216 587-0100
6650 W Snowville Rd Brecksville (44141) *(G-1474)*

Johnson Controls Inc....................................... 513 489-0950
7863 Palace Dr Cincinnati (45249) *(G-2771)*

Johnson Controls Inc....................................... 513 671-6338
11648 Springfield Pike Cincinnati (45246) *(G-2772)*

Johnson Controls Inc....................................... 414 524-1200
1111 Mckinley Rd Saint Marys (45885) *(G-11739)*

Johnson Controls Inc....................................... 614 895-6600
835 Green Crest Dr Westerville (43081) *(G-14267)*

Johnson Controls Inc....................................... 330 270-4385
1044 N Meridian Rd Ste A Youngstown (44509) *(G-14884)*

Johnson Metall Inc... 440 245-6826
1305 Oberlin Ave Lorain (44052) *(G-8559)*

Johnson Mfg Systems LLC................................. 937 866-4744
4505 Infirmary Rd Miamisburg (45342) *(G-9704)*

Johnson Plastic Plus, Findlay *Also Called: Rowmark LLC (G-6914)*

Johnson Prcision Machining Inc.......................... 513 353-4252
5919 Hamilton Cleves Rd Cleves (45002) *(G-4541)*

Johnson-Nash Metal Pdts Inc............................. 513 874-7022
9265 Seward Rd Fairfield (45014) *(G-6748)*

Johnsonite, Solon *Also Called: Tarkett USA Inc (G-12193)*

Johnsonite Inc.. 440 632-3441
16035 Industrial Pkwy Middlefield (44062) *(G-9804)*

Johnsonite Inc.. 440 543-8916
30000 Aurora Rd Solon (44139) *(G-12131)*

Johnsonite Rubber Flooring, Middlefield *Also Called: Johnsonite Inc (G-9804)*

Johnsons Emrgncy Vhcl Slutions, Wellston *Also Called: Johnsons Fire Equipment Co (G-13908)*

Johnsons Fire Equipment Co.............................. 740 357-4916
20213 State Route 93 Wellston (45692) *(G-13908)*

Johnsons Real Ice Cream LLC.. 614 231-0014
   2728 E Main St Columbus (43209) *(G-5042)*

Johnston Mfg Co Inc.. 440 269-1420
   7611 Saint Clair Ave Mentor (44060) *(G-9544)*

Joining Metals Inc.. 440 259-1790
   3314 Blackmore Rd Perry (44081) *(G-11193)*

Jolly Pats, Streetsboro Also Called: HP Enterprise Inc *(G-12503)*

Jomac Ltd.. 330 627-7727
   182 Scio Rd Se Carrollton (44615) *(G-2087)*

Jonashtons LLC... 419 488-2363
   12485 State Route 634 Cloverdale (45827) *(G-4555)*

Jones Industries LLC.. 440 810-1251
   8543 Evergreen Trl Olmsted Twp (44138) *(G-10946)*

Jones Metal Products Co LLC (PA)...................................740 545-6381
   200 N Center St West Lafayette (43845) *(G-14171)*

Jones Metal Products Company.. 740 545-6341
   305 N Center St West Lafayette (43845) *(G-14172)*

Jones Potato Chip Co (PA)... 419 529-9424
   823 Bowman St Mansfield (44903) *(G-8808)*

Jones Propane Supply, Carrollton Also Called: Jomac Ltd *(G-2087)*

Jones-Hamilton Co (PA)...888 858-4425
   570 Longbow Dr Maumee (43537) *(G-9300)*

Jones-Hamilton Co., Maumee Also Called: Jones-Hamilton Co *(G-9300)*

Joneszylon Company LLC.. 740 545-6341
   300 N Center St West Lafayette (43845) *(G-14173)*

Jonmar Gear and Machine Inc.. 330 854-6500
   13786 Warwick Dr Nw Canal Fulton (44614) *(G-1776)*

Jordan Young International, London Also Called: Textiles Inc *(G-8542)*

Jordankelly LLC.. 216 855-8550
   165 Ira Ave Akron (44301) *(G-187)*

Jordon Auto Service & Tire Inc... 216 214-6528
   5201 Carnegie Ave Cleveland (44103) *(G-3891)*

Jos Berning Printing Co... 513 721-0781
   1850 Dalton Ave Cincinnati (45214) *(G-2773)*

Jos-Tech Inc... 330 678-3260
   852 W Main St Kent (44240) *(G-8038)*

Jose Madrid Salsa, Zanesville Also Called: Michael Zakany LLC *(G-15028)*

Joseph Adams Corp.. 330 225-9125
   5740 Grafton Rd Valley City (44280) *(G-13500)*

Joseph Industries Inc... 330 528-0091
   10039 Aurora Hudson Rd Streetsboro (44241) *(G-12507)*

Joseph Sabatino... 330 332-5879
   1834 Depot Rd Salem (44460) *(G-11791)*

Joseph T Snyder Industries Inc... 216 883-6900
   9210 Loren Ave Cleveland (44105) *(G-3892)*

Joslyn Hi-Voltage Company LLC... 216 271-6600
   4000 E 116th St Cleveland (44105) *(G-3893)*

Joslyn Manufacturing Company.. 330 467-8111
   9400 Valley View Rd Macedonia (44056) *(G-8701)*

Joslyn Sunbank Company LLC (DH).. 805 238-2840
   1000 Eaton Blvd Cleveland (44122) *(G-3894)*

Jotco Inc... 513 721-4943
   1400 Park Ave E Mansfield (44905) *(G-8809)*

Joules Angstrom Uv Prtg Inks C (PA)....................................740 964-9113
   104 Heritage Dr Pataskala (43062) *(G-11141)*

Journal Leader, Caldwell Also Called: Southeast Publications Inc *(G-1729)*

Journal Register Company... 440 245-6901
   401 Broadway Ste B Lorain (44052) *(G-8560)*

Journal Register Company... 440 951-0000
   36625 Vine St Willoughby (44094) *(G-14473)*

Journey Electronics Corp... 513 539-9836
   902 N Garver Rd Monroe (45050) *(G-10111)*

Journey Systems LLC... 513 831-6200
   25 Whitney Dr Ste 100 Milford (45150) *(G-9940)*

Joy Global Underground Min LLC.. 440 248-7970
   6160 Cochran Rd Cleveland (44139) *(G-3895)*

Joy Global Underground Min LLC.. 440 248-7970
   6160 Cochran Rd Solon (44139) *(G-12132)*

Joyce Manufacturing Co.. 440 239-9100
   1125 Berea Industrial Pkwy Berea (44017) *(G-1179)*

Joyce Windows, Berea Also Called: Joyce Manufacturing Co *(G-1179)*

Joyce/Dayton Corp... 937 294-6261
   Dayton (45401) *(G-5830)*

Joyce/Dayton Corp (HQ).. 937 294-6261
   3300 S Dixie Dr Ste 101 Dayton (45439) *(G-5831)*

JP Cabinets LLC.. 440 232-9780
   20910 Miles Pkwy Cleveland (44128) *(G-3896)*

JP Industrial, Lisbon Also Called: J P Industrial Products Inc *(G-8473)*

Jpi Coastal LLC.. 330 424-1110
   11988 State Route 45 Lisbon (44432) *(G-8475)*

JPS Technologies Inc (PA)..513 984-6400
   11110 Deerfield Rd Blue Ash (45242) *(G-1291)*

JPS Technologies Inc.. 513 984-6400
   11118 Deerfield Rd Blue Ash (45242) *(G-1292)*

JR Manufacturing Inc (PA).. 419 375-8021
   900 Industrial Dr W Fort Recovery (45846) *(G-6968)*

Jrb Attachments LLC (DH).. 330 734-3000
   820 Glaser Pkwy Akron (44306) *(G-188)*

Jrb Family Holdings Inc
   4255 E Lincoln Way Wooster (44691) *(G-14656)*

Jrb Industries LLC... 567 825-7022
   3425 State Route 571 Greenville (45331) *(G-7344)*

Jrm 2 Company... 513 554-1700
   425 Shepherd Ave Cincinnati (45215) *(G-2774)*

Js Fabrications Inc... 419 333-0323
   1400 E State St Fremont (43420) *(G-7118)*

Jsc Employee Leasing Corp (PA).. 330 773-8971
   1560 Firestone Pkwy Akron (44301) *(G-189)*

Jsh International LLC.. 330 734-0251
   124 Darrow Rd Ste 5 Akron (44305) *(G-190)*

Jsj Sb Holdings Inc.. 216 398-7774
   4653 Spring Rd Cleveland (44131) *(G-3897)*

Jst LLC... 614 423-7815
   6240 Frost Rd Ste C Westerville (43082) *(G-14216)*

JSW Steel USA Ohio Inc.. 740 535-8172
   1500 Commercial St Mingo Junction (43938) *(G-10052)*

Jsw USA, Mingo Junction Also Called: JSW Steel USA Ohio Inc *(G-10052)*

JT Plus Well Service LLC... 740 347-0070
   140 E Main St Corning (43730) *(G-5441)*

Jt Premier Printing Corp... 216 831-8785
   18780 Cranwood Pkwy Cleveland (44128) *(G-3898)*

JTL Enterprises LLC (PA)..937 890-8189
   5700 Webster St Dayton (45414) *(G-5832)*

Jtm Food Group, Harrison Also Called: Jtm Provisions Company Inc *(G-7556)*

Jtm Food Group, Harrison Also Called: Jtm Provisions Company Inc *(G-7557)*

Jtm Products Inc.. 440 287-2302
   31025 Carter St Solon (44139) *(G-12133)*

Jtm Provisions Company Inc (PA).. 513 367-4900
   200 Sales Ave Harrison (45030) *(G-7556)*

Jtm Provisions Company Inc.. 513 367-4900
   270 Industrial Dr Harrison (45030) *(G-7557)*

Juba Industries Inc.. 440 655-9960
   126 W Jefferson St Jefferson (44047) *(G-7973)*

Judith Leiber LLC (PA).. 614 449-4217
   4300 E 5th Ave Columbus (43219) *(G-5043)*

Judo Steel, Dayton Also Called: Judo Steel Company Inc *(G-5833)*

Judo Steel Company Inc
   1526 Nicholas Rd Dayton (45417) *(G-5833)*

Judy Mills Company Inc (PA)... 513 271-4241
   3360 Red Bank Rd Cincinnati (45227) *(G-2775)*

Julie Maynard Inc... 937 443-0408
   4991 Hempstead Station Dr Dayton (45429) *(G-5834)*

Julius Zorn Inc... 330 923-4999
   3690 Zorn Dr Cuyahoga Falls (44223) *(G-5553)*

Junker Inc.. 630 231-3770
   1601 Perry Dr Sw Canton (44706) *(G-1923)*

Juno Enterprises LLC... 419 448-9350
   8146 Us Highway 224 New Riegel (44853) *(G-10470)*

Jupmode... 419 318-2029
   2022 Adams St Toledo (43604) *(G-13013)*

Just Business Inc... 866 577-3303
   1612 Prosser Ave Ste 100 Dayton (45409) *(G-5835)*

(G-0000) Company's Geographic Section entry number

Just Name It Inc..614 626-8662
110 Hedstrom Dr Ashland (44805) *(G-542)*

Just Natural Provision Company...........................216 431-7922
4800 Crayton Ave Cleveland (44104) *(G-3899)*

Just-Ink-Tees, Jamestown *Also Called: Ball Jackets LLC (G-7968)*

Justice..937 435-6928
2700 Miamisburg Centerville Rd Ste 260 Dayton (45459) *(G-5836)*

Justins Delight LLC...567 234-3575
101 W Park St Toledo (43608) *(G-13014)*

Juzo USA, Cuyahoga Falls *Also Called: Julius Zorn Inc (G-5553)*

K & B Acquisitions Inc.......................................937 253-1163
3013 Linden Ave Dayton (45410) *(G-5837)*

K & B Molded Products, Brookville *Also Called: Kuhns Mold & Tool Co Inc (G-1572)*

K & G Machine Company.....................................216 732-7115
26981 Tungsten Rd Cleveland (44132) *(G-3900)*

K & J Machine Inc...740 425-3282
326 Fairmont Ave Barnesville (43713) *(G-845)*

K & K Auto & Truck Parts, Logan *Also Called: Pattons Trck & Hvy Eqp Svc Inc (G-8523)*

K & K Precision Inc...513 336-0032
5001 N Mason Montgomery Rd Mason (45040) *(G-9117)*

K & L Ready Mix Inc..419 293-2937
5511 State Route 613 Mc Comb (45858) *(G-9354)*

K & L Ready Mix Inc (PA)....................................419 523-4376
10391 State Route 15 Ottawa (45875) *(G-11037)*

K A O Brands, West Chester *Also Called: KAO USA Inc (G-14018)*

K B I, Sandusky *Also Called: Kyklos Bearing International Llc (G-11848)*

K B Machine & Tool Inc......................................937 773-1624
1500 S Main St Piqua (45356) *(G-11362)*

K C P, Beachwood *Also Called: Kirtland Capital Partners LP (G-924)*

K D C, Johnstown *Also Called: Tri-Tech Laboratories Inc (G-8000)*

K Davis Inc...419 307-7051
206 Lynn St Fremont (43420) *(G-7119)*

K F T Inc..513 241-5910
726 Mehring Way Cincinnati (45203) *(G-2776)*

K G M, Cincinnati *Also Called: Knoble Glass & Metal Inc (G-2802)*

K K Tool Co...937 325-1373
115 S Center St Springfield (45502) *(G-12333)*

K M I, Cincinnati *Also Called: United Tool Supply Inc (G-2317)*

K Petroleum Inc (PA)..614 532-5420
81 Mill St Ste 205 Gahanna (43230) *(G-7161)*

K S Machine Inc...216 687-0459
3215 Superior Ave E Cleveland (44114) *(G-3901)*

K Ventures Inc...419 678-2308
211 E Main St Coldwater (45828) *(G-4579)*

K Wm Beach Mfg Co Inc.....................................937 399-3838
4655 Urbana Rd Springfield (45502) *(G-12334)*

K-B Plating Inc...216 341-1115
3685 E 78th St Cleveland (44105) *(G-3903)*

K-D Lamp Company..440 293-4064
101 Parker Dr Andover (44003) *(G-457)*

K-M-S Industries Inc...440 243-6680
6519 Eastland Rd Ste 1 Brookpark (44142) *(G-1554)*

K-Mar Structures LLC..231 924-5777
1825 Flagdale Rd S Junction City (43748) *(G-8002)*

K-O-K Products Inc...740 548-0526
700 S 3 Bs And K Rd Galena (43021) *(G-7173)*

K.M.I. Printing, Chardon *Also Called: Key Maneuvers Inc (G-2210)*

K.M.S., Brookpark *Also Called: K-M-S Industries Inc (G-1554)*

K&M Aviation LLC...216 261-9000
355 Richmond Rd Cleveland (44143) *(G-3902)*

Kabab-G Inc..216 476-3335
6676 Rochelle Blvd Cleveland (44130) *(G-3904)*

Kadant Black Clawson Inc (HQ)............................513 229-8100
1425 Kingsview Dr Lebanon (45036) *(G-8270)*

Kadee Industries, Bedford *Also Called: Dribble Creek Inc (G-1029)*

Kaeden Books, Westlake *Also Called: Kaeden Publishing (G-14312)*

Kaeden Publishing..440 617-1400
24700 Center Ridge Rd Ste 170 Westlake (44145) *(G-14312)*

Kaeper Machine Inc...440 974-1010
8680 Twinbrook Rd Mentor (44060) *(G-9545)*

Kaffenbarger Truck Eqp Co..................................513 772-6800
3260 E Kemper Rd Cincinnati (45241) *(G-2777)*

Kaffenbarger Truck Eqp Co (PA)...........................937 845-3804
10991 Ballentine Pike New Carlisle (45344) *(G-10373)*

Kahiki, Gahanna *Also Called: Kahiki Foods Inc (G-7162)*

Kahiki Foods Inc..614 322-3180
1100 Morrison Rd Gahanna (43230) *(G-7162)*

Kahny Printing Inc..513 251-2911
4766 River Rd Cincinnati (45233) *(G-2778)*

Kaiser Aluminum Fab Pdts LLC.............................740 522-1151
600 Kaiser Dr Heath (43056) *(G-7598)*

Kaiser Aluminum Newark Works, Heath *Also Called: Kaiser Aluminum Fab Pdts LLC (G-7598)*

Kaiser Foods Inc (PA)..513 621-2053
500 York St Cincinnati (45214) *(G-2779)*

Kaiser Pickles LLC (HQ).....................................513 621-2053
500 York St Cincinnati (45214) *(G-2780)*

Kaiser Pickles LLC..513 621-2053
422 York St Cincinnati (45214) *(G-2781)*

Kaivac, Hamilton *Also Called: Kaivac Inc (G-7508)*

Kaivac Inc...513 887-4600
2680 Van Hook Ave Hamilton (45015) *(G-7508)*

Kalcor Coatings Company....................................440 946-4700
37721 Stevens Blvd Willoughby (44094) *(G-14474)*

Kaliburn Inc..843 695-4073
22801 Saint Clair Ave Cleveland (44117) *(G-3905)*

Kalida Manufacturing Inc....................................419 532-2026
801 Ottawa St Kalida (45853) *(G-8004)*

Kalinich Fence Company Inc................................440 238-6127
12223 Prospect Rd Strongsville (44149) *(G-12569)*

Kalmbach, Upper Sandusky *Also Called: Kalmbach Feeds Inc (G-13443)*

Kalmbach Feeds Inc (PA)....................................419 294-3838
7148 State Highway 199 Upper Sandusky (43351) *(G-13443)*

Kalron LLC..440 647-3039
143 Erie St Wellington (44090) *(G-13893)*

Kalron LLC..440 647-3039
775 Shiloh Ave Wellington (44090) *(G-13894)*

Kalt Manufacturing Company................................440 327-2102
36700 Sugar Ridge Rd North Ridgeville (44039) *(G-10738)*

Kam Manufacturing Inc......................................419 238-6037
1197 Grill Rd Van Wert (45891) *(G-13538)*

Kamco Industries Inc (HQ)..................................419 924-5511
1001 E Jackson St West Unity (43570) *(G-14196)*

Kamps Inc...937 526-9333
10709 Reed Rd Versailles (45380) *(G-13598)*

Kamps Pallets..616 818-4323
2132 Refugee Rd Columbus (43207) *(G-5044)*

Kanan Enterprises Inc (PA).................................440 248-8484
31900 Solon Rd Solon (44139) *(G-12134)*

Kanan Enterprises Inc..440 248-8484
30600 Carter St Solon (44139) *(G-12135)*

Kanan Enterprises Inc..440 349-0719
6401 Davis Industrial Pkwy Solon (44139) *(G-12136)*

Kando of Cincinnati Inc......................................513 459-7782
2025 Mckinley Blvd Lebanon (45036) *(G-8271)*

Kann Custom Welding LLC...................................330 231-2719
2425 Township Road 414 Dundee (44624) *(G-6366)*

Kantner Ingredients Inc......................................614 766-3638
975 Worthington Woods Loop Rd Columbus (43085) *(G-5045)*

Kanya Industries LLC...330 722-5432
694 W Liberty St Medina (44256) *(G-9416)*

KAO USA Inc (HQ)..513 421-1400
2535 Spring Grove Ave Cincinnati (45214) *(G-2782)*

KAO USA Inc..513 629-5210
312 Plum St Cincinnati (45202) *(G-2783)*

KAO USA Inc..513 341-2630
8778 Le Saint Dr West Chester (45014) *(G-14018)*

Kap Signs, Dayton *Also Called: Blang Acquisition LLC (G-5679)*

Kapco, Kent *Also Called: Kent Adhesive Products Co (G-8039)*

Kapios LLC..567 661-0772
2865 N Reynolds Rd Ste 220d Toledo (43615) *(G-13015)*

Kapios Health, Toledo *Also Called: Kapios LLC (G-13015)*

ALPHABETIC

Kaplan Industries Inc..856 779-8181
6255 Kilby Rd Harrison (45030) *(G-7558)*

Kaps, Willoughby *Also Called: Kelly Arspc Thrmal Systems LLC (G-14476)*

Kar-Del Plastics Inc..419 289-9739
1177 Faultless Dr Ashland (44805) *(G-543)*

Kard Bridge Products, Minster *Also Called: Kard Welding Inc (G-10059)*

Kard Welding Inc...419 628-2598
480 Osterloh Rd Minster (45865) *(G-10059)*

Kardol Quality Products LLC (PA)............................513 933-8206
9933 Alliance Rd Ste 2 Blue Ash (45242) *(G-1293)*

Karen Carson Creations, Dayton *Also Called: Carson-Saeks Inc (G-5694)*

Karg Corporation...330 633-4916
241 Southwest Ave Tallmadge (44278) *(G-12738)*

Karl Kuemmerling Inc
129 Edgewater Ave Nw Massillon (44646) *(G-9209)*

Karma Metal Products Inc.....................................419 524-4371
556 Caldwell Ave Mansfield (44905) *(G-8810)*

Karman Rubber Company.......................................330 864-2161
2331 Copley Rd Akron (44320) *(G-191)*

Karn Meats Inc..614 252-3712
922 Taylor Ave Columbus (43219) *(G-5046)*

Karol-Warner, Lewis Center *Also Called: Kw Acquisition Inc (G-8341)*

Karon C Enold...740 269-3475
45 Monroe St Sherrodsville (44675) *(G-11975)*

Karrikin Spirits Company LLC.................................513 561-5000
3717 Jonlen Dr Cincinnati (45227) *(G-2784)*

Kars Ohio LLC..614 655-1099
6359 Summit Rd Sw Pataskala (43062) *(G-11142)*

Karyall-Telday Inc..216 281-4063
8221 Clinton Rd Cleveland (44144) *(G-3906)*

Kasai North America Inc..614 356-1494
655 Metro Pl S Ste 560 Dublin (43017) *(G-6314)*

Kasai North America Inc..419 209-0399
1111 N Warpole St Upper Sandusky (43351) *(G-13444)*

Kase Equipment Corporation.................................216 642-9040
7400 Hub Pkwy Cleveland (44125) *(G-3907)*

Kasel Engineering LLC..937 854-8875
5911 Wolf Creek Pike Trotwood (45426) *(G-13196)*

Kaskell, Springboro *Also Called: Kaskell Manufacturing Inc (G-12257)*

Kaskell Manufacturing Inc.....................................937 704-9700
240 Hiawatha Trl Springboro (45066) *(G-12257)*

Kasper Enterprises Inc...419 841-6656
7844 W Central Ave Toledo (43617) *(G-13016)*

Katch Kitchen LLC..513 537-8056
4172 Hamilton Ave Cincinnati (45223) *(G-2785)*

Kathom Manufacturing Co Inc................................513 868-8890
1301 Hook Dr Middletown (45042) *(G-9871)*

Kathys Krafts and Kollectibles...............................423 787-3709
3303 Hamilton Rd Medina (44256) *(G-9417)*

Katimex USA Inc..440 338-3500
15241 Hemlock Point Rd Chagrin Falls (44022) *(G-2147)*

Kaufman Container Company (PA)..........................216 898-2000
1000 Keystone Pkwy Ste 100 Cleveland (44135) *(G-3908)*

Kaufman Engineered Systems Inc...........................419 878-9727
1260 Waterville Monclova Rd Waterville (43566) *(G-13837)*

Kawneer Company Inc..216 252-3203
4536 Industrial Pkwy Cleveland (44135) *(G-3909)*

Kaws Inc..513 521-8292
2680 Civic Center Dr Cincinnati (45231) *(G-2786)*

Kay Toledo Tag Inc..419 729-5479
6050 Benore Rd Toledo (43612) *(G-13017)*

Kay-Zee Inc...330 339-1268
1279 Crestview Ave Sw New Philadelphia (44663) *(G-10451)*

Kayden Industries...740 336-7801
2167 State Route 821 Marietta (45750) *(G-8925)*

Kaydon Corporation...231 755-3741
1500 Nagel Rd Avon (44011) *(G-729)*

Kaylo Enterprises LLC..330 535-1860
540 S Main St Ste 115 Akron (44311) *(G-192)*

Kbc Services..513 693-3743
9993 Union Cemetery Rd Loveland (45140) *(G-8634)*

Kbr, Cincinnati *Also Called: Kitchens By Rutenschroer Inc (G-2799)*

Kc Robotics Inc..513 860-4442
9000 Le Saint Dr West Chester (45014) *(G-14019)*

Kci, Middleburg Heights *Also Called: Kinetic Concepts Inc (G-9774)*

Kci Holding USA Inc (DH)......................................937 525-5533
4401 Gateway Blvd Springfield (45502) *(G-12335)*

Kci Works, Canal Winchester *Also Called: Kellogg Cabinets Inc (G-1792)*

Kcn Technologies LLC..440 439-4219
1 W Interstate St # 13 Bedford (44146) *(G-1041)*

Kcs Cleaning Service..740 418-5479
7550 State Route 93 Oak Hill (45656) *(G-10889)*

Kda Manufacturing LLC..330 590-7431
5221 S Cleveland Massillon Rd Norton (44203) *(G-10825)*

Kdc Innovation, New Albany *Also Called: Kdc US Holdings Inc (G-10344)*

Kdc One..614 984-2871
8825 Smiths Mill Rd New Albany (43054) *(G-10343)*

Kdc US Holdings Inc...614 656-1130
8825 Smiths Mill Rd New Albany (43054) *(G-10344)*

KDI Med Supply, Fremont *Also Called: K Davis Inc (G-7119)*

Kdlamp Company, Andover *Also Called: Atc Lighting & Plastics Inc (G-456)*

Kdm Screen Printing, Cincinnati *Also Called: Kdm Signs Inc (G-2787)*

Kdm Signs Inc (PA)...513 769-1932
10450 Medallion Dr Cincinnati (45241) *(G-2787)*

Kdm Signs Inc..513 554-1393
2996 Exon Ave Cincinnati (45241) *(G-2788)*

Kdm Signs Inc..513 769-3900
3000 Exon Ave Cincinnati (45241) *(G-2789)*

Keb Industries Inc...440 953-4623
2166 Joseph Lloyd Pkwy Willoughby (44094) *(G-14475)*

Keban Industries Inc..216 446-0159
1263 Royalwood Rd Broadview Heights (44147) *(G-1503)*

Kebco Prcision Fabricators Inc...............................330 456-0808
2006 Allen Ave Se Canton (44707) *(G-1924)*

Kec America, Covington *Also Called: Hitachi Automation Ohio Inc (G-5494)*

Kecamm LLC..330 527-2918
10404 Industrial Dr Garrettsville (44231) *(G-7222)*

Kecoat LLC..330 527-0215
10610 Freedom St Garrettsville (44231) *(G-7223)*

Kecy Metal Technologies, Wauseon *Also Called: ARC Metal Stamping LLC (G-13845)*

Keebler, Cincinnati *Also Called: Keebler Company (G-2790)*

Keebler Company..513 271-3500
1 Trade St Cincinnati (45227) *(G-2790)*

Keeler Enterprises Inc..330 336-7601
924 Seville Rd Wadsworth (44281) *(G-13646)*

Keen Pump, Ashland *Also Called: Keen Pump Company Inc (G-544)*

Keen Pump Company Inc.......................................419 207-9400
471 E State Rte 250 E Ashland (44805) *(G-544)*

Keene Building Products Co (PA)............................440 605-1020
2926 Chester Ave Cleveland (44114) *(G-3910)*

Keener, Cleveland *Also Called: Keener Printing Inc (G-3911)*

Keener Printing Inc..216 531-7595
401 E 200th St Cleveland (44119) *(G-3911)*

Keener Rubber Company.......................................330 821-1880
14700 Commerce St Ne Alliance (44601) *(G-387)*

KEffs Inc...614 443-0586
2117 S High St Columbus (43207) *(G-5047)*

Kehl-Kolor Inc..419 281-3107
824 Us Highway 42 Ashland (44805) *(G-545)*

Keho Fitness and Nutrition LLC..............................740 587-1313
660 International Dr Hebron (43025) *(G-7621)*

Keithley Instruments LLC (DH)..............................440 248-0400
28775 Aurora Rd Solon (44139) *(G-12137)*

Kel-Eez, Akron *Also Called: Die-Gem Co Inc (G-122)*

Kel-Mar Inc...419 806-4600
436 N Enterprise St Bowling Green (43402) *(G-1423)*

Kel-Par Co Inc..740 344-2627
85 S Williams St Newark (43055) *(G-10513)*

Kelbly's, North Lawrence *Also Called: Kelblys Rifle Range Inc (G-10701)*

Kelblys Rifle Range Inc..330 683-4674
7222 Dalton Fox Lake Rd North Lawrence (44666) *(G-10701)*

Kelchner Inc (DH)..937 704-9890
50 Advanced Dr Springboro (45066) *(G-12258)*

Kelic, Waterville *Also Called: Rimer Enterprises Inc (G-13841)*

Kelko Manufacturing LLC..419 626-2571
2110 George St Sandusky (44870) *(G-11847)*

Kelko Products, Sandusky *Also Called: Kelko Manufacturing LLC (G-11847)*

Kellanova..614 879-9659
125 Enterprise Pkwy West Jefferson (43162) *(G-14163)*

Kellanova..740 453-5501
1675 Fairview Rd Zanesville (43701) *(G-15024)*

Kellermyer Bergensons Svcs LLC.................................419 867-4300
6546 Weatherfield Ct Maumee (43537) *(G-9301)*

Kelley Bible Books, Dayton *Also Called: Kelley Communication Dev (G-5838)*

Kelley Communication Dev...937 298-6132
2312 Candlewood Dr Dayton (45419) *(G-5838)*

Kelleys Island Winery Inc...419 746-2678
418 Woodford Rd Kelleys Island (43438) *(G-8008)*

Kellog, West Jefferson *Also Called: Kellanova (G-14163)*

Kellog, Zanesville *Also Called: Kellanova (G-15024)*

Kellogg Cabinets Inc...614 833-9596
7711 Diley Rd Canal Winchester (43110) *(G-1792)*

Kellstone, Kelleys Island *Also Called: Kellstone Inc (G-8009)*

Kellstone Inc...419 746-2396
Lake Shore Drive Kelleys Island (43438) *(G-8009)*

Kelly Arspc Thrmal Systems LLC..................................440 951-4744
1625 Lost Nation Rd Willoughby (44094) *(G-14476)*

Kelly Duplex, Springfield *Also Called: Duplex Mill & Manufacturing Co (G-12304)*

Kelly Foods Corporation (PA)......................................330 722-8855
3337 Medina Rd Medina (44256) *(G-9418)*

Kelly Plating Co..216 961-1080
10316 Madison Ave Cleveland (44102) *(G-3912)*

Kelly-Creswell Company, Springfield *Also Called: Ernest Industries Inc (G-12307)*

Kellys Wldg & Fabrication Ltd.....................................440 593-6040
285 N Amboy Rd Conneaut (44030) *(G-5406)*

Keltec Inc (PA)...330 425-3100
2300 E Enterprise Pkwy Twinsburg (44087) *(G-13322)*

Keltec-Technolab, Twinsburg *Also Called: Keltec Inc (G-13322)*

Kem Advertising and Prtg LLC.....................................330 818-5061
564 W Tuscarawas Ave Ste 104 Barberton (44203) *(G-816)*

Kempf Surgical Appliances Inc....................................513 984-5758
10567 Montgomery Rd Cincinnati (45242) *(G-2791)*

Kemps Ace Hardware Inc..740 472-1651
218 State Rte 78 Woodsfield (43793) *(G-14614)*

Ken Emerick Machine Products.....................................440 834-4501
14504 Main Market Rd Burton (44021) *(G-1702)*

Ken Forging Inc...440 993-8091
1049 Griggs Rd Jefferson (44047) *(G-7974)*

Ken Ganley Kia, Medina *Also Called: KG Medina LLC (G-9419)*

Ken-Dal Corporation...330 644-7118
644 Killian Rd Coventry Township (44319) *(G-5484)*

Ken-Tools, Akron *Also Called: Summit Tool Company (G-322)*

Kenag Inc...419 281-1204
101 E 7th St Ashland (44805) *(G-546)*

Kenakore Solutions, Perrysburg *Also Called: Depot Direct Inc (G-11215)*

Kenamerican Resources Inc..740 338-3100
46226 National Rd Saint Clairsville (43950) *(G-11694)*

Kenan Advantage Group Inc.......................................614 878-4050
500 Manor Park Dr Columbus (43228) *(G-5048)*

Kenco Products Co Inc...216 351-7610
3204 Sackett Ave Cleveland (44109) *(G-3913)*

Kendall Holdings Ltd (PA)...614 486-4750
2111 Builders Pl Columbus (43204) *(G-5049)*

Kendall/Hunt Publishing Co..877 275-4725
8805 Governors Hill Dr Ste 400 Cincinnati (45249) *(G-2792)*

Kendel Wldg & Fabrication Inc.....................................330 834-2429
1700 Navarre Rd Se Massillon (44646) *(G-9210)*

Kenics, Dayton *Also Called: Chemineer Inc (G-5700)*

Kenlake Foods, Cincinnati *Also Called: Inter American Products Inc (G-2748)*

Kenley Enterprises LLC..419 630-0921
418 N Lynn St Bryan (43506) *(G-1647)*

Kenmore Construction Co Inc......................................330 832-8888
9500 Forty Corners Rd Nw Massillon (44647) *(G-9211)*

Kenmore Development & Mch Co...................................330 753-2274
1395 Kenmore Blvd Akron (44314) *(G-193)*

Kenmore Gear & Machine Co Inc...................................330 753-6671
2129 Jennifer St Akron (44313) *(G-194)*

Kennametal Inc...440 437-5131
180 Penniman Rd Orwell (44076) *(G-11022)*

Kennametal Inc...440 349-5151
6865 Cochran Rd Solon (44139) *(G-12138)*

Kennedy Group Incorporated (HQ)................................440 951-7660
38601 Kennedy Pkwy Willoughby (44094) *(G-14477)*

Kennedy Ink Company Inc (PA)....................................513 871-2515
5230 Wooster Pike Cincinnati (45226) *(G-2793)*

Kennedy Manufacturing, Van Wert *Also Called: KMC Holdings LLC (G-13539)*

Kennedys Bakery Inc...740 432-2301
1025 Wheeling Ave Cambridge (43725) *(G-1746)*

Kenoil Inc...330 262-1144
1537 Blachleyville Rd Wooster (44691) *(G-14657)*

Kens His & Hers Shop Inc...330 872-3190
5 S Milton Blvd Ste C Newton Falls (44444) *(G-10578)*

Kensington Plant, Kensington *Also Called: M3 Midstream LLC (G-8010)*

Kent Adhesive Products Co..330 678-1626
1000 Cherry St Kent (44240) *(G-8039)*

Kent Corporation...440 582-3400
9601 York Alpha Dr North Royalton (44133) *(G-10768)*

Kent Displays Inc (PA)...330 673-8784
343 Portage Blvd Kent (44240) *(G-8040)*

Kent Elastomer Products, Kent *Also Called: Meridian Industries Inc (G-8051)*

Kent Elastomer Products, Winesburg *Also Called: Meridian Industries Inc (G-14607)*

Kent Elastomer Products Inc (HQ).................................330 673-1011
1500 Saint Clair Ave Kent (44240) *(G-8041)*

Kent Elastomer Products Inc.......................................800 331-4762
3890 Mogadore Industrial Pkwy Mogadore (44260) *(G-10079)*

Kent Information Services Inc......................................330 672-2110
6185 2nd Ave Kent (44240) *(G-8042)*

Kent Mold and Manufacturing Co..................................330 673-3469
1190 W Main St Kent (44240) *(G-8043)*

Kent Outdoors, New London *Also Called: Kent Water Sports LLC (G-10412)*

Kent Post Acquisition Inc..330 678-6343
449 Dodge St Kent (44240) *(G-8044)*

Kent Water Sports LLC (PA).......................................419 929-7021
433 Park Ave New London (44851) *(G-10412)*

Kentak Products Company..330 386-3700
1308 Railroad St East Liverpool (43920) *(G-6393)*

Kentak Products Company (PA)....................................330 382-2000
1230 Railroad St Ste 1 East Liverpool (43920) *(G-6394)*

Kenton Iron Products Inc (PA).....................................419 674-4178
13510 S Vision Dr Kenton (43326) *(G-8102)*

Kenton Strl & Orn Ir Works...419 674-4025
100 Cleveland Ave Kenton (43326) *(G-8103)*

Kenton Times, The, Kenton *Also Called: Hardin County Publishing Co (G-8101)*

Kentrox Inc (HQ)...614 798-2000
5800 Innovation Dr Dublin (43016) *(G-6315)*

Kenvue Brands LLC..513 985-1540
8044 Montgomery Rd Ste 510 Cincinnati (45236) *(G-2794)*

Kenwel Printers Inc..614 261-1011
4272 Indianola Ave Columbus (43214) *(G-5050)*

Kenyetta Bagby Enterprise LLC....................................614 584-3426
6629 Penick Dr Reynoldsburg (43068) *(G-11573)*

Kenyon Co, Coshocton *Also Called: Novelty Advertising Co Inc (G-5465)*

Kenyon Review...740 427-5208
209 Chase Ave Gambier (43022) *(G-7211)*

Keough and Associates LLC.......................................440 682-0514
106 Cherry Ave Chardon (44024) *(G-2209)*

Kepcor Inc..330 868-6434
215 Bridge St Minerva (44657) *(G-10040)*

Kerber Sheetmetal Works Inc......................................937 339-6366
104 Foss Way Troy (45373) *(G-13233)*

Kerek Industries Ltd Lblty Co
750 Beta Dr Ste A Cleveland (44143) *(G-3914)*

A
L
P
H
A
B
E
T
I
C

Kern Inc..440 930-7315
755 Alpha Dr Cleveland (44143) *(G-3915)*

Kern-Liebers Usa Inc (HQ)..........................419 865-2437
1510 Albon Rd Holland (43528) *(G-7771)*

Kernells Autmtc Machining Inc......................419 588-2164
10511 State Rte 61 N Berlin Heights (44814) *(G-1205)*

Kerr Lakeside Inc....................................216 261-2100
26841 Tungsten Rd Euclid (44132) *(G-6657)*

Kerry Inc..760 685-2548
100 Hope Ave Byesville (43723) *(G-1715)*

Kerry Inc..440 229-5200
29136 Norman Ave Wickliffe (44092) *(G-14379)*

Kerry Ingredients, Byesville *Also Called: Kerry Inc (G-1715)*

Kessler Outdoor Advertising, Zanesville *Also Called: Kessler Sign Company (G-15025)*

Kessler Sign Company (PA)...........................740 453-0668
2669 National Rd Zanesville (43701) *(G-15025)*

Ketco Inc..937 426-9331
1348 Research Park Dr Dayton (45432) *(G-5615)*

Ketman Corporation...................................330 262-1688
205 W Liberty St Wooster (44691) *(G-14658)*

Kettering Monogramming, Dayton *Also Called: Zimmer Enterprises Inc (G-6090)*

Kettle Creations LLC.................................567 940-9401
651 Commerce Pkwy Lima (45804) *(G-8423)*

Keuchel & Associates Inc............................330 945-9455
175 Muffin Ln Cuyahoga Falls (44223) *(G-5554)*

Keurig Dr Pepper Inc.................................614 237-4201
950 Stelzer Rd Columbus (43219) *(G-5051)*

Kevin Is Always Mixing, Chardon *Also Called: Keough and Associates LLC (G-2209)*

Kevin K Tidd..419 885-5603
5505 Roan Rd Sylvania (43560) *(G-12714)*

Kevin Noesner..614 451-5459
2672 Eastcleft Dr Columbus (43221) *(G-5052)*

Key Finishes LLC....................................614 351-8393
727 Harrison Dr Columbus (43204) *(G-5053)*

Key Maneuvers Inc (PA)..............................440 285-0774
10639 Grant St Ste C Chardon (44024) *(G-2210)*

Key Resin Company (DH)..............................513 943-4225
4050 Clough Woods Dr Batavia (45103) *(G-869)*

Keyah International Trdg LLC (PA)...................937 399-3140
4655 Urbana Rd Springfield (45502) *(G-12336)*

Keyline, North Olmsted *Also Called: Bianchi Usa Inc (G-10718)*

Keynes Bros Inc......................................740 385-6824
1 W Front St Logan (43138) *(G-8517)*

Keysco Tools, Cleveland *Also Called: S & H Industries Inc (G-4266)*

Keystone Auto Glass Inc.............................419 509-0497
2255 Linden Ct Maumee (43537) *(G-9302)*

Keystone Automotive Inds Inc........................614 228-4328
5830 Green Pointe Dr S Groveport (43125) *(G-7440)*

Keystone Bolt & Nut Company.........................216 524-9626
7600 Hub Pkwy Cleveland (44125) *(G-3916)*

Keystone Cooperative Inc............................937 884-5526
141 S Commerce St Verona (45378) *(G-13591)*

Keystone Foods LLC...................................419 257-2341
2208 Grant Rd North Baltimore (45872) *(G-10613)*

Keystone Press Inc..................................419 243-7326
1801 Broadway St Toledo (43609) *(G-13018)*

Keystone Threaded Products, Cleveland *Also Called: Keystone Bolt & Nut Company (G-3916)*

Keytel Systems, Reynoldsburg *Also Called: Town Cntry Technical Svcs Inc (G-11582)*

KG Medina LLC.......................................256 330-4273
2925 Medina Rd Medina (44256) *(G-9419)*

Kg63 LLC...216 941-7766
15501 Chatfield Ave Cleveland (44111) *(G-3917)*

Kgi Holdings, Cincinnati *Also Called: Kost Usa Inc (G-2806)*

Khempco Bldg Sup Co Ltd Partnr (PA)................740 549-0465
130 Johnson Dr Delaware (43015) *(G-6159)*

Kichler Lighting, Solon *Also Called: Kichler Lighting LLC (G-12139)*

Kichler Lighting LLC (DH)...........................216 573-1000
30455 Solon Rd Solon (44139) *(G-12139)*

Kidd Properties LLC.................................513 779-6278
9085 Sutton Pl West Chester (45011) *(G-14020)*

Kidron Inc..330 857-3011
13442 Emerson Rd Kidron (44636) *(G-8129)*

Kiefer Tool & Mold Inc..............................216 251-0076
3855 W 150th St Cleveland (44111) *(G-3918)*

Kiemle-Hankins, Perrysburg *Also Called: Kiemle-Hankins Company (G-11233)*

Kiemle-Hankins Company (PA)........................419 661-2430
94 H St Perrysburg (43551) *(G-11233)*

Kiffer Industries Inc (PA)..........................216 267-1818
4905 Rocky River Dr Cleveland (44135) *(G-3919)*

Kilbarger Construction Inc..........................740 385-6019
450 Gallagher Ave Logan (43138) *(G-8518)*

Kiley Machine Company................................513 875-3223
4196 Anderson State Rd Fayetteville (45118) *(G-6828)*

Killbuck Oil and Gas LLC............................330 447-8423
52 Marvin Ave Akron (44302) *(G-195)*

Killer Brownie Company, The, Miamisburg *Also Called: Killer Brownie Ltd (G-9705)*

Killer Brownie Company, The, Miamisburg *Also Called: Killer Brownie Ltd (G-9706)*

Killer Brownie Ltd (PA)............................937 535-5690
2495 Technical Dr Miamisburg (45342) *(G-9705)*

Killer Brownie Ltd...................................937 530-8600
675 Precision Ct Ste A Miamisburg (45342) *(G-9706)*

Killian Latex Inc....................................330 644-6746
2064 Killian Rd Akron (44312) *(G-196)*

Kilroy Company (PA).................................440 951-8700
17325 Euclid Ave Ste 2042 Cleveland (44112) *(G-3920)*

Kimball Midwest, Columbus *Also Called: Midwest Motor Supply Co (G-5100)*

Kimble Clay & Limestone, Dover *Also Called: Kimble Company (G-6250)*

Kimble Company (PA)................................330 343-1226
3596 State Route 39 Nw Dover (44622) *(G-6250)*

Kimble Custom Chassis Company......................877 546-2537
1951 Reiser Ave Se New Philadelphia (44663) *(G-10452)*

Kimble Machines Inc.................................419 485-8449
124 S Jonesville St Montpelier (43543) *(G-10129)*

Kimble Manufacturing Company, New Philadelphia *Also Called: Kimble Custom Chassis Company (G-10452)*

Kimble Mixer Company................................330 308-6700
1951 Reiser Ave Se New Philadelphia (44663) *(G-10453)*

Kimmatt Corp...937 228-3811
4459 Preble County Line Rd S West Alexandria (45381) *(G-13920)*

Kimpton Printing & Spc Co...........................330 467-1640
400 Highland Rd E Macedonia (44056) *(G-8702)*

Kimpton Prtg & Specialities, Macedonia *Also Called: Kimpton Printing & Spc Co (G-8702)*

Kinetic Concepts Inc................................440 234-8590
6751 Engle Rd Middleburg Heights (44130) *(G-9774)*

Kinetico Incorporated (HQ)..........................440 564-9111
10845 Kinsman Rd Newbury (44065) *(G-10556)*

Kinetics Noise Control Inc (PA)....................614 889-0480
6300 Irelan Pl Dublin (43017) *(G-6316)*

King Bag and Manufacturing Co (PA).................513 541-5440
1500 Spring Lawn Ave Cincinnati (45223) *(G-2795)*

King Bros Feed & Supply, Bristolville *Also Called: M B K Inc (G-1498)*

King Castings, Akron *Also Called: King Model Company (G-197)*

King Force & Machine, Twinsburg *Also Called: King Forge and Machine Company (G-13323)*

King Forge and Machine Company.....................330 963-0600
8250 Boyle Pkwy Twinsburg (44087) *(G-13323)*

King Kold Inc..937 836-2731
331 N Main St Englewood (45322) *(G-6617)*

King Kutter II Inc..................................740 446-0351
2150 Eastern Ave Gallipolis (45631) *(G-7207)*

King Luminaire, Jefferson *Also Called: Stress-Crete Company (G-7983)*

King Luminaire Company Inc (HQ)....................440 576-9073
1153 State Route 46 N Jefferson (44047) *(G-7975)*

King Machine and Tool Co............................330 833-7217
1237 Sanders Ave Sw Massillon (44647) *(G-9212)*

King Media Enterprises Inc..........................216 588-6700
11800 Shaker Blvd Cleveland (44120) *(G-3921)*

King Model Company..................................330 633-0491
365 Kenmore Blvd Akron (44301) *(G-197)*

King Nut Companies, Solon *Also Called: Kanan Enterprises Inc (G-12134)*

King Nut Companies, Solon *Also Called: Kanan Enterprises Inc (G-12135)*

King Nut Companies, Plant 2, Solon *Also Called: Kanan Enterprises Inc (G-12136)*

King of The Road, Troy *Also Called: Crowe Manufacturing Services (G-13207)*

King-Indiana Forge Inc...630 425-4250
8250 Boyle Pkwy Twinsburg (44087) *(G-13324)*

Kings Welding and Fabg Inc..330 738-3592
5259 Bane Rd Ne Mechanicstown (44651) *(G-9368)*

Kingsly Compression, Cambridge *Also Called: Kingsly Compression Inc (G-1747)*

Kingsly Compression Inc..740 439-0772
3956 Glenn Hwy Cambridge (43725) *(G-1747)*

Kingspan Benchmark, Columbus *Also Called: Benchmark Archtectural Systems (G-4751)*

Kingspan Insulation LLC..800 433-5551
1010 Brice St Newark (43055) *(G-10514)*

Kingswood Company, The, Columbus *Also Called: Glister Inc (G-4957)*

Kinko's, Cleveland *Also Called: Kinkos Inc (G-3922)*

Kinkos Inc..216 661-9950
4832 Ridge Rd Cleveland (44144) *(G-3922)*

Kinnemeyers Cornerstone Cab Co, Cleves *Also Called: Kinnemyers Cornerstone Cab Inc (G-4542)*

Kinnemyers Cornerstone Cab Inc....................................513 353-3030
6000 Hamilton Cleves Rd Cleves (45002) *(G-4542)*

Kinninger Prod Wldg Co Inc...419 629-3491
710 Kuenzel Dr New Bremen (45869) *(G-10361)*

Kinoly Signs..740 451-7446
2485 County Road 1 South Point (45680) *(G-12225)*

Kinsella Manufacturing Co Inc...513 561-5285
7880 Camargo Rd Cincinnati (45243) *(G-2796)*

Kinstle Strlng/Wstern Star Trc, Wapakoneta *Also Called: Kinstle Truck & Auto Svc Inc (G-13718)*

Kinstle Truck & Auto Svc Inc..419 738-7493
1770 Wapakoneta Fisher Rd Wapakoneta (45895) *(G-13718)*

Kinzua Environmental Inc..216 881-4040
1176 E 38th St Ste 1 Cleveland (44114) *(G-3923)*

Kip-Craft Incorporated (PA)..216 898-5500
4747 W 160th St Cleveland (44135) *(G-3924)*

Kiraly Tool and Die Inc..330 744-5773
1250 Crescent St Youngstown (44502) *(G-14885)*

Kirby and Sons Inc...419 927-2260
4876 County Highway 43 Upper Sandusky (43351) *(G-13445)*

Kirby Sand & Gravel, Upper Sandusky *Also Called: Kirby and Sons Inc (G-13445)*

Kirbys Auto and Truck Repr Inc......................................513 934-3999
875 Columbus Ave Lebanon (45036) *(G-8272)*

Kirchhoff Auto Waverly Inc (DH).....................................740 947-7763
611 W 2nd St Waverly (45690) *(G-13866)*

Kirk & Blum Manufacturing Co (DH)................................513 458-2600
4625 Red Bank Rd Ste 200 Cincinnati (45227) *(G-2797)*

Kirk Excavating & Construction.......................................614 444-4008
1399 Stimmel Rd Columbus (43223) *(G-5054)*

Kirk Key Interlock Company LLC......................................330 833-8223
9048 Meridian Cir Nw North Canton (44720) *(G-10648)*

Kirk Williams Company Inc..614 875-9023
2734 Home Rd Grove City (43123) *(G-7393)*

Kirkwood Holding Inc (PA)..216 267-6200
1239 Rockside Rd Cleveland (44134) *(G-3925)*

Kirtland Capital Partners LP (PA)....................................216 593-0100
3201 Enterprise Pkwy Ste 200 Beachwood (44122) *(G-924)*

Kirtland Plastics Inc...440 951-4466
7955 Euclid Chardon Rd Kirtland (44094) *(G-8145)*

Kirwan Industries Inc..513 333-0766
8390 Ridge Rd Cincinnati (45236) *(G-2798)*

Kish Company Inc (PA)...440 205-9970
8020 Tyler Blvd Ste 100 Mentor (44060) *(G-9546)*

Kitchen Designs Plus Inc..419 536-6605
2725 N Reynolds Rd Toledo (43615) *(G-13019)*

Kitchenaid Inc..937 316-4782
1700 Kitchen Aid Way Greenville (45331) *(G-7345)*

Kitchens By Rutenschroer Inc (PA).................................513 251-8333
950 Laidlaw Ave Cincinnati (45237) *(G-2799)*

Kitto Katsu Inc..818 256-6997
7445 Lockwood St Clayton (45315) *(G-3274)*

Kittyhawk Molding Company Inc......................................937 746-3663
10 Eagle Ct Carlisle (45005) *(G-2067)*

Kiwi Promotional AP & Prtg Co..330 487-5115
2170 E Aurora Rd Twinsburg (44087) *(G-13325)*

Klarity Medical Products LLC...740 788-8107
600 Industrial Pkwy Ste A Heath (43056) *(G-7599)*

Kleen Test Products, Beach City *Also Called: Meridian Industries Inc (G-904)*

Kleen Test Products Corp..330 878-5586
216 12th St Ne Strasburg (44680) *(G-12479)*

Klenk, Canton *Also Called: Klenk Industries Inc (G-1925)*

Klenk Industries Inc...330 453-7857
1016 9th St Sw Canton (44707) *(G-1925)*

Klinger Thermoseal, Sidney *Also Called: Thermoseal Inc (G-12057)*

Klingshirn Winery Inc...440 933-6666
33050 Webber Rd Avon Lake (44012) *(G-762)*

Klingstedt Brothers Company...330 456-8319
425 Schroyer Ave Sw Canton (44702) *(G-1926)*

KLm Manufacturing Co Inc..740 666-5171
56 Huston St Ostrander (43061) *(G-11027)*

Klosterman Baking Co LLC..513 242-5667
1000 E Ross Ave Cincinnati (45217) *(G-2800)*

Klosterman Baking Co LLC..513 398-2707
1130 Reading Rd Mason (45040) *(G-9118)*

Klutch Cannabis, Akron *Also Called: Atcpc of Ohio LLC (G-63)*

Klw Plastics Inc (DH)..513 539-2673
980 Deneen Ave Monroe (45050) *(G-10112)*

Klx Energy Services LLC..740 922-1155
3571 Brighwood Rd Midvale (44653) *(G-9912)*

Kmak Group LLC...937 308-1023
480 E High St London (43140) *(G-8538)*

KMC Holdings LLC...419 238-2442
1260 Industrial Dr Van Wert (45891) *(G-13539)*

Kmgrafx Inc...513 248-4100
394 Wards Corner Rd Ste 100 Loveland (45140) *(G-8635)*

Kmj Leasing Ltd...614 871-3883
7001 Harrisburg Pike Orient (43146) *(G-10971)*

Kml Acquisitions Ltd...614 732-9777
10325 Spicebrush Dr Plain City (43064) *(G-11411)*

KMS 2000 Inc (PA)..330 454-9444
315 12th St Nw Canton (44703) *(G-1927)*

Kn Rubber LLC (HQ)...419 739-4200
1400 Lunar Dr Wapakoneta (45895) *(G-13719)*

Kn8designs LLC..859 380-5926
4016 Allston St Cincinnati (45209) *(G-2801)*

Knape Industries Inc...614 885-3016
6592 Proprietors Rd Worthington (43085) *(G-14717)*

Knapke Cabinets Inc...937 335-8383
2 E Main St Troy (45373) *(G-13234)*

Knapke Custom Cabinetry, Versailles *Also Called: Knapke Custom Cabinetry Ltd (G-13599)*

Knapke Custom Cabinetry Ltd...937 459-8866
9306 Kelch Rd Versailles (45380) *(G-13599)*

Knappco Corporation..513 870-3100
9393 Princeton Glendale Rd Hamilton (45011) *(G-7509)*

Knb Tools of America Inc...614 733-0400
8440 Rausch Dr Plain City (43064) *(G-11412)*

Knight Ergonomics Inc..440 746-0044
6650 W Snowville Rd Ste G Brecksville (44141) *(G-1475)*

Knight Industries Corp..419 478-8550
5949 Telegraph Rd Toledo (43612) *(G-13020)*

Knight Line Signature AP Corp..330 545-8108
16 W Liberty St Girard (44420) *(G-7273)*

Knight Manufacturing Co Inc...740 676-5516
E 40th St Shadyside (43947) *(G-11922)*

Knight Manufacturing Co Inc (PA)...................................740 676-9532
399 E 40th St Shadyside (43947) *(G-11923)*

Knight Material Tech LLC (PA)...330 488-1651
5385 Orchardview Dr Se East Canton (44730) *(G-6378)*

Knippen Chrysler Ddge Jeep Inc.....................................419 695-4976
800 W 5th St Delphos (45833) *(G-6188)*

Knippen Chrysler Dodge Jeep, Delphos *Also Called: Knippen Chrysler Ddge Jeep Inc (G-6188)*

Knitting Machinery Co Amer LLC.....................................937 548-2338
607 Riffle Ave Greenville (45331) *(G-7346)*

A L P H A B E T I C

Knoble Glass & Metal Inc (PA)..............................513 753-1246
8650 Green Rd Cincinnati (45255) *(G-2802)*

Knott Brake Company..800 566-8887
144 West Dr Lodi (44254) *(G-8503)*

Knotty Pallet LLC...330 451-9838
4801 Munson St Nw Canton (44718) *(G-1928)*

Knowlton Machine Inc..419 281-6802
726 Virginia Ave Ashland (44805) *(G-547)*

Knowlton Manufacturing Co Inc...............................513 631-7353
2524 Leslie Ave Cincinnati (45212) *(G-2803)*

Knox Energy Inc (PA)...740 927-6731
11872 Worthington Rd Nw Pataskala (43062) *(G-11143)*

Knox Machine & Tool..740 392-3133
250 Columbus Rd Mount Vernon (43050) *(G-10248)*

Knudsen & Sons Inc..330 682-3000
1 Strawberry Ln Orrville (44667) *(G-10991)*

Knutsen Machine Products Inc.................................216 751-6500
15020 Miles Ave Cleveland (44128) *(G-3926)*

Kobelco Stewart Bolling Inc.....................................330 655-3111
1600 Terex Rd Hudson (44236) *(G-7848)*

Kodak, Dayton *Also Called: Eastman Kodak Company (G-5758)*

Kodak, Kettering *Also Called: Eastman Kodak Company (G-8119)*

Koebbe Products Inc (PA)..513 753-4200
1132 Ferris Rd Amelia (45102) *(G-430)*

Koebbe Products Inc...513 735-1400
4226 Grissom Dr Batavia (45103) *(G-870)*

Koenig Equipment Inc..937 653-5281
3130 E Us Highway 36 Urbana (43078) *(G-13472)*

Koester Corporation (PA)..419 599-0291
813 N Perry St Napoleon (43545) *(G-10289)*

Koester Machined Products Co.................................419 782-0291
136 Fox Run Dr Defiance (43512) *(G-6117)*

Kohl & Madden Inc...513 326-6900
5000 Spring Grove Ave Cincinnati (45232) *(G-2804)*

KOHLER COATING, Canton *Also Called: Kohler Coating Inc (G-1929)*

Kohler Coating Inc...330 499-1407
1205 5th St Sw Canton (44707) *(G-1929)*

Koki Laboratories Inc..330 773-7669
1081 Rosemary Blvd Akron (44306) *(G-198)*

Kokosing Materials Inc...740 694-5872
11624 Hyatt Rd Fredericktown (43019) *(G-7081)*

Kokosing Materials Inc...419 522-2715
215 Oak St Mansfield (44907) *(G-8811)*

Kokosing Materials Inc...740 745-3341
9134 Mount Vernon Rd Saint Louisville (43071) *(G-11729)*

Kokosing Materials Inc...614 491-1199
4755 S High St Columbus (43207) *(G-5055)*

Kokosing Materials Inc (HQ).....................................740 694-9585
17531 Waterford Rd Fredericktown (43019) *(G-7082)*

Kol-Cap Manufacturing Co, Brunswick *Also Called: Walest Incorporated (G-1623)*

Kolhfab Cstm Plstic Fbrication.................................937 237-2098
2025 Webster St Dayton (45404) *(G-5839)*

Kolinahr Systems Inc...513 745-9401
6840 Ashfield Dr Blue Ash (45242) *(G-1294)*

Kolpin Outdoors Corporation....................................330 328-0772
3479 State Rd Cuyahoga Falls (44223) *(G-5555)*

Koltcz Concrete Block Co...440 232-3630
7660 Oak Leaf Rd Bedford (44146) *(G-1042)*

Komatsu Mining Corp...216 503-5029
981 Keynote Cir Ste 8 Independence (44131) *(G-7906)*

Kona Blackbird Inc...440 285-3189
11730 Ravenna Rd Chardon (44024) *(G-2211)*

Konecranes Inc..440 461-8400
331 Treeworth Blvd Broadview Heights (44147) *(G-1504)*

Konecranes Inc..614 863-0150
1110 Claycraft Rd Ste C Gahanna (43230) *(G-7163)*

Konecranes Inc..937 328-5100
4505 Gateway Blvd Springfield (45502) *(G-12337)*

Konecranes Inc (HQ)...937 525-5533
4401 Gateway Blvd Springfield (45502) *(G-12338)*

Konecranes Inc..419 382-7575
2221 Tedrow Rd Toledo (43614) *(G-13021)*

Konecranes Inc..513 755-2800
4866 Duff Dr West Chester (45246) *(G-14130)*

Koneta Inc..419 739-4200
1400 Lunar Dr Wapakoneta (45895) *(G-13720)*

Koneta Rubber, Wapakoneta *Also Called: Kn Rubber LLC (G-13719)*

Kongsberg Actation Systems LLC.............................440 639-8778
301 Olive St Grand River (44045) *(G-7311)*

Kongsberg Automotive, Grand River *Also Called: Kongsberg Actation Systems LLC (G-7311)*

Kongsberg Prcsion Cctng Systems............................937 800-2169
1983 Byers Rd Miamisburg (45342) *(G-9707)*

Kontron America Incorporated..................................937 324-2420
202 N Limestone St Springfield (45503) *(G-12339)*

Konys, Mark Glass Design, Cleveland *Also Called: Bruening Glass Works Inc (G-3445)*

Koop Diamond Cutters Inc.......................................513 621-2838
214 E 8th St Fl 4 Cincinnati (45202) *(G-2805)*

Kopco Graphics Inc (PA)..513 874-7230
9750 Crescent Park Dr West Chester (45069) *(G-14021)*

Korda Manufacturing LLC..330 262-1555
3927 E Lincoln Way Wooster (44691) *(G-14659)*

Korff Holdings LLC...330 332-1566
310 E Euclid Ave Salem (44460) *(G-11792)*

Kosei St Marys Corporation.....................................419 394-7840
1100 Mckinley Rd Saint Marys (45885) *(G-11740)*

Koski Construction Co (PA).......................................440 997-5337
5841 Woodman Ave Ashtabula (44004) *(G-601)*

Kost Usa Inc (DH)...513 583-7070
1000 Tennessee Ave Cincinnati (45229) *(G-2806)*

Kotobuki-Reliable Die Casting Inc............................937 347-1111
851 Bellbrook Ave Xenia (45385) *(G-14768)*

Kottler Metal Products Co Inc..................................440 946-7473
1595 Lost Nation Rd Willoughby (44094) *(G-14478)*

Kovatch Castings, Uniontown *Also Called: Kovatch Castings Inc (G-13421)*

Kovatch Castings Inc...330 896-9944
3743 Tabs Dr Uniontown (44685) *(G-13421)*

Kowalski Heat Treating Co.......................................216 631-4411
3611 Detroit Ave Cleveland (44113) *(G-3927)*

Krafft and Associates Inc...937 325-4671
991 W Leffel Ln Springfield (45506) *(G-12340)*

Kraft Electrical Contg Inc...614 836-9300
5710 Green Pointe Dr N Groveport (43125) *(G-7441)*

Kraft Heinz Company..330 837-8331
1301 Oberlin Ave Sw Massillon (44647) *(G-9213)*

Kraft Heinz Company, Massillon *Also Called: Kraft Heinz Company (G-9213)*

Kraft Heinz Foods Company......................................740 622-0523
1660 S 2nd St Coshocton (43812) *(G-5458)*

Kraft Heinz Foods Company......................................419 332-7357
1200n N 5th St Fremont (43420) *(G-7120)*

Kraft Heinz Foods Company......................................513 339-0045
7325 Snider Rd Mason (45040) *(G-9119)*

Kraftmaid Cabinetry, Middlefield *Also Called: Cabinetwrks Group Mddlfield LLC (G-9784)*

Kraftmaid Cabinetry, Orwell *Also Called: Cabinetwrks Group Mddlfield LLC (G-11020)*

Kraftmaid Trucking Inc (PA).....................................440 632-2531
16052 Industrial Pkwy Middlefield (44062) *(G-9805)*

Krafts Exotika LLC..216 563-1178
3553 Bosworth Rd Cleveland (44111) *(G-3928)*

Kram Precision Machining Inc..................................937 849-1301
1751 Dalton Dr New Carlisle (45344) *(G-10374)*

Kramer & Kiefer Inc...330 336-8742
2662 Valley Side Ave Wadsworth (44281) *(G-13647)*

Kramer Graphics Inc..937 296-9600
2408 W Dorothy Ln Moraine (45439) *(G-10172)*

Kramer Power Equipment Co....................................937 456-2232
2388 State Route 726 N Eaton (45320) *(G-6457)*

Kramer Printing, Mentor *Also Called: J & L Management Corporation (G-9537)*

Kraton Corporation...740 423-7571
2419 State Route 618 Belpre (45714) *(G-1148)*

Kraton Emplyees Recreation CLB.............................740 423-7571
2419 State Route 618 Belpre (45714) *(G-1149)*

Kraton Polymers, Belpre *Also Called: Kraton Polymers US LLC (G-1150)*

Kraton Polymers US LLC..740 423-7571
2419 State Route 618 Belpre (45714) *(G-1150)*

Krausher Machining Inc.. 440 839-2828
   4267 Butler Rd Wakeman (44889) *(G-13681)*

Krazy Glue, West Jefferson *Also Called: Toagosei America Inc (G-14168)*

Kreager Co LLC.. 740 345-1605
   1045 Brice St Newark (43055) *(G-10515)*

Kreate Industries, Findlay *Also Called: Nickolas Plastics LLC (G-6899)*

Krehbiel Holdings Inc.. 513 271-6035
   3962 Virginia Ave Cincinnati (45227) *(G-2807)*

Kreider Corp... 937 325-8787
   400 Harrison St Springfield (45505) *(G-12341)*

Krema Group Inc.. 614 889-4824
   8415 Rausch Dr Plain City (43064) *(G-11413)*

Krema Nut Co, Columbus *Also Called: Brilista Foods Company Inc (G-4780)*

Krendl Machine Company.. 419 692-3060
   1201 Spencerville Rd Delphos (45833) *(G-6189)*

Krendl Rack Co Inc... 419 667-4800
   18413 Haver Rd Venedocia (45894) *(G-13586)*

Krengel Equipment LLC.. 440 946-3570
   34580 Lakeland Blvd Eastlake (44095) *(G-6434)*

Krengel Manufacturing, Eastlake *Also Called: Krengel Equipment LLC (G-6434)*

Krenz Precision Machining Inc.. 440 237-1800
   9801 York Alpha Dr North Royalton (44133) *(G-10769)*

Krigbaum Inc.. 614 478-6472
   373 Vista Dr Columbus (43230) *(G-5056)*

Krin USA, Lakeville *Also Called: 1200 Feet Limited (G-8159)*

Krisdale, Valley City *Also Called: Krisdale Inc (G-13501)*

Krisdale Inc... 330 225-2392
   649 Marks Rd Valley City (44280) *(G-13501)*

Krispy Kreme, Columbus *Also Called: Krispy Kreme Doughnut Corp (G-5058)*

Krispy Kreme 322, Columbus *Also Called: Krispy Kreme Doughnut Corp (G-5057)*

Krispy Kreme Doughnut Corp... 614 798-0812
   3690 W Dublin Granville Rd Columbus (43235) *(G-5057)*

Krispy Kreme Doughnut Corp... 614 876-0058
   2557 Westbelt Dr Columbus (43228) *(G-5058)*

Kriss Kreations.. 330 405-6102
   9224 Darrow Rd Twinsburg (44087) *(G-13326)*

Krista Messer.. 734 459-1952
   15301 E State Route 37 Sunbury (43074) *(G-12668)*

Kroner Publications Inc (PA).. 330 544-5500
   1123 W Park Ave Niles (44446) *(G-10594)*

Kross Acquisition Company LLC.. 513 554-0555
   10690 Loveland Madeira Rd Loveland (45140) *(G-8636)*

Kroy LLC... 800 837-4323
   3830 Kelley Ave Cleveland (44114) *(G-3929)*

Krumor Inc... 216 328-9802
   7655 Hub Pkwy Ste 206 Cleveland (44125) *(G-3930)*

Krupp Rubber Machinery.. 330 864-0800
   103 Western Ave Akron (44313) *(G-199)*

Krusinski's Meat Market, Cleveland *Also Called: John Krusinski (G-3889)*

Kruz Inc... 330 878-5595
   6332 Columbia Rd Nw Dover (44622) *(G-6251)*

KSA Limited Partnership.. 740 776-3238
   6501 Pershing Ave Portsmouth (45662) *(G-11468)*

Kse Manufacturing... 937 409-9831
   175 S Lester Ave Sidney (45365) *(G-12027)*

Ksm Metal Fabrication.. 937 339-6366
   104 Foss Way Troy (45373) *(G-13235)*

Ksm Metal Fabrications, Troy *Also Called: Kerber Sheetmetal Works Inc (G-13233)*

Kth Parts Industries Inc (HQ)..937 663-5941
   1111 State Route 235 N Saint Paris (43072) *(G-11758)*

Ktm North America Inc (PA)...855 215-6360
   1119 Milan Ave Amherst (44001) *(G-447)*

Ktri Holdings Inc (DH).. 216 400-9308
   127 Public Sq Ste 5110 Cleveland (44114) *(G-3931)*

Kts Cstm Lgs/Xclsvely You Inc... 440 285-9803
   602 South St Ste C-2 Chardon (44024) *(G-2212)*

Kts Custom Logos.. 440 285-9803
   602 South St Ste C-2 Chardon (44024) *(G-2213)*

Kts Equipment Inc... 440 647-2015
   47117 State Route 18 Wellington (44090) *(G-13895)*

Kts Met-Bar Products Inc... 440 288-9308
   967 G St Lorain (44052) *(G-8561)*

Ktsdi LLC.. 330 783-2000
   801 E Middletown Rd North Lima (44452) *(G-10709)*

Kubota Authorized Dealer, Athens *Also Called: All Power Equipment LLC (G-632)*

Kubota Tractor Corporation.. 614 835-3800
   6300 At One Kubota Way Groveport (43125) *(G-7442)*

Kuhlman Construction Products, Maumee *Also Called: Kuhlman Corporation (G-9303)*

Kuhlman Corporation.. 330 724-9900
   999 Swartz Rd Coventry Township (44319) *(G-5485)*

Kuhlman Corporation (PA)..419 897-6000
   1845 Indian Wood Cir Maumee (43537) *(G-9303)*

Kuhlman Corporation.. 419 321-1670
   444 Kuhlman Dr Toledo (43609) *(G-13022)*

Kuhlman Engineering Co.. 419 243-2196
   840 Champlain St Toledo (43604) *(G-13023)*

Kuhlman Instrument Company.. 419 668-9533
   54 Summit St Norwalk (44857) *(G-10849)*

Kuhls Hot Sportspot... 513 474-2282
   6701 Beechmont Ave Cincinnati (45230) *(G-2808)*

Kuhn Fabricating Inc.. 440 277-4182
   1637 E 28th St Lorain (44055) *(G-8562)*

Kuhns Mold & Tool Co Inc.. 937 833-2178
   9360 National Rd Brookville (45309) *(G-1572)*

Kuka Tledo Prdction Oprtons LL.. 419 727-5500
   3770 Stickney Ave Toledo (43608) *(G-13024)*

Kundel, Vienna *Also Called: Kundel Industries Inc (G-13609)*

Kundel Industries Inc (PA).. 330 469-6147
   1510 Ridge Rd Vienna (44473) *(G-13609)*

Kurtz Bros Compost Services... 330 864-2621
   2677 Riverview Rd Akron (44313) *(G-200)*

Kurtz Tool & Die Co Inc... 330 755-7723
   164 State St Struthers (44471) *(G-12619)*

Kurz-Kasch, Newcomerstown *Also Called: Kurz-Kasch Inc (G-10572)*

Kurz-Kasch Inc (DH)..740 498-8343
   199 E State St Newcomerstown (43832) *(G-10572)*

Kutol Products Company Inc (PA)...................................... 513 527-5500
   100 Partnership Way Sharonville (45241) *(G-11946)*

Kutol Products Company Inc... 513 527-5500
   11955 Enterprise Dr Sharonville (45241) *(G-11947)*

Kutrite Manufacturing, Tremont City *Also Called: Mike Loppe (G-13189)*

Kuzma Industries LLC... 419 701-7005
   1541 N Township Road 101 Fostoria (44830) *(G-6986)*

Kw Acquisition Inc.. 740 548-7298
   7975 N Central Dr Lewis Center (43035) *(G-8341)*

KWD Automotive Inc.. 419 344-8232
   6700 Cemetery Rd Whitehouse (43571) *(G-14362)*

Kween and Co.. 440 724-4342
   994 Valley Belt Rd Brooklyn Heights (44131) *(G-1534)*

Kwik Kopy Printing, Blue Ash *Also Called: Larmax Inc (G-1296)*

Kyklos Bearing International Llc.. 419 627-7000
   2509 Hayes Ave Sandusky (44870) *(G-11848)*

Kyle Media Inc... 877 775-2538
   7862 W Central Ave Ste F Toledo (43617) *(G-13025)*

Kyntronics Inc (PA)..440 220-5990
   6565 Davis Industrial Pkwy Ste R Solon (44139) *(G-12140)*

Kyocera Hardcoating Tech Ltd.. 330 686-2136
   220 Marc Dr Cuyahoga Falls (44223) *(G-5556)*

Kyocera Precision Tools, Cuyahoga Falls *Also Called: Kyocera SGS Precision Tls Inc*
(G-5557)

Kyocera Senco Indus Tls Inc (HQ)...................................... 513 388-2000
   8450 Broadwell Rd Cincinnati (45244) *(G-2809)*

Kyocera SGS Precision Tls Inc (PA)..................................... 330 688-6667
   150 Marc Dr Cuyahoga Falls (44223) *(G-5557)*

Kyocera SGS Precision Tls Inc.. 330 922-1953
   238 Marc Dr Cuyahoga Falls (44223) *(G-5558)*

Kyron Tool & Machine Co Inc... 614 231-6000
   2900 Banwick Rd Columbus (43232) *(G-5059)*

L & F Products... 937 498-4710
   1810 Progress Way Sidney (45365) *(G-12028)*

L & J Cable Inc.. 937 526-9445
   102 Industrial Dr Russia (45363) *(G-11675)*

L & L Machine Inc..............................419 272-5000
2919 County Road 2l Edon (43518) *(G-6474)*

L & L Ornamental Iron Co......................513 353-1930
6024 Hamilton Cleves Rd Cleves (45002) *(G-4543)*

L & L Plastics, Felicity *Also Called: L C Liming & Sons Inc (G-6830)*

L & L Railings, Cleves *Also Called: L & L Ornamental Iron Co (G-4543)*

L & M Mineral Co..............................330 852-3696
2010 County Road 144 Sugarcreek (44681) *(G-12640)*

L & R Racing Inc..............................330 220-3102
1261 Industrial Pkwy N Ste 1a Brunswick (44212) *(G-1601)*

L & S Home Improvement.......................330 906-3199
549 Saunders Ave Coventry Township (44319) *(G-5486)*

L & T Collins Inc.............................740 345-4494
44 S 4th St Newark (43055) *(G-10516)*

L & W Inc...................................734 397-6300
1190 Jaycox Rd Avon (44011) *(G-730)*

L & W Investments Inc.........................937 492-4171
2005 Campbell Rd Sidney (45365) *(G-12029)*

L and J Woodworking...........................330 359-3216
9035 Senff Rd Dundee (44624) *(G-6367)*

L B Foster Company............................330 652-1461
1193 Salt Springs Rd Mineral Ridge (44440) *(G-10030)*

L B L Printing, Painesville *Also Called: LBL Lithographers Inc (G-11096)*

L B Manufacturing, Byesville *Also Called: Famous Industries Inc (G-1711)*

L Brown Loans & Investments..................216 308-1820
1879 Colonnade Rd Cleveland (44112) *(G-3932)*

L C F Inc...................................330 877-3322
114 S Prospect Ave Hartville (44632) *(G-7579)*

L C Liming & Sons Inc.........................513 876-2555
3200 State Route 756 Felicity (45120) *(G-6830)*

L D C, Independence *Also Called: Liquid Development Company (G-7907)*

L Haberny Co Inc..............................440 543-5999
10115 Queens Way Chagrin Falls (44023) *(G-2168)*

L J Manufacturing Inc.........................440 352-1979
9436 Mercantile Dr Mentor (44060) *(G-9547)*

L J Publishing LLC............................888 749-5994
1287 Ridge Rd Ste B Hinckley (44233) *(G-7734)*

L J Smith Stair System, Bowerston *Also Called: Novo Manufacturing LLC (G-1401)*

L J Star Incorporated.........................330 405-3040
2396 Edison Blvd Twinsburg (44087) *(G-13327)*

L M Animal Farms, Pleasant Plain *Also Called: Hartz Mountain Corporation (G-11432)*

L M Engineering Inc...........................330 270-2400
3760 Oakwood Ave Austintown (44515) *(G-706)*

L N Brut Manufacturing Co.....................330 833-9045
7300 State Route 754 Shreve (44676) *(G-11984)*

L P S I, Cleveland *Also Called: Laser Printing Solutions Inc (G-3944)*

L T V Steel Company Inc........................216 622-5000
200 Public Sq Cleveland (44114) *(G-3933)*

L W G Finishing, West Chester *Also Called: Hard Surface Technology Inc (G-14013)*

L-3 Cmmncations Nova Engrg Inc................877 282-1168
4393 Digital Way Mason (45040) *(G-9120)*

L.A.m Wldg & Met Fabrication, East Sparta *Also Called: William Niccum (G-6413)*

L.E.M. Products, West Chester *Also Called: Lem Products Holding LLC (G-14023)*

L&H Threaded Rods Corp........................937 294-6666
3050 Dryden Rd Moraine (45439) *(G-10173)*

L&W Cleveland, Avon *Also Called: L & W Inc (G-730)*

L3 Technologies Inc...........................513 943-2000
3975 Mcmann Rd Cincinnati (45245) *(G-2309)*

L3 Technologies Inc...........................937 257-8501
47 Alf/ Raythoen Arospace Bld 201 Area C 5 Dayton (45433) *(G-5616)*

L3 Technologies Inc...........................937 223-3285
3155 Research Blvd Ste 101 Dayton (45420) *(G-5840)*

L3harris Cincinnati Elec Corp (DH).............513 573-6100
7500 Innovation Way Mason (45040) *(G-9121)*

L3harris Electrodynamics Inc..................847 259-0740
3975 Mcmann Rd Cincinnati (45245) *(G-2310)*

L3harris Fzing Ord Systems Inc................513 943-2000
3975 Mcmann Rd Cincinnati (45245) *(G-2311)*

La Boit Specialty Vehicles....................614 231-7640
700 Cross Pointe Rd Gahanna (43230) *(G-7164)*

La Chatelaine, Columbus *Also Called: La Marquise Inc (G-5060)*

La Grange Elec Assemblies Co..................440 355-5388
349 S Center St Lagrange (44050) *(G-8149)*

La Marquise Inc...............................614 488-1911
1550 W Lane Ave Columbus (43221) *(G-5060)*

La Mfg Inc...................................513 577-7200
9483 Reading Rd Cincinnati (45215) *(G-2810)*

La Perla Inc (PA).............................419 534-2074
2742 Hill Ave Toledo (43607) *(G-13026)*

La Prensa Publications Inc....................419 870-6565
616 Adams St Toledo (43604) *(G-13027)*

LA Rose Paving Co.............................440 632-0330
16590 Nauvoo Rd Middlefield (44062) *(G-9806)*

Laad Sign & Lighting Inc......................330 379-2297
3097 State Route 59 Ravenna (44266) *(G-11529)*

Lab Quality Machining Inc.....................513 625-0219
6311 Roudebush Rd Goshen (45122) *(G-7297)*

Lab-Pro Inc..................................937 434-9600
845 N Main St Miamisburg (45342) *(G-9708)*

Labcraft Inc.................................419 878-4400
1070 Disher Dr Waterville (43566) *(G-13838)*

Label Aid, Huron *Also Called: Label Aid Inc (G-7876)*

Label Aid Inc................................419 433-2888
608 Rye Beach Rd Huron (44839) *(G-7876)*

Label Print Technologies, LLC, Mogadore *Also Called: Tpl Holdings LLC (G-10090)*

Label Technique Southeast LLC.................440 951-7660
38601 Kennedy Pkwy Willoughby (44094) *(G-14479)*

Labelmatch, Hudson *Also Called: Mabis Shipping Solutions Inc (G-7850)*

Labeltek Inc.................................330 335-3110
985 Seville Rd Wadsworth (44281) *(G-13648)*

Laborie Enterprises, Portage *Also Called: Laborie Enterprises LLC (G-11458)*

Laborie Enterprises LLC.......................419 686-6245
10892 S Dixie Hwy Portage (43451) *(G-11458)*

Lacal Equipment Inc...........................937 596-6106
901 W Pike St Jackson Center (45334) *(G-7964)*

Lachina Creative Inc..........................216 292-7959
3791 Green Rd Cleveland (44122) *(G-3934)*

Lacrema Coffee Company, West Chester *Also Called: Kidd Properties LLC (G-14020)*

Lafferty Chipping, Kimbolton *Also Called: Calvin W Lafferty (G-8136)*

Lagonda Investments III Inc...................937 325-7305
2145 Airpark Dr Springfield (45502) *(G-12342)*

Lahlouh Inc..................................650 692-6600
150 Lawton Ave Monroe (45050) *(G-10113)*

Lahm Tool, Dayton *Also Called: Lahm-Trosper Inc (G-5841)*

Lahm-Trosper Inc.............................937 252-8791
1030 Springfield St Dayton (45403) *(G-5841)*

Laipplys Prtg Mktg Sltions Inc................740 387-9282
270 E Center St Marion (43302) *(G-8975)*

Laird Plastics, Columbus *Also Called: Plastics Family Holdings Inc (G-5196)*

Laird Technologies, Cleveland *Also Called: Thermagon Inc (G-4390)*

Laird Technologies Inc........................330 434-7929
50 S Main St Ste 1100 Akron (44308) *(G-201)*

Laird Technologies Inc........................216 939-2300
4707 Detroit Ave Cleveland (44102) *(G-3935)*

Laird Technologies Inc........................234 806-0105
655 N River Rd Nw Warren (44483) *(G-13776)*

Lake Building Products Inc....................216 486-1500
1361 Chardon Rd Ste 4 Cleveland (44117) *(G-3936)*

Lake City Plating, Ashtabula *Also Called: Lake City Plating LLC (G-602)*

Lake City Plating LLC (PA)....................440 964-3555
1701 Lake Ave Ashtabula (44004) *(G-602)*

Lake City Plating LLC.........................440 964-3555
108 S Sycamore St Jefferson (44047) *(G-7976)*

Lake Cnty Dprtmntal Rtrdtion D, Willoughby *Also Called: County of Lake (G-14443)*

Lake Community News...........................440 946-2577
36081 Lake Shore Blvd Ste 5 Willoughby (44095) *(G-14480)*

Lake County Plating Corp......................440 255-8835
7790 Division Dr Mentor (44060) *(G-9548)*

Lake Erie Frozen Foods Mfg Co.................419 289-9204
1830 Orange Rd Ashland (44805) *(G-548)*

Lake Erie Graphics Inc.................................. 216 575-1333
5372 W 130th St Brookpark (44142) *(G-1555)*

Lake Erie Iron and Metal, Cleveland *Also Called: Welders Supply Inc (G-4500)*

Lake Erie Ship Repr Fbrction L................... 440 228-7110
1459 State Route 46 S Jefferson (44047) *(G-7977)*

Lake Metals, Ravenna *Also Called: A C Williams Co Inc (G-11511)*

Lake Park Tool & Machine, Youngstown *Also Called: Lake Park Tool & Machine LLC*
(G-14886)

Lake Park Tool & Machine LLC.................... 330 788-2437
1221 Velma Ct Youngstown (44512) *(G-14886)*

Lake Publishing Inc..................................... 440 299-8500
9930 Johnnycake Ridge Rd Mentor (44060) *(G-9549)*

Lake Region Oil Inc..................................... 330 828-8420
26 N Cochran St Dalton (44618) *(G-5587)*

Lake Screen Printing Inc............................. 440 244-5707
1924 Broadway Lorain (44052) *(G-8563)*

Lake Shore Cryotronics Inc (PA).................614 891-2243
480 Olde Worthington Rd Westerville (43082) *(G-14217)*

Lake Shore Electric Corp............................. 440 232-0200
205 Willis St Bedford (44146) *(G-1043)*

Lake Shore Graphic Inds Inc....................... 419 626-8631
2111 Cleveland Rd Sandusky (44870) *(G-11849)*

Lake Township Trustees.............................. 419 836-1143
3800 Ayers Rd Millbury (43447) *(G-9963)*

Lakecraft, Port Clinton *Also Called: Lakecraft Inc (G-11444)*

Lakecraft Inc (PA)....................................... 419 734-2828
1010 W Lakeshore Dr Port Clinton (43452) *(G-11444)*

Lakepark Industries Inc............................... 419 752-4471
40 Seminary St Greenwich (44837) *(G-7363)*

Lakeside Cabins Ltd.................................... 419 896-2299
7389 State Route 13 N Shiloh (44878) *(G-11978)*

Lakeside Sand & Gravel Inc........................ 330 274-2569
3498 Frost Rd Mantua (44255) *(G-8870)*

Lakeview Farms LLC (PA)........................... 419 695-9925
1600 Gressel Dr Delphos (45833) *(G-6190)*

Lakeway Mfg Inc (PA)..................................419 433-3030
730 River Rd Huron (44839) *(G-7877)*

Lako Tool & Manufacturing Inc.................... 419 662-5256
7400 Ponderosa Rd Perrysburg (43551) *(G-11234)*

Lalac - Hanlon LLC...................................... 216 261-7056
1280 E 286th St Euclid (44132) *(G-6658)*

Lalac One LLC... 216 432-4422
18451 Euclid Ave Cleveland (44112) *(G-3937)*

Lam Pro Inc... 216 426-0661
4701 Crayton Ave Ste A Cleveland (44104) *(G-3938)*

Lam Research, Eaton *Also Called: Lam Research Corporation (G-6458)*

Lam Research Corporation........................... 937 472-3311
960 S Franklin St Eaton (45320) *(G-6458)*

Lam Tech, Tiffin *Also Called: Laminate Technologies Inc (G-12786)*

Lambert Sheet Metal Inc............................. 614 237-0384
1625 W Mound St Columbus (43223) *(G-5061)*

Laminate Shop... 740 749-3536
1145 Klinger Rd Waterford (45786) *(G-13827)*

Laminate Technologies Inc (PA)..................800 231-2523
161 Maule Rd Tiffin (44883) *(G-12786)*

Laminated Concepts Inc.............................. 216 475-4141
14300 Industrial Ave N Maple Heights (44137) *(G-8885)*

Lancaster Colony Corporation...................... 614 792-9774
280 Cramer Creek Ct Dublin (43017) *(G-6317)*

Lancaster Colony Corporation (PA)..............614 224-7141
380 Polaris Pkwy Ste 400 Westerville (43082) *(G-14218)*

Lancaster Colony Design Group, Dublin *Also Called: Lancaster Colony Corporation (G-6317)*

Lancaster Commercial Pdts LLC.................. 844 324-1444
2353 Westbrooke Dr Columbus (43228) *(G-5062)*

Lancaster Glass Corporation........................ 614 224-7141
380 Polaris Pkwy Ste 400 Westerville (43082) *(G-14219)*

Lancaster Metal Products Inc...................... 740 653-3421
520 Slocum St Lancaster (43130) *(G-8206)*

Lancaster Municipal Gas, Lancaster *Also Called: City of Lancaster (G-8188)*

Lancaster W Side Coal Co Inc (PA)..............740 862-4713
700 Van Buren Ave Lancaster (43130) *(G-8207)*

Lancer Dispersions Inc
1680 E Market St Akron (44305) *(G-202)*

Land O'Lakes, Kent *Also Called: Land OLakes Inc (G-8045)*

Land O'Lakes, Massillon *Also Called: Land OLakes Inc (G-9214)*

Land OLakes Inc.. 330 678-1578
2001 Mogadore Rd Kent (44240) *(G-8045)*

Land OLakes Inc.. 330 879-2158
8485 Navarre Rd Sw Massillon (44646) *(G-9214)*

Land Specialties LLC................................... 330 663-6974
2293 Ullet St Sw East Sparta (44626) *(G-6412)*

Landerwood Industries Inc.......................... 440 233-4234
4245 Hamann Pkwy Willoughby (44094) *(G-14481)*

Landis Machine Division, Cleveland *Also Called: Barth Industries Co LLC (G-3407)*

Landmark Plastic Corporation (PA)..............330 785-2200
1331 Kelly Ave Akron (44306) *(G-203)*

Landon Vault Company................................ 614 443-5505
1477 Frebis Ave Columbus (43206) *(G-5063)*

Landrum & Brown, Blue Ash *Also Called: Landrum Brown Wrldwide Svcs LL (G-1295)*

Landrum Brown Wrldwide Svcs LL............... 513 530-5333
4445 Lake Forest Dr Ste 700 Blue Ash (45242) *(G-1295)*

Lane Field Materials Inc.............................. 330 526-8082
530 Walnut Ave Ne Canton (44702) *(G-1930)*

Lang Stone Company Inc (PA)..................... 614 235-4099
4099 E 5th Ave Columbus (43219) *(G-5064)*

Langa Tool & Machine Inc........................... 440 953-1138
36430 Reading Ave Ste 1 Willoughby (44094) *(G-14482)*

Langdon Inc... 513 733-5955
9865 Wayne Ave Cincinnati (45215) *(G-2811)*

Lange Grinding & Machining Inc.................. 330 463-3500
10165 Philipp Pkwy Streetsboro (44241) *(G-12508)*

Lange Precision Inc..................................... 513 530-9500
865 S Us Route 42 Lebanon (45036) *(G-8273)*

Langenau Manufacturing Company...............216 651-3400
7306 Madison Ave Cleveland (44102) *(G-3939)*

Lanier & Associates Inc.............................. 216 391-7735
1814 E 40th St Ste 1c Cleveland (44103) *(G-3940)*

Lanko Industries Inc.................................... 440 269-1641
7301 Industrial Park Blvd Mentor (44060) *(G-9550)*

Lanly Company.. 216 731-1115
26201 Tungsten Rd Cleveland (44132) *(G-3941)*

Lantek Systems Inc (DH).............................877 805-1028
5412 Courseview Dr Ste 205 Mason (45040) *(G-9122)*

Lanxess Corporation.................................... 440 324-6060
110 Liberty Ct Elyria (44035) *(G-6557)*

Lapham-Hickey Steel Corp.......................... 614 443-4881
753 Marion Rd Columbus (43207) *(G-5065)*

Lapham-Hickey Steel Corp.......................... 419 399-4803
815 W Gasser Rd Paulding (45879) *(G-11158)*

Largemachining.com, West Chester *Also Called: Gedico International Inc (G-14007)*

Lariccias Italian Foods Inc.......................... 330 729-0222
7438 Southern Blvd Youngstown (44512) *(G-14887)*

Larmax Inc.. 513 984-0783
10945 Reed Hartman Hwy Ste 210 Blue Ash (45242) *(G-1296)*

Larmco Windows Inc (PA)............................216 502-2832
8400 Sweet Valley Dr Ste 404 Cleveland (44125) *(G-3942)*

Larsen Packaging Products Inc.................... 937 644-5511
16789 Square Dr Marysville (43040) *(G-9034)*

Las Americas Inc... 440 459-2030
5722 Mayfield Rd Cleveland (44124) *(G-3943)*

Lasaint Logistics, West Chester *Also Called: Multi Fittings Corporation (G-14032)*

Lasenor Usa LLC... 800 754-1228
600 Snyder Rd Salem (44460) *(G-11793)*

Laser Automation Inc................................... 440 543-9291
16771 Hilltop Park Pl Chagrin Falls (44023) *(G-2169)*

Laser Cartridge Express, Bowling Green *Also Called: Wood County Ohio (G-1448)*

Laser Label Technologies, Stow *Also Called: Electronic Printing Pdts Inc (G-12428)*

Laser Printing Solutions Inc........................ 216 351-4444
6040 Hillcrest Dr Cleveland (44125) *(G-3944)*

Laserfab Technologies Inc........................... 937 493-0800
2339 Industrial Dr Sidney (45365) *(G-12030)*

Laserlinc Inc... 937 318-2440
777 Zapata Dr Fairborn (45324) *(G-6695)*

A
L
P
H
A
B
E
T
I
C

Laspina Tool and Die Inc..330 923-9996
4282 Hudson Dr Stow (44224) *(G-12437)*

Last Arrow Manufacturing LLC....................................330 683-7777
8991 Lincoln Way E Orrville (44667) *(G-10992)*

Lastar Inc..937 224-0639
3555 Kettering Blvd Moraine (45439) *(G-10174)*

Laszeray Technology LLC..440 582-8430
12315 York Delta Dr North Royalton (44133) *(G-10770)*

Latanick Equipment Inc...419 433-2200
720 River Rd Huron (44839) *(G-7878)*

Late For Sky Production Co..513 531-4400
1292 Glendale Milford Rd Cincinnati (45215) *(G-2812)*

Latham Limestone LLC..740 493-2677
6424 State Route 124 Latham (45646) *(G-8235)*

Latrobe Spcialty Mtls Dist Inc (HQ)...........................330 609-5137
1551 Vienna Pkwy Vienna (44473) *(G-13610)*

Latrobe Specialty Mtls Co LLC.......................................419 335-8010
14614 County Road H Wauseon (43567) *(G-13854)*

Lattice Composites LLC..440 759-2082
29001 Solon Rd Unit S Solon (44139) *(G-12141)*

Lau Holdings LLC (HQ)..216 486-4000
16900 S Waterloo Rd Cleveland (44110) *(G-3945)*

Lau Holdings LLC...937 476-6500
4509 Springfield St Dayton (45431) *(G-5617)*

Lau Industries Inc..937 476-6500
4509 Springfield St Dayton (45431) *(G-5618)*

Lauber Manufacturing Co...419 446-2450
3751 County Road 26 Archbold (43502) *(G-499)*

Launch Scout LLC...513 449-6940
5910 Hamilton Ave Cincinnati (45224) *(G-2813)*

Lauren International Ltd (PA)...234 303-2400
143 Garland Dr Sw New Philadelphia (44663) *(G-10454)*

Lauren Manufacturing...330 339-3373
2228 Reiser Ave Se New Philadelphia (44663) *(G-10455)*

Laurenco Systems of Ohio LLC
4255 W Market St Leavittsburg (44430) *(G-8240)*

Laurenee Ltd..513 662-2225
3509 Harrison Ave Cincinnati (45211) *(G-2814)*

Laurentia Winery...440 296-9170
6869 River Rd Madison (44057) *(G-8731)*

Lawbre Co...330 637-3363
3311 Warren Meadville Rd Cortland (44410) *(G-5446)*

Lawrence Industries Inc (PA)...216 518-7000
4500 Lee Rd Ste 120 Cleveland (44128) *(G-3946)*

Lawrence Industries Inc..216 518-1400
4500 Lee Rd Ste 120 Cleveland (44128) *(G-3947)*

Lawrence Machine, Massillon *Also Called: Gary Lawrence Enterprises Inc (G-9194)*

Lawrence Technologies Inc..937 274-7771
2571 Timber Ln Dayton (45414) *(G-5842)*

Lawson Twing Auto Wrecking LLC.................................216 883-9050
14114 Miles Ave Cleveland (44128) *(G-3948)*

Layerzero Power Systems Inc (PA)................................440 399-9000
1500 Danner Dr Aurora (44202) *(G-676)*

Lazars Art Gllery Crtive Frmng.......................................330 477-8351
2940 Woodlawn Ave Nw Canton (44708) *(G-1931)*

Lba Custom Printing..419 535-3151
207 Arco Dr Toledo (43607) *(G-13028)*

LBC Clay Co LLC...330 674-0674
4501 Township Road 307 Millersburg (44654) *(G-9991)*

LBL Lithographers Inc (PA)..440 350-0106
365 W Prospect St Painesville (44077) *(G-11096)*

Lbzb Restaurants Inc..567 413-4700
132 E Wooster St Bowling Green (43402) *(G-1424)*

Lc, Cleveland *Also Called: Logan Clutch Corporation (G-3966)*

Lcas, Lorain *Also Called: Lorain County Auto Systems Inc (G-8565)*

Lckbm Company (HQ)...419 636-4555
1030 E Wilson St Bryan (43506) *(G-1648)*

Le Gourmet Chef, Chillicothe *Also Called: The Kitchen Collection LLC (G-2284)*

Leadec Corp (HQ)..513 731-3590
9395 Kenwood Rd Ste 200 Cincinnati (45242) *(G-2815)*

Leadec Services, Cincinnati *Also Called: Leadec Corp (G-2815)*

Leader Engnrng-Fabrication Inc......................................419 636-1731
County Rd D-50 Bryan (43506) *(G-1649)*

Leader Printing, Newark *Also Called: Ryans Newark Leader Ex Prtg Co (G-10532)*

Leader Publications Inc..330 665-9595
3075 Smith Rd Ste 204 Fairlawn (44333) *(G-6806)*

Leak Finder Inc...440 735-0130
6583 Wooded View Dr Hudson (44236) *(G-7849)*

Lear Corporation...740 928-4358
180 N High St Hebron (43025) *(G-7622)*

Lear Corporation...419 335-6010
447 E Walnut St Wauseon (43567) *(G-13855)*

Lear Mfg Co Inc..440 324-1111
147 Freedom Ct Elyria (44035) *(G-6558)*

Lear Romec, Elyria *Also Called: Hydro-Aire Inc (G-6543)*

Learn21 A Flxble Lrng Cllbrtiv..513 402-2121
11802 Conrey Rd Cincinnati (45249) *(G-2816)*

Leather Resource of America Inc....................................440 262-5761
494 E Main Rd Conneaut (44030) *(G-5407)*

Lectroetch Co...440 934-1249
9200 Tyler Blvd Mentor (44060) *(G-9551)*

Lectroetch Company, The, Mentor *Also Called: Monode Marking Products Inc (G-9567)*

Led Lighting Center Inc (PA)...714 271-2633
5500 Enterprise Blvd Toledo (43612) *(G-13029)*

Led Lighting Center LLC...888 988-6533
5500 Enterprise Blvd Toledo (43612) *(G-13030)*

Led-Andon, Columbus *Also Called: American Led-Gible Inc (G-4699)*

Ledex & Dormeyer Products, Vandalia *Also Called: Saia-Burgess Lcc (G-13576)*

Lee Corporation...513 771-3602
12055 Mosteller Rd Cincinnati (45241) *(G-2817)*

Lee Plastic Company LLC..937 456-5720
1100 Us Route 35 Eaton (45320) *(G-6459)*

Lee Printers, Cincinnati *Also Called: Lee Corporation (G-2817)*

Lee Saylor Logging LLC..740 682-0479
565 Cress Rd Oak Hill (45656) *(G-10890)*

Lee Williams Meats Inc (PA)...419 729-3893
3002 131st St Toledo (43611) *(G-13031)*

Lees Grinding Inc..440 572-4610
15620 Foltz Pkwy Strongsville (44149) *(G-12570)*

Leesburg Loom & Supply, Van Wert *Also Called: Leesburg Looms Incorporated (G-13540)*

Leesburg Looms Incorporated...419 238-2738
201 N Cherry St Van Wert (45891) *(G-13540)*

Lefeld Supplies Rental, Coldwater *Also Called: Lefeld Welding & Stl Sups Inc (G-4580)*

Lefeld Welding & Stl Sups Inc (PA).................................419 678-2397
600 N 2nd St Coldwater (45828) *(G-4580)*

Legacy Farmers Cooperative (PA)..................................419 423-2611
6566 County Road 236 Findlay (45840) *(G-6884)*

Legacy Finishing Inc..937 743-7278
415 Oxford Rd Franklin (45005) *(G-7030)*

Legacy Stwr LLC..937 440-2505
1040 S Dorset Rd Troy (45373) *(G-13236)*

Legacy Supplies Inc...330 405-4565
8252 Darrow Rd Ste E Twinsburg (44087) *(G-13328)*

Legal News Publishing Co..216 696-3322
2935 Prospect Ave E Cleveland (44115) *(G-3949)*

Legalcraft Inc...330 494-1261
302 Hallum St Sw Canton (44720) *(G-1932)*

Legend Metal and Rubber LLC..513 874-8020
9388 Sutton Pl West Chester (45011) *(G-14022)*

Legrand AV Inc...574 267-8101
11500 Williamson Rd Blue Ash (45241) *(G-1297)*

Legrand North America LLC..937 224-0639
6500 Poe Ave Dayton (45414) *(G-5843)*

Lehman's, Dalton *Also Called: Robura LLC (G-5593)*

Lehner Screw Machine LLC...330 688-6616
1169 Brittain Rd Akron (44305) *(G-204)*

Lehner Signs Inc...614 258-0500
133 Salinger Dr Lithopolis (43136) *(G-8483)*

Lehr Awning Co, Mansfield *Also Called: PCR Restorations Inc (G-8844)*

Leica Biosystems - TAS..513 864-9671
300 E Business Way Fl 5 Cincinnati (45241) *(G-2818)*

Leiden Cabinet Co..330 425-8555
  1842 Enterprise Pkwy Twinsburg (44087) *(G-13329)*

Leiden Cabinet Company LLC................................330 425-8555
  1230 Hensel Ave Ne Strasburg (44680) *(G-12480)*

Leiden Cabinet Company LLC (PA)...........................330 425-8555
  2385 Edison Blvd Twinsburg (44087) *(G-13330)*

Leiden Company, Twinsburg *Also Called: Leiden Cabinet Company LLC (G-13330)*

Leidos Inc...937 656-8433
  3745 Pentagon Blvd Beavercreek (45431) *(G-977)*

Leimkuehler Inc (PA)...440 899-7842
  4625 Detroit Ave Cleveland (44102) *(G-3950)*

Leisure Time Pdts Design Corp..............................440 934-1032
  1284 Miller Rd Avon (44011) *(G-731)*

Leitner Fabrication LLC......................................330 721-7374
  935 Heritage Dr Medina (44256) *(G-9420)*

Leland-Gifford Inc..330 785-9730
  1029 Arlington Cir Akron (44306) *(G-205)*

Lem Products Holding LLC (PA)..............................513 202-1188
  4440 Muhlhauser Rd Ste 300 West Chester (45011) *(G-14023)*

Lemsco Inc...419 242-4005
  2056 Canton Ave Toledo (43620) *(G-13032)*

Lemsco-Girkins, Toledo *Also Called: Lemsco Inc (G-13032)*

Lennox, Cleveland *Also Called: Lennox Industries Inc (G-3951)*

Lennox Industries Inc..216 739-1909
  4562 Hinckley Industrial Pkwy Unit 8 Cleveland (44109) *(G-3951)*

Lennox Machine Inc..419 525-1020
  1471 Sprang Pkwy Mansfield (44903) *(G-8812)*

Lennox Machine Shop, Mansfield *Also Called: Lennox Machine Inc (G-8812)*

Lenz Inc..937 277-9364
  3301 Klepinger Rd Dayton (45406) *(G-5844)*

Lenz Company, Dayton *Also Called: Lenz Inc (G-5844)*

Leon Newswanger..419 896-3336
  7828 Planktown North Rd Shiloh (44878) *(G-11979)*

Leonardo Drs Arbr Intllgnce Sy, Beavercreek *Also Called: Drs Leonardo Inc (G-971)*

Leonhardt Plating Company.................................513 242-1410
  5753 Este Ave Cincinnati (45232) *(G-2819)*

Leroi Compressors, Sidney *Also Called: G Denver and Co LLC (G-12021)*

Lesch Boat Cover Canvas Co LLC...........................419 668-6374
  43 1/2 Saint Marys St Norwalk (44857) *(G-10850)*

Lesco Inc...740 633-6366
  100 Picoma Rd Martins Ferry (43935) *(G-9010)*

Lesco Service Center, Martins Ferry *Also Called: Lesco Inc (G-9010)*

Lester Miller, Owner, West Farmington *Also Called: Millertech Energy Solutions (G-14159)*

Lettergraphics Inc...330 683-3903
  400 W Market St Orrville (44667) *(G-10993)*

Letterman Printing Inc.......................................513 523-1111
  310 S College Ave Oxford (45056) *(G-11083)*

Levan Enterprises Inc (PA)..................................330 923-9797
  4585 Allen Rd Stow (44224) *(G-12438)*

Levison Enterprises LLC.....................................419 838-7365
  4470 Moline Martin Rd Millbury (43447) *(G-9964)*

Lewark Metal Spinning Inc...................................937 275-3303
  2746 Keenan Ave Dayton (45414) *(G-5845)*

Lewart Plastics LLC..216 281-2333
  3562 W 69th St Cleveland (44102) *(G-3952)*

Lewco Inc (PA)..419 625-4014
  706 Lane St Sandusky (44870) *(G-11850)*

Lewis Unlimited Inc..216 514-8282
  3690 Orange Pl Ste 340 Beachwood (44122) *(G-925)*

Lewisburg Container Company (DH).........................937 962-2681
  275 W Clay St Lewisburg (45338) *(G-8360)*

Lexington Concrete & Sup Inc (PA)..........................419 529-3232
  362 N Trimble Rd Mansfield (44906) *(G-8813)*

Lexington Rubber Group Inc (PA)............................330 425-8472
  1700 Highland Rd Twinsburg (44087) *(G-13331)*

Lexisnexis, Miamisburg *Also Called: Relx Inc (G-9731)*

Lexisnexis Group (DH)..937 865-6800
  9443 Springboro Pike Miamisburg (45342) *(G-9709)*

Lexisnexis Group, Miamisburg *Also Called: Lexisnexis Group (G-9709)*

Lextech Industries Ltd.......................................216 883-7900
  6800 Union Ave Cleveland (44105) *(G-3953)*

Ley Industries Inc..419 238-6742
  121 S Walnut St Van Wert (45891) *(G-13541)*

Lfe Instruments, Bluffton *Also Called: Triplett Bluffton Corporation (G-1367)*

Lfg Specialties LLC..419 424-4999
  16406 E Us Route 224 Findlay (45840) *(G-6885)*

Lg Chem Ohio Petrochemical Inc............................470 792-5127
  310 Rayann Pkwy Ravenna (44266) *(G-11530)*

LH Marshall Company..614 294-6433
  1601 Woodland Ave Columbus (43219) *(G-5066)*

Lhpc Inc (PA)...330 527-2696
  11964 State Route 88 Garrettsville (44231) *(G-7224)*

Lhy Powertrain Corporation (DH)............................330 533-6801
  5089 W Western Reserve Rd Canfield (44406) *(G-1812)*

Lib Therapeutics Inc...859 240-7764
  5375 Medpace Way Cincinnati (45227) *(G-2820)*

Libbey, Toledo *Also Called: Libbey Glass LLC (G-13033)*

Libbey, Toledo *Also Called: Libbey Inc (G-13035)*

Libbey America, Toledo *Also Called: Libbey Glass LLC (G-13034)*

Libbey Glass LLC (HQ)..419 325-2100
  300 Madison Ave Toledo (43604) *(G-13033)*

Libbey Glass LLC...419 727-2211
  940 Ash St Toledo (43611) *(G-13034)*

Libbey Inc (PA)...419 325-2100
  300 Madison Ave Toledo (43604) *(G-13035)*

Liberty Casting Company LLC (PA)...........................740 363-1941
  550 Liberty Rd Delaware (43015) *(G-6160)*

Liberty Die Cast Molds Inc...................................740 666-7492
  57 2nd St Ostrander (43061) *(G-11028)*

Liberty Iron & Metal Inc......................................724 347-4534
  27 Furnace Ln Girard (44420) *(G-7274)*

Liberty Outdoors, Uniontown *Also Called: Liberty Outdoors LLC (G-13422)*

Liberty Outdoors LLC..330 791-3149
  1519 Boettler Rd Ste A Uniontown (44685) *(G-13422)*

Liberty Pattern and Mold Inc.................................330 788-9463
  1131 Meadowbrook Ave Youngstown (44512) *(G-14888)*

Liberty Sportswear LLC.......................................513 755-8740
  5573 Eureka Dr Hamilton (45011) *(G-7510)*

Liberty Tire Recycling Inc....................................614 871-8097
  3041 Jackson Pike Grove City (43123) *(G-7394)*

LIBERTY TIRE RECYCLING, LLC, Grove City *Also Called: Liberty Tire Recycling LLC (G-7394)*

Libra Guaymas LLC...440 974-7770
  7770 Division Dr Mentor (44060) *(G-9552)*

Libra Industries, Dayton *Also Called: Gem City Engineering Co (G-5792)*

Libra Industries LLC (DH)....................................440 974-7770
  7770 Division Dr Mentor (44060) *(G-9553)*

License Ad Plate Company....................................216 265-4200
  13110 Enterprise Ave Side B Cleveland (44135) *(G-3954)*

Liebert Field Services Inc.....................................614 841-5763
  610 Executive Campus Dr Westerville (43082) *(G-14220)*

Liechty Specialties, Archbold *Also Called: Nef Ltd (G-505)*

Liechty Specialties Inc.......................................419 445-6696
  1901 S Defiance St Archbold (43502) *(G-500)*

Liette L & S Express LLC......................................419 394-7077
  2286 Celina Rd Saint Marys (45885) *(G-11741)*

Life Is Sweet LLC (PA)..330 342-0172
  6926 Main St Cincinnati (45244) *(G-2821)*

Life Sciences - Vandalia LLC (HQ)...........................937 387-0880
  4201 Little York Rd Dayton (45414) *(G-5846)*

Life Support Development Ltd................................614 221-1765
  777 Dearborn Park Ln Ste R Columbus (43085) *(G-5067)*

Lifeformations, Bowling Green *Also Called: Lifeformations Inc (G-1425)*

Lifeformations Inc...419 352-2101
  2029 Wood Bridge Blvd Bowling Green (43402) *(G-1425)*

Lifeline Mobile Inc...614 497-8300
  2050 Mcgaw Rd Columbus (43207) *(G-5068)*

Lifestyle Media Group LLC...................................954 377-9470
  3550 Embassy Pkwy Akron (44333) *(G-206)*

Lifetime Products Inc..614 272-1255
  4364 Sullivant Ave Columbus (43228) *(G-5069)*

Lift-Tech International Inc....................................330 424-7248
  240 Pennsylvania Ave Salem (44460) *(G-11794)*

Light Craft Direct, Fremont *Also Called: Light Craft Manufacturing Inc (G-7121)*

Light Craft Manufacturing Inc..419 332-0536
220 Sullivan Rd Fremont (43420) *(G-7121)*

Light Vision..513 351-9444
1776 Mentor Ave Cincinnati (45212) *(G-2822)*

Lighting Products Inc..440 293-4064
101 Parker Dr Andover (44003) *(G-458)*

Lightning Bolt Fastners, Mount Gilead *Also Called: Lilly Industries Inc (G-10211)*

Lightning Mold & Machine, Conneaut *Also Called: Lightning Mold & Machine Inc (G-5408)*

Lightning Mold & Machine Inc..440 593-6460
509 W Main Rd Conneaut (44030) *(G-5408)*

Lilly Industries Inc (PA)..419 946-7908
6437 County Road 20 Mount Gilead (43338) *(G-10211)*

Lily Ann Cabinets..419 360-2455
2939 Douglas Rd Toledo (43606) *(G-13036)*

Lima Armature Works Inc..419 222-4010
142 E Pearl St Lima (45801) *(G-8424)*

Lima Millwork Inc..419 331-3303
4251 East Rd Elida (45807) *(G-6483)*

Lima Pallet Company Inc..419 229-5736
1470 Neubrecht Rd Lima (45801) *(G-8425)*

Lima Sheet Metal, Lima *Also Called: Lima Sheet Metal Mch & Mfg Inc (G-8426)*

Lima Sheet Metal Mch & Mfg Inc..419 229-1161
1001 Bowman Rd Lima (45804) *(G-8426)*

Lima Sporting Goods Inc..419 222-1036
1404 Allentown Rd Lima (45805) *(G-8427)*

Liminal Data, Gates Mills *Also Called: Liminal Esports LLC (G-7230)*

Liminal Esports LLC..440 423-5856
1500 Chagrin River Rd Unit 361 Gates Mills (44040) *(G-7230)*

Liming Printing Inc..937 374-2646
1450 S Patton St Xenia (45385) *(G-14769)*

Linamar Strctures USA Mich Inc..260 636-7030
507 W Indiana St Edon (43518) *(G-6475)*

Linamar Strctures USA Mich Inc..567 249-0838
201 Leanne St Edon (43518) *(G-6476)*

Lincoln Center Manufacturing, Cardington *Also Called: Marengo Fabricated Steel Ltd (G-2055)*

LINCOLN ELECTRIC, Cleveland *Also Called: Lincoln Electric Holdings Inc (G-3956)*

Lincoln Electric Automtn Inc..419 678-4877
911 N 2nd St Coldwater (45828) *(G-4581)*

Lincoln Electric Automtn Inc..614 471-5926
1700 Jetway Blvd Columbus (43219) *(G-5070)*

Lincoln Electric Automtn Inc (HQ)..937 295-2120
407 S Main St Fort Loramie (45845) *(G-6950)*

Lincoln Electric Company (HQ)..216 481-8100
22801 Saint Clair Ave Cleveland (44117) *(G-3955)*

Lincoln Electric Holdings Inc (PA)..216 481-8100
22801 Saint Clair Ave Cleveland (44117) *(G-3956)*

Lincoln Foodservice Products, Cleveland *Also Called: Lincoln Foodservice Products LLC (G-3957)*

Lincoln Foodservice Products LLC..260 459-8200
1333 E 179th St Cleveland (44110) *(G-3957)*

Lincoln Manufacturing Inc..330 878-7772
310 Railroad Ave Se Strasburg (44680) *(G-12481)*

LINCOLN MANUFACTURING, INC., Strasburg *Also Called: Lincoln Manufacturing Inc (G-12481)*

Lincoln Way Vineyards Inc..330 804-9463
9050 W Old Lincoln Way Wooster (44691) *(G-14660)*

Linde Gas & Equipment Inc..513 821-2192
8376 Reading Rd Cincinnati (45237) *(G-2823)*

Linde Gas & Equipment Inc..614 443-7687
450 Greenlawn Ave Columbus (43223) *(G-5071)*

Linde Gas & Equipment Inc..419 729-7732
6055 Brent Dr Toledo (43611) *(G-13037)*

Linde Gas & Equipment Inc..440 944-8844
1140 Lloyd Rd Wickliffe (44092) *(G-14380)*

Linde Gas USA LLC..330 425-3989
2045 E Aurora Rd Twinsburg (44087) *(G-13332)*

Linde Hydraulics Corporation, Canfield *Also Called: Lhy Powertrain Corporation (G-1812)*

Linde Inc..440 994-1000
3102 Lake Rd E Ashtabula (44004) *(G-603)*

Linde Inc..330 825-4449
4805 Fairland Rd Barberton (44203) *(G-817)*

Linde Inc..440 237-8690
14788 York Rd Cleveland (44133) *(G-3958)*

Linde Inc..419 698-8005
3742 Cedar Point Rd Oregon (43616) *(G-10962)*

Linden-Two Inc..330 928-4064
137 Ascot Pkwy Cuyahoga Falls (44223) *(G-5559)*

Lindsay Precast LLC (PA)..800 837-7788
6845 Erie Ave Nw Canal Fulton (44614) *(G-1777)*

Line Drive Sportz-Lcrc LLC..419 794-7150
2901 Key St Ste 1 Maumee (43537) *(G-9304)*

Line-X of Akron/Medina, North Royalton *Also Called: X-Treme Finishes Inc (G-10790)*

Linear Acoustic Inc..717 735-3611
1241 Superior Ave E Cleveland (44114) *(G-3959)*

Linear Asics Inc..330 474-3920
2061 Case Pkwy S Twinsburg (44087) *(G-13333)*

Linear It Solutions LLC..614 306-0761
639 Gallop Ln Marysville (43040) *(G-9035)*

Linear Technology LLC..440 239-0817
7550 Lucerne Dr Ste 106 Cleveland (44130) *(G-3960)*

Linestream Technologies Inc..216 862-7874
1468 W 9th St Ste 435 Cleveland (44113) *(G-3961)*

Link Systems Inc..800 321-8770
28925 Fountain Pkwy Solon (44139) *(G-12142)*

Link To Success Inc..888 959-4203
23 Stoutenburg Dr Norwalk (44857) *(G-10851)*

Linnea's, Kent *Also Called: Linneas Candy Supplies Inc (G-8046)*

Linneas Candy Supplies Inc (PA)..330 678-7112
4149 Karg Industrial Pkwy Kent (44240) *(G-8046)*

Linsalata Cpitl Prtners Fund I..440 684-1400
5900 Landerbrook Dr Ste 280 Cleveland (44124) *(G-3962)*

Lintech Electronics LLC..513 528-6190
4435 Aicholtz Rd Ste 500 Cincinnati (45245) *(G-2312)*

Lintern Corporation (PA)..440 255-9333
8685 Station St Mentor (44060) *(G-9554)*

Lion Apparel Inc (DH)..937 898-1949
7200 Poe Ave Ste 400 Dayton (45414) *(G-5847)*

Lion Apparel Inc..937 898-1949
6450 Poe Ave Ste 300 Dayton (45414) *(G-5848)*

Lion First Responder Ppe Inc..937 898-1949
7200 Poe Ave Ste 400 Dayton (45414) *(G-5849)*

Lion Group Inc (HQ)..800 421-2926
7200 Poe Ave Ste 400 Dayton (45414) *(G-5850)*

Lion Industries LLC..740 676-1100
423 53rd St Bellaire (43906) *(G-1089)*

Lipari Foods Operating Co LLC..330 893-2479
6597 County Road 625 Millersburg (44654) *(G-9992)*

Lipari Foods Operating Co LLC..330 674-9199
316 S Mad Anthony St Millersburg (44654) *(G-9993)*

Lipo Technologies Inc..937 264-1222
707 Harco Dr Englewood (45315) *(G-6618)*

Lippert Components Inc..574 537-8900
407 N Maple St Payne (45880) *(G-11164)*

Lippincott and Peto Inc..330 864-2122
1741 Akron Peninsula Rd Akron (44313) *(G-207)*

Liqui-Box Corporation..419 289-9696
1817 Masters Ave Ashland (44805) *(G-549)*

Liqui-Box Corporation..419 294-3884
519 Raybestos Dr Upper Sandusky (43351) *(G-13446)*

Liquid Control, North Canton *Also Called: Graco Ohio Inc (G-10644)*

Liquid Development Company (PA)..216 641-9366
5708 E Schaaf Rd Independence (44131) *(G-7907)*

Liquid Image Corp America..216 458-9800
3700 Prospect Ave E Cleveland (44115) *(G-3963)*

Liquid Luggers LLC..330 426-2538
183 Edgeworth Ave East Palestine (44413) *(G-6404)*

Liquid Manufacturing Solutions..937 401-0821
401 Shotwell Dr Franklin (45005) *(G-7031)*

Lisbon Powder Coating..234 567-1324
6191 Lisbon Rd Lisbon (44432) *(G-8476)*

(G-0000) Company's Geographic Section entry number

Listermann Brewery Supply, Cincinnati *Also Called: Listermann Mfg Co Inc (G-2824)*

Listermann Mfg Co Inc.. 513 731-1130
4120 Forest Ave Cincinnati (45212) *(G-2824)*

Litco Corner Protection LLC... 330 539-5433
1000 Tuscarawas St E Vienna (44473) *(G-13611)*

Litco Cornerguard, LLC, Vienna *Also Called: Litco Corner Protection LLC (G-13611)*

Litco International Inc (PA)... 330 539-5433
1 Litco Dr Vienna (44473) *(G-13612)*

Litco Manufacturing LLC.. 330 539-5433
1512 Phoenix Rd Ne Warren (44483) *(G-13777)*

Litco Wood Products, Apple Creek *Also Called: Millwood Inc (G-471)*

Lite Magnesium Products Inc....................................... 330 296-6110
700 N Walnut St Ravenna (44266) *(G-11531)*

Lite Metals Company... 330 296-6110
700 N Walnut St Ravenna (44266) *(G-11532)*

Liteflex Disc LLC... 937 836-7025
3251 Mccall St Dayton (45417) *(G-5851)*

Litehouse Pools & Spas, Strongsville *Also Called: Litehouse Products LLC (G-12571)*

Litehouse Products LLC (PA).. 440 638-2350
10883 Pearl Rd Ste 301 Strongsville (44136) *(G-12571)*

Lithchem, Lancaster *Also Called: Cirba Solutions Us Inc (G-8186)*

Lithium Innovations Co LLC.. 419 725-3525
3171 N Republic Blvd Ste 101 Toledo (43615) *(G-13038)*

Litho-Print Ltd.. 937 222-4351
848 E Monument Ave Dayton (45402) *(G-5852)*

Little Busy Beez Erly Lrng Chl...................................... 216 477-1965
10578 Northfield Rd Northfield (44067) *(G-10795)*

Little Mountain Precision LLC....................................... 440 290-2903
8677 Tyler Blvd Mentor (44060) *(G-9555)*

Little Printing Company.. 937 773-4595
4317 W Us Route 36 Piqua (45356) *(G-11363)*

Little Tikes, Hudson *Also Called: The Little Tikes Company (G-7860)*

Littlern Corporation.. 330 848-8847
1006 Bunker Dr Apt 207 Fairlawn (44333) *(G-6807)*

Liturgical Publications Inc... 216 325-6825
4560 E 71st St Cleveland (44105) *(G-3964)*

Live Off Loyalty Inc.. 513 413-2401
12019 Hitchcock Dr Cincinnati (45240) *(G-2825)*

Liverpool Township... 330 483-4747
6700 Center Rd Valley City (44280) *(G-13502)*

Liverpool-Coil-Processing, Valley City *Also Called: Shl Liquidation Liverpool Inc (G-13518)*

Lkd Aerospace Holdings Inc (PA).................................. 216 262-8481
25101 Chagrin Blvd Ste 350 Cleveland (44122) *(G-3965)*

LLC Bowman Leather... 330 893-1954
6705 Private Road 387 Millersburg (44654) *(G-9994)*

LLC Ring Masters... 330 832-1511
240 6th St Nw Massillon (44647) *(G-9215)*

Lm Cases, Austintown *Also Called: L M Engineering Inc (G-706)*

LMC, Akron *Also Called: Logan Machine Company (G-210)*

Lmg Holdings Inc (PA).. 905 829-3541
4290 Glendale Milford Rd Blue Ash (45242) *(G-1298)*

Lmp, Hartville *Also Called: Louisville Molded Products Inc (G-7580)*

Lmp Machine LLC... 740 596-4559
115 E Chestnut St Zaleski (45698) *(G-14979)*

Load32 LLC... 614 984-6648
265 N Oakley Ave Columbus (43204) *(G-5072)*

Loadmaster Scale, Findlay *Also Called: Holtgreven Scale & Elec Corp (G-6881)*

Loadmaster Trailer Company Ltd................................... 419 732-3434
2354 East Harbor Rd Port Clinton (43452) *(G-11445)*

Loadmaster Trailers Mfg, Port Clinton *Also Called: Loadmaster Trailer Company Ltd (G-11445)*

Lochard Inc... 937 492-8811
903 Wapakoneta Ave Sidney (45365) *(G-12031)*

Locher Inc... 740 654-8888
422 Quarry Rd Se Lancaster (43130) *(G-8208)*

Lock 15 Brewing Company LLC..................................... 234 900-8277
21 W North St Akron (44304) *(G-208)*

Lock 27 Brewing LLC.. 937 433-2739
1024 Quail Run Dr Dayton (45458) *(G-5853)*

Lock Joint Tube Ohio LLC.. 210 278-3757
135 Penniman Rd Orwell (44076) *(G-11023)*

Lockfast LLC.. 800 543-7157
107 Northeast Dr Loveland (45140) *(G-8637)*

Lockheed Mrtin Intgrted System................................... 330 796-2800
1210 Massillon Rd Akron (44315) *(G-209)*

Lockrey Manufacturing, Toledo *Also Called: Raka Corporation (G-13110)*

Loctite, Westlake *Also Called: Henkel US Operations Corp (G-14305)*

Loft Violin Shop... 614 267-7221
4604 N High St Columbus (43214) *(G-5073)*

Logan Clutch Corporation.. 440 808-4258
28855 Ranney Pkwy Cleveland (44145) *(G-3966)*

Logan Coatings LLC.. 740 380-0047
2255 E Front St Logan (43138) *(G-8519)*

Logan Foundry & Machine, Logan *Also Called: Clay Logan Products Company (G-8511)*

Logan Machine Company (PA)....................................... 330 633-6163
1405 Home Ave Akron (44310) *(G-210)*

Logan Welding Inc.. 740 385-9651
37062 Hocking Dr Logan (43138) *(G-8520)*

Logisync, Avon *Also Called: Logisync Corporation (G-732)*

Logisync Corporation.. 440 937-0388
1313 Lear Industrial Pkwy Avon (44011) *(G-732)*

Logitech Inc.. 614 871-2822
6423 Seeds Rd Grove City (43123) *(G-7395)*

Logo This.. 419 445-1355
301 Ditto St Ste E Archbold (43502) *(G-501)*

Lokring Technology LLC... 440 942-0880
38376 Apollo Pkwy Willoughby (44094) *(G-14483)*

Loma Systems... 740 274-9047
151 Discovery Dr Chillicothe (45601) *(G-2262)*

Lomar Enterprises Inc... 614 409-9104
5905 Green Pointe Dr S Ste G Groveport (43125) *(G-7443)*

Long View Steel Corp.. 419 747-1108
1555 W Longview Ave Mansfield (44906) *(G-8814)*

Long-Lok LLC (PA)... 336 343-7319
10630 Chester Rd Cincinnati (45215) *(G-2826)*

Long-Lok Fasteners Corporation................................... 513 772-1880
10630 Chester Rd Cincinnati (45215) *(G-2827)*

Long-Stanton Mfg Company.. 513 874-8020
9388 Sutton Pl West Chester (45011) *(G-14024)*

Lonolife Inc... 614 296-2250
432 W 2nd Ave Columbus (43201) *(G-5074)*

Lonz Winery, Cleveland *Also Called: Paramount Distillers Inc (G-4134)*

Lonz Winery LLC.. 419 625-5474
917 Bardshar Rd Sandusky (44870) *(G-11851)*

Lorain County Auto Systems Inc................................... 248 442-6800
3400 River Industrial Park Rd Lorain (44052) *(G-8564)*

Lorain County Auto Systems Inc (HQ)............................ 440 960-7470
7470 Industrial Parkway Dr Lorain (44053) *(G-8565)*

Lorain Modern Pattern Inc... 440 365-6780
159 Woodbury St Elyria (44035) *(G-6559)*

Lorain Rled Die Pdts Indus Sup.................................... 440 281-8607
6287 Lear Nagle Rd Ste 4 North Ridgeville (44039) *(G-10739)*

Lord Corporation.. 937 278-9431
4644 Wadsworth Rd Dayton (45414) *(G-5854)*

Lorenz Corporation (PA).. 937 228-6118
501 E 3rd St Dayton (45402) *(G-5855)*

Lori Holding Co (PA)... 740 342-3230
1400 Commerce Dr New Lexington (43764) *(G-10403)*

Loris Printing Inc... 419 626-6648
2111 Cleveland Rd Sandusky (44870) *(G-11852)*

Loris Printing & Party Center, Sandusky *Also Called: Loris Printing Inc (G-11852)*

Loroco Industries Inc.. 513 891-9544
10600 Evendale Dr Cincinnati (45241) *(G-2828)*

Losantiville Winery LLC... 513 918-3015
38 W Mcmicken Ave Cincinnati (45202) *(G-2829)*

Lost Tech, West Chester *Also Called: Lost Technology LLP (G-14025)*

Lost Technology LLP... 513 685-0054
9501 Woodland Hills Dr West Chester (45011) *(G-14025)*

Lotus Love LLC.. 614 964-8477
1091 Fountain Ln Apt B Columbus (43213) *(G-5075)*

Lotus Pipes & Rockdrills USA....................................... 516 209-6995
1700 E 12th St Cleveland (44114) *(G-3967)*

A
L
P
H
A
B
E
T
I
C

Lou's Sausage, Cleveland *Also Called: Lous Sausage Ltd (G-3968)*

Louis Arthur Steel Company (PA)..............................440 997-5545
185 Water St Geneva (44041) *(G-7241)*

Louis Arthur Steel Company..440 997-5545
200 North Ave E Geneva (44041) *(G-7242)*

Louis Instantwhip-St Inc..614 488-2536
2200 Cardigan Ave Columbus (43215) *(G-5076)*

Louisville Molded Products Inc....................................330 877-9740
13122 Duquette Ave Ne Hartville (44632) *(G-7580)*

Lous Machine Company Inc...513 856-9199
102 Hastings Ave Hamilton (45011) *(G-7511)*

Lous Sausage Ltd..216 752-5060
14723 Miles Ave Cleveland (44128) *(G-3968)*

Love Laugh & Laundry...567 377-1951
5333 Secor Rd Toledo (43623) *(G-13039)*

Love Chocolate Factory, Hartville *Also Called: L C F Inc (G-7579)*

Love Yueh LLC...614 408-8677
9126 Calverton Ter Pickerington (43147) *(G-11295)*

Love. Laugh. Laundry., Toledo *Also Called: Love Laugh & Laundry (G-13039)*

Loveland Graphics, Cincinnati *Also Called: Eastgate Custom Graphics Ltd (G-2575)*

Loveman Steel Corporation...440 232-6200
5455 Perkins Rd Bedford (44146) *(G-1044)*

Lowry Furnace Co Inc...330 745-4822
663 Flora Ave Akron (44314) *(G-211)*

Lowry Tool & Die Inc..330 332-1722
986 Salem Pkwy Salem (44460) *(G-11795)*

LPI, Cleveland *Also Called: Liturgical Publications Inc (G-3964)*

Lrb Tool & Die Ltd..330 898-5783
3303 Parkman Rd Nw Warren (44481) *(G-13778)*

Lrbg Chemicals USA Inc..419 244-5856
2112 Sylvan Ave Toledo (43606) *(G-13040)*

Lri Post-Acquisition Inc (PA).......................................419 227-2200
893 Shawnee Rd Lima (45805) *(G-8428)*

LS Starrett Company...440 835-0005
24500 Detroit Rd Westlake (44145) *(G-14313)*

Lsc Communications Inc...419 935-0111
1145 S Conwell Ave Willard (44890) *(G-14403)*

LSI Graphic Solutions Plus, Akron *Also Called: Grady McCauley Inc (G-165)*

LSI Industries, Cincinnati *Also Called: LSI Industries Inc (G-2830)*

LSI Industries Inc...913 281-1100
10000 Alliance Rd Blue Ash (45242) *(G-1299)*

LSI Industries Inc (PA)...513 793-3200
10000 Alliance Rd Cincinnati (45242) *(G-2830)*

LSI Lightron Inc..845 562-5500
10000 Alliance Rd Blue Ash (45242) *(G-1300)*

Lsmi, Columbus *Also Called: Lambert Sheet Metal Inc (G-5061)*

Lsp Technologies Inc...614 718-3000
6161 Shamrock Ct Dublin (43016) *(G-6318)*

Lsp Tubes Inc..216 378-2092
135 Penniman Rd Orwell (44076) *(G-11024)*

Lsq Manufacturing Inc..330 725-4905
1140 Industrial Pkwy Medina (44256) *(G-9421)*

Lt Enterprises of Ohio LLC..330 526-6908
334 Orchard Ave Ne North Canton (44720) *(G-10649)*

Lt Moses Willard Inc..513 248-5500
3972 Bach Buxton Rd Amelia (45102) *(G-431)*

Lt Wright Handcrafted Knife Co.....................................740 317-1404
130 Warren Ln Unit B Steubenville (43953) *(G-12405)*

LTI Power Systems Inc..440 327-5050
10800 Middle Ave Hngr B Elyria (44035) *(G-6560)*

Lube & Chem Products, Cincinnati *Also Called: Interlube Corporation (G-2750)*

Luber-Finer, Cleveland *Also Called: First Bmds Group Intrmdate LL (G-3720)*

Lubricant Additives, Wickliffe *Also Called: The Lubrizol Corporation (G-14395)*

Lubrication Specialties LLC...800 341-6516
3975 Morrow Meadows Dr Mount Gilead (43338) *(G-10212)*

Lubriplate Lubricants Company......................................419 691-2491
1500 Oakdale Ave Toledo (43605) *(G-13041)*

Lubriquip Inc..216 581-2000
18901 Cranwood Pkwy Cleveland (44128) *(G-3969)*

Lubrisource Inc..937 432-9292
2900 Cincinnati Dayton Rd Middletown (45044) *(G-9872)*

Lubrizol, Cleveland *Also Called: Lubrizol Global Management Inc (G-3970)*

Lubrizol Advanced Mtls Inc (HQ)...................................216 447-5000
9911 Brecksville Rd Brecksville (44141) *(G-1476)*

Lubrizol Global Management...419 352-5565
1142 N Main St Bowling Green (43402) *(G-1426)*

Lubrizol Global Management Inc....................................440 933-0400
550 Moore Rd Avon Lake (44012) *(G-763)*

Lubrizol Global Management Inc (DH)............................216 447-5000
9911 Brecksville Rd Cleveland (44141) *(G-3970)*

LUBRIZOL GLOBAL MANAGEMENT, INC, Bowling Green *Also Called: Lubrizol Global Management (G-1426)*

Lubrizol Holdings LLC..440 943-4200
29400 Lakeland Blvd Wickliffe (44092) *(G-14381)*

Lubrizol Production Plant, Painesville *Also Called: The Lubrizol Corporation (G-11117)*

Luc Ice Inc..419 734-2201
10020 River Rd Huron (44839) *(G-7879)*

Lucas Sumitomo Brakes Inc..513 934-0024
1650 Kingsview Dr Lebanon (45036) *(G-8274)*

Lucius Fence and Decking, New Riegel *Also Called: Juno Enterprises LLC (G-10470)*

Lucky Thirteen Inc...216 631-0013
7413 Associate Ave Cleveland (44144) *(G-3971)*

Lucky Thirteen Laser, Cleveland *Also Called: Lucky Thirteen Inc (G-3971)*

Ludlow Composites Corporation.....................................419 332-5531
2100 Commerce Dr Fremont (43420) *(G-7122)*

Ludowici Roof Tile Inc..740 342-1995
4757 Tile Plant Rd Se New Lexington (43764) *(G-10404)*

Ludy Greenhouse Mfg Corp (PA)....................................800 255-5839
122 Railroad St New Madison (45346) *(G-10422)*

Luk Clutch Systems, Wooster *Also Called: Luk Clutch Systems LLC (G-14661)*

Luk Clutch Systems LLC (DH)...330 264-4383
3401 Old Airport Rd Wooster (44691) *(G-14661)*

Luke Engineering & Mfg, Wadsworth *Also Called: Luke Engineering & Mfg Corp (G-13649)*

Luke Engineering & Mfg Corp..330 925-3344
11 Pipestone Rd Rittman (44270) *(G-11624)*

Luke Engineering & Mfg Corp (PA).................................330 335-1501
456 South Blvd Wadsworth (44281) *(G-13649)*

Lukens Inc..937 440-2500
1040 S Dorset Rd Troy (45373) *(G-13237)*

Lukjan Metal Pdts Holdg Co Inc.....................................440 599-8127
645 Industry Rd Conneaut (44030) *(G-5409)*

Lukjan Metal Products Inc (PA).....................................440 599-8127
645 Industry Rd Conneaut (44030) *(G-5410)*

Lumacurve Airfield Signs, Macedonia *Also Called: Standard Signs Incorporated (G-8716)*

Lumenforce Led LLC...330 330-8962
5411 Market St Youngstown (44512) *(G-14889)*

Lumenomics Inc..614 798-3500
8333 Green Meadows Dr N Ste B Lewis Center (43035) *(G-8342)*

Lumi Craft, Norwich *Also Called: Lumi-Lite Candle Company (G-10864)*

Lumi-Lite Candle Company..740 872-3248
102 Sundale Rd Norwich (43767) *(G-10864)*

Luminance, Cuyahoga Falls *Also Called: American De Rosa Lamparts LLC (G-5522)*

Luminaud Inc..440 255-9082
8688 Tyler Blvd Mentor (44060) *(G-9556)*

Luminex HD&f Company, Cincinnati *Also Called: Luminex HM Dcor Frgrnce Hldg C (G-2831)*

Luminex HM Dcor Frgrnce Hldg C (PA)...........................513 563-1113
10521 Millington Ct Cincinnati (45242) *(G-2831)*

Lumitex, Strongsville *Also Called: Lumitex Inc (G-12572)*

Lumitex Inc (PA)..440 243-8401
8443 Dow Cir Strongsville (44136) *(G-12572)*

Lunar Tool & Mold Inc...440 237-2141
9860 York Alpha Dr North Royalton (44133) *(G-10771)*

Lund Equipment Company...330 659-4800
2400 N Cleveland Massillon Rd Akron (44333) *(G-212)*

Lustrous Metal Coatings Inc..330 478-4653
1541 Raff Rd Sw Canton (44710) *(G-1933)*

Luther Machine Inc..440 259-5014
4604 Davis Rd Perry (44081) *(G-11194)*

Luvata, Delaware *Also Called: Luvata Ohio Inc (G-6161)*

Luvata Ohio Inc (HQ)..740 363-1981
1376 Pittsburgh Dr Delaware (43015) *(G-6161)*

Luxaire Cushion Co.. 330 872-0995
2410 S Center St Newton Falls (44444) *(G-10579)*

Luxco Inc.. 216 671-6300
3116 Berea Rd Cleveland (44111) *(G-3972)*

Luxfer Magtech Inc (HQ).. 513 772-3066
2940 Highland Ave Ste 210 Cincinnati (45212) *(G-2832)*

Luxus Arms, Mount Orab *Also Called: Luxus Products LLC (G-10218)*

Luxus Products LLC... 937 444-6500
222 Homan Way Mount Orab (45154) *(G-10218)*

Lvd Acquisition LLC (HQ).. 614 861-1350
222 E Campus View Blvd Columbus (43235) *(G-5077)*

Lwhs Ltd... 419 407-5454
2145 Tedrow Rd Toledo (43614) *(G-13042)*

Lyco Corporation.. 412 973-9176
1089 N Hubbard Rd Lowellville (44436) *(G-8663)*

Lyle Printing & Publishing Co (PA)........................... 330 337-3419
185 E State St Salem (44460) *(G-11796)*

Lynk Packaging Inc (PA).. 330 562-8080
1250 Page Rd Aurora (44202) *(G-677)*

Lyondell Chemical Company...................................... 513 530-4000
11530 Northlake Dr Cincinnati (45249) *(G-2833)*

Lyondell Chemical Company...................................... 440 352-9393
110 3rd St Fairport Harbor (44077) *(G-6818)*

Lyondllbsell Advnced Plymers I.................................. 330 773-2700
1353 Exeter Rd Akron (44306) *(G-213)*

Lyondllbsell Advnced Plymers I.................................. 330 630-0308
790 E Tallmadge Ave Akron (44310) *(G-214)*

Lyondllbsell Advnced Plymers I.................................. 330 630-3315
1183 Home Ave Akron (44310) *(G-215)*

Lyondllbsell Advnced Plymers I.................................. 440 224-7291
3365 E Center St Conneaut (44030) *(G-5411)*

Lyondllbsell Advnced Plymers I.................................. 440 224-7544
110 N Eagle St Geneva (44041) *(G-7243)*

Lyondllbsell Advnced Plymers I.................................. 419 872-1408
12600 Eckel Rd Perrysburg (43551) *(G-11235)*

Lyondllbsell Advnced Plymers I.................................. 419 682-3311
103 Railroad Ave Stryker (43557) *(G-12624)*

Lyons.. 440 224-0676
5231 State Route 193 Kingsville (44048) *(G-8138)*

M & B Asphalt Company Inc...................................... 419 992-4236
1525 W County Road 42 Old Fort (44861) *(G-10934)*

M & B Asphalt Company Inc (PA)............................... 419 992-4235
1525 W County Road 42 Tiffin (44883) *(G-12787)*

M & H Fabricating Co Inc... 937 325-8708
823 Mound St Springfield (45505) *(G-12343)*

M & H Fabricating Co Inc (PA)................................... 937 325-8708
717 Mound St Springfield (45505) *(G-12344)*

M & H Screen Printing... 740 522-1957
1486 Hebron Rd Newark (43056) *(G-10517)*

M & J Machine Company... 330 645-0042
2420 Pickle Rd Akron (44312) *(G-216)*

M & J Tooling, Dayton *Also Called: M & J Tooling Ltd (G-5856)*

M & J Tooling Ltd.. 937 951-3527
420 Davis Ave Dayton (45403) *(G-5856)*

M & M Certified Welding Inc..................................... 330 467-1729
556 Highland Rd E Ste 3 Macedonia (44056) *(G-8703)*

M & M Concepts Inc.. 937 355-1115
2633 State Route 292 West Mansfield (43358) *(G-14179)*

M & M Dies Inc.. 216 883-6628
3502 Beyerle Rd Cleveland (44105) *(G-3973)*

M & M Fabrication Inc... 740 779-3071
18828 Us Highway 50 Chillicothe (45601) *(G-2263)*

M & M Hardwoods, Sugarcreek *Also Called: Tusco Hardwoods LLC (G-12655)*

M & R Electric Motor, Dayton *Also Called: M & R Electric Motor Svc Inc (G-5857)*

M & R Electric Motor Svc Inc.................................... 937 701-0475
1516 E 5th St Dayton (45403) *(G-5857)*

M & R Phillips Enterprises....................................... 740 323-0580
6242 Jacksontown Rd Newark (43056) *(G-10518)*

M & R Redi Mix Inc (PA).. 419 445-7771
521 Commercial St Pettisville (43553) *(G-11284)*

M & S AG Solutions LLC... 419 598-8675
755 American Rd Napoleon (43545) *(G-10290)*

M & W Trailers Inc.. 419 453-3331
525 East Main St Ottoville (45876) *(G-11055)*

M A C, Vandalia *Also Called: Nimers & Woody II Inc (G-13574)*

M A C Machine... 410 944-6171
1111 Faircrest St Se Canton (44707) *(G-1934)*

M A Harrison Mfg Co Inc.. 440 965-4306
14307 State Route 113 Wakeman (44889) *(G-13682)*

M Argueso & Co Inc.. 216 252-4122
12651 Elmwood Ave Cleveland (44111) *(G-3974)*

M B K Inc.. 330 889-3451
1306 State Route 88 Bristolville (44402) *(G-1498)*

M B Saxon Co Inc... 440 229-5006
47 Alpha Park Cleveland (44143) *(G-3975)*

M B Trucking, Dover *Also Called: Sugarcreek Lime Service (G-6264)*

M C D Plastics & Manufacturing, Piqua *Also Called: Miami Specialties Inc (G-11366)*

M D Tool, Dayton *Also Called: Dayton Machine Tool Company (G-5730)*

M F Y Inc.. 330 747-1334
1640 Wilson Ave Youngstown (44506) *(G-14890)*

M G Q Inc.. 419 992-4236
1525 W County Road 42 Tiffin (44883) *(G-12788)*

M H Woodworking LLC... 330 893-3929
2789 County Rd Ste 600 Millersburg (44654) *(G-9995)*

M I P Inc... 330 744-0215
701 Jones St Youngstown (44502) *(G-14891)*

M K Metals.. 330 482-3351
41659 Esterly Dr Leetonia (44431) *(G-8303)*

M K Morse Company (PA).. 330 453-8187
1101 11th St Se Canton (44707) *(G-1935)*

M N A, Toledo *Also Called: Ohio Module Manufacturing Company LLC (G-13074)*

M P G, Maumee *Also Called: Magnesium Products Group Inc (G-9306)*

M P I Label Systems, Sebring *Also Called: Miller Products Inc (G-11897)*

M P I Labeltek, Wadsworth *Also Called: Miller Products Inc (G-13652)*

M P I Logistics, Massillon *Also Called: Mpi Logistics and Service Inc (G-9225)*

M PI Label Systems.. 330 938-2134
450 Courtney Rd Sebring (44672) *(G-11896)*

M R I Education Foundation...................................... 513 281-3400
5400 Kennedy Ave Cincinnati (45213) *(G-2834)*

M R S, Columbus *Also Called: MRS Industrial Inc (G-5115)*

M R T, Middletown *Also Called: 3d Sales & Consulting Inc (G-9838)*

M R Trailer Sales Inc... 330 339-7701
1565 Steele Hill Rd Nw New Philadelphia (44663) *(G-10456)*

M Rosenthal Company.. 513 563-0081
3125 Exon Ave Cincinnati (45241) *(G-2835)*

M S B Machine Inc.. 330 686-7740
36 Castle Dr Munroe Falls (44262) *(G-10271)*

M T, Elmore *Also Called: Machining Technologies Inc (G-6489)*

M T D Service Division, Shelby *Also Called: Mtd Products Inc (G-11971)*

M T M Molded Products Company............................... 937 890-7461
3370 Obco Ct Dayton (45414) *(G-5858)*

M T O, Saint Marys *Also Called: Murotech Ohio Corporation (G-11743)*

M T S I, Fairfield *Also Called: Mendenhall Technical Services Inc (G-6754)*

M T Systems Inc... 330 453-4646
400 Schroyer Ave Sw Canton (44702) *(G-1936)*

M Technologies Inc... 330 477-9009
1818 Hopple Ave Sw Canton (44706) *(G-1937)*

M W Solutions LLC.. 419 782-1611
1802 Baltimore St Ste B Defiance (43512) *(G-6118)*

M-Boss Inc.. 216 441-6080
4510 E 71st St Cleveland (44105) *(G-3976)*

M-D Building Products Inc.. 513 539-2255
100 Westheimer Dr Middletown (45044) *(G-9873)*

M-D Building Products Inc.. 513 539-2255
100 Westheimer Dr Middletown (45044) *(G-9874)*

M-D Metal Source, Middletown *Also Called: M-D Building Products Inc (G-9874)*

M.S. Barkin Company, Cleveland *Also Called: Em Es Be Company LLC (G-3665)*

M/W International Inc.. 440 526-6900
3839 Heron Dr Lorain (44053) *(G-8566)*

M&D Machine LLC... 419 214-0201
42 W Sylvania Ave Toledo (43612) *(G-13043)*

A
L
P
H
A
B
E
T
I
C

M&H Medical Holdings Inc (PA)........................ 419 727-8421
1670 Indian Wood Cir Maumee (43537) *(G-9305)*

M&Ms Autosales LLC.. 234 334-7022
2203 Manchester Rd Akron (44314) *(G-217)*

M21 Industries LLC.. 937 781-1377
721 Springfield St Dayton (45403) *(G-5859)*

M3 Midstream LLC.. 330 223-2220
11543 State Route 644 Kensington (44427) *(G-8010)*

M3 Midstream LLC.. 330 679-5580
10 E Main St Salineville (43945) *(G-11818)*

M3 Midstream LLC.. 740 945-1170
37950 Crimm Rd Scio (43988) *(G-11888)*

M3 Technologies Inc... 216 898-9936
13910 Enterprise Ave Cleveland (44135) *(G-3977)*

M4 Knick LLC... 513 833-2500
55 W Techne Center Dr Ste C Milford (45150) *(G-9941)*

M7 Hrp LLC.. 330 923-3256
75 E Market St Akron (44308) *(G-218)*

M7 Technologies, Youngstown Also Called: Garvey Corporation *(G-14860)*

Maag Automatik Inc... 330 677-2225
235 Progress Blvd Kent (44240) *(G-8047)*

Maag Reduction Inc.. 704 716-9000
235 Progress Blvd Kent (44240) *(G-8048)*

Maag Reduction Engineering, Kent Also Called: Maag Automatik Inc *(G-8047)*

Maag's Automotive, Sandusky Also Called: Maags Automotive & Mch Inc *(G-11853)*

Maags Automotive & Mch Inc............................ 419 626-1539
1640 Columbus Ave Sandusky (44870) *(G-11853)*

Maass Midwest Mfg Inc.................................... 419 894-6424
19710 State Route 12 Arcadia (44804) *(G-482)*

Mabis Shipping Solutions Inc........................... 330 650-1788
126 W Streetsboro St Hudson (44236) *(G-7850)*

Mabsc, Akron Also Called: Meggitt Arcft Brking Systems C *(G-228)*

Mac, Alliance Also Called: Mac Manufacturing Inc *(G-388)*

Mac Instruments, Sandusky Also Called: Machine Applications Corp *(G-11854)*

Mac Its LLC (PA).. 937 454-0722
1625 Fieldstone Way Vandalia (45377) *(G-13565)*

Mac Lean J S Co.. 614 878-5454
5454 Alkire Rd Columbus (43228) *(G-5078)*

Mac Manufacturing Inc (HQ)............................. 330 823-9900
14599 Commerce St Ne Alliance (44601) *(G-388)*

Mac Manufacturing Inc...................................... 330 829-1680
1453 Allen Rd Salem (44460) *(G-11797)*

Mac Mfg and Test Facilities, Youngstown Also Called: Magnetic Analysis Corporation *(G-14893)*

Mac Oil Field Service Inc.................................. 330 674-7371
7861 Township Road 306 Millersburg (44654) *(G-9996)*

Mac Steel Trailer Ltd.. 330 823-9900
14599 Commerce St Ne Alliance (44601) *(G-389)*

Mac Tools, Dublin Also Called: Stanley Industrial & Auto LLC *(G-6349)*

Mac Tools Inc... 614 755-7039
505 N Cleveland Ave Ste 200 Westerville (43082) *(G-14221)*

Mac Trailer Manufacturing Inc (PA).................... 800 795-8454
14599 Commerce St Ne Alliance (44601) *(G-390)*

Mac Trailer Service Inc...................................... 330 823-9190
14504 Commerce St Ne Alliance (44601) *(G-391)*

Macdivitt Rubber Company LLC......................... 440 259-5937
3291 Center Rd Perry (44081) *(G-11195)*

Mace, Cleveland Also Called: Mace Security Intl Inc *(G-3979)*

Mace Personal Def & SEC Inc (HQ)................... 440 424-5321
4400 Carnegie Ave Cleveland (44103) *(G-3978)*

Mace Security Intl Inc (PA)................................ 440 424-5325
4400 Carnegie Ave Cleveland (44103) *(G-3979)*

Machine Applications Corp................................. 419 621-2322
3410 Tiffin Ave Sandusky (44870) *(G-11854)*

Machine Concepts Inc....................................... 419 628-3498
2167 State Route 66 Minster (45865) *(G-10060)*

Machine Development Corp................................ 513 825-5885
7707 Affinity Pl Cincinnati (45240) *(G-2836)*

Machine Drive Company.................................... 513 793-7077
2513 Crescentville Rd Cincinnati (45241) *(G-2837)*

Machine Dynamics & Engrg Inc......................... 330 868-5603
9312 Arrow Rd Nw Minerva (44657) *(G-10041)*

Machine Products, Loveland Also Called: Macpro Inc *(G-8638)*

Machine Products Company............................... 937 890-6600
5660 Webster St Dayton (45414) *(G-5860)*

Machine Shop, Toledo Also Called: M&D Machine LLC *(G-13043)*

Machine Tek Systems Inc.................................. 330 527-4450
10400 Industrial Dr Garrettsville (44231) *(G-7225)*

Machine Tool Design & Fab LLC........................ 419 435-7676
226 Heritage Dr Tiffin (44883) *(G-12789)*

Machine Tool Division, Bluffton Also Called: Grob Systems Inc *(G-1361)*

Machine Tools Supply, Huber Heights Also Called: Updike Supply Company *(G-7825)*

Machine-Pro Technologies Inc........................... 419 584-0086
1321 W Market St Celina (45822) *(G-2113)*

Machined Glass Specialist Inc........................... 937 743-6166
245 Hiawatha Trl Springboro (45066) *(G-12259)*

Machining Technologies Inc (PA)....................... 419 862-3110
468 Maple St Elmore (43416) *(G-6489)*

Machintek Co.. 513 551-1000
3721 Port Union Rd Fairfield (45014) *(G-6749)*

Mack Concrete Industries Inc............................ 330 784-7008
124 Darrow Rd Ste 7 Akron (44305) *(G-219)*

Mack Concrete Industries Inc (HQ).................... 330 483-3111
201 Columbia Rd Valley City (44280) *(G-13503)*

Mack Industries.. 419 353-7081
507 Derby Ave Bowling Green (43402) *(G-1427)*

Mack Industries Inc.. 740 393-1121
400 Howard St Mount Vernon (43050) *(G-10249)*

Mack Industries PA Inc (HQ)............................. 330 483-3111
201 Columbia Rd Valley City (44280) *(G-13504)*

Mack Industries PA Inc..................................... 330 638-7680
2207 Sodom Hutchings Rd Ne Vienna (44473) *(G-13613)*

Mack Iron Works Company................................ 419 626-3712
124 Warren St Sandusky (44870) *(G-11855)*

Mack Ready-Mix, Akron Also Called: Mack Concrete Industries Inc *(G-219)*

Macke Brothers Inc... 513 771-7500
10355 Spartan Dr Cincinnati (45215) *(G-2838)*

Macmillan Graphics, Milford Also Called: Gregg Macmillan *(G-9937)*

Macpherson & Company, Warren Also Called: Macpherson Engineering Inc *(G-13779)*

Macpherson Engineering Inc............................. 440 243-6565
2809 Mahoning Ave Nw Warren (44483) *(G-13779)*

Macpro Inc... 513 575-3000
1456 Fay Rd Unit B Loveland (45140) *(G-8638)*

Macray Co LLC... 937 325-1726
100 W North St Springfield (45504) *(G-12345)*

Macro Meric, Aurora Also Called: Saco Aei Polymers Inc *(G-688)*

Mactac, Stow Also Called: Mactac Americas LLC *(G-12439)*

Mactac, Stow Also Called: Morgan Adhesives Company LLC *(G-12441)*

Mactac Americas LLC (DH)............................... 800 762-2822
4560 Darrow Rd Stow (44224) *(G-12439)*

Macton Corporation.. 330 259-8555
3200 Innovation Pl Youngstown (44509) *(G-14892)*

Mad River Steel Ltd.. 937 845-4046
2141 N Dayton Lakeview Rd New Carlisle (45344) *(G-10375)*

Mad River Steel Company, New Carlisle Also Called: Mad River Steel Ltd *(G-10375)*

Made Men Circle LLC.. 216 501-0414
2883 Mayfield Rd Apt 2 Cleveland Heights (44118) *(G-4529)*

Mader Automotive Center Inc (PA)..................... 937 339-2681
225 S Walnut St Troy (45373) *(G-13238)*

Mader Dampers, Lagrange Also Called: Mader Machine Co Inc *(G-8150)*

Mader Elc Mtr Pwr Trnsmssons L...................... 937 325-5576
205 E Main St Springfield (45503) *(G-12346)*

Mader Machine Co Inc...................................... 440 355-4505
422 Commerce Dr E Lagrange (44050) *(G-8150)*

Madison Electric Products Inc (HQ).................... 216 391-7776
30575 Bainbridge Rd Ste 130 Solon (44139) *(G-12143)*

Madison Messenger, Columbus Also Called: Columbus Messenger Company *(G-4830)*

Madison Mine Supply Co, Jackson Also Called: Waterloo Coal Company Inc *(G-7955)*

Madison Property Holdings Inc........................... 800 215-3210
5055 Madison Rd Cincinnati (45227) *(G-2839)*

Madisono's Gelato, Cincinnati Also Called: Cfgsc LLC *(G-2454)*

Mae Fence LLC... 614 929-3526
109 E Main St Fulton (43321) *(G-7151)*

(G-0000) Company's Geographic Section entry number

Mae Materials LLC.. 740 778-2242
8336 Bennett School House Rd South Webster (45682) *(G-12231)*

Mag Resources LLC... 330 294-0494
711 Wooster Rd W Barberton (44203) *(G-818)*

Mag-Nif Inc.. 440 255-9366
8820 East Ave Mentor (44060) *(G-9557)*

Magellan Arospc Middletown Inc (HQ)..................... 513 422-2751
2320 Wedekind Dr Middletown (45042) *(G-9875)*

Magic Dragon Machine Inc...................................... 614 539-8004
3451 Grant Ave Grove City (43123) *(G-7396)*

Magic Rack, Ashville *Also Called: Production Plus Corp (G-630)*

Magic Wok Inc (PA).. 419 531-1818
3352 W Laskey Rd Toledo (43623) *(G-13044)*

Magic Wok Enterprises, Toledo *Also Called: Magic Wok Inc (G-13044)*

Magna, Northwood *Also Called: Norplas Industries Inc (G-10805)*

Magna Machine Co (PA).. 513 851-6900
11180 Southland Rd Cincinnati (45240) *(G-2840)*

Magna Modular Systems LLC (DH)........................... 419 324-3387
1800 Jason St Toledo (43611) *(G-13045)*

Magna Seating America Inc..................................... 330 824-3101
3637 Mallard Run Sheffield Village (44054) *(G-11960)*

Magna Seating America Inc..................................... 419 410-4780
428 Church St Swanton (43558) *(G-12686)*

Magna Three LLC.. 513 389-0776
2668 Cyclorama Dr Cincinnati (45211) *(G-2841)*

Magna Visual Inc... 314 843-9000
28271 Cedar Park Blvd Ste 1 Perrysburg (43551) *(G-11236)*

Magnaco Industries Inc.. 216 961-3636
140 West Dr Lodi (44254) *(G-8504)*

Magneco/Metrel Inc... 330 426-9468
51365 State Route 154 Negley (44441) *(G-10315)*

Magneforce Inc... 330 856-9300
155 Shaffer Dr Ne Warren (44484) *(G-13780)*

Magnesium Products Group Inc............................... 310 971-5799
3928 Azalea Cir Maumee (43537) *(G-9306)*

Magnesium Refining Technologies Inc...................... 419 483-9199
29695 Pettibone Rd Cleveland (44139) *(G-3980)*

Magnetech, Massillon *Also Called: 3-D Service Ltd (G-9168)*

Magnetech Industrial Services, Massillon *Also Called: Magnetech Industrial Svcs Inc (G-9217)*

Magnetech Industrial Svcs Inc................................. 330 830-3500
800 Nave Rd Se Massillon (44646) *(G-9216)*

Magnetech Industrial Svcs Inc (DH)......................... 330 830-3500
800 Nave Rd Se Massillon (44646) *(G-9217)*

Magnetech Industrial Svcs Inc................................. 330 830-3500
800 Nave Rd Se Massillon (44646) *(G-9218)*

Magnetic Analysis Corporation................................ 330 758-1367
675 Mcclurg Rd Youngstown (44512) *(G-14893)*

Magnetic Screw Machine Pdts................................. 937 348-2807
23241 State Route 37 Marysville (43040) *(G-9036)*

Magnetic Source, Marietta *Also Called: Tengam Pro Inc (G-8952)*

Magni Fab & Magnetic, Wooster *Also Called: Magni-Power Company (G-14662)*

Magni-Power Company (PA)..................................... 330 264-3637
5511 E Lincoln Way Wooster (44691) *(G-14662)*

Magnum Asset Acquisition LLC................................ 330 915-2382
5675 Hudson Industrial Pkwy # 3 Hudson (44236) *(G-7851)*

Magnum Computers Inc.. 216 781-1757
868 Montford Rd Cleveland (44121) *(G-3981)*

Magnum Inks & Coatings, Marietta *Also Called: Magnum Magnetics Corporation (G-8926)*

Magnum Innovations, Hudson *Also Called: Magnum Asset Acquisition LLC (G-7851)*

Magnum Magnetics Corporation............................... 740 516-6237
17289 Industrial Hwy Caldwell (43724) *(G-1725)*

Magnum Magnetics Corporation (PA)........................ 740 373-7770
801 Masonic Park Rd Marietta (45750) *(G-8926)*

Magnum Magnetics Corporation............................... 513 360-0790
355 Wright Dr Middletown (45044) *(G-9876)*

Magnum Molding Inc.. 937 368-3040
7435 N Bollinger Rd Conover (45317) *(G-5421)*

Magnum Piering Inc... 513 759-3348
156 Circle Freeway Dr West Chester (45246) *(G-14131)*

Magnum Press, Columbus *Also Called: Resilient Holdings Inc (G-5227)*

Magnum Tapes Films.. 877 460-8402
17289 Industrial Hwy Caldwell (43724) *(G-1726)*

Magnum Tool Corp... 937 228-0900
1407 Stanley Ave Dayton (45404) *(G-5861)*

Magnus Engineered Eqp LLC................................... 440 942-8488
4500 Beidler Rd Willoughby (44094) *(G-14484)*

Magnus Equipment, Willoughby *Also Called: Reid Asset Management Company (G-14516)*

Magnus International Group Inc (PA)......................... 216 592-8355
679 Hardy Rd Painesville (44077) *(G-11097)*

Mahle Behr Dayton LLC.. 937 369-2000
1600 Webster St Dayton (45404) *(G-5862)*

Mahle Behr Dayton LLC (DH)................................... 937 369-2900
1600 Webster St Dayton (45404) *(G-5863)*

Mahle Behr Dayton LLC.. 937 369-2900
1720 Webster St Dayton (45404) *(G-5864)*

Mahle Behr Dayton LLC.. 937 356-2001
250 Northwoods Blvd Bldg 47 Vandalia (45377) *(G-13566)*

Mahle Behr USA Inc... 937 356-2001
250 Northwoods Blvd Bldg 47 Vandalia (45377) *(G-13567)*

Mahle Behr USA Inc... 937 369-2610
1003 Bellbrook Ave Xenia (45385) *(G-14770)*

Mahle Eng Components USA Inc.............................. 740 962-8004
5130 N State Route 60 Nw Mcconnelsville (43756) *(G-9363)*

Mahle Industries Incorporated................................. 937 890-2739
1600 Webster St Dayton (45404) *(G-5865)*

Mahoning Valley Mfg Inc... 330 537-4492
17796 Rte 62 Beloit (44609) *(G-1145)*

MAI Manufacturing, Marysville *Also Called: Straight 72 Inc (G-9051)*

MAI-Weave LLC... 937 322-1698
1800 E Pleasant St Springfield (45505) *(G-12347)*

Mailposts By Mike, Cleveland *Also Called: Stiber Fabricating Inc (G-4332)*

Main Awning & Tent Inc.. 513 621-6947
415 W Seymour Ave Cincinnati (45216) *(G-2842)*

Main Street Cambritt Cookies, Cuyahoga Falls *Also Called: Main Street Gourmet LLC (G-5560)*

Main Street Gourmet LLC....................................... 330 929-0000
170 Muffin Ln Cuyahoga Falls (44223) *(G-5560)*

Main Street Lighting Standards, Medina *Also Called: Msls Group LLC (G-9428)*

Mainline Contracting LLC.. 513 202-1408
10860 Paddys Run Rd Harrison (45030) *(G-7559)*

Mainstream Waterjet LLC.. 513 683-5426
108 Northeast Dr Loveland (45140) *(G-8639)*

Maintenance + Inc... 330 264-6262
1051 W Liberty St Wooster (44691) *(G-14663)*

Maintenance Repair Supply Inc............................... 740 922-3006
5539 Gundy Dr Midvale (44653) *(G-9913)*

Maiweave, Springfield *Also Called: Intertape Polymer Corp (G-12330)*

Majestic Fireplace Distr.. 440 439-1040
7500 Northfield Rd Bedford (44146) *(G-1045)*

Majestic Manufacturing Inc..................................... 330 457-2447
4536 State Route 7 New Waterford (44445) *(G-10488)*

Majestic Plastics Inc.. 937 593-9500
811 N Main St Bellefontaine (43311) *(G-1112)*

Majestic Tool and Machine Inc................................ 440 248-5058
30700 Carter St Ste C Solon (44139) *(G-12144)*

Major Metals Company.. 419 886-4600
844 Kochheiser Rd Mansfield (44904) *(G-8815)*

MAK Fabricating Inc... 330 747-0040
1609 Wilson Ave Youngstown (44506) *(G-14894)*

Mak Magic Inc.. 614 591-3551
3900 Fisher Rd Ste G Columbus (43228) *(G-5079)*

Makergear LLC.. 216 765-0030
23632 Mercantile Rd Ste I Beachwood (44122) *(G-926)*

Makers Supply LLC.. 937 203-8245
6665 N Spiker Rd Piqua (45356) *(G-11364)*

Makino Inc (HQ).. 513 573-7200
7680 Innovation Way Mason (45040) *(G-9123)*

Mako Finished Products Inc.................................... 740 357-0839
708 Fairground Rd Lucasville (45648) *(G-8667)*

Malabar.. 419 866-6301
1 Air Cargo Pkwy E Swanton (43558) *(G-12687)*

Malabar International, Swanton *Also Called: Malabar (G-12687)*

Malabar Properties LLC... 419 884-0071
300 S Mill St Mansfield (44904) *(G-8816)*

Malco Products, Barberton *Also Called: Malco Products Inc (G-819)*

Malco Products Inc (PA)..330 753-0361
361 Fairview Ave Barberton (44203) *(G-819)*

Malcuit Racing Engines, Strasburg *Also Called: B A Malcuit Racing Inc (G-12476)*

Malik Media LLC.. 614 933-0328
7591 Lambton Park Rd New Albany (43054) *(G-10345)*

Malin Co... 216 267-9080
5400 Smith Rd Cleveland (44142) *(G-3982)*

Malin Company, Cleveland *Also Called: Brushes Inc (G-3447)*

Malish, Mentor *Also Called: Malish Corporation (G-9558)*

Malish Corporation (PA)...440 951-5356
7333 Corporate Blvd Mentor (44060) *(G-9558)*

Malley's Chocolates, Cleveland *Also Called: Malleys Candies LLC (G-3983)*

Malleys Candies LLC (PA)...216 362-8700
13400 Brookpark Rd Cleveland (44135) *(G-3983)*

Mallory Pattern Works Inc... 419 726-8001
5340 Enterprise Blvd Toledo (43612) *(G-13046)*

Malone Specialty Inc... 440 255-4200
8900 East Ave Mentor (44060) *(G-9559)*

Malta Dynamics LLC (PA).. 740 749-3512
405 Watertown Rd Waterford (45786) *(G-13828)*

Mama Jo Homestyle Pies, Amherst *Also Called: Papa Joes Pies Inc (G-451)*

Mama Rosas's, Sidney *Also Called: Schwans Mama Rosass LLC (G-12049)*

Mamabees HM Gds Lifestyle LLC... 419 277-2914
2186 Mccutchenville Rd Fostoria (44830) *(G-6987)*

Mameco International Inc... 216 752-4400
4475 E 175th St Cleveland (44128) *(G-3984)*

Mammana Custom Woodworking Inc... 216 581-9059
14400 Industrial Ave N Maple Heights (44137) *(G-8886)*

Mammoth Labels & Packaging, Grove City *Also Called: Boehm Inc (G-7374)*

Manairco Inc... 419 524-2121
28 Industrial Pkwy Mansfield (44903) *(G-8817)*

Manco Manufacturing Co.. 419 925-4152
2411 Rolfes Rd Maria Stein (45860) *(G-8899)*

Mancor Ohio Inc (HQ)..937 228-6141
1008 Leonhard St Dayton (45404) *(G-5866)*

Mancor Ohio Inc.. 937 228-6141
600 Kiser St Dayton (45404) *(G-5867)*

Mandrax Technologies, Westerville *Also Called: David Chojnacki (G-14254)*

Mandrel Group LLC... 330 881-1266
105 Ohio Ave Mc Donald (44437) *(G-9359)*

Mane Inc... 513 248-9876
10261 Chester Rd Cincinnati (45215) *(G-2843)*

Mane Inc... 513 248-9876
1093 Mane Way Lebanon (45036) *(G-8275)*

Mane Inc (DH)..513 248-9876
2501 Henkle Dr Lebanon (45036) *(G-8276)*

Mane Calafornia, Lebanon *Also Called: Mane Inc (G-8276)*

Manifold & Phalor Inc... 614 920-1200
10385 Busey Rd Nw Canal Winchester (43110) *(G-1793)*

Manitwoc Ovens Advnced Cooking, Cleveland *Also Called: Cleveland Range LLC (G-3522)*

Mannings Packing Co.. 937 446-3278
100 College Ave Sardinia (45171) *(G-11885)*

Manoranjan Shaffer & Heidkamp, Dayton *Also Called: Watson Haran & Company Inc (G-6076)*

Mansfield Brass & Aluminum Corporation.................................. 419 492-2154
636 S Center St New Washington (44854) *(G-10480)*

Mansfield Brew Works LLC... 419 631-3153
131 N Diamond St Mansfield (44902) *(G-8818)*

Mansfield Castings, New Washington *Also Called: Mansfield Brass & Aluminum Corporation (G-10480)*

Mansfield Engineered Components LLC...................................... 419 524-1300
1776 Harrington Memorial Rd Mansfield (44903) *(G-8819)*

Mansfield Fabricated Products, Mansfield *Also Called: The Mansfield Strl & Erct Co (G-8859)*

Mansfield Graphics, Mansfield *Also Called: Five Handicap Inc (G-8788)*

Mansfield Industries Inc... 419 524-1300
1776 Harrington Memorial Rd Mansfield (44903) *(G-8820)*

Mansfield Operations, Mansfield *Also Called: Cleveland-Cliffs Steel Corp (G-8775)*

Mansfield Paint Co Inc... 330 725-2436
525 W Liberty St Medina (44256) *(G-9422)*

Mansfield Plumbing Pdts LLC (HQ).. 419 938-5211
1430 George Rd Perrysville (44864) *(G-11282)*

Mansfield Welding Service LLC.. 419 594-2738
20027 State Route 613 Oakwood (45873) *(G-10898)*

Mansion Homes, Bryan *Also Called: Manufactured Housing Entps Inc (G-1650)*

Mantaline, Hiram *Also Called: Mantaline Corporation (G-7740)*

Mantaline Corporation... 330 569-3147
6969 Constance Rd Hiram (44234) *(G-7740)*

Mantaline Corporation... 330 274-2264
4754 E High St Mantua (44255) *(G-8871)*

Mantaline Corporation (PA)... 330 274-2264
4754 E High St Mantua (44255) *(G-8872)*

Mantua Bed Frames, Glenwillow *Also Called: Rize Home LLC (G-7288)*

Mantych Metalworking Inc... 937 258-1373
3175 Plainfield Rd Dayton (45432) *(G-5619)*

Manufactured Housing Entps Inc... 419 636-4511
9302 Us Highway 6 Bryan (43506) *(G-1650)*

Manufacturers Equipment Co... 513 424-3573
35 Enterprise Dr Middletown (45044) *(G-9877)*

Manufacturers Repdirect Distr, Hudson *Also Called: Starbright Lighting USA LLC (G-7859)*

Manufacturers Service Inc... 216 267-3771
11440 Brookpark Rd Cleveland (44130) *(G-3985)*

Manufacturers Wholesale Lumber, Cleveland *Also Called: Flagship Trading Corporation (G-3722)*

Manufacturing, Beavercreek Township *Also Called: Fluid Applied Roofing LLC (G-998)*

Manufacturing, Twinsburg *Also Called: Phoenix Mtal Sls Fbrcation LLC (G-13356)*

Manufacturing, West Chester *Also Called: DA Precision Products Inc (G-13981)*

Manufacturing Animal Food Phrm, Batavia *Also Called: Ingredient Masters Inc (G-868)*

Manufacturing Company LLC.. 414 708-7583
3468 Cornell Pl Cincinnati (45220) *(G-2844)*

Manufacturing Concepts.. 330 784-9054
409 Munroe Falls Rd Tallmadge (44278) *(G-12739)*

Manufacturing Division, Willard *Also Called: Lsc Communications Inc (G-14403)*

Manufacturing Process Tech, Ashland *Also Called: Mp Technologies Inc (G-554)*

Manufctred Assemblies Corp LLC.. 937 454-0722
1625 Fieldstone Way Vandalia (45377) *(G-13568)*

Manufctring Bus Dev Sltons LLC... 419 294-1313
1950 Industrial Dr Findlay (45840) *(G-6886)*

Mapco, Mansfield *Also Called: Midwest Aircraft Products Co (G-8826)*

Mapcs, Akron *Also Called: Millers Aplus Cmpt Svcs LLC (G-234)*

Maple City Rubber Co, Norwalk *Also Called: MCR of Norwalk Inc (G-10852)*

Maple City Rubber Company, The, Norwalk *Also Called: Goodlevel Enterprises LLC (G-10843)*

Maple Grove Companies, Tiffin *Also Called: M G Q Inc (G-12788)*

Maple Grove Materials Inc... 419 992-4235
1525 W City Rd Ste 42 Tiffin (44883) *(G-12790)*

Maple Grove Stone, Old Fort *Also Called: M & B Asphalt Company Inc (G-10934)*

Maple Valley Cleaners, Akron *Also Called: Norkaam Industries LLC (G-247)*

Mapledale Farm Inc... 440 286-3389
12613 Woodin Rd Chardon (44024) *(G-2214)*

Mapledale Landscaping, Chardon *Also Called: Mapledale Farm Inc (G-2214)*

Mapvision Inc.. 513 400-1038
5601 Creek Rd Ste C Blue Ash (45242) *(G-1301)*

Mar-Bal Inc (PA).. 440 543-7526
10095 Queens Way Chagrin Falls (44023) *(G-2170)*

Mar-Bal Pultrusion Inc.. 440 953-0456
38310 Apollo Pkwy Willoughby (44094) *(G-14485)*

Mar-Con Tool Company... 937 299-2244
2301 Arbor Blvd Moraine (45439) *(G-10175)*

Mar-Flex Systems LLC... 513 422-7285
500 Business Pkwy Carlisle (45005) *(G-2068)*

Mar-Flex Wtrproofing Bldg Pdts, Carlisle *Also Called: Mar-Flex Systems LLC (G-2068)*

Mar-Metal Mfg Inc... 419 447-1102
420 N Warpole St Upper Sandusky (43351) *(G-13447)*

Mar-Vel Tool Co... 937 223-2137
858 Hall Ave Dayton (45404) *(G-5868)*

2025 Harris Ohio
Industrial Directory

(G-0000) Company's Geographic Section entry number

Mar-Zane Inc (HQ)...740 453-0721
3570 S River Rd Zanesville (43701) *(G-15026)*

Mar-Zane Materials, Zanesville Also Called: Mar-Zane Inc *(G-15026)*

Maradyne Corporation (HQ).................................216 362-0755
4540 W 160th St Cleveland (44135) *(G-3986)*

Maramor Chocolates, Columbus Also Called: Hake Head LLC *(G-4967)*

Marathon At Sawmill...614 734-0836
7200 Sawmill Rd Columbus (43235) *(G-5080)*

Marathon Canton Refinery, Canton Also Called: Mplx Terminals LLC *(G-1952)*

Marathon Intl Pdts Sup LLC................................419 422-2121
539 S Main St Findlay (45840) *(G-6887)*

Marathon Oil, Doylestown Also Called: Adapt Oil *(G-6269)*

Marathon Oil Company..419 422-2121
539 S Main St Findlay (45840) *(G-6888)*

Marathon Petroleum, Findlay Also Called: Marathon Petroleum Corporation *(G-6890)*

Marathon Petroleum Company LP (HQ)...............419 422-2121
539 S Main St Findlay (45840) *(G-6889)*

Marathon Petroleum Corporation (PA)................419 422-2121
539 S Main St Findlay (45840) *(G-6890)*

Marathon Special Products Corp........................419 352-8441
427 Van Camp Rd Bowling Green (43402) *(G-1428)*

Marbee Inc...419 422-9441
2703 N Main St Ste 1 Findlay (45840) *(G-6891)*

Marbee Printing & Graphic Art, Findlay Also Called: Marbee Inc *(G-6891)*

Marble Arch Products Inc...................................937 746-8388
263 Industrial Dr Franklin (45005) *(G-7032)*

Marc V Concepts Inc..419 782-6505
401 Agnes St Defiance (43512) *(G-6119)*

March First Brewing, Cincinnati Also Called: March First Manufacturing LLC *(G-2845)*

March First Manufacturing LLC (PA)...................513 266-3076
7885 E Kemper Rd Cincinnati (45249) *(G-2845)*

Marcus Jewelers, Cincinnati Also Called: Markus Jewelers LLC *(G-2848)*

Marcus Uppe Inc..216 263-4000
815 Superior Ave E Ste 714 Cleveland (44114) *(G-3987)*

Marengo Fabricated Steel Ltd (PA).....................800 919-2652
2896 State Route 61 Cardington (43315) *(G-2055)*

Marfo Company (PA)...614 276-3352
799 N Hague Ave Columbus (43204) *(G-5081)*

Margo Tool Technology Inc................................740 653-8115
2616 Setter Ct Nw Lancaster (43130) *(G-8209)*

Marich Machine and Tool Co..............................216 391-5502
3815 Lakeside Ave E Cleveland (44114) *(G-3988)*

Marie Noble Wine Company................................216 633-0025
1891 Idlehurst Dr Euclid (44117) *(G-6659)*

Marie's Candies, West Liberty Also Called: Maries Candies LLC *(G-14176)*

Maries Candies LLC..937 465-3061
311 Zanesfield Rd West Liberty (43357) *(G-14176)*

Marietta Coal Co Inc...740 695-2197
67705 Friends Church Rd Saint Clairsville (43950) *(G-11695)*

Marietta Martin Materials Inc..............................740 247-2211
50427 State Route 124 Racine (45771) *(G-11505)*

Marietta Martin Materials Inc..............................937 335-8313
250 Dye Mill Rd Troy (45373) *(G-13239)*

Marietta Resources Corporation........................740 373-6305
704 Pike St Marietta (45750) *(G-8927)*

Marietta Times, Marietta Also Called: Gannett Stllite Info Ntwrk LLC *(G-8918)*

Marik Spring Inc..330 564-0617
121 Northeast Ave Tallmadge (44278) *(G-12740)*

Marine Development, Cincinnati Also Called: Machine Development Corp *(G-2836)*

Marine Jet Power Inc..614 759-9000
6740 Commerce Court Dr Blacklick (43004) *(G-1224)*

Mariner's Landing Marina, Cincinnati Also Called: Mariners Landing Inc *(G-2846)*

Mariners Landing Inc...513 941-3625
7405 Forbes Rd Cincinnati (45233) *(G-2846)*

Marino Maintenance Co, Canton Also Called: Phase II Enterprises Inc *(G-1975)*

Marion Cnty Coal Resources Inc........................740 338-3100
46226 National Rd Saint Clairsville (43950) *(G-11696)*

Marion County Coal Company.............................740 338-3100
46226 National Rd Saint Clairsville (43950) *(G-11697)*

Marion Dofasco Inc..740 382-3979
686 W Fairground St Marion (43302) *(G-8976)*

Marion Industries LLC..740 223-0075
999 Kellogg Pkwy Marion (43302) *(G-8977)*

Mariotti Printing Co LLC.....................................440 245-4120
513 E 28th St Lorain (44055) *(G-8567)*

Mark Advertising Agency Inc..............................419 626-9000
1600 5th St Sandusky (44870) *(G-11856)*

Mark Grzianis St Treats Ex Inc (PA)...................330 414-6266
1294 Windward Ln Kent (44240) *(G-8049)*

Mark J Myers...513 753-7300
80 W Main St Amelia (45102) *(G-432)*

Mark Knupp Muffler & Tire Inc...........................937 773-1334
950 S College St Piqua (45356) *(G-11365)*

Mark W Thruman..614 754-5500
85 Mcnaughten Rd Columbus (43213) *(G-5082)*

Mark West Energy, Cadiz Also Called: Markwest Energy Partners LP *(G-1719)*

Mark-All Enterprises LLC...................................800 433-3615
888 W Waterloo Rd Akron (44314) *(G-220)*

Markers Inc..440 933-5927
33490 Pin Oak Pkwy Avon Lake (44012) *(G-764)*

Market Garden Brewery, Cleveland Also Called: Bar 25 LLC *(G-3403)*

Market Garden Brewery, Cleveland Also Called: Bar 25 LLC *(G-3404)*

Market Media Creations, Coshocton Also Called: Sprint Print Inc *(G-5473)*

Market Ready...513 289-9231
1129 Avalon Dr Maineville (45039) *(G-8741)*

Markethtch Inc D/B/A Mh Eye CA.......................330 376-6363
91 E Voris St Akron (44311) *(G-221)*

Marketing Essentials LLC...................................419 629-0080
14 N Washington St New Bremen (45869) *(G-10362)*

Markham Machine Company Inc..........................330 762-7676
160 N Union St Akron (44304) *(G-222)*

Marking Devices Inc...216 861-4498
3110 Payne Ave Cleveland (44114) *(G-3989)*

Markley Enterprises LLC....................................513 771-1290
1705 Magnolia Dr Cincinnati (45215) *(G-2847)*

Markt LLC..740 397-5900
314 W Burgess St Mount Vernon (43050) *(G-10250)*

Markus Jewelers LLC...513 474-4950
2022 8 Mile Rd Cincinnati (45244) *(G-2848)*

Markwest Energy Partners LP.............................740 942-0463
78405 Cadiz New Athens Rd Cadiz (43907) *(G-1719)*

Markwest Energy Partners LP.............................800 730-8388
46700 Giacobbi Rd Jewett (43986) *(G-7989)*

Markwest Energy Partners LP.............................740 838-1434
26645 Zep Rd E Summerfield (43788) *(G-12660)*

Marlboro Manufacturing Inc...............................330 935-2221
11750 Marlboro Ave Ne Alliance (44601) *(G-392)*

Marlen, Bedford Also Called: Marlen Manufacturing & Dev Co *(G-1046)*

Marlen Manufacturing & Dev Co (PA).................216 292-7060
5150 Richmond Rd Bedford (44146) *(G-1046)*

Marlen Manufacturing & Dev Co.........................216 292-7546
5156 Richmond Rd Bedford (44146) *(G-1047)*

Marlin Manufacturing Corp (PA).........................216 676-1340
12800 Corporate Dr Cleveland (44130) *(G-3990)*

Marlin Thermocouple Wire Inc...........................440 835-1950
847 Canterbury Rd Westlake (44145) *(G-14314)*

Marlite Inc (DH)...330 343-6621
1 Marlite Dr Dover (44622) *(G-6252)*

Marlow-2000 Inc...216 362-8500
13811 Enterprise Ave Cleveland (44135) *(G-3991)*

Marmax Machine Co..937 698-9900
2425 S State Route 48 Ludlow Falls (45339) *(G-8672)*

Marne Plastics LLC..614 732-4666
3655 Brookham Dr Ste F Grove City (43123) *(G-7397)*

Marrow County Sentinel, Mount Gilead Also Called: Hirt Publishing Co Inc *(G-10210)*

Mars Horsecare, Dalton Also Called: Mars Horsecare Us Inc *(G-5588)*

Mars Horsecare Us Inc.......................................330 828-2251
330 E Schultz St Dalton (44618) *(G-5588)*

Mars Petcare Us Inc...614 878-7242
5115 Fisher Rd Columbus (43228) *(G-5083)*

Mars Petcare Us Inc...419 943-4280
3700 State Route 65 Leipsic (45856) *(G-8307)*

Marsam Metalfab Inc.................................... 330 405-1520
1870 Enterprise Pkwy Twinsburg (44087) *(G-13334)*

Marsh Technologies Inc................................. 330 545-0085
30 W Main St Ste A Girard (44420) *(G-7275)*

Marsh Valley Forest Pdts Ltd......................... 440 632-1889
14141 Old State Rd Middlefield (44062) *(G-9807)*

Marshall Cnty Coal Rsurces Inc...................... 740 338-3100
46226 National Rd Saint Clairsville (43950) *(G-11698)*

Marshall Plastics Inc.................................... 937 653-4740
590 S Edgewood Ave Urbana (43078) *(G-13473)*

Marshalltown Packaging Inc........................... 641 753-5272
601 N Hague Ave Columbus (43204) *(G-5084)*

Marshallville Packing Co Inc.......................... 330 855-2871
50 E Market St Marshallville (44645) *(G-9007)*

Marshas Buckeyes LLC................................. 419 872-7666
25631 Fort Meigs Rd Ste E Perrysburg (43551) *(G-11237)*

Marsulex Inc.. 419 698-8181
1400 Otter Creek Rd Oregon (43616) *(G-10963)*

Mart Plus Fuel.. 216 261-0420
21820 Lake Shore Blvd Euclid (44123) *(G-6660)*

Martin Allen Trailer LLC................................ 330 942-0217
837 N Cleveland Massillon Rd Akron (44333) *(G-223)*

Martin Cab Div, Cleveland *Also Called: Martin Sheet Metal Inc (G-3993)*

Martin Diesel Inc.. 419 782-9911
27809 County Road 424 Defiance (43512) *(G-6120)*

Martin Industrial Truck, Cleveland *Also Called: Marlow-2000 Inc (G-3991)*

Martin Industries Inc................................... 419 862-2694
473 Maple St Elmore (43416) *(G-6490)*

Martin Machine, Bowling Green *Also Called: Aeropact Manufacturing LLC (G-1406)*

Martin Marietta Aggragate, West Chester *Also Called: Martin Marietta Materials Inc (G-14026)*

Martin Marietta Aggregates, Mason *Also Called: Martin Marietta Materials Inc (G-9124)*

Martin Marietta Aggregates, Racine *Also Called: Marietta Martin Materials Inc (G-11505)*

Martin Marietta Materials Inc......................... 513 701-1120
4900 Parkway Dr Mason (45040) *(G-9124)*

Martin Marietta Materials Inc......................... 513 701-1140
9277 Centre Pointe Dr Ste 250 West Chester (45069) *(G-14026)*

Martin Pultrusion Group Inc.......................... 440 439-9130
20801 Miles Rd Ste B Cleveland (44128) *(G-3992)*

Martin Sheet Metal Inc................................. 216 377-8200
7108 Madison Ave Cleveland (44102) *(G-3993)*

Martin Welding LLC (PA)............................... 937 687-3602
1472 W Main St New Lebanon (45345) *(G-10400)*

Martin Wheel, Tallmadge *Also Called: Americana Development Inc (G-12730)*

Martin-Brower Company LLC.......................... 513 773-2301
4260 Port Union Rd West Chester (45011) *(G-14027)*

Martin-Palmer Tool, Dayton *Also Called: Edfa LLC (G-5760)*

Martina Metal LLC....................................... 614 291-9700
1575 Shawnee Ave Columbus (43211) *(G-5085)*

Martindale Electric Company.......................... 216 521-8567
1375 Hird Ave Cleveland (44107) *(G-3994)*

Martins Partitions, Lancaster *Also Called: Thorwald Holdings Inc (G-8229)*

Martins Steel Fabrication Inc.......................... 330 882-4311
2115 Center Rd New Franklin (44216) *(G-10390)*

Marwil, Fort Loramie *Also Called: Rol - Tech Inc (G-6953)*

Mary Ann Donut Shoppe Inc (PA)..................... 330 478-1655
5032 Yukon St Nw Canton (44708) *(G-1938)*

Mary Ann Donuts, Canton *Also Called: Mary Ann Donut Shoppe Inc (G-1938)*

Marysville Auto Plant, Marysville *Also Called: Honda Dev & Mfg Amer LLC (G-9026)*

Marysville Newspaper Inc (PA)........................ 937 644-9111
207 N Main St Marysville (43040) *(G-9037)*

Marysville Steel Inc..................................... 937 642-5971
323 E 8th St Marysville (43040) *(G-9038)*

Marz Direct, Monroe *Also Called: R & L Software LLC (G-10115)*

Marzano Inc.. 216 459-2051
4147 Pearl Rd Cleveland (44109) *(G-3995)*

Mason Color Works Inc................................. 330 385-4400
250 E 2nd St East Liverpool (43920) *(G-6395)*

Mason Company LLC.................................... 937 780-2321
260 Depot Ln Leesburg (45135) *(G-8299)*

Mason Steel, Walton Hills *Also Called: Mssi Group Inc (G-13701)*

Mason Structural Steel LLC............................ 440 439-1040
7500 Northfield Rd Walton Hills (44146) *(G-13699)*

Masonite Corporation................................... 937 454-9207
3250 Old Springfield Rd Ste 1 Vandalia (45377) *(G-13569)*

Masonite International Corp............................ 937 454-9308
875 Center Dr Vandalia (45377) *(G-13570)*

Masons Sand and Gravel Co........................... 614 491-3611
2385 Rathmell Rd Obetz (43207) *(G-10924)*

Mass-Marketing Inc (PA)............................... 513 860-6200
7209 Dixie Hwy Fairfield (45014) *(G-6750)*

Massageblocks.com, Powell *Also Called: Summit Online Products LLC (G-11495)*

Massillon Container Co.................................. 330 879-5653
49 Ohio St Sw Navarre (44662) *(G-10306)*

Massillon Feed Mill, Massillon *Also Called: Case Farms LLC (G-9178)*

Massillon Machine & Die Inc.......................... 330 833-8913
3536 17th St Sw Massillon (44647) *(G-9219)*

Massillon Materials Inc (PA)........................... 330 837-4767
26 N Cochran St Dalton (44618) *(G-5589)*

Mast Farm Service Ltd.................................. 330 893-2972
3585 State Rte 39 Walnut Creek (44687) *(G-13694)*

Mast Mini Barn, Junction City *Also Called: K-Mar Structures LLC (G-8002)*

Masteller Electric Motor Svc........................... 937 492-8500
122 Lane St Sidney (45365) *(G-12032)*

Master Bldrs Sltons Admxtres U (PA).............. 216 839-7500
23700 Chagrin Blvd Beachwood (44122) *(G-927)*

Master Bolt LLC.. 440 323-5529
811 Taylor St Elyria (44035) *(G-6561)*

Master Builders LLC (HQ).............................. 800 228-3318
23700 Chagrin Blvd Beachwood (44122) *(G-928)*

Master Carbide Tools Company....................... 440 352-1112
3529 Lane Rd Ext Perry (44081) *(G-11196)*

Master Caster Company, Cleveland *Also Called: Master Mfg Co Inc (G-3997)*

Master Chemical Corporation (PA)................... 419 874-7902
501 W Boundary St Perrysburg (43551) *(G-11238)*

Master Communications Inc............................ 208 821-3473
2692 Madison Rd Ste N1-307 Cincinnati (45208) *(G-2849)*

Master Craft Products Inc.............................. 216 281-5910
10621 Briggs Rd Cleveland (44111) *(G-3996)*

Master Draw Lubricants, Chagrin Falls *Also Called: Etna Products Incorporated (G-2161)*

Master Fluid Solutions, Perrysburg *Also Called: Master Chemical Corporation (G-11238)*

Master Mfg Co Inc....................................... 216 641-0500
9200 Inman Ave Cleveland (44105) *(G-3997)*

Master Print Center, Cincinnati *Also Called: Gerald L Herrmann Company Inc (G-2669)*

Master Printing & Mailing, Berea *Also Called: Master Printing Group Inc (G-1180)*

Master Printing Group Inc.............................. 216 351-2246
95 Pelret Industrial Pkwy Berea (44017) *(G-1180)*

Master Products Company.............................. 216 341-1740
6400 Park Ave Cleveland (44105) *(G-3998)*

Master Swaging Inc..................................... 937 596-6171
210 Washington St Jackson Center (45334) *(G-7965)*

Master-Halco Inc... 513 869-7600
620 Commerce Center Dr Fairfield (45011) *(G-6751)*

Masterbrand, Beachwood *Also Called: Masterbrand Inc (G-929)*

Masterbrand Inc (PA).................................... 877 622-4782
3300 Enterprise Pkwy Ste 300 Beachwood (44122) *(G-929)*

Masterfoods USA, Columbus *Also Called: Mars Petcare Us Inc (G-5083)*

Masterpiece Signs Graphics Inc....................... 419 358-0077
902 N Main St Bluffton (45817) *(G-1362)*

Masters Pharmaceutical Inc............................ 513 290-2969
8695 Seward Rd Fairfield (45011) *(G-6752)*

Masters Prcision Machining Inc....................... 330 419-1933
4465 Crystal Pkwy Kent (44240) *(G-8050)*

Mastertech Diamond Products Co, Perry *Also Called: Master Carbide Tools Company (G-11196)*

Mastropietro Winery Inc................................ 330 547-2151
14558 Ellsworth Rd Berlin Center (44401) *(G-1201)*

Mat Basics Incorporated................................ 513 793-0313
4546 Cornell Rd Blue Ash (45241) *(G-1302)*

Matalco (us) Inc (HQ)................................... 330 452-4760
4420 Louisville St Ne Canton (44705) *(G-1939)*

Matalco (us) Inc.. 234 806-0600
  5120 Tod Ave Sw Warren (44481) *(G-13781)*

Match Mold & Machine Inc.................................. 330 830-5503
  1100 Nova Dr Se Massillon (44646) *(G-9220)*

Matco Tools, Stow Also Called: Matco Tools Corporation *(G-12440)*

Matco Tools Corporation (HQ).............................. 330 929-4949
  4403 Allen Rd Stow (44224) *(G-12440)*

Matdan Corporation... 513 794-0500
  10855 Millington Ct Blue Ash (45242) *(G-1303)*

Material Holdings Inc... 513 583-5500
  185 Commerce Dr Loveland (45140) *(G-8640)*

Material Processing & Hdlg Co.............................. 419 436-9562
  1150 State St Fostoria (44830) *(G-6988)*

Material Sciences Corporation.............................. 330 702-3882
  460 W Main St Canfield (44406) *(G-1813)*

Material Sciences Corporation.............................. 419 661-5905
  30610 E Broadway St Walbridge (43465) *(G-13685)*

Materials Science Intl Inc.................................... 614 870-0400
  1660 Georgesville Rd Columbus (43228) *(G-5086)*

Materion, Mayfield Heights Also Called: Materion Brush Inc *(G-9336)*

Materion Advnced Mtls Tech Svc (HQ).................... 216 486-4200
  6070 Parkland Blvd Mayfield Heights (44124) *(G-9335)*

Materion Brush Inc.. 419 862-2745
  14710 W Portage River South Rd Elmore (43416) *(G-6491)*

Materion Brush Inc (HQ)..................................... 216 486-4200
  6070 Parkland Blvd Ste 1 Mayfield Heights (44124) *(G-9336)*

Materion Corporation (PA)................................... 216 486-4200
  6070 Parkland Blvd Mayfield Heights (44124) *(G-9337)*

Materion Microelectronics Svcs, Mayfield Heights Also Called: Materion Advnced Mtls Tech Svc *(G-9335)*

Matern Metal Works Inc...................................... 419 529-3100
  210 N Adams St Mansfield (44902) *(G-8821)*

Matheson Gas Products, Twinsburg Also Called: Matheson Tri-Gas Inc *(G-13335)*

Matheson Tri-Gas Inc... 419 865-8881
  1720 Trade Rd Holland (43528) *(G-7772)*

Matheson Tri-Gas Inc... 330 425-4407
  1650 Enterprise Pkwy Twinsburg (44087) *(G-13335)*

Matlock Electric Co Inc....................................... 513 731-9600
  2780 Highland Ave Cincinnati (45212) *(G-2850)*

Matplus, Painesville Also Called: Matplus Ltd *(G-11098)*

Matplus Ltd... 440 352-7201
  76 Burton St Painesville (44077) *(G-11098)*

Matrix Management Solutions............................... 330 470-3700
  5200 Stoneham Rd Canton (44720) *(G-1940)*

Matrix Meats Inc.. 614 602-1846
  5164 Blazer Pkwy Dublin (43017) *(G-6319)*

Matrix Research Inc... 937 427-8433
  3844 Research Blvd Dayton (45430) *(G-5869)*

Matrix Sys Auto Finishes LLC............................... 248 668-8135
  600 Nova Dr Se Massillon (44646) *(G-9221)*

Matrix Tool & Machine Inc................................... 440 255-0300
  7870 Division Dr Mentor (44060) *(G-9560)*

Matsu Ohio Inc.. 419 298-2394
  228 E Morrison St Edgerton (43517) *(G-6467)*

Matteo Aluminum Inc... 440 585-5213
  1261 E 289th St Wickliffe (44092) *(G-14382)*

Matthew Bender & Company, Miamisburg Also Called: Matthew Bender & Company Inc *(G-9710)*

Matthew Bender & Company Inc............................ 518 487-3000
  9443 Springboro Pike Miamisburg (45342) *(G-9710)*

Matthew Brun Enterprises Inc.............................. 937 604-0057
  3600 Valley St Dayton (45424) *(G-5870)*

Matthew Warren Inc... 614 418-0250
  2000 Jetway Blvd Columbus (43219) *(G-5087)*

Matting Products Div, Fairlawn Also Called: Rjf International Corporation *(G-6809)*

Mattmark Drilling Company, Cambridge Also Called: Mattmark Partners Inc *(G-1748)*

Mattmark Partners Inc.. 740 439-3109
  61234 Southgate Rd Cambridge (43725) *(G-1748)*

Mattr US Inc... 513 683-7800
  173 Commerce Dr Loveland (45140) *(G-8641)*

Mattress Mart, Plain City Also Called: Quilting Inc *(G-11417)*

Maumee Assembly & Stamping LLC........................ 419 304-2887
  920 Illinois Ave Maumee (43537) *(G-9307)*

Maumee Bay Brewing Company............................. 419 243-1253
  27 Broadway St Ste A Toledo (43604) *(G-13047)*

Maumee Hose & Belting Co, Maumee Also Called: Maumee Hose & Fitting Inc *(G-9308)*

Maumee Hose & Fitting Inc.................................. 419 893-7252
  720 Illinois Ave Ste H Maumee (43537) *(G-9308)*

Maumee Machine & Tool Corp............................... 419 385-2501
  2960 South Ave Toledo (43609) *(G-13048)*

Maumee Pattern Company.................................... 419 693-4968
  1019 Hazelwood St Toledo (43605) *(G-13049)*

Maumee Valley Fabricators Inc............................. 419 476-1411
  4801 Bennett Rd Toledo (43612) *(G-13050)*

Maumee Valley Memorials Inc (DH)........................ 419 878-9030
  111 Anthony Wayne Trl Waterville (43566) *(G-13839)*

Mauser Usa LLC... 513 398-1300
  1229 Castle Dr Mason (45040) *(G-9125)*

Mauser Usa LLC... 740 397-1762
  219 Commerce Dr Mount Vernon (43050) *(G-10251)*

Maval Industries LLC (PA).................................... 330 405-1600
  1555 Enterprise Pkwy Twinsburg (44087) *(G-13336)*

Maval Manufacturing, Twinsburg Also Called: Maval Industries LLC *(G-13336)*

Maverick Corporation... 513 469-9919
  11285 Grooms Rd Blue Ash (45242) *(G-1304)*

Maverick Electronics, Cleveland Also Called: Heilind Electronics Inc *(G-3818)*

Maverick Innvtive Slutions LLC............................. 419 281-7944
  532 County Road 1600 Ashland (44805) *(G-550)*

Maverick Molding Co.. 513 387-6100
  11359 Grooms Rd Blue Ash (45242) *(G-1305)*

Mavericks Stainless, Mansfield Also Called: Mk Metal Products Entps Inc *(G-8830)*

Max - Pro Tools Inc... 800 456-0931
  8999 W Pleasant Valley Rd Cleveland (44130) *(G-3999)*

Maxfield Candy Company, Columbus Also Called: International Confections Company LLC *(G-5019)*

Maxim Integrated Products LLC............................. 216 375-1057
  9000 Yale Ave Cleveland (44108) *(G-4000)*

Maxion Wheels Sedalia LLC.................................. 330 794-2300
  428 Seiberling St Akron (44306) *(G-224)*

Maxx Iron LLC... 614 753-9697
  287 E North St Worthington (43085) *(G-14718)*

May Conveyor Inc... 440 237-8012
  9981 York Theta Dr North Royalton (44133) *(G-10772)*

May Industries of Ohio Inc.................................. 440 237-8012
  9981 York Theta Dr North Royalton (44133) *(G-10773)*

May Lin Silicone Products Inc.............................. 330 825-9019
  955 Wooster Rd W Barberton (44203) *(G-820)*

May Tool & Die Co.. 440 237 8012
  9981 York Theta Dr Ste 1 Cleveland (44133) *(G-4001)*

Mayco Colors, Hilliard Also Called: Coloramics LLC *(G-7678)*

Mayfair Granite Co Inc....................................... 216 382-8150
  4202 Mayfield Rd Cleveland (44121) *(G-4002)*

Mayfair Memorial, Cleveland Also Called: Mayfair Granite Co Inc *(G-4002)*

Mayfran International Inc (HQ).............................. 440 461-4100
  6650 Beta Dr Cleveland (44143) *(G-4003)*

Maynard Company, The, Cleveland Also Called: Bud May Inc *(G-3449)*

Mayo, R A Industries, East Palestine Also Called: Robert Mayo Industries *(G-6406)*

Maysville Ready Mix Con Co, Aberdeen Also Called: Hilltop Basic Resources Inc *(G-1)*

Mazzella Jhh Company Inc................................... 440 239-7000
  21000 Aerospace Pkwy Cleveland (44142) *(G-4004)*

Mazzella Lifting Tech Inc (HQ).............................. 440 239-7000
  21000 Aerospace Pkwy Cleveland (44142) *(G-4005)*

MB Dynamics Inc.. 216 292-5850
  25865 Richmond Rd Cleveland (44146) *(G-4006)*

MB Manufacturing Corp....................................... 513 682-1461
  2904 Symmes Rd Fairfield (45014) *(G-6753)*

MB Renovations & Designs LLC............................. 614 772-6139
  4449 Easton Way Ste 200 Columbus (43219) *(G-5088)*

MBA Design, Peninsula Also Called: X44 Corp *(G-11188)*

Mbas Printing Inc... 513 489-3000
  11401 Deerfield Rd Blue Ash (45242) *(G-1306)*

Mbcc Admixtures, Beachwood *Also Called: Master Bldrs Sltons Admxtres U (G-927)*

Mbds, Findlay *Also Called: Manufctring Bus Dev Sltons LLC (G-6886)*

Mbs Acquisition, Mason *Also Called: Remtec Engineering (G-9142)*

Mc Alarney Pool Spas and Blld..................................740 373-6698
908 Pike St Marietta (45750) *(G-8928)*

Mc Brown Industries Inc...419 963-2800
10534 Township Road 128 Findlay (45840) *(G-6892)*

Mc Cartney Industries, Mentor *Also Called: Semper Quality Industry Inc (G-9613)*

Mc Concepts Llc..330 933-6402
2459 55th St Ne Canton (44721) *(G-1941)*

Mc Connells Market..740 765-4300
2189 State Route 43 Richmond (43944) *(G-11604)*

Mc Elwain Industries Inc.......................................419 532-3126
17941 Road L Ottawa (45875) *(G-11038)*

Mc Graw-Hill Educational Pubg, Ashland *Also Called: McGraw-Hill Schl Edcatn Hldngs (G-551)*

Mc Group, Mentor *Also Called: Stratus Unlimited LLC (G-9629)*

Mc Happy's Bake Shoppe, Belpre *Also Called: Wal-Bon of Ohio Inc (G-1156)*

Mc Happys Donuts, Athens *Also Called: McHappys Dnuts Parkersburg Inc (G-643)*

Mc Machine Llc..216 398-3666
9000 Brookpark Rd Cleveland (44129) *(G-4007)*

MCA Industries, Massillon *Also Called: The Massillon-Cleveland-Akronsign Company (G-9247)*

McAfee Tool & Die Inc...330 896-9555
1717 Boettler Rd Uniontown (44685) *(G-13423)*

McAlarney Pols Spas Blld More, Marietta *Also Called: Mc Alamey Pool Spas and Blld (G-8928)*

McC - Mason W&S (DH)...513 459-1100
5510 Courseview Dr Mason (45040) *(G-9126)*

McC-Norway LLC..513 381-1480
4053 Clough Woods Dr Batavia (45103) *(G-871)*

McCann, Canton *Also Called: McCann Plastics LLC (G-1943)*

McCann Color Inc..330 498-4840
8562 Port Jackson Ave Nw Canton (44720) *(G-1942)*

McCann Plastics LLC...330 499-1515
5600 Mayfair Rd Canton (44720) *(G-1943)*

McCann Tool & Die Inc...330 264-8820
3230 Columbus Rd Wooster (44691) *(G-14664)*

McCc Sportswear Inc (PA).....................................513 583-9210
501 Techne Center Dr Milford (45150) *(G-9942)*

McClelland Inc (PA)..740 452-3036
98 E La Salle St Zanesville (43701) *(G-15027)*

McConnell's Farm Market, Richmond *Also Called: Mc Connells Market (G-11604)*

McCoy Group Inc..330 753-1041
1020 Eagon St Barberton (44203) *(G-821)*

McCrary, Port Jefferson *Also Called: McCrary Metal Polishing Co Inc (G-11454)*

McCrary Metal Polishing Co Inc...............................937 492-1979
207 Pasco Montra Rd Port Jefferson (45360) *(G-11454)*

McCullough Industries, Kenton *Also Called: Mcl Inc (G-8106)*

McCullough Industries Inc.......................................419 673-0767
13047 County Road 175 Kenton (43326) *(G-8104)*

McDaniel Products Inc (PA)......................................419 524-5841
50 Industrial Pkwy Mansfield (44903) *(G-8822)*

McDaniel Products Inc...419 524-5841
433 Springmill St Mansfield (44903) *(G-8823)*

McDonald Steel Corporation (PA)..............................330 530-9118
100 Ohio Ave Mc Donald (44437) *(G-9360)*

McDonald Steel Plate Inc..216 883-4200
3344 E 80th St Cleveland (44127) *(G-4008)*

McDonalds..513 753-6100
1261 W Ohio Pike Amelia (45102) *(G-433)*

McDonalds..513 752-2008
812 Eastgate North Dr Cincinnati (45245) *(G-2313)*

McDonalds..216 226-7754
16407 Detroit Ave Lakewood (44107) *(G-8169)*

McDonalds..513 336-0820
5301 Kings Island Dr Mason (45040) *(G-9127)*

McDonalds..740 753-4018
21 Watkins St Nelsonville (45764) *(G-10318)*

McDonalds..419 935-1414
207 E Walton St Willard (44890) *(G-14404)*

McDonalds...,.........330 792-0527
1709 S Raccoon Rd Youngstown (44515) *(G-14895)*

McElroy Coal Company (DH)....................................724 485-4000
46226 National Rd Saint Clairsville (43950) *(G-11699)*

McElroy Contract Packaging Inc...............................330 682-2155
301 Collins Blvd Orrville (44667) *(G-10994)*

McF Industries..330 526-6337
1206 N Main St North Canton (44720) *(G-10650)*

McFlusion Inc...800 341-8616
2112 Case Pkwy Ste 8 Twinsburg (44087) *(G-13337)*

McGean, Cleveland *Also Called: McGean-Rohco Inc (G-4009)*

McGean-Rohco Inc..216 441-4900
2910 Harvard Ave Newburgh Heights (44105) *(G-10545)*

McGean-Rohco Inc (PA)...216 441-4900
2910 Harvard Ave Cleveland (44105) *(G-4009)*

McGill Airclean, Columbus *Also Called: McGill Airclean LLC (G-5089)*

McGill Airclean LLC...614 829-1200
1777 Refugee Rd Columbus (43207) *(G-5089)*

McGill Airflow LLC...614 829-1200
2400 Fairwood Ave Columbus (43207) *(G-5090)*

McGill Corporation (PA)..614 829-1200
1 Mission Park Groveport (43125) *(G-7444)*

McGill Septic Tank Co..330 876-2171
8913 State St Kinsman (44428) *(G-8141)*

McGinnis Inc (HQ)..740 377-4391
502 2nd St E South Point (45680) *(G-12226)*

McGlennon Metal Products Inc................................614 252-7114
940 N 20th St Columbus (43219) *(G-5091)*

McGovney Ready Mix Inc..740 353-4111
55 River Ave Portsmouth (45662) *(G-11469)*

McGovney River Terminal, Portsmouth *Also Called: McGovney Ready Mix Inc (G-11469)*

McGraw-Hill Education Inc......................................760 931-1290
860 Taylor Station Rd Blacklick (43004) *(G-1225)*

McGraw-Hill Global Educatn LLC..............................614 755-4151
860 Taylor Station Rd Blacklick (43004) *(G-1226)*

McGraw-Hill Schl Edcatn Hldngs...............................419 207-7400
1250 George Rd Ashland (44805) *(G-551)*

McGraw-Hill Schl Edcatn Hldngs...............................614 430-4000
8787 Orion Pl Columbus (43240) *(G-4642)*

McGregor & Associates Inc....................................937 629-4346
365 Carr Dr Brookville (45309) *(G-1573)*

McGregor Metal National Works LLC..........................937 882-6347
5573 W National Rd Springfield (45504) *(G-12348)*

McGregor Metalworking, Springfield *Also Called: McGregor Mtal Yllow Sprng Wrks (G-12351)*

McGregor Mtal Innsfllen Wrks L.................................937 322-3880
1305 Innisfallen Ave Springfield (45506) *(G-12349)*

McGregor Mtal Leffel Works LLC...............................937 325-5561
900 W Leffel Ln Springfield (45506) *(G-12350)*

McGregor Mtal Yllow Sprng Wrks (PA).........................937 325-5561
2100 S Yellow Springs St Springfield (45506) *(G-12351)*

McGregor Surmount, Brookville *Also Called: McGregor & Associates Inc (G-1573)*

McGuire Machine,, North Lawrence *Also Called: Sjk Machine LLC (G-10702)*

McHael D Goronok String Instrs...............................216 421-4227
10823 Magnolia Dr Cleveland (44106) *(G-4010)*

McHappys Dnuts Parkersburg Inc.............................740 593-8744
384 Richland Ave Athens (45701) *(G-643)*

McHenry Industries Inc..330 799-8930
85 Victoria Rd Youngstown (44515) *(G-14896)*

Mcl Inc...800 245-9490
13047 County Road 175 Kenton (43326) *(G-8105)*

Mcl Inc...800 245-9490
13047 County Road 175 Kenton (43326) *(G-8106)*

McIntosh Manufacturing LLC...................................513 424-5307
3350 Yankee Rd Middletown (45044) *(G-9878)*

McIntosh Safe Corp...937 222-7008
603 Leo St Dayton (45404) *(G-5871)*

McKechnie Arospc Holdings Inc................................216 706-2960
1301 E 9th St Ste 3000 Cleveland (44114) *(G-4011)*

McKinley Leather, Marion *Also Called: Williams Leather Products Inc (G-9004)*

McKinley Packaging Company...................................216 663-3344
16645 Granite Rd Maple Heights (44137) *(G-8887)*

McKnight Industries Inc.................937 592-9010
Orchard & Elm Street Bellefontaine (43311) *(G-1113)*

McL Inc.................614 861-6259
5240 E Main St Columbus (43213) *(G-5092)*

McL Whitehall, Columbus *Also Called: McL Inc (G-5092)*

McM Ind Co Inc (PA).................216 292-4506
22901 Millcreek Blvd Ste 250 Cleveland (44122) *(G-4012)*

McM Ind Co Inc.................216 641-6300
7800 Finney Ave Cleveland (44105) *(G-4013)*

McM Industries, Cleveland *Also Called: McM Ind Co Inc (G-4012)*

McM Precision Castings Inc.................419 669-3226
13133 Beech St Weston (43569) *(G-14349)*

McNational Inc (PA).................740 377-4391
502 2nd St E South Point (45680) *(G-12227)*

McNeal Enterprises LLC.................740 703-7108
807 E 2nd St Chillicothe (45601) *(G-2264)*

McNeil & Nrm Inc (HQ).................330 761-1855
96 E Crosier St Akron (44311) *(G-225)*

McNeil & Nrm Intl Inc (PA).................330 253-2525
96 E Crosier St Akron (44311) *(G-226)*

McNeil Group Inc.................614 298-0300
1701 Woodland Ave Columbus (43219) *(G-5093)*

McNeil Holdings LLC.................614 298-0300
1701 Woodland Ave Columbus (43219) *(G-5094)*

McNeil Industries Inc.................440 951-7756
835 Richmond Rd Ste 2 Painesville (44077) *(G-11099)*

McNeilus Truck and Mfg Inc.................614 868-0760
1130 Morrison Rd Gahanna (43230) *(G-7165)*

McNerney & Associates LLC (PA).................513 241-9951
5443 Duff Dr West Chester (45246) *(G-14132)*

McNish Corporation.................614 899-2282
214 Hoff Rd Unit M Westerville (43082) *(G-14222)*

McO Inc (PA).................216 341-8914
7555 Bessemer Ave Cleveland (44127) *(G-4014)*

McOn Inds Inc (HQ).................937 294-2681
2221 Arbor Blvd Moraine (45439) *(G-10176)*

McPp, Bellevue *Also Called: Mitsubishi Chemical Amer Inc (G-1126)*

McPp-Detroit, Bellevue *Also Called: Mitsubishi Chemical Amer Inc (G-1127)*

MCR of Norwalk Inc.................419 668-8261
55 Newton St Norwalk (44857) *(G-10852)*

McRd Enterprises LLC.................740 775-2377
337 E Main St Chillicothe (45601) *(G-2265)*

McRon Finance Corp.................513 487-5000
3010 Disney St Cincinnati (45209) *(G-2851)*

MCS Mfg LLC.................419 923-0169
15210 County Road 10 3 Lyons (43533) *(G-8674)*

MCS Midwest LLC (PA).................513 217-0805
3876 Hendrickson Rd Franklin (45005) *(G-7033)*

McSwain Manufacturing LLC.................513 619-1222
189 Container Pl Cincinnati (45246) *(G-2852)*

McSweeneys Inc.................740 894-3353
235 Commerce Dr South Point (45680) *(G-12228)*

McWane Inc.................740 622-6651
2266 S 6th St Coshocton (43812) *(G-5459)*

Mdf Tool, North Royalton *Also Called: Mdf Tool Corporation (G-10774)*

Mdf Tool Corporation.................440 237-2277
10166 Royalton Rd North Royalton (44133) *(G-10774)*

Mdi of Ohio Inc (HQ).................937 866-2345
802 N 4th St Miamisburg (45342) *(G-9711)*

Meador Supply Company Inc.................330 405-4403
20437 Hannan Pkwy Ste 5 Walton Hills (44146) *(G-13700)*

Meadow Burke Products, West Chester *Also Called: Merchants Metals LLC (G-14028)*

Measurement Computing Corp (DH).................440 439-4091
25971 Cannon Rd Cleveland (44146) *(G-4015)*

Measurement Specialties, Miamisburg *Also Called: Advanced Indus Msrment Systems (G-9660)*

Measurement Specialties Inc.................330 659-3312
2236 N Cleveland Massillon Rd Ste A Akron (44333) *(G-227)*

Measurement Specialties Inc.................937 427-1231
2670 Indian Ripple Rd Dayton (45440) *(G-5872)*

Meccas Lounge LLC.................419 239-6918
2614 Pioneer Trl Apt 606 Sandusky (44870) *(G-11857)*

Mechanical Dynamics Analis LLC.................440 946-0082
1250 E 222nd St Euclid (44117) *(G-6661)*

Mechanical Finishers Inc LLC.................513 641-5419
6350 Este Ave Cincinnati (45232) *(G-2853)*

Mechanical Finishing Inc.................513 641-5419
6350 Este Ave Cincinnati (45232) *(G-2854)*

Mechanical Galv-Plating Corp.................937 492-3143
933 Oak Ave Sidney (45365) *(G-12033)*

Mechanical Rubber Ohio LLC.................845 986-2271
12312 Alameda Dr Strongsville (44149) *(G-12573)*

Mechanicsburg Sand & Gravel.................937 834-2606
5734 State Route 4 Mechanicsburg (43044) *(G-9367)*

Meco, Middletown *Also Called: Manufacturers Equipment Co (G-9877)*

Medallion Lighting Corporation.................440 255-8383
9345 Progress Pkwy Mentor (44060) *(G-9561)*

Meder Special-Tees Ltd.................513 921-3800
618 Delhi Ave Cincinnati (45204) *(G-2855)*

Medex, Dublin *Also Called: Saint-Gobain Prfmce Plas Corp (G-6342)*

Mediajacked Sound Studio LLC.................330 391-3123
2903 Mahoning Ave Youngstown (44509) *(G-14897)*

Medical & Home Health, Westlake *Also Called: Applied Marketing Services Inc (G-14289)*

Medical Device Bus Svcs Inc.................937 274-5850
2747 Armstrong Ln Dayton (45414) *(G-5873)*

Medical Quant USA Inc.................440 542-0761
6521 Davis Industrial Pkwy Solon (44139) *(G-12145)*

Medical Resources, Lewis Center *Also Called: Eoi Inc (G-8333)*

Medina County.................330 723-3641
144 N Broadway St Ste 117 Medina (44256) *(G-9423)*

Medina County Recorders, Medina *Also Called: Medina County (G-9423)*

Medina Foods Inc.................330 725-1390
9706 Crow Rd Litchfield (44253) *(G-8481)*

Medina Fuel, Coshocton *Also Called: MFC Drilling Inc (G-5460)*

Medina Hntngton RE Group II LL.................330 591-2777
635 N Huntington St Medina (44256) *(G-9424)*

Medina Supply Co, Twinsburg *Also Called: Medina Supply Company (G-13338)*

Medina Supply Company.................440 234-1321
661 Front St Berea (44017) *(G-1181)*

Medina Supply Company.................330 364-4411
820 W Smith Rd Medina (44256) *(G-9425)*

Medina Supply Company (DH).................330 723-3681
230 E Smith Rd Medina (44256) *(G-9426)*

Medina Supply Company.................330 425-0752
1516 Highland Rd Twinsburg (44087) *(G-13338)*

Medina Tool & Die, Wadsworth *Also Called: Kramer & Kiefer Inc (G-13647)*

Mediview Xr Inc.................419 270-2774
10000 Cedar Ave Cleveland (44106) *(G-4016)*

Medline Industries LP.................614 879-9728
1040 Enterprise Pkwy West Jefferson (43162) *(G-14164)*

Medpace, Cincinnati *Also Called: Medpace Holdings Inc (G-2857)*

Medpace Core Laboratories LLC.................513 579-9911
5375 Medpace Way Cincinnati (45227) *(G-2856)*

Medpace Holdings Inc (PA).................513 579-9911
5375 Medpace Way Cincinnati (45227) *(G-2857)*

Medrano USA, Columbus *Also Called: Medrano Usa Inc (G-5095)*

Medrano Usa Inc (PA).................614 272-5856
4311 Janitrol Rd Ste 500 Columbus (43228) *(G-5095)*

Medtrace, Akron *Also Called: Vertical Data LLC (G-353)*

Medtronic, Cleveland *Also Called: Medtronic Inc (G-4017)*

Medtronic, Independence *Also Called: Cardioinsight Technologies Inc (G-7890)*

Medtronic, Independence *Also Called: Medtronic Inc (G-7908)*

Medtronic Inc.................216 642-1977
5005 Rockside Rd Ste 1160 Cleveland (44131) *(G-4017)*

Medtronic Inc.................763 526-2566
3 Summit Park Dr Ste 400 Independence (44131) *(G-7908)*

Medway Tool Corp.................937 335-7717
2100 Corporate Dr Troy (45373) *(G-13240)*

Meech Sttic Elminators USA Inc.................330 564-2000
1298 Centerview Cir Copley (44321) *(G-5434)*

Meeks Pastry Shop.................419 782-4871
315 Clinton St Defiance (43512) *(G-6121)*

Meese Inc.. 440 998-1202
4920 State Rd Ashtabula (44004) *(G-604)*

Mega Plastics Co....................................... 330 527-2211
10610 Freedom St Garrettsville (44231) *(G-7226)*

Mega Techway Inc (PA)............................. 440 605-0700
760 Beta Dr Ste F Cleveland (44143) *(G-4018)*

Megadyne Medical Products Inc................. 801 576-9669
4545 Creek Rd Blue Ash (45242) *(G-1307)*

Megalift, Grove City *Also Called: Megalift LLC (G-7398)*

Megalift LLC.. 614 696-9086
2087 Hendrix Dr Grove City (43123) *(G-7398)*

Meggitt (erlanger) LLC.............................. 513 851-5550
10293 Burlington Rd Cincinnati (45231) *(G-2858)*

Meggitt Arcft Brking Systems C (DH)......... 330 796-4400
1204 Massillon Rd Akron (44306) *(G-228)*

Meggitt Polymers & Composites................. 513 851-5550
10293 Burlington Rd Cincinnati (45231) *(G-2859)*

Megna Plastics, Cleveland *Also Called: Dal-Little Fabricating Inc (G-3598)*

Mehaffie Pie Company, Dayton *Also Called: K & B Acquisitions Inc (G-5837)*

MEI, Wapakoneta *Also Called: Midwest Elastomers Inc (G-13722)*

Meierjohan-Wengler Inc............................ 513 771-6074
10340 Julian Dr Cincinnati (45215) *(G-2860)*

Meiers Wine Cellars Inc............................ 513 891-2900
6955 Plainfield Rd Cincinnati (45236) *(G-2861)*

Meigs County Coal Company..................... 740 338-3100
46226 National Rd Saint Clairsville (43950) *(G-11700)*

Meiring Precision, Ludlow Falls *Also Called: Marmax Machine Co (G-8672)*

Meister Media Worldwide, Willoughby *Also Called: Meister Media Worldwide Inc (G-14486)*

Meister Media Worldwide Inc (PA).............. 440 942-2000
4420 Sherwin Rd Ste 4 Willoughby (44094) *(G-14486)*

Meistermatic Inc....................................... 216 481-7773
12446 Bentbrook Dr Chesterland (44026) *(G-2235)*

Mek Van Wert Inc..................................... 419 203-4902
595 Fox Rd Van Wert (45891) *(G-13542)*

Mel Heitkamp Builders Ltd......................... 419 375-0405
635 Secret Judy Rd Fort Recovery (45846) *(G-6969)*

Mel Wacker Signs Inc............................... 330 832-1726
13076 Barrs St Sw Massillon (44647) *(G-9222)*

Meldrum Mechanical Services.................... 419 535-3500
4455 South Ave Toledo (43615) *(G-13051)*

Melin Tool Company Inc............................ 216 362-4200
5565 Venture Dr Ste C Cleveland (44130) *(G-4019)*

Melink Corporation.................................... 513 685-0958
5140 River Valley Rd Milford (45150) *(G-9943)*

Melinz Industries Inc (PA)......................... 440 946-3512
34099 Melinz Pkwy Unit D Willoughby (44095) *(G-14487)*

Mellott Bronze Inc.................................... 330 435-6304
4634 E Sterling Rd Creston (44217) *(G-5507)*

Melnor Graphics LLC................................ 419 476-8808
5225 Telegraph Rd Toledo (43612) *(G-13052)*

Melvin Stone Co LLC................................ 513 771-0820
11641 Mosteller Rd Ste 2 Cincinnati (45241) *(G-2862)*

Memac Industries Inc................................ 740 653-4815
324 Quarry Rd Se Lancaster (43130) *(G-8210)*

Memphis Smokehouse Inc......................... 216 351-5321
8463 Memphis Ave Cleveland (44144) *(G-4020)*

Menard Inc... 513 250-4566
2789 Cunningham Rd Cincinnati (45241) *(G-2863)*

Menard Inc... 419 998-4348
2614 N Eastown Rd Lima (45807) *(G-8429)*

Menard Inc... 513 583-1444
3787 W State Route 22 3 Loveland (45140) *(G-8642)*

Menards, Loveland *Also Called: Menard Inc (G-8642)*

Menasha, West Jefferson *Also Called: Menasha Packaging Company LLC (G-14165)*

Menasha Packaging Company LLC............. 614 202-4084
131 Enterprise Pkwy West Jefferson (43162) *(G-14165)*

Mendenhall Technical Services Inc............. 513 860-1280
9175 Seward Rd Fairfield (45014) *(G-6754)*

Mennel Milling Company............................ 419 436-5130
320 Findlay St Fostoria (44830) *(G-6989)*

Mennel Milling Company............................ 419 435-8151
611 N Corporate Dr W Fostoria (44830) *(G-6990)*

Mennel Milling Company............................ 419 307-9657
425 S Union St Fostoria (44830) *(G-6991)*

Mennel Milling Company............................ 740 385-6824
1 W Front St Logan (43138) *(G-8521)*

Mennel Milling Company............................ 419 294-2337
7097 County Highway 47 Upper Sandusky (43351) *(G-13448)*

Mennel Milling Company............................ 419 458-3041
110 Railroad St Wharton (43359) *(G-14351)*

Mennel Milling Logan, Logan *Also Called: Mennel Milling Company (G-8521)*

Mennex Processing & Packing, Fostoria *Also Called: Mennel Milling Company (G-6991)*

Mercer Color Corporation.......................... 419 678-8273
425 Hardin St Coldwater (45828) *(G-4582)*

Mercer Tool Corporation............................ 419 394-7277
311 S Park Dr Saint Marys (45885) *(G-11742)*

Merchants Metals LLC............................... 513 942-0268
8760 Global Way Bldg 1 West Chester (45069) *(G-14028)*

Mercury Iron and Steel Co........................ 440 349-1500
6275 Cochran Rd Solon (44139) *(G-12146)*

Mercury Machine Co................................. 440 349-3222
30250 Carter St Solon (44139) *(G-12147)*

Mercury Plastics LLC................................ 440 632-5281
15760 Madison Rd Middlefield (44062) *(G-9808)*

Meriam Instrument, Cleveland *Also Called: Adalet/Scott Fetzer Company (G-3295)*

Meridian, Aurora *Also Called: Meridian LLC (G-678)*

Meridian Arts and Graphics....................... 330 759-9099
16 Belgrade St Youngstown (44505) *(G-14898)*

Meridian Bioscience, Cincinnati *Also Called: Meridian Bioscience Inc (G-2864)*

Meridian Bioscience Inc (PA)..................... 513 271-3700
3471 River Hills Dr Cincinnati (45244) *(G-2864)*

Meridian Industries Inc.............................. 330 359-5809
9901 Chestnut Ridge Rd Nw Beach City (44608) *(G-904)*

Meridian Industries Inc.............................. 330 673-1011
1500 Saint Clair Ave Kent (44240) *(G-8051)*

Meridian Industries Inc.............................. 330 359-5447
7369 Peabody Kent Rd Winesburg (44690) *(G-14607)*

Meridian Life Science Inc (HQ).................. 513 271-3700
3471 River Hills Dr Cincinnati (45244) *(G-2865)*

Meridian LLC.. 330 995-0371
325 Harris Dr Aurora (44202) *(G-678)*

Meridienne International Inc....................... 330 274-8317
125 Lena Dr Aurora (44202) *(G-679)*

Merillat Racing LLC.................................. 419 376-4833
22670 County Road H Archbold (43502) *(G-502)*

Meristem Crop Prfmce Group LLC.............. 833 637-4783
489 Village Park Dr Powell (43065) *(G-11490)*

Merit Brass, Cleveland *Also Called: Merit Brass Co (G-4021)*

Merit Brass Co (PA).................................. 216 261-9800
1 Merit Dr Cleveland (44143) *(G-4021)*

Meritech, Painesville *Also Called: Ohio Associated Entps LLC (G-11101)*

Meritor Inc... 740 348-3270
4009 Columbus Rd Unit 111 Granville (43023) *(G-7317)*

Merksteijn, Warren *Also Called: Reinforcement Systems of Ohio LLC (G-13793)*

Merle Norman Cosmetics Inc..................... 419 282-0630
893 Park Ave W Mansfield (44906) *(G-8824)*

Merritt, Mentor *Also Called: Profac Inc (G-9593)*

Merritt Woodwork, Mentor *Also Called: Profac Inc (G-9594)*

Merryweather, Barberton *Also Called: Merryweather Foam Inc (G-822)*

Merryweather Foam Inc (PA)...................... 330 753-0353
11 Brown St Barberton (44203) *(G-822)*

Mes Painting & Graphics Ltd...................... 614 496-1696
8298 Harlem Rd Westerville (43081) *(G-14268)*

Mes Painting and Graphics........................ 614 496-1696
8298 Harlem Rd Westerville (43081) *(G-14269)*

Mesa Industries Inc (PA)........................... 513 321-2950
4027 Eastern Ave Cincinnati (45226) *(G-2866)*

Mesa Industries Inc.................................. 513 999-9781
4141 Airport Rd Cincinnati (45226) *(G-2867)*

Mesocoat Inc.. 216 453-0866
24112 Rockwell Dr Euclid (44117) *(G-6662)*

Mesocoat Advanced Coating Tech, Euclid *Also Called: Mesocoat Inc (G-6662)*

(G-0000) Company's Geographic Section entry number

Messenger Press, Celina *Also Called: Heitkamp & Kremer Printing Inc (G-2109)*

Messenger Publishing Company.................................. 740 592-6612
9300 Johnson Hollow Rd Athens (45701) *(G-644)*

Messer LLC.. 216 533-7256
6300 Halle Dr Cleveland (44125) *(G-4022)*

Messer LLC.. 419 822-3909
6744 County Road 10 Delta (43515) *(G-6211)*

Messer LLC.. 614 539-2259
1699 Feddern Ave Grove City (43123) *(G-7399)*

Messer LLC.. 419 227-95d5
961 Industry Ave Lima (45804) *(G-8430)*

Messer LLC.. 419 221-5043
1680 Buckeye Rd Lima (45804) *(G-8431)*

Messer LLC.. 513 831-4742
State Road 126160 Glendale-Milford Road Miamiville (45147) *(G-9763)*

Messer LLC.. 330 394-4541
2000 Pine Ave Se Warren (44483) *(G-13782)*

Messinger Press, Celina *Also Called: Society of The Precious Blood (G-2120)*

Mestek Inc.. 419 288-2703
219 S Church St # 200 Bowling Green (43402) *(G-1429)*

Mestek Inc.. 419 288-2703
120 Plin St Bradner (43406) *(G-1454)*

Met Fab Fabrication and Mch...................................... 513 724-3715
2974 Waitensburg Pike Batavia (45103) *(G-872)*

Met-Pro Technologies LLC (HQ).................................. 513 458-2600
4625 Red Bank Rd Cincinnati (45277) *(G-2868)*

Meta Manufacturing Corporation................................ 513 793-6382
8901 Blue Ash Rd Ste 1 Blue Ash (45242) *(G-1308)*

Metal & Wire Products Company.................................. 330 332-1015
1069 Salem Pkwy Salem (44460) *(G-11798)*

Metal & Wire Products Company (PA).......................... 330 332-9448
1065 Salem Pkwy Salem (44460) *(G-11799)*

Metal Building Intr Pdts Co.. 440 322-6500
750 Adams St Elyria (44035) *(G-6562)*

Metal Coaters.. 740 432-7351
530 N 2nd St Cambridge (43725) *(G-1749)*

Metal Coating Company, Lima *Also Called: JM Hamilton Group Inc (G-8422)*

Metal Fabricating Corporation...................................... 216 631-8121
10408 Berea Rd Cleveland (44102) *(G-4023)*

Metal Finishing Divison, Ravenna *Also Called: Allen Aircraft Products Inc (G-11515)*

Metal Forming & Coining LLC (PA).............................. 419 893-8748
1007 Illinois Ave Maumee (43537) *(G-9309)*

Metal Improvement Company LLC................................ 513 489-6484
11131 Luschek Dr Blue Ash (45241) *(G-1309)*

Metal Improvement Company LLC................................ 330 425-1490
1652 Highland Rd Twinsburg (44087) *(G-13339)*

Metal Maintenance Inc.. 513 661-3300
322 N Finley St Cleves (45002) *(G-4544)*

Metal Man Inc.. 614 830-0968
4681 Homer Ohio Ln Ste A Groveport (43125) *(G-7445)*

Metal Manufacturing, Elyria *Also Called: Elyria Metal Spinning Fabg Co (G-6531)*

Metal Marker Manufacturing, North Ridgeville *Also Called: Metal Marker Manufacturing Co (G-10740)*

Metal Marker Manufacturing Co.................................. 440 327-2300
6225 Lear Nagle Rd North Ridgeville (44039) *(G-10740)*

Metal Panel Systems, Cincinnati *Also Called: Metal Panel Systems LLC (G-2869)*

Metal Panel Systems LLC.. 513 554-6120
11401 Rockfield Ct Cincinnati (45241) *(G-2869)*

Metal Products Company (PA)...................................... 330 652-2558
9455 Concord Rd Powell (43065) *(G-11491)*

Metal Sales Manufacturing Corp.................................. 440 319-3779
352 E Erie St Jefferson (44047) *(G-7978)*

Metal Seal & Products Inc.. 440 946-8500
7333 Corporate Blvd Mentor (44060) *(G-9562)*

Metal Seal Precision Ltd (PA)...................................... 440 255-8888
8687 Tyler Blvd Mentor (44060) *(G-9563)*

Metal Seal Precision Ltd.. 440 255-8888
4369 Hamann Pkwy Willoughby (44094) *(G-14488)*

Metal Shredders Inc.. 937 866-0777
5101 Farmersville W Carrollton Rd Miamisburg (45342) *(G-9712)*

Metal Stamping, Cleveland *Also Called: Precision Metal Products Inc (G-4185)*

Metal Stampings Unlimited Inc.................................... 937 328-0206
552 W Johnny Lytle Ave Springfield (45506) *(G-12352)*

Metal-Max Inc.. 330 673-9926
1540 Enterprise Way Kent (44240) *(G-8052)*

Metalbrite Polishing LLC.. 937 278-9739
2445 Neff Rd Unit 4 Dayton (45414) *(G-5874)*

Metalcraft Industries, Northfield *Also Called: Nor-Fab Inc (G-10796)*

Metalcraft Solutions, Akron *Also Called: Acro Tool & Die Company (G-16)*

Metalcrafts, Youngstown *Also Called: P & L Metalcrafts LLC (G-14908)*

Metalex Manufacturing Inc (PA).................................. 513 489-0507
5750 Cornell Rd Blue Ash (45242) *(G-1310)*

Metalfab Group.. 440 543-6234
10145 Philipp Pkwy Streetsboro (44241) *(G-12509)*

Metalico Akron Inc (HQ).. 330 376-1400
943 Hazel St Akron (44305) *(G-229)*

Metalico Annaco, Akron *Also Called: Metalico Akron Inc (G-229)*

Metallic Resources Inc.. 330 425-3155
2368 E Enterprise Pkwy Twinsburg (44087) *(G-13340)*

Metallics, Cleveland *Also Called: Ironunits LLC (G-3871)*

Metallurgical Service Inc.. 937 294-2681
2221 Arbor Blvd Moraine (45439) *(G-10177)*

Metallus Inc (PA).. 330 471-7000
1835 Dueber Ave Sw Canton (44706) *(G-1944)*

Metallus Inc.. 216 825-2533
2311 Shepler Church Ave Sw Canton (44706) *(G-1945)*

Metallus Inc.. 800 967-1218
4748 Navarre Rd Sw Canton (44706) *(G-1946)*

Metallus Inc.. 330 471-7000
1835 Dueber Ave Sw Canton (44706) *(G-1947)*

Metallus Inc.. 330 471-7000
4511 Faircrest St Sw Canton (44706) *(G-1948)*

Metalphoto of Cincinnati Inc.. 513 772-8281
1080 Skillman Dr Cincinnati (45215) *(G-2870)*

Metaltek Industries Inc.. 937 342-1750
829 Pauline St Springfield (45503) *(G-12353)*

Metaltek International, Sandusky *Also Called: Metaltek International Inc (G-11858)*

Metaltek International Inc.. 419 626-5340
615 W Market St Sandusky (44870) *(G-11858)*

Metalworking Group, The, Cincinnati *Also Called: Mwgh LLC (G-2892)*

Metaullics Systems, Solon *Also Called: Metaullics Systems LP (G-12148)*

Metaullics Systems LP.. 509 926-6212
31935 Aurora Rd Solon (44139) *(G-12148)*

Metcut Research Associates Inc (PA).......................... 513 271-5100
3980 Rosslyn Dr Cincinnati (45209) *(G-2871)*

Metcut Research, Inc., Cincinnati *Also Called: Metcut Research Associates Inc (G-2871)*

Meteor Automotive, Dover *Also Called: Meteor Sealing Systems LLC (G-6253)*

Meteor Creative Inc (DH).. 800 273-1535
1414 Commerce Park Dr Tipp City (45371) *(G-12830)*

Meteor Sealing Systems LLC...................................... 330 343-9595
400 S Tuscarawas Ave Dover (44622) *(G-6253)*

Metokote Corporation.. 937 233-1565
8040 Center Point 70 Blvd Dayton (45424) *(G-5875)*

Metokote Corporation (HQ).. 419 996-7800
1340 Neubrecht Rd Lima (45801) *(G-8432)*

Metro Containers Inc.. 513 351-6800
4927 Beech St Cincinnati (45212) *(G-2872)*

Metro Design Inc.. 440 458-4200
10740 Middle Ave Elyria (44035) *(G-6563)*

Metro Design Inc.. 440 324-4700
7515 W Ridge Rd Elyria (44035) *(G-6564)*

Metro Flex Inc.. 937 299-5360
3304 Encrete Ln Moraine (45439) *(G-10178)*

Metro Press, Millbury *Also Called: Douthit Communications Inc (G-9959)*

Metromedia Technologies Inc...................................... 330 264-2501
1061 Venture Blvd Wooster (44691) *(G-14665)*

Metron Instruments Inc.. 216 332-0592
5198 Richmond Rd Bedford Heights (44146) *(G-1079)*

Mettler Footwear Inc.. 330 703-0079
704 Westbrook Way Hudson (44236) *(G-7852)*

METTLER-TOLEDO, Columbus *Also Called: Mettler-Toledo Intl Inc (G-4643)*

Mettler-Toledo LLC..614 841-7300
6600 Huntley Rd Columbus (43229) *(G-5096)*

Mettler-Toledo LLC..614 438-4511
720 Dearborn Park Ln Worthington (43085) *(G-14719)*

Mettler-Toledo LLC..614 438-4390
1150 Dearborn Dr Worthington (43085) *(G-14720)*

Mettler-Toledo Intl Inc (PA)...................................614 438-4511
1900 Polaris Pkwy Columbus (43240) *(G-4643)*

Mettler-Toledo LLC (HQ).......................................614 438-4511
1900 Polaris Pkwy Columbus (43240) *(G-4644)*

Mettlr-Tledo Globl Hldings LLC (HQ).....................614 438-4511
1900 Polaris Pkwy Columbus (43240) *(G-4645)*

Metzenbaum Sheltered Inds Inc............................440 729-1919
8090 Cedar Rd Chesterland (44026) *(G-2236)*

Metzger Machine Co..513 241-3360
2165 Spring Grove Ave Cincinnati (45214) *(G-2873)*

Metzgers..419 861-8611
150 Arco Dr Toledo (43607) *(G-13053)*

Metzgers, Toledo *Also Called: Tj Metzgers Inc (G-13143)*

Mexichem Specialty Resins Inc (HQ).....................440 930-1435
33653 Walker Rd Avon Lake (44012) *(G-765)*

Meyer Company (PA)...216 587-3400
7180 Sugar Bush Ln Chagrin Falls (44022) *(G-2148)*

Meyer Design Inc...330 434-9176
100 N High St Akron (44308) *(G-230)*

Meyer Products LLC...216 486-1313
18513 Euclid Ave Cleveland (44112) *(G-4024)*

Meyer Products LLC...216 486-1313
324 N 7th St Steubenville (43952) *(G-12406)*

Meyer Tool Inc (PA)...513 681-7362
3055 Colerain Ave Cincinnati (45225) *(G-2874)*

Meyerpt, Hudson *Also Called: Boxout LLC (G-7835)*

Meyers Printing & Design Inc................................937 461-6000
254 Leo St Dayton (45404) *(G-5876)*

MFC Drilling Inc...740 622-5600
46281 Us Highway 36 Coshocton (43812) *(G-5460)*

Mfg Composite Systems Company.........................440 997-5851
2925 Mfg Pl Ashtabula (44004) *(G-605)*

Mfg CSC, Ashtabula *Also Called: Mfg Composite Systems Company (G-605)*

Mfh Partners Inc (PA)..440 461-4100
6650 Beta Dr Cleveland (44143) *(G-4025)*

Mfi, Cincinnati *Also Called: Mechanical Finishers Inc LLC (G-2853)*

Mfm Building Products Corp..................................740 622-2645
425 Brewer Ln Coshocton (43812) *(G-5461)*

Mfm Building Products Corp (PA)..........................740 622-2645
525 Orange St Coshocton (43812) *(G-5462)*

Mfs Supply LLC (PA)...800 607-0541
31100 Solon Rd Ste 16 Solon (44139) *(G-12149)*

MGF Sourcing, Columbus *Also Called: MGF Sourcing US LLC (G-5097)*

MGF Sourcing US LLC (HQ)....................................614 904-3300
4200 Regent St Ste 205 Columbus (43219) *(G-5097)*

MGM Construction Inc...440 234-7660
1480 W Bagley Rd Ste 1 Berea (44017) *(G-1182)*

MGM Roofing, Berea *Also Called: MGM Construction Inc (G-1182)*

MH & Son Machining & Wldg Co............................419 621-0690
210 W Perkins Ave Ste 10 Sandusky (44870) *(G-11859)*

Mhi, Cincinnati *Also Called: Micropyretics Heaters Intl Inc (G-2877)*

Miami Control Systems Inc.....................................937 233-8146
4433 Interpoint Blvd Dayton (45424) *(G-5877)*

Miami Graphics Services Inc..................................937 698-4013
225 N Jay St West Milton (45383) *(G-14183)*

Miami Ice Machine Inc...513 863-6707
4251 Riverside Dr Overpeck (45055) *(G-11060)*

Miami Machine, Cleves *Also Called: Pohl Machining Inc (G-4546)*

Miami Machine Corporation...................................513 863-6707
4251 Riverside Dr Overpeck (45055) *(G-11061)*

Miami Specialties Inc...937 778-1850
172 Robert M Davis Pkwy Piqua (45356) *(G-11366)*

Miami Valley Eductl Cmpt Assn.............................937 767-1468
888 Dayton St Unit 102 Yellow Springs (45387) *(G-14789)*

Miami Valley Lighting LLC.....................................937 224-6000
1065 Woodman Dr Dayton (45432) *(G-5620)*

Miami Valley Meals Inc..937 938-7141
428 S Edwin C Moses Blvd Dayton (45402) *(G-5878)*

Miami Valley Plastics Inc.......................................937 273-3200
310 S Main St Eldorado (45321) *(G-6480)*

Miami Valley Polishing LLC....................................937 615-9353
211 S Lester Ave Sidney (45365) *(G-12034)*

Miami Valley Precision Inc.....................................937 866-1804
1944 Byers Rd Miamisburg (45342) *(G-9713)*

Miami Valley Publishing LLC..................................937 879-5678
678 Yellow Springs Fairfield Rd Fairborn (45324) *(G-6696)*

Miami Vly Counters & Spc Inc...............................937 865-0562
8515 Dayton Cincinnati Pike Miamisburg (45342) *(G-9714)*

Miami Vly Mfg & Assembly Inc..............................937 254-6665
1889 Radio Rd Dayton (45431) *(G-5621)*

Miami Vly Packg Solutions Inc..............................937 224-1800
1752 Stanley Ave Dayton (45404) *(G-5879)*

Miami-Cast Inc..937 866-2951
901 N Main St Miamisburg (45342) *(G-9715)*

Miamisburg Coating..937 866-1323
925 N Main St Miamisburg (45342) *(G-9716)*

Miamisburg News, Miamisburg *Also Called: Cox Newspapers LLC (G-9684)*

Miba Bearings US LLC...740 962-4242
5037 N State Route 60 Nw Mcconnelsville (43756) *(G-9364)*

Miba Sinter USA LLC..740 962-4242
5045 N State Route 60 Nw Mcconnelsville (43756) *(G-9365)*

Mic-Ray Metal Products Inc...................................216 791-2206
9016 Manor Ave Cleveland (44104) *(G-4026)*

Micc Manufacturing Corporation...........................567 331-0101
26695 Eckel Rd Perrysburg (43551) *(G-11239)*

Miceli Dairy Products Co (PA)................................216 791-6222
2721 E 90th St Cleveland (44104) *(G-4027)*

Michael Byrne Manufacturing Co Inc.....................419 525-1214
1855 Earth Boring Rd Mansfield (44903) *(G-8825)*

Michael Day Enterprises LLC.................................330 335-5100
9774 Trease Rd Wadsworth (44281) *(G-13650)*

Michael Kaufman Companies Inc...........................330 673-4881
845 Overholt Rd Kent (44240) *(G-8053)*

Michael W Hyes Desgr Goldsmith..........................440 519-0889
28200 Miles Rd Unit F Solon (44139) *(G-12150)*

Michael W Newton...740 352-9334
768 Fairground Rd Lucasville (45648) *(G-8668)*

Michael Zakany LLC...740 221-3934
601 Putnam Ave Zanesville (43701) *(G-15028)*

Michaels Pre-Cast Con Pdts Inc.............................513 683-1292
1917 Adams Rd Loveland (45140) *(G-8643)*

Michalek Manufacturing LLC.................................740 763-0910
160 Obannon Ave Newark (43055) *(G-10519)*

Michel Tires Plus 227565, Cincinnati *Also Called: Bridgestone Ret Operations LLC (G-2426)*

Michele Caldwell...937 505-7744
3421 Olive Rd Dayton (45426) *(G-5880)*

Michelman, Cincinnati *Also Called: Michelman Inc (G-2875)*

Michelman Inc (PA)...513 793-7766
9080 Shell Rd Cincinnati (45236) *(G-2875)*

Michigan Silkscreen Inc..419 885-1163
5354 Whiteford Rd Sylvania (43560) *(G-12715)*

Michigan Sugar Company......................................419 332-9931
1101 N Front St Fremont (43420) *(G-7123)*

Miconvi Properties Inc...440 954-3500
37200 Research Dr Eastlake (44095) *(G-6435)*

Micro Industries Corporation (PA)..........................740 548-7878
8399 Green Meadows Dr N Westerville (43081) *(G-14270)*

Micro Laboratories Inc..440 918-0001
7158 Industrial Park Blvd Mentor (44060) *(G-9564)*

Micro Machine Ltd...330 438-7078
275 7th St Sw Brewster (44613) *(G-1492)*

Micro Machine Works Inc.......................................740 678-8471
8900 State Route 339 Vincent (45784) *(G-13622)*

Micro Metal Finishing LLC.....................................513 541-3095
3448 Spring Grove Ave Cincinnati (45225) *(G-2876)*

Micro Products Co Inc..440 943-0258
26653 Curtiss Wright Pkwy Willoughby Hills (44092) *(G-14560)*

(G-0000) Company's Geographic Section entry number

Micro-Pise Msrment Systems LLC.................... 330 541-9100
555 Mondial Pkwy Streetsboro (44241) *(G-12510)*

Microcom Corporation.................... 740 548-6262
855 Corduroy Rd Lewis Center (43035) *(G-8343)*

Microfinish, Vandalia *Also Called: Microfinish LLC (G-13571)*

Microfinish LLC.................... 937 264-1598
865 Scholz Dr Vandalia (45377) *(G-13571)*

Micromd.................... 850 217-7412
790 Boardman Canfield Rd Youngstown (44512) *(G-14899)*

Micron Manufacturing Inc.................... 440 355-4200
186 Commerce Dr Lagrange (44050) *(G-8151)*

Microplex Inc.................... 330 498-0600
7568 Whipple Ave Nw North Canton (44720) *(G-10651)*

Microplex Printware Corp.................... 440 374-2424
30300 Solon Industrial Pkwy Ste E Solon (44139) *(G-12151)*

Micropower Group US Inc.................... 937 606-2793
150 Marybill Dr S Troy (45373) *(G-13241)*

Micropower LLC.................... 937 606-2793
150 Marybill Dr S Troy (45373) *(G-13242)*

Micropure Filtration Inc.................... 952 472-2323
837 E 79th St Cleveland (44103) *(G-4028)*

Micropyretics Heaters Intl Inc.................... 513 772-0404
750 Redna Ter Cincinnati (45215) *(G-2877)*

Microsheen Corporation.................... 216 481-5610
1100 E 222nd St Ste 1 Cleveland (44117) *(G-4029)*

Microsoft, Cleveland *Also Called: Microsoft Corporation (G-4030)*

Microsoft, Columbus *Also Called: Microsoft Corporation (G-4646)*

Microsoft Corporation.................... 216 986-1440
6050 Oak Tree Blvd Ste 300 Cleveland (44131) *(G-4030)*

Microsoft Corporation.................... 614 719-5900
8800 Lyra Dr Ste 400 Columbus (43240) *(G-4646)*

Microsun Lamps LLC.................... 888 328-8701
7890 Center Point 70 Blvd Dayton (45424) *(G-5881)*

Microtek Finishing LLC.................... 513 766-5600
5579 Spellmire Dr West Chester (45246) *(G-14133)*

Mid, Columbus *Also Called: Minimally Invasive Devices Inc (G-5104)*

Mid America Tire of Hillsboro Inc.................... 937 393-3520
108 Willetsville Pike Hillsboro (45133) *(G-7720)*

Mid American Publishing.................... 419 822-5662
7227 County Road D Delta (43515) *(G-6212)*

Mid American Ventures Inc.................... 216 524-0974
7600 Wall St Ste 205 Cleveland (44125) *(G-4031)*

Mid Ohio Net, Delaware *Also Called: Delaware Gazette Company (G-6143)*

Mid Ohio Wood Products Inc.................... 740 323-0427
535 Franklin Ave Newark (43056) *(G-10520)*

Mid Ohio Wood Recycling Inc.................... 419 673-8470
16289 State Route 31 Kenton (43326) *(G-8107)*

Mid West Fabricating Co, Amanda *Also Called: Mid-West Fabricating Co (G-424)*

Mid-America Chemical Corp.................... 216 749-0100
4701 Spring Rd Cleveland (44131) *(G-4032)*

Mid-America Packaging LLC.................... 330 963-4199
2127 Reiser Ave Se New Philadelphia (44663) *(G-10457)*

Mid-America Stainless, Cleveland *Also Called: Mid-America Steel Corp (G-4033)*

Mid-America Steel Corp.................... 800 282-3466
20900 Saint Clair Ave Rear Cleveland (44117) *(G-4033)*

Mid-America Store Fixtures, Columbus *Also Called: Global Retail Partners LLC (G-4958)*

Mid-American Publishing, Delta *Also Called: Mid American Publishing (G-6212)*

Mid-Continent Minerals Corp (PA).................... 216 283-5700
20600 Chagrin Blvd Ste 850 Cleveland (44122) *(G-4034)*

Mid-Ohio Electric Co.................... 614 274-8000
1170 Mckinley Ave Columbus (43222) *(G-5098)*

Mid-Ohio Products Inc.................... 614 771-2795
4329 Reynolds Dr Hilliard (43026) *(G-7686)*

Mid-Ohio Screen Print Inc.................... 614 875-1774
4163 Kelnor Dr Grove City (43123) *(G-7400)*

Mid-State Sales, Columbus *Also Called: Mid-State Sales Inc (G-5099)*

Mid-State Sales Inc.................... 330 744-2158
519 N Meridian Rd Youngstown (44509) *(G-14900)*

Mid-State Sales Inc (PA).................... 614 864-1811
1101 Gahanna Pkwy Columbus (43230) *(G-5099)*

Mid-West Fabricating Co (PA).................... 740 969-4411
313 N Johns St Amanda (43102) *(G-424)*

Mid-West Fabricating Co.................... 740 277-7021
885 Mill Park Dr Lancaster (43130) *(G-8211)*

Mid-West Forge Corporation (PA).................... 216 481-3030
2778 Som Center Rd Ste 200 Willoughby (44094) *(G-14489)*

Mid-Wood Inc.................... 419 257-3331
101 E State St North Baltimore (45872) *(G-10614)*

Mid's Spaghetti Sauce, Navarre *Also Called: RC Industries Inc (G-10313)*

Middaugh Enterprises Inc.................... 330 852-2471
211 Yoder Ave Ne Sugarcreek (44681) *(G-12641)*

Middlebury Cheese Company LLC.................... 330 893-2500
5060 State Route 557 Millersburg (44654) *(G-9997)*

Middlefield Glass Incorporated.................... 440 632-5699
17447 Kinsman Rd Middlefield (44062) *(G-9809)*

Middlefield Pallet Inc.................... 440 632-0553
15940 Burton Windsor Rd Middlefield (44062) *(G-9810)*

Middlefield Plastics Inc.................... 440 834-4638
15235 Burton Windsor Rd Middlefield (44062) *(G-9811)*

Middleton Llyd Dolls Inc (PA).................... 740 989-2082
23689 Mountain Bell Rd Coolville (45723) *(G-5426)*

Middleton Enterprises Inc.................... 614 885-2514
7100 N High St Worthington (43085) *(G-14721)*

Middleton Printing Co Inc.................... 614 294-7277
81 Mill St Ste 300 Gahanna (43230) *(G-7166)*

Middletown License Agency Inc.................... 513 422-7225
3232 Roosevelt Blvd Middletown (45044) *(G-9879)*

Middlfeld Original Cheese Coop.................... 440 632-5567
16942 Kinsman Rd Middlefield (44062) *(G-9812)*

Middlton Lloyd Doll Fctry Outl, Coolville *Also Called: Middleton Llyd Dolls Inc (G-5426)*

Midlake Products & Mfg Co.................... 330 875-4202
819 N Nickelplate St Louisville (44641) *(G-8608)*

Midland Engineering, Canton *Also Called: Decision Systems Inc (G-1879)*

Midlands Millroom Supply Inc.................... 330 453-9100
1911 36th St Ne Canton (44705) *(G-1949)*

Midmark Corporation (PA).................... 937 528-7500
10170 Penny Ln Ste 300 Miamisburg (45342) *(G-9717)*

Midmark Corporation.................... 937 526-3662
60 Vista Dr Versailles (45380) *(G-13600)*

Midmark Corporation.................... 937 526-8387
160 Industrial Pkwy Versailles (45380) *(G-13601)*

Midstate Machine, Cincinnati *Also Called: McSwain Manufacturing LLC (G-2852)*

Midstate Machine Ohio Facility.................... 513 619-1222
189 Container Pl Cincinnati (45246) *(G-2878)*

Midtown Pallet & Recycling Inc.................... 419 241-1311
1987 Hawthorne St Toledo (43606) *(G-13054)*

Midway Machining Inc.................... 740 373 0076
1060 Gravel Bank Rd Marietta (45750) *(G-8929)*

Midway Products, Findlay *Also Called: P & A Industries Inc (G-6906)*

Midway Products Group, Greenwich *Also Called: Lakepark Industries Inc (G-7363)*

Midway Products Group Inc.................... 419 422-7070
2045 Industrial Dr Findlay (45840) *(G-6893)*

Midwest Aircraft Products Co.................... 419 884-2164
125 S Mill St Mansfield (44904) *(G-8826)*

Midwest Box Company.................... 216 281-9021
9801 Walford Ave Ste C Cleveland (44102) *(G-4035)*

Midwest Centerless Grinding, Cincinnati *Also Called: A and V Grinding Inc (G-2324)*

Midwest Commercial Mllwk Inc.................... 419 224-5001
514 N Union St Lima (45801) *(G-8433)*

Midwest Composites LLC.................... 419 738-2431
302 Krein Ave Wapakoneta (45895) *(G-13721)*

Midwest Compost Inc.................... 419 547-7979
7250 State Route 101 E Clyde (43410) *(G-4560)*

Midwest Conveyor Products Inc.................... 419 281-1235
1919 Cellar Dr Ashland (44805) *(G-552)*

Midwest Curtainwalls Inc.................... 216 641-7900
5171 Grant Ave Cleveland (44125) *(G-4036)*

Midwest Cylinder, Harrison *Also Called: Kaplan Industries Inc (G-7558)*

Midwest Die Supply Company.................... 419 729-7141
6240 American Rd Ste A Toledo (43612) *(G-13055)*

Midwest Distribution Center, Columbus *Also Called: BASF Corporation (G-4745)*

Midwest Division, Hebron *Also Called: Diebold Nixdorf Incorporated (G-7612)*

Midwest Elastomers Inc.. 419 738-8844
700 Industrial Dr Wapakoneta (45895) *(G-13722)*

Midwest Fabrications Inc.. 330 633-0191
516 Commerce St Tallmadge (44278) *(G-12741)*

Midwest Filtration LLC... 513 874-6510
9775 International Blvd Cincinnati (45246) *(G-2879)*

Midwest Glycol Services LLC.. 419 946-3326
116 Lawrence Ave Marion (43302) *(G-8978)*

Midwest Knife Grinding Inc... 330 854-1030
492 Elm Ridge Ave Ste 4 Canal Fulton (44614) *(G-1778)*

Midwest Laser Systems Inc.. 419 424-0062
4777 S Us Highway 23 Alvada (44802) *(G-422)*

Midwest Machine Service Inc.. 216 631-8151
4700 Train Ave Ste 1 Cleveland (44102) *(G-4037)*

Midwest Marketing, Newark *Also Called: Midwest Menu Mate Inc (G-10521)*

Midwest Menu Mate Inc.. 740 323-2599
1065 Lizabeth Cir Newark (43056) *(G-10521)*

Midwest Metal Fabricators... 419 739-7077
712 Maple St Wapakoneta (45895) *(G-13723)*

Midwest Metal Fabricators Ltd....................................... 419 739-7077
712 Maple St Wapakoneta (45895) *(G-13724)*

Midwest Metal Products LLC... 614 539-7322
3945 Brookham Dr Grove City (43123) *(G-7401)*

Midwest Mold & Texture Corp....................................... 513 732-1300
4270 Armstrong Blvd Batavia (45103) *(G-873)*

Midwest Motoplex LLC.. 740 772-5300
98 Consumer Center Dr Chillicothe (45601) *(G-2266)*

Midwest Motor Supply Co (PA)...................................800 233-1294
4800 Roberts Rd Columbus (43228) *(G-5100)*

Midwest Muffler Pros & More.. 937 293-2450
3061 Dryden Rd Moraine (45439) *(G-10179)*

Midwest Plastics, Lima *Also Called: W T Inc (G-8458)*

Midwest Precision... 216 658-0058
1000 Valley Belt Rd Brooklyn Heights (44131) *(G-1535)*

Midwest Precision Holdings Inc (HQ)............................440 497-4086
34700 Lakeland Blvd Eastlake (44095) *(G-6436)*

Midwest Precision LLC.. 440 951-2333
34700 Lakeland Blvd Eastlake (44095) *(G-6437)*

Midwest Retail Services Inc.. 800 576-7577
7920 Industrial Pkwy Plain City (43064) *(G-11414)*

Midwest Rlwy Prsrvtion Soc Inc.................................... 216 781-3629
2800 W 3rd St Cleveland (44113) *(G-4038)*

Midwest Sea Salt Company LLC.................................... 513 770-9177
8694 Rite Track Way West Chester (45069) *(G-14029)*

Midwest Security Services... 937 853-9000
4050 Benfield Dr Dayton (45429) *(G-5882)*

Midwest Service, Middletown *Also Called: Vail Rubber Works Inc (G-9901)*

Midwest Specialties Inc.. 800 837-2503
705 Commerce Rd Wapakoneta (45895) *(G-13725)*

Midwest Specialty Pdts Co Inc...................................... 513 874-7070
280 Northpointe Dr Fairfield (45014) *(G-6755)*

Midwest Strapping Products.. 614 527-1454
1819 Walcutt Rd Ste 13 Columbus (43228) *(G-5101)*

Midwest Tool & Engineering Co
112 Webster St Dayton (45402) *(G-5883)*

Midwest Wood Trim Inc... 419 592-3389
1650 Commerce Dr Napoleon (43545) *(G-10291)*

Midwestern Industries Inc (PA)..................................... 330 837-4203
915 Oberlin Ave Sw Massillon (44648) *(G-9223)*

Mielke Furniture Repair Inc... 419 625-4572
3209 Columbus Ave Sandusky (44870) *(G-11860)*

Miiler Brewing Company.. 513 896-9200
2525 Wayne Madison Rd Trenton (45067) *(G-13193)*

Mika Metal Fabricating, Willoughby *Also Called: Weybridge LLC (G-14549)*

Mike Loppe... 937 969-8102
2 W Main St Tremont City (45372) *(G-13189)*

Mike-Sells Potato Chip Co.. 937 228-9400
1610 Stanley Ave Dayton (45404) *(G-5884)*

Mike-Sells Potato Chip Co (HQ)................................... 937 228-9400
333 Leo St Dayton (45404) *(G-5885)*

Mike-Sells Potato Chip Co.. 937 228-9400
155 N College St Sabina (45169) *(G-11679)*

Mike-Sells West Virginia Inc (PA)................................ 937 228-9400
333 Leo St Dayton (45404) *(G-5886)*

Mikes Transm & Auto Svc LLC..................................... 330 799-8266
202 S Meridian Rd Youngstown (44509) *(G-14901)*

Mikesells Snack Fd Co Dist Ctr, Dayton *Also Called: Mike-Sells Potato Chip Co (G-5884)*

Mikron Industries Inc.. 859 623-2643
388 S Main St Ste 700 Akron (44311) *(G-231)*

Mikron Industries Inc (HQ)...713 961-4600
388 S Main St Ste 700 Akron (44311) *(G-232)*

Mil-Mar Century Corporation.. 937 275-4860
8641 Washington Church Rd Miamisburg (45342) *(G-9718)*

Milacron, Batavia *Also Called: Milacron Holdings Corp (G-874)*

Milacron Holdings Corp (HQ).. 513 487-5000
4165 Half Acre Rd Batavia (45103) *(G-874)*

Milacron LLC (DH).. 513 487-5000
10200 Alliance Rd Ste 200 Cincinnati (45242) *(G-2880)*

Milacron Marketing Company LLC (DH).......................... 513 536-2000
4165 Half Acre Rd Batavia (45103) *(G-875)*

Milacron Plas Tech Group LLC (DH)............................... 513 536-2000
4165 Half Acre Rd Batavia (45103) *(G-876)*

Milacron Plas Tech Group LLC...................................... 937 444-2532
418 W Main St Mount Orab (45154) *(G-10219)*

Milan Tool Corp.. 216 661-1078
8989 Brookpark Rd Cleveland (44129) *(G-4039)*

Milark Industries, Mansfield *Also Called: Hayford Technologies Inc (G-8800)*

Milark Industries Inc... 419 524-7627
520 S Airport Rd Mansfield (44903) *(G-8827)*

Milark Industries Inc (PA)..419 524-7627
536 S Airport Rd Mansfield (44903) *(G-8828)*

Milathan Wholesalers.. 614 697-1458
423 N Front St 237 Columbus (43215) *(G-5102)*

Miles Folding Box Co Div, Cleveland *Also Called: Sobel Corrugated Containers Inc (G-4311)*

Miles Midprint Inc... 216 860-4770
1215 W 10th St Ste B Cleveland (44113) *(G-4040)*

Miles Rubber & Packing Company (PA).......................... 330 425-3888
9020 Dutton Dr Twinsburg (44087) *(G-13341)*

Milestone Services Corp... 330 374-9988
551 Beacon St Akron (44311) *(G-233)*

Milford Printers (PA)..513 831-6630
317 Main St Milford (45150) *(G-9944)*

Military Spec Packaging, Columbus *Also Called: Tri-W Group Inc (G-5332)*

Milk Hney Cndy Soda Shoppe LLC............................... 330 492-5884
3400 Cleveland Ave Nw Ste 1 Canton (44709) *(G-1950)*

Mill & Motion Inc.. 216 524-4000
5415 E Schaaf Rd Independence (44131) *(G-7909)*

Mill & Motion Properties Ltd... 216 524-4000
5415 E Schaaf Rd Independence (44131) *(G-7910)*

Mill Brook, Euclid *Also Called: Schwebel Baking Company (G-6678)*

Mill Rose Laboratories Inc.. 440 974-6730
7310 Corp Blvd Mentor (44060) *(G-9565)*

Mill-Rose, Mentor *Also Called: Mill-Rose Company (G-9566)*

Mill-Rose Company (PA)...440 255-9171
7995 Tyler Blvd Mentor (44060) *(G-9566)*

Millat Industries Corp... 937 535-1500
7611 Center Point 70 Blvd Dayton (45424) *(G-5887)*

Millat Industries Corp (PA)... 937 434-6666
4901 Croftshire Dr Dayton (45440) *(G-5888)*

Millcraft Group LLC (PA)..216 441-5500
9000 Rio Nero Dr Independence (44131) *(G-7911)*

Millcraft Purchasing Corp... 216 441-5505
6800 Grant Ave Cleveland (44105) *(G-4041)*

Millennium, Ashtabula *Also Called: Ineos Pigments USA Inc (G-598)*

Millennium Adhesive Pdts LLC..................................... 440 708-1212
178 E Washington St Ste 1 Chagrin Falls (44022) *(G-2149)*

Millennium Machine Tech LLC...................................... 440 269-8080
38323 Apollo Pkwy Ste 7 Willoughby (44094) *(G-14490)*

Millennium Plant, Massillon *Also Called: Shearers Foods LLC (G-9242)*

Millennium Printing LLC.. 513 489-3000
11401 Deerfield Rd Blue Ash (45242) *(G-1311)*

Miller Bearing Company Inc.. 330 678-8844
420 Portage Blvd Kent (44240) *(G-8054)*

Miller Bros Paving Inc (HQ)... 419 445-1015
1613 S Defiance St Archbold (43502) *(G-503)*

Miller Cabinet Ltd... 614 873-4221
6217 Converse Huff Rd Plain City (43064) *(G-11415)*

Miller Castings Inc... 330 482-2923
1634 Lower Elkton Rd Columbiana (44408) *(G-4622)*

Miller Consolidated Inds Inc, Moraine Also Called: McOn Inds Inc *(G-10176)*

Miller Core II Inc.. 330 359-0500
9823 Chestnut Ridge Rd Nw Beach City (44608) *(G-905)*

Miller Engine & Machine Co, Springfield Also Called: Muller Engine & Machine Co *(G-12354)*

Miller Express Inc.. 330 714-6751
828 Dogwood Ter Copley (44321) *(G-5435)*

Miller Logging Inc.. 330 279-4721
8373 State Route 83 Holmesville (44633) *(G-7802)*

Miller Lumber Co Inc.. 330 674-0273
7101 State Route 39 Millersburg (44654) *(G-9998)*

Miller Manufacturing Inc.. 330 852-0689
2705 Shetler Rd Nw Sugarcreek (44681) *(G-12642)*

Miller Plating LLC.. 330 952-2550
940 Lafayette Rd Medina (44256) *(G-9427)*

Miller Precision Manufacturing Industries Inc................. 419 453-3251
131 Progressive Dr Ottoville (45876) *(G-11056)*

Miller Printing Co, Springfield Also Called: Graphic Paper Products Corp *(G-12315)*

Miller Products Inc.. 330 308-5934
642 Wabash Ave Nw New Philadelphia (44663) *(G-10458)*

Miller Products Inc.. 330 335-3110
985 Seville Rd Wadsworth (44281) *(G-13651)*

Miller Products Inc.. 330 335-3110
985 Seville Rd Wadsworth (44281) *(G-13652)*

Miller Products Inc (PA).. 330 938-2134
450 Courtney Rd Sebring (44672) *(G-11897)*

Miller Studio Inc.. 330 339-1100
734 Fair Ave Nw New Philadelphia (44663) *(G-10459)*

Miller Weldmaster Corporation (PA).............................. 330 833-6739
4220 Alabama Ave Sw Navarre (44662) *(G-10307)*

Miller Wood Design, Sugarcreek Also Called: Miller Manufacturing Inc *(G-12642)*

Miller-Holzwarth Inc.. 330 342-7224
450 W Pershing St Salem (44460) *(G-11800)*

Miller, Jim Furniture, Springfield Also Called: Hallmark Industries Inc *(G-12316)*

Millers Aplus Cmpt Svcs LLC.. 330 620-5288
1067 Mercer Ave Akron (44320) *(G-234)*

Millers Storage Barns LLC.. 330 893-3293
4230 State Route 39 Millersburg (44654) *(G-9999)*

Millersburg Ice Company.. 330 674-3016
25 S Grant St Millersburg (44654) *(G-10000)*

Millertech Energy Solutions.. 855 629-5484
17795 Farmington Rd West Farmington (44491) *(G-14159)*

Millprint, Blue Ash Also Called: Millennium Printing LLC *(G-1311)*

Mills Metal Finishing, Columbus Also Called: Mmf Incorporated *(G-5106)*

Mills Partition Company LLC.. 740 375-0770
3007 Harding Hwy E Bldg 201 Marion (43302) *(G-8979)*

Mills Pride Premier Inc.. 740 941-1300
423 Hopewell Rd Waverly (45690) *(G-13867)*

Millstone Coffee Inc (HQ)... 513 983-1100
1 Procter And Gamble Plz Cincinnati (45202) *(G-2881)*

Milltree Lumber Holdings... 740 226-2090
535 Coal Dock Rd Waverly (45690) *(G-13868)*

Millwood Inc.. 330 857-3075
8208 S Kohler Rd Apple Creek (44606) *(G-471)*

Millwood Inc.. 216 881-1414
4201 Lakeside Ave E Cleveland (44114) *(G-4042)*

Millwood Inc.. 330 359-5220
18279 Dover Rd Dundee (44624) *(G-6368)*

Millwood Inc.. 440 914-0540
30311 Emerald Valley Pkwy Ste 300 Solon (44139) *(G-12152)*

Millwood Inc.. 330 609-0220
1328 Ridge Rd Vienna (44473) *(G-13614)*

Millwood Inc.. 740 226-2090
535 Coal Dock Rd Waverly (45690) *(G-13869)*

Millwood Inc.. 513 860-4567
4438 Muhlhauser Rd Ste 100 West Chester (45011) *(G-14030)*

Millwood Incorporated... 330 704-6707
13407 Dover Rd Apple Creek (44606) *(G-472)*

Millwood Logging, Gnadenhutten Also Called: Millwood Lumber Inc *(G-7291)*

Millwood Lumber Inc... 740 254-4681
2400 Larson Rd Se Gnadenhutten (44629) *(G-7291)*

Millwood Natural LLC.. 330 393-4400
3708 International Blvd Vienna (44473) *(G-13615)*

Millwood Pallet Co, Dundee Also Called: Millwood Inc *(G-6368)*

Millwood Wholesale Inc... 330 359-6109
7969 Township Road 662 Dundee (44624) *(G-6369)*

Millwork Elements LLC.. 614 905-8163
6663 Huntley Rd Ste A Columbus (43229) *(G-5103)*

Millwright, Spring Valley Also Called: PMRservices LLC *(G-12242)*

Milos Whole World Gourmet LLC................................... 740 589-6456
296 S Harper St Nelsonville (45764) *(G-10319)*

Milsek Furniture Polish Inc... 330 542-2700
1351 Quaker Cir Salem (44460) *(G-11801)*

Mim Software Inc (HQ).. 216 455-0600
25800 Science Park Dr Ste 180 Beachwood (44122) *(G-930)*

Minco Group, Vandalia Also Called: Minco Tool and Mold Inc *(G-13572)*

Minco Group, The, Dayton Also Called: Minco Tool and Mold Inc *(G-5889)*

Minco Tool and Mold Inc (PA)....................................... 937 890-7905
5690 Webster St Dayton (45414) *(G-5889)*

Minco Tool and Mold Inc... 937 890-0322
900 Falls Creek Dr Vandalia (45377) *(G-13572)*

Mindful, Akron Also Called: Virtual Hold Tech Slutions LLC *(G-354)*

Miner's Bishop Tractor Sales, Rootstown Also Called: Miners Tractor Sales Inc *(G-11649)*

Mineral Processing Company... 419 396-3501
1855 County Highway 99 Carey (43316) *(G-2059)*

Miners Tractor Sales Inc (PA)....................................... 330 325-9914
6941 Tallmadge Rd Rootstown (44272) *(G-11649)*

Minerva Dairy Inc.. 330 868-4196
430 Radloff Ave Minerva (44657) *(G-10042)*

Minerva Maid, Minerva Also Called: Minerva Dairy Inc *(G-10042)*

Minerva Manufacturing Facility, Minerva Also Called: American Axle & Mfg Inc *(G-10033)*

Minerva Operations, Minerva Also Called: Colfor Manufacturing Inc *(G-10036)*

Minerva Tube Plant, Minerva Also Called: Caraustar Indus Cnsmr Pdts Gro *(G-10035)*

Minerva Welding and Fabg Inc...................................... 330 868-7731
22133 Us Route 30 Minerva (44657) *(G-10043)*

Minimally Invasive Devices Inc...................................... 614 484-5036
1275 Kinnear Rd Columbus (43212) *(G-5104)*

Minnich Manufacturing Co Inc....................................... 419 903-0010
1444 State Route 42 Mansfield (44903) *(G-8829)*

Minster Farmers, Minster Also Called: Sunrise Cooperative Inc *(G-10066)*

Minster Farmers Co-Op Exchange, Minster Also Called: Minster Farmers Coop Exch *(G-10061)*

Minster Farmers Coop Exch.. 419 628-4705
292 W 4th St Minster (45865) *(G-10061)*

Minster Machine, Minster Also Called: NIDEC MINSTER CORPORATION *(G-10062)*

Minteq International Inc... 419 636-4561
719 E High St Bryan (43506) *(G-1651)*

Minteq International Inc... 330 343-8821
5864 Crown Street Ext Nw Dover (44622) *(G-6254)*

Minuteman of Heath, Newark Also Called: L & T Collins Inc *(G-10516)*

Minuteman Press, Cincinnati Also Called: Minuteman Press Inc *(G-2882)*

Minuteman Press, Cincinnati Also Called: Mmp Printing Inc *(G-2883)*

Minuteman Press, Columbus Also Called: Capehart Enterprises LLC *(G-4795)*

Minuteman Press, Fairlawn Also Called: Frisby Printing Company *(G-6801)*

Minuteman Press, Kettering Also Called: Jasper Printing Co LLC *(G-8121)*

Minuteman Press, Maumee Also Called: Stepping Stone Enterprises Inc *(G-9320)*

Minuteman Press Inc... 513 741-9056
9904 Colerain Ave Cincinnati (45251) *(G-2882)*

Miracle, Moraine Also Called: Heading4ward Investment Co *(G-10169)*

Miracle Air, Franklin Also Called: Miracle Welding Inc *(G-7034)*

Miracle Welding Inc... 937 746-9977
141 Industrial Dr Ste 200 Franklin (45005) *(G-7034)*

Mirion Technologies Ist Corp.. 614 367-2050
12954 Stonecreek Dr Ste C Pickerington (43147) *(G-11296)*

Mirror Publishing Co Inc.. 419 893-8135
113 W Wayne St Maumee (43537) *(G-9310)*

Mirror, The, Maumee *Also Called: Mirror Publishing Co Inc (G-9310)*

Mirus Adapted Tech LLC...................................... 614 402-4585
288 Cramer Creek Ct Dublin (43017) *(G-6320)*

Mis, Ashland *Also Called: Maverick Innvtive Slutions LLC (G-550)*

Misco Refractometer, Solon *Also Called: Mercury Iron and Steel Co (G-12146)*

Miscor Group, Massillon *Also Called: Magnetech Industrial Svcs Inc (G-9216)*

Miscor Group Ltd... 330 830-3500
800 Nave Rd Se Massillon (44646) *(G-9224)*

Mission Industrial Group LLC.............................. 740 387-2287
3602 Harding Hwy E Marion (43302) *(G-8980)*

Mitchell, Youngstown *Also Called: George A Mitchell Company (G-14866)*

Mitchell Bros Tire Rtread Svc............................. 740 353-1551
1205 Findlay St Portsmouth (45662) *(G-11470)*

Mitchell Brothers Retread Svc, Portsmouth *Also Called: Mitchell Bros Tire Rtread Svc (G-11470)*

Mitchell Piping LLC... 330 245-0258
1101 Sunnyside St Sw Hartville (44632) *(G-7581)*

Mitchell Plastics Inc... 330 825-2461
130 31st St Nw Barberton (44203) *(G-823)*

Mitchellace Inc (PA).. 740 354-2813
830 Murray St Portsmouth (45662) *(G-11471)*

Mitchs Welding & Hitches.................................... 419 893-3117
802 Kingsbury St Maumee (43537) *(G-9311)*

Mitec Powertrain Inc... 567 525-5606
4000 Fostoria Ave Findlay (45840) *(G-6894)*

Mitsubishi Chemical Amer Inc.............................. 419 483-2931
350 N Buckeye St Bellevue (44811) *(G-1126)*

Mitsubishi Chemical Amer Inc.............................. 586 755-1660
350 N Buckeye St Bellevue (44811) *(G-1127)*

Mitsubishi Elc Auto Amer Inc (DH)...................... 513 573-6614
4773 Bethany Rd Mason (45040) *(G-9128)*

Mitsubishi Elc Automtn Inc.................................. 937 492-3058
213 N Ohio Ave Sidney (45365) *(G-12035)*

Mix-Masters Inc.. 513 228-2800
2726 Henkle Dr Lebanon (45036) *(G-8277)*

Mixed Logic LLC.. 440 826-1676
5907 E Law Rd Valley City (44280) *(G-13505)*

Mixmill, Cincinnati *Also Called: Processall Inc (G-2986)*

Mj Bornhorst Enterprises LLC.............................. 937 295-3469
400 Enterprise Dr Fort Loramie (45845) *(G-6951)*

MJB Toledo Inc (HQ)...419 531-2121
3115 Frenchmens Rd Toledo (43607) *(G-13056)*

Mjc Enterprise Inc.. 330 669-3744
7820 Blough Rd Sterling (44276) *(G-12398)*

Mjcj Holdings Inc.. 937 885-0800
2580 Kohnle Dr Miamisburg (45342) *(G-9719)*

MJM Industries Inc... 440 350-1230
1200 East St Fairport Harbor (44077) *(G-6819)*

Mjo Industries Inc (PA)... 800 590-4055
8000 Technology Blvd Huber Heights (45424) *(G-7822)*

Mk Metal Products Inc.. 330 669-2631
301 W Prospect St Smithville (44677) *(G-12066)*

Mk Metal Products Entps Inc (PA)........................419 756-3644
90 Sawyer Pkwy Mansfield (44903) *(G-8830)*

Mk Welding & Fabrication Inc............................... 937 603-4430
1824 E Lower Springboro Rd Waynesville (45068) *(G-13880)*

Mkfour Inc... 620 629-1120
108 Hawks Cove Ct Granville (43023) *(G-7318)*

Mkgs Corp... 937 254-8181
1712 Springfield St Ste 2 Dayton (45403) *(G-5890)*

ML Advertising & Design LLC............................... 419 447-6523
185 Jefferson St Tiffin (44883) *(G-12791)*

ML Erectors LLC.. 440 328-3227
827 Walnut St Elyria (44035) *(G-6565)*

Mlad Graphic Design Services, Tiffin *Also Called: ML Advertising & Design LLC (G-12791)*

Mlb Molded Urethane Pdts LLC............................ 419 825-9140
1680 Us Highway 20a Swanton (43558) *(G-12688)*

MLS Systems, Alvada *Also Called: Midwest Laser Systems Inc (G-422)*

Mm Industries Inc... 330 332-5947
36135 Salem Grange Rd Salem (44460) *(G-11802)*

Mm Outsourcing LLC... 937 661-4300
355 S South St Leesburg (45135) *(G-8300)*

Mm Service.. 330 626-2520
8936 State Route 14 Streetsboro (44241) *(G-12511)*

Mmei, Middlefield *Also Called: Molten Mtal Eqp Innvations LLC (G-9813)*

Mmelo Btq Confectioners LLC.............................. 614 822-9530
6475 E Main St Ste 128 Reynoldsburg (43068) *(G-11574)*

Mmf Inc... 614 252-2522
1977 Mcallister Ave Columbus (43205) *(G-5105)*

Mmf Incorporated (PA)... 614 252-0078
1977 Mcallister Ave Columbus (43205) *(G-5106)*

Mmi Textiles Inc (PA).. 440 899-8050
1 American Rd Ste 950 Brooklyn (44144) *(G-1523)*

Mmp Printing, Moraine *Also Called: Andrin Enterprises Inc (G-10146)*

Mmp Printing Inc.. 513 381-0990
10570 Chester Rd Cincinnati (45215) *(G-2883)*

Mmp Toledo... 419 472-0505
5847 Secor Rd Toledo (43623) *(G-13057)*

Mn8-Foxfire, Cincinnati *Also Called: Evp International LLC (G-2607)*

Mo-Trim Inc... 740 439-2725
240 Steubenville Ave Cambridge (43725) *(G-1750)*

Mob Apparel, Grove City *Also Called: Vandava Inc (G-7421)*

Mobex Global, Edon *Also Called: Linamar Strctures USA Mich Inc (G-6475)*

Mobex Global, Edon *Also Called: Linamar Strctures USA Mich Inc (G-6476)*

Mobile Conversions Inc.. 513 797-1991
3354 State Route 132 Amelia (45102) *(G-434)*

Mobile Operations, Van Wert *Also Called: Eaton Corporation (G-13534)*

Mobile Solutions LLC.. 614 286-3944
149 N Hamilton Rd Columbus (43213) *(G-5107)*

Mock Woodworking Company LLC.......................... 740 452-2701
4400 West Pike Zanesville (43701) *(G-15029)*

MODE Industries Inc... 614 504-8008
3000 E Main St Ste 134 Columbus (43209) *(G-5108)*

Model Graphics, West Chester *Also Called: Model GRAphics& Media Inc (G-14031)*

Model GRAphics& Media Inc................................. 513 541-2355
2614 Crescentville Rd West Chester (45069) *(G-14031)*

Model Medical LLC.. 216 972-0573
3429 Lee Rd Apt 12 Shaker Heights (44120) *(G-11931)*

Model Pattern & Foundry Co.................................. 513 542-2322
3242 Spring Grove Ave Cincinnati (45225) *(G-2884)*

Modern Builders Supply Inc.................................. 419 526-0002
85 Smith Ave Mansfield (44905) *(G-8831)*

Modern Builders Supply Inc (PA).......................... 419 241-3961
3500 Phillips Ave Toledo (43608) *(G-13058)*

Modern China Company Inc (PA)........................... 330 938-6104
550 E Ohio Ave Sebring (44672) *(G-11898)*

Modern Designs Inc.. 330 644-1771
310 Killian Rd Green (44232) *(G-7323)*

Modern Engineering Inc.. 440 593-5414
527 W Adams St Conneaut (44030) *(G-5412)*

Modern Ice Equipment & Sup Co (PA)...................513 367-2101
5709 Harrison Ave Cincinnati (45248) *(G-2885)*

Modern Industries Inc... 216 432-2855
6610 Metta Ave Cleveland (44103) *(G-4043)*

Modern Machine Development............................... 937 253-4576
400 Linden Ave Ste 3 Dayton (45403) *(G-5891)*

Modern Mold Corporation...................................... 440 236-9600
27684 Royalton Rd Columbia Station (44028) *(G-4594)*

Modern Retail Solutions LLC................................. 330 527-4308
10421 Industrial Dr Garrettsville (44231) *(G-7227)*

Modern Safety Techniques, Hicksville *Also Called: Mst Inc (G-7648)*

Modern Sheet Metal Works Inc............................. 513 353-3666
6037 Hamilton Cleves Rd Cleves (45002) *(G-4545)*

Modern Time Dealer, Uniontown *Also Called: Bbm Fairway Inc (G-13417)*

Modern Tour, Cincinnati *Also Called: Modern Ice Equipment & Sup Co (G-2885)*

Modern Transmission Dev Co
5903 Grafton Rd Valley City (44280) *(G-13506)*

Modern Welding Co Ohio Inc................................. 740 344-9425
1 Modern Way Newark (43055) *(G-10522)*

Modernfold, Youngstown *Also Called: W B Becherer Inc (G-14965)*

Modroto..440 998-1202
4920 State Rd Ashtabula (44004) *(G-606)*

Modula Inc (DH)..207 440-5100
5000 Commerce Center Dr Franklin (45005) *(G-7035)*

Modular Assmbly Invvations LLC (PA).........614 389-4860
600 Stonehenge Pkwy Ste 100 Dublin (43017) *(G-6321)*

Module 21 Bldg Company, Dayton *Also Called: M21 Industries LLC (G-5859)*

Moen, North Olmsted *Also Called: Moen Incorporated (G-10722)*

Moen Incorporated (HQ)............................800 289-6636
25300 Al Moen Dr North Olmsted (44070) *(G-10722)*

Mohawk Industries Inc...............................800 837-3812
3565 Urbancrest Industrial Dr Grove City (43123) *(G-7402)*

Mohawk Manufacturing Inc........................860 632-2345
306 E Gambier St Mount Vernon (43050) *(G-10252)*

Mohican Industries Inc..............................330 869-0500
1225 W Market St Akron (44313) *(G-235)*

Mohler Lumber Company...........................330 499-5461
4214 Portage St Nw North Canton (44720) *(G-10652)*

Mohr Stamping Inc....................................440 647-4316
22038 Fairgrounds Rd Wellington (44090) *(G-13896)*

Mojonnier Usa LLC...................................844 665-6664
10325 State Route 43 Ste N Streetsboro (44241) *(G-12512)*

Mold Masters Intl LLC...............................440 953-0220
34000 Melinz Pkwy Eastlake (44095) *(G-6438)*

Mold Shop Inc...419 829-2041
8520 Central Ave Sylvania (43560) *(G-12716)*

Mold Surface Textures Inc.........................330 678-8590
4485 Crystal Pkwy Ste 300 Kent (44240) *(G-8055)*

Mold Tech, Painesville *Also Called: Xponet Inc (G-11123)*

Mold-Rite Plastics LLC..............................330 405-7739
2300 Highland Rd Twinsburg (44087) *(G-13342)*

Mold-Rite Plastics LLC..............................330 405-7739
2222 Highland Rd Twinsburg (44087) *(G-13343)*

Molded Fiber Glass Companies (PA)............440 997-5851
2925 Mfg Pl Ashtabula (44004) *(G-607)*

Molded Fiber Glass Companies...................440 997-5851
4401 Benefit Ave Ashtabula (44004) *(G-608)*

Molded Fiber Glass Companies...................440 994-5100
1315 W 47th St Ashtabula (44004) *(G-609)*

Molding Dynamics Inc...............................440 786-8100
7009 Krick Rd Bedford (44146) *(G-1048)*

Molding Technologies, Hebron *Also Called: Molding Technologies Ltd (G-7623)*

Molding Technologies Ltd..........................740 929-2065
85 N. High Street Hebron (43025) *(G-7623)*

Moldmakers Inc...419 673-0902
13608 Us Highway 68 Kenton (43326) *(G-8108)*

Molson Coors Bev Co USA LLC...................513 896-9200
2525 Wayne Madison Rd Trenton (45067) *(G-13194)*

Molten Metals, Middlefield *Also Called: Pckd Enterprises Inc (G-9820)*

Molten Mtal Eqp Invvations LLC..................440 632-9119
15510 Old State Rd Middlefield (44062) *(G-9813)*

Molten North America Corp (DH).................419 425-2700
1835 Industrial Dr Findlay (45840) *(G-6895)*

Momentive Perf Mtrls Quartz.....................408 436-6221
22557 Lunn Rd Strongsville (44149) *(G-12574)*

Momentive Performance Mtls, Richmond Heights *Also Called: Momentive Performance Mtls Inc (G-11611)*

Momentive Performance Mtls Inc.................614 986-2495
180 E Broad St Columbus (43215) *(G-5109)*

Momentive Performance Mtls Inc.................740 928-7010
611 O Neill Dr Hebron (43025) *(G-7624)*

Momentive Performance Mtls Inc.................440 878-5705
24400 Highland Rd Richmond Heights (44143) *(G-11611)*

Momentive Performance Mtls Inc.................740 929-8732
4901 Campbell Rd Willoughby (44094) *(G-14491)*

Momentive Prfmce Mtls Qrtz Inc (HQ).........440 878-5700
22557 Lunn Rd Strongsville (44149) *(G-12575)*

Momentive Technologies, Strongsville *Also Called: Momentive Prfmce Mtls Qrtz Inc (G-12575)*

Momentum Fleet MGT Group Inc..................440 759-2219
24481 Detroit Rd Westlake (44145) *(G-14315)*

Momma Js Blazing Kitchen LLC...................216 551-8791
2281 S Overlook Rd Cleveland Heights (44106) *(G-4530)*

Momq Holding Company (PA)......................440 878-5700
22557 Lunn Rd Strongsville (44149) *(G-12576)*

Mon-Say Corp..419 720-0163
2735 Dorr St Toledo (43607) *(G-13059)*

Monaco Plating Inc....................................216 206-2360
3555 E 91st St Cleveland (44105) *(G-4044)*

Monaghan & Associates Inc........................937 253-7706
30 N Clinton St Dayton (45402) *(G-5892)*

Monaghan Tooling Group, Dayton *Also Called: Monaghan & Associates Inc (G-5892)*

Monarch, Cleveland *Also Called: Integrated Power Services LLC (G-3863)*

Monarch, Cleveland *Also Called: Monarch Steel Company Inc (G-4045)*

Monarch Plastic Inc...................................330 683-0822
516 Jefferson Ave Orrville (44667) *(G-10995)*

Monarch Products Co.................................330 868-7717
105 Short St Minerva (44657) *(G-10044)*

Monarch Steel Company Inc.......................216 587-8000
4650 Johnston Pkwy Cleveland (44128) *(G-4045)*

Monarch Water Systems Inc.......................937 426-5773
689 Greystone Dr Beavercreek (45434) *(G-978)*

Mondo Polymer Technologies Inc (PA).........740 376-9396
27620 State Route 7 Marietta (45750) *(G-8930)*

Monique Bath and Body Ltd........................513 440-7370
6545 Market Ave N Canton (44721) *(G-1951)*

Monitor Mold & Machine Co.......................330 697-7800
3393 Industry Rd Rootstown (44272) *(G-11650)*

Monks Copy Shop Inc................................614 461-6438
47 E Gay St Columbus (43215) *(G-5110)*

Monode Marking Products Inc (PA)..............440 975-8802
9200 Tyler Blvd Mentor (44060) *(G-9567)*

Monode Marking Products Inc.....................419 929-0346
149 High St New London (44851) *(G-10413)*

Monode Steel Stamp Inc............................440 975-8802
7620 Tyler Blvd Mentor (44060) *(G-9568)*

Monroe Tool and Mfg Co............................216 883-7360
3900 E 93rd St Cleveland (44105) *(G-4046)*

Monsanto, Greenville *Also Called: Monsanto Company (G-7347)*

Monsanto Company....................................937 548-7858
1051 Landsdowne Ave Greenville (45331) *(G-7347)*

Montgomery & Montgomery LLC..................330 858-9533
80 N Pershing Ave Akron (44313) *(G-236)*

Montgomery Ellis LLC................................614 226-7976
4151 Executive Pkwy Ste 300 Westerville (43081) *(G-14271)*

Montgomery License Bureau, Montgomery *Also Called: D J Klingler Inc (G-10124)*

Montgomery Mch Fabrication Inc.................740 286-2863
206 Watts Blevins Rd Jackson (45640) *(G-7948)*

Montgomerys Pallet Service Inc...................330 297-6677
7937 State Route 44 Ravenna (44266) *(G-11533)*

Monti Incorporated (PA).............................513 761-7775
4510 Reading Rd Cincinnati (45229) *(G-2886)*

Montville Plastics, Parkman *Also Called: Montville Plastics & Rubber Inc (G-11128)*

Montville Plastics & Rbr LLC......................440 548-2005
15567 Main Market Rd Parkman (44080) *(G-11127)*

Montville Plastics & Rubber Inc...................440 548-3211
15567 Main Market Rd Parkman (44080) *(G-11128)*

Moog Inc...330 682-0010
1701 N Main St Orrville (44667) *(G-10996)*

Moorchild LLC...513 649-8867
6 S Broad St Middletown (45044) *(G-9880)*

Moore Mc Millen Holdings (PA)...................330 745-3075
1850 Front St Cuyahoga Falls (44221) *(G-5561)*

Moore Chrome Products Company...............419 843-3510
3525 Silica Rd Sylvania (43560) *(G-12717)*

Moore Industries Inc..................................419 485-5572
1317 Henricks Dr Montpelier (43543) *(G-10130)*

Moore Metal Finishing, Sylvania *Also Called: Moore Chrome Products Company (G-12717)*

Moore Mr Specialty Company......................330 332-1229
1050 Pennsylvania Ave Salem (44460) *(G-11803)*

Moore Outdoor Sign Craftsman, Westerville *Also Called: Ohio Shelterall Inc (G-14272)*

Moore Well Services Inc.............................330 650-4443
246 N Cleveland Ave Mogadore (44260) *(G-10080)*

ALPHABETIC

Mor-X Plastics, Youngstown *Also Called: Jamen Tool & Die Co* *(G-14880)*

Morbark LLC... 330 264-8699
4255 E Lincoln Way Wooster (44691) *(G-14666)*

Morbern USA... 937 298-2176
3265 Dryden Rd Dayton (45439) *(G-5893)*

Mordies Inc... 330 758-8050
556 Bev Rd Youngstown (44512) *(G-14902)*

More Manufacturing LLC.................................. 937 233-3898
4025 Lisa Dr Ste A Tipp City (45371) *(G-12831)*

More Than Gourmet, Akron *Also Called: Ajinomoto Hlth Ntrtn N Amer In* *(G-23)*

More Than Gourmet Holdings Inc....................... 330 762-6652
929 Home Ave Akron (44310) *(G-237)*

Morel Landscaping LLC................................... 216 551-4395
9396 Broadview Rd Broadview Heights (44147) *(G-1505)*

Morgan Adhesives Company LLC (DH)............... 330 688-1111
4560 Darrow Rd Stow (44224) *(G-12441)*

Morgan Advanced Ceramics Inc........................ 330 405-1033
2181 Pinnacle Pkwy Twinsburg (44087) *(G-13344)*

Morgan Advanced Materials.............................. 419 435-8182
200 N Town St Fostoria (44830) *(G-6992)*

Morgan Advanced Materials, Twinsburg *Also Called: Morgan Advanced Ceramics Inc* *(G-13344)*

Morgan AM&t... 419 435-8182
200 N Town St Fostoria (44830) *(G-6993)*

Morgan County Herald, Mcconnelsville *Also Called: Morgan County Publishing Co* *(G-9366)*

Morgan County Publishing Co............................ 740 962-3377
25 N 5th St Mcconnelsville (43756) *(G-9366)*

Morgan Engineering Systems Inc....................... 330 821-4721
1182 E Summit St Alliance (44601) *(G-393)*

Morgan Engineering Systems Inc (PA)............... 330 823-6130
1049 S Mahoning Ave Alliance (44601) *(G-394)*

Morgan Engineering Systems Inc....................... 330 545-9731
700 Dot St Girard (44420) *(G-7276)*

Morgan Litho, Cleveland *Also Called: T D Dynamics Inc* *(G-4362)*

Morgan Mfg Plant No 3, Girard *Also Called: Morgan Engineering Systems Inc* *(G-7276)*

Morgan Site Services Inc.................................. 330 823-6120
1049 S Mahoning Ave Alliance (44601) *(G-395)*

Morgan Wood Products Inc................................ 614 336-4000
9761 Fairway Dr Powell (43065) *(G-11492)*

Morgan4140 LLC... 513 873-1426
4760 Paddock Rd Ste B Cincinnati (45229) *(G-2887)*

Mori Shuji... 614 459-1296
3755 Mountview Rd Columbus (43220) *(G-5111)*

Moriroku Technology N Amer Inc (HQ)............... 937 548-3217
15000 Industrial Pkwy Marysville (43040) *(G-9039)*

Moritz Concrete Inc... 419 529-3232
362 N Trimble Rd Mansfield (44906) *(G-8832)*

Moritz International Inc..................................... 419 526-5222
665 N Main St Mansfield (44902) *(G-8833)*

Moritz Materials Inc (PA).................................. 419 281-0575
859 Faultless Dr Ashland (44805) *(G-553)*

Moritz Ready Mix Inc....................................... 419 253-0001
4083 Bennington Way Marengo (43334) *(G-8898)*

Morlan & Associates Inc.................................. 614 889-6152
4970 Scioto Darby Rd Ste D Hilliard (43026) *(G-7687)*

Morlock Asphalt Ltd... 419 419-4772
9362 Mermill Rd Portage (43451) *(G-11459)*

Morning Journal, The, Lorain *Also Called: Journal Register Company* *(G-8560)*

Morning Pride Mfg LLC (HQ)............................. 937 264-2662
1 Innovation Ct Dayton (45414) *(G-5894)*

Morning Pride Mfg LLC.................................... 937 264-1726
4978 Riverton Dr Dayton (45414) *(G-5895)*

Morris Bean & Company.................................. 937 767-7301
777 E Hyde Rd Yellow Springs (45387) *(G-14790)*

Morris Furniture Co Inc (PA)............................. 937 874-7100
2377 Commerce Center Blvd Ste A Fairborn (45324) *(G-6697)*

Morris Home Furnishing, Fairborn *Also Called: Morris Furniture Co Inc* *(G-6697)*

Morris Technologies Inc................................... 513 733-1611
11988 Tramway Dr Cincinnati (45241) *(G-2888)*

Morrison Custom Welding, Wooster *Also Called: Iron Gate Industries LLC* *(G-14652)*

Morrison Products Inc (PA)............................... 216 486-4000
16900 S Waterloo Rd Cleveland (44110) *(G-4047)*

Morrison Sign Company Inc.............................. 614 276-1181
2757 Scioto Pkwy Columbus (43221) *(G-5112)*

Morrow Gravel, Morrow *Also Called: Valley Asphalt Corporation* *(G-10203)*

Morrow Gravel Company Inc (PA)...................... 513 771-0820
11641 Mosteller Rd Cincinnati (45241) *(G-2889)*

Morrow Gravel Company Inc............................. 513 899-2000
4850 Stubbs Mills Rd Morrow (45152) *(G-10202)*

Morse Enterprises Inc..................................... 513 229-3600
6678 Tri Way Dr Mason (45040) *(G-9129)*

Morton Buildings Inc.. 419 399-4549
14623 State Route 31 Kenton (43326) *(G-8109)*

Morton Buildings Inc.. 419 675-2311
14483 State Route 31 Kenton (43326) *(G-8110)*

Morton Buildings Inc.. 330 345-6188
1055 Columbus Avenue Ext Wooster (44691) *(G-14667)*

Morton Buildings Plant, Kenton *Also Called: Morton Buildings Inc* *(G-8110)*

Morton Salt, Cincinnati *Also Called: Morton Salt Inc* *(G-2890)*

Morton Salt Inc... 513 941-1578
5336 River Rd Cincinnati (45233) *(G-2890)*

Morton Salt Inc... 216 664-0728
2100 W 3rd St Cleveland (44113) *(G-4048)*

Morton Salt Inc... 330 925-3015
151 Industrial Ave Rittman (44270) *(G-11625)*

Mosher Machine & Tool Co Inc.......................... 937 258-8070
2201 Valley Springs Rd Beavercreek Township (45434) *(G-999)*

Mosser Glass Inc.. 740 439-1827
9279 Cadiz Rd Cambridge (43725) *(G-1751)*

Mossing Machine and Tool Inc.......................... 419 476-5657
5225 Telegraph Rd Toledo (43612) *(G-13060)*

Motherson Ychiyo Auto Tech PDT (HQ).............. 614 876-3220
2285 Walcutt Rd Columbus (43228) *(G-5113)*

Motherson Ychiyo US Auto Syste...................... 740 375-4687
1177 Kellogg Pkwy Marion (43302) *(G-8981)*

Motion Mobility & Design Inc............................. 330 244-9723
6490 Promler St Nw North Canton (44720) *(G-10653)*

Motionsource International LLC.......................... 440 287-7037
31200 Solon Rd Ste 7 Solon (44139) *(G-12153)*

Moto-Electric Inc... 419 668-7894
262 Cleveland Rd Norwalk (44857) *(G-10853)*

Motors & Drives Division, Norwood *Also Called: Siemens Industry Inc* *(G-10873)*

Mound Laser Photonics Center, Kettering *Also Called: Resonetics LLC* *(G-8123)*

Mound Manufacturing Center Inc....................... 937 236-8387
33 Commerce Park Dr Dayton (45404) *(G-5896)*

Mound Printing Company Inc............................. 937 866-2872
2455 Belvo Rd Miamisburg (45342) *(G-9720)*

Mound Technologies Inc................................... 937 748-2937
25 Mound Park Dr Springboro (45066) *(G-12260)*

Mount Eaton Division, Mount Eaton *Also Called: Flex Technologies Inc* *(G-10207)*

Mount Vernon News, Mount Vernon *Also Called: Progrssive Communications Corp* *(G-10261)*

Mount Vernon Packaging Inc............................. 740 397-3221
135 Progress Dr Mount Vernon (43050) *(G-10253)*

Mount Vernon Steel, Mount Vernon *Also Called: Mt Vernon Machine & Tool Inc* *(G-10254)*

Mountain Tarp, Ravenna *Also Called: Tarped Out Inc* *(G-11545)*

Mountain Top Frozen Pies Div, Columbus *Also Called: Quality Bakery Company Inc* *(G-5218)*

Move Ez Inc... 844 466-8339
855 Grandview Ave Ste 140 Columbus (43215) *(G-5114)*

Moveeasy, Columbus *Also Called: Move Ez Inc* *(G-5114)*

Mowhawk Lumber Ltd...................................... 330 698-5333
2931 S Carr Rd Apple Creek (44606) *(G-473)*

Mp Biomedicals LLC....................................... 440 337-1200
29525 Fountain Pkwy Solon (44139) *(G-12154)*

Mp Technologies Inc.. 440 838-4466
532 County Road 1600 Ashland (44805) *(G-554)*

Mpac Switchback, Cleveland *Also Called: Switchback Group Inc* *(G-4358)*

MPC Plastics Inc... 216 881-7220
1859 E 63rd St Cleveland (44103) *(G-4049)*

MPC Plating LLC... 216 881-7220
9921 Clinton Rd Cleveland (44144) *(G-4050)*

Mpc Plating Inc... 216 881-7220
9921 Clinton Rd Brooklyn (44144) *(G-1524)*

(G-0000) Company's Geographic Section entry number

Mpe Aeroengines Inc..937 878-3800
7700 New Carlisle Pike Huber Heights (45424) *(G-7823)*

Mpi Label Systems., Sebring *Also Called: Mpi Labels of Baltimore Inc (G-11899)*

Mpi Labels of Baltimore Inc (HQ)............................330 938-2134
450 Courtney Rd Sebring (44672) *(G-11899)*

Mpi Logistics and Service Inc.................................330 832-5309
1414 Industrial Ave Sw Massillon (44647) *(G-9225)*

Mplx GP LLC..419 422-2121
539 S Main St Findlay (45840) *(G-6896)*

Mplx Terminals LLC..330 479-5539
2408 Gambrinus Ave Sw Canton (44706) *(G-1952)*

Mpp Legacy Inc...440 237-9500
9940 York Alpha Dr North Royalton (44133) *(G-10775)*

MPS Manufacturing Company LLC..........................330 343-1435
326 Pearl Ave Ne New Philadelphia (44663) *(G-10460)*

MPW Industrial Svcs Group Inc (PA)......................740 927-8790
9711 Lancaster Rd Hebron (43025) *(G-7625)*

Mr Box, Mansfield *Also Called: Skybox Packaging LLC (G-8853)*

Mr Emblem Inc..419 697-1888
3209 Navarre Ave Oregon (43616) *(G-10964)*

Mr Heater, Cleveland *Also Called: Enerco Group Inc (G-3671)*

Mr Heater Inc..216 916-3000
4560 W 160th St Cleveland (44135) *(G-4051)*

Mr Label Inc...513 681-2088
5018 Gray Rd Cincinnati (45232) *(G-2891)*

Mr. Heater, Cleveland *Also Called: Enerco Technical Products Inc (G-3672)*

MRC & Associates, Dayton *Also Called: Michele Caldwell (G-5880)*

Mrl, Xenia *Also Called: Mrl Materials Resources LLC (G-14771)*

Mrl Materials Resources LLC.................................937 531-6657
123 Fairground Rd Xenia (45385) *(G-14771)*

Mro Built LLC..330 526-0555
6410 Promway Ave Nw North Canton (44720) *(G-10654)*

Mro Built, Inc., North Canton *Also Called: Mro Built LLC (G-10654)*

Mrpicker..440 354-6497
595 Miner Rd Cleveland (44143) *(G-4052)*

Mrs Electronic Inc...937 660-6767
6680 Poe Ave Ste 100 Dayton (45414) *(G-5897)*

MRS Industrial Inc...614 308-1070
2583 Harrison Rd Columbus (43204) *(G-5115)*

Mrs Mllers Hmmade Noodles Ltd...........................330 694-5814
9140 County Road 192 Fredericksburg (44627) *(G-7065)*

Ms Murcko & Sons LLC..724 854-4907
8090 Chestnut Ridge Rd Hubbard (44425) *(G-7814)*

Ms Welding LLC..419 925-4141
8070 Flyer Dr Maria Stein (45860) *(G-8900)*

MSC Industries Inc..440 474-8788
6131 Ireland Rd Romo (44086) *(C 11645)*

MSC Walbridge Coatings Inc.................................419 666-6130
30610 E Broadway St Walbridge (43465) *(G-13686)*

Msg Premier Molded Fiber, Ashtabula *Also Called: Molded Fiber Glass Companies (G-608)*

MSI, Chesterland *Also Called: Metzenbaum Sheltered Inds Inc (G-2236)*

Msls Group LLC..330 723-4431
1080 Industrial Pkwy Medina (44256) *(G-9428)*

Mssi Group Inc...440 439-1040
7500 Northfield Rd Walton Hills (44146) *(G-13701)*

Mssk Manufacturing Inc.......................................330 393-6624
400 Dietz Rd Ne Warren (44483) *(G-13783)*

MST, Kent *Also Called: Mold Surface Textures Inc (G-8055)*

Mst Inc..419 542-6645
11370 Breininger Rd Hicksville (43526) *(G-7648)*

Mt Eaton Pallet Ltd...330 893-2986
4761 County Road 207 Millersburg (44654) *(G-10001)*

Mt Perry Foods Inc...740 743-3890
5705 State Route 204 Ne Mount Perry (43760) *(G-10225)*

Mt Pleasant Blacktopping Inc................................513 874-3777
3199 Production Dr Fairfield (45014) *(G-6756)*

Mt Vernon Machine & Tool Inc..............................740 397-0311
8585 Blackjack Road Ext Mount Vernon (43050) *(G-10254)*

Mt Vernon Mold Works Inc...................................618 242-6040
2200 Massillon Rd Akron (44312) *(G-238)*

Mt.pleasant Blacktopping, Fairfield *Also Called: Mt Pleasant Blacktopping Inc (G-6756)*

Mtd Consumer Group Inc (DH)..............................330 225-2600
5965 Grafton Rd Valley City (44280) *(G-13507)*

Mtd Consumer Products Supply, Valley City *Also Called: Mtd Products Inc (G-13511)*

Mtd Holdings Inc (HQ)...330 225-2600
5965 Grafton Rd Valley City (44280) *(G-13508)*

Mtd International Operations (DH)..........................330 225-2600
5965 Grafton Rd Valley City (44280) *(G-13509)*

Mtd Products Inc..419 342-6455
305 Mansfield Ave Shelby (44875) *(G-11971)*

Mtd Products Inc (DH)...330 225-2600
5965 Grafton Rd Valley City (44280) *(G-13510)*

Mtd Products Inc..330 225-1940
5903 Grafton Rd Valley City (44280) *(G-13511)*

Mtd Products Inc..330 225-9127
680 Liverpool Dr Valley City (44280) *(G-13512)*

Mtd Products Inc..419 951-9779
810 Theo Moll Dr Willard (44890) *(G-14405)*

Mtd Products Inc..419 935-6611
979 S Conwell Ave Willard (44890) *(G-14406)*

Mto Suncoke, Middletown *Also Called: Suncoke Energy Inc (G-9895)*

Mudbrook Golf Ctr At Thndrbird............................419 433-2945
1609 Mudbrook Rd Huron (44839) *(G-7880)*

Mueller Art Cover & Binding Co.............................440 238-3303
12005 Alameda Dr Strongsville (44149) *(G-12577)*

Mueller Electric Company Inc (HQ).........................216 771-5225
2850 Gilchrist Rd Ste 5 Akron (44305) *(G-239)*

Mueller Electric Company Inc................................614 888-8855
7795 Walton Pkwy Ste 175 New Albany (43054) *(G-10346)*

Muhlenberg County Coal Co LLC...........................740 338-3100
46226 National Rd Saint Clairsville (43950) *(G-11701)*

Mulch Manufacturing Inc (HQ)..............................614 864-4004
6747 Taylor Rd Sw Reynoldsburg (43068) *(G-11575)*

Mulch Masters of Ohio, Miamisburg *Also Called: Gayston Corporation (G-9693)*

Mulhern Belting Inc...201 337-5700
310 Osborne Dr Fairfield (45014) *(G-6757)*

Mull Iron, Rittman *Also Called: Rittman Inc (G-11627)*

Muller Engine & Machine Co.................................937 322-1861
1414 S Yellow Springs St Springfield (45506) *(G-12354)*

Muller Pipe Organ Co..740 893-1700
122 N High St Croton (43013) *(G-5514)*

Muller Pipe Organ Company, Croton *Also Called: Muller Pipe Organ Co (G-5514)*

Mullet Cabinets Inc...330 674-9646
6086 State Route 241 Millersburg (44654) *(G-10002)*

Mullet Enterprises Inc (PA)..................................330 852-4681
138 2nd St Nw Sugarcreek (44681) *(G-12643)*

Mullins Rubber Products Inc.................................937 233-4211
2949 Valley Pike Dayton (45404) *(G-5898)*

Multi Cast LLC...419 335-0010
225 E Linfoot St Wauseon (43567) *(G-13856)*

Multi Fittings Corporation.....................................513 942-9910
4507 Le Saint Ct West Chester (45014) *(G-14032)*

Multi Galvanizing LLC..330 453-1441
825 Navarre Rd Sw Canton (44707) *(G-1953)*

Multi Lapping Service Inc.....................................440 944-7592
30032 Lakeland Blvd Wickliffe (44092) *(G-14383)*

Multi Products Company.......................................330 674-5981
7188 State Route 39 Millersburg (44654) *(G-10003)*

Multi Radiance Medical, Solon *Also Called: Medical Quant USA Inc (G-12145)*

Multi-Color, Batavia *Also Called: Verstrete In Mold Lbels USA In (G-896)*

Multi-Color, Mason *Also Called: McC - Mason W&S (G-9126)*

Multi-Color Australia LLC (DH).............................513 381-1480
4053 Clough Woods Dr Batavia (45103) *(G-877)*

Multi-Color Corporation.......................................513 381-1480
4053 Clough Woods Dr Batavia (45103) *(G-878)*

Multi-Color Corporation.......................................513 459-3283
5510 Courseview Dr Mason (45040) *(G-9130)*

Multi-Craft Litho Inc..859 581-2754
4440 Creek Rd Blue Ash (45242) *(G-1312)*

Multi-Form Plastics, Batavia *Also Called: Plastikos Corporation (G-882)*

A L P H A B E T I C

Multi-Plastics Inc (PA) 740 548-4894
7770 N Central Dr Lewis Center (43035) *(G-8344)*

Multi-Wing America Inc 440 834-9400
15030 Berkshire Industrial Pkwy Middlefield (44062) *(G-9814)*

Multibase Inc 330 666-0505
3835 Copley Rd Akron (44321) *(G-240)*

Multifab, Elyria Also Called: Multilink Inc *(G-6566)*

Multilink Inc 440 366-6966
580 Ternes Ln Elyria (44035) *(G-6566)*

Multiple Products Company, Cleveland Also Called: Kg63 LLC *(G-3917)*

Mum Industries Inc (PA) 440 269-4966
8989 Tyler Blvd Mentor (44060) *(G-9569)*

Mumford's Potato Chip, Urbana Also Called: Mumfords Potato Chips & Deli *(G-13474)*

Mumfords Potato Chips & Deli 937 653-3491
325 N Main St Urbana (43078) *(G-13474)*

Muncy Corporation 937 346-0800
2020 Progress Rd Springfield (45505) *(G-12355)*

Munson Machine Company Inc 740 967-6867
80 E College Ave Johnstown (43031) *(G-7996)*

Murotech Ohio Corporation 419 394-6529
550 Mckinley Rd Saint Marys (45885) *(G-11743)*

Murphy Dog LLC 614 755-4278
225 Business Center Dr Blacklick (43004) *(G-1227)*

Murphy Tractor & Eqp Co Inc 330 220-4999
1550 Industrial Pkwy Brunswick (44212) *(G-1602)*

Murphy Tractor & Eqp Co Inc 330 477-9304
1509 Raff Rd Sw Canton (44710) *(G-1954)*

Murphy Tractor & Eqp Co Inc 614 876-1141
2121 Walcutt Rd Columbus (43228) *(G-5116)*

Murphy Tractor & Eqp Co Inc 419 221-3666
3550 Saint Johns Rd Lima (45804) *(G-8434)*

Murphy Tractor & Eqp Co Inc 937 898-4198
1015 Industrial Park Dr Vandalia (45377) *(G-13573)*

Murphy's Landing Casual Dining, Middletown Also Called: Moorchild LLC *(G-9880)*

Murr Corporation 330 264-2223
201 N Buckeye St Wooster (44691) *(G-14668)*

Murr Printing and Graphics, Wooster Also Called: Murr Corporation *(G-14668)*

Murray American Energy Inc (DH) 740 338-3100
46226 National Rd Saint Clairsville (43950) *(G-11702)*

Murray Display Fixtures Ltd 614 875-1594
2300 Southwest Blvd Grove City (43123) *(G-7403)*

Murray Fabrics Inc (PA) 216 881-4041
837 E 79th St Cleveland (44103) *(G-4053)*

Murray Kentucky Energy Inc (HQ) 740 338-3100
46226 National Rd Saint Clairsville (43950) *(G-11703)*

Murray Machine and Tool Inc 216 267-1126
17801 Sheldon Rd Side Cleveland (44130) *(G-4054)*

Murrubber Technologies Inc
1350 Commerce Dr Stow (44224) *(G-12442)*

Muscle Feast LLC (PA) 740 877-8808
1320 Boston Rd Nashport (43830) *(G-10301)*

Muskingum Grinding and Mch Co 740 622-4741
2155 Otsego Ave Coshocton (43812) *(G-5463)*

Muskingum Tire Company Inc 740 453-8473
758 Putnam Ave Zanesville (43701) *(G-15030)*

Mustang Dynamometer, Twinsburg Also Called: Ganzcorp Investments Inc *(G-13307)*

Mustang Printing 419 592-2746
119 W Washington St Napoleon (43545) *(G-10292)*

Mustard Seed Health Fd Mkt Inc 440 519-3663
6025 Kruse Dr Ste 100 Solon (44139) *(G-12155)*

Muster Rdu Inc 614 537-5440
1450 E Walnut St Lancaster (43130) *(G-8212)*

Mutual Tool LLC 937 667-5818
1350 Commerce Park Dr Tipp City (45371) *(G-12832)*

Mveca, Yellow Springs Also Called: Miami Valley Eductl Cmpt Assn *(G-14789)*

Mvgg Inc 937 228-0781
1222 E 3rd St Dayton (45402) *(G-5899)*

Mvp Pharmacy 614 449-8000
1931 Parsons Ave Columbus (43207) *(G-5117)*

Mvp Plastics Inc (PA) 440 834-1790
15005 Enterprise Way Middlefield (44062) *(G-9815)*

Mvp Plastics Sa LLC 440 834-1790
15005 Enterprise Way Middlefield (44062) *(G-9816)*

Mw Metals Group LLC 937 222-5992
461 Homestead Ave Dayton (45417) *(G-5900)*

Mwgh LLC 513 521-4114
9070 Pippin Rd Cincinnati (45251) *(G-2892)*

Mwi Dmntable Office Partitions, Lorain Also Called: M/W International Inc *(G-8566)*

Mxr Imaging Inc 614 219-2011
4770 Northwest Pkwy Hilliard (43026) *(G-7688)*

My Alarm, Franklin Also Called: Valued Relationships Inc *(G-7054)*

My Floors By Prints and Paints, Galion Also Called: Prints & Paints Flr Cvg Co Inc *(G-7197)*

My Second Home Early Lrng Schl, Marysville Also Called: New Republic Industries LLC *(G-9040)*

My Splash Pad 330 705-1802
6565 Saint Peters Church Rd Ne Louisville (44641) *(G-8609)*

Mye Automotive Inc 330 253-5592
1293 S Main St Akron (44301) *(G-241)*

Myers and Lasch Inc 440 235-2050
2530 Wyndgate Ct Westlake (44145) *(G-14316)*

Myers Controlled Power LLC 909 923-1800
133 Taft Ave Ne Canton (44720) *(G-1955)*

Myers FSI, North Canton Also Called: Myers Power Products Inc *(G-10655)*

MYERS INDUSTRIES, Akron Also Called: Myers Industries Inc *(G-243)*

Myers Industries Inc 330 253-5592
1293 S Main St Akron (44301) *(G-242)*

Myers Industries Inc (PA) 330 253-5592
1293 S Main St Akron (44301) *(G-243)*

Myers Industries Inc 330 821-4700
2290 W Main St Alliance (44601) *(G-396)*

Myers Industries Inc 440 632-1006
15150 Madison Rd Middlefield (44062) *(G-9817)*

Myers Industries Inc 330 336-6621
250 Seville Rd Wadsworth (44281) *(G-13653)*

Myers Machining Inc 330 874-3005
11789 Strasburg Bolivar Rd Nw Bolivar (44612) *(G-1385)*

Myers Power Products Inc (PA) 330 834-3200
219 E Maple St Ste 100/200e North Canton (44720) *(G-10655)*

Myers Precision Grinding Inc 216 587-3737
19500 S Miles Rd Cleveland (44128) *(G-4055)*

Myfootshopcom LLC 740 522-5681
1159 Cherry Valley Rd Se Newark (43055) *(G-10523)*

Myrlen, Cincinnati Also Called: Ep Bollinger LLC *(G-2594)*

Mysta Equipment Co 330 879-5353
6434 Werstler Ave Sw Navarre (44662) *(G-10308)*

Mytee, Solon Also Called: Mytee Products Inc *(G-12156)*

Mytee Products Inc 888 705-8277
30701 Carter St Solon (44139) *(G-12156)*

N & W Machining & Fabg Inc 937 695-5582
8 Mathias Rd Winchester (45697) *(G-14599)*

N A C, Findlay Also Called: Nichidai America Corporation *(G-6898)*

N A D, Cincinnati Also Called: National Access Design LLC *(G-2893)*

N E C Columbus, Columbus Also Called: National Electric Coil Inc *(G-5120)*

N F M, Massillon Also Called: Nfm/Welding Engineers Inc *(G-9226)*

N G C, North Royalton Also Called: Next Gerenation Crimping *(G-10776)*

N J E M A Magazine, Cincinnati Also Called: Sesh Communications *(G-3084)*

N M Hansen Machine and Tool, Toledo Also Called: Rogar International Inc *(G-13118)*

N N I, Cleveland Also Called: Norman Noble Inc *(G-4081)*

N S B, Cincinnati Also Called: National Scoreboards LLC *(G-2895)*

N W P Manufacturing, Waldo Also Called: Nwp Manufacturing Inc *(G-13690)*

N Wasserstrom & Sons Inc (HQ) 614 228-5550
2300 Lockbourne Rd Columbus (43207) *(G-5118)*

N Wasserstrom & Sons Inc 614 737-5410
862 E Jenkins Ave Columbus (43207) *(G-5119)*

N-Molecular Inc 440 439-5356
7650 First Pl Ste B Oakwood Village (44146) *(G-10907)*

N-Viro, Toledo Also Called: N-Viro International Corp *(G-13061)*

N-Viro International Corp 419 535-6374
2254 Centennial Rd Toledo (43617) *(G-13061)*

N2 Publishing 937 641-8277
3634 Watertower Ln Ste 4 West Carrollton (45449) *(G-13930)*

N2 Publishing, Pickerington *Also Called: Cbus Inc (G-11291)*

NA Financial Service Center, Cleveland *Also Called: Eaton Corporation (G-3651)*

Nabco Entrances, Sylvania *Also Called: Nabco Entrances Inc (G-12718)*

Nabco Entrances Inc..419 842-0484
3407 Silica Rd Sylvania (43560) *(G-12718)*

Nacco Industries Inc (PA)..440 229-5151
22901 Millcreek Blvd Ste 600 Cleveland (44122) *(G-4056)*

Nachurs Alpine Solutions LLC (HQ)..740 382-5701
421 Leader St Marion (43302) *(G-8982)*

Nachurs Alpine Solutions Corp, Marion *Also Called: Nachurs Alpine Solutions LLC (G-8982)*

Nagase Chemtex America LLC...740 362-4444
100 Innovation Ct Delaware (43015) *(G-6162)*

Nagele Manufacturing Company...216 433-1100
5201 W 164th St Cleveland (44142) *(G-4057)*

Namoh Ohio Holdings Inc (PA)   5612 Carthage Ave Norwood (45212) *(G-10869)*

Nancy Blanket, Mount Sterling *Also Called: Watershed Mangement LLC (G-10230)*

Nanofiber Solutions LLC..614 319-3075
5164 Blazer Pkwy Dublin (43017) *(G-6322)*

Nanogate North America LLC...419 522-7745
515 Newman St Mansfield (44902) *(G-8834)*

Nanogate North America LLC...419 747-1096
1555 W Longview Ave Mansfield (44906) *(G-8835)*

Nanolap Technologies LLC..877 658-4949
85 Harrisburg Dr Englewood (45322) *(G-6619)*

Nanosperse LLC...937 296-5030
2000 Composite Dr Kettering (45420) *(G-8122)*

Nanotronics, Cuyahoga Falls *Also Called: Nanotronics Imaging Inc (G-5562)*

Nanotronics Imaging Inc (PA)...330 926-9809
2251 Front St Ste 110 Cuyahoga Falls (44221) *(G-5562)*

Napoleon Machine LLC..419 591-7010
476 E Riverview Ave Napoleon (43545) *(G-10293)*

Napoleon Spring Works Inc (HQ)..419 445-1010
111 Weires Dr Archbold (43502) *(G-504)*

Napoli's Pizza, Belpre *Also Called: Wal-Bon of Ohio Inc (G-1155)*

Narrow Way Custom Tech Inc...937 743-1611
100 Industry Dr Carlisle (45005) *(G-2069)*

Nasg Auto-Seat Tec LLC..419 359-5954
19911 County Rd T Ridgeville Corners (43555) *(G-11615)*

Nasg Ohio LLC...419 634-3125
605 E Montford Ave Ada (45810) *(G-4)*

Nasg Seating Bryan LLC...419 633-0662
633 Commerce Dr Bryan (43506) *(G-1652)*

Nasg Seating Paulding LLC...419 399-4500
810 W Gasser Rd Paulding (45879) *(G-11159)*

Nasg Sting Rdgvlle Corners LLC (HQ).....................................419 267-5240
19911 County Rd T Ridgeville Corners (43555) *(G-11616)*

Natz Inc (PA)..614 270-2507
8754 Cotter St Lewis Center (43035) *(G-8345)*

Nate's Nectar, De Graff *Also Called: Nates Nectar LLC (G-6092)*

Nates Nectar LLC..937 935-3289
4684 Township Road 53 De Graff (43318) *(G-6092)*

Nation Coating Systems Inc..937 746-7632
501 Shotwell Dr Franklin (45005) *(G-7036)*

Nation Tool & Die Ltd..419 822-5939
5226 County Road 6 Delta (43515) *(G-6213)*

National Access Design LLC..513 351-3400
1871 Summit Rd Cincinnati (45237) *(G-2893)*

National Aerospace Proc LLC...234 900-6497
1330 Commerce Dr Stow (44224) *(G-12443)*

National Aviation Products Inc (DH)...330 688-6494
4880 Hudson Dr Stow (44224) *(G-12444)*

National Beef Ohio LLC..800 449-2333
2208 Grant Rd North Baltimore (45872) *(G-10615)*

National Beef Packing Co LLC..419 257-5500
2208 Grant Rd North Baltimore (45872) *(G-10616)*

National Beverage, Obetz *Also Called: Shasta Beverages Inc (G-10926)*

National Beverage Corp...614 491-5415
4685 Groveport Rd Obetz (43207) *(G-10925)*

National Bias Fabric Co..216 361-0530
4516 Saint Clair Ave Cleveland (44103) *(G-4058)*

National Biological Corp...216 831-0600
23700 Mercantile Rd Beachwood (44122) *(G-931)*

National Bios Fabric Company, Cleveland *Also Called: Db Rediheat Inc (G-3604)*

National Bronze Mtls Ohio Inc...440 277-1226
5311 W River Rd Lorain (44055) *(G-8568)*

National Bullet Co..800 317-9506
34971 Glen Dr Eastlake (44095) *(G-6439)*

National Carton & Coating Company..937 347-1042
1439 Lavelle Dr Xenia (45385) *(G-14772)*

National Colloid Company...740 282-1171
11 Technology Way Steubenville (43952) *(G-12407)*

National Compressor Svcs LLC (PA)..419 868-4980
10349 Industrial St Holland (43528) *(G-7773)*

National Diamond TI & Coating, Westlake *Also Called: Diamond Reserve Inc (G-14298)*

National Door and Trim Inc..419 238-9345
1189 Grill Rd Van Wert (45891) *(G-13543)*

National Electric Coil Inc (PA)..614 488-1151
800 King Ave Columbus (43212) *(G-5120)*

National Electro-Coatings Inc..216 898-0080
15655 Brookpark Rd Cleveland (44142) *(G-4059)*

National Engrg Archtctral Svcs, Columbus *Also Called: Barr Engineering Incorporated (G-4744)*

National Extrusion & Mfg Co, Bellefontaine *Also Called: McKnight Industries Inc (G-1113)*

National Fleet Svcs Ohio LLC...440 930-5177
607 Miller Rd Avon Lake (44012) *(G-766)*

National Foods Packaging Inc..216 622-2740
8200 Madison Ave Cleveland (44102) *(G-4060)*

National Frt Vgtable Tech Corp...740 400-4055
250 Civic Center Dr Columbus (43215) *(G-5121)*

National Gas & Oil Corporation (DH)..740 344-2102
1500 Granville Rd Newark (43055) *(G-10524)*

National Glass Service Group, Dublin *Also Called: National Glass Svc Group LLC (G-6323)*

National Glass Svc Group LLC..614 652-3699
5500 Frantz Rd Ste 120 Dublin (43017) *(G-6323)*

National Illmination Sign Corp...419 866-1666
6525 Angola Rd Holland (43528) *(G-7774)*

National Indus Concepts Inc..615 989-9101
170 N Park Dr Chillicothe (45601) *(G-2267)*

National Lien Digest, Highland Heights *Also Called: C & S Associates Inc (G-7655)*

National Lime and Stone Co..419 562-0771
4580 Bethel Rd Bucyrus (44820) *(G-1684)*

National Lime and Stone Co..419 396-7671
370 N Patterson St Carey (43316) *(G-2060)*

National Lime and Stone Co..740 548-4206
2406 S Section Line Rd Delaware (43015) *(G-6163)*

National Lime and Stone Co..419 423-3400
9860 County Road 313 Findlay (45840) *(G-6897)*

National Lime and Stone Co..419 228-3434
1314 Findlay Rd Lima (45801) *(G-8435)*

National Lime and Stone Co..614 497-0083
5911 Lockbourne Rd Lockbourne (43137) *(G-8491)*

National Lime and Stone Co..740 387-3485
700 Likens Rd Marion (43302) *(G-8983)*

National Lime and Stone Co..330 966-4836
5377 Lauby Rd North Canton (44720) *(G-10656)*

National Lime and Stone Co..419 657-6745
18430 Main Street Rd Wapakoneta (45895) *(G-13726)*

National Lime Stone Clmbus Reg, Delaware *Also Called: National Lime and Stone Co (G-6163)*

National Machine Co...330 688-2584
1330 Commerce Dr Stow (44224) *(G-12445)*

NATIONAL MACHINE CO (INC), Stow *Also Called: National Machine Co (G-12445)*

National Machine Company (HQ)..330 688-6494
4880 Hudson Dr Stow (44224) *(G-12446)*

National Machine Company, Mansfield *Also Called: Buckler Industries Inc (G-8769)*

National Machine Tool Company..513 541-6682
2013 E Galbraith Rd Cincinnati (45215) *(G-2894)*

National Machinery LLC (HQ)...419 447-5211
161 Greenfield St Tiffin (44883) *(G-12792)*

National Metal Shapes Inc...740 363-9559
425 S Sandusky St Ste 1 Delaware (43015) *(G-6164)*

National Molded Products Inc................................ 440 365-3400
  131 Samuel St Elyria (44035) *(G-6567)*

National Office Services, Cleveland *Also Called: National Electro-Coatings Inc (G-4059)*

National Oil Products, Hamilton *Also Called: Wallover Oil Hamilton Inc (G-7537)*

National Oilwell Varco LP.................................... 937 454-4660
  5870 Poe Ave Dayton (45414) *(G-5901)*

National Pallet & Mulch LLC................................ 937 237-1643
  3550 Intercity Dr Dayton (45424) *(G-5902)*

National Pat Anlytical Systems............................. 419 526-6727
  2090 Harrington Memorial Rd Mansfield (44903) *(G-8836)*

National Pattern Mfgco....................................... 330 682-6871
  1200 N Main St Orrville (44667) *(G-10997)*

National Peening.. 216 342-9155
  23800 Corbin Dr Unit B Bedford Heights (44128) *(G-1080)*

National Plating Corporation................................ 216 341-6707
  6701 Hubbard Ave Ste 1 Cleveland (44127) *(G-4061)*

National Polishing Systems Inc............................. 330 659-6547
  9299 Market Pl Broadview Heights (44147) *(G-1506)*

National Polymer Inc... 440 708-1245
  10200 Gottschalk Pkwy Chagrin Falls (44023) *(G-2171)*

National Power Coating Ohio................................ 330 405-5587
  2020 Case Pkwy Twinsburg (44087) *(G-13345)*

National Pride Equipment, Mansfield *Also Called: National Pride Equipment Inc (G-8837)*

National Pride Equipment Inc.............................. 419 289-2886
  905 Hickory Ln Ste 101 Mansfield (44905) *(G-8837)*

National Roller Die Inc...................................... 440 951-3850
  4750 Beidler Rd Unit 4 Willoughby (44094) *(G-14492)*

National Safety Apparel LLC (HQ)..........................800 553-0672
  15825 Industrial Pkwy Cleveland (44135) *(G-4062)*

National Scoreboards LLC................................... 513 791-5244
  8044 Montgomery Rd Ste 700 Cincinnati (45236) *(G-2895)*

National Screen Production, Cleveland *Also Called: Charizma Corp (G-3485)*

National Sign Systems Inc................................... 614 850-2540
  4200 Lyman Ct Hilliard (43026) *(G-7689)*

National Skilled Trades Netwrk............................. 614 230-2852
  5950 Sharon Woods Blvd Columbus (43229) *(G-5122)*

National Smallwares, Columbus *Also Called: Wasserstrom Company (G-5356)*

National Stair Corp... 937 325-1347
  20 Zischler St Springfield (45504) *(G-12356)*

National Super Service Co, Toledo *Also Called: MJB Toledo Inc (G-13056)*

National Tool & Equipment Inc.............................. 330 629-8665
  60 Karago Ave Youngstown (44512) *(G-14903)*

National Welding, Grove City *Also Called: National Wldg Tanker Repr LLC (G-7404)*

National Wldg Tanker Repr LLC............................. 614 875-3399
  2036 Hendrix Dr Grove City (43123) *(G-7404)*

Nationwide Belting Sls Svc LLC (PA)...................... 419 287-7092
  504 E Front St Pemberville (43450) *(G-11177)*

Nationwide Chemical Products.............................. 419 714-7075
  24851 E Broadway Rd Perrysburg (43551) *(G-11240)*

Natreeola Soap Company LLC............................... 513 390-2247
  2367 Bendel Dr Middletown (45044) *(G-9881)*

Natural Beauty Hc Express.................................. 440 459-1776
  6809 Mayfield Rd Apt 550 Mayfield Heights (44124) *(G-9338)*

Natural Beauty Products Inc................................ 513 420-9400
  104 Charles St Middletown (45042) *(G-9882)*

Natural Essentials Inc....................................... 330 562-8022
  115 Lena Dr Aurora (44202) *(G-680)*

Natural Essentials Inc (PA)................................. 330 562-8022
  1830 Miller Pkwy Streetsboro (44241) *(G-12513)*

Natural Optons Armatherapy LLC.......................... 419 886-3736
  610 State Route 97 W Bellville (44813) *(G-1140)*

Nature Pure LLC (PA).. 937 358-2364
  26586 State Route 739 Raymond (43067) *(G-11553)*

Nature Pure LLC.. 937 358-2364
  26560 Storms Rd West Mansfield (43358) *(G-14180)*

Natures Health Food LLC.................................... 419 260-9265
  21561 County Road 190 Mount Victory (43340) *(G-10269)*

Natures Own Source LLC.................................... 440 838-5135
  7033 Mill Rd Brecksville (44141) *(G-1477)*

Natures Way Bird Products LLC............................. 440 554-6166
  9054 Washington St Chagrin Falls (44023) *(G-2172)*

Nautical Needle LLC... 419 732-2990
  2853 East Harbor Rd Ste B Port Clinton (43452) *(G-11446)*

Nauticus Inc.. 440 746-1290
  8080 Snowville Rd Brecksville (44141) *(G-1478)*

Navage, Brooklyn *Also Called: Rhinosystems Inc (G-1525)*

Navidea, Dublin *Also Called: Navidea Biopharmaceuticals Inc (G-6324)*

Navidea Biopharmaceuticals Inc (PA)...................... 614 793-7500
  4995 Bradenton Ave Ste 240 Dublin (43017) *(G-6324)*

Navistar, Cincinnati *Also Called: International Motors LLC (G-2752)*

Navistar, Springfield *Also Called: International Motors LLC (G-12328)*

Navistone Inc.. 844 677-3667
  231 W 12th St Ste 200w Cincinnati (45202) *(G-2896)*

Nbw Inc... 216 377-1700
  4556 Industrial Pkwy Cleveland (44135) *(G-4063)*

NC Works Inc.. 937 514-7781
  3500 Commerce Center Dr Franklin (45005) *(G-7037)*

Ncc, Cleveland *Also Called: North Coast Container LLC (G-4083)*

Nccd, Wooster *Also Called: North Central Con Designs Inc (G-14669)*

Ncf Cim Fabricators LLC.................................... 863 425-1000
  1310 W 4th St Ontario (44906) *(G-10950)*

NCM, Cleveland *Also Called: North Coast Media LLC (G-4087)*

NCR Technology Center...................................... 937 445-1936
  1560 S Patterson Blvd Dayton (45409) *(G-5903)*

Ncrformscom.. 800 709-1938
  137 Owen Brown St Hudson (44236) *(G-7853)*

Ncs, Brookpark *Also Called: North Coast Seal Incorporated (G-1556)*

Nct Technologies Group, New Carlisle *Also Called: Nct Technologies Group Inc (G-10376)*

Nct Technologies Group Inc (PA)..........................937 882-6800
  7867 W National Rd New Carlisle (45344) *(G-10376)*

ND Paper Inc.. 937 528-3822
  7777 Washington Village Dr Ste 210 Dayton (45459) *(G-5904)*

NDC Technologies, Dayton *Also Called: NDC Technologies Inc (G-5906)*

NDC Technologies Inc.. 937 233-9935
  8001 Technology Blvd Dayton (45424) *(G-5905)*

NDC Technologies Inc (HQ)..................................937 233-9935
  8001 Technology Blvd Dayton (45424) *(G-5906)*

Ndi Medical LLC (PA)..216 378-9106
  22901 Millcreek Blvd Ste 110 Cleveland (44122) *(G-4064)*

Ndw Textiles, Brooklyn *Also Called: Mmi Textiles Inc (G-1523)*

Nease Performance Chemicals, Harrison *Also Called: Catexel Nease LLC (G-7544)*

Nease Performance Chemicals, West Chester *Also Called: Catexel Nease LLC (G-13955)*

Neatlysmart, Lima *Also Called: United States Plastic Corp (G-8457)*

Neaton Auto Products Mfg Inc (HQ)........................ 937 456-7103
  975 S Franklin St Eaton (45320) *(G-6460)*

Nebc Inc.. 440 992-5500
  1726 Griswold Ave Ashtabula (44004) *(G-610)*

Neer's Engineering Labs, Bellefontaine *Also Called: Arden J Neer Sr (G-1099)*

Nef Ltd... 419 445-6696
  1901 S Defiance St Archbold (43502) *(G-505)*

Neff Machinery and Supplies................................ 740 454-0128
  112 S Shawnee Ave Zanesville (43701) *(G-15031)*

Neff Motivation Inc (DH)..................................... 937 548-3194
  645 Pine St Greenville (45331) *(G-7348)*

Neff Parts, Zanesville *Also Called: Neff Machinery and Supplies (G-15031)*

Neff-Perkins Company (PA)...................................440 632-1658
  16080 Industrial Pkwy Middlefield (44062) *(G-9818)*

Nehemiah Manufacturing Co LLC........................... 513 351-5700
  1907 South St Cincinnati (45204) *(G-2897)*

Neher Burial Vault Company................................. 937 399-4494
  1903 Saint Paris Pike Springfield (45504) *(G-12357)*

Neider, F A Co, Norwood *Also Called: Namoh Ohio Holdings Inc (G-10869)*

Neidert Fabricating Inc...................................... 330 753-3331
  712 Wooster Rd W Barberton (44203) *(G-824)*

Neil R Scholl Inc... 740 653-6593
  54 Snoke Hill Rd Ne Lancaster (43130) *(G-8213)*

Nelson, Oak Harbor *Also Called: C Nelson Mfg Co (G-10884)*

Nelson Aluminum Foundry Inc.............................. 440 543-1941
  17093 Munn Rd Chagrin Falls (44023) *(G-2173)*

Nelson Companies One LLC................................. 330 239-4370
  6935 Ridge Rd Wadsworth (44281) *(G-13654)*

Nelson Company... 614 444-1164
2160 Refugee Rd Columbus (43207) *(G-5123)*

Nelson Labs Fairfield Inc................................... 973 227-6882
9100 S Hills Blvd Broadview Heights (44147) *(G-1507)*

Nelson Manufacturing Company.......................... 419 523-5321
6448 State Route 224 Ottawa (45875) *(G-11039)*

Nelson Sand & Gravel Inc.................................. 440 224-0198
5720 State Route 193 Kingsville (44048) *(G-8139)*

Nelson Stud Welding Inc (HQ)............................ 440 329-0400
7900 W Ridge Rd Elyria (44035) *(G-6568)*

Nelson Tool Corporation.................................... 740 965-1894
388 N County Line Rd Sunbury (43074) *(G-12669)*

Nemco Food Equipment Ltd (PA).........................419 542-7751
301 Meuse Argonne St Hicksville (43526) *(G-7649)*

Neograf Solutions LLC...................................... 216 529-3777
11709 Madison Ave Lakewood (44107) *(G-8170)*

Neon... 216 541-5600
15201 Euclid Ave Cleveland (44112) *(G-4065)*

Neon Health Services Inc................................... 216 231-7700
4800 Payne Ave Cleveland (44103) *(G-4066)*

Neptune Equipment Company.............................. 513 851-8008
11082 Southland Rd Cincinnati (45240) *(G-2898)*

Nervive, Cleveland *Also Called: Nervive Inc (G-4067)*

Nervive Inc... 847 274-1790
5900 Landerbrook Dr Ste 350 Cleveland (44124) *(G-4067)*

Nesco Inc (PA).. 440 461-6000
6140 Parkland Blvd Ste 110 Cleveland (44124) *(G-4068)*

Nesco Resource, Cleveland *Also Called: Nesco Inc (G-4068)*

Nestaway LLC.. 216 587-1500
9100 Bank St Ste 1 Cleveland (44125) *(G-4069)*

Nestle, Solon *Also Called: Nestle Prepared Foods Company (G-12158)*

Nestle Brands Company, Solon *Also Called: Nestle Usa Inc (G-12160)*

Nestle Food Service Factory, Cleveland *Also Called: Nestle Usa Inc (G-4070)*

Nestle Prepared Foods Company.......................... 440 349-5757
5750 Harper Rd Solon (44139) *(G-12157)*

Nestle Prepared Foods Company (DH).................... 440 248-3600
30003 Bainbridge Rd Solon (44139) *(G-12158)*

Nestle Purina Petcare Company.......................... 740 454-8575
5 N 2nd St Zanesville (43701) *(G-15032)*

Nestle Usa Inc.. 216 861-8350
2621 W 25th St Cleveland (44113) *(G-4070)*

Nestle Usa Inc.. 440 349-5757
30003 Bainbridge Rd Solon (44139) *(G-12159)*

Nestle Usa Inc.. 440 264-6600
30000 Bainbridge Rd Solon (44139) *(G-12160)*

Nestle Usa Inc.. 440 349-5757
30500 Bainbridge Rd Solon (44139) *(G-12161)*

Net Braze LLC... 937 444-1444
351 Apple St Mount Orab (45154) *(G-10220)*

Netform, Maumee *Also Called: Metal Forming & Coining LLC (G-9309)*

Netherland Rubber Company (PA).........................513 733-0883
2931 Exon Ave Cincinnati (45241) *(G-2899)*

Nettleton Steel Treating Div, Wickliffe *Also Called: Thermal Treatment Center Inc (G-14396)*

Neturen America Corporation.............................. 513 863-1900
2995 Moser Ct Hamilton (45011) *(G-7512)*

Network Polymers Inc....................................... 330 773-2700
1353 Exeter Rd Akron (44306) *(G-244)*

Network Printing & Graphics.............................. 614 230-2084
443 Crestview Rd Columbus (43202) *(G-5124)*

Network Technologies Inc.................................. 330 562-7070
1275 Danner Dr Aurora (44202) *(G-681)*

Neundorfer Inc.. 440 942-8990
4590 Hamann Pkwy Willoughby (44094) *(G-14493)*

Neundorfer Engineering Service, Willoughby *Also Called: Neundorfer Inc (G-14493)*

Neurologix Technologies Inc.............................. 512 914-7941
10000 Cedar Ave Ste 3-160 Cleveland (44106) *(G-4071)*

Neuronoff Inc.. 216 505-1818
11000 Cedar Ave Ste 290 Cleveland (44106) *(G-4072)*

Neuros Medical Inc... 440 951-2565
35010 Chardon Rd Ste 210 Willoughby Hills (44094) *(G-14561)*

New Age Design & Tool Inc................................. 440 355-5400
162 Commerce Dr Lagrange (44050) *(G-8152)*

New Aqua LLC... 614 265-9000
3707 Interchange Rd Columbus (43204) *(G-5125)*

NEW AQUA LLC, Columbus *Also Called: New Aqua LLC (G-5125)*

New Bloomer Candy Company LLC........................ 740 452-7501
1445 Deercreek Dr Zanesville (43701) *(G-15033)*

New Bltmore Ice Cream Pdts Inc.......................... 330 904-6687
2932 Clearview Ave Nw Canton (44718) *(G-1956)*

New Bremen Machine & Tool Co.......................... 419 629-3295
705 Kuenzel Dr New Bremen (45869) *(G-10363)*

New Castings Inc... 330 645-6653
2200 Massillon Rd Akron (44312) *(G-245)*

New Cut Tool and Mfg Corp................................ 740 676-1666
1 New Cut Road Shadyside (43947) *(G-11924)*

New Dairy Cincinnati LLC................................... 214 258-1200
415 John St Cincinnati (45215) *(G-2900)*

New Dairy Ohio LLC.. 214 258-1200
3068 W 106th St Cleveland (44111) *(G-4073)*

New Dairy Ohio Transport LLC............................ 214 258-1200
3068 W 106th St Cleveland (44111) *(G-4074)*

New Dawn Designs, Girard *Also Called: New Dawn Distribution Inc (G-7277)*

New Dawn Distribution Inc................................. 330 759-3500
1282 Trumbull Ave Ste E Girard (44420) *(G-7277)*

New Dawn Labs LLC.. 203 675-5644
102 S Main St Union (45322) *(G-13410)*

New Die Inc.. 419 726-7581
2828 E Manhattan Blvd Toledo (43611) *(G-13062)*

New Diry Cincinnati Trnspt LLC........................... 214 258-1200
415 John St Cincinnati (45215) *(G-2901)*

New Eezy-Gro Inc... 419 927-6110
9841 County Highway 49 Upper Sandusky (43351) *(G-13449)*

New Horizons Baking Co LLC (PA)........................ 419 668-8226
211 Woodlawn Ave Norwalk (44857) *(G-10854)*

New Horizons Fd Solutions LLC (PA).................... 614 861-3639
2300 Citygate Dr Columbus (43219) *(G-5126)*

New Life Chapel.. 513 298-2980
10195 Giverny Blvd Cincinnati (45241) *(G-2902)*

New Life Sustainable Solutions, Leetonia *Also Called: Hamilton Polymers Company (G-8302)*

New Mansfield Brass & Alum Co.......................... 419 492-2166
636 S Center St New Washington (44854) *(G-10481)*

New Page Corporation....................................... 877 855-7243
8540 Gander Creek Dr Miamisburg (45342) *(G-9721)*

New Path International LLC................................. 614 410-3974
1476 Manning Pkwy Ste A Powell (43065) *(G-11493)*

New Pme Inc... 513 671-1717
518 W Crescentville Rd Cincinnati (45246) *(G-2903)*

New Publishing Holdings LLC.............................. 513 531-2690
10151 Carver Rd Ste 200 Blue Ash (45242) *(G-1313)*

New Republic Industries LLC (PA)....................... 614 580-9927
497 Bridle Dr Marysville (43040) *(G-9040)*

New Sabina Industries Inc................................. 937 584-2433
3650 Brookham Dr Ste A Grove City (43123) *(G-7405)*

New Sabina Industries Inc (HQ).......................... 937 584-2433
12555 Us Highway 22 And 3 Sabina (45169) *(G-11680)*

New Stone Age, North Ridgeville *Also Called: Rock Hard Industries LLC (G-10748)*

New Tech Plastics LLC...................................... 937 473-3011
1300 Mote Dr Covington (45318) *(G-5496)*

New Transcon LLC.. 440 255-7600
8824 Twinbrook Rd Mentor (44060) *(G-9570)*

New Vulco Mfg & Sales Co LLC........................... 513 242-2672
5353 Spring Grove Ave Cincinnati (45217) *(G-2904)*

New Waste Concepts Inc.................................... 877 736-6924
26624 Glenwood Rd Perrysburg (43551) *(G-11241)*

New Wayne Inc.. 740 453-3454
1555 Ritchey Pkwy Zanesville (43701) *(G-15034)*

New World Energy Resources (PA).......................740 344-4087
1500 Granville Rd Newark (43055) *(G-10525)*

New York Frozen Foods Inc (DH)......................... 216 292-5655
25900 Fargo Ave Bedford (44146) *(G-1049)*

New York Frozen Foods Inc................................. 626 338-3000
380 Polaris Pkwy Ste 400 Westerville (43082) *(G-14223)*

New York Frozen Foods Inc................................. 614 846-2232
380 Polaris Pkwy Ste 400 Westerville (43082) *(G-14224)*

Newact Inc.. 513 321-5177
2084 James E Sauls Sr Dr Batavia (45103) *(G-879)*

Newall Electronics Inc.. 614 771-0213
1803 Obrien Rd Columbus (43228) *(G-5127)*

Newark Water Plant, Newark *Also Called: City of Newark (G-10497)*

Neway Stamping & Mfg Inc.. 440 951-8500
4820 E 345th St Willoughby (44094) *(G-14494)*

Newberry Wood Enterprises Inc (PA)........................... 440 238-6127
12223 Prospect Rd Strongsville (44149) *(G-12578)*

Newbury Sandblasting & Pntg, Newbury *Also Called: Newbury Sndblst & Pntg Inc (G-10557)*

Newbury Sndblst & Pntg Inc....................................... 440 564-7204
9992 Kinsman Rd Newbury (44065) *(G-10557)*

Newbury Woodworks.. 440 564-5273
10958 Kinsman Rd Unit 2 Newbury (44065) *(G-10558)*

Newco Industries... 717 566-9560
4057 Glenmoor Rd Nw Canton (44718) *(G-1957)*

Newell - Psn LLC (PA)... 304 387-2700
235 E State Route 14 Ste 104 Columbiana (44408) *(G-4623)*

Newell Brands Inc... 330 733-1184
212 Progress Blvd Kent (44240) *(G-8056)*

Newell Brands Inc... 330 733-7771
3200 Gilchrist Rd Mogadore (44260) *(G-10081)*

Newell Holdings Delaware Inc..................................... 740 681-6461
1115 W 5th Ave Lancaster (43130) *(G-8214)*

Newell Rubbermaid, Mogadore *Also Called: Newell Brands Inc (G-10081)*

Newman Brothers Inc
5609 Center Hill Ave Cincinnati (45216) *(G-2905)*

Newman Diaphragms LLC.. 513 932-7379
964 W Main St Lebanon (45036) *(G-8278)*

Newman Sanitary Gasket Company............................. 513 932-7379
964 W Main St Lebanon (45036) *(G-8279)*

Newman Technology Inc (HQ)..................................... 419 525-1856
100 Cairns Rd Mansfield (44903) *(G-8838)*

Newpage Group Inc.. 937 242-9500
8540 Gander Creek Dr Miamisburg (45342) *(G-9722)*

News Tribune, Hicksville *Also Called: Tribune Printing Inc (G-7654)*

News Watchman & Paper.. 740 947-2149
860 W Emmitt Ave Ste 5 Waverly (45690) *(G-13870)*

Newsome & Work Metalizing Co................................... 330 376-7144
258 Kenmore Blvd Akron (44301) *(G-246)*

Newspaper Network Central OH.................................. 419 524-3545
70 W 4th St Mansfield (44903) *(G-8839)*

Newswanger Machine, Shiloh *Also Called: Leon Newswanger (G-11979)*

Newton Materion Inc... 216 692-3990
21801 Tungsten Rd Euclid (44117) *(G-6663)*

Newton's Paint & Body, Lucasville *Also Called: Michael W Newton (G-8668)*

Nexceris, Lewis Center *Also Called: Nextech Materials Ltd (G-8346)*

Next, Cincinnati *Also Called: Nilpeter Usa Inc (G-2909)*

Next Generation Crimping.. 440 237-6300
9880 York Alpha Dr North Royalton (44133) *(G-10776)*

Next Resins, Sylvania *Also Called: Next Specialty Resins Inc (G-12719)*

Next Sales LLC.. 330 704-4126
3258 Dogwood Ln Nw Dover (44622) *(G-6255)*

Next Specialty Resins Inc (PA)................................... 419 843-4600
3315 Centennial Rd Ste J Sylvania (43560) *(G-12719)*

Next Surface Inc.. 440 576-0194
223 S Spruce St Jefferson (44047) *(G-7979)*

Next Wave Automation LLC.. 419 491-4520
600 W Boundary St Perrysburg (43551) *(G-11242)*

Nextant Aerospace, Cleveland *Also Called: Nextant Aerospace LLC (G-4075)*

Nextant Aerospace LLC.. 216 898-4800
18601 Cleveland Pkwy Dr Cleveland (44135) *(G-4075)*

Nextant Aerospace Holdings LLC, Cleveland *Also Called: K&M Aviation LLC (G-3902)*

Nextech Materials Ltd... 614 842-6606
404 Enterprise Dr Lewis Center (43035) *(G-8346)*

Nextgen Fiber Optics LLC (PA)................................... 513 549-4691
720 E Pete Rose Way Ste 410 Cincinnati (45202) *(G-2906)*

Nextmed Systems Inc (PA).. 216 674-0511
16 Triangle Park Dr Cincinnati (45246) *(G-2907)*

Nextstep Networking, Blue Ash *Also Called: Eaj Services LLC (G-1269)*

Neyra Interstate Inc (PA)... 513 733-1000
10700 Evendale Dr Cincinnati (45241) *(G-2908)*

Nfi Industries Inc... 740 928-9522
111 Enterprise Dr Hebron (43025) *(G-7626)*

Nfm/Welding Engineers Inc (PA)................................. 330 837-3868
577 Oberlin Ave Sw Massillon (44647) *(G-9226)*

Ngo Development Corporation..................................... 740 622-9560
504 N 3rd St Coshocton (43812) *(G-5464)*

Ngts, Beavercreek Township *Also Called: Northrop Grmman Tchncal Svcs I (G-1000)*

Nhvs International Inc... 440 527-8610
7600 Tyler Blvd Mentor (44060) *(G-9571)*

Niagara Custombilt Mfg, Cleveland *Also Called: S A Langmack Company (G-4267)*

Nic Global, Chillicothe *Also Called: National Indus Concepts Inc (G-2267)*

Nice Body Automotive, Elyria *Also Called: Nice Body Automotive LLC (G-6569)*

Nice Body Automotive LLC.. 440 752-5568
818 Cleveland St Elyria (44035) *(G-6569)*

Nichidai America Corporation..................................... 419 423-7511
15630 E State Route 12 Ste 4 Findlay (45840) *(G-6898)*

Nichols Mold Inc... 330 297-9719
222 W Lake St Ravenna (44266) *(G-11534)*

Nick Kostecki Excavating Inc..................................... 330 242-0706
10644 Chatham Rd Spencer (44275) *(G-12234)*

Nickles Bakery 45, Zanesville *Also Called: Alfred Nickles Bakery Inc (G-14985)*

Nickolas Plastics LLC.. 419 423-1213
814 W Lima St Findlay (45840) *(G-6899)*

Nicks Plating Co.. 937 773-3175
6980 Free Rd Piqua (45356) *(G-11367)*

Nidec Avtron Automation Corporation......................... 216 642-1230
7555 E Pleasant Valley Rd Independence (44131) *(G-7912)*

Nidec Industrial Solutions, Cleveland *Also Called: Nidec Motor Corporation (G-4076)*

Nidec Industrial Solutions, Cleveland *Also Called: Nidec Motor Corporation (G-4077)*

NIDEC MINSTER CORPORATION (DH)......................... 419 628-2331
240 W 5th St Minster (45865) *(G-10062)*

Nidec Motor Corporation... 216 642-1230
243 Tuxedo Ave Cleveland (44131) *(G-4076)*

Nidec Motor Corporation... 216 642-1230
7555 E Pleasant Valley Rd Cleveland (44131) *(G-4077)*

Nielsen Jewelers, Lorain *Also Called: H P Nielsen Inc (G-8557)*

Niese Farms... 419 347-1204
7506 Cole Rd Crestline (44827) *(G-5504)*

Nifco America Corporation (HQ)................................. 614 920-6800
8015 Dove Pkwy Canal Winchester (43110) *(G-1794)*

Nifco America Corporation.. 614 836-3808
7877 Robinett Way Canal Winchester (43110) *(G-1795)*

Nifco America Corporation.. 614 836-8691
4485 S Hamilton Rd Groveport (43125) *(G-7446)*

Niftech, Mentor *Also Called: R J K Enterprises Inc (G-9604)*

Niftech Inc... 440 257-6018
5565 Wilson Dr Mentor (44060) *(G-9572)*

Niftech Precision Race Pdts, Mentor *Also Called: Niftech Inc (G-9572)*

Nifty Promo Products, Middletown *Also Called: Backyard Scoreboards LLC (G-9842)*

Nihon Company, Urbana *Also Called: Parker Trutec Incorporated (G-13476)*

Nikke Kureha America Co Ltd....................................... 513 771-6788
4591 Brate Dr West Chester (45011) *(G-14033)*

Nikola Labs, Westerville *Also Called: Assetwatch Inc (G-14243)*

Niktec Inc.. 513 282-3747
127 Industrial Dr Franklin (45005) *(G-7038)*

Niles Building Products Company (PA)......................... 330 544-0880
1600 Hunter Ave Niles (44446) *(G-10595)*

Niles Expanded Metals & Plas, Niles *Also Called: Nmc Metals Inc (G-10599)*

Niles Manufacturing & Finshg...................................... 330 544-0402
465 Walnut St Niles (44446) *(G-10596)*

Niles Mirror & Glass Inc.. 330 652-6277
234 Robbins Ave Ste 1 Niles (44446) *(G-10597)*

Niles Roll Service Inc (PA).. 330 544-0026
704 Warren Ave Niles (44446) *(G-10598)*

Nilodor Inc.. 800 443-4321
10966 Industrial Pkwy Nw Bolivar (44612) *(G-1386)*

Nilpeter Usa Inc.. 513 489-4400
11550 Goldcoast Dr Cincinnati (45249) *(G-2909)*

(G-0000) Company's Geographic Section entry number

Nimers & Woody II Inc (PA)...937 454-0722
1625 Fieldstone Way Vandalia (45377) *(G-13574)*

Nine Giant Brewing LLC..510 220-5104
6095 Montgomery Rd Cincinnati (45213) *(G-2910)*

Niobium Microsystems Inc...937 203-8117
444 E 2nd St Dayton (45402) *(G-5907)*

Nippon Paint (usa) Inc...216 651-5900
11110 Berea Rd Ste 1 Cleveland (44102) *(G-4078)*

Nippon Stl Intgrted Crnkshaft...419 435-0411
1815 Sandusky St Fostoria (44830) *(G-6994)*

Nissen Chemitec America, London *Also Called: Nissen Chemitec America Inc (G-8539)*

Nissen Chemitec America Inc..740 852-3200
350 E High St London (43140) *(G-8539)*

Nissin Precision N Amer Inc...937 836-1910
375 Union Blvd Englewood (45322) *(G-6620)*

Nitrojection..440 729-2711
8430 Mayfield Rd Chesterland (44026) *(G-2237)*

Nitto Inc...937 773-4820
220 Fox Dr Piqua (45356) *(G-11368)*

Nitto Inc...937 773-4820
1620 S Main St Piqua (45356) *(G-11369)*

Njf Manufacturing LLC..419 294-0400
7387 Township Highway 104 Upper Sandusky (43351) *(G-13450)*

Njm Furniture Outlet Inc...330 893-3514
6899 County Road 672 Millersburg (44654) *(G-10004)*

Nk Machine Inc..513 737-8035
1550 Pleasant Ave Hamilton (45015) *(G-7513)*

Nkh-Safety Inc..513 771-3839
1375 Kemper Meadow Dr Ste 12 Cincinnati (45240) *(G-2911)*

Nmc Metals Inc (PA)...330 652-2501
310 N Pleasant Ave Niles (44446) *(G-10599)*

Nmg Aerospace, Stow *Also Called: National Machine Company (G-12446)*

Nmgg Ctg LLC (HQ)..419 447-5211
161 Greenfield St Tiffin (44883) *(G-12793)*

Nn Inc..440 647-4711
125 Bennett St Wellington (44090) *(G-13897)*

Nn Autocam Precision Component...440 647-4711
125 Bennett St Wellington (44090) *(G-13898)*

Nn Metal Stampings LLC (PA)..419 737-2311
510 S Maple St Pioneer (43554) *(G-11322)*

Nnodum Pharmaceuticals Corp...513 861-2329
483 Northland Blvd Cincinnati (45240) *(G-2912)*

No Burn Inc...330 336-1500
1255 High St Ste 200 Wadsworth (44281) *(G-13655)*

No Name Lumber LLC..740 289-3722
165 No Name Rd Piketon (45661) *(G-11309)*

No Rinse Laboratories LLC..937 746-7357
868 Pleasant Valley Dr Springboro (45066) *(G-12261)*

Noble Beast Brewing LLC..570 809-6405
1864 W 45th St Cleveland (44102) *(G-4079)*

Noble Denim Workshop..513 560-5640
2929 Spring Grove Ave Cincinnati (45225) *(G-2913)*

Noble Tool Corp...937 461-4040
1535 Stanley Ave Dayton (45404) *(G-5908)*

Nock and Son Company...740 682-7741
4138 Monroe Hollow Rd Oak Hill (45656) *(G-10891)*

Noco, Glenwillow *Also Called: Noco Company (G-7286)*

Noco Company (PA)...216 464-8131
30339 Diamond Pkwy Ste 102 Glenwillow (44139) *(G-7286)*

Nof Metal Coatings N Amer Inc (HQ).....................................440 285-2231
275 Industrial Pkwy Chardon (44024) *(G-2215)*

Nofziger Door Sales Inc..419 445-2961
111 Taylor Pkwy Archbold (43502) *(G-506)*

Nofziger Door Sales Inc (PA)..419 337-9900
320 Sycamore St Wauseon (43567) *(G-13857)*

Nolan Company...740 269-1512
300 Boyce Dr Bowerston (44695) *(G-1400)*

Nolan Company (HQ)...330 453-7922
1016 9th St Sw Canton (44707) *(G-1958)*

Nolte Precise Manufacturing Inc..513 923-3100
6850 Colerain Ave Cincinnati (45239) *(G-2914)*

Nomac Drilling LLC...724 324-2205
67090 Executive Dr Saint Clairsville (43950) *(G-11704)*

Nomis Publications Inc..330 965-2380
8570 Foxwood Ct Youngstown (44514) *(G-14904)*

Non-Ferrous Casting Company...937 228-1162
736 Albany St Dayton (45417) *(G-5909)*

Non-Ferrous Heat Treating, Maple Heights *Also Called: Dewitt Inc (G-8882)*

Non-Injectable Manufacturing, Columbus *Also Called: Hikma Pharmaceuticals USA Inc (G-4986)*

Nook Industries LLC (DH)..216 271-7900
4950 E 49th St Cleveland (44125) *(G-4080)*

Nor-Fab Inc...330 467-6580
231 Beechwood Dr Northfield (44067) *(G-10796)*

Noramco, Euclid *Also Called: North American Plas Chem Inc (G-6666)*

Noramco Inc..216 531-3400
1400 E 222nd St Euclid (44117) *(G-6664)*

Norbar Torque Tools Inc..440 953-1175
36400 Biltmore Pl Willoughby (44094) *(G-14495)*

Norcia Bakery..330 454-1077
624 Belden Ave Ne Canton (44704) *(G-1959)*

Norcold LLC (HQ)..800 543-1219
1440 N Vandemark Rd Sidney (45365) *(G-12036)*

Nordec Inc...330 940-3700
900 Hampshire Rd Stow (44224) *(G-12447)*

Norden Mfg LLC..440 693-4630
4210 Kinsman Rd Nw North Bloomfield (44450) *(G-10625)*

Nordic Light America Inc...614 981-9497
6320 Winchester Blvd Canal Winchester (43110) *(G-1796)*

Nordson, Westlake *Also Called: Nordson Corporation (G-14317)*

Nordson Corporation...440 985-4496
300 Nordson Dr Amherst (44001) *(G-448)*

Nordson Corporation...440 985-4458
444 Gordon Ave Dock C1-C3 Amherst (44001) *(G-449)*

Nordson Corporation...440 985-4000
100 Nordson Dr M 81 Amherst (44001) *(G-450)*

Nordson Corporation (PA)...440 892-1580
28601 Clemens Rd Westlake (44145) *(G-14317)*

Nordson MCS, Dayton *Also Called: NDC Technologies Inc (G-5905)*

Nordson Medical Corporation..440 892-1580
28601 Clemens Rd Westlake (44145) *(G-14318)*

Norgren LLC..937 833-4033
325 Carr Dr Brookville (45309) *(G-1574)*

Norkaam Industries LLC..330 873-9793
1477 Copley Rd Akron (44320) *(G-247)*

Norlab, Lorain *Also Called: Norlab Inc (G-8569)*

Norlab Inc...440 282-5265
7465 Industrial Parkway Dr Lorain (44053) *(G-8569)*

Norlake, North Ridgeville *Also Called: Norlake Manufacturing Company (G-10741)*

Norlake Manufacturing Company (PA)...................................440 353-3200
39301 Taylor Pkwy North Ridgeville (44035) *(G-10741)*

Norman Noble Inc..216 761-5387
5507 Avion Park Dr Cleveland (44143) *(G-4081)*

Norman Noble Inc..216 851-4007
931 E 228th St Euclid (44123) *(G-6665)*

Norman Noble Inc (PA)...216 761-5387
5507 Avion Park Dr Highland Heights (44143) *(G-7660)*

Normandy Products Co..440 632-5050
16125 Industrial Pkwy Middlefield (44062) *(G-9819)*

Norplas Industries Inc (DH)..419 662-3200
7825 Caple Blvd Northwood (43619) *(G-10805)*

Norris Manufacturing LLC...330 602-5005
317 E Broadway St Dover (44622) *(G-6256)*

Norris North Manufacturing...330 691-0449
1500 Henry Ave Sw Canton (44706) *(G-1960)*

Norse Dairy Systems, Columbus *Also Called: Interbake Foods LLC (G-5018)*

Norse Dairy Systems Inc...614 294-4931
1700 E 17th Ave Columbus (43219) *(G-5128)*

Norse Dairy Systems LP..614 294-4931
1740 Joyce Ave Columbus (43219) *(G-5129)*

North Amercn Kit Solutions Inc (PA).....................................800 854-3267
172 Reaser Ct Elyria (44035) *(G-6570)*

North American Assemblies LLC.................... 843 420-5354
600 Stonehenge Pkwy Dublin (43017) *(G-6325)*

North American Cast Stone Inc.................... 440 286-1999
11546 Claridon Troy Rd Chardon (44024) *(G-2216)*

North American Coating Labs, Mentor *Also Called: Wilson Optical Labs Inc (G-9652)*

North American Composites.................... 440 930-0602
33660 Pin Oak Pkwy Avon Lake (44012) *(G-767)*

North American Dist Ctr, Cambridge *Also Called: Ridge Tool Company (G-1758)*

North American Plas Chem Inc (PA).................... 216 531-3400
1400 E 222nd St Euclid (44117) *(G-6666)*

North American Stamping Group, Ada *Also Called: Nasg Ohio LLC (G-4)*

North Cape Manufacturing, Streetsboro *Also Called: Technology House Ltd (G-12527)*

North Central Con Designs Inc.................... 419 606-1908
3331 E Lincoln Way Wooster (44691) *(G-14669)*

North Central Insulation Inc (PA).................... 419 886-2030
7539 State Route 13 Bellville (44813) *(G-1141)*

North Coast Composites Inc.................... 216 398-8550
4605 Spring Rd Cleveland (44131) *(G-4082)*

North Coast Container LLC (HQ).................... 216 441-6214
8806 Crane Ave Cleveland (44105) *(G-4083)*

North Coast Custom Molding Inc.................... 419 905-6447
211 W Geneva St Dunkirk (45836) *(G-6375)*

North Coast Exotics Inc.................... 216 651-5512
3159 W 68th St Cleveland (44102) *(G-4084)*

North Coast Instruments Inc.................... 216 251-2353
14615 Lorain Ave Cleveland (44111) *(G-4085)*

North Coast Litho Inc.................... 216 881-1952
4701 Manufacturing Ave Cleveland (44135) *(G-4086)*

North Coast Media LLC.................... 216 706-3700
1360 E 9th St Ste 1070 Cleveland (44114) *(G-4087)*

North Coast Medical Eqp Inc.................... 440 243-6189
96 Lincoln Ave Berea (44017) *(G-1183)*

North Coast Minority Media LLC.................... 216 407-4327
1360 E 9th St Cleveland (44114) *(G-4088)*

North Coast Publications, Cleveland *Also Called: North Coast Minority Media LLC (G-4088)*

North Coast Rivet Inc.................... 440 366-6829
700 Sugar Ln Elyria (44035) *(G-6571)*

North Coast Seal Incorporated.................... 216 898-5000
5163 W 137th St Brookpark (44142) *(G-1556)*

North Coast Theatrical Inc.................... 330 762-1768
2181 Killian Rd Akron (44312) *(G-248)*

North Coast Tire Co Inc.................... 216 447-1690
7810 Old Rockside Rd Cleveland (44131) *(G-4089)*

North East Fuel Inc.................... 330 264-4454
3927 Cleveland Rd Wooster (44691) *(G-14670)*

North End Press Incorporated.................... 740 653-6514
235 S Columbus St Lancaster (43130) *(G-8215)*

North Hill Marble & Granite Co.................... 330 253-2179
448 N Howard St Akron (44310) *(G-249)*

North Ridge Enterprises Inc.................... 440 965-5300
62 Firelands Blvd Norwalk (44857) *(G-10855)*

North Shore Printing LLC.................... 740 876-9066
1105 Gallia St Portsmouth (45662) *(G-11472)*

North Shore Safety, Mentor *Also Called: Tecmark Corporation (G-9633)*

North Shore Strapping Company (PA).................... 216 661-5200
1400 Valley Belt Rd Brooklyn Heights (44131) *(G-1536)*

North Star Building Pdts LLC.................... 216 431-1000
1281 E 38th St Cleveland (44114) *(G-4090)*

North Toledo Graphics LLC.................... 419 476-8808
5225 Telegraph Rd Toledo (43612) *(G-13063)*

Northast Ohio Nghbrhood Hlth S.................... 216 751-3100
13301 Miles Ave Cleveland (44105) *(G-4091)*

Northcoast Advertising, Ashland *Also Called: Heritage Press Inc (G-539)*

Northcoast Environmental Labs.................... 330 342-3377
10100 Wellman Rd Streetsboro (44241) *(G-12514)*

Northcoast Pmm LLC.................... 419 540-8667
4725 Southbridge Rd Toledo (43623) *(G-13064)*

Northcoast Valve and Gate Inc.................... 440 392-9910
9437 Mercantile Dr Mentor (44060) *(G-9573)*

Northcoast Woodcraft Inc.................... 330 677-1189
939 Treat Blvd Tallmadge (44278) *(G-12742)*

Northeast Blueprint and Sup Co.................... 216 261-7500
1230 E 286th St Cleveland (44132) *(G-4092)*

Northeast Cabinet Co LLC.................... 614 759-0800
6063 Taylor Rd Columbus (43230) *(G-5130)*

Northeast Coatings Inc.................... 330 784-7773
415 Munroe Falls Rd Tallmadge (44278) *(G-12743)*

Northeast Fabricators LLC.................... 330 747-3484
365 E Boardman St Youngstown (44503) *(G-14905)*

Northeast Tubular Inc.................... 330 567-2690
426 S Grant St Wooster (44691) *(G-14671)*

Northeastern Plastics Inc.................... 330 453-5925
112 Navarre Rd Sw Canton (44707) *(G-1961)*

Northeastern Process Cooling, Willoughby *Also Called: Nrc Inc (G-14497)*

Northeastern Rfrgn Corp.................... 440 942-7676
38274 Western Pkwy Willoughby (44094) *(G-14496)*

Northend Gear and Machine Inc.................... 513 860-4334
475 Security Dr Fairfield (45014) *(G-6758)*

Northern Bank Note Company, Harrison *Also Called: Sekuworks LLC (G-7566)*

Northern Chem Blnding Corp Inc.................... 216 781-7799
360 Literary Rd Cleveland (44113) *(G-4093)*

Northern Concrete Pipe Inc.................... 419 841-3361
3756 Centennial Rd Sylvania (43560) *(G-12720)*

Northern Manufacturing Co Inc.................... 419 898-2821
150 N Lake Winds Pkwy Oak Harbor (43449) *(G-10886)*

Northern Mobile Electric, Canton *Also Called: M Technologies Inc (G-1937)*

Northern Ohio Printing Inc.................... 216 398-0000
4721 Hinckley Industrial Pkwy Cleveland (44109) *(G-4094)*

Northern Precision Inc.................... 513 860-4701
3245 Production Dr Fairfield (45014) *(G-6759)*

Northern Stamping, Cleveland *Also Called: Northern Stamping Co (G-4096)*

Northern Stamping Co.................... 216 883-8888
5900 Harvard Ave Cleveland (44105) *(G-4095)*

Northern Stamping Co (HQ).................... 216 883-8888
6600 Chapek Pkwy Cleveland (44125) *(G-4096)*

Northern Stamping Co.................... 216 642-8081
7750 Hub Pkwy Cleveland (44125) *(G-4097)*

Northern Stamping Plant 2, Cleveland *Also Called: Northern Stamping Co (G-4097)*

Northhill T-Shirt Print Dsign.................... 330 208-0338
509 E Glenwood Ave Akron (44310) *(G-250)*

Northlake Steel Corporation.................... 330 220-7717
5455 Wegman Dr Valley City (44280) *(G-13513)*

Northrop Grmman Innvtion Syste.................... 937 429-9261
1365 Technology Ct Beavercreek (45430) *(G-993)*

Northrop Grmman Tchncal Svcs I.................... 937 320-3100
4065 Colonel Glenn Hwy Beavercreek Township (45431) *(G-1000)*

Northrop Grmmn Spce & Mssn Sys.................... 937 259-4956
1900 Founders Dr Ste 202 Dayton (45420) *(G-5910)*

Northrop Grumman Systems Corp.................... 937 490-4111
1365 Technology Ct Beavercreek (45430) *(G-994)*

Northrop Grumman Systems Corp.................... 937 429-6450
4065 Colonel Glenn Hwy Beavercreek Township (45431) *(G-1001)*

Northrop Grumman Systems Corp.................... 513 881-3296
460 W Crescentville Rd West Chester (45246) *(G-14134)*

Northshore Mold Inc.................... 440 838-8212
2861 E Royalton Rd Cleveland (44147) *(G-4098)*

Northstar Asphalt, Canton *Also Called: Stark Materials Inc (G-2014)*

Northstar Plastics Inc.................... 216 340-7109
27200 Tinkers Ct Glenwillow (44139) *(G-7287)*

Northstar Publishing Inc.................... 330 721-9126
437 Lafayette Rd Ste 310 Medina (44256) *(G-9429)*

Northwest Installations Inc.................... 419 423-5738
1903 Blanchard Ave Findlay (45840) *(G-6900)*

Northwest Molded Plastics.................... 419 459-4414
14372 County Road 4 Edon (43518) *(G-6477)*

Northwest Products, Stryker *Also Called: Quadco Rehabilitation Ctr Inc (G-12626)*

Northwestern Tools Inc.................... 937 298-9994
4800 Hempstead Station Dr Dayton (45429) *(G-5911)*

Northwind Industries Inc.................... 216 433-0666
11324 Brookpark Rd Cleveland (44130) *(G-4099)*

Northwood Energy Corporation.................... 614 457-1024
941 Chatham Ln Ste 100 Columbus (43221) *(G-5131)*

Northwood Industries Inc.. 419 666-2100
  7650 Ponderosa Rd Perrysburg (43551) *(G-11243)*

Norton Industries Inc... 888 357-2345
  1366 W 117th St Lakewood (44107) *(G-8171)*

Norton Manufacturing Co Inc... 419 435-0411
  455 W 4th St Fostoria (44830) *(G-6995)*

Norton Outdoor Advertising.. 513 631-4864
  5280 Kennedy Ave Cincinnati (45213) *(G-2915)*

Norwalk Concrete Inds Inc (PA).. 419 668-8167
  80 Commerce Dr Norwalk (44857) *(G-10856)*

Norwalk Precast Molds, Inc., Norwalk *Also Called: Precast Products LLC (G-10859)*

Norwalk Reflector, Norwalk *Also Called: Herald Reflector Inc (G-10847)*

Norwalk Reflector, Norwalk *Also Called: Ogden News Publishing Ohio Inc (G-10858)*

Norwalk Wastewater Eqp Co.. 419 668-4471
  220 Republic St Norwalk (44857) *(G-10857)*

Norweco, Norwalk *Also Called: Norwalk Wastewater Eqp Co (G-10857)*

Norwesco Inc... 740 654-6402
  3111 Wilson Rd Lancaster (43130) *(G-8216)*

Norwood Medical, Dayton *Also Called: Norwood Medical LLC (G-5912)*

Norwood Medical LLC (DH).. 937 228-4101
  2122 Winners Cir Dayton (45404) *(G-5912)*

Norwood Medical LLC... 937 228-4101
  2101 Winners Cir Dayton (45404) *(G-5913)*

Norwood Tool Company... 937 228-4101
  2055 Winners Cir Dayton (45404) *(G-5914)*

NORWOOD TOOL COMPANY, Dayton *Also Called: Norwood Tool Company (G-5914)*

Noshok Inc (PA).. 440 243-0838
  1010 W Bagley Rd Berea (44017) *(G-1184)*

Nostalgic Images Inc... 419 784-1728
  26012 Nostalgic Rd Defiance (43512) *(G-6122)*

Nostrum Laboratories Inc... 419 636-1168
  705 E Mulberry St Unit A Bryan (43506) *(G-1653)*

Nov Inc... 937 454-3200
  5870 Poe Ave Dayton (45414) *(G-5915)*

Nov Process & Flow Tech US Inc... 937 454-3300
  5870 Poe Ave Dayton (45414) *(G-5916)*

Nova, Middleburg Heights *Also Called: Nova Machine Products Inc (G-9775)*

Nova Machine Products Inc.. 216 267-3200
  18001 Sheldon Rd Middleburg Heights (44130) *(G-9775)*

Nova Metal Products, Mentor *Also Called: Nova Metal Products Inc (G-9574)*

Nova Metal Products Inc.. 440 269-1741
  7500 Clover Ave Mentor (44060) *(G-9574)*

Nova Structural Steel Inc.. 216 938-7476
  900 E 69th St Cleveland (44103) *(G-4100)*

Novacel Inc.. 937 335-5611
  421 Union St Troy (45373) *(G-13243)*

Novacel Prfmce Coatings Inc... 937 552-4932
  421 Union St Troy (45373) *(G-13244)*

Novagard Solutions Inc (PA).. 216 881-8111
  5109 Hamilton Ave Cleveland (44114) *(G-4101)*

Novak J F Manufacturing Co LLC... 216 741-5112
  2701 Meyer Ave Cleveland (44109) *(G-4102)*

Novatex North America Inc.. 419 282-4264
  1070 Faultless Dr Ashland (44805) *(G-555)*

Novation Solutions LLC... 330 620-6721
  25 Foundation Pl Barberton (44203) *(G-825)*

Novavision LLC (PA).. 419 354-1427
  524 E Woodland Cir Bowling Green (43402) *(G-1430)*

Novel Writing Workshop, Blue Ash *Also Called: F+w Media Inc (G-1274)*

Novelis Alr Almnum-Alabama LLC.. 256 353-1550
  25825 Science Park Dr Ste 400 Beachwood (44122) *(G-932)*

Novelis Alr Aluminum LLC.. 216 910-3400
  25825 Science Park Dr Ste 400 Beachwood (44122) *(G-933)*

Novelis Alr Recycling Ohio LLC.. 740 922-2373
  7335 Newport Rd Se Uhrichsville (44683) *(G-13404)*

Novelis Alr Rolled Pdts LLC.. 740 983-2571
  1 Reynolds Rd Ashville (43103) *(G-627)*

Novelis Alr Rolled Pdts LLC (DH).. 216 910-3400
  25825 Science Park Dr Ste 400 Beachwood (44122) *(G-934)*

Novelis Corporation.. 740 983-2571
  1 Reynolds Rd Ashville (43103) *(G-628)*

Novelis Corporation.. 330 841-3456
  390 Griswold St Ne Warren (44483) *(G-13784)*

Novelty Advertising Co Inc.. 740 622-3113
  1148 Walnut St Coshocton (43812) *(G-5465)*

Noveon Fcc Inc.. 440 943-4200
  29400 Lakeland Blvd Wickliffe (44092) *(G-14384)*

Novex Operating Company LLC... 330 335-2371
  74 Robinson Ave Barberton (44203) *(G-826)*

Novex Products Inc.. 440 244-3330
  2707 Toledo Ave Ste A Lorain (44055) *(G-8570)*

Novo Manufacturing LLC (DH).. 740 269-2221
  35280 Scio Bowerston Rd Bowerston (44695) *(G-1401)*

Novoco LLC... 330 359-5315
  4041 Township Road 606 Fredericksburg (44627) *(G-7066)*

Novolyte Performance, Cleveland *Also Called: Novolyte Technologies Inc (G-4103)*

Novolyte Technologies Inc... 216 867-1040
  8001 E Pleasant Valley Rd Cleveland (44131) *(G-4103)*

Noxgear LLC.. 937 317-0199
  966 Proprietors Rd Worthington (43085) *(G-14722)*

Npa Coatings, Cleveland *Also Called: Npa Coatings Inc (G-4104)*

Npa Coatings Inc... 216 651-5900
  11110 Berea Rd Ste 1 Cleveland (44102) *(G-4104)*

Npas Inc... 614 595-6916
  2090 Harrington Memorial Rd Mansfield (44903) *(G-8840)*

Npk Construction Equipment Inc (HQ)................................. 440 232-7900
  7550 Independence Dr Bedford (44146) *(G-1050)*

Npl Homecare LLC.. 440 365-8581
  13500 Darice Pkwy Ste A Strongsville (44149) *(G-12579)*

NPS, Broadview Heights *Also Called: National Polishing Systems Inc (G-1506)*

Nrc Inc... 440 975-9449
  38160 Western Pkwy Willoughby (44094) *(G-14497)*

NRG Industrial Lighting Mfg Co.. 419 354-8207
  7458 Linwood Rd Bowling Green (43402) *(G-1431)*

Nrka Corp... 440 817-0700
  1100 W Royalton Rd Ste A Broadview Heights (44147) *(G-1508)*

Nsg Glass North America Inc... 734 755-5816
  21705 Pemberville Rd Luckey (43443) *(G-8671)*

Nsg Glass North America Inc (PA)....................................... 419 247-4800
  811 Madison Ave Toledo (43604) *(G-13065)*

Nsi Crankshaft, Fostoria *Also Called: Nippon Stl Intgrted Crnkshaft (G-6994)*

NSK Industries Inc (PA)... 330 923-4112
  150 Ascot Pkwy Cuyahoga Falls (44223) *(G-5563)*

NSM, Cleveland *Also Called: Flexrack By Qcells LLC (G-3725)*

Nt, Toledo *Also Called: North Toledo Graphics LLC (G-13063)*

Nta Graphics Inc.. 419 476-8808
  5225 Telegraph Rd Toledo (43612) *(G-13066)*

Ntb, Cleveland *Also Called: Tbc Retail Group Inc (G-4303)*

Ntech Industries Inc... 707 467-3747
  5475 Kellenburger Rd Dayton (45424) *(G-5917)*

Nu Pet Company (HQ)... 330 682-3000
  1 Strawberry Ln Orrville (44667) *(G-10998)*

Nu Stream Filtration Inc... 937 949-3174
  1257 Stanley Ave Dayton (45404) *(G-5918)*

Nu-Di, Cleveland *Also Called: Nu-Di Products Co Inc (G-4105)*

Nu-Di Products Co Inc... 216 251-9070
  12730 Triskett Rd Cleveland (44111) *(G-4105)*

Nu-Tech Polymers Co Inc.. 513 942-6003
  3220 E Sharon Rd Cincinnati (45241) *(G-2916)*

Nu-Tool Industries Inc.. 440 237-9240
  9920 York Alpha Dr North Royalton (44133) *(G-10777)*

Nuance Company.. 740 964-0367
  17 Amanda Dr Granville (43023) *(G-7319)*

Nucam, Twinsburg *Also Called: Semtorq Inc (G-13377)*

Nucon International Inc (PA).. 614 846-5710
  7000 Huntley Rd Columbus (43229) *(G-5132)*

Nucor Corporation... 937 390-2300
  3000 Presidential Dr Ste 110 Beavercreek (45324) *(G-979)*

Nucor Corporation... 407 855-2990
  Cincinnati (45201) *(G-2917)*

Nucor Corporation... 901 275-3826
  300 Pike St Fl 4 Cincinnati (45202) *(G-2918)*

A
L
P
H
A
B
E
T
I
C

Nucor Load Center, Cincinnati *Also Called: Nucor Corporation (G-2918)*

Nucor Logistics LLC... 901 275-3826
  300 Pike St Cincinnati (45202) *(G-2919)*

Nucor Steel Marion Inc.. 740 383-6068
  400 Bartram Ave Marion (43302) *(G-8984)*

Nucor Steel Marion Inc (HQ)... 740 383-4011
  912 Cheney Ave Marion (43302) *(G-8985)*

Nuevue Solutions Inc.. 440 836-4772
  4209 State Route 44 D-134 Rootstown (44272) *(G-11651)*

Nufacturing Inc... 330 814-5259
  2845 Center Rd Brunswick (44212) *(G-1603)*

Numerics Unlimited Inc.. 937 849-0100
  1700 Dalton Dr New Carlisle (45344) *(G-10377)*

Nunzios Cabinet Shop, Cleveland *Also Called: Marzano Inc (G-3995)*

Nupco Inc... 419 629-2259
  06561 County Road 66a New Bremen (45869) *(G-10364)*

Nupro Company.. 440 951-9729
  4800 E 345th St Willoughby (44094) *(G-14498)*

Nutone Inc.. 888 336-3948
  9825 Kenwood Rd Ste 301 Blue Ash (45242) *(G-1314)*

Nutri-Force Nutrition, Delaware *Also Called: Vitamin Shoppe Florida LLC (G-6178)*

Nutrien AG Solutions Inc... 614 873-4253
  9972 State Route 38 Milford Center (43045) *(G-9958)*

Nutritional Medicinals LLC.. 937 433-4673
  9277 Centre Pointe Dr Ste 220 West Chester (45069) *(G-14034)*

Nutro Corporation... 440 572-3800
  11515 Alameda Dr Strongsville (44149) *(G-12580)*

Nutro Inc.. 440 572-3800
  11515 Alameda Dr Strongsville (44149) *(G-12581)*

Nutro Machinery, Strongsville *Also Called: Nutro Corporation (G-12580)*

Nuts Are Good Inc (PA)... 586 619-2400
  Busch Blvd Columbus (43229) *(G-5133)*

Nuvo Packaging LLC... 216 400-9676
  845 Kaderly Dr Columbus (43228) *(G-5134)*

Nvent Management Company... 440 248-0100
  6800 Arnold Miller Pkwy Solon (44139) *(G-12162)*

Nwp Manufacturing Inc.. 419 894-6871
  2862 County Road 146 Waldo (43356) *(G-13690)*

O C I, Waverly *Also Called: Oak Chips Inc (G-13871)*

O Connor Office Pdts & Prtg... 740 852-2209
  60 W High St London (43140) *(G-8540)*

O D M, Mason *Also Called: Oakley Die & Mold Co (G-9131)*

O E Meyer Co.. 614 428-5656
  5677 Chantry Dr Columbus (43232) *(G-5135)*

O E Meyer Co.. 419 332-6931
  1005 Everett Rd Fremont (43420) *(G-7124)*

O G Bell, Avon Lake *Also Called: Wolff Tool & Mfg Company Inc (G-774)*

O Gauge Railroading, Hilliard *Also Called: Ogr Publishing Inc (G-7690)*

O J C Publishing Co Inc.. 614 337-2055
  2862 Johnstown Rd Columbus (43219) *(G-5136)*

O K Coal & Concrete, Zanesville *Also Called: McClelland Inc (G-15027)*

O S C, Columbus *Also Called: Octsys Security Corp (G-5138)*

O-1, Perrysburg *Also Called: Owens-Illinois General Inc (G-11253)*

O-I, Perrysburg *Also Called: O-I Glass Inc (G-11244)*

O-I Glass Inc (PA).. 567 336-5000
  1 Michael Owens Way Perrysburg (43551) *(G-11244)*

O'Reilly Precision Tool, Russia *Also Called: OReilly Precision Pdts Inc (G-11676)*

Oak Chips Inc.. 740 947-4159
  9329 State Route 220 Ste A Waverly (45690) *(G-13871)*

Oak Hills Carton Co.. 513 948-4200
  6310 Este Ave Cincinnati (45232) *(G-2920)*

Oak Industrial Inc... 440 263-2780
  12955 York Delta Dr Ste G North Royalton (44133) *(G-10778)*

Oak Pointe Legacy LLC... 740 498-9820
  96 New Pace Rd Newcomerstown (43832) *(G-10573)*

Oak View Enterprises Inc... 513 860-4446
  100 Crossroads Blvd Bucyrus (44820) *(G-1685)*

Oakbridge Timber Framing.. 419 994-1052
  9001 Township Road 461 Loudonville (44842) *(G-8592)*

Oakes Foundry Inc... 330 372-4010
  700 Bronze Rd Ne Warren (44483) *(G-13785)*

Oakley Inc.. 949 672-6560
  1421 Springfield St Unit 2 Dayton (45403) *(G-5919)*

Oakley Die & Mold Co... 513 754-8500
  4393 Digital Way Mason (45040) *(G-9131)*

Oakley Inds Sub Assmbly Div In.................................... 419 661-8888
  6317 Fairfield Dr Northwood (43619) *(G-10806)*

Oaks Welding Inc.. 330 482-4216
  201 Prospect St Columbiana (44408) *(G-4624)*

Oaktree Wireline LLC.. 330 352-7250
  1825 E High Ave New Philadelphia (44663) *(G-10461)*

Oakwood Industries Inc (PA).. 440 232-8700
  7250 Division St Bedford (44146) *(G-1051)*

Oakwood Laboratories LLC (PA)..................................... 440 359-0000
  7670 First Pl Ste A Oakwood Village (44146) *(G-10908)*

Oakwood Laboratories LLC.. 440 505-2011
  27070 Miles Rd Solon (44139) *(G-12163)*

Oakwood Register, The, Dayton *Also Called: Winkler Co Inc (G-6082)*

Oase North America Inc.. 800 365-3880
  125 Lena Dr Aurora (44202) *(G-682)*

Oasis Consumer Healthcare LLC..................................... 216 394-0544
  425 Literary Rd Apt 100 Cleveland (44113) *(G-4106)*

Oasis International, Columbus *Also Called: Lvd Acquisition LLC (G-5077)*

Oasis Mditerranean Cuisine Inc...................................... 419 269-1459
  1520 W Laskey Rd Toledo (43612) *(G-13067)*

Oatey, Cleveland *Also Called: Oatey Supply Chain Svcs Inc (G-4108)*

Oatey Co (PA)... 800 203-1155
  20600 Emerald Pkwy Cleveland (44135) *(G-4107)*

Oatey Supply Chain Svcs Inc (HQ)................................. 216 267-7100
  20600 Emerald Pkwy Cleveland (44135) *(G-4108)*

Oats Overnight Inc.. 602 492-1751
  7757 Union Centre Blvd Ste 400 West Chester (45011) *(G-14035)*

Obars Machine and Tool Company (PA)........................... 419 535-6307
  115 N Westwood Ave # 125 Toledo (43607) *(G-13068)*

Obars Welding & Fabg Div, Toledo *Also Called: Obars Machine and Tool Company (G-13068)*

Oberfields LLC... 614 252-0955
  1165 Alum Creek Dr Columbus (43209) *(G-5137)*

Oberfields LLC... 937 885-3711
  10075 Sheehan Rd Dayton (45458) *(G-5920)*

Oberfields LLC (HQ).. 740 369-7644
  528 London Rd Delaware (43015) *(G-6165)*

Oberfields LLC... 740 369-7644
  471 Kintner Pkwy Sunbury (43074) *(G-12670)*

Obersons Nurs & Landscapes LLC.................................. 513 687-7379
  2389 Hamilton Cleves Rd Hamilton (45013) *(G-7514)*

Obersons Snow and Ice MGT, Hamilton *Also Called: Obersons Nurs & Landscapes LLC (G-7514)*

Obhc Inc... 440 236-5112
  33549 E Royalton Rd Unit 9 Columbia Station (44028) *(G-4595)*

Obic LLC... 419 633-3147
  525 Winzeler Dr # 1 Bryan (43506) *(G-1654)*

Obr Cooling Companies, Northwood *Also Called: Obr Cooling Towers LLC (G-10807)*

Obr Cooling Towers LLC... 419 243-3443
  2845 Crane Way Northwood (43619) *(G-10807)*

Obron Atlantic Corporation.. 440 954-7600
  830 E Erie St Painesville (44077) *(G-11100)*

Obs Inc... 330 453-3725
  1324 Tuscarawas St W Canton (44702) *(G-1962)*

Obs Specialty Vehicles, Canton *Also Called: Obs Inc (G-1962)*

Occassionaly Yours, Beavercreek *Also Called: Shops By Todd Inc (G-982)*

Occv1 Inc... 419 248-8000
  1 Owens Corning Pkwy Toledo (43659) *(G-13069)*

Occv2 LLC.. 419 248-8000
  1 Owens Corning Prkwy Toledo (43659) *(G-13070)*

Ochc, Cleveland *Also Called: Oasis Consumer Healthcare LLC (G-4106)*

Ocm LLC... 937 247-2700
  4500 Lyons Rd Miamisburg (45342) *(G-9723)*

Ocs Intellitrak Inc... 513 742-5600
  8660 Seward Rd Fairfield (45011) *(G-6760)*

Ocsial LLC (PA).. 415 906-5271
  950 Taylor Station Rd Ste W Gahanna (43230) *(G-7167)*

Octal Extrusion Corp... 513 881-6100
  5399 E Provident Dr West Chester (45246) *(G-14135)*

(G-0000) Company's Geographic Section entry number

Octopus Express Inc.. 614 412-1222
470 Olde Worthington Rd Westerville (43082) *(G-14225)*

Octsys Security Corp.. 614 470-4510
341 S 3rd St Ste 100-42 Columbus (43215) *(G-5138)*

Oculii Corp... 937 912-9261
829 Space Dr Beavercreek Township (45434) *(G-1002)*

Odawara Automation Inc... 937 667-8433
4805 S County Road 25a Tipp City (45371) *(G-12833)*

Odell Electronic Cleaning Stns, Westlake *Also Called: Aerocase Incorporated (G-14284)*

Odi, Elyria *Also Called: Ohio Displays Inc (G-6572)*

Odom, Milford *Also Called: Odom Industries Inc (G-9945)*

Odom Industries Inc... 513 248-0287
1262 Us Route 50 Milford (45150) *(G-9945)*

Odyssey Machine Company Ltd.................................. 419 455-6621
26675 Eckel Rd # 5 Perrysburg (43551) *(G-11245)*

Odyssey Printwear, Chagrin Falls *Also Called: Odyssey Spirits Inc (G-2174)*

Odyssey Spirits Inc.. 330 562-1523
7409 Pettibone Rd Chagrin Falls (44023) *(G-2174)*

Oe Exchange LLC (PA)... 440 266-1639
7750 Tyler Blvd Mentor (44060) *(G-9575)*

OEM, Cincinnati *Also Called: Ctl-Aerospace Inc (G-2530)*

Oerlikon Blzers Cating USA Inc................................. 330 343-9892
120 Deeds Dr Dover (44622) *(G-6257)*

Oerlikon Frction Systems US In................................. 937 233-9191
240 Detrick St Dayton (45404) *(G-5921)*

Oerlikon Friction Systems.. 937 449-4000
14 Heid Ave Dayton (45404) *(G-5922)*

Oerlikon Friction Systems (HQ)................................. 937 449-4000
240 Detrick St Dayton (45404) *(G-5923)*

Ofco Inc... 740 622-5922
111 N 14th St Coshocton (43812) *(G-5466)*

Off Contact Inc... 419 255-5546
4756 W Bancroft St Toledo (43615) *(G-13071)*

Off Contact Productions, Toledo *Also Called: Off Contact Inc (G-13071)*

Office Furniture Solution, North Canton *Also Called: Document Concepts Inc (G-10636)*

Office Magic Inc (PA)... 510 782-6100
2290 Wilbur Rd Medina (44256) *(G-9430)*

Ogc Industries Inc... 330 456-1500
934 Wells Ave Nw Canton (44703) *(G-1963)*

Ogden News Publishing Ohio Inc............................... 567 743-9843
34 E Main St Norwalk (44857) *(G-10858)*

Ogden News Publishing Ohio Inc (DH)........................ 419 625-5500
314 W Market St Sandusky (44870) *(G-11861)*

Ogden Newspapers Inc.. 304 748-0606
401 Herald Sq Steubenville (43952) *(G-12408)*

Ogden Newspapers Ohio Inc..................................... 419 448-3200
320 Nelson St Tiffin (44883) *(G-12794)*

Ogg Garick, Cleveland *Also Called: Garick LLC (G-3755)*

Oglebay Norton Mar Svcs Co LLC.............................. 216 861-3300
1001 Lakeside Ave E 15th Fl Cleveland (44114) *(G-4109)*

Ogonek Custom Hardwood Inc (PA)............................ 833 718-2531
61 E State St Barberton (44203) *(G-827)*

Ogr Publishing Inc... 330 757-3020
5825 Redsand Rd Hilliard (43026) *(G-7690)*

Ogs Industries, Akron *Also Called: Ohio Gasket and Shim Co Inc (G-252)*

Ohashi Technica USA Inc (HQ)................................... 740 965-5115
111 Burrer Dr Sunbury (43074) *(G-12671)*

Ohashi Technica USA Mfg Inc.................................... 740 965-9002
99 Burrer Dr Sunbury (43074) *(G-12672)*

Ohigro Inc (PA).. 740 726-2429
6720 Gillette Rd Waldo (43356) *(G-13691)*

Ohio Aluminum Chemicals LLC.................................. 513 860-3842
4544 Mulhauser Rd West Chester (45011) *(G-14036)*

Ohio Aluminum Industries Inc................................... 216 641-8865
4840 Warner Rd Cleveland (44125) *(G-4110)*

Ohio Art Company (PA)... 419 636-3141
1 Toy St Bryan (43506) *(G-1655)*

Ohio Asphaltic Limestone Corp................................. 937 364-2191
8591 Mad River Rd Hillsboro (45133) *(G-7721)*

Ohio Associated Entps LLC....................................... 440 354-3148
72 Corwin Dr Painesville (44077) *(G-11101)*

Ohio Associated Entps LLC....................................... 440 354-3148
1359 W Jackson St Painesville (44077) *(G-11102)*

Ohio Auto Supply Company....................................... 330 454-5105
1128 Tuscarawas St W Canton (44702) *(G-1964)*

Ohio Awning & Manufacturing Co............................... 216 861-2400
5777 Grant Ave Cleveland (44105) *(G-4111)*

Ohio Beauty Cut Stone, Akron *Also Called: Ohio Beauty Cut Stone II Inc (G-251)*

Ohio Beauty Cut Stone II Inc..................................... 330 644-2241
40 W Turkeyfoot Lake Rd Akron (44319) *(G-251)*

Ohio Beef USA LLC.. 419 257-5536
2208 Grant Rd North Baltimore (45872) *(G-10617)*

Ohio Belt Control Supply Co, Wadsworth *Also Called: D & J Electric Motor Repair Co (G-13634)*

Ohio Beverage Systems Inc....................................... 216 475-3900
9200 Midwest Ave Cleveland (44125) *(G-4112)*

Ohio Biosystems Coop Inc.. 419 980-7663
134 S Adams St Loudonville (44842) *(G-8593)*

Ohio Blenders Inc (PA)... 419 726-2655
2404 N Summit St Toledo (43611) *(G-13072)*

Ohio Blow Pipe, Cleveland *Also Called: Ohio Blow Pipe Company (G-4113)*

Ohio Blow Pipe Company (PA).................................... 216 681-7379
446 E 131st St Cleveland (44108) *(G-4113)*

Ohio Box & Crate Inc... 440 526-3133
16751 Tavern Rd Burton (44021) *(G-1703)*

Ohio Box and Crate Co, Burton *Also Called: Ohio Box & Crate Inc (G-1703)*

Ohio Bridge Corporation... 740 432-6334
201 Wheeling Ave Cambridge (43725) *(G-1752)*

Ohio Broach & Machine Company............................... 440 946-1040
35264 Topps Industrial Pkwy Willoughby (44094) *(G-14499)*

Ohio Brush Works, Plain City *Also Called: Delaware Paint Company Ltd (G-11403)*

Ohio Building Restoration Inc (PA)............................. 419 244-7372
830 Mill St Toledo (43609) *(G-13073)*

Ohio Carbon Blank Inc... 440 953-9302
38403 Pelton Rd Willoughby (44094) *(G-14500)*

Ohio Carbon Industries Inc....................................... 888 248-5029
1201 Jacobson Ave Ashland (44805) *(G-556)*

Ohio Cbd Guy LLC... 513 417-9806
7875 Montgomery Rd Cincinnati (45236) *(G-2921)*

Ohio City Pasta, Cleveland *Also Called: Food Designs Inc (G-3733)*

Ohio Cllbrtive Lrng Sltons Inc (PA)............................. 216 595-5289
17171 Golden Star Dr Strongsville (44136) *(G-12582)*

Ohio Coatings Company.. 740 859-5500
2100 Tin Plate Pl Yorkville (43971) *(G-14798)*

Ohio Coffee Collaborative Ltd.................................... 614 564-9852
745 N High St Columbus (43215) *(G-5139)*

Ohio Community Media, Miamisburg *Also Called: Ocm LLC (G-9723)*

Ohio Construction News, Cincinnati *Also Called: 400 3W 7th Street Partners Ltd (G-2320)*

Ohio Crafted Malt House LLC..................................... 614 961-7805
7775 Walton Pkwy New Albany (43054) *(G-10347)*

Ohio Crankshaft Div, Newburgh Heights *Also Called: Park-Ohio Industries Inc (G-10546)*

Ohio Custom Dies LLC... 330 538-3396
293 Rosemont Rd North Jackson (44451) *(G-10691)*

Ohio Custom Door LLC... 330 695-6301
9141 County Road 201 Fredericksburg (44627) *(G-7067)*

Ohio Cut Sheet, Strongsville *Also Called: Dupli-Systems Inc (G-12555)*

Ohio Dalley Press, Belpre *Also Called: Ovp Inc (G-1152)*

Ohio Decorative Products LLC (PA)............................. 419 647-9033
220 S Elizabeth St Spencerville (45887) *(G-12238)*

Ohio Department Transportation................................ 614 351-2898
1606 W Broad St Columbus (43223) *(G-5140)*

Ohio Designer Craftsmen Entps (HQ).......................... 614 486-7119
1665 W 5th Ave Columbus (43212) *(G-5141)*

Ohio Displays Inc.. 216 961-5600
825 Leona St Elyria (44035) *(G-6572)*

Ohio Distinctive Enterprises...................................... 614 459-0453
6500 Fiesta Dr Columbus (43235) *(G-5142)*

Ohio Distinctive Software, Columbus *Also Called: Ohio Distinctive Enterprises (G-5142)*

Ohio Drill & Tool Co (PA).. 330 525-7717
23255 Georgetown Rd Homeworth (44634) *(G-7806)*

Ohio Eagle Distributing LLC...................................... 513 539-8483
9300 Allen Rd West Chester (45069) *(G-14037)*

A
L
P
H
A
B
E
T
I
C

Ohio Electric Control, Ashland *Also Called: Precision Design Inc (G-566)*

Ohio Electric Motor Service Center Inc.............. 614 444-1451
1854 S High St Columbus (43207) *(G-5143)*

Ohio Electric Motor Svc LLC (PA).............. 614 444-1451
1909 E Livingston Ave Columbus (43209) *(G-5144)*

Ohio Electro-Polishing Co Inc.............. 419 667-2281
15085 Main St Venedocia (45894) *(G-13587)*

Ohio Embroidery LLC.............. 330 479-0029
1321 Davis St Sw Canton (44706) *(G-1965)*

Ohio Engineering and Mfg Co, Wadsworth *Also Called: Hutnik Company (G-13643)*

Ohio Envelope Manufacturing Co.............. 216 267-2920
5161 W 164th St Cleveland (44142) *(G-4114)*

Ohio Fabricators, Coshocton *Also Called: Ofco Inc (G-5466)*

Ohio Fabricators Company.............. 740 622-5922
1321 Elm St Coshocton (43812) *(G-5467)*

Ohio Feather Company Inc.............. 513 921-3373
1910 South St Cincinnati (45204) *(G-2922)*

Ohio Flame Hardening Company (PA).............. 513 336-6160
3944 Miami Rd Apt 106 Cincinnati (45227) *(G-2923)*

Ohio Flexible Packaging Co.............. 513 494-1800
512 S Main St South Lebanon (45065) *(G-12220)*

Ohio Foam Corporation.............. 614 252-4877
1513 Alum Creek Dr Columbus (43209) *(G-5145)*

Ohio Foam Corporation.............. 419 492-2151
529 S Kibler St New Washington (44854) *(G-10482)*

Ohio Foam Corporation.............. 330 799-4553
1201 Ameritech Blvd Youngstown (44509) *(G-14906)*

Ohio Fresh Eggs LLC (PA).............. 740 893-7200
11212 Croton Rd Croton (43013) *(G-5515)*

Ohio Galvanizing LLC.............. 740 387-6474
467 W Fairground St Marion (43302) *(G-8986)*

Ohio Gasket and Shim Co Inc (PA).............. 330 630-0626
976 Evans Ave Akron (44305) *(G-252)*

Ohio Gratings Inc (PA).............. 800 321-9800
5299 Southway St Sw Canton (44706) *(G-1966)*

Ohio Gravure Technologies, Miamisburg *Also Called: Ohio Gravure Technologies Inc (G-9724)*

Ohio Gravure Technologies Inc.............. 937 439-1582
4401 Lyons Rd Miamisburg (45342) *(G-9724)*

Ohio Hckry Hrvest Brnd Pdts In.............. 330 644-6266
90 Logan Pkwy Akron (44319) *(G-253)*

Ohio Hd Video.............. 614 656-1162
1355 Bingham Mills Dr New Albany (43054) *(G-10348)*

Ohio Heat Transfer.............. 513 870-5323
3400 Port Union Rd Hamilton (45014) *(G-7515)*

Ohio Heat Transfer Ltd.............. 877 633-0391
66721 Executive Dr Saint Clairsville (43950) *(G-11705)*

Ohio Hydraulics Inc.............. 513 771-2590
2510 E Sharon Rd Cincinnati (45241) *(G-2924)*

Ohio Industrial Coating Corp.............. 567 230-6719
880 S Bon Aire Ave Tiffin (44883) *(G-12795)*

Ohio Irish American News.............. 216 647-1144
14615 Triskett Rd Cleveland (44111) *(G-4115)*

Ohio Knitting Mills, Cleveland *Also Called: Okm LLC (G-4117)*

Ohio Label Inc.............. 614 777-0180
5005 Transamerica Dr Columbus (43228) *(G-5146)*

Ohio Laminating & Binding Inc.............. 614 771-4868
4364 Reynolds Dr Hilliard (43026) *(G-7691)*

Ohio Lumex Co Inc.............. 440 264-2500
30350 Bruce Industrial Pkwy Solon (44139) *(G-12164)*

Ohio Machinery Co (PA).............. 440 526-6200
3993 E Royalton Rd Broadview Heights (44147) *(G-1509)*

Ohio Made Tires LLC.............. 740 421-4934
47063 Black Walnut Pkwy Woodsfield (43793) *(G-14615)*

Ohio Magnetics Inc.............. 216 662-8484
5400 Dunham Rd Maple Heights (44137) *(G-8888)*

Ohio Metal Fabricating Inc.............. 937 233-2400
6057 Milo Rd Dayton (45414) *(G-5924)*

Ohio Metal Processing LLC.............. 740 912-2057
16064 Beaver Pike Jackson (45640) *(G-7949)*

Ohio Metal Products Company.............. 937 228-6101
35 Bates St Dayton (45402) *(G-5925)*

Ohio Metal Technologies Inc.............. 740 928-8288
470 John Alford Pkwy Hebron (43025) *(G-7627)*

Ohio Metallurgical Service Inc.............. 440 365-4104
1033 Clark St Elyria (44035) *(G-6573)*

Ohio Mill Supply, Cleveland *Also Called: Ohio Mills Corporation (G-4116)*

Ohio Mills Corporation (PA).............. 216 431-3979
1719 E 39th St Cleveland (44114) *(G-4116)*

Ohio Mirror Technologies Inc (PA).............. 419 399-5903
114 W Jackson St Paulding (45879) *(G-11160)*

Ohio Model Products LLC.............. 614 808-4488
4180 Fisher Rd Columbus (43228) *(G-5147)*

Ohio Module Manufacturing Company LLC.............. 419 729-6700
3900 Stickney Ave Toledo (43608) *(G-13074)*

Ohio Moulding Corporation (HQ).............. 440 944-2100
30396 Lakeland Blvd Wickliffe (44092) *(G-14385)*

Ohio Mulch, Lewis Center *Also Called: Ohio Mulch Supply Inc (G-8347)*

Ohio Mulch Supply Inc.............. 740 548-6242
6673 Columbus Pike Lewis Center (43035) *(G-8347)*

Ohio News Network.............. 614 460-3700
770 Twin Rivers Dr Columbus (43215) *(G-5148)*

Ohio News Network, Columbus *Also Called: Ohio News Network (G-5148)*

Ohio Newspaper Services Inc.............. 614 486-6677
1335 Dublin Rd Ste 216b Columbus (43215) *(G-5149)*

Ohio Newspapers Inc (DH).............. 937 225-2000
1611 S Main St Dayton (45409) *(G-5926)*

Ohio Newspapers Inc.............. 937 335-3997
131 S Market St Troy (45373) *(G-13245)*

Ohio Newspapers Foundation.............. 614 486-6677
1335 Dublin Rd Ste 216b Columbus (43215) *(G-5150)*

Ohio Nitrogen Co.............. 216 839-5485
25800 Science Park Dr Beachwood (44122) *(G-935)*

Ohio Nut & Bolt Company Div, Berea *Also Called: Fastener Industries Inc (G-1172)*

Ohio Ordnance Works Inc.............. 440 285-3481
310 Park Dr Chardon (44024) *(G-2217)*

Ohio Packing Company.............. 614 445-0627
1306 Harmon Ave Columbus (43223) *(G-5151)*

Ohio Paper Tube Co.............. 330 478-5171
3422 Navarre Rd Sw Canton (44706) *(G-1967)*

Ohio Pet Foods Inc (HQ).............. 330 424-1431
38251 Industrial Park Rd Lisbon (44432) *(G-8477)*

Ohio Pickling & Processing, Toledo *Also Called: Ohio Steel Processing LLC (G-13075)*

Ohio Plastics & Belting Co LLC.............. 330 882-6764
6140 Manchester Rd New Franklin (44319) *(G-10391)*

Ohio Power Systems LLC.............. 419 396-4041
807 E Findlay St Carey (43316) *(G-2061)*

Ohio Precision Inc.............. 330 453-9710
1239 Market Ave S Canton (44707) *(G-1968)*

Ohio Precision Molding Inc.............. 330 745-9393
122 E Tuscarawas Ave Barberton (44203) *(G-828)*

Ohio Pulp Mills Inc.............. 513 631-7400
2100 Losantiville Ave Ste 3 Cincinnati (45237) *(G-2925)*

Ohio Pure Foods Inc (HQ).............. 330 753-2293
681 W Waterloo Rd Akron (44314) *(G-254)*

Ohio Refining Company LLC.............. 614 210-2300
5550 Blazer Pkwy Ste 200 Dublin (43017) *(G-6326)*

Ohio Report, Columbus *Also Called: Gongwer News Service Inc (G-4962)*

Ohio Rights Group.............. 614 300-0529
1021 E Broad St Columbus (43205) *(G-5152)*

Ohio River Valley Cabinet.............. 740 975-8846
4 Waterworks Rd Newark (43055) *(G-10526)*

Ohio Roll Grinding Inc.............. 330 453-1884
5165 Louisville St Louisville (44641) *(G-8610)*

Ohio Rotational Molding LLC.............. 419 608-5040
2330 Heatherwood Dr Findlay (45840) *(G-6901)*

Ohio Screw Products Inc.............. 440 322-6341
818 Lowell St Elyria (44035) *(G-6574)*

Ohio Select Imprinted Fabrics, Reynoldsburg *Also Called: Ohio State Institute Fin Inc (G-11576)*

Ohio Semitronics Inc.............. 614 777-1005
4242 Reynolds Dr Hilliard (43026) *(G-7692)*

Ohio Shelterall Inc.............. 614 882-1110
6060 Westerville Rd Westerville (43081) *(G-14272)*

Ohio Specialty Dies LLC.............................330 538-3396
  293 Rosemont Rd North Jackson (44451) *(G-10692)*

Ohio Standard Bread, Medina *Also Called: Trogdon Publishing Inc (G-9458)*

Ohio Star Forge Co (HQ).............................330 847-6360
  3991 Mahoning Ave Nw Warren (44483) *(G-13786)*

Ohio State Institute Fin Inc.........................614 861-8811
  7394 E Main St Reynoldsburg (43068) *(G-11576)*

Ohio State Pallet Corp..............................614 332-3961
  2175 Broehm Rd Homer (43027) *(G-7804)*

Ohio State Plastics.................................614 299-5618
  1917 Joyce Ave Columbus (43219) *(G-5153)*

Ohio Steel Industries Inc...........................740 927-9500
  13792 Broad St Sw Pataskala (43062) *(G-11144)*

Ohio Steel Industries Inc (PA)......................614 471-4800
  2575 Ferris Rd Columbus (43224) *(G-5154)*

Ohio Steel Processing LLC...........................419 241-9601
  1149 Campbell St Toledo (43607) *(G-13075)*

Ohio Steel Sheet and Plate Inc......................800 827-2401
  7845 Chestnut Ridge Rd Hubbard (44425) *(G-7815)*

Ohio Table Pad Co Georgia Div, Perrysburg *Also Called: Ohio Table Pad Company (G-11246)*

Ohio Table Pad Company (PA).........................419 872-6400
  350 3 Meadows Dr Perrysburg (43551) *(G-11246)*

Ohio Table Pad Company..............................419 872-6400
  350 3 Meadows Dr Perrysburg (43551) *(G-11247)*

Ohio Table Pad of Indiana...........................419 872-6400
  350 3 Meadows Dr Perrysburg (43551) *(G-11248)*

Ohio Tile & Marble Co...............................513 541-4211
  3809 Spring Grove Ave Cincinnati (45223) *(G-2926)*

Ohio Timberland Products Inc........................419 682-6322
  102 Railroad Ave Stryker (43557) *(G-12625)*

Ohio Tool & Jig Grind Inc...........................937 415-0692
  6948 Clearview Ct Springboro (45066) *(G-12262)*

Ohio Tool Work LLC..................................419 281-3700
  1374 Township Road 743 Ashland (44805) *(G-557)*

Ohio Tool Works LLC.................................419 281-3700
  1374 Township Road 743 743 Ashland (44805) *(G-558)*

Ohio Trailer Inc....................................330 392-4444
  1899 Tod Ave Sw Warren (44485) *(G-13787)*

Ohio Trailer Supply Inc.............................614 471-9121
  2966 Westerville Rd Columbus (43224) *(G-5155)*

Ohio Transitional Mch & TI Inc......................419 476-0820
  3940 Castener St Toledo (43612) *(G-13076)*

Ohio Valley Alloy Services Inc......................740 373-1900
  100 Westview Ave Marietta (45750) *(G-8931)*

Ohio Valley Coal Company............................740 926-1351
  46226 National Rd Saint Clairsville (43950) *(G-11706)*

Ohio Valley Manufacturing Inc.......................419 522-5818
  1501 Harrington Memorial Rd Mansfield (44903) *(G-8841)*

Ohio Valley Specialty Company.......................740 373-2276
  115 Industry Rd Marietta (45750) *(G-8932)*

Ohio Valley Trackwork Inc...........................740 446-0181
  39 Fairview Rd Bidwell (45614) *(G-1213)*

Ohio Valley Truss Company (PA)......................937 393-3995
  6000 Us Highway 50 Hillsboro (45133) *(G-7722)*

Ohio Valley Veneer Inc..............................740 289-4979
  165 No Name Rd Piketon (45661) *(G-11310)*

Ohio Valley Veneer Inc (PA).........................740 493-2901
  16523 State Route 124 Piketon (45661) *(G-11311)*

Ohio Valley Veneer Co, Piketon *Also Called: Ohio Valley Veneer Inc (G-11311)*

Ohio Vly Stmpng-Assemblies Inc......................419 522-0983
  500 Newman St Mansfield (44902) *(G-8842)*

Ohio Willow Wood Company, The, Mount Sterling *Also Called: Willowwood Global LLC (G-10231)*

Ohio Wire Cloth, Englewood *Also Called: Unified Scrning Crshing - OH I (G-6627)*

Ohio Wire Form & Spring Co..........................614 444-3676
  2270 S High St Columbus (43207) *(G-5156)*

Ohio Wire Harness LLC...............................937 292-7355
  225 Lincoln Ave Bellefontaine (43311) *(G-1114)*

Ohio Wood Fabrication, Sandusky *Also Called: Gary L Gast (G-11835)*

Ohio Woodworking Co Inc.............................513 631-0870
  5035 Beech St Cincinnati (45212) *(G-2927)*

Ohio's Country Journal, Columbus *Also Called: Agri Communicators Inc (G-4679)*

Ohiohealth Imaging Services.........................740 420-7925
  1434 Circleville Plaza Dr Circleville (43113) *(G-3261)*

Ohiomet, Elyria *Also Called: Ohio Metallurgical Service Inc (G-6573)*

Ohios Best Juice Company LLC........................440 258-0834
  299 Pathfinder Dr Ste 103 Reynoldsburg (43068) *(G-11577)*

Ohlinger Dev & Editorial Co.........................614 261-5360
  28 W Henderson Rd Columbus (43214) *(G-5157)*

Ohlinger Publishing Svcs Inc........................614 261-5360
  28 W Henderson Rd Columbus (43214) *(G-5158)*

Ohlinger Studios, Columbus *Also Called: Ohlinger Dev & Editorial Co (G-5157)*

Ohlinger Studios, Columbus *Also Called: Ohlinger Publishing Svcs Inc (G-5158)*

Ohmart Vega, Lebanon *Also Called: Vega Americas Inc (G-8295)*

Ohta Press US Inc...................................937 374-3382
  1125 S Patton St Xenia (45385) *(G-14773)*

Oi, Perrysburg *Also Called: Owens-Illinois Inc (G-11255)*

Oil Enterprises, Logan *Also Called: Ralph Robinson Inc (G-8524)*

Oil Kraft Div, Cincinnati *Also Called: US Industrial Lubricants Inc (G-3189)*

Oil Skimmers, North Royalton *Also Called: OSI Environmental LLC (G-10779)*

Oil Tooling and Stamping, Ontario *Also Called: Cole Tool & Die Company (G-10948)*

OK Brugmann Jr & Sons Inc...........................330 274-2106
  4083 Mennonite Rd Mantua (44255) *(G-8873)*

OK Industries Inc...................................419 435-2361
  2307 W Corporate Dr W Fostoria (44830) *(G-6996)*

Okamoto Sandusky Mfg LLC............................419 626-1633
  3130 W Monroe St Sandusky (44870) *(G-11862)*

Okamoto USA, Sandusky *Also Called: Okamoto Sandusky Mfg LLC (G-11862)*

OKL Can Line Inc....................................
  11235 Sebring Dr Cincinnati (45240) *(G-2928)*

Okm LLC...216 272-6375
  4701 Perkins Ave Cleveland (44103) *(G-4117)*

Olan Plastics Inc...................................614 834-6526
  6550 Olan Dr Canal Winchester (43110) *(G-1797)*

Olberding Brand Family, Cincinnati *Also Called: The Photo-Type Engraving Company (G-3149)*

Old Classic Delight Inc.............................419 394-7955
  310 S Park Dr Saint Marys (45885) *(G-11744)*

Old Firehouse Cellars, Geneva *Also Called: Old Firehouse Winery Inc (G-7244)*

Old Firehouse Winery Inc............................440 466-9300
  5499 Lake Rd E Geneva (44041) *(G-7244)*

Old Mason Winery Inc................................937 698-1122
  4199 S Iddings Rd West Milton (45383) *(G-14184)*

Old Rar Inc...216 545-7249
  3700 Park East Dr Ste 300 Beachwood (44122) *(G-936)*

Old Smo Inc...419 394-3346
  323 S Park Dr Saint Marys (45885) *(G-11745)*

Old Smo Inc (PA)....................................419 394-3346
  405 E South St Saint Marys (45885) *(G-11746)*

Old Trail Printing Co, Columbus *Also Called: Old Trail Printing Company (G-5159)*

Old Trail Printing Company..........................614 443-4852
  100 Fornoff Rd Columbus (43207) *(G-5159)*

Old West Woods, Waynesfield *Also Called: Aca Millworks Inc (G-13877)*

Oldcastle Apg Midwest Inc...........................440 949-1815
  5190 Oster Rd Sheffield Village (44054) *(G-11961)*

Oldcastle Buildingenvelope Inc......................800 537-4064
  291 M St Perrysburg (43551) *(G-11249)*

Oldcastle Infrastructure Inc........................419 592-2309
  1675 Industrial Dr Napoleon (43545) *(G-10294)*

Olde Man Granola LLC................................419 819-9576
  7227 W State Route 12 Findlay (45840) *(G-6902)*

Olde Schlhuse Vnyrd Winery LLC......................937 472-9463
  152 State Route 726 N Eaton (45320) *(G-6461)*

Olde Wood Ltd.......................................330 866-1441
  7557 Willowdale Ave Se Magnolia (44643) *(G-8735)*

Oldkor Inc..216 631-7800
  10410 Berea Rd Cleveland (44102) *(G-4118)*

Olen Corporation....................................419 294-2611
  6326 County Highway 61 Upper Sandusky (43351) *(G-13451)*

Oliver Healthcare Packaging Co......................513 860-6880
  3840 Symmes Rd Hamilton (45015) *(G-7516)*

A
L
P
H
A
B
E
T
I
C

Oliver Inc., Cleveland Also Called: Chilcote Company **(G-3495)**

Oliver Inc., Twinsburg Also Called: Oliver Printing & Packg Co LLC **(G-13346)**

Oliver Printing & Packg Co LLC (HQ)..................330 425-7890
1760 Enterprise Pkwy Twinsburg (44087) **(G-13346)**

Oliver Rubber Co...419 420-6235
701 Lima Ave Findlay (45840) **(G-6903)**

Oliver Steel Plate, Bedford Also Called: AM Castle & Co **(G-1011)**

Oliver Steel Plate Co.....................................330 425-7000
7851 Bavaria Rd Twinsburg (44087) **(G-13347)**

Oliver-Tolas Healthcare Packg, Hamilton Also Called: Oliver Healthcare Packaging Co
(G-7516)

Olson Sheet Metal Cnstr Co.........................330 745-8225
465 Glenn St Barberton (44203) **(G-829)**

Olymco, Canton Also Called: Delta Plating Inc **(G-1880)**

Olympia Candies, Strongsville Also Called: Robert E McGrath Inc **(G-12593)**

Olympic Forest Products Co.........................216 421-2775
2280 W 11th St Cleveland (44113) **(G-4119)**

Olympus Surgical Technologies, Norwalk Also Called: Gyrus Acmi LP **(G-10845)**

Om Group, Westlake Also Called: Borchers Americas Inc **(G-14295)**

Om Group Inc...216 781-0083
127 Public Sq Ste 3900 Cleveland (44114) **(G-4120)**

Omar Associates LLC..................................419 426-0610
625 N State Route 4 Attica (44807) **(G-657)**

Omco Holdings Inc (PA)..............................440 944-2100
30396 Lakeland Blvd Wickliffe (44092) **(G-14386)**

Omco Usa LLC...740 588-1722
1000 Linden Ave Zanesville (43701) **(G-15035)**

Omega 1 Inc..216 663-8424
38373 Pelton Rd Willoughby (44094) **(G-14501)**

Omega Cementing Co...................................330 695-7147
3776 S Millborne Rd Apple Creek (44606) **(G-474)**

Omega Engineering Inc................................740 965-9340
149 Stelzer Ct Sunbury (43074) **(G-12673)**

Omega Machine & Tool Inc..........................440 946-6846
7590 Jenther Dr Mentor (44060) **(G-9576)**

Omega Polymer Technologies Inc (PA)..........330 562-5201
1331 S Chillicothe Rd Aurora (44202) **(G-683)**

Omega Pultrusions Incorporated..................330 562-5201
1331 S Chillicothe Rd Aurora (44202) **(G-684)**

Omega Tek Inc...419 756-9580
649 Old Mill Run Rd Mansfield (44906) **(G-8843)**

Omegadyne, Sunbury Also Called: Omega Engineering Inc **(G-12673)**

Omegadyne, Sunbury Also Called: Omegadyne Inc **(G-12674)**

Omegadyne Inc..740 965-9340
149 Stelzer Ct Sunbury (43074) **(G-12674)**

Omegaone, Willoughby Also Called: Amfm Inc **(G-14419)**

Omer J Smith Inc...513 921-4717
9112 Le Saint Dr West Chester (45014) **(G-14038)**

Ometek LLC...614 861-6729
790 Cross Pointe Rd Columbus (43230) **(G-5160)**

OMI Surgical Products.................................513 561-2241
4900 Charlemar Dr Cincinnati (45227) **(G-2929)**

Omni Die Casting Inc...................................330 830-5500
1100 Nova Dr Se Massillon (44646) **(G-9227)**

Omni Manufacturing Inc (PA).......................419 394-7424
901 Mckinley Rd Saint Marys (45885) **(G-11747)**

Omni Manufacturing Inc..............................419 394-7424
220 Cleveland Ave Saint Marys (45885) **(G-11748)**

Omni Systems LLC (PA)...............................216 377-5160
701 Beta Dr Mayfield Village (44143) **(G-9345)**

Omni Tech Electronics, Columbus Also Called: Accuscan Instruments Inc **(G-4670)**

Omni Technical Products Inc........................216 433-1970
15300 Industrial Pkwy Cleveland (44135) **(G-4121)**

Omni USA Inc..330 830-5500
1100 Nova Dr Se Massillon (44646) **(G-9228)**

Omnipresence Cleaning LLC........................937 250-4749
302 W Fairview Ave Dayton (45405) **(G-5927)**

Omnitec, Painesville Also Called: Ohio Associated Entps LLC **(G-11102)**

Omnova Wallcovering USA Inc......................216 682-7000
25435 Harvard Rd Beachwood (44122) **(G-937)**

Omwp Company..330 453-8438
3620 Progress St Ne Canton (44705) **(G-1969)**

Omya, Mason Also Called: Omya Industries Inc **(G-9133)**

Omya Distribution LLC (DH).........................513 387-4600
4605 Duke Dr Mason (45040) **(G-9132)**

Omya Inc (DH)...513 387-4600
9987 Carver Rd Ste 300 Cincinnati (45242) **(G-2930)**

Omya Industries Inc (HQ)............................513 387-4600
4605 Duke Dr Ste 700 Mason (45040) **(G-9133)**

On Display Ltd...513 841-1600
1250 Clough Pike Batavia (45103) **(G-880)**

On The Mantle LLC......................................740 702-1803
20 E Water St Chillicothe (45601) **(G-2268)**

On US LLC..330 286-3436
315 Gougler Ave Kent (44240) **(G-8057)**

Onbase, Westlake Also Called: Hyland Software Inc **(G-14307)**

One Cloud Services LLC..............................513 231-9500
1080 Nimitzview Dr Ste 400 Cincinnati (45230) **(G-2931)**

One Line Coffee, Columbus Also Called: Ohio Coffee Collaborative Ltd **(G-5139)**

One Three Energy Inc..................................513 996-6973
1311 Vine St Cincinnati (45202) **(G-2932)**

One Time, Eastlake Also Called: Bond Distributing LLC **(G-6420)**

One Wish LLC..800 505-6883
23700 Aurora Rd Bedford (44146) **(G-1052)**

Oneil, Miamisburg Also Called: ONeil & Associates Inc **(G-9725)**

ONeil & Associates Inc (PA).........................937 865-0800
495 Byers Rd Miamisburg (45342) **(G-9725)**

Onesource Water LLC..................................866 917-7873
812 Warehouse Rd Ste F Toledo (43615) **(G-13077)**

Onetouchpoint East Corp.............................513 421-1600
1441 Western Ave Cincinnati (45214) **(G-2933)**

Onix Corporation..800 844-0076
27100 Oakmead Dr Perrysburg (43551) **(G-11250)**

Online Engineering Corp..............................513 561-8878
6732 High Meadows Dr Cincinnati (45230) **(G-2934)**

Online Mega Sellers Corp (PA).....................888 384-6468
4236 W Alexis Rd Toledo (43623) **(G-13078)**

Onpower Inc..513 228-2100
3525 Grant Ave Ste A Lebanon (45036) **(G-8280)**

Onstage Publications, Dayton Also Called: Just Business Inc **(G-5835)**

Onstation, Cleveland Also Called: Projitech Inc **(G-4201)**

Onx Acquisition LLC....................................440 569-2300
5910 Landerbrook Dr Ste 250 Mayfield Heights (44124) **(G-9339)**

Onx Enterprise Solutions, Cincinnati Also Called: Onx Holdings LLC **(G-2935)**

Onx Enterprise Solutions, Mayfield Heights Also Called: Onx Acquisition LLC **(G-9339)**

Onx Holdings LLC (DH)................................866 587-2287
221 E 4th St Cincinnati (45202) **(G-2935)**

Ooteksofpak, Columbus Also Called: Tarigma Corporation **(G-5309)**

Op Dawg Logistics LLC...............................937 844-3135
1700 Shroyer Rd Apt 4 Dayton (45419) **(G-5928)**

Opal Diamond LLC.......................................330 653-5876
20033 Detroit Rd N Ridge Annex 2nd Fl Rocky River (44116) **(G-11635)**

Opc Inc..419 531-2222
419 N Reynolds Rd Toledo (43615) **(G-13079)**

OPC Polymers, Columbus Also Called: OPC Polymers LLC **(G-5161)**

OPC Polymers LLC......................................614 253-8511
1920 Leonard Ave Columbus (43219) **(G-5161)**

Open Additive LLC......................................937 306-6140
2750 Indian Ripple Rd Dayton (45440) **(G-5929)**

Open Text, Hilliard Also Called: Open Text Inc **(G-7693)**

Open Text Inc..614 658-3588
3671 Ridge Mill Dr Hilliard (43026) **(G-7693)**

Operational Support Svcs LLC.....................419 425-0889
1850 Industrial Dr Findlay (45840) **(G-6904)**

Opm, Barberton Also Called: Ohio Precision Molding Inc **(G-828)**

Opp, Toledo Also Called: Opp Dissolution LLC **(G-13080)**

Opp Dissolution LLC...................................419 241-9601
1149 Campbell St Toledo (43607) **(G-13080)**

Ops Wireless, Carey Also Called: Ohio Power Systems LLC **(G-2061)**

Optem, Medina Also Called: Ovation Plymr Tech Engnred Mtl **(G-9432)**

Opti, Aurora *Also Called: Omega Polymer Technologies Inc (G-683)*

Optical Display Engrg Inc.. 440 995-6555
375 Alpha Park Highland Heights (44143) *(G-7661)*

Optics Incorporated... 800 362-1337
2936 Westway Dr Brunswick (44212) *(G-1604)*

Optimal Led, Toledo *Also Called: Led Lighting Center Inc (G-13029)*

Optimalled, Toledo *Also Called: Led Lighting Center LLC (G-13030)*

Optimum Graphics, Westerville *Also Called: Optimum System Products Inc (G-14273)*

Optimum Surgical.. 216 870-8526
2524 Medina Rd Ste 600 Medina (44256) *(G-9431)*

Optimum System Products Inc (PA)................................... 614 885-4464
921 Eastwind Dr Ste 133 Westerville (43081) *(G-14273)*

Option Advisor, The, Blue Ash *Also Called: Schaeffers Investment Research Inc (G-1331)*

Options Plus, Fredericktown *Also Called: Options Plus Incorporated (G-7083)*

Options Plus Incorporated... 740 694-9811
143 Tuttle Ave Fredericktown (43019) *(G-7083)*

Optum Infusion Svcs 550 LLC (DH)................................... 866 442-4679
7167 E Kemper Rd Cincinnati (45249) *(G-2936)*

Opw Engineered Systems, West Chester *Also Called: Opw Fueling Components Inc (G-14040)*

Opw Engineered Systems Inc (DH).................................. 888 771-9438
9393 Princeton Glendale Rd West Chester (45011) *(G-14039)*

Opw Fueling Components Inc (HQ)................................... 800 422-2525
9393 Princeton Glendale Rd West Chester (45011) *(G-14040)*

Or-Tec Inc... 216 475-5225
5445 Dunham Rd Maple Heights (44137) *(G-8889)*

Oracle America Inc.. 650 506-7000
4378 Tuller Rd Dublin (43017) *(G-6327)*

Oracle Corporation.. 216 706-1500
1300 E 9th St Ste 1600 Cleveland (44114) *(G-4122)*

Orange Barrel Media LLC.. 614 294-4898
250 N Hartford Ave Columbus (43222) *(G-5162)*

Orange Blossom Press Inc... 216 781-8655
38005 Brown Ave Willoughby (44094) *(G-14502)*

Orange Frazer Press Inc.. 937 382-3196
37 1/2 W Main St Wilmington (45177) *(G-14585)*

Orbis Corporation... 262 560-5000
232 J St Perrysburg (43551) *(G-11251)*

Orbis Corporation... 937 652-1361
200 Elm St Urbana (43078) *(G-13475)*

Orbis Rpm LLC... 419 307-8511
592 Claycraft Rd Columbus (43230) *(G-5163)*

Orbis Rpm LLC... 419 355-8310
2100 Cedar St Fremont (43420) *(G-7125)*

Orbit Manufacturing Inc... 513 732-6097
4291 Armstrong Blvd Batavia (45103) *(G-881)*

Orbytel, Cleveland *Also Called: Orbytel Print and Packg Inc (G-4123)*

Orbytel Print and Packg Inc.. 216 267-8734
4901 Johnston Pkwy Cleveland (44128) *(G-4123)*

Oregon Printing, Dayton *Also Called: Oregon Vlg Print Shoppe Inc (G-5930)*

Oregon Vlg Print Shoppe Inc.. 937 222-9418
29 N June St Dayton (45403) *(G-5930)*

OReilly Equipment LLC.. 440 564-1234
14555 Ravenna Rd Newbury (44065) *(G-10559)*

OReilly Precision Pdts Inc.. 937 526-4677
560 E Main St Russia (45363) *(G-11676)*

Oren Elliot Products LLC.. 419 298-0015
128 W Vine St Edgerton (43517) *(G-6468)*

Orflex Inc
470 Northland Blvd Cincinnati (45240) *(G-2937)*

Organic Technologies, Coshocton *Also Called: Wiley Companies (G-5476)*

Organic Technologies, Coshocton *Also Called: Wiley Companies (G-5477)*

Organized Lightning LLC.. 407 965-2730
5601 Belleview Ave Blue Ash (45242) *(G-1315)*

Organized Living.. 513 277-3700
12115 Ellington Ct Cincinnati (45249) *(G-2938)*

Organized Living, Cincinnati *Also Called: Organized Living Inc (G-2939)*

Organized Living Inc (PA).. 513 489-9300
3100 E Kemper Rd Cincinnati (45241) *(G-2939)*

Organon Inc.. 440 729-2290
7407 Cedar Rd Chesterland (44026) *(G-2238)*

Orick Stamping Inc... 419 331-0600
614 E Kiracofe Ave Elida (45807) *(G-6484)*

Original Beverage Holder Co, Columbia Station *Also Called: Obhc Inc (G-4595)*

Original Mattress Factory, Columbus *Also Called: Ahmf Inc (G-4681)*

Orion Engineered Carbons LLC.. 740 423-9571
11135 State Route 7 Belpre (45714) *(G-1151)*

Orion Engineered Carbons LLC.. 985 312-7406
1300 Blue Knob Rd Marietta (45750) *(G-8933)*

Orlando, Cleveland *Also Called: Orlando Baking Company (G-4124)*

Orlando Baking Company (PA)... 216 361-1872
7777 Grand Ave Cleveland (44104) *(G-4124)*

Ormet Corporation.. 740 483-1381
43840 State Rte 7 Hannibal (43931) *(G-7540)*

Ormet Primary Aluminum Corp.. 740 483-1381
43840 State Rt 7 Hannibal (43931) *(G-7541)*

ORourke Sales Company.. 877 599-6548
3319 Southwest Blvd Grove City (43123) *(G-7406)*

Orrville Bronze & Aluminum Co.. 330 682-4015
Central Ct Orrville (44667) *(G-10999)*

Orrville Trucking & Grading Co (PA).................................. 330 682-4010
475 Orr St Orrville (44667) *(G-11000)*

Orrvilon Inc... 330 684-9400
1400 Dairy Ln Orrville (44667) *(G-11001)*

Orthotic & Prosthetic Spc Inc.. 216 531-2773
20650 Lakeland Blvd Euclid (44119) *(G-6667)*

Orthotics Prsthtics Rhblttion... 330 856-2553
700 Howland Wilson Rd Se Warren (44484) *(G-13788)*

Orton Edward Jr Crmic Fndation....................................... 614 895-2663
6991 S Old 3c Hwy Westerville (43082) *(G-14226)*

Orval Kent Food Company LLC.. 419 695-5015
1600 Gressel Dr Delphos (45833) *(G-6191)*

Orwell Printing... 440 285-2233
10639 Grant St Ste C Chardon (44024) *(G-2218)*

OS Kelly Corporation.. 937 322-4921
318 E North St Springfield (45503) *(G-12358)*

Osair Inc (PA)... 440 974-6500
7001 Center St Mentor (44060) *(G-9577)*

Osb Software Inc.. 440 542-9145
6240 Som Center Rd Ste 230 Solon (44139) *(G-12165)*

Osborne Inc.. 440 232-1440
26481 Cannon Rd Cleveland (44146) *(G-4125)*

Osborne Inc (PA)... 440 942-7000
7954 Reynolds Rd Mentor (44060) *(G-9578)*

Osborne Co... 440 942-7000
7954 Reynolds Rd Mentor (44060) *(G-9579)*

Osborne Coinage Company LLC (PA)................................ 877 480-0456
4362 Glendale Milford Rd Blue Ash (45242) *(G-1316)*

Osburn Associates Inc (PA)... 740 385-5732
9383 Vanatta Rd Logan (43138) *(G-8522)*

Oscar Brugmann Sand & Gravel...................................... 330 274-8224
3828 Dudley Rd Mantua (44255) *(G-8874)*

Osco Industries Inc.. 740 286-5004
165 Athens St Jackson (45640) *(G-7950)*

Osco Industries Inc (PA).. 740 354-3183
734 11th St Portsmouth (45662) *(G-11473)*

Osg-Sterling Die Inc... 216 267-1300
12502 Plaza Dr Parma (44130) *(G-11133)*

OSI, Hilliard *Also Called: Ohio Semitronics Inc (G-7692)*

OSI Environmental LLC.. 440 237-4600
12800 York Rd North Royalton (44133) *(G-10779)*

OSI Global Sourcing LLC.. 614 471-4800
2575 Ferris Rd Columbus (43224) *(G-5164)*

Osmans Pies Inc.. 330 607-9083
3678 Elm Rd Stow (44224) *(G-12448)*

Osram Sylvania Inc... 800 463-9275
6400 Rockside Rd Independence (44131) *(G-7913)*

Osteonovus Inc.. 419 530-5940
1510 N Westwood Ave Ste 1080 Toledo (43606) *(G-13081)*

Osteonovus Inc.. 419 530-5940
1510 N Westwood Ave # 2040 Toledo (43606) *(G-13082)*

Osteosymbionics LLC.. 216 881-8500
1768 E 25th St Ste 316 Cleveland (44114) *(G-4126)*

ALPHABETIC

Oster Enterprises, Massillon *Also Called: Oster Sand and Gravel Inc* *(G-9229)*

Oster Sand and Gravel Inc..................................330 874-3322
3467 Dover Zoar Rd Ne Bolivar (44612) *(G-1387)*

Oster Sand and Gravel Inc (PA)..........................330 494-5472
5947 Whipple Ave Nw Canton (44720) *(G-1970)*

Oster Sand and Gravel Inc..................................330 833-2649
1955 Riverside Dr Nw Massillon (44647) *(G-9229)*

Otc Industrial Technologies (PA)........................800 837-6827
1900 Jetway Blvd Columbus (43219) *(G-5165)*

Otc Services Inc..330 871-2444
1776 Constitution Ave Louisville (44641) *(G-8611)*

Other Styles - See Operation, Cleveland *Also Called: Lubriquip Inc (G-3969)*

Otis Elevator Company......................................216 573-2333
9800 Rockside Rd Ste 1200 Cleveland (44125) *(G-4127)*

Otp Holding LLC...614 733-0979
8000 Corporate Blvd Plain City (43064) *(G-11416)*

Ots, Columbus *Also Called: Ohio Trailer Supply Inc (G-5155)*

Ottawa Defense Logistics LLC...........................419 596-3202
804 N Pratt St Ottawa (45875) *(G-11040)*

Ottawa Oil Co Inc..419 425-3301
1100 Trenton Ave Findlay (45840) *(G-6905)*

Ottawa Products Co..419 836-5115
1602 N Curtice Rd Ste A Curtice (43412) *(G-5517)*

Ottawa Rubber Company (PA).............................419 865-1378
1600 Commerce Rd Holland (43528) *(G-7775)*

Otterbacher Trailers LLC..................................419 462-1975
352 South St Galion (44833) *(G-7196)*

Otto Konigslow Mfg Co......................................216 851-7900
13300 Coit Rd Cleveland (44110) *(G-4128)*

Ottokee Group Inc...419 636-1932
17768 County Road H 50 Bryan (43506) *(G-1656)*

Ournashonisme Ent LLC....................................689 276-0367
1423 E 263rd St Euclid (44132) *(G-6668)*

Outhouse Paper Etc Inc.....................................937 382-2800
319 Collett Rd Waynesville (45068) *(G-13881)*

Outlook Tool Inc...937 235-6330
360 Fame Rd Dayton (45449) *(G-5931)*

Outotec North America, Strongsville *Also Called: Outotec Oyj (G-12583)*

Outotec Oyj..440 783-3336
11288 Alameda Dr Strongsville (44149) *(G-12583)*

Ovase Manufacturing LLC..................................937 275-0617
1990 Berwyck Ave Dayton (45414) *(G-5932)*

Ovation Plymr Tech Engnred Mtl.........................330 723-5686
1030 W Smith Rd Medina (44256) *(G-9432)*

Overhead Door Company, Toledo *Also Called: Overhead Inc (G-13083)*

Overhead Door Corporation................................440 593-5226
1001 Chamberlain Blvd Conneaut (44030) *(G-5413)*

Overhead Door Corporation................................330 828-2291
14512 Lincoln Way E Dalton (44618) *(G-5590)*

Overhead Door Corporation................................740 383-6376
1332 E Fairground Rd Marion (43302) *(G-8987)*

Overhead Door Corporation................................419 294-3874
781 Rt 30w Upper Sandusky (43351) *(G-13452)*

Overhead Door of Pike County............................740 289-3925
4237 Us Highway 23 Piketon (45661) *(G-11312)*

Overhead Inc...419 476-0300
340 New Towne Square Dr Toledo (43612) *(G-13083)*

Overhoff Technology Corp..................................513 248-2400
1160 Us Route 50 Milford (45150) *(G-9946)*

Overly Hautz Company.......................................513 932-0025
285 S West St Lebanon (45036) *(G-8281)*

Overseas Packing LLC.......................................440 232-2917
19800 Alexander Rd Bedford (44146) *(G-1053)*

Ovp Inc...740 423-5171
305 Washington Blvd Belpre (45714) *(G-1152)*

Ovs Knife Co., Mogadore *Also Called: Wise Edge LLC (G-10094)*

Owens Corning...614 754-4098
2050 Integrity Dr S Columbus (43209) *(G-5166)*

Owens Corning...419 248-8000
9318 Erie Ave Sw Navarre (44662) *(G-10309)*

Owens Corning (PA)..419 248-8000
1 Owens Corning Pkwy Toledo (43659) *(G-13084)*

Owens Corning, Ashville *Also Called: Owens Corning Sales LLC (G-629)*

Owens Corning, Grove City *Also Called: Owens Corning Sales LLC (G-7407)*

Owens Corning, Hebron *Also Called: Owens Corning Sales LLC (G-7628)*

Owens Corning, Mount Vernon *Also Called: Owens Corning Sales LLC (G-10255)*

Owens Corning, Swanton *Also Called: Owens Corning Sales LLC (G-12689)*

Owens Corning, Tallmadge *Also Called: Owens Corning Sales LLC (G-12745)*

Owens Corning Corp Svcs LLC............................419 248-8000
1 Owens Corning Pkwy Toledo (43659) *(G-13085)*

Owens Corning Ht Inc..419 248-8000
Owens Corning World Headquar Toledo (43659) *(G-13086)*

Owens Corning Pink, Toledo *Also Called: Owens Corning (G-13084)*

Owens Corning Roofg & Asp LLC (HQ)..................877 858-3855
1 Owens Corning Pkwy Toledo (43659) *(G-13087)*

Owens Corning Sales LLC..................................740 983-1300
1 Reynolds Rd Ashville (43103) *(G-629)*

Owens Corning Sales LLC..................................614 539-0830
3750 Brookham Dr Ste K Grove City (43123) *(G-7407)*

Owens Corning Sales LLC..................................740 928-6620
341 O Neill Dr Bldg 6 Hebron (43025) *(G-7628)*

Owens Corning Sales LLC..................................614 399-3915
100 Blackjack Road Ext Mount Vernon (43050) *(G-10255)*

Owens Corning Sales LLC..................................419 248-5751
11451 W Airport Service Rd Swanton (43558) *(G-12689)*

Owens Corning Sales LLC..................................330 634-0460
170 South Ave Tallmadge (44278) *(G-12744)*

Owens Corning Sales LLC..................................330 633-6735
275 Southwest Ave Tallmadge (44278) *(G-12745)*

Owens Corning Sales LLC (HQ)...........................419 248-8000
1 Owens Corning Pkwy Toledo (43659) *(G-13088)*

Owens Crning Inslting Systm.............................740 328-2300
400 Case Ave Newark (43055) *(G-10527)*

Owens Crning Tchncal Fbrics LL.........................419 248-5535
1 Owens Corning Pkwy Toledo (43659) *(G-13089)*

Owens Foods Inc
8111 Smiths Mill Rd New Albany (43054) *(G-10349)*

Owens-Brockway Glass Cntrs, Perrysburg *Also Called: Owens-Brockway Glass Cont Inc* *(G-11252)*

Owens-Brockway Glass Cont Inc (DH)...................567 336-8449
1 Michael Owens Way Perrysburg (43551) *(G-11252)*

Owens-Brockway Glass Cont Inc.........................740 455-4516
1700 State St Zanesville (43701) *(G-15036)*

Owens-Illinois General Inc................................567 336-5000
1 Michael Owens Way Perrysburg (43551) *(G-11253)*

Owens-Illinois Group Inc (HQ)...........................567 336-5000
1 Michael Owens Way Perrysburg (43551) *(G-11254)*

Owens-Illinois Inc..567 336-5000
1 Michael Owens Way Perrysburg (43551) *(G-11255)*

Oxford Mining Company Inc (DH).........................740 622-6302
544 Chestnut St Coshocton (43812) *(G-5468)*

Oxford Mining Company Inc................................740 588-0190
1855 Kemper Ct Zanesville (43701) *(G-15037)*

Oxford Mining Company LLC (DH)........................740 622-6302
544 Chestnut St Coshocton (43812) *(G-5469)*

Oxford Mining Company - KY LLC........................740 622-6302
544 Chestnut St Coshocton (43812) *(G-5470)*

Oxford Press, Oxford *Also Called: Cox Newspapers LLC (G-11062)*

Oxyrase Inc...419 589-8800
3000 Park Ave W Ontario (44906) *(G-10951)*

P & A Industries Inc (HQ)...................................419 422-7070
600 Crystal Ave Findlay (45840) *(G-6906)*

P & J Industries Inc (PA)....................................419 726-2675
4934 Lewis Ave Toledo (43612) *(G-13090)*

P & L Heat Trting Grinding Inc............................330 746-1339
313 E Wood St Youngstown (44503) *(G-14907)*

P & L Metalcrafts LLC.......................................330 793-2178
1050 Ohio Works Dr Youngstown (44510) *(G-14908)*

P & L Precision Grinding Llc...............................330 746-8081
948 Poland Ave Youngstown (44502) *(G-14909)*

P & P Machine Tool Inc......................................440 232-7404
26189 Broadway Ave Cleveland (44146) *(G-4129)*

P & P Mold & Die Inc...330 784-8333
1034 S Munroe Rd Tallmadge (44278) *(G-12746)*

2025 Harris Ohio
Industrial Directory

(G-0000) Company's Geographic Section entry number

P & R Specialty Inc................................ 937 773-0263
1835 W High St Piqua (45356) *(G-11370)*

P & T Millwork Inc............................... 440 543-2151
10090 Queens Way Chagrin Falls (44023) *(G-2175)*

P & T Products Inc............................... 419 621-1966
472 Industrial Pkwy Sandusky (44870) *(G-11863)*

P A I, Blue Ash *Also Called: Precision Anlytical Instrs Inc (G-1323)*

P C M Co (PA)...................................... 330 336-8040
291 W Bergey St Wadsworth (44281) *(G-13656)*

P C Workshop Inc................................. 419 399-4805
900 W Caroline St Paulding (45879) *(G-11161)*

P Graham Dunn Inc............................... 330 828-2105
630 Henry St Dalton (44618) *(G-5591)*

P H I, Toledo *Also Called: Pilkington Holdings Inc (G-13097)*

P J McNerney & Associates, West Chester *Also Called: McNerney & Associates LLC (G-14132)*

P J Tool Company Inc............................ 937 254-2817
1115 Springfield St Dayton (45403) *(G-5933)*

P M C, Blue Ash *Also Called: Plastic Moldings Company Llc (G-1319)*

P M C, Wickliffe *Also Called: Precision McHning Cnnction LLC (G-14392)*

P M I Food Equipment Group, Piqua *Also Called: Hobart LLC (G-11355)*

P M R Inc.. 440 937-6241
4661 Jaycox Rd Avon (44011) *(G-733)*

P O McIntire Company (PA)..................... 440 269-1848
29191 Anderson Rd Wickliffe (44092) *(G-14387)*

P P F, Bradford *Also Called: Production Paint Finishers Inc (G-1452)*

P P G, Milford *Also Called: PPG Industries Inc (G-9948)*

P P G Refinishing Group, Delaware *Also Called: PPG Industries Inc (G-6166)*

P P I Graphics, Canton *Also Called: KMS 2000 Inc (G-1927)*

P R Machine Works Inc.......................... 419 529-5748
1825 Nussbaum Pkwy Ontario (44906) *(G-10952)*

P S Awards, Cleveland *Also Called: PS Superior Inc (G-4204)*

P S C Inc.. 216 531-3375
21761 Tungsten Rd Cleveland (44117) *(G-4130)*

P S Graphics Inc.................................. 440 356-9656
20284 Orchard Grove Ave Rocky River (44116) *(G-11636)*

P T C, Lima *Also Called: Precision Thrmplstic Cmpnnts I (G-8461)*

P T I Inc.. 419 445-2800
100 Taylor Pkwy Archbold (43502) *(G-507)*

P-Americas LLC.................................... 614 253-8771
1241 Gibbard Ave Columbus (43219) *(G-5167)*

P-Americas LLC.................................... 440 323-5524
925 Lorain Blvd Elyria (44035) *(G-6575)*

P-Americas LLC.................................... 419 227-3541
1750 Greely Chapel Rd Lima (45804) *(G-8436)*

P-Americas LLC.................................... 330 837-4224
815 Oberlin Ave Sw Massillon (44647) *(G-9230)*

P-Americas LLC.................................... 740 266-6121
729 Main St Steubenville (43953) *(G-12409)*

P-Americas LLC.................................... 330 746-7652
500 Pepsi Pl Youngstown (44502) *(G-14910)*

P.E. Labellers, Cincinnati *Also Called: PE Usa LLC (G-2950)*

P&E Sales Ltd...................................... 330 829-0100
1595 W Main St Alliance (44601) *(G-397)*

P&G, Cincinnati *Also Called: Procter & Gamble Company (G-2999)*

P&The Mfg Acquisition LLC..................... 937 492-4134
815 Oak Ave Sidney (45365) *(G-12037)*

P3 Infrastructure Inc............................ 330 408-9504
2146 Entp Pkwy Ste C Twinsburg (44087) *(G-13348)*

PA MA Inc.. 440 846-3799
11288 Alameda Dr Strongsville (44149) *(G-12584)*

PA Technologies LLC............................. 513 800-3541
10176 Evendale Commons Dr Cincinnati (45241) *(G-2940)*

Paarlo Plastics Inc............................... 330 494-3798
7720 Tim Ave Nw North Canton (44720) *(G-10657)*

Pac, Loveland *Also Called: Powder Alloy Corporation (G-8646)*

Pac Manufacturing, Monroe *Also Called: Pac Worldwide Corporation (G-10114)*

Pac Worldwide Corporation..................... 800 535-0039
575 Gateway Blvd Monroe (45050) *(G-10114)*

Paccar Inc.. 740 774-5111
65 Kenworth Dr Chillicothe (45601) *(G-2269)*

Pace Consolidated Inc (PA)..................... 440 942-1234
4800 Beidler Rd Willoughby (44094) *(G-14503)*

Pace Engineering, Willoughby *Also Called: Pace Consolidated Inc (G-14503)*

Pace Engineering Inc............................. 440 942-1234
4800 Beidler Rd Willoughby (44094) *(G-14504)*

Pace Mold & Machine LLC....................... 330 879-1777
8225 Navarre Rd Sw Massillon (44646) *(G-9231)*

Pacific Highway Products LLC................... 740 914-5217
324 Barnhart St Marion (43302) *(G-8988)*

Pacific Industries USA Inc....................... 513 860-3900
8955 Seward Rd Fairfield (45011) *(G-6761)*

Pacific Manufacturing Ohio Inc................. 513 860-3900
8955 Seward Rd Fairfield (45011) *(G-6762)*

Pacific Manufacturing Ohio Inc................. 513 860-3900
8935 Seward Rd Fairfield (45011) *(G-6763)*

Pacific Piston Ring Co Inc....................... 513 387-6100
11379 Grooms Rd Blue Ash (45242) *(G-1317)*

Pacific Valve, Piqua *Also Called: Crane Pumps & Systems Inc (G-11340)*

Pack Line Corp..................................... 212 564-0664
22900 Miles Rd Cleveland (44128) *(G-4131)*

Packaging Corporation America................ 419 282-5809
929 Faultless Dr Ashland (44805) *(G-559)*

Packaging Corporation America................ 330 644-9542
708 Killian Rd Coventry Township (44319) *(G-5487)*

Packaging Corporation America................ 513 424-3542
1824 Baltimore St Middletown (45044) *(G-9883)*

Packaging Corporation America................ 740 344-1126
205 S 21st St Newark (43055) *(G-10528)*

Packaging Department, Ashland *Also Called: Pioneer National Latex Inc (G-563)*

Packaging Materials Inc.......................... 740 432-6337
62805 Bennett Ave Cambridge (43725) *(G-1753)*

Packaging Specialties Inc........................ 330 723-6000
300 Lake Rd Medina (44256) *(G-9433)*

Pacs Industries Inc............................... 740 397-5021
8405 Blackjack Road Ext Mount Vernon (43050) *(G-10256)*

Pactiv LLC.. 614 771-5400
2120 Westbelt Dr Columbus (43228) *(G-5168)*

Padco Industries LLC............................. 440 564-7160
10357 Kinsman Rd Unit D Newbury (44065) *(G-10560)*

Paddock Enterprises LLC (HQ).................. 567 336-5000
1 Michael Owens Way 2 Perrysburg (43551) *(G-11256)*

Page One Group.................................. 740 397-4240
10 E Vine St Ste C Mount Vernon (43050) *(G-10257)*

Pahl Ready Mix Concrete, Bryan *Also Called: Pahl Ready Mix Concrete Inc (G-1657)*

Pahl Ready Mix Concrete Inc (PA).............. 419 636-4238
14586 Us Highway 127 Ew Bryan (43506) *(G-1657)*

Painesville Pride, Willoughby *Also Called: Lake Community News (G-14480)*

Painesville Publishing Inc....................... 440 354-4142
2883 Industrial Park Dr Austinburg (44010) *(G-701)*

Painted Hill Inv Group Inc....................... 937 339-1756
402 E Main St Troy (45373) *(G-13246)*

Pak Master LLC................................... 330 523-5319
3778 Timberlake Dr Richfield (44286) *(G-11595)*

Paklab, Batavia *Also Called: Universal Packg Systems Inc (G-894)*

Paklab, Cincinnati *Also Called: Universal Packg Systems Inc (G-3186)*

Pako Inc.. 440 946-8030
7615 Jenther Dr Mentor (44060) *(G-9580)*

Pakra LLC... 614 477-6965
449 E Mound St Columbus (43215) *(G-5169)*

Palisin & Associates Inc (PA).................... 216 252-3930
10003 Memphis Ave Cleveland (44144) *(G-4132)*

Pallet Distributors Inc........................... 330 852-3531
10343 Copperhead Rd Nw Sugarcreek (44681) *(G-12644)*

Pallet Solutions, Apple Creek *Also Called: Dutch Legacy Company LLC (G-466)*

Pallet Specs Plus LLC............................ 513 351-3200
1701 Mills Ave Norwood (45212) *(G-10870)*

Pallet World Inc................................... 419 874-9333
8272 Fremont Pike Perrysburg (43551) *(G-11257)*

Pallets-Fam-In-place-packaging, Versailles *Also Called: Kamps Inc (G-13598)*

Palm Harbor Homes Inc.......................... 937 725-9465
11004 State Route 28 New Vienna (45159) *(G-10475)*

A
L
P
H
A
B
E
T
I
C

Palm Plastics Ltd.. 561 776-6700
  843 Miller Dr Bowling Green (43402) *(G-1432)*

Palmer Bros Transit Mix Con (PA)..........................419 352-4681
  12205 E Gypsy Lane Rd Bowling Green (43402) *(G-1433)*

Palmer Bros Transit Mix Con.............................. 419 686-2366
  12580 Greensburg Pike Portage (43451) *(G-11460)*

Palmer Donavin Manufacturing............................ 740 527-1111
  1120 O Neill Dr Hebron (43025) *(G-7629)*

Palmer Products, Akron *Also Called: Palmer Products Inc (G-255)*

Palmer Products Inc... 330 630-9397
  920 Moe Dr Akron (44310) *(G-255)*

Palpac Industries Inc... 419 523-3230
  610 N Agner St Ottawa (45875) *(G-11041)*

Palstar Inc.. 937 773-6255
  9676 Looney Rd Piqua (45356) *(G-11371)*

Pama Tool & Die, Strongsville *Also Called: PA MA Inc (G-12584)*

Pamee LLC... 216 232-9255
  18500 Lake Rd Rocky River (44116) *(G-11637)*

Pan-Glo, Mansfield *Also Called: Russell T Bundy Associates Inc (G-8851)*

Panacea Products Corporation............................. 614 429-6320
  1825 Joyce Ave Columbus (43219) *(G-5170)*

Panacea Products Corporation (PA).......................614 850-7000
  2711 International St Columbus (43228) *(G-5171)*

Panam Imaging Systems, Cleveland *Also Called: Horizons Incorporated (G-3838)*

Pandrol Inc... 419 592-5050
  25 Interstate Dr Napoleon (43545) *(G-10295)*

Panel Master LLC.. 440 355-4442
  191 Commerce Dr Lagrange (44050) *(G-8153)*

Panel-Fab Inc.. 513 771-1462
  10520 Taconic Ter Cincinnati (45215) *(G-2941)*

Panelmatic Inc.. 330 782-8007
  1125 Meadowbrook Ave Youngstown (44512) *(G-14911)*

Panelmatic Bldg Solutions Inc.............................. 330 619-5235
  6882 Parkway Dr Brookfield (44403) *(G-1517)*

Panelmatic Youngstown, Youngstown *Also Called: Panelmatic Inc (G-14911)*

Panelmatic Youngstown Inc................................. 330 782-8007
  1125 Meadowbrook Ave Youngstown (44512) *(G-14912)*

Paneltech LLC... 440 516-1300
  17525 Haskins Rd Chagrin Falls (44023) *(G-2176)*

Pang Rubber Company, Johnstown *Also Called: Truflex Rubber Products Co (G-8001)*

Panhandle Olfld Svc Cmpnies In........................... 330 340-9525
  62787 Philips Rd Cambridge (43725) *(G-1754)*

Pantrybag Inc.. 614 812-8073
  769 Sullivant Ave Columbus (43222) *(G-5172)*

Papa Joes Pies Inc (PA)...................................... 440 960-7437
  1969 Cooper Foster Park Rd Amherst (44001) *(G-451)*

Papel Couture... 614 848-5700
  6522 Singletree Dr Columbus (43229) *(G-5173)*

Paper Products Company, West Chester *Also Called: Omer J Smith Inc (G-14038)*

Paper Service Inc.. 330 227-3546
  12022 Leslie Rd Lisbon (44432) *(G-8478)*

Paper Systems Incorporated, Springboro *Also Called: Psix LLC (G-12264)*

Papertech, Findlay *Also Called: Pressed Paperboard Tech LLC (G-6909)*

Papyrus, Cincinnati *Also Called: Schurman Fine Papers (G-3068)*

Papyrus-Recycled Greetings Inc........................... 773 348-6410
  1 American Blvd Westlake (44145) *(G-14319)*

Paragon Integrated Svcs Group, Newcomerstown *Also Called: Paragon Intgrted Svcs Group LL (G-10574)*

Paragon Intgrted Svcs Group LL........................... 724 639-5126
  200 Enterprise Dr Newcomerstown (43832) *(G-10574)*

Paragon Machine Company, Bedford *Also Called: Done-Rite Bowling Service Co (G-1028)*

Paragon Robotics LLC.. 216 313-9299
  2234 E Enterprise Pkwy Twinsburg (44087) *(G-13349)*

Paragon Tempered Glass LLC............................... 419 258-5531
  5406 County Road 424 Antwerp (45813) *(G-463)*

Paragraphics Inc... 330 493-1074
  2011 29th St Nw Canton (44709) *(G-1971)*

Parallel Technologies Inc.................................... 614 798-9700
  4868 Blazer Pkwy Dublin (43017) *(G-6328)*

Paramelt, Cleveland *Also Called: M Argueso & Co Inc (G-3974)*

Paramelt, Cleveland *Also Called: Paramelt Argueso Kindt Inc (G-4133)*

Paramelt Argueso Kindt Inc................................. 216 252-4122
  12651 Elmwood Ave Cleveland (44111) *(G-4133)*

Paramount Distillers, Cleveland *Also Called: Luxco Inc (G-3972)*

Paramount Distillers Inc..................................... 216 671-6300
  3116 Berea Rd Cleveland (44111) *(G-4134)*

Paramount Tube, Apple Creek *Also Called: Precision Products Group Inc (G-475)*

Paratus Supply Inc.. 330 745-3600
  30 2nd St Sw Barberton (44203) *(G-830)*

Pardson Inc... 740 373-5285
  149 Acme St Marietta (45750) *(G-8934)*

Park Corporation (PA)... 216 267-4870
  3555 Reserve Commons Dr Medina (44256) *(G-9434)*

Park Place Technologies LLC (PA) 747 Alpha Dr Cleveland (44143) *(G-4135)*

Park PLC Prntg Cpyg & Dgtl IMG........................... 330 799-1739
  3410 Canfield Rd Ste B Youngstown (44511) *(G-14913)*

Park Press Direct.. 419 626-4426
  2143 Sherman St Sandusky (44870) *(G-11864)*

Park-Ohio, Cleveland *Also Called: Park-Ohio Industries Inc (G-4137)*

Park-Ohio Holdings Corp (PA).............................. 440 947-2000
  6065 Parkland Blvd Ste 1 Cleveland (44124) *(G-4136)*

Park-Ohio Industries Inc (HQ).............................. 440 947-2000
  6065 Parkland Blvd Ste 1 Cleveland (44124) *(G-4137)*

Park-Ohio Industries Inc..................................... 216 341-2300
  3800 Harvard Ave Newburgh Heights (44105) *(G-10546)*

Park-Ohio Products Inc....................................... 216 961-7200
  7000 Denison Ave Cleveland (44102) *(G-4138)*

Parker, Cleveland *Also Called: Parker-Hannifin Corporation (G-4143)*

Parker Aerospace.. 216 225-2721
  19600 Five Points Rd Cleveland (44135) *(G-4139)*

Parker Fabricating Co... 330 379-0112
  20 E North St Akron (44304) *(G-256)*

Parker Hannifin, Berlin Center *Also Called: Parker-Hannifin Corporation (G-1202)*

Parker Hannifin Partner B LLC.............................. 216 896-3000
  6035 Parkland Blvd Cleveland (44124) *(G-4140)*

Parker Meggitt.. 513 851-5550
  10293 Burlington Rd Cincinnati (45231) *(G-2942)*

Parker Precision Inc... 440 951-6501
  8950 Tyler Blvd Mentor (44060) *(G-9581)*

Parker Royalty Partnership.................................. 216 896-3000
  6035 Parkland Blvd Cleveland (44124) *(G-4141)*

Parker Rst-Proof Cleveland Inc............................. 216 481-6680
  1688 Arabella Rd Cleveland (44112) *(G-4142)*

Parker Trutec, Springfield *Also Called: Parker Trutec Incorporated (G-12359)*

Parker Trutec Incorporated (HQ)........................... 937 323-8833
  4700 Gateway Blvd Springfield (45502) *(G-12359)*

Parker Trutec Incorporated.................................. 937 653-8500
  4795 Upper Valley Pike Urbana (43078) *(G-13476)*

Parker-Hannifin Corporation................................ 440 937-6211
  1160 Center Rd Avon (44011) *(G-734)*

Parker-Hannifin Corporation................................ 330 261-1618
  14010 Ellsworth Rd Berlin Center (44401) *(G-1202)*

Parker-Hannifin Corporation (PA).......................... 216 896-3000
  6035 Parkland Blvd Cleveland (44124) *(G-4143)*

Parker-Hannifin Corporation................................ 216 433-1795
  19600 Five Points Rd Cleveland (44135) *(G-4144)*

Parker-Hannifin Corporation................................ 614 279-7070
  3885 Gateway Blvd Columbus (43228) *(G-5174)*

Parker-Hannifin Corporation................................ 937 456-5571
  725 N Beech St Eaton (45320) *(G-6462)*

Parker-Hannifin Corporation................................ 440 284-6277
  711 Taylor St Elyria (44035) *(G-6576)*

Parker-Hannifin Corporation................................ 419 542-6611
  373 Meuse Argonne St Hicksville (43526) *(G-7650)*

Parker-Hannifin Corporation................................ 937 644-3915
  14249 Industrial Pkwy Marysville (43040) *(G-9041)*

Parker-Hannifin Corporation................................ 440 266-2300
  8940 Tyler Blvd Mentor (44060) *(G-9582)*

Parker-Hannifin Corporation................................ 419 644-4311
  16810 County Road 2 Metamora (43540) *(G-9658)*

Parker-Hannifin Corporation................................ 513 831-2340
  50 W Techne Center Dr Ste H Milford (45150) *(G-9947)*

(G-0000) Company's Geographic Section entry number

Parker-Hannifin Corporation.................. 330 335-6740
135 Quadral Dr Wadsworth (44281) *(G-13657)*

Parker-Hannifin Corporation.................. 330 336-3511
135 Quadral Dr Wadsworth (44281) *(G-13658)*

Parker-Hannifin Corporation.................. 330 336-3511
135 Quadral Dr Wadsworth (44281) *(G-13659)*

Parker-Hannifin Corporation.................. 513 847-1758
9050 Centre Pointe Dr Ste 310 West Chester (45069) *(G-14041)*

Parker-Hannifin Corporation.................. 704 637-1190
30240 Lakeland Blvd Wickliffe (44092) *(G-14388)*

Parker-Hannifin Corporation.................. 440 943-5700
30240 Lakeland Blvd Wickliffe (44092) *(G-14389)*

Parker-Hannifin Corporation.................. 330 740-8366
1911 Logan Ave Youngstown (44505) *(G-14914)*

Parking & Traffic Control SEC.................. 440 243-7565
13651 Newton Rd Cleveland (44130) *(G-4145)*

Parking Facilities, Cleveland *Also Called: City of Cleveland (G-3500)*

Parkn Manufacturing LLC.................. 330 723-8172
8035 Norwalk Rd Ste 107 Litchfield (44253) *(G-8482)*

Parkohio Worldwide LLC (HQ).................. 440 947-2000
6065 Parkland Blvd Ste 1 Cleveland (44124) *(G-4146)*

Parksite Inc.................. 330 455-3782
3934 Jeffries Cir Louisville (44641) *(G-8612)*

Parlex USA LLC (DH).................. 937 898-3621
801 Scholz Dr Vandalia (45377) *(G-13575)*

Parma Heights License Bureau.................. 440 888-0388
6339 Olde York Rd Cleveland (44130) *(G-4147)*

Parmed Pharmaceuticals, Dublin *Also Called: Cardinal Health 110 LLC (G-6287)*

Paro Services Co (PA).................. 330 467-1300
1755 Enterprise Pkwy Ste 100 Twinsburg (44087) *(G-13350)*

Parobek Trucking Co.................. 419 869-7500
192 State Route 42 West Salem (44287) *(G-14189)*

Part 2 Screen Prtg Design Inc.................. 614 294-4429
935 King Ave Columbus (43212) *(G-5175)*

Partitions Plus Incorporated.................. 419 422-2600
12517 County Road 99 Findlay (45840) *(G-6907)*

Partitions Plus, Inc., Findlay *Also Called: Partitions Plus Incorporated (G-6907)*

Partners In Recognition Inc.................. 937 420-2150
405 S Main St Fort Loramie (45845) *(G-6952)*

Party Animal Inc.................. 440 471-1030
909 Crocker Rd Westlake (44145) *(G-14320)*

Pas Technologies Inc.................. 937 840-1053
214 Hobart Dr Hillsboro (45133) *(G-7723)*

Pataskala Post.................. 740 964-6226
190 E Broad St Ste 2 # E Pataskala (43062) *(G-11145)*

Patent Construction Systems, Marion *Also Called: Enviri Corporation (G-8969)*

Path Robotics Inc.................. 330 808-2788
3950 Business Park Dr Columbus (43204) *(G-5176)*

Path Technologies Inc.................. 440 358-1500
437 W Prospect St Painesville (44077) *(G-11103)*

Patheon Pharmaceuticals Inc.................. 513 948-9111
4750 Lake Forest Dr Blue Ash (45242) *(G-1318)*

Patheon Pharmaceuticals Inc.................. 513 948-9111
2110 E Galbraith Rd Cincinnati (45237) *(G-2943)*

Pathfinder Cmpt Systems Inc.................. 330 928-1961
345 5th St Ne Barberton (44203) *(G-831)*

Patio Enclosures (PA).................. 513 733-4646
11949 Tramway Dr Cincinnati (45241) *(G-2944)*

Patio Enclsures Stanek Windows, Macedonia *Also Called: Great Day Improvements LLC (G-8695)*

Patio Print & Promotions, Columbus *Also Called: Patio Printing Inc (G-5177)*

Patio Printing Inc.................. 614 785-9553
6663 Huntley Rd Ste S Columbus (43229) *(G-5177)*

Patrick J Burke & Co.................. 513 455-8200
901 Adams Crossing Fl 1 Cincinnati (45202) *(G-2945)*

Patrick M Davidson.................. 513 897-2971
6490 Corwin Ave Waynesville (45068) *(G-13882)*

Patrick Products Inc.................. 419 943-4137
150 S Werner St Leipsic (45856) *(G-8308)*

Patriot Armor, West Chester *Also Called: Patriot Armored Systems LLC (G-14042)*

Patriot Armored Systems LLC.................. 413 637-1060
9113 Le Saint Dr West Chester (45014) *(G-14042)*

Patriot Mfg Group Inc.................. 937 746-2117
512 Linden Ave Carlisle (45005) *(G-2070)*

Patriot Mobility, Holland *Also Called: Patriot Products Inc (G-7776)*

Patriot Products Inc.................. 419 865-9712
1133 Corporate Dr Ste B Holland (43528) *(G-7776)*

Patriot Signage Inc.................. 859 655-9009
5725 Dragon Way Cincinnati (45227) *(G-2946)*

Patriot Software LLC.................. 877 968-7147
4883 Dressler Rd Nw Ste 301 Canton (44718) *(G-1972)*

Patriot Special Metals Inc.................. 330 580-9600
2201 Harrison Ave Sw Canton (44706) *(G-1973)*

Patriot Stainless Welding.................. 740 297-6040
1555 Fairview Rd Zanesville (43701) *(G-15038)*

Patterson-Britton Printing Inc.................. 216 781-7997
7805 Saint James Dr Mentor (44060) *(G-9583)*

Patton Aluminum Products Inc.................. 937 845-9404
65 Quick Rd New Carlisle (45344) *(G-10378)*

Pattons Trck & Hvy Eqp Svc Inc.................. 740 385-4067
35640 Hocking Dr Logan (43138) *(G-8523)*

Paul Blausey Farms, Genoa *Also Called: Rcr Partnership (G-7249)*

Paul J Tatulinski Ltd.................. 330 584-8251
1595 W Main St North Benton (44449) *(G-10623)*

Paul Martin and Sons, Napoleon *Also Called: M & S AG Solutions LLC (G-10290)*

Paul Peterson Company (PA).................. 614 486-4375
950 Dublin Rd Columbus (43215) *(G-5178)*

Paul Peterson Safety Div Inc.................. 614 486-4375
950 Dublin Rd Columbus (43215) *(G-5179)*

Paul R Lipp & Son Inc.................. 330 227-9614
47563 Pancake Clarkson Rd Rogers (44455) *(G-11642)*

Paul Shovlin.................. 330 757-0032
807 Mulberry Ln Youngstown (44512) *(G-14915)*

Paul Wilke & Son Inc.................. 513 921-3163
1965 Grand Ave Cincinnati (45214) *(G-2947)*

Paul Yoder.................. 740 439-5811
13051 Deerfield Rd Senecaville (43780) *(G-11906)*

Paulin Industries Inc.................. 216 433-7633
12400 Plaza Dr U 1 Parma (44130) *(G-11134)*

Paulo Products Company.................. 440 942-0153
4428 Hamann Pkwy Willoughby (44094) *(G-14505)*

Pauls Tire Company, Youngstown *Also Called: Paul Shovlin (G-14915)*

Pave Technology Co.................. 937 890-1100
2751 Thunderhawk Ct Dayton (45414) *(G-5934)*

Pavestone LLC.................. 513 474-3783
8479 Broadwell Rd Cincinnati (45244) *(G-2948)*

Pawnee Maintenance Inc.................. 740 373-6861
101 Rathbone Rd Marietta (45750) *(G-8935)*

Pax Corrugated Products, Inc., Lebanon *Also Called: Georgia-Pacific Pcpi Inc (G-8260)*

Pax Machine Works Inc.................. 419 586-2337
5139 Monroe Rd Celina (45822) *(G-2114)*

Pax Products Inc.................. 419 586-2337
5097 Monroe Rd Celina (45822) *(G-2115)*

Paxos Plating Inc.................. 330 479-0022
4631 Navarre Rd Sw Canton (44706) *(G-1974)*

Paycor, Cincinnati *Also Called: Paycor Hcm Inc (G-2949)*

Paycor Hcm Inc (HQ).................. 800 381-0053
4811 Montgomery Rd Cincinnati (45212) *(G-2949)*

PB Fbrction Mech Contrs Corp.................. 419 478-4869
750 W Laskey Rd Toledo (43612) *(G-13091)*

Pbf Holding Company LLC.................. 419 698-6600
1819 Woodville Rd Oregon (43616) *(G-10965)*

PBM Covington LLC.................. 937 473-2050
400 Hazel St Covington (45318) *(G-5497)*

PC, Columbus *Also Called: Papel Couture (G-5173)*

PC Campana Inc.................. 800 321-0151
3000 Leavitt Rd Frnt Lorain (44052) *(G-8571)*

PC Campana Inc (PA).................. 800 321-0151
6155 Park Square Dr Ste 1 Lorain (44053) *(G-8572)*

PC Treats, Waverly *Also Called: Robert A Malone (G-13873)*

PCA/Akron 312, Coventry Township *Also Called: Packaging Corporation America (G-5487)*

Pca/Ashland 307, Ashland *Also Called: Packaging Corporation America (G-559)*

**A
L
P
H
A
B
E
T
I
C**

Pca/Fairfielde 329, Fairfield *Also Called: Dixie Container Corporation (G-6728)*

Pca/Middletown 353, Middletown *Also Called: Packaging Corporation America (G-9883)*

PCA/Newark 365, Newark *Also Called: Packaging Corporation America (G-10528)*

PCC, Painesville *Also Called: Precision Castparts Corp (G-11106)*

PCC Airfoils LLC (DH).. 216 831-3590
3401 Enterprise Pkwy Ste 200 Beachwood (44122) *(G-938)*

PCC Airfoils LLC.. 216 692-7900
1781 Octavia Rd Cleveland (44112) *(G-4148)*

PCC Airfoils LLC.. 740 982-6025
101 China St Crooksville (43731) *(G-5511)*

PCC Airfoils LLC.. 440 585-8247
34300 Melinz Pkwy Eastlake (44095) *(G-6440)*

PCC Airfoils LLC.. 440 255-9770
8607 Tyler Blvd Mentor (44060) *(G-9584)*

PCC Airfoils LLC.. 330 868-6441
3860 Union Ave Se Minerva (44657) *(G-10045)*

PCC Airfoils LLC.. 440 350-6150
870 Renaissance Pkwy Painesville (44077) *(G-11104)*

PCC Airfoils LLC.. 216 766-6206
25201 Chagrin Blvd Ste 290 Beachwood (44122) *(G-939)*

PCC Ceramic Group 1.. 440 516-3672
1470 E 289th St Wickliffe (44092) *(G-14390)*

PCI, West Chester *Also Called: Professional Case Inc (G-14139)*

Pckd Enterprises Inc.. 440 632-9119
15510 Old State Rd Middlefield (44062) *(G-9820)*

Pcna, Cincinnati *Also Called: Peter Cremer North America LP (G-2958)*

PCR Restorations Inc.. 419 747-7957
933 W Longview Ave Mansfield (44906) *(G-8844)*

Pcs Nitrogen Inc... 419 226-1200
1900 Fort Amanda Rd Lima (45804) *(G-8437)*

Pcs Phosphate Company Inc.................................. 513 738-1261
10818 Paddys Run Rd Harrison (45030) *(G-7560)*

Pct Industries, Perry *Also Called: Precision Conveyor Technology (G-11197)*

PD&b, Toledo *Also Called: Projects Designed & Built (G-13104)*

Pdi, Cleveland *Also Called: Pile Dynamics Inc (G-4165)*

Pdi Ground Support Systems Inc............................. 216 271-7344
6225 Cochran Rd Solon (44139) *(G-12166)*

Pdi Group, The, Solon *Also Called: Pdi Ground Support Systems Inc (G-12166)*

PDQ Printing Service... 216 241-5443
29003 Brockway Dr Westlake (44145) *(G-14321)*

PDQ Technologies Inc.. 937 274-4958
2500 Us Route 40 Tipp City (45371) *(G-12834)*

Pdsi, Groveport *Also Called: Pinnacle Data Systems Inc (G-7449)*

Pdsi Technical Services, Dayton *Also Called: Production Design Services Inc (G-5962)*

PE Usa LLC.. 513 771-7374
89 Partnership Way Cincinnati (45241) *(G-2950)*

Peaceful Fruits LLC.. 330 356-8515
101 E Tuscarawas Ave Barberton (44203) *(G-832)*

Peak Electric, Toledo *Also Called: Peak Electric Inc (G-13092)*

Peak Electric Inc... 419 726-4848
320 N Byrne Rd Toledo (43607) *(G-13092)*

Peak Foods Llc... 937 440-0707
1903 W Main St Troy (45373) *(G-13247)*

Pearce Inc.. 216 252-0550
1935 Stone Ridge Dr Hinckley (44233) *(G-7735)*

Pearl Valley Cheese Inc....................................... 740 545-6002
54760 Township Road 90 Fresno (43824) *(G-7147)*

Pearson Education Inc... 614 876-0371
4350 Equity Dr Columbus (43228) *(G-5180)*

Pearson Education Inc... 614 841-3700
800 N High St Columbus (43215) *(G-5181)*

Pease Enterprises Inc... 513 871-8907
1402 Riverside Dr Cincinnati (45202) *(G-2951)*

Pease Industies Inc.. 513 870-3600
7100 Dixie Hwy Fairfield (45014) *(G-6764)*

PEC Biofuels LLC... 419 542-8210
210 Wendell Ave Hicksville (43526) *(G-7651)*

Peco Holdings Corp (PA)...................................... 937 667-5705
6555 S State Route 202 Tipp City (45371) *(G-12835)*

Peco Welding Services LLC, Tipp City *Also Called: Process Eqp Co Wldg Svcs LLC (G-12837)*

Peebles - Herzog Inc... 614 279-2211
50 Hayden Ave Columbus (43222) *(G-5182)*

Peebles Creative Group Inc................................... 614 487-2011
4260 Tuller Rd Ste 200 Dublin (43017) *(G-6329)*

Peebles Messenger Newspaper............................... 937 587-1451
58 S Main St Peebles (45660) *(G-11171)*

Peerless Food Equipment LLC, Sidney *Also Called: Coperion Food Equipment LLC (G-12009)*

Peerless Foods Inc... 937 492-4158
500 S Vandemark Rd Sidney (45365) *(G-12038)*

Peerless Foods Equipment, Sidney *Also Called: Peerless Foods Inc (G-12038)*

Peerless Laser Processors Inc............................... 614 836-5790
4353 Directors Blvd Groveport (43125) *(G-7447)*

Peerless Metal Products Inc.................................. 216 431-6905
6017 Superior Ave Cleveland (44103) *(G-4149)*

Peerless Printing Company.................................... 513 721-4657
2250 Gilbert Ave Ste 1 Cincinnati (45206) *(G-2952)*

Peerless Prof Cooking Eqp, Sandusky *Also Called: Peerless Stove & Mfg Co (G-11865)*

Peerless Pump Clveland Svc Ctr, Cleveland *Also Called: Wm Plotz Machine and Forge Co (G-4512)*

Peerless Saw Company (PA)................................... 614 836-5790
4353 Directors Blvd Groveport (43125) *(G-7448)*

Peerless Stove & Mfg Co....................................... 419 625-4514
334 Harrison St Sandusky (44870) *(G-11865)*

Peerless-Winsmith Inc... 330 399-3651
5200 Upper Metro Pl Ste 110 Dublin (43017) *(G-6330)*

Pei Liquidation Company....................................... 330 467-4267
700 Highland Rd E Macedonia (44056) *(G-8704)*

Pelletier Brothers Mfg Inc..................................... 740 774-4704
4000 Sulphur Lick Rd Chillicothe (45601) *(G-2270)*

Pelton Environmental Pdts Inc............................... 440 838-1221
8638 Cotter St Lewis Center (43035) *(G-8348)*

Pemco Inc... 216 524-2990
5663 Brecksville Rd Cleveland (44131) *(G-4150)*

Pemco North Canton Division, North Canton *Also Called: Powell Electrical Systems Inc (G-10660)*

Pemro Corporation... 800 440-5441
125 Alpha Park Cleveland (44143) *(G-4151)*

Pemro Distribution, Cleveland *Also Called: Pemro Corporation (G-4151)*

Pen-Ann Corporation... 740 373-2054
2343 State Route 821 Ste A Marietta (45750) *(G-8936)*

Penguin Enterprises Inc....................................... 440 899-5112
869 Canterbury Rd Ste 2 Westlake (44145) *(G-14322)*

Pengywn, Columbus *Also Called: Y O H Inc (G-5377)*

Peninsula Publishing LLC...................................... 330 524-3359
2 Summit Park Dr Ste 300 Independence (44131) *(G-7914)*

Penn Machine Company LLC.................................. 814 288-1547
2182 E Aurora Rd Twinsburg (44087) *(G-13351)*

Pennant, Pioneer *Also Called: Nn Metal Stampings LLC (G-11322)*

Pennant Inc... 937 584-5411
401 N Front St Ste 350 Columbus (43215) *(G-5183)*

Pennant Companies (PA)....................................... 614 451-1782
12381 Us Highway 22 And 3 Sabina (45169) *(G-11681)*

Pennant Manufacturing, Columbus *Also Called: Pennant Inc (G-5183)*

Pennant Moldings Inc.. 937 584-5411
12381 Us Highway 22 And 3 Sabina (45169) *(G-11682)*

Pennex Aluminum Company LLC.............................. 330 427-6704
1 Commerce Ave Leetonia (44431) *(G-8304)*

Penny Fab, Columbus *Also Called: Penny Fab LLC (G-5184)*

Penny Fab LLC.. 740 967-3669
1055 Gibbard Ave Columbus (43201) *(G-5184)*

Pentaflex Inc... 937 325-5551
4981 Gateway Blvd Springfield (45502) *(G-12360)*

Pentagear Products LLC.. 937 660-8182
6161 Webster St Dayton (45414) *(G-5935)*

Pentagon Protection Usa LLC................................. 614 734-7240
5500 Frantz Rd Ste 120 Dublin (43017) *(G-6331)*

Pentair.. 440 248-0100
34600 Solon Rd Solon (44139) *(G-12167)*

Pentair Pump Group Inc....................................... 419 281-9918
740 E 9th St Ashland (44805) *(G-560)*

Penwood Mfg.. 330 359-5600
30505 Township Road 212 Fresno (43824) *(G-7148)*

Pepcon Concrete, Bradford *Also Called: C F Poeppelman Inc (G-1451)*

Pepi, North Canton *Also Called: Portage Electric Products Inc (G-10659)*

Pepperidge Farm Incorporated............................... 419 933-2611
3320 State Route 103 E Willard (44890) *(G-14407)*

Pepperl + Fuchs Inc (DH)............................... 330 425-3555
1600 Enterprise Pkwy Twinsburg (44087) *(G-13352)*

Pepsi Cola Bottling Co, Lima *Also Called: Consolidated Bottling Company (G-8396)*

Pepsi-Cola, Athens *Also Called: G & J Pepsi-Cola Bottlers Inc (G-640)*

Pepsi-Cola, Cincinnati *Also Called: G & J Pepsi-Cola Bottlers Inc (G-2644)*

Pepsi-Cola, Dayton *Also Called: Pepsi-Cola Metro Btlg Co Inc (G-5936)*

Pepsi-Cola, Elyria *Also Called: Pepsi-Cola Metro Btlg Co Inc (G-6577)*

Pepsi-Cola, Hamilton *Also Called: G & J Pepsi-Cola Bottlers Inc (G-7492)*

Pepsi-Cola, Springfield *Also Called: Pepsi-Cola Metro Btlg Co Inc (G-12361)*

Pepsi-Cola, Twinsburg *Also Called: Pepsi-Cola Metro Btlg Co Inc (G-13353)*

Pepsi-Cola Metro Btlg Co Inc............................... 614 261-8193
2553 N High St Columbus (43202) *(G-5185)*

Pepsi-Cola Metro Btlg Co Inc............................... 937 461-4664
526 Milburn Ave Dayton (45404) *(G-5936)*

Pepsi-Cola Metro Btlg Co Inc............................... 440 323-5524
925 Lorain Blvd Elyria (44035) *(G-6577)*

Pepsi-Cola Metro Btlg Co Inc............................... 937 328-6750
233 Dayton Ave Springfield (45506) *(G-12361)*

Pepsi-Cola Metro Btlg Co Inc............................... 419 534-2186
3245 Hill Ave Toledo (43607) *(G-13093)*

Pepsi-Cola Metro Btlg Co Inc............................... 330 425-8236
1999 Enterprise Pkwy Twinsburg (44087) *(G-13353)*

Pepsi-Cola Metro Btlg Co Inc............................... 330 963-5300
1999 Enterprise Pkwy Twinsburg (44087) *(G-13354)*

Pepsico, Chillicothe *Also Called: G & J Pepsi-Cola Bottlers Inc (G-2252)*

Pepsico, Columbus *Also Called: G & J Pepsi-Cola Bottlers Inc (G-4942)*

Pepsico, Columbus *Also Called: G & J Pepsi-Cola Bottlers Inc (G-4943)*

Pepsico, Columbus *Also Called: P-Americas LLC (G-5167)*

Pepsico, Columbus *Also Called: Pepsi-Cola Metro Btlg Co Inc (G-5185)*

Pepsico, Elyria *Also Called: P-Americas LLC (G-6575)*

Pepsico, Franklin Furnace *Also Called: G & J Pepsi-Cola Bottlers Inc (G-7058)*

Pepsico, Lima *Also Called: P-Americas LLC (G-8436)*

Pepsico, Massillon *Also Called: P-Americas LLC (G-9230)*

Pepsico, Steubenville *Also Called: P-Americas LLC (G-12409)*

Pepsico, Toledo *Also Called: Pepsi-Cola Metro Btlg Co Inc (G-13093)*

Pepsico, Twinsburg *Also Called: Pepsi-Cola Metro Btlg Co Inc (G-13354)*

Pepsico, Youngstown *Also Called: P-Americas LLC (G-14910)*

Pepsico, Zanesville *Also Called: G & J Pepsi-Cola Bottlers Inc (G-15017)*

Per-Tech Inc............................... 330 833-8824
113 Erie St S Massillon (44646) *(G-9232)*

Percuvision LLC............................... 614 891-4800
2030 Dividend Dr Columbus (43228) *(G-5186)*

Perdatum Inc............................... 614 761-1578
4098 Main St Hilliard (43026) *(G-7694)*

Perennial Vineyards LLC............................... 330 832-3677
11877 Poorman St Sw Navarre (44662) *(G-10310)*

Perfect Prcision Machining Ltd............................... 330 475-0324
920 Clay St Akron (44311) *(G-257)*

Perfect Probate............................... 513 791-4100
2036 8 Mile Rd Cincinnati (45244) *(G-2953)*

Perfect Products Company
265 Morges Rd Malvern (44644) *(G-8752)*

Perfect Score, The, Bedford Heights *Also Called: the Perfect Score Company (G-1082)*

Perfection Fabricators Inc............................... 440 365-5850
680 Sugar Ln Elyria (44035) *(G-6578)*

Perfection Fine Products, Cleveland *Also Called: Gwj Liquidation Inc (G-3802)*

Perfection Finishers Inc............................... 419 337-8015
1151 N Ottokee St Wauseon (43567) *(G-13858)*

Perfection In Carbide, Canfield *Also Called: Advetech Inc (G-1801)*

Perfection Printing............................... 513 874-2173
9560 Le Saint Dr Fairfield (45014) *(G-6765)*

Perfecto Industries Inc............................... 937 778-1900
1729 W High St Piqua (45356) *(G-11372)*

Performace Diesel Inc............................... 740 392-3693
16901 Mcvay Rd Mount Vernon (43050) *(G-10258)*

Performance Elastomers, Ravenna *Also Called: Performance Elastomers Corporation (G-11535)*

Performance Elastomers Corporation............................... 330 297-2255
7162 State Route 88 Ravenna (44266) *(G-11535)*

Performance Electronics Ltd............................... 513 777-5233
11529 Goldcoast Dr Cincinnati (45249) *(G-2954)*

Performance Health, Akron *Also Called: Hygenic Company LLC (G-181)*

Performance Motorsports Inc............................... 440 951-6600
7201 Industrial Park Blvd Mentor (44060) *(G-9585)*

Performance Packaging Inc............................... 419 478-8805
5219 Telegraph Rd Toledo (43612) *(G-13094)*

Performance Plastics, Cincinnati *Also Called: Performance Plastics Ltd (G-2955)*

Performance Plastics Ltd............................... 513 321-8404
4435 Brownway Ave Cincinnati (45209) *(G-2955)*

Performance Research Inc............................... 614 475-8300
3328 Westerville Rd Columbus (43224) *(G-5187)*

Performance Results Plus Inc............................... 614 297-9877
1700 Joyce Ave Columbus (43219) *(G-5188)*

Performance Superabrasives LLC............................... 440 946-7171
7255 Industrial Park Blvd Ste A Mentor (44060) *(G-9586)*

Performance Tank Sales Inc............................... 330 602-8800
424 W 3rd St Dover (44622) *(G-6258)*

Performance Technologies LLC............................... 330 875-1216
3690 Tulane Ave Louisville (44641) *(G-8613)*

Performance Wraps LLC............................... 937 535-2400
229 S 3rd St Miamisburg (45342) *(G-9726)*

Performanx Specialty Chem LLC............................... 614 300-7001
479 Industrial Park Dr Waverly (45690) *(G-13872)*

Performnce Plymr Solutions Inc............................... 937 298-3713
2711 Lance Dr Moraine (45409) *(G-10180)*

Peritec Biosciences, Cleveland *Also Called: Peritec Biosciences Ltd (G-4152)*

Peritec Biosciences Ltd............................... 216 445-3756
3291 Bremerton Rd Cleveland (44124) *(G-4152)*

Perkins Motor Service Ltd (PA)............................... 440 277-1256
1864 E 28th St Lorain (44055) *(G-8573)*

Perma Edge Industries LLC............................... 937 623-7819
8579 N Dixie Dr Dayton (45414) *(G-5937)*

Perma-Fix of Dayton Inc............................... 937 268-6501
300 Cherokee Dr Dayton (45417) *(G-5938)*

Permatex, Solon *Also Called: Illinois Tool Works Inc (G-12126)*

Permco Inc............................... 330 626-2801
1500 Frost Rd Streetsboro (44241) *(G-12515)*

Permian Oil & Gas Division, Newark *Also Called: National Gas & Oil Corporation (G-10524)*

Perrigo............................... 937 473-2050
400 Hazel St Covington (45318) *(G-5498)*

Perrons Printing Company Inc............................... 440 236-8870
27500 Royalton Rd Ste D Columbia Station (44028) *(G-4596)*

Perry County Tribune............................... 740 342-4121
399 Lincoln Park Dr Ste A New Lexington (43764) *(G-10405)*

Perry Welding Service Inc............................... 330 425-2211
2075 Case Pkwy S Twinsburg (44087) *(G-13355)*

Perrysburg Messenger-Journal, Perrysburg *Also Called: Welch Publishing Co (G-11279)*

Persistence of Vision Inc............................... 440 591-5443
16715 W Park Circle Dr Chagrin Falls (44023) *(G-2177)*

Personal Defense & Tactics LLC............................... 513 571-7163
2200 Ernestine Dr Middletown (45042) *(G-9884)*

Personal Plumber Service Corp............................... 440 324-4321
42343 N Ridge Rd Elyria (44035) *(G-6579)*

Personaliteez LLC............................... 614 354-9108
144 1/2 Brunson Ave Columbus (43203) *(G-5189)*

Personnel Selection Services............................... 440 835-3255
31517 Walker Rd Cleveland (44140) *(G-4153)*

Perstorp Polyols Inc............................... 419 729-5448
600 Matzinger Rd Toledo (43612) *(G-13095)*

Peska Inc (PA)............................... 440 998-4664
3600 N Ridge Rd E Ashtabula (44004) *(G-611)*

Pet Goods Mfg, Columbus *Also Called: Tarahill Inc (G-5308)*

Pet Processors LLc............................... 440 354-4321
1350 Bacon Rd Painesville (44077) *(G-11105)*

Pete Gaietto & Associates Inc............................... 513 771-0903
1900 Section Rd Cincinnati (45237) *(G-2956)*

Peter Cremer N Amer Enrgy Inc..................... 513 557-3943
3131 River Rd Cincinnati (45204) *(G-2957)*

Peter Cremer North America, Cincinnati *Also Called: Peter Cremer N Amer Enrgy Inc*
(G-2957)

Peter Cremer North America LP (DH)............... 513 471-7200
3131 River Rd Cincinnati (45204) *(G-2958)*

Peter Graham Dunn Inc............................. 330 816-0035
1417 Zuercher Rd Dalton (44618) *(G-5592)*

Peter LI Education Group, Moraine *Also Called: Pjl Enterprise Inc (G-10182)*

Peters Family Enterprises Inc..................... 419 339-0555
5959 Allentown Rd Elida (45807) *(G-6485)*

Peterson American Corporation.................... 419 867-8711
1625 Commerce Rd Holland (43528) *(G-7777)*

Petfiber LLC...................................... 216 767-4535
17000 Saint Clair Ave Ste 105 Cleveland (44110) *(G-4154)*

Petnet Solutions Inc.............................. 865 218-2000
2139 Auburn Ave Cincinnati (45219) *(G-2959)*

Petnet Solutions Cleveland LLC.................... 865 218-2000
2035 E 86th St Rm Jb122 Cleveland (44106) *(G-4155)*

Petro Gear Corporation (PA)....................... 216 431-2820
3901 Hamilton Ave Cleveland (44114) *(G-4156)*

Petro Quest Inc (PA).............................. 740 593-3800
3 W Stimson Ave Athens (45701) *(G-645)*

Petro Ware Inc.................................... 740 982-1302
713 Keystone St Crooksville (43731) *(G-5512)*

Petrox Inc.. 330 653-5526
10005 Ellsworth Rd Streetsboro (44241) *(G-12516)*

Pettisville Grain Co (PA)......................... 419 446-2547
18251 County Road D-E Pettisville (43553) *(G-11285)*

Pettisville Meats Incorporated.................... 419 445-0921
3082 Main St Pettisville (43553) *(G-11286)*

Pettit W T & Sons Co Inc.......................... 330 539-6100
1670 Keefer Rd Girard (44420) *(G-7278)*

Pettits Pallets Inc............................... 614 351-4920
1891 Dauphin Dr Galloway (43119) *(G-7210)*

Pexco Packaging Corp.............................. 419 470-5935
795 Berdan Ave Toledo (43610) *(G-13096)*

Pf Management Inc................................. 513 874-8741
9990 Princeton Glendale Rd West Chester (45246) *(G-14136)*

Pfi Displays Inc (PA)............................. 330 925-9015
40 Industrial St Rittman (44270) *(G-11626)*

Pfi Precision Inc................................. 937 845-3563
2011 N Dayton Lakeview Rd New Carlisle (45344) *(G-10379)*

Pfi Precision Machining, New Carlisle *Also Called: Pfi Precision Inc (G-10379)*

Pfi USA... 937 547-0413
5963 Jaysville Saint Johns Rd Greenville (45331) *(G-7349)*

Pfizer, Franklin *Also Called: Pfizer Inc (G-7039)*

Pfizer Inc.. 937 746-3603
160 Industrial Dr Franklin (45005) *(G-7039)*

Pflaum Publishing Group........................... 937 293-1415
3055 Kettering Blvd Ste 100 Moraine (45439) *(G-10181)*

Pfmi, West Chester *Also Called: Pf Management Inc (G-14136)*

Pfp Holdings LLC.................................. 419 647-4191
220 S Elizabeth St Spencerville (45887) *(G-12239)*

Pfpc Enterprises Inc.............................. 513 941-6200
5750 Hillside Ave Cincinnati (45233) *(G-2960)*

Pg Square LLC..................................... 216 896-3000
6035 Parkland Blvd Cleveland (44124) *(G-4157)*

Pgc Feeds, Pettisville *Also Called: Pettisville Grain Co (G-11285)*

Phantasm Dsgns Sprtsn More Ltd.................... 419 538-6737
112 W Main St Ottawa (45875) *(G-11042)*

Phantom Fireworks, Youngstown *Also Called: Phantom Fireworks Wstn Reg LLC (G-14916)*

Phantom Fireworks Wstn Reg LLC.................... 330 746-1064
2445 Belmont Ave Youngstown (44505) *(G-14916)*

Phantom Sound..................................... 513 759-4477
11865 Enyart Rd Loveland (45140) *(G-8644)*

Phantom Technology LLC............................ 614 710-0074
4179 Lyman Dr Hilliard (43026) *(G-7695)*

Pharmacia Hepar LLC............................... 937 746-3603
160 Industrial Dr Franklin (45005) *(G-7040)*

Pharmaforce Inc
960 Crupper Ave Columbus (43229) *(G-5190)*

Phase Array Company LLC........................... 513 785-0801
9472 Meridian Way West Chester (45069) *(G-14043)*

Phase II Enterprises Inc.......................... 330 484-2113
2154 Bolivar Rd Sw Canton (44706) *(G-1975)*

PHC Divison Bic Manufacturing, Euclid *Also Called: Precision Hydrlic Cnnctors Inc (G-6673)*

Phe Manufacturing, Franklin *Also Called: Phe Manufacturing Inc (G-7041)*

Phe Manufacturing Inc............................. 937 790-1582
331 Industrial Dr Franklin (45005) *(G-7041)*

PHI Werkes LLC.................................... 419 586-9222
1201 Havemann Rd Celina (45822) *(G-2116)*

Phil Vedda & Sons Inc............................. 216 671-2222
12000 Berea Rd Cleveland (44111) *(G-4158)*

Phil-Matic Screw Products Inc..................... 440 942-7290
1457 E 357th St Willoughby (44095) *(G-14506)*

Philadelphia Instantwhip Inc...................... 614 488-2536
2200 Cardigan Ave Columbus (43215) *(G-5191)*

Philips Healthcare, Cleveland *Also Called: Philips Med Systems Clvland In (G-4159)*

Philips Med Systems Clvland In.................... 617 245-5510
100 Park Ave Ste 300 Beachwood (44122) *(G-940)*

Philips Med Systems Clvland In (HQ)............... 440 483-3000
595 Miner Rd Cleveland (44143) *(G-4159)*

Phillips Companies (PA)........................... 937 426-5461
620 Phillips Dr Beavercreek Township (45434) *(G-1003)*

Phillips Electric, Cleveland *Also Called: Phillips Electric Co (G-4160)*

Phillips Electric Co.............................. 216 361-0014
4126 Saint Clair Ave Cleveland (44103) *(G-4160)*

Phillips Manufacturing Co......................... 330 652-4335
504 Walnut St Niles (44446) *(G-10600)*

Phillips Mch & Stamping Corp...................... 330 882-6714
5290 S Main St New Franklin (44319) *(G-10392)*

Phillips Meat Processing LLC...................... 740 453-3337
2790 Ridge Rd Zanesville (43701) *(G-15039)*

Phillips Mfg & Mch Corp........................... 330 823-9178
118 1/2 E Ely St Alliance (44601) *(G-398)*

Phillips Mfg and Tower Co (PA).................... 419 347-1720
5578 State Route 61 N Shelby (44875) *(G-11972)*

Phillips Syrup, Westlake *Also Called: Innovtive Cnfction Sltions LLC (G-14311)*

Phillips Syrup LLC................................ 440 835-8001
28025 Ranney Pkwy Westlake (44145) *(G-14323)*

Phillips Tube Group Inc........................... 205 338-4771
2201 Trine St Middletown (45044) *(G-9885)*

Phillips Tube Group, LLC, Middletown *Also Called: Phillips Tube Group Inc (G-9885)*

Philpott Rubber and Plastics, Aurora *Also Called: Philpott Rubber LLC (G-685)*

Philpott Rubber Company, Brunswick *Also Called: Philpott Rubber LLC (G-1605)*

Philpott Rubber LLC............................... 330 225-3344
375 Gentry Dr Aurora (44202) *(G-685)*

Philpott Rubber LLC (HQ).......................... 330 225-3344
1010 Industrial Pkwy N Brunswick (44212) *(G-1605)*

Philway Products Inc.............................. 419 281-7777
521 E 7th St Ashland (44805) *(G-561)*

Phoenix Asphalt Company Inc....................... 330 339-4935
18025 Imperial Rd Magnolia (44643) *(G-8736)*

Phoenix Associates................................ 440 543-9701
16760 W Park Circle Dr Chagrin Falls (44023) *(G-2178)*

Phoenix Brewing, Mansfield *Also Called: Mansfield Brew Works LLC (G-8818)*

Phoenix Door Systems Inc (PA)..................... 513 492-8213
7390 Union Centre Blvd West Chester (45014) *(G-14044)*

Phoenix Forge Group LLC........................... 800 848-6125
1501 W Main St West Jefferson (43162) *(G-14166)*

Phoenix Graphix Inc............................... 513 751-4433
817 W Court St Cincinnati (45203) *(G-2961)*

Phoenix Hydraulic Presses Inc..................... 614 850-8940
4329 Reynolds Dr Hilliard (43026) *(G-7696)*

Phoenix Inds & Apparatus Inc...................... 513 722-1085
6466 Snider Rd Apt C Loveland (45140) *(G-8645)*

Phoenix Metal Fabricators, Dayton *Also Called: Phoenix Metal Works Inc (G-5939)*

Phoenix Metal Works Inc........................... 937 274-5555
2528 Ashcraft Rd Dayton (45414) *(G-5939)*

Phoenix Mtal Sls Fbrcation LLC.................... 330 562-0585
2201 Pinnacle Pkwy Ste A Twinsburg (44087) *(G-13356)*

(G-0000) Company's Geographic Section entry number

Phoenix Quality Mfg LLC..............................705 279-0538
16064 Beaver Pike # 888 Jackson (45640) *(G-7951)*

Phoenix Safety Outfitters LLC.....................614 361-0544
19 S Fostoria Ave Springfield (45505) *(G-12362)*

Phoenix Technologies Intl LLC (HQ)...........419 353-7738
1098 Fairview Ave Bowling Green (43402) *(G-1434)*

Phoenix Tool Company...................................330 372-4627
1351 Phoenix Rd Ne Warren (44483) *(G-13789)*

Photo Journals, Sandusky *Also Called: Douthit Communications Inc (G-11828)*

Photography and Publishing, Mansfield *Also Called: Universal Ch Directories LLC (G-8862)*

Phpk Technologies, Columbus *Also Called: Kendall Holdings Ltd (G-5049)*

Phunkenship - Platform Beer Co...................216 417-7743
3137 Sackett Ave Cleveland (44109) *(G-4161)*

Phyllis Ann's, Columbus *Also Called: Roy Retrac Incorporated (G-5236)*

Phymet Inc...937 743-8061
75 N Pioneer Blvd Springboro (45066) *(G-12263)*

Pi-Tech, Dayton *Also Called: Proficient Info Tech Inc (G-5964)*

Pickens Plastics Inc.......................................440 576-4001
149 S Cucumber St Jefferson (44047) *(G-7980)*

Pickens Window Service Inc.........................513 931-4432
7824 Hamilton Ave Cincinnati (45231) *(G-2962)*

Pickett Concrete, Chesapeake *Also Called: G Big Inc (G-2229)*

Pieco Inc (PA)...419 422-5335
2151 Industrial Dr Findlay (45840) *(G-6908)*

Pieco Inc..937 399-5100
5225 Prosperity Dr Springfield (45502) *(G-12363)*

Piedmont Water Services LLC.......................216 554-4747
21400 Lorain Rd Cleveland (44126) *(G-4162)*

Pier Tool & Die Inc...440 236-3188
27369 Royalton Rd Columbia Station (44028) *(G-4597)*

Pierce Signs, Sylvania *Also Called: Pierce Signs & Displays Inc (G-12721)*

Pierce Signs & Displays Inc.........................408 292-3500
5648 Bent Oak Rd Sylvania (43560) *(G-12721)*

Pierce-Wright Precision Inc...........................216 362-2870
13606 Enterprise Ave Cleveland (44135) *(G-4163)*

Pierre Holding Corp (HQ)...............................513 874-8741
9990 Princeton Glendale Rd West Chester (45246) *(G-14137)*

Pierres Ice Cream Company Inc.....................216 432-1144
6200 Euclid Ave Cleveland (44103) *(G-4164)*

Pietra Naturale Inc...937 438-8882
2425 Stanley Ave Dayton (45404) *(G-5940)*

Pigments Division, Cincinnati *Also Called: Sun Chemical Corporation (G-3127)*

Pile Dynamics Inc...216 831-6131
30725 Aurora Rd Cleveland (44139) *(G-4165)*

Pilington Libbey-Owens-Ford Co, Rossford *Also Called: Pilkington North America Inc (G-11660)*

Pilkington Holdings Inc (DH) 811 Madison Ave Fl 1 Toledo (43604) *(G-13097)*

Pilkington North America Inc.........................800 547-9280
2401 E Broadway St Northwood (43619) *(G-10808)*

Pilkington North America Inc.........................419 247-3211
140 Dixie Hwy Rossford (43460) *(G-11660)*

Pilkington North America Inc (DH)................419 247-3731
811 Madison Ave Fl 3 Toledo (43604) *(G-13098)*

Pilkington North America Inc.........................419 247-3731
3440 Centerpoint Dr Urbancrest (43123) *(G-13483)*

Pillsbury, Caledonia *Also Called: Pillsbury Company LLC (G-1733)*

Pillsbury, Wellston *Also Called: Pillsbury Company LLC (G-13909)*

Pillsbury Company LLC..................................419 845-3751
4136 Martel Rd Caledonia (43314) *(G-1733)*

Pillsbury Company LLC..................................740 286-2170
2403 S Pennsylvania Ave Wellston (45692) *(G-13909)*

Pilorusso Construction Div, Lowellville *Also Called: Lyco Corporation (G-8663)*

Pilot Chemical Company, West Chester *Also Called: Pilot Chemical Company Ohio (G-14045)*

Pilot Chemical Company Ohio (PA)...............513 326-0600
9075 Centre Pointe Dr Ste 400 West Chester (45069) *(G-14045)*

Pilot Chemical Corp..513 424-9700
3439 Yankee Rd Middletown (45044) *(G-9886)*

Pilot Chemical Corp (HQ)...............................513 326-0600
9075 Centre Pointe Dr Ste 400 West Chester (45069) *(G-14046)*

Pilot Plastics, Peninsula *Also Called: Preformed Line Products Co (G-11183)*

Pilot Polymer Technologies...........................412 735-4799
9075 Centre Pointe Dr Ste 400 West Chester (45069) *(G-14047)*

Pima Valve LLC...330 337-9535
1913 E State St Salem (44460) *(G-11804)*

Pin Oak Energy Partners LLC (PA)................888 748-0763
388 S Main St Ste 401b Akron (44311) *(G-258)*

Pines Manufacturing Inc (PA).......................440 835-5553
29100 Lakeland Blvd Westlake (44145) *(G-14324)*

Pines Technology, Westlake *Also Called: Pines Manufacturing Inc (G-14324)*

Pines Technology, Westlake *Also Called: Risk Industries LLC (G-14328)*

Pink Pages, Cincinnati *Also Called: Printery Inc (G-2983)*

Pinnacle Data Systems Inc...........................614 748-1150
6600 Port Rd Groveport (43125) *(G-7449)*

Pinnacle Industrial Entps Inc.......................419 352-8688
513 Napoleon Rd Bowling Green (43402) *(G-1435)*

Pinnacle Metal Products, Columbus *Also Called: McNeil Group Inc (G-5093)*

Pinnacle Plastic Products, Bowling Green *Also Called: Pinnacle Industrial Entps Inc (G-1435)*

Pinnacle Press Inc...330 453-7060
2960 Harrisburg Rd Ne Canton (44705) *(G-1976)*

Pinnacle Roller Co..513 369-4830
2147 Spring Grove Ave Cincinnati (45214) *(G-2963)*

Pinney Dock & Transport LLC........................440 964-7186
1149 E 5th St Ashtabula (44004) *(G-612)*

Pioneer Athletics, Cleveland *Also Called: Pioneer Manufacturing Inc (G-4167)*

Pioneer Automotive Tech Inc (DH)................937 746-2293
10100 Innovation Dr Ste 150 Miamisburg (45342) *(G-9727)*

Pioneer City Casting Company......................740 423-7533
904 Campus Dr Belpre (45714) *(G-1153)*

Pioneer Cldding Glzing Systems...................216 816-4242
2550 Brookpark Rd Cleveland (44134) *(G-4166)*

Pioneer Custom Coating LLC.........................419 737-3152
255 Industrial Ave Bldg D Pioneer (43554) *(G-11323)*

Pioneer Custom Molding Inc.........................419 737-3252
3 Kexon Dr Pioneer (43554) *(G-11324)*

Pioneer Forge Div, Pioneer *Also Called: Powers and Sons LLC (G-11325)*

Pioneer Frge A Div Pwers Sons, Montpelier *Also Called: Powers and Sons LLC (G-10132)*

Pioneer Group, Marietta *Also Called: Pioneer Pipe Inc (G-8937)*

Pioneer Industrial Systems LLC (PA)...........419 737-9506
1815 Magda Dr Montpelier (43543) *(G-10131)*

Pioneer Labels Inc..618 546-5418
9290 Le Saint Dr West Chester (45014) *(G-14048)*

Pioneer Machine Inc.......................................330 948-6500
104 S Prospect St Lodi (44254) *(G-8505)*

Pioneer Manufacturing Inc (PA)...................216 671-5500
4529 Industrial Pkwy Cleveland (44135) *(G-4167)*

Pioneer National Latex Inc............................419 289-3300
114 E 7th St Ashland (44805) *(G-562)*

Pioneer National Latex Inc............................419 289-3300
244 Commercial Ave Ashland (44805) *(G-563)*

Pioneer Packing Co..419 352-5283
510 Napoleon Rd Bowling Green (43402) *(G-1436)*

Pioneer Pipe Inc...740 376-2400
2021 Hanna Rd Marietta (45750) *(G-8937)*

Pioneer Plastics Corporation.........................330 896-2356
3330 Massillon Rd Akron (44312) *(G-259)*

Pioneer Solutions LLC...................................216 383-3400
1090 E 222nd St Euclid (44117) *(G-6669)*

Pioneer Table Pad, Cleveland *Also Called: A & W Table Pad Co (G-3278)*

PIP Printing, Columbus *Also Called: Preisser Inc (G-5203)*

Pipe Line Development Company....................440 871-5700
11792 Alameda Dr Strongsville (44149) *(G-12585)*

Pipe Products Inc...513 587-7532
5122 Rialto Rd West Chester (45069) *(G-14049)*

Piqua, Piqua *Also Called: Piqua Champion Foundry Inc (G-11373)*

Piqua Champion Foundry Inc
918 S Main St Piqua (45356) *(G-11373)*

Piqua Chocolate Company Inc (PA)...............937 773-1981
310 Spring St Piqua (45356) *(G-11374)*

Piqua Emery Cutter & Fndry Co.....................937 773-4134
821 S Downing St Piqua (45356) *(G-11375)*

A
L
P
H
A
B
E
T
I
C

Piqua Emery Foundry, Piqua *Also Called: Piqua Emery Cutter & Fndry Co (G-11375)*

Piqua Granite & Marble Co Inc (PA).................... 937 773-2000
123 N Main St Piqua (45356) *(G-11376)*

Piqua Materials Inc (PA).................... 513 771-0820
11641 Mosteller Rd Ste 1 Cincinnati (45241) *(G-2964)*

Piqua Materials Inc.................... 937 773-4824
1750 W Statler Rd Piqua (45356) *(G-11377)*

Piqua Mineral Division, Piqua *Also Called: Piqua Materials Inc (G-11377)*

Piqua Paper Box Company.................... 937 773-0313
616 Covington Ave Piqua (45356) *(G-11378)*

Pique Stripping Division, Moraine *Also Called: Rack Processing Company Inc (G-10190)*

Piston Automotive LLC.................... 313 541-8674
37988 Avon Commerce Pkwy Avon (44011) *(G-735)*

Piston Automotive LLC.................... 740 223-0075
999 Kellogg Pkwy Marion (43302) *(G-8989)*

Piston Automotive LLC.................... 419 464-0250
1212 E Alexis Rd Toledo (43612) *(G-13099)*

Piston Group, Toledo *Also Called: Piston Automotive LLC (G-13099)*

Pita Wrap LLC.................... 330 886-8091
4721 Market St Boardman (44512) *(G-1375)*

Pitt Plastics Inc (DH).................... 614 868-8660
3980 Groves Rd Ste A Columbus (43232) *(G-5192)*

Pittman Engineering Inc.................... 330 821-4365
15835 Armour St Ne Alliance (44601) *(G-399)*

Pittsbrgh Crning Corp Asb Per, Toledo *Also Called: Pittsburgh Corning LLC (G-13100)*

Pittsburgh Corning LLC (HQ).................... 724 327-6100
1 Owens Corning Pkwy Toledo (43659) *(G-13100)*

Pittsburgh Paints Co.................... 740 774-7600
848 Southern Ave Chillicothe (45601) *(G-2271)*

Pittsburgh Paints Co.................... 513 242-3050
4600 Reading Rd Cincinnati (45229) *(G-2965)*

Pittsburgh Paints Co.................... 513 563-0220
2960 Exon Ave Cincinnati (45241) *(G-2966)*

Pittsburgh Paints Co.................... 419 433-5664
300 Sprowl Rd Huron (44839) *(G-7881)*

Pittsburgh Paints Co.................... 440 826-5100
16651 W Sprague Rd Strongsville (44136) *(G-12586)*

Pixelle Spcialty Solutions LLC.................... 740 772-3111
232 E 8th St Chillicothe (45601) *(G-2272)*

Pixelle Spcialty Solutions LLC.................... 419 333-6700
2275 Commerce Dr Fremont (43420) *(G-7126)*

Pizza Hut, Celina *Also Called: Buckeye Valley Pizza Hut Ltd (G-2098)*

PJ Bush Associates Inc.................... 216 362-6700
15901 Industrial Pkwy Cleveland (44135) *(G-4168)*

Pj's, Canton *Also Called: PJs Fabricating Inc (G-1977)*

Pjl Enterprise Inc (DH).................... 937 293-1415
3055 Kettering Blvd Ste 100 Moraine (45439) *(G-10182)*

Pjl Enterprise Inc.................... 937 293-1415
2019 Springboro W Moraine (45439) *(G-10183)*

Pjs Corrugated Inc.................... 419 644-3383
2330 Us Highway 20 Swanton (43558) *(G-12690)*

PJs Fabricating Inc.................... 330 478-1120
1511 Linwood Ave Sw Canton (44710) *(G-1977)*

Pjs Wholesale Inc.................... 614 402-9363
2551 Westbelt Dr Columbus (43228) *(G-5193)*

Pk Controls, Plain City *Also Called: Otp Holding LLC (G-11416)*

Pki Inc.................... 513 832-8749
4500 Reading Rd Cincinnati (45229) *(G-2967)*

Plabell Rubber Products Corp (PA).................... 419 691-5878
300 S Saint Clair St # 324 Toledo (43604) *(G-13101)*

Placecrete Inc.................... 937 298-2121
2475 Arbor Blvd Moraine (45439) *(G-10184)*

Plaid Hat Games.................... 419 552-5490
1172 State Route 96 Ashland (44805) *(G-564)*

Plaid Hat Games LLC.................... 419 552-5490
1172 State Route 96 Ashland (44805) *(G-565)*

Plank and Hide Co.................... 888 462-6852
2721 E Sharon Rd Cincinnati (45241) *(G-2968)*

Plant 1, Celina *Also Called: S & K Products Company (G-2118)*

Plant 2, Ashtabula *Also Called: Iten Industries Inc (G-599)*

Plant 2, Columbus *Also Called: Fred D Pfening Company (G-4940)*

Plant 2, Wooster *Also Called: Wooster Products Inc (G-14702)*

Plant 5, Dayton *Also Called: Oerlikon Frction Systems US In (G-5921)*

Plant 8, Sugarcreek *Also Called: Belden Brick Company LLC (G-12632)*

Plant Maintenance Engineering, Cincinnati *Also Called: New Pme Inc (G-2903)*

Plant Plant Co.................... 303 809-9588
630 Kaiser Dr Heath (43056) *(G-7600)*

Plant Two, Cleveland *Also Called: Falls Stamping & Welding Co (G-3705)*

Plas-Mac Corp.................... 440 349-3222
30250 Carter St Solon (44139) *(G-12168)*

Plas-Tanks Industries Inc (PA).................... 513 942-3800
39 Standen Dr Hamilton (45015) *(G-7517)*

Plas-TEC Corp.................... 419 272-2731
601 W Indiana St Edon (43518) *(G-6478)*

Plaskolite LLC (PA).................... 614 294-3281
400 W Nationwide Blvd Ste 400 Columbus (43215) *(G-5194)*

Plaskolite LLC.................... 614 294-3281
400 W Nationwide Blvd Ste 400 Columbus (43215) *(G-5195)*

Plaskolite LLC.................... 740 450-1109
1175 5 Bs Dr Zanesville (43701) *(G-15040)*

Plasman AB LP.................... 216 252-2995
3000 W 121st St Cleveland (44111) *(G-4169)*

Plasman Cleveland Mfg, Cleveland *Also Called: Plasman AB LP (G-4169)*

Plaster Process Castings Co.................... 216 663-1814
19800 Miles Rd Cleveland (44128) *(G-4170)*

Plasti-Kote Co Inc.................... 330 725-4511
1000 Lake Rd Medina (44256) *(G-9435)*

Plastic Card Inc (PA).................... 330 896-5555
3711 Boettler Oaks Dr Uniontown (44685) *(G-13424)*

Plastic Color Division, Minerva *Also Called: General Color Investments Inc (G-10038)*

Plastic Compounders Inc.................... 740 432-7371
1125 Utica Dr Cambridge (43725) *(G-1755)*

Plastic Enterprises Inc (PA).................... 440 324-3240
41520 Schadden Rd Elyria (44035) *(G-6580)*

Plastic Enterprises Inc.................... 440 366-0220
1150 Taylor St Elyria (44035) *(G-6581)*

Plastic Extrusion Tech Ltd.................... 440 632-5611
15229 S State Ave Middlefield (44062) *(G-9821)*

Plastic Forming Company Inc.................... 330 830-5167
201 Vista Ave Se Massillon (44646) *(G-9233)*

Plastic Materials Inc.................... 330 468-5706
775 Highland Rd E Macedonia (44056) *(G-8705)*

Plastic Mold Technology Inc.................... 330 848-4921
40 Stuver Pl Barberton (44203) *(G-833)*

Plastic Moldings Company Llc (PA).................... 513 921-5040
9825 Kenwood Rd Ste 302 Blue Ash (45242) *(G-1319)*

Plastic Process Equipment Inc (PA).................... 216 367-7000
8303 Corporate Park Dr Macedonia (44056) *(G-8706)*

Plastic Works Inc.................... 440 331-5575
19851 Ingersoll Dr Cleveland (44116) *(G-4171)*

Plasticards Inc (PA).................... 330 896-5555
3711 Boettler Oaks Dr Uniontown (44685) *(G-13425)*

Plasticraft Usa LLC.................... 513 761-2999
3101 Exon Ave Cincinnati (45241) *(G-2969)*

Plastics -R- Unique Inc.................... 330 334-4820
330 Grandview Ave Wadsworth (44281) *(G-13660)*

Plastics Division, Stow *Also Called: Esterle Mold & Machine Co Inc (G-12429)*

Plastics Family Holdings Inc.................... 440 891-1140
17851 Englewood Dr Ste A Cleveland (44130) *(G-4172)*

Plastics Family Holdings Inc.................... 614 272-0777
2220 International St Columbus (43228) *(G-5196)*

Plastics Machinery Magazine, Independence *Also Called: Peninsula Publishing LLC (G-7914)*

Plastiform Tool & Die, Port Clinton *Also Called: Rexles Inc (G-11451)*

Plastigraphics Inc.................... 513 771-8848
722 Redna Ter Cincinnati (45215) *(G-2970)*

Plastikos Corporation.................... 513 732-0961
700 Kent Rd Batavia (45103) *(G-882)*

Plastilene Inc.................... 614 592-8699
1010 Mead St Washington Court Hou (43160) *(G-13822)*

Plastipak Packaging Inc.................... 740 928-4435
610 O Neill Dr Bldg 22 Hebron (43025) *(G-7630)*

2025 Harris Ohio
Industrial Directory

(G-0000) Company's Geographic Section entry number

Plastipak Packaging Inc 937 596-6142
18015 State Route 65 Jackson Center (45334) *(G-7966)*

Plate Engraving Corporation 330 239-2155
2324 Sharon Copley Rd Medina (44256) *(G-9436)*

Plate-All Metal Company Inc 330 633-6166
1210 Devalera St Akron (44310) *(G-260)*

Platform Beer, Cleveland *Also Called: Platform Beers LLC (G-4173)*

Platform Beers LLC 440 539-3245
4125 Lorain Ave Cleveland (44113) *(G-4173)*

Plating Perceptions Inc 330 425-4180
8815 Herrick Rd Twinsburg (44087) *(G-13357)*

Plating Process Systems Inc
7561 Tyler Blvd Ste 5 Mentor (44060) *(G-9587)*

Plating Technology Inc 937 268-6882
1525 W River Rd Dayton (45417) *(G-5941)*

Platinum Industries, Ironton *Also Called: Platinum Industries LLC (G-7932)*

Platinum Industries LLC 740 285-2641
541 Private Road 908 Ironton (45638) *(G-7932)*

Play Mor, Millersburg *Also Called: Hershberger Lawn Structures (G-9983)*

Playtex Manufacturing Inc 937 498-4710
1905 Progress Way Sidney (45365) *(G-12039)*

PLC Connections, Columbus *Also Called: Plcc2 LLC (G-5197)*

Plcc2 LLC 614 279-1796
673 N Wilson Rd Columbus (43204) *(G-5197)*

Pleasant Precision Inc 419 675-0556
13840 Us Highway 68 Kenton (43326) *(G-8111)*

Pleasant Valley Ready Mix Inc 330 852-2613
559 Pleasant Valley Rd Nw Sugarcreek (44681) *(G-12645)*

Plibrico Company LLC 740 682-7755
1627 Pyro Rd Oak Hill (45656) *(G-10892)*

Plidco Ppline Repr Ppline Mint, Strongsville *Also Called: Pipe Line Development Company (G-12585)*

Plrs Legacy Inc 440 365-7333
38830 Taylor Pkwy North Ridgeville (44039) *(G-10742)*

Plug Power Inc 518 605-5703
219 S Alex Rd West Carrollton (45449) *(G-13931)*

Plumb Builders Inc 937 293-1111
2367 S Dixie Dr Dayton (45409) *(G-5942)*

Plus Mark LLC 216 252-6770
1 American Rd Cleveland (44144) *(G-4174)*

Ply-Trim Inc (PA) 330 799-7876
550 N Meridian Rd Youngstown (44509) *(G-14917)*

Plymouth Foam LLC 740 254-1188
1 Southern Gateway Dr Gnadenhutten (44629) *(G-7292)*

PM Graphics Inc 330 650-0861
10170 Philipp Pkwy Streetsboro (44241) *(G-12517)*

PM Motor Fan Blade Company, North Ridgeville *Also Called: Beckett Air Incorporated (G-10725)*

PM Power Products LLC 614 652-6509
4393 Tuller Rd Ste A Dublin (43017) *(G-6332)*

Pmbp Legacy Co Inc 330 253-8148
219 E Miller Ave Akron (44301) *(G-261)*

Pmbp Legacy Co Inc (PA) 330 253-8148
485 Kenmore Blvd Akron (44301) *(G-262)*

PMC Gage Inc (PA) 440 953-1672
38383 Willoughby Pkwy Willoughby (44094) *(G-14507)*

PMC Industries Corp 440 943-3300
29100 Lakeland Blvd Wickliffe (44092) *(G-14391)*

PMC Lonestar, Willoughby *Also Called: PMC Gage Inc (G-14507)*

PMC Smart Solutions LLC 513 921-5040
9825 Kenwood Rd Ste 300 Blue Ash (45242) *(G-1320)*

PMC Specialties Group Inc (DH) 513 242-3300
501 Murray Rd Cincinnati (45217) *(G-2971)*

PMC Specialties Group Inc 513 242-3300
5220 Vine St Cincinnati (45217) *(G-2972)*

PMC Systems Limited 330 538-2268
12155 Commissioner Dr North Jackson (44451) *(G-10693)*

Pmcsg, Cincinnati *Also Called: PMC Specialties Group Inc (G-2971)*

PME of Ohio Inc (PA) 513 671-1717
518 W Crescentville Rd Cincinnati (45246) *(G-2973)*

PME- Babbit Bearings, Cincinnati *Also Called: PME of Ohio Inc (G-2973)*

Pmp Industries Inc 513 563-3028
4460 Lake Forest Dr Ste 228 Blue Ash (45242) *(G-1321)*

PMRservices LLC 937 219-0062
2543 Us Route 42 Spring Valley (45370) *(G-12242)*

Pneumatic Scale Angelus, Cuyahoga Falls *Also Called: Pneumatic Scale Corporation (G-5564)*

Pneumatic Scale Corporation (DH) 330 923-0491
10 Ascot Pkwy Cuyahoga Falls (44223) *(G-5564)*

Pneumatic Specialties Inc 440 729-4400
11677 Chillicothe Rd Unit 1 Chesterland (44026) *(G-2239)*

Podnar Plastics Inc (PA) 1510 Mogadore Rd Kent (44240) *(G-8058)*

Podnar Plastics Inc 330 673-2255
343 Portage Blvd Unit 3 Kent (44240) *(G-8059)*

Poet Biorefining, Marion *Also Called: Poet Biorefining Marion LLC (G-8990)*

Poet Biorefining - Leipsic LLC 419 943-7447
3875 State Route 65 Leipsic (45856) *(G-8309)*

Poet Biorefining Marion LLC 740 383-4400
1660 Hillman Ford Rd Marion (43302) *(G-8990)*

Poet Biorefining-Leipsic, Leipsic *Also Called: Poet Biorefining - Leipsic LLC (G-8309)*

Poet Borefining - Fostoria LLC 419 436-0954
2111 Sandusky St Fostoria (44830) *(G-6997)*

Poet Brfining- Fostoria 23200, Fostoria *Also Called: Poet Borefining - Fostoria LLC (G-6997)*

Pohl Machining Inc (PA) 513 353-2929
4901 Hamilton Cleves Rd Cleves (45002) *(G-4546)*

Pohlman, Massillon *Also Called: Pohlman Precision LLC (G-9234)*

Pohlman Precision LLC 636 537-1909
999 Oberlin Ave Sw Massillon (44647) *(G-9234)*

Point Source Inc 937 855-6020
7996 N Butter St Germantown (45327) *(G-7252)*

Poland Print Shop, North Lima *Also Called: Print Factory Pll (G-10711)*

Polar Inc 937 297-0911
2297 N Moraine Dr Moraine (45439) *(G-10185)*

Polar Air, Englewood *Also Called: Eaton Comprsr Fabrication Inc (G-6613)*

Polar Products Inc 330 253-9973
3380 Cavalier Trl Stow (44224) *(G-12449)*

Polaris Technologies, Toledo *Also Called: Modern Builders Supply Inc (G-13058)*

Polarpics, Etna *Also Called: Yankee Candle Company Inc (G-6636)*

Pole/Zero Acquisition, Inc., West Chester *Also Called: Pole/Zero LLC (G-14050)*

Pole/Zero LLC 513 870-9060
5558 Union Centre Dr West Chester (45069) *(G-14050)*

Polimeros Usa LLC 216 591-0175
1052 Mahoning Ave Nw Warren (44483) *(G-13790)*

Poling Group, Akron *Also Called: Akron Steel Fabricators Co (G-42)*

Poling Group, The, Akron *Also Called: Akron Special Machinery Inc (G-41)*

Pollock Research & Design Inc 330 332-3300
1134 Salem Pkwy Salem (44460) *(G-11805)*

Poly Flex, Baltic *Also Called: Flex Technologies Inc (G-777)*

Poly Products Inc 216 391-7659
837 E 79th St Cleveland (44103) *(G-4175)*

Poly TEC East Inc 330 799-7876
550 N Meridian Rd Youngstown (44509) *(G-14918)*

Poly-Carb Inc 440 248-1223
9456 Freeway Dr Macedonia (44056) *(G-8707)*

Polycase Division, Avon *Also Called: Ecp Corporation (G-724)*

Polychem LLC 419 547-1400
202 Watertower Dr Clyde (43410) *(G-4561)*

Polychem LLC (HQ) 440 357-1500
6277 Heisley Rd Mentor (44060) *(G-9588)*

Polychem Dispersions Inc 800 545-3530
16066 Industrial Pkwy Middlefield (44062) *(G-9822)*

Polycom Inc 937 245-1853
35 Rockridge Rd Ste A Englewood (45322) *(G-6621)*

Polyfill LLC 937 493-0041
960 N Vandemark Rd Sidney (45365) *(G-12040)*

Polyflex, Willoughby *Also Called: Polyflex LLC (G-14508)*

Polyflex LLC 440 946-0758
4803 E 345th St Willoughby (44094) *(G-14508)*

Polymer & Steel Tech Inc 440 510-0108
34899 Curtis Blvd Eastlake (44095) *(G-6441)*

Polymer Additives Holdings Inc (PA) 216 875-7200
7500 E Pleasant Valley Rd Independence (44131) *(G-7915)*

Polymer Concepts Inc..440 953-9605
7555 Tyler Blvd Ste 1 Mentor (44060) *(G-9589)*

Polymer Diagnostics Inc...440 930-1361
33587 Walker Rd Avon Lake (44012) *(G-768)*

Polymer Engineering Pilot Ctr, Akron *Also Called: Firestone Polymers LLC (G-148)*

Polymer Packaging Inc (PA)....................................330 832-2000
7755 Freedom Ave Nw North Canton (44720) *(G-10658)*

Polymer Tech & Svcs Inc (HQ).................................740 929-5500
1835 James Pkwy Heath (43056) *(G-7601)*

Polymera Inc...740 527-2069
511 Milliken Dr Hebron (43025) *(G-7631)*

Polymerics Inc (PA)..330 928-2210
2828 2nd St Cuyahoga Falls (44221) *(G-5565)*

Polymerics Inc..330 677-1131
1540 Saint Clair Ave Kent (44240) *(G-8060)*

Polymet Corporation..513 874-3586
7397 Union Centre Blvd West Chester (45014) *(G-14051)*

Polymet Recovery LLC..330 630-9006
1280 Devalera St Akron (44310) *(G-263)*

Polynew Inc..330 897-3202
3557 State Route 93 Baltic (43804) *(G-780)*

Polynt Composites USA Inc.....................................816 391-6000
1321 First St Sandusky (44870) *(G-11866)*

Polyone, Greenville *Also Called: Avient Corporation (G-7335)*

Polyone Corporation..216 622-0100
680 N Rocky River Dr Berea (44017) *(G-1185)*

Polyone Corporation..330 467-8108
775 Highland Rd E Macedonia (44056) *(G-8708)*

POLYONE CORPORATION, Berea *Also Called: Polyone Corporation (G-1185)*

Polyone LLC..440 930-1000
33587 Walker Rd Avon Lake (44012) *(G-769)*

Polyplastex International, Kent *Also Called: Schneller LLC (G-8073)*

Polysource LLC..937 778-9500
555 E Statler Rd Piqua (45356) *(G-11379)*

Polystar Inc..330 963-5100
1676 Commerce Dr Stow (44224) *(G-12450)*

Polytech America LLC...904 728-7458
3021 Saratoga Ave Sw Canton (44706) *(G-1978)*

Polytech Component Corp.......................................330 726-3235
8469 Southern Blvd Youngstown (44512) *(G-14919)*

Pomacon Inc...330 273-1576
2996 Interstate Pkwy Brunswick (44212) *(G-1606)*

Pompili Precast Concrete, Cleveland *Also Called: E Pompili Sons Inc (G-3645)*

Pool Office Manager, Hilliard *Also Called: Phantom Technology LLC (G-7695)*

Pops Printed Apparel LLC.......................................614 372-5651
1758 N High St Unit 2 Columbus (43201) *(G-5198)*

Porath Business Services Inc..................................216 626-0060
21000 Miles Pkwy Cleveland (44128) *(G-4176)*

Porath Printing, Cleveland *Also Called: Porath Business Services Inc (G-4176)*

Porcelain Enamels, Cleveland *Also Called: Vibrantz Corporation (G-4467)*

Porcelain Steel Buildings Company..........................614 228-5781
555 W Goodale St Columbus (43215) *(G-5199)*

Port Clinton Manufacturing LLC...............................419 734-2141
328 W Perry St Port Clinton (43452) *(G-11447)*

Porta-Kleen, Lancaster *Also Called: Pro-Kleen Industrial Svcs Inc (G-8218)*

Portable Crushing LLC..330 618-5251
4237 State Park Dr New Franklin (44319) *(G-10393)*

Portage Electric Products Inc.................................330 499-2727
7700 Freedom Ave Nw North Canton (44720) *(G-10659)*

Portage Knife Company, Akron *Also Called: Portage Machine Concepts Inc (G-264)*

Portage Machine Concepts Inc................................330 628-2343
75 Skelton Rd Akron (44312) *(G-264)*

Portage Packaging Systems Inc...............................330 274-8295
5933 State Route 82 Hiram (44234) *(G-7741)*

Porter, Cincinnati *Also Called: Porter Precision Products Co (G-2974)*

Porter Paints, Chillicothe *Also Called: Pittsburgh Paints Co (G-2271)*

Porter Precision Products Co (PA)...........................513 385-1569
2734 Banning Rd Cincinnati (45239) *(G-2974)*

Porter-Guertin Co Inc..513 241-7663
2150 Colerain Ave Cincinnati (45214) *(G-2975)*

Porters Welding Inc (PA)..740 452-4181
601 Linden Ave Zanesville (43701) *(G-15041)*

Portico Merchandising, Cincinnati *Also Called: Catalog Merchandiser Inc (G-2443)*

Portion Pac Inc (DH)...513 398-0400
7325 Snider Rd Mason (45040) *(G-9134)*

Portsmouth Block Inc..740 353-4113
2700 Gallia St Portsmouth (45662) *(G-11474)*

Portsmouth Block & Brick, Portsmouth *Also Called: Portsmouth Block Inc (G-11474)*

Portsmouth Division, Portsmouth *Also Called: Osco Industries Inc (G-11473)*

Positech Corp...513 942-7411
11310 Williamson Rd Blue Ash (45241) *(G-1322)*

Positive Images, Newton Falls *Also Called: Kens His & Hers Shop Inc (G-10578)*

Positrol Inc..513 272-0500
3890 Virginia Ave Cincinnati (45227) *(G-2976)*

Positrol Workholding, Cincinnati *Also Called: Positrol Inc (G-2976)*

Posm Software LLC..859 274-0041
2145 Millsboro Rd Mansfield (44906) *(G-8845)*

Post Business Properties Inc (PA)...........................419 628-2321
205 W 4th St Minster (45865) *(G-10063)*

Post Products Inc...330 678-0048
1600 Franklin Ave Kent (44240) *(G-8061)*

Posterservice Incorporated (PA).............................513 577-7100
225 Northland Blvd Cincinnati (45246) *(G-2977)*

Postle Industries Inc (PA).....................................216 265-9000
5500 W 164th St Cleveland (44142) *(G-4177)*

Potemkin Industries Inc (PA)..................................740 397-4888
8043 Columbus Rd Mount Vernon (43050) *(G-10259)*

Potters Industries LLC..216 621-0840
2380 W 3rd St Cleveland (44113) *(G-4178)*

Pov Print Communications, Chagrin Falls *Also Called: Persistence of Vision Inc (G-2177)*

Powder Alloy Corporation......................................513 984-4016
9401 Union Cemetery Rd Loveland (45140) *(G-8646)*

Powder Coatings, Strongsville *Also Called: PPG Industries Inc (G-12588)*

Powder Kote Industries, Cincinnati *Also Called: Pki Inc (G-2967)*

Powdermet Inc (PA)..216 404-0053
24112 Rockwell Dr Euclid (44117) *(G-6670)*

Powdermet Powder Prod Inc...................................216 404-0053
24112 Rockwell Dr Ste D Euclid (44117) *(G-6671)*

Powell Electrical Systems Inc.................................330 966-1750
8967 Pleasantwood Ave Nw North Canton (44720) *(G-10660)*

Powell Valve, Cincinnati *Also Called: William Powell Company (G-3224)*

Power Acquisition LLC...614 228-5000
5025 Bradenton Ave Ste 130 Dublin (43017) *(G-6333)*

Power Distributors LLC (PA)..................................614 876-3533
3700 Paragon Dr Columbus (43228) *(G-5200)*

Power Media Inc...330 475-0500
152 Hunt Club Dr Apt 3c Copley (44321) *(G-5436)*

Power Shelf LLC...419 775-6125
500 Industrial Park Dr Plymouth (44865) *(G-11433)*

Power Source Service LLC......................................513 607-4555
5400 Belle Meade Dr Batavia (45103) *(G-883)*

Powerbilt Mtl Hdlg Sltions LLC (PA).........................937 592-5660
230 Reynolds Ave Bellefontaine (43311) *(G-1115)*

Powerbuff Inc...419 241-2156
1001 Brown Ave Toledo (43607) *(G-13102)*

Powerclean Equipment Company.............................513 202-0001
5945 Dry Fork Rd Cleves (45002) *(G-4547)*

Powerex, Harrison *Also Called: Powerex-Iwata Air Tech Inc (G-7561)*

Powerex-Iwata Air Tech Inc...................................888 769-7979
150 Production Dr Harrison (45030) *(G-7561)*

Powers and Sons LLC (DH)....................................419 485-3151
1613 Magda Dr Montpelier (43543) *(G-10132)*

Powers and Sons LLC..419 737-2373
101 Industrial Ave Pioneer (43554) *(G-11325)*

Powersonic Industries LLC.....................................513 429-2329
5406 Spellmire Dr West Chester (45246) *(G-14138)*

Powersteps, Wadsworth *Also Called: Stable Step LLC (G-13673)*

Powrkleen, Medina *Also Called: Woodbine Products Company (G-9465)*

Ppafco Inc...614 488-7259
1096 Ridge St Columbus (43215) *(G-5201)*

Ppd, West Chester *Also Called: Thermo Fisher Scientific Inc (G-14154)*

Ppe, Macedonia *Also Called: Plastic Process Equipment Inc (G-8706)*

PPG Aerospace, Chillicothe *Also Called: PPG Industries Inc (G-2275)*

PPG AF US, Strongsville *Also Called: PPG Industries Ohio Inc (G-12589)*

PPG Architectural Coatings LLC..................................... 440 297-8000
15885 W Sprague Rd Strongsville (44136) *(G-12587)*

PPG Chillicothe, Chillicothe *Also Called: PPG Industries Inc (G-2273)*

PPG Coating Services, Lima *Also Called: Crown Group Co (G-8397)*

PPG Deco USA, Cleveland *Also Called: PPG Industries Ohio Inc (G-4181)*

PPG Industries Inc.. 330 825-0831
4829 Fairland Rd Barberton (44203) *(G-834)*

PPG Industries Inc.. 740 774-8734
7012 Chillicoth Chillicothe (45601) *(G-2273)*

PPG Industries Inc.. 740 774-7600
848 Southern Ave Chillicothe (45601) *(G-2274)*

PPG Industries Inc.. 740 774-7600
848 Southern Ave Chillicothe (45601) *(G-2275)*

PPG Industries Inc.. 740 474-3161
559 Pittsburgh Rd Circleville (43113) *(G-3262)*

PPG Industries Inc.. 216 671-7793
14800 Emery Ave Cleveland (44135) *(G-4179)*

PPG Industries Inc.. 740 363-9610
760 Pittsburgh Dr Delaware (43015) *(G-6166)*

PPG Industries Inc.. 419 331-2011
2599 Shawnee Industrial Dr Lima (45804) *(G-8438)*

PPG Industries Inc.. 513 576-0360
500 Techne Center Dr Milford (45150) *(G-9948)*

PPG Industries Inc.. 440 572-2800
19699 Progress Dr Strongsville (44149) *(G-12588)*

PPG Industries Ohio Inc (HQ).. 216 671-0050
3800 W 143rd St Cleveland (44111) *(G-4180)*

PPG Industries Ohio Inc... 412 434-3888
Cleveland (44101) *(G-4181)*

PPG Industries Ohio Inc... 740 363-9610
760 Pittsburgh Dr Delaware (43015) *(G-6167)*

PPG Industries Ohio Inc... 412 434-1542
23000 Saint Clair Ave Euclid (44117) *(G-6672)*

PPG Industries Ohio Inc... 440 572-6777
9699 Progress Dr Strongsville (44149) *(G-12589)*

PPG Oak Creek, Cleveland *Also Called: PPG Industries Ohio Inc (G-4180)*

PPG Regional Support Center, Chillicothe *Also Called: PPG Industries Inc (G-2274)*

Ppg-Metokote, Lima *Also Called: Metokote Corporation (G-8432)*

Pr-Weld & Manufacturing Ltd.. 419 633-9204
18258 County Road H50 West Unity (43570) *(G-14197)*

Pragmatic Mfg LLC.. 330 222-6051
2774 Nationwide Pkwy Unit 18 Brunswick (44212) *(G-1607)*

Prairie Builders Supply Inc... 419 332-7546
2114 Hayes Ave Fremont (43420) *(G-7127)*

Prairie Lane Corporation... 330 262-3322
4489 Prairie Ln Wooster (44691) *(G-14672)*

Prairie Lane Gravel Co, Wooster *Also Called: Prairie Lane Corporation (G-14672)*

Prasco LLC (PA).. 513 204-1100
6125 Commerce Ct Mason (45040) *(G-9135)*

Prasco Laboratories, Mason *Also Called: Prasco LLC (G-9135)*

Pratt (jet Corr) Inc.. 937 390-7100
1515 Baker Rd Springfield (45504) *(G-12364)*

Pratt (target Container) Inc... 513 770-0851
4700 Duke Dr Ste 140 Mason (45040) *(G-9136)*

Pratt Industries Inc... 513 262-6253
98 Quality Ln Dayton (45449) *(G-5943)*

Pratt Industries Inc... 937 583-4990
301 W Clay St Lewisburg (45338) *(G-8361)*

Pratt Industries USA, Springfield *Also Called: Pratt (jet Corr) Inc (G-12364)*

Pratt Paper (oh) LLC... 567 320-3353
602 Leon Pratt Dr Wapakoneta (45895) *(G-13727)*

Praxair, Barberton *Also Called: Linde Inc (G-817)*

Praxair, Cincinnati *Also Called: Linde Gas & Equipment Inc (G-2823)*

Praxair, Oregon *Also Called: Linde Inc (G-10962)*

Praxair, Toledo *Also Called: Linde Gas & Equipment Inc (G-13037)*

Praxair, Wickliffe *Also Called: Linde Gas & Equipment Inc (G-14380)*

Prc-Saltillo, Wooster *Also Called: Prentke Romich Company (G-14673)*

Prcc Holdings Inc.. 330 798-4790
175 Montrose West Ave Ste 200 Copley (44321) *(G-5437)*

Precast Products LLC.. 419 668-1639
205 Industrial Pkwy Norwalk (44857) *(G-10859)*

Precise Custom Millwork Inc... 614 539-7855
6145 Enterprise Pkwy Grove City (43123) *(G-7408)*

Precise Metal Form Inc.. 419 636-5221
810 Commerce Dr Bryan (43506) *(G-1658)*

Precise Models Inc.. 440 365-5701
195 Canterbury Rd Elyria (44035) *(G-6582)*

Precise Tool & Die Company Inc.................................... 440 951-9173
38128 Willoughby Pkwy Willoughby (44094) *(G-14509)*

Precise Tool & Mfg Corp... 216 524-1500
5755 Canal Rd Cleveland (44125) *(G-4182)*

Precision Aggregates, Portage *Also Called: Palmer Bros Transit Mix Con (G-11460)*

Precision Anlytical Instrs Inc.. 513 984-1600
10857 Millington Ct Blue Ash (45242) *(G-1323)*

Precision Arcft Components Inc..................................... 937 278-0265
2787 Armstrong Ln Dayton (45414) *(G-5944)*

Precision Assemblies Inc.. 330 549-2630
11233 South Ave North Lima (44452) *(G-10710)*

Precision Bending Tech Inc (PA)................................... 440 974-2500
7350 Production Dr Mentor (44060) *(G-9590)*

Precision Brush Co.. 440 542-9600
6700 Parkland Blvd Solon (44139) *(G-12169)*

Precision Business Solutions... 419 661-8700
668 1st St Perrysburg (43551) *(G-11258)*

Precision Castparts Corp.. 440 350-6150
870 Renaissance Pkwy Painesville (44077) *(G-11106)*

Precision Cnc.. 614 496-1048
192 Fox Glen Dr E Pickerington (43147) *(G-11297)*

Precision Cnc LLC... 740 689-9009
1858 Cedar Hill Rd Lancaster (43130) *(G-8217)*

Precision Coatings Inc.. 216 441-0805
3289 E 80th St Cleveland (44104) *(G-4183)*

Precision Coatings Systems.. 937 642-4727
948 Columbus Ave Marysville (43040) *(G-9042)*

Precision Component & Mch Inc.................................... 740 867-6366
17 Rosslyn Rd Chesapeake (45619) *(G-2230)*

Precision Component Inds LLC...................................... 330 477-6287
5325 Southway St Sw Canton (44706) *(G-1979)*

Precision Conveyor Technology..................................... 440 352-6100
3785 Ln Rd Perry (44081) *(G-11197)*

Precision Cut Fabricating Inc.. 440 877-1260
9921 York Alpha Dr North Royalton (44133) *(G-10780)*

Precision Cutoff LLC... 419 866-8000
7400 Airport Hwy Holland (43528) *(G-7778)*

Precision Design Inc... 419 289-1553
2221 Ford Dr Ashland (44805) *(G-566)*

Precision Details Inc... 937 596-0068
104 Washington St Jackson Center (45334) *(G-7967)*

Precision Die & Stamping Inc.. 513 942-8220
9800 Harwood Ct West Chester (45014) *(G-14052)*

Precision Duct Fabrication LLC...................................... 614 580-9385
182 N Yale Ave Columbus (43222) *(G-5202)*

Precision Engineered Plas Inc....................................... 216 334-1105
7000 Denison Ave Cleveland (44102) *(G-4184)*

Precision Fab Products Inc.. 937 526-5681
10061 Old State Route 121 Versailles (45380) *(G-13602)*

Precision Fabg & Stamping Inc...................................... 740 453-7310
1755 Kemper Ct Zanesville (43701) *(G-15042)*

Precision Finishing Systems.. 937 415-5794
6101 Webster St Dayton (45414) *(G-5945)*

Precision Fittings LLC.. 440 647-4143
709 N Main St Wellington (44090) *(G-13899)*

Precision Foam Fabrication Inc...................................... 330 270-2440
3760 Oakwood Ave Ste B Austintown (44515) *(G-707)*

Precision Forged Products, Gallipolis *Also Called: GKN Sinter Metals LLC (G-7206)*

Precision Gage & Tool Company.................................... 937 866-9666
375 Gargrave Rd Dayton (45449) *(G-5946)*

Precision Gear LLC..330 487-0888
1900 Midway Dr Twinsburg (44087) *(G-13358)*

Precision Geophysical Inc (PA)............................330 674-2198
2695 State Route 83 Millersburg (44654) *(G-10005)*

Precision Hydrlic Cnnctors Inc............................440 953-3778
26420 Century Corners Pkwy Euclid (44132) *(G-6673)*

Precision Impacts LLC (PA)..................................937 530-8254
721 Richard St Miamisburg (45342) *(G-9728)*

Precision Imprint..740 592-5916
26 E State St Athens (45701) *(G-646)*

Precision International LLC..................................330 793-0900
7000 S Edgerton Rd Ste 106 Brecksville (44141) *(G-1479)*

Precision Laser & Forming Inc.............................419 943-4350
6500 Road 5 Leipsic (45856) *(G-8310)*

Precision Machine & Tool Co...............................419 334-8405
142 W Wilcox Rd Port Clinton (43452) *(G-11448)*

Precision Machining Services..............................937 222-4608
365 Leo St Dayton (45404) *(G-5947)*

Precision Manufacturing Co Inc...........................937 236-2170
2149 Valley Pike Dayton (45404) *(G-5948)*

Precision McHning Cnnction LLC.........................440 943-3300
29100 Lakeland Blvd Wickliffe (44092) *(G-14392)*

Precision McHning Srfacing Inc...........................440 439-9850
20637 Krick Rd Bedford (44146) *(G-1054)*

Precision Metal Products Inc...............................216 447-1900
5745 Canal Rd Cleveland (44125) *(G-4185)*

Precision Metal Products Inc...............................614 526-7000
5200 Upper Metro Pl Dublin (43017) *(G-6334)*

Precision Metal Products Inc...............................216 447-1900
9005 Bank St Cleveland (44125) *(G-4186)*

Precision Metalforming Assn................................216 901-8800
6363 Oak Tree Blvd Independence (44131) *(G-7916)*

Precision Metals Group LLC.................................440 255-8888
8687 Tyler Blvd Mentor (44060) *(G-9591)*

Precision Mfg & Assembly LLC............................937 252-3507
2240 Richard St Dayton (45403) *(G-5949)*

Precision Mtal Fabrication Inc (PA)......................937 235-9261
191 Heid Ave Dayton (45404) *(G-5950)*

Precision Polymer Casting...................................440 205-1900
4304 Maple St Ste 3 Perry (44081) *(G-11198)*

Precision Polymers Inc..614 322-9951
6919 Americana Pkwy Reynoldsburg (43068) *(G-11578)*

Precision Powder Coating Inc..............................330 478-0741
1530 Raff Rd Sw Canton (44710) *(G-1980)*

Precision Pressed Powdered Met.........................937 433-6802
295 S Alex Rd Dayton (45449) *(G-5951)*

Precision Production, Strongsville *Also Called: Precision Production LLC (G-12590)*

Precision Production LLC.....................................216 252-0372
8250 Dow Cir Strongsville (44136) *(G-12590)*

Precision Products Group Inc..............................330 698-4711
339 Mill St Apple Creek (44606) *(G-475)*

Precision Quincy Inds Inc....................................888 312-5442
4600 N Mason Montgomery Rd Mason (45040) *(G-9137)*

Precision Reflex Inc...419 629-2603
710 Streine Dr New Bremen (45869) *(G-10365)*

Precision Replacement LLC.................................330 908-0410
9009 Freeway Dr Unit 7 Macedonia (44056) *(G-8709)*

Precision Strip Inc..419 674-4186
190 Bales Rd Kenton (43326) *(G-8112)*

Precision Strip Inc..937 667-6255
315 Park Ave Tipp City (45371) *(G-12836)*

Precision Swiss LLC..513 716-7000
9580 Wayne Ave Cincinnati (45215) *(G-2978)*

Precision Tek Manufacturing, Mason *Also Called: Ashley F Ward Inc (G-9067)*

Precision Temp, Cincinnati *Also Called: RAD Technologies Incorporated (G-3030)*

Precision Thrmplstic Cmpnnts I..........................419 227-4500
3765 Saint Johns Rd Lima (45806) *(G-8461)*

Precision Tool Grinding Inc.................................419 339-9959
216 S Greenlawn Ave Ste 5a Elida (45807) *(G-6486)*

Precision Welding & Mfg Inc (PA)........................937 444-6925
101 Day Rd Mount Orab (45154) *(G-10221)*

Precision Welding Corporation.............................216 524-6110
7900 Exchange St Cleveland (44125) *(G-4187)*

Precision Wldg & Installation, Zanesville *Also Called: Precision Wldg Instllation LLC*
(G-15043)

Precision Wldg Instllation LLC............................740 995-0613
3445 Church Hill Rd Zanesville (43701) *(G-15043)*

Precision Wood Products Inc (PA).......................937 787-3523
2456 Aukerman Creek Rd Camden (45311) *(G-1768)*

Precisions Paint Systems LLC.............................740 894-6224
5852 County Road 1 South Point (45680) *(G-12229)*

Precison Coating Technology, Cleveland *Also Called: Precision Coatings Inc (G-4183)*

Predicor LLC...419 460-1831
2728 Euclid Ave Ste 300 Cleveland (44115) *(G-4188)*

Preferred Compounding, Barberton *Also Called: Hexpol Compounding Pc Inc (G-810)*

Preferred Compounding, Copley *Also Called: Prcc Holdings Inc (G-5437)*

Preferred Printing (PA).......................................937 492-6961
3700 Michigan St Sidney (45365) *(G-12041)*

Preferred Solutions Inc.......................................216 642-1200
5000 Rockside Rd Ste 230 Independence (44131) *(G-7917)*

Preformed Line Products Co (PA)........................440 461-5200
660 Beta Dr Mayfield Village (44143) *(G-9346)*

Preformed Line Products Co................................330 920-1718
200 Cuyahoga Falls Industrial Pkwy Peninsula (44264) *(G-11183)*

Preisser Inc..614 345-0199
3560 Millikin Ct Ste A Columbus (43228) *(G-5203)*

Premere Enterprises Inc......................................330 874-3000
10882 Fort Laurens Rd Nw Bolivar (44612) *(G-1388)*

Premere Precast Products...................................740 533-3333
317 Hecla St Ironton (45638) *(G-7933)*

Premier Aerospace Group LLC............................937 233-8300
2127 Troy St Dayton (45404) *(G-5952)*

Premier Bandag 8 Inc..330 823-3822
1469 W Main St Alliance (44601) *(G-400)*

Premier Building Solutions LLC (PA)...................330 244-2907
480 Nova Dr Se Massillon (44646) *(G-9235)*

Premier Construction Company...........................513 874-2611
7092 Champions Ln West Chester (45069) *(G-14053)*

Premier Container, Cleveland *Also Called: Premier Container Inc (G-4189)*

Premier Container Inc (PA)..................................800 230-7132
4500 Crayton Ave Cleveland (44104) *(G-4189)*

Premier Enrgy Systems Ohio LLC.......................304 252-1918
2099 E State St Ste D Athens (45701) *(G-647)*

Premier Farnell Corp (HQ)...................................330 659-0459
4180 Highlander Pkwy Richfield (44286) *(G-11596)*

Premier Farnell Holding Inc (DH)........................330 523-4273
4180 Highlander Pkwy Richfield (44286) *(G-11597)*

Premier Feeds LLC (HQ)......................................937 584-2411
292 N Howard St Sabina (45169) *(G-11683)*

Premier Grain LLC...937 584-6552
5827 E Xenia St Bowersville (45307) *(G-1402)*

Premier Grain LLC (PA).......................................937 584-6552
1 Solutions Ave Sabina (45169) *(G-11684)*

Premier Industries Inc...513 271-2550
5721 Dragon Way Ste 113 Cincinnati (45227) *(G-2979)*

Premier Ink Systems Inc (PA)..............................513 367-2300
10420 N State St Harrison (45030) *(G-7562)*

Premier Inv Cast Group LLC................................937 299-7333
3034 Dryden Rd Moraine (45439) *(G-10186)*

Premier Manufacturing Corp (HQ).......................216 941-9700
3003 Priscilla Ave Cleveland (44134) *(G-4190)*

Premier O.E.M., Cuyahoga Falls *Also Called: Kolpin Outdoors Corporation (G-5555)*

Premier Pallet and Recycl Inc.............................330 767-2221
11361 Lawndell Rd Sw Navarre (44662) *(G-10311)*

Premier Printing, Cleveland *Also Called: Jt Premier Printing Corp (G-3898)*

Premier Printing Corporation...............................216 478-9720
18780 Cranwood Pkwy Cleveland (44128) *(G-4191)*

Premier Prtg Centl Ohio Ltd.................................937 642-0988
16710 Square Dr Marysville (43040) *(G-9043)*

Premier Seals Mfg, Akron *Also Called: Premier Seals Mfg LLC (G-265)*

Premier Seals Mfg LLC..330 861-1060
909 W Waterloo Rd Akron (44314) *(G-265)*

(G-0000) Company's Geographic Section entry number

Premier Shot Company 330 405-0583
1666 Enterprise Pkwy Twinsburg (44087) *(G-13359)*

Premier Southern Ticket, Cincinnati *Also Called: Gtlp Holdings LLC (G-2696)*

Premier Southern Ticket Co Inc 513 489-6700
7911 School Rd Cincinnati (45249) *(G-2980)*

Premier Tanning & Nutrition 419 342-6259
35 Mansfield Ave Shelby (44875) *(G-11973)*

Premiere Con Solutions LLC 419 737-9808
508 Cedar St Pioneer (43554) *(G-11326)*

Premiere Mold and Machine Co 330 874-3000
10882 Fort Laurens Rd Nw Bolivar (44612) *(G-1389)*

Premium Balloon ACC Inc 330 239-4547
6935 Ridge Rd Wadsworth (44281) *(G-13661)*

Premium Balloon Accessories, Wadsworth *Also Called: Premium Balloon ACC Inc (G-13661)*

Premium Wood & Garden Products, Jackson *Also Called: Summers Organization LLC (G-7954)*

Premix-Hadlock Composites LLC (DH) 440 335-4301
3365 E Center St Conneaut (44030) *(G-5414)*

Premix-Hadlock Composites LLC 440 335-4301
110 N Eagle St Geneva (44041) *(G-7245)*

Prentke Romich Company (PA) 330 262-1984
1022 Heyl Rd Wooster (44691) *(G-14673)*

Presque Isle Medical Tech, Cleveland *Also Called: Presque Isle Orthtics Prsthtic (G-4192)*

Presque Isle Orthtics Prsthtic 216 371-0660
14055 Cedar Rd Ste 107 Cleveland (44118) *(G-4192)*

Presrite Corporation (PA) 216 441-5990
3665 E 78th St Cleveland (44105) *(G-4193)*

Presrite Corporation 440 576-0015
322 S Cucumber St Jefferson (44047) *(G-7981)*

Press of Ohio Inc 330 678-5868
3765 Sunnybrook Rd Kent (44240) *(G-8062)*

Press Technology & Mfg Inc 937 327-0755
1401 Fotler St Springfield (45504) *(G-12365)*

Pressco, Cleveland *Also Called: Pressco Technology Inc (G-4194)*

Pressco Technology Inc (PA) 440 498-2600
29200 Aurora Rd Cleveland (44139) *(G-4194)*

Pressed Coffee Bar & Eatery 330 746-8030
215 Lincoln Ave Youngstown (44503) *(G-14920)*

Pressed Paperboard Tech LLC 419 423-4030
115 Bentley Ct Findlay (45840) *(G-6909)*

Presslers Meats Inc 330 644-5636
2553 Pressler Rd Akron (44312) *(G-266)*

Pressure Connections Corp 614 863-6930
610 Claycraft Rd Columbus (43230) *(G-5204)*

Pressure Technology Ohio Inc 215 628-1975
7996 Auburn Rd Concord Township (44077) *(G-5393)*

Pressworks, Plain City *Also Called: Bindery & Spc Pressworks Inc (G-11398)*

Prestige Display and Packaging LLC 513 285-1040
420 Distribution Cir Fairfield (45014) *(G-6766)*

Prestige Enterprise Intl Inc 513 469-6044
11343 Grooms Rd Blue Ash (45242) *(G-1324)*

Prestige Store Interiors Inc 419 476-2106
427 W Dussel Dr # 209 Maumee (43537) *(G-9312)*

Presto Labels, Tipp City *Also Called: Repacorp Inc (G-12841)*

Preston 740 788-8208
42 Sandalwood Dr Newark (43055) *(G-10529)*

Prestress Services Inds LLC (PA) 859 299-0461
3400 Southwest Blvd Grove City (43123) *(G-7409)*

Pretreatment & Specialty Pdts, Euclid *Also Called: PPG Industries Ohio Inc (G-6672)*

PRI Marine, Columbus *Also Called: Performance Research Inc (G-5187)*

Price Farms Organics Ltd 740 369-1000
4838 Warrensburg Rd Delaware (43015) *(G-6168)*

Pride 821 LLC 330 754-6320
401 Cherry Ave Ne Canton (44702) *(G-1981)*

Pride Cast Metals Inc 513 541-1295
2737 Colerain Ave Cincinnati (45225) *(G-2981)*

Pride Investments LLC 937 461-1121
1346 Morris Ave Dayton (45417) *(G-5953)*

Pride of The Hills Manufacturing Inc 330 567-3108
8275 State Route 514 Big Prairie (44611) *(G-1217)*

Pridecraft Enterprises, Cincinnati *Also Called: Standard Textile Co Inc (G-3112)*

Priest Services Inc (PA) 440 333-1123
1127 Linda St 5885 Landerbrook Dr Ste 140 Mayfield Heights (44124) *(G-9340)*

Primal Life Organics LLC 800 260-4946
405 Rothrock Rd Ste 105 Copley (44321) *(G-5438)*

Primal Screen Inc 330 677-1766
1021 Mason Ave Kent (44240) *(G-8063)*

Primary Pdts Ingrdnts Amrcas L 937 235-4074
5584 Webster St Dayton (45414) *(G-5954)*

Primary Pdts Ingrdnts Amrcas L 937 236-5906
5600 Brentlinger Dr Dayton (45414) *(G-5955)*

Prime Conduit Inc (PA) 216 464-3400
23240 Chagrin Blvd Ste 405 Beachwood (44122) *(G-941)*

Prime Engineered Plastics Corp 330 452-5110
1505 Howington Cir Se Canton (44707) *(G-1982)*

Prime Equipment Group LLC 614 253-8590
2001 Courtright Rd Columbus (43232) *(G-5205)*

Prime Industries Inc
1817 Iowa Ave Lorain (44052) *(G-8574)*

Prime Instruments Inc 216 651-0400
9805 Walford Ave Cleveland (44102) *(G-4195)*

Prime Printing Inc (PA) 937 438-3707
8929 Kingsridge Dr Dayton (45458) *(G-5956)*

Primex 513 831-9959
400 Techne Center Dr Ste 104 Milford (45150) *(G-9949)*

Primo Services LLC 513 725-7888
1937 Clarion Ave Cincinnati (45207) *(G-2982)*

Prince & Izant LLC (PA) 216 362-7000
12999 Plaza Dr Cleveland (44130) *(G-4196)*

Princeton Precision Group, Mentor *Also Called: Princeton Tool Inc (G-9592)*

Princeton Tool Inc (PA) 440 290-8666
7830 Division Dr Mentor (44060) *(G-9592)*

Principle Business Entps Inc (PA) 419 352-1551
20189 Pine Lake Rd Bowling Green (43402) *(G-1437)*

Principled Dynamics Inc 419 351-6303
6920 Hall St Holland (43528) *(G-7779)*

Print All Inc 419 534-2880
380 S Erie St Toledo (43604) *(G-13103)*

Print Centers of Ohio Inc 419 526-4139
36 W 3rd St Mansfield (44902) *(G-8846)*

Print Digital, Stow *Also Called: Print-Digital Incorporated (G-12451)*

Print Direct For Less 2 Inc 440 236-8870
27500 Royalton Rd Columbia Station (44028) *(G-4598)*

Print Factory PII 330 549-9640
11471 South Ave North Lima (44452) *(G-10711)*

Print Shop of Canton Inc 330 497-3212
6536 Promler St Nw Canton (44720) *(G-1983)*

Print Shop, The, Wshngtn Ct Hs *Also Called: Brass Bull 1 LLC (G-14735)*

Print Syndicate Inc 617 290-9550
2282 Westbrooke Dr Columbus (43228) *(G-5206)*

Print-Digital Incorporated 330 686-5945
4688 Darrow Rd Stow (44224) *(G-12451)*

Printed Image 614 221-1412
41 S Grant Ave Columbus (43215) *(G-5207)*

Printed Image, The, Columbus *Also Called: V & C Enterprises Co (G-5343)*

Printer Components Inc 585 924-5190
4236 Thunderbird Ln Fairfield (45014) *(G-6767)*

Printers Bindery, Batavia *Also Called: Printers Bindery Services Inc (G-884)*

Printers Bindery Services Inc 513 821-8039
4564 Winners Cir Batavia (45103) *(G-884)*

Printers Devil Inc 330 650-1218
77 Maple Dr Hudson (44236) *(G-7854)*

Printers Edge Inc 330 372-2232
4965 Mahoning Ave Nw Warren (44483) *(G-13791)*

Printery Inc 513 574-1099
4460 Bridgetown Rd Cincinnati (45211) *(G-2983)*

Printex Incorporated (PA) 740 773-0088
185 E Main St Chillicothe (45601) *(G-2276)*

Printex-Same Day Printing, Chillicothe *Also Called: Printex Incorporated (G-2276)*

Printing & Reproduction Div, Cleveland *Also Called: City of Cleveland (G-3499)*

Printing Arts Press Inc 740 397-6106
8028 Newark Rd Mount Vernon (43050) *(G-10260)*

Printing Concepts, Stow *Also Called: Traxium LLC (G-12466)*

Printing Dimensions Inc.. 937 256-0044
500 N Irwin St Dayton (45403) *(G-5957)*

Printing Express... 937 276-7794
3350 Kettering Blvd Moraine (45439) *(G-10187)*

Printing Graphics, Maumee *Also Called: B & B Printing Graphics Inc (G-9263)*

Printing Partners, Solon *Also Called: Allen Graphics Inc (G-12075)*

Printing Plant, Fairfield *Also Called: Tech/III Inc (G-6781)*

Printing Service Company.. 937 425-6100
3233 S Tech Blvd Miamisburg (45342) *(G-9729)*

Printink Inc.. 513 943-0599
3976 Bach Buxton Rd Amelia (45102) *(G-435)*

Printpoint Inc.. 937 223-9041
150 S Patterson Blvd Dayton (45402) *(G-5958)*

Prints & Paints Flr Cvg Co Inc....................................... 419 462-5663
888 Bucyrus Rd Galion (44833) *(G-7197)*

Prism Powder Coatings Ltd... 330 225-5626
2890 Carquest Dr Brunswick (44212) *(G-1608)*

Pro A V of Ohio.. 877 812-5350
120 6th Dr Sw New Philadelphia (44663) *(G-10462)*

Pro Audio... 513 752-7500
671 Cincinnati Batavia Pike Cincinnati (45245) *(G-2314)*

Pro Cal, Twinsburg *Also Called: Hc Companies Inc (G-13315)*

Pro Line Collision and Pnt LLC (PA).............................. 937 223-7611
1 Armor Pl Dayton (45417) *(G-5959)*

Pro Mach Inc.. 513 771-7374
89 Partnership Way Cincinnati (45241) *(G-2984)*

Pro Oncall Technologies LLC.. 614 761-1400
4374 Tuller Rd Ste B Dublin (43017) *(G-6335)*

Pro Press Inc.. 216 631-8200
3135 Berea Rd Ste 1 Cleveland (44111) *(G-4197)*

Pro Tire Inc.. 614 864-8662
61 N Brice Rd Columbus (43213) *(G-5208)*

Pro-Decal Inc... 330 484-0089
3638 Cleveland Ave S Canton (44707) *(G-1984)*

Pro-Fab Inc... 330 644-0044
2570 Pressler Rd Akron (44312) *(G-267)*

Pro-Gram Engineering Corp... 330 745-1004
1680 Hampton Rd Akron (44305) *(G-268)*

Pro-Kleen Industrial Svcs Inc... 740 689-1886
1030 Mill Park Dr Lancaster (43130) *(G-8218)*

Pro-Pak Industries Inc (PA).. 419 729-0751
1125 Ford St Maumee (43537) *(G-9313)*

Pro-Pet LLC.. 419 394-3374
1601 Mckinley Rd Saint Marys (45885) *(G-11749)*

Pro-TEC Coating Company Inc (PA)............................... 419 943-1100
5500 Pro Tec Pkwy Leipsic (45856) *(G-8311)*

Pro-TEC Coating Company LLC...................................... 419 943-1100
4500 Protec Pkwy Leipsic (45856) *(G-8312)*

Pro-TEC Coating Company LLC...................................... 419 943-1100
5000 Pro Tec Pkwy Leipsic (45856) *(G-8313)*

Pro-tec Coating Company, Llc, Leipsic *Also Called: Pro-TEC Coating Company LLC (G-8312)*

Pro-tec Coating Company, Llc, Leipsic *Also Called: Pro-TEC Coating Company LLC (G-8313)*

Pro-TEC Industries Inc... 440 937-4142
1384 Lear Industrial Pkwy Avon (44011) *(G-736)*

Pro-Tech Manufacturing Inc.. 937 444-6484
14944 Hillcrest Rd Mount Orab (45154) *(G-10222)*

Proampac, Cincinnati *Also Called: Ampac Holdings LLC (G-2365)*

Proampac, Cincinnati *Also Called: Proampac LLC (G-2985)*

Proampac LLC.. 513 671-1777
12025 Tricon Rd Cincinnati (45246) *(G-2985)*

Process Dynamics Inc.. 330 686-2597
1659 Commerce Dr Stow (44224) *(G-12452)*

Process Eqp Co Wldg Svcs LLC...................................... 937 667-4451
319 S 1st St Tipp City (45371) *(G-12837)*

Process Equipment Co Tipp City (HQ)............................. 937 667-5705
319 S 1st St Tipp City (45371) *(G-12838)*

Process Equipment Company, Tipp City *Also Called: Process Equipment Co Tipp City (G-12838)*

Process Innovations Inc... 330 856-5192
4219 King Graves Rd Vienna (44473) *(G-13616)*

Process Technology, Willoughby *Also Called: Tom Richards Inc (G-14541)*

Processall Inc.. 513 771-2266
4600 N Mason Montgomery Road Cincinnati (45215) *(G-2986)*

Procoat Painting Inc... 513 735-2500
601 W Main St Batavia (45103) *(G-885)*

Procter & Gamble, Blue Ash *Also Called: Procter & Gamble Company (G-1325)*

Procter & Gamble, Cincinnati *Also Called: Procter & Gamble Company (G-2987)*

Procter & Gamble, Cincinnati *Also Called: Procter & Gamble Company (G-2988)*

Procter & Gamble, Cincinnati *Also Called: Procter & Gamble Company (G-2989)*

Procter & Gamble, Cincinnati *Also Called: Procter & Gamble Company (G-2990)*

Procter & Gamble, Cincinnati *Also Called: Procter & Gamble Company (G-2991)*

Procter & Gamble, Cincinnati *Also Called: Procter & Gamble Company (G-2992)*

Procter & Gamble, Cincinnati *Also Called: Procter & Gamble Company (G-2993)*

Procter & Gamble, Cincinnati *Also Called: Procter & Gamble Company (G-2994)*

Procter & Gamble, Cincinnati *Also Called: Procter & Gamble Company (G-2995)*

Procter & Gamble, Cincinnati *Also Called: Procter & Gamble Company (G-2996)*

Procter & Gamble, Cincinnati *Also Called: Procter & Gamble Company (G-2997)*

Procter & Gamble, Cincinnati *Also Called: Procter & Gamble Mfg Co (G-3002)*

Procter & Gamble, Cincinnati *Also Called: Procter & Gamble Paper Pdts Co (G-3003)*

Procter & Gamble, Cincinnati *Also Called: Procter & Gamble Paper Pdts Co (G-3004)*

Procter & Gamble, Lima *Also Called: Procter & Gamble Mfg Co (G-8439)*

Procter & Gamble, Mason *Also Called: Procter & Gamble Company (G-9138)*

Procter & Gamble, Union *Also Called: Procter & Gamble Distrg LLC (G-13411)*

Procter & Gamble, West Chester *Also Called: Procter & Gamble Company (G-14054)*

Procter & Gamble, West Chester *Also Called: Procter & Gamble Company (G-14055)*

Procter & Gamble Company.. 513 626-2500
11530 Reed Hartman Hwy Blue Ash (45241) *(G-1325)*

Procter & Gamble Company.. 513 983-1100
6210 Center Hill Ave Cincinnati (45224) *(G-2987)*

Procter & Gamble Company.. 513 266-4375
5280 Vine St Cincinnati (45217) *(G-2988)*

Procter & Gamble Company.. 513 871-7557
654 Wilmer Ave Hngr 4 Cincinnati (45226) *(G-2989)*

Procter & Gamble Company.. 513 983-1100
5299 Spring Grove Ave Cincinnati (45217) *(G-2990)*

Procter & Gamble Company.. 513 482-6789
4460 Kings Run Rd. Cincinnati (45232) *(G-2991)*

Procter & Gamble Company.. 513 634-5069
6300 Center Hill Ave Fl 2 Cincinnati (45224) *(G-2992)*

Procter & Gamble Company.. 513 983-3000
1 Plaza Cincinnati (45246) *(G-2993)*

Procter & Gamble Company.. 513 627-7115
5348 Vine St Cincinnati (45217) *(G-2994)*

Procter & Gamble Company.. 513 658-9853
1340 Clay St Cincinnati (45202) *(G-2995)*

Procter & Gamble Company.. 513 983-1100
2 Procter And Gamble Plz Cincinnati (45202) *(G-2996)*

Procter & Gamble Company.. 513 945-0340
6280 Center Hill Ave Cincinnati (45224) *(G-2997)*

Procter & Gamble Company.. 513 242-5752
5289 Vine St Cincinnati (45217) *(G-2998)*

Procter & Gamble Company (PA)..................................... 513 983-1100
1 Procter And Gamble Plz Cincinnati (45202) *(G-2999)*

Procter & Gamble Company.. 513 622-1000
8700 S Mason Montgomery Rd Mason (45040) *(G-9138)*

Procter & Gamble Company.. 513 634-9600
8256 Union Centre Blvd West Chester (45069) *(G-14054)*

Procter & Gamble Company.. 513 634-9110
8611 Beckett Rd West Chester (45069) *(G-14055)*

Procter & Gamble Distrg LLC.. 937 387-5189
1800 Union Airpark Blvd Union (45377) *(G-13411)*

Procter & Gamble Far East Inc (HQ)............................... 513 983-1100
1 Procter And Gamble Plz Cincinnati (45202) *(G-3000)*

Procter & Gamble Hair Care LLC..................................... 513 983-4502
1 Procter And Gamble Plz Cincinnati (45202) *(G-3001)*

Procter & Gamble Mfg Co (HQ).. 513 983-1100
1 Procter And Gamble Plz Cincinnati (45202) *(G-3002)*

Procter & Gamble Mfg Co.. 419 226-5500
3875 Reservoir Rd Lima (45801) *(G-8439)*

Procter & Gamble Paper Pdts Co (HQ).................... 513 983-1100
  1 Procter And Gamble Plz Cincinnati (45202) *(G-3003)*

Procter & Gamble Paper Pdts Co.......................... 513 983-2222
  301 E 6th St Cincinnati (45202) *(G-3004)*

Prodigy Print Inc
  884 Valley St Dayton (45404) *(G-5960)*

Prodigy Print Ink, Dayton *Also Called: Prodigy Print Inc (G-5960)*

Produce Packaging Inc.. 216 391-6129
  27853 Chardon Rd Willoughby Hills (44092) *(G-14562)*

Producers Service Corporation.............................. 740 454-6253
  109 Graham St Zanesville (43701) *(G-15044)*

Production, Cuyahoga Falls *Also Called: Gojo Industries Inc (G-5545)*

Production Control Units Inc................................... 937 299-5594
  2280 W Dorothy Ln Dayton (45439) *(G-5961)*

Production Design Services Inc (PA)......................937 866-3377
  313 Mound St Dayton (45402) *(G-5962)*

Production Div, Youngstown *Also Called: Gasser Chair Co Inc (G-14862)*

Production Manufacturing Inc................................. 513 892-2331
  870 Hanover St Bldg A Hamilton (45011) *(G-7518)*

Production Paint Finishers Inc................................. 937 448-2627
  140 Center St Bradford (45308) *(G-1452)*

Production Pattern Company, Cleveland *Also Called: TW Manufacturing Co (G-4434)*

Production Plant, Dayton *Also Called: U S Chrome Corporation Ohio (G-6068)*

Production Plus Corp... 740 983-5178
  101 S Business Pl Ashville (43103) *(G-630)*

Production Products Inc... 734 241-7242
  200 Sugar Grove Ln Columbus Grove (45830) *(G-5384)*

Production Screw Machine, Dayton *Also Called: Gmd Industries LLC (G-5801)*

Production Support Inc.. 937 526-3897
  105 Francis St Russia (45363) *(G-11677)*

Production TI Co Cleveland Inc.............................. 330 425-4466
  9002 Dutton Dr Twinsburg (44087) *(G-13360)*

Production Tube Cutting Inc................................... 937 254-6138
  1100 S Smithville Rd Dayton (45403) *(G-5963)*

Products Chemical Company LLC........................... 216 218-1155
  4005 Clark Ave Cleveland (44109) *(G-4198)*

Profac Inc (PA).. 440 942-0205
  7198 Industrial Park Blvd Mentor (44060) *(G-9593)*

Profac Inc... 440 942-0205
  7171 Industrial Park Blvd Mentor (44060) *(G-9594)*

Professional Award Service................................... 513 389-3600
  3901 N Bend Rd Cincinnati (45211) *(G-3005)*

Professional Case Inc.. 513 682-2520
  4954 Provident Dr West Chester (45246) *(G-14139)*

Professional Detailing Pdts, Canton *Also Called: Ohio Auto Supply Company (G-1964)*

Professional Marine Repair LLC............................. 440 409-9957
  1163 Dover Cntr Rd Ashtabula (44004) *(C-613)*

Professional Plastics Corp..................................... 614 336-2498
  4863 Rays Cir Dublin (43016) *(G-6336)*

Professional Screen Printing.................................. 740 687-0760
  731 N Pierce Ave Lancaster (43130) *(G-8219)*

Professional Supply Inc... 419 332-7373
  504 Liberty St Fremont (43420) *(G-7128)*

Proficient Info Tech Inc... 937 470-1300
  301 W 1st St Dayton (45402) *(G-5964)*

Proficient Machining Co... 440 942-4942
  7522 Tyler Blvd Unit B-G Mentor (44060) *(G-9595)*

Proficient Plastics Inc... 440 205-9700
  7777 Saint Clair Ave Mentor (44060) *(G-9596)*

Profile Digital Printing LLC.................................... 937 866-4241
  5449 Marina Dr Dayton (45449) *(G-5965)*

Profile Discovery, Columbus *Also Called: Profile Imaging Columbus LLC (G-5209)*

Profile Grinding Inc.. 216 351-0600
  4593 Spring Rd Cleveland (44131) *(G-4199)*

Profile Imaging Columbus LLC.............................. 614 301-3444
  815 Grandview Ave Ste 650 Columbus (43215) *(G-5209)*

Profile Plastics Inc... 330 452-7000
  1226 Prospect Ave Sw Canton (44706) *(G-1985)*

Profiles In Design Inc.. 513 751-2212
  860 Dellway St Cincinnati (45229) *(G-3006)*

Profiles In Diversity Journal, Westlake *Also Called: Rector Inc (G-14327)*

Proform Group Inc.. 614 332-9654
  1715 Georgesville Rd Columbus (43228) *(G-5210)*

Proforma, Cortland *Also Called: Howland Printing Inc (G-5445)*

Proforma Buckeye, Columbus *Also Called: Buckeye Business Forms Inc (G-4784)*

Proforma Signature Solutions, Brooklyn Heights *Also Called: R&D Marketing Group Inc (G-1537)*

Proforma Systems Advantage................................ 419 224-8747
  1207 Findlay Rd Lima (45801) *(G-8440)*

Profound Logic Software Inc (PA)...........................937 439-7925
  396 Congress Park Dr Dayton (45459) *(G-5966)*

Proft & Gamble... 513 945-0340
  6280 Center Hill Ave Cincinnati (45224) *(G-3007)*

Profusion Industries LLC (PA)................................800 938-2858
  822 Kumho Dr Ste 202 Fairlawn (44333) *(G-6808)*

Profusion Industries LLC....................................... 740 374-6400
  700 Bf Goodrich Rd Marietta (45750) *(G-8938)*

Progage, Mentor *Also Called: Progage Inc (G-9597)*

Progage Inc... 440 951-4477
  7555 Tyler Blvd Ste 6 Mentor (44060) *(G-9597)*

Program Managers Inc.. 937 431-1982
  1138 Richfield Ctr Beavercreek (45430) *(G-995)*

Progress Rail Services Corp................................... 216 641-4000
  6600 Bessemer Ave Cleveland (44127) *(G-4200)*

Progress Rail Services Corp................................... 614 850-1730
  2351 Westbelt Dr Columbus (43228) *(G-5211)*

Progress Tool & Stamping Inc................................ 419 628-2384
  207 Southgate Minster (45865) *(G-10064)*

Progress Tool Co, Minster *Also Called: Progress Tool & Stamping Inc (G-10064)*

Progressive Foam Tech Inc.................................... 330 756-3200
  6753 Chestnut Ridge Rd Nw Beach City (44608) *(G-906)*

Progressive Furniture Inc (HQ).............................. 419 446-4500
  502 Middle St Archbold (43502) *(G-508)*

Progressive International, Archbold *Also Called: Progressive Furniture Inc (G-508)*

Progressive Mfg Co Inc... 330 784-4717
  300 Massillon Rd Akron (44312) *(G-269)*

Progressive Molding Tech...................................... 330 220-7030
  2620 Medina Rd Medina (44256) *(G-9437)*

Progressive Plastics, Cleveland *Also Called: Alpha Packaging Holdings Inc (G-3332)*

Progressive Powder Coating Inc.............................. 440 974-3478
  7742 Tyler Blvd Mentor (44060) *(G-9598)*

Progressive Printers Inc.. 937 222-1267
  6700 Homestretch Rd Dayton (45414) *(G-5967)*

Progressive Ribbon Inc (PA).................................. 513 705-9319
  1533 Central Ave Middletown (45044) *(G-9887)*

Progressive Stamping Inc...................................... 419 453-1111
  200 Progressive Dr Ottoville (45876) *(G-11057)*

Progressive Supply LLC.. 570 000-9030
  38601 Kennedy Pkwy Willoughby (44094) *(G-14510)*

Progressive Tool Division, Delphos *Also Called: Van Wert Machine Inc (G-6198)*

Progressor Times... 419 396-7567
  1198 E Findlay St Carey (43316) *(G-2062)*

Progrssive Communications Corp............................ 740 397-5333
  18 E Vine St Mount Vernon (43050) *(G-10261)*

Progrssive Molding Bolivar Inc.............................. 330 874-3000
  10882 Fort Laurens Rd Nw Bolivar (44612) *(G-1390)*

Progrssive Mtllizing Machining, Akron *Also Called: Progressive Mfg Co Inc (G-269)*

Prohos Inc.. 419 877-0153
  10755 Logan St Whitehouse (43571) *(G-14363)*

Prohos Manufacturing Co Inc................................. 419 877-0153
  10755 Logan St Whitehouse (43571) *(G-14364)*

Project Engineering Company................................. 937 743-9114
  9874 Eby Rd Germantown (45327) *(G-7253)*

Projects Designed & Built...................................... 419 726-7400
  5949 American Rd E Toledo (43612) *(G-13104)*

Projects Unlimited Inc (PA)....................................937 918-2200
  6300 Sand Lake Rd Dayton (45414) *(G-5968)*

Projitech Inc.. 216 999-6228
  2310 Superior Ave E Ste 200 Cleveland (44114) *(G-4201)*

Proklean Services LLC (PA)................................... 330 273-0122
  3041 Nationwide Pkwy Brunswick (44212) *(G-1609)*

Prolamina, Cincinnati *Also Called: Jen-Coat Inc (G-2764)*

Prolease, Solon *Also Called: Link Systems Inc (G-12142)*

Proline Finishing, Dayton *Also Called: Pro Line Collision and Pnt LLC (G-5959)*

Promac Inc..937 864-1961
350 Conley Dr Enon (45323) *(G-6632)*

Promatch Solutions LLC...................................877 299-0185
2251 Arbor Blvd Moraine (45439) *(G-10188)*

Prominence Energy Corporation.........................513 818-8329
1325 Spring St Cincinnati (45202) *(G-3008)*

Promold Inc...330 633-3532
487 Commerce St Tallmadge (44278) *(G-12747)*

Promold Gauer, Tallmadge *Also Called: Promold Inc (G-12747)*

Promospark Inc...513 844-2211
300 Osborne Dr Fairfield (45014) *(G-6768)*

Promote-U-Graphics, Cleveland *Also Called: Bizall Inc (G-3419)*

Promotional Fixtures, Rittman *Also Called: Pfi Displays Inc (G-11626)*

Promotional Spring, Miamisburg *Also Called: Mound Printing Company Inc (G-9720)*

Proof RES Advnced Cmpsites Div, Moraine *Also Called: Performnce Plymr Solutions Inc (G-10180)*

Prospect Mold, Cuyahoga Falls *Also Called: Prospect Mold & Die Company (G-5566)*

Prospect Mold & Die Company..........................330 929-3311
1100 Main St Cuyahoga Falls (44221) *(G-5566)*

Prospect Rock LLC..740 512-0542
98 N Market St Ste 4 Saint Clairsville (43950) *(G-11707)*

Prospiant Inc (HQ)...513 242-0310
5513 Vine St Cincinnati (45217) *(G-3009)*

Prospira America Corporation (DH).....................419 423-9552
2030 Production Dr Findlay (45839) *(G-6910)*

Prospira America Corporation............................419 294-6989
235 Commerce Way Upper Sandusky (43351) *(G-13453)*

Prostar LLC..419 225-8806
4610 S Dixie Hwy Ste D Lima (45806) *(G-8462)*

Protech Industries, Avon *Also Called: Pro-TEC Industries Inc (G-736)*

Protech Pet LLC..419 552-4617
3595 State Route 51 Gibsonburg (43431) *(G-7258)*

Protech Powder Coatings Inc.............................216 244-2761
11110 Berea Rd Cleveland (44102) *(G-4202)*

Protective Industrial Polymers...........................440 327-0015
7875 Bliss Pkwy North Ridgeville (44039) *(G-10743)*

Protective Packg Solutions LLC.........................513 769-5777
10345 S Medallion Dr Cincinnati (45241) *(G-3010)*

Protectoplas Div, Streetsboro *Also Called: Ebco Inc (G-12500)*

Protein Technologies Ltd...................................513 769-0840
4015 Executive Park Dr Cincinnati (45241) *(G-3011)*

Proteus Electronics Inc.....................................419 886-2296
161 Spayde Rd Bellville (44813) *(G-1142)*

Proto Circuit Inc..330 572-3400
7 Ascot Pkwy Cuyahoga Falls (44223) *(G-5567)*

Proto Machine & Mfg Inc...................................330 677-1700
2190 State Route 59 Kent (44240) *(G-8064)*

Proto Plastics Inc..937 667-8416
316 Park Ave Tipp City (45371) *(G-12839)*

Proto Prcsion Mfg Slutions LLC.........................614 771-0080
4101 Leap Rd Hilliard (43026) *(G-7697)*

Proto Precision Fabricators, Hilliard *Also Called: Proto Prcsion Mfg Slutions LLC (G-7697)*

Proto Precision Fabricators, Hilliard *Also Called: Vicart Prcsion Fabricators Inc (G-7710)*

Proto-Mold Products Co Inc...............................937 778-1959
1750 Commerce Dr Piqua (45356) *(G-11380)*

Proto-Vest Inc...623 872-3495
5462 Walnut Ridge Ln Sheffield Village (44054) *(G-11962)*

Prototype Fabricators Co...................................216 252-0080
10911 Briggs Rd Cleveland (44111) *(G-4203)*

Prout Boiler Htg & Wldg Inc...............................330 744-0293
3124 Temple St Youngstown (44510) *(G-14921)*

Proveyance Group, Holland *Also Called: Woodsage LLC (G-7792)*

Provia - Heritage Stone, Sugarcreek *Also Called: Provia Holdings Inc (G-12646)*

Provia Holdings Inc (PA)...................................330 852-4711
2150 State Route 39 Sugarcreek (44681) *(G-12646)*

Providence REES Inc.......................................614 833-6231
2111 Builders Pl Columbus (43204) *(G-5212)*

Provimi North America Inc (HQ)..........................937 770-2400
6571 State Route 503 N Lewisburg (45338) *(G-8362)*

Provimi North America Inc.................................937 770-2400
6531 State Route 503 N Lewisburg (45338) *(G-8363)*

Provimi North America Inc.................................937 770-2400
6571 State Route 503 N Lewisburg (45338) *(G-8364)*

Prp, Columbus *Also Called: Performance Results Plus Inc (G-5188)*

PRU Industries Inc...937 746-8702
8401 Claude Thomas Rd Ste 57 Franklin (45005) *(G-7042)*

PS Copy, Westlake *Also Called: Penguin Enterprises Inc (G-14322)*

PS Superior Inc...216 587-1000
9257 Midwest Ave Cleveland (44125) *(G-4204)*

Psb Company, Columbus *Also Called: Porcelain Steel Buildings Company (G-5199)*

PSC 272 TRC Pbf...419 466-7129
1819 Woodville Rd Oregon (43616) *(G-10966)*

PSC Holdings Inc (PA)......................................740 454-6253
109 Graham St Zanesville (43701) *(G-15045)*

PSI, Chesterland *Also Called: Pneumatic Specialties Inc (G-2239)*

Psix LLC..937 746-6841
185 S Pioneer Blvd Springboro (45066) *(G-12264)*

PSK Steel Corp...330 759-1251
2960 Gale Dr Hubbard (44425) *(G-7816)*

Pt Metals LLC...330 767-3003
10384 Navarre Rd Sw Navarre (44662) *(G-10312)*

Pt Tech LLC (HQ)...330 239-4933
1441 Wolf Creek Trl Wadsworth (44281) *(G-13662)*

Ptc Alliance LLC..330 821-5700
640 Keystone St Alliance (44601) *(G-401)*

Ptc Enterprises Inc..419 272-2524
3047 County Road K Edon (43518) *(G-6479)*

Ptc Industries, Cleveland *Also Called: Parking & Traffic Control SEC (G-4145)*

Pti, Bowling Green *Also Called: Phoenix Technologies Intl LLC (G-1434)*

Ptmj Enterprises Inc..440 543-8000
32000 Aurora Rd Solon (44139) *(G-12170)*

Ptp of Mississippi, Cincinnati *Also Called: Cindus Corporation (G-2491)*

Pts, Heath *Also Called: Polymer Tech & Svcs Inc (G-7601)*

Pts Prfssnal Technical Svc Inc...........................513 642-0111
503 Commercial Dr West Chester (45014) *(G-14056)*

Pubco Corporation (PA).....................................216 881-5300
3830 Kelley Ave Cleveland (44114) *(G-4205)*

Public Safety Ohio Department...........................440 943-5545
31517 Vine St Willoughby (44095) *(G-14511)*

Publishing Group Ltd..614 572-1240
781 Northwest Blvd Ste 202 Columbus (43212) *(G-5213)*

Pucel Enterprises Inc.......................................216 881-4604
1440 E 36th St Cleveland (44114) *(G-4206)*

Pucel Enterprises Inc.......................................800 336-4986
1401 E 34th St Cleveland (44114) *(G-4207)*

Pughs Designer Jewelers Inc.............................740 344-9259
12 W Main St Newark (43055) *(G-10530)*

Pukka LLC (DH)...419 429-7808
337 S Main St Fl 4 Findlay (45840) *(G-6911)*

Pukka, Inc., Findlay *Also Called: Pukka LLC (G-6911)*

Pullman Company...419 499-2541
33 Lockwood Rd Milan (44846) *(G-9917)*

Pullman Company...419 592-2055
11800 County Road 424 Napoleon (43545) *(G-10296)*

Pulsar Ecoproducts LLC....................................216 861-8800
3615 Superior Ave E Ste 4402a Cleveland (44114) *(G-4208)*

Pulsar Products, Cleveland *Also Called: Pulsar Ecoproducts LLC (G-4208)*

Pulse Worldwide Ltd...513 234-7829
7554 Central Parke Blvd Mason (45040) *(G-9139)*

Pumpco Concrete Pumping LLC.........................740 809-1473
7230 Johnstown Utica Rd Johnstown (43031) *(G-7997)*

Pumphrey Machine Corp....................................440 417-0481
7240 N Ridge Rd Madison (44057) *(G-8732)*

Pumps Group, Toledo *Also Called: Airtex Industries LLC (G-12868)*

Punch Components Inc......................................419 224-1242
505 N Cable Rd Lima (45805) *(G-8441)*

Pur Hair Extensions LLC...................................330 786-5772
1088 E Tallmadge Ave Akron (44310) *(G-270)*

Pure Foods LLC...303 358-8375
675 Alpha Dr Ste E Highland Heights (44143) *(G-7662)*

Pure Water Technology NW Ohio, Toledo *Also Called: Onesource Water LLC (G-13077)*

Purebuttonscom LLC................................... 330 721-1600
4930 Chippewa Rd Unit A Medina (44256) *(G-9438)*

Puremonics, Cleveland *Also Called: CPI Group Limited (G-3573)*

Pureti Group LLC....................................... 513 708-3631
10931 Reed Hartman Hwy Ste C Cincinnati (45242) *(G-3012)*

Purina Mills, Orrville *Also Called: Purina Mills LLC (G-11002)*

Purina Mills LLC....................................... 330 682-1951
635 Collins Blvd Orrville (44667) *(G-11002)*

Puritas Metal Products Inc........................... 440 353-1917
39097 Center Ridge Rd North Ridgeville (44039) *(G-10744)*

Purple Orchid Boutique LLC.......................... 614 554-7686
1535 Cunard Rd Columbus (43227) *(G-5214)*

Purushealth LLC.. 800 601-0580
3558 Lee Rd Shaker Heights (44120) *(G-11932)*

Purvis Milling Co, West Union *Also Called: Dinsmore Inc (G-14190)*

Putnam Aggregrates Co................................ 419 523-6004
7053 Road M Ottawa (45875) *(G-11043)*

Putnam Plastics Inc.................................... 937 866-6261
255 S Alex Rd Dayton (45449) *(G-5969)*

Puttmann Industries Inc............................... 513 202-9444
320 N State St Harrison (45030) *(G-7563)*

Pvm Incorporated....................................... 614 871-0302
3515 Grove City Rd Grove City (43123) *(G-7410)*

PVS Chemical Solutions Inc.......................... 330 666-0888
3149 Copley Rd Copley (44321) *(G-5439)*

PVS Plastics Technology Corp........................ 937 233-4376
6290 Executive Blvd Huber Heights (45424) *(G-7824)*

Pwp Inc... 216 251-2181
532 County Road 1600 Ashland (44805) *(G-567)*

Pyramid Industries LLC................................ 614 783-1543
327 Briarwood Dr Columbus (43213) *(G-5215)*

Pyramid Mold & Machine Co Inc...................... 330 673-5200
222 Martinel Dr Kent (44240) *(G-8065)*

Pyramid Mold & Machine Company, Kent *Also Called: Pyramid Mold & Machine Co Inc (G-8065)*

Pyramid Plastics Inc................................... 216 641-5904
9202 Reno Ave Cleveland (44105) *(G-4209)*

Pyro-Chem Corporation................................ 740 377-2244
2491 County Road 1 South Point (45680) *(G-12230)*

Pyromatics Corp (PA).................................. 440 352-3500
9321 Pineneedle Dr Mentor (44060) *(G-9599)*

Pyros Pharmaceuticals Inc............................ 201 743-9468
470 Olde Worthington Rd Ste 200 Westerville (43082) *(G-14227)*

Q Holding Company (HQ).............................. 440 903-1827
1700 Highland Rd Twinsburg (44087) *(G-13361)*

Q Holding Mexico, Twinsburg *Also Called: Q Holding Company (G-13361)*

Q M P, Cleves *Also Called: Stock Mfg & Design Co Inc (G-4549)*

Q Model Inc.. 330 733-6545
3414 E Waterloo Rd Akron (44312) *(G-271)*

Q S I Fabrication Inc.................................. 419 832-1680
10333 S River Rd Grand Rapids (43522) *(G-7308)*

Q T Columbus LLC...................................... 800 758-2410
1330 Stimmel Rd Columbus (43223) *(G-5216)*

Q-Lab, Westlake *Also Called: Q-Lab Corporation (G-14325)*

Q-Lab Corporation (PA)................................ 440 835-8700
800 Canterbury Rd Westlake (44145) *(G-14325)*

Q&D Indrustrial Floors, Farmersville *Also Called: Quality Durable Indus Floors (G-6823)*

Qaf Technologies Inc................................... 440 941-4348
1212 E Dublin Granville Rd Ste 105 Columbus (43229) *(G-5217)*

Qc LLC.. 847 682-9072
730 Miley Rd North Lima (44452) *(G-10712)*

Qc Software LLC.. 513 469-1424
50 E Business Way Cincinnati (45241) *(G-3013)*

Qca Inc... 513 681-8400
2832 Spring Grove Ave Cincinnati (45225) *(G-3014)*

Qcforge.com, Cincinnati *Also Called: Queen City Forging Company (G-2315)*

Qcp, Holland *Also Called: Quality Care Products LLC (G-7780)*

Qcp Pallet Services, Cincinnati *Also Called: Queen City Pallets Inc (G-3023)*

Qcsm LLC... 216 650-8731
9335 Mccracken Blvd Cleveland (44125) *(G-4210)*

Qfm Stamping Inc...................................... 330 337-3311
400 W Railroad St Ste 1 Columbiana (44408) *(G-4625)*

Qibco Buffing Pads Inc (PA)........................... 937 743-0805
301 Industry Dr Ste B Carlisle (45005) *(G-2071)*

Qlog Corp.. 513 874-1211
33 Standen Dr Hamilton (45015) *(G-7519)*

Qnnect LLC (PA)....................................... 864 275-8970
1382 W Jackson St Painesville (44077) *(G-11107)*

Qrp Inc.. 910 371-0700
1000 W Bagley Rd Ste 101 Berea (44017) *(G-1186)*

Qsi, Fairport Harbor *Also Called: Quartz Scientific Inc (G-6820)*

Qsr, Twinsburg *Also Called: Lexington Rubber Group Inc (G-13331)*

QT Equipment Company (PA)........................... 330 724-3055
151 W Dartmore Ave Akron (44301) *(G-272)*

Quad Fluid Dynamics Inc.............................. 330 220-3005
2826 Westway Dr Brunswick (44212) *(G-1610)*

Quadco Rehabilitation Ctr Inc (PA)................... 419 682-1011
427 N Defiance St Stryker (43557) *(G-12626)*

Quadrel Inc.. 440 602-4700
7670 Jenther Dr Mentor (44060) *(G-9600)*

Quadrel Labeling Systems, Mentor *Also Called: Quadrel Inc (G-9600)*

Quadriga Americas LLC (PA)........................... 614 890-6090
480 Olde Worthington Rd Ste 350 Westerville (43082) *(G-14228)*

Quaker Chemical Corporation (HQ)................... 513 422-9600
3431 Yankee Rd Middletown (45044) *(G-9888)*

Quaker City Casting, Salem *Also Called: Korff Holdings LLC (G-11792)*

Quaker City Castings Inc.............................. 330 332-1566
310 E Euclid Ave Salem (44460) *(G-11806)*

Quaker City Concrete Pdts LLC....................... 330 427-2239
290 E High St Leetonia (44431) *(G-8305)*

Quaker Houghton, Middletown *Also Called: Quaker Chemical Corporation (G-9888)*

Quaker Houghton Pa Inc............................... 513 422-9600
3431 Yankee Rd Middletown (45044) *(G-9889)*

Quaker Mfg, Salem *Also Called: Quaker Mfg Corp (G-11807)*

Quaker Mfg Corp....................................... 330 332-4631
187 Georgetown Rd Salem (44460) *(G-11807)*

Qual-Fab Inc... 440 327-5000
34250 Mills Rd Avon (44011) *(G-737)*

Qualiform Inc.. 330 336-6777
689 Weber Dr Wadsworth (44281) *(G-13663)*

Qualitee Design Sportswear Co (PA).................. 740 333-8337
1270 Us Highway 22 Nw Ste 9 Wshngtn Ct Hs (43160) *(G-14742)*

Qualitor Inc (DH)...................................... 248 204-8600
127 Public Sq Ste 5300 Cleveland (44114) *(G-4211)*

Qualitor Subsidiary H Inc............................. 419 562-7987
1232 Whetstone St Bucyrus (44820) *(G-1686)*

Qualiturn Inc.. 513 808-3333
9081 Le Saint Dr West Chester (45014) *(G-14057)*

Quality Architectural and Fabr........................ 937 743-2923
8 Shotwell Dr Franklin (45005) *(G-7043)*

Quality Assurance, Fremont *Also Called: Kraft Heinz Foods Company (G-7120)*

Quality Bakery Company Inc........................... 614 224-1424
50 N Glenwood Ave Columbus (43222) *(G-5218)*

Quality Bar Inc.. 330 755-0000
17 Union St Ste 7 Struthers (44471) *(G-12620)*

Quality Block & Supply Inc (DH)...................... 330 364-4411
Rte 250 Mount Eaton (44659) *(G-10208)*

Quality Blow Molding Inc.............................. 440 458-6550
635 Oberlin Elyria Rd Elyria (44035) *(G-6583)*

Quality Borate Co LLC................................. 216 896-1949
3690 Orange Pl Ste 495 Cleveland (44122) *(G-4212)*

Quality Care Products LLC............................. 734 847-2704
6920 Hall St Holland (43528) *(G-7780)*

Quality Castings Company (PA)........................ 330 682-6010
1200 N Main St Orrville (44667) *(G-11003)*

Quality CNC Machining Inc............................ 440 953-0723
38195 Airport Pkwy Willoughby (44094) *(G-14512)*

Quality Components Inc................................ 440 255-0606
8825 East Ave Mentor (44060) *(G-9601)*

Quality Controls Inc................................... 513 272-3900
3411 Church St Cincinnati (45244) *(G-3015)*

Quality Custom Signs LLC.................... 614 580-7233
651 Lakeview Plaza Blvd Ste F Worthington (43085) *(G-14723)*

Quality Cutter Grinding Co.................... 216 362-6444
15501 Commerce Park Dr Cleveland (44142) *(G-4213)*

Quality Design Machining Inc.................... 440 352-7290
64 Penniman Rd Orwell (44076) *(G-11025)*

Quality Durable Indus Floors.................... 937 696-2833
5005 Farmersville Germantn Pike Farmersville (45325) *(G-6823)*

Quality Electrodynamics LLC.................... 440 638-5106
6655 Beta Dr Ste 100 Mayfield Village (44143) *(G-9347)*

Quality Envelope Inc.................... 513 942-7578
9792 Inter Ocean Dr West Chester (45246) *(G-14140)*

Quality Fabricated Metals Inc
14000 W Middletown Rd Salem (44460) *(G-11808)*

Quality Forms, Piqua *Also Called: Little Printing Company (G-11363)*

Quality Gold, Fairfield *Also Called: Quality Gold Inc (G-6769)*

Quality Gold Inc (PA).................... 513 942-7659
500 Quality Blvd Fairfield (45014) *(G-6769)*

Quality Industries Inc.................... 216 961-5566
3716 Clark Ave Cleveland (44109) *(G-4214)*

Quality Liquid Feeds Inc.................... 330 532-4635
2402 Clark Ave Wellsville (43968) *(G-13913)*

Quality Machine Systems LLC.................... 440 223-2217
7875 Enterprise Dr Mentor (44060) *(G-9602)*

Quality Machining and Mfg Inc.................... 419 899-2543
14168 State Route 18 Sherwood (43556) *(G-11976)*

Quality Mechanicals Inc.................... 513 559-0998
1225 Streng St Cincinnati (45223) *(G-3016)*

Quality Mfg Company Inc.................... 513 921-4500
4323 Spring Grove Ave Cincinnati (45223) *(G-3017)*

Quality Molded, Akron *Also Called: New Castings Inc (G-245)*

Quality Office Products, Dayton *Also Called: SPAOS Inc (G-6014)*

Quality Parts, Jackson Center *Also Called: A G Parts Inc (G-7957)*

Quality Plastics, Fredericksburg *Also Called: Yoders Produce Inc (G-7073)*

Quality Plastics LLC.................... 330 695-5920
9620 S Apple Creek Rd Fredericksburg (44627) *(G-7068)*

Quality Plating Co.................... 216 361-0151
1443 E 40th St Cleveland (44103) *(G-4215)*

Quality Printing & Publishing, Hamilton *Also Called: Quality Publishing Co (G-7520)*

Quality Printing Co, Bucyrus *Also Called: Bucyrus Graphics Inc (G-1673)*

Quality Publishing Co.................... 513 863-8210
3200 Symmes Rd Hamilton (45015) *(G-7520)*

Quality Quartz Engineering Inc.................... 937 236-3250
802 Orchard Ln Beavercreek Township (45434) *(G-1004)*

Quality Quartz Engineering Inc (PA).................... 510 791-1013
802 Orchard Ln Beavercreek Township (45434) *(G-1005)*

Quality Ready Mix Inc (PA).................... 419 394-8870
16672 County Road 66a Saint Marys (45885) *(G-11750)*

Quality Reproductions Inc.................... 330 335-5000
127 Hartman Rd Wadsworth (44281) *(G-13664)*

Quality Rubber Stamp Inc.................... 614 235-2700
1777 Victor Rd Nw Lancaster (43130) *(G-8220)*

Quality Solutions Inc.................... 440 933-9946
Cleveland (44140) *(G-4216)*

QUALITY SOLUTIONS INC, Cleveland *Also Called: Quality Solutions Inc (G-4216)*

Quality Specialists Inc.................... 440 946-9129
1428 E 363rd St Willoughby (44095) *(G-14513)*

Quality Stamping, Toledo *Also Called: Quality Tool Company (G-13105)*

Quality Stamping Products Co (PA).................... 216 441-2700
5322 Bragg Rd Cleveland (44127) *(G-4217)*

Quality Steel Fabrication.................... 937 492-9503
2500 Fair Rd Sidney (45365) *(G-12042)*

Quality Switch Inc.................... 330 872-5707
715 Arlington Blvd Newton Falls (44444) *(G-10580)*

Quality Synthetic Rubber Co, Twinsburg *Also Called: TAC Materials Inc (G-13382)*

Quality Tool Company.................... 419 476-8228
577 Mel Simon Dr Toledo (43612) *(G-13105)*

Quality Tooling Systems Inc.................... 330 722-5025
5352 Lance Rd Medina (44256) *(G-9439)*

Quality Welding Inc.................... 419 483-6067
104 Ronald Ln Bellevue (44811) *(G-1128)*

Quality Woodproducts LLC.................... 330 279-2217
8216 Township Road 568 Fredericksburg (44627) *(G-7069)*

Qualtech NP, Cincinnati *Also Called: Curtiss-Wright Flow Ctrl Corp (G-2300)*

Qualtech Technologies Inc.................... 440 946-8081
1685b Joseph Lloyd Pkwy Willoughby (44094) *(G-14514)*

Qualtek Electronics Corp.................... 440 951-3300
7610 Jenther Dr Mentor (44060) *(G-9603)*

Quanex Building Products, Akron *Also Called: Quanex Ig Systems Inc (G-273)*

Quanex Building Products, Cambridge *Also Called: Quanex Ig Systems Inc (G-1757)*

Quanex Custom Mixing, Cambridge *Also Called: Quanex Ig Systems Inc (G-1756)*

Quanex Ig Systems Inc (HQ).................... 216 910-1500
388 S Main St Ste 700 Akron (44311) *(G-273)*

Quanex Ig Systems Inc.................... 740 435-0444
804 Byesville Rd Cambridge (43725) *(G-1756)*

Quanex Ig Systems Inc.................... 740 439-2338
800 Cochran Ave Cambridge (43725) *(G-1757)*

Quanta International LLC.................... 513 354-3639
1 Landy Ln Cincinnati (45215) *(G-3018)*

Quantum.................... 740 328-2548
400 Case Ave Newark (43055) *(G-10531)*

Quantum Energy LLC (PA).................... 440 285-7381
10405 Locust Grove Dr Chardon (44024) *(G-2219)*

Quantum Solutions Group.................... 614 442-0664
1555 Bethel Rd Columbus (43220) *(G-5219)*

Quarrymasters Inc.................... 330 612-0474
1644 Berna Rd Akron (44312) *(G-274)*

Quarter Century Design LLC.................... 937 434-5127
2555 S Dixie Dr Ste 232 Dayton (45409) *(G-5970)*

Quartz, Mentor *Also Called: Aco Inc (G-9468)*

Quartz Scientific Inc (PA).................... 360 574-6254
819 East St Fairport Harbor (44077) *(G-6820)*

Quasonix, West Chester *Also Called: Quasonix Inc (G-14058)*

Quasonix Inc (PA).................... 513 942-1287
6025 Schumacher Park Dr West Chester (45069) *(G-14058)*

Quass Sheet Metal Inc.................... 330 477-4841
5018 Yukon St Nw Canton (44708) *(G-1986)*

Qube Corporation.................... 440 543-2393
16744 W Park Circle Dr Chagrin Falls (44023) *(G-2179)*

Quebecor World Johnson Hardin.................... 614 326-0299
3600 Red Bank Rd Cincinnati (45227) *(G-3019)*

Queen City Awning, Cincinnati *Also Called: Queen City Awning & Tent Co (G-3020)*

Queen City Awning & Tent Co.................... 513 530-9660
7225 E Kemper Rd Cincinnati (45249) *(G-3020)*

Queen City Carpets LLC.................... 513 823-8238
6539 Harrison Ave 304 Cincinnati (45247) *(G-3021)*

Queen City Forging Company.................... 513 321-2003
1019 Seabrook Way Cincinnati (45245) *(G-2315)*

Queen City Mascots and Logos, Cincinnati *Also Called: Queen City Spirit LLC (G-3026)*

Queen City Office Machine.................... 513 251-7200
3984 Trevor Ave Cincinnati (45211) *(G-3022)*

Queen City Pallets Inc.................... 513 821-6700
7744 Reinhold Dr Cincinnati (45237) *(G-3023)*

Queen City Polymers Inc (PA).................... 513 779-0990
6101 Schumacher Park Dr West Chester (45069) *(G-14059)*

Queen City Reprographics.................... 513 326-2300
2863 E Sharon Rd Cincinnati (45241) *(G-3024)*

Queen City Sausage, Cincinnati *Also Called: Queen City Sausage & Prov Inc (G-3025)*

Queen City Sausage & Prov Inc.................... 513 541-5581
1136 Straight St Cincinnati (45214) *(G-3025)*

Queen City Spirit LLC.................... 513 533-2662
8211 Blue Ash Rd Cincinnati (45236) *(G-3026)*

Queen City Steel Treating Co, Cincinnati *Also Called: Fbf Limited (G-2615)*

Queen City Tool Works Inc.................... 513 874-0111
125 Constitution Dr Ste 2 Fairfield (45014) *(G-6770)*

Queen Exhibits LLC.................... 937 615-6051
1707 Commerce Dr Piqua (45356) *(G-11381)*

Ques Industries Inc.................... 216 267-8989
5420 W 140th St Cleveland (44142) *(G-4218)*

Quest Diagnostics, Mason *Also Called: Quest Diagnostics Incorporated (G-9140)*

Quest Diagnostics Incorporated.................... 513 229-5500
4690 Parkway Dr Mason (45040) *(G-9140)*

Quest Lasercut, Franklin *Also Called: Quest Technologies Inc (G-7044)*

Quest Service Labs, Twinsburg *Also Called: A E Wilson Holdings Inc (G-13265)*

Quest Service Labs Inc.. 330 405-0316
2307 E Aurora Rd Unit B10 Twinsburg (44087) *(G-13362)*

Quest Software Inc... 614 336-9223
6500 Emerald Pkwy Ste 400 Dublin (43016) *(G-6337)*

Quest Solutions Group LLC.. 513 703-4520
8046 Green Lake Dr Liberty Township (45044) *(G-8378)*

Quest Technologies Inc.. 937 743-1200
600 Commerce Center Dr Franklin (45005) *(G-7044)*

Questline Inc... 614 255-3166
5500 Frantz Rd Ste 156 Dublin (43017) *(G-6338)*

Quez Media, Independence *Also Called: Quez Media Marketing Inc (G-7918)*

Quez Media Marketing Inc.. 216 910-0202
6100 Oak Tree Blvd Ste 200 Independence (44131) *(G-7918)*

Quick Loadz Container Sys LLC................................... 888 304-3946
5850 Industrial Park Rd Athens (45701) *(G-648)*

Quick Print, Cambridge *Also Called: Taylor Quick Print (G-1763)*

Quick Print, Canton *Also Called: USA Quickprint Inc (G-2040)*

Quick Service Welding & Mch Co.................................. 330 673-3818
117 E Summit St Kent (44240) *(G-8066)*

Quick Tab II Inc (PA)... 419 448-6622
241 Heritage Dr Tiffin (44883) *(G-12796)*

Quick Tech Business Forms Inc................................... 937 743-5952
408 Sharts Dr Springboro (45066) *(G-12265)*

Quick Tech Graphics Inc.. 937 743-5952
408 Sharts Dr Frnt Springboro (45066) *(G-12266)*

Quickdraft Inc... 330 477-4574
1525 Perry Dr Sw Canton (44710) *(G-1987)*

Quickloadz, Athens *Also Called: Quick Loadz Container Sys LLC (G-648)*

Quidel Corporation.. 858 552-1100
2005 E State St # 100 Athens (45701) *(G-649)*

Quidel Corporation.. 740 589-3300
1055 E State St Ste 100 Athens (45701) *(G-650)*

Quidel Dhi... 740 589-3300
2005 E State St Athens (45701) *(G-651)*

Quikey Manufacturing Co Inc (PA).............................. 330 633-8106
1500 Industrial Pkwy Akron (44310) *(G-275)*

Quikrete Cincinnati, Harrison *Also Called: Quikrete Companies LLC (G-7564)*

Quikrete Companies LLC.. 614 885-4406
6225 Huntley Rd Columbus (43229) *(G-5220)*

Quikrete Companies LLC.. 513 367-6135
5425 Kilby Rd Harrison (45030) *(G-7564)*

Quikrete Companies LLC.. 330 296-6080
2693 Lake Rockwell Rd Ravenna (44266) *(G-11536)*

Quikrete Companies LLC.. 419 241-1148
070 Western Ave Toledo (43009) *(G-13100)*

Quikrete of Cleveland, Ravenna *Also Called: Quikrete Companies LLC (G-11536)*

Quikspray, Port Clinton *Also Called: Quikstir Inc (G-11449)*

Quikstir Inc... 419 732-2601
2105 W Lakeshore Dr Port Clinton (43452) *(G-11449)*

Quilting Inc (PA)... 614 504-5971
7600 Industrial Pkwy Plain City (43064) *(G-11417)*

Quinami LLC... 419 797-4445
3845 E Wine Cellar Rd Port Clinton (43452) *(G-11450)*

Quintus Technologies LLC... 614 891-2732
8270 Green Meadows Dr N Lewis Center (43035) *(G-8349)*

Qxsoft LLC... 740 777-9609
759 Carle Ave Lewis Center (43035) *(G-8350)*

R & A Sports Inc.. 216 289-2254
23780 Lakeland Blvd Euclid (44132) *(G-6674)*

R & C Monument Company LLC.................................. 216 297-5444
5146 Warrensville Center Rd Maple Heights (44137) *(G-8890)*

R & D Custom Machine & TI Inc.................................. 419 727-1700
5961 American Rd E Toledo (43612) *(G-13107)*

R & D Equipment Inc... 419 668-8439
206 Republic St Norwalk (44857) *(G-10860)*

R & D Hilltop Lumber Inc... 740 342-3051
2126 State Route 93 Se New Lexington (43764) *(G-10406)*

R & D Logging LLC.. 740 259-6127
2218 Cramer Rd Lucasville (45648) *(G-8669)*

R & D Machine Inc... 937 339-2545
1204 S Crawford St Troy (45373) *(G-13248)*

R & D Nestle Center Inc.. 440 349-5757
5750 Harper Rd Solon (44139) *(G-12171)*

R & F Franchise Group LLC.. 440 942-7140
37333 Euclid Ave Willoughby (44094) *(G-14515)*

R & H Enterprises Llc.. 216 702-4449
4933 Karen Isle Dr Richmond Heights (44143) *(G-11612)*

R & J AG Manufacturing Inc.. 419 962-4707
821 State Route 511 Ashland (44805) *(G-568)*

R & J Bardon Inc.. 614 457-5500
4676 Larwell Dr Columbus (43220) *(G-5221)*

R & J Cylinder & Machine Inc...................................... 330 364-8263
464 Robinson Dr Se New Philadelphia (44663) *(G-10463)*

R & J Tool Inc... 937 833-3200
10550 Upper Lewisburg Salem Rd Brookville (45309) *(G-1575)*

R & L Software LLC (PA).. 513 847-4942
421 Breaden Dr Ste 3 Monroe (45050) *(G-10115)*

R & L Truss Inc.. 419 587-3440
17985 Road 60 Grover Hill (45849) *(G-7459)*

R & M Fluid Power Inc... 330 758-2766
7953 Southern Blvd Youngstown (44512) *(G-14922)*

R & R Engine & Machine, Coventry Township *Also Called: Chemequip Sales Inc (G-5481)*

R & R Fabrications Inc... 419 678-4831
601 E Washington St Saint Henry (45883) *(G-11723)*

R & R Tool Inc.. 937 783-8665
1449a Middleboro Rd Blanchester (45107) *(G-1237)*

R & S Data Products, Hillsboro *Also Called: Highland Computer Forms Inc (G-7718)*

R & S Label, Oberlin *Also Called: R R Donnelley & Sons Company (G-10920)*

R & S Monitions Inc... 614 846-0597
181 Rosslyn Ave Columbus (43214) *(G-5222)*

R & T Estate LLC.. 216 862-0822
17001 Euclid Ave Cleveland (44112) *(G-4219)*

R A Hamed International Inc... 330 247-0190
8400 Darrow Rd Twinsburg (44087) *(G-13363)*

R A Heller Company.. 513 771-6100
10530 Chester Rd Cincinnati (45215) *(G-3027)*

R A M Plastics Co Inc.. 330 549-3107
11401 South Ave North Lima (44452) *(G-10713)*

R A M Precision Tool, Dayton *Also Called: Ram Precision Industries Inc (G-5972)*

R and J Corporation... 440 871-6009
24142 Detroit Rd Westlake (44145) *(G-14326)*

R and S Technologies Inc... 419 483-3691
2474 State Route 4 Bellevue (44811) *(G-1129)*

R Anthony Enterprises LLC... 419 341-0961
2626 Whetstone River Rd S Marion (43302) *(G-8991)*

R C M, Akron *Also Called: Rubber City Machinery Corp (G-293)*

R C Moore Lumber Co... 740 732-4950
820 Miller St Caldwell (43724) *(G-1727)*

R C Musson Rubber Co.. 330 773-7651
1320 E Archwood Ave Akron (44306) *(G-276)*

R D Baker Enterprises Inc... 937 461-5225
765 Liberty Ln Dayton (45449) *(G-5971)*

R D Holder Oil Co Inc.. 740 522-3136
1000 Keller Dr Heath (43056) *(G-7602)*

R E H Inc.. 330 876-2775
St Rt 5 Kinsman (44428) *(G-8142)*

R E May Inc.. 216 771-6332
1401 E 24th St Cleveland (44114) *(G-4220)*

R E Smith Inc... 513 771-0645
10330 Chester Rd Cincinnati (45215) *(G-3028)*

R F Cook Manufacturing Co, Stow *Also Called: Levan Enterprises Inc (G-12438)*

R F I.. 740 654-4502
276 Bremen Rd Lancaster (43130) *(G-8221)*

R F W, Cleveland *Also Called: RFW Holdings Inc (G-4239)*

R G Barry Corporation... 212 244-3145
13405 Yarmouth Dr Pickerington (43147) *(G-11298)*

R G Smith Company (PA).. 330 456-3415
1249 Dueber Ave Sw Canton (44706) *(G-1988)*

R H Industries Inc.. 216 281-5210
3155 W 33rd St Cleveland (44109) *(G-4221)*

ALPHABETIC

R H Little Co.. 330 477-3455
   4434 Southway St Sw Canton (44706) *(G-1989)*

R J Displays, Toledo *Also Called: Hill John (G-12993)*

R J K Enterprises Inc....................................... 440 257-6018
   5565 Wilson Dr Mentor (44060) *(G-9604)*

R J Manray Inc... 330 559-6716
   7320 Akron Canfield Rd Ste B Canfield (44406) *(G-1814)*

R K Industries Inc.. 419 523-5001
   725 N Locust St Ottawa (45875) *(G-11044)*

R K Metals Ltd.. 513 874-6055
   3235 Homeward Way Fairfield (45014) *(G-6771)*

R L Industries Inc.. 513 874-2800
   9355 Le Saint Dr West Chester (45014) *(G-14060)*

R L Rush Tool & Pattern Inc............................. 419 562-9849
   1620 Whetstone St Bucyrus (44820) *(G-1687)*

R L S Corporation... 740 773-1440
   990 Eastern Ave Chillicothe (45601) *(G-2277)*

R L S Recycling, Chillicothe *Also Called: R L S Corporation (G-2277)*

R L Torbeck Industries Inc............................... 513 367-0080
   355 Industrial Dr Harrison (45030) *(G-7565)*

R L Waller Construction Inc.............................. 740 772-6185
   645 Alum Cliff Rd Chillicothe (45601) *(G-2278)*

R M Tool & Die Inc... 440 238-6459
   19768 Progress Dr Strongsville (44149) *(G-12591)*

R R Donnelley, Hebron *Also Called: R R Donnelley & Sons Company (G-7632)*

R R Donnelley, Streetsboro *Also Called: R R Donnelley & Sons Company (G-12518)*

R R Donnelley & Sons Company....................... 740 928-6110
   190 Milliken Dr Hebron (43025) *(G-7632)*

R R Donnelley & Sons Company....................... 440 774-2101
   450 Sterns Rd Oberlin (44074) *(G-10920)*

R R Donnelley & Sons Company....................... 330 562-5250
   10400 Danner Dr Streetsboro (44241) *(G-12518)*

R R Donnelley & Sons Company....................... 513 552-1512
   8720 Global Way West Chester (45069) *(G-14061)*

R R Donnelley & Sons Company....................... 513 870-4040
   8740 Global Way West Chester (45069) *(G-14062)*

R R R Development Co (PA)............................... 330 966-8855
   8817 Pleasantwood Ave Nw North Canton (44720) *(G-10661)*

R S C, Columbus *Also Called: Safecor Health LLC (G-5242)*

R S Hanline and Co Inc (PA)............................. 419 347-8077
   17 Republic Ave Shelby (44875) *(G-11974)*

R T & T Machining, Mentor *Also Called: R T & T Machining Co Inc (G-9605)*

R T & T Machining Co Inc................................. 440 974-8479
   8195 Tyler Blvd Mentor (44060) *(G-9605)*

R Vandewalle Inc... 513 921-2657
   4030 Delhi Ave Cincinnati (45204) *(G-3029)*

R W Long Lumber & Box Co Inc......................... 513 932-5124
   1840 Cornett Rd Ste 1 Lebanon (45036) *(G-8282)*

R W Machine & Tool Inc.................................. 330 296-5211
   7944 State Route 44 Ravenna (44266) *(G-11537)*

R W Screw Products Inc.................................. 330 837-9211
   999 Oberlin Ave Sw Massillon (44647) *(G-9236)*

R W Sidley Inc.. 440 224-2664
   105 Maple Shade Dr Marietta (45750) *(G-8939)*

R W Sidley Incorporated................................. 330 499-5616
   7545 Pittsburg Ave Nw Canton (44720) *(G-1990)*

R W Sidley Incorporated................................. 440 564-2221
   10688 Kinsman Rd Newbury (44065) *(G-10561)*

R W Sidley Incorporated................................. 440 352-9343
   436 Casement Ave Painesville (44077) *(G-11108)*

R W Sidley Incorporated (PA)............................ 440 352-9343
   436 Casement Ave Painesville (44077) *(G-11109)*

R W Sidley Incorporated................................. 440 298-3232
   7123 Madison Rd Thompson (44086) *(G-12762)*

R W Sidley Incorporated................................. 440 298-3232
   6900 Madison Rd Thompson (44086) *(G-12763)*

R W Sidley Incorporated................................. 330 392-2721
   425 N River Rd Nw Warren (44483) *(G-13792)*

R W Sidley Incorporated................................. 330 793-7374
   3424 Oregon Ave Youngstown (44509) *(G-14923)*

R-K Electronics Inc.. 513 204-6060
   7405 Industrial Row Dr Mason (45040) *(G-9141)*

R. W. Sidley, Painesville *Also Called: R W Sidley Incorporated (G-11109)*

R.W., Willoughby *Also Called: Spence Technologies Inc (G-14531)*

R&D Marketing Group Inc................................. 216 398-9100
   4597 Van Epps Rd Brooklyn Heights (44131) *(G-1537)*

Ra Consultants LLC....................................... 513 469-6600
   10856 Kenwood Rd Blue Ash (45242) *(G-1326)*

Raber Lumber Co... 330 893-2797
   4112 State Rte 557 Charm (44617) *(G-2227)*

Rable Machine Inc... 740 689-9009
   1858 Cedar Hill Rd Lancaster (43130) *(G-8222)*

Rable Machine Inc... 419 525-2255
   30 Paragon Pkwy Mansfield (44903) *(G-8847)*

Race Winning Brands Inc (PA)........................... 440 951-6600
   7201 Industrial Park Blvd Mentor (44060) *(G-9606)*

Racelite Southcoast Inc.................................. 216 581-4600
   16518 Broadway Ave Maple Heights (44137) *(G-8891)*

Raceway, Lorain *Also Called: Raceway Petroleum Inc (G-8575)*

Raceway Petroleum Inc................................... 440 989-2660
   3040 Oberlin Ave Lorain (44052) *(G-8575)*

Rack Processing Company Inc (PA)..................... 937 294-1911
   2350 Arbor Blvd Moraine (45439) *(G-10189)*

Rack Processing Company Inc.......................... 937 294-1911
   2350 Arbor Blvd Moraine (45439) *(G-10190)*

RAD Technologies Incorporated........................ 513 641-0523
   3428 Hauck Rd Ste G Cincinnati (45241) *(G-3030)*

Radar Love Co.. 419 951-4750
   5500 Fostoria Ave Findlay (45840) *(G-6912)*

Radcliffe Steel, Berea *Also Called: Rads LLC (G-1187)*

Radco Fire Protection Inc................................ 419 476-0102
   444 W Laskey Rd Ste S Toledo (43612) *(G-13108)*

Radco Industries Inc...................................... 419 531-4731
   3226 Frenchmens Rd Toledo (43607) *(G-13109)*

Radici Plastics Usa Inc (DH)............................ 330 336-7611
   960 Seville Rd Wadsworth (44281) *(G-13665)*

Radioshack, Cuyahoga Falls *Also Called: 4r Enterprises Incorporated (G-5519)*

Radix Wire, Solon *Also Called: Radix Wire & Cable LLC (G-12172)*

Radix Wire & Cable LLC.................................. 216 731-9191
   30333 Emerald Valley Pkwy Solon (44139) *(G-12172)*

Radix Wire Co.. 330 995-3677
   350 Harris Dr Aurora (44202) *(G-686)*

Radix Wire Co (PA).. 216 731-9191
   30333 Emerald Valley Pkwy Solon (44139) *(G-12173)*

Radix Wire Co.. 216 731-9191
   30333 Emerald Valley Pkwy Solon (44139) *(G-12174)*

Radix Wire Company, The, Solon *Also Called: Radix Wire Co (G-12173)*

Radocy Inc.. 419 666-4400
   30652 East River Rd Rossford (43551) *(G-11661)*

Radon Eliminator LLC..................................... 330 844-0703
   5046 Stoney Creek Ln North Canton (44720) *(G-10662)*

Rads LLC.. 330 671-0464
   135 Blaze Industrial Pkwy Berea (44017) *(G-1187)*

Raf Acquisition Co.. 440 572-5999
   5478 Grafton Rd Valley City (44280) *(G-13514)*

Rafter Equipment Company LLC........................ 440 572-3700
   12430 Alameda Dr Strongsville (44149) *(G-12592)*

Rage Corporation (PA).................................... 614 771-4771
   3949 Lyman Dr Hilliard (43026) *(G-7698)*

Rage Plastics, Hilliard *Also Called: Rage Corporation (G-7698)*

Ragon House Collection, Bolivar *Also Called: Rhc Inc (G-1391)*

Rah Investment Holding Inc............................. 330 832-8124
   1320 Sanders Ave Sw Massillon (44647) *(G-9237)*

Rail Bearing Service Inc, North Canton *Also Called: Rail Bearing Service LLC (G-10663)*

Rail Bearing Service LLC................................. 234 262-3000
   4500 Mount Pleasant St Nw North Canton (44720) *(G-10663)*

Railroad Tools & Solutions Inc......................... 513 533-7070
   4729 Red Bank Rd Cincinnati (45227) *(G-3031)*

Rain Drop Products Llc................................... 419 207-1229
   2121 Cottage St Ashland (44805) *(G-569)*

Rainbow Industries Inc................................... 937 323-6493
   5975 E National Rd Springfield (45505) *(G-12366)*

Rainbow Master Mixing Inc.................................. 330 374-1810
   467 Dan St Akron (44310) *(G-277)*

Rainbow Printing, Uniontown *Also Called: Plastic Card Inc (G-13424)*

Rainbow Printing, Uniontown *Also Called: Plasticards Inc (G-13425)*

Rainbow Tarp, Springfield *Also Called: Rainbow Industries Inc (G-12366)*

Rainin Instrument LLC....................................... 510 564-1600
   1900 Polaris Pkwy Columbus (43240) *(G-4647)*

Raka Corporation.. 419 476-6572
   203 Matzinger Rd Toledo (43612) *(G-13110)*

Ralph Robinson Inc... 740 385-2747
   700 Ohio Ave Logan (43138) *(G-8524)*

Ralphie Gianni Mfg & Co Ltd.............................. 216 507-3873
   250 E 271st St Euclid (44132) *(G-6675)*

Ralston Food, Lancaster *Also Called: Treehouse Private Brands Inc (G-8231)*

Ralston Instruments LLC................................... 440 564-1430
   15035 Cross Creek Pkwy Newbury (44065) *(G-10562)*

Ram Innovative Tech LLC................................... 330 956-4056
   3969 Jeffries Cir Louisville (44641) *(G-8614)*

Ram Machining Inc... 740 333-5522
   806 Delaware St Wshngtn Ct Hs (43160) *(G-14743)*

Ram Precision Industries Inc........................... 937 885-7700
   11125 Yankee St Ste A Dayton (45458) *(G-5972)*

Ram Products Inc.. 614 443-4634
   19250 Unger Rd Logan (43138) *(G-8525)*

Ram Sensors Inc... 440 835-3540
   875 Canterbury Rd Cleveland (44145) *(G-4222)*

Ram Tool Inc... 937 277-0717
   1944 Neva Dr Dayton (45414) *(G-5973)*

Rambasek Realty Inc.. 937 228-1189
   827 S Patterson Blvd Dayton (45402) *(G-5974)*

Ramco Electric Motors Inc............................... 937 548-2525
   5763 Jaysville Saint Johns Rd Greenville (45331) *(G-7350)*

Ramco Specialties Inc (PA)................................ 330 653-5135
   5445 Hudson Industrial Pkwy Hudson (44236) *(G-7855)*

Rampe Manufacturing Company......................... 440 352-8995
   .1246 High St Fairport Harbor (44077) *(G-6821)*

Rampp Company (PA).. 740 373-7886
   20445 State Route 550 Ofc Marietta (45750) *(G-8940)*

Ramsey Stairs & Wdwkg LLC............................ 614 694-2101
   4134 Little Pine Dr Columbus (43230) *(G-5223)*

Rance Industries Inc.. 330 482-1745
   1361 Heck Rd Columbiana (44408) *(G-4626)*

Randall, Lima *Also Called: Randall Bearings Inc (G-8442)*

Randall Richard & Moore Inc........................... 330 455-8873
   3710 Progress St Ne Canton (44705) *(G-1991)*

Randall Bearings Inc.. 419 678-2486
   821 Weis St Coldwater (45828) *(G-4583)*

Randall Bearings Inc (DH)................................ 419 223-1075
   240 Jay Begg Pkwy Lima (45804) *(G-8442)*

Randd Assoc Prtg & Promotions........................ 937 294-1874
   330 Progress Rd Dayton (45449) *(G-5975)*

Randolph Tool Company Inc............................. 330 877-4923
   750 Wales Dr Hartville (44632) *(G-7582)*

Randy Gray.. 513 533-3200
   4142 Airport Rd Unit 1 Cincinnati (45226) *(G-3032)*

Randys Pickles LLC.. 440 864-6611
   2203 Superior Ave E Cleveland (44114) *(G-4223)*

Randys Tire & Auto Repair Inc.......................... 419 562-2926
   1000 N Sandusky Ave Bucyrus (44820) *(G-1688)*

Range Impact Inc (PA)...................................... 216 304-6556
   200 Park Ave Ste 400 Cleveland (44122) *(G-4224)*

Range Kleen Mfg Inc.. 419 331-8000
   4240 East Rd Elida (45807) *(G-6487)*

Rankin Mfg Inc... 419 929-8338
   201 N Main St New London (44851) *(G-10414)*

Ranpak Holdings Corp (PA)............................... 440 354-4445
   7990 Auburn Rd Concord Township (44077) *(G-5394)*

Ransom & Randolph LLC (PA)........................... 419 865-9497
   520 Illinois Ave Maumee (43537) *(G-9314)*

Rantek Products LLC.. 419 485-2421
   1826 Magda Dr Ste A Montpelier (43543) *(G-10133)*

Rapid Machine Inc.. 419 737-2377
   610 N State St Pioneer (43554) *(G-11327)*

Rapid Mr International LLC............................... 614 486-6300
   1500 Lake Shore Dr Ste 310 Columbus (43204) *(G-5224)*

Rapid Quality Manufacturing, West Chester *Also Called: GE Aviation Systems LLC (G-14005)*

Rapiscan Systems High Enrgy In....................... 937 879-4200
   514 E Dayton Yellow Springs Rd Fairborn (45324) *(G-6698)*

Ratliff Metal Spinning Company........................ 937 836-3900
   40 Harrisburg Dr Englewood (45322) *(G-6622)*

Rauh Polymers Inc... 330 376-1120
   420 Kenmore Blvd Akron (44301) *(G-278)*

Ravago Americas LLC.. 330 825-2505
   5192 Lake Rd Medina (44256) *(G-9440)*

Ravago Chemical Dist Inc.................................. 330 920-8023
   1665 Enterprise Pkwy Twinsburg (44087) *(G-13364)*

Ravana Industries Inc.. 330 536-4015
   6170 Center Rd Lowellville (44436) *(G-8664)*

Raven Concealment Systems LLC...................... 440 508-9000
   7889 Root Rd North Ridgeville (44039) *(G-10745)*

Ravens Sales & Service, Dover *Also Called: Kruz Inc (G-6251)*

Ravenworks Deer Skin.. 937 354-5151
   34477 Shertzer Rd Mount Victory (43340) *(G-10270)*

Ray C Sprosty Bag Co Inc.................................. 330 669-0045
   5857 Applecreek Rd Smithville (44677) *(G-12067)*

Ray Communications Inc.................................. 330 686-0226
   1337 Commerce Dr Ste 11 Stow (44224) *(G-12453)*

Ray Fogg Construction Inc................................ 216 351-7976
   981 Keynote Cir Ste 15 Cleveland (44131) *(G-4225)*

Ray Meyer Sign Company Inc............................ 513 984-5446
   8942 Glendale Milford Rd Loveland (45140) *(G-8647)*

Ray-Tech Industries LLC.................................... 419 923-0169
   15210 County Road 10 3 Lyons (43533) *(G-8675)*

Raydar Inc of Ohio.. 330 334-6111
   1734 Wall Rd Ste B Wadsworth (44281) *(G-13666)*

Rayhaven Group, Richfield *Also Called: Rayhaven Group Inc (G-11598)*

Rayhaven Group Inc... 330 659-3183
   3842 Congress Pkwy Ste A Richfield (44286) *(G-11598)*

Rayle Coal Co.. 740 695-2197
   67705 Friends Church Rd Saint Clairsville (43950) *(G-11708)*

Raymar Holdings Corporation............................ 614 497-3033
   3700 Lockbourne Rd Columbus (43207) *(G-5225)*

Raymath, Troy *Also Called: Raymath Company (G-13249)*

Raymath Company.. 937 335-1860
   2323 W State Route 55 Troy (45373) *(G-13249)*

Rays Sausage Inc... 216 921-8782
   3146 E 123rd St Cleveland (44120) *(G-4226)*

Raytec Systems, Stow *Also Called: Ray Communications Inc (G-12453)*

Raytheon, Beavercreek *Also Called: Raytheon Company (G-980)*

Raytheon, Dayton *Also Called: L3 Technologies Inc (G-5616)*

Raytheon Company... 937 429-5429
   2970 Presidential Dr Ste 300 Beavercreek (45324) *(G-980)*

RB Sigma LLC.. 440 290-0577
   6111 Heisley Rd Mentor (44060) *(G-9607)*

RB Tool & Mfg. Co., Cincinnati *Also Called: Kaws Inc (G-2786)*

RB&w Manufacturing LLC (HQ)......................... 234 380-8540
   10080 Wellman Rd Streetsboro (44241) *(G-12519)*

Rba Inc.. 330 336-6700
   487 College St Wadsworth (44281) *(G-13667)*

Rbb Systems Inc.. 330 263-4502
   1909 Old Mansfield Rd Ste A Wooster (44691) *(G-14674)*

Rbm Environmental & Cnstr Inc........................ 419 693-5840
   4526 Bayshore Rd Oregon (43616) *(G-10967)*

Rbr Enterprises LLC.. 866 437-9327
   6910 Miller Rd Brecksville (44141) *(G-1480)*

Rbs Manufacturing Inc..................................... 330 426-9486
   145 E Martin St East Palestine (44413) *(G-6405)*

RC Industries Inc... 330 879-5486
   620 Main St N Navarre (44662) *(G-10313)*

RCE Heat Exchangers LLC................................ 330 627-0300
   3165 Folsam Rd Nw Carrollton (44615) *(G-2088)*

Rcf Kitchens Indiana LLC................................. 765 478-6600
   87 Shelford Way Dayton (45440) *(G-5976)*

A
L
P
H
A
B
E
T
I
C

Rci, Sidney *Also Called: Ross Casting & Innovation LLC (G-12047)*

Rcl Benziger, Cincinnati *Also Called: Kendall/Hunt Publishing Co (G-2792)*

Rcl Publishing Group LLC... 972 390-6400
8805 Governors Hill Dr Ste 400 Cincinnati (45249) *(G-3033)*

RCM Engineering Company... 330 666-0575
2089 N Cleveland Massillon Rd Akron (44333) *(G-279)*

Rcr Partnership... 419 340-1202
424 N Martin Williston Rd Genoa (43430) *(G-7249)*

Rct Industries Inc.. 937 602-1100
1314 Farr Dr Dayton (45404) *(G-5977)*

RDM Equipment Company Inc...................................... 330 264-8808
1141 Mechanicsburg Rd Wooster (44691) *(G-14675)*

RE Connors Construction Ltd...................................... 740 644-0261
13352 Forrest Rd Ne Thornville (43076) *(G-12767)*

REA Elektronik Inc... 440 232-0555
7307 Young Dr Ste B Walton Hills (44146) *(G-13702)*

REA Polishing Inc.. 419 470-0216
1606 W Laskey Rd Toledo (43612) *(G-13111)*

Reactive Resin Products Co.. 419 666-6119
327 5th St Perrysburg (43551) *(G-11259)*

Reading Rock Incorporated (PA)................................ 513 874-2345
4600 Devitt Dr Cincinnati (45246) *(G-3034)*

Ready 2 Ride Trnsp LLC.. 614 207-2683
12435 Thoroughbred Dr Pickerington (43147) *(G-11299)*

Ready Field Solutions LLC... 330 562-0550
1240 Ethan Ave Streetsboro (44241) *(G-12520)*

Ready For Flight, Westerville *Also Called: Garage Scenes Ltd (G-14211)*

Ready Media LLC... 614 441-8178
1491 Polaris Pkwy Ste 81 Columbus (43240) *(G-4648)*

Ready Rigs LLC... 740 963-9203
2321 Taylor Park Dr Reynoldsburg (43068) *(G-11579)*

Ready Technology Inc (HQ).. 937 866-7200
333 Progress Rd Dayton (45449) *(G-5978)*

Real Alloy Recycling LLC (DH).................................. 216 755-8900
3700 Park East Dr Ste 300 Beachwood (44122) *(G-942)*

Real Alloy Specialty Pdts LLC (DH)............................ 844 732-5087
3700 Park East Dr Ste 300 Beachwood (44122) *(G-943)*

Real Alloy Specialty Pdts LLC.................................... 440 322-0072
320 Huron St Elyria (44035) *(G-6584)*

Realeflow LLC.. 855 545-2095
150 Pearl Rd Brunswick (44212) *(G-1611)*

Really Cool Foods, Dayton *Also Called: Rcf Kitchens Indiana LLC (G-5976)*

Ream and Haager Laboratory Inc................................ 330 343-3711
179 W Broadway St Dover (44622) *(G-6259)*

Rebecca Benston.. 937 360-0669
2130 W Possum Rd Springfield (45506) *(G-12367)*

Reberland Equipment Inc.. 330 698-5883
5963 Fountain Nook Rd Apple Creek (44606) *(G-476)*

Rebiltco Inc... 513 424-2024
8775 Thomas Rd Middletown (45042) *(G-9890)*

Rebiz LLC... 844 467-3249
1925 Saint Clair Ave Ne Cleveland (44114) *(G-4227)*

Rebsco Inc.. 937 548-2246
4362 Us Route 36 Greenville (45331) *(G-7351)*

Reclamation Technologies Inc.................................... 800 372-1301
1100 Haskins Rd Bowling Green (43402) *(G-1438)*

Recognition Robotics Inc (PA).................................. 440 590-0499
141 Innovation Dr Pmb 306 Elyria (44035) *(G-6585)*

Recon... 740 609-3050
54382 National Rd Bridgeport (43912) *(G-1495)*

Recon Systems LLC.. 330 488-0368
330 Wood St S East Canton (44730) *(G-6379)*

Record Herald, Cincinnati *Also Called: Record Herald Publishing Co (G-3035)*

Record Herald Publishing Co (DH).............................. 717 762-2151
5050 Kingsley Dr Cincinnati (45227) *(G-3035)*

Record Publishing Co... 330 688-0088
1619 Commerce Dr Stow (44224) *(G-12454)*

Recto Molded Products Inc.. 513 871-5544
4425 Appleton St Cincinnati (45209) *(G-3036)*

Rector Inc... 440 892-0444
1991 Crocker Rd Ste 320 Westlake (44145) *(G-14327)*

Recycled Systems Furniture Inc.................................. 614 880-9110
401 E Wilson Bridge Rd Worthington (43085) *(G-14724)*

Recycling Eqp Solutions Corp.................................... 330 920-1500
276 Remington Rd Ste C Cuyahoga Falls (44224) *(G-5568)*

Red Barakuda LLC... 614 596-5432
4439 Shoupmill Dr Columbus (43230) *(G-5226)*

Red Diamond Plant, Mc Arthur *Also Called: Austin Powder Company (G-9348)*

Red Head Brass, Shreve *Also Called: Rhba Acquisitions LLC (G-11986)*

Red Head Brass Inc.. 330 567-2903
643 Legion Dr Shreve (44676) *(G-11985)*

Red Seal Electric Company.. 216 941-3900
3835 W 150th St Cleveland (44111) *(G-4228)*

Red Tie Group Inc (PA)   4521 Industrial Pkwy Cleveland (44135) *(G-4229)*

Redex Industries Inc (PA).. 330 332-9800
1176 Salem Pkwy Salem (44460) *(G-11809)*

Redhawk Energy Systems LLC................................... 740 927-8244
10340 Palmer Rd Sw Pataskala (43062) *(G-11146)*

Redland Quarries NY Inc... 216 566-0545
560 Harrison Street Cleveland (44113) *(G-4230)*

Reds Auto Glass Shop, Warren *Also Called: J W Goss Company (G-13773)*

Reduction Engineering Inc... 330 677-2225
235 Progress Blvd Kent (44240) *(G-8067)*

Reebar Die Casting Inc.. 419 878-7591
1177 Farnsworth Rd Waterville (43566) *(G-13840)*

Reed Gowdey Company.. 401 723-6114
101 Glenshire Dr Granville (43023) *(G-7320)*

Reed Minerals LLC.. 216 652-2002
412 Mckees Ln Niles (44446) *(G-10601)*

Reese Machine Company Inc...................................... 440 992-3942
2501 State Rd Ashtabula (44004) *(G-614)*

Reflexis Systems Inc.. 614 948-1931
579 Executive Campus Dr Ste 310 Westerville (43082) *(G-14229)*

Refocus Holdings Inc... 216 751-8384
2310 Superior Ave E Ste 210 Cleveland (44114) *(G-4231)*

Refractory Coating Tech Inc...................................... 800 807-7464
2421 E 28th St Lorain (44055) *(G-8576)*

Refractory Specialties Inc.. 330 938-2101
230 W California Ave Sebring (44672) *(G-11900)*

Refresco North America, Carlisle *Also Called: Refresco Us Inc (G-2072)*

Refresco Us Inc.. 937 790-1400
300 Industry Dr Carlisle (45005) *(G-2072)*

Refurb-World LLC.. 440 471-9030
33888 Center Ridge Rd North Ridgeville (44039) *(G-10746)*

Regal, Tipp City *Also Called: Regal Beloit America Inc (G-12840)*

Regal Beloit America Inc.. 419 352-8441
427 Van Camp Rd Bowling Green (43402) *(G-1439)*

Regal Beloit America Inc.. 608 364-8800
200 E Chapman Rd Lima (45801) *(G-8443)*

Regal Beloit America Inc.. 937 667-2431
531 N 4th St Tipp City (45371) *(G-12840)*

Regal Diamond Products Corp.................................... 440 944-7700
1405 E 286th St Wickliffe (44092) *(G-14393)*

Regal Metal Products Co (PA).................................... 330 868-6343
3615 Union Ave Se Minerva (44657) *(G-10046)*

Regency Office Furniture, Akron *Also Called: Regency Seating Inc (G-280)*

Regency Seating Inc... 330 848-3700
2375 Romig Rd Akron (44320) *(G-280)*

Regional Sheetmetal Mfg L.. 937 425-6972
4401 Springfield St Dayton (45431) *(G-5622)*

Rego Manufacturing Co Inc.. 419 562-0466
1870 E Mansfield St Bucyrus (44820) *(G-1689)*

Regol-G Industries, Cleveland *Also Called: DCW Acquisition Inc (G-3607)*

Reid Asset Management Company................................ 440 942-8488
4500 Beidler Rd Willoughby (44094) *(G-14516)*

Reifel Industries Inc... 419 737-2138
201 Ohio St Pioneer (43554) *(G-11328)*

Reighart Steel Products, Willoughby *Also Called: Sticker Corporation (G-14534)*

Reinalt-Thomas Corporation...................................... 330 863-1936
5125 Canton Rd Nw Carrollton (44615) *(G-2089)*

Reinforcement Systems of Ohio LLC........................... 330 469-6958
3121 W Market St Warren (44485) *(G-13793)*

Reisbeck Fd Mkts St Clirsville, Saint Clairsville *Also Called: Riesbeck Food Markets Inc (G-11709)*

Reiter Dairy, Springfield *Also Called: Reiter Dairy of Akron Inc (G-12369)*

Reiter Dairy LLC Dean Foods.. 937 323-5777
1941 Commerce Cir Springfield (45504) *(G-12368)*

Reiter Dairy of Akron Inc... 937 323-5777
1961 Commerce Cir Springfield (45504) *(G-12369)*

Rek Associates LLC.. 419 294-3838
11218 County Highway 44 Upper Sandusky (43351) *(G-13454)*

Rel Enterprises Inc (DH).. 216 741-1700
4760 Van Epps Rd Brooklyn Heights (44131) *(G-1538)*

Reladyne Reliability Svcs Inc (HQ)....................................... 888 478-6996
3713 Progress St Ne Canton (44705) *(G-1992)*

Relay Rail Div., Mineral Ridge *Also Called: L B Foster Company (G-10030)*

Reliable Castings Corporation (PA)....................................... 513 541-2627
3530 Spring Grove Ave Cincinnati (45223) *(G-3037)*

Reliable Castings Corporation.. 937 497-5217
1521 W Michigan St Sidney (45365) *(G-12043)*

Reliable Hermetic Seals LLC.. 888 747-3250
4156 Dayton Xenia Rd Beavercreek (45432) *(G-981)*

Reliable Manufacturing LLC.. 740 756-9373
5594 Winchester Rd Carroll (43112) *(G-2077)*

Reliable Metal Buildings LLC... 419 737-1300
16570 Us Highway 20ns Pioneer (43554) *(G-11329)*

Reliable Mfg Co LLC.. 740 756-9373
4411 Carroll Southern Rd Carroll (43112) *(G-2078)*

Reliable Pattern Works Inc.. 440 232-8820
590 Golden Oak Pkwy Cleveland (44146) *(G-4232)*

Reliable Products Co.. 419 394-5854
315 S Park Dr Saint Marys (45885) *(G-11751)*

Reliable Ready Mix Co.. 330 453-8266
1606 Allen Ave Se Canton (44706) *(G-1993)*

Reliable Wheelchair Trans.. 216 390-3999
28899 Harvard Rd Beachwood (44122) *(G-944)*

Reliacheck Manufacturing Inc.. 440 933-6162
6550 Eastland Rd Brookpark (44142) *(G-1557)*

Reliance Medical Products, Mason *Also Called: Haag-Streit Usa Inc (G-9107)*

Reliant Worth Corp.. 440 232-1422
20638 Krick Rd Bedford (44146) *(G-1055)*

Relx Inc.. 937 865-6800
4700 Lyons Rd Miamisburg (45342) *(G-9730)*

Relx Inc.. 937 865-6800
9333 Springboro Pike Miamisburg (45342) *(G-9731)*

Rely-On Manufacturing Inc... 937 254-0118
955 Springfield St Dayton (45403) *(G-5979)*

Remel Products, Oakwood Village *Also Called: Thermo Fisher Scientific Inc (G-10910)*

Remington Engrg Machining Inc... 513 965-8999
5105 River Valley Rd Milford (45150) *(G-9950)*

Remington Products Company (PA).. 330 335-1571
3366 Riverside Dr Ste 103 Upper Arlington (43221) *(G-13432)*

Remington Steel, Springfield *Also Called: Westfield Steel Inc (G-12392)*

Remington Steel Inc... 937 322-2414
1120 S Burnett Rd Springfield (45505) *(G-12370)*

Remlinger Manufacturing Co Inc.. 419 532-3647
16394 Us 224 Kalida (45853) *(G-8005)*

Remodeling, Cincinnati *Also Called: Superior Property Restoration (G-3129)*

Remram Recovery LLC (PA)... 740 667-0092
49705 East Park Dr Tuppers Plains (45783) *(G-13262)*

Remtec Engineering.. 513 860-4299
6049 Hi Tek Ct Mason (45040) *(G-9142)*

Remtec International, Bowling Green *Also Called: Reclamation Technologies Inc (G-1438)*

Remtron, Warren *Also Called: Cattron North America Inc (G-13749)*

Renascent Prtction Sltions LLC... 678 910-0412
5500 Frantz Rd Ste 100 Dublin (43017) *(G-6339)*

Renee Grace Bridal, Cincinnati *Also Called: Renee Grace LLC (G-3038)*

Renee Grace LLC.. 513 399-5616
11176 Main St Cincinnati (45241) *(G-3038)*

Renegade Brands LLC.. 216 342-4347
3201 Enterprise Pkwy Ste 490 Cleveland (44122) *(G-4233)*

Renegade Candle Company, New Albany *Also Called: Faith Guiding Cafe LLC (G-10340)*

Renegade Materials Corporation.. 937 350-5274
3363 S Tech Blvd Miamisburg (45342) *(G-9732)*

Renewal By Andersen LLC... 614 781-9600
400 Lazelle Rd Ste 1 Columbus (43240) *(G-4649)*

Renewal Parts Maintenance, Euclid *Also Called: Mechanical Dynamics Analis LLC (G-6661)*

Rennco Automation Systems Inc... 419 861-2340
971 Hamilton Dr Holland (43528) *(G-7781)*

Renosol Seating, Hebron *Also Called: Lear Corporation (G-7622)*

Rent-A-John, Columbus *Also Called: BJ Equipment Ltd (G-4758)*

Repacorp Inc (PA).. 937 667-8496
31 Industry Park Ct Tipp City (45371) *(G-12841)*

Repko Machine Inc... 216 267-1144
5081 W 164th St Cleveland (44142) *(G-4234)*

Replex Mirror Company.. 740 397-5535
11 Mount Vernon Ave Mount Vernon (43050) *(G-10262)*

Replex Plastics, Mount Vernon *Also Called: Replex Mirror Company (G-10262)*

Reporter Newspaper Inc... 330 535-7061
1088 S Main St Akron (44301) *(G-281)*

Repository, Canton *Also Called: Copley Ohio Newspapers Inc (G-1871)*

Repro Acquisition Company LLC.. 216 738-3800
25001 Rockwell Dr Cleveland (44117) *(G-4235)*

Reprocenter, The, Cleveland *Also Called: Repro Acquisition Company LLC (G-4235)*

Republic Anode Fabricators, Valley City *Also Called: Raf Acquisition Co (G-13514)*

Republic Engineered Products.. 440 277-2000
1807 E 28th St Lorain (44055) *(G-8577)*

Republic Metals, Cleveland *Also Called: Vwm-Republic Inc (G-4484)*

Republic Mills Inc.. 419 758-3511
888 School St Okolona (43545) *(G-10932)*

Republic Powdered Metals Inc (HQ)...................................... 330 225-3192
2628 Pearl Rd Medina (44256) *(G-9441)*

Republic Steel.. 330 438-5533
2633 8th St Ne Canton (44704) *(G-1994)*

Republic Steel (DH).. 330 438-5435
2633 8th St Ne Canton (44704) *(G-1995)*

Republic Steel.. 440 277-2000
1807 E 28th St Lorain (44055) *(G-8578)*

Republic Steel, Lorain *Also Called: Republic Engineered Products (G-8577)*

Republic Steel Wire Proc LLC... 440 996-0740
31000 Solon Rd Solon (44139) *(G-12175)*

Republic Storage Systems LLC... 330 438-5800
1038 Belden Ave Ne Canton (44705) *(G-1996)*

Republic Wire Inc... 513 860-1800
5525 Union Centre Dr West Chester (45069) *(G-14063)*

Requarth Lumber Co., Dayton *Also Called: The F A Requarth Company (G-6048)*

Resco Products Inc.. 330 488-1226
6878 Osnaburg St Se East Canton (44730) *(G-6380)*

Resco Products Inc.. 740 682-7794
3542 State Route 93 Oak Hill (45656) *(G-10893)*

Research & Development Div, Bedford *Also Called: Hikma Pharmaceuticals USA Inc (G-1035)*

Research & Development II, Mentor *Also Called: Steris Corporation (G-9623)*

Research Abrasive Products Inc.. 440 944-3200
1400 E 286th St Wickliffe (44092) *(G-14394)*

Research Organics LLC.. 216 883-8025
4353 E 49th St Cleveland (44125) *(G-4236)*

Research Technologies Intl, Cleveland *Also Called: Detrex Corporation (G-3611)*

Reserve Energy Exploration Co.. 440 543-0770
10155 Gottschalk Pkwy Ste 1 Chagrin Falls (44023) *(G-2180)*

Reserve Millwork LLC.. 216 531-6982
26881 Cannon Rd Bedford (44146) *(G-1056)*

Resideo LLC... 440 439-7002
7710 First Pl Ste A Bedford (44146) *(G-1057)*

Resideo LLC... 513 772-1851
5601 Creek Rd Ste A Cincinnati (45242) *(G-3039)*

Resilience Fund III LP (PA).. 216 292-0200
25101 Chagrin Blvd Ste 350 Cleveland (44122) *(G-4237)*

Resilience Us Inc.. 513 645-2600
8814 Trade Port Dr West Chester (45011) *(G-14064)*

Resilient Holdings Inc.. 614 847-5600
6155 Huntley Rd Ste F Columbus (43229) *(G-5227)*

Resinoid Engineering Corp (PA)... 740 928-6115
251 O Neill Dr Hebron (43025) *(G-7633)*

Resonant Sciences LLC.. 937 431-8180
　3975 Research Blvd Dayton (45430) *(G-5980)*

Resonetics LLC.. 937 865-4070
　2941 College Dr Kettering (45420) *(G-8123)*

Resource Mtl Hdlg & Recycl Inc (PA).........................440 834-0727
　14970 Berkshire Industrial Pkwy Middlefield (44062) *(G-9823)*

Resource Recycling Inc.. 419 222-2702
　1596 Neubrecht Rd Lima (45801) *(G-8444)*

Resource Systems, New Concord *Also Called: Cerner Corporation (G-10386)*

Respironics Novametrix LLC...................................... 800 345-6443
　9570 Logistics Ct Columbus (43217) *(G-5228)*

Response Metal Fabricators....................................... 937 222-9000
　521 Kiser St Dayton (45404) *(G-5981)*

Responsible Products Limited.................................... 888 988-6627
　6101 Schumacher Park Dr West Chester (45069) *(G-14065)*

Restortion Parts Unlimited Inc (PA).......................... 513 934-0815
　2175 Deerfield Rd Lebanon (45036) *(G-8283)*

Retail Display Group, Columbus *Also Called: Plaskolite LLC (G-5195)*

Retail Management Products Ltd................................. 740 548-1725
　8851 Whitney Dr Lewis Center (43035) *(G-8351)*

Retain Loyalty LLC... 330 830-0839
　1250 Sanders Ave Sw Massillon (44647) *(G-9238)*

Retalix Inc.. 937 384-2277
　2490 Technical Dr Miamisburg (45342) *(G-9733)*

Retention Knob Supply & Mfg Co................................ 937 686-6405
　4905 State Route 274 W Huntsville (43324) *(G-7865)*

Retterbush Fiberglass Corp.. 937 778-1936
　719 Long St Piqua (45356) *(G-11382)*

Retterbush Graphics Packg Corp................................ 513 779-4466
　6392 Gano Rd West Chester (45069) *(G-14066)*

Rettig Family Pallets Inc.. 419 439-0776
　12484 State Route 110 Napoleon (43545) *(G-10297)*

Return Polymers Inc... 419 289-1998
　400 Westlake Dr Ashland (44805) *(G-570)*

Reuter-Stokes LLC... 330 425-3755
　8499 Darrow Rd Ste 1 Twinsburg (44087) *(G-13365)*

Reuther Mold & Manufacturing, Cuyahoga Falls *Also Called: Reuther Mold & Mfg Co Inc (G-5569)*

Reuther Mold & Mfg Co Inc.. 330 923-5266
　1225 Munroe Falls Ave Cuyahoga Falls (44221) *(G-5569)*

Rev38 LLC.. 937 572-4000
　8888 Beckett Rd West Chester (45069) *(G-14067)*

Revair LLC... 440 462-6100
　1333 Highland Rd E Ste E Macedonia (44056) *(G-8710)*

Revere Building Products, Cuyahoga Falls *Also Called: Gentek Building Products Inc (G-5544)*

Revere Plas Systems Group LLC (HQ)........................419 547-6918
　401 Elm St Clyde (43410) *(G-4562)*

Revere Plastics Systems LLC..................................... 573 785-0871
　401 Elm St Clyde (43410) *(G-4563)*

Review, The, Alliance *Also Called: Alliance Publishing Co Inc (G-372)*

Revlis Corporation (PA)... 330 535-2100
　255 Fountain St Akron (44304) *(G-282)*

Revlis Corporation... 330 535-2108
　2845 Newpark Dr Barberton (44203) *(G-835)*

Revlon, Barberton *Also Called: Revlis Corporation (G-835)*

Revolution Group Inc.. 614 212-1111
　670 Meridian Way Westerville (43082) *(G-14230)*

Revolution Machine Works Inc.................................... 706 505-6525
　5613 Cloverleaf Pkwy Cleveland (44125) *(G-4238)*

Revvity Health Sciences Inc....................................... 330 825-4525
　520 S Main St Ste 2423 Akron (44311) *(G-283)*

Rex, Dayton *Also Called: Rex American Resources Corp (G-5982)*

Rex American Resources Corp (PA)............................937 276-3931
　7720 Paragon Rd Dayton (45459) *(G-5982)*

Rex International USA Inc.. 800 321-7950
　3744 Jefferson Rd Ashtabula (44004) *(G-615)*

Rex Welding Inc.. 740 387-1650
　1410 E Center St Marion (43302) *(G-8992)*

Rexam Closure Systems, Perrysburg *Also Called: Bprex Halthcare Brookville Inc (G-11206)*

Rexam Plastic Packaging, Toledo *Also Called: Bprex Plastic Packaging Inc (G-12902)*

Rexam PLC... 330 893-2451
　5091 County Road 120 Millersburg (44654) *(G-10006)*

Rexarc International Inc.. 937 839-4604
　35 E 3rd St West Alexandria (45381) *(G-13921)*

Rexles Inc.. 419 732-8188
　1850 W Lakeshore Dr Port Clinton (43452) *(G-11451)*

Rexon Components Inc... 216 292-7373
　24500 Highpoint Rd Beachwood (44122) *(G-945)*

Reymond Products Intl Inc... 330 339-3583
　2066 Brightwood Rd Se New Philadelphia (44663) *(G-10464)*

Reynolds and Reynolds Company............................... 419 584-7000
　824 Murlin Ave Celina (45822) *(G-2117)*

Reynolds Cabinetry & Millwork, Cincinnati *Also Called: Village Cabinet Shop Inc (G-3205)*

Reynolds Industries Group LLC.................................. 614 363-9149
　97 Hallowell Dr Blacklick (43004) *(G-1228)*

Reynolds Machinery Inc... 937 847-8121
　760 Liberty Ln Dayton (45449) *(G-5983)*

Rez Stone, Toledo *Also Called: Hoover & Wells Inc (G-12995)*

Rez-Tech Corporation.. 330 673-4009
　1510 Mogadore Rd Kent (44240) *(G-8068)*

RFW Holdings Inc... 440 331-8300
　1200 Smith Ct Cleveland (44116) *(G-4239)*

Rgs, Canton *Also Called: R G Smith Company (G-1988)*

Rh Enterprises, Richmond Heights *Also Called: R & H Enterprises Llc (G-11612)*

Rh Seals, Beavercreek *Also Called: Reliable Hermetic Seals LLC (G-981)*

Rhba Acquisitions LLC... 330 567-2903
　643 Legion Dr Shreve (44676) *(G-11986)*

Rhc Inc... 330 874-3750
　10841 Fisher Rd Nw Bolivar (44612) *(G-1391)*

Rheaco Builders Inc... 330 425-3090
　1941 E Aurora Rd Twinsburg (44087) *(G-13366)*

Rhein Chemie Corporation... 440 279-2367
　145 Parker Ct Chardon (44024) *(G-2220)*

Rhenium Alloys, North Ridgeville *Also Called: Rhenium Alloys Inc (G-10747)*

Rhenium Alloys Inc (PA)...440 365-7388
　38683 Taylor Pkwy North Ridgeville (44035) *(G-10747)*

Rhetech Colors, Sandusky *Also Called: Thermocolor LLC (G-11875)*

Rhgs Company.. 513 721-6299
　1150 W 8th St Ste 111 Cincinnati (45203) *(G-3040)*

Rhi US Ltd (DH)..513 527-6160
　3956 Virginia Ave Cincinnati (45227) *(G-3041)*

Rhinegeist Holding Company Inc................................ 513 381-1367
　1910 Elm St Cincinnati (45202) *(G-3042)*

Rhinestahl AMG, Mason *Also Called: Rhinestahl Corporation (G-9144)*

Rhinestahl Corporation.. 513 229-5300
　7687 Innovation Way Mason (45040) *(G-9143)*

Rhinestahl Corporation (PA)......................................513 489-1317
　1111 Western Row Rd Mason (45040) *(G-9144)*

Rhinestahl CTS, Mason *Also Called: Rhinestahl Corporation (G-9143)*

Rhino Linings, Toledo *Also Called: Zie Bart Rhino Linings Toledo (G-13184)*

Rhinosystems Inc... 216 351-6262
　1 American Rd Ste 1100 Brooklyn (44144) *(G-1525)*

Rhoads Print Center Inc.. 330 678-2042
　564 Washburn Rd Tallmadge (44278) *(G-12748)*

Rhodes Manufacturing Co Inc..................................... 740 743-2614
　7045 Buckeye Valley Rd Ne Somerset (43783) *(G-12210)*

RI Alto Mfg Inc... 740 914-4230
　1632 Cascade Dr Marion (43302) *(G-8993)*

Ribbon Technology Corporation.................................. 614 864-5444
　825 Taylor Station Rd Gahanna (43230) *(G-7168)*

Ribbon Warehouse, Cleveland *Also Called: Discount Floral Supply Inc (G-3617)*

Ribs King Inc.. 513 791-1942
　9406 Main St Cincinnati (45242) *(G-3043)*

Ribtec, Gahanna *Also Called: Ribbon Technology Corporation (G-7168)*

Riceland Cabinet Inc.. 330 601-1071
　326 N Hillcrest Dr Ste A Wooster (44691) *(G-14676)*

Riceland Cabinet Corporation..................................... 330 601-1071
　326 N Hillcrest Dr Ste A Wooster (44691) *(G-14677)*

Rich Industries Inc... 330 339-4113
　2384 Brightwood Rd Se New Philadelphia (44663) *(G-10465)*

(G-0000) Company's Geographic Section entry number

Rich Products Corporation................................ 614 771-1117
4600 Northwest Pkwy Hilliard (43026) *(G-7699)*

Richard Steel Company Inc.............................. 216 520-6390
11110 Avon Ave Cleveland (44105) *(G-4240)*

Richard's Fence Company, Akron *Also Called: Richards Whl Fence Co Inc (G-284)*

Richards Industrials, Cincinnati *Also Called: Richards Industrials Inc (G-3044)*

Richards Industrials Inc (PA).............................513 533-5600
3170 Wasson Rd Cincinnati (45209) *(G-3044)*

Richards Intrors Bldg Cmpnents, Youngstown *Also Called: Youngstown Shade & Alum LLC (G-14975)*

Richards Maple Products Inc............................ 440 286-4160
545 Water St Chardon (44024) *(G-2221)*

Richards Whl Fence Co Inc............................... 330 773-0423
1600 Firestone Pkwy Akron (44301) *(G-284)*

Richardson Printing Corp (PA)........................... 800 848-9752
201 Acme St Marietta (45750) *(G-8941)*

Richardson Publishing Company........................ 330 753-1068
70 4th St Nw Ste 1 Barberton (44203) *(G-836)*

Richardson Supply Ltd................................... 614 539-3033
2080 Hardy Parkway St Grove City (43123) *(G-7411)*

Richardson Woodworking................................. 614 893-8850
3834 Mann Rd Blacklick (43004) *(G-1229)*

Richelieu Foods Inc.................................... 740 335-4813
1104 Clinton Ave Wshngtn Ct Hs (43160) *(G-14744)*

Richland Laminated Columns LLC....................... 419 895-0036
8252 State Route 13 Greenwich (44837) *(G-7364)*

Richland Newhope Inds Inc (PA)........................ 419 774-4400
150 E 4th St Mansfield (44902) *(G-8848)*

Richland Screw Mch Pdts Inc............................ 419 524-1272
531 Grant St Mansfield (44903) *(G-8849)*

Richland Source.. 419 610-2100
40 W 4th St Mansfield (44902) *(G-8850)*

Richland Township Bd Trustees......................... 419 358-4897
8435 Dixie Hwy Bluffton (45817) *(G-1363)*

Richmond Builders Supply, Saint Henry *Also Called: St Henry Tile Co Inc (G-11724)*

Richmond Machine Co.................................... 419 485-5740
1528 Travis Dr Montpelier (43543) *(G-10134)*

Richtech Industries Inc.................................. 440 937-4401
34000 Lear Industrial Pkwy Avon (44011) *(G-738)*

Richwood Gazette, Marysville *Also Called: Marysville Newspaper Inc (G-9037)*

Ricking Holding Co...................................... 513 825-3551
5800 Grant Ave Cleveland (44105) *(G-4241)*

Rickly Hydrological Co.................................. 614 297-9877
1700 Joyce Ave Columbus (43219) *(G-5229)*

Ricks Graphic Accents Inc.............................. 330 896-4700
3554 S Arlington Rd Unit B Akron (44312) *(G-285)*

Ridge Corporation (PA)................................. 614 421-7434
1201 Etna Pkwy Pataskala (43062) *(G-11147)*

Ridge Engineering Inc.................................. 513 681-5500
1700 Blue Rock St Cincinnati (45223) *(G-3045)*

Ridge Machine & Welding Co............................ 740 537-2821
1015 Railroad St Toronto (43964) *(G-13186)*

Ridge Tool Company..................................... 740 432-8782
9877 Brick Church Rd Cambridge (43725) *(G-1758)*

Ridge Tool Company (HQ)............................... 440 323-5581
400 Clark St Elyria (44035) *(G-6586)*

Ridge Tool Company..................................... 440 329-4737
321 Sumner St Elyria (44035) *(G-6587)*

Ridge Tool Manufacturing Co........................... 440 323-5581
400 Clark St Elyria (44035) *(G-6588)*

Ridge Township Stone Quarry.......................... 419 968-2222
16905 Middle Point Rd Van Wert (45891) *(G-13544)*

Ridgid, Elyria *Also Called: Ridge Tool Company (G-6586)*

Ridley USA Inc.. 800 837-8222
104 Oak St Botkins (45306) *(G-1398)*

Riesbeck Food Markets Inc............................. 740 695-3401
104 Plaza Dr Saint Clairsville (43950) *(G-11709)*

Rieter Automotive-Oregon Plant, Oregon *Also Called: Autoneum North America Inc (G-10957)*

Riffle & Sons, Chillicothe *Also Called: Riffle Machine Works Inc (G-2279)*

Riffle Machine Works Inc (PA).......................... 740 775-2838
5746 State Route 159 Chillicothe (45601) *(G-2279)*

Right Away Division, Blue Ash *Also Called: Baxters North America Inc (G-1247)*

Riker Products Inc..................................... 419 729-1626
4901 Stickney Ave Toledo (43612) *(G-13112)*

Riley Creek Holdings Inc............................... 419 358-6946
8950 Dixie Hwy Bluffton (45817) *(G-1364)*

Rimeco Products Inc................................... 440 918-1220
2002 Joseph Lloyd Pkwy Willoughby (44094) *(G-14517)*

Rimer Enterprises Inc.................................. 419 878-8156
916 Rimer Dr Waterville (43566) *(G-13841)*

Rimm Kleen Systems, West Unity *Also Called: Hardline International Inc (G-14195)*

Rimrock Corporation.................................... 614 471-5926
1700 Jetway Blvd Columbus (43219) *(G-5230)*

Rimrock Holdings Corporation.......................... 614 471-5926
1700 Jetway Blvd Columbus (43219) *(G-5231)*

Rina Systems LLC...................................... 513 469-7462
8180 Corporate Park Dr Ste 140 Cincinnati (45242) *(G-3046)*

Ring Container Tech LLC................................ 937 492-0961
603 Oak Ave Sidney (45365) *(G-12044)*

Ring Masters, Brunswick *Also Called: Alternative Surface Grinding (G-1579)*

Ringer Screen Print, North Kingsville *Also Called: Wholesale Imprints Inc (G-10700)*

Ringneck Brewing Company, Strongsville *Also Called: Brew Kettle Inc (G-12546)*

Rinos Woodworking Shop Inc............................ 440 946-1718
36475 Biltmore Pl Willoughby (44094) *(G-14518)*

Ripley Metalworks LLC.................................. 937 392-4992
111 Waterworks Rd Ripley (45167) *(G-11619)*

Rise Holdings LLC...................................... 440 946-9646
4839 E 345th St Willoughby (44094) *(G-14519)*

Risher & Co.. 216 732-8351
27011 Tungsten Rd Euclid (44132) *(G-6676)*

Risk Industries LLC.................................... 440 835-5553
30505 Clemens Rd Westlake (44145) *(G-14328)*

Rite Track, West Chester *Also Called: Rite Track Equipment Services LLC (G-14068)*

Rite Track Equipment Services LLC (PA)............... 513 881-7820
8655 Rite Track Way West Chester (45069) *(G-14068)*

Riten Industries Incorporated.......................... 740 335-5353
1100 Lakeview Ave Wshngtn Ct Hs (43160) *(G-14745)*

Ritime Incorporated.................................... 330 273-3443
6363 York Rd Ste 104 Cleveland (44130) *(G-4242)*

Rittman Inc.. 330 927-6855
10 Mull Dr Rittman (44270) *(G-11627)*

Rivals Sports Grille LLC................................ 216 267-0005
6710 Smith Rd Middleburg Heights (44130) *(G-9776)*

River City Body Company............................... 513 772-9317
2660 Commerce Blvd Cincinnati (45241) *(G-3047)*

River City Pharma..................................... 513 870-1680
8695 Seward Rd Fairfield (45011) *(G-6772)*

River East Custom Cabinets Inc........................ 419 244-3228
221 S Saint Clair St Toledo (43602) *(G-13113)*

River Valley Paper, Akron *Also Called: River Valley Paper Company LLC (G-286)*

River Valley Paper Company LLC........................ 330 535-1001
131 N Summit St Akron (44304) *(G-286)*

Riverbend Sand Rock and Gravel, Miamisburg *Also Called: Hilltop Basic Resources Inc (G-9699)*

Riverside, Genoa *Also Called: Riverside Mch & Automtn Inc (G-7250)*

Riverside Cnstr Svcs Inc............................... 513 723-0900
218 W Mcmicken Ave Cincinnati (45214) *(G-3048)*

Riverside Drives, Cleveland *Also Called: Riverside Drives Inc (G-4243)*

Riverside Drives Inc................................... 216 362-1211
4509 W 160th St Cleveland (44135) *(G-4243)*

Riverside Marine Inds Inc.............................. 419 729-1621
2824 N Summit St Toledo (43611) *(G-13114)*

Riverside Mch & Automtn Inc (PA)......................419 855-8308
1240 N Genoa Clay Center Rd Genoa (43430) *(G-7250)*

Riverside Mch & Automtn Inc............................ 419 855-8308
28701 E Broadway St Walbridge (43465) *(G-13687)*

Riverside Mfg Acquisition LLC.......................... 585 458-2090
5344 Bragg Rd Cleveland (44127) *(G-4244)*

Riverside Steel Inc.................................... 330 856-5299
3102 Warren Sharon Rd Vienna (44473) *(G-13617)*

Riverview Indus WD Pdts Inc (PA)...................... 330 669-8509
179 S Gilbert Dr Smithville (44677) *(G-12068)*

ALPHABETIC

Riverview Packaging Inc.................................. 937 743-9530
101 Shotwell Dr Franklin (45005) *(G-7045)*

Riverview Productions Inc............................... 740 441-1150
652 Jackson Pike Gallipolis (45631) *(G-7208)*

Riverview Raquetball Club, Willoughby *Also Called: Melinz Industries Inc (G-14487)*

Riverview Transport LLC................................. 330 669-8509
179 Gilbert Dr Smithville (44677) *(G-12069)*

Riverview Transport, Inc., Smithville *Also Called: Riverview Transport LLC (G-12069)*

Rixan Associates Inc..................................... 937 438-3005
7560 Paragon Rd Dayton (45459) *(G-5984)*

Rize Home LLC (PA)...................................... 800 333-8333
31050 Diamond Pkwy Glenwillow (44139) *(G-7288)*

Rjf International Corporation........................... 330 668-2069
3875 Embassy Pkwy Fairlawn (44333) *(G-6809)*

Rjm Stamping Co... 614 443-1191
9151 Cotswold Dr Pickerington (43147) *(G-11300)*

Rjs, Akron *Also Called: Rjs Corporation (G-287)*

Rjs Corporation.. 330 896-2387
3400 Massillon Rd Akron (44312) *(G-287)*

Rjw Trucking Company Ltd.............................. 740 363-5343
124 Henderson Ct Delaware (43015) *(G-6169)*

Rki Inc (PA)... 888 953-9400
8901 Tyler Blvd Mentor (44060) *(G-9608)*

RL Craig Inc.. 330 424-1525
6496 State Route 45 Lisbon (44432) *(G-8479)*

Rl Smith Graphics, Youngstown *Also Called: Rl Smith Graphics LLC (G-14924)*

Rl Smith Graphics LLC.................................. 330 629-8616
493 Bev Rd Bldg 7b Youngstown (44512) *(G-14924)*

Rld Transportation LLC................................. 234 334-7777
3060 Brookline Rd North Canton (44720) *(G-10664)*

RLM Fabricating Inc...................................... 419 729-6130
4801 Bennett Rd Toledo (43612) *(G-13115)*

Rm Advisory Group Inc.................................. 513 242-2100
5300 Vine St Cincinnati (45217) *(G-3049)*

RMC USA Incorporation................................. 440 992-4906
149 S Cucumber St Jefferson (44047) *(G-7982)*

Rmi Titanium Company LLC............................ 330 471-1844
208 15th St Sw Canton (44707) *(G-1997)*

Rmi Titanium Company LLC............................ 330 453-2118
1550 Marietta Ave Se Canton (44707) *(G-1998)*

Rmi Titanium Company LLC............................ 330 455-4010
1935 Warner Rd Se Canton (44707) *(G-1999)*

Rmi Titanium Company LLC............................ 330 544-9470
2000 Warren Ave Niles (44446) *(G-10602)*

Rmi Titanium Company LLC............................ 330 652-9955
1000 Warren Ave Niles (44446) *(G-10603)*

Rmi Titanium Company LLC (HQ).................... 330 652-9952
1000 Warren Ave Niles (44446) *(G-10604)*

RMS Equipment LLC...................................... 330 564-1360
1 Vision Ln Cuyahoga Falls (44223) *(G-5570)*

RMS Equipment Company, Cuyahoga Falls *Also Called: RMS Equipment LLC (G-5570)*

Rmt Acquisition Inc....................................... 513 241-5566
3111 Spring Grove Ave Cincinnati (45225) *(G-3050)*

Rmt Corporation... 937 274-2121
2552 Titus Ave Dayton (45414) *(G-5985)*

Rmt Holdings Inc.. 419 221-1168
1025 Findlay Rd Lima (45801) *(G-8445)*

Rnm Holdings Inc... 614 444-5556
2350 Refugee Park Columbus (43207) *(G-5232)*

Rnm Holdings Inc (PA).................................. 937 704-9900
550 Conover Dr Franklin (45005) *(G-7046)*

Rnm Holdings Inc... 419 867-8712
1810 Eber Rd Ste C Holland (43528) *(G-7782)*

Rnp Inc
8014 Linden Dr Sw Dellroy (44620) *(G-6182)*

Rnr Enterprises LLC...................................... 330 852-3022
1361 County Road 108 Sugarcreek (44681) *(G-12647)*

Rnw Holdings Inc.. 330 792-0600
200 Division Street Ext Youngstown (44510) *(G-14925)*

Ro-MAI Industries Inc.................................... 330 425-9090
1605 Enterprise Pkwy Twinsburg (44087) *(G-13367)*

Roach Studios LLC....................................... 614 725-1405
441 E Hudson St Columbus (43202) *(G-5233)*

Roach Wood Products & Plas Inc.................... 740 532-4855
25 Township Road 328 Ironton (45638) *(G-7934)*

Road Apple Music.. 513 217-4444
65 S Main St Middletown (45044) *(G-9891)*

Roadsafe Traffic Systems Inc......................... 614 274-9782
1350 Stimmel Rd Columbus (43223) *(G-5234)*

Rob's Welding Technologies, Dayton *Also Called: Robs Welding Technologies Ltd (G-5987)*

Roban Inc... 330 794-1059
1319 Main St Lakemore (44250) *(G-8156)*

Robbins & Myers Inc..................................... 937 454-3200
5870 Poe Ave Ste A Dayton (45414) *(G-5986)*

Robbins Company, The, Solon *Also Called: Global TBM Company (G-12117)*

Robbins Industrial Frnc Co Inc....................... 440 949-2292
3739 Colorado Ave Sheffield Village (44054) *(G-11963)*

Robbins Sports Surfaces, Cincinnati *Also Called: Robbins Sports Surfaces LLC (G-3051)*

Robbins Sports Surfaces LLC (PA)................. 513 871-8988
4777 Eastern Ave Cincinnati (45226) *(G-3051)*

Robeck, Aurora *Also Called: Robeck Fluid Power Co (G-687)*

Robeck Fluid Power Co.................................. 330 562-1140
350 Lena Dr Aurora (44202) *(G-687)*

Roberds Converting Co Inc............................ 513 683-6667
113 Northeast Dr Loveland (45140) *(G-8648)*

Robert A Malone.. 740 947-2859
450 State Route 551 Waverly (45690) *(G-13873)*

Robert Becker Impressions Inc....................... 419 385-5303
4646 Angola Rd Toledo (43615) *(G-13116)*

Robert E McGrath Inc.................................... 440 572-7747
11606 Pearl Rd Strongsville (44136) *(G-12593)*

Robert Long Manufacturing Co........................ 330 678-0911
4192 Karg Industrial Pkwy Kent (44240) *(G-8069)*

Robert Mayo Industries................................. 330 426-2587
157 E Martin St East Palestine (44413) *(G-6406)*

Robert Rothschild Farm LLC.......................... 855 969-8050
9958 Crescent Park Dr West Chester (45069) *(G-14069)*

Robert Rothschild Market Cafe, West Chester *Also Called: Robert Rothschild Farm LLC (G-14069)*

Robert Smart Inc.. 330 454-8881
1100 High Ave Sw Canton (44707) *(G-2000)*

Robert W Johnson Inc (PA)............................ 614 336-4545
6280 Sawmill Rd Dublin (43017) *(G-6340)*

Robert's Men's Shop, Dellroy *Also Called: Rnp Inc (G-6182)*

ROBERTS BROTHERS, Steubenville *Also Called: Fort Stben Burial Estates Assn (G-12403)*

Roberts Demand No 3 Corp............................ 216 641-0660
4008 E 89th St Cleveland (44105) *(G-4245)*

Roberts Machine Products LLC....................... 937 682-4015
270 Rush St Rushsylvania (43347) *(G-11666)*

Roberts Manufacturing Co Inc......................... 419 594-2712
24338 Road 148 Oakwood (45873) *(G-10899)*

Roberts Screw Products, Rushsylvania *Also Called: Dayton Superior Corporation (G-11665)*

Robertson Cabinets Inc................................. 937 698-3755
1090 S Main St West Milton (45383) *(G-14185)*

Robertson Manufacturing Co.......................... 216 531-8222
10150 Colton Ave Concord Township (44077) *(G-5395)*

Robin Enterprises Company............................ 614 891-0250
111 N Otterbein Ave Westerville (43081) *(G-14274)*

Robin Industries Inc..................................... 330 893-3501
5200 County Rd 120 Berlin (44610) *(G-1199)*

Robin Industries Inc..................................... 330 695-9300
300 W Clay St Fredericksburg (44627) *(G-7070)*

Robin Industries Inc..................................... 330 359-5418
7227 State Route 515 Winesburg (44690) *(G-14608)*

Robin Industries Inc (PA).............................. 216 631-7000
6500 Rockside Rd Ste 230 North Canton (44720) *(G-10665)*

Robinson Fin Machines Inc............................ 419 674-4152
13670 Us Highway 68 Kenton (43326) *(G-8113)*

Robs Welding Technologies Ltd....................... 937 890-4963
2920 Production Ct Dayton (45414) *(G-5987)*

Robura Inc.. 330 857-7404
3328 S Kohler Rd Orrville (44667) *(G-11004)*

Robura LLC (PA)...800 438-5346
  4779 Kidron Rd Dalton (44618) *(G-5593)*

Robura, Inc., Orrville *Also Called: Robura Inc (G-11004)*

Rocal Inc (PA)...740 998-2122
  3186 County Road 550 Frankfort (45628) *(G-7005)*

Rochester Manufacturing Inc..............................440 647-2463
  24765 Quarry Rd Wellington (44090) *(G-13900)*

Rochling Automotive USA LLP.............................330 400-5785
  2275 Picton Pkwy Akron (44312) *(G-288)*

Rochling Glastic Composites, Cleveland *Also Called: Roechling Indus Cleveland LP (G-4248)*

Rock Away Capital Inc..216 432-9465
  3092 Rockefeller Ave Cleveland (44115) *(G-4246)*

Rock Decor Company...330 830-9760
  167 Maple St Apple Creek (44606) *(G-477)*

Rock Em Sock Em Retro LLC (PA)........................419 575-9309
  5902 Moline Martin Rd Walbridge (43465) *(G-13688)*

Rock Hard Industries LLC....................................440 327-3077
  34555 Mills Rd North Ridgeville (44039) *(G-10748)*

Rock Lite, Maple Heights *Also Called: Charles Svec Inc (G-8879)*

Rock Tenn, Ravenna *Also Called: Westrock Rkt LLC (G-11550)*

Rocket Ventures LLC..419 530-6083
  300 Madison Ave Ste 270 Toledo (43604) *(G-13117)*

Rockport Ready Mix, Cleveland *Also Called: Rock Away Capital Inc (G-4246)*

Rocks General Maintenance LLC..........................740 323-4711
  10019 Jacksontown Rd Thornville (43076) *(G-12768)*

Rockstedt Tool & Die Inc.....................................330 273-9000
  2974 Interstate Pkwy Brunswick (44212) *(G-1612)*

Rocktenn Merchandising Display, West Chester *Also Called: Westrock Rkt LLC (G-14093)*

Rockwell Automation Inc.....................................440 646-7900
  6680 Beta Dr Cleveland (44143) *(G-4247)*

Rockwell Automation Inc.....................................440 646-5000
  1 Allen Bradley Dr Mayfield Heights (44124) *(G-9341)*

Rockwell Automation Inc.....................................330 425-3211
  8440 Darrow Rd Twinsburg (44087) *(G-13368)*

Rockwell Automation Inc.....................................513 942-9828
  9355 Allen Rd West Chester (45069) *(G-14070)*

Rockwell Metals Company LLC............................440 242-2420
  3709 W Erie Ave Lorain (44053) *(G-8579)*

Rockwood Door & Millwork, Millersburg *Also Called: Rockwood Products Ltd (G-10007)*

Rockwood Products Ltd.......................................330 893-2392
  5264 Township Road 401 Millersburg (44654) *(G-10007)*

Rocky Brands Inc (PA)...740 753-1951
  39 E Canal St Nelsonville (45764) *(G-10320)*

Rocky Hinge Inc...330 539-6296
  1660 Harding Ave Girard (44420) *(G-7279)*

Rocky River Brewing Co......................................440 895-2739
  21290 Center Ridge Rd Rocky River (44116) *(G-11638)*

Rocla Concrete Tie Inc..740 776-3238
  6501 Pershing Ave Portsmouth (45662) *(G-11475)*

ROCLA CONCRETE TIE, INC, Portsmouth *Also Called: Rocla Concrete Tie Inc (G-11475)*

Rod McLellan Company..937 578-5284
  14111 Scottslawn Rd Marysville (43040) *(G-9044)*

Rodney Wells...740 425-2266
  34225 Holland Rd Barnesville (43713) *(G-846)*

Rods Welding and Rebuilding, Barnesville *Also Called: Rodney Wells (G-846)*

Roe Transportation Entps Inc..............................937 497-7161
  3680 Michigan St Sidney (45365) *(G-12045)*

Roechling Indus Cleveland LP (DH)......................216 486-0100
  4321 Glenridge Rd Cleveland (44121) *(G-4248)*

Roemer Industries Inc...330 448-2000
  1555 Masury Rd Masury (44438) *(G-9256)*

Roerig Machine...440 647-4718
  27348 State Route 511 New London (44851) *(G-10415)*

Roessner Holdings Inc..419 356-2123
  482 State Route 119 Fort Recovery (45846) *(G-6970)*

Roetmans Welding LLC.......................................216 385-5938
  155 Beaver St Akron (44304) *(G-289)*

Roettger Hardwood Inc.......................................937 693-6811
  17066 Kettlersville Rd Kettlersville (45336) *(G-8125)*

Rogar International Inc..419 476-5500
  4015 Dewey St Toledo (43612) *(G-13118)*

Rogers Company, The, Mentor *Also Called: Rogers Display Inc (G-9609)*

Rogers Display Inc (HQ)......................................440 951-9200
  7550 Tyler Blvd Mentor (44060) *(G-9609)*

Rogers Industrial Products Inc.............................330 535-3331
  532 S Main St Akron (44311) *(G-290)*

Rohrer Corporation (HQ)......................................330 335-1541
  717 Seville Rd Wadsworth (44282) *(G-13668)*

Roki America Co Ltd...419 424-9713
  2001 Production Dr Findlay (45839) *(G-6913)*

Rol - Tech Inc...214 905-8050
  4814 Calvert Dr Fort Loramie (45845) *(G-6953)*

Rol- Fab Inc...216 662-2500
  4949 Johnston Pkwy Cleveland (44128) *(G-4249)*

Rolcon Inc...513 821-7259
  510 Station Ave Cincinnati (45215) *(G-3052)*

Roll-In Saw Inc..216 459-9001
  15851 Commerce Park Dr Brookpark (44142) *(G-1558)*

Roll-Kraft, Mentor *Also Called: Rki Inc (G-9608)*

Rolled Alloys Inc (PA)...800 521-0332
  6630 Monclova Rd Maumee (43537) *(G-9315)*

Roller Source Inc..440 748-4033
  34100 E Royalton Rd Columbia Station (44028) *(G-4599)*

Rolling Enterprises Inc..937 866-4917
  2701 Lance Dr Moraine (45409) *(G-10191)*

Rolls-Royce Energy Systems Inc..........................703 834-1700
  105 N Sandusky St Mount Vernon (43050) *(G-10263)*

Romar Metal Fabricating Inc...............................740 682-7731
  201 Zane Oak Rd Oak Hill (45656) *(G-10894)*

Romline Express LLC..234 855-1905
  1572 Brownlee Ave Youngstown (44514) *(G-14926)*

Ron-Al Mold & Machine Inc.................................330 673-7919
  1057 Mason Ave Kent (44240) *(G-8070)*

Rona Enterprises Inc...740 927-9971
  30 W Broad St Pataskala (43062) *(G-11148)*

Ronald T Dodge Co...937 439-4497
  55 Westpark Rd Dayton (45459) *(G-5988)*

Rondy & Co., Ashland *Also Called: Tahoma Rubber & Plastics Inc (G-579)*

Ronfeldt Manufacturing LLC (HQ).......................419 382-5641
  2345 S Byrne Rd Toledo (43614) *(G-13119)*

Ronlen Industries Inc..330 273-6468
  2809 Nationwide Pkwy Brunswick (44212) *(G-1613)*

Roof Maxx, Westerville *Also Called: Roof Maxx Technologies LLC (G-14231)*

Roof Maxx Technologies LLC...............................855 766-3629
  7385 State Route 3 Westerville (43082) *(G-14231)*

Roofing Annex LLC...513 942-0555
  4866 Duff Dr Ste E West Chester (45246) *(G-14141)*

Root Candles, Medina *Also Called: Al Root Company (G-9372)*

Roots Meat Market LLC.......................................419 332-0041
  3721 W State St Fremont (43420) *(G-7129)*

Roots Poultry Inc...419 332-0041
  3721 W State St Fremont (43420) *(G-7130)*

Roppe Corporation...419 435-8546
  1602 N Union St Fostoria (44830) *(G-6998)*

Roppe Holding Company (PA)..............................419 435-8546
  1602 N Union St Fostoria (44830) *(G-6999)*

Roppe Holding Company......................................419 435-6601
  106 N Main St Fostoria (44830) *(G-7000)*

Rosati Windows, Columbus *Also Called: Rosatis Window Co LLC (G-5235)*

Rosatis Window Co LLC.......................................614 777-4806
  4200 Roberts Rd Columbus (43228) *(G-5235)*

Rose Metal Industries, Cleveland *Also Called: Rose Properties Inc (G-4252)*

Rose Metal Industries LLC (PA)...........................216 881-3355
  1536 E 43rd St Cleveland (44103) *(G-4250)*

Rose Metal Industries LLC...................................216 426-8615
  1155 Marquette St Cleveland (44114) *(G-4251)*

Rose Properties Inc..216 881-6000
  1536 E 43rd St Cleveland (44103) *(G-4252)*

Rosebud Mining Company...................................740 768-2275
  9076 County Road 53 Bergholz (43908) *(G-1196)*

Rosebud Mining Company...................................740 658-4217
  28490 Birmingham Rd Freeport (43973) *(G-7089)*

Rosebud's Real Food, Covington *Also Called: Rosebuds Ranch and Garden LLC (G-5499)*

Rosebuds Ranch and Garden LLC........................ 937 214-1801
473 E Troy Pike Covington (45318) *(G-5499)*

Rosenfeld Jewelry Inc... 440 446-0099
5668 Mayfield Rd Cleveland (44124) *(G-4253)*

Ross Aluminum, Sidney *Also Called: P&The Mfg Acquisition LLC (G-12037)*

Ross Aluminum Castings LLC............................... 937 492-4134
815 Oak Ave Sidney (45365) *(G-12046)*

Ross Casting & Innovation LLC............................. 937 497-4500
402 S Kuther Rd Sidney (45365) *(G-12047)*

Ross County License Bureau, Willoughby *Also Called: Public Safety Ohio Department (G-14511)*

Ross Group Inc.. 937 427-3069
4555 Lake Forest Dr Ste 650 Blue Ash (45242) *(G-1327)*

Ross Hx, Middletown *Also Called: Ross Hx LLC (G-9892)*

Ross Hx LLC (PA).. 513 217-1565
2722 Cincinnati Dayton Rd Middletown (45044) *(G-9892)*

Ross Special Products Inc.................................... 937 335-8406
2500 W State Route 55 Troy (45373) *(G-13250)*

Ross-Co Redi-Mix Co Inc (PA).............................. 740 775-4466
6430 State Route 159 Chillicothe (45601) *(G-2280)*

Rossborough Automotive Corp.............................. 216 941-6115
3425 Service Rd Cleveland (44111) *(G-4254)*

Rossborough Supply Co....................................... 216 941-6115
3425 Service Rd Cleveland (44111) *(G-4255)*

Rotadyne, Franklin *Also Called: Finzer Roller Inc (G-7021)*

Rotary Forms Press Inc (PA)................................. 937 393-3426
835 S High St Hillsboro (45133) *(G-7724)*

Rotary Products Inc... 740 747-2623
202 W High St Ashley (43003) *(G-583)*

Rotary Products Inc (PA)...................................... 740 747-2623
117 E High St Ashley (43003) *(G-584)*

Rotary Smer Spcalist Group LLC........................... 330 299-8210
635 Wooster Rd W Barberton (44203) *(G-837)*

Rotek, Aurora *Also Called: Thyssnkrupp Rothe Erde USA Inc (G-689)*

Rotex Global LLC.. 513 541-1236
1230 Knowlton St Cincinnati (45223) *(G-3053)*

Rothenbuhler Cheese Chalet LLC.......................... 800 327-9477
15815 Nauvoo Rd Middlefield (44062) *(G-9824)*

Rothenbuhler Holding Company............................ 440 632-6000
15815 Nauvoo Rd Middlefield (44062) *(G-9825)*

Roto Met Rice, West Chester *Also Called: Roto-Die Company Inc (G-14071)*

Roto Mold, Mentor *Also Called: Interpak Inc (G-9535)*

Roto Solutions Inc.. 330 279-2424
8300 County Rd 189 Holmesville (44633) *(G-7803)*

Roto-Die Company Inc... 513 942-3500
4430 Mulhauser Rd West Chester (45011) *(G-14071)*

Rotocast Technologies Inc.................................... 330 798-9091
1900 Englewood Ave Akron (44312) *(G-291)*

Rotoline USA LLC... 330 677-3223
4429 Crystal Pkwy Ste B Kent (44240) *(G-8071)*

Rotopolymers.. 216 645-0333
1052 Mahoning Ave Nw Warren (44483) *(G-13794)*

Rotopolymers, Warren *Also Called: Polimeros Usa LLC (G-13790)*

Rotosolutions Inc.. 419 903-0800
1401 Jacobson Ave Ashland (44805) *(G-571)*

Rough Brothers Mfg Inc....................................... 513 242-0310
5513 Vine St Cincinnati (45217) *(G-3054)*

Round Mate Systems.. 419 675-3334
13840 Us Highway 68 Kenton (43326) *(G-8114)*

Rouster Lfting Rgging A Mzzlla, Cleveland *Also Called: Mazzella Lifting Tech Inc (G-4005)*

Rowe Premix Inc... 937 678-9015
10107 Us Rr 127 N West Manchester (45382) *(G-14177)*

Rowend Industries Inc... 419 333-8300
1035 Napoleon St Ste 101 Fremont (43420) *(G-7131)*

Rowmark LLC (PA).. 419 425-8974
5409 Hamlet Dr Findlay (45840) *(G-6914)*

Roxane Laboratories, Columbus *Also Called: Hikma Labs Inc (G-4984)*

Roy I Kaufman Inc... 740 382-0643
1672 Marion Upper Sandusky Rd Marion (43302) *(G-8994)*

Roy Retrac Incorporated....................................... 740 564-5552
100 E Campus View Blvd Ste 250 Columbus (43235) *(G-5236)*

Royal Acme Corporation (PA)................................ 216 241-1477
3110 Payne Ave Cleveland (44114) *(G-4256)*

Royal Adhesives & Sealants LLC........................... 440 708-1212
17340 Munn Rd Chagrin Falls (44023) *(G-2181)*

Royal Appliance Intl Co.. 440 996-2000
7005 Cochran Rd Cleveland (44139) *(G-4257)*

Royal Building Products, Columbus *Also Called: Westlake Ryal Bldg Pdts USA In (G-5365)*

Royal Cabinet Design Co Inc................................. 216 267-5330
15800 Commerce Park Dr Cleveland (44142) *(G-4258)*

Royal Chemical Company Ltd................................. 330 467-1300
1755 Enterprise Pkwy Ste 100 Twinsburg (44087) *(G-13369)*

Royal Chemical Company Ltd (HQ).......................... 330 467-1300
8679 Freeway Dr Macedonia (44056) *(G-8711)*

Royal Docks Brewing Co LLC................................ 330 353-9103
5646 Wales Ave Nw Massillon (44646) *(G-9239)*

Royal Group, The, Marion *Also Called: Schwarz Partners Packaging LLC (G-8996)*

Royal Metal Products LLC..................................... 740 397-8842
325 Commerce Dr Mount Vernon (43050) *(G-10264)*

Royal Pad Products, Cincinnati *Also Called: Loroco Industries Inc (G-2828)*

Royal Plastics Inc... 440 352-1357
9410 Pineneedle Dr Mentor (44060) *(G-9610)*

Royal Powder Corporation.................................... 216 898-0074
4800 Briar Rd Cleveland (44135) *(G-4259)*

Royal Wire Products Inc (PA)................................ 440 237-8787
13450 York Delta Dr North Royalton (44133) *(G-10781)*

Royalton Archtctral Fbrication.............................. 440 582-0400
13155 York Delta Dr North Royalton (44133) *(G-10782)*

Royalton Industries Inc.. 440 748-9900
12450 Eaton Commerce Pkwy Ste 1 Columbia Station (44028) *(G-4600)*

Royalton Manufacturing Inc.................................. 440 237-2233
1169 Brittain Rd Akron (44305) *(G-292)*

Roys Mueller Box Co.. 216 464-1191
5140 Richmond Rd Cleveland (44146) *(G-4260)*

Royster-Clark Inc.. 513 941-4100
10743 Brower Rd North Bend (45052) *(G-10621)*

Rozzi Company, Loveland *Also Called: Rozzi Company Inc (G-8649)*

Rozzi Company Inc (PA)....................................... 513 683-0620
10059 Loveland Madeira Rd Loveland (45140) *(G-8649)*

Rozzi Company Inc.. 513 683-0620
6047 State Route 350 Martinsville (45146) *(G-9013)*

RP Hoskins Inc... 216 631-1000
3033 W 44th St Cleveland (44113) *(G-4261)*

Rp Manufacturing LLC.. 419 468-5095
3424 State Rte 309 Iberia (43325) *(G-7884)*

Rpg Industries Inc... 937 698-9801
3571 Ginghamsburg Frederick Rd Tipp City (45371) *(G-12842)*

RPI Color Service Inc... 513 471-4040
1950 Radcliff Dr Cincinnati (45204) *(G-3055)*

RPI Graphic Data Solutions, Cincinnati *Also Called: RPI Color Service Inc (G-3055)*

RPM, Arcadia *Also Called: RPM Carbide Die Inc (G-483)*

RPM Carbide Die Inc.. 419 894-6426
202 E South St Arcadia (44804) *(G-483)*

RPM International Inc (PA)..................................... 330 273-5090
2628 Pearl Rd Medina (44258) *(G-9442)*

Rpmi, Lebanon *Also Called: Rpmi Packaging Inc (G-8284)*

Rpmi Packaging Inc... 513 398-4040
3899 S Us Route 42 Lebanon (45036) *(G-8284)*

Rpp Containers, Cincinnati *Also Called: Dadco Inc (G-2539)*

Rpui, Lebanon *Also Called: Restortion Parts Unlimited Inc (G-8283)*

RR Donnelley, West Chester *Also Called: R R Donnelley & Sons Company (G-14061)*

RR Donnelley & Sons Company.............................. 614 221-8385
41 S High St Ste 3750 Columbus (43215) *(G-5237)*

RS Industries Inc... 216 351-8200
1455 E Schaaf Rd Brooklyn Heights (44131) *(G-1539)*

Rs Manufacturing Inc... 440 946-8002
8878 East Ave Mentor (44060) *(G-9611)*

RS&b Industries LLC.. 330 255-6000
1147 Akron Rd Wooster (44691) *(G-14678)*

(G-0000) Company's Geographic Section entry number

Rsb Spine LLC...216 241-2804
2530 Superior Ave E Ste 703 Cleveland (44114) *(G-4262)*

Rsfi Office Furniture, Worthington *Also Called: Recycled Systems Furniture Inc (G-14724)*

RSI Company (PA)...216 360-9800
24050 Commerce Park Ste 200 Beachwood (44122) *(G-946)*

Rsl LLC..330 392-8900
1160 Paige Ave Ne Warren (44483) *(G-13795)*

Rsp Industries Inc...440 823-4502
415 Hazelwood Dr Chagrin Falls (44022) *(G-2150)*

Rss Maclin, Barberton *Also Called: Rotary Smer Spcalist Group LLC (G-837)*

Rsv Wlding Fbrction McHning In.........................419 592-0993
M063 County Road 12 Napoleon (43545) *(G-10298)*

Rsw Distributors LLC.......................................502 587-8877
4700 Ashwood Dr Ste 200 Blue Ash (45241) *(G-1328)*

Rsw Technologies LLC.....................................419 662-8100
135 Dixie Hwy Rossford (43460) *(G-11662)*

RT Industries Inc (PA)......................................937 335-5784
110 Foss Way Troy (45373) *(G-13251)*

RTC Converters Inc...937 743-2300
300 Shotwell Dr Franklin (45005) *(G-7047)*

RTD Electronics Inc...330 487-0716
1632 Enterprise Pkwy Ste D Twinsburg (44087) *(G-13370)*

Rti, Niles *Also Called: Rmi Titanium Company LLC (G-10602)*

Rti Alloys...330 652-9952
1000 Warren Ave Niles (44446) *(G-10605)*

Rti Alloys, Canton *Also Called: Rmi Titanium Company LLC (G-1998)*

Rti Alloys Tpd, Canton *Also Called: Rmi Titanium Company LLC (G-1999)*

Rti International Metals Inc
1000 Warren Ave Niles (44446) *(G-10606)*

Rti Niles, Niles *Also Called: Rmi Titanium Company LLC (G-10604)*

Rti Remmele Engineering Inc.............................651 635-4179
5801 Postal Rd Cleveland (44181) *(G-4263)*

Rti Securex LLC...937 859-5290
20 S 1st St Miamisburg (45342) *(G-9734)*

RTS Companies (us) Inc...................................440 275-3077
2900 Industrial Park Dr Austinburg (44010) *(G-702)*

Rtsi LLC..440 542-3066
6161 Cochran Rd Ste G Solon (44139) *(G-12176)*

Rtx Corporation...330 784-5477
6051 W Airport Dr North Canton (44720) *(G-10666)*

RTZ Manufacturing Co.....................................614 848-8366
12755 Fairview Rd Heath (43056) *(G-7603)*

Rubber & Plastics News, Cuyahoga Falls *Also Called: Crain Communications Inc (G-5536)*

Rubber Associates Inc.....................................330 745-2186
1522 Turkeyfoot Lake Rd New Franklin (44203) *(G-10394)*

Rubber City Industries Inc................................330 990-9641
471 E Bergey St Wadsworth (44281) *(G-13089)*

Rubber City Machinery Corp..............................330 434-3500
One Thousand Sweitzer Avenue Akron (44311) *(G-293)*

Rubber Duck 4x4 Inc..513 889-1735
1622 Smith Rd Hamilton (45013) *(G-7521)*

Rubber Grinding Inc...419 692-3000
1430 N Main St Delphos (45833) *(G-6192)*

Rubber Seal Products, Dayton *Also Called: Teknol Inc (G-6043)*

Rubber World Magazine, Akron *Also Called: Lippincott and Peto Inc (G-207)*

Rubber World Magazine Inc...............................330 864-2122
1741 Akron Peninsula Rd Akron (44313) *(G-294)*

Rubber-Tech Inc..937 274-1114
5208 Wadsworth Rd Dayton (45414) *(G-5989)*

Rubbermaid, Kent *Also Called: Newell Brands Inc (G-8056)*

Rubbermaid, Mogadore *Also Called: Rubbermaid Home Products (G-10082)*

Rubbermaid Home Products..............................330 733-7771
3200 Gilchrist Rd Mogadore (44260) *(G-10082)*

Rubbermaid Incorporated.................................330 733-7771
3200 Gilchrist Rd Mogadore (44260) *(G-10083)*

Rubbertec Industrial Pdts Co............................740 657-3345
7580 Commerce Ct Lewis Center (43035) *(G-8352)*

Rubex Inc..614 875-6343
3709 Grove City Rd Grove City (43123) *(G-7412)*

Rubicon Rubber LLC...234 678-0078
276 W Greenwich Rd Seville (44273) *(G-11920)*

Rubix LLC..330 577-8249
2310 Township Road 444 Sugarcreek (44681) *(G-12648)*

Rudd Equipment Company Inc..........................513 321-7833
11807 Enterprise Dr Cincinnati (45241) *(G-3056)*

Rudolph Foods, Lima *Also Called: Rudolph Foods Company Inc (G-8446)*

Rudolph Foods Company Inc (PA).....................909 383-7463
6575 Bellefontaine Rd Lima (45804) *(G-8446)*

Rudy's Strudel & Bakery, Cleveland *Also Called: Rudys Strudel Shop (G-4264)*

Rudys Strudel Shop..440 886-4430
5580 Ridge Rd Cleveland (44129) *(G-4264)*

Ruff Neon & Lighting Maint Inc..........................440 350-6267
295 W Prospect St Painesville (44077) *(G-11110)*

Ruhe Sales Inc..419 943-3357
5450 State Route 109 Leipsic (45856) *(G-8314)*

Rultract Inc...330 856-9808
8598 Kimblewick Ln Ne Warren (44484) *(G-13796)*

Rumford Paper Company...................................937 242-9230
8540 Gander Creek Dr Miamisburg (45342) *(G-9735)*

Rumpke Container Service, Cincinnati *Also Called: Rumpke Transportation Co LLC (G-3057)*

Rumpke Transportation Co LLC.........................513 242-4600
553 Vine St Cincinnati (45202) *(G-3057)*

Rumpke Transportation Co LLC (HQ)..................513 851-0122
10795 Hughes Rd Cincinnati (45251) *(G-3058)*

Runkles Sawmill LLC..937 663-0115
2534 Dialton Rd Saint Paris (43072) *(G-11759)*

Ruple Trucking, Willoughby Hills *Also Called: Chagrin Vly Stl Erectors Inc (G-14557)*

Rupp Construction Inc......................................330 855-2781
18228 Fulton Rd Marshallville (44645) *(G-9008)*

Rural-Urban Record Inc....................................440 236-8982
24487 Squire Rd Columbia Station (44028) *(G-4601)*

Ruscilli Real Estate Services............................614 923-6400
5100 Parkcenter Ave Ste 100 Dublin (43017) *(G-6341)*

Rusco Design Center, Youngstown *Also Called: Rusco Products Inc (G-14927)*

Rusco Products Inc..330 758-0378
423 E Western Reserve Rd Youngstown (44514) *(G-14927)*

Ruscoe, Akron *Also Called: Pmbp Legacy Co Inc (G-262)*

Ruscoe Company...330 253-8148
485 Kenmore Blvd Akron (44301) *(G-295)*

Rush Fixture & Millwork Co................................216 241-9100
1978 W 3rd St Cleveland (44113) *(G-4265)*

Rush, R L Tool & Pattern, Bucyrus *Also Called: R L Rush Tool & Pattern Inc (G-1687)*

Russ Jr Enterprises Inc....................................440 237-4642
6165 Royalton Rd North Royalton (44133) *(G-10783)*

Russel Hunt Total Land Care, Steubenville *Also Called: Russell Hunt (G-12410)*

Russel Upholstery, Ashtabula *Also Called: Custom Craft Collection Inc (G-589)*

Russell Cast Stone Inc.....................................856 753-4000
4600 Devitt Dr West Chester (45246) *(G-14142)*

Russell Group United LLC.................................614 353-6853
1250 Arthur E Adams Dr Ste 205 Columbus (43221) *(G-5238)*

Russell Hunt..740 264-1196
175 Detmar Rd Steubenville (43953) *(G-12410)*

Russell L Garber (PA).......................................937 548-6224
4891 Clark Station Rd Greenville (45331) *(G-7352)*

Russell Products Co Inc....................................330 535-9246
275 N Forge St Ste 1 Akron (44304) *(G-296)*

Russell Products Co Inc....................................330 535-3391
1066 Home Ave Akron (44310) *(G-297)*

Russell Products Co Inc (PA).............................330 535-9246
275 N Forge St Akron (44304) *(G-298)*

Russell Standard Corporation............................330 733-9400
990 Hazel St Akron (44305) *(G-299)*

Russell T Bundy Associates Inc........................419 526-4454
1711 N Main St Mansfield (44903) *(G-8851)*

Russell T Bundy Associates Inc........................740 965-3008
601 W Cherry St Sunbury (43074) *(G-12675)*

Rust Belt Broncos LLC......................................330 533-0048
6145 State Route 446 Canfield (44406) *(G-1815)*

Ruthman Pump and Engineering.........................937 783-2411
459 E Fancy St Blanchester (45107) *(G-1238)*

Rutland Township...740 742-2805
33325 Jessie Creek Rd Bidwell (45614) *(G-1214)*

(PA)=Parent Co (HQ)=Headquarters (DH)=Div Headquarters

Rv Mobile Power LLC (PA)................................ 855 427-7978
  830 Kinnear Rd Columbus (43212) *(G-5239)*

Rv Xpress Inc.. 937 418-0127
  501 East St Piqua (45356) *(G-11383)*

Rvmp, Columbus *Also Called: Rv Mobile Power LLC (G-5239)*

Rvtronix Corporation.................................... 440 359-7200
  34099 Melinz Pkwy Unit E Eastlake (44095) *(G-6442)*

RW Beckett Corporation (PA)............................. 440 327-1060
  38251 Center Ridge Rd North Ridgeville (44039) *(G-10749)*

Rw Screw LLC.. 330 837-9211
  999 Oberlin Ave Sw Massillon (44647) *(G-9240)*

Rxscan, Lewis Center *Also Called: Retail Management Products Ltd (G-8351)*

Ryans Newark Leader Ex Prtg Co.......................... 740 522-2149
  56 Westgate Dr Newark (43055) *(G-10532)*

Ryanworks Inc... 937 438-1282
  175 E Alex Bell Rd Ste 264 Dayton (45459) *(G-5990)*

Ryder Engraving Inc..................................... 740 927-7193
  1029 Hazelton Etna Rd Sw Pataskala (43062) *(G-11149)*

Ryder-Heil Bronze Inc................................... 419 562-2841
  126 E Irving St Bucyrus (44820) *(G-1690)*

Ryse Aero Holdco Inc.................................... 513 318-9907
  6951 Cintas Blvd Mason (45040) *(G-9145)*

S & A Industries Corporation............................ 330 733-6040
  1500 Exeter Rd Akron (44306) *(G-300)*

S & A Industries Corporation (DH)....................... 330 733-6040
  1471 Exeter Rd Akron (44306) *(G-301)*

S & D Architectural Metals.............................. 440 582-2560
  12955 York Delta Dr North Royalton (44133) *(G-10784)*

S & G Manufacturing Group LLC (PA)...................... 614 529-0100
  4830 Northwest Pkwy Hilliard (43026) *(G-7700)*

S & H Automation & Eqp Co Inc........................... 419 636-0020
  815 Commerce Dr Bryan (43506) *(G-1659)*

S & H Industries Inc.................................... 216 831-0550
  5200 Richmond Rd Cleveland (44146) *(G-4266)*

S & H Industries Inc (PA)............................... 216 831-0550
  5200 Richmond Rd Bedford (44146) *(G-1058)*

S & J Lumber, Thurman *Also Called: S & J Lumber Company LLC (G-12771)*

S & J Lumber Company LLC................................ 740 245-5804
  3667 Garners Ford Rd Thurman (45685) *(G-12771)*

S & K Metal Polsg & Buffing............................. 513 732-6662
  4194 Taylor Rd Batavia (45103) *(G-886)*

S & K Products Company.................................. 419 268-2244
  4540 St Rt 127 Celina (45822) *(G-2118)*

S & S Aggregates Inc.................................... 419 938-5604
  4540 State Route 39 Perrysville (44864) *(G-11283)*

S & S Aggregates Inc (HQ)............................... 740 453-0721
  3570 S River Rd Zanesville (43701) *(G-15046)*

S & W Express Inc....................................... 330 683-2747
  8849 Lincoln Way E Orrville (44667) *(G-11005)*

S A Langmack Company.................................... 216 541-0500
  13400 Glenside Rd Cleveland (44110) *(G-4267)*

S A Oma-U Inc... 330 487-0602
  9329 Ravenna Rd Ste A Twinsburg (44087) *(G-13371)*

S A S Rubber, Painesville *Also Called: Yokohama Tire Corporation (G-11125)*

S and S Tool Inc....................................... 440 593-4000
  576 Blair St Conneaut (44030) *(G-5415)*

S Beckman Print Grphic Sltons.......................... 614 864-2232
  376 Morrison Rd Ste D Columbus (43213) *(G-5240)*

S C Fastening Systems, Macedonia *Also Called: SC Fire Protection Ltd (G-8712)*

S C Industries Inc..................................... 216 732-9000
  24460 Lakeland Blvd Euclid (44132) *(G-6677)*

S F Mock & Associates LLC.............................. 937 438-0196
  105 Westpark Rd Dayton (45459) *(G-5991)*

S Holley Lumber LLC.................................... 440 272-5315
  7143 Noble Rd Windsor (44099) *(G-14603)*

S I Distributing Inc................................... 419 647-4909
  13540 Spencerville Rd Spencerville (45887) *(G-12240)*

S I T Strings Co Inc................................... 330 434-8010
  2493 Romig Rd Akron (44320) *(G-302)*

S J Roth Enterprises Inc............................... 513 543-1140
  900 Kieley Pl Cincinnati (45217) *(G-3059)*

S J T Enterprises Inc.................................. 440 617-1100
  28045 Ranney Pkwy Ste B Westlake (44145) *(G-14329)*

S Lehman Central Warehouse............................. 330 828-8828
  289 Kurzen Rd N Dalton (44618) *(G-5594)*

S M C, Upper Sandusky *Also Called: Schmidt Machine Company (G-13455)*

S O I T A, Dayton *Also Called: Southwstern Ohio Instrctnal Te (G-6013)*

S O S Shades, Lewis Center *Also Called: Inside Outfitters Inc (G-8338)*

S P E Inc.. 330 733-0101
  3300 Gilchrist Rd Mogadore (44260) *(G-10084)*

S R Door Inc (PA)...................................... 740 927-3558
  1120 O Neill Dr Hebron (43025) *(G-7634)*

S R P M Inc.. 440 248-8440
  30300 Bruce Industrial Pkwy Ste B Cleveland (44139) *(G-4268)*

S T C, Canton *Also Called: Stark Truss Company Inc (G-2017)*

S Toys Holdings LLC.................................... 330 656-0440
  10010 Aurora Hudson Rd Streetsboro (44241) *(G-12521)*

S-P Company Inc (PA)................................... 330 782-5651
  400 W Railroad St Ste 1 Columbiana (44408) *(G-4627)*

S-Tek Inc (PA)... 440 439-8232
  2095 Midway Dr Twinsburg (44087) *(G-13373)*

S.E.S. Engineering, Alliance *Also Called: Steel Eqp Specialists Inc (G-406)*

S.H. BELL COMPANY, East Liverpool *Also Called: SH Bell Company (G-6396)*

S&B Metal Pdts Twinsburg LLC (PA)...................... 330 487-5790
  2060 Case Pkwy Twinsburg (44087) *(G-13372)*

S&G Distribution, Hilliard *Also Called: S & G Manufacturing Group LLC (G-7700)*

S&L Fleet Services Inc................................. 740 549-2722
  670 Meridian Way Ste 252 Westerville (43082) *(G-14232)*

S&M Trucking LLC....................................... 661 310-2585
  5700 Gateway Ste 400 Mason (45040) *(G-9146)*

S&Ps, Warren *Also Called: Aptiv Services Us LLC (G-13739)*

S&R Lumber LLC... 740 352-6135
  207 Sugar Run Rd Piketon (45661) *(G-11313)*

S&S Sign Service....................................... 614 279-9722
  485 Ternstedt Ln Columbus (43228) *(G-5241)*

S&V Industries Inc (PA)................................ 330 666-1986
  5054 Paramount Dr Medina (44256) *(G-9443)*

Sabatino Cabinet, Salem *Also Called: Joseph Sabatino (G-11791)*

Sabco Industries Inc................................... 419 531-5347
  5242 Angola Rd Ste 150 Toledo (43615) *(G-13120)*

Sabin Robbins Paper Company, Mansfield *Also Called: Eagles Nest Holdings LLC (G-8782)*

Sabre Industries Inc................................... 419 542-1420
  761 W High St Hicksville (43526) *(G-7652)*

Saco Aei Polymers Inc.................................. 330 995-1600
  1395 Danner Dr Aurora (44202) *(G-688)*

Saco Lowell Parts LLC.................................. 330 794-1535
  1395 Triplett Blvd Akron (44306) *(G-303)*

Sadler Corporation..................................... 330 688-0009
  4600 Hudson Dr Stow (44224) *(G-12455)*

Saehwa IMC Na Inc (PA)................................. 330 645-6653
  2200 Massillon Rd Akron (44312) *(G-304)*

Saf-Holland Inc.. 513 874-7888
  105 Mercantile Dr Fairfield (45014) *(G-6773)*

Safc Cleveland, Cleveland *Also Called: Research Organics LLC (G-4236)*

Safe Grain Max Tronix, Dayton *Also Called: Safe-Grain Inc (G-5992)*

Safe Haven Brands LLC.................................. 937 550-9407
  217 S Pioneer Blvd Springboro (45066) *(G-12267)*

Safe-Grain Inc... 513 398-2500
  10522 Success Ln Dayton (45458) *(G-5992)*

Safe-Grain Inc (PA).................................... 513 398-2500
  417 Wards Corner Rd Ste B Loveland (45140) *(G-8650)*

Safecor Health LLC (PA)................................ 800 447-1006
  4060 Business Park Dr Ste B Columbus (43204) *(G-5242)*

Safecor Health LLC..................................... 614 351-6117
  4000 Business Park Dr Columbus (43204) *(G-5243)*

Safeguard, Streetsboro *Also Called: Safeguard Technology Inc (G-12522)*

Safeguard Technology Inc............................... 330 995-5200
  1460 Miller Pkwy Streetsboro (44241) *(G-12522)*

Safelite Autoglass, Columbus *Also Called: Safelite Group Inc (G-5244)*

Safelite Group Inc (DH)................................ 614 210-9000
  7400 Safelite Way Columbus (43235) *(G-5244)*

(G-0000) Company's Geographic Section entry number

Safeway Packaging Inc (PA)................................419 629-3200
300 White Mountain Dr New Bremen (45869) *(G-10366)*

Safeway Safety Step LLC................................513 942-7837
5242 Rialto Rd West Chester (45069) *(G-14072)*

Safran Usa Inc................................513 247-7000
300 E Business Way Sharonville (45241) *(G-11948)*

Sage Integration Holdings LLC (PA)................................330 733-8183
4075 Karg Industrial Pkwy Ste B Kent (44240) *(G-8072)*

Sagequest LLC................................216 896-7243
31500 Bainbridge Rd Ste 1 Solon (44139) *(G-12177)*

Saia-Burgess Lcc................................937 898-3621
801 Scholz Dr Vandalia (45377) *(G-13576)*

Saica, Hamilton *Also Called: Saica Pack US LLC (G-7522)*

Saica Pack US LLC................................513 399-5602
2995 Mcbride Ct Hamilton (45011) *(G-7522)*

Sailors Tailor Inc................................937 862-7781
1480 Spring Valley Painters Rd Spring Valley (45370) *(G-12243)*

Saint Ctherines Metalworks Inc................................216 409-0576
1985 W 68th St Cleveland (44102) *(G-4269)*

Saint Gobain Crystals, Newbury *Also Called: Saint-Gobain Ceramics Plas Inc (G-10563)*

Saint-Gobain Ceramics Plas Inc................................440 542-2712
12359 Kinsman Rd Newbury (44065) *(G-10563)*

Saint-Gobain Ceramics Plas Inc................................440 564-8000
12345 Kinsman Rd Newbury (44065) *(G-10564)*

Saint-Gobain Ceramics Plas Inc................................330 673-5860
3840 Fishcreek Rd Stow (44224) *(G-12456)*

Saint-Gobain Ceramics Plas Inc (DH)................................610 893-6000
3840 Fishcreek Rd Stow (44224) *(G-12457)*

Saint-Gobain Hycomp LLC................................440 234-2002
17960 Englewood Dr Cleveland (44130) *(G-4270)*

Saint-Gobain Norpro, Stow *Also Called: Saint-Gobain Ceramics Plas Inc (G-12456)*

Saint-Gobain Norpro Corp (HQ)................................330 673-5860
3840 Fishcreek Rd Stow (44224) *(G-12458)*

Saint-Gobain Prfmce Plas Corp................................330 798-6981
2664 Gilchrist Rd Akron (44305) *(G-305)*

Saint-Gobain Prfmce Plas Corp................................614 889-2220
6250 Shier Rings Rd Dublin (43016) *(G-6342)*

Saint-Gobain Prfmce Plas Corp................................330 296-9948
335 N Diamond St Ravenna (44266) *(G-11538)*

Saint-Gobain Prfmce Plas Corp................................440 836-6900
31500 Solon Rd Solon (44139) *(G-12178)*

Sairam Oil Inc................................440 289-8232
4610 Milford Ave Parma (44134) *(G-11135)*

Sajar Plastics, Inc., Middlefield *Also Called: SPI Liquidation Inc (G-9828)*

Sakamura USA Inc................................740 223-7777
970 Kellogg Pkwy Marion (43302) *(G-8995)*

Sakroto Inc................................513 242 3644
5155 Fischer Ave Cincinnati (45217) *(G-3060)*

Salco Machine Inc................................330 456-8281
3822 Victory Ave Louisville (44641) *(G-8615)*

Salem Manufacturing & Sls Inc................................614 572-4242
171 N Hamilton Rd Columbus (43213) *(G-5245)*

Salem Mill & Cabinet Co................................330 337-9568
1455 Quaker Cir Salem (44460) *(G-11810)*

Salem Welding & Supply Company................................330 332-4517
475 Prospect St Salem (44460) *(G-11811)*

Salem-Republic Rubber Company................................877 425-5079
475 W California Ave Sebring (44672) *(G-11901)*

Sales Office Rob Jordan Vp Sls, Hilliard *Also Called: Textiles Inc (G-7706)*

Salient Systems Inc................................614 792-5800
4393 Tuller Rd Ste K Dublin (43017) *(G-6343)*

Salineville Office, Salineville *Also Called: M3 Midstream LLC (G-11818)*

Salt Creek Lumber Company Inc................................330 695-3500
11657 Salt Creek Rd Fredericksburg (44627) *(G-7071)*

Saltillo Corporation (PA)................................330 674-6722
2143 Township Road 112 Millersburg (44654) *(G-10008)*

Salus Enterprises North Amer, Mason *Also Called: Salus North America Inc (G-9147)*

Salus North America Inc................................888 387-2587
4700 Duke Dr Ste 200 Mason (45040) *(G-9147)*

Sam Americas Inc................................330 628-1118
3555 Gilchrist Rd Mogadore (44260) *(G-10085)*

Sam Dong America Inc................................740 363-1985
801 Pittsburgh Dr Delaware (43015) *(G-6170)*

Sam Dong Ohio Inc................................740 363-1985
801 Pittsburgh Dr Delaware (43015) *(G-6171)*

Sam Oht Services LLC................................330 225-3117
620 E Smith Rd Enterprise Ctr Ste D Medina (44256) *(G-9444)*

Samegoal Inc................................216 766-5713
3401 Enterprise Pkwy Ste 340 Beachwood (44122) *(G-947)*

Samhain Publishing Ltd (llc)................................513 453-4688
11821 Mason Montgomery Rd # 2 Cincinnati (45249) *(G-3061)*

Sammy S Auto Detail................................614 263-2728
3514 Cleveland Ave Columbus (43224) *(G-5246)*

Sample Machining Inc................................937 258-3338
220 N Jersey St Dayton (45403) *(G-5993)*

Sams Graphic Industries................................330 821-4710
611 Homeworth Rd Alliance (44601) *(G-402)*

Samsco Corp................................216 400-8207
837 E 79th St Cleveland (44103) *(G-4271)*

Samsel Rope & Marine Supply Co (PA)................................216 241-0333
1285 Old River Rd Uppr Cleveland (44113) *(G-4272)*

Samsel Supply Company, Cleveland *Also Called: Samsel Rope & Marine Supply Co (G-4272)*

Samson................................614 504-8038
772 N High St Ste 101 Columbus (43215) *(G-5247)*

Samuel Son & Co (usa) Inc................................740 522-2500
1455 James Pkwy Heath (43056) *(G-7604)*

Samuel Adams Brewery Company Ltd................................513 412-3200
1625 Central Pkwy Cincinnati (45214) *(G-3062)*

Samuel L Peters LLC................................513 745-1500
10001 Alliance Rd Ste 1 Blue Ash (45242) *(G-1329)*

Samuel Steel Pickling Company, Twinsburg *Also Called: Worthngton Smuel Coil Proc LLC (G-13398)*

Samuels Products Inc................................513 891-4456
9851 Redhill Dr Blue Ash (45242) *(G-1330)*

San-Fab Conveyor and Automtn, Sandusky *Also Called: Sandusky Fabricating & Sls Inc (G-11867)*

Sancap Liner Technology Inc................................330 821-1166
16125 Armour St Ne Alliance (44601) *(G-403)*

Sancast Inc................................740 622-8660
535 Clow Ln Coshocton (43812) *(G-5471)*

Sanctuary Software Studio Inc................................330 666-9690
3090 W Market St Ste 300 Fairlawn (44333) *(G-6810)*

Sandco Industries................................419 547-3273
567 Premier Dr Clyde (43410) *(G-4564)*

Sandpiper, Mansfield *Also Called: Warren Rupp Inc (G-8863)*

Sandra Weddington................................740 417-4286
1400 Stratford Rd Delaware (43015) *(G-6172)*

Sandusky Fabricating & Sls Inc (PA)................................419 626-4465
2000 Superior St Sandusky (44870) *(G-11867)*

Sandusky International Inc................................419 626-5340
510 W Water St Sandusky (44870) *(G-11868)*

Sandusky Machine & Tool Inc................................419 626-8359
2223 Tiffin Ave Sandusky (44870) *(G-11869)*

Sandusky Newspaper Group, Sandusky *Also Called: Isaac Foster Mack Co (G-11843)*

Sandusky Packaging Corporation................................419 626-8520
2016 George St Sandusky (44870) *(G-11870)*

Sandvik Inc................................614 438-6579
6325 Huntley Rd Columbus (43229) *(G-5248)*

Sandvik Hyperion, Columbus *Also Called: Sandvik Inc (G-5248)*

Sandvik Rock Proc Sltons N AME................................216 431-2600
1214 Marquette St Cleveland (44114) *(G-4273)*

Sandvik Rock Proc Sltons N AME (HQ)................................216 431-2600
3900 Kelley Ave Cleveland (44114) *(G-4274)*

Sandwisch Enterprises Inc (PA)................................419 944-6446
1644 Campbell St Toledo (43607) *(G-13121)*

Sanger Holdings LLC................................513 784-9046
501 Chestnut St Cincinnati (45203) *(G-3063)*

Sangraf International Inc................................216 543-3288
159 Crocker Park Blvd Ste 100 Westlake (44145) *(G-14330)*

Sanoh America Inc (HQ)................................419 425-2600
1849 Industrial Dr Findlay (45840) *(G-6915)*

Sanreed Management Group LLC................................513 722-1037
1132 Ferris Rd Amelia (45102) *(G-436)*

A L P H A B E T I C

Santos Industrial Ltd (PA)...................................937 299-7333
 3034 Dryden Rd Dayton (45439) *(G-5994)*

Sapphire Creek Wnery Grdns LLC..........................440 543-7777
 16965 Park Circle Dr Chagrin Falls (44023) *(G-2182)*

Sara Wood Pharmaceuticals, Mason *Also Called: Sara Wood Pharmaceuticals LLC (G-9148)*

Sara Wood Pharmaceuticals LLC............................513 833-5502
 4518 Margaret Ct Mason (45040) *(G-9148)*

Sarahs Vineyard Inc..330 929-8057
 1204 W Steels Corners Rd Cuyahoga Falls (44223) *(G-5571)*

Sarasota Quality Products..................................440 899-9820
 27330 Center Ridge Rd Westlake (44145) *(G-14331)*

Sarcom Inc..614 854-1300
 8337a Green Meadows Dr N Lewis Center (43035) *(G-8353)*

Sardinia Concrete Company (PA).............................513 248-0090
 911 Us Route 50 Milford (45150) *(G-9951)*

Sardinia Ready Mix Inc.....................................937 446-2523
 9 Oakdale Ave Sardinia (45171) *(G-11886)*

Sare Plastics, Alliance *Also Called: Stuchell Products LLC (G-407)*

Sarepta Therapeutics Inc...................................380 324-3973
 4201 Easton Cmns Columbus (43219) *(G-5249)*

Sarica, Urbana *Also Called: Sarica Manufacturing Company (G-13477)*

Sarica Manufacturing Company..............................937 484-4030
 240 W Twain Ave Urbana (43078) *(G-13477)*

Sarka Bros Machining Inc...................................419 532-2393
 607 Ottawa St Kalida (45853) *(G-8006)*

Sarka Conveyor, Tiffin *Also Called: Sarka Shtmtl & Fabrication Inc (G-12797)*

Sarka Shtmtl & Fabrication Inc.............................419 447-4377
 70 Clinton Ave Tiffin (44883) *(G-12797)*

Sasha Electronics Inc......................................419 662-8100
 135 Dixie Hwy Rossford (43460) *(G-11663)*

Satco Inc...513 707-6150
 457 Wards Corner Rd Loveland (45140) *(G-8651)*

Satelytics Inc...419 372-0160
 6330 Levis Commons Blvd Perrysburg (43551) *(G-11260)*

Sattler Companies Inc......................................330 239-2552
 1455 Wolf Creek Trl Wadsworth (44281) *(G-13670)*

Sattler Machine Products, Wadsworth *Also Called: Sattler Companies Inc (G-13670)*

Saturday Knight Ltd (PA)...................................513 641-1400
 4330 Winton Rd Cincinnati (45232) *(G-3064)*

Sauder, Archbold *Also Called: Sauder Woodworking Co (G-511)*

Sauder Manufacturing Co (HQ)...............................419 445-7670
 930 W Barre Rd Archbold (43502) *(G-509)*

Sauder Manufacturing Co....................................419 682-3061
 201 Horton St Stryker (43557) *(G-12627)*

Sauder Woodworking Co......................................419 446-2711
 330 N Clydes Way Archbold (43502) *(G-510)*

Sauder Woodworking Co (PA).................................419 446-2711
 502 Middle St Archbold (43502) *(G-511)*

Sauerwein Welding...513 563-2979
 605 Wayne Park Dr Cincinnati (45215) *(G-3065)*

Sausser Steel Company Inc..................................419 422-9632
 230 Crystal Ave Findlay (45840) *(G-6916)*

Savant Technologies LLC (HQ)...............................800 435-4448
 1975 Noble Rd East Cleveland (44112) *(G-6382)*

Save Edge Inc...937 376-8268
 360 W Church St Xenia (45385) *(G-14774)*

Save Edge USA, Xenia *Also Called: Save Edge Inc (G-14774)*

Savko Plastic Pipe & Fittings..............................614 885-8420
 683 E Lincoln Ave Columbus (43229) *(G-5250)*

Savor Seasonings LLC......................................513 732-2333
 4292 Armstrong Blvd Batavia (45103) *(G-887)*

Savory Foods Inc..740 354-6655
 2240 6th St Portsmouth (45662) *(G-11476)*

Saw Dust Ltd..740 862-0612
 4799 Refugee Rd Nw Baltimore (43105) *(G-787)*

Sawmill 9721 LLC..614 937-4400
 9721 Sawmill Rd Powell (43065) *(G-11494)*

Sawmill Marathon, Columbus *Also Called: Marathon At Sawmill (G-5080)*

Sawmill Road Management Co LLC (PA)........................937 342-9071
 370 S 5th St Columbus (43215) *(G-5251)*

Sawyer Crystal Systems, Willoughby *Also Called: Sawyer Technical Materials LLC (G-14520)*

Sawyer Technical Materials LLC (HQ)........................440 951-8770
 35400 Lakeland Blvd Willoughby (44095) *(G-14520)*

Saxon Jewelers, Cleveland *Also Called: M B Saxon Co Inc (G-3975)*

Saxon Products Inc..419 241-6771
 2283 Fulton St Toledo (43620) *(G-13122)*

Say Security Group USA LLC (PA)............................419 634-0004
 520 E Montford Ave Ada (45810) *(G-5)*

Saylor Products Corporation................................419 832-2125
 17484 Saylor Ln Grand Rapids (43522) *(G-7309)*

Sb Trans LLC..407 477-2545
 300 E Business Way Ste 200 Cincinnati (45241) *(G-3066)*

SBC, Columbus *Also Called: Ameritech Publishing Inc (G-4704)*

SBC, Uniontown *Also Called: Ameritech Publishing Inc (G-13416)*

SC Fire Protection Ltd.....................................330 468-3300
 8531 Freeway Dr Macedonia (44056) *(G-8712)*

SC Liquidation Company LLC (DH)............................937 332-6500
 550 Summit Ave Troy (45373) *(G-13252)*

SC Strategic Solutions LLC.................................567 424-6054
 600 Industrial Pkwy Norwalk (44857) *(G-10861)*

Scanacon Incorporated.....................................330 877-7600
 950 Wales Dr Hartville (44632) *(G-7583)*

Scandinavian Tob Group Ln Ltd.............................770 934-4594
 1424 Diagonal Rd Akron (44320) *(G-306)*

Scarefactory Inc..614 565-3590
 350 Mccormick Blvd # C Columbus (43213) *(G-5252)*

Scarlett Kitty LLC..678 438-3796
 2786 Wilmington Pike Dayton (45419) *(G-5995)*

Scarlett Ktty Bath Made Pretty, Dayton *Also Called: Scarlett Kitty LLC (G-5995)*

Scenic Solutions Ltd Lblty Co..............................937 866-5062
 355 Gargrave Rd Dayton (45449) *(G-5996)*

Scenic Wood Products, Sugarcreek *Also Called: Pallet Distributors Inc (G-12644)*

Scepter Publishers..212 354-0670
 21510 Drake Rd Strongsville (44149) *(G-12594)*

Scepter Supply LLC..307 634-6074
 1500 Greene St Marietta (45750) *(G-8942)*

Schaaf Co Inc...513 241-7044
 2440 Spring Grove Ave Cincinnati (45214) *(G-3067)*

Schaefer Box & Pallet Co...................................513 738-2500
 11875 Paddys Run Rd Hamilton (45013) *(G-7523)*

Schaefer Equipment Inc.....................................330 372-4006
 1590 Phoenix Rd Ne Warren (44483) *(G-13797)*

Schaeffer Metal Products Inc...............................330 296-6226
 357 Commerce St Ravenna (44266) *(G-11539)*

Schaeffers Investment Research Inc.........................513 589-3800
 5151 Pfeiffer Rd Ste 450 Blue Ash (45242) *(G-1331)*

Schaeffler Group USA Inc...................................800 274-5001
 5370 Wegman Dr Valley City (44280) *(G-13515)*

Schaeffler Group USA Inc...................................330 202-6752
 3571 Old Airport Rd Wooster (44691) *(G-14679)*

Schaeffler Transm Systems LLC..............................330 202-6212
 3177 Old Airport Rd Wooster (44691) *(G-14680)*

Schaeffler Transm Systems LLC (DH).........................330 264-4383
 3401 Old Airport Rd Wooster (44691) *(G-14681)*

Schaeffler Transmission Llc (DH)...........................330 264-4383
 3401 Old Airport Rd Wooster (44691) *(G-14682)*

Schafer Driveline LLC (HQ).................................740 694-2055
 123 Phoenix Pl Fredericktown (43019) *(G-7084)*

Schafer Industries, Fredericktown *Also Called: Schafer Driveline LLC (G-7084)*

Schaffer Grinding Co Inc...................................323 724-4476
 8470 Chamberlin Rd Twinsburg (44087) *(G-13374)*

Schaffner Publication Inc..................................419 732-2154
 4340 Mckenna Ln Port Clinton (43452) *(G-11452)*

Schantz Custom Woodworking, Orrville *Also Called: Schantz Organ Company (G-11006)*

Schantz Organ Company (PA).................................330 682-6065
 626 S Walnut St Orrville (44667) *(G-11006)*

Schauer Battery Chargers, Cincinnati *Also Called: Brookwood Group Inc (G-2430)*

Scheel Publishing LLC......................................216 731-8616
 5900 Som Center Rd Willoughby (44094) *(G-14521)*

Scheiders Foods LLC (PA)...................................740 404-6641
 5705 State Route 204 Ne Mount Perry (43760) *(G-10226)*

Schell Scenic Studio Inc...................................614 444-9550
 2140 Refugee St Millersport (43046) *(G-10024)*

Scherba Industries Inc..330 273-3200
2880 Interstate Pkwy Brunswick (44212) *(G-1614)*

Scherer Industrial Group, Springfield *Also Called: Horner Industrial Services Inc (G-12325)*

Schilling Graphics Inc (PA).....................................419 468-1037
275 Gelsanliter Rd Galion (44833) *(G-7198)*

Schilling Truss Inc..740 984-2396
230 Stony Run Rd Beverly (45715) *(G-1208)*

Schindler, Sidney *Also Called: Schindler Elevator Corporation (G-12048)*

Schindler Elevator, Holland *Also Called: Schindler Elevator Corporation (G-7783)*

Schindler Elevator Corporation...............................419 861-5900
1530 Timber Wolf Dr Ste B Holland (43528) *(G-7783)*

Schindler Elevator Corporation...............................937 492-3186
920 S Vandemark Rd Sidney (45365) *(G-12048)*

Schindler Logistics Center, Holland *Also Called: Adams Elevator Equipment Co (G-7743)*

Schindlers Broad Run Chshuse I............................330 343-4108
6011 Old Route 39 Nw Dover (44622) *(G-6260)*

Schlabach Printers, Sugarcreek *Also Called: Schlabach Printers LLC (G-12649)*

Schlabach Printers LLC..330 852-4687
798 State Route 93 Nw Sugarcreek (44681) *(G-12649)*

Schlabach Woodworks Ltd.....................................330 674-7488
6678 State Route 241 Millersburg (44654) *(G-10009)*

Schlessman Seed Co (PA)......................................419 499-2572
11513 Us Highway 250 N Milan (44846) *(G-9918)*

Schlezinger Metals, Columbus *Also Called: I H Schlezinger Inc (G-4996)*

Schmelzer Industries Inc.......................................740 743-2866
7970 Wesley Chapel Rd Ne Somerset (43783) *(G-12211)*

Schmidt Machine Company....................................419 294-3814
7013 State Highway 199 Upper Sandusky (43351) *(G-13455)*

Schmidt Progressive LLC.......................................513 934-2600
360 Harmon Ave Lebanon (45036) *(G-8285)*

Schmitmeyer Inc..937 295-2091
195 Ben St Fort Loramie (45845) *(G-6954)*

Schneider Automation Inc......................................612 426-0709
5855 Union Centre Blvd Fairfield (45014) *(G-6774)*

Schneider Electric, Oxford *Also Called: Schneider Electric Usa Inc (G-11064)*

Schneider Electric, West Chester *Also Called: Schneider Electric Usa Inc (G-14073)*

Schneider Electric Usa Inc....................................513 523-4171
5735 College Corner Pike Oxford (45056) *(G-11064)*

Schneider Electric Usa Inc....................................513 777-4445
9870 Crescent Park Dr West Chester (45069) *(G-14073)*

Schneller LLC (HQ)...330 673-1400
6019 Powdermill Rd Kent (44240) *(G-8073)*

Schnider Pallet LLC...440 632-5346
9782 Bundysburg Rd Middlefield (44062) *(G-9826)*

Schodorf Truck Body & Eqp Co..............................614 228-6793
885 Harmon Ave Columbus (43223) *(G-5253)*

School Pride Limited...614 568-0697
3511 Johnny Appleseed Ct Columbus (43231) *(G-5254)*

School Uniforms and More Inc................................216 365-1957
13721 Lorain Ave Cleveland (44111) *(G-4275)*

Schoolbelles, Cleveland *Also Called: Kip-Craft Incorporated (G-3924)*

Schoonover Industries Inc.....................................419 289-8332
1440 Simonton Rd Ashland (44805) *(G-572)*

Schott Metal Products Company.............................330 773-7873
2225 Lee Dr Akron (44306) *(G-307)*

Schrock John...937 544-8457
99 Fugate Rd Peebles (45660) *(G-11172)*

Schuck Mtal Fbrction Dsign Inc..............................419 586-1054
8319 Us 127 N Celina (45822) *(G-2119)*

Schuerholz Inc...937 294-5218
3540 Marshall Rd Dayton (45429) *(G-5997)*

Schulers Bakery Inc (PA).......................................937 323-4154
1911 S Limestone St Springfield (45505) *(G-12371)*

Schumann Enterprises Inc.....................................216 267-6850
12340 Plaza Dr Cleveland (44130) *(G-4276)*

Schurman Fine Papers...513 791-5554
7875 Montgomery Rd Spc 81 Cincinnati (45236) *(G-3068)*

Schutz Container Systems Inc................................419 872-2477
2105 S Wilkinson Way Perrysburg (43551) *(G-11261)*

Schwab Industries, Berea *Also Called: Medina Supply Company (G-1181)*

Schwab Industries Inc (HQ)...................................330 364-4411
2301 Progress St Dover (44622) *(G-6261)*

Schwab Machine Inc..419 626-0245
3120 Venice Rd Sandusky (44870) *(G-11871)*

Schwans Mama Rosass LLC (DH)...........................937 498-4511
1910 Fair Rd Sidney (45365) *(G-12049)*

Schwarz Partners Packaging LLC...........................740 387-3700
2135 Innovation Dr Marion (43302) *(G-8996)*

Schwarz Partners Packaging LLC...........................317 290-1140
2450 Campbell Rd Sidney (45365) *(G-12050)*

Schwebel Baking Co-Solon Bky, Solon *Also Called: Schwebel Baking Company (G-12179)*

Schwebel Baking Company....................................216 481-1880
345 E 200th St Euclid (44119) *(G-6678)*

Schwebel Baking Company....................................330 783-2860
121 O Neill Dr Hebron (43025) *(G-7635)*

Schwebel Baking Company....................................330 926-9410
7382 Whipple Ave Nw North Canton (44720) *(G-10667)*

Schwebel Baking Company....................................440 248-1500
6250 Camp Industrial Rd Solon (44139) *(G-12179)*

Schwebel Baking Company....................................440 846-1921
22626 Royalton Rd Strongsville (44149) *(G-12595)*

Schwebel Baking Company (PA).............................330 783-2860
965 E Midlothian Blvd Youngstown (44502) *(G-14928)*

Schwebel Baking Company....................................330 783-2860
920 E Midlothian Blvd Youngstown (44502) *(G-14929)*

Schwebel Bkg Co N Canton Agcy, North Canton *Also Called: Schwebel Baking Company (G-10667)*

Schweizer Dipple Inc...440 786-8090
7227 Division St Cleveland (44146) *(G-4277)*

SCI, Columbus *Also Called: SCI Engineered Materials Inc (G-5255)*

SCI Engineered Materials Inc.................................614 486-0261
2839 Charter St Columbus (43228) *(G-5255)*

Sciath Aim Forge Inc...574 933-3479
11560 Goldcoast Dr Cincinnati (45249) *(G-3069)*

Science/Electronics Inc...937 224-4444
521 Kiser St Dayton (45404) *(G-5998)*

Scientific Molding Corp Ltd....................................330 342-7800
2374 Edison Blvd Twinsburg (44087) *(G-13375)*

Scientific Plastics Ltd...305 557-3737
7154 State Route 88 Ravenna (44266) *(G-11540)*

Scioto Fleet Services LLC......................................614 749-2318
659 Marion Rd Columbus (43207) *(G-5256)*

Scioto Ready Mix LLC..740 924-9273
6214 Taylor Rd Sw Pataskala (43062) *(G-11150)*

Scioto Sand & Gravel, Prospect *Also Called: Fleming Construction Co (G-11501)*

Scioto Sign Co Inc...419 673-1261
6047 Us Highway 68 Kenton (43326) *(G-8115)*

Scorecards Unlimited LLC.....................................614 885-0796
1820 W Dublin Granville Rd Columbus (43085) *(G-5257)*

Scot Industries Inc..330 262-7585
6578 Ashland Rd Wooster (44691) *(G-14683)*

Scots...215 370-9498
3875 S Elyria Rd Shreve (44676) *(G-11987)*

Scott Bader Inc...330 920-4410
4280 Hudson Dr Stow (44224) *(G-12459)*

Scott Fetzer Company...216 267-9000
4801 W 150th St Cleveland (44135) *(G-4278)*

Scott Fetzer Company...216 252-1190
3881 W 150th St Cleveland (44111) *(G-4279)*

Scott Models Inc...513 771-8005
607 Redna Ter Ste 400 Cincinnati (45215) *(G-3070)*

Scott Molders Incorporated...................................330 673-5777
7180 State Route 43 Kent (44240) *(G-8074)*

Scott Process Systems Inc....................................330 877-2350
1160 Sunnyside St Sw Hartville (44632) *(G-7584)*

Scott Thomas Furniture, Twinsburg *Also Called: R A Hamed International Inc (G-13363)*

Scottcare Corporation (HQ)...................................216 362-0550
4791 W 150th St Cleveland (44135) *(G-4280)*

Scottcare Crdvscular Solutions, Cleveland *Also Called: Scottcare Corporation (G-4280)*

Scottdel Cushion Inc...419 825-0432
400 Church St Swanton (43558) *(G-12691)*

A
L
P
H
A
B
E
T
I
C

Scottrods LLC.................................... 419 499-2705
2512 Higbee Rd Monroeville (44847) *(G-10120)*

Scotts Company LLC................................ 937 454-2782
20 Innovation Ct Dayton (45414) *(G-5999)*

Scotts Company LLC (HQ).......................... 937 644-0011
14111 Co Hwy 105 Marysville (43040) *(G-9045)*

Scotts Miracle-Gro, Marysville *Also Called: Scotts Miracle-Gro Company (G-9046)*

Scotts Miracle-Gro Company (PA).................. 937 644-0011
14111 Scottslawn Rd Marysville (43041) *(G-9046)*

Scotts Miracle-Gro Company........................ 937 578-5065
14101 Industrial Pkwy Marysville (43040) *(G-9047)*

Scotts Miracle-Gro Company........................ 330 684-0421
1220 Schrock Rd Orrville (44667) *(G-11007)*

Scotts Miracle-Gro Products, Marysville *Also Called: Scotts Company LLC (G-9045)*

Scotts Temecula Operations LLC.................. 800 221-1760
14111 Scottslawn Rd Marysville (43040) *(G-9048)*

Scotts- Hyponex, Marysville *Also Called: Hyponex Corporation (G-9031)*

Scotts- Hyponex, Shreve *Also Called: Hyponex Corporation (G-11982)*

Scovil Hanna LLC................................... 216 581-1500
4545 Johnston Pkwy Cleveland (44128) *(G-4281)*

Scram Systems, Blue Ash *Also Called: Lmg Holdings Inc (G-1298)*

Scratch Off Works LLC............................ 440 333-4302
19537 Lake Rd Rocky River (44116) *(G-11639)*

Scratch-Off Systems Inc........................... 216 649-7800
2457 Edison Blvd Twinsburg (44087) *(G-13376)*

Screen Machine, Pataskala *Also Called: SMI Holdings Inc (G-11151)*

Screen Works Inc (PA)............................ 937 264-9111
3970 Image Dr Dayton (45414) *(G-6000)*

Screenplay Printing, Xenia *Also Called: Liming Printing Inc (G-14769)*

Scrip-Safe International, Loveland *Also Called: Scrip-Safe Security Products (G-8652)*

Scrip-Safe Security Products...................... 513 697-7789
136 Commerce Dr Loveland (45140) *(G-8652)*

Scriptel Corporation.............................. 877 848-6824
2222 Dividend Dr Columbus (43228) *(G-5258)*

Scriptype Publishing Inc.......................... 330 659-0303
4300 W Streetsboro Rd Richfield (44286) *(G-11599)*

Scs Construction Services Inc..................... 513 929-0260
2130 Western Ave Cincinnati (45214) *(G-3071)*

Scs Gearbox Inc.................................. 419 483-7278
739 W Main St Bellevue (44811) *(G-1130)*

Sdg Inc... 440 893-0771
10000 Cedar Ave Cleveland (44106) *(G-4282)*

Sdg News Group Inc............................... 419 929-3411
43 E Main St New London (44851) *(G-10416)*

Sdi Industries.................................... 513 561-4032
8561 New England Ct Cincinnati (45236) *(G-3072)*

Sdk Associates Inc............................... 330 745-3648
2044 Wadsworth Rd Unit B Norton (44203) *(G-10826)*

Sdmk LLC... 330 965-0970
7340 Market St Youngstown (44512) *(G-14930)*

Sdo Sports Ltd................................... 440 546-9998
10250 Brecksville Rd Cleveland (44141) *(G-4283)*

SDS Logistics Services, Boardman *Also Called: SDS National LLC (G-1376)*

SDS National LLC................................. 330 759-8066
143 Boardman Canfield Rd Pmb 333 Boardman (44512) *(G-1376)*

Seabiscuit Motorsports Inc (HQ).................. 440 951-6600
7201 Industrial Park Blvd Mentor (44060) *(G-9612)*

Seacor Painting Corporation...................... 330 755-6361
98 Creed Cir Campbell (44405) *(G-1770)*

Seaforth Mineral & Ore Co Inc (PA).............. 216 292-5820
3690 Orange Pl Ste 495 Beachwood (44122) *(G-948)*

Seagate Plastics, Waterville *Also Called: Seagate Plastics Company LLC (G-13842)*

Seagate Plastics Company LLC (PA)............... 419 878-5010
1110 Disher Dr Waterville (43566) *(G-13842)*

Seal Master Corporation.......................... 330 673-8410
340 Martinel Dr Kent (44240) *(G-8075)*

Seal Master Corporation (PA)..................... 330 673-8410
368 Martinel Dr Kent (44240) *(G-8076)*

Seal Tite, Hillsboro *Also Called: Seal Tite LLC (G-7725)*

Seal Tite LLC.................................... 937 393-4268
120 Moore Rd Hillsboro (45133) *(G-7725)*

Seal-Rite Door, Hebron *Also Called: S R Door Inc (G-7634)*

Sealco, Uhrichsville *Also Called: Sealco Inc (G-13405)*

Sealco Inc.. 740 922-4122
6566 Superior Rd Se Uhrichsville (44683) *(G-13405)*

Sealmaster, Kent *Also Called: Seal Master Corporation (G-8075)*

Sealmaster, Kent *Also Called: Seal Master Corporation (G-8076)*

Sealmaster, Sandusky *Also Called: Thorworks Industries Inc (G-11876)*

Sealock, Bowling Green *Also Called: Novavision LLC (G-1430)*

Sealtron Inc...................................... 513 733-8400
9705 Reading Rd Cincinnati (45215) *(G-3073)*

Sealy Mattress Mfg Co LLC........................ 800 697-3259
1070 Lake Rd Medina (44256) *(G-9445)*

Seaman Corporation (PA).......................... 330 262-1111
1000 Venture Blvd Wooster (44691) *(G-14684)*

Seapine Software Inc (HQ)........................ 513 754-1655
6960 Cintas Blvd Mason (45040) *(G-9149)*

Seaport Mold & Casting Company.................. 419 243-1422
1309 W Bancroft St Toledo (43606) *(G-13123)*

Seaside Retailer, Medina *Also Called: Breakwall Publishing LLC (G-9385)*

Seaway, Columbia Station *Also Called: Seaway Bolt And Specials Company (G-4602)*

Seaway Bolt And Specials Company................ 440 236-5015
11561 Station Rd Columbia Station (44028) *(G-4602)*

Seaway Enterprises, Toledo *Also Called: Initial Designs Inc (G-13004)*

Seaway Pattern Mfg Inc........................... 419 865-5724
5749 Angola Rd Toledo (43615) *(G-13124)*

Seawin Inc.. 419 355-9111
728 Graham Dr Fremont (43420) *(G-7132)*

Sebring Fluid Power Corp.......................... 330 938-9984
513 N Johnson Rd Sebring (44672) *(G-11902)*

Seco Machine Inc.................................. 330 499-2150
5335 Mayfair Rd North Canton (44720) *(G-10668)*

Secondary Machining Svcs Inc..................... 440 593-3040
539 Center Rd Conneaut (44030) *(G-5416)*

Securastock LLC.................................. 844 732-8727
11470 Euclid Ave Cleveland (44106) *(G-4284)*

Securcom, Minster *Also Called: Securcom Inc (G-10065)*

Securcom Inc...................................... 419 628-1049
307 W 1st St Minster (45865) *(G-10065)*

Secure Pak, Perrysburg *Also Called: Glassline Corporation (G-11225)*

Security Designs, Cleveland *Also Called: Technlogy Install Partners LLC (G-4371)*

Security Fence Group Inc (PA).................... 513 681-3700
4260 Dane Ave Cincinnati (45223) *(G-3074)*

Sedona Office, Chagrin Falls *Also Called: Fmx 2018 Inc (G-2144)*

See Ya There Inc................................. 614 856-9037
12710 W Bank Dr Ne Millersport (43046) *(G-10025)*

See Ya There Vacation and Trvl, Millersport *Also Called: See Ya There Inc (G-10025)*

Seekirk Inc....................................... 614 278-9200
2420 Scioto Harper Dr Columbus (43204) *(G-5259)*

Seemless Printing LLC............................ 513 871-2366
717 Linn St Cincinnati (45203) *(G-3075)*

Seemray LLC...................................... 440 536-8705
261 Alpha Park Cleveland (44143) *(G-4285)*

Seepex Inc.. 937 864-7150
511 Speedway Dr Enon (45323) *(G-6633)*

Segna Inc... 937 335-6700
1316 Barnhart Rd Ste 1316 Troy (45373) *(G-13253)*

Seilkop Industries Inc............................ 513 679-5680
7211 Market Pl Cincinnati (45216) *(G-3076)*

Seilkop Industries Inc (PA)....................... 513 761-1035
425 W North Bend Rd Cincinnati (45216) *(G-3077)*

Seilkop Industries Inc............................ 513 353-3090
5927 State Route 128 Miamitown (45041) *(G-9760)*

Seislove Brial Vlts Sptic Tnks, Tiffin *Also Called: Seislove Vault & Septic Tanks (G-12798)*

Seislove Vault & Septic Tanks.................... 419 447-5473
2168 S State Route 100 Tiffin (44883) *(G-12798)*

Sekuworks LLC.................................... 513 202-1210
9487 Dry Fork Rd Harrison (45030) *(G-7566)*

Selas Heat Technology Co LLC (HQ)............... 800 523-6500
11012 Aurora Hudson Rd Streetsboro (44241) *(G-12523)*

Selby Service/Roxy Press Inc..................... 513 241-3445
2020 Elm St Cincinnati (45202) *(G-3078)*

Selco Industries Inc.. 419 861-0336
1590 Albon Rd Ste 1 Holland (43528) *(G-7784)*

Select Industries Corporation............................... 937 233-9191
60 Heid Ave Dayton (45404) *(G-6001)*

Select Machine Inc.. 330 678-7676
4125 Karg Industrial Pkwy Kent (44240) *(G-8077)*

Select Mattress Co Inc... 419 244-3645
8125 Kevin Ln Sylvania (43560) *(G-12722)*

Select Seating, Columbus *Also Called: N Wasserstrom & Sons Inc (G-5119)*

Select Signs.. 937 262-7095
1755 Spaulding Rd Dayton (45432) *(G-5623)*

Select Tool & Production, Toledo *Also Called: Hedges Selective Tl & Prod Inc (G-12991)*

Select-Arc Inc (PA)...937 295-5215
600 Enterprise Dr Fort Loramie (45845) *(G-6955)*

Selecteon Corporation.. 614 710-1132
2041 Arlingate Ln Columbus (43228) *(G-5260)*

Self Made Holdings LLC.. 330 477-1052
5325 Southway St Sw Canton (44706) *(G-2001)*

Self-Srvice PDT Dist Shipg Ctr, Hebron *Also Called: Diebold Nixdorf Incorporated (G-7613)*

Selling Precision, Stow *Also Called: Hydraulic Manifolds USA LLC (G-12436)*

Selling Precision Inc.. 973 728-1214
4540 Boyce Pkwy Stow (44224) *(G-12460)*

Selmco Metal Fabricators Inc................................. 937 498-1331
1615 Ferguson Ct Sidney (45365) *(G-12051)*

Sem-Com Company Inc (PA)................................. 419 537-8813
1040 N Westwood Ave Toledo (43607) *(G-13125)*

Semco Inc... 800 848-5764
1025 Pole Lane Rd Marion (43302) *(G-8997)*

Semco Carbon, Lorain *Also Called: Sentinel Management Inc (G-8580)*

Semco Ceramics, Uhrichsville *Also Called: Stebbins Engineering & Mfg Co (G-13407)*

Semper Quality Industry Inc.................................. 440 352-8111
9411 Mercantile Dr Mentor (44060) *(G-9613)*

Semtorq Inc.. 330 487-0600
1780 Enterprise Pkwy Twinsburg (44087) *(G-13377)*

Senator International Inc (HQ)...............................419 887-5806
4111 N Jerome Rd Maumee (43537) *(G-9316)*

Seneca, Bellevue *Also Called: Seneca Railroad & Mining Co (G-1131)*

Seneca Enterprises Inc... 814 432-7890
4053 Clough Woods Dr Batavia (45103) *(G-888)*

Seneca Environmental Products Inc........................ 419 447-1282
1685 S County Road 1 Tiffin (44883) *(G-12799)*

Seneca Label Inc... 440 237-1600
1120 W 130th St Brunswick (44212) *(G-1615)*

Seneca Millwork Inc.. 419 435-6671
300 Court Pl Fostoria (44830) *(G-7001)*

Seneca Petroleum Co Inc..................................... 419 691-3581
1441 Woodville Rd Toledo (43606) *(G-13126)*

Seneca Petroleum Co Inc..................................... 419 691-3581
2563 Front St Toledo (43605) *(G-13127)*

Seneca Processing Facility, Summerfield *Also Called: Markwest Energy Partners LP (G-12660)*

Seneca Railroad & Mining Co................................ 419 483-7764
1075 W Main St Bellevue (44811) *(G-1131)*

Seneca Sheet Metal Company................................ 419 447-8434
277 Water St Tiffin (44883) *(G-12800)*

Seneca Wire & Manufacturing Co Inc (HQ).............. 419 435-9261
319 S Vine St Fostoria (44830) *(G-7002)*

Seneca Wires, Fostoria *Also Called: Seneca Wire & Manufacturing Co Inc (G-7002)*

Senior Impact Publications LLC............................. 513 791-8800
5980 Kugler Mill Rd Cincinnati (45236) *(G-3079)*

Senior Times, Columbus *Also Called: O J C Publishing Co Inc (G-5136)*

Senneca Holdings Inc (HQ)...................................800 543-4455
10021 Commerce Park Dr Cincinnati (45246) *(G-3080)*

Sense Diagnostics Inc.. 513 702-0376
1776 Mentor Ave Ste 426 Cincinnati (45212) *(G-3081)*

Sensible Products Inc... 330 659-4212
3857 Brecksville Rd Richfield (44286) *(G-11600)*

Sensical Inc.. 216 641-1141
31115 Aurora Rd Solon (44139) *(G-12180)*

Sensience, Westerville *Also Called: Therm-O-Disc Incorporated (G-14236)*

Sensor Technology Systems, Miamisburg *Also Called: Steiner Eoptics Inc (G-9740)*

Sensorwerks, Hilliard *Also Called: Sensotec LLC (G-7701)*

Sensory Robotics Inc... 513 545-9501
9711 Winton Hills Ln Cincinnati (45215) *(G-3082)*

Sensoryffcts Powdr Systems Inc............................ 419 783-5518
136 Fox Run Dr Defiance (43512) *(G-6123)*

Sensotec LLC.. 614 481-8616
3450 Cemetery Rd Hilliard (43026) *(G-7701)*

Sensus LLC... 513 892-7100
2991 Hamilton Mason Rd Hamilton (45011) *(G-7524)*

Sentek Corporation.. 614 586-1123
1300 Memory Ln N Columbus (43209) *(G-5261)*

Sentient Studios Ltd.. 330 204-8636
2894 Chamberlain Rd Apt 6 Fairlawn (44333) *(G-6811)*

Sentinel Management Inc...................................... 440 821-7372
3000 Leavitt Rd Unit 1 Lorain (44052) *(G-8580)*

Sentrilock LLC... 513 618-5800
7701 Service Center Dr West Chester (45069) *(G-14074)*

Sentro Tech Corporation....................................... 440 260-0364
21294 Drake Rd Strongsville (44149) *(G-12596)*

Sentronic, Brunswick *Also Called: Controlled Access Inc (G-1586)*

Sentry Products, Canton *Also Called: Canton Sterilized Wiping Cloth (G-1860)*

Seppi M SPA... 513 443-6339
8880 Beckett Rd West Chester (45011) *(G-14075)*

Septic Products Inc... 419 282-5933
1378 Township Road 743 Ashland (44805) *(G-573)*

Sequa Can Machinery Inc..................................... 330 493-0444
4150 Belden Village St Nw Ste 504 Canton (44718) *(G-2002)*

Serappers Gallery, Newark *Also Called: M & R Phillips Enterprises (G-10518)*

Sermonix Pharmaceuticals Inc............................... 614 864-4919
250 E Broad St Ste 250 Columbus (43215) *(G-5262)*

Sertek LLC.. 614 504-5828
6399 Shier Rings Rd Dublin (43016) *(G-6344)*

Servatii Inc... 513 271-5040
3774 Paxton Ave Cincinnati (45209) *(G-3083)*

Service Express LLC.. 513 942-6170
10004 International Blvd West Chester (45246) *(G-14143)*

Service Spring Corp... 419 867-0212
6615 Maumee Western Rd Maumee (43537) *(G-9317)*

Service Spring Corp (PA)...................................... 419 838-6081
1703 Toll Gate Dr Maumee (43537) *(G-9318)*

Service Stampings Inc.. 440 946-2330
4700 Hamann Pkwy Willoughby (44094) *(G-14522)*

Service Station Equipment Co (PA)........................ 216 431-6100
1294 E 55th St Cleveland (44103) *(G-4286)*

Services Acquisition Co LLC.................................. 330 479-9267
4412 Pleasant Valley Rd Se Dennison (44621) *(G-6218)*

Serving Veterans Mobility Inc................................ 937 746-4788
303 Conover Dr Franklin (45005) *(G-7048)*

Sesh Communications... 513 851-1693
3440 Burnet Ave Ste 130 Cincinnati (45229) *(G-3084)*

Sest Inc... 440 777-9777
24509 Annie Ln Westlake (44145) *(G-14332)*

Setco Industries Inc.. 513 941-5110
5880 Hillside Ave Cincinnati (45233) *(G-3085)*

Setex Inc.. 419 394-7800
1111 Mckinley Rd Saint Marys (45885) *(G-11752)*

Seth Enterprises, Zanesville *Also Called: Buckeye Energy Resources Inc (G-15001)*

Seven Lakeway Refractories LLC........................... 419 433-3030
730 River Rd Huron (44839) *(G-7882)*

Seven Ranges Mfg Corp.. 330 627-7155
330 Industrial Dr Sw Carrollton (44615) *(G-2090)*

Seventh Son Brewing, Columbus *Also Called: Green Room Brewing LLC (G-4966)*

Severn River Publishing LLC................................. 703 819-4686
Kings Mills (45034) *(G-8137)*

Seville Bronze, Seville *Also Called: Jj Seville LLC (G-11919)*

Seville Sand & Gravel Inc..................................... 330 948-0168
12663 Bristol Ln Strongsville (44149) *(G-12597)*

Sew & Sew Embroidery Inc................................... 330 676-1600
881 Tallmadge Rd Ste C Kent (44240) *(G-8078)*

Sew It Seams, Woodsfield *Also Called: J C L S Enterprises LLC (G-14613)*

ALPHABETIC

Sew-Eurodrive Inc.. 937 335-0036
2001 W Main St Troy (45373) *(G-13254)*

Sewah Studios Inc.. 740 373-2087
190 Mill Creek Rd Marietta (45750) *(G-8943)*

Sewer Rodding Equipment Co.............................. 419 991-2065
3434 S Dixie Hwy Lima (45804) *(G-8447)*

Sexton Industrial Inc... 513 530-5555
366 Circle Freeway Dr West Chester (45246) *(G-14144)*

Seyekcub Inc.. 330 324-1394
615 W 4th St Uhrichsville (44683) *(G-13406)*

Sfc Graphic Arts Div, Toledo *Also Called: Sfc Graphics Cleveland Ltd (G-13128)*

Sfc Graphics Cleveland Ltd.................................. 419 255-1283
110 E Woodruff Ave Toledo (43604) *(G-13128)*

SFM Corp... 440 951-5500
4530 Hamann Pkwy Willoughby (44094) *(G-14523)*

Sfs Group Usa Inc... 330 239-7100
5201 Portside Dr Medina (44256) *(G-9446)*

Sfs Intec, Medina *Also Called: Sfs Group Usa Inc (G-9446)*

Sfs Intec Inc.. 330 239-7100
5201 Portside Dr Medina (44256) *(G-9447)*

Sfs Truck Sales & Parts, Gallipolis *Also Called: King Kutter II Inc (G-7207)*

SGB Usa Inc (DH).. 330 472-1187
180 South Ave Tallmadge (44278) *(G-12749)*

Sgi Matrix LLC (PA)... 937 438-9033
1041 Byers Rd Miamisburg (45342) *(G-9736)*

Sgl, Warren *Also Called: Stadium Grow Lighting Inc (G-13798)*

Sgl Carbon Technic LLC....................................... 440 572-3600
21945 Drake Rd Strongsville (44149) *(G-12598)*

Sgm Co Inc... 440 255-1190
9000 Tyler Blvd Mentor (44060) *(G-9614)*

SGS Cincinnati, Cincinnati *Also Called: Stevenson Color Inc (G-3119)*

SH Bell Company.. 412 963-9910
2217 Michigan Ave East Liverpool (43920) *(G-6396)*

Shadow Holdings LLC (HQ).................................. 614 741-7458
9200 Smiths Mill Rd N New Albany (43054) *(G-10350)*

Shafer Valve Company, Ontario *Also Called: Emerson Process Management (G-10949)*

Shaffer Metal Fab Inc... 937 492-1384
2031 Commerce Dr Sidney (45365) *(G-12052)*

Shafts Mfg.. 440 942-6012
1585 E 361st St Unit G1 Willoughby (44095) *(G-14524)*

Shaheen Oriental Rug Co Inc (PA)....................... 330 493-9000
4120 Whipple Ave Nw Canton (44718) *(G-2003)*

Shaker Numeric Mfg, Euclid *Also Called: Tech-Med Inc (G-6679)*

Shaker Workshops, Blue Ash *Also Called: Tappan Chairs LLC (G-1340)*

Shalix Inc... 216 941-3546
10910 Briggs Rd Cleveland (44111) *(G-4287)*

Shalmet Corporation... 440 236-8840
164 Freedom Ct Elyria (44035) *(G-6589)*

Shamrock Acquisition Company, Westlake *Also Called: Shamrock Companies Inc (G-14333)*

Shamrock Companies Inc (PA)............................. 440 899-9510
24090 Detroit Rd Westlake (44145) *(G-14333)*

Shamrock Materials Inc.. 513 988-0647
11641 Mosteller Rd Cincinnati (45241) *(G-3086)*

Shamrock Molded Products, Holland *Also Called: Doyle Manufacturing Inc (G-7756)*

Shanafelt Manufacturing Co (PA)......................... 330 455-0315
2633 Winfield Way Ne Canton (44705) *(G-2004)*

Shape Supply Inc.. 513 863-6695
700 S Erie Hwy Hamilton (45011) *(G-7525)*

Shaq Inc... 770 427-0402
22901 Millcreek Blvd Ste 650 Beachwood (44122) *(G-949)*

Sharon Manufacturing Inc.................................... 330 239-1561
6867 Ridge Rd Sharon Center (44274) *(G-11942)*

Sharon Stone Inc... 740 732-7100
44895 Sharon Stone Rd Caldwell (43724) *(G-1728)*

Sharonco Inc.. 419 882-3443
5651 Main St Sylvania (43560) *(G-12723)*

Sharp Enterprises Inc... 937 295-2965
400 Enterprise Dr Fort Loramie (45845) *(G-6956)*

Sharp Tool Service Inc.. 330 273-4114
4735 W 150th St Unit H Cleveland (44135) *(G-4288)*

Shasta Beverages Inc... 614 491-5415
4685 Groveport Rd Obetz (43207) *(G-10926)*

Shasta Beverges, Obetz *Also Called: National Beverage Corp (G-10925)*

Shaw Industries Inc.. 513 942-3692
8580 Seward Rd Ste 400 Fairfield (45011) *(G-6775)*

Shaw Stainless, Beachwood *Also Called: Shaq Inc (G-949)*

Shawadi LLC... 614 839-0698
20 S State St Ste B Westerville (43081) *(G-14275)*

Shawn Fleming Ind Trckg LLC.............................. 937 707-8539
4982 Aquilla Dr Dayton (45415) *(G-6002)*

Shawne Springs Winery.. 740 623-0744
20093 County Road 6 Coshocton (43812) *(G-5472)*

Shawnee Molds, Eaton *Also Called: Camden Concrete Products LLC (G-6451)*

Shawnee Systems Inc.. 513 561-9932
4221 Brandonmore Dr Cincinnati (45255) *(G-3087)*

Shear Service Inc.. 216 341-2700
3175 E 81st St Cleveland (44104) *(G-4289)*

Shear Service, The, Cleveland *Also Called: Shear Service Inc (G-4289)*

Shearer Farm Inc... 330 345-9023
7762 Cleveland Rd Wooster (44691) *(G-14685)*

Shearer's Snacks, Brewster *Also Called: Shearers Foods LLC (G-1493)*

Shearer's Snacks, Massillon *Also Called: Shearers Foods LLC (G-9241)*

Shearers Foods LLC... 330 767-3426
692 Wabash Ave N Brewster (44613) *(G-1493)*

Shearers Foods LLC (HQ).................................... 800 428-6843
100 Lincoln Way E Massillon (44646) *(G-9241)*

Shearers Foods LLC... 330 767-7969
4100 Millennium Blvd Se Massillon (44646) *(G-9242)*

Sheet Metal Fabricator, Tiffin *Also Called: Seneca Sheet Metal Company (G-12800)*

Sheet Metal Products Co Inc................................ 440 392-9000
5950 Pinecone Dr Mentor (44060) *(G-9615)*

Sheetmetal Crafters Inc.. 330 452-6700
325 5th St Se Canton (44702) *(G-2005)*

Sheffield Bronze Paint Corp................................. 216 481-8330
17814 S Waterloo Rd Cleveland (44119) *(G-4290)*

Sheffield Metals Cleveland LLC (PA)................... 800 283-5262
5467 Evergreen Pkwy Sheffield Village (44054) *(G-11964)*

Sheffield Metals International, Sheffield Village *Also Called: Sheffield Metals Cleveland LLC (G-11964)*

Sheffield Metals Intl Inc.. 440 934-8500
5467 Evergreen Pkwy Sheffield Village (44054) *(G-11965)*

Sheffield Oldcastle, Sheffield Village *Also Called: Oldcastle Apg Midwest Inc (G-11961)*

Sheiban Jewelry Inc.. 440 238-0616
16938 Pearl Rd Strongsville (44136) *(G-12599)*

Shelar Inc... 419 729-9756
5335 Enterprise Blvd Toledo (43612) *(G-13129)*

Shelby Company... 440 871-9901
865 Canterbury Rd Westlake (44145) *(G-14334)*

Shelby County Review, Wapakoneta *Also Called: Horizon Ohio Publications Inc (G-13715)*

Shelby Welded Tube Div, Shelby *Also Called: Phillips Mfg and Tower Co (G-11972)*

Shelfgenie, Medina *Also Called: Dje Management Consulting LLC (G-9397)*

Shelley Company, Maumee *Also Called: Stoneco Inc (G-9321)*

Shelly & Sands Zanesville OH, Perrysville *Also Called: S & S Aggregates Inc (G-11283)*

Shelly and Sands Inc.. 740 859-2104
1731 Old State Route 7 Rayland (43943) *(G-11552)*

Shelly and Sands Inc (PA).................................... 740 453-0721
3570 S River Rd Zanesville (43701) *(G-15047)*

Shelly Company... 216 688-0684
4431 W 130th St Cleveland (44135) *(G-4291)*

Shelly Company, The, Thornville *Also Called: Shelly Materials Inc (G-12770)*

Shelly Liquid Division, Toledo *Also Called: Shelly Materials Inc (G-13130)*

Shelly Materials Inc.. 740 775-4567
1177 Hopetown Rd Chillicothe (45601) *(G-2281)*

Shelly Materials Inc.. 419 622-2101
2364 Richey Rd Convoy (45832) *(G-5425)*

Shelly Materials Inc.. 614 871-6704
3300 Jackson Pike Grove City (43123) *(G-7413)*

Shelly Materials Inc.. 330 723-3681
820 W Smith Rd Medina (44256) *(G-9448)*

Shelly Materials Inc.. 740 666-5841
8328 Watkins Rd Ostrander (43061) *(G-11029)*

(G-0000) Company's Geographic Section entry number

Shelly Materials Inc.. 740 247-2311
49947 State Route 338 Racine (45771) *(G-11506)*

Shelly Materials Inc.. 937 325-7386
4301 S Charleston Pike Springfield (45502) *(G-12372)*

Shelly Materials Inc.. 740 246-5009
8775 Blackbird Ln Thornville (43076) *(G-12769)*

Shelly Materials Inc.. 740 246-6315
352 George Hardy Dr Toledo (43605) *(G-13130)*

Shelly Materials Inc.. 330 963-5180
1749 Highland Rd Twinsburg (44087) *(G-13378)*

Shelly Materials Inc.. 937 358-2224
20620 Spangler Rd West Mansfield (43358) *(G-14181)*

Shelly Materials Inc.. 419 273-2510
3798 State Route 53 Forest (45843) *(G-6941)*

Shelly Materials Inc (DH)... 740 246-6315
80 Park Dr Thornville (43076) *(G-12770)*

Shelter Studios, Blue Ash *Also Called: Organized Lightning LLC (G-1315)*

Shelves West LLC.. 928 692-1449
510 S Main St Findlay (45840) *(G-6917)*

Shepherd Material Science Co (PA)............................ 513 731-1110
4900 Beech St Norwood (45212) *(G-10871)*

Shepherd Widnes Ltd.. 513 731-1110
4900 Beech St Norwood (45212) *(G-10872)*

Sher International, Middletown *Also Called: Sher International Inc (G-9893)*

Sher International Inc... 800 895-9581
2608 Oxford State Rd Middletown (45044) *(G-9893)*

Sherbrooke Corporation.. 440 942-3520
36490 Reading Ave Willoughby (44094) *(G-14525)*

Sherbrooke Metals... 440 542-3066
37552 N Industrial Pkwy Willoughby (44094) *(G-14526)*

Sheridan Mfg, Wauseon *Also Called: Lear Corporation (G-13855)*

Sheridan One Stop Carryout Inc.................................. 740 687-1300
1510 Sheridan Dr Lancaster (43130) *(G-8223)*

Sheridan Woodworks Inc... 216 663-9333
17801 S Miles Rd Cleveland (44128) *(G-4292)*

Sherwin-Williams, Cleveland *Also Called: Sherwin-Williams Company (G-4293)*

Sherwin-Williams, Hudson *Also Called: Sherwin-Williams Company (G-7856)*

Sherwin-Williams, Strongsville *Also Called: Sherwin-Williams Company (G-12600)*

Sherwin-Williams Company (PA)................................ 216 566-2000
101 W Prospect Ave Ste 1020 Cleveland (44115) *(G-4293)*

Sherwin-Williams Company.. 330 528-0124
5860 Darrow Rd Hudson (44236) *(G-7856)*

Sherwin-Williams Company.. 330 830-6000
600 Nova Dr Se Massillon (44646) *(G-9243)*

Sherwin-Williams Company.. 440 846-4328
11410 Alameda Dr Strongsville (44149) *(G-12600)*

Sherwin Williams Mfg Co... 216 566-2000
101 W Prospect Ave Ste 1020 Cleveland (44115) *(G-4294)*

Sherwn-Wlams Auto Fnshes Corp (HQ)....................... 216 332-8330
4440 Warrensville Center Rd Cleveland (44128) *(G-4295)*

Sherwood Refractores, Cleveland *Also Called: PCC Airfoils LLC (G-4148)*

Sherwood Rtm Corp.. 330 875-7151
4043 Beck Ave Louisville (44641) *(G-8616)*

Sherwood Valve LLC... 216 264-5023
7900 Hub Pkwy Cleveland (44125) *(G-4296)*

Shi Shi Events... 440 623-3822
26758 Russell Rd Bay Village (44140) *(G-903)*

Shield Laminating, Hilliard *Also Called: The Guardtower Inc (G-7707)*

Shiffler Equipment Sales Inc (PA).............................. 440 285-9175
745 South St Chardon (44024) *(G-2222)*

Shilling Transport Inc.. 330 948-1105
9718 Avon Lake Rd Lodi (44254) *(G-8506)*

Shiloh Inds Inc Mdina Blnking, Valley City *Also Called: Shl Liquidation Medina Inc (G-13519)*

Shiloh Inds Wellington Mfg Div, Wellington *Also Called: Shl Liquidation Industries Inc (G-13901)*

Shiloh Industries, Valley City *Also Called: Grouper Acquisition Co LLC (G-13498)*

Shiloh Industries, Valley City *Also Called: Shl Liquidation Industries Inc (G-13517)*

Shiloh Industries, Wellington *Also Called: Grouper Acquisition Co LLC (G-13892)*

Shiloh Industries Inc... 937 236-5100
5988 Executive Blvd Ste B Dayton (45424) *(G-6003)*

Shiloh Industries Inc... 330 558-2000
5569 Innovation Dr Valley City (44280) *(G-13516)*

Shim Shack... 877 557-3930
105 May Dr Harrison (45030) *(G-7567)*

Shin-Etsu Silicones Amer Inc.................................... 330 630-9860
963 Evans Ave Akron (44305) *(G-308)*

Shin-Etsu Silicones of America Inc (HQ)...................... 330 630-9460
1150 Damar Dr Akron (44305) *(G-309)*

Shinagawa, Mogadore *Also Called: Shinagawa Inc (G-10086)*

Shinagawa Inc.. 330 628-1118
3555 Gilchrist Rd Mogadore (44260) *(G-10086)*

Shincor Silicones Inc... 330 630-9460
1030 Evans Ave Akron (44305) *(G-310)*

Shirley KS LLC... 740 331-7934
1150 Newark Rd Zanesville (43701) *(G-15048)*

Shirley KS Storage Trays LLC.................................... 740 868-8140
1150 Newark Rd Zanesville (43701) *(G-15049)*

Shl Liquidation Industries Inc (PA)............................ 330 558-2600
880 Steel Dr Valley City (44280) *(G-13517)*

Shl Liquidation Industries Inc................................... 440 647-2100
350 Maple St Wellington (44090) *(G-13901)*

Shl Liquidation Liverpool Inc.................................... 330 558-2600
880 Steel Dr Valley City (44280) *(G-13518)*

Shl Liquidation Medina Inc (PA)   5580 Wegman Dr Valley City (44280) *(G-13519)*

Shl Liquidation Mfg LLC (HQ)..................................... 330 558-2600
880 Steel Dr Valley City (44280) *(G-13520)*

Shoals Tubular, Mason *Also Called: Shoals Tubular Inc (G-9150)*

Shoals Tubular Inc.. 256 767-7171
4501 Quality Pl Mason (45040) *(G-9150)*

Shoemaker Electric Company..................................... 614 294-5626
831 Bonham Ave Columbus (43211) *(G-5263)*

Shoemaker Industrial Solutions, Columbus *Also Called: Shoemaker Electric Company (G-5263)*

Shook Manufactured Pdts Inc (PA).............................. 330 848-9780
1017 Kenmore Blvd Akron (44314) *(G-311)*

Shook Manufactured Pdts Inc..................................... 440 247-9130
3801 Wiltshire Rd Chagrin Falls (44022) *(G-2151)*

Shoot-A-Way Inc... 419 294-4654
7157 County Highway 134 Nevada (44849) *(G-10323)*

Shops By Todd Inc (PA).. 937 458-3192
2727 Fairfield Commons Blvd Spc W273 Beavercreek (45431) *(G-982)*

Shore To Shore Inc (DH)... 937 866-1908
8170 Washington Village Dr Dayton (45458) *(G-6004)*

Shoreline Machine Products Co (PA)........................... 216 481-8033
19301 Saint Clair Ave Cleveland (44117) *(G-4297)*

Shorr Packaging, Cincinnati *Also Called: Hanchett Paper Company (G-2703)*

Short Run Machine Products Inc.................................. 440 969-1313
4744 Kister Ct Ashtabula (44004) *(G-616)*

Shousha Trucking LLC.. 937 270-4471
3695 Barbarosa Dr Dayton (45416) *(G-6005)*

Shout Out Loud Prints... 614 432-8990
809 Phillipi Rd Columbus (43228) *(G-5264)*

Show What You Know, Dayton *Also Called: Lorenz Corporation (G-5855)*

Shrader Tire & Oil Inc.. 419 420-8435
3511 Genoa Rd Perrysburg (43551) *(G-11262)*

Shrader Tire Oil Fleet Tire S, Perrysburg *Also Called: Shrader Tire & Oil Inc (G-11262)*

Shreiner Sole Company Inc.. 330 276-6135
1 Taylor Dr Killbuck (44637) *(G-8133)*

Shrock Engineering, Loudonville *Also Called: Shrock Prefab LLC (G-8594)*

Shrock Prefab LLC... 419 994-1900
614 N Spring St Loudonville (44842) *(G-8594)*

Shuler Pewter, Chagrin Falls *Also Called: EL Ostendorf Inc (G-2143)*

Shur-Fit Distributors Inc.. 937 746-0567
221 N Main St Franklin (45005) *(G-7049)*

Shur-Form Laminates Division, Franklin *Also Called: Shur-Fit Distributors Inc (G-7049)*

Sibg, Cleveland *Also Called: Snyder Intl Brewing Group LLC (G-4310)*

Sid-Mar Foods Inc... 330 743-0112
1481 South Ave Ste 182 Youngstown (44502) *(G-14931)*

Sidari's Italian Foods, Cleveland *Also Called: Gsi of Ohio LLC (G-3799)*

Sidley Truck & Equipment, Thompson *Also Called: R W Sidley Incorporated (G-12762)*

A
L
P
H
A
B
E
T
I
C

Sidney Manufacturing Company.................................. 937 492-4154
  405 N Main Ave Sidney (45365) *(G-12053)*

Sidney Plant, Sidney *Also Called: Advanced Composites Inc (G-11990)*

Sidwell Materials Inc... 740 849-2422
  4200 Maysville Pike Zanesville (43701) *(G-15050)*

Sidwell Materials Inc... 740 968-4313
  72607 Gun Club Rd Saint Clairsville (43950) *(G-11710)*

Sieb & Meyer America Inc... 513 563-0860
  4884 Duff Dr Ste D West Chester (45246) *(G-14145)*

Sieb & Meyer America USA, West Chester *Also Called: Sieb & Meyer America Inc (G-14145)*

Siebtechnik Tema Inc... 513 489-7811
  7806 Redsky Dr Cincinnati (45249) *(G-3088)*

Siefker Sawmill LLC.. 419 339-8523
  8705 W State Rd Lima (45807) *(G-8448)*

Siemens AG.. 513 576-2451
  6693 Summer Field Dr Mason (45040) *(G-9151)*

Siemens Energy Inc.. 740 504-1947
  105 N Sandusky St Mount Vernon (43050) *(G-10265)*

Siemens Industry Inc.. 937 593-6010
  811 N Main St Bellefontaine (43311) *(G-1116)*

Siemens Industry Inc.. 513 576-2088
  2000 Eastman Dr Milford (45150) *(G-9952)*

Siemens Industry Inc.. 513 841-3100
  4620 Forest Ave Norwood (45212) *(G-10873)*

Siemens Power and Gas, Mount Vernon *Also Called: Siemens Energy Inc (G-10265)*

Siemer Distributing, New Lexington *Also Called: Lori Holding Co (G-10403)*

Sierra Nevada Corporation.. 937 431-2800
  2611 Commons Blvd Beavercreek (45431) *(G-983)*

SIERRA NEVADA CORPORATION, Beavercreek *Also Called: Sierra Nevada Corporation (G-983)*

Sifco, Cleveland *Also Called: Sifco Industries Inc (G-4299)*

Sifco Applied Srfc Cncepts LLC (PA)............................ 216 524-0099
  5708 E Schaaf Rd Cleveland (44131) *(G-4298)*

Sifco ASC, Cleveland *Also Called: Sifco Applied Srfc Cncepts LLC (G-4298)*

Sifco Industries Inc (PA).. 216 881-8600
  970 E 64th St Cleveland (44103) *(G-4299)*

Sightgain, Mason *Also Called: Sightgain Inc (G-9152)*

Sightgain Inc.. 202 494-9317
  5325 Deerfield Blvd Mason (45040) *(G-9152)*

Sigma Div, Newburgh Heights *Also Called: Howmet Aluminum Casting Inc (G-10544)*

Sigma T E K, Cincinnati *Also Called: Sigmatek Systems LLC (G-3089)*

Sigma Tube Company.. 419 729-9756
  1050 Progress Ave Toledo (43612) *(G-13131)*

Sigma-Aldrich, Miamisburg *Also Called: Aldrich Chemical (G-9663)*

Sigma-Aldrich Corporation.. 216 206-5424
  4353 E 49th St Cleveland (44125) *(G-4300)*

Sigmatek Systems LLC (HQ)..................................... 513 674-0005
  1445 Kemper Meadow Dr Cincinnati (45240) *(G-3089)*

Sign America Incorporated.. 740 765-5555
  3887 State Route 43 Richmond (43944) *(G-11605)*

Sign Connection Inc.. 937 435-4070
  90 Compark Rd Ste B Dayton (45459) *(G-6006)*

Sign Design, Wooster *Also Called: Sign Design Wooster Inc (G-14686)*

Sign Design Wooster Inc... 330 262-8838
  1537 W Old Lincoln Way Wooster (44691) *(G-14686)*

Sign Gypsies, Bedford Heights *Also Called: Sign Gypsies Cleveland LLC (G-1081)*

Sign Gypsies Cleveland LLC....................................... 216 202-2093
  5940 Lehman Dr Bedford Heights (44146) *(G-1081)*

Sign Source USA Inc... 419 224-1130
  1700 S Dixie Hwy Lima (45804) *(G-8449)*

Sign Technologies LLC... 937 439-3970
  2001 Kuntz Rd Dayton (45404) *(G-6007)*

Sign-A-Rama, Columbus *Also Called: Business Idntfction Systems In (G-4789)*

Sign-A-Rama, South Point *Also Called: Kinoly Signs (G-12225)*

Signal Interactive.. 614 360-3938
  401 W Town St # B Columbus (43215) *(G-5265)*

Signalysis Inc... 513 528-6164
  539 Glenrose Ln Cincinnati (45244) *(G-3090)*

Signature 4 Image, Coldwater *Also Called: Signature Partners Inc (G-4584)*

Signature Cabinetry Inc.. 614 252-2227
  1285 Alum Creek Dr Columbus (43209) *(G-5266)*

Signature Control Systems, Columbus *Also Called: Tiba LLC (G-5324)*

Signature Flexible Packg LLC..................................... 614 252-2121
  2901 E 4th Ave Columbus (43219) *(G-5267)*

Signature Partners Inc... 419 678-1400
  149 Harvest Dr Coldwater (45828) *(G-4584)*

Signature Printing, Dayton *Also Called: Dayton Legal Blank Inc (G-5729)*

Signature Sign Co Inc... 216 426-1234
  1776 E 43rd St Cleveland (44103) *(G-4301)*

Signature Store Fixtures, Columbus *Also Called: A-Display Service Corp (G-4657)*

Signature Technologies Inc (DH)................................. 937 859-6323
  3728 Benner Rd Miamisburg (45342) *(G-9737)*

Signcom Incorporated... 614 228-9999
  527 W Rich St Columbus (43215) *(G-5268)*

Signet Enterprises LLC (PA)...................................... 330 762-9102
  19 N High St Akron (44308) *(G-312)*

Signet Group Inc... 330 668-5000
  375 Ghent Rd Fairlawn (44333) *(G-6812)*

Signet Group Services US Inc..................................... 330 668-5000
  375 Ghent Rd Fairlawn (44333) *(G-6813)*

Signetics, Dayton *Also Called: Sign Technologies LLC (G-6007)*

Signme LLC.. 614 221-7803
  39 E Gay St Columbus (43215) *(G-5269)*

Signode Industrial Group LLC..................................... 513 248-2990
  396 Wards Corner Rd Ste 100 Loveland (45140) *(G-8653)*

Signs By Tomorrow, Columbus *Also Called: Krigbaum Inc (G-5056)*

Signs Limited LLC.. 740 282-7715
  356 Technology Way Steubenville (43952) *(G-12411)*

Signs Now Dayton, Dayton *Also Called: Doxie Inc (G-5611)*

Signs Ohio Inc.. 419 228-7446
  57 Town Sq Lima (45801) *(G-8450)*

Signs Unlmted The Grphic Advnt (PA)........................... 614 836-7446
  21313 State Route 93 S Logan (43138) *(G-8526)*

Signwire Worldwide Inc.. 937 428-6189
  2781 Thunderhawk Ct Dayton (45414) *(G-6008)*

Signwire.com, Dayton *Also Called: Signwire Worldwide Inc (G-6008)*

Silcor Oilfield Services Inc.. 330 448-8500
  6874 Strimbu Dr Brookfield (44403) *(G-1518)*

Siler Excavation Services.. 513 400-8628
  6025 Catherine Dr Milford (45150) *(G-9953)*

Silfex Inc (HQ).. 937 472-3311
  950 S Franklin St Eaton (45320) *(G-6463)*

Silfex Inc.. 937 324-2487
  1000 Titus Rd Springfield (45502) *(G-12373)*

Silgan, Ottawa *Also Called: Silgan Plastics LLC (G-11045)*

Silgan Dispensing Systems Corp................................. 330 425-4260
  1244 Highland Rd E Macedonia (44056) *(G-8713)*

Silgan Plastics LLC... 419 523-3737
  690 Woodland Dr Ottawa (45875) *(G-11045)*

Silicon Processors Inc... 740 373-2252
  1988 Masonic Park Rd Marietta (45750) *(G-8944)*

Silicone Solutions Inc.. 330 920-3125
  338 Remington Rd Cuyahoga Falls (44224) *(G-5572)*

Silly Brandz Global LLC... 419 697-8324
  148 Main St Toledo (43605) *(G-13132)*

Silmarillion Partners Inc (PA)..................................... 330 821-4700
  2290 W Main St Alliance (44601) *(G-404)*

Silmix Division, Canton *Also Called: Wacker Chemical Corporation (G-2044)*

Silver Line Building Pdts LLC...................................... 740 382-5595
  2549 Innovation Dr Marion (43302) *(G-8998)*

Silver Machine Co, Elyria *Also Called: Ultra Machine Inc (G-6597)*

Silvesco Inc... 740 373-6661
  2985 State Route 26 Marietta (45750) *(G-8945)*

Simcote Inc.. 740 382-5000
  250 N Greenwood St Marion (43302) *(G-8999)*

Simcote of Ohio Division, Marion *Also Called: Simcote Inc (G-8999)*

Simet, Hudson *Also Called: Sintered Metal Industries Inc (G-7857)*

Simmers Crane Design & Svcs, Salem *Also Called: Flatiron Crane Oper Co LLC (G-11780)*

Simmons Feed & Supply LLC...................................... 800 754-1228
  600 Snyder Rd Salem (44460) *(G-11812)*

Simmons Grain Company, Salem *Also Called: Simmons Feed & Supply LLC (G-11812)*

Simon De Young Corporation.................................... 440 834-3000
15010 Berkshire Industrial Pkwy Middlefield (44062) *(G-9827)*

Simon Ellis Superabrasives Inc.................................. 937 226-0683
501 Progress Rd Dayton (45449) *(G-6009)*

Simon Roofing, Youngstown *Also Called: Simon Roofing and Shtmtl Corp (G-14932)*

Simon Roofing and Shtmtl Corp (PA)........................ 330 629-7392
70 Karago Ave Youngstown (44512) *(G-14932)*

Simona Boltaron Inc... 740 498-5900
1 General St Newcomerstown (43832) *(G-10575)*

Simona PMC LLC.. 419 429-0042
2040 Industrial Dr Findlay (45840) *(G-6918)*

Simple Times LLC... 614 504-3551
750 Cross Pointe Rd Ste M Columbus (43230) *(G-5270)*

Simplevms LLC.. 888 255-8918
7373 Beechmont Ave Ste 130 Cincinnati (45230) *(G-3091)*

Simply Bags, Canfield *Also Called: R J Manray Inc (G-1814)*

Simply Unique Snacks LLC...................................... 513 223-7736
4420 Haight Ave Cincinnati (45223) *(G-3092)*

Simpson & Sons Inc.. 513 367-0152
10220 Harrison Ave Harrison (45030) *(G-7568)*

Simpson Strong-Tie Company Inc........................... 614 876-8060
2600 International St Columbus (43228) *(G-5271)*

Sims Bros Inc (PA)... 740 387-9041
1011 S Prospect St Marion (43302) *(G-9000)*

Sims Brothers Recycling, Marion *Also Called: Sims Bros Inc (G-9000)*

Sims-Lohman Inc... 440 799-8285
1500 Valley Belt Rd Brooklyn Heights (44131) *(G-1540)*

Sims-Lohman Inc (PA)... 513 651-3510
6325 Este Ave Cincinnati (45232) *(G-3093)*

Sims-Lohman Fine Kitchens Gran, Cincinnati *Also Called: Sims-Lohman Inc (G-3093)*

Sinbon Ohio LLC.. 937 415-2070
815 S Brown School Rd Vandalia (45377) *(G-13577)*

Sinbon Usa LLC... 937 667-8999
4265 Gibson Dr Tipp City (45371) *(G-12843)*

Sinel Company Inc.. 937 433-4772
4811 Pamela Sue Dr Dayton (45429) *(G-6010)*

Singleton Corporation... 216 651-7800
3280 W 67th Pl Cleveland (44102) *(G-4302)*

Singleton Reels Inc... 330 274-2961
4612 Lynn Rd Rootstown (44272) *(G-11652)*

Sinico Mtm US Inc.. 216 264-8344
7007 Engle Rd Ste C Middleburg Heights (44130) *(G-9777)*

Sintered Metal Industries Inc................................ 330 650-4000
1890 Georgetown Rd Hudson (44236) *(G-7857)*

Sir Steak Machinery Inc... 419 526-9181
40 Baird Pkwy Mansfield (44903) *(G-8852)*

Siraj Recovery LLC.. 614 893-3507
4088 Seigman Ave Columbus (43213) *(G-5272)*

Sirius Steel Services Inc.. 937 797-3975
1985 Henderson Rd Ste 2211 Columbus (43220) *(G-5273)*

Sirrus Inc.. 513 448-0308
422 Wards Corner Rd Loveland (45140) *(G-8654)*

Sister Schbrts Hmmade Rlls Inc (DH)................... 334 335-2232
380 Polaris Pkwy Ste 400 Westerville (43082) *(G-14233)*

Sister Schubert's, Westerville *Also Called: Sister Schbrts Hmmade Rlls Inc (G-14233)*

Sisters Tanning, Wshngtn Ct Hs *Also Called: Sisters Tanning Inc (G-14746)*

Sisters Tanning Inc... 740 636-0303
1568 State Route 41 Ne Wshngtn Ct Hs (43160) *(G-14746)*

Sit Inc.. 330 758-8468
1305 Boardman Canfield Rd Youngstown (44512) *(G-14933)*

Sitler Printer Inc.. 330 482-4463
707 E Park Ave Columbiana (44408) *(G-4628)*

Six C Fabrication Inc... 330 296-5594
5245 S Prospect St Ravenna (44266) *(G-11541)*

Sixteen Brcks Artsan Bakehouse, Cincinnati *Also Called: Morgan4140 LLC (G-2887)*

Sjbs, Akron *Also Called: Standard Jig Boring Svc LLC (G-315)*

Sje Rhombus Controls.. 419 281-5767
2221 Ford Dr Ashland (44805) *(G-574)*

Sjk Machine LLC... 330 868-3072
1862 Ben Fulton Rd North Lawrence (44666) *(G-10702)*

Sjv Investment Inc... 330 452-9711
722 Mulberry Rd Se Canton (44707) *(G-2006)*

Sk, Cincinnati *Also Called: Sk Textile Inc (G-3094)*

Sk Mold & Tool Inc (PA)... 937 339-0299
955 N 3rd St Tipp City (45371) *(G-12844)*

Sk Mold & Tool Inc... 937 339-0299
2120 Corporate Dr Troy (45373) *(G-13255)*

Sk Tech Inc... 937 836-3535
200 Metro Dr Englewood (45315) *(G-6623)*

Sk Textile Inc... 800 888-9112
1 Knollcrest Dr Cincinnati (45237) *(G-3094)*

SK Wellman Corp... 440 528-4000
6180 Cochran Rd Solon (44139) *(G-12181)*

Skaggs Trlr & Tire Repr Co Inc............................... 440 986-7470
516 W Main St Amherst (44001) *(G-452)*

SKF Machine Tool Services, Cleveland *Also Called: SKF USA Inc (G-4303)*

SKF Machine Tools Service, Cleveland *Also Called: American Precision Spindles (G-3347)*

SKF USA Inc... 800 589-5563
670 Alpha Dr Cleveland (44143) *(G-4303)*

Skid Guard, Cleveland *Also Called: Sure-Foot Industries Corp (G-4352)*

Skidmore-Wilhelm Mfg Company........................... 216 481-4774
30340 Solon Industrial Pkwy Ste B Solon (44139) *(G-12182)*

Skiff Craft, Plain City *Also Called: W of Ohio Inc (G-11426)*

Skinner Firestone Inc... 740 984-4247
232 5th St Beverly (45715) *(G-1209)*

Skinner Machining Co... 216 486-6636
38127 Willoughby Pkwy Willoughby (44094) *(G-14527)*

Skl Home, Cincinnati *Also Called: Saturday Knight Ltd (G-3064)*

Skladany Enterprises Inc.. 614 823-6882
695 Mccorkle Blvd Westerville (43082) *(G-14234)*

Skladany Printing Center, Westerville *Also Called: Skladany Enterprises Inc (G-14234)*

Skok Industries, Bedford *Also Called: E J Skok Industries (G-1030)*

Skrl Die Casting Inc... 440 946-7200
34580 Lakeland Blvd Willoughby (44095) *(G-14528)*

Skuld LLC... 330 423-7339
918 S Main St Piqua (45356) *(G-11384)*

Skuttle Indoor Air Qulty Pdts, Marietta *Also Called: Skuttle Mfg Co (G-8946)*

Skuttle Mfg Co.. 740 373-9169
101 Margaret St Marietta (45750) *(G-8946)*

Sky Climber Fabricating LLC.................................. 740 990-9430
1600 Pittsburgh Dr Delaware (43015) *(G-6173)*

Sky Climber Wind Solutions LLC........................... 740 203-3900
1800 Pittsburgh Dr Delaware (43015) *(G-6174)*

Sky Wireless and Smoke Sp LLC........................... 513 488-5992
100 S Cooper Ave Cincinnati (45215) *(G-3095)*

Skybox Packaging LLC... 419 525-7209
1275 Pollock Pkwy Mansfield (44905) *(G-8853)*

Skybryte Company Inc.. 216 771-1590
3125 Perkins Ave Cleveland (44114) *(G-4304)*

Skylift Inc... 440 960-2100
3000 Leavitt Rd Ste 6 Lorain (44052) *(G-8581)*

Skyline Cem Holdings LLC (PA)............................. 513 874-1188
4180 Thunderbird Ln Fairfield (45014) *(G-6776)*

Skyline Chili, Fairfield *Also Called: Skyline Cem Holdings LLC (G-6776)*

Skyline Corporation... 330 852-2483
580 Mill St Nw Sugarcreek (44681) *(G-12650)*

SKYLINE CORPORATION, Sugarcreek *Also Called: Skyline Corporation (G-12650)*

Skyline Material Sales LLC.................................... 937 981-5505
12325 Pommert Rd Greenfield (45123) *(G-7331)*

Skyline Steel LLC.. 740 423-8544
12355 State Route 7 Belpre (45714) *(G-1154)*

Skyline Trisource Exhibits, Cleveland *Also Called: Ternion Inc (G-4375)*

Skyliner... 740 738-0874
225 Main St Bridgeport (43912) *(G-1496)*

Skymark Refuelers LLC... 419 957-1709
1525 Lima Ave Findlay (45840) *(G-6919)*

SL Endmills Inc.. 513 851-6363
133 Circle Freeway Dr West Chester (45246) *(G-14146)*

Slabe.. 440 298-3693
8000 Plank Rd Thompson (44086) *(G-12764)*

Slabe Machine Products LLC.................................. 440 946-6555
4659 Hamann Pkwy Willoughby (44094) *(G-14529)*

A
L
P
H
A
B
E
T
I
C

Slater Builders Supply, The Plains Also Called: Tyjen Inc (G-12760)

Slater Road Mills Inc.. 330 332-9951
11000 Youngstown Salem Rd Salem (44460) *(G-11813)*

Slicechief, Toledo Also Called: CM Slicechief Co (G-12926)

Slimans Printery Inc... 330 454-9141
624 5th St Nw Canton (44703) *(G-2007)*

Slimline Surgical Devices LLC................................. 937 335-0496
1990 W Stanfield Rd Troy (45373) *(G-13256)*

Sloat Inc... 440 951-9554
34099 Melinz Pkwy Unit A Willoughby (44095) *(G-14530)*

Slone Gear International Inc.................................... 507 401-4327
207 S 1st St Tipp City (45371) *(G-12845)*

Sls Machining Group LLC.. 330 428-2094
2642 Gilchrist Rd Akron (44305) *(G-313)*

Slush Puppie.. 513 771-0940
44 Carnegie Way West Chester (45246) *(G-14147)*

Sluterbeck Tool & Die Co Inc.................................. 937 836-5736
7540 Jacks Ln Clayton (45315) *(G-3275)*

Sluterbeck Tool Co, Clayton Also Called: Sluterbeck Tool & Die Co Inc (G-3275)

Sly Inc (PA).. 800 334-2957
8300 Dow Cir Ste 600 Strongsville (44136) *(G-12601)*

Small Sand & Gravel Inc.. 740 427-3130
10229 Killduff Rd Gambier (43022) *(G-7212)*

Small's Ready-Mixed Concrete, Gambier Also Called: Smalls Inc (G-7213)

Smalls Inc.. 740 427-3633
10229 Killduff Rd Gambier (43022) *(G-7213)*

Smalls Asphalt Paving Inc....................................... 740 427-4096
10229 Killduff Rd Gambier (43022) *(G-7214)*

Smart Business Magazine, Cleveland Also Called: Smart Business Network Inc (G-4305)

Smart Business Network Inc (PA)............................ 440 250-7000
835 Sharon Dr Ste 200 Cleveland (44145) *(G-4305)*

Smart Microsystems Ltd.. 440 366-4257
141 Innovation Dr Elyria (44035) *(G-6590)*

Smart Snic Stencil Clg Systems, Cleveland Also Called: Smart Sonic Corporation (G-4306)

Smart Solutions, Strongsville Also Called: Ohio Cllbrtive Lrng Sltons Inc (G-12582)

Smart Sonic Corporation.. 818 610-7900
837 E 79th St Cleveland (44103) *(G-4306)*

Smartbill Ltd... 740 928-6909
1050 O Neill Dr Hebron (43025) *(G-7636)*

Smartsoda Holdings Inc (PA).................................. 888 998-9668
6095 Parkland Blvd Cleveland (44124) *(G-4307)*

SMC Corporation of America................................... 330 659-2006
4160 Highlander Pkwy Ste 200 Richfield (44286) *(G-11601)*

SMC Ltd Product Design & Dev, Twinsburg Also Called: Scientific Molding Corp Ltd (G-13375)

Smead Manufacturing Company............................... 740 385-5601
851 Smead Rd Logan (43138) *(G-8527)*

Smg Growing Media Inc (HQ).................................. 937 644-0011
14111 Scottslawn Rd Marysville (43041) *(G-9049)*

Smgm LLC.. 937 644-0011
14111 Scottslawn Rd Marysville (43040) *(G-9050)*

SMI Holdings Inc.. 740 927-3464
10685 Columbus Pkwy Pataskala (43062) *(G-11151)*

Smith & Thompson Entps LLC................................. 330 386-9345
46368 Y And O Rd East Liverpool (43920) *(G-6397)*

Smith and Thompson Enterprise, East Liverpool Also Called: Smith & Thompson Entps LLC (G-6397)

Smith Carl E Cnslting Engneers, Bath Also Called: Warmus and Associates Inc (G-898)

Smith Concrete... 740 439-7714
61539 Southgate Rd Cambridge (43725) *(G-1759)*

Smith Concrete Co.. 740 593-5633
5240 Hebbardsville Rd Athens (45701) *(G-652)*

Smith Concrete Co (PA)... 740 373-7441
2301 Progress St Dover (44622) *(G-6262)*

Smith Electro Chemical Co....................................... 513 351-7227
5936 Carthage Ct Cincinnati (45212) *(G-3096)*

Smith Machine Inc.. 330 821-9898
20651 Lake Park Blvd Alliance (44601) *(G-405)*

Smith Rn Sheet Metal Shop Inc............................... 740 653-5011
1312 Campground Rd Lancaster (43130) *(G-8224)*

Smithco Distributing... 419 367-7685
T480 County Road 7 Liberty Center (43532) *(G-8376)*

Smithers Group Inc... 330 833-8548
1845 Harsh Ave Se Massillon (44646) *(G-9244)*

Smithers-Oasis Company... 330 673-5831
919 Marvin St Kent (44240) *(G-8079)*

Smithers-Oasis Company (PA)................................ 330 945-5100
295 S Water St Ste 201 Kent (44240) *(G-8080)*

Smithersoasis North America, Kent Also Called: Smithers-Oasis Company (G-8080)

Smithfield Direct LLC... 419 422-2233
4411 Township Road 142 Findlay (45840) *(G-6920)*

Smithfield Packaged Meats Corp (DH)..................... 513 782-3800
805 E Kemper Rd Cincinnati (45246) *(G-3097)*

Smithfoods Inc (HQ).. 330 683-8710
1381 Dairy Ln Orrville (44667) *(G-11008)*

Smiths Medical Asd Inc... 800 796-8701
5200 Upper Metro Pl Ste 200 Dublin (43017) *(G-6345)*

Smiths Medical Asd Inc... 614 889-2220
6250 Shier Rings Rd Dublin (43016) *(G-6346)*

Smiths Medical North America................................. 614 210-7300
5200 Upper Metro Pl Ste 200 Dublin (43017) *(G-6347)*

Smithville Mfg Co... 330 345-5818
6563 Cleveland Rd Wooster (44691) *(G-14687)*

Smoke-Rings Inc.. 419 420-9966
1928 Tiffin Ave Findlay (45840) *(G-6921)*

Smp Welding LLC... 440 205-9353
8171 Tyler Blvd Mentor (44060) *(G-9616)*

SMS Technologies Inc.. 419 465-4175
3531 Everingin Rd Monroeville (44847) *(G-10121)*

Smucker Foodservice Inc... 877 858-3855
1 Strawberry Ln Orrville (44667) *(G-11009)*

Smucker International Inc... 330 682-3000
1 Strawberry Ln Orrville (44667) *(G-11010)*

Smucker Manufacturing Inc..................................... 888 550-9555
1 Strawberry Ln Orrville (44667) *(G-11011)*

Smucker Natural Foods Inc...................................... 330 682-3000
Strawberry Lane Orrville (44667) *(G-11012)*

Smucker Retail Foods Inc.. 330 684-1500
333 Wadsworth Rd Orrville (44667) *(G-11013)*

Smucker's, Orrville Also Called: J M Smucker Company (G-10987)

Smucker's, Orrville Also Called: Smucker International Inc (G-11010)

Smyrna Ready Mix Concrete LLC............................. 937 855-0410
9151 Township Park Dr Germantown (45327) *(G-7254)*

Smyrna Ready Mix Concrete LLC............................. 937 773-0841
8395 Piqua Lockington Rd Piqua (45356) *(G-11385)*

Smyrna Ready Mix Concrete LLC............................. 937 698-7229
555 Old Springfield Rd Vandalia (45377) *(G-13578)*

Snack Alliance Inc (DH)... 330 767-3426
100 Lincoln Way E Massillon (44646) *(G-9245)*

Snap Rite Manufacturing Inc.................................... 910 897-4080
14300 Darley Ave Cleveland (44110) *(G-4308)*

Snap-On Business Solutions Inc (HQ)...................... 330 659-1600
4025 Kinross Lakes Pkwy Richfield (44286) *(G-11602)*

Snaps Inc... 419 477-5100
2557 Township Road 35 Mount Cory (45868) *(G-10205)*

Sneller Machine Tool Division, Cleveland Also Called: Grand Harbor Yacht Sales & Svc (G-3784)

Snider General Tire, Cambridge Also Called: Snider Tire Inc (G-1760)

Snider Tire Inc... 740 439-2741
9501 Sunrise Rd Cambridge (43725) *(G-1760)*

Snook Advertising Al Publisher............................... 614 866-3333
1567 Alar Ave Reynoldsburg (43068) *(G-11580)*

Snook Al Advertising/Publisher, Reynoldsburg Also Called: Snook Advertising Al Publisher (G-11580)

Snow Aviation Intl Inc.. 614 588-2452
949 Creek Dr Gahanna (43230) *(G-7169)*

Snow Dragon LLC... 440 295-0238
1441 Chardon Rd Cleveland (44117) *(G-4309)*

Snow Printing Co Inc.. 419 229-7669
1000 W Grand Ave Frnt Lima (45801) *(G-8451)*

Snows Wood Shop Inc (PA)..................................... 419 836-3805
7220 Brown Rd Oregon (43616) *(G-10968)*

Snowville Creamery LLC... 740 698-2301
32623 State Route 143 Pomeroy (45769) *(G-11438)*

Snyder Brick & Block, Troy *Also Called: Snyder Concrete Products Inc (G-13257)*

Snyder Brick and Block, Dayton *Also Called: Snyder Concrete Products Inc (G-6011)*

Snyder Brick and Block, Moraine *Also Called: Snyder Concrete Products Inc (G-10192)*

Snyder Concrete Products Inc................................. 937 224-1433
1433 S Euclid Ave Dayton (45417) *(G-6011)*

Snyder Concrete Products Inc (PA)....................... 937 885-5176
2301 W Dorothy Ln Moraine (45439) *(G-10192)*

Snyder Concrete Products Inc................................. 937 339-7577
3246 N County Road 25a Troy (45373) *(G-13257)*

Snyder Hot Shot, Wooster *Also Called: H & H Equipment Inc (G-14647)*

Snyder Intl Brewing Group LLC (PA)...................... 216 619-7424
1940 E 6th St Ste 200 Cleveland (44114) *(G-4310)*

Snyder Manufacturing Inc.. 330 343-4456
3001 Progress St Dover (44622) *(G-6263)*

So-Low Environmental Eqp Co................................. 513 772-9410
10310 Spartan Dr Cincinnati (45215) *(G-3098)*

Soaring Software Solutions Inc.............................. 419 442-7676
110 W Airport Hwy Ste 1 Swanton (43558) *(G-12692)*

Sobel Corrugated Containers Inc........................... 216 475-2100
1111 Superior Ave E Ste 1111 Cleveland (44114) *(G-4311)*

Socar of Ohio Inc (PA)... 419 596-3100
21739 Road E16 Continental (45831) *(G-5423)*

Society of The Precious Blood................................. 419 925-4516
2860 Us Route 127 Celina (45822) *(G-2120)*

Soelter Corporation.. 800 838-8984
385 Carr Dr Brookville (45309) *(G-1576)*

Soemhejee Inc... 419 298-2306
128 W Vine St Edgerton (43517) *(G-6469)*

Sofie, Oakwood Village *Also Called: N-Molecular Inc (G-10907)*

Soft Touch Wood LLC... 330 545-4204
1560 S State St Girard (44420) *(G-7280)*

Soft Tuch Furn Repr Rfinishing, Girard *Also Called: Soft Touch Wood LLC (G-7280)*

Softbox Systems Inc... 513 360-7189
675 Gateway Blvd Monroe (45050) *(G-10116)*

Software Solutions Inc (PA)..................................... 513 932-6667
8534 Yankee St Ste 2b Dayton (45458) *(G-6012)*

Sojourners Truth Inc... 419 243-0007
7 E Bancroft St Toledo (43620) *(G-13133)*

Solae LLC.. 419 483-0400
300 Great Lakes Pkwy Bellevue (44811) *(G-1132)*

Solae Central Soya, Bellevue *Also Called: Solae LLC (G-1132)*

Solae LLC.. 419 483-5340
605 Goodrich Rd Bellevue (44811) *(G-1133)*

Solar Arts Graphic Designs...................................... 330 744-0535
824 Tod Ave Youngstown (44502) *(G-14934)*

Solarflo Corporation... 440 439-1680
22001 Aurora Rd Cleveland (44140) *(G-4312)*

Solas Ltd.. 650 501-0889
33587 Streamview Dr Avon (44011) *(G-739)*

Solas Global Solutions, Avon *Also Called: Solas Ltd (G-739)*

Sole Choice Inc.. 740 354-2813
2415 Scioto Trl Portsmouth (45662) *(G-11477)*

Soleo Health Inc.. 844 467-8200
6190 Shamrock Ct Ste 100 Dublin (43016) *(G-6348)*

Solid Dimensions Inc... 419 663-1134
720 Townline Road 151 Norwalk (44857) *(G-10862)*

Solid Dimensions Line, Norwalk *Also Called: Solid Dimensions Inc (G-10862)*

Solid Surface Concepts Inc...................................... 513 948-8677
7660 Production Dr Cincinnati (45237) *(G-3099)*

Solid Surfaces Plus, Cleveland *Also Called: Wdi Group Inc (G-4495)*

Solidstate Controls LLC (HQ).................................. 614 846-7500
875 Dearborn Dr Columbus (43085) *(G-5274)*

Solmet Technologies Inc.. 330 915-4160
2716 Shepler Church Ave Sw Canton (44706) *(G-2008)*

Solo Products Inc.. 513 321-7884
838 Reedy St Cincinnati (45202) *(G-3100)*

Solon Glass Center Inc... 440 248-5018
33001 Station St Cleveland (44139) *(G-4313)*

Solon Glass Ctr, Cleveland *Also Called: Solon Glass Center Inc (G-4313)*

Solon Manufacturing Company............................... 440 286-7149
425 Center St Chardon (44024) *(G-2223)*

Solon Specialty Wire Co... 440 248-7600
30000 Solon Rd Solon (44139) *(G-12183)*

Solstice Sleep Products Inc (PA)............................. 614 279-8850
3720 W Broad St Columbus (43228) *(G-5275)*

Solut, Lewis Center *Also Called: Solut Inc (G-8354)*

Solut Inc (PA).. 740 549-3336
7787 Graphics Way Lewis Center (43035) *(G-8354)*

Solution Industries LLC... 440 816-9500
21555 Drake Rd Strongsville (44149) *(G-12602)*

Solutions In Polycarbonate LLC............................. 330 572-2860
6353 Norwalk Rd Medina (44256) *(G-9449)*

Solvay Advanced Polymers LLC.............................. 740 373-9242
17005 State Route 7 Marietta (45750) *(G-8947)*

Solvay Spclty Polymers USA LLC........................... 740 373-9242
17005 State Route 7 Marietta (45750) *(G-8948)*

Somerville Manufacturing Inc................................. 740 336-7847
15 Townhall Rd Marietta (45750) *(G-8949)*

Sonalysts Inc... 937 429-9711
2940 Presidential Dr Ste 160 Beavercreek (45324) *(G-984)*

Sonic Drive-In... 937 717-6917
40 S Tuttle Rd Springfield (45505) *(G-12374)*

Sonoco Products Company...................................... 937 429-0040
761 Space Dr Beavercreek Township (45434) *(G-1006)*

Sonoco Products Company...................................... 614 759-8470
444 Mccormick Blvd Columbus (43213) *(G-5276)*

Sonoco Products Company...................................... 330 688-8247
59 N Main St Munroe Falls (44262) *(G-10272)*

Sonoco Products Company...................................... 513 870-3985
4633 Dues Dr West Chester (45246) *(G-14148)*

Sonogage Inc... 216 464-1119
26650 Renaissance Pkwy Ste 3 Cleveland (44128) *(G-4314)*

Sonoma Grinding Machining Inc............................. 440 918-7990
9330 Progress Pkwy Mentor (44060) *(G-9617)*

Sonosite Inc... 425 951-1200
236 High St Hamilton (45011) *(G-7526)*

Soondook LLC.. 614 389-5757
6344 Nicholas Dr Columbus (43235) *(G-5277)*

Soprema USA Inc (HQ).. 330 334-0066
310 Quadral Dr Wadsworth (44281) *(G-13671)*

Sorbothane Inc (PA).. 330 678-9444
2144 State Route 59 Kent (44240) *(G-8081)*

Sound Communications Inc..................................... 614 875-8500
3474 Park St Grove City (43123) *(G-7414)*

Sound Laboratory LLC.. 330 968-4060
109 S Water St Kent (44240) *(G-8082)*

Sound Solutions Cnstr Svcs, Bedford *Also Called: Baswa Acoustics North Amer LLC (G-1014)*

Soundex Communications Group, Dayton *Also Called: Dcm Soundex Inc (G-5744)*

Soundtrace Inc.. 513 278-5288
408 4th Ave Mason (45040) *(G-9153)*

Soundwich Inc... 216 249-4900
17000 Saint Clair Ave Cleveland (44110) *(G-4315)*

Soundwich Inc (PA).. 216 486-2666
881 Wayside Rd Cleveland (44110) *(G-4316)*

Source3media Inc.. 330 467-9003
6470 Som Center Rd Solon (44139) *(G-12184)*

South Akron Awning Co (PA).................................... 330 848-7611
763 Kenmore Blvd Akron (44314) *(G-314)*

South Central Industrial LLC.................................. 740 333-5401
1825 Old Us 35 Se Wshngtn Ct Hs (43160) *(G-14747)*

South Plant, Barberton *Also Called: PPG Industries Inc (G-834)*

South Shore Controls Inc... 440 259-2500
9395 Pinecone Dr Mentor (44060) *(G-9618)*

South Shore Finishers Inc.. 216 664-1792
1720 Willey Ave Cleveland (44113) *(G-4317)*

South Side Drive Thru... 937 295-2927
9204 Hilgefort Rd Fort Loramie (45845) *(G-6957)*

Southast Diesl Acquisition Sub, Greenville *Also Called: Stateline Power Corp (G-7356)*

Southeast Health Center, Cleveland *Also Called: Northast Ohio Nghbrhood Hlth S (G-4091)*

Southeast Publications Inc...................................... 740 732-2341
309 Main St Caldwell (43724) *(G-1729)*

A
L
P
H
A
B
E
T
I
C

Southeastern Container Inc................... 419 352-6300
307 Industrial Pkwy Bowling Green (43402) *(G-1440)*

Southeastern Shafting Mfg Inc................... 740 342-4629
402 W Broadway St New Lexington (43764) *(G-10407)*

Southern Bag, Wilmington *Also Called: Hood Packaging Corporation (G-14584)*

Southern Cabinetry Inc................... 740 245-5992
41 International Blvd Bidwell (45614) *(G-1215)*

Southern Champion Tray LP................... 513 755-7200
7100 Dixie Hwy Fairfield (45014) *(G-6777)*

Southern Champion Tray, L.P., Fairfield *Also Called: Southern Champion Tray LP (G-6777)*

Southern Division, Perrysburg *Also Called: Ohio Table Pad Company (G-11247)*

Southern Graphic Systems LLC................... 513 648-4641
9435 Waterstone Blvd Ste 300 Cincinnati (45249) *(G-3101)*

Southern Ohio Kitchens, Dayton *Also Called: C-Link Enterprises LLC (G-5692)*

Southern Ohio Lumber, Peebles *Also Called: Southern Ohio Lumber LLC (G-11173)*

Southern Ohio Lumber LLC................... 614 436-4472
11855 State Route 73 Peebles (45660) *(G-11173)*

Southern Ohio Mfg Inc................... 513 943-2555
3214 Marshall Dr Amelia (45102) *(G-437)*

Southern Ohio Printing................... 513 241-5150
2230 Gilbert Ave Cincinnati (45206) *(G-3102)*

Southern Ohio Vault Co Inc................... 740 456-5898
502 Shale Dr Portsmouth (45662) *(G-11478)*

Southern Wholesale, Millersburg *Also Called: Affordable Barn Co Ltd (G-9966)*

Southpaw Enterprises Inc................... 937 252-7676
2350 Dryden Rd Moraine (45439) *(G-10193)*

Southstern McHning Feld Svc In (PA)................... 740 689-1147
500 Lincoln Ave Lancaster (43130) *(G-8225)*

Southwest Ohio Computer Assn, Fairfield Township *Also Called: Butler Tech (G-6795)*

Southwood Pallet LLC................... 330 682-3747
8849 Lincoln Way E Orrville (44667) *(G-11014)*

Southwestern Ohio Instrctnal Te................... 937 746-6333
1205 E 5th St Dayton (45402) *(G-6013)*

Sovac, Portsmouth *Also Called: Southern Ohio Vault Co Inc (G-11478)*

Sovereign Circuits Inc................... 330 538-3900
12080 Debartolo Dr North Jackson (44451) *(G-10694)*

SP Mount Printing Company................... 216 881-3316
1306 E 55th St Cleveland (44103) *(G-4318)*

Sp3 Winco LLC................... 937 667-4476
835 N Hyatt St Tipp City (45371) *(G-12846)*

Space & Sensors, Mason *Also Called: L3harris Cincinnati Elec Corp (G-9121)*

Space Exploration Tech Corp................... 559 593-2731
4555 Creekside Pkwy Lockbourne (43137) *(G-8492)*

Spacelinks Enterprises Inc................... 330 788-2401
1110 Thalia Ave Youngstown (44512) *(G-14935)*

Spalding................... 440 286-5717
12860 Mayfield Rd Chardon (44024) *(G-2224)*

Spallinger Millwright Svc Co................... 419 225-5830
1155 E Hanthorn Rd Lima (45804) *(G-8452)*

Spallnger Atclave Systms/US MI, Lima *Also Called: Spallinger Millwright Svc Co (G-8452)*

Spang & Company................... 440 350-6108
9305 Progress Pkwy Mentor (44060) *(G-9619)*

Spangler Candy Company (PA)................... 419 636-4221
400 N Portland St Bryan (43506) *(G-1660)*

SPAOS Inc (PA)................... 937 890-0783
6012 N Dixie Dr Dayton (45414) *(G-6014)*

Sparoom, Bedford Heights *Also Called: Unitrex Ltd (G-1083)*

Sparta Embroidery Inc................... 330 484-8484
3611 Cleveland Ave S Canton (44707) *(G-2009)*

Spartech LLC................... 937 548-1395
1050 Landsdowne Ave Greenville (45331) *(G-7353)*

Spartech LLC................... 419 399-4050
925 W Gasser Rd Paulding (45879) *(G-11162)*

Spartech Mexico Holding Co Two................... 440 930-3619
33587 Walker Rd Avon Lake (44012) *(G-770)*

Spartech Plastics, Paulding *Also Called: Spartech LLC (G-11162)*

Sparton Enterprises LLC................... 877 772-7866
3717 Clark Mill Rd Barberton (44203) *(G-838)*

Spartronics Strongsville Inc................... 440 878-4630
22740 Lunn Rd Strongsville (44149) *(G-12603)*

Spear Application Systems, Mason *Also Called: Spear Inc (G-9154)*

Spear Inc................... 513 459-1100
5510 Courseview Dr Mason (45040) *(G-9154)*

Special Design Products Inc................... 614 272-6700
520 Industrial Mile Rd Columbus (43228) *(G-5278)*

Special Machined Components................... 513 459-1113
7626 Easy St Mason (45040) *(G-9155)*

Special Metal Stamping, Independence *Also Called: Triad Capital Group LLC (G-7922)*

Special Pack Inc................... 330 458-3204
5555 Massillon Rd Canton (44720) *(G-2010)*

Specialized Castings Ltd................... 937 669-5620
1569 Martindale Rd Greenville (45331) *(G-7354)*

Specialties Unlimited, Mentor *Also Called: J & P Products Inc (G-9539)*

Specialty Ceramics Inc................... 330 482-0800
41995 State Route 344 Columbiana (44408) *(G-4629)*

Specialty Fab, North Lima *Also Called: Bird Equipment LLC (G-10704)*

Specialty Hardware Inc................... 216 291-1160
2200 Kerwin Rd Apt 710 Cleveland (44118) *(G-4319)*

Specialty Lithographing Co................... 513 621-0222
1035 W 7th St Cincinnati (45203) *(G-3103)*

Specialty Machines Inc................... 937 837-8852
5370 Salem Ave Dayton (45426) *(G-6015)*

Specialty Metals Proc Inc................... 330 656-2767
837 Seasons Rd Hudson (44224) *(G-7858)*

Specialty Nameplate Corp................... 614 444-6876
4670 Groves Rd Columbus (43232) *(G-5279)*

Specialty Packg Licensing Ltd, Toledo *Also Called: Bprex Plastic Services Co Inc (G-12903)*

Specialty Printing and Proc................... 614 322-9035
4670 Groves Rd Columbus (43232) *(G-5280)*

Specialty Svcs Cabinetry Inc................... 614 421-1599
1253 Essex Ave Columbus (43201) *(G-5281)*

Specialty Switch Company LLC................... 330 427-3000
525 Mcclurg Rd Youngstown (44512) *(G-14936)*

Specialty Technology & Res................... 614 870-0744
1150 Milepost Dr Columbus (43228) *(G-5282)*

Specialty Trans Components, Youngstown *Also Called: Specialty Switch Company LLC (G-14936)*

Specialty Wine-Spirits, Sandusky *Also Called: Lonz Winery LLC (G-11851)*

Specialty Wood Products, Cincinnati *Also Called: Wjf Enterprises LLC (G-3228)*

Specified Structures Inc................... 330 753-0693
643 Holmes Ave Barberton (44203) *(G-839)*

Spectex LLC................... 603 330-3334
6156 Wesselman Rd Cincinnati (45248) *(G-3104)*

Spectra Group Limited Inc................... 419 837-9783
27800 Lemoyne Rd Ste J Millbury (43447) *(G-9965)*

Spectra Photopolymers, Millbury *Also Called: Formlabs Ohio Inc (G-9961)*

Spectra Photopolymers, Millbury *Also Called: Spectra Group Limited Inc (G-9965)*

Spectra-Tech Manufacturing Inc................... 513 735-9300
4013 Borman Dr Batavia (45103) *(G-889)*

Spectracam Ltd................... 937 223-3805
1112 East Race Dr Dayton (45404) *(G-6016)*

Spectre Industries LLC................... 440 665-2600
10185 Gottschalk Pkwy Ste 1 Chagrin Falls (44023) *(G-2183)*

Spectre Sensors Inc................... 440 250-0372
2392 Georgia Dr Westlake (44145) *(G-14335)*

Spectron Inc................... 937 461-5590
132 S Terry St Dayton (45403) *(G-6017)*

Spectrum Adhesives Inc................... 740 763-2886
11047 Lambs Ln Newark (43055) *(G-10533)*

Spectrum Brands, Orrville *Also Called: United Industries Incorporated (G-11015)*

Spectrum Dispersions Inc................... 330 296-0600
225 W Lake St Ravenna (44266) *(G-11542)*

Spectrum Machine Inc (PA)................... 330 626-3666
1668 Frost Rd Streetsboro (44241) *(G-12524)*

Spectrum Metal Finishing Inc................... 330 758-8358
535 Bev Rd Youngstown (44512) *(G-14937)*

Spectrum News Ohio................... 614 384-2640
580 N 4th St Ste 350 Columbus (43215) *(G-5283)*

Spectrum Plastics Corporation................... 330 926-9766
99 E Ascot Ln Cuyahoga Falls (44223) *(G-5573)*

Spectrum Printing & Design, Dayton *Also Called: Eugene Stewart (G-5770)*

Spectrum Surgical Instruments, Stow *Also Called: Steris Instrument MGT Svcs Inc (G-12464)*

Spectrum Textiles Inc.. 513 933-8346
5883 Casaway Rd Lebanon (45036) *(G-8286)*

Speed North America Inc.. 330 202-7775
1700a Old Mansfield Rd Wooster (44691) *(G-14688)*

Speed-O-Print, Crooksville *Also Called: Temple Oil and Gas LLC (G-5513)*

Speedpro Imaging.. 513 771-4776
2888 E Kemper Rd Cincinnati (45241) *(G-3105)*

Spence Technologies Inc... 440 946-3035
4752 Topps Industrial Pkwy Willoughby (44094) *(G-14531)*

Spencer Feed & Supply LLC... 330 648-2111
227 N Main St Spencer (44275) *(G-12235)*

Spencer Forge & Manufacturing, Spencer *Also Called: Alta Mira Corporation (G-12233)*

Spencer Forge & Manufacturing, Spencer *Also Called: Spencer Manufacturing Company Inc (G-12236)*

Spencer Manufacturing Company Inc... 330 648-2461
225 N Main St Spencer (44275) *(G-12236)*

Sperling Railway Services Inc.. 330 479-2004
4313 Southway St Sw Canton (44706) *(G-2011)*

Sperry & Rice, Killbuck *Also Called: Sperry & Rice LLC (G-8135)*

Sperry & Rice LLC... 330 276-2801
1088 N Main St Killbuck (44637) *(G-8134)*

Sperry & Rice LLC (PA).. 765 647-4141
1088 N Main St Killbuck (44637) *(G-8135)*

SPI Liquidation Inc
15285 S State Ave Middlefield (44062) *(G-9828)*

SPI Mailing, Canton *Also Called: Slimans Printery Inc (G-2007)*

Spiegelberg Manufacturing Inc (HQ).. 440 324-3042
12200 Alameda Dr Strongsville (44149) *(G-12604)*

Spiegler Brake Systems USA, Dayton *Also Called: Spiegler Brake Systems USA LLC (G-6018)*

Spiegler Brake Systems USA LLC.. 937 291-1735
1699 Thomas Paine Pkwy Dayton (45459) *(G-6018)*

Spinal Balance Inc... 419 530-5935
11360 S Airfield Rd Swanton (43558) *(G-12693)*

Spinnaker Coating, Troy *Also Called: SC Liquidation Company LLC (G-13252)*

Spinnker Prssure Snstive Pdts.. 800 543-9452
550 Summit Ave Troy (45373) *(G-13258)*

Spintech, Miamisburg *Also Called: Spintech Holdings Inc (G-9738)*

Spintech Holdings Inc.. 937 912-3250
1964 Byers Rd Miamisburg (45342) *(G-9738)*

Spiral Brushes Inc... 330 686-2861
1355 Commerce Dr Stow (44224) *(G-12461)*

Spiralcool Company... 419 483-2510
186 Sheffield St Ste 188 Bellevue (44811) *(G-1134)*

Opirex Corporation... 330 726-1166
375 Victoria Rd Ste 1 Youngstown (44515) *(G-14938)*

Spirit Aeronautics, Columbus *Also Called: Spirit Avionics Ltd (G-5284)*

Spirit Avionics Ltd (PA).. 614 237-4271
465 Waterbury Ct Ste C Columbus (43230) *(G-5284)*

Spirol Shim Corporation (DH)... 330 920-3655
321 Remington Rd Stow (44224) *(G-12462)*

Splendid LLC.. 614 396-6481
1415 E Dublin Granville Rd Ste 219 Columbus (43229) *(G-5285)*

Spoerr Precast Concrete Inc.. 419 625-9132
2020 Caldwell St Sandusky (44870) *(G-11872)*

Sponseller Group Inc (PA)... 419 861-3000
1600 Timber Wolf Dr Holland (43528) *(G-7785)*

Sponseller Group Inc... 937 492-9949
1516 Target Dr Sidney (45365) *(G-12054)*

Sports & Sports, Ashtabula *Also Called: Peska Inc (G-611)*

Sports Imports Incorporated.. 614 771-0246
6950 Worthington Galena Rd Worthington (43085) *(G-14725)*

Sportsco Imprinting.. 513 641-5111
8277 Wicklow Ave Cincinnati (45236) *(G-3106)*

Sportsmans Haven Inc... 740 432-7243
14695 E Pike Rd Cambridge (43725) *(G-1761)*

Sportwing, Cleveland *Also Called: Dawn Enterprises Inc (G-3601)*

Sposie LLC... 888 977-2229
4064 Technology Dr Maumee (43537) *(G-9319)*

Spot On Main LLC.. 740 285-0441
91 Harding Ave Jackson (45640) *(G-7952)*

Spot On Main Coffee Roastery, Jackson *Also Called: Spot On Main LLC (G-7952)*

Spradlin Bros Welding Co.. 800 219-2182
2131 Quality Ln Springfield (45505) *(G-12375)*

Sprague Products, Brecksville *Also Called: Curtiss-Wright Flow Ctrl Corp (G-1461)*

Spring Grove Manufacturing Inc.. 513 542-6900
2838 Spring Grove Ave Cincinnati (45225) *(G-3107)*

Spring Hlthcare Dagnostics LLC... 866 201-9503
16064 Beaver Pike Jackson (45640) *(G-7953)*

Spring Team Inc... 440 275-5981
2851 Industrial Park Dr Austinburg (44010) *(G-703)*

Spring Works Incorporated.. 614 351-9345
3201 Alberta St Columbus (43204) *(G-5286)*

Springco Metal Coatings Inc... 216 941-0020
12500 Elmwood Ave Cleveland (44111) *(G-4320)*

Springdot, Cincinnati *Also Called: Springdot Inc (G-3108)*

Springdot Inc (PA)... 513 542-4000
2611 Colerain Ave Cincinnati (45214) *(G-3108)*

Springfield News Sun, Springfield *Also Called: Springfield Newspapers Inc (G-12376)*

Springfield Newspapers Inc... 937 323-5533
137 E Main St Springfield (45502) *(G-12376)*

Springfield Plastics Inc... 937 322-6071
15 N Bechtle Ave Springfield (45504) *(G-12377)*

Springhill Dimensions... 330 359-5972
4530 Mount Eaton Rd S Dalton (44618) *(G-5595)*

Springseal Inc... 330 626-0673
800 Enterprise Pkwy Ravenna (44266) *(G-11543)*

Sprint Print Inc.. 740 622-4429
520 Main St Coshocton (43812) *(G-5473)*

Sprinter Marking Inc.. 740 453-1000
1805 Chandlersville Rd Zanesville (43701) *(G-15051)*

Sprosty, Smithville *Also Called: Ray C Sprosty Bag Co Inc (G-12067)*

Spsi, Hartville *Also Called: Scott Process Systems Inc (G-7584)*

Spunfab, Cuyahoga Falls *Also Called: Keuchel & Associates Inc (G-5554)*

Spurlino Materials LLC.. 513 202-1111
6600 Dry Fork Rd Cleves (45002) *(G-4548)*

Spurlino Materials LLC (PA).. 513 705-0111
4000 Oxford State Rd Middletown (45044) *(G-9894)*

Spz Machine Company LLC.. 330 848-3286
2871 Newpark Dr Norton (44203) *(G-10827)*

Square One Solutions LLC.. 419 425-5445
130 Bentley Ct Findlay (45840) *(G-6922)*

Squeaky Clean Cincinnati Inc.. 513 729-2712
1500 Goodman Ave Cincinnati (45224) *(G-3109)*

Squeaky Clean Off & Coml Clg, Cincinnati *Also Called: Squeaky Clean Cincinnati Inc (C 3100)*

Sr Products... 330 998-6500
70 Karago Ave Youngstown (44512) *(G-14939)*

SRC & Company... 216 417-7477
3214 Prospect Ave E Cleveland (44115) *(G-4321)*

SRC Liquidation LLC (PA).. 937 221-1000
111 W 1st St Dayton (45402) *(G-6019)*

SRC Worldwide, Cleveland *Also Called: Buckingham Src Inc (G-3448)*

SRC Worldwide Inc (HQ)... 216 941-6115
3425 Service Rd Cleveland (44111) *(G-4322)*

Sreco Flexible, Lima *Also Called: Sewer Rodding Equipment Co (G-8447)*

SRI Healthcare LLC.. 513 398-6406
7086 Industrial Row Dr Mason (45040) *(G-9156)*

SRI Ohio Inc.. 740 653-5800
1061 Mill Park Dr Lancaster (43130) *(G-8226)*

Srico Inc... 614 799-0664
2724 Sawbury Blvd Columbus (43235) *(G-5287)*

Srm Concrete, Piqua *Also Called: Smyrna Ready Mix Concrete LLC (G-11385)*

Sroufe Healthcare Products LLC... 260 894-4171
961 Seville Rd Wadsworth (44281) *(G-13672)*

SRS Die Casting Holdings LLC (HQ).. 330 467-0750
635 Highland Rd E Macedonia (44056) *(G-8714)*

SRS Light Metals Inc (PA).. 330 467-0750
635 Highland Rd E Macedonia (44056) *(G-8715)*

SRS Manufacturing Corp...937 746-3086
  395 Industrial Dr Franklin (45005) *(G-7050)*

Ss Industries, Dayton *Also Called: Stanco Precision Mfg Inc (G-6022)*

SSC Controls Company..440 205-1600
  8909 East Ave Mentor (44060) *(G-9620)*

Sseco Solutions, Cleveland *Also Called: Service Station Equipment Co (G-4286)*

Ssi Tiles, Minerva *Also Called: Kepcor Inc (G-10040)*

SSP, Twinsburg *Also Called: SSP Fittings Corp (G-13379)*

SSP Fittings Corp (PA)...330 425-4250
  8250 Boyle Pkwy Twinsburg (44087) *(G-13379)*

SSP Industrial Group Inc...330 665-2900
  3560 W Market St Ste 300 Fairlawn (44333) *(G-6814)*

St Henry Tile Co Inc...937 548-1101
  5410 S State Route 49 Greenville (45331) *(G-7355)*

St Henry Tile Co Inc (PA)...419 678-4841
  281 W Washington St Saint Henry (45883) *(G-11724)*

St Lawrence Holdings LLC..330 562-9000
  16500 Rockside Rd Maple Heights (44137) *(G-8892)*

St Lawrence Steel Corporation.......................................330 562-9000
  16500 Rockside Rd Maple Heights (44137) *(G-8893)*

St Media Group International, Blue Ash *Also Called: St Media Group Intl Inc (G-1332)*

St Media Group Intl Inc..513 421-2050
  11262 Cornell Park Dr Blue Ash (45242) *(G-1332)*

ST Tool & Design Inc...440 357-1250
  9452 Mercantile Dr Mentor (44060) *(G-9621)*

STA-Warm Electric Company...330 296-6461
  553 N Chestnut St Ravenna (44266) *(G-11544)*

Staber Industries Inc...614 836-5995
  4800 Homer Ohio Ln Groveport (43125) *(G-7450)*

Stable Step LLC...800 491-1571
  961 Seville Rd Wadsworth (44281) *(G-13673)*

Staci Lagrange, Lagrange *Also Called: Inservco Inc (G-8148)*

Stack Construction Tech Inc (PA)....................................513 445-5122
  9999 Carver Rd Blue Ash (45242) *(G-1333)*

Stack Constructyion Technology, Mason *Also Called: To Scale Software LLC (G-9162)*

Staco Energy Products Co..937 253-1191
  301 Gaddis Blvd Dayton (45403) *(G-6020)*

Staco Energy Products Co (HQ).......................................937 253-1191
  2425 Technical Dr Miamisburg (45342) *(G-9739)*

Stadco Inc..937 878-0911
  632 Yellow Springs Fairfield Rd Fairborn (45324) *(G-6699)*

Stadco Automatics, Fairborn *Also Called: Stadco Inc (G-6699)*

Stadium Grow Lighting Inc..855 346-9403
  108 Main Ave Sw Ste 500 Warren (44481) *(G-13798)*

Staely Custom Crating, Conover *Also Called: Conover Lumber Company Inc (G-5420)*

Stafast Products Inc (PA)...440 357-5546
  505 Lakeshore Blvd Painesville (44077) *(G-11111)*

Stafast West, Painesville *Also Called: Stafast Products Inc (G-11111)*

Stafford Gage & Tool Inc..937 277-9944
  4606 Webster St Dayton (45414) *(G-6021)*

Stafford Gravel Inc..419 298-2440
  4225 Co Rd 79 Edgerton (43517) *(G-6470)*

Stahl Gear & Machine Co...216 431-2820
  3901 Hamilton Ave Cleveland (44114) *(G-4323)*

Stahl/Scott Fetzer Company (HQ).....................................800 277-8245
  3201 W Old Lincoln Way Wooster (44691) *(G-14689)*

Stainless Automation..216 961-4550
  1978 W 74th St Cleveland (44102) *(G-4324)*

Stainless Crafts Inc...513 353-4578
  6660 Russell Heights Dr Cincinnati (45248) *(G-3110)*

Stainless Specialties Inc..440 942-4242
  33240 Lakeland Blvd Eastlake (44095) *(G-6443)*

Stakes Manufacturing LLC..216 245-4752
  34440 Vine St Willowick (44095) *(G-14567)*

Stakes Mfg, Willowick *Also Called: Stakes Manufacturing LLC (G-14567)*

Stalder Spring Works Inc..937 322-6120
  2345 Springfield Xenia Rd Springfield (45506) *(G-12378)*

Stam, Mentor *Also Called: Precision Bending Tech Inc (G-9590)*

Stam, Mentor *Also Called: Stam Inc (G-9622)*

Stam Inc..440 974-2500
  7350 Production Dr Mentor (44060) *(G-9622)*

Stamco Industries Inc..216 731-9333
  26650 Lakeland Blvd Cleveland (44132) *(G-4325)*

Stamm Contracting Company Inc.....................................330 274-8230
  4566 Orchard St Mantua (44255) *(G-8875)*

Stamp & Flash Inc (PA)..419 335-3015
  135 E Linfoot St Wauseon (43567) *(G-13859)*

Stamped Steel Products Inc..330 538-3951
  151 S Bailey Rd North Jackson (44451) *(G-10695)*

Stamtex Metal Stampings, Powell *Also Called: Metal Products Company (G-11491)*

Stan-Kell LLC..440 998-1116
  2621 West Ave Ashtabula (44004) *(G-617)*

Stanco Precision Mfg Inc..937 274-1785
  1 Walbrook Ave Dayton (45405) *(G-6022)*

Standard Aero Inc..937 840-1053
  214 Hobart Dr Hillsboro (45133) *(G-7726)*

Standard Bariatrics Inc..513 620-7751
  4300 Glendale Milford Rd Blue Ash (45242) *(G-1334)*

Standard Die Supply, Dayton *Also Called: Ready Technology Inc (G-5978)*

Standard Engineering Group Inc......................................330 494-4300
  3516 Highland Park Nw North Canton (44720) *(G-10669)*

Standard Jig Boring Svc LLC (HQ)....................................330 896-9530
  3360 Miller Park Rd Akron (44312) *(G-315)*

Standard Jig Boring Svc LLC...330 644-5405
  3194 Massillon Rd Akron (44312) *(G-316)*

Standard Machine Inc...216 631-4440
  1952 W 93rd St Cleveland (44102) *(G-4326)*

Standard Printing Co Inc...419 586-2371
  123 E Market St Celina (45822) *(G-2121)*

Standard Printing Co of Canton.......................................330 453-8247
  1115 Cherry Ave Ne Canton (44704) *(G-2012)*

Standard Printing Company, Canton *Also Called: Standard Printing Co of Canton (G-2012)*

Standard Publishing LLC...513 931-4050
  8805 Governors Hill Dr Ste 400 Cincinnati (45249) *(G-3111)*

Standard Register, Coldwater *Also Called: Taylor Communications Inc (G-4585)*

Standard Register Technologies..937 443-1000
  600 Albany St Dayton (45417) *(G-6023)*

Standard Signs Incorporated (PA)....................................330 467-2030
  9115 Freeway Dr Macedonia (44056) *(G-8716)*

Standard Technologies, Fremont *Also Called: Standard Technologies LLC (G-7133)*

Standard Technologies LLC...419 332-6434
  2641 Hayes Ave Fremont (43420) *(G-7133)*

Standard Textile Co Inc (PA)...513 761-9255
  1 Knollcrest Dr Cincinnati (45237) *(G-3112)*

Standard Welding & Lift Truck, Lorain *Also Called: Perkins Motor Service Ltd (G-8573)*

Standard Wellness Company LLC......................................330 931-1037
  105 Commerce Dr Gibsonburg (43431) *(G-7259)*

Standard Wldg & Stl Pdts Inc..330 273-2777
  260 S State Rd Medina (44256) *(G-9450)*

Standardaero, Hillsboro *Also Called: Pas Technologies Inc (G-7723)*

Standby Screw Machine Pdts Co......................................440 243-8200
  1122 W Bagley Rd Berea (44017) *(G-1188)*

Standex Electronics Inc (HQ)...513 871-3777
  4150 Thunderbird Ln Fairfield (45014) *(G-6778)*

Standex International Corp...513 533-7171
  4150 Thunderbird Ln Fairfield (45014) *(G-6779)*

Standex-Meder Electronics, Fairfield *Also Called: Standex Electronics Inc (G-6778)*

Standout Stickers Inc...877 449-7703
  2991 Interstate Pkwy Brunswick (44212) *(G-1616)*

Standridge Color Corporation..770 464-3362
  1122 Integrity Dr Defiance (43512) *(G-6124)*

Stanek E F and Assoc Inc...216 341-7700
  700 Highland Rd E Macedonia (44056) *(G-8717)*

Stanek Windows, Macedonia *Also Called: Stanek E F and Assoc Inc (G-8717)*

Stanley Bittinger...740 942-4302
  81331 Hines Rd Cadiz (43907) *(G-1720)*

Stanley Electric US Co Inc (HQ)..740 852-5200
  420 E High St London (43140) *(G-8541)*

Stanley Engineered Fasten..440 657-3537
  7900 W Ridge Rd Elyria (44035) *(G-6591)*

Stanley Industrial & Auto LLC (HQ)...................................614 755-7000
  5195 Blazer Pkwy Dublin (43017) *(G-6349)*

Stanley Industries Inc...................................216 475-4000
19120 Cranwood Pkwy Cleveland (44128) *(G-4327)*

Stanley Steemer Carpet Cleaner, Dublin *Also Called: Stanley Steemer Intl Inc (G-6350)*

Stanley Steemer Intl Inc (PA)...................614 764-2007
5800 Innovation Dr Dublin (43016) *(G-6350)*

Stansley Mineral Resources Inc (PA)..........419 843-2813
3793 Silica Rd # B Sylvania (43560) *(G-12724)*

Stanwade Metal Products Inc.....................330 772-2421
6868 State Rt 305 Hartford (44424) *(G-7573)*

Stanwade Tanks and Equipment, Hartford *Also Called: Stanwade Metal Products Inc (G-7573)*

Staq Pharma of Ohio LLC..........................833 397-0106
255 Phillipi Rd Columbus (43228) *(G-5288)*

Star, Columbus *Also Called: Specialty Technology & Res (G-5282)*

Star, Marion *Also Called: Steam Trbine Altrntive Rsrces (G-9001)*

Star Brite Express Car WA.........................330 674-0062
887 S Washington St Millersburg (44654) *(G-10010)*

Star Calendar & Printing Inc......................216 741-3223
4354 Pearl Rd Cleveland (44109) *(G-4328)*

Star Distribution and Mfg LLC...................513 860-3573
10179 Commerce Park Dr West Chester (45246) *(G-14149)*

Star Dynamics Corporation (PA).................614 334-4510
4455 Reynolds Dr Hilliard (43026) *(G-7702)*

Star Engineering LLC................................740 342-3514
701 Madison St New Lexington (43764) *(G-10408)*

Star Extruded Shapes LLC.........................330 533-98J3
7055 Herbert Rd Canfield (44406) *(G-1816)*

Star Fab Inc..330 482-1601
400 W Railroad St Ste 8 Columbiana (44408) *(G-4630)*

Star Fab LLC (HQ)...................................330 533-9863
7055 Herbert Rd Canfield (44406) *(G-1817)*

STAR FAB, INC., Columbiana *Also Called: Star Fab Inc (G-4630)*

Star Fire Distributing, Akron *Also Called: Thermo-Rite Mfg Company (G-336)*

Star Jet LLC...614 338-4379
4130 E 5th Ave Columbus (43219) *(G-5289)*

Star Manufacturing LLC............................330 740-8300
1775 Logan Ave Youngstown (44505) *(G-14940)*

Star Manufacturring, West Chester *Also Called: Star Distribution and Mfg LLC (G-14149)*

Star Metal Products Co Inc........................440 899-7000
30405 Clemens Rd Westlake (44145) *(G-14336)*

Star Printing Company Inc.........................330 376-0514
125 N Union St Akron (44304) *(G-317)*

Starbright Lighting USA LLC.......................330 650-2000
5136 Darrow Rd Hudson (44236) *(G-7859)*

Stark Cnty Fdrtion Cnsrvtion C...................330 268-1652
6323 Richville Dr Sw Canton (44706) *(G-2013)*

Stark Forest Products, Canton *Also Called: Stark Truss Company Inc (G-2015)*

Stark Industrial LLC.................................330 966-8108
5103 Stoneham Rd North Canton (44720) *(G-10670)*

Stark Materials Inc...................................330 497-1648
7345 Sunset Strip Ave Nw Canton (44720) *(G-2014)*

Stark Truss Beach City Lumber, Beach City *Also Called: Stark Truss Company Inc (G-907)*

Stark Truss Company Inc...........................330 756-3050
6855 Chestnut Ridge Rd Nw Beach City (44608) *(G-907)*

Stark Truss Company Inc...........................330 478-2100
4933 Southway St Sw Canton (44706) *(G-2015)*

Stark Truss Company Inc...........................330 478-6063
1601 Perry Dr Sw Canton (44706) *(G-2016)*

Stark Truss Company Inc (PA)....................330 478-2100
109 Miles Ave Sw Canton (44710) *(G-2017)*

Stark Truss Company Inc...........................419 298-3777
400 Component Dr Edgerton (43517) *(G-6471)*

Stark Truss Company Inc...........................740 335-4156
2000 Landmark Blvd Washington Court Hou (43160) *(G-13823)*

Starkey Machinery Inc..............................419 468-2560
254 S Washington St Galion (44833) *(G-7199)*

Starks Plastics LLC..................................513 541-4591
11236 Sebring Dr Cincinnati (45240) *(G-3113)*

Starr Fabricating Inc................................330 394-9891
4175 Warren Sharon Rd Vienna (44473) *(G-13618)*

Starr Machine Inc....................................740 753-0184
226 Sylvania Ave Nelsonville (45764) *(G-10321)*

Starr Services Inc....................................513 241-7708
3625 Spring Grove Ave Cincinnati (45223) *(G-3114)*

Starwin Industries LLC.............................937 293-8568
3387 Woodman Dr Dayton (45429) *(G-6024)*

Stat Index Tab, Chillicothe *Also Called: Stat Industries Inc (G-2282)*

Stat Index Tab Company, Chillicothe *Also Called: Stat Industries Inc (G-2283)*

Stat Industries Inc (PA)............................740 779-6561
137 Stone Rd Chillicothe (45601) *(G-2282)*

Stat Industries Inc...................................740 779-6561
137 Stone Rd Chillicothe (45601) *(G-2283)*

Stat Industries Inc...................................513 860-4482
3269 Profit Dr Hamilton (45014) *(G-7527)*

State 8 Motorcycle & Atv, Peninsula *Also Called: Wholecycle Inc (G-11186)*

State Chemical Manufacturing, Cleveland *Also Called: State Industrial Products Corp (G-4329)*

State Chemical Manufacturing, Hebron *Also Called: State Industrial Products Corp (G-7637)*

State Industrial Products Corp (PA).............877 747-6986
5915 Landerbrook Dr Ste 300 Cleveland (44124) *(G-4329)*

State Industrial Products Corp....................740 929-6370
383 N High St Hebron (43025) *(G-7637)*

State Metal Hose Inc................................614 527-4700
4171 Lyman Dr Hilliard (43026) *(G-7703)*

Stateline Power Corp................................937 547-1006
650 Pine St Greenville (45331) *(G-7356)*

Status Mens Accessories...........................440 786-9394
7650 First Pl Ste F Oakwood Village (44146) *(G-10909)*

Status Solutions, Westerville *Also Called: Status Solutions LLC (G-14235)*

Status Solutions LLC................................434 296-1789
999 County Line Rd W # A Westerville (43082) *(G-14235)*

Staub Laser Cutting Inc.............................937 890-4486
2501 Thunderhawk Ct Dayton (45414) *(G-6025)*

Staub Manufacturing Solutions, Dayton *Also Called: Staub Laser Cutting Inc (G-6025)*

Staufs Coffee Roasters Limited...................614 486-4479
705 Hadley Dr Columbus (43228) *(G-5290)*

Stays Lighting Inc....................................440 328-3254
936 Taylor St Elyria (44035) *(G-6592)*

STC International Co Ltd (PA).....................561 308-6002
1499 Shaker Run Blvd Lebanon (45036) *(G-8287)*

Std Liquidation Inc...................................937 492-6121
1950 Campbell Rd Sidney (45365) *(G-12055)*

Stealth Arms LLC....................................419 925-7005
4939 Kittle Rd Celina (45822) *(G-2122)*

Steam Trbine Altrntive Rsrces....................740 387-5535
370 W Fairground St Marion (43302) *(G-9001)*

Stebbins Engineering & Mfg Co...................740 922-3012
4778 Belden Dr Se Uhrichsville (44683) *(G-13407)*

Steck Manufacturing Co LLC......................937 222-0002
1200 Leo St Dayton (45404) *(G-6026)*

Steel & Alloy Utility Pdts Inc......................330 530-2220
110 Ohio Ave Mc Donald (44437) *(G-9361)*

Steel Aviation Aircraft Sales......................937 332-7587
4433 E State Route 55 Casstown (45312) *(G-2092)*

Steel Ceilings Inc.....................................740 967-1063
451 E Coshocton St Johnstown (43031) *(G-7998)*

Steel City Contractors LLC........................330 519-8873
419 Blossom Ave Campbell (44405) *(G-1771)*

Steel City Corporation (PA)........................330 792-7663
100 Hedstrom Dr Ashland (44805) *(G-575)*

Steel Eqp Specialists Inc (PA)....................330 823-8260
1507 Beeson St Ne Alliance (44601) *(G-406)*

Steel Forming Inc....................................714 532-6321
1775 Logan Ave Youngstown (44505) *(G-14941)*

Steel It LLC...513 253-3111
250 Mccullough St Cincinnati (45226) *(G-3115)*

Steel Products Corp Akron........................330 688-6633
2288 Samira Rd Stow (44224) *(G-12463)*

Steel Quest Inc.......................................513 772-5030
8180 Corporate Park Dr Ste 250 Cincinnati (45242) *(G-3116)*

Steel Technologies LLC.............................419 523-5199
740 E Williamstown Rd Ottawa (45875) *(G-11046)*

Steel Technologies LLC.............................440 946-8666
2220 Joseph Lloyd Pkwy Willoughby (44094) *(G-14532)*

Steel Valley Tank & Welding................................. 740 598-4994
24 County Road 7e Brilliant (43913) *(G-1497)*

Steel Warehouse Division, Columbus *Also Called: Columbus Pipe and Equipment Co*
(G-4831)

Steelastic Company LLC................................. 330 633-0505
1 Vision Ln Cuyahoga Falls (44223) *(G-5574)*

Steelcon LLC................................. 330 457-4003
47161 Oh-558 Rogers (44455) *(G-11643)*

Steelial Cnstr Met Fabrication, Vinton *Also Called: Steelial Wldg Met Fbrction Inc (G-13624)*

Steelial Wldg Met Fbrction Inc................................. 740 669-5300
70764 State Route 124 Vinton (45686) *(G-13624)*

Steeltec Products LLC................................. 216 681-1114
13000 Saint Clair Ave Cleveland (44108) *(G-4330)*

Steer & Gear Inc................................. 614 231-4064
1000 Barnett Rd Columbus (43227) *(G-5291)*

Steer & Geer, Columbus *Also Called: Steer & Gear Inc (G-5291)*

Steer America, Uniontown *Also Called: Steeramerica Inc (G-13426)*

Steeramerica Inc................................. 330 563-4407
1525 Corporate Woods Pkwy Ste 500 Uniontown (44685) *(G-13426)*

Steere Enterprises Inc................................. 330 633-4926
303 Tacoma Ave Tallmadge (44278) *(G-12750)*

Steere Enterprises Inc (PA)................................. 330 633-4926
285 Commerce St Tallmadge (44278) *(G-12751)*

Stefan Restoration, Broadview Heights *Also Called: Keban Industries Inc (G-1503)*

Stefra Inc................................. 440 846-8240
18021 Cliffside Dr Strongsville (44136) *(G-12605)*

Stegemeyer Machine Inc................................. 513 321-5651
212 Mccullough St Cincinnati (45226) *(G-3117)*

Stehlin, John & Sons Meats, Cincinnati *Also Called: John Stehlin & Sons Co (G-2769)*

Stein LLC................................. 216 883-7444
2032 Campbell Rd Cleveland (44105) *(G-4331)*

Stein LLC (DH)................................. 440 526-9301
3 Summit Park Dr Ste 425 Independence (44131) *(G-7919)*

Stein Holdings Inc................................. 440 526-9301
3 Summit Park Dr Ste 425 Independence (44131) *(G-7920)*

Stein Inc................................. 419 747-2611
1490 Old Bowman St Mansfield (44903) *(G-8854)*

Stein-Palmer Printing Co................................. 740 633-3894
1 Westwood Dr Unit 202 Saint Clairsville (43950) *(G-11711)*

Stein-Way Equipment................................. 330 857-8700
12335 Emerson Rd Apple Creek (44606) *(G-478)*

Steinbarger Precision Cnc Inc................................. 937 376-0322
634 Cincinnati Ave Xenia (45385) *(G-14775)*

Steiner Eoptics Inc (PA)................................. 937 426-2341
3475 Newmark Dr Miamisburg (45342) *(G-9740)*

Steinert Industries Inc................................. 330 678-0028
1507 Franklin Ave Kent (44240) *(G-8083)*

Stelfast LLC (HQ)................................. 440 879-0077
22979 Stelfast Pkwy Strongsville (44149) *(G-12606)*

Stellar Group Inc................................. 330 769-8484
4935 Enterprise Pkwy Seville (44273) *(G-11921)*

Stellar Systems Inc................................. 513 921-8748
1944 Harrison Ave Cincinnati (45214) *(G-3118)*

Stelter and Brinck Inc................................. 513 367-9300
201 Sales Ave Harrison (45030) *(G-7569)*

Step 2, Streetsboro *Also Called: Step2 Company LLC (G-12525)*

Step In Time, Youngstown *Also Called: Sit Inc (G-14933)*

Step2 Company LLC (HQ)................................. 866 429-5200
10010 Aurora Hudson Rd Streetsboro (44241) *(G-12525)*

Stephen Andrews Inc................................. 330 725-2672
7634 Lafayette Rd Lodi (44254) *(G-8507)*

Stephen M Trudick................................. 440 834-1891
13813 Station Road Burton (44021) *(G-1704)*

Stephens Pipe & Steel LLC................................. 740 869-2257
10732 Schadel Ln Mount Sterling (43143) *(G-10229)*

Stepp Sewing Service, Milford *Also Called: Chris Stepp (G-9928)*

Stepping Stone Enterprises Inc................................. 419 472-0505
1689 Lance Pointe Rd Maumee (43537) *(G-9320)*

Sterilite, Massillon *Also Called: Sterilite Corporation (G-9246)*

Sterilite Corporation................................. 330 830-2204
4495 Sterilite St Se Massillon (44646) *(G-9246)*

Steris Corporation................................. 440 354-2600
5900 Heisley Rd Mentor (44060) *(G-9623)*

Steris Corporation (DH)................................. 440 354-2600
5960 Heisley Rd Mentor (44060) *(G-9624)*

Steris Corporation................................. 330 696-9946
6515 Hopkins Rd Mentor (44060) *(G-9625)*

Steris Corporation................................. 440 392-8079
6100 Heisley Rd Mentor (44060) *(G-9626)*

Steris Corporation................................. 440 354-2600
9325 Pinecone Dr Mentor (44060) *(G-9627)*

Steris Instrument MGT Svcs Inc................................. 800 783-9251
4575 Hudson Dr Stow (44224) *(G-12464)*

Steris-IMS................................. 330 686-4557
4575 Hudson Dr Stow (44224) *(G-12465)*

Sterling Associates Inc................................. 330 630-3500
1783 Brittain Rd Akron (44310) *(G-318)*

Sterling Coating................................. 513 942-4900
9048 Port Union Rialto Rd West Chester (45069) *(G-14076)*

Sterling Commerce LLC................................. 614 798-2192
4600 Lakehurst Ct Dublin (43016) *(G-6351)*

Sterling Industries Inc................................. 419 523-3788
740 E Main St Ottawa (45875) *(G-11047)*

Sterling Mining Corporation (HQ)................................. 330 549-2165
10900 South Ave North Lima (44452) *(G-10714)*

Sterling Pipe & Tube, Toledo *Also Called: Sigma Tube Company (G-13131)*

Sterling Process Equipment & Services Inc (PA)................................. 614 868-5151
333 Mccormick Blvd Columbus (43213) *(G-5292)*

Stevco, Wellsville *Also Called: Stevenson Mfg Co (G-13914)*

Steve Vore Welding and Steel................................. 419 375-4087
3234 State Route 49 Fort Recovery (45846) *(G-6971)*

Steve's Vans Auto Sales, Marietta *Also Called: Steves Vans ACC Unlimited LLC (G-8950)*

Steven A Esnbrown Lk Lure Qprt................................. 740 965-2200
4909 Harlem Rd Galena (43021) *(G-7174)*

Stevenson Color Inc................................. 513 321-7500
535 Wilmer Ave Cincinnati (45226) *(G-3119)*

Stevenson Mfg Co................................. 330 532-1581
1 1st St Wellsville (43968) *(G-13914)*

Steves Sports Inc................................. 440 735-0044
10333 Northfield Rd Unit 136 Northfield (44067) *(G-10797)*

Steves Vans ACC Unlimited LLC................................. 740 374-3154
221 Pike St Marietta (45750) *(G-8950)*

Steward Edge Bus Solutions................................. 614 826-5305
23 N Westgate Ave Columbus (43204) *(G-5293)*

Stewart Acquisition LLC (PA)................................. 330 963-0322
2146 Enterprise Pkwy Twinsburg (44087) *(G-13380)*

Stewart Filmscreen Corp................................. 513 753-0800
3919 Bach Buxton Rd Amelia (45102) *(G-438)*

Stewart Manufacturing Corp................................. 937 390-3333
5230 Prosperity Dr Springfield (45502) *(G-12379)*

Stewart McDnalds Guitar Sp Sup, Athens *Also Called: Stewart-Macdonald Mfg Co (G-653)*

Stewart-Macdonald Mfg Co (PA)................................. 740 592-3021
21 N Shafer St Athens (45701) *(G-653)*

Stg Lane, Akron *Also Called: Scandinavian Tob Group Ln Ltd (G-306)*

STI Liquidation Inc................................. 614 733-0099
7710 Corporate Blvd Plain City (43064) *(G-11418)*

Stiber Fabricating Inc................................. 216 771-7210
1678 Leonard St Cleveland (44113) *(G-4332)*

Sticker Corporation................................. 440 942-4700
37941 Elm St Willoughby (44094) *(G-14533)*

Sticker Corporation (PA)................................. 440 946-2100
37877 Elm St Willoughby (44094) *(G-14534)*

Sticktite Lenses LLC................................. 571 276-9508
5195 Hampsted Village Center Way New Albany (43054) *(G-10351)*

Stiger Pre Cast Inc................................. 740 482-2313
17793 State Highway 231 Nevada (44849) *(G-10324)*

Stirling Ultracold, Athens *Also Called: Global Cooling Inc (G-641)*

Stitches Usa LLC................................. 330 852-0500
3149 State Rte 39 Walnut Creek (44687) *(G-13695)*

Stock, Chagrin Falls *Also Called: Stock Equipment Company Inc (G-2184)*

Stock Equipment Company, Solon *Also Called: Stock Fairfield Corporation (G-12185)*

Stock Equipment Company Inc................................. 440 543-6000
16490 Chillicothe Rd Chagrin Falls (44023) *(G-2184)*

2025 Harris Ohio
Industrial Directory

(G-0000) Company's Geographic Section entry number

Stock Fairfield Corporation.................................. 440 543-6000
30825 Aurora Rd # 150 Solon (44139) *(G-12185)*

Stock Mfg & Design Co Inc (PA)......................... 513 353-3600
10040 Cilley Rd Cleves (45002) *(G-4549)*

Stocker & Sitler Oil Company (HQ)..................... 614 888-9588
4770 Indianola Ave Columbus (43214) *(G-5294)*

Stocker Concrete Company................................. 740 254-4626
7574 Us Hwy 36 Se Gnadenhutten (44629) *(G-7293)*

Stocker Sand & Gravel Co (PA)........................... 740 254-4635
Rte 36 Gnadenhutten (44629) *(G-7294)*

Stoepfel Drilling Co... 419 532-3307
12245 State Route 115 Ottawa (45875) *(G-11048)*

Stolle Machinery Company LLC........................... 330 244-0555
1007 High Ave Sw Canton (44707) *(G-2018)*

Stolle Machinery Company LLC........................... 937 497-5400
7425 Webster St Dayton (45414) *(G-6027)*

Stolle Machinery Company LLC........................... 937 497-5400
2900 Campbell Rd Sidney (45365) *(G-12056)*

Stolle Machinery-Sidney, Sidney Also Called: Stolle Machinery Company LLC *(G-12056)*

Stolle Milk Biologics Inc.................................... 513 489-7997
4735 Devitt Dr West Chester (45246) *(G-14150)*

Stolle Properties Inc.. 513 932-8664
6954 Cornell Rd Ste 100 Blue Ash (45242) *(G-1335)*

Stone Center, Cincinnati Also Called: Blu Bird LLC *(G-2413)*

Stone Center, Columbus Also Called: Blu Bird LLC *(G-4766)*

Stone Center of Dayton, Moraine Also Called: 3jd Inc *(G-10141)*

Stone Statements Incorporated........................... 513 489-7866
7451 Fields Ertel Rd Cincinnati (45241) *(G-3120)*

Stoneco, Carey Also Called: Wyandot Dolomite Inc *(G-2064)*

Stoneco Inc (DH).. 419 422-8854
1700 Fostoria Ave Ste 200 Findlay (45840) *(G-6923)*

Stoneco Inc.. 419 893-7645
1360 Ford St Maumee (43537) *(G-9321)*

Stoneco Inc.. 419 393-2555
13762 Road 179 Oakwood (45873) *(G-10900)*

Stoneco Inc.. 419 686-3311
11580 S Dixie Hwy Portage (43451) *(G-11461)*

Stoneco Inc.. 419 693-3933
352 George Hardy Dr Toledo (43605) *(G-13134)*

Stonecote, Norton Also Called: E L Stone Company *(G-10820)*

Stoneridge Inc... 419 884-1219
345 S Mill St Lexington (44904) *(G-8374)*

Stony Hill Mixing Ltd.. 330 674-0814
5526 Township Road 127 Millersburg (44654) *(G-10011)*

Stonyridge Inc... 937 845-9482
570 S Dayton Lakeview Rd New Carlisle (45344) *(G-10380)*

Stop Stick Ltd.. 513 202-5500
365 Industrial Dr Harrison (45030) *(G-7570)*

Stop Stick, Liability Company, Harrison Also Called: Stop Stick Ltd *(G-7570)*

Storetek Engineering Inc................................... 330 294-0678
399 Commerce St Tallmadge (44278) *(G-12752)*

Storopack Inc (DH).. 513 874-0314
4758 Devitt Dr Cincinnati (45246) *(G-3121)*

Storopack Inc... 513 874-0314
4600 Brate Dr West Chester (45011) *(G-14077)*

Stouffer Corporation (DH)................................. 440 349-5757
30003 Bainbridge Rd Solon (44139) *(G-12186)*

Stoutheart Corporation....................................... 800 556-6470
7205 Chagrin Rd Ste 4 Chagrin Falls (44023) *(G-2185)*

Stover International Inc...................................... 740 363-5251
222 Stover Dr Delaware (43015) *(G-6175)*

Straight 72 Inc.. 740 943-5730
20078 State Route 4 Marysville (43040) *(G-9051)*

Straightaway Fabrications Ltd............................ 419 281-9440
481us Highway 250 E Ashland (44805) *(G-576)*

Strassells Machine Inc...................................... 419 747-1088
1015 Springmill St Mansfield (44906) *(G-8855)*

Strata Mine Services Inc................................... 740 695-6880
68000 Bayberry Dr Unit 103 Saint Clairsville (43950) *(G-11712)*

Strata Mine Services LLC.................................. 740 695-0488
67925 Bayberry Dr Saint Clairsville (43950) *(G-11713)*

Strategic Materials Inc...................................... 740 349-9523
101 S Arch St Newark (43055) *(G-10534)*

Strategic Technology Entp................................. 440 354-2600
5960 Heisley Rd Mentor (44060) *(G-9628)*

Stratton Creek Wood Works LLC........................ 330 876-0005
5915 Burnett East Rd Kinsman (44428) *(G-8143)*

Stratus Unlimited LLC (PA)................................ 440 209-6200
8959 Tyler Blvd Mentor (44060) *(G-9629)*

Strawn Oil Field Service, Salem Also Called: Everflow Eastern Partners LP *(G-11778)*

Strawser Steel Drum Ohio Ltd........................... 614 856-5982
219 Commerce Dr Mount Vernon (43050) *(G-10266)*

Streamline Media & Pubg LLC........................... 614 822-1817
2699 Prendergast Pl Reynoldsburg (43068) *(G-11581)*

Streamside Materials, Findlay Also Called: Streamside Materials Llc *(G-6924)*

Streamside Materials Llc................................... 419 423-1290
7440 Township Road 95 Findlay (45840) *(G-6924)*

Streetsboro Operations, Twinsburg Also Called: Facil North America Inc *(G-13302)*

Stress-Crete Company....................................... 440 576-9073
1153 State Route 46 N Jefferson (44047) *(G-7983)*

Stresscrete, Jefferson Also Called: King Luminaire Company Inc *(G-7975)*

Stretchtape Inc.. 216 486-9400
3100 Hamilton Ave Cleveland (44114) *(G-4333)*

Stricker Refinishing Inc.................................... 216 696-2906
2060 Hamilton Ave Cleveland (44114) *(G-4334)*

Strictly Stitchery Inc.. 440 543-7128
13801 Shaker Blvd Apt 4a Cleveland (44120) *(G-4335)*

Stride Out Rnch N Rodeo Sp LLC...................... 937 539-1537
4122 Laybourne Rd Springfield (45505) *(G-12380)*

Stride Tool LLC... 440 247-4600
30333 Emerald Valley Pkwy Glenwillow (44139) *(G-7289)*

Striker Hydraulic Breakers, Willoughby Also Called: Toku America Inc *(G-14540)*

Stripmatic Products Inc..................................... 216 241-7143
5301 Grant Ave Ste 200 Cleveland (44125) *(G-4336)*

Strohecker Incorporated.................................... 330 426-9496
213 N Pleasant Dr East Palestine (44413) *(G-6407)*

Strong Bindery Inc.. 216 231-0001
13015 Larchmere Blvd Cleveland (44120) *(G-4337)*

Strong-Coat LLC.. 440 299-2068
4420 Sherwin Rd Willoughby (44094) *(G-14535)*

Structural Steel Fabrication, Cleveland Also Called: Nova Structural Steel Inc *(G-4100)*

Structural Steel Fabrication, Pataskala Also Called: Ohio Steel Industries Inc *(G-11144)*

Struers Inc (DH).. 440 871-0071
24766 Detroit Rd Westlake (44145) *(G-14337)*

Struggle Grind Success LLC.............................. 330 834-6738
6414 Market St Boardman (44512) *(G-1377)*

Stryker Orthopedic.. 614 766-2990
4420 Tuller Rd Dublin (43017) *(G-6352)*

Stryker Plant, Stryker Also Called: Sauder Manufacturing Co *(G-12627)*

Stryver Mfg Inc... 937 854-3048
15 N Broadway St Dayton (45426) *(G-6028)*

Stuart Burial Vault Co Inc................................. 740 569-4158
527 Ford St Bremen (43107) *(G-1487)*

Stuart-Dean Co Inc... 412 765-2752
2615 Saint Clair Ave Ne Cleveland (44114) *(G-4338)*

Stuchell Products LLC....................................... 330 821-4299
12240 Rockhill Ave Ne Alliance (44601) *(G-407)*

Stud Welding, Strongsville Also Called: Stud Welding Associates Inc *(G-12607)*

Stud Welding Associates.................................... 216 392-7808
101 Liberty Ct Elyria (44035) *(G-6593)*

Stud Welding Associates, Strongsville Also Called: Spiegelberg Manufacturing Inc *(G-12604)*

Stud Welding Associates Inc.............................. 440 783-3160
12200 Alameda Dr Strongsville (44149) *(G-12607)*

Studgionsgroup LLC.. 216 804-1561
10413 Way Ave Cleveland (44105) *(G-4339)*

Studio Arts and Glass Inc.................................. 330 494-9779
7495 Strauss Ave Nw Canton (44720) *(G-2019)*

Studio Eleven Inc (PA)....................................... 937 295-2225
301 S Main St Fort Loramie (45845) *(G-6958)*

Studio Foundry, Cleveland Also Called: Foundry Artists Inc *(G-3739)*

Stull Woodworks Inc.. 937 698-8181
155 Marybill Dr S Troy (45373) *(G-13259)*

A
L
P
H
A
B
E
T
I
C

Stumps Converting Inc 419 492-2542
742 W Mansfield St New Washington (44854) *(G-10483)*

Stumptown Lbr Pallet Mills Ltd 740 757-2275
55613 Washington St Somerton (43713) *(G-12212)*

Stutzman Manufacturing Ltd 330 674-4359
7727 Township Road 604 Millersburg (44654) *(G-10012)*

Style Crest Enterprises Inc (PA) 419 355-8586
2450 Enterprise St Fremont (43420) *(G-7134)*

Style-Line Incorporated (PA) 614 291-0600
901 W 3rd Ave Ste A Columbus (43212) *(G-5295)*

Suburban Communications Inc 440 632-0130
14905 N State Ave Middlefield (44062) *(G-9829)*

Suburban Manufacturing Co 440 953-2024
1924 E 337th St Eastlake (44095) *(G-6444)*

Suburban Metal Products, Circleville *Also Called: Cline Machine and Automtn Inc (G-3252)*

Suburban Metal Products Inc 740 474-4237
1050 Tarlton Rd Circleville (43113) *(G-3263)*

Suburban Plastics Co (PA) 847 741-4900
509 Water St Sw Bolivar (44612) *(G-1392)*

Suburban Press Incorporated 216 961-0766
3818 Lorain Ave Cleveland (44113) *(G-4340)*

Suburban Steel of Indiana, Columbus *Also Called: Suburban Stl Sup Co Ltd Partnr (G-5296)*

Suburban Steel Supply Co Limited Partnership (PA) 614 737-5501
1900 Deffenbaugh Ct Gahanna (43230) *(G-7170)*

Suburban Stl Sup Co Ltd Partnr 317 783-6555
1900 Deffenbaugh Ct Columbus (43230) *(G-5296)*

Suburbanite Inc 419 756-4390
1552 W Cook Rd Mansfield (44906) *(G-8856)*

Subway, Circleville *Also Called: Circleville Oil Co (G-3251)*

Suelos Sweetz LLC 440 478-1301
35560 Vine St Willowick (44095) *(G-14568)*

Sugar Creek, Cincinnati *Also Called: Sugar Creek Packing Co (G-3122)*

Sugar Creek Packing Co (PA) 513 551-5280
4320 Indeco Ct Cincinnati (45241) *(G-3122)*

Sugar Creek Packing Co 937 268-6601
1241 N Gettysburg Ave Dayton (45417) *(G-6029)*

Sugarcreek Lime Service 330 364-4460
2068 Gordon Rd Nw Dover (44622) *(G-6264)*

Sugarcreek Ready Mix, Bellbrook *Also Called: Ernst Enterprises Inc (G-1091)*

Sugarcreek Shavings LLC 330 763-4239
3121 Winklepleck Rd Nw Sugarcreek (44681) *(G-12651)*

Sulecki Precision Products Inc 440 255-5454
8785 East Ave Mentor (44060) *(G-9630)*

Sullivan Company, The, Westerville *Also Called: Bluelogos Inc (G-14247)*

Sumiriko Ohio Inc (DH) 419 358-2121
320 Snider Rd Bluffton (45817) *(G-1365)*

Sumitomo Elc Carbide Mfg Inc (DH) 440 354-0600
210 River St Grand River (44045) *(G-7312)*

Sumitomo Elc Wirg Systems Inc 937 642-7579
14800 Industrial Pkwy Marysville (43040) *(G-9052)*

Summer Garden Food Mfg, Boardman *Also Called: Zidian Manufacturing LLC (G-1380)*

Summers Acquisition Corp (DH) 216 941-7700
12555 Berea Rd Cleveland (44111) *(G-4341)*

Summers Organization LLC 740 286-1322
345 E Main St Ste H Jackson (45640) *(G-7954)*

Summers Rubber Company, Cleveland *Also Called: Summers Acquisition Corp (G-4341)*

Summit Avionics Inc 330 425-1440
2225 E Enterprise Pkwy # 1a Twinsburg (44087) *(G-13381)*

Summit Container Corporation (PA) 719 481-8400
8080 Beckett Center Dr Ste 203 West Chester (45069) *(G-14078)*

Summit County 330 865-8065
1828 Smith Rd Akron (44313) *(G-319)*

Summit Design and Tech Inc 330 733-6662
1147 Sweitzer Ave Akron (44301) *(G-320)*

Summit Engineered Products Inc 330 854-5388
516 Elm Ridge Ave Canal Fulton (44614) *(G-1779)*

Summit Machine Ltd 330 628-2663
3991 Mogadore Rd Mogadore (44260) *(G-10087)*

Summit Machine Solutions LLC 330 785-0781
1029 Arlington Cir Akron (44306) *(G-321)*

Summit Machining Co Ltd 330 628-2663
3991 Mogadore Rd Mogadore (44260) *(G-10088)*

Summit Millwork LLC 330 920-4000
1619 Main St Cuyahoga Falls (44221) *(G-5575)*

Summit Online Products LLC 800 326-1972
3982 Powell Rd Ste 137 Powell (43065) *(G-11495)*

Summit Packaging Solutions LLC (PA) 719 481-8400
8080 Beckett Center Dr Ste 203 West Chester (45069) *(G-14079)*

Summit Tool Company (HQ) 330 535-7177
768 E North St Akron (44305) *(G-322)*

Summit Trailer Sales & Svcs, Coventry Township *Also Called: Friess Welding Inc (G-5482)*

Summitville Laboratories, Summitville *Also Called: Summitville Tiles Inc (G-12661)*

Summitville Labs, Minerva *Also Called: Summitville Tiles Inc (G-10048)*

Summitville Tiles Inc 330 868-6771
1310 Alliance Rd Nw Minerva (44657) *(G-10047)*

Summitville Tiles Inc 330 868-6463
81 Arbor Rd Ne Minerva (44657) *(G-10048)*

Summitville Tiles Inc (DH) 330 223-1511
15364 State Rte 644 Summitville (43962) *(G-12661)*

Sun America LLC 330 821-6300
46 N Rockhill Ave Alliance (44601) *(G-408)*

Sun Art Decals Inc 440 234-9045
83 Dorland Ave Berea (44017) *(G-1189)*

Sun Chemical Corporation 513 753-9550
3922 Bach Buxton Rd Amelia (45102) *(G-439)*

Sun Chemical Corporation 513 671-0407
12049 Centron Pl Cincinnati (45246) *(G-3123)*

Sun Chemical Corporation 513 681-5950
5020 Spring Grove Ave Cincinnati (45232) *(G-3124)*

Sun Chemical Corporation 513 681-5950
5020 Spring Grove Ave Cincinnati (45232) *(G-3125)*

Sun Chemical Corporation 513 830-8667
5000 Spring Grove Ave Cincinnati (45232) *(G-3126)*

Sun Chemical Corporation 513 681-5950
4526 Chickering Ave Cincinnati (45232) *(G-3127)*

Sun Chemical Corporation 419 891-3514
1380 Ford St Maumee (43537) *(G-9322)*

Sun Chemical US Rycoline, Cincinnati *Also Called: Sun Chemical Corporation (G-3124)*

Sun Newspaper Div, Cleveland *Also Called: Comcorp Inc (G-3550)*

Sun Polishing Corp 440 237-5525
13800 Progress Pkwy Ste E Cleveland (44133) *(G-4342)*

Sun Shine Awards 740 425-2504
36099 Bethesda Street Ext Barnesville (43713) *(G-847)*

Sun State Plastics Inc 330 494-5220
4045 Kevin St Nw Canton (44720) *(G-2020)*

Sunamericaconverting LLC 330 821-6300
46 N Rockhill Ave Alliance (44601) *(G-409)*

Suncoke Energy Inc 513 727-5571
3353 Yankee Rd Middletown (45044) *(G-9895)*

Sunfield Inc 740 928-0405
116 Enterprise Dr Hebron (43025) *(G-7638)*

Sunless, Macedonia *Also Called: Innove Inc (G-8697)*

Sunnest Service LLC 740 283-2815
619 Slack St Steubenville (43952) *(G-12412)*

Sunny Brook Prest Concrete Co 330 673-7667
3586 Sunnybrook Rd Kent (44240) *(G-8084)*

Sunpower Inc 740 594-2221
2005 E State St Ste 104 Athens (45701) *(G-654)*

Sunrise Cooperative Inc 419 628-4705
292 W 4th St Minster (45865) *(G-10066)*

Sunrise Foods, Columbus *Also Called: Sunrise Foods Inc (G-5297)*

Sunrise Foods Inc 614 276-2880
2097 Corvair Blvd Columbus (43207) *(G-5297)*

Sunset Golf LLC 419 994-5563
71 West Ave Ste 6 Tallmadge (44278) *(G-12753)*

Sunset Industries Inc 440 306-8284
7567 Tyler Blvd Mentor (44060) *(G-9631)*

Sunshine Farms Dairy, Elyria *Also Called: Consun Food Industries Inc (G-6514)*

Sunshine Products 303 478-4913
760 Warehouse Rd Ste O Toledo (43615) *(G-13135)*

Sunstar, Springboro *Also Called: Sunstar Engrg Americas Inc (G-12268)*

Sunstar Engrg Americas Inc 937 743-9049
700 Watkins Glen Dr Franklin (45005) *(G-7051)*

Sunstar Engrg Americas Inc (HQ)..................... 937 746-8575
85 S Pioneer Blvd Springboro (45066) *(G-12268)*

Sunstar Sprockets, Franklin Also Called: Sunstar Engrg Americas Inc *(G-7051)*

Sup-R-Die, Cleveland Also Called: Palisin & Associates Inc *(G-4132)*

Super Suppers, Bay Village Also Called: Generations Ace Inc *(G-902)*

Super Systems Inc (PA)................................ 513 772-0060
7205 Edington Dr Cincinnati (45249) *(G-3128)*

Superalloy Mfg Solutions Corp..................... 513 605-8380
11495 Deerfield Rd Blue Ash (45242) *(G-1336)*

Superalloy Mfg Solutions Corp..................... 513 489-9800
11230 Deerfield Rd Blue Ash (45242) *(G-1337)*

Superb Bakehouse Inc.................................. 614 302-7242
4395 Marketing Pl Groveport (43125) *(G-7451)*

Superb Industries Inc................................... 330 852-0500
330 3rd St Nw Sugarcreek (44681) *(G-12652)*

Superfine Manufacturing Inc........................ 330 897-9024
33715 County Road 10 Fresno (43824) *(G-7149)*

Superfinishers Inc....................................... 330 467-2125
380 Highland Rd E Macedonia (44056) *(G-8718)*

Superion Inc... 937 374-0033
1285 S Patton St Xenia (45385) *(G-14776)*

Superior Bar Products Inc............................ 419 784-2590
1710 Spruce St Defiance (43512) *(G-6125)*

Superior Caster Inc..................................... 513 539-8980
455 Wright Dr Middletown (45044) *(G-9896)*

Superior Casters, Middletown Also Called: Superior Caster Inc *(G-9896)*

Superior Clay Corporation............................ 740 922-4122
6566 Superior Rd Se Uhrichsville (44683) *(G-13408)*

Superior Dairy Inc....................................... 330 477-4515
4719 Navarre Rd Sw Canton (44706) *(G-2021)*

Superior Die Tool & Machine Co, Columbus Also Called: Superior Production LLC *(G-5299)*

Superior Energy Group Ltd.......................... 216 282-4440
34469 Scotch Ln Apt 4 Willoughby Hills (44094) *(G-14563)*

Superior Energy Systems LLC...................... 440 236-6009
13660 Station Rd Columbia Station (44028) *(G-4603)*

Superior Fibers Inc...................................... 740 394-2491
9702 Iron Point Rd Se Shawnee (43782) *(G-11952)*

Superior Flux & Mfg Co................................ 440 349-3000
6615 Parkland Blvd Cleveland (44139) *(G-4343)*

Superior Forge & Steel Corp (PA)................. 419 222-4412
1820 Mcclain Rd Lima (45804) *(G-8453)*

Superior Hardwoods Cambridge, Cambridge Also Called: Superior Hardwoods Ohio Inc *(G-1762)*

Superior Hardwoods Ohio Inc....................... 740 439-2727
9911 Ohio Ave Cambridge (43725) *(G-1762)*

Superior Hardwoods Ohio Inc....................... 740 596-2561
62581 Us Highway 50 Mc Arthur (45651) *(G-9350)*

Superior Hardwoods Ohio Inc (PA)............... 740 384-5677
134 Wellston Industrial Park Rd Wellston (45692) *(G-13910)*

Superior Holding LLC (DH).......................... 216 651-9400
3786 Ridge Rd Cleveland (44144) *(G-4344)*

Superior Image Embroidery LLC................... 513 991-7543
10152 International Blvd West Chester (45246) *(G-14151)*

Superior Impressions Inc............................. 419 244-8676
327 12th St Toledo (43604) *(G-13136)*

Superior Label Systems Inc (DH).................. 513 336-0825
7500 Industrial Row Dr Mason (45040) *(G-9157)*

Superior Machine Co, Canton Also Called: Robert Smart Inc *(G-2000)*

Superior Machine Systems, Mason Also Called: Superior Label Systems Inc *(G-9157)*

Superior Machine Tool LLC.......................... 419 675-2363
13606 Us Highway 68 Kenton (43326) *(G-8116)*

Superior Machining Inc................................ 937 236-9619
2946 Lindale Ave Dayton (45414) *(G-6030)*

Superior Marine Ways Inc............................ 740 894-6224
5852 County Rd 1 Suoth Pt Proctorville (45669) *(G-11499)*

Superior Metal Products Inc (PA).................. 419 228-1145
1005 W Grand Ave Lima (45801) *(G-8454)*

Superior Metal Worx LLC............................. 614 879-9400
1239 Alum Creek Dr Columbus (43209) *(G-5298)*

Superior Mold & Die Co............................... 330 688-8251
449 N Main St Munroe Falls (44262) *(G-10273)*

Superior Packaging...................................... 419 380-3335
2930 Airport Hwy Toledo (43609) *(G-13137)*

Superior Plastics Inc (PA)............................ 614 733-0307
8175 Business Way Plain City (43064) *(G-11419)*

Superior Plastics Inc................................... 614 733-0307
8163 Business Way Plain City (43064) *(G-11420)*

Superior Plastics Intl Inc............................. 419 424-3113
1116 Glen Meadow Dr Findlay (45840) *(G-6925)*

Superior Precision Pdts Inc.......................... 216 881-3696
968 E 69th Pl Cleveland (44103) *(G-4345)*

Superior Printing Ink Co Inc......................... 216 328-1720
7655 Hub Pkwy Ste 205 Cleveland (44125) *(G-4346)*

Superior Production LLC (PA)....................... 614 444-2181
2301 Fairwood Ave Columbus (43207) *(G-5299)*

Superior Products LLC................................. 216 651-9400
3786 Ridge Rd Cleveland (44144) *(G-4347)*

Superior Property Restoration...................... 513 509-6849
2144 Schappelle Ln Cincinnati (45240) *(G-3129)*

Superior Soda Service LLC........................... 937 657-9700
3626 Napanee Dr Beavercreek (45430) *(G-996)*

Superior Steel Service LLC.......................... 513 724-7888
2760 Old State Route 32 Batavia (45103) *(G-890)*

Superior Street Holding Inc (PA).................. 419 626-5757
2105 Superior St Sandusky (44870) *(G-11873)*

Superior Street Holding Inc......................... 419 626-5757
2020 Superior St Sandusky (44870) *(G-11874)*

Superior Tool Company, Cleveland Also Called: Superior Tool Corporation *(G-4348)*

Superior Tool Corporation............................ 216 398-8600
100 Hayes Dr Ste C Cleveland (44131) *(G-4348)*

Superior Trim, Findlay Also Called: Pieco Inc *(G-6908)*

Superior Trim Formed Products, Findlay Also Called: Radar Love Co *(G-6912)*

Superior Trims Springfield Div, Springfield Also Called: Pieco Inc *(G-12363)*

Superior Walls, Warren Also Called: Superior Walls of Ohio Inc *(G-13799)*

Superior Walls of Ohio Inc.......................... 330 393-4101
1401 Pine Ave Se Warren (44483) *(G-13799)*

Superior Water Conditioning Co, Moraine Also Called: Enting Water Conditioning Inc *(G-10160)*

Superior Weld and Fabg Co Inc.................... 216 249-5122
15002 Woodworth Rd Cleveland (44110) *(G-4349)*

Superior Welding Co.................................... 614 252-8539
906 S Nelson Rd Columbus (43205) *(G-5300)*

Superior's Brand Meats, Massillon Also Called: Fresh Mark Inc *(G-9192)*

Superkids Reading Program, Columbus Also Called: Zaner-Bloser Inc *(G-5380)*

Supertrapp, Cleveland Also Called: Supertrapp Industries Inc *(G-4350)*

Supertrapp Industries Inc............................ 216 265-8400
4540 W 160th St Cleveland (44135) *(G-4350)*

Supplier Inspection Svcs Inc (PA)................. 877 263-7097
2941 S Gettysburg Ave Dayton (45439) *(G-6031)*

Supply One Corporation............................... 937 297-1111
4146 Woodedge Dr Bellbrook (45305) *(G-1093)*

Supply Technologies LLC (HQ)..................... 440 947-2100
6065 Parkland Blvd Ste 1 Cleveland (44124) *(G-4351)*

Supply Technologies LLC............................. 614 759-9939
590 Claycraft Rd Columbus (43230) *(G-5301)*

Supply Technologies LLC............................. 937 898-5795
4704 Wadsworth Rd Dayton (45414) *(G-6032)*

Supplyone Retail, Cleveland Also Called: Cleveland Supplyone Inc *(G-3527)*

Support Service, Lexington Also Called: Support Svc LLC *(G-8375)*

Support Svc LLC.. 419 617-0660
25 Walnut St Ste 4 Lexington (44904) *(G-8375)*

Suppressor Co LLC...................................... 330 749-5234
2004 State Route 60 Ashland (44805) *(G-577)*

Supreme Fan/Industrial Air, Dayton Also Called: Lau Industries Inc *(G-5618)*

Supro Spring & Wire Forms Inc.................... 330 722-5628
9085 Coon Club Rd Medina (44256) *(G-9451)*

Sur-Seal LLC (PA)....................................... 513 574-8500
6156 Wesselman Rd Cincinnati (45248) *(G-3130)*

Sure Tool & Manufacturing Co..................... 937 253-9111
429 Winston Ave Dayton (45403) *(G-6033)*

Sure-Foot Industries Corp........................... 440 234-4446
20260 1st Ave Cleveland (44130) *(G-4352)*

A L P H A B E T I C

Surface Combustion Inc (PA)................................... 419 891-7150
1700 Indian Wood Cir Maumee (43537) *(G-9323)*

Surface Enhancement Tech LLC........................... 513 561-1520
3929 Virginia Ave Cincinnati (45227) *(G-3131)*

Surface Recovery Tech LLC................................... 937 879-5864
833 Zapata Dr Fairborn (45324) *(G-6700)*

Surftech, Austinburg *Also Called: Euclid Refinishing Compnay Inc (G-698)*

Surgical Appliance Inds Inc (PA)........................... 513 271-4594
3960 Rosslyn Dr Cincinnati (45209) *(G-3132)*

Surgical Recovery Systems LLC........................... 513 833-6868
4130 Tylersville Rd Hamilton (45011) *(G-7528)*

Surgical Theater Inc... 216 452-2177
30559 Pinetree Rd Ste 206 Pepper Pike (44124) *(G-11189)*

Surgrx Inc... 650 482-2400
4545 Creek Rd Blue Ash (45242) *(G-1338)*

Surili Couture LLC... 440 600-1456
29961 Persimmon Dr Westlake (44145) *(G-14338)*

Surplus Freight Inc (PA)..................................... 614 235-7660
501 Morrison Rd Ste 100 Gahanna (43230) *(G-7171)*

Survitec Group (usa) Inc (DH)........................... 330 239-4331
1420 Wolfcreek Trl Sharon Center (44274) *(G-11943)*

Sushi On The Roll, Medina *Also Called: Alsatian Llc (G-9374)*

Suspension Feeder, Fort Recovery *Also Called: Roessner Holdings Inc (G-6970)*

Suspension Feeder Corporation........................... 419 763-1377
482 State Route 119 Fort Recovery (45846) *(G-6972)*

Sustainment Actions LLC................................... 330 805-3468
20 S 3rd St Ste 210 Columbus (43215) *(G-5302)*

Sutphen, Dublin *Also Called: Sutphen Corporation (G-6353)*

Sutphen Corporation (PA)................................... 800 726-7030
6450 Eiterman Rd Dublin (43016) *(G-6353)*

Sutphen Towers Inc... 614 876-1262
4500 Sutphen Ct Hilliard (43026) *(G-7704)*

Sutter Llc... 513 891-2261
11105 Deerfield Rd Blue Ash (45242) *(G-1339)*

Sutterlin Machine & TI Co Inc........................... 440 357-0817
9445 Pineneedle Dr Mentor (44060) *(G-9632)*

Swagelok Co, Willoughby Hills *Also Called: Swagelok Company (G-14564)*

Swagelok Company... 440 461-7714
358 Bishop Rd Cleveland (44143) *(G-4353)*

Swagelok Company... 440 473-1050
318 Bishop Rd Cleveland (44143) *(G-4354)*

Swagelok Company... 440 442-6611
328 Bishop Rd Cleveland (44143) *(G-4355)*

Swagelok Company... 440 248-4600
31400 Aurora Rd Solon (44139) *(G-12187)*

Swagelok Company (PA)..................................... 440 248-4600
29500 Solon Rd Solon (44139) *(G-12188)*

Swagelok Company... 440 349-5652
6100 Cochran Rd Solon (44139) *(G-12189)*

Swagelok Company... 440 349-5836
29495 F A Lennon Dr Solon (44139) *(G-12190)*

Swagelok Company... 440 349-5934
29495 F A Lennon Dr Solon (44139) *(G-12191)*

Swagelok Company... 440 248-4600
26653 Curtiss Wright Pkwy Willoughby Hills (44092) *(G-14564)*

Swagg Productions2015llc................................. 614 601-7414
628 Arborway Ct Worthington (43085) *(G-14726)*

Swan Creek Candle Co., Swanton *Also Called: Ambrosia Inc (G-12676)*

Swanton Wldg Machining Co Inc (PA)............... 419 826-4816
407 Bdwy Ave Swanton (43558) *(G-12694)*

Swapil Inc
2740 Airport Dr Ste 310 Columbus (43219) *(G-5303)*

Sweet Manufacturing Company........................... 937 325-1511
2000 E Leffel Ln Springfield (45505) *(G-12381)*

Sweet Packaing, Cleveland *Also Called: The Apex Paper Box Company (G-4377)*

Sweet Persuasions LLC..................................... 614 216-9052
9636 Circle Dr Pickerington (43147) *(G-11301)*

Sweeties Olympia Treats LLC........................... 440 572-7747
11606 Pearl Rd Strongsville (44136) *(G-12608)*

Sweets & Meats Bbq, Cincinnati *Also Called: Sweets and Meats LLC (G-3133)*

Sweets and Meats LLC..................................... 513 888-4227
2249 Beechmont Ave Cincinnati (45230) *(G-3133)*

Swift Filters Inc... 877 887-9438
24040 Forbes Rd Bedford (44146) *(G-1059)*

Swift Manufacturing Co Inc............................... 740 237-4405
700 Lorain St Ironton (45638) *(G-7935)*

Swiger Coil Systems Ltd..................................... 216 362-7500
4677 Manufacturing Ave Cleveland (44135) *(G-4356)*

Swihart Industries Inc....................................... 937 277-4796
5111 Webster St Dayton (45414) *(G-6034)*

Swimmer Printing Inc....................................... 216 623-1005
1215 Superior Ave E Ste 110 Cleveland (44114) *(G-4357)*

Swingle Countertops... 740 454-7368
18 Beaumont St Zanesville (43701) *(G-15052)*

Swingle Drilling, Crooksville *Also Called: Petro Ware Inc (G-5512)*

Swiss Woodcraft Inc... 330 925-1807
15 Industrial St Rittman (44270) *(G-11628)*

Switchback Group Inc (HQ)............................... 216 290-6040
5638 Transportation Blvd Cleveland (44125) *(G-4358)*

Swp Legacy Ltd... 330 340-9663
10143 Copperhead Rd Nw Sugarcreek (44681) *(G-12653)*

Sycamore Tire & Auto Repair........................... 513 793-0726
9372 Kenwood Rd Cincinnati (45242) *(G-3134)*

Sylvan Studio, Sylvania *Also Called: Sharonco Inc (G-12723)*

Sylvan Studios Inc... 419 882-3423
5651 Main St Sylvania (43560) *(G-12725)*

Sylvania Advantage... 419 725-2695
5655 Main St Apt 1 Sylvania (43560) *(G-12726)*

SYLVANIA MOOSE LODGE 1579, Sylvania *Also Called: Sylvania Mose Ldge No 1579 Lya (G-12727)*

Sylvania Mose Ldge No 1579 Lya....................... 419 885-4953
6072 Main St Sylvania (43560) *(G-12727)*

Symantec, Akron *Also Called: Gen Digital Inc (G-159)*

Symantec, Columbus *Also Called: Gen Digital Inc (G-4947)*

Symatic Inc... 330 225-1510
803 E Washington St Ste 200 Medina (44256) *(G-9452)*

Symbol Tool & Die Inc..................................... 440 582-5989
11000 Industrial First Ave North Royalton (44133) *(G-10785)*

Syme Inc (PA)... 330 723-6000
300 Lake Rd Medina (44256) *(G-9453)*

Symrise Inc... 440 324-6060
110 Liberty Ct Elyria (44035) *(G-6594)*

Synagro Midwest Inc... 937 384-0669
4515 Infirmary Rd Miamisburg (45342) *(G-9741)*

Synergy Manufacturing LLC............................... 740 352-5933
4239 Us Highway 23 Piketon (45661) *(G-11314)*

Syntec LLC... 440 229-6262
20525 Center Ridge Rd Ste 512 Rocky River (44116) *(G-11640)*

Synteko, Strongsville *Also Called: PPG Architectural Coatings LLC (G-12587)*

Synthomer Adhesive Tech LLC........................... 216 682-7000
25435 Harvard Rd Beachwood (44122) *(G-950)*

Synthomer Inc... 330 734-1237
1380 Tech Way Akron (44306) *(G-323)*

Synthomer Inc (HQ)... 216 682-7000
25435 Harvard Rd Beachwood (44122) *(G-951)*

Synthomer USA LLC (HQ)................................. 678 400-6655
25435 Harvard Rd Beachwood (44122) *(G-952)*

Syracuse China Company, Toledo *Also Called: Syracuse China LLC (G-13138)*

Syracuse China LLC (DH)................................. 419 325-2100
300 Madison Ave Toledo (43604) *(G-13138)*

Sysco Guest Supply LLC................................... 440 960-2515
7395 Industrial Parkway Dr Lorain (44052) *(G-8582)*

Syscom Advanced Materials Inc......................... 614 487-3626
1305 Kinnear Rd Columbus (43212) *(G-5304)*

Systech Handling Inc... 419 445-8226
120 Taylor Pkwy Archbold (43502) *(G-512)*

Systecon LLC... 513 777-7722
6121 Schumacher Park Dr West Chester (45069) *(G-14080)*

System EDM of Ohio, Mason *Also Called: Hi-Tek Manufacturing Inc (G-9108)*

System Packaging of Glassline........................... 419 666-9712
28905 Glenwood Rd Perrysburg (43551) *(G-11263)*

System Seals Inc... 216 220-1800
6600 W Snowville Rd Brecksville (44141) *(G-1481)*

System Seals LLC (HQ).................... 440 735-0200
9505 Midwest Ave Cleveland (44125) *(G-4359)*

System Seals, Inc., Brecksville *Also Called: System Seals Inc (G-1481)*

Systemax Manufacturing Inc.................... 937 368-2300
6450 Poe Ave Ste 200 Dayton (45414) *(G-6035)*

Systems Advantage, Lima *Also Called: Proforma Systems Advantage (G-8440)*

Systems Kit LLC MB.................... 330 945-4500
925 Glaser Pkwy Akron (44306) *(G-324)*

Systems Pack Inc.................... 330 467-5729
649 Highland Rd E Macedonia (44056) *(G-8719)*

T & B Foundry Company.................... 216 391-4200
2469 E 71st St Cleveland (44104) *(G-4360)*

T & CS Repairs & Retail LLC.................... 704 964-7325
1153 Marcy St Akron (44301) *(G-325)*

T & D Fabricating, Eastlake *Also Called: T & D Fabricating Inc (G-6445)*

T & D Fabricating Inc.................... 440 951-5646
1489 E 363rd St Eastlake (44095) *(G-6445)*

T & D Thompson Inc.................... 740 332-8515
15952 State Route 56 E Laurelville (43135) *(G-8238)*

T & L Custom Screening Inc.................... 937 237-3121
3464 Successful Way Dayton (45414) *(G-6036)*

T & R Welding Systems Inc.................... 937 228-7517
1 Janney Rd Dayton (45404) *(G-6037)*

T & S Machine Inc.................... 419 453-2101
712 Maple St Wapakoneta (45895) *(G-13728)*

T & W Forge, Alliance *Also Called: T & W Forge Inc (G-410)*

T & W Forge Inc
562 W Ely St Alliance (44601) *(G-410)*

T A Bacon Co.................... 216 595-1310
235 E 131st St Cleveland (44108) *(G-4361)*

T C F C, Cleveland *Also Called: Those Chrcters From Clvland LL (G-4394)*

T C I, Greenville *Also Called: Treaty City Industries Inc (G-7358)*

T C Redi Mix Youngstown Inc (PA).................... 330 755-2143
2400 Poland Ave Youngstown (44502) *(G-14942)*

T C Service Co.................... 440 954-7500
38285 Pelton Rd Willoughby (44094) *(G-14536)*

T D Dynamics Inc.................... 216 881-0800
4101 Commerce Ave Cleveland (44103) *(G-4362)*

T E Q HI Inc.................... 877 448-3701
1525 Alum Creek Dr Columbus (43209) *(G-5305)*

T F O, Jeffersonville *Also Called: Tfo Tech Co Ltd (G-7988)*

T J Davies Company Inc.................... 440 248-5510
11823 State Route 44 Mantua (44255) *(G-8876)*

T J F Inc.................... 419 878-4400
1070 Disher Dr Waterville (43566) *(G-13843)*

T L Squire and Company Inc.................... 330 668-2604
1040 Embassy Pkwy Ste 300 Akron (44333) *(G-326)*

T S I, Englewood *Also Called: Tom Smith Industries Inc (G-6626)*

T W Corporation.................... 440 461-3234
99 S Seiberling St Akron (44305) *(G-327)*

T-Mac Machine Inc.................... 330 673-0621
924 Overholt Rd Kent (44240) *(G-8085)*

T-Shirt Co.................... 513 821-7100
413 Northland Blvd Cincinnati (45240) *(G-3135)*

T.E.A.M. Systems, Toledo *Also Called: Magna Modular Systems LLC (G-13045)*

T&R Wood Products, Middle Point *Also Called: Traveling Recycle WD Pdts Inc (G-9764)*

T&T Graphics Inc.................... 937 847-6000
2563 Technical Dr Miamisburg (45342) *(G-9742)*

T&T Machine Inc.................... 440 354-0605
892 Callendar Blvd Painesville (44077) *(G-11112)*

Tabco, Cleveland *Also Called: T A Bacon Co (G-4361)*

Tablox Inc.................... 440 953-1951
4821 E 345th St Willoughby (44094) *(G-14537)*

Tabtronics, Dayton *Also Called: Blue Creek Enterprises Inc (G-5680)*

TAC Industries Inc (PA).................... 937 328-5200
2160 Old Selma Rd Springfield (45505) *(G-12382)*

TAC Materials Inc.................... 330 425-8472
1700 Highland Rd Twinsburg (44087) *(G-13382)*

Tack-Anew Inc.................... 419 734-4212
451 W Lakeshore Dr Port Clinton (43452) *(G-11453)*

Tacoma Energy LLC.................... 614 899-8990
697 Green Crest Dr Westerville (43081) *(G-14276)*

Tadd Spring Co Inc.................... 440 572-1313
15060 Foltz Pkwy Strongsville (44149) *(G-12609)*

Taft Tool & Production Co.................... 419 385-2576
756 S Byrne Rd Ste 1 Toledo (43609) *(G-13139)*

Taft's Ale House, Cincinnati *Also Called: Dswdwk LLC (G-2564)*

Tahoma Engineered Solutions, Ashland *Also Called: Tahoma Engineered Solutions Inc (G-578)*

Tahoma Engineered Solutions Inc.................... 330 345-6169
532 County Road 1600 Ashland (44805) *(G-578)*

Tahoma Enterprises Inc (PA).................... 330 745-9016
255 Wooster Rd N Barberton (44203) *(G-840)*

Tahoma Rubber & Plastics Inc (HQ).................... 330 745-9016
532 County Road 1600 Ashland (44805) *(G-579)*

Taiho, Tiffin *Also Called: Taiho Corporation of America (G-12801)*

Taiho Corporation of America.................... 419 443-1645
194 Heritage Dr Tiffin (44883) *(G-12801)*

Taikisha Usa Inc.................... 614 444-5602
1939 Refugee Rd Columbus (43207) *(G-5306)*

Tailored Systems Inc.................... 937 299-3900
2853 Springboro W Moraine (45439) *(G-10194)*

Tailwind Technologies Inc (PA).................... 937 778-4200
1 Propeller Pl Piqua (45356) *(G-11386)*

Taiyo America Inc (HQ).................... 419 300-8811
1702 E Spring St Saint Marys (45885) *(G-11753)*

Take It For Granite LLC.................... 513 735-0555
3898 Mcmann Rd Cincinnati (45245) *(G-2316)*

Takk Industries Inc.................... 513 353-4306
5838a Hamilton Cleves Rd Cleves (45002) *(G-4550)*

Takumi Stamping Inc.................... 513 642-0081
8585 Seward Rd Fairfield (45011) *(G-6780)*

Talan Products Inc.................... 216 458-0170
18800 Cochran Ave Cleveland (44110) *(G-4363)*

Talent Tool & Die Inc.................... 440 239-8777
777 Berea Industrial Pkwy Berea (44017) *(G-1190)*

Talisman Racing, Cincinnati *Also Called: All Craft Manufacturing Co (G-2348)*

Tallmadge Spinning & Metal Co.................... 330 794-2277
2783 Gilchrist Rd Unit A Akron (44305) *(G-328)*

Tally Ho Slipcovers.................... 614 448-6170
2019 Andover Rd Columbus (43212) *(G-5307)*

Talus Renewables Inc (PA).................... 650 248-5374
3762 Bainbridge Rd Cleveland Heights (44118) *(G-4531)*

Tamarron Technology Inc.................... 800 277-3207
8044 Montgomery Rd Cincinnati (45236) *(G-3136)*

Tambrands Sales Corp (HQ).................... 513 983-1100
1 Procter And Gamble Plz Cincinnati (45202) *(G-3137)*

Tampax, Cincinnati *Also Called: Tambrands Sales Corp (G-3137)*

Tangent Air Inc.................... 740 474-1114
127 Edison Ave Circleville (43113) *(G-3264)*

Tangent Company LLC.................... 440 543-2775
10175 Queens Way Ste 1 Chagrin Falls (44023) *(G-2186)*

Tangible Solutions Inc.................... 937 912-4603
678 Yellow Springs Fairfield Rd Fairborn (45324) *(G-6701)*

Tango Products Inc.................... 440 353-2605
4915 Mills Industrial Pkwy North Ridgeville (44039) *(G-10750)*

Tank Services, Dennison *Also Called: Services Acquisition Co LLC (G-6218)*

Tappan Chairs LLC.................... 800 840-9121
9115 Blue Ash Rd Blue Ash (45242) *(G-1340)*

Tarahill Inc.................... 706 864-0808
3985 Groves Rd Columbus (43232) *(G-5308)*

Target Holdings Inc.................... 513 474-4409
2300 E Kemper Rd Unit 5 Cincinnati (45241) *(G-3138)*

Target World, Cincinnati *Also Called: Target Holdings Inc (G-3138)*

Targeted Cmpund Monitoring LLC.................... 937 825-0842
2790 Indian Ripple Rd Ste A Dayton (45440) *(G-6038)*

Tarigma Corporation.................... 614 436-3734
6161 Busch Blvd Ste 110 Columbus (43229) *(G-5309)*

Tark Inc (PA).................... 937 434-6766
9273 Byers Rd Miamisburg (45342) *(G-9743)*

Tarkett Inc.................... 440 543-8916
16910 Munn Rd Chagrin Falls (44023) *(G-2187)*

A
L
P
H
A
B
E
T
I
C

Tarkett Inc..800 771-7476
16035 Industrial Pkwy Middlefield (44062) *(G-9830)*

Tarkett Inc (DH)..................................800 899-8916
30000 Aurora Rd Solon (44139) *(G-12192)*

Tarkett Inc..614 349-1565
1050 Gateway Park Dr West Jefferson (43162) *(G-14167)*

Tarkett North America, Solon Also Called: Tarkett Inc *(G-12192)*

Tarkett USA, Solon Also Called: Johnsonite Inc *(G-12131)*

Tarkett USA Inc...................................440 543-8916
16910 Munn Rd Chagrin Falls (44023) *(G-2188)*

Tarkett USA Inc (DH)...........................877 827-5388
30000 Aurora Rd Solon (44139) *(G-12193)*

Tarman Machine Company Inc..............614 834-4010
8215 Dove Pkwy Canal Winchester (43110) *(G-1798)*

Tarpco, Kent Also Called: Hapco Inc *(G-8035)*

Tarpco Inc...330 677-8277
390 Portage Blvd Kent (44240) *(G-8086)*

Tarped Out Inc....................................330 325-7722
4442 State Route 14 Ravenna (44266) *(G-11545)*

Tarpstop LLC (PA)...............................419 873-7867
12000 Williams Rd Perrysburg (43551) *(G-11264)*

Tarrier, Columbus Also Called: Tarrier Foods Corp *(G-5310)*

Tarrier Foods Corp..............................614 876-8594
2700 International St Columbus (43228) *(G-5310)*

Tarrier Steel Company Inc....................614 444-4000
1379 S 22nd St Columbus (43206) *(G-5311)*

Tastemorr Snacks, Coldwater Also Called: Basic Grain Products Inc *(G-4568)*

Tat Machine & Tool Ltd........................419 836-7706
1313 S Cousino Rd Curtice (43412) *(G-5518)*

Tata America Intl Corp..........................513 677-6500
1000 Summit Dr Unit 1 Milford (45150) *(G-9954)*

Tata Consultancy Services, Milford Also Called: Tata America Intl Corp *(G-9954)*

Tate & Lyle, Dayton Also Called: Primary Pdts Ingrdnts Amrcas L *(G-5954)*

Tatham Schulz Incorporated.................216 861-4431
11400 Brookpark Rd Cleveland (44130) *(G-4364)*

Tavens Container Inc............................216 883-3333
22475 Aurora Rd Bedford (44146) *(G-1060)*

Tavens Packg Display Solutions, Bedford Also Called: Tavens Container Inc *(G-1060)*

Taylor - Winfield Corporation................330 259-8500
3200 Innovation Place Hubbard (44425) *(G-7817)*

Taylor & Moore Co...............................513 733-5530
807 Wachendorf St Cincinnati (45215) *(G-3139)*

Taylor Communications Inc...................419 678-6000
515 W Sycamore St Coldwater (45828) *(G-4585)*

Taylor Communications Inc...................614 351-6868
3950 Business Park Dr Columbus (43204) *(G-5312)*

Taylor Communications Inc...................937 221-1000
600 Albany St Dayton (45417) *(G-6039)*

Taylor Communications Inc...................732 356-0081
7755 Paragon Rd Ste 101 Dayton (45459) *(G-6040)*

Taylor Communications Inc...................937 221-3347
3545 Urbancrest Industrial Dr Grove City (43123) *(G-7415)*

Taylor Communications Inc...................216 265-1800
4125 Highlander Pkwy Ste 230 Richfield (44286) *(G-11603)*

Taylor Communications Inc...................614 277-7500
3125 Lewis Centre Way Urbancrest (43123) *(G-13484)*

Taylor Lumber, Piketon Also Called: Taylor Lumber Worldwide Inc *(G-11315)*

Taylor Lumber Worldwide Inc................740 259-6222
16523 State Route 124 Piketon (45661) *(G-11315)*

Taylor Made Glass Systems, Payne Also Called: Taylor Products Inc *(G-11166)*

Taylor Manufacturing Co Inc.................937 322-8622
1101 W Main St Springfield (45504) *(G-12383)*

Taylor Metal Products Co......................419 522-3471
700 Springmill St Mansfield (44903) *(G-8857)*

Taylor Mtl Hdlg & Conveyor, Toledo Also Called: Bobco Enterprises Inc *(G-12899)*

Taylor Products Inc..............................419 263-2313
230 S Laura St Payne (45880) *(G-11165)*

Taylor Products Inc..............................419 263-2313
407 N Maple St Payne (45880) *(G-11166)*

Taylor Quick Print...............................740 439-2208
1008 Woodlawn Ave # A Cambridge (43725) *(G-1763)*

Taylor Tool & Die Inc...........................937 845-1491
306 N Main St New Carlisle (45344) *(G-10381)*

Taylor Winfield Indus Wldg Eqp, Youngstown Also Called: Taylor-Winfield Tech Inc *(G-14943)*

Taylor-Winfield Tech Inc.......................330 259-8500
3200 Innovation Pl Youngstown (44509) *(G-14943)*

Tb Backstop Inc..................................330 434-4442
4478 Regal Dr Akron (44321) *(G-329)*

Tbc Retail Group Inc............................216 267-8040
5370 W 130th St Cleveland (44142) *(G-4365)*

Tbec, Painesville Also Called: Thirion Brothers Eqp Co LLC *(G-11118)*

Tbk Holdings LLC (PA).........................313 584-0400
232 J St Perrysburg (43551) *(G-11265)*

Tbone Sales, Baltic Also Called: Tbone Sales LLC *(G-781)*

Tbone Sales LLC..................................330 897-6131
410 N Ray St Baltic (43804) *(G-781)*

Tbt Hauling LLC...................................904 635-7631
500 Lehman Ave Ste 103 Bowling Green (43402) *(G-1441)*

Tca Graphics, Fairborn Also Called: Tee Creations *(G-6702)*

Tcb Automation LLC.............................330 556-6444
601 W 15th St Dover (44622) *(G-6265)*

Tce International Ltd.............................800 962-2376
4843 N Ridge Rd Perry (44081) *(G-11199)*

TCH Industries Incorporated.................330 487-5155
2307 E Aurora Rd Twinsburg (44087) *(G-13383)*

TCS Schindler & Co LLC.......................937 836-9473
36 Haas Dr Englewood (45322) *(G-6624)*

TD Landscape Inc................................740 694-0244
16780 Pinkley Rd Fredericktown (43019) *(G-7085)*

Td Synnex Corporation.........................614 669-6889
5350 Centerpoint Pkwy Groveport (43125) *(G-7452)*

Td Synnex Corporation, Groveport Also Called: Td Synnex Corporation *(G-7452)*

Tdb Associates Inc..............................937 459-5730
1014 Front St Greenville (45331) *(G-7357)*

Tdi Co..937 898-9600
6800 Poe Ave Dayton (45414) *(G-6041)*

Tdl Tool Inc...937 374-0055
1296 S Patton St Xenia (45385) *(G-14777)*

TDS Custom Cabinets LLC....................614 850-7590
1819 Walcutt Rd Ste 9 Columbus (43228) *(G-5313)*

TDS-Bf/Ls Holdings Inc........................440 327-5800
38900 Taylor Industrial Pkwy North Ridgeville (44039) *(G-10751)*

Te Connectivity Corporation..................419 521-9500
175 N Diamond St Mansfield (44902) *(G-8858)*

Te-Co Inc..937 836-0961
100 Quinter Farm Rd Union (45322) *(G-13412)*

Te-Co Manufacturing LLC.....................937 836-0961
100 Quinter Farm Rd Englewood (45322) *(G-6625)*

Teachers Publishing Group...................614 486-0631
4200 Parkway Ct Hilliard (43026) *(G-7705)*

Team Inc...614 263-1808
3005 Silver Dr Columbus (43224) *(G-5314)*

Team Cobra Products, North Ridgeville Also Called: H & S Distributing Inc *(G-10733)*

Team Plastics Inc................................216 251-8270
3901 W 150th St Cleveland (44111) *(G-4366)*

Team Ppi, Kenton Also Called: Pleasant Precision Inc *(G-8111)*

Team Remington Cadillac, Canton Also Called: McCann Color Inc *(G-1942)*

Team Systems, Toledo Also Called: Decoma Systems Integration Gro *(G-12940)*

Team Wendy LLC.................................216 738-2518
17000 Saint Clair Ave Bldg 1 Cleveland (44110) *(G-4367)*

Teamcentral Inc...................................513 382-1497
7875 Montgomery Rd Cincinnati (45236) *(G-3140)*

Teca, Dayton Also Called: Troy Engnred Cmpnnts Assmblies *(G-6065)*

Tech Art Productions, Columbus Also Called: Technical Artistry Inc *(G-5316)*

Tech Data, Groveport Also Called: Vertiv Corporation *(G-7456)*

Tech Development, Dayton Also Called: GE Aviation Systems LLC *(G-5791)*

Tech Dynamics Inc...............................419 666-1666
361 D St Ste B Perrysburg (43551) *(G-11266)*

Tech Industries Inc..............................216 861-7337
1313 Washington Ave Cleveland (44113) *(G-4368)*

Tech International, Johnstown Also Called: Technical Rubber Company Inc *(G-7999)*

Tech Mold and Tool Co.. 937 667-8851
4333 Lisa Dr Tipp City (45371) *(G-12847)*

Tech Products Corporation (DH).............................. 937 438-1100
2215 Lyons Rd Miamisburg (45342) *(G-9744)*

Tech Ready Mix Inc... 216 361-5000
5000 Crayton Ave Cleveland (44104) *(G-4369)*

Tech Solutions LLC... 419 852-7190
658 N Main St Celina (45822) *(G-2123)*

Tech-Med Inc.. 216 486-0900
1080 E 222nd St Euclid (44117) *(G-6679)*

Tech-Sonic Inc (PA).. 614 792-3117
4330 Tuller Rd Dublin (43017) *(G-6354)*

Tech-Way Industries Inc.. 937 746-1004
301 Industrial Dr Franklin (45005) *(G-7052)*

Tech/III Inc... 513 482-7500
2594 Mack Rd Fairfield (45014) *(G-6781)*

Tech4imaging LLC.. 614 214-2655
1910 Crown Park Ct Ste B Columbus (43235) *(G-5315)*

Techmetals Inc (PA)... 937 253-5311
345 Springfield St Dayton (45403) *(G-6042)*

Techneglas Inc... 419 873-2000
25875 Dixie Hwy Bldg 52 Perrysburg (43551) *(G-11267)*

Techneglas LLC (HQ)... 419 873-2000
2100 N Wilkinson Way Perrysburg (43551) *(G-11268)*

TECHNEGLAS, INC., Perrysburg Also Called: Techneglas Inc *(G-11267)*

Technibus Inc.. 330 479-4202
1501 Raff Rd Sw Ste 6 Canton (44710) *(G-2022)*

Technical Artistry Inc.. 614 299-7777
1340b Emig Rd Columbus (43207) *(G-5316)*

Technical Glass Products Inc (PA)........................ 440 639-6399
881 Callendar Blvd Painesville (44077) *(G-11113)*

Technical Glass Products Inc............................... 425 396-8420
7460 Ponderosa Rd Perrysburg (43551) *(G-11269)*

Technical Machine Products Inc
5500 Walworth Ave Cleveland (44102) *(G-4370)*

Technical Rubber Company Inc (PA)..................... 740 967-9015
200 E Coshocton St Johnstown (43031) *(G-7999)*

Technical Tool & Gauge Inc................................... 330 273-1778
2914 Westway Dr Brunswick (44212) *(G-1617)*

Technicolor Usa Inc... 614 474-8821
24200 Us Highway 23 S Circleville (43113) *(G-3265)*

Technicote, Miamisburg Also Called: Technicote Inc *(G-9745)*

Technicote Inc.. 330 928-1476
70 Marc Dr Cuyahoga Falls (44223) *(G-5576)*

Technicote Inc (PA).. 800 358-4448
222 Mound Ave Miamisburg (45342) *(G-9745)*

Technidrill Systems Inc... 330 678-9980
429 Portage Blvd Kent (44240) *(G-8087)*

Technifab Inc (PA).. 440 934-8324
1355 Chester Industrial Pkwy Avon (44011) *(G-740)*

Technifab Engineered Products, Avon Also Called: Technifab Inc *(G-740)*

Techniprint Inc.. 614 899-1403
515 S State St Westerville (43081) *(G-14277)*

Techniques Surfaces Usa Inc................................ 937 323-2556
2015 Progress Rd Springfield (45505) *(G-12384)*

Technlogy Install Partners LLC............................. 888 586-7040
13701 Enterprise Ave Cleveland (44135) *(G-4371)*

Techno Adhesives Co.. 513 771-1584
12113 Mosteller Rd Cincinnati (45241) *(G-3141)*

Technoform GL Insul N Amer Inc........................... 330 487-6600
1755 Enterprise Pkwy Ste 300 Twinsburg (44087) *(G-13384)*

Technology Explortation Pdts, Mentor Also Called: Gdj Inc *(G-9523)*

Technology House Ltd.. 440 248-3025
30700 Carter St Solon (44139) *(G-12194)*

Technology House Ltd.. 440 248-3025
10036 Aurora Hudson Rd Streetsboro (44241) *(G-12526)*

Technology House Ltd (PA).................................... 440 248-3025
10036 Aurora Hudson Rd Streetsboro (44241) *(G-12527)*

Technosoft Inc.. 513 985-9877
11180 Reed Hartman Hwy Ste 200 Blue Ash (45242) *(G-1341)*

Techstar, Findlay Also Called: DS Techstar Inc *(G-6861)*

Techtron Systems Inc.. 440 505-2990
29500 Fountain Pkwy Solon (44139) *(G-12195)*

Tecmark Corporation.. 440 205-9188
7335 Production Dr Mentor (44060) *(G-9633)*

Tecmark Corporation (PA)...................................... 440 205-7600
7745 Metric Dr Mentor (44060) *(G-9634)*

Tecnocap LLC... 330 392-7222
2100 Griswold Street Ext Ne Warren (44483) *(G-13800)*

Teco, Toledo Also Called: Toledo Engineering Co Inc *(G-13151)*

Tectum Inc.. 740 345-9691
105 S 6th St Newark (43055) *(G-10535)*

Tecumseh Packg Solutions Inc............................. 419 238-1122
1275 Industrial Dr Van Wert (45891) *(G-13545)*

Ted Bolle Millwork Inc.. 937 325-8779
2834 Hustead Rd Springfield (45502) *(G-12385)*

Ted M Figgins... 740 277-3750
347 S Columbus St Pmb 634 Lancaster (43130) *(G-8227)*

Tee Creations... 937 878-2822
701 N Broad St Ste C Fairborn (45324) *(G-6702)*

Tegam, Geneva Also Called: Tegam Inc *(G-7246)*

Tegam Inc (HQ).. 440 466-6100
10 Tegam Way Geneva (44041) *(G-7246)*

Tegr Inc... 419 678-4991
191 N Eastern Ave Saint Henry (45883) *(G-11725)*

Teh Investments Inc.. 330 782-1127
4605 Lake Park Rd Youngstown (44512) *(G-14944)*

Teijin Automotive Tech Inc.................................... 419 396-1980
2915 County Highway 96 Carey (43316) *(G-2063)*

Teijin Automotive Tech Inc.................................... 440 945-4800
333 Gore Rd Conneaut (44030) *(G-5417)*

Teijin Automotive Tech Inc.................................... 419 257-2231
100 S Poe Rd North Baltimore (45872) *(G-10618)*

Teijin Automotive Tech Inc.................................... 419 238-4628
1276 Industrial Dr Van Wert (45891) *(G-13546)*

Teikoku USA Inc... 304 699-1156
27881 State Route 7 Marietta (45750) *(G-8951)*

Teikuro Corporation... 937 327-3955
4500 Gateway Blvd Springfield (45502) *(G-12386)*

Tek Gear & Machine Inc... 330 455-3331
1220 Camden Ave Sw Canton (44706) *(G-2023)*

Tek Group International.. 330 706-0000
567 Elm Ridge Ave Canal Fulton (44614) *(G-1780)*

Tek Manufacturing, Canal Fulton Also Called: Tek Group International *(G-1780)*

Tekfor Inc... 330 202-7420
3690 Long Rd Wooster (44691) *(G-14690)*

Tekfor USA, Wooster Also Called: Tekfor Inc *(G-14690)*

Tekmar-Dohrmann, Mason Also Called: Teledyne Tekmar Company *(G-9160)*

Tekni-Plex Inc.. 419 491-2399
1445 Timber Wolf Dr Holland (43528) *(G-7786)*

Teknol Inc (PA)... 937 264-0190
5751 Webster St Dayton (45414) *(G-6043)*

Tekraft Industries Inc.. 440 352-8321
244 Latimore St Painesville (44077) *(G-11114)*

Tektronix, Solon Also Called: Tektronix Inc *(G-12196)*

Tektronix, West Chester Also Called: Tektronix Inc *(G-14152)*

Tektronix Inc.. 440 248-0400
28775 Aurora Rd Solon (44139) *(G-12196)*

Tektronix Inc.. 248 305-5200
9639 Inter Ocean Dr West Chester (45246) *(G-14152)*

Tekworx LLC... 513 533-4777
3094 Madison Rd Cincinnati (45209) *(G-3142)*

Telcon LLC... 330 562-5566
1677 Miller Pkwy Streetsboro (44241) *(G-12528)*

Teledoor LLC.. 419 227-3000
1075 Prosperity Rd Lima (45801) *(G-8455)*

Teledyne Defense Elec LLC.................................... 866 539-5916
1100 Vanguard Blvd Miamisburg (45342) *(G-9746)*

Teledyne Instruments Inc...................................... 513 229-7000
4736 Socialville Foster Rd Mason (45040) *(G-9158)*

Teledyne Instruments Inc...................................... 603 886-8400
4736 Socialville Foster Rd Mason (45040) *(G-9159)*

A L P H A B E T I C

Teledyne Leeman Labs, Mason *Also Called: Teledyne Instruments Inc* **(G-9159)**

Teledyne Qptiq Eltrnic Sltions, Miamisburg *Also Called: Teledyne Defense Elec LLC* **(G-9746)**

Teledyne Tekmar, Mason *Also Called: Teledyne Instruments Inc* **(G-9158)**

Teledyne Tekmar Company (DH)..............................513 229-7000
4736 Socialville Foster Rd Mason (45040) *(G-9160)*

Telehealth Care Solutions LLC..............................440 823-6023
2551 Sweetwater Dr Brecksville (44141) *(G-1482)*

Telempu N Hayashi Amer Corp..............................513 932-9319
1500 Kingsview Dr Lebanon (45036) *(G-8288)*

Telesis Marking Systems, Circleville *Also Called: Telesis Technologies Inc* **(G-3266)**

Telesis Technologies Inc (DH)..............................740 477-5000
28181 River Dr Circleville (43113) *(G-3266)*

Telex Communications Inc..............................419 865-0972
5660 Southwyck Blvd Ste 150 Toledo (43614) *(G-13140)*

Telling Industries LLC..............................740 435-8900
2105 Larrick Rd Cambridge (43725) *(G-1764)*

Telling Industries LLC (PA)..............................440 974-3370
4420 Sherwin Rd Ste 4 Willoughby (44094) *(G-14538)*

Telos Alliance, The, Cleveland *Also Called: Tls Corp* **(G-4396)**

Telos Systems, Cleveland *Also Called: Cutting Edge Technologies Inc* **(G-3589)**

Tembec Btlsr Inc..............................419 244-5856
2112 Sylvan Ave Toledo (43606) *(G-13141)*

Tempcraft Corporation..............................216 391-3885
3960 S Marginal Rd Cleveland (44114) *(G-4372)*

Temperature Controls Co Inc..............................330 773-6633
5729 Dailey Rd New Franklin (44319) *(G-10395)*

Tempest Inc..............................216 883-6500
12750 Berea Rd Cleveland (44111) *(G-4373)*

Temple Inland..............................513 425-0830
912 Nelbar St Middletown (45042) *(G-9897)*

Temple Israel..............................330 762-8617
91 Springside Dr Akron (44333) *(G-330)*

Temple Oil and Gas LLC..............................740 452-7878
6626 Ceramic Rd Ne Crooksville (43731) *(G-5513)*

Tempo Manufacturing Company..............................937 773-6613
727 E Ash St Piqua (45356) *(G-11387)*

Tempo Trophy Mfg, Piqua *Also Called: Tempo Manufacturing Company* **(G-11387)**

Temprecision Intl Corp (PA)..............................855 891-7732
777 Stow St Kent (44240) *(G-8088)*

Ten Mfg LLC..............................440 487-1100
7675 Saint Clair Ave Mentor (44060) *(G-9635)*

Tenacity Manufacturing Company..............................513 821-0201
4455 Mulhauser Rd West Chester (45011) *(G-14081)*

Tenaxoltechnologies, Wickliffe *Also Called: Chemtool Incorporated* **(G-14369)**

Tencom Ltd..............................419 865-5877
7134 Railroad St Holland (43528) *(G-7787)*

Tendon Manufacturing Inc..............................216 663-3200
20805 Aurora Rd Cleveland (44146) *(G-4374)*

Tengam Pro Inc..............................740 373-0909
108 Industry Rd Marietta (45750) *(G-8952)*

Tenneco, Milan *Also Called: Pullman Company* **(G-9917)**

Tenneco, Napoleon *Also Called: Pullman Company* **(G-10296)**

Tenneplas Div Wndsr Mold USA, Bellevue *Also Called: ABC Technologies Wmg Usa Inc* **(G-1117)**

Tennessee Rand, Fort Loramie *Also Called: Lincoln Electric Automtn Inc* **(G-6950)**

Tenpoint Crossbow Technologies, Mogadore *Also Called: Hunters Manufacturing Co Inc* **(G-10077)**

Teradyne Inc..............................937 427-1280
2689 Commons Blvd Ste 201 Beavercreek (45431) *(G-985)*

Terex USA, Solon *Also Called: Demag Cranes & Components Corp* **(G-12100)**

Terex Utilities Inc..............................419 470-8408
25661 Fort Meigs Rd Ste A Perrysburg (43551) *(G-11270)*

Terminal Equipment Inds Inc..............................330 468-0322
64 Privet Ln Northfield (44067) *(G-10798)*

Terminal Ready-Mix Inc..............................440 288-0181
524 Colorado Ave Lorain (44052) *(G-8583)*

Ternion Inc (PA)..............................216 642-6180
12400 Plaza Dr Cleveland (44130) *(G-4375)*

Teron Lighting, Fairfield *Also Called: Damak 1 LLC* **(G-6725)**

Terra Sonic International LLC..............................740 374-6608
27825 State Route 7 Marietta (45750) *(G-8953)*

Terra Surfaces LLC..............................937 836-1900
6350 Frederick Pike Dayton (45414) *(G-6044)*

Terradyn Corporation..............................614 805-0897
6457 Reflections Dr Ste 200 Dublin (43017) *(G-6355)*

Terrasmart LLC..............................239 362-0211
1000 Buckeye Park Rd Columbus (43207) *(G-5317)*

Terreal North America LLC..............................888 582-9052
4757 Tile Plant Rd Se New Lexington (43764) *(G-10409)*

Terry Asphalt Materials Inc (DH)..............................513 874-6192
8600 Bilstein Blvd Hamilton (45015) *(G-7529)*

Terry Lumber and Supply Co..............................330 659-6800
1710 Mill St W Peninsula (44264) *(G-11184)*

Terydon Inc..............................330 879-2448
7260 Erie Ave Sw Navarre (44662) *(G-10314)*

Tes Therapy, Fairlawn *Also Called: Total Education Solutions Inc* **(G-6815)**

Tesa Inc..............................614 847-8200
544 Enterprise Dr Ste A Lewis Center (43035) *(G-8355)*

Tessa Precision Product Inc..............................440 392-3470
850 Callendar Blvd Painesville (44077) *(G-11115)*

Tessec, Dayton *Also Called: Tessec Manufacturing Svcs LLC* **(G-6046)**

Tessec LLC..............................937 576-0010
5621 Webster St Dayton (45414) *(G-6045)*

Tessec Manufacturing Svcs LLC..............................937 985-3552
5621 Webster St Dayton (45414) *(G-6046)*

Tessec Technology Services LLC..............................513 240-5601
5621 Webster St Dayton (45414) *(G-6047)*

Test Mark Industries Inc..............................330 426-2200
995 N Market St East Palestine (44413) *(G-6408)*

Test Measurement Systems Inc..............................888 867-4872
9073 Pleasantwood Ave Nw North Canton (44720) *(G-10671)*

Test-Fuchs Corporation..............................440 708-3505
10325 Brecksville Rd Brecksville (44141) *(G-1483)*

Testlink Usa Inc..............................513 272-1081
11445 Century Cir W Cincinnati (45246) *(G-3143)*

Tetra Mold & Tool Inc..............................937 845-1651
51 Quick Rd New Carlisle (45344) *(G-10382)*

Tetrad Electronics Inc (PA)..............................440 946-6443
2048 Joseph Lloyd Pkwy Willoughby (44094) *(G-14539)*

Teva Pharmaceuticals Usa Inc..............................513 731-9900
5040 Duramed Rd Cincinnati (45213) *(G-3144)*

Teva Womens Health LLC (DH)..............................513 731-9900
5040 Duramed Rd Cincinnati (45213) *(G-3145)*

Texas Tile Manufacturing LLC..............................713 869-5811
30000 Aurora Rd Solon (44139) *(G-12197)*

Textiles Inc..............................614 529-8642
5892 Heritage Lakes Dr Hilliard (43026) *(G-7706)*

Textiles Inc (PA)..............................740 852-0782
23 Old Springfield Rd London (43140) *(G-8542)*

Tfi Manufacturing LLC..............................440 290-9411
8989 Tyler Blvd Mentor (44060) *(G-9636)*

Tfo Tech Co Ltd..............................740 426-6381
221 State St Jeffersonville (43128) *(G-7988)*

Tfp Corporation (PA)..............................330 725-7741
460 Lake Rd Medina (44256) *(G-9454)*

Tgm LLC..............................419 636-8567
401 N Union St Bryan (43506) *(G-1661)*

Tgm Holdings Company..............................419 885-3769
5439 Roan Rd Sylvania (43560) *(G-12728)*

Tgs Industries Inc..............................330 339-2211
406 Mill Ave Sw New Philadelphia (44663) *(G-10466)*

Tgs International Inc..............................330 893-4828
4464 Oh-39 Berlin (44610) *(G-1200)*

Th Magnesium Inc..............................513 285-7568
9435 Waterstone Blvd Ste 290 Cincinnati (45249) *(G-3146)*

Th Manufacturing Inc..............................330 893-3572
4674 County Road 120 Millersburg (44654) *(G-10013)*

Th Plastics Inc..............................419 352-2770
843 Miller Dr Bowling Green (43402) *(G-1442)*

Th Plastics Inc..............................419 425-5825
101 Bentley Ct Findlay (45840) *(G-6926)*

Tha Presidential Suite LLC..............................216 338-7287
3863 E 112th St Cleveland (44105) *(G-4376)*

Thaler Machine Company LLC 937 550-2400
216 Tahlequah Trl Springboro (45066) *(G-12269)*

Thaler Machine Holdings LLC (PA) 937 550-2400
216 Tahlequah Trl Springboro (45066) *(G-12270)*

The Andersons Clymers Ethanol LLC 574 722-2627
1947 Briarfield Blvd Maumee (43537) *(G-9324)*

The Apex Paper Box Company (PA) 216 631-4000
5601 Walworth Ave Cleveland (44102) *(G-4377)*

The Armor Group Inc (PA) 513 923-5260
4600 N Mason Montgomery Rd Mason (45040) *(G-9161)*

The Basic Aluminum Castings Co 216 481-5606
1325 E 168th St Cleveland (44110) *(G-4378)*

The Belden Brick Company LLC (HQ) 330 456-0031
700 Tuscarawas St W Uppr Canton (44702) *(G-2024)*

The Blonder Company 216 431-3560
3950 Prospect Ave E Cleveland (44115) *(G-4379)*

The China Hall Company 330 385-2900
1 Anna St East Liverpool (43920) *(G-6398)*

The Cleveland Jewish Publ Co 216 454-8300
23880 Commerce Park Ste 1 Beachwood (44122) *(G-953)*

The Cleveland-Cliffs Iron Co 216 694-5700
1100 Superior Ave E Ste 1500 Cleveland (44114) *(G-4380)*

The Columbus Show Case Company
4401 Equity Dr Columbus (43228) *(G-5318)*

The Cornwell Quality Tools Company (PA) 330 336-3506
667 Seville Rd Wadsworth (44281) *(G-13674)*

The County Classified's, Bellefontaine *Also Called: County Classifieds (G-1102)*

The Crane Group Companies Limited (HQ) 614 754-3000
330 W Spring St Ste 200 Columbus (43215) *(G-5319)*

The Cyril-Scott Company 740 654-2112
3950 Lancaster New Lexington Rd Se Lancaster (43130) *(G-8228)*

The D B Hess Company 330 678-5868
3765 Sunnybrook Rd Kent (44240) *(G-8089)*

The D S Brown Company (HQ) 419 257-3561
300 E Cherry St North Baltimore (45872) *(G-10619)*

The Dupps Company (PA) 937 855-6555
548 N Cherry St Germantown (45327) *(G-7255)*

The Dyson Corporation 440 946-3500
53 Freedom Rd Painesville (44077) *(G-11116)*

The Ellenbee-Leggett Company Inc 513 874-3200
3765 Port Union Rd Fairfield (45014) *(G-6782)*

The F A Requarth Company 937 224-1141
447 E Monument Ave Dayton (45402) *(G-6048)*

The F L Emmert Co Inc 513 721-5808
2007 Dunlap St Cincinnati (45214) *(G-3147)*

The Fechheimer Brothers Co (HQ) 513 793-5400
4545 Malsbary Rd Blue Ash (45242) *(G-1342)*

The Fischer & Jirouch Company 216 361-3840
9105 Sapphire Ct Cleveland (44130) *(G-4381)*

The Florand Company 330 747-8986
4404 Lake Park Rd Youngstown (44512) *(G-14945)*

The Fremont Kraut Company 419 332-6481
724 N Front St Fremont (43420) *(G-7135)*

The Galehouse Companies Inc 330 658-2023
12667 Portage St Doylestown (44230) *(G-6270)*

The Garland Company Inc (HQ) 216 641-7500
3800 E 91st St Cleveland (44105) *(G-4382)*

The Gazette Printing Co Inc 440 593-6030
218 Washington St Conneaut (44030) *(G-5418)*

The Gazette Printing Co Inc (PA) 440 576-9125
46 W Jefferson St Jefferson (44047) *(G-7984)*

The General's Books, Columbus *Also Called: Generals Books (G-4949)*

The Great Lakes Towing Company (PA) 216 621-4854
4500 Division Ave Cleveland (44102) *(G-4383)*

The Guardtower Inc 614 488-4311
5514 Nike Dr Hilliard (43026) *(G-7707)*

The Hamilton Caster & Mfg Company 513 863-3300
1637 Dixie Hwy Hamilton (45011) *(G-7530)*

The Hartman Corp 614 475-5035
3216 Morse Rd Columbus (43231) *(G-5320)*

The Hattenbach Company 216 881-5200
5309 Hamilton Ave Cleveland (44114) *(G-4384)*

The Holtkamp Organ Co 216 741-5180
2909 Meyer Ave Cleveland (44109) *(G-4385)*

The Hooven - Dayton Corp 937 233-4473
511 Byers Rd Miamisburg (45342) *(G-9747)*

The Ideal Builders Supply & Fuel Co Inc (PA) 216 741-1600
4720 Brookpark Rd Cleveland (44134) *(G-4386)*

The Kindt-Collins Company LLC 216 252-4122
12651 Elmwood Ave Cleveland (44111) *(G-4387)*

The Kitchen Collection LLC 740 773-9150
71 E Water St Chillicothe (45601) *(G-2284)*

The Kordenbrock Tool and Die Co 513 326-4390
10250 Wayne Ave Cincinnati (45215) *(G-3148)*

The Label Team Inc 330 332-1067
1251 Quaker Cir Salem (44460) *(G-11814)*

The Little Tikes Company (PA) 330 650-3000
2180 Barlow Rd Hudson (44236) *(G-7860)*

The Louis G Freeman Company LLC (DH) 419 334-9709
911 Graham Dr Fremont (43420) *(G-7136)*

The Lubrizol Corporation 216 447-6212
1779 Marvo Dr Akron (44306) *(G-331)*

The Lubrizol Corporation 440 357-7064
155 Freedom Rd Painesville (44077) *(G-11117)*

The Lubrizol Corporation (HQ) 440 943-4200
29400 Lakeland Blvd Wickliffe (44092) *(G-14395)*

The Mansfield Strl & Erct Co (PA) 419 522-5911
429 Park Ave E Mansfield (44905) *(G-8859)*

The Massillon-Cleveland-Akronsign Company 330 833-3165
681 1st St Sw Massillon (44646) *(G-9247)*

The Mead Corporation 937 495-6323
4751 Hempstead Station Dr Dayton (45429) *(G-6049)*

The Mennel Milling Company (PA) 419 435-8151
319 S Vine St Fostoria (44830) *(G-7003)*

The Mobility Store, Westerville *Also Called: Columbus Prescr Rehabilitation (G-14250)*

The National Lime and Stone Company (PA) 419 422-4341
551 Lake Cascade Pkwy Findlay (45840) *(G-6927)*

The National Telephone Supply Company 216 361-0221
5100 Superior Ave Cleveland (44103) *(G-4388)*

The Olen Corporation (PA) 614 491-1515
4755 S High St Columbus (43207) *(G-5321)*

the Perfect Score Company 440 439-9320
25801 Solon Rd Bedford Heights (44146) *(G-1082)*

The Photo-Type Engraving Company (PA) 513 281-0999
2141 Gilbert Ave Cincinnati (45206) *(G-3149)*

The Pioneer Tool and Die Co 330 724-5572
1363 Triplett Blvd Akron (44306) *(G-332)*

The Plastic Works Inc, Cleveland *Also Called: Plastic Works Inc (G-4171)*

The Press of Ohio Inc 330 678-5868
3765 Sunnybrook Rd Kent (44240) *(G-8090)*

The Printed Image, Columbus *Also Called: Printed Image (G-5207)*

The Q-P Manufacturing Co Inc 440 946-2120
215 5th Ave Chardon (44024) *(G-2225)*

The R C A Rubber Company 330 784-1291
1833 E Market St Akron (44305) *(G-333)*

The Ransohoff Company 513 870-0100
4933 Provident Dr West Chester (45246) *(G-14153)*

The Reliable Spring Wire Frms 440 365-7400
910 Taylor St Elyria (44035) *(G-6595)*

The Schaefer Group Inc (PA) 937 253-3342
1300 Grange Hall Rd Beavercreek (45430) *(G-997)*

The Sharon Companies Ltd 614 438-3210
200 W Old Wilson Bridge Rd Worthington (43085) *(G-14727)*

The Sheffer Corporation (HQ) 513 489-9770
6990 Cornell Rd Cincinnati (45242) *(G-3150)*

The Shepherd Chemical Company (HQ) 513 731-1110
4900 Beech St Norwood (45212) *(G-10874)*

The Shepherd Color Company (PA) 513 874-0714
4539 Dues Dr Cincinnati (45246) *(G-3151)*

The Smead Manufacturing Company, Logan *Also Called: Smead Manufacturing Company (G-8527)*

The Vindicator Printing Company (PA) 330 747-1471
107 Vindicator Sq Youngstown (44503) *(G-14946)*

ALPHABETIC

The Vulcan Tool Company................................ 937 253-6194
730 Lorain Ave Dayton (45410) *(G-6050)*

The Wagner-Smith Company.............................. 866 338-0398
3201 Encrete Ln Moraine (45439) *(G-10195)*

The Western States Machine Company............... 513 863-4758
625 Commerce Center Dr Fairfield (45011) *(G-6783)*

The Wooster Brush Company (PA)....................... 330 264-4440
604 Madison Ave Wooster (44691) *(G-14691)*

The-Fischer-Group... 513 285-1281
2028- 2052 Bohlke Blvd Fairfield (45014) *(G-6784)*

The419... 855 451-1018
201 W Market St Lima (45801) *(G-8456)*

Theb Inc... 216 391-4800
3700 Kelley Ave Cleveland (44114) *(G-4389)*

Thees Machine & Tool Company........................ 419 586-4766
2007 State Route 703 Celina (45822) *(G-2124)*

Theiss Uav Solutions LLC................................ 330 584-2070
10881 Johnson Rd North Benton (44449) *(G-10624)*

Theken Companies LLC.................................... 330 733-7600
1800 Triplett Blvd Akron (44306) *(G-334)*

Theken Port Park LLC...................................... 330 733-7600
1800 Triplett Blvd Akron (44306) *(G-335)*

Theken Spine LLC... 330 773-7677
1153 Medina Rd Ste 100 Medina (44256) *(G-9455)*

Therm-All, Westlake *Also Called: Therm-All Inc (G-14339)*

Therm-All Inc (PA).. 440 779-9494
830 Canterbury Rd Ste A Westlake (44145) *(G-14339)*

Therm-O-Disc Incorporated (HQ)....................... 419 525-8500
570 Polaris Pkwy Ste 500 Westerville (43082) *(G-14236)*

Therm-O-Link Inc (PA)..................................... 330 527-2124
10513 Freedom St Garrettsville (44231) *(G-7228)*

Therm-O-Link Inc.. 330 393-7600
621 Dana St Ne Ste 5 Warren (44483) *(G-13801)*

Thermafab Alloy Inc.. 216 861-0540
25367 Water St Olmsted Falls (44138) *(G-10941)*

Thermafiber Inc (HQ)....................................... 260 563-2111
1 Owens Corning Pkwy Toledo (43659) *(G-13142)*

Thermagon Inc.. 216 939-2300
4707 Detroit Ave Cleveland (44102) *(G-4390)*

Thermal Solutions Inc...................................... 614 263-1808
3005 Silver Dr Columbus (43224) *(G-5322)*

Thermal Solutions Mfg Inc................................ 800 776-4225
15600 Commerce Park Dr Brookpark (44142) *(G-1559)*

Thermal Treatment Center Inc (HQ).................... 216 881-8100
28910 Lakeland Blvd Wickliffe (44092) *(G-14396)*

Thermalgraphics, Cincinnati *Also Called: Agnone-Kelly Enterprises Inc (G-2343)*

Thermeq Co, Waterville *Also Called: T J F Inc (G-13843)*

Thermo Fisher Scientific Inc............................. 513 948-6290
4750 Lake Forest Dr Ste 114 Blue Ash (45242) *(G-1343)*

Thermo Fisher Scientific Inc............................. 800 955-6288
2110 E Galbraith Rd Cincinnati (45237) *(G-3152)*

Thermo Fisher Scientific Inc............................. 800 871-8909
1 Thermo Fisher Way Oakwood Village (44146) *(G-10910)*

Thermo Fisher Scientific Inc............................. 513 659-7945
10085 International Blvd West Chester (45246) *(G-14154)*

Thermo Fsher Scntfic Ashvlle L......................... 740 373-4763
401 Mill Creek Rd Marietta (45750) *(G-8954)*

Thermo Gamma-Metrics LLC (HQ)...................... 858 450-9811
1 Thermo Fisher Way Bedford (44146) *(G-1061)*

Thermo King Corporation.................................. 567 280-9243
1750 E State St Fremont (43420) *(G-7137)*

Thermo King Corporation, Fremont *Also Called: Thermo King Corporation (G-7137)*

Thermo Systems Technology Inc........................ 216 292-8250
2000 Auburn Dr Ste 200 Cleveland (44122) *(G-4391)*

Thermo-Rite Mfg Company................................ 330 633-8680
1355 Evans Ave Akron (44305) *(G-336)*

Thermocolor LLC (DH)...................................... 419 626-5677
2901 W Monroe St Sandusky (44870) *(G-11875)*

Thermoid, Bellefontaine *Also Called: Hbd/Thermoid Inc (G-1108)*

Thermoprene Inc... 440 543-8660
5718 Transportation Blvd Cleveland (44125) *(G-4392)*

Thermoseal Inc (PA).. 937 498-2222
2350 Campbell Rd Sidney (45365) *(G-12057)*

Thermotion Corp... 440 639-8325
6520 Hopkins Rd Mentor (44060) *(G-9637)*

Thermotion-Madison, Mentor *Also Called: Thermotion Corp (G-9637)*

Thermtrol, North Canton *Also Called: Thermtrol Corporation (G-10672)*

Thermtrol Corporation..................................... 330 497-4148
8914 Pleasantwood Ave Nw North Canton (44720) *(G-10672)*

Thieman Quality Metal Fab Inc.......................... 419 629-2612
05140 Dicke Rd New Bremen (45869) *(G-10367)*

Thieman Tailgates Inc...................................... 419 586-7727
600 E Wayne St Celina (45822) *(G-2125)*

Thinkcsc, Worthington *Also Called: Ideal Integrations LLC (G-14713)*

Thinkware Incorporated................................... 513 598-3300
4055 Executive Park Dr Ste 240 Cincinnati (45241) *(G-3153)*

Third Millennium Materials LLC......................... 740 947-1023
974 Prosperity Rd Waverly (45690) *(G-13874)*

Third Salvo Company....................................... 740 818-9669
16355 Tick Ridge Rd Amesville (45711) *(G-443)*

Third Wave Water LLC...................................... 855 590-4500
251 Bellbrook Ave Xenia (45385) *(G-14778)*

Thirion Brothers Eqp Co LLC............................ 440 357-8004
340 W Prospect St Painesville (44077) *(G-11118)*

This Is L Inc.. 415 630-5172
1100 Sycamore St Ste 300 Cincinnati (45202) *(G-3154)*

Thk Manufacturing America Inc.......................... 740 928-1415
471 N High St Hebron (43025) *(G-7639)*

Thogus Products Company................................ 440 933-8850
33490 Pin Oak Pkwy Avon Lake (44012) *(G-771)*

Thomas Cabinet Shop Inc................................. 937 847-8239
321 Gargrave Rd Dayton (45449) *(G-6051)*

Thomas Creative Apparel Inc............................ 419 929-1506
1 Harmony Pl New London (44851) *(G-10417)*

Thomas D Epperson.. 937 855-3300
7440 Weaver Rd Germantown (45327) *(G-7256)*

Thomas Do-It Center Inc (PA)............................ 740 446-2002
176 Mccormick Rd Gallipolis (45631) *(G-7209)*

Thomas J Weaver Inc (PA)................................ 740 622-2040
1501 Kenilworth Ave Coshocton (43812) *(G-5474)*

Thomas Products Co Inc (PA)............................ 513 756-9009
3625 Spring Grove Ave Cincinnati (45223) *(G-3155)*

Thomas Rental, Gallipolis *Also Called: Thomas Do-It Center Inc (G-7209)*

Thomas Steel Inc.. 419 483-7540
305 Elm St Bellevue (44811) *(G-1135)*

Thomas Tool & Mold Company........................... 614 890-4978
271 Broad St Westerville (43081) *(G-14278)*

Thompson Aluminum Casting Co........................ 216 206-2781
5161 Canal Rd Cleveland (44125) *(G-4393)*

Thompson Bros Mining Co................................ 330 549-3979
3379 E Garfield Rd New Springfield (44443) *(G-10474)*

Thompson Brothers Mining, New Springfield *Also Called: Thompson Bros Mining Co (G-10474)*

Thompson Castings, Cleveland *Also Called: Thompson Aluminum Casting Co (G-4393)*

Thomson Higher Education, Mason *Also Called: Cengage Learning Inc (G-9080)*

Thornton Powder Coatings Inc........................... 419 522-7183
2300 N Main St Mansfield (44903) *(G-8860)*

Thorwald Holdings Inc..................................... 740 756-9271
866 Mill Park Dr Lancaster (43130) *(G-8229)*

Thorworks Industries Inc (PA)........................... 419 626-4375
2520 Campbell St Sandusky (44870) *(G-11876)*

Those Chrcters From Clvland LL......................... 216 252-7300
1 American Rd Cleveland (44144) *(G-4394)*

Thread Works Custom Embroidery...................... 937 478-5231
2630 Colonel Glenn Hwy Beavercreek (45324) *(G-986)*

Thread Wrks EMB Screenprinting, Beavercreek *Also Called: Thread Works Custom Embroidery (G-986)*

Three Bond International Inc.............................. 937 610-3000
101 Daruma Pkwy Dayton (45439) *(G-6052)*

Three Bond International Inc (DH)....................... 513 779-7300
6184 Schumacher Park Dr West Chester (45069) *(G-14082)*

Thrift Tool Inc... 937 275-3600
5916 Milo Rd Dayton (45414) *(G-6053)*

(G-0000) Company's Geographic Section entry number

Tht Presses, Dayton *Also Called: THT Presses Inc (G-6054)*

THT Presses Inc.. 937 898-2012
7475 Webster St Dayton (45414) *(G-6054)*

Thurns Bakery & Deli.. 614 221-9246
541 S 3rd St Columbus (43215) *(G-5323)*

Thyme Inc.. 484 872-8430
3245 Pickle Rd Akron (44312) *(G-337)*

Thyssenkrupp Bilstein Amer Inc (HQ)............................. 513 881-7600
8685 Bilstein Blvd Hamilton (45015) *(G-7531)*

Thyssenkrupp Materials NA Inc....................................... 216 883-8100
6050 Oak Tree Blvd Ste 110 Independence (44131) *(G-7921)*

Thyssnkrupp Rothe Erde USA Inc (DH)........................... 330 562-4000
1400 S Chillicothe Rd Aurora (44202) *(G-689)*

Ti Inc... 419 332-8484
2107 Hayes Ave Fremont (43420) *(G-7138)*

TI Group Auto Systems LLC.. 740 929-2049
3600 Hebron Rd Hebron (43025) *(G-7640)*

TI Marie Candle Company LLC... 513 746-7798
311 Elm St Ste 270 Cincinnati (45202) *(G-3156)*

Tiama Americas Inc.. 269 274-3107
6500 Weatherfield Ct Maumee (43537) *(G-9325)*

Tiba LLC (DH).. 614 328-2040
2228 Citygate Dr Columbus (43219) *(G-5324)*

Tierra-Derco International LLC.. 419 929-2240
40 S Main St New London (44851) *(G-10418)*

Tiffin Foundry & Machine Inc.. 419 447-3991
423 W Adams St Tiffin (44883) *(G-12802)*

Tiffin Metal Products Co (PA)... 419 447-8414
450 Wall St Tiffin (44883) *(G-12803)*

Tiffin Paper Company (PA).. 419 447-2121
401 Wall St Tiffin (44883) *(G-12804)*

Tiffin Scenic Studios Inc (PA)... 800 445-1546
146 Riverside Dr Tiffin (44883) *(G-12805)*

Tiger Cat Furniture.. 330 220-7232
294 Marks Rd Brunswick (44212) *(G-1618)*

Tiger General LLC.. 330 239-4949
6867 Wooster Pike Medina (44256) *(G-9456)*

Tiger Lebanese Bakery, Toledo *Also Called: Investors United Inc (G-13008)*

Tiger Sand & Gravel LLC.. 330 833-6325
411 Oberlin Ave Sw Massillon (44647) *(G-9248)*

Tigerpoly Manufacturing Inc.. 614 871-0045
6231 Enterprise Pkwy Grove City (43123) *(G-7416)*

Tii Treeman Industries, Boardman *Also Called: Treemen Industries Inc (G-1378)*

Tilden Mining Company LC (HQ)..................................... 216 694-5700
200 Public Sq Ste 3300 Cleveland (44114) *(G-4395)*

Tiller Foods, Dayton *Also Called: Instantwhip-Dayton Inc (G-5823)*

Tiller Foods, Dayton *Also Called: Instantwhip-Dayton Inc (G-5824)*

Tilt 15 Inc... 330 239-4192
1440 Wolf Creek Trl Sharon Center (44274) *(G-11944)*

Tilt-Or-Lift Inc (PA)... 419 893-6944
124 E Dudley St Maumee (43537) *(G-9326)*

Tim Calvin Access Controls.. 740 494-4200
7585 Taway Rd Radnor (43066) *(G-11507)*

Tim Calvin Enterprises, Radnor *Also Called: Tim Calvin Access Controls (G-11507)*

Timac Manufacturing Company....................................... 937 372-3305
825 Bellbrook Ave Xenia (45385) *(G-14779)*

Timbertech, Wilmington *Also Called: Cpg International LLC (G-14577)*

Timbertech, Wilmington *Also Called: Timbertech Limited (G-14586)*

Timbertech Limited.. 937 655-8766
894 Prairie Rd Wilmington (45177) *(G-14586)*

Timco Inc.. 740 685-2594
57051 Marietta Rd Byesville (43723) *(G-1716)*

Timco Rubber Products Inc (PA)..................................... 216 267-6242
125 Blaze Industrial Pkwy Berea (44017) *(G-1191)*

Timekap Inc... 330 747-2122
2315 Belmont Ave Youngstown (44505) *(G-14947)*

Timekap Indus Sls Svc & Mch, Youngstown *Also Called: Timekap Inc (G-14947)*

Timekeeping Systems Inc... 216 595-0890
30700 Bainbridge Rd Ste H Solon (44139) *(G-12198)*

Times Reporter/Midwest Offset, New Philadelphia *Also Called: Copley Ohio Newspapers Inc (G-10439)*

Timet Toronto, Toronto *Also Called: Titanium Metals Corporation (G-13187)*

Timken, North Canton *Also Called: Timken Company (G-10673)*

Timken Company.. 614 836-3337
3782 Potomac St Groveport (43125) *(G-7453)*

Timken Company (PA).. 234 262-3000
4500 Mount Pleasant St Nw North Canton (44720) *(G-10673)*

Timken Newco I LLC.. 234 262-3000
4500 Mount Pleasant St Nw North Canton (44720) *(G-10674)*

Timken Receivables Corporation..................................... 234 262-3000
4500 Mount Pleasant St Nw North Canton (44720) *(G-10675)*

Timkensteel Fircrest Stl Plant, Canton *Also Called: Metallus Inc (G-1948)*

Timkensteel Material Svcs LLC....................................... 281 449-0319
1835 Dueber Ave Sw Canton (44706) *(G-2025)*

Timothy Whatman.. 419 883-2443
6617 Stoffer Rd Bellville (44813) *(G-1143)*

Tin Wizard Heating & Coolg Inc...................................... 330 467-9826
8853 Robinwood Ter Macedonia (44056) *(G-8720)*

Tinker Omega Sinto LLC.. 937 322-2272
2424 Columbus Rd Springfield (45503) *(G-12387)*

Tinnerman Palnut Engineered PR.................................... 330 220-5100
1060 W 130th St Brunswick (44212) *(G-1619)*

Tiny Lion Music Groups.. 419 874-7353
144 E 5th St Perrysburg (43551) *(G-11271)*

Tinycircuits.. 330 329-5753
540 S Main St Akron (44311) *(G-338)*

Tip Products Inc.. 216 252-2535
106 Industrial Dr New London (44851) *(G-10419)*

Tipco Punch Inc.. 513 874-9140
6 Rowe Ct Hamilton (45015) *(G-7532)*

Tipp Machine & Tool Inc... 937 890-8428
4201 Little York Rd Dayton (45414) *(G-6055)*

Tipton Environmental Intl Inc... 513 735-2777
4446 State Route 132 Batavia (45103) *(G-891)*

Tire Tread Development Inc.. 330 628-5666
1460 Martin Rd Mogadore (44260) *(G-10089)*

Tisch Environmental Inc (PA)... 513 467-9000
145 S Miami Ave Cleves (45002) *(G-4551)*

Titan Tire Corporation... 419 633-4221
927 S Union St Bryan (43506) *(G-1662)*

Titan Tire Corporation Bryan... 419 633-4224
927 S Union St Bryan (43506) *(G-1663)*

Titan Tire Corporation Bryan, Bryan *Also Called: Titan Tire Corporation (G-1662)*

Titanium Metals Corporation.. 740 537-1571
100 Titanium Way Toronto (43964) *(G-13187)*

Titans Packaging LLC... 513 449-0014
33 Circle Freeway Dr West Chester (45246) *(G-14155)*

TJ Clark International LLC.. 614 398 8860
320 London Rd Ste 608 Delaware (43015) *(G-6176)*

Tj Metzgers Inc... 419 861-8611
207 Arco Dr Toledo (43607) *(G-13143)*

TJ Oil & Gas Inc.. 740 623-0190
27353 State Route 621 Fresno (43824) *(G-7150)*

Tjar Innovations LLC.. 937 347-1999
1004 Cincinnati Ave Xenia (45385) *(G-14780)*

Tk America, West Chester *Also Called: Nikke Kureha America Co Ltd (G-14033)*

Tk Gas Services Inc... 740 826-0303
2303 John Glenn Hwy New Concord (43762) *(G-10387)*

Tkf Conveyor Systems LLC... 513 621-5260
5298 River Rd Cincinnati (45233) *(G-3157)*

Tkm Print Solutions Inc.. 330 237-4029
3455 Forest Lake Dr Uniontown (44685) *(G-13427)*

Tkn Oilfield Services LLC.. 740 516-2583
108 Woodcrest Dr Marietta (45750) *(G-8955)*

TL Industries Inc (PA).. 419 666-8144
28271 Cedar Park Blvd Ste 8 Perrysburg (43551) *(G-11272)*

Tl Krieg Offset LLC.. 513 542-1522
10600 Chester Rd Cincinnati (45215) *(G-3158)*

TLC Products, Westlake *Also Called: TLC Products Inc (G-14340)*

TLC Products Inc... 216 472-3030
26100 1st St Westlake (44145) *(G-14340)*

Tlg Cochran Inc (PA)... 440 914-1122
2026 Summit Commerce Park Twinsburg (44087) *(G-13385)*

Tls Corp (PA)..216 574-4759
1241 Superior Ave E Cleveland (44114) *(G-4396)*

Tlt-Babcock Inc..330 867-8540
260 Springside Dr Akron (44333) *(G-339)*

Tlt-Turbo Inc...330 776-5115
2693 Wingate Ave Akron (44314) *(G-340)*

Tm Machine & Tool Inc................................419 478-0310
521 Mel Simon Dr Toledo (43612) *(G-13144)*

Tmarzetti Company (HQ)..............................614 846-2232
380 Polaris Pkwy Ste 400 Westerville (43082) *(G-14237)*

Tmd, Toledo *Also Called: Toledo Molding & Die LLC (G-13153)*

Tmd Inc..419 476-4581
4 E Laskey Rd Toledo (43612) *(G-13145)*

Tmd Wek North LLC....................................440 576-6940
1085 Jefferson Eagleville Rd Jefferson (44047) *(G-7985)*

Tmg Performance Products LLC....................440 891-0999
140 Blaze Industrial Pkwy Berea (44017) *(G-1192)*

TMI, Cincinnati *Also Called: Win Plastic Extrusions LLC (G-3226)*

Tmi Inc...330 270-9780
6475 Victoria East Rd Youngstown (44515) *(G-14948)*

Tmk Farm Service, Sugarcreek *Also Called: Mullet Enterprises Inc (G-12643)*

Tmm, Waverly *Also Called: Third Millennium Materials LLC (G-13874)*

Tms International LLC..................................216 441-9702
4300 E 49th St Cleveland (44125) *(G-4397)*

Tms International LLC..................................513 425-6462
1801 Crawford St Middletown (45044) *(G-9898)*

Tms International LLC..................................513 422-4572
3018 Oxford State Rd Middletown (45044) *(G-9899)*

Tmsi, North Canton *Also Called: Tmsi LLC (G-10676)*

Tmsi LLC (HQ)..888 867-4872
8817 Pleasantwood Ave Nw North Canton (44720) *(G-10676)*

Tmt Inc..419 592-1041
655 D St Perrysburg (43551) *(G-11273)*

Tmt Logistics, Perrysburg *Also Called: Tmt Inc (G-11273)*

TNT Solid Solutions LLC.............................419 262-6228
6120 N Detroit Ave Toledo (43612) *(G-13146)*

To Scale Software LLC................................513 253-0053
6398 Thornberry Ct Mason (45040) *(G-9162)*

TOA Technologies Inc (PA)..........................216 925-5950
3333 Richmond Rd Ste 420 Beachwood (44122) *(G-954)*

Toagosei America Inc..................................614 718-3855
1450 W Main St West Jefferson (43162) *(G-14168)*

Toast With Cake LLC..................................937 554-5900
9231 Towering Pine Dr Apt L Miamisburg (45342) *(G-9748)*

Toastmasters International...........................937 429-2680
1854 Redleaf Ct Dayton (45432) *(G-5624)*

Tobacco Company, Cleveland *Also Called: Memphis Smokehouse Inc (G-4020)*

Tobal Products, Columbus *Also Called: Abbott Laboratories (G-4662)*

Tod Thin Brushes Inc.................................440 576-6859
1152 State Route 46 N Jefferson (44047) *(G-7986)*

Todco...740 223-2542
1295 E Fairground Rd Marion (43302) *(G-9002)*

Todco, Upper Sandusky *Also Called: Overhead Door Corporation (G-13452)*

Todd Industries Inc.....................................440 439-2900
7300 Northfield Rd Ste 1 Cleveland (44146) *(G-4398)*

Toft Dairy Inc...419 625-4376
3717 Venice Rd Sandusky (44870) *(G-11877)*

Toga-Pak Inc..937 294-7311
2208 Sandridge Dr Dayton (45439) *(G-6056)*

Toku America Inc..440 954-9923
3900 Ben Hur Ave Ste 3 Willoughby (44094) *(G-14540)*

Tolco, Toledo *Also Called: Tolco Corporation (G-13147)*

Tolco Corporation (PA).................................419 241-1113
1920 Linwood Ave Toledo (43604) *(G-13147)*

Toledo Alfalfa Mills Inc...............................419 836-3705
861 S Stadium Rd Oregon (43616) *(G-10969)*

Toledo Blade Company................................419 724-6000
541 N Superior St Toledo (43660) *(G-13148)*

Toledo Business Journals, Toledo *Also Called: Telex Communications Inc (G-13140)*

Toledo City Paper, Toledo *Also Called: Adams Street Publishing Co Inc (G-12864)*

Toledo Controls...419 474-2537
3550 Maxwell Rd Toledo (43606) *(G-13149)*

Toledo Cut Stone Inc..................................419 531-1623
4011 South Ave Toledo (43615) *(G-13150)*

Toledo Cutting Tools, Perrysburg *Also Called: Imco Carbide Tool Inc (G-11230)*

Toledo Deburring Co, Northwood *Also Called: Toledo Metal Finishing Inc (G-10809)*

Toledo Division, Perrysburg *Also Called: Terex Utilities Inc (G-11270)*

Toledo Driveline, Toledo *Also Called: Dana Light Axle Mfg LLC (G-12938)*

Toledo Electromotive Inc.............................419 874-7751
28765 White Rd Perrysburg (43551) *(G-11274)*

Toledo Engineering Co Inc (PA)...................419 537-9711
3400 Executive Pkwy Toledo (43606) *(G-13151)*

Toledo Express, Swanton *Also Called: Toledo Jet Center LLC (G-12695)*

Toledo Grmtor Blffton Mtr Wrks, Sylvania *Also Called: Tgm Holdings Company (G-12728)*

Toledo Integrated Systems, Maumee *Also Called: Toledo Transducers Inc (G-9327)*

Toledo Jet Center LLC (PA)..........................419 866-9050
11591 W Airport Service Rd Swanton (43558) *(G-12695)*

Toledo Metal Finishing Inc..........................419 661-1422
7880 Caple Blvd Northwood (43619) *(G-10809)*

Toledo Metal Spinning Company...................419 535-5931
1819 Clinton St Toledo (43607) *(G-13152)*

Toledo Molding & Die LLC...........................419 354-6050
515 E Gypsy Lane Rd Bowling Green (43402) *(G-1443)*

Toledo Molding & Die LLC...........................419 692-6022
24086 State Route 697 Delphos (45833) *(G-6193)*

Toledo Molding & Die LLC...........................419 692-6022
900 Gressel Dr Delphos (45833) *(G-6194)*

Toledo Molding & Die LLC...........................419 443-9031
1441 Maule Rd Tiffin (44883) *(G-12806)*

Toledo Molding & Die LLC (DH).....................419 470-3950
1429 Coining Dr Toledo (43612) *(G-13153)*

Toledo Molding & Die LLC...........................419 476-0581
4 E Laskey Rd Toledo (43612) *(G-13154)*

Toledo Optical, Toledo *Also Called: Toledo Optical Laboratory Inc (G-13155)*

Toledo Optical Laboratory Inc......................419 248-3384
1201 Jefferson Ave Toledo (43604) *(G-13155)*

Toledo Pro Fiberglass Inc............................419 241-9390
210 Wade St Toledo (43604) *(G-13156)*

Toledo Scales & Systems, Worthington *Also Called: Mettler-Toledo LLC (G-14719)*

Toledo Sign Company Inc (PA)......................419 244-4444
2021 Adams St Toledo (43604) *(G-13157)*

Toledo Solar Inc...567 202-4145
1775 Progress Dr Perrysburg (43551) *(G-11275)*

Toledo Spirits Company LLC.........................419 704-3705
1301 N Summit St Toledo (43604) *(G-13158)*

Toledo Tarp Service Inc...............................419 837-5098
3273 Genoa Rd Perrysburg (43551) *(G-11276)*

Toledo Ticket Company.................................419 476-5424
3963 Catawba St Toledo (43612) *(G-13159)*

Toledo Tool & Die, Toledo *Also Called: Toledo Tool and Die Co Inc (G-13161)*

Toledo Tool and Die Co Inc.........................419 476-9066
2 Kexon Dr Pioneer (43554) *(G-11330)*

Toledo Tool and Die Co Inc.........................419 476-4422
5639 Telegraph Rd Toledo (43612) *(G-13160)*

Toledo Tool and Die Co Inc (PA)...................419 476-4422
105 W Alexis Rd Toledo (43612) *(G-13161)*

Toledo Transducers Inc...............................419 724-4170
1345 Ford St Maumee (43537) *(G-9327)*

Toledo Window & Awning Inc.......................419 474-3396
3035 W Sylvania Ave Toledo (43613) *(G-13162)*

Toli Vault...866 998-8654
2035 Crocker Rd Ste 103 Westlake (44145) *(G-14341)*

Tolloti Pipe LLC..330 364-6627
102 Barnhill Rd Se New Philadelphia (44663) *(G-10467)*

Tolloti Plastic Pipe Inc (PA).........................330 364-6627
102 Barnhill Rd Se New Philadelphia (44663) *(G-10468)*

Tolson Pallet Mfg Inc..................................937 787-3511
10240 State Rte 122 Gratis (45330) *(G-7321)*

Tom Barbour Auto Parts Inc (PA)..................740 354-4654
915 11th St Portsmouth (45662) *(G-11479)*

(G-0000) Company's Geographic Section entry number

Tom Richards Inc (PA)..440 974-1300
  38809 Mentor Ave Willoughby (44094) *(G-14541)*

Tom Smith Industries Inc...937 832-1555
  500 Smith Dr Englewood (45315) *(G-6626)*

Tom Thumb Clip Co Inc...440 953-9606
  36300 Lakeland Blvd Unit 2 Willoughby (44095) *(G-14542)*

Tom Tire & Automotive, Lorain *Also Called: Certified Auto & Trck Repr Inc (G-8550)*

Tomahawk Entrmt Group LLC......................................216 505-0548
  26870 Drakefield Ave Euclid (44132) *(G-6680)*

Tomahawk Tool Supply...419 485-8737
  1604 Magda Dr Montpelier (43543) *(G-10135)*

Tomak Precision, Lebanon *Also Called: Aws Industries Inc (G-8245)*

Tomco Machining Inc..937 264-1943
  10950 Industry Ln Miamisburg (45342) *(G-9749)*

Tomco Tool Inc...937 322-5768
  203 S Wittenberg Ave Springfield (45506) *(G-12388)*

Tomlinson Industries, Chagrin Falls *Also Called: Meyer Company (G-2148)*

Tomlinson Industries LLC..216 587-3400
  4350 Renaissance Pkwy Cleveland (44128) *(G-4399)*

Tomson Steel Company...513 420-8600
  1400 Made Dr Middletown (45044) *(G-9900)*

Toney Tool, Dayton *Also Called: Toney Tool Manufacturing Inc (G-6057)*

Toney Tool Manufacturing Inc.....................................937 890-8535
  3488 Stop 8 Rd Dayton (45414) *(G-6057)*

Tonys Wldg & Fabrication LLC.....................................740 333-4000
  2305 Robinson Rd Se Wshngtn Ct Hs (43160) *(G-14748)*

Tool and Die Systems..440 327-5800
  38900 Taylor Pkwy Elyria (44035) *(G-6596)*

Tool Tech LLC..614 893-5876
  4901 Urbana Rd Springfield (45502) *(G-12389)*

Tool Technologies Van Dyke.......................................937 349-4900
  639 Clymer Rd Marysville (43040) *(G-9053)*

Toolbold Corporation (PA)..216 676-9840
  5330 Commerce Pkwy W Cleveland (44130) *(G-4400)*

Toolbold Corporation...440 543-1660
  5330 Commerce Pkwy W Cleveland (44130) *(G-4401)*

Toolcomp, Toledo *Also Called: Tooling & Components Corp (G-13163)*

Toolcraft Products Inc..937 223-8271
  1265 Mccook Ave Dayton (45404) *(G-6058)*

Tooling & Components Corp..419 478-9122
  5261 Tractor Rd Toledo (43612) *(G-13163)*

Tooling Components Division, Cleveland *Also Called: Jergens Inc (G-3885)*

Tooling Connection Inc..419 594-3339
  State Rte 66 N Ste 12603 Oakwood (45873) *(G-10901)*

Tooling Tech Group, Fort Loramie *Also Called: Tooling Technology LLC (G-6960)*

Tooling Tech Holdings LLC (HQ)...................................937 295-3672
  100 Enterprise Dr Fort Loramie (45845) *(G-6960)*

Tooling Technology LLC (PA)......................................937 381-9211
  100 Enterprise Dr Fort Loramie (45845) *(G-6960)*

Tooling Zone Inc...937 550-4180
  285 S Pioneer Blvd Springboro (45066) *(G-12271)*

Toolrite Manufacturing Inc...937 278-1962
  2608 Nordic Rd Dayton (45414) *(G-6059)*

Tooltex Inc...614 539-3222
  17287 Florence Chapel Pike Circleville (43113) *(G-3267)*

Top Cat Air Tools, Willoughby *Also Called: T C Service Co (G-14536)*

Top Knotch Products Inc...419 543-2266
  819 Colonel Dr Cleveland (44109) *(G-4402)*

Top Shot Ammunition, Akron *Also Called: TS Sales LLC (G-347)*

Top Tool & Die Inc...216 267-5878
  15500 Brookpark Rd Cleveland (44135) *(G-4403)*

Tope Printing Inc...330 674-4993
  1056 S Washington St Millersburg (44654) *(G-10014)*

Topkote Inc...440 428-0525
  404 N Lake St Madison (44057) *(G-8733)*

Topps Products Inc..913 685-2500
  3201 E 66th St Cleveland (44127) *(G-4404)*

Torax Medical Inc..651 361-8900
  4545 Creek Rd Blue Ash (45242) *(G-1344)*

Torbeck Industries, Harrison *Also Called: R L Torbeck Industries Inc (G-7565)*

Torbot Group Inc...419 724-1475
  3461 Curtice Rd Northwood (43619) *(G-10810)*

Torque 2020 CMA Acqisition LLC (PA)............................330 874-2900
  10896 Industrial Pkwy Nw Bolivar (44612) *(G-1393)*

Torque Transmission, Fairport Harbor *Also Called: Rampe Manufacturing Company (G-6821)*

Torrmetal LLC..216 671-1616
  12125 Bennington Ave Cleveland (44135) *(G-4405)*

Torrmetal Corporation..216 671-1616
  12125 Bennington Ave Cleveland (44135) *(G-4406)*

Torsion Control Products Inc.......................................248 537-1900
  1441 Wolf Creek Trl Wadsworth (44281) *(G-13675)*

Tortilla Factory, Toledo *Also Called: La Perla Inc (G-13026)*

Tortilleria La Bamba LLC..216 515-1600
  12119 Bennington Ave Cleveland (44135) *(G-4407)*

Tosoh America Inc (HQ)..614 539-8622
  3600 Gantz Rd Grove City (43123) *(G-7417)*

Tosoh SMD Inc (DH)..614 875-7912
  3600 Gantz Rd Grove City (43123) *(G-7418)*

Total Automation, Columbia Station *Also Called: Columbia Stamping Inc (G-4591)*

Total Baking Solutions LLC
  474 S Nelson Ave Wilmington (45177) *(G-14587)*

Total Call Center Solutions..330 869-9844
  1014 Margate Dr Ste 200 Akron (44313) *(G-341)*

Total Education Solutions Inc......................................330 668-4041
  3428 W Market St Fairlawn (44333) *(G-6815)*

Total Engine Airflow...330 634-2155
  285 West Ave Tallmadge (44278) *(G-12754)*

Total Life Safety LLC..866 955-2318
  6228 Centre Park Dr Ste C West Chester (45069) *(G-14083)*

Total Maintenance MGT Inc..513 228-2345
  320 Harmon Ave Lebanon (45036) *(G-8289)*

Total Manufacturing Co Inc...440 205-9700
  7777 Saint Clair Ave Mentor (44060) *(G-9638)*

Total Plastics International, Cleveland *Also Called: Plastics Family Holdings Inc (G-4172)*

Total Tennis Inc..614 488-5004
  1733 Cardiff Rd Columbus (43221) *(G-5325)*

Total Tennis Inc..614 504-7446
  321 W Bigelow Ave Plain City (43064) *(G-11421)*

Total Touch LLC...800 726-2117
  250 W Huron Rd Ste 400 Cleveland (44113) *(G-4408)*

Totally Promotional, Coldwater *Also Called: Casad Company Inc (G-4570)*

Totes Isotoner, Cincinnati *Also Called: Indra Holdings Corp (G-2743)*

Totes Isotoner Corporation (PA)...................................513 682-8200
  9655 International Blvd Cincinnati (45246) *(G-3159)*

Totes Isotoner Holdings LLC (PA).................................513 682-8200
  9655 International Blvd Cincinnati (45246) *(G-3160)*

Toth Industries Inc...419 729-4669
  5102 Enterprise Blvd Toledo (43612) *(G-13164)*

Toth Mold & Die Inc...440 232-8530
  380 Solon Rd Ste 6 Bedford (44146) *(G-1062)*

Touch Bionics Inc (DH)...800 233-6263
  6640 Riverside Dr Dublin (43017) *(G-6356)*

Touch Print Solution, Cincinnati *Also Called: Onetouchpoint East Corp (G-2933)*

Touchmark, Dublin *Also Called: Advanced Prgrm Resources Inc (G-6273)*

Tow Path Ready Mix, Jackson *Also Called: D G M Inc (G-7943)*

Tower Atmtive Oprtons USA I LL..................................419 483-1500
  630 Southwest St Bellevue (44811) *(G-1136)*

Tower Atmtive Oprtons USA I LL..................................419 358-8966
  18717 County Road 15 Bluffton (45817) *(G-1366)*

Tower Automotive, Bluffton *Also Called: Tower Atmtive Oprtons USA I LL (G-1366)*

Tower Countertops, Massillon *Also Called: Tower Industries Ltd (G-9249)*

Tower Industries Ltd...330 837-2216
  2101 9th St Sw Massillon (44647) *(G-9249)*

Town Cntry Technical Svcs Inc.....................................614 866-7700
  6200 Eastgreen Blvd Reynoldsburg (43068) *(G-11582)*

Toxco Inc...740 653-6290
  265 Quarry Rd Se Lancaster (43130) *(G-8230)*

Tpam Inc...567 315-8694
  5915 Jason St Toledo (43611) *(G-13165)*

TPC Food Service, Tiffin *Also Called: Tiffin Paper Company (G-12804)*

**A
L
P
H
A
B
E
T
I
C**

Tpf Inc..513 761-9968
313 S Wayne Ave Cincinnati (45215) *(G-3161)*

Tpl Holdings LLC..800 475-4030
3380 Gilchrist Rd Mogadore (44260) *(G-10090)*

Tpo Hess Holdings Inc.................................815 334-6140
3765 Sunnybrook Rd Kent (44240) *(G-8091)*

Tq Manufacturing Company Inc....................440 255-9000
7345 Production Dr Mentor (44060) *(G-9639)*

Tr Boes Holdings Inc....................................419 595-2255
14 N Perry St New Riegel (44853) *(G-10471)*

Tracer Specialties Inc...................................216 696-2363
1842 Columbus Rd Cleveland (44113) *(G-4409)*

Tracewell Systems Inc (PA)...........................614 846-6175
567 Enterprise Dr Lewis Center (43035) *(G-8356)*

Tracker Management Systems........................800 445-2438
10091 Brecksville Rd Brecksville (44141) *(G-1484)*

Trademark Designs Inc..................................419 628-3897
17 Jackson St Minster (45865) *(G-10067)*

Trades Restore LLC.......................................440 614-0480
405 N Brice Rd Blacklick (43004) *(G-1230)*

Tradewinds Prin Twear..................................740 214-5005
35 E Athens Rd Roseville (43777) *(G-11654)*

Trading Corp of America, Columbus *Also Called: Marfo Company (G-5081)*

Tradye Machine & Tool Inc.............................740 625-7550
3116a Wilson Rd Centerburg (43011) *(G-2128)*

Traffic Cntrl Sgnls Signs & MA.......................740 670-7763
1195 E Main St Newark (43055) *(G-10536)*

Traffic Detectors & Signs, Youngstown *Also Called: Traffic Detectors & Signs Inc (G-14949)*

Traffic Detectors & Signs Inc.........................330 707-9060
7521 Forest Hill Ave Youngstown (44514) *(G-14949)*

Traffic Engineering Department, Canton *Also Called: City of Canton (G-1866)*

Traichal Construction Company (PA)...............800 255-3667
332 Plant St Niles (44446) *(G-10607)*

Trail Sprayer & Service LLC............................330 720-2966
2830 Cleveland Ave Nw Canton (44709) *(G-2026)*

Trailer Component Mfg Inc..............................440 255-2888
8120 Tyler Blvd Mentor (44060) *(G-9640)*

Trailer One Inc...330 723-7474
1030 W Liberty St Medina (44256) *(G-9457)*

Trailstar, Alliance *Also Called: Trailstar International Inc (G-412)*

Trailstar International Inc...............................330 823-9900
14599 Commerce St Ne Alliance (44601) *(G-411)*

Trailstar International Inc (PA).......................330 821-9900
20700 Harrisburg Westville Rd Alliance (44601) *(G-412)*

Tramonte & Sons LLC....................................513 770-5501
3850 Welden Dr Lebanon (45036) *(G-8290)*

Trane, Cincinnati *Also Called: Trane US Inc (G-3163)*

Trane, Groveport *Also Called: Trane US Inc (G-7454)*

Trane Cleveland, Cleveland *Also Called: Trane Inc (G-4410)*

Trane Inc..440 946-7823
9555 Rockside Rd Ste 350 Cleveland (44125) *(G-4410)*

Trane National Account Service, Columbus *Also Called: Trane US Inc (G-5327)*

Trane Technologies Company LLC...................419 636-4242
1 Aro Ctr Bryan (43506) *(G-1664)*

Trane Technologies Company LLC...................419 633-6800
209 N Main St Bryan (43506) *(G-1665)*

Trane Technologies Company LLC...................513 459-4580
10300 Springfield Pike Cincinnati (45215) *(G-3162)*

Trane US Inc...513 771-8884
10300 Springfield Pike Cincinnati (45215) *(G-3163)*

Trane US Inc...614 473-3131
2300 Citygate Dr Ste 100 Columbus (43219) *(G-5326)*

Trane US Inc...614 473-8701
2300 Citygate Dr Ste 250 Columbus (43219) *(G-5327)*

Trane US Inc...614 497-6300
6600 Port Rd Ste 200 Groveport (43125) *(G-7454)*

Trane US Inc...419 491-2278
1001 Hamilton Dr Holland (43528) *(G-7788)*

Tranquility, Bowling Green *Also Called: Principle Business Entps Inc (G-1437)*

Trans Ash Inc..859 341-1528
360 S Wayne Ave Cincinnati (45215) *(G-3164)*

Trans-Acc Inc (PA)..513 793-6410
11167 Deerfield Rd Cincinnati (45242) *(G-3165)*

Trans-Foam Inc...330 630-9444
281 Southwest Ave Tallmadge (44278) *(G-12755)*

Transcat Inc..440 853-1907
9325 Progress Pkwy Mentor (44060) *(G-9641)*

Transcendia Inc...740 929-5100
3700 Hebron Rd Hebron (43025) *(G-7641)*

Transcendia Inc...440 638-2000
22889 Lunn Rd Strongsville (44149) *(G-12610)*

Transco Railway Products Inc..........................330 872-0934
2310 S Center St Newton Falls (44444) *(G-10581)*

Transcon Conveyor, Mentor *Also Called: New Transcon LLC (G-9570)*

Transdigm, Cleveland *Also Called: Transdigm Group Incorporated (G-4413)*

Transdigm Inc...216 291-6025
4223 Monticello Blvd Cleveland (44121) *(G-4411)*

Transdigm Inc (HQ).......................................216 706-2960
1350 Euclid Ave Ste 1601 Cleveland (44115) *(G-4412)*

Transdigm Inc...330 676-7147
2146 State Route 59 Kent (44240) *(G-8092)*

Transdigm Inc...440 352-6182
313 Gillett St Painesville (44077) *(G-11119)*

Transdigm Group Incorporated (PA)...............216 706-2960
1350 Euclid Ave Ste 1601 Cleveland (44115) *(G-4413)*

Transducers Direct, Cincinnati *Also Called: Transducers Direct Llc (G-3166)*

Transducers Direct Llc...................................513 247-0601
12115 Ellington Ct Cincinnati (45249) *(G-3166)*

Transfer Express Inc......................................440 918-1900
7650 Tyler Blvd Mentor (44060) *(G-9642)*

Transformer Associates Limited......................330 430-0750
831 Market Ave N Canton (44702) *(G-2027)*

Transit Fittings N Amer Inc............................330 797-2516
295 S Meridian Rd Youngstown (44509) *(G-14950)*

Transit Sittings of NA....................................330 797-2516
295 S Meridian Rd Youngstown (44509) *(G-14951)*

Transmet Corporation....................................614 276-5522
4290 Perimeter Dr Columbus (43228) *(G-5328)*

Transnorm System Inc...................................972 606-0303
7901 Innovation Way Mason (45040) *(G-9163)*

Transport Buff Intl Inc...................................419 332-5110
1099 County Road 126 Fremont (43420) *(G-7139)*

Transportation Group, Mantua *Also Called: Mantaline Corporation (G-8871)*

Transtar Holding Company LLC (PA)...............800 359-3339
7350 Young Dr Walton Hills (44146) *(G-13703)*

Transue & Williams Stampg Corp....................330 821-5777
207 N Four Mile Run Rd Austintown (44515) *(G-708)*

Tranzonic Companies.....................................440 446-0643
26301 Curtiss Wright Pkwy Ste 200 Cleveland (44143) *(G-4414)*

Tranzonic Companies, Richmond Heights *Also Called: Tz Acquisition Corp (G-11613)*

Travelers Custom Case Inc.............................216 621-8447
7444 Tyler Blvd Ste C Mentor (44060) *(G-9643)*

Travelers Vacation Guide................................440 582-4949
10143 Royalton Rd North Royalton (44133) *(G-10786)*

Traveling Recycle WD Pdts Inc.......................419 968-2649
19590 Bellis Rd Middle Point (45863) *(G-9764)*

Travis Products Mfg Inc.................................234 759-3741
80 Eastgate Dr North Lima (44452) *(G-10715)*

Traxium LLC..330 572-8200
4246 Hudson Dr Stow (44224) *(G-12466)*

Traxler Printing...614 593-1270
310 W Pacemont Rd Apt A Columbus (43202) *(G-5329)*

Treadway Manufacturing LLC.........................937 266-3423
8800 Frederick Pike Dayton (45414) *(G-6060)*

Treality Svs LLC (PA).....................................937 372-7579
600 Bellbrook Ave Xenia (45385) *(G-14781)*

Treaty City Industries Inc..............................937 548-9000
945 Sater St Greenville (45331) *(G-7358)*

Trebnick Systems LLC....................................937 743-1550
215 S Pioneer Blvd Springboro (45066) *(G-12272)*

Trebnick Tags and Labels, Springboro *Also Called: Trebnick Systems LLC (G-12272)*

Trec Industries Inc..216 741-4114
4713 Spring Rd Cleveland (44131) *(G-4415)*

Treehouse Private Brands Inc 740 654-8880
3775 Lancaster New Lexington Rd Se Lancaster (43130) *(G-8231)*

Treehouse Private Brands Inc 740 654-8880
276 Bremen Rd Lancaster (43130) *(G-8232)*

Treemen Industries Inc 330 965-3777
691 Mcclurg Rd Boardman (44513) *(G-1378)*

Trek Diagnostics Inc 440 808-0000
982 Keynote Cir Brooklyn Heights (44131) *(G-1541)*

Trellborg Sling Prfiles US Inc 330 995-9725
285 Lena Dr Aurora (44202) *(G-690)*

Trelleborg, Aurora *Also Called: Trellborg Sling Prfiles US Inc (G-690)*

Tremcar USA Inc 330 878-7708
436 12th St Ne Strasburg (44680) *(G-12482)*

Tremco Cpg Inc 419 289-2050
1451 Jacobson Ave Ashland (44805) *(G-580)*

Tremco Cpg Inc 216 514-7783
23150 Commerce Park Beachwood (44122) *(G-955)*

Tremco Incorporated (HQ) 216 292-5000
3735 Green Rd Beachwood (44122) *(G-956)*

Tremont Electric Incorporated 888 214-3137
2112 W 7th St Cleveland (44113) *(G-4416)*

Trenchless Rsrces Globl Hldngs 419 419-6498
420 Industrial Pkwy Bowling Green (43402) *(G-1444)*

Trent Manufacturing Company 216 391-1551
7310 Corporate Blvd Mentor (44060) *(G-9644)*

Tresslers Plumbing LLC 419 784-2142
9170 State Route 15 Defiance (43512) *(G-6126)*

Treved Exteriors 513 771-3888
10235 Spartan Dr Ste T Cincinnati (45215) *(G-3167)*

Trevor Clatterbuck 330 359-2129
927 Us Route 62 Wilmot (44689) *(G-14595)*

Trewbric III Inc 614 444-2184
1701 Moler Rd Columbus (43207) *(G-5330)*

Trexler Rubber Co Inc (PA) 330 296-9677
503 N Diamond St Ravenna (44266) *(G-11546)*

Trey Corrugated Inc 513 942-4800
9048 Port Union Rialto Rd West Chester (45069) *(G-14084)*

Trg United, Columbus *Also Called: Russell Group United LLC (G-5238)*

Tri - Flex of Ohio Inc (PA) 330 705-7084
2701 Applegrove St Nw North Canton (44720) *(G-10677)*

Tri Cast Limited Partnership 330 733-8718
2128 Killian Rd Akron (44312) *(G-342)*

Tri County Concrete Inc 330 425-4464
10155 Royalton Rd Cleveland (44133) *(G-4417)*

Tri County Concrete Inc (PA) 330 425-4464
9423 Darrow Rd Twinsburg (44087) *(G-13386)*

Tri County Eggs, Versailles *Also Called: Weaver Bros Inc (G-13605)*

Tri County Locksmith, Cincinnati *Also Called: AB Bonded Locksmiths Inc (G-2330)*

Tri County Ready Mixed Con Co, Cleveland *Also Called: Tri County Concrete Inc (G-4417)*

Tri County Tarp LLC (PA) 419 288-3350
13100 Us Highway 23 Gibsonburg (43431) *(G-7260)*

Tri State Dairy LLC (PA) 330 897-5555
9946 Fiat Rd Sw Baltic (43804) *(G-782)*

Tri State Dairy LLC 419 542-8788
210 Wendell Ave Hicksville (43526) *(G-7653)*

Tri State Equipment Company 513 738-7227
5009 Cincinnati-Brookville Rd Shandon (45063) *(G-11935)*

Tri State Media LLC 513 933-0101
325 Davids Dr Wilmington (45177) *(G-14588)*

Tri State Pallet Inc (PA) 937 746-8702
8401 Claude Thomas Rd Franklin (45005) *(G-7053)*

Tri-America Contractors, Wheelersburg *Also Called: Tri-America Contractors Inc (G-14355)*

Tri-America Contractors Inc (PA) 740 574-0148
1664 State Route 522 Wheelersburg (45694) *(G-14354)*

Tri-America Contractors Inc 740 574-0148
1664 State Route 522 Wheelersburg (45694) *(G-14355)*

Tri-Cast Inc (PA) 330 733-8718
2128 Killian Rd Akron (44312) *(G-343)*

Tri-County Block and Brick Inc 419 826-7060
1628 Us Highway 20a Swanton (43558) *(G-12696)*

Tri-Craft Inc 440 826-1050
17941 Englewood Dr Cleveland (44130) *(G-4418)*

Tri-Fab Inc 330 337-3425
10372 W South Range Rd Salem (44460) *(G-11815)*

Tri-K Enterprises Inc 330 832-7380
935 Mckinley Ave Sw Canton (44707) *(G-2028)*

Tri-Mac Mfg & Serv, Hamilton *Also Called: Tri-Mac Mfg & Svcs Co (G-7533)*

Tri-Mac Mfg & Svcs Co 513 896-4445
860 Belle Ave Hamilton (45015) *(G-7533)*

Tri-R Dies, Youngstown *Also Called: Mordies Inc (G-14902)*

Tri-R Tooling Inc 419 522-8665
220 Piper Rd Mansfield (44905) *(G-8861)*

Tri-State Archtctural Panl Sls, Toledo *Also Called: Toledo Cut Stone Inc (G-13150)*

Tri-State Asphalt Co, Rayland *Also Called: Shelly and Sands Inc (G-11552)*

Tri-State Fabricators Inc 513 752-5005
1146 Ferris Rd Amelia (45102) *(G-440)*

Tri-State Paper Inc 937 885-3365
9000 Kenrick Rd Dayton (45458) *(G-6061)*

Tri-State Plating & Polishing 304 529-2579
187 Township Road 1204 Proctorville (45669) *(G-11500)*

Tri-State Printing, Steubenville *Also Called: Tri-State Publishing Company (G-12413)*

Tri-State Publishing Company (PA) 740 283-3686
157 N 3rd St Steubenville (43952) *(G-12413)*

Tri-State Supply Co Inc 614 272-6767
3840 Fisher Rd Columbus (43228) *(G-5331)*

Tri-State Wilbert Vault Co, Ironton *Also Called: Allen Enterprises Inc (G-7928)*

Tri-State Wire Rope Supply Inc (HQ) 513 871-8656
5246 Wooster Pike Cincinnati (45226) *(G-3168)*

Tri-Tech, Baltimore *Also Called: Tri-Tech Led Systems LLC (G-788)*

Tri-Tech Laboratories Inc 740 927-2817
8825 Smiths Mill Rd N Johnstown (43031) *(G-8000)*

Tri-Tech Led Systems LLC 614 593-2868
600 W Market St Baltimore (43105) *(G-788)*

Tri-W Group Inc 614 228-5000
835 Goodale Blvd Columbus (43212) *(G-5332)*

Triad Capital Group LLC 440 236-6677
4641 Spring Rd Cleveland (44131) *(G-4419)*

Triad Capital Group LLC (PA) 440 236-6677
4641 Spring Rd Independence (44131) *(G-7922)*

Triad Energy Corporation 740 374-2940
125 Putnam St Marietta (45750) *(G-8956)*

Triad Governmental Systems 937 376-5446
358 S Monroe St Xenia (45385) *(G-14782)*

Triage Ortho Group 937 653-6431
132 Lafayette Ave Urbana (43078) *(G-13478)*

Triangle Machine Products Co 216 524-5872
6055 Hillcrest Dr Cleveland (44125) *(G-4420)*

Triangle Precision Inds Inc 937 299-6776
1050 Delco Park Dr Dayton (45420) *(G-0001)*

Triangle Sign Co LLC 513 266-1009
221 N B St Hamilton (45013) *(G-7534)*

Tribco Incorporated 216 486-2000
18901 Cranwood Pkwy Cleveland (44128) *(G-4421)*

TRIBORO QUILT MANUFACTURING CORPORATION, Vandalia *Also Called: Triboro Quilt Mfg Corp (G-13579)*

Triboro Quilt Mfg Corp 937 222-2132
303 Corporate Center Dr Ste 108 Vandalia (45377) *(G-13579)*

Tribotech Composites Inc 216 901-1300
7800 Exchange St Cleveland (44125) *(G-4422)*

Tribune , The, Jefferson *Also Called: The Gazette Printing Co Inc (G-7984)*

Tribune Printing Inc 419 542-7764
147 E High St Hicksville (43526) *(G-7654)*

Tribune Shopping News, The, New Lexington *Also Called: Perry County Tribune (G-10405)*

Trico, Cleveland *Also Called: Trico Products Corporation (G-4425)*

Trico Enterprises LLC 216 970-9984
17717 Hilliard Rd Lakewood (44107) *(G-8172)*

Trico Holding Corporation (DH) 216 589-0198
127 Public Sq Ste 5110 Cleveland (44114) *(G-4423)*

Trico Machine Products Corp 216 662-4194
5081 Corbin Dr Cleveland (44128) *(G-4424)*

Trico Products Corporation (DH) 800 388-7428
127 Public Sq Cleveland (44114) *(G-4425)*

A
L
P
H
A
B
E
T
I
C

Tricor Industrial Inc (PA).. 330 264-3299
  3225 W Old Lincoln Way Wooster (44691) *(G-14692)*

Tricor Metals, Wooster *Also Called: Tricor Industrial Inc (G-14692)*

Trifecta Tool and Engrg LLC.. 937 291-0933
  4648 Gateway Cir Dayton (45440) *(G-6063)*

Trilogy Plastics, Alliance *Also Called: Myers Industries Inc (G-396)*

Trilogy Plastics, Alliance *Also Called: Trilogy Plastics Alliance Inc (G-413)*

Trilogy Plastics Alliance Inc.. 330 821-4700
  2290 W Main St Alliance (44601) *(G-413)*

Trim Parts Inc.. 513 934-0815
  2175 Deerfield Rd Lebanon (45036) *(G-8291)*

Trim Systems Operating Corp.. 740 772-5998
  75 Chamber Dr Chillicothe (45601) *(G-2285)*

Trim Systems Operating Corp (HQ)............................... 614 289-5360
  7800 Walton Pkwy New Albany (43054) *(G-10352)*

Trim Tool & Machine Inc.. 216 889-1916
  3431 Service Rd Cleveland (44111) *(G-4426)*

Trimble Engineering & Cnstr, Tipp City *Also Called: Trimble Inc (G-12848)*

Trimble Inc.. 937 233-8921
  5475 Kellenburger Rd Dayton (45424) *(G-6064)*

Trimble Inc.. 937 233-8921
  4450 Gibson Dr Tipp City (45371) *(G-12848)*

Trimble Trnsp Entp Sltions Inc (HQ)............................ 216 831-6606
  6085 Parkland Blvd Mayfield Heights (44124) *(G-9342)*

Trimco.. 614 679-3931
  7265 Park Bend Dr Westerville (43082) *(G-14238)*

Trimline Die Corporation... 440 355-6900
  421 Commerce Dr E Lagrange (44050) *(G-8154)*

Trimold LLC... 740 474-7591
  200 Pittsburgh Rd Circleville (43113) *(G-3268)*

Trimtec Systems Ltd... 614 820-0340
  2455 Harrisburg Pike Grove City (43123) *(G-7419)*

Trinel Inc... 216 265-9190
  5251 W 137th St Cleveland (44142) *(G-4427)*

Trinity Specialty Compounding Inc............................... 419 924-9090
  600 Oak St West Unity (43570) *(G-14198)*

Trinity Water Solutions LLC... 740 318-0585
  17226 Industrial Hwy Caldwell (43724) *(G-1730)*

Trionetics Inc.. 216 812-3570
  4924 Schaaf Ln Brooklyn Heights (44131) *(G-1542)*

Trionix Research Lab Inc... 330 425-9055
  8037 Bavaria Rd Twinsburg (44087) *(G-13387)*

Triple A Builders Inc... 216 249-0327
  540 E 105th St Cleveland (44108) *(G-4428)*

Triple Arrow Industries Inc... 614 437-5588
  13311 Industrial Pkwy Marysville (43040) *(G-9054)*

Triplett Bluffton Corporation... 419 358-8750
  1 Triplett Dr Bluffton (45817) *(G-1367)*

Trisource Exhibits.. 800 229-8600
  12400 Plaza Dr Ste 1 Parma (44130) *(G-11136)*

Tristan Rubber Molding Inc (PA).................................. 330 499-4055
  7255 Whipple Ave Nw North Canton (44720) *(G-10678)*

Tristate Steel Contractors LLC...................................... 513 648-9000
  2508 Civic Center Dr Ste A Cincinnati (45231) *(G-3169)*

Triton Duro Werks Inc.. 407 497-9116
  3475 W Bath Rd Akron (44333) *(G-344)*

Triton Duro Werks Inc.. 216 267-1117
  12200 Sprecher Ave Cleveland (44135) *(G-4429)*

Triton Global Products Inc.. 440 248-5480
  30700 Carter St Ste D Solon (44139) *(G-12199)*

Triton Products, Solon *Also Called: Triton Global Products Inc (G-12199)*

Triumph Signs & Consulting Inc................................... 513 576-8090
  480 Milford Pkwy Milford (45150) *(G-9955)*

Triumph Thermal Systems LLC (HQ)............................ 419 273-2511
  200 Railroad St Forest (45843) *(G-6942)*

Triumphant Enterprises Inc... 513 617-1668
  7096 Hill Station Rd Goshen (45122) *(G-7298)*

Trivium Alum Packg USA Corp (DH).............................. 330 744-2267
  1 Performance Pl Youngstown (44502) *(G-14952)*

TRM Manufacturing Inc (PA)... 330 769-2600
  607 Munroe Falls Ave Cuyahoga Falls (44221) *(G-5577)*

TRM Manufacturing Inc.. 330 769-2600
  601 Munroe Falls Ave Cuyahoga Falls (44221) *(G-5578)*

Trogdon Publishing Inc.. 330 721-7678
  5164 Normandy Park Dr Ste 100 Medina (44256) *(G-9458)*

Tronair Inc (DH).. 419 866-6301
  1 Air Cargo Pkwy E Swanton (43558) *(G-12697)*

Trophy Nut Co (PA)... 937 667-8478
  320 N 2nd St Tipp City (45371) *(G-12849)*

Trophy Nut Co.. 937 669-5513
  1567 Harmony Dr Tipp City (45371) *(G-12850)*

Trophy's Unlimited, Wheelersburg *Also Called: Greg Blume (G-14353)*

Tropical Nut & Fruit, Grove City *Also Called: Hayden Valley Foods Inc (G-7390)*

Trotwood Corporation... 937 854-3047
  11 N Broadway St Trotwood (45426) *(G-13197)*

Troy, Burton *Also Called: Troy Manufacturing Co (G-1706)*

Troy Chemical, Burton *Also Called: Troy Chemical Industries Inc (G-1705)*

Troy Chemical Industries Inc (PA)................................ 440 834-4408
  17040 Rapids Rd Burton (44021) *(G-1705)*

Troy Engnred Cmpnnts Assmblies............................... 937 335-8070
  4900 Webster St Dayton (45414) *(G-6065)*

Troy Filters Ltd... 614 777-8222
  1680 Westbelt Dr Columbus (43228) *(G-5333)*

Troy Innovative Instrs Inc... 440 834-9567
  15111 White Rd Middlefield (44062) *(G-9831)*

Troy Manufacturing Co.. 440 834-8262
  17090 Rapids Rd Burton (44021) *(G-1706)*

Troy Precision Carbide, Burton *Also Called: Troy Precision Carbide Die Inc (G-1707)*

Troy Precision Carbide Die Inc..................................... 440 834-4477
  17720 Claridon Troy Rd Burton (44021) *(G-1707)*

Troy Sand and Gravel, Troy *Also Called: Marietta Martin Materials Inc (G-13239)*

Troy Water Treatment Plant, Troy *Also Called: City of Troy (G-13205)*

Troyer Cheese, Inc., Millersburg *Also Called: Cheese Holdings Inc (G-9977)*

Troyer Manufacturing, Millersburg *Also Called: Lipari Foods Operating Co LLC (G-9992)*

Troyer Manufacturing, Millersburg *Also Called: Lipari Foods Operating Co LLC (G-9993)*

Troyer Signs Incorporated.. 330 263-1400
  2740 S Honeytown Rd Wooster (44691) *(G-14693)*

Troyers Cabinet Shop Ltd... 937 464-7702
  9442 County Road 101 Belle Center (43310) *(G-1097)*

Troyers Trail Bologna Inc.. 330 893-2414
  6552 State Route 515 Dundee (44624) *(G-6370)*

Troyke Manufacturing Company.................................... 513 769-4242
  11294 Orchard St Cincinnati (45241) *(G-3170)*

Troymill Lumber Company... 440 632-6353
  7000 Granger Rd Ste 1 Independence (44131) *(G-7923)*

Troymill Manufacturing Inc (PA)................................... 440 632-5580
  17055 Kinsman Rd Middlefield (44062) *(G-9832)*

Troymill Wood Products, Middlefield *Also Called: Troymill Manufacturing Inc (G-9832)*

Troyridge Mfg.. 330 893-7516
  3998 County Road 168 Millersburg (44654) *(G-10015)*

Tru Comfort Mattress... 614 595-8600
  8994 Mediterra Pl Dublin (43016) *(G-6357)*

Tru Form Metal Products Inc.. 216 252-3700
  12305 Grimsby Ave Cleveland (44135) *(G-4430)*

Tru-Bore Machine Co Inc... 330 928-6215
  1220 Orlen Ave Cuyahoga Falls (44221) *(G-5579)*

Tru-Fab Inc.. 937 435-1733
  2225 Lyons Rd Miamisburg (45342) *(G-9750)*

Tru-Fab Technology Inc.. 440 954-9760
  34820 Lakeland Blvd Willoughby (44095) *(G-14543)*

Tru-Form Steel & Wire Inc... 765 348-5001
  5509 Telegraph Rd Toledo (43612) *(G-13166)*

Tru-Tex International Corp... 513 825-8844
  11050 Southland Rd Cincinnati (45240) *(G-3171)*

Tru-Weld Stud Welding Div, Medina *Also Called: Tfp Corporation (G-9454)*

Truax Printing Inc... 419 994-4166
  425 E Haskell St Loudonville (44842) *(G-8595)*

Trucast Inc.. 440 942-4923
  4382 Hamann Pkwy Willoughby (44094) *(G-14544)*

Truck & Parts of Ohio, New Paris *Also Called: Trucks & Parts of Tampa LLC (G-10427)*

Truck Cab Manufacturers Inc (PA)............................... 513 922-1300
  2420 Anderson Ferry Rd Cincinnati (45238) *(G-3172)*

2025 Harris Ohio
Industrial Directory

(G-0000) Company's Geographic Section entry number

Truck Fax Inc..216 921-8866
  17700 S Woodland Rd Cleveland (44120) *(G-4431)*

Truckcorp LLC...234 666-5702
  3026 Saratoga Ave Sw Canton (44706) *(G-2029)*

Trucks & Parts of Tampa LLC..............................937 437-0377
  9206 Us Route 40 W New Paris (45347) *(G-10427)*

Trucut Incorporated (PA)....................................330 938-9806
  1145 Allied Dr Sebring (44672) *(G-11903)*

True Dinero Records & Tech LLC..........................513 428-4610
  2611 Kemper Ln Uppr Level1 Cincinnati (45206) *(G-3173)*

True Industries Inc...330 296-4342
  666 Pratt St Ravenna (44266) *(G-11547)*

True North Energy LLC.......................................440 442-0060
  6411 Mayfield Rd Mayfield Heights (44124) *(G-9343)*

True Step LLC..513 933-0933
  1105 S Us Route 42 Lebanon (45036) *(G-8292)*

True Value, North Baltimore *Also Called: Mid-Wood Inc (G-10614)*

True Value, Woodsfield *Also Called: Kemps Ace Hardware Inc (G-14614)*

Truechoicepack Corp..937 630-3832
  9565 Cincinnati Columbus Rd West Chester (45069) *(G-14085)*

Truenorth Energy, Mayfield Heights *Also Called: True North Energy LLC (G-9343)*

Truex Tool & Die Div, Youngstown *Also Called: Jamen Tool & Die Co (G-14879)*

Trufast, Bryan *Also Called: Altenloh Brinck & Co US Inc (G-1628)*

Truflex Rubber Products Co................................740 967-9015
  200 E Coshocton St Johnstown (43031) *(G-8001)*

Trulil Inc...937 652-1242
  625 S Edgewood Ave Urbana (43078) *(G-13479)*

Truline Industries Inc.......................................440 729-0140
  1400 Silver St Wickliffe (44092) *(G-14397)*

Trulite GL Alum Solutions LLC............................740 929-2443
  160 N High St Hebron (43025) *(G-7642)*

Trulou Holdings Inc..513 347-0100
  5311 Robert Ave Ste A Cincinnati (45248) *(G-3174)*

Trumbull Asphalt, Toledo *Also Called: Owens Corning Roofg & Asp LLC (G-13087)*

Trumbull Cement Products Co.............................330 372-4342
  2185 Larchmont Ave Ne Warren (44483) *(G-13802)*

Trumbull County Hardwoods...............................440 632-0555
  9446 Bundysburg Rd Middlefield (44062) *(G-9833)*

Trumbull Industries Inc.....................................330 434-6174
  209 Perkins St Akron (44304) *(G-345)*

Trumbull Manufacturing Inc................................330 270-7888
  3850 Hendricks Rd Youngstown (44515) *(G-14953)*

Trumbull Mobile Meals......................................330 394-2538
  323 E Market St Warren (44481) *(G-13803)*

Trupoint Products LLC.......................................330 204-3302
  Uknown Sugarcreek (44681) *(G-12654)*

Truseal Technologies Inc (HQ)............................216 910-1500
  388 S Main St Ste 700 Akron (44311) *(G-346)*

Trusscore USA Inc..888 418-4679
  6161 Ventnor Ave Dayton (45414) *(G-6066)*

Trust Manufacturing LLC (PA).............................216 531-8787
  20080 Saint Clair Ave Euclid (44117) *(G-6681)*

Trust Technologies, Cleveland *Also Called: Kilroy Company (G-3920)*

Trutech Cabinetry LLC.......................................614 338-0680
  2121 S James Rd Columbus (43232) *(G-5334)*

Trv LLC...440 951-7722
  4860 E 345th St Willoughby (44094) *(G-14545)*

TS Sales LLC...727 804-8060
  847 Pier Dr Akron (44307) *(G-347)*

TS Tech Americas Inc (HQ).................................614 575-4100
  8458 E Broad St Reynoldsburg (43068) *(G-11583)*

TS Tech Co Ltd...740 420-5617
  200 Pittsburgh Rd Circleville (43113) *(G-3269)*

TS Tech USA Corporation (DH)............................614 577-1088
  8400 E Broad St Reynoldsburg (43068) *(G-11584)*

TS Trim Industries Inc (DH)................................614 837-4114
  6380 Canal St Canal Winchester (43110) *(G-1799)*

Tsjmedia, Blue Ash *Also Called: Gate West Coast Ventures LLC (G-1276)*

Tsk America Co Ltd...513 942-4002
  9668 Inter Ocean Dr West Chester (45246) *(G-14156)*

Tsp Inc...513 732-8900
  2009 Glenn Pkwy Batavia (45103) *(G-892)*

TSR Machinery Services Inc................................513 874-9697
  100 Security Dr Fairfield (45014) *(G-6785)*

TSS Acquisition Company...................................513 772-7000
  1201 Hill Smith Dr Cincinnati (45215) *(G-3175)*

TSS Technologies, West Chester *Also Called: Cbn Westside Holdings Inc (G-13956)*

TSS Technologies, West Chester *Also Called: Cbn Westside Technologies Inc (G-13957)*

Tsw Industries Inc..440 572-7200
  14960 Foltz Pkwy Strongsville (44149) *(G-12611)*

TT Electronics IMS, Perry *Also Called: TT Electronics Integrated Manufacturing Services Inc (G-11200)*

TT Electronics Integrated Manufacturing Services Inc....................440 352-8961
  3700 Lane Rd Ext Perry (44081) *(G-11200)*

TTI Sports Equipment, Columbus *Also Called: Total Tennis Inc (G-5325)*

Ttm, North Jackson *Also Called: Cleveland Coretec Inc (G-10685)*

Ttm Technologies, North Jackson *Also Called: Ttm Technologies North America LLC (G-10697)*

Ttm Technologies Inc..330 538-3900
  12080 Debartolo Dr North Jackson (44451) *(G-10696)*

Ttm Technologies North America LLC....................330 572-3400
  12080 Debartolo Dr North Jackson (44451) *(G-10697)*

Tubar Eureka Industrial Group, Canton *Also Called: Uhrden Inc (G-2030)*

Tube Fittings Division, Columbus *Also Called: Parker-Hannifin Corporation (G-5174)*

Tubetech Inc (PA)...330 426-9476
  900 E Taggart St East Palestine (44413) *(G-6409)*

Tubetech North America, East Palestine *Also Called: Tubetech Inc (G-6409)*

Tuboscope, Youngstown *Also Called: Varco LP (G-14959)*

Tubular Techniques Inc......................................614 529-4130
  3025 Scioto Darby Executive Ct Hilliard (43026) *(G-7708)*

Tucker Printers Inc...585 359-3030
  8740 Global Way West Chester (45069) *(G-14086)*

Tuf-N-Lite, Liberty Twp *Also Called: Feather Lite Innovations Inc (G-8383)*

Tuf-N-Lite, Springboro *Also Called: Feather Lite Innovations Inc (G-12252)*

Tuf-Tug Inc..937 299-1213
  3434 Encrete Ln Dayton (45439) *(G-6067)*

Tuffco Sand and Gravel Inc.................................614 873-3977
  8195 Old State Route 161 Plain City (43064) *(G-11422)*

Tuffy Manufacturing..330 940-2356
  360 Massillon Rd Akron (44312) *(G-348)*

Tuffy Pad Company...330 688-0043
  454 Seasons Rd Stow (44224) *(G-12467)*

Tugz International LLC.......................................216 621-4854
  4500 Division Ave Cleveland (44102) *(G-4432)*

Tulkoff Food Products Ohio LLC...........................410 864-0523
  3015 E Kemper Rd Cincinnati (45241) *(G-3176)*

Tune Town, Sandusky *Also Called: Tune Town Car Audio (G-11878)*

Tune Town Car Audio...419 627-1100
  2345 E Perkins Ave Sandusky (44870) *(G-11878)*

Tungsten and Capital, Solon *Also Called: Bowes Manufacturing Inc (G-12087)*

Turbine Eng Cmpnents Tech Corp.........................216 692-5200
  23555 Euclid Ave Cleveland (44117) *(G-4433)*

Turbine Standard Ltd (PA)..................................419 865-0355
  1750 Eber Rd Ste A Holland (43528) *(G-7789)*

Turf Care Supply LLC (PA)..................................877 220-1014
  50 Pearl Rd Ste 200 Brunswick (44212) *(G-1620)*

Turkeyfoot Printing, Napoleon *Also Called: Mustang Printing (G-10292)*

Turn-All Machine & Gear Co.................................937 342-8710
  5499 Tremont Ln Springfield (45502) *(G-12390)*

Turn-Key Industrial Svcs LLC..............................614 274-1128
  4512 Harrisburg Pike Grove City (43123) *(G-7420)*

Turn-Key Tunneling Inc......................................614 275-4832
  1247 Stimmel Rd Columbus (43223) *(G-5335)*

Turner Concrete Products...................................419 662-9007
  2121 Tracy Rd Northwood (43619) *(G-10811)*

Turner Machine Co..330 332-5821
  1433 Salem Pkwy Salem (44460) *(G-11816)*

Turner Vault Co..419 537-1133
  2121 Tracy Rd Northwood (43619) *(G-10812)*

Turning Technologies LLC (PA)............................330 746-3015
  6000 Mahoning Ave Youngstown (44515) *(G-14954)*

Turtle Plastics, Lorain *Also Called: Cleveland Reclaim Inds Inc (G-8551)*

Turtlecreek Township.................... 513 932-4080
670 N State Route 123 Lebanon (45036) *(G-8293)*

Tuscarora Wood Midwest LLC.................... 937 603-8882
6506 W Us Route 36 Covington (45318) *(G-5500)*

Tusco Display, Gnadenhutten *Also Called: Tusco Limited Partnership (G-7295)*

Tusco Hardwoods LLC.................... 330 852-4281
10887 Gerber Valley Rd Nw Sugarcreek (44681) *(G-12655)*

Tusco Limited Partnership.................... 740 254-4343
239 S Chestnut St Gnadenhutten (44629) *(G-7295)*

Tvh Parts Co.................... 877 755-7311
8756 Global Way West Chester (45069) *(G-14087)*

Tvone Ncsa.................... 859 282-7303
621 Wilmer Ave Cincinnati (45226) *(G-3177)*

Tvone Ncsa - N Centl & S Amer, Cincinnati *Also Called: Tvone Ncsa (G-3177)*

TW Manufacturing Co.................... 440 439-3243
6065 Parkland Blvd Cleveland (44124) *(G-4434)*

Twb Company LLC.................... 330 558-2026
5569 Innovation Dr Valley City (44280) *(G-13521)*

Twenty One Barrels Ltd.................... 937 467-4498
9717 Horatio Harris Creek Rd Bradford (45308) *(G-1453)*

Twin Cities Concrete Co.................... 330 627-2158
1031 Kensington Rd Ne Carrollton (44615) *(G-2091)*

Twin Cities Concrete Co (DH).................... 330 343-4491
141 S Tuscarawas Ave Dover (44622) *(G-6266)*

Twin Oaks Barns LLC.................... 330 893-3126
3337 Us Route 62 Dundee (44624) *(G-6371)*

Twin Point Inc (PA).................... 419 923-7525
11955 County Road 10-2 Delta (43515) *(G-6214)*

Twin Rivers Technologies Mfg, Painesville *Also Called: Twin Rvers Tech - Pnsville LLC (G-11120)*

Twin Rvers Tech - Pnsville LLC.................... 440 350-6300
679 Hardy Rd Painesville (44077) *(G-11120)*

Twin Sisters Productions LLC.................... 330 631-0361
4710 Hudson Dr Stow (44224) *(G-12468)*

Twin Valley Metalcraft, West Alexandria *Also Called: Twin Valley Metalcraft Asm LLC (G-13922)*

Twin Valley Metalcraft Asm LLC.................... 937 787-4634
4739 Enterprise Rd West Alexandria (45381) *(G-13922)*

Twin Ventures Inc.................... 330 405-3838
2457 Edison Blvd Twinsburg (44087) *(G-13388)*

Twinsource LLC.................... 440 248-6800
32333 Aurora Rd Ste 50 Solon (44139) *(G-12200)*

Twist Inc (PA).................... 937 675-9581
47 S Limestone St Jamestown (45335) *(G-7969)*

Twist Inc.................... 937 675-9581
5100 Waynesville Jamestown (45335) *(G-7970)*

Twisted Vine Family Vinyrd LLC.................... 740 256-1923
1375 Carter Rd Patriot (45658) *(G-11152)*

Twister Cleaning Tech Inc.................... 865 521-3976
3115 Frenchmens Rd Toledo (43607) *(G-13167)*

Twister Displays, East Liverpool *Also Called: Delta Manufacturing Inc (G-6392)*

Two Grndmthers Gourmet Kit LLC.................... 614 746-0888
9127 Firstgate Dr Reynoldsburg (43068) *(G-11585)*

Two M Precision Co Inc.................... 440 946-2120
1747 Joseph Lloyd Pkwy Unit 3 Willoughby (44094) *(G-14546)*

Tyco Fire Products LP.................... 216 265-0505
5565 Venture Dr Ste A Cleveland (44130) *(G-4435)*

Tyco Fire Protection Products, Cleveland *Also Called: Tyco Fire Products LP (G-4435)*

Tyjen Inc.................... 740 797-4064
8 Slater Dr The Plains (45780) *(G-12760)*

Tykma Inc.................... 740 779-9918
370 Gateway Dr Chillicothe (45601) *(G-2286)*

Tykma Electrox, Chillicothe *Also Called: Tykma Inc (G-2286)*

Tyler Elevator Products, Twinsburg *Also Called: Wittur Usa Inc (G-13396)*

Tyler Grain & Fertilizer Co.................... 330 669-2341
3388 Eby Rd Smithville (44677) *(G-12070)*

Tyler Haver Inc (DH).................... 440 974-1047
8570 Tyler Blvd Mentor (44060) *(G-9645)*

Tyler Technologies Inc.................... 800 800-2581
1 Tyler Way Moraine (45439) *(G-10196)*

Tylok International Inc.................... 216 261-7310
1061 E 260th St Cleveland (44132) *(G-4436)*

Tymex Plastics Inc.................... 216 429-8950
5300 Harvard Ave Cleveland (44105) *(G-4437)*

Tymoca Partners LLC.................... 440 946-4327
33220 Lakeland Blvd Eastlake (44095) *(G-6446)*

Tyson, West Chester *Also Called: Advancepierre Foods Inc (G-14097)*

Tyson Foods Inc.................... 440 960-0146
1833 Cooper Foster Park Rd Amherst (44001) *(G-453)*

Tz Acquisition Corp.................... 216 535-4300
26301 Curtiss Wright Pkwy 2nd Fl Richmond Heights (44143) *(G-11613)*

U D F, Cincinnati *Also Called: United Dairy Farmers Inc (G-3181)*

U M D, Fredericktown *Also Called: Umd Automated Systems Inc (G-7086)*

U P I, Cleveland *Also Called: Urethane Polymers Intl (G-4450)*

U S Alloy Die Corp.................... 216 749-9700
4007 Brookpark Rd Cleveland (44134) *(G-4438)*

U S Chemical & Plastics.................... 330 830-6000
600 Nova Dr Se Massillon (44646) *(G-9250)*

U S Chrome Corporation Ohio.................... 877 872-7716
107 Westboro St Dayton (45417) *(G-6068)*

U S Hair Inc.................... 614 235-5190
3727 E Broad St Columbus (43213) *(G-5336)*

U S M, Wickliffe *Also Called: Usm Precision Products Inc (G-14400)*

U S Molding Machinery Co Inc.................... 440 918-1701
38294 Pelton Rd Willoughby (44094) *(G-14547)*

U S Weatherford L P.................... 330 746-2502
1100 Performance Pl Youngstown (44502) *(G-14955)*

U.S. Bridge, Cambridge *Also Called: Ohio Bridge Corporation (G-1752)*

U.S. Casting Company, Canton *Also Called: Sjv Investment Inc (G-2006)*

UAS, Blue Ash *Also Called: United Air Specialists Inc (G-1345)*

Ucan Test Instruments LLC.................... 330 696-6624
388 S Main St Akron (44311) *(G-349)*

UCAR Carbon, Brooklyn Heights *Also Called: Graftech Intl Holdings Inc (G-1532)*

UCI, Toledo *Also Called: United Components LLC (G-13168)*

UCI Controls Inc (PA).................... 216 398-0330
1111 Brookpark Rd Cleveland (44109) *(G-4439)*

UCI International LLC (DH).................... 330 899-0340
2100 International Pkwy North Canton (44720) *(G-10679)*

Udderly Smooth, Salem *Also Called: Redex Industries Inc (G-11809)*

Udecx LLC.................... 877 698-3329
320 N 4th St Tipp City (45371) *(G-12851)*

Ufo Bikes LLC.................... 724 986-1417
9930 Hidden Hollow Trl Broadview Heights (44147) *(G-1510)*

Ugly Bunny Winery LLC.................... 330 988-9057
16104 State Route 39 Loudonville (44842) *(G-8596)*

UGN Inc.................... 513 360-3500
201 Exploration Dr Lebanon (45036) *(G-8294)*

Uhrden Inc.................... 330 456-0031
700 Tuscarawas St W Canton (44702) *(G-2030)*

Uhrichsville Carbide Inc.................... 740 922-9197
410 N Water St Uhrichsville (44683) *(G-13409)*

UIC West Chester Plant, West Chester *Also Called: Usui International Corporation (G-14089)*

Ulterior Products LLC.................... 614 441-9465
3142 N Section Line Rd Radnor (43066) *(G-11508)*

Ultimate Chem Solutions Inc.................... 440 998-6751
1800 E 21st St Ashtabula (44004) *(G-618)*

Ultimate Printing Inc.................... 330 847-2941
6090 Mahoning Ave Nw Ste C Warren (44481) *(G-13804)*

Ultimate Rb Inc (DH).................... 419 692-3000
1430 N Main St Delphos (45833) *(G-6195)*

Ultimate Systems Ltd.................... 419 692-3005
1430 N Main St Delphos (45833) *(G-6196)*

Ultium Cells Holdings LLC.................... 313 818-6324
7400 Tod Ave Sw Warren (44481) *(G-13805)*

Ultium Cells LLC (HQ).................... 313 818-6324
7400 Tod Ave Sw Warren (44481) *(G-13806)*

Ultra Machine Inc.................... 440 323-7632
530 Lowell St Elyria (44035) *(G-6597)*

Ultra Punch, Dayton *Also Called: Stolle Machinery Company LLC (G-6027)*

Ultra Tech Machinery Inc.................... 330 929-5544
297 Ascot Pkwy Cuyahoga Falls (44223) *(G-5580)*

Ultra-Met, Urbana *Also Called: Ultra-Met Company (G-13481)*

2025 Harris Ohio
Industrial Directory

(G-0000) Company's Geographic Section entry number

Ultra-Met Company..937 653-7133
120 Fyffe St Urbana (43078) *(G-13480)*

Ultra-Met Company..937 653-7133
720 N Main St Urbana (43078) *(G-13481)*

Ultrabuilt Play Systems Inc................................419 652-2294
1114 Us Highway 224 Nova (44859) *(G-10878)*

Ultraedit Inc...216 464-7465
5559 Eureka Dr Ste B Hamilton (45011) *(G-7535)*

Umd Automated Systems Inc...............................740 694-8614
9855 Salem Rd Fredericktown (43019) *(G-7086)*

Umd Contractors Inc..740 694-8614
9855 Salem Rd Fredericktown (43019) *(G-7087)*

Uncle Jays Cakes LLC...513 882-3433
2516 Clifton Ave Cincinnati (45219) *(G-3178)*

Under Pressure Systems Inc...............................330 602-4466
322 North Ave Ne New Philadelphia (44663) *(G-10469)*

Underground Sports Shop Inc.............................513 751-1662
1233 Findlay St Ste Frnt Cincinnati (45214) *(G-3179)*

UNI Corp..800 782-3296
1300 Market Ave N Canton (44714) *(G-2031)*

UNI-Facs, Columbus *Also Called: Universal Fabg Cnstr Svcs Inc (G-5338)*

Unibat, Cleveland *Also Called: Cleanlife Energy LLC (G-3503)*

Unibilt Industries Inc...937 890-7570
8005 Johnson Station Rd Vandalia (45377) *(G-13580)*

Unified Scrning Crshing - OH I............................937 836-3201
200 Cass Dr Englewood (45315) *(G-6627)*

Unifin Chesapeake, Salem *Also Called: Cardinal Pumps Exchangers Inc (G-11767)*

Unifrax Sebring S Operations, Sebring *Also Called: Refractory Specialties Inc (G-11900)*

Uniloy Century LLC...419 332-2693
215 N Stone St Fremont (43420) *(G-7140)*

Uniloy Milacron Inc...513 487-5000
4165 Half Acre Rd Batavia (45103) *(G-893)*

Uninterrupted LLC...216 771-2323
3800 Embassy Pkwy Ste 360 Akron (44333) *(G-350)*

Union America, Cincinnati *Also Called: United Precision Services Inc (G-3184)*

Union Carbide Corporation..................................216 529-3784
11709 Madison Ave Cleveland (44107) *(G-4440)*

Union Fabricating and Mch Co.............................419 626-5963
3427 Venice Rd Sandusky (44870) *(G-11879)*

Union Gospel Press Division, Middleburg Heights *Also Called: Incorprted Trstees of The Gspl (G-9773)*

Union Metal Corporation......................................330 456-7653
1432 Maple Ave Ne Canton (44705) *(G-2032)*

Union Metal Industries Corp................................330 456-7653
1432 Maple Ave Ne Canton (44705) *(G-2033)*

Union Rome Sewer System, Chesapeake *Also Called: Aqua Ohio Inc (G-2228)*

Uniontown Septic Tanks Inc.................................330 600-3386
2781 Raber Rd Uniontown (44685) *(G-13428)*

Uniontown Stone...740 968-4313
72607 Gun Club Rd Flushing (43977) *(G-6937)*

Unipac Inc...740 929-2000
2109 National Rd Sw Hebron (43025) *(G-7643)*

Unique Awards & Signs, Saint Marys *Also Called: Behrco Inc (G-11731)*

UNIQUE EXPRESSIONS, Gallipolis *Also Called: Riverview Productions Inc (G-7208)*

Unique Fabrications Inc.......................................419 355-1700
2520 Hayes Ave Fremont (43420) *(G-7141)*

Unique Packaging & Printing................................440 785-6730
9086 Goldfinch Ct Mentor (44060) *(G-9646)*

Unique Solutions, Newark *Also Called: Holophane Corporation (G-10506)*

Unisand Incorporated..330 722-0222
1097 Industrial Pkwy Medina (44256) *(G-9459)*

Unison Industries LLC...937 426-0621
2070 Heller Rd Alpha (45301) *(G-419)*

Unison Industries LLC...904 667-9904
2455 Dayton Xenia Rd Dayton (45434) *(G-5625)*

Unison UCI Inc
1111 Brookpark Rd Cleveland (44109) *(G-4441)*

Unisport Inc...419 529-4727
2254 Stumbo Rd Ontario (44906) *(G-10953)*

Unit Sets Inc..937 840-6123
835 S High St Hillsboro (45133) *(G-7727)*

Unitec, Canton *Also Called: UNI Corp (G-2031)*

United - Maier Signs Inc......................................513 681-6600
1030 Straight St Cincinnati (45214) *(G-3180)*

United Air Specialists Inc.....................................513 891-0400
4440 Creek Rd Blue Ash (45242) *(G-1345)*

United Candle Company LLC................................740 872-3248
102 N Sundale Rd Norwich (43767) *(G-10865)*

United Chart Processors Inc.................................740 373-5801
1461 Masonic Park Rd Marietta (45750) *(G-8957)*

United Components LLC (DH)...............................330 899-0340
6056 Deer Park Ct Toledo (43614) *(G-13168)*

United Dairy Inc..740 373-4121
1701 Greene St Marietta (45750) *(G-8958)*

United Dairy Inc (PA)..740 633-1451
300 N 5th St Martins Ferry (43935) *(G-9011)*

United Dairy Company, Martins Ferry *Also Called: United Dairy Inc (G-9011)*

United Dairy Farmers Inc (PA).............................513 396-8700
3955 Montgomery Rd Cincinnati (45212) *(G-3181)*

United Dental Laboratories (PA)..........................330 253-1810
261 South Ave Tallmadge (44278) *(G-12756)*

United Die & Mfg Sales Co...................................330 938-6141
100 S 17th St Sebring (44672) *(G-11904)*

United Engineering & Fndry Co............................330 456-2761
1400 Grace Ave Ne Canton (44705) *(G-2034)*

United Engraving, Cincinnati *Also Called: Wood Graphics Inc (G-3230)*

United Envelope LLC...513 542-4700
4890 Spring Grove Ave Cincinnati (45232) *(G-3182)*

United Extrusion Dies Inc....................................330 533-2915
5171 W Western Reserve Rd Canfield (44406) *(G-1818)*

United Feed Screws Ltd.......................................330 798-5532
487 Wellington Ave Akron (44305) *(G-351)*

United Finshg & Die Cutng Inc.............................216 881-0239
3875 King Ave Cleveland (44114) *(G-4442)*

United Grinding and Machine Co...........................330 453-7402
2315 Ellis Ave Ne Canton (44705) *(G-2035)*

United Group Services Inc (PA)............................800 633-9690
9740 Near Dr Cincinnati (45246) *(G-3183)*

United Hardwoods Ltd...330 878-9510
5508 Hilltop Dr Nw Strasburg (44680) *(G-12483)*

United Hydraulics..440 585-0906
29627 Lakeland Blvd Wickliffe (44092) *(G-14398)*

United Hydraulics, Willoughby *Also Called: Two M Precision Co Inc (G-14546)*

United Ignition Wire Corp.....................................216 898-1112
15620 Industrial Pkwy Cleveland (44135) *(G-4443)*

United Industries Incorporated.............................330 682-5010
2308 S Crown Hill Rd Orrville (44667) *(G-11015)*

United Initiators Inc (HQ).....................................440 323-3112
555 Garden St Elyria (44035) *(G-6598)*

United Machine and Tool Inc................................440 946-7677
1956 E 337th St Eastlake (44095) *(G-6447)*

United McGill Corporation (HQ)............................614 829-1200
1 Mission Park Groveport (43125) *(G-7455)*

United McGill Corporation....................................614 920-1267
122 E Columbus St Lithopolis (43136) *(G-8484)*

United Medical Supply Company...........................866 678-8633
2948 Nationwide Pkwy Brunswick (44212) *(G-1621)*

United Metal Fabricators Inc................................216 662-2000
14301 Industrial Ave S Maple Heights (44137) *(G-8894)*

United Packaging Supply Co Div, Bedford *Also Called: Overseas Packing LLC (G-1053)*

United Plastic Film, Cleveland *Also Called: A Aabaco Plastics Inc (G-3279)*

United Precast Inc..740 393-1121
400 Howard St Mount Vernon (43050) *(G-10267)*

United Precision Services Inc...............................513 851-6900
11183 Southland Rd Cincinnati (45240) *(G-3184)*

United Ready Mix Inc...216 696-1600
7820 Carnegie Ave Cleveland (44103) *(G-4444)*

United Refractories Inc..330 372-3716
1929 Larchmont Ave Ne Warren (44483) *(G-13807)*

United Roller Co LLC...440 564-9698
14910 Cross Creek Pkwy Newbury (44065) *(G-10565)*

United Rolls Inc (DH)   1400 Grace Ave Ne Canton (44705) *(G-2036)*

ALPHABETIC

United Rotary Brush Inc.. 937 644-3515
  8150 Business Way Plain City (43064) *(G-11423)*

United Seal Company, Columbus *Also Called: United Security Seals Inc (G-5337)*

United Security Seals Inc (PA).................................614 443-7633
  2000 Fairwood Ave Columbus (43207) *(G-5337)*

United Sport Apparel... 330 722-0818
  229 Harding St Ste B Medina (44256) *(G-9460)*

United States Drill Head Co..................................... 513 941-0300
  5298 River Rd Cincinnati (45233) *(G-3185)*

United States Gypsum Company............................. 419 734-3161
  121 S Lake St Gypsum (43433) *(G-7460)*

United States Plastic Corp...................................... 419 228-2242
  1390 Neubrecht Rd Lima (45801) *(G-8457)*

United Sttes Endscopy Group In (DH).................... 440 639-4494
  5976 Heisley Rd Mentor (44060) *(G-9647)*

United Surface Finishing Inc................................... 330 453-2786
  2202 Gilbert Ave Ne Canton (44705) *(G-2037)*

United Titanium, Wooster *Also Called: United Titanium Inc (G-14694)*

United Titanium Inc (PA)... 330 264-2111
  3450 Old Airport Rd Wooster (44691) *(G-14694)*

United Tool and Machine Inc.................................... 937 843-5603
  490 N Main St Lakeview (43331) *(G-8158)*

United Tool Supply Inc.. 513 752-6000
  851 Ohio Pike Ste 101 Cincinnati (45245) *(G-2317)*

United Trade Printers LLC....................................... 614 326-4829
  94 N High St Ste 290 Dublin (43017) *(G-6358)*

United Tube Corporation... 330 725-4196
  960 Lake Rd Medina (44256) *(G-9461)*

Unitrex Ltd... 216 831-1900
  5060 Taylor Dr Ste D Bedford Heights (44128) *(G-1083)*

Unitus, Solon *Also Called: Sensical Inc (G-12180)*

Unity Tube Inc.. 330 426-4282
  1862 State Route 165 East Palestine (44413) *(G-6410)*

Univar Solutions USA LLC....................................... 800 531-7106
  6000 Parkwood Pl Dublin (43016) *(G-6359)*

Univar Solutions USA LLC....................................... 513 714-5264
  4600 Dues Dr West Chester (45246) *(G-14157)*

Universal Black Oxiding, Aurora *Also Called: Universal Heat Treating Inc (G-691)*

Universal Cargo, Cleveland *Also Called: Acme Lifting Products Inc (G-3290)*

Universal Ch Directories LLC.................................. 419 522-5011
  1150 National Pkwy Mansfield (44906) *(G-8862)*

Universal Clay Products, Sandusky *Also Called: Ethima Inc (G-11834)*

Universal Coatings Division, Twinsburg *Also Called: Universal Rack & Eqp Co Inc (G-13390)*

Universal Creative Concepts, North Royalton *Also Called: Universal North Inc (G-10787)*

Universal Direct Fulfillment Corp............................ 330 650-5000
  5581 Hudson Industrial Pkwy Hudson (44236) *(G-7861)*

Universal Dsign Fbrication LLC............................... 419 202-5269
  7319 Portland Rd Sandusky (44870) *(G-11880)*

Universal Electronics Inc.. 330 487-1110
  1864 Enterprise Pkwy Ste B Twinsburg (44087) *(G-13389)*

Universal Fabg Cnstr Svcs Inc................................ 614 274-1128
  1241 Mckinley Ave Columbus (43222) *(G-5338)*

Universal Forest Products, Dayton *Also Called: Idx Dayton LLC (G-5818)*

Universal Grinding Corporation............................... 216 631-9410
  1234 W 78th St Cleveland (44102) *(G-4445)*

Universal Heat Treating Inc..................................... 216 641-2000
  60 Samantha Dr Aurora (44202) *(G-691)*

Universal Hydraulik USA Corp................................. 419 873-6340
  25651 Fort Meigs Rd Perrysburg (43551) *(G-11277)*

Universal Industrial Pdts Inc................................... 419 737-9584
  1 Coreway Dr Pioneer (43554) *(G-11331)*

Universal J&Z Machine LLC..................................... 216 486-2220
  4781 E 355th St Willoughby (44094) *(G-14548)*

Universal Lettering Inc.. 419 238-9320
  1197 Grill Rd # B Van Wert (45891) *(G-13547)*

Universal Lettering Company, Van Wert *Also Called: Universal Lettering Inc (G-13547)*

Universal Manufacturing... 816 396-0101
  9900 Clinton Rd Cleveland (44144) *(G-4446)*

Universal Metal Products Inc................................... 419 287-3223
  850 W Front St Pemberville (43450) *(G-11178)*

Universal Metal Products Inc (PA)........................... 440 943-3040
  29980 Lakeland Blvd Wickliffe (44092) *(G-14399)*

Universal Metals Cutting Inc................................... 330 580-5192
  2656 Harrison Ave Sw Canton (44706) *(G-2038)*

Universal North Inc.. 440 230-1366
  10143 Royalton Rd Ste E North Royalton (44133) *(G-10787)*

Universal Oil Inc.. 216 771-4300
  265 Jefferson Ave Cleveland (44113) *(G-4447)*

Universal Packg Systems Inc................................... 513 732-2000
  5055 State Route 276 Batavia (45103) *(G-894)*

Universal Packg Systems Inc................................... 513 735-4777
  5069 State Route 276 Batavia (45103) *(G-895)*

Universal Packg Systems Inc................................... 513 674-9400
  470 Northland Blvd Cincinnati (45240) *(G-3186)*

Universal Pallets Inc.. 614 444-1095
  611 Marion Rd Columbus (43207) *(G-5339)*

Universal Plastics, North Canton *Also Called: UPL International Inc (G-10680)*

Universal Polymer & Rubber Ltd (PA)...................... 440 632-1691
  15730 Madison Rd Middlefield (44062) *(G-9834)*

Universal Polymer & Rubber Ltd.............................. 330 633-1666
  165 Northeast Ave Tallmadge (44278) *(G-12757)*

Universal Production Corp....................................... 740 522-1147
  1776 Tamarack Rd Newark (43055) *(G-10537)*

Universal Rack & Eqp Co Inc................................... 330 963-6776
  8511 Tower Dr Twinsburg (44087) *(G-13390)*

Universal Rubber & Plastics, Tallmadge *Also Called: Universal Polymer & Rubber Ltd (G-12757)*

Universal Scientific Inc... 440 428-1777
  6210 Campbell Dr Madison (44057) *(G-8734)*

Universal Steel Company... 216 883-4972
  6600 Grant Ave Cleveland (44105) *(G-4448)*

Universal Tool Co, Dayton *Also Called: Precision Machining Services (G-5947)*

Universal Tool Technology LLC................................ 937 222-4608
  3488 Stop 8 Rd Dayton (45414) *(G-6069)*

Universal Urethane Pdts Inc.................................... 419 693-7400
  410 1st St Toledo (43605) *(G-13169)*

Universal Veneer Mill Corp...................................... 740 522-1147
  1776 Tamarack Rd Newark (43055) *(G-10538)*

Universal Veneer Sales Corp (PA)........................... 740 522-1147
  1776 Tamarack Rd Newark (43055) *(G-10539)*

Universal Well Services Inc..................................... 814 333-2656
  11 S Washington St Millersburg (44654) *(G-10016)*

University Hring Aid Assctions, Cincinnati *Also Called: Communications Aid Inc (G-2505)*

University of Toledo... 419 530-2311
  2801 W Bancroft St Toledo (43606) *(G-13170)*

Uniwall Mfg Co (HQ).. 330 875-1444
  3750 Beck Ave Louisville (44641) *(G-8617)*

Unlimited Energy Services LLC............................... 304 517-7097
  19371 State Route 60 Beverly (45715) *(G-1210)*

Unlimited Machine and Tool LLC............................. 419 269-1730
  5139 Tractor Rd Ste C Toledo (43612) *(G-13171)*

Unlimted Rcovery Solutions LLC............................. 419 868-4888
  2701 S Eberd Rd Ste B Wauseon (43567) *(G-13860)*

Unverferth, Kalida *Also Called: Unverferth Mfg Co Inc (G-8007)*

Unverferth Mfg Co Inc (PA)..................................... 419 532-3121
  601 S Broad St Kalida (45853) *(G-8007)*

UPA Technology Inc... 513 755-1380
  8963 Cincinnati Columbus Rd West Chester (45069) *(G-14088)*

Updike Supply Company.. 937 482-4000
  8241 Expansion Way Huber Heights (45424) *(G-7825)*

UPL International Inc... 330 433-2860
  7661 Freedom Ave Nw North Canton (44720) *(G-10680)*

Upper Arlington Crew Inc.. 614 485-0089
  5257 Sinclair Rd Columbus (43229) *(G-5340)*

Upright Steel LLC.. 216 923-0852
  9110 George Ave Cleveland (44105) *(G-4449)*

Uprising Food Inc.. 513 313-1087
  4200 Plainville Rd Cincinnati (45227) *(G-3187)*

UPS Store 7395, Cincinnati *Also Called: Cree Logistics LLC (G-2524)*

Upshift, Cincinnati *Also Called: Upshift Work LLC (G-3188)*

Upshift Work LLC.. 513 813-5695
  2300 Montana Ave Ste 301 Cincinnati (45211) *(G-3188)*

Uptown Dog The Inc.. 740 592-4600	
9 W Union St Athens (45701) *(G-655)*	
Uptown Graphics, Norwood *Also Called: Blt Inc (G-10866)*	
Urban Industries, Galion *Also Called: Urban Industries of Ohio Inc (G-7200)*	
Urban Industries of Ohio Inc.................................... 419 468-3578	
525 King Ave Galion (44833) *(G-7200)*	
Urbn Timber LLC.. 614 981-3043	
29 Kingston Ave Columbus (43207) *(G-5341)*	
Urc, Chagrin Falls *Also Called: Utility Relay Co Ltd (G-2189)*	
Urethane Polymers Intl (HQ).................................... 216 430-3655	
3800 E 91st St Cleveland (44105) *(G-4450)*	
Urra Co Inc.. 330 673-8473	
1897 State Route 59 Kent (44240) *(G-8093)*	
US Aeroteam Inc.. 937 458-0344	
2601 W Stroop Rd Ste 60 Dayton (45439) *(G-6070)*	
US Coexcell Inc.. 419 897-9110	
640 Mingo Dr Maumee (43537) *(G-9328)*	
US Cotton LLC.. 216 676-6400	
15501 Industrial Pkwy Cleveland (44135) *(G-4451)*	
US Development Corp.. 330 673-6900	
900 W Main St Kent (44240) *(G-8094)*	
US Die & Mold, Canal Winchester *Also Called: Manifold & Phalor Inc (G-1793)*	
US Endoscopy, Mentor *Also Called: United Sttes Endoscopy Group In (G-9647)*	
US Filter, Pickerington *Also Called: Evoqua Water Technologies LLC (G-11294)*	
US Fittings Inc.. 234 212-9420	
2182 E Aurora Rd Twinsburg (44087) *(G-13391)*	
US Footwear Holdings LLC.. 740 753-9100	
39 E Canal St Nelsonville (45764) *(G-10322)*	
US Group, East Palestine *Also Called: E R Advanced Ceramics Inc (G-6402)*	
US Industrial Lubricants Inc.................................... 513 541-2225	
3330 Beekman St Cincinnati (45223) *(G-3189)*	
US Kondo Corporation.. 937 916-3045	
233 1st St Piqua (45356) *(G-11388)*	
US Lighting Group Inc.. 216 896-7000	
1148 E 222nd St Euclid (44117) *(G-6682)*	
US Metalcraft Inc.. 419 692-4962	
101 S Franklin St Delphos (45833) *(G-6197)*	
US Refractory Products LLC...................................... 440 386-4580	
7660 Race Rd North Ridgeville (44039) *(G-10752)*	
US Technology Corporation...................................... 330 455-1181	
4200 Munson St Nw Canton (44718) *(G-2039)*	
US Technology Media Inc.. 330 874-3094	
509 Water St Sw Bolivar (44612) *(G-1394)*	
US Tsubaki Power Transm LLC.................................. 419 626-4560	
1010 Edgewater Ave Sandusky (44870) *(G-11881)*	
US Tubular Products Inc.. 330 832-1734	
14852 Lincoln Way W North Lawrence (44666) *(G-10703)*	
US Water Company LLC.. 740 453-0604	
1115 Newark Rd Zanesville (43701) *(G-15053)*	
US Welding Training LLC.. 440 669-9380	
518 5th St Fairport Harbor (44077) *(G-6822)*	
US Wellness LLC.. 216 772-3364	
1200 E 55th St Ste A Cleveland (44103) *(G-4452)*	
US Yachiyo Inc., Marion *Also Called: Motherson Ychiyo US Auto Syste (G-8981)*	
USA Heat Treating Inc.. 216 587-4700	
4500 Lee Rd Ste B Cleveland (44128) *(G-4453)*	
USA Instruments Inc.. 330 562-1000	
1515 Danner Dr Aurora (44202) *(G-692)*	
USA Label Express Inc.. 330 874-1001	
11206 Industrial Pkwy Nw Bolivar (44612) *(G-1395)*	
USA Precast Concrete Limited.................................. 330 854-9600	
801 Elm Ridge Ave Canal Fulton (44614) *(G-1781)*	
USA Quickprint Inc (PA).. 330 455-5119	
409 3rd St Sw Canton (44702) *(G-2040)*	
USA Rolls, Canfield *Also Called: Alstart Enterprises LLC (G-1803)*	
Usalco, Fairfield *Also Called: Usalco Michigan City Plant LLC (G-6787)*	
Usalco Fairfield Plant LLC.. 513 737-7100	
3700 Dixie Hwy Fairfield (45014) *(G-6786)*	
Usalco Michigan City Plant LLC................................ 440 992-7039	
1741 W 47th St Ashtabula (44004) *(G-619)*	

Usalco Michigan City Plant LLC................................ 513 737-7100	
3700 Dixie Hwy Fairfield (45014) *(G-6787)*	
USB Corporation.. 216 765-5000	
26111 Miles Rd Cleveland (44128) *(G-4454)*	
Usm Precision Products Inc...................................... 440 975-8600	
1340 Lloyd Rd Ste D Wickliffe (44092) *(G-14400)*	
Ustek Incorporated.. 614 538-8000	
4663 Executive Dr Ste 3 Columbus (43220) *(G-5342)*	
Usui International Corporation.................................. 513 448-0410	
88 Partnership Way Sharonville (45241) *(G-11949)*	
Usui International Corporation.................................. 734 354-3626	
8748 Jacquemin Dr Ste 100 West Chester (45069) *(G-14089)*	
Utahamerican Energy Inc.. 435 888-4000	
153 Highway 7 S Powhatan Point (43942) *(G-11498)*	
Utica East Ohio Midstream LLC................................ 740 431-4168	
8349 Azalea Rd Sw Dennison (44621) *(G-6219)*	
Utilco Div, Blue Ash *Also Called: Ilsco LLC (G-1287)*	
Utility Relay Co Ltd.. 440 708-1000	
10100 Queens Way Chagrin Falls (44023) *(G-2189)*	
Utility Wire Products Inc.. 216 441-2180	
3302 E 87th St Cleveland (44127) *(G-4455)*	
V & A Process Inc.. 440 288-8137	
2345 E 28th St Lorain (44055) *(G-8584)*	
V & C Enterprises Co.. 614 221-1412	
41 S Grant Ave Columbus (43215) *(G-5343)*	
V & M Star LP.. 330 742-6300	
2669 Martin Luther King Jr Blvd Youngstown (44510) *(G-14956)*	
V & S Schuler Engineering Inc (DH)..........................330 452-5200	
2240 Allen Ave Se Canton (44707) *(G-2041)*	
V & S Schuler Engineering Inc.................................. 330 452-5200	
15175 Kinsman Rd Middlefield (44062) *(G-9835)*	
V H Cooper & Co Inc (HQ).. 419 375-4116	
2321 State Route 49 Fort Recovery (45846) *(G-6973)*	
V H Cooper & Co Inc.. 419 678-4853	
1 Cooper Farm Dr Saint Henry (45883) *(G-11726)*	
V H Cooper & Co Inc.. 419 678-4853	
1 Cooper Farm Dr Saint Henry (45883) *(G-11727)*	
V M Systems Inc.. 419 535-1044	
3125 Hill Ave Toledo (43607) *(G-13172)*	
V P, Newton Falls *Also Called: Venture Plastics Inc (G-10582)*	
V S I, Massillon *Also Called: Vehicle Systems Inc (G-9251)*	
V-I-S-c-e-r-o-t-o-n-i-c Inc.. 330 690-3355	
118 W Market St Akron (44303) *(G-352)*	
VA Technology, Solon *Also Called: Versatile Automation Tech Ltd (G-12202)*	
Vacono America LLC.. 216 938-7428	
1163 E 40th St Ste 301 Cleveland (44114) *(G-4456)*	
Vacuform Inc.. 330 938-9674	
500 Courtney Rd Sebring (44672) *(G-11905)*	
Vacuum Electric Switch Co Inc (PA).......................... 330 374-5156	
3900 Mogadore Industrial Pkwy Mogadore (44260) *(G-10091)*	
Vagabond Creations Inc.. 937 298-1124	
2560 Lance Dr Moraine (45409) *(G-10197)*	
Vail Rubber Works Inc.. 513 705-2060	
605 Clark St Middletown (45042) *(G-9901)*	
Val Casting Inc.. 419 562-2499	
108 E Rensselaer St Bucyrus (44820) *(G-1691)*	
Val Products, Coldwater *Also Called: Val-Co Pax Inc (G-4586)*	
Val-Co Pax Inc (DH).. 717 354-4586	
210 E Main St Coldwater (45828) *(G-4586)*	
Val-Con Inc.. 440 357-1898	
7201 Hermitage Rd Concord Township (44077) *(G-5396)*	
Valco Cincinnati Inc (PA)..513 874-6550	
411 Circle Freeway Dr Cincinnati (45246) *(G-3190)*	
Valco Division, North Royalton *Also Called: Valley Tool & Die Inc (G-10788)*	
Valco Industries LLC.. 937 399-7400	
625 Burt St Springfield (45505) *(G-12391)*	
Valco Melton, Cincinnati *Also Called: Valco Cincinnati Inc (G-3190)*	
Valco Melton Inc.. 513 874-6550	
497 Circle Freeway Dr Ste 490 West Chester (45246) *(G-14158)*	
Valence Industrial, Sidney *Also Called: Valence Industrial LLC (G-12058)*	
Valence Industrial LLC.. 877 330-2354	
1661 Saint Marys Rd Sidney (45365) *(G-12058)*	

A
L
P
H
A
B
E
T
I
C

Valensil Technologies LLC........................440 937-8181
34910 Commerce Way Avon (44011) *(G-741)*

Valentine Research Inc...............................513 984-8900
10280 Alliance Rd Blue Ash (45242) *(G-1346)*

Valgroup LLC...419 423-6500
3441 N Main St Findlay (45840) *(G-6928)*

Valgroup North America Inc (PA)...............419 423-6500
3441 N Main St Findlay (45840) *(G-6929)*

Valley, Toronto *Also Called: Valley Converting Co Inc (G-13188)*

Valley Asphalt, Morrow *Also Called: Morrow Gravel Company Inc (G-10202)*

Valley Asphalt Corporation (HQ)...............513 771-0820
11641 Mosteller Rd Cincinnati (45241) *(G-3191)*

Valley Asphalt Corporation........................513 381-0652
4850 Stubbs Mills Rd Morrow (45152) *(G-10203)*

Valley Concrete, Carrollton *Also Called: Ernst Enterprises Inc (G-2082)*

Valley Concrete Division, Fairborn *Also Called: Ernst Enterprises Inc (G-6690)*

Valley Containers Inc.................................330 544-2244
3515 Union St Mineral Ridge (44440) *(G-10031)*

Valley Converting Co Inc (PA)....................740 537-2152
405 Daniels St Toronto (43964) *(G-13188)*

Valley Electric Company.............................419 332-6405
432 N Wood St Fremont (43420) *(G-7142)*

Valley List LLC..740 760-6411
11 Watertown Rd Unit C Waterford (45786) *(G-13829)*

Valley Machine Tool Inc..............................513 899-2737
9773 Morrow Cozaddale Rd Morrow (45152) *(G-10204)*

Valley Metal Works Inc................................513 554-1022
698 W Columbia Ave Cincinnati (45215) *(G-3192)*

Valley Mining Inc..740 922-3942
4412 Pleasant Valley Rd Se Dennison (44621) *(G-6220)*

Valley Plastics Company Inc.......................419 666-2349
399 Phillips Ave Toledo (43612) *(G-13173)*

Valley Tool & Die Inc (PA)..........................440 237-0160
10020 York Theta Dr North Royalton (44133) *(G-10788)*

Valley Trailers, Leesburg *Also Called: Creative Fab & Welding LLC (G-8298)*

Valley View Pallets LLC..............................740 599-0010
22414 Hostetler Rd Danville (43014) *(G-5600)*

Valley View Pallets Partners, Danville *Also Called: Valley View Pallets LLC (G-5600)*

Valley Vitamins II Inc..................................330 533-0051
4449 Easton Way Fl 2 Columbus (43219) *(G-5344)*

Vallourec Star LP..330 742-6227
706 S State St Girard (44420) *(G-7281)*

Vallourec Star LP (HQ)...............................330 742-6300
2669 Martin Luther King Jr Blvd Youngstown (44510) *(G-14957)*

Valmac Industries Inc..................................937 890-5558
825 Scholz Dr Vandalia (45377) *(G-13581)*

Valspar, Medina *Also Called: Plasti-Kote Co Inc (G-9435)*

Valtris, Independence *Also Called: Polymer Additives Holdings Inc (G-7915)*

Valtris Specialty Chemicals.......................216 875-7200
7050 Krick Rd Walton Hills (44146) *(G-13704)*

Valtronic Technology Inc.............................440 349-1239
29200 Fountain Pkwy Solon (44139) *(G-12201)*

Value Added Packaging Inc.........................937 832-9595
44 Lau Pkwy Englewood (45315) *(G-6628)*

Value-Rooter, Elyria *Also Called: Personal Plumber Service Corp (G-6579)*

Valued Relationships Inc............................800 860-4230
1400 Commerce Center Dr Ste B Franklin (45005) *(G-7054)*

Valv-Trol LLC..330 686-2800
1340 Commerce Dr Stow (44224) *(G-12469)*

Valve Related Controls Inc..........................513 677-8724
143 Commerce Dr Loveland (45140) *(G-8655)*

Valvsys LLC...513 870-1234
2 Rowe Ct Hamilton (45015) *(G-7536)*

Vam Usa Llc..330 742-3130
1053 Ohio Works Dr Youngstown (44510) *(G-14958)*

Van Dyke Custom Iron Inc...........................614 860-9300
700 Janice Ln Pickerington (43147) *(G-11302)*

Van Engineering Co, Cincinnati *Also Called: R Vandewalle Inc (G-3029)*

Van Tilburg Farms Inc.................................419 586-3077
8398 Celina Mendon Rd Celina (45822) *(G-2126)*

Van Wert Division, Van Wert *Also Called: Tecumseh Packg Solutions Inc (G-13545)*

Van Wert Machine Inc..................................419 692-6836
210 E Cleveland St Delphos (45833) *(G-6198)*

Van-Griner LLC...419 733-7951
1009 Delta Ave Cincinnati (45208) *(G-3193)*

Vanamatic Company.....................................419 692-6085
701 Ambrose Dr Delphos (45833) *(G-6199)*

Vance's Wonder Store, Manchester *Also Called: Vances Department Store (G-8755)*

Vances Department Store (PA).....................937 549-2188
37 E 2nd St Manchester (45144) *(G-8755)*

Vances Department Store............................937 549-3033
600 Washington St Manchester (45144) *(G-8756)*

Vandalia Massage Therapy..........................937 890-8660
147 W National Rd Vandalia (45377) *(G-13582)*

Vandava Inc...614 277-8003
4094 Broadway Grove City (43123) *(G-7421)*

Vanex Tube Corporation..............................330 544-9500
301 Mckees Ln Ste 2 Niles (44446) *(G-10608)*

Vanguard Paints and Finishes Inc...............740 373-5261
1409 Greene St Marietta (45750) *(G-8959)*

Vanner, Hilliard *Also Called: Vanner Holdings Inc (G-7709)*

Vanner Holdings Inc....................................614 771-2718
4282 Reynolds Dr Hilliard (43026) *(G-7709)*

Vanscoyk Sheet Metal Corp.........................937 845-0581
475 Quick Rd New Carlisle (45344) *(G-10383)*

Vantage Orthopedics Inc.............................513 563-1690
41 Techview Dr Cincinnati (45215) *(G-3194)*

Vantage Spclty Ingredients Inc....................937 264-1222
707 Harco Dr Englewood (45315) *(G-6629)*

Vantilburg Farms, Celina *Also Called: Van Tilburg Farms Inc (G-2126)*

Varbros LLC (PA)...216 267-5200
16025 Brookpark Rd Cleveland (44142) *(G-4457)*

Varco LP..330 746-2922
2669 Martin Luther King Jr Blvd Youngstown (44510) *(G-14959)*

Vari-Wall Tube Specialists Inc.....................330 482-0000
1350 Wardingsley Ave Columbiana (44408) *(G-4631)*

Varian Medical Systems Inc.........................888 827-4265
7777 Yankee Rd Liberty Township (45044) *(G-8379)*

Variety Glass Inc...740 432-3643
201 Foster Ave Cambridge (43725) *(G-1765)*

Varland Metal Service Inc............................513 861-0555
3231 Fredonia Ave Cincinnati (45229) *(G-3195)*

Varland Plating Company, Cincinnati *Also Called: Varland Metal Service Inc (G-3195)*

Varmland Inc...216 741-1510
1200 Brookpark Rd Cleveland (44109) *(G-4458)*

Varouh Oil Inc...440 482-8686
970 Griswold Rd Elyria (44035) *(G-6599)*

Vasil Co Inc...419 562-2901
119 E Mary St Bucyrus (44820) *(G-1692)*

Vasil Fashions, Bucyrus *Also Called: Vasil Co Inc (G-1692)*

Ve Global Vending Inc..................................216 785-2611
8700 Brookpark Rd Cleveland (44129) *(G-4459)*

Vector Electromagnetics LLC.......................937 478-5904
1245 Airport Rd Wilmington (45177) *(G-14589)*

Vector International Corp.............................440 942-2002
7404 Tyler Blvd Mentor (44060) *(G-9648)*

Vector Mechanical LLC................................216 337-4042
10917 Dale Ave Cleveland (44111) *(G-4460)*

Vector Screenprinting & EMB, Mentor *Also Called: Vector International Corp (G-9648)*

Vectra Inc..614 351-6868
3950 Business Park Dr Columbus (43204) *(G-5345)*

Vectra Visual, Columbus *Also Called: Vectra Inc (G-5345)*

Vectron Inc..440 323-3369
201 Perry Ct Elyria (44035) *(G-6600)*

Vedda Printing, Cleveland *Also Called: Phil Vedda & Sons Inc (G-4158)*

Veeam Government Solutions LLC.................614 339-8200
8800 Lyra Dr Ste 350 Columbus (43240) *(G-4650)*

Veelo Technologies, Cincinnati *Also Called: General Nano LLC (G-2664)*

Veepak OH LLC..740 927-9002
9040 Smiths Mill Rd New Albany (43054) *(G-10353)*

2025 Harris Ohio
Industrial Directory

(G-0000) Company's Geographic Section entry number

Vega Americas Inc (HQ)... 513 272-0131
  3877 Mason Research Pkwy Lebanon (45036) *(G-8295)*

Vegv, Cleveland *Also Called: Ve Global Vending Inc (G-4459)*

Vehicle Systems Inc... 330 854-0535
  7130 Lutz Ave Nw Massillon (44646) *(G-9251)*

Vehtek Systems Inc.. 419 373-8741
  2125 Wood Bridge Blvd Bowling Green (43402) *(G-1445)*

Veitsch-Radex America LLC... 717 793-7122
  4741 Kister Ct Ashtabula (44004) *(G-620)*

Velocity Concept Dev Group LLC....................................... 740 685-2637
  8824 Clay Pike Byesville (43723) *(G-1717)*

Velocity Concept Dev Group LLC (PA)............................... 513 204-2100
  4393 Digital Way Mason (45040) *(G-9164)*

Velocys Inc.. 614 733-3300
  8520 Warner Rd Plain City (43064) *(G-11424)*

Velvet Ice Cream Company... 419 562-2009
  1233 Whetstone St Bucyrus (44820) *(G-1693)*

Velvet Ice Cream Company (PA).......................................740 892-3921
  11324 Mount Vernon Rd Utica (43080) *(G-13488)*

Velvetflow, Hannibal *Also Called: Ormet Primary Aluminum Corp (G-7541)*

Venco Manufacturing Inc.. 513 772-8448
  12110 Best Pl Cincinnati (45241) *(G-3196)*

Venco Venturo Industries LLC (PA)................................... 513 772-8448
  12110 Best Pl Cincinnati (45241) *(G-3197)*

Venco/Venturo Div, Cincinnati *Also Called: Venco Venturo Industries LLC (G-3197)*

Ventco Inc... 440 834-8888
  66 Windward Way Chagrin Falls (44023) *(G-2190)*

Ventek Solutions LLC... 419 420-0029
  1900 Industrial Dr Findlay (45840) *(G-6930)*

Venti-Now... 513 334-3375
  9891 Montgomery Rd Ste 302 Montgomery (45242) *(G-10125)*

Ventilation Systems Jsc... 513 348-3853
  400 Murray Rd Cincinnati (45217) *(G-3198)*

Ventra Sandusky LLC... 419 627-3600
  3020 Tiffin Ave Sandusky (44870) *(G-11882)*

Vents - US, Cincinnati *Also Called: Ventilation Systems Jsc (G-3198)*

Vents US, Cincinnati *Also Called: Bodor Vents Inc (G-2415)*

Venture, Dayton *Also Called: Venture Mfg Co (G-6071)*

Venture Medical, Plain City *Also Called: Bahler Medical Inc (G-11396)*

Venture Mfg Co.. 937 233-8792
  3636 Dayton Park Dr Dayton (45414) *(G-6071)*

Venture Packaging Inc... 419 465-2534
  311 Monroe St Monroeville (44847) *(G-10122)*

Venture Packaging Midwest Inc.. 419 465-2534
  311 Monroe St Monroeville (44847) *(G-10123)*

Venture Plastics Inc (PA)...330 872-5774
  4000 Warren Ravonna Rd Newton Falls (44444) *(C-10582)*

Venture Products Inc... 330 683-0075
  500 Venture Dr Orrville (44667) *(G-11016)*

Venturo Manufacturing Inc.. 513 772-8448
  12110 Best Pl Cincinnati (45241) *(G-3199)*

Venue Lifestyle & Event Guide... 513 405-6822
  11959 Tramway Dr Cincinnati (45241) *(G-3200)*

Veolia Wts Systems Usa Inc.. 513 794-1010
  11799 Enterprise Dr Cincinnati (45241) *(G-3201)*

Veolia Wts Systems Usa Inc.. 330 929-1639
  887 Hampshire Rd Ste I Stow (44224) *(G-12470)*

Veoneer Brake Systems LLC.. 419 425-6725
  2001 Industrial Dr Findlay (45840) *(G-6931)*

Ver-Mac Industries Inc.. 740 397-6511
  100 Progress Dr Mount Vernon (43050) *(G-10268)*

Verantis Corporation (PA).. 440 243-0700
  7251 Engle Rd Ste 300 Middleburg Heights (44130) *(G-9778)*

Verdin Company, Cincinnati *Also Called: I T Verdin Co (G-2738)*

Verhoff Alfalfa Mills Inc (PA)... 419 523-4767
  1188 Sugar Mill Dr Ottawa (45875) *(G-11049)*

Verhoff Machine & Welding Inc.. 419 596-3202
  7300 Road 18 Continental (45831) *(G-5424)*

Veriano Fine Foods Spirits Ltd.. 614 745-7705
  5175 Zarley St Ste A New Albany (43054) *(G-10354)*

Verifone Inc.. 800 837-4366
  855 Grandview Ave Ste 110 Columbus (43215) *(G-5346)*

Veritiv.. 614 323-3335
  2344 Limestone Way Columbus (43228) *(G-5347)*

Verizon Business, Kenton *Also Called: Mci Inc (G-8105)*

Vernay Manufacturing Inc (HQ).. 404 994-2000
  120 E South College St Yellow Springs (45387) *(G-14791)*

Verona Agriculture Center, Verona *Also Called: Keystone Cooperative Inc (G-13591)*

Versa Tech Technologies, Apple Creek *Also Called: Versi-Tech Incorporated (G-479)*

Versa-Pak Ltd.. 419 586-5466
  500 Staeger Rd Celina (45822) *(G-2127)*

Versailles Building Supply.. 937 526-3238
  741 N Center St Versailles (45380) *(G-13603)*

Versalift East Inc.. 610 866-1400
  4884 Corporate St Sw Canton (44706) *(G-2042)*

VERSALIFT EAST, INC., Canton *Also Called: Versalift East Inc (G-2042)*

Versatile Automation Tech Corp.. 330 220-2600
  2853 Westway Dr Brunswick (44212) *(G-1622)*

Versatile Automation Tech Ltd.. 440 589-6700
  30355 Solon Industrial Pkwy Solon (44139) *(G-12202)*

Versatile Machine... 330 618-9895
  402 Commerce St Tallmadge (44278) *(G-12758)*

Versi-Tech Incorporated... 586 944-2230
  32 Hunter St Apple Creek (44606) *(G-479)*

Versitec Manufacturing Inc.. 440 354-4283
  152 Elevator Ave Painesville (44077) *(G-11121)*

Versitech Mold Div, Akron *Also Called: Saehwa IMC Na Inc (G-304)*

Verso Paper, West Chester *Also Called: Billerud Americas Corporation (G-13952)*

Verso Paper Inc.. 901 369-4100
  8540 Gander Creek Dr Miamisburg (45342) *(G-9751)*

Verstrete In Mold Lbels USA In... 513 943-0080
  4101 Founders Blvd Batavia (45103) *(G-896)*

Vertex Inc... 330 628-6230
  3956 Mogadore Industrial Pkwy Mogadore (44260) *(G-10092)*

Vertical Data LLC.. 330 289-0313
  2169 Chuckery Ln Akron (44333) *(G-353)*

Vertiflo Pump Company... 513 530-0888
  7807 Redsky Dr Cincinnati (45249) *(G-3202)*

Vertiv, Ironton *Also Called: Vertiv Corporation (G-7936)*

Vertiv, Lorain *Also Called: Vertiv Energy Systems Inc (G-8585)*

Vertiv, Westerville *Also Called: Vertiv Holdings Co (G-14241)*

Vertiv Co., Westerville *Also Called: Vertiv Group Corporation (G-14240)*

Vertiv Corporation... 614 841-6078
  975 Pittsburgh Dr Delaware (43015) *(G-6177)*

Vertiv Corporation... 614 491-9286
  5350 Centerpoint Pkwy Groveport (43125) *(G-7456)*

Vertiv Corporation... 740 547-5100
  3040 S 9th St Ironton (45638) *(G-7936)*

Vertiv Corporation (DH)... 614 888-0246
  505 N Cleveland Ave Westerville (43082) *(G-14239)*

Vertiv Energy Systems Inc... 440 288-1122
  1510 Kansas Ave Lorain (44052) *(G-8585)*

Vertiv Group Corporation... 440 460-3600
  5900 Landerbrook Dr Ste 300 Cleveland (44124) *(G-4461)*

Vertiv Group Corporation... 440 288-1122
  1510 Kansas Ave Lorain (44052) *(G-8586)*

Vertiv Group Corporation (DH).. 614 888-0246
  505 N Cleveland Ave Westerville (43082) *(G-14240)*

Vertiv Holdings Co (PA)..614 888-0246
  505 N Cleveland Ave Westerville (43082) *(G-14241)*

Vertiv JV Holdings LLC.. 614 888-0246
  1050 Dearborn Dr Columbus (43085) *(G-5348)*

Vesco LLC... 330 374-5156
  3900 Mogadore Industrial Pkwy Mogadore (44260) *(G-10093)*

Vesco Medical LLC.. 614 914-5991
  60 Collegeview Rd Ste 144 Westerville (43081) *(G-14279)*

Vesi, Cincinnati *Also Called: Vesi Incorporated (G-3203)*

Vesi Incorporated... 513 563-6002
  7289 Kirkridge Dr Cincinnati (45233) *(G-3203)*

Vestcom Retail Solutions, Lewis Center *Also Called: Electronic Imaging Svcs Inc (G-8332)*

Vesuvius U S A Corporation... 440 593-1161
  1100 Maple Ave Conneaut (44030) *(G-5419)*

Veterans Representative Co LLC................................330 779-0768
1584 Tamarisk Trl Youngstown (44514) *(G-14960)*

Veterans Steel Inc................................216 938-7476
900 E 69th St Cleveland (44103) *(G-4462)*

Vexos Inc................................440 284-2500
110 Commerce Dr Lagrange (44050) *(G-8155)*

Vexos Electronic Mfg Svcs, Lagrange *Also Called: Vexos Inc (G-8155)*

Vgs Inc................................216 431-7800
2239 E 55th St Cleveland (44103) *(G-4463)*

Vgu Industries Inc................................216 676-9093
4747 Manufacturing Ave Cleveland (44135) *(G-4464)*

Viavi Solutions Inc................................316 522-4981
8740 Orion Pl Ste 100 Columbus (43240) *(G-4651)*

Vib-ISO, Wooster *Also Called: Vib-Iso LLC (G-14695)*

Vib-Iso LLC................................800 735-9645
449 Freedlander Rd Wooster (44691) *(G-14695)*

Vibra Finish Co................................513 870-6300
8411 Seward Rd Fairfield (45011) *(G-6788)*

Vibrantz Color Solutions Inc (DH)................................440 997-5137
2600 Michigan Ave Ashtabula (44004) *(G-621)*

Vibrantz Corporation................................724 207-2152
4150 E 56th St Cleveland (44105) *(G-4465)*

Vibrantz Corporation................................442 224-6100
6060 Parkland Blvd Ste 250 Cleveland (44124) *(G-4466)*

Vibrantz Corporation................................216 875-5600
6060 Parkland Blvd Cleveland (44124) *(G-4467)*

Vibrantz Corporation................................216 875-6213
4150 E 56th St Cleveland (44105) *(G-4468)*

Vibrantz Corporation................................732 287-4925
6060 Parkland Blvd Cleveland (44124) *(G-4469)*

Vibrantz Corporation (DH)................................216 875-5600
6060 Parkland Blvd Ste 250 Mayfield Heights (44124) *(G-9344)*

Vibrantz Technologies Inc................................330 765-4378
1560 N Main St Orrville (44667) *(G-11017)*

Vibrodyne Division, Moraine *Also Called: Tailored Systems Inc (G-10194)*

Vic Maroscher................................330 332-4958
36135 Salem Grange Rd Salem (44460) *(G-11817)*

Vicart Prcsion Fabricators Inc................................614 771-0080
4101 Leap Rd Hilliard (43026) *(G-7710)*

Vicas Manufacturing Co Inc................................513 791-7741
8407 Monroe Ave Cincinnati (45236) *(G-3204)*

Vickers International Inc................................419 867-2200
3000 Strayer Rd Maumee (43537) *(G-9329)*

Vicon Fabricating Company Ltd................................440 205-6700
7200 Justin Way Mentor (44060) *(G-9649)*

Vics Turning Coinc................................216 531-5016
16911 Saint Clair Ave Cleveland (44110) *(G-4470)*

Victor Bodie Tire Co................................216 431-1700
1750 E 55th St Cleveland (44103) *(G-4471)*

Victor Organ Company................................330 792-1321
5340 Mahoning Ave Youngstown (44515) *(G-14961)*

Victorias Secret Service Co, Reynoldsburg *Also Called: Vs Service Company LLC (G-11586)*

Victory Direct LLC................................614 626-0000
750 Cross Pointe Rd Ste M Gahanna (43230) *(G-7172)*

Victory Postcards Inc................................614 764-8975
6129 Balmoral Dr Dublin (43017) *(G-6360)*

Victory Postcards & Souvenirs, Dublin *Also Called: Victory Postcards Inc (G-6360)*

Victory White Metal Company (PA)................................216 271-1400
6100 Roland Ave Cleveland (44127) *(G-4472)*

Victory White Metal Company................................216 641-2575
7930 Jones Rd Cleveland (44105) *(G-4473)*

Victory White Metal Company................................216 271-1400
3027 E 55th St Cleveland (44127) *(G-4474)*

Video Products Inc................................330 562-2622
1275 Danner Dr Aurora (44202) *(G-693)*

Viewpoint Graphic Design................................419 447-6073
132 S Washington St Tiffin (44883) *(G-12807)*

Viewray Inc (PA)................................440 703-3210
2 Thermo Fisher Way Oakwood Village (44146) *(G-10911)*

Viewray Technologies Inc (HQ)................................440 703-3210
2 Thermo Fisher Way Oakwood Village (44146) *(G-10912)*

Vigilante Love LLC................................380 258-5983
191 Broad Meadows Blvd Columbus (43214) *(G-5349)*

Viking Fabricators Inc................................740 374-5246
2021 Hanna Rd Marietta (45750) *(G-8960)*

Viking Forge LLC................................330 562-3366
4500 Crane Centre Dr Streetsboro (44241) *(G-12529)*

Viking Paper Company (PA)................................419 729-4951
5148 Stickney Ave Toledo (43612) *(G-13174)*

Viking Well Service Inc................................681 205-1999
64201 Wintergreen Rd Lore City (43755) *(G-8589)*

Village Cabinet Shop Inc................................704 966-0801
1820 Loisview Ln Cincinnati (45255) *(G-3205)*

Village Controls LLC................................614 600-8880
9349 Westview Dr Powell (43065) *(G-11496)*

Village of Grafton................................440 926-2075
1013 Chestnut St Grafton (44044) *(G-7305)*

Village Plastics Co................................330 753-0100
23610 Saint Clair Ave Euclid (44117) *(G-6683)*

Vindicator................................330 841-1600
240 Franklin St Se Warren (44483) *(G-13808)*

Vindicator Printing Company................................330 744-8611
101 W Boardman St Youngstown (44503) *(G-14962)*

Vineyards At Pine Lake Inc................................330 549-0195
14101 Market St Columbiana (44408) *(G-4632)*

Vino Di Piccin LLC................................740 738-0261
55155 National Rd Lansing (43934) *(G-8234)*

Vinoklet Winery Inc................................513 385-9309
11069 Colerain Rd Cincinnati (45252) *(G-3206)*

Vintage Automotive Elc Inc................................419 472-9349
3335 Mcgregor Ln Toledo (43623) *(G-13175)*

Vintage Heating and Air, Toledo *Also Called: Vintage Automotive Elc Inc (G-13175)*

Vintage Wine Distributor Inc................................513 443-4300
9422 Meridian Way West Chester (45069) *(G-14090)*

Vinyl Design Corporation................................419 283-4009
7856 Hill Ave Holland (43528) *(G-7790)*

Vinyl Graphics, Cleveland *Also Called: Vgu Industries Inc (G-4464)*

Vinyl Profiles Acquisition LLC................................330 538-0660
11675 Mahoning Ave North Jackson (44451) *(G-10698)*

Vinyl Tool & Die Company................................330 782-0254
1144 Meadowbrook Ave Youngstown (44512) *(G-14963)*

Vinylmng LLC................................440 261-5799
8001 Krueger Ave Cleveland (44105) *(G-4475)*

Vinyltech Inc................................330 538-0369
11635 Mahoning Ave North Jackson (44451) *(G-10699)*

Vinylume Products Inc................................330 799-2000
3745 Hendricks Rd Youngstown (44515) *(G-14964)*

Viral Antigens, Cincinnati *Also Called: Meridian Life Science Inc (G-2865)*

Virginia Air Distributors Inc................................614 262-1129
2821 Silver Dr Columbus (43211) *(G-5350)*

Virtual Hold Tech Slutions LLC (DH)................................330 670-2200
3875 Embassy Pkwy Ste 350 Akron (44333) *(G-354)*

Visi-Trak Worldwide LLC (PA)................................216 524-2363
8400 Sweet Valley Dr Ste 406 Cleveland (44125) *(G-4476)*

Visimax Technologies Inc................................330 405-8330
9177 Dutton Dr Ste 2 Twinsburg (44087) *(G-13392)*

Vision Color LLC................................419 924-9450
214 S Defiance St West Unity (43570) *(G-14199)*

Vision Graphix Inc................................440 835-6540
29275 Clemens Rd Westlake (44145) *(G-14342)*

Vision Manufacturing Inc................................937 332-1801
513 Garfield Ave Troy (45373) *(G-13260)*

Vision Press Inc................................440 357-6362
1634 W Jackson St Painesville (44077) *(G-11122)*

Vision Projects Inc................................937 667-8648
1350 Commerce Park Dr Tipp City (45371) *(G-12852)*

Visionmark Nameplate Co LLC................................419 977-3131
100 White Mountain Dr New Bremen (45869) *(G-10368)*

Vista Community Church................................614 718-2294
8500 Memorial Dr Ste C Plain City (43064) *(G-11425)*

Vista Creations LLC................................440 954-9191
7896 Tyler Blvd Mentor (44060) *(G-9650)*

Vista Industrial Packaging LLC (PA)................800 454-6117
4700 Fisher Rd Columbus (43228) *(G-5351)*

Vista Packaging & Logistics, Columbus *Also Called: Vista Industrial Packaging LLC (G-5351)*

Vistech, Fairfield *Also Called: Vistech Mfg Solutions LLC (G-6789)*

Vistech Mfg Solutions LLC..........................513 860-1408
4274 Thunderbird Ln Fairfield (45014) *(G-6789)*

Vistech Mfg Solutions LLC..........................513 933-9300
265 S West St Lebanon (45036) *(G-8296)*

Visual Marking Systems Inc (PA)..................330 425-7100
2097 E Aurora Rd Twinsburg (44087) *(G-13393)*

Vita-Mix Manufacturing Corporation (PA)......440 235-4840
8615 Usher Rd Olmsted Falls (44138) *(G-10942)*

Vitakraft Sun Seed Inc..............................419 832-1641
20584 Long Judson Rd Weston (43569) *(G-14350)*

Vital & Fhr North America LLC......................650 405-9975
1201 Brim Rd Bowling Green (43402) *(G-1446)*

Vitals Matter LLC....................................937 848-8871
1398 Nature Ct Dayton (45440) *(G-6072)*

Vitamin Shoppe Florida LLC (DH) 109 Innovation Ct Ste J Delaware (43015) *(G-6178)*

Vitamin Shoppe Industries LLC (DH) 109 Innovation Ct Ste J Delaware (43015) *(G-6179)*

Vitamin Shoppe, The, Delaware *Also Called: Vitamin Shoppe Industries LLC (G-6179)*

Vitamix, Olmsted Falls *Also Called: Vita-Mix Manufacturing Corporation (G-10942)*

Vitatoe Industries Inc (PA)..........................740 773-2425
100 Chamber Dr Chillicothe (45601) *(G-2287)*

Vitec Inc..216 464-4670
26901 Cannon Rd Bedford (44146) *(G-1063)*

Vitex Corporation....................................216 883-0920
2960 Broadway Ave Cleveland (44115) *(G-4477)*

Vivo Brothers LLC....................................330 629-8686
1387 Columbiana Lisbon Rd Columbiana (44408) *(G-4633)*

Vmaxx Inc..419 738-4044
323 Commerce Rd Wapakoneta (45895) *(G-13729)*

Vmi Americas Inc (HQ)..............................330 929-6800
4670 Allen Rd Stow (44224) *(G-12471)*

Vmi Liquidating Inc..................................937 492-3100
2309 Industrial Dr Sidney (45365) *(G-12059)*

Vndly LLC..513 572-2500
4900 Parkway Dr Ste 125 Mason (45040) *(G-9165)*

Vocational Services Inc............................216 431-8085
2239 E 55th St Cleveland (44103) *(G-4478)*

Voice Products Inc..................................216 360-0433
23715 Mercantile Rd Ste A200 Cleveland (44122) *(G-4479)*

Voigt & Schweitzer LLC (HQ)......................614 449-8281
987 Buckeye Park Rd Columbus (43207) *(G-5352)*

Voisard Manufacturing Inc........................419 896-3191
60 Scott St Shiloh (44878) *(G-11980)*

Volant Performance, Berea *Also Called: Tmg Performance Products LLC (G-1192)*

Volens LLC..216 544-1200
480 Highland Rd E Macedonia (44056) *(G-8721)*

Volk Corporation....................................513 621-1052
635 Main St Ste 1 Cincinnati (45202) *(G-3207)*

Volk Optical, Mentor *Also Called: Volk Optical Inc (G-9651)*

Volk Optical Inc......................................440 942-6161
7893 Enterprise Dr Mentor (44060) *(G-9651)*

Volpe Millwork Inc..................................216 581-0200
4500 Lee Rd Cleveland (44128) *(G-4480)*

Von Roll Isola, Cleveland *Also Called: Von Roll Usa Inc (G-4481)*

Von Roll Usa Inc....................................216 433-7474
4853 W 130th St Cleveland (44135) *(G-4481)*

Vores Steve Welding & Steel, Fort Recovery *Also Called: Steve Vore Welding and Steel (G-6971)*

Vortec and Paxton Products......................513 891-7474
10125 Carver Rd Blue Ash (45242) *(G-1347)*

Vortec Corporation..................................513 891-7485
10125 Carver Rd Blue Ash (45242) *(G-1348)*

Vortec-An Illinois TI Works Co, Blue Ash *Also Called: Vortec Corporation (G-1348)*

Vorti-Siv, Salem *Also Called: Mm Industries Inc (G-11802)*

Voss Industries LLC................................216 771-7655
1000 W Bagley Rd Berea (44017) *(G-1193)*

Voss Industries LLC (DH)..........................216 771-7655
2168 W 25th St Cleveland (44113) *(G-4482)*

Voyale Minority Enterprise LLC..................216 271-3661
5855 Grant Ave Cleveland (44105) *(G-4483)*

Voyant Beauty, New Albany *Also Called: Veepak OH LLC (G-10353)*

VPI, Aurora *Also Called: Video Products Inc (G-693)*

Vpl LLC..330 549-0195
14101 Market St Columbiana (44408) *(G-4634)*

Vpp Industries Inc..................................937 526-3775
960 E Main St Versailles (45380) *(G-13604)*

Vr Assets LLC..440 600-2963
5265 Naiman Pkwy Ste J Solon (44139) *(G-12203)*

Vrc, Loveland *Also Called: Valve Related Controls Inc (G-8655)*

Vrc Inc..440 243-6666
696 W Bagley Rd Berea (44017) *(G-1194)*

Vrc Manufacturers, Berea *Also Called: Vrc Inc (G-1194)*

Vs Service Company LLC..........................614 415-2348
4 Limited Pkwy E Reynoldsburg (43068) *(G-11586)*

Vscorp LLC..937 305-3562
4754 Us Route 40 Tipp City (45371) *(G-12853)*

Vsp Lab Columbus..................................614 409-8900
2605 Rohr Rd Lockbourne (43137) *(G-8493)*

VT Industries LLC....................................614 804-6904
1999 Friston Blvd Hilliard (43026) *(G-7711)*

Vtd Systems Inc......................................440 323-4122
7600 W River Rd S Elyria (44035) *(G-6601)*

Vts Co Ltd..419 273-4010
607 E Lima St Forest (45843) *(G-6943)*

Vulcan International Corp..........................513 621-2850
30 Garfield Pl Ste 1000 Cincinnati (45202) *(G-3208)*

Vulcan Machinery Corporation....................330 376-6025
20 N Case Ave Akron (44305) *(G-355)*

Vulcan Oil Company, Cincinnati *Also Called: New Vulco Mfg & Sales Co LLC (G-2904)*

Vulcan Products Co Inc............................419 468-1039
208 S Washington St Galion (44833) *(G-7201)*

Vulcraft, Beavercreek *Also Called: Nucor Corporation (G-979)*

Vulkor, Warren *Also Called: Therm-O-Link Inc (G-13801)*

Vulkor Incorporated (PA)..........................330 393-7600
621 Dana St Ne Ste V Warren (44483) *(G-13809)*

Vurvey Labs Inc......................................513 379-3595
1008 Race St Ste 4 Cincinnati (45202) *(G-3209)*

Vwm Republic Metals, Cleveland *Also Called: Victory White Metal Company (G-4473)*

Vwm-Republic Inc....................................216 641-2575
7930 Jones Rd Cleveland (44105) *(G-4484)*

VWR Chemicals LLC (DH)..........................800 448-4442
28600 Fountain Pkwy Solon (44139) *(G-12204)*

VWR Part of Avantor (DH)..........................440 349-1199
28600 Fountain Pkwy Solon (44139) *(G-12205)*

Vya Inc..513 772-5400
1325 Glendale Milford Rd Cincinnati (45215) *(G-3210)*

Vylon Pipe, Bowling Green *Also Called: Trenchless Rsrces Globl Hldngs (G-1444)*

Vyral LLC..937 993-7765
2078 E Dorothy Ln Dayton (45420) *(G-6073)*

W & W Automotive, Beavercreek Township *Also Called: W&W Automotive & Towing Inc (G-1007)*

W & W Custom Fabrication Inc....................513 353-4617
4801 Hamilton Cleves Rd Cleves (45002) *(G-4552)*

W B, Marion *Also Called: Wilson Bohannan Company (G-9005)*

W B Becherer Inc....................................330 758-6616
7905 Southern Blvd Youngstown (44512) *(G-14965)*

W C Bunting Co Inc..................................330 385-2050
1425 Globe St East Liverpool (43920) *(G-6399)*

W C R, Fairborn *Also Called: Wcr Incorporated (G-6703)*

W E Lott Company....................................419 563-9400
1432 Isaac Beal Rd Bucyrus (44820) *(G-1694)*

W H Patten Drilling Co Inc..........................330 674-3046
6336 County Road 207 Millersburg (44654) *(G-10017)*

W J Egli Company Inc (PA)........................330 823-3666
205 E Columbia St Alliance (44601) *(G-414)*

W M Dauch Concrete Inc............................419 562-6917
900 Nevada Rd Bucyrus (44820) *(G-1695)*

W of Ohio Inc (PA)..................................614 873-4664
225 Guy St Plain City (43064) *(G-11426)*

W P Brown Enterprises Inc.................................. 740 685-2594
57051 Marietta Rd Byesville (43723) *(G-1718)*

W Pole Contracting Inc...................................... 330 325-7177
4188 State Route 14 Ravenna (44266) *(G-11548)*

W R G Inc.. 216 351-8494
631 Parkside Dr Avon Lake (44012) *(G-772)*

W S Tyler, Mentor *Also Called: Tyler Haver Inc (G-9645)*

W T Inc.. 419 224-6942
606 N Jackson St Lima (45801) *(G-8458)*

W W Cross Industries Inc................................. 330 588-8400
2510 Allen Ave Se Canton (44707) *(G-2043)*

W.britain Model Figures, Chillicothe *Also Called: On The Mantle LLC (G-2268)*

W.T.nickell Co., Batavia *Also Called: D&D Design Concepts Inc (G-860)*

W/S Packaging Group Inc................................... 513 459-8800
7400 Industrial Row Dr Mason (45040) *(G-9166)*

W&W Automotive & Towing Inc......................... 937 429-1699
680 Orchard Ln Beavercreek Township (45434) *(G-1007)*

W&W Rock Sand and Gravel............................. 513 266-3708
1451 Maple Grove Rd Williamsburg (45176) *(G-14410)*

WA Hammond Drierite Co Ltd............................ 937 376-2927
138 Dayton Ave Xenia (45385) *(G-14783)*

Wabash National Corporation........................... 419 434-9409
2000 Fostoria Ave Findlay (45840) *(G-6932)*

Wabtec Corporation.. 216 362-7500
4677 Manufacturing Ave Cleveland (44135) *(G-4485)*

Wabtec Global Services, Mansfield *Also Called: Westinghouse A Brake Tech Corp (G-8866)*

Wabush Mnes Clffs Min Mnging A...................... 216 694-5700
200 Public Sq Ste 3300 Cleveland (44114) *(G-4486)*

Wacker Chemical Corporation........................... 330 899-0847
2215 International Pkwy Canton (44720) *(G-2044)*

Wacker Sign, Massillon *Also Called: Mel Wacker Signs Inc (G-9222)*

Waco Scaffolding & Equipment Inc..................... 216 749-8900
4545 Spring Rd Cleveland (44131) *(G-4487)*

Waddell A Div GMI Companies, Greenfield *Also Called: GMI Companies Inc (G-7328)*

Wade Dynamics Inc.. 216 431-8484
1411 E 39th St Cleveland (44114) *(G-4488)*

Wades Woodworking Inc................................. 937 374-6470
1427 Bellbrook Ave Xenia (45385) *(G-14784)*

Wagner Farms Sawmill Ltd Lblty....................... 419 653-4126
13201 Road X Leipsic (45856) *(G-8315)*

Wagner Machine Inc....................................... 330 706-0700
5151 Wooster Rd W Norton (44203) *(G-10828)*

Wagner Quarries Company................................ 419 625-8141
4203 Milan Rd Sandusky (44870) *(G-11883)*

Wahl, Fremont *Also Called: Wahl Refractory Solutions LLC (G-7143)*

Wahl Refractory Solutions LLC........................ 419 334-2658
767 S State Route 19 Fremont (43420) *(G-7143)*

Waibel Electric Co Inc..................................... 740 964-2956
133 Humphries Dr Etna (43068) *(G-6634)*

Wal Plax, Bedford *Also Called: Walton Plastics Inc (G-1064)*

Wal-Bon of Ohio Inc (PA)................................ 740 423-6351
210 Main St Belpre (45714) *(G-1155)*

Wal-Bon of Ohio Inc....................................... 740 423-8178
708 Main St Belpre (45714) *(G-1156)*

Walbridge Coatings, Walbridge *Also Called: Material Sciences Corporation (G-13685)*

Walbridge Coatings, Walbridge *Also Called: MSC Walbridge Coatings Inc (G-13686)*

Walden Industries Inc..................................... 740 633-5971
101 Walden Ave Tiltonsville (43963) *(G-12810)*

Waldorf Marking Devices, New London *Also Called: Monode Marking Products Inc (G-10413)*

Walest Incorporated.. 216 362-8110
306 Aynesly Way Brunswick (44212) *(G-1623)*

Walker National Inc.. 614 492-1614
2195 Wright Brothers Ave Columbus (43217) *(G-5353)*

Walker Printing Co., Mentor *Also Called: Jack Walker Printing Co (G-9540)*

Walker Tool & Machine Company........................ 419 661-8000
7700 Ponderosa Rd Perrysburg (43551) *(G-11278)*

Wall Colmonoy Corporation.............................. 513 842-4200
940 Redna Ter Cincinnati (45215) *(G-3211)*

Wall Technology Inc.. 715 532-5548
1 Owens Corning Pkwy Toledo (43659) *(G-13176)*

Wallace Forge Company.................................... 330 488-1203
3700 Georgetown Rd Ne Canton (44704) *(G-2045)*

Waller Brothers Stone Company........................ 740 858-1948
744 Mcdermott Rushtown Rd Mc Dermott (45652) *(G-9356)*

Walleye Investments Ltd.................................. 440 564-7210
6750 Arnold Miller Pkwy Solon (44139) *(G-12206)*

Wallover Enterprises Inc (DH)........................... 440 238-9250
21845 Drake Rd Strongsville (44149) *(G-12612)*

Wallover Oil Company Inc (DH).......................... 440 238-9250
21845 Drake Rd Strongsville (44149) *(G-12613)*

Wallover Oil Hamilton Inc................................ 513 896-6692
1000 Forest Ave Hamilton (45015) *(G-7537)*

Wallseye Concrete Corp.................................... 419 483-2738
8802 Portland Rd Castalia (44824) *(G-2096)*

Wallseye Concrete Corp (PA)............................. 440 235-1800
26000 Sprague Rd Cleveland (44138) *(G-4489)*

Walnut Creek Planing Ltd................................. 330 893-3244
5778 State Route 515 Millersburg (44654) *(G-10018)*

Walor North America Inc................................... 614 445-6060
2230 S 3rd St Columbus (43207) *(G-5354)*

Walsh Manufacturing, Cleveland *Also Called: Herman Manufacturing LLC (G-3827)*

Waltco Lift Corp (PA)....................................... 330 633-9191
1777 Miller Pkwy Streetsboro (44241) *(G-12530)*

Waltek & Company, Cincinnati *Also Called: Wt Acquisition Company Ltd (G-3234)*

Walter F Stephens Jr Inc................................. 937 746-0521
415 South Ave Franklin (45005) *(G-7055)*

Walter H Drane Co Inc...................................... 216 514-1022
23811 Chagrin Blvd Ste 344 Beachwood (44122) *(G-957)*

Walter North... 937 204-6050
900 Pimlico Dr Apt 2a Dayton (45459) *(G-6074)*

Walters Buildings, Urbana *Also Called: Jack Walters & Sons Corp (G-13470)*

Walther EMC, Franklin *Also Called: Walther Engrg & Mfg Co Inc (G-7056)*

Walther Engrg & Mfg Co Inc............................. 937 743-8125
3501 Shotwell Dr Franklin (45005) *(G-7056)*

Walton Hills, Walton Hills *Also Called: Controllix Corporation (G-13696)*

Walton Plastics Inc.. 440 786-7711
20493 Hannan Pkwy Bedford (44146) *(G-1064)*

Wan Dynamics Inc.. 877 400-9490
303 N Court St Unit 1758 Medina (44258) *(G-9462)*

Wannemacher Enterprises Inc.......................... 419 771-1101
422 W Guthrie Dr Upper Sandusky (43351) *(G-13456)*

Wannemacher Packaging, Upper Sandusky *Also Called: Wannemacher Enterprises Inc (G-13456)*

Wanner Metal Worx Inc................................... 740 369-4034
525 London Rd Delaware (43015) *(G-6180)*

Wappoo Wood Products Inc............................. 937 492-1166
12877 Kirkwood Rd Sidney (45365) *(G-12060)*

Ward Construction Co (PA)............................... 419 943-2450
385 Oak St Leipsic (45856) *(G-8316)*

Ward Engineering Inc....................................... 614 442-8063
2041 Arlingate Ln Columbus (43228) *(G-5355)*

Ward/Kraft Forms of Ohio Inc........................... 740 694-0015
700 Salem Ave Ext Fredericktown (43019) *(G-7088)*

Warehouse, Mansfield *Also Called: Gorman-Rupp Company (G-8795)*

Warehouse, Painesville *Also Called: De Nora Tech LLC (G-11077)*

Warfighter Fcsed Logistics Inc.......................... 740 513-4692
8800 Global Way Ste 100a West Chester (45069) *(G-14091)*

Warmus and Associates Inc............................. 330 659-4440
2324 N Cleveland Massillon Rd Bath (44210) *(G-898)*

Warner Fabricating Inc.................................... 330 848-3191
7812 Hartman Rd Wadsworth (44281) *(G-13676)*

Warren Castings Inc.. 216 883-2520
2934 E 55th St Cleveland (44127) *(G-4490)*

Warren Concrete and Supply Co......................... 330 393-1581
1113 Parkman Rd Nw Warren (44485) *(G-13810)*

Warren Door, Niles *Also Called: Traichal Construction Company (G-10607)*

Warren Drilling Co Inc..................................... 740 783-2775
305 Smithson St Dexter City (45727) *(G-6225)*

Warren Fabricating Corporation (PA)................... 330 534-5017
7845 Chestnut Ridge Rd Hubbard (44425) *(G-7818)*

Warren Metal Lithography, Warren *Also Called: Tecnocap LLC (G-13800)*

Warren Printing & Off Pdts Inc.................... 419 523-3635
250 E Main St Ottawa (45875) *(G-11050)*

Warren Rupp Inc.. 419 524-8388
800 N Main St Mansfield (44902) *(G-8863)*

Warren Screw Machine Inc............................ 330 609-6020
3869 Niles Rd Se Warren (44484) *(G-13811)*

Warren Steel Holdings LLC.......................... 330 847-0487
4000 Mahoning Ave Nw Warren (44483) *(G-13812)*

Warren Trucking, Dexter City Also Called: Warren Drilling Co Inc *(G-6225)*

Warren Welding and Fabrication, Lebanon Also Called: Kirbys Auto and Truck Repr Inc *(G-8272)*

Warrior Imports Inc...................................... 954 935-5536
112 S Meridian Rd Youngstown (44509) *(G-14966)*

Warther Cutlery, Dover Also Called: E Warther & Sons Inc *(G-6244)*

Warthman Drilling Inc.................................... 740 746-9950
7525 Lancaster Logan Rd Sugar Grove (43155) *(G-12630)*

Warwick Products Company.......................... 216 334-1200
5350 Tradex Pkwy Cleveland (44102) *(G-4491)*

Wasca LLC.. 937 723-9031
750 Rosedale Dr Dayton (45402) *(G-6075)*

Washing Systems LLC (HQ).......................... 800 272-1974
167 Commerce Dr Loveland (45140) *(G-8656)*

Washington County Coal Company................ 740 338-3100
46226 National Rd Saint Clairsville (43950) *(G-11714)*

Washington Crt Hse Converting, Wshngtn Ct Hs Also Called: Weyerhaeuser Company *(G-14751)*

Washington Group, Oregon Also Called: Aecom Energy & Cnstr Inc *(G-10956)*

Washington Products Inc (PA)...................... 330 837-5101
1875 Harsh Ave Se Ste 1 Massillon (44646) *(G-9252)*

Washita Valley Enterprises Inc...................... 330 510-1568
3707 Tulane Ave Bldg 9 Louisville (44641) *(G-8618)*

Wasserstrom Company (PA)..........................614 228-6525
4500 E Broad St Columbus (43213) *(G-5356)*

Wasserstrom Marketing Division, Columbus Also Called: N Wasserstrom & Sons Inc *(G-5118)*

Waste King, North Olmsted Also Called: Anaheim Manufacturing Company *(G-10717)*

Waste Water Plant, The, Ravenna Also Called: City of Ravenna *(G-11521)*

Waste Water Treatment Plant, Madison Also Called: County of Lake *(G-8728)*

Watch-Us Inc.. 513 829-8870
3400 Port Union Rd Fairfield (45014) *(G-6790)*

Water & Sewer, Chardon Also Called: City of Chardon *(G-2201)*

Water & Waste Water Dept., Mount Vernon Also Called: City of Mount Vernon *(G-10240)*

Water & Waste Water Eqp Co........................ 440 542-0972
32100 Solon Rd Ste 101a Solon (44139) *(G-12207)*

Water Star Inc.. 440 996-0800
7590 Discovery Ln Concord Township (44077) *(G-5397)*

Water Treatment, Middletown Also Called: City of Middletown *(G-9844)*

Waterco of The Central States...................... 937 294-0375
3215 Homeward Way Fairfield (45014) *(G-6791)*

Waterford Tank Fabrication Ltd...................... 740 984-4100
203 State Route 83 Beverly (45715) *(G-1211)*

Waterloo Coal Company Inc (PA).................. 740 286-0004
235 E Main St Jackson (45640) *(G-7955)*

Waterloo Industries Inc................................ 800 833-8851
12487 Plaza Dr Cleveland (44130) *(G-4492)*

Waterlox Coatings Corporation...................... 216 641-4877
9808 Meech Ave Cleveland (44105) *(G-4493)*

Watershed Distillery LLC.............................. 614 357-1936
1145 Chesapeake Ave Ste D Columbus (43212) *(G-5357)*

Watershed Mangement LLC.......................... 740 852-5607
10460 State Route 56 Se Mount Sterling (43143) *(G-10230)*

Watersource LLC.. 419 747-9552
1225 W Longview Ave Mansfield (44906) *(G-8864)*

Waterville Sheet Metal Co Inc...................... 419 878-5050
1210 Waterville Monclova Rd Waterville (43566) *(G-13844)*

Watkins Printing Company............................ 614 297-8270
1401 E 17th Ave Columbus (43211) *(G-5358)*

Watson Gravel Inc (PA)................................ 513 863-0070
2728 Hamilton Cleves Rd Hamilton (45013) *(G-7538)*

Watson Gravel Inc.. 513 422-3781
2100 S Main St Middletown (45044) *(G-9902)*

Watson Haran & Company Inc...................... 937 436-1414
1500 Yankee Park Pl Dayton (45458) *(G-6076)*

Watt Printers, Olmsted Falls Also Called: Gergel-Kellem Company Inc *(G-10940)*

Watteredge, Avon Lake Also Called: Watteredge LLC *(G-773)*

Watteredge LLC (DH)....................................440 933-6110
567 Miller Rd Avon Lake (44012) *(G-773)*

Watters Manufacturing Co Inc...................... 216 281-8600
1931 W 47th St Cleveland (44102) *(G-4494)*

Watts Antenna Company................................ 740 797-9380
70 N Plains Rd Ste H The Plains (45780) *(G-12761)*

Watts Water.. 614 491-5143
6201 Green Pointe Dr S Groveport (43125) *(G-7457)*

Wausau Mosinee Paper, Middletown Also Called: Wausau Paper Corp *(G-9903)*

Wausau Paper Corp...................................... 513 217-3623
700 Columbia Ave Middletown (45042) *(G-9903)*

Wauseon Machine & Mfg, Wauseon Also Called: Cornerstone Wauseon Inc *(G-13847)*

Wauseon Precast, Wauseon Also Called: Wauseon Silo & Coal Company *(G-13861)*

Wauseon Silo & Coal Company
535 Wood St Wauseon (43567) *(G-13861)*

Wavy Ticket LLC.. 513 827-0886
3748 State Line Rd Okeana (45053) *(G-10929)*

Waxco International Inc.................................. 937 746-4845
727 Dayton Oxford Rd Miamisburg (45342) *(G-9752)*

Waxman Industries Inc (PA)..........................440 439-1830
5386 Majestic Pkwy Bedford (44146) *(G-1065)*

Waygate Technologies Usa LP...................... 866 243-2638
1 Neumann Way Cincinnati (45215) *(G-3212)*

Wayne - Dalton Plastics, Conneaut Also Called: Overhead Door Corporation *(G-5413)*

Wayne A Whaley.. 330 525-7779
4466 12th St Homeworth (44634) *(G-7807)*

Wayne Builders Supply, Greenville Also Called: St Henry Tile Co Inc *(G-7355)*

Wayne Concrete Company LLC...................... 937 545-9919
223 Western Dr Medway (45341) *(G-9466)*

Wayne County Rubber Inc............................ 330 264-5553
1205 E Bowman St Wooster (44691) *(G-14696)*

Wayne Manufacturing, Zanesville Also Called: New Wayne Inc *(G-15034)*

Wayne Tire Service, Homeworth Also Called: Wayne A Whaley *(G-7807)*

Wayne Water Systems Inc............................ 800 237-0987
101 Production Dr Harrison (45030) *(G-7571)*

Wayne/Scott Fetzer Company, Harrison Also Called: Wayne Water Systems Inc *(G-7571)*

Waynedale Truss and Panel Co...................... 330 698-7373
8971 Dover Rd Apple Creek (44606) *(G-480)*

Waytek Corporation...................................... 937 743-6142
400 Shotwell Dr Franklin (45005) *(G-7057)*

Wccv Floor Coverings LLC (PA).................... 330 688-0114
4535 State Rd Peninsula (44264) *(G-11185)*

Wch Molding LLC.. 740 335-6320
1850 Lowes Blvd Wshngtn Ct Hs (43160) *(G-14749)*

Wcm Holdings Inc.. 513 705-2100
11500 Canal Rd Cincinnati (45241) *(G-3213)*

Wcr Incorporated (PA)..................................937 223-0703
2377 Commerce Center Blvd Ste B Fairborn (45324) *(G-6703)*

Wcr Incorporated.. 740 333-3448
809 Delaware St Wshngtn Ct Hs (43160) *(G-14750)*

Wdi Group Inc.. 216 251-5509
4031 W 150th St Cleveland (44135) *(G-4495)*

Wear Magic, Cincinnati Also Called: Cincinnati Advg Pdts LLC *(G-2467)*

Wear Technology, Batavia Also Called: Milacron Marketing Company LLC *(G-875)*

Weastec Incorporated (HQ).......................... 937 393-6800
1600 N High St Hillsboro (45133) *(G-7728)*

Weather King Heating & AC.......................... 330 908-0281
51 Meadow Ln Ste E Northfield (44067) *(G-10799)*

Weatherchem Corporation............................ 330 425-4206
2222 Highland Rd Twinsburg (44087) *(G-13394)*

Weaver Barns Ltd.. 330 852-2103
1696 State Route 39 Sugarcreek (44681) *(G-12656)*

Weaver Bros Inc (PA).................................... 937 526-3907
895 E Main St Versailles (45380) *(G-13605)*

Weaver Craft of Sugarcreek, Sugarcreek Also Called: Weavers Furniture Ltd *(G-12657)*

Weaver Fab & Finishing, Akron Also Called: Bogie Industries Inc Ltd *(G-81)*

**A
L
P
H
A
B
E
T
I
C**

Weaver Leather LLC (HQ)..330 674-7548
7540 County Road 201 Millersburg (44654) *(G-10019)*

Weaver Lumber Co...330 359-5091
1925 Us Route 62 Wilmot (44689) *(G-14596)*

Weaver Propack - Marc Drive.....................................330 379-3660
129 Marc Dr Cuyahoga Falls (44223) *(G-5581)*

Weaver Woodcraft L L C...330 695-2150
9652 Harrison Rd Apple Creek (44606) *(G-481)*

Weavers Furniture Ltd...330 852-2701
7011 Old Route 39 Nw Sugarcreek (44681) *(G-12657)*

Weber Ready Mix Inc..419 394-9097
16672 County Road 66a Saint Marys (45885) *(G-11754)*

Weber Sand & Gravel Inc..419 636-7920
14586 Us Highway 127 Ew Bryan (43506) *(G-1666)*

Webers Body & Frame Inc...937 839-5946
2017 State Route 503 N West Alexandria (45381) *(G-13923)*

Webster Industries Inc (PA).......................................419 447-8232
325 Hall St Tiffin (44883) *(G-12808)*

Webster Manufacturing Company, Tiffin *Also Called: Webster Industries Inc (G-12808)*

Wecall Inc...440 437-8202
510 Center St Chardon (44024) *(G-2226)*

Wecan Fabricators LLC...740 667-0731
49425 E Park Dr Tuppers Plains (45783) *(G-13263)*

Wedco LLC..513 309-0781
716 N High St Mount Orab (45154) *(G-10223)*

Wedge Hardwood Products...330 525-7775
2137 Knox School Rd Alliance (44601) *(G-415)*

Wedge Products Inc...330 405-4477
2181 Enterprise Pkwy Twinsburg (44087) *(G-13395)*

Wedgeworks Mch Tl Boring Inc...................................216 441-1200
3169 E 80th St Cleveland (44104) *(G-4496)*

Wedron Silica LLC...815 433-2449
3 Summit Park Dr Ste 700 Independence (44131) *(G-7924)*

Weekly Division, Stow *Also Called: Record Publishing Co (G-12454)*

Weidmann, Cleveland *Also Called: Weidmann Electrical Tech Inc (G-4497)*

Weidmann Electrical Tech Inc.....................................937 508-2112
1300 E 9th St Cleveland (44114) *(G-4497)*

Weighing Division, Ashville *Also Called: Interface Logic Systems Inc (G-626)*

Weirton Daily Times, The, Steubenville *Also Called: Ogden Newspapers Inc (G-12408)*

Weiskopf Industries Corp...440 442-4400
54 Alpha Park Cleveland (44143) *(G-4498)*

Weiss Industries Inc..419 526-2480
2480 N Main St Mansfield (44903) *(G-8865)*

Weiss Metallurgical Services, Mansfield *Also Called: Weiss Industries Inc (G-8865)*

Wek Industries, Jefferson *Also Called: Tmd Wek North LLC (G-7985)*

Wek Industries, Inc., Akron *Also Called: WI Inc (G-357)*

Welage Corporation...513 681-2300
7712 Reinhold Dr Cincinnati (45237) *(G-3214)*

Welch Foods, Cincinnati *Also Called: Welch Foods Inc A Cooperative (G-3215)*

Welch Foods Inc A Cooperative...................................513 632-5610
720 E Pete Rose Way Cincinnati (45202) *(G-3215)*

Welch Holdings Inc..513 353-3220
8953 E Miami River Rd Cincinnati (45247) *(G-3216)*

Welch Packaging Columbus, Columbus *Also Called: Welch Packaging Group Inc (G-5359)*

Welch Packaging Group Inc..614 870-2000
4700 Alkire Rd Columbus (43228) *(G-5359)*

Welch Publishing Co (PA)...419 874-2528
117 E 2nd St Perrysburg (43551) *(G-11279)*

Welch Publishing Co....419 666-5344
215 Osborne St Rossford (43460) *(G-11664)*

Welch Sand & Gravel Inc...513 353-3220
8953 E Miami River Rd Cincinnati (45247) *(G-3217)*

Weld Tech LLC...419 357-3214
12316 Berlin Rd Berlin Heights (44814) *(G-1206)*

Weld-Action Company Inc...330 372-1063
2100 N River Rd Ne Warren (44483) *(G-13813)*

Weldco Inc...513 744-9353
2121 Spring Grove Ave Cincinnati (45214) *(G-3218)*

Weldcraft Products Co, Tipp City *Also Called: Wpc Successor Inc (G-12855)*

Welded Ring Products Co (PA).....................................216 961-3800
2180 W 114th St Cleveland (44102) *(G-4499)*

Welded Tubes, Orwell *Also Called: Lock Joint Tube Ohio LLC (G-11023)*

Welded Tubes, Inc., Orwell *Also Called: Lsp Tubes Inc (G-11024)*

Welders Supply Inc..216 267-4470
5575 Engle Rd Brookpark (44142) *(G-1560)*

Welders Supply Inc (HQ)..216 241-1696
2020 Train Ave Cleveland (44113) *(G-4500)*

Welding and Fabrication, Bergholz *Also Called: Witts Services LLC (G-1197)*

Welding Consultants Inc..614 258-7018
889 N 22nd St Columbus (43219) *(G-5360)*

Welding Consultants LLC..614 258-7018
889 N 22nd St Columbus (43219) *(G-5361)*

Welding Improvement Company...................................330 424-9666
10070 Stookesberry Rd Lisbon (44432) *(G-8480)*

Weldments Inc...937 235-9261
167 Heid Ave Dayton (45404) *(G-6077)*

Weldon Ice Cream Company..740 467-2400
2887 Canal Dr Millersport (43046) *(G-10026)*

Weldon Pump, Cleveland *Also Called: Bergstrom Company Ltd Partnr (G-3415)*

Weldon Pump, Oakwood Village *Also Called: Weldon Pump LLC (G-10913)*

Weldon Pump LLC..440 232-2282
640 Golden Oak Pkwy Oakwood Village (44146) *(G-10913)*

Weldon Technologies, Columbus *Also Called: Akron Brass Company (G-4682)*

Wellex AMG...513 734-1700
3214 Marshall Dr Amelia (45102) *(G-441)*

Wellex Manufacturing Inc..513 734-1700
3214 Marshall Dr Amelia (45102) *(G-442)*

Wellman Container Corporation...................................513 860-3040
412 S Cooper Ave Cincinnati (45215) *(G-3219)*

Wellman Friction Products, Solon *Also Called: SK Wellman Corp (G-12181)*

Wellman Products LLC...855 403-9083
920 Lake Rd Medina (44256) *(G-9463)*

Wellnitz, Columbus *Also Called: Hazelbaker Industries Ltd (G-4973)*

Wellpoint..614 771-9600
6740 N High St Worthington (43085) *(G-14728)*

Wells Group LLC..740 532-9240
487 Gallia Pike Ironton (45638) *(G-7937)*

Wells Inc...419 457-2611
8176 Us Highway 23 Risingsun (43457) *(G-11620)*

Wells Manufacturing Llc..937 987-2481
280 W Main St New Vienna (45159) *(G-10476)*

Wellston Aerosol Mfg Co..740 384-2320
105 W A St Wellston (45692) *(G-13911)*

Welser Profile North Amer LLC (DH)............................330 225-2500
5535 Wegman Dr Valley City (44280) *(G-13522)*

Wengerd Wood Inc..330 359-4300
1760 County Road 200 Dundee (44624) *(G-6372)*

Wenrick Machine, Tipp City *Also Called: Wenrick Machine and Tool Corp (G-12854)*

Wenrick Machine and Tool Corp..................................937 667-7307
4685 Us Route 40 Tipp City (45371) *(G-12854)*

Wentworth Mold Inc Electra.......................................937 898-8460
852 Scholz Dr Vandalia (45377) *(G-13583)*

Wentworth Solutions...440 212-7696
1265 Ridge Rd Hinckley (44233) *(G-7736)*

Weprintquick.com, Cleveland *Also Called: Eveready Printing Inc (G-3693)*

Werk-Brau, Findlay *Also Called: Werk-Brau Company (G-6933)*

Werk-Brau Company (HQ)...419 422-2912
2800 Fostoria Ave Findlay (45840) *(G-6933)*

Werk-Brau Company..419 422-2912
616 N Blanchard St Findlay (45840) *(G-6934)*

Werks Kraft Engineering LLC......................................330 721-7374
935 Heritage Dr Medina (44256) *(G-9464)*

Werling and Sons Inc...937 338-3281
100 Plum St Burkettsville (45310) *(G-1698)*

Werlor...419 784-4285
1420 Ralston Ave Defiance (43512) *(G-6127)*

Werlor Waste Control, Defiance *Also Called: Werlor Inc (G-6127)*

Werner G Smith Inc..216 861-3676
1730 Train Ave Cleveland (44113) *(G-4501)*

Wernet Inc...330 452-2200
606 Cherry Ave Ne Canton (44702) *(G-2046)*

Wernke Wldg & Stl Erection Co............................513 353-4173
3150 State Line Rd North Bend (45052) *(G-10622)*

Wes-Garde Components Group Inc......................614 885-0319
300 Enterprise Dr Westerville (43081) *(G-14280)*

Weschler Instruments, Strongsville *Also Called: Hughes Corporation (G-12564)*

Wesco Distribution, Northwood *Also Called: Wesco Distribution Inc (G-10813)*

Wesco Distribution Inc..................................419 666-1670
6519 Fairfield Dr Northwood (43619) *(G-10813)*

Wesco Machine Inc.......................................330 688-6973
2304 Roberts Journey Ravenna (44266) *(G-11549)*

West & Barker Inc...330 652-9923
950 Summit Ave Niles (44446) *(G-10609)*

West 6th Products Company (PA).....................330 467-7446
60 Meadow Ln Northfield (44067) *(G-10800)*

West Bend Printing & Pubg Inc........................419 258-2000
101 N Main St Antwerp (45813) *(G-464)*

West Carrollton Converting Inc.......................937 859-3621
400 E Dixie Dr West Carrollton (45449) *(G-13932)*

West Carrollton Mfg Fcilty, West Carrollton *Also Called: Domtar Corporation (G-13927)*

West Chester Holdings LLC.............................513 705-2100
11500 Canal Rd Cincinnati (45241) *(G-3220)*

West Chester Protective Gear, Cincinnati *Also Called: West Chester Holdings LLC (G-3220)*

West Crrllton Prchment Cnvrtin.......................513 594-3341
400 E Dixie Dr West Carrollton (45449) *(G-13933)*

West Equipment Company Inc (PA)..................419 698-1601
1545 E Broadway St Toledo (43605) *(G-13177)*

West Liberty Commons, Medina *Also Called: Al Root Company (G-9371)*

West Ohio Tool Co...937 842-6688
7311 World Class Dr Russells Point (43348) *(G-11670)*

West Reserve Controls, Akron *Also Called: Summit Design and Tech Inc (G-320)*

West Side Leader, Fairlawn *Also Called: Leader Publications Inc (G-6806)*

West-Camp Press Inc....................................216 426-2660
1538 E 41st St Cleveland (44103) *(G-4502)*

West-Camp Press Inc....................................614 895-0233
5178 Sinclair Rd Columbus (43229) *(G-5362)*

West-Camp Press Inc (PA).............................614 882-2378
39 Collegeview Rd Westerville (43081) *(G-14281)*

West-Ward Columbus Inc................................614 276-4000
1809 Wilson Rd Columbus (43228) *(G-5363)*

Westar Plastics, Bryan *Also Called: Westar Plastics Llc (G-1667)*

Westar Plastics Llc.......................................419 636-1333
4271 County Road 15d Bryan (43506) *(G-1667)*

Westbrook Manufacturing, Dayton *Also Called: Westbrook Mfg Inc (G-6078)*

Westbrook Mfg Inc..937 254-2004
600 N Irwin St Dayton (45403) *(G-6078)*

Westendorf Printing, Dayton *Also Called: Fmh Enterprises LLC (G-5781)*

Westerman Inc (PA)......................................800 338-8265
245 N Broad St Bremen (43107) *(G-1488)*

WESTERN & SOUTHERN, Cincinnati *Also Called: Western & Southern Lf Insur Co (G-3221)*

Western & Southern Lf Insur Co (DH)...............513 629-1800
400 Broadway St Stop G Cincinnati (45202) *(G-3221)*

Western Branch Diesel LLC............................330 454-8800
1616 Metric Ave Sw Canton (44706) *(G-2047)*

Western Enterprises, Westlake *Also Called: Western/Scott Fetzer Company (G-14344)*

Western Kentucky Coal Co LLC........................740 338-3334
46226 National Rd Saint Clairsville (43950) *(G-11715)*

Western KY Cnsld Resources LLC (DH).............740 338-3100
46226 National Rd Saint Clairsville (43950) *(G-11716)*

Western KY Coal Resources LLC (DH)...............740 338-3100
46226 National Rd Saint Clairsville (43950) *(G-11717)*

Western KY Resources Fing LLC (DH)...............740 338-3100
46226 National Rd Saint Clairsville (43950) *(G-11718)*

Western Ohio Cut Stone Ltd............................937 492-4722
1130 Dingman Slagle Rd Sidney (45365) *(G-12061)*

Western Ohio Graphics, Troy *Also Called: Painted Hill Inv Group Inc (G-13246)*

Western Ohio Technologies LLC.......................937 947-8810
105 Commerce Dr Russia (45363) *(G-11678)*

Western Reserve Distillers LLC.......................330 780-9599
14221 Madison Ave Lakewood (44107) *(G-8173)*

Western Reserve Sleeve Inc...........................440 238-8850
22360 Royalton Rd Strongsville (44149) *(G-12614)*

Western Reserve Wire Products, Twinsburg *Also Called: Wrwp LLC (G-13399)*

Western Roto Engravers Inc............................330 336-7636
668 Seville Rd Wadsworth (44281) *(G-13677)*

Western States Envelope Co...........................419 666-7480
6859 Commodore Dr Walbridge (43465) *(G-13689)*

Western States Envelope Label, Walbridge *Also Called: Western States Envelope Co (G-13689)*

Western/Scott Fetzer Company (HQ)................440 892-3000
28800 Clemens Rd Westlake (44145) *(G-14343)*

Western/Scott Fetzer Company.......................440 871-2160
875 Bassett Rd Westlake (44145) *(G-14344)*

Westfield Steel Inc..937 322-2414
1120 S Burnett Rd Springfield (45505) *(G-12392)*

Westinghouse A Brake Tech Corp.....................419 526-5323
472 Rembrandt St Mansfield (44902) *(G-8866)*

Westlake Corporation....................................614 986-2497
180 E Broad St Columbus (43215) *(G-5364)*

Westlake Dimex LLC......................................800 334-3776
28305 State Route 7 Marietta (45750) *(G-8961)*

Westlake Epoxy, Columbus *Also Called: Westlake Corporation (G-5364)*

Westlake Ryal Bldg Pdts USA In (DH)..............800 366-8472
1441 Universal Rd Columbus (43207) *(G-5365)*

Westlake Tool & Die Mfg Co............................440 934-5305
1280 Moore Rd Avon (44011) *(G-742)*

Westmont Inc...330 862-3080
3035 Union Ave Ne Minerva (44657) *(G-10049)*

Westmoreland Resources Gp LLC.....................740 622-6302
544 Chestnut St Coshocton (43812) *(G-5475)*

Weston Brands Inc..800 814-4895
7575 E Pleasant Valley Rd Ste 100 Independence (44131) *(G-7925)*

Westrock Commercial LLC..............................419 476-9101
1635 Coining Dr Toledo (43612) *(G-13178)*

Westrock Converting LLC...............................513 860-0225
9266 Meridian Way West Chester (45069) *(G-14092)*

Westrock Mwv LLC..937 495-6323
10 W 2nd St Dayton (45402) *(G-6079)*

Westrock Rkt LLC...330 296-5155
975 N Freedom St Ravenna (44266) *(G-11550)*

Westrock Rkt LLC...513 860-5546
9245 Meridian Way West Chester (45069) *(G-14093)*

Westshore Metal Finishing LLC.......................440 892-0774
26891 Kenley Ct Westlake (44145) *(G-14345)*

Westview Concrete Corp.................................440 458-5800
40105 Butternut Ridge Rd Elyria (44035) *(G-6602)*

Westview Concrete Corp (PA)..........................440 235-1800
26000 Sprague Rd Olmsted Falls (44138) *(G-10943)*

Westwood Fbrction Shtmetal Inc.....................937 837-0494
1752 Stanley Ave Dayton (45404) *(G-6080)*

Westwood Finishing Company..........................937 837-1488
1118 Neeld Dr Xenia (45385) *(G-14785)*

Wetsu Group Inc...937 324-9353
125 W North St Springfield (45504) *(G-12393)*

Weybridge LLC...440 951-5500
4530 Hamann Pkwy Willoughby (44094) *(G-14549)*

Weyerhaeuser Company..................................740 335-4480
1803 Lowes Blvd Wshngtn Ct Hs (43160) *(G-14751)*

Wfmj-Tv21, Youngstown *Also Called: Vindicator Printing Company (G-14962)*

Wfs Filter Co, Cleveland *Also Called: Micropure Filtration Inc (G-4028)*

Wfsr Holdings LLC..877 735-4966
220 E Monument Ave Dayton (45402) *(G-6081)*

Wharton Grain, Wharton *Also Called: Mennel Milling Company (G-14351)*

Whatifsportscom Inc.....................................513 333-0313
10200 Alliance Rd Ste 301 Blue Ash (45242) *(G-1349)*

Wheat Ridge Pallet & Lumber, Peebles *Also Called: Schrock John (G-11172)*

Wheatland Tube LLC......................................724 342-6851
1800 Hunter Ave Niles (44446) *(G-10610)*

Wheatland Tube LLC......................................330 372-6611
901 Dietz Rd Ne Warren (44483) *(G-13814)*

Wheatland Tube Company, Cambridge *Also Called: Zekelman Industries Inc (G-1766)*

Wheatland Tube Company, Niles *Also Called: Wheatland Tube LLC (G-10610)*

Wheatland Tube Company, Warren *Also Called: Wheatland Tube LLC (G-13814)*

ALPHABETIC

Wheatley Electric Service Co.. 513 531-4951
2046 Ross Ave Cincinnati (45212) *(G-3222)*

Wheel Group Holdings LLC.. 614 253-6247
2901 E 4th Ave Ste 3 Columbus (43219) *(G-5366)*

Wheel One, Columbus *Also Called: Wheel Group Holdings LLC (G-5366)*

Wheeler Manufacturing, Ashtabula *Also Called: Rex International USA Inc (G-615)*

Wheeling Coffee & Spice Co.. 304 232-0141
117 Pinecrest Dr Saint Clairsville (43950) *(G-11719)*

Whelco Industrial Ltd... 419 385-4627
28210 Cedar Park Blvd Perrysburg (43551) *(G-11280)*

Whemco, Canton *Also Called: United Rolls Inc (G-2036)*

Whemco, Lima *Also Called: Whemco-Ohio Foundry Inc (G-8459)*

Whemco-Ohio Foundry Inc... 419 222-2111
1600 Mcclain Rd Lima (45804) *(G-8459)*

Whempys Corp.. 614 888-6670
6969 Worthington Galena Rd Ste P Worthington (43085) *(G-14729)*

Whip Guide Co.. 440 543-5151
16829 Park Circle Dr Chagrin Falls (44023) *(G-2191)*

Whirlaway Corporation.. 440 647-4711
125 Bennett St Wellington (44090) *(G-13902)*

Whirlaway Corporation.. 440 647-4711
125 Bennett St Wellington (44090) *(G-13903)*

Whirlaway Corporation (HQ).. 440 647-4711
720 Shiloh Ave Wellington (44090) *(G-13904)*

Whirlpool, Clyde *Also Called: Whirlpool Corporation (G-4565)*

Whirlpool, Clyde *Also Called: Whirlpool Corporation (G-4566)*

Whirlpool, Lockbourne *Also Called: Whirlpool Corporation (G-8494)*

Whirlpool Corporation... 419 547-7711
119 Birdseye St Clyde (43410) *(G-4565)*

Whirlpool Corporation... 419 547-2610
1081 W Mcpherson Hwy Clyde (43410) *(G-4566)*

Whirlpool Corporation... 419 423-8123
4901 N Main St Findlay (45840) *(G-6935)*

Whirlpool Corporation... 937 548-4126
1701 Kitchen Aid Way Greenville (45331) *(G-7359)*

Whirlpool Corporation... 614 409-4340
6241 Shook Rd Lockbourne (43137) *(G-8494)*

Whirlpool Corporation... 740 383-7122
1300 Marion Agosta Rd Marion (43302) *(G-9003)*

Whirlwind Propellers, Piqua *Also Called: Hartzell Propeller Inc (G-11353)*

Whitacre Engineering Company (PA)................................. 330 455-8505
4645 Rebar Ave Ne Canton (44705) *(G-2048)*

Whitacre Enterprises Inc... 740 934-2331
35651 State Route 537 Graysville (45734) *(G-7322)*

Whitacre Greer Company (PA).. 330 823-1610
1400 S Mahoning Ave Alliance (44601) *(G-416)*

Whitaker Finishing LLC... 419 666-7746
2707 Tracy Rd Northwood (43619) *(G-10814)*

Whitcraft Cleveland, Cleveland *Also Called: Turbine Eng Cmpnents Tech Corp (G-4433)*

White Castle, Columbus *Also Called: White Castle System Inc (G-5367)*

White Castle System Inc... 513 563-2290
3126 Exon Ave Cincinnati (45241) *(G-3223)*

White Castle System Inc (PA)... 614 228-5781
555 Edgar Waldo Way Columbus (43215) *(G-5367)*

White Dove Mattress, Newburgh Heights *Also Called: H Goodman Inc (G-10542)*

White Feather Foods Inc... 419 738-8975
13845 Cemetery Rd Wapakoneta (45895) *(G-13730)*

White Industrial Tool Inc... 330 773-6889
102 W Wilbeth Rd Akron (44301) *(G-356)*

White Jewelers Inc.. 330 264-3324
516 N Bever St Apt 1 Wooster (44691) *(G-14697)*

White Machine Inc... 440 237-3282
9621 York Alpha Dr Side North Royalton (44133) *(G-10789)*

White Machine & Mfg Co (PA).. 740 453-5451
120 Graham St Zanesville (43701) *(G-15054)*

White Mule Company.. 740 382-9008
2420 W 4th St Ontario (44906) *(G-10954)*

White Tiger Inc.. 740 852-4873
131 S Oak St London (43140) *(G-8543)*

White Tiger Graphics, London *Also Called: White Tiger Inc (G-8543)*

White Tool, Akron *Also Called: White Industrial Tool Inc (G-356)*

White Water Forest, Batavia *Also Called: Whitewater Forest Products LLC (G-897)*

Whitefeather Foods, Wapakoneta *Also Called: White Feather Foods Inc (G-13730)*

Whitehouse Bros Inc... 513 621-2259
4393 Creek Rd Blue Ash (45241) *(G-1350)*

Whiterock Pigments Inc... 216 391-7765
1768 E 25th St Cleveland (44114) *(G-4503)*

Whiteside Manufacturing Co... 740 363-1179
309 Hayes St Delaware (43015) *(G-6181)*

Whitewater Forest Products LLC...................................... 513 724-0157
1970 Clark Ln Batavia (45103) *(G-897)*

Whitewater Processing LLC.. 513 367-4133
10964 Campbell Rd Harrison (45030) *(G-7572)*

Whitman Corporation.. 513 541-3223
2530 Joyce Ln Okeana (45053) *(G-10930)*

Whitmer Woodworks Inc.. 614 873-1196
8490 Carters Mill Rd Plain City (43064) *(G-11427)*

Whitmore Productions Inc... 216 752-3960
20209 Harvard Ave Warrensville Heights (44122) *(G-13819)*

Whitmore's Bbq, Warrensville Heights *Also Called: Whitmore Productions Inc (G-13819)*

Whitney Stained GL Studio Inc... 216 348-1616
5939 Broadway Ave Cleveland (44127) *(G-4504)*

Whitt Machine Inc.. 513 423-7624
806 Central Ave Middletown (45044) *(G-9904)*

Whole Shop Inc... 330 630-5305
181 S Thomas Rd Tallmadge (44278) *(G-12759)*

Wholecycle Inc... 330 929-8123
100 Cuyahoga Falls Industrial Pkwy Peninsula (44264) *(G-11186)*

Wholesale, Cincinnati *Also Called: Hen of Woods LLC (G-2716)*

Wholesale and Manufacturer, Toledo *Also Called: Estone Group LLC (G-12957)*

Wholesale Bait Co Inc... 513 863-2380
2619 Bobmeyer Rd Fairfield (45014) *(G-6792)*

Wholesale Channel Letters.. 440 256-3200
8603 Euclid Chardon Rd Kirtland (44094) *(G-8146)*

Wholesale Imprints Inc.. 440 224-3527
6259 Hewitt Lane North Kingsville (44068) *(G-10700)*

Wholesome Valley Farm, Wilmot *Also Called: Trevor Clatterbuck (G-14595)*

WI Inc.. 440 576-6940
1293 S Main St Akron (44301) *(G-357)*

Wicked Premiums LLC.. 216 364-0322
8748 Brecksville Rd Ste 224 Brecksville (44141) *(G-1485)*

Wicom Services, Lisbon *Also Called: Welding Improvement Company (G-8480)*

Wieland, Archbold *Also Called: Sauder Manufacturing Co (G-509)*

Wieland Metal Svcs Foils LLC.. 330 823-1700
2081 Mccrea St Alliance (44601) *(G-417)*

Wifi-Plus Inc.. 330 273-3665
2950 Westway Dr Ste 101 Brunswick (44212) *(G-1624)*

Wiholi Inc... 440 543-8233
17050 Munn Rd Chagrin Falls (44023) *(G-2192)*

WIKA Sensor Technlgy LP... 614 430-0683
6957 Green Meadows Dr Lewis Center (43035) *(G-8357)*

Wikoff Color Corporation.. 513 423-0727
1392 Oxford State Rd Middletown (45044) *(G-9905)*

Wilcox Awning & Sign, Perrysburg *Also Called: Toledo Tarp Service Inc (G-11276)*

Wilcoxon, James H Jr, Columbus *Also Called: Johnsons Real Ice Cream LLC (G-5042)*

Wild Berry Incense Inc.. 513 523-8583
5475 College Corner Pike Oxford (45056) *(G-11065)*

Wild Berry Incense Factory, Oxford *Also Called: Wild Berry Incense Inc (G-11065)*

Wild Fire Systems.. 440 442-8999
535 Ransome Rd Cleveland (44143) *(G-4505)*

Wild Ohio Brewing Company... 614 262-0000
2025 S High St Columbus (43207) *(G-5368)*

Wildcat Creek Farms Inc... 419 263-2549
4633 Road 94 Payne (45880) *(G-11167)*

Wildcat Creek Popcorn, Payne *Also Called: Wildcat Creek Farms Inc (G-11167)*

Wiley Companies (PA).. 740 622-0755
545 Walnut St Coshocton (43812) *(G-5476)*

Wiley Companies.. 740 622-0755
1245 S 6th St Coshocton (43812) *(G-5477)*

Wileys Finest LLC (PA).. 740 622-1072
545 Walnut St Coshocton (43812) *(G-5478)*

(G-0000) Company's Geographic Section entry number

Will-Burt Company (PA).................................. 330 682-7015
401 Collins Blvd Orrville (44667) *(G-11018)*

Will-Burt Company... 330 682-7015
312 Collins Blvd Orrville (44667) *(G-11019)*

Willard Machine & Welding Inc...................... 330 467-0642
556 Highland Rd E Ste 3 Macedonia (44056) *(G-8722)*

William Dauch Concrete Company.................. 419 562-6917
900 Nevada Wynford Rd Bucyrus (44820) *(G-1696)*

William Dauch Concrete Company (PA).......... 419 668-4458
84 Cleveland Rd Norwalk (44857) *(G-10863)*

William Exline Inc.. 216 941-0800
12301 Bennington Ave Cleveland (44135) *(G-4506)*

William J Bergen & Co..................................... 440 248-6132
32520 Arthur Rd Solon (44139) *(G-12208)*

William Niccum.. 330 415-0154
11882 Sandyville Ave Se East Sparta (44626) *(G-6413)*

William Powell Company (PA).......................... 513 852-2000
3261 Spring Grove Ave Cincinnati (45225) *(G-3224)*

William R Hague Inc.. 614 836-2115
4343 S Hamilton Rd Groveport (43125) *(G-7458)*

William S Miller Inc... 330 223-1794
11250 Montgomery Rd Kensington (44427) *(G-8011)*

Williams Concrete Inc..................................... 419 893-3251
1350 Ford St Maumee (43537) *(G-9330)*

Williams Industrial, Bowling Green *Also Called: Williams Industrial Svc Inc (G-1447)*

Williams Industrial Svc Inc............................. 419 353-2120
2120 Wood Bridge Blvd Bowling Green (43402) *(G-1447)*

Williams Leather Products Inc......................... 740 223-1604
1476 Likens Rd Ste 104 Marion (43302) *(G-9004)*

Williams Partners LP.. 330 414-6201
7235 Whipple Ave Nw North Canton (44720) *(G-10681)*

Williams Pork Co Op.. 419 682-9022
18487 County Road F Stryker (43557) *(G-12628)*

Williams Steel Rule Die Co.............................. 216 431-3232
1633 E 40th St Cleveland (44103) *(G-4507)*

Williamson Safe Inc... 937 393-9919
5631 State Route 73 Hillsboro (45133) *(G-7729)*

Willis Cnc... 440 926-0434
1008 Commerce Dr Grafton (44044) *(G-7306)*

Willis Music Company...................................... 513 671-3288
11700 Princeton Pike Unit E209 Cincinnati (45246) *(G-3225)*

Willoughby Brewing Company LLC.................. 440 975-0202
4057 Erie St Willoughby (44094) *(G-14550)*

Willoughby Printing Co Inc.............................. 440 946-0800
37946 Elm St Willoughby (44094) *(G-14551)*

Willowwood Global LLC (PA)...........................740 869-3377
15441 Scioto Darby Rd Mount Sterling (43143) *(G-10231)*

Willy's Fresh Salsa, Swanton *Also Called: Willys Inc (G-12698)*

Willys Inc... 419 823-3200
11305 W Airport Service Rd Swanton (43558) *(G-12698)*

Wilmington Forest Products............................ 937 382-7813
5562 S Us Highway 68 Wilmington (45177) *(G-14590)*

Wilmington Prcsion McHning Inc.................... 937 382-3700
397 Starbuck Rd Wilmington (45177) *(G-14591)*

Wilmington Precision Machining, Wilmington *Also Called: Wilmington Prcsion McHning Inc (G-14591)*

Wilson Blacktop Corp...................................... 740 635-3566
915 Carlisle St Rear Martins Ferry (43935) *(G-9012)*

Wilson Bohannan Company.............................. 740 382-3639
621 Buckeye St Marion (43302) *(G-9005)*

Wilson Electronic Displays, Germantown *Also Called: Wilson Sign Co Inc (G-7257)*

Wilson Optical Labs Inc................................... 440 357-7000
9450 Pineneedle Dr Mentor (44060) *(G-9652)*

Wilson Sign Co Inc... 937 253-2246
2623 Dayton Germantown Pike Germantown (45327) *(G-7257)*

Wilson Specialties, North Jackson *Also Called: Canfield Manufacturing Co Inc (G-10684)*

Wilson Sporting Goods Co............................... 419 634-9901
217 Liberty St Ada (45810) *(G-6)*

Wilsonart LLC... 614 876-1515
2500 International St Columbus (43228) *(G-5369)*

Win Cd Inc.. 330 929-1999
3333 Win St Cuyahoga Falls (44223) *(G-5582)*

Win Plastic Extrusions LLC............................. 330 929-1999
11502 Century Blvd Cincinnati (45246) *(G-3226)*

Win Plex, Cuyahoga Falls *Also Called: Win Cd Inc (G-5582)*

Winans Chocolate and Coffee, Piqua *Also Called: Piqua Chocolate Company Inc (G-11374)*

Winco Industries, Inc., Tipp City *Also Called: Sp3 Winco LLC (G-12846)*

Windsor Airmotive, West Chester *Also Called: Barnes Group Inc (G-13946)*

Windsor Tool Inc.. 216 671-1900
10714 Bellaire Rd Cleveland (44111) *(G-4508)*

Wine Cellar Innovations LLC........................... 513 321-3733
4575 Eastern Ave Cincinnati (45226) *(G-3227)*

Wine Mill.. 234 571-2594
4964 Akron Cleveland Rd Peninsula (44264) *(G-11187)*

Winery At Wilcox Inc.. 937 526-3232
6572 State Route 47 Versailles (45380) *(G-13606)*

Winery At Wolf Creek....................................... 330 666-9285
2637 S Cleveland Massillon Rd Barberton (44203) *(G-841)*

Winesburg Meats Inc....................................... 330 359-5092
2181 Us Route 62 Winesburg (44690) *(G-14609)*

Winkle Industries Inc....................................... 330 823-9730
2080 W Main St Alliance (44601) *(G-418)*

Winkler Co Inc.. 937 294-2662
435 Patterson Rd Dayton (45419) *(G-6082)*

Winner Corporation (PA).................................. 419 582-4321
8544 State Route 705 Yorkshire (45388) *(G-14797)*

Winner's Meat Service, Yorkshire *Also Called: Winner Corporation (G-14797)*

Winston Heat Treating Inc............................... 937 226-0110
711 E 2nd St Dayton (45402) *(G-6083)*

Winston Oil Co Inc... 740 373-9664
1 Court House Ln Ste 3 Marietta (45750) *(G-8962)*

Winter Equipment Company Incorporated....... 440 946-8377
1900 Joseph Lloyd Pkwy Willoughby (44094) *(G-14552)*

Winters Concrete, Jackson *Also Called: Winters Products Inc (G-7956)*

Winters Products Inc.. 740 286-4149
109 Athens St Jackson (45640) *(G-7956)*

Winzeler Couplings & Mtls LLC....................... 419 485-3147
910 E Main St Montpelier (43543) *(G-10136)*

Winzeler Manufacturing Company (PA)............ 419 485-8147
129 W Wabash St Montpelier (43543) *(G-10137)*

Winzeler Stamping Co (HQ)............................. 419 485-3147
129 W Wabash St Montpelier (43543) *(G-10138)*

Wipe Out Enterprises Inc................................. 937 497-9473
6523 Dawson Rd Sidney (45365) *(G-12062)*

Wire Lab Company, Cleveland *Also Called: Omni Technical Products Inc (G-4121)*

Wire Products Company Inc............................. 216 267-0777
14700 Industrial Pkwy Cleveland (44135) *(G-4509)*

Wire Products Company LLC (PA).................... 216 267-0777
14601 Industrial Pkwy Cleveland (44135) *(O-4510)*

WIRE PRODUCTS COMPANY, INC., Cleveland *Also Called: Wire Products Company Inc (G-4509)*

Wire Shop Inc.. 440 354-6842
5959 Pinecone Dr Mentor (44060) *(G-9653)*

Wireless Retail LLC.. 614 657-5182
6750 Commerce Court Dr Blacklick (43004) *(G-1231)*

Wiremax A Heico Company, Toledo *Also Called: Connectronics Corp (G-12930)*

Wiremax Ltd... 419 531-9500
705 Wamba Ave Toledo (43607) *(G-13179)*

Wisco Products Incorporated.......................... 937 228-2101
109 Commercial St Dayton (45402) *(G-6084)*

Wisconsin Indus Sand Co LLC......................... 715 235-0942
3 Summit Park Dr Ste 700 Independence (44131) *(G-7926)*

Wise Edge LLC... 330 208-0889
491 Roland Hills Dr Mogadore (44260) *(G-10094)*

Wiseco, Mentor *Also Called: Race Winning Brands Inc (G-9606)*

Wiseman Bros Fabg & Stl Ltd........................... 740 988-5121
2598 Glade Rd Beaver (45613) *(G-961)*

Wismar Prcsion Toling Prod Inc...................... 440 296-0487
7505 Tyler Blvd Ste 2 Mentor (44060) *(G-9654)*

Witt Enterprises Inc... 440 992-8333
2024 Aetna Rd Ashtabula (44004) *(G-622)*

Witt Industries Inc (HQ)...................................513 871-5700
4600 N Mason Montgomery Rd Mason (45040) *(G-9167)*

Witt Products, Mason *Also Called: Witt Industries Inc (G-9167)*

Wittrock Wdwkg & Mfg Co Inc.................... 513 891-5800
4201 Malsbary Rd Blue Ash (45242) *(G-1351)*

Witts Services LLC.................... 740 543-8526
553 County Road 59 Bergholz (43908) *(G-1197)*

Wittur Usa Inc.................... 216 524-0100
7852 Bavaria Rd Twinsburg (44087) *(G-13396)*

Wiwa LLC.................... 419 757-0141
107 N Main St Alger (45812) *(G-363)*

Wjf Enterprises LLC.................... 513 871-7320
1347 Custer Ave Cincinnati (45208) *(G-3228)*

Wls Stamping & Fabricating, Cleveland *Also Called: WLS Stamping Co (G-4511)*

WLS Stamping Co (PA).................... 216 271-5100
3292 E 80th St Cleveland (44104) *(G-4511)*

Wm Lang & Sons Company.................... 513 541-3304
3280 Beekman St Cincinnati (45223) *(G-3229)*

Wm Plotz Machine and Forge Co.................... 216 861-0441
2514 Center St Cleveland (44113) *(G-4512)*

Wober Muster, Springfield *Also Called: Crowning Food Company (G-12296)*

Woco, Strongsville *Also Called: Wallover Oil Company Inc (G-12613)*

Wodin Inc.................... 440 439-4222
5441 Perkins Rd Cleveland (44146) *(G-4513)*

Woeber Mustard Mfg Co (PA).................... 937 323-6281
1966 Commerce Cir Springfield (45504) *(G-12394)*

Woeber Mustard Mfg Co.................... 937 342-9601
5103 Urbana Rd Springfield (45502) *(G-12395)*

Wolf Composite Solutions.................... 614 219-6990
3991 Fondorf Dr Columbus (43228) *(G-5370)*

Wolf G T Awning & Tent Co.................... 937 548-4161
3352 State Route 571 Greenville (45331) *(G-7360)*

Wolf Machine Company (PA).................... 513 791-5194
5570 Creek Rd Blue Ash (45242) *(G-1352)*

Wolf Metals Inc.................... 614 461-6361
1625 W Mound St Columbus (43223) *(G-5371)*

Wolfe Grinding Inc.................... 330 929-6677
4582 Allen Rd Stow (44224) *(G-12472)*

Wolff Bros Supply Inc.................... 440 327-1650
38777 Taylor Industrial Pkwy North Ridgeville (44035) *(G-10753)*

Wolff Tool & Mfg Company Inc.................... 440 933-7797
139 Lear Rd Avon Lake (44012) *(G-774)*

Wolters Kluwer Clinical Drug Information Inc.................... 330 650-6506
1100 Terex Rd Hudson (44236) *(G-7862)*

Wonder Machine Services Inc.................... 440 937-7500
35340 Avon Commerce Pkwy Avon (44011) *(G-743)*

Wonder-Shirts Inc.................... 917 679-2336
7695 Crawley Dr Dublin (43017) *(G-6361)*

Wonderly Trucking & Excvtg LLC.................... 419 837-6294
3939 Fremont Pike Perrysburg (43551) *(G-11281)*

Wood County Ohio.................... 419 353-1227
991 S Main St Bowling Green (43402) *(G-1448)*

Wood Creations.................... 419 692-2624
12805 State Rd Delphos (45833) *(G-6200)*

Wood Graphics Inc (PA).................... 513 771-6300
8075 Reading Rd Ste 301 Cincinnati (45237) *(G-3230)*

Wood Recovery, Newark *Also Called: Hope Timber & Marketing Group (G-10507)*

Wood Working, Troy *Also Called: Stull Woodworks Inc (G-13259)*

Wood-Sebring Corporation.................... 216 267-3191
13800 Enterprise Ave Cleveland (44135) *(G-4514)*

Woodbine Products Company.................... 330 725-0165
915 W Smith Rd Medina (44256) *(G-9465)*

Woodbridge, Fremont *Also Called: Woodbridge Group (G-7144)*

Woodbridge Englewood Inc.................... 937 540-9889
300 Lau Pkwy Englewood (45315) *(G-6630)*

Woodbridge Group.................... 419 334-3666
827 Graham Dr Fremont (43420) *(G-7144)*

Woodburn Press Ltd.................... 937 293-9245
405 Littell Ave Dayton (45419) *(G-6085)*

Woodco US, Waverly *Also Called: Clarksville Stave & Veneer Co (G-13864)*

Woodcraft, Dayton *Also Called: Ryanworks Inc (G-5990)*

Woodcraft Industries Inc.................... 440 632-9655
15351 S State Ave Middlefield (44062) *(G-9836)*

WOODCRAFT INDUSTRIES, INC., Middlefield *Also Called: Woodcraft Industries Inc (G-9836)*

Wooden Horse.................... 740 503-5243
204 N Main St Baltimore (43105) *(G-789)*

Woodford Logistics.................... 513 417-8453
15 Sprague Rd South Charleston (45368) *(G-12214)*

Woodhill Plating Works Company.................... 216 883-1344
9114 Reno Ave Cleveland (44105) *(G-4515)*

Woodlawn Rubber Co.................... 513 489-1718
11268 Williamson Rd Blue Ash (45241) *(G-1353)*

Woodman Agitator Inc.................... 440 937-9865
1404 Lear Industrial Pkwy Avon (44011) *(G-744)*

Woodrow Manufacturing Inc.................... 937 399-9333
4300 River Rd Springfield (45502) *(G-12396)*

Woodsage Industries LLC.................... 419 866-8000
7400 Airport Hwy Holland (43528) *(G-7791)*

Woodsage LLC.................... 419 866-8000
7400 Airport Hwy Holland (43528) *(G-7792)*

Woodstock Products Inc.................... 216 641-3811
2914 Broadway Ave Cleveland (44115) *(G-4516)*

Woodworking Shop LLC.................... 513 330-9663
1195 Mound Rd Miamisburg (45342) *(G-9753)*

Woodworks Design.................... 440 693-4414
9005 N Girdle Rd Middlefield (44062) *(G-9837)*

Wooldridge Lumber Co.................... 740 289-4912
3264 Laurel Ridge Rd Piketon (45661) *(G-11316)*

Wooster Abruzzi Company (PA).................... 330 345-3968
3310 Columbus Rd Wooster (44691) *(G-14698)*

Wooster Book Company, The, Wooster *Also Called: Ketman Corporation (G-14658)*

Wooster Brush Company.................... 440 322-8081
870 Infirmary Rd Elyria (44035) *(G-6603)*

Wooster Brush Company.................... 330 264-4440
2550 Daisy Way Wooster (44691) *(G-14699)*

Wooster Daily Record Inc LLC (HQ).................... 330 264-1125
212 E Liberty St Wooster (44691) *(G-14700)*

Wooster Products Inc (PA).................... 330 264-2844
1000 Spruce St Wooster (44691) *(G-14701)*

Wooster Products Inc.................... 330 264-2854
1000 Spruce St Wooster (44691) *(G-14702)*

Worker Automation Inc.................... 937 473-2111
953 Belfast Dr Dayton (45440) *(G-6086)*

Workflowone LLC.................... 877 735-4966
220 E Monument Ave Dayton (45402) *(G-6087)*

Workhorse Group Inc (PA).................... 888 646-5205
3600 Park 42 Dr Ste 160e Sharonville (45241) *(G-11950)*

Workhorse Technologies Inc.................... 888 646-5205
3600 Park 42 Dr Ste 160 Sharonville (45241) *(G-11951)*

Workman Electronic Pdts Inc.................... 419 923-7525
11955 County Road 10-2 Delta (43515) *(G-6215)*

Workman Electronics, Delta *Also Called: Twin Point Inc (G-6214)*

Works In Progress Inc (PA).................... 802 658-3797
3825 Edwards Rd Ste 800 Cincinnati (45209) *(G-3231)*

Workstream Inc (HQ).................... 513 870-4400
3158 Production Dr Fairfield (45014) *(G-6793)*

World Book Company.................... 440 892-3000
28800 Clemens Rd Westlake (44145) *(G-14346)*

World Book/Scott Fetzer Co, Westlake *Also Called: World Book Company (G-14346)*

World Class Carriages LLC.................... 330 857-7811
5090 Mount Eaton Rd S Dalton (44618) *(G-5596)*

World Class Plastics Inc.................... 937 843-3003
7695 State Route 708 Russells Point (43348) *(G-11671)*

World Connections Corps.................... 419 363-2681
10803 Erastus Durbin Rd Rockford (45882) *(G-11631)*

World Digital Imaging, Beavercreek *Also Called: Program Managers Inc (G-995)*

World Harvest Church Inc (PA).................... 614 837-1990
4595 Gender Rd Canal Winchester (43110) *(G-1800)*

World Resource Solutons Corp.................... 614 733-3737
8485 Estates Ct Plain City (43064) *(G-11428)*

World Wide Recyclers Inc.................... 614 554-3296
3755 S High St Columbus (43207) *(G-5372)*

Worldclass Processing Corp
1400 Enterprise Pkwy Twinsburg (44087) *(G-13397)*

Worldmark, Strongsville *Also Called: Donprint Inc (G-12554)*

Worldwide Brands Direct LLC.................................... 937 991-0999
2609 Nordic Rd Dayton (45414) *(G-6088)*

Worldwide Graphics and Sign, Blue Ash *Also Called: Beebe Worldwide Graphics Sign (G-1250)*

Wornick Company, The, West Chester *Also Called: Baxters North America Inc (G-14106)*

Wornick Foods, Blue Ash *Also Called: Baxters North America Inc (G-1249)*

Wornick Foods, Cincinnati *Also Called: Baxters North America Inc (G-2404)*

Wornick Holding Company Inc................................. 513 794-9800
4700 Creek Rd Blue Ash (45242) *(G-1354)*

Worthignton Products Inc...................................... 330 452-7400
1520 Wood Ave Se East Canton (44730) *(G-6381)*

Worthington, Beachwood *Also Called: RSI Company (G-946)*

WORTHINGTON, Worthington *Also Called: Worthington Enterprises Inc (G-14731)*

Worthington Cylinder, Worthington *Also Called: Worthington Cylinder Corp (G-14730)*

Worthington Cylinder Corp.................................... 740 569-4143
245 N Broad St Bremen (43107) *(G-1489)*

Worthington Cylinder Corp.................................... 614 438-7900
1085 Dearborn Dr Columbus (43085) *(G-5373)*

Worthington Cylinder Corp.................................... 440 576-5847
863 State Route 307 E Jefferson (44047) *(G-7987)*

Worthington Cylinder Corp.................................... 614 840-3800
333 Maxtown Rd Westerville (43082) *(G-14242)*

Worthington Cylinder Corp.................................... 330 262-1762
899 Venture Blvd Wooster (44691) *(G-14703)*

Worthington Cylinder Corp (HQ)............................. 614 840-3210
200 W Old Wilson Bridge Rd Worthington (43085) *(G-14730)*

Worthington Energy Innovations, Fremont *Also Called: Professional Supply Inc (G-7128)*

Worthington Enterprises Inc (PA)........................... 614 438-3210
200 W Old Wilson Bridge Rd Worthington (43085) *(G-14731)*

Worthington Foods Inc... 740 453-5501
1675 Fairview Rd Zanesville (43701) *(G-15055)*

Worthington Industries, Cleveland *Also Called: Worthington Mid-Rise Cnstr Inc (G-4517)*

Worthington Mid-Rise Cnstr Inc (HQ)...................... 216 472-1511
3100 E 45th St Ste 400 Cleveland (44127) *(G-4517)*

WORTHINGTON STEEL, Columbus *Also Called: Worthington Steel Inc (G-5374)*

Worthington Steel, Worthington *Also Called: Worthington Steel Company (G-14732)*

Worthington Steel Inc (PA).................................... 614 840-3462
100 W Old Wilson Bridge Rd Columbus (43085) *(G-5374)*

Worthington Steel Company (PA)............................ 800 944-2255
100 W Old Wilson Bridge Rd Worthington (43085) *(G-14732)*

Worthngton Smuel Coil Proc LLC (HQ).................... 330 963-3777
1400 Enterprise Pkwy Twinsburg (44087) *(G-13398)*

Worthngton Stelpac Systems LLC (HQ).................... 614 438-3205
1205 Dearborn Dr Columbus (43085) *(G-5375)*

Worthngton Stl Mexico SA De Cv............................ 800 944-2255
200 W Old Wlson Bridge Rd Worthington (43085) *(G-14733)*

Wpc Successor Inc.. 937 233-6141
6555 Oh 202 Tipp City (45371) *(G-12855)*

Wrap-Tite, Solon *Also Called: B D G Wrap-Tite Inc (G-12081)*

Wray Precision Products Inc................................. 513 228-5000
3650 Turtlecreek Rd Lebanon (45036) *(G-8297)*

Wrayco Industries Inc... 330 688-5617
858 Seasons Rd Stow (44224) *(G-12473)*

Wrayco Manufacturing In..................................... 330 688-5617
5010 Hudson Dr Stow (44224) *(G-12474)*

Wrc, Akron *Also Called: Wrc Holdings Inc (G-358)*

Wrc Holdings Inc... 330 733-6662
1485 Exeter Rd Akron (44306) *(G-358)*

Wre Color Tech, Wadsworth *Also Called: Western Roto Engravers Inc (G-13677)*

Wright Brothers Inc (PA)..................................... 513 731-2222
7825 Cooper Rd Cincinnati (45242) *(G-3232)*

Wright Brothers Global Gas LLC............................ 513 731-2222
7825 Cooper Rd Cincinnati (45242) *(G-3233)*

Wright Enrichment Incorporated............................ 337 783-3096
8000 Memorial Dr Plain City (43064) *(G-11429)*

Wright Group, The, Plain City *Also Called: Wright Enrichment Incorporated (G-11429)*

Wright Tool Company.. 330 848-0600
1 Wright Pl Barberton (44203) *(G-842)*

Wrights Well Service LLC..................................... 740 380-9602
37940 Scout Rd Logan (43138) *(G-8528)*

Wrkco Inc... 216 663-3344
16645 Granite Rd Cleveland (44137) *(G-4518)*

Wrwp, Twinsburg *Also Called: C C M Wire Inc (G-13283)*

Wrwp LLC.. 330 425-3421
1920 Case Pkwy S Twinsburg (44087) *(G-13399)*

Ws Thermal Process Tech Inc............................... 440 385-6829
8301 W Erie Ave Lorain (44053) *(G-8587)*

Wsi Seller Inc... 330 379-0270
323 N Arlington St Akron (44305) *(G-359)*

Wt Acquisition Company Ltd................................. 513 577-7980
2130 Waycross Rd Cincinnati (45240) *(G-3234)*

Wtd Real Estate Inc.. 440 934-5305
1280 Moore Rd Avon (44011) *(G-745)*

Wulco Inc (PA).. 513 679-2600
6899 Steger Dr Ste A Cincinnati (45237) *(G-3235)*

Wulco Inc... 513 679-2600
6900 Steger Dr Cincinnati (45237) *(G-3236)*

Wulco Inc... 513 379-6115
1010 Eaton Ave Ste B # B Hamilton (45013) *(G-7539)*

Wurms Woodworking Company.............................. 419 492-2184
725 W Mansfield St New Washington (44854) *(G-10484)*

Wurtec Manufacturing Service.............................. 419 726-1066
6200 Brent Dr Toledo (43611) *(G-13180)*

Wurth Elecktronik, Miamisburg *Also Called: Wurth Electronics Ics Inc (G-9754)*

Wurth Electronics Ics Inc.................................... 937 415-7700
1982 Byers Rd Miamisburg (45342) *(G-9754)*

WW Williams Company LLC (PA)............................ 614 228-5000
400 Metro Pl N Ste 201 Dublin (43017) *(G-6362)*

Www.slidepartsexpress.com, Willoughby *Also Called: Quality Specialists Inc (G-14513)*

Wyandot Dolomite Inc... 419 396-7641
1794 County Highway 99 Carey (43316) *(G-2064)*

Wyandot Snacks, Marion *Also Called: Wyandot Usa LLC (G-9006)*

Wyandot Usa LLC (PA).. 740 383-4031
135 Wyandot Ave Marion (43302) *(G-9006)*

Wyandotte Winery LLC.. 614 357-7522
4640 Wyandotte Dr Columbus (43230) *(G-5376)*

Wyatt Industries LLC.. 330 954-1790
965 Cascades Dr Aurora (44202) *(G-694)*

Wyman Gordon, Cleveland *Also Called: Wyman-Gordon Company (G-4519)*

Wyman-Gordon Company...................................... 216 341-0085
3097 E 61st St Cleveland (44127) *(G-4519)*

Wyoming Casing Service Inc................................. 330 479-8785
1414 Raff Rd Sw Canton (44710) *(G-2049)*

Wyse Industrial Carts Inc.................................... 419 923-7353
10510 County Road 12 Wauseon (43567) *(G-13862)*

Wysong Gravel Co Inc... 937 452-1523
120 Camden College Corner Rd Camden (45311) *(G-1769)*

Wysong Gravel Co Inc (PA).................................. 937 456-4539
2332 State Route 503 N West Alexandria (45381) *(G-13924)*

Wysong Gravel Co Inc... 937 839-5497
2032 State Route 503 N West Alexandria (45381) *(G-13925)*

X L Sand and Gravel Co...................................... 330 426-9876
9289 Jackman Rd Negley (44441) *(G-10316)*

X M C, Sylvania *Also Called: Don-Ell Corporation (G-12705)*

X M C Division, Sylvania *Also Called: Don-Ell Corporation (G-12704)*

X-Mil Inc... 937 444-1323
220 Homan Way Mount Orab (45154) *(G-10224)*

X-Treme Finishes Inc.. 330 474-0614
4821 Brookhaven Dr North Royalton (44133) *(G-10790)*

X44 Corp.. 330 657-2335
1601 Mill St W Peninsula (44264) *(G-11188)*

Xact Spec Industries LLC.................................... 440 543-8157
16959 Munn Rd Chagrin Falls (44023) *(G-2193)*

Xact Spec Industries LLC (PA).............................. 440 543-8157
16959 Munn Rd Chagrin Falls (44023) *(G-2194)*

Xaloy LLC (PA).. 330 726-4000
375 Victoria Rd Ste 1 Austintown (44515) *(G-709)*

Xapc Co... 216 362-4100
15583 Brookpark Rd Cleveland (44142) *(G-4520)*

XCEL Mold and Machine Inc................................. 330 499-8450
7661 Freedom Ave Nw Canton (44720) *(G-2050)*

ALPHABETIC

Xchanging... 440 914-2000
  31500 Solon Rd Solon (44139) *(G-12209)*

Xcite Systems Corporation............................. 513 965-0300
  675 Cincinnati Batavia Pike Cincinnati (45245) *(G-2318)*

Xellia Pharmaceuticals, Beachwood *Also Called: Xellia Pharmaceuticals Inc (G-958)*

Xellia Pharmaceuticals Inc (DH)....................... 847 947-0200
  2000 Auburn Dr Ste 200 Beachwood (44122) *(G-958)*

Xenia City Water Treatment Div, Xenia *Also Called: City of Xenia (G-14758)*

Xerion Advanced Battery Corp.......................... 720 229-0697
  3100 Research Blvd Ste 320 Kettering (45420) *(G-8124)*

Xgs.it, West Chester *Also Called: It XCEL Consulting LLC (G-14016)*

Xomox Corporation...................................... 513 745-6000
  4477 Malsbary Rd Blue Ash (45242) *(G-1355)*

Xomox Corporation...................................... 936 271-6500
  4444 Cooper Rd Cincinnati (45242) *(G-3237)*

Xomox Pft Corp.. 936 271-6500
  4444 Cooper Rd Cincinnati (45242) *(G-3238)*

Xorb Corporation.. 419 354-6021
  455 W Woodland Cir Bowling Green (43402) *(G-1449)*

Xperion E & E USA LLC.................................. 740 788-9560
  1475 James Pkwy Heath (43056) *(G-7605)*

Xponet Inc.. 440 354-6617
  20 Elberta Rd Painesville (44077) *(G-11123)*

XS Smith Inc (PA)....................................... 252 940-5060
  5513 Vine St Ste 1 Cincinnati (45217) *(G-3239)*

Xtek Inc (PA)... 513 733-7800
  11451 Reading Rd Cincinnati (45241) *(G-3240)*

Xto Energy, Bellaire *Also Called: Xto Energy Inc (G-1090)*

Xto Energy Inc.. 740 671-9901
  2358 W 23rd St Bellaire (43906) *(G-1090)*

Xtreme Outdoors LLC.................................... 330 731-4137
  1519 Boettler Rd Ste A Uniontown (44685) *(G-13429)*

Xunlight Corporation.................................... 419 469-8600
  3145 Nebraska Ave Toledo (43607) *(G-13181)*

Xylem Inc.. 937 767-7241
  1700 Brannum Ln Ste 1725 Yellow Springs (45387) *(G-14792)*

Xylem Ysi, A Xylem Brand, Yellow Springs *Also Called: Ysi Environmental Inc (G-14795)*

Y City Recycling LLC.................................... 740 452-2500
  4005 All American Way Zanesville (43701) *(G-15056)*

Y O H Inc.. 614 488-2861
  2550 W 5th Ave Columbus (43204) *(G-5377)*

Yachiyo Manufacturing America, Columbus *Also Called: Motherson Ychiyo Auto Tech PDT (G-5113)*

Yamada North America Inc.............................. 937 462-7111
  9000 Columbus Cincinnati Rd South Charleston (45368) *(G-12215)*

Yanfeng Intl Auto Tech US I LL......................... 419 633-1873
  918 S Union St Bryan (43506) *(G-1668)*

Yanfeng Intl Auto Tech US I LL......................... 616 834-9422
  715 E South St Bryan (43506) *(G-1669)*

Yanfeng Intl Auto Tech US I LL......................... 419 662-4905
  7560 Arbor Dr Northwood (43619) *(G-10815)*

Yanfeng Intl Auto Tech US II L......................... 419 636-4211
  918 S Union St Bryan (43506) *(G-1670)*

Yanke Bionics Inc (PA)................................. 330 762-6411
  303 W Exchange St Akron (44302) *(G-360)*

Yankee Candle Company Inc............................ 413 712-9416
  175 Heritage Dr Etna (43062) *(G-6636)*

Yankee Wire Cloth Products Inc........................ 740 545-9129
  221 W Main St West Lafayette (43845) *(G-14174)*

YAR Corporation.. 330 652-1222
  406 S Main St Niles (44446) *(G-10611)*

Yarder Manufacturing Company (PA).................... 419 476-3933
  722 Phillips Ave Toledo (43612) *(G-13182)*

Yaskawa America Inc.................................... 937 847-6200
  100 Automation Way Miamisburg (45342) *(G-9755)*

Yaskawa America Inc.................................... 937 440-2600
  1050 S Dorset Rd Troy (45373) *(G-13261)*

Yaya's, Kent *Also Called: Mark Grzianis St Treats Ex Inc (G-8049)*

Ye Olde Mille Shoppe, Utica *Also Called: Velvet Ice Cream Company (G-13488)*

Yellow Creek Casting Co Inc............................ 330 532-4608
  18141 Fife Coal Rd Wellsville (43968) *(G-13915)*

Yellow Springs International, Yellow Springs *Also Called: Ysi Incorporated (G-14796)*

Yellow Springs Pottery LLC............................. 937 767-1666
  222 Xenia Ave Ste 1 Yellow Springs (45387) *(G-14793)*

Yespress Graphics LLC.................................. 614 899-1403
  515 S State St Westerville (43081) *(G-14282)*

Yipes Stripes, Englewood *Also Called: TCS Schindler & Co LLC (G-6624)*

Yizumi-HPM Corporation................................ 740 382-5600
  3424 State Rt 309 Iberia (43325) *(G-7885)*

YKK AP America Inc.................................... 513 942-7200
  8748 Jacquemin Dr Ste 400 West Chester (45069) *(G-14094)*

YKK USA, West Chester *Also Called: YKK AP America Inc (G-14094)*

Yockey Group Inc....................................... 513 860-9053
  9053 Le Saint Dr West Chester (45014) *(G-14095)*

Yoder & Frey Inc....................................... 419 445-2070
  3649 County Road 24 Archbold (43502) *(G-513)*

Yoder Industries Inc (PA).............................. 937 278-5769
  2520 Needmore Rd Dayton (45414) *(G-6089)*

Yoder Lumber Co Inc (PA).............................. 330 893-3121
  4515 Township Road 367 Millersburg (44654) *(G-10020)*

Yoder Lumber Co Inc.................................... 330 674-1435
  7100 County Road 407 Millersburg (44654) *(G-10021)*

Yoder Lumber Co Inc.................................... 330 893-3131
  3799 County Road 70 Sugarcreek (44681) *(G-12658)*

Yoder Sharpening Ltd.................................. 330 359-0767
  14280 Durstine Rd Dundee (44624) *(G-6373)*

Yoder Window & Siding Ltd (PA)........................ 330 695-6960
  7846 Harrison Rd Fredericksburg (44627) *(G-7072)*

Yoder Window and Siding, Fredericksburg *Also Called: Yoder Window & Siding Ltd (G-7072)*

Yoder's Cider Barn, Gambier *Also Called: Yoders Fine Foods LLC (G-7215)*

Yoders Fine Foods LLC.................................. 740 668-4961
  3361 Martinsburg Rd Gambier (43022) *(G-7215)*

Yoders Produce Inc (PA)................................ 330 695-5900
  9599 S Apple Creek Rd Fredericksburg (44627) *(G-7073)*

Yokohama Inds Amricas Ohio Inc........................ 440 352-3321
  474 Newell St Painesville (44077) *(G-11124)*

Yokohama Tire Corporation............................. 440 352-3321
  474 Newell St Painesville (44077) *(G-11125)*

Yokohama Tws North America Inc (DH)................... 330 436-5168
  1501 Exeter Rd Akron (44306) *(G-361)*

Yonezawa Usa Inc...................................... 614 799-2210
  7920 Corporate Blvd Ste A Plain City (43064) *(G-11430)*

Yost Labs Inc.. 740 876-4936
  630 2nd St Portsmouth (45662) *(G-11480)*

Yost Superior Co....................................... 937 323-7591
  300 S Center St Ste 1 Springfield (45501) *(G-12397)*

Yotec, South Charleston *Also Called: Yamada North America Inc (G-12215)*

Young & Bertke Air Systems Co., Cincinnati *Also Called: Rmt Acquisition Inc (G-3050)*

Young Regulator Company Inc........................... 440 232-9452
  7100 Krick Rd Ste A Bedford (44146) *(G-1066)*

Youngs Jersey Dairy Inc................................ 937 325-0629
  6880 Springfield Xenia Rd Yellow Springs (45387) *(G-14794)*

Youngs Locker Serv & Meat Proc, Danville *Also Called: Youngs Locker Service Inc (G-5601)*

Youngs Locker Service Inc.............................. 740 599-6833
  16201 Nashville Rd Danville (43014) *(G-5601)*

Youngs Publishing Inc.................................. 937 259-6575
  4130 Linden Ave Ste 150 Dayton (45432) *(G-5626)*

Youngs Sand & Gravel Co Inc........................... 419 994-3040
  689 State Route 39 Loudonville (44842) *(G-8597)*

Youngstown Bolt & Supply Co........................... 330 799-3201
  340 N Meridian Rd Youngstown (44509) *(G-14967)*

Youngstown Burial Vault Co............................. 330 782-0015
  316 Forsythe Ave Girard (44420) *(G-7282)*

Youngstown Curve Form Inc............................. 330 744-3028
  1102 Rigby St Youngstown (44506) *(G-14968)*

Youngstown Fence Incorporated........................ 330 788-8110
  235 E Indianola Ave Youngstown (44507) *(G-14969)*

Youngstown Hard Chrome Pltg Gr....................... 330 758-9721
  8451 Southern Blvd Youngstown (44512) *(G-14970)*

Youngstown Heat Trting Ntrding......................... 330 788-3025
  1118 Meadowbrook Ave Youngstown (44512) *(G-14971)*

Youngstown Letter Shop Inc............................ 330 793-4935
  3650 Connecticut Ave Youngstown (44515) *(G-14972)*

2025 Harris Ohio
Industrial Directory

(G-0000) Company's Geographic Section entry number

Youngstown Metal Fabricating, Youngstown *Also Called: M F Y Inc (G-14890)*

Youngstown Plastic Tooling (PA)................................330 782-7222
1209 Velma Ct Youngstown (44512) *(G-14973)*

Youngstown Pre-Press Inc................................330 793-3690
3691 Leharps Dr Youngstown (44515) *(G-14974)*

Youngstown Rubber Products, Youngstown *Also Called: Mid-State Sales Inc (G-14900)*

Youngstown Shade & Alum LLC................................330 782-2313
3335 South Ave Youngstown (44502) *(G-14975)*

Youngstown Specialty Mtls Inc................................330 259-1110
571 Andrews Ave Youngstown (44505) *(G-14976)*

Youngstown Tool & Die Company................................330 747-4464
2572 Salt Springs Rd Youngstown (44509) *(G-14977)*

Youngstown Tube Co................................330 743-7414
401 Andrews Ave Youngstown (44505) *(G-14978)*

Youngstown-Kenworth Inc (PA)................................330 534-9761
7255 Hubbard Masury Rd Hubbard (44425) *(G-7819)*

Your Carpenter Inc................................216 621-2166
2403 Saint Clair Ave Ne Cleveland (44114) *(G-4521)*

Yourway Coatings LLC................................216 651-9022
8617 Clinton Rd Brooklyn (44144) *(G-1526)*

Ysi, Yellow Springs *Also Called: Xylem Inc (G-14792)*

Ysi Environmental Inc................................937 767-7241
1725 Brannum Ln Yellow Springs (45387) *(G-14795)*

Ysi Incorporated (HQ)................................937 767-7241
1700 Brannum Ln # 1725 Yellow Springs (45387) *(G-14796)*

Ysk Corporation................................740 774-7315
1 Colomet Rd Chillicothe (45601) *(G-2288)*

Yukon Industries Inc................................440 478-4174
7665 Mentor Ave Ste 113 Mentor (44060) *(G-9655)*

Yusa Corporation (HQ)................................740 335-0335
151 Jamison Rd Nw Washington Court Hou (43160) *(G-13824)*

Yutzy Woodworking Ltd................................330 359-6166
2441 Us Route 62 Dundee (44624) *(G-6374)*

Yz Enterprises Inc................................419 893-8777
1930 Indian Wood Cir Ste 100 Maumee (43537) *(G-9331)*

Z & Z Manufacturing Inc................................440 953-2800
4765 E 355th St Willoughby (44094) *(G-14553)*

Z Line Kitchen and Bath, Marysville *Also Called: Z Line Kitchen and Bath LLC (G-9055)*

Z Line Kitchen and Bath LLC (PA)................................614 777-5004
916 Delaware Ave Marysville (43040) *(G-9055)*

Z M O Company (PA)................................614 875-0230
2140 Eakin Rd Columbus (43223) *(G-5378)*

Z M O Oil, Columbus *Also Called: Z M O Company (G-5378)*

Zaclon LLC................................216 271-1601
2981 Independence Rd Cleveland (44115) *(G-4522)*

Zaenkert Srvying Essntials Inc................................513 738-2917
7461a Cincinnati Brookville Rd Okeana (45053) *(G-10931)*

Zane Petroleum Inc................................740 454-8779
575 S 3rd St Columbus (43215) *(G-5379)*

Zaner-Bloser Inc (HQ)................................614 486-0221
1800 Watermark Dr Columbus (43215) *(G-5380)*

Zanesville Fabricators Inc................................740 452-2439
2981 E Military Rd Zanesville (43701) *(G-15057)*

Zanesville Pallet Co Inc................................740 454-3700
2235 Licking Rd Zanesville (43701) *(G-15058)*

Zarbana Alum Extrusions LLC................................330 482-5092
41738 Esterly Dr Columbiana (44408) *(G-4635)*

Zarbana Industries Inc................................330 482-5092
41738 Esterly Dr Columbiana (44408) *(G-4636)*

Zaytran Inc................................440 324-2814
41535 Schadden Rd Elyria (44035) *(G-6604)*

Zebco Industries Inc................................740 654-4510
211 N Columbus St Lancaster (43130) *(G-8233)*

Zebec of North America Inc................................513 829-5533
210 Donald Dr Fairfield (45014) *(G-6794)*

Zed Digital, Columbus *Also Called: IPA Ltd (G-5024)*

Zed Industries Inc................................937 667-8407
3580 Lightner Rd Vandalia (45377) *(G-13584)*

Zeda Inc................................513 966-4633
11560 Goldcoast Dr Cincinnati (45249) *(G-3241)*

Zehrco-Giancola Composites Inc (PA)................................440 994-6317
1501 W 47th St Ashtabula (44004) *(G-623)*

Zeiger Industries Inc................................330 484-4413
4704 Wiseland Ave Se Canton (44707) *(G-2051)*

Zekelman Industries Inc................................216 910-3700
3201 Entp Pkwy Ste 150 Beachwood (44122) *(G-959)*

Zekelman Industries Inc................................740 432-2146
9208 Jeffrey Dr Cambridge (43725) *(G-1766)*

Zelaya Stoneworks LLC................................513 777-8030
7590 Wyandot Ln Ste 1 Liberty Township (45044) *(G-8380)*

Zen Industries Inc................................216 432-3240
6200 Harvard Ave Cleveland (44105) *(G-4523)*

Zena Baby Soap Company................................216 317-6433
6651 Hedgeline Dr Bedford Heights (44146) *(G-1084)*

Zenex International................................440 232-4155
7777 First Pl Bedford (44146) *(G-1067)*

Zenni Usa Inc................................614 439-9850
4531 Industrial Center Dr Columbus (43207) *(G-5381)*

Zenni USA LLC, Columbus *Also Called: Zenni Usa Inc (G-5381)*

Zephyr Industries Inc................................419 281-4485
600 Township Road 1500 Ashland (44805) *(G-581)*

Zeres Inc................................419 354-5555
2018 Clearwater Cir Bowling Green (43402) *(G-1450)*

Zero-D Products Inc................................440 942-5005
37939 Stevens Blvd Willoughby (44094) *(G-14554)*

ZF Active Safety & Elec US LLC................................216 750-2400
8333 Rockside Rd Cleveland (44125) *(G-4524)*

ZF Active Safety & Elec US LLC................................419 726-5599
5915 Jason St Toledo (43611) *(G-13183)*

ZF Active Safety US Inc................................419 237-2511
705 N Fayette St Fayette (43521) *(G-6825)*

Zide Screen Printing, Marietta *Also Called: Zide Sport Shop of Ohio Inc (G-8963)*

Zide Sport Shop of Ohio Inc................................740 373-8199
118 Industry Rd Marietta (45750) *(G-8963)*

Zidian Management LLC (PA)................................330 743-6050
574 Mcclurg Rd Boardman (44512) *(G-1379)*

Zidian Manufacturing LLC................................330 965-8455
500 Mcclurg Rd Boardman (44512) *(G-1380)*

Zidian Specialty Foods, Youngstown *Also Called: John Zidian Company (G-14883)*

Zie Bart Rhino Linings Toledo................................419 841-2886
3343 N Holland Sylvania Rd Toledo (43615) *(G-13184)*

Ziegler Oil Co, Dover *Also Called: Ziegler Tire and Supply Co (G-6267)*

Ziegler Tire and Supply Co................................330 434-7126
547 Wolf Ledges Pkwy Akron (44311) *(G-362)*

Ziegler Tire and Supply Co................................330 477-3463
4300 Tuscarawas St W Canton (44708) *(G-2052)*

Ziegler Tire and Supply Co................................330 343-7739
411 Commercial Pkwy Dover (44622) *(G-6267)*

Ziegler Tire Oil, Akron *Also Called: Ziegler Tire and Supply Co (G-363)*

Zilla................................614 763-5311
6728 Liggett Rd Ste 110 Dublin (43016) *(G-6363)*

Zimcom Internet Solutions, Cincinnati *Also Called: One Cloud Services LLC (G-2931)*

Zimmer Enterprises Inc (PA)................................937 428-1057
911 Senate Dr Dayton (45459) *(G-6090)*

Zimmer Orthopaedic Surgical, Dover *Also Called: Zimmer Surgical Inc (G-6268)*

Zimmer Surgical Inc................................800 321-5533
200 W Ohio Ave Dover (44622) *(G-6268)*

Zimmerman Steel & Sup Co LLC................................330 828-1010
18543 Davis Rd Dalton (44618) *(G-5597)*

Zinkan Enterprises Inc (PA)................................330 487-1500
1919 Case Pkwy Twinsburg (44087) *(G-13400)*

Zion Industries Inc (PA)................................330 483-4650
6229 Grafton Rd Valley City (44280) *(G-13523)*

Zip Center, The-Division, Marietta *Also Called: Richardson Printing Corp (G-8941)*

Zippitycom Print LLC................................216 438-0001
1600 E 23rd St Cleveland (44114) *(G-4525)*

Zipscene, Cincinnati *Also Called: Zipscene LLC (G-3242)*

Zipscene LLC................................513 201-5174
615 Main St Fl 5 Cincinnati (45202) *(G-3242)*

Zircoa Inc (PA)................................440 248-0500
31501 Solon Rd Cleveland (44139) *(G-4526)*

Zoia, Cleveland *Also Called: Artistic Metal Spinning Inc (G-3372)*

Zook Enterprises LLC (PA).. 440 543-1010
  16809 Park Circle Dr Chagrin Falls (44023) *(G-2195)*

Zorich Industries Inc.. 330 482-9803
  1400 Wardingsley Ave Columbiana (44408) *(G-4637)*

Zsi Manufacturing Inc... 440 266-0701
  8059 Crile Rd Concord Township (44077) *(G-5398)*

Zts Inc... 513 271-2557
  5628 Wooster Pike Cincinnati (45227) *(G-3243)*

Zullix LLC.. 440 536-9300
  18500 Lake Rd Rocky River (44116) *(G-11641)*

Zurn Industries LLC... 814 455-0921
  4501 Sutphen Ct Hilliard (43026) *(G-7712)*

Zwanenberg Food Group (usa) Inc (DH)............................ 513 682-6000
  3640 Muddy Creek Rd Cincinnati (45238) *(G-3244)*

Zygo Inc.. 513 281-0888
  2832 Jefferson Ave Cincinnati (45219) *(G-3245)*

A

ABRASIVES
ABRASIVES: Coated
ACCELERATION INDICATORS & SYSTEM COMPONENTS: Aerospace
ACIDS
ACIDS: Hydrochloric
ACIDS: Inorganic
ACIDS: Sulfuric, Oleum
ACOUSTICAL BOARD & TILE
ACRYLIC RESINS
ACTUATORS: Indl, NEC
ADAPTERS: Well
ADDITIVE BASED PLASTIC MATERIALS: Plasticizers
ADDRESSING SVCS
ADHESIVES
ADHESIVES & SEALANTS
ADHESIVES & SEALANTS WHOLESALERS
ADHESIVES: Adhesives, plastic
ADHESIVES: Epoxy
ADVERTISING AGENCIES
ADVERTISING AGENCIES: Consultants
ADVERTISING DISPLAY PRDTS
ADVERTISING REPRESENTATIVES: Electronic Media
ADVERTISING REPRESENTATIVES: Newspaper
ADVERTISING SPECIALTIES, WHOLESALE
ADVERTISING SVCS: Direct Mail
ADVERTISING SVCS: Display
ADVERTISING SVCS: Outdoor
ADVERTISING SVCS: Sample Distribution
AERIAL WORK PLATFORMS
AEROSOLS
AGRICULTURAL EQPT: BARN, SILO, POULTRY, DAIRY/ LIVESTOCK MACH
AGRICULTURAL EQPT: Elevators, Farm
AGRICULTURAL EQPT: Fertilizing Machinery
AGRICULTURAL EQPT: Grounds Mowing Eqpt
AGRICULTURAL EQPT: Tractors, Farm
AGRICULTURAL EQPT: Turf & Grounds Eqpt
AGRICULTURAL MACHINERY & EQPT: Wholesalers
AIR CLEANING SYSTEMS
AIR CONDITIONERS: Motor Vehicle
AIR CONDITIONING & VENTILATION EQPT & SPLYS: Wholesales
AIR CONDITIONING EQPT
AIR CONDITIONING REPAIR SVCS
AIR CONDITIONING UNITS: Complete, Domestic Or Indl
AIR DUCT CLEANING SVCS
AIR MATTRESSES: Plastic
AIR PURIFICATION EQPT
AIRCRAFT & AEROSPACE FLIGHT INSTRUMENTS & GUIDANCE SYSTEMS
AIRCRAFT & HEAVY EQPT REPAIR SVCS
AIRCRAFT ASSEMBLY PLANTS
AIRCRAFT CONTROL SYSTEMS:
AIRCRAFT ELECTRICAL EQPT REPAIR SVCS
AIRCRAFT ENGINES & ENGINE PARTS: Airfoils
AIRCRAFT ENGINES & ENGINE PARTS: Nonelectric Starters
AIRCRAFT ENGINES & ENGINE PARTS: Pumps
AIRCRAFT ENGINES & ENGINE PARTS: Research & Development, Mfr
AIRCRAFT ENGINES & PARTS
AIRCRAFT EQPT & SPLYS WHOLESALERS
AIRCRAFT MAINTENANCE & REPAIR SVCS
AIRCRAFT PARTS & AUXILIARY EQPT: Assys, Subassemblies/Parts
AIRCRAFT PARTS & AUXILIARY EQPT: Body & Wing Assys & Parts
AIRCRAFT PARTS & AUXILIARY EQPT: Body Assemblies & Parts
AIRCRAFT PARTS & AUXILIARY EQPT: Brakes
AIRCRAFT PARTS & AUXILIARY EQPT: Landing Assemblies & Brakes
AIRCRAFT PARTS & AUXILIARY EQPT: Lighting/Landing Gear Assy
AIRCRAFT PARTS & AUXILIARY EQPT: Military Eqpt & Armament

AIRCRAFT PARTS & AUXILIARY EQPT: Research & Development, Mfr
AIRCRAFT PARTS & AUXILIARY EQPT: Tanks, Fuel
AIRCRAFT PARTS & EQPT, NEC
AIRCRAFT PARTS WHOLESALERS
AIRCRAFT PROPELLERS & PARTS
AIRCRAFT SERVICING & REPAIRING
AIRCRAFT TURBINES
AIRCRAFT WHEELS
AIRCRAFT: Airplanes, Fixed Or Rotary Wing
AIRCRAFT: Motorized
AIRCRAFT: Research & Development, Manufacturer
AIRPORTS, FLYING FIELDS & SVCS
ALARMS: Fire
ALCOHOL: Ethyl & Ethanol
ALKALIES & CHLORINE
ALLOYS: Additive, Exc Copper Or Made In Blast Furnaces
ALTERNATORS & GENERATORS: Battery Charging
ALTERNATORS: Automotive
ALUMINUM
ALUMINUM PRDTS
ALUMINUM: Coil & Sheet
ALUMINUM: Ingots & Slabs
ALUMINUM: Pigs
ALUMINUM: Rolling & Drawing
AMMUNITION: Arming & Fusing Devices
AMMUNITION: Shot, Steel
AMMUNITION: Small Arms
AMPLIFIERS
AMUSEMENT & RECREATION SVCS: Exhibition Operation
AMUSEMENT & RECREATION SVCS: Exposition Operation
AMUSEMENT & RECREATION SVCS: Golf Club, Membership
AMUSEMENT & RECREATION SVCS: Physical Fitness Instruction
AMUSEMENT PARK DEVICES & RIDES
ANALYZERS: Network
ANIMAL FEED & SUPPLEMENTS: Livestock & Poultry
ANIMAL FEED: Wholesalers
ANIMAL FOOD & SUPPLEMENTS: Bird Food, Prepared
ANIMAL FOOD & SUPPLEMENTS: Cat
ANIMAL FOOD & SUPPLEMENTS: Dog
ANIMAL FOOD & SUPPLEMENTS: Dog & Cat
ANIMAL FOOD & SUPPLEMENTS: Feed Premixes
ANIMAL FOOD & SUPPLEMENTS: Feed Supplements
ANIMAL FOOD & SUPPLEMENTS: Livestock
ANIMAL FOOD & SUPPLEMENTS: Pet, Exc Dog & Cat, Canned
ANIMAL FOOD & SUPPLEMENTS: Pet, Exc Dog & Cat, Dry
ANIMAL FOOD & SUPPLEMENTS: Poultry
ANIMAL FOOD/SUPPLEMENTS: Feeds Fm Meat/Meat/Veg Combnd Meals
ANNEALING: Metal
ANODIZING EQPT
ANODIZING SVC
ANTENNA REPAIR & INSTALLATION SVCS
ANTENNAS: Radar Or Communications
ANTENNAS: Receiving
ANTIBIOTICS
ANTIFREEZE
ANTIQUE REPAIR & RESTORATION SVCS, EXC FURNITURE & AUTOS
APPAREL ACCESS STORES
APPAREL DESIGNERS: Commercial
APPLIANCE PARTS: Porcelain Enameled
APPLIANCES, HOUSEHOLD OR COIN OPERATED: Laundry Dryers
APPLIANCES, HOUSEHOLD: Kitchen, Major, Exc Refrigs & Stoves
APPLIANCES, HOUSEHOLD: Laundry Machines, Incl CoinOperated
APPLIANCES, HOUSEHOLD: Refrigs, Mechanical & Absorption
APPLIANCES: Household, Refrigerators & Freezers
APPLIANCES: Major, Cooking
APPLIANCES: Small, Electric
APPLICATIONS SOFTWARE PROGRAMMING

APPRAISAL SVCS, EXC REAL ESTATE
APRONS: Rubber, Vulcanized Or Rubberized Fabric
AQUARIUMS & ACCESS: Plastic
ARCHITECTURAL SVCS
ARMATURE REPAIRING & REWINDING SVC
ART DEALERS & GALLERIES
ART MARBLE: Concrete
ARTS & CRAFTS SCHOOL
ASBESTOS PRDTS: Roofing, Felt Roll
ASBESTOS PRODUCTS
ASPHALT & ASPHALT PRDTS
ASPHALT COATINGS & SEALERS
ASPHALT MIXTURES WHOLESALERS
ASPHALT PLANTS INCLUDING GRAVEL MIX TYPE
ASSEMBLING SVC: Plumbing Fixture Fittings, Plastic
ASSOCIATION FOR THE HANDICAPPED
ASSOCIATIONS: Business
ASSOCIATIONS: Real Estate Management
ASSOCIATIONS: Scientists'
ASSOCIATIONS: Trade
ATOMIZERS
AUDIO & VIDEO EQPT, EXC COMMERCIAL
AUDIO COMPONENTS
AUDIO ELECTRONIC SYSTEMS
AUTO & HOME SUPPLY STORES: Auto & Truck Eqpt & Parts
AUTO & HOME SUPPLY STORES: Automotive Access
AUTO & HOME SUPPLY STORES: Automotive parts
AUTO & HOME SUPPLY STORES: Batteries, Automotive & Truck
AUTO & HOME SUPPLY STORES: Trailer Hitches, Automotive
AUTO & HOME SUPPLY STORES: Truck Eqpt & Parts
AUTO SPLYS & PARTS, NEW, WHSLE: Exhaust Sys, Mufflers, Etc
AUTOMATIC REGULATING CONTROL: Building Svcs Monitoring, Auto
AUTOMATIC REGULATING CONTROLS: AC & Refrigeration
AUTOMATIC REGULATING CONTROLS: Appliance, Exc AirCond/Refr
AUTOMATIC REGULATING CONTROLS: Hardware, Environmental Reg
AUTOMATIC REGULATING CTRLS: Damper, Pneumatic Or Electric
AUTOMATIC TELLER MACHINES
AUTOMOBILE FINANCE LEASING
AUTOMOBILES & OTHER MOTOR VEHICLES WHOLESALERS
AUTOMOBILES: Wholesalers
AUTOMOTIVE & TRUCK GENERAL REPAIR SVC
AUTOMOTIVE BODY SHOP
AUTOMOTIVE BODY, PAINT & INTERIOR REPAIR & MAINTENANCE SVC
AUTOMOTIVE CUSTOMIZING SVCS, NONFACTORY BASIS
AUTOMOTIVE GLASS REPLACEMENT SHOPS
AUTOMOTIVE PAINT SHOP
AUTOMOTIVE PARTS, ACCESS & SPLYS
AUTOMOTIVE PARTS: Plastic
AUTOMOTIVE PRDTS: Rubber
AUTOMOTIVE RADIATOR REPAIR SHOPS
AUTOMOTIVE REPAIR SHOPS: Diesel Engine Repair
AUTOMOTIVE REPAIR SHOPS: Electrical Svcs
AUTOMOTIVE REPAIR SHOPS: Engine Rebuilding
AUTOMOTIVE REPAIR SHOPS: Engine Repair
AUTOMOTIVE REPAIR SHOPS: Machine Shop
AUTOMOTIVE REPAIR SHOPS: Muffler Shop, Sale/Rpr/ Installation
AUTOMOTIVE REPAIR SHOPS: Rebuilding & Retreading Tires
AUTOMOTIVE REPAIR SHOPS: Tire Recapping
AUTOMOTIVE REPAIR SHOPS: Tire Repair Shop
AUTOMOTIVE REPAIR SHOPS: Trailer Repair
AUTOMOTIVE REPAIR SHOPS: Truck Engine Repair, Exc Indl
AUTOMOTIVE REPAIR SVC
AUTOMOTIVE SPLYS & PARTS, NEW, WHOL: Auto Servicing Eqpt

AUTOMOTIVE SPLYS & PARTS, NEW, WHOLESALE:
Clutches
AUTOMOTIVE SPLYS & PARTS, NEW, WHOLESALE:
Engines/Eng Parts
AUTOMOTIVE SPLYS & PARTS, NEW, WHOLESALE:
Filters, Air & Oil
AUTOMOTIVE SPLYS & PARTS, NEW, WHOLESALE: Splys
AUTOMOTIVE SPLYS & PARTS, NEW, WHOLESALE:
Stampings
AUTOMOTIVE SPLYS & PARTS, NEW, WHOLESALE: Tools
& Eqpt
AUTOMOTIVE SPLYS & PARTS, NEW, WHOLESALE: Trailer
Parts
AUTOMOTIVE SPLYS & PARTS, NEW, WHOLESALE:
Wheels
AUTOMOTIVE SPLYS & PARTS, WHOLESALE, NEC
AUTOMOTIVE SPLYS/PART, NEW, WHOL: Spring, Shock
Absorb/Strut
AUTOMOTIVE SVCS, EXC REPAIR & CARWASHES:
Lubrication
AUTOMOTIVE SVCS, EXC REPAIR & CARWASHES: Trailer
Maintenance
AUTOMOTIVE SVCS, EXC RPR/CARWASHES: High Perf
Auto Rpr/Svc
AUTOMOTIVE TRANSMISSION REPAIR SVC
AUTOMOTIVE WELDING SVCS
AUTOMOTIVE: Bodies
AUTOMOTIVE: Seat Frames, Metal
AUTOMOTIVE: Seating
AUTOTRANSFORMERS: Electric
AVIATION SCHOOL
AWNINGS & CANOPIES: Awnings, Fabric, From Purchased
Matls
AWNINGS: Fiberglass
AWNINGS: Metal
AXLES

B

BACKHOES
BADGES: Identification & Insignia
BAGS & CONTAINERS: Textile, Exc Sleeping
BAGS & SACKS: Shipping & Shopping
BAGS: Canvas
BAGS: Cellophane
BAGS: Duffle, Canvas, Made From Purchased Materials
BAGS: Food Storage & Frozen Food, Plastic
BAGS: Food Storage & Trash, Plastic
BAGS: Paper
BAGS: Paper, Made From Purchased Materials
BAGS: Plastic
BAGS: Plastic & Pliofilm
BAGS: Plastic, Made From Purchased Materials
BAGS: Rubber Or Rubberized Fabric
BAGS: Shipping
BAGS: Shopping, Made From Purchased Materials
BAGS: Textile
BAKERIES, COMMERCIAL: On Premises Baking Only
BAKERIES: On Premises Baking & Consumption
BAKERY MACHINERY
BAKERY PRDTS: Bakery Prdts, Partially Cooked, Exc frozen
BAKERY PRDTS: Bread, All Types, Fresh Or Frozen
BAKERY PRDTS: Buns, Bread Type, Fresh Or Frozen
BAKERY PRDTS: Cakes, Bakery, Exc Frozen
BAKERY PRDTS: Cakes, Bakery, Frozen
BAKERY PRDTS: Cones, Ice Cream
BAKERY PRDTS: Cookies
BAKERY PRDTS: Cookies & crackers
BAKERY PRDTS: Doughnuts, Exc Frozen
BAKERY PRDTS: Dry
BAKERY PRDTS: Frozen
BAKERY PRDTS: Pastries, Exc Frozen
BAKERY PRDTS: Pies, Bakery, Frozen
BAKERY PRDTS: Pies, Exc Frozen
BAKERY PRDTS: Pretzels
BAKERY PRDTS: Rice Cakes
BAKERY PRDTS: Wholesalers
BAKERY: Wholesale Or Wholesale & Retail Combined
BALLOONS: Toy & Advertising, Rubber
BANNERS: Fabric
BANQUET HALL FACILITIES
BAR
BAR FIXTURES: Wood

BAR JOISTS & CONCRETE REINFORCING BARS:
Fabricated
BARBECUE EQPT
BARGES BUILDING & REPAIR
BARRICADES: Metal
BARS & BAR SHAPES: Copper & Copper Alloy
BARS & BAR SHAPES: Steel, Hot-Rolled
BARS, COLD FINISHED: Steel, From Purchased Hot-Rolled
BARS: Concrete Reinforcing, Fabricated Steel
BARS: Iron, Made In Steel Mills
BASEMENT WINDOW AREAWAYS: Concrete
BASES, BEVERAGE
BASKETS: Steel Wire
BATHROOM ACCESS & FITTINGS: Vitreous China &
Earthenware
BATHROOM FIXTURES: Plastic
BATTERIES, EXC AUTOMOTIVE: Wholesalers
BATTERIES: Alkaline, Cell Storage
BATTERIES: Lead Acid, Storage
BATTERIES: Rechargeable
BATTERIES: Storage
BATTERIES: Wet
BATTERY CASES: Plastic Or Plastics Combination
BATTERY CHARGERS
BATTERY CHARGERS: Storage, Motor & Engine Generator
Type
BEARINGS & PARTS Ball
BEARINGS: Ball & Roller
BEARINGS: Railroad Car Journal
BEARINGS: Roller & Parts
BEAUTY & BARBER SHOP EQPT
BEAUTY & BARBER SHOP EQPT & SPLYS WHOLESALERS
BEAUTY SALONS
BEDDING & BEDSPRINGS STORES
BEDDING, BEDSPREADS, BLANKETS & SHEETS
BEDS: Institutional
BEDSPREADS, COTTON
BEER & ALE WHOLESALERS
BEER, WINE & LIQUOR STORES: Beer, Packaged
BELLOWS
BELTING: Rubber
BELTS & BELT PRDTS
BELTS: Conveyor, Made From Purchased Wire
BERYLLIUM
BEVERAGE BASES & SYRUPS
BEVERAGE PRDTS: Brewers' Grain
BEVERAGE PRDTS: Malt, Barley
BEVERAGES, ALCOHOLIC: Ale
BEVERAGES, ALCOHOLIC: Applejack
BEVERAGES, ALCOHOLIC: Beer
BEVERAGES, ALCOHOLIC: Beer & Ale
BEVERAGES, ALCOHOLIC: Bourbon Whiskey
BEVERAGES, ALCOHOLIC: Distilled Liquors
BEVERAGES, ALCOHOLIC: Near Beer
BEVERAGES, ALCOHOLIC: Wines
BEVERAGES, NONALCOHOLIC: Bottled & canned soft drinks
BEVERAGES, NONALCOHOLIC: Carbonated
BEVERAGES, NONALCOHOLIC: Carbonated, Canned &
Bottled, Etc
BEVERAGES, NONALCOHOLIC: Flavoring extracts &
syrups, nec
BEVERAGES, NONALCOHOLIC: Fruit Drnks, Under 100%
Juice, Can
BEVERAGES, NONALCOHOLIC: Soft Drinks, Canned &
Bottled, Etc
BEVERAGES, NONALCOHOLIC: Tea, Iced, Bottled &
Canned, Etc
BEVERAGES, WINE & DISTILLED ALCOHOLIC,
WHOLESALE: Liquor
BEVERAGES, WINE & DISTILLED ALCOHOLIC,
WHOLESALE: Wine
BICYCLES, PARTS & ACCESS
BILLING & BOOKKEEPING SVCS
BINDING SVC: Books & Manuals
BINDING SVC: Pamphlets
BINDINGS: Bias, Made From Purchased Materials
BIOLOGICAL PRDTS: Exc Diagnostic
BIOLOGICAL PRDTS: Vaccines & Immunizing
BIOLOGICAL PRDTS: Veterinary
BLACKBOARDS & CHALKBOARDS
BLADES: Knife
BLADES: Saw, Hand Or Power
BLANKBOOKS & LOOSELEAF BINDERS

BLANKBOOKS: Albums, Record
BLANKBOOKS: Passbooks, Bank, Etc
BLANKETS & BLANKETING, COTTON
BLAST FURNACE & RELATED PRDTS
BLASTING SVC: Sand, Metal Parts
BLINDS & SHADES: Vertical
BLINDS : Window
BLOCKS & BRICKS: Concrete
BLOCKS: Landscape Or Retaining Wall, Concrete
BLOCKS: Paving
BLOCKS: Paving, Concrete
BLOCKS: Standard, Concrete Or Cinder
BLOOD BANK
BLOWERS & FANS
BLOWERS & FANS
BLUEPRINTING SVCS
BOAT & BARGE COMPONENTS: Metal, Prefabricated
BOAT BUILDING & REPAIR
BOAT BUILDING & REPAIRING: Motorized
BOAT DEALERS
BOAT DEALERS: Marine Splys & Eqpt
BOAT REPAIR SVCS
BODIES: Truck & Bus
BODY PARTS: Automobile, Stamped Metal
BOILER & HEATING REPAIR SVCS
BOILERS: Low-Pressure Heating, Steam Or Hot Water
BOLTS: Metal
BOOK STORES
BOOK STORES: Children's
BOOKS, WHOLESALE
BOTTLED GAS DEALERS: Propane
BOTTLES: Plastic
BOWLING CENTERS
BOWLING EQPT & SPLYS
BOXES & CRATES: Rectangular, Wood
BOXES & SHOOK: Nailed Wood
BOXES: Corrugated
BOXES: Filing, Paperboard Made From Purchased Materials
BOXES: Packing & Shipping, Metal
BOXES: Paperboard, Folding
BOXES: Paperboard, Set-Up
BOXES: Wooden
BRAKES & BRAKE PARTS
BRAKES: Bicycle, Friction Clutch & Other
BRAKES: Metal Forming
BRASS & BRONZE PRDTS: Die-casted
BRASS FOUNDRY, NEC
BRAZING SVCS
BRAZING: Metal
BRICK, STONE & RELATED PRDTS WHOLESALERS
BRICKS & BLOCKS: Structural
BRICKS : Ceramic Glazed, Clay
BRICKS : Flooring, Clay
BRICKS : Paving, Clay
BRICKS: Clay
BRIDGE COMPONENTS: Bridge sections, prefabricated,
highway
BROACHING MACHINES
BROADCASTING & COMMS EQPT: Antennas, Transmitting/
Comms
BROADCASTING & COMMS EQPT: Rcvr-Transmitter Unt,
Transceiver
BROADCASTING & COMMUNICATIONS EQPT: Light
Comms Eqpt
BROKERS' SVCS
BROKERS: Food
BROKERS: Log & Lumber
BROKERS: Printing
BRONZE FOUNDRY, NEC
BRONZE ROLLING & DRAWING
BROOMS
BROOMS & BRUSHES
BROOMS & BRUSHES: Household Or Indl
BROOMS & BRUSHES: Paint & Varnish
BUCKETS: Plastic
BUILDING & OFFICE CLEANING SVCS
BUILDING & STRUCTURAL WOOD MEMBERS
BUILDING CLEANING & MAINTENANCE SVCS
BUILDING COMPONENTS: Structural Steel
BUILDING MAINTENANCE SVCS, EXC REPAIRS
BUILDING PRDTS & MATERIALS DEALERS
BUILDING PRDTS: Concrete
BUILDING PRDTS: Stone

BUILDING SCALES MODELS
BUILDINGS & COMPONENTS: Prefabricated Metal
BUILDINGS: Mobile, For Commercial Use
BUILDINGS: Portable
BUILDINGS: Prefabricated, Metal
BUILDINGS: Prefabricated, Wood
BULLETIN BOARDS: Wood
BULLETPROOF VESTS
BUMPERS: Motor Vehicle
BUOYS: Plastic
BURIAL VAULTS: Concrete Or Precast Terrazzo
BURNERS: Gas, Domestic
BURNERS: Gas, Indl
BURNERS: Oil, Domestic Or Indl
BUS BARS: Electrical
BUSHINGS & BEARINGS
BUSHINGS & BEARINGS: Brass, Exc Machined
BUSINESS ACTIVITIES: Non-Commercial Site
BUSINESS FORMS WHOLESALERS
BUSINESS FORMS: Printed, Continuous
BUSINESS FORMS: Printed, Manifold
BUSINESS MACHINE REPAIR, ELECTRIC
BUSINESS TRAINING SVCS
BUTTER WHOLESALERS
BUTTONS

C

CABINETS & CASES: Show, Display & Storage, Exc Wood
CABINETS: Bathroom Vanities, Wood
CABINETS: Entertainment
CABINETS: Entertainment Units, Household, Wood
CABINETS: Factory
CABINETS: Kitchen, Metal
CABINETS: Kitchen, Wood
CABINETS: Office, Wood
CABINETS: Show, Display, Etc, Wood, Exc Refrigerated
CABLE & OTHER PAY TELEVISION DISTRIBUTION
CABLE TELEVISION
CABLE: Fiber
CABLE: Fiber Optic
CABLE: Noninsulated
CABLE: Ropes & Fiber
CABLE: Steel, Insulated Or Armored
CABS: Indl Trucks & Tractors
CAFES
CAFETERIAS
CALCULATING & ACCOUNTING EQPT
CALIBRATING SVCS, NEC
CAMSHAFTS
CANDLES
CANDY & CONFECTIONS: Cake Ornaments
CANDY & CONFECTIONS: Candy Bars, Including Chocolate
  Covered
CANDY & CONFECTIONS: Chocolate Candy, Exc Solid
  Chocolate
CANDY & CONFECTIONS: Popcorn Balls/Other Trtd
  Popcorn Prdts
CANDY, NUT & CONFECTIONERY STORES: Candy
CANDY: Chocolate From Cacao Beans
CANNED SPECIALTIES
CANS: Aluminum
CANS: Metal
CANS: Tin
CANVAS PRDTS
CANVAS PRDTS: Convertible Tops, Car/Boat, Fm Purchased
  Mtrl
CAPACITORS: NEC
CAPS & PLUGS: Electric, Attachment
CAPS: Plastic
CAR WASH EQPT
CAR WASH EQPT & SPLYS WHOLESALERS
CARBON & GRAPHITE PRDTS, NEC
CARBON BLACK
CARBON PAPER & INKED RIBBONS
CARDIOVASCULAR SYSTEM DRUGS, EXC DIAGNOSTIC
CARDS: Beveled
CARDS: Color
CARDS: Greeting
CARDS: Identification
CARPET & UPHOLSTERY CLEANING SVCS
CARPET & UPHOLSTERY CLEANING SVCS: Carpet/
  Furniture, On Loc
CARPETS & RUGS: Tufted

CARPETS, RUGS & FLOOR COVERING
CARS: Electric
CARTONS: Egg, Molded Pulp, Made From Purchased
  Materials
CASES: Carrying
CASES: Carrying, Clothing & Apparel
CASES: Plastic
CASKETS & ACCESS
CAST STONE: Concrete
CASTINGS GRINDING: For The Trade
CASTINGS: Aerospace Investment, Ferrous
CASTINGS: Aerospace, Aluminum
CASTINGS: Aerospace, Nonferrous, Exc Aluminum
CASTINGS: Aluminum
CASTINGS: Brass, NEC, Exc Die
CASTINGS: Bronze, NEC, Exc Die
CASTINGS: Commercial Investment, Ferrous
CASTINGS: Die, Aluminum
CASTINGS: Die, Magnesium & Magnesium-Base Alloy
CASTINGS: Die, Nonferrous
CASTINGS: Ductile
CASTINGS: Gray Iron
CASTINGS: Lead
CASTINGS: Machinery, Aluminum
CASTINGS: Machinery, Nonferrous, Exc Die or Aluminum
  Copper
CASTINGS: Magnesium
CASTINGS: Precision
CASTINGS: Steel
CASTINGS: Titanium
CATALOG & MAIL-ORDER HOUSES
CATALYSTS: Chemical
CATAPULTS
CATCH BASIN COVERS: Concrete
CATERERS
CATTLE WHOLESALERS
CAULKING COMPOUNDS
CEILING SYSTEMS: Luminous, Commercial
CELLULOSE DERIVATIVE MATERIALS
CEMENT & CONCRETE RELATED PRDTS & EQPT:
  Bituminous
CEMENT ROCK: Crushed & Broken
CEMENT, EXC LINOLEUM & TILE
CEMENT: Hydraulic
CEMENT: Masonry
CEMENT: Natural
CEMENT: Portland
CERAMIC FIBER
CHARCOAL
CHARCOAL: Activated
CHASSIS: Motor Vehicle
CHEESE WHOLESALERS
CHEMICAL CLEANING SVCS
CHEMICAL ELEMENTS
CHEMICAL PROCESSING MACHINERY & EQPT
CHEMICALS & ALLIED PRDTS WHOLESALERS, NEC
CHEMICALS & ALLIED PRDTS, WHOLESALE: Chemical
  Additives
CHEMICALS & ALLIED PRDTS, WHOLESALE: Chemicals,
  Indl
CHEMICALS & ALLIED PRDTS, WHOLESALE: Chemicals,
  Indl & Heavy
CHEMICALS & ALLIED PRDTS, WHOLESALE: Detergent/
  Soap
CHEMICALS & ALLIED PRDTS, WHOLESALE: Detergents
CHEMICALS & ALLIED PRDTS, WHOLESALE: Plastics Film
CHEMICALS & ALLIED PRDTS, WHOLESALE: Plastics
  Materials, NEC
CHEMICALS & ALLIED PRDTS, WHOLESALE: Plastics
  Prdts, NEC
CHEMICALS & ALLIED PRDTS, WHOLESALE: Plastics
  Sheets & Rods
CHEMICALS & ALLIED PRDTS, WHOLESALE: Resins
CHEMICALS & ALLIED PRDTS, WHOLESALE: Resins,
  Plastics
CHEMICALS & ALLIED PRDTS, WHOLESALE: Rubber,
  Synthetic
CHEMICALS & ALLIED PRDTS, WHOLESALE: Spec Clean/
  Sanitation
CHEMICALS & ALLIED PRDTS, WHOLESALE: Syn Resin,
  Rub/Plastic
CHEMICALS & OTHER PRDTS DERIVED FROM COKING
CHEMICALS, AGRICULTURE: Wholesalers

CHEMICALS: Agricultural
CHEMICALS: Alkalies
CHEMICALS: Aluminum Compounds
CHEMICALS: Aluminum Oxide
CHEMICALS: Anhydrous Ammonia
CHEMICALS: Bleaching Powder, Lime Bleaching Compounds
CHEMICALS: Caustic Potash & Potassium Hydroxide
CHEMICALS: Caustic Soda
CHEMICALS: Fire Retardant
CHEMICALS: High Purity Grade, Organic
CHEMICALS: High Purity, Refined From Technical Grade
CHEMICALS: Inorganic, NEC
CHEMICALS: Lithium Compounds, Inorganic
CHEMICALS: Medicinal
CHEMICALS: Medicinal, Organic, Uncompounded, Bulk
CHEMICALS: NEC
CHEMICALS: Phenol
CHEMICALS: Phosphates, Defluorinated/Ammoniated, Exc
  Fertlr
CHEMICALS: Reagent Grade, Refined From Technical Grade
CHEMICALS: Silica Compounds
CHEMICALS: Silver Compounds Or Salts, Inorganic
CHEMICALS: Sodium Bicarbonate
CHEMICALS: Water Treatment
CHICKEN SLAUGHTERING & PROCESSING
CHILD DAY CARE SVCS
CHILD RESTRAINT SEATS, AUTOMOTIVE, WHOLESALE
CHILDREN'S WEAR STORES
CHOCOLATE, EXC CANDY FROM BEANS: Chips, Powder,
  Block, Syrup
CHOCOLATE, EXC CANDY FROM PURCH CHOC: Chips,
  Powder, Block
CHUCKS
CHURCHES
CIGARETTE & CIGAR PRDTS & ACCESS
CIGARETTE LIGHTERS
CIRCUIT BOARD REPAIR SVCS
CIRCUIT BOARDS: Wiring
CIRCUITS: Electronic
CLAMPS & COUPLINGS: Hose
CLAMPS: Metal
CLEANING EQPT: Commercial
CLEANING EQPT: Floor Washing & Polishing, Commercial
CLEANING OR POLISHING PREPARATIONS, NEC
CLEANING PRDTS: Automobile Polish
CLEANING PRDTS: Bleaches, Household, Dry Or Liquid
CLEANING PRDTS: Degreasing Solvent
CLEANING PRDTS: Deodorants, Nonpersonal
CLEANING PRDTS: Drain Pipe Solvents Or Cleaners
CLEANING PRDTS: Laundry Preparations
CLEANING PRDTS: Sanitation Preparations
CLEANING PRDTS: Sanitation Preps, Disinfectants/
  Deodorants
CLEANING PRDTS: Specialty
CLEANING PRDTS: Stain Removers
CLEANING SVCS: Industrial Or Commercial
CLIPS & FASTENERS, MADE FROM PURCHASED WIRE
CLOSURES: Closures, Stamped Metal
CLOSURES: Plastic
CLOTHING & ACCESS, WOMEN, CHILDREN & INFANT,
  WHOL: Uniforms
CLOTHING & ACCESS: Costumes, Theatrical
CLOTHING & ACCESS: Men's Miscellaneous Access
CLOTHING & APPAREL STORES: Custom
CLOTHING & FURNISHINGS, MEN'S & BOYS',
  WHOLESALE: Uniforms
CLOTHING & FURNISHINGS, MENS & BOYS,
  WHOLESALE: Apprl Belts
CLOTHING ACCESS STORES: Umbrellas
CLOTHING STORES: T-Shirts, Printed, Custom
CLOTHING STORES: Uniforms & Work
CLOTHING STORES: Unisex
CLOTHING STORES: Work
CLOTHING/ACCESS, WOMEN, CHILDREN/INFANT, WHOL:
  Apparel Belt
CLOTHING/ACCESS, WOMEN, CHILDREN/INFANT, WHOL:
  Hosp Gowns
CLOTHING: Access, Women's & Misses'
CLOTHING: Aprons, Exc Rubber/Plastic, Women, Misses,
  Junior
CLOTHING: Aprons, Harness
CLOTHING: Athletic & Sportswear, Men's & Boys'
CLOTHING: Athletic & Sportswear, Women's & Girls'

CLOTHING: Blouses, Women's & Girls'
CLOTHING: Blouses, Womens & Juniors, From Purchased Mtrls
CLOTHING: Bridal Gowns
CLOTHING: Caps, Baseball
CLOTHING: Children & Infants'
CLOTHING: Coats & Suits, Men's & Boys'
CLOTHING: Costumes
CLOTHING: Disposable
CLOTHING: Dresses
CLOTHING: Hospital, Men's
CLOTHING: Jerseys, Knit
CLOTHING: Mens & Boys Jackets, Sport, Suede, Leatherette
CLOTHING: Outerwear, Knit
CLOTHING: Outerwear, Lthr, Wool/Down-Filled, Men, Youth/Boy
CLOTHING: Outerwear, Women's & Misses' NEC
CLOTHING: Robes & Dressing Gowns
CLOTHING: Shirts, Dress, Men's & Boys'
CLOTHING: Socks
CLOTHING: Sweatshirts & T-Shirts, Men's & Boys'
CLOTHING: T-Shirts & Tops, Knit
CLOTHING: Underwear, Women's & Children's
CLOTHING: Uniforms & Vestments
CLOTHING: Uniforms, Ex Athletic, Women's, Misses' & Juniors'
CLOTHING: Uniforms, Firemen's, From Purchased Materials
CLOTHING: Uniforms, Men's & Boys'
CLOTHING: Uniforms, Military, Men/Youth, Purchased Materials
CLOTHING: Uniforms, Work
CLOTHING: Waterproof Outerwear
CLOTHING: Work, Waterproof, Exc Raincoats
CLUTCHES, EXC VEHICULAR
COAL & OTHER MINERALS & ORES WHOLESALERS
COAL MINING SERVICES
COAL MINING: Anthracite
COAL MINING: Bituminous & Lignite Surface
COAL MINING: Bituminous Coal & Lignite-Surface Mining
COAL MINING: Bituminous, Strip
COAL MINING: Bituminous, Surface, NEC
COAL MINING: Lignite, Surface, NEC
COAL TAR CRUDES: Derived From Chemical Recovery Coke Oven
COATING COMPOUNDS: Tar
COATING SVC: Metals, With Plastic Or Resins
COATINGS: Epoxy
COATINGS: Polyurethane
COILS & TRANSFORMERS
COILS, WIRE: Aluminum, Made In Rolling Mills
COILS: Pipe
COLOR LAKES OR TONERS
COLOR PIGMENTS
COLORS: Pigments, Inorganic
COMBINED ELEMENTARY & SECONDARY SCHOOLS, PUBLIC
COMMERCIAL & OFFICE BUILDINGS RENOVATION & REPAIR
COMMERCIAL ART & GRAPHIC DESIGN SVCS
COMMERCIAL ART & ILLUSTRATION SVCS
COMMERCIAL CONTAINERS WHOLESALERS
COMMERCIAL EQPT WHOLESALERS, NEC
COMMERCIAL EQPT, WHOLESALE: Display Eqpt, Exc Refrigerated
COMMERCIAL EQPT, WHOLESALE: Restaurant, NEC
COMMERCIAL EQPT, WHOLESALE: Store Fixtures & Display Eqpt
COMMERCIAL PHOTOGRAPHIC STUDIO
COMMERCIAL PRINTING & NEWSPAPER PUBLISHING
COMMON SAND MINING
COMMUNICATIONS EQPT WHOLESALERS
COMMUNICATIONS SVCS: Data
COMMUNICATIONS SVCS: Internet Connectivity Svcs
COMMUNICATIONS SVCS: Online Svc Providers
COMMUNICATIONS SVCS: Telephone, Local & Long Distance
COMMUTATORS: Electronic
COMPACT LASER DISCS: Prerecorded
COMPOSITION STONE: Plastic
COMPOST
COMPRESSORS: Air & Gas
COMPRESSORS: Air & Gas, Including Vacuum Pumps
COMPRESSORS: Refrigeration & Air Conditioning Eqpt

COMPUTER & COMPUTER SOFTWARE STORES
COMPUTER & COMPUTER SOFTWARE STORES: Peripheral Eqpt
COMPUTER & COMPUTER SOFTWARE STORES: Software & Access
COMPUTER & COMPUTER SOFTWARE STORES: Software, Bus/Non-Game
COMPUTER & COMPUTER SOFTWARE STORES: Software, Computer Game
COMPUTER & OFFICE MACHINE MAINTENANCE & REPAIR
COMPUTER FACILITIES MANAGEMENT SVCS
COMPUTER FORMS
COMPUTER GRAPHICS SVCS
COMPUTER PERIPHERAL EQPT REPAIR & MAINTENANCE
COMPUTER PERIPHERAL EQPT, NEC
COMPUTER PERIPHERAL EQPT, WHOLESALE
COMPUTER PERIPHERAL EQPT: Decoders
COMPUTER PERIPHERAL EQPT: Input Or Output
COMPUTER PROCESSING SVCS
COMPUTER PROGRAMMING SVCS: Custom
COMPUTER RELATED MAINTENANCE SVCS
COMPUTER SERVICE BUREAU
COMPUTER SOFTWARE DEVELOPMENT
COMPUTER SOFTWARE DEVELOPMENT & APPLICATIONS
COMPUTER SOFTWARE SYSTEMS ANALYSIS & DESIGN: Custom
COMPUTER STORAGE DEVICES, NEC
COMPUTER STORAGE UNITS: Auxiliary
COMPUTER SYSTEM SELLING SVCS
COMPUTER SYSTEMS ANALYSIS & DESIGN
COMPUTER TERMINALS
COMPUTER TIME-SHARING
COMPUTERS, NEC
COMPUTERS, PERIPHERALS & SOFTWARE, WHOLESALE: Printers
COMPUTERS, PERIPHERALS & SOFTWARE, WHOLESALE: Software
COMPUTERS: Mainframe
COMPUTERS: Personal
CONCENTRATES, DRINK
CONCENTRATES, FLAVORING, EXC DRINK
CONCRETE BUILDING PRDTS WHOLESALERS
CONCRETE CURING & HARDENING COMPOUNDS
CONCRETE PRDTS
CONCRETE PRDTS, PRECAST, NEC
CONCRETE: Asphaltic, Not From Refineries
CONCRETE: Bituminous
CONCRETE: Dry Mixture
CONCRETE: Ready-Mixed
CONDENSERS: Heat Transfer Eqpt, Evaporative
CONDENSERS: Refrigeration
CONDUITS & FITTINGS: Electric
CONNECTORS: Cord, Electric
CONNECTORS: Electronic
CONSTRUCTION & MINING MACHINERY WHOLESALERS
CONSTRUCTION EQPT REPAIR SVCS
CONSTRUCTION EQPT: Attachments, Snow Plow
CONSTRUCTION EQPT: Roofing Eqpt
CONSTRUCTION MATERIALS, WHOLESALE: Architectural Metalwork
CONSTRUCTION MATERIALS, WHOLESALE: Awnings
CONSTRUCTION MATERIALS, WHOLESALE: Brick, Exc Refractory
CONSTRUCTION MATERIALS, WHOLESALE: Building Stone
CONSTRUCTION MATERIALS, WHOLESALE: Building Stone, Marble
CONSTRUCTION MATERIALS, WHOLESALE: Building, Exterior
CONSTRUCTION MATERIALS, WHOLESALE: Building, Interior
CONSTRUCTION MATERIALS, WHOLESALE: Cement
CONSTRUCTION MATERIALS, WHOLESALE: Concrete Mixtures
CONSTRUCTION MATERIALS, WHOLESALE: Door Frames
CONSTRUCTION MATERIALS, WHOLESALE: Doors, Garage
CONSTRUCTION MATERIALS, WHOLESALE: Doors, Sliding
CONSTRUCTION MATERIALS, WHOLESALE: Glass
CONSTRUCTION MATERIALS, WHOLESALE: Gravel
CONSTRUCTION MATERIALS, WHOLESALE: Limestone

CONSTRUCTION MATERIALS, WHOLESALE: Masons' Materials
CONSTRUCTION MATERIALS, WHOLESALE: Molding, All Materials
CONSTRUCTION MATERIALS, WHOLESALE: Pallets, Wood
CONSTRUCTION MATERIALS, WHOLESALE: Particleboard
CONSTRUCTION MATERIALS, WHOLESALE: Paving Materials
CONSTRUCTION MATERIALS, WHOLESALE: Prefabricated Structures
CONSTRUCTION MATERIALS, WHOLESALE: Roofing & Siding Material
CONSTRUCTION MATERIALS, WHOLESALE: Sand
CONSTRUCTION MATERIALS, WHOLESALE: Septic Tanks
CONSTRUCTION MATERIALS, WHOLESALE: Sewer Pipe, Clay
CONSTRUCTION MATERIALS, WHOLESALE: Siding, Exc Wood
CONSTRUCTION MATERIALS, WHOLESALE: Stone, Crushed Or Broken
CONSTRUCTION MATERIALS, WHOLESALE: Windows
CONSTRUCTION SAND MINING
CONSTRUCTION: Athletic & Recreation Facilities
CONSTRUCTION: Bridge
CONSTRUCTION: Commercial & Office Building, New
CONSTRUCTION: Commercial & Office Buildings, Prefabricated
CONSTRUCTION: Food Prdts Manufacturing or Packing Plant
CONSTRUCTION: Foundation & Retaining Wall
CONSTRUCTION: Heavy Highway & Street
CONSTRUCTION: Indl Buildings, New, NEC
CONSTRUCTION: Indl Plant
CONSTRUCTION: Land Preparation
CONSTRUCTION: Oil & Gas Pipeline Construction
CONSTRUCTION: Pipeline, NEC
CONSTRUCTION: Power Plant
CONSTRUCTION: Residential, Nec
CONSTRUCTION: Scaffolding
CONSTRUCTION: Sewer Line
CONSTRUCTION: Single-Family Housing
CONSTRUCTION: Single-family Housing, New
CONSTRUCTION: Street Sign Installation & Mntnce
CONSTRUCTION: Swimming Pools
CONSTRUCTION: Waste Water & Sewage Treatment Plant
CONSULTING SVC: Business, NEC
CONSULTING SVC: Financial Management
CONSULTING SVC: Human Resource
CONSULTING SVC: Management
CONSULTING SVCS, BUSINESS: Communications
CONSULTING SVCS, BUSINESS: Energy Conservation
CONSULTING SVCS, BUSINESS: Environmental
CONSULTING SVCS, BUSINESS: Safety Training Svcs
CONSULTING SVCS, BUSINESS: Sys Engnrg, Exc Computer/ Prof
CONSULTING SVCS, BUSINESS: Systems Analysis & Engineering
CONSULTING SVCS, BUSINESS: Systems Analysis Or Design
CONSULTING SVCS: Scientific
CONTACT LENSES
CONTAINERS, GLASS: Food
CONTAINERS, GLASS: Water Bottles
CONTAINERS: Cargo, Wood & Metal Combination
CONTAINERS: Food & Beverage
CONTAINERS: Food, Folding, Made From Purchased Materials
CONTAINERS: Food, Liquid Tight, Including Milk
CONTAINERS: Food, Metal
CONTAINERS: Glass
CONTAINERS: Ice Cream, Made From Purchased Materials
CONTAINERS: Laminated Phenolic & Vulcanized Fiber
CONTAINERS: Metal
CONTAINERS: Plastic
CONTAINERS: Sanitary, Food
CONTAINERS: Shipping, Bombs, Metal Plate
CONTAINERS: Wood
CONTRACTOR: Rigging & Scaffolding
CONTRACTORS: Acoustical & Insulation Work
CONTRACTORS: Asbestos Removal & Encapsulation
CONTRACTORS: Boiler Maintenance Contractor
CONTRACTORS: Building Site Preparation
CONTRACTORS: Carpentry Work
CONTRACTORS: Carpentry, Cabinet & Finish Work

CONTRACTORS: Closet Organizers, Installation & Design
CONTRACTORS: Coating, Caulking & Weather, Water & Fire
CONTRACTORS: Commercial & Office Building
CONTRACTORS: Communications Svcs
CONTRACTORS: Concrete Block Masonry Laying
CONTRACTORS: Concrete Reinforcement Placing
CONTRACTORS: Core Drilling & Cutting
CONTRACTORS: Corrosion Control Installation
CONTRACTORS: Decontamination Svcs
CONTRACTORS: Directional Oil & Gas Well Drilling Svc
CONTRACTORS: Electric Power Systems
CONTRACTORS: Electronic Controls Installation
CONTRACTORS: Energy Management Control
CONTRACTORS: Erection & Dismantling, Poured Concrete
  Forms
CONTRACTORS: Fence Construction
CONTRACTORS: Fiber Optic Cable Installation
CONTRACTORS: Floor Laying & Other Floor Work
CONTRACTORS: Foundation & Footing
CONTRACTORS: Gas Field Svcs, NEC
CONTRACTORS: General Electric
CONTRACTORS: Glass Tinting, Architectural & Automotive
CONTRACTORS: Heating & Air Conditioning
CONTRACTORS: Heating Systems Repair & Maintenance
  Svc
CONTRACTORS: Highway & Street Construction, General
CONTRACTORS: Highway & Street Paving
CONTRACTORS: Hydraulic Eqpt Installation & Svcs
CONTRACTORS: Machine Rigging & Moving
CONTRACTORS: Machinery Installation
CONTRACTORS: Marble Installation, Interior
CONTRACTORS: Masonry & Stonework
CONTRACTORS: Office Furniture Installation
CONTRACTORS: Oil & Gas Building, Repairing &
  Dismantling Svc
CONTRACTORS: Oil & Gas Field Geological Exploration Svcs
CONTRACTORS: Oil & Gas Field Geophysical Exploration
  Svcs
CONTRACTORS: Oil & Gas Field Tools Fishing Svcs
CONTRACTORS: Oil & Gas Well Plugging & Abandoning
  Svcs
CONTRACTORS: Oil & Gas Well Redrilling
CONTRACTORS: Oil & Gas Wells Pumping Svcs
CONTRACTORS: Oil & Gas Wells Svcs
CONTRACTORS: Oil Field Mud Drilling Svcs
CONTRACTORS: Oil Field Pipe Testing Svcs
CONTRACTORS: Ornamental Metal Work
CONTRACTORS: Painting, Commercial
CONTRACTORS: Painting, Commercial, Exterior
CONTRACTORS: Painting, Indl
CONTRACTORS: Petroleum Storage Tanks, Pumping &
  Draining
CONTRACTORS: Plumbing
CONTRACTORS: Pollution Control Eqpt Installation
CONTRACTORS: Power Generating Eqpt Installation
CONTRACTORS: Prefabricated Window & Door Installation
CONTRACTORS: Process Piping
CONTRACTORS: Refractory or Acid Brick Masonry
CONTRACTORS: Roustabout Svcs
CONTRACTORS: Septic System
CONTRACTORS: Sheet Metal Work, NEC
CONTRACTORS: Siding
CONTRACTORS: Skylight Installation
CONTRACTORS: Structural Iron Work, Structural
CONTRACTORS: Structural Steel Erection
CONTRACTORS: Tile Installation, Ceramic
CONTRACTORS: Underground Utilities
CONTRACTORS: Ventilation & Duct Work
CONTRACTORS: Warm Air Heating & Air Conditioning
CONTRACTORS: Water Well Drilling
CONTRACTORS: Well Logging Svcs
CONTRACTORS: Windows & Doors
CONTRACTORS: Wood Floor Installation & Refinishing
CONTRACTORS: Wrecking & Demolition
CONTROL EQPT: Electric
CONTROL EQPT: Electric Buses & Locomotives
CONTROL EQPT: Noise
CONTROLS & ACCESS: Indl, Electric
CONTROLS & ACCESS: Motor
CONTROLS: Automatic Temperature
CONTROLS: Electric Motor
CONTROLS: Environmental
CONTROLS: Hydronic

CONTROLS: Thermostats, Built-in
CONVENIENCE STORES
CONVERTERS: Frequency
CONVEYOR SYSTEMS
CONVEYOR SYSTEMS: Belt, General Indl Use
CONVEYOR SYSTEMS: Bucket Type
CONVEYOR SYSTEMS: Bulk Handling
CONVEYOR SYSTEMS: Pneumatic Tube
CONVEYOR SYSTEMS: Robotic
CONVEYORS & CONVEYING EQPT
COOKING & FOODWARMING EQPT: Commercial
COOKING EQPT, HOUSEHOLD: Ranges, Gas
COOLING TOWERS: Metal
COPPER: Rolling & Drawing
CORRECTION FLUID
CORRUGATING MACHINES
COSMETIC PREPARATIONS
COSMETICS & TOILETRIES
COSMETOLOGY & PERSONAL HYGIENE SALONS
COUNTER & SINK TOPS
COUNTERS OR COUNTER DISPLAY CASES, EXC WOOD
COUNTERS OR COUNTER DISPLAY CASES, WOOD
COUNTING DEVICES: Controls, Revolution & Timing
COUNTING DEVICES: Tachometer, Centrifugal
COUNTRY CLUBS
COUPLINGS: Hose & Tube, Hydraulic Or Pneumatic
COUPLINGS: Pipe
COUPLINGS: Shaft
COVERS: Automobile Seat
CRANE & AERIAL LIFT SVCS
CRANES & MONORAIL SYSTEMS
CRANES: Indl Plant
CRANES: Indl Truck
CRANES: Overhead
CROWNS & CLOSURES
CRUDE PETROLEUM & NATURAL GAS PRODUCTION
CRUDE PETROLEUM PRODUCTION
CRYOGENIC COOLING DEVICES: Infrared Detectors,
  Masers
CULVERTS: Sheet Metal
CUPS: Paper, Made From Purchased Materials
CURBING: Granite Or Stone
CURTAIN WALLS: Building, Steel
CURTAINS: Window, From Purchased Materials
CUSHIONS & PILLOWS
CUSHIONS & PILLOWS: Bed, From Purchased Materials
CUSHIONS: Carpet & Rug, Foamed Plastics
CUSTOM COMPOUNDING OF RUBBER MATERIALS
CUT STONE & STONE PRODUCTS
CUTLERY
CYCLIC CRUDES & INTERMEDIATES
CYLINDER & ACTUATORS: Fluid Power
CYLINDERS: Pressure
CYLINDERS: Pump

D

DAIRY PRDTS STORE: Cheese
DAIRY PRDTS STORE: Ice Cream, Packaged
DAIRY PRDTS STORES
DAIRY PRDTS: Butter
DAIRY PRDTS: Canned Milk, Whole
DAIRY PRDTS: Cheese
DAIRY PRDTS: Cheese, Cottage
DAIRY PRDTS: Condensed Milk
DAIRY PRDTS: Cream Substitutes
DAIRY PRDTS: Dietary Supplements, Dairy & Non-Dairy
  Based
DAIRY PRDTS: Evaporated Milk
DAIRY PRDTS: Ice Cream & Ice Milk
DAIRY PRDTS: Ice Cream, Bulk
DAIRY PRDTS: Ice Cream, Packaged, Molded, On Sticks,
  Etc.
DAIRY PRDTS: Milk, Condensed & Evaporated
DAIRY PRDTS: Milk, Fluid
DAIRY PRDTS: Natural Cheese
DAIRY PRDTS: Powdered Milk
DAIRY PRDTS: Processed Cheese
DAIRY PRDTS: Whipped Topping, Exc Frozen Or Dry Mix
DATA PROCESSING & PREPARATION SVCS
DATA PROCESSING SVCS
DECORATIVE WOOD & WOODWORK
DEFENSE SYSTEMS & EQPT
DEGREASING MACHINES

DENTAL EQPT & SPLYS
DENTAL EQPT & SPLYS WHOLESALERS
DENTAL EQPT & SPLYS: Impression Materials
DENTAL EQPT & SPLYS: Orthodontic Appliances
DEODORANTS: Personal
DEPARTMENT STORES
DEPARTMENT STORES: Army-Navy Goods
DEPARTMENT STORES: Country General
DEPILATORIES, COSMETIC
DESIGN SVCS, NEC
DESIGN SVCS: Commercial & Indl
DESIGN SVCS: Computer Integrated Systems
DETECTION APPARATUS: Electronic/Magnetic Field, Light/
  Heat
DETECTION EQPT: Magnetic Field
DIAGNOSTIC SUBSTANCES
DIAGNOSTIC SUBSTANCES OR AGENTS: Radioactive
DIAGNOSTIC SUBSTANCES OR AGENTS: Veterinary
DIE CUTTING SVC: Paper
DIE SETS: Presses, Metal Stamping
DIES & TOOLS: Special
DIES: Cutting, Exc Metal
DIES: Extrusion
DIES: Paper Cutting
DIES: Plastic Forming
DIES: Steel Rule
DIODES & RECTIFIERS
DIODES: Light Emitting
DIODES: Solid State, Germanium, Silicon, Etc
DIRECT SELLING ESTABLISHMENTS, NEC
DISCS & TAPE: Optical, Blank
DISPLAY FIXTURES: Wood
DISPLAY ITEMS: Corrugated, Made From Purchased
  Materials
DISPLAY ITEMS: Solid Fiber, Made From Purchased
  Materials
DISTRIBUTORS: Motor Vehicle Engine
DOCK EQPT & SPLYS, INDL
DOLOMITE: Crushed & Broken
DOOR FRAMES: Wood
DOOR MATS: Rubber
DOORS & WINDOWS: Screen & Storm
DOORS & WINDOWS: Storm, Metal
DOORS: Combination Screen & Storm, Wood
DOORS: Fiberglass
DOORS: Folding, Plastic Or Plastic Coated Fabric
DOORS: Garage, Overhead, Metal
DOORS: Garage, Overhead, Wood
DOORS: Glass
DRAPERIES & CURTAINS
DRAPERIES: Plastic & Textile, From Purchased Materials
DRAPERY & UPHOLSTERY STORES: Draperies
DRILL BITS
DRILLING MACHINERY & EQPT: Oil & Gas
DRILLS & DRILLING EQPT: Mining
DRINK MIXES, NONALCOHOLIC: Cocktail
DRINKING FOUNTAINS: Metal, Nonrefrigerated
DRINKING PLACES: Bars & Lounges
DRINKING PLACES: Beer Garden
DRINKING WATER COOLERS WHOLESALERS: Mechanical
DRUGS & DRUG PROPRIETARIES, WHOLESALE
DRUGS & DRUG PROPRIETARIES, WHOLESALE: Patent
  Medicines
DRUGS & DRUG PROPRIETARIES, WHOLESALE:
  Pharmaceuticals
DRUGS & DRUG PROPRIETARIES, WHOLESALE: Vitamins
  & Minerals
DRUMS: Fiber
DRUMS: Shipping, Metal
DUCTS: Sheet Metal
DUMPSTERS: Garbage
DUST OR FUME COLLECTING EQPT: Indl
DYES & PIGMENTS: Organic
DYES OR COLORS: Food, Synthetic

E

EATING PLACES
EDUCATIONAL SVCS
ELECTRIC MOTOR REPAIR SVCS
ELECTRIC SERVICES
ELECTRICAL APPARATUS & EQPT WHOLESALERS
ELECTRICAL DEVICE PARTS: Porcelain, Molded
ELECTRICAL DISCHARGE MACHINING, EDM

ELECTRICAL EQPT REPAIR SVCS
ELECTRICAL EQPT REPAIR SVCS: High Voltage
ELECTRICAL EQPT: Automotive, NEC
ELECTRICAL GOODS, WHOLESALE: Boxes & Fittings
ELECTRICAL GOODS, WHOLESALE: Cable Conduit
ELECTRICAL GOODS, WHOLESALE: Electronic Parts
ELECTRICAL GOODS, WHOLESALE: Fittings &
  Construction Mat
ELECTRICAL GOODS, WHOLESALE: Generators
ELECTRICAL GOODS, WHOLESALE: Household
  Appliances, NEC
ELECTRICAL GOODS, WHOLESALE: Lighting Fittings &
  Access
ELECTRICAL GOODS, WHOLESALE: Modems, Computer
ELECTRICAL GOODS, WHOLESALE: Security Control Eqpt
  & Systems
ELECTRICAL GOODS, WHOLESALE: Switches, Exc
  Electronic, NEC
ELECTRICAL GOODS, WHOLESALE: Telephone Eqpt
ELECTRICAL GOODS, WHOLESALE: Wire & Cable
ELECTRICAL MEASURING INSTRUMENT REPAIR &
  CALIBRATION SVCS
ELECTRICAL SPLYS
ELECTRICAL SUPPLIES: Porcelain
ELECTRODES: Thermal & Electrolytic
ELECTROMEDICAL EQPT
ELECTROMEDICAL EQPT WHOLESALERS
ELECTROMETALLURGICAL PRDTS
ELECTRONIC DEVICES: Solid State, NEC
ELECTRONIC EQPT REPAIR SVCS
ELECTRONIC LOADS & POWER SPLYS
ELECTRONIC PARTS & EQPT WHOLESALERS
ELECTRONIC SHOPPING
ELECTRONIC TRAINING DEVICES
ELECTROPLATING & PLATING SVC
ELEVATORS & EQPT
ELEVATORS WHOLESALERS
ELEVATORS: Installation & Conversion
EMBLEMS: Embroidered
EMBROIDERY ADVERTISING SVCS
EMERGENCY ALARMS
ENAMELS
ENCLOSURES: Electronic
ENCLOSURES: Screen
ENCODERS: Digital
ENGINE REBUILDING: Diesel
ENGINEERING SVCS
ENGINEERING SVCS: Acoustical
ENGINEERING SVCS: Building Construction
ENGINEERING SVCS: Chemical
ENGINEERING SVCS: Civil
ENGINEERING SVCS: Construction & Civil
ENGINEERING SVCS: Electrical Or Electronic
ENGINEERING SVCS: Machine Tool Design
ENGINEERING SVCS: Mechanical
ENGINES: Diesel & Semi-Diesel Or Duel Fuel
ENGINES: Gasoline, NEC
ENGINES: Internal Combustion, NEC
ENGINES: Jet Propulsion
ENGINES: Marine
ENGRAVING SVC, NEC
ENGRAVING SVCS
ENVELOPES
ENVELOPES WHOLESALERS
ENZYMES
EPOXY RESINS
EQUIPMENT: Rental & Leasing, NEC
ETCHING & ENGRAVING SVC
ETHYLENE
ETHYLENE-PROPYLENE RUBBERS: EPDM Polymers
EXHAUST HOOD OR FAN CLEANING SVCS
EXHAUST SYSTEMS: Eqpt & Parts
EXPLOSIVES
EXPLOSIVES, FUSES & DETONATORS: Primary explosives
EXTENSION CORDS
EXTRACTS, FLAVORING

F

FABRICS & CLOTHING: Rubber Coated
FABRICS: Apparel & Outerwear, Cotton
FABRICS: Automotive, From Manmade Fiber
FABRICS: Cotton, Narrow
FABRICS: Decorative Trim & Specialty, Including Twist Weave

FABRICS: Denims
FABRICS: Fiberglass, Broadwoven
FABRICS: Glass & Fiberglass, Broadwoven
FABRICS: Nonwoven
FABRICS: Nylon, Broadwoven
FABRICS: Resin Or Plastic Coated
FABRICS: Rubber & Elastic Yarns & Fabrics
FABRICS: Rubberized
FABRICS: Scrub Cloths
FABRICS: Shoe Laces, Exc Leather
FABRICS: Umbrella Cloth, Cotton
FABRICS: Upholstery, Wool
FACILITIES SUPPORT SVCS
FAMILY CLOTHING STORES
FANS, BLOWING: Indl Or Commercial
FANS, EXHAUST: Indl Or Commercial
FANS, VENTILATING: Indl Or Commercial
FANS: Ceiling
FARM & GARDEN MACHINERY WHOLESALERS
FARM MACHINERY REPAIR SVCS
FARM SPLYS WHOLESALERS
FARM SPLYS, WHOLESALE: Feed
FARM SPLYS, WHOLESALE: Fertilizers & Agricultural
  Chemicals
FARM SPLYS, WHOLESALE: Garden Splys
FASTENERS WHOLESALERS
FASTENERS: Metal
FASTENERS: Metal
FAUCETS & SPIGOTS: Metal & Plastic
FEATHERS & FEATHER PRODUCTS
FENCE POSTS: Iron & Steel
FENCES OR POSTS: Ornamental Iron Or Steel
FENCING MATERIALS: Docks & Other Outdoor Prdts, Wood
FENCING MATERIALS: Wood
FENCING: Chain Link
FERROALLOYS
FERROMANGANESE, NOT MADE IN BLAST FURNACES
FERROSILICON, EXC MADE IN BLAST FURNACES
FERROUS METALS: Reclaimed From Clay
FERTILIZER, AGRICULTURAL: Wholesalers
FERTILIZERS: Nitrogen Solutions
FERTILIZERS: Nitrogenous
FERTILIZERS: Phosphatic
FIBER & FIBER PRDTS: Elastomeric
FIBER & FIBER PRDTS: Protein
FIBER & FIBER PRDTS: Vinyl
FIBER OPTICS
FIBERS: Carbon & Graphite
FILM BASE: Cellulose Acetate Or Nitrocellulose Plastics
FILTER ELEMENTS: Fluid & Hydraulic Line
FILTERS
FILTERS & SOFTENERS: Water, Household
FILTERS & STRAINERS: Pipeline
FILTERS: Air
FILTERS: Air Intake, Internal Combustion Engine, Exc Auto
FILTERS: General Line, Indl
FILTERS: Oil, Internal Combustion Engine, Exc Auto
FILTRATION DEVICES: Electronic
FINISHING AGENTS
FIRE ALARM MAINTENANCE & MONITORING SVCS
FIRE ARMS, SMALL: Guns Or Gun Parts, 30 mm & Below
FIRE ARMS, SMALL: Rifles Or Rifle Parts, 30 mm & below
FIRE CONTROL EQPT REPAIR SVCS, MILITARY
FIRE CONTROL OR BOMBING EQPT: Electronic
FIRE DETECTION SYSTEMS
FIRE EXTINGUISHERS, WHOLESALE
FIRE EXTINGUISHERS: Portable
FIRE OR BURGLARY RESISTIVE PRDTS
FIREARMS & AMMUNITION, EXC SPORTING, WHOLESALE
FIREFIGHTING APPARATUS
FIREPLACE EQPT & ACCESS
FIREWORKS
FIRST AID SPLYS, WHOLESALE
FISH & SEAFOOD WHOLESALERS
FISH FOOD
FITTINGS & ASSEMBLIES: Hose & Tube, Hydraulic Or
  Pneumatic
FITTINGS: Pipe
FITTINGS: Pipe, Fabricated
FIXTURES & EQPT: Kitchen, Metal, Exc Cast Aluminum
FIXTURES & EQPT: Kitchen, Porcelain Enameled
FLAGS: Fabric
FLAT GLASS: Construction

FLAT GLASS: Float
FLAT GLASS: Picture
FLAT GLASS: Plate, Polished & Rough
FLAT GLASS: Window, Clear & Colored
FLAVORS OR FLAVORING MATERIALS: Synthetic
FLIGHT RECORDERS
FLOOR COVERING STORES
FLOOR COVERING STORES: Carpets
FLOOR COVERINGS WHOLESALERS
FLOOR COVERINGS: Aircraft & Automobile
FLOOR COVERINGS: Rubber
FLOORING & SIDING: Metal
FLOORING: Hardwood
FLOORING: Rubber
FLORIST: Flowers, Fresh
FLOWERS, FRESH, WHOLESALE
FLUID METERS & COUNTING DEVICES
FLUID POWER PUMPS & MOTORS
FLUID POWER VALVES & HOSE FITTINGS
FOAM RUBBER
FOAMS & RUBBER, WHOLESALE
FOIL & LEAF: Metal
FOOD PRDTS, BREAKFAST: Cereal, Oatmeal
FOOD PRDTS, BREAKFAST: Cereal, Wheat Flakes
FOOD PRDTS, CANNED OR FRESH PACK: Fruit Juices
FOOD PRDTS, CANNED: Baby Food
FOOD PRDTS, CANNED: Barbecue Sauce
FOOD PRDTS, CANNED: Beans & Bean Sprouts
FOOD PRDTS, CANNED: Fruit Juices, Fresh
FOOD PRDTS, CANNED: Fruits
FOOD PRDTS, CANNED: Fruits
FOOD PRDTS, CANNED: Jams, Including Imitation
FOOD PRDTS, CANNED: Jams, Jellies & Preserves
FOOD PRDTS, CANNED: Jellies, Edible, Including Imitation
FOOD PRDTS, CANNED: Puddings, Exc Meat
FOOD PRDTS, CANNED: Spaghetti & Other Pasta Sauce
FOOD PRDTS, CANNED: Tomato Sauce.
FOOD PRDTS, CANNED: Vegetables
FOOD PRDTS, CONFECTIONERY, WHOLESALE: Candy
FOOD PRDTS, CONFECTIONERY, WHOLESALE: Pretzels
FOOD PRDTS, CONFECTIONERY, WHOLESALE: Snack
  Foods
FOOD PRDTS, FROZEN: Ethnic Foods, NEC
FOOD PRDTS, FROZEN: Fruit Juice, Concentrates
FOOD PRDTS, FROZEN: Fruit Juices
FOOD PRDTS, FROZEN: Fruits
FOOD PRDTS, FROZEN: Fruits & Vegetables
FOOD PRDTS, FROZEN: Fruits, Juices & Vegetables
FOOD PRDTS, WHOLESALE: Baking Splys
FOOD PRDTS, WHOLESALE: Beverages, Exc Coffee & Tea
FOOD PRDTS, WHOLESALE: Chocolate
FOOD PRDTS, WHOLESALE: Coffee, Green Or Roasted
FOOD PRDTS, WHOLESALE: Condiments
FOOD PRDTS, WHOLESALE: Cookies
FOOD PRDTS, WHOLESALE: Dried or Canned Foods
FOOD PRDTS, WHOLESALE: Grain Elevators
FOOD PRDTS, WHOLESALE: Grains
FOOD PRDTS, WHOLESALE: Juices
FOOD PRDTS, WHOLESALE: Salt, Edible
FOOD PRDTS, WHOLESALE: Specialty
FOOD PRDTS, WHOLESALE: Water, Distilled
FOOD PRDTS: Animal & marine fats & oils
FOOD PRDTS: Bread Crumbs, Exc Made In Bakeries
FOOD PRDTS: Chicken, Processed, Cooked
FOOD PRDTS: Chicken, Processed, Fresh
FOOD PRDTS: Chicken, Processed, Frozen
FOOD PRDTS: Chocolate Bars, Solid
FOOD PRDTS: Cocoa, Powdered
FOOD PRDTS: Coffee
FOOD PRDTS: Corn Oil Prdts
FOOD PRDTS: Dips, Exc Cheese & Sour Cream Based
FOOD PRDTS: Dough, Pizza, Prepared
FOOD PRDTS: Doughs, Frozen Or Refrig From Purchased
  Flour
FOOD PRDTS: Dressings, Salad, Raw & Cooked Exc Dry
  Mixes
FOOD PRDTS: Dried & Dehydrated Fruits, Vegetables &
  Soup Mix
FOOD PRDTS: Edible fats & oils
FOOD PRDTS: Emulsifiers
FOOD PRDTS: Flour
FOOD PRDTS: Flour & Other Grain Mill Products
FOOD PRDTS: Flour Mixes & Doughs

FOOD PRDTS: Flour, Blended From Purchased Flour
FOOD PRDTS: Flours & Flour Mixes, From Purchased Flour
FOOD PRDTS: Fruits & Vegetables, Pickled
FOOD PRDTS: Ice, Cubes
FOOD PRDTS: Mixes, Cake, From Purchased Flour
FOOD PRDTS: Mixes, Flour
FOOD PRDTS: Mixes, Sauces, Dry
FOOD PRDTS: Mustard, Prepared
FOOD PRDTS: Oils & Fats, Animal
FOOD PRDTS: Olive Oil
FOOD PRDTS: Pasta, Uncooked, Packaged With Other
   Ingredients
FOOD PRDTS: Peanut Butter
FOOD PRDTS: Pizza Doughs From Purchased Flour
FOOD PRDTS: Pork Rinds
FOOD PRDTS: Potato Chips & Other Potato-Based Snacks
FOOD PRDTS: Poultry, Processed, Frozen
FOOD PRDTS: Salad Oils, Refined Vegetable, Exc Corn
FOOD PRDTS: Sandwiches
FOOD PRDTS: Seasonings & Spices
FOOD PRDTS: Shortening & Solid Edible Fats
FOOD PRDTS: Starch, Corn
FOOD PRDTS: Sugar
FOOD PRDTS: Sugar, Beet
FOOD PRDTS: Syrup, Maple
FOOD PRDTS: Syrups
FOOD PRDTS: Tea
FOOD PRDTS: Tofu, Exc Frozen Desserts
FOOD PRDTS: Turkey, Slaughtered & Dressed
FOOD PRDTS: Vinegar
FOOD PRODUCTS MACHINERY
FOOD STORES: Convenience, Chain
FOOD STORES: Convenience, Independent
FOOD STORES: Delicatessen
FOOD STORES: Grocery, Independent
FOOD STORES: Supermarkets, Chain
FOOTWEAR, WHOLESALE: Boots
FOOTWEAR, WHOLESALE: Shoes
FOOTWEAR: Cut Stock
FORESTRY RELATED EQPT
FORGINGS: Aircraft, Ferrous
FORGINGS: Aluminum
FORGINGS: Automotive & Internal Combustion Engine
FORGINGS: Construction Or Mining Eqpt, Ferrous
FORGINGS: Iron & Steel
FORGINGS: Machinery, Ferrous
FORGINGS: Machinery, Nonferrous
FORGINGS: Metal , Ornamental, Ferrous
FORGINGS: Nonferrous
FORGINGS: Nuclear Power Plant, Ferrous
FORGINGS: Plumbing Fixture, Nonferrous
FORMS: Concrete, Sheet Metal
FOUNDRIES: Aluminum
FOUNDRIES: Gray & Ductile Iron
FOUNDRIES: Iron
FOUNDRIES: Nonferrous
FOUNDRIES: Steel
FOUNDRIES: Steel Investment
FOUNDRY MACHINERY & EQPT
FOUNTAINS: Concrete
FRACTIONATION PRDTS OF CRUDE PETROLEUM,
   HYDROCARBONS, NEC
FRANCHISES, SELLING OR LICENSING
FREIGHT FORWARDING ARRANGEMENTS
FRICTION MATERIAL, MADE FROM POWDERED METAL
FRUIT STANDS OR MARKETS
FRUITS & VEGETABLES WHOLESALERS: Fresh
FUEL ADDITIVES
FUEL CELLS: Solid State
FUEL OIL DEALERS
FUEL TREATING
FUELS: Diesel
FUNGICIDES OR HERBICIDES
FURNACES & OVENS: Indl
FURNACES: Indl, Electric
FURNACES: Indl, Electric
FURNACES: Warm Air, Electric
FURNITURE PARTS: Metal
FURNITURE REFINISHING SVCS
FURNITURE REPAIR & MAINTENANCE SVCS
FURNITURE STOCK & PARTS: Hardwood
FURNITURE STORES
FURNITURE WHOLESALERS

FURNITURE, HOUSEHOLD: Wholesalers
FURNITURE, MATTRESSES: Wholesalers
FURNITURE, OFFICE: Wholesalers
FURNITURE, WHOLESALE: Chairs
FURNITURE, WHOLESALE: Lockers
FURNITURE, WHOLESALE: Racks
FURNITURE, WHOLESALE: Shelving
FURNITURE: Bedroom, Wood
FURNITURE: Beds, Household, Incl Folding & Cabinet, Metal
FURNITURE: Cabinets & Filing Drawers, Office, Exc Wood
FURNITURE: Cabinets & Vanities, Medicine, Metal
FURNITURE: Chairs, Household Upholstered
FURNITURE: Chairs, Household Wood
FURNITURE: Chairs, Office Wood
FURNITURE: Church
FURNITURE: Console Tables, Wood
FURNITURE: Dining Room, Wood
FURNITURE: Fiberglass & Plastic
FURNITURE: Hotel
FURNITURE: Household, Metal
FURNITURE: Household, Upholstered, Exc Wood Or Metal
FURNITURE: Juvenile, Metal
FURNITURE: Lawn & Garden, Metal
FURNITURE: Lawn, Exc Wood, Metal, Stone Or Concrete
FURNITURE: Living Room, Upholstered On Wood Frames
FURNITURE: Mattresses & Foundations
FURNITURE: Mattresses, Box & Bedsprings
FURNITURE: Mattresses, Innerspring Or Box Spring
FURNITURE: Office, Exc Wood
FURNITURE: Office, Wood
FURNITURE: Picnic Tables Or Benches, Park
FURNITURE: Play Pens, Children's, Wood
FURNITURE: School
FURNITURE: Table Tops, Marble
FURNITURE: Upholstered
FURNITURE: Vehicle
FUSE MOUNTINGS: Electric Power
FUSES & FUSE EQPT

G

GAMES & TOYS: Board Games, Children's & Adults'
GAMES & TOYS: Child Restraint Seats, Automotive
GARBAGE CONTAINERS: Plastic
GARBAGE DISPOSERS & COMPACTORS: Commercial
GAS & OIL FIELD EXPLORATION SVCS
GAS & OIL FIELD SVCS, NEC
GAS FIELD MACHINERY & EQPT
GASES: Acetylene
GASES: Carbon Dioxide
GASES: Indl
GASES: Nitrogen
GASES: Oxygen
GASKET MATERIALS
GASKETS
GASKETS & SEALING DEVICES
GASOLINE FILLING STATIONS
GASOLINE WHOLESALERS
GEARS
GEARS & GEAR UNITS: Reduction, Exc Auto
GEARS: Power Transmission, Exc Auto
GENERATING APPARATUS & PARTS: Electrical
GENERATION EQPT: Electronic
GENERATORS: Electrochemical, Fuel Cell
GENERATORS: Gas
GIFT SHOP
GIFT WRAP: Paper, Made From Purchased Materials
GIFT, NOVELTY & SOUVENIR STORES: Gifts & Novelties
GIFTS & NOVELTIES: Wholesalers
GLASS & GLASS CERAMIC PRDTS, PRESSED OR
   BLOWN: Tableware
GLASS PRDTS, FROM PURCHASED GLASS: Glassware
GLASS PRDTS, FROM PURCHASED GLASS: Insulating
GLASS PRDTS, FROM PURCHASED GLASS: Mirrored
GLASS PRDTS, FROM PURCHASED GLASS: Sheet, Bent
GLASS PRDTS, FROM PURCHASED GLASS: Windshields
GLASS PRDTS, FROM PURCHD GLASS: Strengthened Or
   Reinforced
GLASS PRDTS, PRESSED OR BLOWN: Furnishings &
   Access
GLASS PRDTS, PRESSED OR BLOWN: Glass Fibers, Textile
GLASS PRDTS, PRESSED OR BLOWN: Glassware, Art Or
   Decorative
GLASS PRDTS, PRESSED OR BLOWN: Scientific Glassware

GLASS PRDTS, PRESSED OR BLOWN: Yarn, Fiberglass
GLASS, AUTOMOTIVE: Wholesalers
GLASS: Fiber
GLASS: Flat
GLASS: Pressed & Blown, NEC
GLASS: Tempered
GLOVES: Safety
GLOVES: Work
GLOVES: Woven Or Knit, From Purchased Materials
GLYCOL ETHERS
GOLF COURSES: Public
GOLF DRIVING RANGES
GOLF EQPT
GOURMET FOOD STORES
GOVERNMENT, GENERAL: Administration
GRADING SVCS
GRAIN & FIELD BEANS WHOLESALERS
GRANITE: Crushed & Broken
GRANITE: Cut & Shaped
GRAPHIC ARTS & RELATED DESIGN SVCS
GRAPHITE MINING SVCS
GRATINGS: Open Steel Flooring
GRAVE VAULTS, METAL
GRAVEL MINING
GREASES: Lubricating
GREENHOUSES: Prefabricated Metal
GRINDING SVC: Precision, Commercial Or Indl
GROCERIES, GENERAL LINE WHOLESALERS
GUIDED MISSILES & SPACE VEHICLES
GUM & WOOD CHEMICALS
GUTTERS: Sheet Metal
GYPSUM PRDTS
GYROSCOPES

H

HAIR & HAIR BASED PRDTS
HAIR CARE PRDTS
HAND TOOLS, NEC: Wholesalers
HANDBAGS
HANDBAGS: Women's
HANDYMAN SVCS
HARD RUBBER PRDTS, NEC
HARDWARE
HARDWARE & BUILDING PRDTS: Plastic
HARDWARE & EQPT: Stage, Exc Lighting
HARDWARE STORES
HARDWARE STORES: Builders'
HARDWARE STORES: Pumps & Pumping Eqpt
HARDWARE STORES: Tools
HARDWARE WHOLESALERS
HARDWARE, WHOLESALE: Bolts
HARDWARE, WHOLESALE: Builders', NEC
HARDWARE, WHOLESALE: Nuts
HARDWARE, WHOLESALE: Power Tools & Access
HARDWARE, WHOLESALE: Screws
HARDWARE: Aircraft
HARDWARE: Aircraft & Marine, Incl Pulleys & Similar Items
HARDWARE: Builders'
HARDWARE: Casket
HARDWARE: Furniture, Builders' & Other Household
HARNESS ASSEMBLIES: Cable & Wire
HARNESS WIRING SETS: Internal Combustion Engines
HEALTH & WELFARE COUNCIL
HEARING AIDS
HEAT EMISSION OPERATING APPARATUS
HEAT EXCHANGERS: After Or Inter Coolers Or Condensers,
   Etc
HEAT TREATING: Metal
HEATERS: Swimming Pool, Electric
HEATING & AIR CONDITIONING UNITS, COMBINATION
HEATING APPARATUS: Steam
HEATING EQPT: Complete
HEATING EQPT: Induction
HEATING UNITS & DEVICES: Indl, Electric
HEAVY DISTILLATES
HELMETS: Steel
HELP SUPPLY SERVICES
HOBBY, TOY & GAME STORES: Toys & Games
HOISTING SLINGS
HOISTS
HOLDING COMPANIES: Investment, Exc Banks
HOLDING COMPANIES: Personal, Exc Banks
HOME FOR THE MENTALLY HANDICAPPED

HOMEFURNISHING STORES: Beddings & Linens
HOMEFURNISHING STORES: Brushes
HOMEFURNISHING STORES: Cutlery
HOMEFURNISHING STORES: Pottery
HOMEFURNISHINGS, WHOLESALE: Blinds, Vertical
HOMEFURNISHINGS, WHOLESALE: Decorating Splys
HOMEFURNISHINGS, WHOLESALE: Draperies
HOMEFURNISHINGS, WHOLESALE: Grills, Barbecue
HOMEFURNISHINGS, WHOLESALE: Kitchenware
HOMES: Log Cabins
HOODS: Range, Sheet Metal
HORSESHOES
HOSE: Automobile, Rubber
HOSE: Flexible Metal
HOSE: Plastic
HOSE: Rubber
HOSPITALS: Medical & Surgical
HOTELS & MOTELS
HOUSEHOLD ARTICLES, EXC KITCHEN: Pottery
HOUSEHOLD ARTICLES: Metal
HOUSEHOLD FURNISHINGS, NEC
HOUSEWARES, ELECTRIC: Air Purifiers, Portable
HOUSEWARES, ELECTRIC: Cooking Appliances
HOUSEWARES, ELECTRIC: Fans, Exhaust & Ventilating
HOUSEWARES: Food Dishes & Utensils, Pressed & Molded
  Pulp
HUMIDIFIERS & DEHUMIDIFIERS
HYDRAULIC EQPT REPAIR SVC

I

ICE
ICE CREAM & ICES WHOLESALERS
IDENTIFICATION TAGS, EXC PAPER
IGNITION SYSTEMS: High Frequency
INCINERATORS
INCUBATORS & BROODERS: Farm
INDL & PERSONAL SVC PAPER WHOLESALERS
INDL & PERSONAL SVC PAPER, WHOLESALE: Boxes &
  Containers
INDL & PERSONAL SVC PAPER, WHOLESALE: Shipping
  Splys
INDL CONTRACTORS: Exhibit Construction
INDL DIAMONDS WHOLESALERS
INDL EQPT SVCS
INDL GASES WHOLESALERS
INDL HELP SVCS
INDL MACHINERY & EQPT WHOLESALERS
INDL PATTERNS: Foundry Cores
INDL PATTERNS: Foundry Patternmaking
INDL PROCESS INSTRUMENTS: Chromatographs
INDL PROCESS INSTRUMENTS: Control
INDL SPLYS WHOLESALERS
INDL SPLYS, WHOLESALE: Abrasives
INDL SPLYS, WHOLESALE: Bearings
INDL SPLYS, WHOLESALE: Bins & Containers, Storage
INDL SPLYS, WHOLESALE: Drums, New Or Reconditioned
INDL SPLYS, WHOLESALE: Gaskets & Seals
INDL SPLYS, WHOLESALE: Gears
INDL SPLYS, WHOLESALE: Glass Bottles
INDL SPLYS, WHOLESALE: Power Transmission, Eqpt &
  Apparatus
INDL SPLYS, WHOLESALE: Rubber Goods, Mechanical
INDL SPLYS, WHOLESALE: Seals
INDL SPLYS, WHOLESALE: Tools
INDL SPLYS, WHOLESALE: Valves & Fittings
INDUSTRIAL & COMMERCIAL EQPT INSPECTION SVCS
INFORMATION RETRIEVAL SERVICES
INFRARED OBJECT DETECTION EQPT
INGOT: Aluminum
INK OR WRITING FLUIDS
INK: Gravure
INK: Printing
INSECTICIDES
INSECTICIDES & PESTICIDES
INSPECTION & TESTING SVCS
INSTRUMENTS & METERS: Measuring, Electric
INSTRUMENTS, LABORATORY: Analyzers, Automatic
  Chemical
INSTRUMENTS, LABORATORY: Spectrometers
INSTRUMENTS, MEASURING & CNTRL: Geophysical &
  Meteorological
INSTRUMENTS, MEASURING & CNTRL: Radiation &
  Testing, Nuclear

INSTRUMENTS, MEASURING & CNTRLG: Aircraft & Motor
  Vehicle
INSTRUMENTS, MEASURING & CNTRLNG: Nuclear
  Instrument Modules
INSTRUMENTS, MEASURING & CONTROLLING:
  Breathalyzers
INSTRUMENTS, MEASURING & CONTROLLING: Cable
  Testing
INSTRUMENTS, MEASURING & CONTROLLING:
  Magnetometers
INSTRUMENTS, MEASURING & CONTROLLING: Ultrasonic
  Testing
INSTRUMENTS, OPTICAL: Mirrors
INSTRUMENTS, SURGICAL & MED: Needles & Syringes,
  Hypodermic
INSTRUMENTS, SURGICAL & MEDICAL: Blood & Bone
  Work
INSTRUMENTS, SURGICAL & MEDICAL: Inhalation Therapy
INSTRUMENTS, SURGICAL & MEDICAL: IV Transfusion
INSTRUMENTS, SURGICAL & MEDICAL: Operating Tables
INSTRUMENTS, SURGICAL/MED: Microsurgical, Exc
  Electromedical
INSTRUMENTS: Analytical
INSTRUMENTS: Combustion Control, Indl
INSTRUMENTS: Electrocardiographs
INSTRUMENTS: Endoscopic Eqpt, Electromedical
INSTRUMENTS: Flow, Indl Process
INSTRUMENTS: Indl Process Control
INSTRUMENTS: Infrared, Indl Process
INSTRUMENTS: Laser, Scientific & Engineering
INSTRUMENTS: Liquid Level, Indl Process
INSTRUMENTS: Measurement, Indl Process
INSTRUMENTS: Measuring, Electrical Energy
INSTRUMENTS: Measuring, Electrical Power
INSTRUMENTS: Medical & Surgical
INSTRUMENTS: Particle Size Analyzers
INSTRUMENTS: Pressure Measurement, Indl
INSTRUMENTS: Radio Frequency Measuring
INSTRUMENTS: Signal Generators & Averagers
INSTRUMENTS: Temperature Measurement, Indl
INSTRUMENTS: Test, Electrical, Engine
INSTRUMENTS: Test, Electronic & Electric Measurement
INSULATION & ROOFING MATERIALS: Wood, Reconstituted
INSULATION MATERIALS WHOLESALERS
INSULATION: Fiberglass
INSULATORS & INSULATION MATERIALS: Electrical
INSULATORS, PORCELAIN: Electrical
INSURANCE BROKERS, NEC
INSURANCE CARRIERS: Life
INSURANCE CLAIM PROCESSING, EXC MEDICAL
INSURANCE: Agents, Brokers & Service
INTEGRATED CIRCUITS, SEMICONDUCTOR NETWORKS,
  ETC
INTERIOR DESIGN SVCS, NEC
INTRAVENOUS SOLUTIONS
INVERTERS: Nonrotating Electrical
INVESTMENT ADVISORY SVCS
INVESTMENT FIRM: General Brokerage
INVESTORS, NEC
IRON & STEEL PRDTS: Hot-Rolled
IRON ORE MINING
IRON ORES

J

JACKS: Hydraulic
JEWELERS' FINDINGS & MATERIALS
JEWELRY REPAIR SVCS
JEWELRY STORES
JEWELRY STORES: Precious Stones & Precious Metals
JEWELRY STORES: Silverware
JEWELRY, PRECIOUS METAL: Settings & Mountings
JEWELRY, WHOLESALE
JEWELRY: Precious Metal
JIGS & FIXTURES
JOB PRINTING & NEWSPAPER PUBLISHING COMBINED
JOINTS: Expansion, Pipe
JOINTS: Swivel & Universal, Exc Aircraft & Auto
JOISTS: Long-Span Series, Open Web Steel

K

KILNS & FURNACES: Ceramic
KITCHEN CABINETS WHOLESALERS

KITCHEN UTENSILS: Food Handling & Processing Prdts,
  Wood
KITCHENWARE STORES
KITCHENWARE: Plastic
KNIVES: Agricultural Or indl

L

LABELS: Paper, Made From Purchased Materials
LABELS: Woven
LABORATORIES, TESTING: Food
LABORATORIES, TESTING: Metallurgical
LABORATORIES, TESTING: Pollution
LABORATORIES, TESTING: Product Testing
LABORATORIES, TESTING: Product Testing, Safety/
  Performance
LABORATORIES: Biological Research
LABORATORIES: Biotechnology
LABORATORIES: Dental, Crown & Bridge Production
LABORATORIES: Electronic Research
LABORATORIES: Medical
LABORATORIES: Noncommercial Research
LABORATORIES: Physical Research, Commercial
LABORATORIES: Testing
LABORATORIES: Testing
LABORATORY APPARATUS & FURNITURE
LABORATORY APPARATUS, EXC HEATING & MEASURING
LABORATORY APPARATUS: Freezers
LABORATORY APPARATUS: Pipettes, Hemocytometer
LABORATORY CHEMICALS: Organic
LABORATORY EQPT, EXC MEDICAL: Wholesalers
LABORATORY EQPT: Chemical
LABORATORY EQPT: Clinical Instruments Exc Medical
LABORATORY EQPT: Incubators
LABORATORY EQPT: Measuring
LABORATORY EQPT: Sterilizers
LABORATORY INSTRUMENT REPAIR SVCS
LADDERS: Metal
LADLES: Metal Plate
LAMINATED PLASTICS: Plate, Sheet, Rod & Tubes
LAMINATING SVCS
LAMP & LIGHT BULBS & TUBES
LAMP BULBS & TUBES/PARTS, ELECTRIC: Generalized
  Applications
LAMP SHADES: Glass
LAMPS: Fluorescent
LAMPS: Table, Residential
LAND SUBDIVISION & DEVELOPMENT
LASER SYSTEMS & EQPT
LASERS: Welding, Drilling & Cutting Eqpt
LATEX: Foamed
LATH: Expanded Metal
LAUNDRY EQPT: Commercial
LAUNDRY EQPT: Household
LAWN & GARDEN EQPT
LAWN & GARDEN EQPT: Grass Catchers, Lawn Mower
LAWN & GARDEN EQPT: Lawnmowers, Residential, Hand
  Or Power
LAWN & GARDEN EQPT: Rototillers
LAWN & GARDEN EQPT: Tractors & Eqpt
LEAD & ZINC ORES
LEAD PENCILS & ART GOODS
LEASING & RENTAL SVCS: Cranes & Aerial Lift Eqpt
LEASING & RENTAL SVCS: Oil Field Eqpt
LEASING & RENTAL SVCS: Oil Well Drilling
LEASING & RENTAL: Construction & Mining Eqpt
LEASING & RENTAL: Medical Machinery & Eqpt
LEASING & RENTAL: Trucks, Indl
LEASING & RENTAL: Trucks, Without Drivers
LEATHER & CUT STOCK WHOLESALERS
LEATHER GOODS, EXC FOOTWEAR, GLOVES,
  LUGGAGE/ BELTING, WHOL
LEATHER GOODS: Garments
LEATHER GOODS: Holsters
LEATHER GOODS: Personal
LEATHER GOODS: Wallets
LEATHER TANNING & FINISHING
LEGAL OFFICES & SVCS
LEGAL SVCS: General Practice Attorney or Lawyer
LICENSE TAGS: Automobile, Stamped Metal
LIGHTING EQPT: Flashlights
LIGHTING EQPT: Motor Vehicle
LIGHTING EQPT: Motor Vehicle, Headlights
LIGHTING EQPT: Motor Vehicle, NEC

LIGHTING EQPT: Outdoor
LIGHTING FIXTURES WHOLESALERS
LIGHTING FIXTURES, NEC
LIGHTING FIXTURES: Decorative Area
LIGHTING FIXTURES: Fluorescent, Commercial
LIGHTING FIXTURES: Indl & Commercial
LIGHTING FIXTURES: Motor Vehicle
LIGHTING FIXTURES: Ornamental, Commercial
LIGHTING FIXTURES: Public
LIGHTING FIXTURES: Residential, Electric
LIGHTING FIXTURES: Street
LIME
LIME ROCK: Ground
LIMESTONE: Crushed & Broken
LIMESTONE: Cut & Shaped
LIMESTONE: Dimension
LIMESTONE: Ground
LINENS & TOWELS WHOLESALERS
LINERS & COVERS: Fabric
LINERS & LINING
LININGS: Fabric, Apparel & Other, Exc Millinery
LIQUEFIED PETROLEUM GAS DEALERS
LIQUEFIED PETROLEUM GAS WHOLESALERS
LIQUID CRYSTAL DISPLAYS
LITHOGRAPHIC PLATES
LIVESTOCK WHOLESALERS, NEC
LOADS: Electronic
LOCKERS
LOCKSMITHS
LOCOMOTIVES & PARTS
LOGGING
LOGGING CAMPS & CONTRACTORS
LOGGING: Timber, Cut At Logging Camp
LOGGING: Wooden Logs
LOGS: Gas, Fireplace
LOTIONS OR CREAMS: Face
LUBRICANTS: Corrosion Preventive
LUBRICATING EQPT: Indl
LUBRICATING OIL & GREASE WHOLESALERS
LUBRICATION SYSTEMS & EQPT
LUGGAGE & BRIEFCASES
LUGGAGE & LEATHER GOODS STORES
LUGGAGE: Traveling Bags
LUMBER & BLDG MATLS DEALER, RET: Garage Doors, Sell/Install
LUMBER & BLDG MATRLS DEALERS, RET: Bath Fixtures, Eqpt/Sply
LUMBER & BLDG MATRLS DEALERS, RETAIL: Doors, Wood/Metal
LUMBER & BLDG MTRLS DEALERS, RET: Planing Mill Prdts/Lumber
LUMBER & BUILDING MATERIALS DEALER, RET: Door & Window Prdts
LUMBER & BUILDING MATERIALS DEALER, RET: Masonry Matls/Splys
LUMBER & BUILDING MATERIALS DEALERS, RET: Solar Heating Eqpt
LUMBER & BUILDING MATERIALS DEALERS, RETAIL: Brick
LUMBER & BUILDING MATERIALS DEALERS, RETAIL: Cement
LUMBER & BUILDING MATERIALS DEALERS, RETAIL: Modular Homes
LUMBER & BUILDING MATERIALS DEALERS, RETAIL: Tile, Ceramic
LUMBER & BUILDING MATERIALS RET DEALERS: Millwork & Lumber
LUMBER & BUILDING MATLS DEALERS, RET: Concrete/Cinder Block
LUMBER: Dimension, Hardwood
LUMBER: Fiberboard
LUMBER: Flooring, Dressed, Softwood
LUMBER: Hardwood Dimension
LUMBER: Hardwood Dimension & Flooring Mills
LUMBER: Kiln Dried
LUMBER: Plywood, Hardwood
LUMBER: Plywood, Softwood
LUMBER: Treated
LUMBER: Veneer, Softwood

M

MACHINE PARTS: Stamped Or Pressed Metal
MACHINE TOOL ACCESS: Drill Bushings, Drilling Jig
MACHINE TOOL ACCESS: Drills

MACHINE TOOL ACCESS: Tools & Access
MACHINE TOOL ATTACHMENTS & ACCESS
MACHINE TOOLS & ACCESS
MACHINE TOOLS, METAL CUTTING: Drilling
MACHINE TOOLS, METAL CUTTING: Drilling & Boring
MACHINE TOOLS, METAL CUTTING: Exotic, Including Explosive
MACHINE TOOLS, METAL CUTTING: Home Workshop
MACHINE TOOLS, METAL CUTTING: Numerically Controlled
MACHINE TOOLS, METAL CUTTING: Pipe Cutting & Threading
MACHINE TOOLS, METAL CUTTING: Plasma Process
MACHINE TOOLS, METAL CUTTING: Tool Replacement & Rpr Parts
MACHINE TOOLS, METAL FORMING: Bending
MACHINE TOOLS, METAL FORMING: Die Casting & Extruding
MACHINE TOOLS, METAL FORMING: Marking
MACHINE TOOLS, METAL FORMING: Mechanical, Pneumatic Or Hyd
MACHINE TOOLS, METAL FORMING: Pressing
MACHINE TOOLS, METAL FORMING: Rebuilt
MACHINE TOOLS: Metal Cutting
MACHINE TOOLS: Metal Forming
MACHINERY & EQPT FINANCE LEASING
MACHINERY & EQPT, AGRICULTURAL, WHOLESALE: Lawn & Garden
MACHINERY & EQPT, INDL, WHOLESALE: Chemical Process
MACHINERY & EQPT, INDL, WHOLESALE: Conveyor Systems
MACHINERY & EQPT, INDL, WHOLESALE: Cranes
MACHINERY & EQPT, INDL, WHOLESALE: Engines & Parts, Diesel
MACHINERY & EQPT, INDL, WHOLESALE: Engs & Parts, Air-Cooled
MACHINERY & EQPT, INDL, WHOLESALE: Engs/Transportation Eqpt
MACHINERY & EQPT, INDL, WHOLESALE: Fans
MACHINERY & EQPT, INDL, WHOLESALE: Food Product Manufacturng
MACHINERY & EQPT, INDL, WHOLESALE: Heat Exchange
MACHINERY & EQPT, INDL, WHOLESALE: Hydraulic Systems
MACHINERY & EQPT, INDL, WHOLESALE: Indl Machine Parts
MACHINERY & EQPT, INDL, WHOLESALE: Instruments & Cntrl Eqpt
MACHINERY & EQPT, INDL, WHOLESALE: Lift Trucks & Parts
MACHINERY & EQPT, INDL, WHOLESALE: Machine Tools & Access
MACHINERY & EQPT, INDL, WHOLESALE: Packaging
MACHINERY & EQPT, INDL, WHOLESALE: Paint Spray
MACHINERY & EQPT, INDL, WHOLESALE: Paper Manufacturing
MACHINERY & EQPT, INDL, WHOLESALE: Petroleum Industry
MACHINERY & EQPT, INDL, WHOLESALE: Processing & Packaging
MACHINERY & EQPT, INDL, WHOLESALE: Pulp Manufacturing, Wood
MACHINERY & EQPT, INDL, WHOLESALE: Recycling
MACHINERY & EQPT, INDL, WHOLESALE: Safety Eqpt
MACHINERY & EQPT, INDL, WHOLESALE: Trailers, Indl
MACHINERY & EQPT, INDL, WHOLESALE: Water Pumps
MACHINERY & EQPT, WHOLESALE: Construction, General
MACHINERY & EQPT, WHOLESALE: Oil Field Eqpt
MACHINERY & EQPT, WHOLESALE: Road Construction & Maintenance
MACHINERY & EQPT: Electroplating
MACHINERY & EQPT: Farm
MACHINERY & EQPT: Liquid Automation
MACHINERY, CALCULATING: Calculators & Adding
MACHINERY, EQPT & SUPPLIES: Parking Facility
MACHINERY, FOOD PRDTS: Beverage
MACHINERY, FOOD PRDTS: Cutting, Chopping, Grinding, Mixing
MACHINERY, FOOD PRDTS: Food Processing, Smokers
MACHINERY, FOOD PRDTS: Oilseed Crushing & Extracting
MACHINERY, FOOD PRDTS: Ovens, Bakery
MACHINERY, FOOD PRDTS: Processing, Poultry
MACHINERY, METALWORKING: Coiling

MACHINERY, OFFICE: Paper Handling
MACHINERY, PACKAGING: Canning, Food
MACHINERY, PACKAGING: Packing & Wrapping
MACHINERY, PACKAGING: Vacuum
MACHINERY, PAPER INDUSTRY: Converting, Die Cutting & Stampng
MACHINERY, PAPER INDUSTRY: Paper Mill, Plating, Etc
MACHINERY, PAPER INDUSTRY: Pulp Mill
MACHINERY, PRINTING TRADES: Plates
MACHINERY, SEWING: Sewing & Hat & Zipper Making
MACHINERY, TEXTILE: Printing
MACHINERY: Ammunition & Explosives Loading
MACHINERY: Automotive Related
MACHINERY: Concrete Prdts
MACHINERY: Construction
MACHINERY: Cryogenic, Industrial
MACHINERY: Custom
MACHINERY: Electronic Component Making
MACHINERY: Gas Separators
MACHINERY: Ice Cream
MACHINERY: Metalworking
MACHINERY: Mining
MACHINERY: Pack-Up Assemblies, Wheel Overhaul
MACHINERY: Packaging
MACHINERY: Paint Making
MACHINERY: Plastic Working
MACHINERY: Printing Presses
MACHINERY: Recycling
MACHINERY: Road Construction & Maintenance
MACHINERY: Robots, Molding & Forming Plastics
MACHINERY: Rubber Working
MACHINERY: Screening Eqpt, Electric
MACHINERY: Semiconductor Manufacturing
MACHINERY: Separation Eqpt, Magnetic
MACHINERY: Sifting & Screening
MACHINERY: Textile
MACHINERY: Tire Retreading
MACHINERY: Wire Drawing
MACHINERY: Woodworking
MACHINISTS' TOOLS & MACHINES: Measuring, Metalworking Type
MACHINISTS' TOOLS: Measuring, Precision
MACHINISTS' TOOLS: Precision
MAGNESIUM
MAGNESIUM
MAGNETIC INK & OPTICAL SCANNING EQPT
MAGNETS: Permanent
MAIL-ORDER HOUSE, NEC
MAIL-ORDER HOUSES: Educational Splys & Eqpt
MAIL-ORDER HOUSES: Food
MAILING & MESSENGER SVCS
MAILING LIST: Compilers
MAILING SVCS, NEC
MANAGEMENT CONSULTING SVCS: Automation & Robotics
MANAGEMENT CONSULTING SVCS: Business
MANAGEMENT CONSULTING SVCS: Business Planning & Organizing
MANAGEMENT CONSULTING SVCS: Construction Project
MANAGEMENT CONSULTING SVCS: Corporation Organizing
MANAGEMENT CONSULTING SVCS: Distribution Channels
MANAGEMENT CONSULTING SVCS: General
MANAGEMENT CONSULTING SVCS: Hospital & Health
MANAGEMENT CONSULTING SVCS: Industrial
MANAGEMENT CONSULTING SVCS: Industry Specialist
MANAGEMENT CONSULTING SVCS: Information Systems
MANAGEMENT CONSULTING SVCS: Manufacturing
MANAGEMENT CONSULTING SVCS: Training & Development
MANAGEMENT CONSULTING SVCS: Transportation
MANAGEMENT SERVICES
MANAGEMENT SVCS: Administrative
MANAGEMENT SVCS: Business
MANAGEMENT SVCS: Construction
MANPOWER POOLS
MANUFACTURING INDUSTRIES, NEC
MARBLE, BUILDING: Cut & Shaped
MARINE CARGO HANDLING SVCS
MARINE HARDWARE
MARINE SPLYS WHOLESALERS
MARKETS: Meat & fish
MARKING DEVICES

MARKING DEVICES: Canceling Stamps, Hand, Rubber Or Metal
MARKING DEVICES: Embossing Seals & Hand Stamps
MARKING DEVICES: Embossing Seals, Corporate & Official
MATS OR MATTING, NEC: Rubber
MATS, MATTING & PADS: Nonwoven
MEAT MARKETS
MEAT PRDTS: Bacon, Side & Sliced, From Purchased Meat
MEAT PRDTS: Boxed Beef, From Slaughtered Meat
MEAT PRDTS: Cooked Meats, From Purchased Meat
MEAT PRDTS: Frozen
MEAT PRDTS: Luncheon Meat, From Purchased Meat
MEAT PRDTS: Prepared Beef Prdts From Purchased Beef
MEAT PRDTS: Sausages & Related Prdts, From Purchased Meat
MEAT PRDTS: Sausages, From Purchased Meat
MEAT PRDTS: Snack Sticks, Incl Jerky, From Purchased Meat
MEDIA: Magnetic & Optical Recording
MEDICAL & HOSPITAL EQPT WHOLESALERS
MEDICAL & SURGICAL SPLYS: Bandages & Dressings
MEDICAL & SURGICAL SPLYS: Braces, Elastic
MEDICAL & SURGICAL SPLYS: Braces, Orthopedic
MEDICAL & SURGICAL SPLYS: Clothing, Fire Resistant & Protect
MEDICAL & SURGICAL SPLYS: Foot Appliances, Orthopedic
MEDICAL & SURGICAL SPLYS: Grafts, Artificial
MEDICAL & SURGICAL SPLYS: Gynecological Splys & Appliances
MEDICAL & SURGICAL SPLYS: Limbs, Artificial
MEDICAL & SURGICAL SPLYS: Orthopedic Appliances
MEDICAL & SURGICAL SPLYS: Prosthetic Appliances
MEDICAL & SURGICAL SPLYS: Splints, Pneumatic & Wood
MEDICAL & SURGICAL SPLYS: Stretchers
MEDICAL EQPT REPAIR SVCS, NON-ELECTRIC
MEDICAL EQPT: Diagnostic
MEDICAL EQPT: Electromedical Apparatus
MEDICAL EQPT: Sterilizers
MEDICAL EQPT: Ultrasonic Scanning Devices
MEDICAL EQPT: X-Ray Apparatus & Tubes, Radiographic
MEDICAL INSURANCE CLAIM PROCESSING: Contract Or Fee Basis
MEDICAL SUNDRIES: Rubber
MEDICAL, DENTAL & HOSP EQPT, WHOLESALE: X-ray Film & Splys
MEDICAL, DENTAL & HOSPITAL EQPT, WHOL: Hospital Eqpt & Splys
MEDICAL, DENTAL & HOSPITAL EQPT, WHOL: Surgical Eqpt & Splys
MEDICAL, DENTAL & HOSPITAL EQPT, WHOLESALE: Artificial Limbs
MELAMINE RESINS: Melamine-Formaldehyde
MEMBERSHIP ORGANIZATIONS, NEC: Personal Interest
MEMBERSHIP ORGS, RELIGIOUS: Non-Denominational Church
MEN'S & BOYS' CLOTHING ACCESS STORES
MEN'S & BOYS' CLOTHING STORES
MEN'S & BOYS' CLOTHING WHOLESALERS, NEC
METAL & STEEL PRDTS: Abrasive
METAL COMPONENTS: Prefabricated
METAL DETECTORS
METAL FABRICATORS: Plate
METAL FINISHING SVCS
METAL MINING SVCS
METAL SERVICE CENTERS & OFFICES
METAL STAMPING, FOR THE TRADE
METAL STAMPINGS: Perforated
METAL TREATING COMPOUNDS
METAL, TITANIUM: Sponge & Granules
METAL: Battery
METALS SVC CENTERS & WHOLESALERS: Cable, Wire
METALS SVC CENTERS & WHOLESALERS: Ferrous Metals
METALS SVC CENTERS & WHOLESALERS: Flat Prdts, Iron Or Steel
METALS SVC CENTERS & WHOLESALERS: Pipe & Tubing, Steel
METALS SVC CENTERS & WHOLESALERS: Sheets, Metal
METALS SVC CENTERS & WHOLESALERS: Steel
METALS SVC CENTERS & WHOLESALERS: Tubing, Metal
METALS: Precious NEC
METALS: Precious, Secondary
METALS: Primary Nonferrous, NEC
METALWORK: Miscellaneous

METALWORK: Ornamental
METALWORKING MACHINERY WHOLESALERS
METERING DEVICES: Flow Meters, Impeller & Counter Driven
METERING DEVICES: Water Quality Monitoring & Control Systems
METERS: Pyrometers, Indl Process
MICROCIRCUITS, INTEGRATED: Semiconductor
MICROPHONES
MICROPROCESSORS
MICROWAVE COMPONENTS
MILITARY INSIGNIA
MILL PRDTS: Structural & Rail
MILLWORK
MINE & QUARRY SVCS: Nonmetallic Minerals
MINE DEVELOPMENT SVCS: Nonmetallic Minerals
MINE PREPARATION SVCS
MINERAL WOOL
MINERAL WOOL INSULATION PRDTS
MINERALS: Ground Or Otherwise Treated
MINERALS: Ground or Treated
MINIATURES
MINING EXPLORATION & DEVELOPMENT SVCS
MINING MACHINERY & EQPT WHOLESALERS
MINING MACHINES & EQPT: Crushers, Stationary
MIXTURES & BLOCKS: Asphalt Paving
MOBILE COMMUNICATIONS EQPT
MOBILE HOMES
MOBILE HOMES, EXC RECREATIONAL
MOBILE HOMES: Personal Or Private Use
MODELS: General, Exc Toy
MODULES: Computer Logic
MOLDED RUBBER PRDTS
MOLDING COMPOUNDS
MOLDINGS & TRIM: Metal, Exc Automobile
MOLDINGS & TRIM: Wood
MOLDINGS OR TRIM: Automobile, Stamped Metal
MOLDS: Gray, Ingot, Cast Iron
MOLDS: Indl
MOLYBDENUM SILICON, EXC MADE IN BLAST FURNACES
MOPS: Floor & Dust
MORTAR: High Temperature, Nonclay
MOTOR & GENERATOR PARTS: Electric
MOTOR CONTROL CENTERS
MOTOR HOMES
MOTOR SCOOTERS & PARTS
MOTOR VEHICLE ASSEMBLY, COMPLETE: Ambulances
MOTOR VEHICLE ASSEMBLY, COMPLETE: Buses, All Types
MOTOR VEHICLE ASSEMBLY, COMPLETE: Fire Department Vehicles
MOTOR VEHICLE ASSEMBLY, COMPLETE: Military Motor Vehicle
MOTOR VEHICLE ASSEMBLY, COMPLETE: Wreckers, Tow Truck
MOTOR VEHICLE DEALERS: Automobiles, New & Used
MOTOR VEHICLE DEALERS: Vans, New & Used
MOTOR VEHICLE PARTS & ACCESS: Acceleration Eqpt
MOTOR VEHICLE PARTS & ACCESS: Air Conditioner Parts
MOTOR VEHICLE PARTS & ACCESS: Ball Joints
MOTOR VEHICLE PARTS & ACCESS: Bearings
MOTOR VEHICLE PARTS & ACCESS: Body Components & Frames
MOTOR VEHICLE PARTS & ACCESS: Brakes, Air
MOTOR VEHICLE PARTS & ACCESS: Clutches
MOTOR VEHICLE PARTS & ACCESS: Connecting Rods
MOTOR VEHICLE PARTS & ACCESS: Electrical Eqpt
MOTOR VEHICLE PARTS & ACCESS: Engines & Parts
MOTOR VEHICLE PARTS & ACCESS: Fuel Pumps
MOTOR VEHICLE PARTS & ACCESS: Fuel Systems & Parts
MOTOR VEHICLE PARTS & ACCESS: Gas Tanks
MOTOR VEHICLE PARTS & ACCESS: Gears
MOTOR VEHICLE PARTS & ACCESS: Heaters
MOTOR VEHICLE PARTS & ACCESS: Instrument Board Assemblies
MOTOR VEHICLE PARTS & ACCESS: Lubrication Systems & Parts
MOTOR VEHICLE PARTS & ACCESS: Mufflers, Exhaust
MOTOR VEHICLE PARTS & ACCESS: Oil Strainers
MOTOR VEHICLE PARTS & ACCESS: Power Steering Eqpt
MOTOR VEHICLE PARTS & ACCESS: Propane Conversion Eqpt
MOTOR VEHICLE PARTS & ACCESS: Pumps, Hydraulic Fluid Power

MOTOR VEHICLE PARTS & ACCESS: Rear Axel Housings
MOTOR VEHICLE PARTS & ACCESS: Sanders, Safety
MOTOR VEHICLE PARTS & ACCESS: Tire Valve Cores
MOTOR VEHICLE PARTS & ACCESS: Trailer Hitches
MOTOR VEHICLE PARTS & ACCESS: Transmission Housings Or Parts
MOTOR VEHICLE PARTS & ACCESS: Transmissions
MOTOR VEHICLE PARTS & ACCESS: Water Pumps
MOTOR VEHICLE PARTS & ACCESS: Wiring Harness Sets
MOTOR VEHICLE SPLYS & PARTS WHOLESALERS: New
MOTOR VEHICLE SPLYS & PARTS WHOLESALERS: Used
MOTOR VEHICLE: Hardware
MOTOR VEHICLE: Radiators
MOTOR VEHICLE: Shock Absorbers
MOTOR VEHICLE: Wheels
MOTOR VEHICLES & CAR BODIES
MOTOR VEHICLES, WHOLESALE: Fire Trucks
MOTOR VEHICLES, WHOLESALE: Truck tractors
MOTOR VEHICLES, WHOLESALE: Trucks, commercial
MOTORCYCLE ACCESS
MOTORCYCLE PARTS: Wholesalers
MOTORCYCLES & RELATED PARTS
MOTORS: Electric
MOTORS: Generators
MOTORS: Pneumatic
MOUTHWASHES
MULTIPLEXERS: Telephone & Telegraph
MUSICAL INSTRUMENTS & ACCESS: Carrying Cases
MUSICAL INSTRUMENTS & ACCESS: NEC
MUSICAL INSTRUMENTS WHOLESALERS
MUSICAL INSTRUMENTS: Guitars & Parts, Electric & Acoustic

N

NAME PLATES: Engraved Or Etched
NATURAL GAS DISTRIBUTION TO CONSUMERS
NATURAL GAS LIQUID FRACTIONATING SVC
NATURAL GAS LIQUIDS PRODUCTION
NATURAL GAS PRODUCTION
NATURAL GAS TRANSMISSION
NATURAL GAS TRANSMISSION & DISTRIBUTION
NATURAL GASOLINE PRODUCTION
NATURAL PROPANE PRODUCTION
NAVIGATIONAL SYSTEMS & INSTRUMENTS
NETS: Launderers & Dyers
NEWS SYNDICATES
NICKEL
NONCURRENT CARRYING WIRING DEVICES
NONFERROUS: Rolling & Drawing, NEC
NOTEBOOKS, MADE FROM PURCHASED MATERIALS
NOVELTIES
NOVELTIES: Plastic
NOZZLES: Fire Fighting
NOZZLES: Spray, Aerosol, Paint Or Insecticide
NUCLEAR SHIELDING: Metal Plate
NURSERIES & LAWN & GARDEN SPLY STORES, RETAIL: Fertilizer
NURSING CARE FACILITIES: Skilled
NUTS: Metal
NYLON FIBERS

O

OFFICE EQPT WHOLESALERS
OFFICE FURNITURE REPAIR & MAINTENANCE SVCS
OFFICE SPLY & STATIONERY STORES: Office Forms & Splys
OFFICE SPLYS, NEC, WHOLESALE
OIL & GAS FIELD EQPT: Drill Rigs
OIL & GAS FIELD MACHINERY
OIL FIELD MACHINERY & EQPT
OIL FIELD SVCS, NEC
OIL TREATING COMPOUNDS
OILS & ESSENTIAL OILS
OILS: Cutting
OILS: Lubricating
OILS: Mineral, Natural
OLEFINS
OPERATOR TRAINING, COMPUTER
OPHTHALMIC GOODS
OPHTHALMIC GOODS WHOLESALERS
OPHTHALMIC GOODS: Frames, Lenses & Parts, Eyeglasses
OPHTHALMIC GOODS: Lenses, Ophthalmic
OPTICAL GOODS STORES

OPTICAL INSTRUMENTS & APPARATUS
OPTICAL INSTRUMENTS & LENSES
OPTICAL ISOLATORS
ORGANIZATIONS: Medical Research
ORGANIZATIONS: Physical Research, Noncommercial
ORGANIZATIONS: Religious
ORNAMENTS: Christmas Tree, Exc Electrical & Glass
OVENS: Laboratory

P

PACKAGE DESIGN SVCS
PACKAGING & LABELING SVCS
PACKAGING MATERIALS, WHOLESALE
PACKAGING MATERIALS: Paper
PACKAGING MATERIALS: Paper, Coated Or Laminated
PACKAGING MATERIALS: Plastic Film, Coated Or Laminated
PACKAGING: Blister Or Bubble Formed, Plastic
PACKING & CRATING SVC
PACKING MATERIALS: Mechanical
PADDING: Foamed Plastics
PAINTS & ADDITIVES
PAINTS & ALLIED PRODUCTS
PAINTS, VARNISHES & SPLYS WHOLESALERS
PAINTS, VARNISHES & SPLYS, WHOLESALE: Paints
PAINTS: Oil Or Alkyd Vehicle Or Water Thinned
PALLET REPAIR SVCS
PALLETIZERS & DEPALLETIZERS
PALLETS & SKIDS: Wood
PALLETS: Plastic
PALLETS: Wood & Metal Combination
PANEL & DISTRIBUTION BOARDS & OTHER RELATED
  APPARATUS
PANEL & DISTRIBUTION BOARDS: Electric
PANELS: Building, Plastic, NEC
PAPER & BOARD: Die-cut
PAPER & PAPER PRDTS: Crepe, Made From Purchased
  Materials
PAPER PRDTS: Infant & Baby Prdts
PAPER PRDTS: Molded Pulp Prdts
PAPER PRDTS: Napkins, Sanitary, Made From Purchased
  Material
PAPER PRDTS: Sanitary
PAPER PRDTS: Tampons, Sanitary, Made From Purchased
  Material
PAPER, WHOLESALE: Printing
PAPER: Adhesive
PAPER: Book
PAPER: Building, Insulating & Packaging
PAPER: Cardboard
PAPER: Cloth, Lined, Made From Purchased Materials
PAPER: Coated & Laminated, NEC
PAPER: Coated, Exc Photographic, Carbon Or Abrasive
PAPER: Fine
PAPER: Packaging
PAPER: Specialty
PAPER: Specialty Or Chemically Treated
PAPER: Wrapping & Packaging
PAPERBOARD PRDTS: Folding Boxboard
PAPERBOARD PRDTS: Packaging Board
PARTICLEBOARD: Laminated, Plastic
PARTITIONS & FIXTURES: Except Wood
PARTITIONS: Solid Fiber, Made From Purchased Materials
PARTITIONS: Wood & Fixtures
PARTS: Metal
PATTERNS: Indl
PAVERS
PAVING MIXTURES
PENCILS & PENS WHOLESALERS
PERFUME: Perfumes, Natural Or Synthetic
PERFUMES
PERISCOPES
PEST CONTROL IN STRUCTURES SVCS
PEST CONTROL SVCS
PESTICIDES
PET SPLYS
PETROLEUM & PETROLEUM PRDTS, WHOLESALE: Bulk
  Stations
PHARMACEUTICAL PREPARATIONS: Adrenal
PHARMACEUTICAL PREPARATIONS: Druggists'
  Preparations
PHARMACEUTICAL PREPARATIONS: Pills
PHARMACEUTICAL PREPARATIONS: Proprietary Drug
PHARMACEUTICAL PREPARATIONS: Solutions

PHARMACEUTICALS
PHARMACEUTICALS: Mail-Order Svc
PHOSPHATES
PHOTOCOPYING & DUPLICATING SVCS
PHOTOGRAPHIC EQPT & SPLYS
PHOTOGRAPHIC EQPT & SPLYS WHOLESALERS
PHOTOGRAPHIC EQPT & SPLYS: Film, Sensitized
PHOTOGRAPHIC EQPT & SPLYS: Graphic Arts Plates,
  Sensitized
PHOTOGRAPHIC EQPT & SPLYS: Printing Eqpt
PHOTOGRAPHY SVCS: Commercial
PHYSICIANS' OFFICES & CLINICS: Medical doctors
PICTURE FRAMES: Metal
PICTURE FRAMES: Wood
PICTURE FRAMING SVCS, CUSTOM
PIECE GOODS & NOTIONS WHOLESALERS
PIGMENTS, INORGANIC: Metallic & Mineral, NEC
PILOT SVCS: Aviation
PINS
PINS: Dowel
PIPE & FITTINGS: Cast Iron
PIPE & TUBES: Seamless
PIPE FITTINGS: Plastic
PIPE SECTIONS, FABRICATED FROM PURCHASED PIPE
PIPE, CYLINDER: Concrete, Prestressed Or Pretensioned
PIPE, SEWER: Concrete
PIPE: Concrete
PIPE: Plastic
PIPE: Sheet Metal
PIPELINES: Crude Petroleum
PIPELINES: Natural Gas
PIPES & TUBES
PIPES & TUBES: Steel
PIPES & TUBES: Welded
PIPES: Steel & Iron
PISTONS & PISTON RINGS
PLACER GOLD MINING
PLAQUES: Picture, Laminated
PLASTICIZERS, ORGANIC: Cyclic & Acyclic
PLASTICS FILM & SHEET
PLASTICS FILM & SHEET: Polyethylene
PLASTICS FILM & SHEET: Polypropylene
PLASTICS FILM & SHEET: Polyvinyl
PLASTICS FILM & SHEET: Vinyl
PLASTICS FINISHED PRDTS: Laminated
PLASTICS MATERIAL & RESINS
PLASTICS MATERIALS, BASIC FORMS & SHAPES
  WHOLESALERS
PLASTICS PROCESSING
PLASTICS SHEET: Packing Materials
PLASTICS: Blow Molded
PLASTICS: Extruded
PLASTICS: Finished Injection Molded
PLASTICS: Molded
PLASTICS: Polystyrene Foam
PLASTICS: Thermoformed
PLATE WORK: Metalworking Trade
PLATES: Steel
PLATING & POLISHING SVC
PLATING COMPOUNDS
PLATING SVC: Chromium, Metals Or Formed Prdts
PLAYGROUND EQPT
PLEATING & STITCHING FOR THE TRADE: Decorative &
  Novelty
PLEATING & STITCHING SVC
PLUGS: Electric
PLUMBING FIXTURES
PLUMBING FIXTURES: Plastic
PLUMBING FIXTURES: Vitreous
PLUMBING FIXTURES: Vitreous China
POINT OF SALE DEVICES
POLE LINE HARDWARE
POLISHING SVC: Metals Or Formed Prdts
POLYESTERS
POLYETHYLENE RESINS
POLYMETHYL METHACRYLATE RESINS: Plexiglas
POLYSTYRENE RESINS
POLYURETHANE RESINS
POLYVINYL CHLORIDE RESINS
POULTRY & POULTRY PRDTS WHOLESALERS
POULTRY & SMALL GAME SLAUGHTERING &
  PROCESSING
POULTRY SLAUGHTERING & PROCESSING

POWDER: Iron
POWDER: Metal
POWER GENERATORS
POWER SPLY CONVERTERS: Static, Electronic Applications
POWER SUPPLIES: All Types, Static
POWER SWITCHING EQPT
PRECAST TERRAZZO OR CONCRETE PRDTS
PRECIOUS METALS
PRECIPITATORS: Electrostatic
PRESSED FIBER & MOLDED PULP PRDTS, EXC FOOD
PRESTRESSED CONCRETE PRDTS
PRIMARY ROLLING MILL EQPT
PRINT CARTRIDGES: Laser & Other Computer Printers
PRINTED CIRCUIT BOARDS
PRINTERS & PLOTTERS
PRINTERS' SVCS: Folding, Collating, Etc
PRINTERS: Computer
PRINTERS: Magnetic Ink, Bar Code
PRINTING & BINDING: Books
PRINTING & EMBOSSING: Plastic Fabric Articles
PRINTING & ENGRAVING: Financial Notes & Certificates
PRINTING & STAMPING: Fabric Articles
PRINTING & WRITING PAPER WHOLESALERS
PRINTING MACHINERY
PRINTING, COMMERCIAL: Bags, Plastic, NEC
PRINTING, COMMERCIAL: Business Forms, NEC
PRINTING, COMMERCIAL: Calendars, NEC
PRINTING, COMMERCIAL: Decals, NEC
PRINTING, COMMERCIAL: Envelopes, NEC
PRINTING, COMMERCIAL: Imprinting
PRINTING, COMMERCIAL: Labels & Seals, NEC
PRINTING, COMMERCIAL: Letterpress & Screen
PRINTING, COMMERCIAL: Literature, Advertising, NEC
PRINTING, COMMERCIAL: Magazines, NEC
PRINTING, COMMERCIAL: Periodicals, NEC
PRINTING, COMMERCIAL: Promotional
PRINTING, COMMERCIAL: Screen
PRINTING, COMMERCIAL: Stationery, NEC
PRINTING, LITHOGRAPHIC: Advertising Posters
PRINTING, LITHOGRAPHIC: Calendars
PRINTING, LITHOGRAPHIC: Circulars
PRINTING, LITHOGRAPHIC: Color
PRINTING, LITHOGRAPHIC: Forms, Business
PRINTING, LITHOGRAPHIC: Offset & photolithographic
  printing
PRINTING, LITHOGRAPHIC: Posters
PRINTING, LITHOGRAPHIC: Tags
PRINTING, LITHOGRAPHIC: Tickets
PRINTING: Books
PRINTING: Books
PRINTING: Commercial, NEC
PRINTING: Flexographic
PRINTING: Gravure, Forms, Business
PRINTING: Gravure, Labels
PRINTING: Gravure, Rotogravure
PRINTING: Laser
PRINTING: Letterpress
PRINTING: Lithographic
PRINTING: Offset
PRINTING: Photo-Offset
PRINTING: Photolithographic
PRINTING: Rotogravure
PRINTING: Screen, Broadwoven Fabrics, Cotton
PRINTING: Screen, Fabric
PRINTING: Screen, Manmade Fiber & Silk, Broadwoven
  Fabric
PRINTING: Thermography
PROFESSIONAL EQPT & SPLYS, WHOLESALE: Analytical
  Instruments
PROFESSIONAL EQPT & SPLYS, WHOLESALE: Engineers',
  NEC
PROFESSIONAL EQPT & SPLYS, WHOLESALE: Optical
  Goods
PROFESSIONAL INSTRUMENT REPAIR SVCS
PROFILE SHAPES: Unsupported Plastics
PROTECTION EQPT: Lightning
PROTECTIVE FOOTWEAR: Rubber Or Plastic
PUBLIC RELATIONS & PUBLICITY SVCS
PUBLISHERS: Music Book & Sheet Music
PUBLISHERS: Music, Book
PUBLISHERS: Sheet Music
PUBLISHERS: Telephone & Other Directory
PUBLISHING & BROADCASTING: Internet Only

PUBLISHING & PRINTING: Art Copy
PUBLISHING & PRINTING: Book Music
PUBLISHING & PRINTING: Books
PUBLISHING & PRINTING: Directories, NEC
PUBLISHING & PRINTING: Directories, Telephone
PUBLISHING & PRINTING: Guides
PUBLISHING & PRINTING: Magazines: publishing & printing
PUBLISHING & PRINTING: Newsletters, Business Svc
PUBLISHING & PRINTING: Newspapers
PUBLISHING & PRINTING: Pamphlets
PUBLISHING & PRINTING: Textbooks
PUBLISHING & PRINTING: Trade Journals
PULLEYS: Metal
PULLEYS: Power Transmission
PULP MILLS
PULP MILLS: Mechanical & Recycling Processing
PUMPS & PARTS: Indl
PUMPS & PUMPING EQPT REPAIR SVCS
PUMPS & PUMPING EQPT WHOLESALERS
PUMPS: Domestic, Water Or Sump
PUMPS: Fluid Power
PUMPS: Gasoline, Measuring Or Dispensing
PUMPS: Hydraulic Power Transfer
PUMPS: Measuring & Dispensing
PUMPS: Oil Well & Field
PUMPS: Oil, Measuring Or Dispensing
PUNCHES: Forming & Stamping
PURIFICATION & DUST COLLECTION EQPT

R

RACEWAYS
RADAR SYSTEMS & EQPT
RADIO & TELEVISION COMMUNICATIONS EQUIPMENT
RADIO BROADCASTING & COMMUNICATIONS EQPT
RADIO BROADCASTING STATIONS
RADIO COMMUNICATIONS: Airborne Eqpt
RADIO COMMUNICATIONS: Carrier Eqpt
RADIO, TV & CONSUMER ELEC STORES: High Fidelity
   Stereo Eqpt
RADIO, TV/CONSUMER ELEC STORES: Antennas, Satellite
   Dish
RAILINGS: Prefabricated, Metal
RAILINGS: Wood
RAILROAD CAR REPAIR SVCS
RAILROAD EQPT
RAILROAD EQPT & SPLYS WHOLESALERS
RAILROAD EQPT: Brakes, Air & Vacuum
RAILROAD MAINTENANCE & REPAIR SVCS
RAILROAD RELATED EQPT: Railway Track
RAMPS: Prefabricated Metal
RAZORS, RAZOR BLADES
RAZORS: Electric
REAL ESTATE AGENCIES & BROKERS
REAL ESTATE AGENTS & MANAGERS
REAL ESTATE INVESTMENT TRUSTS
RECEIVERS: Radio Communications
RECORDS & TAPES: Prerecorded
RECOVERY SVC: Iron Ore, From Open Hearth Slag
RECREATIONAL VEHICLE PARTS & ACCESS STORES
REFINERS & SMELTERS: Copper
REFINERS & SMELTERS: Silicon, Primary, Over 99% Pure
REFINING: Petroleum
REFRACTORIES: Brick
REFRACTORIES: Cement
REFRACTORIES: Clay
REFRACTORIES: Foundry, Clay
REFRACTORIES: Graphite, Carbon Or Ceramic Bond
REFRACTORIES: Nonclay
REFRACTORIES: Tile & Brick, Exc Plastic
REFRIGERATION & HEATING EQUIPMENT
REFRIGERATION EQPT & SPLYS WHOLESALERS
REFRIGERATION EQPT: Complete
REFRIGERATION REPAIR SVCS
REFRIGERATION SVC & REPAIR
REFUSE SYSTEMS
REGISTERS: Air, Metal
REGULATORS: Power
REHABILITATION SVCS
RELAYS & SWITCHES: Indl, Electric
RELAYS: Control Circuit, Ind
RELIGIOUS SPLYS WHOLESALERS
REMOVERS & CLEANERS
REMOVERS: Paint

RENTAL SVCS: Costume
RENTAL SVCS: Sign
RENTAL SVCS: Sound & Lighting Eqpt
RENTAL SVCS: Tent & Tarpaulin
RENTAL SVCS: Vending Machine
RENTAL SVCS: Work Zone Traffic Eqpt, Flags, Cones, Etc
RENTAL: Portable Toilet
RENTAL: Video Tape & Disc
RESEARCH & DEVELOPMENT SVCS, COMMERCIAL:
   Engineering Lab
RESEARCH, DEVELOPMENT & TESTING SVCS,
   COMMERCIAL: Energy
RESEARCH, DEVELOPMENT & TESTING SVCS,
   COMMERCIAL: Medical
RESEARCH, DEVELOPMENT & TESTING SVCS,
   COMMERCIAL: Physical
RESINS: Custom Compound Purchased
RESISTORS & RESISTOR UNITS
RESPIRATORS
RESTAURANT EQPT: Carts
RESTAURANT EQPT: Sheet Metal
RESTAURANTS:Full Svc, American
RETAIL BAKERY: Bread
RETAIL BAKERY: Cakes
RETAIL BAKERY: Cookies
RETAIL BAKERY: Doughnuts
RETAIL BAKERY: Pastries
RETAIL STORES: Alcoholic Beverage Making Eqpt & Splys
RETAIL STORES: Audio-Visual Eqpt & Splys
RETAIL STORES: Batteries, Non-Automotive
RETAIL STORES: Cake Decorating Splys
RETAIL STORES: Christmas Lights & Decorations
RETAIL STORES: Cleaning Eqpt & Splys
RETAIL STORES: Communication Eqpt
RETAIL STORES: Concrete Prdts, Precast
RETAIL STORES: Cosmetics
RETAIL STORES: Educational Aids & Electronic Training Mat
RETAIL STORES: Electronic Parts & Eqpt
RETAIL STORES: Flags
RETAIL STORES: Hair Care Prdts
RETAIL STORES: Ice
RETAIL STORES: Medical Apparatus & Splys
RETAIL STORES: Orthopedic & Prosthesis Applications
RETAIL STORES: Pet Splys
RETAIL STORES: Religious Goods
RETAIL STORES: Safety Splys & Eqpt
RETAIL STORES: Swimming Pools, Above Ground
RETAIL STORES: Telephone & Communication Eqpt
RETAIL STORES: Tents
RETAIL STORES: Water Purification Eqpt
RETAIL STORES: Welding Splys
REUPHOLSTERY & FURNITURE REPAIR
RIBBONS & BOWS
RIVETS: Metal
ROAD CONSTRUCTION EQUIPMENT WHOLESALERS
ROBOTS: Assembly Line
ROBOTS: Indl Spraying, Painting, Etc
RODS: Rolled, Aluminum
RODS: Steel & Iron, Made In Steel Mills
ROLL FORMED SHAPES: Custom
ROLLING MILL EQPT: Finishing
ROLLING MILL MACHINERY
ROLLING MILL ROLLS: Cast Steel
ROLLS: Rubber, Solid Or Covered
ROOFING MATERIALS: Asphalt
ROOFING MEMBRANE: Rubber
RUBBER BANDS
RUBBER PRDTS: Appliance, Mechanical
RUBBER PRDTS: Automotive, Mechanical
RUBBER PRDTS: Medical & Surgical Tubing, Extrudd &
   Lathe-Cut
RUBBER PRDTS: Oil & Gas Field Machinery, Mechanical
RUBBER PRDTS: Silicone
RUBBER PRDTS: Sponge
RUBBER STRUCTURES: Air-Supported
RUST RESISTING

S

SAFE DEPOSIT BOXES
SAFES & VAULTS: Metal
SAFETY EQPT & SPLYS WHOLESALERS
SAFETY INSPECTION SVCS
SALT

SAND & GRAVEL
SAND LIME PRDTS
SAND MINING
SANDBLASTING EQPT
SANITARY SVC, NEC
SANITARY SVCS: Hazardous Waste, Collection & Disposal
SANITARY SVCS: Liquid Waste Collection & Disposal
SANITARY SVCS: Refuse Collection & Disposal Svcs
SANITARY SVCS: Rubbish Collection & Disposal
SANITARY SVCS: Waste Materials, Recycling
SASHES: Door Or Window, Metal
SATELLITES: Communications
SAW BLADES
SAWDUST & SHAVINGS
SCAFFOLDS: Mobile Or Stationary, Metal
SCALES & BALANCES, EXC LABORATORY
SCALES: Indl
SCIENTIFIC EQPT REPAIR SVCS
SCIENTIFIC INSTRUMENTS WHOLESALERS
SCRAP & WASTE MATERIALS, WHOLESALE: Ferrous Metal
SCRAP & WASTE MATERIALS, WHOLESALE: Junk & Scrap
SCRAP & WASTE MATERIALS, WHOLESALE: Metal
SCRAP & WASTE MATERIALS, WHOLESALE: Nonferrous
   Metals Scrap
SCRAP & WASTE MATERIALS, WHOLESALE: Paper
SCRAP STEEL CUTTING
SCREENS: Projection
SCREENS: Window, Metal
SCREENS: Woven Wire
SCREW MACHINE PRDTS
SCREWS: Metal
SEALANTS
SEALING COMPOUNDS: Sealing, synthetic rubber or plastic
SEALS: Hermetic
SEARCH & NAVIGATION SYSTEMS
SEATING: Stadium
SECURITY CONTROL EQPT & SYSTEMS
SECURITY DEVICES
SECURITY SYSTEMS SERVICES
SEMICONDUCTOR CIRCUIT NETWORKS
SEMICONDUCTORS & RELATED DEVICES
SENSORS: Temperature, Exc Indl Process
SEPARATORS: Metal Plate
SEPTIC TANK CLEANING SVCS
SEPTIC TANKS: Concrete
SEPTIC TANKS: Plastic
SEWAGE & WATER TREATMENT EQPT
SEWER CLEANING EQPT: Power
SHADES: Window
SHAPES & PILINGS, STRUCTURAL: Steel
SHAPES: Extruded, Aluminum, NEC
SHAVING PREPARATIONS
SHEET METAL SPECIALTIES, EXC STAMPED
SHEETS: Hard Rubber
SHELVING, MADE FROM PURCHASED WIRE
SHIMS: Metal
SHOE STORES
SHOE STORES: Boots, Men's
SHOE STORES: Men's
SHOES: Men's
SHOES: Men's, Work
SHOES: Plastic Or Rubber
SHOES: Women's
SHOT PEENING SVC
SHOWCASES & DISPLAY FIXTURES: Office & Store
SHOWER STALLS: Plastic & Fiberglass
SHREDDERS: Indl & Commercial
SHUTTERS, DOOR & WINDOW: Metal
SHUTTERS, DOOR & WINDOW: Plastic
SIDING MATERIALS
SIDING: Plastic
SIDING: Sheet Metal
SIGN PAINTING & LETTERING SHOP
SIGNALS: Traffic Control, Electric
SIGNS & ADVERTISING SPECIALTIES
SIGNS & ADVERTISING SPECIALTIES: Artwork, Advertising
SIGNS & ADVERTISING SPECIALTIES: Displays, Paint
   Process
SIGNS & ADVERTISING SPECIALTIES: Letters For Signs,
   Metal
SIGNS & ADVERTISING SPECIALTIES: Novelties
SIGNS & ADVERTISING SPECIALTIES: Scoreboards,
   Electric

SIGNS, ELECTRICAL: Wholesalers
SIGNS, EXC ELECTRIC, WHOLESALE
SIGNS: Electrical
SIGNS: Neon
SILICA MINING
SILICON WAFERS: Chemically Doped
SILICON: Pure
SILICONE RESINS
SILICONES
SILK SCREEN DESIGN SVCS
SILVERWARE & PLATED WARE
SIMULATORS: Flight
SINTER: Iron
SLAG: Crushed Or Ground
SMOKE DETECTORS
SOFT DRINKS WHOLESALERS
SOFTWARE PUBLISHERS: Home Entertainment
SOFTWARE PUBLISHERS: Operating Systems
SOFTWARE TRAINING, COMPUTER
SOLAR CELLS
SOLAR HEATING EQPT
SOLES, BOOT OR SHOE: Rubber, Composition Or Fiber
SOLID CONTAINING UNITS: Concrete
SOLVENTS: Organic
SONAR SYSTEMS & EQPT
SOUND EFFECTS & MUSIC PRODUCTION: Motion Picture
SOUND EQPT: Electric
SOUND REPRODUCING EQPT
SPEAKER SYSTEMS
SPECIALTY FOOD STORES: Coffee
SPECIALTY FOOD STORES: Eggs & Poultry
SPECIALTY FOOD STORES: Health & Dietetic Food
SPECIALTY FOOD STORES: Vitamin
SPORTING & ATHLETIC GOODS: Basketball Eqpt & Splys,
   NEC
SPORTING & ATHLETIC GOODS: Camping Eqpt & Splys
SPORTING & ATHLETIC GOODS: Cases, Gun & Rod
SPORTING & ATHLETIC GOODS: Hunting Eqpt
SPORTING & ATHLETIC GOODS: Shafts, Golf Club
SPORTING & ATHLETIC GOODS: Team Sports Eqpt
SPORTING & ATHLETIC GOODS: Water Sports Eqpt
SPORTING & RECREATIONAL GOODS, WHOLESALE:
   Athletic Goods
SPORTING & RECREATIONAL GOODS, WHOLESALE:
   Boat Access & Part
SPORTING GOODS STORES: Firearms
SPORTING GOODS STORES: Playground Eqpt
SPORTS APPAREL STORES
SPRINGS: Clock, Precision
SPRINGS: Coiled Flat
SPRINGS: Leaf, Automobile, Locomotive, Etc
SPRINGS: Mechanical, Precision
SPRINGS: Precision
SPRINGS: Steel
SPRINGS: Torsion Bar
SPRINGS: Wire
SPROCKETS: Power Transmission
STAINLESS STEEL
STAINLESS STEEL WARE
STAIRCASES & STAIRS, WOOD
STAMPINGS: Automotive
STAMPINGS: Metal
STARTERS & CONTROLLERS: Motor, Electric
STATIONERY & OFFICE SPLYS WHOLESALERS
STATIONERY: Made From Purchased Materials
STATUARY & OTHER DECORATIVE PRDTS: Nonmetallic
STEEL & ALLOYS: Tool & Die
STEEL, COLD-ROLLED: Flat Bright, From Purchased
   HotRolled
STEEL, COLD-ROLLED: Sheet Or Strip, From Own HotRolled
STEEL, COLD-ROLLED: Strip NEC, From Purchased
   HotRolled
STEEL, COLD-ROLLED: Strip Or Wire
STEEL, HOT-ROLLED: Sheet Or Strip
STOCK SHAPES: Plastic
STONE: Dimension, NEC
STONE: Quarrying & Processing, Own Stone Prdts
STONEWARE PRDTS: Pottery
STORE FIXTURES: Exc Wood
STORE FIXTURES: Wood
STORES: Auto & Home Supply
STRAINERS: Line, Piping Systems
STRAWS: Drinking, Made From Purchased Materials

STRUCTURAL SUPPORT & BUILDING MATERIAL: Concrete
STUDS & JOISTS: Sheet Metal
SUNDRIES & RELATED PRDTS: Medical & Laboratory,
   Rubber
SUNGLASSES, WHOLESALE
SURFACE ACTIVE AGENTS
SURGICAL APPLIANCES & SPLYS
SURGICAL APPLIANCES & SPLYS
SURGICAL IMPLANTS
SURGICAL INSTRUMENT REPAIR SVCS
SURVEYING INSTRUMENTS WHOLESALERS
SUSPENSION SYSTEMS: Acoustical, Metal
SVC ESTABLISHMENT EQPT, WHOLESALE: Firefighting
   Eqpt
SVC ESTABLISHMENT EQPT, WHOLESALE: Laundry Eqpt
   & Splys
SVC ESTABLISHMENT EQPT, WHOLESALE: Restaurant
   Splys
SWEEPING COMPOUNDS
SWIMMING POOL EQPT: Filters & Water Conditioning
   Systems
SWIMMING POOLS, EQPT & SPLYS: Wholesalers
SWITCHBOARDS & PARTS: Power
SWITCHES: Electric Power
SWITCHES: Electric Power, Exc Snap, Push Button, Etc
SWITCHES: Electronic
SWITCHES: Electronic Applications
SWITCHES: Time, Electrical Switchgear Apparatus
SWITCHGEAR & SWITCHBOARD APPARATUS
SWITCHGEAR & SWITCHGEAR ACCESS, NEC
SYNTHETIC RESIN FINISHED PRDTS, NEC
SYRUPS, DRINK
SYSTEMS ENGINEERING: Computer Related
SYSTEMS INTEGRATION SVCS
SYSTEMS INTEGRATION SVCS: Local Area Network
SYSTEMS SOFTWARE DEVELOPMENT SVCS

T

TABLE OR COUNTERTOPS, PLASTIC LAMINATED
TABLETS: Bronze Or Other Metal
TABLEWARE: Vitreous China
TAGS & LABELS: Paper
TANK REPAIR & CLEANING SVCS
TANK REPAIR SVCS
TANK TOWERS: Metal Plate
TANKS & OTHER TRACKED VEHICLE CMPNTS
TANKS: Concrete
TANKS: Cryogenic, Metal
TANKS: For Tank Trucks, Metal Plate
TANKS: Fuel, Including Oil & Gas, Metal Plate
TANKS: Lined, Metal
TANKS: Military, Including Factory Rebuilding
TANKS: Plastic & Fiberglass
TANKS: Standard Or Custom Fabricated, Metal Plate
TANKS: Storage, Farm, Metal Plate
TAPE DRIVES
TAPES: Pressure Sensitive, Rubber
TARGET DRONES
TARPAULINS
TARPAULINS, WHOLESALE
TECHNICAL MANUAL PREPARATION SVCS
TELECOMMUNICATION EQPT REPAIR SVCS, EXC
   TELEPHONES
TELEMETERING EQPT
TELEPHONE BOOTHS, EXC WOOD
TELEPHONE EQPT: Modems
TELEPHONE EQPT: NEC
TELEPHONE SVCS
TELEVISION BROADCASTING & COMMUNICATIONS EQPT
TELEVISION BROADCASTING STATIONS
TELEVISION: Closed Circuit Eqpt
TELEVISION: Monitors
TEMPORARY HELP SVCS
TERMINAL BOARDS
TESTERS: Battery
TESTERS: Physical Property
TESTING SVCS
TEXTILE DESIGNERS
TEXTILE FINISHING: Napping, Manmade Fiber & Silk,
   Broadwoven
TEXTILES: Linen Fabrics
THEATRICAL PRODUCTION SVCS
THEATRICAL SCENERY

THERMISTORS, EXC TEMPERATURE SENSORS
THERMOCOUPLES
THERMOPLASTIC MATERIALS
THERMOSETTING MATERIALS
TILE: Brick & Structural, Clay
TILE: Clay, Drain & Structural
TILE: Wall & Floor, Ceramic
TIN
TIRE & INNER TUBE MATERIALS & RELATED PRDTS
TIRE & TUBE REPAIR MATERIALS, WHOLESALE
TIRE CORD & FABRIC
TIRE SUNDRIES OR REPAIR MATERIALS: Rubber
TIRES & INNER TUBES
TIRES & TUBES WHOLESALERS
TIRES & TUBES, WHOLESALE: Automotive
TIRES: Plastic
TOBACCO & TOBACCO PRDTS WHOLESALERS
TOBACCO: Chewing & Snuff
TOBACCO: Cigarettes
TOBACCO: Smoking
TOILET PREPARATIONS
TOILETRIES, WHOLESALE: Hair Preparations
TOILETRIES, WHOLESALE: Perfumes
TOILETRIES, WHOLESALE: Toiletries
TOOL & DIE STEEL
TOOLS: Hand, Mechanics
TOWELS: Fabric & Nonwoven, Made From Purchased
   Materials
TOWELS: Paper
TOWERS, SECTIONS: Transmission, Radio & Television
TOWING SVCS: Marine
TOYS & HOBBY GOODS & SPLYS, WHOLESALE: Balloons,
   Novelty
TOYS & HOBBY GOODS & SPLYS, WHOLESALE: Toys &
   Games
TOYS & HOBBY GOODS & SPLYS, WHOLESALE: Toys,
   NEC
TOYS: Rubber
TRADE SHOW ARRANGEMENT SVCS
TRAILERS & PARTS: Boat
TRAILERS & TRAILER EQPT
TRAILERS: Semitrailers, Missile Transportation
TRAILERS: Semitrailers, Truck Tractors
TRANSDUCERS: Electrical Properties
TRANSDUCERS: Pressure
TRANSFORMERS: Distribution
TRANSFORMERS: Distribution, Electric
TRANSFORMERS: Instrument
TRANSFORMERS: Specialty
TRANSFORMERS: Voltage Regulating
TRANSMISSIONS: Motor Vehicle
TRANSPORTATION EQPT & SPLYS WHOLESALERS, NEC
TRANSPORTATION SVCS, AIR, NONSCHEDULED: Air
   Cargo Carriers
TRAVEL TRAILERS & CAMPERS
TROPHIES, NEC
TROPHIES, WHOLESALE
TROPHIES: Metal, Exc Silver
TRUCK & BUS BODIES: Cement Mixer
TRUCK & BUS BODIES: Motor Vehicle, Specialty
TRUCK & BUS BODIES: Truck Beds
TRUCK & BUS BODIES: Utility Truck
TRUCK BODIES: Body Parts
TRUCK BODY SHOP
TRUCK GENERAL REPAIR SVC
TRUCK PARTS & ACCESSORIES: Wholesalers
TRUCKING & HAULING SVCS: Contract Basis
TRUCKING & HAULING SVCS: Lumber & Log, Local
TRUCKING: Except Local
TRUCKING: Local, With Storage
TRUCKING: Local, Without Storage
TRUCKS & TRACTORS: Industrial
TRUCKS: Forklift
TRUCKS: Indl
TRUSSES & FRAMING: Prefabricated Metal
TRUSSES: Wood, Floor
TUBES: Paper
TUBES: Steel & Iron
TUBES: Wrought, Welded Or Lock Joint
TUBING: Copper
TUBING: Flexible, Metallic
TUBING: Glass
TUBING: Rubber

TUGBOAT SVCS
TURBINES & TURBINE GENERATOR SETS
TURBINES: Gas, Mechanical Drive
TURBINES: Hydraulic, Complete
TURBINES: Steam
TYPESETTING SVC
TYPESETTING SVC: Computer

U

UNIFORM SPLY SVCS: Indl
UNIFORM STORES
UNSUPPORTED PLASTICS: Floor Or Wall Covering
UPHOLSTERY WORK SVCS
URANIUM ORE MINING, NEC
USED CAR DEALERS
UTENSILS: Cast Aluminum, Cooking Or Kitchen
UTILITY TRAILER DEALERS

V

VACUUM CLEANERS: Indl Type
VALUE-ADDED RESELLERS: Computer Systems
VALVES
VALVES & PARTS: Gas, Indl
VALVES & PIPE FITTINGS
VALVES & REGULATORS: Pressure, Indl
VALVES: Aerosol, Metal
VALVES: Aircraft, Control, Hydraulic & Pneumatic
VALVES: Aircraft, Fluid Power
VALVES: Aircraft, Hydraulic
VALVES: Control, Automatic
VALVES: Electrohydraulic Servo, Metal
VALVES: Fluid Power, Control, Hydraulic & pneumatic
VALVES: Gas Cylinder, Compressed
VALVES: Indl
VALVES: Plumbing & Heating
VALVES: Regulating, Process Control
VAN CONVERSIONS
VARNISHES, NEC
VAULTS & SAFES WHOLESALERS
VEHICLES: Recreational
VENDING MACHINE REPAIR SVCS
VENDING MACHINES & PARTS
VENTILATING EQPT: Metal
VENTILATING EQPT: Sheet Metal
VENTURE CAPITAL COMPANIES
VETERINARY PHARMACEUTICAL PREPARATIONS
VIDEO & AUDIO EQPT, WHOLESALE
VIDEO TAPE PRODUCTION SVCS
VIDEO TAPE WHOLESALERS, RECORDED
VIDEO TRIGGERS: Remote Control TV Devices
VINYL RESINS, NEC
VISUAL COMMUNICATIONS SYSTEMS
VITAMINS: Natural Or Synthetic, Uncompounded, Bulk
VOCATIONAL REHABILITATION AGENCY
VOCATIONAL TRAINING AGENCY

W

WALL COVERINGS WHOLESALERS
WALL COVERINGS: Rubber
WALLPAPER & WALL COVERINGS
WALLPAPER: Made From Purchased Paper
WALLS: Curtain, Metal
WAREHOUSING & STORAGE FACILITIES, NEC
WAREHOUSING & STORAGE, REFRIGERATED: Cold
    Storage Or Refrig
WAREHOUSING & STORAGE, REFRIGERATED: Frozen Or
    Refrig Goods
WAREHOUSING & STORAGE: General
WAREHOUSING & STORAGE: Refrigerated
WAREHOUSING & STORAGE: Self Storage
WARM AIR HEATING/AC EQPT/SPLYS, WHOL Warm Air
    Htg Eqpt/Splys
WASHERS
WASHERS: Metal
WATCH & CLOCK STORES
WATCH REPAIR SVCS
WATER HEATERS
WATER PURIFICATION EQPT: Household
WATER SOFTENING WHOLESALERS
WATER SUPPLY
WATER TREATMENT EQPT: Indl
WATER: Distilled
WATER: Pasteurized, Canned & Bottled, Etc
WATERPROOFING COMPOUNDS
WAXES: Petroleum, Not Produced In Petroleum Refineries
WEATHER STRIP: Sponge Rubber
WEATHER STRIPS: Metal
WEIGHING MACHINERY & APPARATUS
WELDING & CUTTING APPARATUS & ACCESS, NEC
WELDING EQPT
WELDING EQPT & SPLYS WHOLESALERS
WELDING EQPT & SPLYS: Gas
WELDING EQPT & SPLYS: Generators, Arc Welding, AC &
    DC
WELDING EQPT REPAIR SVCS
WELDING EQPT: Electric
WELDING EQPT: Electrical
WELDING MACHINES & EQPT: Ultrasonic
WELDING REPAIR SVC
WELDING SPLYS, EXC GASES: Wholesalers
WELDING TIPS: Heat Resistant, Metal
WELDMENTS
WET CORN MILLING
WHEELCHAIR LIFTS
WHEELCHAIRS
WHEELS & PARTS
WHEELS, GRINDING: Artificial
WHEELS: Abrasive
WHEELS: Disc, Wheelbarrow, Stroller, Etc, Stamped Metal
WHEELS: Iron & Steel, Locomotive & Car
WHEELS: Railroad Car, Cast Steel
WHITING MINING: Crushed & Broken

WINCHES
WINDMILLS: Electric Power Generation
WINDOW & DOOR FRAMES
WINDOW FRAMES & SASHES: Plastic
WINDOW FRAMES, MOLDING & TRIM: Vinyl
WINDOW SCREENING: Plastic
WINDOWS: Wood
WINDSHIELD WIPER SYSTEMS
WINDSHIELDS: Plastic
WIRE
WIRE & CABLE: Aluminum
WIRE & CABLE: Nonferrous, Building
WIRE & WIRE PRDTS
WIRE CLOTH & WOVEN WIRE PRDTS, MADE FROM
    PURCHASED
WIRE MATERIALS: Aluminum
WIRE MATERIALS: Copper
WIRE MATERIALS: Steel
WIRE PRDTS: Ferrous Or Iron, Made In Wiredrawing Plants
WIRE PRDTS: Steel & Iron
WIRE WINDING OF PURCHASED WIRE
WIRE, FLAT: Strip, Cold-Rolled, Exc From Hot-Rolled Mills
WIRE: Communication
WIRE: Magnet
WIRE: Mesh
WIRE: Nonferrous
WIRE: Steel, Insulated Or Armored
WIRE: Wire, Ferrous Or Iron
WIRING DEVICES WHOLESALERS
WOMEN'S & CHILDREN'S CLOTHING WHOLESALERS,
    NEC
WOMEN'S & GIRLS' SPORTSWEAR WHOLESALERS
WOMEN'S CLOTHING STORES
WOOD & WOOD BY-PRDTS, WHOLESALE
WOOD CHIPS, PRODUCED AT THE MILL
WOOD FENCING WHOLESALERS
WOOD PRDTS: Laundry
WOOD PRDTS: Moldings, Unfinished & Prefinished
WOOD PRDTS: Mulch Or Sawdust
WOOD PRDTS: Mulch, Wood & Bark
WOOD PRDTS: Plugs
WOOD PRDTS: Signboards
WOOD PRDTS: Trophy Bases
WOOD TREATING: Millwork
WOOD TREATING: Structural Lumber & Timber
WOODWORK & TRIM: Exterior & Ornamental
WOODWORK & TRIM: Interior & Ornamental
WOODWORK: Interior & Ornamental, NEC
WORK EXPERIENCE CENTER
WOVEN WIRE PRDTS, NEC
WRENCHES

X

X-RAY EQPT & TUBES
X-RAY EQPT REPAIR SVCS

PRODUCT SECTION

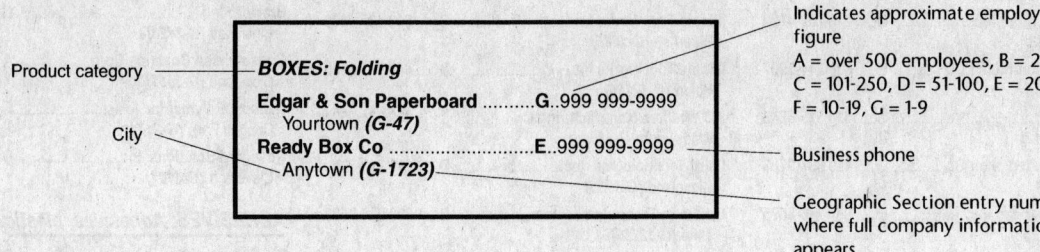

Product category — **BOXES: Folding**

Edgar & Son Paperboard ....G..999 999-9999
City — Yourtown **(G-47)**
Ready Box Co ....E..999 999-9999
Anytown **(G-1723)**

Indicates approximate employment figure
A = over 500 employees, B = 251-500
C = 101-250, D = 51-100, E = 20-50
F = 10-19, G = 1-9

— Business phone

— Geographic Section entry number where full company information appears

See footnotes for symbols and codes identification.
- Refer to the Industrial Product Index preceding this section to locate product headings.

ABRASIVES

Abrasive Products........................G..... 513 502-9150
Cincinnati *(G-2335)*

Abrasive Source Inc....................F 937 526-9753
Russia *(G-11672)*

Abrasive Supply Company Inc.............F 330 894-2818
Minerva *(G-10032)*

Abrasive Technology Lapidary ... G 740 548-4855
Lewis Center *(G-8318)*

Alb Tyler Holdings Inc...............G 440 946-7171
Mentor *(G-9475)*

Ali Industries LLC.......................B 937 878-3946
Fairborn *(G-6685)*

Alliance Abrasives LLC.................F 330 823-7957
Alliance *(G-368)*

ARC Abrasives Inc.......................D 800 888-4885
Troy *(G-13201)*

Belanger Inc...............................D 517 870-3206
West Chester *(G-13948)*

Buffalo Abrasives Inc..................E 614 891-6450
Westerville *(G-14248)*

Diamond Innovations Inc..............B 614 438-2000
Columbus *(G-4880)*

Enterprise Machine Inc................G 513 681-4409
Cincinnati *(G-2592)*

Even Cut Abrasive Company.............F 216 881-9595
Cleveland *(G-3692)*

Hec Investments Inc.....................C 937 278-9123
Dayton *(G-5808)*

Lawrence Industries Inc...............E 216 518-7000
Cleveland *(G-3946)*

Mill-Rose Company......................C 440 255-9171
Mentor *(G-9566)*

National Lime and Stone Co..........E 419 396-7671
Carey *(G-2060)*

Sure-Foot Industries Corp.............E 440 234-4446
Cleveland *(G-4352)*

US Technology Corporation.............E 330 455-1181
Canton *(G-2039)*

US Technology Media Inc...............F 330 874-3094
Bolivar *(G-1394)*

Vibra Finish Co...........................E 513 870-6300
Fairfield *(G-6788)*

ABRASIVES: Coated

Nanolap Technologies LLC.............G 877 658-4949
Englewood *(G-6619)*

ACCELERATION INDICATORS & SYSTEM COMPONENTS: Aerospace

Midwest Precision Holdings Inc........... F 440 497-4086
Eastlake *(G-6436)*

Nhvs International Inc................B 440 527-8610
Mentor *(G-9571)*

ACIDS

Emery Oleochemicals LLC....................E 513 762-2500
Cincinnati *(G-2584)*

ACIDS: Hydrochloric

Jones-Hamilton Co........................D 888 858-4425
Maumee *(G-9300)*

ACIDS: Inorganic

Capital Resin Corporation.............D 614 445-7177
Columbus *(G-4798)*

Detrex Corporation.....................F 216 749-2605
Cleveland *(G-3611)*

ACIDS: Sulfuric, Oleum

Marsulex Inc...............................E 419 698-8181
Oregon *(G-10963)*

ACOUSTICAL BOARD & TILE

Essi Acoustical Products................F 216 251-7888
Cleveland *(G-3686)*

ACRYLIC RESINS

Capital Resin Corporation.............D 614 445-7177
Columbus *(G-4798)*

Plaskolite LLC.............................D 614 294-3281
Columbus *(G-5195)*

Plaskolite LLC.............................C 740 450-1109
Zanesville *(G-15040)*

ACTUATORS: Indl, NEC

Automation Technology Inc..............E 937 233-6084
Dayton *(G-5670)*

Norgren LLC...............................C 937 833-4033
Brookville *(G-1574)*

SMC Corporation of America..............F 330 659-2006
Richfield *(G-11601)*

Thermotion Corp..........................F 440 639-8325
Mentor *(G-9637)*

Venture Mfg Co...........................E 937 233-8792
Dayton *(G-6071)*

ADAPTERS: Well

Wells Inc...................................F 419 457-2611
Risingsun *(G-11620)*

ADDITIVE BASED PLASTIC MATERIALS: Plasticizers

Aerosport Modeling Design LLC...........F 614 834-5227
Canal Winchester *(G-1783)*

Mum Industries Inc.......................D 440 269-4966
Mentor *(G-9569)*

Nanofiber Solutions LLC...............F 614 319-3075
Dublin *(G-6322)*

ADDRESSING SVCS

Franklin Printing Company..................F 740 452-6375
Zanesville *(G-15016)*

Gerald L Herrmann Company Inc..........F 513 661-1818
Cincinnati *(G-2669)*

Hecks Direct Mail Prtg Svc Inc................F 419 697-3505
Toledo *(G-12990)*

ADHESIVES

Adchem Adhesives Inc...................F 440 526-1976
Cleveland *(G-3296)*

Akzo Nobel Paints LLC...................A 440 297-8000
Strongsville *(G-12533)*

Certon Technologies Inc..................F 440 786-7185
Bedford *(G-1021)*

Chemspec Usa Inc........................D 330 669-8512
Orrville *(G-10977)*

Choice Brands Adhesives Ltd...............E 800 330-5566
Cincinnati *(G-2462)*

Conversion Tech Intl Inc.................E 419 924-5566
West Unity *(G-14193)*

Edge Adhesives Inc.......................E 614 875-6343
Grove City *(G-7383)*

Entrochem Inc.............................F 614 046-7602
Columbus *(G-4904)*

Evans Adhesive Corporation..............E 614 451-2665
Columbus *(G-4912)*

Evans Adhesive Corporation Ltd..........E 614 451-2665
Columbus *(G-4913)*

Franklin International Inc..................B 614 443-0241
Columbus *(G-4938)*

HB Fuller Company.......................D 513 719-3600
Blue Ash *(G-1282)*

HB Fuller Company.......................F 513 719-3600
Blue Ash *(G-1283)*

HB Fuller Company.......................F 440 708-1212
Chagrin Falls *(G-2164)*

Henkel US Operations Corp...............E 513 830-0260
Cincinnati *(G-2717)*

Henkel US Operations Corp...............C 216 475-3600
Cleveland *(G-3821)*

Henkel US Operations Corp...............C 440 255-8900
Mentor *(G-9528)*

Imperial Adhesives......................G 513 351-1300
Cincinnati *(G-2741)*

Mitsubishi Chemical Amer Inc..............D 419 483-2931
Bellevue *(G-1126)*

Morgan Adhesives Company LLC.........B 330 688-1111
Stow *(G-12441)*

P
R
O
D
U
C
T

Nagase Chemtex America LLC............ E 740 362-4444
Delaware *(G-6162)*

Paramelt Argueso Kindt Inc................. G ... 216 252-4122
Cleveland *(G-4133)*

Premier Building Solutions LLC............ E ... 330 244-2907
Massillon *(G-9235)*

Rubex Inc.. G ... 614 875-6343
Grove City *(G-7412)*

Spectra Group Limited Inc................... G ... 419 837-9783
Millbury *(G-9965)*

Sunstar Engrg Americas Inc................. E ... 937 746-8575
Springboro *(G-12268)*

Synthomer Adhesive Tech LLC.............. F ... 216 682-7000
Beachwood *(G-950)*

Synthomer USA LLC........................... E ... 678 400-6655
Beachwood *(G-952)*

Technicote Inc................................... E ... 330 928-1476
Cuyahoga Falls *(G-5576)*

Techno Adhesives Co.......................... G ... 513 771-1584
Cincinnati *(G-3141)*

Three Bond International Inc................. E ... 937 610-3000
Dayton *(G-6052)*

Three Bond International Inc................. D ... 513 779-7300
West Chester *(G-14082)*

Toagosei America Inc.......................... D ... 614 718-3855
West Jefferson *(G-14168)*

ADHESIVES & SEALANTS

Akron Paint & Varnish Inc................... D ... 330 773-8911
Akron *(G-36)*

Alpha Coatings Inc............................. C ... 419 435-5111
Fostoria *(G-6974)*

Arclin USA LLC.................................. F ... 419 726-5013
Toledo *(G-12885)*

Avery Dennison Corporation................. B ... 440 358-2564
Painesville *(G-11069)*

Bostik Inc.. E ... 419 289-9588
Ashland *(G-524)*

Bostik Inc.. E ... 614 232-8510
Columbus *(G-4770)*

Brewer Company............................... G ... 513 576-6300
Cincinnati *(G-2422)*

Cardinal Rubber Company.................... E ... 330 745-2191
Barberton *(G-801)*

Chemspec Ltd................................... F ... 330 364-4422
New Philadelphia *(G-10437)*

Chemspec Ltd................................... E ... 330 896-0355
Canton *(G-1864)*

Cincinnati Assn For The Blind.............. C ... 513 221-8558
Cincinnati *(G-2469)*

Consolidated Coatings Corp................. A ... 216 514-7596
Cleveland *(G-3561)*

Ddp Specialty Electronic MA................ G ... 937 839-4612
West Alexandria *(G-13918)*

Elmers Products Inc........................... C ... 614 225-4000
Columbus *(G-4900)*

Engineered Conductive Mtl LLC............ G ... 740 362-4444
Delaware *(G-6146)*

Foam Seal Inc................................... C ... 216 881-8111
Cleveland *(G-3730)*

Gdc Inc... F ... 574 533-3128
Wooster *(G-14642)*

Glenrock Company............................. G ... 513 489-6710
Blue Ash *(G-1277)*

HB Fuller Company............................ G ... 833 672-1482
Bellevue *(G-1124)*

Henkel US Operations Corp.................. D ... 440 250-7700
Westlake *(G-14305)*

Hexpol Cmpnding Amrcas Mfg LLC....... C ... 440 632-0901
Middlefield *(G-9799)*

Hexpol Compounding LLC.................... C ... 440 834-4644
Burton *(G-1699)*

Hoover & Wells Inc............................ C ... 419 691-9220
Toledo *(G-12995)*

Illinois Tool Works Inc........................ C ... 513 489-7600
Blue Ash *(G-1286)*

Illinois Tool Works Inc........................ D ... 440 914-3100
Solon *(G-12126)*

J C Whitlam Manufacturing Co............. E ... 330 334-2524
Wadsworth *(G-13644)*

Laird Technologies Inc........................ D ... 216 939-2300
Cleveland *(G-3935)*

Laminate Technologies Inc.................. D ... 800 231-2523
Tiffin *(G-12786)*

Laurenco Systems of Ohio LLC............. G
Leavittsburg *(G-8240)*

Lubrizol Global Management Inc........... F ... 216 447-5000
Cleveland *(G-3970)*

M Argueso & Co Inc........................... C ... 216 252-4122
Cleveland *(G-3974)*

Mactac Americas LLC......................... D ... 800 762-2822
Stow *(G-12439)*

Marlen Manufacturing & Dev Co........... F ... 216 292-7546
Bedford *(G-1047)*

Merryweather Foam Inc....................... E ... 330 753-0353
Barberton *(G-822)*

Millennium Adhesive Pdts LLC............. F ... 440 708-1212
Chagrin Falls *(G-2149)*

Neyra Interstate Inc........................... E ... 513 733-1000
Cincinnati *(G-2908)*

Pmbp Legacy Co Inc.......................... E ... 330 253-8148
Akron *(G-262)*

Polymerics Inc.................................. E ... 330 928-2210
Cuyahoga Falls *(G-5565)*

PPG Architectural Coatings LLC........... D ... 440 297-8000
Strongsville *(G-12587)*

Priest Services Inc............................ G ... 440 333-1123
Mayfield Heights *(G-9340)*

Quest Solutions Group LLC................. G ... 513 703-4520
Liberty Township *(G-8378)*

Republic Powdered Metals Inc.............. D ... 330 225-3192
Medina *(G-9441)*

RPM International Inc.......................... D ... 330 273-5090
Medina *(G-9442)*

Ruscoe Company............................... E ... 330 253-8148
Akron *(G-295)*

Sem-Com Company Inc....................... F ... 419 537-8813
Toledo *(G-13125)*

Sherwin-Williams Company.................. C ... 330 830-6000
Massillon *(G-9243)*

Shincor Silicones Inc......................... E ... 330 630-9460
Akron *(G-310)*

Signature Flexible Packg LLC.............. F ... 614 252-2121
Columbus *(G-5267)*

Silicone Solutions Inc........................ F ... 330 920-3125
Cuyahoga Falls *(G-5572)*

Simona Boltaron Inc........................... D ... 740 498-5900
Newcomerstown *(G-10575)*

Sirrus Inc.. E ... 513 448-0308
Loveland *(G-8654)*

Sonoco Products Company.................. E ... 937 429-0040
Beavercreek Township *(G-1006)*

Thermagon Inc.................................. D ... 216 939-2300
Cleveland *(G-4390)*

Thorworks Industries Inc..................... C ... 419 626-4375
Sandusky *(G-11876)*

Tremco Cpg Inc................................. C ... 419 289-2050
Ashland *(G-580)*

United McGill Corporation.................... E ... 614 829-1200
Groveport *(G-7455)*

Valco Cincinnati Inc........................... C ... 513 874-6550
Cincinnati *(G-3190)*

Waytek Corporation............................ E ... 937 743-6142
Franklin *(G-7057)*

ADHESIVES & SEALANTS WHOLESALERS

Brewpro Inc...................................... G ... 513 577-7200
Cincinnati *(G-2423)*

Consolidated Coatings Corp................. A ... 216 514-7596
Cleveland *(G-3561)*

National Polymer Inc.......................... F ... 440 708-1245
Chagrin Falls *(G-2171)*

Novagard Solutions Inc....................... D ... 216 881-8111
Cleveland *(G-4101)*

ADHESIVES: Adhesives, plastic

Durez Corporation.............................. D ... 567 295-6400
Kenton *(G-8097)*

National Polymer Inc.......................... F ... 440 708-1245
Chagrin Falls *(G-2171)*

ADHESIVES: Epoxy

Nanosperse LLC................................ G ... 937 296-5030
Kettering *(G-8122)*

Renegade Materials Corporation........... D ... 937 350-5274
Miamisburg *(G-9732)*

Summitville Tiles Inc.......................... D ... 330 868-6463
Minerva *(G-10048)*

ADVERTISING AGENCIES

Aardvark Screen Prtg & EMB LLC........ F ... 419 354-6686
Bowling Green *(G-1404)*

Advertising Joe LLC Mean................... G ... 440 247-8200
Chagrin Falls *(G-2135)*

Black River Group Inc........................ E ... 419 524-6699
Mansfield *(G-8765)*

Buckeye Business Forms Inc................ G ... 614 882-1890
Columbus *(G-4784)*

Dee Printing Inc................................ F ... 614 777-8700
Columbus *(G-4874)*

Mark Advertising Agency Inc................ F ... 419 626-9000
Sandusky *(G-11856)*

Pro Press Inc.................................... F ... 216 631-8200
Cleveland *(G-4197)*

ADVERTISING AGENCIES: Consultants

Airmate Co Inc.................................. D ... 419 636-3184
Bryan *(G-1625)*

Just Business Inc.............................. F ... 866 577-3303
Dayton *(G-5835)*

Kyle Media Inc.................................. F ... 877 775-2538
Toledo *(G-13025)*

ADVERTISING DISPLAY PRDTS

Aster Industries Inc........................... E ... 330 762-7965
Akron *(G-62)*

Edi Custom Interiors Inc...................... F ... 513 829-3895
Fairfield *(G-6731)*

Indispenser Ltd................................. E ... 419 625-5825
Sandusky *(G-11841)*

On Display Ltd.................................. E ... 513 841-1600
Batavia *(G-880)*

Power Media Inc................................ G ... 330 475-0500
Copley *(G-5436)*

ADVERTISING REPRESENTATIVES: Electronic Media

Retain Loyalty LLC............................ G ... 330 830-0839
Massillon *(G-9238)*

ADVERTISING REPRESENTATIVES: Newspaper

American City Bus Journals Inc............ C ... 937 528-4400
Dayton *(G-5651)*

Copley Ohio Newspapers Inc............... C ... 330 364-5577
New Philadelphia *(G-10439)*

Gazette Publishing Company................ D 419 335-2010
Napoleon (G-10280)

News Watchman & Paper................... F 740 947-2149
Waverly (G-13870)

Ohio Newspaper Services Inc.............. G 614 486-6677
Columbus (G-5149)

Progressor Times............................ G 419 396-7567
Carey (G-2062)

ADVERTISING SPECIALTIES, WHOLESALE

Ace Plastics Company...................... G 330 928-7720
Stow (G-12414)

American Business Forms Inc............. E 513 312-2522
West Chester (G-14101)

Associated Premium Corporation......... E 513 679-4444
Cincinnati (G-2381)

Auto Dealer Designs Inc................... E 330 374-7666
Akron (G-65)

Baker Plastics Inc.......................... G 330 743-3142
Youngstown (G-14817)

Bluelogos Inc............................... F 614 898-9971
Westerville (G-14247)

Bottomline Ink Corporation................ E 419 897-8000
Perrysburg (G-11205)

Cal Sales Embroidery...................... G 440 236-3820
Columbia Station (G-4590)

Capehart Enterprises LLC.................. F 614 769-7746
Columbus (G-4795)

Charizma Corp.............................. G 216 621-2220
Cleveland (G-3485)

Custom Sporstwear Imprints LLC......... G 330 335-8326
Wadsworth (G-13633)

Flashions Sportswear Ltd.................. F 937 323-5885
Springfield (G-12312)

Galaxy Balloons Incorporated............. C 216 476-3360
Cleveland (G-3753)

Gary Lawrence Enterprises Inc............ G 330 833-7181
Massillon (G-9194)

Gq Business Products Inc.................. G 513 792-4750
Loveland (G-8627)

Identity Group LLC......................... G 614 337-6167
Westerville (G-14213)

Mr Emblem Inc............................. G 419 697-1888
Oregon (G-10964)

Novelty Advertising Co Inc................ E 740 622-3113
Coshocton (G-5465)

Ohio State Institute Fin Inc................ G 614 861-8811
Reynoldsburg (G-11570)

Peter Graham Dunn Inc.................... G 330 816-0035
Dalton (G-5592)

PS Superior Inc............................ G 216 587-1000
Cleveland (G-4204)

Publishing Group Ltd....................... F 614 572-1240
Columbus (G-5213)

Randd Assoc Prtg & Promotions.......... G 937 294-1874
Dayton (G-5975)

Screen Works Inc.......................... E 937 264-9111
Dayton (G-6000)

Sew & Sew Embroidery Inc................ F 330 676-1600
Kent (G-8078)

Shamrock Companies Inc.................. D 440 899-9510
Westlake (G-14333)

Solar Arts Graphic Designs................ G 330 744-0535
Youngstown (G-14934)

Star Calendar & Printing Inc............... G 216 741-3223
Cleveland (G-4328)

T & L Custom Screening Inc............... G 937 237-3121
Dayton (G-6036)

Traichal Construction Company............ E 800 255-3667
Niles (G-10607)

Underground Sports Shop Inc.............. F 513 751-1662
Cincinnati (G-3179)

White Tiger Inc............................. F 740 852-4873
London (G-8543)

ADVERTISING SVCS: Direct Mail

Amsive OH LLC............................. D 937 885-8000
Miamisburg (G-9665)

Baesman Group Inc......................... D 614 771-2300
Hilliard (G-7674)

Consolidated Graphics Group Inc......... C 216 881-9191
Cleveland (G-3559)

Digital Color Intl LLC....................... F
Akron (G-123)

Hecks Direct Mail & Prtg Svc.............. E 419 661-6028
Toledo (G-12989)

Laipplys Prtg Mktg Sltions Inc............. G 740 387-9282
Marion (G-8975)

Malik Media LLC............................ G 614 933-0328
New Albany (G-10345)

Network Printing & Graphics............... F 614 230-2084
Columbus (G-5124)

Quez Media Marketing Inc................. F 216 910-0202
Independence (G-7918)

Retain Loyalty LLC......................... G 330 830-0839
Massillon (G-9238)

Traxium LLC............................... E 330 572-8200
Stow (G-12466)

ADVERTISING SVCS: Display

A Sign Above Inc........................... F 330 425-7832
Twinsburg (G-13266)

Cgs Imaging Inc............................ F 419 897-3000
Holland (G-7749)

Design Masters Inc......................... G 513 772-7175
Cincinnati (G-2547)

Digital Color Intl LLC....................... F
Akron (G-123)

Display Dynamics Inc....................... F 937 832-2830
Englewood (G-6612)

Kyle Media Inc............................. F 877 775-2538
Toledo (G-13025)

Performance Packaging Inc................ F 419 478-8805
Toledo (G-13094)

ADVERTISING SVCS: Outdoor

Ike Smart City............................. E 614 294-4898
Columbus (G-5000)

Kessler Sign Company..................... E 740 453-0668
Zanesville (G-15025)

Ohio Shelterall LLC........................ F 614 882-1110
Westerville (G-14272)

Orange Barrel Media LLC.................. D 614 294-4898
Columbus (G-5162)

ADVERTISING SVCS: Sample Distribution

Aztech Printing & Promotions.............. G 937 339-0100
Troy (G-13202)

AERIAL WORK PLATFORMS

G & T Manufacturing Co.................... F 440 639-7777
Mentor (G-9522)

Powerbilt Mtl Hdlg Sltions LLC............. D 937 592-5660
Bellefontaine (G-1115)

AEROSOLS

C A P Industries Inc....................... F 937 773-1824
Piqua (G-11338)

Eveready Products Corporation............ F 216 661-2755
Cleveland (G-3694)

Wellston Aerosol Mfg Co................... G 740 384-2320
Wellston (G-13911)

Zenex International......................... G 440 232-4155
Bedford (G-1067)

AGRICULTURAL EQPT: BARN, SILO, POULTRY, DAIRY/LIVESTOCK MACH

Fort Recovery Equipment Inc............... G 419 375-1006
Fort Recovery (G-6962)

Stein-Way Equipment....................... G 330 857-8700
Apple Creek (G-478)

AGRICULTURAL EQPT: Elevators, Farm

Afs Technology LLC........................ F 937 545-0627
Dayton (G-5641)

Gerald Grain Center Inc.................... F 419 445-2451
Archbold (G-495)

Sweet Manufacturing Company............ E 937 325-1511
Springfield (G-12381)

AGRICULTURAL EQPT: Fertilizing Machinery

Shearer Farm Inc.......................... C 330 345-9023
Wooster (G-14685)

AGRICULTURAL EQPT: Grounds Mowing Eqpt

TD Landscape Inc.......................... F 740 694-0244
Fredericktown (G-7085)

AGRICULTURAL EQPT: Tractors, Farm

Miners Tractor Sales Inc................... F 330 325-9914
Rootstown (G-11649)

AGRICULTURAL EQPT: Turf & Grounds Eqpt

Randall Richard & Moore LLC.............. E 330 455-8873
Canton (G-1991)

Rhinestahl Corporation..................... D 513 489-1317
Mason (G-9144)

AGRICULTURAL MACHINERY & EQPT: Wholesalers

Bortnick Tractor Sales Inc.................. E 330 924-2555
Cortland (G-5442)

Buckeye Companies......................... E 740 452-3641
Zanesville (G-15000)

Reberland Equipment Inc................... F 330 698-5883
Apple Creek (G-476)

S I Distributing Inc........................ F 419 647-4909
Spencerville (G-12240)

Yoder & Frey Inc........................... F 419 445-2070
Archbold (G-313)

AIR CLEANING SYSTEMS

H-P Products Inc........................... C 330 875-5556
Louisville (G-8602)

United Air Specialists Inc.................. C 513 891-0400
Blue Ash (G-1345)

AIR CONDITIONERS: Motor Vehicle

Jbar A/C Inc............................... F 216 447-4294
Cleveland (G-3884)

AIR CONDITIONING & VENTILATION EQPT & SPLYS: Wholesales

Weather King Heating & AC................ G 330 908-0281
Northfield (G-10799)

AIR CONDITIONING EQPT

Bard Manufacturing Company Inc.......... D 419 636-1194
Bryan (G-1631)

Hydro-Thrift Corporation................... E 330 837-5141
Massillon (G-9205)

JD Indoor Comfort Inc...................... F 440 949-8758
Sheffield Lake (G-11954)

PRODUCT

Snap Rite Manufacturing Inc.................. E 910 897-4080
Cleveland *(G-4308)*

Vertiv Corporation................................. A 614 888-0246
Westerville *(G-14239)*

AIR CONDITIONING REPAIR SVCS

Air-Rite Inc....................................... E 216 228-8200
Cleveland *(G-3316)*

Weather King Heating & AC.............. G 330 908-0281
Northfield *(G-10799)*

Wsi Seller Inc.................................... F 330 379-0270
Akron *(G-359)*

AIR CONDITIONING UNITS: Complete, Domestic Or Indl

Air Enterprises Inc.......................... A 330 794-9770
Akron *(G-22)*

Ecu Corporation................................. F 513 898-9294
Cincinnati *(G-2579)*

Fred D Pfening Company.................... E 614 294-5361
Columbus *(G-4939)*

Hdt Ep Inc... C 216 438-6111
Solon *(G-12120)*

Hdt Expeditionary Systems Inc......... F 440 466-6640
Geneva *(G-7239)*

Lintern Corporation........................... E 440 255-9333
Mentor *(G-9554)*

Taylor & Moore Co............................. F 513 733-5530
Cincinnati *(G-3139)*

Vertiv Corporation............................. C 614 841-6078
Delaware *(G-6177)*

Vertiv Group Corporation................... A 614 888-0246
Westerville *(G-14240)*

Vertiv JV Holdings LLC....................... A 614 888-0246
Columbus *(G-5348)*

Whirlpool Corporation......................... E 614 409-4340
Lockbourne *(G-8494)*

AIR DUCT CLEANING SVCS

Indoor Envmtl Specialists Inc............... E 937 433-5202
Dayton *(G-5821)*

AIR MATTRESSES: Plastic

Fiber -Tech Industries Inc.................... D 740 335-9400
Wshngtn Ct Hs *(G-14739)*

Kmak Group LLC................................. F 937 308-1023
London *(G-8538)*

AIR PURIFICATION EQPT

Airecon Manufacturing Corp............... E 513 561-5522
Cincinnati *(G-2345)*

Allied Separation Tech Inc................... G 704 736-0420
Twinsburg *(G-13273)*

Extreme Microbial Tech LLC................ E 844 885-0088
Moraine *(G-10162)*

Guardian Technologies LLC................. E 866 603-5900
Euclid *(G-6652)*

Indoor Envmtl Specialists Inc............... E 937 433-5202
Dayton *(G-5821)*

Met-Pro Technologies LLC.................... F 513 458-2600
Cincinnati *(G-2868)*

AIRCRAFT & AEROSPACE FLIGHT INSTRUMENTS & GUIDANCE SYSTEMS

Consoldted Precision Pdts Corp........... C 216 453-4800
Cleveland *(G-3560)*

Landrum Brown Wrldwide Svcs LL........ G 513 530-5333
Blue Ash *(G-1295)*

Ryse Aero Holdco Inc.......................... E 513 318-9907
Mason *(G-9145)*

AIRCRAFT & HEAVY EQPT REPAIR SVCS

Apph Wichita Inc................................ E 316 943-5752
Strongsville *(G-12537)*

Grimes Aerospace Company................ D 937 484-2001
Urbana *(G-13464)*

K & J Machine Inc.............................. G 740 425-3282
Barnesville *(G-845)*

Karon C Enold.................................... E 740 269-3475
Sherrodsville *(G-11975)*

McNational Inc.................................... D 740 377-4391
South Point *(G-12227)*

Ohio Machinery Co.............................. C 440 526-6200
Broadview Heights *(G-1509)*

Pas Technologies Inc........................... D 937 840-1053
Hillsboro *(G-7723)*

Tri State Equipment Company.............. G 513 738-7227
Shandon *(G-11935)*

AIRCRAFT ASSEMBLY PLANTS

Avari Aero LLC................................... G 513 828-0860
Cincinnati *(G-2392)*

Executive Wings Inc............................ G 440 254-1812
Painesville *(G-11084)*

Goodrich Corporation.......................... A 937 339-3811
Troy *(G-13219)*

Hii Mission Technologies Corp.............. G 937 426-3421
Beavercreek *(G-992)*

K&M Aviation LLC.............................. D 216 261-9000
Cleveland *(G-3902)*

Nextant Aerospace LLC....................... E 216 898-4800
Cleveland *(G-4075)*

Powder Alloy Corporation.................... E 513 984-4016
Loveland *(G-8646)*

Ruhe Sales Inc................................... F 419 943-3357
Leipsic *(G-8314)*

Snow Aviation Intl Inc......................... G 614 588-2452
Gahanna *(G-7169)*

Star Jet LLC...................................... G 614 338-4379
Columbus *(G-5289)*

Technology House Ltd.......................... F 440 248-3025
Streetsboro *(G-12526)*

Tessec Manufacturing Svcs LLC........... E 937 985-3552
Dayton *(G-6046)*

Theiss Uav Solutions LLC.................... G 330 584-2070
North Benton *(G-10624)*

Toledo Jet Center LLC......................... G 419 866-9050
Swanton *(G-12695)*

AIRCRAFT CONTROL SYSTEMS:

Esterline Technologies Corp................. E 216 706-2960
Cleveland *(G-3687)*

AIRCRAFT ELECTRICAL EQPT REPAIR SVCS

General Electric Company.................... E 513 977-1500
Cincinnati *(G-2662)*

Karon C Enold.................................... E 740 269-3475
Sherrodsville *(G-11975)*

Spirit Avionics Ltd.............................. F 614 237-4271
Columbus *(G-5284)*

AIRCRAFT ENGINES & ENGINE PARTS: Airfoils

PCC Airfoils LLC................................ C 440 255-9770
Mentor *(G-9584)*

Turbine Eng Cmpnents Tech Corp........ B 216 692-5200
Cleveland *(G-4433)*

AIRCRAFT ENGINES & ENGINE PARTS: Nonelectric Starters

Dreison International Inc..................... C 216 362-0755
Cleveland *(G-3632)*

AIRCRAFT ENGINES & ENGINE PARTS: Pumps

At Holdings Corporation...................... A 216 692-6000
Cleveland *(G-3382)*

Eaton Industrial Corporation................ B 216 523-4205
Cleveland *(G-3656)*

AIRCRAFT ENGINES & ENGINE PARTS: Research & Development, Mfr

Defense Research Assoc Inc................. E 937 431-1644
Dayton *(G-5609)*

AIRCRAFT ENGINES & PARTS

Advanced Ground Systems.................... F 513 402-7226
Cincinnati *(G-2338)*

Aero Jet Wash Llc.............................. F 866 381-7955
Dayton *(G-5637)*

American Aero Components Llc............ G 937 367-5068
Dayton *(G-5649)*

Avidyne... G 800 284-3963
Dublin *(G-6280)*

Barnes Group Inc................................ F 513 779-6888
West Chester *(G-13946)*

CFM International Inc.......................... F 513 563-4180
Cincinnati *(G-2455)*

CFM International Inc.......................... F 513 563-4180
Cincinnati *(G-2456)*

CFM International Inc.......................... E 513 552-2787
West Chester *(G-13959)*

Drt Aerospace LLC.............................. E 937 492-6121
Sidney *(G-12013)*

Enjet Aero Dayton Inc......................... E 937 878-3800
Huber Heights *(G-7821)*

Ferrotherm Corporation....................... C 216 883-9350
Cleveland *(G-3714)*

General Electric Company.................... G 513 948-4170
Cincinnati *(G-2660)*

Heico Aerospace Parts Corp................. B 954 987-6101
Highland Heights *(G-7659)*

Henry Tools Inc................................. G 216 291-1011
Cleveland *(G-3824)*

Hi-Tek Manufacturing Inc.................... C 513 459-1094
Mason *(G-9108)*

Honeywell International I...................... F 513 282-5519
Mason *(G-9109)*

Honeywell International Inc.................. E 440 329-9000
Elyria *(G-6542)*

Honeywell Lebow Products.................. C 614 850-5000
Columbus *(G-4991)*

Lsp Technologies Inc........................... E 614 718-3000
Dublin *(G-6318)*

Magellan Arospc Middletown Inc........... D 513 422-2751
Middletown *(G-9875)*

Meyer Tool Inc.................................... A 513 681-7362
Cincinnati *(G-2874)*

Miba Bearings US LLC......................... B 740 962-4242
Mcconnelsville *(G-9364)*

Optical Display Engrg Inc.................... F 440 995-6555
Highland Heights *(G-7661)*

Otto Konigslow Mfg Co......................... F 216 851-7900
Cleveland *(G-4128)*

Pako Inc... C 440 946-8030
Mentor *(G-9580)*

Parker-Hannifin Corporation............... C 440 284-6277
Elyria (G-6576)

Pas Technologies Inc.......................... D 937 840-1053
Hillsboro (G-7723)

Precision Castparts Corp..................... F 440 350-6150
Painesville (G-11106)

Sifco Industries Inc........................... D 216 881-8600
Cleveland (G-4299)

Snow Aviation Intl Inc........................ G 614 588-2452
Gahanna (G-7169)

Spirit Avionics Ltd............................. F 614 237-4271
Columbus (G-5284)

Superalloy Mfg Solutions Corp............. C 513 489-9800
Blue Ash (G-1337)

Tessec LLC....................................... D 937 576-0010
Dayton (G-6045)

Turbine Standard Ltd.......................... G 419 865-0355
Holland (G-7789)

Welded Ring Products Co..................... D 216 961-3800
Cleveland (G-4499)

AIRCRAFT EQPT & SPLYS WHOLESALERS

Transdigm Group Incorporated.............. B 216 706-2960
Cleveland (G-4413)

AIRCRAFT MAINTENANCE & REPAIR SVCS

Malta Dynamics LLC........................... F 740 749-3512
Waterford (G-13828)

Toledo Jet Center LLC........................ G 419 866-9050
Swanton (G-12695)

AIRCRAFT PARTS & AUXILIARY EQPT:
Assys, Subassemblies/Parts

Ctl-Aerospace Inc.............................. C 513 874-7900
Cincinnati (G-2530)

Electronic Concepts Engrg Inc.............. F 419 861-9000
Holland (G-7763)

Esterline Technologies Corp................. E 216 706-2960
Cleveland (G-3687)

Master Swaging Inc............................ G 937 596-6171
Jackson Center (G-7965)

Parker-Hannifin Corporation............... C 440 284-6277
Elyria (G-6576)

Snow Aviation Intl Inc........................ G 614 588-2452
Gahanna (G-7169)

AIRCRAFT PARTS & AUXILIARY EQPT:
Body & Wing Assys & Parts

Achilles Aerospace Pdts Inc................. E 330 425-8444
Twinsburg (G-13268)

Columbus Jack Corporation.................. E 614 443-7492
Swanton (G-12680)

GSE Production and Support LLC.......... G 419 866-6301
Swanton (G-12685)

Industrial Mfg Co LLC......................... F 440 838-4700
Brecksville (G-1472)

AIRCRAFT PARTS & AUXILIARY EQPT:
Body Assemblies & Parts

Magellan Arospc Middletown Inc........... D 513 422-2751
Middletown (G-9875)

Milan Tool Corp................................. E 216 661-1078
Cleveland (G-4039)

Pacific Piston Ring Co Inc.................... E 513 387-6100
Blue Ash (G-1317)

AIRCRAFT PARTS & AUXILIARY EQPT:
Brakes

Meggitt Arcft Brking Systems C........... A 330 796-4400
Akron (G-228)

AIRCRAFT PARTS & AUXILIARY EQPT:
Landing Assemblies & Brakes

Friction Products Co........................... B 330 725-4941
Medina (G-9406)

Goodrich Corporation.......................... A 937 339-3811
Troy (G-13219)

AIRCRAFT PARTS & AUXILIARY EQPT:
Lighting/Landing Gear Assy

Hdi Landing Gear USA Inc.................... E 937 325-1586
Strongsville (G-12563)

Hdi Landing Gear USA Inc.................... D 937 325-1586
Springfield (G-12318)

AIRCRAFT PARTS & AUXILIARY EQPT:
Military Eqpt & Armament

Dircksen and Associates Inc................ G 614 238-0413
Columbus (G-4881)

Test-Fuchs Corporation....................... G 440 708-3505
Brecksville (G-1483)

AIRCRAFT PARTS & AUXILIARY EQPT:
Research & Development, Mfr

Drt Aerospace LLC............................. E 937 492-6121
Sidney (G-12013)

Long-Lok LLC.................................... E 336 343-7319
Cincinnati (G-2826)

Weldon Pump LLC.............................. E 440 232-2282
Oakwood Village (G-10913)

AIRCRAFT PARTS & AUXILIARY EQPT:
Tanks, Fuel

Bosserman Aviation Equipment Inc....... E 419 722-2879
Carey (G-2056)

AIRCRAFT PARTS & EQPT, NEC

Advanced Fuel Systems Inc................. G 614 252-8422
Columbus (G-4676)

Aero Tech Tool & Mold Inc.................. G 440 942-3327
Mentor (G-9471)

Aerospace LLC.................................. F 937 561-1104
Moraine (G-10143)

Aerospace Maint Solutions LLC........... E 440 729-7703
Solon (G-12074)

Aim International................................ G 513 831-2938
Miamiville (G-9761)

Allen Aircraft Products Inc.................. E 330 296-9621
Ravenna (G-11514)

Allen Aircraft Products Inc.................. D 330 296-9621
Ravenna (G-11516)

American Aero Components Llc............ G 937 367-5068
Dayton (G-5649)

Apph Wichita Inc............................... E 316 943-5752
Strongsville (G-12537)

Arctos Mission Solutions LLC.............. E 813 609-5591
Beavercreek (G-965)

At Holdings Corporation...................... A 216 692-6000
Cleveland (G-3382)

Auto-Valve Inc.................................. E 937 854-3037
Dayton (G-5668)

Aviation Cmpnent Solutions Inc........... F 440 295-6590
Richmond Heights (G-11607)

Avtron Aerospace Inc......................... C 216 750-5152
Cleveland (G-3393)

Aws Industries Inc............................. E 513 932-7941
Lebanon (G-8245)

Barnes Group Inc............................... D 513 779-6888
West Chester (G-13947)

Ctl-Aerospace Inc.............................. E 513 874-7900
West Chester (G-14112)

Danfoss Power Solutions II LLC........... F 419 238-1190
Van Wert (G-13533)

Drt Holdings LLC............................... D 937 298-7391
Dayton (G-5753)

Dukes Aerospace Inc......................... D 818 998-9811
Painesville (G-11080)

Eaton Aeroquip LLC........................... C 440 523-5000
Cleveland (G-3650)

Eaton Industrial Corporation............... C 216 692-5456
Cleveland (G-3657)

Eaton Industrial Corporation............... B 216 523-4205
Cleveland (G-3656)

Enjet Aero LLC.................................. F 937 878-3800
Huber Heights (G-7820)

Enjet Aero Dayton Inc........................ E 937 878-3800
Huber Heights (G-7821)

Eti Tech LLC..................................... F 937 832-4200
Kettering (G-8120)

Exito Manufacturing LLC..................... G 937 291-9871
Beavercreek (G-991)

Federal Equipment Company................ D 513 621-5260
Cincinnati (G-2616)

Ferco Tech LLC................................. C 937 746-6696
Franklin (G-7020)

Field Aviation Inc.............................. E 513 792-2282
Cincinnati (G-2622)

GE Aviation Systems LLC................... B 937 898-5881
Vandalia (G-13558)

GE Engine Services LLC..................... B 513 977-1500
Cincinnati (G-2656)

GE Military Systems........................... E 513 243-2000
Cincinnati (G-2658)

General Dynamics-Ots Inc................... C 937 746-8500
Springboro (G-12253)

General Electric Company.................... E 513 977-1500
Cincinnati (G-2662)

Goodrich Corporation.......................... G 440 262-1400
Brecksville (G-1469)

Goodrich Corporation.......................... G 330 374-2358
North Canton (G-10643)

Goodrich Corporation.......................... F 216 429-4378
Troy (G-13220)

Grimes Aerospace Company................ D 937 484-2000
Urbana (G-13463)

Grimes Aerospace Company................ A 937 484-2000
Urbana (G-13462)

Heller Machine Products Inc................ G 216 281-2951
Cleveland (G-3820)

Heroux-Devtek Inc............................. F 937 325-1586
Springfield (G-12321)

Hydro-Aire Inc.................................. C 440 323-3211
Elyria (G-6543)

Hydro-Aire Aerospace Corp................. C 440 323-3211
Elyria (G-6544)

Kelly Arspc Thrmal Systems LLC......... E 440 951-4744
Willoughby (G-14476)

Lawrence Technologies Inc.................. G 937 274-7771
Dayton (G-5842)

Lincoln Electric Automtn Inc................ B 937 295-2120
Fort Loramie (G-6950)

Lkd Aerospace Holdings Inc................. F 216 262-8481
Cleveland (G-3965)

Logan Machine Company...................... D 330 633-6163
Akron (G-210)

Malabar.. E 419 866-6301
Swanton (G-12687)

Mar-Con Tool Company........................ E 937 299-2244
Moraine (G-10175)

Maverick Molding Co........................... F 513 387-6100
Blue Ash (G-1305)

Employee Codes: A=Over 500 employees, B=251-500
C=101-250, D=51-100, E=20-50, F=10-19, G=1-9

2025 Harris Ohio
Industrial Directory

1221

PRODUCT

McKechnie Arospc Holdings Inc............ G 216 706-2960
  Cleveland *(G-4011)*

Meggitt Polymers & Composites........... F 513 851-5550
  Cincinnati *(G-2859)*

Middleton Enterprises Inc................... G 614 885-2514
  Worthington *(G-14721)*

Midwest Aircraft Products Co............... F 419 884-2164
  Mansfield *(G-8826)*

Pako Inc... C 440 946-8030
  Mentor *(G-9580)*

Parker Meggitt.................................. F 513 851-5550
  Cincinnati *(G-2942)*

PCC Airfoils LLC............................... B 740 982-6025
  Crooksville *(G-5511)*

Skidmore-Wilhelm Mfg Company......... G 216 481-4774
  Solon *(G-12182)*

Starwin Industries LLC....................... E 937 293-8568
  Dayton *(G-6024)*

Summit Avionics Inc.......................... G 330 425-1440
  Twinsburg *(G-13381)*

Taylor Manufacturing Co Inc............... F 937 322-8622
  Springfield *(G-12383)*

Tessec Technology Services LLC......... E 513 240-5601
  Dayton *(G-6047)*

Tracewell Systems Inc....................... D 614 846-6175
  Lewis Center *(G-8356)*

Transdigm Group Incorporated........... B 216 706-2960
  Cleveland *(G-4413)*

Triumph Thermal Systems LLC........... D 419 273-2511
  Forest *(G-6942)*

Tronair Inc....................................... D 419 866-6301
  Swanton *(G-12697)*

Truline Industries Inc........................ D 440 729-0140
  Wickliffe *(G-14397)*

Turbine Eng Cmpnents Tech Corp....... B 216 692-5200
  Cleveland *(G-4433)*

Unison Industries LLC....................... B 904 667-9904
  Dayton *(G-5625)*

US Aeroteam Inc.............................. E 937 458-0344
  Dayton *(G-6070)*

US Technology Corporation................ E 330 455-1181
  Canton *(G-2039)*

White Machine Inc............................ G 440 237-3282
  North Royalton *(G-10789)*

AIRCRAFT PARTS WHOLESALERS

Grimes Aerospace Company............... D 937 484-2001
  Urbana *(G-13464)*

AIRCRAFT PROPELLERS & PARTS

Hartzell Propeller Inc........................ C 937 778-4200
  Piqua *(G-11353)*

Spectrum Textiles Inc....................... F 513 933-8346
  Lebanon *(G-8286)*

AIRCRAFT SERVICING & REPAIRING

Spirit Avionics Ltd............................ F 614 237-4271
  Columbus *(G-5284)*

Unison Industries LLC....................... B 904 667-9904
  Dayton *(G-5625)*

AIRCRAFT TURBINES

Honeywell International Inc................. F 216 459-6048
  Brookpark *(G-1552)*

AIRCRAFT WHEELS

Aircraft Wheel & Brake LLC................ D 440 937-6211
  Avon *(G-713)*

Jay-Em Aerospace Corporation........... E 330 923-0333
  Cuyahoga Falls *(G-5551)*

Parker-Hannifin Corporation............... C 440 937-6211
  Avon *(G-734)*

AIRCRAFT: Airplanes, Fixed Or Rotary Wing

Boeing Company............................... E 740 788-4000
  Heath *(G-7594)*

Steel Aviation Aircraft Sales............... G 937 332-7587
  Casstown *(G-2092)*

AIRCRAFT: Motorized

Tessec LLC...................................... D 937 576-0010
  Dayton *(G-6045)*

AIRCRAFT: Research & Development, Manufacturer

Aerovation Tech Holdings LLC............ G 567 208-5525
  Forest *(G-6938)*

Consoldted Precision Pdts Corp.......... C 216 453-4800
  Cleveland *(G-3560)*

AIRPORTS, FLYING FIELDS & SVCS

Grand Aire Inc.................................. E 419 861-6700
  Swanton *(G-12684)*

Ruhe Sales Inc................................. F 419 943-3357
  Leipsic *(G-8314)*

ALARMS: Fire

Honeywell International Inc................. A 937 484-2000
  Urbana *(G-13466)*

ALCOHOL: Ethyl & Ethanol

Andersons Mrathon Holdings LLC........ E 937 316-3700
  Greenville *(G-7334)*

Guardian Lima LLC............................ E 567 940-9500
  Lima *(G-8412)*

Poet Biorefining - Leipsic LLC............ E 419 943-7447
  Leipsic *(G-8309)*

Poet Biorefining Marion LLC.............. E 740 383-4400
  Marion *(G-8990)*

Poet Borefining - Fostoria LLC........... E 419 436-0954
  Fostoria *(G-6997)*

The Andersons Clymers Ethanol LLC... E 574 722-2627
  Maumee *(G-9324)*

ALKALIES & CHLORINE

Eltech Systems Corporation............... G 440 285-0380
  Concord Township *(G-5390)*

GFS Chemicals Inc............................ E 740 881-5501
  Powell *(G-11488)*

National Colloid Company................... E 740 282-1171
  Steubenville *(G-12407)*

National Lime and Stone Co............... E 419 396-7671
  Carey *(G-2060)*

ALLOYS: Additive, Exc Copper Or Made In Blast Furnaces

GE Aviation Systems LLC................... E 620 218-5237
  Springdale *(G-12273)*

GE Aviation Systems LLC................... G 513 889-5150
  West Chester *(G-14005)*

Morris Technologies Inc..................... E 513 733-1611
  Cincinnati *(G-2888)*

Theken Port Park LLC........................ D 330 733-7600
  Akron *(G-335)*

ALTERNATORS & GENERATORS: Battery Charging

Asidaco LLC..................................... G 800 204-1544
  Dayton *(G-5666)*

Rv Mobile Power LLC......................... E 855 427-7978
  Columbus *(G-5239)*

ALTERNATORS: Automotive

Cuyahoga Rebuilders Inc.................... G 216 635-0659
  Cleveland *(G-3592)*

Hitachi Astemo Americas Inc.............. B 740 965-1133
  Sunbury *(G-12666)*

M W Solutions LLC............................ F 419 782-1611
  Defiance *(G-6118)*

ALUMINUM

Alcan Primary Products Corp.............. C
  Independence *(G-7889)*

Boggs Recycling Inc.......................... G 800 837-8101
  Newbury *(G-10547)*

Kaiser Aluminum Fab Pdts LLC........... C 740 522-1151
  Heath *(G-7598)*

Ormet Corporation............................ A 740 483-1381
  Hannibal *(G-7540)*

P&The Mfg Acquisition LLC................ D 937 492-4134
  Sidney *(G-12037)*

ALUMINUM PRDTS

Accu-Tek Tool & Die Inc.................... G 330 726-1946
  Salem *(G-11760)*

Alanod Westlake Metal Ind Inc............ E 440 327-8184
  North Ridgeville *(G-10723)*

Alufab Inc.. G 513 528-7281
  Cincinnati *(G-2296)*

Aluminum Extruded Shapes Inc.......... C 513 563-2205
  Cincinnati *(G-2354)*

American Aluminum Extrusions........... C 330 458-0300
  Canton *(G-1830)*

AMG Aluminum North America LLC...... F 659 348-3620
  Cambridge *(G-1735)*

Arem Co.. G 440 974-6740
  Willoughby *(G-14426)*

Astro Aluminum Enterprises Inc.......... G 330 755-1414
  Struthers *(G-12616)*

Astro-Coatings Inc............................ G 330 755-1414
  Struthers *(G-12617)*

Bidwell Family Corporation................. C 513 988-6351
  Trenton *(G-13191)*

BRT Extrusions Inc............................ C 330 544-0177
  Niles *(G-10584)*

Central Aluminum Company LLC......... E 614 491-5700
  Obetz *(G-10922)*

Da Investments Inc........................... D 330 781-6100
  Youngstown *(G-14845)*

Extrudex Aluminum Inc...................... C 330 538-4444
  North Jackson *(G-10687)*

Fom USA Incorporated....................... G 234 248-4400
  Medina *(G-9404)*

H-P Products Inc............................... C 330 875-5556
  Louisville *(G-8602)*

Hydro Aluminum Fayetteville.............. G 937 492-9194
  Sidney *(G-12024)*

Industrial Mold Inc............................ E 330 425-7374
  Twinsburg *(G-13320)*

Isaiah Industries Inc.......................... G 937 778-2246
  Piqua *(G-11357)*

Isaiah Industries Inc.......................... E 937 773-9840
  Piqua *(G-11358)*

Knoble Glass & Metal Inc................... G 513 753-1246
  Cincinnati *(G-2802)*

L & L Ornamental Iron Co................... F 513 353-1930
  Cleves *(G-4543)*

M-D Building Products Inc.................. F 513 539-2255
  Middletown *(G-9874)*

McKnight Industries Inc...................... F 937 592-9010
  Bellefontaine *(G-1113)*

National Metal Shapes Inc.................. E 740 363-9559
  Delaware *(G-6164)*

Orrvilon Inc...................................... C 330 684-9400
  Orrville *(G-11001)*

Owens Corning Sales LLC.................... F 740 983-1300
Ashville (G-629)

Pennex Aluminum Company LLC.......... C 330 427-6704
Leetonia (G-8304)

Star Extruded Shapes LLC.................... B 330 533-9863
Canfield (G-1816)

Star Fab Inc... E 330 482-1601
Columbiana (G-4630)

Star Fab LLC.. C 330 533-9863
Canfield (G-1817)

T & D Fabricating Inc........................... E 440 951-5646
Eastlake (G-6445)

Tecnocap LLC.. C 330 392-7222
Warren (G-13800)

Tri County Tarp LLC.............................. E 419 288-3350
Gibsonburg (G-7260)

Trivium Alum Packg USA Corp.............. E 330 744-2267
Youngstown (G-14952)

Urban Industries of Ohio Inc................ E 419 468-3578
Galion (G-7200)

Youngstown Tool & Die Company......... D 330 747-4464
Youngstown (G-14977)

Zarbana Alum Extrusions LLC.............. E 330 482-5092
Columbiana (G-4635)

Zarbana Industries Inc......................... E 330 482-5092
Columbiana (G-4636)

ALUMINUM: Coil & Sheet

Monarch Steel Company Inc................. E 216 587-8000
Cleveland (G-4045)

Polytech America LLC........................... G 904 728-7458
Canton (G-1978)

ALUMINUM: Ingots & Slabs

Homan Metals LLC................................ G 513 721-5010
Cincinnati (G-2728)

Ormet Primary Aluminum Corp............. A 740 483-1381
Hannibal (G-7541)

ALUMINUM: Pigs

Real Alloy Specialty Pdts LLC.............. D 844 732-5087
Beachwood (G-943)

ALUMINUM: Rolling & Drawing

Aleris Rm Inc... B 216 910-3400
Beachwood (G-909)

Eastman Kodak Company...................... E 937 259-3000
Dayton (G-5758)

Howmet Aerospace Inc......................... E 330 544-7633
Niles (G-10590)

Novelis Alr Aluminum LLC.................... A 216 910-3400
Beachwood (G-933)

Novelis Alr Rolled Pdts LLC................. A 740 983-2571
Ashville (G-627)

Novelis Alr Rolled Pdts LLC................. E 216 910-3400
Beachwood (G-934)

Novelis Corporation.............................. D 330 841-3456
Warren (G-13784)

Real Alloy Specialty Pdts LLC.............. E 440 322-0072
Elyria (G-6584)

AMMUNITION: Arming & Fusing Devices

L3harris Fzing Ord Systems Inc............ A 513 943-2000
Cincinnati (G-2311)

AMMUNITION: Shot, Steel

Premier Shot Company........................... G 330 405-0583
Twinsburg (G-13359)

AMMUNITION: Small Arms

Ares Inc... D 419 635-2175
Port Clinton (G-11439)

BTR Enterprises LLC............................. G 740 975-2526
Newark (G-10495)

Galion LLC... C 419 468-5214
Galion (G-7190)

National Bullet Co.................................. G 800 317-9506
Eastlake (G-6439)

R & S Monitions Inc.............................. G 614 846-0597
Columbus (G-5222)

AMPLIFIERS

Dare Electronics Inc............................. E 937 335-0031
Troy (G-13208)

Dr Z Amps Inc....................................... F 216 475-1444
Maple Heights (G-8883)

AMUSEMENT & RECREATION SVCS: Exhibition Operation

Asm International.................................. D 440 338-5151
Novelty (G-10879)

AMUSEMENT & RECREATION SVCS: Exposition Operation

Park Corporation................................... B 216 267-4870
Medina (G-9434)

AMUSEMENT & RECREATION SVCS: Golf Club, Membership

Hilltop Recreation Inc........................... G 937 549-2904
Manchester (G-8754)

AMUSEMENT & RECREATION SVCS: Physical Fitness Instruction

Building Block Performance LLC........... G 614 918-7476
Plain City (G-11400)

AMUSEMENT PARK DEVICES & RIDES

Advanced Indus Machining Inc.............. F 614 596-4183
Powell (G-11481)

ARM (usa) Inc.. E 740 264-6599
Wintersville (G-14611)

Cutting Dynamics LLC........................... D 440 249-4666
Avon (G-722)

Delta Manufacturing Inc........................ F 330 386-1270
East Liverpool (G-6392)

Enterprise Machine Inc......................... G 513 681-4409
Cincinnati (G-2592)

Hearn Plating Co Ltd............................ F 419 473-9773
Toledo (G-12988)

Karon C Enold...................................... E 740 269-3475
Sherrodsville (G-11975)

OReilly Precision Pdts Inc.................... G 937 526-4677
Russia (G-11676)

Wavy Ticket LLC.................................... E 513 827-0886
Okeana (G-10929)

ANALYZERS: Network

Community Care Network Inc................. E 216 671-0977
Cleveland (G-3554)

ANIMAL FEED & SUPPLEMENTS: Livestock & Poultry

Archer-Daniels-Midland Company......... G 330 852-3025
Sugarcreek (G-12631)

Archer-Daniels-Midland Company......... G 419 705-3292
Toledo (G-12884)

Cargill Incorporated............................. D 330 745-0031
Akron (G-90)

Cargill Incorporated............................. C 216 651-7200
Cleveland (G-3470)

Cargill Incorporated............................. G 419 394-3374
Saint Marys (G-11735)

Cargill Incorporated............................. F 937 497-4848
Sidney (G-11999)

Cooper Hatchery Inc............................. C 419 594-3325
Oakwood (G-10897)

Granville Milling Co.............................. G 740 345-1305
Newark (G-10505)

Hamlet Protein Inc................................ E 567 525-5627
Findlay (G-6876)

Hartz Mountain Corporation................. D 513 877-2131
Pleasant Plain (G-11432)

Legacy Farmers Cooperative............... F 419 423-2611
Findlay (G-6884)

Magnus International Group Inc............ G 216 592-8355
Painesville (G-11097)

Mennel Milling Company....................... G 419 458-3041
Wharton (G-14351)

Mid-Wood Inc.. F 419 257-3331
North Baltimore (G-10614)

Ohio Blenders Inc................................. F 419 726-2655
Toledo (G-13072)

Pettisville Grain Co.............................. E 419 446-2547
Pettisville (G-11285)

Premier Feeds LLC............................... G 937 584-2411
Sabina (G-11683)

Premier Grain LLC................................ G 937 584-6552
Bowersville (G-1402)

Premier Grain LLC................................ G 937 584-6552
Sabina (G-11684)

Pro-Pet LLC... D 419 394-3374
Saint Marys (G-11749)

Provimi North America Inc.................... E 937 770-2400
Lewisburg (G-8363)

Provimi North America Inc.................... F 937 770-2400
Lewisburg (G-8364)

Provimi North America Inc.................... B 937 770-2400
Lewisburg (G-8362)

Quality Liquid Feeds Inc....................... F 330 532-4635
Wellsville (G-13913)

Rek Associates LLC.............................. F 419 294-3838
Upper Sandusky (G-13454)

The F L Emmert Co Inc......................... F 513 721-5808
Cincinnati (G-3147)

The Mennel Milling Company................ E 419 435-8151
Fostoria (G-7003)

ANIMAL FEED: Wholesalers

Gerald Grain Center Inc....................... F 419 445-2451
Archbold (G-495)

Granville Milling Co.............................. G 740 345-1305
Newark (G-10505)

Land OLakes Inc................................... D 330 879-2158
Massillon (G-9214)

Provimi North America Inc.................... B 937 770-2400
Lewisburg (G-8362)

Ridley USA Inc...................................... F 800 837-8222
Botkins (G-1398)

ANIMAL FOOD & SUPPLEMENTS: Bird Food, Prepared

Centerra Co-Op..................................... E 419 281-2153
Ashland (G-526)

Four Natures Keepers Inc..................... F 740 363-8007
Delaware (G-6148)

Natures Way Bird Products LLC........... E 440 554-6166
Chagrin Falls (G-2172)

Stony Hill Mixing Ltd............................ G 330 674-0814
Millersburg (G-10011)

Vitakraft Sun Seed Inc......................... D 419 832-1641
Weston (G-14350)

PRODUCT

ANIMAL FOOD & SUPPLEMENTS: Cat

Hartz Mountain Corporation.................... D 513 877-2131
Pleasant Plain *(G-11432)*

Pro-Pet LLC.. D 419 394-3374
Saint Marys *(G-11749)*

ANIMAL FOOD & SUPPLEMENTS: Dog

Bil-Jac Foods Inc.. E 330 722-7888
Medina *(G-9380)*

Bravo LLC.. F 866 922-9222
Moraine *(G-10151)*

Foster Canning Inc..................................... E 419 841-6755
Toledo *(G-12968)*

G & C Raw LLC... G 937 827-0010
Versailles *(G-13595)*

JM Smucker LLC... D 330 682-3000
Orrville *(G-10990)*

Mars Petcare Us Inc.................................. E 614 878-7242
Columbus *(G-5083)*

Mars Petcare Us Inc.................................. E 419 943-4280
Leipsic *(G-8307)*

Ohio Pet Foods Inc.................................... E 330 424-1431
Lisbon *(G-8477)*

ANIMAL FOOD & SUPPLEMENTS: Dog & Cat

Cargill Incorporated................................... G 419 394-3374
Saint Marys *(G-11735)*

Kelly Foods Corporation........................... E 330 722-8855
Medina *(G-9418)*

Land OLakes Inc... D 330 879-2158
Massillon *(G-9214)*

Nestle Purina Petcare Company............. C 740 454-8575
Zanesville *(G-15032)*

Ohio Blenders Inc...................................... F 419 726-2655
Toledo *(G-13072)*

Purina Mills LLC... G 330 682-1951
Orrville *(G-11002)*

Vitakraft Sun Seed Inc............................. D 419 832-1641
Weston *(G-14350)*

ANIMAL FOOD & SUPPLEMENTS: Feed Premixes

Ggc Feeds LLC... E 419 445-2451
Archbold *(G-496)*

Rowe Premix Inc... G 937 678-9015
West Manchester *(G-14177)*

ANIMAL FOOD & SUPPLEMENTS: Feed Supplements

Direct Action Co Inc.................................. F 330 364-3219
Dover *(G-6236)*

ANIMAL FOOD & SUPPLEMENTS: Livestock

Gerber & Sons Inc...................................... E 330 897-6201
Baltic *(G-778)*

Hanby Farms Inc... E 740 763-3554
Nashport *(G-10299)*

Kalmbach Feeds Inc................................... C 419 294-3838
Upper Sandusky *(G-13443)*

Land OLakes Inc... D 330 879-2158
Massillon *(G-9214)*

Republic Mills Inc...................................... F 419 758-3511
Okolona *(G-10932)*

Ridley USA Inc.. F 800 837-8222
Botkins *(G-1398)*

Spencer Feed & Supply LLC..................... F 330 648-2111
Spencer *(G-12235)*

ANIMAL FOOD & SUPPLEMENTS: Pet, Exc Dog & Cat, Canned

Brightpet Nutrition Group LLC................. E 330 424-1431
Lisbon *(G-8464)*

ANIMAL FOOD & SUPPLEMENTS: Pet, Exc Dog & Cat, Dry

Kelly Foods Corporation........................... E 330 722-8855
Medina *(G-9418)*

ANIMAL FOOD & SUPPLEMENTS: Poultry

Cooper Farms Inc....................................... D 419 594-3325
Oakwood *(G-10896)*

Nature Pure LLC... F 937 358-2364
Raymond *(G-11553)*

ANIMAL FOOD/SUPPLEMENTS: Feeds Fm Meat/Meat/Veg Combnd Meals

G A Wintzer and Son Company................. D 419 739-4913
Wapakoneta *(G-13712)*

G A Wintzer and Son Company................. F 419 739-4900
Wapakoneta *(G-13711)*

ANNEALING: Metal

Atmosphere Annealing LLC...................... D 330 478-0314
Kenton *(G-8095)*

FB Acquisition LLC..................................... E 513 459-7782
Lebanon *(G-8255)*

Northlake Steel Corporation.................... D 330 220-7717
Valley City *(G-13513)*

Pro-TEC Coating Company LLC............... D 419 943-1100
Leipsic *(G-8313)*

Youngstown Heat Trting Ntrding............. G 330 788-3025
Youngstown *(G-14971)*

ANODIZING EQPT

Singleton Corporation................................ F 216 651-7800
Cleveland *(G-4302)*

ANODIZING SVC

Allen Aircraft Products Inc....................... D 330 296-9621
Ravenna *(G-11516)*

Amac Enterprises Inc................................ F 216 362-1880
Cleveland *(G-3337)*

Anomatic Corporation................................ B 740 522-2203
Newark *(G-10491)*

Anomatic Corporation................................ E 740 522-2203
New Albany *(G-10328)*

Commercial Anodizing Co......................... F 440 942-8384
Willoughby *(G-14440)*

Luke Engineering & Mfg Corp................. E 330 335-1501
Wadsworth *(G-13649)*

Russell Products Co Inc............................ F 330 535-9246
Akron *(G-296)*

Russell Products Co Inc............................ F 330 535-9246
Akron *(G-298)*

Sifco Industries Inc................................... D 216 881-8600
Cleveland *(G-4299)*

ANTENNA REPAIR & INSTALLATION SVCS

Central USA Wireless LLC........................ G 513 469-1500
Cincinnati *(G-2453)*

Dss Installations Ltd................................. G 513 761-7000
Cincinnati *(G-2563)*

ANTENNAS: Radar Or Communications

Circle Prime Manufacturing Inc.............. E 330 923-0019
Cuyahoga Falls *(G-5534)*

Editencom Ltd.. E 419 865-5877
Holland *(G-7762)*

Quasonix Inc.. E 513 942-1287
West Chester *(G-14058)*

ANTENNAS: Receiving

Focus Manufacturing LLC......................... F 440 946-8766
Mentor *(G-9517)*

Gem City Engineering Co.......................... C 937 223-5544
Dayton *(G-5792)*

Sinbon Usa LLC.. E 937 667-8999
Tipp City *(G-12843)*

Wifi-Plus Inc... G 330 273-3665
Brunswick *(G-1624)*

ANTIBIOTICS

Pfizer Inc... F 937 746-3603
Franklin *(G-7039)*

ANTIFREEZE

BASF Corporation....................................... D 614 662-5682
Columbus *(G-4745)*

Kost Usa Inc.. E 513 583-7070
Cincinnati *(G-2806)*

ANTIQUE REPAIR & RESTORATION SVCS, EXC FURNITURE & AUTOS

Midwest Rlwy Prsrvtion Soc Inc............. G 216 781-3629
Cleveland *(G-4038)*

APPAREL ACCESS STORES

Indra Holdings Corp................................... C 513 682-8200
Cincinnati *(G-2743)*

APPAREL DESIGNERS: Commercial

Struggle Grind Success LLC..................... G 330 834-6738
Boardman *(G-1377)*

APPLIANCE PARTS: Porcelain Enameled

Destiny Manufacturing Inc....................... E 330 273-9000
Brunswick *(G-1588)*

Whirlaway Corporation.............................. C 440 647-4711
Wellington *(G-13904)*

APPLIANCES, HOUSEHOLD OR COIN OPERATED: Laundry Dryers

Whirlpool Corporation............................... D 740 383-7122
Marion *(G-9003)*

APPLIANCES, HOUSEHOLD: Kitchen, Major, Exc Refrigs & Stoves

ABC Appliance Inc...................................... E 419 693-4414
Oregon *(G-10955)*

New Path International LLC....................... F 614 410-3974
Powell *(G-11493)*

Robura LLC.. D 800 438-5346
Dalton *(G-5593)*

Sandco Industries...................................... E 419 547-3273
Clyde *(G-4564)*

APPLIANCES, HOUSEHOLD: Laundry Machines, Incl CoinOperated

Whirlpool Corporation............................... E 614 409-4340
Lockbourne *(G-8494)*

APPLIANCES, HOUSEHOLD: Refrigs, Mechanical & Absorption

Norcold LLC... G 800 543-1219
Sidney *(G-12036)*

Whirlpool Corporation.................... E 614 409-4340
　Lockbourne *(G-8494)*

APPLIANCES: Household, Refrigerators & Freezers

Dover Corporation........................... D 513 870-3206
　West Chester *(G-13985)*

Whirlpool Corporation.................... D 419 423-8123
　Findlay *(G-6935)*

Whirlpool Corporation.................... D 740 383-7122
　Marion *(G-9003)*

APPLIANCES: Major, Cooking

Garland Commercial Industries LLC...... G 800 338-2204
　Cleveland *(G-3756)*

APPLIANCES: Small, Electric

Ces Nationwide............................... G 937 322-0771
　Springfield *(G-12289)*

Cleveland Range LLC....................... C 216 481-4900
　Cleveland *(G-3522)*

Dyoung Enterprise Inc..................... C 440 918-0505
　Willoughby *(G-14452)*

Glo-Quartz Electric Htr Co Inc............ E 440 255-9701
　Mentor *(G-9524)*

Johnson Bros Rubber Co Inc............. E 419 752-4814
　Greenwich *(G-7362)*

Nutone Inc...................................... A 888 336-3948
　Blue Ash *(G-1314)*

Qualtek Electronics Corp.................. C 440 951-3300
　Mentor *(G-9603)*

Vita-Mix Manufacturing Corporation...... C 440 235-4840
　Olmsted Falls *(G-10942)*

APPLICATIONS SOFTWARE PROGRAMMING

Analytica Usa Inc............................ G 513 348-2333
　Dayton *(G-5658)*

Cerkl Incorporated.......................... D 513 813-8425
　Blue Ash *(G-1261)*

Foundation Software LLC.................. B 330 220-8383
　Strongsville *(G-12559)*

NCR Technology Center.................... G 937 445-1936
　Dayton *(G-5903)*

Profound Logic Software Inc............. E 937 439-7925
　Dayton *(G-5966)*

Qxsoft LLC..................................... G 740 777-9609
　Lewis Center *(G-8350)*

APPRAISAL SVCS, EXC REAL ESTATE

Amos Media Company...................... C 937 498-2121
　Sidney *(G-11992)*

Pughs Designer Jewelers Inc............ G 740 344-9259
　Newark *(G-10530)*

APRONS: Rubber, Vulcanized Or Rubberized Fabric

Leisure Time Pdts Design Corp.......... G 440 934-1032
　Avon *(G-731)*

AQUARIUMS & ACCESS: Plastic

Th Plastics Inc............................... D 419 425-5825
　Findlay *(G-6926)*

ARCHITECTURAL SVCS

Ceso Inc.. E 937 435-8584
　Miamisburg *(G-9681)*

Dlz Ohio Inc................................... C 614 888-0040
　Columbus *(G-4887)*

Garland Industries Inc..................... G 216 641-7500
　Cleveland *(G-3757)*

Garland/Dbs Inc............................. C 216 641-7500
　Cleveland *(G-3758)*

Golden Angle Archtctral Group.......... G 614 531-7932
　Columbus *(G-4960)*

ARMATURE REPAIRING & REWINDING SVC

City Machine Technologies Inc.......... F 330 747-2639
　Youngstown *(G-14836)*

Horner Industrial Services Inc........... G 513 874-8722
　West Chester *(G-14125)*

Kcn Technologies LLC...................... G 440 439-4219
　Bedford *(G-1041)*

Rel Enterprises Inc.......................... E 216 741-1700
　Brooklyn Heights *(G-1538)*

Yaskawa America Inc....................... C 937 847-6200
　Miamisburg *(G-9755)*

ART DEALERS & GALLERIES

Fenwick Gallery of Fine Arts............. G 419 475-1651
　Toledo *(G-12962)*

Lazars Art Gllery Crtive Frmng........... G 330 477-8351
　Canton *(G-1931)*

ART MARBLE: Concrete

Agean Marble Manufacturing Inc......... G 513 874-1475
　West Chester *(G-14099)*

ARTS & CRAFTS SCHOOL

Studio Arts and Glass Inc................. F 330 494-9779
　Canton *(G-2019)*

Wooden Horse................................ G 740 503-5243
　Baltimore *(G-789)*

ASBESTOS PRDTS: Roofing, Felt Roll

American Way Exteriors LLC.............. G 937 221-8860
　Dayton *(G-5656)*

ASBESTOS PRODUCTS

Owens Corning................................ A 419 248-8000
　Toledo *(G-13084)*

Owens Corning Corp Svcs LLC........... F 419 248-8000
　Toledo *(G-13085)*

Owens Crning Tchncal Fbrics LL......... G 419 248-5535
　Toledo *(G-13089)*

ASPHALT & ASPHALT PRDTS

Central Allied Enterprises Inc............ E 330 477-6751
　Canton *(G-1862)*

Central Oil Asphalt Corp.................. G 614 224-8111
　Columbus *(G-4803)*

Gerken Materials Inc....................... E 419 533-2421
　Napoleon *(G-10281)*

Heidelberg Mtls Mdwest Agg Inc......... G 419 878-2006
　Waterville *(G-13834)*

Heritage Group Inc.......................... A 330 875-5566
　Louisville *(G-8603)*

Kokosing Materials Inc..................... F 740 694-5872
　Fredericktown *(G-7081)*

Kokosing Materials Inc..................... F 419 522-2715
　Mansfield *(G-8811)*

Kokosing Materials Inc..................... F 740 745-3341
　Saint Louisville *(G-11729)*

Kokosing Materials Inc..................... G 614 491-1199
　Columbus *(G-5055)*

Kokosing Materials Inc..................... F 740 694-9585
　Fredericktown *(G-7082)*

Koski Construction Co...................... G 440 997-5337
　Ashtabula *(G-601)*

M & B Asphalt Company Inc............... F 419 992-4235
　Tiffin *(G-12787)*

Maintenance + Inc........................... F 330 264-6262
　Wooster *(G-14663)*

Morrow Gravel Company Inc.............. E 513 771-0820
　Cincinnati *(G-2889)*

Mt Pleasant Blacktopping Inc............. G 513 874-3777
　Fairfield *(G-6756)*

Seneca Petroleum Co Inc.................. F 419 691-3581
　Toledo *(G-13126)*

Shelly and Sands Inc....................... F 740 453-0721
　Zanesville *(G-15047)*

Shelly Materials Inc......................... E 740 666-5841
　Ostrander *(G-11029)*

Stoneco Inc.................................... E 419 422-8854
　Findlay *(G-6923)*

Valley Asphalt Corporation............... E 513 771-0820
　Cincinnati *(G-3191)*

Wilson Blacktop Corp....................... F 740 635-3566
　Martins Ferry *(G-9012)*

Wyandot Dolomite Inc...................... E 419 396-7641
　Carey *(G-2064)*

ASPHALT COATINGS & SEALERS

Atlas Roofing Corporation................ C 937 746-9941
　Franklin *(G-7010)*

CIC Old Corporation......................... E 330 457-2367
　New Waterford *(G-10487)*

Hy-Grade Corporation...................... E 216 341-7711
　Cleveland *(G-3846)*

Hyload Inc...................................... G 330 336-6604
　Seville *(G-11917)*

Isaiah Industries Inc........................ E 937 773-9840
　Piqua *(G-11358)*

M & B Asphalt Company Inc............... F 419 992-4235
　Tiffin *(G-12787)*

Metal Sales Manufacturing Corp......... E 440 319-3779
　Jefferson *(G-7978)*

Mfm Building Products Corp............... E 740 622-2645
　Coshocton *(G-5461)*

National Tool & Equipment Inc........... F 330 629-8665
　Youngstown *(G-14903)*

Owens Corning Sales LLC................. A 419 248-8000
　Toledo *(G-13088)*

Pioneer Manufacturing Inc................ D 216 671-5500
　Cleveland *(G-4167)*

Roof Maxx Technologies LLC.............. G 855 766-3629
　Westerville *(G-14231)*

Simon Roofing and Shtmtl Corp.......... C 330 629-7392
　Youngstown *(G-14932)*

Sr Products.................................... F 330 998-6500
　Youngstown *(G-14939)*

State Industrial Products Corp........... B 877 747-6986
　Cleveland *(G-4329)*

Terry Asphalt Materials Inc............... E 513 874-6192
　Hamilton *(G-7529)*

Thorworks Industries Inc.................. C 419 626-4375
　Sandusky *(G-11876)*

Transtar Holding Company LLC........... G 800 359-3339
　Walton Hills *(G-13703)*

ASPHALT MIXTURES WHOLESALERS

Hy-Grade Corporation...................... E 216 341-7711
　Cleveland *(G-3846)*

Russell Standard Corporation............ G 330 733-9400
　Akron *(G-299)*

ASPHALT PLANTS INCLUDING GRAVEL MIX TYPE

Geauga Highway Co.......................... F 440 834-4580
　Windham *(G-14600)*

ASSEMBLING SVC: Plumbing Fixture Fittings, Plastic

PRODUCT

Langenau Manufacturing Company....... F 216 651-3400
Cleveland *(G-3939)*

ASSOCIATION FOR THE HANDICAPPED

Cincinnati Assn For The Blind................ C 513 221-8558
Cincinnati *(G-2469)*

ASSOCIATIONS: Business

Cox Newspapers LLC.......................... G
Franklin *(G-7015)*

Hirzel Canning Company...................... E 419 693-0531
Northwood *(G-10803)*

Interstate Contractors LLC.................... E 513 372-5393
Mason *(G-9115)*

Superior Clay Corporation.................... D 740 922-4122
Uhrichsville *(G-13408)*

ASSOCIATIONS: Real Estate Management

Elite Property Group LLC...................... F 216 356-7469
Elyria *(G-6527)*

Nesco Inc.. E 440 461-6000
Cleveland *(G-4068)*

ASSOCIATIONS: Scientists'

American Ceramic Society.................... E 614 890-4700
Westerville *(G-14202)*

ASSOCIATIONS: Trade

Precision Metalforming Assn................. E 216 901-8800
Independence *(G-7916)*

ATOMIZERS

Automtve Rfnish Clor Sltons I.............. E 330 461-6067
Medina *(G-9378)*

Ferguson Fire Fabrication Inc................ E 614 299-2070
Columbus *(G-4923)*

Jrb Industries LLC............................. E 567 825-7022
Greenville *(G-7344)*

Triboro Quilt Mfg Corp....................... F 937 222-2132
Vandalia *(G-13579)*

Truck Fax Inc.................................... G 216 921-8866
Cleveland *(G-4431)*

Velocity Concept Dev Group LLC.......... G 513 204-2100
Mason *(G-9164)*

Woodsage Industries LLC.................... G 419 866-8000
Holland *(G-7791)*

Zorich Industries Inc.......................... G 330 482-9803
Columbiana *(G-4637)*

AUDIO & VIDEO EQPT, EXC COMMERCIAL

5 Core Inc.. F 951 386-6372
Bellefontaine *(G-1098)*

Eprad Inc... G 419 666-3266
Perrysburg *(G-11219)*

Fellhauer Mechanical Systems.............. E 419 734-3674
Port Clinton *(G-11441)*

Floyd Bell Inc................................... D 614 294-4000
Columbus *(G-4930)*

Mitsubishi Elc Auto Amer Inc............... B 513 573-6614
Mason *(G-9128)*

Ohio Hd Video.................................. F 614 656-1162
New Albany *(G-10348)*

Pioneer Automotive Tech Inc................ C 937 746-2293
Miamisburg *(G-9727)*

Tech Products Corporation................... F 937 438-1100
Miamisburg *(G-9744)*

Technicolor Usa Inc........................... A 614 474-8821
Circleville *(G-3265)*

Tls Corp.. D 216 574-4759
Cleveland *(G-4396)*

Tune Town Car Audio.......................... G 419 627-1100
Sandusky *(G-11878)*

AUDIO COMPONENTS

Avtek International Inc........................ G 330 633-7500
Silver Lake *(G-12063)*

Bose Corporation.............................. G 513 891-4384
Cincinnati *(G-2418)*

China Enterprises Inc......................... G 419 885-1485
Toledo *(G-12920)*

AUDIO ELECTRONIC SYSTEMS

Andersound PA Service....................... G 216 401-4631
Cleveland *(G-3359)*

Db Unlimited LLC.............................. G 937 401-2602
Dayton *(G-5743)*

Pro Audio.. G 513 752-7500
Cincinnati *(G-2314)*

AUTO & HOME SUPPLY STORES: Auto & Truck Eqpt & Parts

Abutilon Company Inc......................... F 419 536-6123
Toledo *(G-12862)*

Horizon Global Corporation................. E 734 656-3000
Cleveland *(G-3837)*

Tbone Sales LLC................................ G 330 897-6131
Baltic *(G-781)*

AUTO & HOME SUPPLY STORES: Automotive Access

Bucyrus Precision Tech Inc.................. C 419 563-9950
Bucyrus *(G-1674)*

Cequent Consumer Products Inc........... D 440 498-0001
Solon *(G-12092)*

Epix Tube Co Inc............................... F 937 529-4858
Dayton *(G-5766)*

Front Pocket Innovations LLC............... G 330 441-2365
Wadsworth *(G-13639)*

Steves Vans ACC Unlimited LLC........... G 740 374-3154
Marietta *(G-8950)*

Superior Production LLC..................... C 614 444-2181
Columbus *(G-5299)*

AUTO & HOME SUPPLY STORES: Automotive parts

American Cold Forge LLC..................... E 419 836-1062
Northwood *(G-10802)*

K-M-S Industries Inc.......................... G 440 243-6680
Brookpark *(G-1554)*

M Technologies Inc............................ F 330 477-9009
Canton *(G-1937)*

Mader Automotive Center Inc............... F 937 339-2681
Troy *(G-13238)*

Mark Knupp Muffler & Tire Inc.............. G 937 773-1334
Piqua *(G-11365)*

Ohio Auto Supply Company.................. G 330 454-5105
Canton *(G-1964)*

Rust Belt Broncos LLC........................ E 330 533-0048
Canfield *(G-1815)*

Tom Barbour Auto Parts Inc................. F 740 354-4654
Portsmouth *(G-11479)*

AUTO & HOME SUPPLY STORES: Batteries, Automotive & Truck

Battery Unlimited.............................. G 740 452-5030
Zanesville *(G-14993)*

J & J Tire & Alignment........................ G 330 424-5200
Lisbon *(G-8471)*

AUTO & HOME SUPPLY STORES: Trailer Hitches, Automotive

Overhead Door of Pike County.............. G 740 289-3925
Piketon *(G-11312)*

AUTO & HOME SUPPLY STORES: Truck Eqpt & Parts

Ace Truck Equipment Co...................... E 740 453-0551
Zanesville *(G-14981)*

Crown Equipment Corporation.............. A 419 629-2311
New Bremen *(G-10358)*

Galion-Godwin Truck Bdy Co LLC.......... F 330 359-5495
Dundee *(G-6365)*

H & H Truck Parts LLC........................ E 216 642-4540
Cleveland *(G-3804)*

Kaffenbarger Truck Eqp Co.................. E 513 772-6800
Cincinnati *(G-2777)*

Marlow-2000 Inc............................... F 216 362-8500
Cleveland *(G-3991)*

Martin Diesel Inc............................... E 419 782-9911
Defiance *(G-6120)*

Perkins Motor Service Ltd.................... F 440 277-1256
Lorain *(G-8573)*

River City Body Company.................... F 513 772-9317
Cincinnati *(G-3047)*

Trucks & Parts of Tampa LLC............... E 937 437-0377
New Paris *(G-10427)*

Western Branch Diesel LLC.................. F 330 454-8800
Canton *(G-2047)*

X-Treme Finishes Inc.......................... F 330 474-0614
North Royalton *(G-10790)*

AUTO SPLYS & PARTS, NEW, WHSLE: Exhaust Sys, Mufflers, Etc

Dreison International Inc...................... C 216 362-0755
Cleveland *(G-3632)*

AUTOMATIC REGULATING CONTROL: Building Svcs Monitoring, Auto

A & P Tool Inc................................... E 419 542-6681
Hicksville *(G-7644)*

Evokes LLC...................................... E 513 947-8433
Mason *(G-9099)*

AUTOMATIC REGULATING CONTROLS: AC & Refrigeration

Air Enterprises Inc............................ A 330 794-9770
Akron *(G-22)*

Young Regulator Company Inc.............. E 440 232-9452
Bedford *(G-1066)*

AUTOMATIC REGULATING CONTROLS: Appliance, Exc AirCond/Refr

K Davis Inc...................................... G 419 307-7051
Fremont *(G-7119)*

Melink Corporation............................ D 513 685-0958
Milford *(G-9943)*

Portage Electric Products Inc............... C 330 499-2727
North Canton *(G-10659)*

AUTOMATIC REGULATING CONTROLS: Hardware, Environmental Reg

Ecopro Solutions LLC......................... E 216 232-4040
Independence *(G-7900)*

Mestek Inc....................................... F 419 288-2703
Bradner *(G-1454)*

West 6th Products Company................. D 330 467-7446
Northfield *(G-10800)*

AUTOMATIC REGULATING CTRLS: Damper, Pneumatic Or Electric

Mader Machine Co Inc............................ E 440 355-4505
Lagrange *(G-8150)*

Tlt-Babcock Inc....................................D 330 867-8540
Akron *(G-339)*

AUTOMATIC TELLER MACHINES

Atm Nerds LLC................................. F 614 983-3056
Columbus *(G-4733)*

Diebold Nixdorf Incorporated.................D 330 490-4000
Canton *(G-1882)*

Diebold Nixdorf Incorporated.................D 740 928-0200
Hebron *(G-7613)*

Diebold Nixdorf Incorporated.................A 330 490-4000
North Canton *(G-10635)*

Ginko Voting Systems LLC................... E 937 291-4060
Dayton *(G-5795)*

Glenn Michael Brick........................... F 740 391-5735
Flushing *(G-6936)*

Testlink Usa Inc................................ E 513 272-1081
Cincinnati *(G-3143)*

AUTOMOBILE FINANCE LEASING

Momentum Fleet MGT Group Inc............D 440 759-2219
Westlake *(G-14315)*

AUTOMOBILES & OTHER MOTOR VEHICLES WHOLESALERS

Btw LLC.. G 419 382-4443
Toledo *(G-12907)*

Doug Marine Motors Inc....................... F 740 335-3700
Wshngtn Ct Hs *(G-14738)*

Interstate Truckway Inc....................... F 614 771-1220
Columbus *(G-5022)*

AUTOMOBILES: Wholesalers

Tpam Inc.. E 567 315-8694
Toledo *(G-13165)*

AUTOMOTIVE & TRUCK GENERAL REPAIR SVC

AB Tire & Repair................................ G 440 543-2929
Chagrin Falls *(G-2152)*

Abutilon Company Inc.......................... F 419 536-6123
Tuledu *(G-12802)*

Automtve Rfnish Clor Sltons I..............E 330 461-6067
Medina *(G-9378)*

Bob Sumerel Tire Co Inc...................... F 330 769-9092
Seville *(G-11914)*

Bowman Tire Repr Ctr Bxley LLC...........G 740 928-7000
Hebron *(G-7609)*

Bridgestone Ret Operations LLC............ F 440 299-6126
Mentor *(G-9493)*

Bridgestone Ret Operations LLC............G 419 625-6571
Sandusky *(G-11823)*

C & F Tire & Truck Repair.....................G 419 526-1412
Ontario *(G-10947)*

Certified Auto & Trck Repr Inc...............G 440 288-2029
Lorain *(G-8550)*

Doug Marine Motors Inc....................... F 740 335-3700
Wshngtn Ct Hs *(G-14738)*

Goodyear Tire & Rubber Company........ A 330 796-2121
Akron *(G-164)*

Grismer Tire Company......................... E 937 643-2526
Centerville *(G-2132)*

Hutter Racing Engines Ltd..................... F 440 285-2175
Chardon *(G-2208)*

J & J Tire & Alignment..........................G 330 424-5200
Lisbon *(G-8471)*

Kirbys Auto and Truck Repr Inc.............G 513 934-3999
Lebanon *(G-8272)*

Nice Body Automotive LLC....................G 440 752-5568
Elyria *(G-6569)*

Ohio Trailer Inc.................................G 330 392-4444
Warren *(G-13787)*

Pattons Trck & Hvy Eqp Svc Inc............ F 740 385-4067
Logan *(G-8523)*

Randys Tire & Auto Repair Inc...............G 419 562-2926
Bucyrus *(G-1688)*

Sammy S Auto Detail.......................... F 614 263-2728
Columbus *(G-5246)*

Skaggs Trlr & Tire Repr Co Inc.............. F 440 986-7470
Amherst *(G-452)*

Sycamore Tire & Auto Repair................G 513 793-0726
Cincinnati *(G-3134)*

Youngstown-Kenworth Inc..................... F 330 534-9761
Hubbard *(G-7819)*

AUTOMOTIVE BODY SHOP

Chardon Square Auto & Body Inc.......... F 440 286-7600
Chardon *(G-2199)*

Obs Inc.. F 330 453-3725
Canton *(G-1962)*

W&W Automotive & Towing Inc.............. F 937 429-1699
Beavercreek Township *(G-1007)*

Webers Body & Frame Inc....................G 937 839-5946
West Alexandria *(G-13923)*

AUTOMOTIVE BODY, PAINT & INTERIOR REPAIR & MAINTENANCE SVC

Bobbart Industries Inc.........................G 419 350-5477
Sylvania *(G-12702)*

Willard Machine & Welding Inc.............. F 330 467-0642
Macedonia *(G-8722)*

AUTOMOTIVE CUSTOMIZING SVCS, NONFACTORY BASIS

Afg Industries Inc...............................D 614 322-4580
Grove City *(G-7368)*

AUTOMOTIVE GLASS REPLACEMENT SHOPS

A Service Glass Inc............................ F 937 426-4920
Beavercreek *(G-963)*

J W Goss Company............................. F 330 395-0739
Warren *(G-13773)*

Keystone Auto Glass Inc.......................D 419 509-0497
Maumee *(G-9302)*

Safelite Group Inc.............................. A 614 210-9000
Columbus *(G-5244)*

Support Svc LLC................................G 419 617-0660
Lexington *(G-8375)*

Webers Body & Frame Inc....................G 937 839-5946
West Alexandria *(G-13923)*

AUTOMOTIVE PAINT SHOP

Michael W Newton..............................G 740 352-9334
Lucasville *(G-8668)*

Newbury Sndblst & Pntg Inc..................G 440 564-7204
Newbury *(G-10557)*

Precision Coatings Systems.................. F 937 642-4727
Marysville *(G-9042)*

AUTOMOTIVE PARTS, ACCESS & SPLYS

A G Parts Inc.................................... F 937 596-6448
Jackson Center *(G-7957)*

ABC Technologies Dlhb Inc...................B 330 478-2503
Canton *(G-1821)*

Accel Performance Group LLC.............. C 216 658-6413
Independence *(G-7887)*

Ach LLC...G 419 621-5748
Sandusky *(G-11819)*

Ad Industries Inc............................... A 303 744-1911
Dayton *(G-5634)*

Adient US LLC.................................. C 937 981-2176
Greenfield *(G-7324)*

Adient US LLC.................................. C 419 662-4900
Northwood *(G-10801)*

Adient US LLC.................................. E 419 394-7800
Saint Marys *(G-11730)*

Airstream Inc.....................................B 937 596-6111
Jackson Center *(G-7958)*

Airtex Industries LLC.......................... F 330 899-0340
Toledo *(G-12868)*

American Axle & Mfg Inc......................G 330 863-7500
Malvern *(G-8746)*

American Axle & Mfg Inc...................... C 330 486-3200
Twinsburg *(G-13275)*

American Manufacturing & Eqp..............G 513 829-2248
Fairfield *(G-6711)*

Amsoil Inc...G 614 274-9851
Urbancrest *(G-13482)*

Amsted Industries Incorporated.............B 614 836-2323
Groveport *(G-7422)*

Aptiv Services Us LLC........................ C 330 367-6000
Vienna *(G-13607)*

Aptiv Services Us LLC........................ A 330 505-3150
Warren *(G-13740)*

Arlington Rack & Packaging Co..............G 419 476-7700
Toledo *(G-12886)*

Atc Lighting & Plastics Inc.................... C 440 466-7670
Andover *(G-456)*

Atwood Mobile Products LLC.................D 419 258-5531
Antwerp *(G-462)*

Auria Fremont LLC.............................B 419 332-1587
Fremont *(G-7092)*

Auria Holmesville LLC.........................B 330 279-4505
Holmesville *(G-7794)*

Auria Sidney LLC...............................B 937 492-1225
Sidney *(G-11994)*

Autoneum North America Inc.................B 419 693-0511
Oregon *(G-10957)*

Autoneum North America Inc.................D 419 690-8924
Oregon *(G-10958)*

B A Malcuit Racing Inc.........................G 330 878-7111
Strasburg *(G-12476)*

B&C Machine Co LLC.......................... F 330 745-4013
Barberton *(G-796)*

Beach Manufacturing Co...................... C 937 882-6372
Donnelsville *(G-6227)*

Beijing West Industries.........................G 937 455-5281
Dayton *(G-5675)*

Better Brake Parts Inc......................... E 419 227-0685
Lima *(G-8390)*

Bobbart Industries Inc.........................G 419 350-5477
Sylvania *(G-12702)*

Boler Company.................................. C 330 445-6728
Canton *(G-1841)*

Bores Manufacturing Inc......................G 419 465-2606
Monroeville *(G-10118)*

Bowden Manufacturing Corp.................. E 440 946-1770
Willoughby *(G-14432)*

Buyers Products Company.................... C 440 974-8888
Mentor *(G-9496)*

Bwi Chassis Dynamics NA Inc............... F 937 455-5100
Kettering *(G-8117)*

Bwi North America Inc......................... E 614 394-5983
Moraine *(G-10153)*

PRODUCT

Cequent Consumer Products Inc........... D .... 440 498-0001 Solon *(G-12092)*	Dana World Trade Corporation............... F .... 419 887-3000 Maumee *(G-9289)*	Hendrickson Usa LLC........................... C .... 630 910-2800 North Canton *(G-10646)*
Champion Spark Plug Company............ D .... 419 535-2567 Toledo *(G-12915)*	Dayton Clutch & Joint Inc...................... F .... 937 236-9770 Dayton *(G-5724)*	Hfi LLC... B .... 614 491-0700 Canal Winchester *(G-1791)*
Cleveland Ignition Co Inc...................... G .... 440 439-3688 Cleveland *(G-3513)*	Dcm Manufacturing Inc......................... E .... 216 265-8006 Cleveland *(G-3606)*	Hi-Tek Manufacturing Inc...................... C .... 513 459-1094 Mason *(G-9108)*
CMI Holding Company Crawford............ D .... 419 468-9122 Galion *(G-7183)*	Doug Marine Motors Inc........................ F .... 740 335-3700 Wshngtn Ct Hs *(G-14738)*	Honda Dev & Mfg Amer LLC................. A .... 937 843-5555 Russells Point *(G-11667)*
Crown Div of Allen Gr........................... G .... 330 263-4919 Wooster *(G-14632)*	Driveline 1 Inc..................................... G .... 614 279-7734 Columbus *(G-4890)*	Hp2g LLC... G .... 419 906-1525 Napoleon *(G-10286)*
Cummins Filtration Inc.......................... C Findlay *(G-6858)*	Ebco Inc... E .... 330 562-8265 Streetsboro *(G-12500)*	Igw USA... G .... 740 588-1722 Zanesville *(G-15022)*
Cummins Inc.. F .... 614 604-6004 Grove City *(G-7379)*	Ebog Legacy Inc.................................. D .... 330 239-4933 Sharon Center *(G-11940)*	Illinois Tool Works Inc.......................... C .... 513 489-7600 Blue Ash *(G-1286)*
Custer Products Limited........................ F .... 330 490-3158 Massillon *(G-9184)*	Edgerton Forge Inc.............................. D .... 419 298-2333 Edgerton *(G-6466)*	Illinois Tool Works Inc.......................... E .... 262 248-8277 Bryan *(G-1645)*
Custom Floaters LLC............................ G .... 216 536-8979 Brookpark *(G-1546)*	Egr Products Company Inc..................... F .... 330 833-6554 Dalton *(G-5584)*	Imasen Bucyrus Technology Inc............ C .... 419 563-9590 Bucyrus *(G-1683)*
Cvg National Seating Co LLC................ F .... 219 872-7295 New Albany *(G-10338)*	Ernie Green Industries Inc..................... E .... 740 420-5252 Circleville *(G-3257)*	Industry Products Co............................ B .... 937 778-0585 Piqua *(G-11356)*
Cwd LLC... E .... 310 218-1082 Cleveland *(G-3594)*	Exito Manufacturing LLC....................... G .... 937 291-9871 Beavercreek *(G-991)*	Interntnal Auto Cmpnnts Group............ D .... 419 335-1000 Wauseon *(G-13852)*
D-Terra Solutions LLC.......................... G .... 614 450-1040 Powell *(G-11486)*	Falls Stamping & Welding Co................. C .... 330 928-1191 Cuyahoga Falls *(G-5541)*	Interntnal Auto Cmpnnts Group............ A .... 419 433-5653 Wauseon *(G-13853)*
D4 Industries Inc................................. G .... 419 523-9555 Ottawa *(G-11032)*	Farin Industries Inc.............................. G .... 440 275-2755 Austinburg *(G-699)*	Inteva Products LLC............................. C .... 937 280-8500 Vandalia *(G-13563)*
Daido Metal Bellefontaine LLC............... F .... 937 592-5010 Bellefontaine *(G-1104)*	Flex Technologies Inc........................... D .... 330 359-5415 Mount Eaton *(G-10207)*	Jake Sweeney Mazda Tri-County........... G .... 513 782-1150 Cincinnati *(G-2757)*
Dana... E .... 419 887-3000 Toledo *(G-12937)*	Florida Production Engrg Inc................. D .... 937 996-4361 New Madison *(G-10421)*	Johnson Controls Inc............................ G .... 414 524-1200 Saint Marys *(G-11739)*
Dana Auto Systems Group LLC............. E .... 419 887-3000 Maumee *(G-9270)*	Force Control Industries Inc.................. E .... 513 868-0900 Fairfield *(G-6737)*	Joseph Industries Inc........................... D .... 330 528-0091 Streetsboro *(G-12507)*
Dana Automotive Mfg Inc...................... C .... 419 887-3000 Maumee *(G-9271)*	Ford Motor Company............................ C .... 216 676-7918 Brookpark *(G-1550)*	Julie Maynard Inc................................ F .... 937 443-0408 Dayton *(G-5834)*
Dana Brazil Holdings I LLC................... C .... 419 887-3000 Maumee *(G-9272)*	Fram Group... G .... 479 271-7934 Cleveland *(G-3741)*	K Wm Beach Mfg Co Inc....................... C .... 937 399-3838 Springfield *(G-12334)*
Dana Commercial Vhcl Pdts LLC........... G .... 419 887-3000 Maumee *(G-9273)*	Fram Group Operations LLC.................. E .... 419 436-5827 Fostoria *(G-6983)*	Kalida Manufacturing Inc...................... C .... 419 532-2026 Kalida *(G-8004)*
Dana Driveshaft Products LLC.............. E .... 419 887-3000 Maumee *(G-9274)*	Fremont Plastic Products Inc................. C .... 419 332-6407 Fremont *(G-7111)*	Kasai North America Inc........................ E .... 614 356-1494 Dublin *(G-6314)*
Dana Global Products Inc...................... D .... 419 887-3000 Maumee *(G-9275)*	Freudenberg-Nok Sealing Tech.............. F .... 877 331-8427 Milan *(G-9915)*	Kasai North America Inc........................ C .... 419 209-0399 Upper Sandusky *(G-13444)*
Dana Hvy Vhcl Systems Group LL........ E .... 419 887-3000 Maumee *(G-9276)*	Ftech R&D North America Inc................. E .... 937 339-2777 Troy *(G-13217)*	Kenley Enterprises LLC........................ G .... 419 630-0921 Bryan *(G-1647)*
Dana Incorporated................................ A .... 419 887-3000 Maumee *(G-9277)*	Fuserashi Intl Tech Inc.......................... E .... 330 273-0140 Valley City *(G-13496)*	Keystone Auto Glass Inc....................... D .... 419 509-0497 Maumee *(G-9302)*
Dana Light Axle Mfg LLC...................... B .... 419 887-3000 Toledo *(G-12938)*	General Metals Powder Co LLC.............. E .... 330 633-1226 Akron *(G-160)*	KG Medina LLC................................... E .... 256 330-4273 Medina *(G-9419)*
Dana Light Axle Mfg LLC...................... G .... 419 346-4528 Maumee *(G-9278)*	General Motors LLC.............................. A .... 216 265-5000 Cleveland *(G-3767)*	Knippen Chrysler Ddge Jeep Inc............ F .... 419 695-4976 Delphos *(G-6188)*
Dana Limited....................................... D .... 419 866-7253 Holland *(G-7754)*	General Motors LLC.............................. C .... 330 824-5840 Warren *(G-13768)*	Kongsberg Actation Systems LLC......... E .... 440 639-8778 Grand River *(G-7311)*
Dana Limited....................................... E .... 419 887-3000 Maumee *(G-9279)*	GKN Driveline North Amer Inc............... D .... 419 354-3955 Bowling Green *(G-1422)*	Kth Parts Industries Inc........................ A .... 937 663-5941 Saint Paris *(G-11758)*
Dana Limited....................................... E .... 419 887-3000 Maumee *(G-9280)*	Gra-Mag Truck Intr Systems LLC........... E .... 740 490-1000 London *(G-8536)*	Ktri Holdings Inc................................. B .... 216 400-9308 Cleveland *(G-3931)*
Dana Limited....................................... D .... 419 482-2000 Maumee *(G-9281)*	Grand-Rock Company Inc...................... E .... 440 639-2000 Painesville *(G-11089)*	KWD Automotive Inc............................ G .... 419 344-8232 Whitehouse *(G-14362)*
Dana Limited....................................... B .... 419 887-3000 Maumee *(G-9282)*	Green Rdced Emssons Netwrk LLC....... G .... 330 340-0941 Strasbur *(G-12478)*	Lacal Equipment Inc............................ E .... 937 596-6106 Jackson Center *(G-7964)*
Dana Off Highway Products LLC........... E .... 419 887-3000 Maumee *(G-9283)*	Green Tokai Co Ltd............................... C .... 937 237-1630 Dayton *(G-5804)*	Lawrence Technologies Inc................... G .... 937 274-7771 Dayton *(G-5842)*
Dana Sac USA Inc............................... G .... 419 887-3550 Maumee *(G-9284)*	Hall-Toledo Inc.................................... F .... 419 893-4334 Maumee *(G-9294)*	Leadec Corp.. E .... 513 731-3590 Cincinnati *(G-2815)*
Dana Sealing Manufacturing LLC........... F Maumee *(G-9285)*	Hendrickson....................................... G .... 740 678-8033 Vincent *(G-13621)*	Lear Corporation.................................. D .... 740 928-4358 Hebron *(G-7622)*
Dana Sealing Products LLC................... F .... 419 887-3000 Maumee *(G-9286)*	Hendrickson International Corp.............. D .... 740 929-5600 Hebron *(G-7617)*	Lear Corporation.................................. E .... 419 335-6010 Wauseon *(G-13855)*
Dana Structural Products LLC.............. G .... 419 887-3000 Maumee *(G-9287)*	Hendrickson Usa LLC........................... C .... 330 456-7288 Canton *(G-1911)*	Lhy Powertrain Corporation................... E .... 330 533-6801 Canfield *(G-1812)*
Dana Thermal Products LLC................. F .... 419 887-3000 Maumee *(G-9288)*	Hendrickson Usa LLC........................... C .... 740 929-5600 Hebron *(G-7618)*	Lippert Components Inc........................ G .... 574 537-8900 Payne *(G-11164)*

Maags Automotive & Mch Inc..............G 419 626-1539
Sandusky *(G-11853)*

Magna Seating America Inc...................C 330 824-3101
Sheffield Village *(G-11960)*

Magna Seating America Inc...................E 419 410-4780
Swanton *(G-12686)*

Magnaco Industries Inc...........................E 216 961-3636
Lodi *(G-8504)*

Mahle Behr Dayton LLC..........................B 937 356-2001
Vandalia *(G-13566)*

Mahle Behr Dayton LLC..........................D 937 369-2900
Dayton *(G-5863)*

Mahle Behr USA Inc................................C 937 356-2001
Vandalia *(G-13567)*

Mahle Eng Components USA Inc...........F 740 962-8004
Mcconnelsville *(G-9363)*

Mahle Industries Incorporated.............E 937 890-2739
Dayton *(G-5865)*

Maxion Wheels Sedalia LLC....................A 330 794-2300
Akron *(G-224)*

Merillat Racing LLC.................................G 419 376-4833
Archbold *(G-502)*

Milark Industries Inc..............................D 419 524-7627
Mansfield *(G-8827)*

Milark Industries Inc..............................E 419 524-7627
Mansfield *(G-8828)*

Millat Industries Corp...........................F 937 535-1500
Dayton *(G-5887)*

Millat Industries Corp...........................D 937 434-6666
Dayton *(G-5888)*

Mitec Powertrain Inc...............................C 567 525-5606
Findlay *(G-6894)*

Mitsubishi Elc Auto Amer Inc.................B 513 573-6614
Mason *(G-9128)*

Monarch Plastic Inc...............................F 330 683-0822
Orrville *(G-10995)*

Namoh Ohio Holdings Inc......................G
Norwood *(G-10869)*

Nanogate North America LLC..................B 419 522-7745
Mansfield *(G-8834)*

Nitto Inc...D 937 773-4820
Piqua *(G-11368)*

Nitto Inc...C 937 773-4820
Piqua *(G-11369)*

Norlake Manufacturing Company...........D 440 353-3200
North Ridgeville *(G-10741)*

Norplas Industries Inc............................C 419 662-3200
Northwood *(G-10805)*

North Coast Exotics Inc........................G 216 651-5512
Cleveland *(G-4084)*

Northern Stamping Co.............................F 216 642-8081
Cleveland *(G-4097)*

Norton Manufacturing Co Inc.................F 419 435-0411
Fostoria *(G-6995)*

Ohio Auto Supply Company.....................G 330 454-5105
Canton *(G-1964)*

Ohta Press US Inc.................................F 937 374-3382
Xenia *(G-14773)*

Pacific Manufacturing Ohio Inc.............B 513 860-3900
Fairfield *(G-6762)*

Pako Inc...C 440 946-8030
Mentor *(G-9580)*

Parker-Hannifin Corporation...................B 440 943-5700
Wickliffe *(G-14389)*

Performance Motorsports Inc................F 440 951-6600
Mentor *(G-9585)*

Pioneer Automotive Tech Inc..................C 937 746-2293
Miamisburg *(G-9727)*

Piston Automotive LLC..........................D 313 541-8674
Avon *(G-735)*

Piston Automotive LLC..........................A 419 464-0250
Toledo *(G-13099)*

Powers and Sons LLC..............................G 419 737-2373
Pioneer *(G-11325)*

Powers and Sons LLC..............................C 419 485-3151
Montpelier *(G-10132)*

Quality Reproductions Inc.....................G 330 335-5000
Wadsworth *(G-13664)*

Race Winning Brands Inc.......................B 440 951-6600
Mentor *(G-9606)*

Radar Love Co...G 419 951-4750
Findlay *(G-6912)*

Ramco Specialties Inc...........................D 330 653-5135
Hudson *(G-7855)*

Reactive Resin Products Co....................F 419 666-6119
Perrysburg *(G-11259)*

Restortion Parts Unlimited Inc..............F 513 934-0815
Lebanon *(G-8283)*

Rubber Duck 4x4 Inc..............................G 513 889-1735
Hamilton *(G-7521)*

Saia-Burgess Lcc....................................D 937 898-3621
Vandalia *(G-13576)*

Sanoh America Inc..................................D 419 425-2600
Findlay *(G-6915)*

Schaeffler Transm Systems LLC............A 330 202-6212
Wooster *(G-14680)*

Schaeffler Transm Systems LLC............E 330 264-4383
Wooster *(G-14681)*

Schott Metal Products Company.............G 330 773-7873
Akron *(G-307)*

Seabiscuit Motorsports Inc...................B 440 951-6600
Mentor *(G-9612)*

Sew-Eurodrive Inc..................................D 937 335-0036
Troy *(G-13254)*

Sfs Group Usa Inc..................................C 330 239-7100
Medina *(G-9446)*

Sfs Intec Inc..E 330 239-7100
Medina *(G-9447)*

Steck Manufacturing Co LLC..................F 937 222-0062
Dayton *(G-6026)*

Steere Enterprises Inc............................D 330 633-4926
Tallmadge *(G-12751)*

Sumiriko Ohio Inc..................................D 419 358-2121
Bluffton *(G-1365)*

Tdi Co...G 937 898-9600
Dayton *(G-6041)*

Teijin Automotive Tech Inc.....................B 419 396-1980
Carey *(G-2063)*

Teijin Automotive Tech Inc.....................B 419 257-2231
North Baltimore *(C 10610)*

Teijin Automotive Tech Inc.....................B 419 238-4628
Van Wert *(G-13546)*

Tetra Mold & Tool Inc............................E 937 845-1651
New Carlisle *(G-10382)*

Tfo Tech Co Ltd......................................C 740 426-6381
Jeffersonville *(G-7988)*

TI Group Auto Systems LLC....................E 740 929-2049
Hebron *(G-7640)*

Tigerpoly Manufacturing Inc..................B 614 871-0045
Grove City *(G-7416)*

Toledo Molding & Die LLC......................C 419 692-6022
Delphos *(G-6193)*

Toledo Molding & Die LLC......................C 419 692-6022
Delphos *(G-6194)*

Toledo Pro Fiberglass Inc......................E 419 241-9390
Toledo *(G-13156)*

Tom Smith Industries Inc......................D 937 832-1555
Englewood *(G-6626)*

Total Engine Airflow...............................G 330 634-2155
Tallmadge *(G-12754)*

Tower Atmtive Oprtons USA I LL.............C 419 483-1500
Bellevue *(G-1136)*

Trailer Component Mfg Inc......................E 440 255-2888
Mentor *(G-9640)*

Tri-Mac Mfg & Svcs Co............................F 513 896-4445
Hamilton *(G-7533)*

Trico Holding Corporation.......................G 216 589-0198
Cleveland *(G-4423)*

Trim Parts Inc...E 513 934-0815
Lebanon *(G-8291)*

Trim Systems Operating Corp.................D 614 289-5360
New Albany *(G-10352)*

Trucks & Parts of Tampa LLC.................E 937 437-0377
New Paris *(G-10427)*

TS Trim Industries Inc............................B 614 837-4114
Canal Winchester *(G-1799)*

Ucan Test Instruments LLC....................G 330 696-6624
Akron *(G-349)*

UCI International LLC.............................E 330 899-0340
North Canton *(G-10679)*

UGN Inc...C 513 360-3500
Lebanon *(G-8294)*

Unison Industries LLC...........................B 904 667-9904
Dayton *(G-5625)*

United Components LLC.........................E 330 899-0340
Toledo *(G-13168)*

US Kondo Corporation.............................F 937 916-3045
Piqua *(G-11388)*

US Tsubaki Power Transm LLC................C 419 626-4560
Sandusky *(G-11881)*

Usui International Corporation................D 734 354-3626
West Chester *(G-14089)*

Varbros LLC...D 216 267-5200
Cleveland *(G-4457)*

Vari-Wall Tube Specialists Inc...............D 330 482-0000
Columbiana *(G-4631)*

Venco Manufacturing Inc.......................E 513 772-8448
Cincinnati *(G-3196)*

Venco Venturo Industries LLC.................E 513 772-8448
Cincinnati *(G-3197)*

Ventra Sandusky LLC.............................C 419 627-3600
Sandusky *(G-11882)*

Walor North America Inc.........................B 614 445-6060
Columbus *(G-5354)*

Walther Engrg & Mfg Co Inc....................E 937 743-8125
Franklin *(G-7056)*

West & Barker Inc..................................F 330 652-9923
Niles *(G-10609)*

Westbrook Mfg Inc...................................B 937 254-2004
Dayton *(G-6078)*

Western Branch Diesel LLC....................F 330 454-8800
Canton *(G-2047)*

Whirlaway Corporation............................D 440 647-4711
Wellington *(G-13902)*

Whirlaway Corporation............................D 440 647-4711
Wellington *(G-13903)*

Winzeler Stamping Co.............................E 419 485-3147
Montpelier *(G-10138)*

Woodbridge Group...................................C 419 334-3666
Fremont *(G-7144)*

Workhorse Group Inc...............................D 888 646-5205
Sharonville *(G-11950)*

Workhorse Technologies Inc...................E 888 646-5205
Sharonville *(G-11951)*

Yanfeng Intl Auto Tech US I LL................D 419 633-1873
Bryan *(G-1668)*

Yanfeng Intl Auto Tech US I LL................D 616 834-9422
Bryan *(G-1669)*

ZF Active Safety & Elec US LLC...............D 216 750-2400
Cleveland *(G-4524)*

ZF Active Safety & Elec US LLC...............E 419 726-5599
Toledo *(G-13183)*

ZF Active Safety US Inc..........................F 419 237-2511
Fayette *(G-6825)*

PRODUCT

AUTOMOTIVE PARTS: Plastic

Cpp Group Holdings LLC........................ E 216 453-4800
Cleveland (G-3574)

Fpe Inc.. C 740 420-5252
Circleville (G-3259)

Greenville Techniology Inc..................... G 937 642-6744
Marysville (G-9022)

M W Solutions LLC................................ F 419 782-1611
Defiance (G-6118)

Molten North America Corp.................... C 419 425-2700
Findlay (G-6895)

National Fleet Svcs Ohio LLC................. F 440 930-5177
Avon Lake (G-766)

Nifco America Corporation..................... D 614 836-3808
Canal Winchester (G-1795)

Nifco America Corporation..................... E 614 836-8691
Groveport (G-7446)

Nifco America Corporation..................... B 614 920-6800
Canal Winchester (G-1794)

Polyfill LLC.. E 937 493-0041
Sidney (G-12040)

Precision Engineered Plas Inc................ E 216 334-1105
Cleveland (G-4184)

Precision Mfg & Assembly LLC............... D 937 252-3507
Dayton (G-5949)

Reinalt-Thomas Corporation.................. G 330 863-1936
Carrollton (G-2089)

Toledo Molding & Die LLC..................... C 419 443-9031
Tiffin (G-12806)

Trifecta Tool and Engrg LLC.................. G 937 291-0933
Dayton (G-6063)

Woodbridge Englewood Inc.................... E 937 540-9889
Englewood (G-6630)

Xaloy LLC.. C 330 726-4000
Austintown (G-709)

AUTOMOTIVE PRDTS: Rubber

Green Tokai Co Ltd............................... A 937 833-5444
Brookville (G-1570)

Kn Rubber LLC..................................... C 419 739-4200
Wapakoneta (G-13719)

Myers Industries Inc............................. C 330 336-6621
Wadsworth (G-13653)

Myers Industries Inc............................. E 330 253-5592
Akron (G-243)

S P E Inc... E 330 733-0101
Mogadore (G-10084)

AUTOMOTIVE RADIATOR REPAIR SHOPS

Albright Radiator Inc............................ G 330 264-8886
Wooster (G-14622)

Brock RAD Wldg Fabrication Inc............. G 740 773-2540
Chillicothe (G-2246)

Cincinnati Radiator Inc.......................... F 513 874-5555
Fairfield (G-6722)

Friess Welding Inc................................ G 330 644-8160
Coventry Township (G-5482)

Perkins Motor Service Ltd...................... F 440 277-1256
Lorain (G-8573)

AUTOMOTIVE REPAIR SHOPS: Diesel Engine Repair

Cummins Inc.. F 614 771-1000
Hilliard (G-7679)

Power Acquisition LLC........................... A 614 228-5000
Dublin (G-6333)

Tri-W Group Inc.................................... A 614 228-5000
Columbus (G-5332)

WW Williams Company LLC.................... D 614 228-5000
Dublin (G-6362)

AUTOMOTIVE REPAIR SHOPS: Electrical Svcs

Entratech Systems LLC.......................... G 419 433-7683
Sandusky (G-11832)

Miscor Group Ltd.................................. B 330 830-3500
Massillon (G-9224)

Vintage Automotive Elc Inc.................... F 419 472-9349
Toledo (G-13175)

AUTOMOTIVE REPAIR SHOPS: Engine Rebuilding

Maags Automotive & Mch Inc................. G 419 626-1539
Sandusky (G-11853)

AUTOMOTIVE REPAIR SHOPS: Engine Repair

Heisley Tire & Brake Inc........................ G 440 357-9797
Mentor (G-9527)

AUTOMOTIVE REPAIR SHOPS: Machine Shop

Mc Machine Llc.................................... E 216 398-3666
Cleveland (G-4007)

Tuf-Tug Inc.. F 937 299-1213
Dayton (G-6067)

AUTOMOTIVE REPAIR SHOPS: Muffler Shop, Sale/Rpr/Installation

Mark Knupp Muffler & Tire Inc............... G 937 773-1334
Piqua (G-11365)

AUTOMOTIVE REPAIR SHOPS: Rebuilding & Retreading Tires

Bell Tire Co... F 440 234-8022
Olmsted Falls (G-10937)

Bridgestone Ret Operations LLC............. G 740 592-3075
Athens (G-635)

Bridgestone Ret Operations LLC............. G 330 454-9478
Canton (G-1845)

Bridgestone Ret Operations LLC............. G 440 461-4747
Cleveland (G-3437)

Bridgestone Ret Operations LLC............. G 216 229-2550
Cleveland (G-3438)

Bridgestone Ret Operations LLC............. G 216 382-8970
Cleveland (G-3439)

Bridgestone Ret Operations LLC............. F 614 864-3350
Columbus (G-4777)

Bridgestone Ret Operations LLC............. F 614 491-8062
Columbus (G-4778)

Bridgestone Ret Operations LLC............. G 614 224-4221
Columbus (G-4779)

Bridgestone Ret Operations LLC............. G 440 324-3327
Elyria (G-6504)

Bridgestone Ret Operations LLC............. G 440 365-8308
Elyria (G-6505)

Bridgestone Ret Operations LLC............. G 937 548-1197
Greenville (G-7336)

Bridgestone Ret Operations LLC............. G 513 868-7399
Hamilton (G-7473)

Bridgestone Ret Operations LLC............. G 330 673-1700
Kent (G-8020)

Bridgestone Ret Operations LLC............. G 614 861-7994
Reynoldsburg (G-11560)

Bridgestone Ret Operations LLC............. G 724 346-2621
Warren (G-13744)

Bridgestone Ret Operations LLC............. G 330 758-0921
Youngstown (G-14825)

Bridgestone Ret Operations LLC............. G 330 759-3697
Youngstown (G-14826)

Grismer Tire Company........................... E 937 643-2526
Centerville (G-2132)

Heartland Retreaders Inc....................... F 740 472-0558
Woodsfield (G-14612)

Ziegler Tire and Supply Co.................... E 330 343-7739
Dover (G-6267)

AUTOMOTIVE REPAIR SHOPS: Tire Recapping

Best One Tire & Svc Lima Inc................. G 419 425-3322
Findlay (G-6843)

Best One Tire & Svc Lima Inc................. E 419 229-2380
Lima (G-8389)

Central Ohio Bandag LP......................... F 740 454-9728
Zanesville (G-15007)

Custom Recapping Inc........................... G 937 324-4331
Springfield (G-12297)

JTL Enterprises LLC.............................. E 937 890-8189
Dayton (G-5832)

Mitchell Bros Tire Rtread Svc................. G 740 353-1551
Portsmouth (G-11470)

Skinner Firestone Inc............................ G 740 984-4247
Beverly (G-1209)

Victor Bodie Tire Co............................. G 216 431-1700
Cleveland (G-4471)

AUTOMOTIVE REPAIR SHOPS: Tire Repair Shop

Associates Tire and Svc Inc................... F 937 436-4692
Centerville (G-2129)

Bob Sumerel Tire Company Inc............... G 740 927-2811
Reynoldsburg (G-11559)

Bridgestone Ret Operations LLC............. G 440 842-3200
Cleveland (G-3436)

Bridgestone Ret Operations LLC............. F 740 397-5601
Mount Vernon (G-10237)

Exit 11 Truck Tire Service Inc................. G 330 659-6372
Richfield (G-11591)

Fleet Relief Company............................ G 419 525-2625
Mansfield (G-8789)

Forklift Tire East Mich Inc..................... F 586 771-1330
Toledo (G-12967)

Goodyear Tire & Rubber Company.......... G 330 966-1274
Canton (G-1904)

Goodyear Tire & Rubber Company.......... G 330 759-9343
Youngstown (G-14869)

Gt Tire Service Inc................................ G 740 927-7226
Pataskala (G-11139)

Heisley Tire & Brake Inc........................ G 440 357-9797
Mentor (G-9527)

Mark Knupp Muffler & Tire Inc............... G 937 773-1334
Piqua (G-11365)

Muskingum Tire Company Inc................. G 740 453-8473
Zanesville (G-15030)

North Coast Tire Co Inc......................... G 216 447-1690
Cleveland (G-4089)

Paul Shovlin.. G 330 757-0032
Youngstown (G-14915)

Urra Co Inc.. G 330 673-8473
Kent (G-8093)

Wayne A Whaley................................... G 330 525-7779
Homeworth (G-7807)

Ziegler Tire and Supply Co.................... G 330 434-7126
Akron (G-362)

AUTOMOTIVE REPAIR SHOPS: Trailer Repair

Capitol City Trailers Inc......................... D 614 491-2616
Obetz (G-10921)

Greggs Specialty Services...................... F 419 478-0803
Toledo *(G-12977)*

J & L Body Inc.................................... F 216 661-2323
Brooklyn Heights *(G-1533)*

M & W Trailers Inc............................. F 419 453-3331
Ottoville *(G-11055)*

Mac Trailer Manufacturing Inc................ A 800 795-8454
Alliance *(G-390)*

Nelson Manufacturing Company............ D 419 523-5321
Ottawa *(G-11039)*

AUTOMOTIVE REPAIR SHOPS: Truck Engine Repair, Exc Indl

Kaffenbarger Truck Eqp Co.................... E 513 772-6800
Cincinnati *(G-2777)*

Kinstle Truck & Auto Svc Inc................. G 419 738-7493
Wapakoneta *(G-13718)*

Sutphen Towers Inc............................. D 614 876-1262
Hilliard *(G-7704)*

AUTOMOTIVE REPAIR SVC

AB Tire & Repair................................. G 440 543-2929
Chagrin Falls *(G-2152)*

Bowman Tire Repr Ctr Bxley LLC............ G 740 928-7000
Hebron *(G-7609)*

C & F Tire & Truck Repair...................... G 419 526-1412
Ontario *(G-10947)*

Certified Auto & Trck Repr Inc................ G 440 288-2029
Lorain *(G-8550)*

East Trailers LLC................................ E 330 325-9921
Randolph *(G-11510)*

Goodyear Tire & Rubber Company........ A 330 796-2121
Akron *(G-164)*

J & J Tire & Alignment.......................... G 330 424-5200
Lisbon *(G-8471)*

Jordon Auto Service & Tire Inc............... G 216 214-6528
Cleveland *(G-3891)*

Kirbys Auto and Truck Repr Inc.............. G 513 934-3999
Lebanon *(G-8272)*

Maags Automotive & Mch Inc................ G 419 626-1539
Sandusky *(G-11853)*

Midwest Muffler Pros & More................. G 937 293-2450
Moraine *(G-10179)*

Mikes Transm & Auto Svc LLC............. F 330 799-8266
Youngstown *(G-14901)*

Randys Tire & Auto Repair Inc............... G 419 562-2926
Bucyrus *(G-1688)*

Skaggs Trlr & Tire Repr Co Inc............... F 440 986-7470
Amherst *(G-452)*

Sycamore Tire & Auto Repair................. G 513 793-0726
Cincinnati *(G-3134)*

AUTOMOTIVE SPLYS & PARTS, NEW, WHOL: Auto Servicing Eqpt

D & J Electric Motor Repair Co.............. F 330 336-4343
Wadsworth *(G-13634)*

Tuffy Manufacturing............................. F 330 940-2356
Akron *(G-348)*

AUTOMOTIVE SPLYS & PARTS, NEW, WHOLESALE: Clutches

All Wright Enterprises LLC.................... G 440 259-5656
Perry *(G-11190)*

AUTOMOTIVE SPLYS & PARTS, NEW, WHOLESALE: Engines/Eng Parts

Interstate Diesel Service Inc.................. C 216 881-0015
Cleveland *(G-3865)*

Ultra-Met Company.............................. F 937 653-7133
Urbana *(G-13480)*

AUTOMOTIVE SPLYS & PARTS, NEW, WHOLESALE: Filters, Air & Oil

OSI Environmental LLC......................... E 440 237-4600
North Royalton *(G-10779)*

AUTOMOTIVE SPLYS & PARTS, NEW, WHOLESALE: Splys

Autobody Supply Company Inc............. D 614 228-4328
Columbus *(G-4735)*

Finale Products Inc............................. G 419 874-2662
Perrysburg *(G-11221)*

Keystone Automotive Inds Inc............... G 614 228-4328
Groveport *(G-7440)*

Nelson Companies One LLC................ E 330 239-4370
Wadsworth *(G-13654)*

AUTOMOTIVE SPLYS & PARTS, NEW, WHOLESALE: Stampings

Namoh Ohio Holdings Inc..................... G
Norwood *(G-10869)*

T A Bacon Co..................................... G 216 595-1310
Cleveland *(G-4361)*

AUTOMOTIVE SPLYS & PARTS, NEW, WHOLESALE: Tools & Eqpt

Cedar Elec Holdings Corp..................... D 773 804-6288
West Chester *(G-13958)*

Matco Tools Corporation....................... B 330 929-4949
Stow *(G-12440)*

Myers Industries Inc........................... E 330 253-5592
Akron *(G-243)*

AUTOMOTIVE SPLYS & PARTS, NEW, WHOLESALE: Trailer Parts

Frontier Tank Center Inc....................... G 330 659-3888
Richfield *(G-11593)*

Ohio Trailer Supply Inc....................... G 614 471-9121
Columbus *(G-5155)*

AUTOMOTIVE SPLYS & PARTS, NEW, WHOLESALE: Wheels

The Hamilton Caster & Mfg Company.... D 513 863-3300
Hamilton *(G-7530)*

AUTOMOTIVE SPLYS & PARTS, WHOLESALE, NEC

Accel Performance Group LLC.............. C 216 658-6413
Independence *(G-7887)*

Alegre Inc.. F 937 885-6786
Miamisburg *(G-9664)*

Bendix Coml Vhcl Systems LLC............ B 440 329-9000
Avon *(G-716)*

Brookville Roadster Inc......................... G 937 833-4605
Brookville *(G-1563)*

Florence Alloys Inc............................. G 330 745-9141
Barberton *(G-805)*

Gmelectric Inc.................................... G 330 477-3392
Canton *(G-1902)*

Hite Parts Exchange Inc...................... G 614 272-5115
Chillicothe *(G-2258)*

Mader Automotive Center Inc................ F 937 339-2681
Troy *(G-13238)*

Martin Diesel Inc............................... E 419 782-9911
Defiance *(G-6120)*

Ohashi Technica USA Inc...................... E 740 965-5115
Sunbury *(G-12671)*

Ohio Auto Supply Company.................. G 330 454-5105
Canton *(G-1964)*

Pioneer Automotive Tech Inc................. C 937 746-2293
Miamisburg *(G-9727)*

Qualitor Subsidiary H Inc..................... E 419 562-7987
Bucyrus *(G-1686)*

Sims Bros Inc..................................... D 740 387-9041
Marion *(G-9000)*

TS Trim Industries Inc.......................... B 614 837-4114
Canal Winchester *(G-1799)*

Vintage Automotive Elc Inc................... F 419 472-9349
Toledo *(G-13175)*

AUTOMOTIVE SPLYS/PART, NEW, WHOL: Spring, Shock Absorb/Strut

Thyssenkrupp Bilstein Amer Inc............ C 513 881-7600
Hamilton *(G-7531)*

AUTOMOTIVE SVCS, EXC REPAIR & CARWASHES: Lubrication

Lubrication Specialties LLC.................. E 800 341-6516
Mount Gilead *(G-10212)*

AUTOMOTIVE SVCS, EXC REPAIR & CARWASHES: Trailer Maintenance

J & L Body Inc.................................... F 216 661-2323
Brooklyn Heights *(G-1533)*

AUTOMOTIVE SVCS, EXC RPR/ CARWASHES: High Perf Auto Rpr/Svc

Mikes Transm & Auto Svc LLC............. F 330 799-8266
Youngstown *(G-14901)*

AUTOMOTIVE TRANSMISSION REPAIR SVC

Bob Sumerel Tire Co Inc...................... F 330 769-9092
Seville *(G-11914)*

Mikes Transm & Auto Svc LLC............. F 330 799-8266
Youngstown *(G-14901)*

Power Acquisition LLC......................... A 614 228-5000
Dublin *(G-6333)*

Rumpke Transportation Co LLC............. F 513 851-0122
Cincinnati *(G-3058)*

Tri-W Group Inc................................... A 614 228-5000
Columbus *(G-5332)*

WW Williams Company LLC................. D 614 228-5000
Dublin *(G-6362)*

AUTOMOTIVE WELDING SVCS

Brock RAD Wldg Fabrication Inc............ G 740 773-2540
Chillicothe *(G-2246)*

Brown Industrial Inc........................... E 937 693-3838
Botkins *(G-1397)*

Industry Products Co........................... B 937 778-0585
Piqua *(G-11356)*

McGregor Mtal Leffel Works LLC........... D 937 325-5561
Springfield *(G-12350)*

Perkins Motor Service Ltd..................... F 440 277-1256
Lorain *(G-8573)*

Process Eqp Co Wldg Svcs LLC........... G 937 667-4451
Tipp City *(G-12837)*

R K Industries Inc............................. D 419 523-5001
Ottawa *(G-11044)*

Turn-Key Industrial Svcs LLC................ D 614 274-1128
Grove City *(G-7420)*

AUTOMOTIVE: Bodies

Monarch Plastic Inc........................... F 330 683-0822
Orrville *(G-10995)*

Scottrods LLC................................... G 419 499-2705
Monroeville *(G-10120)*

PRODUCT

AUTOMOTIVE: Seat Frames, Metal

Camaco LLC.................................. A 440 288-4444
Lorain (G-8549)

Jay Mid-South LLC..................... G 256 439-6600
Mansfield (G-8807)

Pfi USA... F 937 547-0413
Greenville (G-7349)

AUTOMOTIVE: Seating

Clarios LLC.................................. E 419 636-4211
Bryan (G-1636)

Clarios LLC.................................. E 440 205-7221
Mentor (G-9499)

Commercial Vehicle Group Inc............. B 614 289-5360
New Albany (G-10336)

Evenflo Company Inc.................. A 937 415-3300
Miamisburg (G-9692)

Jay Industries Inc...................... A 419 747-4161
Mansfield (G-8806)

Johnson Controls Inc................ D 216 587-0100
Brecksville (G-1474)

Johnson Controls Inc................ D 513 489-0950
Cincinnati (G-2771)

Johnson Controls Inc................ F 513 671-6338
Cincinnati (G-2772)

Johnson Controls Inc................ D 614 895-6600
Westerville (G-14267)

Johnson Controls Inc................ E 330 270-4385
Youngstown (G-14884)

Magna Seating America Inc.............. C 330 824-3101
Sheffield Village (G-11960)

Setex Inc..................................... B 419 394-7800
Saint Marys (G-11752)

AUTOTRANSFORMERS: Electric

SGB Usa Inc................................ G 330 472-1187
Tallmadge (G-12749)

AVIATION SCHOOL

Flightsafety International Inc.............. C 614 324-3500
Columbus (G-4929)

AWNINGS & CANOPIES: Awnings, Fabric, From Purchased Matls

ABC Signs Inc............................ F 513 407-4367
Cincinnati (G-2331)

Awning Fabri Caters Inc.................... G 216 476-4888
Cleveland (G-3397)

Canvas Specialty Mfg Co.................. G 216 881-0647
Cleveland (G-3465)

Capital City Awning Co Inc.............. E 614 221-5404
Columbus (G-4796)

Fabric Forms Inc........................ G 513 281-6300
Cincinnati (G-2610)

Glawe Manufacturing Co Inc.............. G 937 754-0064
Fairborn (G-6694)

Independent Awning & Canvas Co......... G 937 223-9661
Dayton (G-5820)

Main Awning & Tent Inc.................. G 513 621-6947
Cincinnati (G-2842)

Ohio Awning & Manufacturing Co......... E 216 861-2400
Cleveland (G-4111)

Queen City Awning & Tent Co.............. E 513 530-9660
Cincinnati (G-3020)

Schaaf Co Inc............................. G 513 241-7044
Cincinnati (G-3067)

South Akron Awning Co................. F 330 848-7611
Akron (G-314)

Tarped Out Inc........................... E 330 325-7722
Ravenna (G-11545)

AWNINGS: Fiberglass

PCR Restorations Inc.................. G 419 747-7957
Mansfield (G-8844)

Superior Fibers Inc.................... B 740 394-2491
Shawnee (G-11952)

AWNINGS: Metal

Alumetal Manufacturing Company......... E 419 268-2311
Coldwater (G-4567)

Crest Products Inc...................... F 440 942-5770
Mentor (G-9508)

General Awning Company Inc.............. G 216 749-0110
Cleveland (G-3762)

Joyce Manufacturing Co................ D 440 239-9100
Berea (G-1179)

Toledo Window & Awning Inc.............. F 419 474-3396
Toledo (G-13162)

Youngstown Shade & Alum LLC......... G 330 782-2373
Youngstown (G-14975)

AXLES

Alta Mira Corporation.................. D 330 648-2461
Spencer (G-12233)

Meritor Inc.................................. C 740 348-3270
Granville (G-7317)

Schafer Driveline LLC.................. F 740 694-2055
Fredericktown (G-7084)

Spencer Manufacturing Company Inc... D 330 648-2461
Spencer (G-12236)

BACKHOES

Brian Hosher Backhoe Plum.............. G 740 503-4434
Baltimore (G-783)

BADGES: Identification & Insignia

Identiphoto Co Ltd...................... F 440 306-9000
Willoughby (G-14467)

BAGS & CONTAINERS: Textile, Exc Sleeping

Baggallini Inc............................. F 800 448-8753
Pickerington (G-11289)

BAGS & SACKS: Shipping & Shopping

Pantrybag Inc............................. F 614 812-8073
Columbus (G-5172)

BAGS: Canvas

American Made Bags LLC................ F 330 475-1385
Akron (G-56)

Capital City Awning Co Inc.............. E 614 221-5404
Columbus (G-4796)

Hdt Expeditionary Systems Inc........... E 216 438-6111
Solon (G-12121)

BAGS: Cellophane

Buckeye Boxes Inc...................... D 614 274-8484
Columbus (G-4783)

BAGS: Duffle, Canvas, Made From Purchased Materials

R J Manray Inc............................ G 330 559-6716
Canfield (G-1814)

BAGS: Food Storage & Frozen Food, Plastic

Global Plastic Tech Inc.................. G 440 879-6045
Lorain (G-8556)

BAGS: Food Storage & Trash, Plastic

American Plastics LLC.................. C 419 423-1213
Findlay (G-6836)

BAGS: Paper

A To Z Paper Box Company............... G 330 325-8722
Rootstown (G-11646)

Dazpak Flexible Packaging Corp......... C 614 252-2121
Columbus (G-4872)

Ray C Sprosty Bag Co Inc................ F 330 669-0045
Smithville (G-12067)

Ricking Holding Co...................... F 513 825-3551
Cleveland (G-4241)

BAGS: Paper, Made From Purchased Materials

Duro Bag Manufacturing Company......... D 800 879-3876
Cincinnati (G-2565)

Ecopac LLC................................. E 513 795-6002
Fairfield (G-6730)

Greif Inc..................................... E 740 657-6500
Delaware (G-6150)

Greif Inc..................................... E 740 549-6000
Delaware (G-6149)

BAGS: Plastic

Automated Packg Systems Inc.............. E 330 342-2000
Bedford (G-1013)

Buckeye Packaging Co Inc............... D 330 935-0301
Alliance (G-373)

Command Plastic Corporation......... F 800 321-8001
Bedford (G-1022)

Dayton Industrial Drum Inc.............. E 937 253-8933
Dayton (G-5608)

Flavorseal LLC........................... D 440 937-3900
Avon (G-726)

Hood Packaging Corporation........... C 937 382-6681
Wilmington (G-14584)

Kennedy Group Incorporated............. D 440 951-7660
Willoughby (G-14477)

Noramco Inc............................... D 216 531-3400
Euclid (G-6664)

Packaging Materials Inc................ E 740 432-6337
Cambridge (G-1753)

Pitt Plastics Inc......................... D 614 868-8660
Columbus (G-5192)

Safeway Packaging Inc.................. E 419 629-3200
New Bremen (G-10366)

Signature Flexible Packg LLC.............. F 614 252-2121
Columbus (G-5267)

BAGS: Plastic & Pliofilm

Charter Nex Films - Delaware Oh Inc..... E 740 369-2770
Delaware (G-6137)

Engineered Films Division Inc.............. D 419 884-8150
Lexington (G-8373)

General Films Inc........................ D 888 436-3456
Covington (G-5493)

North American Plas Chem Inc........... E 216 531-3400
Euclid (G-6666)

BAGS: Plastic, Made From Purchased Materials

Ampac Holdings LLC.................... A 513 671-1777
Cincinnati (G-2365)

B K Plastics Inc......................... G 937 473-2087
Covington (G-5490)

Cpg - Ohio LLC............................ D 513 825-4800
Cincinnati (G-2521)

Crayex Corporation..................... D 937 773-7000
Piqua (G-11342)

Custom Poly Bag LLC.................... D 330 935-2408
Alliance (G-378)

Dazpak Flexible Packaging Corp............ C 614 252-2121
Columbus **(G-4872)**

Liqui-Box Corporation............................ E 419 289-9696
Ashland **(G-549)**

Pexco Packaging Corp............................ E 419 470-5935
Toledo **(G-13096)**

BAGS: Rubber Or Rubberized Fabric

Timco Rubber Products Inc.................... E 216 267-6242
Berea **(G-1191)**

BAGS: Shipping

Hood Packaging Corporation.................. C 937 382-6681
Wilmington **(G-14584)**

BAGS: Shopping, Made From Purchased Materials

Ampac Holdings LLC............................... A 513 671-1777
Cincinnati **(G-2365)**

BAGS: Textile

Baggallini Inc... F 800 448-8753
Pickerington **(G-11289)**

BAKERIES, COMMERCIAL: On Premises Baking Only

Amish Door Inc...................................... C 330 359-5464
Wilmot **(G-14592)**

Arlington Valley Farms LLC.................... E 216 426-5000
Hudson **(G-7833)**

Blf Enterprises Inc................................. F 937 642-6425
Westerville **(G-14246)**

Bread Kneads Inc.................................. G 419 422-3863
Findlay **(G-6845)**

Buns of Delaware Inc............................. F 740 363-2867
Delaware **(G-6135)**

Fragapane Bakeries Inc.......................... G 440 779-6050
North Olmsted **(G-10721)**

Gardner Pie Company............................ C 330 245-2030
Coventry Township **(G-5483)**

Garys Chesecakes Fine Desserts........... G 513 574-1700
Cincinnati **(G-2652)**

Graeters Ice Cream Company................. D 513 721-3323
Cincinnati **(G-2687)**

Harvest Commissary LLC........................ E 513 706-1951
Granville **(G-7315)**

Heinens Inc.. C 330 562-5297
Aurora **(G-673)**

Hostess Brands Inc............................... D 816 701-4600
Orrville **(G-10984)**

Interbake Foods LLC.............................. D 614 294-4931
Columbus **(G-5018)**

Kennedys Bakery Inc.............................. G 740 432-2301
Cambridge **(G-1746)**

Klosterman Baking Co LLC..................... C 513 242-5667
Cincinnati **(G-2800)**

La Marquise Inc...................................... D 614 488-1911
Columbus **(G-5060)**

Main Street Gourmet LLC....................... C 330 929-0000
Cuyahoga Falls **(G-5560)**

Meeks Pastry Shop................................. G 419 782-4871
Defiance **(G-6121)**

Morgan4140 LLC..................................... F 513 873-1426
Cincinnati **(G-2887)**

Mustard Seed Health Fd Mkt Inc............ E 440 519-3663
Solon **(G-12155)**

Osmans Pies Inc..................................... E 330 607-9083
Stow **(G-12448)**

Pf Management Inc................................. G 513 874-1111
West Chester **(G-14136)**

Pierre Holding Corp................................ G 513 874-8741
West Chester **(G-14137)**

Quality Bakery Company Inc.................... C 614 224-1424
Columbus **(G-5218)**

Rich Products Corporation...................... C 614 771-1117
Hilliard **(G-7699)**

Riesbeck Food Markets Inc.................... C 740 695-3401
Saint Clairsville **(G-11709)**

Schulers Bakery Inc............................... E 937 323-4154
Springfield **(G-12371)**

Schwebel Baking Company..................... F 216 481-1880
Euclid **(G-6678)**

Schwebel Baking Company..................... E 330 783-2860
Hebron **(G-7635)**

Schwebel Baking Company..................... F 330 926-9410
North Canton **(G-10667)**

Schwebel Baking Company..................... C 440 248-1500
Solon **(G-12179)**

Schwebel Baking Company..................... E 330 783-2860
Youngstown **(G-14929)**

Schwebel Baking Company..................... B 330 783-2860
Youngstown **(G-14928)**

Servatii Inc.. G 513 271-5040
Cincinnati **(G-3083)**

Thurns Bakery & Deli............................. G 614 221-9246
Columbus **(G-5323)**

Uprising Food Inc.................................. G 513 313-1087
Cincinnati **(G-3187)**

White Castle System Inc........................ B 614 228-5781
Columbus **(G-5367)**

BAKERIES: On Premises Baking & Consumption

Alfred Nickles Bakery Inc....................... E 740 453-6522
Zanesville **(G-14985)**

Buns of Delaware Inc............................. F 740 363-2867
Delaware **(G-6135)**

Crumbs Inc.. F 740 592-3803
Athens **(G-637)**

Fragapane Bakeries Inc.......................... G 440 779-6050
North Olmsted **(G-10721)**

La Marquise Inc...................................... D 614 488-1911
Columbus **(G-5060)**

Osmans Pies Inc..................................... E 330 607-9083
Stow **(G-12448)**

Pepperidge Farm Incorporated............... G 419 933-2611
Willard **(G-14407)**

Thurns Bakery & Deli............................. G 614 221-9246
Columbus **(G-5323)**

BAKERY MACHINERY

Coperion Food Equipment LLC............... E 937 492-4158
Sidney **(G-12009)**

Fred D Pfening Company......................... G 614 294-5361
Columbus **(G-4940)**

Ingredient Masters Inc........................... G 513 231-7432
Batavia **(G-868)**

Magna Machine Co.................................. G 513 851-6900
Cincinnati **(G-2840)**

Peerless Foods Inc................................. D 937 492-4158
Sidney **(G-12038)**

the Perfect Score Company.................... F 440 439-9320
Bedford Heights **(G-1082)**

BAKERY PRDTS: Bakery Prdts, Partially Cooked, Exc frozen

Suelos Sweetz LLC................................ G 440 478-1301
Willowick **(G-14568)**

Toast With Cake LLC.............................. G 937 554-5900
Miamisburg **(G-9748)**

BAKERY PRDTS: Bread, All Types, Fresh Or Frozen

Angelic Bakehouse LLC.......................... E 414 312-7300
Westerville **(G-14203)**

Brooks Pastries Inc................................ G 614 274-4880
Plain City **(G-11399)**

Hostess Brands LLC............................... D 816 701-4600
Orrville **(G-10985)**

New York Frozen Foods Inc.................... B 216 292-5655
Bedford **(G-1049)**

Orlando Baking Company........................ C 216 361-1872
Cleveland **(G-4124)**

BAKERY PRDTS: Buns, Bread Type, Fresh Or Frozen

B & J Baking Company............................ F 513 541-2386
Cincinnati **(G-2394)**

New Horizons Baking Co LLC.................. C 419 668-8226
Norwalk **(G-10854)**

New York Frozen Foods Inc.................... E 626 338-3000
Westerville **(G-14223)**

BAKERY PRDTS: Cakes, Bakery, Exc Frozen

Cake House Cleveland LLC..................... F 216 870-4659
Cleveland **(G-3460)**

Cake In A Cup Inc.................................. G 419 491-1104
Toledo **(G-12909)**

Uncle Jays Cakes LLC............................ G 513 882-3433
Cincinnati **(G-3178)**

BAKERY PRDTS: Cakes, Bakery, Frozen

Keough and Associates LLC................... G 440 682-0514
Chardon **(G-2209)**

BAKERY PRDTS: Cones, Ice Cream

Norse Dairy Systems LP......................... B 614 294-4931
Columbus **(G-5129)**

BAKERY PRDTS: Cookies

Hearthside Food Solutions LLC.............. A 419 293-2911
Mc Comb **(G-9353)**

Interbake Foods LLC.............................. D 614 294-4931
Columbus **(G-5018)**

Keebler Company................................... C 513 271-3500
Cincinnati **(G-2790)**

Pepperidge Farm Incorporated............... G 419 933-2611
Willard **(G-14407)**

Yz Enterprises Inc.................................. E 419 893-8777
Maumee **(G-9331)**

BAKERY PRDTS: Cookies & crackers

Blf Enterprises Inc................................. F 937 642-6425
Westerville **(G-14246)**

Cheryl & Co.. F 614 776-1500
Obetz **(G-10923)**

Cookie Bouquets Inc.............................. G 614 888-2171
Columbus **(G-4847)**

Ditsch Usa LLC....................................... E 513 782-8888
Cincinnati **(G-2551)**

Kennedys Bakery Inc.............................. G 740 432-2301
Cambridge **(G-1746)**

La Marquise Inc...................................... D 614 488-1911
Columbus **(G-5060)**

Main Street Gourmet LLC....................... C 330 929-0000
Cuyahoga Falls **(G-5560)**

Mmelo Btq Confectioners LLC................ G 614 822-9530
Reynoldsburg **(G-11574)**

Norcia Bakery.. G 330 454-1077
Canton **(G-1959)**

Osmans Pies Inc......................................E 330 607-9083
Stow (G-12448)

Rudys Strudel Shop................................G 440 886-4430
Cleveland (G-4264)

Schulers Bakery Inc...............................E 937 323-4154
Springfield (G-12371)

BAKERY PRDTS: Doughnuts, Exc Frozen

Crispie Creme Chillicothe Inc.................G 740 774-3770
Chillicothe (G-2249)

Dandi Enterprises Inc............................G 419 516-9070
Solon (G-12099)

Mary Ann Donut Shoppe Inc..................G 330 478-1655
Canton (G-1938)

McHappys Dnuts Parkersburg Inc..........D 740 593-8744
Athens (G-643)

Wal-Bon of Ohio Inc..............................E 740 423-8178
Belpre (G-1156)

BAKERY PRDTS: Dry

Brand Castle LLC...................................E 216 292-7700
Bedford Heights (G-1070)

Imagine Baking Buyer LLC.....................F 419 502-9000
Sandusky (G-11840)

BAKERY PRDTS: Frozen

Main Street Gourmet LLC.......................C 330 929-0000
Cuyahoga Falls (G-5560)

Pepperidge Farm Incorporated..............G 419 933-2611
Willard (G-14407)

BAKERY PRDTS: Pastries, Exc Frozen

Krispy Kreme Doughnut Corp.................E 614 798-0812
Columbus (G-5057)

Krispy Kreme Doughnut Corp.................D 614 876-0058
Columbus (G-5058)

BAKERY PRDTS: Pies, Bakery, Frozen

Gardner Pie Company.............................C 330 245-2030
Coventry Township (G-5483)

BAKERY PRDTS: Pies, Exc Frozen

K & B Acquisitions Inc...........................F 937 253-1163
Dayton (G-5837)

Papa Joes Pies Inc................................F 440 960-7437
Amherst (G-451)

BAKERY PRDTS: Pretzels

Ditsch Usa LLC......................................G 513 782-8888
Cincinnati (G-2552)

BAKERY PRDTS: Rice Cakes

Basic Grain Products Inc.......................D 419 678-2304
Coldwater (G-4568)

BAKERY PRDTS: Wholesalers

Busken Bakery Inc.................................D 513 871-2114
Cincinnati (G-2434)

Ditsch Usa LLC......................................G 513 782-8888
Cincinnati (G-2552)

Food Plant Engineering LLC...................F 513 618-3165
Blue Ash (G-1275)

Klosterman Baking Co LLC....................C 513 242-5667
Cincinnati (G-2800)

Osmans Pies Inc...................................E 330 607-9083
Stow (G-12448)

Thurns Bakery & Deli.............................G 614 221-9246
Columbus (G-5323)

BAKERY: Wholesale Or Wholesale & Retail Combined

Alfred Nickles Bakery Inc.......................E 740 453-6522
Zanesville (G-14985)

Bimbo Qsr Us LLC.................................G 740 562-4188
Zanesville (G-14996)

Crumbs Inc...F 740 592-3803
Athens (G-637)

Evans Bakery Inc..................................G 937 228-4151
Dayton (G-5771)

Gawa Traders LLC.................................E 614 697-1440
Columbus (G-4946)

Home Bakery..F 419 678-3018
Coldwater (G-4578)

Killer Brownie Ltd..................................D 937 530-8600
Miamisburg (G-9706)

Killer Brownie Ltd..................................E 937 535-5690
Miamisburg (G-9705)

Klosterman Baking Co LLC....................F 513 398-2707
Mason (G-9118)

McL Inc..E 614 861-6259
Columbus (G-5092)

Norcia Bakery.......................................G 330 454-1077
Canton (G-1959)

Rudys Strudel Shop...............................G 440 886-4430
Cleveland (G-4264)

Scheiders Foods LLC.............................F 740 404-6641
Mount Perry (G-10226)

Schwebel Baking Company....................F 440 846-1921
Strongsville (G-12595)

Skyliner...G 740 738-0874
Bridgeport (G-1496)

Studgionsgroup LLC..............................E 216 804-1561
Cleveland (G-4339)

Sweet Persuasions LLC.........................G 614 216-9052
Pickerington (G-11301)

Wal-Bon of Ohio Inc..............................F 740 423-6351
Belpre (G-1155)

BALLOONS: Toy & Advertising, Rubber

Goodlevel Enterprises LLC.....................G 419 668-8261
Norwalk (G-10843)

MCR of Norwalk Inc...............................E 419 668-8261
Norwalk (G-10852)

Nelson Companies One LLC...................E 330 239-4370
Wadsworth (G-13654)

Perfect Products Company....................E
Malvern (G-8752)

Scherba Industries Inc..........................D 330 273-3200
Brunswick (G-1614)

BANNERS: Fabric

Party Animal Inc....................................F 440 471-1030
Westlake (G-14320)

BANQUET HALL FACILITIES

Buns of Delaware Inc.............................F 740 363-2867
Delaware (G-6135)

Mustard Seed Health Fd Mkt Inc............E 440 519-3663
Solon (G-12155)

Vulcan Machinery Corporation...............F 330 376-6025
Akron (G-355)

BAR

Great Lakes Brewing Co.........................C 216 771-4404
Cleveland (G-3789)

BAR FIXTURES: Wood

Ingle-Barr Inc.......................................D 740 702-6117
Chillicothe (G-2261)

BAR JOISTS & CONCRETE REINFORCING BARS: Fabricated

Foundation Systems Anchors Inc...........F 330 454-1700
Canton (G-1893)

Worthington Enterprises Inc...................C 614 438-3210
Worthington (G-14731)

BARBECUE EQPT

Gosun Inc...F 888 868-6154
Cincinnati (G-2684)

BARGES BUILDING & REPAIR

McGinnis Inc...C 740 377-4391
South Point (G-12226)

McNational Inc......................................D 740 377-4391
South Point (G-12227)

Superior Marine Ways Inc......................C 740 894-6224
Proctorville (G-11499)

BARRICADES: Metal

Df Supply Inc...E 330 650-9226
Twinsburg (G-13294)

BARS & BAR SHAPES: Copper & Copper Alloy

Avtron Aerospace Inc............................C 216 750-5152
Cleveland (G-3393)

BARS & BAR SHAPES: Steel, Hot-Rolled

McDonald Steel Corporation..................D 330 530-9118
Mc Donald (G-9360)

BARS, COLD FINISHED: Steel, From Purchased Hot-Rolled

Telling Industries LLC............................E 740 435-8900
Cambridge (G-1764)

Telling Industries LLC............................F 440 974-3370
Willoughby (G-14538)

BARS: Concrete Reinforcing, Fabricated Steel

Akron Rebar Co.....................................E 330 745-7100
Akron (G-40)

Barsplice Products Inc...........................E 937 275-8700
Dayton (G-5674)

Bridge Components Incorporated...........G 614 873-0777
Columbus (G-4775)

Gateway Con Forming Svcs Inc..............D 513 353-2000
Miamitown (G-9758)

Industrial Millwright Svcs LLC................E 419 523-9147
Ottawa (G-11035)

Ncf Cim Fabricators LLC........................E 863 425-1000
Ontario (G-10950)

Ohio Bridge Corporation........................C 740 432-6334
Cambridge (G-1752)

Sky Climber Fabricating LLC..................G 740 990-9430
Delaware (G-6173)

Veterans Steel Inc.................................F 216 938-7476
Cleveland (G-4462)

BARS: Iron, Made In Steel Mills

Republic Engineered Products...............E 440 277-2000
Lorain (G-8577)

Republic Steel.......................................E 330 438-5435
Canton (G-1995)

BASEMENT WINDOW AREAWAYS: Concrete

Bilco Company......................................E 740 455-9020
Zanesville (G-14995)

BASES, BEVERAGE

Third Wave Water LLC .... F 855 590-4500
Xenia **(G-14778)**

BASKETS: Steel Wire

Cherokee Manufacturing LLC .... G 800 777-5030
Perry **(G-11191)**

BATHROOM ACCESS & FITTINGS: Vitreous China & Earthenware

Crane Plumbing LLC .... A 419 522-4211
Mansfield **(G-8778)**

BATHROOM FIXTURES: Plastic

American Platinum Door LLC .... G 440 497-6213
Solon **(G-12078)**

Marble Arch Products Inc .... G 937 746-8388
Franklin **(G-7032)**

BATTERIES, EXC AUTOMOTIVE: Wholesalers

Ametek Inc .... F 937 440-0800
Troy **(G-13200)**

Battery Unlimited .... G 740 452-5030
Zanesville **(G-14993)**

D C Systems Inc .... F 330 273-3030
Brunswick **(G-1587)**

One Wish LLC .... F 800 505-6883
Bedford **(G-1052)**

BATTERIES: Alkaline, Cell Storage

Energizer Manufacturing Inc .... F
Westlake **(G-14301)**

Transdigm Inc .... E 216 291-6025
Cleveland **(G-4411)**

BATTERIES: Lead Acid, Storage

All Power Battery Inc .... G 330 453-5236
Canton **(G-1828)**

Enersys .... C 216 252-4242
Cleveland **(G-3673)**

BATTERIES: Rechargeable

Cirba Solutions Us Inc .... D 740 653-6290
Lancaster **(G-8187)**

Clarios LLC .... A 419 865-0542
Holland **(G-7750)**

Graywacke Inc .... G 419 884-7014
Mansfield **(G-8798)**

Millertech Energy Solutions .... F 855 629-5484
West Farmington **(G-14159)**

Toxco Inc .... E 740 653-6290
Lancaster **(G-8230)**

Xerion Advanced Battery Corp .... F 720 229-0697
Kettering **(G-8124)**

BATTERIES: Storage

Acculon Energy Inc .... E 614 259-7792
Columbus **(G-4669)**

Crown Battery Manufacturing Co .... G 330 425-3308
Fremont **(G-7101)**

Crown Battery Manufacturing Co .... B 419 334-7181
Fremont **(G-7100)**

Glx Power Systems Inc .... G 440 338-6526
Chagrin Falls **(G-2145)**

Micropower Group US Inc .... G 937 606-2793
Troy **(G-13241)**

Micropower LLC .... G 937 606-2793
Troy **(G-13242)**

Reliant Worth Corp .... G 440 232-1422
Bedford **(G-1055)**

BATTERIES: Wet

Glx Power Systems Inc .... G 440 338-6526
Chagrin Falls **(G-2145)**

Inventus Power (ohio) Inc .... F 614 351-2191
Dublin **(G-6312)**

BATTERY CASES: Plastic Or Plastics Combination

Rjf International Corporation .... A 330 668-2069
Fairlawn **(G-6809)**

BATTERY CHARGERS

Asg Division Jergens Inc .... E 888 486-6163
Cleveland **(G-3377)**

Brookwood Group Inc .... F 513 791-3030
Cincinnati **(G-2430)**

D C Systems Inc .... F 330 273-3030
Brunswick **(G-1587)**

Exide Technologies LLC .... G 614 863-3866
Gahanna **(G-7157)**

Noco Company .... D 216 464-8131
Glenwillow **(G-7286)**

TL Industries Inc .... C 419 666-8144
Perrysburg **(G-11272)**

BATTERY CHARGERS: Storage, Motor & Engine Generator Type

Brinkley Technology Group LLC .... F 330 830-2498
Massillon **(G-9175)**

One Three Energy Inc .... F 513 996-6973
Cincinnati **(G-2932)**

BEARINGS & PARTS Ball

Bearings Manufacturing Company .... F 440 846-5517
Strongsville **(G-12544)**

Jay Dee Service Corporation .... G 330 425-1546
Macedonia **(G-8699)**

Kaydon Corporation .... D 231 755-3741
Avon **(G-729)**

Miller Bearing Company Inc .... E 330 678-8844
Kent **(G-8054)**

Nn Inc .... E 440 647-4711
Wellington **(G-13897)**

Thyssnkrupp Rothe Erde USA Inc .... C 330 562-4000
Aurora **(G-689)**

Tsk America Co Ltd .... F 513 942-4002
West Chester **(G-14156)**

BEARINGS: Ball & Roller

Gt Technologies Inc .... E 419 782-8955
Defiance **(G-6109)**

Schaeffler Group USA Inc .... E 800 274-5001
Valley City **(G-13515)**

Schaeffler Group USA Inc .... E 330 202-6752
Wooster **(G-14679)**

Timken Company .... F 614 836-3337
Groveport **(G-7453)**

Timken Company .... A 234 262-3000
North Canton **(G-10673)**

Timken Newco I LLC .... G 234 262-3000
North Canton **(G-10674)**

BEARINGS: Railroad Car Journal

Rail Bearing Service LLC .... B 234 262-3000
North Canton **(G-10663)**

BEARINGS: Roller & Parts

HMS Industries LLC .... F 440 899-0001
Westlake **(G-14306)**

BEAUTY & BARBER SHOP EQPT

Aluminum Line Products Company .... D 440 835-8880
Westlake **(G-14285)**

Carroll Hills Industries .... G 330 627-5524
Carrollton **(G-2080)**

Clarity Retail Services LLC .... D 513 800-9369
West Chester **(G-13965)**

Clearsonic Manufacturing Inc .... G 828 772-9809
Akron **(G-103)**

Dayton Armor LLC .... G 937 723-8675
Dayton **(G-5720)**

Downing Enterprises Inc .... D 330 666-3888
Akron **(G-126)**

Duraflow Industries Inc .... G 440 965-5047
Wakeman **(G-13680)**

Excalibur Barber LLC .... F 330 729-9006
Boardman **(G-1371)**

Foundation Industries Inc .... E 330 564-1250
Akron **(G-152)**

GKN Driveline Bowl Green Inc .... E 419 373-7700
Bowling Green **(G-1421)**

Ideal Image Inc .... D 937 832-1660
Englewood **(G-6615)**

K K Tool Co .... E 937 325-1373
Springfield **(G-12333)**

Lincoln Manufacturing Inc .... F 330 878-7772
Strasburg **(G-12481)**

MPS Manufacturing Company LLC ...... G 330 343-1435
New Philadelphia **(G-10460)**

Pacific Manufacturing Ohio Inc .... G 513 860-3900
Fairfield **(G-6763)**

Premier Seals Mfg LLC .... G 330 861-1060
Akron **(G-265)**

Production Tl Co Cleveland Inc .... F 330 425-4466
Twinsburg **(G-13360)**

Quick Tech Business Forms Inc .... G 937 743-5952
Springboro **(G-12265)**

RB Sigma LLC .... D 440 290-0577
Mentor **(G-9607)**

Rowend Industries Inc .... G 419 333-8300
Fremont **(G-7131)**

T J Davies Company Inc .... G 440 248-5510
Mantua **(G-8876)**

Tango Products Inc .... G 440 353-2605
North Ridgeville **(G-10750)**

TLC Products Inc .... F 216 472-3030
Westlake **(G-14340)**

Vistech Mfg Solutions LLC .... F 513 860-1408
Fairfield **(G-6789)**

BEAUTY & BARBER SHOP EQPT & SPLYS WHOLESALERS

Beaute Asylum LLC .... F 419 377-9933
Toledo **(G-12894)**

Excalibur Barber LLC .... F 330 729-9006
Boardman **(G-1371)**

BEAUTY SALONS

James C Robinson .... G 513 969-7482
Cincinnati **(G-2760)**

BEDDING & BEDSPRINGS STORES

Ahmf Inc .... E 614 921-1223
Columbus **(G-4681)**

BEDDING, BEDSPREADS, BLANKETS & SHEETS

Fluvitex USA Inc .... C 614 610-1199
Groveport **(G-7433)**

Employee Codes: A=Over 500 employees, B=251-500
C=101-250, D=51-100, E=20-50, F=10-19, G=1-9

2025 Harris Ohio
Industrial Directory

1235

PRODUCT

BEDS: Institutional

Belmont Community Hospital................ E 740 671-1216
Bellaire *(G-1085)*

BEDSPREADS, COTTON

Sk Textile Inc... C 800 888-9112
Cincinnati *(G-3094)*

BEER & ALE WHOLESALERS

Wild Ohio Brewing Company.................. G 614 262-0000
Columbus *(G-5368)*

BEER, WINE & LIQUOR STORES: Beer, Packaged

Currier Richard & James....................... G 440 988-4132
Amherst *(G-445)*

Millersburg Ice Company....................... E 330 674-3016
Millersburg *(G-10000)*

BELLOWS

Alloy Precision Tech Inc........................ D 440 266-7700
Mentor *(G-9477)*

International Bellows............................. F 937 294-6261
Englewood *(G-6616)*

BELTING: Rubber

Fenner Dunlop (toledo) LLC .... F 419 531-5300
Toledo *(G-12961)*

Novex Operating Company LLC............ F 330 335-2371
Barberton *(G-826)*

BELTS & BELT PRDTS

Nationwide Belting Sls Svc LLC........... E 419 287-7092
Pemberville *(G-11177)*

BELTS: Conveyor, Made From Purchased Wire

Akron Belting & Supply Company.......... G 330 633-8212
Akron *(G-25)*

May Conveyor Inc................................ G 440 237-8012
North Royalton *(G-10772)*

BERYLLIUM

Materion Brush Inc............................... A 419 862-2745
Elmore *(G-6491)*

Materion Brush Inc............................... D 216 486-4200
Mayfield Heights *(G-9336)*

Materion Corporation............................ C 216 486-4200
Mayfield Heights *(G-9337)*

BEVERAGE BASES & SYRUPS

Hen of Woods LLC.............................. G 513 954-8871
Cincinnati *(G-2716)*

J M Smucker Company.......................... A 330 682-3000
Orrville *(G-10987)*

Mapledale Farm Inc.............................. F 440 286-3389
Chardon *(G-2214)*

Nu Pet Company.................................. E 330 682-3000
Orrville *(G-10998)*

BEVERAGE PRDTS: Brewers' Grain

Wedco LLC.. G 513 309-0781
Mount Orab *(G-10223)*

BEVERAGE PRDTS: Malt, Barley

Ohio Crafted Malt House LLC................ G 614 961-7805
New Albany *(G-10347)*

BEVERAGES, ALCOHOLIC: Ale

Wild Ohio Brewing Company.................. G 614 262-0000
Columbus *(G-5368)*

BEVERAGES, ALCOHOLIC: Applejack

Toledo Spirits Company LLC.................. F 419 704-3705
Toledo *(G-13158)*

BEVERAGES, ALCOHOLIC: Beer

Anheuser-Busch LLC............................ B 614 847-6213
Columbus *(G-4718)*

Artisan Ales LLC.................................. G 216 544-8703
Cleveland *(G-3369)*

Bar 25 LLC.. E 216 373-3700
Cleveland *(G-3404)*

Bar 25 LLC.. G 216 621-4000
Cleveland *(G-3403)*

Branch & Bone Artisan Ales LLC........... F 937 723-7608
Dayton *(G-5683)*

Brew Kettle Inc.................................... F 440 234-8788
Strongsville *(G-12546)*

Brewdog Brewing Company LLC............ F 614 908-3051
Canal Winchester *(G-1786)*

Bummin Beaver Brewery LLC................ G 440 543-9900
Chagrin Falls *(G-2156)*

Cincinnati Beverage Company............... E 513 904-8910
Cincinnati *(G-2470)*

Dayton Heidelberg Distrg Co................ C 440 989-1027
Lorain *(G-8554)*

District Brewing Company Inc............... E 614 224-3626
Columbus *(G-4886)*

Dvdbrew LLC....................................... F 513 677-2739
Loveland *(G-8624)*

Fifty West Brewing Company LLC.......... E 740 775-2337
Chillicothe *(G-2251)*

Great Lakes Brewing Co........................ C 216 771-4404
Cleveland *(G-3789)*

Lock 27 Brewing LLC........................... F 937 433-2739
Dayton *(G-5853)*

Mansfield Brew Works LLC.................... F 419 631-3153
Mansfield *(G-8818)*

Maumee Bay Brewing Company............. E 419 243-1253
Toledo *(G-13047)*

Miiler Brewing Company........................ E 513 896-9200
Trenton *(G-13193)*

Molson Coors Bev Co USA LLC............. C 513 896-9200
Trenton *(G-13194)*

Phunkenship - Platform Beer Co............ F 216 417-7743
Cleveland *(G-4161)*

Samuel Adams Brewery Company Ltd.. D 513 412-3200
Cincinnati *(G-3062)*

Snyder Intl Brewing Group LLC............. E 216 619-7424
Cleveland *(G-4310)*

South Side Drive Thru.......................... G 937 295-2927
Fort Loramie *(G-6957)*

Willoughby Brewing Company LLC........ G 440 975-0202
Willoughby *(G-14550)*

BEVERAGES, ALCOHOLIC: Beer & Ale

Brew Kettle Strongsville LLC................ G 440 915-7074
Medina *(G-9386)*

Brewpub Restaurant Corporation........... F 614 228-2537
Columbus *(G-4774)*

Columbus Kombucha Company LLC..... G 614 262-0000
Columbus *(G-4828)*

Dswdwk LLC.. G 513 853-5021
Cincinnati *(G-2564)*

Great Lakes Brewing Co........................ E 216 771-4404
Cleveland *(G-3788)*

Great Lakes Brewing Co........................ E 216 771-4404
Strongsville *(G-12561)*

Lock 15 Brewing Company LLC............. E 234 900-8277
Akron *(G-208)*

Nine Giant Brewing LLC........................ G 510 220-5104
Cincinnati *(G-2910)*

Noble Beast Brewing LLC...................... G 570 809-6405
Cleveland *(G-4079)*

Rhinegeist Holding Company Inc............ G 513 381-1367
Cincinnati *(G-3042)*

Rocky River Brewing Co........................ G 440 895-2739
Rocky River *(G-11638)*

Royal Docks Brewing Co LLC................ D 330 353-9103
Massillon *(G-9239)*

BEVERAGES, ALCOHOLIC: Bourbon Whiskey

Brain Brew Ventures 30 Inc................... F 513 310-6374
Newtown *(G-10583)*

Luxco Inc... G 216 671-6300
Cleveland *(G-3972)*

BEVERAGES, ALCOHOLIC: Distilled Liquors

Karrikin Spirits Company LLC................ F 513 561-5000
Cincinnati *(G-2784)*

March First Manufacturing LLC.............. G 513 266-3076
Cincinnati *(G-2845)*

Paramount Distillers Inc........................ B 216 671-6300
Cleveland *(G-4134)*

Veriano Fine Foods Spirits Ltd............... F 614 745-7705
New Albany *(G-10354)*

Watershed Distillery LLC....................... E 614 357-1936
Columbus *(G-5357)*

Western Reserve Distillers LLC.............. G 330 780-9599
Lakewood *(G-8173)*

BEVERAGES, ALCOHOLIC: Near Beer

Georgetown Vineyards Inc..................... E 740 435-3222
Cambridge *(G-1744)*

Green Room Brewing LLC...................... G 614 421-2337
Columbus *(G-4966)*

Platform Beers LLC.............................. F 440 539-3245
Cleveland *(G-4173)*

BEVERAGES, ALCOHOLIC: Wines

Amani Vines LLC.................................. F 440 335-5432
Cleveland *(G-3338)*

Barrel Run Crssing Wnery Vnyrd........... G 330 325-1075
Rootstown *(G-11647)*

Breitenbach Wine Cellars Inc................. G 330 343-3603
Dover *(G-6232)*

Buckeye Lake Winery........................... F 614 439-7576
Thornville *(G-12765)*

Cask 307 LLC....................................... F 440 307-9586
Madison *(G-8724)*

Chalet Debonne Vineyards Inc............... F 440 466-3485
Madison *(G-8725)*

Delaware City Vineyard......................... F 740 362-6383
Delaware *(G-6141)*

E & J Gallo Winery............................... E 513 381-4050
Cincinnati *(G-2568)*

Ferrante Wine Farm Inc......................... F 440 466-8466
Geneva *(G-7237)*

Gillig Custom Winery Inc....................... G 419 202-6057
Findlay *(G-6871)*

Glenn Ravens Winery........................... G 740 545-1000
West Lafayette *(G-14170)*

Hillside Winery.................................... G 419 456-3434
Gilboa *(G-7261)*

J E Nicolozakes Co.............................. G 740 310-1606
Cambridge *(G-1745)*

John Christ Winery Inc.......................... G 440 933-9672
Avon Lake *(G-761)*

Kelleys Island Winery Inc...................... G 419 746-2678
Kelleys Island *(G-8008)*

Klingshirn Winery Inc .... G 440 933-6666
Avon Lake *(G-762)*

Laurentia Winery .... F 440 296-9170
Madison *(G-8731)*

Lonz Winery LLC .... E 419 625-5474
Sandusky *(G-11851)*

Losantiville Winery LLC .... G 513 918-3015
Cincinnati *(G-2829)*

Mastropietro Winery Inc .... G 330 547-2151
Berlin Center *(G-1201)*

Meiers Wine Cellars Inc .... E 513 891-2900
Cincinnati *(G-2861)*

Old Mason Winery Inc .... G 937 698-1122
West Milton *(G-14184)*

Olde Schlhuse Vnyrd Winery LLC .... F 937 472-9463
Eaton *(G-6461)*

Paramount Distillers Inc .... B 216 671-6300
Cleveland *(G-4134)*

Perennial Vineyards LLC .... F 330 832-3677
Navarre *(G-10310)*

Quinami LLC .... G 419 797-4445
Port Clinton *(G-11450)*

R & T Estate LLC .... F 216 862-0822
Cleveland *(G-4219)*

Sandra Weddington .... F 740 417-4286
Delaware *(G-6172)*

Sapphire Creek Wnery Grdns LLC .... F 440 543-7777
Chagrin Falls *(G-2182)*

Sarahs Vineyard Inc .... G 330 929-8057
Cuyahoga Falls *(G-5571)*

Shawne Springs Winery .... G 740 623-0744
Coshocton *(G-5472)*

Tramonte & Sons LLC .... F 513 770-5501
Lebanon *(G-8290)*

Twenty One Barrels Ltd .... G 937 467-4498
Bradford *(G-1453)*

Twisted Vine Family Vinyrd LLC .... G 740 256-1923
Patriot *(G-11152)*

Ugly Bunny Winery LLC .... F 330 988-9057
Loudonville *(G-8596)*

Vineyards At Pine Lake Inc .... E 330 549-0195
Columbiana *(G-4632)*

Vinoklet Winery Inc .... E 513 385-9309
Cincinnati *(G-3206)*

Vintage Wine Distributor Inc .... F 513 443-4300
West Chester *(G-14090)*

Vpl LLC .... F 330 549-0195
Columbiana *(G-1631)*

Wine Mill .... G 234 571-2594
Peninsula *(G-11187)*

Winery At Wilcox Inc .... G 937 526-3232
Versailles *(G-13606)*

Winery At Wolf Creek .... F 330 666-9285
Barberton *(G-841)*

Wyandotte Winery LLC .... F 614 357-7522
Columbus *(G-5376)*

BEVERAGES, NONALCOHOLIC: Bottled & canned soft drinks

Abbott Laboratories .... A 614 624-3191
Columbus *(G-4660)*

Akron Coca-Cola Bottling Co .... A 330 784-2653
Akron *(G-27)*

Belton Foods LLC .... E 937 890-7768
Dayton *(G-5676)*

Borden Dairy Co Cincinnati LLC .... E 513 948-8811
Cleveland *(G-3428)*

Ccbcc Operations LLC .... D 304 203-8647
Lockbourne *(G-8487)*

Central Coca-Cola Btlg Co Inc .... E 330 875-1487
Akron *(G-95)*

Central Coca-Cola Btlg Co Inc .... E 740 474-2180
Circleville *(G-3250)*

Central Coca-Cola Btlg Co Inc .... E 440 324-3335
Elyria *(G-6511)*

Central Coca-Cola Btlg Co Inc .... C 614 863-7200
Lockbourne *(G-8488)*

Central Coca-Cola Btlg Co Inc .... E 419 522-2653
Mansfield *(G-8773)*

Central Coca-Cola Btlg Co Inc .... C 419 476-6622
Toledo *(G-12913)*

Central Coca-Cola Btlg Co Inc .... C 330 425-4401
Twinsburg *(G-13285)*

Central Coca-Cola Btlg Co Inc .... E 440 269-1433
Willoughby *(G-14438)*

Central Coca-Cola Btlg Co Inc .... E 330 783-1982
Youngstown *(G-14833)*

Central Coca-Cola Btlg Co Inc .... E 740 452-3608
Zanesville *(G-15006)*

Cleveland Coca-Cola Btlg Inc .... C 216 690-2653
Bedford Heights *(G-1073)*

Coca-Cola Company .... E 614 491-6305
Columbus *(G-4815)*

Coca-Cola Consolidated Inc .... A 513 527-6600
Cincinnati *(G-2503)*

Coca-Cola Consolidated Inc .... A 937 878-5000
Dayton *(G-5704)*

Coca-Cola Consolidated Inc .... G 419 422-3743
Lima *(G-8395)*

Coca-Cola Consolidated Inc .... C 740 353-3133
Portsmouth *(G-11464)*

Currier Richard & James .... G 440 988-4132
Amherst *(G-445)*

Fbg Bottling Group LLC .... E 614 580-7063
Columbus *(G-4920)*

Gordon Brothers Btlg Group Inc .... G 330 337-8754
Salem *(G-11782)*

Hornell Brewing Co Inc .... G 516 812-0384
Cincinnati *(G-2732)*

Meiers Wine Cellars Inc .... E 513 891-2900
Cincinnati *(G-2861)*

P-Americas LLC .... C 419 227-3541
Lima *(G-8436)*

Pepsi-Cola Metro Btlg Co Inc .... C 330 425-8236
Twinsburg *(G-13353)*

Smucker International Inc .... F 330 682-3000
Orrville *(G-11010)*

Smucker Natural Foods Inc .... A 330 682-3000
Orrville *(G-11012)*

BEVERAGES, NONALCOHOLIC: Carbonated

Central Investment LLC .... F 513 563-4700
Cincinnati *(G-2450)*

Consolidated Bottling Company .... C 419 227-3541
Lima *(G-8396)*

G & J Pepsi-Cola Bottlers Inc .... E 740 593-3366
Athens *(G-640)*

G & J Pepsi-Cola Bottlers Inc .... E 740 774-2148
Chillicothe *(G-2252)*

G & J Pepsi-Cola Bottlers Inc .... E 866 647-2734
Columbus *(G-4942)*

G & J Pepsi-Cola Bottlers Inc .... A 614 253-8771
Columbus *(G-4943)*

G & J Pepsi-Cola Bottlers Inc .... B 740 354-9191
Franklin Furnace *(G-7058)*

G & J Pepsi-Cola Bottlers Inc .... D 513 896-3700
Hamilton *(G-7492)*

G & J Pepsi-Cola Bottlers Inc .... E 740 354-9191
Zanesville *(G-15017)*

G & J Pepsi-Cola Bottlers Inc .... F 513 785-6060
Cincinnati *(G-2644)*

P-Americas LLC .... E 614 253-8771
Columbus *(G-5167)*

P-Americas LLC .... F 440 323-5524
Elyria *(G-6575)*

P-Americas LLC .... E 330 837-4224
Massillon *(G-9230)*

P-Americas LLC .... E 740 266-6121
Steubenville *(G-12409)*

P-Americas LLC .... E 330 746-7652
Youngstown *(G-14910)*

Pepsi-Cola Metro Btlg Co Inc .... F 614 261-8193
Columbus *(G-5185)*

Pepsi-Cola Metro Btlg Co Inc .... F 440 323-5524
Elyria *(G-6577)*

Pepsi-Cola Metro Btlg Co Inc .... G 937 328-6750
Springfield *(G-12361)*

Pepsi-Cola Metro Btlg Co Inc .... D 419 534-2186
Toledo *(G-13093)*

Pepsi-Cola Metro Btlg Co Inc .... G 330 963-5300
Twinsburg *(G-13354)*

BEVERAGES, NONALCOHOLIC: Carbonated, Canned & Bottled, Etc

Gehm & Sons Limited .... G 330 724-8423
Akron *(G-158)*

BEVERAGES, NONALCOHOLIC: Flavoring extracts & syrups, nec

Abbott Laboratories .... A 614 624-3191
Columbus *(G-4660)*

Agrana Fruit Us Inc .... C 937 693-3821
Anna *(G-459)*

Agrana Fruit Us Inc .... E 440 546-1199
Brecksville *(G-1456)*

Cargill Incorporated .... E 937 236-1971
Dayton *(G-5693)*

Flavor Systems Intl Inc .... E 513 870-4900
Cincinnati *(G-2626)*

Givaudan Flavors Corporation .... G 513 948-8000
Cincinnati *(G-2674)*

Givaudan Flavors Corporation .... C 513 948-8000
Cincinnati *(G-2673)*

Givaudan Fragrances Corp .... D 513 948-3428
Cincinnati *(G-2675)*

Joseph Adams Corp .... F 330 225-9125
Valley City *(G-13500)*

Mane Inc .... D 513 248-9876
Cincinnati *(G-2843)*

Mane Inc .... D 513 240-9070
Lebanon *(G-8275)*

Phillips Syrup LLC .... F 440 835-8001
Westlake *(G-14323)*

Primary Pdts Ingrdnts Amrcas L .... D 937 236-5906
Dayton *(G-5955)*

BEVERAGES, NONALCOHOLIC: Fruit Drnks, Under 100% Juice, Can

Beverages Holdings LLC .... A 513 483-3300
Blue Ash *(G-1252)*

Country Pure Foods Inc .... C 330 753-2293
Akron *(G-108)*

Life Support Development Ltd .... G 614 221-1765
Columbus *(G-5067)*

Ohio Beverage Systems Inc .... F 216 475-3900
Cleveland *(G-4112)*

Ohio Pure Foods Inc .... D 330 753-2293
Akron *(G-254)*

BEVERAGES, NONALCOHOLIC: Soft Drinks, Canned & Bottled, Etc

American Bottling Company .... E 330 733-3830
Akron *(G-55)*

American Bottling Company.................. D 513 381-4891
Cincinnati *(G-2356)*

American Bottling Company.................. D 513 242-5151
Cincinnati *(G-2357)*

American Bottling Company.................. D 614 237-4201
Columbus *(G-4692)*

American Bottling Company.................. C 614 237-4201
Columbus *(G-4693)*

American Bottling Company.................. C 937 236-0333
Dayton *(G-5650)*

American Bottling Company.................. D 419 229-7777
Lima *(G-8387)*

American Bottling Company.................. E 740 423-9230
Little Hocking *(G-8486)*

American Bottling Company.................. E 740 922-5253
Midvale *(G-9906)*

American Bottling Company.................. D 740 377-4371
South Point *(G-12222)*

American Bottling Company.................. D 419 535-0777
Toledo *(G-12873)*

Cincinnati Marlins Inc...................... G 513 761-3320
Cincinnati *(G-2480)*

Dr Pepper Bottlers Associates............. G 330 746-7651
Youngstown *(G-14849)*

Dr Pepper Snapple Group.................. G 419 223-0072
Lima *(G-8402)*

Dr Pepper/Seven Up Inc.................... F 513 875-2466
Fayetteville *(G-6827)*

Dr Pepper/Seven Up Inc.................... F 419 229-7777
Lima *(G-8403)*

Gem Beverages Inc......................... F 740 384-2411
Wellston *(G-13906)*

Keurig Dr Pepper Inc....................... D 614 237-4201
Columbus *(G-5051)*

National Beverage Corp.................... F 614 491-5415
Obetz *(G-10925)*

Pepsi-Cola Metro Btlg Co Inc.............. D 937 461-4664
Dayton *(G-5936)*

Shasta Beverages Inc...................... D 614 491-5415
Obetz *(G-10926)*

BEVERAGES, NONALCOHOLIC: Tea, Iced, Bottled & Canned, Etc

Ohio Eagle Distributing LLC............... E 513 539-8483
West Chester *(G-14037)*

BEVERAGES, WINE & DISTILLED ALCOHOLIC, WHOLESALE: Liquor

Blue Collar M LLC.......................... F 216 209-5666
Solon *(G-12086)*

Veriano Fine Foods Spirits Ltd............. F 614 745-7705
New Albany *(G-10354)*

BEVERAGES, WINE & DISTILLED ALCOHOLIC, WHOLESALE: Wine

Old Firehouse Winery Inc.................. E 440 466-9300
Geneva *(G-7244)*

Paramount Distillers Inc................... B 216 671-6300
Cleveland *(G-4134)*

Sandra Weddington........................ F 740 417-4286
Delaware *(G-6172)*

Watershed Distillery LLC.................. E 614 357-1936
Columbus *(G-5357)*

Wedco LLC................................. G 513 309-0781
Mount Orab *(G-10223)*

BICYCLES, PARTS & ACCESS

Safe Haven Brands LLC.................... F 937 550-9407
Springboro *(G-12267)*

BILLING & BOOKKEEPING SVCS

Michele Caldwell.......................... G 937 505-7744
Dayton *(G-5880)*

Steward Edge Bus Solutions............... F 614 826-5305
Columbus *(G-5293)*

BINDING SVC: Books & Manuals

A-A Blueprint Co Inc....................... E 330 794-8803
Akron *(G-10)*

AAA Laminating and Bindery Inc.......... G 513 860-2680
Fairfield *(G-6705)*

Activities Press Inc........................ E 440 953-1200
Mentor *(G-9469)*

AGS Custom Graphics Inc................. D 330 963-7770
Macedonia *(G-8676)*

Allen Graphics Inc......................... G 440 349-4100
Solon *(G-12075)*

American Printing & Lithog Co............. F 513 867-0602
Hamilton *(G-7463)*

Anderson Graphics Inc..................... E 330 745-2165
Barberton *(G-793)*

Andrin Enterprises Inc..................... F 937 276-7794
Moraine *(G-10146)*

Baesman Group Inc........................ D 614 771-2300
Hilliard *(G-7674)*

Barnhart Printing Corp..................... G 330 456-2279
Canton *(G-1837)*

Bindery & Spc Pressworks Inc............. D 614 873-4623
Plain City *(G-11398)*

Bindusa................................... B 513 247-3000
Blue Ash *(G-1253)*

Black River Group Inc...................... E 419 524-6699
Mansfield *(G-8765)*

Bookfactory LLC........................... E 937 226-7100
Dayton *(G-5682)*

Century Graphics Inc...................... G 614 895-7698
Westerville *(G-14206)*

Classic Laminations Inc................... E 440 735-1333
Oakwood Village *(G-10904)*

Clints Printing Inc......................... G 937 426-2771
Dayton *(G-5703)*

Consolidated Graphics Group Inc.......... C 216 881-9191
Cleveland *(G-3559)*

Copley Ohio Newspapers Inc.............. C 330 364-5577
New Philadelphia *(G-10439)*

COS Blueprint Inc......................... E 330 376-0022
Akron *(G-107)*

Cox Printing Company...................... G 937 382-2312
Wilmington *(G-14576)*

Crossbridge Mktg & Media Inc............. G 330 682-5066
Orrville *(G-10979)*

Davis Printing Company.................... E 330 745-3113
Barberton *(G-803)*

Dayton Bindery Service Inc................ E 937 235-3111
Dayton *(G-5722)*

Dayton Legal Blank Inc.................... G 937 435-4405
Dayton *(G-5729)*

Earl D Arnold Printing Company........... E 513 533-6900
Cincinnati *(G-2574)*

Eugene Stewart........................... G 937 898-1117
Dayton *(G-5770)*

Folks Creative Printers Inc................ G 740 383-6326
Marion *(G-8970)*

Franklin Printing Company................. F 740 452-6375
Zanesville *(G-15016)*

Gli Holdings Inc........................... D 216 651-1500
Stow *(G-12433)*

Golden Graphics Ltd....................... F 419 673-6260
Kenton *(G-8099)*

Greg Blume................................ G 740 574-2308
Wheelersburg *(G-14353)*

Harris Paper Crafts Inc.................... F 614 299-2141
Columbus *(G-4971)*

Hecks Direct Mail Prtg Svc Inc............ F 419 697-3505
Toledo *(G-12990)*

Hf Group LLC.............................. C 440 729-9411
Newbury *(G-10553)*

HP Industries Inc.......................... E 419 478-0695
Toledo *(G-12997)*

Innmark Communications LLC............. D 937 454-5555
Miamisburg *(G-9701)*

Jack Walker Printing Co.................... F 440 352-4222
Mentor *(G-9540)*

Kehl-Kolor Inc............................. E 419 281-3107
Ashland *(G-545)*

Kenwel Printers Inc........................ E 614 261-1011
Columbus *(G-5050)*

Kevin K Tidd.............................. G 419 885-5603
Sylvania *(G-12714)*

Keystone Press Inc........................ G 419 243-7326
Toledo *(G-13018)*

Laipplys Prtg Mktg Sltions Inc............ G 740 387-9282
Marion *(G-8975)*

Lam Pro Inc............................... F 216 426-0661
Cleveland *(G-3938)*

Lee Corporation........................... G 513 771-3602
Cincinnati *(G-2817)*

Legal News Publishing Co.................. E 216 696-3322
Cleveland *(G-3949)*

Liturgical Publications Inc................. D 216 325-6825
Cleveland *(G-3964)*

Mmp Printing Inc.......................... F 513 381-0990
Cincinnati *(G-2883)*

Multi-Craft Litho Inc...................... E 859 581-2754
Blue Ash *(G-1312)*

Network Printing & Graphics.............. F 614 230-2084
Columbus *(G-5124)*

North End Press Incorporated............. G 740 653-6514
Lancaster *(G-8215)*

Ohio Laminating & Binding Inc............ G 614 771-4868
Hilliard *(G-7691)*

Old Trail Printing Company................ C 614 443-4852
Columbus *(G-5159)*

Onetouchpoint East Corp.................. D 513 421-1600
Cincinnati *(G-2933)*

Orange Blossom Press Inc................. G 216 781-8655
Willoughby *(G-14502)*

Painesville Publishing Inc................. G 440 354-4142
Austinburg *(G-701)*

Penguin Enterprises Inc................... E 440 899-5112
Westlake *(G-14322)*

Prime Printing Inc......................... E 937 438-3707
Dayton *(G-5956)*

Print-Digital Incorporated................. G 330 686-5945
Stow *(G-12451)*

Printed Image............................. F 614 221-1412
Columbus *(G-5207)*

Prodigy Print Inc.......................... F
Dayton *(G-5960)*

Promatch Solutions LLC................... F 877 299-0185
Moraine *(G-10188)*

Quick Tab II Inc........................... D 419 448-6622
Tiffin *(G-12796)*

Repro Acquisition Company LLC........... G 216 738-3800
Cleveland *(G-4235)*

Robin Enterprises Company................ C 614 891-0250
Westerville *(G-14274)*

RT Industries Inc.......................... G 937 335-5784
Troy *(G-13251)*

Ryans Newark Leader Ex Prtg Co.......... F 740 522-2149
Newark *(G-10532)*

Standard Printing Co of Canton............ D 330 453-8247
Canton *(G-2012)*

Star Printing Company Inc.................... E 330 376-0514
Akron *(G-317)*

Suburban Press Incorporated................ F 216 961-0766
Cleveland *(G-4340)*

The D B Hess Company........................ E 330 678-5868
Kent *(G-8089)*

Tj Metzgers Inc.................................... D 419 861-8611
Toledo *(G-13143)*

Tl Krieg Offset LLC.............................. E 513 542-1522
Cincinnati *(G-3158)*

Traxium LLC.. E 330 572-8200
Stow *(G-12466)*

Watkins Printing Company.................... E 614 297-8270
Columbus *(G-5358)*

West-Camp Press Inc........................... D 614 882-2378
Westerville *(G-14281)*

Wfsr Holdings LLC............................... A 877 735-4966
Dayton *(G-6081)*

BINDING SVC: Pamphlets

Macke Brothers Inc.............................. G 513 771-7500
Cincinnati *(G-2838)*

BINDINGS: Bias, Made From Purchased Materials

National Bias Fabric Co......................... G 216 361-0530
Cleveland *(G-4058)*

BIOLOGICAL PRDTS: Exc Diagnostic

ABI Inc... F 800 847-8950
Cleveland *(G-3288)*

Algix LLC.. G 706 207-3425
Stow *(G-12417)*

Bio-Blood Components Inc.................... D 614 294-3183
Columbus *(G-4754)*

EMD Millipore Corporation.................... C 513 631-0445
Norwood *(G-10868)*

Ferro Corporation................................ D 216 577-7144
Bedford *(G-1032)*

Forge Biologics Inc.............................. G 216 401-7611
Grove City *(G-7387)*

Jsh International LLC............................ G 330 734-0251
Akron *(G-190)*

PEC Biofuels LLC................................ G 419 542-8210
Hicksville *(G-7651)*

Powder Alloy Corporation..................... E 513 984-4016
Loveland *(G-8646)*

Protein Technologies Ltd...................... G 513 769-0840
Cincinnati *(G-3011)*

Revvity Health Sciences Inc................. D 330 825-4525
Akron *(G-283)*

BIOLOGICAL PRDTS: Vaccines & Immunizing

Decaria Brothers Inc............................ G 330 385-0825
East Liverpool *(G-6391)*

BIOLOGICAL PRDTS: Veterinary

No Rinse Laboratories LLC................... G 937 746-7357
Springboro *(G-12261)*

BLACKBOARDS & CHALKBOARDS

1914 Mi Inc... D 800 426-4244
New Philadelphia *(G-10429)*

GMI Companies Inc.............................. F 937 981-0244
Greenfield *(G-7327)*

GMI Companies Inc.............................. F 513 932-3445
Lebanon *(G-8263)*

GMI Companies Inc.............................. C 513 932-3445
Lebanon *(G-8262)*

Tri-State Supply Co Inc........................ F 614 272-6767
Columbus *(G-5331)*

BLADES: Knife

Advetech Inc....................................... E 330 533-2227
Canfield *(G-1801)*

American Quicksilver Company............. G 513 871-4517
Cincinnati *(G-2362)*

Busse Knife Co.................................... G 419 923-6471
Wauseon *(G-13846)*

BLADES: Saw, Hand Or Power

M K Morse Company............................ B 330 453-8187
Canton *(G-1935)*

Peerless Saw Company........................ E 614 836-5790
Groveport *(G-7448)*

BLANKBOOKS & LOOSELEAF BINDERS

Deluxe Corporation.............................. D 330 342-1500
Streetsboro *(G-12497)*

Dupli-Systems Inc............................... C 440 234-9415
Strongsville *(G-12555)*

Graphic Imaginations............................ G 216 781-4880
Cleveland *(G-3786)*

Quick Tech Graphics Inc...................... F 937 743-5952
Springboro *(G-12266)*

BLANKBOOKS: Albums, Record

Live Off Loyalty Inc............................. G 513 413-2401
Cincinnati *(G-2825)*

BLANKBOOKS: Passbooks, Bank, Etc

William Exline Inc................................ G 216 941-0800
Cleveland *(G-4506)*

BLANKETS & BLANKETING, COTTON

R J Manray Inc.................................... G 330 559-6716
Canfield *(G-1814)*

BLAST FURNACE & RELATED PRDTS

Custom Blast & Coat Inc...................... G 419 225-6024
Lima *(G-8399)*

Rmi Titanium Company LLC.................. B 330 471-1844
Canton *(G-1997)*

BLASTING SVC: Sand, Metal Parts

American Indus Maintenance................ C 937 261-3400
Dayton *(G-5653)*

Badboy Blasters Incorporated............... F 330 454-2699
Canton *(G-1835)*

Boville Indus Coatings Inc.................... E 330 669-8558
Smithville *(G-12064)*

Derrick Company Inc........................... E 513 321-8122
Cincinnati *(G-2546)*

Industrial Mill Maintenance................... F 330 746-1155
Youngstown *(G-14876)*

Newbury Sndblst & Pntg Inc................ G 440 564-7204
Newbury *(G-10557)*

Newsome & Work Metalizing Co........... G 330 376-7144
Akron *(G-246)*

Pki Inc... F 513 832-8749
Cincinnati *(G-2967)*

Witt Enterprises Inc............................. G 440 992-8333
Ashtabula *(G-622)*

BLINDS & SHADES: Vertical

11 92 Holdings LLC.............................. F 216 920-7790
Chagrin Falls *(G-2134)*

BLINDS : Window

Designer Window Treatments Inc.......... G 419 822-4967
Delta *(G-6204)*

Golden Drapery Supply Inc................... E 216 351-3283
Cleveland *(G-3779)*

Mag Resources LLC............................. F 330 294-0494
Barberton *(G-818)*

BLOCKS & BRICKS: Concrete

Charles Svec Inc................................. E 216 662-5200
Maple Heights *(G-8879)*

Midwest Specialties Inc........................ D 800 837-2503
Wapakoneta *(G-13725)*

Oberfields LLC.................................... F 614 252-0955
Columbus *(G-5137)*

R W Sidley Incorporated....................... E 440 564-2221
Newbury *(G-10561)*

RE Connors Construction Ltd............... G 740 644-0261
Thornville *(G-12767)*

S & S Aggregates Inc........................... F 740 453-0721
Zanesville *(G-15046)*

Stocker Concrete Company.................. F 740 254-4626
Gnadenhutten *(G-7293)*

The Ideal Builders Supply & Fuel Co Inc F 216 741-1600
Cleveland *(G-4386)*

Triple A Builders Inc............................ G 216 249-0327
Cleveland *(G-4428)*

William Dauch Concrete Company......... F 419 668-4458
Norwalk *(G-10863)*

BLOCKS: Landscape Or Retaining Wall, Concrete

Benchmark Land Management LLC....... G 513 310-7850
West Chester *(G-13949)*

Green Impressions LLC......................... D 440 240-8508
Sheffield Village *(G-11958)*

Green Vision Materials Inc.................... F 440 564-5500
Newbury *(G-10552)*

Meridienne International Inc.................. G 330 274-8317
Aurora *(G-679)*

Ready Field Solutions LLC.................... E 330 562-0550
Streetsboro *(G-12520)*

BLOCKS: Paving

LA Rose Paving Co.............................. G 440 632-0330
Middlefield *(G-9806)*

BLOCKS: Paving, Concrete

E C S Corp.. G 440 323-1707
Elyria *(G-6524)*

BLOCKS: Standard, Concrete Or Cinder

American Concrete Products Inc............ G 937 224-1433
Dayton *(G-5652)*

Beazer East Inc................................... F 740 474-3169
Circleville *(G-3248)*

Cantelli Block and Brick Inc................. E 419 433-0102
Sandusky *(G-11826)*

Cement Products Inc............................ E 419 524-4342
Mansfield *(G-8772)*

Dearth Resources Inc........................... G 937 663-4171
Springfield *(G-12299)*

Dearth Resources Inc........................... G 937 325-0651
Springfield *(G-12298)*

Hazelbaker Industries Ltd..................... G
Columbus *(G-4973)*

Koltcz Concrete Block Co..................... E 440 232-3630
Bedford *(G-1042)*

National Lime and Stone Co.................. F 614 497-0083
Lockbourne *(G-8491)*

Osborne Inc.. E 440 942-7000
Mentor *(G-9578)*

Portsmouth Block Inc........................... F 740 353-4113
Portsmouth *(G-11474)*

PRODUCT

Prairie Builders Supply Inc...................... G 419 332-7546
Fremont (G-7127)

Quality Block & Supply Inc...................... E 330 364-4411
Mount Eaton (G-10208)

Reading Rock Incorporated................... D 513 874-2345
Cincinnati (G-3034)

Snyder Concrete Products Inc............... G 937 224-1433
Dayton (G-6011)

Snyder Concrete Products Inc............... G 937 339-7577
Troy (G-13257)

Snyder Concrete Products Inc............... E 937 885-5176
Moraine (G-10192)

St Henry Tile Co Inc............................... G 937 548-1101
Greenville (G-7355)

St Henry Tile Co Inc............................... E 419 678-4841
Saint Henry (G-11724)

Stiger Pre Cast Inc................................ G 740 482-2313
Nevada (G-10324)

Stocker Sand & Gravel Co...................... F 740 254-4635
Gnadenhutten (G-7294)

Tri-County Block and Brick Inc............... E 419 826-7060
Swanton (G-12696)

Trumbull Cement Products Co................ G 330 372-4342
Warren (G-13802)

Tyjen Inc.. G 740 797-4064
The Plains (G-12760)

BLOOD BANK

Bio-Blood Components Inc..................... D 614 294-3183
Columbus (G-4754)

BLOWERS & FANS

Air Enterprises Inc................................ A 330 794-9770
Akron (G-22)

Air-Rite Inc... E 216 228-8200
Cleveland (G-3316)

American Manufacturing & Eqp............. G 513 829-2248
Fairfield (G-6711)

Atmos360 Inc.. E 513 772-4777
West Chester (G-14105)

Beckett Air Incorporated....................... D 440 327-9999
North Ridgeville (G-10725)

Bry-Air Inc.. E 740 965-2974
Sunbury (G-12662)

Famous Industries Inc............................ F 740 685-2592
Byesville (G-1711)

Flex Technologies Inc............................ D 330 359-5415
Mount Eaton (G-10207)

FM AF LLC.. C 866 771-6266
Fairfield (G-6736)

Howden North America Inc.................... C 513 874-2400
Fairfield (G-6742)

Illinois Tool Works Inc............................ E 262 248-8277
Bryan (G-1645)

Kirk Williams Company Inc..................... D 614 875-9023
Grove City (G-7393)

Langdon Inc.. E 513 733-5955
Cincinnati (G-2811)

Mestek Inc... F 419 288-2703
Bradner (G-1454)

Midwestern Industries Inc...................... D 330 837-4203
Massillon (G-9223)

Nupro Company..................................... E 440 951-9729
Willoughby (G-14498)

Ohio Blow Pipe Company....................... E 216 681-7379
Cleveland (G-4113)

OSI Environmental LLC........................... E 440 237-4600
North Royalton (G-10779)

Plas-Tanks Industries Inc....................... E 513 942-3800
Hamilton (G-7517)

Qualtek Electronics Corp........................ C 440 951-3300
Mentor (G-9603)

Quickdraft Inc....................................... E 330 477-4574
Canton (G-1987)

Rmt Acquisition Inc................................ E 513 241-5566
Cincinnati (G-3050)

Selas Heat Technology Co LLC................ E 800 523-6500
Streetsboro (G-12523)

Starr Fabricating Inc.............................. D 330 394-9891
Vienna (G-13618)

Stelter and Brinck Inc............................ E 513 367-9300
Harrison (G-7569)

Tisch Environmental Inc......................... E 513 467-9000
Cleves (G-4551)

Tosoh America Inc.................................. B 614 539-8622
Grove City (G-7417)

Americraft Mfg Co Inc............................ F 513 489-1047
Cincinnati (G-2363)

Buckeye BOP LLC................................... F 740 498-9898
Newcomerstown (G-10569)

Hartzell Fan Inc..................................... C 937 773-7411
Piqua (G-11350)

Tlt-Babcock Inc...................................... D 330 867-8540
Akron (G-339)

Verantis Corporation.............................. E 440 243-0700
Middleburg Heights (G-9778)

Vortec and Paxton Products.................... F 513 891-7474
Blue Ash (G-1347)

BLUEPRINTING SVCS

Northeast Blueprint and Sup Co............. G 216 261-7500
Cleveland (G-4092)

Profile Digital Printing LLC..................... E 937 866-4241
Dayton (G-5965)

Queen City Reprographics...................... C 513 326-2300
Cincinnati (G-3024)

Robert Becker Impressions Inc............... F 419 385-5303
Toledo (G-13116)

BOAT & BARGE COMPONENTS: Metal, Prefabricated

PC Campana Inc..................................... E 800 321-0151
Lorain (G-8572)

BOAT BUILDING & REPAIR

Checkmate Marine Inc............................ G 419 562-3881
Bucyrus (G-1675)

Don Wartko Construction Inc.................. D 330 673-5252
Kent (G-8026)

Mariners Landing Inc.............................. G 513 941-3625
Cincinnati (G-2846)

Racelite Southcoast Inc.......................... F 216 581-4600
Maple Heights (G-8891)

Tugz International LLC............................ F 216 621-4854
Cleveland (G-4432)

W of Ohio Inc.. G 614 873-4664
Plain City (G-11426)

BOAT BUILDING & REPAIRING: Motorized

Nauticus Inc.. G 440 746-1290
Brecksville (G-1478)

BOAT DEALERS

Dynamic Plastics Inc.............................. G 937 437-7261
New Paris (G-10426)

Mariners Landing Inc.............................. G 513 941-3625
Cincinnati (G-2846)

BOAT DEALERS: Marine Splys & Eqpt

Hydromotive Engineering Co.................. G 330 425-4266
Twinsburg (G-13317)

Sailors Tailor Inc................................... F 937 862-7781
Spring Valley (G-12243)

BOAT REPAIR SVCS

Superior Marine Ways Inc...................... C 740 894-6224
Proctorville (G-11499)

BODIES: Truck & Bus

Abutilon Company Inc............................ F 419 536-6123
Toledo (G-12862)

Ace Truck Equipment Co......................... E 740 453-0551
Zanesville (G-14981)

Airstream Inc... B 937 596-6111
Jackson Center (G-7958)

Atc Lighting & Plastics Inc..................... C 440 466-7670
Andover (G-456)

Bores Manufacturing Inc........................ G 419 465-2606
Monroeville (G-10118)

Cascade Corporation.............................. E 937 327-0300
Springfield (G-12287)

Field Gymmy Inc.................................... G 419 538-6511
Glandorf (G-7283)

Hendrickson International Corp.............. D 740 929-5600
Hebron (G-7617)

Joseph Industries Inc............................. D 330 528-0091
Streetsboro (G-12507)

King Kutter II Inc.................................... E 740 446-0351
Gallipolis (G-7207)

Kuka Tledo Prdction Oprtons LL............. C 419 727-5500
Toledo (G-13024)

Martin Sheet Metal Inc........................... E 216 377-8200
Cleveland (G-3993)

Meritor Inc.. C 740 348-3270
Granville (G-7317)

Paccar Inc... D 740 774-5111
Chillicothe (G-2269)

Radar Love Co.. G 419 951-4750
Findlay (G-6912)

Skymark Refuelers LLC........................... D 419 957-1709
Findlay (G-6919)

Tarpstop LLC... F 419 873-7867
Perrysburg (G-11264)

Trucks & Parts of Tampa LLC.................. E 937 437-0377
New Paris (G-10427)

Vitatoe Industries Inc............................. D 740 773-2425
Chillicothe (G-2287)

Wallace Forge Company.......................... D 330 488-1203
Canton (G-2045)

Youngstown-Kenworth Inc...................... F 330 534-9761
Hubbard (G-7819)

BODY PARTS: Automobile, Stamped Metal

Antique Auto Sheet Metal Inc................. F 937 833-4422
Brookville (G-1562)

Aptiv Services Us LLC............................. A 330 373-3568
Warren (G-13739)

Artiflex Manufacturing Inc...................... B 330 262-2015
Wooster (G-14623)

Buyers Products Company...................... B 440 974-8888
Mentor (G-9497)

Clevelnd-Clffs Tling Stmping H............... F 519 969-4632
West Chester (G-13967)

Clevelnd-Clffs Toling Stamping.............. C 216 694-5700
West Chester (G-13968)

Decoma Systems Integration Gro........... D 419 324-3387
Toledo (G-12940)

General Motors LLC................................ A 216 265-5000
Cleveland (G-3767)

Matsu Ohio Inc...................................... C 419 298-2394
Edgerton (G-6467)

Murotech Ohio Corporation.................... C 419 394-6529
Saint Marys (G-11743)

Trellborg Sling Prfiles US Inc.................. C 330 995-9725
Aurora (G-690)

Valco Industries LLC.............................. E 937 399-7400
Springfield *(G-12391)*

Vehtek Systems Inc............................... A 419 373-8741
Bowling Green *(G-1445)*

BOILER & HEATING REPAIR SVCS

Air-Rite Inc... E 216 228-8200
Cleveland *(G-3316)*

Babcock & Wilcox Company.................. A 330 753-4511
Akron *(G-67)*

Nbw Inc... E 216 377-1700
Cleveland *(G-4063)*

Weather King Heating & AC.................. G 330 908-0281
Northfield *(G-10799)*

BOILERS: Low-Pressure Heating, Steam Or Hot Water

Weather King Heating & AC.................. G 330 908-0281
Northfield *(G-10799)*

BOLTS: Metal

Airfasco Inc.. E 330 430-6190
Canton *(G-1824)*

Auto Bolt Company............................... D 216 881-3913
Cleveland *(G-3388)*

Bowes Manufacturing Inc...................... F 216 378-2110
Solon *(G-12087)*

Cold Headed Fas Assemblies Inc.......... F 330 833-0800
Massillon *(G-9180)*

Consolidated Metal Pdts Inc................. D 513 251-2624
Cincinnati *(G-2511)*

Curtiss-Wright Flow Ctrl Corp............... D 216 267-3200
Cleveland *(G-3583)*

Gray America Corp................................ E 937 293-9313
Moraine *(G-10166)*

Jacodar Inc... F 330 832-9557
Massillon *(G-9208)*

Jacodar Fsa LLC................................... E 330 454-1832
Canton *(G-1920)*

Keystone Bolt & Nut Company.............. D 216 524-9626
Cleveland *(G-3916)*

Matdan Corporation.............................. E 513 794-0500
Blue Ash *(G-1303)*

Mid-West Fabricating Co....................... E 740 277-7021
Lancaster *(G-8211)*

Nova Machine Products Inc................... C 216 267-3200
Middleburg Heights *(G-9775)*

Qrp Inc... D 910 371-0700
Berea *(G-1186)*

Rs Manufacturing Inc............................ G 440 946-8002
Mentor *(G-9611)*

Stelfast LLC.. E 440 879-0077
Strongsville *(G-12606)*

BOOK STORES

Bookfactory LLC................................... E 937 226-7100
Dayton *(G-5682)*

BOOK STORES: Children's

Auguste Moone Enterprises Ltd............ E 216 333-9248
Cleveland Heights *(G-4527)*

BOOKS, WHOLESALE

CSS Publishing Company...................... F 419 227-1818
Lima *(G-8398)*

Hubbard Company................................ E 419 784-4455
Defiance *(G-6111)*

Zaner-Bloser Inc.................................. C 614 486-0221
Columbus *(G-5380)*

BOTTLED GAS DEALERS: Propane

Brightstar Propane & Fuels................... G 614 891-8395
Westerville *(G-14204)*

Jomac Ltd.. E 330 627-7727
Carrollton *(G-2087)*

Ngo Development Corporation............... G 740 622-9560
Coshocton *(G-5464)*

Welders Supply Inc.............................. E 216 267-4470
Brookpark *(G-1560)*

BOTTLES: Plastic

Al Root Company.................................. E 330 725-6677
Medina *(G-9372)*

Al Root Company.................................. C 330 723-4359
Medina *(G-9371)*

Alpha Packaging Holdings Inc............... B 216 252-5595
Cleveland *(G-3332)*

Eco-Groupe Inc.................................... F 937 898-2603
Dayton *(G-5759)*

Encon Inc... C 937 898-2603
Dayton *(G-5765)*

Graham Packaging Pet Tech Inc............ G 419 334-4197
Fremont *(G-7116)*

Graham Packg Plastic Pdts Inc............. C 419 421-8037
Findlay *(G-6873)*

Novatex North America Inc................... D 419 282-4264
Ashland *(G-555)*

Phoenix Technologies Intl LLC.............. E 419 353-7738
Bowling Green *(G-1434)*

Plastipak Packaging Inc........................ C 740 928-4435
Hebron *(G-7630)*

Plastipak Packaging Inc........................ B 937 596-6142
Jackson Center *(G-7966)*

Rexam PLC... F 330 893-2451
Millersburg *(G-10006)*

Ring Container Tech LLC....................... F 937 492-0961
Sidney *(G-12044)*

Silly Brandz Global LLC........................ D 419 697-8324
Toledo *(G-13132)*

Southeastern Container Inc................... D 419 352-6300
Bowling Green *(G-1440)*

BOWLING CENTERS

Greater Cincinnati Bowl Assn............... E 513 761-7387
Cincinnati *(G-2689)*

BOWLING EQPT & SPLYS

Done-Rite Bowling Service Co.............. E 440 232-3280
Bedford *(G-1028)*

H & S Distributing Inc.......................... G 800 336-7784
North Ridgeville *(G-10733)*

BOXES & CRATES: Rectangular, Wood

Cassis Packaging Co............................ F 937 223-8868
Dayton *(G-5696)*

Cima Inc... G 513 382-8976
Hamilton *(G-7476)*

Custom Built Crates Inc........................ E
Milford *(G-9932)*

J & L Wood Products Inc...................... E 937 667-4064
Tipp City *(G-12829)*

Schaefer Box & Pallet Co..................... E 513 738-2500
Hamilton *(G-7523)*

Silvesco Inc... F 740 373-6661
Marietta *(G-8945)*

Terry Lumber and Supply Co................ F 330 659-6800
Peninsula *(G-11184)*

BOXES & SHOOK: Nailed Wood

Caravan Packaging Inc......................... G 440 243-4100
Cleveland *(G-3469)*

Cassady Woodworks Inc....................... F 937 256-7948
Dayton *(G-5605)*

Clark Rm Inc... F 419 425-9889
Findlay *(G-6853)*

Hann Manufacturing Inc........................ E 740 962-3752
Mcconnelsville *(G-9362)*

J & L Wood Products Inc...................... E 937 667-4064
Tipp City *(G-12829)*

Kennedy Group Incorporated................ D 440 951-7660
Willoughby *(G-14477)*

Lima Pallet Company Inc...................... E 419 229-5736
Lima *(G-8425)*

Quadco Rehabilitation Ctr Inc............... C 419 682-1011
Stryker *(G-12626)*

Schaefer Box & Pallet Co..................... E 513 738-2500
Hamilton *(G-7523)*

BOXES: Corrugated

A-Kobak Container Company Inc........... F 330 225-7791
Hinckley *(G-7730)*

Action Specialty Packaging LLC............ G
West Chester *(G-14096)*

Adapt-A-Pak Inc................................... E 937 845-0386
Fairborn *(G-6684)*

Akers Packaging Service Inc................ C 513 422-6312
Middletown *(G-9839)*

Akers Packaging Solutions Inc.............. D 513 422-6312
Middletown *(G-9840)*

American Corrugated Products Inc........ C 614 870-2000
Columbus *(G-4696)*

American Made Crrgted Pckg Inc.......... G 937 981-2111
Greenfield *(G-7325)*

Archbold Container Corp...................... C 800 446-2520
Archbold *(G-487)*

B & B Box Company Inc........................ F 419 872-5600
Perrysburg *(G-11204)*

BBH Holdings Inc.................................. E 513 870-3000
Lebanon *(G-8246)*

Billerud Americas Corporation.............. D 901 369-4105
West Chester *(G-13952)*

Brimar Packaging Inc........................... E 440 934-3080
Avon *(G-717)*

Bryan Packaging Inc............................. F 419 636-2600
Bryan *(G-1633)*

Buckeye Boxes Inc............................... D 614 274-8484
Columbus *(G-4783)*

Buckeye Corrugated Inc....................... D 330 264-6336
Wooster *(G-14628)*

Buckeye Corrugated Inc....................... G 330 576-0590
Fairlawn *(G-6797)*

Cambridge Packaging Inc..................... E 740 432-3351
Cambridge *(G-1738)*

Cameron Packaging Inc........................ G 419 222-9404
Lima *(G-8394)*

Chillicothe Packaging Corp................... E 740 773-5800
Chillicothe *(G-2247)*

Clecorr Inc... E 216 961-5500
Cleveland *(G-3505)*

Corpad Company Inc............................ D 419 522-7818
Mansfield *(G-8777)*

Creative Packaging LLC........................ E 740 452-8497
Zanesville *(G-15009)*

Family Packaging Inc............................ G 937 325-4106
Springfield *(G-12310)*

Gatton Packaging Inc........................... G 419 886-2577
Bellville *(G-1138)*

Georgia-Pacific LLC.............................. C 740 477-3347
Circleville *(G-3260)*

Georgia-Pacific Pcpi Inc....................... D 513 932-9855
Lebanon *(G-8260)*

Graphic Paper Products Corp................ D 937 325-5503
Springfield *(G-12315)*

Green Bay Packaging Inc...................... C 419 332-5593
Fremont *(G-7117)*

Employee Codes: A=Over 500 employees, B=251-500
C=101-250, D=51-100, E=20-50, F=10-19, G=1-9

2025 Harris Ohio
Industrial Directory

1241

PRODUCT

Green Bay Packaging Inc............................ D 513 489-8700
  Lebanon (G-8266)

Greif Inc.. E 740 657-6500
  Delaware (G-6150)

Greif Inc.. E 740 549-6000
  Delaware (G-6149)

International Paper Company.................... C 740 369-7691
  Delaware (G-6158)

International Paper Company.................... C 740 522-3123
  Newark (G-10512)

International Paper Company.................... D 330 626-7300
  Streetsboro (G-12505)

International Paper Company.................... D 330 264-1322
  Wooster (G-14651)

Jamestown Cont Cleveland Inc................. B 216 831-3700
  Cleveland (G-3882)

Jeff Lori Jed Holdings Inc........................ E 513 423-0319
  Middletown (G-9869)

Jet Container Company............................ D 614 444-2133
  Columbus (G-5038)

Larsen Packaging Products Inc................ F 937 644-5511
  Marysville (G-9034)

Lewisburg Container Company................. C 937 962-2681
  Lewisburg (G-8360)

Marshalltown Packaging Inc.................... G 641 753-5272
  Columbus (G-5084)

McKinley Packaging Company.................. F 216 663-3344
  Maple Heights (G-8887)

Menasha Packaging Company LLC......... E 614 202-4084
  West Jefferson (G-14165)

Metro Containers Inc............................... D 513 351-6800
  Cincinnati (G-2872)

Miami Vly Packg Solutions Inc................. F 937 224-1800
  Dayton (G-5879)

Midwest Box Company............................ E 216 281-9021
  Cleveland (G-4035)

Mount Vernon Packaging Inc.................... F 740 397-3221
  Mount Vernon (G-10253)

Nebc Inc.. D 440 992-5500
  Ashtabula (G-610)

Omer J Smith Inc.................................... E 513 921-4717
  West Chester (G-14038)

Packaging Corporation America................ C 419 282-5809
  Ashland (G-559)

Packaging Corporation America................ E 330 644-9542
  Coventry Township (G-5487)

Packaging Corporation America................ D 513 424-3542
  Middletown (G-9883)

Packaging Corporation America................ C 740 344-1126
  Newark (G-10528)

Piqua Paper Box Company....................... E 937 773-0313
  Piqua (G-11378)

Pjs Corrugated Inc.................................. F 419 644-3383
  Swanton (G-12690)

Pratt (jet Corr) Inc.................................. A 937 390-7100
  Springfield (G-12364)

Pratt Industries Inc................................. F 513 262-6253
  Dayton (G-5943)

Pro-Pak Industries Inc............................ D 419 729-0751
  Maumee (G-9313)

Protective Packg Solutions LLC................ E 513 769-5777
  Cincinnati (G-3010)

Raymar Holdings Corporation.................. E 614 497-3033
  Columbus (G-5225)

Riverview Packaging Inc.......................... E 937 743-9530
  Franklin (G-7045)

Safeway Packaging Inc........................... E 419 629-3200
  New Bremen (G-10366)

Schwarz Partners Packaging LLC.......... D 740 387-3700
  Marion (G-8996)

Schwarz Partners Packaging LLC........ F 317 290-1140
  Sidney (G-12050)

Skybox Packaging LLC............................ C 419 525-7209
  Mansfield (G-8853)

Sobel Corrugated Containers Inc........... C 216 475-2100
  Cleveland (G-4311)

Square One Solutions LLC....................... E 419 425-5445
  Findlay (G-6922)

Summit Container Corporation.................. F 719 481-8400
  West Chester (G-14078)

Tavens Container Inc............................... D 216 883-3333
  Bedford (G-1060)

Tecumseh Packg Solutions Inc................ F 419 238-1122
  Van Wert (G-13545)

Temple Inland.. G 513 425-0830
  Middletown (G-9897)

The Mead Corporation............................. B 937 495-6323
  Dayton (G-6049)

Trey Corrugated Inc................................ D 513 942-4800
  West Chester (G-14084)

Tri-State Paper Inc.................................. F 937 885-3365
  Dayton (G-6061)

Unipac Inc.. E 740 929-2000
  Hebron (G-7643)

Valley Containers Inc.............................. F 330 544-2244
  Mineral Ridge (G-10031)

Value Added Packaging Inc..................... F 937 832-9595
  Englewood (G-6628)

Viking Paper Company............................ E 419 729-4951
  Toledo (G-13174)

Wellman Container Corporation................ E 513 860-3040
  Cincinnati (G-3219)

Westrock Converting LLC........................ E 513 860-0225
  West Chester (G-14092)

Westrock Rkt LLC................................... E 330 296-5155
  Ravenna (G-11550)

Westrock Rkt LLC................................... C 513 860-5546
  West Chester (G-14093)

Weyerhaeuser Company.......................... G 740 335-4480
  Wshngtn Ct Hs (G-14751)

BOXES: Filing, Paperboard Made From Purchased Materials

A To Z Paper Box Company..................... G 330 325-8722
  Rootstown (G-11646)

BOXES: Packing & Shipping, Metal

Karyall-Telday Inc................................... G 216 281-4063
  Cleveland (G-3906)

Yarder Manufacturing Company............. E 419 476-3933
  Toledo (G-13182)

BOXES: Paperboard, Folding

American Corrugated Products Inc........ C 614 870-2000
  Columbus (G-4696)

Boxit Corporation................................... E 216 416-9475
  Cleveland (G-3430)

Boxit Corporation................................... F 216 631-6900
  Cleveland (G-3431)

Brimar Packaging Inc.............................. E 440 934-3080
  Avon (G-717)

Cardpak Incorporated............................. C 440 542-3100
  Solon (G-12091)

Chilcote Company.................................. C 216 781-6000
  Cleveland (G-3495)

Gpi Ohio LLC... F 605 332-6721
  Groveport (G-7437)

Graphic Packaging Intl LLC.................... C 513 424-4200
  Middletown (G-9863)

Graphic Packaging Intl LLC.................... C 440 248-4370
  Solon (G-12118)

Jefferson Smurfit Corporation................. G 440 248-4370
  Solon (G-12129)

Oak Hills Carton Co................................ E 513 948-4200
  Cincinnati (G-2920)

R R Donnelley & Sons Company.............. E 513 870-4040
  West Chester (G-14062)

Roys Mueller Box Co.............................. G 216 464-1191
  Cleveland (G-4260)

Saica Pack US LLC................................. E 513 399-5602
  Hamilton (G-7522)

Sandusky Packaging Corporation.......... E 419 626-8520
  Sandusky (G-11870)

Shelby Company.................................... E 440 871-9901
  Westlake (G-14334)

The Apex Paper Box Company............... G 216 631-4000
  Cleveland (G-4377)

Unipac Inc.. E 740 929-2000
  Hebron (G-7643)

BOXES: Paperboard, Set-Up

Boxit Corporation................................... E 216 416-9475
  Cleveland (G-3430)

Boxit Corporation................................... F 216 631-6900
  Cleveland (G-3431)

Brimar Packaging Inc.............................. E 440 934-3080
  Avon (G-717)

Chilcote Company.................................. C 216 781-6000
  Cleveland (G-3495)

Clarke-Boxit Corporation......................... E 716 487-1950
  Cleveland (G-3502)

Graphic Paper Products Corp.................. D 937 325-5503
  Springfield (G-12315)

Sandusky Packaging Corporation.......... E 419 626-8520
  Sandusky (G-11870)

The Apex Paper Box Company............... G 216 631-4000
  Cleveland (G-4377)

BOXES: Wooden

Aslan Worldwide..................................... F 513 671-0671
  West Chester (G-13943)

Buckeye Diamond Logistics Inc............. C 937 462-8361
  South Charleston (G-12213)

Built-Rite Box & Crate Inc....................... E 330 263-0936
  Wooster (G-14630)

Cedar Craft Products Inc......................... G 614 759-1600
  Blacklick (G-1222)

Damar Products Inc................................ F 937 492-9023
  Sidney (G-12010)

Forest City Companies Inc....................... E 216 586-5279
  Cleveland (G-3735)

Lalac One LLC.. E 216 432-4422
  Cleveland (G-3937)

Ohio Box & Crate Inc.............................. G 440 526-3133
  Burton (G-1703)

Sterling Industries Inc............................ F 419 523-3788
  Ottawa (G-11047)

Thomas J Weaver Inc.............................. F 740 622-2040
  Coshocton (G-5474)

Traveling Recycle WD Pdts Inc.............. G 419 968-2649
  Middle Point (G-9764)

BRAKES & BRAKE PARTS

Advics Manufacturing Ohio Inc.............. A 513 932-7878
  Lebanon (G-8242)

Bendix Coml Vhcl Systems LLC............ B 440 329-9000
  Avon (G-716)

Brake Parts Inc China LLC...................... G 216 589-0198
  Cleveland (G-3433)

Buckeye Brake Mfg Inc........................... F 740 782-1379
  Morristown (G-10200)

Cooper-Standard Automotive Inc.......... D 740 342-3523
  New Lexington (G-10401)

Friction Products Co............................... B 330 725-4941
  Medina (G-9406)

Harco Manufacturing Group LLC.......... C 937 528-5000
   Moraine *(G-10168)*

Harco Manufacturing Group LLC.......... C 937 528-5000
   Moraine *(G-10167)*

Hitachi Astemo Americas Inc.................... C 419 425-1259
   Findlay *(G-6880)*

Knott Brake Company.............................. E 800 566-8887
   Lodi *(G-8503)*

Lucas Sumitomo Brakes Inc.................... F 513 934-0024
   Lebanon *(G-8274)*

Qualitor Subsidiary H Inc......................... E 419 562-7987
   Bucyrus *(G-1686)*

Vehicle Systems Inc................................. G 330 854-0535
   Massillon *(G-9251)*

Veoneer Brake Systems LLC.................... C 419 425-6725
   Findlay *(G-6931)*

Whirlaway Corporation.............................. C 440 647-4711
   Wellington *(G-13904)*

BRAKES: Bicycle, Friction Clutch & Other

Cmbf Products Inc................................... C 855 403-9083
   Medina *(G-9388)*

BRAKES: Metal Forming

Eaton Corporation.................................... C 216 281-2211
   Cleveland *(G-3653)*

Ebog Legacy Inc...................................... D 330 239-4933
   Sharon Center *(G-11940)*

Pioneer Solutions LLC.............................. E 216 383-3400
   Euclid *(G-6669)*

BRASS & BRONZE PRDTS: Die-casted

American De Rosa Lamparts LLC.......... D
   Cuyahoga Falls *(G-5522)*

Hamilton Brass & Alum Castings.......... G
   Hamilton *(G-7500)*

Model Pattern & Foundry Co.................... G 513 542-2322
   Cincinnati *(G-2884)*

The Kindt-Collins Company LLC............. D 216 252-4122
   Cleveland *(G-4387)*

BRASS FOUNDRY, NEC

Brost Foundry Company............................ E 419 522-1133
   Mansfield *(G-8768)*

Bunting Bearings LLC.............................. D 419 866-7000
   Holland *(G-7747)*

Maass Midwest Mfg Inc............................ G 419 894-6424
   Arcadia *(G-482)*

Non-Ferrous Casting Company............. G 937 228-1162
   Dayton *(G-5909)*

BRAZING SVCS

Alexy Metals Ltd....................................... F 216 410-8661
   Willoughby *(G-14416)*

Braze Solutions LLC................................ F 440 349-5100
   Solon *(G-12089)*

Paulo Products Company.......................... E 440 942-0153
   Willoughby *(G-14505)*

Prince & Izant LLC.................................. E 216 362-7000
   Cleveland *(G-4196)*

BRAZING: Metal

American Metal Treating Co..................... E 216 431-4492
   Cleveland *(G-3346)*

Fbf Limited.. E 513 541-6300
   Cincinnati *(G-2615)*

HI Tecmetal Group Inc............................. E 216 881-8100
   Wickliffe *(G-14378)*

Kando of Cincinnati Inc............................ E 513 459-7782
   Lebanon *(G-8271)*

Ohio Flame Hardening Company............. E 513 336-6160
   Cincinnati *(G-2923)*

Surface Enhancement Tech LLC............. F 513 561-1520
   Cincinnati *(G-3131)*

Zion Industries Inc.................................. E 330 483-4650
   Valley City *(G-13523)*

BRICK, STONE & RELATED PRDTS WHOLESALERS

Collinwood Shale Brick Sup Co............. E 216 587-2700
   Cleveland *(G-3545)*

Exhibit Concepts Inc................................ D 937 890-7000
   Vandalia *(G-13557)*

Grafton Ready Mix Concret Inc............. C 440 926-2911
   Grafton *(G-7303)*

Kuhlman Corporation.............................. E 419 897-6000
   Maumee *(G-9303)*

Lancaster W Side Coal Co Inc................. F 740 862-4713
   Lancaster *(G-8207)*

Modern Builders Supply Inc..................... E 419 526-0002
   Mansfield *(G-8831)*

Modern Builders Supply Inc..................... C 419 241-3961
   Toledo *(G-13058)*

R W Sidley Incorporated.......................... E 330 793-7374
   Youngstown *(G-14923)*

Sidwell Materials Inc................................ C 740 849-2422
   Zanesville *(G-15050)*

Stamm Contracting Company Inc.......... F 330 274-8230
   Mantua *(G-8875)*

Trumbull Cement Products Co.................. G 330 372-4342
   Warren *(G-13802)*

Wallseye Concrete Corp........................... F 419 483-2738
   Castalia *(G-2096)*

Warren Concrete and Supply Co............. G 330 393-1581
   Warren *(G-13810)*

William Dauch Concrete Company.......... F 419 668-4458
   Norwalk *(G-10863)*

BRICKS & BLOCKS: Structural

Belden Brick Company LLC..................... D 330 456-0031
   Sugarcreek *(G-12632)*

Belden Brick Company LLC..................... D 330 265-2030
   Sugarcreek *(G-12633)*

Glen-Gery Corporation.............................. E 419 468-5002
   Iberia *(G-7883)*

The Belden Brick Company LLC............. E 330 456-0031
   Canton *(G-2024)*

BRICKS : Ceramic Glazed, Clay

Nutro Inc... E 440 572-3800
   Strongsville *(G-12581)*

BRICKS : Flooring, Clay

Kona Blackbird Inc.................................. E 440 285-3189
   Chardon *(G-2211)*

BRICKS : Paving, Clay

Whitacre Greer Company.......................... E 330 823-1610
   Alliance *(G-416)*

BRICKS: Clay

Bowerston Shale Company..................... C 740 763-3921
   Newark *(G-10494)*

Bowerston Shale Company..................... E 740 269-2921
   Bowerston *(G-1399)*

Glen-Gery Corporation.............................. D 419 845-3321
   Caledonia *(G-1731)*

BRIDGE COMPONENTS: Bridge sections, prefabricated, highway

DS Techstar Inc....................................... G 419 424-0888
   Findlay *(G-6861)*

BROACHING MACHINES

Ohio Broach & Machine Company.......... E 440 946-1040
   Willoughby *(G-14499)*

BROADCASTING & COMMS EQPT: Antennas, Transmitting/Comms

Central USA Wireless LLC....................... G 513 469-1500
   Cincinnati *(G-2453)*

Electro-Magwave Inc................................ G 216 453-1160
   Twinsburg *(G-13298)*

Tencom Ltd... G 419 865-5877
   Holland *(G-7787)*

Watts Antenna Company.......................... G 740 797-9380
   The Plains *(G-12761)*

BROADCASTING & COMMS EQPT: Rcvr-Transmitter Unt, Transceiver

Control Industries Inc.............................. G 937 653-7694
   Findlay *(G-6855)*

BROADCASTING & COMMUNICATIONS EQPT: Light Comms Eqpt

LSI Industries Inc.................................... C 513 793-3200
   Cincinnati *(G-2830)*

BROKERS' SVCS

Shamrock Companies Inc......................... D 440 899-9510
   Westlake *(G-14333)*

BROKERS: Food

Comber Holdings Inc................................ E 216 961-8600
   Cleveland *(G-3549)*

BROKERS: Log & Lumber

Dale R Adkins.. G 740 682-7312
   Oak Hill *(G-10887)*

Hochstetler Milling LLC............................ E 419 368-0004
   Loudonville *(G-8591)*

Southwood Pallet LLC.............................. D 330 682-3747
   Orrville *(G-11014)*

BROKERS: Printing

Depot Direct Inc....................................... E 419 661-1233
   Perrysburg *(G-11215)*

Scrip-Safe Security Products.................. E 513 697-7789
   Loveland *(G-8652)*

BRONZE FOUNDRY, NEC

Advance Bronzehubco Div....................... E 304 232-4414
   Lodi *(G-8497)*

Foundry Artists Inc.................................. G 216 391-9030
   Cleveland *(G-3739)*

Meierjohan-Wengler Inc............................ E 513 771-6074
   Cincinnati *(G-2860)*

BRONZE ROLLING & DRAWING

Jj Seville LLC.. E 330 769-2071
   Seville *(G-11919)*

BROOMS

Delaware Paint Company Ltd.................. F 740 368-9981
   Plain City *(G-11403)*

BROOMS & BRUSHES

Deco Tools Inc.. E 419 476-9321
   Toledo *(G-12939)*

Designetics Inc....................................... D 419 866-0700
   Holland *(G-7755)*

PRODUCT

Fimm USA Inc.............................F 614 568-4874
Lancaster *(G-8202)*

Mill Rose Laboratories Inc.................E 440 974-6730
Mentor *(G-9565)*

Stephen M Trudick............................E 440 834-1891
Burton *(G-1704)*

Unique Packaging & Printing..............F 440 785-6730
Mentor *(G-9646)*

Wooster Brush Company....................B 330 264-4440
Wooster *(G-14699)*

BROOMS & BRUSHES: Household Or Indl

Brushes Inc.....................................G 216 267-8084
Cleveland *(G-3446)*

Malish Corporation...........................D 440 951-5356
Mentor *(G-9558)*

Mill-Rose Company...........................C 440 255-9171
Mentor *(G-9566)*

Precision Brush Co............................F 440 542-9600
Solon *(G-12169)*

Spiral Brushes Inc............................E 330 686-2861
Stow *(G-12461)*

Tod Thin Brushes Inc........................F 440 576-6859
Jefferson *(G-7986)*

Trent Manufacturing Company............G 216 391-1551
Mentor *(G-9644)*

United Rotary Brush Inc.....................E 937 644-3515
Plain City *(G-11423)*

BROOMS & BRUSHES: Paint & Varnish

The Wooster Brush Company...............C 330 264-4440
Wooster *(G-14691)*

Wooster Brush Company....................G 440 322-8081
Elyria *(G-6603)*

BUCKETS: Plastic

Graham Packaging Pet Tech Inc..........G 513 398-5000
Mason *(G-9105)*

Impact Products LLC..........................C 419 841-2891
Toledo *(G-13001)*

BUILDING & OFFICE CLEANING SVCS

High-TEC Industrial Services..............D 937 667-1772
Tipp City *(G-12827)*

Image By J & K LLC...........................F 888 667-6929
Maumee *(G-9297)*

BUILDING & STRUCTURAL WOOD MEMBERS

Carter-Jones Lumber Company............G 330 674-9060
Millersburg *(G-9975)*

Holmes Lumber & Bldg Ctr Inc............E 330 479-8314
Canton *(G-1912)*

Holmes Lumber & Bldg Ctr Inc............C 330 674-9060
Millersburg *(G-9989)*

Laminate Technologies Inc.................D 800 231-2523
Tiffin *(G-12786)*

Socar of Ohio Inc..............................D 419 596-3100
Continental *(G-5423)*

BUILDING CLEANING & MAINTENANCE SVCS

All Pack Services LLC........................G 614 935-0964
Grove City *(G-7370)*

Contract Lumber Inc..........................F 614 751-1109
Columbus *(G-4844)*

Green Impressions LLC.......................D 440 240-8508
Sheffield Village *(G-11958)*

Obersons Nurs & Landscapes LLC........E 513 687-7379
Hamilton *(G-7514)*

Omnipresence Cleaning LLC................F 937 250-4749
Dayton *(G-5927)*

Phase II Enterprises Inc.....................G 330 484-2113
Canton *(G-1975)*

Richland Newhope Inds Inc.................C 419 774-4400
Mansfield *(G-8848)*

BUILDING COMPONENTS: Structural Steel

Applied Engneered Surfaces Inc...........F 440 366-0440
Elyria *(G-6497)*

Boardman Steel Inc............................D 330 758-0951
Columbiana *(G-4606)*

Fabx LLC...F 614 565-5835
Columbus *(G-4918)*

Frederick Steel Company LLC..............D 513 821-6400
Cincinnati *(G-2641)*

GL Nause Co Inc...............................E 513 722-9500
Loveland *(G-8626)*

J A McMahon Incorporated.................A 330 652-2588
Niles *(G-10593)*

JJ&pl Services-Consulting LLC.............G 330 923-5783
Cuyahoga Falls *(G-5552)*

Judo Steel Company Inc.....................F
Dayton *(G-5833)*

Kirwan Industries Inc.........................G 513 333-0766
Cincinnati *(G-2798)*

Lake Building Products Inc..................E 216 486-1500
Cleveland *(G-3936)*

Louis Arthur Steel Company................G 440 997-5545
Geneva *(G-7241)*

M & M Fabrication Inc........................F 740 779-3071
Chillicothe *(G-2263)*

Mad River Steel Ltd...........................G 937 845-4046
New Carlisle *(G-10375)*

Mc Elwain Industries Inc....................F 419 532-3126
Ottawa *(G-11038)*

Mound Technologies Inc.....................E 937 748-2937
Springboro *(G-12260)*

Niles Building Products Company.........F 330 544-0880
Niles *(G-10595)*

Nova Structural Steel Inc....................E 216 938-7476
Cleveland *(G-4100)*

R L Waller Construction Inc.................G 740 772-6185
Chillicothe *(G-2278)*

Rol- Fab Inc.....................................E 216 662-2500
Cleveland *(G-4249)*

Sirius Steel Services Inc.....................F 937 797-3975
Columbus *(G-5273)*

Steelcon LLC....................................E 330 457-4003
Rogers *(G-11643)*

Thomas Steel Inc..............................E 419 483-7540
Bellevue *(G-1135)*

Turn-Key Industrial Svcs LLC..............D 614 274-1128
Grove City *(G-7420)*

Unique Fabrications Inc......................F 419 355-1700
Fremont *(G-7141)*

Universal Fabg Cnstr Svcs Inc.............F 614 274-1128
Columbus *(G-5338)*

Waterford Tank Fabrication Ltd............D 740 984-4100
Beverly *(G-1211)*

Wm Lang & Sons Company..................F 513 541-3304
Cincinnati *(G-3229)*

BUILDING MAINTENANCE SVCS, EXC REPAIRS

Lima Sheet Metal Mch & Mfg Inc..........F 419 229-1161
Lima *(G-8426)*

BUILDING PRDTS & MATERIALS DEALERS

Adams Brothers Inc...........................G 740 819-0323
Zanesville *(G-14983)*

Building Concepts Inc........................F 419 298-2371
Edgerton *(G-6464)*

Carter-Jones Lumber Company............G 330 674-9060
Millersburg *(G-9975)*

Consumeracq Inc..............................E 440 277-9305
Lorain *(G-8552)*

Consumers Builders Supply Co............G 440 277-9306
Lorain *(G-8553)*

Contract Lumber Inc..........................F 614 751-1109
Columbus *(G-4844)*

Counter Concepts Inc.........................F 330 848-4848
Wadsworth *(G-13632)*

Dearth Resources Inc.........................G 937 325-0651
Springfield *(G-12298)*

Dowel Yoder & Molding.......................G 330 231-2962
Fredericksburg *(G-7063)*

E P Gerber & Sons Inc........................D 330 857-2021
Kidron *(G-8126)*

Great Lakes Window Inc......................A 419 666-5555
Walbridge *(G-13684)*

Higgins Construction & Supply Co Inc...F 937 364-2331
Hillsboro *(G-7717)*

Holmes Lumber & Bldg Ctr Inc............E 330 479-8314
Canton *(G-1912)*

Holmes Lumber & Bldg Ctr Inc............C 330 674-9060
Millersburg *(G-9989)*

Holmes Panel LLC.............................G 330 897-5040
Baltic *(G-779)*

Judy Mills Company Inc......................E 513 271-4241
Cincinnati *(G-2775)*

Khempco Bldg Sup Co Ltd Partnr.........D 740 549-0465
Delaware *(G-6159)*

Lancaster W Side Coal Co Inc..............F 740 862-4713
Lancaster *(G-8207)*

Lang Stone Company Inc.....................E 614 235-4099
Columbus *(G-5064)*

M B K Inc..F 330 889-3451
Bristolville *(G-1498)*

Menard Inc......................................C 513 583-1444
Loveland *(G-8642)*

North Star Building Pdts LLC...............G 216 431-1000
Cleveland *(G-4090)*

Osborne Inc.....................................E 440 942-7000
Mentor *(G-9578)*

Portsmouth Block Inc.........................F 740 353-4113
Portsmouth *(G-11474)*

Stamm Contracting Company Inc.........F 330 274-8230
Mantua *(G-8875)*

Stiber Fabricating Inc........................F 216 771-7210
Cleveland *(G-4332)*

T C Redi Mix Youngstown Inc...............E 330 755-2143
Youngstown *(G-14942)*

Terry Lumber and Supply Co................F 330 659-6800
Peninsula *(G-11184)*

The F A Requarth Company..................E 937 224-1141
Dayton *(G-6048)*

Tri-County Block and Brick Inc.............E 419 826-7060
Swanton *(G-12696)*

Trumbull Cement Products Co..............G 330 372-4342
Warren *(G-13802)*

Vances Department Store.....................G 937 549-3033
Manchester *(G-8756)*

Vances Department Store.....................G 937 549-2188
Manchester *(G-8755)*

Warren Concrete and Supply Co............G 330 393-1581
Warren *(G-13810)*

Zaenkert Srvying Essntials Inc.............G 513 738-2917
Okeana *(G-10931)*

BUILDING PRDTS: Concrete

Baswa Acoustics North Amer LLC.........F 216 475-7197
Bedford *(G-1014)*

Olde Wood Ltd..............................E 330 866-1441
Magnolia (G-8735)

One Wish LLC.............................F 800 505-6883
Bedford (G-1052)

Parksite Inc...............................G 330 455-3782
Louisville (G-8612)

Tamarron Technology Inc.............F 800 277-3207
Cincinnati (G-3136)

BUILDING PRDTS: Stone

Jalco Industries Inc.....................F 740 286-3808
Jackson (G-7947)

Toledo Cut Stone Inc..................F 419 531-1623
Toledo (G-13150)

BUILDING SCALES MODELS

3-D Technical Services Company.........E 937 746-2901
Franklin (G-7006)

BUILDINGS & COMPONENTS: Prefabricated Metal

American Ramp Systems...............G 440 336-4988
North Olmsted (G-10716)

Benchmark Archtectural Systems.......E 614 444-0110
Columbus (G-4751)

Benko Products Inc....................E 440 934-2180
Sheffield Village (G-11957)

Cdc Fab Co...............................F 419 866-7705
Maumee (G-9269)

Connect Housing Blocks LLC..........E 614 503-4344
Columbus (G-4841)

Consoldted Anlytcal Systems In.......F 513 542-1200
Cincinnati (G-2510)

Haz-Safe LLC............................F 330 793-0900
Austintown (G-705)

Hoge Lumber Company................E 419 753-2263
New Knoxville (G-10398)

Lab-Pro Inc...............................G 937 434-9600
Miamisburg (G-9708)

Morton Buildings Inc....................G 419 399-4549
Kenton (G-8109)

R L Torbeck Industries Inc.............G 513 367-0080
Harrison (G-7565)

Rebsco Inc...............................F 937 548-2246
Greenville (G-7351)

Reliable Metal Buildings LLC..........G 419 737-1300
Pioneer (G-11329)

Skyline Corporation.....................C 330 852-2483
Sugarcreek (G-12650)

BUILDINGS: Mobile, For Commercial Use

Muster Rdu Inc..........................G 614 537-5440
Lancaster (G-8212)

BUILDINGS: Portable

Affordable Barn Co Ltd.................G 330 674-3001
Millersburg (G-9966)

Golden Giant Inc........................E 419 674-4038
Kenton (G-8098)

Jack Walters & Sons Corp.............E 937 653-8986
Urbana (G-13470)

Morton Buildings Inc....................E 330 345-6188
Wooster (G-14667)

BUILDINGS: Prefabricated, Metal

Cornerstone Bldg Brands Inc..........C 937 584-3300
Middletown (G-9850)

Enclosure Suppliers LLC...............E 513 782-3900
Cincinnati (G-2586)

Great Day Improvements LLC..........B 267 223-1289
Macedonia (G-8695)

Joyce Manufacturing Co................D 440 239-9100
Berea (G-1179)

Pei Liquidation Company................C 330 467-4267
Macedonia (G-8704)

Rayhaven Group Inc....................G 330 659-3183
Richfield (G-11598)

BUILDINGS: Prefabricated, Wood

Beachy Barns Ltd.......................F 614 873-4193
Plain City (G-11397)

Cooper Enterprises Inc.................D 419 347-5232
Shelby (G-11968)

Fifth Avenue Lumber Co................E 614 833-6655
Canal Winchester (G-1790)

J Aaron Weaver.........................G 440 474-9185
Rome (G-11644)

Morton Buildings Inc....................E 419 675-2311
Kenton (G-8110)

Patio Enclosures........................F 513 733-4646
Cincinnati (G-2944)

Rona Enterprises Inc....................G 740 927-9971
Pataskala (G-11148)

Skyline Corporation.....................C 330 852-2483
Sugarcreek (G-12650)

Vinyl Design Corporation................E 419 283-4009
Holland (G-7790)

BULLETIN BOARDS: Wood

1914 Mi Inc...............................D 800 426-4244
New Philadelphia (G-10429)

GMI Companies Inc....................F 513 932-3445
Lebanon (G-8263)

GMI Companies Inc....................C 513 932-3445
Lebanon (G-8262)

Tri-State Supply Co Inc.................F 614 272-6767
Columbus (G-5331)

BULLETPROOF VESTS

Forceone LLC............................G 513 939-1018
Hebron (G-7615)

BUMPERS: Motor Vehicle

Superior Production LLC................C 614 444-2181
Columbus (G-5299)

BUOYS: Plastic

Worthignton Products Inc...............G 330 452-7400
East Canton (G-6381)

BURIAL VAULTS: Concrete Or Precast Terrazzo

Akron Vault Company Inc...............F 330 784-5475
Akron (G-46)

Alexander Wilbert Vault Co.............G 419 468-3477
Galion (G-7177)

Bell Vault and Monu Works Inc.........F 937 866-2444
Miamisburg (G-9668)

Fort Stben Burial Estates Assn.........G 740 266-6101
Steubenville (G-12403)

Landon Vault Company..................F 614 443-5505
Columbus (G-5063)

Mack Industries.........................F 419 353-7081
Bowling Green (G-1427)

Mack Industries Inc.....................F 740 393-1121
Mount Vernon (G-10249)

Neher Burial Vault Company............G 937 399-4494
Springfield (G-12357)

Seislove Vault & Septic Tanks..........G 419 447-5473
Tiffin (G-12798)

Southern Ohio Vault Co Inc............G 740 456-5898
Portsmouth (G-11478)

Stuart Burial Vault Co Inc..............F 740 569-4158
Bremen (G-1487)

Toli Vault.................................G 866 998-8654
Westlake (G-14341)

Turner Vault Co.........................E 419 537-1133
Northwood (G-10812)

Youngstown Burial Vault Co............G 330 782-0015
Girard (G-7282)

BURNERS: Gas, Domestic

Solarflo Corporation.....................F 440 439-1680
Cleveland (G-4312)

BURNERS: Gas, Indl

Ws Thermal Process Tech Inc..........G 440 385-6829
Lorain (G-8587)

BURNERS: Oil, Domestic Or Indl

Es Thermal Inc..........................E 440 323-3291
Berea (G-1170)

RW Beckett Corporation................C 440 327-1060
North Ridgeville (G-10749)

BUS BARS: Electrical

Crown Electric Engrg & Mfg LLC........E 513 539-7394
Middletown (G-9852)

Reliable Hermetic Seals LLC............F 888 747-3250
Beavercreek (G-981)

Schneider Electric Usa Inc..............D 513 777-4445
West Chester (G-14073)

BUSHINGS & BEARINGS

Advance Bronze Inc.....................F 330 948-1231
Lodi (G-8496)

Climax Metal Products Company........D 440 943-8898
Mentor (G-9502)

Dupont Specialty Pdts USA LLC........C 216 901-3600
Cleveland (G-3638)

McNeil Industries Inc....................E 440 951-7756
Painesville (G-11099)

S C Industries Inc.......................E 216 732-9000
Euclid (G-6677)

BUSHINGS & BEARINGS: Brass, Exc Machined

D4 Industries Inc........................G 419 523-9555
Ottawa (C 11032)

Johnson Metall Inc......................D 440 245-6826
Lorain (G-8559)

BUSINESS ACTIVITIES: Non-Commercial Site

A Good Mobile Detailing LLC...........G 513 316-3802
Cincinnati (G-2325)

ADSr Ent LLC............................F 773 280-2129
Columbus (G-4674)

Appalachia Freeze Dry Co LLC.........F 740 412-0169
Richmond Dale (G-11606)

As Clean As It Gets Off Brkroo.........E 216 256-1143
South Euclid (G-12218)

Custom Built Crates Inc.................E
Milford (G-9932)

Custom Information Systems Inc.........F 614 875-2245
Grove City (G-7380)

Endless Home Improvements LLC........G 614 599-1799
Columbus (G-4901)

Ergo Desktop LLC.......................E 567 890-3746
Celina (G-2105)

Essential Provisions LLC.................G 937 271-0381
Wilmington (G-14579)

PRODUCT

Express Ground Services Inc................ G 216 870-9374
Cleveland *(G-3700)*

Flexsys Inc... B 212 605-6000
Akron *(G-151)*

Fsqpronet LLC... F 330 942-6014
Youngstown *(G-14859)*

Geauga Highway Co................................. F 440 834-4580
Windham *(G-14600)*

Groundhogs 2000 LLC............................. G 440 653-1647
Bedford *(G-1033)*

Handshakers Construction LLC............. F 513 370-1371
Cincinnati *(G-2704)*

Jason Poffenberger................................. G 937 369-1358
Dayton *(G-5827)*

Jls Funeral Home.................................... F 614 625-1220
Columbus *(G-5040)*

Jnp Group LLC.. F 800 735-9645
Wooster *(G-14655)*

Link To Success Inc................................ G 888 959-4203
Norwalk *(G-10851)*

Millers Aplus Cmpt Svcs LLC................ F 330 620-5288
Akron *(G-234)*

North Shore Printing LLC....................... G 740 876-9066
Portsmouth *(G-11472)*

Op Dawg Logistics LLC........................... E 937 844-3135
Dayton *(G-5928)*

Park Press Direct..................................... G 419 626-4426
Sandusky *(G-11864)*

Paul Shovlin... G 330 757-0032
Youngstown *(G-14915)*

PMRservices LLC...................................... F 937 219-0062
Spring Valley *(G-12242)*

Prospect Rock LLC................................... F 740 512-0542
Saint Clairsville *(G-11707)*

RE Connors Construction Ltd................ G 740 644-0261
Thornville *(G-12767)*

Shousha Trucking LLC............................ F 937 270-4471
Dayton *(G-6005)*

Signalysis Inc.. F 513 528-6164
Cincinnati *(G-3090)*

Siraj Recovery LLC.................................. G 614 893-3507
Columbus *(G-5272)*

Standard Wellness Company LLC......... C 330 931-1037
Gibsonburg *(G-7259)*

Stutzman Manufacturing Ltd................. G 330 674-4359
Millersburg *(G-10012)*

Valley View Pallets LLC.......................... G 740 599-0010
Danville *(G-5600)*

Vitals Matter LLC.................................... G 937 848-8871
Dayton *(G-6072)*

BUSINESS FORMS WHOLESALERS

American Business Forms Inc............... E 513 312-2522
West Chester *(G-14101)*

Bay Business Forms Inc.......................... F 937 322-3000
Springfield *(G-12285)*

Bloch Printing Company......................... G 330 576-6760
Copley *(G-5431)*

GBS Corp.. C 330 494-5330
North Canton *(G-10641)*

Gq Business Products Inc...................... G 513 792-4750
Loveland *(G-8627)*

Highland Computer Forms Inc.............. D 937 393-4215
Hillsboro *(G-7718)*

Optimum System Products Inc............. E 614 885-4464
Westerville *(G-14273)*

Shamrock Companies Inc...................... D 440 899-9510
Westlake *(G-14333)*

William J Bergen & Co............................ G 440 248-6132
Solon *(G-12208)*

BUSINESS FORMS: Printed, Continuous

Rotary Forms Press Inc.......................... E 937 393-3426
Hillsboro *(G-7724)*

BUSINESS FORMS: Printed, Manifold

Anderson Graphics Inc........................... E 330 745-2165
Barberton *(G-793)*

Custom Products Corporation............... D 440 528-7100
Glenwillow *(G-7285)*

Dupli-Systems Inc................................... C 440 234-9415
Strongsville *(G-12555)*

Eleet Cryogenics Inc.............................. E 330 874-4009
Bolivar *(G-1382)*

GBS Corp.. C 330 863-1828
Malvern *(G-8750)*

GBS Corp.. C 330 494-5330
North Canton *(G-10641)*

Glatfelter Corporation............................ G 419 333-6700
Fremont *(G-7115)*

Kroy LLC.. C 800 837-4323
Cleveland *(G-3929)*

Plastilene Inc... F 614 592-8699
Washington Court Hou *(G-13822)*

Print-Digital Incorporated..................... G 330 686-5945
Stow *(G-12451)*

Quick Tech Graphics Inc........................ F 937 743-5952
Springboro *(G-12266)*

Reynolds and Reynolds Company......... F 419 584-7000
Celina *(G-2117)*

S F Mock & Associates LLC.................... F 937 438-0196
Dayton *(G-5991)*

Shawnee Systems Inc............................ D 513 561-9932
Cincinnati *(G-3087)*

SRC Liquidation LLC................................ A 937 221-1000
Dayton *(G-6019)*

Taylor Communications Inc.................... E 937 221-1000
Dayton *(G-6039)*

Taylor Communications Inc.................... F 732 356-0081
Dayton *(G-6040)*

Taylor Communications Inc.................... F 937 221-3347
Grove City *(G-7415)*

Taylor Communications Inc.................... F 216 265-1800
Richfield *(G-11603)*

Thomas Products Co Inc........................ E 513 756-9009
Cincinnati *(G-3155)*

Wfsr Holdings LLC................................... A 877 735-4966
Dayton *(G-6081)*

BUSINESS MACHINE REPAIR, ELECTRIC

Queen City Office Machine..................... F 513 251-7200
Cincinnati *(G-3022)*

BUSINESS TRAINING SVCS

Pakra LLC.. F 614 477-6965
Columbus *(G-5169)*

BUTTER WHOLESALERS

Frank L Harter & Son Inc....................... G 513 574-1330
Cincinnati *(G-2638)*

BUTTONS

Purebuttonscom LLC............................... F 330 721-1600
Medina *(G-9438)*

CABINETS & CASES: Show, Display & Storage, Exc Wood

D Lewis Inc... G 740 695-2615
Saint Clairsville *(G-11690)*

Metal Fabricating Corporation.............. D 216 631-8121
Cleveland *(G-4023)*

Paul Yoder.. G 740 439-5811
Senecaville *(G-11906)*

CABINETS: Bathroom Vanities, Wood

Bison Builders LLC................................... F 614 636-0365
Columbus *(G-4756)*

East Oberlin Cabinets LLC..................... G 440 775-1166
Oberlin *(G-10916)*

Hampshire Co.. F 937 773-3493
Piqua *(G-11348)*

Profiles In Design Inc............................. F 513 751-2212
Cincinnati *(G-3006)*

S & G Manufacturing Group LLC........... D 614 529-0100
Hilliard *(G-7700)*

CABINETS: Entertainment

Innerwood & Company............................ F 513 677-2229
Loveland *(G-8631)*

Kraftmaid Trucking Inc........................... D 440 632-2531
Middlefield *(G-9805)*

CABINETS: Entertainment Units, Household, Wood

Progressive Furniture Inc...................... E 419 446-4500
Archbold *(G-508)*

CABINETS: Factory

Bolons Custom Kitchens Inc.................. G 330 499-0092
Canton *(G-1842)*

Home Idea Center Inc............................. G 419 375-4951
Fort Recovery *(G-6966)*

Kinnemyers Cornerstone Cab Inc......... G 513 353-3030
Cleves *(G-4542)*

Mro Built LLC... D 330 526-0555
North Canton *(G-10654)*

Vivo Brothers LLC.................................... F 330 629-8686
Columbiana *(G-4633)*

Wades Woodworking Inc........................ F 937 374-6470
Xenia *(G-14784)*

Woodworking Shop LLC.......................... F 513 330-9663
Miamisburg *(G-9753)*

CABINETS: Kitchen, Metal

C-Link Enterprises LLC........................... F 937 222-2829
Dayton *(G-5692)*

CABINETS: Kitchen, Wood

1914 Mi Inc.. E 330 308-8667
New Philadelphia *(G-10428)*

4-B Wood Specialties Inc...................... G 330 769-2188
Seville *(G-11908)*

A & J Woodworking Inc.......................... G 419 695-5655
Delphos *(G-6183)*

A-Display Service Corp.......................... F 614 469-1230
Columbus *(G-4657)*

Agean Marble Manufacturing Inc.......... G 513 874-1475
West Chester *(G-14099)*

Ailes Millwork Inc................................... F 330 678-4300
Kent *(G-8015)*

Al-Co Products Inc.................................. G 419 399-3867
Latty *(G-8236)*

Anthony Flottemesch & Son Inc............ F 513 561-1212
Cincinnati *(G-2371)*

Apex Cabinetry Inc................................. E 513 832-7905
Cincinnati *(G-2373)*

Approved Plumbing Co............................ F 216 663-5063
Cleveland *(G-3362)*

As America Inc... D 419 522-4211
Mansfield *(G-8763)*

Bear Cabinetry LLC................................. G 216 481-9282
Euclid *(G-6643)*

Bestwood Cabinetry LLC.......................G 937 661-9621
Xenia *(G-14755)*

Bruewer Woodwork Mfg Co.............. D 513 353-3505
Cleves *(G-4532)*

Cabinet and Granite Depot LLC............ F 513 874-2100
West Chester *(G-13953)*

Cabinet Concepts Inc.........................G 440 232-4644
Oakwood Village *(G-10903)*

Cabinet Shop.....................................G 614 885-9676
Columbus *(G-4639)*

Cabinet Specialties Inc.......................G 330 695-3463
Fredericksburg *(G-7061)*

Cabinetworks Group Mich LLC........... E 440 247-3091
Chagrin Falls *(G-2137)*

Cabinetworks Group Mich LLC........... C 440 632-2547
Middlefield *(G-9783)*

Cabintwrks Group Mddlfield LLC......... C 440 437-8537
Orwell *(G-11020)*

Cabintwrks Group Mddlfield LLC......... A 888 562-7744
Middlefield *(G-9784)*

Carter-Jones Lumber Company.............G 330 674-9060
Millersburg *(G-9975)*

Cedee Cedar Inc............................... F 740 363-3148
Delaware *(G-6136)*

Century Components LLC....................G 330 852-3610
Sugarcreek *(G-12636)*

Clark Son Actn Liquidation Inc............G 330 866-9330
East Sparta *(G-6411)*

Climate Pros LLC.............................. D 216 881-5200
Cleveland *(G-3541)*

Climate Pros LLC.............................. D 330 744-2732
Youngstown *(G-14839)*

Colby Woodworking Inc...................... E 937 224-7676
Dayton *(G-5705)*

Counter-Advice Inc............................G 937 291-1600
Franklin *(G-7014)*

Creative Cabinets Ltd........................ F 740 689-0603
Lancaster *(G-8190)*

Creative Edge Cbnets Wdwkg LLC......G 419 453-3416
Ottoville *(G-11053)*

Crowes Cabinets Inc.......................... E 330 729-9911
Youngstown *(G-14842)*

Custom Woodworking Inc....................G 419 456-3330
Ottawa *(G-11031)*

D Lewis Inc......................................G 740 695-2615
Saint Clairsville *(G-11690)*

Dgl Woodworking Inc......................... F 937 837-7091
Dayton *(G-5747)*

Distinctive Surfaces LLC.................... F 614 431-0898
Columbus *(G-4885)*

Dover Cabinet Industries Inc.............. F 330 343-9074
Dover *(G-6237)*

E J Skok Industries........................... E 216 292-7533
Bedford *(G-1030)*

Fairfield Wood Works Ltd....................G 740 689-1953
Lancaster *(G-8201)*

Fdi Cabinetry LLC..............................G 513 353-4500
Cleves *(G-4537)*

Formware Inc.................................... F 614 231-9387
Columbus *(G-4932)*

Franklin Cabinet Company Inc............ E 937 743-9606
Franklin *(G-7022)*

Gillard Construction Inc..................... F 740 376-9744
Marietta *(G-8919)*

Gross & Sons Custom Millwork............G 419 227-0214
Lima *(G-8411)*

Holmes Lumber & Bldg Ctr Inc............ E 330 479-8314
Canton *(G-1912)*

Holmes Lumber & Bldg Ctr Inc............ C 330 674-9060
Millersburg *(G-9989)*

J & K Cabinetry Inc............................G 513 860-3461
West Chester *(G-14017)*

J L Custom Woodworking LLC.............G 419 704-5181
Sullivan *(G-12659)*

Jacob & Levis Ltd..............................G 330 852-7600
Sugarcreek *(G-12639)*

Johannings Inc..................................G 330 875-1706
Louisville *(G-8607)*

JP Cabinets LLC................................G 440 232-9780
Cleveland *(G-3896)*

Kellogg Cabinets Inc..........................G 614 833-9596
Canal Winchester *(G-1792)*

Kinnemyers Cornerstone Cab Inc.........G 513 353-3030
Cleves *(G-4542)*

Kinsella Manufacturing Co Inc............ F 513 561-5285
Cincinnati *(G-2796)*

Kitchen Designs Plus Inc....................G 419 536-6605
Toledo *(G-13019)*

Kitchens By Rutenschroer Inc..............G 513 251-8333
Cincinnati *(G-2799)*

Knapke Cabinets Inc..........................G 937 335-8383
Troy *(G-13234)*

Knapke Custom Cabinetry Ltd.............G 937 459-8866
Versailles *(G-13599)*

Kreager Co LLC.................................G 740 345-1605
Newark *(G-10515)*

Laminated Concepts Inc..................... F 216 475-4141
Maple Heights *(G-8885)*

Leiden Cabinet Co.............................G 330 425-8555
Twinsburg *(G-13329)*

Lily Ann Cabinets.............................. F 419 360-2455
Toledo *(G-13036)*

Lima Millwork Inc..............................G 419 331-3303
Elida *(G-6483)*

Mac Lean J S Co...............................G 614 878-5454
Columbus *(G-5078)*

Mammana Custom Woodworking Inc.... E 216 581-9059
Maple Heights *(G-8886)*

Marzano Inc.....................................G 216 459-2051
Cleveland *(G-3995)*

Masterbrand Inc................................ A 877 622-4782
Beachwood *(G-929)*

Miami Vly Counters & Spc Inc.............G 937 865-0562
Miamisburg *(G-9714)*

Miller Cabinet Ltd.............................. F 614 873-4221
Plain City *(G-11415)*

Mills Pride Premier Inc.......................G 740 941-1300
Waverly *(G-13867)*

Mock Woodworking Company LLC....... E 740 452-2701
Zanesville *(G-15029)*

Modern Designs Inc...........................G 330 644-1771
Green *(G-7323)*

Mro Built LLC................................... D 330 526-0555
North Canton *(G-10654)*

Mullet Cabinets Inc........................... D 330 674-9646
Millersburg *(G-10002)*

Nagele Manufacturing Company.......... E 216 433-1100
Cleveland *(G-4057)*

North Star Building Pdts LLC...............G 216 431-1000
Cleveland *(G-4090)*

Northeast Cabinet Co LLC..................G 614 759-0800
Columbus *(G-5130)*

Ohio River Valley Cabinet....................G 740 975-8846
Newark *(G-10526)*

Online Mega Sellers Corp....................G 888 384-6468
Toledo *(G-13078)*

Reserve Millwork LLC........................ E 216 531-6982
Bedford *(G-1056)*

Rheaco Builders Inc...........................G 330 425-3090
Twinsburg *(G-13366)*

Riceland Cabinet Inc......................... D 330 601-1071
Wooster *(G-14676)*

Riceland Cabinet Corporation..............D 330 601-1071
Wooster *(G-14677)*

River East Custom Cabinets Inc...........G 419 244-3226
Toledo *(G-13113)*

Riverside Cnstr Svcs Inc.................... E 513 723-0900
Cincinnati *(G-3048)*

Roettger Hardwood Inc.......................G 937 693-6811
Kettlersville *(G-8125)*

Royal Cabinet Design Co Inc.............. F 216 267-5330
Cleveland *(G-4258)*

Salem Mill & Cabinet Co....................G 330 337-9568
Salem *(G-11810)*

Signature Cabinetry Inc..................... F 614 252-2227
Columbus *(G-5266)*

Snows Wood Shop Inc........................G 419 836-3805
Oregon *(G-10968)*

Specified Structures Inc.....................G 330 753-0693
Barberton *(G-839)*

Supply One Corporation...................... F 937 297-1111
Bellbrook *(G-1093)*

TDS Custom Cabinets LLC..................G 614 850-7590
Columbus *(G-5313)*

The Hattenbach Company.................. D 216 881-5200
Cleveland *(G-4384)*

Thomas Cabinet Shop Inc................... F 937 847-8239
Dayton *(G-6051)*

Tiffin Metal Products Co.................... D 419 447-8414
Tiffin *(G-12803)*

Troyers Cabinet Shop Ltd................... F 937 464-7702
Belle Center *(G-1097)*

Trutech Cabinetry LLC.......................G 614 338-0680
Columbus *(G-5334)*

Woodcraft Industries Inc.................... E 440 632-9655
Middlefield *(G-9836)*

Wurms Woodworking Company............ E 419 492-2184
New Washington *(G-10484)*

X44 Corp... F 330 657-2335
Peninsula *(G-11188)*

CABINETS: Office, Wood

Custom Millcraft Corp........................ E 513 874-7080
West Chester *(G-13980)*

East Woodworking Company...............G 216 791-5950
Cleveland *(G-3649)*

Geograph Industries Inc..................... E 513 202-9200
Harrison *(G-7553)*

Hardwood Lumber Company Inc.......... F 440 834-1891
Middlefield *(G-9797)*

Hoge Lumber Company....................... E 419 753-2263
New Knoxville *(G-10398)*

Interior Products Co Inc......................G 216 641-1919
Cleveland *(G-3864)*

Mel Heitkamp Builders Ltd..................G 419 375-0405
Fort Recovery *(G-6969)*

Specialty Svcs Cabinetry Inc...............G 614 421-1599
Columbus *(G-5281)*

CABINETS: Show, Display, Etc, Wood, Exc Refrigerated

A J Construction Co...........................G 330 539-9544
Girard *(G-7262)*

Amtekco Industries LLC..................... D 614 228-6590
Columbus *(G-4708)*

Case Crafters Inc..............................G 937 667-9473
Tipp City *(G-12819)*

Climate Pros LLC.............................. D 216 881-5200
Cleveland *(G-3541)*

Climate Pros LLC.............................. D 330 744-2732
Youngstown *(G-14839)*

Custom Design Cabinets & Tops..........G 440 639-9900
Painesville *(G-11075)*

Designer Cntemporary Laminates.........G 440 946-8207
Painesville *(G-11079)*

PRODUCT

Gary L Gast.................................. G 419 626-5915
Sandusky *(G-11835)*

Kellogg Cabinets Inc.................... G 614 833-9596
Canal Winchester *(G-1792)*

Miller Cabinet Ltd.......................... F 614 873-4221
Plain City *(G-11415)*

Nagele Manufacturing Company........... E 216 433-1100
Cleveland *(G-4057)*

Rinos Woodworking Shop Inc............. F 440 946-1718
Willoughby *(G-14518)*

Robertson Cabinets Inc.................. G 937 698-3755
West Milton *(G-14185)*

The Hattenbach Company................. D 216 881-5200
Cleveland *(G-4384)*

Vances Department Store................. G 937 549-3033
Manchester *(G-8756)*

Vances Department Store................. G 937 549-2188
Manchester *(G-8755)*

Village Cabinet Shop Inc................. G 704 966-0801
Cincinnati *(G-3205)*

CABLE & OTHER PAY TELEVISION DISTRIBUTION

Ohio News Network......................... G 614 460-3700
Columbus *(G-5148)*

CABLE TELEVISION

Block Communications Inc................. F 419 724-6212
Toledo *(G-12898)*

CABLE: Fiber

Core Optix Inc............................. F 855 267-3678
Cincinnati *(G-2517)*

Katimex USA Inc........................... G 440 338-3500
Chagrin Falls *(G-2147)*

CABLE: Fiber Optic

Cbst Acquisition LLC...................... D 513 361-9600
Cincinnati *(G-2445)*

Core Optix Inc............................. F 855 267-3678
Cincinnati *(G-2517)*

Syscom Advanced Materials Inc........... E 614 487-3626
Columbus *(G-5304)*

CABLE: Noninsulated

Assembly Specialty Pdts Inc.............. E 216 676-5600
Cleveland *(G-3381)*

Microplex Inc............................. E 330 498-0600
North Canton *(G-10651)*

CABLE: Ropes & Fiber

Atwood Rope Manufacturing Inc........... E 614 920-0534
Canal Winchester *(G-1784)*

Atwood Rope Manufacturing Inc........... F 614 920-0534
Millersport *(G-10022)*

Automted Cmpnent Spcalists LLC......... E 513 335-4285
Cincinnati *(G-2391)*

Radix Wire & Cable LLC................... D 216 731-9191
Solon *(G-12172)*

CABLE: Steel, Insulated Or Armored

Heilind Electronics Inc................... E 440 473-9600
Cleveland *(G-3818)*

Torque 2020 CMA Acqisition LLC.......... C 330 874-2900
Bolivar *(G-1393)*

CABS: Indl Trucks & Tractors

Martin Sheet Metal Inc.................... E 216 377-8200
Cleveland *(G-3993)*

CAFES

R & T Estate LLC.......................... F 216 862-0822
Cleveland *(G-4219)*

Shawadi LLC............................... E 614 839-0698
Westerville *(G-14275)*

CAFETERIAS

Mark Grzianis St Treats Ex Inc........... F 330 414-6266
Kent *(G-8049)*

CALCULATING & ACCOUNTING EQPT

Diebold Nixdorf Incorporated............. D 336 662-1115
North Canton *(G-10634)*

Thyme Inc................................. F 484 872-8430
Akron *(G-337)*

CALIBRATING SVCS, NEC

Mjcj Holdings Inc......................... G 937 885-0800
Miamisburg *(G-9719)*

CAMSHAFTS

Park-Ohio Industries Inc.................. C 216 341-2300
Newburgh Heights *(G-10546)*

CANDLES

Al Root Company........................... E 330 725-6677
Medina *(G-9372)*

Al Root Company........................... C 330 723-4359
Medina *(G-9371)*

Alene Candles Midwest LLC................ F 614 933-4005
New Albany *(G-10325)*

Ambrosia Inc.............................. G 419 825-3896
Swanton *(G-12676)*

Ambrosia Inc.............................. G 734 529-5024
Swanton *(G-12677)*

Candle Lab................................ G 614 488-2009
Columbus *(G-4793)*

Candle-Lite Company LLC.................. D 937 780-2563
Blue Ash *(G-1258)*

Cleveland Plant and Flower Co............ G 614 478-9900
Columbus *(G-4811)*

Connies Candles........................... G 740 574-1224
Wheelersburg *(G-14352)*

Eleventh Candle Co........................ G 614 530-4853
Worthington *(G-14709)*

Faith Guiding Cafe LLC.................... F 614 245-8451
New Albany *(G-10340)*

Fallen Oak Candles Inc.................... G 419 204-8162
Celina *(G-2106)*

Gorant Chocolatier LLC.................... C 330 726-8821
Boardman *(G-1372)*

Inez Essentials LLC....................... F 216 701-8360
Maple Heights *(G-8884)*

Lumi-Lite Candle Company................. D 740 872-3248
Norwich *(G-10864)*

Tl Marie Candle Company LLC.............. F 513 746-7798
Cincinnati *(G-3156)*

United Candle Company LLC................ G 740 872-3248
Norwich *(G-10865)*

Yankee Candle Company Inc................ G 413 712-9416
Etna *(G-6636)*

CANDY & CONFECTIONS: Cake Ornaments

Superior Street Holding Inc.............. F 419 626-5757
Sandusky *(G-11874)*

Superior Street Holding Inc.............. E 419 626-5757
Sandusky *(G-11873)*

CANDY & CONFECTIONS: Candy Bars, Including Chocolate Covered

Barfections LLC........................... F 330 759-3100
Girard *(G-7266)*

Bucks For Pups Confections LLC.......... F 614 359-4672
Columbus *(G-4787)*

Malleys Candies LLC...................... D 216 362-8700
Cleveland *(G-3983)*

Maries Candies LLC....................... G 937 465-3061
West Liberty *(G-14176)*

CANDY & CONFECTIONS: Chocolate Candy, Exc Solid Chocolate

Executive Sweets East Inc................ G 440 359-9866
Oakwood Village *(G-10905)*

International Confections C............... C 800 288-8002
Columbus *(G-5019)*

New Bloomer Candy Company LLC........... E 740 452-7501
Zanesville *(G-15033)*

CANDY & CONFECTIONS: Popcorn Balls/ Other Trtd Popcorn Prdts

Humphrey Popcorn Company................. F 216 662-6629
Strongsville *(G-12565)*

Jml Holdings Inc.......................... F 419 866-7500
Holland *(G-7770)*

CANDY, NUT & CONFECTIONERY STORES: Candy

Brandts Candies Inc...................... G 440 942-1016
Willoughby *(G-14433)*

Coblentz Family Brands Inc............... E 330 893-2995
Walnut Creek *(G-13693)*

Fannie May Confections Inc............... A 330 494-0833
North Canton *(G-10638)*

Fawn Confectionery Inc................... F 513 574-9612
Cincinnati *(G-2613)*

Gorant Chocolatier LLC................... C 330 726-8821
Boardman *(G-1372)*

Harry London Candies Inc................. E 330 494-0833
North Canton *(G-10645)*

Hartville Chocolates Inc................. G 330 877-1999
Hartville *(G-7576)*

Island Delights Inc...................... G 866 887-4100
Seville *(G-11918)*

Linneas Candy Supplies Inc............... E 330 678-7112
Kent *(G-8046)*

Malleys Candies LLC...................... D 216 362-8700
Cleveland *(G-3983)*

Maries Candies LLC....................... G 937 465-3061
West Liberty *(G-14176)*

New Dawn Distribution Inc................ G 330 759-3500
Girard *(G-7277)*

Piqua Chocolate Company Inc.............. G 937 773-1981
Piqua *(G-11374)*

Robert E McGrath Inc..................... F 440 572-7747
Strongsville *(G-12593)*

Sweeties Olympia Treats LLC.............. F 440 572-7747
Strongsville *(G-12608)*

CANDY: Chocolate From Cacao Beans

Coblentz Family Brands Inc............... E 330 893-2995
Walnut Creek *(G-13693)*

Giannios Candy Co Inc.................... E 330 755-7000
Struthers *(G-12618)*

L C F Inc................................. G 330 877-3322
Hartville *(G-7579)*

Mmelo Btq Confectioners LLC.............. G 614 822-9530
Reynoldsburg *(G-11574)*

CANNED SPECIALTIES

Abbott Laboratories....................... A 614 624-3191
Columbus *(G-4660)*

Baxters North America Inc.................. E 513 552-7463
Blue Ash (G-1247)

Baxters North America Inc.................. C 513 552-7400
Blue Ash (G-1248)

Bittersweet Inc.................................... D 419 875-6986
Whitehouse (G-14358)

Hayden Valley Foods Inc.................... E 614 539-7233
Grove City (G-7390)

Heritage Cooperative Inc................... F 740 828-2215
Nashport (G-10300)

JES Foods/Celina Inc.......................... F 419 586-7446
Celina (G-2112)

Oasis Mditerranean Cuisine Inc.......... E 419 269-1459
Toledo (G-13067)

Robert Rothschild Farm LLC.............. F 855 969-8050
West Chester (G-14069)

Skyline Cem Holdings LLC.................. C 513 874-1188
Fairfield (G-6776)

Trevor Clatterbuck.............................. G 330 359-2129
Wilmot (G-14595)

Wornick Holding Company Inc........... E 513 794-9800
Blue Ash (G-1354)

CANS: Aluminum

Crown Cork & Seal Usa Inc................ B 330 833-1011
Massillon (G-9183)

Trivium Alum Packg USA Corp............ E 330 744-2267
Youngstown (G-14952)

CANS: Metal

Anchor Hocking LLC........................... A 740 687-2500
Columbus (G-4711)

Ball Corporation.................................. D 614 771-9112
Columbus (G-4742)

Buckeye Stamping Company............... D 877 728-0776
Columbus (G-4786)

Cardinal Welding Inc.......................... G 330 426-2404
East Palestine (G-6400)

Cleveland Steel Container Corp.......... E 330 656-5600
Streetsboro (G-12493)

Crown Cork & Seal Usa Inc................ C 937 299-2027
Dayton (G-5715)

Crown Cork & Seal Usa Inc................ D 740 681-6593
Lancaster (G-8192)

Crown Cork & Seal Usa Inc................ D 740 681-3000
Lancaster (G-8193)

Crown Cork & Seal Usa Inc................ C 419 727-8201
Toledo (G-12933)

Drt Holdings LLC................................ G 937 297-6676
West Chester (G-13987)

Eisenhauer Mfg Co LLC...................... D 419 238-0081
Van Wert (G-13535)

Encore Industries Inc......................... C 419 626-8000
Sandusky (G-11830)

Organized Living Inc........................... E 513 489-9300
Cincinnati (G-2939)

Packaging Specialties Inc.................... E 330 723-6000
Medina (G-9433)

Winzeler Stamping Co......................... E 419 485-3147
Montpelier (G-10138)

Witt Industries Inc.............................. D 513 871-5700
Mason (G-9167)

CANS: Tin

Independent Can Company.................. F 440 593-5300
Conneaut (G-5405)

Stolle Machinery Company LLC........... E 330 244-0555
Canton (G-2018)

CANVAS PRDTS

Advantage Tent Fittings Inc................ F 740 773-3015
Chillicothe (G-2241)

Chalfant Sew Fabricators Inc.............. E 216 521-7922
Cleveland (G-3484)

Cleveland Canvas Goods Mfg Co........ E 216 361-4567
Cleveland (G-3508)

Columbus Canvas Products Inc........... F 614 375-1397
Columbus (G-4819)

DCW Acquisition Inc........................... G 216 451-0666
Cleveland (G-3607)

Delphos Tent and Awning Inc............. G 419 692-5776
Delphos (G-6186)

Electra Tarp Inc.................................. F 330 477-7168
Canton (G-1885)

Forest City Companies Inc.................. E 216 586-5279
Cleveland (G-3735)

Galion Canvas Products....................... G 419 468-5333
Galion (G-7191)

Hdt Expeditionary Systems Inc........... E 216 438-6111
Solon (G-12121)

National Bias Fabric Co....................... G 216 361-0530
Cleveland (G-4058)

Samsel Rope & Marine Supply Co........ E 216 241-0333
Cleveland (G-4272)

Scherba Industries Inc........................ D 330 273-3200
Brunswick (G-1614)

Wolf G T Awning & Tent Co................ F 937 548-4161
Greenville (G-7360)

Youngstown Shade & Alum LLC.......... G 330 782-2373
Youngstown (G-14975)

CANVAS PRDTS: Convertible Tops, Car/ Boat, Fm Purchased Mtrl

American Canvas Products Inc............ G 419 382-8450
Toledo (G-12874)

Griffin Fisher Co Inc........................... G 513 961-2110
Cincinnati (G-2692)

CAPACITORS: NEC

CPI Group Limited............................... F 216 525-0046
Cleveland (G-3573)

Oren Elliot Products LLC..................... E 419 298-0015
Edgerton (G-6468)

Soemhejee Inc.................................... E 419 298-2306
Edgerton (G-6469)

Standex International Corp.................. D 513 533-7171
Fairfield (G-6779)

CAPS & PLUGS: Electric, Attachment

Knappco Corporation........................... C 513 870-3100
Hamilton (G-7509)

CAPS: Plastic

Bprex Halthcare Brookville Inc............ C 847 541-9700
Perrysburg (G-11206)

Electro-Cap International Inc............... F 937 456-6099
Eaton (G-6453)

Wisco Products Incorporated.............. E 937 228-2101
Dayton (G-6084)

CAR WASH EQPT

Giant Industries Inc............................ E 419 531-4600
Toledo (G-12975)

National Pride Equipment Inc.............. G 419 289-2886
Mansfield (G-8837)

Proto-Vest Inc.................................... F 623 872-3495
Sheffield Village (G-11962)

Russ Jr Enterprises Inc....................... F 440 237-4642
North Royalton (G-10783)

Sammy S Auto Detail........................... G 614 263-2728
Columbus (G-5246)

CAR WASH EQPT & SPLYS WHOLESALERS

National Pride Equipment Inc.............. G 419 289-2886
Mansfield (G-8837)

Service Station Equipment Co............. G 216 431-6100
Cleveland (G-4286)

CARBON & GRAPHITE PRDTS, NEC

Active Chemical Systems Inc............... F 440 543-7755
Chagrin Falls (G-2154)

American Spring Wire Corp................. C 216 292-4620
Bedford Heights (G-1068)

Applied Sciences Inc........................... E 937 766-2020
Cedarville (G-2097)

Cammann Inc....................................... F 440 965-4051
Wakeman (G-13678)

Ges Graphite Inc................................. E 216 658-6660
Parma (G-11132)

Graftech Holdings Inc......................... D 216 676-2000
Independence (G-7905)

Graftech International Ltd.................... D 216 676-2000
Brooklyn Heights (G-1531)

Graftech Intl Trdg Inc......................... E 216 676-2000
Cleveland (G-3782)

Metaullics Systems LP........................ C 509 926-6212
Solon (G-12148)

Mill-Rose Company.............................. C 440 255-9171
Mentor (G-9566)

Morgan Advanced Materials................ C 419 435-8182
Fostoria (G-6992)

Morgan AM&t....................................... G 419 435-8182
Fostoria (G-6993)

Ocsial LLC... F 415 906-5271
Gahanna (G-7167)

Ohio Carbon Blank Inc........................ E 440 953-9302
Willoughby (G-14500)

Ohio Carbon Industries Inc................. E 888 248-5029
Ashland (G-556)

Randall Bearings Inc........................... F 419 678-2486
Coldwater (G-4583)

Randall Bearings Inc........................... D 419 223-1075
Lima (G-8442)

Sentinel Management Inc.................... E 440 821-7372
Lorain (G-8580)

CARBON BLACK

Chromascape LLC................................ E 330 998-7574
Independence (G-7892)

Jacobi Carbons Inc.............................. D 215 546-3900
Columbus (G-5029)

Orion Engineered Carbons LLC........... E 985 312-7406
Marietta (G-8933)

CARBON PAPER & INKED RIBBONS

Kroy LLC... C 800 837-4323
Cleveland (G-3929)

Pubco Corporation.............................. D 216 881-5300
Cleveland (G-4205)

CARDIOVASCULAR SYSTEM DRUGS, EXC DIAGNOSTIC

Pfizer Inc.. F 937 746-3603
Franklin (G-7039)

CARDS: Beveled

Cott Systems Inc................................ D 614 847-4405
Columbus (G-4853)

CARDS: Color

Dorn Color LLC................................... C 216 634-2252
Cleveland (G-3627)

CARDS: Greeting

CARDS: Greeting

American Greetings Corporation............A 216 252-7300
Cleveland *(G-3344)*

Papyrus-Recycled Greetings Inc............D 773 348-6410
Westlake *(G-14319)*

Plus Mark LLC.............................D 216 252-6770
Cleveland *(G-4174)*

Schurman Fine Papers.....................E 513 791-5554
Cincinnati *(G-3068)*

Those Chrcters From Clvland LL...........G 216 252-7300
Cleveland *(G-4394)*

Vagabond Creations Inc...................G 937 298-1124
Moraine *(G-10197)*

CARDS: Identification

Griffin Technology Inc...................C 585 924-7121
Hudson *(G-7842)*

Identification Systems Inc...............E 614 448-1741
Columbus *(G-4999)*

Octsys Security Corp.....................G 614 470-4510
Columbus *(G-5138)*

Plasticards Inc..........................E 330 896-5555
Uniontown *(G-13425)*

CARPET & UPHOLSTERY CLEANING SVCS

Image By J & K LLC.......................F 888 667-6929
Maumee *(G-9297)*

CARPET & UPHOLSTERY CLEANING SVCS: Carpet/Furniture, On Loc

Shaheen Oriental Rug Co Inc..............F 330 493-9000
Canton *(G-2003)*

Stanley Steemer Intl Inc.................C 614 764-2007
Dublin *(G-6350)*

CARPETS & RUGS: Tufted

Mohawk Industries Inc....................E 800 837-3812
Grove City *(G-7402)*

CARPETS, RUGS & FLOOR COVERING

3359 Kingston LLC........................G 614 871-8989
Grove City *(G-7365)*

4blar LLC................................G 513 576-0441
Milford *(G-9919)*

Alliance Carpet Cushion Co...............E 740 966-5001
Johnstown *(G-7990)*

Boardman Molded Products Inc.............D 330 788-2400
Youngstown *(G-14822)*

Ccp Industries Inc.......................B 216 535-4227
Richmond Heights *(G-11609)*

Dribble Creek Inc........................F 440 439-8650
Bedford *(G-1029)*

Johns Manville Corporation...............C 419 878-8111
Waterville *(G-13835)*

Mat Basics Incorporated..................G 513 793-0313
Blue Ash *(G-1302)*

Shaw Industries Inc......................A 513 942-3692
Fairfield *(G-6775)*

CARS: Electric

Mobile Solutions LLC.....................F 614 286-3944
Columbus *(G-5107)*

CARTONS: Egg, Molded Pulp, Made From Purchased Materials

Tekni-Plex Inc...........................E 419 491-2399
Holland *(G-7786)*

CASES: Carrying

Clipper Products Inc.....................G 513 688-7300
Cincinnati *(G-2299)*

Professional Case Inc....................F 513 682-2520
West Chester *(G-14139)*

Travelers Custom Case Inc................F 216 621-8447
Mentor *(G-9643)*

UNI Corp.................................E 800 782-3296
Canton *(G-2031)*

Whitman Corporation......................G 513 541-3223
Okeana *(G-10930)*

CASES: Carrying, Clothing & Apparel

Made Men Circle LLC......................G 216 501-0414
Cleveland Heights *(G-4529)*

Northhill T-Shirt Print Dsign............G 330 208-0338
Akron *(G-250)*

T & CS Repairs & Retail LLC..............E 704 964-7325
Akron *(G-325)*

CASES: Plastic

Aerocase Incorporated....................F 440 617-9294
Westlake *(G-14284)*

M T M Molded Products Company............D 937 890-7461
Dayton *(G-5858)*

Warwick Products Company.................E 216 334-1200
Cleveland *(G-4491)*

CASKETS & ACCESS

Case Ohio Burial Co......................F 440 779-1992
Cleveland *(G-3474)*

CAST STONE: Concrete

Fibreboard Corporation...................C 419 248-8000
Toledo *(G-12963)*

CASTINGS GRINDING: For The Trade

Cincinnati Grinding Technologies Inc.....G 866 983-1097
Fairfield *(G-6721)*

P & L Heat Trting Grinding Inc...........E 330 746-1339
Youngstown *(G-14907)*

Trinel Inc...............................G 216 265-9190
Cleveland *(G-4427)*

Wise Edge LLC............................G 330 208-0889
Mogadore *(G-10094)*

Youngstown Hard Chrome Pltg Gr...........E 330 758-9721
Youngstown *(G-14970)*

CASTINGS: Aerospace Investment, Ferrous

Aeropact Manufacturing LLC...............F 419 373-1711
Bowling Green *(G-1406)*

Bescast Inc..............................C 440 946-5300
Willoughby *(G-14430)*

Consolidated Foundries Inc...............D 909 595-2252
Cleveland *(G-3562)*

Interntnal Prcsion Cast Sups I...........G 330 342-0407
Hudson *(G-7847)*

CASTINGS: Aerospace, Aluminum

Howmet Aluminum Casting Inc..............E 216 641-4340
Newburgh Heights *(G-10544)*

Htci Co..................................F 937 845-1204
New Carlisle *(G-10372)*

Mpe Aeroengines Inc......................E 937 878-3800
Huber Heights *(G-7823)*

Ransom & Randolph LLC....................G 419 865-9497
Maumee *(G-9314)*

T W Corporation..........................G 440 461-3234
Akron *(G-327)*

Tessec LLC...............................D 937 576-0010
Dayton *(G-6045)*

CASTINGS: Aerospace, Nonferrous, Exc Aluminum

Hydro-Aire Aerospace Corp................C 440 323-3211
Elyria *(G-6544)*

Lite Magnesium Products Inc..............D 330 296-6110
Ravenna *(G-11531)*

Voss Industries LLC......................C 216 771-7655
Cleveland *(G-4482)*

CASTINGS: Aluminum

Brost Foundry Company....................E 216 641-1131
Cleveland *(G-3443)*

Cast Metals Technology Inc...............E 937 968-5460
Union City *(G-13414)*

Castek Inc...............................E 440 365-2333
Elyria *(G-6510)*

General Aluminum Mfg Company.............E 330 297-1020
Ravenna *(G-11526)*

General Aluminum Mfg LLC.................B 440 593-6225
Conneaut *(G-5401)*

General Aluminum Mfg LLC.................D 330 297-1225
Ravenna *(G-11527)*

General Motors LLC.......................A 419 782-7010
Defiance *(G-6107)*

Iabf Inc.................................G 614 279-4498
Columbus *(G-4997)*

Jrm 2 Company............................D 513 554-1700
Cincinnati *(G-2774)*

Morris Bean & Company....................C 937 767-7301
Yellow Springs *(G-14790)*

Multi Cast LLC...........................E 419 335-0010
Wauseon *(G-13856)*

New Mansfield Brass & Alum Co............G 419 492-2166
New Washington *(G-10481)*

P C M Co.................................E 330 336-8040
Wadsworth *(G-13656)*

Piqua Emery Cutter & Fndry Co............D 937 773-4134
Piqua *(G-11375)*

Pride Cast Metals Inc....................D 513 541-1295
Cincinnati *(G-2981)*

Reliable Castings Corporation............D 513 541-2627
Cincinnati *(G-3037)*

Ross Aluminum Castings LLC...............C 937 492-4134
Sidney *(G-12046)*

Rotocast Technologies Inc................E 330 798-9091
Akron *(G-291)*

Specialized Castings Ltd.................F 937 669-5620
Greenville *(G-7354)*

US Metalcraft Inc........................F 419 692-4962
Delphos *(G-6197)*

CASTINGS: Brass, NEC, Exc Die

Accurate Products Company................G 740 498-7202
Newcomerstown *(G-10567)*

CASTINGS: Bronze, NEC, Exc Die

Albco Foundry Inc........................F 330 424-7716
Lisbon *(G-8463)*

Brost Foundry Company....................E 216 641-1131
Cleveland *(G-3443)*

Oakes Foundry Inc........................E 330 372-4010
Warren *(G-13785)*

Piqua Emery Cutter & Fndry Co............D 937 773-4134
Piqua *(G-11375)*

Pride Cast Metals Inc....................D 513 541-1295
Cincinnati *(G-2981)*

CASTINGS: Commercial Investment, Ferrous

B W Grinding Co..........................E 419 923-1376
Lyons *(G-8673)*

Cmt Imports Inc..........................G 513 615-1851
Cincinnati *(G-2502)*

Dd Foundry Inc...........................F 216 362-4100
Brookpark *(G-1548)*

Kovatch Castings Inc.............................C 330 896-9944
Uniontown *(G-13421)*

Rimer Enterprises Inc..........................E 419 878-8156
Waterville *(G-13841)*

CASTINGS: Die, Aluminum

Accro-Cast Corporation..........................G 937 228-0497
Dayton *(G-5630)*

Ahresty Wilmington Corporation...........B 937 382-6112
Wilmington *(G-14570)*

Akron Foundry Co.................................C 330 745-3101
Akron *(G-31)*

American Light Metals LLC....................C 330 908-3065
Macedonia *(G-8677)*

Apex Aluminum Die Cast Co Inc............E 937 773-0432
Piqua *(G-11334)*

Cast Specialties Inc.............................E 216 292-7393
Cleveland *(G-3475)*

Cmt Imports Inc..................................G 513 615-1851
Cincinnati *(G-2502)*

Destin Die Casting LLC........................E 937 347-1111
Xenia *(G-14762)*

Edc Liquidating Inc.............................C 330 467-0750
Macedonia *(G-8688)*

Enterprise Machine Inc.........................G 513 681-4409
Cincinnati *(G-2592)*

Fort Recovery Industries Inc.................C 419 375-4121
Fort Recovery *(G-6964)*

General Die Casters Inc........................D 330 467-6700
Northfield *(G-10793)*

General Die Casters Inc........................E 330 678-2528
Twinsburg *(G-13310)*

Krengel Equipment LLC.........................C 440 946-3570
Eastlake *(G-6434)*

Matalco (us) Inc.................................E 234 806-0600
Warren *(G-13781)*

Matalco (us) Inc.................................E 330 452-4760
Canton *(G-1939)*

Model Pattern & Foundry Co...................G 513 542-2322
Cincinnati *(G-2884)*

Ohio Aluminum Industries Inc................C 216 641-8865
Cleveland *(G-4110)*

Ohio Decorative Products LLC................C 419 647-9033
Spencerville *(G-12238)*

Omni Die Casting Inc...........................E 330 830-5500
Massillon *(G-9227)*

Omni USA Inc.....................................G 330 830-5500
Massillon *(G-9228)*

Park-Ohio Holdings Corp.......................F 440 947-2000
Cleveland *(G-4136)*

Park-Ohio Industries Inc.......................C 440 947-2000
Cleveland *(G-4137)*

Plaster Process Castings Co...................E 216 663-1814
Cleveland *(G-4170)*

Ramco Electric Motors Inc.....................D 937 548-2525
Greenville *(G-7350)*

Ravana Industries Inc..........................G 330 536-4015
Lowellville *(G-8664)*

Reliable Castings Corporation.................D 937 497-5217
Sidney *(G-12043)*

Ross Casting & Innovation LLC...............B 937 497-4500
Sidney *(G-12047)*

Seilkop Industries Inc..........................F 513 679-5680
Cincinnati *(G-3076)*

Seilkop Industries Inc..........................E 513 761-1035
Cincinnati *(G-3077)*

Seyekcub Inc.....................................G 330 324-1394
Uhrichsville *(G-13406)*

SRS Die Casting Holdings LLC................E 330 467-0750
Macedonia *(G-8714)*

SRS Light Metals Inc............................F 330 467-0750
Macedonia *(G-8715)*

The Basic Aluminum Castings Co...........D 216 481-5606
Cleveland *(G-4378)*

The Kindt-Collins Company LLC.............D 216 252-4122
Cleveland *(G-4387)*

Thompson Aluminum Casting Co.............E 216 206-2781
Cleveland *(G-4393)*

Tooling Technology LLC.........................D 937 381-9211
Fort Loramie *(G-6960)*

United States Drill Head Co...................F 513 941-0300
Cincinnati *(G-3185)*

W E Lott Company...............................F 419 563-9400
Bucyrus *(G-1694)*

Yoder Industries Inc............................C 937 278-5769
Dayton *(G-6089)*

CASTINGS: Die, Magnesium & Magnesium-Base Alloy

Thompson Aluminum Casting Co...........E 216 206-2781
Cleveland *(G-4393)*

CASTINGS: Die, Nonferrous

Dd Foundry Inc...................................F 216 362-4100
Brookpark *(G-1548)*

M & M Dies Inc...................................G 216 883-6628
Cleveland *(G-3973)*

Martina Metal LLC..............................E 614 291-9700
Columbus *(G-5085)*

Oakwood Industries Inc........................D 440 232-8700
Bedford *(G-1051)*

Support Svc LLC.................................G 419 617-0660
Lexington *(G-8375)*

Yoder Industries Inc............................C 937 278-5769
Dayton *(G-6089)*

CASTINGS: Ductile

Cmt Imports Inc..................................G 513 615-1851
Cincinnati *(G-2502)*

Sancast Inc.......................................E 740 622-8660
Coshocton *(G-5471)*

CASTINGS: Gray Iron

A C Williams Co Inc.............................E 330 296-6110
Ravenna *(G-11511)*

Barberton Steel Industries Inc...............E 330 745-6837
Barberton *(G-798)*

Brittany Stamping LLC.........................A 216 267-0850
Cleveland *(G-3440)*

Cast-Fab Technologies Inc....................C 513 758-1000
Cincinnati *(G-2442)*

Casting Solutions LLC..........................C 740 452-9371
Zanesville *(G-15005)*

Castings Usa Inc................................C 330 339-3611
New Philadelphia *(G-10436)*

Chris Erhart Foundry & Mch Co..............F 513 421-6550
Cincinnati *(G-2463)*

Col-Pump Company Inc.........................D 330 482-1029
Columbiana *(G-4610)*

Columbiana Foundry Company................C 330 482-3336
Columbiana *(G-4612)*

Ej Usa Inc..F 216 692-3001
South Euclid *(G-12219)*

Elyria Foundry Company LLC..................C 440 322-4657
Elyria *(G-6529)*

General Motors LLC.............................A 419 782-7010
Defiance *(G-6107)*

Liberty Casting Company LLC................D 740 363-1941
Delaware *(G-6160)*

Miami-Cast Inc...................................F 937 866-2951
Miamisburg *(G-9715)*

Old Smo Inc......................................C 419 394-3346
Saint Marys *(G-11746)*

OS Kelly Corporation............................E 937 322-4921
Springfield *(G-12358)*

Osco Industries Inc.............................D 740 286-5004
Jackson *(G-7950)*

Osco Industries Inc.............................B 740 354-3183
Portsmouth *(G-11473)*

Pioneer City Casting Company................E 740 423-7533
Belpre *(G-1153)*

Piqua Champion Foundry Inc..................G
Piqua *(G-11373)*

Quaker City Castings Inc.......................A 330 332-1566
Salem *(G-11806)*

Quality Castings Company......................B 330 682-6010
Orrville *(G-11003)*

T & B Foundry Company........................G 216 391-4200
Cleveland *(G-4360)*

Tri Cast Limited Partnership...................E 330 733-8718
Akron *(G-342)*

Tri-Cast Inc.......................................E 330 733-8718
Akron *(G-343)*

Whemco-Ohio Foundry Inc.....................C 419 222-2111
Lima *(G-8459)*

Yellow Creek Casting Co Inc..................G 330 532-4608
Wellsville *(G-13915)*

CASTINGS: Lead

Cpp-Cleveland Inc...............................C 440 953-0053
Eastlake *(G-6422)*

Cpp-Cleveland Inc...............................D 216 453-4800
Euclid *(G-6646)*

CASTINGS: Machinery, Aluminum

889 Global Solutions Ltd.......................F 614 235-8889
Columbus *(G-4655)*

Enprotech Industrial Tech LLC...............E 216 883-3220
Cleveland *(G-3675)*

General Precision Corporation.................G 440 951-9380
Willoughby *(G-14463)*

Nelson Aluminum Foundry Inc................G 440 543-1941
Chagrin Falls *(G-2173)*

Tri - Flex of Ohio Inc...........................G 330 705-7084
North Canton *(G-10677)*

Zephyr Industries Inc...........................G 419 281-4485
Ashland *(G-581)*

CASTINGS: Machinery, Nonferrous, Exc Die or Aluminum Copper

889 Global Solutions Ltd.......................F 614 235-8889
Columbus *(G-4655)*

Rossborough Supply Co.........................G 216 941-6115
Cleveland *(G-4255)*

CASTINGS: Magnesium

A C Williams Co Inc.............................E 330 296-6110
Ravenna *(G-11511)*

Garfield Alloys Inc..............................F 216 587-4843
Cleveland *(G-3754)*

Thompson Aluminum Casting Co...........E 216 206-2781
Cleveland *(G-4393)*

CASTINGS: Precision

Akron Foundry Co.................................C 330 745-3101
Akron *(G-31)*

Consoldted Precision Pdts Corp.............C 440 953-0053
Eastlake *(G-6421)*

Esco Turbine Technologies -...................C 440 953-0053
Eastlake *(G-6428)*

McM Precision Castings Inc....................E 419 669-3226
Weston *(G-14349)*

PCC Airfoils LLC.................................B 216 692-7900
Cleveland *(G-4148)*

PRODUCT

PCC Airfoils LLC................................. B 740 982-6025
Crooksville (G-5511)

PCC Airfoils LLC................................. B 440 585-8247
Eastlake (G-6440)

PCC Airfoils LLC................................. C 440 255-9770
Mentor (G-9584)

Sam Americas Inc................................ E 330 628-1118
Mogadore (G-10085)

Sandusky International Inc.................... C 419 626-5340
Sandusky (G-11868)

Warren Castings Inc............................. G 216 883-2520
Cleveland (G-4490)

CASTINGS: Steel

Alcon Industries Inc............................. D 216 961-1100
Cleveland (G-3321)

Coronado Steel Co............................... E 330 744-1143
Youngstown (G-14840)

Jrm 2 Company.................................... D 513 554-1700
Cincinnati (G-2774)

Quaker City Castings Inc...................... A 330 332-1566
Salem (G-11806)

Rampp Company................................... E 740 373-7886
Marietta (G-8940)

Sandusky International Inc.................... C 419 626-5340
Sandusky (G-11868)

Sjv Investment Inc............................... E 330 452-9711
Canton (G-2006)

Worthington Enterprises Inc................. C 614 438-3210
Worthington (G-14731)

CASTINGS: Titanium

Rmi Titanium Company LLC.................. G 330 652-9955
Niles (G-10603)

Rmi Titanium Company LLC.................. E 330 652-9952
Niles (G-10604)

Rti International Metals Inc.................... A
Niles (G-10606)

Tailwind Technologies Inc..................... A 937 778-4200
Piqua (G-11386)

Water Star Inc..................................... F 440 996-0800
Concord Township (G-5397)

CATALOG & MAIL-ORDER HOUSES

Hen of Woods LLC................................ G 513 954-8871
Cincinnati (G-2716)

Universal Direct Fulfillment Corp........... F 330 650-5000
Hudson (G-7861)

CATALYSTS: Chemical

BASF Catalysts LLC.............................. A 216 360-5005
Cleveland (G-3408)

BASF Catalysts LLC.............................. A 440 322-3741
Elyria (G-6502)

BLaster Holdings LLC........................... E 216 901-5800
Cleveland (G-3422)

BLaster LLC.. E 216 901-5800
Cleveland (G-3423)

Chemspec Usa Inc............................... D 330 669-8512
Orrville (G-10977)

Christy Catalytics LLC.......................... G 740 982-1302
Crooksville (G-5509)

Essential Elements Usa LLC................. E 513 482-5700
Cincinnati (G-2599)

United Initiators Inc............................. D 440 323-3112
Elyria (G-6598)

CATAPULTS

Universal Fabg Cnstr Svcs Inc.............. F 614 274-1128
Columbus (G-5338)

CATCH BASIN COVERS: Concrete

Wauseon Silo & Coal Company.............. F
Wauseon (G-13861)

CATERERS

Kenyetta Bagby Enterprise LLC............ F 614 584-3426
Reynoldsburg (G-11573)

Mustard Seed Health Fd Mkt Inc........... E 440 519-3663
Solon (G-12155)

CATTLE WHOLESALERS

Gardner Lumber Company Inc............... F 740 254-4664
Tippecanoe (G-12857)

CAULKING COMPOUNDS

Dap Products Inc................................. D 937 667-4461
Tipp City (G-12822)

CEILING SYSTEMS: Luminous, Commercial

Eaton Electric Holdings LLC................. B 440 523-5000
Cleveland (G-3654)

Hercules Led LLC................................ E 844 437-2533
Boardman (G-1374)

M-Boss Inc... E 216 441-6080
Cleveland (G-3976)

Nordic Light America Inc...................... F 614 981-9497
Canal Winchester (G-1796)

Norton Industries Inc........................... E 888 357-2345
Lakewood (G-8171)

CELLULOSE DERIVATIVE MATERIALS

Advanced Fiber LLC............................. E 419 562-1337
Bucyrus (G-1671)

Oak View Enterprises Inc...................... E 513 860-4446
Bucyrus (G-1685)

CEMENT & CONCRETE RELATED PRDTS & EQPT: Bituminous

Mesa Industries Inc............................. F 513 999-9781
Cincinnati (G-2867)

Mesa Industries Inc............................. E 513 321-2950
Cincinnati (G-2866)

CEMENT ROCK: Crushed & Broken

R W Sidley Incorporated....................... E 440 352-9343
Painesville (G-11108)

CEMENT, EXC LINOLEUM & TILE

Hartline Products Coinc........................ G 216 851-7189
Cleveland (G-3811)

CEMENT: Hydraulic

Hartline Products Coinc........................ G 216 851-7189
Cleveland (G-3811)

Holcim (us) Inc................................... G 216 781-9330
Cleveland (G-3833)

Holcim (us) Inc................................... C 419 399-4861
Paulding (G-11156)

Huron Cement Products Company......... E 419 433-4161
Huron (G-7874)

Quikrete Companies LLC...................... D 614 885-4406
Columbus (G-5220)

Quikrete Companies LLC...................... E 330 296-6080
Ravenna (G-11536)

Quikrete Companies LLC...................... F 419 241-1148
Toledo (G-13106)

Redland Quarries NY Inc...................... E 216 566-0545
Cleveland (G-4230)

USA Precast Concrete Limited.............. E 330 854-9600
Canal Fulton (G-1781)

CEMENT: Masonry

Kona Blackbird Inc.............................. E 440 285-3189
Chardon (G-2211)

CEMENT: Natural

Fairborn Cement Company LLC............ C 937 879-8393
Xenia (G-14764)

Independence Cement LLC................... E 216 264-1212
Brecksville (G-1471)

CEMENT: Portland

Wallseye Concrete Corp....................... F 419 483-2738
Castalia (G-2096)

Wallseye Concrete Corp....................... F 440 235-1800
Cleveland (G-4489)

CERAMIC FIBER

Astro Met Inc...................................... F 513 772-1242
Cincinnati (G-2383)

Ceramsource Inc................................. F 732 257-5002
East Palestine (G-6401)

Maverick Corporation........................... F 513 469-9919
Blue Ash (G-1304)

CHARCOAL

Nucon International Inc........................ F 614 846-5710
Columbus (G-5132)

CHARCOAL: Activated

Calgon Carbon Corporation.................. F 614 258-9501
Columbus (G-4791)

CHASSIS: Motor Vehicle

Custom Chassis Inc............................. G 440 839-5574
Wakeman (G-13679)

Falls Stamping & Welding Co............... C 330 928-1191
Cuyahoga Falls (G-5541)

Jefferson Industries Corp..................... C 614 879-5300
West Jefferson (G-14162)

Lippert Components Inc....................... G 574 537-8900
Payne (G-11164)

Ohio Module Manufacturing C.............. A 419 729-6700
Toledo (G-13074)

W&W Automotive & Towing Inc............. F 937 429-1699
Beavercreek Township (G-1007)

CHEESE WHOLESALERS

Bunker Hill Cheese Co Inc................... D 330 893-2131
Millersburg (G-9973)

Food Plant Engineering LLC................. F 513 618-3165
Blue Ash (G-1275)

Grays Orange Barn Inc........................ G 419 568-2718
Wapakoneta (G-13714)

Guggisberg Cheese Inc....................... E 330 893-2550
Millersburg (G-9982)

Schindlers Broad Run Chshuse I.......... F 330 343-4108
Dover (G-6260)

CHEMICAL CLEANING SVCS

Bleachtech LLC................................... E 216 921-1980
Seville (G-11913)

Chemical Solvents Inc.......................... E 216 741-9310
Cleveland (G-3492)

CHEMICAL ELEMENTS

Perstorp Polyols Inc............................ C 419 729-5448
Toledo (G-13095)

CHEMICAL PROCESSING MACHINERY & EQPT

Aquila Pharmatech LLC.........................G..... 419 386-2527
Waterville (G-13830)

Cammann Inc..F..... 440 965-4051
Wakeman (G-13678)

Chemineer Inc.......................................C..... 937 454-3200
Dayton (G-5700)

Guild Associates Inc.............................G..... 843 573-0095
Dublin (G-6299)

Guild Associates Inc.............................D..... 614 798-8215
Dublin (G-6300)

Hydro Systems Company........................F..... 513 271-8800
West Chester (G-14014)

Jbw Systems Inc....................................F..... 614 882-5008
Westerville (G-14215)

Processall Inc..F..... 513 771-2266
Cincinnati (G-2986)

CHEMICALS & ALLIED PRDTS WHOLESALERS, NEC

AIN Industries Inc..................................G..... 440 781-0950
Cleveland (G-3315)

Aquablue Incorporated...........................G..... 330 343-0220
New Philadelphia (G-10430)

Ashland Chemco Inc...............................C..... 614 790-3333
Columbus (G-4727)

Barentz N Amer Intrmdate Hldng...........G..... 440 937-1000
Avon (G-715)

Bleachtech LLC.......................................E..... 216 921-1980
Seville (G-11913)

Calvary Industries Inc............................E..... 513 874-1113
Fairfield (G-6716)

Chem-Sales Inc.......................................F
Toledo (G-12918)

Chemmasters Inc....................................E..... 440 428-2105
Madison (G-8726)

Corrugated Chemicals Inc.......................G..... 513 561-7773
Cincinnati (G-2519)

Dover Chemical Corporation....................C..... 330 343-7711
Dover (G-6238)

Finale Products Inc.................................G..... 419 874-2662
Perrysburg (G-11221)

Formlabs Ohio Inc...................................E..... 419 837-9783
Millbury (G-9961)

Hickman Williams & Company..................F..... 513 621-1946
Cincinnati (G-2721)

Imcd Us LLC..E..... 216 228-8900
Westlake (G-14310)

Knight Material Tech LLC.........................E..... 330 488-1651
East Canton (G-6378)

Netherland Rubber Company....................F..... 513 733-0883
Cincinnati (G-2899)

Polymer Additives Holdings Inc...............C..... 216 875-7200
Independence (G-7915)

PVS Chemical Solutions Inc.....................F..... 330 666-0888
Copley (G-5439)

Quality Borate Co LLC.............................F..... 216 896-1949
Cleveland (G-4212)

Sigma-Aldrich Corporation......................D..... 216 206-5424
Cleveland (G-4300)

Toagosei America Inc..............................D..... 614 718-3855
West Jefferson (G-14168)

Tricor Industrial Inc...............................D..... 330 264-3299
Wooster (G-14692)

CHEMICALS & ALLIED PRDTS, WHOLESALE: Chemical Additives

Chemcore Inc..F..... 937 228-6118
Dayton (G-5699)

Chemstation International Inc...................E..... 937 294-8265
Dayton (G-5701)

CHEMICALS & ALLIED PRDTS, WHOLESALE: Chemicals, Indl

Polar Inc..F..... 937 297-0911
Moraine (G-10185)

Rhein Chemie Corporation.......................C..... 440 279-2367
Chardon (G-2220)

Tembec Btlsr Inc.....................................E..... 419 244-5856
Toledo (G-13141)

Tosoh America Inc..................................B..... 614 539-8622
Grove City (G-7417)

Univar Solutions USA LLC........................F..... 800 531-7106
Dublin (G-6359)

Univar Solutions USA LLC........................E..... 513 714-5264
West Chester (G-14157)

CHEMICALS & ALLIED PRDTS, WHOLESALE: Chemicals, Indl & Heavy

Environmental Chemical Corp...................F..... 330 453-5200
Uniontown (G-13419)

Hexion Inc..C..... 888 443-9466
Columbus (G-4976)

CHEMICALS & ALLIED PRDTS, WHOLESALE: Detergent/Soap

Chemical Solvents Inc.............................E..... 216 741-9310
Cleveland (G-3492)

Love Laugh & Laundry.............................G..... 567 377-1951
Toledo (G-13039)

CHEMICALS & ALLIED PRDTS, WHOLESALE: Detergents

Cleaning Lady Inc...................................G..... 419 589-5566
Mansfield (G-8774)

Washing Systems LLC.............................C..... 800 272-1974
Loveland (G-8656)

CHEMICALS & ALLIED PRDTS, WHOLESALE: Plastics Film

Cleveland Supplyone Inc.........................E..... 216 514-7000
Cleveland (G-3527)

CHEMICALS & ALLIED PRDTS, WHOLESALE: Plastics Materials, NEC

Alro Steel Corporation............................E..... 614 878-7271
Columbus (G-4690)

Alro Steel Corporation............................D..... 419 720-5300
Toledo (G-12871)

Plastics -R- Unique Inc...........................E..... 330 334-4820
Wadsworth (G-13660)

Plastics Family Holdings Inc...................F..... 614 272-0777
Columbus (G-5196)

CHEMICALS & ALLIED PRDTS, WHOLESALE: Plastics Prdts, NEC

Carney Plastics Inc.................................G..... 330 746-8273
Youngstown (G-14831)

Polymer Packaging Inc............................D..... 330 832-2000
North Canton (G-10658)

Queen City Polymers Inc.........................E..... 513 779-0990
West Chester (G-14059)

Tahoma Enterprises Inc..........................D..... 330 745-9016
Barberton (G-840)

Tahoma Rubber & Plastics Inc.................D..... 330 745-9016
Ashland (G-579)

UPL International Inc...............................F..... 330 433-2860
North Canton (G-10680)

CHEMICALS & ALLIED PRDTS, WHOLESALE: Plastics Sheets & Rods

HP Manufacturing Company Inc...............D..... 216 361-6500
Cleveland (G-3841)

Plastics Family Holdings Inc...................G..... 440 891-1140
Cleveland (G-4172)

CHEMICALS & ALLIED PRDTS, WHOLESALE: Resins

Avient Corporation..................................D..... 440 930-1000
Avon Lake (G-748)

Epsilyte Holdings LLC..............................D..... 937 778-9500
Piqua (G-11346)

Hexpol Compounding LLC.........................C..... 440 834-4644
Burton (G-1699)

CHEMICALS & ALLIED PRDTS, WHOLESALE: Resins, Plastics

Network Polymers Inc..............................E..... 330 773-2700
Akron (G-244)

CHEMICALS & ALLIED PRDTS, WHOLESALE: Rubber, Synthetic

Goldsmith & Eggleton Inc........................F..... 330 336-6616
Wadsworth (G-13640)

Goldsmith & Eggleton LLC........................F..... 203 855-6000
Wadsworth (G-13641)

Mantaline Corporation.............................F..... 330 274-2264
Mantua (G-8871)

CHEMICALS & ALLIED PRDTS, WHOLESALE: Spec Clean/Sanitation

Ccp Industries Inc...................................B..... 216 535-4227
Richmond Heights (G-11609)

CHEMICALS & ALLIED PRDTS, WHOLESALE: Syn Resin, Rub/Plastic

Akrochem Corporation.............................D..... 330 535-2100
Akron (G-24)

Flex Technologies Inc.............................D..... 330 897-6311
Baltic (G-777)

Kraton Polymers US LLC..........................B..... 740 423-7571
Belpre (G-1150)

Phoenix Technologies Intl LLC..................E..... 419 353-7738
Bowling Green (G-1434)

CHEMICALS & OTHER PRDTS DERIVED FROM COKING

FBC Chemical Corporation.......................E..... 216 341-2000
Cleveland (G-3707)

Geauga Coatings LLC...............................G..... 440 221-7286
Chardon (G-2206)

Worthington Steel Company......................B..... 800 944-2255
Worthington (G-14732)

CHEMICALS, AGRICULTURE: Wholesalers

Helena Agri-Enterprises LLC.....................G..... 614 275-4200
Columbus (G-4975)

Imcd Us LLC..E..... 216 228-8900
Westlake (G-14310)

Keystone Cooperative Inc........................G..... 937 884-5526
Verona (G-13591)

Tyler Grain & Fertilizer Co........................F..... 330 669-2341
Smithville (G-12070)

CHEMICALS: Agricultural

Employee Codes: A=Over 500 employees, B=251-500
C=101-250, D=51-100, E=20-50, F=10-19, G=1-9

2025 Harris Ohio
Industrial Directory

1253

PRODUCT

BASF Corporation.................................D 614 662-5682
Columbus (G-4745)

Damon Industries Inc..........................D 330 821-5310
Alliance (G-379)

Dupont Wealth Solutions LLC............F 614 384-5246
Dublin (G-6295)

Hawthorne Hydroponics LLC...............F 888 478-6544
Marysville (G-9024)

Keystone Cooperative Inc....................G 937 884-5526
Verona (G-13591)

Meristem Crop Prfmce Group LLC........E 833 637-4783
Powell (G-11490)

Monsanto Company...............................F 937 548-7858
Greenville (G-7347)

Quality Borate Co LLC.........................F 216 896-1949
Cleveland (G-4212)

TLC Products Inc..................................F 216 472-3030
Westlake (G-14340)

CHEMICALS: Alkalies

Valvsys LLC...G 513 870-1234
Hamilton (G-7536)

CHEMICALS: Aluminum Compounds

Drs Industrial LLC...............................G 419 861-0334
Holland (G-7758)

Drs Industries Inc.................................D 419 861-0334
Holland (G-7759)

Gayston Corporation............................C 937 743-6050
Miamisburg (G-9693)

CHEMICALS: Aluminum Oxide

Custom Metal Shearing Inc..................F 937 233-6950
Dayton (G-5718)

CHEMICALS: Anhydrous Ammonia

CF Industries Inc..................................C 330 385-5424
East Liverpool (G-6389)

Talus Renewables Inc...........................F 650 248-5374
Cleveland Heights (G-4531)

CHEMICALS: Bleaching Powder, Lime Bleaching Compounds

Bleachtech LLC.....................................E 216 921-1980
Seville (G-11913)

CHEMICALS: Caustic Potash & Potassium Hydroxide

INEOS KOH INC....................................C 440 997-5221
Ashtabula (G-596)

CHEMICALS: Caustic Soda

National Colloid Company....................E 740 282-1171
Steubenville (G-12407)

CHEMICALS: Fire Retardant

No Burn Inc...G 330 336-1500
Wadsworth (G-13655)

Pyro-Chem Corporation........................F 740 377-2244
South Point (G-12230)

CHEMICALS: High Purity Grade, Organic

Ronald T Dodge Co..............................F 937 439-4497
Dayton (G-5988)

CHEMICALS: High Purity, Refined From Technical Grade

Arboris LLC...E 740 522-9350
Newark (G-10492)

Helena Agri-Enterprises LLC................G 614 275-4200
Columbus (G-4975)

Helena Agri-Enterprises LLC................G 419 596-3806
Continental (G-5422)

Heraeus Epurio LLC.............................E 937 264-1000
Vandalia (G-13559)

Pureti Group LLC.................................G 513 708-3631
Cincinnati (G-3012)

CHEMICALS: Inorganic, NEC

Airgas Usa LLC....................................G 440 232-6397
Twinsburg (G-13270)

Akron Dispersions Inc.........................E 330 666-0045
Copley (G-5428)

Alchem Corporation.............................G 330 725-2436
Medina (G-9373)

Alfrebro LLC..F 513 539-7373
Monroe (G-10095)

Alpha Zeta Holdings Inc......................G 216 271-1601
Cleveland (G-3334)

Aluchem Inc..E 513 733-8519
Cincinnati (G-2353)

Aluchem of Jackson Inc.......................G 740 286-2455
Jackson (G-7938)

Americhem Inc......................................D 330 929-4213
Cuyahoga Falls (G-5523)

BASF Corporation.................................D 614 662-5682
Columbus (G-4745)

Bio-Systems Corporation.....................G 608 365-9550
Bowling Green (G-1410)

Bond Chemicals Inc.............................G 330 725-5935
Medina (G-9382)

Borchers Americas Inc........................D 440 899-2950
Westlake (G-14295)

Calvary Industries Inc..........................E 513 874-1113
Fairfield (G-6716)

Chem Technologies Ltd.......................D 440 632-9311
Middlefield (G-9786)

Chemtrade Logistics Inc......................F 216 566-8070
Cleveland (G-3493)

Chemtrade Refinery Svcs Inc...............F 419 641-4151
Cairo (G-1721)

Cil Isotope Separations LLC................F 937 376-5413
Xenia (G-14757)

Cirba Solutions Us Inc.........................E 740 653-6290
Lancaster (G-8186)

Current Lighting Solutions LLC............E 216 462-4700
Cleveland (G-3581)

Diverseylever Inc.................................G 513 554-4200
Cincinnati (G-2553)

Diversified Brands...............................F 216 595-8777
Bedford (G-1027)

Dover Chemical Corporation................C 330 343-7711
Dover (G-6238)

Dupont Electronic Polymers LP............D 937 268-3411
Dayton (G-5756)

Eagle Chemicals Inc............................F 513 868-9662
Hamilton (G-7487)

Elco Corporation..................................E 440 997-6131
Ashtabula (G-590)

Eliokem Inc...D 330 734-1100
Fairlawn (G-6800)

Evonik Corporation..............................E 513 554-8969
Cincinnati (G-2606)

Ferro Corporation................................D 216 577-7144
Bedford (G-1032)

Ferroglobe USA Mtlurgical Inc.............C 740 984-2361
Waterford (G-13826)

Flexsys Inc..B 212 605-6000
Akron (G-151)

General Electric Company....................G 216 268-3846
Cleveland (G-3763)

GFS Chemicals Inc...............................E 614 351-5347
Columbus (G-4953)

Great River Re Inc...............................E 513 471-8770
Cincinnati (G-2688)

Hilltop Energy Inc.................................F 330 859-2108
Mineral City (G-10028)

Illinois Tool Works Inc.........................D 440 914-3100
Solon (G-12126)

Ineos Pigments Asu LLC......................F 440 994-1999
Ashtabula (G-597)

Ineos Pigments USA Inc......................C 440 994-1400
Ashtabula (G-598)

J R M Chemical Inc..............................F 216 475-8488
Cleveland (G-3878)

Littlern Corporation.............................G 330 848-8847
Fairlawn (G-6807)

Malco Products Inc...............................C 330 753-0361
Barberton (G-819)

McGean-Rohco Inc...............................E 216 441-4900
Newburgh Heights (G-10545)

McGean-Rohco Inc...............................D 216 441-4900
Cleveland (G-4009)

Nachurs Alpine Solutions LLC..............E 740 382-5701
Marion (G-8982)

National Colloid Company....................E 740 282-1171
Steubenville (G-12407)

Norlab Inc...F 440 282-5265
Lorain (G-8569)

Om Group Inc.......................................F 216 781-0083
Cleveland (G-4120)

Omnova Wallcovering USA Inc.............D 216 682-7000
Beachwood (G-937)

PMC Specialties Group Inc..................F 513 242-3300
Cincinnati (G-2972)

PMC Specialties Group Inc..................E 513 242-3300
Cincinnati (G-2971)

Polymerics Inc......................................E 330 928-2210
Cuyahoga Falls (G-5565)

Primary Pdts Ingrdnts Amrcas L...........D 937 236-5906
Dayton (G-5955)

Quanta International LLC......................F 513 354-3639
Cincinnati (G-3018)

Saint-Gobain Ceramics Plas Inc...........C 440 564-8000
Newbury (G-10564)

Saint-Gobain Ceramics Plas Inc...........D 330 673-5860
Stow (G-12456)

Saint-Gobain Ceramics Plas Inc...........A 610 893-6000
Stow (G-12457)

Shepherd Widnes Ltd..........................D 513 731-1110
Norwood (G-10872)

Synthomer Inc......................................F 330 734-1237
Akron (G-323)

Synthomer Inc......................................C 216 682-7000
Beachwood (G-951)

Univar Solutions USA LLC....................E 513 714-5264
West Chester (G-14157)

Usalco Michigan City Plant LLC...........D 440 992-7039
Ashtabula (G-619)

Usalco Michigan City Plant LLC...........F 513 737-7100
Fairfield (G-6787)

Vibrantz Corporation............................F 442 224-6100
Cleveland (G-4466)

VWR Chemicals LLC.............................E 800 448-4442
Solon (G-12204)

WA Hammond Drierite Co Ltd...............E 937 376-2927
Xenia (G-14783)

Zaclon LLC..E 216 271-1601
Cleveland (G-4522)

CHEMICALS: Lithium Compounds, Inorganic

Lithium Innovations Co LLC.................G 419 725-3525
Toledo (G-13038)

CHEMICALS: Medicinal

Pharmacia Hepar LLC........................... G 937 746-3603
Franklin (G-7040)

Polar Products Inc................................ E 330 253-9973
Stow (G-12449)

CHEMICALS: Medicinal, Organic, Uncompounded, Bulk

Nutritional Medicinals LLC.................. F 937 433-4673
West Chester (G-14034)

CHEMICALS: NEC

Akron Dispersions Inc.......................... E 330 666-0045
Copley (G-5428)

Aldrich Chemical.................................. D 937 859-1808
Miamisburg (G-9663)

Alterra Energy LLC............................... G 800 569-6061
Akron (G-53)

Aps-Materials Inc................................. D 937 278-6547
Dayton (G-5662)

Ashland Chemco Inc............................. F 216 961-4690
Cleveland (G-3378)

Ashland Chemco Inc............................. C 614 790-3333
Columbus (G-4727)

Ashland Spcalty Ingredients GP........... C 614 529-3311
Columbus (G-4728)

ASK Chemicals LLC.............................. B 800 848-7485
Dublin (G-6277)

Bernard Laboratories Inc...................... E 513 681-7373
Cincinnati (G-2407)

Bird Control International...................... G 330 425-2377
Twinsburg (G-13281)

BLaster LLC.. E 216 901-5800
Cleveland (G-3423)

Bond Distributing LLC........................... G 440 461-7920
Eastlake (G-6420)

Borchers Americas Inc.......................... D 440 899-2950
Westlake (G-14295)

Buckeye Fabric Finishers Inc................ F 740 622-3251
Coshocton (G-5453)

Cargill Incorporated.............................. C 216 651-7200
Cleveland (G-3470)

Cfo Ntic.. G 216 450-5700
Beachwood (G-911)

Chem Technologies Ltd......................... D 440 632-9311
Middlefield (G-9786)

Chemical Methods Incorporated........... C 210 470-0400
Brunswick (G-1582)

Chemstation International Inc............... E 937 294-8265
Dayton (G-5701)

Cinchempro Inc..................................... C 513 724-6111
Batavia (G-855)

Cincinnati - Vulcan Company............... D 513 242-5300
Cincinnati (G-2465)

CP Chemicals Group LP......................... G 440 833-3000
Wickliffe (G-14372)

Cresset Chemical Co Inc....................... F 419 669-2041
Weston (G-14348)

Cresset Chemical Co Inc....................... F 419 669-2041
Weston (G-14347)

Dayton Superior Corporation................ C 937 866-0711
Miamisburg (G-9687)

Dover Chemical Corporation................. C 330 343-7711
Dover (G-6238)

Elco Corporation................................... E 440 997-6131
Ashtabula (G-590)

EMD Millipore Corporation.................... C 513 631-0445
Norwood (G-10868)

Ensign Product Company Inc................ G 216 341-5911
Cleveland (G-3676)

Enviri Corporation................................ F 330 372-1781
Warren (G-13763)

Environmental Chemical Corp.............. F 330 453-5200
Uniontown (G-13419)

ESP Akron Sub LLC.............................. D 330 374-2242
Akron (G-139)

Essential Elements Usa LLC................. E 513 482-5700
Cincinnati (G-2599)

Etna Products Incorporated.................. E 440 543-9845
Chagrin Falls (G-2161)

Euclid Chemical Company..................... F 216 292-5000
Beachwood (G-918)

Euclid Chemical Company..................... E 800 321-7628
Cleveland (G-3688)

Flexsys America LP.............................. D 330 666-4111
Akron (G-150)

Formlabs Ohio Inc................................ E 419 837-9783
Millbury (G-9961)

Fuchs Lubricants Co............................. F 330 963-0400
Twinsburg (G-13306)

Fusion Ceramics Inc............................. E 330 627-5821
Carrollton (G-2083)

Fusion Incorporated............................. D 440 946-3300
Willoughby (G-14460)

Galapagos Inc...................................... F 937 890-3068
Dayton (G-5789)

General Electric Company..................... G 216 268-3846
Cleveland (G-3763)

GFS Chemicals Inc............................... D 614 224-5345
Columbus (G-4954)

GFS Chemicals Inc............................... E 740 881-5501
Powell (G-11488)

Great River Re Inc............................... E 513 471-8770
Cincinnati (G-2688)

H B Chemical Corporation..................... G 330 920-8023
Twinsburg (G-13313)

H&G Legacy Co..................................... F 513 921-1075
Cincinnati (G-2701)

Hexion LLC... D 614 225-4000
Columbus (G-4977)

Hexpol Compounding LLC...................... C 440 834-4644
Burton (G-1699)

Howard Industries Inc.......................... F 614 444-9900
Columbus (G-4993)

Hunt Imaging LLC................................. E 440 826-0433
Berea (G-1176)

Huntsman Corporation.......................... D 330 374-2418
Akron (G-179)

Illinois Tool Works Inc.......................... D 440 914-3100
Solon (G-12126)

Innovative Food Processors Inc............ G 507 334-2730
Defiance (G-6112)

Intercontinental Chemical Corp........... E 513 541-7100
Cincinnati (G-2749)

Italmatch Sc LLC.................................. F 216 749-2605
Cleveland (G-3873)

J C Whitlam Manufacturing Co.............. E 330 334-2524
Wadsworth (G-13644)

Koki Laboratories Inc........................... E 330 773-7669
Akron (G-198)

Leonhardt Plating Company.................. G 513 242-1410
Cincinnati (G-2819)

Liquid Development Company............... G 216 641-9366
Independence (G-7907)

Lubrizol Advanced Mtls Inc.................. F 216 447-5000
Brecksville (G-1476)

Lubrizol Global Management................. E 419 352-5565
Bowling Green (G-1426)

Lubrizol Global Management Inc........... E 440 933-0400
Avon Lake (G-763)

Lubrizol Global Management Inc........... F 216 447-5000
Cleveland (G-3970)

Lubrizol Holdings LLC........................... F 440 943-4200
Wickliffe (G-14381)

Malco Products Inc............................... C 330 753-0361
Barberton (G-819)

Master Chemical Corporation............... D 419 874-7902
Perrysburg (G-11238)

McGean-Rohco Inc................................ G 216 441-4900
Newburgh Heights (G-10545)

McGean-Rohco Inc................................ D 216 441-4900
Cleveland (G-4009)

Midwest Glycol Services LLC................ E 419 946-3326
Marion (G-8978)

Morgan Advanced Ceramics Inc........... E 330 405-1033
Twinsburg (G-13344)

Morton Salt Inc.................................... C 330 925-3015
Rittman (G-11625)

National Colloid Company..................... E 740 282-1171
Steubenville (G-12407)

New Vulco Mfg & Sales Co LLC............ D 513 242-2672
Cincinnati (G-2904)

Noco Company...................................... D 216 464-8131
Glenwillow (G-7286)

Nof Metal Coatings N Amer Inc............ E 440 285-2231
Chardon (G-2215)

Noveon Fcc Inc..................................... F 440 943-4200
Wickliffe (G-14384)

Ohio Aluminum Chemicals LLC............. E 513 860-3842
West Chester (G-14036)

Parker Trutec Incorporated.................. D 937 653-8500
Urbana (G-13476)

Polymer Additives Holdings Inc............ C 216 875-7200
Independence (G-7915)

Polymerics Inc...................................... E 330 677-1131
Kent (G-8060)

PPG Architectural Coatings LLC............ D 440 297-8000
Strongsville (G-12587)

Premier Ink Systems Inc...................... F 513 367-2300
Harrison (G-7562)

Primary Pdts Ingrdnts Amrcas L........... D 937 236-5906
Dayton (G-5955)

Proklean Services LLC.......................... E 330 273-0122
Brunswick (G-1609)

Quaker Chemical Corporation............... E 513 422-9600
Middletown (G-9888)

Quikrete Companies LLC...................... D 614 885-4406
Columbus (G-5220)

Ravago Chemical Dist Inc..................... E 330 920-8023
Twinsburg (G-13364)

Research Organics LLC.......................... D 216 883-8025
Cleveland (G-4236)

Rhenium Alloys Inc............................... E 440 365-7388
North Ridgeville (G-10747)

Rolled Alloys Inc.................................. D 800 521-0332
Maumee (G-9315)

Rozzi Company Inc............................... F 513 683-0620
Martinsville (G-9013)

Sigma-Aldrich Corporation................... D 216 206-5424
Cleveland (G-4300)

Signet Enterprises LLC......................... E 330 762-9102
Akron (G-312)

State Industrial Products Corp............. B 877 747-6986
Cleveland (G-4329)

Summitville Tiles Inc............................ D 330 868-6463
Minerva (G-10048)

Teknol Inc.. D 937 264-0190
Dayton (G-6043)

The Lubrizol Corporation...................... G 216 447-6212
Akron (G-331)

The Lubrizol Corporation...................... C 440 357-7064
Painesville (G-11117)

U S Chemical & Plastics....................... G 330 830-6000
Massillon (G-9250)

PRODUCT

Univar Solutions USA LLC...................... E 513 714-5264
West Chester *(G-14157)*

Valtris Specialty Chemicals................... F 216 875-7200
Walton Hills *(G-13704)*

Vesuvius U S A Corporation.................. G 440 593-1161
Conneaut *(G-5419)*

Vibrantz Corporation............................ E 216 875-5600
Cleveland *(G-4467)*

Zinkan Enterprises Inc......................... F 330 487-1500
Twinsburg *(G-13400)*

CHEMICALS: Phenol

Altivia Petrochemicals LLC.................... E 740 532-3420
Haverhill *(G-7585)*

CHEMICALS: Phosphates, Defluorinated/ Ammoniated, Exc Fertlr

Pcs Phosphate Company Inc................. C 513 738-1261
Harrison *(G-7560)*

CHEMICALS: Reagent Grade, Refined From Technical Grade

GFS Chemicals Inc............................... D 614 224-5345
Columbus *(G-4954)*

GFS Chemicals Inc............................... E 740 881-5501
Powell *(G-11488)*

CHEMICALS: Silica Compounds

Wisconsin Indus Sand Co LLC............. E 715 235-0942
Independence *(G-7926)*

CHEMICALS: Silver Compounds Or Salts, Inorganic

Materion Advnced Mtls Tech Svc.......... D 216 486-4200
Mayfield Heights *(G-9335)*

CHEMICALS: Sodium Bicarbonate

Church & Dwight Co Inc....................... G 740 852-3621
London *(G-8533)*

Church & Dwight Co Inc....................... G 419 992-4244
Old Fort *(G-10933)*

CHEMICALS: Water Treatment

AP Tech Group Inc............................... F 513 761-8111
West Chester *(G-13940)*

Applied Specialties Innovations LLC... E 440 933-9442
Avon Lake *(G-746)*

Aqua Science Inc................................. E 614 252-5000
Columbus *(G-4723)*

Aquablue Incorporated........................ G 330 343-0220
New Philadelphia *(G-10430)*

Bond Chemicals Inc............................. G 330 725-5935
Medina *(G-9382)*

City of Mount Vernon........................... G 740 393-9508
Mount Vernon *(G-10240)*

Damon Industries Inc........................... D 330 821-5310
Alliance *(G-379)*

Ques Industries Inc............................. F 216 267-8989
Cleveland *(G-4218)*

US Water Company LLC...................... G 740 453-0604
Zanesville *(G-15053)*

Usalco Fairfield Plant LLC................... E 513 737-7100
Fairfield *(G-6786)*

CHICKEN SLAUGHTERING & PROCESSING

Pf Management Inc............................... G 513 874-8741
West Chester *(G-14136)*

Pierre Holding Corp............................. G 513 874-8741
West Chester *(G-14137)*

V H Cooper & Co Inc............................ C 419 375-4116
Fort Recovery *(G-6973)*

CHILD DAY CARE SVCS

Learn21 A Flxble Lrng Cllbrtiv............... F 513 402-2121
Cincinnati *(G-2816)*

CHILD RESTRAINT SEATS, AUTOMOTIVE, WHOLESALE

TS Tech Americas Inc........................... B 614 575-4100
Reynoldsburg *(G-11583)*

CHILDREN'S WEAR STORES

Carters Inc.. G 330 758-0390
Boardman *(G-1369)*

Love Laugh & Laundry.......................... G 567 377-1951
Toledo *(G-13039)*

CHOCOLATE, EXC CANDY FROM BEANS: Chips, Powder, Block, Syrup

Anthony-Thomas Candy Company........ C 614 274-8405
Columbus *(G-4719)*

Brandts Candies Inc............................. G 440 942-1016
Willoughby *(G-14433)*

Brantley Partners IV LP........................ G 216 464-8400
Cleveland *(G-3434)*

Cheryl & Co.. F 614 776-1500
Obetz *(G-10923)*

Chocolate Pig Inc................................. G 440 461-4511
Cleveland *(G-3496)*

Dietsch Brothers Incorporated.............. E 419 422-4474
Findlay *(G-6859)*

Executive Sweets East Inc.................... G 440 359-9866
Oakwood Village *(G-10905)*

Fawn Confectionery Inc........................ F 513 574-9612
Cincinnati *(G-2613)*

Gorant Chocolatier LLC........................ C 330 726-8821
Boardman *(G-1372)*

Graeters Ice Cream Company............... D 513 721-3323
Cincinnati *(G-2687)*

Harry London Candies Inc.................... E 330 494-0833
North Canton *(G-10645)*

Linneas Candy Supplies Inc................. E 330 678-7112
Kent *(G-8046)*

Malleys Candies LLC............................ D 216 362-8700
Cleveland *(G-3983)*

Milk Hney Cndy Soda Shoppe LLC........ G 330 492-5884
Canton *(G-1950)*

Robert E McGrath Inc.......................... F 440 572-7747
Strongsville *(G-12593)*

Sweeties Olympia Treats LLC............... F 440 572-7747
Strongsville *(G-12608)*

CHOCOLATE, EXC CANDY FROM PURCH CHOC: Chips, Powder, Block

Golden Turtle Chocolate Fctry.............. G 513 932-1990
Lebanon *(G-8264)*

Hartville Chocolates Inc....................... G 330 877-1999
Hartville *(G-7576)*

CHUCKS

Flex-E-On Inc...................................... F 330 928-4496
Cuyahoga Falls *(G-5542)*

Hammill Manufacturing Co.................... D 419 476-0789
Maumee *(G-9295)*

Jerry Tools Inc..................................... F 513 242-3211
Cincinnati *(G-2765)*

Shook Manufactured Pdts Inc............... G 440 247-9130
Chagrin Falls *(G-2151)*

Shook Manufactured Pdts Inc............... G 330 848-9780
Akron *(G-311)*

CHURCHES

Christian Missionary Alliance............... C 380 208-6200
Reynoldsburg *(G-11562)*

CIGARETTE & CIGAR PRDTS & ACCESS

Gumbys LLC.. F 740 671-0818
Bellaire *(G-1088)*

CIGARETTE LIGHTERS

Hunters Manufacturing Co Inc............... E 330 628-9245
Mogadore *(G-10077)*

CIRCUIT BOARD REPAIR SVCS

Mid-Ohio Electric Co............................ E 614 274-8000
Columbus *(G-5098)*

CIRCUIT BOARDS: Wiring

Parlex USA LLC................................... E 937 898-3621
Vandalia *(G-13575)*

R-K Electronics Inc.............................. F 513 204-6060
Mason *(G-9141)*

CIRCUITS: Electronic

Accurate Electronics Inc....................... F 330 682-7015
Orrville *(G-10972)*

Alphabet Inc.. D 330 856-3366
Warren *(G-13733)*

Astro Industries Inc............................. E 937 429-5900
Beavercreek *(G-966)*

C E Electronics Inc.............................. D 419 636-6705
Bryan *(G-1635)*

Captor Corporation.............................. D 937 667-8484
Tipp City *(G-12818)*

CEC Electronics Corp.......................... G 330 916-8100
Akron *(G-92)*

Channel Products Inc........................... D 440 423-0113
Solon *(G-12093)*

CMC Electronics Cincinn...................... G 513 573-6316
Mason *(G-9091)*

Cutting Edge Technologies Inc.............. G 216 574-4759
Cleveland *(G-3589)*

Dynalab Ems Inc.................................. C 614 866-9999
Reynoldsburg *(G-11566)*

Dynalab Ff Inc..................................... D 614 866-9999
Reynoldsburg *(G-11567)*

Electro-Line Inc................................... F 937 461-5683
Dayton *(G-5762)*

Electronauts LLC................................. F 859 261-3600
Cincinnati *(G-2581)*

Eti Tech LLC.. F 937 832-4200
Kettering *(G-8120)*

Great Lakes Glasswerks Inc................. G 440 358-0460
Painesville *(G-11090)*

Inservco Inc.. D 847 855-9600
Lagrange *(G-8148)*

Laird Technologies Inc......................... F 330 434-7929
Akron *(G-201)*

Lintech Electronics LLC........................ E 513 528-6190
Cincinnati *(G-2312)*

Mjo Industries Inc................................ D 800 590-4055
Huber Heights *(G-7822)*

Niktec Inc.. G 513 282-3747
Franklin *(G-7038)*

Parker-Hannifin Corporation................. E 937 644-3915
Marysville *(G-9041)*

Performance Electronics Ltd................. G 513 777-5233
Cincinnati *(G-2954)*

Precision Manufacturing Co Inc............ D 937 236-2170
Dayton *(G-5948)*

Qlog Corp..G 513 874-1211
Hamilton (G-7519)

Rct Industries Inc..................................F 937 602-1100
Dayton (G-5977)

Sentrilock LLC.......................................C 513 618-5800
West Chester (G-14074)

Shiloh Industries Inc...........................F 937 236-5100
Dayton (G-6003)

Sovereign Circuits Inc.........................G 330 538-3900
North Jackson (G-10694)

Spectron Inc...937 461-5590
Dayton (G-6017)

Tinycircuits...G 330 329-5753
Akron (G-338)

Tls Corp..D 216 574-4759
Cleveland (G-4396)

Twin Point Inc.......................................G 419 923-7525
Delta (G-6214)

US Lighting Group Inc.........................E 216 896-7000
Euclid (G-6682)

Valley Electric Company.....................G 419 332-6405
Fremont (G-7142)

Workman Electronic Pdts Inc.............G 419 923-7525
Delta (G-6215)

CLAMPS & COUPLINGS: Hose

Bowes Manufacturing Inc....................F 216 378-2110
Solon (G-12087)

Eaton Aeroquip LLC.............................C 440 523-5000
Cleveland (G-3650)

Eaton Corporation................................A 419 238-1190
Van Wert (G-13534)

Voss Industries LLC.............................C 216 771-7655
Cleveland (G-4482)

Winzeler Stamping Co..........................E 419 485-3147
Montpelier (G-10138)

CLAMPS: Metal

Case Maul Clamps Inc.........................G 419 668-6563
Norwalk (G-10832)

Clampco Products Inc..........................C 330 336-8857
Wadsworth (G-13631)

Etl Performance Products Inc.............G 234 575-7226
Salem (G-11777)

Herman Machine Inc............................F 330 633-3261
Tallmadge (G-12736)

Ottawa Products Co.............................E 419 836-5115
Curtice (G-3517)

CLEANING EQPT: Commercial

As Clean As It Gets Off Brkroo............E 216 256-1143
South Euclid (G-12218)

Cold Jet International LLC....................D 513 831-3211
Loveland (G-8622)

Detrex Corporation..............................F 216 749-2605
Cleveland (G-3611)

Evers Enterprises Inc..........................G 513 541-7200
Cincinnati (G-2603)

High-TEC Industrial Services..............D 937 667-1772
Tipp City (G-12827)

Holdren Brothers Inc...........................F 937 465-7050
West Liberty (G-14175)

Kaivac Inc..D 513 887-4600
Hamilton (G-7508)

Kellermyer Bergensons Svcs LLC......D 419 867-4300
Maumee (G-9301)

MPW Industrial Svcs Group Inc..........B 740 927-8790
Hebron (G-7625)

Squeaky Clean Cincinnati Inc.............F 513 729-2712
Cincinnati (G-3109)

CLEANING EQPT: Floor Washing & Polishing, Commercial

Diversey Taski Inc...............................E 419 531-2121
Toledo (G-12945)

Image By J & K LLC..............................F 888 667-6929
Maumee (G-9297)

MJB Toledo Inc.....................................D 419 531-2121
Toledo (G-13056)

Powerbuff Inc..F 419 241-2156
Toledo (G-13102)

CLEANING OR POLISHING PREPARATIONS, NEC

Aromair Fine Fragrance Company.........B 614 984-2900
New Albany (G-10330)

Canberra Corporation..........................C 419 724-4300
Toledo (G-12910)

Chemical Methods Incorporated..........E 216 476-8400
Brunswick (G-1582)

Chempace Corporation.........................F 419 535-0101
Toledo (G-12919)

Chemstation International Inc..............E 937 294-8265
Dayton (G-5701)

Damon Industries Inc...........................D 330 821-5310
Alliance (G-379)

Emes Supply LLC..................................G 216 400-8025
Willowick (G-14566)

Kleen Test Products Corp....................B 330 878-5586
Strasburg (G-12479)

Kona Blackbird Inc...............................E 440 285-3189
Chardon (G-2211)

Ohio Auto Supply Company.................G 330 454-5105
Canton (G-1964)

Paro Services Co...................................F 330 467-1300
Twinsburg (G-13350)

Ventco Inc..F 440 834-8888
Chagrin Falls (G-2190)

Vitex Corporation.................................F 216 883-0920
Cleveland (G-4477)

Woodbine Products Company...............F 330 725-0165
Medina (G-9465)

CLEANING PRDTS: Automobile Polish

BLaster Holdings LLC...........................E 216 901-5800
Cleveland (G-3422)

BLaster LLC..E 216 901-5800
Cleveland (G-3423)

James C Robinson.................................G 513 969-7482
Cincinnati (G-2760)

Jax Wax Inc..F 614 476-6769
Columbus (G-5033)

CLEANING PRDTS: Bleaches, Household, Dry Or Liquid

K-O-K Products Inc...............................F 740 548-0526
Galena (G-7173)

CLEANING PRDTS: Degreasing Solvent

Pneumatic Specialties Inc....................G 440 729-4400
Chesterland (G-2239)

CLEANING PRDTS: Deodorants, Nonpersonal

Fresh Products LLC..............................D 419 531-9741
Perrysburg (G-11224)

Nilodor Inc...E 800 443-4321
Bolivar (G-1386)

CLEANING PRDTS: Drain Pipe Solvents Or Cleaners

Personal Plumber Service Corp............F 440 324-4321
Elyria (G-6579)

CLEANING PRDTS: Laundry Preparations

Clorox Company....................................G 513 445-1840
Mason (G-9089)

Procter & Gamble Far East Inc.............C 513 983-1100
Cincinnati (G-3000)

CLEANING PRDTS: Sanitation Preparations

New Waste Concepts Inc......................F 877 736-6924
Perrysburg (G-11241)

CLEANING PRDTS: Sanitation Preps, Disinfectants/Deodorants

D & J Distributing & Mfg.......................F 419 865-2552
Holland (G-7753)

Ecolab Inc...G 513 932-0830
Lebanon (G-8253)

Tranzonic Companies............................C 440 446-0643
Cleveland (G-4414)

Tz Acquisition Corp..............................F 216 535-4300
Richmond Heights (G-11613)

CLEANING PRDTS: Specialty

Carbonklean Llc....................................G 614 980-9515
Powell (G-11483)

Kinzua Environmental Inc.....................E 216 881-4040
Cleveland (G-3923)

Procter & Gamble Company..................E 513 983-1100
Cincinnati (G-2987)

Procter & Gamble Company..................E 513 266-4375
Cincinnati (G-2988)

Procter & Gamble Company..................F 513 871-7557
Cincinnati (G-2989)

Procter & Gamble Company..................F 513 482-6789
Cincinnati (G-2991)

Procter & Gamble Company..................C 513 983-3000
Cincinnati (G-2993)

Procter & Gamble Company..................D 513 627-7115
Cincinnati (G-2994)

Procter & Gamble Company..................E 513 945-0340
Cincinnati (G-2997)

Procter & Gamble Company..................G 513 622-1000
Mason (G-9138)

Procter & Gamble Company..................C 513 634-9600
West Chester (G-14054)

Procter & Gamble Company..................C 513 634-9110
West Chester (G-14055)

Procter & Gamble Company..................A 513 983-1100
Cincinnati (G-2999)

Republic Powdered Metals Inc.............D 330 225-3192
Medina (G-9441)

RPM International Inc............................D 330 273-5090
Medina (G-9442)

US Industrial Lubricants Inc................E 513 541-2225
Cincinnati (G-3189)

CLEANING PRDTS: Stain Removers

Sherwin-Williams Company..................C 330 830-6000
Massillon (G-9243)

CLEANING SVCS: Industrial Or Commercial

MPW Industrial Svcs Group Inc..........B 740 927-8790
Hebron (G-7625)

Omega Cementing Co...........................G 330 695-7147
Apple Creek (G-474)

PRODUCT

Paro Services Co.............................F 330 467-1300
Twinsburg *(G-13350)*

CLIPS & FASTENERS, MADE FROM PURCHASED WIRE

Pennant Inc...................................F 937 584-5411
Columbus *(G-5183)*

Stud Welding Associates Inc.................D 440 783-3160
Strongsville *(G-12607)*

Tom Thumb Clip Co Inc.....................F 440 953-9606
Willoughby *(G-14542)*

CLOSURES: Closures, Stamped Metal

Crown Cork & Seal Usa Inc.................D 740 681-3000
Lancaster *(G-8193)*

Winzeler Couplings & Mtls LLC...........D 419 485-3147
Montpelier *(G-10136)*

CLOSURES: Plastic

Crown Cork & Seal Usa Inc.................D 740 681-3000
Lancaster *(G-8193)*

Mold-Rite Plastics LLC......................C 330 405-7739
Twinsburg *(G-13343)*

CLOTHING & ACCESS, WOMEN, CHILDREN & INFANT, WHOL: Uniforms

Cintas Sales Corporation....................B 513 459-1200
Cincinnati *(G-2495)*

Digitek Corp....................................F 513 794-3190
Mason *(G-9094)*

CLOTHING & ACCESS: Costumes, Theatrical

Costume Specialists Inc.....................E 614 464-2115
Columbus *(G-4852)*

Snaps Inc..G 419 477-5100
Mount Cory *(G-10205)*

CLOTHING & ACCESS: Men's Miscellaneous Access

Carters Inc.....................................G 330 758-0390
Boardman *(G-1369)*

Indra Holdings Corp..........................C 513 682-8200
Cincinnati *(G-2743)*

Rocky Brands Inc.............................C 740 753-1951
Nelsonville *(G-10320)*

Status Mens Accessories....................G 440 786-9394
Oakwood Village *(G-10909)*

CLOTHING & APPAREL STORES: Custom

Bluelogos Inc..................................F 614 898-9971
Westerville *(G-14247)*

Carols Ultra Stitch & Variety................G 419 935-8991
Willard *(G-14401)*

Indra Holdings Corp..........................C 513 682-8200
Cincinnati *(G-2743)*

CLOTHING & FURNISHINGS, MEN'S & BOYS', WHOLESALE: Uniforms

Cintas Sales Corporation....................B 513 459-1200
Cincinnati *(G-2495)*

Digitek Corp....................................F 513 794-3190
Mason *(G-9094)*

Identity Group LLC...........................G 614 337-6167
Westerville *(G-14213)*

Walter F Stephens Jr Inc...................E 937 746-0521
Franklin *(G-7055)*

CLOTHING & FURNISHINGS, MENS & BOYS, WHOLESALE: Apprl Belts

Rbr Enterprises LLC..........................F 866 437-9327
Brecksville *(G-1480)*

CLOTHING ACCESS STORES: Umbrellas

Totes Isotoner Corporation..................D 513 682-8200
Cincinnati *(G-3159)*

Totes Isotoner Holdings LLC................C 513 682-8200
Cincinnati *(G-3160)*

CLOTHING STORES: T-Shirts, Printed, Custom

Impact Printing and Design LLC...........F 833 522-6200
Columbus *(G-5003)*

Odyssey Spirits Inc...........................F 330 562-1523
Chagrin Falls *(G-2174)*

CLOTHING STORES: Uniforms & Work

Appleheart Inc.................................G 937 384-0430
Miamisburg *(G-9666)*

Markt LLC.......................................G 740 397-5900
Mount Vernon *(G-10250)*

Rbr Enterprises LLC..........................F 866 437-9327
Brecksville *(G-1480)*

CLOTHING STORES: Unisex

Chris Stepp.....................................G 513 248-0822
Milford *(G-9928)*

Ohio Mills Corporation.......................G 216 431-3979
Cleveland *(G-4116)*

CLOTHING STORES: Work

Karl Kuemmerling Inc........................F
Massillon *(G-9209)*

CLOTHING/ACCESS, WOMEN, CHILDREN/ INFANT, WHOL: Apparel Belt

Rbr Enterprises LLC..........................F 866 437-9327
Brecksville *(G-1480)*

CLOTHING/ACCESS, WOMEN, CHILDREN/ INFANT, WHOL: Hosp Gowns

Philips Med Systems Clvland In............B 440 483-3000
Cleveland *(G-4159)*

CLOTHING: Access, Women's & Misses'

Blingflingforever LLC.........................G 216 215-6955
Mentor On The Lake *(G-9657)*

Indra Holdings Corp..........................C 513 682-8200
Cincinnati *(G-2743)*

Rocky Brands Inc.............................C 740 753-1951
Nelsonville *(G-10320)*

CLOTHING: Aprons, Exc Rubber/Plastic, Women, Misses, Junior

Carrera Holdings Inc.........................G 216 687-1311
Cleveland *(G-3472)*

Geauga Group LLC...........................G 440 543-8797
Chagrin Falls *(G-2162)*

CLOTHING: Aprons, Harness

Watershed Mangement LLC.................F 740 852-5607
Mount Sterling *(G-10230)*

CLOTHING: Athletic & Sportswear, Men's & Boys'

Kam Manufacturing Inc......................C 419 238-6037
Van Wert *(G-13538)*

Rocky Brands Inc.............................C 740 753-1951
Nelsonville *(G-10320)*

Vesi Incorporated.............................E 513 563-6002
Cincinnati *(G-3203)*

CLOTHING: Athletic & Sportswear, Women's & Girls'

Bodied Beauties LLC.........................G 216 971-1155
Richmond Heights *(G-11608)*

Columbus Apparel Studio LLC.............F 614 706-7292
Columbus *(G-4817)*

Fluff Boutique.................................G 513 227-6614
Cincinnati *(G-2630)*

CLOTHING: Blouses, Women's & Girls'

Columbus Apparel Studio LLC.............F 614 706-7292
Columbus *(G-4817)*

Kam Manufacturing Inc......................C 419 238-6037
Van Wert *(G-13538)*

Love Laugh & Laundry.......................G 567 377-1951
Toledo *(G-13039)*

Rocky Brands Inc.............................C 740 753-1951
Nelsonville *(G-10320)*

CLOTHING: Blouses, Womens & Juniors, From Purchased Mtrls

J C L S Enterprises LLC....................G 740 472-0314
Woodsfield *(G-14613)*

CLOTHING: Bridal Gowns

Renee Grace LLC.............................G 513 399-5616
Cincinnati *(G-3038)*

Surili Couture LLC............................F 440 600-1456
Westlake *(G-14338)*

CLOTHING: Caps, Baseball

Barbs Graffiti Inc.............................E 216 881-5550
Cleveland *(G-3405)*

CLOTHING: Children & Infants'

Justice...G 937 435-6928
Dayton *(G-5836)*

CLOTHING: Coats & Suits, Men's & Boys'

Bea-Ecc Apparels Inc........................G 216 650-6336
Cleveland *(G-3411)*

CLOTHING: Costumes

Akron Design & Costume LLC..............G 330 644-0425
Coventry Township *(G-5479)*

CLOTHING: Disposable

Direct Disposables LLC......................G 440 717-3335
Brecksville *(G-1463)*

Rich Industries Inc...........................E 330 339-4113
New Philadelphia *(G-10465)*

CLOTHING: Dresses

Purple Orchid Boutique LLC.................G 614 554-7686
Columbus *(G-5214)*

CLOTHING: Hospital, Men's

Model Medical LLC............................F 216 972-0573
Shaker Heights *(G-11931)*

CLOTHING: Jerseys, Knit

Spalding...F 440 286-5717
Chardon *(G-2224)*

CLOTHING: Mens & Boys Jackets, Sport, Suede, Leatherette

Neff Motivation Inc............................... C 937 548-3194
Greenville *(G-7348)*

CLOTHING: Outerwear, Knit

Okm LLC.. G 216 272-6375
Cleveland *(G-4117)*

CLOTHING: Outerwear, Lthr, Wool/Down-Filled, Men, Youth/Boy

Holloway Sportswear Inc..................... D 937 497-7575
Sidney *(G-12023)*

Universal Lettering Inc........................ F 419 238-9320
Van Wert *(G-13547)*

CLOTHING: Outerwear, Women's & Misses' NEC

Barton-Carey Medical Pdts Inc............. E 419 887-1285
Maumee *(G-9265)*

Careismatic Brands LLC...................... G 614 497-5289
Groveport *(G-7429)*

Holloway Sportswear Inc...................... D 937 497-7575
Sidney *(G-12023)*

Kip-Craft Incorporated......................... D 216 898-5500
Cleveland *(G-3924)*

The Fechheimer Brothers Co................. C 513 793-5400
Blue Ash *(G-1342)*

CLOTHING: Robes & Dressing Gowns

Thomas Creative Apparel Inc................ G 419 929-1506
New London *(G-10417)*

CLOTHING: Shirts, Dress, Men's & Boys'

Columbus Apparel Studio LLC............. F 614 706-7292
Columbus *(G-4817)*

CLOTHING: Socks

Hype Socks LLC................................. F 855 497-3769
Columbus *(G-4994)*

Rock Em Sock Em Retro LLC............... G 419 575-9309
Walbridge *(G-13688)*

Smithco Distributing............................ E 419 367-7685
Liberty Center *(G-8376)*

CLOTHING: Sweatshirts & T-Shirts, Men's & Boys'

J C L S Enterprises LLC...................... G 740 472-0314
Woodsfield *(G-14613)*

CLOTHING: T-Shirts & Tops, Knit

Digitek Corp....................................... F 513 794-3190
Mason *(G-9094)*

E Retailing Associates LLC.................. D 614 300-5785
Columbus *(G-4894)*

Pjs Wholesale Inc............................... G 614 402-9363
Columbus *(G-5193)*

Wonder-Shirts Inc............................... G 917 679-2336
Dublin *(G-6361)*

CLOTHING: Underwear, Women's & Children's

Vs Service Company LLC..................... A 614 415-2348
Reynoldsburg *(G-11586)*

CLOTHING: Uniforms & Vestments

Careismatic Brands LLC...................... G 614 497-5289
Groveport *(G-7429)*

Fire-Dex LLC...................................... D 330 723-0000
Medina *(G-9403)*

Walter F Stephens Jr Inc..................... E 937 746-0521
Franklin *(G-7055)*

CLOTHING: Uniforms, Ex Athletic, Women's, Misses' & Juniors'

Cintas Corporation.............................. D 513 631-5750
Cincinnati *(G-2494)*

Cintas Corporation.............................. A 513 459-1200
Mason *(G-9086)*

Cintas Corporation No 2....................... D 330 966-7800
Canton *(G-1865)*

CLOTHING: Uniforms, Firemen's, From Purchased Materials

Lion Apparel Inc................................. C 937 898-1949
Dayton *(G-5847)*

Lion Apparel Inc................................. D 937 898-1949
Dayton *(G-5848)*

Lion First Responder Ppe Inc............... D 937 898-1949
Dayton *(G-5849)*

Lion Group Inc................................... D 800 421-2926
Dayton *(G-5850)*

CLOTHING: Uniforms, Men's & Boys'

Empirical Manufacturing Co Inc............. F 513 948-1616
Cincinnati *(G-2585)*

The Fechheimer Brothers Co................. C 513 793-5400
Blue Ash *(G-1342)*

CLOTHING: Uniforms, Military, Men/Youth, Purchased Materials

Vgs Inc... C 216 431-7800
Cleveland *(G-4463)*

CLOTHING: Uniforms, Work

Cintas Corporation.............................. D 513 631-5750
Cincinnati *(G-2494)*

Cintas Corporation.............................. A 513 459-1200
Mason *(G-9086)*

Cintas Corporation No 2....................... D 330 966-7800
Canton *(G-1865)*

Cintas Sales Corporation...................... B 513 459-1200
Cincinnati *(G-2495)*

School Uniforms and More Inc............. G 216 365-1957
Cleveland *(G-4275)*

Vgs Inc... C 216 431-7800
Cleveland *(G-4463)*

CLOTHING: Waterproof Outerwear

Totes Isotoner Corporation................... D 513 682-8200
Cincinnati *(G-3159)*

CLOTHING: Work, Waterproof, Exc Raincoats

Linsalata Cpitl Prtners Fund I............... G 440 684-1400
Cleveland *(G-3962)*

Tranzonic Companies........................... C 440 446-0643
Cleveland *(G-4414)*

Tz Acquisition Corp............................. F 216 535-4300
Richmond Heights *(G-11613)*

CLUTCHES, EXC VEHICULAR

Eaton Corporation............................... C 216 281-2211
Cleveland *(G-3653)*

Ebog Legacy Inc................................ D 330 239-4933
Sharon Center *(G-11940)*

Force Control Industries Inc................. E 513 868-0900
Fairfield *(G-6737)*

Logan Clutch Corporation.................... E 440 808-4258
Cleveland *(G-3966)*

NIDEC MINSTER CORPORATION.......... C 419 628-2331
Minster *(G-10062)*

COAL & OTHER MINERALS & ORES WHOLESALERS

B & S Transport Inc............................ G 330 767-4319
Navarre *(G-10302)*

Graphel Corporation............................ C 513 779-6166
West Chester *(G-14012)*

Hickman Williams & Company.............. F 513 621-1946
Cincinnati *(G-2721)*

Tosoh America Inc.............................. B 614 539-8622
Grove City *(G-7417)*

COAL MINING SERVICES

American Coal Company....................... D 740 338-3334
Saint Clairsville *(G-11686)*

Appalachian Fuels LLC........................ C 606 928-0460
Dublin *(G-6276)*

Coal Services Inc............................... B 740 795-5220
Powhatan Point *(G-11497)*

Global Coal Sales Group LLC............... G 614 221-0101
Dublin *(G-6298)*

Ohio Valley Coal Company................... B 740 926-1351
Saint Clairsville *(G-11706)*

Rosebud Mining Company.................... D 740 658-4217
Freeport *(G-7089)*

Suncoke Energy Inc............................ E 513 727-5571
Middletown *(G-9895)*

Terradyn Corporation........................... F 614 805-0897
Dublin *(G-6355)*

Western KY Cnsld Resources LLC........ G 740 338-3100
Saint Clairsville *(G-11716)*

Western KY Resources Fing LLC.......... G 740 338-3100
Saint Clairsville *(G-11718)*

COAL MINING: Anthracite

Coal Services Inc............................... B 740 795-5220
Powhatan Point *(G-11497)*

COAL MINING: Bituminous & Lignite Surface

Commercial Minerals Inc...................... G 330 549-2165
North Lima *(G-10706)*

Ivi Mining Group Ltd........................... G 740 418-7745
Vinton *(G-13623)*

J & D Mining Inc................................ G 330 339-4935
New Philadelphia *(G-10450)*

McElroy Coal Company........................ F 724 485-4000
Saint Clairsville *(G-11699)*

Murray American Energy Inc................. C 740 338-3100
Saint Clairsville *(G-11702)*

Washington County Coal Company........ B 740 338-3100
Saint Clairsville *(G-11714)*

COAL MINING: Bituminous Coal & Lignite-Surface Mining

Anthony Mining Co Inc........................ G 740 282-5301
Wintersville *(G-14610)*

Buckingham Coal Company LLC........... D
Zanesville *(G-15002)*

Coal Resources Inc............................ E 216 765-1240
Saint Clairsville *(G-11689)*

Coal Services Inc............................... B 740 795-5220
Powhatan Point *(G-11497)*

D & D Mining Co Inc........................... F 330 549-3127
New Springfield *(G-10472)*

Franklin County Coal Company............. C 740 338-3100
Saint Clairsville *(G-11692)*

Harrison County Coal Company............. F 740 338-3100
Saint Clairsville *(G-11693)*

Kimble Company................................. C 330 343-1226
Dover *(G-6250)*

Employee Codes: A=Over 500 employees, B=251-500
C=101-250, D=51-100, E=20-50, F=10-19, G=1-9   2025 Harris Ohio
Industrial Directory   1259

PRODUCT

L & M Mineral Co.................................. G 330 852-3696
   Sugarcreek *(G-12640)*

Meigs County Coal Company............... C 740 338-3100
   Saint Clairsville *(G-11700)*

Muhlenberg County Coal Co LLC .... D 740 338-3100
   Saint Clairsville *(G-11701)*

Oxford Mining Company Inc................ C 740 588-0190
   Zanesville *(G-15037)*

Oxford Mining Company Inc................ G 740 622-6302
   Coshocton *(G-5468)*

Oxford Mining Company LLC .... F 740 622-6302
   Coshocton *(G-5469)*

Rosebud Mining Company................... D 740 768-2275
   Bergholz *(G-1196)*

Westmoreland Resources Gp LLC ..... E 740 622-6302
   Coshocton *(G-5475)*

COAL MINING: Bituminous, Strip

B&N Coal Inc...................................... E 740 783-3575
   Dexter City *(G-6224)*

Holmes Limestone Co.........................G 330 893-2721
   Berlin *(G-1198)*

Oxford Mining Company - KY LLC ...... E 740 622-6302
   Coshocton *(G-5470)*

Thompson Bros Mining Co.................. F 330 549-3979
   New Springfield *(G-10474)*

Waterloo Coal Company Inc................ D 740 286-0004
   Jackson *(G-7955)*

COAL MINING: Bituminous, Surface, NEC

Marietta Coal Co................................. E 740 695-2197
   Saint Clairsville *(G-11695)*

Rayle Coal Co..................................... F 740 695-2197
   Saint Clairsville *(G-11708)*

COAL MINING: Lignite, Surface, NEC

Nacco Industries Inc........................... E 440 229-5151
   Cleveland *(G-4056)*

COAL TAR CRUDES: Derived From Chemical Recovery Coke Oven

Marion County Coal Company.............. D 740 338-3100
   Saint Clairsville *(G-11697)*

COATING COMPOUNDS: Tar

Brewer Company................................. G 513 576-6300
   Cincinnati *(G-2422)*

Brewer Company................................. G 440 944-3800
   Wickliffe *(G-14368)*

Brewer Company................................. G 800 394-0017
   Milford *(G-9926)*

Neyra Interstate Inc............................ E 513 733-1000
   Cincinnati *(G-2908)*

COATING SVC: Metals, With Plastic Or Resins

Corrotec Inc.. E 937 325-3585
   Springfield *(G-12294)*

Godfrey & Wing Inc.............................. E 330 562-1440
   Aurora *(G-671)*

Harwood Entp Holdings Inc................. F 330 923-3256
   Cuyahoga Falls *(G-5548)*

Perfection Finishers Inc...................... E 419 337-8015
   Wauseon *(G-13858)*

Rack Processing Company Inc............ E 937 294-1911
   Moraine *(G-10190)*

Techneglas LLC.................................. F 419 873-2000
   Perrysburg *(G-11268)*

Universal Rack & Eqp Co Inc.............. G 330 963-6776
   Twinsburg *(G-13390)*

COATINGS: Epoxy

CPI Industrial Co................................. E 614 445-0800
   Mount Sterling *(G-10227)*

Epoxy Systems Blstg Cating Inc........... F 513 924-1800
   Cleves *(G-4535)*

EZ Concrete Supply LLC..................... G 844 393-7699
   Lima *(G-8407)*

Master Builders LLC............................ E 800 228-3318
   Beachwood *(G-928)*

Nanosperse LLC.................................. G 937 296-5030
   Kettering *(G-8122)*

Postle Industries Inc........................... E 216 265-9000
   Cleveland *(G-4177)*

Quality Durable Indus Floors............... F 937 696-2833
   Farmersville *(G-6823)*

The Garland Company Inc.................... D 216 641-7500
   Cleveland *(G-4382)*

X-Treme Finishes Inc........................... F 330 474-0614
   North Royalton *(G-10790)*

COATINGS: Polyurethane

Trexler Rubber Co Inc......................... E 330 296-9677
   Ravenna *(G-11546)*

COILS & TRANSFORMERS

Barnes International LLC..................... E 419 352-7501
   Bowling Green *(G-1407)*

Duca Manufacturing & Consulting Inc... E 330 758-0828
   Youngstown *(G-14850)*

Electromotive Inc................................. E 330 688-6494
   Stow *(G-12427)*

Industrial Quartz Corporation.............. F 440 942-0909
   Mentor *(G-9530)*

Kurz-Kasch Inc.................................... E 740 498-8343
   Newcomerstown *(G-10572)*

Npas Inc.. F 614 595-6916
   Mansfield *(G-8840)*

PCC Airfoils LLC.................................. B 216 692-7900
   Cleveland *(G-4148)*

Rapid Mr International LLC.................. G 614 486-6300
   Columbus *(G-5224)*

Schneider Electric Usa Inc.................. B 513 523-4171
   Oxford *(G-11064)*

Staco Energy Products Co................... G 937 253-1191
   Miamisburg *(G-9739)*

Swiger Coil Systems Ltd...................... C 216 362-7500
   Cleveland *(G-4356)*

USA Instruments Inc........................... C 330 562-1000
   Aurora *(G-692)*

Wabtec Corporation............................. F 216 362-7500
   Cleveland *(G-4485)*

COILS, WIRE: Aluminum, Made In Rolling Mills

Amh Holdings II Inc............................. B 330 929-1811
   Cuyahoga Falls *(G-5525)*

COILS: Pipe

Industrial Power Systems Inc.............. B 419 531-3121
   Rossford *(G-11659)*

COLOR LAKES OR TONERS

Vibrantz Corporation........................... C 216 875-6213
   Cleveland *(G-4468)*

Vibrantz Corporation........................... D 732 287-4925
   Cleveland *(G-4469)*

COLOR PIGMENTS

American Colors Inc............................ E 419 621-4000
   Sandusky *(G-11821)*

Chromascape LLC............................... E 330 998-7574
   Independence *(G-7892)*

Ferro International Svcs Inc................. G 216 875-5600
   Mayfield Heights *(G-9333)*

General Color Investments Inc............. D 330 868-4161
   Minerva *(G-10038)*

Gsdi Specialty Dispersions Inc............ E 330 848-9200
   Massillon *(G-9198)*

McCann Color Inc................................ E 330 498-4840
   Canton *(G-1942)*

Spectrum Dispersions Inc................... F 330 296-0600
   Ravenna *(G-11542)*

Vibrantz Corporation........................... E 724 207-2152
   Cleveland *(G-4465)*

Vibrantz Corporation........................... D 216 875-5600
   Mayfield Heights *(G-9344)*

COLORS: Pigments, Inorganic

Americhem Inc..................................... E 330 926-3185
   Cuyahoga Falls *(G-5524)*

Americhem Inc..................................... D 330 929-4213
   Cuyahoga Falls *(G-5523)*

Ampacet Corporation........................... C 740 929-5521
   Newark *(G-10490)*

Arconic... F 330 471-1844
   Canton *(G-1832)*

Avient Corporation............................... D 419 668-4844
   Norwalk *(G-10829)*

Colormatrix Corporation....................... C 216 622-0100
   Berea *(G-1163)*

Colormatrix Group Inc.......................... C 216 622-0100
   Berea *(G-1164)*

Colormatrix Holdings Inc...................... F 440 930-3162
   Berea *(G-1165)*

Day-Glo Color Corp.............................. F 216 391-7070
   Cleveland *(G-3603)*

Day-Glo Color Corp.............................. F 216 391-7070
   Twinsburg *(G-13291)*

Day-Glo Color Corp.............................. C 216 391-7070
   Cleveland *(G-3602)*

Degussa Incorporated......................... G 513 733-5111
   Cincinnati *(G-2544)*

Eckart America Corporation................. D 440 954-7600
   Painesville *(G-11082)*

Kish Company Inc................................ F 440 205-9970
   Mentor *(G-9546)*

Lancer Dispersions Inc........................ D
   Akron *(G-202)*

Leonhardt Plating Company................. G 513 242-1410
   Cincinnati *(G-2819)*

LyondIlbsell Advnced Plymers I........... D 419 682-3311
   Stryker *(G-12624)*

Mason Color Works Inc........................ F 330 385-4400
   East Liverpool *(G-6395)*

PMC Specialties Group Inc.................. F 513 242-3300
   Cincinnati *(G-2972)*

PMC Specialties Group Inc.................. E 513 242-3300
   Cincinnati *(G-2971)*

Revlis Corporation............................... F 330 535-2108
   Barberton *(G-835)*

Sun Chemical Corporation................... C 513 681-5950
   Cincinnati *(G-3127)*

Thorworks Industries Inc..................... C 419 626-4375
   Sandusky *(G-11876)*

Vibrantz Color Solutions Inc................ C 440 997-5137
   Ashtabula *(G-621)*

Vibrantz Corporation........................... D 732 287-4925
   Cleveland *(G-4469)*

COMBINED ELEMENTARY & SECONDARY SCHOOLS, PUBLIC

Butler Tech.. E 513 867-1028
Fairfield Township *(G-6795)*

COMMERCIAL & OFFICE BUILDINGS RENOVATION & REPAIR

Facility Service Pros LLC........................ G 419 577-6123
Collins *(G-4587)*

Thomas Cabinet Shop Inc...................... F 937 847-8239
Dayton *(G-6051)*

Youngstown Shade & Alum LLC............ G 330 782-2373
Youngstown *(G-14975)*

COMMERCIAL ART & GRAPHIC DESIGN SVCS

Clarity Retail Services LLC..................... D 513 800-9369
West Chester *(G-13965)*

Converters/Prepress Inc......................... F 937 743-0935
Carlisle *(G-2065)*

Enlarging Arts Inc.................................. G 330 434-3433
Akron *(G-136)*

Fx Digital Media Inc............................... F 216 241-4040
Cleveland *(G-3746)*

General Theming Contrs LLC................. C 614 252-6342
Columbus *(G-4948)*

Malik Media LLC.................................... G 614 933-0328
New Albany *(G-10345)*

Midwest Menu Mate Inc.......................... F 740 323-2599
Newark *(G-10521)*

Morse Enterprises Inc............................. G 513 229-3600
Mason *(G-9129)*

Painted Hill Inv Group Inc....................... F 937 339-1756
Troy *(G-13246)*

Quez Media Marketing Inc....................... G 216 910-0202
Independence *(G-7918)*

Sylvan Studios Inc.................................. G 419 882-3423
Sylvania *(G-12725)*

The Photo-Type Engraving Company.... D 513 281-0999
Cincinnati *(G-3149)*

True Dinero Records & Tech LLC........... G 513 428-4610
Cincinnati *(G-3173)*

COMMERCIAL ART & ILLUSTRATION SVCS

ONeil & Associates Inc........................... C 937 865-0800
Miamisburg *(G-9725)*

COMMERCIAL CONTAINERS WHOLESALERS

Brimar Packaging Inc.............................. E 440 934-3080
Avon *(G-717)*

Kaufman Container Company.................. C 216 898-2000
Cleveland *(G-3908)*

COMMERCIAL EQPT WHOLESALERS, NEC

Active Aeration Systems Inc................... G 614 873-3626
Plain City *(G-11390)*

Cgmw Incorporated................................ G 614 236-8388
Columbus *(G-4804)*

Cummins - Allison Corp........................... G 513 469-2924
Blue Ash *(G-1266)*

Cummins - Allison Corp........................... G 440 824-5050
Cleveland *(G-3579)*

General Data Company Inc..................... B 513 752-7978
Cincinnati *(G-2304)*

National Pride Equipment Inc................. G 419 289-2886
Mansfield *(G-8837)*

Rayhaven Group Inc............................... G 330 659-3183
Richfield *(G-11598)*

COMMERCIAL EQPT, WHOLESALE: Display Eqpt, Exc Refrigerated

Abstract Displays Inc.............................. F 513 985-9700
Blue Ash *(G-1241)*

Ternion Inc.. E 216 642-6180
Cleveland *(G-4375)*

COMMERCIAL EQPT, WHOLESALE: Restaurant, NEC

Harry C Lobalzo & Sons Inc.................... E 330 666-6758
Akron *(G-172)*

ITW Food Equipment Group LLC............ C 937 393-4271
Hillsboro *(G-7719)*

ITW Food Equipment Group LLC............ A 937 332-2396
Troy *(G-13231)*

N Wasserstrom & Sons Inc..................... C 614 228-5550
Columbus *(G-5118)*

COMMERCIAL EQPT, WHOLESALE: Store Fixtures & Display Eqpt

Baker Plastics Inc.................................. G 330 743-3142
Youngstown *(G-14817)*

COMMERCIAL PHOTOGRAPHIC STUDIO

Eclipse 3d/Pi LLC.................................. E 614 626-8536
Columbus *(G-4896)*

COMMERCIAL PRINTING & NEWSPAPER PUBLISHING

Belem Group LLC.................................... G 614 604-6870
Columbus *(G-4750)*

Cameco Communications LLC............... G 937 840-9490
Hillsboro *(G-7715)*

Carrollton Publishing Company.............. G 330 627-5591
Carrollton *(G-2081)*

Copley Ohio Newspapers Inc.................. C 330 364-5577
New Philadelphia *(G-10439)*

Copley Ohio Newspapers Inc.................. E 585 598-0030
Canton *(G-1871)*

Daily Chief Union.................................... F 419 294-2331
Upper Sandusky *(G-13438)*

Defiance Publishing Co Ltd..................... B 419 784-5441
Defiance *(G-6106)*

Delaware Gazette Company.................... F 740 363-1161
Delaware *(G-6143)*

Dispatch Printing Company..................... F 740 548-5331
Lewis Center *(G-8331)*

Hamilton Journal News Inc..................... G 513 863-8200
Liberty Township *(G-8377)*

Herald Reflector Inc............................... E 419 668-3771
Norwalk *(G-10847)*

Horizon Ohio Publications Inc................. D 419 738-2128
Wapakoneta *(G-13715)*

Horizon Ohio Publications Inc................. F 419 394-7414
Saint Marys *(G-11738)*

Hubbard Publishing Co........................... G 937 592-3060
Bellefontaine *(G-1110)*

King Media Enterprises Inc..................... F 216 588-6700
Cleveland *(G-3921)*

Kml Acquisitions Ltd.............................. G 614 732-9777
Plain City *(G-11411)*

Kroner Publications Inc.......................... E 330 544-5500
Niles *(G-10594)*

Ohio Newspapers Inc............................. A 937 225-2000
Dayton *(G-5926)*

Progrssive Communications Corp........... F 740 397-5333
Mount Vernon *(G-10261)*

Record Herald Publishing Co.................. E 717 762-2151
Cincinnati *(G-3035)*

Samuel L Peters LLC.............................. G 513 745-1500
Blue Ash *(G-1329)*

Southeast Publications Inc..................... F 740 732-2341
Caldwell *(G-1729)*

Standard Printing Co Inc......................... G 419 586-2371
Celina *(G-2121)*

Toledo Blade Company........................... B 419 724-6000
Toledo *(G-13148)*

Wooster Daily Record Inc LLC................ C 330 264-1125
Wooster *(G-14700)*

COMMON SAND MINING

Demilta Sand and Gravel Inc................... F 440 942-2015
Willoughby *(G-14446)*

Demmy Sand and Gravel LLC................. E
Springfield *(G-12301)*

Feikert Sand & Gravel Co Inc................. E 330 674-0038
Millersburg *(G-9980)*

Kirby and Sons Inc................................. F 419 927-2260
Upper Sandusky *(G-13445)*

Nelson Sand & Gravel Inc....................... F 440 224-0198
Kingsville *(G-8139)*

Stocker Sand & Gravel Co....................... F 740 254-4635
Gnadenhutten *(G-7294)*

Welch Holdings Inc................................ E 513 353-3220
Cincinnati *(G-3216)*

X L Sand and Gravel Co........................... G 330 426-9876
Negley *(G-10316)*

COMMUNICATIONS EQPT WHOLESALERS

Cattron Holdings Inc.............................. E 234 806-0018
Warren *(G-13748)*

Cota International Inc.............................. G 937 526-5520
Versailles *(G-13593)*

Quasonix Inc.. E 513 942-1287
West Chester *(G-14058)*

Ray Communications Inc......................... G 330 686-0226
Stow *(G-12453)*

Securcom Inc.. E 419 628-1049
Minster *(G-10065)*

COMMUNICATIONS SVCS: Data

Springdot Inc.. D 513 542-4000
Cincinnati *(G-3108)*

COMMUNICATIONS SVCS: Internet Connectivity Svcs

DSI Management Holdings LLC............. F 800 645-7002
Kent *(G-8027)*

Great Lakes Telcom Ltd........................... E 330 629-8848
Youngstown *(G-14870)*

Revolution Group Inc.............................. D 614 212-1111
Westerville *(G-14230)*

COMMUNICATIONS SVCS: Online Svc Providers

F+w Media Inc... A 513 531-2690
Blue Ash *(G-1274)*

COMMUNICATIONS SVCS: Telephone, Local & Long Distance

Airwave Communications Cons............. G 419 331-1526
Lima *(G-8385)*

AT&T Enterprises LLC............................ G 513 792-9300
Cincinnati *(G-2384)*

COMMUTATORS: Electronic

Ra Consultants LLC................................ E 513 469-6600
Blue Ash *(G-1326)*

COMPACT LASER DISCS: Prerecorded

Jk Digital Publishing LLC........................ G 937 299-0185
Springboro *(G-12256)*

COMPOSITION STONE: Plastic

Rsl LLC... E 330 392-8900
Warren *(G-13795)*

Silver Line Building Pdts LLC................ A 740 382-5595
Marion *(G-8998)*

COMPOST

Hyponex Corporation............................... C 330 262-1300
Shreve *(G-11982)*

Kurtz Bros Compost Services................ G 330 864-2621
Akron *(G-200)*

Midwest Compost Inc............................... F 419 547-7979
Clyde *(G-4560)*

Opal Diamond LLC..................................... D 330 653-5876
Rocky River *(G-11635)*

Price Farms Organics Ltd....................... F 740 369-1000
Delaware *(G-6168)*

Van Tilburg Farms Inc............................... F 419 586-3077
Celina *(G-2126)*

Werlor Inc... F 419 784-4285
Defiance *(G-6127)*

COMPRESSORS: Air & Gas

Airtx International Ltd............................... F 513 631-0660
Cincinnati *(G-2346)*

Ariel Corporation....................................... F 740 397-0311
Mount Vernon *(G-10235)*

Eaton Comprsr Fabrication Inc.............. D 937 540-1140
Englewood *(G-6613)*

Ernest Industries Inc............................... F 937 325-9851
Springfield *(G-12307)*

Field Gymmy Inc... G 419 538-6511
Glandorf *(G-7283)*

G Denver and Co LLC................................. E 937 498-2555
Sidney *(G-12021)*

General Fabrications Corp....................... E 419 625-6055
Sandusky *(G-11836)*

Kingsly Compression Inc......................... G 740 439-0772
Cambridge *(G-1747)*

Lsq Manufacturing Inc............................. F 330 725-4905
Medina *(G-9421)*

National Compressor Svcs LLC.............. E 419 868-4980
Holland *(G-7773)*

Nordson Corporation............................... B 440 985-4496
Amherst *(G-448)*

Nordson Medical Corporation.............. D 440 892-1580
Westlake *(G-14318)*

Powerex-Iwata Air Tech Inc.................... D 888 769-7979
Harrison *(G-7561)*

Transdigm Inc... E 216 291-6025
Cleveland *(G-4411)*

COMPRESSORS: Air & Gas, Including Vacuum Pumps

Aci Services Inc... E 740 435-0240
Cambridge *(G-1734)*

Airbase Industries LLC............................. F 937 540-1140
Englewood *(G-6606)*

Ariel Corporation....................................... D 330 896-2660
Akron *(G-60)*

Ariel Corporation....................................... C 740 397-0311
Mount Vernon *(G-10236)*

Autobody Supply Company Inc.............. D 614 228-4328
Columbus *(G-4735)*

Ch Transition Company LLC.................... C 800 543-6400
Cincinnati *(G-2457)*

Keystone Automotive Inds Inc............... G 614 228-4328
Groveport *(G-7440)*

Potemkin Industries Inc........................... F 740 397-4888
Mount Vernon *(G-10259)*

COMPRESSORS: Refrigeration & Air Conditioning Eqpt

Copeland Corporation............................. F 937 498-3011
Sidney *(G-12004)*

Copeland LP... A 937 498-3011
Sidney *(G-12005)*

Hanon Systems Usa LLC......................... C 313 920-0583
Carey *(G-2058)*

COMPUTER & COMPUTER SOFTWARE STORES

Copier Resources Inc............................... G 614 268-1100
Columbus *(G-4849)*

Gordons Graphics Inc............................... G 330 863-2322
Malvern *(G-8751)*

Journey Systems LLC............................... F 513 831-6200
Milford *(G-9940)*

COMPUTER & COMPUTER SOFTWARE STORES: Peripheral Eqpt

Computer Products Corporation........... E 513 221-0600
Cincinnati *(G-2508)*

COMPUTER & COMPUTER SOFTWARE STORES: Software & Access

Lantek Systems Inc................................... G 877 805-1028
Mason *(G-9122)*

COMPUTER & COMPUTER SOFTWARE STORES: Software, Bus/Non-Game

RB Sigma LLC... D 440 290-0577
Mentor *(G-9607)*

Retalix Inc... G 937 384-2277
Miamisburg *(G-9733)*

COMPUTER & COMPUTER SOFTWARE STORES: Software, Computer Game

Thyme Inc... F 484 872-8430
Akron *(G-337)*

COMPUTER & OFFICE MACHINE MAINTENANCE & REPAIR

Eaj Services LLC... F 513 792-3400
Blue Ash *(G-1269)*

Government Acquisitions Inc.................. E 513 721-8700
Cincinnati *(G-2685)*

Magnum Computers Inc........................... F 216 781-1757
Cleveland *(G-3981)*

Pinnacle Data Systems Inc...................... C 614 748-1150
Groveport *(G-7449)*

Vr Assets LLC... G 440 600-2963
Solon *(G-12203)*

COMPUTER FACILITIES MANAGEMENT SVCS

Park Place Technologies LLC.................. C
Cleveland *(G-4135)*

COMPUTER FORMS

R R Donnelley & Sons Company........... D 440 774-2101
Oberlin *(G-10920)*

COMPUTER GRAPHICS SVCS

Great Lakes Publishing Company.......... D 216 771-2833
Cleveland *(G-3793)*

IPA Ltd... F 614 523-3974
Columbus *(G-5024)*

Quez Media Marketing Inc....................... G 216 910-0202
Independence *(G-7918)*

COMPUTER PERIPHERAL EQPT REPAIR & MAINTENANCE

Ascendtech Inc... E 216 458-1101
Willoughby *(G-14428)*

Park Place Technologies LLC.................. C
Cleveland *(G-4135)*

COMPUTER PERIPHERAL EQPT, NEC

Airwave Communications Cons.............. G 419 331-1526
Lima *(G-8385)*

AT&T Enterprises LLC............................... G 513 792-9300
Cincinnati *(G-2384)*

Black Box Corporation............................. F 800 676-8850
Brecksville *(G-1460)*

Black Box Corporation............................. G 800 837-7777
Dublin *(G-6282)*

Black Box Corporation............................. E 614 825-7400
Lewis Center *(G-8325)*

Black Box Corporation............................. G 855 324-9909
Westlake *(G-14292)*

Contact Control Interfaces LLC.............. G 609 333-3264
Cincinnati *(G-2512)*

Data Processing Sciences Corporation. D 513 791-7100
Cincinnati *(G-2542)*

Dataq Instruments Inc............................. F 330 668-1444
Akron *(G-115)*

Eastman Kodak Company....................... E 937 259-3000
Dayton *(G-5758)*

Embedded Planet Inc............................... F 216 245-4180
Solon *(G-12104)*

Gleason Metrology Systems Corp.......... E 937 384-8901
Dayton *(G-5796)*

Government Acquisitions Inc.................. E 513 721-8700
Cincinnati *(G-2685)*

Grimes Aerospace Company.................. A 937 484-2000
Urbana *(G-13462)*

Interactive Products Corp....................... G 513 313-3397
Monroe *(G-10110)*

Kern Inc... C 440 930-7315
Cleveland *(G-3915)*

Loma Systems... E 740 274-9047
Chillicothe *(G-2262)*

Parker-Hannifin Corporation.................. F 513 831-2340
Milford *(G-9947)*

Phase Array Company LLC....................... G 513 785-0801
West Chester *(G-14043)*

Qualtek Electronics Corp......................... C 440 951-3300
Mentor *(G-9603)*

Reflexis Systems Inc................................. C 614 948-1931
Westerville *(G-14229)*

Scriptel Corporation................................. F 877 848-6824
Columbus *(G-5258)*

Sierra Nevada Corporation...................... E 937 431-2800
Beavercreek *(G-983)*

Signature Technologies Inc...................... E 937 859-6323
Miamisburg *(G-9737)*

Stellar Systems Inc................................... G 513 921-8748
Cincinnati *(G-3118)*

Superior Label Systems Inc.................... B 513 336-0825
Mason *(G-9157)*

Sutter Llc... F 513 891-2261
Blue Ash *(G-1339)*

COMPUTER TERMINALS *(continued)*

Systemax Manufacturing Inc................G 937 368-2300
Dayton *(G-6035)*

Timekeeping Systems Inc...................F 216 595-0890
Solon *(G-12198)*

Treality Svs LLC..................................E 937 372-7579
Xenia *(G-14781)*

Video Products Inc............................D 330 562-2622
Aurora *(G-693)*

Vyral LLC..F 937 993-7765
Dayton *(G-6073)*

Xponet Inc..G 440 354-6617
Painesville *(G-11123)*

Yonezawa Usa Inc.............................F 614 799-2210
Plain City *(G-11430)*

COMPUTER PERIPHERAL EQPT, WHOLESALE

Ascendtech Inc...................................E 216 458-1101
Willoughby *(G-14428)*

Black Box Corporation.......................G 855 324-9909
Westlake *(G-14292)*

Legrand North America LLC................B 937 224-0639
Dayton *(G-5843)*

Microplex Inc......................................E 330 498-0600
North Canton *(G-10651)*

Systemax Manufacturing Inc................G 937 368-2300
Dayton *(G-6035)*

COMPUTER PERIPHERAL EQPT: Decoders

Harris Mackessy & Brennan Inc...........C 614 221-6831
Westerville *(G-14212)*

COMPUTER PERIPHERAL EQPT: Input Or Output

New Dawn Labs LLC............................F 203 675-5644
Union *(G-13410)*

COMPUTER PROCESSING SVCS

Sightgain Inc......................................F 202 494-9317
Mason *(G-9152)*

COMPUTER PROGRAMMING SVCS: Custom

Corporate Elevator LLC......................G 614 288-1847
Columbus *(G-4851)*

Jasstek Inc...F 614 808-3600
Dublin *(G-6313)*

Teachers Publishing Group.................F 614 486-0631
Hilliard *(G-7705)*

Timekeeping Systems Inc...................F 216 595-0890
Solon *(G-12198)*

COMPUTER RELATED MAINTENANCE SVCS

Ascendtech Inc...................................E 216 458-1101
Willoughby *(G-14428)*

Freedom Usa Inc................................E 216 503-6374
Twinsburg *(G-13305)*

NCR Technology Center......................G 937 445-1936
Dayton *(G-5903)*

Proficient Info Tech Inc.......................G 937 470-1300
Dayton *(G-5964)*

Syntec LLC..F 440 229-6262
Rocky River *(G-11640)*

Wolters Kluwer Clinical Dru................D 330 650-6506
Hudson *(G-7862)*

COMPUTER SERVICE BUREAU

CD Solutions Inc.................................G 937 676-2376
Pleasant Hill *(G-11431)*

COMPUTER SOFTWARE DEVELOPMENT

Auto Des Sys Inc................................F 614 488-8838
Dublin *(G-6278)*

Brainmaster Technologies Inc............G 440 232-6000
Bedford *(G-1018)*

Cincinnati Assn For The Blind............C 513 221-8558
Cincinnati *(G-2469)*

Computer Allied Technology Co..........G 614 457-2292
Columbus *(G-4839)*

Eci Macola/Max LLC............................C 978 539-6186
Dublin *(G-6296)*

Electronic Concepts Engrg Inc............F 419 861-9000
Holland *(G-7763)*

Embedded Planet Inc.........................F 216 245-4180
Solon *(G-12104)*

Fscreations Corporation.....................D 330 746-3015
Youngstown *(G-14858)*

Ganymede Technologies Corp.............G 419 562-5522
Bucyrus *(G-1681)*

Global Realms LLC..............................G 614 828-7284
Gahanna *(G-7158)*

H Mack Charles & Associates Inc.........E 513 791-4456
Blue Ash *(G-1281)*

Intelligrated Systems Inc....................A 866 936-7300
Mason *(G-9113)*

Intelligrated Systems LLC...................A 513 701-7300
West Chester *(G-14128)*

IPA Ltd...F 614 523-3974
Columbus *(G-5024)*

Keithley Instruments LLC....................D 440 248-0400
Solon *(G-12137)*

Leidos Inc...D 937 656-8433
Beavercreek *(G-977)*

Link Systems Inc.................................F 800 321-8770
Solon *(G-12142)*

Navistone Inc......................................D 844 677-3667
Cincinnati *(G-2896)*

Parker-Hannifin Corporation...............F 513 831-2340
Milford *(G-9947)*

Qc Software LLC.................................E 513 469-1424
Cincinnati *(G-3013)*

Sanctuary Software Studio Inc............E 330 666-9690
Fairlawn *(G-6810)*

Stellar Systems Inc.............................G 513 921-8748
Cincinnati *(G-3118)*

Tech4imaging LLC...............................F 614 214-2655
Columbus *(G-5315)*

Thinkware Incorporated......................E 513 598-3300
Cincinnati *(G-3133)*

Thyme Inc...F 484 872-8430
Akron *(G-337)*

Triad Governmental Systems...............F 937 376-5446
Xenia *(G-14782)*

Truck Fax Inc......................................G 216 921-8866
Cleveland *(G-4431)*

Virtual Hold Tech Slutions LLC............E 330 670-2200
Akron *(G-354)*

COMPUTER SOFTWARE DEVELOPMENT & APPLICATIONS

Cott Systems Inc................................D 614 847-4405
Columbus *(G-4853)*

Deemsys Inc.......................................D 614 322-9928
Gahanna *(G-7155)*

Forcam Inc..F 513 878-2780
Cincinnati *(G-2633)*

Generic Systems Inc...........................F 419 841-8460
Holland *(G-7764)*

Hab Inc...G 608 785-7650
Solon *(G-12119)*

Lantek Systems Inc.............................G 877 805-1028
Mason *(G-9122)*

Miles Midprint Inc...............................F 216 860-4770
Cleveland *(G-4040)*

Sest Inc..F 440 777-9777
Westlake *(G-14332)*

Signalysis Inc.....................................F 513 528-6164
Cincinnati *(G-3090)*

Simplevms LLC....................................F 888 255-8918
Cincinnati *(G-3091)*

Tech Solutions LLC.............................G 419 852-7190
Celina *(G-2123)*

COMPUTER SOFTWARE SYSTEMS ANALYSIS & DESIGN: Custom

Airwave Communications Cons............G 419 331-1526
Lima *(G-8385)*

American Power LLC............................F 937 235-0418
Dayton *(G-5654)*

Associated Software Cons Inc.............F 440 826-1010
Lakewood *(G-8162)*

Atr Distributing Company....................G 513 353-1800
Cincinnati *(G-2387)*

Empyracom Inc...................................F 330 744-5570
Boardman *(G-1370)*

Facts Inc...E 330 928-2332
Cuyahoga Falls *(G-5540)*

Online Mega Sellers Corp...................G 888 384-6468
Toledo *(G-13078)*

Quez Media Marketing Inc...................G 216 910-0202
Independence *(G-7918)*

Sightgain Inc......................................F 202 494-9317
Mason *(G-9152)*

Soaring Software Solutions Inc............F 419 442-7676
Swanton *(G-12692)*

Steward Edge Bus Solutions................F 614 826-5305
Columbus *(G-5293)*

COMPUTER STORAGE DEVICES, NEC

Capsa Solutions LLC...........................D 800 437-6633
Canal Winchester *(G-1788)*

Freedom Usa Inc................................E 216 503-6374
Twinsburg *(G-13305)*

Park Place Technologies LLC...............C
Cleveland *(G-4135)*

Quantum..F 740 328-2548
Newark *(G-10531)*

Quantum Solutions Group....................G 614 442-0664
Columbus *(G-5219)*

Sam Oht Services LLC.........................F 330 225-3117
Medina *(G-9444)*

Town Cntry Technical Svcs Inc............F 614 866-7700
Reynoldsburg *(G-11582)*

Tracewell Systems Inc.........................D 614 846-6175
Lewis Center *(G-8356)*

COMPUTER STORAGE UNITS: Auxiliary

Pinnacle Data Systems Inc...................C 614 748-1150
Groveport *(G-7449)*

COMPUTER SYSTEM SELLING SVCS

Lantek Systems Inc.............................G 877 805-1028
Mason *(G-9122)*

R & L Software LLC.............................G 513 847-4942
Monroe *(G-10115)*

COMPUTER SYSTEMS ANALYSIS & DESIGN

David Chojnacki..................................E 303 905-1918
Westerville *(G-14254)*

Sightgain Inc......................................F 202 494-9317
Mason *(G-9152)*

COMPUTER TERMINALS

Freedom Usa Inc.................................... E 216 503-6374
Twinsburg *(G-13305)*

Parker-Hannifin Corporation.................... F 513 831-2340
Milford *(G-9947)*

Pinnacle Data Systems Inc...................... C 614 748-1150
Groveport *(G-7449)*

Td Synnex Corporation.......................... E 614 669-6889
Groveport *(G-7452)*

COMPUTER TIME-SHARING

Miami Valley Eductl Cmpt Assn............. F 937 767-1468
Yellow Springs *(G-14789)*

COMPUTERS, NEC

Ascendtech Inc...................................... E 216 458-1101
Willoughby *(G-14428)*

AT&T Enterprises LLC............................ G 513 792-9300
Cincinnati *(G-2384)*

Dapsco.. F 937 294-5331
Moraine *(G-10155)*

Eaj Services LLC.................................... F 513 792-3400
Blue Ash *(G-1269)*

General Dynmics Mssion Systems........ G 937 723-2001
Dayton *(G-5794)*

Global Realms LLC................................ G 614 828-7284
Gahanna *(G-7158)*

Grimes Aerospace Company.................. A 937 484-2000
Urbana *(G-13462)*

Interntnal Pdts Srcing Group I............... B 614 334-1500
Columbus *(G-5020)*

Journey Systems LLC............................ F 513 831-6200
Milford *(G-9940)*

Magnum Computers Inc.......................... F 216 781-1757
Cleveland *(G-3981)*

Park Place Technologies LLC................ C
Cleveland *(G-4135)*

Parker-Hannifin Corporation.................... F 513 831-2340
Milford *(G-9947)*

Powersonic Industries LLC...................... E 513 429-2329
West Chester *(G-14138)*

Predicor LLC.. G 419 460-1831
Cleveland *(G-4188)*

Systemax Manufacturing Inc.................. G 937 368-2300
Dayton *(G-6035)*

Town Cntry Technical Svcs Inc.............. F 614 866-7700
Reynoldsburg *(G-11582)*

Tracewell Systems Inc............................ D 614 846-6175
Lewis Center *(G-8356)*

Vr Assets LLC.. G 440 600-2963
Solon *(G-12203)*

Walter North.. F 937 204-6050
Dayton *(G-6074)*

COMPUTERS, PERIPHERALS & SOFTWARE, WHOLESALE: Printers

Printer Components Inc........................... G 585 924-5190
Fairfield *(G-6767)*

COMPUTERS, PERIPHERALS & SOFTWARE, WHOLESALE: Software

Eci Macola/Max LLC.............................. C 978 539-6186
Dublin *(G-6296)*

GBS Corp.. C 330 494-5330
North Canton *(G-10641)*

Government Acquisitions Inc.................. E 513 721-8700
Cincinnati *(G-2685)*

Miles Midprint Inc.................................. F 216 860-4770
Cleveland *(G-4040)*

Software Solutions Inc............................ E 513 932-6667
Dayton *(G-6012)*

COMPUTERS: Mainframe

Griffin Technology Inc............................ C 585 924-7121
Hudson *(G-7842)*

COMPUTERS: Personal

Eaton Corporation.................................. B 440 523-5000
Cleveland *(G-3652)*

Inns Holdings Ltd.................................. F 740 345-3700
Newark *(G-10511)*

Polycom Inc.. G 937 245-1853
Englewood *(G-6621)*

CONCENTRATES, DRINK

Belton Foods LLC.................................. E 937 890-7768
Dayton *(G-5676)*

Inter American Products Inc.................. D 800 645-2233
Cincinnati *(G-2748)*

CONCENTRATES, FLAVORING, EXC DRINK

Flavor Producers LLC............................ E 513 771-0777
Cincinnati *(G-2625)*

Wiley Companies.................................... C 740 622-0755
Coshocton *(G-5476)*

CONCRETE BUILDING PRDTS WHOLESALERS

Jalco Industries Inc................................ F 740 286-3808
Jackson *(G-7947)*

Michaels Pre-Cast Con Pdts Inc............. F 513 683-1292
Loveland *(G-8643)*

Moritz Materials Inc................................ E 419 281-0575
Ashland *(G-553)*

Stocker Concrete Company.................... F 740 254-4626
Gnadenhutten *(G-7293)*

Tamarron Technology Inc........................ F 800 277-3207
Cincinnati *(G-3136)*

CONCRETE CURING & HARDENING COMPOUNDS

Blackthorn LLC...................................... F 937 836-9296
Clayton *(G-3272)*

Chemmasters Inc.................................... E 440 428-2105
Madison *(G-8726)*

Master Bldrs Sltons Admxtres U............. C 216 839-7500
Beachwood *(G-927)*

Master Builders LLC.............................. E 800 228-3318
Beachwood *(G-928)*

CONCRETE PRDTS

9/10 Castings Inc.................................. G 216 406-8907
Chardon *(G-2196)*

American Spring Wire Corp.................... C 216 292-4620
Bedford Heights *(G-1068)*

Baxter Burial Vault Svc Inc.................... F 513 641-1010
Cincinnati *(G-2403)*

Carruth Studio Inc.................................. F 419 878-3060
Waterville *(G-13831)*

Cement Products Inc.............................. E 419 524-4342
Mansfield *(G-8772)*

Charles Svec Inc.................................... E 216 662-5200
Maple Heights *(G-8879)*

Contech Bridge Solutions LLC.............. F 937 878-2170
Dayton *(G-5710)*

DCA Construction Products LLC............. E 330 527-4308
Garrettsville *(G-7217)*

Dm2018 LLC.. G 513 893-5483
Liberty Twp *(G-8382)*

Euclid Chemical Company...................... E 800 321-7628
Cleveland *(G-3688)*

Forterra Pipe & Precast LLC.................. F 614 445-3830
Columbus *(G-4933)*

Growco Inc.. G 419 886-4628
Mansfield *(G-8799)*

Hazelbaker Industries Ltd...................... G
Columbus *(G-4973)*

Hilltop Basic Resources Inc.................. C 513 621-1500
Cincinnati *(G-2723)*

Huron Cement Products Company........ E 419 433-4161
Huron *(G-7874)*

Lang Stone Company Inc........................ E 614 235-4099
Columbus *(G-5064)*

Ludowici Roof Tile Inc.......................... D 740 342-1995
New Lexington *(G-10404)*

M B K Inc.. F 330 889-3451
Bristolville *(G-1498)*

Mack Industries PA Inc.......................... D 330 638-7680
Vienna *(G-13613)*

Michaels Pre-Cast Con Pdts Inc............. F 513 683-1292
Loveland *(G-8643)*

Oberfields LLC...................................... F 614 252-0955
Columbus *(G-5137)*

Occv1 Inc.. G 419 248-8000
Toledo *(G-13069)*

OK Brugmann Jr & Sons Inc.................. G 330 274-2106
Mantua *(G-8873)*

Oldcastle Infrastructure Inc.................. E 419 592-2309
Napoleon *(G-10294)*

Orrville Trucking & Grading Co.............. E 330 682-4010
Orrville *(G-11000)*

Pawnee Maintenance Inc........................ G 740 373-6861
Marietta *(G-8935)*

Premiere Con Solutions LLC.................. F 419 737-9808
Pioneer *(G-11326)*

Prestress Services Inds LLC.................. C 859 299-0461
Grove City *(G-7409)*

R W Sidley Incorporated........................ E 440 564-2221
Newbury *(G-10561)*

R W Sidley Incorporated........................ C 440 298-3232
Thompson *(G-12763)*

Rocla Concrete Tie Inc.......................... E 740 776-3238
Portsmouth *(G-11475)*

Russell Cast Stone Inc.......................... D 856 753-4000
West Chester *(G-14142)*

S & S Aggregates Inc............................ F 740 453-0721
Zanesville *(G-15046)*

Snyder Concrete Products Inc.............. E 937 885-5176
Moraine *(G-10192)*

Superior Walls of Ohio Inc.................... D 330 393-4101
Warren *(G-13799)*

Tri County Concrete Inc........................ F 330 425-4464
Twinsburg *(G-13386)*

William Dauch Concrete Company........ F 419 668-4458
Norwalk *(G-10863)*

Wyandot Dolomite Inc............................ E 419 396-7641
Carey *(G-2064)*

CONCRETE PRDTS, PRECAST, NEC

A L D Precast Corp................................ G 614 449-3366
Columbus *(G-4656)*

Aco Inc.. E 440 639-7230
Mentor *(G-9468)*

Carey Precast Concrete Company........ G 419 396-7142
Carey *(G-2057)*

E Pompili Sons Inc................................ G 216 581-8080
Cleveland *(G-3645)*

Eldorado Stone LLC.............................. E 330 698-3931
Apple Creek *(G-467)*

Fin Pan Inc.. F 513 870-9200
Hamilton *(G-7490)*

Mack Concrete Industries Inc.............. F 330 483-3111
Valley City *(G-13503)*

Mack Industries PA Inc.................. D 330 483-3111
Valley City (G-13504)

McGill Septic Tank Co..................... G 330 876-2171
Kinsman (G-8141)

North American Cast Stone Inc........... G 440 286-1999
Chardon (G-2216)

Norwalk Concrete Inds Inc.............. E 419 668-8167
Norwalk (G-10856)

Oberfields LLC................................ G 937 885-3711
Dayton (G-5920)

Oberfields LLC................................ E 740 369-7644
Sunbury (G-12670)

Oberfields LLC................................ D 740 369-7644
Delaware (G-6165)

Oldcastle Apg Midwest Inc.............. E 440 949-1815
Sheffield Village (G-11961)

Premere Precast Products.............. G 740 533-3333
Ironton (G-7933)

Snyder Concrete Products Inc.......... G 937 339-7577
Troy (G-13257)

Spoerr Precast Concrete Inc........... F 419 625-9132
Sandusky (G-11872)

St Henry Tile Co Inc....................... G 937 548-1101
Greenville (G-7355)

Uniontown Septic Tanks Inc............ F 330 699-3386
Uniontown (G-13428)

United Precast Inc........................... C 740 393-1121
Mount Vernon (G-10267)

United Refractories Inc.................... E 330 372-3716
Warren (G-13807)

CONCRETE: Asphaltic, Not From Refineries

Shelly Materials Inc......................... D 740 246-6315
Thornville (G-12770)

CONCRETE: Bituminous

Russell Standard Corporation............ G 330 733-9400
Akron (G-299)

CONCRETE: Dry Mixture

Quikrete Companies LLC.................. D 614 885-4406
Columbus (G-5220)

Quikrete Companies LLC.................. E 513 367-6135
Harrison (G-7564)

Quikrete Companies LLC.................. E 330 296-6080
Ravenna (G-11536)

Quikrete Companies LLC.................. F 419 241-1148
Toledo (G-13100)

Smith Concrete Co........................... E 740 373-7441
Dover (G-6262)

CONCRETE: Ready-Mixed

Ace Ready Mix Concrete Co Inc.......... F 330 745-8125
Norton (G-10817)

Adams Bros Concrete Pdts Ltd......... E 740 452-7566
Zanesville (G-14982)

Adams Brothers Inc......................... G 740 819-0323
Zanesville (G-14983)

Alexis Concrete Enterprise Inc.......... G 440 366-0031
Elyria (G-6494)

Allega Concrete Corp....................... E 216 447-0814
Richfield (G-11587)

Anderson Concrete Corp.................. C 614 443-0123
Columbus (G-4716)

Associated Associates Inc.............. E 330 626-3300
Mantua (G-8867)

Baird Concrete Products Inc............ F 740 623-8600
Coshocton (G-5451)

Baker-Shindler Contracting Co......... E 419 782-5080
Defiance (G-6100)

Barrett Paving Materials Inc............ F 937 293-9033
Moraine (G-10148)

Beazer East Inc............................... F 740 474-3169
Circleville (G-3248)

Beazer East Inc............................... E 937 364-2311
Hillsboro (G-7714)

Beazer East Inc............................... F 740 947-4677
Waverly (G-13863)

Bhi Transition Inc........................... E 937 663-4152
Saint Paris (G-11756)

Brock Corporation........................... G 440 235-1806
Olmsted Falls (G-10939)

Buckeye Ready Mix Concrete.......... G 330 798-5511
Akron (G-85)

Buckeye Ready-Mix LLC.................. E 740 967-4801
Johnstown (G-7993)

Buckeye Ready-Mix LLC.................. G 614 879-6316
West Jefferson (G-14160)

Buckeye Ready-Mix LLC.................. E 740 654-4423
Lancaster (G-8182)

Buckeye Ready-Mix LLC.................. F 937 642-2951
Marysville (G-9015)

Buckeye Ready-Mix LLC.................. E 614 575-2132
Reynoldsburg (G-11561)

C F Poeppelman Inc........................ E 937 448-2191
Bradford (G-1451)

Caldwell Lumber & Supply Co......... F 740 732-2306
Caldwell (G-1724)

Camden Ready Mix Co..................... G 937 456-4539
Camden (G-1767)

Carr Bros Inc................................... E 440 232-3700
Bedford (G-1020)

Carr Bros Bldrs Sup & Coal Co......... E 440 232-3700
Cleveland (G-3471)

Castalia Trenching & Rdymx LLC........ F 419 684-5502
Castalia (G-2094)

Castalia Trenching & Ready Mix........ F 419 684-5502
Castalia (G-2095)

Cemco Construction Corporation........ G 440 567-7708
Concord Township (G-5388)

Cement Products Inc....................... E 419 524-4342
Mansfield (G-8772)

Cemex Cement Inc........................... C 937 873-9858
Fairborn (G-6688)

Cemex Materials LLC....................... C 330 654-2501
Diamond (G-6226)

Center Concrete Inc......................... G 419 782-2495
Defiance (G-6102)

Center Concrete Inc......................... F 800 453-4224
Edgerton (G-6166)

Central Ready Mix LLC.................... E 513 402-5001
Cincinnati (G-2451)

Central Ready-Mix of Ohio LLC......... G 614 252-3452
Cincinnati (G-2452)

Chappell-Zimmerman Inc................. F 330 337-8711
Salem (G-11769)

Cioffi Holdings LLC......................... G 330 794-9448
Akron (G-101)

City Concrete LLc........................... F 330 743-2825
Youngstown (G-14835)

Citywide Materials Inc.................... E 513 533-1111
Cincinnati (G-2496)

Collinwood Shale Brick Sup Co......... E 216 587-2700
Cleveland (G-3545)

Consumeracq Inc............................. E 440 277-9305
Lorain (G-8552)

Consumers Builders Supply Co......... G 440 277-9306
Lorain (G-8553)

D G M Inc.. F 740 286-2131
Jackson (G-7943)

D W Dickey and Son Inc.................. C 330 424-1441
Lisbon (G-8466)

Dearth Resources Inc..................... E 937 663-4171
Springfield (G-12299)

Dearth Resources Inc..................... G 937 325-0651
Springfield (G-12298)

Diano Construction and Sup Co......... F 330 456-7229
Canton (G-1881)

Ellis Brothers Inc Upg.................... F 740 397-9191
Mount Vernon (G-10244)

Elyria Concrete Inc......................... F 440 322-2750
Elyria (G-6528)

Ernst Enterprises Inc..................... E 937 848-6811
Bellbrook (G-1091)

Ernst Enterprises Inc..................... F 937 866-9441
Carrollton (G-2082)

Ernst Enterprises Inc..................... G 513 367-1939
Cleves (G-4536)

Ernst Enterprises Inc..................... F 614 308-0063
Columbus (G-4907)

Ernst Enterprises Inc..................... F 614 308-0063
Columbus (G-4908)

Ernst Enterprises Inc..................... E 614 443-9456
Columbus (G-4909)

Ernst Enterprises Inc..................... F 937 878-9378
Fairborn (G-6690)

Ernst Enterprises Inc..................... E 513 829-8683
Fairfield (G-6733)

Ernst Enterprises Inc..................... E 513 874-8300
Lebanon (G-8254)

Ernst Enterprises Inc..................... F 513 422-3651
Middletown (G-9857)

Ernst Enterprises Inc..................... F 937 339-6249
Troy (G-13212)

Ernst Enterprises Inc..................... F 937 233-7777
West Milton (G-14182)

Ernst Enterprises Inc..................... E 937 233-5555
Vandalia (G-13556)

EZ Concrete Supply LLC.................. G 844 393-7699
Lima (G-8407)

Fairborn Cement Plant..................... G 937 879-8466
Fairborn (G-6691)

Feikert Sand & Gravel Co Inc.......... E 330 674-0038
Millersburg (G-9980)

G Big Inc.. E 740 867-5758
Chesapeake (G-2229)

Geauga Concrete Inc....................... F 440 338-4915
Newbury (G-10551)

Grafton Ready Mix Concret Inc......... C 440 926-2911
Grafton (G-7303)

Heidelberg Materials Us Inc............ E 937 587-2671
Peebles (G-11109)

Heidelberg Materials Us Inc............ E 937 442-6009
Winchester (G-14598)

Heidelberg Mtls US Cem LLC........... F 330 499-9100
Middlebranch (G-9765)

Heidelberg Mtls US Cem LLC........... G 972 653-5500
Sylvania (G-12709)

Hilltop Basic Resources Inc............ F 937 795-2020
Aberdeen (G-1)

Hilltop Basic Resources Inc............ G 513 242-8400
Cincinnati (G-2722)

Hilltop Basic Resources Inc............ C 513 621-1500
Cincinnati (G-2723)

Hilltop Big Bend Quarry LLC........... E 513 651-5000
Cincinnati (G-2724)

Hocking Valley Concrete Inc............ G 740 592-5335
Athens (G-642)

Hocking Valley Concrete Inc............ G 740 342-1948
New Lexington (G-10402)

Hocking Valley Concrete Inc............ F 740 385-2165
Logan (G-8516)

Hull Ready Mix Concrete Inc............ F 419 625-8070
Sandusky (G-11839)

Huron Cement Products Company........ E 419 433-4161
Huron (G-7874)

Huth Ready Mix & Supply Co.................. G 330 833-4191
Massillon (G-9203)

IMI Real Estate LLC.............................. G 513 769-3666
Cincinnati (G-2740)

IMI Real Estate LLC.............................. F 513 844-8444
Hamilton (G-7504)

Integrated Resources Inc...................... E 419 885-7122
Sylvania (G-12713)

Ioppolo Concrete Corporation................ G 440 439-6606
Bedford (G-1040)

K & L Ready Mix Inc............................. F 419 293-2937
Mc Comb (G-9354)

K & L Ready Mix Inc............................. F 419 523-4376
Ottawa (G-11037)

Kuhlman Corporation............................ E 330 724-9900
Coventry Township (G-5485)

Kuhlman Corporation............................ F 419 321-1670
Toledo (G-13022)

Kuhlman Corporation............................ E 419 897-6000
Maumee (G-9303)

Lancaster W Side Coal Co Inc............... F 740 862-4713
Lancaster (G-8207)

Lexington Concrete & Sup Inc............... G 419 529-3232
Mansfield (G-8813)

M & B Asphalt Company Inc.................. G 419 992-4236
Old Fort (G-10934)

M & R Redi Mix Inc.............................. E 419 445-7771
Pettisville (G-11284)

M B K Inc... F 330 889-3451
Bristolville (G-1498)

Mack Concrete Industries Inc............... E 330 784-7008
Akron (G-219)

Market Ready....................................... G 513 289-9231
Maineville (G-8741)

McClelland Inc.................................... E 740 452-3036
Zanesville (G-15027)

McGovney Ready Mix Inc...................... G 740 353-4111
Portsmouth (G-11469)

Medina Supply Company........................ G 440 234-1321
Berea (G-1181)

Medina Supply Company........................ D 330 425-0752
Twinsburg (G-13338)

Medina Supply Company........................ E 330 723-3681
Medina (G-9426)

Moritz Concrete Inc.............................. E 419 529-3232
Mansfield (G-8832)

Moritz Materials Inc............................. E 419 281-0575
Ashland (G-553)

Moritz Ready Mix Inc........................... G 419 253-0001
Marengo (G-8898)

National Lime and Stone Co.................. E 419 423-3400
Findlay (G-6897)

OK Brugmann Jr & Sons Inc.................. G 330 274-2106
Mantua (G-8873)

Olen Corporation................................. F 419 294-2611
Upper Sandusky (G-13451)

Orrville Trucking & Grading Co.............. E 330 682-4010
Orrville (G-11000)

Osborne Inc.. F 440 232-1440
Cleveland (G-4125)

Osborne Inc.. E 440 942-7000
Mentor (G-9578)

Osborne Co... G 440 942-7000
Mentor (G-9579)

Pahl Ready Mix Concrete Inc................ F 419 636-4238
Bryan (G-1657)

Palmer Bros Transit Mix Con................ F 419 686-2366
Portage (G-11460)

Palmer Bros Transit Mix Con................ F 419 352-4681
Bowling Green (G-1433)

Paul R Lipp & Son Inc.......................... F 330 227-9614
Rogers (G-11642)

Placecrete Inc..................................... G 937 298-2121
Moraine (G-10184)

Pleasant Valley Ready Mix Inc............... F 330 852-2613
Sugarcreek (G-12645)

Quality Block & Supply Inc.................... E 330 364-4411
Mount Eaton (G-10208)

Quality Ready Mix Inc.......................... F 419 394-8870
Saint Marys (G-11750)

Quikrete Companies LLC....................... E 513 367-6135
Harrison (G-7564)

Quikrete Companies LLC....................... E 330 296-6080
Ravenna (G-11536)

R W Sidley Inc.................................... G 440 224-2664
Marietta (G-8939)

R W Sidley Incorporated....................... E 330 499-5616
Canton (G-1990)

R W Sidley Incorporated....................... E 440 564-2221
Newbury (G-10561)

R W Sidley Incorporated....................... D 440 298-3232
Thompson (G-12762)

R W Sidley Incorporated....................... E 330 392-2721
Warren (G-13792)

R W Sidley Incorporated....................... E 330 793-7374
Youngstown (G-14923)

Reliable Ready Mix Co.......................... E 330 453-8266
Canton (G-1993)

Rock Away Capital Inc.......................... E 216 432-9465
Cleveland (G-4246)

Ross-Co Redi-Mix Co Inc...................... F 740 775-4466
Chillicothe (G-2280)

S J Roth Enterprises Inc....................... D 513 543-1140
Cincinnati (G-3059)

Sakrete Inc... E 513 242-3644
Cincinnati (G-3060)

Sardinia Concrete Company.................. E 513 248-0090
Milford (G-9951)

Sardinia Ready Mix Inc......................... E 937 446-2523
Sardinia (G-11886)

Schwab Industries Inc.......................... F 330 364-4411
Dover (G-6261)

Scioto Ready Mix LLC........................... D 740 924-9273
Pataskala (G-11150)

Shamrock Materials Inc........................ F 513 988-0647
Cincinnati (G-3086)

Shelly Materials Inc............................. E 740 775-4567
Chillicothe (G-2281)

Shelly Materials Inc............................. E 614 871-6704
Grove City (G-7413)

Shelly Materials Inc............................. F 330 723-3681
Medina (G-9448)

Shelly Materials Inc............................. G 937 325-7386
Springfield (G-12372)

Shelly Materials Inc............................. F 330 963-5180
Twinsburg (G-13378)

Sidwell Materials Inc........................... F 740 968-4313
Saint Clairsville (G-11710)

Small Sand & Gravel Inc....................... E 740 427-3130
Gambier (G-7212)

Smalls Inc... F 740 427-3633
Gambier (G-7213)

Smith Concrete.................................... F 740 439-7714
Cambridge (G-1759)

Smith Concrete Co............................... G 740 593-5633
Athens (G-652)

Smith Concrete Co............................... E 740 373-7441
Dover (G-6262)

Smyrna Ready Mix Concrete LLC........... D 937 855-0410
Germantown (G-7254)

Smyrna Ready Mix Concrete LLC........... D 937 773-0841
Piqua (G-11385)

Smyrna Ready Mix Concrete LLC........... C 937 698-7229
Vandalia (G-13578)

Spurlino Materials LLC......................... G 513 202-1111
Cleves (G-4548)

Spurlino Materials LLC......................... E 513 705-0111
Middletown (G-9894)

St Henry Tile Co Inc............................ E 419 678-4841
Saint Henry (G-11724)

Stamm Contracting Company Inc........... F 330 274-8230
Mantua (G-8875)

Stocker Concrete Company.................... F 740 254-4626
Gnadenhutten (G-7293)

T C Redi Mix Youngstown Inc................ E 330 755-2143
Youngstown (G-14942)

Tech Ready Mix Inc.............................. E 216 361-5000
Cleveland (G-4369)

Terminal Ready-Mix Inc........................ F 440 288-0181
Lorain (G-8583)

The National Lime and Stone Company . E 419 422-4341
Findlay (G-6927)

Tri County Concrete Inc....................... F 330 425-4464
Cleveland (G-4417)

Tri County Concrete Inc....................... F 330 425-4464
Twinsburg (G-13386)

Turner Concrete Products...................... G 419 662-9007
Northwood (G-10811)

Twin Cities Concrete Co....................... B 330 627-2158
Carrollton (G-2091)

Twin Cities Concrete Co....................... F 330 343-4491
Dover (G-6266)

United Ready Mix Inc........................... G 216 696-1600
Cleveland (G-4444)

W M Dauch Concrete Inc....................... G 419 562-6917
Bucyrus (G-1695)

Walden Industries Inc.......................... E 740 633-5971
Tiltonsville (G-12810)

Warren Concrete and Supply Co............. G 330 393-1581
Warren (G-13810)

Weber Ready Mix Inc........................... E 419 394-9097
Saint Marys (G-11754)

Wells Group LLC.................................. F 740 532-9240
Ironton (G-7937)

Westview Concrete Corp........................ F 440 458-5800
Elyria (G-6602)

Westview Concrete Corp........................ E 440 235-1800
Olmsted Falls (G-10943)

William Dauch Concrete Company........... F 419 562-6917
Bucyrus (G-1696)

William Dauch Concrete Company........... F 419 668-4458
Norwalk (G-10863)

Williams Concrete Inc.......................... E 419 893-3251
Maumee (G-9330)

Winters Products Inc........................... F 740 286-4149
Jackson (G-7956)

CONDENSERS: Heat Transfer Eqpt, Evaporative

Hydro-Dyne Inc.................................... F 330 832-5076
Massillon (G-9204)

Lfg Specialties LLC............................. E 419 424-4999
Findlay (G-6885)

CONDENSERS: Refrigeration

Copeland LP....................................... B 937 498-3011
Sidney (G-12006)

Copeland LP....................................... B 937 498-3587
Sidney (G-12007)

CONDUITS & FITTINGS: Electric

Allied Tube & Conduit Corp.................... F 740 928-1018
Hebron (G-7607)

Lagonda Investments III Inc.................. F 937 325-7305
Springfield (G-12342)

Madison Electric Products Inc.............. E 216 391-7776
Solon *(G-12143)*

Saylor Products Corporation................. F 419 832-2125
Grand Rapids *(G-7309)*

CONNECTORS: Cord, Electric

Tip Products Inc.............................. E 216 252-2535
New London *(G-10419)*

CONNECTORS: Electronic

Joslyn Sunbank Company LLC............ F 805 238-2840
Cleveland *(G-3894)*

Mjo Industries Inc........................... D 800 590-4055
Huber Heights *(G-7822)*

CONSTRUCTION & MINING MACHINERY WHOLESALERS

Columbus Pipe and Equipment Co........ F 614 444-7871
Columbus *(G-4831)*

Great Lakes Power Service Co............. F 440 259-0025
Perry *(G-11192)*

JD Power Systems LLC..................... F 614 317-9394
Hilliard *(G-7685)*

Koenig Equipment Inc...................... F 937 653-5281
Urbana *(G-13472)*

La Mfg Inc.................................. G 513 577-7200
Cincinnati *(G-2810)*

Mesa Industries Inc......................... E 513 321-2950
Cincinnati *(G-2866)*

Murphy Tractor & Eqp Co Inc.............. G 330 220-4999
Brunswick *(G-1602)*

Murphy Tractor & Eqp Co Inc.............. G 330 477-9304
Canton *(G-1954)*

Murphy Tractor & Eqp Co Inc.............. G 614 876-1141
Columbus *(G-5116)*

Murphy Tractor & Eqp Co Inc.............. G 419 221-3666
Lima *(G-8434)*

Murphy Tractor & Eqp Co Inc.............. G 937 898-4198
Vandalia *(G-13573)*

Shearer Farm Inc........................... C 330 345-9023
Wooster *(G-14685)*

Simpson Strong-Tie Company Inc.......... B 614 876-8060
Columbus *(G-5271)*

The Wagner-Smith Company................ B 866 338-0398
Moraine *(G-10195)*

CONSTRUCTION EQPT REPAIR SVCS

West Equipment Company Inc............. G 419 698-1601
Toledo *(G-13177)*

CONSTRUCTION EQPT: Attachments, Snow Plow

Ironhawk Industrial Dist LLC............... G 216 502-3700
Euclid *(G-6656)*

Snow Dragon LLC.......................... F 440 295-0238
Cleveland *(G-4309)*

Winter Equipment Company In............. E 440 946-8377
Willoughby *(G-14552)*

Y O H Inc.................................. E 614 488-2861
Columbus *(G-5377)*

CONSTRUCTION EQPT: Roofing Eqpt

A J C Inc.................................. F 800 428-2438
Hudson *(G-7826)*

Dimensional Metals Inc..................... E 740 927-3633
Reynoldsburg *(G-11565)*

CONSTRUCTION MATERIALS, WHOLESALE: Architectural Metalwork

Charles Mfg Co............................. F 330 395-3490
Warren *(G-13751)*

CONSTRUCTION MATERIALS, WHOLESALE: Awnings

PCR Restorations Inc....................... G 419 747-7957
Mansfield *(G-8844)*

CONSTRUCTION MATERIALS, WHOLESALE: Brick, Exc Refractory

Snyder Concrete Products Inc.............. G 937 224-1433
Dayton *(G-6011)*

Snyder Concrete Products Inc.............. G 937 339-7577
Troy *(G-13257)*

Snyder Concrete Products Inc.............. E 937 885-5176
Moraine *(G-10192)*

The Ideal Builders Supply & Fuel Co Inc F 216 741-1600
Cleveland *(G-4386)*

CONSTRUCTION MATERIALS, WHOLESALE: Building Stone

Toledo Cut Stone Inc....................... F 419 531-1623
Toledo *(G-13150)*

CONSTRUCTION MATERIALS, WHOLESALE: Building Stone, Marble

Castelli Marble LLC......................... G 216 361-1222
Cleveland *(G-3477)*

Helmart Company Inc....................... G 513 941-3095
Cincinnati *(G-2715)*

CONSTRUCTION MATERIALS, WHOLESALE: Building, Exterior

Francis-Schulze Co......................... F 937 295-3941
Russia *(G-11674)*

Higgins Construction & Supply Co Inc.. F 937 364-2331
Hillsboro *(G-7717)*

Imex Bz LLC................................ F 786 866-8798
Orrville *(G-10986)*

Orrville Trucking & Grading Co............ E 330 682-4010
Orrville *(G-11000)*

CONSTRUCTION MATERIALS, WHOLESALE: Building, Interior

Youngstown Curve Form Inc................ F 330 744-3028
Youngstown *(G-14968)*

CONSTRUCTION MATERIALS, WHOLESALE: Cement

Huron Cement Products Company........ E 419 433-4161
Huron *(G-7874)*

CONSTRUCTION MATERIALS, WHOLESALE: Concrete Mixtures

Ernst Enterprises Inc....................... F 937 233-7777
West Milton *(G-14182)*

CONSTRUCTION MATERIALS, WHOLESALE: Door Frames

Provia Holdings Inc......................... C 330 852-4711
Sugarcreek *(G-12646)*

CONSTRUCTION MATERIALS, WHOLESALE: Doors, Garage

Alumo Extrusions and Mfg Co.............. E 330 779-3333
Youngstown *(G-14810)*

CONSTRUCTION MATERIALS, WHOLESALE: Doors, Sliding

Alumo Extrusions and Mfg Co.............. E 330 779-3333
Youngstown *(G-14810)*

CONSTRUCTION MATERIALS, WHOLESALE: Glass

A Service Glass Inc......................... F 937 426-4920
Beavercreek *(G-963)*

Dale Kestler................................ G 513 871-9000
Cincinnati *(G-2540)*

Global Glass Block Inc...................... G 216 731-2333
Euclid *(G-6651)*

Machined Glass Specialist Inc............. G 937 743-6166
Springboro *(G-12259)*

Snyder Concrete Products Inc.............. G 937 339-7577
Troy *(G-13257)*

CONSTRUCTION MATERIALS, WHOLESALE: Gravel

Hilltop Basic Resources Inc................ G 937 859-3616
Miamisburg *(G-9699)*

CONSTRUCTION MATERIALS, WHOLESALE: Limestone

Pinney Dock & Transport LLC.............. F 440 964-7186
Ashtabula *(G-612)*

R W Sidley Incorporated................... C 440 298-3232
Thompson *(G-12763)*

CONSTRUCTION MATERIALS, WHOLESALE: Masons' Materials

Koltcz Concrete Block Co................... E 440 232-3630
Bedford *(G-1042)*

CONSTRUCTION MATERIALS, WHOLESALE: Molding, All Materials

Architctral Mllwk Cbinetry Inc............. G 440 708-0086
Chagrin Falls *(G-2155)*

Toledo Molding & Die LLC.................. C 419 692-6022
Delphos *(G-6193)*

CONSTRUCTION MATERIALS, WHOLESALE: Pallets, Wood

Component Solutions Group Inc........... F 937 434-8100
Dayton *(G-5708)*

Universal Pallets Inc........................ E 614 444-1095
Columbus *(G-5339)*

CONSTRUCTION MATERIALS, WHOLESALE: Particleboard

Litco International Inc....................... D 330 539-5433
Vienna *(G-13612)*

CONSTRUCTION MATERIALS, WHOLESALE: Paving Materials

The D S Brown Company.................... C 419 257-3561
North Baltimore *(G-10619)*

CONSTRUCTION MATERIALS, WHOLESALE: Prefabricated Structures

Morton Buildings Inc....................... E 419 675-2311
Kenton *(G-8110)*

Morton Buildings Inc....................... E 330 345-6188
Wooster *(G-14667)*

PRODUCT

Patio Enclosures.................................. F 513 733-4646
Cincinnati (G-2944)

Pease Enterprises Inc......................... F 513 871-8907
Cincinnati (G-2951)

Will-Burt Company.............................. F 330 682-7015
Orrville (G-11019)

Will-Burt Company.............................. C 330 682-7015
Orrville (G-11018)

CONSTRUCTION MATERIALS, WHOLESALE: Roofing & Siding Material

Associated Materials LLC.................... C 330 929-1811
Cuyahoga Falls (G-5528)

Associated Materials Group Inc.......... D 330 929-1811
Cuyahoga Falls (G-5529)

Associated Mtls Holdings LLC............ A 330 929-1811
Cuyahoga Falls (G-5530)

Kingspan Insulation LLC..................... D 800 433-5551
Newark (G-10514)

CONSTRUCTION MATERIALS, WHOLESALE: Sand

Acme Company.................................... D 330 758-2313
Poland (G-11434)

Allied Corporation Inc......................... F 330 425-7861
Twinsburg (G-13272)

Phoenix Asphalt Company Inc............ G 330 339-4935
Magnolia (G-8736)

CONSTRUCTION MATERIALS, WHOLESALE: Septic Tanks

Active Aeration Systems Inc................ G 614 873-3626
Plain City (G-11390)

Allen Enterprises Inc........................... E 740 532-5913
Ironton (G-7928)

CONSTRUCTION MATERIALS, WHOLESALE: Sewer Pipe, Clay

Sewer Rodding Equipment Co............. C 419 991-2065
Lima (G-8447)

CONSTRUCTION MATERIALS, WHOLESALE: Siding, Exc Wood

Alside Inc.. E 419 865-0934
Maumee (G-9258)

Vinyl Design Corporation..................... E 419 283-4009
Holland (G-7790)

CONSTRUCTION MATERIALS, WHOLESALE: Stone, Crushed Or Broken

Olen Corporation................................. F 419 294-2611
Upper Sandusky (G-13451)

Palmer Bros Transit Mix Con............... F 419 686-2366
Portage (G-11460)

Ridge Township Stone Quarry.............. G 419 968-2222
Van Wert (G-13544)

Stoneco Inc... E 419 893-7645
Maumee (G-9321)

CONSTRUCTION MATERIALS, WHOLESALE: Windows

Associated Materials LLC.................... C 330 929-1811
Cuyahoga Falls (G-5528)

Associated Materials Group Inc.......... D 330 929-1811
Cuyahoga Falls (G-5529)

Associated Mtls Holdings LLC............ A 330 929-1811
Cuyahoga Falls (G-5530)

Blockamerica Corporation................... G 614 274-0700
Columbus (G-4765)

Champion Win Co Cleveland LLC......... G..... 440 899-2562
Macedonia (G-8681)

Roofing Annex LLC.............................. G 513 942-0555
West Chester (G-14141)

CONSTRUCTION SAND MINING

Arden J Neer Sr.................................. F 937 585-6733
Bellefontaine (G-1099)

Hocking Valley Concrete Inc................ F 740 385-2165
Logan (G-8516)

Hugo Sand Company........................... G 216 570-1212
Kent (G-8036)

Lakeside Sand & Gravel Inc................ E 330 274-2569
Mantua (G-8870)

Masons Sand and Gravel Co............... G 614 491-3611
Obetz (G-10924)

Mechanicsburg Sand & Gravel............ G 937 834-2606
Mechanicsburg (G-9367)

Morrow Gravel Company Inc................ E 513 771-0820
Cincinnati (G-2889)

National Lime and Stone Co................ F 614 497-0083
Lockbourne (G-8491)

Oscar Brugmann Sand & Gravel.......... E 330 274-8224
Mantua (G-8874)

S & S Aggregates Inc......................... C 419 938-5604
Perrysville (G-11283)

Seville Sand & Gravel Inc.................... E 330 948-0168
Strongsville (G-12597)

Shelly and Sands Inc.......................... F 740 453-0721
Zanesville (G-15047)

CONSTRUCTION: Athletic & Recreation Facilities

MGM Construction Inc......................... G 440 234-7660
Berea (G-1182)

CONSTRUCTION: Bridge

Ohio Bridge Corporation...................... C 740 432-6334
Cambridge (G-1752)

CONSTRUCTION: Commercial & Office Building, New

Fleming Construction Co...................... G 740 494-2177
Prospect (G-11501)

Ingle-Barr Inc...................................... D 740 702-6117
Chillicothe (G-2261)

Kel-Par Co Inc..................................... F 740 344-2627
Newark (G-10513)

Rebsco Inc.. F 937 548-2246
Greenville (G-7351)

Scs Construction Services Inc............. E 513 929-0260
Cincinnati (G-3071)

The Galehouse Companies Inc............ E 330 658-2023
Doylestown (G-6270)

Thomas J Weaver Inc.......................... F 740 622-2040
Coshocton (G-5474)

CONSTRUCTION: Commercial & Office Buildings, Prefabricated

Precision Wldg Instllation LLC............. F 740 995-0613
Zanesville (G-15043)

CONSTRUCTION: Food Prdts Manufacturing or Packing Plant

Milos Whole World Gourmet LLC.......... G 740 589-6456
Nelsonville (G-10319)

CONSTRUCTION: Foundation & Retaining Wall

Third Salvo Company........................... G 740 818-9669
Amesville (G-443)

CONSTRUCTION: Heavy Highway & Street

Central Allied Enterprises Inc............... E 330 477-6751
Canton (G-1862)

G-R Contracting Inc............................. F 740 567-3202
Lewisville (G-8366)

Hull Ready Mix Concrete Inc................ F 419 625-8070
Sandusky (G-11839)

Seneca Petroleum Co Inc.................... F 419 691-3581
Toledo (G-13127)

Smalls Asphalt Paving Inc................... G 740 427-4096
Gambier (G-7214)

CONSTRUCTION: Indl Buildings, New, NEC

Baker-Shindler Contracting Co............. E 419 782-5080
Defiance (G-6100)

Fleming Construction Co...................... G 740 494-2177
Prospect (G-11501)

Thomas J Weaver Inc.......................... F 740 622-2040
Coshocton (G-5474)

CONSTRUCTION: Indl Plant

Advanced Indus Machining Inc............. F 614 596-4183
Powell (G-11481)

Babcock & Wilcox Company................ A 330 753-4511
Akron (G-67)

Htec Systems Inc................................ F 937 438-3010
Dayton (G-5816)

Tri-America Contractors Inc................. E 740 574-0148
Wheelersburg (G-14354)

CONSTRUCTION: Land Preparation

Valley Mining Inc................................. C 740 922-3942
Dennison (G-6220)

CONSTRUCTION: Oil & Gas Pipeline Construction

Terra Sonic International LLC............... E 740 374-6608
Marietta (G-8953)

CONSTRUCTION: Pipeline, NEC

Eastern Automated Piping.................... G 740 535-8184
Mingo Junction (G-10050)

Sterling Process Equipment .... E 614 868-5151
Columbus (G-5292)

CONSTRUCTION: Power Plant

Enerfab LLC... B 513 641-0500
Cincinnati (G-2590)

CONSTRUCTION: Residential, Nec

American Egle Prprty Prsrvtion............. G 855 440-6938
North Ridgeville (G-10724)

Artisan Constructors LLC..................... E 216 800-7641
Cleveland (G-3370)

CONSTRUCTION: Scaffolding

Waco Scaffolding & Equipment Inc........ A 216 749-8900
Cleveland (G-4487)

CONSTRUCTION: Sewer Line

Fleming Construction Co...................... G 740 494-2177
Prospect (G-11501)

Mt Pleasant Blacktopping Inc............... G 513 874-3777
Fairfield (G-6756)

CONSTRUCTION: Single-Family Housing

Building Concepts Inc.......................... F 419 298-2371
Edgerton (G-6464)

Clearview Construction LLC................... G 513 206-6415
Cincinnati (G-2498)

GUTTER TOPPER LTD........................... G 513 797-5800
Batavia (G-866)

Manufactured Housing Entps Inc........... F 419 636-4511
Bryan (G-1650)

Plumb Builders Inc............................. F 937 293-1111
Dayton (G-5942)

Third Salvo Company.......................... G 740 818-9669
Amesville (G-443)

CONSTRUCTION: Single-family Housing, New

Al Yoder Construction Co...................... G 330 359-5726
Millersburg (G-9967)

Hoge Lumber Company........................ E 419 753-2263
New Knoxville (G-10398)

The Galehouse Companies Inc.............. E 330 658-2023
Doylestown (G-6270)

Thomas J Weaver Inc.......................... F 740 622-2040
Coshocton (G-5474)

CONSTRUCTION: Street Sign Installation & Mntnce

A & A Safety Inc................................ F 937 567-9781
Beavercreek (G-987)

A & A Safety Inc................................ E 513 943-6100
Amelia (G-425)

CONSTRUCTION: Swimming Pools

Imperial On-Pece Fibrgls Pools............. F 740 747-2971
Ashley (G-582)

CONSTRUCTION: Waste Water & Sewage Treatment Plant

Artesian of Pioneer Inc........................ F 419 737-2352
Pioneer (G-11318)

CONSULTING SVC: Business, NEC

Apex Control Systems Inc..................... D 330 938-2588
Sebring (G-11891)

Deemsys Inc..................................... D 614 322-9928
Gahanna (G-7135)

Dje Management Consulting LLC........... G 330 760-2990
Medina (G-9397)

E Retailing Associates LLC................... D 614 300-5785
Columbus (G-4894)

Estone Group LLC.............................. E 888 653-2246
Toledo (G-12957)

Ktsdi LLC... G 330 783-2000
North Lima (G-10709)

Lake Publishing Inc............................ G 440 299-8500
Mentor (G-9549)

Magnum Computers Inc....................... F 216 781-1757
Cleveland (G-3981)

Optum Infusion Svcs 550 LLC............... D 866 442-4679
Cincinnati (G-2936)

Ream and Haager Laboratory Inc.......... F 330 343-3711
Dover (G-6259)

Russell Group United LLC.................... F 614 353-6853
Columbus (G-5238)

Simplevms LLC................................. F 888 255-8918
Cincinnati (G-3091)

Sutter Llc.. F 513 891-2261
Blue Ash (G-1339)

CONSULTING SVC: Financial Management

Dco LLC... E 419 931-9086
Perrysburg (G-11213)

Jmac Inc.. E 614 436-2418
Columbus (G-5041)

CONSULTING SVC: Human Resource

Delphia Consulting LLC........................ E 614 421-2000
Columbus (G-4877)

Paycor Hcm Inc................................. F 800 381-0053
Cincinnati (G-2949)

Simplevms LLC................................. F 888 255-8918
Cincinnati (G-3091)

CONSULTING SVC: Management

Advanced Prgrm Resources Inc............. E 614 761-9994
Dublin (G-6273)

American Egle Prprty Prsrvtion.............. G 855 440-6938
North Ridgeville (G-10724)

Amerihua Intl Entps Inc....................... G 740 549-0300
Lewis Center (G-8321)

Dms Inc... C 440 951-9838
Willoughby (G-14449)

EP Ferris & Associates Inc................... E 614 299-2999
Columbus (G-4906)

Equip Business Solutions Co................. G 614 854-9755
Jackson (G-7945)

Harris Mackessy & Brennan Inc............. C 614 221-6831
Westerville (G-14212)

Link To Success Inc............................ G 888 959-4203
Norwalk (G-10851)

Michele Caldwell................................ G 937 505-7744
Dayton (G-5880)

Pakra LLC.. F 614 477-6965
Columbus (G-5169)

Quality Solutions Inc........................... E 440 933-9946
Cleveland (G-4216)

Russell Group United LLC.................... F 614 353-6853
Columbus (G-5238)

Smithco Distributing........................... E 419 367-7685
Liberty Center (G-8376)

SSP Industrial Group Inc...................... G 330 665-2900
Fairlawn (G-6814)

Tdb Associates Inc............................. F 937 459-5730
Greenville (G-7357)

Vehicle Systems Inc............................ G 330 854-0535
Massillon (C-0261)

Welding Consultants Inc....................... G 614 258-7018
Columbus (G-5360)

CONSULTING SVCS, BUSINESS: Communications

Telex Communications Inc.................... F 419 865-0972
Toledo (G-13140)

CONSULTING SVCS, BUSINESS: Energy Conservation

Aeroseal LLC.................................... E 937 428-9300
Dayton (G-5638)

Aeroseal LLC.................................... E 937 428-9300
Miamisburg (G-9662)

Melink Corporation............................. D 513 685-0958
Milford (G-9943)

CONSULTING SVCS, BUSINESS: Environmental

Radon Eliminator LLC.......................... F 330 844-0703
North Canton (G-10662)

CONSULTING SVCS, BUSINESS: Safety Training Svcs

American Apex Corporation................... F 614 652-2000
Delaware (G-6130)

Nkh-Safety Inc.................................. F 513 771-3839
Cincinnati (G-2911)

CONSULTING SVCS, BUSINESS: Sys Engnrg, Exc Computer/ Prof

Fluid Equipment Corporation................. G 419 636-0777
Bryan (G-1641)

Jasstek Inc....................................... F 614 808-3600
Dublin (G-6313)

Millers Aplus Cmpt Svcs LLC................ F 330 620-5288
Akron (G-234)

Tangible Solutions Inc......................... E 937 912-4603
Fairborn (G-6701)

CONSULTING SVCS, BUSINESS: Systems Analysis & Engineering

Defense Research Assoc Inc................. E 937 431-1644
Dayton (G-5609)

Great Lakes Mfg Group Ltd................... G 440 391-8266
Rocky River (G-11634)

Interactive Engineering Corp................. E 330 239-6888
Medina (G-9413)

Sentek Corporation............................. G 614 586-1123
Columbus (G-5261)

Tekworx LLC..................................... F 513 533-4777
Cincinnati (G-3142)

CONSULTING SVCS, BUSINESS: Systems Analysis Or Design

Architctral Identification Inc.................. F 614 868-8400
Gahanna (G-7154)

Qlog Corp... G 513 874-1211
Hamilton (G-7519)

CONSULTING SVCS: Scientific

Advanced Green Tech Inc..................... G 614 397-8130
Plain City (G-11392)

Mrl Materials Resources LLC................. E 937 531-6657
Xenia (G-14771)

CONTACT LENSES

Diversified Ophthalmics Inc.................. E 803 783-3454
Cincinnati (G-2554)

CONTAINERS, GLASS: Food

Bprex Plastic Packaging Inc.................. F 419 247-5000
Toledo (G-12902)

Ghp II LLC.. C 740 687-2500
Lancaster (G-8204)

CONTAINERS, GLASS: Water Bottles

Waterco of The Central States............... E 937 294-0375
Fairfield (G-6791)

CONTAINERS: Cargo, Wood & Metal Combination

Schutz Container Systems Inc............... D 419 872-2477
Perrysburg (G-11261)

CONTAINERS: Food & Beverage

Ball Arosol Specialty Cont Inc............... E 330 534-1903
Hubbard (G-7808)

Ball Corporation................................. E 419 423-3071
Findlay (G-6840)

PRODUCT

CONTAINERS: Food & Beverage

Ball Corporation...................................F 330 244-2313
North Canton *(G-10629)*

Envases Media Inc..............................E 419 636-5461
Bryan *(G-1640)*

Ghp II LLC..C 740 687-2500
Lancaster *(G-8204)*

SSP Industrial Group Inc....................G 330 665-2900
Fairlawn *(G-6814)*

CONTAINERS: Food, Folding, Made From Purchased Materials

Graphic Packaging Intl LLC................E 419 668-1006
Norwalk *(G-10844)*

CONTAINERS: Food, Liquid Tight, Including Milk

Billerud Americas Corporation...........D 901 369-4105
West Chester *(G-13952)*

Island Aseptics LLC............................C 740 685-2548
Byesville *(G-1714)*

Kerry Inc..E 760 685-2548
Byesville *(G-1715)*

Ohio State Plastics.............................F 614 299-5618
Columbus *(G-5153)*

CONTAINERS: Food, Metal

G W Cobb Co.......................................F 216 341-0100
Cleveland *(G-3751)*

CONTAINERS: Glass

Anchor Glass Container Corp..............D 740 452-2743
Zanesville *(G-14987)*

Anchor Hocking LLC.............................A 740 687-2500
Columbus *(G-4711)*

Chantilly Development Corp.................E 419 243-8109
Toledo *(G-12916)*

Dura Temp Corporation.......................F 419 866-4348
Holland *(G-7760)*

O-I Glass Inc.......................................C 567 336-5000
Perrysburg *(G-11244)*

Owens-Brockway Glass Cont Inc........E 740 455-4516
Zanesville *(G-15036)*

Owens-Brockway Glass Cont Inc........C 567 336-8449
Perrysburg *(G-11252)*

Owens-Illinois General Inc.................A 567 336-5000
Perrysburg *(G-11253)*

Owens-Illinois Group Inc....................D 567 336-5000
Perrysburg *(G-11254)*

Owens-Illinois Inc...............................A 567 336-5000
Perrysburg *(G-11255)*

Paddock Enterprises LLC....................E 567 336-5000
Perrysburg *(G-11256)*

Pyromatics Corp..................................F 440 352-3500
Mentor *(G-9599)*

Tiama Americas Inc.............................E 269 274-3107
Maumee *(G-9325)*

CONTAINERS: Ice Cream, Made From Purchased Materials

Huhtamaki Inc......................................D 513 201-1525
Batavia *(G-867)*

Huhtamaki Inc......................................D 937 746-9700
Franklin *(G-7028)*

Norse Dairy Systems LP.....................B 614 294-4931
Columbus *(G-5129)*

CONTAINERS: Laminated Phenolic & Vulcanized Fiber

Polystar Inc...F 330 963-5100
Stow *(G-12450)*

CONTAINERS: Metal

G P Manufacturing Inc........................G 937 544-3190
Peebles *(G-11168)*

Premier Container Inc.........................E 800 230-7132
Cleveland *(G-4189)*

Shanafelt Manufacturing Co................E 330 455-0315
Canton *(G-2004)*

CONTAINERS: Plastic

Alpla Inc..F 419 991-9484
Lima *(G-8460)*

Amcor Rigid Packaging Usa LLC..........G 419 483-4343
Bellevue *(G-1118)*

Axium Packaging LLC...........................A 614 706-5955
New Albany *(G-10331)*

Bakelite N Sumitomo Amer Inc............E 419 675-1282
Kenton *(G-8096)*

Bprex Plastic Packaging Inc...............F 419 247-5000
Toledo *(G-12902)*

Cell-O-Core Co....................................G 800 239-4370
Wadsworth *(G-13630)*

Century Container LLC........................E 330 457-2367
Columbiana *(G-4608)*

Century Container LLC........................F 330 457-2367
New Waterford *(G-10485)*

Century Container Corporation...........C 330 457-2367
New Waterford *(G-10486)*

Composite Technologies Co LLC..........D 937 228-2880
Dayton *(G-5709)*

Dadco Inc..F 513 489-2244
Cincinnati *(G-2539)*

Dester Corporation.............................F 419 362-8020
Lima *(G-8401)*

Dester Corporation.............................F 419 362-8020
Lima *(G-8400)*

Dometic Sanitation Corporation.........E 330 439-5550
Big Prairie *(G-1216)*

Eaton Corporation...............................E 330 274-0743
Aurora *(G-667)*

Ebco Inc..E 330 562-8265
Streetsboro *(G-12500)*

Eliason Corporation............................E 800 828-3655
West Chester *(G-14116)*

Encon Inc..C 937 898-2603
Dayton *(G-5765)*

Enpac LLC..D 440 975-0070
Eastlake *(G-6425)*

Fields Process Technology Inc............G 216 781-4787
Cleveland *(G-3716)*

Flambeau Inc.......................................D 440 632-6131
Middlefield *(G-9794)*

G3 Packaging LLC.................................334 799-0015
Monroe *(G-10106)*

Genpak LLC..E 614 276-5156
Columbus *(G-4950)*

Graham Packaging Pet Tech Inc...........G 419 334-4197
Fremont *(G-7116)*

Greif Inc..E 740 657-6500
Delaware *(G-6150)*

Greif Inc..E 740 549-6000
Delaware *(G-6149)*

Hamilton Custom Molding Inc.............G 513 844-6643
Hamilton *(G-7501)*

Hendrickson International Corp...........D 740 929-5600
Hebron *(G-7617)*

HP Liquidating Inc...............................D 614 861-1791
Blacklick *(G-1223)*

Iml Containers Ohio Inc......................F 330 754-1066
Alliance *(G-385)*

Kennedy Group Incorporated..............D 440 951-7660
Willoughby *(G-14477)*

CONTAINERS: (right column)

Lalac - Hanlon LLC..............................E 216 261-7056
Euclid *(G-6658)*

Landmark Plastic Corporation.............C 330 785-2200
Akron *(G-203)*

Molded Fiber Glass Companies...........D 440 994-5100
Ashtabula *(G-609)*

Olan Plastics Inc.................................E 614 834-6526
Canal Winchester *(G-1797)*

Patrick Products Inc............................C 419 943-4137
Leipsic *(G-8308)*

Plastics -R- Unique Inc.......................E 330 334-4820
Wadsworth *(G-13660)*

Plastipak Packaging Inc......................C 740 928-4435
Hebron *(G-7630)*

Polyflex LLC...F 440 946-0758
Willoughby *(G-14508)*

Polymer & Steel Tech Inc....................E 440 510-0108
Eastlake *(G-6441)*

Premium Balloon ACC Inc....................G 330 239-4547
Wadsworth *(G-13661)*

Resource Mtl Hdlg & Recycl Inc...........E 440 834-0727
Middlefield *(G-9823)*

S Toys Holdings LLC.............................A 330 656-0440
Streetsboro *(G-12521)*

Shirley KS Storage Trays LLC..............G 740 868-8140
Zanesville *(G-15049)*

Silgan Plastics LLC..............................C 419 523-3737
Ottawa *(G-11045)*

Southeastern Container Inc.................D 419 352-6300
Bowling Green *(G-1440)*

Spartech LLC.......................................C 937 548-1395
Greenville *(G-7353)*

Tbk Holdings LLC.................................G 313 584-0400
Perrysburg *(G-11265)*

US Coexcell Inc...................................E 419 897-9110
Maumee *(G-9328)*

CONTAINERS: Sanitary, Food

Nuvo Packaging LLC............................E 216 400-9676
Columbus *(G-5134)*

Solut Inc..E 740 549-3336
Lewis Center *(G-8354)*

Sonoco Products Company..................E 513 870-3985
West Chester *(G-14148)*

The Mead Corporation........................B 937 495-6323
Dayton *(G-6049)*

Washington Products Inc.....................F 330 837-5101
Massillon *(G-9252)*

CONTAINERS: Shipping, Bombs, Metal Plate

Buckeye Stamping Company................D 877 728-0776
Columbus *(G-4786)*

Industrial Repair and Mfg...................E 419 822-4232
Delta *(G-6210)*

CONTAINERS: Wood

Brimar Packaging Inc..........................E 440 934-3080
Avon *(G-717)*

Brown-Forman Corporation.................G 740 384-3027
Wellston *(G-13905)*

Cima Inc...E 513 382-8976
Hamilton *(G-7477)*

Clark Rm Inc..F 419 425-9889
Findlay *(G-6853)*

Dedicated Industries Inc.....................D 440 238-5200
Strongsville *(G-12553)*

Denoon Lumber Company LLC..............D 740 768-2220
Bergholz *(G-1195)*

Haessly Lumber Sales Co....................D 740 373-6681
Marietta *(G-8922)*

Overseas Packing LLC..........................G 440 232-2917
Bedford *(G-1053)*

T & D Thompson Inc................................. F 740 332-8515
Laurelville (G-8238)

Traveling Recycle WD Pdts Inc.............. G 419 968-2649
Middle Point (G-9764)

Wellman Container Corporation........... E 513 860-3040
Cincinnati (G-3219)

CONTRACTOR: Rigging & Scaffolding

Janson Industries.................................... D 330 455-7029
Canton (G-1921)

CONTRACTORS: Acoustical & Insulation Work

Holland Assocts LLC DBA Archou........ F 513 891-0006
Cincinnati (G-2727)

One Wish LLC... F 800 505-6883
Bedford (G-1052)

CONTRACTORS: Asbestos Removal & Encapsulation

American Way Exteriors LLC................... G 937 221-8860
Dayton (G-5656)

CONTRACTORS: Boiler Maintenance Contractor

Holgate Metal Fab Inc........................... F 419 599-2000
Napoleon (G-10285)

Prout Boiler Htg & Wldg Inc.................. E 330 744-0293
Youngstown (G-14921)

CONTRACTORS: Building Site Preparation

Barrett Paving Materials Inc.................. E 973 533-1001
Hamilton (G-7468)

CONTRACTORS: Carpentry Work

Acme Home Improvement Co Inc.......... F 614 252-2129
Columbus (G-4671)

AK Fabrication Inc.................................. F 330 458-1037
Canton (G-1827)

Finelli Ornamental Iron Co..................... E 440 248-0050
Cleveland (G-3717)

Joseph Sabatino.................................... G 330 332-5879
Salem (G-11791)

Millwood Wholesale Inc.......................... F 330 359-6109
Dundee (G-6369)

Overhead Door of Pike County.............. G 740 289-3925
Piketon (G-11312)

Premier Construction Company............ G 513 874-2611
West Chester (G-14053)

Riverside Cnstr Svcs Inc........................ E 513 723-0900
Cincinnati (G-3048)

Triple A Builders Inc.............................. G 216 249-0327
Cleveland (G-4428)

CONTRACTORS: Carpentry, Cabinet & Finish Work

Architctral Mllwk Cbinetry Inc............... G 440 708-0086
Chagrin Falls (G-2155)

Case Crafters Inc................................... G 937 667-9473
Tipp City (G-12819)

Dgl Woodworking Inc.............................. F 937 837-7091
Dayton (G-5747)

Display Dynamics Inc............................. F 937 832-2830
Englewood (G-6612)

Snows Wood Shop Inc........................... E 419 836-3805
Oregon (G-10968)

CONTRACTORS: Closet Organizers, Installation & Design

Ptmj Enterprises Inc.............................. F 440 543-8000
Solon (G-12170)

CONTRACTORS: Coating, Caulking & Weather, Water & Fire

Akay Holdings Inc................................... E 330 753-8458
Barberton (G-790)

CONTRACTORS: Commercial & Office Building

Brenmar Construction Inc...................... D 740 286-2151
Jackson (G-7941)

Commercial Cnstr Group LLC................ G 513 722-8952
Milford (G-9930)

MGM Construction Inc........................... G 440 234-7660
Berea (G-1182)

Stamm Contracting Company Inc.......... F 330 274-8230
Mantua (G-8875)

CONTRACTORS: Communications Svcs

Gatesair Inc.. D 513 459-3400
Mason (G-9102)

Legrand North America LLC.................. B 937 224-0639
Dayton (G-5843)

Vertiv Group Corporation....................... G 440 460-3600
Cleveland (G-4461)

CONTRACTORS: Concrete Block Masonry Laying

G L Pierce Inc.. G 513 772-7202
Cincinnati (G-2647)

North Central Con Designs Inc.............. G 419 606-1908
Wooster (G-14669)

CONTRACTORS: Concrete Reinforcement Placing

Upright Steel LLC................................... E 216 923-0852
Cleveland (G-4449)

CONTRACTORS: Core Drilling & Cutting

Barr Engineering Incorporated.............. E 614 714-0299
Columbus (G-4744)

CONTRACTORS: Corrosion Control Installation

Corrpro Companies Inc.......................... E 770 761-5400
Medina (G-9392)

Mesocoat Inc... F 216 453-0866
Euclid (G-6662)

CONTRACTORS: Decontamination Svcs

Extreme Microbial Tech LLC.................. E 844 885-0088
Moraine (G-10162)

CONTRACTORS: Directional Oil & Gas Well Drilling Svc

Brendel Producing Company................. G 330 854-4151
Canton (G-1844)

Clearpath Utility Solutions LLC............. F 740 661-4240
Hebron (G-7610)

Directional One Svcs Inc USA............... G 740 371-5031
Marietta (G-8913)

Groundhogs 2000 LLC............................ G 440 653-1647
Bedford (G-1033)

Kirk Excavating & Construction............ E 614 444-4008
Columbus (G-5054)

Temple Oil and Gas LLC........................ G 740 452-7878
Crooksville (G-5513)

Warren Drilling Co Inc............................ C 740 783-2775
Dexter City (G-6225)

CONTRACTORS: Electric Power Systems

Asg Division Jergens Inc........................ E 888 486-6163
Cleveland (G-3377)

Asidaco LLC.. G 800 204-1544
Dayton (G-5666)

CONTRACTORS: Electronic Controls Installation

Controls Inc.. E 330 239-4345
Medina (G-9390)

Industrial Electronic Service.................. F 937 746-9750
Carlisle (G-2066)

Safe-Grain Inc.. G 513 398-2500
Loveland (G-8650)

CONTRACTORS: Energy Management Control

Tekworx LLC.. F 513 533-4777
Cincinnati (G-3142)

CONTRACTORS: Erection & Dismantling, Poured Concrete Forms

R W Sidley Incorporated........................ C 440 298-3232
Thompson (G-12763)

CONTRACTORS: Fence Construction

Bowden Fence Co LLC............................ G 614 272-8923
Columbus (G-4771)

Connaughton Wldg & Fence LLC.......... G 513 867-0230
Hamilton (G-7480)

Cuyahoga Fence LLC.............................. F 216 830-2200
Cleveland (G-3591)

Double D D Mtls Instlltion Inc............... G 937 898-2534
Dayton (G-5750)

Fence One Inc... F 216 441-2600
Cleveland (G-3712)

Mae Fence LLC....................................... F 614 929-3526
Fulton (G-7151)

Security Fence Group Inc....................... E 513 681-3700
Cincinnati (G-3074)

Youngstown Fence Incorporated........... G 330 788-8110
Youngstown (G-14969)

CONTRACTORS: Fiber Optic Cable Installation

DSI Management Holdings LLC.............. F 800 645-7002
Kent (G-8027)

CONTRACTORS: Floor Laying & Other Floor Work

Done-Rite Bowling Service Co............... E 440 232-3280
Bedford (G-1028)

Tremco Incorporated............................. C 216 292-5000
Beachwood (G-956)

Triple A Builders Inc.............................. G 216 249-0327
Cleveland (G-4428)

CONTRACTORS: Foundation & Footing

Gateway Con Forming Svcs Inc............. D 513 353-2000
Miamitown (G-9758)

CONTRACTORS: Gas Field Svcs, NEC

Critical Ctrl Enrgy Svcs Inc................... F 330 539-4267
Girard (G-7269)

CONTRACTORS: General Electric

PRODUCT

D & J Electric Motor Repair Co.............. F 330 336-4343
Wadsworth *(G-13634)*

Franks Electric Inc.................................. G 513 313-5883
Cincinnati *(G-2640)*

Industrial Power Systems Inc.................. B 419 531-3121
Rossford *(G-11659)*

Instrmntation Ctrl Systems Inc............... E 513 662-2600
Cincinnati *(G-2747)*

JC Electric Llc... F 330 760-2915
Garrettsville *(G-7221)*

Jeff Bonham Electric Inc......................... E 937 233-7662
Dayton *(G-5828)*

Magnum Computers Inc........................... F 216 781-1757
Cleveland *(G-3981)*

Mikes Transm & Auto Svc LLC................ F 330 799-8266
Youngstown *(G-14901)*

P S C Inc... G 216 531-3375
Cleveland *(G-4130)*

Security Fence Group Inc........................ E 513 681-3700
Cincinnati *(G-3074)*

Tcb Automation LLC................................ F 330 556-6444
Dover *(G-6265)*

The Wagner-Smith Company................... B 866 338-0398
Moraine *(G-10195)*

Valley Electric Company.......................... G 419 332-6405
Fremont *(G-7142)*

Waibel Electric Co Inc............................. F 740 964-2956
Etna *(G-6634)*

CONTRACTORS: Glass Tinting, Architectural & Automotive

Afg Industries Inc................................... D 614 322-4580
Grove City *(G-7368)*

CONTRACTORS: Heating & Air Conditioning

Air-Tech Mechanical Inc.......................... G 419 292-0074
Toledo *(G-12867)*

Hess Advanced Solutions Llc.................. G 937 829-4794
Dayton *(G-5809)*

Northeastern Rfrgn Corp......................... E 440 942-7676
Willoughby *(G-14496)*

CONTRACTORS: Heating Systems Repair & Maintenance Svc

Whempys Corp... G 614 888-6670
Worthington *(G-14729)*

CONTRACTORS: Highway & Street Construction, General

John R Jurgensen Co............................... B 513 771-0820
Cincinnati *(G-2768)*

Kenmore Construction Co Inc................. D 330 832-8888
Massillon *(G-9211)*

Valley Asphalt Corporation...................... E 513 771-0820
Cincinnati *(G-3191)*

Ward Construction Co.............................. F 419 943-2450
Leipsic *(G-8316)*

CONTRACTORS: Highway & Street Paving

Barrett Paving Materials Inc................... E 973 533-1001
Hamilton *(G-7468)*

Gerken Materials Inc............................... E 419 533-2421
Napoleon *(G-10281)*

M & B Asphalt Company Inc.................... F 419 992-4235
Tiffin *(G-12787)*

Terminal Ready-Mix Inc.......................... E 440 288-0181
Lorain *(G-8583)*

Wilson Blacktop Corp.............................. F 740 635-3566
Martins Ferry *(G-9012)*

CONTRACTORS: Hydraulic Eqpt Installation & Svcs

Kcn Technologies LLC............................. G 440 439-4219
Bedford *(G-1041)*

CONTRACTORS: Machine Rigging & Moving

Atlas Industrial Contrs LLC.................... B 614 841-4500
Columbus *(G-4732)*

Chagrin Vly Stl Erectors Inc.................... F 440 975-1556
Willoughby Hills *(G-14557)*

CONTRACTORS: Machinery Installation

Expert Crane Inc..................................... D 216 451-9900
Wellington *(G-13886)*

Intertec Corporation................................ F 419 537-9711
Toledo *(G-13007)*

Northwest Installations Inc..................... E 419 423-5738
Findlay *(G-6900)*

Spallinger Millwright Svc Co................... E 419 225-5830
Lima *(G-8452)*

CONTRACTORS: Marble Installation, Interior

Cutting Edge Countertops Inc................. E 419 873-9500
Perrysburg *(G-11212)*

Distinctive Marble & Gran Inc................. F 614 760-0003
Plain City *(G-11404)*

CONTRACTORS: Masonry & Stonework

Albert Freytag Inc................................... E 419 628-2018
Minster *(G-10053)*

North Hill Marble & Granite Co................ F 330 253-2179
Akron *(G-249)*

Pioneer Cldding Glzing Systems............. E 216 816-4242
Cleveland *(G-4166)*

Rmi Titanium Company LLC.................... E 330 652-9952
Niles *(G-10604)*

CONTRACTORS: Office Furniture Installation

National Electro-Coatings Inc................. D 216 898-0080
Cleveland *(G-4059)*

CONTRACTORS: Oil & Gas Building, Repairing & Dismantling Svc

Dow Cameron Oil & Gas LLC................... G 740 452-1568
Zanesville *(G-15011)*

Formation Cementing Inc........................ G 740 453-6926
Zanesville *(G-15015)*

J-Well Service Inc.................................... G 330 824-2718
Warren *(G-13774)*

Ralph Robinson Inc................................. G 740 385-2747
Logan *(G-8524)*

CONTRACTORS: Oil & Gas Field Geological Exploration Svcs

David R Hill Inc....................................... G 740 685-5168
Byesville *(G-1708)*

New World Energy Resources.................. F 740 344-4087
Newark *(G-10525)*

CONTRACTORS: Oil & Gas Field Geophysical Exploration Svcs

Dlz Ohio Inc.. C 614 888-0040
Columbus *(G-4887)*

Hocking Hlls Enrgy Well Svcs L............. G 740 385-6690
Logan *(G-8515)*

CONTRACTORS: Oil & Gas Field Tools Fishing Svcs

Klx Energy Services LLC......................... E 740 922-1155
Midvale *(G-9912)*

CONTRACTORS: Oil & Gas Well Plugging & Abandoning Svcs

Omega Cementing Co.............................. G 330 695-7147
Apple Creek *(G-474)*

CONTRACTORS: Oil & Gas Well Redrilling

Decker Drilling Inc.................................. G 740 749-3939
Vincent *(G-13620)*

CONTRACTORS: Oil & Gas Wells Pumping Svcs

Ottawa Oil Co Inc.................................... F 419 425-3301
Findlay *(G-6905)*

Stocker & Sitler Oil Company.................. G 614 888-9588
Columbus *(G-5294)*

CONTRACTORS: Oil & Gas Wells Svcs

Bakerwell Inc.. E 330 276-2161
Killbuck *(G-8130)*

Wrights Well Service LLC....................... G 740 380-9602
Logan *(G-8528)*

CONTRACTORS: Oil Field Mud Drilling Svcs

Kelchner Inc.. D 937 704-9890
Springboro *(G-12258)*

CONTRACTORS: Oil Field Pipe Testing Svcs

Leak Finder Inc....................................... G 440 735-0130
Hudson *(G-7849)*

Ream and Haager Laboratory Inc............ F 330 343-3711
Dover *(G-6259)*

CONTRACTORS: Ornamental Metal Work

Spradlin Bros Welding Co........................ F 800 219-2182
Springfield *(G-12375)*

Stuart-Dean Co Inc................................. G 412 765-2752
Cleveland *(G-4338)*

CONTRACTORS: Painting, Commercial

Mes Painting & Graphics Ltd................... E 614 496-1696
Westerville *(G-14268)*

Napoleon Machine LLC............................ E 419 591-7010
Napoleon *(G-10293)*

CONTRACTORS: Painting, Commercial, Exterior

Ohio Building Restoration Inc................. E 419 244-7372
Toledo *(G-13073)*

CONTRACTORS: Painting, Indl

A1 Industrial Painting Inc....................... E 330 750-9441
Youngstown *(G-14801)*

Banks Manufacturing Company............... F 440 458-8661
Grafton *(G-7299)*

Industrial Mill Maintenance.................... F 330 746-1155
Youngstown *(G-14876)*

Js Fabrications Inc.................................. G 419 333-0323
Fremont *(G-7118)*

Kars Ohio LLC... G 614 655-1099
Pataskala *(G-11142)*

Semper Quality Industry Inc................... G 440 352-8111
Mentor *(G-9613)*

CONTRACTORS: Petroleum Storage Tanks, Pumping & Draining

Envirmnntal Cmpliance Tech LLC........... F 216 634-0400
North Royalton *(G-10760)*

CONTRACTORS: Plumbing

Approved Plumbing Co............................ F 216 663-5063
Cleveland *(G-3362)*

Bear Mechanical LLC............................... G 937 288-2316
Hillsboro *(G-7713)*

Dennis Constuction Sanitation.............. G 419 332-8026
Fremont *(G-7104)*

Personal Plumber Service Corp............. F 440 324-4321
Elyria *(G-6579)*

Pioneer Pipe Inc...................................... A 740 376-2400
Marietta *(G-8937)*

CONTRACTORS: Pollution Control Eqpt Installation

L Haberny Co Inc...................................... F 440 543-5999
Chagrin Falls *(G-2168)*

McGill Airclean LLC.................................. D 614 829-1200
Columbus *(G-5089)*

CONTRACTORS: Power Generating Eqpt Installation

Clopay Ames Inc....................................... C 800 282-2260
Mason *(G-9087)*

CONTRACTORS: Prefabricated Window & Door Installation

Alside Inc... E 419 865-0934
Maumee *(G-9258)*

Cabinet Restylers Inc.............................. D 419 281-8449
Ashland *(G-525)*

General Awning Company Inc................. G 216 749-0110
Cleveland *(G-3762)*

Midwest Curtainwalls Inc....................... D 216 641-7900
Cleveland *(G-4036)*

Yoder Window & Siding Ltd.................... F 330 695-6960
Fredericksburg *(G-7072)*

CONTRACTORS: Process Piping

United Group Services Inc...................... C 800 633-9690
Cincinnati *(G-3183)*

CONTRACTORS: Refractory or Acid Brick Masonry

The Schaefer Group Inc.......................... E 937 253-3342
Beavercreek *(G-997)*

CONTRACTORS: Roustabout Svcs

Prospect Rock LLC.................................. F 740 512-0542
Saint Clairsville *(G-11707)*

Ruscilli Real Estate Services.................. F 614 923-6400
Dublin *(G-6341)*

CONTRACTORS: Septic System

AAA Wastewater Services Inc................ F 937 746-6361
Franklin *(G-7009)*

Accurate Mechanical Inc........................ D 740 681-1332
Lancaster *(G-8174)*

Mack Industries....................................... F 419 353-7081
Bowling Green *(G-1427)*

CONTRACTORS: Sheet Metal Work, NEC

All-Type Welding & Fabrication.............. E 440 439-3990
Cleveland *(G-3329)*

Anchor Metal Processing Inc................. F 216 362-6463
Cleveland *(G-3354)*

Anchor Metal Processing Inc................. E 216 362-1850
Cleveland *(G-3355)*

Avon Lake Sheet Metal Co..................... E 440 933-3505
Avon Lake *(G-750)*

Budde Sheet Metal Works Inc................ E 937 224-0868
Dayton *(G-5689)*

Cmt Machining & Fabg LLC..................... F 937 652-3740
Urbana *(G-13459)*

Defabco Inc.. D 614 231-2700
Columbus *(G-4875)*

Dimensional Metals Inc.......................... E 740 927-3633
Reynoldsburg *(G-11565)*

Ducts Inc.. G 216 391-2400
Cleveland *(G-3637)*

Everyday Technologies Inc..................... F 937 497-7774
Sidney *(G-12018)*

Franck and Fric Incorporated................ D 216 524-4451
Cleveland *(G-3742)*

Holgate Metal Fab Inc............................ F 419 599-2000
Napoleon *(G-10285)*

Jim Nier Construction Inc....................... E 740 289-3925
Piketon *(G-11308)*

Kirk & Blum Manufacturing Co............... C 513 458-2600
Cincinnati *(G-2797)*

Martina Metal LLC................................... E 614 291-9700
Columbus *(G-5085)*

Precision Impacts LLC............................ D 937 530-8254
Miamisburg *(G-9728)*

Rmt Acquisition Inc................................. E 513 241-5566
Cincinnati *(G-3050)*

Seneca Sheet Metal Company................ F 419 447-8434
Tiffin *(G-12800)*

Tendon Manufacturing Inc...................... E 216 663-3200
Cleveland *(G-4374)*

CONTRACTORS: Siding

Cardinal Builders Inc.............................. G 614 237-1000
Columbus *(G-4801)*

Champion Opco LLC................................ B 513 327-7338
Cincinnati *(G-2458)*

General Awning Company Inc................. G 216 749-0110
Cleveland *(G-3762)*

Waxco International Inc........................... F 937 746-4845
Miamisburg *(G-9752)*

CONTRACTORS: Skylight Installation

Scs Construction Services Inc............... E 513 929-0260
Cincinnati *(G-3071)*

CONTRACTORS: Structural Iron Work, Structural

Wernke Wldg & Stl Erection Co.............. F 513 353-4173
North Bend *(G-10622)*

White Mule Company............................... E 740 382-9008
Ontario *(G-10954)*

CONTRACTORS: Structural Steel Erection

Affiliated Metal Industries Inc............... F 440 235-3345
Olmsted Falls *(G-10936)*

Atlantic Welding LLC............................... F 937 570-5094
Piqua *(G-11335)*

Chagrin Vly Stl Erectors Inc................... F 440 975-1556
Willoughby Hills *(G-14557)*

Chc Fabricating Corp.............................. D 513 821-7757
Cincinnati *(G-2459)*

Concord Fabricators Inc......................... E 614 875-2500
Grove City *(G-7377)*

Evers Welding Co Inc.............................. G 513 385-7352
Cincinnati *(G-2604)*

Frederick Steel Company LLC................ D 513 821-6400
Cincinnati *(G-2641)*

G & P Construction LLC.......................... E 855 494-4830
North Royalton *(G-10762)*

GL Nause Co Inc...................................... E 513 722-9500
Loveland *(G-8626)*

Lake Building Products Inc..................... E 216 486-1500
Cleveland *(G-3936)*

Marysville Steel Inc................................. E 937 642-5971
Marysville *(G-9038)*

Mound Technologies Inc......................... E 937 748-2937
Springboro *(G-12260)*

Parker Fabricating Co............................. E 330 379-0112
Akron *(G-256)*

Pro-Fab Inc... G 330 644-0044
Akron *(G-267)*

Rex Welding Inc....................................... F 740 387-1650
Marion *(G-8992)*

Rittman Inc... D 330 927-6855
Rittman *(G-11627)*

CONTRACTORS: Tile Installation, Ceramic

Prints & Paints Flr Cvg Co Inc............... E 419 462-5663
Galion *(G-7197)*

CONTRACTORS: Underground Utilities

Great Lakes Crushing Ltd....................... D 440 944-5500
Wickliffe *(G-14376)*

CONTRACTORS: Ventilation & Duct Work

Franck and Fric Incorporated................ D 216 524-4451
Cleveland *(G-3742)*

Jacobs Mechanical Co............................ C 513 681-6800
Cincinnati *(G-2756)*

CONTRACTORS: Warm Air Heating & Air Conditioning

Controls and Sheet Metal Inc................ E 513 721-3610
Cincinnati *(G-2515)*

Daikin Applied Americas Inc.................. G 614 351-9862
Westerville *(G-14252)*

Glt Inc.. F 937 237-0055
Dayton *(G-5800)*

Style Crest Enterprises Inc..................... E 419 355-8586
Fremont *(G-7134)*

Yanfeng Intl Auto Tech US I LL............... E 419 662-4905
Northwood *(G-10815)*

CONTRACTORS: Water Well Drilling

Stoepfel Drilling Co................................ G 419 532-3307
Ottawa *(G-11048)*

CONTRACTORS: Well Logging Svcs

Oaktree Wireline LLC.............................. G 330 352-7250
New Philadelphia *(G-10461)*

CONTRACTORS: Windows & Doors

Artisan Constructors LLC....................... E 216 800-7641
Cleveland *(G-3370)*

Golden Angle Archtctral Group.............. G 614 531-7932
Columbus *(G-4960)*

Seemray LLC.. E 440 536-8705
Cleveland *(G-4285)*

Traichal Construction Company.............. E 800 255-3667
Niles *(G-10607)*

CONTRACTORS: Wood Floor Installation & Refinishing

Hoover & Wells Inc.................................. C 419 691-9220
Toledo *(G-12995)*

CONTRACTORS: Wrecking & Demolition

Allgeier & Son Inc.................................... F 513 574-3735
Cincinnati *(G-2351)*

Rnw Holdings Inc..................................... E 330 792-0600
Youngstown *(G-14925)*

Employee Codes: A=Over 500 employees, B=251-500
C=101-250, D=51-100, E=20-50, F=10-19, G=1-9

2025 Harris Ohio
Industrial Directory

1273

PRODUCT

CONTROL EQPT: Electric

Cincinnati Ctrl Dynamics Inc.................. G 513 242-7300
Cincinnati (G-2473)

Controls Inc.. E 330 239-4345
Medina (G-9390)

Davis Technologies Inc........................... F .. 330 823-2544
Alliance (G-380)

Lake Shore Electric Corp........................ E .. 440 232-0200
Bedford (G-1043)

Machine Drive Company......................... D .. 513 793-7077
Cincinnati (G-2837)

R-K Electronics Inc.................................. F .. 513 204-6060
Mason (G-9141)

Rockwell Automation Inc......................... B 330 425-3211
Twinsburg (G-13368)

Spang & Company.................................. E .. 440 350-6108
Mentor (G-9619)

Superb Industries Inc............................. D .. 330 852-0500
Sugarcreek (G-12652)

Village Controls LLC............................... F .. 614 600-8880
Powell (G-11496)

CONTROL EQPT: Electric Buses & Locomotives

Precision Design Inc............................... G .. 419 289-1553
Ashland (G-566)

CONTROL EQPT: Noise

Acon Inc... G 513 276-2111
Tipp City (G-12814)

Keene Building Products Co.................... E .. 440 605-1020
Cleveland (G-3910)

Kinetics Noise Control Inc...................... C .. 614 889-0480
Dublin (G-6316)

Seneca Environmental Products Inc...... E .. 419 447-1282
Tiffin (G-12799)

Tech Products Corporation..................... F 937 438-1100
Miamisburg (G-9744)

CONTROLS & ACCESS: Indl, Electric

Apex Control Systems Inc....................... D .. 330 938-2588
Sebring (G-11891)

Avtron Holdings LLC................................ E .. 216 642-1230
Cleveland (G-3394)

Corrotec Inc... E .. 937 325-3585
Springfield (G-12294)

Filnor Inc... F .. 330 821-8731
Alliance (G-382)

Miami Control Systems Inc..................... G .. 937 233-8146
Dayton (G-5877)

PMC Systems Limited............................. E .. 330 538-2268
North Jackson (G-10693)

Rockwell Automation Inc......................... D .. 440 646-5000
Mayfield Heights (G-9341)

Tekworx LLC.. F .. 513 533-4777
Cincinnati (G-3142)

CONTROLS & ACCESS: Motor

Eaton Corporation................................... B 440 523-5000
Cleveland (G-3652)

Eaton Electrical...................................... F 787 257-4470
Cleveland (G-3655)

Standex Electronics Inc.......................... D .. 513 871-3777
Fairfield (G-6778)

CONTROLS: Automatic Temperature

Acutemp Thermal Systems...................... F 937 312-0114
Moraine (G-10142)

Building Ctrl Integrators LLC.................. G..... 513 247-6154
Cincinnati (G-2433)

Building Ctrl Integrators LLC.................. G .. 513 860-9600
West Chester (G-14108)

Building Ctrl Integrators LLC.................. E .. 614 334-3300
Powell (G-11482)

Energy & Ctrl Integrators Inc.................. G .. 419 222-0025
Lima (G-8405)

Ignio Systems LLC.................................. G .. 419 708-0503
Toledo (G-12999)

CONTROLS: Electric Motor

Ignio Systems LLC.................................. G .. 419 708-0503
Toledo (G-12999)

Toledo Electromotive Inc......................... G .. 419 874-7751
Perrysburg (G-11274)

TT Electronics Integrated M.................... B .. 440 352-8961
Perry (G-11200)

CONTROLS: Environmental

Alan Manufacturing Inc........................... E .. 330 262-1555
Wooster (G-14621)

Babcock & Wilcox Company................... A 330 753-4511
Akron (G-67)

Bry-Air Inc... E .. 740 965-2974
Sunbury (G-12662)

Cincinnati Air Conditioning Co............... D .. 513 721-5622
Cincinnati (G-2468)

Columbus Controls Inc............................ E .. 614 882-9029
Columbus (G-4820)

Doan/Pyramid Solutions LLC.................. E .. 216 587-9510
Cleveland (G-3622)

Dyoung Enterprise Inc............................. C .. 440 918-0505
Willoughby (G-14452)

Envirnment Ctrl Sthwest Ohio I.............. F .. 937 669-9900
Tipp City (G-12824)

Future Controls Corporation................... E .. 440 275-3191
Austinburg (G-700)

Honeywell International Inc..................... A .. 937 484-2000
Urbana (G-13466)

Hunter Defense Tech Inc......................... E .. 216 438-6111
Solon (G-12124)

Integrated Development & Mfg............... F .. 440 543-2423
Chagrin Falls (G-2167)

Integrated Development & Mfg............... F .. 440 247-5100
Chagrin Falls (G-2146)

Karman Rubber Company........................ D .. 330 864-2161
Akron (G-191)

Logisync Corporation.............................. G .. 440 937-0388
Avon (G-732)

Parker-Hannifin Corporation................... E .. 216 433-1795
Cleveland (G-4144)

Pepperl + Fuchs Inc................................ C .. 330 425-3555
Twinsburg (G-13352)

Premier Enrgy Systems Ohio LLC.......... F .. 304 252-1918
Athens (G-647)

Resideo LLC.. G .. 440 439-7002
Bedford (G-1057)

Resideo LLC.. F .. 513 772-1851
Cincinnati (G-3039)

Sje Rhombus Controls............................. F .. 419 281-5767
Ashland (G-574)

Skuttle Mfg Co... F .. 740 373-9169
Marietta (G-8946)

Ventra Sandusky LLC.............................. C .. 419 627-3600
Sandusky (G-11882)

Vib-Iso LLC... F .. 800 735-9645
Wooster (G-14695)

Vortec Corporation.................................. E .. 513 891-7485
Blue Ash (G-1348)

CONTROLS: Hydronic

Certified Labs & Service Inc................... G .. 419 289-7462
Ashland (G-527)

CONTROLS: Thermostats, Built-in

Therm-O-Disc Incorporated.................... A 419 525-8500
Westerville (G-14236)

CONVENIENCE STORES

Tbone Sales LLC..................................... G .. 330 897-6131
Baltic (G-781)

CONVERTERS: Frequency

R E Smith Inc.. F 513 771-0645
Cincinnati (G-3028)

CONVEYOR SYSTEMS

2e Associates Inc.................................... E .. 440 975-9955
Willoughby (G-14412)

Global TBM Company............................. C .. 440 248-3303
Solon (G-12117)

Hostar International Inc........................... F .. 440 564-5362
Solon (G-12123)

Ulterior Products LLC............................. G .. 614 441-9465
Radnor (G-11508)

CONVEYOR SYSTEMS: Belt, General Indl Use

Allgaier Process Technology................... G 513 402-2566
West Chester (G-13937)

Bavis Fabacraft Inc................................. E .. 513 677-0500
Maineville (G-8738)

Blair Rubber Company............................ D .. 330 769-5583
Seville (G-11911)

Conveyor Solutions LLC......................... F .. 513 367-4845
Cleves (G-4533)

Manufacturers Equipment Co................. F .. 513 424-3573
Middletown (G-9877)

Mayfran International Inc........................ C .. 440 461-4100
Cleveland (G-4003)

Mfh Partners Inc..................................... B .. 440 461-4100
Cleveland (G-4025)

Midwest Conveyor Products Inc............. E .. 419 281-1235
Ashland (G-552)

New Transcon LLC.................................. E .. 440 255-7600
Mentor (G-9570)

CONVEYOR SYSTEMS: Bucket Type

Fenner Dunlop Port Clinton LLC............ C .. 419 635-2191
Port Clinton (G-11442)

Joy Global Underground Min LLC.......... E .. 440 248-7970
Cleveland (G-3895)

CONVEYOR SYSTEMS: Bulk Handling

Air Technical Industries Inc.................... E .. 440 951-5191
Mentor (G-9474)

Bulk Handling Equipment Co.................. G .. 330 468-5703
Northfield (G-10792)

Lewco Inc.. C .. 419 625-4014
Sandusky (G-11850)

Webster Industries Inc............................ B .. 419 447-8232
Tiffin (G-12808)

CONVEYOR SYSTEMS: Pneumatic Tube

American Solving Inc............................... G .. 440 234-7373
Brookpark (G-1543)

Coperion Process Solutions LLC............ F .. 513 576-9200
Solon (G-12098)

Fred D Pfening Company......................... E .. 614 294-5361
Columbus (G-4939)

CONVEYOR SYSTEMS: Robotic

Automation Systems Design Inc............. E .. 937 387-0351
Dayton (G-5669)

Grob Systems Inc............................ A 419 358-9015
Bluffton (G-1361)

Imperial Conveying Systems LLC.......... F .. 330 491-3200
Canton (G-1916)

CONVEYORS & CONVEYING EQPT

Ad Industries Inc............................ A 303 744-1911
Dayton (G-5634)

Advanced Equipment Systems LLC....... G .. 216 289-6505
Euclid (G-6638)

Alan Bortree................................. G 937 585-6962
De Graff (G-6091)

Alba Manufacturing Inc.................... D .. 513 874-0551
Fairfield (G-6708)

Allied Consolidated Inds Inc.............. C .. 330 744-0808
Youngstown (G-14808)

Allied Fabricating & Wldg Co............. E .. 614 868-8680
Columbus (G-4687)

Ambaflex Inc................................. E .. 330 478-1858
Canton (G-1829)

Barth Industries Co LLC................... E .. 216 267-1950
Cleveland (G-3407)

Bobco Enterprises Inc...................... F .. 419 867-3560
Toledo (G-12899)

Bry-Air Inc.................................... E .. 740 965-2974
Sunbury (G-12662)

C A Litzler Co Inc........................... E .. 216 267-8020
Cleveland (G-3457)

Cincinnati Mine Machinery Co............ E .. 513 522-7777
Cincinnati (G-2482)

Coating Systems Group Inc............... F .. 440 816-9306
Middleburg Heights (G-9768)

Con-Belt Inc.................................. F .. 330 273-2003
Valley City (G-13492)

Conveyor Metal Works Inc................. E .. 740 477-8700
Frankfort (G-7004)

Conveyor Technologies Ltd................ G .. 513 248-0663
Milford (G-9931)

Daifuku America Corporation............. C .. 614 863-1888
Reynoldsburg (G-11564)

Decision Systems Inc...................... F .. 330 456-7600
Canton (G-1879)

Defabco Inc.................................. D .. 614 231-2700
Columbus (G-4875)

Dematic Corp................................ D .. 440 526-2770
Brecksville (G-1462)

Dillin Engineered Systems Corp.......... E .. 419 666-6789
Perrysburg (G-11210)

Dover Conveyor Inc......................... E .. 740 922-9390
Midvale (G-9908)

Duplex Mill & Manufacturing Co.......... E .. 937 325-5555
Springfield (G-12304)

Eagle Crusher Co Inc....................... D .. 419 468-2288
Galion (G-7187)

Enviri Corporation.......................... F .. 740 387-1150
Marion (G-8969)

Esco Turbine Tech Cleveland.............. F .. 440 953-0053
Eastlake (G-6427)

Fabacraft Inc................................. E .. 513 677-0500
Maineville (G-8740)

Fabco Inc..................................... D .. 419 422-4533
Findlay (G-6862)

Falcon Industries Inc...................... E .. 330 723-0099
Medina (G-9401)

Federal Equipment Company............. D .. 513 621-5260
Cincinnati (G-2616)

Feedall Inc................................... F .. 440 942-8100
Willoughby (G-14458)

Fki Logistex Automation Inc.............. A .. 513 881-5251
West Chester (G-14120)

Formtek Inc.................................. D .. 216 292-4460
Cleveland (G-3737)

Glassline Corporation...................... E .. 419 666-9712
Perrysburg (G-11225)

Grasan Equipment Company Inc.......... D .. 419 526-4440
Mansfield (G-8797)

Gray-Eering Ltd.............................. G .. 740 498-8816
Tippecanoe (G-12858)

Innovative Controls Corp.................. F .. 419 691-6684
Maumee (G-9298)

Innovative Handling LLC................... E .. 419 882-7480
Sylvania (G-12712)

Ins Robotics Inc............................ G .. 888 293-5325
Hilliard (G-7684)

Intelligrated Inc............................ A .. 513 874-0788
West Chester (G-14127)

Intelligrated Inc............................ E .. 866 936-7300
Mason (G-9111)

Intelligrated Products LLC................ E .. 740 490-0300
London (G-8537)

Intelligrated Sub Holdings Inc............ D .. 513 701-7300
Mason (G-9112)

Intelligrated Systems Inc.................. A .. 866 936-7300
Mason (G-9113)

Intelligrated Systems LLC................. A .. 513 701-7300
West Chester (G-14128)

Intelligrated Systems Ohio LLC.......... G .. 513 682-6600
West Chester (G-14129)

Intelligrated Systems Ohio LLC.......... E .. 513 701-7300
Mason (G-9114)

Jsj Sb Holdings Inc......................... G .. 216 398-7774
Cleveland (G-3897)

Kolinahr Systems Inc...................... F .. 513 745-9401
Blue Ash (G-1294)

Laser Automation Inc...................... C .. 440 543-9291
Chagrin Falls (G-2169)

Logitech Inc.................................. E .. 614 871-2822
Grove City (G-7395)

Material Holdings Inc...................... E .. 513 583-5500
Loveland (G-8640)

Met Fab Fabrication and Mch............. E .. 513 724-3715
Batavia (G-872)

Miller Products Inc......................... E .. 330 308-5934
New Philadelphia (G-10458)

Modula Inc................................... D .. 207 440-5100
Franklin (G-7035)

Mulhern Belting Inc........................ E .. 201 337-5700
Fairfield (G-6757)

Nesco Inc.................................... E .. 440 461-6000
Cleveland (O-4000)

Ocs Intellitrak Inc.......................... F .. 513 742-5600
Fairfield (G-6760)

Ohio Magnetics Inc........................ E .. 216 662-8484
Maple Heights (G-8888)

Opw Engineered Systems Inc............. E .. 888 771-9438
West Chester (G-14039)

Parker-Hannifin Corporation............. G .. 330 336-3511
Wadsworth (G-13658)

PB Fbrction Mech Contrs Corp........... F .. 419 478-4869
Toledo (G-13091)

Pfpc Enterprises Inc....................... G .. 513 941-6200
Cincinnati (G-2960)

Pneumatic Scale Corporation............ D .. 330 923-0491
Cuyahoga Falls (G-5564)

Pomacon Inc................................ F .. 330 273-1576
Brunswick (G-1606)

Precision Conveyor Technology.......... F .. 440 352-6100
Perry (G-11197)

Pro Mach Inc................................ E .. 513 771-7374
Cincinnati (G-2984)

Quickdraft Inc............................... E .. 330 477-4574
Canton (G-1987)

Richmond Machine Co..................... E .. 419 485-5740
Montpelier (G-10134)

Rolcon Inc.................................... F .. 513 821-7259
Cincinnati (G-3052)

Sandusky Fabricating & Sls Inc........... E .. 419 626-4465
Sandusky (G-11867)

Spirex Corporation......................... C .. 330 726-1166
Youngstown (G-14938)

Stock Equipment Company Inc........... C .. 440 543-6000
Chagrin Falls (G-2184)

Stock Fairfield Corporation............... C .. 440 543-6000
Solon (G-12185)

Sweet Manufacturing Company.......... E .. 937 325-1511
Springfield (G-12381)

Tkf Conveyor Systems LLC................ C .. 513 621-5260
Cincinnati (G-3157)

Transnorm System Inc..................... D .. 972 606-0303
Mason (G-9163)

Uhrden Inc................................... E .. 330 456-0031
Canton (G-2030)

Werks Kraft Engineering LLC.............. E .. 330 721-7374
Medina (G-9464)

COOKING & FOODWARMING EQPT: Commercial

Belanger Inc................................. D .. 517 870-3206
West Chester (G-13948)

Cleveland Range LLC....................... C .. 216 481-4900
Cleveland (G-3522)

Lima Sheet Metal Mch & Mfg Inc......... F .. 419 229-1161
Lima (G-8426)

Siebtechnik Tema Inc...................... E .. 513 489-7811
Cincinnati (G-3088)

COOKING EQPT, HOUSEHOLD: Ranges, Gas

Z Line Kitchen and Bath LLC.............. G .. 614 777-5004
Marysville (G-9055)

COOLING TOWERS: Metal

Air-Tech Mechanical Inc................... G .. 419 292-0074
Toledo (G-12867)

COPPER: Rolling & Drawing

Production Tube Cutting Inc............... E .. 937 254-6138
Dayton (G-5963)

T & D Fabricating Inc....................... E .. 440 951-5646
Eastlake (G-6445)

CORRECTION FLUID

Milacron LLC................................. E .. 513 487-5000
Cincinnati (G-2880)

CORRUGATING MACHINES

Rebiltco Inc.................................. G .. 513 424-2024
Middletown (G-9890)

COSMETIC PREPARATIONS

AA Hand Sanitizer........................... G .. 513 506-7575
Cincinnati (G-2328)

B & P Company Inc.......................... G .. 937 298-0265
Centerville (G-2130)

Bonne Bell Inc............................... C .. 440 835-2440
Westlake (G-14293)

Bonne Bell LLC.............................. G .. 440 835-2440
Westlake (G-14294)

KAO USA Inc................................. F .. 513 629-5210
Cincinnati (G-2783)

KAO USA Inc................................. E .. 513 341-2630
West Chester (G-14018)

KAO USA Inc................................. B .. 513 421-1400
Cincinnati (G-2782)

Kdc One Inc.................................. G .. 614 984-2871
New Albany (G-10343)

Merle Norman Cosmetics Inc.............. E 419 282-0630
   Mansfield (G-8824)

Midwest Sea Salt Company Inc.............. F 513 770-9177
   West Chester (G-14029)

Montgomery Ellis LLC.............. C 614 226-7976
   Westerville (G-14271)

Natural Essentials Inc.............. C 330 562-8022
   Streetsboro (G-12513)

Universal Packg Systems Inc.............. C 513 732-2000
   Batavia (G-894)

Universal Packg Systems Inc.............. C 513 735-4777
   Batavia (G-895)

Universal Packg Systems Inc.............. C 513 674-9400
   Cincinnati (G-3186)

Veepak OH LLC.............. F 740 927-9002
   New Albany (G-10353)

COSMETICS & TOILETRIES

Abitec Corporation.............. E 614 429-6464
   Columbus (G-4665)

Bath & Body Works LLC.............. B 614 856-6000
   Reynoldsburg (G-11557)

Brand5 LLC.............. F 614 920-9254
   Pickerington (G-11290)

Cameo Inc.............. G 419 661-9611
   Perrysburg (G-11208)

Colgate-Palmolive Company.............. C 212 310-2000
   Cambridge (G-1739)

French Transit LLC.............. G 650 431-3959
   Mason (G-9101)

Gojo Industries Inc.............. G 330 255-6525
   Stow (G-12435)

Gojo Industries Inc.............. C 330 255-6000
   Akron (G-163)

Interco Division 10 Ohio Inc.............. G 614 875-2959
   Grove City (G-7392)

Luminex HM Dcor Frgrnce Hldg C.......... A 513 563-1113
   Cincinnati (G-2831)

Meridian Industries Inc.............. E 330 359-5809
   Beach City (G-904)

Natural Essentials Inc.............. F 330 562-8022
   Aurora (G-680)

Nehemiah Manufacturing Co LLC.......... D 513 351-5700
   Cincinnati (G-2897)

Primal Life Organics LLC.............. E 800 260-4946
   Copley (G-5438)

Procter & Gamble Mfg Co.............. C 419 226-5500
   Lima (G-8439)

Shadow Holdings LLC.............. B 614 741-7458
   New Albany (G-10350)

Sysco Guest Supply LLC.............. E 440 960-2515
   Lorain (G-8582)

US Cotton LLC.............. D 216 676-6400
   Cleveland (G-4451)

Woodbine Products Company.............. F 330 725-0165
   Medina (G-9465)

Zena Baby Soap Company.............. G 216 317-6433
   Bedford Heights (G-1084)

COSMETOLOGY & PERSONAL HYGIENE SALONS

Pur Hair Extensions LLC.............. G 330 786-5772
   Akron (G-270)

COUNTER & SINK TOPS

3jd Inc.............. F 513 324-9655
   Moraine (G-10141)

American Countertops Inc.............. E 330 495-1915
   Hartville (G-7574)

Cameo Countertops Inc.............. F 419 865-6371
   Holland (G-7748)

Crafted Surface and Stone LLC.............. E 440 658-3799
   Chagrin Falls (G-2157)

Formica Corporation.............. E 513 786-3400
   Cincinnati (G-2635)

Gross & Sons Custom Millwork.............. G 419 227-0214
   Lima (G-8411)

Zanesville Fabricators Inc.............. G 740 452-2439
   Zanesville (G-15057)

COUNTERS OR COUNTER DISPLAY CASES, EXC WOOD

Formatech Inc.............. E 330 273-2800
   Brunswick (G-1590)

Stiber Fabricating Inc.............. F 216 771-7210
   Cleveland (G-4332)

COUNTERS OR COUNTER DISPLAY CASES, WOOD

Counter Concepts Inc.............. F 330 848-4848
   Wadsworth (G-13632)

Formatech Inc.............. E 330 273-2800
   Brunswick (G-1590)

Hardwood Lumber Company Inc.............. F 440 834-1891
   Middlefield (G-9797)

Kinsella Manufacturing Co Inc.............. F 513 561-5285
   Cincinnati (G-2796)

COUNTING DEVICES: Controls, Revolution & Timing

L3harris Electrodynamics Inc.............. C 847 259-0740
   Cincinnati (G-2310)

Thermo Gamma-Metrics LLC.............. E 858 450-9811
   Bedford (G-1061)

COUNTING DEVICES: Tachometer, Centrifugal

Lake Shore Cryotronics Inc.............. D 614 891-2243
   Westerville (G-14217)

COUNTRY CLUBS

Cincinnati Marlins Inc.............. G 513 761-3320
   Cincinnati (G-2480)

COUPLINGS: Hose & Tube, Hydraulic Or Pneumatic

Custom Cltch Jint Hydrlics Inc.............. F 216 431-1630
   Cleveland (G-3584)

Dyna-Flex Inc.............. F 440 946-9424
   Painesville (G-11081)

COUPLINGS: Pipe

B S F Inc.............. F 937 890-6121
   Tipp City (G-12816)

B S F Inc.............. F 937 890-6121
   Dayton (G-5672)

COUPLINGS: Shaft

B S F Inc.............. F 937 890-6121
   Tipp City (G-12816)

B S F Inc.............. F 937 890-6121
   Dayton (G-5672)

Bowes Manufacturing Inc.............. F 216 378-2110
   Solon (G-12087)

Climax Metal Products Company.......... D 440 943-8898
   Mentor (G-9502)

COVERS: Automobile Seat

Besi Manufacturing Inc.............. G 513 874-1460
   West Chester (G-13950)

Besi Manufacturing Inc.............. E 513 874-0232
   West Chester (G-13951)

Griffin Fisher Co Inc.............. G 513 961-2110
   Cincinnati (G-2692)

CRANE & AERIAL LIFT SVCS

IBI Brake Products Inc.............. G 440 543-7962
   Chagrin Falls (G-2166)

Konecranes Inc.............. F 440 461-8400
   Broadview Heights (G-1504)

Pollock Research & Design Inc.............. E 330 332-3300
   Salem (G-11805)

Rex Welding Inc.............. F 740 387-1650
   Marion (G-8992)

CRANES & MONORAIL SYSTEMS

Crane 1 Services Inc.............. E 937 704-9900
   West Chester (G-13977)

Emh Inc.............. D 330 220-8600
   Valley City (G-13495)

CRANES: Indl Plant

Demag Cranes & Components Corp...... C 440 248-2400
   Solon (G-12100)

Hiab USA Inc.............. D 419 482-6000
   Perrysburg (G-11228)

Kci Holding USA Inc.............. C 937 525-5533
   Springfield (G-12335)

Konecranes Inc.............. E 937 328-5100
   Springfield (G-12337)

Konecranes Inc.............. B 937 525-5533
   Springfield (G-12338)

Radocy Inc.............. F 419 666-4400
   Rossford (G-11661)

CRANES: Indl Truck

Hoist Equipment Co Inc.............. E 440 232-0300
   Bedford Heights (G-1078)

Skylift Inc.............. D 440 960-2100
   Lorain (G-8581)

Venturo Manufacturing Inc.............. F 513 772-8448
   Cincinnati (G-3199)

CRANES: Overhead

ACC Automation Co Inc.............. E 330 928-3821
   Akron (G-12)

Altec Industries Inc.............. F 205 408-2341
   Cuyahoga Falls (G-5521)

Morgan Engineering Systems Inc.......... C 330 821-4721
   Alliance (G-393)

Morgan Engineering Systems Inc.......... E 330 823-6130
   Alliance (G-394)

Rnm Holdings Inc.............. F 614 444-5556
   Columbus (G-5232)

CROWNS & CLOSURES

Boardman Molded Products Inc.......... D 330 788-2400
   Youngstown (G-14822)

Eisenhauer Mfg Co LLC.............. D 419 238-0081
   Van Wert (G-13535)

CRUDE PETROLEUM & NATURAL GAS PRODUCTION

Bijoe Development Inc.............. E 330 674-5981
   Millersburg (G-9971)

Exco Resources LLC.............. F 740 254-4061
   Tippecanoe (G-12856)

G-R Contracting Inc.............. F 740 567-3202
   Lewisville (G-8366)

John D Oil and Gas Company.............. G 440 255-6325
   Mentor (G-9543)

Kenoil Inc.. G 330 262-1144
Wooster *(G-14657)*

Pin Oak Energy Partners LLC.............. F 888 748-0763
Akron *(G-258)*

Stocker & Sitler Oil Company.............. G 614 888-9588
Columbus *(G-5294)*

CRUDE PETROLEUM PRODUCTION

Andeavor Logistics LP......................... F 419 421-2414
Findlay *(G-6837)*

Apache Acquisitions LLC..................... G 419 782-8003
Defiance *(G-6096)*

Bakerwell Inc....................................... E 330 276-2161
Killbuck *(G-8130)*

Buckeye Oil Producing Co.................... F 330 264-8847
Wooster *(G-14629)*

Cameron Drilling Co Inc....................... G 740 453-3300
Zanesville *(G-15003)*

Cgas Exploration Inc............................ F 614 436-4631
Worthington *(G-14705)*

Cgas Inc... G 614 975-4697
Worthington *(G-14706)*

Derrick Petroleum Inc.......................... G 740 668-5711
Bladensburg *(G-1232)*

Dome Drilling Company........................ G 440 892-9434
Westlake *(G-14299)*

Elkhead Gas & Oil Co.......................... G 740 763-3966
Newark *(G-10500)*

Exco Resources (pa) LLC..................... F 740 796-5231
Adamsville *(G-7)*

Franklin Gas & Oil Company LLC......... G 330 264-8739
Wooster *(G-14638)*

Green Energy Inc.................................. G 330 262-5112
Wooster *(G-14644)*

Knight Material Tech LLC...................... E 330 488-1651
East Canton *(G-6378)*

Marietta Resources Corporation........... F 740 373-6305
Marietta *(G-8927)*

W H Patten Drilling Co Inc.................... G 330 674-3046
Millersburg *(G-10017)*

W P Brown Enterprises Inc................... G 740 685-2594
Byesville *(G-1718)*

William S Miller Inc.............................. G 330 223-1794
Kensington *(G-8011)*

Xto Energy Inc...................................... G 740 671-9901
Bellaire *(G-1090)*

CRYOGENIC COOLING DEVICES: Infrared Detectors, Masers

Advanced Cryogenic Entps Inc............ F 330 922-0750
Akron *(G-20)*

Drivetrain USA Inc................................ F 614 733-0940
Plain City *(G-11405)*

Lake Shore Cryotronics Inc.................. D 614 891-2243
Westerville *(G-14217)*

CULVERTS: Sheet Metal

Contech Engnered Solutions Inc........... A 513 645-7000
West Chester *(G-13971)*

Edwards Sheet Metal Works Inc........... F 740 694-0010
Fredericktown *(G-7078)*

CUPS: Paper, Made From Purchased Materials

American Greetings Corporation........... A 216 252-7300
Cleveland *(G-3344)*

Graphic Packaging Intl LLC.................. B 419 673-0711
Kenton *(G-8100)*

Ricking Holding Co............................... F 513 825-3551
Cleveland *(G-4241)*

CURBING: Granite Or Stone

Distinctive Marble & Gran Inc............... F 614 760-0003
Plain City *(G-11404)*

CURTAIN WALLS: Building, Steel

Precision Wldg Instllation LLC.............. F 740 995-0613
Zanesville *(G-15043)*

CURTAINS: Window, From Purchased Materials

Style-Line Incorporated....................... E 614 291-0600
Columbus *(G-5295)*

CUSHIONS & PILLOWS

Dorex LLC.. G 216 271-7064
Newburgh Heights *(G-10540)*

Easy Way Leisure Company LLC.......... E 513 731-5640
Cincinnati *(G-2576)*

Greendale Home Fashions LLC............ D 859 916-5475
Cincinnati *(G-2690)*

CUSHIONS & PILLOWS: Bed, From Purchased Materials

Brentwood Originals Inc....................... D 330 793-2255
Youngstown *(G-14824)*

Down-Lite International Inc................... C 513 229-3696
Mason *(G-9095)*

Downhome Inc...................................... E 513 921-3373
Cincinnati *(G-2561)*

Downhome Inc...................................... E 513 921-3373
Cincinnati *(G-2562)*

CUSHIONS: Carpet & Rug, Foamed Plastics

Johnsonite Inc...................................... B 440 632-3441
Middlefield *(G-9804)*

Scottdel Cushion Inc............................ E 419 825-0432
Swanton *(G-12691)*

Solo Products Inc................................. F 513 321-7884
Cincinnati *(G-3100)*

CUSTOM COMPOUNDING OF RUBBER MATERIALS

Bdu Holdings Inc.................................. F 330 374-1810
Akron *(G-73)*

Dnh Mixing Inc..................................... E 330 296-6327
Mogadore *(G-10073)*

Gen-Rubber LLC................................... G 440 655-3643
Galion *(G-7192)*

Hexpol Compounding Pc Inc................ C 330 798-4790
Barberton *(G-810)*

Killian Latex Inc................................... E 330 644-6746
Akron *(G-196)*

Polymerics Inc...................................... E 330 928-2210
Cuyahoga Falls *(G-5565)*

Prcc Holdings Inc................................. C 330 798-4790
Copley *(G-5437)*

Wayne County Rubber Inc.................... E 330 264-5553
Wooster *(G-14696)*

CUT STONE & STONE PRODUCTS

1914 Mi Inc.. E 330 308-8667
New Philadelphia *(G-10428)*

Agean Marble Manufacturing Inc.......... G 513 874-1475
West Chester *(G-14099)*

As America Inc..................................... D 419 522-4211
Mansfield *(G-8763)*

Bell Vault and Monu Works Inc............. F 937 866-2444
Miamisburg *(G-9668)*

Blu Bird LLC... F 513 271-5646
Cincinnati *(G-2413)*

Blu Bird LLC... G 614 276-3585
Columbus *(G-4766)*

Castelli Marble LLC.............................. G 216 361-1222
Cleveland *(G-3477)*

Classic Stone Company Inc.................. F 614 833-3946
Columbus *(G-4810)*

Dutch Quality Stone Inc....................... D 877 359-7866
Mount Eaton *(G-10206)*

Kellstone Inc... E 419 746-2396
Kelleys Island *(G-8009)*

Lang Stone Company Inc...................... G 614 235-4099
Columbus *(G-5064)*

Lima Millwork Inc.................................. G 419 331-3303
Elida *(G-6483)*

Maumee Valley Memorials Inc.............. F 419 878-9030
Waterville *(G-13839)*

Medina Supply Company....................... E 330 723-3681
Medina *(G-9426)*

Melvin Stone Co LLC............................ F 513 771-0820
Cincinnati *(G-2862)*

National Lime and Stone Co................. E 419 562-0771
Bucyrus *(G-1684)*

National Lime and Stone Co................. E 419 396-7671
Carey *(G-2060)*

North Hill Marble & Granite Co............. F 330 253-2179
Akron *(G-249)*

Ohio Beauty Cut Stone II Inc................ G 330 644-2241
Akron *(G-251)*

Pavestone LLC..................................... D 513 474-3783
Cincinnati *(G-2948)*

Riceland Cabinet Inc............................ D 330 601-1071
Wooster *(G-14676)*

Shelly Materials Inc.............................. G 937 358-2224
West Mansfield *(G-14181)*

Sims-Lohman Inc.................................. D 440 799-8285
Brooklyn Heights *(G-1540)*

Solid Surface Concepts Inc.................. E 513 948-8677
Cincinnati *(G-3099)*

Take It For Granite LLC......................... F 513 735-0555
Cincinnati *(G-2316)*

Transtar Holding Company LLC............ G 800 359-3339
Walton Hills *(G-13703)*

Western Ohio Cut Stone Ltd.................. F 937 492-4722
Sidney *(G-12061)*

CUTLERY

American Punch Co............................... E 216 731-4501
Euclid *(G-6642)*

Crescent Manufacturing Company........ D 419 332-6484
Fremont *(G-7099)*

Edgewell Per Care Brands LLC............ F 330 527-2191
Garrettsville *(G-7219)*

Energizer Global Auto Care.................. G 937 742-4500
Vandalia *(G-13555)*

G & S Metal Products Co Inc................ C 216 441-0700
Cleveland *(G-3748)*

General Cutlery Inc............................... F 419 332-2316
Fremont *(G-7114)*

Libbey Glass LLC................................. D 419 727-2211
Toledo *(G-13034)*

Madison Property Holdings Inc............. E 800 215-3210
Cincinnati *(G-2839)*

Northstar Plastics Inc........................... D 216 340-7109
Glenwillow *(G-7287)*

Npk Construction Equipment Inc.......... D 440 232-7900
Bedford *(G-1050)*

CYCLIC CRUDES & INTERMEDIATES

Color Products Inc................................ G 513 860-2749
Hamilton *(G-7479)*

Ferro Corporation.....................E 330 682-8015
Orrville *(G-10980)*

Neyra Interstate Inc.....................E 513 733-1000
Cincinnati *(G-2908)*

Polymerics Inc.....................E 330 928-2210
Cuyahoga Falls *(G-5565)*

Standridge Color Corporation.....................F 770 464-3362
Defiance *(G-6124)*

Sun Chemical Corporation.....................D 513 753-9550
Amelia *(G-439)*

Sun Chemical Corporation.....................C 513 681-5950
Cincinnati *(G-3127)*

CYLINDER & ACTUATORS: Fluid Power

Cascade Corporation.....................E 937 327-0300
Springfield *(G-12287)*

Control Line Equipment Inc.....................F 216 433-7766
Cleveland *(G-3565)*

Custom Hoists Inc.....................C 419 368-4721
Ashland *(G-532)*

Cylinders and Valves Inc.....................G 440 238-7343
Strongsville *(G-12552)*

Dynamic Hydraulic Svcs Co LLC.....................E 330 447-8967
Dover *(G-6243)*

Eaton Aeroquip LLC.....................A 419 891-7775
Maumee *(G-9292)*

Eaton Leasing Corporation.....................B 216 382-2292
Beachwood *(G-916)*

Hydraulic Parts Store Inc.....................G 330 364-6667
New Philadelphia *(G-10449)*

Hydraulic Specialists Inc.....................G 740 922-3343
Midvale *(G-9911)*

Ic-Fluid Power Inc.....................F 419 661-8811
Rossford *(G-11658)*

Moog Inc.....................E 330 682-0010
Orrville *(G-10996)*

North Coast Instruments Inc.....................G 216 251-2353
Cleveland *(G-4085)*

Parker-Hannifin Corporation.....................C 330 336-3511
Wadsworth *(G-13659)*

Parker-Hannifin Corporation.....................A 216 896-3000
Cleveland *(G-4143)*

Robeck Fluid Power Co.....................D 330 562-1140
Aurora *(G-687)*

Sebring Fluid Power Corp.....................G 330 938-9984
Sebring *(G-11902)*

Skidmore-Wilhelm Mfg Company.....................G 216 481-4774
Solon *(G-12182)*

Steel Eqp Specialists Inc.....................D 330 823-8260
Alliance *(G-406)*

Suburban Manufacturing Co.....................D 440 953-2024
Eastlake *(G-6444)*

Swagelok Company.....................D 440 349-5934
Solon *(G-12191)*

Xomox Pft Corp.....................B 936 271-6500
Cincinnati *(G-3238)*

CYLINDERS: Pressure

Gayston Corporation.....................C 937 743-6050
Miamisburg *(G-9693)*

Hutnik Company.....................G 330 336-9700
Wadsworth *(G-13643)*

Toledo Metal Spinning Company.....................E 419 535-5931
Toledo *(G-13152)*

Worthington Cylinder Corp.....................C 740 569-4143
Bremen *(G-1489)*

Worthington Cylinder Corp.....................C 614 438-7900
Columbus *(G-5373)*

Worthington Cylinder Corp.....................C 614 840-3800
Westerville *(G-14242)*

Worthington Cylinder Corp.....................D 330 262-1762
Wooster *(G-14703)*

Worthington Cylinder Corp.....................C 614 840-3210
Worthington *(G-14730)*

CYLINDERS: Pump

Custom Cltch Jint Hydrlics Inc.....................F 216 431-1630
Cleveland *(G-3584)*

Rolcon Inc.....................F 513 821-7259
Cincinnati *(G-3052)*

DAIRY PRDTS STORE: Cheese

Cheese Holdings Inc.....................E 330 893-2479
Millersburg *(G-9977)*

Grays Orange Barn Inc.....................G 419 568-2718
Wapakoneta *(G-13714)*

Great Lakes Cheese Co Inc.....................B 440 834-2500
Hiram *(G-7739)*

Lori Holding Co.....................E 740 342-3230
New Lexington *(G-10403)*

DAIRY PRDTS STORE: Ice Cream, Packaged

Jenis Splendid Ice Creams LLC.....................E 614 488-3224
Columbus *(G-5036)*

Malleys Candies LLC.....................D 216 362-8700
Cleveland *(G-3983)*

Milk Hney Cndy Soda Shoppe LLC.....................G 330 492-5884
Canton *(G-1950)*

DAIRY PRDTS STORES

Hans Rothenbuhler & Son Inc.....................E 440 632-6000
Middlefield *(G-9796)*

United Dairy Inc.....................B 740 373-4121
Marietta *(G-8958)*

United Dairy Farmers Inc.....................C 513 396-8700
Cincinnati *(G-3181)*

Youngs Jersey Dairy Inc.....................B 937 325-0629
Yellow Springs *(G-14794)*

DAIRY PRDTS: Butter

Dairy Farmers America Inc.....................G 330 670-7800
Medina *(G-9395)*

Heavenly Creamery Inc.....................G 440 593-6080
Conneaut *(G-5403)*

Minerva Dairy Inc.....................D 330 868-4196
Minerva *(G-10042)*

New Dairy Cincinnati LLC.....................D 214 258-1200
Cincinnati *(G-2900)*

New Dairy Ohio LLC.....................D 214 258-1200
Cleveland *(G-4073)*

DAIRY PRDTS: Canned Milk, Whole

J M Smucker Company.....................A 330 682-3000
Orrville *(G-10987)*

Nu Pet Company.....................E 330 682-3000
Orrville *(G-10998)*

DAIRY PRDTS: Cheese

Amish Wedding Foods Inc.....................E 330 674-9199
Millersburg *(G-9969)*

Dairy Farmers America Inc.....................G 330 670-7800
Medina *(G-9395)*

Lake Erie Frozen Foods Mfg Co.....................D 419 289-9204
Ashland *(G-548)*

Lakeview Farms LLC.....................C 419 695-9925
Delphos *(G-6190)*

Land OLakes Inc.....................C 330 678-1578
Kent *(G-8045)*

Lipari Foods Operating Co LLC.....................E 330 893-2479
Millersburg *(G-9992)*

Lipari Foods Operating Co LLC.....................E 330 674-9199
Millersburg *(G-9993)*

Tri State Dairy LLC.....................G 330 897-5555
Baltic *(G-782)*

DAIRY PRDTS: Cheese, Cottage

United Dairy Inc.....................B 740 373-4121
Marietta *(G-8958)*

DAIRY PRDTS: Condensed Milk

Eagle Family Foods Group LLC.....................E 330 382-3725
Cleveland *(G-3647)*

DAIRY PRDTS: Cream Substitutes

Instantwhip-Dayton Inc.....................G 937 435-4371
Dayton *(G-5824)*

Instantwhip-Dayton Inc.....................G 937 235-5930
Dayton *(G-5823)*

DAIRY PRDTS: Dietary Supplements, Dairy & Non-Dairy Based

Ai Life LLC.....................F 513 605-1079
Mason *(G-9058)*

All-In Nutritionals LLC.....................F 888 400-0333
Springfield *(G-12278)*

Freedom Health LLC.....................E 330 562-0888
Aurora *(G-670)*

Infinit Nutrition LLC.....................F 513 791-3500
Blue Ash *(G-1288)*

Innovated Health LLC.....................G 330 858-0651
Cuyahoga Falls *(G-5549)*

Instantwhip-Columbus Inc.....................E 614 871-9447
Grove City *(G-7391)*

Muscle Feast LLC.....................F 740 877-8808
Nashport *(G-10301)*

Wileys Finest LLC.....................C 740 622-1072
Coshocton *(G-5478)*

DAIRY PRDTS: Evaporated Milk

Nestle Usa Inc.....................B 440 349-5757
Solon *(G-12159)*

Nestle Usa Inc.....................B 440 264-6600
Solon *(G-12160)*

DAIRY PRDTS: Ice Cream & Ice Milk

Cfgsc LLC.....................G 513 772-5920
Cincinnati *(G-2454)*

International Brand Services.....................G 513 376-8209
Cincinnati *(G-2751)*

Malleys Candies LLC.....................D 216 362-8700
Cleveland *(G-3983)*

Toft Dairy Inc.....................D 419 625-4376
Sandusky *(G-11877)*

United Dairy Farmers Inc.....................C 513 396-8700
Cincinnati *(G-3181)*

DAIRY PRDTS: Ice Cream, Bulk

Country Parlour Ice Cream Co.....................G 440 237-4040
Cleveland *(G-3570)*

Fritzie Freeze Inc.....................G 419 727-0818
Toledo *(G-12969)*

United Dairy Inc.....................C 740 633-1451
Martins Ferry *(G-9011)*

Velvet Ice Cream Company.....................D 740 892-3921
Utica *(G-13488)*

Weldon Ice Cream Company.....................G 740 467-2400
Millersport *(G-10026)*

DAIRY PRDTS: Ice Cream, Packaged, Molded, On Sticks, Etc.

Graeters Ice Cream Company.....................D 513 721-3323
Cincinnati *(G-2687)*

United Dairy Inc.....................B 740 373-4121
Marietta *(G-8958)*

DAIRY PRDTS: Milk, Condensed & Evaporated

Hans Rothenbuhler & Son Inc............E 440 632-6000
Middlefield *(G-9796)*

Ingredia Inc............................E 419 738-4060
Wapakoneta *(G-13716)*

Minerva Dairy Inc.....................D 330 868-4196
Minerva *(G-10042)*

Nestle Usa Inc.........................D 216 861-8350
Cleveland *(G-4070)*

New Diry Cincinnati Trnspt LLC........D 214 258-1200
Cincinnati *(G-2901)*

Rich Products Corporation.............C 614 771-1117
Hilliard *(G-7699)*

DAIRY PRDTS: Milk, Fluid

Arps Dairy Inc........................F 419 782-9116
Defiance *(G-6098)*

Consun Food Industries Inc............E 440 322-6301
Elyria *(G-6514)*

Dairy Farmers America Inc.............G 330 670-7800
Medina *(G-9395)*

Dfa Dairy Brands Ice Cream LLC.........B 419 473-9621
Toledo *(G-12943)*

Green Field Farms Co-Op...............G 330 263-0246
Wooster *(G-14645)*

Instantwhip Foods Inc.................F 614 488-2536
Columbus *(G-5011)*

Reiter Dairy LLC Dean Foods...........G 937 323-5777
Springfield *(G-12368)*

Smithfoods Inc.........................E 330 683-8710
Orrville *(G-11008)*

Snowville Creamery LLC................E 740 698-2301
Pomeroy *(G-11438)*

Superior Dairy Inc.....................C 330 477-4515
Canton *(G-2021)*

DAIRY PRDTS: Natural Cheese

9444 Ohio Holding Co..................E 330 359-6291
Winesburg *(G-14604)*

A&M Cheese Co.........................D 419 476-8369
Toledo *(G-12860)*

Brewster Cheese Company..............C 330 767-3492
Brewster *(G-1490)*

Bunker Hill Cheese Co Inc.............D 330 893-2131
Millersburg *(G-9973)*

Great Lakes Cheese Co Inc.............B 440 834-2500
Hiram *(G-7739)*

Guggisberg Cheese Inc.................E 330 893-2550
Millersburg *(G-9982)*

Hans Rothenbuhler & Son Inc...........E 440 632-6000
Middlefield *(G-9796)*

Holmes Cheese Co......................E 330 674-6451
Millersburg *(G-9986)*

Kathys Krafts and Kollectibles........G 423 787-3709
Medina *(G-9417)*

Krafts Exotika LLC....................G 216 563-1178
Cleveland *(G-3928)*

Miceli Dairy Products Co..............D 216 791-6222
Cleveland *(G-4027)*

Middlfeld Original Cheese Coop.........F 440 632-5567
Middlefield *(G-9812)*

Pearl Valley Cheese Inc...............E 740 545-6002
Fresno *(G-7147)*

Rothenbuhler Cheese Chalet LLC.........G 800 327-9477
Middlefield *(G-9824)*

Rothenbuhler Holding Company..........G 440 632-6000
Middlefield *(G-9825)*

Schindlers Broad Run Chshuse I.........F 330 343-4108
Dover *(G-6260)*

Tri State Dairy LLC...................G 419 542-8788
Hicksville *(G-7653)*

DAIRY PRDTS: Powdered Milk

Stolle Milk Biologics Inc.............G 513 489-7997
West Chester *(G-14150)*

DAIRY PRDTS: Processed Cheese

Alpine Dairy LLC......................E 330 359-6291
Dundee *(G-6364)*

Inter American Products Inc...........D 800 645-2233
Cincinnati *(G-2748)*

Minerva Dairy Inc.....................D 330 868-4196
Minerva *(G-10042)*

DAIRY PRDTS: Whipped Topping, Exc Frozen Or Dry Mix

Instantwhip Connecticut Inc...........F 614 488-2536
Columbus *(G-5010)*

Instantwhip Products Co PA............F 614 488-2536
Columbus *(G-5012)*

Instantwhip-Buffalo Inc...............F 614 488-2536
Columbus *(G-5013)*

Instantwhip-Columbus Inc.............E 614 871-9447
Grove City *(G-7391)*

Instantwhip-Syracuse Inc.............F 614 488-2536
Columbus *(G-5015)*

Louis Instantwhip-St Inc.............F 614 488-2536
Columbus *(G-5076)*

Peak Foods Llc........................D 937 440-0707
Troy *(G-13247)*

Philadelphia Instantwhip Inc..........F 614 488-2536
Columbus *(G-5191)*

DATA PROCESSING & PREPARATION SVCS

Datatrak International Inc............E 440 443-0082
Beachwood *(G-914)*

Gracie Plum Investments Inc...........E 740 355-9029
Portsmouth *(G-11467)*

ITM Marketing Inc.....................C 740 295-3575
Coshocton *(G-5457)*

NCR Technology Center.................G 937 445-1936
Dayton *(G-5903)*

Northrop Grmmn Spce & Mssn Sys.......D 937 259-4956
Dayton *(G-5910)*

Sarcom Inc............................A 614 854-1300
Lewis Center *(G-8353)*

SC Strategic Solutions LLC............C 567 424-6054
Norwalk *(G-10861)*

Thinkware Incorporated................E 513 598-3300
Cincinnati *(G-3153)*

DATA PROCESSING SVCS

Aero Fulfillment Services Corp.........D 800 225-7145
Mason *(G-9056)*

Amsive OH LLC.........................D 937 885-8000
Miamisburg *(G-9665)*

Cpmm Services Group Inc...............G 614 447-0165
Columbus *(G-4857)*

Delaware Data Products Inc............D 740 369-5449
Delaware *(G-6142)*

Vndly LLC.............................E 513 572-2500
Mason *(G-9165)*

DECORATIVE WOOD & WOODWORK

Brown Wood Products Company..........G 330 339-8000
New Philadelphia *(G-10433)*

CM Paula Company......................E 513 759-7473
Mason *(G-9090)*

Grk Manufacturing Co..................E 513 863-3131
Hamilton *(G-7497)*

Hardwood Store Inc....................G 937 864-2899
Enon *(G-6631)*

Insta Plak Inc........................G 419 537-1555
Toledo *(G-13006)*

J R Custom Unlimited Inc..............F 513 894-9800
Hamilton *(G-7507)*

Miller Manufacturing Inc..............G 330 852-0689
Sugarcreek *(G-12642)*

Newbury Woodworks.....................G 440 564-5273
Newbury *(G-10558)*

P & T Millwork Inc....................F 440 543-2151
Chagrin Falls *(G-2175)*

Peters Family Enterprises Inc.........G 419 339-0555
Elida *(G-6485)*

Ryanworks Inc.........................E 937 438-1282
Dayton *(G-5990)*

Walnut Creek Planing Ltd..............D 330 893-3244
Millersburg *(G-10018)*

DEFENSE SYSTEMS & EQPT

IMT Defense Corp......................G 614 891-8812
Westerville *(G-14214)*

Lite Magnesium Products Inc...........D 330 296-6110
Ravenna *(G-11531)*

Mrl Materials Resources LLC...........E 937 531-6657
Xenia *(G-14771)*

Personal Defense & Tactics LLC........G 513 571-7163
Middletown *(G-9884)*

Skuld LLC.............................E 330 423-7339
Piqua *(G-11384)*

Transdigm Inc.........................G 216 706-2960
Cleveland *(G-4412)*

Vector Electromagnetics LLC...........F 937 478-5904
Wilmington *(G-14589)*

DEGREASING MACHINES

Auto-Tap Inc..........................G 216 671-1043
Cleveland *(G-3389)*

Crowne Group LLC......................F 216 589-0198
Cleveland *(G-3577)*

DENTAL EQPT & SPLYS

Boxout LLC............................C 833 462-7746
Hudson *(G-7835)*

Dental Ceramics Inc...................E 330 523-5240
Richfield *(G-11590)*

Midmark Corporation...................G 937 526-3662
Versailles *(G-13600)*

Midmark Corporation...................A 937 528-7500
Miamisburg *(G-9717)*

Palm Plastics Ltd.....................G 561 776-6700
Bowling Green *(G-1432)*

Precision Swiss LLC...................G 513 716-7000
Cincinnati *(G-2978)*

United Dental Laboratories............E 330 253-1810
Tallmadge *(G-12756)*

DENTAL EQPT & SPLYS WHOLESALERS

Dentronix Inc.........................D 330 916-7300
Cuyahoga Falls *(G-5538)*

DENTAL EQPT & SPLYS: Impression Materials

Dentsply Sirona Inc...................E 419 865-9497
Maumee *(G-9291)*

DENTAL EQPT & SPLYS: Orthodontic Appliances

Dentronix Inc.........................D 330 916-7300
Cuyahoga Falls *(G-5538)*

PRODUCT

DEODORANTS: Personal

Dover Wipes Company........................... F 513 983-1100
Cincinnati *(G-2560)*

Procter & Gamble Company.................. E 513 626-2500
Blue Ash *(G-1325)*

Procter & Gamble Company.................. E 513 983-1100
Cincinnati *(G-2987)*

Procter & Gamble Company.................. E 513 266-4375
Cincinnati *(G-2988)*

Procter & Gamble Company.................. F 513 871-7557
Cincinnati *(G-2989)*

Procter & Gamble Company.................. D 513 983-1100
Cincinnati *(G-2990)*

Procter & Gamble Company.................. F 513 482-6789
Cincinnati *(G-2991)*

Procter & Gamble Company.................. E 513 634-5069
Cincinnati *(G-2992)*

Procter & Gamble Company.................. C 513 983-3000
Cincinnati *(G-2993)*

Procter & Gamble Company.................. D 513 627-7115
Cincinnati *(G-2994)*

Procter & Gamble Company.................. G 513 658-9853
Cincinnati *(G-2995)*

Procter & Gamble Company.................. B 513 983-1100
Cincinnati *(G-2996)*

Procter & Gamble Company.................. E 513 945-0340
Cincinnati *(G-2997)*

Procter & Gamble Company.................. E 513 242-5752
Cincinnati *(G-2998)*

Procter & Gamble Company.................. C 513 622-1000
Mason *(G-9138)*

Procter & Gamble Company.................. C 513 634-9600
West Chester *(G-14054)*

Procter & Gamble Company.................. C 513 634-9110
West Chester *(G-14055)*

DEPARTMENT STORES

Siemens Industry Inc........................... F 513 576-2088
Milford *(G-9952)*

DEPARTMENT STORES: Army-Navy Goods

Raven Concealment Systems LLC......... E 440 508-9000
North Ridgeville *(G-10745)*

DEPARTMENT STORES: Country General

John Purdum....................................... G 513 897-9686
Waynesville *(G-13879)*

DEPILATORIES, COSMETIC

Scarlett Kitty LLC.............................. F 678 438-3796
Dayton *(G-5995)*

DESIGN SVCS, NEC

Bollin & Sons Inc............................... E 419 693-6573
Toledo *(G-12900)*

Columbus Design & Mfg LLC.............. G 414 534-3273
Columbus *(G-4822)*

Controls Inc... E 330 239-4345
Medina *(G-9390)*

Dasher Lawless Automation LLC......... E 855 755-7275
Warren *(G-13757)*

Htec Systems Inc................................ F 937 438-3010
Dayton *(G-5816)*

IEC Infrared Systems LLC.................... E 440 234-8000
Middleburg Heights *(G-9772)*

Impact Printing and Design LLC........... F 833 522-6200
Columbus *(G-5003)*

Signs Unlmted The Grphic Advnt......... G 614 836-7446
Logan *(G-8526)*

Universal Dsign Fbrication LLC............. F 419 202-5269
Sandusky *(G-11880)*

Valley List LLC.................................... G 740 760-6411
Waterford *(G-13829)*

DESIGN SVCS: Commercial & Indl

Acreo Inc.. G 513 734-3327
Amelia *(G-426)*

David Wolfe Design Inc........................ F 330 633-6124
Akron *(G-117)*

Electrovations Inc............................... G 330 274-3558
Solon *(G-12103)*

Hutnik Company.................................. G 330 336-9700
Wadsworth *(G-13643)*

Ies Systems Inc.................................. E 330 533-6683
Canfield *(G-1811)*

New Path International LLC................... F 614 410-3974
Powell *(G-11493)*

R and J Corporation............................ E 440 871-6009
Westlake *(G-14326)*

R J K Enterprises Inc........................... G 440 257-6018
Mentor *(G-9604)*

Tugz International LLC.......................... F 216 621-4854
Cleveland *(G-4432)*

Ultra Tech Machinery Inc...................... E 330 929-5544
Cuyahoga Falls *(G-5580)*

DESIGN SVCS: Computer Integrated Systems

Aclara Technologies LLC...................... F 440 528-7200
Solon *(G-12072)*

Applied Experience LLC....................... G 614 943-2970
Plain City *(G-11394)*

Bcs Technologies Ltd.......................... F 513 829-4577
Fairfield *(G-6713)*

Cott Systems Inc................................. D 614 847-4405
Columbus *(G-4853)*

Eaj Services LLC................................. E 513 792-3400
Blue Ash *(G-1269)*

Electronic Concepts Engrg Inc............. F 419 861-9000
Holland *(G-7763)*

IPA Ltd.. F 614 523-3974
Columbus *(G-5024)*

Logisync Corporation........................... G 440 937-0388
Avon *(G-732)*

M T Systems Inc................................. G 330 453-4646
Canton *(G-1936)*

Matrix Management Solutions............... G 330 470-3700
Canton *(G-1940)*

Northrop Grmman Tchncal Svcs I......... C 937 320-3100
Beavercreek Township *(G-1000)*

Sarcom Inc.. A 614 854-1300
Lewis Center *(G-8353)*

Sentient Studios Ltd............................ E 330 204-8636
Fairlawn *(G-6811)*

Sgi Matrix LLC.................................... D 937 438-9033
Miamisburg *(G-9736)*

Software Solutions Inc......................... E 513 932-6667
Dayton *(G-6012)*

Syntec LLC.. F 440 229-6262
Rocky River *(G-11640)*

Tata America Intl Corp.......................... B 513 677-6500
Milford *(G-9954)*

Thyme Inc.. F 484 872-8430
Akron *(G-337)*

Worker Automation Inc......................... G 937 473-2111
Dayton *(G-6086)*

DETECTION APPARATUS: Electronic/ Magnetic Field, Light/Heat

L3harris Cincinnati Elec Corp............... A 513 573-6100
Mason *(G-9121)*

DETECTION EQPT: Magnetic Field

Ceia Usa Ltd....................................... D 330 310-4741
Hudson *(G-7836)*

HBD Industries Inc............................... E 614 526-7000
Dublin *(G-6302)*

DIAGNOSTIC SUBSTANCES

Diagnostic Hybrids Inc........................ C 740 593-1784
Athens *(G-638)*

GE Healthcare Inc............................... F 513 241-5955
Cincinnati *(G-2657)*

John P Ellis Clinic Podiatry.................. G 440 460-0444
Cleveland *(G-3890)*

Meridian Bioscience Inc....................... C 513 271-3700
Cincinnati *(G-2864)*

Nanofiber Solutions LLC...................... G 614 319-3075
Dublin *(G-6322)*

Navidea Biopharmaceuticals Inc........... G 614 793-7500
Dublin *(G-6324)*

Quest Diagnostics Incorporated........... G 513 229-5500
Mason *(G-9140)*

Quidel Corporation............................... E 858 552-1100
Athens *(G-649)*

Quidel Corporation............................... G 740 589-3300
Athens *(G-650)*

Revvity Health Sciences Inc................. D 330 825-4525
Akron *(G-283)*

Thermo Fisher Scientific Inc................. E 800 871-8909
Oakwood Village *(G-10910)*

DIAGNOSTIC SUBSTANCES OR AGENTS: Radioactive

Cardinal Health 414 LLC...................... G 513 759-1900
West Chester *(G-13954)*

Cardinal Health 414 LLC...................... C 614 757-5000
Dublin *(G-6288)*

Petnet Solutions Inc............................ G 865 218-2000
Cincinnati *(G-2959)*

Petnet Solutions Cleveland LLC........... F 865 218-2000
Cleveland *(G-4155)*

USB Corporation................................. F 216 765-5000
Cleveland *(G-4454)*

DIAGNOSTIC SUBSTANCES OR AGENTS: Veterinary

Cleveland AEC West LLC...................... G 216 362-6000
Cleveland *(G-3506)*

Meridian Life Science Inc..................... F 513 271-3700
Cincinnati *(G-2865)*

DIE CUTTING SVC: Paper

Forest Converting Co Inc...................... G 513 631-4190
Cincinnati *(G-2634)*

P & R Specialty Inc............................. E 937 773-0263
Piqua *(G-11370)*

Williams Steel Rule Die Co................... G 216 431-3232
Cleveland *(G-4507)*

DIE SETS: Presses, Metal Stamping

Brassgate Industries Inc...................... G 937 339-2192
Troy *(G-13203)*

Centaur Tool & Die Inc........................ F 419 352-7704
Bowling Green *(G-1412)*

Columbia Stamping Inc........................ G 440 236-6677
Columbia Station *(G-4591)*

Kurtz Tool & Die Co Inc....................... G 330 755-7723
Struthers *(G-12619)*

McAfee Tool & Die Inc......................... E 330 896-9555
Uniontown *(G-13423)*

Toolcraft Products Inc............................ E 937 223-8271
Dayton *(G-6058)*

Western Ohio Technologies LLC.......... G 937 947-8810
Russia *(G-11678)*

DIES & TOOLS: Special

A & B Tool & Manufacturing.................... G 419 382-0215
Toledo *(G-12859)*

Accu-Rite Tool & Die Co Corp................ G 330 497-9959
Canton *(G-1822)*

Accu-Tek Tool & Die Inc........................ G 330 726-1946
Salem *(G-11760)*

Accu-Tool Inc....................................... G 937 667-5878
Tipp City *(G-12813)*

Ace American Wire Die Co..................... F 330 425-7269
Twinsburg *(G-13267)*

Acro Tool & Die Company...................... E 330 773-5173
Akron *(G-16)*

Adept Manufacturing Corp..................... F 937 222-7110
Dayton *(G-5636)*

Afc Tool Co Inc.................................... E 937 275-8700
Dayton *(G-5640)*

Allied Tool & Die Inc............................ F 216 941-6196
Cleveland *(G-3331)*

Alpha Tool & Mold Inc.......................... F 440 473-2343
Cleveland *(G-3333)*

Alpine Gage Inc................................... G 937 669-8665
Tipp City *(G-12815)*

Amcraft Inc... G 419 729-7900
Toledo *(G-12872)*

Amtech Tool & Machine Inc.................... G 330 758-8215
Youngstown *(G-14813)*

Antwerp Tl Die & Engrg Co Inc............... F 419 258-5271
Antwerp *(G-461)*

Apollo Products Inc.............................. F 440 269-8551
Willoughby *(G-14422)*

Arnett Tool Inc.................................... G 937 437-0361
New Paris *(G-10425)*

Artisan Tool & Die Corp........................ F 216 883-2769
Cleveland *(G-3371)*

Athens Mold and Machine Inc................ D 740 593-6613
Athens *(G-633)*

Automation Tool & Die Inc..................... D 330 225-8336
Valley City *(G-13490)*

B-K Tool & Design Inc.......................... D 419 532-3890
Kalida *(G-8003)*

Banner Metals Group Inc....................... E 614 291-3105
Columbus *(G-4743)*

Bk Tool Company Inc............................ G 513 870-9622
Fairfield *(G-6714)*

Bollinger Tool & Die Inc........................ G 419 866-5180
Holland *(G-7746)*

Brinkman Tool & Die Inc........................ E 937 222-1161
Dayton *(G-5685)*

Brothers Tool and Mfg Ltd..................... G 513 353-9700
Miamitown *(G-9757)*

Brw Tool Inc.. F 419 394-3371
Saint Marys *(G-11734)*

Bryan Die-Cast Products Ltd.................. G 419 252-6208
Toledo *(G-12906)*

Capital Precision Machine & Tl.............. G 937 258-1176
Dayton *(G-5604)*

Capital Tool Company........................... E 216 661-5750
Cleveland *(G-3467)*

Chippewa Tool and Mfg Co.................... F 419 849-2790
Woodville *(G-14616)*

Cleveland Metal Processing Inc............. C 440 243-3404
Cleveland *(G-3517)*

Cleveland Roll Forming Co.................... G 216 281-0202
Cleveland *(G-3524)*

Clyde Tool & Die Inc............................ F 419 547-9574
Clyde *(G-4557)*

Coach Tool & Die LLC......................... G 937 890-4716
Springboro *(G-12249)*

Coldwater Machine Company LLC.......... C 419 678-4877
Coldwater *(G-4571)*

Cole Tool & Die Company...................... E 419 522-1272
Ontario *(G-10948)*

Colonial Machine Company Inc.............. D 330 673-5859
Kent *(G-8021)*

Compco Quaker Mfg Inc........................ E 330 482-0200
Salem *(G-11772)*

Condor Tool & Die Inc.......................... E 216 671-6000
Cleveland *(G-3558)*

Cornerstone Manufacturing Inc.............. G 937 456-5930
Eaton *(G-6452)*

Custom Machine Inc............................. E 419 986-5122
Tiffin *(G-12781)*

D A Fitzgerald Co Inc........................... G 937 548-0511
Greenville *(G-7340)*

Darke Precision Inc.............................. G 937 548-2232
Piqua *(G-11343)*

Dayton Progress Intl Corp..................... G 937 859-5111
Dayton *(G-5738)*

DC Legacy Corp.................................. E 330 896-4220
Akron *(G-118)*

Defiance Metal Products Co................... B 419 784-5332
Defiance *(G-6105)*

Die-Mension Corporation...................... F 330 273-5872
Brunswick *(G-1589)*

Direct Wire Service LLP....................... G 937 526-4447
Versailles *(G-13594)*

Diversified Mold Castings LLC.............. E 216 663-1814
Cleveland *(G-3621)*

DMG Tool & Die LLC........................... G 937 407-0810
Bellefontaine *(G-1106)*

Dove Die and Stamping Company.......... E 216 267-3720
Cleveland *(G-3628)*

Drt Mfg Co LLC................................... D 937 297-6670
Dayton *(G-5754)*

Duco Tool & Die Inc............................. F 419 628-2031
Minster *(G-10056)*

Duncan Tool Inc.................................. F 937 667-9364
Tipp City *(G-12823)*

Dyco Manufacturing Inc........................ F 419 485-5525
Montpelier *(G-10128)*

Dynamic Dies Inc................................. E 513 705-9524
Middletown *(G-9855)*

Dynamic Dies Inc................................. E 419 865-0249
Holland *(G-7701)*

Dynamic Tool & Mold Inc...................... G 440 237-8665
Cleveland *(G-3642)*

E D M Fastar Inc................................. G 216 676-0100
Cleveland *(G-3644)*

Eagle Precision Products LLC............... G 440 582-9393
North Royalton *(G-10759)*

Edfa LLC.. G 937 222-1415
Dayton *(G-5760)*

Estee 2 Inc... G 937 224-7853
Dayton *(G-5768)*

Euclid Design and Mfg Inc.................... F 440 942-0066
Willoughby Hills *(G-14558)*

Exco Engineering USA Inc.................... E 419 726-1595
Toledo *(G-12958)*

F & G Tool and Die Co.......................... G 937 294-1405
Moraine *(G-10163)*

Fabrication Shop Inc............................ F 419 435-7934
Fostoria *(G-6978)*

Faith Tool and Mfg Inc.......................... G 440 951-5934
Willoughby *(G-14457)*

Falls Tool and Die Inc.......................... G 330 633-4884
Akron *(G-144)*

Faull & Son LLC.................................. F 330 652-4341
Niles *(G-10588)*

Fc Industries Inc................................. E 937 275-8700
Dayton *(G-5774)*

Feller Tool Co..................................... F 440 324-6277
Elyria *(G-6536)*

First Machine & Tool Corp..................... G 440 269-8644
Willoughby *(G-14459)*

Fremar Industries Inc........................... E 330 220-3700
Brunswick *(G-1592)*

Gasdorf Tool and Mch Co Inc................ E 419 227-0103
Lima *(G-8409)*

Gem City Engineering Co...................... C 937 223-5544
Dayton *(G-5792)*

General Tool Company.......................... C 513 733-5500
Cincinnati *(G-2666)*

Gentzler Tool & Die Corp....................... E 330 896-1941
Akron *(G-161)*

Gokoh Corporation............................... F 937 339-4977
Troy *(G-13218)*

Greenfield Die & Mfg Corp.................... F 734 454-4000
Valley City *(G-13497)*

H G Schneider Company........................ G 614 882-6944
Westerville *(G-14262)*

Hardin Creek Machine & Tl Inc.............. F 419 678-4913
Coldwater *(G-4576)*

Hedges Selective Tl & Prod Inc............. G 419 478-8670
Toledo *(G-12991)*

Herd Manufacturing Inc........................ E 216 651-4221
Cleveland *(G-3826)*

Hess Industries Ltd............................. F 419 525-4000
Mansfield *(G-8802)*

Hi-Tech Wire Inc.................................. D 419 678-8376
Saint Henry *(G-11721)*

Hocker Tool and Die Inc....................... E 937 274-3443
Dayton *(G-5811)*

Hofacker Prcsion Machining LLC........... F 937 832-7712
Clayton *(G-3273)*

Holland Engraving Company.................. G 419 865-2765
Toledo *(G-12994)*

Honda Engineering North America LLC. B 937 642-5000
Marysville *(G-9029)*

Horizon Industries Corporation.............. G 937 323-0801
Springfield *(G-12324)*

Ibycorp... G 330 425-8226
Twinsburg *(G-13318)*

Impact Industries Inc........................... F 440 327-2360
North Ridgeville *(G-10735)*

Imperial Die & Mfg Co.......................... F 440 268-9080
Strongsville *(G-12300)*

Independent Stamping Inc..................... F 216 251-3500
Cleveland *(G-3857)*

Innovative Tool & Die Inc...................... G 419 599-0492
Napoleon *(G-10287)*

Intelitool Mfg Svcs Inc......................... G 440 953-1071
Willoughby *(G-14470)*

Ishmael Precision Tool Corp.................. E 937 335-8070
Troy *(G-13230)*

J & J Tool & Die Inc............................. G 330 343-4721
Dover *(G-6249)*

J Tek Tool & Mold Inc.......................... F 419 547-9476
Clyde *(G-4559)*

J W Harwood Co.................................. F 216 531-6230
Cleveland *(G-3880)*

Jena Tool Inc...................................... D 937 296-1122
Moraine *(G-10171)*

Johnston Mfg Co Inc............................ G 440 269-1420
Mentor *(G-9544)*

K B Machine & Tool Inc........................ G 937 773-1624
Piqua *(G-11362)*

Kalt Manufacturing Company................ D 440 327-2102
North Ridgeville *(G-10738)*

Ken Forging Inc.................................. C 440 993-8091
Jefferson *(G-7974)*

Employee Codes: A=Over 500 employees, B=251-500
C=101-250, D=51-100, E=20-50, F=10-19, G=1-9

2025 Harris Ohio
Industrial Directory

1281

PRODUCT

Kent Mold and Manufacturing Co............ F 330 673-3469
Kent *(G-8043)*

Kiffer Industries Inc.............................. E 216 267-1818
Cleveland *(G-3919)*

Knowlton Manufacturing Co Inc............ F 513 631-7353
Cincinnati *(G-2803)*

Kramer & Kiefer Inc............................... G 330 336-8742
Wadsworth *(G-13647)*

Lako Tool & Manufacturing Inc.............. F 419 662-5256
Perrysburg *(G-11234)*

Lange Precision Inc............................... F 513 530-9500
Lebanon *(G-8273)*

Laspina Tool and Die Inc...................... F 330 923-9996
Stow *(G-12437)*

Lincoln Electric Automtn Inc................. C 419 678-4877
Coldwater *(G-4581)*

Lowry Tool & Die Inc............................. F 330 332-1722
Salem *(G-11795)*

Lrb Tool & Die Ltd................................ F 330 898-5783
Warren *(G-13778)*

Lukens Inc.. D 937 440-2500
Troy *(G-13237)*

Lunar Tool & Mold Inc.......................... E 440 237-2141
North Royalton *(G-10771)*

M & M Dies Inc...................................... G 216 883-6628
Cleveland *(G-3973)*

Machine Tek Systems Inc....................... E 330 527-4450
Garrettsville *(G-7225)*

Machine Tool Design & Fab LLC............ F 419 435-7676
Tiffin *(G-12789)*

Magnum Tool Corp................................. F 937 228-0900
Dayton *(G-5861)*

Manufacturers Service Inc..................... E 216 267-3771
Cleveland *(G-3985)*

Mar-Metal Mfg Inc................................. G 419 447-1102
Upper Sandusky *(G-13447)*

Mar-Vel Tool Co..................................... F 937 223-2137
Dayton *(G-5868)*

Master Craft Products Inc...................... F 216 281-5910
Cleveland *(G-3996)*

Match Mold & Machine Inc.................... G 330 830-5503
Massillon *(G-9220)*

May Industries of Ohio Inc.................... E 440 237-8012
North Royalton *(G-10773)*

Mdf Tool Corporation............................ F 440 237-2277
North Royalton *(G-10774)*

Midwest Tool & Engineering Co............. G
Dayton *(G-5883)*

Mold Shop Inc.. F 419 829-2041
Sylvania *(G-12716)*

Moldmakers Inc...................................... F 419 673-0902
Kenton *(G-8108)*

Monarch Products Co............................. G 330 868-7717
Minerva *(G-10044)*

Mt Vernon Mold Works Inc.................... E 618 242-6040
Akron *(G-238)*

Mtd Holdings Inc................................... B 330 225-2600
Valley City *(G-13508)*

National Roller Die Inc.......................... F 440 951-3850
Willoughby *(G-14492)*

Nelson Tool Corporation........................ F 740 965-1894
Sunbury *(G-12669)*

New Bremen Machine & Tool Co............ E 419 629-3295
New Bremen *(G-10363)*

New Die Inc.. E 419 726-7581
Toledo *(G-13062)*

Noble Tool Corp..................................... E 937 461-4040
Dayton *(G-5908)*

Ohio Custom Dies LLC........................... F 330 538-3396
North Jackson *(G-10691)*

Ohio Specialty Dies LLC........................ F 330 538-3396
North Jackson *(G-10692)*

Omni Manufacturing Inc........................ F 419 394-7424
Saint Marys *(G-11748)*

Omni Manufacturing Inc........................ D 419 394-7424
Saint Marys *(G-11747)*

PA MA Inc.. G 440 846-3799
Strongsville *(G-12584)*

Palisin & Associates Inc....................... E 216 252-3930
Cleveland *(G-4132)*

Phillips Mch & Stamping Corp............... G 330 882-6714
New Franklin *(G-10392)*

Phoenix Tool Company........................... G 330 372-4627
Warren *(G-13789)*

Pier Tool & Die Inc................................ F 440 236-3188
Columbia Station *(G-4597)*

Plrs Legacy Inc...................................... F 440 365-7333
North Ridgeville *(G-10742)*

Porter Precision Products Co................. D 513 385-1569
Cincinnati *(G-2974)*

Precision Details Inc............................. F 937 596-0068
Jackson Center *(G-7967)*

Precision Die & Stamping Inc................ G 513 942-8220
West Chester *(G-14052)*

Pro-Tech Manufacturing Inc.................. F 937 444-6484
Mount Orab *(G-10222)*

Progage Inc.. F 440 951-4477
Mentor *(G-9597)*

Progress Tool & Stamping Inc............... E 419 628-2384
Minster *(G-10064)*

Project Engineering Company................ G 937 743-9114
Germantown *(G-7253)*

PSK Steel Corp....................................... E 330 759-1251
Hubbard *(G-7816)*

Pyramid Mold & Machine Co Inc............ G 330 673-5200
Kent *(G-8065)*

Quaker Mfg Corp.................................... C 330 332-4631
Salem *(G-11807)*

Quality Specialists Inc.......................... G 440 946-9129
Willoughby *(G-14513)*

Quality Tooling Systems Inc.................. F 330 722-5025
Medina *(G-9439)*

Queen City Tool Works Inc.................... E 513 874-0111
Fairfield *(G-6770)*

R M Tool & Die Inc................................ F 440 238-6459
Strongsville *(G-12591)*

Ram Tool Inc.. G 937 277-0717
Dayton *(G-5973)*

Raymath Company................................. C 937 335-1860
Troy *(G-13249)*

Rmt Corporation.................................... F 937 274-2121
Dayton *(G-5985)*

Rockstedt Tool & Die Inc....................... G 330 273-9000
Brunswick *(G-1612)*

Ronlen Industries Inc............................ E 330 273-6468
Brunswick *(G-1613)*

Roto-Die Company Inc........................... E 513 942-3500
West Chester *(G-14071)*

RPM Carbide Die Inc.............................. E 419 894-6426
Arcadia *(G-483)*

Saint-Gobain Ceramics Plas Inc............ D 330 673-5860
Stow *(G-12456)*

Saint-Gobain Ceramics Plas Inc............ A 610 893-6000
Stow *(G-12457)*

Schmitmeyer Inc.................................... E 937 295-2091
Fort Loramie *(G-6954)*

Seilkop Industries Inc............................ E 513 761-1035
Cincinnati *(G-3077)*

Select Industries Corporation................ C 937 233-9191
Dayton *(G-6001)*

Self Made Holdings LLC......................... E 330 477-1052
Canton *(G-2001)*

Shalix Inc.. F 216 941-3546
Cleveland *(G-4287)*

Shl Liquidation Industries Inc............... A 330 558-2600
Valley City *(G-13517)*

Sk Mold & Tool Inc............................... E 937 339-0299
Troy *(G-13255)*

Sk Mold & Tool Inc............................... E 937 339-0299
Tipp City *(G-12844)*

Skrl Die Casting Inc.............................. F 440 946-7200
Willoughby *(G-14528)*

Sluterbeck Tool & Die Co Inc................ F 937 836-5736
Clayton *(G-3275)*

Smithville Mfg Co.................................. F 330 345-5818
Wooster *(G-14687)*

Stanco Precision Mfg Inc....................... G 937 274-1785
Dayton *(G-6022)*

Standard Engineering Group Inc............ G 330 494-4300
North Canton *(G-10669)*

Summit Tool Company........................... D 330 535-7177
Akron *(G-322)*

Superior Production LLC........................ C 614 444-2181
Columbus *(G-5299)*

Sure Tool & Manufacturing Co............... E 937 253-9111
Dayton *(G-6033)*

Sutterlin Machine & Tl Co Inc............... F 440 357-0817
Mentor *(G-9632)*

Symbol Tool & Die Inc........................... G 440 582-5989
North Royalton *(G-10785)*

Taft Tool & Production Co...................... F 419 385-2576
Toledo *(G-13139)*

Taylor Tool & Die Inc............................ G 937 845-1491
New Carlisle *(G-10381)*

Tech Industries Inc................................ F 216 861-7337
Cleveland *(G-4368)*

Tech Mold and Tool Co.......................... G 937 667-8851
Tipp City *(G-12847)*

Technical Tool & Gauge Inc................... F 330 273-1778
Brunswick *(G-1617)*

The Kordenbrock Tool and Die Co......... F 513 326-4390
Cincinnati *(G-3148)*

The Louis G Freeman Company LLC..... D 419 334-9709
Fremont *(G-7136)*

The Pioneer Tool and Die Co................. D 330 724-5572
Akron *(G-332)*

The Vulcan Tool Company....................... G 937 253-6194
Dayton *(G-6050)*

Tipco Punch Inc..................................... E 513 874-9140
Hamilton *(G-7532)*

Tipp Machine & Tool Inc........................ C 937 890-8428
Dayton *(G-6055)*

Tm Machine & Tool Inc.......................... G 419 478-0310
Toledo *(G-13144)*

Toledo Tool and Die Co Inc................... F 419 476-9066
Pioneer *(G-11330)*

Tomahawk Tool Supply........................... G 419 485-8737
Montpelier *(G-10135)*

Toney Tool Manufacturing Inc............... G 937 890-8535
Dayton *(G-6057)*

Tooling Connection Inc.......................... G 419 594-3339
Oakwood *(G-10901)*

Tooling Zone Inc.................................... E 937 550-4180
Springboro *(G-12271)*

Toolrite Manufacturing Inc.................... F 937 278-1962
Dayton *(G-6059)*

Top Tool & Die Inc................................ G 216 267-5878
Cleveland *(G-4403)*

Tradye Machine & Tool Inc.................... G 740 625-7550
Centerburg *(G-2128)*

Trim Tool & Machine Inc....................... E 216 889-1916
Cleveland *(G-4426)*

Trimline Die Corporation....................... E 440 355-6900
Lagrange *(G-8154)*

Troy Precision Carbide Die Inc.............. G 440 834-4477
Burton *(G-1707)*

Trucut Incorporated.................................. D 330 938-9806
Sebring *(G-11903)*

True Industries Inc................................... E 330 296-4342
Ravenna *(G-11547)*

U S Alloy Die Corp.................................... E 216 749-9700
Cleveland *(G-4438)*

United Extrusion Dies Inc........................ F 330 533-2915
Canfield *(G-1818)*

United Finshg & Die Cutng Inc................ G 216 881-0239
Cleveland *(G-4442)*

Universal Tool Technology LLC.............. G 937 222-4608
Dayton *(G-6069)*

Unlimited Machine and Tool LLC............ F 419 269-1730
Toledo *(G-13171)*

Valley Tool & Die Inc.............................. D 440 237-0160
North Royalton *(G-10788)*

Van Wert Machine Inc.............................. G 419 692-6836
Delphos *(G-6198)*

Walest Incorporated................................. G 216 362-8110
Brunswick *(G-1623)*

Walker Tool & Machine Company.......... F 419 661-8000
Perrysburg *(G-11278)*

Weiss Industries Inc................................ E 419 526-2480
Mansfield *(G-8865)*

Wilmington Prcsion McHning Inc........... E 937 382-3700
Wilmington *(G-14591)*

Windsor Tool Inc....................................... F 216 671-1900
Cleveland *(G-4508)*

Wire Shop Inc... E 440 354-6842
Mentor *(G-9653)*

WLS Stamping Co...................................... D 216 271-5100
Cleveland *(G-4511)*

Youngstown Tool & Die Company.......... D 330 747-4464
Youngstown *(G-14977)*

DIES: Cutting, Exc Metal

D & M Saw & Tool Inc.............................. G 513 871-5433
Cincinnati *(G-2535)*

DIES: Extrusion

Amex Dies Inc... F 330 545-9766
Girard *(G-7265)*

Diamond America Corporation................ F 330 762-9269
Akron *(G-119)*

Jamen Tool & Die Co............................... F 330 788-6521
Youngstown *(G-14879)*

Mordies Inc.. F 330 758-8050
Youngstown *(G-1490£)*

Village Plastics Co................................... G 330 753-0100
Euclid *(G-6683)*

Vinyl Tool & Die Company...................... G 330 782-0254
Youngstown *(G-14963)*

DIES: Paper Cutting

Williams Steel Rule Die Co..................... G 216 431-3232
Cleveland *(G-4507)*

DIES: Plastic Forming

National Pattern Mfgco............................ F 330 682-6871
Orrville *(G-10997)*

Progrssive Molding Bolivar Inc.............. G 330 874-3000
Bolivar *(G-1390)*

DIES: Steel Rule

Aukerman J F Steel Rule Die................... G 937 456-4498
Eaton *(G-6448)*

Csw Inc.. E 413 589-1311
Sylvania *(G-12703)*

Customformed Products Inc.................... F 937 388-0480
Miamisburg *(G-9685)*

Die Guys Inc.. F 330 239-3437
Medina *(G-9396)*

Hedalloy Die Corporation........................ G 216 341-3768
Cleveland *(G-3817)*

Lorain Rled Die Pdts Indus Sup.............. G 440 281-8607
North Ridgeville *(G-10739)*

Loroco Industries Inc.............................. D 513 891-9544
Cincinnati *(G-2828)*

DIODES & RECTIFIERS

Materion Corporation............................... C 216 486-4200
Mayfield Heights *(G-9337)*

DIODES: Light Emitting

Ceso Inc.. E 937 435-8584
Miamisburg *(G-9681)*

Cks Solution Incorporated...................... E 513 947-1277
Fairfield *(G-6723)*

Harrison Corporation............................... G 513 681-2420
Cincinnati *(G-2708)*

Hawthorne Hydroponics LLC.................. F 888 478-6544
Marysville *(G-9024)*

Refocus Holdings Inc.............................. F 216 751-8384
Cleveland *(G-4231)*

Tri-Tech Led Systems LLC...................... G 614 593-2868
Baltimore *(G-788)*

DIODES: Solid State, Germanium, Silicon, Etc

Measurement Specialties Inc.................. C 937 427-1231
Dayton *(G-5872)*

DIRECT SELLING ESTABLISHMENTS, NEC

Oats Overnight Inc................................... D 602 492-1751
West Chester *(G-14035)*

DISCS & TAPE: Optical, Blank

Folio Photonics Inc.................................. F 440 420-4500
Solon *(G-12114)*

DISPLAY FIXTURES: Wood

A G Industries Inc................................... G 216 252-7300
Cleveland *(G-3281)*

Cassady Woodworks Inc.......................... F 937 256-7948
Dayton *(G-5605)*

Couch Business Development Inc........... G 937 253-1099
Dayton *(G-5711)*

Gabriel Logan LLC................................... D 740 380-6809
Groveport *(G-7436)*

Kdm Signs Inc... E 513 769-3900
Cincinnati *(G-2789)*

Murray Display Fixtures Ltd.................... F 614 875-1594
Grove City *(G-7403)*

Ohio Woodworking Co Inc....................... G 513 631-0870
Cincinnati *(G-2927)*

Ptmj Enterprises Inc................................ F 440 543-8000
Solon *(G-12170)*

Scenic Solutions Ltd Lblty Co................ F 937 866-5062
Dayton *(G-5996)*

Ultrabuilt Play Systems Inc.................... F 419 652-2294
Nova *(G-10878)*

W J Egli Company Inc.............................. F 330 823-3666
Alliance *(G-414)*

DISPLAY ITEMS: Corrugated, Made From Purchased Materials

Shelby Company...................................... E 440 871-9901
Westlake *(G-14334)*

DISPLAY ITEMS: Solid Fiber, Made From Purchased Materials

Digital Color Intl LLC............................... F
Akron *(G-123)*

DISTRIBUTORS: Motor Vehicle Engine

Brinkley Technology Group LLC............ F 330 830-2498
Massillon *(G-9175)*

Legacy Supplies Inc................................ F 330 405-4565
Twinsburg *(G-13328)*

Power Acquisition LLC............................ A 614 228-5000
Dublin *(G-6333)*

Thirion Brothers Eqp Co LLC.................. G 440 357-8004
Painesville *(G-11118)*

Tri-W Group Inc.. A 614 228-5000
Columbus *(G-5332)*

Weldon Pump LLC.................................... E 440 232-2282
Oakwood Village *(G-10913)*

WW Williams Company LLC.................... D 614 228-5000
Dublin *(G-6362)*

DOCK EQPT & SPLYS, INDL

Rbs Manufacturing Inc............................ E 330 426-9486
East Palestine *(G-6405)*

Tmt Inc.. G 419 592-1041
Perrysburg *(G-11273)*

DOLOMITE: Crushed & Broken

Drummond Dolomite Inc.......................... F 440 942-7000
Mentor *(G-9511)*

DOOR FRAMES: Wood

All Pro Ovrhd Door Systems LLC........... G 614 444-3667
Columbus *(G-4684)*

Rsl LLC... E 330 392-8900
Warren *(G-13795)*

DOOR MATS: Rubber

Ultimate Systems Ltd.............................. E 419 692-3005
Delphos *(G-6196)*

DOORS & WINDOWS: Screen & Storm

Duo-Corp.. F 330 549-2149
North Lima *(G-10707)*

Euclid Jalousies Inc................................ G 440 953-1112
Chardon *(G-2205)*

DOORS & WINDOWS: Storm, Metal

Champion Opco LLC................................. B 513 327-7338
Cincinnati *(G-2458)*

Champion Win Co Cleveland LLC........... G 440 899-2562
Macedonia *(G-8681)*

DOORS: Combination Screen & Storm, Wood

R C Moore Lumber Co.............................. F 740 732-4950
Caldwell *(G-1727)*

DOORS: Fiberglass

Schmidt Progressive LLC........................ G 513 934-2600
Lebanon *(G-8285)*

Toledo Pro Fiberglass Inc....................... G 419 241-9390
Toledo *(G-13156)*

DOORS: Folding, Plastic Or Plastic Coated Fabric

Alumo Extrusions and Mfg Co................ E 330 779-3333
Youngstown *(G-14810)*

Modern Builders Supply Inc.................... E 419 526-0002
Mansfield *(G-8831)*

National Access Design LLC.................... F 513 351-3400
Cincinnati *(G-2893)*

Pease Industies Inc................................. G 513 870-3600
Fairfield *(G-6764)*

PRODUCT

DOORS: Garage, Overhead, Metal

Anderson Door Co... F 216 475-5700
Cleveland *(G-3358)*

Clopay Ames Inc... C 800 282-2260
Mason *(G-9087)*

Division Overhead Door Inc.................... F 513 872-0888
Cincinnati *(G-2556)*

Haas Door Company.............................. C 419 337-9900
Wauseon *(G-13850)*

Hope Holdings Inc................................... G 330 674-7015
Mount Hope *(G-10214)*

Hrh Door Corp... E 513 674-9300
Cincinnati *(G-2734)*

Overhead Door Corporation.................... G 330 828-2291
Dalton *(G-5590)*

Overhead Door Corporation.................... D 740 383-6376
Marion *(G-8987)*

Overhead Door Corporation.................... F 419 294-3874
Upper Sandusky *(G-13452)*

Overhead Door of Pike County.............. G 740 289-3925
Piketon *(G-11312)*

DOORS: Garage, Overhead, Wood

Anderson Door Co... F 216 475-5700
Cleveland *(G-3358)*

Clopay Ames Inc... C 800 282-2260
Mason *(G-9087)*

Clopay Corporation.................................. E 513 770-4800
Mason *(G-9088)*

Division Overhead Door Inc.................... F 513 872-0888
Cincinnati *(G-2556)*

Hope Holdings Inc................................... G 330 674-7015
Mount Hope *(G-10214)*

Hrh Door Corp... E 513 674-9300
Cincinnati *(G-2734)*

DOORS: Glass

A Service Glass Inc................................. F 937 426-4920
Beavercreek *(G-963)*

Basco Manufacturing Company............. C 513 573-1900
Mason *(G-9069)*

Scs Construction Services Inc............... E 513 929-0260
Cincinnati *(G-3071)*

DRAPERIES & CURTAINS

Accent Drapery Co Inc............................ E 614 488-0741
Columbus *(G-4667)*

Ikiriska LLC.. F 614 389-8994
Powell *(G-11489)*

Janson Industries................................... D 330 455-7029
Canton *(G-1921)*

Sk Textile Inc... C 800 888-9112
Cincinnati *(G-3094)*

STI Liquidation Inc................................. E 614 733-0099
Plain City *(G-11418)*

Vocational Services Inc.......................... F 216 431-8085
Cleveland *(G-4478)*

DRAPERIES: Plastic & Textile, From Purchased Materials

Elden Draperies of Toledo Inc............... F 419 535-1909
Toledo *(G-12947)*

Tiffin Scenic Studios Inc........................ E 800 445-1546
Tiffin *(G-12805)*

DRAPERY & UPHOLSTERY STORES: Draperies

Accent Drapery Co Inc............................ E 614 488-0741
Columbus *(G-4667)*

Elden Draperies of Toledo Inc............... F 419 535-1909
Toledo *(G-12947)*

DRILL BITS

Arch Cutng Tls Cincinnati LLC.............. F 513 851-6363
West Chester *(G-14104)*

DRILLING MACHINERY & EQPT: Oil & Gas

Buckeye Oil Equipment Co..................... F 937 387-0671
Dayton *(G-5687)*

Rmi Titanium Company LLC .... E 330 652-9952
Niles *(G-10604)*

Terra Sonic International LLC................. E 740 374-6608
Marietta *(G-8953)*

Tiger General LLC.................................. F 330 239-4949
Medina *(G-9456)*

DRILLS & DRILLING EQPT: Mining

Davey Kent Inc....................................... E 330 673-5400
Kent *(G-8025)*

DRINK MIXES, NONALCOHOLIC: Cocktail

Gwj Liquidation Inc................................ F 216 475-5770
Cleveland *(G-3802)*

DRINKING FOUNTAINS: Metal, Nonrefrigerated

Lvd Acquisition LLC............................... D 614 861-1350
Columbus *(G-5077)*

DRINKING PLACES: Bars & Lounges

Brewdog Brewing Company LLC........... F 614 908-3051
Canal Winchester *(G-1786)*

District Brewing Company Inc............... E 614 224-3626
Columbus *(G-4886)*

Green Room Brewing LLC...................... G 614 421-2337
Columbus *(G-4966)*

Lock 15 Brewing Company LLC........... E 234 900-8277
Akron *(G-208)*

Mansfield Brew Works LLC................... F 419 631-3153
Mansfield *(G-8818)*

DRINKING PLACES: Beer Garden

Bar 25 LLC.. G 216 621-4000
Cleveland *(G-3403)*

Lock 27 Brewing LLC............................ F 937 433-2739
Dayton *(G-5853)*

DRINKING WATER COOLERS WHOLESALERS: Mechanical

Lvd Acquisition LLC............................... D 614 861-1350
Columbus *(G-5077)*

DRUGS & DRUG PROPRIETARIES, WHOLESALE

Buderer Drug Company Inc.................... E 419 627-2800
Sandusky *(G-11824)*

DRUGS & DRUG PROPRIETARIES, WHOLESALE: Patent Medicines

Teva Womens Health LLC...................... C 513 731-9900
Cincinnati *(G-3145)*

DRUGS & DRUG PROPRIETARIES, WHOLESALE: Pharmaceuticals

American Regent Inc............................... D 614 436-2222
Hilliard *(G-7667)*

Cardinal Health Inc................................. E 614 553-3830
Dublin *(G-6285)*

Cardinal Health Inc................................. G 614 757-2863
Lewis Center *(G-8328)*

Cardinal Health Inc................................. A 614 757-5000
Dublin *(G-6286)*

Optum Infusion Svcs 550 LLC.............. D 866 442-4679
Cincinnati *(G-2936)*

River City Pharma................................. G 513 870-1680
Fairfield *(G-6772)*

Xellia Pharmaceuticals Inc.................... G 847 947-0200
Beachwood *(G-958)*

DRUGS & DRUG PROPRIETARIES, WHOLESALE: Vitamins & Minerals

Boxout LLC.. C 833 462-7746
Hudson *(G-7835)*

Direct Action Co Inc.............................. F 330 364-3219
Dover *(G-6236)*

DRUMS: Fiber

Greif Inc.. E 740 657-6500
Delaware *(G-6150)*

Greif Inc.. E 419 238-0565
Van Wert *(G-13536)*

DRUMS: Shipping, Metal

Greif Inc.. E 740 657-6500
Delaware *(G-6150)*

Greif Inc.. E 740 549-6000
Delaware *(G-6149)*

Mauser Usa LLC.................................... D 513 398-1300
Mason *(G-9125)*

North Coast Container LLC.................... E 216 441-6214
Cleveland *(G-4083)*

DUCTS: Sheet Metal

Controls and Sheet Metal Inc................ E 513 721-3610
Cincinnati *(G-2515)*

Eastern Sheet Metal Inc......................... A 513 793-3440
Blue Ash *(G-1270)*

Kerber Sheetmetal Works Inc................ F 937 339-6366
Troy *(G-13233)*

Langdon Inc... E 513 733-5955
Cincinnati *(G-2811)*

Lukjan Metal Products Inc..................... C 440 599-8127
Conneaut *(G-5410)*

McGill Airflow LLC................................. D 614 829-1200
Columbus *(G-5090)*

McGill Corporation.................................. F 614 829-1200
Groveport *(G-7444)*

Precision Duct Fabrication LLC............. F 614 580-9385
Columbus *(G-5202)*

R G Smith Company............................... D 330 456-3415
Canton *(G-1988)*

Technibus Inc... D 330 479-4202
Canton *(G-2022)*

United McGill Corporation...................... E 614 829-1200
Groveport *(G-7455)*

DUMPSTERS: Garbage

Cheap Dumpsters Llc............................. G 614 285-5865
Columbus *(G-4806)*

E-Pak Manufacturing LLC...................... E 330 264-0825
Wooster *(G-14636)*

Giuseppes Concessions LLC................. F 614 554-2551
Marengo *(G-8897)*

DUST OR FUME COLLECTING EQPT: Indl

Coperion Process Solutions LLC........... F 513 576-9200
Solon *(G-12098)*

Envirofab Inc.. G 216 651-1767
Cleveland *(G-3679)*

Herman Manufacturing LLC.................. F 216 251-6400
Cleveland (G-3827)

Jacp Inc.. G 513 353-3660
Miamitown (G-9759)

Sly Inc.. E 800 334-2957
Strongsville (G-12601)

DYES & PIGMENTS: Organic

Avient Corporation.............................. D 419 668-4844
Norwalk (G-10829)

Colormatrix Corporation....................... C 216 622-0100
Berea (G-1163)

Colormatrix Group Inc........................ C 216 622-0100
Berea (G-1164)

Colormatrix Holdings Inc..................... F 440 930-3162
Berea (G-1165)

Hexpol Compounding LLC..................... C 440 834-4644
Burton (G-1699)

Marathon Petroleum Company LP......... F 419 422-2121
Findlay (G-6889)

Republic Powdered Metals Inc.............. D 330 225-3192
Medina (G-9441)

Revlis Corporation.............................. E 330 535-2100
Akron (G-282)

RPM International Inc........................... D 330 273-5090
Medina (G-9442)

Sun Chemical Corporation.................... E 513 830-8667
Cincinnati (G-3126)

DYES OR COLORS: Food, Synthetic

Berghausen Corporation....................... E 513 591-4491
Cincinnati (G-2406)

EATING PLACES

Breitenbach Wine Cellars Inc............... G 330 343-3603
Dover (G-6232)

Bucks For Pups Confections LLC.......... F 614 359-4672
Columbus (G-4787)

Buns of Delaware Inc.......................... F 740 363-2867
Delaware (G-6135)

Ferrante Wine Farm Inc....................... F 440 466-8466
Geneva (G-7237)

Grace Juice Company LLC.................... F 614 398-6879
Westerville (G-14261)

Guggisberg Cheese Inc........................ E 330 893-2550
Millersburg (G-9982)

John Purdum...................................... G 513 897-9686
Waynesville (G-13879)

Karrikin Spirits Company LLC............... F 513 561-5000
Cincinnati (G-2784)

McDonalds.. F 513 753-6100
Amelia (G-433)

McDonalds.. F 513 752-2008
Cincinnati (G-2313)

McDonalds.. F 216 226-7754
Lakewood (G-8169)

McDonalds.. E 513 336-0820
Mason (G-9127)

McDonalds.. F 740 753-4018
Nelsonville (G-10318)

McDonalds.. F 419 935-1414
Willard (G-14404)

McDonalds.. F 330 792-0527
Youngstown (G-14895)

Paramount Distillers Inc....................... B 216 671-6300
Cleveland (G-4134)

Rocky River Brewing Co........................ G 440 895-2739
Rocky River (G-11638)

Willoughby Brewing Company LLC........ G 440 975-0202
Willoughby (G-14550)

EDUCATIONAL SVCS

Auguste Moone Enterprises Ltd............ E 216 333-9248
Cleveland Heights (G-4527)

Dietrich Von Hldbrand Lgacy PR............ G 703 496-7821
Steubenville (G-12402)

Health Sense Inc................................ G 440 354-8057
Painesville (G-11093)

Tangible Solutions Inc......................... E 937 912-4603
Fairborn (G-6701)

ELECTRIC MOTOR REPAIR SVCS

3-D Service Ltd.................................. C 330 830-3500
Massillon (G-9168)

Als High Tech Inc............................... F 440 232-7090
Bedford (G-1010)

American Armature Corporation............ G 419 448-1926
Tiffin (G-12773)

Bennett Electric Inc............................ F 800 874-5405
Norwalk (G-10830)

Big River Electric Inc.......................... G 740 446-4360
Gallipolis (G-7202)

Bornhorst Motor Service Inc................. G 937 773-0426
Piqua (G-11337)

Clark-Fowler Enterprises Inc................ E 330 262-0906
Wooster (G-14631)

D & J Electric Motor Repair Co............. F 330 336-4343
Wadsworth (G-13634)

E M Service Inc.................................. F 440 323-3260
Elyria (G-6525)

E-Z Electric Motor Svc Corp................. G 216 581-8820
Cleveland (G-3646)

Fenton Bros Electric Co....................... E 330 343-0093
New Philadelphia (G-10445)

Franks Electric Inc.............................. G 513 313-5883
Cincinnati (G-2640)

Hackworth Electric Motors Inc.............. G 330 345-6049
Wooster (G-14648)

Hannon Company................................ F 330 343-7758
Dover (G-6246)

Hannon Company................................ F 740 453-0527
Zanesville (G-15019)

Hennings Quality Service Inc............... F 216 941-9120
Cleveland (G-3822)

Horner Industrial Services Inc.............. F 937 390-6667
Springfield (G-12325)

Integrated Power Services LLC............. D 216 433-7808
Cleveland (G-3863)

Integrated Power Services LLC............. E 513 863-8816
Hamilton (G-7506)

Kiemle-Hankins Company..................... E 419 661-2430
Perrysburg (G-11233)

Lemsco Inc.. G 419 242-4005
Toledo (G-13032)

Lima Armature Works Inc..................... G 419 222-4010
Lima (G-8424)

M & R Electric Motor Svc Inc............... E 937 701-0475
Dayton (G-5857)

Mader Elc Mtr Pwr Trnsmssons L......... G 937 325-5576
Springfield (G-12346)

Magnetech Industrial Svcs Inc.............. G 330 830-3500
Massillon (G-9216)

Magnetech Industrial Svcs Inc.............. F 330 830-3500
Massillon (G-9218)

Magnetech Industrial Svcs Inc.............. D 330 830-3500
Massillon (G-9217)

Masteller Electric Motor Svc................. F 937 492-8500
Sidney (G-12032)

Matlock Electric Co Inc........................ E 513 731-9600
Cincinnati (G-2850)

Mid-Ohio Electric Co.......................... E 614 274-8000
Columbus (G-5098)

Moto-Electric Inc................................ G 419 668-7894
Norwalk (G-10853)

National Electric Coil Inc..................... B 614 488-1151
Columbus (G-5120)

Ohio Electric Motor Service Center Inc.. F 614 444-1451
Columbus (G-5143)

Ohio Electric Motor Svc LLC................. F 614 444-1451
Columbus (G-5144)

Phillips Electric Co.............................. F 216 361-0014
Cleveland (G-4160)

Shoemaker Electric Company................ E 614 294-5626
Columbus (G-5263)

Total Maintenance MGT Inc.................. G 513 228-2345
Lebanon (G-8289)

Wheatley Electric Service Co................ G 513 531-4951
Cincinnati (G-3222)

Whelco Industrial Ltd........................... D 419 385-4627
Perrysburg (G-11280)

ELECTRIC SERVICES

National Gas & Oil Corporation............. E 740 344-2102
Newark (G-10524)

Powder Alloy Corporation..................... E 513 984-4016
Loveland (G-8646)

ELECTRICAL APPARATUS & EQPT WHOLESALERS

Acorn Technology Corporation.............. E 216 663-1244
Shaker Heights (G-11925)

Allen Fields Assoc Inc......................... E 513 228-1010
Lebanon (G-8243)

Als High Tech Inc............................... F 440 232-7090
Bedford (G-1010)

Best Lighting Products Inc.................... D 740 964-1198
Pataskala (G-11137)

Black Box Corporation......................... G 855 324-9909
Westlake (G-14292)

Controllix Corporation......................... F 440 232-8757
Walton Hills (G-13696)

Filnor Inc.. F 330 821-8731
Alliance (G-382)

Hughes Corporation............................. E 440 238-2550
Strongsville (G-12564)

Industrial Power Systems Inc............... B 419 531-3121
Rossford (G-11659)

Kirk Key Interlock Company LLC........... E 330 833-8223
North Canton (G-10648)

LSI Lightron Inc.................................. A 845 562-5500
Blue Ash (G-1300)

Machine Drive Company....................... D 513 793-7077
Cincinnati (G-2837)

Peak Electric Inc................................ F 419 726-4848
Toledo (G-13092)

Powell Electrical Systems Inc............... D 330 966-1750
North Canton (G-10660)

Resideo LLC...................................... G 440 439-7002
Bedford (G-1057)

Schneider Electric Usa Inc................... D 513 777-4445
West Chester (G-14073)

Sieb & Meyer America Inc.................... F 513 563-0860
West Chester (G-14145)

Specialty Switch Company LLC............. F 330 427-3000
Youngstown (G-14936)

Tesa Inc.. G 614 847-8200
Lewis Center (G-8355)

Warmus and Associates Inc................. G 330 659-4440
Bath (G-898)

ELECTRICAL DEVICE PARTS: Porcelain, Molded

PRODUCT

Materion Brush Inc................................... D 216 486-4200
　Mayfield Heights *(G-9336)*

ELECTRICAL DISCHARGE MACHINING, EDM

Detroit Diesl Specialty TI Inc.................. E 740 435-4452
　Byesville *(G-1710)*

Morris Technologies Inc.......................... E 513 733-1611
　Cincinnati *(G-2888)*

Padco Industries LLC.............................. E 440 564-7160
　Newbury *(G-10560)*

Skinner Machining Co............................... G 216 486-6636
　Willoughby *(G-14527)*

The Kordenbrock Tool and Die Co........ F 513 326-4390
　Cincinnati *(G-3148)*

U S Alloy Die Corp.................................. F 216 749-9700
　Cleveland *(G-4438)*

ELECTRICAL EQPT REPAIR SVCS

D & J Electric Motor Repair Co.............. F 330 336-4343
　Wadsworth *(G-13634)*

Kiemle-Hankins Company........................ E 419 661-2430
　Perrysburg *(G-11233)*

Miscor Group Ltd.................................... B 330 830-3500
　Massillon *(G-9224)*

ELECTRICAL EQPT REPAIR SVCS: High Voltage

Wilson Sign Co Inc.................................. F 937 253-2246
　Germantown *(G-7257)*

ELECTRICAL EQPT: Automotive, NEC

Commercial Vehicle Group Inc.............. B 614 289-5360
　New Albany *(G-10336)*

Electra Sound Inc.................................... D 216 433-9600
　Avon Lake *(G-754)*

Stanley Electric US Co Inc...................... E 740 852-5200
　London *(G-8541)*

ELECTRICAL GOODS, WHOLESALE: Boxes & Fittings

Akron Foundry Co.................................... C 330 745-3101
　Akron *(G-31)*

Ignio Systems LLC.................................. G 419 708-0503
　Toledo *(G-12999)*

Osburn Associates Inc............................ F 740 385-5732
　Logan *(G-8522)*

ELECTRICAL GOODS, WHOLESALE: Cable Conduit

Legrand North America LLC.................... B 937 224-0639
　Dayton *(G-5843)*

ELECTRICAL GOODS, WHOLESALE: Electronic Parts

Heilind Electronics Inc............................ E 440 473-9600
　Cleveland *(G-3818)*

Kontron America Incorporated............... G 937 324-2420
　Springfield *(G-12339)*

Pemro Corporation.................................. F 800 440-5441
　Cleveland *(G-4151)*

Rixan Associates Inc.............................. E 937 438-3005
　Dayton *(G-5984)*

Wes-Garde Components Group Inc........ G 614 885-0319
　Westerville *(G-14280)*

Wurth Electronics Ics Inc....................... E 937 415-7700
　Miamisburg *(G-9754)*

ELECTRICAL GOODS, WHOLESALE: Fittings & Construction Mat

Schneider Electric Usa Inc..................... B 513 523-4171
　Oxford *(G-11064)*

ELECTRICAL GOODS, WHOLESALE: Generators

Rv Mobile Power LLC.............................. E 855 427-7978
　Columbus *(G-5239)*

Western Branch Diesel LLC.................... F 330 454-8800
　Canton *(G-2047)*

ELECTRICAL GOODS, WHOLESALE: Household Appliances, NEC

World Wide Recyclers Inc....................... G 614 554-3296
　Columbus *(G-5372)*

ELECTRICAL GOODS, WHOLESALE: Lighting Fittings & Access

Current Elec & Enrgy Solutions.............. G 513 575-4600
　Loveland *(G-8623)*

ELECTRICAL GOODS, WHOLESALE: Modems, Computer

Black Box Corporation............................ G 855 324-9909
　Westlake *(G-14292)*

ELECTRICAL GOODS, WHOLESALE: Security Control Eqpt & Systems

H2flow Controls Inc................................ G 419 841-7774
　Toledo *(G-12981)*

Mace Personal Def & SEC Inc................ E 440 424-5321
　Cleveland *(G-3978)*

Sage Integration Holdings LLC.............. E 330 733-8183
　Kent *(G-8072)*

ELECTRICAL GOODS, WHOLESALE: Switches, Exc Electronic, NEC

Wes-Garde Components Group Inc........ G 614 885-0319
　Westerville *(G-14280)*

ELECTRICAL GOODS, WHOLESALE: Telephone Eqpt

ABC Appliance Inc.................................. E 419 693-4414
　Oregon *(G-10955)*

Cbst Acquisition LLC.............................. D 513 361-9600
　Cincinnati *(G-2445)*

Famous Industries Inc............................ E 330 535-1811
　Akron *(G-145)*

Floyd Bell Inc... D 614 294-4000
　Columbus *(G-4930)*

Pro Oncall Technologies LLC.................. F 614 761-1400
　Dublin *(G-6335)*

ELECTRICAL GOODS, WHOLESALE: Wire & Cable

Associated Mtls Holdings LLC................ A 330 929-1811
　Cuyahoga Falls *(G-5530)*

Mjo Industries Inc.................................. D 800 590-4055
　Huber Heights *(G-7822)*

Multilink Inc... C 440 366-6966
　Elyria *(G-6566)*

Noco Company.. D 216 464-8131
　Glenwillow *(G-7286)*

Scott Fetzer Company............................ C 216 267-9000
　Cleveland *(G-4278)*

Sumitomo Elc Wirg Systems Inc............ E 937 642-7579
　Marysville *(G-9052)*

ELECTRICAL MEASURING INSTRUMENT REPAIR & CALIBRATION SVCS

Instrmntation Ctrl Systems Inc.............. E 513 662-2600
　Cincinnati *(G-2747)*

Interface Logic Systems Inc................... G 614 236-8388
　Ashville *(G-626)*

Tegam Inc... E 440 466-6100
　Geneva *(G-7246)*

ELECTRICAL SPLYS

Accurate Mechanical Inc........................ D 740 681-1332
　Lancaster *(G-8174)*

Ces Nationwide....................................... G 937 322-0771
　Springfield *(G-12289)*

Fenton Bros Electric Co.......................... E 330 343-0093
　New Philadelphia *(G-10445)*

ELECTRICAL SUPPLIES: Porcelain

Akron Porcelain & Plastics Co............... C 330 745-2159
　Akron *(G-39)*

CAM-Lem Inc.. G 216 391-7750
　Cleveland *(G-3461)*

Channel Products Inc.............................. D 440 423-0113
　Solon *(G-12093)*

Electrodyne Company Inc....................... F 513 732-2822
　Batavia *(G-862)*

Fram Group Operations LLC................... E 419 436-5827
　Fostoria *(G-6983)*

Petro Ware Inc.. G 740 982-1302
　Crooksville *(G-5512)*

Vibrantz Corporation.............................. C 216 875-6213
　Cleveland *(G-4468)*

Weldco Inc.. E 513 744-9353
　Cincinnati *(G-3218)*

ELECTRODES: Thermal & Electrolytic

De Nora Tech LLC.................................. D 440 710-5334
　Painesville *(G-11078)*

Graftech Intl Holdings Inc....................... C 216 676-2000
　Brooklyn Heights *(G-1532)*

Graphel Corporation............................... C 513 779-6166
　West Chester *(G-14012)*

Graphite Sales Inc.................................. F 419 652-3388
　Nova *(G-10877)*

Neograf Solutions LLC........................... C 216 529-3777
　Lakewood *(G-8170)*

Sangraf International Inc......................... G 216 543-3288
　Westlake *(G-14330)*

Sherbrooke Corporation......................... E 440 942-3520
　Willoughby *(G-14525)*

ELECTROMEDICAL EQPT

Avation Medical Inc................................ F 614 591-4201
　Columbus *(G-4736)*

Brainmaster Technologies Inc................ G 440 232-6000
　Bedford *(G-1018)*

Cardiac Analytics LLC............................ F 614 314-1332
　Powell *(G-11484)*

Checkpoint Surgical Inc......................... D 216 378-9107
　Independence *(G-7891)*

Coopersurgical Inc.................................. G 203 601-5200
　Cincinnati *(G-2516)*

Ctl Analyzers LLC.................................. E 216 791-5084
　Shaker Heights *(G-11929)*

Eoi Inc... F 740 201-3300
　Lewis Center *(G-8333)*

Gyrus Acmi LP.. D 419 668-8201
　Norwalk *(G-10845)*

Lumitex Inc... D 440 243-8401
　Strongsville *(G-12572)*

Mrpicker.. G 440 354-6497
Cleveland *(G-4052)*

Ndi Medical LLC.................................... E 216 378-9106
Cleveland *(G-4064)*

Neuros Medical Inc............................... G 440 951-2565
Willoughby Hills *(G-14561)*

Nkh-Safety Inc...................................... F 513 771-3839
Cincinnati *(G-2911)*

Pemco Inc.. E 216 524-2990
Cleveland *(G-4150)*

Rapiscan Systems High Enrgy In.......... E 937 879-4200
Fairborn *(G-6698)*

Respironics Novametrix LLC.................. A 800 345-6443
Columbus *(G-5228)*

Sonosite Inc.. G 425 951-1200
Hamilton *(G-7526)*

Thermo Fisher Scientific Inc................. F 513 948-6290
Blue Ash *(G-1343)*

Varian Medical Systems Inc.................. G 888 827-4265
Liberty Township *(G-8379)*

Viewray Inc.. D 440 703-3210
Oakwood Village *(G-10911)*

Viewray Technologies Inc...................... F 440 703-3210
Oakwood Village *(G-10912)*

ELECTROMEDICAL EQPT WHOLESALERS

Icu Medical Inc...................................... D 614 210-7300
Dublin *(G-6305)*

ELECTROMETALLURGICAL PRDTS

Rhenium Alloys Inc................................ E 440 365-7388
North Ridgeville *(G-10747)*

ELECTRONIC DEVICES: Solid State, NEC

Burke Products Inc................................ G 937 372-3516
Xenia *(G-14756)*

D F Electronics Inc............................... D 513 772-7792
Cincinnati *(G-2537)*

Dan-Mar Company Inc.......................... E 419 660-8830
Norwalk *(G-10835)*

ELECTRONIC EQPT REPAIR SVCS

Bentronix Corp....................................... G 440 632-0606
Middlefield *(G-9782)*

Electric Service Co Inc.......................... E 513 271-6387
Cincinnati *(G-2580)*

Sasha Electronics Inc........................... G 419 662-8100
Rossford *(G-11663)*

Vacuum Electric Switch Co Inc............. F 330 374-5156
Mogadore *(G-10091)*

Vertiv Corporation................................. A 614 888-0246
Westerville *(G-14239)*

ELECTRONIC LOADS & POWER SPLYS

Vertiv Holdings Co................................. C 614 888-0246
Westerville *(G-14241)*

ELECTRONIC PARTS & EQPT WHOLESALERS

Cartessa Corp....................................... F 513 738-4477
Shandon *(G-11933)*

Certified Comparator Products.............. G 937 426-9677
Miamisburg *(G-9679)*

Electro-Line Inc..................................... F 937 461-5683
Dayton *(G-5762)*

M4 Knick LLC.. G 513 833-2500
Milford *(G-9941)*

Pepperl + Fuchs Inc.............................. C 330 425-3555
Twinsburg *(G-13352)*

Premier Farnell Holding Inc................... E 330 523-4273
Richfield *(G-11597)*

Projects Unlimited Inc............................ C 937 918-2200
Dayton *(G-5968)*

Spirit Avionics Ltd................................. F 614 237-4271
Columbus *(G-5284)*

Standex Electronics Inc........................ D 513 871-3777
Fairfield *(G-6778)*

ELECTRONIC SHOPPING

E Retailing Associates LLC................... D 614 300-5785
Columbus *(G-4894)*

ELECTRONIC TRAINING DEVICES

E-Beam Services Inc............................. E 513 933-0031
Lebanon *(G-8252)*

ELECTROPLATING & PLATING SVC

Krendl Rack Co Inc............................... G 419 667-4800
Venedocia *(G-13586)*

Twist Inc.. C 937 675-9581
Jamestown *(G-7969)*

Worthington Steel Company.................. B 800 944-2255
Worthington *(G-14732)*

ELEVATORS & EQPT

Adams Elevator Equipment Co.............. D 847 581-2900
Holland *(G-7743)*

Avt Beckett Elevators USA Inc.............. G 844 360-0288
Logan *(G-8509)*

Canton Elevator Inc.............................. D 330 833-3600
North Canton *(G-10632)*

Elevator Cncepts By Wurtec LLC.......... F 734 246-4700
Toledo *(G-12950)*

Gray-Eering Ltd.................................... G 740 498-8816
Tippecanoe *(G-12858)*

Otis Elevator Company.......................... E 216 573-2333
Cleveland *(G-4127)*

Schindler Elevator Corporation............. E 419 861-5900
Holland *(G-7783)*

Schindler Elevator Corporation............. C 937 492-3186
Sidney *(G-12048)*

Sweet Manufacturing Company............. E 937 325-1511
Springfield *(G-12381)*

Wittur Usa Inc....................................... E 216 524-0100
Twinsburg *(G-13396)*

ELEVATORS WHOLESALERS

Otis Elevator Company.......................... E 216 573-2333
Cleveland *(G-4127)*

ELEVATORS: Installation & Conversion

Otis Elevator Company.......................... E 216 573-2333
Cleveland *(G-4127)*

EMBLEMS: Embroidered

Atlantis Sportswear Inc......................... E 937 773-0680
Piqua *(G-11336)*

Craco Embroidery Inc............................ G 513 563-6999
Cincinnati *(G-2522)*

Novak J F Manufacturing Co LLC.......... G 216 741-5112
Cleveland *(G-4102)*

R J Manray Inc...................................... G 330 559-6716
Canfield *(G-1814)*

Randy Gray.. G 513 533-3200
Cincinnati *(G-3032)*

Sportsco Imprinting............................... G 513 641-5111
Cincinnati *(G-3106)*

EMBROIDERY ADVERTISING SVCS

City Apparel Inc.................................... F 419 434-1155
Findlay *(G-6852)*

Custom Sporstwear Imprints LLC.......... G 330 335-8326
Wadsworth *(G-13633)*

Screen Works Inc.................................. E 937 264-9111
Dayton *(G-6000)*

Underground Sports Shop Inc............... F 513 751-1662
Cincinnati *(G-3179)*

EMERGENCY ALARMS

Floyd Bell Inc.. D 614 294-4000
Columbus *(G-4930)*

Resideo LLC.. G 440 439-7002
Bedford *(G-1057)*

Resideo LLC.. F 513 772-1851
Cincinnati *(G-3039)*

Status Solutions LLC............................ D 434 296-1789
Westerville *(G-14235)*

ENAMELS

J C Whitlam Manufacturing Co.............. E 330 334-2524
Wadsworth *(G-13644)*

North Shore Strapping Company........... E 216 661-5200
Brooklyn Heights *(G-1536)*

ENCLOSURES: Electronic

American Rugged Enclosures Inc.......... F 513 942-3004
Hamilton *(G-7464)*

Buckeye Stamping Company................. D 877 728-0776
Columbus *(G-4786)*

Ecp Corporation.................................... E 440 934-0444
Avon *(G-724)*

Nn Metal Stampings LLC....................... E 419 737-2311
Pioneer *(G-11322)*

ENCLOSURES: Screen

Patton Aluminum Products Inc.............. F 937 845-9404
New Carlisle *(G-10378)*

ENCODERS: Digital

Garage Scenes Ltd................................ F 614 407-6094
Westerville *(G-14211)*

Liquid Image Corp America................... G 216 458-9800
Cleveland *(G-3963)*

ENGINE REBUILDING: Diesel

Chemequip Sales Inc............................ E 330 724-8300
Coventry Township *(G-5481)*

Detroit Desl Rmnfctrng-Ast Inc............. B 740 439-7701
Byesville *(G-1709)*

Detroit Desl Rmnufacturing LLC............ C 740 439-7701
Cambridge *(G-1741)*

General Engine Products LLC................ D 937 704-0160
Franklin *(G-7024)*

Jatrodiesel Inc....................................... F
Miamisburg *(G-9703)*

Maags Automotive & Mch Inc................ G 419 626-1539
Sandusky *(G-11853)*

Performace Diesel Inc........................... F 740 392-3693
Mount Vernon *(G-10258)*

ENGINEERING SVCS

A+ Engineering Fabrication Inc............. F 419 832-0748
Grand Rapids *(G-7307)*

Alfons Haar Inc...................................... E 937 560-2031
Springboro *(G-12246)*

Applied Experience LLC........................ G 614 943-2970
Plain City *(G-11394)*

Automted Cmpnent Spcalists LLC......... E 513 335-4285
Cincinnati *(G-2391)*

B&N Coal Inc... E 740 783-3575
Dexter City *(G-6224)*

Babcock & Wilcox Holdings LLC........... A 330 453-4511
Akron *(G-69)*

Bender Engineering Company............... G 330 938-2355
Beloit *(G-1144)*

PRODUCT

Beringer Plating Inc.................................... G 330 633-8409
Akron (G-76)

Braze Solutions LLC................................. F 440 349-5100
Solon (G-12089)

Circle Prime Manufacturing Inc............ E 330 923-0019
Cuyahoga Falls (G-5534)

Clarkwestern Dietrich Building.............. D 330 372-5564
Warren (G-13752)

Clarkwstern Dtrich Bldg System........... C 513 870-1100
West Chester (G-13966)

Coal Services Inc...................................... B 740 795-5220
Powhatan Point (G-11497)

Coating Systems Group Inc................... F 440 816-9306
Middleburg Heights (G-9768)

Comtec Incorporated................................ F 330 425-8102
Twinsburg (G-13288)

Control Electric Co.................................... E 216 671-8010
Columbia Station (G-4592)

Corrpro Companies Inc............................ E 770 761-5400
Medina (G-9392)

Corrpro Companies Inc............................ E 330 725-6681
Medina (G-9393)

Custom Craft Controls Inc...................... F 330 630-9599
Akron (G-112)

DA Precision Products Inc...................... F 513 459-1113
West Chester (G-13981)

Decision Systems Inc.............................. F 330 456-7600
Canton (G-1879)

Dms Inc... C 440 951-9838
Willoughby (G-14449)

Donald E Didion II.................................... E 419 483-2226
Bellevue (G-1123)

Dynamic Hydraulic Svcs Co LLC........... E 330 447-8967
Dover (G-6243)

Enprotech Industrial Tech LLC............... E 216 883-3220
Cleveland (G-3675)

Eti Tech LLC.. F 937 832-4200
Kettering (G-8120)

Fishel Company.. C 614 850-4400
Columbus (G-4926)

Frost Engineering Inc.............................. E 513 541-6330
Cincinnati (G-2642)

General Precision Corporation............... G 440 951-9380
Willoughby (G-14463)

Hii Mission Technologies Corp.............. G 937 426-3421
Beavercreek (G-992)

Hunter Defense Tech Inc......................... E 216 438-6111
Solon (G-12124)

Hydro-Dyne Inc... F 330 832-5076
Massillon (G-9204)

Imax Industries Inc.................................. F 440 639-0242
Painesville (G-11095)

Innovative Controls Corp........................ F 419 691-6684
Maumee (G-9298)

Innovtive McHning Slutions LLC........... F 419 925-2060
Celina (G-2110)

Integris Composites Inc.......................... D 740 928-0326
Hebron (G-7619)

Jotco Inc.. G 513 721-4943
Mansfield (G-8809)

Matrix Research Inc................................. D 937 427-8433
Dayton (G-5869)

Mendenhall Technical Services Inc....... E 513 860-1280
Fairfield (G-6754)

Micro Industries Corporation................. D 740 548-7878
Westerville (G-14270)

Modula Inc.. D 207 440-5100
Franklin (G-7035)

Mrl Materials Resources LLC................. E 937 531-6657
Xenia (G-14771)

Nesco Inc... E 440 461-6000
Cleveland (G-4068)

New Path International LLC..................... F 614 410-3974
Powell (G-11493)

Northrop Grmman Tchncal Svcs I......... C 937 320-3100
Beavercreek Township (G-1000)

Ohio Blow Pipe Company........................ E 216 681-7379
Cleveland (G-4113)

PA Technologies LLC............................... F 513 800-3541
Cincinnati (G-2940)

Padco Industries LLC.............................. E 440 564-7160
Newbury (G-10560)

Plate-All Metal Company Inc.................. G 330 633-6166
Akron (G-260)

Plcc2 LLC... G 614 279-1796
Columbus (G-5197)

Process Innovations Inc......................... G 330 856-5192
Vienna (G-13616)

Providence REES Inc............................... G 614 833-6231
Columbus (G-5212)

Quality Plating Co.................................... G 216 361-0151
Cleveland (G-4215)

Rolls-Royce Energy Systems Inc.......... A 703 834-1700
Mount Vernon (G-10263)

Sgi Matrix LLC.. D 937 438-9033
Miamisburg (G-9736)

Star Distribution and Mfg LLC.............. E 513 860-3573
West Chester (G-14149)

Sunpower Inc.. D 740 594-2221
Athens (G-654)

Support Svc LLC....................................... G 419 617-0660
Lexington (G-8375)

Systech Handling Inc.............................. F 419 445-8226
Archbold (G-512)

Tangent Company LLC............................ G 440 543-2775
Chagrin Falls (G-2186)

Tangible Solutions Inc........................... E 937 912-4603
Fairborn (G-6701)

Tfi Manufacturing LLC............................. F 440 290-9411
Mentor (G-9636)

Thermal Treatment Center Inc.............. E 216 881-8100
Wickliffe (G-14396)

Timekeeping Systems Inc...................... F 216 595-0890
Solon (G-12198)

Torsion Control Products Inc................. F 248 537-1900
Wadsworth (G-13675)

Trumbull Industries Inc.......................... D 330 434-6174
Akron (G-345)

Welding Consultants Inc......................... G 614 258-7018
Columbus (G-5360)

Werks Kraft Engineering LLC................. E 330 721-7374
Medina (G-9464)

Xaloy LLC... C 330 726-4000
Austintown (G-709)

Xcite Systems Corporation..................... G 513 965-0300
Cincinnati (G-2318)

ENGINEERING SVCS: Acoustical

Straight 72 Inc... D 740 943-5730
Marysville (G-9051)

ENGINEERING SVCS: Building Construction

Owens Corning Sales LLC..................... F 330 633-6735
Tallmadge (G-12745)

ENGINEERING SVCS: Chemical

Hexion Inc.. C 888 443-9466
Columbus (G-4976)

ENGINEERING SVCS: Civil

Barr Engineering Incorporated.............. E 614 714-0299
Columbus (G-4744)

Ceso Inc... E 937 435-8584
Miamisburg (G-9681)

Ever Secure SEC Systems Inc............... F 937 369-8294
Dayton (G-5772)

JBI Corporation... F 419 855-3389
Genoa (G-7248)

Pollock Research & Design Inc............. E 330 332-3300
Salem (G-11805)

Ra Consultants LLC................................. E 513 469-6600
Blue Ash (G-1326)

ENGINEERING SVCS: Construction & Civil

EP Ferris & Associates Inc.................... E 614 299-2999
Columbus (G-4906)

ENGINEERING SVCS: Electrical Or Electronic

American Controls Inc............................. E 440 944-9735
Wickliffe (G-14366)

CPI Group Limited.................................... F 216 525-0046
Cleveland (G-3573)

Davis Technologies Inc........................... F 330 823-2544
Alliance (G-380)

Electrovations Inc.................................... G 330 274-3558
Solon (G-12103)

Field Apparatus Service & Tstg............ G 513 353-9399
Cincinnati (G-2621)

L-3 Cmmncations Nova Engrg Inc......... F 877 282-1168
Mason (G-9120)

Lintech Electronics LLC.......................... E 513 528-6190
Cincinnati (G-2312)

Mid-Ohio Electric Co................................ E 614 274-8000
Columbus (G-5098)

New Dawn Labs LLC................................ F 203 675-5644
Union (G-13410)

PMC Systems Limited.............................. E 330 538-2268
North Jackson (G-10693)

Stock Fairfield Corporation.................... C 440 543-6000
Solon (G-12185)

TL Industries Inc...................................... C 419 666-8144
Perrysburg (G-11272)

Vector Electromagnetics LLC................. F 937 478-5904
Wilmington (G-14589)

ENGINEERING SVCS: Machine Tool Design

Hahn Automation Group Us Inc............ D 937 886-3232
Miamisburg (G-9694)

Jet Di Inc... G 330 607-7913
Brunswick (G-1600)

Mound Manufacturing Center Inc.......... F 937 236-8387
Dayton (G-5896)

Youngstown Plastic Tooling................... F 330 782-7222
Youngstown (G-14973)

ENGINEERING SVCS: Mechanical

Cbn Westside Technologies Inc............. B 513 772-7000
West Chester (G-13957)

Dillin Engineered Systems Corp............ E 419 666-6789
Perrysburg (G-11216)

Genius Solutions Engrg Co..................... E 419 794-9914
Maumee (G-9293)

Genpact LLC.. E 513 763-7660
Cincinnati (G-2667)

Johnson Mfg Systems LLC..................... F 937 866-4744
Miamisburg (G-9704)

Markley Enterprises LLC......................... E 513 771-1290
Cincinnati (G-2847)

Morris Technologies Inc......................... E 513 733-1611
Cincinnati (G-2888)

Performnce Plymr Solutions Inc........... F 937 298-3713
Moraine (G-10180)

Projects Designed & Built....................... E 419 726-7400
Toledo (G-13104)

Qcsm LLC.. G 216 650-8731
Cleveland *(G-4210)*

Systems Kit LLC MB............................ E 330 945-4500
Akron *(G-324)*

ENGINES: Diesel & Semi-Diesel Or Duel Fuel

Clarke Fire Prtection Pdts Inc............... F 513 771-2200
West Chester *(G-14111)*

Miscor Group Ltd................................... B 330 830-3500
Massillon *(G-9224)*

ENGINES: Gasoline, NEC

Miba Bearings US LLC........................... B 740 962-4242
Mcconnelsville *(G-9364)*

ENGINES: Internal Combustion, NEC

B A Malcuit Racing Inc.......................... G 330 878-7111
Strasburg *(G-12476)*

Bowden Manufacturing Corp................ E 440 946-1770
Willoughby *(G-14432)*

Cummins - Allison Corp......................... G 513 469-2924
Blue Ash *(G-1266)*

Cummins - Allison Corp......................... G 440 824-5050
Cleveland *(G-3579)*

Cummins Inc... F 614 604-6004
Grove City *(G-7379)*

Cummins Inc... F 614 771-1000
Hilliard *(G-7679)*

Ford Motor Company............................ A 419 226-7000
Lima *(G-8408)*

Precision Castparts Corp...................... F 440 350-6150
Painesville *(G-11106)*

Western Branch Diesel LLC.................. F 330 454-8800
Canton *(G-2047)*

ENGINES: Jet Propulsion

Enjet Aero Dayton Inc........................... E 937 878-3800
Huber Heights *(G-7821)*

ENGINES: Marine

Performance Research Inc.................... G 614 475-8300
Columbus *(G-5187)*

ENGRAVING SVC, NEC

Gordons Graphics Inc........................... G 330 863-2322
Malvern *(G-8751)*

Handcrafted Jewelry Inc........................ G 330 650-9011
Hudson *(G-7843)*

Irwin Engraving & Printing Co.............. G 216 391-7300
Cleveland *(G-3872)*

Sams Graphic Industries...................... F 330 821-4710
Alliance *(G-402)*

ENGRAVING SVCS

Engravers Gallery & Sign Co................ G 330 830-1271
Massillon *(G-9190)*

Genius Solutions Engrg Co................... E 419 794-9914
Maumee *(G-9293)*

Hafners Hrdwood Connection LLC........ G 419 726-4828
Toledo *(G-12983)*

Professional Award Service................... G 513 389-3600
Cincinnati *(G-3005)*

Queen City Spirit LLC........................... F 513 533-2662
Cincinnati *(G-3026)*

Ryder Engraving Inc.............................. G 740 927-7193
Pataskala *(G-11149)*

ENVELOPES

American Paper Group Inc.................... B 330 758-4545
Youngstown *(G-14811)*

Ampac Holdings LLC............................. A 513 671-1777
Cincinnati *(G-2365)*

Church-Budget Envelope Company....... E 800 446-9780
Salem *(G-11770)*

E-1 (2012) Holdings Inc........................ C 330 482-3900
Columbiana *(G-4615)*

Envelope 1 Inc....................................... D 330 482-3900
Columbiana *(G-4616)*

Envelope Mart of Ohio Inc.................... F 440 365-8177
Elyria *(G-6535)*

Jbm Packaging Company...................... C 513 933-8333
Lebanon *(G-8269)*

Keene Building Products Co.................. E 440 605-1020
Cleveland *(G-3910)*

Ohio Envelope Manufacturing Co......... E 216 267-2920
Cleveland *(G-4114)*

Pac Worldwide Corporation.................. E 800 535-0039
Monroe *(G-10114)*

Quality Envelope Inc............................. G 513 942-7578
West Chester *(G-14140)*

SRC Liquidation LLC............................. A 937 221-1000
Dayton *(G-6019)*

United Envelope LLC............................. B 513 542-4700
Cincinnati *(G-3182)*

Western States Envelope Co................. E 419 666-7480
Walbridge *(G-13689)*

ENVELOPES WHOLESALERS

Envelope Mart of Ohio Inc.................... F 440 365-8177
Elyria *(G-6535)*

Jbm Packaging Company...................... C 513 933-8333
Lebanon *(G-8269)*

Pac Worldwide Corporation.................. E 800 535-0039
Monroe *(G-10114)*

Western States Envelope Co................. E 419 666-7480
Walbridge *(G-13689)*

ENZYMES

Biowish Technologies Inc..................... G 312 572-6700
Cincinnati *(G-2410)*

Mp Biomedicals LLC.............................. C 440 337-1200
Solon *(G-12154)*

Oxyrase Inc.. F 419 589-8800
Ontario *(G-10951)*

EPOXY RESINS

Hexion Inc.. C 888 443-9466
Columbus *(G-4976)*

Key Resin Company.............................. F 513 943-4225
Batavia *(G-869)*

Lattice Composites LLC........................ F 440 759-2082
Solon *(G-12141)*

Nanosperse LLC.................................... G 937 296-5030
Kettering *(G-8122)*

Renegade Materials Corporation.......... D 937 350-5274
Miamisburg *(G-9732)*

Westlake Corporation........................... D 614 986-2497
Columbus *(G-5364)*

EQUIPMENT: Rental & Leasing, NEC

Aircraft Dynamics Corporation............ F 419 331-0371
Elida *(G-6482)*

Brinkman LLC.. F 419 204-5934
Lima *(G-8392)*

Cattron Holdings Inc............................. E 234 806-0018
Warren *(G-13748)*

De Nora Tech LLC.................................. D 440 710-5334
Painesville *(G-11078)*

Dearing Compressor and Pump............ E 330 783-2258
Youngstown *(G-14847)*

Eaton Leasing Corporation................... B 216 382-2292
Beachwood *(G-916)*

Elliott Tool Technologies Ltd................ D 937 253-6133
Dayton *(G-5763)*

Glawe Manufacturing Co Inc................ G 937 754-0064
Fairborn *(G-6694)*

Great Lakes Crushing Ltd..................... D 440 944-5500
Wickliffe *(G-14376)*

Hansen Scaffolding LLC........................ F 513 574-9000
West Chester *(G-14124)*

Higgins Construction & Supply Co Inc.. F 937 364-2331
Hillsboro *(G-7717)*

Powerclean Equipment Company......... F 513 202-0001
Cleves *(G-4547)*

Rambasek Realty Inc............................. F 937 228-1189
Dayton *(G-5974)*

Thomas Do-It Center Inc....................... E 740 446-2002
Gallipolis *(G-7209)*

Trailer One Inc....................................... F 330 723-7474
Medina *(G-9457)*

Tri State Equipment Company.............. G 513 738-7227
Shandon *(G-11935)*

Waco Scaffolding & Equipment Inc....... A 216 749-8900
Cleveland *(G-4487)*

West Equipment Company Inc............. G 419 698-1601
Toledo *(G-13177)*

ETCHING & ENGRAVING SVC

Canton Galvanizing LLC....................... E 330 685-9060
Canton *(G-1855)*

Cubbison Company................................ D 330 793-2481
Youngstown *(G-14843)*

Hadronics Inc.. D 513 321-9350
Cincinnati *(G-2702)*

Sterling Coating.................................... G 513 942-4900
West Chester *(G-14076)*

Tce International Ltd.............................. F 800 962-2376
Perry *(G-11199)*

Worldclass Processing Corp................. E
Twinsburg *(G-13397)*

X-Treme Finishes Inc............................ F 330 474-0614
North Royalton *(G-10790)*

ETHYLENE

Geon Company....................................... A 216 447-6000
Cleveland *(G-3771)*

ETHYLENE-PROPYLENE RUBBERS: EPDM Polymers

Allied Polymers..................................... G 330 975-4200
Seville *(G-11909)*

Canton OH Rubber Speclty Prods......... G 330 454-3847
Canton *(G-1857)*

Geon Performance Solutions LLC......... F 800 438-4366
Westlake *(G-14304)*

Great Lakes Polymer Proc Inc............. F 313 655-4024
Akron *(G-166)*

Innoplast Inc... F 440 543-8660
Cleveland *(G-3861)*

Key Resin Company.............................. F 513 943-4225
Batavia *(G-869)*

Mexichem Specialty Resins Inc............ E 440 930-1435
Avon Lake *(G-765)*

Protective Industrial Polymers............ F 440 327-0015
North Ridgeville *(G-10743)*

EXHAUST HOOD OR FAN CLEANING SVCS

Link To Success Inc.............................. G 888 959-4203
Norwalk *(G-10851)*

EXHAUST SYSTEMS: Eqpt & Parts

Cardington Yutaka Tech Inc.................. A 419 864-8777
Cardington *(G-2053)*

Dbw Fiber Corporation.......................... D
Wooster *(G-14634)*

Emssons Faurecia Ctrl Systems..........B 937 743-0551
　Franklin *(G-7018)*

Tmg Performance Products LLC...........D 440 891-0999
　Berea *(G-1192)*

EXPLOSIVES

Austin Powder Company.........................G 419 299-3347
　Findlay *(G-6838)*

Austin Powder Company.........................C 740 596-5286
　Mc Arthur *(G-9348)*

Austin Powder Company.........................G 740 968-1555
　Saint Clairsville *(G-11687)*

Austin Powder Company.........................D 216 464-2400
　Cleveland *(G-3386)*

Austin Powder Holdings Company.........D 216 464-2400
　Cleveland *(G-3387)*

Hilltop Energy Inc....................................F 330 859-2108
　Mineral City *(G-10028)*

EXPLOSIVES, FUSES & DETONATORS:

Primary explosives

Sloat Inc...G 440 951-9554
　Willoughby *(G-14530)*

EXTENSION CORDS

Rah Investment Holding Inc...................D 330 832-8124
　Massillon *(G-9237)*

EXTRACTS, FLAVORING

Berghausen Corporation........................E 513 591-4491
　Cincinnati *(G-2406)*

Frutarom USA Inc...................................C 513 870-4900
　Cincinnati *(G-2643)*

Mane Inc...D 513 248-9876
　Lebanon *(G-8276)*

FABRICS & CLOTHING: Rubber Coated

Ansell Healthcare Products LLC............E 740 622-4311
　Coshocton *(G-5449)*

FABRICS: Apparel & Outerwear, Cotton

Heritage Hill LLC....................................G 513 237-0240
　Blue Ash *(G-1285)*

Roach Studios LLC.................................F 614 725-1405
　Columbus *(G-5233)*

Struggle Grind Success LLC..................G 330 834-6738
　Boardman *(G-1377)*

Wonder-Shirts Inc..................................G 917 679-2336
　Dublin *(G-6361)*

FABRICS: Automotive, From Manmade Fiber

Collins & Aikman Auto Mats LLC..........E 330 456-4543
　Canton *(G-1869)*

FABRICS: Cotton, Narrow

US Cotton LLC..D 216 676-6400
　Cleveland *(G-4451)*

FABRICS: Decorative Trim & Specialty, Including Twist Weave

Stitches Usa LLC....................................F 330 852-0500
　Walnut Creek *(G-13695)*

Synthomer Inc...C 216 682-7000
　Beachwood *(G-951)*

FABRICS: Denims

Noble Denim Workshop...........................G 513 560-5640
　Cincinnati *(G-2913)*

FABRICS: Fiberglass, Broadwoven

Schmelzer Industries Inc.......................E 740 743-2866
　Somerset *(G-12211)*

FABRICS: Glass & Fiberglass, Broadwoven

Architectural Fiberglass Inc...................E 216 641-8300
　Cleveland *(G-3364)*

FABRICS: Nonwoven

Amantea Nonwovens LLC.......................G 513 842-6600
　Cincinnati *(G-2355)*

Autoneum North America Inc..................B 419 693-0511
　Oregon *(G-10957)*

Ccp Industries Inc..................................B 216 535-4227
　Richmond Heights *(G-11609)*

Nikke Kureha America Co Ltd................G 513 771-6788
　West Chester *(G-14033)*

FABRICS: Nylon, Broadwoven

Seaman Corporation...............................C 330 262-1111
　Wooster *(G-14684)*

FABRICS: Resin Or Plastic Coated

Biothane Coated Webbing Corp.............E 440 327-0485
　North Ridgeville *(G-10727)*

Diamond Polymers Incorporated............D 330 773-2700
　Akron *(G-121)*

Duracote Corporation.............................E 330 296-9600
　Ravenna *(G-11523)*

Durez Corporation..................................D 567 295-6400
　Kenton *(G-8097)*

Hartco Inc...E 513 771-4430
　Cincinnati *(G-2709)*

Petfiber LLC...F 216 767-4535
　Cleveland *(G-4154)*

Schneller LLC...C 330 673-1400
　Kent *(G-8073)*

FABRICS: Rubber & Elastic Yarns & Fabrics

CT Specialty Polymers Ltd.....................G 440 632-9311
　Middlefield *(G-9789)*

Murrubber Technologies Inc...................E
　Stow *(G-12442)*

FABRICS: Rubberized

Salem-Republic Rubber Company.........E 877 425-5079
　Sebring *(G-11901)*

FABRICS: Scrub Cloths

Akron Cotton Products Inc.....................G 330 434-7171
　Akron *(G-28)*

Canton Sterilized Wiping Cloth...............G 330 455-5179
　Canton *(G-1860)*

Linsalata Cpiti Prtners Fund I.................G 440 684-1400
　Cleveland *(G-3962)*

Tranzonic Companies.............................C 440 446-0643
　Cleveland *(G-4414)*

Tz Acquisition Corp................................F 216 535-4300
　Richmond Heights *(G-11613)*

FABRICS: Shoe Laces, Exc Leather

Mitchellace Inc.......................................D 740 354-2813
　Portsmouth *(G-11471)*

Sole Choice Inc......................................E 740 354-2813
　Portsmouth *(G-11477)*

FABRICS: Umbrella Cloth, Cotton

Totes Isotoner Holdings LLC..................C 513 682-8200
　Cincinnati *(G-3160)*

FABRICS: Upholstery, Wool

Midwest Composites LLC.......................F 419 738-2431
　Wapakoneta *(G-13721)*

FACILITIES SUPPORT SVCS

Facility Service Pros LLC........................G 419 577-6123
　Collins *(G-4587)*

MPW Industrial Svcs Group Inc.............B 740 927-8790
　Hebron *(G-7625)*

Taylor Communications Inc....................E 937 221-1000
　Dayton *(G-6039)*

FAMILY CLOTHING STORES

Odyssey Spirits Inc................................F 330 562-1523
　Chagrin Falls *(G-2174)*

Vances Department Store........................G 937 549-3033
　Manchester *(G-8756)*

Vances Department Store........................G 937 549-2188
　Manchester *(G-8755)*

FANS, BLOWING: Indl Or Commercial

Cincinnati Fan & Ventilator....................D 513 573-1000
　Mason *(G-9083)*

Howden USA Company...........................C 513 874-2400
　Fairfield *(G-6743)*

FANS, EXHAUST: Indl Or Commercial

American Fan Company...........................C 513 874-2400
　Fairfield *(G-6709)*

ARI Phoenix Inc......................................E 513 229-3750
　Sharonville *(G-11945)*

Multi-Wing America Inc...........................E 440 834-9400
　Middlefield *(G-9814)*

FANS, VENTILATING: Indl Or Commercial

Ad Industries Inc....................................A 303 744-1911
　Dayton *(G-5634)*

Humongous Holdings Llc........................F 216 663-8830
　Cleveland *(G-3844)*

Lau Holdings LLC...................................E 937 476-6500
　Dayton *(G-5617)*

Lau Holdings LLC...................................D 216 486-4000
　Cleveland *(G-3945)*

Lau Industries Inc...................................A 937 476-6500
　Dayton *(G-5618)*

Tlt-Turbo Inc...G 330 776-5115
　Akron *(G-340)*

Vector Mechanical LLC...........................G 216 337-4042
　Cleveland *(G-4460)*

FANS: Ceiling

Acorn Technology Corporation................E 216 663-1244
　Shaker Heights *(G-11925)*

Hinkley Lighting Inc................................E 440 653-5500
　Avon Lake *(G-760)*

FARM & GARDEN MACHINERY WHOLESALERS

All Power Equipment LLC........................F 740 593-3279
　Athens *(G-632)*

Smg Growing Media Inc.........................F 937 644-0011
　Marysville *(G-9049)*

FARM MACHINERY REPAIR SVCS

Reberland Equipment Inc.......................F 330 698-5883
　Apple Creek *(G-476)*

FARM SPLYS WHOLESALERS

Andersons Inc...G 419 536-0460
　Toledo *(G-12881)*

Andersons Inc...C 419 893-5050
　Maumee *(G-9261)*

Countyline Co-Op Inc.............................F 419 287-3241
　Pemberville *(G-11174)*

Darling Ingredients Inc............................ G..... 216 651-9300
Cleveland *(G-3599)*

Green Field Farms Co-Op............................ G..... 330 263-0246
Wooster *(G-14645)*

Legacy Farmers Cooperative.................. F..... 419 423-2611
Findlay *(G-6884)*

Minster Farmers Coop Exch.................. D..... 419 628-4705
Minster *(G-10061)*

FARM SPLYS, WHOLESALE: Feed

Cooper Farms Inc.................................... D..... 419 594-3325
Oakwood *(G-10896)*

Keynes Bros Inc.. D..... 740 385-6824
Logan *(G-8517)*

M B K Inc.. F..... 330 889-3451
Bristolville *(G-1498)*

Mennel Milling Company.......................... E..... 740 385-6824
Logan *(G-8521)*

Republic Mills Inc..................................... F..... 419 758-3511
Okolona *(G-10932)*

Stony Hill Mixing Ltd.............................. G..... 330 674-0814
Millersburg *(G-10011)*

Sunrise Cooperative Inc.......................... G..... 419 628-4705
Minster *(G-10066)*

FARM SPLYS, WHOLESALE: Fertilizers & Agricultural Chemicals

Helena Agri-Enterprises LLC.................. G..... 419 596-3806
Continental *(G-5422)*

Nutrien AG Solutions Inc........................ G..... 614 873-4253
Milford Center *(G-9958)*

United Industries Incorporated.............. D..... 330 682-5010
Orrville *(G-11015)*

FARM SPLYS, WHOLESALE: Garden Splys

Matthew Brun Enterprises Inc................ E..... 937 604-0057
Dayton *(G-5870)*

FASTENERS WHOLESALERS

Bamal Corp.. G..... 937 492-9484
Sidney *(G-11995)*

Beckett-Greenhill LLC.............................. F..... 216 861-5730
Cleveland *(G-3413)*

Cardinal Fstener Specialty Inc............... E..... 216 831-3800
Bedford Heights *(G-1072)*

Dimcogray Corporation............................ D..... 937 433-7600
Centerville *(G-2131)*

Dubose Nat Enrgy Fas McHned PR...... F..... 216 362-1700
Middleburg Heights *(G-9769)*

Efg Holdings LLC...................................... A..... 440 325-4337
Berea *(G-1168)*

Erico International Corp.......................... B..... 440 248-0100
Solon *(G-12107)*

ET&f Fastening Systems Inc.................. G..... 800 248-2376
Solon *(G-12108)*

Global Specialties Inc............................ G..... 800 338-0814
Brunswick *(G-1595)*

Master Bolt LLC.. E..... 440 323-5529
Elyria *(G-6561)*

Midwest Motor Supply Co........................ C..... 800 233-1294
Columbus *(G-5100)*

Ohashi Technica USA Mfg Inc................ F..... 740 965-9002
Sunbury *(G-12672)*

Ramco Specialties Inc............................ D..... 330 653-5135
Hudson *(G-7855)*

Stanley Engineered Fasten...................... G..... 440 657-3537
Elyria *(G-6591)*

Stelfast LLC.. E..... 440 879-0077
Strongsville *(G-12606)*

Tfp Corporation.. E..... 330 725-7741
Medina *(G-9454)*

W W Cross Industries Inc........................ F..... 330 588-8400
Canton *(G-2043)*

Wodin Inc.. E..... 440 439-4222
Cleveland *(G-4513)*

Youngstown Bolt & Supply Co................ G..... 330 799-3201
Youngstown *(G-14967)*

FASTENERS: Metal

Wecall Inc.. G..... 440 437-8202
Chardon *(G-2226)*

Contitech Usa LLC.................................... C..... 937 644-8900
Marysville *(G-9016)*

Midwest Motor Supply Co........................ C..... 800 233-1294
Columbus *(G-5100)*

Seaway Bolt And Specials Company..... D..... 440 236-5015
Columbia Station *(G-4602)*

FAUCETS & SPIGOTS: Metal & Plastic

Toolbold Corporation................................ F..... 440 543-1660
Cleveland *(G-4401)*

FEATHERS & FEATHER PRODUCTS

Ohio Feather Company Inc...................... G..... 513 921-3373
Cincinnati *(G-2922)*

FENCE POSTS: Iron & Steel

Msls Group LLC.. E..... 330 723-4431
Medina *(G-9428)*

FENCES OR POSTS: Ornamental Iron Or Steel

Acme Fence LLC.. F..... 330 784-0456
Akron *(G-15)*

Akron Products Company.......................... D..... 330 576-1750
Wadsworth *(G-13627)*

FENCING MATERIALS: Docks & Other Outdoor Prdts, Wood

Juno Enterprises LLC.............................. G..... 419 448-9350
New Riegel *(G-10470)*

FENCING MATERIALS: Wood

Acme Fence LLC.. F..... 330 784-0456
Akron *(G-15)*

Kalinich Fence Company Inc.................. F..... 440 238-6127
Strongsville *(G-12569)*

Youngstown Fence Incorporated.......... G..... 330 788-8110
Youngstown *(G-14969)*

FENCING: Chain Link

Acme Fence LLC.. F..... 330 784-0456
Akron *(G-15)*

Richards Whl Fence Co Inc...................... E..... 330 773-0423
Akron *(G-284)*

FERROALLOYS

ERAMET MARIETTA INC............................ C..... 740 374-1000
Marietta *(G-8916)*

International Metal Supply LLC.............. G..... 330 764-1004
Medina *(G-9414)*

FERROMANGANESE, NOT MADE IN BLAST FURNACES

Real Alloy Specialty Pdts LLC.............. D..... 844 732-5087
Beachwood *(G-943)*

FERROSILICON, EXC MADE IN BLAST FURNACES

Ferroglobe USA Mtlurgical Inc.............. C..... 740 984-2361
Waterford *(G-13826)*

FERROUS METALS: Reclaimed From Clay

A-Gas US Holdings Inc............................ F..... 419 867-8990
Bowling Green *(G-1403)*

FERTILIZER, AGRICULTURAL: Wholesalers

Hanby Farms Inc...................................... E..... 740 763-3554
Nashport *(G-10299)*

Ohigro Inc.. E..... 740 726-2429
Waldo *(G-13691)*

FERTILIZERS: Nitrogen Solutions

Pcs Nitrogen Inc...................................... F..... 419 226-1200
Lima *(G-8437)*

FERTILIZERS: Nitrogenous

Agrium Advanced Tech US Inc................ G..... 614 276-5103
Columbus *(G-4680)*

Keystone Cooperative Inc...................... G..... 937 884-5526
Verona *(G-13591)*

R & J AG Manufacturing Inc.................. F..... 419 962-4707
Ashland *(G-568)*

Royster-Clark Inc.................................... G..... 513 941-4100
North Bend *(G-10621)*

Scotts Miracle-Gro Company.................. G..... 330 684-0421
Orrville *(G-11007)*

Scotts Miracle-Gro Company.................. B..... 937 644-0011
Marysville *(G-9046)*

Smgm LLC.. F..... 937 644-0011
Marysville *(G-9050)*

Synagro Midwest Inc................................ F..... 937 384-0669
Miamisburg *(G-9741)*

Turf Care Supply LLC.............................. D..... 877 220-1014
Brunswick *(G-1620)*

FERTILIZERS: Phosphatic

Andersons Inc.. G..... 419 536-0460
Toledo *(G-12881)*

Andersons Inc.. C..... 419 893-5050
Maumee *(G-9261)*

FIBER & FIBER PRDTS: Elastomeric

Bridge Components Incorporated.......... G..... 614 873-0777
Columbus *(G-4775)*

FIBER & FIBER PRDTS: Protein

Matrix Meats Inc...................................... F..... 614 602-1846
Dublin *(G-6319)*

FIBER & FIBER PRDTS: Vinyl

Mytee Products Inc.................................. D..... 888 705-8277
Solon *(G-12156)*

FIBER OPTICS

Nextgen Fiber Optics LLC........................ G..... 513 549-4691
Cincinnati *(G-2906)*

Sem-Com Company Inc............................ F..... 419 537-8813
Toledo *(G-13125)*

Srico Inc.. G..... 614 799-0664
Columbus *(G-5287)*

FIBERS: Carbon & Graphite

Ges AGM.. E..... 216 658-6528
Cleveland *(G-3773)*

Wolf Composite Solutions........................ F..... 614 219-6990
Columbus *(G-5370)*

Xperion E & E USA LLC............................ E..... 740 788-9560
Heath *(G-7605)*

FILM BASE: Cellulose Acetate Or Nitrocellulose Plastics

PRODUCT

American Insulation Tech LLC............... F 513 733-4248
  Milford *(G-9921)*

Simona Boltaron Inc........................... D 740 498-5900
  Newcomerstown *(G-10575)*

FILTER ELEMENTS: Fluid & Hydraulic Line

Two M Precision Co Inc..................... E 440 946-2120
  Willoughby *(G-14546)*

FILTERS

Abanaki Corporation........................... F 440 543-7400
  Chagrin Falls *(G-2153)*

Allied Separation Tech Inc................. E 704 732-8034
  Twinsburg *(G-13274)*

Columbus Industries Inc.................... D 740 983-2552
  Ashville *(G-624)*

Columbus Industries One LLC........... F 740 983-2552
  Ashville *(G-625)*

Cummins Filtration Inc........................ C
  Findlay *(G-6858)*

Ddp Specialty Electronic MA............... G 937 839-4612
  West Alexandria *(G-13918)*

E R Advanced Ceramics Inc............... E 330 426-9433
  East Palestine *(G-6402)*

Evoqua Water Technologies LLC.......... G 614 861-5440
  Pickerington *(G-11294)*

Filter Technology Inc......................... G 614 921-9801
  Baltimore *(G-785)*

Hdt Tactical Systems Inc.................... C 216 438-6111
  Solon *(G-12122)*

Hunter Defense Tech Inc.................... E 216 438-6111
  Solon *(G-12124)*

Joyce/Dayton Corp............................ E 937 294-6261
  Dayton *(G-5830)*

Lawrence Technologies Inc................. G 937 274-7771
  Dayton *(G-5842)*

OSI Environmental LLC...................... E 440 237-4600
  North Royalton *(G-10779)*

Swift Filters Inc................................. E 877 887-9438
  Bedford *(G-1059)*

FILTERS & SOFTENERS: Water, Household

Amsoil Inc... G 614 274-9851
  Urbancrest *(G-13482)*

Enting Water Conditioning Inc............ E 937 294-5100
  Moraine *(G-10160)*

Monarch Water Systems Inc............... F 937 426-5773
  Beavercreek *(G-978)*

New Aqua LLC.................................. F 614 265-9000
  Columbus *(G-5125)*

Obic LLC.. F 419 633-3147
  Bryan *(G-1654)*

United McGill Corporation.................. F 614 920-1267
  Lithopolis *(G-8484)*

William R Hague Inc.......................... D 614 836-2115
  Groveport *(G-7458)*

FILTERS & STRAINERS: Pipeline

Hellan Strainer Company................... G..... 216 206-4200
  Cleveland *(G-3819)*

FILTERS: Air

Cincinnati A Flter Sls Svc Inc.............. E 513 242-3400
  Cincinnati *(G-2466)*

Swift Filters Inc................................. E 877 887-9438
  Bedford *(G-1059)*

FILTERS: Air Intake, Internal Combustion Engine, Exc Auto

Plas-Mac Corp.................................. D 440 349-3222
  Solon *(G-12168)*

FILTERS: General Line, Indl

1200 Feet Limited.............................. G 419 827-6061
  Lakeville *(G-8159)*

Falls Filtration Tech Inc..................... E 330 928-4100
  Stow *(G-12430)*

Gvs Filtration Inc.............................. B 419 423-9040
  Findlay *(G-6875)*

Metaullics Systems LP....................... C 509 926-6212
  Solon *(G-12148)*

Midwest Filtration LLC....................... D 513 874-6510
  Cincinnati *(G-2879)*

Nupro Company................................ E 440 951-9729
  Willoughby *(G-14498)*

Petro Ware Inc.................................. G 740 982-1302
  Crooksville *(G-5512)*

S A Langmack Company..................... G 216 541-0500
  Cleveland *(G-4267)*

FILTERS: Oil, Internal Combustion Engine, Exc Auto

Brinkley Technology Group LLC........... F 330 830-2498
  Massillon *(G-9175)*

FILTRATION DEVICES: Electronic

Contech Strmwter Solutions LLC.......... G 513 645-7000
  West Chester *(G-13973)*

Fontaine Pieciak Engrg Inc................. G 413 592-2273
  Twinsburg *(G-13304)*

Illinois Tool Works Inc....................... E 262 248-8277
  Bryan *(G-1645)*

Micropure Filtration Inc..................... G 952 472-2323
  Cleveland *(G-4028)*

Nu Stream Filtration Inc.................... F 937 949-3174
  Dayton *(G-5918)*

FINISHING AGENTS

Pilot Chemical Company Ohio............. E 513 326-0600
  West Chester *(G-14045)*

FIRE ALARM MAINTENANCE & MONITORING SVCS

Total Life Safety LLC........................ F 866 955-2318
  West Chester *(G-14083)*

FIRE ARMS, SMALL: Guns Or Gun Parts, 30 mm & Below

Highpoint Firearms............................ G 419 747-9444
  Mansfield *(G-8803)*

Ohio Ordnance Works Inc.................. E 440 285-3481
  Chardon *(G-2217)*

Stealth Arms LLC.............................. G..... 419 925-7005
  Celina *(G-2122)*

TS Sales LLC................................... F 727 804-8060
  Akron *(G-347)*

FIRE ARMS, SMALL: Rifles Or Rifle Parts, 30 mm & below

Kelblys Rifle Range Inc..................... G..... 330 683-4674
  North Lawrence *(G-10701)*

FIRE CONTROL EQPT REPAIR SVCS, MILITARY

Fire Foe Corp................................... E 330 759-9834
  Girard *(G-7271)*

FIRE CONTROL OR BOMBING EQPT: Electronic

Fire-End & Croker Corp........................... E 513 870-0517
  West Chester *(G-14119)*

Highcom Global Security Inc............... G 727 592-9400
  Columbus *(G-4981)*

FIRE DETECTION SYSTEMS

Total Life Safety LLC........................ F 866 955-2318
  West Chester *(G-14083)*

FIRE EXTINGUISHERS, WHOLESALE

A-Gas US Holdings Inc...................... F 419 867-8990
  Bowling Green *(G-1403)*

Fire Safety Services Inc..................... F 937 686-2000
  Huntsville *(G-7864)*

FIRE EXTINGUISHERS: Portable

Fire Safety Services Inc..................... F 937 686-2000
  Huntsville *(G-7864)*

FIRE OR BURGLARY RESISTIVE PRDTS

All Ohio Welding Inc.......................... G 937 663-7116
  Saint Paris *(G-11755)*

Central Machinery Company LLC.......... F 740 387-1289
  Marion *(G-8966)*

Donald E Didion II............................. E 419 483-2226
  Bellevue *(G-1123)*

Fabricating Solutions Inc.................... F 330 486-0998
  Twinsburg *(G-13301)*

MAK Fabricating Inc.......................... F 330 747-0040
  Youngstown *(G-14894)*

Mast Farm Service Ltd...................... F 330 893-2972
  Walnut Creek *(G-13694)*

Penny Fab LLC.................................. F 740 967-3669
  Columbus *(G-5184)*

Quest Technologies Inc...................... F 937 743-1200
  Franklin *(G-7044)*

Tengam Pro Inc................................. F 740 373-0909
  Marietta *(G-8952)*

FIREARMS & AMMUNITION, EXC SPORTING, WHOLESALE

Mabis Shipping Solutions Inc.............. G 330 650-1788
  Hudson *(G-7850)*

FIREFIGHTING APPARATUS

Johnsons Fire Equipment Co............... F 740 357-4916
  Wellston *(G-13908)*

FIREPLACE EQPT & ACCESS

Thermo-Rite Mfg Company.................. E 330 633-8680
  Akron *(G-336)*

FIREWORKS

American Fireworks Inc...................... A 330 650-1776
  Hudson *(G-7829)*

American Fireworks Company............. A 330 650-1776
  Hudson *(G-7830)*

Phantom Fireworks Wstn Reg LLC........ G 330 746-1064
  Youngstown *(G-14916)*

Rozzi Company Inc............................ E 513 683-0620
  Loveland *(G-8649)*

FIRST AID SPLYS, WHOLESALE

Eleven 10 LLC.................................. F 888 216-4049
  Westlake *(G-14300)*

FISH & SEAFOOD WHOLESALERS

Alsatian Llc..................................... G 330 661-0600
  Medina *(G-9374)*

FISH FOOD

(G-0000) Company's Geographic Section entry number

Alsatian Llc .... G 330 661-0600
Medina (G-9374)

FITTINGS & ASSEMBLIES: Hose & Tube, Hydraulic Or Pneumatic

Ace Manufacturing Company .... E 513 541-2490
West Chester (G-13935)

Danfoss Power Solutions II LLC .... F 419 238-1190
Van Wert (G-13533)

Eaton Aeroquip LLC .... C 440 523-5000
Cleveland (G-3650)

Hombre Capital Inc .... F 440 838-5335
Brecksville (G-1470)

Industrial Connections Inc .... G 330 274-2155
Mantua (G-8869)

Malone Specialty Inc .... F 440 255-4200
Mentor (G-9559)

Mid-State Sales Inc .... G 330 744-2158
Youngstown (G-14900)

Mid-State Sales Inc .... D 614 864-1811
Columbus (G-5099)

Netherland Rubber Company .... F 513 733-0883
Cincinnati (G-2899)

Ohio Hydraulics Inc .... E 513 771-2590
Cincinnati (G-2924)

Omega 1 Inc .... F 216 663-8424
Willoughby (G-14501)

State Metal Hose Inc .... G 614 527-4700
Hilliard (G-7703)

Tylok International Inc .... D 216 261-7310
Cleveland (G-4436)

FITTINGS: Pipe

Adaptall America Inc .... F 330 425-4114
Twinsburg (G-13269)

Drainage Pipe & Fittings LLC .... G 419 538-6337
Ottawa (G-11033)

General Plug and Mfg Co .... C 440 926-2411
Grafton (G-7302)

Greater Cleve Pipe Ftting Fund .... F 216 524-8334
Cleveland (G-3795)

Mid-State Sales Inc .... D 614 864-1811
Columbus (G-5099)

Parker-Hannifin Corporation .... C 614 279-7070
Columbus (G-5174)

Parker-Hannifin Corporation .... C 937 456-5571
Eaton (G-6462)

Richards Industrials Inc .... D 513 533-5600
Cincinnati (G-3044)

SSP Fittings Corp .... D 330 425-4250
Twinsburg (G-13379)

Swagelok Company .... D 440 473-1050
Cleveland (G-4354)

Swagelok Company .... E 440 349-5652
Solon (G-12189)

Swagelok Company .... E 440 349-5836
Solon (G-12190)

Swagelok Company .... A 440 248-4600
Solon (G-12188)

TCH Industries Incorporated .... F 330 487-5155
Twinsburg (G-13383)

US Fittings Inc .... F 234 212-9420
Twinsburg (G-13391)

FITTINGS: Pipe, Fabricated

Phoenix Forge Group LLC .... B 800 848-6125
West Jefferson (G-14166)

Pipe Line Development Company .... D 440 871-5700
Strongsville (G-12585)

Pipe Products Inc .... C 513 587-7532
West Chester (G-14049)

FIXTURES & EQPT: Kitchen, Metal, Exc Cast Aluminum

Amtekco Industries LLC .... D 614 228-6590
Columbus (G-4708)

Washington Products Inc .... F 330 837-5101
Massillon (G-9252)

FIXTURES & EQPT: Kitchen, Porcelain Enameled

Anchor Hocking Holdings Inc .... A 740 687-2500
Columbus (G-4713)

FLAGS: Fabric

Annin & Co Inc .... C 740 622-4447
Coshocton (G-5447)

Flag Lady Inc .... G 614 263-1776
Columbus (G-4927)

FLAT GLASS: Construction

Imaging Sciences LLC .... G 440 975-9640
Willoughby (G-14468)

Pilkington North America Inc .... C 419 247-3731
Urbancrest (G-13483)

Pilkington North America Inc .... D 419 247-3731
Toledo (G-13098)

S R Door Inc .... D 740 927-3558
Hebron (G-7634)

Wt Acquisition Company Ltd .... E 513 577-7980
Cincinnati (G-3234)

FLAT GLASS: Float

Pilkington North America Inc .... B 419 247-3211
Rossford (G-11660)

FLAT GLASS: Picture

Knight Industries Corp .... F 419 478-8550
Toledo (G-13020)

FLAT GLASS: Plate, Polished & Rough

Guardian Fabrication LLC .... C 419 855-7706
Millbury (G-9962)

FLAT GLASS: Window, Clear & Colored

Sonalysts Inc .... E 937 429-9711
Beavercreek (G-984)

FLAVORS OR FLAVORING MATERIALS: Synthetic

Frutarom USA Holding Inc .... G 201 861-9500
West Chester (G-14121)

Givaudan Flavors Corporation .... E 513 948-3428
Cincinnati (G-2672)

Givaudan Flavors Corporation .... C 513 948-8000
Cincinnati (G-2673)

Givaudan Fragrances Corp .... D 513 948-3428
Cincinnati (G-2675)

FLIGHT RECORDERS

L3harris Electrodynamics Inc .... C 847 259-0740
Cincinnati (G-2310)

FLOOR COVERING STORES

Armstrong World Industries Inc .... E 614 771-9307
Hilliard (G-7669)

Wccv Floor Coverings LLC .... F 330 688-0114
Peninsula (G-11185)

FLOOR COVERING STORES: Carpets

Prints & Paints Flr Cvg Co Inc .... E 419 462-5663
Galion (G-7197)

Shaheen Oriental Rug Co Inc .... F 330 493-9000
Canton (G-2003)

Stanley Steemer Intl Inc .... C 614 764-2007
Dublin (G-6350)

FLOOR COVERINGS WHOLESALERS

Pfpc Enterprises Inc .... G 513 941-6200
Cincinnati (G-2960)

FLOOR COVERINGS: Aircraft & Automobile

Angstrom Fiber Englewood LLC .... E 734 756-1164
Englewood (G-6607)

FLOOR COVERINGS: Rubber

Dandy Products Inc .... G 513 625-3000
Goshen (G-7296)

Delphos Rubber Company .... E 419 692-3000
Delphos (G-6185)

Johnsonite Inc .... B 440 543-8916
Solon (G-12131)

Mameco International Inc .... F 216 752-4400
Cleveland (G-3984)

FLOORING & SIDING: Metal

Higgins Construction & Supply Co Inc .. F 937 364-2331
Hillsboro (G-7717)

FLOORING: Hardwood

Marsh Valley Forest Pdts Ltd .... G 440 632-1889
Middlefield (G-9807)

Prestige Enterprise Intl Inc .... D 513 469-6044
Blue Ash (G-1324)

Robbins Sports Surfaces LLC .... E 513 871-8988
Cincinnati (G-3051)

Timothy Whatman .... E 419 883-2443
Bellville (G-1143)

FLOORING: Rubber

Roppe Corporation .... B 419 435-8546
Fostoria (G-6998)

Tarkett Inc .... E 440 543-8916
Chagrin Falls (G-2187)

Tarkett Inc .... F 800 771-7476
Middlefield (G-9830)

Tarkett Inc .... F 614 349-1565
West Jefferson (G-14167)

Tarkett Inc .... D 800 899-8916
Solon (G-12192)

FLORIST: Flowers, Fresh

Cleveland Plant and Flower Co .... G 614 478-9900
Columbus (G-4811)

FLOWERS, FRESH, WHOLESALE

Cleveland Plant and Flower Co .... G 614 478-9900
Columbus (G-4811)

FLUID METERS & COUNTING DEVICES

Aqua Technology Group LLC .... G 513 298-1183
West Chester (G-13941)

Exact Equipment Corporation .... F 215 295-2000
Columbus (G-4640)

Reliable Manufacturing LLC .... E 740 756-9373
Carroll (G-2077)

Triplett Bluffton Corporation .... G 419 358-8750
Bluffton (G-1367)

FLUID POWER PUMPS & MOTORS

Aerocontrolex Group Inc .... D 216 291-6025
South Euclid (G-12216)

PRODUCT

Anchor Flange Company..........................D 513 527-3512
Cincinnati (G-2369)

Apph Wichita Inc...................................E 316 943-5752
Strongsville (G-12537)

Bergstrom Company Ltd Partnr.............F 440 232-2282
Cleveland (G-3415)

Dynamic Hydraulic Svcs Co LLC..........E 330 447-8967
Dover (G-6243)

Eaton Aeroquip LLC..............................A 419 891-7775
Maumee (G-9292)

Eaton Leasing Corporation.....................B 216 382-2292
Beachwood (G-916)

Emerson Process Management.............E 419 529-4311
Ontario (G-10949)

Fluid Power Solutions LLC....................G 614 777-8954
Hilliard (G-7682)

Force Control Industries Inc..................E 513 868-0900
Fairfield (G-6737)

Furukawa Rock Drill USA Co Ltd..........F 330 673-5826
Kent (G-8034)

Giant Industries Inc..............................E 419 531-4600
Toledo (G-12975)

Gorman-Rupp Company.........................C 419 755-1011
Mansfield (G-8794)

Hite Parts Exchange Inc.......................G 614 272-5115
Chillicothe (G-2258)

Hy-Production LLC.................................C 330 273-2400
Valley City (G-13499)

Hydraulic Parts Store Inc.....................G 330 364-6667
New Philadelphia (G-10449)

Hydraulic Products Inc..........................G 440 946-4575
Willoughby (G-14466)

Midwest Tool & Engineering Co.............G
Dayton (G-5883)

Parker Hannifin Partner B LLC..............G 216 896-3000
Cleveland (G-4140)

Parker Royalty Partnership....................G 216 896-3000
Cleveland (G-4141)

Parker-Hannifin Corporation..................F 330 261-1618
Berlin Center (G-1202)

Parker-Hannifin Corporation..................C 419 644-4311
Metamora (G-9658)

Parker-Hannifin Corporation..................G 513 847-1758
West Chester (G-14041)

Permco Inc...C 330 626-2801
Streetsboro (G-12515)

Pfpc Enterprises Inc.............................G 513 941-6200
Cincinnati (G-2960)

Quad Fluid Dynamics Inc......................F 330 220-3005
Brunswick (G-1610)

Radocy Inc...F 419 666-4400
Rossford (G-11661)

Robeck Fluid Power Co.........................D 330 562-1140
Aurora (G-687)

Semtorq Inc...F 330 487-0600
Twinsburg (G-13377)

Starkey Machinery Inc...........................E 419 468-2560
Galion (G-7199)

Sunset Industries Inc............................E 440 306-8284
Mentor (G-9631)

Swagelok Company................................E 440 349-5836
Solon (G-12190)

Toth Industries Inc................................D 419 729-4669
Toledo (G-13164)

Trane Technologies Company LLC........E 419 633-6800
Bryan (G-1665)

Y O H Inc...E 614 488-2861
Columbus (G-5377)

FLUID POWER VALVES & HOSE FITTINGS

Alkon Corporation..................................D 419 355-9111
Fremont (G-7090)

Amfm Inc..F 440 953-4545
Willoughby (G-14419)

Cho Bedford Inc.....................................D 330 343-8896
Dover (G-6233)

Dixon Valve & Coupling Co LLC............F 330 425-3000
Twinsburg (G-13296)

Eaton Aeroquip LLC..............................A 419 891-7775
Maumee (G-9292)

Freudenberg-Nok General Partnr...........C 419 427-5221
Findlay (G-6868)

Hydac Technology Corp.........................F 610 266-0100
Wooster (G-14649)

Hydraulic Parts Store Inc.....................G 330 364-6667
New Philadelphia (G-10449)

Ic-Fluid Power Inc.................................F 419 661-8811
Rossford (G-11658)

Kirtland Capital Partners LP..................E 216 593-0100
Beachwood (G-924)

Parker-Hannifin Corporation..................C 937 456-5571
Eaton (G-6462)

Parker-Hannifin Corporation..................B 440 943-5700
Wickliffe (G-14389)

Pima Valve LLC.....................................D 330 337-9535
Salem (G-11804)

Pressure Connections Corp...................D 614 863-6930
Columbus (G-5204)

Quality Machining and Mfg Inc..............F 419 899-2543
Sherwood (G-11976)

SSP Fittings Corp..................................D 330 425-4250
Twinsburg (G-13379)

Superior Holding LLC.............................G 216 651-9400
Cleveland (G-4344)

Superior Products LLC...........................D 216 651-9400
Cleveland (G-4347)

Swagelok Company................................E 440 349-5836
Solon (G-12190)

Thogus Products Company.....................D 440 933-8850
Avon Lake (G-771)

Transdigm Inc..E 216 291-6025
Cleveland (G-4411)

Winzeler Manufacturing Company..........F 419 485-8147
Montpelier (G-10137)

Zaytran Inc...E 440 324-2814
Elyria (G-6604)

FOAM RUBBER

Archem America Inc..............................F 419 294-6304
Upper Sandusky (G-13433)

ISO Technologies Inc............................F 740 928-0084
Hebron (G-7620)

Ohio Foam Corporation.........................G 614 252-4877
Columbus (G-5145)

Ohio Foam Corporation.........................F 419 492-2151
New Washington (G-10482)

Ohio Foam Corporation.........................E 330 799-4553
Youngstown (G-14906)

Pfp Holdings LLC..................................A 419 647-4191
Spencerville (G-12239)

Precision Fab Products Inc...................G 937 526-5681
Versailles (G-13602)

FOAMS & RUBBER, WHOLESALE

Acor Orthopaedic LLC...........................E 216 662-4500
Cleveland (G-3293)

Johnson Bros Rubber Co Inc................E 419 752-4814
Greenwich (G-7362)

Johnson Bros Rubber Co.......................D 419 853-4122
West Salem (G-14188)

Tahoma Enterprises Inc.........................D 330 745-9016
Barberton (G-840)

Tahoma Rubber & Plastics Inc..............D 330 745-9016
Ashland (G-579)

FOIL & LEAF: Metal

Avery Dennison Corporation..................D 440 639-3900
Mentor (G-9490)

Avery Dennison Corporation..................A 440 534-6000
Mentor (G-9489)

CCL Label Inc.......................................E 216 676-2703
Cleveland (G-3480)

CCL Label Inc.......................................D 440 878-7000
Strongsville (G-12548)

Compco Quaker Mfg Inc........................E 330 482-0200
Salem (G-11772)

Quaker Mfg Corp...................................C 330 332-4631
Salem (G-11807)

Wieland Metal Svcs Foils LLC...............D 330 823-1700
Alliance (G-417)

FOOD PRDTS, BREAKFAST: Cereal, Oatmeal

Niese Farms..G 419 347-1204
Crestline (G-5504)

FOOD PRDTS, BREAKFAST: Cereal, Wheat Flakes

General Mills Inc...................................F 419 269-3100
Toledo (G-12974)

FOOD PRDTS, CANNED OR FRESH PACK: Fruit Juices

Fremont Company..................................E 419 363-2924
Rockford (G-11630)

Refresco Us Inc.....................................C 937 790-1400
Carlisle (G-2072)

FOOD PRDTS, CANNED: Baby Food

Baxters North America Inc.....................E 513 552-7728
Blue Ash (G-1249)

Baxters North America Inc.....................D 513 552-7718
West Chester (G-14106)

Baxters North America Inc.....................E 513 552-7485
Cincinnati (G-2404)

FOOD PRDTS, CANNED: Barbecue Sauce

Annarino Foods Ltd...............................E 937 274-3663
Dayton (G-5659)

Dominion Liquid Tech LLC......................E 513 272-2824
Cincinnati (G-2557)

FOOD PRDTS, CANNED: Beans & Bean Sprouts

B&G Foods Inc......................................D 513 482-8226
Cincinnati (G-2397)

FOOD PRDTS, CANNED: Fruit Juices, Fresh

Country Pure Foods Inc.........................C 330 753-2293
Akron (G-108)

Gwj Liquidation Inc...............................F 216 475-5770
Cleveland (G-3802)

Meiers Wine Cellars Inc........................E 513 891-2900
Cincinnati (G-2861)

Ohio Pure Foods Inc.............................D 330 753-2293
Akron (G-254)

FOOD PRDTS, CANNED: Fruits

B&G Foods Inc......................................D 513 482-8226
Cincinnati (G-2397)

Fry Foods Inc..E 419 448-0831
Tiffin (G-12784)

JES Foods Inc.......................................F 216 883-8987
Medina (G-9415)

JES Foods/Celina Inc............................F 419 586-7446
Celina (G-2112)

Milos Whole World Gourmet LLC.......... G 740 589-6456
Nelsonville (G-10319)

Pillsbury Company LLC........................... D 419 845-3751
Caledonia (G-1733)

Pillsbury Company LLC........................... D 740 286-2170
Wellston (G-13909)

Robert Rothschild Farm LLC.................. F 855 969-8050
West Chester (G-14069)

Rosebuds Ranch and Garden LLC........ F 937 214-1801
Covington (G-5499)

Smucker International Inc....................... F 330 682-3000
Orrville (G-11010)

The Fremont Kraut Company .... F 419 332-6481
Fremont (G-7135)

Trevor Clatterbuck................................. G 330 359-2129
Wilmot (G-14595)

Two Grndmthers Gourmet Kit LLC........ G 614 746-0888
Reynoldsburg (G-11585)

Welch Foods Inc A Cooperative.............. D 513 632-5610
Cincinnati (G-3215)

Clovervale Farms LLC........................... D 440 960-0146
Amherst (G-444)

FOOD PRDTS, CANNED: Jams, Including Imitation

Yoders Fine Foods LLC.......................... F 740 668-4961
Gambier (G-7215)

FOOD PRDTS, CANNED: Jams, Jellies & Preserves

Coopers Mill Inc..................................... G 419 562-4215
Bucyrus (G-1676)

J M Smucker Company........................... A 330 682-3000
Orrville (G-10987)

Nu Pet Company.................................... E 330 682-3000
Orrville (G-10998)

Smucker Foodservice Inc....................... G 877 858-3855
Orrville (G-11009)

Smucker Manufacturing Inc................... G 888 550-9555
Orrville (G-11011)

Smucker Retail Foods Inc...................... F 330 684-1500
Orrville (G-11013)

FOOD PRDTS, CANNED: Jellies, Edible, Including Imitation

Inter American Products Inc.................... D 800 645-2233
Cincinnati (G-2748)

FOOD PRDTS, CANNED: Puddings, Exc Meat

Clovervale Farms LLC........................... D 440 960-0146
Amherst (G-444)

FOOD PRDTS, CANNED: Spaghetti & Other Pasta Sauce

Bellisio Foods Inc.................................. C 740 286-5505
Jackson (G-7940)

RC Industries Inc................................... E 330 879-5486
Navarre (G-10313)

FOOD PRDTS, CANNED: Tomato Sauce.

Kraft Heinz Company............................. A 330 837-8331
Massillon (G-9213)

FOOD PRDTS, CANNED: Vegetables

Bfc Inc... E 330 364-6645
Dover (G-6230)

FOOD PRDTS, CONFECTIONERY, WHOLESALE: Candy

Bendon Inc.. D 419 207-3600
Ashland (G-521)

Gorant Chocolatier LLC.......................... C 330 726-8821
Boardman (G-1372)

Robert E McGrath Inc............................ F 440 572-7747
Strongsville (G-12593)

Smithco Distributing.............................. E 419 367-7685
Liberty Center (G-8376)

Sweeties Olympia Treats LLC................. F 440 572-7747
Strongsville (G-12608)

FOOD PRDTS, CONFECTIONERY, WHOLESALE: Pretzels

Mike-Sells West Virginia Inc................... D 937 228-9400
Dayton (G-5886)

FOOD PRDTS, CONFECTIONERY, WHOLESALE: Snack Foods

Hen of Woods LLC................................. G 513 954-8871
Cincinnati (G-2716)

Mike-Sells Potato Chip Co...................... E 937 228-9400
Dayton (G-5885)

Shearers Foods LLC.............................. A 800 428-6843
Massillon (G-9241)

FOOD PRDTS, FROZEN: Ethnic Foods, NEC

Sunrise Foods Inc................................. E 614 276-2880
Columbus (G-5297)

Superb Bakehouse Inc........................... F 614 302-7242
Groveport (G-7451)

FOOD PRDTS, FROZEN: Fruit Juice, Concentrates

Beverages Holdings LLC........................ A 513 483-3300
Blue Ash (G-1252)

Country Pure Foods Inc.......................... C 330 753-2293
Akron (G-108)

FOOD PRDTS, FROZEN: Fruit Juices

Simply Unique Snacks LLC..................... G 513 223-7736
Cincinnati (G-3092)

FOOD PRDTS, FROZEN: Fruits

National Frt Vgtable Tech Corp.............. F 740 400-4055
Columbus (G-5121)

FOOD PRDTS, FROZEN: Fruits & Vegetables

Heinz Foreign Investment Co.................. G 330 837-8331
Massillon (G-9200)

HJ Heinz Company LP............................ D 330 837-8331
Massillon (G-9202)

FOOD PRDTS, FROZEN: Fruits, Juices & Vegetables

Nestle Prepared Foods Company........... B 440 349-5757
Solon (G-12157)

Ohios Best Juice Company LLC............. F 440 258-0834
Reynoldsburg (G-11577)

FOOD PRDTS, WHOLESALE: Baking Splys

Cassanos Inc... E 937 294-8400
Dayton (G-5695)

FOOD PRDTS, WHOLESALE: Beverages, Exc Coffee & Tea

G & J Pepsi-Cola Bottlers Inc................. E 740 593-3366
Athens (G-640)

FOOD PRDTS, WHOLESALE: Chocolate

Coblentz Family Brands Inc.................... E 330 893-2995
Walnut Creek (G-13693)

FOOD PRDTS, WHOLESALE: Coffee, Green Or Roasted

Ohio Coffee Collaborative Ltd................ F 614 564-9852
Columbus (G-5139)

FOOD PRDTS, WHOLESALE: Condiments

Kerry Inc... E 760 685-2548
Byesville (G-1715)

FOOD PRDTS, WHOLESALE: Cookies

Bendon Inc.. D 419 207-3600
Ashland (G-521)

FOOD PRDTS, WHOLESALE: Dried or Canned Foods

James C Robinson................................. G 513 969-7482
Cincinnati (G-2760)

Tarrier Foods Corp................................ E 614 876-8594
Columbus (G-5310)

FOOD PRDTS, WHOLESALE: Grain Elevators

Fort Recovery Equity Inc........................ E 419 375-4119
Fort Recovery (G-6963)

Keystone Cooperative Inc....................... G 937 884-5526
Verona (G-13591)

Minster Farmers Coop Exch................... D 419 628-4705
Minster (G-10061)

Mullet Enterprises Inc............................ G 330 852-4681
Sugarcreek (G-12643)

Pettisville Grain Co............................... E 419 446-2547
Pettisville (G-11285)

Sunrise Cooperative Inc........................ G 419 628-4705
Minster (G-10066)

FOOD PRDTS, WHOLESALE: Grains

Andersons Inc....................................... G 419 536-0460
Toledo (G-12881)

Andersons Inc....................................... C 419 893-5050
Maumee (G-9261)

Cooper Hatchery Inc.............................. C 419 594-3325
Oakwood (G-10897)

Countyline Co-Op Inc............................ F 419 287-3241
Pemberville (G-11174)

Hansen-Mueller Co................................ G 419 729-5535
Toledo (G-12986)

Legacy Farmers Cooperative................ F 419 423-2611
Findlay (G-6884)

Mid-Wood Inc.. F 419 257-3331
North Baltimore (G-10614)

Premier Feeds LLC................................ G 937 584-2411
Sabina (G-11683)

Simmons Feed & Supply LLC................ E 800 754-1228
Salem (G-11812)

Van Tilburg Farms Inc........................... F 419 586-3077
Celina (G-2126)

FOOD PRDTS, WHOLESALE: Juices

Grace Juice Company LLC..................... F 614 398-6879
Westerville (G-14261)

FOOD PRDTS, WHOLESALE: Salt, Edible

Morton Salt Inc...................................... C 330 925-3015
Rittman (G-11625)

FOOD PRDTS, WHOLESALE: Specialty

Amerihua Intl Entps Inc.......................... G 740 549-0300
Lewis Center (G-8321)

PRODUCT

Cheese Holdings Inc..................E 330 893-2479
Millersburg (G-9977)

JM Smucker LLC..........................D 330 682-3000
Orrville (G-10990)

FOOD PRDTS, WHOLESALE: Water, Distilled

Distillata Company.......................D 216 771-2900
Cleveland (G-3619)

Rambasek Realty Inc.....................F 937 228-1189
Dayton (G-5974)

FOOD PRDTS: Animal & marine fats & oils

Archer-Daniels-Midland Company........E 419 435-6633
Fostoria (G-6975)

Cargill Incorporated....................D 937 498-4555
Sidney (G-12000)

Darling Ingredients Inc.................G 972 717-0300
Cincinnati (G-2541)

Darling Ingredients Inc.................G 216 651-9300
Cleveland (G-3599)

Darling Ingredients Inc.................G 216 351-3440
Cleveland (G-3600)

Fiske Brothers Refining Co..............D 419 691-2491
Toledo (G-12965)

Griffin Industries LLC..................F 513 549-0041
Blue Ash (G-1279)

Holmes By-Products Co Inc...............E 330 893-2322
Millersburg (G-9985)

Werner G Smith Inc......................F 216 861-3676
Cleveland (G-4501)

FOOD PRDTS: Bread Crumbs, Exc Made In Bakeries

Pepperidge Farm Incorporated............G 419 933-2611
Willard (G-14407)

FOOD PRDTS: Chicken, Processed, Cooked

Roots Poultry Inc.......................G 419 332-0041
Fremont (G-7130)

FOOD PRDTS: Chicken, Processed, Fresh

Gerber Farm Division LLC................G 800 362-7381
Orrville (G-10982)

Gerber Poultry LLC......................B 330 857-2731
Kidron (G-8127)

Rcf Kitchens Indiana LLC................G 765 478-6600
Dayton (G-5976)

FOOD PRDTS: Chicken, Processed, Frozen

Imex Bz LLC.............................F 786 866-8798
Orrville (G-10986)

FOOD PRDTS: Chocolate Bars, Solid

Fannie May Confections Inc..............A 330 494-0833
North Canton (G-10638)

FOOD PRDTS: Cocoa, Powdered

Benjamin P Forbes Company...............F 440 838-4400
Broadview Heights (G-1499)

FOOD PRDTS: Coffee

Altraserv LLC...........................G 614 889-2500
Plain City (G-11393)

Generations Coffee Company LLC..........F 440 546-0901
Brecksville (G-1467)

Inter American Products Inc.............D 800 645-2233
Cincinnati (G-2748)

Kidd Properties LLC.....................G 513 779-6278
West Chester (G-14020)

Mc Concepts Llc.........................G 330 933-6402
Canton (G-1941)

Ohio Coffee Collaborative Ltd...........F 614 564-9852
Columbus (G-5139)

Rosebuds Ranch and Garden LLC...........F 937 214-1801
Covington (G-5499)

FOOD PRDTS: Corn Oil Prdts

Poet Biorefining Marion LLC.............E 740 383-4400
Marion (G-8990)

FOOD PRDTS: Dips, Exc Cheese & Sour Cream Based

Gomez Salsa LLC.........................F 513 314-1978
Cincinnati (G-2683)

Lakeview Farms LLC......................C 419 695-9925
Delphos (G-6190)

Oasis Mditerranean Cuisine Inc..........E 419 269-1459
Toledo (G-13067)

FOOD PRDTS: Dough, Pizza, Prepared

Crestar Crusts Inc......................F 740 335-4813
Wshngtn Ct Hs (G-14736)

FOOD PRDTS: Doughs, Frozen Or Refrig From Purchased Flour

Mid American Ventures Inc...............F 216 524-0974
Cleveland (G-4031)

FOOD PRDTS: Dressings, Salad, Raw & Cooked Exc Dry Mixes

Annarino Foods Ltd......................E 937 274-3663
Dayton (G-5659)

Consumer Guild Foods Inc................G 419 726-3406
Toledo (G-12931)

Lancaster Colony Corporation............F 614 792-9774
Dublin (G-6317)

Lancaster Colony Corporation............E 614 224-7141
Westerville (G-14218)

Lancaster Glass Corporation.............C 614 224-7141
Westerville (G-14219)

Lbzb Restaurants Inc....................F 567 413-4700
Bowling Green (G-1424)

Mark Grzianis St Treats Ex Inc..........F 330 414-6266
Kent (G-8049)

Tmarzetti Company.......................C 614 846-2232
Westerville (G-14237)

Tulkoff Food Products Ohio LLC..........G 410 864-0523
Cincinnati (G-3176)

FOOD PRDTS: Dried & Dehydrated Fruits, Vegetables & Soup Mix

Appalachia Freeze Dry Co LLC............F 740 412-0169
Richmond Dale (G-11606)

Bosc & Brie.............................F 614 985-2215
Columbus (G-4769)

Hayden Valley Foods Inc.................E 614 539-7233
Grove City (G-7390)

Hirzel Canning Company..................E 419 693-0531
Northwood (G-10803)

FOOD PRDTS: Edible fats & oils

Cincinnati Biorefining Corp.............F 513 482-8800
Cincinnati (G-2471)

Cincinnati Renewable Fuels LLC..........D 513 482-8800
Cincinnati (G-2484)

Wileys Finest LLC.......................C 740 622-1072
Coshocton (G-5478)

FOOD PRDTS: Emulsifiers

Generations Ace Inc.....................G 440 835-4872
Bay Village (G-902)

Lasenor Usa LLC.........................F 800 754-1228
Salem (G-11793)

FOOD PRDTS: Flour

Mennel Milling Company..................F 419 307-9657
Fostoria (G-6991)

Mennel Milling Company..................F 419 294-2337
Upper Sandusky (G-13448)

Mennel Milling Company..................G 419 458-3041
Wharton (G-14351)

The Mennel Milling Company..............E 419 435-8151
Fostoria (G-7003)

FOOD PRDTS: Flour & Other Grain Mill Products

Archer-Daniels-Midland Company........E 419 435-6633
Fostoria (G-6975)

Archer-Daniels-Midland Company........G 419 705-3292
Toledo (G-12884)

Bunge North America East LLC............G 419 483-5340
Bellevue (G-1121)

Cargill Incorporated....................E 937 236-1971
Dayton (G-5693)

Countyline Co-Op Inc....................F 419 287-3241
Pemberville (G-11174)

Dik Jaxon Products Co Inc...............F 937 890-7350
Dayton (G-5748)

Hansen-Mueller Co.......................G 419 729-5535
Toledo (G-12986)

I Dream of Cakes........................G 937 533-6024
Eaton (G-6455)

Legacy Farmers Cooperative..............F 419 423-2611
Findlay (G-6884)

Mennel Milling Company..................D 419 436-5130
Fostoria (G-6989)

Mennel Milling Company..................F 419 435-8151
Fostoria (G-6990)

Minster Farmers Coop Exch...............D 419 628-4705
Minster (G-10061)

Mullet Enterprises Inc..................G 330 852-4681
Sugarcreek (G-12643)

Pettisville Grain Co....................E 419 446-2547
Pettisville (G-11285)

Pillsbury Company LLC...................D 419 845-3751
Caledonia (G-1733)

Pillsbury Company LLC...................D 740 286-2170
Wellston (G-13909)

Premier Feeds LLC.......................G 937 584-2411
Sabina (G-11683)

Sunrise Cooperative Inc.................G 419 628-4705
Minster (G-10066)

FOOD PRDTS: Flour Mixes & Doughs

Abitec Corporation......................E 614 429-6464
Columbus (G-4665)

Athens Foods Inc........................C 216 676-8500
Cleveland (G-3384)

Rich Products Corporation...............C 614 771-1117
Hilliard (G-7699)

FOOD PRDTS: Flour, Blended From Purchased Flour

Busken Bakery Inc.......................D 513 871-2114
Cincinnati (G-2434)

Fleetchem LLC...........................F 513 539-1111
Monroe (G-10105)

FOOD PRDTS: Flours & Flour Mixes, From Purchased Flour

Bakemark USA LLC...................................F 440 323-5100
Elyria (G-6501)

FOOD PRDTS: Fruits & Vegetables, Pickled

Kaiser Pickles LLC...............................F 513 621-2053
Cincinnati (G-2781)

Kaiser Pickles LLC...............................G 513 621-2053
Cincinnati (G-2780)

FOOD PRDTS: Ice, Cubes

Home City Ice Company.......................G 513 851-4040
Cincinnati (G-2729)

Zygo Inc...G 513 281-0888
Cincinnati (G-3245)

FOOD PRDTS: Mixes, Cake, From Purchased Flour

Procter & Gamble Mfg Co....................F 513 983-1100
Cincinnati (G-3002)

FOOD PRDTS: Mixes, Flour

1-2-3 Gluten Free Inc...........................G 216 378-9233
Chagrin Falls (G-2133)

FOOD PRDTS: Mixes, Sauces, Dry

Whitmore Productions Inc.....................G 216 752-3960
Warrensville Heights (G-13819)

FOOD PRDTS: Mustard, Prepared

Woeber Mustard Mfg Co.......................C 937 323-6281
Springfield (G-12394)

FOOD PRDTS: Oils & Fats, Animal

Wileys Finest LLC.................................C 740 622-1072
Coshocton (G-5478)

FOOD PRDTS: Olive Oil

Liquid Manufacturing Solutions............. E 937 401-0821
Franklin (G-7031)

FOOD PRDTS: Pasta, Uncooked, Packaged With Other Ingredients

Food Designs Inc..................................F 216 651-9221
Cleveland (G-3733)

FOOD PRDTS: Peanut Butter

Krema Group Inc...................................F 614 889-4824
Plain City (G-11413)

Procter & Gamble Mfg Co....................F 513 983-1100
Cincinnati (G-3002)

FOOD PRDTS: Pizza Doughs From Purchased Flour

Cassanos Inc..E 937 294-8400
Dayton (G-5695)

FOOD PRDTS: Pork Rinds

Evans Food Group Ltd..........................F 626 636-8110
Portsmouth (G-11465)

Evans Food Group Ltd..........................G 740 285-3078
Portsmouth (G-11466)

Rudolph Foods Company Inc...............C 909 383-7463
Lima (G-8446)

White Feather Foods Inc.......................G 419 738-8975
Wapakoneta (G-13730)

FOOD PRDTS: Potato Chips & Other Potato-Based Snacks

Advanced Green Tech Inc.....................G 614 397-8130
Plain City (G-11392)

Ballreich Bros Inc.................................C 419 447-1814
Tiffin (G-12777)

Conns Potato Chip Co Inc.....................E 740 452-4615
Zanesville (G-15008)

Frito-Lay North America Inc..................D 330 477-7009
Canton (G-1895)

Grippo Potato Chip Co Inc....................F 513 923-1900
Cincinnati (G-2694)

Herr Foods Incorporated.......................D 740 773-8282
Chillicothe (G-2256)

Herr Foods Incorporated.......................F 800 344-3777
Chillicothe (G-2257)

Jones Potato Chip Co............................E 419 529-9424
Mansfield (G-8808)

Mike-Sells Potato Chip Co.....................E 937 228-9400
Dayton (G-5885)

Mike-Sells West Virginia Inc.................D 937 228-9400
Dayton (G-5886)

Mumfords Potato Chips & Deli...............G 937 653-3491
Urbana (G-13474)

FOOD PRDTS: Poultry, Processed, Frozen

Martin-Brower Company LLC................C 513 773-2301
West Chester (G-14027)

FOOD PRDTS: Salad Oils, Refined Vegetable, Exc Corn

Inter American Products Inc..................D 800 645-2233
Cincinnati (G-2748)

FOOD PRDTS: Sandwiches

Advancperre Foods Holdings Inc...........D 513 428-5699
West Chester (G-14098)

Caruso Foods LLC................................D 513 860-9200
Cincinnati (G-2440)

White Castle System Inc.......................D 513 563-2290
Cincinnati (G-3223)

FOOD PRDTS: Seasonings & Spices

Alimento Ventures Inc...........................F 855 510-2866
Blue Ash (G-1245)

Hen of Woods LLC................................G 513 954-8871
Cincinnati (G-2716)

National Foods Packaging Inc...............E 216 622-2740
Cleveland (G-4060)

Rosebuds Ranch and Garden LLC.........F 937 214-1801
Covington (G-5499)

Savor Seasonings LLC..........................F 513 732-2333
Batavia (G-887)

FOOD PRDTS: Shortening & Solid Edible Fats

Procter & Gamble Mfg Co....................F 513 983-1100
Cincinnati (G-3002)

FOOD PRDTS: Starch, Corn

Cargill Incorporated..............................E 937 236-1971
Dayton (G-5693)

FOOD PRDTS: Sugar

Domino Foods Inc.................................C 216 432-3222
Cleveland (G-3625)

FOOD PRDTS: Sugar, Beet

Michigan Sugar Company......................F 419 332-9931
Fremont (G-7123)

FOOD PRDTS: Syrup, Maple

Natures Health Food LLC......................F 419 260-9265
Mount Victory (G-10269)

FOOD PRDTS: Syrups

B&G Foods Inc......................................D 513 482-8226
Cincinnati (G-2397)

J M Smucker Company...........................A 330 682-3000
Orrville (G-10987)

Nu Pet Company....................................E 330 682-3000
Orrville (G-10998)

Smartsoda Holdings Inc........................G 888 998-9668
Cleveland (G-4307)

Smucker International Inc......................F 330 682-3000
Orrville (G-11010)

FOOD PRDTS: Tea

US Wellness LLC...................................G 216 772-3364
Cleveland (G-4452)

FOOD PRDTS: Tofu, Exc Frozen Desserts

Foodies Vegan Ltd................................F 513 487-3037
Cincinnati (G-2632)

FOOD PRDTS: Turkey, Slaughtered & Dressed

Whitewater Processing LLC...................D 513 367-4133
Harrison (G-7572)

FOOD PRDTS: Vinegar

Woeber Mustard Mfg Co.......................C 937 323-6281
Springfield (G-12394)

FOOD PRODUCTS MACHINERY

Abj Equipfix LLC...................................E 419 684-5236
Castalia (G-2093)

Acreo Inc..G 513 734-3327
Amelia (G-426)

American Pan Company.........................C 937 652-3232
Urbana (G-13457)

Binos Inc..G 330 938-0888
Sebring (G-11892)

Biro Manufacturing Company................F 419 798-4451
North Canton (G-10630)

Chemineer Inc.......................................C 937 454-3200
Dayton (G-5700)

Christy Machine Company......................G 419 332-6451
Fremont (G-7098)

Cleveland Range LLC............................C 216 481-4900
Cleveland (G-3522)

Crescent Metal Products Inc..................C 440 350-1100
Mentor (G-9507)

Edge Exponential LLC...........................F 614 226-4421
Columbus (G-4898)

G & S Metal Products Co Inc.................C 216 441-0700
Cleveland (G-3748)

G F Frank and Sons Inc........................F 513 870-9075
West Chester (G-14002)

Gold Medal Products Co........................B 513 769-7676
Cincinnati (G-2680)

Harry C Lobalzo & Sons Inc..................E 330 666-6758
Akron (G-172)

Hobart LLC..D 937 332-2797
Piqua (G-11355)

Hobart LLC..E 937 332-3000
Troy (G-13225)

Hobart LLC..D 937 332-3000
Troy (G-13226)

Innovative Controls Corp.......................F 419 691-6684
Maumee (G-9298)

ITW Food Equipment Group LLC...........C 937 393-4271
Hillsboro (G-7719)

ITW Food Equipment Group LLC...........A 937 332-2396
Troy (G-13231)

PRODUCT

Jbt Marel Corporation.............................. C 513 433-2500
Middletown *(G-9868)*

Jbt Marel Corporation.............................. B 419 626-0304
Sandusky *(G-11846)*

JE Grote Company Inc....................... D 614 868-8414
Columbus *(G-5035)*

Lima Sheet Metal Mch & Mfg Inc............. F 419 229-1161
Lima *(G-8426)*

Maverick Innvtive Slutions LLC............. D 419 281-7944
Ashland *(G-550)*

Meyer Company.................................. C 216 587-3400
Chagrin Falls *(G-2148)*

N Wasserstrom & Sons Inc .... C 614 228-5550
Columbus *(G-5118)*

National Oilwell Varco LP................. C 937 454-4660
Dayton *(G-5901)*

Nemco Food Equipment Ltd................. D 419 542-7751
Hicksville *(G-7649)*

Nestle Usa Inc .... C 440 349-5757
Solon *(G-12161)*

Norse Dairy Systems Inc .... C 614 294-4931
Columbus *(G-5128)*

Omar Associates LLC .... G 419 426-0610
Attica *(G-657)*

Peerless Stove & Mfg Co .... F 419 625-4514
Sandusky *(G-11865)*

Premier Industries Inc...................... E 513 271-2550
Cincinnati *(G-2979)*

Processall Inc.................................. F 513 771-2266
Cincinnati *(G-2986)*

R and J Corporation......................... E 440 871-6009
Westlake *(G-14326)*

RS Industries Inc............................. G 216 351-8200
Brooklyn Heights *(G-1539)*

Sarka Bros Machining Inc .... G 419 532-2393
Kalida *(G-8006)*

Sidney Manufacturing Company.......... E 937 492-4154
Sidney *(G-12053)*

Siebtechnik Tema Inc .... E 513 489-7811
Cincinnati *(G-3088)*

Sir Steak Machinery Inc.................... E 419 526-9181
Mansfield *(G-8852)*

Sterling Process Equipment .... E 614 868-5151
Columbus *(G-5292)*

Tomlinson Industries LLC................. C 216 587-3400
Cleveland *(G-4399)*

Wolf Machine Company..................... E 513 791-5194
Blue Ash *(G-1352)*

FOOD STORES: Convenience, Chain

United Dairy Farmers Inc.................. C 513 396-8700
Cincinnati *(G-3181)*

FOOD STORES: Convenience, Independent

Whitacre Enterprises Inc.................. G 740 934-2331
Graysville *(G-7322)*

FOOD STORES: Delicatessen

Baltic Country Meats........................ G 330 897-7025
Baltic *(G-776)*

Bread Kneads Inc............................. G 419 422-3863
Findlay *(G-6845)*

Fragapane Bakeries Inc.................... G 440 779-6050
North Olmsted *(G-10721)*

Investors United Inc......................... G 419 473-8942
Toledo *(G-13008)*

Mumfords Potato Chips & Deli........... G 937 653-3491
Urbana *(G-13474)*

Zygo Inc.. G 513 281-0888
Cincinnati *(G-3245)*

FOOD STORES: Grocery, Independent

Brinkman Turkey Farms Inc................ F 419 365-5127
Findlay *(G-6846)*

C J Kraft Enterprises Inc................... G..... 740 653-9606
Lancaster *(G-8184)*

Dioguardis Italian Foods Inc............... F 330 492-3777
Canton *(G-1883)*

Lariccias Italian Foods Inc................ F 330 729-0222
Youngstown *(G-14887)*

Troyers Trail Bologna Inc.................. G 330 893-2414
Dundee *(G-6370)*

FOOD STORES: Supermarkets, Chain

Heinens Inc...................................... C 330 562-5297
Aurora *(G-673)*

Riesbeck Food Markets Inc................ C 740 695-3401
Saint Clairsville *(G-11709)*

FOOTWEAR, WHOLESALE: Boots

Hudson Leather Ltd.......................... G 419 485-8531
Pioneer *(G-11321)*

FOOTWEAR, WHOLESALE: Shoes

Careismatic Brands LLC .... G 561 843-8727
Groveport *(G-7428)*

Careismatic Brands LLC .... G..... 614 497-5289
Groveport *(G-7429)*

Georgia-Boot Inc.............................. D 740 753-1951
Nelsonville *(G-10317)*

FOOTWEAR: Cut Stock

Hudson Leather Ltd.......................... G 419 485-8531
Pioneer *(G-11321)*

Remington Products Company............ D 330 335-1571
Upper Arlington *(G-13432)*

FORESTRY RELATED EQPT

Jrb Family Holdings Inc..................... C
Wooster *(G-14656)*

Morbark LLC.................................... C 330 264-8699
Wooster *(G-14666)*

FORGINGS: Aircraft, Ferrous

Sifco Industries Inc.......................... D 216 881-8600
Cleveland *(G-4299)*

FORGINGS: Aluminum

Howmet Aerospace Inc...................... A 216 641-3600
Newburgh Heights *(G-10543)*

Howmet Aerospace Inc...................... E 330 544-7633
Niles *(G-10590)*

FORGINGS: Automotive & Internal Combustion Engine

American Cold Forge LLC................... E 419 836-1062
Northwood *(G-10802)*

Presrite Corporation........................ B 216 441-5990
Cleveland *(G-4193)*

R E H Inc.. G 330 876-2775
Kinsman *(G-8142)*

FORGINGS: Construction Or Mining Eqpt, Ferrous

Dayton Superior Corporation.............. C 937 866-0711
Miamisburg *(G-9687)*

Pumpco Concrete Pumping LLC........... F 740 809-1473
Johnstown *(G-7997)*

Rudd Equipment Company Inc............. E 513 321-7833
Cincinnati *(G-3056)*

FORGINGS: Iron & Steel

Forge Products Corporation................ E 216 231-2600
Cleveland *(G-3736)*

S&V Industries Inc............................ E 330 666-1986
Medina *(G-9443)*

FORGINGS: Machinery, Ferrous

Dayton Forging Heat Treating.............. D 937 253-4126
Dayton *(G-5726)*

Wodin Inc.. E 440 439-4222
Cleveland *(G-4513)*

FORGINGS: Machinery, Nonferrous

Mp Technologies Inc......................... F 440 838-4466
Ashland *(G-554)*

FORGINGS: Metal , Ornamental, Ferrous

Alliance Forging Group LLC................ G 330 680-4861
Akron *(G-52)*

FORGINGS: Nonferrous

Canton Drop Forge Inc...................... B 330 477-4511
Canton *(G-1854)*

Colfor Manufacturing Inc................... B 330 623-7814
Malvern *(G-8748)*

Edward W Daniel LLC........................ F 440 647-1960
Wellington *(G-13885)*

Forge Products Corporation................ E 216 231-2600
Cleveland *(G-3736)*

Powers and Sons LLC....................... G 419 737-2373
Pioneer *(G-11325)*

Thyssnkrupp Rothe Erde USA Inc......... C 330 562-4000
Aurora *(G-689)*

Turbine Eng Cmpnents Tech Corp....... B 216 692-5200
Cleveland *(G-4433)*

Wallace Forge Company..................... D 330 488-1203
Canton *(G-2045)*

Wodin Inc.. E 440 439-4222
Cleveland *(G-4513)*

FORGINGS: Nuclear Power Plant, Ferrous

Advanced FME Products Inc................ G 440 953-0700
Mentor *(G-9470)*

FORGINGS: Plumbing Fixture, Nonferrous

Guarantee Specialties Inc.................. G 216 451-9744
Strongsville *(G-12562)*

Mansfield Plumbing Pdts LLC.............. A 419 938-5211
Perrysville *(G-11282)*

FORMS: Concrete, Sheet Metal

C L W Inc.. G 740 374-8443
Marietta *(G-8905)*

Feather Lite Innovations Inc................ F 513 893-5483
Liberty Twp *(G-8383)*

Feather Lite Innovations Inc................ E 937 743-9008
Springboro *(G-12252)*

FOUNDRIES: Aluminum

Acuity Brands Lighting Inc.................. D 740 349-4343
Newark *(G-10489)*

Air Craft Wheels LLC......................... G 440 937-7903
Ravenna *(G-11513)*

Akron Foundry Co............................. G 330 745-3101
Barberton *(G-791)*

Akron Foundry Co............................. C 330 745-3101
Akron *(G-31)*

Aluminum Line Products Company....... D 440 835-8880
Westlake *(G-14285)*

AMG Aluminum North America LLC....... F 659 348-3620
Cambridge *(G-1735)*

Aztec Manufacturing Inc .... E 330 783-9747
Youngstown (G-14816)

C M M S - Re LLC .... F 513 489-5111
Blue Ash (G-1257)

Dd Foundry Inc .... F 216 362-4100
Brookpark (G-1548)

Durivage Pattern and Mfg Inc .... E 419 836-8655
Williston (G-14411)

Francis Manufacturing Company .... C 937 526-4551
Russia (G-11673)

General Die Casters Inc .... E 330 678-2528
Twinsburg (G-13310)

Kovatch Castings Inc .... C 330 896-9944
Uniontown (G-13421)

Lite Metals Company .... E 330 296-6110
Ravenna (G-11532)

Mansfield Brass & Aluminum .... D 419 492-2154
New Washington (G-10480)

Miba Bearings US LLC .... B 740 962-4242
Mcconnelsville (G-9364)

Miller Castings Inc .... E 330 482-2923
Columbiana (G-4622)

Model Pattern & Foundry Co .... G 513 542-2322
Cincinnati (G-2884)

Reliable Castings Corporation .... D 937 497-5217
Sidney (G-12043)

Seilkop Industries Inc .... F 513 679-5680
Cincinnati (G-3076)

Skuld LLC .... E 330 423-7339
Piqua (G-11384)

Stripmatic Products Inc .... E 216 241-7143
Cleveland (G-4336)

Thompson Aluminum Casting Co .... E 216 206-2781
Cleveland (G-4393)

Tooling Technology LLC .... D 937 381-9211
Fort Loramie (G-6960)

Yoder Industries Inc .... C 937 278-5769
Dayton (G-6089)

FOUNDRIES: Gray & Ductile Iron

Akron Gear & Engineering Inc .... E 330 773-6608
Akron (G-32)

Arcelrmttal Tblar Pdts Shlby L .... A 419 347-2424
Shelby (G-11966)

D Picking & Co .... G 419 562-6891
Bucyrus (G-1677)

Dd Foundry Inc .... F 216 362-4100
Brookpark (G-1548)

Ford Motor Company .... C 216 676-7918
Brookpark (G-1550)

Hamilton Brass & Alum Castings .... G
Hamilton (G-7500)

Hobart LLC .... D 937 332-2797
Piqua (G-11355)

Hobart LLC .... E 937 332-3000
Troy (G-13225)

Hobart LLC .... D 937 332-3000
Troy (G-13226)

Howmet Aerospace Inc .... A 216 641-3600
Newburgh Heights (G-10543)

Korff Holdings LLC .... C 330 332-1566
Salem (G-11792)

Old Smo Inc .... G 419 394-3346
Saint Marys (G-11745)

Skuld LLC .... E 330 423-7339
Piqua (G-11384)

Thyssnkrupp Rothe Erde USA Inc .... C 330 562-4000
Aurora (G-689)

Tiffin Foundry & Machine Inc .... E 419 447-3991
Tiffin (G-12802)

Vanex Tube Corporation .... D 330 544-9500
Niles (G-10608)

W E Lott Company .... F 419 563-9400
Bucyrus (G-1694)

Wallace Forge Company .... D 330 488-1203
Canton (G-2045)

FOUNDRIES: Iron

Cast-Fab Technologies Inc .... C 513 758-1000
Cincinnati (G-2442)

Ej Usa Inc .... F 216 692-3001
South Euclid (G-12219)

Ellwood Engineered Castings Co .... C 330 568-3000
Hubbard (G-7810)

General Motors LLC .... A 419 782-7010
Defiance (G-6107)

Kenton Iron Products Inc .... E 419 674-4178
Kenton (G-8102)

Old Smo Inc .... C 419 394-3346
Saint Marys (G-11746)

Osco Industries Inc .... D 740 286-5004
Jackson (G-7950)

Pioneer City Casting Company .... E 740 423-7533
Belpre (G-1153)

Sancast Inc .... E 740 622-8660
Coshocton (G-5471)

T & B Foundry Company .... G 216 391-4200
Cleveland (G-4360)

Tiffin Foundry & Machine Inc .... E 419 447-3991
Tiffin (G-12802)

Tooling Technology LLC .... D 937 381-9211
Fort Loramie (G-6960)

W E Lott Company .... F 419 563-9400
Bucyrus (G-1694)

Whemco-Ohio Foundry Inc .... C 419 222-2111
Lima (G-8459)

Yellow Creek Casting Co Inc .... G 330 532-4608
Wellsville (G-13915)

FOUNDRIES: Nonferrous

Air Craft Wheels LLC .... G 440 937-7903
Ravenna (G-11513)

Alcon Industries Inc .... C 216 961-1100
Cleveland (G-3321)

Apex Aluminum Die Cast Co Inc .... E 937 773-0432
Piqua (G-11334)

Brost Foundry Company .... E 216 641-1131
Cleveland (G-3443)

Bunting Bearings LLC .... E 419 522-3323
Mansfield (G-8770)

Catania Medallic Specialty Inc .... A 440 933-9595
Avon Lake (G-751)

Columbiana Foundry Company .... C 330 482-3336
Columbiana (G-4612)

Curtiss-Wright Flow Ctrl Corp .... D 216 267-3200
Cleveland (G-3583)

Dd Foundry Inc .... F 216 362-4100
Brookpark (G-1548)

DMK Industries Inc .... F 513 727-4549
Middletown (G-9854)

Durivage Pattern and Mfg Inc .... E 419 836-8655
Williston (G-14411)

Ecm Industries LLC .... F 513 533-6242
Cincinnati (G-2578)

Ellwood Engineered Castings Co .... C 330 568-3000
Hubbard (G-7810)

Elyria Foundry Company LLC .... C 440 322-4657
Elyria (G-6529)

Francis Manufacturing Company .... C 937 526-4551
Russia (G-11673)

Frohn North America Inc .... G 770 819-0089
Bedford Heights (G-1077)

General Aluminum Mfg Company .... E 330 297-1020
Ravenna (G-11526)

General Aluminum Mfg LLC .... B 440 593-6225
Conneaut (G-5401)

General Aluminum Mfg LLC .... D 330 297-1225
Ravenna (G-11527)

General Die Casters Inc .... E 330 678-2528
Twinsburg (G-13310)

General Motors LLC .... A 419 782-7010
Defiance (G-6107)

Harbor Castings Inc .... E 330 499-7178
Cuyahoga Falls (G-5547)

Iabf Inc .... G 614 279-4498
Columbus (G-4997)

Ilsco LLC .... C 513 533-6200
Blue Ash (G-1287)

Jrm 2 Company .... D 513 554-1700
Cincinnati (G-2774)

Kovatch Castings Inc .... C 330 896-9944
Uniontown (G-13421)

Kse Manufacturing .... G 937 409-9831
Sidney (G-12027)

Lite Metals Company .... E 330 296-6110
Ravenna (G-11532)

Materion Advnced Mtls Tech Svc .... D 216 486-4200
Mayfield Heights (G-9335)

Materion Brush Inc .... A 419 862-2745
Elmore (G-6491)

Morris Bean & Company .... C 937 767-7301
Yellow Springs (G-14790)

Nelson Aluminum Foundry Inc .... G 440 543-1941
Chagrin Falls (G-2173)

Nova Machine Products Inc .... C 216 267-3200
Middleburg Heights (G-9775)

Old Smo Inc .... C 419 394-3346
Saint Marys (G-11746)

PCC Airfoils LLC .... C 330 868-6441
Minerva (G-10045)

PCC Airfoils LLC .... C 440 350-6150
Painesville (G-11104)

PCC Airfoils LLC .... E 216 831-3590
Beachwood (G-938)

PCC Airfoils LLC .... D 216 766-6206
Beachwood (G-939)

Piqua Emery Cutter & Fndry Co .... D 937 773-4134
Piqua (G-11375)

Precision Castparts Corp .... F 440 350-6150
Painesville (G-11106)

Reliable Castings Corporation .... D 937 497-5217
Sidney (G-12043)

Rolled Alloys Inc .... D 800 521-0332
Maumee (G-9315)

Ross Aluminum Castings LLC .... C 937 492-4134
Sidney (G-12046)

Seaport Mold & Casting Company .... G 419 243-1422
Toledo (G-13123)

Seilkop Industries Inc .... F 513 679-5680
Cincinnati (G-3076)

T & B Foundry Company .... G 216 391-4200
Cleveland (G-4360)

Technology House Ltd .... G 440 248-3025
Streetsboro (G-12527)

Telcon LLC .... D 330 562-5566
Streetsboro (G-12528)

Yoder Industries Inc .... C 937 278-5769
Dayton (G-6089)

FOUNDRIES: Steel

Brost Foundry Company .... E 216 641-1131
Cleveland (G-3443)

Castings Usa Inc .... G 330 339-3611
New Philadelphia (G-10436)

Columbiana Foundry Company .... C 330 482-3336
Columbiana (G-4612)

Columbus Steel Castings Co.................. A 614 444-2121
Columbus *(G-4834)*

Dd Foundry Inc.. F 216 362-4100
Brookpark *(G-1548)*

Durivage Pattern and Mfg Inc................. E 419 836-8655
Williston *(G-14411)*

Elyria Foundry Company LLC.................. C 440 322-4657
Elyria *(G-6529)*

Evertz Technology Svc USA Inc............. F 513 422-8400
Middletown *(G-9860)*

Harbor Castings Inc................................... E 330 499-7178
Cuyahoga Falls *(G-5547)*

Jmac Inc... E 614 436-2418
Columbus *(G-5041)*

Korff Holdings LLC.................................... C 330 332-1566
Salem *(G-11792)*

Kovatch Castings Inc................................ C 330 896-9944
Uniontown *(G-13421)*

Lakeway Mfg Inc.. E 419 433-3030
Huron *(G-7877)*

Premier Inv Cast Group LLC................... E 937 299-7333
Moraine *(G-10186)*

Shl Liquidation Medina Inc...................... C
Valley City *(G-13519)*

Tiffin Foundry & Machine Inc.................. E 419 447-3991
Tiffin *(G-12802)*

W E Lott Company....................................... F 419 563-9400
Bucyrus *(G-1694)*

Whemco-Ohio Foundry Inc...................... C 419 222-2111
Lima *(G-8459)*

Worthngton Stelpac Systems LLC......... C 614 438-3205
Columbus *(G-5375)*

FOUNDRIES: Steel Investment

Brost Foundry Company........................... E 216 641-1131
Cleveland *(G-3443)*

Castalloy Inc... D 216 961-7990
Cleveland *(G-3476)*

Harbor Castings Inc................................... E 330 499-7178
Cuyahoga Falls *(G-5547)*

Mercury Machine Co.................................. D 440 349-3222
Solon *(G-12147)*

Mold Masters Intl LLC............................... C 440 953-0220
Eastlake *(G-6438)*

PCC Airfoils LLC.. C 440 255-9770
Mentor *(G-9584)*

PCC Airfoils LLC.. C 330 868-6441
Minerva *(G-10045)*

Precision Castparts Corp......................... F 440 350-6150
Painesville *(G-11106)*

Steel Ceilings Inc....................................... E 740 967-1063
Johnstown *(G-7998)*

W E Lott Company....................................... F 419 563-9400
Bucyrus *(G-1694)*

Xapc Co.. C 216 362-4100
Cleveland *(G-4520)*

FOUNDRY MACHINERY & EQPT

A & B Foundry LLC.................................... F 937 412-1900
Tipp City *(G-12811)*

Empire Systems Inc.................................. G 440 653-9300
Avon Lake *(G-755)*

Equipment Mfrs Intl Inc............................ E 216 651-6700
Cleveland *(G-3682)*

Exomet Inc... F 440 593-1161
Conneaut *(G-5400)*

Gokoh Corporation..................................... F 937 339-4977
Troy *(G-13218)*

Skuld LLC... E 330 423-7339
Piqua *(G-11384)*

FOUNTAINS: Concrete

Fountain Specialists Inc.......................... G 513 831-5717
Milford *(G-9934)*

FRACTIONATION PRDTS OF CRUDE PETROLEUM, HYDROCARBONS, NEC

Enrevo Pyro LLC... G 203 517-5002
Brookfield *(G-1514)*

FRANCHISES, SELLING OR LICENSING

Cassanos Inc.. E 937 294-8400
Dayton *(G-5695)*

Chemstation International Inc................. E 937 294-8265
Dayton *(G-5701)*

Gold Star Chili Inc..................................... E 513 231-4541
Cincinnati *(G-2681)*

Instantwhip Foods Inc.............................. F 614 488-2536
Columbus *(G-5011)*

R&D Marketing Group Inc......................... G 216 398-9100
Brooklyn Heights *(G-1537)*

Skyline Cem Holdings LLC...................... C 513 874-1188
Fairfield *(G-6776)*

Stanley Steemer Intl Inc.......................... C 614 764-2007
Dublin *(G-6350)*

The Cornwell Quality Tools Company.... D 330 336-3506
Wadsworth *(G-13674)*

FREIGHT FORWARDING ARRANGEMENTS

Carbon Enterprises Inc............................ G 740 420-6472
Circleville *(G-3249)*

FRICTION MATERIAL, MADE FROM POWDERED METAL

Addup Inc... E 513 745-4510
Blue Ash *(G-1242)*

General Metals Powder Co LLC............. E 330 633-1226
Akron *(G-160)*

Lewark Metal Spinning Inc...................... E 937 275-3303
Dayton *(G-5845)*

Rmi Titanium Company LLC..................... B 330 455-4010
Canton *(G-1999)*

SK Wellman Corp.. C 440 528-4000
Solon *(G-12181)*

Tribco Incorporated................................... E 216 486-2000
Cleveland *(G-4421)*

Wellman Products LLC............................. B 855 403-9083
Medina *(G-9463)*

FRUIT STANDS OR MARKETS

Coopers Mill Inc... G 419 562-4215
Bucyrus *(G-1676)*

Grays Orange Barn Inc............................. G 419 568-2718
Wapakoneta *(G-13714)*

FRUITS & VEGETABLES WHOLESALERS: Fresh

Chefs Garden Inc....................................... C 419 433-4947
Sandusky *(G-11827)*

Frank L Harter & Son Inc......................... G 513 574-1330
Cincinnati *(G-2638)*

Produce Packaging Inc............................. C 216 391-6129
Willoughby Hills *(G-14562)*

FUEL ADDITIVES

BLaster Holdings LLC............................... E 216 901-5800
Cleveland *(G-3422)*

BLaster LLC... E 216 901-5800
Cleveland *(G-3423)*

FUEL CELLS: Solid State

Plug Power Inc.. G 518 605-5703
West Carrollton *(G-13931)*

FUEL OIL DEALERS

Centerra Co-Op... E 419 281-2153
Ashland *(G-526)*

Cincinnati - Vulcan Company................. D 513 242-5300
Cincinnati *(G-2465)*

New Vulco Mfg & Sales Co LLC............. D 513 242-2672
Cincinnati *(G-2904)*

FUEL TREATING

Opw Fueling Components Inc.................. D 800 422-2525
West Chester *(G-14040)*

FUELS: Diesel

PEC Biofuels LLC....................................... G 419 542-8210
Hicksville *(G-7651)*

FUNGICIDES OR HERBICIDES

Scotts Company LLC................................. C 937 644-0011
Marysville *(G-9045)*

Scotts Miracle-Gro Company.................. E 937 578-5065
Marysville *(G-9047)*

FURNACES & OVENS: Indl

A Jacks Manufacturing Co....................... E 216 531-1010
Cleveland *(G-3283)*

Abp Induction LLC..................................... F 262 878-6390
Massillon *(G-9171)*

Armature Coil Equipment Inc.................. F 216 267-6366
Strongsville *(G-12538)*

Benko Products Inc................................... E 440 934-2180
Sheffield Village *(G-11957)*

C A Litzler Co Inc....................................... E 216 267-8020
Cleveland *(G-3457)*

CA Litzler Holding Company................... D 216 267-8020
Cleveland *(G-3458)*

Crescent Metal Products Inc................... C 440 350-1100
Mentor *(G-9507)*

Duca Mfg & Consulting Inc...................... G 330 726-7175
Youngstown *(G-14851)*

Ebner Furnaces Inc................................... D 330 335-2311
Wadsworth *(G-13637)*

Garland Commercial Industries LLC...... G 800 338-2204
Cleveland *(G-3756)*

Hannon Company... D 330 456-4728
Canton *(G-1908)*

I Cerco Inc... C 740 982-2050
Crooksville *(G-5510)*

Kaufman Engineered Systems Inc......... D 419 878-9727
Waterville *(G-13837)*

L Haberny Co Inc....................................... F 440 543-5999
Chagrin Falls *(G-2168)*

Lakeway Mfg Inc.. E 419 433-3030
Huron *(G-7877)*

Micropyretics Heaters Intl Inc................ F 513 772-0404
Cincinnati *(G-2877)*

Resilience Fund III LP............................... F 216 292-0200
Cleveland *(G-4237)*

Robbins Industrial Frnc Co Inc.............. F 440 949-2292
Sheffield Village *(G-11963)*

Selas Heat Technology Co LLC.............. E 800 523-6500
Streetsboro *(G-12523)*

Sentro Tech Corporation.......................... G 440 260-0364
Strongsville *(G-12596)*

Stelter and Brinck Inc.............................. E 513 367-9300
Harrison *(G-7569)*

Strohecker Incorporated.......................... E 330 426-9496
East Palestine *(G-6407)*

Surface Combustion Inc.......................... D 419 891-7150
  Maumee (G-9323)

T E Q HI Inc.. E 877 448-3701
  Columbus (G-5305)

T J F Inc... F 419 878-4400
  Waterville (G-13843)

United McGill Corporation...................... E 614 829-1200
  Groveport (G-7455)

FURNACES: Indl, Electric

Ajax Tocco Magnethermic Corp.............. C 800 547-1527
  Warren (G-13732)

CMI Industry Americas Inc..................... D 330 332-4661
  Salem (G-11771)

Duca Manufacturing & Consulting Inc... E 330 758-0828
  Youngstown (G-14850)

The Schaefer Group Inc......................... E 937 253-3342
  Beavercreek (G-997)

Ajax Tocco Magnethermic Corp.............. C 800 547-1527
  Warren (G-13732)

FURNACES: Warm Air, Electric

Columbus Heating & Vent Co.................. C 614 274-1177
  Columbus (G-4823)

FURNITURE PARTS: Metal

Mansfield Engineered Components LLCC 419 524-1300
  Mansfield (G-8819)

McNeil Group Inc.................................. E 614 298-0300
  Columbus (G-5093)

Pucel Enterprises Inc............................ D 216 881-4604
  Cleveland (G-4206)

Pucel Enterprises Inc............................ G 800 336-4986
  Cleveland (G-4207)

FURNITURE REFINISHING SVCS

Mielke Furniture Repair Inc.................... G 419 625-4572
  Sandusky (G-11860)

Soft Touch Wood LLC............................ E 330 545-4204
  Girard (G-7280)

FURNITURE REPAIR & MAINTENANCE SVCS

Furniture Concepts Inc.......................... F 216 292-9100
  Cleveland (G-3745)

FURNITURE STOCK & PARTS: Hardwood

Ogonok Custom Hardwood Inc............... G 833 718 2531
  Barberton (G-827)

Regency Seating Inc............................. E 330 848-3700
  Akron (G-280)

FURNITURE STORES

Archbold Furniture Co............................ E 567 444-4666
  Archbold (G-488)

Bruening Glass Works Inc...................... G 440 333-4768
  Cleveland (G-3445)

Chagrin Valley Custom Furn LLC........... G 440 591-5511
  Warrensville Heights (G-13816)

Coconis Furniture Inc............................ E 740 452-1231
  South Zanesville (G-12232)

Eoi Inc... F 740 201-3300
  Lewis Center (G-8333)

Fortner Upholstering Inc........................ F 614 475-8282
  Columbus (G-4936)

Furniture By Otmar Inc.......................... F 937 435-2039
  Dayton (G-5788)

Hallmark Industries Inc......................... E 937 864-7378
  Springfield (G-12316)

Home Stor & Off Solutions Inc............... E 216 362-4660
  Cleveland (G-3836)

Ohio Table Pad Company....................... F 419 872-6400
  Perrysburg (G-11246)

Precision Fab Products Inc..................... G 937 526-5681
  Versailles (G-13602)

Sailors Tailor Inc.................................. F 937 862-7781
  Spring Valley (G-12243)

FURNITURE WHOLESALERS

Fabcor Inc.. F 419 628-4428
  Minster (G-10057)

Friends Service Co Inc.......................... F 800 427-1704
  Dayton (G-5785)

Friends Service Co Inc.......................... E 419 427-1704
  Findlay (G-6869)

Sauder Woodworking Co......................... F 419 446-2711
  Archbold (G-510)

Urbn Timber LLC.................................. G 614 981-3043
  Columbus (G-5341)

FURNITURE, HOUSEHOLD: Wholesalers

Sauder Woodworking Co......................... A 419 446-2711
  Archbold (G-511)

FURNITURE, MATTRESSES: Wholesalers

Ahmf Inc.. E 614 921-1223
  Columbus (G-4681)

FURNITURE, OFFICE: Wholesalers

Wasserstrom Company........................... B 614 228-6525
  Columbus (G-5356)

FURNITURE, WHOLESALE: Chairs

Millwood Wholesale Inc......................... F 330 359-6109
  Dundee (G-6369)

FURNITURE, WHOLESALE: Lockers

American Platinum Door LLC.................. G 440 497-6213
  Solon (G-12078)

FURNITURE, WHOLESALE: Racks

KMC Holdings LLC................................ C 419 238-2442
  Van Wert (G-13539)

Partitions Plus Incorporated.................. E 419 422-2600
  Findlay (G-6907)

FURNITURE, WHOLESALE: Shelving

G & P Construction LLC......................... E 855 494-4830
  North Royalton (G-10762)

FURNITURE: Bedroom, Wood

Andal Woodworking................................ F 330 897-8059
  Baltic (G-775)

FURNITURE: Beds, Household, Incl Folding & Cabinet, Metal

Invacare Corporation............................. G 800 333-6900
  Elyria (G-6551)

Invacare Corporation............................. A 440 329-6000
  Elyria (G-6549)

Invacare Holdings Corporation............... B 440 329-6000
  Elyria (G-6554)

FURNITURE: Cabinets & Filing Drawers, Office, Exc Wood

East Woodworking Company.................. G 216 791-5950
  Cleveland (G-3649)

Jsc Employee Leasing Corp................... D 330 773-8971
  Akron (G-189)

FURNITURE: Cabinets & Vanities, Medicine, Metal

Installed Building Pdts LLC.................... B 614 308-9900
  Columbus (G-5009)

FURNITURE: Chairs, Household Upholstered

Buckeye Seating LLC............................ F 330 893-7700
  Millersburg (G-9972)

FURNITURE: Chairs, Household Wood

Anthony Flottemesch & Son Inc............. F 513 561-1212
  Cincinnati (G-2371)

Artistic Finishes Inc............................. G 440 951-7850
  Willoughby (G-14427)

Basic Cases Inc................................... G 216 662-3900
  Cleveland (G-3409)

Cabintwrks Group Mddlfield LLC........... A 888 562-7744
  Middlefield (G-9784)

Carlisle Oak.. G 330 852-8734
  Sugarcreek (G-12634)

Criswell Furniture LLC.......................... F 330 695-2082
  Fredericksburg (G-7062)

Custom Surfaces Inc............................ G 440 439-2310
  Bedford (G-1024)

Diversified Products & Svcs.................. F 740 393-6202
  Mount Vernon (G-10242)

Dje Management Consulting LLC........... G 330 760-2990
  Medina (G-9397)

Dutch Legacy Company LLC.................. G 330 359-0270
  Apple Creek (G-466)

Furniture By Otmar Inc.......................... F 937 435-2039
  Dayton (G-5788)

Gasser Chair Co Inc............................. D 330 759-2234
  Youngstown (G-14862)

Grabo Interiors Inc............................... G 216 391-6677
  Cleveland (G-3780)

Greenway Home Products Inc................ F
  Perrysburg (G-11227)

Grk Manufacturing Co............................ E 513 863-3131
  Hamilton (G-7497)

Guernsey Industries.............................. C 740 439-4452
  Byesville (G-1713)

Hardwood Lumber Company Inc............. F 440 834-1891
  Middlefield (G-9797)

Holmes Panel LLC................................ G 330 897-5040
  Baltic (G-779)

James L Deckebach LLC....................... G 513 321-3733
  Cincinnati (G-2761)

Jeffco Sheltered Workshop.................... G 740 264-4608
  Steubenville (G-12404)

Kitchens By Rutenschroer Inc................ G 513 251-8333
  Cincinnati (G-2799)

Lauber Manufacturing Co....................... G 419 446-2450
  Archbold (G-499)

Lima Millwork Inc................................. G 419 331-3303
  Elida (G-6483)

Mamabees HM Gds Lifestyle LLC.......... G 419 277-2914
  Fostoria (G-6987)

Michaels Pre-Cast Con Pdts Inc............ F 513 683-1292
  Loveland (G-8643)

Mielke Furniture Repair Inc.................... G 419 625-4572
  Sandusky (G-11860)

Miller Cabinet Ltd................................. F 614 873-4221
  Plain City (G-11415)

N Wasserstrom & Sons Inc.................... F 614 737-5410
  Columbus (G-5119)

Nagele Manufacturing Company.............. E 216 433-1100
  Cleveland (G-4057)

Penwood Mfg.. G 330 359-5600
  Fresno (G-7148)

R A Hamed International Inc................... G 330 247-0190
  Twinsburg (G-13363)

Rnr Enterprises LLC............................. F 330 852-3022
  Sugarcreek (G-12647)

PRODUCT

Specialty Svcs Cabinetry Inc.................. G 614 421-1599
Columbus *(G-5281)*

Stark Truss Company Inc...................... D 330 478-2100
Canton *(G-2015)*

Stark Truss Company Inc...................... E 419 298-3777
Edgerton *(G-6471)*

Tappan Chairs LLC............................ G 800 840-9121
Blue Ash *(G-1340)*

Textiles Inc.................................. G 614 529-8642
Hilliard *(G-7706)*

Textiles Inc.................................. G 740 852-0782
London *(G-8542)*

Vocational Services Inc....................... F 216 431-8085
Cleveland *(G-4478)*

Waller Brothers Stone Company............ F 740 858-1948
Mc Dermott *(G-9356)*

Weaver Woodcraft L L C................... G 330 695-2150
Apple Creek *(G-481)*

Wine Cellar Innovations LLC.............. C 513 321-3733
Cincinnati *(G-3227)*

Woodworking Shop LLC..................... F 513 330-9663
Miamisburg *(G-9753)*

FURNITURE: Chairs, Office Wood

Buckeye Seating LLC.......................... F 330 893-7700
Millersburg *(G-9972)*

Buzz Seating Inc.............................. G 877 263-5737
West Chester *(G-14109)*

Gasser Chair Co Inc.......................... E 330 534-2234
Youngstown *(G-14861)*

FURNITURE: Church

Sauder Manufacturing Co..................... C 419 445-7670
Archbold *(G-509)*

FURNITURE: Console Tables, Wood

Dorel Home Furnishings Inc.................. D 419 447-7448
Tiffin *(G-12782)*

FURNITURE: Dining Room, Wood

Canal Dover Furniture LLC.................... D 330 359-5375
Millersburg *(G-9974)*

FURNITURE: Fiberglass & Plastic

Evenflo Company Inc........................... D 937 773-3971
Troy *(G-13213)*

Office Magic Inc.............................. F 510 782-6100
Medina *(G-9430)*

Owens Corning................................ A 419 248-8000
Toledo *(G-13084)*

Sauder Woodworking Co....................... F 419 446-2711
Archbold *(G-510)*

FURNITURE: Hotel

Textiles Inc.................................. G 614 529-8642
Hilliard *(G-7706)*

FURNITURE: Household, Metal

Medallion Lighting Corporation............. E 440 255-8383
Mentor *(G-9561)*

Metal Fabricating Corporation.............. D 216 631-8121
Cleveland *(G-4023)*

FURNITURE: Household, Upholstered, Exc Wood Or Metal

Bulk Carrier Trnsp Eqp Co.................... G 330 339-3333
New Philadelphia *(G-10434)*

John Purdum.................................. G 513 897-9686
Waynesville *(G-13879)*

Kitchens By Rutenschroer Inc.............. G 513 251-8333
Cincinnati *(G-2799)*

Sailors Tailor Inc............................ F 937 862-7781
Spring Valley *(G-12243)*

FURNITURE: Juvenile, Metal

Angels Landing Inc........................... G 513 687-3681
Moraine *(G-10147)*

FURNITURE: Lawn & Garden, Metal

Sunnest Service LLC.......................... E 740 283-2815
Steubenville *(G-12412)*

FURNITURE: Lawn, Exc Wood, Metal, Stone Or Concrete

Hershy Way Ltd............................... G 330 893-2809
Millersburg *(G-9984)*

FURNITURE: Living Room, Upholstered On Wood Frames

Hallmark Industries Inc...................... E 937 864-7378
Springfield *(G-12316)*

Morris Furniture Co Inc....................... C 937 874-7100
Fairborn *(G-6697)*

FURNITURE: Mattresses & Foundations

Ahmf Inc..................................... E 614 921-1223
Columbus *(G-4681)*

H Goodman Inc................................ D 216 341-0200
Newburgh Heights *(G-10542)*

Homecare Mattress Inc........................ F 937 746-2556
Franklin *(G-7027)*

Select Mattress Co Inc....................... F 419 244-3645
Sylvania *(G-12722)*

Tru Comfort Mattress......................... G 614 595-8600
Dublin *(G-6357)*

Walter F Stephens Jr Inc..................... E 937 746-0521
Franklin *(G-7055)*

FURNITURE: Mattresses, Box & Bedsprings

Banner Mattress Co Inc....................... D 419 324-7181
Toledo *(G-12892)*

Coconis Furniture Inc........................ E 740 452-1231
South Zanesville *(G-12232)*

HSP Bedding Solutions LLC.................. E 440 437-4425
Orwell *(G-11021)*

Solstice Sleep Products Inc.................. E 614 279-8850
Columbus *(G-5275)*

V-I-S-c-e-r-o-t-o-n-i-c Inc.................. D 330 690-3355
Akron *(G-352)*

FURNITURE: Mattresses, Innerspring Or Box Spring

Quilting Inc................................. D 614 504-5971
Plain City *(G-11417)*

Sealy Mattress Mfg Co LLC.................. E 800 697-3259
Medina *(G-9445)*

FURNITURE: Office, Exc Wood

1914 Mi Inc.................................. E 330 308-8667
New Philadelphia *(G-10428)*

Americas Mdular Off Specialist............. G 614 277-0216
Grove City *(G-7372)*

Casco Mfg Solutions Inc...................... D 513 681-0003
Cincinnati *(G-2441)*

Custom Craft Collection Inc.................. F 440 998-3000
Ashtabula *(G-589)*

Custom Millcraft Corp........................ E 513 874-7080
West Chester *(G-13980)*

Ergo Desktop LLC............................. E 567 890-3746
Celina *(G-2105)*

Frontier Signs & Displays Inc............... G 513 367-0813
Harrison *(G-7552)*

Gasser Chair Co Inc.......................... D 330 759-2234
Youngstown *(G-14862)*

Infinium Wall Systems Inc.................... E 440 572-5000
Strongsville *(G-12567)*

M/W International Inc......................... F 440 526-6900
Lorain *(G-8566)*

Metal Fabricating Corporation............... D 216 631-8121
Cleveland *(G-4023)*

National Electro-Coatings Inc............... D 216 898-0080
Cleveland *(G-4059)*

Pucel Enterprises Inc........................ D 216 881-4604
Cleveland *(G-4206)*

Recycled Systems Furniture Inc............. E 614 880-9110
Worthington *(G-14724)*

Senator International Inc.................... E 419 887-5806
Maumee *(G-9316)*

Starr Fabricating Inc........................ D 330 394-9891
Vienna *(G-13618)*

Tiffin Metal Products Co..................... D 419 447-8414
Tiffin *(G-12803)*

FURNITURE: Office, Wood

August Incorporated.......................... E 937 434-2520
Dayton *(G-5667)*

Basic Cases Inc.............................. G 216 662-3900
Cleveland *(G-3409)*

Crow Works LLC............................... E 888 811-2769
Killbuck *(G-8132)*

Dvuv LLC..................................... F 216 741-5511
Cleveland *(G-3641)*

Frontier Signs & Displays Inc............... G 513 367-0813
Harrison *(G-7552)*

Gasser Chair Co Inc.......................... D 330 759-2234
Youngstown *(G-14862)*

Lima Millwork Inc............................ G 419 331-3303
Elida *(G-6483)*

Miller Cabinet Ltd........................... F 614 873-4221
Plain City *(G-11415)*

Sauder Manufacturing Co...................... D 419 682-3061
Stryker *(G-12627)*

Senator International Inc.................... E 419 887-5806
Maumee *(G-9316)*

Symatic Inc.................................. G 330 225-1510
Medina *(G-9452)*

Tiffin Metal Products Co..................... D 419 447-8414
Tiffin *(G-12803)*

FURNITURE: Picnic Tables Or Benches, Park

Summit County................................ G 330 865-8065
Akron *(G-319)*

FURNITURE: Play Pens, Children's, Wood

Western & Southern Lf Insur Co............. A 513 629-1800
Cincinnati *(G-3221)*

FURNITURE: School

Shiffler Equipment Sales Inc................. E 440 285-9175
Chardon *(G-2222)*

FURNITURE: Table Tops, Marble

Accent Manufacturing Inc..................... F 330 724-7704
Norton *(G-10816)*

FURNITURE: Upholstered

Custom Craft Collection Inc.................. F 440 998-3000
Ashtabula *(G-589)*

Fortner Upholstering Inc..................... F 614 475-8282
Columbus *(G-4936)*

Franklin Cabinet Company Inc................. E 937 743-9606
Franklin *(G-7022)*

Grk Manufacturing Co.............................E 513 863-3131
Hamilton *(G-7497)*

H Goodman Inc.....................................D 216 341-0200
Newburgh Heights *(G-10542)*

Njm Furniture Outlet Inc........................F 330 893-3514
Millersburg *(G-10004)*

Robert Mayo Industries........................G 330 426-2587
East Palestine *(G-6406)*

Sauder Woodworking Co.......................A 419 446-2711
Archbold *(G-511)*

Weavers Furniture Ltd...........................F 330 852-2701
Sugarcreek *(G-12657)*

FURNITURE: Vehicle

Wurms Woodworking Company............E 419 492-2184
New Washington *(G-10484)*

FUSE MOUNTINGS: Electric Power

Regal Beloit America Inc......................C 419 352-8441
Bowling Green *(G-1439)*

FUSES & FUSE EQPT

Marathon Special Products Corp...........C 419 352-8441
Bowling Green *(G-1428)*

GAMES & TOYS: Board Games, Children's & Adults'

Late For Sky Production Co...................E 513 531-4400
Cincinnati *(G-2812)*

GAMES & TOYS: Child Restraint Seats, Automotive

Evenflo Company Inc............................D 937 773-3971
Troy *(G-13213)*

Rocky Hinge Inc...................................G 330 539-6296
Girard *(G-7279)*

GARBAGE CONTAINERS: Plastic

MCS Midwest LLC.................................G 513 217-0805
Franklin *(G-7033)*

GARBAGE DISPOSERS & COMPACTORS: Commercial

City of Ashland....................................G 419 289-8728
Ashland *(G-529)*

Knight Manufacturing Co Inc..................G 740 676-5516
Shadyside *(G-11922)*

GAS & OIL FIELD EXPLORATION SVCS

AB Resources LLC................................E 440 922-1098
Brecksville *(G-1455)*

Antero Resources Corporation..............E 303 357-7310
Caldwell *(G-1722)*

Antero Resources Corporation..............D 740 760-1000
Marietta *(G-8901)*

BD Oil Gathering Corp...........................E 740 374-9355
Marietta *(G-8903)*

Beck Energy Corporation......................E 330 297-6891
Ravenna *(G-11517)*

Blue Racer Midstream LLC.....................F 740 630-7556
Cambridge *(G-1737)*

Canton Oil Well Service Inc....................F 330 494-1221
Canton *(G-1858)*

Cgas Exploration Inc.............................F 614 436-4631
Worthington *(G-14705)*

Diversified Production LLC.....................C 740 373-8771
Marietta *(G-8914)*

Dome Drilling Company.........................G 440 892-9434
Westlake *(G-14299)*

Elkhead Gas & Oil Co...........................G 740 763-3966
Newark *(G-10500)*

Everflow Eastern Partners LP................G 330 533-2692
Canfield *(G-1809)*

G&O Resources Ltd.............................G 330 253-2525
Akron *(G-153)*

Gonzoil Inc..G 330 497-5888
Canton *(G-1903)*

John D Oil and Gas Company................G 440 255-6325
Mentor *(G-9543)*

K Petroleum Inc...................................F 614 532-5420
Gahanna *(G-7161)*

Knox Energy Inc...................................F 740 927-6731
Pataskala *(G-11143)*

Lake Region Oil Inc..............................G 330 828-8420
Dalton *(G-5587)*

M3 Midstream LLC...............................E 330 223-2220
Kensington *(G-8010)*

M3 Midstream LLC...............................G 330 679-5580
Salineville *(G-11818)*

M3 Midstream LLC...............................F 740 945-1170
Scio *(G-11888)*

MFC Drilling Inc...................................F 740 622-5600
Coshocton *(G-5460)*

Mori Shuji..G 614 459-1296
Columbus *(G-5111)*

Ngo Development Corporation...............G 740 622-9560
Coshocton *(G-5464)*

Northwood Energy Corporation.............F 614 457-1024
Columbus *(G-5131)*

Powder Alloy Corporation.....................E 513 984-4016
Loveland *(G-8646)*

Precision Geophysical Inc.....................E 330 674-2198
Millersburg *(G-10005)*

Prominence Energy Corporation............G 513 818-8329
Cincinnati *(G-3008)*

Quantum Energy LLC............................F 440 285-7381
Chardon *(G-2219)*

Reserve Energy Exploration Co.............G 440 543-0770
Chagrin Falls *(G-2180)*

Silcor Oilfield Services Inc....................G 330 448-8500
Brookfield *(G-1518)*

Triad Energy Corporation......................G 740 374-2940
Marietta *(G-8956)*

True North Energy LLC..........................E 440 442-0060
Mayfield Heights *(G-9343)*

Unlimited Energy Services LLC..............F 304 517-7097
Beverly *(G-1210)*

Utica East Ohio Midstream LLC.............C 740 431-4168
Dennison *(G-6219)*

Whitacre Enterprises Inc......................G 740 934-2331
Graysville *(G-7322)*

Zane Petroleum Inc..............................F 740 454-8779
Columbus *(G-5379)*

GAS & OIL FIELD SVCS, NEC

Adapt Oil..G 330 658-1482
Doylestown *(G-6269)*

Aim Services Company.........................E 800 321-9038
Girard *(G-7263)*

Aj Enterprise LLC.................................F 740 231-2205
Zanesville *(G-14984)*

Gdn Welding LLC.................................E 740 398-6109
Danville *(G-5599)*

Killbuck Oil and Gas LLC......................G 330 447-8423
Akron *(G-195)*

GAS FIELD MACHINERY & EQPT

Jet Rubber Company.............................E 330 325-1821
Rootstown *(G-11648)*

GASES: Acetylene

Delille Oxygen Company........................E 614 444-1177
Columbus *(G-4876)*

GASES: Carbon Dioxide

Linde Gas & Equipment Inc...................G 513 821-2192
Cincinnati *(G-2823)*

GASES: Indl

Airgas Usa LLC...................................G 440 232-6397
Twinsburg *(G-13270)*

Atlantic Welding LLC............................F 937 570-5094
Piqua *(G-11335)*

Delille Oxygen Company........................G 937 325-9595
Springfield *(G-12300)*

Endurance Manufacturing Inc................G 330 628-2600
Akron *(G-133)*

Invacare Corporation............................G 800 333-6900
Elyria *(G-6551)*

Invacare Corporation............................A 440 329-6000
Elyria *(G-6549)*

Linde Gas & Equipment Inc...................E 614 443-7687
Columbus *(G-5071)*

Linde Gas & Equipment Inc...................E 419 729-7732
Toledo *(G-13037)*

Linde Gas & Equipment Inc...................G 440 944-8844
Wickliffe *(G-14380)*

Linde Gas USA LLC..............................G 330 425-3989
Twinsburg *(G-13332)*

Linde Inc...G 330 825-4449
Barberton *(G-817)*

Linde Inc...F 440 237-8690
Cleveland *(G-3958)*

Linde Inc...G 419 698-8005
Oregon *(G-10962)*

Matheson Tri-Gas Inc...........................E 330 425-4407
Twinsburg *(G-13335)*

Messer LLC..G 419 822-3909
Delta *(G-6211)*

Messer LLC..G 614 539-2259
Grove City *(G-7399)*

Messer LLC..F 419 227-9585
Lima *(G-8430)*

National Gas & Oil Corporation.............E 740 344-2102
Newark *(G-10524)*

Plasti-Kote Co Inc................................C 330 725-4511
Medina *(G-0436)*

Reliable Mfg Co LLC.............................G 740 756-9373
Carroll *(G-2078)*

Wright Brothers Inc..............................F 513 731-2222
Cincinnati *(G-3232)*

Wright Brothers Global Gas LLC............F 513 731-2222
Cincinnati *(G-3233)*

GASES: Nitrogen

Matheson Tri-Gas Inc...........................F 419 865-8881
Holland *(G-7772)*

Messer LLC..E 419 221-5043
Lima *(G-8431)*

Messer LLC..F 513 831-4742
Miamiville *(G-9763)*

Messer LLC..G 330 394-4541
Warren *(G-13782)*

Ohio Nitrogen LLC...............................F 216 839-5485
Beachwood *(G-935)*

Osair Inc...G 440 974-6500
Mentor *(G-9577)*

GASES: Oxygen

Airgas Usa LLC....................................E 330 454-1330
Canton *(G-1826)*

Linde Inc..F 440 994-1000
   Ashtabula *(G-603)*

Messer LLC.....................................E 216 533-7256
   Cleveland *(G-4022)*

Welders Supply Inc........................F 216 241-1696
   Cleveland *(G-4500)*

Western/Scott Fetzer Company......E 440 892-3000
   Westlake *(G-14343)*

GASKET MATERIALS

Flow Dry Technology Inc...............C 937 833-2161
   Brookville *(G-1568)*

Forest City Technologies Inc.........C 440 647-2115
   Wellington *(G-13889)*

Forest City Technologies Inc.........C 440 647-2115
   Wellington *(G-13890)*

Thermoseal Inc..............................G 937 498-2222
   Sidney *(G-12057)*

GASKETS

Akalina Associates Inc..................C 440 992-2195
   Ashtabula *(G-586)*

Akron Gasket & Packg Entps Inc...F 330 633-3742
   Tallmadge *(G-12729)*

Blackthorn LLC..............................F 937 836-9296
   Clayton *(G-3272)*

Cincinnati Gasket Pkg Mfg Inc......E 513 761-3458
   Cincinnati *(G-2475)*

Durox Company..............................D 440 238-5350
   Strongsville *(G-12556)*

Epg Inc..D 330 995-5125
   Aurora *(G-669)*

Epg Inc..F 330 995-9725
   Streetsboro *(G-12501)*

Espi Enterprises Inc......................G 440 543-8108
   Chagrin Falls *(G-2160)*

Forest City Technologies Inc.........B 440 647-2115
   Wellington *(G-13891)*

Fouty & Company Inc....................E 419 693-0017
   Oregon *(G-10961)*

Freudenberg-Nok General Partnr....C 419 427-5221
   Findlay *(G-6868)*

G-M-I Inc..G 440 953-8811
   Willoughby *(G-14461)*

Gasko Fabricated Products LLC......E 330 239-1781
   Medina *(G-9407)*

Grand River Rubber & Plasti...........C 440 998-2900
   Ashtabula *(G-594)*

Green Technologies Ohio LLC........G 330 630-3350
   Tallmadge *(G-12735)*

Industry Products Co.....................B 937 778-0585
   Piqua *(G-11356)*

Ishikawa Gasket America Inc........F 419 353-7300
   Maumee *(G-9299)*

James K Green Enterprises Inc......G 614 878-6041
   Columbus *(G-5031)*

Jbc Technologies Inc.....................D 440 327-4522
   North Ridgeville *(G-10737)*

K Wm Beach Mfg Co Inc................C 937 399-3838
   Springfield *(G-12334)*

May Lin Silicone Products Inc........G 330 825-9019
   Barberton *(G-820)*

Mechanical Rubber Ohio LLC.........E 845 986-2271
   Strongsville *(G-12573)*

Miles Rubber & Packing Company....E 330 425-3888
   Twinsburg *(G-13341)*

Mvgg Inc..E 937 228-0781
   Dayton *(G-5899)*

Netherland Rubber Company..........F 513 733-0883
   Cincinnati *(G-2899)*

Newman Diaphragms LLC...............E 513 932-7379
   Lebanon *(G-8278)*

Newman Sanitary Gasket Company.......E 513 932-7379
   Lebanon *(G-8279)*

Ohio Gasket and Shim Co Inc........E 330 630-0626
   Akron *(G-252)*

P & R Specialty Inc........................F 937 773-0263
   Piqua *(G-11370)*

P&E Sales Ltd.................................G 330 829-0100
   Alliance *(G-397)*

Paul J Tatulinski Ltd......................F 330 584-8251
   North Benton *(G-10623)*

Phoenix Associates........................E 440 543-9701
   Chagrin Falls *(G-2178)*

Sur-Seal LLC..................................C 513 574-8500
   Cincinnati *(G-3130)*

GASKETS & SEALING DEVICES

Dana Limited.................................B 419 887-3000
   Maumee *(G-9282)*

Forest City Technologies Inc.........C 440 647-2115
   Wellington *(G-13888)*

Seal Master Corporation................E 330 673-8410
   Kent *(G-8076)*

Superior Plastics Intl Inc...............G 419 424-3113
   Findlay *(G-6925)*

GASOLINE FILLING STATIONS

Shelly and Sands Inc.....................F 740 453-0721
   Zanesville *(G-15047)*

Tbone Sales LLC.............................G 330 897-6131
   Baltic *(G-781)*

True North Energy LLC...................E 440 442-0060
   Mayfield Heights *(G-9343)*

United Dairy Farmers Inc...............C 513 396-8700
   Cincinnati *(G-3181)*

GASOLINE WHOLESALERS

Marathon Petroleum Company LP.........F 419 422-2121
   Findlay *(G-6889)*

Marathon Petroleum Corporation....A 419 422-2121
   Findlay *(G-6890)*

Mplx Terminals LLC........................F 330 479-5539
   Canton *(G-1952)*

GEARS

Cincinnati Gearing Systems Inc.........E 513 527-8634
   Cincinnati *(G-2477)*

Gear Company of America Inc........D 216 671-5400
   Cleveland *(G-3760)*

Landerwood Industries Inc.............E 440 233-4234
   Willoughby *(G-14481)*

GEARS & GEAR UNITS: Reduction, Exc Auto

Hefty Hoist Inc..............................E 740 467-2515
   Millersport *(G-10023)*

GEARS: Power Transmission, Exc Auto

Akron Gear & Engineering Inc........E 330 773-6608
   Akron *(G-32)*

B & B Gear and Machine Co Inc.........E 937 687-1771
   New Lebanon *(G-10399)*

Cage Gear & Machine LLC..............E 330 452-1532
   Canton *(G-1850)*

Canton Gear Mfg Designing Inc.........F 330 455-2771
   Canton *(G-1856)*

Dayton Gear and Tool Co................E 937 866-4327
   Dayton *(G-5727)*

Forge Industries Inc......................A 330 960-2468
   Youngstown *(G-14857)*

Gear Company of America Inc........D 216 671-5400
   Cleveland *(G-3760)*

Geartec Inc....................................E 440 953-3900
   Willoughby *(G-14462)*

Horsburgh & Scott Co.....................C 216 431-3900
   Cleveland *(G-3839)*

Jonmar Gear and Machine Inc........G 330 854-6500
   Canal Fulton *(G-1776)*

Lhy Powertrain Corporation............E 330 533-6801
   Canfield *(G-1812)*

Little Mountain Precision LLC.........E 440 290-2903
   Mentor *(G-9555)*

Petro Gear Corporation..................F 216 431-2820
   Cleveland *(G-4156)*

Robertson Manufacturing Co..........F 216 531-8222
   Concord Township *(G-5395)*

Sew-Eurodrive Inc..........................D 937 335-0036
   Troy *(G-13254)*

Stahl Gear & Machine Co................G 216 431-2820
   Cleveland *(G-4323)*

Tgm Holdings Company...................G 419 885-3769
   Sylvania *(G-12728)*

Timken Newco I LLC......................G 234 262-3000
   North Canton *(G-10674)*

GENERATING APPARATUS & PARTS: Electrical

Turtlecreek Township......................F 513 932-4080
   Lebanon *(G-8293)*

GENERATION EQPT: Electronic

Energy Technologies Inc................D 419 522-4444
   Mansfield *(G-8786)*

Erico Products Inc..........................B 440 248-0100
   Cleveland *(G-3683)*

Eti Tech LLC..................................F 937 832-4200
   Kettering *(G-8120)*

Lubrizol Global Management Inc.........F 216 447-5000
   Cleveland *(G-3970)*

Power Source Service LLC..............G 513 607-4555
   Batavia *(G-883)*

Proteus Electronics Inc..................G 419 886-2296
   Bellville *(G-1142)*

Sarica Manufacturing Company.........E 937 484-4030
   Urbana *(G-13477)*

Spirit Avionics Ltd.........................F 614 237-4271
   Columbus *(G-5284)*

Superior Packaging........................F 419 380-3335
   Toledo *(G-13137)*

Tecmark Corporation......................D 440 205-7600
   Mentor *(G-9634)*

Thermo Fisher Scientific Inc...........F 513 948-6290
   Blue Ash *(G-1343)*

GENERATORS: Electrochemical, Fuel Cell

Plug Power Inc...............................G 518 605-5703
   West Carrollton *(G-13931)*

GENERATORS: Gas

Rexarc International Inc..................E 937 839-4604
   West Alexandria *(G-13921)*

Rti Remmele Engineering Inc.........C 651 635-4179
   Cleveland *(G-4263)*

GIFT SHOP

Amish Door Inc...............................C 330 359-5464
   Wilmot *(G-14592)*

Down Home.....................................G 740 393-1186
   Mount Vernon *(G-10243)*

E Warther & Sons Inc.....................F 330 343-7513
   Dover *(G-6244)*

Handcrafted Jewelry Inc.................G 330 650-9011
   Hudson *(G-7843)*

Odyssey Spirits Inc.........................F 330 562-1523
   Chagrin Falls *(G-2174)*

R J Manray Inc.................................. G 330 559-6716
Canfield *(G-1814)*

S-P Company Inc.............................. D 330 782-5651
Columbiana *(G-4627)*

Schindlers Broad Run Chshuse I.......... F 330 343-4108
Dover *(G-6260)*

Shops By Todd Inc.......................... G 937 458-3192
Beavercreek *(G-982)*

Velvet Ice Cream Company................... D 740 892-3921
Utica *(G-13488)*

Youngs Jersey Dairy Inc................... B 937 325-0629
Yellow Springs *(G-14794)*

GIFT WRAP: Paper, Made From Purchased Materials

American Greetings Corporation........... A 216 252-7300
Cleveland *(G-3344)*

GIFT, NOVELTY & SOUVENIR STORES: Gifts & Novelties

City Apparel Inc............................ F 419 434-1155
Findlay *(G-6852)*

Golden Turtle Chocolate Fctry............ G 513 932-1990
Lebanon *(G-8264)*

GIFTS & NOVELTIES: Wholesalers

Papyrus-Recycled Greetings Inc........... D 773 348-6410
Westlake *(G-14319)*

GLASS & GLASS CERAMIC PRDTS, PRESSED OR BLOWN: Tableware

Anchor Hocking LLC......................... A 740 687-2500
Columbus *(G-4711)*

Ghp II LLC................................. C 740 687-2500
Lancaster *(G-8204)*

Libbey Glass LLC........................... D 419 727-2211
Toledo *(G-13034)*

Libbey Glass LLC........................... C 419 325-2100
Toledo *(G-13033)*

GLASS PRDTS, FROM PURCHASED GLASS: Glassware

Mosser Glass Inc........................... E 740 439-1827
Cambridge *(G-1751)*

GLASS PRDTS, FROM PURCHASED GLASS: Insulating

Intigral Inc............................... G 440 439-0980
Youngstown *(G-14877)*

Intigral Inc............................... C 440 439-0980
Walton Hills *(G-13698)*

GLASS PRDTS, FROM PURCHASED GLASS: Mirrored

Bruening Glass Works Inc................... G 440 333-4768
Cleveland *(G-3445)*

Chantilly Development Corp................. E 419 243-8109
Toledo *(G-12916)*

Installed Building Pdts LLC................ B 614 308-9900
Columbus *(G-5009)*

GLASS PRDTS, FROM PURCHASED GLASS: Sheet, Bent

Glasstech Inc.............................. C 419 661-9500
Perrysburg *(G-11226)*

GLASS PRDTS, FROM PURCHASED GLASS: Windshields

Aag Glass LLC.............................. E 513 286-8268
Batavia *(G-849)*

Safelite Group Inc......................... A 614 210-9000
Columbus *(G-5244)*

GLASS PRDTS, FROM PURCHD GLASS: Strengthened Or Reinforced

Glass Surface Systems Inc.................. D 330 745-8500
Barberton *(G-808)*

Kimmatt Corp............................... G 937 228-3811
West Alexandria *(G-13920)*

GLASS PRDTS, PRESSED OR BLOWN: Furnishings & Access

Libbey Inc................................. C 419 325-2100
Toledo *(G-13035)*

GLASS PRDTS, PRESSED OR BLOWN: Glass Fibers, Textile

Knoble Glass & Metal Inc................... G 513 753-1246
Cincinnati *(G-2802)*

Owens Corning Ht Inc....................... E 419 248-8000
Toledo *(G-13086)*

Owens Corning Sales LLC.................... A 419 248-8000
Toledo *(G-13088)*

GLASS PRDTS, PRESSED OR BLOWN: Glassware, Art Or Decorative

Anchor Hocking Consmr GL Corp............. G 740 653-2527
Lancaster *(G-8176)*

Modern China Company Inc................... E 330 938-6104
Sebring *(G-11898)*

GLASS PRDTS, PRESSED OR BLOWN: Scientific Glassware

Technical Glass Products Inc............... F 425 396-8420
Perrysburg *(G-11269)*

Variety Glass Inc.......................... F 740 432-3643
Cambridge *(G-1765)*

GLASS PRDTS, PRESSED OR BLOWN: Yarn, Fiberglass

Integris Composites Inc.................... D 740 928-0326
Hebron *(G-7619)*

GLASS, AUTOMOTIVE: Wholesalers

Fuyao Glass America Inc.................... B 937 496-5777
Moraine *(G-10164)*

GLASS: Fiber

Dal-Little Fabricating Inc................. G 216 883-3323
Cleveland *(G-3598)*

Industrial Fiberglass Spc Inc............. E 937 222-9000
Vandalia *(G-13561)*

Mfg Composite Systems Company............. B 440 997-5851
Ashtabula *(G-605)*

Midwest Composites LLC..................... F 419 738-2431
Wapakoneta *(G-13721)*

Scottrods LLC.............................. G 419 499-2705
Monroeville *(G-10120)*

GLASS: Flat

Custom Glass Solutions LLC................. E 248 340-1800
Upper Sandusky *(G-13437)*

Nsg Glass North America Inc................ C 734 755-5816
Luckey *(G-8671)*

Nsg Glass North America Inc................ E 419 247-4800
Toledo *(G-13065)*

Pilkington Holdings Inc.................... B
Toledo *(G-13097)*

Pilkington North America Inc.............. C 800 547-9280
Northwood *(G-10808)*

Rsl LLC.................................... E 330 392-8900
Warren *(G-13795)*

Schodorf Truck Body & Eqp Co.............. F 614 228-6793
Columbus *(G-5253)*

Taylor Products Inc........................ E 419 263-2313
Payne *(G-11166)*

Vinylume Products Inc...................... F 330 799-2000
Youngstown *(G-14964)*

GLASS: Pressed & Blown, NEC

Anchor Hocking Corporation................ G 614 633-4247
Columbus *(G-4712)*

Anderson Glass Co Inc...................... G 614 476-4877
Columbus *(G-4717)*

Eickholt Glass Inc......................... F 614 638-4903
Columbus *(G-4899)*

General Electric Company................... G 740 385-2114
Logan *(G-8514)*

General Electric Company................... G 330 373-1400
Warren *(G-13767)*

Interntnal Auto Cmpnnts Group............. A 419 433-5653
Wauseon *(G-13853)*

Jack Pine Studio LLC....................... G 740 332-2223
Laurelville *(G-8237)*

Johns Manville Corporation................ C 419 878-8111
Waterville *(G-13835)*

Pittsburgh Corning LLC..................... B 724 327-6100
Toledo *(G-13100)*

Rocket Ventures LLC........................ F 419 530-6083
Toledo *(G-13117)*

Technical Glass Products Inc.............. F 440 639-6399
Painesville *(G-11113)*

Wilson Optical Labs Inc.................... E 440 357-7000
Mentor *(G-9652)*

GLASS: Tempered

Cardinal CT Company........................ E 740 892-2324
Utica *(G-13486)*

Cardinal Glass Industries Inc............. E 740 892-2324
Utica *(G-13487)*

Glasstech Inc.............................. C 419 661-9500
Perrysburg *(G-11226)*

Machined Glass Specialist Inc............. G 937 743-6166
Springboro *(G-12259)*

Trulite GL Alum Solutions LLC............. D 740 929-2443
Hebron *(G-7642)*

GLOVES: Safety

Ansell Healthcare Products LLC............ C 740 622-4369
Coshocton *(G-5448)*

Ansell Healthcare Products LLC............ E 740 622-4311
Coshocton *(G-5449)*

Enespro LLC................................ G 630 332-2801
Cleveland *(G-3674)*

National Safety Apparel LLC............... D 800 553-0672
Cleveland *(G-4062)*

GLOVES: Work

Wcm Holdings Inc........................... C 513 705-2100
Cincinnati *(G-3213)*

West Chester Holdings LLC.................. C 513 705-2100
Cincinnati *(G-3220)*

PRODUCT

GLOVES: Woven Or Knit, From Purchased Materials

Totes Isotoner Holdings LLC................ C 513 682-8200
Cincinnati *(G-3160)*

GLYCOL ETHERS

Catexel Nease LLC........................... D 513 738-1255
Harrison *(G-7544)*

GOLF COURSES: Public

McClelland Inc................................ E 740 452-3036
Zanesville *(G-15027)*

GOLF DRIVING RANGES

Mudbrook Golf Ctr At Thndrbird........... G 419 433-2945
Huron *(G-7880)*

GOLF EQPT

Dayton Stencil Works Company........... F 937 223-3233
Dayton *(G-5739)*

Golf Galaxy Golfworks Inc.................. C 740 328-4193
Newark *(G-10504)*

Steven A Esnbrown Lk Lure Qprt......... G 740 965-2200
Galena *(G-7174)*

Sunset Golf LLC.............................. G 419 994-5563
Tallmadge *(G-12753)*

GOURMET FOOD STORES

Mustard Seed Health Fd Mkt Inc.......... E 440 519-3663
Solon *(G-12155)*

GOVERNMENT, GENERAL: Administration

City of Cleveland............................. E 216 664-3013
Cleveland *(G-3499)*

Turtlecreek Township........................ F 513 932-4080
Lebanon *(G-8293)*

GRADING SVCS

Great Lakes Crushing Ltd................... D 440 944-5500
Wickliffe *(G-14376)*

GRAIN & FIELD BEANS WHOLESALERS

Imex Bz LLC.................................. F 786 866-8798
Orrville *(G-10986)*

GRANITE: Crushed & Broken

Bradley Stone Industries LLC............. F 440 519-3277
Solon *(G-12088)*

Martin Marietta Materials Inc.............. F 513 701-1140
West Chester *(G-14026)*

The National Lime and Stone Company. E 419 422-4341
Findlay *(G-6927)*

GRANITE: Cut & Shaped

Creative Countertops Ohio Inc............ F 937 540-9450
Englewood *(G-6610)*

Cutting Edge Countertops Inc............. E 419 873-9500
Perrysburg *(G-11212)*

Quarrymasters Inc........................... G 330 612-0474
Akron *(G-274)*

Zelaya Stoneworks LLC..................... F 513 777-8030
Liberty Township *(G-8380)*

GRAPHIC ARTS & RELATED DESIGN SVCS

Abstract Displays Inc....................... F 513 985-9700
Blue Ash *(G-1241)*

Academy Graphic Comm Inc............... F 216 661-2550
Cleveland *(G-3289)*

Alonovus Corp................................ E 330 674-2300
Millersburg *(G-9968)*

Container Graphics Corp..................... E 419 531-5133
Toledo *(G-12932)*

Coyne Graphic Finishing Inc............... E 740 397-6232
Mount Vernon *(G-10241)*

Envoi Design Inc............................. G 513 651-4229
Cincinnati *(G-2593)*

Golden Graphics Ltd......................... F 419 673-6260
Kenton *(G-8099)*

Great Lakes Graphics Inc................... G 216 391-0077
Cleveland *(G-3791)*

Gregg Macmillan.............................. G 513 248-2121
Milford *(G-9937)*

Insignia Signs Inc............................ G 937 866-2341
Moraine *(G-10170)*

Laipplys Prtg Mktg Sltions Inc............. G 740 387-9282
Marion *(G-8975)*

ML Advertising & Design LLC.............. G 419 447-6523
Tiffin *(G-12791)*

Mueller Art Cover & Binding Co........... E 440 238-3303
Strongsville *(G-12577)*

Perrons Printing Company Inc............. G 440 236-8870
Columbia Station *(G-4596)*

Phantasm Dsgns Sprtsn More Ltd........ G 419 538-6737
Ottawa *(G-11042)*

Rba Inc.. G 330 336-6700
Wadsworth *(G-13667)*

Sanger Holdings LLC........................ F 513 784-9046
Cincinnati *(G-3063)*

Schuerholz Inc............................... G 937 294-5218
Dayton *(G-5997)*

White Tiger Inc............................... F 740 852-4873
London *(G-8543)*

Youngstown Pre-Press Inc.................. G 330 793-3690
Youngstown *(G-14974)*

GRAPHITE MINING SVCS

Graftech Holdings Inc........................ D 216 676-2000
Independence *(G-7905)*

GRATINGS: Open Steel Flooring

Ohio Gratings Inc............................. B 800 321-9800
Canton *(G-1966)*

GRAVE VAULTS, METAL

American Steel Grave Vault Co............. F 419 468-6715
Galion *(G-7178)*

GRAVEL MINING

Beck Sand & Gravel Inc..................... G 330 626-3863
Ravenna *(G-11518)*

Fleming Construction Co.................... G 740 494-2177
Prospect *(G-11501)*

Fouremans Sand & Gravel Inc............. G 937 547-1005
Greenville *(G-7341)*

Morrow Gravel Company Inc............... F 513 899-2000
Morrow *(G-10202)*

Oster Sand and Gravel Inc................. G 330 494-5472
Canton *(G-1970)*

Stansley Mineral Resources Inc........... E 419 843-2813
Sylvania *(G-12724)*

Watson Gravel Inc........................... G 513 422-3781
Middletown *(G-9902)*

Watson Gravel Inc........................... E 513 863-0070
Hamilton *(G-7538)*

Weber Sand & Gravel Inc................... G 419 636-7920
Bryan *(G-1666)*

Wysong Gravel Co Inc....................... G 937 452-1523
Camden *(G-1769)*

Wysong Gravel Co Inc....................... G 937 839-5497
West Alexandria *(G-13925)*

Wysong Gravel Co Inc....................... F 937 456-4539
West Alexandria *(G-13924)*

GREASES: Lubricating

Foam Seal Inc................................ C 216 881-8111
Cleveland *(G-3730)*

GREENHOUSES: Prefabricated Metal

Cropking Incorporated....................... F 330 302-4203
Lodi *(G-8500)*

Ludy Greenhouse Mfg Corp................ D 800 255-5839
New Madison *(G-10422)*

Prospiant Inc................................. D 513 242-0310
Cincinnati *(G-3009)*

Rough Brothers Mfg Inc.................... D 513 242-0310
Cincinnati *(G-3054)*

XS Smith Inc................................. E 252 940-5060
Cincinnati *(G-3239)*

GRINDING SVC: Precision, Commercial Or Indl

Advanced Cryogenic Entps Inc............ F 330 922-0750
Akron *(G-20)*

G H Cutter Services Inc..................... E 419 476-0476
Toledo *(G-12971)*

Herman Machine Inc......................... F 330 633-3261
Tallmadge *(G-12736)*

Micro Products Co Inc....................... E 440 943-0258
Willoughby Hills *(G-14560)*

P & L Precision Grinding Llc............... F 330 746-8081
Youngstown *(G-14909)*

S C Industries Inc........................... E 216 732-9000
Euclid *(G-6677)*

Sandwisch Enterprises Inc.................. G 419 944-6446
Toledo *(G-13121)*

Tipp Machine & Tool Inc..................... C 937 890-8428
Dayton *(G-6055)*

GROCERIES, GENERAL LINE WHOLESALERS

Brantley Partners IV LP..................... G 216 464-8400
Cleveland *(G-3434)*

Imex Bz LLC.................................. F 786 866-8798
Orrville *(G-10986)*

La Perla Inc................................... G 419 534-2074
Toledo *(G-13026)*

R S Hanline and Co Inc..................... C 419 347-8077
Shelby *(G-11974)*

Ricking Holding Co........................... F 513 825-3551
Cleveland *(G-4241)*

The Ellenbee-Leggett Company Inc....... C 513 874-3200
Fairfield *(G-6782)*

Zwanenberg Food Group (usa) Inc........ F 513 682-6000
Cincinnati *(G-3244)*

GUIDED MISSILES & SPACE VEHICLES

Space Exploration Tech Corp.............. C 559 593-2731
Lockbourne *(G-8492)*

Tessec Manufacturing Svcs LLC........... E 937 985-3552
Dayton *(G-6046)*

GUM & WOOD CHEMICALS

Damon Industries Inc........................ D 330 821-5310
Alliance *(G-379)*

PPG Architectural Coatings LLC........... D 440 297-8000
Strongsville *(G-12587)*

GUTTERS: Sheet Metal

GUTTER TOPPER LTD........................ G 513 797-5800
Batavia *(G-866)*

Matteo Aluminum Inc........................ E 440 585-5213
Wickliffe *(G-14382)*

Roofing Annex LLC........................... G 513 942-0555
West Chester *(G-14141)*

GYPSUM PRDTS

Caraustar Industries Inc.......................... E 330 665-7700
Copley (G-5432)

Ernst Enterprises Inc............................. F 419 222-2015
Lima (G-8406)

Mineral Processing Company.................. G 419 396-3501
Carey (G-2059)

Owens Corning Sales LLC...................... C 330 634-0460
Tallmadge (G-12744)

Priest Services Inc................................. G 440 333-1123
Mayfield Heights (G-9340)

United States Gypsum Company........... B 419 734-3161
Gypsum (G-7460)

Wall Technology Inc................................ G 715 532-5548
Toledo (G-13176)

GYROSCOPES

Atlantic Inertial Systems Inc.................. C 740 788-3800
Heath (G-7593)

HAIR & HAIR BASED PRDTS

Aajaj Hair Company LLC......................... F 216 309-0816
Cleveland (G-3285)

Ariezhair Collection LLC......................... F 614 964-5748
Columbus (G-4725)

Crownme Coil Care LLC.......................... F 937 797-2070
Trotwood (G-13195)

Pur Hair Extensions LLC......................... G 330 786-5772
Akron (G-270)

U S Hair Inc... G 614 235-5190
Columbus (G-5336)

HAIR CARE PRDTS

John Frieda Prof Hair Care Inc.............. E 800 521-3189
Cincinnati (G-2767)

Natural Beauty Products Inc.................. F 513 420-9400
Middletown (G-9882)

Pfizer Inc... F 937 746-3603
Franklin (G-7039)

Procter & Gamble Company.................. A 513 983-1100
Cincinnati (G-2999)

HAND TOOLS, NEC: Wholesalers

Elliott Tool Technologies Ltd.................. D 937 253-6133
Dayton (G-5763)

National Tool & Equipment Inc.............. F 330 629-8665
Youngstown (G-14903)

Norbar Torque Tools Inc......................... F 440 953-1175
Willoughby (G-14495)

HANDBAGS

Judith Leiber LLC................................... E 614 449-4217
Columbus (G-5043)

Ravenworks Deer Skin........................... G 937 354-5151
Mount Victory (G-10270)

HANDBAGS: Women's

Hugo Bosca Company Inc...................... F 937 323-5523
Springfield (G-12327)

HANDYMAN SVCS

Handshakers Construction LLC............. F 513 370-1371
Cincinnati (G-2704)

HARD RUBBER PRDTS, NEC

International Automotive Compo............ F 330 279-6557
Holmesville (G-7801)

HARDWARE

A JC Inc... F 800 428-2438
Hudson (G-7826)

AB Bonded Locksmiths Inc.................... G 513 531-7334
Cincinnati (G-2330)

Action Coupling & Eqp Inc..................... D 330 279-4242
Holmesville (G-7793)

Aluminum Bearing Co of America......... G 216 267-8560
Cleveland (G-3336)

Ampex Metal Products Company........... D 216 267-9242
Brookpark (G-1544)

Annin & Co Inc.. C 740 622-4447
Coshocton (G-5447)

Arnco Corporation.................................. F 800 847-7661
Elyria (G-6498)

Boardman Molded Products Inc............ D 330 788-2400
Youngstown (G-14822)

Chantilly Development Corp................... E 419 243-8109
Toledo (G-12916)

Conform Automotive LLC....................... B 937 492-2708
Sidney (G-12002)

Curtiss-Wright Flow Ctrl Corp............... D 216 267-3200
Cleveland (G-3583)

Custom Metal Works Inc........................ F 419 668-7831
Norwalk (G-10834)

Dayton Superior Corporation................. F 937 682-4015
Rushsylvania (G-11665)

Desco Corporation.................................. G 614 888-8855
New Albany (G-10339)

Die Co Inc... E 440 942-8856
Eastlake (G-6423)

Eaton Corporation.................................. E 330 274-0743
Aurora (G-667)

Edward W Daniel LLC............................. F 440 647-1960
Wellington (G-13885)

Elster Perfection Corporation................ D 440 428-1171
Geneva (G-7236)

Faull & Son LLC...................................... F 330 652-4341
Niles (G-10588)

Federal Equipment Company................. D 513 621-5260
Cincinnati (G-2616)

Feitl Manufacturing Co Inc.................... F 330 405-6600
Macedonia (G-8690)

First Francis Company Inc..................... E 440 352-8927
Painesville (G-11087)

Flex-Strut Inc.. D 330 372-9999
Warren (G-13765)

Florida Production Engrg Inc................. D 937 996-4361
New Madison (G-10421)

Fort Recovery Industries Inc................. C 419 375-4121
Fort Recovery (G-8904)

Gateway Con Forming Svcs Inc............ D 513 353-2000
Miamitown (G-9758)

Group Industries Inc.............................. E 216 271-0702
Cleveland (G-3796)

Hbd/Thermoid Inc................................... C 800 543-8070
Bellefontaine (G-1108)

Hdt Expeditionary Systems Inc............ F 513 943-1111
Cincinnati (G-2306)

Heller Machine Products Inc................. G 216 281-2951
Cleveland (G-3820)

Hfi LLC... B 614 491-0700
Canal Winchester (G-1791)

Interntnal Auto Cmpnnts Group........... A 419 433-5653
Wauseon (G-13853)

Kasai North America Inc........................ E 614 356-1494
Dublin (G-6314)

L & W Inc... D 734 397-6300
Avon (G-730)

Linear It Solutions LLC.......................... F 614 306-0761
Marysville (G-9035)

Matdan Corporation............................... E 513 794-0500
Blue Ash (G-1303)

McGregor Mtal Yllow Sprng Wrks......... D 937 325-5561
Springfield (G-12351)

Meese Inc.. F 440 998-1202
Ashtabula (G-604)

Midlake Products & Mfg Co................... D 330 875-4202
Louisville (G-8608)

Miller Studio Inc..................................... G 330 339-1100
New Philadelphia (G-10459)

Netherland Rubber Company................. F 513 733-0883
Cincinnati (G-2899)

Nova Machine Products Inc................... C 216 267-3200
Middleburg Heights (G-9775)

Ohio Hydraulics Inc............................... E 513 771-2590
Cincinnati (G-2924)

Parker-Hannifin Corporation................. G 704 637-1190
Wickliffe (G-14388)

Peterson American Corporation............ E 419 867-8711
Holland (G-7777)

Qualitor Subsidiary H Inc...................... E 419 562-7987
Bucyrus (G-1686)

R & R Tool Inc... E 937 783-8665
Blanchester (G-1237)

S & K Products Company........................ E 419 268-2244
Celina (G-2118)

S Lehman Central Warehouse............... G 330 828-8828
Dalton (G-5594)

Samsel Rope & Marine Supply Co......... E 216 241-0333
Cleveland (G-4272)

Sarasota Quality Products..................... G 440 899-9820
Westlake (G-14331)

Sheet Metal Products Co Inc................. E 440 392-9000
Mentor (G-9615)

Summers Acquisition Corp.................... E 216 941-7700
Cleveland (G-4341)

Superior Metal Products Inc.................. E 419 228-1145
Lima (G-8454)

Te-Co Manufacturing LLC...................... D 937 836-0961
Englewood (G-6625)

Technoform GL Insul N Amer Inc.......... E 330 487-6600
Twinsburg (G-13384)

Trim Parts Inc... E 513 934-0815
Lebanon (G-8291)

United Die & Mfg Sales Co.................... E 330 938-6141
Sebring (G-11904)

Universal Industrial Pdts Inc................ F 419 737-9584
Pioneer (G-11331)

Verhoff Machine & Welding Inc............. C 419 596-3202
Continental (G-5424)

Voss Industries LLC............................... D 216 771-7655
Berea (G-1193)

Washington Products Inc....................... F 330 837-5101
Massillon (G-9252)

Whiteside Manufacturing Co................. E 740 363-1179
Delaware (G-6181)

HARDWARE & BUILDING PRDTS: Plastic

Associated Materials LLC....................... C 330 929-1811
Cuyahoga Falls (G-5528)

Associated Materials Group Inc............ D 330 929-1811
Cuyahoga Falls (G-5529)

Axion International Inc........................... G 740 452-2500
Zanesville (G-14989)

Blackthorn LLC.. F 937 836-9296
Clayton (G-3272)

Buckeye Stamping Company................. D 877 728-0776
Columbus (G-4786)

Calorplast USA LLC................................ G 513 576-6333
Milford (G-9927)

Cosmo Plastics Company....................... C 440 498-7500
Cleveland (G-3569)

Cpg International LLC.............................. B 937 655-8766
Wilmington (G-14577)

Dayton Superior Corporation................. C 937 866-0711
Miamisburg (G-9687)

Fox Lite Inc................................E 937 864-1966
Fairborn *(G-6692)*

Gorell Enterprises Inc........................B 724 465-1800
Streetsboro *(G-12502)*

Harbor Industrial Corp......................F 440 599-8366
Conneaut *(G-5402)*

Pro-TEC Industries Inc......................G 440 937-4142
Avon *(G-736)*

Stonyridge Inc..................................F 937 845-9482
New Carlisle *(G-10380)*

Style Crest Enterprises Inc................E 419 355-8586
Fremont *(G-7134)*

Timbertech Limited.............................B 937 655-8766
Wilmington *(G-14586)*

Trusscore USA Inc...........................E 888 418-4679
Dayton *(G-6066)*

West & Barker Inc.............................F 330 652-9923
Niles *(G-10609)*

Westlake Dimex LLC...........................C 800 334-3776
Marietta *(G-8961)*

HARDWARE & EQPT: Stage, Exc Lighting

Beck Studios Inc................................E 513 831-6650
Milford *(G-9925)*

Janson Industries.............................D 330 455-7029
Canton *(G-1921)*

Millers Aplus Cmpt Svcs LLC..............F 330 620-5288
Akron *(G-234)*

Tiffin Scenic Studios Inc...................E 800 445-1546
Tiffin *(G-12805)*

HARDWARE STORES

Caldwell Lumber & Supply Co..............F 740 732-2306
Caldwell *(G-1724)*

E P Gerber & Sons Inc......................D 330 857-2021
Kidron *(G-8126)*

Hyde Park Lumber Company................E 513 271-1500
Cincinnati *(G-2736)*

Judy Mills Company Inc......................E 513 271-4241
Cincinnati *(G-2775)*

Kemps Ace Hardware Inc.....................F 740 472-1651
Woodsfield *(G-14614)*

Lochard Inc.....................................D 937 492-8811
Sidney *(G-12031)*

Matco Tools Corporation.....................B 330 929-4949
Stow *(G-12440)*

Mid-Wood Inc....................................F 419 257-3331
North Baltimore *(G-10614)*

Rocky Hinge Inc................................G 330 539-6296
Girard *(G-7279)*

S Lehman Central Warehouse..............G 330 828-8828
Dalton *(G-5594)*

Spencer Feed & Supply LLC...............F 330 648-2111
Spencer *(G-12235)*

Terry Lumber and Supply Co................F 330 659-6800
Peninsula *(G-11184)*

Thomas Do-It Center Inc....................E 740 446-2002
Gallipolis *(G-7209)*

HARDWARE STORES: Builders'

Wauseon Silo & Coal Company............F
Wauseon *(G-13861)*

HARDWARE STORES: Pumps & Pumping Eqpt

Fountain Specialists Inc....................G 513 831-5717
Milford *(G-9934)*

Graco Ohio Inc................................D 330 494-1313
North Canton *(G-10644)*

Oase North America Inc......................G 800 365-3880
Aurora *(G-682)*

HARDWARE STORES: Tools

Cammel Saw Company........................F 330 477-3764
Canton *(G-1851)*

Gordon Tool Inc................................F 419 263-3151
Payne *(G-11163)*

National Tool & Equipment Inc.............F 330 629-8665
Youngstown *(G-14903)*

Stanley Industrial & Auto LLC.............D 614 755-7000
Dublin *(G-6349)*

HARDWARE WHOLESALERS

Atlas Bolt & Screw Company LLC.........C 419 289-6171
Ashland *(G-519)*

Barnes Group Inc.............................C 419 891-9292
Maumee *(G-9264)*

Chrisnik Inc....................................G 513 738-2920
Okeana *(G-10927)*

Custer Products Limited.....................F 330 490-3158
Massillon *(G-9184)*

Diy Holster LLC................................G 419 921-2168
Elyria *(G-6520)*

DL Schwartz Co LLC.........................G 260 692-1464
Hicksville *(G-7647)*

G & S Metal Products Co Inc...............C 216 441-0700
Cleveland *(G-3748)*

Khempco Bldg Sup Co Ltd Partnr.........D 740 549-0465
Delaware *(G-6159)*

Matco Tools Corporation.....................B 330 929-4949
Stow *(G-12440)*

Ohashi Technica USA Inc....................G 740 965-5115
Sunbury *(G-12671)*

Paulin Industries Inc.........................E 216 433-7633
Parma *(G-11134)*

Shook Manufactured Pdts Inc...............G 330 848-9780
Akron *(G-311)*

Specialty Hardware Inc......................G 216 291-1160
Cleveland *(G-4319)*

Superior Caster Inc...........................E 513 539-8980
Middletown *(G-9896)*

Twin Ventures Inc.............................F 330 405-3838
Twinsburg *(G-13388)*

Waxman Industries Inc.......................C 440 439-1830
Bedford *(G-1065)*

HARDWARE, WHOLESALE: Bolts

Akko Fastener Inc.............................F 513 489-8300
Middletown *(G-9841)*

HARDWARE, WHOLESALE: Builders', NEC

Lckbm Company................................D 419 636-4555
Bryan *(G-1648)*

Twin Cities Concrete Co.....................F 330 343-4491
Dover *(G-6266)*

HARDWARE, WHOLESALE: Nuts

Facil North America Inc......................C 330 487-2500
Twinsburg *(G-13302)*

HARDWARE, WHOLESALE: Power Tools & Access

Noco Company..................................D 216 464-8131
Glenwillow *(G-7286)*

HARDWARE, WHOLESALE: Screws

Maumee Machine & Tool Corp..............E 419 385-2501
Toledo *(G-13048)*

HARDWARE: Aircraft

Esterline Technologies Corp................E 216 706-2960
Cleveland *(G-3687)*

Tessec LLC......................................D 937 576-0010
Dayton *(G-6045)*

Twin Valley Metalcraft Asm LLC...........G 937 787-4634
West Alexandria *(G-13922)*

HARDWARE: Aircraft & Marine, Incl Pulleys & Similar Items

Acorn Technology Corporation..............E 216 663-1244
Shaker Heights *(G-11925)*

HARDWARE: Builders'

Arrow Tru-Line Inc...........................G 419 636-7013
Bryan *(G-1630)*

Cleveland Steel Specialty Co...............E 216 464-9400
Bedford Heights *(G-1074)*

Endura Products LLC.........................F 419 248-8911
Toledo *(G-12952)*

Napoleon Spring Works Inc..................C 419 445-1010
Archbold *(G-504)*

HARDWARE: Casket

Langenau Manufacturing Company........F 216 651-3400
Cleveland *(G-3939)*

HARDWARE: Furniture, Builders' & Other Household

Dudick Inc......................................E 330 562-1970
Streetsboro *(G-12499)*

Fortner Upholstering Inc....................F 614 475-8282
Columbus *(G-4936)*

Master Mfg Co Inc............................E 216 641-0500
Cleveland *(G-3997)*

HARNESS ASSEMBLIES: Cable & Wire

American Advnced Assmblies LLC.........E 937 339-6267
Troy *(G-13199)*

Ankim Enterprises Incorporated............G 937 599-1121
Sidney *(G-11993)*

C C M Wire Inc................................F 330 425-3421
Twinsburg *(G-13283)*

Co-Ax Technology Inc........................C 440 914-9200
Solon *(G-12096)*

Connective Design Incorporated...........F 937 746-8252
Miamisburg *(G-9683)*

D H S LLC.......................................F 937 599-2485
Bellefontaine *(G-1103)*

Deca Mfg Co....................................F 419 884-0071
Mansfield *(G-8780)*

Dynalab Inc.....................................D 614 866-9999
Reynoldsburg *(G-11568)*

Ewh Spectrum LLC...........................D 937 593-8010
Bellefontaine *(G-1107)*

Gmelectric Inc..................................G 330 477-3392
Canton *(G-1902)*

L & J Cable Inc................................F 937 526-9445
Russia *(G-11675)*

La Grange Elec Assemblies Co.............E 440 355-5388
Lagrange *(G-8149)*

Malabar Properties LLC......................F 419 884-0071
Mansfield *(G-8816)*

Mega Techway Inc.............................D 440 605-0700
Cleveland *(G-4018)*

Microplex Inc...................................E 330 498-0600
North Canton *(G-10651)*

MJM Industries Inc...........................C 440 350-1230
Fairport Harbor *(G-6819)*

Mueller Electric Company Inc...............G 614 888-8855
New Albany *(G-10346)*

Nimers & Woody II Inc.......................C 937 454-0722
Vandalia *(G-13574)*

Ogc Industries Inc.................................. F 330 456-1500
Canton (G-1963)

Ohio Wire Harness LLC........................ F 937 292-7355
Bellefontaine (G-1114)

Per-Tech Inc....................................... E 330 833-8824
Massillon (G-9232)

Projects Unlimited Inc......................... C 937 918-2200
Dayton (G-5968)

RTD Electronics Inc............................. G 330 487-0716
Twinsburg (G-13370)

Russell Group United LLC .... F 614 353-6853
Columbus (G-5238)

Thermtrol Corporation......................... A 330 497-4148
North Canton (G-10672)

Westbrook Mfg Inc.............................. B 937 254-2004
Dayton (G-6078)

Wetsu Group Inc................................. F 937 324-9353
Springfield (G-12393)

HARNESS WIRING SETS: Internal Combustion Engines

Electripack LLC................................... E 937 433-2602
Moraine (G-10159)

Mueller Electric Company Inc.............. D 216 771-5225
Akron (G-239)

HEALTH & WELFARE COUNCIL

Alscommunity....................................... F 215 478-5095
Coventry Township (G-5480)

HEARING AIDS

Communications Aid Inc....................... F 513 475-8453
Cincinnati (G-2505)

Soundtrace Inc.................................... F 513 278-5288
Mason (G-9153)

HEAT EMISSION OPERATING APPARATUS

Hanon Systems Usa LLC..................... C 313 920-0583
Carey (G-2058)

HEAT EXCHANGERS: After Or Inter Coolers Or Condensers, Etc

Ohio Heat Transfer Ltd........................ F 877 633-0391
Saint Clairsville (G-11705)

Universal Hydraulik USA Corp............. G 419 873-6340
Perrysburg (G-11277)

HEAT TREATING: Metal

Akron Steel Treating Co....................... E 330 773-8211
Akron (G-43)

Al Fe Heat Treating-Ohio Inc............... E 330 336-0211
Wadsworth (G-13628)

Al-Fe Heat Treating LLC....................... F 419 782-7200
Defiance (G-6095)

AM Castle & Co................................... F 330 425-7000
Bedford (G-1011)

Amac Enterprises Inc.......................... C 216 362-1880
Parma (G-11129)

American Quality Stripping Inc............. E 419 625-6288
Sandusky (G-11822)

American Steel Treating Inc................. D 419 874-2044
Perrysburg (G-11202)

ATI Flat Rlled Pdts Hldngs LLC........... F 330 875-2244
Louisville (G-8598)

B&C Machine Co LLC.......................... F 330 745-4013
Barberton (G-796)

Bekaert Corporation............................ E 330 683-5060
Orrville (G-10975)

Berkshire Road Holdings Inc............... F 216 883-4200
Cleveland (G-3416)

Bob Lanes Welding Inc........................ G 740 373-3567
Marietta (G-8904)

Bodycote Imt Inc................................. F 740 852-5000
London (G-8531)

Bodycote Srfc Tech Prperty LLC........ C 513 770-4900
Mason (G-9072)

Bodycote Surfc Tech Mexico LLC....... C 513 770-4900
Mason (G-9075)

Bodycote Thermal Proc Inc................. E 513 921-2300
Cincinnati (G-2416)

Bodycote Thermal Proc Inc................. E 440 473-2020
Cleveland (G-3425)

Bodycote Thermal Proc Inc................. G 740 852-4955
London (G-8532)

Bolttech Mannings LLC........................ G 614 836-0021
Groveport (G-7426)

Bowdil Company................................. F 800 356-8663
Canton (G-1843)

Carpe Diem Industries LLC................. D 419 358-0129
Bluffton (G-1359)

Carpe Diem Industries LLC................. D 419 659-5639
Columbus Grove (G-5382)

Certified Heat Treating Inc.................. G 937 866-0245
Dayton (G-5697)

Cincinnati Gearing Systems Inc.......... D 513 527-8600
Cincinnati (G-2476)

Cincinnati Stl Treating Co LLC............ E 513 271-3173
Cincinnati (G-2487)

Cleveland-Cliffs Columbus LLC.......... C 614 492-6800
Richfield (G-11589)

Clifton Steel Company......................... D 216 662-6111
Maple Heights (G-8881)

Commercial Steel Treating Co............. F 216 431-8204
Cleveland (G-3553)

Curtiss-Wright Surfc Tech LLC........... F 330 425-1490
Twinsburg (G-13290)

Dayton Forging Heat Treating............. D 937 253-4126
Dayton (G-5726)

Derrick Company Inc.......................... E 513 321-8122
Cincinnati (G-2546)

Detroit Flame Hardening Co................ F 513 942-1400
Fairfield (G-6727)

Dewitt Inc.. G 216 662-0800
Maple Heights (G-8882)

Die Co Inc.. E 440 942-8856
Eastlake (G-6423)

Dowa Tht America Inc......................... E 419 354-4144
Dowling Green (G-1410)

Erie Steel Ltd..................................... E 419 478-3743
Toledo (G-12956)

Euclid Heat Treating Co...................... D 216 481-8444
Euclid (G-6650)

Flynn Inc.. G 419 478-3743
Toledo (G-12966)

Fusion Incorporated........................... D 440 946-3300
Willoughby (G-14460)

Gerdau McSteel Atmsphere Annli........ E 330 478-0314
Canton (G-1900)

Gt Technologies Inc............................ E 419 782-8955
Defiance (G-6109)

H & M Metal Processing Co................. G 330 745-3075
Akron (G-168)

Heat Treating Inc................................ E 937 325-3121
Springfield (G-12319)

Heat Treating Equipment Inc............... E 740 549-3700
Lewis Center (G-8335)

Heat Treating Inc................................ E 614 759-9963
Gahanna (G-7159)

Heat-Treating Technologies Inc........... E 419 224-8324
Lima (G-8413)

Hmt Inc.. E 440 599-7005
Conneaut (G-5404)

Kowalski Heat Treating Co.................. F 216 631-4411
Cleveland (G-3927)

Lapham-Hickey Steel Corp.................. D 614 443-4881
Columbus (G-5065)

Lapham-Hickey Steel Corp.................. D 419 399-4803
Paulding (G-11158)

McDonald Steel Plate Inc.................... F 216 883-4200
Cleveland (G-4008)

McOn Inds Inc.................................... E 937 294-2681
Moraine (G-10176)

Metallurgical Service Inc..................... F 937 294-2681
Moraine (G-10177)

Moore Mc Millen Holdings................... E 330 745-3075
Cuyahoga Falls (G-5561)

Neturen America Corporation.............. F 513 863-1900
Hamilton (G-7512)

Northwind Industries Inc..................... G 216 433-0666
Cleveland (G-4099)

Ohio Metallurgical Service Inc............. D 440 365-4104
Elyria (G-6573)

Oliver Steel Plate Co.......................... D 330 425-7000
Twinsburg (G-13347)

P & L Heat Trting Grinding Inc............ E 330 746-1339
Youngstown (G-14907)

P & L Precision Grinding Llc............... F 330 746-8081
Youngstown (G-14909)

Parker Trutec Incorporated................. D 937 323-8833
Springfield (G-12359)

Precision Powder Coating Inc.............. F 330 478-0741
Canton (G-1980)

Pressure Technology Ohio Inc............. E 215 628-1975
Concord Township (G-5393)

Pride Investments LLC........................ F 937 461-1121
Dayton (G-5953)

Ridge Machine & Welding Co.............. G 740 537-2821
Toronto (G-13186)

Team Inc.. F 614 263-1808
Columbus (G-5314)

Techniques Surfaces Usa Inc.............. G 937 323-2556
Springfield (G-12384)

Thermal Solutions Inc......................... E 614 263-1808
Columbus (G-5322)

Thermal Treatment Center Inc............. E 216 881-8100
Wickliffe (G-14396)

Universal Heat Treating Inc................. E 216 641-2000
Aurora (G-691)

USA Heat Treating Inc......................... E 216 587-4700
Cleveland (G-4453)

Vicon Fabricating Company Ltd............ F 440 205-6700
Mentor (G-9649)

Weiss Industries Inc........................... E 419 526-2480
Mansfield (G-8865)

Winston Heat Treating Inc................... E 937 226-0110
Dayton (G-6083)

Worthngton Smuel Coil Proc LLC........ E 330 963-3777
Twinsburg (G-13398)

Xtek Inc... B 513 733-7800
Cincinnati (G-3240)

HEATERS: Swimming Pool, Electric

Aquapro Systems LLC......................... F 877 278-2797
Oakwood (G-10895)

Siemens Industry Inc.......................... F 513 576-2088
Milford (G-9952)

HEATING & AIR CONDITIONING UNITS, COMBINATION

Crawford Ae LLC................................ D 330 794-9770
Akron (G-109)

Energy Labs LLC................................ B 619 671-0100
Westerville (G-14208)

Famous Realty Cleveland Inc................ F 740 685-2533
Byesville *(G-1712)*

J&I Duct Fab Llc.................................... F 937 473-2121
Covington *(G-5495)*

HEATING APPARATUS: Steam

Grid Industrial Heating Inc.................... G 330 332-9931
Salem *(G-11783)*

HEATING EQPT: Complete

Chilltex LLC.. F 937 710-3308
Anna *(G-460)*

Sticker Corporation............................... F 440 946-2100
Willoughby *(G-14534)*

Trane US Inc....................................... F 419 491-2278
Holland *(G-7788)*

Yukon Industries Inc............................. E 440 478-4174
Mentor *(G-9655)*

HEATING EQPT: Induction

Induction Tooling Inc............................ F 440 237-0711
North Royalton *(G-10765)*

Magneforce Inc.................................... F 330 856-9300
Warren *(G-13780)*

Park-Ohio Holdings Corp...................... F 440 947-2000
Cleveland *(G-4136)*

Park-Ohio Industries Inc....................... C 440 947-2000
Cleveland *(G-4137)*

Taylor - Winfield Corporation................. C 330 259-8500
Hubbard *(G-7817)*

HEATING UNITS & DEVICES: Indl, Electric

Furnace Technologies Inc...................... G 419 878-2100
Waterville *(G-13833)*

Glenro Inc... G 606 564-4778
Ripley *(G-11618)*

Glo-Quartz Electric Htr Co Inc............... E 440 255-9701
Mentor *(G-9524)*

Heat Sensor Technologie LLC................ D 513 228-0481
Lebanon *(G-8267)*

Lanly Company.................................... E 216 731-1115
Cleveland *(G-3941)*

Lewco Inc... C 419 625-4014
Sandusky *(G-11850)*

Thermo Systems Technology Inc........... G 216 292-8250
Cleveland *(G-4391)*

Williams Industrial Svc Inc.................... E 419 353-2120
Bowling Green *(G-1447)*

HEAVY DISTILLATES

Ineos Neal LLC................................... E 610 790-3333
Dublin *(G-6308)*

HELMETS: Steel

Armorsource LLC................................. E 740 928-0070
Hebron *(G-7608)*

HELP SUPPLY SERVICES

Fluff Boutique..................................... G 513 227-6614
Cincinnati *(G-2630)*

Industrial Repair and Mfg..................... F 419 822-0314
Delta *(G-6209)*

HOBBY, TOY & GAME STORES: Toys & Games

Anime Palace...................................... G 408 858-1918
Lewis Center *(G-8322)*

Intrism Inc.. G 614 787-4631
Worthington *(G-14716)*

Ohio Art Company............................... D 419 636-3141
Bryan *(G-1655)*

HOISTING SLINGS

Acme Lifting Products Inc..................... G 440 838-4430
Cleveland *(G-3290)*

HOISTS

ARI Phoenix Inc................................... E 513 229-3750
Sharonville *(G-11945)*

Drc Acquisition Inc.............................. E 330 656-1600
Streetsboro *(G-12498)*

Hoist Equipment Co Inc........................ E 440 232-0300
Bedford Heights *(G-1078)*

Lift-Tech International Inc...................... B 330 424-7248
Salem *(G-11794)*

Rp Manufacturing LLC.......................... G 419 468-5095
Iberia *(G-7884)*

HOLDING COMPANIES: Investment, Exc Banks

Ampac Holdings LLC............................ A 513 671-1777
Cincinnati *(G-2365)*

Armor Consolidated Inc........................ A 513 923-5260
Mason *(G-9064)*

Brake Parts Holdings Inc...................... B 216 589-0198
Cleveland *(G-3432)*

Cpp Group Holdings LLC...................... E 216 453-4800
Cleveland *(G-3574)*

Crane Carrier Holdings LLC.................. C 918 286-2889
New Philadelphia *(G-10441)*

Drt Holdings LLC................................. D 937 298-7391
Dayton *(G-5753)*

Elite Property Group LLC...................... F 216 356-7469
Elyria *(G-6527)*

Hexion Topco LLC............................... D 614 225-4000
Columbus *(G-4978)*

Hexpol Holding Inc.............................. F 440 834-4644
Burton *(G-1701)*

Indra Holdings Corp............................. C 513 682-8200
Cincinnati *(G-2743)*

Lion Group Inc.................................... D 800 421-2926
Dayton *(G-5850)*

Norse Dairy Systems Inc...................... C 614 294-4931
Columbus *(G-5128)*

Vertiv JV Holdings LLC........................ A 614 888-0246
Columbus *(G-5348)*

HOLDING COMPANIES: Personal, Exc Banks

Hartzell Industries Inc.......................... F 937 773-6295
Piqua *(G-11352)*

HOME FOR THE MENTALLY HANDICAPPED

Bittersweet Inc.................................... D 419 875-6986
Whitehouse *(G-14358)*

RT Industries Inc................................. G 937 335-5784
Troy *(G-13251)*

HOMEFURNISHING STORES: Beddings & Linens

Morris Furniture Co Inc........................ C 937 874-7100
Fairborn *(G-6697)*

HOMEFURNISHING STORES: Brushes

Buckeye BOP LLC............................... F 740 498-9898
Newcomerstown *(G-10569)*

HOMEFURNISHING STORES: Cutlery

Handy Twine Knife Co........................... G 419 294-3424
Upper Sandusky *(G-13442)*

HOMEFURNISHING STORES: Pottery

All Fired Up Pnt Your Own Pot............... G 330 865-5858
Copley *(G-5429)*

HOMEFURNISHINGS, WHOLESALE: Blinds, Vertical

Custom Blind Corporation...................... F 937 643-2907
Dayton *(G-5717)*

HOMEFURNISHINGS, WHOLESALE: Decorating Splys

Rhc Inc.. E 330 874-3750
Bolivar *(G-1391)*

HOMEFURNISHINGS, WHOLESALE: Draperies

Accent Drapery Co Inc......................... E 614 488-0741
Columbus *(G-4667)*

Inside Outfitters Inc............................. E 614 798-3500
Lewis Center *(G-8338)*

Lumenomics Inc.................................. E 614 798-3500
Lewis Center *(G-8342)*

HOMEFURNISHINGS, WHOLESALE: Grills, Barbecue

S I Distributing Inc.............................. F 419 647-4909
Spencerville *(G-12240)*

HOMEFURNISHINGS, WHOLESALE: Kitchenware

G & S Metal Products Co Inc................. C 216 441-0700
Cleveland *(G-3748)*

Walter F Stephens Jr Inc...................... E 937 746-0521
Franklin *(G-7055)*

HOMES: Log Cabins

Al Yoder Construction Co...................... G 330 359-5726
Millersburg *(G-9967)*

Gillard Construction Inc........................ F 740 376-9744
Marietta *(G-8919)*

Hochstetler Milling LLC........................ E 419 368-0004
Loudonville *(G-8591)*

HOODS: Range, Sheet Metal

Z Line Kitchen and Bath LLC................. G 614 777-5004
Marysville *(G-9055)*

HORSESHOES

Horseshoe Express Inc......................... G 330 692-1209
Canfield *(G-1810)*

HOSE: Automobile, Rubber

Cooper-Standard Automotive Inc............ D 419 352-3533
Bowling Green *(G-1416)*

Mm Outsourcing LLC............................ F 937 661-4300
Leesburg *(G-8300)*

Myers Industries Inc............................. C 330 336-6621
Wadsworth *(G-13653)*

Myers Industries Inc............................. E 330 253-5592
Akron *(G-243)*

Sumiriko Ohio Inc................................ D 419 358-2121
Bluffton *(G-1365)*

HOSE: Flexible Metal

Ace Manufacturing Company................. E 513 541-2490
West Chester *(G-13935)*

Federal Hose Manufacturing LLC........... E 800 346-4673
Cleveland *(G-3710)*

First Francis Company Inc.................... E 440 352-8927
Painesville *(G-11087)*

Hose Master LLC.................................. B 216 481-2020
Cleveland *(G-3840)*

HOSE: Plastic

Kentak Products Company.................... D 330 386-3700
East Liverpool *(G-6393)*

Kentak Products Company.................... E 330 382-2000
East Liverpool *(G-6394)*

HOSE: Rubber

Danfoss Power Solutions II LLC............ F 419 238-1190
Van Wert *(G-13533)*

Eaton Aeroquip LLC............................ A 419 891-7775
Maumee *(G-9292)*

Eaton Aeroquip LLC............................ C 440 523-5000
Cleveland *(G-3650)*

Eaton Corporation.............................. A 419 238-1190
Van Wert *(G-13534)*

HBD Industries Inc............................. E 614 526-7000
Dublin *(G-6302)*

Parker-Hannifin Corporation................ G 704 637-1190
Wickliffe *(G-14388)*

Salem-Republic Rubber Company......... E 877 425-5079
Sebring *(G-11901)*

HOSPITALS: Medical & Surgical

Dan Allen Surgical LLC........................ F 800 261-9953
Newbury *(G-10549)*

HOTELS & MOTELS

Amish Door Inc.................................. C 330 359-5464
Wilmot *(G-14592)*

John Purdum..................................... G 513 897-9686
Waynesville *(G-13879)*

HOUSEHOLD ARTICLES, EXC KITCHEN: Pottery

Bodycote Imt Inc............................... F 740 852-5000
London *(G-8531)*

HOUSEHOLD ARTICLES: Metal

R L Torbeck Industries Inc................... G 513 367-0080
Harrison *(G-7565)*

Voyale Minority Enterprise LLC............ E 216 271-3661
Cleveland *(G-4483)*

HOUSEHOLD FURNISHINGS, NEC

Casco Mfg Solutions Inc...................... D 513 681-0003
Cincinnati *(G-2441)*

Ccp Industries Inc.............................. B 216 535-4227
Richmond Heights *(G-11609)*

Columbus Canvas Products Inc............ F 614 375-1397
Columbus *(G-4819)*

DCW Acquisition Inc........................... G 216 451-0666
Cleveland *(G-3607)*

Integrant LLC.................................... G 440 628-9550
North Royalton *(G-10767)*

Master Mfg Co Inc.............................. E 216 641-0500
Cleveland *(G-3997)*

Nestaway LLC.................................... D 216 587-1500
Cleveland *(G-4069)*

Ohio Table Pad Company..................... F 419 872-6400
Perrysburg *(G-11246)*

STI Liquidation Inc............................. E 614 733-0099
Plain City *(G-11418)*

HOUSEWARES, ELECTRIC: Air Purifiers, Portable

Hmi Industries Inc.............................. E 440 846-7800
Brooklyn *(G-1522)*

HOUSEWARES, ELECTRIC: Cooking Appliances

ORourke Sales Company...................... F 877 599-6548
Grove City *(G-7406)*

Whirlpool Corporation......................... D 937 548-4126
Greenville *(G-7359)*

HOUSEWARES, ELECTRIC: Fans, Exhaust & Ventilating

Ad Industries Inc............................... A 303 744-1911
Dayton *(G-5634)*

Ventilation Systems Jsc...................... F 513 348-3853
Cincinnati *(G-3198)*

HOUSEWARES: Food Dishes & Utensils, Pressed & Molded Pulp

Pressed Paperboard Tech LLC.............. C 419 423-4030
Findlay *(G-6909)*

HUMIDIFIERS & DEHUMIDIFIERS

Guardian Technologies LLC.................. E 866 603-5900
Euclid *(G-6652)*

HYDRAULIC EQPT REPAIR SVC

American Hydraulic Svcs Inc................ E 606 739-8680
Ironton *(G-7929)*

Dynamic Hydraulic Svcs Co LLC........... E 330 447-8967
Dover *(G-6243)*

Fluid System Service Inc...................... G 216 651-2450
Cleveland *(G-3728)*

Hunger Hydraulics CC Ltd.................... F 419 666-4510
Rossford *(G-11657)*

Hunter Hydraulics Inc......................... G 330 455-3983
Canton *(G-1913)*

Hydraulic Products Inc........................ G 440 946-4575
Willoughby *(G-14466)*

Hydraulic Specialists Inc..................... G 740 922-3343
Midvale *(G-9911)*

Ic-Fluid Power Inc.............................. F 419 661-8811
Rossford *(G-11658)*

Perkins Motor Service Ltd.................... F 440 277-1256
Lorain *(G-8573)*

Quad Fluid Dynamics Inc..................... F 330 220-3005
Brunswick *(G-1610)*

ICE

Haller Enterprises Inc......................... F 330 733-9693
Akron *(G-169)*

Home City Ice Company....................... G 440 439-5001
Bedford *(G-1036)*

Home City Ice Company....................... G 937 461-6028
Dayton *(G-5812)*

Home City Ice Company....................... F 419 562-4953
Delaware *(G-6157)*

Home City Ice Company....................... F 614 836-2877
Groveport *(G-7438)*

Home City Ice Company....................... F 513 353-9346
Harrison *(G-7555)*

Lori Holding Co.................................. E 740 342-3230
New Lexington *(G-10403)*

Millersburg Ice Company..................... E 330 674-3016
Millersburg *(G-10000)*

Velvet Ice Cream Company.................. E 419 562-2009
Bucyrus *(G-1693)*

ICE CREAM & ICES WHOLESALERS

United Dairy Farmers Inc..................... C 513 396-8700
Cincinnati *(G-3181)*

Velvet Ice Cream Company.................. E 419 562-2009
Bucyrus *(G-1693)*

IDENTIFICATION TAGS, EXC PAPER

Silly Brandz Global LLC....................... D 419 697-8324
Toledo *(G-13132)*

IGNITION SYSTEMS: High Frequency

Altronic LLC...................................... C 330 545-9768
Girard *(G-7264)*

INCINERATORS

Novagard Solutions Inc....................... D 216 881-8111
Cleveland *(G-4101)*

INCUBATORS & BROODERS: Farm

Chick Master Incubator Company.......... D 330 722-5591
Medina *(G-9387)*

INDL & PERSONAL SVC PAPER WHOLESALERS

Buckeye Paper Co Inc......................... E 330 477-5925
Canton *(G-1847)*

CJ Dannemiller Co.............................. E 330 825-7808
Norton *(G-10819)*

Cleveland Supplyone Inc...................... C 216 514-7000
Cleveland *(G-3527)*

Dayton Industrial Drum Inc.................. E 937 253-8933
Dayton *(G-5608)*

Gt Industrial Supply Inc....................... F 513 771-7000
Cincinnati *(G-2695)*

Gvs Industries Inc.............................. G 513 851-3606
Hamilton *(G-7498)*

Millcraft Group LLC............................ D 216 441-5500
Independence *(G-7911)*

Putnam Plastics Inc............................ G 937 866-6261
Dayton *(G-5969)*

Zebco Industries Inc........................... F 740 654-4510
Lancaster *(G-8233)*

INDL & PERSONAL SVC PAPER, WHOLESALE: Boxes & Containers

Deufol Worldwide Packaging LLC.......... E 440 232-1100
Bedford *(G-1026)*

Responsible Products Limited............... F 888 988-6627
West Chester *(G-14065)*

INDL & PERSONAL SVC PAPER, WHOLESALE: Shipping Splys

Adapt-A-Pak Inc................................ E 937 845-0386
Fairborn *(G-6684)*

Systems Pack Inc............................... E 330 467-5729
Macedonia *(G-8719)*

INDL CONTRACTORS: Exhibit Construction

Abstract Displays Inc......................... F 513 985-9700
Blue Ash *(G-1241)*

Benchmark Craftsman Inc.................... E 866 313-4700
Seville *(G-11910)*

Display Dynamics Inc.......................... F 937 832-2830
Englewood *(G-6612)*

Exhibit Concepts Inc........................... D 937 890-7000
Vandalia *(G-13557)*

INDL DIAMONDS WHOLESALERS

Chardon Tool & Supply Co Inc.............. E 440 286-6440
Chardon *(G-2200)*

INDL EQPT SVCS

P
R
O
D
U
C
T

3-D Service Ltd.................................... C 330 830-3500
Massillon *(G-9168)*

Aerosport Modeling Design LLC........... F 614 834-5227
Canal Winchester *(G-1783)*

Commercial Electric Pdts Corp.............. E 216 241-2886
Cleveland *(G-3552)*

Dayton Industrial Drum Inc.................. E 937 253-8933
Dayton *(G-5608)*

Forge Industries Inc............................ A 330 960-2468
Youngstown *(G-14857)*

GL Nause Co Inc.................................. E 513 722-9500
Loveland *(G-8626)*

Graphic Systems Services Inc.............. E 937 746-0708
Springboro *(G-12254)*

Grob Systems Inc............................... A 419 358-9015
Bluffton *(G-1361)*

Lubrisource Inc................................... F 937 432-9292
Middletown *(G-9872)*

Magnetech Industrial Svcs Inc.............. F 330 830-3500
Massillon *(G-9218)*

Mesocoat Inc...................................... F 216 453-0866
Euclid *(G-6662)*

Northwood Industries Inc..................... F 419 666-2100
Perrysburg *(G-11243)*

Obr Cooling Towers LLC...................... E 419 243-3443
Northwood *(G-10807)*

Quintus Technologies LLC................... E 614 891-2732
Lewis Center *(G-8349)*

Slater Road Mills Inc........................... E 330 332-9951
Salem *(G-11813)*

U S Molding Machinery Co Inc.............. E 440 918-1701
Willoughby *(G-14547)*

Walker National Inc............................. E 614 492-1614
Columbus *(G-5353)*

INDL GASES WHOLESALERS

Airgas Usa LLC................................... G 440 232-6397
Twinsburg *(G-13270)*

INDL HELP SVCS

Aqua Technology Group LLC................ G 513 298-1183
West Chester *(G-13941)*

INDL MACHINERY & EQPT WHOLESALERS

2e Associates Inc................................ E 440 975-9955
Willoughby *(G-14412)*

Addition Manufacturing Tech................ C 513 228-7000
Lebanon *(G-8241)*

Aerocontrolex Group Inc...................... D 216 291-6025
South Euclid *(G-12216)*

Alkon Corporation............................... F 614 799-6650
Dublin *(G-6274)*

Alkon Corporation............................... D 419 355-9111
Fremont *(G-7090)*

Ats Systems Oregon Inc....................... F 541 738-0932
Lewis Center *(G-8324)*

Bionix Safety Technologies Ltd............. E 419 727-0552
Maumee *(G-9267)*

Brown Industrial Inc............................ E 937 693-3838
Botkins *(G-1397)*

Combined Tech Group Inc.................... E 937 274-4866
Dayton *(G-5706)*

Contitech Usa LLC.............................. C 937 644-8900
Marysville *(G-9016)*

Cortest Inc... F 440 942-1235
Willoughby *(G-14442)*

Country Sales & Service LLC............... F 330 683-2500
Orrville *(G-10978)*

Ctm Integration Incorporated............... E 330 332-1800
Salem *(G-11774)*

Dengensha America Corporation........... F 440 439-8081
Bedford *(G-1025)*

Dura Magnetics Inc.............................. F 419 882-0591
Sylvania *(G-12706)*

Eltool Corporation............................... G 513 723-1772
Mansfield *(G-8785)*

EMI Corp... D 937 596-5511
Jackson Center *(G-7963)*

Equipment Guys Inc............................ F 614 871-9220
Newark *(G-10501)*

Equipment Mfrs Intl Inc........................ E 216 651-6700
Cleveland *(G-3682)*

Exomet Inc... F 440 593-1161
Conneaut *(G-5400)*

Freeman Manufacturing & Sup Co......... E 440 934-1902
Avon *(G-727)*

G & P Construction LLC....................... E 855 494-4830
North Royalton *(G-10762)*

G W Cobb Co...................................... F 216 341-0100
Cleveland *(G-3751)*

Ged Holdings Inc................................ G 330 963-5401
Twinsburg *(G-13309)*

Glavin Industries Inc........................... E 440 349-0049
Solon *(G-12115)*

Gokoh Corporation.............................. F 937 339-4977
Troy *(G-13218)*

Grand Harbor Yacht Sales & Svc.......... G 440 442-2919
Cleveland *(G-3784)*

Grenga Machine & Welding................... F 330 743-1113
Youngstown *(G-14871)*

Hannon Company................................ D 330 456-4728
Canton *(G-1908)*

Hendrickson International Corp.............. D 740 929-5600
Hebron *(G-7617)*

Hickman Williams & Company.............. F 513 621-1946
Cincinnati *(G-2721)*

Hydrotech Inc..................................... D 888 651-5712
West Chester *(G-14126)*

IBI Brake Products Inc......................... G 440 543-7962
Chagrin Falls *(G-2166)*

Intelligrated Inc.................................. A 513 874-0788
West Chester *(G-14127)*

Intelligrated Systems Inc..................... A 866 936-7300
Mason *(G-9113)*

Intelligrated Systems Ohio LLC............ A 513 701-7300
Mason *(G-9114)*

Jcl Equipment Co Inc........................... G 937 374-1010
Xenia *(G-14767)*

Jed Industries Inc............................... F 440 639-9973
Grand River *(G-7310)*

JPS Technologies Inc.......................... F 513 984-6400
Blue Ash *(G-1292)*

JPS Technologies Inc.......................... F 513 984-6400
Blue Ash *(G-1291)*

Jsh International LLC........................... G 330 734-0251
Akron *(G-190)*

Kinetics Noise Control Inc.................... C 614 889-0480
Dublin *(G-6316)*

Kolinahr Systems Inc........................... F 513 745-9401
Blue Ash *(G-1294)*

Kyocera SGS Precision Tls Inc.............. E 330 688-6667
Cuyahoga Falls *(G-5557)*

Linden-Two Inc................................... E 330 928-4064
Cuyahoga Falls *(G-5559)*

Mfh Partners Inc................................. B 440 461-4100
Cleveland *(G-4025)*

Minerva Welding and Fabg Inc.............. E 330 868-7731
Minerva *(G-10043)*

Monaghan & Associates Inc................. F 937 253-7706
Dayton *(G-5892)*

Multi Products Company....................... F 330 674-5981
Millersburg *(G-10003)*

Neil R Scholl Inc................................. F 740 653-6593
Lancaster *(G-8213)*

Off Contact Inc................................... F 419 255-5546
Toledo *(G-13071)*

Park Corporation................................ B 216 267-4870
Medina *(G-9434)*

Pfpc Enterprises Inc............................ G 513 941-6200
Cincinnati *(G-2960)*

Pines Manufacturing Inc...................... E 440 835-5553
Westlake *(G-14324)*

Plastic Process Equipment Inc.............. E 216 367-7000
Macedonia *(G-8706)*

Progressive Mfg Co Inc....................... G 330 784-4717
Akron *(G-269)*

Prospect Mold & Die Company.............. C 330 929-3311
Cuyahoga Falls *(G-5566)*

Reduction Engineering Inc.................... E 330 677-2225
Kent *(G-8067)*

Rubber City Machinery Corp................. E 330 434-3500
Akron *(G-293)*

Samuel Son & Co (usa) Inc................... G 740 522-2500
Heath *(G-7604)*

Sequa Can Machinery Inc..................... E 330 493-0444
Canton *(G-2002)*

Stanley Bittinger.................................. G 740 942-4302
Cadiz *(G-1720)*

Starkey Machinery Inc.......................... E 419 468-2560
Galion *(G-7199)*

Super Systems Inc.............................. E 513 772-0060
Cincinnati *(G-3128)*

Tilt-Or-Lift Inc.................................... G 419 893-6944
Maumee *(G-9326)*

Tooltex Inc... F 614 539-3222
Circleville *(G-3267)*

Tri State Equipment Company............... E 513 738-7227
Shandon *(G-11935)*

United Hydraulics................................ G 440 585-0906
Wickliffe *(G-14398)*

Valv-Trol LLC..................................... F 330 686-2800
Stow *(G-12469)*

Valve Related Controls Inc.................... F 513 677-8724
Loveland *(G-8655)*

Venturo Manufacturing Inc................... E 513 772-8448
Cincinnati *(G-3199)*

INDL PATTERNS: Foundry Cores

Founders Service & Mfg Inc................. G 330 584-7759
Deerfield *(G-6093)*

Humtown Pattern Company................... D 330 482-5555
Columbiana *(G-4619)*

PCC Airfoils LLC................................ B 216 692-7900
Cleveland *(G-4148)*

Sinel Company Inc.............................. F 937 433-4772
Dayton *(G-6010)*

TW Manufacturing Co.......................... G 440 439-3243
Cleveland *(G-4434)*

INDL PATTERNS: Foundry Patternmaking

Accuform Manufacturing Inc................. E 330 797-9291
Youngstown *(G-14803)*

Cincinnati Pattern Company Inc............ G 513 241-9872
Cincinnati *(G-2483)*

National Pattern Mfgco......................... F 330 682-6871
Orrville *(G-10997)*

Plas-Mac Corp.................................... D 440 349-3222
Solon *(G-12168)*

Seilkop Industries Inc.......................... F 513 679-5680
Cincinnati *(G-3076)*

INDL PROCESS INSTRUMENTS: Chromatographs

Consoldted Anlytcal Systems In........... F 513 542-1200
Cincinnati *(G-2510)*

INDL PROCESS INSTRUMENTS: Control

Bay Controls LLC .... E 419 891-4390
Holland *(G-7745)*

Dalton Corporation .... E 419 682-6328
Stryker *(G-12621)*

Gc Controls Inc .... G 440 779-4777
Westlake *(G-14303)*

INDL SPLYS WHOLESALERS

Alb Tyler Holdings Inc .... G 440 946-7171
Mentor *(G-9475)*

Alkon Corporation .... F 614 799-6650
Dublin *(G-6274)*

All Ohio Threaded Rod Co Inc .... E 216 426-1800
Cleveland *(G-3326)*

Allied Shipping and Packagi .... F 937 222-7422
Moraine *(G-10144)*

Alro Steel Corporation .... E 614 878-7271
Columbus *(G-4690)*

Alro Steel Corporation .... D 419 720-5300
Toledo *(G-12871)*

Anchor Flange Company .... D 513 527-3512
Cincinnati *(G-2369)*

Aqua Technology Group LLC .... G 513 298-1183
West Chester *(G-13941)*

Ci Disposition Co .... F 216 587-5200
Brooklyn Heights *(G-1530)*

Cmt Machining & Fabg LLC .... F 937 652-3740
Urbana *(G-13459)*

Cornwell Quality Tools Company ..... D 330 628-2627
Mogadore *(G-10071)*

Dayton Stencil Works Company .... F 937 223-3233
Dayton *(G-5739)*

Dearing Compressor and Pump ...... E 330 783-2258
Youngstown *(G-14847)*

Dynatech Systems Inc .... F 440 365-1774
Elyria *(G-6523)*

Eagle Industrial Truck Mfg LLC ...... E 419 866-6301
Swanton *(G-12683)*

Edward W Daniel LLC .... F 440 647-1960
Wellington *(G-13885)*

Fcx Performance Inc .... E 614 253-1996
Columbus *(G-4922)*

Ges Graphite Inc .... E 216 658-6660
Parma *(G-11132)*

Gokoh Corporation .... F 937 339-4977
Troy *(G-13218)*

H3d Tool Corporation .... E 740 498-5181
Newcomerstown *(G-10570)*

HMS Industries LLC .... F 440 899-0001
Westlake *(G-14306)*

Indelco Custom Products Inc .... G 216 797-7300
Euclid *(G-6654)*

Industrial Mold Inc .... E 330 425-7374
Twinsburg *(G-13320)*

Japo Inc .... E 614 263-2850
Columbus *(G-5032)*

Lancaster Commercial Pdts LLC ..... E 844 324-1444
Columbus *(G-5062)*

Lawrence Industries Inc .... E 216 518-7000
Cleveland *(G-3946)*

Logan Clutch Corporation .... E 440 808-4258
Cleveland *(G-3966)*

Lynk Packaging Inc .... E 330 562-8080
Aurora *(G-677)*

Maintenance Repair Supply Inc ...... G 740 922-3006
Midvale *(G-9913)*

McWane Inc .... B 740 622-6651
Coshocton *(G-5459)*

Metzger Machine Co .... F 513 241-3360
Cincinnati *(G-2873)*

Mill-Rose Company .... C 440 255-9171
Mentor *(G-9566)*

Newact Inc .... F 513 321-5177
Batavia *(G-879)*

Orbytel Print and Packg Inc .... G 216 267-8734
Cleveland *(G-4123)*

Plastic Process Equipment Inc .... E 216 367-7000
Macedonia *(G-8706)*

Pressure Connections Corp .... D 614 863-6930
Columbus *(G-5204)*

Samsel Rope & Marine Supply Co .... E 216 241-0333
Cleveland *(G-4272)*

Samuel Son & Co (usa) Inc .... D 740 522-2500
Heath *(G-7604)*

Service Spring Corp .... G 419 867-0212
Maumee *(G-9317)*

SSP Fittings Corp .... D 330 425-4250
Twinsburg *(G-13379)*

Steam Trbine Altrntive Rsrces .... E 740 387-5535
Marion *(G-9001)*

Superior Holding LLC .... G 216 651-9400
Cleveland *(G-4344)*

The Cornwell Quality Tools Company .... D 330 336-3506
Wadsworth *(G-13674)*

The Dyson Corporation .... C 440 946-3500
Painesville *(G-11116)*

The Kindt-Collins Company LLC ...... D 216 252-4122
Cleveland *(G-4387)*

Tlg Cochran Inc .... E 440 914-1122
Twinsburg *(G-13385)*

Toledo Tarp Service Inc .... E 419 837-5098
Perrysburg *(G-11276)*

United Tool Supply Inc .... G 513 752-6000
Cincinnati *(G-2317)*

Watteredge LLC .... D 440 933-6110
Avon Lake *(G-773)*

Wesco Distribution Inc .... F 419 666-1670
Northwood *(G-10813)*

Wulco Inc .... D 513 379-6115
Hamilton *(G-7539)*

Wulco Inc .... D 513 679-2600
Cincinnati *(G-3235)*

INDL SPLYS, WHOLESALE: Abrasives

ARC Abrasives Inc .... D 800 888-4885
Troy *(G-13201)*

Cincinnati Abrasive Supply Co .... G 513 941-8866
Hamilton *(G-7478)*

Hickman Williams & Company .... F 513 621-1946
Cincinnati *(G-2721)*

INDL SPLYS, WHOLESALE: Bearings

Forge Industries Inc .... A 330 960-2468
Youngstown *(G-14857)*

Miba Bearings US LLC .... B 740 962-4242
Mcconnelsville *(G-9364)*

INDL SPLYS, WHOLESALE: Bins & Containers, Storage

Creative Plastic Concepts LLC .... F 419 927-9588
Sycamore *(G-12699)*

Dadco Inc .... F 513 489-2244
Cincinnati *(G-2539)*

Modroto .... G 440 998-1202
Ashtabula *(G-606)*

INDL SPLYS, WHOLESALE: Drums, New Or Reconditioned

Dayton Industrial Drum Inc .... E 937 253-8933
Dayton *(G-5608)*

Horwitz & Pintis Co .... F 419 666-2220
Toledo *(G-12996)*

INDL SPLYS, WHOLESALE: Gaskets & Seals

North Coast Seal Incorporated .... F 216 898-5000
Brookpark *(G-1556)*

P&E Sales Ltd .... G 330 829-0100
Alliance *(G-397)*

INDL SPLYS, WHOLESALE: Gears

Ig Watteeuw Usa LLC .... F 740 588-1722
Zanesville *(G-15021)*

INDL SPLYS, WHOLESALE: Glass Bottles

Cleveland Supplyone Inc .... E 216 514-7000
Cleveland *(G-3527)*

INDL SPLYS, WHOLESALE: Power Transmission, Eqpt & Apparatus

Commercial Electric Pdts Corp .... E 216 241-2886
Cleveland *(G-3552)*

Great Lakes Power Products Inc ...... D 440 951-5111
Madison *(G-8730)*

INDL SPLYS, WHOLESALE: Rubber Goods, Mechanical

Akalina Associates Inc .... C 440 992-2195
Ashtabula *(G-586)*

Alloy Extrusion Company .... E 330 677-4946
Kent *(G-8016)*

ARC Rubber Inc .... F 440 466-4555
Geneva *(G-7233)*

Brp Manufacturing Company .... E 800 858-0482
Lima *(G-8393)*

C & M Rubber Co Inc .... F 937 299-2782
Dayton *(G-5690)*

Chardon Custom Polymers LLC .... F 440 285-2161
Chardon *(G-2197)*

Clark Rubber & Plastic Company ...... C 440 255-9793
Mentor *(G-9500)*

Colonial Rubber Company .... E 330 296-2831
Ravenna *(G-11522)*

Contitech North America Inc .... F 330 664-7180
Fairlawn *(G-6798)*

Datwyler Sling Sltions USA Inc .... D 937 387-2800
Vandalia *(G-13554)*

Dayton Molded Urethanes LLC .... E 937 279-1910
Dayton *(G-5733)*

Dybrook Products Inc .... E 330 392-7665
Warren *(G-13761)*

Epg Inc .... D 330 995-5125
Aurora *(G-669)*

Epg Inc .... F 330 995-9725
Streetsboro *(G-12501)*

Extruded Slcone Pdts Gskets In .... E 330 733-0101
Mogadore *(G-10075)*

Frankes Wood Products LLC .... E 937 642-0706
Marysville *(G-9020)*

Harwood Entp Holdings Inc .... F 330 923-3256
Cuyahoga Falls *(G-5548)*

Hygenic Acquisition Co .... C 330 633-8460
Akron *(G-180)*

Hygenic Company LLC .... B 330 633-8460
Akron *(G-181)*

Ier Fujikura Inc .... C 330 425-7121
Macedonia *(G-8696)*

Jakmar Incorporated .... G 513 631-4303
Cincinnati *(G-2758)*

Johnson Bros Rubber Co .... D 419 853-4122
West Salem *(G-14188)*

PRODUCT

Karman Rubber Company.................... D 330 864-2161
Akron (G-191)

Macdivitt Rubber Company LLC........... E 440 259-5937
Perry (G-11195)

Mantaline Corporation...................... F 330 569-3147
Hiram (G-7740)

Mantaline Corporation...................... F 330 274-2264
Mantua (G-8871)

Mantaline Corporation...................... C 330 274-2264
Mantua (G-8872)

Martin Industries Inc...................... G 419 862-2694
Elmore (G-6490)

Meridian Industries Inc.................... D 330 673-1011
Kent (G-8051)

Midlands Millroom Supply Inc............ E 330 453-9100
Canton (G-1949)

Namoh Ohio Holdings Inc.................. G
Norwood (G-10869)

Performance Elastomers Corporation... D 330 297-2255
Ravenna (G-11535)

Plabell Rubber Products Corp............ E 419 691-5878
Toledo (G-13101)

Q Holding Company........................ B 440 903-1827
Twinsburg (G-13361)

Qualiform Inc............................... E 330 336-6777
Wadsworth (G-13663)

Quanex Ig Systems Inc.................... E 740 439-2338
Cambridge (G-1757)

Quanex Ig Systems Inc.................... C 216 910-1500
Akron (G-273)

Robin Industries Inc....................... E 330 893-3501
Berlin (G-1199)

Robin Industries Inc....................... C 330 695-9300
Fredericksburg (G-7070)

Robin Industries Inc....................... D 330 359-5418
Winesburg (G-14608)

Robin Industries Inc....................... F 216 631-7000
North Canton (G-10665)

Rubber-Tech Inc........................... F 937 274-1114
Dayton (G-5989)

Shreiner Sole Company Inc............... F 330 276-6135
Killbuck (G-8133)

Sperry & Rice LLC......................... F 330 276-2801
Killbuck (G-8134)

Sperry & Rice LLC......................... G 765 647-4141
Killbuck (G-8135)

TAC Materials Inc.......................... C 330 425-8472
Twinsburg (G-13382)

The D S Brown Company................... C 419 257-3561
North Baltimore (G-10619)

Tigerpoly Manufacturing Inc............. B 614 871-0045
Grove City (G-7416)

Universal Urethane Pdts Inc.............. D 419 693-7400
Toledo (G-13169)

Vertex Inc.................................. E 330 628-6230
Mogadore (G-10092)

Woodlawn Rubber Co....................... F 513 489-1718
Blue Ash (G-1353)

Yokohama Tire Corporation................ D 440 352-3321
Painesville (G-11125)

INDL SPLYS, WHOLESALE: Seals

Datwyler Sling Sltions USA Inc.............. D 937 387-2800
Vandalia (G-13554)

McNeil Industries Inc...................... E 440 951-7756
Painesville (G-11099)

INDL SPLYS, WHOLESALE: Tools

B W Grinding Co........................... E 419 923-1376
Lyons (G-8673)

H & D Steel Service Inc................... E 800 666-3390
North Royalton (G-10764)

High Quality Tools Inc..................... F 440 975-9684
Eastlake (G-6433)

Ohio Drill & Tool Co....................... E 330 525-7717
Homeworth (G-7806)

Save Edge Inc.............................. E 937 376-8268
Xenia (G-14774)

TCH Industries Incorporated............. F 330 487-5155
Twinsburg (G-13383)

INDL SPLYS, WHOLESALE: Valves & Fittings

Crane Pumps & Systems Inc.............. F 937 773-2442
Piqua (G-11340)

Pipe Products Inc.......................... C 513 587-7532
West Chester (G-14049)

Quad Fluid Dynamics Inc.................. F 330 220-3005
Brunswick (G-1610)

Ruthman Pump and Engineering........... G 937 783-2411
Blanchester (G-1238)

Shaq Inc.................................... D 770 427-0402
Beachwood (G-949)

Victory White Metal Company............. D 216 271-1400
Cleveland (G-4472)

INDUSTRIAL & COMMERCIAL EQPT INSPECTION SVCS

4r Enterprises Incorporated.............. G 330 923-9799
Cuyahoga Falls (G-5519)

Quintus Technologies LLC................. E 614 891-2732
Lewis Center (G-8349)

INFORMATION RETRIEVAL SERVICES

Advant-E Corporation...................... F 937 429-4288
Beavercreek (G-964)

AGS Custom Graphics Inc.................. D 330 963-7770
Macedonia (G-8676)

Hkm Drect Mkt Cmmnications Inc......... C 800 860-4456
Cleveland (G-3832)

Promatch Solutions LLC................... F 877 299-0185
Moraine (G-10188)

Repro Acquisition Company LLC.......... G 216 738-3800
Cleveland (G-4235)

Welch Publishing Co....................... E 419 874-2528
Perrysburg (G-11279)

INFRARED OBJECT DETECTION EQPT

IEC Infrared Systems Inc.................. E 440 234-8000
Middleburg Heights (G-9771)

INGOT: Aluminum

Homan Metals LLC.......................... G 513 721-5010
Cincinnati (G-2728)

INK OR WRITING FLUIDS

Color Resolutions International LLC...... C 513 552-7200
Fairfield (G-6724)

Sun Chemical Corporation................. D 513 671-0407
Cincinnati (G-3123)

INK: Gravure

Superior Printing Ink Co Inc.............. G 216 328-1720
Cleveland (G-4346)

INK: Printing

American Inks and Coatings Co........... G 513 552-7200
Fairfield (G-6710)

Eckart America Corporation............... D 440 954-7600
Painesville (G-11082)

Flint CPS Inks North Amer LLC........... E 513 619-2089
Cincinnati (G-2628)

Glass Coatings & Concepts LLC.......... E 513 539-5300
Monroe (G-10107)

Ink Technology Corporation............... E 216 486-6720
Cleveland (G-3860)

INX International Ink Co................... F 440 239-1766
Cleveland (G-3867)

INX International Ink Co................... F 707 693-2990
Lebanon (G-8268)

Joules Angstrom Uv Prtg Inks C.......... E 740 964-9113
Pataskala (G-11141)

Kennedy Ink Company Inc................. F 513 871-2515
Cincinnati (G-2793)

Kohl & Madden Inc......................... G 513 326-6900
Cincinnati (G-2804)

Magnum Magnetics Corporation........... E 740 516-6237
Caldwell (G-1725)

Magnum Magnetics Corporation........... E 513 360-0790
Middletown (G-9876)

Premier Ink Systems Inc.................. F 513 367-2300
Harrison (G-7562)

Printink Inc................................ G 513 943-0599
Amelia (G-435)

Red Tie Group Inc.......................... E
Cleveland (G-4229)

Sun Chemical Corporation................. D 513 753-9550
Amelia (G-439)

Sun Chemical Corporation................. D 513 671-0407
Cincinnati (G-3123)

Sun Chemical Corporation................. E 513 681-5950
Cincinnati (G-3124)

Sun Chemical Corporation................. E 513 681-5950
Cincinnati (G-3125)

Sun Chemical Corporation................. E 513 830-8667
Cincinnati (G-3126)

Sun Chemical Corporation................. D 419 891-3514
Maumee (G-9322)

Vibrantz Corporation...................... C 216 875-6213
Cleveland (G-4468)

Wikoff Color Corporation................. G 513 423-0727
Middletown (G-9905)

Zeres Inc.................................. E 419 354-5555
Bowling Green (G-1450)

INSECTICIDES

Abbott Laboratories....................... D 847 937-6100
Columbus (G-4662)

INSECTICIDES & PESTICIDES

A Best Trmt & Pest Ctrl Sups............. G 330 434-5555
Akron (G-9)

Advanced Biological Mktg Inc............. E 419 232-2461
Van Wert (G-13525)

Scotts Miracle-Gro Company.............. B 937 644-0011
Marysville (G-9046)

INSPECTION & TESTING SVCS

Brown Company of Findlay Ltd............ E 419 425-3002
Findlay (G-6847)

Cleveland Spclty Insptn Svc In........... F 440 974-1818
Mentor (G-9501)

Leak Finder Inc............................ G 440 735-0130
Hudson (G-7849)

National Wldg Tanker Repr LLC........... G 614 875-3399
Grove City (G-7404)

Pioneer Solutions LLC..................... E 216 383-3400
Euclid (G-6669)

Supplier Inspection Svcs Inc............. F 877 263-7097
Dayton (G-6031)

Vista Industrial Packaging LLC........... E 800 454-6117
Columbus (G-5351)

INSTRUMENTS & METERS: Measuring, Electric

Lake Shore Cryotronics Inc..................D 614 891-2243
Westerville (G-14217)

INSTRUMENTS, LABORATORY: Analyzers, Automatic Chemical

Prospira America Corporation..............F 419 423-9552
Findlay (G-6910)

Targeted Cmpund Monitoring LLC........G 937 825-0842
Dayton (G-6038)

INSTRUMENTS, LABORATORY: Spectrometers

Teledyne Instruments Inc.....................D 603 886-8400
Mason (G-9159)

INSTRUMENTS, MEASURING & CNTRL: Geophysical & Meteorological

Electric Speed Indicator Co..................F 216 251-2540
Aurora (G-668)

INSTRUMENTS, MEASURING & CNTRL: Radiation & Testing, Nuclear

Fluke Biomedical LLC...........................C 440 248-9300
Solon (G-12113)

Nucon International Inc.........................F 614 846-5710
Columbus (G-5132)

Reuter-Stokes LLC................................B 330 425-3755
Twinsburg (G-13365)

INSTRUMENTS, MEASURING & CNTRLG: Aircraft & Motor Vehicle

Nidec Avtron Automation Corporation...C 216 642-1230
Independence (G-7912)

Nidec Motor Corporation.......................E 216 642-1230
Cleveland (G-4077)

INSTRUMENTS, MEASURING & CNTRLNG: Nuclear Instrument Modules

Babcock & Wilcox Entps Inc.................C 330 753-4511
Akron (G-68)

Overhoff Technology Corp......................F 513 248-2400
Milford (G-9946)

INSTRUMENTS, MEASURING & CONTROLLING: Breathalyzers

National Pat Anlytical Systems.............E 419 526-6727
Mansfield (G-8836)

INSTRUMENTS, MEASURING & CONTROLLING: Cable Testing

Multilink Inc...C 440 366-6966
Elyria (G-6566)

INSTRUMENTS, MEASURING & CONTROLLING: Magnetometers

Ceia Usa Ltd..D 330 310-4741
Hudson (G-7836)

INSTRUMENTS, MEASURING & CONTROLLING: Ultrasonic Testing

Waygate Technologies Usa LP..............D 866 243-2638
Cincinnati (G-3212)

INSTRUMENTS, OPTICAL: Mirrors

Bruening Glass Works Inc.....................G 440 333-4768
Cleveland (G-3445)

Dale Kestler...G 513 871-9000
Cincinnati (G-2540)

INSTRUMENTS, SURGICAL & MED: Needles & Syringes, Hypodermic

Hgi Holdings Inc...................................A 330 963-6996
Twinsburg (G-13316)

INSTRUMENTS, SURGICAL & MEDICAL: Blood & Bone Work

Findlay Amrcn Prsthtic Orthtic..............G 419 424-1622
Findlay (G-6863)

Mediview Xr Inc....................................F 419 270-2774
Cleveland (G-4016)

Nervive Inc..F 847 274-1790
Cleveland (G-4067)

Resonetics LLC....................................D 937 865-4070
Kettering (G-8123)

Troy Innovative Instrs Inc.....................E 440 834-9567
Middlefield (G-9831)

INSTRUMENTS, SURGICAL & MEDICAL: Inhalation Therapy

Invacare Holdings Corporation...............B 440 329-6000
Elyria (G-6554)

Rhinosystems Inc.................................F 216 351-6262
Brooklyn (G-1525)

INSTRUMENTS, SURGICAL & MEDICAL: IV Transfusion

Smiths Medical Asd Inc........................C 614 889-2220
Dublin (G-6346)

INSTRUMENTS, SURGICAL & MEDICAL: Operating Tables

Midmark Corporation.............................G 937 526-3662
Versailles (G-13600)

Midmark Corporation.............................A 937 528-7500
Miamisburg (G-9717)

INSTRUMENTS, SURGICAL/MED: Microsurgical, Exc Electromedical

Norman Noble Inc.................................E 216 851-4007
Euclid (G-6665)

Norman Noble Inc.................................B 216 761-5367
Highland Heights (G-7660)

INSTRUMENTS: Analytical

Affymetrix Inc.......................................D 800 321-9322
Cleveland (G-3313)

Affymetrix Inc.......................................E 419 887-1233
Maumee (G-9257)

American Scientific LLC.........................G 614 764-9002
Columbus (G-4702)

Apera Instruments LLC..........................F 614 285-3080
Columbus (G-4720)

Bionix Safety Technologies Ltd..............E 419 727-0552
Maumee (G-9267)

Bridge Analyzers Inc.............................F 216 332-0592
Bedford Heights (G-1071)

Columbus Instruments LLC....................E 614 276-0861
Columbus (G-4825)

Columbus Instruments Intl Corp.............E 614 276-0593
Columbus (G-4826)

Consoldted Anlytcal Systems In.............F 513 542-1200
Cincinnati (G-2510)

Dentronix Inc.......................................D 330 916-7300
Cuyahoga Falls (G-5538)

Environmental Sample Technology Inc.E 513 642-0100
West Chester (G-13993)

Laserlinc Inc..E 937 318-2440
Fairborn (G-6695)

Metron Instruments Inc.........................G 216 332-0592
Bedford Heights (G-1079)

Mettler-Toledo Intl Inc...........................A 614 438-4511
Columbus (G-4643)

Mettlr-Tledo Globl Hldings LLC...............E 614 438-4511
Columbus (G-4645)

Nanotronics Imaging Inc........................G 330 926-9809
Cuyahoga Falls (G-5562)

NDC Technologies Inc...........................C 937 233-9935
Dayton (G-5905)

Ohio Lumex Co Inc...............................E 440 264-2500
Solon (G-12164)

Orton Edward Jr Crmic Fndation.............E 614 895-2663
Westerville (G-14226)

PMC Gage Inc......................................E 440 953-1672
Willoughby (G-14507)

Precision Anlytical Instrs Inc.................G 513 984-1600
Blue Ash (G-1323)

Pts Prfssnal Technical Svc Inc...............D 513 642-0111
West Chester (G-14056)

Q-Lab Corporation................................D 440 835-8700
Westlake (G-14325)

Teledyne Instruments Inc.....................E 513 229-7000
Mason (G-9158)

Teledyne Tekmar Company.....................E 513 229-7000
Mason (G-9160)

Test-Fuchs Corporation.........................G 440 708-3505
Brecksville (G-1483)

Thermo Fisher Scientific Inc..................F 513 948-6290
Blue Ash (G-1343)

Thermo Fisher Scientific Inc..................F 800 955-6288
Cincinnati (G-3152)

Thermo Fisher Scientific Inc..................F 513 659-7945
West Chester (G-14154)

Thermo Fsher Scntfic Ashvlle L..............A 740 373-4763
Marietta (G-8954)

Trek Diagnostics Inc.............................F 440 808-0000
Brooklyn Heights (G-1541)

Viavi Solutions Inc................................F 316 522-4981
Columbus (G-4651)

Weidmann Electrical Tech Inc.................G 937 508-2112
Cleveland (G-4497)

Xorb Corporation..................................G 419 354-6021
Bowling Green (G-1449)

Ysi Environmental Inc...........................E 937 767-7241
Yellow Springs (G-14795)

INSTRUMENTS: Combustion Control, Indl

Catacel Corp...F
Ravenna (G-11520)

Cleveland Controls Inc..........................F 216 398-0330
Cleveland (G-3510)

Unison UCI Inc......................................G
Cleveland (G-4441)

INSTRUMENTS: Electrocardiographs

Cardioinsight Technologies Inc...............G 216 274-2221
Independence (G-7890)

INSTRUMENTS: Endoscopic Eqpt, Electromedical

Steris Corporation................................A 440 354-2600
Mentor (G-9624)

INSTRUMENTS: Flow, Indl Process

Ernst Flow Industries LLC......................F 732 938-5641
Strongsville (G-12558)

PRODUCT

L J Star Incorporated.............................. E 330 405-3040
   Twinsburg *(G-13327)*

INSTRUMENTS: Indl Process Control

Aqua Technology Group LLC................. G 513 298-1183
   West Chester *(G-13941)*

Clark-Reliance LLC................................. C 440 572-1500
   Strongsville *(G-12550)*

Facts Inc... E 330 928-2332
   Cuyahoga Falls *(G-5540)*

Jbt Marel Corporation............................ E 614 891-2732
   Lewis Center *(G-8340)*

Journey Electronics Corp....................... G 513 539-9836
   Monroe *(G-10111)*

Production Control Units Inc.................. D 937 299-5594
   Dayton *(G-5961)*

INSTRUMENTS: Infrared, Indl Process

L3harris Cincinnati Elec Corp................ A 513 573-6100
   Mason *(G-9121)*

INSTRUMENTS: Laser, Scientific & Engineering

Tech4imaging LLC.................................. F 614 214-2655
   Columbus *(G-5315)*

INSTRUMENTS: Liquid Level, Indl Process

Dixon Bayco USA................................... G 513 874-8499
   Fairfield *(G-6729)*

INSTRUMENTS: Measurement, Indl Process

Beaumont Machine LLC.......................... F 513 701-0421
   Mason *(G-9070)*

Command Alkon Incorporated................ E 614 799-0600
   Dublin *(G-6290)*

Crawford United Corporation................. E 216 243-2614
   Cleveland *(G-3576)*

Meech Sttic Elminators USA Inc............ F 330 564-2000
   Copley *(G-5434)*

Nextech Materials Ltd............................ D 614 842-6606
   Lewis Center *(G-8346)*

Rickly Hydrological Co.......................... E 614 297-9877
   Columbus *(G-5229)*

Slone Gear International Inc.................. G 507 401-4327
   Tipp City *(G-12845)*

INSTRUMENTS: Measuring, Electrical Energy

Drs Signal Technologies Inc................. G 937 429-7470
   Beavercreek *(G-972)*

Tacoma Energy LLC............................... C 614 899-8990
   Westerville *(G-14276)*

Westerman Inc....................................... C 800 338-8265
   Bremen *(G-1488)*

INSTRUMENTS: Measuring, Electrical Power

F Squared Inc.. G 419 752-7273
   Greenwich *(G-7361)*

INSTRUMENTS: Medical & Surgical

Abbott Laboratories.............................. D 847 937-6100
   Columbus *(G-4662)*

Applied Medical Technology Inc............ F 440 717-4000
   Brecksville *(G-1457)*

Atc Group Inc.. D 440 293-4064
   Andover *(G-455)*

Avalign - Integrated LLC....................... F 440 269-6984
   Mentor *(G-9487)*

Aws Industries Inc................................ E 513 932-7941
   Lebanon *(G-8245)*

Axon Medical Llc.................................. E 216 276-0262
   Medina *(G-9379)*

Beam Technologies Inc.......................... B 800 648-1179
   Columbus *(G-4746)*

Becton Dickinson and Company........... G 858 617-4272
   Groveport *(G-7424)*

Bowden Manufacturing Corp................. E 440 946-1770
   Willoughby *(G-14432)*

Buckeye Medical Tech LLC.................... G 330 719-9868
   Warren *(G-13745)*

Butler Cnty Surgical Prpts LLC............. G 513 844-2200
   Hamilton *(G-7475)*

Care Fusion.. G 216 521-1220
   Lakewood *(G-8164)*

Casco Mfg Solutions Inc...................... D 513 681-0003
   Cincinnati *(G-2441)*

Cmd Medtech LLC................................. F 614 364-4243
   Columbus *(G-4814)*

Codonics Inc... C 800 444-1198
   Cleveland *(G-3544)*

Coopersurgical Inc................................ G 203 601-5200
   Cincinnati *(G-2516)*

Covidien Holding Inc............................. C 513 948-7219
   Cincinnati *(G-2520)*

Cqt Kennedy LLC.................................. D 419 238-2442
   Van Wert *(G-13532)*

Dentronix Inc.. D 330 916-7300
   Cuyahoga Falls *(G-5538)*

Devicor Med Pdts Holdings Inc............. A 513 864-9000
   Cincinnati *(G-2548)*

Elite Biomedical Solutions LLC............. F 513 207-0602
   Cincinnati *(G-2302)*

Encore Industries Inc............................ C 419 626-8000
   Sandusky *(G-11830)*

Frantz Medical Development Ltd............ G 440 255-1155
   Mentor *(G-9519)*

General Data Company Inc.................... B 513 752-7978
   Cincinnati *(G-2304)*

Gentherm Medical LLC.......................... C 513 772-8810
   Cincinnati *(G-2668)*

Gyrus Acmi LP...................................... D 419 668-8201
   Norwalk *(G-10845)*

Haag-Streit Usa Inc.............................. D 513 398-3937
   Mason *(G-9107)*

Howmedica Osteonics Corp.................. D 937 291-3900
   Dayton *(G-5814)*

Inspyre Health Systems LLC................ G 440 412-7916
   Grafton *(G-7304)*

Interntnal Cutng Solutions Inc.............. G 440 786-1700
   Streetsboro *(G-12506)*

Johnson & Johnson.............................. E 513 786-7000
   Blue Ash *(G-1290)*

Kinetic Concepts Inc............................ F 440 234-8590
   Middleburg Heights *(G-9774)*

Klarity Medical Products LLC................ F 740 788-8107
   Heath *(G-7599)*

KMC Holdings LLC................................ C 419 238-2442
   Van Wert *(G-13539)*

Leica Biosystems - TAS........................ E 513 864-9671
   Cincinnati *(G-2818)*

Life Sciences - Vandalia LLC................ C 937 387-0880
   Dayton *(G-5846)*

M&H Medical Holdings Inc.................... E 419 727-8421
   Maumee *(G-9305)*

Markethtch Inc D/B/A Mh Eye CA.......... F 330 376-6363
   Akron *(G-221)*

Medical Quant USA Inc......................... F 440 542-0761
   Solon *(G-12145)*

Medtronic Inc.. F 216 642-1977
   Cleveland *(G-4017)*

Medtronic Inc.. G 763 526-2566
   Independence *(G-7908)*

Meridian LLC... G 330 995-0371
   Aurora *(G-678)*

Micromd.. G 850 217-7412
   Youngstown *(G-14899)*

Minimally Invasive Devices Inc............. G 614 484-5036
   Columbus *(G-5104)*

Morris Technologies Inc........................ E 513 733-1611
   Cincinnati *(G-2888)*

National Biological Corp....................... E 216 831-0600
   Beachwood *(G-931)*

Norwood Medical LLC........................... D 937 228-4101
   Dayton *(G-5912)*

Nuevue Solutions Inc............................ G 440 836-4772
   Rootstown *(G-11651)*

Ohiohealth Imaging Services................ F 740 420-7925
   Circleville *(G-3261)*

OMI Surgical Products.......................... G 513 561-2241
   Cincinnati *(G-2929)*

Patriot Products Inc.............................. F 419 865-9712
   Holland *(G-7776)*

Pemco Inc... E 216 524-2990
   Cleveland *(G-4150)*

Percuvision LLC.................................... E 614 891-4800
   Columbus *(G-5186)*

Peritec Biosciences Ltd........................ G 216 445-3756
   Cleveland *(G-4152)*

Phoenix Quality Mfg LLC...................... E 705 279-0538
   Jackson *(G-7951)*

Pulse Worldwide Ltd............................. G 513 234-7829
   Mason *(G-9139)*

Quality Electrodynamics LLC................ C 440 638-5106
   Mayfield Village *(G-9347)*

Respironics Novametrix LLC................. A 800 345-6443
   Columbus *(G-5228)*

Rultract Inc... G 330 856-9808
   Warren *(G-13796)*

Scientific Molding Corp Ltd.................. G 330 342-7800
   Twinsburg *(G-13375)*

Smiths Medical Asd Inc........................ E 800 796-8701
   Dublin *(G-6345)*

Smiths Medical North America.............. G 614 210-7300
   Dublin *(G-6347)*

Spartronics Strongsville Inc................. D 440 878-4630
   Strongsville *(G-12603)*

Spring Hlthcare Dagnostics LLC........... D 866 201-9503
   Jackson *(G-7953)*

SRI Healthcare LLC............................... G 513 398-6406
   Mason *(G-9156)*

Standard Bariatrics Inc......................... E 513 620-7751
   Blue Ash *(G-1334)*

Steris Corporation................................ D 440 354-2600
   Mentor *(G-9623)*

Steris Instrument MGT Svcs Inc........... C 800 783-9251
   Stow *(G-12464)*

Stryker Orthopedic................................ G 614 766-2990
   Dublin *(G-6352)*

Summit Online Products LLC................ G 800 326-1972
   Powell *(G-11495)*

Surgical Theater Inc............................. E 216 452-2177
   Pepper Pike *(G-11189)*

Surgrx Inc... F 650 482-2400
   Blue Ash *(G-1338)*

Theken Companies LLC......................... F 330 733-7600
   Akron *(G-334)*

Thermo Fisher Scientific Inc................. E 800 871-8909
   Oakwood Village *(G-10910)*

Torbot Group Inc.................................. F 419 724-1475
   Northwood *(G-10810)*

United Medical Supply Company........... F 866 678-8633
   Brunswick *(G-1621)*

United Sttes Endscopy Group In........... C 440 639-4494
   Mentor *(G-9647)*

Valensil Technologies LLC.................... E 440 937-8181
   Avon *(G-741)*

Vesco Medical LLC............................... F 614 914-5991
Westerville (G-14279)

Ward Engineering Inc............................ G 614 442-8063
Columbus (G-5355)

INSTRUMENTS: Particle Size Analyzers

Rotex Global LLC................................. C 513 541-1236
Cincinnati (G-3053)

INSTRUMENTS: Pressure Measurement, Indl

Cincinnati Test Systems Inc.................. D 513 202-5100
Harrison (G-7546)

Koester Corporation.............................. E 419 599-0291
Napoleon (G-10289)

Solon Manufacturing Company............ E 440 286-7149
Chardon (G-2223)

INSTRUMENTS: Radio Frequency Measuring

Dss Installations Ltd............................. G 513 761-7000
Cincinnati (G-2563)

Resonant Sciences LLC........................ E 937 431-8180
Dayton (G-5980)

INSTRUMENTS: Signal Generators & Averagers

Adams Elevator Equipment Co............. D 847 581-2900
Holland (G-7743)

Palstar Inc.. F 937 773-6255
Piqua (G-11371)

INSTRUMENTS: Temperature Measurement, Indl

Thermo King Corporation...................... F 567 280-9243
Fremont (G-7137)

INSTRUMENTS: Test, Electrical, Engine

Nu-Di Products Co Inc.......................... D 216 251-9070
Cleveland (G-4105)

INSTRUMENTS: Test, Electronic & Electric Measurement

Advanced Integration LLC.................... E 614 863-2433
Reynoldsburg (G-11554)

Advanced Kiffer Systems Inc................ E 216 267-8181
Cleveland (G-3306)

Bionix Safety Technologies Ltd .... F 419 727-0552
Maumee (G-9267)

Bird Electronic Corporation.................. C 440 248-1200
Solon (G-12084)

Bird Technologies Group Inc................ C 440 248-1200
Solon (G-12085)

Field Apparatus Service & Tstg........... G 513 353-9399
Cincinnati (G-2621)

Keithley Instruments LLC..................... D 440 248-0400
Solon (G-12137)

Mueller Electric Company Inc.............. G 614 888-8855
New Albany (G-10346)

Paneltech LLC..................................... G 440 516-1300
Chagrin Falls (G-2176)

INSULATION & ROOFING MATERIALS: Wood, Reconstituted

Bmca Insulation Products Inc.............. F 330 335-2501
Wadsworth (G-13629)

INSULATION MATERIALS WHOLESALERS

Denizen Inc... F 937 615-9561
Piqua (G-11344)

Tlg Cochran Inc.................................... E 440 914-1122
Twinsburg (G-13385)

INSULATION: Fiberglass

American Insulation Tech LLC.............. F 513 733-4248
Milford (G-9921)

Blackthorn LLC.................................... F 937 836-9296
Clayton (G-3272)

Johns Manville Corporation.................. D 419 784-7000
Defiance (G-6114)

Johns Manville Corporation.................. E 419 784-7000
Defiance (G-6115)

Johns Manville Corporation.................. E 419 878-8111
Defiance (G-6116)

Johns Manville Corporation.................. C 419 878-8111
Waterville (G-13835)

Johns Manville Corporation.................. D 419 878-8112
Waterville (G-13836)

Metal Building Intr Pdts Co.................. F 440 322-6500
Elyria (G-6562)

Owens Corning..................................... G 614 754-4098
Columbus (G-5166)

Owens Corning..................................... G 419 248-8000
Navarre (G-10309)

Owens Corning Roofg & Asp LLC......... E 877 858-3855
Toledo (G-13087)

Owens Corning Sales LLC.................... E 614 539-0830
Grove City (G-7407)

Owens Corning Sales LLC.................... E 740 928-6620
Hebron (G-7628)

Owens Corning Sales LLC.................... E 419 248-5751
Swanton (G-12689)

Owens Corning Sales LLC.................... A 419 248-8000
Toledo (G-13088)

Owens Crning Inslting Systm............... A 740 328-2300
Newark (G-10527)

Thermafiber Inc.................................... D 260 563-2111
Toledo (G-13142)

INSULATORS & INSULATION MATERIALS: Electrical

Bourbon Plastics Inc............................ E 574 342-0893
Cuyahoga Falls (G-5533)

Koebbe Products Inc............................ D 513 753-4200
Amelia (G-430)

Monti Incorporated............................... D 513 761-7775
Cincinnati (G-2886)

Mueller Electric Company Inc.............. D 216 771-5225
Akron (G-239)

Red Seal Electric Company.................. E 216 941-3900
Cleveland (G-4228)

Von Roll Usa Inc.................................. D 216 433-7474
Cleveland (G-4481)

INSULATORS, PORCELAIN: Electrical

Ethima Inc.. D 419 626-4912
Sandusky (G-11834)

Newell - Psn LLC................................. G 304 387-2700
Columbiana (G-4623)

INSURANCE BROKERS, NEC

Forge Industries Inc............................. A 330 960-2468
Youngstown (G-14857)

INSURANCE CARRIERS: Life

Western & Southern Lf Insur Co........... A 513 629-1800
Cincinnati (G-3221)

INSURANCE CLAIM PROCESSING, EXC MEDICAL

Safelite Group Inc................................ A 614 210-9000
Columbus (G-5244)

INSURANCE: Agents, Brokers & Service

Beam Technologies Inc......................... B 800 648-1179
Columbus (G-4746)

Move Ez Inc.. D 844 466-8339
Columbus (G-5114)

INTEGRATED CIRCUITS, SEMICONDUCTOR NETWORKS, ETC

Leidos Inc.. D 937 656-8433
Beavercreek (G-977)

INTERIOR DESIGN SVCS, NEC

Nordic Light America Inc...................... F 614 981-9497
Canal Winchester (G-1796)

INTRAVENOUS SOLUTIONS

Clinical Specialties Inc........................ D 888 873-7888
Hudson (G-7840)

INVERTERS: Nonrotating Electrical

Myers Controlled Power LLC................ C 909 923-1800
Canton (G-1955)

Vanner Holdings Inc............................. D 614 771-2718
Hilliard (G-7709)

INVESTMENT ADVISORY SVCS

Linsalata Cpitl Prtners Fund I.............. G 440 684-1400
Cleveland (G-3962)

INVESTMENT FIRM: General Brokerage

Western & Southern Lf Insur Co........... A 513 629-1800
Cincinnati (G-3221)

INVESTORS, NEC

Alpha Zeta Holdings Inc....................... G 216 271-1601
Cleveland (G-3334)

Brantley Partners IV LP........................ G 216 464-8400
Cleveland (G-3434)

Edgewater Capital Partners LP............. G 216 292-3838
Independence (G-7901)

Kinetico Incorporated........................... B 440 564-9111
Newbury (G-10556)

Resilience Fund III LP.......................... F 216 292-0200
Cleveland (G-4237)

IRON & STEEL PRDTS: Hot-Rolled

Nucor Steel Marion Inc......................... B 740 383-4011
Marion (G-8985)

IRON ORE MINING

The Cleveland-Cliffs Iron Co................ C 216 694-5700
Cleveland (G-4380)

Tilden Mining Company LC................... A 216 694-5700
Cleveland (G-4395)

Wabush Mnes Clffs Min Mnging A........ F 216 694-5700
Cleveland (G-4486)

IRON ORES

Cliffs & Associates Ltd......................... C 216 694-5700
Cleveland (G-3538)

Cliffs Mining Company......................... F 216 694-5700
Cleveland (G-3539)

JACKS: Hydraulic

Joyce/Dayton Corp............................... E 937 294-6261
Dayton (G-5831)

JEWELERS' FINDINGS & MATERIALS

Zero-D Products Inc.............................. G 440 942-5005
Willoughby (G-14554)

PRODUCT

JEWELRY REPAIR SVCS

Bensan Jewelers Inc................................. G 216 221-1434
Lakewood *(G-8163)*

Gustave Julian Jewelers Inc..................... G 440 888-1100
Cleveland *(G-3801)*

H P Nielsen Inc....................................... G 440 244-4255
Lorain *(G-8557)*

Koop Diamond Cutters Inc........................ F 513 621-2838
Cincinnati *(G-2805)*

Michael W Hyes Desgr Goldsmith.......... G 440 519-0889
Solon *(G-12150)*

Pughs Designer Jewelers Inc................... G 740 344-9259
Newark *(G-10530)*

JEWELRY STORES

Farah Jewelers Inc.................................. G 614 438-6140
Westerville *(G-14210)*

Markus Jewelers LLC............................... G 513 474-4950
Cincinnati *(G-2848)*

Michael W Hyes Desgr Goldsmith.......... G 440 519-0889
Solon *(G-12150)*

Rosenfeld Jewelry Inc............................. G 440 446-0099
Cleveland *(G-4253)*

JEWELRY STORES: Precious Stones & Precious Metals

Bensan Jewelers Inc................................. G 216 221-1434
Lakewood *(G-8163)*

D & J Manufacturing Jeweler.................. G 513 541-5200
Cincinnati *(G-2534)*

Em Es Be Company LLC........................... G 216 761-9500
Cleveland *(G-3665)*

Goyal Enterprises Inc............................... F 513 874-9303
Cincinnati *(G-2686)*

H P Nielsen Inc....................................... G 440 244-4255
Lorain *(G-8557)*

Handcrafted Jewelry Inc........................... G 330 650-9011
Hudson *(G-7843)*

James C Free Inc................................... G 513 793-0133
Cincinnati *(G-2759)*

James C Free Inc................................... E 937 298-0171
Dayton *(G-5826)*

M B Saxon Co Inc................................... G 440 229-5006
Cleveland *(G-3975)*

Pughs Designer Jewelers Inc................... G 740 344-9259
Newark *(G-10530)*

Robert W Johnson Inc............................. D 614 336-4545
Dublin *(G-6340)*

Sheiban Jewelry Inc................................. F 440 238-0616
Strongsville *(G-12599)*

White Jewelers Inc.................................. G 330 264-3324
Wooster *(G-14697)*

JEWELRY STORES: Silverware

Gustave Julian Jewelers Inc..................... G 440 888-1100
Cleveland *(G-3801)*

JEWELRY, PRECIOUS METAL: Settings & Mountings

Prince & Izant LLC.................................. E 216 362-7000
Cleveland *(G-4196)*

JEWELRY, WHOLESALE

Goyal Enterprises Inc............................... F 513 874-9303
Cincinnati *(G-2686)*

M B Saxon Co Inc................................... G 440 229-5006
Cleveland *(G-3975)*

Marfo Company...................................... D 614 276-3352
Columbus *(G-5081)*

Sheiban Jewelry Inc................................. F 440 238-0616
Strongsville *(G-12599)*

JEWELRY: Precious Metal

Associated Premium Corporation.......... E 513 679-4444
Cincinnati *(G-2381)*

D & J Manufacturing Jeweler.................. G 513 541-5200
Cincinnati *(G-2534)*

Diamond Designs Inc.............................. G 330 434-6776
Akron *(G-120)*

Don Basch Jewelers Inc.......................... F 330 467-2116
Macedonia *(G-8687)*

Em Es Be Company LLC........................... G 216 761-9500
Cleveland *(G-3665)*

Ginos Awards Inc.................................... E 216 831-6565
Warrensville Heights *(G-13818)*

Gustave Julian Jewelers Inc..................... G 440 888-1100
Cleveland *(G-3801)*

H P Nielsen Inc....................................... G 440 244-4255
Lorain *(G-8557)*

Im Greenberg Inc.................................... G 440 461-4464
Cleveland *(G-3849)*

James C Free Inc................................... G 513 793-0133
Cincinnati *(G-2759)*

James C Free Inc................................... E 937 298-0171
Dayton *(G-5826)*

Koop Diamond Cutters Inc........................ F 513 621-2838
Cincinnati *(G-2805)*

M B Saxon Co Inc................................... G 440 229-5006
Cleveland *(G-3975)*

Markus Jewelers LLC............................... G 513 474-4950
Cincinnati *(G-2848)*

Michael W Hyes Desgr Goldsmith.......... G 440 519-0889
Solon *(G-12150)*

Robert W Johnson Inc............................. D 614 336-4545
Dublin *(G-6340)*

Rosenfeld Jewelry Inc............................. G 440 446-0099
Cleveland *(G-4253)*

Sheiban Jewelry Inc................................. F 440 238-0616
Strongsville *(G-12599)*

Signet Group Inc.................................... E 330 668-5000
Fairlawn *(G-6812)*

Signet Group Services US Inc................. F 330 668-5000
Fairlawn *(G-6813)*

Val Casting Inc...................................... G 419 562-2499
Bucyrus *(G-1691)*

White Jewelers Inc.................................. G 330 264-3324
Wooster *(G-14697)*

Whitehouse Bros Inc.............................. G 513 621-2259
Blue Ash *(G-1350)*

JIGS & FIXTURES

Cmt Machining & Fabg LLC..................... F 937 652-3740
Urbana *(G-13459)*

Delta Tool & Die Stl Block Inc................ E 419 822-5939
Delta *(G-6203)*

First Tool Corp...................................... E 937 254-6197
Dayton *(G-5777)*

Homeworth Fabrication Mch Inc............. F 330 525-5459
Homeworth *(G-7805)*

JBI Corporation...................................... F 419 855-3389
Genoa *(G-7248)*

Jergens Inc... C 216 486-5540
Cleveland *(G-3885)*

Kilroy Company...................................... D 440 951-8700
Cleveland *(G-3920)*

Krisdale Inc... G 330 225-2392
Valley City *(G-13501)*

Nation Tool & Die Ltd............................. E 419 822-5939
Delta *(G-6213)*

Northwestern Tools Inc........................... F 937 298-9994
Dayton *(G-5911)*

P O McIntire Company............................. E 440 269-1848
Wickliffe *(G-14387)*

JOB PRINTING & NEWSPAPER PUBLISHING COMBINED

Bluffton News Pubg & Prtg Co................ F 419 358-8010
Bluffton *(G-1357)*

County Classifieds.................................. G 937 592-8847
Bellefontaine *(G-1102)*

Douthit Communications Inc.................... D 419 855-7465
Millbury *(G-9959)*

Douthit Communications Inc.................... D 419 625-5825
Sandusky *(G-11828)*

Hardin County Publishing Co.................. E 419 674-4066
Kenton *(G-8101)*

Springfield Newspapers Inc.................... F 937 323-5533
Springfield *(G-12376)*

Welch Publishing Co.............................. E 419 874-2528
Perrysburg *(G-11279)*

JOINTS: Expansion, Pipe

Bosch Rexroth Corporation..................... C 330 263-3300
Wooster *(G-14627)*

JOINTS: Swivel & Universal, Exc Aircraft & Auto

Excel Loading Systems LLC..................... G 513 504-1069
Hamilton *(G-7489)*

JOISTS: Long-Span Series, Open Web Steel

Socar of Ohio Inc................................... D 419 596-3100
Continental *(G-5423)*

KILNS & FURNACES: Ceramic

Harrop Industries Inc.............................. E 614 231-3621
Columbus *(G-4972)*

I Cerco Inc... C 330 567-2145
Shreve *(G-11983)*

Star Engineering LLC.............................. E 740 342-3514
New Lexington *(G-10408)*

KITCHEN CABINETS WHOLESALERS

Bison Builders LLC.................................. F 614 636-0365
Columbus *(G-4756)*

Clark Wood Specialties Inc..................... G 330 499-8711
Clinton *(G-4553)*

Custom Design Cabinets & Tops............. G 440 639-9900
Painesville *(G-11075)*

Kitchen Designs Plus Inc........................ G 419 536-6605
Toledo *(G-13019)*

Modern Builders Supply Inc.................... E 419 526-0002
Mansfield *(G-8831)*

Sims-Lohman Inc.................................... E 513 651-3510
Cincinnati *(G-3093)*

KITCHEN UTENSILS: Food Handling & Processing Prdts, Wood

Alfrebro LLC... F 513 539-7373
Monroe *(G-10095)*

Katch Kitchen LLC.................................. E 513 537-8056
Cincinnati *(G-2785)*

Mt Perry Foods Inc.................................. D 740 743-3890
Mount Perry *(G-10225)*

KITCHENWARE STORES

The Kitchen Collection LLC..................... A 740 773-9150
Chillicothe *(G-2284)*

Wasserstrom Company............................. B 614 228-6525
Columbus *(G-5356)*

KITCHENWARE: Plastic

HI Lite Plastic Products............................ G 614 235-9050
Columbus (G-4980)

KNIVES: Agricultural Or indl

Advetech Inc... E 330 533-2227
Canfield (G-1802)

Advetech Inc... E 330 533-2227
Canfield (G-1801)

C B Mfg & Sls Co Inc............................. D 937 866-5986
Miamisburg (G-9678)

Hamilton Industrial Grinding Inc............ E 513 863-1221
Hamilton (G-7502)

Handy Twine Knife Co.......................... G 419 294-3424
Upper Sandusky (G-13442)

Randolph Tool Company Inc................. F 330 877-4923
Hartville (G-7582)

Superion Inc.. E 937 374-0033
Xenia (G-14776)

LABELS: Paper, Made From Purchased Materials

CCL Label Inc...................................... E 216 676-2703
Cleveland (G-3480)

General Data Company Inc.................. B 513 752-7978
Cincinnati (G-2304)

Label Aid Inc....................................... E 419 433-2888
Huron (G-7876)

Label Technique Southeast LLC........... F 440 951-7660
Willoughby (G-14479)

Mabis Shipping Solutions Inc.............. G 330 650-1788
Hudson (G-7850)

Multi-Color Corporation....................... C 513 381-1480
Batavia (G-878)

Multi-Color Corporation....................... G 513 459-3283
Mason (G-9130)

Scratch-Off Systems Inc...................... E 216 649-7800
Twinsburg (G-13376)

Shore To Shore Inc............................. D 937 866-1908
Dayton (G-6004)

T&T Graphics Inc................................ G 937 847-6000
Miamisburg (G-9742)

Tri State Media LLC............................. F 513 933-0101
Wilmington (G-14588)

Verstrete In Mold Lbels USA In............ F 513 943-0080
Batavia (G-896)

LABELS: Woven

Crane Consumables Inc....................... E 513 539-9980
Middletown (G-9851)

Shore To Shore Inc............................. D 937 866-1908
Dayton (G-6004)

LABORATORIES, TESTING: Food

Agrana Fruit Us Inc............................. C 937 693-3821
Anna (G-459)

LABORATORIES, TESTING: Metallurgical

Metcut Research Associates Inc............ D 513 271-5100
Cincinnati (G-2871)

Mrl Materials Resources LLC................ E 937 531-6657
Xenia (G-14771)

Phymet Inc.. F 937 743-8061
Springboro (G-12263)

LABORATORIES, TESTING: Pollution

Nucon International Inc......................... F 614 846-5710
Columbus (G-5132)

LABORATORIES, TESTING: Product Testing

Wallover Enterprises Inc...................... E 440 238-9250
Strongsville (G-12612)

LABORATORIES, TESTING: Product Testing, Safety/Performance

Chemsultants International Inc............. G 440 974-3080
Mentor (G-9498)

Smithers Group Inc.............................. D 330 833-8548
Massillon (G-9244)

LABORATORIES: Biological Research

Mp Biomedicals LLC............................ C 440 337-1200
Solon (G-12154)

LABORATORIES: Biotechnology

EMD Millipore Corporation................... C 513 631-0445
Norwood (G-10868)

LABORATORIES: Dental, Crown & Bridge Production

Dental Ceramics Inc............................. E 330 523-5240
Richfield (G-11590)

LABORATORIES: Electronic Research

Barco Inc.. E 937 372-7579
Xenia (G-14753)

Electronic Concepts Engrg Inc............. F 419 861-9000
Holland (G-7763)

Point Source Inc.................................. F 937 855-6020
Germantown (G-7252)

Sierra Nevada Corporation.................. E 937 431-2800
Beavercreek (G-983)

Srico Inc... G 614 799-0664
Columbus (G-5287)

Steiner Eoptics Inc.............................. D 937 426-2341
Miamisburg (G-9740)

LABORATORIES: Medical

Cellular Technology Limited.................. E 216 791-5084
Shaker Heights (G-11928)

Mp Biomedicals LLC............................ C 440 337-1200
Solon (G-12154)

Smithers Group Inc.............................. D 330 833-8548
Massillon (G-9244)

LABORATORIES: Noncommercial Research

Sdg Inc... F 440 893-0771
Cleveland (G-4282)

Tangent Company LLC......................... G 440 543-2775
Chagrin Falls (G-2186)

LABORATORIES: Physical Research, Commercial

BASF Catalysts LLC............................. A 216 360-5005
Cleveland (G-3408)

Borchers Americas Inc......................... D 440 899-2950
Westlake (G-14295)

Circle Prime Manufacturing Inc............ E 330 923-0019
Cuyahoga Falls (G-5534)

Curtiss-Wright Ds Inc.......................... E 937 252-5601
Fairborn (G-6689)

Defense Research Assoc Inc................ E 937 431-1644
Dayton (G-5609)

Flexsys America LP............................. D 330 666-4111
Akron (G-150)

Lyondell Chemical Company................. C 513 530-4000
Cincinnati (G-2833)

Medpace Holdings Inc......................... C 513 579-9911
Cincinnati (G-2857)

Northcoast Environmental Labs............ G 330 342-3377
Streetsboro (G-12514)

Open Additive LLC.............................. F 937 306-6140
Dayton (G-5929)

Owens Corning Sales LLC.................... F 330 633-6735
Tallmadge (G-12745)

Range Impact Inc................................ G 216 304-6556
Cleveland (G-4224)

Specialty Technology & Res................. G 614 870-0744
Columbus (G-5282)

Sunpower Inc...................................... D 740 594-2221
Athens (G-654)

Trico Products Corporation................... C 800 388-7428
Cleveland (G-4425)

Vehicle Systems Inc............................ G 330 854-0535
Massillon (G-9251)

Wiley Companies................................. C 740 622-0755
Coshocton (G-5476)

LABORATORIES: Testing

Personnel Selection Services............... F 440 835-3255
Cleveland (G-4153)

Quest Diagnostics Incorporated........... G 513 229-5500
Mason (G-9140)

Balancing Company Inc........................ E 937 898-9111
Vandalia (G-13550)

Barr Engineering Incorporated............. E 614 714-0299
Columbus (G-4744)

Curtiss-Wright Flow Ctrl Corp.............. D 513 528-7900
Cincinnati (G-2300)

Fischer Engineering Co LLC................. G 937 754-1750
Dayton (G-5778)

Godfrey & Wing Inc............................. E 330 562-1440
Aurora (G-671)

JBI Corporation................................... F 419 855-3389
Genoa (G-7248)

Jci Jones Chemicals Inc....................... F 330 825-2531
Barberton (G-814)

Micro Laboratories Inc......................... G 440 918-0001
Mentor (G-9564)

National Polymer Inc........................... F 440 708-1245
Chagrin Falls (G-2171)

Nelson Labs Fairfield Inc..................... F 973 227-6882
Broadview Heights (G-1507)

Ohio Lumex Co Inc.............................. E 440 264-2500
Solon (G-12164)

Sample Machining Inc.......................... E 937 258-3338
Dayton (G-5993)

Tangent Company LLC......................... G 440 543-2775
Chagrin Falls (G-2186)

Trico Products Corporation................... C 800 388-7428
Cleveland (G-4425)

Welding Consultants Inc...................... G 614 258-7018
Columbus (G-5360)

Yoder Industries Inc............................ C 937 278-5769
Dayton (G-6089)

LABORATORY APPARATUS & FURNITURE

Chemsultants International Inc............. G 513 860-1598
West Chester (G-13962)

Chemsultants International Inc............. G 440 974-3080
Mentor (G-9498)

Cortest Inc.. F 440 942-1235
Willoughby (G-14442)

Dentronix Inc....................................... D 330 916-7300
Cuyahoga Falls (G-5538)

Gilson Company Inc............................. E 740 548-7298
Lewis Center (G-8334)

Ies Systems Inc................................... E 330 533-6683
Canfield (G-1811)

Philips Med Systems Clvland In........... B 440 483-3000
Cleveland (G-4159)

PRODUCT

So-Low Environmental Eqp Co............ E 513 772-9410
Cincinnati *(G-3098)*

Teledyne Instruments Inc................... E 513 229-7000
Mason *(G-9158)*

Teledyne Tekmar Company................. E 513 229-7000
Mason *(G-9160)*

Waller Brothers Stone Company.......... F 740 858-1948
Mc Dermott *(G-9356)*

LABORATORY APPARATUS, EXC HEATING & MEASURING

Accuscan Instruments Inc.................... F 614 878-6644
Columbus *(G-4670)*

Caron Products and Svcs Inc............... E 740 373-6809
Marietta *(G-8906)*

LABORATORY APPARATUS: Freezers

Global Cooling Inc............................... C 740 274-7900
Athens *(G-641)*

LABORATORY APPARATUS: Pipettes, Hemocytometer

Mettler-Toledo LLC............................. A 614 438-4511
Columbus *(G-4644)*

LABORATORY CHEMICALS: Organic

Nationwide Chemical Products.............. G 419 714-7075
Perrysburg *(G-11240)*

Polymer Diagnostics Inc...................... E 440 930-1361
Avon Lake *(G-768)*

The Shepherd Chemical Company........ C 513 731-1110
Norwood *(G-10874)*

LABORATORY EQPT, EXC MEDICAL: Wholesalers

Revvity Health Sciences Inc................. D 330 825-4525
Akron *(G-283)*

Teledyne Instruments Inc.................... E 513 229-7000
Mason *(G-9158)*

Teledyne Tekmar Company................. E 513 229-7000
Mason *(G-9160)*

Test Mark Industries Inc...................... F 330 426-2200
East Palestine *(G-6408)*

LABORATORY EQPT: Chemical

Cheminstruments Inc........................... G 513 860-1598
West Chester *(G-13960)*

LABORATORY EQPT: Clinical Instruments Exc Medical

Cellular Technology Limited.................. E 216 791-5084
Shaker Heights *(G-11928)*

Strategic Technology Entp.................... G 440 354-2600
Mentor *(G-9628)*

LABORATORY EQPT: Incubators

Health Aid of Ohio Inc......................... E 216 252-3900
Cleveland *(G-3814)*

Malta Dynamics LLC............................ F 740 749-3512
Waterford *(G-13828)*

LABORATORY EQPT: Measuring

4r Enterprises Incorporated................. G 330 923-9799
Cuyahoga Falls *(G-5519)*

Mettler-Toledo Intl Inc......................... A 614 438-4511
Columbus *(G-4643)*

LABORATORY EQPT: Sterilizers

American Sterilizer Company................ E 440 392-8328
Mentor *(G-9480)*

LABORATORY INSTRUMENT REPAIR SVCS

Tektronix Inc...................................... F 248 305-5200
West Chester *(G-14152)*

LADDERS: Metal

Bauer Corporation............................... E 800 321-4760
Wooster *(G-14624)*

Bc Investment Corporation................... C 330 262-3070
Wooster *(G-14625)*

LADLES: Metal Plate

Lincoln Electric Automtn Inc................ E 614 471-5926
Columbus *(G-5070)*

Rimrock Corporation............................ E 614 471-5926
Columbus *(G-5230)*

Rimrock Holdings Corporation.............. C 614 471-5926
Columbus *(G-5231)*

Rose Metal Industries LLC................... F 216 881-3355
Cleveland *(G-4250)*

LAMINATED PLASTICS: Plate, Sheet, Rod & Tubes

Advanced Drainage Systems Inc........... E 419 424-8324
Findlay *(G-6835)*

Advanced Drainage Systems Inc........... E 419 599-9565
Napoleon *(G-10274)*

Advanced Drainage Systems Inc........... E 330 264-4949
Wooster *(G-14618)*

Applied Medical Technology Inc........... F 440 717-4000
Brecksville *(G-1457)*

Arthur Corporation.............................. D 419 433-7202
Huron *(G-7868)*

Biothane Coated Webbing Corp............ E 440 327-0485
North Ridgeville *(G-10727)*

Brr Bear Ltd....................................... F 419 666-1111
Perrysburg *(G-11207)*

Duracote Corporation.......................... E 330 296-9600
Ravenna *(G-11523)*

Durivage Pattern and Mfg Inc.............. E 419 836-8655
Williston *(G-14411)*

Elster Perfection Corporation.............. D 440 428-1171
Geneva *(G-7236)*

Flex Technologies Inc.......................... E 740 922-5992
Midvale *(G-9910)*

Fowler Products Inc............................ G 419 683-4057
Crestline *(G-5502)*

Hancor Inc... B 614 658-0050
Hilliard *(G-7683)*

Iko Production Inc............................... E 937 746-4561
Franklin *(G-7029)*

Laminate Shop.................................... F 740 749-3536
Waterford *(G-13827)*

Lwhs Ltd.. F 419 407-5454
Toledo *(G-13042)*

Meridian Industries Inc....................... D 330 673-1011
Kent *(G-8051)*

Meridienne International Inc................. G 330 274-8317
Aurora *(G-679)*

Organized Living Inc........................... E 513 489-9300
Cincinnati *(G-2939)*

Overhead Door Corporation.................. F 440 593-5226
Conneaut *(G-5413)*

Plaskolite LLC..................................... D 614 294-3281
Columbus *(G-5195)*

Production Tube Cutting Inc................. E 937 254-6138
Dayton *(G-5963)*

Recto Molded Products Inc.................. D 513 871-5544
Cincinnati *(G-3036)*

Resinoid Engineering Corp................... D 740 928-6115
Hebron *(G-7633)*

Rowmark LLC...................................... D 419 425-8974
Findlay *(G-6914)*

Saint-Gobain Prfmce Plas Corp............ C 330 798-6981
Akron *(G-305)*

Snyder Manufacturing Inc.................... D 330 343-4456
Dover *(G-6263)*

Spartech LLC...................................... D 419 399-4050
Paulding *(G-11162)*

TS Trim Industries Inc......................... B 614 837-4114
Canal Winchester *(G-1799)*

Wurms Woodworking Company............ E 419 492-2184
New Washington *(G-10484)*

LAMINATING SVCS

Conversion Tech Intl Inc...................... E 419 924-5566
West Unity *(G-14193)*

Kent Adhesive Products Co.................. D 330 678-1626
Kent *(G-8039)*

Ohio Laminating & Binding Inc............. G 614 771-4868
Hilliard *(G-7691)*

Urban Industries of Ohio Inc................ E 419 468-3578
Galion *(G-7200)*

LAMP & LIGHT BULBS & TUBES

Carlisle and Finch Company................. E 513 681-6080
Cincinnati *(G-2439)*

Current Elec & Enrgy Solutions............ G 513 575-4600
Loveland *(G-8623)*

Current Lighting Solutions LLC............. E 216 462-4700
Cleveland *(G-3581)*

General Electric Company.................... F 440 593-1156
Mc Donald *(G-9358)*

Kichler Lighting LLC............................ B 216 573-1000
Solon *(G-12139)*

Lumitex Inc.. D 440 243-8401
Strongsville *(G-12572)*

Medallion Lighting Corporation............ E 440 255-8383
Mentor *(G-9561)*

Osram Sylvania Inc............................. D 800 463-9275
Independence *(G-7913)*

Savant Technologies LLC..................... F 800 435-4448
East Cleveland *(G-6382)*

LAMP BULBS & TUBES/PARTS, ELECTRIC: Generalized Applications

Advanced Lighting Tech LLC................. D 888 440-2358
Solon *(G-12073)*

LAMP SHADES: Glass

A Service Glass Inc............................. F 937 426-4920
Beavercreek *(G-963)*

All State GL Block Fctry Inc................. G 440 205-8410
Mentor *(G-9476)*

Blockamerica Corporation.................... G 614 274-0700
Columbus *(G-4765)*

Dale Kestler...................................... G 513 871-9000
Cincinnati *(G-2540)*

Niles Mirror & Glass Inc...................... E 330 652-6277
Niles *(G-10597)*

Oldcastle Buildingenvelope Inc............ C 800 537-4064
Perrysburg *(G-11249)*

LAMPS: Fluorescent

General Electric Company.................... E 419 563-1200
Bucyrus *(G-1682)*

LAMPS: Table, Residential

J Schrader Company............................ G 216 961-2890
Cleveland *(G-3879)*

Medallion Lighting Corporation............ E 440 255-8383
Mentor *(G-9561)*

LAND SUBDIVISION & DEVELOPMENT

Phillips Companies.......................... E 937 426-5461
Beavercreek Township *(G-1003)*

Stonyridge Inc................................ F 937 845-9482
New Carlisle *(G-10380)*

LASER SYSTEMS & EQPT

Eagle Welding & Fabg Inc...................... E 440 946-0692
Willoughby *(G-14453)*

FM Manufacturing Inc........................ G 419 445-0700
Archbold *(G-493)*

Resonetics LLC.............................. D 937 865-4070
Kettering *(G-8123)*

LASERS: Welding, Drilling & Cutting Eqpt

Great Lakes Power Service Co.............. F 440 259-0025
Perry *(G-11192)*

Innovar Systems Limited.................... E 330 538-3942
North Jackson *(G-10689)*

Laser Automation Inc........................ G 440 543-9291
Chagrin Falls *(G-2169)*

Lucky Thirteen Inc.......................... G 216 631-0013
Cleveland *(G-3971)*

Peerless Laser Processors Inc.............. F 614 836-5790
Groveport *(G-7447)*

Pt Metals LLC.............................. E 330 767-3003
Navarre *(G-10312)*

LATEX: Foamed

Firestone Polymers LLC...................... D 330 379-7000
Akron *(G-148)*

Trexler Rubber Co Inc........................ E 330 296-9677
Ravenna *(G-11546)*

LATH: Expanded Metal

Nmc Metals Inc.............................. E 330 652-2501
Niles *(G-10599)*

LAUNDRY EQPT: Commercial

Ha-International LLC.......................... E 419 537-0096
Toledo *(G-12982)*

Whirlpool Corporation........................ C 419 547-7711
Clyde *(G-4565)*

LAUNDRY EQPT: Household

Kitchenaid Inc.............................. F 937 316-4782
Greenville *(G-7345)*

Staber Industries Inc........................ E 614 836-5995
Groveport *(G-7450)*

Whirlpool Corporation........................ G 419 547-2610
Clyde *(G-4566)*

LAWN & GARDEN EQPT

Cannon Salt & Supply Inc.................... G 440 232-1700
Bedford *(G-1019)*

Commercial Turf Products Ltd.............. F 330 995-7000
Streetsboro *(G-12494)*

Dinsmore Inc.............................. G 937 544-3332
West Union *(G-14190)*

Elan Designs Inc............................ G 614 985-5600
Westerville *(G-14258)*

Erosion Control Products Corp.............. F 302 815-6500
West Chester *(G-13994)*

Extrudex Limited Partnership................ E 440 352-7101
Painesville *(G-11085)*

Finn Corporation............................ E 513 874-2818
West Chester *(G-13997)*

Franklin Equipment LLC...................... E 614 228-2014
Groveport *(G-7435)*

Gardner Inc................................ C 614 456-4000
Columbus *(G-4945)*

Karl Kuemmerling Inc........................ F
Massillon *(G-9209)*

Koenig Equipment Inc........................ F 937 653-5281
Urbana *(G-13472)*

Mm Service................................ G 330 626-2520
Streetsboro *(G-12511)*

Mtd Holdings Inc............................ B 330 225-2600
Valley City *(G-13508)*

Mtd International Operations................ G 330 225-2600
Valley City *(G-13509)*

Mtd Products Inc............................ C 419 342-6455
Shelby *(G-11971)*

Mtd Products Inc............................ G 330 225-1940
Valley City *(G-13511)*

Mtd Products Inc............................ G 419 951-9779
Willard *(G-14405)*

Mtd Products Inc............................ B 330 225-2600
Valley City *(G-13510)*

Oase North America Inc...................... G 800 365-3880
Aurora *(G-682)*

Power Distributors LLC...................... D 614 876-3533
Columbus *(G-5200)*

Scotts Company LLC.......................... C 937 644-0011
Marysville *(G-9045)*

Scotts Temecula Operations LLC.......... G 800 221-1760
Marysville *(G-9048)*

Smg Growing Media Inc...................... F 937 644-0011
Marysville *(G-9049)*

Tierra-Derco International LLC.............. G 419 929-2240
New London *(G-10418)*

LAWN & GARDEN EQPT: Grass Catchers, Lawn Mower

Cub Cadet Corporation Sales................ D 330 273-4550
Valley City *(G-13494)*

LAWN & GARDEN EQPT: Lawnmowers, Residential, Hand Or Power

Johnson & Johnson Services LLC.......... F 513 289-4514
Cincinnati *(G-2770)*

Mtd Products Inc............................ C 330 225-9127
Valley City *(G-13512)*

LAWN & GARDEN EQPT: Rototillers

Rotoline USA LLC............................ G 330 677-3223
Kent *(G-8071)*

LAWN & GARDEN EQPT: Tractors & Eqpt

Hawthorne Gardening Company.......... E 360 883-8846
Marysville *(G-9023)*

Mo-Trim Inc................................ G 740 439-2725
Cambridge *(G-1750)*

Mtd Consumer Group Inc.................... C 330 225-2600
Valley City *(G-13507)*

Park-Ohio Holdings Corp.................... F 440 947-2000
Cleveland *(G-4136)*

Park-Ohio Industries Inc.................... C 440 947-2000
Cleveland *(G-4137)*

Venture Products Inc........................ D 330 683-0075
Orrville *(G-11016)*

LEAD & ZINC ORES

Abatement Lead Tstg Risk Assss.......... G 330 785-6420
Akron *(G-11)*

LEAD PENCILS & ART GOODS

North Shore Strapping Company.......... E 216 661-5200
Brooklyn Heights *(G-1536)*

Pulsar Ecoproducts LLC...................... F 216 861-8800
Cleveland *(G-4208)*

LEASING & RENTAL SVCS: Cranes & Aerial Lift Eqpt

Rnm Holdings Inc............................ F 614 444-5556
Columbus *(G-5232)*

LEASING & RENTAL SVCS: Oil Field Eqpt

Eleet Cryogenics Inc........................ E 330 874-4009
Bolivar *(G-1382)*

Terra Sonic International LLC................ E 740 374-6608
Marietta *(G-8953)*

LEASING & RENTAL SVCS: Oil Well Drilling

Dover Fabrication and Burn Inc.............. G 330 339-1057
Dover *(G-6239)*

LEASING & RENTAL: Construction & Mining Eqpt

Brewpro Inc................................ G 513 577-7200
Cincinnati *(G-2423)*

Ioppolo Concrete Corporation................ G 440 439-6606
Bedford *(G-1040)*

Lefeld Welding & Stl Sups Inc.............. E 419 678-2397
Coldwater *(G-4580)*

Ohio Machinery Co.......................... C 440 526-6200
Broadview Heights *(G-1509)*

Pollock Research & Design Inc.............. E 330 332-3300
Salem *(G-11805)*

The Wagner-Smith Company................ B 866 338-0398
Moraine *(G-10195)*

LEASING & RENTAL: Medical Machinery & Eqpt

Columbus Prescr Rehabilitation.............. G 614 294-1600
Westerville *(G-14250)*

Health Aid of Ohio Inc...................... E 216 252-3900
Cleveland *(G-3814)*

Kempf Surgical Appliances Inc.............. G 513 984-5758
Cincinnati *(G-2791)*

LEASING & RENTAL: Trucks, Indl

Hull Ready Mix Concrete Inc................ F 419 625-8070
Sandusky *(G-11839)*

LEASING & RENTAL: Trucks, Without Drivers

Knippen Chrysler Ddge Jeep Inc.......... F 419 695-4976
Delphos *(G-8188)*

Marlow-2000 Inc............................ F 216 362-8500
Cleveland *(G-3991)*

LEATHER & CUT STOCK WHOLESALERS

Weaver Leather LLC.......................... D 330 674-7548
Millersburg *(G-10019)*

LEATHER GOODS, EXC FOOTWEAR, GLOVES, LUGGAGE/ BELTING, WHOL

B D G Wrap-Tite Inc.......................... E 440 349-5400
Solon *(G-12081)*

LEATHER GOODS: Garments

LLC Bowman Leather........................ G 330 893-1954
Millersburg *(G-9994)*

LEATHER GOODS: Holsters

Diy Holster LLC.............................. G 419 921-2168
Elyria *(G-6520)*

LEATHER GOODS: Personal

Bison Leather Co............................ G 419 517-1737
Toledo *(G-12897)*

PRODUCT

Down Home.. G 740 393-1186
Mount Vernon *(G-10243)*

Ravenworks Deer Skin.......................... G 937 354-5151
Mount Victory *(G-10270)*

Total Education Solutions Inc................. D 330 668-4041
Fairlawn *(G-6815)*

Weaver Leather LLC............................... D 330 674-7548
Millersburg *(G-10019)*

Williams Leather Products Inc............... G 740 223-1604
Marion *(G-9004)*

LEATHER GOODS: Wallets

Hugo Bosca Company Inc....................... F 937 323-5523
Springfield *(G-12327)*

LEATHER TANNING & FINISHING

Premier Tanning & Nutrition.................. G 419 342-6259
Shelby *(G-11973)*

Sisters Tanning Inc............................... G 740 636-0303
Wshngtn Ct Hs *(G-14746)*

LEGAL OFFICES & SVCS

Akron Legal News Inc............................ F 330 296-7578
Akron *(G-33)*

Bigmar Inc... E 740 966-5800
Johnstown *(G-7992)*

Gongwer News Service Inc..................... F 614 221-1992
Columbus *(G-4962)*

Perfect Probate.................................... G 513 791-4100
Cincinnati *(G-2953)*

LEGAL SVCS: General Practice Attorney or Lawyer

Petro Quest Inc.................................... G 740 593-3800
Athens *(G-645)*

LICENSE TAGS: Automobile, Stamped Metal

Barbara A Lieurance.............................. G 937 382-2864
Wilmington *(G-14573)*

Clemens License Agency........................ G 614 288-8007
Pickerington *(G-11292)*

D J Klingler Inc.................................... G 513 891-2284
Montgomery *(G-10124)*

Middletown License Agency Inc............. G 513 422-7225
Middletown *(G-9879)*

Parma Heights License Bureau.............. G 440 888-0388
Cleveland *(G-4147)*

Public Safety Ohio Department............. G 440 943-5545
Willoughby *(G-14511)*

Suburbanite Inc................................... G 419 756-4390
Mansfield *(G-8856)*

LIGHTING EQPT: Flashlights

Fulton Industries LLC........................... D 419 270-3937
Wauseon *(G-13849)*

Stamp & Flash Inc................................ D 419 335-3015
Wauseon *(G-13859)*

LIGHTING EQPT: Motor Vehicle

Atc Lighting & Plastics Inc.................... C 440 466-7670
Andover *(G-456)*

Lighting Products Inc............................ F 440 293-4064
Andover *(G-458)*

LIGHTING EQPT: Motor Vehicle, Headlights

K-D Lamp Company................................ E 440 293-4064
Andover *(G-457)*

LIGHTING EQPT: Motor Vehicle, NEC

Rvtronix Corporation............................. E 440 359-7200
Eastlake *(G-6442)*

Stanley Electric US Co Inc..................... E 740 852-5200
London *(G-8541)*

Washington Products Inc....................... F 330 837-5101
Massillon *(G-9252)*

LIGHTING EQPT: Outdoor

Holophane Corporation.......................... C 866 759-1577
Granville *(G-7316)*

Stadium Grow Lighting Inc.................... G 855 346-9403
Warren *(G-13798)*

LIGHTING FIXTURES WHOLESALERS

American De Rosa Lamparts LLC......... D
Cuyahoga Falls *(G-5522)*

Architectural Busstrut Corp.................. F 614 933-8695
New Albany *(G-10329)*

B2d Solutions Inc................................. G 855 484-1145
Cleveland *(G-3402)*

Cleanlife Energy LLC............................. F 800 316-2532
Cleveland *(G-3503)*

Gt Industrial Supply Inc........................ F 513 771-7000
Cincinnati *(G-2695)*

LSI Industries Inc................................. C 913 281-1100
Blue Ash *(G-1299)*

Technical Artistry Inc............................ G 614 299-7777
Columbus *(G-5316)*

LIGHTING FIXTURES, NEC

Aat USA LLC... G 614 388-8866
Columbus *(G-4658)*

Acuity Brands Lighting Inc.................... D 740 349-4343
Newark *(G-10489)*

Advanced Lighting Tech LLC................. D 888 440-2358
Solon *(G-12073)*

Akron Brass Company........................... E 614 529-7230
Columbus *(G-4682)*

Atc Lighting & Plastics Inc.................... C 440 466-7670
Andover *(G-456)*

Avid Lighting LLC................................. G 614 502-2843
Hilliard *(G-7670)*

Brightguy Inc....................................... G 440 942-8318
Willoughby *(G-14434)*

Cooper Lighting LLC............................. G 800 334-6871
Columbus *(G-4848)*

Delta Power Supply Inc......................... F 513 771-3835
Cincinnati *(G-2545)*

Ericson Manufacturing Co..................... D 440 951-8000
Willoughby *(G-14456)*

General Electric Company...................... G 330 373-1400
Warren *(G-13767)*

Genesis Lamp Corp............................... F 440 354-0095
Painesville *(G-11088)*

Global Lighting Tech Inc....................... E 440 922-4584
Brecksville *(G-1468)*

Hughey & Phillips LLC........................... E 937 652-3500
Urbana *(G-13467)*

Kichler Lighting LLC.............................. B 216 573-1000
Solon *(G-12139)*

LSI Industries Inc................................. C 513 793-3200
Cincinnati *(G-2830)*

Lumitex Inc.. D 440 243-8401
Strongsville *(G-12572)*

Midmark Corporation............................ G 937 526-3662
Versailles *(G-13600)*

Midmark Corporation............................ E 937 526-8387
Versailles *(G-13601)*

Midmark Corporation............................ A 937 528-7500
Miamisburg *(G-9717)*

Starbright Lighting USA LLC................. G 330 650-2000
Hudson *(G-7859)*

Vanner Holdings Inc.............................. D 614 771-2718
Hilliard *(G-7709)*

Will-Burt Company................................ C 330 682-7015
Orrville *(G-11018)*

LIGHTING FIXTURES: Decorative Area

B2d Solutions Inc................................. G 855 484-1145
Cleveland *(G-3402)*

LIGHTING FIXTURES: Fluorescent, Commercial

Damak 1 LLC.. E 513 858-6004
Fairfield *(G-6725)*

Magnum Asset Acquisition LLC............. E 330 915-2382
Hudson *(G-7851)*

LIGHTING FIXTURES: Indl & Commercial

Acuity Brands Lighting Inc.................... C 800 754-0463
Granville *(G-7313)*

Acuity Brands Lighting Inc.................... D 740 349-4343
Newark *(G-10489)*

Acuity Brands Lighting Inc.................... C 740 892-2011
Utica *(G-13485)*

Advanced Lighting Tech LLC................. D 888 440-2358
Solon *(G-12073)*

Besa Lighting Co Inc............................. E 614 475-7046
Blacklick *(G-1220)*

Best Lighting Products Inc..................... D 740 964-1198
Pataskala *(G-11137)*

Bock Company LLC................................ G 216 912-7050
Twinsburg *(G-13282)*

Current Lighting Solutions LLC............. B 216 266-4416
Cleveland *(G-3580)*

Current Lighting Solutions LLC............. E 216 462-4700
Cleveland *(G-3581)*

Etherium Lighting LLC........................... G 614 388-9893
Columbus *(G-4911)*

Evp International LLC............................. G 513 761-7614
Cincinnati *(G-2607)*

GE Lighting Inc..................................... D 216 266-2121
Cleveland *(G-3759)*

General Electric Company...................... F 330 458-3200
Canton *(G-1899)*

Genesis Lamp Corp............................... F 440 354-0095
Painesville *(G-11088)*

Grimes Aerospace Company................... A 937 484-2000
Urbana *(G-13462)*

Hinkley Lighting Inc.............................. E 440 653-5500
Avon Lake *(G-760)*

Holophane Corporation.......................... F 740 349-4194
Newark *(G-10506)*

Holophane Corporation.......................... C 866 759-1577
Granville *(G-7316)*

J Schrader Company.............................. E 216 961-2890
Cleveland *(G-3879)*

JB Machining Concepts LLC................... G 419 523-0096
Ottawa *(G-11036)*

Led Lighting Center Inc......................... G 714 271-2633
Toledo *(G-13029)*

Led Lighting Center LLC........................ F 888 988-6533
Toledo *(G-13030)*

Light Craft Manufacturing Inc............... F 419 332-0536
Fremont *(G-7121)*

LSI Industries Inc................................. C 913 281-1100
Blue Ash *(G-1299)*

LSI Lightron Inc.................................... A 845 562-5500
Blue Ash *(G-1300)*

Lumenforce Led LLC.............................. E 330 330-8962
Youngstown *(G-14889)*

Lumitex Inc.. D 440 243-8401
Strongsville *(G-12572)*

NRG Industrial Lighting Mfg Co............ G 419 354-8207
Bowling Green *(G-1431)*

Power Source Service LLC.................... G 513 607-4555
Batavia *(G-883)*

SMS Technologies Inc......................... F 419 465-4175
Monroeville *(G-10121)*

Stress-Crete Company...................... E 440 576-9073
Jefferson *(G-7983)*

Treemen Industries Inc....................... E 330 965-3777
Boardman *(G-1378)*

LIGHTING FIXTURES: Motor Vehicle

Advanced Technology Corp................ F 440 293-4064
Andover *(G-454)*

Akron Brass Company........................ E 614 529-7230
Columbus *(G-4682)*

Akron Brass Company........................ E 800 228-1161
Wooster *(G-14619)*

Akron Brass Company........................ B 330 264-5678
Wooster *(G-14620)*

Atc Group Inc.................................... D 440 293-4064
Andover *(G-455)*

Grimes Aerospace Company.............. D 937 484-2001
Urbana *(G-13464)*

Grimes Aerospace Company.............. A 937 484-2000
Urbana *(G-13462)*

Treemen Industries Inc....................... E 330 965-3777
Boardman *(G-1378)*

LIGHTING FIXTURES: Ornamental, Commercial

King Luminaire Company Inc............... E 440 576-9073
Jefferson *(G-7975)*

LIGHTING FIXTURES: Public

Union Metal Corporation..................... B 330 456-7653
Canton *(G-2032)*

LIGHTING FIXTURES: Residential, Electric

Architectural Busstrut Corp................ F 614 933-8695
New Albany *(G-10329)*

LIGHTING FIXTURES: Street

Miami Valley Lighting LLC................... G 937 224-6000
Dayton *(G-5620)*

LIME

Ayers Limestone Quarry Inc............... F 740 633-2958
Martins Ferry *(G-9000)*

Bluffton Stone Co.............................. F 419 358-6941
Bluffton *(G-1358)*

Graymont Dolime (oh) Inc................... D 419 855-8682
Genoa *(G-7247)*

Mineral Processing Company.............. G 419 396-3501
Carey *(G-2059)*

National Lime and Stone Co................ E 419 396-7671
Carey *(G-2060)*

Piqua Materials Inc............................ D 937 773-4824
Piqua *(G-11377)*

Shelly Materials Inc........................... E 740 666-5841
Ostrander *(G-11029)*

Sugarcreek Lime Service.................... G 330 364-4460
Dover *(G-6264)*

LIME ROCK: Ground

National Lime and Stone Co................ E 419 396-7671
Carey *(G-2060)*

LIMESTONE: Crushed & Broken

Acme Company.................................. D 330 758-2313
Poland *(G-11434)*

Allgeier & Son Inc............................. F 513 574-3735
Cincinnati *(G-2351)*

Beazer East Inc................................ E 937 364-2311
Hillsboro *(G-7714)*

Bluffton Stone Co.............................. F 419 358-6941
Bluffton *(G-1358)*

Carmeuse Lime Inc............................ D 419 986-5200
Bettsville *(G-1207)*

Carmeuse Lime Inc............................ F 419 638-2511
Millersville *(G-10027)*

Cumberland Limestone LLC................ E 740 638-3942
Cumberland *(G-5516)*

Custar Stone Co................................ E 419 669-4327
Napoleon *(G-10277)*

Duff Quarry Inc................................. F 419 273-2518
Forest *(G-6940)*

Duff Quarry Inc................................. F 937 686-2811
Huntsville *(G-7863)*

Feikert Sand & Gravel Co Inc............. E 330 674-0038
Millersburg *(G-9980)*

Heidelberg Mtls Mdwest Agg Inc......... F 419 882-0123
Sylvania *(G-12708)*

Kellstone Inc.................................... E 419 746-2396
Kelleys Island *(G-8009)*

Lang Stone Company Inc.................... E 614 235-4099
Columbus *(G-5064)*

Marietta Martin Materials Inc.............. G 740 247-2211
Racine *(G-11505)*

Marietta Martin Materials Inc.............. G 937 335-8313
Troy *(G-13239)*

Martin Marietta Materials Inc.............. F 513 701-1120
Mason *(G-9124)*

Martin Marietta Materials Inc.............. F 513 701-1140
West Chester *(G-14026)*

National Lime and Stone Co................ E 419 562-0771
Bucyrus *(G-1684)*

National Lime and Stone Co................ E 740 548-4206
Delaware *(G-6163)*

National Lime and Stone Co................ E 419 423-3400
Findlay *(G-6897)*

National Lime and Stone Co................ F 419 228-3434
Lima *(G-8435)*

National Lime and Stone Co................ F 330 966-4836
North Canton *(G-10656)*

National Lime and Stone Co................ G 419 657-6745
Wapakoneta *(G-13726)*

Oglebay Norton Mar Svcs Co LLC........ A 216 861-3300
Cleveland *(G-4109)*

Omya Industries Inc........................... D 513 387-4600
Mason *(G-9133)*

Oster Sand and Gravel Inc................. G 330 833-2649
Massillon *(G-9229)*

Ridge Township Stone Quarry............. G 419 968-2222
Van Wert *(G-13544)*

Shelly Company................................. G 216 688-0684
Cleveland *(G-4291)*

Shelly Materials Inc........................... E 740 666-5841
Ostrander *(G-11029)*

Shelly Materials Inc........................... E 740 246-6315
Toledo *(G-13130)*

Shelly Materials Inc........................... D 740 246-6315
Thornville *(G-12770)*

Sidwell Materials Inc.......................... C 740 849-2422
Zanesville *(G-15050)*

Stoneco Inc...................................... E 419 893-7645
Maumee *(G-9321)*

Stoneco Inc...................................... E 419 393-2555
Oakwood *(G-10900)*

Stoneco Inc...................................... G 419 686-3311
Portage *(G-11461)*

The National Lime and Stone Company. E 419 422-4341
Findlay *(G-6927)*

Uniontown Stone................................ G 740 968-4313
Flushing *(G-6937)*

Wyandot Dolomite Inc........................ E 419 396-7641
Carey *(G-2064)*

LIMESTONE: Cut & Shaped

Maple Grove Materials Inc.................. G 419 992-4235
Tiffin *(G-12790)*

National Lime and Stone Co................ G 419 657-6745
Wapakoneta *(G-13726)*

LIMESTONE: Dimension

Gregory Stone Co Inc......................... G 937 275-7455
Dayton *(G-5805)*

National Lime and Stone Co................ E 419 562-0771
Bucyrus *(G-1684)*

Stoneco Inc...................................... E 419 422-8854
Findlay *(G-6923)*

Waterloo Coal Company Inc................ D 740 286-0004
Jackson *(G-7955)*

Wyandot Dolomite Inc........................ E 419 396-7641
Carey *(G-2064)*

LIMESTONE: Ground

Conag Inc... G 419 394-8870
Saint Marys *(G-11736)*

Heidelberg Mtls Mdwest Agg Inc......... G 419 983-2211
Bloomville *(G-1240)*

Latham Limestone LLC........................ G 740 493-2677
Latham *(G-8235)*

National Lime and Stone Co................ E 740 387-3485
Marion *(G-8983)*

Ohio Asphaltic Limestone Corp........... F 937 364-2191
Hillsboro *(G-7721)*

Piqua Materials Inc............................ D 937 773-4824
Piqua *(G-11377)*

Piqua Materials Inc............................ E 513 771-0820
Cincinnati *(G-2964)*

Sharon Stone Inc.............................. G 740 732-7100
Caldwell *(G-1728)*

Wagner Quarries Company.................. E 419 625-8141
Sandusky *(G-11883)*

LINENS & TOWELS WHOLESALERS

Standard Textile Co Inc...................... B 513 761-9255
Cincinnati *(G-3112)*

LINERS & COVERS: Fabric

Custom Canvas & Boat Repr Inc.......... G 419 732-3314
Lakeside *(G-8157)*

Sailors Tailor Inc.............................. F 937 862-7781
Spring Valley *(G-12243)*

LINERS & LINING

Flow-Liner Systems Ltd...................... E 800 348-0020
Zanesville *(G-15014)*

Ridge Corporation............................. D 614 421-7434
Pataskala *(G-11147)*

LININGS: Fabric, Apparel & Other, Exc Millinery

Fortner Upholstering Inc..................... F 614 475-8282
Columbus *(G-4936)*

Indra Holdings Corp........................... C 513 682-8200
Cincinnati *(G-2743)*

Promospark Inc................................. F 513 844-2211
Fairfield *(G-6768)*

LIQUEFIED PETROLEUM GAS DEALERS

Legacy Farmers Cooperative............... F 419 423-2611
Findlay *(G-6884)*

Employee Codes: A=Over 500 employees, B=251-500
C=101-250, D=51-100, E=20-50, F=10-19, G=1-9

PRODUCT

LIQUEFIED PETROLEUM GAS WHOLESALERS

Centerra Co-Op...................................E 419 281-2153
Ashland (G-526)

LIQUID CRYSTAL DISPLAYS

Cks Solution Incorporated.....................E 513 947-1277
Fairfield (G-6723)

Cleanlife Energy LLC...........................F 800 316-2532
Cleveland (G-3503)

Kent Displays Inc..............................D 330 673-8784
Kent (G-8040)

S-Tek Inc......................................G 440 439-8232
Twinsburg (G-13373)

LITHOGRAPHIC PLATES

Gli Holdings Inc...............................D 440 892-7760
Stow (G-12434)

Gli Holdings Inc...............................D 216 651-1500
Stow (G-12433)

Kehl-Kolor Inc.................................E 419 281-3107
Ashland (G-545)

R E May Inc....................................G 216 771-6332
Cleveland (G-4220)

LIVESTOCK WHOLESALERS, NEC

Werling and Sons Inc...........................F 937 338-3281
Burkettsville (G-1698)

LOADS: Electronic

Omega Engineering Inc..........................E 740 965-9340
Sunbury (G-12673)

Omegadyne Inc..................................D 740 965-9340
Sunbury (G-12674)

TL Industries Inc..............................C 419 666-8144
Perrysburg (G-11272)

LOCKERS

Industrial Mfg Co Intl LLC.....................G 440 838-4555
Upper Arlington (G-13431)

Industrial Mfg Co LLC..........................F 440 838-4700
Brecksville (G-1472)

Republic Storage Systems LLC...................B 330 438-5800
Canton (G-1996)

Tiffin Metal Products Co.......................D 419 447-8414
Tiffin (G-12803)

LOCKSMITHS

Esmet Inc......................................E 330 452-9132
Canton (G-1888)

Kirk Key Interlock Company LLC.................E 330 833-8223
North Canton (G-10648)

LOCOMOTIVES & PARTS

B&C Machine Co LLC.............................F 330 745-4013
Barberton (G-796)

LOGGING

Dale R Adkins..................................G 740 682-7312
Oak Hill (G-10887)

Haessly Lumber Sales Co........................D 740 373-6681
Marietta (G-8922)

Miller Logging Inc.............................G 330 279-4721
Holmesville (G-7802)

Stark Truss Company Inc........................E 419 298-3777
Edgerton (G-6471)

LOGGING CAMPS & CONTRACTORS

Beachs Trees Slctive Hrvstg LL.................G 513 289-5976
Cincinnati (G-2297)

Biedenbach Logging.............................G 740 732-6477
Sarahsville (G-11884)

Blair Logging.................................G 740 934-2730
Lower Salem (G-8665)

Blankenship Logging LLC........................G 740 372-3833
Otway (G-11058)

Border Lumber & Logging Ltd....................G 330 897-0177
Fresno (G-7145)

Craig Saylor...................................G 740 352-8363
Portland (G-11462)

Custom Material Hdlg Eqp LLC...................G 513 235-5336
Cincinnati (G-2531)

David Adkins Logging...........................G 740 533-0297
Kitts Hill (G-8147)

HK Logging & Lumber Ltd........................G 440 632-1997
Middlefield (G-9801)

R & D Logging LLC..............................G 740 259-6127
Lucasville (G-8669)

LOGGING: Timber, Cut At Logging Camp

Oakbridge Timber Framing.......................G 419 994-1052
Loudonville (G-8592)

LOGGING: Wooden Logs

Lee Saylor Logging LLC.........................G 740 682-0479
Oak Hill (G-10890)

LOGS: Gas, Fireplace

Specialty Ceramics Inc.........................D 330 482-0800
Columbiana (G-4629)

LOTIONS OR CREAMS: Face

Beautyavenues LLC..............................F 614 856-6000
Reynoldsburg (G-11558)

Beiersdorf Inc.................................C 513 682-7300
West Chester (G-14107)

Bright Holdco LLC..............................C 614 741-7458
New Albany (G-10333)

Innove Inc.....................................D 440 836-0199
Macedonia (G-8697)

Redex Industries Inc...........................F 330 332-9800
Salem (G-11809)

LUBRICANTS: Corrosion Preventive

Apex Advanced Technologies LLC.................G 216 898-1595
Cleveland (G-3361)

Dinol US Inc...................................E 740 548-1656
Lewis Center (G-8330)

Stellar Group Inc..............................F 330 769-8484
Seville (G-11921)

LUBRICATING EQPT: Indl

Motionsource International LLC.................F 440 287-7037
Solon (G-12153)

LUBRICATING OIL & GREASE WHOLESALERS

Aerospace Lubricants LLC.......................F 614 878-3600
Columbus (G-4678)

American Ultra Specialties Inc.................F 330 656-5000
Hudson (G-7831)

Digilube Systems Inc...........................F 937 748-2209
Springboro (G-12250)

Functional Products Inc........................F 330 963-3060
Macedonia (G-8692)

Groeneveld-Beka Usa Inc........................G 330 225-4949
Sharon Center (G-11941)

Lubriplate Lubricants Company..................G 419 691-2491
Toledo (G-13041)

Varouh Oil Inc.................................F 440 482-8686
Elyria (G-6599)

LUBRICATION SYSTEMS & EQPT

Cleveland Gear Company Inc.....................D 216 641-9000
Cleveland (G-3511)

Digilube Systems Inc...........................F 937 748-2209
Springboro (G-12250)

Koester Corporation............................E 419 599-0291
Napoleon (G-10289)

Pax Products Inc...............................F 419 586-2337
Celina (G-2115)

LUGGAGE & BRIEFCASES

Buckeye Stamping Company.......................D 877 728-0776
Columbus (G-4786)

Cleveland Canvas Goods Mfg Co..................E 216 361-4567
Cleveland (G-3508)

Kam Manufacturing Inc..........................E 419 238-6037
Van Wert (G-13538)

Plastic Forming Company Inc....................E 330 830-5167
Massillon (G-9233)

Weaver Leather LLC.............................D 330 674-7548
Millersburg (G-10019)

LUGGAGE & LEATHER GOODS STORES

Baggallini Inc.................................F 800 448-8753
Pickerington (G-11289)

LUGGAGE: Traveling Bags

Belaire Products Inc...........................E 330 253-3116
Akron (G-75)

Eagle Creek Inc................................D 513 385-4442
Cincinnati (G-2572)

LUMBER & BLDG MATLS DEALER, RET: Garage Doors, Sell/Install

A L Callahan Door Sales........................G 419 884-3667
Mansfield (G-8757)

Jerry Harolds Doors Unlimited..................G 740 635-4949
Bridgeport (G-1494)

Nofziger Door Sales Inc........................F 419 445-2961
Archbold (G-506)

Overhead Inc...................................G 419 476-0300
Toledo (G-13083)

LUMBER & BLDG MATRLS DEALERS, RET: Bath Fixtures, Eqpt/Sply

Agean Marble Manufacturing Inc.................G 513 874-1475
West Chester (G-14099)

Marble Arch Products Inc.......................G 937 746-8388
Franklin (G-7032)

LUMBER & BLDG MATRLS DEALERS, RETAIL: Doors, Wood/Metal

Nofziger Door Sales Inc........................C 419 337-9900
Wauseon (G-13857)

Pease Enterprises Inc..........................F 513 871-8907
Cincinnati (G-2951)

LUMBER & BLDG MTRLS DEALERS, RET: Planing Mill Prdts/Lumber

1914 Mi Inc....................................E 330 308-8667
New Philadelphia (G-10428)

Cox Wood Product Inc...........................F 740 372-4735
Otway (G-11059)

Yoder Lumber Co Inc............................E 330 893-3131
Sugarcreek (G-12658)

LUMBER & BUILDING MATERIALS DEALER, RET: Door & Window Prdts

Dale Kestler.................................G.....513 871-9000
Cincinnati (G-2540)

P & T Millwork Inc.........................F.....440 543-2151
Chagrin Falls (G-2175)

Rockwood Products Ltd..................E.....330 893-2392
Millersburg (G-10007)

Seemray LLC...............................E.....440 536-8705
Cleveland (G-4285)

Waxco International Inc..................F.....937 746-4845
Miamisburg (G-9752)

LUMBER & BUILDING MATERIALS DEALER, RET: Masonry Matls/Splys

Associated Associates Inc..............E.....330 626-3300
Mantua (G-8867)

Feather Lite Innovations Inc...........E.....937 743-9008
Springboro (G-12252)

Grafton Ready Mix Concret Inc.........C.....440 926-2911
Grafton (G-7303)

Gregory Stone Co Inc.....................G.....937 275-7455
Dayton (G-5805)

Hazelbaker Industries Ltd...............G
Columbus (G-4973)

Koltcz Concrete Block Co................E.....440 232-3630
Bedford (G-1042)

Mack Industries............................F.....419 353-7081
Bowling Green (G-1427)

Pleasant Valley Ready Mix Inc.........F.....330 852-2613
Sugarcreek (G-12645)

Quikrete Companies LLC.................E.....330 296-6080
Ravenna (G-11536)

St Henry Tile Co Inc......................G.....937 548-1101
Greenville (G-7355)

St Henry Tile Co Inc......................E.....419 678-4841
Saint Henry (G-11724)

Stocker Concrete Company.............F.....740 254-4626
Gnadenhutten (G-7293)

Westview Concrete Corp.................F.....440 458-5800
Elyria (G-6602)

Westview Concrete Corp.................E.....440 235-1800
Olmsted Falls (G-10943)

LUMBER & BUILDING MATERIALS DEALERS, RET: Solar Heating Eqpt

Gopowerx Inc...............................E.....440 707-6029
Richfield (G-11594)

LUMBER & BUILDING MATERIALS DEALERS, RETAIL: Brick

American Concrete Products Inc.......G.....937 224-1433
Dayton (G-5652)

Glen-Gery Corporation...................D.....419 845-3321
Caledonia (G-1731)

Huth Ready Mix & Supply Co............G.....330 833-4191
Massillon (G-9203)

Medina Supply Company..................E.....330 723-3681
Medina (G-9426)

Snyder Concrete Products Inc..........G.....937 339-7577
Troy (G-13257)

The Ideal Builders Supply & Fuel Co Inc F.....216 741-1600
Cleveland (G-4386)

LUMBER & BUILDING MATERIALS DEALERS, RETAIL: Cement

Ernst Enterprises Inc....................E.....614 443-9456
Columbus (G-4909)

Scioto Ready Mix LLC.....................D.....740 924-9273
Pataskala (G-11150)

Smyrna Ready Mix Concrete LLC........D.....937 855-0410
Germantown (G-7254)

LUMBER & BUILDING MATERIALS DEALERS, RETAIL: Modular Homes

Everything In America....................G.....347 871-6872
Cleveland (G-3695)

LUMBER & BUILDING MATERIALS DEALERS, RETAIL: Tile, Ceramic

Ohio Tile & Marble Co....................E.....513 541-4211
Cincinnati (G-2926)

Saint-Gobain Norpro Corp...............C.....330 673-5860
Stow (G-12458)

LUMBER & BUILDING MATERIALS RET DEALERS: Millwork & Lumber

Laborie Enterprises LLC.................G.....419 686-6245
Portage (G-11458)

Mohler Lumber Company..................E.....330 499-5461
North Canton (G-10652)

The Galehouse Companies Inc..........E.....330 658-2023
Doylestown (G-6270)

Walnut Creek Planing Ltd................D.....330 893-3244
Millersburg (G-10018)

LUMBER & BUILDING MATLS DEALERS, RET: Concrete/Cinder Block

Encore Precast LLC.......................D.....513 726-5678
Seven Mile (G-11907)

Ernst Enterprises Inc....................F.....419 222-2015
Lima (G-8406)

OK Brugmann Jr & Sons Inc.............G.....330 274-2106
Mantua (G-8873)

Prairie Builders Supply Inc.............G.....419 332-7546
Fremont (G-7127)

LUMBER: Dimension, Hardwood

Halliday Holdings Inc.....................E.....740 335-1430
Washington Court Hou (G-13821)

J McCoy Lumber Co Ltd...................F.....937 587-3423
Peebles (G-11170)

Stephen M Trudick........................E.....440 834-1891
Burton (G-1704)

Woodcraft Industries Inc................E.....440 632-9655
Middlefield (G-9836)

LUMBER: Fiberboard

Frankes Wood Products LLC............E.....937 642-0706
Marysville (G-9020)

Tectum Inc..................................C.....740 345-9691
Newark (G-10535)

LUMBER: Flooring, Dressed, Softwood

Conover Lumber Company Inc..........F.....937 368-3010
Conover (G-5420)

LUMBER: Hardwood Dimension

Canfield Manufacturing Co Inc..........G.....330 533-3333
North Jackson (G-10684)

Itl LLC.......................................G.....216 831-3140
Beachwood (G-923)

Ohio Valley Veneer Inc...................F.....740 289-4979
Piketon (G-11310)

Ohio Valley Veneer Inc...................E.....740 493-2901
Piketon (G-11311)

Siefker Sawmill LLC.......................G.....419 339-8523
Lima (G-8448)

LUMBER: Hardwood Dimension & Flooring Mills

Armstrong Custom Moulding Inc........G.....740 922-5931
Uhrichsville (G-13401)

Baillie Lumber Co LP......................E.....419 462-2000
Galion (G-7179)

Beaver Wood Products....................G.....740 226-6211
Beaver (G-960)

Carter-Jones Lumber Company.........G.....330 674-9060
Millersburg (G-9975)

Cherokee Hardwoods Inc................G.....440 632-0322
Middlefield (G-9787)

Crownover Lumber Company Inc........D.....740 596-5229
Mc Arthur (G-9349)

Denoon Lumber Company LLC...........D.....740 768-2220
Bergholz (G-1195)

Gross Lumber Inc..........................G.....330 683-2055
Apple Creek (G-469)

Haessly Lumber Sales Co.................D.....740 373-6681
Marietta (G-8922)

Hartzell Hardwoods Inc..................D.....937 773-7054
Piqua (G-11351)

Holmes Lumber & Bldg Ctr Inc..........E.....330 479-8314
Canton (G-1912)

Holmes Lumber & Bldg Ctr Inc..........C.....330 674-9060
Millersburg (G-9989)

Itl Corp......................................E.....216 831-3140
Cleveland (G-3874)

Mid Ohio Wood Products Inc............G.....740 323-0427
Newark (G-10520)

Mohler Lumber Company..................E.....330 499-5461
North Canton (G-10652)

Roppe Holding Company..................B.....419 435-8546
Fostoria (G-6999)

Superior Hardwoods Ohio Inc...........E.....740 439-2727
Cambridge (G-1762)

Superior Hardwoods Ohio Inc...........G.....740 596-2561
Mc Arthur (G-9350)

Superior Hardwoods Ohio Inc...........D.....740 384-5677
Wellston (G-13910)

T & D Thompson Inc.......................F.....740 332-8515
Laurelville (G-8238)

Trumbull County Hardwoods.............E.....440 632-0555
Middlefield (G-9833)

Wagner Farms Sawmill Ltd Lblty........G.....419 653-4126
Leipsic (G-8315)

Walnut Creek Planing Ltd................D.....330 893-3244
Millersburg (G-10018)

Wappoo Wood Products Inc.............E.....937 492-1166
Sidney (G-12060)

Wooden Horse..............................G.....740 503-5243
Baltimore (G-789)

Yoder Lumber Co Inc......................E.....330 893-3131
Sugarcreek (G-12658)

Yoder Lumber Co Inc......................D.....330 893-3121
Millersburg (G-10020)

LUMBER: Kiln Dried

Blaney Hardwoods Ohio Inc.............D.....740 678-8288
Vincent (G-13619)

Itl Corp......................................E.....216 831-3140
Cleveland (G-3874)

Miller Lumber Co Inc......................G.....330 674-0273
Millersburg (G-9998)

LUMBER: Plywood, Hardwood

Automated Bldg Components Inc........E.....419 257-2152
North Baltimore (G-10612)

Beaver Wood Products....................G.....740 226-6211
Beaver (G-960)

Bruewer Woodwork Mfg Co...............D.....513 353-3505
Cleves (G-4532)

Dimension Hardwood Veneers Inc......E.....419 272-2245
Edon (G-6473)

PRODUCT

Exhibit Concepts Inc.............................. D 937 890-7000
Vandalia *(G-13557)*

Fifth Avenue Lumber Co.......................... E 614 833-6655
Canal Winchester *(G-1790)*

Fryburg Door Inc..................................... D 330 674-5252
Millersburg *(G-9981)*

Haessly Lumber Sales Co....................... D 740 373-6681
Marietta *(G-8922)*

Mac Lean J S Co..................................... G 614 878-5454
Columbus *(G-5078)*

Miller Manufacturing Inc........................ G 330 852-0689
Sugarcreek *(G-12642)*

Mohler Lumber Company......................... E 330 499-5461
North Canton *(G-10652)*

Ohio Valley Veneer Inc........................... E 740 493-2901
Piketon *(G-11311)*

S & G Manufacturing Group LLC........... D 614 529-0100
Hilliard *(G-7700)*

Sims-Lohman Inc.................................... E 513 651-3510
Cincinnati *(G-3093)*

Universal Veneer Mill Corp..................... C 740 522-1147
Newark *(G-10538)*

Wappoo Wood Products Inc.................... E 937 492-1166
Sidney *(G-12060)*

Yoder Lumber Co Inc............................. E 330 893-3131
Sugarcreek *(G-12658)*

LUMBER: Plywood, Softwood

Clopay Corporation.................................. E 513 770-4800
Mason *(G-9088)*

LUMBER: Treated

ISK Americas Incorporated..................... F 440 357-4600
Concord Township *(G-5392)*

The F A Requarth Company..................... E 937 224-1141
Dayton *(G-6048)*

LUMBER: Veneer, Softwood

American Veneer Edgebanding Co......... G 740 928-2700
Heath *(G-7592)*

MACHINE PARTS: Stamped Or Pressed Metal

Abbott Tool Inc....................................... E 419 476-6742
Toledo *(G-12861)*

Artisan Equipment Inc............................ F 740 756-9135
Carroll *(G-2073)*

Diamond America Corporation................ F 330 762-9269
Akron *(G-119)*

Gb Manufacturing Company.................... D 419 822-5323
Delta *(G-6207)*

Gdn Welding LLC.................................... E 740 398-6109
Danville *(G-5599)*

Hidaka Usa Inc....................................... E 614 889-8611
Dublin *(G-6303)*

Independent Power Cons Inc................. G 419 476-8383
Toledo *(G-13002)*

Modern Engineering Inc......................... G 440 593-5414
Conneaut *(G-5412)*

MSC Industries Inc................................. G 440 474-8788
Rome *(G-11645)*

Northwood Industries Inc....................... F 419 666-2100
Perrysburg *(G-11243)*

PE Usa LLC.. F 513 771-7374
Cincinnati *(G-2950)*

Perry Welding Service Inc...................... F 330 425-2211
Twinsburg *(G-13355)*

Plating Technology Inc........................... D 937 268-6882
Dayton *(G-5941)*

Saco Lowell Parts LLC........................... G 330 794-1535
Akron *(G-303)*

Spectrum Machine Inc............................ F 330 626-3666
Streetsboro *(G-12524)*

Tech-Med Inc.. F 216 486-0900
Euclid *(G-6679)*

Tenacity Manufacturing Company.......... G 513 821-0201
West Chester *(G-14081)*

Thk Manufacturing America Inc.............. C 740 928-1415
Hebron *(G-7639)*

Voss Industries LLC............................... C 216 771-7655
Cleveland *(G-4482)*

Ysk Corporation..................................... B 740 774-7315
Chillicothe *(G-2288)*

MACHINE TOOL ACCESS: Drill Bushings, Drilling Jig

Jergens Inc... C 216 486-5540
Cleveland *(G-3885)*

MACHINE TOOL ACCESS: Drills

Sp3 Winco LLC....................................... E 937 667-4476
Tipp City *(G-12846)*

MACHINE TOOL ACCESS: Tools & Access

Atalys Ottoville LLC............................... E 419 453-3376
Ottoville *(G-11052)*

Cowles Industrial Tool Co LLC............... E 330 799-9100
Austintown *(G-704)*

Furukawa Rock Drill USA Co Ltd........... F 330 673-5826
Kent *(G-8034)*

H & S Tool Inc.. F 330 335-1536
Wadsworth *(G-13642)*

HI Carb Corp.. G 216 486-5000
Eastlake *(G-6432)*

High Quality Tools Inc........................... F 440 975-9684
Eastlake *(G-6433)*

Imco Carbide Tool Inc............................ D 419 661-6313
Perrysburg *(G-11230)*

MSC Industries Inc................................. G 440 474-8788
Rome *(G-11645)*

Oakley Die & Mold Co............................ E 513 754-8500
Mason *(G-9131)*

Red Head Brass Inc............................... F 330 567-2903
Shreve *(G-11985)*

Tomco Tool Inc....................................... G 937 322-5768
Springfield *(G-12388)*

MACHINE TOOL ATTACHMENTS & ACCESS

Allied Machine & Engrg Corp................ C 330 343-4283
Dover *(G-6228)*

Carbide Probes Inc................................ E 937 429-9123
Beavercreek *(G-967)*

D C Morrison Company Inc..................... E 859 581-7511
Cincinnati *(G-2536)*

Frecon Technologies Inc........................ F 513 874-8981
West Chester *(G-14001)*

Positrol Inc... E 513 272-0500
Cincinnati *(G-2976)*

Retention Knob Supply & Mfg Co.......... F 937 686-6405
Huntsville *(G-7865)*

Riten Industries Incorporated................. E 740 335-5353
Wshngtn Ct Hs *(G-14745)*

Te-Co Inc... F 937 836-0961
Union *(G-13412)*

Te-Co Manufacturing LLC....................... D 937 836-0961
Englewood *(G-6625)*

MACHINE TOOLS & ACCESS

Able Tool Corporation............................ E 513 733-8989
Cincinnati *(G-2334)*

Akron Gear & Engineering Inc............... E 330 773-6608
Akron *(G-32)*

Anchor Lamina America Inc.................... F 330 952-1595
Medina *(G-9375)*

Antwerp TI Die & Engrg Co Inc.............. F 419 258-5271
Antwerp *(G-461)*

Apollo Products Inc................................ F 440 269-8551
Willoughby *(G-14422)*

Ata Tools Inc.. C 330 928-7744
Cuyahoga Falls *(G-5531)*

B & R Machine Co.................................. F 216 961-7370
Cleveland *(G-3399)*

Bender Engineering Company................ G 330 938-2355
Beloit *(G-1144)*

Big Chief Manufacturing Ltd.................. E 513 934-3888
Lebanon *(G-8247)*

Capital Tool Company............................ E 216 661-5750
Cleveland *(G-3467)*

Coldwater Machine Company LLC.......... C 419 678-4877
Coldwater *(G-4571)*

Covert Manufacturing Inc....................... C 419 468-1761
Galion *(G-7185)*

Dayton Progress Corporation................. A 937 859-5111
Dayton *(G-5737)*

Diamond Products Limited..................... G 440 323-4616
Elyria *(G-6516)*

Diamond Products Limited..................... G 440 323-4616
Elyria *(G-6517)*

Diamond Products Limited..................... B 440 323-4616
Elyria *(G-6518)*

Drt Mfg Co LLC...................................... D 937 297-6670
Dayton *(G-5754)*

E & J Demark Inc................................... E 419 337-5866
Wauseon *(G-13848)*

Eversharpe-Deburring Tool Co.............. G 513 988-6240
Trenton *(G-13192)*

Fischer Special Tooling Corp................. G 440 951-8411
Mentor *(G-9516)*

Gleason Metrology Systems Corp.......... E 937 384-8901
Dayton *(G-5796)*

Greentec Precision Inc........................... G 937 431-1840
Beavercreek *(G-976)*

Hudson Supply Company Inc................. G 216 518-3000
Cleveland *(G-3843)*

Jbm Technologies of Ohio LLC............. G 216 264-1270
Willoughby *(G-14472)*

Johnson Bros Rubber Co Inc................. E 419 752-4814
Greenwich *(G-7362)*

Kalt Manufacturing Company.................. D 440 327-2102
North Ridgeville *(G-10738)*

Kiffer Industries Inc............................... E 216 267-1818
Cleveland *(G-3919)*

Kilroy Company...................................... D 440 951-8700
Cleveland *(G-3920)*

Kongsberg Prcsion Ctng Systems......... F 937 800-2169
Miamisburg *(G-9707)*

Lange Precision Inc................................ F 513 530-9500
Lebanon *(G-8273)*

Lincoln Electric Automtn Inc.................. C 419 678-4877
Coldwater *(G-4581)*

Lord Corporation.................................... C 937 278-9431
Dayton *(G-5854)*

Luther Machine Inc................................. G 440 259-5014
Perry *(G-11194)*

M & J Tooling Ltd................................... F 937 951-3527
Dayton *(G-5856)*

Matrix Tool & Machine Inc..................... E 440 255-0300
Mentor *(G-9560)*

Mdf Tool Corporation............................. F 440 237-2277
North Royalton *(G-10774)*

Medway Tool Corp.................................. G 937 335-7717
Troy *(G-13240)*

Metalex Manufacturing Inc..................... C 513 489-0507
Blue Ash *(G-1310)*

Midwest Tool & Engineering Co............. G
Dayton *(G-5883)*

Obars Machine and Tool Company........ E 419 535-6307
Toledo *(G-13068)*

Ohio Broach & Machine Company........ E 440 946-1040
Willoughby *(G-14499)*

Ohio Drill & Tool Co.......................... E 330 525-7717
Homeworth *(G-7806)*

Omwp Company.................................. E 330 453-8438
Canton *(G-1969)*

Pemco Inc.. E 216 524-2990
Cleveland *(G-4150)*

Plrs Legacy Inc .... F 440 365-7333
North Ridgeville *(G-10742)*

R T & T Machining Co Inc .... F 440 974-8479
Mentor *(G-9605)*

Rex International USA Inc .... E 800 321-7950
Ashtabula *(G-615)*

Rhgs Company.................................... G 513 721-6299
Cincinnati *(G-3040)*

Ridge Tool Manufacturing Co.............. F 440 323-5581
Elyria *(G-6588)*

Rol - Tech Inc..................................... G 214 905-8050
Fort Loramie *(G-6953)*

Setco Industries Inc............................ D 513 941-5110
Cincinnati *(G-3085)*

Shl Liquidation Medina Inc................. C
Valley City *(G-13519)*

Skidmore-Wilhelm Mfg Company .... G 216 481-4774
Solon *(G-12182)*

SL Endmills Inc................................... F 513 851-6363
West Chester *(G-14146)*

Sorbothane Inc................................... E 330 678-9444
Kent *(G-8081)*

Spectrum Machine Inc......................... F 330 626-3666
Streetsboro *(G-12524)*

Stanley Bittinger .... G 740 942-4302
Cadiz *(G-1720)*

STC International Co Ltd..................... G 561 308-6002
Lebanon *(G-8287)*

Sumitomo Elc Carbide Mfg Inc............ F 440 354-0600
Grand River *(G-7312)*

Superion Inc....................................... E 937 374-0033
Xenia *(G-14776)*

Supplier Inspection Svcs Inc.............. F 877 263-7097
Dayton *(G-6031)*

Technidrill Systems Inc....................... E 330 678-9980
Kent *(G-8087)*

Troyke Manufacturing Company........... F 513 769-4242
Cincinnati *(O-3170)*

Wise Edge LLC.................................... G 330 208-0889
Mogadore *(G-10094)*

MACHINE TOOLS, METAL CUTTING: Drilling

Cincinnati Gilbert Mch TI LLC............. G 513 541-4815
Cincinnati *(G-2478)*

MACHINE TOOLS, METAL CUTTING: Drilling & Boring

Barbco Inc.. E 330 488-9400
East Canton *(G-6377)*

Bor-It Mfg Co Inc............................... E 419 289-6639
Ashland *(G-523)*

Global TBM Company.......................... C 440 248-3303
Solon *(G-12117)*

Grt Utilicorp Inc .... E 330 264-8444
Wooster *(G-14646)*

Leland-Gifford Inc.............................. E 330 785-9730
Akron *(G-205)*

Technidrill Systems Inc....................... E 330 678-9980
Kent *(G-8087)*

MACHINE TOOLS, METAL CUTTING: Exotic, Including Explosive

C M M S - Re LLC.............................. F 513 489-5111
Blue Ash *(G-1257)*

Fischer Special Tooling Corp................ G 440 951-8411
Mentor *(G-9516)*

National Machine Tool Company........... G 513 541-6682
Cincinnati *(G-2894)*

MACHINE TOOLS, METAL CUTTING: Home Workshop

H & D Steel Service Inc...................... E 800 666-3390
North Royalton *(G-10764)*

MACHINE TOOLS, METAL CUTTING: Numerically Controlled

Masters Prcision Machining Inc............ F 330 419-1933
Kent *(G-8050)*

MACHINE TOOLS, METAL CUTTING: Pipe Cutting & Threading

Rex International USA Inc .... E 800 321-7950
Ashtabula *(G-615)*

Ridge Tool Company............................ A 440 323-5581
Elyria *(G-6586)*

MACHINE TOOLS, METAL CUTTING: Plasma Process

Cutting Systems Inc............................ F 216 928-0500
Cleveland *(G-3590)*

Dbcr Inc... E 330 920-1900
Cuyahoga Falls *(G-5537)*

MACHINE TOOLS, METAL CUTTING: Tool Replacement & Rpr Parts

Ald Group LLC.................................... G 440 942-9800
Willoughby *(G-14415)*

Cardinal Builders Inc.......................... G 614 237-1000
Columbus *(G-4801)*

Drake Manufacturing Services Co.......... D 330 847-7291
Warren *(G-13760)*

Eagle Machinery & Supply Inc.............. E 330 852-1300
Sugarcreek *(G-12637)*

More Manufacturing LLC...................... F 937 233-3898
Tipp City *(G-12831)*

Ravana Industries Inc.......................... G 330 536-4015
Lowellville *(G-8664)*

MACHINE TOOLS, METAL FORMING: Bending

Addition Manufacturing Tech................ C 513 228-7000
Lebanon *(G-8241)*

American Fluid Power Inc...................... G 877 223-8742
Elyria *(G-6495)*

Bendco Machine & Tool Inc.................. F 419 628-3802
Minster *(G-10054)*

Pines Manufacturing Inc...................... E 440 835-5553
Westlake *(G-14324)*

Ready Technology Inc.......................... F 937 866-7200
Dayton *(G-5978)*

MACHINE TOOLS, METAL FORMING: Die Casting & Extruding

Tfi Manufacturing LLC.......................... F 440 290-9411
Mentor *(G-9636)*

MACHINE TOOLS, METAL FORMING: Marking

Monode Marking Products Inc.............. F 419 929-0346
New London *(G-10413)*

Monode Marking Products Inc.............. E 440 975-8802
Mentor *(G-9567)*

Monode Steel Stamp Inc...................... F 440 975-8802
Mentor *(G-9568)*

MACHINE TOOLS, METAL FORMING: Mechanical, Pneumatic Or Hyd

Apeks LLC... E 740 809-1174
Johnstown *(G-7991)*

Compass Systems & Sales LLC........... D 330 733-2111
Barberton *(G-802)*

Recycling Eqp Solutions Corp.............. G 330 920-1500
Cuyahoga Falls *(G-5568)*

MACHINE TOOLS, METAL FORMING: Pressing

Technical Machine Products Inc............ F
Cleveland *(G-4370)*

MACHINE TOOLS, METAL FORMING: Rebuilt

Advanced Tech Utilization Co................ F 440 238-3770
Strongsville *(G-12532)*

MACHINE TOOLS: Metal Cutting

5 Axis Grinding Inc............................. G 937 312-9797
Dayton *(G-5628)*

A & P Tool Inc.................................... E 419 542-6681
Hicksville *(G-7644)*

Acro Tool & Die Company.................... E 330 773-5173
Akron *(G-16)*

Advanced Innovative Mfg Inc............... D 330 562-2468
Aurora *(G-660)*

Advetech Inc....................................... E 330 533-2227
Canfield *(G-1801)*

Alcon Tool Company........................... E 330 773-9171
Akron *(G-48)*

Arch Cutting Tls - Mentor LLC............. F 440 350-9393
Mentor *(G-9486)*

Barth Industries Co LLC...................... E 216 267-1950
Cleveland *(G-3407)*

Beverly Dove Inc................................. G 740 495-5200
New Holland *(G-10397)*

Butech Inc.. D 330 337-0000
Salem *(G-11764)*

Butech Inc.. D 330 337-0000
Salem *(G-11765)*

Butech Inc.. D 330 337-0000
Salem *(G-11766)*

Callahan Cutting Tools Inc.................. G 614 294-1649
Columbus *(G-4792)*

Cammann Inc...................................... F 440 965-4051
Wakeman *(G-13678)*

Carter Manufacturing Co Inc................ F 513 398-7303
Mason *(G-9077)*

Channel Products Inc.......................... D 440 423-0113
Solon *(G-12093)*

Chart-Tech Tool Inc............................ F 937 667-3543
Tipp City *(G-12820)*

Cincinnati Mine Machinery Co.............. E 513 522-7777
Cincinnati *(G-2482)*

Cincinnati Radiator Inc........................ F 513 874-5555
Fairfield *(G-6722)*

Columbus Design & Mfg LLC................ G 414 534-3273
Columbus *(G-4822)*

Employee Codes: A=Over 500 employees, B=251-500
C=101-250, D=51-100, E=20-50, F=10-19, G=1-9

2025 Harris Ohio
Industrial Directory

1327

PRODUCT

Commercial Grinding Svcs Inc	E	330 273-5040
Medina *(G-9389)*		
Competetive Carbide Inc	E	440 350-9393
Madison *(G-8727)*		
Criterion Tool & Die Inc	E	216 267-1733
Brookpark *(G-1545)*		
Dayton Machine Tool Company	G	937 222-6444
Dayton *(G-5730)*		
Desmond-Stephan Mfgcompany	E	937 653-7181
Urbana *(G-13461)*		
Dixie Machinery Inc	F	513 360-0091
Monroe *(G-10103)*		
Dmg Mori Usa Inc	F	440 546-7088
West Chester *(G-13984)*		
Elliott Tool Technologies Ltd	D	937 253-6133
Dayton *(G-5763)*		
Esi-Extrusion Services Inc	E	330 374-3388
Akron *(G-138)*		
Falcon Industries Inc	E	330 723-0099
Medina *(G-9401)*		
Falcon Tool & Machine Inc	G	937 534-9999
Dayton *(G-5773)*		
Frazier Machine and Prod Inc	E	419 874-7321
Perrysburg *(G-11223)*		
General Electric Company	C	513 341-0214
West Chester *(G-14008)*		
George A Mitchell Company	E	330 758-5777
Youngstown *(G-14866)*		
Glassline Corporation	E	419 666-9712
Perrysburg *(G-11225)*		
Glt Inc	F	937 237-0055
Dayton *(G-5800)*		
Gzjb Holdings Inc	E	216 731-0500
Cleveland *(G-3803)*		
Herco Inc	G	740 498-5181
Newcomerstown *(G-10571)*		
Houston Machine Products Inc	E	937 322-8022
Springfield *(G-12326)*		
Industrial Paper Shredders Inc	F	888 637-4733
North Lima *(G-10708)*		
Innovtive McHning Slutions LLC	F	419 925-2060
Celina *(G-2110)*		
Interstate Tool Corporation	E	216 671-1077
Cleveland *(G-3866)*		
J & S Tool Corporation	G	216 676-8330
Lorain *(G-8558)*		
Jilco LLC	G	330 270-9780
Youngstown *(G-14882)*		
Kilroy Company	D	440 951-8700
Cleveland *(G-3920)*		
KLm Manufacturing Co Inc	G	740 666-5171
Ostrander *(G-11027)*		
Lahm-Trosper Inc	F	937 252-8791
Dayton *(G-5841)*		
Levan Enterprises Inc	E	330 923-9797
Stow *(G-12438)*		
Lincoln Electric Automtn Inc	E	614 471-5926
Columbus *(G-5070)*		
Makino Inc	B	513 573-7200
Mason *(G-9123)*		
Martindale Electric Company	E	216 521-8567
Cleveland *(G-3994)*		
Max - Pro Tools Inc	F	800 456-0931
Cleveland *(G-3999)*		
Melin Tool Company Inc	D	216 362-4200
Cleveland *(G-4019)*		
Michael Byrne Manufacturing Co Inc	E	419 525-1214
Mansfield *(G-8825)*		
Midwest Knife Grinding Inc	F	330 854-1030
Canal Fulton *(G-1778)*		
Milacron Marketing Company LLC	E	513 536-2000
Batavia *(G-875)*		

Monaghan & Associates Inc	F	937 253-7706
Dayton *(G-5892)*		
Nesco Inc	E	440 461-6000
Cleveland *(G-4068)*		
Northwood Industries Inc	F	419 666-2100
Perrysburg *(G-11243)*		
Obars Machine and Tool Company	E	419 535-6307
Toledo *(G-13068)*		
P M R Inc	G	440 937-6241
Avon *(G-733)*		
Peerless Saw Company	E	614 836-5790
Groveport *(G-7448)*		
Phillips Manufacturing Co	D	330 652-4335
Niles *(G-10600)*		
Portage Machine Concepts Inc	F	330 628-2343
Akron *(G-264)*		
Rafter Equipment Company LLC	E	440 572-3700
Strongsville *(G-12592)*		
Reliable Products Co	G	419 394-5854
Saint Marys *(G-11751)*		
Ridge Tool Company	D	740 432-8782
Cambridge *(G-1758)*		
Ridge Tool Company	C	440 329-4737
Elyria *(G-6587)*		
Ridge Tool Manufacturing Co	F	440 323-5581
Elyria *(G-6588)*		
Rimrock Corporation	E	614 471-5926
Columbus *(G-5230)*		
Rimrock Holdings Corporation	C	614 471-5926
Columbus *(G-5231)*		
Sinico Mtm US Inc	F	216 264-8344
Middleburg Heights *(G-9777)*		
Specialty Metals Proc Inc	G	330 656-2767
Hudson *(G-7858)*		
Stadco Inc	E	937 878-0911
Fairborn *(G-6699)*		
STC International Co Ltd	G	561 308-6002
Lebanon *(G-8287)*		
Sumitomo Elc Carbide Mfg Inc	F	440 354-0600
Grand River *(G-7312)*		
Superion Inc	E	937 374-0033
Xenia *(G-14776)*		
The Vulcan Tool Company	G	937 253-6194
Dayton *(G-6050)*		
Tooling Connection Inc	G	419 594-3339
Oakwood *(G-10901)*		
Tykma Inc	D	740 779-9918
Chillicothe *(G-2286)*		
U S Alloy Die Corp	F	216 749-9700
Cleveland *(G-4438)*		
Updike Supply Company	E	937 482-4000
Huber Heights *(G-7825)*		
West Ohio Tool Co	F	937 842-6688
Russells Point *(G-11670)*		
Wise Edge LLC	G	330 208-0889
Mogadore *(G-10094)*		
Wonder Machine Services Inc	E	440 937-7500
Avon *(G-743)*		

MACHINE TOOLS: Metal Forming

Aida-America Corporation	F	937 237-2382
Dayton *(G-5643)*		
Anderson & Vreeland Inc	D	419 636-5002
Bryan *(G-1629)*		
Barclay Machine Inc	F	330 337-9541
Salem *(G-11763)*		
Barth Industries Co LLC	E	216 267-1950
Cleveland *(G-3407)*		
Brilex Industries Inc	D	330 744-1114
Youngstown *(G-14827)*		
Columbus Water Section Permit	G	614 645-8039
Columbus *(G-4837)*		

D C Morrison Company Inc	E	859 581-7511
Cincinnati *(G-2536)*		
Decked LLC	F	208 806-0251
Defiance *(G-6104)*		
Elliott Tool Technologies Ltd	D	937 253-6133
Dayton *(G-5763)*		
Exito Manufacturing LLC	G	937 291-9871
Beavercreek *(G-991)*		
F & G Tool and Die Co	G	937 746-3658
Franklin *(G-7019)*		
First Tool Corp	E	937 254-6197
Dayton *(G-5777)*		
Gem City Metal Tech LLC	E	937 252-8998
Dayton *(G-5793)*		
H&G Legacy Co	F	513 921-1075
Cincinnati *(G-2701)*		
High Production Technology LLC	G	419 599-1511
Napoleon *(G-10283)*		
J & S Tool Corporation	G	216 676-8330
Lorain *(G-8558)*		
Kiraly Tool and Die Inc	F	330 744-5773
Youngstown *(G-14885)*		
Levan Enterprises Inc	E	330 923-9797
Stow *(G-12438)*		
Madison Property Holdings Inc	E	800 215-3210
Cincinnati *(G-2839)*		
McNeil & Nrm Inc	D	330 761-1855
Akron *(G-225)*		
Metal & Wire Products Company	E	330 332-9448
Salem *(G-11799)*		
Rafter Equipment Company LLC	E	440 572-3700
Strongsville *(G-12592)*		
Risk Industries LLC	D	440 835-5553
Westlake *(G-14328)*		
Ritime Incorporated	G	330 273-3443
Cleveland *(G-4242)*		
Semtorq Inc	F	330 487-0600
Twinsburg *(G-13377)*		
Spencer Manufacturing Company Inc	D	330 648-2461
Spencer *(G-12236)*		
Starkey Machinery Inc	E	419 468-2560
Galion *(G-7199)*		
Stolle Machinery Company LLC	C	937 497-5400
Sidney *(G-12056)*		
Stover International LLC	E	740 363-5251
Delaware *(G-6175)*		
Taylor - Winfield Corporation	G	330 259-8500
Hubbard *(G-7817)*		
Terminal Equipment Inds Inc	G	330 468-0322
Northfield *(G-10798)*		
The Vulcan Tool Company	G	937 253-6194
Dayton *(G-6050)*		
Trucut Incorporated	D	330 938-9806
Sebring *(G-11903)*		
Turner Machine Co	G	330 332-5821
Salem *(G-11816)*		
Twist Inc	G	937 675-9581
Jamestown *(G-7970)*		
Twist Inc	C	937 675-9581
Jamestown *(G-7969)*		
Uhrichsville Carbide Inc	F	740 922-9197
Uhrichsville *(G-13409)*		
Valley Tool & Die Inc	D	440 237-0160
North Royalton *(G-10788)*		

MACHINERY & EQPT FINANCE LEASING

Ohio Machinery Co	C	440 526-6200
Broadview Heights *(G-1509)*		

MACHINERY & EQPT, AGRICULTURAL, WHOLESALE: Lawn & Garden

Arnold Corporation...............................C 330 225-2600
Valley City (G-13489)

Hawthorne Gardening Company...........E 360 883-8846
Marysville (G-9023)

Karl Kuemmerling Inc..............................F
Massillon (G-9209)

MACHINERY & EQPT, INDL, WHOLESALE:
Chemical Process

Aldrich Chemical.....................................D 937 859-1808
Miamisburg (G-9663)

MACHINERY & EQPT, INDL, WHOLESALE:
Conveyor Systems

Alba Manufacturing Inc............................D 513 874-0551
Fairfield (G-6708)

Digilube Systems Inc..............................F 937 748-2209
Springboro (G-12250)

Logitech Inc..E 614 871-2822
Grove City (G-7395)

Midwest Conveyor Products Inc.............E 419 281-1235
Ashland (G-552)

Mitsubishi Elc Automtn Inc......................E 937 492-3058
Sidney (G-12035)

Pomacon Inc...F 330 273-1576
Brunswick (G-1606)

Transnorm System Inc............................D 972 606-0303
Mason (G-9163)

MACHINERY & EQPT, INDL, WHOLESALE:
Cranes

Expert Crane Inc.....................................D 216 451-9900
Wellington (G-13886)

Hiab USA Inc...D 419 482-6000
Perrysburg (G-11228)

Rnm Holdings Inc.....................................F 614 444-5556
Columbus (G-5232)

Rnm Holdings Inc.....................................F 419 867-8712
Holland (G-7782)

Venco Venturo Industries LLC.................E 513 772-8448
Cincinnati (G-3197)

MACHINERY & EQPT, INDL, WHOLESALE:
Engines & Parts, Diesel

Cummins Inc..F 614 771-1000
Hilliard (G-7679)

Industrial Parts Depot LLC.......................G.... 440 237-9164
North Royalton (G-10766)

Martin Diesel Inc......................................E 419 782-9911
Defiance (G-6120)

Western Branch Diesel LLC......................F 330 454-8800
Canton (G-2047)

MACHINERY & EQPT, INDL, WHOLESALE:
Engs & Parts, Air-Cooled

Power Distributors LLC.............................D 614 876-3533
Columbus (G-5200)

MACHINERY & EQPT, INDL, WHOLESALE:
Engs/Transportation Eqpt

Bulk Carriers Service Inc..........................G.... 330 339-3333
New Philadelphia (G-10435)

MACHINERY & EQPT, INDL, WHOLESALE:
Fans

National Tool & Equipment Inc.................F 330 629-8665
Youngstown (G-14903)

MACHINERY & EQPT, INDL, WHOLESALE:
Food Product Manufacturng

Chemineer Inc...C 937 454-3200
Dayton (G-5700)

Marengo Fabricated Steel Ltd..................F 800 919-2652
Cardington (G-2055)

MACHINERY & EQPT, INDL, WHOLESALE:
Heat Exchange

Gerow Equipment Company Inc..............G.... 216 383-8800
Cleveland (G-3772)

Process Dynamics Inc.............................G.... 330 686-2597
Stow (G-12452)

Rayhaven Group Inc.................................G.... 330 659-3183
Richfield (G-11598)

MACHINERY & EQPT, INDL, WHOLESALE:
Hydraulic Systems

Breaker Technology Inc............................F 440 248-7168
Solon (G-12090)

Control Line Equipment Inc......................F 216 433-7766
Cleveland (G-3565)

Depot Direct Inc......................................E 419 661-1233
Perrysburg (G-11215)

Eaton Corporation...................................F 216 523-5000
Willoughby (G-14455)

Fluid Power Solutions LLC.......................G.... 614 777-8954
Hilliard (G-7682)

Hydraulic Manifolds USA LLC...................E 973 728-1214
Stow (G-12436)

Hydraulic Parts Store Inc.........................G.... 330 364-6667
New Philadelphia (G-10449)

Hydro Supply Co.....................................G.... 740 454-3842
Zanesville (G-15020)

Ic-Fluid Power Inc....................................F 419 661-8811
Rossford (G-11658)

Jay Dee Service Corporation....................G.... 330 425-1546
Macedonia (G-8699)

Lubrisource Inc.......................................F 937 432-9292
Middletown (G-9872)

Mid-State Sales Inc.................................D 614 864-1811
Columbus (G-5099)

Ohio Hydraulics Inc.................................E 513 771-2590
Cincinnati (G-2924)

Parker-Hannifin Corporation....................F 216 433-1795
Cleveland (G-4144)

R & M Fluid Power Inc.............................E 330 758-2766
Youngstown (G-14922)

Robeck Fluid Power Co............................D 330 562-1140
Aurora (G-687)

Rumpke Transportation Co LLC...............F 513 851-0122
Cincinnati (G-3058)

System Seals Inc.....................................E 216 220-1800
Brecksville (G-1481)

System Seals LLC....................................E 440 735-0200
Cleveland (G-4359)

Taiyo America Inc....................................F 419 300-8811
Saint Marys (G-11753)

MACHINERY & EQPT, INDL, WHOLESALE:
Indl Machine Parts

Grt Utilicorp Inc.......................................E 330 264-8444
Wooster (G-14646)

Transducers Direct Llc.............................F 513 247-0601
Cincinnati (G-3166)

MACHINERY & EQPT, INDL, WHOLESALE:
Instruments & Cntrl Eqpt

Fcx Performance Inc................................E 614 253-1996
Columbus (G-4922)

Groeneveld-Beka Usa Inc........................G.... 330 225-4949
Sharon Center (G-11941)

Instrumentors Inc....................................G.... 440 238-3430
Strongsville (G-12568)

South Shore Controls Inc.........................E 440 259-2500
Mentor (G-9618)

MACHINERY & EQPT, INDL, WHOLESALE:
Lift Trucks & Parts

Fastener Industries Inc............................E 440 891-2031
Berea (G-1172)

Fastener Industries Inc............................G.... 440 243-0034
Berea (G-1173)

Joseph Industries Inc..............................D 330 528-0091
Streetsboro (G-12507)

MACHINERY & EQPT, INDL, WHOLESALE:
Machine Tools & Access

Imco Carbide Tool Inc.............................D 419 661-6313
Perrysburg (G-11230)

Interstate Tool Corporation......................E 216 671-1077
Cleveland (G-3866)

J & S Tool Corporation............................G.... 216 676-8330
Lorain (G-8558)

Jergens Inc...C 216 486-5540
Cleveland (G-3885)

Jis Distribution LLC.................................F 216 706-6552
Cleveland (G-3888)

Neff Machinery and Supplies....................G.... 740 454-0128
Zanesville (G-15031)

Wolf Machine Company............................E 513 791-5194
Blue Ash (G-1352)

MACHINERY & EQPT, INDL, WHOLESALE:
Packaging

Alfons Haar Inc..E 937 560-2031
Springboro (G-12246)

Bollin & Sons Inc....................................E 419 693-6573
Toledo (G-12900)

Millwood Inc..E 513 860-4567
West Chester (G-14030)

PE Usa LLC...F 513 771-7374
Cincinnati (G-2950)

Toga-Pak Inc...E 937 294-7311
Dayton (G-6056)

MACHINERY & EQPT, INDL, WHOLESALE:
Paint Spray

Kecamm LLC...G.... 330 527-2918
Garrettsville (G-7222)

MACHINERY & EQPT, INDL, WHOLESALE:
Paper Manufacturing

Oak View Enterprises Inc.........................E 513 860-4446
Bucyrus (G-1685)

MACHINERY & EQPT, INDL, WHOLESALE:
Petroleum Industry

Stanwade Metal Products Inc...................E 330 772-2421
Hartford (G-7573)

MACHINERY & EQPT, INDL, WHOLESALE:
Processing & Packaging

Ampac Packaging LLC.............................C 513 671-1777
Cincinnati (G-2366)

Employee Codes: A=Over 500 employees, B=251-500
C=101-250, D=51-100, E=20-50, F=10-19, G=1-9

2025 Harris Ohio
Industrial Directory

1329

PRODUCT

Kingsly Compression Inc.......................... G 740 439-0772
Cambridge *(G-1747)*

MACHINERY & EQPT, INDL, WHOLESALE: Pulp Manufacturing, Wood

Advanced Green Tech Inc....................... G 614 397-8130
Plain City *(G-11392)*

MACHINERY & EQPT, INDL, WHOLESALE: Recycling

Axion International Inc........................ G 740 452-2500
Zanesville *(G-14989)*

MACHINERY & EQPT, INDL, WHOLESALE: Safety Eqpt

A & A Safety Inc............................... F 937 567-9781
Beavercreek *(G-987)*

A & A Safety Inc............................... E 513 943-6100
Amelia *(G-425)*

American Rescue Technology Inc.......... F 937 293-6240
Dayton *(G-5655)*

Cintas Corporation............................. D 513 631-5750
Cincinnati *(G-2494)*

Cintas Corporation............................. A 513 459-1200
Mason *(G-9086)*

Cintas Corporation No 2....................... D 330 966-7800
Canton *(G-1865)*

Impact Products LLC........................... C 419 841-2891
Toledo *(G-13001)*

Paul Peterson Company........................ F 614 486-4375
Columbus *(G-5178)*

MACHINERY & EQPT, INDL, WHOLESALE: Trailers, Indl

Martin Allen Trailer LLC....................... G 330 942-0217
Akron *(G-223)*

MACHINERY & EQPT, INDL, WHOLESALE: Water Pumps

Hawthorne Hydroponics LLC.................. F 888 478-6544
Marysville *(G-9024)*

MACHINERY & EQPT, WHOLESALE: Construction, General

Baswa Acoustics North Amer LLC.......... F 216 475-7197
Bedford *(G-1014)*

Npk Construction Equipment Inc.......... D 440 232-7900
Bedford *(G-1050)*

Ohio Machinery Co............................. C 440 526-6200
Broadview Heights *(G-1509)*

Thirion Brothers Eqp Co LLC................. G 440 357-8004
Painesville *(G-11118)*

West Equipment Company Inc............... G 419 698-1601
Toledo *(G-13177)*

MACHINERY & EQPT, WHOLESALE: Oil Field Eqpt

Global Energy Partners LLC.................. E 419 756-8027
Mansfield *(G-8792)*

Petrox Inc.. F 330 653-5526
Streetsboro *(G-12516)*

MACHINERY & EQPT, WHOLESALE: Road Construction & Maintenance

Terry Asphalt Materials Inc.................... E 513 874-6192
Hamilton *(G-7529)*

MACHINERY & EQPT: Electroplating

Corrotec Inc..................................... E 937 325-3585
Springfield *(G-12294)*

Liquid Development Company................ G 216 641-9366
Independence *(G-7907)*

Universal Rack & Eqp Co Inc................. G 330 963-6776
Twinsburg *(G-13390)*

MACHINERY & EQPT: Farm

American Baler Co.............................. D 419 483-5790
Bellevue *(G-1119)*

Cailin Development LLC....................... F 216 408-6261
Cleveland *(G-3459)*

Country Manufacturing Inc................... F 740 694-9926
Fredericktown *(G-7075)*

Creamer Metal Products Inc.................. F 740 852-1752
London *(G-8534)*

Empire Plow Company Inc.................... E 216 641-2290
Berea *(G-1169)*

Fecon LLC.. E 513 696-4430
Lebanon *(G-8256)*

Fecon LLC.. D 513 696-4430
Lebanon *(G-8257)*

Field Gymmy Inc................................ G 419 538-6511
Glandorf *(G-7283)*

Finn Corporation................................ E 513 874-2818
West Chester *(G-13997)*

Fremont Plastic Products Inc................. C 419 332-6407
Fremont *(G-7111)*

Hog Slat Incorporated......................... E 937 968-3890
Union City *(G-13415)*

Intertec Corporation........................... F 419 537-9711
Toledo *(G-13007)*

J & M Manufacturing Co Inc.................. C 419 375-2376
Fort Recovery *(G-6967)*

Kts Equipment Inc.............................. E 440 647-2015
Wellington *(G-13895)*

Ley Industries Inc.............................. G 419 238-6742
Van Wert *(G-13541)*

M & S AG Solutions LLC....................... F 419 598-8675
Napoleon *(G-10290)*

Norden Mfg LLC................................. E 440 693-4630
North Bloomfield *(G-10625)*

Ntech Industries Inc........................... G 707 467-3747
Dayton *(G-5917)*

Ohio Machinery Co............................. C 440 526-6200
Broadview Heights *(G-1509)*

Precision Assemblies Inc..................... F 330 549-2630
North Lima *(G-10710)*

Rld Transportation LLC........................ F 234 334-7777
North Canton *(G-10664)*

Safe-Grain Inc.................................. G 513 398-2500
Dayton *(G-5992)*

Stephens Pipe & Steel LLC................... C 740 869-2257
Mount Sterling *(G-10229)*

Unverferth Mfg Co Inc......................... C 419 532-3121
Kalida *(G-8007)*

Yoder & Frey Inc................................ G 419 445-2070
Archbold *(G-513)*

MACHINERY & EQPT: Liquid Automation

Dosmatic USA Inc.............................. E 972 245-9765
Cincinnati *(G-2559)*

Fluid Automation Inc........................... E 248 912-1970
North Canton *(G-10640)*

Nov Inc... D 937 454-3200
Dayton *(G-5915)*

Nutro Corporation.............................. D 440 572-3800
Strongsville *(G-12580)*

MACHINERY, CALCULATING: Calculators & Adding

Ganymede Technologies Corp............... G 419 562-5522
Bucyrus *(G-1681)*

MACHINERY, EQPT & SUPPLIES: Parking Facility

Amano Cincinnati Incorporated............. F 513 697-9000
Loveland *(G-8619)*

City of Cleveland............................... E 216 664-2711
Cleveland *(G-3500)*

Innoplast Inc.................................... F 440 543-8660
Cleveland *(G-3861)*

Integrity Parking LLC.......................... F 440 543-4123
Aurora *(G-675)*

Tiba LLC.. E 614 328-2040
Columbus *(G-5324)*

MACHINERY, FOOD PRDTS: Beverage

Drink Modern Technologies LLC............. G 216 577-1536
Cleveland *(G-3633)*

Mojonnier Usa LLC............................. E 844 665-6664
Streetsboro *(G-12512)*

MACHINERY, FOOD PRDTS: Cutting, Chopping, Grinding, Mixing

Lem Products Holding LLC.................... E 513 202-1188
West Chester *(G-14023)*

MACHINERY, FOOD PRDTS: Food Processing, Smokers

Frost Engineering Inc.......................... E 513 541-6330
Cincinnati *(G-2642)*

MACHINERY, FOOD PRDTS: Oilseed Crushing & Extracting

Simmons Feed & Supply LLC................ E 800 754-1228
Salem *(G-11812)*

MACHINERY, FOOD PRDTS: Ovens, Bakery

Garland Commercial Industries LLC...... G 800 338-2204
Cleveland *(G-3756)*

Lincoln Foodservice Products LLC........ B 260 459-8200
Cleveland *(G-3957)*

Total Baking Solutions LLC................... E
Wilmington *(G-14587)*

MACHINERY, FOOD PRDTS: Processing, Poultry

Prime Equipment Group LLC................. D 614 253-8590
Columbus *(G-5205)*

MACHINERY, METALWORKING: Coiling

Formtek Inc...................................... D 216 292-4460
Cleveland *(G-3737)*

Guild International Inc......................... E 440 232-5887
Bedford *(G-1034)*

Kent Corporation............................... E 440 582-3400
North Royalton *(G-10768)*

Perfecto Industries Inc........................ E 937 778-1900
Piqua *(G-11372)*

MACHINERY, OFFICE: Paper Handling

Symatic Inc...................................... G 330 225-1510
Medina *(G-9452)*

MACHINERY, PACKAGING: Canning, Food

Scanacon Incorporated................ G 330 877-7600
Hartville *(G-7583)*

MACHINERY, PACKAGING: Packing & Wrapping

Able Tool Corporation................. E 513 733-8989
Cincinnati *(G-2334)*

Audion Automation Ltd................. F 216 267-1911
Berea *(G-1160)*

MACHINERY, PACKAGING: Vacuum

Precision Replacement LLC................. G 330 908-0410
Macedonia *(G-8709)*

MACHINERY, PAPER INDUSTRY: Converting, Die Cutting & Stampng

Erd Specialty Graphics Inc................. G 419 242-9545
Toledo *(G-12955)*

Jen-Coat Inc................. C 513 671-1777
Cincinnati *(G-2764)*

Nilpeter Usa Inc................. C 513 489-4400
Cincinnati *(G-2909)*

Spectex LLC................. F 603 330-3334
Cincinnati *(G-3104)*

MACHINERY, PAPER INDUSTRY: Paper Mill, Plating, Etc

Miami Machine Corporation................. F 513 863-6707
Overpeck *(G-11061)*

Press Technology & Mfg Inc................. G 937 327-0755
Springfield *(G-12365)*

MACHINERY, PAPER INDUSTRY: Pulp Mill

Andritz Inc................. D 513 677-5620
Loveland *(G-8621)*

Fq Sale Inc................. E 937 324-0352
Springfield *(G-12314)*

MACHINERY, PRINTING TRADES: Plates

Dynamic Dies Inc................. E 419 865-0249
Holland *(G-7761)*

E C Shaw Company of Ohio................. E 513 721-6334
Cincinnati *(G-2569)*

Flexotech Graphics Inc................. F 330 929-4743
Stow *(G-12432)*

MACHINERY, SEWING: Sewing & Hat & Zipper Making

Production Design Services Inc................. D 937 866-3377
Dayton *(G-5962)*

Velocys Inc................. D 614 733-3300
Plain City *(G-11424)*

MACHINERY, TEXTILE: Printing

Alley Cat Designs Inc................. G 937 291-8803
Dayton *(G-5645)*

MACHINERY: Ammunition & Explosives Loading

Omco Usa LLC................. F 740 588-1722
Zanesville *(G-15035)*

Roberts Machine Products LLC................. F 937 682-4015
Rushsylvania *(G-11666)*

MACHINERY: Automotive Related

Autotool Inc................. E 614 733-0222
Plain City *(G-11395)*

Buddy Backyard Inc................. E 800 837-9353
Warren *(G-13746)*

Cornerstone Wauseon Inc................. C 419 337-0940
Wauseon *(G-13847)*

Dengensha America Corooration................. F 440 439-8081
Bedford *(G-1025)*

Designetics Inc................. D 419 866-0700
Holland *(G-7755)*

Ganzcorp Investments Inc................. E 330 963-5400
Twinsburg *(G-13307)*

M W Solutions LLC................. F 419 782-1611
Defiance *(G-6118)*

Manufctring Bus Dev Sltons LLC................. D 419 294-1313
Findlay *(G-6886)*

Modular Assmbly Innvations LLC................. E 614 389-4860
Dublin *(G-6321)*

Steelastic Company LLC................. E 330 633-0505
Cuyahoga Falls *(G-5574)*

Toney Tool Manufacturing Inc................. G 937 890-8535
Dayton *(G-6057)*

MACHINERY: Concrete Prdts

Ernest Industries Inc................. E 937 325-9851
Lowellville *(G-8660)*

MACHINERY: Construction

1062 Technologies Inc................. G 303 453-9251
Youngstown *(G-14799)*

Allied Consolidated Inds Inc................. C 330 744-0808
Youngstown *(G-14808)*

Allied Industrial Dev Corp................. E 724 346-1984
Youngstown *(G-14809)*

Altec Industries................. G 419 289-6066
Ashland *(G-515)*

American Alloy Corporation................. E 216 642-9638
Cleveland *(G-3340)*

Ballinger Industries Inc................. E 419 422-4533
Findlay *(G-6842)*

Basetek LLC................. F 877 712-2273
Middlefield *(G-9781)*

Caterpillar Industrial Inc................. G 440 247-8484
Chagrin Falls *(G-2138)*

Chemineer Inc................. C 937 454-3200
Dayton *(G-5700)*

Cityscapes International Inc................. C 614 850-2540
Hilliard *(G-7677)*

Coe Manufacturing Company................. E 440 352-9381
Painesville *(G-11072)*

Curtis Industires................. F 216 430-5759
Cloveland *(C-3502)*

CW Machine Worx Ltd................. F 740 654-5304
Carroll *(G-2074)*

DA Precision Products Inc................. F 513 459-1113
West Chester *(G-13981)*

Desco Corporation................. G 614 888-8855
New Albany *(G-10339)*

Dragon Products LLC................. G 330 345-3968
Wooster *(G-14635)*

Dynamic Plastics Inc................. G 937 437-7261
New Paris *(G-10426)*

E R Advanced Ceramics Inc................. E 330 426-9433
East Palestine *(G-6402)*

E Z Grout Corporation................. E 740 749-3512
Malta *(G-8744)*

Eagle Crusher Co Inc................. D 419 562-1183
Bucyrus *(G-1679)*

Eagle Crusher Co Inc................. D 419 468-2288
Galion *(G-7187)*

Enviri Corporation................. F 740 387-1150
Marion *(G-8969)*

Fecon LLC................. D 513 696-4430
Lebanon *(G-8257)*

Field Gymmy Inc................. G 419 538-6511
Glandorf *(G-7283)*

Fives St Corp................. E 234 217-9070
Wadsworth *(G-13638)*

Gradall Industries LLC................. D 330 339-2211
New Philadelphia *(G-10448)*

Grand Harbor Yacht Sales & Svc................. G 440 442-2919
Cleveland *(G-3784)*

Grasan Equipment Company Inc................. D 419 526-4440
Mansfield *(G-8797)*

Hickmans Construction Co LLC................. F 866 271-2565
Euclid *(G-6653)*

Jbw Systems Inc................. F 614 882-5008
Westerville *(G-14215)*

Jlg Industries Inc................. E 330 684-0132
Orrville *(G-10988)*

Jlg Industries Inc................. E 330 684-0200
Orrville *(G-10989)*

Jordankelly LLC................. F 216 855-8550
Akron *(G-187)*

Kaffenbarger Truck Eqp Co................. E 513 772-6800
Cincinnati *(G-2777)*

Kubota Tractor Corporation................. E 614 835-3800
Groveport *(G-7442)*

Kundel Industries Inc................. D 330 469-6147
Vienna *(G-13609)*

Meyer Products LLC................. E 216 486-1313
Cleveland *(G-4024)*

Murphy Tractor & Eqp Co Inc................. G 330 220-4999
Brunswick *(G-1602)*

Murphy Tractor & Eqp Co Inc................. G 330 477-9304
Canton *(G-1954)*

Murphy Tractor & Eqp Co Inc................. G 614 876-1141
Columbus *(G-5116)*

Murphy Tractor & Eqp Co Inc................. G 419 221-3666
Lima *(G-8434)*

Murphy Tractor & Eqp Co Inc................. G 937 898-4198
Vandalia *(G-13573)*

Norris Manufacturing LLC................. F 330 602-5005
Dover *(G-6256)*

Nov Inc................. D 937 454-3200
Dayton *(G-5915)*

Npk Construction Equipment Inc................. D 440 232-7900
Bedford *(G-1050)*

Otc Industrial Technologies................. F 800 837-6827
Columbus *(G-5165)*

Pace Consolidated Inc................. D 440 942-1234
Willoughby *(G-14503)*

Pace Engineering Inc................. C 440 942-1234
Willoughby *(G-14504)*

Pubco Corporation................. D 216 881-5300
Cleveland *(G-4205)*

Roadsafe Traffic Systems Inc................. G 614 274-9782
Columbus *(G-5234)*

Sandvik Rock Proc Sltons N AME................. F 216 431-2600
Cleveland *(G-4273)*

Sciath Aim Forge Inc................. G 574 933-3479
Cincinnati *(G-3069)*

Terex Utilities Inc................. F 419 470-8408
Perrysburg *(G-11270)*

The Wagner-Smith Company................. B 866 338-0398
Moraine *(G-10195)*

Thorworks Industries Inc................. C 419 626-4375
Sandusky *(G-11876)*

Uhrden Inc................. E 330 456-0031
Canton *(G-2030)*

Valence Industrial LLC................. E 877 330-2354
Sidney *(G-12058)*

MACHINERY: Cryogenic, Industrial

Chart International Inc................. D 440 753-1490
Cleveland *(G-3489)*

Eden Cryogenics LLC................. E 614 873-3949
Columbus *(G-4897)*

PRODUCT

JC Carter LLC... G 440 569-1818
   Richmond Heights *(G-11610)*

MACHINERY: Custom

A & R Machine Co Inc............................... G 330 832-4631
   Massillon *(G-9169)*

Alfons Haar Inc.. E 937 560-2031
   Springboro *(G-12246)*

Alliance Automation LLC......................... D 419 238-2520
   Van Wert *(G-13526)*

Artisan Equipment Inc............................ F 740 756-9135
   Carroll *(G-2073)*

Astro Technical Services Inc.................. E 330 394-4747
   Warren *(G-13742)*

Autotec Corporation................................. E 419 885-2529
   Toledo *(G-12889)*

Berran Industrial Group Inc..................... E 330 253-5800
   Akron *(G-77)*

Bomen Marking Products Inc.................. G 440 582-0053
   Cleveland *(G-3426)*

Bonnot Company....................................... E 330 896-6544
   Akron *(G-82)*

Bowdil Company....................................... F 800 356-8663
   Canton *(G-1843)*

East End Welding LLC.............................. C 330 677-6000
   Kent *(G-8028)*

Enprotech Industrial Tech LLC............... E 216 883-3220
   Cleveland *(G-3675)*

F & G Tool and Die Co............................. E 937 294-1405
   Moraine *(G-10163)*

Farr Automation Inc................................ G 419 289-1883
   Ashland *(G-534)*

Ferry Industries Inc................................. D 330 920-9200
   Stow *(G-12431)*

Fostoria MT&f Corp................................. F 419 435-7676
   Fostoria *(G-6982)*

Fredon Corporation.................................. D 440 951-5200
   Mentor *(G-9520)*

Gasdorf Tool and Mch Co Inc.................. E 419 227-0103
   Lima *(G-8409)*

Global Srcing Support Svcs LLC............ G 800 645-2986
   Cincinnati *(G-2677)*

Hahn Automation Group Us Inc.............. D 937 886-3232
   Miamisburg *(G-9694)*

Heisler Tool Company.............................. F 440 951-2424
   Willoughby *(G-14464)*

Herd Manufacturing Inc.......................... E 216 651-4221
   Cleveland *(G-3826)*

Htec Systems Inc..................................... F 937 438-3010
   Dayton *(G-5816)*

Inovent Engineering Inc.......................... G 330 468-0019
   Macedonia *(G-8698)*

Interscope Manufacturing Inc................. E 513 423-8866
   Middletown *(G-9867)*

JF Martt and Associates Inc................... F 330 938-4000
   Sebring *(G-11895)*

Keban Industries Inc............................... G 216 446-0159
   Broadview Heights *(G-1503)*

Kiffer Industries Inc................................ E 216 267-1818
   Cleveland *(G-3919)*

Kimble Machines Inc................................ G 419 485-8449
   Montpelier *(G-10129)*

Last Arrow Manufacturing LLC............... D 330 683-7777
   Orrville *(G-10992)*

Latanick Equipment Inc.......................... E 419 433-2200
   Huron *(G-7878)*

Lightning Mold & Machine Inc................. F 440 593-6460
   Conneaut *(G-5408)*

Logan Machine Company......................... D 330 633-6163
   Akron *(G-210)*

Massillon Machine & Die Inc.................. G 330 833-8913
   Massillon *(G-9219)*

Matrix Tool & Machine Inc....................... E 440 255-0300
   Mentor *(G-9560)*

McNeil & Nrm Inc...................................... D 330 761-1855
   Akron *(G-225)*

McNeil & Nrm Intl Inc............................... D 330 253-2525
   Akron *(G-226)*

Metalex Manufacturing Inc..................... C 513 489-0507
   Blue Ash *(G-1310)*

Metro Design Inc...................................... F 440 458-4200
   Elyria *(G-6563)*

Michael Byrne Manufacturing Co Inc..... E 419 525-1214
   Mansfield *(G-8825)*

Midwest Laser Systems Inc.................... E 419 424-0062
   Alvada *(G-422)*

Modern Machine Development................. F 937 253-4576
   Dayton *(G-5891)*

Narrow Way Custom Tech Inc.................. E 937 743-1611
   Carlisle *(G-2069)*

Neil R Scholl Inc...................................... F 740 653-6593
   Lancaster *(G-8213)*

Odawara Automation Inc......................... E 937 667-8433
   Tipp City *(G-12833)*

Odyssey Machine Company Ltd............. G 419 455-6621
   Perrysburg *(G-11245)*

Path Robotics Inc..................................... C 330 808-2788
   Columbus *(G-5176)*

Perfecto Industries Inc............................ E 937 778-1900
   Piqua *(G-11372)*

Perry Welding Service Inc....................... F 330 425-2211
   Twinsburg *(G-13355)*

Production Design Services Inc............... D 937 866-3377
   Dayton *(G-5962)*

Projects Designed & Built........................ E 419 726-7400
   Toledo *(G-13104)*

Quality Specialists Inc............................ G 440 946-9129
   Willoughby *(G-14513)*

R J K Enterprises Inc............................... F 440 257-6018
   Mentor *(G-9604)*

Richmond Machine Co.............................. E 419 485-5740
   Montpelier *(G-10134)*

Royalton Industries Inc........................... F 440 748-9900
   Columbia Station *(G-4600)*

RTZ Manufacturing Co.............................. G 614 848-8366
   Heath *(G-7603)*

S-P Company Inc....................................... D 330 782-5651
   Columbiana *(G-4627)*

Sample Machining Inc.............................. E 937 258-3338
   Dayton *(G-5993)*

Sequa Can Machinery Inc........................ E 330 493-0444
   Canton *(G-2002)*

Siebtechnik Tema Inc............................... E 513 489-7811
   Cincinnati *(G-3088)*

Steel Eqp Specialists Inc........................ D 330 823-8260
   Alliance *(G-406)*

Systech Handling Inc............................... F 419 445-8226
   Archbold *(G-512)*

Terydon Inc... G 330 879-2448
   Navarre *(G-10314)*

Ti Inc... E 419 332-8484
   Fremont *(G-7138)*

Tru-Bore Machine Co Inc......................... G 330 928-6215
   Cuyahoga Falls *(G-5579)*

Tru-Fab Technology Inc............................ F 440 954-9760
   Willoughby *(G-14543)*

MACHINERY: Electronic Component Making

Inpower LLC.. F 740 548-0965
   Lewis Center *(G-8337)*

Storetek Engineering Inc......................... E 330 294-0678
   Tallmadge *(G-12752)*

Summit Design and Tech Inc................... F 330 733-6662
   Akron *(G-320)*

MACHINERY: Gas Separators

H P E Inc... G 330 833-3161
   Massillon *(G-9199)*

MACHINERY: Ice Cream

Heavenly Creamery Inc............................ G 440 593-6080
   Conneaut *(G-5403)*

Norse Dairy Systems LP......................... B 614 294-4931
   Columbus *(G-5129)*

MACHINERY: Metalworking

Addition Manufacturing Tech.................. C 513 228-7000
   Lebanon *(G-8241)*

ADS Machinery Corp................................. D 330 399-3601
   Warren *(G-13731)*

Advance Manufacturing Corp.................. E 216 333-1684
   Cleveland *(G-3302)*

Bardons & Oliver Inc............................... C 440 498-5800
   Solon *(G-12082)*

Barth Industries Co LLC.......................... E 216 267-1950
   Cleveland *(G-3407)*

Berran Industrial Group Inc..................... E 330 253-5800
   Akron *(G-77)*

Brilex Industries Inc................................ D 330 744-1114
   Youngstown *(G-14827)*

C A Litzler Co Inc..................................... E 216 267-8020
   Cleveland *(G-3457)*

Cammann Inc.. F 440 965-4051
   Wakeman *(G-13678)*

Cincinnati Incorporated........................... C 513 367-7100
   Harrison *(G-7545)*

Cline Machine and Automtn Inc.............. E 740 474-4237
   Circleville *(G-3252)*

Ctm Integration Incorporated.................. E 330 332-1800
   Salem *(G-11774)*

Dayton Machine Tool Company.............. G 937 222-6444
   Dayton *(G-5730)*

Esi-Extrusion Services Inc...................... E 330 374-3388
   Akron *(G-138)*

Forrest Machine Pdts Co Ltd.................. E 419 589-3774
   Mansfield *(G-8790)*

Gem City Engineering Co......................... C 937 223-5544
   Dayton *(G-5792)*

Gilson Machine & Tool Co Inc................. E 419 592-2911
   Napoleon *(G-10282)*

Glunt Industries Inc................................ C 330 399-7585
   Warren *(G-13770)*

Hahn Manufacturing Company............... E 216 391-9300
   Cleveland *(G-3807)*

Heisler Tool Company.............................. F 440 951-2424
   Willoughby *(G-14464)*

Holdren Brothers Inc............................... F 937 465-7050
   West Liberty *(G-14175)*

J Horst Manufacturing Co....................... D 330 828-2216
   Dalton *(G-5586)*

Junker Inc... G 630 231-3770
   Canton *(G-1923)*

Kalt Manufacturing Company.................. D 440 327-2102
   North Ridgeville *(G-10738)*

Kilroy Company.. D 440 951-8700
   Cleveland *(G-3920)*

Midwest Laser Systems Inc.................... E 419 424-0062
   Alvada *(G-422)*

Milacron LLC... E 513 487-5000
   Cincinnati *(G-2880)*

Pines Manufacturing Inc......................... E 440 835-5553
   Westlake *(G-14324)*

Rafter Equipment Company LLC............. E 440 572-3700
   Strongsville *(G-12592)*

Riverside Mch & Automtn Inc.................. D 419 855-8308
   Genoa *(G-7250)*

(G-0000) Company's Geographic Section entry number

South Shore Controls Inc....................E 440 259-2500
Mentor (G-9618)

Stainless Automation...........................G 216 961-4550
Cleveland (G-4324)

Stein LLC..D 216 883-7444
Cleveland (G-4331)

Sticker Corporation.............................F 440 946-2100
Willoughby (G-14534)

Todd Industries Inc.............................E 440 439-2900
Cleveland (G-4398)

Tri-Mac Mfg & Svcs Co........................F 513 896-4445
Hamilton (G-7533)

MACHINERY: Mining

Bowdil Company.................................F 800 356-8663
Canton (G-1843)

Breaker Technology Inc........................F 440 248-7168
Solon (G-12090)

Cailin Development LLC........................F 216 408-6261
Cleveland (G-3459)

Carr Tool Company.............................F 513 825-2900
Fairfield (G-6717)

Cleveland Vibrator Company.................G 800 221-3298
Cleveland (G-3529)

Cool Machines Inc..............................F 419 232-4871
Van Wert (G-13529)

Engines Inc of Ohio............................E 740 377-9874
South Point (G-12223)

Epiroc USA LLC.................................F 717 552-8488
Akron (G-137)

Joy Global Underground Min LLC..........C 440 248-7970
Solon (G-12132)

Kaffenbarger Truck Eqp Co...................E 513 772-6800
Cincinnati (G-2777)

Kennametal Inc..................................F 440 349-5151
Solon (G-12138)

Komatsu Mining Corp..........................C 216 503-5029
Independence (G-7906)

Nolan Company..................................G 740 269-1512
Bowerston (G-1400)

Nolan Company..................................F 330 453-7922
Canton (G-1958)

Npk Construction Equipment Inc............D 440 232-7900
Bedford (G-1050)

Penn Machine Company LLC..................D 814 288-1547
Twinsburg (G-13351)

Strata Mine Services Inc.......................G 740 695-6880
Saint Clairsville (G-11712)

Uhrden Inc..E 330 456-0031
Canton (G-2030)

Warren Fabricating Corporation..............D 330 534-5017
Hubbard (G-7818)

Zen Industries Inc...............................E 216 432-3240
Cleveland (G-4523)

MACHINERY: Pack-Up Assemblies, Wheel Overhaul

Aot LLC..F 937 323-9669
Springfield (G-12280)

Haeco Inc..G 513 722-1030
Loveland (G-8629)

MACHINERY: Packaging

Advanced Poly-Packaging Inc.................C 330 785-4000
Akron (G-21)

Apackaging Group Ohio Inc...................F 419 785-8600
Defiance (G-6097)

Atlas Vac Machine Co LLC....................G 513 407-3513
Cincinnati (G-2386)

Atmos360 Inc.....................................E 513 772-4777
West Chester (G-14105)

Audion Automation Ltd........................E 216 267-1911
Berea (G-1159)

Automated Packaging Systems LLC......C 330 528-2000
Streetsboro (G-12490)

Automated Packg Systems Inc...............E 330 342-2000
Bedford (G-1013)

Automated Packg Systems Inc...............G 330 626-2313
Streetsboro (G-12491)

Barry-Wehmiller Companies Inc.............F 330 923-0491
Cuyahoga Falls (G-5532)

Boggs Graphics Equipment LLC.............E 888 837-8101
Maple Heights (G-8878)

Combi Packaging Systems Llc................D 330 456-9333
Canton (G-1870)

Crown Closures Machinery.....................E 740 681-6593
Lancaster (G-8191)

Ctm Integration Incorporated.................E 330 332-1800
Salem (G-11774)

Ctm Labeling Systems..........................E 330 332-1800
Salem (G-11775)

Darifill Inc...F 614 890-3274
Westerville (G-14253)

Exact Equipment Corporation.................F 215 295-2000
Columbus (G-4640)

Expo Packaging Inc.............................G 216 267-9700
Cleveland (G-3699)

Food Equipment Mfg Corp.....................F 216 672-5859
Bedford Heights (G-1076)

G and J Automatic Systems Inc.............E 216 741-6070
Cleveland (G-3749)

GL Industries Inc................................E 513 874-1233
Hamilton (G-7494)

Gunnison Associates Llc.......................G 330 562-5230
Aurora (G-672)

H & G Equipment Inc..........................F 513 761-2060
Blue Ash (G-1280)

H&G Legacy Co..................................F 513 921-1075
Cincinnati (G-2701)

Kaufman Engineered Systems Inc..........D 419 878-9727
Waterville (G-13837)

Kennedy Group Incorporated.................D 440 951-7660
Willoughby (G-14477)

Kolinahr Systems Inc...........................F 513 745-9401
Blue Ash (G-1294)

Millwood Inc......................................E 513 860-4567
West Chester (G-14030)

Millwood Natural LLC...........................F 330 393-4400
Vienna (G-13615)

Nilpeter Usa Inc..................................C 513 489-4400
Cincinnati (G-2909)

Norse Dairy Systems Inc.......................C 614 294-4931
Columbus (G-5128)

Pack Line Corp...................................G 212 564-0664
Cleveland (G-4131)

Pak Master LLC..................................E 330 523-5319
Richfield (G-11595)

PE Usa LLC..F 513 771-7374
Cincinnati (G-2950)

Portage Packaging Systems Inc.............G 330 274-8295
Hiram (G-7741)

Precision Products Group Inc.................G 330 698-4711
Apple Creek (G-475)

Reactive Resin Products Co...................F 419 666-6119
Perrysburg (G-11259)

Recon Systems LLC.............................G 330 488-0368
East Canton (G-6379)

Rpmi Packaging Inc.............................F 513 398-4040
Lebanon (G-8284)

Switchback Group Inc..........................E 216 290-6040
Cleveland (G-4358)

System Packaging of Glassline...............D 419 666-9712
Perrysburg (G-11263)

Titans Packaging LLC...........................F 513 449-0014
West Chester (G-14155)

Vistech Mfg Solutions LLC.....................F 513 933-9300
Lebanon (G-8296)

Vmi Americas Inc................................E 330 929-6800
Stow (G-12471)

MACHINERY: Paint Making

Bethel Engineering and Eqp Inc.............E 419 568-1100
New Hampshire (G-10396)

Cohesant Inc......................................E 216 910-1700
Beachwood (G-913)

Fawcett Co Inc...................................G 330 659-4187
Richfield (G-11592)

General Fabrications Corp......................E 419 625-6055
Sandusky (G-11836)

Nutro Corporation...............................D 440 572-3800
Strongsville (G-12580)

Nutro Inc...E 440 572-3800
Strongsville (G-12581)

Woodman Agitator Inc..........................F 440 937-9865
Avon (G-744)

MACHINERY: Plastic Working

Alstart Enterprises LLC........................F 330 533-3222
Canfield (G-1803)

American Plastic Tech Inc.....................C 440 632-5203
Middlefield (G-9780)

Budget Molders Supply Inc....................F 216 367-7050
Macedonia (G-8680)

DRG Hydraulics Inc.............................E 216 663-9747
Twinsburg (G-13297)

Encore Industries Inc...........................C 419 626-8000
Sandusky (G-11830)

Esi-Extrusion Services Inc.....................E 330 374-3388
Akron (G-138)

Jaco Manufacturing Company.................E 440 234-4000
Berea (G-1177)

Linden-Two Inc...................................E 330 928-4064
Cuyahoga Falls (G-5559)

Plastic Process Equipment Inc...............E 216 367-7000
Macedonia (G-8706)

Tooltex Inc..F 614 539-3222
Circleville (G-3267)

Vulcan Machinery Corporation................F 330 376-6025
Akron (G-355)

Wentworth Mold Inc Electra...................D 937 898-8460
Vandalia (G-13583)

Wesco Machine Inc.............................F 330 688-6973
Ravenna (G-11549)

Youngstown Plastic Tooling....................F 330 782-7222
Youngstown (G-14973)

Zed Industries Inc...............................D 937 667-8407
Vandalia (G-13584)

MACHINERY: Printing Presses

Boggs Graphics Equipment LLC.............E 888 837-8101
Maple Heights (G-8878)

Desco Equipment Corp.........................F 330 405-1581
Twinsburg (G-13292)

Graphic Systems Services Inc.................E 937 746-0708
Springboro (G-12254)

MACHINERY: Recycling

Agmet Metals Inc................................E 440 439-7400
Oakwood Village (G-10902)

ARS Recycling Systems LLC..................F 330 536-8210
Lowellville (G-8658)

Glenn Hunter & Associates Inc..............D 419 533-0925
Delta (G-6208)

Grasan Equipment Company Inc............D 419 526-4440
Mansfield (G-8797)

Employee Codes: A=Over 500 employees, B=251-500
C=101-250, D=51-100, E=20-50, F=10-19, G=1-9

2025 Harris Ohio
Industrial Directory

1333

PRODUCT

RSI Company... F 216 360-9800
Beachwood (G-946)

SDS National LLC..................................... G 330 759-8066
Boardman (G-1376)

MACHINERY: Road Construction & Maintenance

2e Associates Inc.................................... E 440 975-9955
Willoughby (G-14412)

American Highway Products LLC........... F 330 874-3270
Bolivar (G-1381)

Concord Road Equipment Mfg Inc......... E 440 357-5344
Painesville (G-11073)

Concord Road Equipment Mfg LLC....... E 440 357-5344
Mentor (G-9504)

Forge Industries Inc............................... A 330 960-2468
Youngstown (G-14857)

Gledhill Road Machinery Co.................... E 419 468-4400
Galion (G-7193)

Jcl Equipment Co Inc.............................. G 937 374-1010
Xenia (G-14767)

Lake Township Trustees.......................... E 419 836-1143
Millbury (G-9963)

Liverpool Township.................................. G 330 483-4747
Valley City (G-13502)

Richland Township Bd Trustees.............. F 419 358-4897
Bluffton (G-1363)

MACHINERY: Robots, Molding & Forming Plastics

CAM-Lem Inc.. G 216 391-7750
Cleveland (G-3461)

Lifeformations Inc.................................... E 419 352-2101
Bowling Green (G-1425)

Technology House Ltd.............................. F 440 248-3025
Streetsboro (G-12526)

MACHINERY: Rubber Working

Anderson International Corp.................... D 216 641-1112
Stow (G-12418)

Conviber Inc.. F 330 723-6006
Medina (G-9391)

Kobelco Stewart Bolling Inc.................... D 330 655-3111
Hudson (G-7848)

McNeil & Nrm Inc.................................... D 330 761-1855
Akron (G-225)

McNeil & Nrm Intl Inc............................. D 330 253-2525
Akron (G-226)

Rjs Corporation....................................... E 330 896-2387
Akron (G-287)

RMS Equipment LLC.............................. A 330 564-1360
Cuyahoga Falls (G-5570)

Rubber City Machinery Corp.................... E 330 434-3500
Akron (G-293)

Technical Machine Products Inc............. F
Cleveland (G-4370)

MACHINERY: Screening Eqpt, Electric

Midwestern Industries Inc....................... D 330 837-4203
Massillon (G-9223)

Mjcj Holdings Inc.................................... G 937 885-0800
Miamisburg (G-9719)

Mm Industries Inc................................... E 330 332-5947
Salem (G-11802)

MACHINERY: Semiconductor Manufacturing

Eaton Corporation................................... B 440 523-5000
Cleveland (G-3652)

Rite Track Equipment Services LLC....... D 513 881-7820
West Chester (G-14068)

MACHINERY: Separation Eqpt, Magnetic

Decision Systems Inc.............................. F 330 456-7600
Canton (G-1879)

Ohio Magnetics Inc................................. E 216 662-8484
Maple Heights (G-8888)

MACHINERY: Sifting & Screening

Rotex Global LLC.................................... C 513 541-1236
Cincinnati (G-3053)

MACHINERY: Textile

C A Litzler Co Inc................................... E 216 267-8020
Cleveland (G-3457)

Open Additive LLC.................................. F 937 306-6140
Dayton (G-5929)

Randy Gray.. G 513 533-3200
Cincinnati (G-3032)

Slater Road Mills Inc.............................. E 330 332-9951
Salem (G-11813)

Wise Edge LLC.. G 330 208-0889
Mogadore (G-10094)

Wolf Machine Company........................... E 513 791-5194
Blue Ash (G-1352)

MACHINERY: Tire Retreading

American Manufacturing & Eqp............... G 513 829-2248
Fairfield (G-6711)

MACHINERY: Wire Drawing

Lanko Industries Inc................................ G 440 269-1641
Mentor (G-9550)

MACHINERY: Woodworking

Axiom Tool Group Inc.............................. G 844 642-4902
Westerville (G-14245)

Diamond Machinery LLC.......................... G 216 312-1235
Cleveland (G-3613)

General Intl Pwr Pdts LLC...................... E 419 877-5234
Whitehouse (G-14360)

Trico Enterprises LLC............................. F 216 970-9984
Lakewood (G-8172)

MACHINISTS' TOOLS & MACHINES: Measuring, Metalworking Type

Karma Metal Products Inc....................... F 419 524-4371
Mansfield (G-8810)

PMC Gage Inc... E 440 953-1672
Willoughby (G-14507)

MACHINISTS' TOOLS: Measuring, Precision

Thaler Machine Company LLC................. C 937 550-2400
Springboro (G-12269)

Thaler Machine Holdings LLC................. F 937 550-2400
Springboro (G-12270)

MACHINISTS' TOOLS: Precision

Angstrom Precision Metals LLC.............. F 440 255-6700
Mentor (G-9481)

Chippewa Tool and Mfg Co..................... F 419 849-2790
Woodville (G-14616)

DA Precision Products Inc...................... F 513 459-1113
West Chester (G-13981)

Kaeper Machine Inc................................ E 440 974-1010
Mentor (G-9545)

Keb Industries Inc.................................. G 440 953-4623
Willoughby (G-14475)

Levan Enterprises Inc............................. E 330 923-9797
Stow (G-12438)

M A Harrison Mfg Co Inc......................... E 440 965-4306
Wakeman (G-13682)

Machining Technologies Inc.................... E 419 862-3110
Elmore (G-6489)

Sjk Machine LLC..................................... F 330 868-3072
North Lawrence (G-10702)

Tessa Precision Product Inc................... E 440 392-3470
Painesville (G-11115)

MAGNESIUM

Magnesium Refining Technologies Inc.. D 419 483-9199
Cleveland (G-3980)

Air Craft Wheels LLC.............................. G 440 937-7903
Ravenna (G-11513)

Lite Metals Company............................... E 330 296-6110
Ravenna (G-11532)

Th Magnesium Inc................................... G 513 285-7568
Cincinnati (G-3146)

MAGNETIC INK & OPTICAL SCANNING EQPT

Applied Vision Corporation..................... D 330 926-2222
Cuyahoga Falls (G-5526)

MAGNETS: Permanent

Dura Magnetics Inc................................. F 419 882-0591
Sylvania (G-12706)

Flexmag Industries Inc............................ D 740 373-3492
Marietta (G-8917)

Magnum Magnetics Corporation.............. D 740 373-7770
Marietta (G-8926)

Ohio Magnetics Inc................................. E 216 662-8484
Maple Heights (G-8888)

Walker National Inc................................ E 614 492-1614
Columbus (G-5353)

Winkle Industries Inc.............................. D 330 823-9730
Alliance (G-418)

MAIL-ORDER HOUSE, NEC

American Frame Corporation................... E 419 893-5595
Maumee (G-9259)

Communication Concepts Inc.................. G 937 426-8600
Beavercreek (G-968)

Pardson Inc... F 740 373-5285
Marietta (G-8934)

MAIL-ORDER HOUSES: Educational Splys & Eqpt

Bendon Inc.. D 419 207-3600
Ashland (G-521)

E-Z Grader Company............................... G 440 247-7511
Chagrin Falls (G-2141)

Twin Sisters Productions LLC................. E 330 631-0361
Stow (G-12468)

MAIL-ORDER HOUSES: Food

Tech Solutions LLC.................................. G 419 852-7190
Celina (G-2123)

MAILING & MESSENGER SVCS

Delaware Data Products Inc.................... G 740 369-5449
Delaware (G-6142)

Richardson Printing Corp........................ D 800 848-9752
Marietta (G-8941)

MAILING LIST: Compilers

Cpmm Services Group Inc....................... G 614 447-0165
Columbus (G-4857)

MAILING SVCS, NEC

Aero Fulfillment Services Corp............... D 800 225-7145
Mason (G-9056)

American Paper Group Inc..................... B 330 758-4545
Youngstown (G-14811)

Bindery & Spc Pressworks Inc.............. D 614 873-4623
Plain City (G-11398)

Buckeye Business Forms Inc................ G 614 882-1890
Columbus (G-4784)

Covap Inc.. F 513 793-1855
Blue Ash (G-1264)

Dayton Mailing Services Inc................. E 937 222-5056
Dayton (G-5731)

Directconnectgroup Ltd....................... G 216 281-2866
Cleveland (G-3616)

Eg Enterprise Services Inc.................. G 216 431-3300
Cleveland (G-3658)

Fine Line Graphics Corp...................... C 614 486-0276
Columbus (G-4924)

Hkm Drect Mkt Cmmnications Inc......... C 800 860-4456
Cleveland (G-3832)

Macke Brothers Inc............................. G 513 771-7500
Cincinnati (G-2838)

Master Printing Group Inc.................... F 216 351-2246
Berea (G-1180)

Northcoast Pmm LLC........................... F 419 540-8667
Toledo (G-13064)

Porath Business Services Inc............... F 216 626-0060
Cleveland (G-4176)

Print All Inc.. G 419 534-2880
Toledo (G-13103)

Victory Direct LLC.............................. G 614 626-0000
Gahanna (G-7172)

Youngstown Letter Shop Inc................ G 330 793-4935
Youngstown (G-14972)

MANAGEMENT CONSULTING SVCS:
Automation & Robotics

Projects Designed & Built.................... E 419 726-7400
Toledo (G-13104)

Recognition Robotics Inc.................... F 440 590-0499
Elyria (G-6585)

MANAGEMENT CONSULTING SVCS:
Business

5me LLC... E 513 719-1600
Cincinnati (G-2289)

Crimson Gate Consulting Co................ G 614 805-0897
Dublin (G-6292)

Crohm LLC... G 513 921-9400
Cincinnati (G-2526)

Salient Systems Inc............................ E 614 792-5800
Dublin (G-6343)

Sightgain Inc..................................... F 202 494-9317
Mason (G-9152)

Tha Presidential Suite LLC................... G 216 338-7287
Cleveland (G-4376)

MANAGEMENT CONSULTING SVCS:
Business Planning & Organizing

Mag Resources LLC............................. F 330 294-0494
Barberton (G-818)

MANAGEMENT CONSULTING SVCS:
Construction Project

Elite Property Group LLC..................... F 216 356-7469
Elyria (G-6527)

Kbc Services...................................... F 513 693-3743
Loveland (G-8634)

MANAGEMENT CONSULTING SVCS:
Corporation Organizing

Comex North America Inc..................... D 303 307-2100
Cleveland (G-3551)

MANAGEMENT CONSULTING SVCS:
Distribution Channels

Tramonte & Sons LLC.......................... F 513 770-5501
Lebanon (G-8290)

MANAGEMENT CONSULTING SVCS: General

Faith Guiding Cafe LLC........................ F 614 245-8451
New Albany (G-10340)

Quarrymasters Inc.............................. G 330 612-0474
Akron (G-274)

MANAGEMENT CONSULTING SVCS:
Hospital & Health

Health Sense Inc................................ G 440 354-8057
Painesville (G-11093)

MANAGEMENT CONSULTING SVCS:
Industrial

4r Enterprises Incorporated................. G 330 923-9799
Cuyahoga Falls (G-5519)

Alloy Extrusion Company..................... E 330 677-4946
Kent (G-8016)

MANAGEMENT CONSULTING SVCS:
Industry Specialist

Applied Specialties Innovations LLC..... E 440 933-9442
Avon Lake (G-746)

Chemsultants International Inc.............. G 440 974-3080
Mentor (G-9498)

Ketman Corporation............................ G 330 262-1688
Wooster (G-14658)

Telex Communications Inc................... F 419 865-0972
Toledo (G-13140)

MANAGEMENT CONSULTING SVCS:
Information Systems

Millers Aplus Cmpt Svcs LLC............... F 330 620-5288
Akron (G-234)

Neurologix Technologies Inc................ F 512 914-7941
Cleveland (G-4071)

MANAGEMENT CONSULTING SVCS:
Manufacturing

889 Global Solutions Ltd...................... F 614 235-8889
Columbus (G-4655)

MANAGEMENT CONSULTING SVCS:
Training & Development

Honda Dev & Mfg Amer LLC.................. C 937 644-0724
Marysville (G-9028)

Leidos Inc.. D 937 656-8433
Beavercreek (G-977)

MANAGEMENT CONSULTING SVCS:
Transportation

Integrity Parking LLC.......................... F 440 543-4123
Aurora (G-675)

MANAGEMENT SERVICES

Babcock & Wilcox Company................. A 330 753-4511
Akron (G-67)

Cardinal Health Inc............................. E 614 553-3830
Dublin (G-6285)

Cardinal Health Inc............................. G 614 757-2863
Lewis Center (G-8328)

Cardinal Health Inc............................. A 614 757-5000
Dublin (G-6286)

Central Coca-Cola Btlg Co Inc............. E 330 875-1487
Akron (G-95)

Central Coca-Cola Btlg Co Inc............. E 740 474-2180
Circleville (G-3250)

Coal Services Inc................................ B 740 795-5220
Powhatan Point (G-11497)

Eleet Cryogenics Inc........................... E 330 874-4009
Bolivar (G-1382)

Instantwhip-Columbus Inc................... E 614 871-9447
Grove City (G-7391)

Integrated Resources Inc.................... E 419 885-7122
Sylvania (G-12713)

Kenyetta Bagby Enterprise LLC........... F 614 584-3426
Reynoldsburg (G-11573)

Kurtz Bros Compost Services.............. G 330 864-2621
Akron (G-200)

Leadec Corp....................................... E 513 731-3590
Cincinnati (G-2815)

Momentum Fleet MGT Group Inc.......... D 440 759-2219
Westlake (G-14315)

Ohio Designer Craftsmen Entps........... F 614 486-7119
Columbus (G-5141)

Pf Management Inc.............................. G 513 874-8741
West Chester (G-14136)

RB Sigma LLC..................................... D 440 290-0577
Mentor (G-9607)

Revolution Group Inc.......................... D 614 212-1111
Westerville (G-14230)

TAC Industries Inc.............................. B 937 328-5200
Springfield (G-12382)

MANAGEMENT SVCS: Administrative

Instantwhip Foods Inc......................... F 614 488-2536
Columbus (G-5011)

Renascent Prtction Sltions LLC............ D 678 910-0412
Dublin (G-6339)

MANAGEMENT SVCS: Business

Ironhawk Industrial Dist LLC................ G 216 502-3700
Euclid (G-6656)

Ohio Cllbrtive Lrng Sltons Inc.............. E 216 595-5289
Strongsville (G-12582)

Steward Edge Bus Solutions................ F 614 826-5305
Columbus (G-5293)

MANAGEMENT SVCS: Construction

Ameridian Specialty Services............... E 513 769-0150
Cincinnati (G-2364)

Elite Property Group LLC..................... F 216 356-7469
Elyria (G-6527)

Ingle-Barr Inc..................................... D 740 702-6117
Chillicothe (G-2261)

Mel Heitkamp Builders Ltd................... G 419 375-0405
Fort Recovery (G-6969)

Protective Industrial Polymers.............. F 440 327-0015
North Ridgeville (G-10743)

MANPOWER POOLS

Channel Products Inc.......................... D 440 423-0113
Solon (G-12093)

MANUFACTURING INDUSTRIES, NEC

4S Company.. F 330 792-5518
Youngstown (G-14800)

Actual Industries LLC......................... G 614 379-2739
Columbus (G-4673)

Agile Manufacturing Tech LLC.............. F 937 258-3338
Dayton (G-5642)

AMG Industries Inc............................. F 740 397-4044
Mount Vernon (G-10232)

PRODUCT

ARS Recycling Systems 2019 LLC......... E 330 536-8210
Lowellville *(G-8659)*

Axalta Coating Systems USA LLC......... D 614 777-7230
Hilliard *(G-7673)*

B&M Underground LLC.......................... G 740 505-3096
Wilmington *(G-14572)*

Blackstar International Inc.................... G 917 510-5482
Columbus *(G-4763)*

Carapa Industries Inc........................... G 330 307-1890
Masury *(G-9255)*

D Jacob Industries LLC........................ G 440 292-7277
Cleveland *(G-3596)*

Desco Machine Company LLC.............. G 330 405-5181
Twinsburg *(G-13293)*

Digimanufacturing Tech LLC............... G 419 212-6414
Bryan *(G-1638)*

DLAC Industries Inc.............................. G 330 519-4789
Canfield *(G-1808)*

Elaire Corporation................................ G 419 843-2192
Toledo *(G-12946)*

Endurance Industries LLC.................... F 513 285-8503
Cincinnati *(G-2588)*

Essentialware....................................... G 888 975-0405
Kirtland *(G-8144)*

FB Acquisition LLC.............................. E 513 459-7782
Lebanon *(G-8255)*

Five Star Fabrication LLC..................... F 440 666-0427
Wellington *(G-13887)*

Front Pocket Innovations LLC............. G 330 441-2365
Wadsworth *(G-13639)*

Honda Transmission Manufacturi........ F 937 843-5555
Marysville *(G-9030)*

Housing & Emrgncy Lgstcs Plnnr....... E 209 201-7511
Lisbon *(G-8470)*

Item NA... G 216 271-7241
Akron *(G-184)*

Jbs Industries Ltd................................. G 513 314-5599
Columbus *(G-5034)*

Jones Industries LLC............................ F 440 810-1251
Olmsted Twp *(G-10946)*

Juba Industries Inc.............................. G 440 655-9960
Jefferson *(G-7973)*

Kanya Industries LLC........................... G 330 722-5432
Medina *(G-9416)*

Kayden Industries................................ G 740 336-7801
Marietta *(G-8925)*

Kitto Katsu Inc...................................... G 818 256-6997
Clayton *(G-3274)*

Lauren Manufacturing.......................... D 330 339-3373
New Philadelphia *(G-10455)*

Mako Finished Products Inc................. E 740 357-0839
Lucasville *(G-8667)*

Manufacturing Company LLC.............. F 414 708-7583
Cincinnati *(G-2844)*

Manufctred Assemblies Corp LLC....... F 937 454-0722
Vandalia *(G-13568)*

MCS Mfg LLC.. G 419 923-0169
Lyons *(G-8674)*

MODE Industries Inc............................ G 614 504-8008
Columbus *(G-5108)*

Morgan Site Services Inc.................... E 330 823-6120
Alliance *(G-395)*

My Splash Pad...................................... G 330 705-1802
Louisville *(G-8609)*

New Republic Industries LLC.............. G 614 580-9927
Marysville *(G-9040)*

Nfi Industries Inc................................. F 740 928-9522
Hebron *(G-7626)*

Njf Manufacturing LLC......................... G 419 294-0400
Upper Sandusky *(G-13450)*

Norkaam Industries LLC...................... G 330 873-9793
Akron *(G-247)*

Norris North Manufacturing................. F 330 691-0449
Canton *(G-1960)*

Palmer Donavin Manufacturing............ F 740 527-1111
Hebron *(G-7629)*

Perma Edge Industries LLC................. G 937 623-7819
Dayton *(G-5937)*

Platinum Industries LLC...................... F 740 285-2641
Ironton *(G-7932)*

Pragmatic Mfg LLC.............................. G 330 222-6051
Brunswick *(G-1607)*

Proto Prcsion Mfg Slutions LLC.......... F 614 771-0080
Hilliard *(G-7697)*

Pyramid Industries LLC....................... G 614 783-1543
Columbus *(G-5215)*

Rable Machine Inc................................ E 740 689-9009
Lancaster *(G-8222)*

RS&b Industries LLC............................ E 330 255-6000
Wooster *(G-14678)*

Rubber City Industries Inc................... G 330 990-9641
Wadsworth *(G-13669)*

Sdi Industries...................................... G 513 561-4032
Cincinnati *(G-3072)*

Shafts Mfg.. G 440 942-6012
Willoughby *(G-14524)*

Spectre Industries LLC........................ G 440 665-2600
Chagrin Falls *(G-2183)*

Suppressor Co LLC.............................. G 330 749-5234
Ashland *(G-577)*

Travis Products Mfg Inc....................... G 234 759-3741
North Lima *(G-10715)*

Troyridge Mfg....................................... G 330 893-7516
Millersburg *(G-10015)*

Tuffy Manufacturing............................. F 330 940-2356
Akron *(G-348)*

Universal Manufacturing...................... G 816 396-0101
Cleveland *(G-4446)*

Vic Maroscher...................................... F 330 332-4958
Salem *(G-11817)*

VT Industries LLC................................ G 614 804-6904
Hilliard *(G-7711)*

Waterloo Industries Inc....................... G 800 833-8851
Cleveland *(G-4492)*

Weaver Propack - Marc Drive.............. G 330 379-3660
Cuyahoga Falls *(G-5581)*

Wrayco Manufacturing In..................... F 330 688-5617
Stow *(G-12474)*

MARBLE, BUILDING: Cut & Shaped

Accent Manufacturing Inc................... F 330 724-7704
Akron *(G-13)*

Al-Co Products Inc............................... G 419 399-3867
Latty *(G-8236)*

Engineered Marble Inc......................... G 614 308-0041
Columbus *(G-4902)*

Ohio Tile & Marble Co.......................... E 513 541-4211
Cincinnati *(G-2926)*

Pietra Naturale Inc............................... F 937 438-8882
Dayton *(G-5940)*

Piqua Granite & Marble Co Inc............ G 937 773-2000
Piqua *(G-11376)*

MARINE CARGO HANDLING SVCS

McGinnis Inc... C 740 377-4391
South Point *(G-12226)*

McNational Inc...................................... D 740 377-4391
South Point *(G-12227)*

Rayle Coal Co.. F 740 695-2197
Saint Clairsville *(G-11708)*

MARINE HARDWARE

Hydromotive Engineering Co................ G 330 425-4266
Twinsburg *(G-13317)*

Racelite Southcoast Inc....................... F 216 581-4600
Maple Heights *(G-8891)*

Worthignton Products Inc.................... G 330 452-7400
East Canton *(G-6381)*

MARINE SPLYS WHOLESALERS

Hydromotive Engineering Co................ G 330 425-4266
Twinsburg *(G-13317)*

Werner G Smith Inc.............................. F 216 861-3676
Cleveland *(G-4501)*

MARKETS: Meat & fish

D & H Meats Inc.................................... G 419 387-7767
Vanlue *(G-13585)*

Riesbeck Food Markets Inc................. C 740 695-3401
Saint Clairsville *(G-11709)*

MARKING DEVICES

Akron Paint & Varnish Inc.................... D 330 773-8911
Akron *(G-36)*

Bishop Machine Tool & Die................. F 740 453-8818
Zanesville *(G-14997)*

Dayton Stencil Works Company........... F 937 223-3233
Dayton *(G-5739)*

E C Shaw Company of Ohio.................. E 513 721-6334
Cincinnati *(G-2569)*

Hathaway Stamp Idntfction Cncn........ G 513 621-1052
Cincinnati *(G-2713)*

Magna Visual Inc.................................. E 314 843-9000
Perrysburg *(G-11236)*

Metal Marker Manufacturing Co........... F 440 327-2300
North Ridgeville *(G-10740)*

Microcom Corporation.......................... E 740 548-6262
Lewis Center *(G-8343)*

Monode Marking Products Inc............. F 419 929-0346
New London *(G-10413)*

REA Elektronik Inc............................... F 440 232-0555
Walton Hills *(G-13702)*

Visual Marking Systems Inc................. D 330 425-7100
Twinsburg *(G-13393)*

Volk Corporation.................................. G 513 621-1052
Cincinnati *(G-3207)*

MARKING DEVICES: Canceling Stamps, Hand, Rubber Or Metal

Telesis Technologies Inc..................... C 740 477-5000
Circleville *(G-3266)*

MARKING DEVICES: Embossing Seals & Hand Stamps

Hathaway Stamp Co.............................. F 513 621-1052
Cincinnati *(G-2712)*

Marking Devices Inc............................. G 216 861-4498
Cleveland *(G-3989)*

Royal Acme Corporation....................... E 216 241-1477
Cleveland *(G-4256)*

System Seals Inc.................................. E 216 220-1800
Brecksville *(G-1481)*

System Seals LLC................................ E 440 735-0200
Cleveland *(G-4359)*

MARKING DEVICES: Embossing Seals, Corporate & Official

Williams Steel Rule Die Co.................. G 216 431-3232
Cleveland *(G-4507)*

MATS OR MATTING, NEC: Rubber

Durable Corporation............................. D 800 537-1603
Norwalk *(G-10836)*

2025 Harris Ohio
Industrial Directory

(G-0000) Company's Geographic Section entry number

Garro Tread Corporation...................... G 330 376-3125
Akron (G-156)

Ludlow Composites Corporation........... C 419 332-5531
Fremont (G-7122)

R C Musson Rubber Co........................ E 330 773-7651
Akron (G-276)

Rubber Grinding Inc............................ D 419 692-3000
Delphos (G-6192)

Ultimate Rb Inc................................... F 419 692-3000
Delphos (G-6195)

Westlake Dimex LLC............................ C 800 334-3776
Marietta (G-8961)

MATS, MATTING & PADS: Nonwoven

Durable Corporation............................ D 800 537-1603
Norwalk (G-10836)

Spacelinks Enterprises Inc.................. E 330 788-2401
Youngstown (G-14935)

Tranzonic Companies........................... C 440 446-0643
Cleveland (G-4414)

MEAT MARKETS

Dee-Jays Cstm Btchring Proc LL.......... F 740 694-7492
Fredericktown (G-7076)

Foris Extraordinary Meats LLC............ F 614 670-5726
Columbus (G-4931)

Hoffman Meat Processing..................... G 419 864-3994
Cardington (G-2054)

Honeybaked Ham Company.................. E 513 583-9700
Cincinnati (G-2730)

John Krusinski.................................... F 216 441-0100
Cleveland (G-3889)

John Stehlin & Sons Co....................... G 513 385-6164
Cincinnati (G-2769)

Lee Williams Meats Inc....................... E 419 729-3893
Toledo (G-13031)

Marshallville Packing Co Inc............... G 330 855-2871
Marshallville (G-9007)

Mc Connells Market............................. G 740 765-4300
Richmond (G-11604)

Pettisville Meats Incorporated............. F 419 445-0921
Pettisville (G-11286)

Queen City Sausage & Prov Inc........... E 513 541-5581
Cincinnati (G-3025)

Winesburg Meats Inc........................... G 330 359-5092
Winesburg (G-14609)

MEAT PRDTS: Bacon, Side & Sliced, From Purchased Meat

Foris Extraordinary Meats LLC............ F 614 670-5726
Columbus (G-4931)

Honeybaked Foods Inc......................... A 567 703-0002
Holland (G-7767)

Sugar Creek Packing Co....................... G 937 268-6601
Dayton (G-6029)

Sugar Creek Packing Co....................... B 513 551-5280
Cincinnati (G-3122)

MEAT PRDTS: Boxed Beef, From Slaughtered Meat

National Beef Ohio LLC........................ C 800 449-2333
North Baltimore (G-10615)

MEAT PRDTS: Cooked Meats, From Purchased Meat

King Kold Inc...................................... E 937 836-2731
Englewood (G-6617)

MEAT PRDTS: Frozen

A To Z Portion Ctrl Meats Inc.............. E 419 358-2926
Bluffton (G-1356)

Dee-Jays Cstm Btchring Proc LL.......... F 740 694-7492
Fredericktown (G-7076)

Frank Brunckhorst Company LLC......... G 614 662-5300
Groveport (G-7434)

The Ellenbee-Leggett Company Inc...... C 513 874-3200
Fairfield (G-6782)

White Castle System Inc...................... B 614 228-5781
Columbus (G-5367)

MEAT PRDTS: Luncheon Meat, From Purchased Meat

Fink Meat Company Inc........................ G 937 390-2750
Springfield (G-12311)

MEAT PRDTS: Prepared Beef Prdts From Purchased Beef

Advancepierre Foods Inc..................... B 513 874-8741
West Chester (G-14097)

Brinkman Turkey Farms Inc................. F 419 365-5127
Findlay (G-6846)

Fresh Mark Inc.................................... B 330 832-7491
Massillon (G-9192)

Pierre Holding Corp............................ G 513 874-8741
West Chester (G-14137)

MEAT PRDTS: Sausages & Related Prdts, From Purchased Meat

Owens Foods Inc.................................. B
New Albany (G-10349)

Queen City Sausage & Prov Inc........... E 513 541-5581
Cincinnati (G-3025)

MEAT PRDTS: Sausages, From Purchased Meat

Lous Sausage Ltd................................ G 216 752-5060
Cleveland (G-3968)

Rays Sausage Inc................................ G 216 921-8782
Cleveland (G-4226)

MEAT PRDTS: Snack Sticks, Incl Jerky, From Purchased Meat

Simply Unique Snacks LLC................... G 513 223-7736
Cincinnati (G-3092)

MEDIA: Magnetic & Optical Recording

CD Solutions Inc.................................. G 937 676-2376
Pleasant Hill (G-11431)

MEDICAL & HOSPITAL EQPT WHOLESALERS

Boxout LLC.. C 833 462-7746
Hudson (G-7835)

Homecare Mattress Inc........................ F 937 746-2556
Franklin (G-7027)

Optum Infusion Svcs 550 LLC.............. D 866 442-4679
Cincinnati (G-2936)

Smiths Medical North America............. G 614 210-7300
Dublin (G-6347)

MEDICAL & SURGICAL SPLYS: Bandages & Dressings

Beiersdorf Inc..................................... C 513 682-7300
West Chester (G-14107)

MEDICAL & SURGICAL SPLYS: Braces, Elastic

Motion Mobility & Design Inc............... F 330 244-9723
North Canton (G-10653)

Myfootshopcom LLC............................. G 740 522-5681
Newark (G-10523)

MEDICAL & SURGICAL SPLYS: Braces, Orthopedic

ABI Orthtc/Prosthetic Labs Ltd............ E 330 758-1143
Youngstown (G-14802)

Akron Orthotic Solutions Inc............... G 330 253-3002
Akron (G-35)

Anatomical Concepts Inc..................... F 330 757-3569
Youngstown (G-14815)

Cole Orthotics Prosthetic Ctr.............. G 419 476-4248
Toledo (G-12927)

Cranial Technologies Inc..................... G 844 447-5894
Cincinnati (G-2523)

Faretec Inc... F 440 350-9510
Painesville (G-11086)

Findlay Amrcn Prsthtic Orthtic............ G 419 424-1622
Findlay (G-6863)

Opc Inc... G 419 531-2222
Toledo (G-13079)

Orthotics Prsthtics Rhblttion............... G 330 856-2553
Warren (G-13788)

Vantage Orthopedics Inc..................... F 513 563-1690
Cincinnati (G-3194)

MEDICAL & SURGICAL SPLYS: Clothing, Fire Resistant & Protect

Barton-Carey Medical Pdts Inc............ E 419 887-1285
Maumee (G-9265)

Lion First Responder Ppe Inc.............. D 937 898-1949
Dayton (G-5849)

Wcm Holdings Inc................................ C 513 705-2100
Cincinnati (G-3213)

West Chester Holdings LLC................. C 513 705-2100
Cincinnati (G-3220)

MEDICAL & SURGICAL SPLYS: Foot Appliances, Orthopedic

Stable Step LLC.................................. C 800 491-1571
Wadsworth (G-13673)

MEDICAL & SURGICAL SPLYS: Grafts, Artificial

Osteonovus Inc................................... F 419 530-5940
Toledo (G-13081)

Osteonovus Inc................................... G 419 530-5940
Toledo (G-13082)

MEDICAL & SURGICAL SPLYS: Gynecological Splys & Appliances

Coopersurgical Inc.............................. G 203 601-5200
Cincinnati (G-2516)

MEDICAL & SURGICAL SPLYS: Limbs, Artificial

Capital Prsthtic Orthtic Ctr I............... F 614 451-0446
Columbus (G-4797)

Fidelity Orthopedic Inc....................... G 937 228-0682
Dayton (G-5776)

Luminaud Inc...................................... G 440 255-9082
Mentor (G-9556)

PRODUCT

Willowwood Global LLC............................ C 740 869-3377
Mount Sterling *(G-10231)*

Yanke Bionics Inc.................................. E 330 762-6411
Akron *(G-360)*

MEDICAL & SURGICAL SPLYS: Orthopedic Appliances

Acor Orthopaedic Inc.............................. F 440 532-0117
Cleveland *(G-3292)*

Gottfried Medical Inc.............................. F 419 474-2973
Toledo *(G-12976)*

Matplus Ltd.. G 440 352-7201
Painesville *(G-11098)*

Medical Device Bus Svcs Inc................... E 937 274-5850
Dayton *(G-5873)*

Orthotic & Prosthetic Spc Inc................. E 216 531-2773
Euclid *(G-6667)*

Sroufe Healthcare Products LLC........... G 260 894-4171
Wadsworth *(G-13672)*

Zimmer Surgical Inc................................ B 800 321-5533
Dover *(G-6268)*

MEDICAL & SURGICAL SPLYS: Prosthetic Appliances

Acor Orthopaedic LLC............................ E 216 662-4500
Cleveland *(G-3293)*

American Orthopedics Inc....................... F 614 291-6454
Columbus *(G-4700)*

Form5 Prosthetics Inc............................ F 614 226-1141
New Albany *(G-10341)*

Presque Isle Orthtics Prsthtic................. G 216 371-0660
Cleveland *(G-4192)*

Touch Bionics Inc................................. G 800 233-6263
Dublin *(G-6356)*

MEDICAL & SURGICAL SPLYS: Splints, Pneumatic & Wood

Ferno-Washington Inc............................. C 877 733-0911
Wilmington *(G-14580)*

MEDICAL & SURGICAL SPLYS: Stretchers

Midmark Corporation.............................. G 937 526-3662
Versailles *(G-13600)*

Midmark Corporation.............................. A 937 528-7500
Miamisburg *(G-9717)*

MEDICAL EQPT REPAIR SVCS, NON-ELECTRIC

Elite Biomedical Solutions LLC............... F 513 207-0602
Cincinnati *(G-2302)*

MEDICAL EQPT: Diagnostic

Quidel Dhi.. E 740 589-3300
Athens *(G-651)*

MEDICAL EQPT: Electromedical Apparatus

Cleveland Medical Devices Inc............... E 216 619-5928
Cleveland *(G-3515)*

Furniss Corporation Ltd.......................... F 614 871-1470
Mount Sterling *(G-10228)*

Great Lkes Nrotechnologies Inc............. E 855 456-3876
Cleveland *(G-3794)*

Imalux Corporation................................. F 216 502-0755
Cleveland *(G-3851)*

Norwood Medical LLC............................ D 937 228-4101
Dayton *(G-5912)*

Torax Medical Inc.................................. F 651 361-8900
Blue Ash *(G-1344)*

MEDICAL EQPT: Sterilizers

Steris Corporation................................. D 330 696-9946
Mentor *(G-9625)*

Steris Corporation................................. A 440 354-2600
Mentor *(G-9624)*

MEDICAL EQPT: Ultrasonic Scanning Devices

Canary Health Technologies Inc............. F 617 784-4021
Cleveland *(G-3462)*

MEDICAL EQPT: X-Ray Apparatus & Tubes, Radiographic

General Electric Company....................... F 216 663-2110
Cleveland *(G-3765)*

Waygate Technologies Usa LP................ D 866 243-2638
Cincinnati *(G-3212)*

MEDICAL INSURANCE CLAIM PROCESSING: Contract Or Fee Basis

Acu-Serve Corp.................................... C 330 923-5258
Akron *(G-17)*

Mxr Imaging Inc.................................... G 614 219-2011
Hilliard *(G-7688)*

MEDICAL SUNDRIES: Rubber

Philpott Rubber LLC............................... G 330 225-3344
Aurora *(G-685)*

Philpott Rubber LLC............................... E 330 225-3344
Brunswick *(G-1605)*

MEDICAL, DENTAL & HOSP EQPT, WHOLESALE: X-ray Film & Splys

Philips Med Systems Clvland In............. B 440 483-3000
Cleveland *(G-4159)*

MEDICAL, DENTAL & HOSPITAL EQPT, WHOL: Hospital Eqpt & Splys

Kempf Surgical Appliances Inc............... G 513 984-5758
Cincinnati *(G-2791)*

MEDICAL, DENTAL & HOSPITAL EQPT, WHOL: Surgical Eqpt & Splys

Cardinal Health Inc................................ E 614 553-3830
Dublin *(G-6285)*

Cardinal Health Inc................................ G 614 757-2863
Lewis Center *(G-8328)*

Cardinal Health Inc................................ A 614 757-5000
Dublin *(G-6286)*

MEDICAL, DENTAL & HOSPITAL EQPT, WHOLESALE: Artificial Limbs

Blatchford Inc...................................... D 937 291-3636
Miamisburg *(G-9673)*

MELAMINE RESINS: Melamine-Formaldehyde

Bakelite Chemicals LLC.......................... D 404 652-4000
Columbus *(G-4741)*

Next Specialty Resins Inc....................... E 419 843-4600
Sylvania *(G-12719)*

MEMBERSHIP ORGANIZATIONS, NEC: Personal Interest

American Gild of English Hndbe............. G 937 438-0085
Cincinnati *(G-2359)*

MEMBERSHIP ORGS, RELIGIOUS: Non-Denominational Church

New Life Chapel.................................... F 513 298-2980
Cincinnati *(G-2902)*

MEN'S & BOYS' CLOTHING ACCESS STORES

Rnp Inc... G
Dellroy *(G-6182)*

MEN'S & BOYS' CLOTHING STORES

City Apparel Inc.................................... F 419 434-1155
Findlay *(G-6852)*

S F Mock & Associates LLC................... F 937 438-0196
Dayton *(G-5991)*

MEN'S & BOYS' CLOTHING WHOLESALERS, NEC

McCc Sportswear Inc............................. G 513 583-9210
Milford *(G-9942)*

West Chester Holdings LLC................... C 513 705-2100
Cincinnati *(G-3220)*

METAL & STEEL PRDTS: Abrasive

Cleveland Granite & Marble LLC............. E 216 291-7637
Cleveland *(G-3512)*

Innovation Sales LLC............................. G 330 239-0400
Medina *(G-9412)*

Libra Guaymas LLC............................... C 440 974-7770
Mentor *(G-9552)*

Tomson Steel Company.......................... E 513 420-8600
Middletown *(G-9900)*

METAL COMPONENTS: Prefabricated

Iron Works Inc...................................... F 937 420-2100
Fort Loramie *(G-6949)*

Pioneer Cldding Glzing Systems............. E 216 816-4242
Cleveland *(G-4166)*

METAL DETECTORS

Ceia Usa Ltd.. D 330 310-4741
Hudson *(G-7836)*

Ohio Magnetics Inc................................ E 216 662-8484
Maple Heights *(G-8888)*

METAL FABRICATORS: Plate

Krendl Rack Co Inc................................ G 419 667-4800
Venedocia *(G-13586)*

Loveman Steel Corporation..................... D 440 232-6200
Bedford *(G-1044)*

METAL FINISHING SVCS

Broco Products Inc................................ G 216 531-0880
Cleveland *(G-3441)*

Conforming Matrix Corporation............... E 419 729-3777
Toledo *(G-12929)*

Luke Engineering & Mfg Corp................. E 330 335-1501
Wadsworth *(G-13649)*

Taikisha Usa Inc................................... D 614 444-5602
Columbus *(G-5306)*

Tom Richards Inc.................................. C 440 974-1300
Willoughby *(G-14541)*

METAL MINING SVCS

Western Kentucky Coal Co LLC............. D 740 338-3334
Saint Clairsville *(G-11715)*

METAL SERVICE CENTERS & OFFICES

American Tank & Fabricating Co........... D 216 252-1500
Cleveland *(G-3348)*

Atlas Bolt & Screw Company LLC........... C 419 289-6171
Ashland *(G-519)*

Canfield Coating LLC........................... E 330 533-3311
Canfield *(G-1806)*

Canfield Metal Coating Corp................. D 330 702-3876
Canfield *(G-1807)*

EPI of Cleveland Inc........................... G 330 468-2872
Twinsburg *(G-13299)*

Kirtland Capital Partners LP.................. E 216 593-0100
Beachwood *(G-924)*

Lake Building Products Inc.................... E 216 486-1500
Cleveland *(G-3936)*

Merit Brass Co................................... C 216 261-9800
Cleveland *(G-4021)*

Modern Welding Co Ohio Inc................. E 740 344-9425
Newark *(G-10522)*

Nucor Steel Marion Inc........................ E 740 383-6068
Marion *(G-8984)*

Ohio Steel Sheet and Plate Inc............. E 800 827-2401
Hubbard *(G-7815)*

Oliver Steel Plate Co........................... D 330 425-7000
Twinsburg *(G-13347)*

Omega 1 Inc..................................... F 216 663-8424
Willoughby *(G-14501)*

Panacea Products Corporation.............. E 614 850-7000
Columbus *(G-5171)*

The Mansfield Strl & Erct Co................. F 419 522-5911
Mansfield *(G-8859)*

Tricor Industrial Inc............................ D 330 264-3299
Wooster *(G-14692)*

Tsk America Co Ltd............................. F 513 942-4002
West Chester *(G-14156)*

Watteredge LLC.................................. D 440 933-6110
Avon Lake *(G-773)*

Wieland Metal Svcs Foils LLC............... D 330 823-1700
Alliance *(G-417)*

Worthngton Smuel Coil Proc LLC........... E 330 963-3777
Twinsburg *(G-13398)*

Worthngton Stelpac Systems LLC........... C 614 438-3205
Columbus *(G-5375)*

METAL STAMPING, FOR THE TRADE

AAA Stamping Inc............................... E 216 749-4494
Cleveland *(G-3284)*

Acro Tool & Die Company..................... E 330 773-5173
Akron *(G-18)*

Agb LLC.. G 419 924-5216
West Unity *(G-14191)*

AJD Holding Co.................................. D 330 405-4477
Twinsburg *(G-13271)*

Allied Tool & Die Inc........................... F 216 941-6196
Cleveland *(G-3331)*

Amaroq Inc....................................... G 419 747-2110
Mansfield *(G-8760)*

Amclo Group Inc................................ F 216 791-8400
North Royalton *(G-10754)*

American Tool and Die Inc................... F 419 726-5394
Toledo *(G-12879)*

Ampex Metal Products Company........... D 216 267-9242
Brookpark *(G-1544)*

Andre Corporation.............................. E 574 293-0207
Mason *(G-9061)*

Arbor Industries Inc............................ D 440 255-4720
Mentor *(G-9485)*

ARC Metal Stamping LLC..................... D 517 448-8954
Wauseon *(G-13845)*

Art Technologies LLC.......................... E 513 942-8800
Hamilton *(G-7466)*

Artistic Metal Spinning Inc................... G 216 961-3336
Cleveland *(G-3372)*

Atlantic Tool & Die Company................. C 440 238-6931
Strongsville *(G-12539)*

Atra Metal Spinning Inc....................... F 440 354-9525
Painesville *(G-11067)*

Automatic Stamp Products Inc.............. G 216 781-7933
Cleveland *(G-3390)*

Banner Metals Group Inc..................... E 614 291-3105
Columbus *(G-4743)*

Bayloff Stmped Pdts Knsman Inc.......... D 330 876-4511
Kinsman *(G-8140)*

Bennett Machine & Stamping Co........... E 440 415-0401
Geneva *(G-7234)*

Boehm Pressed Steel Company............. E 330 220-8000
Valley City *(G-13491)*

Brainerd Industries Inc........................ E 937 228-0488
Miamisburg *(G-9676)*

Buckley Manufacturing Company........... F 513 821-4444
Cincinnati *(G-2432)*

Central Ohio Met Stmping Fbrct............. E 614 861-3332
New Albany *(G-10335)*

Cleveland Die & Mfg Co....................... C 440 243-3404
Middleburg Heights *(G-9767)*

Cleveland Metal Stamping Co............... F 440 234-0010
Berea *(G-1162)*

Com-Corp Industries Inc...................... D 216 431-6266
Cleveland *(G-3548)*

Continental Business Entps Inc............. F 440 439-4400
Bedford *(G-1023)*

Dayton Rogers of Ohio Inc................... D 614 491-1477
Columbus *(G-4871)*

Deerfield Manufacturing Inc................. E 513 398-2010
Mason *(G-9093)*

Defiance Stamping Co......................... D 419 782-5781
Napoleon *(G-10278)*

Dependable Stamping Company............ E 216 486-5522
Cleveland *(G-3609)*

Die Co Inc.. E 440 942-8856
Eastlake *(G-6423)*

Die-Matic Corporation......................... D 216 749-4656
Independence *(G-7897)*

Dove Die and Stamping Company.......... E 216 267-3720
Cleveland *(G-3628)*

Dyco Manufacturing Inc....................... F 419 485-5525
Montpelier *(G-10128)*

Eagle Precision Products LLC............... G 440 582-9393
North Royalton *(G-10759)*

Eisenhauer Mfg Co LLC....................... D 419 238-0081
Van Wert *(G-13333)*

Elyria Spring Spclty Holdg Inc.............. G 440 323-5502
Cleveland *(G-3664)*

Ernst Metal Technologies LLC............... D 937 434-3133
Moraine *(G-10161)*

Ernst Metal Technologies LLC............... E 937 434-3133
Dayton *(G-5767)*

F C Brengman and Assoc LLC............... D 740 756-4308
Carroll *(G-2075)*

Fairfield Manufacturing Inc................... B 513 642-0081
Fairfield *(G-6734)*

Falls Stamping & Welding Co................. C 330 928-1191
Cuyahoga Falls *(G-5541)*

Falls Tool and Die Inc......................... D 330 633-4884
Akron *(G-144)*

Famous Industries Inc......................... F 740 685-2592
Byesville *(G-1711)*

Faull & Son LLC................................. F 330 652-4341
Niles *(G-10588)*

Five Handicap Inc............................... F 419 525-2511
Mansfield *(G-8788)*

Gentzler Tool & Die Corp..................... E 330 896-1941
Akron *(G-161)*

Grenada Stamping Assembly Inc........... E 419 842-3600
Sylvania *(G-12707)*

Guarantee Specialties Inc.................... G 216 451-9744
Strongsville *(G-12562)*

H&M Mtal Stamping Assembly Inc......... F 216 898-9030
Brook Park *(G-1513)*

Hamlin Newco LLC............................. D 330 753-7791
Akron *(G-170)*

Hamlin Steel Products LLC................... F 330 753-7791
Akron *(G-171)*

Hashier & Hashier Mfg........................ G 440 933-4883
Avon Lake *(G-758)*

Herd Manufacturing Inc....................... E 216 651-4221
Cleveland *(G-3826)*

Hill Manufacturing Inc......................... E 419 335-5006
Wauseon *(G-13851)*

Ice Industries Inc............................... E 419 842-3600
Sylvania *(G-12710)*

Impact Industries Inc.......................... F 440 327-2360
North Ridgeville *(G-10735)*

Imperial Die & Mfg Co......................... G 440 268-9080
Strongsville *(G-12566)*

Imperial Metal Spinning Co................... G 216 524-5020
Cleveland *(G-3855)*

Independent Stamping Inc.................... F 216 251-3500
Cleveland *(G-3857)*

Interlake Stamping Ohio Inc................. E 440 942-0800
Willoughby *(G-14471)*

J B Stamping Inc................................ E 216 631-0013
Cleveland *(G-3877)*

Kg63 LLC.. F 216 941-7766
Cleveland *(G-3917)*

Knowlton Manufacturing Co Inc............. F 513 631-7353
Cincinnati *(G-2803)*

Kreider Corp..................................... D 937 325-8787
Springfield *(G-12341)*

L & W Inc... D 734 397-6300
Avon *(G-730)*

Lakepark Industries Inc....................... C 419 752-4471
Greenwich *(G-7363)*

Lextech Industries Ltd......................... G 216 883-7900
Cleveland *(G-3953)*

Lippert Components Inc....................... G 574 537-8900
Payne *(G-11164)*

Mahoning Valley Mfg Inc...................... E 330 537-4492
Beloit *(G-1145)*

Mansfield Industries Inc....................... F 419 524-1300
Mansfield *(G-8820)*

Marc V Concepts Inc........................... F 419 782-6505
Defiance *(G-6119)*

Master Products Company.................... D 216 341-1740
Cleveland *(G-3998)*

Maumee Assembly & Stamping LLC....... C 419 304-2887
Maumee *(G-9307)*

May Industries of Ohio Inc................... E 440 237-8012
North Royalton *(G-10773)*

McGlennon Metal Products Inc.............. F 614 252-7114
Columbus *(G-5091)*

McGregor Mtal Innsfllen Wrks L............. C 937 322-3880
Springfield *(G-12349)*

McGregor Mtal Yllow Sprng Wrks........... D 937 325-5561
Springfield *(G-12351)*

Metal & Wire Products Company........... F 330 332-1015
Salem *(G-11798)*

Metal & Wire Products Company........... E 330 332-9448
Salem *(G-11799)*

Metal Fabricating Corporation............... D 216 631-8121
Cleveland *(G-4023)*

Metal Products Company...................... E 330 652-2558
Powell *(G-11491)*

Metal Stampings Unlimited Inc.............. F 937 328-0206
Springfield *(G-12352)*

Mohawk Manufacturing Inc................... G 860 632-2345
Mount Vernon *(G-10252)*

PRODUCT

Nasg Auto-Seat Tec LLC.............. E 419 359-5954
Ridgeville Corners (G-11615)

Nasg Ohio LLC................................ F 419 634-3125
Ada (G-4)

Nasg Seating Bryan LLC............... D 419 633-0662
Bryan (G-1652)

Neway Stamping & Mfg Inc .... D 440 951-8500
Willoughby (G-14494)

Niles Manufacturing & Finshg................ C 330 544-0402
Niles (G-10596)

Ohio Gasket and Shim Co Inc............... E 330 630-0626
Akron (G-252)

Ohio Valley Manufacturing Inc............... D 419 522-5818
Mansfield (G-8841)

Omni Manufacturing Inc............... F 419 394-7424
Saint Marys (G-11748)

Omni Manufacturing Inc............... D 419 394-7424
Saint Marys (G-11747)

Orick Stamping Inc....................... D 419 331-0600
Elida (G-6484)

Pax Machine Works Inc................ D 419 586-2337
Celina (G-2114)

Peerless Metal Products Inc.........G 216 431-6905
Cleveland (G-4149)

Pennant Moldings Inc................... C 937 584-5411
Sabina (G-11682)

Pentaflex Inc................................. C 937 325-5551
Springfield (G-12360)

Phillips Mch & Stamping Corp............... G 330 882-6714
New Franklin (G-10392)

Precision Metal Products Inc............... E 216 447-1900
Cleveland (G-4185)

Precision Metal Products Inc............... F 216 447-1900
Cleveland (G-4186)

Qfm Stamping Inc.........................G 330 337-3311
Columbiana (G-4625)

Quality Fabricated Metals Inc............... F
Salem (G-11808)

Quality Stamping Products Co............... F 216 441-2700
Cleveland (G-4217)

Quality Tool Company.................... E 419 476-8228
Toledo (G-13105)

R K Metals Ltd.............................. E 513 874-6055
Fairfield (G-6771)

R L Rush Tool & Pattern Inc............... G 419 562-9849
Bucyrus (G-1687)

Ratliff Metal Spinning Company.......... E 937 836-3900
Englewood (G-6622)

RB&w Manufacturing LLC................ G 234 380-8540
Streetsboro (G-12519)

Rjm Stamping Co.......................... F 614 443-1191
Pickerington (G-11300)

Ronfeldt Manufacturing LLC........... F 419 382-5641
Toledo (G-13119)

Ronlen Industries Inc.................... E 330 273-6468
Brunswick (G-1613)

Sadler Corporation........................G 330 688-0009
Stow (G-12455)

Schott Metal Products Company........... G 330 773-7873
Akron (G-307)

Service Stampings Inc................... E 440 946-2330
Willoughby (G-14522)

Seven Ranges Mfg Corp................ E 330 627-7155
Carrollton (G-2090)

Shl Liquidation Industries Inc............... D 440 647-2100
Wellington (G-13901)

Smithville Mfg Co.......................... F 330 345-5818
Wooster (G-14687)

Spirol Shim Corporation................ E 330 920-3655
Stow (G-12462)

Stamp & Flash Inc......................... D 419 335-3015
Wauseon (G-13859)

Stamped Steel Products Inc................ F 330 538-3951
North Jackson (G-10695)

Stolle Machinery Company LLC........... C 937 497-5400
Sidney (G-12056)

Stripmatic Products Inc................. E 216 241-7143
Cleveland (G-4336)

Sunfield Inc.................................. D 740 928-0405
Hebron (G-7638)

Supply Technologies LLC................ G 937 898-5795
Dayton (G-6032)

Supply Technologies LLC................ C 440 947-2100
Cleveland (G-4351)

Takumi Stamping Inc..................... C 513 642-0081
Fairfield (G-6780)

Talan Products Inc........................ D 216 458-0170
Cleveland (G-4363)

Taylor Metal Products Co............... C 419 522-3471
Mansfield (G-8857)

The Kordenbrock Tool and Die Co........ F 513 326-4390
Cincinnati (G-3148)

The Pioneer Tool and Die Co.......... D 330 724-5572
Akron (G-332)

The Reliable Spring Wire Frms....... E 440 365-7400
Elyria (G-6595)

Toledo Tool and Die Co Inc............. C 419 476-4422
Toledo (G-13161)

Torrmetal LLC............................... E 216 671-1616
Cleveland (G-4405)

Torrmetal Corporation................... E 216 671-1616
Cleveland (G-4406)

Transue & Williams Stampg Corp........ E 330 821-5777
Austintown (G-708)

United Die & Mfg Sales Co............. E 330 938-6141
Sebring (G-11904)

Universal Metal Products Inc.......... E 419 287-3223
Pemberville (G-11178)

Universal Metal Products Inc.......... C 440 943-3040
Wickliffe (G-14399)

Varbros LLC.................................. D 216 267-5200
Cleveland (G-4457)

Wedge Products Inc....................... B 330 405-4477
Twinsburg (G-13395)

Westlake Tool & Die Mfg Co........... D 440 934-5305
Avon (G-742)

WLS Stamping Co.......................... D 216 271-5100
Cleveland (G-4511)

Wtd Real Estate Inc....................... D 440 934-5305
Avon (G-745)

METAL STAMPINGS: Perforated

A J Rose Mfg Co........................... C 216 631-4645
Avon (G-710)

METAL TREATING COMPOUNDS

Broco Products Inc....................... G 216 531-0880
Cleveland (G-3441)

Ferrum Industries Inc................... G 440 519-1768
Twinsburg (G-13303)

Northern Chem Blnding Corp Inc........ G 216 781-7799
Cleveland (G-4093)

METAL, TITANIUM: Sponge & Granules

Advance Materials Products Inc............ G 330 650-4000
Hudson (G-7827)

METAL: Battery

Cleanlife Energy LLC..................... F 800 316-2532
Cleveland (G-3503)

METALS SVC CENTERS & WHOLESALERS: Cable, Wire

Nimers & Woody II Inc................... C 937 454-0722
Vandalia (G-13574)

Radix Wire Co............................... D 216 731-9191
Solon (G-12173)

METALS SVC CENTERS & WHOLESALERS: Ferrous Metals

Curtis Steel & Supply Inc.............. F 330 376-7141
Akron (G-110)

METALS SVC CENTERS & WHOLESALERS: Flat Prdts, Iron Or Steel

H & D Steel Service Inc................. E 800 666-3390
North Royalton (G-10764)

Major Metals Company................... E 419 886-4600
Mansfield (G-8815)

METALS SVC CENTERS & WHOLESALERS: Pipe & Tubing, Steel

McWane Inc................................... B 740 622-6651
Coshocton (G-5459)

Pipe Products Inc.......................... C 513 587-7532
West Chester (G-14049)

Shaq Inc....................................... D 770 427-0402
Beachwood (G-949)

METALS SVC CENTERS & WHOLESALERS: Sheets, Metal

Rockwell Metals Company LLC........... F 440 242-2420
Lorain (G-8579)

METALS SVC CENTERS & WHOLESALERS: Steel

Alro Steel Corporation................... E 614 878-7271
Columbus (G-4690)

Alro Steel Corporation................... E 937 253-6121
Dayton (G-5648)

Alro Steel Corporation................... D 419 720-5300
Toledo (G-12871)

Aluminum Line Products Company....... D 440 835-8880
Westlake (G-14285)

AM Castle & Co............................. F 330 425-7000
Bedford (G-1011)

American Ir Met Cleveland LLC........... E 216 266-0509
Cleveland (G-3345)

American Posts LLC....................... D 419 720-0652
Toledo (G-12877)

B&A Ison Steel Inc......................... F 216 663-4300
Cleveland (G-3400)

Berkshire Road Holdings Inc............... F 216 883-4200
Cleveland (G-3416)

Bico Akron Inc.............................. D 330 794-1716
Mogadore (G-10070)

Clifton Capital Holdings LLC............ F 330 562-9000
Maple Heights (G-8880)

Clifton Steel Company.................... D 216 662-6111
Maple Heights (G-8881)

Contractors Steel Company............ D 330 425-3050
Twinsburg (G-13289)

Coventry Steel Services Inc........... G 216 883-4477
Cleveland (G-3571)

Grenga Machine & Welding............. F 330 743-1113
Youngstown (G-14871)

Hickman Williams & Company............ F 513 621-1946
Cincinnati (G-2721)

JSW Steel USA Ohio Inc................. B 740 535-8172
Mingo Junction (G-10052)

Lapham-Hickey Steel Corp............. D 614 443-4881
Columbus (G-5065)

Latrobe Spcialty Mtls Dist Inc............... D 330 609-5137
Vienna *(G-13610)*

Louis Arthur Steel Company.................. G 440 997-5545
Geneva *(G-7241)*

Master-Halco Inc............................... F 513 869-7600
Fairfield *(G-6751)*

McDonald Steel Plate Inc.................... F 216 883-4200
Cleveland *(G-4008)*

McOn Inds Inc.................................... E 937 294-2681
Moraine *(G-10176)*

Mid-America Steel Corp....................... E 800 282-3466
Cleveland *(G-4033)*

Monarch Steel Company Inc................. E 216 587-8000
Cleveland *(G-4045)*

Remington Steel Inc........................... D 937 322-2414
Springfield *(G-12370)*

Rex Welding Inc................................ F 740 387-1650
Marion *(G-8992)*

Rolled Alloys Inc............................... D 800 521-0332
Maumee *(G-9315)*

Samuel Son & Co (usa) Inc.................. D 740 522-2500
Heath *(G-7604)*

Sausser Steel Company Inc................. G 419 422-9632
Findlay *(G-6916)*

Scot Industries Inc............................. C 330 262-7585
Wooster *(G-14683)*

St Lawrence Holdings LLC.................. E 330 562-9000
Maple Heights *(G-8892)*

St Lawrence Steel Corporation............ E 330 562-9000
Maple Heights *(G-8893)*

Thyssenkrupp Materials NA Inc............ D 216 883-8100
Independence *(G-7921)*

Tomson Steel Company...................... E 513 420-8600
Middletown *(G-9900)*

Universal Steel Company.................... D 216 883-4972
Cleveland *(G-4448)*

Westfield Steel Inc............................. D 937 322-2414
Springfield *(G-12392)*

Youngstown Specialty Mtls Inc............ G 330 259-1110
Youngstown *(G-14976)*

METALS SVC CENTERS & WHOLESALERS: Tubing, Metal

Swagelok Company............................. D 440 349-5934
Solon *(G-12191)*

Tubular Techniques Inc....................... G 614 529-4130
Hilliard *(G-7708)*

METALS: Precious NEC

Metallic Resources Inc....................... E 330 425-3155
Twinsburg *(G-13340)*

METALS: Precious, Secondary

Auris Noble LLC................................ E 330 321-6649
Akron *(G-64)*

Elemetal Refining LLC........................ C 740 286-6457
Jackson *(G-7944)*

Materion Brush Inc............................. D 216 486-4200
Mayfield Heights *(G-9336)*

Materion Corporation.......................... C 216 486-4200
Mayfield Heights *(G-9337)*

Mek Van Wert Inc.............................. G 419 203-4902
Van Wert *(G-13542)*

Ohio Metal Processing LLC................. G 740 912-2057
Jackson *(G-7949)*

METALS: Primary Nonferrous, NEC

Aci Industries Ltd.............................. E 740 368-4160
Delaware *(G-6128)*

American Friction Tech LLC................. D 216 823-0861
Cleveland *(G-3343)*

American Spring Wire Corp.................. C 216 292-4620
Bedford Heights *(G-1068)*

AMG Aluminum North America LLC....... F 659 348-3620
Cambridge *(G-1735)*

Elemetal Refining LLC........................ C 740 286-6457
Jackson *(G-7944)*

Elmet Euclid LLC............................... D 216 692-3990
Euclid *(G-6648)*

Elmet Technologies Inc....................... F 216 692-3990
Cleveland *(G-3663)*

Galt Alloys Inc Main Ofc...................... G 330 453-4678
Canton *(G-1897)*

Rhenium Alloys Inc............................ E 440 365-7388
North Ridgeville *(G-10747)*

Swift Manufacturing Co Inc.................. G 740 237-4405
Ironton *(G-7935)*

METALWORK: Miscellaneous

Active Metal and Molds Inc.................. F 419 281-9623
Ashland *(G-514)*

Advance Industrial Mfg Inc.................. E 614 871-3333
Grove City *(G-7367)*

Arrow Tru-Line Inc............................. G 419 636-7013
Bryan *(G-1630)*

Buckeye Stamping Company................ D 877 728-0776
Columbus *(G-4786)*

Burghardt Metal Fabg Inc.................... F 330 794-1830
Akron *(G-87)*

Custom Control Tech LLC................... G 419 342-5593
Shelby *(G-11969)*

Fc Industries Inc............................... E 937 275-8700
Dayton *(G-5774)*

Fortin Welding & Mfg Inc..................... E 614 291-4342
Columbus *(G-4934)*

Kenton Strl & Orn Ir Works.................. D 419 674-4025
Kenton *(G-8103)*

Markley Enterprises LLC..................... E 513 771-1290
Cincinnati *(G-2847)*

Matteo Aluminum Inc.......................... E 440 585-5213
Wickliffe *(G-14382)*

Metal Sales Manufacturing Corp........... E 440 319-3779
Jefferson *(G-7978)*

Metalfab Group.................................. G 440 543-6234
Streetsboro *(G-12509)*

Ohio Moulding Corporation................... E 440 944-2100
Wickliffe *(G-14385)*

Precision Impacts LLC........................ D 937 530-8254
Miamisburg *(G-9728)*

Simcote Inc...................................... F 740 382-5000
Marion *(G-8999)*

T J F Inc.. F 419 878-4400
Waterville *(G-13843)*

Ver-Mac Industries Inc....................... E 740 397-6511
Mount Vernon *(G-10268)*

Watteredge LLC................................ D 440 933-6110
Avon Lake *(G-773)*

Will-Burt Company............................. F 330 682-7015
Orrville *(G-11019)*

Will-Burt Company............................. C 330 682-7015
Orrville *(G-11018)*

METALWORK: Ornamental

Cozmyk Enterprises Inc...................... F 614 231-1370
Columbus *(G-4856)*

Finelli Ornamental Iron Co................... E 440 248-0050
Cleveland *(G-3717)*

Fortin Welding & Mfg Inc..................... E 614 291-4342
Columbus *(G-4934)*

L & L Ornamental Iron Co................... E 513 353-1930
Cleves *(G-4543)*

Newman Brothers Inc.......................... G
Cincinnati *(G-2905)*

P & L Metalcrafts LLC........................ F 330 793-2178
Youngstown *(G-14908)*

Tarrier Steel Company Inc................... E 614 444-4000
Columbus *(G-5311)*

METALWORKING MACHINERY WHOLESALERS

Advanced Tech Utilization Co............... F 440 238-3770
Strongsville *(G-12532)*

METERING DEVICES: Flow Meters, Impeller & Counter Driven

Bif Co LLC....................................... F 330 564-0941
Akron *(G-79)*

METERING DEVICES: Water Quality Monitoring & Control Systems

American Water Services Inc................ G 440 243-9840
Strongsville *(G-12536)*

METERS: Pyrometers, Indl Process

Marlin Manufacturing Corp................... D 216 676-1340
Cleveland *(G-3990)*

MICROCIRCUITS, INTEGRATED: Semiconductor

Smart Microsystems Ltd...................... F 440 366-4257
Elyria *(G-6590)*

MICROPHONES

Cochran 6573 LLC............................. F 440 349-4900
Solon *(G-12097)*

MICROPROCESSORS

AT&T Enterprises LLC........................ G 513 792-9300
Cincinnati *(G-2384)*

Salient Systems Inc............................ E 614 792-5800
Dublin *(G-6343)*

MICROWAVE COMPONENTS

Berry Investments Inc......................... G 937 293-0398
Moraine *(G-10150)*

MILITARY INSIGNIA

Gayston Corporation........................... C 937 743-6050
Miamisburg *(G-9693)*

MILL PRDTS: Structural & Rail

Bd Laplace LLC................................. B 985 652-4900
Cleveland *(G-3410)*

MILLWORK

1914 Mi Inc...................................... E 330 308-8667
New Philadelphia *(G-10428)*

A & J Woodworking Inc....................... G 419 695-5655
Delphos *(G-6183)*

Aca Millworks Inc.............................. F 419 339-7600
Waynesfield *(G-13877)*

Ace Lumber Company........................ F 330 744-3167
Youngstown *(G-14804)*

Advantage Tent Fittings Inc................. F 740 773-3015
Chillicothe *(G-2241)*

Ailes Millwork Inc.............................. F 330 678-4300
Kent *(G-8015)*

Anthony Flottemesch & Son Inc........... F 513 561-1212
Cincinnati *(G-2371)*

Art Woodworking & Mfg Co.................. E 513 681-2986
Cincinnati *(G-2379)*

Automated Bldg Components Inc........... E 419 257-2152
North Baltimore *(G-10612)*

PRODUCT

Bruewer Woodwork Mfg Co D .... 513 353-3505 Cleves *(G-4532)*	**Menard Inc** C .... 513 583-1444 Loveland *(G-8642)*	**Trimco** G .... 614 679-3931 Westerville *(G-14238)*
C & W Custom Wdwkg Co Inc G .... 513 891-6340 Cincinnati *(G-2435)*	**Midwest Commercial Mllwk Inc** F .... 419 224-5001 Lima *(G-8433)*	**Tuscarora Wood Midwest LLC** G .... 937 603-8882 Covington *(G-5500)*
Carter-Jones Lumber Company G .... 330 674-9060 Millersburg *(G-9975)*	**Miller Manufacturing Inc** G .... 330 852-0689 Sugarcreek *(G-12642)*	**Volpe Millwork Inc** G .... 216 581-0200 Cleveland *(G-4480)*
Cassady Woodworks Inc F .... 937 256-7948 Dayton *(G-5605)*	**Millwood Wholesale Inc** F .... 330 359-6109 Dundee *(G-6369)*	**Wengerd Wood Inc** F .... 330 359-4300 Dundee *(G-6372)*
Cincinnati Stair & Handrail F .... 513 722-3947 Cincinnati *(G-2486)*	**Millwork Elements LLC** G .... 614 905-8163 Columbus *(G-5103)*	**Whitmer Woodworks Inc** G .... 614 873-1196 Plain City *(G-11427)*
Cindoco Wood Products Co G .... 937 444-2504 Mount Orab *(G-10216)*	**Nagele Manufacturing Company** E .... 216 433-1100 Cleveland *(G-4057)*	**Wittrock Wdwkg & Mfg Co Inc** D .... 513 891-5800 Blue Ash *(G-1351)*
Cox Interior Inc G .... 614 473-9169 Columbus *(G-4855)*	**National Door and Trim Inc** E .... 419 238-9345 Van Wert *(G-13543)*	**Wood Creations** G .... 419 692-2624 Delphos *(G-6200)*
Decker Custom Wood Llc G .... 419 332-3464 Fremont *(G-7103)*	**Oak Pointe Legacy LLC** E .... 740 498-9820 Newcomerstown *(G-10573)*	**Woodcraft Industries Inc** E .... 440 632-9655 Middlefield *(G-9836)*
Dendratec Ltd G .... 330 473-4878 Dalton *(G-5583)*	**Ogonek Custom Hardwood Inc** G .... 833 718-2531 Barberton *(G-827)*	**Woodworks Design** G .... 440 693-4414 Middlefield *(G-9837)*
Denoon Lumber Company LLC D .... 740 768-2220 Bergholz *(G-1195)*	**Ohio Woodworking Co Inc** G .... 513 631-0870 Cincinnati *(G-2927)*	**Yoder Lumber Co Inc** D .... 330 893-3121 Millersburg *(G-10020)*
Display Dynamics Inc F .... 937 832-2830 Englewood *(G-6612)*	**P & T Millwork Inc** F .... 440 543-2151 Chagrin Falls *(G-2175)*	**Youngstown Shade & Alum LLC** G .... 330 782-2373 Youngstown *(G-14975)*
Dublin Millwork Co Inc F .... 614 889-7776 Dublin *(G-6294)*	**Ply-Trim Inc** E .... 330 799-7876 Youngstown *(G-14917)*	**Yutzy Woodworking Ltd** E .... 330 359-6166 Dundee *(G-6374)*
Encompass Woodworking LLC G .... 513 569-2841 Cincinnati *(G-2587)*	**Precise Custom Millwork Inc** G .... 614 539-7855 Grove City *(G-7408)*	
Fdi Cabinetry LLC G .... 513 353-4500 Cleves *(G-4537)*	**Profac Inc** D .... 440 942-0205 Mentor *(G-9594)*	## MINE & QUARRY SVCS: Nonmetallic Minerals
Fifth Avenue Lumber Co E .... 614 833-6655 Canal Winchester *(G-1790)*	**Profac Inc** C .... 440 942-0205 Mentor *(G-9593)*	**M G Q Inc** E .... 419 992-4236 Tiffin *(G-12788)*
Fixture Dimensions Inc E .... 513 360-7512 Liberty Twp *(G-8384)*	**Ramsey Stairs & Wdwkg LLC** G .... 614 694-2101 Columbus *(G-5223)*	**Stoepfel Drilling Co** G .... 419 532-3307 Ottawa *(G-11048)*
Forum Works LLC E .... 937 349-8685 Milford Center *(G-9957)*	**Rebsco Inc** F .... 937 548-2246 Greenville *(G-7351)*	## MINE DEVELOPMENT SVCS: Nonmetallic Minerals
Gerstenslager Construction G .... 330 832-3604 Massillon *(G-9195)*	**Renewal By Andersen LLC** G .... 614 781-9600 Columbus *(G-4649)*	**Robin Industries Inc** E .... 330 893-3501 Berlin *(G-1199)*
Greenhart Rstoration Mllwk LLC G .... 330 502-6050 Boardman *(G-1373)*	**Rinos Woodworking Shop Inc** F .... 440 946-1718 Willoughby *(G-14518)*	## MINE PREPARATION SVCS
Gross & Sons Custom Millwork G .... 419 227-0214 Lima *(G-8411)*	**Riverside Cnstr Svcs Inc** E .... 513 723-0900 Cincinnati *(G-3048)*	**Strata Mine Services LLC** F .... 740 695-0488 Saint Clairsville *(G-11713)*
Hardwood Lumber Company Inc F .... 440 834-1891 Middlefield *(G-9797)*	**Robertson Cabinets Inc** G .... 937 698-3755 West Milton *(G-14185)*	## MINERAL WOOL
Heartland Stairways Inc G .... 330 279-2554 Holmesville *(G-7796)*	**Roettger Hardwood Inc** G .... 937 693-6811 Kettlersville *(G-8125)*	**Autoneum North America Inc** B .... 419 693-0511 Oregon *(G-10957)*
Hj Systems Inc F .... 614 351-9777 Columbus *(G-4989)*	**Rush Fixture & Millwork Co** F .... 216 241-9100 Cleveland *(G-4265)*	**ICP Adhesives and Sealants Inc** E .... 330 753-4585 Norton *(G-10823)*
Holmes Custom Moulding Ltd E .... 330 893-3598 Millersburg *(G-9988)*	**S Holley Lumber LLC** S .... 440 272-5315 Windsor *(G-14603)*	**Johns Manville Corporation** D .... 419 782-0180 Defiance *(G-6113)*
Holmes Lumber & Bldg Ctr Inc E .... 330 479-8314 Canton *(G-1912)*	**Salem Mill & Cabinet Co** G .... 330 337-9568 Salem *(G-11810)*	**Kinetics Noise Control Inc** C .... 614 889-0480 Dublin *(G-6316)*
Holmes Lumber & Bldg Ctr Inc C .... 330 674-9060 Millersburg *(G-9989)*	**Sheridan Woodworks Inc** G .... 216 663-9333 Cleveland *(G-4292)*	**Owens Corning Sales LLC** E .... 614 399-3915 Mount Vernon *(G-10255)*
Hyde Park Lumber Company E .... 513 271-1500 Cincinnati *(G-2736)*	**Solid Surface Concepts Inc** E .... 513 948-8677 Cincinnati *(G-3099)*	**Premier Manufacturing Corp** C .... 216 941-9700 Cleveland *(G-4190)*
Judy Mills Company Inc E .... 513 271-4241 Cincinnati *(G-2775)*	**Stein Inc** F .... 419 747-2611 Mansfield *(G-8854)*	**Refractory Specialties Inc** E .... 330 938-2101 Sebring *(G-11900)*
L and J Woodworking F .... 330 359-3216 Dundee *(G-6367)*	**Stephen M Trudick** E .... 440 834-1891 Burton *(G-1704)*	**Sorbothane Inc** E .... 330 678-9444 Kent *(G-8081)*
Liechty Specialties Inc G .... 419 445-6696 Archbold *(G-500)*	**Stratton Creek Wood Works LLC** F .... 330 876-0005 Kinsman *(G-8143)*	**Tectum Inc** C .... 740 345-9691 Newark *(G-10535)*
Lima Millwork Inc G .... 419 331-3303 Elida *(G-6483)*	**Summit Millwork LLC** G .... 330 920-4000 Cuyahoga Falls *(G-5575)*	## MINERAL WOOL INSULATION PRDTS
M H Woodworking LLC F .... 330 893-3929 Millersburg *(G-9995)*	**T & D Thompson Inc** F .... 740 332-8515 Laurelville *(G-8238)*	**Fibreboard Corporation** C .... 419 248-8000 Toledo *(G-12963)*
Mac Lean J S Co G .... 614 878-5454 Columbus *(G-5078)*	**Ted Bolle Millwork Inc** F .... 937 325-8779 Springfield *(G-12385)*	## MINERALS: Ground Or Otherwise Treated
McCoy Group Inc G .... 330 753-1041 Barberton *(G-821)*	**The F A Requarth Company** E .... 937 224-1141 Dayton *(G-6048)*	**Cimbar Performance Mnrl WV LLC** E .... 330 532-2034 Wellsville *(G-13912)*
Menard Inc F .... 513 250-4566 Cincinnati *(G-2863)*	**The Galehouse Companies Inc** E .... 330 658-2023 Doylestown *(G-6270)*	**Covia Solutions LLC** G .... 440 214-3200 Independence *(G-7895)*
Menard Inc D .... 419 998-4348 Lima *(G-8429)*	**Todco** F .... 740 223-2542 Marion *(G-9002)*	

Kish Company Inc.............................F 440 205-9970
Mentor (G-9546)

MINERALS: Ground or Treated

Acme Company.................................D 330 758-2313
Poland (G-11434)

Aquablok Ltd....................................F 419 825-1325
Swanton (G-12679)

Continental Mineral Process.............E 513 771-7190
Cincinnati (G-2513)

Edw C Levy Co.................................G 330 484-6328
Canton (G-1884)

Edw C Levy Co.................................G 419 822-8286
Delta (G-6205)

EMD Millipore Corporation................C 513 631-0445
Norwood (G-10868)

Ethima Inc.......................................D 419 626-4912
Sandusky (G-11834)

GRB Holdings Inc..............................G 937 236-3250
Dayton (G-5802)

Harbison Walker Intl Mnrl Inc..........G 513 251-1010
Cincinnati (G-2705)

Howard Industries Inc.......................F 614 444-9900
Columbus (G-4993)

Industrial Quartz Corporation...........F 440 942-0909
Mentor (G-9530)

Reed Minerals LLC.............................E 216 652-2002
Niles (G-10601)

Seaforth Mineral & Ore Co Inc...........F 216 292-5820
Beachwood (G-948)

MINIATURES

Country Lane Custom Buildings...........G 740 485-8481
Danville (G-5598)

On The Mantle LLC............................G 740 702-1803
Chillicothe (G-2268)

Precise Models Inc............................G 440 365-5701
Elyria (G-6582)

MINING EXPLORATION & DEVELOPMENT SVCS

Galt Alloys Enterprise........................F 330 309-8194
Canton (G-1896)

Omega Cementing Co.........................G 330 695-7147
Apple Creek (G-474)

MINING MACHINERY & EQPT WHOLESALERS

Unified Scrning Crshing - OH I............G 937 836-3201
Englewood (G-6627)

Valence Industrial LLC.......................E 877 330-2354
Sidney (G-12058)

MINING MACHINES & EQPT: Crushers, Stationary

Grasan Equipment Company Inc..........D 419 526-4440
Mansfield (G-8797)

MIXTURES & BLOCKS: Asphalt Paving

Advanced Fiber LLC............................E 419 562-1337
Bucyrus (G-1671)

All Coatings Co Inc............................G 330 821-3806
Alliance (G-367)

Allied Corporation Inc........................F 330 425-7861
Twinsburg (G-13272)

Asphalt Fabrics & Specialties.............E 440 786-1077
Solon (G-12080)

Atlas Roofing Corporation..................C 937 746-9941
Franklin (G-7010)

Bluffton Stone Co..............................F 419 358-6941
Bluffton (G-1358)

Bowerston Shale Company..................E 740 269-2921
Bowerston (G-1399)

Brewer Company................................G 800 394-0017
Milford (G-9926)

Crafco Inc..F 330 270-3034
Youngstown (G-14841)

Extendit Company.............................G 330 743-4343
New Springfield (G-10473)

Gbr Property Maintenance LLC............F 937 879-0200
Fairborn (G-6693)

Heidelberg Mtls Mdwest Agg Inc.........G 419 983-2211
Bloomville (G-1240)

Holmes Supply Corp..........................G 330 279-2634
Holmesville (G-7799)

Hy-Grade Corporation.......................E 216 341-7711
Cleveland (G-3846)

Image Pavement Maintenance.............G 937 833-9200
Brookville (G-1571)

Mae Materials LLC.............................E 740 778-2242
South Webster (G-12231)

Mar-Zane Inc....................................F 740 453-0721
Zanesville (G-15026)

Miller Bros Paving Inc........................F 419 445-1015
Archbold (G-503)

Mplx Terminals LLC............................F 330 479-5539
Canton (G-1952)

Reading Rock Incorporated.................D 513 874-2345
Cincinnati (G-3034)

Rutland Township.............................G 740 742-2805
Bidwell (G-1214)

Seal Master Corporation.....................E 330 673-8410
Kent (G-8075)

Shelly and Sands Inc..........................E 740 859-2104
Rayland (G-11552)

Shelly Materials Inc...........................F 419 622-2101
Convoy (G-5425)

Shelly Materials Inc...........................E 740 246-5009
Thornville (G-12769)

Shelly Materials Inc...........................G 419 273-2510
Forest (G-6941)

Sidwell Materials Inc.........................C 740 849-2422
Zanesville (G-15050)

Smalls Asphalt Paving Inc...................G 740 427-4096
Gambier (G-7214)

Smith & Thompson Entps LLC..............F 330 386-9345
East Liverpool (G-6397)

Stark Materials Inc............................F 330 497-1648
Canton (G-2014)

Stoneco Inc......................................E 419 393-2555
Oakwood (G-10900)

Thorworks Industries Inc....................C 419 626-4375
Sandusky (G-11876)

Valley Asphalt Corporation.................G 513 381-0652
Morrow (G-10203)

MOBILE COMMUNICATIONS EQPT

Eei Acquisition Corp..........................E 440 564-5484
Middlefield (G-9793)

Engineered Endeavors Inc...................E 440 564-5484
Newbury (G-10550)

Estone Group LLC..............................E 888 653-2246
Toledo (G-12957)

Sagequest LLC..................................D 216 896-7243
Solon (G-12177)

Wireless Retail LLC............................F 614 657-5182
Blacklick (G-1231)

MOBILE HOMES

Clayton Homes...................................F 937 592-3039
Bellefontaine (G-1101)

Mobile Conversions Inc......................F 513 797-1991
Amelia (G-434)

Skyline Corporation...........................C 330 852-2483
Sugarcreek (G-12650)

MOBILE HOMES, EXC RECREATIONAL

Manufactured Housing Entps Inc.........F 419 636-4511
Bryan (G-1650)

MOBILE HOMES: Personal Or Private Use

Palm Harbor Homes Inc......................G 937 725-9465
New Vienna (G-10475)

MODELS: General, Exc Toy

3-D Technical Services Company...........E 937 746-2901
Franklin (G-7006)

Anza Inc...G 513 542-7337
Cincinnati (G-2372)

King Model Company..........................E 330 633-0491
Akron (G-197)

MODULES: Computer Logic

Ezurio LLC..D 330 434-7929
Akron (G-141)

MOLDED RUBBER PRDTS

Action Rubber Co Inc..........................F 937 866-5975
Dayton (G-5633)

American Rubber Pdts Co Inc...............G 440 461-0900
Solon (G-12079)

ARC Rubber Inc..................................F 440 466-4555
Geneva (G-7233)

Cardinal Rubber Company...................E 330 745-2191
Barberton (G-801)

Chardon Custom Polymers LLC............F 440 285-2161
Chardon (G-2197)

Clark Rubber & Plastic Company..........C 440 255-9793
Mentor (G-9500)

Contitech Usa Llc...............................F 330 664-7000
Akron (G-105)

Cooper-Standard Holdings Inc.............G 800 683-0676
New Philadelphia (G-10438)

Custom Rubber Corporation................D 216 391-2928
Cleveland (G-3587)

Datwyler Sling Sltions USA Inc.............D 937 387-2800
Vandalia (G-13554)

Eaton Aeroquip LLC............................C 440 523-5000
Cleveland (G-3650)

Enduro Rubber Company.....................G 330 296-9603
Ravenna (G-11524)

Hytech Silicone Products Inc...............G 330 297-1888
Ravenna (G-11528)

Ier Fujikura Inc..................................C 330 425-7121
Macedonia (G-8696)

James K Green Enterprises Inc............G 614 878-6041
Columbus (G-5031)

Jet Rubber Company..........................E 330 325-1821
Rootstown (G-11648)

Karman Rubber Company....................D 330 864-2161
Akron (G-191)

Lauren International Ltd......................C 234 303-2400
New Philadelphia (G-10454)

Macdivitt Rubber Company LLC...........E 440 259-5937
Perry (G-11195)

May Lin Silicone Products Inc..............G 330 825-9019
Barberton (G-820)

Mullins Rubber Products Inc................D 937 233-4211
Dayton (G-5898)

Neff-Perkins Company........................D 440 632-1658
Middlefield (G-9818)

Newact Inc..F 513 321-5177
Batavia (G-879)

Ottawa Rubber Company...................... F 419 865-1378
Holland *(G-7775)*

Park-Ohio Holdings Corp....................... F 440 947-2000
Cleveland *(G-4136)*

Park-Ohio Industries Inc......................... C 440 947-2000
Cleveland *(G-4137)*

Park-Ohio Products Inc........................... D 216 961-7200
Cleveland *(G-4138)*

Parkohio Worldwide LLC.......................... E 440 947-2000
Cleveland *(G-4146)*

Plabell Rubber Products Corp............... E 419 691-5878
Toledo *(G-13101)*

Q Model Inc.. F 330 733-6545
Akron *(G-271)*

Qualiform Inc... E 330 336-6777
Wadsworth *(G-13663)*

Raydar Inc of Ohio.................................. G 330 334-6111
Wadsworth *(G-13666)*

Robin Industries Inc............................... E 330 893-3501
Berlin *(G-1199)*

Robin Industries Inc............................... C 330 695-9300
Fredericksburg *(G-7070)*

Robin Industries Inc............................... D 330 359-5418
Winesburg *(G-14608)*

Robin Industries Inc............................... F 216 631-7000
North Canton *(G-10665)*

Rubber Associates Inc........................... D 330 745-2186
New Franklin *(G-10394)*

Rubber-Tech Inc...................................... F 937 274-1114
Dayton *(G-5989)*

Sorbothane Inc....................................... E 330 678-9444
Kent *(G-8081)*

Sumiriko Ohio Inc................................... D 419 358-2121
Bluffton *(G-1365)*

Sur-Seal LLC... C 513 574-8500
Cincinnati *(G-3130)*

The R C A Rubber Company.................. D 330 784-1291
Akron *(G-333)*

Tmi Inc... E 330 270-9780
Youngstown *(G-14948)*

Tristan Rubber Molding Inc.................... F 330 499-4055
North Canton *(G-10678)*

Universal Polymer & Rubber Ltd........... F 330 633-1666
Tallmadge *(G-12757)*

Universal Polymer & Rubber Ltd........... C 440 632-1691
Middlefield *(G-9834)*

Universal Urethane Pdts Inc.................. D 419 693-7400
Toledo *(G-13169)*

Vernay Manufacturing Inc...................... E 404 994-2000
Yellow Springs *(G-14791)*

Woodlawn Rubber Co............................. F 513 489-1718
Blue Ash *(G-1353)*

Yokohama Inds Amricas Ohio Inc......... D 440 352-3321
Painesville *(G-11124)*

MOLDING COMPOUNDS

Ada Solutions Inc................................... G 440 576-0423
Jefferson *(G-7971)*

Clyde Tool & Die Inc............................... F 419 547-9574
Clyde *(G-4557)*

Dentsply Sirona Inc................................ E 419 865-9497
Maumee *(G-9291)*

Flex Technologies Inc............................. D 330 897-6311
Baltic *(G-777)*

Hpc Holdings LLC.................................. F 330 666-3751
Fairlawn *(G-6804)*

Incredible Solutions Inc......................... F 330 898-3878
Warren *(G-13772)*

Industrial Thermoset Plas Inc............... F 440 975-0411
Mentor *(G-9531)*

Jain America Foods Inc.......................... G 614 850-9400
Columbus *(G-5030)*

JMS Industries Inc.................................. F 937 325-3502
Springfield *(G-12332)*

Lyondllbsell Advnced Plymers I............. C 330 773-2700
Akron *(G-213)*

Lyondllbsell Advnced Plymers I............. C 330 630-0308
Akron *(G-214)*

Lyondllbsell Advnced Plymers I............. D 330 630-3315
Akron *(G-215)*

Meggitt (erlanger) LLC........................... D 513 851-5550
Cincinnati *(G-2858)*

Michael Day Enterprises LLC................ E 330 335-5100
Wadsworth *(G-13650)*

Ohio Rotational Molding LLC................. E 419 608-5040
Findlay *(G-6901)*

Pace Mold & Machine LLC..................... G 330 879-1777
Massillon *(G-9231)*

Resinoid Engineering Corp.................... D 740 928-6115
Hebron *(G-7633)*

Roechling Indus Cleveland LP............... E 216 486-0100
Cleveland *(G-4248)*

Uniloy Century LLC................................ D 419 332-2693
Fremont *(G-7140)*

Yoders Produce Inc................................ F 330 695-5900
Fredericksburg *(G-7073)*

MOLDINGS & TRIM: Metal, Exc Automobile

Aluminum Color Industries Inc.............. E 330 536-6295
Lowellville *(G-8657)*

MOLDINGS & TRIM: Wood

Armstrong Custom Moulding Inc........... G 740 922-5931
Uhrichsville *(G-13401)*

Dowel Yoder & Molding.......................... G 330 231-2962
Fredericksburg *(G-7063)*

Fairfield Wood Works Ltd....................... G 740 689-1953
Lancaster *(G-8201)*

Round Mate Systems.............................. G 419 675-3334
Kenton *(G-8114)*

MOLDINGS OR TRIM: Automobile, Stamped Metal

American Trim LLC.................................. A 419 228-1145
Sidney *(G-11991)*

Florida Production Engrg Inc................. D 937 996-4361
New Madison *(G-10421)*

Kasai North America Inc........................ C 419 209-0399
Upper Sandusky *(G-13444)*

Pennant Companies................................ E 614 451-1782
Sabina *(G-11681)*

TS Trim Industries Inc............................ B 614 837-4114
Canal Winchester *(G-1799)*

MOLDS: Gray, Ingot, Cast Iron

Anchor Glass Container Corp................ D 740 452-2743
Zanesville *(G-14987)*

Ellwood Engineered Castings Co.......... C 330 568-3000
Hubbard *(G-7810)*

Kenton Iron Products Inc....................... E 419 674-4178
Kenton *(G-8102)*

MOLDS: Indl

Aero Tech Tool & Mold Inc.................... G 440 942-3327
Mentor *(G-9471)*

Akron Centl Engrv Mold Mch Inc.......... E 330 794-8704
Akron *(G-26)*

American Cube Mold Inc........................ G 330 558-0044
Brunswick *(G-1580)*

Amerimold Inc... G 800 950-8020
Mogadore *(G-10069)*

Apollo Plastics Inc................................. F 440 951-7774
Mentor *(G-9484)*

Caliber Mold and Machine Inc............... E 330 633-8171
Akron *(G-88)*

Camden Concrete Products LLC............ G 937 456-1229
Eaton *(G-6451)*

Deca Mfg Co.. F 419 884-0071
Mansfield *(G-8780)*

Durivage Pattern and Mfg Inc............... E 419 836-8655
Williston *(G-14411)*

Esterle Mold & Machine Co Inc............. E 330 686-1685
Stow *(G-12429)*

Ferriot Inc... C 330 786-3000
Akron *(G-147)*

H&M Machine & Tool LLC...................... E 419 776-9220
Toledo *(G-12980)*

Herbert Usa Inc...................................... D 330 929-4297
Akron *(G-173)*

High-Tech Mold & Machine Inc.............. F 330 896-4466
Uniontown *(G-13420)*

J M Mold Inc.. G 937 778-0077
Piqua *(G-11360)*

Jamen Tool & Die Co.............................. E 330 782-6731
Youngstown *(G-14880)*

Kuhns Mold & Tool Co Inc..................... D 937 833-2178
Brookville *(G-1572)*

Liberty Die Cast Molds Inc.................... F 740 666-7492
Ostrander *(G-11028)*

Lightning Mold & Machine Inc............... F 440 593-6460
Conneaut *(G-5408)*

Magnum Molding Inc............................... G 937 368-3040
Conover *(G-5421)*

Mallory Pattern Works Inc..................... G 419 726-8001
Toledo *(G-13046)*

Maumee Pattern Company...................... E 419 693-4968
Toledo *(G-13049)*

Mercury Machine Co............................... D 440 349-3222
Solon *(G-12147)*

Midwest Mold & Texture Corp............... E 513 732-1300
Batavia *(G-873)*

Milacron Holdings Corp.......................... B 513 487-5000
Batavia *(G-874)*

Mold Surface Textures Inc..................... G 330 678-8590
Kent *(G-8055)*

Monitor Mold & Machine Co................... F 330 697-7800
Rootstown *(G-11650)*

New Castings Inc.................................... E 330 645-6653
Akron *(G-245)*

Nichols Mold Inc..................................... G 330 297-9719
Ravenna *(G-11534)*

Numerics Unlimited Inc.......................... E 937 849-0100
New Carlisle *(G-10377)*

Oakley Die & Mold Co............................ E 513 754-8500
Mason *(G-9131)*

Plastic Mold Technology Inc.................. G 330 848-4921
Barberton *(G-833)*

Precast Products LLC............................. E 419 668-1639
Norwalk *(G-10859)*

Reuther Mold & Mfg Co Inc................... D 330 923-5266
Cuyahoga Falls *(G-5569)*

Ron-Al Mold & Machine Inc.................... F 330 673-7919
Kent *(G-8070)*

Saehwa IMC Na Inc................................ D 330 645-6653
Akron *(G-304)*

Seaway Pattern Mfg Inc.......................... F 419 865-5724
Toledo *(G-13124)*

Stan-Kell LLC.. F 440 998-1116
Ashtabula *(G-617)*

Superior Mold & Die Co.......................... F 330 688-8251
Munroe Falls *(G-10273)*

Tempcraft Corporation........................... D 216 391-3885
Cleveland *(G-4372)*

Tom Smith Industries Inc....................... D 937 832-1555
Englewood *(G-6626)*

Tooling Technology LLC.........................D 937 381-9211
Fort Loramie *(G-6960)*

TW Manufacturing Co.............................G 440 439-3243
Cleveland *(G-4434)*

Velocity Concept Dev Group LLC..........G 740 685-2637
Byesville *(G-1717)*

XCEL Mold and Machine Inc..................F 330 499-8450
Canton *(G-2050)*

MOLYBDENUM SILICON, EXC MADE IN BLAST FURNACES

Newton Materion Inc...............................B 216 692-3990
Euclid *(G-6663)*

MOPS: Floor & Dust

Impact Products LLC...............................C 419 841-2891
Toledo *(G-13001)*

Twister Cleaning Tech Inc.......................G 865 521-3976
Toledo *(G-13167)*

MORTAR: High Temperature, Nonclay

Minteq International Inc...........................F 419 636-4561
Bryan *(G-1651)*

MOTOR & GENERATOR PARTS: Electric

Electrocraft Arkansas Inc.......................G 501 268-4203
Gallipolis *(G-7203)*

Global Innovative Products LLC.............G 513 701-0441
Lebanon *(G-8261)*

Parker-Hannifin Corporation...................C 330 336-3511
Wadsworth *(G-13659)*

Swiger Coil Systems Ltd........................C 216 362-7500
Cleveland *(G-4356)*

Wabtec Corporation................................F 216 362-7500
Cleveland *(G-4485)*

MOTOR CONTROL CENTERS

Sdk Associates Inc.................................G 330 745-3648
Norton *(G-10826)*

MOTOR HOMES

Advanced Rv LLC....................................E 440 283-0405
Willoughby *(G-14414)*

Airstream Inc...B 937 596-6111
Jackson Center *(G-7958)*

MOTOR SCOOTERS & PARTS

Dco LLC..E 419 931-9086
Perrysburg *(G-11213)*

MOTOR VEHICLE ASSEMBLY, COMPLETE: Ambulances

Braun Industries Inc...............................B 419 232-7020
Van Wert *(G-13528)*

La Boit Specialty Vehicles......................D 614 231-7640
Gahanna *(G-7164)*

MOTOR VEHICLE ASSEMBLY, COMPLETE: Buses, All Types

Eldorado National Kansas Inc.................C 937 596-6849
Jackson Center *(G-7962)*

MOTOR VEHICLE ASSEMBLY, COMPLETE: Fire Department Vehicles

Copley Fire & Rescue Assn.....................F 330 666-6464
Copley *(G-5433)*

Reberland Equipment Inc........................F 330 698-5883
Apple Creek *(G-476)*

Sutphen Corporation...............................C 800 726-7030
Dublin *(G-6353)*

MOTOR VEHICLE ASSEMBLY, COMPLETE: Military Motor Vehicle

Warfighter Fcsed Logistics Inc...............E 740 513-4692
West Chester *(G-14091)*

MOTOR VEHICLE ASSEMBLY, COMPLETE: Wreckers, Tow Truck

Horizon Global Corporation....................E 734 656-3000
Cleveland *(G-3837)*

Lawson Twing Auto Wrecking LLC..........F 216 883-9050
Cleveland *(G-3948)*

MOTOR VEHICLE DEALERS: Automobiles, New & Used

Doug Marine Motors Inc.........................F 740 335-3700
Wshngtn Ct Hs *(G-14738)*

Ford Motor Company..............................C 440 933-1215
Avon Lake *(G-756)*

Ford Motor Company..............................A 419 226-7000
Lima *(G-8408)*

General Motors LLC................................A 216 265-5000
Cleveland *(G-3767)*

General Motors LLC................................C 330 824-5840
Warren *(G-13768)*

Honda Dev & Mfg Amer LLC...................C 937 644-0724
Marysville *(G-9028)*

Jmac Inc..E 614 436-2418
Columbus *(G-5041)*

Knippen Chrysler Ddge Jeep Inc............F 419 695-4976
Delphos *(G-6188)*

Mitsubishi Chemical Amer Inc................D 419 483-2931
Bellevue *(G-1126)*

Mitsubishi Elc Auto Amer Inc.................B 513 573-6614
Mason *(G-9128)*

Mitsubishi Elc Automtn Inc.....................E 937 492-3058
Sidney *(G-12035)*

MOTOR VEHICLE DEALERS: Vans, New & Used

Steves Vans ACC Unlimited LLC............G 740 374-3154
Marietta *(G-8950)*

MOTOR VEHICLE PARTS & ACCESS: Acceleration Eqpt

Motherson Ychiyo Auto Tech PDT..........D 614 876-3220
Columbus *(G-5113)*

Oerlikon Friction Systems.......................E 937 449-4000
Dayton *(G-5922)*

MOTOR VEHICLE PARTS & ACCESS: Air Conditioner Parts

Aptiv Services Us LLC.............................B 330 306-1000
Warren *(G-13741)*

Ftd Investments LLC................................A 937 833-2161
Brookville *(G-1569)*

Hanon Systems Usa LLC.........................C 313 920-0583
Carey *(G-2058)*

Mahle Behr Dayton LLC...........................A 937 369-2900
Dayton *(G-5864)*

Taiho Corporation of America.................C 419 443-1645
Tiffin *(G-12801)*

MOTOR VEHICLE PARTS & ACCESS: Ball Joints

Torque 2020 CMA Acqisition LLC...........C 330 874-2900
Bolivar *(G-1393)*

MOTOR VEHICLE PARTS & ACCESS: Bearings

Green Acquisition LLC.............................F 440 930-7600
Avon *(G-728)*

Kyklos Bearing International Llc..............A 419 627-7000
Sandusky *(G-11848)*

MOTOR VEHICLE PARTS & ACCESS: Body Components & Frames

ARE Inc...A 330 830-7800
Massillon *(G-9172)*

Classic Reproductions.............................G 937 548-9839
Greenville *(G-7338)*

Frontier Tank Center Inc.........................G 330 659-3888
Richfield *(G-11593)*

Green Tokai Co Ltd..................................A 937 833-5444
Brookville *(G-1570)*

Magna Modular Systems LLC..................D 419 324-3387
Toledo *(G-13045)*

Oakley Inds Sub Assmbly Div In..............E 419 661-8888
Northwood *(G-10806)*

TS Tech USA Corporation........................B 614 577-1088
Reynoldsburg *(G-11584)*

MOTOR VEHICLE PARTS & ACCESS: Brakes, Air

Eaton Corporation...................................C 216 281-2211
Cleveland *(G-3653)*

Trulil Inc...C 937 652-1242
Urbana *(G-13479)*

MOTOR VEHICLE PARTS & ACCESS: Clutches

Luk Clutch Systems LLC.........................E 330 264-4383
Wooster *(G-14661)*

Pt Tech LLC..D 330 239-4933
Wadsworth *(G-13662)*

Remington Steel Inc................................D 937 322-2414
Springfield *(G-12370)*

Westfield Steel Inc..................................D 937 322-2414
Springfield *(G-12392)*

MOTOR VEHICLE PARTS & ACCESS: Connecting Rods

Usui International Corporation.................G 513 448-0410
Sharonville *(G-11949)*

MOTOR VEHICLE PARTS & ACCESS: Electrical Eqpt

Eaton Corporation...................................B 440 523-5000
Beachwood *(G-915)*

Maradyne Corporation.............................D 216 362-0755
Cleveland *(G-3986)*

Mrs Electronic Inc...................................F 937 660-6767
Dayton *(G-5897)*

Stoneridge Inc...A 419 884-1219
Lexington *(G-8374)*

Weastec Incorporated.............................C 937 393-6800
Hillsboro *(G-7728)*

MOTOR VEHICLE PARTS & ACCESS: Engines & Parts

Alegre Inc..F 937 885-6786
Miamisburg *(G-9664)*

Areway LLC..D 216 651-9022
Brooklyn *(G-1520)*

Bucyrus Precision Tech Inc.................... C 419 563-9950
   Bucyrus *(G-1674)*

Detroit Toledo Fiber LLC...................... F 248 647-0400
   Toledo *(G-12942)*

Eaton Corporation.................................. B 440 523-5000
   Cleveland *(G-3652)*

Flaming River Industries Inc.................. F 440 826-4488
   Berea *(G-1174)*

Ft Precision Inc...................................... A 740 694-1500
   Fredericktown *(G-7079)*

Gt Technologies Inc............................... E 419 782-8955
   Defiance *(G-6109)*

Gt Technologies Inc............................... D 419 324-7300
   Toledo *(G-12978)*

Hite Parts Exchange Inc........................ G 614 272-5115
   Chillicothe *(G-2258)*

Linamar Strctures USA Mich Inc........... D 260 636-7030
   Edon *(G-6475)*

Linamar Strctures USA Mich Inc........... C 567 249-0838
   Edon *(G-6476)*

Lorain County Auto Systems Inc........... A 248 442-6800
   Lorain *(G-8564)*

Lorain County Auto Systems Inc........... E 440 960-7470
   Lorain *(G-8565)*

Neaton Auto Products Mfg Inc............... E 937 456-7103
   Eaton *(G-6460)*

Pullman Company.................................. C 419 592-2055
   Napoleon *(G-10296)*

Qualitor Inc... G 248 204-8600
   Cleveland *(G-4211)*

Rochling Automotive USA LLP.............. D 330 400-5785
   Akron *(G-288)*

Schaeffler Transmission Llc................... B 330 264-4383
   Wooster *(G-14682)*

Soundwich Inc....................................... E 216 249-4900
   Cleveland *(G-4315)*

Soundwich Inc....................................... D 216 486-2666
   Cleveland *(G-4316)*

MOTOR VEHICLE PARTS & ACCESS: Fuel Pumps

Bergstrom Company Ltd Partnr.............. F 440 232-2282
   Cleveland *(G-3415)*

MOTOR VEHICLE PARTS & ACCESS: Fuel Systems & Parts

Interstate Diesel Service Inc.................. C 216 881-0015
   Cleveland *(G-3865)*

MOTOR VEHICLE PARTS & ACCESS: Gas Tanks

Buckley Manufacturing Company.......... F 513 821-4444
   Cincinnati *(G-2432)*

MOTOR VEHICLE PARTS & ACCESS: Gears

All Wright Enterprises LLC.................... G 440 259-5656
   Perry *(G-11190)*

Gear Company of America Inc.............. D 216 671-5400
   Cleveland *(G-3760)*

Ig Watteeuw Usa LLC............................ F 740 588-1722
   Zanesville *(G-15021)*

Scs Gearbox Inc.................................... F 419 483-7278
   Bellevue *(G-1130)*

MOTOR VEHICLE PARTS & ACCESS: Heaters

Hdt Tactical Systems Inc....................... C 216 438-6111
   Solon *(G-12122)*

Jbar A/C Inc.. F 216 447-4294
   Cleveland *(G-3884)*

Lintern Corporation............................... E 440 255-9333
   Mentor *(G-9554)*

MOTOR VEHICLE PARTS & ACCESS: Instrument Board Assemblies

New Sabina Industries Inc..................... G 937 584-2433
   Grove City *(G-7405)*

New Sabina Industries Inc..................... E 937 584-2433
   Sabina *(G-11680)*

MOTOR VEHICLE PARTS & ACCESS: Lubrication Systems & Parts

Lubriquip Inc... B 216 581-2000
   Cleveland *(G-3969)*

MOTOR VEHICLE PARTS & ACCESS: Mufflers, Exhaust

Emssons Faurecia Ctrl Systems............. C 812 341-2000
   Toledo *(G-12951)*

Midwest Muffler Pros & More................. G 937 293-2450
   Moraine *(G-10179)*

Newman Technology Inc........................ A 419 525-1856
   Mansfield *(G-8838)*

Riker Products Inc................................. D 419 729-1626
   Toledo *(G-13112)*

Supertrapp Industries Inc...................... D 216 265-8400
   Cleveland *(G-4350)*

MOTOR VEHICLE PARTS & ACCESS: Oil Strainers

Allied Separation Tech Inc..................... G 704 736-0420
   Twinsburg *(G-13273)*

MOTOR VEHICLE PARTS & ACCESS: Power Steering Eqpt

Maval Industries LLC............................ C 330 405-1600
   Twinsburg *(G-13336)*

Steer & Gear Inc.................................... G 614 231-4064
   Columbus *(G-5291)*

MOTOR VEHICLE PARTS & ACCESS: Propane Conversion Eqpt

Superior Energy Systems LLC.............. F 440 236-6009
   Columbia Station *(G-4603)*

MOTOR VEHICLE PARTS & ACCESS: Pumps, Hydraulic Fluid Power

Eaton Corporation.................................. F 216 523-5000
   Willoughby *(G-14455)*

MOTOR VEHICLE PARTS & ACCESS: Rear Axel Housings

American Axle & Mfg Inc........................ D 330 868-5761
   Minerva *(G-10033)*

MOTOR VEHICLE PARTS & ACCESS: Sanders, Safety

Doran Mfg LLC....................................... D 866 816-7233
   Blue Ash *(G-1267)*

MOTOR VEHICLE PARTS & ACCESS: Tire Valve Cores

31 Inc.. D 800 438-3302
   Newcomerstown *(G-10566)*

Haltec Corporation................................ C 330 222-1501
   Salem *(G-11784)*

MOTOR VEHICLE PARTS & ACCESS: Trailer Hitches

Horizon Global Corporation................... E 734 656-3000
   Cleveland *(G-3837)*

Liberty Outdoors LLC............................ F 330 791-3149
   Uniontown *(G-13422)*

Saf-Holland Inc..................................... G 513 874-7888
   Fairfield *(G-6773)*

White Mule Company............................. E 740 382-9008
   Ontario *(G-10954)*

MOTOR VEHICLE PARTS & ACCESS: Transmission Housings Or Parts

Oerlikon Friction Systems..................... D 937 449-4000
   Dayton *(G-5923)*

Torsion Control Products Inc................. F 248 537-1900
   Wadsworth *(G-13675)*

MOTOR VEHICLE PARTS & ACCESS: Transmissions

Capco Automotive Products Corp.......... A 216 523-5000
   Cleveland *(G-3466)*

Florence Alloys Inc............................... G 330 745-9141
   Barberton *(G-805)*

MOTOR VEHICLE PARTS & ACCESS: Water Pumps

ASC Industries Inc................................ D 800 253-6009
   North Canton *(G-10628)*

MOTOR VEHICLE PARTS & ACCESS: Wiring Harness Sets

Connective Design Incorporated........... F 937 746-8252
   Miamisburg *(G-9683)*

Designed Harness Systems Inc............ F 937 599-2485
   Bellefontaine *(G-1105)*

GSW Manufacturing Inc........................ C 419 423-7111
   Findlay *(G-6874)*

Sumitomo Elc Wirg Systems Inc............ E 937 642-7579
   Marysville *(G-9052)*

MOTOR VEHICLE SPLYS & PARTS WHOLESALERS: New

Anest Iwata Usa Inc.............................. F 513 755-3100
   West Chester *(G-14102)*

ARE Inc... A 330 830-7800
   Massillon *(G-9172)*

Chemspec Usa Inc................................ D 330 669-8512
   Orrville *(G-10977)*

Custer Products Limited........................ F 330 490-3158
   Massillon *(G-9184)*

Doran Mfg LLC....................................... D 866 816-7233
   Blue Ash *(G-1267)*

Emssons Faurecia Ctrl Systems............. C 812 341-2000
   Toledo *(G-12951)*

Gear Star Amrcn Prfmce Trnsmss......... E 330 434-5216
   Akron *(G-157)*

Goodyear Tire & Rubber Company........ A 330 796-2121
   Akron *(G-164)*

Keystone Auto Glass Inc....................... D 419 509-0497
   Maumee *(G-9302)*

Legacy Supplies Inc.............................. F 330 405-4565
   Twinsburg *(G-13328)*

Mac Trailer Manufacturing Inc............... A 800 795-8454
   Alliance *(G-390)*

Neff Machinery and Supplies................. G 740 454-0128
   Zanesville *(G-15031)*

Qualitor Inc... G 248 204-8600
Cleveland (G-4211)

MOTOR VEHICLE SPLYS & PARTS WHOLESALERS: Used

Lucas Sumitomo Brakes Inc.................... F 513 934-0024
Lebanon (G-8274)

Mac Trailer Manufacturing Inc............... A 800 795-8454
Alliance (G-390)

MOTOR VEHICLE: Hardware

R H Industries Inc................................. E 216 281-5210
Cleveland (G-4221)

MOTOR VEHICLE: Radiators

Albright Radiator Inc............................. G 330 264-8886
Wooster (G-14622)

Thermal Solutions Mfg Inc..................... G 800 776-4225
Brookpark (G-1559)

MOTOR VEHICLE: Shock Absorbers

Infinity Engineered Pdts LLC.................. E 234 466-7200
Fairlawn (G-6805)

Pullman Company.................................. C 419 499-2541
Milan (G-9917)

Thyssenkrupp Bilstein Amer Inc............ C 513 881-7600
Hamilton (G-7531)

MOTOR VEHICLE: Wheels

Accuride Corporation.............................. F 937 323-9669
Springfield (G-12275)

Dayton Wheel Concepts Inc.................... E 937 438-0100
Dayton (G-5740)

Forgeline Motorsports LLC..................... E 800 886-0093
Dayton (G-5782)

Goodrich Corporation............................. A 937 339-3811
Troy (G-13219)

Honda Transmission Manufact............... A 937 843-5555
Russells Point (G-11668)

Kosei St Marys Corporation.................... A 419 394-7840
Saint Marys (G-11740)

Oe Exchange LLC................................... G 440 266-1639
Mentor (G-9575)

MOTOR VEHICLES & CAR BODIES

Airstream Inc.. B 937 596-6111
Jackson Center (G-7938)

Antique Auto Sheet Metal Inc................. F 937 833-4422
Brookville (G-1562)

Autowax Inc.. G 440 334-4417
Strongsville (G-12542)

Bae Systems Survivability S.................. A 513 881-9800
West Chester (G-13945)

Bobbart Industries Inc........................... G 419 350-5477
Sylvania (G-12702)

D&D Clssic Auto Rstoration Inc.............. G 937 473-2229
Covington (G-5492)

Electro Prime Group LLC........................ E 419 476-0100
Toledo (G-12948)

Ford Motor Company.............................. C 440 933-1215
Avon Lake (G-756)

FOXCONN EV SYSTEM LLC..................... B 234 285-4001
Warren (G-13766)

Galion-Godwin Truck Bdy Co LLC........... F 330 359-5495
Dundee (G-6365)

Halcore Group Inc.................................. C 614 539-8181
Grove City (G-7389)

Honda Dev & Mfg Amer LLC.................. C 937 644-0724
Marysville (G-9028)

Honda Dev & Mfg Amer LLC.................. A 937 642-5000
Marysville (G-9026)

Toledo Pro Fiberglass Inc....................... G 419 241-9390
Toledo (G-13156)

Tpam Inc.. E 567 315-8694
Toledo (G-13165)

Tremcar USA Inc.................................... D 330 878-7708
Strasburg (G-12482)

Workhorse Technologies Inc.................. E 888 646-5205
Sharonville (G-11951)

MOTOR VEHICLES, WHOLESALE: Fire Trucks

Fire Safety Services Inc......................... F 937 686-2000
Huntsville (G-7864)

MOTOR VEHICLES, WHOLESALE: Truck tractors

Kinstle Truck & Auto Svc Inc.................. G 419 738-7493
Wapakoneta (G-13718)

MOTOR VEHICLES, WHOLESALE: Trucks, commercial

Cvg National Seating Co LLC.................. F 219 872-7295
New Albany (G-10338)

Youngstown-Kenworth Inc...................... F 330 534-9761
Hubbard (G-7819)

MOTORCYCLE ACCESS

B&D Truck Parts Sls & Svcs LLC............ G 419 701-7041
Fostoria (G-6976)

Colony Machine & Tool Inc..................... G 330 225-3410
Brunswick (G-1583)

Custom Cycle ACC Mfg Dstrg Inc............ F 440 585-2200
Wickliffe (G-14373)

Newman Technology Inc......................... A 419 525-1856
Mansfield (G-8838)

Thomas D Epperson................................ G 937 855-3300
Germantown (G-7256)

MOTORCYCLE PARTS: Wholesalers

L & R Racing Inc.................................... E 330 220-3102
Brunswick (G-1601)

MOTORCYCLES & RELATED PARTS

Cobra Motorcycles Mfg........................... G 330 207-3844
North Lima (G-10705)

Sunstar Engrg Americas Inc................... F 937 746-8575
Springboro (G-12268)

MOTORS: Electric

Allied Motion At Dayton.......................... E 937 228-3171
Dayton (G-5646)

Ametek Tchnical Indus Pdts Inc............. D 330 673-3451
Kent (G-8017)

Dcm Manufacturing Inc.......................... E 216 265-8006
Cleveland (G-3606)

Dreison International Inc......................... C 216 362-0755
Cleveland (G-3632)

Globe Motors Inc................................... C 334 983-3542
Dayton (G-5798)

Hannon Company................................... D 330 456-4728
Canton (G-1908)

Imperial Electric Company...................... B 330 734-3600
North Canton (G-10647)

Ramco Electric Motors Inc...................... D 937 548-2525
Greenville (G-7350)

Regal Beloit America Inc........................ C 937 667-2431
Tipp City (G-12840)

Siemens Industry Inc............................. C 513 841-3100
Norwood (G-10873)

MOTORS: Generators

American Armature Corporation.............. G 419 448-1926
Tiffin (G-12773)

Ametek Inc.. G 302 636-5401
Columbus (G-4705)

Ares Inc... D 419 635-2175
Port Clinton (G-11439)

Battle Motors Inc.................................. C 888 328-5443
New Philadelphia (G-10432)

Carter Carburetor LLC........................... A 216 314-2711
Cleveland (G-3473)

Chemequip Sales Inc............................. E 330 724-8300
Coventry Township (G-5481)

City Machine Technologies Inc............... F 330 747-2639
Youngstown (G-14836)

Crescent & Sprague............................... F 740 373-2331
Marietta (G-8912)

Dayton-Phoenix Group Inc...................... C 937 496-3900
Dayton (G-5742)

Energy Technologies Inc........................ D 419 522-4444
Mansfield (G-8786)

General Electric Company....................... E 216 883-1000
Cleveland (G-3766)

Gleason Metrology Systems Corp........... E 937 384-8901
Dayton (G-5796)

Grand-Rock Company Inc........................ E 440 639-2000
Painesville (G-11089)

HBD Industries Inc................................. E 614 526-7000
Dublin (G-6302)

Industrial and Mar Eng Svc Co............... F 740 694-0791
Fredericktown (G-7080)

JD Power Systems LLC........................... F 614 317-9394
Hilliard (G-7685)

Lake Shore Electric Corp........................ E 440 232-0200
Bedford (G-1043)

Lhy Powertrain Corporation.................... E 330 533-6801
Canfield (G-1812)

Ohio Magnetics Inc................................ E 216 662-8484
Maple Heights (G-8888)

Ohio Semitronics Inc............................. D 614 777-1005
Hilliard (G-7692)

Peerless-Winsmith Inc........................... B 330 399-3651
Dublin (G-6330)

Regal Beloit America Inc........................ E 608 364-8800
Lima (G-8443)

Safran Usa Inc...................................... C 513 247-7000
Sharonville (G-11948)

Stateline Power Corp............................. F 937 547-1006
Greenville (G-7356)

Tigerpoly Manufacturing Inc................... B 614 871-0045
Grove City (G-7416)

Tremont Electric Incorporated................ G 888 214-3137
Cleveland (G-4416)

Triton Duro Werks Inc............................ G 407 497-9116
Akron (G-344)

Vanner Holdings Inc............................... D 614 771-2718
Hilliard (G-7709)

Waibel Electric Co Inc............................ F 740 964-2956
Etna (G-6634)

MOTORS: Pneumatic

Vickers International Inc......................... G 419 867-2200
Maumee (G-9329)

MOUTHWASHES

Oasis Consumer Healthcare LLC............ G 216 394-0544
Cleveland (G-4106)

MULTIPLEXERS: Telephone & Telegraph

7signal Inc... E 216 777-2900
Independence (G-7886)

AT&T Enterprises LLC..............................G..... 513 792-9300
Cincinnati *(G-2384)*

Cutting Edge Technologies Inc...............G..... 216 574-4759
Cleveland *(G-3589)*

DTE Inc...E..... 419 522-3428
Mansfield *(G-8781)*

Dynalab Inc..D.... 614 866-9999
Reynoldsburg *(G-11568)*

Floyd Bell Inc...D..... 614 294-4000
Columbus *(G-4930)*

Fremont Plastic Products Inc..................C..... 419 332-6407
Fremont *(G-7111)*

Pro Oncall Technologies LLC..................F..... 614 761-1400
Dublin *(G-6335)*

Tls Corp...D..... 216 574-4759
Cleveland *(G-4396)*

Vertiv Energy Systems Inc.......................A..... 440 288-1122
Lorain *(G-8585)*

Vertiv Group Corporation.........................G..... 440 460-3600
Cleveland *(G-4461)*

Vertiv Group Corporation.........................G..... 440 288-1122
Lorain *(G-8586)*

Wan Dynamics Inc...................................F..... 877 400-9490
Medina *(G-9462)*

MUSICAL INSTRUMENTS & ACCESS: Carrying Cases

L M Engineering Inc.................................E..... 330 270-2400
Austintown *(G-706)*

MUSICAL INSTRUMENTS & ACCESS: NEC

Bbb Music LLC...G..... 740 772-2262
Chillicothe *(G-2244)*

Belco Works Inc.......................................D..... 740 695-0500
Saint Clairsville *(G-11688)*

D Picking & Co...G..... 419 562-6891
Bucyrus *(G-1677)*

Grover Musical Products Inc....................E..... 216 391-1188
Cleveland *(G-3797)*

Jatiga Inc...D..... 859 817-7100
Cincinnati *(G-2762)*

Loft Violin Shop.......................................G..... 614 267-7221
Columbus *(G-5073)*

Muller Pipe Organ Co..............................F..... 740 893-1700
Croton *(G-5514)*

MUSICAL INSTRUMENTS WHOLESALERS

Jatiga Inc...D..... 859 817-7100
Cincinnati *(G-2762)*

McHael D Goronok String Instrs.............G..... 216 421-4227
Cleveland *(G-4010)*

MUSICAL INSTRUMENTS: Guitars & Parts, Electric & Acoustic

Conn-Selmer Inc......................................C..... 440 946-6100
Willoughby *(G-14441)*

Earthquaker Devices LLC.........................E..... 330 252-9220
Akron *(G-129)*

S I T Strings Co Inc.................................E..... 330 434-8010
Akron *(G-302)*

NAME PLATES: Engraved Or Etched

Etched Metal Company.............................E..... 440 248-0240
Solon *(G-12109)*

Hathaway Stamp Idntfction Cncn.............G..... 513 621-1052
Cincinnati *(G-2713)*

Industrial and Mar Eng Svc Co.................F..... 740 694-0791
Fredericktown *(G-7080)*

Roemer Industries Inc..............................D..... 330 448-2000
Masury *(G-9256)*

Ryder Engraving Inc.................................G..... 740 927-7193
Pataskala *(G-11149)*

Signature Partners Inc.............................D..... 419 678-1400
Coldwater *(G-4584)*

Visionmark Nameplate Co LLC.................E..... 419 977-3131
New Bremen *(G-10368)*

NATURAL GAS DISTRIBUTION TO CONSUMERS

City of Lancaster.....................................E..... 740 687-6670
Lancaster *(G-8188)*

National Gas & Oil Corporation................E..... 740 344-2102
Newark *(G-10524)*

NATURAL GAS LIQUID FRACTIONATING SVC

Markwest Energy Partners LP..................G..... 800 730-8388
Jewett *(G-7989)*

Markwest Energy Partners LP..................F..... 740 838-1434
Summerfield *(G-12660)*

NATURAL GAS LIQUIDS PRODUCTION

Husky Marketing and Supply Co..............E..... 419 993-8000
Lima *(G-8417)*

Markwest Energy Partners LP..................F..... 740 942-0463
Cadiz *(G-1719)*

NATURAL GAS PRODUCTION

D & L Energy Inc.....................................G..... 330 270-1201
Canton *(G-1876)*

Interstate Gas Supply LLC.......................C..... 877 995-4447
Dublin *(G-6311)*

RCM Engineering Company.......................G..... 330 666-0575
Akron *(G-279)*

Temple Oil and Gas LLC..........................G..... 740 452-7878
Crooksville *(G-5513)*

Williams Partners LP...............................D..... 330 414-6201
North Canton *(G-10681)*

NATURAL GAS TRANSMISSION

Knight Material Tech LLC..........................E..... 330 488-1651
East Canton *(G-6378)*

National Gas & Oil Corporation................E..... 740 344-2102
Newark *(G-10524)*

NATURAL GAS TRANSMISSION & DISTRIBUTION

Ngo Development Corporation...................G..... 740 622-9560
Coshocton *(G-5464)*

NATURAL GASOLINE PRODUCTION

RCM Engineering Company.......................G..... 330 666-0575
Akron *(G-279)*

NATURAL PROPANE PRODUCTION

Consolidated Gas Coop Inc.......................G..... 419 946-6600
Mount Gilead *(G-10209)*

NAVIGATIONAL SYSTEMS & INSTRUMENTS

Cedar Elec Holdings Corp........................D..... 773 804-6288
West Chester *(G-13958)*

Drs Advanced Isr LLC..............................C..... 937 429-7408
Beavercreek *(G-970)*

L3 Technologies Inc.................................G..... 937 223-3285
Dayton *(G-5840)*

Trimble Inc..F..... 937 233-8921
Dayton *(G-6064)*

Trimble Inc..F..... 937 233-8921
Tipp City *(G-12848)*

NETS: Launderers & Dyers

TAC Industries Inc...................................B..... 937 328-5200
Springfield *(G-12382)*

NEWS SYNDICATES

Ohio News Network...................................G..... 614 460-3700
Columbus *(G-5148)*

NICKEL

Allied Mask and Tooling Inc.....................G..... 419 470-2555
Toledo *(G-12870)*

NONCURRENT CARRYING WIRING DEVICES

Akron Foundry Co....................................G..... 330 745-3101
Barberton *(G-791)*

Arnco Corporation....................................F..... 800 847-7661
Elyria *(G-6498)*

Barracuda Technologies Inc......................G..... 216 469-1566
Aurora *(G-663)*

Danco Metal Products LLC........................D..... 440 871-2300
Avon Lake *(G-753)*

Eaton Electric Holdings LLC......................B..... 440 523-5000
Cleveland *(G-3654)*

Erico Inc..E..... 440 248-0100
Solon *(G-12105)*

Erico Products Inc....................................B..... 440 248-0100
Cleveland *(G-3683)*

Power Shelf LLC.......................................G..... 419 775-6125
Plymouth *(G-11433)*

Regal Beloit America Inc...........................C..... 419 352-8441
Bowling Green *(G-1439)*

Roechling Indus Cleveland LP...................C..... 216 486-0100
Cleveland *(G-4248)*

Standex International Corp........................D..... 513 533-7171
Fairfield *(G-6779)*

Vertiv Energy Systems Inc.......................A..... 440 288-1122
Lorain *(G-8585)*

Vertiv Group Corporation.........................G..... 440 288-1122
Lorain *(G-8586)*

Zekelman Industries Inc...........................C..... 740 432-2146
Cambridge *(G-1766)*

NONFERROUS: Rolling & Drawing, NEC

BCi and V Investments Inc........................G..... 330 538-0660
North Jackson *(G-10683)*

Bunting Bearings LLC...............................E..... 419 522-3323
Mansfield *(G-8770)*

Canton Drop Forge Inc.............................B..... 330 477-4511
Canton *(G-1854)*

Consolidated Metal Pdts Inc.....................D..... 513 251-2624
Cincinnati *(G-2511)*

Contour Forming Inc.................................F..... 740 345-9777
Newark *(G-10499)*

Curtiss-Wright Flow Ctrl Corp...................D..... 216 267-3200
Cleveland *(G-3583)*

Elemetal Refining LLC..............................C..... 740 286-6457
Jackson *(G-7944)*

ESAB Group Incorporated.........................G..... 440 813-2506
Ashtabula *(G-591)*

G & S Titanium Inc..................................E..... 330 263-0564
Wooster *(G-14641)*

G A Avril Company...................................F..... 513 641-0566
Cincinnati *(G-2645)*

Gem City Metal Tech LLC.........................E..... 937 252-8998
Dayton *(G-5793)*

Kilroy Company.......................................D..... 440 951-8700
Cleveland *(G-3920)*

Materion Advnced Mtls Tech Svc..............D..... 216 486-4200
Mayfield Heights *(G-9335)*

Mestek Inc...F..... 419 288-2703
Bradner *(G-1454)*

Nova Machine Products Inc................ C 216 267-3200
  Middleburg Heights (G-9775)

Patriot Special Metals Inc.................. D 330 580-9600
  Canton (G-1973)

Titanium Metals Corporation.............. A 740 537-1571
  Toronto (G-13187)

NOTEBOOKS, MADE FROM PURCHASED MATERIALS

Avery Dennison Corporation.............. A 440 534-6000
  Mentor (G-9489)

CCL Label Inc................................. D 440 878-7000
  Strongsville (G-12548)

NOVELTIES

Tiger Cat Furniture.......................... G 330 220-7232
  Brunswick (G-1618)

NOVELTIES: Plastic

Baker Plastics Inc........................... G 330 743-3142
  Youngstown (G-14817)

CM Paula Company......................... E 513 759-7473
  Mason (G-9090)

Motherson Ychiyo Auto Tech PDT........ D 614 876-3220
  Columbus (G-5113)

NOZZLES: Fire Fighting

Premier Farnell Holding Inc................ E 330 523-4273
  Richfield (G-11597)

Sensible Products Inc....................... G 330 659-4212
  Richfield (G-11600)

NOZZLES: Spray, Aerosol, Paint Or Insecticide

Exair LLC.................................... E 513 671-3322
  Cincinnati (G-2608)

Vortec Corporation.......................... E 513 891-7485
  Blue Ash (G-1348)

NUCLEAR SHIELDING: Metal Plate

Laird Technologies Inc..................... E 234 806-0105
  Warren (G-13776)

NURSERIES & LAWN & GARDEN SPLY STORES, RETAIL: Fertilizer

Centerra Co Op.............................. E 410 281 2163
  Ashland (G-526)

Insta-Gro Manufacturing Inc............... G 419 845-3046
  Caledonia (G-1732)

Keystone Cooperative Inc.................. G 937 884-5526
  Verona (G-13591)

M B K Inc................................... F 330 889-3451
  Bristolville (G-1498)

Mid-Wood Inc............................... F 419 257-3331
  North Baltimore (G-10614)

New Eezy-Gro Inc.......................... F 419 927-6110
  Upper Sandusky (G-13449)

Nutrien AG Solutions Inc................... G 614 873-4253
  Milford Center (G-9958)

Ohigro Inc.................................. E 740 726-2429
  Waldo (G-13691)

Premier Feeds LLC.......................... G 937 584-2411
  Sabina (G-11683)

NURSING CARE FACILITIES: Skilled

Optum Infusion Svcs 550 LLC............. D 866 442-4679
  Cincinnati (G-2936)

NUTS: Metal

Facil North America Inc..................... C 330 487-2500
  Twinsburg (G-13302)

Industrial Nut Corp.......................... D 419 625-8543
  Sandusky (G-11842)

Jerry Tools Inc.............................. F 513 242-3211
  Cincinnati (G-2765)

Lear Mfg Co Inc............................. F 440 324-1111
  Elyria (G-6558)

Ramco Specialties Inc...................... D 330 653-5135
  Hudson (G-7855)

The Dyson Corporation..................... C 440 946-3500
  Painesville (G-11116)

Wheel Group Holdings LLC................. G 614 253-6247
  Columbus (G-5366)

NYLON FIBERS

Cast Nylons Co Ltd.......................... D 440 269-2300
  Willoughby (G-14437)

Dowco LLC.................................. E 330 773-6654
  Akron (G-125)

OFFICE EQPT WHOLESALERS

Friends Service Co Inc...................... F 800 427-1704
  Dayton (G-5785)

Friends Service Co Inc...................... E 419 427-1704
  Findlay (G-6869)

Symatic Inc................................. G 330 225-1510
  Medina (G-9452)

OFFICE FURNITURE REPAIR & MAINTENANCE SVCS

American Office Services Inc............... G 440 899-6888
  Westlake (G-14287)

National Electro-Coatings Inc.............. D 216 898-0080
  Cleveland (G-4059)

Recycled Systems Furniture Inc........... E 614 880-9110
  Worthington (G-14724)

OFFICE SPLY & STATIONERY STORES: Office Forms & Splys

Avon Lake Printing.......................... G 440 933-2078
  Avon Lake (G-749)

COS Blueprint Inc........................... E 330 376-0022
  Akron (G-107)

Gordons Graphics Inc....................... G 330 863-2322
  Malvern (G-8751)

Hathaway Stamp Co......................... F 513 621-1052
  Cincinnati (G-2712)

Hubbard Company............................ E 419 784-4455
  Defiance (G-6111)

Murr Corporation............................ G 330 264-2223
  Wooster (G-14668)

O Connor Office Pdts & Prtg................ G 740 852-2209
  London (G-8540)

Quick Tech Graphics Inc.................... F 937 743-5952
  Springboro (G-12266)

Warren Printing & Off Pdts Inc............. F 419 523-3635
  Ottawa (G-11050)

OFFICE SPLYS, NEC, WHOLESALE

Dewitt Group Inc............................ F 614 847-5919
  Columbus (G-4879)

Queen City Office Machine.................. F 513 251-7200
  Cincinnati (G-3022)

Wasserstrom Company....................... B 614 228-6525
  Columbus (G-5356)

OIL & GAS FIELD EQPT: Drill Rigs

Buckeye Companies.......................... E 740 452-3641
  Zanesville (G-15000)

OIL & GAS FIELD MACHINERY

Allied Machine Works Inc................... G 740 454-2534
  Zanesville (G-14986)

Black Gold Capital LLC..................... E 614 348-7460
  Columbus (G-4761)

Cameron International Corp................. E 740 654-4260
  Lancaster (G-8185)

Edi Holding Company LLC................... G 740 401-4000
  Belpre (G-1146)

Electrnic Dsign For Indust Inc............. E 740 401-4000
  Belpre (G-1147)

H P E Inc.................................... G 330 833-3161
  Massillon (G-9199)

OSI Environmental LLC...................... E 440 237-4600
  North Royalton (G-10779)

Pride of The Hills Manufacturing Inc...... D 330 567-3108
  Big Prairie (G-1217)

Reberland Equipment Inc.................... F 330 698-5883
  Apple Creek (G-476)

Robbins & Myers Inc........................ G 937 454-3200
  Dayton (G-5986)

Saint-Gobain Norpro Corp.................. C 330 673-5860
  Stow (G-12458)

Timco Inc.................................. G 740 685-2594
  Byesville (G-1716)

OIL FIELD MACHINERY & EQPT

Multi Products Company..................... F 330 674-5981
  Millersburg (G-10003)

OIL FIELD SVCS, NEC

Altier Brothers Inc......................... G 740 347-4329
  Corning (G-5440)

Appalachian Oilfield Svcs LLC............. F 337 216-0066
  Sardis (G-11887)

Appalachian Well Surveys Inc.............. G 740 255-7652
  Cambridge (G-1736)

Bijoe Development Inc....................... E 330 674-5981
  Millersburg (G-9971)

Bishop Well Services Corp.................. G 330 264-2023
  Wooster (G-14626)

CDK Perforating LLC........................ D 817 862-9834
  Marietta (G-8908)

Complete Energy Services Inc.............. F 440 577-1070
  Pierpont (G-11304)

Completeenergy Services.................... F 440 576-6000
  Pierpont (G-11305)

Crescent Services LLC...................... G 405 603-1200
  Cambridge (G-1740)

Everflow Eastern Partners LP.............. G 330 537-3863
  Salem (G-11778)

Express Energy Svcs Oper LP............... E 740 337-4530
  Toronto (G-13185)

Full Circle Oil Field Svcs Inc............ G 740 371-5422
  Whipple (G-14356)

Genco...................................... G 419 207-7648
  Ashland (G-536)

Global Energy Partners LLC................. E 419 756-8027
  Mansfield (G-8792)

Halliburton Energy Svcs Inc............... F 740 617-2917
  Zanesville (G-15018)

Inland Tarp & Liner LLC.................... E 419 436-6001
  Fostoria (G-6984)

JT Plus Well Service LLC................... F 740 347-0070
  Corning (G-5441)

Mac Oil Field Service Inc.................. G 330 674-7371
  Millersburg (G-9996)

Panhandle Olfld Svc Cmpnies In............ E 330 340-9525
  Cambridge (G-1754)

Paragon Intgrted Svcs Group LL........... E 724 639-5126
  Newcomerstown (G-10574)

Employee Codes: A=Over 500 employees, B=251-500
C=101-250, D=51-100, E=20-50, F=10-19, G=1-9

2025 Harris Ohio
Industrial Directory

1349

PRODUCT

Performance Technologies LLC............ D 330 875-1216
Louisville *(G-8613)*

Petrox Inc... F 330 653-5526
Streetsboro *(G-12516)*

RDM Equipment Company Inc............ F 330 264-8808
Wooster *(G-14675)*

Recon... F 740 609-3050
Bridgeport *(G-1495)*

Superior Energy Group Ltd................. E 216 282-4440
Willoughby Hills *(G-14563)*

Tk Gas Services Inc........................... E 740 826-0303
New Concord *(G-10387)*

Tkn Oilfield Services LLC................... F 740 516-2583
Marietta *(G-8955)*

U S Weatherford L P........................... C 330 746-2502
Youngstown *(G-14955)*

United Chart Processors Inc.............. G 740 373-5801
Marietta *(G-8957)*

Universal Well Services Inc............... D 814 333-2656
Millersburg *(G-10016)*

Vam Usa Llc.. E 330 742-3130
Youngstown *(G-14958)*

W Pole Contracting Inc....................... F 330 325-7177
Ravenna *(G-11548)*

Westerman Inc.................................... C 800 338-8265
Bremen *(G-1488)*

Wyoming Casing Service Inc............. D 330 479-8785
Canton *(G-2049)*

OIL TREATING COMPOUNDS

The Lubrizol Corporation..................... A 440 943-4200
Wickliffe *(G-14395)*

OILS & ESSENTIAL OILS

Lg Chem Ohio Petrochemical Inc.......... F 470 792-5127
Ravenna *(G-11530)*

Natural Essentials Inc........................ C 330 562-8022
Streetsboro *(G-12513)*

Peter Cremer North America LP.......... D 513 471-7200
Cincinnati *(G-2958)*

Unitrex Ltd.. D 216 831-1900
Bedford Heights *(G-1083)*

OILS: Cutting

Chemtool Incorporated........................ C 815 957-4140
Wickliffe *(G-14369)*

OILS: Lubricating

Functional Products Inc...................... F 330 963-3060
Macedonia *(G-8692)*

Varouh Oil Inc.................................... F 440 482-8686
Elyria *(G-6599)*

OILS: Mineral, Natural

Gfl Environmental Svcs USA Inc............ E 614 441-4001
Columbus *(G-4952)*

OLEFINS

Lyondell Chemical Company................ C 513 530-4000
Cincinnati *(G-2833)*

OPERATOR TRAINING, COMPUTER

Computer Workshop Inc....................... E 614 798-9505
Dublin *(G-6291)*

Millers Aplus Cmpt Svcs LLC............... F 330 620-5288
Akron *(G-234)*

OPHTHALMIC GOODS

Classic Optical Labs Inc..................... C 330 759-8245
Youngstown *(G-14838)*

DMV Corporation................................. G 740 452-4787
Zanesville *(G-15010)*

Malta Dynamics LLC........................... F 740 749-3512
Waterford *(G-13828)*

Oakley Inc... F 949 672-6560
Dayton *(G-5919)*

Steiner Eoptics Inc............................. D 937 426-2341
Miamisburg *(G-9740)*

OPHTHALMIC GOODS WHOLESALERS

Haag-Streit Usa Inc............................ D 513 398-3937
Mason *(G-9107)*

OPHTHALMIC GOODS: Frames, Lenses & Parts, Eyeglasses

Essilor of America Inc........................ F 513 765-6000
Mason *(G-9098)*

OPHTHALMIC GOODS: Lenses, Ophthalmic

Sticktite Lenses LLC.......................... F 571 276-9508
New Albany *(G-10351)*

Volk Optical Inc.................................. D 440 942-6161
Mentor *(G-9651)*

OPTICAL GOODS STORES

Central-1-Optical LLC......................... D 330 783-9660
Youngstown *(G-14834)*

Zenni Usa Inc..................................... D 614 439-9850
Columbus *(G-5381)*

OPTICAL INSTRUMENTS & APPARATUS

Greenlight Optics LLC......................... E 513 247-9777
Loveland *(G-8628)*

OPTICAL INSTRUMENTS & LENSES

Cincinnati Eye Inst - Estgate.............. G 513 984-5133
Cincinnati *(G-2298)*

Genvac Aerospace Inc........................ F 440 646-9986
Highland Heights *(G-7657)*

Gooch & Housego (ohio) LLC............... D 216 486-6100
Highland Heights *(G-7658)*

Krendl Machine Company.................... D 419 692-3060
Delphos *(G-6189)*

Mercury Iron and Steel Co.................. F 440 349-1500
Solon *(G-12146)*

Optics Incorporated............................ E 800 362-1337
Brunswick *(G-1604)*

Point Source Inc................................ F 937 855-6020
Germantown *(G-7252)*

Punch Components Inc....................... E 419 224-1242
Lima *(G-8441)*

Sticktite Lenses LLC.......................... F 571 276-9508
New Albany *(G-10351)*

Volk Optical Inc.................................. D 440 942-6161
Mentor *(G-9651)*

Vsp Lab Columbus.............................. G 614 409-8900
Lockbourne *(G-8493)*

Wilson Optical Labs Inc...................... E 440 357-7000
Mentor *(G-9652)*

OPTICAL ISOLATORS

Viavi Solutions Inc............................. F 316 522-4981
Columbus *(G-4651)*

ORGANIZATIONS: Medical Research

Mp Biomedicals LLC............................ C 440 337-1200
Solon *(G-12154)*

Valensil Technologies LLC.................. E 440 937-8181
Avon *(G-741)*

ORGANIZATIONS: Physical Research, Noncommercial

Quasonix Inc....................................... E 513 942-1287
West Chester *(G-14058)*

Sunpower Inc...................................... D 740 594-2221
Athens *(G-654)*

ORGANIZATIONS: Religious

Saint Ctherines Metalworks Inc........... G 216 409-0576
Cleveland *(G-4269)*

Vista Community Church...................... F 614 718-2294
Plain City *(G-11425)*

ORNAMENTS: Christmas Tree, Exc Electrical & Glass

Rhc Inc... E 330 874-3750
Bolivar *(G-1391)*

OVENS: Laboratory

Ignio Systems LLC.............................. G 419 708-0503
Toledo *(G-12999)*

PACKAGE DESIGN SVCS

Amatech Inc.. E 614 252-2506
Columbus *(G-4691)*

PACKAGING & LABELING SVCS

Amros Industries Inc........................... F 216 433-0010
Cleveland *(G-3351)*

Baumfolder Corporation....................... E 937 492-1281
Sidney *(G-11996)*

Bernard Laboratories Inc.................... E 513 681-7373
Cincinnati *(G-2407)*

C A P Industries Inc........................... F 937 773-1824
Piqua *(G-11338)*

Crane Consumables Inc...................... E 513 539-9980
Middletown *(G-9851)*

Custom Products Corporation.............. D 440 528-7100
Glenwillow *(G-7285)*

Domino Foods Inc............................... C 216 432-3222
Cleveland *(G-3625)*

Expo Packaging Inc............................ E 216 267-9700
Cleveland *(G-3699)*

First Choice Packaging Inc................. C 419 333-4100
Fremont *(G-7107)*

G and J Automatic Systems Inc........... E 216 741-6070
Cleveland *(G-3749)*

G S K Inc... G 937 547-1611
Greenville *(G-7342)*

GL Industries Inc............................... E 513 874-1233
Hamilton *(G-7494)*

Howard Industries Inc......................... F 614 444-9900
Columbus *(G-4993)*

Joseph T Snyder Industries Inc........... G 216 883-6900
Cleveland *(G-3892)*

Magnaco Industries Inc...................... E 216 961-3636
Lodi *(G-8504)*

Metzenbaum Sheltered Inds Inc............ E 440 729-1919
Chesterland *(G-2236)*

Ohio Gasket and Shim Co Inc............. E 330 630-0626
Akron *(G-252)*

Pactiv LLC.. C 614 771-5400
Columbus *(G-5168)*

Precision Products Group Inc.............. G 330 698-4711
Apple Creek *(G-475)*

Pro-Pet LLC.. D 419 394-3374
Saint Marys *(G-11749)*

Production Support Inc........................ F 937 526-3897
Russia *(G-11677)*

Richland Newhope Inds Inc................. C 419 774-4400
Mansfield *(G-8848)*

Safecor Health LLC............................ G 614 351-6117
Columbus *(G-5243)*

Systems Pack Inc .... E 330 467-5729
Macedonia *(G-8719)*

Tekni-Plex Inc .... E 419 491-2399
Holland *(G-7786)*

Teva Womens Health LLC .... C 513 731-9900
Cincinnati *(G-3145)*

Unique Packaging & Printing .... F 440 785-6730
Mentor *(G-9646)*

Universal Packg Systems Inc .... C 513 732-2000
Batavia *(G-894)*

Universal Packg Systems Inc .... C 513 735-4777
Batavia *(G-895)*

Universal Packg Systems Inc .... C 513 674-9400
Cincinnati *(G-3186)*

Welch Packaging Group Inc .... C 614 870-2000
Columbus *(G-5359)*

PACKAGING MATERIALS, WHOLESALE

Advanced Poly-Packaging Inc .... C 330 785-4000
Akron *(G-21)*

Allied Shipping and Packagi .... F 937 222-7422
Moraine *(G-10144)*

B B Bradley Company Inc .... G 614 777-5600
Columbus *(G-4740)*

BP 10 Inc .... E 513 346-3900
Hamilton *(G-7472)*

Bryan Packaging Inc .... F 419 636-2600
Bryan *(G-1633)*

Cambridge Packaging Inc .... E 740 432-3351
Cambridge *(G-1738)*

Custom Products Corporation .... D 440 528-7100
Glenwillow *(G-7285)*

Diversified Products & Svcs .... F 740 393-6202
Mount Vernon *(G-10242)*

Global-Pak Inc .... E 330 482-1993
Lisbon *(G-8467)*

Gt Industrial Supply Inc .... F 513 771-7000
Cincinnati *(G-2695)*

Kopco Graphics Inc .... E 513 874-7230
West Chester *(G-14021)*

Protective Packg Solutions LLC .... E 513 769-5777
Cincinnati *(G-3010)*

Putnam Plastics Inc .... G 937 866-6261
Dayton *(G-5969)*

Samuel Son & Co (usa) Inc .... D 740 522-2500
Heath *(G-7604)*

Skybox Packaging LLC .... C 419 525-7209
Mansfield *(G-8853)*

Storopack Inc .... F 513 874-0314
West Chester *(G-14077)*

Storopack Inc .... E 513 874-0314
Cincinnati *(G-3121)*

Systems Pack Inc .... E 330 467-5729
Macedonia *(G-8719)*

Toga-Pak Inc .... E 937 294-7311
Dayton *(G-6056)*

Tri-State Paper Inc .... F 937 885-3365
Dayton *(G-6061)*

Versa-Pak Ltd .... E 419 586-5466
Celina *(G-2127)*

PACKAGING MATERIALS: Paper

American Corrugated Products Inc .... C 614 870-2000
Columbus *(G-4696)*

Austin Tape and Label Inc .... D 330 928-7999
Stow *(G-12420)*

Bollin & Sons Inc .... E 419 693-6573
Toledo *(G-12900)*

Colepak LLC .... D 937 652-3910
Urbana *(G-13460)*

Creative Packaging LLC .... E 740 452-8497
Zanesville *(G-15009)*

Custom Products Corporation .... D 440 528-7100
Glenwillow *(G-7285)*

Dubose Strapping Inc .... E 419 221-0626
Lima *(G-8404)*

Georgia-Pacific LLC .... C 740 477-3347
Circleville *(G-3260)*

Gt Industrial Supply Inc .... F 513 771-7000
Cincinnati *(G-2695)*

Joseph T Snyder Industries Inc .... G 216 883-6900
Cleveland *(G-3892)*

Kay Toledo Tag Inc .... D 419 729-5479
Toledo *(G-13017)*

Kroy LLC .... C 800 837-4323
Cleveland *(G-3929)*

Linneas Candy Supplies Inc .... E 330 678-7112
Kent *(G-8046)*

Liqui-Box Corporation .... E 419 289-9696
Ashland *(G-549)*

Loroco Industries Inc .... D 513 891-9544
Cincinnati *(G-2828)*

Marlen Manufacturing & Dev Co .... F 216 292-7546
Bedford *(G-1047)*

National Glass Svc Group LLC .... F 614 652-3699
Dublin *(G-6323)*

Nilpeter Usa Inc .... C 513 489-4400
Cincinnati *(G-2909)*

Norse Dairy Systems Inc .... C 614 294-4931
Columbus *(G-5128)*

North American Plas Chem Inc .... E 216 531-3400
Euclid *(G-6666)*

Novacel Inc .... C 937 335-5611
Troy *(G-13243)*

Orflex Inc .... B
Cincinnati *(G-2937)*

Pioneer Labels Inc .... C 618 546-5418
West Chester *(G-14048)*

Plastic Works Inc .... F 440 331-5575
Cleveland *(G-4171)*

Plastipak Packaging Inc .... B 937 596-6142
Jackson Center *(G-7966)*

Prime Industries Inc .... F
Lorain *(G-8574)*

Responsible Products Limited .... F 888 988-6627
West Chester *(G-14065)*

Safeway Packaging Inc .... E 419 629-3200
New Bremen *(G-10366)*

Schilling Graphics Inc .... E 419 468-1037
Galion *(G-7198)*

Schwarz Partners Packaging LLC .... F 317 290-1140
Sidney *(G-12050)*

Signode Industrial Group LLC .... C 513 248-2990
Loveland *(G-8653)*

Sonoco Products Company .... E 614 759-8470
Columbus *(G-5276)*

Springdot Inc .... D 513 542-4000
Cincinnati *(G-3108)*

Storopack Inc .... F 513 874-0314
West Chester *(G-14077)*

Storopack Inc .... E 513 874-0314
Cincinnati *(G-3121)*

Stretchtape Inc .... E 216 486-9400
Cleveland *(G-4333)*

Sun America LLC .... E 330 821-6300
Alliance *(G-408)*

Superior Label Systems Inc .... B 513 336-0825
Mason *(G-9157)*

Tce International Ltd .... F 800 962-2376
Perry *(G-11199)*

Tech/III Inc .... C 513 482-7500
Fairfield *(G-6781)*

The Hooven - Dayton Corp .... C 937 233-4473
Miamisburg *(G-9747)*

Thomas Products Co Inc .... E 513 756-9009
Cincinnati *(G-3155)*

Visual Marking Systems Inc .... D 330 425-7100
Twinsburg *(G-13393)*

Zebco Industries Inc .... F 740 654-4510
Lancaster *(G-8233)*

PACKAGING MATERIALS: Paper, Coated Or Laminated

Ampac Plastics LLC .... B 513 671-1777
Cincinnati *(G-2367)*

Central Coated Products LLC .... D 330 821-9830
Alliance *(G-376)*

Central Ohio Paper & Packg Inc .... F 419 621-9239
Huron *(G-7870)*

Diversipak Inc .... E 513 321-7884
Cincinnati *(G-2555)*

Octal Extrusion Corp .... D 513 881-6100
West Chester *(G-14135)*

Proampac LLC .... A 513 671-1777
Cincinnati *(G-2985)*

Retterbush Graphics Packg Corp .... G 513 779-4466
West Chester *(G-14066)*

PACKAGING MATERIALS: Plastic Film, Coated Or Laminated

Amatech Inc .... E 614 252-2506
Columbus *(G-4691)*

Charter Next Generation Inc .... C 740 369-2770
Delaware *(G-6138)*

Charter Next Generation Inc .... C 419 884-8150
Lexington *(G-8367)*

Charter Next Generation Inc .... C 419 884-8150
Lexington *(G-8368)*

Charter Next Generation Inc .... C 419 884-8150
Lexington *(G-8369)*

Charter Next Generation Inc .... C 419 884-8150
Lexington *(G-8370)*

Charter Next Generation Inc .... C 419 884-8150
Lexington *(G-8371)*

Charter Next Generation Inc .... C 330 830-6030
Massillon *(G-9179)*

Command Plastic Corporation .... F 800 321-8001
Bedford *(G-1022)*

Cpg - Ohio LLC .... D 513 825-4800
Cincinnati *(G-2521)*

Crayex Corporation .... D 937 773-7000
Piqua *(G-11342)*

Engineered Films Division Inc .... D 419 884-8150
Lexington *(G-8373)*

Future Polytech Inc .... E 614 942-1209
Columbus *(G-4941)*

Polychem LLC .... C 440 357-1500
Mentor *(G-9588)*

Universal Packg Systems Inc .... C 513 732-2000
Batavia *(G-894)*

Universal Packg Systems Inc .... C 513 735-4777
Batavia *(G-895)*

Universal Packg Systems Inc .... C 513 674-9400
Cincinnati *(G-3186)*

Valgroup North America Inc .... C 419 423-6500
Findlay *(G-6929)*

Versa-Pak Ltd .... E 419 586-5466
Celina *(G-2127)*

PACKAGING: Blister Or Bubble Formed, Plastic

A Aabaco Plastics Inc .... F 216 663-9494
Cleveland *(G-3279)*

Employee Codes: A=Over 500 employees, B=251-500
C=101-250, D=51-100, E=20-50, F=10-19, G=1-9

2025 Harris Ohio
Industrial Directory

PRODUCT

1351

Forrest Enterprises Inc.............. F .... 937 773-1714 Piqua *(G-11347)*	PPG Architectural Coatings LLC.......... D .... 440 297-8000 Strongsville *(G-12587)*	Mid-America Chemical Corp............... G .... 216 749-0100 Cleveland *(G-4032)*
Rohrer Corporation..................... C .... 330 335-1541 Wadsworth *(G-13668)*	PPG Industries Inc....................... E .... 330 825-0831 Barberton *(G-834)*	Npa Coatings Inc........................ C .... 216 651-5900 Cleveland *(G-4104)*
Truechoicepack Corp.................. F .... 937 630-3832 West Chester *(G-14085)*	PPG Industries Ohio Inc................. C .... 412 434-3888 Cleveland *(G-4181)*	Parker Trutec Incorporated............... D .... 937 653-8500 Urbana *(G-13476)*
Ventek Solutions LLC.................. F .... 419 420-0029 Findlay *(G-6930)*	PPG Industries Ohio Inc................. D .... 440 572-6777 Strongsville *(G-12589)*	Perstorp Polyols Inc.................... C .... 419 729-5448 Toledo *(G-13095)*

PACKING & CRATING SVC

	PPG Industries Ohio Inc................. A .... 216 671-0050 Cleveland *(G-4180)*	Pittsburgh Paints Co................... E .... 740 774-7600 Chillicothe *(G-2271)*
Bates Metal Products Inc.............. D .... 740 498-8371 Port Washington *(G-11455)*	Sheffield Bronze Paint Corp............. E .... 216 481-8330 Cleveland *(G-4290)*	Pittsburgh Paints Co................... F .... 513 242-3050 Cincinnati *(G-2965)*
Forrest Enterprises Inc.............. F .... 937 773-1714 Piqua *(G-11347)*	Sherwin-Williams Company............... C .... 330 830-6000 Massillon *(G-9243)*	Pittsburgh Paints Co................... F .... 513 563-0220 Cincinnati *(G-2966)*
Lalac One LLC......................... E .... 216 432-4422 Cleveland *(G-3937)*	Spectrum Dispersions Inc............... F .... 330 296-0600 Ravenna *(G-11542)*	Pittsburgh Paints Co................... C .... 419 433-5664 Huron *(G-7881)*
Vista Industrial Packaging LLC......... E .... 800 454-6117 Columbus *(G-5351)*		Pittsburgh Paints Co................... B .... 440 826-5100 Strongsville *(G-12586)*

PAINTS & ALLIED PRODUCTS

PACKING MATERIALS: Mechanical

Fibercore LLC......................... F .... 216 249-2100 Cleveland *(G-3715)*	Akzo Nobel Coatings Inc................ C .... 614 294-3361 Columbus *(G-4683)*	Plasti-Kote Co Inc..................... C .... 330 725-4511 Medina *(G-9435)*
	Akzo Nobel Coatings Inc................ E .... 419 433-9143 Huron *(G-7866)*	Pmbp Legacy Co Inc.................... E .... 330 253-8148 Akron *(G-262)*

PADDING: Foamed Plastics

	Americhem Inc......................... D .... 330 929-4213 Cuyahoga Falls *(G-5523)*	Polymerics Inc........................ E .... 330 928-2210 Cuyahoga Falls *(G-5565)*
20/20 Custom Molded Plas LLC.......... D .... 419 506-5788 Holiday City *(G-7742)*	Aps-Materials Inc..................... D .... 937 278-6547 Dayton *(G-5662)*	Polynt Composites USA Inc.............. E .... 816 391-6000 Sandusky *(G-11866)*
Aqua Lily Products LLC................ G .... 951 322-0981 Willoughby *(G-14425)*	Avient Corporation.................... D .... 419 668-4844 Norwalk *(G-10829)*	PPG Industries Inc.................... F .... 740 774-8734 Chillicothe *(G-2273)*
J P Industrial Products Inc........... E .... 330 424-3388 Lisbon *(G-8474)*	Basic Coatings LLC.................... F .... 419 241-2156 Bowling Green *(G-1408)*	PPG Industries Inc.................... E .... 740 774-7600 Chillicothe *(G-2274)*
Team Wendy LLC........................ D .... 216 738-2518 Cleveland *(G-4367)*	Bollin & Sons Inc..................... E .... 419 693-6573 Toledo *(G-12900)*	PPG Industries Inc.................... F .... 740 774-7600 Chillicothe *(G-2275)*

PAINTS & ADDITIVES

	Buckeye Fabric Finishers Inc.......... F .... 740 622-3251 Coshocton *(G-5453)*	PPG Industries Inc.................... D .... 740 474-3161 Circleville *(G-3262)*
Aexcel Corporation.................... E .... 440 974-3800 Mentor *(G-9472)*	Cansto Coatings Ltd................... F .... 216 231-6115 Cleveland *(G-3463)*	PPG Industries Inc.................... G .... 216 671-7793 Cleveland *(G-4179)*
Akrochem Corporation.................. D .... 330 535-2100 Akron *(G-24)*	Chemmasters Inc....................... E .... 440 428-2105 Madison *(G-8726)*	PPG Industries Inc.................... G .... 740 363-9610 Delaware *(G-6166)*
Akron Paint & Varnish Inc............. D .... 330 773-8911 Akron *(G-36)*	Consolidated Coatings Corp............ A .... 216 514-7596 Cleveland *(G-3561)*	PPG Industries Inc.................... G .... 419 331-2011 Lima *(G-8438)*
Akzo Nobel Paints LLC................. A .... 440 297-8000 Strongsville *(G-12533)*	CTS National Corporation.............. E .... 216 566-2000 Cleveland *(G-3578)*	PPG Industries Inc.................... D .... 440 572-2800 Strongsville *(G-12588)*
All Coatings Co Inc................... G .... 330 821-3806 Alliance *(G-367)*	Epsilon Management Corporation........ C .... 216 634-2500 Cleveland *(G-3681)*	PPG Industries Ohio Inc............... C .... 740 363-9610 Delaware *(G-6167)*
Axalt Powde Coati Syste Usa I......... G .... 614 921-8000 Hilliard *(G-7671)*	Fuchs Lubricants Co................... F .... 330 963-0400 Twinsburg *(G-13306)*	PPG Industries Ohio Inc............... D .... 412 434-1542 Euclid *(G-6672)*
Axalt Powde Coati Syste Usa I......... G .... 614 600-4104 Hilliard *(G-7672)*	General Electric Company.............. G .... 216 268-3846 Cleveland *(G-3763)*	Priest Services Inc................... G .... 440 333-1123 Mayfield Heights *(G-9340)*
Brinkman LLC.......................... F .... 419 204-5934 Lima *(G-8392)*	Harrison Paint Company................ E .... 330 455-5120 Canton *(G-1909)*	Republic Powdered Metals Inc.......... D .... 330 225-3192 Medina *(G-9441)*
Cansto Paint and Varnish Co........... G Cleveland *(G-3464)*	Henkel US Operations Corp............. C .... 216 475-3600 Cleveland *(G-3821)*	Rolled Alloys Inc..................... D .... 800 521-0332 Maumee *(G-9315)*
Certon Technologies Inc............... F .... 440 786-7185 Bedford *(G-1021)*	Hexpol Compounding LLC................ C .... 440 834-4644 Burton *(G-1699)*	Sherwin-Williams Company.............. G .... 330 528-0124 Hudson *(G-7856)*
Chemspec Usa LLC...................... D .... 330 669-8512 Orrville *(G-10976)*	Hoover & Wells Inc.................... C .... 419 691-9220 Toledo *(G-12995)*	Sherwin-Williams Company.............. F .... 440 846-4328 Strongsville *(G-12600)*
Coloramics LLC........................ E .... 614 876-1171 Hilliard *(G-7678)*	Ineos Neal LLC........................ E .... 610 790-3333 Dublin *(G-6308)*	Sherwin-Williams Company.............. A .... 216 566-2000 Cleveland *(G-4293)*
Comex North America Inc............... D .... 303 307-2100 Cleveland *(G-3551)*	Ineos Solvents Sales US Corp.......... B .... 614 790-3333 Dublin *(G-6309)*	Sherwin-Williams Mfg Co............... F .... 216 566-2000 Cleveland *(G-4294)*
CPC Holding Inc....................... E .... 216 383-3932 Cleveland *(G-3572)*	Kardol Quality Products LLC........... G .... 513 933-8206 Blue Ash *(G-1293)*	Sherwn-Wllams Auto Fnshes Corp........ E .... 216 332-8330 Cleveland *(G-4295)*
Dap Products Inc...................... D .... 937 667-4461 Tipp City *(G-12822)*	Leonhardt Plating Company............. E .... 513 242-1410 Cincinnati *(G-2819)*	Strong-Coat LLC....................... G .... 440 299-2068 Willoughby *(G-14535)*
Kalcor Coatings Company............... E .... 440 946-4700 Willoughby *(G-14474)*	Mameco International Inc.............. F .... 216 752-4400 Cleveland *(G-3984)*	Teknol Inc............................ D .... 937 264-0190 Dayton *(G-6043)*
Karyall-Telday Inc.................... G .... 216 281-4063 Cleveland *(G-3906)*	Matrix Sys Auto Finishes LLC.......... B .... 248 668-8135 Massillon *(G-9221)*	Tremco Incorporated................... C .... 216 292-5000 Beachwood *(G-956)*
Nippon Paint (usa) Inc................ C .... 216 651-5900 Cleveland *(G-4078)*	McCann Color Inc...................... E .... 330 498-4840 Canton *(G-1942)*	Universal Urethane Pdts Inc........... D .... 419 693-7400 Toledo *(G-13169)*
OPC Polymers LLC...................... D .... 614 253-8511 Columbus *(G-5161)*	Meggitt (erlanger) LLC................ D .... 513 851-5550 Cincinnati *(G-2858)*	Urethane Polymers Intl................ F .... 216 430-3655 Cleveland *(G-4450)*

Vanguard Paints and Finishes Inc............ E 740 373-5261
Marietta *(G-8959)*

Vibrantz Corporation............................ D 216 875-5600
Mayfield Heights *(G-9344)*

Wooster Products Inc............................ D 330 264-2844
Wooster *(G-14701)*

Zircoa Inc.. C 440 248-0500
Cleveland *(G-4526)*

PAINTS, VARNISHES & SPLYS WHOLESALERS

Autobody Supply Company Inc............ D 614 228-4328
Columbus *(G-4735)*

Keystone Automotive Inds Inc............ G 614 228-4328
Groveport *(G-7440)*

Teknol Inc.. D 937 264-0190
Dayton *(G-6043)*

PAINTS, VARNISHES & SPLYS, WHOLESALE: Paints

C A P Industries Inc............................ F 937 773-1824
Piqua *(G-11338)*

Comex North America Inc.................... D 303 307-2100
Cleveland *(G-3551)*

Jmac Inc.. E 614 436-2418
Columbus *(G-5041)*

Matrix Sys Auto Finishes LLC............ B 248 668-8135
Massillon *(G-9221)*

PAINTS: Oil Or Alkyd Vehicle Or Water Thinned

Akzo Nobel Coatings Inc.................... E 937 322-2671
Springfield *(G-12277)*

Mansfield Paint Co Inc........................ G 330 725-2436
Medina *(G-9422)*

Waterlox Coatings Corporation............ F 216 641-4877
Cleveland *(G-4493)*

PALLET REPAIR SVCS

Able Pallet Mfg & Repr...................... G 614 444-2115
Columbus *(G-4666)*

Mpi Logistics and Service Inc............ E 330 832-5309
Massillon *(G-9225)*

PALLETIZERS & DEPALLETIZERS

Intelligrated Systems Ohio LLC............ A 513 701-7300
Mason *(G-9114)*

PALLETS & SKIDS: Wood

Able Pallet Mfg & Repr...................... G 614 444-2115
Columbus *(G-4666)*

Aero Pallets Inc................................ E 330 260-7107
Carrollton *(G-2079)*

Belco Works Inc................................ D 740 695-0500
Saint Clairsville *(G-11688)*

Boscowood Ventures Inc.................... F 800 526-1816
Lorain *(G-8548)*

Brookhill Center Inds Inc.................... C 419 876-3932
Ottawa *(G-11030)*

Clark Rm Inc.................................... F 419 425-9889
Findlay *(G-6853)*

Guernsey Industries.......................... C 740 439-4452
Byesville *(G-1713)*

Haessly Lumber Sales Co.................... D 740 373-6681
Marietta *(G-8922)*

Hann Manufacturing Inc...................... E 740 962-3752
Mcconnelsville *(G-9362)*

Makers Supply LLC............................ G 937 203-8245
Piqua *(G-11364)*

PRU Industries Inc............................ F 937 746-8702
Franklin *(G-7042)*

Quadco Rehabilitation Ctr Inc............ C 419 682-1011
Stryker *(G-12626)*

Richland Newhope Inds Inc................ C 419 774-4400
Mansfield *(G-8848)*

Southwood Pallet LLC........................ D 330 682-3747
Orrville *(G-11014)*

Troymill Manufacturing Inc................ F 440 632-5580
Middlefield *(G-9832)*

Tusco Hardwoods LLC........................ G 330 852-4281
Sugarcreek *(G-12655)*

Wjf Enterprises LLC.......................... G 513 871-7320
Cincinnati *(G-3228)*

Yoder Lumber Co Inc........................ D 330 674-1435
Millersburg *(G-10021)*

PALLETS: Plastic

Carbon Polymers Company................ D 330 948-3007
Lodi *(G-8499)*

Mye Automotive Inc.......................... D 330 253-5592
Akron *(G-241)*

Myers Industries Inc.......................... E 330 253-5592
Akron *(G-243)*

PALLETS: Wood & Metal Combination

Satco Inc.. D 513 707-6150
Loveland *(G-8651)*

PANEL & DISTRIBUTION BOARDS & OTHER RELATED APPARATUS

Acorn Technology Corporation............ E 216 663-1244
Shaker Heights *(G-11925)*

Eaton Electric Holdings LLC................ B 440 523-5000
Cleveland *(G-3654)*

Jeff Bonham Electric Inc.................... E 937 233-7662
Dayton *(G-5828)*

PANEL & DISTRIBUTION BOARDS: Electric

Assembly Works Inc.......................... G 419 433-5010
Huron *(G-7869)*

Industrial Solutions Inc...................... E 614 431-8118
Lewis Center *(G-8336)*

Osborne Coinage Company LLC............ D 877 480-0456
Blue Ash *(G-1316)*

Spectra-Tech Manufacturing Inc............ E 513 735-9300
Batavia *(G-880)*

PANELS: Building, Plastic, NEC

Ad Industries Inc.............................. A 303 744-1911
Dayton *(G-5634)*

Fiberglass Technology Inds Inc............ E 740 335-9400
Wshngtn Ct Hs *(G-14740)*

Remram Recovery LLC...................... F 740 667-0092
Tuppers Plains *(G-13262)*

PAPER & BOARD: Die-cut

Art Guild Binders Inc........................ E 513 242-3000
Cincinnati *(G-2378)*

Buckeye Boxes Inc............................ D 614 274-8484
Columbus *(G-4783)*

Chilcote Company.............................. C 216 781-6000
Cleveland *(G-3495)*

Commercial Cutng Graphics LLC............ D 419 526-4800
Mansfield *(G-8776)*

Foldedpak Inc.................................. G 740 527-1090
Hebron *(G-7614)*

Georgia-Pacific LLC............................ C 740 477-3347
Circleville *(G-3260)*

Harris Paper Crafts Inc...................... F 614 299-2141
Columbus *(G-4971)*

Honeymoon Paper Products Inc............ D 513 755-7200
Fairfield *(G-6741)*

Kent Adhesive Products Co................ D 330 678-1626
Kent *(G-8039)*

Keyah International Trdg LLC................ E 937 399-3140
Springfield *(G-12336)*

Lam Pro Inc.................................... F 216 426-0661
Cleveland *(G-3938)*

McElroy Contract Packaging Inc............ F 330 682-2155
Orrville *(G-10994)*

Multi-Craft Litho Inc.......................... E 859 581-2754
Blue Ash *(G-1312)*

Nordec Inc...................................... D 330 940-3700
Stow *(G-12447)*

Printers Bindery Services Inc............ D 513 821-8039
Batavia *(G-884)*

Rohrer Corporation............................ C 330 335-1541
Wadsworth *(G-13668)*

Southern Champion Tray LP................ D 513 755-7200
Fairfield *(G-6777)*

Springdot Inc.................................. D 513 542-4000
Cincinnati *(G-3108)*

Vya Inc.. E 513 772-5400
Cincinnati *(G-3210)*

PAPER & PAPER PRDTS: Crepe, Made From Purchased Materials

Cindus Corporation............................ D 513 948-9951
Cincinnati *(G-2491)*

PAPER PRDTS: Infant & Baby Prdts

Sposie LLC...................................... F 888 977-2229
Maumee *(G-9319)*

PAPER PRDTS: Molded Pulp Prdts

Gr8 News Packaging LLC.................... F 314 739-1202
Lockbourne *(G-8489)*

PAPER PRDTS: Napkins, Sanitary, Made From Purchased Material

Health Care Products Inc.................... E 419 678-9620
Coldwater *(G-4577)*

Procter & Gamble Far East Inc............ C 513 983-1100
Cincinnati *(G-3000)*

Tranzonic Companies.......................... C 440 446-0643
Cleveland *(G-4414)*

Tz Acquisition Corp............................ F 216 535-4300
Richmond Heights *(G-11613)*

PAPER PRDTS: Sanitary

Attends Healthcare Pdts Inc................ G 740 368-7880
Delaware *(G-6133)*

Eleeo Brands LLC.............................. G 513 572-8100
Cincinnati *(G-2582)*

Giant Industries Inc............................ E 419 531-4600
Toledo *(G-12975)*

Johnson & Johnson............................ E 513 786-7000
Blue Ash *(G-1290)*

Linsalata Cpitl Prtners Fund I................ G 440 684-1400
Cleveland *(G-3962)*

Playtex Manufacturing Inc.................. E 937 498-4710
Sidney *(G-12039)*

PAPER PRDTS: Tampons, Sanitary, Made From Purchased Material

Tambrands Sales Corp........................ C 513 983-1100
Cincinnati *(G-3137)*

This Is L Inc.................................... G 415 630-5172
Cincinnati *(G-3154)*

PAPER, WHOLESALE: Printing

Millcraft Group LLC..................................D 216 441-5500
   Independence *(G-7911)*

Phoenix Graphix Inc................................G 513 751-4433
   Cincinnati *(G-2961)*

PAPER: Adhesive

Acpo Ltd...D 419 898-8273
   Oak Harbor *(G-10881)*

Avery Dennison Corporation....................G 216 267-8700
   Cleveland *(G-3391)*

Avery Dennison Corporation....................B 440 358-4691
   Concord Township *(G-5385)*

Avery Dennison Corporation....................D 440 639-3900
   Mentor *(G-9490)*

Avery Dennison Corporation....................F 937 865-2439
   Miamisburg *(G-9667)*

Avery Dennison Corporation....................B 440 358-2564
   Painesville *(G-11069)*

Avery Dennison Corporation....................B 440 878-7000
   Strongsville *(G-12543)*

Avery Dennison Corporation....................A 440 534-6000
   Mentor *(G-9489)*

Avery Dnnison G Holdings I LLC...............G 440 534-6000
   Mentor *(G-9492)*

Bollin & Sons Inc....................................E 419 693-6573
   Toledo *(G-12900)*

CCL Label Inc...E 216 676-2703
   Cleveland *(G-3480)*

CCL Label Inc...D 440 878-7000
   Strongsville *(G-12548)*

GBS Corp..C 330 863-1828
   Malvern *(G-8750)*

Kent Adhesive Products Co.......................D 330 678-1626
   Kent *(G-8039)*

Linneas Candy Supplies Inc.....................E 330 678-7112
   Kent *(G-8046)*

Magnum Tapes Films................................G 877 460-8402
   Caldwell *(G-1726)*

Miller Products Inc..................................C 330 938-2134
   Sebring *(G-11897)*

Miller Studio Inc.....................................G 330 339-1100
   New Philadelphia *(G-10459)*

Morgan Adhesives Company LLC.........B 330 688-1111
   Stow *(G-12441)*

Novavision LLC.......................................D 419 354-1427
   Bowling Green *(G-1430)*

Stretchtape Inc.......................................E 216 486-9400
   Cleveland *(G-4333)*

Technicote Inc...E 800 358-4448
   Miamisburg *(G-9745)*

PAPER: Book

Glatfelter Corporation.............................G 740 772-3893
   Chillicothe *(G-2253)*

Glatfelter Corporation.............................F 740 775-6119
   Chillicothe *(G-2254)*

Glatfelter Corporation.............................D 740 772-3111
   Chillicothe *(G-2255)*

PAPER: Building, Insulating & Packaging

Avery Dennison Corporation....................B 440 358-4691
   Concord Township *(G-5385)*

Avery Dennison Corporation....................D 440 639-3900
   Mentor *(G-9490)*

PAPER: Cardboard

Valley Converting Co Inc.........................E 740 537-2152
   Toronto *(G-13188)*

PAPER: Cloth, Lined, Made From Purchased Materials

Tekni-Plex Inc...E 419 491-2399
   Holland *(G-7786)*

PAPER: Coated & Laminated, NEC

3 Sigma LLC...D 937 440-3400
   Troy *(G-13198)*

Adcraft Decals Incorporated....................E 216 524-2934
   Cleveland *(G-3297)*

Admiral Products Company Inc................E 216 671-0600
   Cleveland *(G-3299)*

Avery Dennison Corporation....................F 440 534-6527
   Mentor *(G-9488)*

Avery Dennison Corporation....................F 419 898-8273
   Oak Harbor *(G-10882)*

Avery Dennison Corporation....................C 440 358-3466
   Painesville *(G-11068)*

BMC Growth Fund LLC............................C 937 291-4110
   Miamisburg *(G-9674)*

Central Coated Products LLC...................D 330 821-9830
   Alliance *(G-376)*

Deco Tools Inc..E 419 476-9321
   Toledo *(G-12939)*

Glatfelter Corporation.............................F 419 333-6700
   Fremont *(G-7115)*

Hall Company...E 937 652-1376
   Urbana *(G-13465)*

Kardol Quality Products LLC...................G 513 933-8206
   Blue Ash *(G-1293)*

Label Technique Southeast LLC...........F 440 951-7660
   Willoughby *(G-14479)*

Lam Pro Inc..F 216 426-0661
   Cleveland *(G-3938)*

Laminate Technologies Inc......................D 800 231-2523
   Tiffin *(G-12786)*

Loroco Industries Inc..............................D 513 891-9544
   Cincinnati *(G-2828)*

Marlen Manufacturing & Dev Co.............F 216 292-7546
   Bedford *(G-1047)*

Mr Label Inc...E 513 681-2088
   Cincinnati *(G-2891)*

Nilpeter Usa Inc......................................C 513 489-4400
   Cincinnati *(G-2909)*

Ohio Laminating & Binding Inc................G 614 771-4868
   Hilliard *(G-7691)*

Pioneer Labels Inc..................................C 618 546-5418
   West Chester *(G-14048)*

R R Donnelley & Sons Company..............D 440 774-2101
   Oberlin *(G-10920)*

Roemer Industries Inc.............................D 330 448-2000
   Masury *(G-9256)*

Sensical Inc..D 216 641-1141
   Solon *(G-12180)*

Superior Label Systems Inc......................B 513 336-0825
   Mason *(G-9157)*

Thomas Products Co Inc..........................E 513 756-9009
   Cincinnati *(G-3155)*

Waytek Corporation.................................E 937 743-6142
   Franklin *(G-7057)*

PAPER: Coated, Exc Photographic, Carbon Or Abrasive

Domtar Corporation................................B 937 859-8261
   West Carrollton *(G-13928)*

Novacel Prfmce Coatings Inc..................D 937 552-4932
   Troy *(G-13244)*

PAPER: Fine

Billerud US Prod Holdg LLC....................B 877 855-7243
   Miamisburg *(G-9672)*

Blue Ridge Paper Products LLC...............E 440 235-7200
   Olmsted Falls *(G-10938)*

PAPER: Packaging

Ampac Plastics LLC................................B 513 671-1777
   Cincinnati *(G-2367)*

Graphic Paper Products Corp..................D 937 325-5503
   Springfield *(G-12315)*

Solut Inc..E 740 549-3336
   Lewis Center *(G-8354)*

Special Pack Inc.....................................E 330 458-3204
   Canton *(G-2010)*

PAPER: Specialty

Billerud Commercial LLC.........................F 877 855-7243
   Miamisburg *(G-9670)*

PAPER: Specialty Or Chemically Treated

Gvs Industries Inc...................................G 513 851-3606
   Hamilton *(G-7498)*

Novolyte Technologies Inc.......................B 216 867-1040
   Cleveland *(G-4103)*

Pixelle Spcialty Solutions LLC................A 740 772-3111
   Chillicothe *(G-2272)*

Pixelle Spcialty Solutions LLC................B 419 333-6700
   Fremont *(G-7126)*

PAPER: Wrapping & Packaging

Corrchoice Cincinnati..............................G 330 833-2884
   Massillon *(G-9181)*

Polymer Packaging Inc............................D 330 832-2000
   North Canton *(G-10658)*

Welch Packaging Group Inc.....................C 614 870-2000
   Columbus *(G-5359)*

PAPERBOARD PRDTS: Folding Boxboard

Caraustar Industries Inc.........................E 330 665-7700
   Copley *(G-5432)*

Graphic Packaging Intl LLC......................C 513 424-4200
   Middletown *(G-9863)*

Graphic Packaging Intl LLC......................C 440 248-4370
   Solon *(G-12118)*

PAPERBOARD PRDTS: Packaging Board

National Carton & Coating Company.....D 937 347-1042
   Xenia *(G-14772)*

Saica Pack US LLC..................................E 513 399-5602
   Hamilton *(G-7522)*

Thorwald Holdings Inc.............................F 740 756-9271
   Lancaster *(G-8229)*

PARTICLEBOARD: Laminated, Plastic

Miller Manufacturing Inc.........................G 330 852-0689
   Sugarcreek *(G-12642)*

PARTITIONS & FIXTURES: Except Wood

3-D Technical Services Company...........E 937 746-2901
   Franklin *(G-7006)*

Accel Group Inc......................................D 330 336-0317
   Wadsworth *(G-13625)*

B-R-O-T Incorporated..............................E 216 267-5335
   Cleveland *(G-3401)*

Benko Products Inc.................................E 440 934-2180
   Sheffield Village *(G-11957)*

Cdc Corporation.....................................G 715 532-5548
   Maumee *(G-9268)*

Communication Exhibits Inc....................D 330 854-4040
   Canal Fulton *(G-1775)*

Component Systems Inc..........................E 216 252-9292
   Cleveland *(G-3556)*

Control Electric Co.................................. E 216 671-8010
Columbia Station (G-4592)

Crescent Metal Products Inc.................. C 440 350-1100
Mentor (G-9507)

Custom Millcraft Corp........................... E 513 874-7080
West Chester (G-13980)

Danco Metal Products LLC..................... D 440 871-2300
Avon Lake (G-753)

Display Dynamics Inc............................ F 937 832-2830
Englewood (G-6612)

HP Manufacturing Company Inc............. D 216 361-6500
Cleveland (G-3841)

Idx Dayton LLC...................................... C 937 401-3460
Dayton (G-5818)

Kellogg Cabinets Inc.............................. G 614 833-9596
Canal Winchester (G-1792)

Mac Lean J S Co................................... G 614 878-5454
Columbus (G-5078)

Marlite Inc... C 330 343-6621
Dover (G-6252)

Midmark Corporation............................. G 937 526-3662
Versailles (G-13600)

Midmark Corporation............................. A 937 528-7500
Miamisburg (G-9717)

Midwest Retail Services Inc.................... F 800 576-7577
Plain City (G-11414)

Modern Retail Solutions LLC.................. E 330 527-4308
Garrettsville (G-7227)

Mro Built LLC... D 330 526-0555
North Canton (G-10654)

Myers Industries Inc.............................. C 330 336-6621
Wadsworth (G-13653)

Ohio Displays Inc.................................. F 216 961-5600
Elyria (G-6572)

Organized Living Inc.............................. E 513 489-9300
Cincinnati (G-2939)

Panacea Products Corporation.............. E 614 429-6320
Columbus (G-5170)

Panacea Products Corporation.............. E 614 850-7000
Columbus (G-5171)

Pfi Displays Inc..................................... E 330 925-9015
Rittman (G-11626)

Prestige Store Interiors Inc.................... G 419 476-2106
Maumee (G-9312)

Pucel Enterprises Inc............................ D 216 881-4604
Cleveland (G-4206)

Rack Processing Company Inc............... E 937 294-1911
Moraine (G-10189)

Rogers Display Inc................................. E 440 951-9200
Mentor (G-9609)

Stein Holdings Inc.................................. E 440 526-9301
Independence (G-7920)

Ternion Inc.. E 216 642-6180
Cleveland (G-4375)

Tusco Limited Partnership...................... C 740 254-4343
Gnadenhutten (G-7295)

Valley Plastics Company Inc.................. E 419 666-2349
Toledo (G-13173)

W B Becherer Inc.................................. G 330 758-6616
Youngstown (G-14965)

W J Egli Company Inc............................ F 330 823-3666
Alliance (G-414)

PARTITIONS: Solid Fiber, Made From Purchased Materials

Colepak LLC... D 937 652-3910
Urbana (G-13460)

PARTITIONS: Wood & Fixtures

A & J Woodworking Inc.......................... G 419 695-5655
Delphos (G-6183)

Accent Manufacturing Inc...................... F 330 724-7704
Norton (G-10816)

Amtekco Industries Inc.......................... E 614 228-6525
Columbus (G-4709)

As America Inc...................................... D 419 522-4211
Mansfield (G-8763)

Automated Bldg Components Inc........... E 419 257-2152
North Baltimore (G-10612)

Creative Products Inc............................ G 419 866-5501
Holland (G-7752)

D Lewis Inc... H 740 695-2615
Saint Clairsville (G-11690)

Diversified Products & Svcs................... F 740 393-6202
Mount Vernon (G-10242)

Geograph Industries Inc........................ E 513 202-9200
Harrison (G-7553)

Global Retail Partners LLC..................... E 614 409-9850
Columbus (G-4958)

Home Stor & Off Solutions Inc............... E 216 362-4660
Cleveland (G-3836)

Kitchens By Rutenschroer Inc................ G 513 251-8333
Cincinnati (G-2799)

Lckbm Company..................................... D 419 636-4555
Bryan (G-1648)

Leiden Cabinet Company LLC................ G 330 425-8555
Strasburg (G-12480)

Lima Millwork Inc................................... G 419 331-3303
Elida (G-6483)

Partitions Plus Incorporated.................. E 419 422-2600
Findlay (G-6907)

R & R Fabrications Inc........................... E 419 678-4831
Saint Henry (G-11723)

Reserve Millwork LLC............................ E 216 531-6982
Bedford (G-1056)

Riceland Cabinet Inc.............................. D 330 601-1071
Wooster (G-14676)

Romline Express LLC............................ G 234 855-1905
Youngstown (G-14926)

Solid Surface Concepts Inc.................... E 513 948-8677
Cincinnati (G-3099)

Symatic Inc.. G 330 225-1510
Medina (G-9452)

Thomas Cabinet Shop Inc...................... F 937 847-8239
Dayton (G-6051)

Trumbull Industries Inc.......................... D 330 434-6174
Akron (G-345)

Tusco Limited Partnership...................... C 740 254-4343
Gnadenhutten (G-7295)

Wine Cellar Innovations LLC.................. C 513 321-3733
Cincinnati (G-3227)

PARTS: Metal

Allpass Corporation............................... F 440 998-6300
Madison (G-8723)

Cleveland Steel Specialty Co................. E 216 464-9400
Bedford Heights (G-1074)

Clifton Steel Company........................... D 216 662-6111
Maple Heights (G-8881)

Diller Metals Inc.................................... G 419 943-3364
Leipsic (G-8306)

Sharon Manufacturing Inc...................... E 330 239-1561
Sharon Center (G-11942)

Strohecker Incorporated........................ E 330 426-9496
East Palestine (G-6407)

PATTERNS: Indl

Advantic Building Group LLC................. E 513 290-4796
Miamisburg (G-9661)

Air Power Dynamics LLC........................ C 440 701-2100
Mentor (G-9473)

Anchor Pattern Company........................ G 614 443-2221
Columbus (G-4714)

API Pattern Works Inc............................ F 440 269-1766
Willoughby (G-14421)

Cascade Pattern Company Inc............... E 440 323-4300
Elyria (G-6509)

Clinton Foundry Ltd............................... F 419 243-6885
Toledo (G-12924)

Clinton Pattern Works Inc...................... G 419 243-0855
Toledo (G-12925)

Colonial Patterns Inc............................. G 330 673-6475
Kent (G-8022)

Dayton Pattern Inc................................ G 937 277-0761
Dayton (G-5735)

Design Pattern Works Inc...................... G 937 252-0797
Dayton (G-5746)

Elyria Pattern Co Inc............................. G 440 323-1526
Elyria (G-6532)

Freeman Manufacturing & Sup Co......... E 440 934-1902
Avon (G-727)

H&M Machine & Tool LLC...................... E 419 776-9220
Toledo (G-12980)

Industrial Pattern & Mfg Co................... F 614 252-0934
Columbus (G-5004)

Industrial Technologies Inc.................... G 330 434-2033
Akron (G-182)

J-Lenco Inc... F 740 499-2260
Morral (G-10199)

Ketco Inc.. E 937 426-9331
Dayton (G-5615)

Liberty Pattern and Mold Inc................. G 330 788-9463
Youngstown (G-14888)

Lorain Modern Pattern Inc..................... F 440 365-6780
Elyria (G-6559)

Maumee Pattern Company..................... E 419 693-4968
Toledo (G-13049)

R L Rush Tool & Pattern Inc.................. G 419 562-9849
Bucyrus (G-1687)

Reliable Castings Corporation................ D 513 541-2627
Cincinnati (G-3037)

Reliable Pattern Works Inc..................... G 440 232-8820
Cleveland (G-4232)

Ross Aluminum Castings LLC................ C 937 492-4134
Sidney (G-12046)

Seaport Mold & Casting Company......... G 419 243-1422
Toledo (G-13123)

Seaway Pattern Mfg Inc......................... F 419 865-5724
Toledo (G-13124)

Sherwood Rtm Corp............................... G 330 875-7151
Louisville (G-8616)

Spectracam Ltd...................................... G 937 223-3805
Dayton (G-6016)

Tempcraft Corporation........................... D 216 391-3885
Cleveland (G-4372)

Th Manufacturing Inc............................. G 330 893-3572
Millersburg (G-10013)

Transducers Direct Llc.......................... F 513 247-0601
Cincinnati (G-3166)

United States Drill Head Co................... F 513 941-0300
Cincinnati (G-3185)

PAVERS

JB Pavers and Hardscapes LLC............ G 937 454-1145
Vandalia (G-13564)

PAVING MIXTURES

Specialty Technology & Res.................. G 614 870-0744
Columbus (G-5282)

Stoneco Inc... G 419 693-3933
Toledo (G-13134)

PENCILS & PENS WHOLESALERS

Identity Group LLC................................ G 614 337-6167
Westerville (G-14213)

PRODUCT

PERFUME: Perfumes, Natural Or Synthetic

Aeroscena LLC.................................. G 800 671-1890
Cleveland *(G-3311)*

PERFUMES

IMH LLC.. F 513 800-9830
Columbus *(G-5001)*

IMH LLC.. G 614 436-0991
Columbus *(G-5002)*

PERISCOPES

Miller-Holzwarth Inc..................... D 330 342-7224
Salem *(G-11800)*

PEST CONTROL IN STRUCTURES SVCS

A Best Trmt & Pest Ctrl Sups.............. G 330 434-5555
Akron *(G-9)*

PEST CONTROL SVCS

Hawthorne Gardening Company........... E 360 883-8846
Marysville *(G-9023)*

Scotts Miracle-Gro Company.............. B 937 644-0011
Marysville *(G-9046)*

PESTICIDES

A Best Trmt & Pest Ctrl Sups.............. G 330 434-5555
Akron *(G-9)*

PET SPLYS

Aquatic Technology........................ F 440 236-8330
Columbia Station *(G-4588)*

Canine Creations Inc..................... G 937 667-8576
Tipp City *(G-12817)*

Fibercore LLC................................ F 216 249-2100
Cleveland *(G-3715)*

Hartz Mountain Corporation.............. D 513 877-2131
Pleasant Plain *(G-11432)*

Heading4ward Investment Co.............. D 937 293-9994
Moraine *(G-10169)*

Worldwide Brands Direct LLC............. F 937 991-0999
Dayton *(G-6088)*

PETROLEUM & PETROLEUM PRDTS, WHOLESALE: Bulk Stations

Cincinnati - Vulcan Company.............. D 513 242-5300
Cincinnati *(G-2465)*

New Vulco Mfg & Sales Co LLC............ D 513 242-2672
Cincinnati *(G-2904)*

Universal Oil Inc........................... E 216 771-4300
Cleveland *(G-4447)*

PHARMACEUTICAL PREPARATIONS: Adrenal

Amgen Inc..................................... F 805 447-1000
New Albany *(G-10327)*

Pharmaforce Inc............................ C
Columbus *(G-5190)*

PHARMACEUTICAL PREPARATIONS: Druggists' Preparations

Abbott Laboratories........................ A 614 624-7677
Columbus *(G-4664)*

CMC Pharmaceuticals Inc.................. G 216 600-9430
Solon *(G-12095)*

Flow Dry Technology Inc................... C 937 833-2161
Brookville *(G-1568)*

Ftd Investments LLC........................ A 937 833-2161
Brookville *(G-1569)*

Hikma Labs Inc.............................. C 614 276-4000
Columbus *(G-4985)*

Soleo Health Inc............................ E 844 467-8200
Dublin *(G-6348)*

West-Ward Columbus Inc................... A 614 276-4000
Columbus *(G-5363)*

PHARMACEUTICAL PREPARATIONS: Pills

Sermonix Pharmaceuticals Inc............ F 614 864-4919
Columbus *(G-5262)*

PHARMACEUTICAL PREPARATIONS: Proprietary Drug

Buderer Drug Company Inc................. E 419 627-2800
Sandusky *(G-11824)*

Camargo Phrm Svcs LLC.................... F 513 561-3329
Cincinnati *(G-2436)*

Cardinal Health 110 LLC.................. E 800 727-6331
Dublin *(G-6287)*

Cardinal Health 414 LLC.................. C 614 757-5000
Dublin *(G-6288)*

PHARMACEUTICAL PREPARATIONS: Solutions

Sara Wood Pharmaceuticals LLC........... G 513 833-5502
Mason *(G-9148)*

PHARMACEUTICALS

2 Retrievers LLC............................ G 216 200-9040
Cleveland *(G-3276)*

Abbott.. G 608 931-1057
Columbus *(G-4659)*

Abbott Laboratories........................ A 614 624-3191
Columbus *(G-4660)*

Abbott Laboratories........................ F 614 624-3192
Columbus *(G-4661)*

Abbott Laboratories........................ D 847 937-6100
Columbus *(G-4662)*

Abbott Laboratories........................ C 800 551-5838
Columbus *(G-4663)*

Abbott Laboratories........................ F 937 503-3405
Tipp City *(G-12812)*

Abeona Therapeutics Inc.................. D 646 813-4701
Cleveland *(G-3287)*

Abitec Corporation........................ E 614 429-6464
Columbus *(G-4665)*

Adare Pharmaceuticals Inc................ C 937 898-9669
Vandalia *(G-13548)*

Aerpio Therapeutics LLC.................. E 513 985-1920
Blue Ash *(G-1244)*

Alkermes Inc................................ E 937 382-5642
Wilmington *(G-14571)*

Allergan Sales LLC........................ C 513 271-6800
Cincinnati *(G-2349)*

Allergan Sales LLC........................ F 513 271-6800
Cincinnati *(G-2350)*

American Regent Inc....................... D 614 436-2222
Columbus *(G-4701)*

American Regent Inc....................... D 614 436-2222
Hilliard *(G-7667)*

American Regent Inc....................... D 614 436-2222
New Albany *(G-10326)*

Amylin Ohio................................. E 512 592-8710
West Chester *(G-13938)*

Analiza Inc.................................. G 216 432-9050
Cleveland *(G-3352)*

Andelyn Biosciences Inc.................. C 614 332-0554
Dublin *(G-6275)*

Andelyn Biosciences Inc.................. E 844 228-2366
Columbus *(G-4715)*

Aprecia Pharmaceuticals LLC............. F 513 984-5000
Mason *(G-9062)*

Astrazeneca Pharmaceuticals LP........... D 513 645-2600
West Chester *(G-13944)*

Axalta.. G 855 629-2582
Toledo *(G-12890)*

Barr Laboratories Inc..................... A 513 731-9900
Cincinnati *(G-2400)*

BASF Corporation........................... D 614 662-5682
Columbus *(G-4745)*

Bayer.. G 513 336-6600
Fairfield *(G-6712)*

Ben Venue Laboratories Inc............... A 800 989-3320
Bedford *(G-1016)*

Bigmar Inc.................................. E 740 966-5800
Johnstown *(G-7992)*

Biosortia Pharmaceuticals Inc............ F 614 636-4850
Dublin *(G-6281)*

Cardinal Health 414 LLC.................. G 513 759-1900
West Chester *(G-13954)*

Chester Labs Inc........................... E 513 458-3871
Cincinnati *(G-2461)*

Diasome Pharmaceuticals Inc............. F 216 444-7110
Cleveland *(G-3614)*

Encapsulation Technologies LLC........... G 419 819-6319
Austinburg *(G-697)*

Galenas LLC................................. F 330 208-9423
Akron *(G-155)*

Ganeden Biotech Inc....................... E 440 229-5200
Mayfield Heights *(G-9334)*

Gebauer Company........................... E 216 581-3030
Cleveland *(G-3761)*

Girindus America Inc...................... E 513 679-3000
Cincinnati *(G-2671)*

Glaxosmithkline LLC........................ G 937 623-2680
Columbus *(G-4955)*

Glaxosmithkline LLC........................ G 614 570-5970
Columbus *(G-4956)*

Hikma Labs Inc.............................. G 614 276-4000
Columbus *(G-4984)*

Hikma Pharmaceuticals USA Inc........... E 732 542-1191
Bedford *(G-1035)*

Hikma Pharmaceuticals USA Inc........... E 614 276-4000
Columbus *(G-4986)*

Hikma Pharmaceuticals USA Inc........... E 732 542-1191
Lockbourne *(G-8490)*

Hikma Specialty USA Inc................... F 856 489-2110
Columbus *(G-4987)*

Imcd Us LLC................................. E 216 228-8900
Westlake *(G-14310)*

Invirsa Inc.................................. G 614 344-1765
Columbus *(G-5023)*

Isp Chemicals LLC.......................... D 614 876-3637
Columbus *(G-5026)*

Johnson & Johnson........................ E 513 786-7000
Blue Ash *(G-1290)*

Kdc US Holdings Inc....................... B 614 656-1130
New Albany *(G-10344)*

Kenvue Brands LLC......................... F 513 985-1540
Cincinnati *(G-2794)*

Lib Therapeutics Inc....................... F 859 240-7764
Cincinnati *(G-2820)*

Lubrizol Global Management Inc........... F 216 447-5000
Cleveland *(G-3970)*

Masters Pharmaceutical Inc................ G 513 290-2969
Fairfield *(G-6752)*

Medpace Core Laboratories LLC........... F 513 579-9911
Cincinnati *(G-2856)*

Medpace Holdings Inc...................... C 513 579-9911
Cincinnati *(G-2857)*

Meridian Bioscience Inc.................... C 513 271-3700
Cincinnati *(G-2864)*

Mp Biomedicals LLC......................... C 440 337-1200
Solon *(G-12154)*

Mvp Pharmacy................................. G 614 449-8000
  Columbus (G-5117)

N-Molecular Inc.............................. F 440 439-5356
  Oakwood Village (G-10907)

Navidea Biopharmaceuticals Inc........... G 614 793-7500
  Dublin (G-6324)

Nnodum Pharmaceuticals Corp............ F 513 861-2329
  Cincinnati (G-2912)

Oakwood Laboratories LLC................ E 440 359-0000
  Oakwood Village (G-10908)

Optum Infusion Svcs 550 LLC............. D 866 442-4679
  Cincinnati (G-2936)

Organon Inc................................. F 440 729-2290
  Chesterland (G-2238)

Patheon Pharmaceuticals Inc............. A 513 948-9111
  Blue Ash (G-1318)

Patheon Pharmaceuticals Inc............. A 513 948-9111
  Cincinnati (G-2943)

Performanx Specialty Chem LLC........... G 614 300-7001
  Waverly (G-13872)

Perrigo...................................... E 937 473-2050
  Covington (G-5498)

Petnet Solutions Cleveland LLC........... F 865 218-2000
  Cleveland (G-4155)

Pharmacia Hepar LLC....................... G 937 746-3603
  Franklin (G-7040)

Prasco LLC................................. E 513 204-1100
  Mason (G-9135)

Principled Dynamics Inc.................... G 419 351-6303
  Holland (G-7779)

Pyros Pharmaceuticals Inc................. E 201 743-9468
  Westerville (G-14227)

Quality Care Products LLC................ E 734 847-2704
  Holland (G-7780)

Resilience Us Inc........................... B 513 645-2600
  West Chester (G-14064)

River City Pharma.......................... G 513 870-1680
  Fairfield (G-6772)

Safecor Health LLC........................ G 614 351-6117
  Columbus (G-5243)

Safecor Health LLC........................ D 800 447-1006
  Columbus (G-5242)

Sarepta Therapeutics Inc................. D 380 324-3973
  Columbus (G-5249)

Staq Pharma of Ohio LLC.................. F 833 397-0106
  Columbus (G-5288)

Teva Pharmaceuticals Usa Inc............ C 513 731-9900
  Cincinnati (G-3144)

Teva Womens Health LLC.................. C 513 731-9900
  Cincinnati (G-3145)

Tri-Tech Laboratories Inc.................. E 740 927-2817
  Johnstown (G-8000)

USB Corporation........................... F 216 765-5000
  Cleveland (G-4454)

Xellia Pharmaceuticals Inc................ G 847 947-0200
  Beachwood (G-958)

PHARMACEUTICALS: Mail-Order Svc

Vitamin Shoppe Industries LLC............ A
  Delaware (G-6179)

PHOSPHATES

Scotts Company LLC....................... C 937 644-0011
  Marysville (G-9045)

PHOTOCOPYING & DUPLICATING SVCS

A Grade Notes Inc......................... G 614 299-9999
  Dublin (G-6271)

A-A Blueprint Co Inc....................... E 330 794-8803
  Akron (G-10)

Aztech Printing & Promotions............. G 937 339-0100
  Troy (G-13202)

Bethart Enterprises Inc.................... F 513 863-6161
  Hamilton (G-7470)

Capitol Citicom Inc........................ E 614 472-2679
  Columbus (G-4799)

Cincinnati Print Solutions LLC............. G 513 943-9500
  Milford (G-9929)

Colortech Graphics & Printing............. F 614 766-2400
  Columbus (G-4816)

Corporate Dcment Solutions Inc........... G 513 595-8200
  Cincinnati (G-2518)

Eg Enterprise Services Inc................. G 216 431-3300
  Cleveland (G-3658)

Hoster Graphics Company Inc............. F 614 299-9770
  Columbus (G-4992)

J & J Tire & Alignment..................... G 330 424-5200
  Lisbon (G-8471)

Monks Copy Shop Inc...................... F 614 461-6438
  Columbus (G-5110)

Morse Enterprises Inc...................... G 513 229-3600
  Mason (G-9129)

Print-Digital Incorporated................. G 330 686-5945
  Stow (G-12451)

Printers Devil Inc.......................... F 330 650-1218
  Hudson (G-7854)

Rhoads Print Center Inc.................... G 330 678-2042
  Tallmadge (G-12748)

Techniprint Inc............................ G 614 899-1403
  Westerville (G-14277)

PHOTOGRAPHIC EQPT & SPLYS

AGFA Corporation.......................... E 513 829-6292
  Fairfield (G-6706)

Dupont Specialty Pdts USA LLC........... E 740 474-0220
  Circleville (G-3255)

Eastman Kodak Company.................. E 937 259-3000
  Kettering (G-8119)

Kg63 LLC................................... F 216 941-7766
  Cleveland (G-3917)

Miller-Holzwarth Inc....................... D 330 342-7224
  Salem (G-11800)

Ohio Hd Video............................. F 614 656-1162
  New Albany (G-10348)

Pulsar Ecoproducts LLC................... F 216 861-8800
  Cleveland (G-4208)

PHOTOGRAPHIC EQPT & SPLYS WHOLESALERS

Identiphoto Co Ltd......................... F 440 306-9000
  Willoughby (G-14467)

PHOTOGRAPHIC EQPT & SPLYS: Film, Sensitized

Stretchtape Inc............................ E 216 486-9400
  Cleveland (G-4333)

PHOTOGRAPHIC EQPT & SPLYS: Graphic Arts Plates, Sensitized

Plastigraphics Inc.......................... F 513 771-8848
  Cincinnati (G-2970)

PHOTOGRAPHIC EQPT & SPLYS: Printing Eqpt

Printer Components Inc.................... G 585 924-5190
  Fairfield (G-6767)

PHOTOGRAPHY SVCS: Commercial

Golden Graphics Ltd....................... F 419 673-6260
  Kenton (G-8099)

Queen City Reprographics.................. C 513 326-2300
  Cincinnati (G-3024)

The Photo-Type Engraving Company.... D 513 281-0999
  Cincinnati (G-3149)

Universal Ch Directories LLC.............. G 419 522-5011
  Mansfield (G-8862)

PHYSICIANS' OFFICES & CLINICS: Medical doctors

Community Action Program Corp......... F 740 374-8501
  Marietta (G-8911)

Eye Surgery Center Ohio Inc.............. E 614 228-3937
  Columbus (G-4917)

Francisco Jaume........................... G 740 622-1200
  Coshocton (G-5455)

Nutritional Medicinals LLC................ F 937 433-4673
  West Chester (G-14034)

Orthotics Prsthtics Rhbltion............... G 330 856-2553
  Warren (G-13788)

Volk Optical Inc........................... D 440 942-6161
  Mentor (G-9651)

PICTURE FRAMES: Metal

Black Squirrel Holdings Inc................ E 513 577-7107
  Cincinnati (G-2412)

Frame Warehouse.......................... G 614 861-4582
  Reynoldsburg (G-11570)

Nostalgic Images Inc....................... E 419 784-1728
  Defiance (G-6122)

PICTURE FRAMES: Wood

Bonfoey Co................................. F 216 621-0178
  Cleveland (G-3427)

Cass Frames Inc........................... G 419 468-2863
  Galion (G-7181)

Fenwick Gallery of Fine Arts.............. G 419 475-1651
  Toledo (G-12962)

Frame Warehouse.......................... G 614 861-4582
  Reynoldsburg (G-11570)

Lazars Art Gllery Crtive Frmng............ G 330 477-8351
  Canton (G-1931)

PICTURE FRAMING SVCS, CUSTOM

American Frame Corporation.............. E 419 893-5595
  Maumee (G-9259)

PIECE GOODS & NOTIONS WHOLESALERS

Sysco Guest Supply LLC................... E 440 960-2515
  Lorain (G-8582)

PIGMENTS, INORGANIC: Metallic & Mineral, NEC

Enviri Corporation......................... F 330 372-1781
  Warren (G-13763)

Obron Atlantic Corporation................ D 440 954-7600
  Painesville (G-11100)

The Shepherd Color Company............. C 513 874-0714
  Cincinnati (G-3151)

PILOT SVCS: Aviation

Theiss Uav Solutions LLC.................. G 330 584-2070
  North Benton (G-10624)

PINS

Altenloh Brinck & Co Inc.................. C 419 636-6715
  Bryan (G-1627)

PINS: Dowel

Dayton Superior Corporation.............. C 937 866-0711
  Miamisburg (G-9687)

PIPE & FITTINGS: Cast Iron

McWane Inc.................................. B 740 622-6651
Coshocton *(G-5459)*

Tangent Air Inc............................. E 740 474-1114
Circleville *(G-3264)*

PIPE & TUBES: Seamless

Dom Tube Corp.............................. A 412 299-2616
Alliance *(G-381)*

Reliacheck Manufacturing Inc.............. E 440 933-6162
Brookpark *(G-1557)*

PIPE FITTINGS: Plastic

Bay Corporation............................ E 440 835-2212
Westlake *(G-14290)*

Cantex Inc................................. D 330 995-3665
Aurora *(G-665)*

Elster Perfection Corporation............. D 440 428-1171
Geneva *(G-7236)*

Gad-Jets Investments Inc.................. G 937 274-2111
Franklin *(G-7023)*

Indelco Custom Products Inc............... G 216 797-7300
Euclid *(G-6654)*

Lenz Inc.................................. E 937 277-9364
Dayton *(G-5844)*

Osburn Associates Inc..................... F 740 385-5732
Logan *(G-8522)*

Ppafco Inc................................ F 614 488-7259
Columbus *(G-5201)*

PIPE SECTIONS, FABRICATED FROM PURCHASED PIPE

Kottler Metal Products Co Inc............. E 440 946-7473
Willoughby *(G-14478)*

Pioneer Pipe Inc.......................... A 740 376-2400
Marietta *(G-8937)*

Scott Process Systems Inc................. C 330 877-2350
Hartville *(G-7584)*

PIPE, CYLINDER: Concrete, Prestressed Or Pretensioned

Complete Cylinder Service Inc............. G 513 772-1500
Cincinnati *(G-2506)*

PIPE, SEWER: Concrete

Ash Sewer & Drain Service................. G 330 376-9714
Akron *(G-61)*

PIPE: Concrete

Haviland Culvert Company.................. G 419 622-6951
Haviland *(G-7588)*

Northern Concrete Pipe Inc................ F 419 841-3361
Sylvania *(G-12720)*

PIPE: Plastic

ADS....................................... G 419 422-6521
Findlay *(G-6832)*

ADS International Inc..................... G 614 658-0050
Hilliard *(G-7663)*

Advanced Drainage of Ohio Inc............. G 614 658-0050
Hilliard *(G-7665)*

Advanced Drainage Systems Inc............. G 419 424-8222
Findlay *(G-6834)*

Advanced Drainage Systems Inc............. E 419 424-8324
Findlay *(G-6835)*

Advanced Drainage Systems Inc............. D 513 863-1384
Hamilton *(G-7462)*

Advanced Drainage Systems Inc............. C 740 852-2980
London *(G-8529)*

Advanced Drainage Systems Inc............. E 419 599-9565
Napoleon *(G-10274)*

Advanced Drainage Systems Inc............. E 330 264-4949
Wooster *(G-14618)*

Advanced Drainage Systems Inc............. D 614 658-0050
Hilliard *(G-7666)*

Baughman Tile Company.................... D 800 837-3160
Paulding *(G-11153)*

Cantex Inc................................ D 330 995-3665
Aurora *(G-665)*

Contech Engnered Solutions Inc............ A 513 645-7000
West Chester *(G-13971)*

Contech Engnered Solutions LLC............ C 513 645-7000
West Chester *(G-13972)*

Drainage Products Inc..................... G 419 622-6951
Haviland *(G-7587)*

Dura-Line Services LLC.................... D 440 322-1000
Elyria *(G-6521)*

Dura-Line Services LLC.................... E 440 322-1000
Elyria *(G-6522)*

Elster Perfection Corporation............. D 440 428-1171
Geneva *(G-7236)*

Flex Technologies Inc..................... E 740 922-5992
Midvale *(G-9910)*

Fowler Products Inc....................... G 419 683-4057
Crestline *(G-5502)*

Geon Performance Solutions LLC............ F 800 438-4366
Westlake *(G-14304)*

Hancor Inc................................ E 419 424-8222
Findlay *(G-6878)*

Hancor Inc................................ E 419 424-8225
Findlay *(G-6879)*

Hancor Inc................................ B 614 658-0050
Hilliard *(G-7683)*

Harrison Mch & Plastic Corp............... E 330 527-5641
Garrettsville *(G-7220)*

Heritage Plastics Liquidation Inc......... D 330 627-8002
Carrollton *(G-2085)*

Ipex USA LLC.............................. G 513 942-9910
Fairfield *(G-6745)*

Nupco Inc................................. G 419 629-2259
New Bremen *(G-10364)*

Plas-Tanks Industries Inc................. E 513 942-3800
Hamilton *(G-7517)*

Savko Plastic Pipe & Fittings............. F 614 885-8420
Columbus *(G-5250)*

Tolloti Pipe LLC.......................... F 330 364-6627
New Philadelphia *(G-10467)*

Tolloti Plastic Pipe Inc.................. E 330 364-6627
New Philadelphia *(G-10468)*

PIPE: Sheet Metal

Shape Supply Inc.......................... G 513 863-6695
Hamilton *(G-7525)*

PIPELINES: Crude Petroleum

Andeavor Logistics LP..................... F 419 421-2414
Findlay *(G-6837)*

PIPELINES: Natural Gas

Markwest Energy Partners LP............... F 740 838-1434
Summerfield *(G-12660)*

PIPES & TUBES

George Manufacturing Inc.................. F 513 932-1067
Lebanon *(G-8258)*

Lokring Technology LLC.................... C 440 942-0880
Willoughby *(G-14483)*

Phillips Tube Group Inc................... E 205 338-4771
Middletown *(G-9885)*

Prime Conduit Inc......................... F 216 464-3400
Beachwood *(G-941)*

Sigma Tube Company........................ F 419 729-9756
Toledo *(G-13131)*

Trenchless Rsrces Globl Hldngs............ F 419 419-6498
Bowling Green *(G-1444)*

PIPES & TUBES: Steel

Alro Steel Corporation.................... E 937 253-6121
Dayton *(G-5648)*

Arcelrmttal Tblar Pdts Shlby L............ A 419 347-2424
Shelby *(G-11966)*

Arcelrmttal Tblar Pdts USA LLC............ A 419 347-2424
Shelby *(G-11967)*

Busch & Thiem Inc......................... E 419 625-7515
Sandusky *(G-11825)*

Caparo Bull Moose Inc..................... G 330 448-4878
Masury *(G-9254)*

Chart International Inc................... D 440 753-1490
Cleveland *(G-3489)*

Clevelnd-Clffs Tblar Cmpnnts L............ D 419 661-4150
Walbridge *(G-13683)*

Commercial Honing LLC..................... D 330 343-8896
Dover *(G-6235)*

Conduit Pipe Products Company............. D 614 879-9114
West Jefferson *(G-14161)*

Contech Engnered Solutions Inc............ A 513 645-7000
West Chester *(G-13971)*

Contech Engnered Solutions LLC............ C 513 645-7000
West Chester *(G-13972)*

Crest Bending Inc......................... E 419 492-2108
New Washington *(G-10478)*

Fd Rolls Corp............................. G 216 916-1922
Solon *(G-12110)*

Grae-Con Process Piping LLC............... E 740 282-6830
Marietta *(G-8920)*

H-P Products Inc.......................... C 330 875-5556
Louisville *(G-8602)*

Jackson Tube Service Inc.................. C 937 773-8550
Piqua *(G-11361)*

Kenco Products Co Inc..................... G 216 351-7610
Cleveland *(G-3913)*

Kirtland Capital Partners LP.............. E 216 593-0100
Beachwood *(G-924)*

Major Metals Company...................... E 419 886-4600
Mansfield *(G-8815)*

Mattr US Inc.............................. E 513 683-7800
Loveland *(G-8641)*

Metallus Inc.............................. E 330 471-7000
Canton *(G-1948)*

Phillips Mfg and Tower Co................. D 419 347-1720
Shelby *(G-11972)*

PMC Industries Corp....................... D 440 943-3300
Wickliffe *(G-14391)*

Ptc Alliance LLC.......................... C 330 821-5700
Alliance *(G-401)*

Rolled Alloys Inc......................... D 800 521-0332
Maumee *(G-9315)*

Shelar Inc................................ C 419 729-9756
Toledo *(G-13129)*

T & D Fabricating Inc..................... E 440 951-5646
Eastlake *(G-6445)*

TI Group Auto Systems LLC................. E 740 929-2049
Hebron *(G-7640)*

Unison Industries LLC..................... B 904 667-9904
Dayton *(G-5625)*

Vallourec Star LP......................... C 330 742-6227
Girard *(G-7281)*

Wheatland Tube LLC........................ C 724 342-6851
Niles *(G-10610)*

Wheatland Tube LLC........................ C 330 372-6611
Warren *(G-13814)*

Woodsage LLC.............................. C 419 866-8000
Holland *(G-7792)*

Zekelman Industries Inc................... E 216 910-3700
Beachwood *(G-959)*

PIPES & TUBES: Welded

Atlantic Welding LLC............................. F 937 570-5094
Piqua *(G-11335)*

Lock Joint Tube Ohio LLC..................... C 210 278-3757
Orwell *(G-11023)*

PIPES: Steel & Iron

Hickman Williams & Company............... F 513 621-1946
Cincinnati *(G-2721)*

JSW Steel USA Ohio Inc........................ B 740 535-8172
Mingo Junction *(G-10052)*

Youngstown Tube Co............................. E 330 743-7414
Youngstown *(G-14978)*

PISTONS & PISTON RINGS

Ad Piston Ring LLC................................ F 216 781-5200
Cleveland *(G-3294)*

Celina Alum Precision Tech Inc............ B 419 586-2278
Celina *(G-2099)*

Quaker City Castings Inc....................... A 330 332-1566
Salem *(G-11806)*

Race Winning Brands Inc...................... B 440 951-6600
Mentor *(G-9606)*

Seabiscuit Motorsports Inc.................... B 440 951-6600
Mentor *(G-9612)*

PLACER GOLD MINING

Ivi Mining Group Ltd............................. G 740 418-7745
Vinton *(G-13623)*

PLAQUES: Picture, Laminated

Gerber Wood Products Inc..................... D 330 857-9007
Kidron *(G-8128)*

Hafners Hrdwood Connection LLC......... G 419 726-4828
Toledo *(G-12983)*

Neff Motivation Inc................................ C 937 548-3194
Greenville *(G-7348)*

PLASTICIZERS, ORGANIC: Cyclic & Acyclic

Chemionics Corporation......................... E 330 733-8834
Tallmadge *(G-12731)*

OPC Polymers LLC................................. D 614 253-8511
Columbus *(G-5161)*

PLASTICS FILM & SHEET

Advanced Polymer Coatings Ltd............ E 440 937-6218
Avon *(G-712)*

Berry Film Products Co Inc.................... D 800 225-6729
Mason *(G-9071)*

Berry Plastics Filmco Inc....................... F 330 562-6111
Aurora *(G-664)*

Clopay Ames Inc.................................... C 800 282-2260
Mason *(G-9087)*

Entrotech Inc... F 614 946-7602
Columbus *(G-4905)*

Renegade Materials Corporation............ D 937 350-5274
Miamisburg *(G-9732)*

Simona PMC LLC................................... D 419 429-0042
Findlay *(G-6918)*

Tsp Inc.. F 513 732-8900
Batavia *(G-892)*

Valgroup LLC.. E 419 423-6500
Findlay *(G-6928)*

PLASTICS FILM & SHEET: Polyethylene

General Films Inc................................... D 888 436-3456
Covington *(G-5493)*

Magnum Tapes Films............................. G 877 460-8402
Caldwell *(G-1726)*

New Tech Plastics LLC........................... D 937 473-3011
Covington *(G-5496)*

Putnam Plastics Inc............................... G 937 866-6261
Dayton *(G-5969)*

PLASTICS FILM & SHEET: Polypropylene

Crown Plastics Co LLC.......................... D 513 367-0238
Harrison *(G-7548)*

PLASTICS FILM & SHEET: Polyvinyl

Jain America Foods Inc.......................... G 614 850-9400
Columbus *(G-5030)*

PLASTICS FILM & SHEET: Vinyl

Clarkwestern Dietrich Building.............. D 330 372-5564
Warren *(G-13752)*

Clarkwstern Dtrich Bldg System............ C 513 870-1100
West Chester *(G-13966)*

Ludlow Composites Corporation............ C 419 332-5531
Fremont *(G-7122)*

Mikron Industries Inc............................ D 713 961-4600
Akron *(G-232)*

Rotary Products Inc............................... F 740 747-2623
Ashley *(G-584)*

Scherba Industries Inc.......................... D 330 273-3200
Brunswick *(G-1614)*

Walton Plastics Inc................................ E 440 786-7711
Bedford *(G-1064)*

World Connections Corps...................... G 419 363-2681
Rockford *(G-11631)*

PLASTICS FINISHED PRDTS: Laminated

Blt Inc.. F 513 631-5050
Norwood *(G-10866)*

Bruewer Woodwork Mfg Co................... D 513 353-3505
Cleves *(G-4532)*

Counter Concepts Inc............................ F 330 848-4848
Wadsworth *(G-13632)*

Designed Images Inc............................. G 440 708-2526
Chagrin Falls *(G-2158)*

Designer Cntemporary Laminates......... G 440 946-8207
Painesville *(G-11079)*

Fdi Cabinetry LLC.................................. G 513 353-4500
Cleves *(G-4537)*

Franklin Cabinet Company Inc............... E 937 743-9606
Franklin *(G-7022)*

General Electric Company...................... G 740 623-5379
Coshocton *(G-5456)*

Mkgs Corp... G 937 254-8181
Dayton *(G-5890)*

Quality Rubber Stamp Inc..................... G 614 235-2700
Lancaster *(G-8220)*

Southern Cabinetry Inc......................... E 740 245-5992
Bidwell *(G-1215)*

PLASTICS MATERIAL & RESINS

A R E Logistics LLC............................... G 330 327-7315
Massillon *(G-9170)*

Al-Co Products Inc................................. G 419 399-3867
Latty *(G-8236)*

American Polymers Corporation............ G 330 666-6048
Akron *(G-57)*

Americas Styrenics LLC......................... D 740 302-8667
Ironton *(G-7930)*

Ampacet Corporation............................. E 513 247-5403
Mason *(G-9060)*

Aptiv Services Us LLC........................... D 330 373-7614
Warren *(G-13738)*

Arclin USA LLC...................................... F 419 726-5013
Toledo *(G-12885)*

Avient Corporation................................ E 440 930-3727
Avon Lake *(G-747)*

Avient Corporation................................ F 440 930-1000
Elyria *(G-6499)*

Avient Corporation................................ E 800 727-4338
Greenville *(G-7335)*

Avient Corporation................................ E 330 834-3812
Massillon *(G-9173)*

Axiom International Inc.......................... G 330 396-5942
Akron *(G-66)*

Benvic Trinity LLC................................. F 609 520-0000
West Unity *(G-14192)*

Biobent Holdings LLC............................ G 513 658-5560
Columbus *(G-4755)*

Biothane Coated Webbing Corp............. E 440 327-0485
North Ridgeville *(G-10727)*

C4 Polymers Inc.................................... G 440 543-3866
Chagrin Falls *(G-2136)*

Cameo Countertops Inc......................... F 419 865-6371
Holland *(G-7748)*

Chem-Materials Inc............................... F 440 455-9465
Westlake *(G-14297)*

Chemionics Corporation......................... E 330 733-8834
Tallmadge *(G-12731)*

Chevron Phillips Chem Ltd Prtnr........... E 740 374-2500
Marietta *(G-8909)*

Chroma Color Corporation..................... D 740 363-6622
Delaware *(G-6139)*

Concrete Sealants Inc........................... E 937 845-8776
Tipp City *(G-12821)*

Covestro LLC... C 740 929-2015
Hebron *(G-7611)*

Crown Plastics Co LLC.......................... D 513 367-0238
Harrison *(G-7548)*

Cuyahoga Molded Plastics Co (inc)....... E 216 261-2744
Euclid *(G-6647)*

Ddp Specialty Electronic MA................. G 937 839-4612
West Alexandria *(G-13918)*

Diamond Polymers Incorporated............ D 330 773-2700
Akron *(G-121)*

Dow Chemical Company......................... F 937 839-4612
West Alexandria *(G-13919)*

Dupont Specialty Pdts USA LLC............ D 740 474-0635
Circleville *(G-3254)*

Durez Corporation................................. D 567 295-6400
Kenton *(G-8097)*

E C Shaw Company of Ohio.................. E 513 721-6334
Cincinnati *(G-2569)*

E P S Specialists Ltd Inc....................... G 513 489-3676
Cincinnati *(G-2571)*

Eagle Elastomer Inc.............................. E 330 923-7070
Peninsula *(G-11182)*

Elyria Foundry Company LLC................. C 440 322-4657
Elyria *(G-6529)*

Ep Bollinger LLC................................... A 513 941-1101
Cincinnati *(G-2594)*

Evans Adhesive Corporation Ltd........... E 614 451-2665
Columbus *(G-4913)*

Fibre Glast Dvlpments Corp LLC........... F 937 833-5200
Brookville *(G-1567)*

Flexsys America LP............................... D 330 666-4111
Akron *(G-150)*

Fortis Parent Inc................................... D 614 790-9299
Columbus *(G-4935)*

Franklin International Inc....................... B 614 443-0241
Columbus *(G-4938)*

Freeman Manufacturing & Sup Co........ E 440 934-1902
Avon *(G-727)*

Freudenberg-Nok General Partnr.......... E 937 335-3306
Troy *(G-13216)*

Gabriel Phenoxies Inc........................... E 704 499-9801
Akron *(G-154)*

Geo-Tech Polymers LLC......................... F 614 797-2300
Waverly *(G-13865)*

Geon Performance Solutions LLC.......... D 440 987-4553
Elyria *(G-6540)*

PRODUCT

Goldsmith & Eggleton Inc.......................... F 330 336-6616
Wadsworth *(G-13640)*

Goldsmith & Eggleton LLC.......................... F 203 855-6000
Wadsworth *(G-13641)*

Gsh Industries Inc.......................... E 440 238-3009
Cleveland *(G-3798)*

Hamilton Polymers Company.......................... F 484 245-4557
Leetonia *(G-8302)*

Hancor Inc.......................... E 419 424-8225
Findlay *(G-6879)*

Hexion US Finance Corp.......................... F 614 225-4000
Columbus *(G-4979)*

Hexpol Holding Inc.......................... F 440 834-4644
Burton *(G-1701)*

Hggc Citadel Plas Holdings Inc.......................... F 330 666-3751
Fairlawn *(G-6803)*

Huntsman Advnced Mtls Amrcas L..... E 330 374-2424
Akron *(G-177)*

Huntsman Advnced Mtls Amrcas L..... E 866 800-2436
Akron *(G-178)*

Huntsman Corporation.......................... D 330 374-2418
Akron *(G-179)*

ICP Adhesives and Sealants Inc............ E 330 753-4585
Norton *(G-10823)*

Ier Fujikura Inc.......................... C 330 425-7121
Macedonia *(G-8696)*

Ineos LLC.......................... D 419 226-1200
Lima *(G-8419)*

Ineos ABS (usa) LLC.......................... C 513 467-2400
Addyston *(G-8)*

Ineos Joliet LLC.......................... F 815 314-4317
Dublin *(G-6307)*

Ineos Neal LLC.......................... E 610 790-3333
Dublin *(G-6308)*

Ineos Nitriles USA LLC.......................... F 281 535-6600
Lima *(G-8420)*

Ineos Solvents Sales US Corp.............. B 614 790-3333
Dublin *(G-6309)*

Integrated Chem Concepts Inc.............. G 440 838-5666
Brecksville *(G-1473)*

Intergroup International Ltd.................. D 216 965-0257
Akron *(G-183)*

Interntnal Tchncal Plymr Syste.......... E 330 505-1218
Niles *(G-10591)*

J P Industrial Products Inc.................. F 330 627-1377
Carrollton *(G-2086)*

J P Industrial Products Inc.................. G 330 424-1110
Lisbon *(G-8473)*

JB Polymers Inc.......................... G 216 941-7041
Oberlin *(G-10919)*

Jeg Associates Inc.......................... G 614 882-1295
Westerville *(G-14266)*

Jerico Plastic Industries Inc.............. F 330 868-4600
Minerva *(G-10039)*

Jerico Plastic Industries Inc.............. E 330 868-4600
Wadsworth *(G-13645)*

Kardol Quality Products LLC.............. G 513 933-8206
Blue Ash *(G-1293)*

Kathom Manufacturing Co Inc.......... E 513 868-8890
Middletown *(G-9871)*

Kraton Corporation.......................... E 740 423-7571
Belpre *(G-1148)*

Kraton Polymers US LLC.......................... B 740 423-7571
Belpre *(G-1150)*

Lrbg Chemicals USA Inc.......................... E 419 244-5856
Toledo *(G-13040)*

Lubrizol Global Management Inc............ E 440 933-0400
Avon Lake *(G-763)*

Lyondell Americas Company.................. C 440 352-9393
Fairport Harbor *(G-6818)*

Lyondllbsell Advnced Plymers I............ D 440 224-7544
Geneva *(G-7243)*

Lyondllbsell Advnced Plymers I............ D 419 872-1408
Perrysburg *(G-11235)*

Lyondllbsell Advnced Plymers I............ D 419 682-3311
Stryker *(G-12624)*

Material Processing & Hdlg Co .... F 419 436-9562
Fostoria *(G-6988)*

Mitsubishi Chemical Amer Inc.............. C 586 755-1660
Bellevue *(G-1127)*

Multi-Plastics Inc.......................... D 740 548-4894
Lewis Center *(G-8344)*

Multibase Inc.......................... D 330 666-0505
Akron *(G-240)*

Network Polymers Inc.......................... E 330 773-2700
Akron *(G-244)*

North American Composites.................. G 440 930-0602
Avon Lake *(G-767)*

Nu-Tech Polymers Co Inc.................. G 513 942-6003
Cincinnati *(G-2916)*

Ohio Foam Corporation.......................... F 419 492-2151
New Washington *(G-10482)*

Ohio Plastics & Belting Co LLC.......... G 330 882-6764
New Franklin *(G-10391)*

OK Industries Inc.......................... E 419 435-2361
Fostoria *(G-6996)*

OPC Polymers LLC.......................... D 614 253-8511
Columbus *(G-5161)*

OSI Global Sourcing LLC.................. G 614 471-4800
Columbus *(G-5164)*

Ovation Plymr Tech Engnred Mtl.......... E 330 723-5686
Medina *(G-9432)*

Owens Corning Sales LLC.................. F 330 633-6735
Tallmadge *(G-12745)*

Performnce Plymr Solutions Inc............ F 937 298-3713
Moraine *(G-10180)*

Perstorp Polyols Inc.......................... C 419 729-5448
Toledo *(G-13095)*

Pilot Polymer Technologies.................. G 412 735-4799
West Chester *(G-14047)*

Plaskolite LLC.......................... C 614 294-3281
Columbus *(G-5194)*

Plastic Compounders Inc.................. E 740 432-7371
Cambridge *(G-1755)*

Plastic Materials Inc.......................... E 330 468-5706
Macedonia *(G-8705)*

Polimeros Usa LLC.......................... G 216 591-0175
Warren *(G-13790)*

Polymer Packaging Inc.......................... D 330 832-2000
North Canton *(G-10658)*

Polymer Tech & Svcs Inc.................. F 740 929-5500
Heath *(G-7601)*

Polymerics Inc.......................... E 330 677-1131
Kent *(G-8060)*

Polymerics Inc.......................... E 330 928-2210
Cuyahoga Falls *(G-5565)*

Polynew Inc.......................... G 330 897-3202
Baltic *(G-780)*

Polyone Corporation.......................... G 216 622-0100
Berea *(G-1185)*

Polyone Corporation.......................... D 330 467-8108
Macedonia *(G-8708)*

Prime Industries Inc.......................... F
Lorain *(G-8574)*

Protech Pet LLC.......................... F 419 552-4617
Gibsonburg *(G-7258)*

Quality Plastics LLC.......................... F 330 695-5920
Fredericksburg *(G-7068)*

Rauh Polymers Inc.......................... F 330 376-1120
Akron *(G-278)*

Ravago Americas LLC.......................... D 330 825-2505
Medina *(G-9440)*

Ray Fogg Construction Inc.................. G 216 351-7976
Cleveland *(G-4225)*

Return Polymers Inc.......................... D 419 289-1998
Ashland *(G-570)*

Rotopolymers.......................... G 216 645-0333
Warren *(G-13794)*

Saco Aei Polymers Inc.......................... F 330 995-1600
Aurora *(G-688)*

Saint-Gobain Prfmce Plas Corp.......... C 614 889-2220
Dublin *(G-6342)*

Saint-Gobain Prfmce Plas Corp.......... C 330 296-9948
Ravenna *(G-11538)*

Scott Bader Inc.......................... G 330 920-4410
Stow *(G-12459)*

Scott Molders Incorporated.................. D 330 673-5777
Kent *(G-8074)*

Sherwood Rtm Corp.......................... G 330 875-7151
Louisville *(G-8616)*

Soelter Corporation.......................... F 800 838-8984
Brookville *(G-1576)*

Solvay Spclty Polymers USA LLC.......... F 740 373-9242
Marietta *(G-8948)*

Sorbothane Inc.......................... E 330 678-9444
Kent *(G-8081)*

Spartech Mexico Holding Co Two.......... F 440 930-3619
Avon Lake *(G-770)*

STC International Co Ltd.................. G 561 308-6002
Lebanon *(G-8287)*

Tembec Btlsr Inc.......................... E 419 244-5856
Toledo *(G-13141)*

Thermocolor LLC.......................... E 419 626-5677
Sandusky *(G-11875)*

Transdigm Inc.......................... G 330 676-7147
Kent *(G-8092)*

Tribotech Composites Inc.................. G 216 901-1300
Cleveland *(G-4422)*

Triple Arrow Industries Inc.................. G 614 437-5588
Marysville *(G-9054)*

Uniloy Milacron Inc.......................... E 513 487-5000
Batavia *(G-893)*

Univar Solutions USA LLC.................. F 800 531-7106
Dublin *(G-6359)*

Urethane Polymers Intl.......................... F 216 430-3655
Cleveland *(G-4450)*

V & A Process Inc.......................... F 440 288-8137
Lorain *(G-8584)*

Ventek Solutions LLC.......................... F 419 420-0029
Findlay *(G-6930)*

Vinylmng LLC.......................... E 440 261-5799
Cleveland *(G-4475)*

Wilsonart LLC.......................... E 614 876-1515
Columbus *(G-5369)*

Win Cd Inc.......................... F 330 929-1999
Cuyahoga Falls *(G-5582)*

PLASTICS MATERIALS, BASIC FORMS & SHAPES WHOLESALERS

Allied Shipping and Packagi.................. F 937 222-7422
Moraine *(G-10144)*

Ampacet Corporation.......................... F 513 247-5400
Cincinnati *(G-2368)*

Morbern USA.......................... F 937 298-2176
Dayton *(G-5893)*

Skybox Packaging LLC.......................... C 419 525-7209
Mansfield *(G-8853)*

United States Plastic Corp.................. D 419 228-2242
Lima *(G-8457)*

Univar Solutions USA LLC.................. F 800 531-7106
Dublin *(G-6359)*

PLASTICS PROCESSING

American Plastics LLC.......................... C 419 423-1213
Findlay *(G-6836)*

AMS Global Ltd............................... G..... 937 620-1036
  West Alexandria (G-13916)

Apogee Plastics Corp............................. G..... 937 864-1966
  Fairborn (G-6687)

Apollo Plastics Inc.................................. F..... 440 951-7774
  Mentor (G-9484)

Bc Investment Corporation.................. C..... 330 262-3070
  Wooster (G-14625)

Bmf Devices Inc................................... F..... 937 866-3451
  Miamisburg (G-9675)

C A Joseph Co....................................... G..... 330 385-6869
  East Liverpool (G-6387)

David Wolfe Design Inc......................... F..... 330 633-6124
  Akron (G-117)

Fountain Specialists Inc........................ G..... 513 831-5717
  Milford (G-9934)

G I Plastek Inc...................................... G..... 440 230-1942
  Westlake (G-14302)

JPS Technologies Inc............................ F..... 513 984-6400
  Blue Ash (G-1292)

JPS Technologies Inc............................ F..... 513 984-6400
  Blue Ash (G-1291)

Liqui-Box Corporation........................... E..... 419 289-9696
  Ashland (G-549)

Lotus Pipes & Rockdrills USA.............. F..... 516 209-6995
  Cleveland (G-3967)

Mega Plastics Co................................. E..... 330 527-2211
  Garrettsville (G-7226)

P T I Inc.. F..... 419 445-2800
  Archbold (G-507)

Preferred Solutions Inc......................... F..... 216 642-1200
  Independence (G-7917)

Radici Plastics Usa Inc......................... E..... 330 336-7611
  Wadsworth (G-13665)

Rexles Inc... G..... 419 732-8188
  Port Clinton (G-11451)

Samuel Son & Co (usa) Inc.................. D..... 740 522-2500
  Heath (G-7604)

Starks Plastics LLC.............................. F..... 513 541-4591
  Cincinnati (G-3113)

Steere Enterprises Inc.......................... D..... 330 633-4926
  Tallmadge (G-12751)

Tahoma Enterprises Inc........................ D..... 330 745-9016
  Barberton (G-840)

Tahoma Rubber & Plastics Inc.............. D..... 330 745-9016
  Ashland (G-579)

Trinity Specialty Compounding Inc........ F..... 419 924-9090
  West Unity (O-14190)

United Security Seals Inc...................... E..... 614 443-7633
  Columbus (G-5337)

United States Plastic Corp.................... D..... 419 228-2242
  Lima (G-8457)

Wyatt Industries LLC............................ G..... 330 954-1790
  Aurora (G-694)

Y City Recycling LLC............................ G..... 740 452-2500
  Zanesville (G-15056)

PLASTICS SHEET: Packing Materials

Automated Packaging Systems LLC...... C..... 330 528-2000
  Streetsboro (G-12490)

Automated Packg Systems Inc.............. G..... 330 626-2313
  Streetsboro (G-12491)

Avery Dennison Corporation................. D..... 440 639-3900
  Mentor (G-9490)

Brr Bear Ltd.. F..... 419 666-1111
  Perrysburg (G-11207)

Buckeye Packaging Co Inc.................... D..... 330 935-0301
  Alliance (G-373)

MAI-Weave LLC.................................... D..... 937 322-1698
  Springfield (G-12347)

Western Reserve Sleeve Inc................. G..... 440 238-8850
  Strongsville (G-12614)

PLASTICS: Blow Molded

Fremont Plastic Products Inc................ C..... 419 332-6407
  Fremont (G-7111)

Klw Plastics Inc.................................. G..... 513 539-2673
  Monroe (G-10112)

Paarlo Plastics Inc.............................. D..... 330 494-3798
  North Canton (G-10657)

Plastic Forming Company Inc............... E..... 330 830-5167
  Massillon (G-9233)

Tigerpoly Manufacturing Inc................. B..... 614 871-0045
  Grove City (G-7416)

Tmd Wek North LLC............................. C..... 440 576-6940
  Jefferson (G-7985)

PLASTICS: Extruded

Akron Polymer Products Inc................. D..... 330 628-5551
  Akron (G-38)

Axion Strl Innovations LLC.................... F..... 740 452-2500
  Zanesville (G-14990)

Cell-O-Core Co.................................... E..... 330 239-4370
  Sharon Center (G-11939)

Clark Rubber & Plastic Company.......... C..... 440 255-9793
  Mentor (G-9500)

Cleveland Specialty Pdts Inc................ E..... 216 281-8300
  Cleveland (G-3525)

Custom Poly Bag LLC........................... D..... 330 935-2408
  Alliance (G-378)

D and D Plastics Inc............................ F..... 330 376-0668
  Akron (G-114)

Extrudex Limited Partnership................ E..... 440 352-7101
  Painesville (G-11085)

Fowler Products Inc............................. G..... 419 683-4057
  Crestline (G-5502)

HP Enterprise Inc................................ E..... 800 232-7950
  Streetsboro (G-12503)

Malish Corporation.............................. D..... 440 951-5356
  Mentor (G-9558)

Merryweather Foam Inc........................ E..... 330 753-0353
  Barberton (G-822)

Meteor Creative Inc............................. E..... 800 273-1535
  Tipp City (G-12830)

Middlefield Plastics Inc........................ E..... 440 834-4638
  Middlefield (G-9811)

Mikron Industries Inc........................... C..... 859 623-2643
  Akron (G-231)

Mikron Industries Inc........................... D..... 713 961-4600
  Akron (G-232)

Montville Plastics & Rubber Inc............ E..... 440 548-3211
  Parkman (G-11128)

North Coast Seal Incorporated............. F..... 216 898-5000
  Brookpark (G-1556)

Overhead Door Corporation.................. F..... 440 593-5226
  Conneaut (G-5413)

Plastic Extrusion Tech Ltd.................... E..... 440 632-5611
  Middlefield (G-9821)

Profile Plastics Inc.............................. E..... 330 452-7000
  Canton (G-1985)

Profusion Industries LLC...................... G..... 800 938-2858
  Fairlawn (G-6808)

Roppe Holding Company....................... G..... 419 435-6601
  Fostoria (G-7000)

Rowmark LLC....................................... D..... 419 425-8974
  Findlay (G-6914)

Spartech LLC....................................... D..... 419 399-4050
  Paulding (G-11162)

The Crane Group Companies Limited.... E..... 614 754-3000
  Columbus (G-5319)

Trellborg Sling Prfiles US Inc............... C..... 330 995-9725
  Aurora (G-690)

Universal Polymer & Rubber Ltd........... E..... 440 632-1691
  Middlefield (G-9834)

Vts Co Ltd... G..... 419 273-4010
  Forest (G-6943)

PLASTICS: Finished Injection Molded

ABC Plastics Inc.................................. E..... 330 948-3322
  Lodi (G-8495)

Akron Porcelain & Plastics Co.............. C..... 330 745-2159
  Akron (G-39)

Alliance-Mcalpin Ny LLC...................... B..... 585 426-5310
  Clyde (G-4556)

Allied Moulded Products Inc................. C..... 419 636-4217
  Bryan (G-1626)

Atc Group Inc...................................... D..... 440 293-4064
  Andover (G-455)

B & B Molded Products Inc................... E..... 419 592-8700
  Defiance (G-6099)

Bourbon Plastics Inc............................ E..... 574 342-0893
  Cuyahoga Falls (G-5533)

Brake Parts Holdings Inc...................... B..... 216 589-0198
  Cleveland (G-3432)

Caraustar Industries Inc....................... E..... 330 665-7700
  Copley (G-5432)

Design Molded Plastics Inc.................. C..... 330 963-4400
  Macedonia (G-8683)

Design Molded Products LLC................ F..... 330 963-4400
  Macedonia (G-8684)

DJM Plastics Ltd................................. F..... 419 424-5250
  Findlay (G-6860)

Edge Plastics Inc................................ C..... 419 522-6696
  Mansfield (G-8784)

Encore Industries Inc.......................... C..... 419 626-8000
  Sandusky (G-11830)

Illinois Tool Works Inc......................... E..... 937 332-2839
  Troy (G-13227)

Interntnal Auto Cmpnnts Group............ A..... 419 433-5653
  Wauseon (G-13853)

Jaco Manufacturing Company............... E..... 440 234-4000
  Berea (G-1177)

Jdh Holdings Inc.................................. C..... 330 963-4400
  Macedonia (G-8700)

Kamco Industries Inc........................... B..... 419 924-5511
  West Unity (G-14196)

Kasai North America Inc...................... E..... 614 356-1494
  Dublin (G-6314)

Kirtland Plastics Inc............................ D..... 440 951-4466
  Kirtland (G-8145)

Kuhns Mold & Tool Co Inc.................... D..... 937 833-2178
  Brookville (G-1572)

Magna Visual Inc................................. E..... 314 843-9000
  Perrysburg (G-11236)

Marne Plastics LLC.............................. F..... 614 732-4666
  Grove City (G-7397)

Mdi of Ohio Inc................................... E..... 937 866-2345
  Miamisburg (G-9711)

Meese Inc... F..... 440 998-1202
  Ashtabula (G-604)

Moriroku Technology N Amer Inc........... A..... 937 548-3217
  Marysville (G-9039)

Myers Industries Inc............................ E..... 440 632-1006
  Middlefield (G-9817)

Novatex North America Inc................... D..... 419 282-4264
  Ashland (G-555)

Reebar Die Casting Inc........................ F..... 419 878-7591
  Waterville (G-13840)

Scientific Plastics Ltd......................... F..... 305 557-3737
  Ravenna (G-11540)

Sonoco Products Company.................... E..... 614 759-8470
  Columbus (G-5276)

Stuchell Products LLC.......................... E..... 330 821-4299
  Alliance (G-407)

Toledo Molding & Die LLC.................... C..... 419 476-0581
  Toledo (G-13154)

PRODUCT

Toledo Molding & Die LLC..................... D 419 470-3950
  Toledo *(G-13153)*

Tom Smith Industries Inc....................... D 937 832-1555
  Englewood *(G-6626)*

Toth Mold & Die Inc.............................. F 440 232-8530
  Bedford *(G-1062)*

Tri-Craft Inc... E 440 826-1050
  Cleveland *(G-4418)*

Venture Packaging Inc.......................... F 419 465-2534
  Monroeville *(G-10122)*

PLASTICS: Molded

Alpha Packaging Holdings Inc............. B 216 252-5595
  Cleveland *(G-3332)*

Astro Manufacturing & Design Inc....... C 888 215-1746
  Eastlake *(G-6417)*

Cuyahoga Molded Plastics Co (inc)...... E 216 261-2744
  Euclid *(G-6647)*

Don-Ell Corporation.............................. E 419 841-7114
  Sylvania *(G-12704)*

Flex Technologies Inc........................... E 740 922-5992
  Midvale *(G-9910)*

Fortis Plastics LLC............................... G 937 382-0966
  Wilmington *(G-14581)*

G S K Inc.. G 937 547-1611
  Greenville *(G-7342)*

Industrial Farm Tank Inc....................... E 937 843-2972
  Lewistown *(G-8365)*

Liqui-Box Corporation........................... E 419 294-3884
  Upper Sandusky *(G-13446)*

Mar-Bal Inc.. D 440 543-7526
  Chagrin Falls *(G-2170)*

Meggitt (erlanger) LLC......................... D 513 851-5550
  Cincinnati *(G-2858)*

Molded Fiber Glass Companies............ D 440 997-5851
  Ashtabula *(G-608)*

Molded Fiber Glass Companies............ A 440 997-5851
  Ashtabula *(G-607)*

Myers Industries Inc............................. E 330 253-5592
  Akron *(G-242)*

North Coast Custom Molding Inc......... F 419 905-6447
  Dunkirk *(G-6375)*

Palpac Industries Inc........................... F 419 523-3230
  Ottawa *(G-11041)*

Plasticraft Usa LLC.............................. G 513 761-2999
  Cincinnati *(G-2969)*

Podnar Plastics Inc.............................. G 330 673-2255
  Kent *(G-8059)*

R and S Technologies Inc..................... F 419 483-3691
  Bellevue *(G-1129)*

RMC USA Incorporation........................ D 440 992-4906
  Jefferson *(G-7982)*

Step2 Company LLC............................. B 866 429-5200
  Streetsboro *(G-12525)*

Superior Plastics Inc............................ F 614 733-0307
  Plain City *(G-11420)*

US Development Corp............................ D 330 673-6900
  Kent *(G-8094)*

Wch Molding LLC................................. E 740 335-6320
  Wshngtn Ct Hs *(G-14749)*

PLASTICS: Polystyrene Foam

Acor Orthopaedic LLC.......................... E 216 662-4500
  Cleveland *(G-3293)*

ADS Worldwide Inc............................... G 614 658-0050
  Hilliard *(G-7664)*

Advanced Drainage Systems Inc........... D 614 658-0050
  Hilliard *(G-7666)*

All Foam Products Co........................... G 330 849-3636
  Middlefield *(G-9779)*

Allied Shipping and Packagi................. F 937 222-7422
  Moraine *(G-10144)*

Amatech Inc... E 614 252-2506
  Columbus *(G-4691)*

American Corrugated Products Inc........ C 614 870-2000
  Columbus *(G-4696)*

Arkay Industries Inc............................. E 513 360-0390
  Monroe *(G-10096)*

Armaly LLC.. E 740 852-3621
  London *(G-8530)*

Creative Foam Dayton Mold................... F 937 279-9987
  Dayton *(G-5713)*

Ddp Specialty Electronic MA................ G 937 839-4612
  West Alexandria *(G-13918)*

Deufol Worldwide Packaging LLC......... E 440 232-1100
  Bedford *(G-1026)*

Extol of Ohio Inc.................................. F 419 668-2072
  Norwalk *(G-10838)*

Gdc Inc.. F 574 533-3128
  Wooster *(G-14642)*

Hedstrom Plastics LLC.......................... E 419 289-9310
  Ashland *(G-538)*

Hfi LLC... B 614 491-0700
  Canal Winchester *(G-1791)*

ICP Adhesives and Sealants Inc............ E 330 753-4585
  Norton *(G-10823)*

ISO Technologies Inc............................ E 740 928-0084
  Heath *(G-7597)*

IVEX Protective Packaging LLC.............. E 937 498-9298
  Sidney *(G-12026)*

Jain America Foods Inc......................... G 614 850-9400
  Columbus *(G-5030)*

Merryweather Foam Inc.......................... E 330 753-0353
  Barberton *(G-822)*

Mlb Molded Urethane Pdts LLC.............. E 419 825-9140
  Swanton *(G-12688)*

Myers Industries Inc............................. E 330 253-5592
  Akron *(G-243)*

Ohio Decorative Products LLC............... C 419 647-9033
  Spencerville *(G-12238)*

Ohio Foam Corporation.......................... G 614 252-4877
  Columbus *(G-5145)*

Owens Corning Sales LLC.................... C 330 634-0460
  Tallmadge *(G-12744)*

Palpac Industries Inc........................... F 419 523-3230
  Ottawa *(G-11041)*

Plastic Forming Company Inc............... E 330 830-5167
  Massillon *(G-9233)*

Prime Industries Inc............................. F
  Lorain *(G-8574)*

S & A Industries Corporation................. E 330 733-6040
  Akron *(G-300)*

S & A Industries Corporation................. D 330 733-6040
  Akron *(G-301)*

Smithers-Oasis Company........................ F 330 673-5831
  Kent *(G-8079)*

Temprecision Intl Corp.......................... G 855 891-7732
  Kent *(G-8088)*

Ventek Solutions LLC............................ F 419 420-0029
  Findlay *(G-6930)*

Wellman Container Corporation............. E 513 860-3040
  Cincinnati *(G-3219)*

PLASTICS: Thermoformed

AMD Plastics Inc.................................. F 216 289-4862
  Euclid *(G-6640)*

Arthur Corporation................................ D 419 433-7202
  Huron *(G-7868)*

Brittany Stamping LLC........................... A 216 267-0850
  Cleveland *(G-3440)*

Comdess Company Inc.......................... F 330 769-2094
  Seville *(G-11916)*

Corvac Composites LLC........................ D 248 807-0969
  Greenfield *(G-7326)*

Encore Industries Inc............................ E 419 626-8000
  Cambridge *(G-1743)*

First Choice Packaging Inc................... C 419 333-4100
  Fremont *(G-7107)*

Kurz-Kasch Inc..................................... E 740 498-8343
  Newcomerstown *(G-10572)*

Maverick Corporation............................ F 513 469-9919
  Blue Ash *(G-1304)*

Neff-Perkins Company........................... D 440 632-1658
  Middlefield *(G-9818)*

Plastikos Corporation........................... E 513 732-0961
  Batavia *(G-882)*

Progrssive Molding Bolivar Inc............. G 330 874-3000
  Bolivar *(G-1390)*

Replex Mirror Company.......................... E 740 397-5535
  Mount Vernon *(G-10262)*

Roechling Indus Cleveland LP............... C 216 486-0100
  Cleveland *(G-4248)*

Rubbermaid Home Products.................. G 330 733-7771
  Mogadore *(G-10082)*

Saint-Gobain Prfmce Plas Corp............ B 440 836-6900
  Solon *(G-12178)*

Scott Molders Incorporated.................. D 330 673-5777
  Kent *(G-8074)*

Tooling Tech Holdings LLC.................... E 937 295-3672
  Fort Loramie *(G-6959)*

PLATE WORK: Metalworking Trade

Alloy Engineering Company................... D 440 243-6800
  Berea *(G-1158)*

Mercury Iron and Steel Co..................... F 440 349-1500
  Solon *(G-12146)*

PLATES: Steel

Churchill Steel Plate Ltd....................... E 330 425-9000
  Twinsburg *(G-13286)*

Evolve Solutions LLC........................... E 440 357-8964
  Painesville *(G-11083)*

Global Metal Services Ltd..................... G 440 591-1264
  Chagrin Falls *(G-2163)*

PLATING & POLISHING SVC

Allen Aircraft Products Inc................... E 330 296-9621
  Ravenna *(G-11514)*

Aluminum Extruded Shapes Inc............ C 513 563-2205
  Cincinnati *(G-2354)*

Arem Co... G 440 974-6740
  Willoughby *(G-14426)*

ATI Flat Rlled Pdts Hldngs LLC............. F 330 875-2244
  Louisville *(G-8598)*

Carlisle and Finch Company.................. E 513 681-6080
  Cincinnati *(G-2439)*

Chemical Methods Incorporated........... E 216 476-8400
  Brunswick *(G-1582)*

Chromium Corporation........................... E 216 271-4910
  Cleveland *(G-3498)*

Cincinnati Gearing Systems Inc............ D 513 527-8600
  Cincinnati *(G-2476)*

Cleveland-Cliffs Columbus LLC............. C 614 492-6800
  Richfield *(G-11589)*

Commercial Honing LLC........................ D 330 343-8896
  Dover *(G-6235)*

Commercial Steel Treating Co............... F 216 431-8204
  Cleveland *(G-3553)*

Die Co Inc.. E 440 942-8856
  Eastlake *(G-6423)*

E L Stone Company............................... E 330 825-4565
  Norton *(G-10820)*

Etched Metal Company.......................... E 440 248-0240
  Solon *(G-12109)*

GRB Holdings Inc................................. G 937 236-3250
  Dayton *(G-5802)*

Hall Company.................................. E 937 652-1376
Urbana (G-13465)

Hartzell Mfg Co LLC....................... E 937 859-5955
Miamisburg (G-9696)

Industrial Paint & Strip Inc.............. E 419 568-2222
Waynesfield (G-13878)

J Horst Manufacturing Co............... D 330 828-2216
Dalton (G-5586)

JM Hamilton Group Inc................... F 419 229-4010
Lima (G-8422)

McGean-Rohco Inc.......................... G 216 441-4900
Newburgh Heights (G-10545)

McGean-Rohco Inc.......................... D 216 441-4900
Cleveland (G-4009)

Metal Seal & Products Inc............... C 440 946-8500
Mentor (G-9562)

Miba Bearings US LLC..................... B 740 962-4242
Mcconnelsville (G-9364)

Milestone Services Corp.................. G 330 374-9988
Akron (G-233)

Niles Manufacturing & Finshg.......... C 330 544-0402
Niles (G-10596)

Ohio Decorative Products LLC.......... C 419 647-9033
Spencerville (G-12238)

Ohio Metal Products Company.......... F 937 228-6101
Dayton (G-5925)

Ohio Roll Grinding Inc..................... E 330 453-1884
Louisville (G-8610)

P & L Heat Trting Grinding Inc.......... E 330 746-1339
Youngstown (G-14907)

Parker Rst-Proof Cleveland Inc........ E 216 481-6680
Cleveland (G-4142)

Parker Trutec Incorporated.............. D 937 653-8500
Urbana (G-13476)

Polymet Recovery LLC..................... G 330 630-9006
Akron (G-263)

Rack Processing Company Inc......... E 937 294-1911
Moraine (G-10189)

Reifel Industries Inc........................ D 419 737-2138
Pioneer (G-11328)

Sawyer Technical Materials LLC....... E 440 951-8770
Willoughby (G-14520)

Scot Industries Inc......................... C 330 262-7585
Wooster (G-14683)

Springco Metal Coatings Inc............ C 216 941-0020
Cleveland (G-4320)

Stuart-Dean Co Inc......................... G 412 765-2752
Cleveland (G-4338)

Tri-State Fabricators Inc.................. E 513 752-5005
Amelia (G-440)

Vectron Inc.................................... F 440 323-3369
Elyria (G-6600)

Wieland Metal Svcs Foils LLC.......... D 330 823-1700
Alliance (G-417)

Worthngton Smuel Coil Proc LLC...... E 330 963-3777
Twinsburg (G-13398)

Yoder Industries Inc....................... C 937 278-5769
Dayton (G-6089)

PLATING COMPOUNDS

Asterion LLC.................................. E 317 875-0051
Cincinnati (G-2382)

Plating Process Systems Inc............ G
Mentor (G-9587)

PLATING SVC: Chromium, Metals Or Formed Prdts

Chrome Deposit Corporation............ E 330 773-7800
Akron (G-98)

Chrome Deposit Corporation............ E 513 539-8486
Monroe (G-10098)

Hale Performance Coatings Inc......... E 419 244-6451
Toledo (G-12984)

Plate-All Metal Company Inc............ G 330 633-6166
Akron (G-260)

Quality Plating Co........................... G 216 361-0151
Cleveland (G-4215)

R A Heller Company........................ F 513 771-6100
Cincinnati (G-3027)

Raf Acquisition Co........................... E 440 572-5999
Valley City (G-13514)

Youngstown Hard Chrome Pltg Gr.... E 330 758-9721
Youngstown (G-14970)

PLAYGROUND EQPT

Adventurous Child Inc..................... G 513 531-7700
Cincinnati (G-2339)

Funtown Playgrounds Inc................. G 513 871-8585
Cincinnati (G-2303)

Meyer Design Inc............................ F 330 434-9176
Akron (G-230)

Ultrabuilt Play Systems Inc.............. F 419 652-2294
Nova (G-10878)

PLEATING & STITCHING FOR THE TRADE: Decorative & Novelty

Ideal Drapery Company Inc.............. F 330 745-9873
Barberton (G-813)

PLEATING & STITCHING SVC

Barbs Graffiti Inc............................ E 216 881-5550
Cleveland (G-3405)

Big Kahuna Graphics LLC................. G 330 455-2625
Canton (G-1840)

Catania Medallic Specialty Inc.......... E 440 933-9595
Avon Lake (G-751)

Design Original Inc......................... F 937 596-5121
Jackson Center (G-7961)

Fineline Imprints Inc....................... G 740 453-1083
Zanesville (G-15013)

Finn Graphics Inc........................... E 513 941-6161
Cincinnati (G-2624)

Shamrock Companies Inc................ D 440 899-9510
Westlake (G-14333)

PLUGS: Electric

Cooper Wiring Devices Inc.............. D 440 523-5000
Cleveland (G-3566)

PLUMBING FIXTURES

As America Inc.............................. F 330 332-9954
Salem (G-11762)

Atlantic Co.................................... F 440 944-8988
Willoughby Hills (G-14555)

Ferguson Enterprises LLC............... G 216 635-2493
Parma (G-11131)

Field Stone Inc.............................. G 937 898-3236
Tipp City (G-12825)

Fort Recovery Industries Inc........... D 419 375-3005
Fort Recovery (G-6965)

Fort Recovery Industries Inc........... C 419 375-4121
Fort Recovery (G-6964)

Krendl Machine Company................ D 419 692-3060
Delphos (G-6189)

Lsq Manufacturing Inc..................... F 330 725-4905
Medina (G-9421)

Maass Midwest Mfg Inc.................. G 419 894-6424
Arcadia (G-482)

Mansfield Plumbing Pdts LLC........... A 419 938-5211
Perrysville (G-11282)

Merit Brass Co.............................. C 216 261-9800
Cleveland (G-4021)

Mssk Manufacturing Inc.................. F 330 393-6624
Warren (G-13783)

Multi Fittings Corporation................ C 513 942-9910
West Chester (G-14032)

Next Gerenation Crimping................ G 440 237-6300
North Royalton (G-10776)

Waxman Industries Inc.................... C 440 439-1830
Bedford (G-1065)

Wolff Bros Supply Inc..................... F 440 327-1650
North Ridgeville (G-10753)

Wsi Seller Inc................................ F 330 379-0270
Akron (G-359)

Zekelman Industries Inc.................. C 740 432-2146
Cambridge (G-1766)

PLUMBING FIXTURES: Plastic

Add-A-Trap LLC............................. G 330 750-0417
Struthers (G-12615)

Bobbart Industries Inc.................... G 419 350-5477
Sylvania (G-12702)

Cincinnati Machines Inc.................. G 513 536-2432
Batavia (G-856)

Cultured Marble Inc........................ G 330 549-2282
Poland (G-11435)

Hancor Inc.................................... B 614 658-0050
Hilliard (G-7683)

Lubrizol Global Management Inc....... F 216 447-5000
Cleveland (G-3970)

Mansfield Plumbing Pdts LLC........... A 419 938-5211
Perrysville (G-11282)

Meese Inc..................................... F 440 998-1202
Ashtabula (G-604)

Tower Industries Ltd...................... E 330 837-2216
Massillon (G-9249)

PLUMBING FIXTURES: Vitreous

Accent Manufacturing Inc............... F 330 724-7704
Norton (G-10816)

As America Inc.............................. F 330 332-9954
Salem (G-11762)

East Woodworking Company........... G 216 791-5950
Cleveland (G-3649)

Mansfield Plumbing Pdts LLC........... A 419 938-5211
Perrysville (G-11282)

PLUMBING FIXTURES: Vitreous China

As America Inc.............................. D 419 522-4211
Mansfield (G-8763)

Watersource LLC............................ G 419 747-9552
Mansfield (G-8864)

POINT OF SALE DEVICES

NCR Technology Center................... G 937 445-1936
Dayton (G-5903)

Total Touch LLC............................. F 800 726-2117
Cleveland (G-4408)

Verifone Inc.................................. C 800 837-4366
Columbus (G-5346)

POLE LINE HARDWARE

Preformed Line Products Co............ B 440 461-5200
Mayfield Village (G-9346)

POLISHING SVC: Metals Or Formed Prdts

A & B Deburring Company............... F 513 723-0444
Cincinnati (G-2323)

Areway Acquisition Inc.................... D 216 651-9022
Brooklyn (G-1519)

Epsilon Management Corporation...... C 216 634-2500
Cleveland (G-3681)

Gei of Columbiana Inc..................... E 330 783-0270
Youngstown (G-14863)

PRODUCT

General Extrusions Intl LLC................... C 330 783-0270
   Youngstown (*G-14864*)

Hy-Blast Inc.................................... F 513 424-0704
   Middletown (*G-9864*)

Microtek Finishing LLC........................ E 513 766-5600
   West Chester (*G-14133*)

Shalmet Corporation........................... E 440 236-8840
   Elyria (*G-6589*)

Sun Polishing Corp............................ G 440 237-5525
   Cleveland (*G-4342*)

POLYESTERS

Dupont Specialty Pdts USA LLC............... E 740 474-0220
   Circleville (*G-3255*)

Illinois Tool Works Inc........................ C 513 489-7600
   Blue Ash (*G-1286*)

Maintenance Repair Supply Inc.............. G 740 922-3006
   Midvale (*G-9913*)

Mar-Bal Inc................................... D 440 543-7526
   Chagrin Falls (*G-2170*)

Pet Processors Llc............................ D 440 354-4321
   Painesville (*G-11105*)

Polynt Composites USA Inc.................... E 816 391-6000
   Sandusky (*G-11866*)

POLYETHYLENE RESINS

Etna Products Incorporated................... E 440 543-9845
   Chagrin Falls (*G-2161*)

Pitt Plastics Inc.............................. D 614 868-8660
   Columbus (*G-5192*)

POLYMETHYL METHACRYLATE RESINS: Plexiglas

Mexichem Specialty Resins Inc.............. E 440 930-1435
   Avon Lake (*G-765*)

POLYSTYRENE RESINS

Deltech Polymers LLC......................... G 937 339-3150
   Troy (*G-13210*)

Epsilyte Holdings LLC......................... D 937 778-9500
   Piqua (*G-11346*)

Evergreen Recycling LLC...................... E 419 547-1400
   Clyde (*G-4558*)

Progressive Foam Tech Inc.................... C 330 756-3200
   Beach City (*G-906*)

POLYURETHANE RESINS

Hfi LLC.. B 614 491-0700
   Canal Winchester (*G-1791*)

Louisville Molded Products Inc.............. G 330 877-9740
   Hartville (*G-7580*)

Polymer Concepts Inc......................... G 440 953-9605
   Mentor (*G-9589*)

POLYVINYL CHLORIDE RESINS

Aurora Plastics LLC........................... E 330 422-0700
   Streetsboro (*G-12488*)

Carlisle Plastics Company.................... G 937 845-9411
   New Carlisle (*G-10369*)

Crane Blending Center........................ E 614 542-1199
   Columbus (*G-4858*)

Geon Company................................ A 216 447-6000
   Cleveland (*G-3771*)

Prime Conduit Inc............................. F 216 464-3400
   Beachwood (*G-941*)

Win Plastic Extrusions LLC................... G 330 929-1999
   Cincinnati (*G-3226*)

POULTRY & POULTRY PRDTS WHOLESALERS

Borden Dairy Co Cincinnati LLC............. E 513 948-8811
   Cleveland (*G-3428*)

Just Natural Provision Company............. G 216 431-7922
   Cleveland (*G-3899*)

Roots Poultry Inc............................. G 419 332-0041
   Fremont (*G-7130*)

POULTRY & SMALL GAME SLAUGHTERING & PROCESSING

Cal-Maine Foods Inc.......................... D 937 337-9576
   Rossburg (*G-11655*)

Case Farms LLC............................... D 330 832-0030
   Massillon (*G-9178*)

Case Farms Processing Inc................... E 330 455-0241
   Winesburg (*G-14606*)

Cooper Foods.................................. E 419 232-2440
   Van Wert (*G-13530*)

Daylay Egg Farm Inc.......................... C 937 355-6531
   West Mansfield (*G-14178*)

Sid-Mar Foods Inc............................ G 330 743-0112
   Youngstown (*G-14931*)

The Ellenbee-Leggett Company Inc....... C 513 874-3200
   Fairfield (*G-6782*)

Weaver Bros Inc.............................. D 937 526-3907
   Versailles (*G-13605*)

POULTRY SLAUGHTERING & PROCESSING

Case Farms of Ohio Inc....................... C 330 359-7141
   Winesburg (*G-14605*)

Cooper Hatchery Inc.......................... C 419 238-4869
   Van Wert (*G-13531*)

Just Natural Provision Company............. G 216 431-7922
   Cleveland (*G-3899*)

POWDER: Iron

Truck Fax Inc................................. G 216 921-8866
   Cleveland (*G-4431*)

POWDER: Metal

Additive Metal Alloys Ltd.................... G 800 687-6110
   Holland (*G-7744*)

Bogie Industries Inc Ltd..................... E 330 745-3105
   Akron (*G-81*)

Duffee Finishing Inc.......................... G 740 965-4848
   Sunbury (*G-12663*)

Eckart America Corporation.................. D 440 954-7600
   Painesville (*G-11082*)

Key Finishes LLC............................. G 614 351-8393
   Columbus (*G-5053*)

Obron Atlantic Corporation.................. D 440 954-7600
   Painesville (*G-11100*)

Powdermet Inc................................ E 216 404-0053
   Euclid (*G-6670*)

Precision Pressed Powdered Met........... F 937 433-6802
   Dayton (*G-5951*)

Rmi Titanium Company LLC.................. E 330 652-9952
   Niles (*G-10604*)

POWER GENERATORS

Babcock & Wilcox Entps Inc.................. C 330 753-4511
   Akron (*G-68*)

Qaf Technologies Inc......................... E 440 941-4348
   Columbus (*G-5217*)

POWER SPLY CONVERTERS: Static, Electronic Applications

Bennett & Bennett Inc........................ G 937 324-1100
   Yellow Springs (*G-14786*)

POWER SUPPLIES: All Types, Static

Dare Electronics Inc.......................... E 937 335-0031
   Troy (*G-13208*)

Kontron America Incorporated.............. G 937 324-2420
   Springfield (*G-12339*)

Vertiv Group Corporation..................... A 614 888-0246
   Westerville (*G-14240*)

Vertiv JV Holdings LLC....................... A 614 888-0246
   Columbus (*G-5348*)

POWER SWITCHING EQPT

Layerzero Power Systems Inc............... F 440 399-9000
   Aurora (*G-676*)

Te Connectivity Corporation.................. C 419 521-9500
   Mansfield (*G-8858*)

UCI Controls Inc.............................. E 216 398-0330
   Cleveland (*G-4439*)

PRECAST TERRAZZO OR CONCRETE PRDTS

Clark Grave Vault Company................... C 614 294-3761
   Columbus (*G-4809*)

PRECIOUS METALS

Alexy Metals Ltd.............................. F 216 410-8661
   Willoughby (*G-14416*)

PRECIPITATORS: Electrostatic

McGill Airclean LLC........................... D 614 829-1200
   Columbus (*G-5089*)

McGill Corporation............................ F 614 829-1200
   Groveport (*G-7444*)

Neundorfer Inc............................... F 440 942-8990
   Willoughby (*G-14493*)

United McGill Corporation.................... E 614 829-1200
   Groveport (*G-7455*)

PRESSED FIBER & MOLDED PULP PRDTS, EXC FOOD

Vista Industrial Packaging LLC.............. E 800 454-6117
   Columbus (*G-5351*)

PRESTRESSED CONCRETE PRDTS

Fabcon Companies LLC........................ D 614 875-8601
   Grove City (*G-7386*)

PRIMARY ROLLING MILL EQPT

Rki Inc....................................... C 888 953-9400
   Mentor (*G-9608*)

PRINT CARTRIDGES: Laser & Other Computer Printers

All Write Ribbon Inc.......................... F 513 753-8300
   Amelia (*G-428*)

Printer Components Inc....................... G 585 924-5190
   Fairfield (*G-6767*)

Wood County Ohio............................ G 419 353-1227
   Bowling Green (*G-1448*)

PRINTED CIRCUIT BOARDS

Accurate Electronics Inc..................... F 330 682-7015
   Orrville (*G-10972*)

Alektronics Inc............................... F 937 429-2118
   Beavercreek (*G-988*)

Avcom Smt Inc................................ F 614 882-8176
   Westerville (*G-14244*)

Blue Creek Enterprises Inc................... F 937 222-9969
   Dayton (*G-5680*)

Blue Creek Enterprises Inc................... F 937 364-2920
   Manchester (*G-8753*)

C E Electronics Inc..............................D 419 636-6705
Bryan *(G-1635)*

Cartessa Corp..................................F 513 738-4477
Shandon *(G-11933)*

Circle Prime Manufacturing Inc...............E 330 923-0019
Cuyahoga Falls *(G-5534)*

Cleveland Circuits Corp.......................E 216 267-9020
Cleveland *(G-3509)*

Cleveland Coretec Inc.........................G 314 727-2087
North Jackson *(G-10685)*

Co-Ax Technology Inc.........................C 440 914-9200
Solon *(G-12096)*

Ddi North Jackson Corp.......................G 330 538-3900
North Jackson *(G-10686)*

Deca Mfg Co...................................F 419 884-0071
Mansfield *(G-8780)*

Dynalab Inc...................................D 614 866-9999
Reynoldsburg *(G-11568)*

Flex Fab LLC..................................G 330 757-8720
Poland *(G-11436)*

Flextronics Intl USA Inc......................E 513 755-2500
Middletown *(G-9861)*

Interactive Engineering Corp.................E 330 239-6888
Medina *(G-9413)*

Journey Electronics Corp.....................G 513 539-9836
Monroe *(G-10111)*

L3 Technologies Inc...........................E 513 943-2000
Cincinnati *(G-2309)*

Levison Enterprises LLC.......................E 419 838-7365
Millbury *(G-9964)*

Libra Industries LLC..........................C 440 974-7770
Mentor *(G-9553)*

Logisync Corporation.........................G 440 937-0388
Avon *(G-732)*

McGregor & Associates Inc...................C 937 629-4346
Brookville *(G-1573)*

Metzenbaum Sheltered Inds Inc..............E 440 729-1919
Chesterland *(G-2236)*

Npas Inc.......................................F 614 595-6916
Mansfield *(G-8840)*

Philway Products Inc..........................C 419 281-7777
Ashland *(G-561)*

Projects Unlimited Inc.........................C 937 918-2200
Dayton *(G-5968)*

Proto Circuit Inc..............................G 330 572-3400
Cuyahoga Falls *(G-5567)*

Qualtech Technologies Inc....................E 440 946-8081
Willoughby *(G-14514)*

Quarter Century Design LLC..................G 937 434-5127
Dayton *(G-5970)*

Sinbon Ohio LLC..............................C 937 415-2070
Vandalia *(G-13577)*

Techtron Systems Inc.........................E 440 505-2990
Solon *(G-12195)*

Tetrad Electronics Inc.........................D 440 946-6443
Willoughby *(G-14539)*

Ttm Technologies Inc..........................C 330 538-3900
North Jackson *(G-10696)*

Ttm Technologies North America LLC ....D 330 572-3400
North Jackson *(G-10697)*

Valtronic Technology Inc......................D 440 349-1239
Solon *(G-12201)*

Versitec Manufacturing Inc....................F 440 354-4283
Painesville *(G-11121)*

Vexos Inc......................................B 440 284-2500
Lagrange *(G-8155)*

Wurth Electronics Ics Inc.....................E 937 415-7700
Miamisburg *(G-9754)*

PRINTERS & PLOTTERS

Gameday Vision...............................F 330 830-4550
Massillon *(G-9193)*

PRINTERS' SVCS: Folding, Collating, Etc

Bookmasters Inc..............................C 419 281-1802
Ashland *(G-522)*

Capitol Citicom Inc............................E 614 472-2679
Columbus *(G-4799)*

Erd Specialty Graphics Inc....................G 419 242-9545
Toledo *(G-12955)*

PRINTERS: Computer

Microcom Corporation........................E 740 548-6262
Lewis Center *(G-8343)*

PRINTERS: Magnetic Ink, Bar Code

Hunkar Technologies Inc......................C 513 272-1010
Cincinnati *(G-2735)*

ID Images Inc..................................E 330 220-7300
Brunswick *(G-1597)*

PRINTING & BINDING: Books

Hf Group LLC..................................C 440 729-9411
Newbury *(G-10554)*

PRINTING & EMBOSSING: Plastic Fabric Articles

Akron Felt Chenille Mfg Co Inc................F 330 733-7778
Akron *(G-30)*

Personaliteez LLC..............................F 614 354-9108
Columbus *(G-5189)*

Plastic Card Inc................................D 330 896-5555
Uniontown *(G-13424)*

Solar Arts Graphic Designs....................G 330 744-0535
Youngstown *(G-14934)*

PRINTING & ENGRAVING: Financial Notes & Certificates

Mabis Shipping Solutions Inc.................G 330 650-1788
Hudson *(G-7850)*

Quick Tech Business Forms Inc................G 937 743-5952
Springboro *(G-12265)*

Watson Haran & Company Inc.................G 937 436-1414
Dayton *(G-6076)*

PRINTING & STAMPING: Fabric Articles

City Apparel Inc................................F 419 434-1155
Findlay *(G-6852)*

Erd Specialty Graphics Inc....................G 419 242-9545
Toledo *(G-12955)*

Hollywood Imprints LLC.......................F 614 501-6040
Gahanna *(G-7160)*

Wholesale Imprints Inc........................E 440 224-3527
North Kingsville *(G-10700)*

PRINTING & WRITING PAPER WHOLESALERS

Gvs Industries Inc.............................G 513 851-3606
Hamilton *(G-7498)*

Microcom Corporation........................E 740 548-6262
Lewis Center *(G-8343)*

PRINTING MACHINERY

Alchem Aluminum Europe Inc................G 216 910-3400
Beachwood *(G-908)*

Anderson & Vreeland Inc......................D 419 636-5002
Bryan *(G-1629)*

Armor...G 614 459-1414
Columbus *(G-4726)*

Beehex Inc....................................G 512 633-5304
Columbus *(G-4748)*

Container Graphics Corp......................E 937 746-5666
Franklin *(G-7013)*

Gedico International Inc.......................G 937 274-2167
West Chester *(G-14007)*

Gew Inc.......................................G 440 237-4439
Cleveland *(G-3774)*

Hadronics Inc..................................D 513 321-9350
Cincinnati *(G-2702)*

Imco Recycling of Indiana Inc.................G 216 910-3400
Beachwood *(G-922)*

Kase Equipment Corporation..................D 216 642-9040
Cleveland *(G-3907)*

Nilpeter Usa Inc...............................C 513 489-4400
Cincinnati *(G-2909)*

Pearce Inc.....................................F 216 252-0550
Hinckley *(G-7735)*

R & D Equipment Inc..........................F 419 668-8439
Norwalk *(G-10860)*

Roessner Holdings Inc........................G 419 356-2123
Fort Recovery *(G-6970)*

Schilling Graphics Inc.........................E 419 468-1037
Galion *(G-7198)*

Suspension Feeder Corporation...............F 419 763-1377
Fort Recovery *(G-6972)*

Wise Edge LLC................................G 330 208-0889
Mogadore *(G-10094)*

Wood Graphics Inc............................E 513 771-6300
Cincinnati *(G-3230)*

PRINTING, COMMERCIAL: Bags, Plastic, NEC

Ray C Sprosty Bag Co Inc.....................F 330 669-0045
Smithville *(G-12067)*

Trebnick Systems LLC.........................E 937 743-1550
Springboro *(G-12272)*

PRINTING, COMMERCIAL: Business Forms, NEC

Carbonless Cut Sheet Forms Inc..............F 740 826-1700
New Concord *(G-10385)*

PJ Bush Associates Inc........................F 216 362-6700
Cleveland *(G-4168)*

R R Donnelley & Sons Company...............B 740 928-6110
Hebron *(G-7632)*

S F Mock & Associates LLC....................F 937 438-0196
Dayton *(G-5991)*

Smartbill Ltd..................................F 740 928-6909
Hebron *(G-7636)*

PRINTING, COMMERCIAL: Calendars, NEC

Haman Enterprises Inc........................F 614 888-7574
Columbus *(G-4968)*

Proforma Systems Advantage..................G 419 224-8747
Lima *(G-8440)*

PRINTING, COMMERCIAL: Decals, NEC

Boehm Inc.....................................E 614 875-9010
Grove City *(G-7374)*

Commercial Decal Ohio Inc....................G 330 385-7178
East Liverpool *(G-6390)*

T&T Graphics Inc..............................D 937 847-6000
Miamisburg *(G-9742)*

PRINTING, COMMERCIAL: Envelopes, NEC

Ohio Envelope Manufacturing Co..............E 216 267-2920
Cleveland *(G-4114)*

PRINTING, COMMERCIAL: Imprinting

Ableprint / Toucan Inc........................F 419 522-9742
Mansfield *(G-8758)*

Better Living Concepts Inc.....................G 330 494-2213
Canton *(G-1839)*

PRODUCT

Fair Publishing House Inc................ E 419 668-3746
Norwalk *(G-10841)*

Middaugh Enterprises Inc................ G 330 852-2471
Sugarcreek *(G-12641)*

PRINTING, COMMERCIAL: Labels & Seals, NEC

CCL Label Inc.................................... E 856 273-0700
New Albany *(G-10334)*

CCL Label Inc.................................... B 440 878-7277
Strongsville *(G-12549)*

Century Marketing Corporation.......... C 419 354-2591
Bowling Green *(G-1413)*

CMC Group Inc.................................. D 419 354-2591
Bowling Green *(G-1415)*

Collotype Labels Usa Inc.................. D 513 381-1480
Batavia *(G-858)*

Contemprary Image Labeling Inc.......... G 513 583-5699
Lebanon *(G-8250)*

D&D Design Concepts Inc.................. F 513 752-2191
Batavia *(G-860)*

Donprint Inc...................................... E 847 573-7777
Strongsville *(G-12554)*

Innovtive Lbling Solutions Inc............ D 513 860-2457
Hamilton *(G-7505)*

Jamac Inc.. E 419 625-9790
Sandusky *(G-11845)*

Label Aid Inc.................................... E 419 433-2888
Huron *(G-7876)*

Label Technique Southeast LLC........ F 440 951-7660
Willoughby *(G-14479)*

Labeltek Inc...................................... D 330 335-3110
Wadsworth *(G-13648)*

M PI Label Systems.......................... G 330 938-2134
Sebring *(G-11896)*

McC-Norway LLC.............................. G 513 381-1480
Batavia *(G-871)*

Miller Products Inc............................ F 330 335-3110
Wadsworth *(G-13651)*

Miller Products Inc............................ D 330 335-3110
Wadsworth *(G-13652)*

Model GRAphics& Media Inc............ E 513 541-2355
West Chester *(G-14031)*

Mpi Labels of Baltimore Inc.............. E 330 938-2134
Sebring *(G-11899)*

Multi-Color Corporation.................... C 513 381-1480
Batavia *(G-878)*

Multi-Color Corporation.................... G 513 459-3283
Mason *(G-9130)*

Ohio Label Inc.................................. F 614 777-0180
Columbus *(G-5146)*

Performance Packaging Inc.............. F 419 478-8805
Toledo *(G-13094)*

Scratch-Off Systems Inc.................. E 216 649-7800
Twinsburg *(G-13376)*

Seneca Label Inc.............................. E 440 237-1600
Brunswick *(G-1615)*

Tech/III Inc.. E 513 482-7500
Fairfield *(G-6781)*

The Hooven - Dayton Corp................ C 937 233-4473
Miamisburg *(G-9747)*

The Label Team Inc.......................... F 330 332-1067
Salem *(G-11814)*

USA Label Express Inc...................... E 330 874-1001
Bolivar *(G-1395)*

Verstrete In Mold Lbels USA In.......... F 513 943-0080
Batavia *(G-896)*

W/S Packaging Group Inc.................. E 513 459-8800
Mason *(G-9166)*

PRINTING, COMMERCIAL: Letterpress & Screen

Club 513 LLC.................................... G 800 530-2574
Cincinnati *(G-2501)*

PRINTING, COMMERCIAL: Literature, Advertising, NEC

Bottomline Ink Corporation................ E 419 897-8000
Perrysburg *(G-11205)*

Multi-Color Australia LLC.................. D 513 381-1480
Batavia *(G-877)*

PRINTING, COMMERCIAL: Magazines, NEC

Quebecor World Johnson Hardin.......... G 614 326-0299
Cincinnati *(G-3019)*

PRINTING, COMMERCIAL: Periodicals, NEC

400 SW 7th Street Partners Ltd.......... E 440 826-4700
Cincinnati *(G-2320)*

AGS Custom Graphics Inc................ D 330 963-7770
Macedonia *(G-8676)*

Center For Inquiry Inc...................... G 330 671-7192
Peninsula *(G-11181)*

Crain Communications Inc................ E 330 836-9180
Cuyahoga Falls *(G-5536)*

Dominion Enterprises........................ F 216 472-1870
Cleveland *(G-3624)*

Greater Cincinnati Bowl Assn............ E 513 761-7387
Cincinnati *(G-2689)*

Kent Information Services Inc............ G 330 672-2110
Kent *(G-8042)*

Legal News Publishing Co................ E 216 696-3322
Cleveland *(G-3949)*

Liturgical Publications Inc................ D 216 325-6825
Cleveland *(G-3964)*

Matthew Bender & Company Inc.......... C 518 487-3000
Miamisburg *(G-9710)*

Pearson Education Inc...................... G 614 876-0371
Columbus *(G-5180)*

Pearson Education Inc...................... E 614 841-3700
Columbus *(G-5181)*

Relx Inc.. G 937 865-6800
Miamisburg *(G-9730)*

Rubber World Magazine Inc.............. G 330 864-2122
Akron *(G-294)*

Schaeffers Investment Research Inc...... D 513 589-3800
Blue Ash *(G-1331)*

Sesh Communications...................... F 513 851-1693
Cincinnati *(G-3084)*

Sterling Associates Inc.................... G 330 630-3500
Akron *(G-318)*

Telex Communications Inc................ F 419 865-0972
Toledo *(G-13140)*

Welch Publishing Co........................ E 419 874-2528
Perrysburg *(G-11279)*

PRINTING, COMMERCIAL: Promotional

Ad-Sensations Inc............................ F 419 841-5395
Sylvania *(G-12700)*

American Business Forms Inc............ E 513 312-2522
West Chester *(G-14101)*

American Imprssions Sportswear.......... G 614 848-6677
Columbus *(G-4697)*

Everythings Image Inc...................... G 513 469-6727
Blue Ash *(G-1273)*

Sensical Inc...................................... D 216 641-1141
Solon *(G-12180)*

SRC Liquidation LLC........................ A 937 221-1000
Dayton *(G-6019)*

PRINTING, COMMERCIAL: Screen

Aardvark Screen Prtg & EMB LLC.......... F 419 354-6686
Bowling Green *(G-1404)*

Absolute Impressions Inc.................. F 614 840-0599
Lewis Center *(G-8319)*

Ace Transfer Company...................... G 937 398-1103
Springfield *(G-12276)*

Adcraft Decals Incorporated.............. E 216 524-2934
Cleveland *(G-3297)*

Advanced Incentives Inc.................. G 419 471-9088
Toledo *(G-12865)*

Airwaves LLC.................................... C 740 548-1200
Lewis Center *(G-8320)*

Albany Screen Printing LLC.............. F 614 585-3279
Reynoldsburg *(G-11555)*

Alberts Screen Print Inc.................... C 330 753-7559
Norton *(G-10818)*

Allied Silk Screen Inc...................... G 937 223-4921
Dayton *(G-5647)*

Ares Sportswear Ltd.......................... D 614 767-1950
Hilliard *(G-7668)*

Art Works.. G 740 425-5765
Barnesville *(G-843)*

Ashton LLC.. F 614 833-4165
Pickerington *(G-11288)*

Ashton LLC.. F 336 447-4951
Pickerington *(G-11287)*

Assocted Vsual Cmmncations Inc...... E 330 452-4449
Canton *(G-1833)*

Aztech Printing & Promotions............ G 937 339-0100
Troy *(G-13202)*

Badlime Promo and Apparel LLC.......... G 330 425-7100
Twinsburg *(G-13277)*

Ball Jackets LLC.............................. E 937 572-1114
Jamestown *(G-7968)*

Big Kahuna Graphics LLC.................. G 330 455-2625
Canton *(G-1840)*

Bluelogos Inc.................................... F 614 898-9971
Westerville *(G-14247)*

Campbell Signs & Apparel LLC.......... G 330 386-4768
East Liverpool *(G-6388)*

Casad Company Inc.......................... F 419 586-9457
Coldwater *(G-4570)*

Clear Images LLC.............................. G 419 241-9347
Toledo *(G-12923)*

Cleveland Printwear Inc.................... G 216 521-5500
Cleveland *(G-3521)*

Columbus Custom Tees...................... F 614 573-5556
Columbus *(G-4821)*

Concept 9 Inc.................................... G 614 294-3743
Columbus *(G-4840)*

Custom Apparel LLC.......................... G 330 633-2626
Akron *(G-111)*

Custom Deco LLC.............................. E 419 698-2900
Toledo *(G-12935)*

Custom Sportswear Imprints LLC.......... G 330 335-8326
Wadsworth *(G-13633)*

Drycal Inc.. G 440 974-1999
Mentor *(G-9512)*

Dynamic Design & Systems Inc.......... G 440 708-1010
Chagrin Falls *(G-2159)*

Erd Specialty Graphics Inc................ G 419 242-9545
Toledo *(G-12955)*

Four Ambition LLC............................ G 937 239-4479
Dayton *(G-5783)*

Fulton Sign & Decal Inc.................... G 440 951-1515
Mentor *(G-9521)*

Glavin Industries Inc........................ E 440 349-0049
Solon *(G-12115)*

Glen D Lala.. G 937 274-7770
Dayton *(G-5797)*

Got Graphix Llc.................................. F 330 703-9047
   Fairlawn *(G-6802)*

Grady McCauley Inc............................ D 330 494-9444
   Akron *(G-165)*

Green Leaf Printing and Design.......... G 937 222-3634
   Dayton *(G-5803)*

Hartman Distributing LLC................... D 740 616-7764
   Heath *(G-7596)*

Hill Sign Company Inc......................... G 614 367-9227
   Columbus *(G-4988)*

Industrial Screen Prcess Svc I........... F 419 255-4900
   Toledo *(G-13003)*

Jason Schirmer................................... G 937 433-3023
   Miamisburg *(G-9702)*

Jupmode... E 419 318-2029
   Toledo *(G-13013)*

Just Name It Inc.................................. G 614 626-8662
   Ashland *(G-542)*

Kaufman Container Company............... C 216 898-2000
   Cleveland *(G-3908)*

Kdm Signs Inc..................................... C 513 769-1932
   Cincinnati *(G-2787)*

Kens His & Hers Shop Inc................... G 330 872-3190
   Newton Falls *(G-10578)*

Knight Line Signature AP Corp............ G 330 545-8108
   Girard *(G-7273)*

Lake Screen Printing Inc..................... G 440 244-5707
   Lorain *(G-8563)*

Liberty Sportswear LLC....................... G 513 755-8740
   Hamilton *(G-7510)*

License Ad Plate Company.................. F 216 265-4200
   Cleveland *(G-3954)*

Lima Sporting Goods Inc..................... E 419 222-1036
   Lima *(G-8427)*

Loris Printing Inc................................. G 419 626-6648
   Sandusky *(G-11852)*

M & H Screen Printing......................... G 740 522-1957
   Newark *(G-10517)*

Markt LLC.. G 740 397-5900
   Mount Vernon *(G-10250)*

McC - Mason W&S............................... C 513 459-1100
   Mason *(G-9126)*

Meder Special-Tees Ltd...................... G 513 921-3800
   Cincinnati *(G-2855)*

Metro Flex Inc..................................... G 937 299-5360
   Moraine *(G-10178)*

Mid-Ohio Screen Print Inc................... G 614 875-1774
   Grove City *(G-7400)*

Morrison Sign Company Inc................. E 614 276-1181
   Columbus *(G-5112)*

Murphy Dog LLC.................................. E 614 755-4278
   Blacklick *(G-1227)*

Neff Motivation Inc.............................. C 937 548-3194
   Greenville *(G-7348)*

New Dawn Distribution Inc.................. G 330 759-3500
   Girard *(G-7277)*

Nordec Inc... D 330 940-3700
   Stow *(G-12447)*

Northeastern Plastics Inc.................... G 330 453-5925
   Canton *(G-1961)*

Odyssey Spirits Inc............................. F 330 562-1523
   Chagrin Falls *(G-2174)*

Off Contact Inc.................................... F 419 255-5546
   Toledo *(G-13071)*

P S Graphics Inc................................. G 440 356-9656
   Rocky River *(G-11636)*

Painted Hill Inv Group Inc................... F 937 339-1756
   Troy *(G-13246)*

Part 2 Screen Prtg Design Inc............ G 614 294-4429
   Columbus *(G-5175)*

Patio Printing Inc................................ G 614 785-9553
   Columbus *(G-5177)*

Pops Printed Apparel LLC................... G 614 372-5651
   Columbus *(G-5198)*

Precision Imprint................................. G 740 592-5916
   Athens *(G-646)*

Primal Screen Inc................................ G 330 677-1766
   Kent *(G-8063)*

Prodigy Print Inc................................. F
   Dayton *(G-5960)*

Qualitee Design Sportswear Co........... F 740 333-8337
   Wshngtn Ct Hs *(G-14742)*

Queen City Spirit LLC.......................... F 513 533-2662
   Cincinnati *(G-3026)*

Richardson Supply Ltd........................ G 614 539-3033
   Grove City *(G-7411)*

Schlabach Printers LLC....................... E 330 852-4687
   Sugarcreek *(G-12649)*

Sit Inc... E 330 758-8468
   Youngstown *(G-14933)*

Spear Inc... D 513 459-1100
   Mason *(G-9154)*

Specialty Nameplate Corp................... F 614 444-6876
   Columbus *(G-5279)*

Specialty Printing and Proc................. F 614 322-9035
   Columbus *(G-5280)*

SRI Ohio Inc.. E 740 653-5800
   Lancaster *(G-8226)*

Standout Stickers Inc.......................... G 877 449-7703
   Brunswick *(G-1616)*

Steves Sports Inc................................ G 440 735-0044
   Northfield *(G-10797)*

Studio Eleven Inc................................ F 937 295-2225
   Fort Loramie *(G-6958)*

T & L Custom Screening Inc................ G 937 237-3121
   Dayton *(G-6036)*

T-Shirt Co.. G 513 821-7100
   Cincinnati *(G-3135)*

Transfer Express Inc........................... D 440 918-1900
   Mentor *(G-9642)*

Underground Sports Shop Inc............. F 513 751-1662
   Cincinnati *(G-3179)*

Unisport Inc.. F 419 529-4727
   Ontario *(G-10953)*

United Sport Apparel........................... F 330 722-0818
   Medina *(G-9460)*

Uptown Dog The Inc............................ G 740 592-4600
   Athens *(G-655)*

Vgu Industries Inc............................... E 216 676-9093
   Cleveland *(G-4464)*

Viewpoint Graphic Design................... G 419 447-6073
   Tiffin *(G-12807)*

PRINTING, COMMERCIAL: Stationery, NEC

CCL Label Inc...................................... E 216 676-2703
   Cleveland *(G-3480)*

Keeler Enterprises Inc......................... G 330 336-7601
   Wadsworth *(G-13646)*

Westrock Mwv LLC.............................. D 937 495-6323
   Dayton *(G-6079)*

PRINTING, LITHOGRAPHIC: Advertising Posters

Sky Wireless and Smoke Sp LLC......... E 513 488-5992
   Cincinnati *(G-3095)*

PRINTING, LITHOGRAPHIC: Calendars

Novelty Advertising Co Inc.................. E 740 622-3113
   Coshocton *(G-5465)*

PRINTING, LITHOGRAPHIC: Circulars

Melnor Graphics LLC........................... E 419 476-8808
   Toledo *(G-13052)*

PRINTING, LITHOGRAPHIC: Color

Fx Digital Media Inc............................ F 216 241-4040
   Cleveland *(G-3746)*

PRINTING, LITHOGRAPHIC: Forms, Business

GBS Corp.. C 330 863-1828
   Malvern *(G-8750)*

Quick Tab II Inc................................... D 419 448-6622
   Tiffin *(G-12796)*

PRINTING, LITHOGRAPHIC: Offset & photolithographic printing

Capitol Citicom Inc.............................. E 614 472-2679
   Columbus *(G-4799)*

Corporate Dcment Solutions Inc.......... G 513 595-8200
   Cincinnati *(G-2518)*

Hecks Direct Mail & Prtg Svc.............. E 419 661-6028
   Toledo *(G-12989)*

M Rosenthal Company.......................... F 513 563-0081
   Cincinnati *(G-2835)*

SMI Holdings Inc................................. D 740 927-3464
   Pataskala *(G-11151)*

PRINTING, LITHOGRAPHIC: Posters

Frame Warehouse................................ G 614 861-4582
   Reynoldsburg *(G-11570)*

PRINTING, LITHOGRAPHIC: Tags

Trebnick Systems LLC......................... E 937 743-1550
   Springboro *(G-12272)*

PRINTING, LITHOGRAPHIC: Tickets

Premier Southern Ticket Co Inc........... E 513 489-6700
   Cincinnati *(G-2980)*

PRINTING: Books

American Printing & Lithog Co............. F 513 867-0602
   Hamilton *(G-7463)*

Hf Group LLC....................................... F 440 729-2445
   Aurora *(G-674)*

Hubbard Company............................... E 419 784-4455
   Defiance *(G-6111)*

J & L Management Corporation............ G 440 205-1199
   Mentor *(G-9537)*

Multi-Craft Litho Inc............................ E 050 501-2754
   Blue Ash *(G-1312)*

The Press of Ohio Inc......................... B 330 678-5868
   Kent *(G-8090)*

Lsc Communications Inc...................... A 419 935-0111
   Willard *(G-14403)*

Quebecor World Johnson Hardin......... G 614 326-0299
   Cincinnati *(G-3019)*

PRINTING: Commercial, NEC

4 Over LLC.. E 937 610-0629
   Dayton *(G-5627)*

A E Wilson Holdings Inc...................... G 330 405-0316
   Twinsburg *(G-13265)*

A To Z Paper Box Company................. G 330 325-8722
   Rootstown *(G-11646)*

Advertising Joe LLC Mean................... G 440 247-8200
   Chagrin Falls *(G-2135)*

Aero Fulfillment Services Corp............ D 800 225-7145
   Mason *(G-9056)*

Agnone-Kelly Enterprises Inc.............. G 800 634-6503
   Cincinnati *(G-2343)*

AGS Custom Graphics Inc................... D 330 963-7770
   Macedonia *(G-8676)*

PRODUCT

American Printing & Lithog Co............ F 513 867-0602
   Hamilton *(G-7463)*

Anderson Graphics Inc..................... E 330 745-2165
   Barberton *(G-793)*

Appleheart Inc............................. G 937 384-0430
   Miamisburg *(G-9666)*

Austin Tape and Label Inc.............. D 330 928-7999
   Stow *(G-12420)*

Bates Printing Inc......................... F 330 833-5830
   Massillon *(G-9174)*

Bindery & Spc Pressworks Inc.......... D 614 873-4623
   Plain City *(G-11398)*

Bizall Inc.................................. G 216 939-9580
   Cleveland *(G-3419)*

Bollin & Sons Inc......................... E 419 693-6573
   Toledo *(G-12900)*

Brass Bull 1 LLC.......................... G 740 335-8030
   Wshngtn Ct Hs *(G-14735)*

Broadway Printing LLC................... G 513 621-3429
   Cincinnati *(G-2427)*

Brook & Whittle Limited.................. E 513 860-2457
   Hamilton *(G-7474)*

BSN Sports................................ G 513 821-7575
   Cincinnati *(G-2431)*

Buckeye Packaging Co Inc............... D 330 935-0301
   Alliance *(G-373)*

Carey Color Inc........................... D 330 239-1835
   Sharon Center *(G-11938)*

Century Graphics Inc..................... G 614 895-7698
   Westerville *(G-14206)*

Charles Huffman & Associates.......... G 216 295-0850
   Warrensville Heights *(G-13817)*

Cincinnati Print Solutions LLC.......... G 513 943-9500
   Milford *(G-9929)*

Consolidated Graphics Group Inc....... C 216 881-9191
   Cleveland *(G-3559)*

Corporate Dcment Solutions Inc........ G 513 595-8200
   Cincinnati *(G-2518)*

Creative Dcument Solutions LLC........ G 740 389-4252
   Marion *(G-8968)*

Culaine Inc............................... G 419 345-4984
   Toledo *(G-12934)*

Custom Products Corporation........... D 440 528-7100
   Glenwillow *(G-7285)*

Dayton Legal Blank Inc................... G 937 435-4405
   Dayton *(G-5729)*

Dayton Mailing Services Inc............. E 937 222-5056
   Dayton *(G-5731)*

Dietrich Von Hldbrand Lgacy PR........ G 703 496-7821
   Steubenville *(G-12402)*

Dlh Enterprises LLC...................... G 330 253-6960
   Akron *(G-124)*

DSC Supply Company LLC................ G 614 891-1100
   Westerville *(G-14257)*

Dupli-Systems Inc........................ C 440 234-9415
   Strongsville *(G-12555)*

Electronic Imaging Svcs Inc............. F 740 549-2487
   Lewis Center *(G-8332)*

Engineered Imaging LLC.................. F 419 255-1283
   Toledo *(G-12953)*

Equip Business Solutions Co............ G 614 854-9755
   Jackson *(G-7945)*

Folks Creative Printers Inc.............. G 740 383-6326
   Marion *(G-8970)*

Galactic Printing LLC.................... G
   Columbus *(G-4944)*

Gb Liquidating Company Inc............. E 513 248-7600
   Milford *(G-9935)*

GBS Corp.................................. C 330 494-5330
   North Canton *(G-10641)*

General Data Company Inc................ B 513 752-7978
   Cincinnati *(G-2304)*

General Theming Contrs LLC............. C 614 252-6342
   Columbus *(G-4948)*

Golden Graphics Ltd....................... F 419 673-6260
   Kenton *(G-8099)*

Gq Business Products Inc................ G 513 792-4750
   Loveland *(G-8627)*

Grafisk Maskinfabrik Amer LLC.......... G 630 432-4370
   Lebanon *(G-8265)*

Graphic Stitch Inc........................ G 937 642-6707
   Marysville *(G-9021)*

Harper Engraving & Printing Co.......... D 614 276-0700
   Columbus *(G-4970)*

Hecks Direct Mail Prtg Svc Inc......... F 419 697-3505
   Toledo *(G-12990)*

Hkm Drect Mkt Cmmnications Inc....... F 440 934-3060
   Sheffield Village *(G-11959)*

Hkm Drect Mkt Cmmnications Inc....... F 330 395-9538
   Warren *(G-13771)*

Hkm Drect Mkt Cmmnications Inc....... C 800 860-4456
   Cleveland *(G-3832)*

Horizon Ohio Publications Inc........... D 419 738-2128
   Wapakoneta *(G-13715)*

HP Industries Inc........................ E 419 478-0695
   Toledo *(G-12997)*

Humtown Pattern Company............... D 330 482-5555
   Columbiana *(G-4619)*

Imagine This Renovations............... G 330 833-6739
   Navarre *(G-10305)*

Innomark Communications LLC.......... D 513 285-1040
   Fairfield *(G-6744)*

Jack Walker Printing Co.................. F 440 352-4222
   Mentor *(G-9540)*

Kay Toledo Tag Inc....................... D 419 729-5479
   Toledo *(G-13017)*

Kdm Signs Inc............................ E 513 554-1393
   Cincinnati *(G-2788)*

Kenwel Printers Inc...................... E 614 261-1011
   Columbus *(G-5050)*

Letterman Printing Inc................... G 513 523-1111
   Oxford *(G-11063)*

Liming Printing Inc....................... F 937 374-2646
   Xenia *(G-14769)*

Lsc Communications Inc.................. A 419 935-0111
   Willard *(G-14403)*

Marbee Inc................................ G 419 422-9441
   Findlay *(G-6891)*

Marcus Uppe Inc......................... E 216 263-4000
   Cleveland *(G-3987)*

Miami Graphics Services Inc............ F 937 698-4013
   West Milton *(G-14183)*

Middleton Printing Co Inc................ G 614 294-7277
   Gahanna *(G-7166)*

ML Advertising & Design LLC............ G 419 447-6523
   Tiffin *(G-12791)*

Mmp Printing Inc......................... F 513 381-0990
   Cincinnati *(G-2883)*

Multi-Craft Litho Inc..................... E 859 581-2754
   Blue Ash *(G-1312)*

Mustang Printing......................... F 419 592-2746
   Napoleon *(G-10292)*

Ncrformscom.............................. G 800 709-1938
   Hudson *(G-7853)*

Network Printing & Graphics............ F 614 230-2084
   Columbus *(G-5124)*

Nilpeter Usa Inc.......................... C 513 489-4400
   Cincinnati *(G-2909)*

Nomis Publications Inc................... F 330 965-2380
   Youngstown *(G-14904)*

Old Trail Printing Company.............. G 614 443-4852
   Columbus *(G-5159)*

Onetouchpoint East Corp................ D 513 421-1600
   Cincinnati *(G-2933)*

Packaging Materials Inc.................. E 740 432-6337
   Cambridge *(G-1753)*

Park PLC Prntg Cpyg & Dgtl IMG.......... G 330 799-1739
   Youngstown *(G-14913)*

Peebles Creative Group Inc............. G 614 487-2011
   Dublin *(G-6329)*

Penguin Enterprises Inc.................. E 440 899-5112
   Westlake *(G-14322)*

Pexco Packaging Corp.................... E 419 470-5935
   Toledo *(G-13096)*

Precision Business Solutions............ F 419 661-8700
   Perrysburg *(G-11258)*

Press of Ohio Inc........................ F 330 678-5868
   Kent *(G-8062)*

Printing Dimensions Inc.................. F 937 256-0044
   Dayton *(G-5957)*

Profile Digital Printing LLC.............. E 937 866-4241
   Dayton *(G-5965)*

Progressive Printers Inc................. D 937 222-1267
   Dayton *(G-5967)*

Quest Service Labs Inc................... G 330 405-0316
   Twinsburg *(G-13362)*

R R Donnelley & Sons Company.......... G 513 552-1512
   West Chester *(G-14061)*

R&D Marketing Group Inc................. G 216 398-9100
   Brooklyn Heights *(G-1537)*

Repacorp Inc.............................. D 937 667-8496
   Tipp City *(G-12841)*

Reynolds and Reynolds Company........ F 419 584-7000
   Celina *(G-2117)*

Ryans Newark Leader Ex Prtg Co.......... F 740 522-2149
   Newark *(G-10532)*

Schilling Graphics Inc.................... E 419 468-1037
   Galion *(G-7198)*

Sekuworks LLC............................ G 513 202-1210
   Harrison *(G-7566)*

Springdot Inc............................. D 513 542-4000
   Cincinnati *(G-3108)*

Standard Register Technologies.......... E 937 443-1000
   Dayton *(G-6023)*

Stephen Andrews Inc..................... G 330 725-2672
   Lodi *(G-8507)*

Stolle Machinery Company LLC.......... C 937 497-5400
   Sidney *(G-12056)*

Suburban Press Incorporated........... F 216 961-0766
   Cleveland *(G-4340)*

Taylor Communications Inc.............. E 419 678-6000
   Coldwater *(G-4585)*

Taylor Communications Inc.............. E 937 221-1000
   Dayton *(G-6039)*

Taylor Communications Inc.............. E 614 277-7500
   Urbancrest *(G-13484)*

The Cyril-Scott Company................. C 740 654-2112
   Lancaster *(G-8228)*

The D B Hess Company................... E 330 678-5868
   Kent *(G-8089)*

Tj Metzgers Inc........................... D 419 861-8611
   Toledo *(G-13143)*

Toledo Ticket Company................... E 419 476-5424
   Toledo *(G-13159)*

Tpo Hess Holdings Inc.................... D 815 334-6140
   Kent *(G-8091)*

Universal North Inc...................... F 440 230-1366
   North Royalton *(G-10787)*

Visual Marking Systems Inc.............. D 330 425-7100
   Twinsburg *(G-13393)*

Vya Inc.................................... E 513 772-5400
   Cincinnati *(G-3210)*

Ward/Kraft Forms of Ohio Inc............ E 740 694-0015
   Fredericktown *(G-7088)*

West-Camp Press Inc..................... D 614 882-2378
   Westerville *(G-14281)*

PRINTING: Flexographic — continued

Western Roto Engravers Inc.............. E 330 336-7636
  Wadsworth (G-13677)

Wfsr Holdings LLC............................ A 877 735-4966
  Dayton (G-6081)

Williams Steel Rule Die Co.............. G 216 431-3232
  Cleveland (G-4507)

Workflowone LLC............................. A 877 735-4966
  Dayton (G-6087)

Yockey Group Inc............................. G 513 860-9053
  West Chester (G-14095)

PRINTING: Flexographic

Admiral Products Company Inc......... E 216 671-0600
  Cleveland (G-3299)

Custom Poly Bag LLC........................ D 330 935-2408
  Alliance (G-378)

Ebel-Binder Printing Co Inc............. G 513 471-1067
  Cincinnati (G-2577)

Hawks & Associates Inc.................. E 513 752-4311
  Cincinnati (G-2305)

HI Tech Printing Co Inc.................... E 513 874-5325
  Fairfield (G-6739)

Kopco Graphics Inc.......................... E 513 874-7230
  West Chester (G-14021)

Mr Label Inc..................................... E 513 681-2088
  Cincinnati (G-2891)

Ohio Flexible Packaging Co............. F 513 494-1800
  South Lebanon (G-12220)

Omni Systems LLC............................ D 216 377-5160
  Mayfield Village (G-9345)

Samuels Products Inc...................... E 513 891-4456
  Blue Ash (G-1330)

Superior Label Systems Inc............. B 513 336-0825
  Mason (G-9157)

Thomas Products Co Inc.................. E 513 756-9009
  Cincinnati (G-3155)

Warren Printing & Off Pdts Inc........ F 419 523-3635
  Ottawa (G-11050)

West Crrllton Prchment Cnvrtin....... E 513 594-3341
  West Carrollton (G-13933)

PRINTING: Gravure, Forms, Business

Dupli-Systems Inc............................ C 440 234-9415
  Strongsville (G-12555)

Workflowone LLC............................. A 877 735-4966
  Dayton (G-6087)

PRINTING: Gravure, Labels

Admiral Products Company Inc......... E 216 671-0600
  Cleveland (G-3299)

M PI Label Systems.......................... G 330 938-2134
  Sebring (G-11896)

Mpi Labels of Baltimore Inc............ E 330 938-2134
  Sebring (G-11899)

Pioneer Labels Inc........................... C 618 546-5418
  West Chester (G-14048)

Retterbush Graphics Packg Corp..... G 513 779-4466
  West Chester (G-14066)

Scratch-Off Systems Inc.................. E 216 649-7800
  Twinsburg (G-13376)

PRINTING: Gravure, Rotogravure

Brook & Whittle Limited.................... E 513 860-2457
  Hamilton (G-7474)

Commercial Cutng Graphics LLC...... D 419 526-4800
  Mansfield (G-8776)

Diversfied Lbling Slutions Inc.......... F 630 625-1225
  Harrison (G-7549)

Multi-Color Australia LLC................ D 513 381-1480
  Batavia (G-877)

Ohio Gravure Technologies Inc........ F 937 439-1582
  Miamisburg (G-9724)

Sekuworks LLC................................. E 513 202-1210
  Harrison (G-7566)

Shamrock Companies Inc................. D 440 899-9510
  Westlake (G-14333)

The Photo-Type Engraving Company.... D 513 281-0999
  Cincinnati (G-3149)

Wfsr Holdings LLC............................ A 877 735-4966
  Dayton (G-6081)

PRINTING: Laser

Laser Printing Solutions Inc............ G 216 351-4444
  Cleveland (G-3944)

Microplex Printware Corp................. F 440 374-2424
  Solon (G-12151)

Queen City Office Machine............... F 513 251-7200
  Cincinnati (G-3022)

True Dinero Records & Tech LLC....... G 513 428-4610
  Cincinnati (G-3173)

PRINTING: Letterpress

A-A Blueprint Co Inc......................... E 330 794-8803
  Akron (G-10)

Akron Litho-Print Company Inc........ F 330 434-3145
  Akron (G-34)

All Points Printing Inc..................... G 440 585-1125
  Wickliffe (G-14365)

Barnhart Printing Corp..................... G 330 456-2279
  Canton (G-1837)

Berea Printing Company................... G 440 243-1080
  Berea (G-1161)

Bramkamp Printing Company Inc...... G 513 241-1865
  Blue Ash (G-1255)

Brothers Printing Co Inc.................. G 216 621-6050
  Cleveland (G-3444)

Cox Printing Company...................... G 937 382-2312
  Wilmington (G-14576)

Dee Printing Inc............................... F 614 777-8700
  Columbus (G-4874)

Diocesan Publications Inc............... E 614 718-9500
  Dublin (G-6293)

Earl D Arnold Printing Company....... E 513 533-6900
  Cincinnati (G-2574)

Eci Macola/Max LLC......................... C 978 539-6186
  Dublin (G-6296)

Empire Printing Inc.......................... G 513 242-3900
  Fairfield (G-6732)

Foote Printing Company Inc............. F 216 431-1757
  Cleveland (G-3734)

Heskamp Printing Co Inc................. G 513 871-6770
  Cincinnati (G-2720)

Jarman Printing LLC......................... G 330 823-8585
  Alliance (G-386)

Keystone Press Inc.......................... G 419 243-7326
  Toledo (G-13018)

KMS 2000 Inc.................................. F 330 454-9444
  Canton (G-1927)

Lee Corporation............................... G 513 771-3602
  Cincinnati (G-2817)

Lyle Printing & Publishing Co.......... E 330 337-3419
  Salem (G-11796)

M Rosenthal Company...................... F 513 563-0081
  Cincinnati (G-2835)

Mariotti Printing Co LLC.................. G 440 245-4120
  Lorain (G-8567)

Post Business Properties Inc........... D 419 628-2321
  Minster (G-10063)

Printex Incorporated........................ F 740 773-0088
  Chillicothe (G-2276)

R R Donnelley & Sons Company........ D 440 774-2101
  Oberlin (G-10920)

Selby Service/Roxy Press Inc.......... G 513 241-3445
  Cincinnati (G-3078)

Sitler Printer Inc.............................. G 330 482-4463
  Columbiana (G-4628)

Slimans Printery Inc........................ F 330 454-9141
  Canton (G-2007)

Snow Printing Co Inc........................ F 419 229-7669
  Lima (G-8451)

Star Calendar & Printing Inc............ G 216 741-3223
  Cleveland (G-4328)

Star Printing Company Inc............... E 330 376-0514
  Akron (G-317)

Starr Services Inc............................ G 513 241-7708
  Cincinnati (G-3114)

Tope Printing Inc.............................. G 330 674-4993
  Millersburg (G-10014)

Traxium LLC..................................... E 330 572-8200
  Stow (G-12466)

William J Bergen & Co...................... G 440 248-6132
  Solon (G-12208)

PRINTING: Lithographic

1one Stop Printing Inc..................... F 614 216-1438
  Columbus (G-4652)

7 7 Print Solutions LLC................... G 513 600-4597
  Fairfield (G-6704)

Adcraft Decals Incorporated........... E 216 524-2934
  Cleveland (G-3297)

Akron Thermography Inc.................. F 330 896-9712
  Akron (G-44)

Alberts Screen Print Inc.................. C 330 753-7559
  Norton (G-10818)

Alliance Publishing Co Inc............... C 330 453-1304
  Alliance (G-372)

Allu Inc.. G 513 624-9333
  Cincinnati (G-2352)

AlphaGraphics................................. G 513 204-6070
  Mason (G-9059)

AlphaGraphics 507 Inc.................... G 440 878-9700
  Strongsville (G-12535)

American Printing & Lithog Co......... F 513 867-0602
  Hamilton (G-7463)

Amsive OH LLC................................. D 937 885-8000
  Miamisburg (G-9665)

Auld Corporation............................. G 614 454-1010
  Columbus (G-4734)

Baesman Group Inc.......................... D 614 771-2300
  Hilliard (G-7674)

Banbury Investments Inc................. G 513 677-4500
  Cincinnati (G-2399)

BCT Alarm Services Inc................... G 440 669-8153
  Lorain (G-8546)

Best Graphics & Printing Inc........... G 513 535-3529
  Cincinnati (G-2409)

Black River Group Inc...................... E 419 524-6699
  Mansfield (G-8765)

Bloch Printing Company................... G 330 576-6760
  Copley (G-5431)

Blue Crescent Enterprises Inc......... G 440 878-9700
  Strongsville (G-12545)

Bookmasters Inc.............................. C 419 281-1802
  Ashland (G-522)

BP 10 Inc... E 513 346-3900
  Hamilton (G-7472)

Brandon Screen Printing.................. F 419 229-9837
  Lima (G-8391)

Capehart Enterprises LLC................ F 614 769-7746
  Columbus (G-4795)

Cardpak Incorporated...................... C 440 542-3100
  Solon (G-12091)

Cincinnati Convertors Inc................. G 513 731-6600
  Cincinnati (G-2472)

City of Cleveland............................. E 216 664-3013
  Cleveland (G-3499)

PRODUCT

County Classifieds............................ G .... 937 592-8847 Bellefontaine *(G-1102)*	Horizon Ohio Publications Inc.............. D .... 419 738-2128 Wapakoneta *(G-13715)*	Promatch Solutions LLC.................... F ..... 877 299-0185 Moraine *(G-10188)*
Covap Inc... F .... 513 793-1855 Blue Ash *(G-1264)*	Identity Group LLC.......................... G .... 614 337-6167 Westerville *(G-14213)*	Quick Tech Graphics Inc.................. F ..... 937 743-5952 Springboro *(G-12266)*
Coyne Graphic Finishing Inc.............. E .... 740 397-6232 Mount Vernon *(G-10241)*	Imprint LLC...................................... G .... 216 233-0066 Cleveland *(G-3856)*	R R Donnelley & Sons Company.......... D ..... 440 774-2101 Oberlin *(G-10920)*
Culaine Inc....................................... G .... 419 345-4984 Toledo *(G-12934)*	Innovative Graphics Ltd.................... F .... 877 406-3636 Columbus *(G-5007)*	R R Donnelley & Sons Company.......... D ..... 330 562-5250 Streetsboro *(G-12518)*
Custom Imprint................................. F .... 440 238-4488 Strongsville *(G-12551)*	Isaac Foster Mack Co....................... C .... 419 625-5500 Sandusky *(G-11843)*	R&D Marketing Group Inc.................. G ..... 216 398-9100 Brooklyn Heights *(G-1537)*
Davis Printing Company...................... E .... 330 745-3113 Barberton *(G-803)*	It XCEL Consulting LLC...................... F .... 513 847-8261 West Chester *(G-14016)*	Record Herald Publishing Co.............. E ..... 717 762-2151 Cincinnati *(G-3035)*
Dayton Legal Blank Inc...................... G .... 937 435-4405 Dayton *(G-5729)*	J Solutions LLC................................ G .... 614 732-4857 Columbus *(G-5028)*	Reynolds and Reynolds Company....... F ..... 419 584-7000 Celina *(G-2117)*
DC Reprographics Co........................ F .... 614 297-1200 Columbus *(G-4873)*	Jasper Printing Co LLC...................... G .... 937 294-5218 Kettering *(G-8121)*	RI Smith Graphics LLC...................... G ..... 330 629-8616 Youngstown *(G-14924)*
Delaware Data Products Inc................ G .... 740 369-5449 Delaware *(G-6142)*	Jay Tees LLC................................... E .... 740 405-1579 Thornville *(G-12766)*	Rotary Forms Press Inc.................... E ..... 937 393-3426 Hillsboro *(G-7724)*
Digital Color Intl LLC......................... F Akron *(G-123)*	Jk Digital Publishing LLC.................. G .... 937 299-0185 Springboro *(G-12256)*	Schlabach Printers LLC.................... D ..... 330 852-4687 Sugarcreek *(G-12649)*
Dla Document Services...................... F .... 937 257-6014 Dayton *(G-5610)*	Joe The Printer Guy LLC.................... G .... 216 651-3880 Lakewood *(G-8168)*	Sdg News Group Inc........................ F ..... 419 929-3411 New London *(G-10416)*
Duck-T Printing LLC.......................... F .... 216 312-0838 Cleveland *(G-3635)*	Kem Advertising and Prtg LLC............ G .... 330 818-5061 Barberton *(G-816)*	Sdo Sports Ltd............................... G ..... 440 546-9998 Cleveland *(G-4283)*
Dupli-Systems Inc............................ C .... 440 234-9415 Strongsville *(G-12555)*	Kevin Noesner................................. E .... 614 451-5459 Columbus *(G-5052)*	Sekuworks LLC............................... E ..... 513 202-1210 Harrison *(G-7566)*
Electronic Printing Pdts Inc................ E .... 800 882-4050 Stow *(G-12428)*	Kinkos Inc...................................... G .... 216 661-9950 Cleveland *(G-3922)*	Sensical Inc.................................... D ..... 216 641-1141 Solon *(G-12180)*
Enlarging Arts Inc............................. G .... 330 434-3433 Akron *(G-136)*	Liturgical Publications Inc................. D .... 216 325-6825 Cleveland *(G-3964)*	Shawnee Systems Inc...................... D ..... 513 561-9932 Cincinnati *(G-3087)*
Ennis Inc... E .... 800 537-8648 Toledo *(G-12954)*	Loris Printing Inc............................. G .... 419 626-6648 Sandusky *(G-11852)*	Shout Out Loud Prints...................... G ..... 614 432-8990 Columbus *(G-5264)*
Envoi Design Inc.............................. G .... 513 651-4229 Cincinnati *(G-2593)*	Lsc Communications Inc.................... A .... 419 935-0111 Willard *(G-14403)*	Soondook LLC................................ E ..... 614 389-5757 Columbus *(G-5277)*
Etched Metal Company...................... E .... 440 248-0240 Solon *(G-12109)*	Malik Media LLC.............................. G .... 614 933-0328 New Albany *(G-10345)*	Southeast Publications Inc................ F ..... 740 732-2341 Caldwell *(G-1729)*
Eugene Stewart................................ G .... 937 898-1117 Dayton *(G-5770)*	Master Printing Group Inc.................. F .... 216 351-2246 Berea *(G-1180)*	SRC & Company.............................. F ..... 216 417-7477 Cleveland *(G-4321)*
Fair Publishing House Inc.................. E .... 419 668-3746 Norwalk *(G-10841)*	Minuteman Press Inc........................ G .... 513 741-9056 Cincinnati *(G-2882)*	Stephen Andrews Inc........................ G ..... 330 725-2672 Lodi *(G-8507)*
Far Corner....................................... G .... 330 767-3734 Navarre *(G-10303)*	Mj Bornhorst Enterprises LLC............ E .... 937 295-3469 Fort Loramie *(G-6951)*	Stevenson Color Inc........................ C ..... 513 321-7500 Cincinnati *(G-3119)*
Fleet Graphics Inc............................ G .... 937 252-2552 Dayton *(G-5779)*	Mmp Printing Inc.............................. F .... 513 381-0990 Cincinnati *(G-2883)*	Taylor Communications Inc................ F ..... 614 351-6868 Columbus *(G-5312)*
Fmh Enterprises LLC........................ F .... 937 478-2739 Dayton *(G-5781)*	Monks Copy Shop Inc...................... F .... 614 461-6438 Columbus *(G-5110)*	Taylor Communications Inc................ E ..... 937 221-1000 Dayton *(G-6039)*
Follow Print Club On Facebook........... G .... 216 707-2579 Cleveland *(G-3732)*	Morse Enterprises Inc...................... G .... 513 229-3600 Mason *(G-9129)*	Tce International Ltd........................ F ..... 800 962-2376 Perry *(G-11199)*
Fremont Printing Inc.......................... F .... 480 272-3443 Fremont *(G-7112)*	Multi-Color Australia LLC.................. D .... 513 381-1480 Batavia *(G-877)*	Techniprint Inc............................... F ..... 614 899-1403 Westerville *(G-14277)*
Friends Service Co Inc...................... F .... 800 427-1704 Dayton *(G-5785)*	North Shore Printing LLC.................. G .... 740 876-9066 Portsmouth *(G-11472)*	Tpl Holdings LLC............................. E ..... 800 475-4030 Mogadore *(G-10090)*
Frisby Printing Company.................... F .... 330 665-4565 Fairlawn *(G-6801)*	Northcoast Pmm LLC........................ F .... 419 540-8667 Toledo *(G-13064)*	Tribune Printing Inc........................ G ..... 419 542-7764 Hicksville *(G-7654)*
Gannett Sttlite Info Ntwrk LLC............ E .... 419 334-1012 Fremont *(G-7113)*	Northeast Blueprint and Sup Co.......... G .... 216 261-7500 Cleveland *(G-4092)*	United Trade Printers LLC.................. E ..... 614 326-4829 Dublin *(G-6358)*
Gazette Publishing Company.............. E .... 419 483-4190 Oberlin *(G-10917)*	Ohio Art Company............................ D .... 419 636-3141 Bryan *(G-1655)*	Vectra Inc...................................... C ..... 614 351-6868 Columbus *(G-5345)*
Gordon Bernard Company LLC............ E .... 513 248-7600 Milford *(G-9936)*	Onetouchpoint East Corp.................. D .... 513 421-1600 Cincinnati *(G-2933)*	Vision Graphix Inc.......................... G ..... 440 835-6540 Westlake *(G-14342)*
Graphic Paper Products Corp.............. D .... 937 325-5503 Springfield *(G-12315)*	Ovp Inc.. G .... 740 423-5171 Belpre *(G-1152)*	Vya Inc.. E ..... 513 772-5400 Cincinnati *(G-3210)*
Hawks & Associates Inc.................... E .... 513 752-4311 Cincinnati *(G-2305)*	Premier Prtg Centl Ohio Ltd.............. E .... 937 642-0988 Marysville *(G-9043)*	Welch Publishing Co........................ E ..... 419 874-2528 Perrysburg *(G-11279)*
Headlee Enterprises Ltd.................... G .... 614 785-1476 Columbus *(G-4641)*	Print Syndicate Inc.......................... F .... 617 290-9550 Columbus *(G-5206)*	Westrock Commercial LLC................ E ..... 419 476-9101 Toledo *(G-13178)*
Hh Associates US Inc....................... F .... 937 644-7492 Marysville *(G-9025)*	Printers Edge Inc............................. F .... 330 372-2232 Warren *(G-13791)*	Wfsr Holdings LLC.......................... A ..... 877 735-4966 Dayton *(G-6081)*
Highland Computer Forms Inc............ D .... 937 393-4215 Hillsboro *(G-7718)*	Professional Screen Printing.............. D .... 740 687-0760 Lancaster *(G-8219)*	Wicked Premiums LLC...................... G ..... 216 364-0322 Brecksville *(G-1485)*
Hkm Drect Mkt Cmmnications Inc........ C .... 800 860-4456 Cleveland *(G-3832)*	Profile Digital Printing LLC................ G .... 937 866-4241 Dayton *(G-5965)*	Woodrow Manufacturing Co.............. E ..... 937 399-9333 Springfield *(G-12396)*

Workflowone LLC.............................A 877 735-4966
Dayton *(G-6087)*

PRINTING: Offset

A F Krainz Co..................................G 216 431-4341
Cleveland *(G-3280)*

A Grade Notes Inc..........................G 614 299-9999
Dublin *(G-6271)*

A Z Printing Inc..............................G 513 733-3900
Cincinnati *(G-2326)*

A-A Blueprint Co Inc......................E 330 794-8803
Akron *(G-10)*

Academy Graphic Comm Inc...........F 216 661-2550
Cleveland *(G-3289)*

Acme Duplicating Co Inc.................G 216 241-1241
Westlake *(G-14283)*

Activities Press Inc.......................E 440 953-1200
Mentor *(G-9469)*

Admark Printing Inc........................G 937 833-5111
Brookville *(G-1561)*

Admiral Products Company Inc........E 216 671-0600
Cleveland *(G-3299)*

Advantage Print Solutions LLC........G 614 519-2392
Columbus *(G-4677)*

AGS Custom Graphics Inc...............D 330 963-7770
Macedonia *(G-8676)*

Akland Printing.............................F 330 467-8292
Northfield *(G-10791)*

Akron Thermography Inc.................G 330 896-9712
Akron *(G-45)*

All Points Printing Inc....................G 440 585-1125
Wickliffe *(G-14365)*

Allen Graphics Inc........................G 440 349-4100
Solon *(G-12075)*

American Printing Inc.....................F 330 630-1121
Akron *(G-58)*

Anderson Graphics Inc...................E 330 745-2165
Barberton *(G-793)*

Andrin Enterprises Inc...................F 937 276-7794
Moraine *(G-10146)*

Angel Prtg & Reproduction Co.........F 216 631-5225
Cleveland *(G-3360)*

Arens Corporation.........................G 937 473-2028
Covington *(G-5489)*

Arens Corporation.........................F 937 473-2028
Covington *(G-5488)*

Armstrong Stationery Co Corp.........G 513 891-0667
Cincinnati *(G-2376)*

Avon Lake Printing........................G 440 933-2078
Avon Lake *(G-749)*

B & B Printing Graphics Inc............F 419 893-7068
Maumee *(G-9263)*

B R Printers Inc............................D 513 271-6035
Cincinnati *(G-2396)*

Bansal Enterprises Inc...................F 330 633-9355
Akron *(G-72)*

Barnhart Printing Corp...................G 330 456-2279
Canton *(G-1837)*

Bates Printing Inc.........................F 330 833-5830
Massillon *(G-9174)*

Bay Business Forms Inc.................F 937 322-3000
Springfield *(G-12285)*

Beckman Xmo................................G 614 864-2232
Columbus *(G-4747)*

Berea Printing Company..................G 440 243-1080
Berea *(G-1161)*

Bethart Enterprises Inc..................F 513 863-6161
Hamilton *(G-7470)*

Bindery & Spc Pressworks Inc.........D 614 873-4623
Plain City *(G-11398)*

Bis Printing..................................G 440 951-2606
Willoughby *(G-14431)*

Bizzy Bee Printing Inc....................G 614 771-1222
Columbus *(G-4757)*

Blooms Printing Inc.......................G 740 922-1765
Dennison *(G-6216)*

Blt Inc...F 513 631-5050
Norwood *(G-10866)*

Bodnar Printing Co Inc...................F 440 277-8295
Lorain *(G-8547)*

Bornhorst Printing Company Inc.......G 419 738-5901
Wapakoneta *(G-13707)*

Bramkamp Printing Company Inc......G 513 241-1865
Blue Ash *(G-1255)*

Brass Bull 1 LLC...........................G 740 335-8030
Wshngtn Ct Hs *(G-14735)*

Brentwood Printing & Sty...............G 513 522-2679
Cincinnati *(G-2421)*

Brothers Printing Co Inc.................G 216 621-6050
Cleveland *(G-3444)*

Buckeye Business Forms Inc...........G 614 882-1890
Columbus *(G-4784)*

Bucyrus Graphics Inc.....................F 419 562-2906
Bucyrus *(G-1673)*

Bush Inc......................................G 216 362-6700
Cleveland *(G-3454)*

C Massouh Printing Co Inc.............F 330 408-7330
Canal Fulton *(G-1774)*

Capitol Square Printing Inc.............G 614 221-2850
Columbus *(G-4800)*

Carbon Web Print LLC....................E 216 402-3504
Willoughby Hills *(G-14556)*

Carbonless On Demandcom LLC......F 330 837-8611
Massillon *(G-9177)*

Cardinal Printing Inc......................G 330 773-7300
Akron *(G-89)*

CB Graphics LLC...........................G 216 749-5577
Cleveland *(G-3478)*

Cbp Co Inc...................................F 513 860-9053
Cincinnati *(G-2444)*

Century Graphics Inc.....................G 614 895-7698
Westerville *(G-14206)*

Cincinnati Print Solutions LLC.........G 513 943-9500
Milford *(G-9929)*

City Printing Co Inc.......................F 330 747-5691
Youngstown *(G-14837)*

Clints Printing Inc.........................G 937 426-2771
Dayton *(G-5703)*

Color Bar Printing Centers Inc.........G 216 595-3939
Cleveland *(G-3646)*

Color Process Inc.........................E 440 268-7100
Seville *(G-11915)*

Commercial Prtg Greenville Inc........G 937 548-3835
Greenville *(G-7339)*

Consoldated Graphics Group Inc......C 216 881-9191
Cleveland *(G-3559)*

Consolidated Graphics Inc..............C 740 654-2112
Lancaster *(G-8189)*

Copley Ohio Newspapers Inc...........C 330 364-5577
New Philadelphia *(G-10439)*

Copy King Inc...............................F 216 861-3377
Cleveland *(G-3567)*

COS Blueprint Inc.........................E 330 376-0022
Akron *(G-107)*

Cox Printing Company....................G 937 382-2312
Wilmington *(G-14576)*

Cpmm Services Group Inc..............G 614 447-0165
Columbus *(G-4857)*

Creative Impressions Inc................F 937 435-5296
Dayton *(G-5714)*

Crest Graphics Inc........................F 513 271-2200
Blue Ash *(G-1265)*

Crossbridge Mktg & Media Inc.........G 330 682-5066
Orrville *(G-10979)*

Curless Printing Company...............E 937 783-2403
Blanchester *(G-1235)*

Curv Imaging LLC..........................G 614 890-2878
Westerville *(G-14251)*

Custom Graphics Inc.....................D 330 963-7770
Macedonia *(G-8682)*

Cwh Graphics LLC.........................G 866 241-8515
Bedford Heights *(G-1075)*

D & J Printing Inc..........................C 330 678-5868
Kent *(G-8024)*

Daubenmires Printing Co LLC..........G 513 425-7223
Middletown *(G-9853)*

David A and Mary A Mathis..............G 330 837-8611
Massillon *(G-9185)*

Deerfield Ventures Inc...................G 614 875-0688
Grove City *(G-7381)*

Delphos Herald Inc........................D 419 695-0015
Delphos *(G-6184)*

Dewitt Group Inc...........................F 614 847-5919
Columbus *(G-4879)*

Direct Digital Graphics Inc..............G 330 405-3770
Twinsburg *(G-13295)*

Directconnectgroup Ltd..................G 216 281-2866
Cleveland *(G-3616)*

Distributor Graphics Inc.................G 440 260-0024
Cleveland *(G-3620)*

Docmann Printing & Assoc Inc.........G 440 975-1775
Solon *(G-12101)*

Document Concepts Inc..................F 330 575-5685
North Canton *(G-10636)*

Doll Inc..G 419 586-7880
Celina *(G-2103)*

Donnelley Financial LLC..................G 216 621-8384
Cleveland *(G-3626)*

Dsk Imaging LLC............................F 513 554-1797
Blue Ash *(G-1268)*

Duke Graphics Inc.........................E 440 946-0606
Willoughby *(G-14450)*

Duncan Press Corporation...............E 330 477-4529
North Canton *(G-10637)*

E Bee Printing Inc.........................G 614 224-0416
Columbus *(G-4893)*

Earl D Arnold Printing Company........E 513 533-6900
Cincinnati *(G-2574)*

Eg Enterprise Services Inc..............G 216 431-3300
Cleveland *(G-3658)*

Empire Printing Inc........................G 513 242-3900
Fairfield *(G-6703)*

Engler Printing Co.........................G 419 332-2181
Fremont *(G-7106)*

Enquirer Printing Co Inc.................F 513 241-1956
Cincinnati *(G-2591)*

Eurostampa North America Inc.........C 513 821-2275
Cincinnati *(G-2601)*

Eveready Printing Inc.....................E 216 587-2389
Cleveland *(G-3693)*

Excelsior Printing Co.....................G 740 927-2934
Pataskala *(G-11138)*

Express Grphics Prtg Dsign Inc........G 513 728-3344
Cincinnati *(G-2609)*

Feld Printing Co............................G 513 271-6806
Cincinnati *(G-2619)*

Fgs-Wi LLC...................................E 630 375-8597
Newark *(G-10502)*

Fine Line Graphics Corp.................C 614 486-0276
Columbus *(G-4924)*

Finn Graphics Inc..........................E 513 941-6161
Cincinnati *(G-2624)*

Folks Creative Printers Inc..............G 740 383-6326
Marion *(G-8970)*

Foote Printing Company Inc.............F 216 431-1757
Cleveland *(G-3734)*

P
R
O
D
U
C
T

Franklin Printing Company ...... F 740 452-6375	**Image Concepts Inc** .... F ... 216 524-9000	**Letterman Printing Inc** .... G 513 523-1111
Zanesville *(G-15016)*	Cleveland *(G-3850)*	Oxford *(G-11063)*
Freeport Press Inc .... C 330 308-3300	**Image Print Inc** .... G ... 614 776-3985	**Liming Printing Inc** .... F ... 937 374-2646
New Philadelphia *(G-10447)*	Westerville *(G-14264)*	Xenia *(G-14769)*
Fx Digital Media Inc .... G 216 241-4040	**Ink Inc** .... G ... 330 875-4789	**Litho-Print Ltd** .... F ... 937 222-4351
Cleveland *(G-3747)*	Louisville *(G-8605)*	Dayton *(G-5852)*
Galaxy Balloons Incorporated ..... C ... 216 476-3360	**Innomark Communications LLC** ..... D ... 937 454-5555	**Little Printing Company** ...... G ... 937 773-4595
Cleveland *(G-3753)*	Miamisburg *(G-9701)*	Piqua *(G-11363)*
Galley Printing Inc .... E ... 330 220-5577	**Inskeep Brothers Inc** .... G ... 614 898-6620	**Lyle Printing & Publishing Co** ..... E ... 330 337-3419
Brunswick *(G-1593)*	Columbus *(G-5008)*	Salem *(G-11796)*
Gaspar Services LLC .... G ... 330 467-8292	**Irwin Engraving & Printing Co** ..... G ... 216 391-7300	**Marbee Inc** .... G ... 419 422-9441
Macedonia *(G-8694)*	Cleveland *(G-3872)*	Findlay *(G-6891)*
GCI Digital Imaging Inc ...... F ... 513 521-7446	**J & L Management Corporation** ..... G ... 440 205-1199	**Mariotti Printing Co LLC** ...... G ... 440 245-4120
Cincinnati *(G-2653)*	Mentor *(G-9537)*	Lorain *(G-8567)*
Gergel-Kellem Company Inc ..... D ... 216 398-2000	**J & P Investments Inc** .... F ... 513 821-2299	**Mark Advertising Agency Inc** ..... F ... 419 626-9000
Olmsted Falls *(G-10940)*	Cincinnati *(G-2755)*	Sandusky *(G-11856)*
Gli Holdings Inc .... D ... 440 892-7760	**Jack Walker Printing Co** ...... F ... 440 352-4222	**Mass-Marketing Inc** .... C ... 513 860-6200
Stow *(G-12434)*	Mentor *(G-9540)*	Fairfield *(G-6750)*
Gli Holdings Inc .... D ... 216 651-1500	**Jakprints Inc** .... C ... 877 246-3132	**Mbas Printing Inc** .... G ... 513 489-3000
Stow *(G-12433)*	Cleveland *(G-3881)*	Blue Ash *(G-1306)*
Globus Printing & Packg Co Inc ..... D ... 419 628-2381	**Jbnovember LLC** .... E ... 513 272-7000	**McNerney & Associates LLC** ..... E ... 513 241-9951
Minster *(G-10058)*	Cincinnati *(G-2763)*	West Chester *(G-14132)*
Golden Graphics Ltd .... F ... 419 673-6260	**Jos Berning Printing Co** ...... F ... 513 721-0781	**Mercer Color Corporation** ..... G ... 419 678-8273
Kenton *(G-8099)*	Cincinnati *(G-2773)*	Coldwater *(G-4582)*
Gordons Graphics Inc ...... G ... 330 863-2322	**Jt Premier Printing Corp** ...... G ... 216 831-8785	**Messenger Publishing Company** ..... C ... 740 592-6612
Malvern *(G-8751)*	Cleveland *(G-3898)*	Athens *(G-644)*
Graphic Info Systems Inc ..... F ... 513 948-1300	**Kahny Printing Inc** .... E ... 513 251-2911	**Metzgers** .... D ... 419 861-8611
Mason *(G-9106)*	Cincinnati *(G-2778)*	Toledo *(G-13053)*
Graphic Village LLC .... C ... 513 241-1865	**Kay Toledo Tag Inc** .... D ... 419 729-5479	**Meyers Printing & Design Inc** ..... F ... 937 461-6000
Blue Ash *(G-1278)*	Toledo *(G-13017)*	Dayton *(G-5876)*
Graphtech Communications Inc ..... F ... 216 676-1020	**Keener Printing Inc** .... G ... 216 531-7595	**Miami Valley Publishing LLC** ..... C ... 937 879-5678
Strongsville *(G-12560)*	Cleveland *(G-3911)*	Fairborn *(G-6696)*
Greg Blume .... G ... 740 574-2308	**Kehl-Kolor Inc** .... G ... 419 281-3107	**Middaugh Enterprises Inc** ..... G ... 330 852-2471
Wheelersburg *(G-14353)*	Ashland *(G-545)*	Sugarcreek *(G-12641)*
Gregg Macmillan .... G ... 513 248-2121	**Kenwel Printers Inc** .... E ... 614 261-1011	**Middleton Printing Co Inc** ..... G ... 614 294-7277
Milford *(G-9937)*	Columbus *(G-5050)*	Gahanna *(G-7166)*
Haman Enterprises Inc ...... F ... 614 888-7574	**Kevin K Tidd** .... G ... 419 885-5603	**Milford Printers** .... E ... 513 831-6630
Columbus *(G-4968)*	Sylvania *(G-12714)*	Milford *(G-9944)*
Harper Engraving & Printing Co ..... D ... 614 276-0700	**Key Maneuvers Inc** .... G ... 440 285-0774	**Millennium Printing LLC** ...... G ... 513 489-3000
Columbus *(G-4970)*	Chardon *(G-2210)*	Blue Ash *(G-1311)*
Hartco Printing Company ..... G ... 614 761-1292	**Keystone Press Inc** .... G ... 419 243-7326	**Mmp Toledo** .... G ... 419 472-0505
Dublin *(G-6301)*	Toledo *(G-13018)*	Toledo *(G-13057)*
Hecks Direct Mail Prtg Svc Inc ..... F ... 419 697-3505	**Kimpton Printing & Spc Co** ..... F ... 330 467-1640	**Mound Printing Company Inc** ..... E ... 937 866-2872
Toledo *(G-12990)*	Macedonia *(G-8702)*	Miamisburg *(G-9720)*
Heeter Printing Company Inc ..... E ... 440 946-0606	**Klingstedt Brothers Company** ..... F ... 330 456-8319	**Multi-Craft Litho Inc** .... E ... 859 581-2754
Eastlake *(G-6431)*	Canton *(G-1926)*	Blue Ash *(G-1312)*
Heitkamp & Kremer Printing Inc ..... G ... 419 925-4121	**KMS 2000 Inc** .... G ... 330 454-9444	**Murr Corporation** .... G ... 330 264-2223
Celina *(G-2109)*	Canton *(G-1927)*	Wooster *(G-14668)*
Herald Inc .... E ... 419 492-2133	**Kramer Graphics Inc** .... E ... 937 296-9600	**Network Printing & Graphics** ..... F ... 614 230-2084
New Washington *(G-10479)*	Moraine *(G-10172)*	Columbus *(G-5124)*
Heritage Press Inc .... E ... 419 289-9209	**Krehbiel Holdings Inc** .... D ... 513 271-6035	**Nomis Publications Inc** ...... F ... 330 965-2380
Ashland *(G-539)*	Cincinnati *(G-2807)*	Youngstown *(G-14904)*
Heskamp Printing Co Inc ..... G ... 513 871-6770	**L & T Collins Inc** .... G ... 740 345-4494	**North Coast Litho Inc** .... E ... 216 881-1952
Cincinnati *(G-2720)*	Newark *(G-10516)*	Cleveland *(G-4086)*
Hi-Point Graphics LLC .... G ... 937 407-6524	**Lahlouh Inc** .... G ... 650 692-6600	**North Toledo Graphics LLC** ..... D ... 419 476-8808
Bellefontaine *(G-1109)*	Monroe *(G-10113)*	Toledo *(G-13063)*
Hilltop Printing .... G ... 419 782-9898	**Lake Shore Graphic Inds Inc** ..... G ... 419 626-8631	**Northern Ohio Printing Inc** ..... E ... 216 398-0000
Defiance *(G-6110)*	Sandusky *(G-11849)*	Cleveland *(G-4094)*
Holmes W & Sons Printing ..... G ... 937 325-1509	**Larmax Inc** .... G ... 513 984-0783	**Nta Graphics Inc** .... G ... 419 476-8808
Springfield *(G-12323)*	Blue Ash *(G-1296)*	Toledo *(G-13066)*
Hoster Graphics Company Inc ..... F ... 614 299-9770	**Laurenee Ltd** .... G ... 513 662-2225	**O Connor Office Pdts & Prtg** ..... G ... 740 852-2209
Columbus *(G-4992)*	Cincinnati *(G-2814)*	London *(G-8540)*
HOT Graphic Services Inc ..... E ... 419 242-7000	**Lba Custom Printing** .... G ... 419 535-3151	**Old Trail Printing Company** ..... C ... 614 443-4852
Northwood *(G-10804)*	Toledo *(G-13028)*	Columbus *(G-5159)*
Howland Printing Inc .... G ... 330 637-8255	**LBL Lithographers Inc** .... G ... 440 350-0106	**Oliver Printing & Packg Co LLC** ..... D ... 330 425-7890
Cortland *(G-5445)*	Painesville *(G-11096)*	Twinsburg *(G-13346)*
HP Industries Inc .... E ... 419 478-0695	**Lee Corporation** .... G ... 513 771-3602	**Orange Blossom Press Inc** ..... G ... 216 781-8655
Toledo *(G-12997)*	Cincinnati *(G-2817)*	Willoughby *(G-14502)*
Hubbard Company .... E ... 419 784-4455	**Legal News Publishing Co** ..... E ... 216 696-3322	**Oregon Vlg Print Shoppe Inc** ..... F ... 937 222-9418
Defiance *(G-6111)*	Cleveland *(G-3949)*	Dayton *(G-5930)*
Hubbard Publishing Co .... G ... 937 592-3060	**Legalcraft Inc** .... G ... 330 494-1261	**Orwell Printing** .... G ... 440 285-2233
Bellefontaine *(G-1110)*	Canton *(G-1932)*	Chardon *(G-2218)*

2025 Harris Ohio
Industrial Directory

(G-0000) Company's Geographic Section entry number

Page One Group......................... G .... 740 397-4240 Mount Vernon *(G-10257)*	Printing Service Company...................... D .. 937 425-6100 Miamisburg *(G-9729)*	Specialty Lithographing Co.................. F .. 513 621-0222 Cincinnati *(G-3103)*
Painesville Publishing Inc...................... G .. 440 354-4142 Austinburg *(G-701)*	Printpoint Inc........................... G .. 937 223-9041 Dayton *(G-5958)*	Springdot Inc.......................... D .. 513 542-4000 Cincinnati *(G-3108)*
Painted Hill Inv Group Inc.................. F .... 937 339-1756 Troy *(G-13246)*	Program Managers Inc...................... G .. 937 431-1982 Beavercreek *(G-995)*	Sprint Print Inc.......................... G ..... 740 622-4429 Coshocton *(G-5473)*
Paragraphics Inc.......................... E .... 330 493-1074 Canton *(G-1971)*	Progressive Printers Inc................. D .. 937 222-1267 Dayton *(G-5967)*	Standard Printing Co of Canton.......... D ..... 330 453-8247 Canton *(G-2012)*
Park Press Direct......................... G .. 419 626-4426 Sandusky *(G-11864)*	Progrssive Communications Corp........ F .. 740 397-5333 Mount Vernon *(G-10261)*	Star Calendar & Printing Inc.................. G .. 216 741-3223 Cleveland *(G-4328)*
Patio Printing Inc......................... G .. 614 785-9553 Columbus *(G-5177)*	Quality Publishing Co................. G .. 513 863-8210 Hamilton *(G-7520)*	Star Printing Company Inc.................. E .. 330 376-0514 Akron *(G-317)*
Patterson-Britton Printing Inc.......... G .. 216 781-7997 Mentor *(G-9583)*	Quebecor World Johnson Hardin......... G .. 614 326-0299 Cincinnati *(G-3019)*	Starr Services Inc....................... G .. 513 241-7708 Cincinnati *(G-3114)*
PDQ Printing Service................. F .... 216 241-5443 Westlake *(G-14321)*	Quez Media Marketing Inc............... G .. 216 910-0202 Independence *(G-7918)*	Stein-Palmer Printing Co...................... G .. 740 633-3894 Saint Clairsville *(G-11711)*
Peerless Printing Company............. F .. 513 721-4657 Cincinnati *(G-2952)*	R & J Bardon Inc........................ G .. 614 457-5500 Columbus *(G-5221)*	Stepping Stone Enterprises Inc.......... F .. 419 472-0505 Maumee *(G-9320)*
Pen-Ann Corporation................. G .. 740 373-2054 Marietta *(G-8936)*	Randd Assoc Prtg & Promotions........ G .. 937 294-1874 Dayton *(G-5975)*	Suburban Press Incorporated.......... F .. 216 961-0766 Cleveland *(G-4340)*
Penguin Enterprises Inc.............. E .. 440 899-5112 Westlake *(G-14322)*	Rba Inc................................ G .. 330 336-6700 Wadsworth *(G-13667)*	Superior Impressions Inc................ G .. 419 244-8676 Toledo *(G-13136)*
Perfection Printing................. G .. 513 874-2173 Fairfield *(G-6765)*	Repro Acquisition Company LLC........ G .. 216 738-3800 Cleveland *(G-4235)*	Swimmer Printing Inc................. G .. 216 623-1005 Cleveland *(G-4357)*
Perrons Printing Company Inc.......... G .. 440 236-8870 Columbia Station *(G-4596)*	Resilient Holdings Inc................. F .. 614 847-5600 Columbus *(G-5227)*	T D Dynamics Inc....................... F .. 216 881-0800 Cleveland *(G-4362)*
Persistence of Vision Inc.............. G .. 440 591-5443 Chagrin Falls *(G-2177)*	Rhoads Print Center Inc................ G .. 330 678-2042 Tallmadge *(G-12748)*	Taylor Quick Print..................... G .. 740 439-2208 Cambridge *(G-1763)*
Phil Vedda & Sons Inc................. G .. 216 671-2222 Cleveland *(G-4158)*	Richardson Printing Corp................ D .. 800 848-9752 Marietta *(G-8941)*	The Gazette Printing Co Inc.............. G .. 440 593-6030 Conneaut *(G-5418)*
Phoenix Graphix Inc................. G .. 513 751-4433 Cincinnati *(G-2961)*	Robert Becker Impressions Inc.......... F .. 419 385-5303 Toledo *(G-13116)*	Theb Inc............................... G .. 216 391-4800 Cleveland *(G-4389)*
Pinnacle Press Inc................... G .. 330 453-7060 Canton *(G-1976)*	Robin Enterprises Company.............. C .. 614 891-0250 Westerville *(G-14274)*	Tj Metzgers Inc....................... D .. 419 861-8611 Toledo *(G-13143)*
PM Graphics Inc..................... E .. 330 650-0861 Streetsboro *(G-12517)*	RPI Color Service Inc.................. D .. 513 471-4040 Cincinnati *(G-3055)*	Tkm Print Solutions Inc................ F .. 330 237-4029 Uniontown *(G-13427)*
Porath Business Services Inc........... F .. 216 626-0060 Cleveland *(G-4176)*	Ryans Newark Leader Ex Prtg Co........ F .. 740 522-2149 Newark *(G-10532)*	TI Krieg Offset LLC..................... E .. 513 542-1522 Cincinnati *(G-3158)*
Post Business Properties Inc........... D .. 419 628-2321 Minster *(G-10063)*	S Beckman Print Grphic Sltons.......... G .. 614 864-2232 Columbus *(G-5240)*	Tope Printing Inc..................... G .. 330 674-4993 Millersburg *(G-10014)*
Preferred Printing................... G .. 937 492-6961 Sidney *(G-12041)*	Schuerholz Inc........................ G .. 937 294-5218 Dayton *(G-5997)*	Tradewinds Prin Twear................. G .. 740 214-5005 Roseville *(G-11654)*
Preisser Inc......................... G .. 614 345-0199 Columbus *(G-5203)*	Scorecards Unlimited LLC.............. G .. 614 885-0796 Columbus *(G-5257)*	Traxium LLC.......................... G .. 330 572-8200 Stow *(G-12466)*
Premier Printing Corporation.......... F .. 216 478-9720 Cleveland *(G-4191)*	Scratch Off Works LLC................ G .. 440 333-4302 Rocky River *(G-11639)*	Traxler Printing..................... G .. 614 593-1270 Columbus *(G-5329)*
Prime Printing Inc.................... E .. 937 438-3707 Dayton *(G-5956)*	Scrip-Safe Security Products........... E .. 513 697-7789 Loveland *(G-8852)*	Tri-State Publishing Company.......... E .. 740 283-3686 Steubenville *(G-12413)*
Print All Inc......................... G .. 419 534-2880 Toledo *(G-13103)*	Seemless Printing LLC................ G .. 513 871-2366 Cincinnati *(G-3075)*	Truax Printing Inc.................... E .. 419 994-4166 Loudonville *(G-8595)*
Print Centers of Ohio Inc.............. F .. 419 526-4139 Mansfield *(G-8846)*	Selby Service/Roxy Press Inc........... G .. 513 241-3445 Cincinnati *(G-3078)*	True Dinero Records & Tech LLC.......... G .. 513 428-4610 Cincinnati *(G-3173)*
Print Direct For Less 2 Inc............. F .. 440 236-8870 Columbia Station *(G-4598)*	Sfc Graphics Cleveland Ltd............. F .. 419 255-1283 Toledo *(G-13128)*	Tucker Printers Inc.................... D .. 585 359-3030 West Chester *(G-14086)*
Print Factory PII.................... G .. 330 549-9640 North Lima *(G-10711)*	Sharp Enterprises Inc................. G .. 937 295-2965 Fort Loramie *(G-6956)*	Ultimate Printing Inc.................. G .. 330 847-2941 Warren *(G-13804)*
Print Shop of Canton Inc.............. F .. 330 497-3212 Canton *(G-1983)*	Sitler Printer Inc.................... G .. 330 482-4463 Columbiana *(G-4628)*	USA Quickprint Inc.................... F .. 330 455-5119 Canton *(G-2040)*
Print-Digital Incorporated........... G .. 330 686-5945 Stow *(G-12451)*	Skladany Enterprises Inc.............. G .. 614 823-6882 Westerville *(G-14234)*	V & C Enterprises Co.................. G .. 614 221-1412 Columbus *(G-5343)*
Printed Image....................... F .. 614 221-1412 Columbus *(G-5207)*	Slimans Printery Inc................. G .. 330 454-9141 Canton *(G-2007)*	Vision Press Inc...................... G .. 440 357-6362 Painesville *(G-11122)*
Printers Devil Inc.................... F .. 330 650-1218 Hudson *(G-7854)*	Snow Printing Co Inc................. F .. 419 229-7669 Lima *(G-8451)*	Vpp Industries Inc.................... F .. 937 526-3775 Versailles *(G-13604)*
Printex Incorporated................. F .. 740 773-0088 Chillicothe *(G-2276)*	Source3media Inc.................... E .. 330 467-9003 Solon *(G-12184)*	Warren Printing & Off Pdts Inc.......... F .. 419 523-3635 Ottawa *(G-11050)*
Printing Arts Press Inc............... F .. 740 397-6106 Mount Vernon *(G-10260)*	Southern Ohio Printing............... G .. 513 241-5150 Cincinnati *(G-3102)*	Watkins Printing Company............. E .. 614 297-8270 Columbus *(G-5358)*
Printing Dimensions Inc.............. F .. 937 256-0044 Dayton *(G-5957)*	SP Mount Printing Company........... E .. 216 881-3316 Cleveland *(G-4318)*	Wernet Inc........................... G .. 330 452-2200 Canton *(G-2046)*
Printing Express.................... G .. 937 276-7794 Moraine *(G-10187)*	SPAOS Inc........................... G .. 937 890-0783 Dayton *(G-6014)*	West Bend Printing & Pubg Inc.......... G .. 419 258-2000 Antwerp *(G-464)*

West-Camp Press Inc...................D 614 882-2378
Westerville (G-14281)

White Tiger Inc...................F 740 852-4873
London (G-8543)

William J Bergen & Co...................G 440 248-6132
Solon (G-12208)

Willoughby Printing Co Inc...................G 440 946-0800
Willoughby (G-14551)

Yespress Graphics LLC...................G 614 899-1403
Westerville (G-14282)

Youngstown Letter Shop Inc...................G 330 793-4935
Youngstown (G-14972)

Zippitycom Print LLC...................F 216 438-0001
Cleveland (G-4525)

PRINTING: Photo-Offset

Deshea Printing Company...................G 330 336-7601
Wadsworth (G-13635)

Gerald L Herrmann Company Inc...................F 513 661-1818
Cincinnati (G-2669)

PRINTING: Photolithographic

Friends Service Co Inc...................E 419 427-1704
Findlay (G-6869)

PRINTING: Rotogravure

Western Roto Engravers Inc...................E 330 336-7636
Wadsworth (G-13677)

PRINTING: Screen, Broadwoven Fabrics, Cotton

Atlantis Sportswear Inc...................E 937 773-0680
Piqua (G-11336)

Image Group Inc...................E 419 866-3300
Holland (G-7769)

Phantasm Dsgns Sprtsn More Ltd...................G 419 538-6737
Ottawa (G-11042)

Precision Imprint...................G 740 592-5916
Athens (G-646)

Uptown Dog The Inc...................G 740 592-4600
Athens (G-655)

West-Camp Press Inc...................D 216 426-2660
Cleveland (G-4502)

PRINTING: Screen, Fabric

American Imprssions Sportswear...................G 614 848-6677
Columbus (G-4697)

Brandon Screen Printing...................F 419 229-9837
Lima (G-8391)

Cal Sales Embroidery...................G 440 236-3820
Columbia Station (G-4590)

Charizma Corp...................G 216 621-2220
Cleveland (G-3485)

Fineline Imprints Inc...................G 740 453-1083
Zanesville (G-15013)

Greenfield Research Inc...................C 937 981-7763
Greenfield (G-7330)

Kiwi Promotional AP & Prtg Co...................E 330 487-5115
Twinsburg (G-13325)

Michigan Silkscreen Inc...................G 419 885-1163
Sylvania (G-12715)

Mr Emblem Inc...................G 419 697-1888
Oregon (G-10964)

Ohio State Institute Fin Inc...................G 614 861-8811
Reynoldsburg (G-11576)

Painted Hill Inv Group Inc...................F 937 339-1756
Troy (G-13246)

Peska Inc...................F 440 998-4664
Ashtabula (G-611)

Quality Rubber Stamp Inc...................G 614 235-2700
Lancaster (G-8220)

R & A Sports Inc...................E 216 289-2254
Euclid (G-6674)

Roach Studios LLC...................F 614 725-1405
Columbus (G-5233)

Sroufe Healthcare Products LLC...................G 260 894-4171
Wadsworth (G-13672)

Stakes Manufacturing LLC...................D 216 245-4752
Willowick (G-14567)

Tee Creations...................G 937 878-2822
Fairborn (G-6702)

Triage Ortho Group...................G 937 653-6431
Urbana (G-13478)

Vandava Inc...................G 614 277-8003
Grove City (G-7421)

Vasil Co Inc...................G 419 562-2901
Bucyrus (G-1692)

Vector International Corp...................G 440 942-2002
Mentor (G-9648)

Zide Sport Shop of Ohio Inc...................F 740 373-8199
Marietta (G-8963)

PRINTING: Screen, Manmade Fiber & Silk, Broadwoven Fabric

717 Inc...................G 440 925-0402
Lakewood (G-8161)

Cincinnati Advg Pdts LLC...................C 513 346-7310
Cincinnati (G-2467)

Dwr Graphics Inc...................E 614 863-6966
Columbus (G-4892)

Flashions Sportswear Ltd...................G 937 323-5885
Springfield (G-12312)

Kaylo Enterprises LLC...................G 330 535-1860
Akron (G-192)

Phantasm Dsgns Sprtsn More Ltd...................G 419 538-6737
Ottawa (G-11042)

Sportsco Imprinting...................G 513 641-5111
Cincinnati (G-3106)

PRINTING: Thermography

A C Hadley - Printing Inc...................G 937 426-0952
Beavercreek (G-962)

PROFESSIONAL EQPT & SPLYS, WHOLESALE: Analytical Instruments

Consoldted Anlytcal Systems In...................F 513 542-1200
Cincinnati (G-2510)

Gilson Company Inc...................E 740 548-7298
Lewis Center (G-8334)

Mettler-Toledo LLC...................A 614 438-4511
Columbus (G-4644)

PROFESSIONAL EQPT & SPLYS, WHOLESALE: Engineers', NEC

S&V Industries Inc...................E 330 666-1986
Medina (G-9443)

US Tsubaki Power Transm LLC...................C 419 626-4560
Sandusky (G-11881)

PROFESSIONAL EQPT & SPLYS, WHOLESALE: Optical Goods

Diversified Ophthalmics Inc...................E 803 783-3454
Cincinnati (G-2554)

PROFESSIONAL INSTRUMENT REPAIR SVCS

Certon Technologies Inc...................F 440 786-7185
Bedford (G-1021)

Cleveland Electric Labs Co...................E 800 447-2207
Twinsburg (G-13287)

Mettler-Toledo LLC...................A 614 438-4511
Columbus (G-4644)

UPA Technology Inc...................F 513 755-1380
West Chester (G-14088)

PROFILE SHAPES: Unsupported Plastics

Advanced Composites Inc...................C 937 575-9800
Sidney (G-11990)

Alkon Corporation...................F 614 799-6650
Dublin (G-6274)

Bobbart Industries Inc...................G 419 350-5477
Sylvania (G-12702)

Cosmo Plastics Company...................C 440 498-7500
Cleveland (G-3569)

Dayton Technologies...................G 513 539-5474
Monroe (G-10101)

Deceuninck North America LLC...................E 513 539-4444
Monroe (G-10102)

Duracote Corporation...................E 330 296-9600
Ravenna (G-11523)

HP Manufacturing Company Inc...................D 216 361-6500
Cleveland (G-3841)

Machining Technologies Inc...................E 419 862-3110
Elmore (G-6489)

Meridian Industries Inc...................D 330 673-1011
Kent (G-8051)

Pexco Packaging Corp...................E 419 470-5935
Toledo (G-13096)

Roach Wood Products & Plas Inc...................G 740 532-4855
Ironton (G-7934)

Wurms Woodworking Company...................E 419 492-2184
New Washington (G-10484)

PROTECTION EQPT: Lightning

Innovest Energy Group LLC...................G 440 644-1027
Chesterland (G-2234)

PROTECTIVE FOOTWEAR: Rubber Or Plastic

Advantage Products Corporation...................G 513 489-2283
Blue Ash (G-1243)

PUBLIC RELATIONS & PUBLICITY SVCS

Marketing Essentials LLC...................E 419 629-0080
New Bremen (G-10362)

PUBLISHERS: Music Book & Sheet Music

Road Apple Music...................G 513 217-4444
Middletown (G-9891)

PUBLISHERS: Music, Sheet

American Gild of English Hndbe...................G 937 438-0085
Cincinnati (G-2359)

Lorenz Corporation...................D 937 228-6118
Dayton (G-5855)

PUBLISHERS: Sheet Music

Willis Music Company...................F 513 671-3288
Cincinnati (G-3225)

PUBLISHERS: Telephone & Other Directory

ITM Marketing Inc...................C 740 295-3575
Coshocton (G-5457)

Mid American Publishing...................G 419 822-5662
Delta (G-6212)

Pro Press Inc...................F 216 631-8200
Cleveland (G-4197)

PUBLISHING & BROADCASTING: Internet Only

Ahalogy...................E 314 974-5599
Cincinnati (G-2344)

Alscommunity.................................. F 215 478-5095
Coventry Township (G-5480)

Cerkl Incorporated............................. D 513 813-8425
Blue Ash (G-1261)

Clark Optimization LLC....................... E 330 417-2164
Canton (G-1867)

Deemsys Inc..................................... D 614 322-9928
Gahanna (G-7155)

Dotcentral LLC................................... F 330 809-0112
Massillon (G-9186)

Evans Creative Group LLC................... G 614 657-9439
Columbus (G-4914)

Intelacomm Inc.................................. G 888 610-9250
Newbury (G-10555)

IPA Ltd... F 614 523-3974
Columbus (G-5024)

Marketing Essentials LLC................... E 419 629-0080
New Bremen (G-10362)

Organized Lightning LLC..................... G 407 965-2730
Blue Ash (G-1315)

Quadriga Americas LLC...................... G 614 890-6090
Westerville (G-14228)

PUBLISHING & PRINTING: Art Copy

Publishing Group Ltd.......................... F 614 572-1240
Columbus (G-5213)

PUBLISHING & PRINTING: Book Music

Swagg Productions2015llc.................. F 614 601-7414
Worthington (G-14726)

PUBLISHING & PRINTING: Books

Bearing Precious Seed Intl Inc............. G 513 575-1706
Milford (G-9924)

Gardner Business Media Inc................ F 513 527-8800
Cincinnati (G-2650)

Kendall/Hunt Publishing Co................. C 877 275-4725
Cincinnati (G-2792)

Marysville Newspaper Inc.................... E 937 644-9111
Marysville (G-9037)

McGraw-Hill Schl Edcatn Hldngs........... A 419 207-7400
Ashland (G-551)

World Harvest Church Inc.................... C 614 837-1990
Canal Winchester (G-1800)

PUBLISHING & PRINTING: Directories, NEC

Haines Publishing Inc......................... F 330 494-9111
Canton (G-1907)

Lsc Communications Inc...................... A 419 935-0111
Willard (G-14403)

PUBLISHING & PRINTING: Directories, Telephone

Berry Company.................................. G 513 768-7800
Cincinnati (G-2408)

PUBLISHING & PRINTING: Guides

Trogdon Publishing Inc....................... E 330 721-7678
Medina (G-9458)

PUBLISHING & PRINTING: Magazines: publishing & printing

614 Media Group LLC.......................... F 614 488-4400
Columbus (G-4654)

Bluffton News Pubg & Prtg Co.............. F 419 358-8010
Bluffton (G-1357)

Breakwall Publishing LLC..................... F 813 575-2570
Medina (G-9385)

Carmel Publishing Inc......................... G 330 478-9200
Canton (G-1861)

Cars and Parts Magazine...................... D 937 498-0803
Sidney (G-12001)

Cincinnati Media LLC........................... G 513 562-2755
Cincinnati (G-2481)

Cruisin Times Magazine....................... G 440 331-4615
Rocky River (G-11633)

Ertel Publishing Inc............................ G 937 767-1433
Yellow Springs (G-14788)

Family Motor Coach Assn Inc............... E 513 474-3622
Cincinnati (G-2611)

Highlights For Children Inc................... C 614 486-0631
Columbus (G-4983)

Insights Sccess Media Tech LLC........... E 614 602-1754
Dublin (G-6310)

Kenyon Review.................................. G 740 427-5208
Gambier (G-7211)

Lifestyle Media Group LLC................... F 954 377-9470
Akron (G-206)

North Coast Minority Media LLC........... G 216 407-4327
Cleveland (G-4088)

Peninsula Publishing LLC..................... G 330 524-3359
Independence (G-7914)

Publishing Group Ltd........................... F 614 572-1240
Columbus (G-5213)

Venue Lifestyle & Event Guide.............. G 513 405-6822
Cincinnati (G-3200)

Youngs Publishing Inc......................... G 937 259-6575
Dayton (G-5626)

PUBLISHING & PRINTING: Newsletters, Business Svc

Omnipresence Cleaning LLC................. F 937 250-4749
Dayton (G-5927)

Quality Solutions Inc.......................... E 440 933-9946
Cleveland (G-4216)

Questline Inc.................................... E 614 255-3166
Dublin (G-6338)

PUBLISHING & PRINTING: Newspapers

Alliance Publishing Co Inc.................... C 330 453-1304
Alliance (G-372)

American Community Newspapers......... G 614 888-4567
Columbus (G-4695)

American Israelite Company Inc............ G 513 621-3145
Cincinnati (G-2360)

Amos Media Company......................... C 937 498-2121
Sidney (G-11992)

Ashland Publishing Co......................... A 419 281-0581
Ashland (G-517)

Atrium At Anna Maria Inc..................... F 330 562-7777
Aurora (G-661)

Beacon Journal Publishing Co............... C 330 996-3600
Akron (G-74)

Block Communications Inc.................... F 419 724-6212
Toledo (G-12898)

Boardman News.................................. G 330 758-6397
Boardman (G-1368)

Bryan Publishing Company................... D 419 636-1111
Bryan (G-1634)

Business Journal............................... E 330 744-5023
Youngstown (G-14830)

Chagrin Valley Publishing Co................ F 440 247-5335
Chagrin Falls (G-2139)

Cincinnati Enquirer............................ C 513 721-2700
Cincinnati (G-2474)

Cincinnati Ftn Sq News Inc................... F 513 421-4049
Mason (G-9084)

Cincinnati Site Solutions LLC............... G 513 373-5001
Cincinnati (G-2485)

Cleveland Jewish Publ Co..................... E 216 454-8300
Cleveland (G-3514)

Cleveland Jewish Publ Co Fdn............... F 216 454-8300
Beachwood (G-912)

Columbus Messenger Company............ E 614 272-5422
Columbus (G-4830)

Columbus-Sports Publications.............. G 614 486-2202
Columbus (G-4838)

Cox Newspapers LLC........................... G
Franklin (G-7015)

Cox Newspapers LLC........................... F 937 866-3331
Miamisburg (G-9684)

Cox Newspapers LLC........................... G 513 523-4139
Oxford (G-11062)

Daily Fantasy Circuit Inc..................... G 614 989-8689
Columbus (G-4868)

Daily Growler Inc............................... G 614 656-2337
Upper Arlington (G-13430)

Daily Reporter.................................. E 614 224-4835
Columbus (G-4869)

Dayton City Paper Group Llc................ F 937 222-8855
Dayton (G-5723)

Delphos Herald Inc............................. G 419 399-4015
Paulding (G-11154)

Delphos Herald Inc............................. D 419 695-0015
Delphos (G-6184)

Dispatch Consumer Services................ C 740 687-1893
Lancaster (G-8199)

Dispatch Printing Company................... F 614 461-5000
Columbus (G-4884)

Dispatch Printing Company................... A 614 220-5833
Columbus (G-4883)

Dow Jones & Company Inc.................... E 419 352-4696
Bowling Green (G-1417)

Euclid Media Group LLC....................... F 216 241-7550
Cleveland (G-3690)

Fremont Discover Ltd.......................... G 419 332-8696
Fremont (G-7110)

Funny Times Inc................................ G 216 371-8600
Cleveland (G-3744)

Gannett Stllite Info Ntwrk LLC.............. F 513 768-8451
Cincinnati (G-2648)

Gannett Stllite Info Ntwrk LLC.............. F 419 334-1012
Fremont (G-7113)

Gannett Stllite Info Ntwrk LLC.............. E 304 485-1891
Marietta (G-8918)

Gate West Coast Ventures LLC............. F 513 891-1000
Blue Ash (G-1276)

Gazette Publishing Company................ F 419 483-4190
Oberlin (C 10017)

Greenworld Enterprises Inc.................. G 800 525-6999
West Chester (G-14123)

Hirt Publishing Co Inc......................... E 419 946-3010
Mount Gilead (G-10210)

Holmes County Hub Inc....................... G 330 674-1811
Millersburg (G-9987)

Journal Register Company.................... D 440 245-6901
Lorain (G-8560)

Journal Register Company.................... B 440 951-0000
Willoughby (G-14473)

Lake Community News.......................... G 440 946-2577
Willoughby (G-14480)

Legal News Publishing Co.................... E 216 696-3322
Cleveland (G-3949)

Marysville Newspaper Inc.................... E 937 644-9111
Marysville (G-9037)

Medina Hntngton RE Group II LL........... E 330 591-2777
Medina (G-9424)

Messenger Publishing Company............ C 740 592-6612
Athens (G-644)

Morgan County Publishing Co............... G 740 962-3377
Mcconnelsville (G-9366)

News Watchman & Paper....................... F 740 947-2149
Waverly (G-13870)

Newspaper Network Central OH............. G 419 524-3545
Mansfield (G-8839)

Ogden Newspapers Ohio Inc................. F 419 448-3200
Tiffin (G-12794)

Ohio Irish American News...................... G 216 647-1144
Cleveland (G-4115)

Ohio Newspaper Services Inc................ G 614 486-6677
Columbus (G-5149)

Ohio Newspapers Inc............................ C 937 335-3997
Troy (G-13245)

Ohio Newspapers Foundation................ G 614 486-6677
Columbus (G-5150)

Ohio Rights Group................................. G 614 300-0529
Columbus (G-5152)

Pataskala Post...................................... F 740 964-6226
Pataskala (G-11145)

Perry County Tribune............................ F 740 342-4121
New Lexington (G-10405)

Premier Prtg Centl Ohio Ltd.................. E 937 642-0988
Marysville (G-9043)

Record Publishing Co............................ D 330 688-0088
Stow (G-12454)

Rural-Urban Record Inc........................ G 440 236-8982
Columbia Station (G-4601)

Schaffner Publication Inc...................... G 419 732-2154
Port Clinton (G-11452)

Sesh Communications........................... F 513 851-1693
Cincinnati (G-3084)

Sojourners Truth Inc............................. F 419 243-0007
Toledo (G-13133)

Spectrum News Ohio............................. F 614 384-2640
Columbus (G-5283)

Stark Cnty Fdrtion Cnsrvtion C............. E 330 268-1652
Canton (G-2013)

Streamline Media & Pubg LLC.............. G 614 822-1817
Reynoldsburg (G-11581)

Sylvania Advantage............................... G 419 725-2695
Sylvania (G-12726)

Syracuse China LLC.............................. C 419 325-2100
Toledo (G-13138)

The Cleveland Jewish Publ Co.............. E 216 454-8300
Beachwood (G-953)

The Gazette Printing Co Inc.................. D 440 576-9125
Jefferson (G-7984)

The Vindicator Printing Company.......... B 330 747-1471
Youngstown (G-14946)

Upper Arlington Crew Inc...................... G 614 485-0089
Columbus (G-5340)

Vindicator.. G 330 841-1600
Warren (G-13808)

Vindicator Printing Company................. E 330 744-8611
Youngstown (G-14962)

PUBLISHING & PRINTING: Pamphlets

Equipping Ministries Intl Inc................. G 513 742-1100
Cincinnati (G-2597)

J S C Publishing................................... G 614 424-6911
Columbus (G-5027)

Liturgical Publications Inc..................... D 216 325-6825
Cleveland (G-3964)

PUBLISHING & PRINTING: Textbooks

Cengage Learning Inc........................... B 415 839-2300
Mason (G-9080)

Cengage Lrng Holdings II Inc............... E 617 289-7700
Mason (G-9081)

PUBLISHING & PRINTING: Trade Journals

Benjamin Media Inc.............................. E 330 467-7588
Brecksville (G-1459)

PULLEYS: Metal

J L R Products Inc................................ G 330 832-9557
Massillon (G-9207)

PULLEYS: Power Transmission

J L R Products Inc................................ G 330 832-9557
Massillon (G-9207)

PULP MILLS

Billerud Americas Corporation.............. D 901 369-4105
West Chester (G-13952)

Caraustar Industries Inc....................... D 740 862-4167
Baltimore (G-784)

Polymer Tech & Svcs Inc...................... F 740 929-5500
Heath (G-7601)

Rumpke Transportation Co LLC............. B 513 242-4600
Cincinnati (G-3057)

The Mead Corporation........................... B 937 495-6323
Dayton (G-6049)

PULP MILLS: Mechanical & Recycling Processing

Riverview Productions Inc..................... G 740 441-1150
Gallipolis (G-7208)

World Wide Recyclers Inc...................... G 614 554-3296
Columbus (G-5372)

PUMPS & PARTS: Indl

A & F Machine Products Co................... E 440 826-0959
Berea (G-1157)

Ayling and Reichert Co Consent............ G 419 898-2471
Oak Harbor (G-10883)

Cima Inc... G 513 382-8976
Hamilton (G-7476)

Columbia Industrial Pdts Inc................. F 216 431-6633
Cleveland (G-3547)

Crane Pumps & Systems LLC............... E 937 773-2442
Piqua (G-11341)

E R Advanced Ceramics Inc.................. E 330 426-9433
East Palestine (G-6402)

Flowserve Corporation........................... D 937 226-4000
Dayton (G-5780)

Flowserve Corporation........................... G 513 874-6990
Loveland (G-8625)

Fluid Automation Inc............................. E 248 912-1970
North Canton (G-10640)

Gerow Equipment Company Inc............. G 216 383-8800
Cleveland (G-3772)

Gorman-Rupp Company.......................... B 419 755-1011
Mansfield (G-8793)

Gorman-Rupp Company.......................... C 419 755-1011
Mansfield (G-8794)

Molten Mtal Eqp Innvations LLC............ E 440 632-9119
Middlefield (G-9813)

Pckd Enterprises Inc............................. G 440 632-9119
Middlefield (G-9820)

Process Dynamics Inc........................... G 330 686-2597
Stow (G-12452)

Thieman Tailgates Inc........................... D 419 586-7727
Celina (G-2125)

Valco Cincinnati Inc.............................. C 513 874-6550
Cincinnati (G-3190)

Warren Rupp Inc................................... C 419 524-8388
Mansfield (G-8863)

PUMPS & PUMPING EQPT REPAIR SVCS

Certified Labs & Service Inc.................. G 419 289-7462
Ashland (G-527)

Eaton Industrial Corporation................. C 216 692-5456
Cleveland (G-3657)

Thirion Brothers Eqp Co LLC................ G 440 357-8004
Painesville (G-11118)

Wm Plotz Machine and Forge Co........... F 216 861-0441
Cleveland (G-4512)

PUMPS & PUMPING EQPT WHOLESALERS

Advanced Fuel Systems Inc................... G 614 252-8422
Columbus (G-4676)

Ashland Water Group Inc...................... G 877 326-3561
Ashland (G-518)

Bergstrom Company Ltd Partnr.............. F 440 232-2282
Cleveland (G-3415)

Bowden Manufacturing Corp................. E 440 946-1770
Willoughby (G-14432)

Chaos Entertainment.............................. G 937 520-5260
Dayton (G-5698)

Dreison International Inc........................ C 216 362-0755
Cleveland (G-3632)

Eaton Aeroquip LLC............................... A 419 891-7775
Maumee (G-9292)

Fill-Rite Company.................................. E 419 755-1011
Mansfield (G-8787)

General Electric Company...................... E 216 883-1000
Cleveland (G-3766)

Giant Industries Inc.............................. E 419 531-4600
Toledo (G-12975)

Gorman-Rupp Company.......................... E 419 755-1245
Mansfield (G-8795)

Hydromatic Pumps Inc.......................... E 419 289-1144
Ashland (G-541)

Idex Corporation................................... G 419 526-7222
Mansfield (G-8805)

Indelco Custom Products Inc................. E 216 797-7300
Euclid (G-6654)

Interstate Pump Company Inc................ G 330 222-1006
Salem (G-11789)

Keen Pump Company Inc....................... E 419 207-9400
Ashland (G-544)

Lubrisource Inc..................................... F 937 432-9292
Middletown (G-9872)

M T Systems Inc................................... G 330 453-4646
Canton (G-1936)

Maag Reduction Inc.............................. E 704 716-9000
Kent (G-8048)

Magnum Piering Inc.............................. E 513 759-3348
West Chester (G-14131)

Metaullics Systems LP.......................... C 509 926-6212
Solon (G-12148)

Pentair... E 440 248-0100
Solon (G-12167)

Pentair Pump Group Inc........................ F 419 281-9918
Ashland (G-560)

Quikstir Inc.. G 419 732-2601
Port Clinton (G-11449)

Rumpke Transportation Co LLC............. F 513 851-0122
Cincinnati (G-3058)

Seepex Inc.. C 937 864-7150
Enon (G-6633)

Stahl Gear & Machine Co...................... G 216 431-2820
Cleveland (G-4323)

Suburban Manufacturing Co.................. D 440 953-2024
Eastlake (G-6444)

Systecon LLC.. D 513 777-7722
West Chester (G-14080)

Tark Inc.. E 937 434-6766
Miamisburg (G-9743)

Teikoku USA Inc.................................... F 304 699-1156
Marietta (G-8951)

TJ Clark International LLC...................... F 614 388-8869
Delaware (G-6176)

Tolco Corporation.................................. E 419 241-1113
Toledo (G-13147)

Trane Technologies Company LLC........ F 419 636-4242
Bryan *(G-1664)*

Trane Technologies Company LLC........ E 419 633-6800
Bryan *(G-1665)*

Trane Technologies Company LLC........ E 513 459-4580
Cincinnati *(G-3162)*

Transdigm Inc.................................. E 216 291-6025
Cleveland *(G-4411)*

Transdigm Inc.................................. E 440 352-6182
Painesville *(G-11119)*

Uhrden Inc...................................... E 330 456-0031
Canton *(G-2030)*

Vertiflo Pump Company..................... F 513 530-0888
Cincinnati *(G-3202)*

Vickers International Inc.................... G 419 867-2200
Maumee *(G-9329)*

PUMPS: Domestic, Water Or Sump

Certified Labs & Service Inc.............. G 419 289-7462
Ashland *(G-527)*

City of Newark................................ E 740 349-6765
Newark *(G-10497)*

Crane Pumps & Systems Inc............. E 937 778-8947
Piqua *(G-11339)*

Lakecraft Inc.................................. G 419 734-2828
Port Clinton *(G-11444)*

Wayne Water Systems Inc................. C 800 237-0987
Harrison *(G-7571)*

PUMPS: Fluid Power

Alkid Corporation............................ E 216 896-3000
Cleveland *(G-3323)*

Custom Cltch Jint Hydrlics Inc.......... F 216 431-1630
Cleveland *(G-3584)*

Danfoss Power Solutions II LLC......... F 419 238-1190
Van Wert *(G-13533)*

Oase North America Inc.................... G 800 365-3880
Aurora *(G-682)*

Parker-Hannifin Corporation............. E 440 266-2300
Mentor *(G-9582)*

Parker-Hannifin Corporation............. G 330 740-8366
Youngstown *(G-14914)*

Parker-Hannifin Corporation............. A 216 896-3000
Cleveland *(G-4143)*

Suburban Manufacturing Co.............. D 440 953-2024
Eastlake *(G-6444)*

Vertiflo Pump Company..................... F 513 530-0888
Cinoinnati *(G 3202)*

PUMPS: Gasoline, Measuring Or Dispensing

Field Stone Inc................................ G 937 898-3236
Tipp City *(G-12825)*

PUMPS: Hydraulic Power Transfer

Bosch Rexroth Corporation............... C 330 263-3300
Wooster *(G-14627)*

Eaton Corporation........................... B 440 523-5000
Cleveland *(G-3652)*

Lhy Powertrain Corporation.............. E 330 533-6801
Canfield *(G-1812)*

Parker-Hannifin Corporation............. E 937 644-3915
Marysville *(G-9041)*

PUMPS: Measuring & Dispensing

Bergstrom Company Ltd Partnr.......... F 440 232-2282
Cleveland *(G-3415)*

Cohesant Inc.................................. E 216 910-1700
Beachwood *(G-913)*

Gojo Industries Inc.......................... G 330 255-6525
Stow *(G-12435)*

Gojo Industries Inc.......................... C 330 255-6000
Akron *(G-163)*

Graco Ohio Inc................................ D 330 494-1313
North Canton *(G-10644)*

Precision Conveyor Technology.......... F 440 352-6100
Perry *(G-11197)*

Seepex Inc..................................... C 937 864-7150
Enon *(G-6633)*

Tolco Corporation............................ E 419 241-1113
Toledo *(G-13147)*

Valco Cincinnati Inc......................... C 513 874-6550
Cincinnati *(G-3190)*

PUMPS: Oil Well & Field

GE Vernova International LLC............. G 330 963-2066
Twinsburg *(G-13308)*

PUMPS: Oil, Measuring Or Dispensing

Energy Manufacturing Ltd................. G 419 355-9304
Fremont *(G-7105)*

Lubrisource Inc............................... F 937 432-9292
Middletown *(G-9872)*

PUNCHES: Forming & Stamping

Cleveland Steel Tool Company........... E 216 681-7400
Cleveland *(G-3526)*

Dayton Progress Corporation............. A 937 859-5111
Dayton *(G-5737)*

Stolle Machinery Company LLC.......... C 937 497-5400
Dayton *(G-6027)*

PURIFICATION & DUST COLLECTION EQPT

Ceco Environmental Corp.................. F 513 458-2606
Blue Ash *(G-1259)*

Ceco Group Global Holdings LLC........ F 513 458-2600
Cincinnati *(G-2448)*

Dreison International Inc................... C 216 362-0755
Cleveland *(G-3632)*

Effox-Flextor-Mader Inc................... F 513 874-8915
West Chester *(G-14115)*

Seneca Environmental Products Inc.... E 419 447-1282
Tiffin *(G-12799)*

RACEWAYS

Raceway Petroleum Inc..................... G 440 989-2660
Lorain *(G-8575)*

RADAR SYSTEMS & EQPT

Decibel Research Inc........................ E 256 705-3341
Beavercreek *(G-969)*

Dedrone Defense Inc........................ F 614 948-2002
Westerville *(G-14255)*

Dragoon Technologies Inc................. G 937 439-9223
Dayton *(G-5751)*

Escort Inc...................................... C 513 870-8500
West Chester *(G-13995)*

Oculii Corp..................................... E 937 912-9261
Beavercreek Township *(G-1002)*

Valentine Research Inc..................... E 513 984-8900
Blue Ash *(G-1346)*

RADIO & TELEVISION COMMUNICATIONS EQUIPMENT

Pole/Zero LLC................................. C 513 870-9060
West Chester *(G-14050)*

RADIO BROADCASTING & COMMUNICATIONS EQPT

Circle Prime Manufacturing Inc.......... E 330 923-0019
Cuyahoga Falls *(G-5534)*

Gatesair Inc................................... D 513 459-3400
Mason *(G-9102)*

Imagine Communications Corp........... G 513 459-3400
Mason *(G-9110)*

RADIO BROADCASTING STATIONS

Iheartcommunications Inc................. G 419 223-2060
Lima *(G-8418)*

Isaac Foster Mack Co....................... C 419 625-5500
Sandusky *(G-11843)*

RADIO COMMUNICATIONS: Airborne Eqpt

Quasonix Inc................................... E 513 942-1287
West Chester *(G-14058)*

RADIO COMMUNICATIONS: Carrier Eqpt

L-3 Cmmncations Nova Engrg Inc........ F 877 282-1168
Mason *(G-9120)*

RADIO, TV & CONSUMER ELEC STORES: High Fidelity Stereo Eqpt

ABC Appliance Inc........................... E 419 693-4414
Oregon *(G-10955)*

Bose Corporation............................ G 513 891-4384
Cincinnati *(G-2418)*

Tune Town Car Audio........................ G 419 627-1100
Sandusky *(G-11878)*

RADIO, TV/CONSUMER ELEC STORES: Antennas, Satellite Dish

Dish One Up Satellite Inc.................. D 216 482-3875
Cleveland *(G-3618)*

Dss Installations Ltd........................ G 513 761-7000
Cincinnati *(G-2563)*

RAILINGS: Prefabricated, Metal

AT&f Advanced Metals LLC................ F 330 684-1122
Orrville *(G-10973)*

AT&f Advanced Metals LLC................ E 330 684-1122
Cleveland *(G-3383)*

Beacon Metal Fabricators Inc............ G 216 391-7444
Cleveland *(G-3412)*

Glas Ornamental Metals Inc.............. G 330 753-0215
Barberton *(G-807)*

Hayes Bros Orna Ir Works Inc............ F 419 531-1491
Toledo *(G-12987)*

RAILINGS: Wood

L & L Ornamental Iron Co.................. F 513 353-1930
Cleves *(G-4543)*

RAILROAD CAR REPAIR SVCS

Andersons Inc................................. G 419 536-0460
Toledo *(G-12881)*

Andersons Inc................................. C 419 893-5050
Maumee *(G-9261)*

Jk-Co LLC...................................... E 419 422-5240
Findlay *(G-6883)*

RAILROAD EQPT

A Stucki Company........................... D 412 424-0560
North Canton *(G-10626)*

Alliance Castings Company LLC.......... E 330 829-5600
Alliance *(G-369)*

Amsted Industries Incorporated......... D 614 836-2323
Groveport *(G-7422)*

Buck Equipment Inc......................... E 614 539-3039
Grove City *(G-7375)*

Dayton-Phoenix Group Inc................ C 937 496-3900
Dayton *(G-5742)*

Gunderson Rail Services LLC............. D 330 792-6521
Youngstown *(G-14872)*

PRODUCT

Johnson Bros Rubber Co Inc............... E 419 752-4814
Greenwich *(G-7362)*

K & G Machine Company................. F 216 732-7115
Cleveland *(G-3900)*

L B Foster Company................. F 330 652-1461
Mineral Ridge *(G-10030)*

Midwest Rlwy Prsrvtion Soc Inc ..... G 216 781-3629
Cleveland *(G-4038)*

Nolan Company................. G 740 269-1512
Bowerston *(G-1400)*

Nolan Company................. F 330 453-7922
Canton *(G-1958)*

Ohio Valley Trackwork Inc............... G 740 446-0181
Bidwell *(G-1213)*

Progress Rail Services Corp............... B 216 641-4000
Cleveland *(G-4200)*

Progress Rail Services Corp............... F 614 850-1730
Columbus *(G-5211)*

R H Little Co................. G 330 477-3455
Canton *(G-1989)*

Sperling Railway Services Inc........... F 330 479-2004
Canton *(G-2011)*

Transco Railway Products Inc............... E 330 872-0934
Newton Falls *(G-10581)*

RAILROAD EQPT & SPLYS WHOLESALERS

Amsted Industries Incorporated........... D 614 836-2323
Groveport *(G-7422)*

Buck Equipment Inc............... E 614 539-3039
Grove City *(G-7375)*

RAILROAD EQPT: Brakes, Air & Vacuum

Westinghouse A Brake Tech Corp......... G 419 526-5323
Mansfield *(G-8866)*

RAILROAD MAINTENANCE & REPAIR SVCS

Simpson & Sons Inc............... G 513 367-0152
Harrison *(G-7568)*

Tmt Inc................. G 419 592-1041
Perrysburg *(G-11273)*

RAILROAD RELATED EQPT: Railway Track

Railroad Tools & Solutions Inc............... G 513 533-7070
Cincinnati *(G-3031)*

RAMPS: Prefabricated Metal

Homecare Mattress Inc............... F 937 746-2556
Franklin *(G-7027)*

Jh Industries Inc............... E 330 963-4105
Twinsburg *(G-13321)*

Overhead Door Corporation............... F 419 294-3874
Upper Sandusky *(G-13452)*

Wyse Industrial Carts Inc............... G 419 923-7353
Wauseon *(G-13862)*

RAZORS, RAZOR BLADES

Edgewell Personal Care Company......... G 740 374-1905
Marietta *(G-8915)*

Gillette Company LLC................. D 513 983-1100
Cincinnati *(G-2670)*

Procter & Gamble Company............... E 513 983-1100
Cincinnati *(G-2987)*

Procter & Gamble Company............... E 513 266-4375
Cincinnati *(G-2988)*

Procter & Gamble Company............... F 513 871-7557
Cincinnati *(G-2989)*

Procter & Gamble Company............... F 513 482-6789
Cincinnati *(G-2991)*

Procter & Gamble Company............... C 513 983-3000
Cincinnati *(G-2993)*

Procter & Gamble Company............... D 513 627-7115
Cincinnati *(G-2994)*

Procter & Gamble Company............... E 513 945-0340
Cincinnati *(G-2997)*

Procter & Gamble Company............... C 513 622-1000
Mason *(G-9138)*

Procter & Gamble Company............... C 513 634-9600
West Chester *(G-14054)*

Procter & Gamble Company............... C 513 634-9110
West Chester *(G-14055)*

Procter & Gamble Company............... A 513 983-1100
Cincinnati *(G-2999)*

RAZORS: Electric

Procter & Gamble Company............... A 513 983-1100
Cincinnati *(G-2999)*

REAL ESTATE AGENCIES & BROKERS

Lenz Inc................. E 937 277-9364
Dayton *(G-5844)*

Stonyridge Inc................. F 937 845-9482
New Carlisle *(G-10380)*

Wedco LLC................. G 513 309-0781
Mount Orab *(G-10223)*

REAL ESTATE AGENTS & MANAGERS

Hitti Enterprises Inc............... F 440 243-4100
Cleveland *(G-3831)*

Kenyetta Bagby Enterprise LLC........... F 614 584-3426
Reynoldsburg *(G-11573)*

Rona Enterprises Inc............... G 740 927-9971
Pataskala *(G-11148)*

REAL ESTATE INVESTMENT TRUSTS

Infinitaire Industries LLC................. G 216 600-2051
Euclid *(G-6655)*

RECEIVERS: Radio Communications

CDI Industries Inc................. E 440 243-1100
Cleveland *(G-3481)*

RECORDS & TAPES: Prerecorded

Cuttercroix LLC................. E 330 289-6185
Cleveland *(G-3588)*

Fluid Handling Dynamics Ltd................. F 419 633-0560
Bryan *(G-1642)*

RECOVERY SVC: Iron Ore, From Open Hearth Slag

Stein LLC................. D 216 883-7444
Cleveland *(G-4331)*

Stein LLC................. F 440 526-9301
Independence *(G-7919)*

Waterford Tank Fabrication Ltd............... D 740 984-4100
Beverly *(G-1211)*

RECREATIONAL VEHICLE PARTS & ACCESS STORES

Mitchs Welding & Hitches................. G 419 893-3117
Maumee *(G-9311)*

Steves Vans ACC Unlimited LLC........... G 740 374-3154
Marietta *(G-8950)*

REFINERS & SMELTERS: Copper

Sam Dong Ohio Inc................. D 740 363-1985
Delaware *(G-6171)*

REFINERS & SMELTERS: Silicon, Primary, Over 99% Pure

Ferroglobe USA Mtllurgical Inc............... C 740 984-2361
Waterford *(G-13826)*

Silicon Processors Inc................. G 740 373-2252
Marietta *(G-8944)*

REFINING: Petroleum

Aecom Energy & Cnstr Inc................. G 419 698-6277
Oregon *(G-10956)*

Blaster Corporation................. F 216 901-5800
Medina *(G-9381)*

BP Products North America Inc............... E 419 537-9540
Toledo *(G-12901)*

Cyberutility LLC................. G 216 291-8723
Cleveland *(G-3595)*

Eidp Inc................. F 440 934-6444
Avon *(G-725)*

Gfl Environmental Svcs USA Inc........... E 281 486-4182
Norwalk *(G-10842)*

Giant Industries Inc................. D 419 421-2121
Findlay *(G-6870)*

Isp Lima LLC................. E 419 998-8700
Lima *(G-8421)*

Knight Material Tech LLC................. E 330 488-1651
East Canton *(G-6378)*

Marathon Intl Pdts Sup LLC................. G 419 422-2121
Findlay *(G-6887)*

Marathon Oil Company................. E 419 422-2121
Findlay *(G-6888)*

Marathon Petroleum Corporation............... A 419 422-2121
Findlay *(G-6890)*

Mkfour Inc................. G 620 629-1120
Granville *(G-7318)*

Mplx GP LLC................. G 419 422-2121
Findlay *(G-6896)*

Ohio Refining Company LLC................. A 614 210-2300
Dublin *(G-6326)*

Pbf Holding Company LLC................. D 419 698-6600
Oregon *(G-10965)*

PSC 272 TRC Pbf................. E 419 466-7129
Oregon *(G-10966)*

Seneca Petroleum Co Inc................. F 419 691-3581
Toledo *(G-13126)*

REFRACTORIES: Brick

Allied Mineral Products LLC................. B 614 876-0244
Columbus *(G-4688)*

Minteq International Inc................. E 330 343-8821
Dover *(G-6254)*

Plibrico Company LLC................. F 740 682-7755
Oak Hill *(G-10892)*

REFRACTORIES: Cement

Castruction Company Inc................. F 330 332-9622
Salem *(G-11768)*

REFRACTORIES: Clay

Bowerston Shale Company................. E 740 269-2921
Bowerston *(G-1399)*

Glen-Gery Corporation................. D 419 845-3321
Caledonia *(G-1731)*

Glen-Gery Corporation................. E 419 468-5002
Iberia *(G-7883)*

I Cerco Inc................. C 740 982-2050
Crooksville *(G-5510)*

Industrial Ceramic Products Inc................. D 937 642-3897
Marysville *(G-9032)*

Lakeway Mfg Inc................. E 419 433-3030
Huron *(G-7877)*

Magneco/Metrel Inc................. C 330 426-9468
Negley *(G-10315)*

Minteq International Inc................. E 330 343-8821
Dover *(G-6254)*

Nock and Son Company................. F 740 682-7741
Oak Hill *(G-10891)*

Resco Products Inc.................................. G.... 330 488-1226
East Canton (G-6380)

Selas Heat Technology Co LLC............ E..... 800 523-6500
Streetsboro (G-12523)

Specialty Ceramics Inc.......................... D..... 330 482-0800
Columbiana (G-4629)

Stebbins Engineering & Mfg Co............ G..... 740 922-3012
Uhrichsville (G-13407)

Summitville Tiles Inc............................. D..... 330 868-6463
Minerva (G-10048)

United Refractories Inc.......................... E..... 330 372-3716
Warren (G-13807)

Whitacre Greer Company........................ E..... 330 823-1610
Alliance (G-416)

REFRACTORIES: Foundry, Clay

Ethima Inc.. D..... 419 626-4912
Sandusky (G-11834)

REFRACTORIES: Graphite, Carbon Or Ceramic Bond

E I Ceramics LLC................................... D..... 513 772-7001
Cincinnati (G-2570)

Refractory Specialties Inc...................... E..... 330 938-2101
Sebring (G-11900)

REFRACTORIES: Nonclay

A & M Refractories Inc.......................... E..... 740 456-8020
New Boston (G-10355)

Ethima Inc.. D..... 419 626-4912
Sandusky (G-11834)

Ets Schaefer LLC.................................. F..... 330 468-6600
Macedonia (G-8689)

Ets Schaefer LLC.................................. E..... 330 468-6600
Beachwood (G-917)

I Cerco Inc... C..... 740 982-2050
Crooksville (G-5510)

Impact Armor Technologies LLC............ F..... 216 706-2024
Cleveland (G-3853)

Industrial Ceramic Products Inc............ D..... 937 642-3897
Marysville (G-9032)

Johns Manville Corporation.................... C..... 419 878-8111
Waterville (G-13835)

Magneco/Metrel Inc.............................. C..... 330 426-9468
Negley (G-10315)

Martin Marietta Materials Inc................ F..... 513 701-1140
West Chester (G-14026)

Momentive Prfmce Mtls Qrtz Inc........... E..... 440 878-5700
Strongsville (G-12575)

Ohio Vly Stmpng-Assemblies Inc........... F..... 419 522-0983
Mansfield (G-8842)

Ormet Primary Aluminum Corp.............. A..... 740 483-1381
Hannibal (G-7541)

Pmbp Legacy Co Inc............................. E..... 330 253-8148
Akron (G-262)

Pyromatics Corp................................... F..... 440 352-3500
Mentor (G-9599)

Resco Products Inc............................... G..... 740 682-7794
Oak Hill (G-10893)

Saint-Gobain Ceramics Plas Inc............ D..... 330 673-5860
Stow (G-12456)

Saint-Gobain Ceramics Plas Inc............ A..... 610 893-6000
Stow (G-12457)

US Refractory Products LLC.................. E..... 440 386-4580
North Ridgeville (G-10752)

Vacuform Inc.. E..... 330 938-9674
Sebring (G-11905)

Zircoa Inc.. C..... 440 248-0500
Cleveland (G-4526)

REFRACTORIES: Tile & Brick, Exc Plastic

Seven Lakeway Refractories LLC........... F.... 419 433-3030
Huron (G-7882)

REFRIGERATION & HEATING EQUIPMENT

Beckett Air Incorporated...................... D..... 440 327-9999
North Ridgeville (G-10725)

Bessamaire Sales Inc........................... E..... 440 439-1200
Twinsburg (G-13279)

Bodor Vents Inc................................... G..... 513 348-3853
Cincinnati (G-2415)

Briskheat Corporation........................... C..... 614 294-3376
Columbus (G-4781)

C Nelson Mfg Co.................................. E..... 419 898-3305
Oak Harbor (G-10884)

Cryogenic Equipment & Svcs Inc.......... F..... 513 761-4200
Hamilton (G-7481)

Csafe LLC.. G..... 513 360-7189
Monroe (G-10100)

Daikin Applied Americas Inc.................. G..... 614 351-9862
Westerville (G-14252)

Dyoung Enterprise Inc.......................... C..... 440 918-0505
Willoughby (G-14452)

Elitaire LLC.. D..... 513 475-3803
Blue Ash (G-1271)

Ellis & Watts Global Inds Inc................ E..... 513 752-9000
Batavia (G-863)

Emerson Network Power........................ G..... 614 841-8054
Ironton (G-7931)

Famous Industries Inc........................... F..... 740 685-2592
Byesville (G-1711)

Fire From Ice Ventures LLC.................... F..... 419 944-6705
Solon (G-12112)

Jnp Group LLC..................................... F..... 800 735-9645
Wooster (G-14655)

Lennox Industries Inc............................ G..... 216 739-1909
Cleveland (G-3951)

Mahle Behr Dayton LLC........................ A..... 937 369-2000
Dayton (G-5862)

Mahle Behr USA Inc............................. G..... 937 369-2610
Xenia (G-14770)

Maverick Innvtive Slutions LLC............. D..... 419 281-7944
Ashland (G-550)

Professional Supply Inc......................... F..... 419 332-7373
Fremont (G-7128)

Royal Metal Products LLC..................... C..... 740 397-8842
Mount Vernon (G-10264)

RSI Company.. F..... 216 360-9800
Beachwood (O-940)

Rtx Corporation.................................... B..... 330 784-5477
North Canton (G-10666)

T J F Inc.. F..... 419 878-4400
Waterville (G-13843)

Taiho Corporation of America............... C..... 419 443-1645
Tiffin (G-12801)

Tempest Inc.. E..... 216 883-6500
Cleveland (G-4373)

Trane Inc.. E..... 440 946-7823
Cleveland (G-4410)

Trane US Inc.. C..... 513 771-8884
Cincinnati (G-3163)

Trane US Inc.. C..... 614 473-3131
Columbus (G-5326)

Trane US Inc.. G..... 614 473-8701
Columbus (G-5327)

Trane US Inc.. G..... 614 497-6300
Groveport (G-7454)

Vertiv Corporation................................. G..... 614 491-9286
Groveport (G-7456)

Vortec Corporation................................ E..... 513 891-7485
Blue Ash (G-1348)

REFRIGERATION EQPT & SPLYS WHOLESALERS

Modern Ice Equipment & Sup Co........... E..... 513 367-2101
Cincinnati (G-2885)

REFRIGERATION EQPT: Complete

Hobart LLC... D..... 937 332-2797
Piqua (G-11355)

Hobart LLC... E..... 937 332-3000
Troy (G-13225)

Hobart LLC... G..... 937 332-3000
Troy (G-13226)

Northeastern Rfrgn Corp....................... E..... 440 942-7676
Willoughby (G-14496)

Nrc Inc... E..... 440 975-9449
Willoughby (G-14497)

So-Low Environmental Eqp Co............... E..... 513 772-9410
Cincinnati (G-3098)

REFRIGERATION REPAIR SVCS

Northeastern Rfrgn Corp....................... E..... 440 942-7676
Willoughby (G-14496)

REFRIGERATION SVC & REPAIR

Bell Industrial Services LLC................... F..... 937 507-9193
Sidney (G-11997)

REFUSE SYSTEMS

A & B Iron & Metal Co Inc.................... F..... 937 228-1561
Dayton (G-5629)

Capital City Oil Inc.............................. G..... 740 397-4483
Mount Vernon (G-10238)

Metalico Akron Inc............................... F..... 330 376-1400
Akron (G-229)

Rumpke Transportation Co LLC............. F..... 513 851-0122
Cincinnati (G-3058)

Unlimited Energy Services LLC............. F..... 304 517-7097
Beverly (G-1210)

REGISTERS: Air, Metal

Hart & Cooley LLC............................... D..... 937 832-7800
Englewood (G-6614)

REGULATORS: Power

Vertiv Corporation................................. A..... 614 888-0246
Westerville (G-14239)

REHABILITATION SVCS

Clovernook Ctr For Blind Vslly............. C..... 513 522-3860
Cincinnati (G-2500)

RELAYS & SWITCHES: Indl, Electric

Control Electric Co............................... E..... 216 671-8010
Columbia Station (G-4592)

Controllix Corporation........................... F..... 440 232-8757
Walton Hills (G-13696)

Rogers Industrial Products Inc.............. E..... 330 535-3331
Akron (G-290)

Utility Relay Co Ltd............................. E..... 440 708-1000
Chagrin Falls (G-2189)

RELAYS: Control Circuit, Ind

Industrial and Mar Eng Svc Co............. F..... 740 694-0791
Fredericktown (G-7080)

Omega Tek Inc..................................... G..... 419 756-9580
Mansfield (G-8843)

RELIGIOUS SPLYS WHOLESALERS

Novak J F Manufacturing Co LLC.......... G..... 216 741-5112
Cleveland (G-4102)

PRODUCT

REMOVERS & CLEANERS

Grand Archt Etrnl Eye 314 LLC.............. F 800 377-8147
Cleveland *(G-3783)*

REMOVERS: Paint

Treved Exteriors....................................... G 513 771-3888
Cincinnati *(G-3167)*

RENTAL SVCS: Costume

Akron Design & Costume LLC.............. G 330 644-0425
Coventry Township *(G-5479)*

Costume Specialists Inc....................... E 614 464-2115
Columbus *(G-4852)*

RENTAL SVCS: Sign

ABC Signs Inc.. F 513 407-4367
Cincinnati *(G-2331)*

RENTAL SVCS: Sound & Lighting Eqpt

Technical Artistry Inc............................ G 614 299-7777
Columbus *(G-5316)*

RENTAL SVCS: Tent & Tarpaulin

Galion Canvas Products........................ G 419 468-5333
Galion *(G-7191)*

Rainbow Industries Inc.......................... G 937 323-6493
Springfield *(G-12366)*

South Akron Awning Co......................... F 330 848-7611
Akron *(G-314)*

Tarpco Inc.. F 330 677-8277
Kent *(G-8086)*

Wolf G T Awning & Tent Co.................... F 937 548-4161
Greenville *(G-7360)*

RENTAL SVCS: Vending Machine

Cuyahoga Vending Co Inc...................... C 440 353-9595
North Ridgeville *(G-10728)*

RENTAL SVCS: Work Zone Traffic Eqpt, Flags, Cones, Etc

A & A Safety Inc.................................... F 937 567-9781
Beavercreek *(G-987)*

A & A Safety Inc.................................... E 513 943-6100
Amelia *(G-425)*

Paul Peterson Company........................ F 614 486-4375
Columbus *(G-5178)*

Paul Peterson Safety Div Inc................. E 614 486-4375
Columbus *(G-5179)*

RENTAL: Portable Toilet

AAA Wastewater Services Inc............... F 937 746-6361
Franklin *(G-7009)*

BJ Equipment Ltd.................................. F 614 497-1188
Columbus *(G-4758)*

Pro-Kleen Industrial Svcs Inc............... E 740 689-1886
Lancaster *(G-8218)*

RENTAL: Video Tape & Disc

Ohio Hd Video....................................... F 614 656-1162
New Albany *(G-10348)*

RESEARCH & DEVELOPMENT SVCS, COMMERCIAL: Engineering Lab

Iconic Labs LLC.................................... F 216 759-4040
Westlake *(G-14308)*

Moog Inc... E 330 682-0010
Orrville *(G-10996)*

Morris Technologies Inc........................ E 513 733-1611
Cincinnati *(G-2888)*

RESEARCH, DEVELOPMENT & TESTING SVCS, COMMERCIAL: Energy

Tacoma Energy LLC.............................. C 614 899-8990
Westerville *(G-14276)*

RESEARCH, DEVELOPMENT & TESTING SVCS, COMMERCIAL: Medical

Applied Medical Technology Inc............ F 440 717-4000
Brecksville *(G-1457)*

RESEARCH, DEVELOPMENT & TESTING SVCS, COMMERCIAL: Physical

Ftech R&D North America Inc................ E 937 339-2777
Troy *(G-13217)*

Ion Vacuum Ivac Tech Corp.................. F 216 662-5158
Cleveland *(G-3868)*

Leidos Inc... D 937 656-8433
Beavercreek *(G-977)*

Velocys Inc.. D 614 733-3300
Plain City *(G-11424)*

RESINS: Custom Compound Purchased

Accel Corporation.................................. D 440 934-7711
Avon *(G-711)*

Advanced Composites Inc...................... C 937 575-9800
Sidney *(G-11990)*

Aurora Plastics LLC.............................. E 330 422-0700
Streetsboro *(G-12488)*

Avient Corporation................................ D 419 668-4844
Norwalk *(G-10829)*

Avient Corporation................................ D 440 930-1000
Avon Lake *(G-748)*

Bay State Polymer Distribution Inc........ F 440 892-8500
Westlake *(G-14291)*

Chemionics Corporation........................ E 330 733-8834
Tallmadge *(G-12731)*

Deltech Polymers LLC........................... D 937 339-3150
Troy *(G-13210)*

Flex Technologies Inc............................ D 330 897-6311
Baltic *(G-777)*

Flex Technologies Inc............................ E 740 922-5992
Midvale *(G-9910)*

Freeman Manufacturing & Sup Co........ E 440 934-1902
Avon *(G-727)*

General Color Investments Inc............... D 330 868-4161
Minerva *(G-10038)*

Hexpol Compounding LLC...................... C 440 834-4644
Burton *(G-1699)*

Hexpol Compounding LLC...................... C 440 632-1962
Middlefield *(G-9800)*

Hexpol Compounding LLC...................... C 440 834-4644
Burton *(G-1700)*

Hexpol Holding Inc................................ F 440 834-4644
Burton *(G-1701)*

Howard Industries Inc............................ F 614 444-9900
Columbus *(G-4993)*

Jpi Coastal LLC..................................... G 330 424-1110
Lisbon *(G-8475)*

Killian Latex Inc.................................... E 330 644-6746
Akron *(G-196)*

Lancer Dispersions Inc.......................... D
Akron *(G-202)*

McCann Plastics LLC............................. D 330 499-1515
Canton *(G-1943)*

Nanosperse LLC.................................... G 937 296-5030
Kettering *(G-8122)*

Polymera Inc.. G 740 527-2069
Hebron *(G-7631)*

Polyone Corporation.............................. D 330 467-8108
Macedonia *(G-8708)*

Radici Plastics Usa Inc......................... E 330 336-7611
Wadsworth *(G-13665)*

Sherwin-Williams Company.................... C 330 830-6000
Massillon *(G-9243)*

Thermafab Alloy Inc.............................. G 216 861-0540
Olmsted Falls *(G-10941)*

Tymex Plastics Inc................................ E 216 429-8950
Cleveland *(G-4437)*

Vibrantz Color Solutions Inc.................. C 440 997-5137
Ashtabula *(G-621)*

RESISTORS & RESISTOR UNITS

Asco Power Technologies LP................ C 216 573-7600
Cleveland *(G-3374)*

Avtron Loadbank Inc.............................. C 216 573-7600
Cleveland *(G-3395)*

RESPIRATORS

Morning Pride Mfg LLC.......................... A 937 264-1726
Dayton *(G-5895)*

Morning Pride Mfg LLC.......................... A 937 264-2662
Dayton *(G-5894)*

RESTAURANT EQPT: Carts

Darpro Storage Solutions LLC............... E 567 233-3190
Marengo *(G-8896)*

Modroto... G 440 998-1202
Ashtabula *(G-606)*

RESTAURANT EQPT: Sheet Metal

Captive-Aire Systems Inc...................... G 513 860-5555
Cincinnati *(G-2437)*

DBs Stnless Stl Fbrctors Inc................. G 513 856-9600
Hamilton *(G-2434)*

Porcelain Steel Buildings Company....... D 614 228-5781
Columbus *(G-5199)*

RESTAURANTS: Full Svc, American

Brewpub Restaurant Corporation.......... F 614 228-2537
Columbus *(G-4774)*

Great Lakes Brewing Co........................ C 216 771-4404
Cleveland *(G-3789)*

Velvet Ice Cream Company.................... D 740 892-3921
Utica *(G-13488)*

RETAIL BAKERY: Bread

Angelic Bakehouse LLC......................... E 414 312-7300
Westerville *(G-14203)*

Blf Enterprises Inc................................ F 937 642-6425
Westerville *(G-14246)*

Brooks Pastries Inc............................... G 614 274-4880
Plain City *(G-11399)*

Busken Bakery Inc................................. D 513 871-2114
Cincinnati *(G-2434)*

Investors United Inc.............................. G 419 473-8942
Toledo *(G-13008)*

Norcia Bakery....................................... G 330 454-1077
Canton *(G-1959)*

Schwebel Baking Company.................... E 330 783-2860
Hebron *(G-7635)*

Schwebel Baking Company.................... C 440 248-1500
Solon *(G-12179)*

RETAIL BAKERY: Cakes

Cake In A Cup Inc.................................. G 419 491-1104
Toledo *(G-12909)*

Hostess Brands Inc............................... D 816 701-4600
Orrville *(G-10984)*

I Dream of Cakes.................................. G 937 533-6024
Eaton *(G-6455)*

RETAIL BAKERY: Cookies

Cookie Bouquets Inc..G 614 888-2171
Columbus *(G-4847)*

RETAIL BAKERY: Doughnuts

Crispie Creme Chillicothe Inc...............G 740 774-3770
Chillicothe *(G-2249)*

Dandi Enterprises Inc...........................G 419 516-9070
Solon *(G-12099)*

Evans Bakery Inc...................................G 937 228-4151
Dayton *(G-5771)*

Kennedys Bakery Inc.............................G 740 432-2301
Cambridge *(G-1746)*

Krispy Kreme Doughnut Corp..............E 614 798-0812
Columbus *(G-5057)*

Krispy Kreme Doughnut Corp..............D 614 876-0058
Columbus *(G-5058)*

Mary Ann Donut Shoppe Inc................G 330 478-1655
Canton *(G-1938)*

McHappys Dnuts Parkersburg Inc..........D 740 593-8744
Athens *(G-643)*

Schulers Bakery Inc..............................E 937 323-4154
Springfield *(G-12371)*

Wal-Bon of Ohio Inc.............................E 740 423-8178
Belpre *(G-1156)*

RETAIL BAKERY: Pastries

Meeks Pastry Shop................................G 419 782-4871
Defiance *(G-6121)*

RETAIL STORES: Alcoholic Beverage Making Eqpt & Splys

Chappell-Zimmerman Inc......................F 330 337-8711
Salem *(G-11769)*

Pomacon Inc...F 330 273-1576
Brunswick *(G-1606)*

RETAIL STORES: Audio-Visual Eqpt & Splys

Educational Direction Inc.....................G 330 836-8439
Fairlawn *(G-6799)*

Findaway World LLC.............................E 440 893-0808
Solon *(G-12111)*

RETAIL STORES: Batteries, Non-Automotive

Battery Unlimited...................................G 740 452-5030
Zanesville *(G-14993)*

One Wish LLC..F 800 505-6883
Bedford *(G-1052)*

RETAIL STORES: Cake Decorating Splys

Hartville Chocolates Inc........................G 330 877-1999
Hartville *(G-7576)*

RETAIL STORES: Christmas Lights & Decorations

Rhc Inc..E 330 874-3750
Bolivar *(G-1391)*

RETAIL STORES: Cleaning Eqpt & Splys

Akron Cotton Products Inc....................G 330 434-7171
Akron *(G-28)*

RETAIL STORES: Communication Eqpt

Communications Aid Inc........................F 513 475-8453
Cincinnati *(G-2505)*

RETAIL STORES: Concrete Prdts, Precast

Michaels Pre-Cast Con Pdts Inc............F 513 683-1292
Loveland *(G-8643)*

RETAIL STORES: Cosmetics

Boxout LLC...C 833 462-7746
Hudson *(G-7835)*

Primal Life Organics LLC......................E 800 260-4946
Copley *(G-5438)*

Studgionsgroup LLC..............................E 216 804-1561
Cleveland *(G-4339)*

RETAIL STORES: Educational Aids & Electronic Training Mat

Bendon Inc..D 419 207-3600
Ashland *(G-521)*

Health Nuts Media LLC..........................G 818 802-5222
Cleveland *(G-3815)*

RETAIL STORES: Electronic Parts & Eqpt

Mixed Logic LLC....................................G 440 826-1676
Valley City *(G-13505)*

Precision Replacement LLC...................G 330 908-0410
Macedonia *(G-8709)*

RETAIL STORES: Flags

Flag Lady Inc..G 614 263-1776
Columbus *(G-4927)*

Mel Wacker Signs Inc............................G 330 832-1726
Massillon *(G-9222)*

RETAIL STORES: Hair Care Prdts

Natural Beauty Products Inc..................F 513 420-9400
Middletown *(G-9882)*

RETAIL STORES: Ice

Haller Enterprises Inc............................F 330 733-9693
Akron *(G-169)*

Home City Ice Company.........................G 440 439-5001
Bedford *(G-1036)*

Home City Ice Company.........................G 937 461-6028
Dayton *(G-5812)*

Home City Ice Company.........................F 614 836-2877
Groveport *(G-7438)*

RETAIL STORES: Medical Apparatus & Splys

Health Aid of Ohio Inc...........................E 216 252-3900
Cleveland *(G-3814)*

Johnson & Johnson................................E 513 786-7000
Blue Ash *(G-1290)*

RETAIL STORES: Orthopedic & Prosthesis Applications

Akron Orthotic Solutions Inc.................G 330 253-3002
Akron *(G-35)*

Blatchford Inc...D 937 291-3636
Miamisburg *(G-9673)*

Leimkuehler Inc.....................................E 440 899-7842
Cleveland *(G-3950)*

Presque Isle Orthtics Prsthtic................G 216 371-0660
Cleveland *(G-4192)*

Stable Step LLC.....................................C 800 491-1571
Wadsworth *(G-13673)*

RETAIL STORES: Pet Splys

Heading4ward Investment Co................D 937 293-9994
Moraine *(G-10169)*

RETAIL STORES: Religious Goods

Incorprted Trstees of The Gspl..............D 216 749-2100
Middleburg Heights *(G-9773)*

Strictly Stitchery Inc.............................F 440 543-7128
Cleveland *(G-4335)*

RETAIL STORES: Safety Splys & Eqpt

Paul Peterson Safety Div Inc.................E 614 486-4375
Columbus *(G-5179)*

Pneumatic Specialties Inc......................G 440 729-4400
Chesterland *(G-2239)*

RETAIL STORES: Swimming Pools, Above Ground

Litehouse Products LLC.........................E 440 638-2350
Strongsville *(G-12571)*

RETAIL STORES: Telephone & Communication Eqpt

Securcom Inc..E 419 628-1049
Minster *(G-10065)*

RETAIL STORES: Tents

Rainbow Industries Inc..........................G 937 323-6493
Springfield *(G-12366)*

RETAIL STORES: Water Purification Eqpt

Enting Water Conditioning Inc..............E 937 294-5100
Moraine *(G-10160)*

US Water Company LLC.........................G 740 453-0604
Zanesville *(G-15053)*

William R Hague Inc...............................D 614 836-2115
Groveport *(G-7458)*

RETAIL STORES: Welding Splys

ARC Solutions LLC.................................E 419 542-9272
Hicksville *(G-7646)*

Fischer Engineering Co LLC...................G 937 754-1750
Dayton *(G-5778)*

Linde Gas & Equipment Inc....................G 513 821-2192
Cincinnati *(G-2823)*

Mt Vernon Machine & Tool Inc...............E 740 397-0311
Mount Vernon *(G-10254)*

Welders Supply Inc................................E 216 267-4470
Brookpark *(G-1560)*

Welders Supply Inc................................F 216 241-1696
Cleveland *(G-4500)*

REUPHOLSTERY & FURNITURE REPAIR

Custom Craft Collection Inc..................F 440 998-3000
Ashtabula *(G-589)*

Fortnor Upholstoring Inc.......................F 614 475-8282
Columbus *(G-4936)*

Robert Mayo Industries..........................G 330 426-2587
East Palestine *(G-6406)*

RIBBONS & BOWS

Discount Floral Supply Inc.....................G
Cleveland *(G-3617)*

Sylvan Studios Inc.................................G 419 882-3423
Sylvania *(G-12725)*

RIVETS: Metal

North Coast Rivet Inc.............................F 440 366-6829
Elyria *(G-6571)*

ROAD CONSTRUCTION EQUIPMENT WHOLESALERS

Brewpro Inc..G 513 577-7200
Cincinnati *(G-2423)*

Winter Equipment Company In...............E 440 946-8377
Willoughby *(G-14552)*

ROBOTS: Assembly Line

PRODUCT

Advanced Design Industries Inc............ F 440 277-4141
Sheffield Village **(G-11956)**

Air Technical Industries Inc................... E 440 951-5191
Mentor **(G-9474)**

Amatrol Inc... E 812 288-8285
Mansfield **(G-8761)**

Ats Systems Oregon Inc...................... F 541 738-0932
Lewis Center **(G-8324)**

Computer Allied Technology Co............ G 614 457-2292
Columbus **(G-4839)**

Hitachi Automation Ohio Inc................. F 937 753-1148
Covington **(G-5494)**

Kc Robotics Inc.................................... E 513 860-4442
West Chester **(G-14019)**

Lincoln Electric Automtn Inc................. E 614 471-5926
Columbus **(G-5070)**

Process Innovations Inc....................... G 330 856-5192
Vienna **(G-13616)**

Recognition Robotics Inc...................... F 440 590-0499
Elyria **(G-6585)**

Rennco Automation Systems Inc.......... E 419 861-2340
Holland **(G-7781)**

Rimrock Corporation............................ E 614 471-5926
Columbus **(G-5230)**

Rimrock Holdings Corporation.............. C 614 471-5926
Columbus **(G-5231)**

Rixan Associates Inc............................ E 937 438-3005
Dayton **(G-5984)**

Sensory Robotics Inc........................... G 513 545-9501
Cincinnati **(G-3082)**

Sentient Studios Ltd............................. E 330 204-8636
Fairlawn **(G-6811)**

Versatile Automation Tech Corp........... G 330 220-2600
Brunswick **(G-1622)**

Versatile Automation Tech Ltd.............. G 440 589-6700
Solon **(G-12202)**

Yaskawa America Inc........................... C 937 440-2600
Troy **(G-13261)**

ROBOTS: Indl Spraying, Painting, Etc

Ats Ohio Inc... C 614 888-2344
Lewis Center **(G-8323)**

RODS: Rolled, Aluminum

Kaiser Aluminum Fab Pdts LLC............ C 740 522-1151
Heath **(G-7598)**

RODS: Steel & Iron, Made In Steel Mills

American Posts LLC.............................. D 419 720-0652
Toledo **(G-12877)**

Buschman Corporation......................... F 216 431-6633
Cleveland **(G-3453)**

Charter Manufacturing Co Inc.............. D 216 883-3800
Cleveland **(G-3490)**

L&H Threaded Rods Corp..................... C 937 294-6666
Moraine **(G-10173)**

ROLL FORMED SHAPES: Custom

American Roll Formed Pdts Corp.......... C 440 352-0753
Youngstown **(G-14812)**

Cdh Custom Roll Form LLC................... E 330 984-0555
Warren **(G-13750)**

Ej Usa Inc.. F 330 782-3900
Youngstown **(G-14852)**

Formasters Corporation........................ F 440 639-9206
Mentor **(G-9518)**

Hynes Holding Company....................... G 330 799-3221
Youngstown **(G-14873)**

Hynes Industries Inc............................ D 800 321-9257
Youngstown **(G-14874)**

Lion Industries LLC.............................. E 740 676-1100
Bellaire **(G-1089)**

Welser Profile North Amer LLC............. E 330 225-2500
Valley City **(G-13522)**

ROLLING MILL EQPT: Finishing

Bardons & Oliver Inc............................ C 440 498-5800
Solon **(G-12082)**

Fives Bronx Inc.................................... D 330 244-1960
North Canton **(G-10639)**

ROLLING MILL MACHINERY

Addition Manufacturing Tech................ C 513 228-7000
Lebanon **(G-8241)**

ADS Machinery Corp............................ D 330 399-3601
Warren **(G-13731)**

Bendco Machine & Tool Inc.................. F 419 628-3802
Minster **(G-10054)**

Circle Machine Rolls Inc....................... E 330 938-9010
Sebring **(G-11893)**

Cornerstone Wauseon Inc.................... E 419 337-0940
Wauseon **(G-13847)**

E R Advanced Ceramics Inc................. E 330 426-9433
East Palestine **(G-6402)**

Element Machinery LLC......................... G 855 447-7648
Toledo **(G-12949)**

Enprotech Industrial Tech LLC.............. E 216 883-3220
Cleveland **(G-3675)**

Formtek Metal Forming Inc................... D 216 292-4460
Cleveland **(G-3738)**

George A Mitchell Company.................. E 330 758-5777
Youngstown **(G-14866)**

H P E Inc.. G 330 833-3161
Massillon **(G-9199)**

Hydranamics Inc.................................. D 419 468-3530
Galion **(G-7195)**

J Horst Manufacturing Co..................... D 330 828-2216
Dalton **(G-5586)**

Kottler Metal Products Co Inc.............. E 440 946-7473
Willoughby **(G-14478)**

Park Corporation.................................. B 216 267-4870
Medina **(G-9434)**

Perfecto Industries Inc......................... E 937 778-1900
Piqua **(G-11372)**

Pines Manufacturing Inc....................... E 440 835-5553
Westlake **(G-14324)**

Rafter Equipment Company LLC........... E 440 572-3700
Strongsville **(G-12592)**

Ridge Tool Company............................ A 440 323-5581
Elyria **(G-6586)**

Ridge Tool Manufacturing Co............... F 440 323-5581
Elyria **(G-6588)**

Steel Eqp Specialists Inc..................... D 330 823-8260
Alliance **(G-406)**

Sticker Corporation.............................. F 440 946-2100
Willoughby **(G-14534)**

Turner Machine Co............................... G 330 332-5821
Salem **(G-11816)**

United Rolls Inc.................................... D
Canton **(G-2036)**

Warren Fabricating Corporation............ D 330 534-5017
Hubbard **(G-7818)**

Xtek Inc... B 513 733-7800
Cincinnati **(G-3240)**

ROLLING MILL ROLLS: Cast Steel

United Engineering & Fndry Co............ G 330 456-2761
Canton **(G-2034)**

ROLLS: Rubber, Solid Or Covered

United Roller Co LLC............................ F 440 564-9698
Newbury **(G-10565)**

ROOFING MATERIALS: Asphalt

Modern Builders Supply Inc................. E 419 526-0002
Mansfield **(G-8831)**

ROOFING MEMBRANE: Rubber

Batman Enterprises LLC....................... F 513 600-3079
Milford **(G-9923)**

Clearview Construction LLC.................. G 513 206-6415
Cincinnati **(G-2498)**

Hyload Inc.. G 330 336-6604
Seville **(G-11917)**

Republic Powdered Metals Inc............. D 330 225-3192
Medina **(G-9441)**

RPM International Inc........................... D 330 273-5090
Medina **(G-9442)**

Soprema USA Inc................................. E 330 334-0066
Wadsworth **(G-13671)**

Synthomer Inc...................................... C 216 682-7000
Beachwood **(G-951)**

Topps Products Inc.............................. F 913 685-2500
Cleveland **(G-4404)**

RUBBER BANDS

Keener Rubber Company....................... F 330 821-1880
Alliance **(G-387)**

RUBBER PRDTS: Appliance, Mechanical

Canton OH Rubber Speclty Prods......... G 330 454-3847
Canton **(G-1857)**

Yokohama Tws North America Inc......... E 330 436-5168
Akron **(G-361)**

RUBBER PRDTS: Automotive, Mechanical

Cardinal Rubber Company.................... E 330 745-2191
Barberton **(G-801)**

Koneta Inc.. D 419 739-4200
Wapakoneta **(G-13720)**

Mm Outsourcing LLC............................ F 937 661-4300
Leesburg **(G-8300)**

Prospira America Corporation............... D 419 294-6989
Upper Sandusky **(G-13453)**

RUBBER PRDTS: Medical & Surgical Tubing, Extrudd & Lathe-Cut

Saint-Gobain Prfmce Plas Corp............ C 330 798-6981
Akron **(G-305)**

RUBBER PRDTS: Oil & Gas Field Machinery, Mechanical

United Feed Screws Ltd........................ F 330 798-5532
Akron **(G-351)**

V & M Star LP....................................... F 330 742-6300
Youngstown **(G-14956)**

RUBBER PRDTS: Silicone

Blair Sales Inc...................................... D 330 769-5586
Seville **(G-11912)**

Brain Child Products LLC...................... F 419 698-4020
Toledo **(G-12904)**

North Coast Seal Incorporated............. F 216 898-5000
Brookpark **(G-1556)**

Novagard Solutions Inc........................ D 216 881-8111
Cleveland **(G-4101)**

S P E Inc.. E 330 733-0101
Mogadore **(G-10084)**

Shin-Etsu Silicones of America Inc........ C 330 630-9460
Akron **(G-309)**

Shincor Silicones Inc........................... E 330 630-9460
Akron **(G-310)**

RUBBER PRDTS: Sponge

Chalfant Sew Fabricators Inc.................. E 216 521-7922
Cleveland (G-3484)

Merryweather Foam Inc......................... E 330 753-0353
Barberton (G-822)

Miles Rubber & Packing Company........ E 330 425-3888
Twinsburg (G-13341)

North Coast Seal Incorporated............. F 216 898-5000
Brookpark (G-1556)

RUBBER STRUCTURES: Air-Supported

Truflex Rubber Products Co.................. C 740 967-9015
Johnstown (G-8001)

RUST RESISTING

Chemtool Incorporated......................... C 815 957-4140
Wickliffe (G-14369)

SAFE DEPOSIT BOXES

Hamilton Safe Co.................................. F 513 874-3733
Milford (G-9938)

Hamilton Security Products Co............. E 513 874-3733
Milford (G-9939)

Williamson Safe Inc.............................. G 937 393-9919
Hillsboro (G-7729)

SAFES & VAULTS: Metal

Diebold Nixdorf Incorporated............... C 740 928-1010
Hebron (G-7612)

Diebold Nixdorf Incorporated............... A 330 490-4000
North Canton (G-10635)

Linsalata Cpitl Prtners Fund I.............. G 440 684-1400
Cleveland (G-3962)

McIntosh Safe Corp.............................. F 937 222-7008
Dayton (G-5871)

Target Holdings Inc.............................. E 513 474-4409
Cincinnati (G-3138)

SAFETY EQPT & SPLYS WHOLESALERS

All-American Fire Eqp Inc.....................F 800 972-6035
Wshngtn Ct Hs (G-14734)

Netherland Rubber Company................ F 513 733-0883
Cincinnati (G-2899)

Wcm Holdings Inc................................ C 513 705-2100
Cincinnati (G-3213)

West Chester Holdings LLC................. C 513 705-2100
Cincinnati (G-3220)

SAFETY INSPECTION SVCS

Industrial Power Systems Inc.............. B 419 531-3121
Rossford (G-11659)

SALT

CJ Salt World....................................... G 440 343-5661
Wickliffe (G-14370)

Morton Salt Inc.................................... G 513 941-1578
Cincinnati (G-2890)

Morton Salt Inc.................................... E 216 664-0728
Cleveland (G-4048)

Obersons Nurs & Landscapes LLC...... E 513 687-7379
Hamilton (G-7514)

SAND & GRAVEL

Bonsal American Inc............................ E 513 398-7300
Cincinnati (G-2417)

Broadway Sand and Gravel LLC........... G 937 853-5555
Dayton (G-5686)

C F Poeppelman Inc............................. E 937 448-2191
Bradford (G-1451)

Canton Asphalt Co............................... G 330 499-6888
Canton (G-1852)

Central Allied Enterprises Inc.............. E 330 477-6751
Canton (G-1862)

Constrction Aggrgtes Corp Mich.......... E 616 842-7900
Independence (G-7893)

Fisher Sand & Gravel Inc..................... G 330 745-9239
Norton (G-10822)

FML Terminal Logistics LLC................ F 440 214-3200
Independence (G-7904)

Foundry Sand Service LLC.................. F 330 823-6152
Sebring (G-11894)

Hanson Aggregates East...................... G 513 353-1100
Cleves (G-4538)

Hilltop Basic Resources Inc................. E 513 621-1500
Cincinnati (G-2723)

Hilltop Basic Resources Inc................. G 937 859-3616
Miamisburg (G-9699)

Hilltop Basic Resources Inc................. G 937 882-6357
Springfield (G-12322)

Holmes Redimix Inc............................ E 330 674-0865
Holmesville (G-7797)

Holmes Supply Corp............................ G 330 279-2634
Holmesville (G-7799)

James Bunnell Inc............................... F 513 353-1100
Cleves (G-4540)

Kenmore Construction Co Inc............. D 330 832-8888
Massillon (G-9211)

Martin Marietta Materials Inc.............. F 513 701-1140
West Chester (G-14026)

McClelland Inc..................................... E 740 452-3036
Zanesville (G-15027)

Medina Supply Company...................... E 330 723-3681
Medina (G-9426)

National Lime and Stone Co................. E 419 396-7671
Carey (G-2060)

Oster Sand and Gravel Inc................... G 330 874-3322
Bolivar (G-1387)

Oster Sand and Gravel Inc................... G 330 833-2649
Massillon (G-9229)

Phoenix Asphalt Company Inc.............. G 330 339-4935
Magnolia (G-8736)

Portable Crushing LLC......................... G 330 618-5251
New Franklin (G-10393)

Prairie Lane Corporation...................... G 330 262-3322
Wooster (G-14672)

Putnam Aggregates Co........................ G 419 523-6004
Ottawa (G-11043)

R W Sidley Incorporated...................... E 440 564-2221
Newbury (G-10561)

Rjw Trucking Company Ltd................... E 740 363-5343
Delaware (G-6169)

Rupp Construction Inc......................... F 330 855-2781
Marshallville (G-9008)

Shelly Materials Inc............................. F 740 247-2311
Racine (G-11506)

Shelly Materials Inc............................. D 740 246-6315
Thornville (G-12770)

Smith Concrete Co.............................. E 740 373-7441
Dover (G-6262)

Stafford Gravel Inc.............................. G 419 298-2440
Edgerton (G-6470)

Stocker Concrete Company.................. F 740 254-4626
Gnadenhutten (G-7293)

Streamside Materials Llc.................... G 419 423-1290
Findlay (G-6924)

The Olen Corporation........................... D 614 491-1515
Columbus (G-5321)

Tiger Sand & Gravel LLC..................... F 330 833-6325
Massillon (G-9248)

Tri County Concrete Inc....................... F 330 425-4464
Twinsburg (G-13386)

Tuffco Sand and Gravel Inc.................. G 614 873-3977
Plain City (G-11422)

W&W Rock Sand and Gravel................. G 513 266-3708
Williamsburg (G-14410)

Wayne Concrete Company LLC............. F 937 545-9919
Medway (G-9466)

Welch Sand & Gravel Inc..................... F 513 353-3220
Cincinnati (G-3217)

Youngs Sand & Gravel Co Inc.............. F 419 994-3040
Loudonville (G-8597)

SAND LIME PRDTS

Holmes Supply Corp............................ G 330 279-2634
Holmesville (G-7799)

SAND MINING

Central Ready Mix LLC........................ E 513 402-5001
Cincinnati (G-2451)

Covia Solutions LLC............................ G 440 214-3200
Independence (G-7895)

D H Bowman & Sons Inc...................... F 419 886-2711
Bellville (G-1137)

John R Jurgensen Co........................... B 513 771-0820
Cincinnati (G-2768)

Massillon Materials Inc....................... F 330 837-4767
Dalton (G-5589)

Phillips Companies.............................. E 937 426-5461
Beavercreek Township (G-1003)

S & S Aggregates Inc.......................... F 740 453-0721
Zanesville (G-15046)

The National Lime and Stone Company. E 419 422-4341
Findlay (G-6927)

Ward Construction Co.......................... F 419 943-2450
Leipsic (G-8316)

SANDBLASTING EQPT

L N Brut Manufacturing Co................... G 330 833-9045
Shreve (G-11984)

SANITARY SVC, NEC

Ash Sewer & Drain Service................... G 330 376-9714
Akron (G-61)

N-Viro International Corp...................... F 419 535-6374
Toledo (G-13061)

SANITARY SVCS: Hazardous Waste, Collection & Disposal

Advanced Drainage Systems Inc........... D 614 658-0050
Hilliard (G-7666)

SANITARY SVCS: Liquid Waste Collection & Disposal

Koski Construction Co.......................... G 440 997-5337
Ashtabula (G-601)

SANITARY SVCS: Refuse Collection & Disposal Svcs

Montgomerys Pallet Service Inc............ G 330 297-6677
Ravenna (G-11533)

SANITARY SVCS: Rubbish Collection & Disposal

Sidwell Materials Inc........................... C 740 849-2422
Zanesville (G-15050)

SANITARY SVCS: Waste Materials, Recycling

Auris Noble LLC.................................. E 330 321-6649
Akron (G-64)

Cirba Solutions Us Inc......................... E 740 653-6290
Lancaster (G-8186)

Fpt Cleveland LLC............................... C 216 441-3800
Cleveland (G-3740)

PRODUCT

Garden Street Iron & Metal Inc............. E 513 721-4660
Cincinnati *(G-2649)*

Grasan Equipment Company Inc.......... D 419 526-4440
Mansfield *(G-8797)*

Green Vision Materials Inc................... F 440 564-5500
Newbury *(G-10552)*

H Hafner & Sons Inc............................. E 513 321-1895
Cincinnati *(G-2698)*

Homan Metals LLC................................ G 513 721-5010
Cincinnati *(G-2728)*

Hope Timber Pallet Recycl LLC............. E 740 344-1788
Newark *(G-10509)*

Innovation Plastics LLC........................ E 513 818-1771
Fostoria *(G-6985)*

Magnus International Group Inc............ G 216 592-8355
Painesville *(G-11097)*

Mondo Polymer Technologies Inc.......... E 740 376-9396
Marietta *(G-8930)*

Novelis Alr Recycling Ohio LLC............. C 740 922-2373
Uhrichsville *(G-13404)*

Perma-Fix of Dayton Inc....................... F 937 268-6501
Dayton *(G-5938)*

Polychem LLC....................................... D 419 547-1400
Clyde *(G-4561)*

Pratt Paper (oh) LLC............................. D 567 320-3353
Wapakoneta *(G-13727)*

Resource Recycling Inc......................... F 419 222-2702
Lima *(G-8444)*

Roe Transportation Entps Inc................ G 937 497-7161
Sidney *(G-12045)*

Rumpke Transportation Co LLC............ B 513 242-4600
Cincinnati *(G-3057)*

Synagro Midwest Inc............................ F 937 384-0669
Miamisburg *(G-9741)*

Werlor Inc... F 419 784-4285
Defiance *(G-6127)*

SASHES: Door Or Window, Metal

Rsl LLC... E 330 392-8900
Warren *(G-13795)*

YKK AP America Inc.............................. E 513 942-7200
West Chester *(G-14094)*

SATELLITES: Communications

Great Lakes Telcom Ltd......................... E 330 629-8848
Youngstown *(G-14870)*

SAW BLADES

Cammel Saw Company........................... F 330 477-3764
Canton *(G-1851)*

Uhrichsville Carbide Inc........................ F 740 922-9197
Uhrichsville *(G-13409)*

SAWDUST & SHAVINGS

Sugarcreek Shavings LLC..................... G 330 763-4239
Sugarcreek *(G-12651)*

SCAFFOLDS: Mobile Or Stationary, Metal

Bil-Jax Inc.. F 419 445-8915
Archbold *(G-490)*

Hansen Scaffolding LLC........................ F 513 574-9000
West Chester *(G-14124)*

Haulotte North America Mfg LLC........... G 419 445-8915
Archbold *(G-497)*

Sky Climber Wind Solutions LLC.......... E 740 203-3900
Delaware *(G-6174)*

Waco Scaffolding & Equipment Inc........ A 216 749-8900
Cleveland *(G-4487)*

SCALES & BALANCES, EXC LABORATORY

Etched Metal Company.......................... E 440 248-0240
Solon *(G-12109)*

Interface Logic Systems Inc................... G 614 236-8388
Ashville *(G-626)*

K Davis Inc... G 419 307-7051
Fremont *(G-7119)*

Rainin Instrument LLC.......................... G 510 564-1600
Columbus *(G-4647)*

SCALES: Indl

Cgmw Incorporated............................... G 614 236-8388
Columbus *(G-4804)*

Exact Equipment Corporation................ F 215 295-2000
Columbus *(G-4640)*

Holtgreven Scale & Elec Corp................ F 419 422-4779
Findlay *(G-6881)*

Mettler-Toledo LLC.............................. C 614 841-7300
Columbus *(G-5096)*

Mettler-Toledo LLC.............................. D 614 438-4511
Worthington *(G-14719)*

Mettler-Toledo LLC.............................. E 614 438-4390
Worthington *(G-14720)*

Mettler-Toledo Intl Inc......................... A 614 438-4511
Columbus *(G-4643)*

Mettler-Toledo LLC.............................. A 614 438-4511
Columbus *(G-4644)*

SCIENTIFIC EQPT REPAIR SVCS

Instrumentors Inc.................................. G 440 238-3430
Strongsville *(G-12568)*

SCIENTIFIC INSTRUMENTS WHOLESALERS

Science/Electronics Inc......................... G 937 224-4444
Dayton *(G-5998)*

SCRAP & WASTE MATERIALS, WHOLESALE: Ferrous Metal

Agmet LLC.. F 216 663-8200
Cleveland *(G-3314)*

Cohen Brothers Inc............................... E 513 217-5200
Middletown *(G-9849)*

Cohen Brothers Inc............................... E 513 422-3696
Middletown *(G-9848)*

Fpt Cleveland LLC................................ C 216 441-3800
Cleveland *(G-3740)*

Franklin Iron & Metal Corp.................... C 937 253-8184
Dayton *(G-5784)*

Homan Metals LLC................................ G 513 721-5010
Cincinnati *(G-2728)*

I H Schlezinger Inc............................... E 614 252-1188
Columbus *(G-4996)*

Metalico Akron Inc................................ F 330 376-1400
Akron *(G-229)*

R L S Corporation................................. G 740 773-1440
Chillicothe *(G-2277)*

Rm Advisory Group Inc......................... E 513 242-2100
Cincinnati *(G-3049)*

SCRAP & WASTE MATERIALS, WHOLESALE: Junk & Scrap

Lawson Twing Auto Wrecking LLC......... F 216 883-9050
Cleveland *(G-3948)*

SCRAP & WASTE MATERIALS, WHOLESALE: Metal

A & B Iron & Metal Co Inc.................... F 937 228-1561
Dayton *(G-5629)*

Fex LLC.. F 412 604-0400
Mingo Junction *(G-10051)*

Nucor Steel Marion Inc......................... E 740 383-6068
Marion *(G-8984)*

Triple Arrow Industries Inc.................... G 614 437-5588
Marysville *(G-9054)*

SCRAP & WASTE MATERIALS, WHOLESALE: Nonferrous Metals Scrap

Auris Noble LLC................................... E 330 321-6649
Akron *(G-64)*

W R G Inc... E 216 351-8494
Avon Lake *(G-772)*

SCRAP & WASTE MATERIALS, WHOLESALE: Paper

Sims Bros Inc....................................... D 740 387-9041
Marion *(G-9000)*

SCRAP STEEL CUTTING

Geneva Liberty Steel Ltd...................... E 330 740-0103
Youngstown *(G-14865)*

Precision Cut Fabricating Inc................ F 440 877-1260
North Royalton *(G-10780)*

SCREENS: Projection

Stewart Filmscreen Corp....................... E 513 753-0800
Amelia *(G-438)*

SCREENS: Window, Metal

Dale Kestler... G 513 871-9000
Cincinnati *(G-2540)*

M-D Building Products Inc..................... F 513 539-2255
Middletown *(G-9874)*

Renewal By Andersen LLC..................... G 614 781-9600
Columbus *(G-4649)*

SCREENS: Woven Wire

Kimmatt Corp.. G 937 228-3811
West Alexandria *(G-13920)*

Yankee Wire Cloth Products Inc............. F 740 545-9129
West Lafayette *(G-14174)*

SCREW MACHINE PRDTS

Abco Bar & Tube Cutng Svc Inc............ E 513 697-9487
Maineville *(G-8737)*

Abel Fbrction Prcsion Pdts Inc.............. F 513 681-5000
Cincinnati *(G-2332)*

Abel Manufacturing Company................ F 513 681-5000
Cincinnati *(G-2333)*

Acme Machine Automatics Inc............... E 419 453-0010
Ottoville *(G-11051)*

Adams Automatic Inc............................ F 440 235-4416
Olmsted Falls *(G-10935)*

Alco Manufacturing Corp LLC................ E 440 458-5165
Elyria *(G-6493)*

Amco Products Inc................................ F 937 433-7982
Dayton *(G-5603)*

Amerascrew Inc.................................... E 419 522-2232
Mansfield *(G-8762)*

American Aero Components Llc.............. F 937 367-5068
Dayton *(G-5649)*

American Micro Products Inc................. C 513 732-2674
Batavia *(G-850)*

Amt Machine Systems Limited............... F 740 965-2693
Columbus *(G-4707)*

Ashley F Ward Inc................................ C 513 398-1414
Mason *(G-9067)*

Atlas Machine Products Co.................... G 216 228-3688
Oberlin *(G-10914)*

Ban Inc.. E 937 325-5539
Springfield *(G-12284)*

Bront Machining Inc............................. E 937 228-4551
Moraine *(G-10152)*

Chardon Metal Products Co.............. E 440 285-2147
Chardon (G-2198)

Clear Creek Screw Machine Co.............. G 740 969-2113
Amanda (G-423)

Condo Incorporated.............. D 330 609-6021
Warren (G-13755)

Dunham Products Inc.............. F 440 232-0885
Walton Hills (G-13697)

Eastlake Machine Products LLC.............. G 440 953-1014
Willoughby (G-14454)

Ecm Industries LLC.............. F 513 533-6242
Cincinnati (G-2578)

Elyria Manufacturing Corp.............. E 440 365-4171
Elyria (G-6530)

Enterprise Machine Inc.............. G 513 681-4409
Cincinnati (G-2592)

Eureka Screw Machine Pdts Co.............. G 216 883-1715
Cleveland (G-3691)

Fairfield Machined Pdts Inc.............. G 740 756-4409
Carroll (G-2076)

Falmer Screw Pdts & Mfg Inc.............. F 330 758-0593
Youngstown (G-14854)

Forrest Machine Pdts Co Ltd.............. E 419 589-3774
Mansfield (G-8790)

Gent Machine Company.............. E 216 481-2334
Cleveland (G-3770)

H & W Screw Products Inc.............. E 937 866-2577
Franklin (G-7026)

Helix Operating Company LLC.............. G 855 435-4958
Beachwood (G-921)

Heller Machine Products Inc.............. G 216 281-2951
Cleveland (G-3820)

Houston Machine Products Inc.............. E 937 322-8022
Springfield (G-12326)

Hy-Production LLC.............. C 330 273-2400
Valley City (G-13499)

Hyland Machine Company.............. E 937 233-8600
Dayton (G-5817)

Ilsco LLC.............. C 513 533-6200
Blue Ash (G-1287)

Integrity Manufacturing Corp.............. F 937 233-6792
Dayton (G-5825)

JAD Machine Company Inc.............. F 419 256-6332
Malinta (G-8743)

Karma Metal Products Inc.............. F 419 524-4371
Mansfield (G-8810)

Ken Emerick Machine Products.............. G 440 834-4501
Burton (G-1702)

Kernells Autmtc Machining Inc.............. E 419 588-2164
Berlin Heights (G-1205)

Kerr Lakeside Inc.............. D 216 261-2100
Euclid (G-6657)

Krausher Machining Inc.............. G 440 839-2828
Wakeman (G-13681)

Kts Met-Bar Products Inc.............. G 440 288-9308
Lorain (G-8561)

Lehner Screw Machine LLC.............. E 330 688-6616
Akron (G-204)

Machine Tek Systems Inc.............. E 330 527-4450
Garrettsville (G-7225)

Magnetic Screw Machine Pdts.............. G 937 348-2807
Marysville (G-9036)

Maumee Machine & Tool Corp.............. E 419 385-2501
Toledo (G-13048)

McDaniel Products Inc.............. F 419 524-5841
Mansfield (G-8823)

McDaniel Products Inc.............. G 419 524-5841
Mansfield (G-8822)

McGregor Metal National Works LLC.... E 937 882-6347
Springfield (G-12348)

McGregor Mtal Yllow Sprng Wrks.............. D 937 325-5561
Springfield (G-12351)

Meistermatic Inc.............. G 216 481-7773
Chesterland (G-2235)

Metal Seal & Products Inc.............. C 440 946-8500
Mentor (G-9562)

Mettlr-Tledo Globl Hldings LLC.............. E 614 438-4511
Columbus (G-4645)

Midwest Precision LLC.............. D 440 951-2333
Eastlake (G-6437)

Mosher Machine & Tool Co Inc.............. E 937 258-8070
Beavercreek Township (G-999)

Murray Machine and Tool Inc.............. G 216 267-1126
Cleveland (G-4054)

Nolte Precise Manufacturing Inc.............. D 513 923-3100
Cincinnati (G-2914)

Nook Industries LLC.............. C 216 271-7900
Cleveland (G-4080)

NSK Industries Inc.............. D 330 923-4112
Cuyahoga Falls (G-5563)

Obars Machine and Tool Company.............. E 419 535-6307
Toledo (G-13068)

Ohio Metal Products Company.............. F 937 228-6101
Dayton (G-5925)

Ohio Screw Products Inc.............. D 440 322-6341
Elyria (G-6574)

Pfi Precision Inc.............. E 937 845-3563
New Carlisle (G-10379)

Pohlman Precision LLC.............. E 636 537-1909
Massillon (G-9234)

Port Clinton Manufacturing LLC.............. E 419 734-2141
Port Clinton (G-11447)

Precision Fittings LLC.............. E 440 647-4143
Wellington (G-13899)

Premier Farnell Corp.............. D 330 659-0459
Richfield (G-11596)

Profile Grinding Inc.............. F 216 351-0600
Cleveland (G-4199)

Qcsm LLC.............. G 216 650-8731
Cleveland (G-4210)

Qualitor Subsidiary H Inc.............. E 419 562-7987
Bucyrus (G-1686)

Quality Machining and Mfg Inc.............. F 419 899-2543
Sherwood (G-11976)

R T & T Machining Co Inc.............. F 440 974-8479
Mentor (G-9605)

R W Screw Products Inc.............. C 330 837-9211
Massillon (G-9236)

Rable Machine Inc.............. D 419 525-2255
Mansfield (G-8847)

Raka Corporation.............. D 419 476-6572
Toledo (G-13110)

Rely-On Manufacturing Inc.............. G 937 254-0118
Dayton (G-5979)

Richland Screw Mch Pdts Inc.............. E 419 524-1272
Mansfield (G-8849)

Rtsi LLC.............. G 440 542-3066
Solon (G-12176)

Semtorq Inc.............. F 330 487-0600
Twinsburg (G-13377)

Shanafelt Manufacturing Co.............. E 330 455-0315
Canton (G-2004)

Soemhejee Inc.............. E 419 298-2306
Edgerton (G-6469)

Stadco Inc.............. E 937 878-0911
Fairborn (G-6699)

Superior Bar Products Inc.............. G 419 784-2590
Defiance (G-6125)

Tri-K Enterprises Inc.............. G 330 832-7380
Canton (G-2028)

Triangle Machine Products Co.............. E 216 524-5872
Cleveland (G-4420)

Twin Valley Metalcraft Asm LLC.............. G 937 787-4634
West Alexandria (G-13922)

Usm Precision Products Inc.............. D 440 975-8600
Wickliffe (G-14400)

Valley Tool & Die Inc.............. D 440 237-0160
North Royalton (G-10788)

Vanamatic Company.............. D 419 692-6085
Delphos (G-6199)

Vulcan Products Co Inc.............. G 419 468-1039
Galion (G-7201)

Watters Manufacturing Co Inc.............. G 216 281-8600
Cleveland (G-4494)

Whirlaway Corporation.............. D 440 647-4711
Wellington (G-13902)

Whirlaway Corporation.............. D 440 647-4711
Wellington (G-13903)

Whirlaway Corporation.............. D 440 647-4711
Wellington (G-13904)

Wood-Sebring Corporation.............. G 216 267-3191
Cleveland (G-4514)

SCREWS: Metal

Agrati - Medina LLC.............. C 330 725-8853
Medina (G-9370)

Agrati - Tiffin LLC.............. D 419 447-2221
Tiffin (G-12772)

Akko Fastener Inc.............. F 513 489-8300
Middletown (G-9841)

Altenloh Brinck & Co US Inc.............. E 419 737-2381
Pioneer (G-11317)

Altenloh Brinck & Co US Inc.............. E 419 636-6715
Bryan (G-1628)

General Plastex Inc.............. E 330 745-7775
Barberton (G-806)

Hexagon Industries Inc.............. E 216 249-0200
Cleveland (G-3829)

Tinnerman Palnut Engineered PR.............. F 330 220-5100
Brunswick (G-1619)

SEALANTS

Chemmasters Inc.............. E 440 428-2105
Madison (G-8726)

CIC Old Corporation.............. E 330 457-2367
New Waterford (G-10487)

Concrete Sealants Inc.............. E 937 845-8776
Tipp City (G-12821)

Egc Operating Company LLC.............. D 440 285-5835
Chardon (G-2204)

ICP Adhesives and Sealants Inc.............. E 330 753-4585
Norton (G-10823)

Jetcoat LLC.............. E 800 394-0047
Columbus (G-5039)

Mameco International Inc.............. F 216 752-4400
Cleveland (G-3984)

P & T Products Inc.............. E 419 621-1966
Sandusky (G-11863)

Royal Adhesives & Sealants LLC.............. F 440 708-1212
Chagrin Falls (G-2181)

Teknol Inc.............. D 937 264-0190
Dayton (G-6043)

Tremco Cpg Inc.............. E 216 514-7783
Beachwood (G-955)

Tremco Incorporated.............. C 216 292-5000
Beachwood (G-956)

Truseal Technologies Inc.............. E 216 910-1500
Akron (G-346)

SEALING COMPOUNDS: Sealing, synthetic rubber or plastic

FedPro Inc.............. E 216 464-6440
Cleveland (G-3711)

Technical Rubber Company Inc.............. C 740 967-9015
Johnstown (G-7999)

PRODUCT

SEALS: Hermetic

Aeroseal LLC.. E 937 428-9300
Dayton *(G-5638)*

Aeroseal LLC.. E 937 428-9300
Miamisburg *(G-9662)*

Reliable Hermetic Seals LLC............... F 888 747-3250
Beavercreek *(G-981)*

SEARCH & NAVIGATION SYSTEMS

Accurate Electronics Inc...................... F 330 682-7015
Orrville *(G-10972)*

ADB Safegate Americas LLC.............. C 614 861-1304
Gahanna *(G-7152)*

Aero-Instruments Co LLC.................... E 216 671-3133
Cleveland *(G-3309)*

Atk Space Systems LLC...................... C 937 490-4121
Beavercreek *(G-989)*

Atk Systems... G 937 429-8632
Beavercreek *(G-990)*

Boeing Company.................................. E 740 788-4000
Heath *(G-7594)*

Btc Inc... F 740 549-2722
Lewis Center *(G-8326)*

Btc Technology Services Inc................ G 740 549-2722
Lewis Center *(G-8327)*

Drs Leonardo Inc................................ E 937 429-7408
Beavercreek *(G-971)*

Drs Leonardo Inc................................ E 513 943-1111
Cincinnati *(G-2301)*

Enjet Aero Dayton Inc......................... E 937 878-3800
Huber Heights *(G-7821)*

Eti Tech LLC.. F 937 832-4200
Kettering *(G-8120)*

Ferrotherm Corporation....................... C 216 883-9350
Cleveland *(G-3714)*

General Dynmics Mssion Systems....... F 513 253-4770
Beavercreek *(G-975)*

General Electric Company.................... E 513 956-9051
Cincinnati *(G-2661)*

Grimes Aerospace Company................ D 937 484-2001
Urbana *(G-13464)*

Heller Machine Products Inc................ G 216 281-2951
Cleveland *(G-3820)*

Hunter Defense Tech Inc...................... E 513 943-7880
Cincinnati *(G-2307)*

Lake Shore Cryotronics Inc................. D 614 891-2243
Westerville *(G-14217)*

Lockheed Mrtin Intgrted System.......... C 330 796-2800
Akron *(G-209)*

Northrop Grmman Innvtion Syste........ C 937 429-9261
Beavercreek *(G-993)*

Northrop Grmman Tchncal Svcs I....... C 937 320-3100
Beavercreek Township *(G-1000)*

Northrop Grumman Systems Corp........ C 937 490-4111
Beavercreek *(G-994)*

Northrop Grumman Systems Corp........ D 937 429-6450
Beavercreek Township *(G-1001)*

Northrop Grumman Systems Corp........ B 513 881-3296
West Chester *(G-14134)*

Parker Aerospace................................ G 216 225-2721
Cleveland *(G-4139)*

PCC Airfoils LLC.................................. B 216 692-7900
Cleveland *(G-4148)*

Reuter-Stokes LLC.............................. B 330 425-3755
Twinsburg *(G-13365)*

S&L Fleet Services Inc........................ E 740 549-2722
Westerville *(G-14232)*

Star Dynamics Corporation.................. D 614 334-4510
Hilliard *(G-7702)*

Sunset Industries Inc........................... E 440 306-8284
Mentor *(G-9631)*

Te Connectivity Corporation................. C 419 521-9500
Mansfield *(G-8858)*

Wall Colmonoy Corporation................. D 513 842-4200
Cincinnati *(G-3211)*

Watts Antenna Company...................... G 740 797-9380
The Plains *(G-12761)*

Yost Labs Inc....................................... F 740 876-4936
Portsmouth *(G-11480)*

SEATING: Stadium

American Office Services Inc................ G 440 899-6888
Westlake *(G-14287)*

SECURITY CONTROL EQPT & SYSTEMS

Checkpoint Systems Inc....................... C 330 456-7776
Canton *(G-1863)*

Diebold Nixdorf Incorporated.............. A 330 490-4000
North Canton *(G-10635)*

Emx Industries LLC............................. F 216 518-9888
Cleveland *(G-3669)*

Everon LLC.. D 513 258-2409
Cincinnati *(G-2602)*

Global Security Tech Inc...................... G 614 890-6400
Westerville *(G-14260)*

Honeywell International Inc................... A 937 484-2000
Urbana *(G-13466)*

Midwest Security Services.................... E 937 853-9000
Dayton *(G-5882)*

Pentagon Protection Usa LLC.............. F 614 734-7240
Dublin *(G-6331)*

R F I... G 740 654-4502
Lancaster *(G-8221)*

Securcom Inc....................................... E 419 628-1049
Minster *(G-10065)*

Technlogy Install Partners LLC............ E 888 586-7040
Cleveland *(G-4371)*

SECURITY DEVICES

Ever Secure SEC Systems Inc............. F 937 369-8294
Dayton *(G-5772)*

Everon LLC.. E 440 397-4428
Broadview Heights *(G-1502)*

Invue Security Products Inc.................. E 330 456-7776
Canton *(G-1919)*

Lindsay Precast LLC............................ E 800 837-7788
Canal Fulton *(G-1777)*

Mace Security Intl Inc........................... E 440 424-5325
Cleveland *(G-3979)*

Sage Integration Holdings LLC............. E 330 733-8183
Kent *(G-8072)*

Say Security Group USA LLC............... F 419 634-0004
Ada *(G-5)*

SECURITY SYSTEMS SERVICES

Fellhauer Mechanical Systems............. E 419 734-3674
Port Clinton *(G-11441)*

Johnson Controls Inc........................... F 513 671-6338
Cincinnati *(G-2772)*

Sage Integration Holdings LLC............. E 330 733-8183
Kent *(G-8072)*

Say Security Group USA LLC............... F 419 634-0004
Ada *(G-5)*

Securcom Inc....................................... E 419 628-1049
Minster *(G-10065)*

Sound Communications Inc.................. E 614 875-8500
Grove City *(G-7414)*

SEMICONDUCTOR CIRCUIT NETWORKS

Micro Industries Corporation............... D 740 548-7878
Westerville *(G-14270)*

SEMICONDUCTORS & RELATED DEVICES

Brocade Cmmnctions Systems LLC...... G 614 232-8015
Columbus *(G-4782)*

Communication Concepts Inc............... G 937 426-8600
Beavercreek *(G-968)*

Darrah Electric Company...................... F 216 631-0912
Chesterland *(G-2233)*

Em4 LLC.. E 608 240-4800
Cleveland *(G-3667)*

Gen Digital Inc..................................... G 330 252-1171
Akron *(G-159)*

Gen Digital Inc..................................... G 614 418-1700
Columbus *(G-4947)*

Gopowerx Inc....................................... F 440 707-6029
Richfield *(G-11594)*

Greenfield Solar Corp.......................... G 216 535-9200
North Ridgeville *(G-10732)*

Heraeus Electro-Nite Co LLC.............. G 330 725-1419
Medina *(G-9408)*

Honeywell International Inc................... E 302 327-8920
Columbus *(G-4990)*

Hyper Tech Research Inc...................... F 614 481-8050
Columbus *(G-4995)*

Illuminate USA LLC.............................. A 614 598-9742
Pataskala *(G-11140)*

Lam Research Corporation................... F 937 472-3311
Eaton *(G-6458)*

Linear Asics Inc................................... G 330 474-3920
Twinsburg *(G-13333)*

Linear Technology LLC......................... G 440 239-0817
Cleveland *(G-3960)*

Materion Brush Inc............................... D 216 486-4200
Mayfield Heights *(G-9336)*

Monti Incorporated............................... D 513 761-7775
Cincinnati *(G-2886)*

Niobium Microsystems Inc.................... G 937 203-8117
Dayton *(G-5907)*

Ohio Semitronics Inc............................ D 614 777-1005
Hilliard *(G-7692)*

Pepperl + Fuchs Inc............................. C 330 425-3555
Twinsburg *(G-13352)*

Rexon Components Inc......................... E 216 292-7373
Beachwood *(G-945)*

Saint-Gobain Ceramics Plas Inc.......... B 440 542-2712
Newbury *(G-10563)*

SCI Engineered Materials Inc.............. E 614 486-0261
Columbus *(G-5255)*

Signature Technologies Inc.................. E 937 859-6323
Miamisburg *(G-9737)*

Silfex Inc... B 937 324-2487
Springfield *(G-12373)*

Silfex Inc... E 937 472-3311
Eaton *(G-6463)*

Spang & Company................................ E 440 350-6108
Mentor *(G-9619)*

Tosoh SMD Inc..................................... D 614 875-7912
Grove City *(G-7418)*

Ustek Incorporated.............................. F 614 538-8000
Columbus *(G-5342)*

SENSORS: Temperature, Exc Indl Process

Krumor Inc... F 216 328-9802
Cleveland *(G-3930)*

Lake Shore Cryotronics Inc................. D 614 891-2243
Westerville *(G-14217)*

Safe-Grain Inc..................................... G 513 398-2500
Loveland *(G-8650)*

SEPARATORS: Metal Plate

Allgaier Process Technology................. G 513 402-2566
West Chester *(G-13937)*

(G-0000) Company's Geographic Section entry number

SEPTIC TANK CLEANING SVCS

AAA Wastewater Services Inc.............F 937 746-6361
Franklin (G-7009)

Pro-Kleen Industrial Svcs Inc.............E 740 689-1886
Lancaster (G-8218)

SEPTIC TANKS: Concrete

Allen Enterprises Inc.............E 740 532-5913
Ironton (G-7928)

Dennis Constuction Sanitation.............G 419 332-8026
Fremont (G-7104)

E A Cox Inc.............G 740 858-4400
Lucasville (G-8666)

Encore Precast LLC.............D 513 726-5678
Seven Mile (G-11907)

J K Precast LLC.............G 740 335-2188
Wshngtn Ct Hs (G-14741)

Lindsay Precast LLC.............E 800 837-7788
Canal Fulton (G-1777)

Quaker City Concrete Pdts LLC.............G 330 427-2239
Leetonia (G-8305)

Riley Creek Holdings Inc.............E 419 358-6946
Bluffton (G-1364)

Septic Products Inc.............G 419 282-5933
Ashland (G-573)

Stiger Pre Cast Inc.............G 740 482-2313
Nevada (G-10324)

SEPTIC TANKS: Plastic

Hancor Inc.............E 419 424-8225
Findlay (G-6879)

Hancor Inc.............B 614 658-0050
Hilliard (G-7683)

J K Precast LLC.............G 740 335-2188
Wshngtn Ct Hs (G-14741)

SEWAGE & WATER TREATMENT EQPT

Aqua Ohio Inc.............F 740 867-8700
Chesapeake (G-2228)

Artesian of Pioneer Inc.............F 419 737-2352
Pioneer (G-11318)

City of Chardon.............E 440 286-2657
Chardon (G-2201)

City of Troy.............F 937 339-4826
Troy (G-13205)

De Nora Tech LLC.............D 440 710-5334
Painesville (G-11078)

Eagle Crusher Co Inc.............D 419 468-2288
Galion (G-7187)

Greene County.............G 937 429-0127
Dayton (G-5613)

Pelton Environmental Pdts Inc.............G 440 838-1221
Lewis Center (G-8348)

Smart Sonic Corporation.............G 818 610-7900
Cleveland (G-4306)

Tangent Company LLC.............G 440 543-2775
Chagrin Falls (G-2186)

SEWER CLEANING EQPT: Power

Best Equipment Co Inc.............E 440 237-3515
North Royalton (G-10755)

Electric Eel Mfg Co Inc.............E 937 323-4644
Springfield (G-12306)

SHADES: Window

Cincinnati Window Shade Inc.............F 513 631-7200
Cincinnati (G-2489)

SHAPES & PILINGS, STRUCTURAL: Steel

A-1 Welding & Fabrication.............F 440 233-8474
Lorain (G-8544)

Brenmar Construction Inc.............D 740 286-2151
Jackson (G-7941)

Nova Structural Steel Inc.............E 216 938-7476
Cleveland (G-4100)

Steve Vore Welding and Steel.............F 419 375-4087
Fort Recovery (G-6971)

SHAPES: Extruded, Aluminum, NEC

Gei of Columbiana Inc.............E 330 783-0270
Youngstown (G-14863)

General Extrusions Intl LLC.............C 330 783-0270
Youngstown (G-14864)

Novelis Alr Aluminum LLC.............A 216 910-3400
Beachwood (G-933)

Patton Aluminum Products Inc.............F 937 845-9404
New Carlisle (G-10378)

Systems Kit LLC MB.............E 330 945-4500
Akron (G-324)

Teh Investments Inc.............D 330 782-1127
Youngstown (G-14944)

Vari-Wall Tube Specialists Inc.............D 330 482-0000
Columbiana (G-4631)

SHAVING PREPARATIONS

Edgewell Personal Care LLC.............C 937 492-1057
Sidney (G-12015)

SHEET METAL SPECIALTIES, EXC STAMPED

Ahner Fabricating & Shtmtl Inc.............E 419 626-6641
Sandusky (G-11820)

All Metal Fabricators Inc.............F 216 267-0033
Cleveland (G-3324)

Allen County Fabrication Inc.............E 419 227-7447
Lima (G-8386)

Allied Fabricating & Wldg Co.............E 614 868-8680
Columbus (G-4687)

Buckeye Metal Works Inc.............G 614 239-8000
Columbus (G-4785)

C & R Inc.............E 614 497-1130
Groveport (G-7427)

Columbus Steelmasters Inc.............F 614 231-2141
Columbus (G-4835)

Cramers Inc.............E 330 477-4571
Canton (G-1873)

Crown Electric Engrg & Mfg LLC.............E 513 539-7394
Middletown (G-9852)

Flood Heliarc Inc.............F 614 835-3929
Groveport (G-7432)

G T Metal Fabricators Inc.............F 440 237-8745
Cleveland (G-3750)

Hartzell Mfg Co LLC.............E 937 859-5955
Miamisburg (G-9696)

I-M-A Enterprises Inc.............F 330 948-3535
Lodi (G-8502)

Kirk & Blum Manufacturing Co.............C 513 458-2600
Cincinnati (G-2797)

Kuhlman Engineering Co.............F 419 243-2196
Toledo (G-13023)

Kuhn Fabricating Inc.............G 440 277-4182
Lorain (G-8562)

Lambert Sheet Metal Inc.............F 614 237-0384
Columbus (G-5061)

M3 Technologies Inc.............F 216 898-9936
Cleveland (G-3977)

Metal-Max Inc.............G 330 673-9926
Kent (G-8052)

Midwest Fabrications Inc.............F 330 633-0191
Tallmadge (G-12741)

Midwest Metal Fabricators Ltd.............F 419 739-7077
Wapakoneta (G-13724)

National Indus Concepts Inc.............F 615 989-9101
Chillicothe (G-2267)

Paul Wilke & Son Inc.............F 513 921-3163
Cincinnati (G-2947)

S&B Metal Pdts Twinsburg LLC.............E 330 487-5790
Twinsburg (G-13372)

Selmco Metal Fabricators Inc.............F 937 498-1331
Sidney (G-12051)

Seneca Sheet Metal Company.............F 419 447-8434
Tiffin (G-12800)

SFM Corp.............E 440 951-5500
Willoughby (G-14523)

Sheet Metal Products Co Inc.............E 440 392-9000
Mentor (G-9615)

Valley Metal Works Inc.............E 513 554-1022
Cincinnati (G-3192)

Varmland Inc.............F 216 741-1510
Cleveland (G-4458)

Vicart Prcsion Fabricators Inc.............E 614 771-0080
Hilliard (G-7710)

Waterville Sheet Metal Co Inc.............E 419 878-5050
Waterville (G-13844)

Weybridge LLC.............E 440 951-5500
Willoughby (G-14549)

Wolf Metals Inc.............G 614 461-6361
Columbus (G-5371)

SHEETS: Hard Rubber

Novex Operating Company LLC.............F 330 335-2371
Barberton (G-826)

SHELVING, MADE FROM PURCHASED WIRE

Interntnal Tchncal Catings Inc.............C 800 567-6592
Columbus (G-5021)

KEffs Inc.............G 614 443-0586
Columbus (G-5047)

SHIMS: Metal

Die-Cut Products Co.............F 216 771-6994
Cleveland (G-3615)

Ohio Gasket and Shim Co Inc.............E 330 630-0626
Akron (G-252)

Shim Shack.............G 877 557-3930
Harrison (G-7567)

SHOE STORES

Vances Department Store.............G 937 549-3033
Manchester (G-8756)

Vances Department Store.............G 937 549-2188
Manchester (G-8755)

SHOE STORES: Boots, Men's

Cobblers Corner LLC.............G 330 482-4005
Columbiana (G-4609)

Hudson Leather Ltd.............G 419 485-8531
Pioneer (G-11321)

SHOE STORES: Men's

Rnp Inc.............G
Dellroy (G-6182)

SHOES: Men's

Acor Orthopaedic LLC.............E 216 662-4500
Cleveland (G-3293)

Careismatic Brands LLC.............G 561 843-8727
Groveport (G-7428)

Careismatic Brands LLC.............G 614 497-5289
Groveport (G-7429)

Georgia-Boot Inc.............D 740 753-1951
Nelsonville (G-10317)

Rocky Brands Inc.............C 740 753-1951
Nelsonville (G-10320)

Employee Codes: A=Over 500 employees, B=251-500
C=101-250, D=51-100, E=20-50, F=10-19, G=1-9

2025 Harris Ohio
Industrial Directory

1387

PRODUCT

SHOES: Men's, Work

Rbr Enterprises LLC...............................F 866 437-9327
Brecksville *(G-1480)*

SHOES: Plastic Or Rubber

Cobblers Corner LLC.............................G 330 482-4005
Columbiana *(G-4609)*

Georgia-Boot Inc..................................D 740 753-1951
Nelsonville *(G-10317)*

Mettler Footwear Inc.............................G 330 703-0079
Hudson *(G-7852)*

Mulhern Belting Inc...............................E 201 337-5700
Fairfield *(G-6757)*

Totes Isotoner Holdings LLC..................C 513 682-8200
Cincinnati *(G-3160)*

US Footwear Holdings LLC....................C 740 753-9100
Nelsonville *(G-10322)*

SHOES: Women's

Acor Orthopaedic LLC...........................E 216 662-4500
Cleveland *(G-3293)*

Careismatic Brands LLC.........................G 561 843-8727
Groveport *(G-7428)*

Careismatic Brands LLC.........................G 614 497-5289
Groveport *(G-7429)*

Georgia-Boot Inc..................................D 740 753-1951
Nelsonville *(G-10317)*

Rocky Brands Inc..................................C 740 753-1951
Nelsonville *(G-10320)*

SHOT PEENING SVC

Metal Improvement Company LLC........D 513 489-6484
Blue Ash *(G-1309)*

Metal Improvement Company LLC........E 330 425-1490
Twinsburg *(G-13339)*

National Peening....................................G 216 342-9155
Bedford Heights *(G-1080)*

SHOWCASES & DISPLAY FIXTURES: Office & Store

CSM Concepts LLC................................F 330 483-1320
Valley City *(G-13493)*

E-B Display Company Inc........................C 330 833-4101
Massillon *(G-9188)*

Pete Gaietto & Associates Inc.................D.... 513 771-0903
Cincinnati *(G-2956)*

SHOWER STALLS: Plastic & Fiberglass

Crane Plumbing LLC..............................A 419 522-4211
Mansfield *(G-8778)*

SHREDDERS: Indl & Commercial

Accushred LLC.....................................F 419 244-7473
Toledo *(G-12863)*

SHUTTERS, DOOR & WINDOW: Metal

Installed Building Pdts LLC......................B 614 308-9900
Columbus *(G-5009)*

SHUTTERS, DOOR & WINDOW: Plastic

Dinesol Building Products Ltd..................E 330 270-0212
Youngstown *(G-14848)*

SIDING MATERIALS

C Green & Sons Incorporated.................F 740 745-2998
Saint Louisville *(G-11728)*

Westlake Ryal Bldg Pdts USA In.............E 800 366-8472
Columbus *(G-5365)*

SIDING: Plastic

Alside Inc...E 419 865-0934
Maumee *(G-9258)*

Exterior Portfolio LLC.............................C 614 754-3400
Columbus *(G-4916)*

Fibreboard Corporation..........................C 419 248-8000
Toledo *(G-12963)*

Gentek Building Products Inc..................F 800 548-4542
Cuyahoga Falls *(G-5544)*

SIDING: Sheet Metal

Gentek Building Products Inc..................F 800 548-4542
Cuyahoga Falls *(G-5544)*

Metal Sales Manufacturing Corp.............E 440 319-3779
Jefferson *(G-7978)*

Owens Corning Sales LLC......................F 740 983-1300
Ashville *(G-629)*

SIGN PAINTING & LETTERING SHOP

Freds Sign Service Inc...........................G 937 335-1901
Troy *(G-13215)*

General Theming Contrs LLC..................C 614 252-6342
Columbus *(G-4948)*

Ohio Shelterall Inc................................F 614 882-1110
Westerville *(G-14272)*

Triangle Sign Co LLC.............................G 513 266-1009
Hamilton *(G-7534)*

SIGNALS: Traffic Control, Electric

Athens Technical Specialists...................F 740 592-2874
Athens *(G-634)*

City Elyria Communication......................G 440 322-3329
Elyria *(G-6513)*

City of Canton......................................E 330 489-3370
Canton *(G-1866)*

Intelligent Signal Tech Intl......................G 614 530-4784
Loveland *(G-8632)*

Paul Peterson Company.........................F 614 486-4375
Columbus *(G-5178)*

Security Fence Group Inc.......................E 513 681-3700
Cincinnati *(G-3074)*

Union Metal Industries Corp...................E 330 456-7653
Canton *(G-2033)*

SIGNS & ADVERTISING SPECIALTIES

A & A Safety Inc....................................F 937 567-9781
Beavercreek *(G-987)*

A & A Safety Inc....................................E 513 943-6100
Amelia *(G-425)*

A Sign Above Inc...................................F 330 425-7832
Twinsburg *(G-13266)*

A&E Signs and Lighting LLC....................F 513 541-0024
Cincinnati *(G-2327)*

Abbott Image Solutions LLC...................F 937 382-6677
Wilmington *(G-14569)*

Accent Signage Systems Inc...................E 612 377-9156
Findlay *(G-6831)*

Adcraft Decals Incorporated...................E 216 524-2934
Cleveland *(G-3297)*

Affinity Disp Expositions Inc...................F 513 771-2339
Cincinnati *(G-2340)*

Agile Sign & Ltg Maint Inc......................E 440 918-1311
Eastlake *(G-6415)*

Alberts Screen Print Inc.........................C 330 753-7559
Norton *(G-10818)*

Allied Sign Co......................................G 614 443-9656
Columbus *(G-4689)*

Apex Signs Inc.....................................G 330 952-2626
Medina *(G-9376)*

Archer Corporation...............................E 330 455-9995
Canton *(G-1831)*

Asi Visual Display Pdts Inc.....................E 330 308-8667
New Philadelphia *(G-10431)*

Associated Premium Corporation............E 513 679-4444
Cincinnati *(G-2381)*

Atlantic Sign Company Inc......................E 513 383-1504
Cincinnati *(G-2385)*

Auto Dealer Designs Inc........................E 330 374-7666
Akron *(G-65)*

Avid Signs Plus LLC..............................G 513 932-7446
Lebanon *(G-8244)*

Baker Plastics Inc.................................G 330 743-3142
Youngstown *(G-14817)*

Barnes Advertising Corporation..............F 740 453-6836
Zanesville *(G-14992)*

Bates Metal Products Inc.......................D 740 498-8371
Port Washington *(G-11455)*

Becker Signs Inc...................................G 330 659-4504
Hudson *(G-7834)*

Belco Works Inc....................................D 740 695-0500
Saint Clairsville *(G-11688)*

Blang Acquisition LLC............................G 937 223-2155
Dayton *(G-5679)*

Brandon Screen Printing........................F 419 229-9837
Lima *(G-8391)*

Brown Cnty Bd Mntal Rtardation.............G 937 378-4891
Georgetown *(G-7251)*

Buckeye Boxes Inc................................D 614 274-8484
Columbus *(G-4783)*

Busch & Thiem Inc................................E 419 625-7515
Sandusky *(G-11825)*

Business Idntfction Systems In.................G 614 841-1255
Columbus *(G-4789)*

C JS Signs...G 330 821-7446
Alliance *(G-374)*

Casad Company Inc...............................F 419 586-9457
Coldwater *(G-4570)*

Cgs Imaging Inc....................................F 419 897-3000
Holland *(G-7749)*

Chase Sign & Lighting Svc Inc.................G 567 128-3444
Toledo *(G-12917)*

Columbus Graphics Inc..........................G 614 577-9360
Reynoldsburg *(G-11563)*

Communication Exhibits Inc.....................D 330 854-4040
Canal Fulton *(G-1775)*

CSP Group Inc......................................E 513 984-9500
Cincinnati *(G-2528)*

Custom Sign Center...............................F 614 279-6035
Columbus *(G-4864)*

Davis Printing Company.........................E 330 745-3113
Barberton *(G-803)*

Dayton Wire Products Inc.......................E 937 236-8000
Dayton *(G-5741)*

Dee Sign Usa LLC.................................F 513 779-3333
West Chester *(G-13983)*

Dern Trophies Corp...............................G 614 895-3260
Westerville *(G-14207)*

Digital Factory Tech Inc..........................E 513 560-4074
Cincinnati *(G-2549)*

Digital Sign Graphics Inc........................G 937 492-9550
Sidney *(G-12012)*

Djmc Partners Inc.................................G 614 890-3821
Westerville *(G-14256)*

Doxie Inc...G 937 427-3431
Dayton *(G-5611)*

Dualite Inc...C 513 724-7100
Williamsburg *(G-14408)*

Eaglestone Products LLC........................G 440 463-8715
Brecksville *(G-1464)*

Eighth Floor Promotions LLC...................C 419 586-6433
Celina *(G-2104)*

Enlarging Arts Inc.................................G 330 434-3433
Akron *(G-136)*

Etched Metal Company...........................E 440 248-0240
Solon *(G-12109)*

Fair Publishing House Inc............... E 419 668-3746
Norwalk (G-10841)

Fast Signs............................ F 614 710-1312
Hilliard (G-7681)

Fastsigns.............................. G 330 952-2626
Medina (G-9402)

Fastsigns.............................. G 440 954-9191
Mentor (G-9515)

Fdi Cabinetry LLC...................... G 513 353-4500
Cleves (G-4537)

Fineline Imprints Inc.................. G 740 453-1083
Zanesville (G-15013)

Folks Creative Printers Inc........... G 740 383-6326
Marion (G-8970)

Forty Nine Degrees LLC................ F 419 678-0100
Coldwater (G-4575)

Fourteen Ventures Group LLC.......... G 937 866-2341
West Carrollton (G-13929)

Frontier Signs & Displays Inc......... G 513 367-0813
Harrison (G-7552)

Galaxy Balloons Incorporated.......... C 216 476-3360
Cleveland (G-3753)

Gary Lawrence Enterprises Inc......... G 330 833-7181
Massillon (G-9194)

Geograph Industries Inc............... E 513 202-9200
Harrison (G-7553)

Ginos Awards Inc...................... E 216 831-6565
Warrensville Heights (G-13818)

Glavin Industries Inc................. E 440 349-0049
Solon (G-12115)

Global Lighting Tech Inc.............. E 440 922-4584
Brecksville (G-1468)

Hall Company.......................... E 937 652-1376
Urbana (G-13465)

Ham Signs LLC DBA Fastsigns........... F 937 890-6770
Dayton (G-5807)

Highrise Creative LLC................. F 614 890-3821
Westerville (G-14263)

Hill Sign Company Inc./............... G 614 367-9227
Columbus (G-4988)

Hlsigns............................... G 513 703-6363
Cincinnati (G-2725)

HP Manufacturing Company Inc.......... D 216 361-6500
Cleveland (G-3841)

Hy-Ko Products Company LLC............ F 330 467-7446
Northfield (G-10794)

Identitek Systems Inc................. D 330 832-9844
Massillon (G-9206)

Ike Smart City........................ E 614 294-4898
Columbus (G-5000)

Industrial and Mar Eng Svc Co......... F 740 694-0791
Fredericktown (G-7080)

Innomark Group LLC.................... G 419 720-8102
Toledo (G-13005)

J Best Inc............................ G 513 943-7000
Cincinnati (G-2308)

Kdm Signs Inc......................... C 513 769-1932
Cincinnati (G-2787)

Kinoly Signs.......................... G 740 451-7446
South Point (G-12225)

Kmgrafx Inc........................... G 513 248-4100
Loveland (G-8635)

Krigbaum Inc.......................... E 614 478-6472
Columbus (G-5056)

Laad Sign & Lighting Inc.............. F 330 379-2297
Ravenna (G-11529)

Lake Erie Graphics Inc................ E 216 575-1333
Brookpark (G-1555)

Lehner Signs Inc...................... G 614 258-0500
Lithopolis (G-8483)

Macray Co LLC......................... G 937 325-1726
Springfield (G-12345)

Magna Visual Inc...................... E 314 843-9000
Perrysburg (G-11236)

Masterpiece Signs Graphics Inc........ F 419 358-0077
Bluffton (G-1362)

Mayfair Granite Co Inc................ G 216 382-8150
Cleveland (G-4002)

Megalift LLC.......................... G 614 696-9086
Grove City (G-7398)

Mes Painting & Graphics Ltd........... E 614 496-1696
Westerville (G-14268)

Mes Painting and Graphics............. G 614 496-1696
Westerville (G-14269)

Mitchell Plastics Inc................. E 330 825-2461
Barberton (G-823)

National Sign Systems Inc............. D 614 850-2540
Hilliard (G-7689)

North Coast Theatrical Inc............ G 330 762-1768
Akron (G-248)

Norton Outdoor Advertising............ E 513 631-4864
Cincinnati (G-2915)

Nrka Corp............................. G 440 817-0700
Broadview Heights (G-1508)

Ohio Shelterall Inc................... F 614 882-1110
Westerville (G-14272)

Orange Barrel Media LLC............... D 614 294-4898
Columbus (G-5162)

Painted Hill Inv Group Inc............ F 937 339-1756
Troy (G-13246)

Performance Wraps LLC................. G 937 535-2400
Miamisburg (G-9726)

Pierce Signs & Displays Inc........... G 408 292-3500
Sylvania (G-12721)

Pro A V of Ohio....................... G 877 812-5350
New Philadelphia (G-10462)

Pro-Decal Inc......................... G 330 484-0089
Canton (G-1984)

Quality Custom Signs LLC.............. G 614 580-7233
Worthington (G-14723)

Queen Exhibits LLC.................... G 937 615-6051
Piqua (G-11381)

Ray Meyer Sign Company Inc............ E 513 984-5446
Loveland (G-8647)

Retain Loyalty LLC.................... G 330 830-0839
Massillon (G-9238)

Ricks Graphic Accents Inc............. G 330 896-4700
Akron (G-285)

Roemer Industries Inc................. G 330 448-2000
Masury (G-9256)

Royal Acme Corporation................ E 216 241-1477
Cleveland (G-4256)

S&S Sign Service...................... G 614 279-9722
Columbus (G-5241)

Sabco Industries Inc.................. E 419 531-5347
Toledo (G-13120)

Screen Works Inc...................... E 937 264-9111
Dayton (G-6000)

Sdmk LLC.............................. G 330 965-0970
Youngstown (G-14930)

Select Signs.......................... E 937 262-7095
Dayton (G-5623)

Sensical Inc.......................... D 216 641-1141
Solon (G-12180)

Sign America Incorporated............. G 740 765-5555
Richmond (G-11605)

Sign Gypsies Cleveland LLC............ F 216 202-2093
Bedford Heights (G-1081)

Sign Source USA Inc................... D 419 224-1130
Lima (G-8449)

Sign Technologies LLC................. G 937 439-3970
Dayton (G-6007)

Signs Ohio Inc........................ G 419 228-7446
Lima (G-8450)

Signs Unlmted The Grphic Advnt........ G 614 836-7446
Logan (G-8526)

Signwire Worldwide Inc................ G 937 428-6189
Dayton (G-6008)

Speedpro Imaging...................... G 513 771-4776
Cincinnati (G-3105)

Stratus Unlimted LLC.................. C 440 209-6200
Mentor (G-9629)

Superior Label Systems Inc............ B 513 336-0825
Mason (G-9157)

Tce International Ltd................. F 800 962-2376
Perry (G-11199)

TCS Schindler & Co LLC................ G 937 836-9473
Englewood (G-6624)

Ternion Inc........................... E 216 642-6180
Cleveland (G-4375)

The Hartman Corp...................... G 614 475-5035
Columbus (G-5320)

The Massillon-Cleveland-Akr........... C 330 833-3165
Massillon (G-9247)

Toledo Sign Company Inc............... E 419 244-4444
Toledo (G-13157)

Traffic Cntrl Sgnls Signs & MA........ G 740 670-7763
Newark (G-10536)

Traffic Detectors & Signs Inc......... G 330 707-9060
Youngstown (G-14949)

Triumph Signs & Consulting Inc........ F 513 576-8090
Milford (G-9955)

Troyer Signs Incorporated............. G 330 263-1400
Wooster (G-14693)

Vista Creations LLC................... G 440 954-9191
Mentor (G-9650)

Visual Marking Systems Inc............ D 330 425-7100
Twinsburg (G-13393)

West 6th Products Company............. D 330 467-7446
Northfield (G-10800)

Williams Steel Rule Die Co............ G 216 431-3232
Cleveland (G-4507)

Zilla................................. G 614 763-5311
Dublin (G-6363)

SIGNS & ADVERTISING SPECIALTIES: Artwork, Advertising

1157 Designconcepts LLC............... F 937 497-1157
Sidney (G-11988)

T&T Graphics Inc...................... D 937 847-6000
Miamisburg (G-9742)

Vision Graphix Inc.................... G 440 835-6540
Westlake (G-14342)

SIGNS & ADVERTISING SPECIALTIES: Displays, Paint Process

Custom Retail Group LLC............... G 614 409-9720
Columbus (G-4863)

Ohio Displays Inc..................... F 216 961-5600
Elyria (G-6572)

SIGNS & ADVERTISING SPECIALTIES: Letters For Signs, Metal

Engravers Gallery & Sign Co........... G 330 830-1271
Massillon (G-9190)

Interstate Sign Products Inc.......... G 419 683-1962
Crestline (G-5503)

SIGNS & ADVERTISING SPECIALTIES: Novelties

E P Gerber & Sons Inc................. D 330 857-2021
Kidron (G-8126)

Finn Graphics Inc..................... E 513 941-6161
Cincinnati (G-2624)

PRODUCT

Gerber Wood Products Inc.................. D 330 857-9007
Kidron (G-8128)

License Ad Plate Company..................... F 216 265-4200
Cleveland (G-3954)

Power Media Inc.................................. G 330 475-0500
Copley (G-5436)

Quikey Manufacturing Co Inc............. C 330 633-8106
Akron (G-275)

W C Bunting Co Inc............................. G 330 385-2050
East Liverpool (G-6399)

SIGNS & ADVERTISING SPECIALTIES:
Scoreboards, Electric

Industrial Electronic Service.................. F 937 746-9750
Carlisle (G-2066)

National Scoreboards LLC.................... G 513 791-5244
Cincinnati (G-2895)

Obhc Inc.. G 440 236-5112
Columbia Station (G-4595)

SIGNS, ELECTRICAL: Wholesalers

Sign America Incorporated.................... G 740 765-5555
Richmond (G-11605)

SIGNS, EXC ELECTRIC, WHOLESALE

K Ventures Inc...................................... F 419 678-2308
Coldwater (G-4579)

Macray Co LLC..................................... G 937 325-1726
Springfield (G-12345)

SIGNS: Electrical

ABC Signs Inc....................................... F 513 407-4367
Cincinnati (G-2331)

Advance Sign Group LLC...................... E 614 429-2111
Columbus (G-4675)

All Signs of Chillicothe Inc.................... G 740 773-5016
Chillicothe (G-2242)

All Star Sign Company......................... G 614 461-9052
Columbus (G-4685)

Allen Industries Inc............................... D 567 408-7538
Toledo (G-12869)

American Led-Gible Inc......................... F 614 851-1100
Columbus (G-4699)

Architctral Identification Inc.................. F 614 868-8400
Gahanna (G-7154)

Behrco Inc.. G 419 394-1612
Saint Marys (G-11731)

Brilliant Electric Sign Co Ltd................. D 216 741-3800
Brooklyn Heights (G-1529)

Custom Sign Center Inc........................ E 614 279-6700
Columbus (G-4865)

Danite Holdings Ltd.............................. E 614 444-3333
Columbus (G-4870)

Ellet Neon Sales & Service Inc.............. E 330 628-9907
Akron (G-131)

Federal Heath Sign Company LLC......... D 740 369-0999
Delaware (G-6147)

Gardner Signs Inc................................. F 419 385-6669
Toledo (G-12972)

Grady McCauley Inc.............................. D 330 494-9444
Akron (G-165)

Gus Holthaus Signs Inc......................... E 513 861-0060
Cincinnati (G-2697)

Hendricks Vacuum Forming Inc............. F 330 837-2040
Massillon (G-9201)

Insignia Signs Inc................................. G 937 866-2341
Moraine (G-10170)

Lettergraphics Inc................................. G 330 683-3903
Orrville (G-10993)

LSI Industries Inc.................................. C 513 793-3200
Cincinnati (G-2830)

National Illmination Sign Corp.............. G 419 866-1666
Holland (G-7774)

Ohio Awning & Manufacturing Co.......... E 216 861-2400
Cleveland (G-4111)

Signs Limited LLC................................. G 740 282-7715
Steubenville (G-12411)

United - Maier Signs Inc....................... D 513 681-6600
Cincinnati (G-3180)

Wilson Sign Co Inc............................... F 937 253-2246
Germantown (G-7257)

SIGNS: Neon

Cicogna Electric and Sign Co................ D 440 998-2637
Ashtabula (G-587)

Columbus Sign Company...................... E 614 252-3133
Columbus (G-4833)

Kasper Enterprises Inc.......................... G 419 841-6656
Toledo (G-13016)

Ruff Neon & Lighting Maint Inc............. F 440 350-6267
Painesville (G-11110)

Signcom Incorporated.......................... F 614 228-9999
Columbus (G-5268)

Triangle Sign Co LLC............................ G 513 266-1009
Hamilton (G-7534)

Wholesale Channel Letters................... G 440 256-3200
Kirtland (G-8146)

SILICA MINING

Covia Holdings LLC............................... D 800 243-9004
Independence (G-7894)

SILICON WAFERS: Chemically Doped

Techneglas LLC.................................... F 419 873-2000
Perrysburg (G-11268)

SILICON: Pure

Ohio Valley Specialty Company............. F 740 373-2276
Marietta (G-8932)

SILICONE RESINS

Poly-Carb Inc....................................... F 440 248-1223
Macedonia (G-8707)

SILICONES

Canton OH Rubber Speclty Prods.......... G 330 454-3847
Canton (G-1857)

Hexion Topco LLC................................ D 614 225-4000
Columbus (G-4978)

Momentive Performance Mtls Inc.......... A 614 986-2495
Columbus (G-5109)

Momentive Performance Mtls Inc.......... B 740 928-7010
Hebron (G-7624)

Momentive Performance Mtls Inc.......... C 440 878-5705
Richmond Heights (G-11611)

Momentive Prfmce Mtls Qrtz Inc........... E 440 878-5700
Strongsville (G-12575)

Novagard Solutions Inc......................... D 216 881-8111
Cleveland (G-4101)

Silicone Solutions Inc........................... F 330 920-3125
Cuyahoga Falls (G-5572)

Wacker Chemical Corporation............... C 330 899-0847
Canton (G-2044)

SILK SCREEN DESIGN SVCS

Eastgate Custom Graphics Ltd.............. G 513 528-7922
Cincinnati (G-2575)

Galaxy Balloons Incorporated............... C 216 476-3360
Cleveland (G-3753)

Hollywood Imprints LLC........................ F 614 501-6040
Gahanna (G-7160)

Kimpton Printing & Spc Co.................... F 330 467-1640
Macedonia (G-8702)

Liming Printing Inc................................ F 937 374-2646
Xenia (G-14769)

Professional Screen Printing.................. G 740 687-0760
Lancaster (G-8219)

Qualitee Design Sportswear Co............. F 740 333-8337
Wshngtn Ct Hs (G-14742)

Roban Inc.. G 330 794-1059
Lakemore (G-8156)

Screen Works Inc.................................. E 937 264-9111
Dayton (G-6000)

Woodrow Manufacturing Co.................. E 937 399-9333
Springfield (G-12396)

SILVERWARE & PLATED WARE

Professional Award Service.................... G 513 389-3600
Cincinnati (G-3005)

SIMULATORS: Flight

Flightsafety International Inc................. C 614 324-3500
Columbus (G-4929)

SINTER: Iron

GKN Sinter Metals LLC.......................... C 740 441-3203
Gallipolis (G-7206)

Miba Sinter USA LLC............................. F 740 962-4242
Mcconnelsville (G-9365)

SLAG: Crushed Or Ground

Enviri Corporation................................ G 740 367-7322
Cheshire (G-2231)

Trans Ash Inc....................................... F 859 341-1528
Cincinnati (G-3164)

SMOKE DETECTORS

Voice Products Inc................................ F 216 360-0433
Cleveland (G-4479)

SOFT DRINKS WHOLESALERS

P-Americas LLC.................................... C 419 227-3541
Lima (G-8436)

Pepsi-Cola Metro Btlg Co Inc................ F 440 323-5524
Elyria (G-6577)

SOFTWARE PUBLISHERS: Home Entertainment

Cake LLC... G 614 592-7681
Dublin (G-6284)

Cerner Corporation............................... D 740 826-7678
New Concord (G-10386)

Mirus Adapted Tech LLC....................... E 614 402-4585
Dublin (G-6320)

Whatifsportscom Inc............................. G 513 333-0313
Blue Ash (G-1349)

SOFTWARE PUBLISHERS: Operating Systems

Seapine Software Inc............................ F 513 754-1655
Mason (G-9149)

Steward Edge Bus Solutions.................. F 614 826-5305
Columbus (G-5293)

SOFTWARE TRAINING, COMPUTER

Computer Workshop Inc........................ G 216 901-0106
Cleveland (G-3557)

SOLAR CELLS

First Solar Inc....................................... F 419 661-1478
Perrysburg (G-11222)

Isofoton North America Inc................... F 419 591-4330
Napoleon (G-10288)

Redhawk Energy Systems LLC............G.....740 927-8244
Pataskala (G-11146)

Rv Mobile Power LLC.........................E.....855 427-7978
Columbus (G-5239)

Toledo Solar Inc..............................F.....567 202-4145
Perrysburg (G-11275)

SOLAR HEATING EQPT

Iosil Energy Corporation.........................F
Groveport (G-7439)

Xunlight Corporation..............................D.....419 469-8600
Toledo (G-13181)

SOLES, BOOT OR SHOE: Rubber, Composition Or Fiber

Shreiner Sole Company Inc..................F.....330 276-6135
Killbuck (G-8133)

SOLID CONTAINING UNITS: Concrete

K-Mar Structures LLC.......................F.....231 924-5777
Junction City (G-8002)

SOLVENTS: Organic

Mid-America Chemical Corp.................G.....216 749-0100
Cleveland (G-4032)

SONAR SYSTEMS & EQPT

Raytheon Company...........................F.....937 429-5429
Beavercreek (G-980)

SOUND EFFECTS & MUSIC PRODUCTION: Motion Picture

Ournashonisme Ent LLC....................F.....689 276-0367
Euclid (G-6668)

Swagg Productions2015llc..................F.....614 601-7414
Worthington (G-14726)

SOUND EQPT: Electric

Fernandes Enterprises LLC..................F.....937 890-6444
Dayton (G-5775)

Holland Assocts LLC DBA Archou........F.....513 891-0006
Cincinnati (G-2727)

Mixed Logic LLC...............................G.....440 826-1676
Valley City (G-13505)

SOUND REPRODUCING EQPT

Background Music & Sound Inc............G.....937 898-9871
Dayton (G-5673)

SPEAKER SYSTEMS

Althar LLC.......................................F.....216 408-9860
Cleveland (G-3335)

J & C Group Inc of Ohio......................G.....440 205-9658
Mentor (G-9536)

Phantom Sound................................G.....513 759-4477
Loveland (G-8644)

Technical Artistry Inc.........................G.....614 299-7777
Columbus (G-5316)

SPECIALTY FOOD STORES: Coffee

Boston Stoker Inc..............................F.....937 890-6401
Vandalia (G-13551)

Crimson Cup Inc...............................F.....614 252-3335
Columbus (G-4860)

Generations Coffee Company LLC........F.....440 546-0901
Brecksville (G-1467)

Ohio Coffee Collaborative Ltd...............F.....614 564-9852
Columbus (G-5139)

SPECIALTY FOOD STORES: Eggs & Poultry

Roots Poultry Inc..............................G.....419 332-0041
Fremont (G-7130)

SPECIALTY FOOD STORES: Health & Dietetic Food

Premier Tanning & Nutrition.................G.....419 342-6259
Shelby (G-11973)

SPECIALTY FOOD STORES: Vitamin

Vitamin Shoppe Industries LLC.............A
Delaware (G-6179)

SPORTING & ATHLETIC GOODS: Basketball Eqpt & Splys, NEC

Huffy Sports Washington Inc.................G.....937 865-2800
Miamisburg (G-9700)

SPORTING & ATHLETIC GOODS: Camping Eqpt & Splys

Leisure Time Pdts Design Corp.............G.....440 934-1032
Avon (G-731)

SPORTING & ATHLETIC GOODS: Cases, Gun & Rod

Raven Concealment Systems LLC........E.....440 508-9000
North Ridgeville (G-10745)

SPORTING & ATHLETIC GOODS: Hunting Eqpt

Lem Products Holding LLC...................E.....513 202-1188
West Chester (G-14023)

SPORTING & ATHLETIC GOODS: Shafts, Golf Club

Board of Park Commissioners..............G.....216 635-3200
Cleveland (G-3424)

SPORTING & ATHLETIC GOODS: Team Sports Eqpt

Backyard Scoreboards LLC..................G.....513 702-6561
Middletown (G-9842)

Shoot-A-Way Inc..............................F.....419 294-4654
Nevada (G-10323)

SPORTING & ATHLETIC GOODS: Water Sports Eqpt

Kent Water Sports LLC.......................D.....419 929-7021
New London (G-10412)

Litehouse Products LLC......................E.....440 638-2350
Strongsville (G-12571)

Rain Drop Products Llc.......................E.....419 207-1229
Ashland (G-569)

SPORTING & RECREATIONAL GOODS, WHOLESALE: Athletic Goods

Garick LLC......................................E.....216 581-0100
Cleveland (G-3755)

SPORTING & RECREATIONAL GOODS, WHOLESALE: Boat Access & Part

Atwood Rope Manufacturing Inc...........E.....614 920-0534
Canal Winchester (G-1784)

SPORTING GOODS STORES: Firearms

Area 419 Firearms LLC.......................F.....419 830-8353
Delta (G-6201)

R & S Monitions Inc...........................G.....614 846-0597
Columbus (G-5222)

Sportsmans Haven Inc.......................G.....740 432-7243
Cambridge (G-1761)

Target Holdings Inc............................E.....513 474-4409
Cincinnati (G-3138)

TS Sales LLC...................................F.....727 804-8060
Akron (G-347)

SPORTING GOODS STORES: Playground Eqpt

Hershberger Lawn Structures................F.....330 674-3900
Millersburg (G-9983)

SPORTS APPAREL STORES

Shoot-A-Way Inc..............................F.....419 294-4654
Nevada (G-10323)

Tee Creations..................................G.....937 878-2822
Fairborn (G-6702)

Unisport Inc.....................................F.....419 529-4727
Ontario (G-10953)

Uptown Dog The Inc...........................G.....740 592-4600
Athens (G-655)

SPRINGS: Clock, Precision

Allied Shipping and Packagi.................F.....937 222-7422
Moraine (G-10144)

Malabar..E.....419 866-6301
Swanton (G-12687)

SPRINGS: Coiled Flat

Golden Spring Company Inc.................F.....937 848-2513
Bellbrook (G-1092)

SPRINGS: Leaf, Automobile, Locomotive, Etc

Liteflex Disc LLC...............................D.....937 836-7025
Dayton (G-5851)

SPRINGS: Mechanical, Precision

Kern-Liebers Usa Inc.........................D.....419 865-2437
Holland (G-7771)

Spring Works Incorporated..................E.....614 351-9345
Columbus (G-5286)

Stalder Spring Works Inc.....................G.....937 322-6120
Springfield (G-12378)

The Reliable Spring Wire Frms..............E.....440 365-7400
Elyria (G 6505)

Twist Inc..G.....937 675-9581
Jamestown (G-7970)

Twist Inc..C.....937 675-9581
Jamestown (G-7969)

Wire Products Company Inc.................F.....216 267-0777
Cleveland (G-4509)

Yost Superior Co...............................E.....937 323-7591
Springfield (G-12397)

SPRINGS: Precision

B & P Spring Prod Co Inc.....................F.....216 486-4260
Cleveland (G-3398)

Tadd Spring Co Inc............................G.....440 572-1313
Strongsville (G-12609)

SPRINGS: Steel

Dayton Progress Corporation................A.....937 859-5111
Dayton (G-5737)

Hendrickson International Corp..............D.....740 929-5600
Hebron (G-7617)

Jamestown Industries Inc....................D.....330 779-0670
Youngstown (G-14881)

Kern-Liebers Usa Inc.........................D.....419 865-2437
Holland (G-7771)

Matthew Warren Inc............................. E 614 418-0250
Columbus (G-5087)

Peterson American Corporation............ E 419 867-8711
Holland (G-7777)

Service Spring Corp............................. G 419 867-0212
Maumee (G-9317)

Service Spring Corp............................. D 419 838-6081
Maumee (G-9318)

Tadd Spring Co Inc.............................. G 440 572-1313
Strongsville (G-12609)

Zsi Manufacturing Inc.......................... F 440 266-0701
Concord Township (G-5398)

SPRINGS: Torsion Bar

Napoleon Spring Works Inc................... C 419 445-1010
Archbold (G-504)

SPRINGS: Wire

Aswpengg LLC..................................... F 216 292-4620
Bedford Heights (G-1069)

Barnes Group Inc................................. G 440 526-5900
Brecksville (G-1458)

Barnes Group Inc................................. C 419 891-9292
Maumee (G-9264)

Betts Company..................................... E 330 533-0111
Canfield (G-1805)

Bloomngburg Spring Wire Form I........ E 740 437-7614
Bloomingburg (G-1239)

Dayton Progress Corporation............... A ... 937 859-5111
Dayton (G-5737)

Elyria Spring Spclty Holdg Inc.............. G 440 323-5502
Cleveland (G-3664)

Euclid Spring Co.................................. E 440 943-3213
Wickliffe (G-14375)

Matthew Warren Inc............................. E 614 418-0250
Columbus (G-5087)

Ohio Wire Form & Spring Co................ F 614 444-3676
Columbus (G-5156)

Six C Fabrication Inc........................... B 330 296-5594
Ravenna (G-11541)

Solon Manufacturing Company............. E 440 286-7149
Chardon (G-2223)

Spring Team Inc.................................. D 440 275-5981
Austinburg (G-703)

Supro Spring & Wire Forms Inc............ E 330 722-5628
Medina (G-9451)

Timac Manufacturing Company............ G 937 372-3305
Xenia (G-14779)

Trupoint Products LLC......................... F 330 204-3302
Sugarcreek (G-12654)

SPROCKETS: Power Transmission

Akron Gear & Engineering Inc............. E 330 773-6608
Akron (G-32)

Robertson Manufacturing Co................ F 216 531-8222
Concord Township (G-5395)

STAINLESS STEEL

Acme Surface Dynamics Inc................. F 330 821-3900
Alliance (G-366)

Aco Inc.. E 440 639-7230
Mentor (G-9468)

ATI Flat Rlled Pdts Hldngs LLC............ F 330 875-2244
Louisville (G-8598)

Cleveland-Cliffs Steel Corp.................. B 419 755-3011
Mansfield (G-8775)

Cleveland-Cliffs Steel Corp.................. B 513 425-3694
Middletown (G-9847)

Fulton County Processing Ltd.............. C 419 822-9266
Delta (G-6206)

Great Lakes Mfg Group Ltd.................. G 440 391-8266
Rocky River (G-11634)

Kda Manufacturing LLC........................ F 330 590-7431
Norton (G-10825)

Latrobe Spcialty Mtls Dist Inc.............. D 330 609-5137
Vienna (G-13610)

McIntosh Manufacturing LLC................ D 513 424-5307
Middletown (G-9878)

Quaker City Castings Inc..................... A 330 332-1566
Salem (G-11806)

Qual-Fab Inc....................................... E 440 327-5000
Avon (G-737)

Quality Bar Inc................................... E 330 755-0000
Struthers (G-12620)

Shaq Inc.. D 770 427-0402
Beachwood (G-949)

STAINLESS STEEL WARE

Online Engineering Corp...................... G 513 561-8878
Cincinnati (G-2934)

STAIRCASES & STAIRS, WOOD

Amcan Stair & Rail LLC....................... G 937 781-3084
Springfield (G-12279)

Carolina Stair Supply Inc.................... E 740 922-3333
Uhrichsville (G-13402)

Great Lakes Stair & Mllwk Co.............. G 330 225-2005
Hinckley (G-7731)

Hinckley Wood Products Ltd................ G 330 220-9999
Hinckley (G-7732)

STAMPINGS: Automotive

Anchor Tool & Die Co........................... B 216 362-1850
Cleveland (G-3356)

Cleveland Metal Processing Inc............ C 440 243-3404
Cleveland (G-3517)

Cole Tool & Die Company..................... E 419 522-1272
Ontario (G-10948)

Compco Quaker Mfg Inc....................... E 330 482-0200
Salem (G-11772)

Exact-Tool & Die Inc............................ E 216 676-9140
Cleveland (G-3696)

Falls Stamping & Welding Co............... F 216 771-9635
Cleveland (G-3705)

Falls Stamping & Welding Co............... C 330 928-1191
Cuyahoga Falls (G-5541)

Falls Tool and Die Inc......................... G 330 633-4884
Akron (G-144)

Feintool Cincinnati Inc......................... C 513 247-0110
Cincinnati (G-2617)

Feintool US Operations Inc.................. C 513 247-0110
Cincinnati (G-2618)

Findlay Products Corporation............... C 419 423-3324
Findlay (G-6866)

Fulton Industries LLC.......................... D 419 270-3937
Wauseon (G-13849)

Grouper Acquisition Co LLC................. D 248 299-7500
Valley City (G-13498)

Grouper Acquisition Co LLC................. D 330 558-2600
Wellington (G-13892)

Gt Technologies Inc............................ D 419 324-7300
Toledo (G-12978)

Guarantee Specialties Inc.................... G 216 451-9744
Strongsville (G-12562)

Hayford Technologies Inc.................... D 419 524-7627
Mansfield (G-8800)

Honda Dev & Mfg Amer LLC................ C 937 644-0724
Marysville (G-9028)

Hydro Extrusion Usa LLC.................... C 888 935-5759
Sidney (G-12025)

Interntnal Cutng Solutions Inc............. G 440 786-1700
Streetsboro (G-12506)

JA Acquisition Corp............................. F 419 287-3223
Pemberville (G-11176)

Kirchhoff Auto Waverly Inc.................. F 740 947-7763
Waverly (G-13866)

L & W Inc.. D 734 397-6300
Avon (G-730)

Lakepark Industries Inc....................... C 419 752-4471
Greenwich (G-7363)

Langenau Manufacturing Company....... F 216 651-3400
Cleveland (G-3939)

Milark Industries Inc........................... D 419 524-7627
Mansfield (G-8827)

Milark Industries Inc........................... D 419 524-7627
Mansfield (G-8828)

Motherson Ychiyo Auto Tech PDT........ D 614 876-3220
Columbus (G-5113)

Muncy Corporation.............................. D 937 346-0800
Springfield (G-12355)

Namoh Ohio Holdings Inc.................... G
Norwood (G-10869)

Nasg Seating Paulding LLC.................. F 419 399-4500
Paulding (G-11159)

Nn Metal Stampings LLC...................... E 419 737-2311
Pioneer (G-11322)

Northern Stamping Co......................... F 216 883-8888
Cleveland (G-4095)

Northern Stamping Co......................... F 216 642-8081
Cleveland (G-4097)

Northern Stamping Co......................... D 216 883-8888
Cleveland (G-4096)

Oerlikon Frction Systems US In............ E 937 233-9191
Dayton (G-5921)

P & A Industries Inc............................ D 419 422-7070
Findlay (G-6906)

Quaker Mfg Corp................................. C 330 332-4631
Salem (G-11807)

R K Industries Inc............................... D 419 523-5001
Ottawa (G-11044)

Regal Metal Products Co..................... E 330 868-6343
Minerva (G-10046)

Shiloh Industries Inc........................... A 330 558-2000
Valley City (G-13516)

Shl Liquidation Industries Inc.............. A 330 558-2600
Valley City (G-13517)

Shl Liquidation Mfg LLC...................... E 330 558-2600
Valley City (G-13520)

SSP Industrial Group Inc..................... G 330 665-2900
Fairlawn (G-6814)

Stamco Industries Inc.......................... E 216 731-9333
Cleveland (G-4325)

Stripmatic Products Inc....................... E 216 241-7143
Cleveland (G-4336)

T A Bacon Co...................................... G 216 595-1310
Cleveland (G-4361)

Taylor Metal Products Co..................... C 419 522-3471
Mansfield (G-8857)

Tfo Tech Co Ltd................................... C 740 426-6381
Jeffersonville (G-7988)

Tower Atmtive Oprtons USA I LL........... B 419 358-8966
Bluffton (G-1366)

Triton Duro Werks Inc.......................... F 216 267-1117
Cleveland (G-4429)

Trucut Incorporated............................. D 330 938-9806
Sebring (G-11903)

Twb Company LLC................................ E 330 558-2026
Valley City (G-13521)

Valley Tool & Die Inc........................... D 440 237-0160
North Royalton (G-10788)

Winzeler Stamping Co.......................... E 419 485-3147
Montpelier (G-10138)

Yanfeng Intl Auto Tech US I LL............. D 419 633-1873
Bryan (G-1668)

STAMPINGS: Metal

Stamped Steel Products Inc.................. F 330 538-3951
North Jackson *(G-10695)*

STARTERS & CONTROLLERS: Motor, Electric

Helm Instrument Company Inc.............. E 419 893-4356
Maumee *(G-9296)*

STATIONERY & OFFICE SPLYS WHOLESALERS

AW Faber-Castell Usa Inc..................... D 216 643-4660
Cleveland *(G-3396)*

Covap Inc.. F 513 793-1855
Blue Ash *(G-1264)*

Equip Business Solutions Co................ G 614 854-9755
Jackson *(G-7945)*

Friends Service Co Inc........................ F 800 427-1704
Dayton *(G-5785)*

Friends Service Co Inc........................ E 419 427-1704
Findlay *(G-6869)*

Gvs Industries Inc.............................. G 513 851-3606
Hamilton *(G-7498)*

Pulsar Ecoproducts LLC...................... F 216 861-8800
Cleveland *(G-4208)*

Quick Tab II Inc.................................. D 419 448-6622
Tiffin *(G-12796)*

Scratch-Off Systems Inc..................... E 216 649-7800
Twinsburg *(G-13376)*

Westrock Commercial LLC................... E 419 476-9101
Toledo *(G-13178)*

STATIONERY: Made From Purchased Materials

American Greetings Corporation........... A 216 252-7300
Cleveland *(G-3344)*

CM Paula Company.............................. E 513 759-7473
Mason *(G-9090)*

STATUARY & OTHER DECORATIVE PRDTS: Nonmetallic

Aquablok Ltd...................................... G 419 402-4170
Swanton *(G-12678)*

Aquablok Ltd...................................... F 419 825-1325
Swanton *(G-12679)*

Fireline Inc.. C 330 743-1164
Youngstown *(G-14855)*

STEEL & ALLOYS: Tool & Die

American Steel & Alloys LLC................ G 330 847-0487
Warren *(G-13735)*

CPM Tool Co LLC................................ G 937 258-1176
Dayton *(G-5606)*

Ernst Metal Technologies LLC............. E 937 434-3133
Dayton *(G-5767)*

Mercer Tool Corporation...................... E 419 394-7277
Saint Marys *(G-11742)*

Rmi Titanium Company LLC................. B 330 453-2118
Canton *(G-1998)*

Thrift Tool Inc.................................... G 937 275-3600
Dayton *(G-6053)*

Unlimited Machine and Tool LLC.......... F 419 269-1730
Toledo *(G-13171)*

STEEL, COLD-ROLLED: Flat Bright, From Purchased HotRolled

Clark Grave Vault Company................. C 614 294-3761
Columbus *(G-4809)*

Geneva Liberty Steel Ltd..................... E 330 740-0103
Youngstown *(G-14865)*

STEEL, COLD-ROLLED: Sheet Or Strip, From Own HotRolled

American Hvy Plate Sltions LLC............ C 740 331-4620
Clarington *(G-3270)*

Nucor Steel Marion Inc....................... E 740 383-6068
Marion *(G-8984)*

Steel Technologies LLC....................... E 419 523-5199
Ottawa *(G-11046)*

Suburban Steel Supply Co Li............... D 614 737-5501
Gahanna *(G-7170)*

STEEL, COLD-ROLLED: Strip NEC, From Purchased HotRolled

Heidtman Steel Products Inc............... E 419 691-4646
Toledo *(G-12992)*

Sandvik Inc.. C 614 438-6579
Columbus *(G-5248)*

Worthngton Stl Mexico SA De Cv.......... G 800 944-2255
Worthington *(G-14733)*

STEEL, COLD-ROLLED: Strip Or Wire

Bekaert Corporation............................ E 330 683-5060
Orrville *(G-10975)*

Worthington Steel Inc......................... B 614 840-3462
Columbus *(G-5374)*

Worthington Steel Company................. B 800 944-2255
Worthington *(G-14732)*

STEEL, HOT-ROLLED: Sheet Or Strip

Cleveland-Cliffs Steel Corp.................. D 216 694-5700
Cleveland *(G-3533)*

Clevelnd-Cliffs Stl Holdg Corp.............. B 216 694-5700
Cleveland *(G-3537)*

Heidtman Steel Products Inc............... E 419 691-4646
Toledo *(G-12992)*

L T V Steel Company Inc...................... A 216 622-5000
Cleveland *(G-3933)*

Ohio Steel Sheet and Plate Inc............ E 800 827-2401
Hubbard *(G-7815)*

Precision Cut Fabricating Inc............... F 440 877-1260
North Royalton *(G-10780)*

STOCK SHAPES: Plastic

Swapil Inc.. D
Columbus *(G-5303)*

STONE: Dimension, NEC

North Hill Marble & Granite Co............. F 330 253-2179
Akron *(G-249)*

Ohio Beauty Cut Stone II Inc................ G 330 644-2241
Akron *(G-251)*

Solid Surface Concepts Inc.................. E 513 948-8677
Cincinnati *(G-3099)*

STONE: Quarrying & Processing, Own Stone Prdts

Beazer East Inc.................................. E 937 364-2311
Hillsboro *(G-7714)*

Briar Hill Stone Co Inc........................ D 216 377-5100
Glenmont *(G-7284)*

Cardinal Aggregate Inc........................ F 419 872-4380
Perrysburg *(G-11209)*

Terra Surfaces LLC............................. G 937 836-1900
Dayton *(G-6044)*

Waller Brothers Stone Company........... F 740 858-1948
Mc Dermott *(G-9356)*

STONEWARE PRDTS: Pottery

Beaumont Bros Stoneware Inc............. E 740 982-0055
Crooksville *(G-5508)*

Brittany Stamping LLC......................... A 216 267-0850
Cleveland *(G-3440)*

Clay Burley Products Co...................... E 740 452-3633
Roseville *(G-11653)*

STORE FIXTURES: Exc Wood

Cap & Associates Inc.......................... C 614 863-3363
Columbus *(G-4794)*

Heat Seal LLC.................................... C 216 341-2022
Cleveland *(G-3816)*

STORE FIXTURES: Wood

Artistic Finishes Inc........................... G 440 951-7850
Willoughby *(G-14427)*

Baker Store Equipment Company......... F
Shaker Heights *(G-11926)*

Cap & Associates Inc.......................... C 614 863-3363
Columbus *(G-4794)*

CIP International Inc........................... D 513 874-9925
West Chester *(G-13964)*

Display Dynamics Inc.......................... F 937 832-2830
Englewood *(G-6612)*

Leiden Cabinet Company LLC.............. D 330 425-8555
Twinsburg *(G-13330)*

Mac Lean J S Co................................ G 614 878-5454
Columbus *(G-5078)*

Norton Industries Inc.......................... E 888 357-2345
Lakewood *(G-8171)*

STORES: Auto & Home Supply

Allen Aircraft Products Inc................... D 330 296-9621
Ravenna *(G-11516)*

Doug Marine Motors Inc...................... F 740 335-3700
Wshngtn Ct Hs *(G-14738)*

Finale Products Inc............................. G 419 874-2662
Perrysburg *(G-11221)*

Keystone Auto Glass Inc..................... D 419 509-0497
Maumee *(G-9302)*

Knippen Chrysler Ddge Jeep Inc.......... F 419 695-4976
Delphos *(G-6188)*

Pattons Trck & Hvy Eqp Svc Inc.......... F 740 385-4067
Logan *(G-8523)*

Support Svc LLC................................ G 419 617-0660
Lexington *(C-8375)*

Vintage Automotive Elc Inc.................. F 419 472-9349
Toledo *(G-13175)*

STRAINERS: Line, Piping Systems

16363 Sca Inc.................................... G 330 448-0000
Masury *(G-9253)*

Insulpro Inc....................................... F 614 262-3768
Columbus *(G-5016)*

STRAWS: Drinking, Made From Purchased Materials

Nelson Companies One LLC................. E 330 239-4370
Wadsworth *(G-13654)*

Solas Ltd... E 650 501-0889
Avon *(G-739)*

STRUCTURAL SUPPORT & BUILDING MATERIAL: Concrete

High Concrete Group LLC.................... B 937 748-2412
Springboro *(G-12255)*

Jet Stream International Inc.................. D 330 505-9988
Hubbard *(G-7813)*

PRODUCT

STUDS & JOISTS: Sheet Metal

Clarkwestern Dietrich Building.............. D 330 372-5564
Warren (G-13752)

Clarkwstern Dtrich Bldg System........... C 513 870-1100
West Chester (G-13966)

SUNDRIES & RELATED PRDTS: Medical & Laboratory, Rubber

American Ntrile Operations LLC............ G 614 425-5211
Grove City (G-7371)

Duramax Marine LLC.......................... D 440 834-5400
Hiram (G-7737)

Elastostar Rubber Corp....................... E 614 841-4400
Plain City (G-11407)

Elbex Corporation.............................. D 330 673-3233
Kent (G-8029)

Express Pharmacy & Dme LLC............. G 210 981-9690
Columbus (G-4915)

Finzer Roller Inc............................... F 937 746-4069
Franklin (G-7021)

Gdc Inc... F 574 533-3128
Wooster (G-14642)

Guardian Manufacturing Co LLC........... E 419 933-2711
Willard (G-14402)

Hexpol Compounding LLC.................... C 440 682-4038
Akron (G-175)

Hygenic Acquisition Co...................... C 330 633-8460
Akron (G-180)

Hygenic Company LLC....................... B 330 633-8460
Akron (G-181)

Kent Elastomer Products Inc.............. C 330 673-1011
Kent (G-8041)

Newell Brands Inc............................ F 330 733-1184
Kent (G-8056)

Plymouth Foam LLC........................... D 740 254-1188
Gnadenhutten (G-7292)

Rainbow Master Mixing Inc................. E 330 374-1810
Akron (G-277)

Roller Source Inc............................. F 440 748-4033
Columbia Station (G-4599)

Vulcan International Corp................... G 513 621-2850
Cincinnati (G-3208)

SUNGLASSES, WHOLESALE

Smithco Distributing.......................... E 419 367-7685
Liberty Center (G-8376)

SURFACE ACTIVE AGENTS

BASF Corporation.............................. D 614 662-5682
Columbus (G-4745)

Peter Cremer N Amer Enrgy Inc........... E 513 557-3943
Cincinnati (G-2957)

Pilot Chemical Corp........................... C 513 326-0600
West Chester (G-14046)

SURGICAL APPLIANCES & SPLYS

American Power LLC.......................... F 937 235-0418
Dayton (G-5654)

Axon Medical Llc.............................. E 216 276-0262
Medina (G-9379)

Cardinal Health Inc........................... E 614 553-3830
Dublin (G-6285)

Cardinal Health Inc........................... G 614 757-2863
Lewis Center (G-8328)

Cardinal Health Inc........................... A 614 757-5000
Dublin (G-6286)

Cleveland Medical Devices Inc............. E 216 619-5928
Cleveland (G-3515)

Deco Tools Inc................................. E 419 476-9321
Toledo (G-12939)

Dentronix Inc.................................. D 330 916-7300
Cuyahoga Falls (G-5538)

Depuy Synthes Inc........................... G 614 472-8008
Columbus (G-4878)

Ethicon Inc..................................... C 513 786-7000
Blue Ash (G-1272)

Florida Invacare Holdings LLC.............. F 800 333-6900
Elyria (G-6537)

Francisco Jaume............................... G 740 622-1200
Coshocton (G-5455)

Frohock-Stewart Inc.......................... E 440 329-6000
North Ridgeville (G-10731)

Gelok International Corp..................... G 419 352-1482
Bowling Green (G-1420)

Gendron Inc.................................... E 419 636-0848
Bryan (G-1643)

Guardian Manufacturing Co LLC........... E 419 933-2711
Willard (G-14402)

Hdwt Holdings Inc............................ D 440 269-6984
Mentor (G-9526)

Invacare Canadian Holdings Inc........... G 440 329-6000
Elyria (G-6546)

Invacare Canadian Holdings LLC........... G 440 329-6000
Elyria (G-6547)

Invacare Continuing Care Inc.............. G 800 668-2337
Elyria (G-6548)

Invacare Corporation......................... F 440 329-6000
North Ridgeville (G-10736)

Invacare Corporation......................... A 440 329-6000
Elyria (G-6549)

Invacare Hcs LLC............................. F 330 634-9925
Elyria (G-6552)

Invacare Holdings LLC....................... G 440 329-6000
Elyria (G-6553)

Johnson & Johnson........................... E 513 786-7000
Blue Ash (G-1290)

Jones Metal Products Co LLC............... E 740 545-6381
West Lafayette (G-14171)

Jones Metal Products Company............ E 740 545-6341
West Lafayette (G-14172)

Kempf Surgical Appliances Inc............. G 513 984-5758
Cincinnati (G-2791)

Leimkuehler Inc............................... E 440 899-7842
Cleveland (G-3950)

Marlen Manufacturing & Dev Co........... F 216 292-7546
Bedford (G-1047)

Medline Industries LP........................ E 614 879-9728
West Jefferson (G-14164)

Meridian Industries Inc...................... D 330 673-1011
Kent (G-8051)

Philips Med Systems Clvland In............ B 440 483-3000
Cleveland (G-4159)

Steris-IMS...................................... G 330 686-4557
Stow (G-12465)

Surgical Recovery Systems LLC........... E 513 833-6868
Hamilton (G-7528)

Thomas Products Co Inc..................... E 513 756-9009
Cincinnati (G-3155)

Tilt 15 Inc...................................... D 330 239-4192
Sharon Center (G-11944)

Dan Allen Surgical LLC...................... F 800 261-9953
Newbury (G-10549)

Marlen Manufacturing & Dev Co........... G 216 292-7060
Bedford (G-1046)

Steris Corporation............................ D 440 392-8079
Mentor (G-9626)

Steris Corporation............................ C 440 354-2600
Mentor (G-9627)

Surgical Appliance Inds Inc................. C 513 271-4594
Cincinnati (G-3132)

SURGICAL IMPLANTS

Bahler Medical Inc............................ G 614 873-7600
Plain City (G-11396)

Hammill Manufacturing Co.................. D 419 476-0789
Maumee (G-9295)

Osteosymbionics LLC........................ F 216 881-8500
Cleveland (G-4126)

Spinal Balance Inc............................ F 419 530-5935
Swanton (G-12693)

Theken Spine LLC............................ F 330 773-7677
Medina (G-9455)

SURGICAL INSTRUMENT REPAIR SVCS

Optimum Surgical.............................. F 216 870-8526
Medina (G-9431)

SURVEYING INSTRUMENTS WHOLESALERS

Zaenkert Srvying Essntials Inc.............. G 513 738-2917
Okeana (G-10931)

SUSPENSION SYSTEMS: Acoustical, Metal

Bowden Fence Co LLC........................ G 614 272-8923
Columbus (G-4771)

Kinetics Noise Control Inc................... C 614 889-0480
Dublin (G-6316)

One Wish LLC.................................. F 800 505-6883
Bedford (G-1052)

Wall Technology Inc.......................... G 715 532-5548
Toledo (G-13176)

SVC ESTABLISHMENT EQPT, WHOLESALE: Firefighting Eqpt

A-1 Sprinkler Company Inc.................. D 937 859-6198
Miamisburg (G-9659)

Action Coupling & Eqp Inc.................. D 330 279-4242
Holmesville (G-7793)

Fire Safety Services Inc..................... F 937 686-2000
Huntsville (G-7864)

Johnsons Fire Equipment Co............... F 740 357-4916
Wellston (G-13908)

Sutphen Corporation......................... C 800 726-7030
Dublin (G-6353)

SVC ESTABLISHMENT EQPT, WHOLESALE: Laundry Eqpt & Splys

Pneumatic Specialties Inc................... G 440 729-4400
Chesterland (G-2239)

SVC ESTABLISHMENT EQPT, WHOLESALE: Restaurant Splys

Martin-Brower Company LLC................ C 513 773-2301
West Chester (G-14027)

Wasserstrom Company....................... B 614 228-6525
Columbus (G-5356)

SWEEPING COMPOUNDS

B&D Water Inc................................. E 330 771-3318
Quaker City (G-11503)

Nwp Manufacturing Inc...................... F 419 894-6871
Waldo (G-13690)

SWIMMING POOL EQPT: Filters & Water Conditioning Systems

Aquapro Systems LLC........................ F 877 278-2797
Oakwood (G-10895)

Hammersmith Bros Invstmnts Inc.......... E 513 353-3000
North Bend (G-10620)

Onesource Water LLC........................ F 866 917-7873
Toledo (G-13077)

SWIMMING POOLS, EQPT & SPLYS: Wholesalers

Bradley Enterprises Inc.......................G 330 875-1444
Louisville *(G-8599)*

Hammersmith Bros Invstmnts Inc.........E 513 353-3000
North Bend *(G-10620)*

Litehouse Products LLC......................E 440 638-2350
Strongsville *(G-12571)*

Mc Alarney Pool Spas and Billd............F 740 373-6698
Marietta *(G-8928)*

SWITCHBOARDS & PARTS: Power

Vacuum Electric Switch Co Inc.............F 330 374-5156
Mogadore *(G-10091)*

SWITCHES: Electric Power

Temple Israel....................................G 330 762-8617
Akron *(G-330)*

Wes-Garde Components Group Inc.......G 614 885-0319
Westerville *(G-14280)*

SWITCHES: Electric Power, Exc Snap, Push Button, Etc

Lake Shore Electric Corp.....................E 440 232-0200
Bedford *(G-1043)*

SWITCHES: Electronic

Black Box Corporation........................E 614 825-7400
Lewis Center *(G-8325)*

Black Box Corporation........................G 855 324-9909
Westlake *(G-14292)*

Don-Ell Corporation...........................E 419 841-7114
Sylvania *(G-12704)*

Hall Company...................................E 937 652-1376
Urbana *(G-13465)*

Quality Switch Inc.............................E 330 872-5707
Newton Falls *(G-10580)*

Specialty Switch Company LLC............F 330 427-3000
Youngstown *(G-14936)*

SWITCHES: Electronic Applications

Bwi Eagle LLC..................................E 724 283-4681
Warren *(G-13747)*

Contact Industries Inc........................E 419 884-9788
Lexington *(G-8372)*

Twinsource LLC.................................F 440 248-6800
Solon *(G-12200)*

SWITCHES: Time, Electrical Switchgear Apparatus

All Pack Services LLC.........................G 614 935-0964
Grove City *(G-7370)*

SWITCHGEAR & SWITCHBOARD APPARATUS

ABB Inc...F 614 818-6300
Westerville *(G-14201)*

Asco Power Technologies LP................C 216 573-7600
Cleveland *(G-3374)*

Avtron Loadbank Inc...........................C 216 573-7600
Cleveland *(G-3395)*

CDI Industries Inc..............................E 440 243-1100
Cleveland *(G-3481)*

Delta Systems Inc.............................B 330 626-2811
Streetsboro *(G-12496)*

Emerson Network Power......................G 614 841-8054
Ironton *(G-7931)*

Flood Heliarc Inc...............................F 614 835-3929
Groveport *(G-7432)*

General Electric Company....................E 216 883-1000
Cleveland *(G-3766)*

Joslyn Hi-Voltage Company LLC...........F 216 271-6600
Cleveland *(G-3893)*

Mercury Iron and Steel Co...................F 440 349-1500
Solon *(G-12146)*

Myers Power Products Inc...................C 330 834-3200
North Canton *(G-10655)*

Npas Inc...F 614 595-6916
Mansfield *(G-8840)*

Roemer Industries Inc.........................D 330 448-2000
Masury *(G-9256)*

Schneider Electric Usa Inc..................D 513 777-4445
West Chester *(G-14073)*

Siemens Industry Inc.........................E 937 593-6010
Bellefontaine *(G-1116)*

Spang & Company..............................E 440 350-6108
Mentor *(G-9619)*

Toledo Transducers Inc.......................E 419 724-4170
Maumee *(G-9327)*

Westbrook Mfg Inc.............................B 937 254-2004
Dayton *(G-6078)*

SWITCHGEAR & SWITCHGEAR ACCESS, NEC

Ideal Electric Power Co.......................E 419 522-3611
Mansfield *(G-8804)*

Pacs Industries Inc............................D 740 397-5021
Mount Vernon *(G-10256)*

SYNTHETIC RESIN FINISHED PRDTS, NEC

Orbis Corporation..............................B 937 652-1361
Urbana *(G-13475)*

Reactive Resin Products Co..................F 419 666-6119
Perrysburg *(G-11259)*

SYRUPS, DRINK

Central Coca-Cola Btlg Co Inc.............C 419 476-6622
Toledo *(G-12913)*

Dominion Liquid Tech LLC...................E 513 272-2824
Cincinnati *(G-2557)*

Innovtive Cnfction Sltions LLC.............G 440 835-8001
Westlake *(G-14311)*

Slush Puppie....................................G 513 771-0940
West Chester *(G-14147)*

SYSTEMS ENGINEERING: Computer Related

Freedom Usa Inc...............................E 216 503-6374
Twinsburg *(G-13305)*

Leidos Inc.......................................D 937 656-8433
Beavercreek *(G-977)*

SYSTEMS INTEGRATION SVCS

Advanced Prgrm Resources Inc............E 614 761-9994
Dublin *(G-6273)*

Creative Microsystems Inc...................D 937 836-4499
Englewood *(G-6611)*

Data Processing Sciences Corporation. D 513 791-7100
Cincinnati *(G-2542)*

Generic Systems Inc..........................F 419 841-8460
Holland *(G-7764)*

Kc Robotics Inc.................................E 513 860-4442
West Chester *(G-14019)*

Systemax Manufacturing Inc.................G 937 368-2300
Dayton *(G-6035)*

SYSTEMS INTEGRATION SVCS: Local Area Network

Town Cntry Technical Svcs Inc.............F 614 866-7700
Reynoldsburg *(G-11582)*

SYSTEMS SOFTWARE DEVELOPMENT SVCS

CHI Corporation................................G 440 498-2300
Cleveland *(G-3494)*

Cincinnati Ctrl Dynamics Inc................G 513 242-7300
Cincinnati *(G-2473)*

Deemsys Inc....................................D 614 322-9928
Gahanna *(G-7155)*

Dewesoft LLC...................................D 855 339-3669
Whitehouse *(G-14359)*

Drb Holdings LLC..............................B 330 645-3299
Akron *(G-127)*

Drb Systems LLC..............................C 330 645-3299
Akron *(G-128)*

Online Mega Sellers Corp....................G 888 384-6468
Toledo *(G-13078)*

Pinnacle Data Systems Inc..................C 614 748-1150
Groveport *(G-7449)*

TABLE OR COUNTERTOPS, PLASTIC LAMINATED

Archer Counter Design Inc...................G 513 396-7526
Cincinnati *(G-2374)*

Customworks Inc...............................G 614 262-1002
Columbus *(G-4866)*

E J Skok Industries............................E 216 292-7533
Bedford *(G-1030)*

Helmart Company Inc.........................G 513 941-3095
Cincinnati *(G-2715)*

Laminated Concepts Inc......................F 216 475-4141
Maple Heights *(G-8885)*

Rusco Products Inc............................G 330 758-0378
Youngstown *(G-14927)*

Shur-Fit Distributors Inc......................F 937 746-0567
Franklin *(G-7049)*

Swingle Countertops..........................F 740 454-7368
Zanesville *(G-15052)*

Wdi Group Inc...................................D 216 251-5509
Cleveland *(G-4495)*

Wilsonart LLC...................................E 614 876-1515
Columbus *(G-5369)*

Youngstown Curve Form Inc.................F 330 744-3028
Youngstown *(G-14968)*

TABLETS: Bronze Or Other Metal

Rise Holdings LLC.............................F 440 946-9646
Willoughby *(G-14519)*

TABLEWARE: Vitreous China

Libbey Inc..C 419 325-2100
Toledo *(G-13035)*

TAGS & LABELS: Paper

Kay Toledo Tag Inc............................D 419 729-5479
Toledo *(G-13017)*

Kennedy Group Incorporated................D 440 951-7660
Willoughby *(G-14477)*

Orbytel Print and Packg Inc.................G 216 267-8734
Cleveland *(G-4123)*

The Hooven - Dayton Corp...................C 937 233-4473
Miamisburg *(G-9747)*

Warren Printing & Off Pdts Inc.............F 419 523-3635
Ottawa *(G-11050)*

TANK REPAIR & CLEANING SVCS

Amko Service Company.......................E 330 364-8857
Midvale *(G-9907)*

Kars Ohio LLC..................................G 614 655-1099
Pataskala *(G-11142)*

PRODUCT

National Wldg Tanker Repr LLC............ G 614 875-3399
  Grove City *(G-7404)*

Ohio Hydraulics Inc............................... E 513 771-2590
  Cincinnati *(G-2924)*

Sabco Industries Inc............................. E 419 531-5347
  Toledo *(G-13120)*

TANK REPAIR SVCS

Corrotec Inc.. E 937 325-3585
  Springfield *(G-12294)*

Frontier Tank Center Inc........................ G 330 659-3888
  Richfield *(G-11593)*

Schaeffer Metal Products Inc................ G 330 296-6226
  Ravenna *(G-11539)*

TANK TOWERS: Metal Plate

Complete Mechanical Svcs LLC............. D 513 489-3080
  Cincinnati *(G-2507)*

TANKS & OTHER TRACKED VEHICLE CMPNTS

American Apex Corporation.................... F 614 652-2000
  Delaware *(G-6130)*

Integris Composites Inc........................ D 740 928-0326
  Hebron *(G-7619)*

Motherson Ychiyo US Auto Syste......... C 740 375-4687
  Marion *(G-8981)*

Performance Tank Sales Inc.................. G 330 602-8800
  Dover *(G-6258)*

Tessec Manufacturing Svcs LLC........... E 937 985-3552
  Dayton *(G-6046)*

Weldon Pump LLC................................. E 440 232-2282
  Oakwood Village *(G-10913)*

TANKS: Concrete

Star Manufacturing LLC........................ C 330 740-8300
  Youngstown *(G-14940)*

TANKS: Cryogenic, Metal

Amko Service Company.......................... E 330 364-8857
  Midvale *(G-9907)*

Eleet Cryogenics Inc............................. E 330 874-4009
  Bolivar *(G-1382)*

Fiba Technologies Inc........................... F 330 602-7300
  Midvale *(G-9909)*

TANKS: For Tank Trucks, Metal Plate

Elliott Machine Works Inc...................... E 419 468-4709
  Galion *(G-7189)*

Jacp Inc.. G 513 353-3660
  Miamitown *(G-9759)*

Liquid Luggers LLC............................... E 330 426-2538
  East Palestine *(G-6404)*

TANKS: Fuel, Including Oil & Gas, Metal Plate

Convault of Ohio Inc.............................. G 614 252-8422
  Columbus *(G-4846)*

Stanwade Metal Products Inc................ E 330 772-2421
  Hartford *(G-7573)*

TANKS: Lined, Metal

Hamilton Tanks LLC.............................. F 614 445-8446
  Columbus *(G-4969)*

Modern Welding Co Ohio Inc................. E 740 344-9425
  Newark *(G-10522)*

TANKS: Military, Including Factory Rebuilding

General Dynmics Land Systems I........... B 419 221-7000
  Lima *(G-8410)*

TANKS: Plastic & Fiberglass

Aco Inc... E 440 639-7230
  Mentor *(G-9468)*

Alliance Equipment Company Inc.......... F 330 821-2291
  Alliance *(G-370)*

Kar-Del Plastics Inc.............................. G 419 289-9739
  Ashland *(G-543)*

Norwesco Inc.. F 740 654-6402
  Lancaster *(G-8216)*

R L Industries Inc................................. D 513 874-2800
  West Chester *(G-14060)*

Wasca LLC.. E 937 723-9031
  Dayton *(G-6075)*

TANKS: Standard Or Custom Fabricated, Metal Plate

Buckeye Fabricating Company............... E 937 746-9822
  Springboro *(G-12248)*

Central Fabricators Inc.......................... E 513 621-1240
  Cincinnati *(G-2449)*

Compco Columbiana Company.............. D 330 482-0200
  Columbiana *(G-4613)*

Compco Youngstown Company............. D 330 482-6488
  Columbiana *(G-4614)*

Dabar Industries LLC............................ F 614 873-3949
  Columbus *(G-4867)*

Enerfab LLC.. B 513 641-0500
  Cincinnati *(G-2590)*

Gaspar Inc.. D 330 477-2222
  Canton *(G-1898)*

Hason USA Corp................................... G 513 248-0287
  Cincinnati *(G-2711)*

M & H Fabricating Co Inc...................... G 937 325-8708
  Springfield *(G-12343)*

Odom Industries Inc.............................. E 513 248-0287
  Milford *(G-9945)*

Rebsco Inc.. F 937 548-2246
  Greenville *(G-7351)*

S-P Company Inc................................... D 330 782-5651
  Columbiana *(G-4627)*

Seneca Environmental Products Inc...... E 419 447-1282
  Tiffin *(G-12799)*

TANKS: Storage, Farm, Metal Plate

Industrial Farm Tank Inc....................... E 937 843-2972
  Lewistown *(G-8365)*

Rcr Partnership..................................... G 419 340-1202
  Genoa *(G-7249)*

TAPE DRIVES

CHI Corporation.................................... G 440 498-2300
  Cleveland *(G-3494)*

TAPES: Pressure Sensitive, Rubber

3M Company.. D 330 725-1444
  Medina *(G-9369)*

Austin Tape and Label Inc..................... D 330 928-7999
  Stow *(G-12420)*

Beiersdorf Inc.. C 513 682-7300
  West Chester *(G-14107)*

Cortape Inc.. F 330 929-6700
  Cuyahoga Falls *(G-5535)*

Lockfast LLC.. G 800 543-7157
  Loveland *(G-8637)*

Progressive Supply LLC........................ G 570 688-9636
  Willoughby *(G-14510)*

The Hooven - Dayton Corp.................... C 937 233-4473
  Miamisburg *(G-9747)*

TARGET DRONES

Drone Express Inc................................. F 513 577-5152
  Dayton *(G-5752)*

TARPAULINS

Custom Tarpaulin Products Inc............. F 330 758-1801
  Youngstown *(G-14844)*

Lesch Boat Cover Canvas Co LLC......... G 419 668-6374
  Norwalk *(G-10850)*

Rainbow Industries Inc.......................... G 937 323-6493
  Springfield *(G-12366)*

Tarpco Inc... F 330 677-8277
  Kent *(G-8086)*

Toledo Tarp Service Inc......................... E 419 837-5098
  Perrysburg *(G-11276)*

Tri County Tarp LLC.............................. E 419 288-3350
  Gibsonburg *(G-7260)*

TARPAULINS, WHOLESALE

Berlin Truck Caps & Tarps Ltd.............. F 330 893-2811
  Millersburg *(G-9970)*

TECHNICAL MANUAL PREPARATION SVCS

ONeil & Associates Inc.......................... C 937 865-0800
  Miamisburg *(G-9725)*

TELECOMMUNICATION EQPT REPAIR SVCS, EXC TELEPHONES

Cbst Acquisition LLC............................ D 513 361-9600
  Cincinnati *(G-2445)*

Town Cntry Technical Svcs Inc.............. F 614 866-7700
  Reynoldsburg *(G-11582)*

Vertiv Energy Systems Inc..................... A 440 288-1122
  Lorain *(G-8585)*

Vertiv Group Corporation....................... G 440 288-1122
  Lorain *(G-8586)*

TELEMETERING EQPT

L3 Technologies Inc.............................. G 937 257-8501
  Dayton *(G-5616)*

TELEPHONE BOOTHS, EXC WOOD

Ray Communications Inc....................... G 330 686-0226
  Stow *(G-12453)*

TELEPHONE EQPT: Modems

Black Box Corporation........................... E 614 825-7400
  Lewis Center *(G-8325)*

Black Box Corporation........................... G 855 324-9909
  Westlake *(G-14292)*

TELEPHONE EQPT: NEC

Arnco Corporation................................. F 800 847-7661
  Elyria *(G-6498)*

Commercial Electric Pdts Corp.............. E 216 241-2886
  Cleveland *(G-3552)*

Siemens AG... G 513 576-2451
  Mason *(G-9151)*

TELEPHONE SVCS

Total Call Center Solutions.................... F 330 869-9844
  Akron *(G-341)*

TELEVISION BROADCASTING & COMMUNICATIONS EQPT

Nissin Precision N Amer Inc.................. D 937 836-1910
  Englewood *(G-6620)*

Punch Components Inc.......................... E 419 224-1242
  Lima *(G-8441)*

(G-0000) Company's Geographic Section entry number

TELEVISION BROADCASTING STATIONS

Block Communications Inc.................. F 419 724-6212
Toledo (G-12898)

Dispatch Printing Company.................. F 740 548-5331
Lewis Center (G-8331)

TELEVISION: Closed Circuit Eqpt

Diamond Electronics Inc........................ G 740 652-9222
Lancaster (G-8196)

TELEVISION: Monitors

Edl Displays Inc................................... E 937 429-7423
Beavercreek (G-974)

TEMPORARY HELP SVCS

Cima Inc... G 513 382-8976
Hamilton (G-7476)

Upshift Work LLC................................ E 513 813-5695
Cincinnati (G-3188)

TERMINAL BOARDS

Osborne Coinage Company LLC........... D 877 480-0456
Blue Ash (G-1316)

TESTERS: Battery

Battery Unlimited................................. G 740 452-5030
Zanesville (G-14993)

Zts Inc... F 513 271-2557
Cincinnati (G-3243)

TESTERS: Physical Property

Advanced Gauging Tech LLC................ F 936 443-7129
Plain City (G-11391)

Kw Acquisition Inc............................... G 740 548-7298
Lewis Center (G-8341)

Pressco Technology Inc........................ D 440 498-2600
Cleveland (G-4194)

Test Mark Industries Inc....................... F 330 426-2200
East Palestine (G-6408)

TESTING SVCS

Alpha Technologies Svcs LLC.............. D 330 745-1641
Hudson (G-7828)

Orton Edward Jr Crmic Fndation........... E 614 895-2663
Westerville (G-14226)

Pease Enterprises Inc.......................... F 513 871-8907
Cincinnati (G-2951)

TEXTILE DESIGNERS

Standard Textile Co Inc........................ B 513 761-9255
Cincinnati (G-3112)

TEXTILE FINISHING: Napping, Manmade Fiber & Silk, Broadwoven

Tranzonic Companies........................... C 440 446-0643
Cleveland (G-4414)

Tz Acquisition Corp.............................. F 216 535-4300
Richmond Heights (G-11613)

TEXTILES: Linen Fabrics

Standard Textile Co Inc........................ B 513 761-9255
Cincinnati (G-3112)

THEATRICAL PRODUCTION SVCS

North Coast Theatrical Inc.................... G 330 762-1768
Akron (G-248)

THEATRICAL SCENERY

Erie Street Thea Svcs Inc..................... G 216 426-0050
Cleveland (G-3684)

Scarefactory Inc.................................. F 614 565-3590
Columbus (G-5252)

Schell Scenic Studio Inc....................... G 614 444-9550
Millersport (G-10024)

THERMISTORS, EXC TEMPERATURE SENSORS

Measurement Specialties Inc................ C 937 427-1231
Dayton (G-5872)

THERMOCOUPLES

Blaze Technical Services Inc................ E 330 923-0409
Stow (G-12422)

Heraeus Electro-Nite Co LLC............... G 330 725-1419
Medina (G-9408)

THERMOPLASTIC MATERIALS

Amros Industries Inc............................ F 216 433-0010
Cleveland (G-3351)

Avient Corporation............................... D 440 930-1000
Avon Lake (G-748)

Genius Solutions Engrg Co................... E 419 794-9914
Maumee (G-9293)

Geon Performance Solutions LLC......... D 440 930-1000
Avon Lake (G-757)

Hexpol Compounding LLC..................... E 440 834-4644
Burton (G-1700)

Integra Enclosures Limited................... D 440 269-4966
Mentor (G-9533)

Polyone LLC.. F 440 930-1000
Avon Lake (G-769)

THERMOSETTING MATERIALS

Current Inc.. G 330 392-5151
Warren (G-13756)

Hexion LLC... D 614 225-4000
Columbus (G-4977)

Hexion Topco LLC............................... D 614 225-4000
Columbus (G-4978)

TILE: Brick & Structural, Clay

Armstrong World Industries Inc............. E 614 771-9307
Hilliard (G-7669)

Glen-Gery Corporation......................... E 419 468-4890
Galion (G-7194)

Kepcor Inc.. F 330 868-6434
Minerva (G-10040)

LBC Clay Co LLC................................ G 330 674-0674
Millersburg (G-9991)

Minteq International Inc........................ E 330 343-8821
Dover (G-6254)

Resco Products Inc............................. G 740 682-7794
Oak Hill (G-10893)

Stebbins Engineering & Mfg Co........... F 740 922-3012
Uhrichsville (G-13407)

TILE: Clay, Drain & Structural

Haviland Drainage Products Co............ F 800 860-6294
Haviland (G-7589)

TILE: Wall & Floor, Ceramic

Wccv Floor Coverings LLC................... F 330 688-0114
Peninsula (G-11185)

TIN

Tin Wizard Heating & Coolg Inc........... G 330 467-9826
Macedonia (G-8720)

TIRE & INNER TUBE MATERIALS & RELATED PRDTS

Grove Engineered Products.................. G 419 659-5939
Columbus Grove (G-5383)

Troy Engnred Cmpnnts Assmblies........ G 937 335-8070
Dayton (G-6065)

Truflex Rubber Products Co.................. C 740 967-9015
Johnstown (G-8001)

TIRE & TUBE REPAIR MATERIALS, WHOLESALE

Mark Knupp Muffler & Tire Inc.............. G 937 773-1334
Piqua (G-11365)

Myers Industries Inc............................ E 330 253-5592
Akron (G-243)

Technical Rubber Company Inc............. C 740 967-9015
Johnstown (G-7999)

TIRE CORD & FABRIC

ARC Abrasives Inc.............................. D 800 888-4885
Troy (G-13201)

Cleveland Canvas Goods Mfg Co......... E 216 361-4567
Cleveland (G-3508)

Mfh Partners Inc................................. B 440 461-4100
Cleveland (G-4025)

TIRE SUNDRIES OR REPAIR MATERIALS: Rubber

31 Inc.. D 800 438-3302
Newcomerstown (G-10566)

Technical Rubber Company Inc............. C 740 967-9015
Johnstown (G-7999)

TIRES & INNER TUBES

B & S Transport Inc............................. G 330 767-4319
Navarre (G-10302)

Bkt USA Inc.. F 330 836-1090
Copley (G-5430)

Bridgstone Amrcas Tire Oprtons.......... D 330 379-3714
Akron (G-83)

North American Assemblies LLC.......... E 843 420-5354
Dublin (G-6325)

Oliver Rubber Co................................. F 419 420-6235
Findlay (G-6903)

Titan Tire Corporation.......................... B 419 633-4221
Bryan (G-1662)

Titan Tire Corporation Bryan................ E 419 633-4224
Bryan (G-1663)

Umd Contractors Inc........................... F 740 094-0014
Fredericktown (G-7087)

TIRES & TUBES WHOLESALERS

B & S Transport Inc............................. G 330 767-4319
Navarre (G-10302)

Best One Tire & Svc Lima Inc.............. G 419 425-3322
Findlay (G-6843)

Bob Sumerel Tire Co Inc...................... F 614 527-9700
Columbus (G-4768)

Bob Sumerel Tire Co Inc...................... G 740 432-5200
Lore City (G-8588)

Bob Sumerel Tire Company Inc............ G 740 927-2811
Reynoldsburg (G-11559)

Forklift Tire East Mich Inc.................... F 586 771-1330
Toledo (G-12967)

Gt Tire Service Inc.............................. G 740 927-7226
Pataskala (G-11139)

Victor Bodie Tire Co............................ G 216 431-1700
Cleveland (G-4471)

TIRES & TUBES, WHOLESALE: Automotive

AB Tire & Repair................................. G 440 543-2929
Chagrin Falls (G-2152)

PRODUCT

Associates Tire and Svc Inc.................... F 937 436-4692
Centerville (G-2129)

Bell Tire Co.. F 440 234-8022
Olmsted Falls (G-10937)

Best One Tire & Svc Lima Inc................ G 419 425-3322
Findlay (G-6843)

Best One Tire & Svc Lima Inc................ E 419 229-2380
Lima (G-8389)

Bkt USA Inc....................................... F 330 836-1090
Copley (G-5430)

Bob Sumerel Tire Co Inc..................... G 937 235-0062
Dayton (G-5681)

Bob Sumerel Tire Co Inc..................... G 740 432-5200
Lore City (G-8588)

Bob Sumerel Tire Co Inc..................... F 330 769-9092
Seville (G-11914)

Bob Sumerel Tire Co Inc..................... G 740 454-9728
Zanesville (G-14999)

Bob Sumerel Tire Company Inc........... G 740 927-2811
Reynoldsburg (G-11559)

Bowman Tire Repr Ctr Bxley LLC........... G 740 928-7000
Hebron (G-7609)

Boy-Rad Inc....................................... G 614 766-1228
Dublin (G-6283)

Bridgestone Ret Operations LLC........... G 740 592-3075
Athens (G-635)

Bridgestone Ret Operations LLC........... G 614 834-3672
Canal Winchester (G-1787)

Bridgestone Ret Operations LLC........... G 330 454-9478
Canton (G-1845)

Bridgestone Ret Operations LLC........... G 513 793-4550
Cincinnati (G-2424)

Bridgestone Ret Operations LLC........... G 513 677-5200
Cincinnati (G-2425)

Bridgestone Ret Operations LLC........... G 513 681-7682
Cincinnati (G-2426)

Bridgestone Ret Operations LLC........... G 440 842-3200
Cleveland (G-3436)

Bridgestone Ret Operations LLC........... G 440 461-4747
Cleveland (G-3437)

Bridgestone Ret Operations LLC........... G 216 229-2550
Cleveland (G-3438)

Bridgestone Ret Operations LLC........... G 216 382-8970
Cleveland (G-3439)

Bridgestone Ret Operations LLC........... F 614 864-3350
Columbus (G-4777)

Bridgestone Ret Operations LLC........... F 614 491-8062
Columbus (G-4778)

Bridgestone Ret Operations LLC........... G 614 224-4221
Columbus (G-4779)

Bridgestone Ret Operations LLC........... G 440 324-3327
Elyria (G-6504)

Bridgestone Ret Operations LLC........... G 440 365-8308
Elyria (G-6505)

Bridgestone Ret Operations LLC........... G 937 548-1197
Greenville (G-7336)

Bridgestone Ret Operations LLC........... G 513 868-7399
Hamilton (G-7473)

Bridgestone Ret Operations LLC........... G 330 673-1700
Kent (G-8020)

Bridgestone Ret Operations LLC........... F 440 299-6126
Mentor (G-9493)

Bridgestone Ret Operations LLC........... F 740 397-5601
Mount Vernon (G-10237)

Bridgestone Ret Operations LLC........... G 614 861-7994
Reynoldsburg (G-11560)

Bridgestone Ret Operations LLC........... G 419 625-6571
Sandusky (G-11823)

Bridgestone Ret Operations LLC........... F 937 325-4638
Springfield (G-12286)

Bridgestone Ret Operations LLC........... G 724 346-2621
Warren (G-13744)

Bridgestone Ret Operations LLC........... G 330 758-0921
Youngstown (G-14825)

Bridgestone Ret Operations LLC........... G 330 759-3697
Youngstown (G-14826)

C & F Tire & Truck Repair..................... G 419 526-1412
Ontario (G-10947)

Canton Bandag Co............................. G 330 454-3025
Canton (G-1853)

Capital Tire Inc.................................. E 330 364-4731
Toledo (G-12911)

Custom Recapping Inc......................... G 937 324-4331
Springfield (G-12297)

Exit 11 Truck Tire Service Inc................ G 330 659-6372
Richfield (G-11591)

Garro Tread Corporation....................... G 330 376-3125
Akron (G-156)

Goodyear Tire & Rubber Company....... F 419 643-8273
Beaverdam (G-1008)

Goodyear Tire & Rubber Company....... G 330 966-1274
Canton (G-1904)

Goodyear Tire & Rubber Company....... G 330 759-9343
Youngstown (G-14869)

Goodyear Tire & Rubber Company....... A 330 796-2121
Akron (G-164)

Grismer Tire Company......................... E 937 643-2526
Centerville (G-2132)

JTL Enterprises LLC........................... E 937 890-8189
Dayton (G-5832)

Mid America Tire of Hillsboro Inc........... E 937 393-3520
Hillsboro (G-7720)

Mid-Wood Inc.................................... F 419 257-3331
North Baltimore (G-10614)

Mitchell Bros Tire Rtread Svc................ G 740 353-1551
Portsmouth (G-11470)

Muskingum Tire Company Inc............... G 740 453-8473
Zanesville (G-15030)

Paul Shovlin..................................... G 330 757-0032
Youngstown (G-14915)

Q T Columbus LLC............................. G 800 758-2410
Columbus (G-5216)

QT Equipment Company....................... E 330 724-3055
Akron (G-272)

Randys Tire & Auto Repair Inc.............. G 419 562-2926
Bucyrus (G-1688)

Shrader Tire & Oil Inc.......................... G 419 420-8435
Perrysburg (G-11262)

Skaggs Trlr & Tire Repr Co Inc............. F 440 986-7470
Amherst (G-452)

Skinner Firestone Inc.......................... G 740 984-4247
Beverly (G-1209)

Snider Tire Inc.................................. F 740 439-2741
Cambridge (G-1760)

Sycamore Tire & Auto Repair................ G 513 793-0726
Cincinnati (G-3134)

Tbc Retail Group Inc.......................... E 216 267-8040
Cleveland (G-4365)

Urra Co Inc....................................... G 330 673-8473
Kent (G-8093)

Victor Bodie Tire Co........................... G 216 431-1700
Cleveland (G-4471)

Wayne A Whaley.................................. G 330 525-7779
Homeworth (G-7807)

Ziegler Tire and Supply Co................... G 330 434-7126
Akron (G-362)

Ziegler Tire and Supply Co................... G 330 477-3463
Canton (G-2052)

Ziegler Tire and Supply Co................... E 330 343-7739
Dover (G-6267)

TIRES: Plastic

Tire Tread Development Inc.................... E 330 628-5666
Mogadore (G-10089)

TOBACCO & TOBACCO PRDTS WHOLESALERS

Scandinavian Tob Group Ln Ltd............. C 770 934-4594
Akron (G-306)

TOBACCO: Chewing & Snuff

Smoke-Rings Inc................................ G 419 420-9966
Findlay (G-6921)

TOBACCO: Cigarettes

Discount Smokes & Gifts Xenia............. G 937 372-0259
Xenia (G-14763)

Memphis Smokehouse Inc.................... G 216 351-5321
Cleveland (G-4020)

TOBACCO: Smoking

Scandinavian Tob Group Ln Ltd............. C 770 934-4594
Akron (G-306)

TOILET PREPARATIONS

Barbasol LLC.................................... E 419 903-0738
Ashland (G-520)

Bocchi Laboratories Ohio LLC............... B 614 741-7458
New Albany (G-10332)

Procter & Gamble Far East Inc.............. C 513 983-1100
Cincinnati (G-3000)

Procter & Gamble Mfg Co..................... F 513 983-1100
Cincinnati (G-3002)

TOILETRIES, WHOLESALE: Hair Preparations

ICM Distributing Company Inc............... E 234 212-3030
Twinsburg (G-13319)

TOILETRIES, WHOLESALE: Perfumes

Beautyavenues LLC............................. F 614 856-6000
Reynoldsburg (G-11558)

TOILETRIES, WHOLESALE: Toiletries

Nehemiah Manufacturing Co LLC........... D 513 351-5700
Cincinnati (G-2897)

Walter F Stephens Jr Inc....................... E 937 746-0521
Franklin (G-7055)

TOOL & DIE STEEL

B & G Tool Company........................... G 614 451-2538
Columbus (G-4739)

Latrobe Specialty Mtls Co LLC............... E 419 335-8010
Wauseon (G-13854)

New Age Design & Tool Inc.................. G 440 355-5400
Lagrange (G-8152)

Nichidai America Corporation................ G 419 423-7511
Findlay (G-6898)

OReilly Precision Pdts Inc.................... E 937 526-4677
Russia (G-11676)

Quality Tool Company......................... E 419 476-8228
Toledo (G-13105)

R & D Machine Inc............................. F 937 339-2545
Troy (G-13248)

Robs Welding Technologies Ltd............. G 937 890-4963
Dayton (G-5987)

Seilkop Industries Inc........................ F 513 353-3090
Miamitown (G-9760)

TOOLS: Hand, Mechanics

S & H Industries Inc........................... E 216 831-0550
Cleveland (G-4266)

S & H Industries Inc........................... F 216 831-0550
Bedford (G-1058)

The Cornwell Quality Tools Company.... D 330 336-3506
Wadsworth (G-13674)

TOWELS: Fabric & Nonwoven, Made From Purchased Materials

Saturday Knight Ltd.............................D..... 513 641-1400
Cincinnati (G-3064)

TOWELS: Paper

Aci Industries Converting Ltd................F..... 740 368-4160
Delaware (G-6129)

TOWERS, SECTIONS: Transmission, Radio & Television

Warmus and Associates Inc...................G..... 330 659-4440
Bath (G-898)

TOWING SVCS: Marine

Great Lakes Group...............................C..... 216 621-4854
Cleveland (G-3792)

TOYS & HOBBY GOODS & SPLYS, WHOLESALE: Balloons, Novelty

Galaxy Balloons Incorporated................C..... 216 476-3360
Cleveland (G-3753)

TOYS & HOBBY GOODS & SPLYS, WHOLESALE: Toys & Games

Party Animal Inc..................................F..... 440 471-1030
Westlake (G-14320)

TOYS & HOBBY GOODS & SPLYS, WHOLESALE: Toys, NEC

Advance Novelty Incorporated...............G..... 419 424-0363
Findlay (G-6833)

ICM Distributing Company Inc...............E..... 234 212-3030
Twinsburg (G-13319)

TOYS: Rubber

Pioneer National Latex Inc.....................D..... 419 289-3300
Ashland (G-562)

Pioneer National Latex Inc.....................E..... 419 289-3300
Ashland (G-563)

TRADE SHOW ARRANGEMENT SVCS

Downing Enterprises Inc.......................D..... 330 666-3888
Akron (G-126)

Publishing Group Ltd............................F..... 614 572-1240
Columbus (G-5213)

TRAILERS & PARTS: Boat

Hitch-Hiker Mfg Inc.............................F..... 330 542-3052
New Middletown (G-10424)

Loadmaster Trailer Company Ltd...........F..... 419 732-3434
Port Clinton (G-11445)

TRAILERS & TRAILER EQPT

Hawkline Nevada LLC...........................G..... 937 444-4295
Mount Orab (G-10217)

Interstate Truckway Inc.........................F..... 614 771-1220
Columbus (G-5022)

Malabar...E..... 419 866-6301
Swanton (G-12687)

Otterbacher Trailers LLC.......................F..... 419 462-1975
Galion (G-7196)

Performance Tank Sales Inc...................G..... 330 602-8800
Dover (G-6258)

Prostar LLC...F..... 419 225-8806
Lima (G-8462)

Rankin Mfg Inc....................................G..... 419 929-8338
New London (G-10414)

TRAILERS: Semitrailers, Missile Transportation

Pdi Ground Support Systems Inc...........D..... 216 271-7344
Solon (G-12166)

TRAILERS: Semitrailers, Truck Tractors

4w Services...F..... 614 554-5427
Hebron (G-7606)

Nelson Manufacturing Company............D..... 419 523-5321
Ottawa (G-11039)

TRANSDUCERS: Electrical Properties

Dcm Soundex Inc.................................F..... 937 522-0371
Dayton (G-5744)

Ohio Semitronics Inc............................D..... 614 777-1005
Hilliard (G-7692)

TRANSDUCERS: Pressure

Honeywell International Inc....................E..... 302 327-8920
Columbus (G-4990)

Omega Engineering Inc.........................E..... 740 965-9340
Sunbury (G-12673)

Omegadyne Inc....................................D..... 740 965-9340
Sunbury (G-12674)

Sensotec LLC......................................G..... 614 481-8616
Hilliard (G-7701)

TRANSFORMERS: Distribution

Darrah Electric Company.......................F..... 216 631-0912
Chesterland (G-2233)

TRANSFORMERS: Distribution, Electric

Clark Substations LLC...........................G..... 330 452-5200
Canton (G-1868)

Tesa Inc..G..... 614 847-8200
Lewis Center (G-8355)

TRANSFORMERS: Instrument

Staco Energy Products Co.....................E..... 937 253-1191
Dayton (G-6020)

TRANSFORMERS: Specialty

LTI Power Systems Inc..........................E..... 440 327-5050
Elyria (G-6560)

TRANSFORMERS: Voltage Regulating

Transformer Associates Limited.............G..... 330 430-0750
Canton (G-2027)

TRANSMISSIONS: Motor Vehicle

Ada Technologies Inc............................C..... 419 634-7000
Ada (G-2)

Comprehensive Logistics Co Inc............E..... 440 934-3517
Avon (G-720)

Custom Cltch Jint Hydrlics Inc...............F..... 216 431-1630
Cleveland (G-3584)

FCA US LLC...B..... 419 661-3500
Perrysburg (G-11220)

Gear Star Amrcn Prfmce Trnsmss..........E..... 330 434-5216
Akron (G-157)

Modern Transmission Dev Co.................C
Valley City (G-13506)

RTC Converters Inc..............................F..... 937 743-2300
Franklin (G-7047)

TRANSPORTATION EQPT & SPLYS WHOLESALERS, NEC

American Power LLC.............................F..... 937 235-0418
Dayton (G-5654)

Dircksen and Associates Inc..................G..... 614 238-0413
Columbus (G-4881)

TRANSPORTATION SVCS, AIR, NONSCHEDULED: Air Cargo Carriers

Grand Aire Inc.....................................E..... 419 861-6700
Swanton (G-12684)

TRAVEL TRAILERS & CAMPERS

Airstream Inc.......................................B..... 937 596-6111
Jackson Center (G-7958)

ARE Inc..A..... 330 830-7800
Massillon (G-9172)

Capitol City Trailers Inc.........................D..... 614 491-2616
Obetz (G-10921)

Xtreme Outdoors LLC...........................E..... 330 731-4137
Uniontown (G-13429)

TROPHIES, NEC

Ginos Awards Inc.................................E..... 216 831-6565
Warrensville Heights (G-13818)

Tempo Manufacturing Company.............G..... 937 773-6613
Piqua (G-11387)

TROPHIES, WHOLESALE

Behrco Inc...G..... 419 394-1612
Saint Marys (G-11731)

Dern Trophies Corp..............................G..... 614 895-3260
Westerville (G-14207)

Sharonco Inc.......................................G..... 419 882-3443
Sylvania (G-12723)

TROPHIES: Metal, Exc Silver

Dern Trophies Corp..............................G..... 614 895-3260
Westerville (G-14207)

Hit Trophy Inc......................................G..... 419 445-5356
Archbold (G-498)

PS Superior Inc....................................G..... 216 587-1000
Cleveland (G-4204)

TRUCK & BUS BODIES: Cement Mixer

Kimble Mixer Company..........................D..... 330 308-6700
New Philadelphia (G-10453)

McNeilus Truck and Mfg Inc..................G..... 614 868-0760
Gahanna (G-7165)

TRUCK & BUS BODIES: Motor Vehicle, Specialty

Bush Specialty Vehicles Inc...................F..... 937 382-5502
Wilmington (G-14574)

Lifeline Mobile Inc................................D..... 614 497-8300
Columbus (G-5068)

Willard Machine & Welding Inc...............F..... 330 467-0642
Macedonia (G-8722)

TRUCK & BUS BODIES: Truck Beds

Zie Bart Rhino Linings Toledo.................G..... 419 841-2886
Toledo (G-13184)

TRUCK & BUS BODIES: Utility Truck

Custom Truck One Source LP.................D..... 330 409-7291
Canton (G-1874)

Q T Columbus LLC...............................G..... 800 758-2410
Columbus (G-5216)

QT Equipment Company........................E..... 330 724-3055
Akron (G-272)

TRUCK BODIES: Body Parts

ARE Inc..A..... 330 830-7800
Massillon (G-9172)

PRODUCT

Brothers Body and Eqp LLC.................. F 419 462-1975
Galion *(G-7180)*

Cota International Inc............................... G 937 526-5520
Versailles *(G-13593)*

Crane Carrier Company LLC................... C 918 286-2889
New Philadelphia *(G-10440)*

Crane Carrier Holdings LLC.................. C 918 286-2889
New Philadelphia *(G-10441)*

Dan Patrick Enterprises Inc.................... G 740 477-1006
Circleville *(G-3253)*

H & H Truck Parts LLC........................... E 216 642-4540
Cleveland *(G-3804)*

Kaffenbarger Truck Eqp Co................... E 513 772-6800
Cincinnati *(G-2777)*

Kimble Custom Chassis Company........ D 877 546-2537
New Philadelphia *(G-10452)*

Mancor Ohio Inc..................................... C 937 228-6141
Dayton *(G-5867)*

Mancor Ohio Inc..................................... E 937 228-6141
Dayton *(G-5866)*

Sutphen Towers Inc................................ D 614 876-1262
Hilliard *(G-7704)*

TRUCK BODY SHOP

Q T Columbus LLC................................. G 800 758-2410
Columbus *(G-5216)*

QT Equipment Company......................... E 330 724-3055
Akron *(G-272)*

TRUCK GENERAL REPAIR SVC

Dan Patrick Enterprises Inc.................... G 740 477-1006
Circleville *(G-3253)*

Knippen Chrysler Ddge Jeep Inc........... F 419 695-4976
Delphos *(G-6188)*

M & W Trailers Inc.................................. F 419 453-3331
Ottoville *(G-11055)*

TRUCK PARTS & ACCESSORIES:
Wholesalers

Adelmans Truck Parts Corp.................... E 330 456-0206
Canton *(G-1823)*

Buyers Products Company...................... C 440 974-8888
Mentor *(G-9496)*

Crane Carrier Company LLC................... C 918 286-2889
New Philadelphia *(G-10440)*

Crane Carrier Holdings LLC.................. C 918 286-2889
New Philadelphia *(G-10441)*

Dan Patrick Enterprises Inc.................... G 740 477-1006
Circleville *(G-3253)*

East Trailers LLC................................... E 330 325-9921
Randolph *(G-11510)*

Kaffenbarger Truck Eqp Co................... C 937 845-3804
New Carlisle *(G-10373)*

Malone Specialty Inc.............................. F 440 255-4200
Mentor *(G-9559)*

Mytee Products Inc................................ D 888 705-8277
Solon *(G-12156)*

Perkins Motor Service Ltd....................... F 440 277-1256
Lorain *(G-8573)*

Youngstown-Kenworth Inc...................... F 330 534-9761
Hubbard *(G-7819)*

TRUCKING & HAULING SVCS: Contract
Basis

Kmj Leasing Ltd...................................... G 614 871-3883
Orient *(G-10971)*

TRUCKING & HAULING SVCS: Lumber &
Log, Local

Dale R Adkins.. G 740 682-7312
Oak Hill *(G-10887)*

TRUCKING: Except Local

American Power LLC............................... F 937 235-0418
Dayton *(G-5654)*

Barrett Paving Materials Inc................... E 973 533-1001
Hamilton *(G-7468)*

Bc Investment Corporation..................... C 330 262-3070
Wooster *(G-14625)*

Buckeye Energy Resources Inc.............. G 740 452-9506
Zanesville *(G-15001)*

Chagrin Vly Stl Erectors Inc................... F 440 975-1556
Willoughby Hills *(G-14557)*

Custom Built Crates Inc......................... E
Milford *(G-9932)*

Euclid Chemical Company...................... E 800 321-7628
Cleveland *(G-3688)*

Mpi Logistics and Service Inc................. E 330 832-5309
Massillon *(G-9225)*

Parobek Trucking Co.............................. G 419 869-7500
West Salem *(G-14189)*

Sandwisch Enterprises Inc..................... G 419 944-6446
Toledo *(G-13121)*

Shawn Fleming Ind Trckg LLC............... G 937 707-8539
Dayton *(G-6002)*

Tk Gas Services Inc............................... E 740 826-0303
New Concord *(G-10387)*

TRUCKING: Local, With Storage

M G Q Inc... E 419 992-4236
Tiffin *(G-12788)*

Resource Recycling Inc.......................... F 419 222-2702
Lima *(G-8444)*

TRUCKING: Local, Without Storage

Corbett R Caudill Chipping Inc............... G 740 596-5984
Hamden *(G-7461)*

Demilta Sand and Gravel Inc.................. F 440 942-2015
Willoughby *(G-14446)*

Hershberger Manufacturing..................... E 440 272-5555
Windsor *(G-14601)*

M & R Redi Mix Inc................................ E 419 445-7771
Pettisville *(G-11284)*

Mm Outsourcing LLC.............................. F 937 661-4300
Leesburg *(G-8300)*

Parobek Trucking Co.............................. G 419 869-7500
West Salem *(G-14189)*

Rjw Trucking Company Ltd..................... G 740 363-5343
Delaware *(G-6169)*

S&M Trucking LLC.................................. F 661 310-2585
Mason *(G-9146)*

Shawn Fleming Ind Trckg LLC............... G 937 707-8539
Dayton *(G-6002)*

Tk Gas Services Inc............................... E 740 826-0303
New Concord *(G-10387)*

Ward Construction Co............................. F 419 943-2450
Leipsic *(G-8316)*

Wooster Abruzzi Company...................... E 330 345-3968
Wooster *(G-14698)*

TRUCKS & TRACTORS: Industrial

Back In Black Co.................................... E 419 425-5555
Findlay *(G-6839)*

Canton Elevator Inc................................ D 330 833-3600
North Canton *(G-10632)*

City Machine Technologies Inc............... F 330 747-2639
Youngstown *(G-14836)*

Crescent Metal Products Inc................... C 440 350-1100
Mentor *(G-9507)*

Crown Equipment Corporation................ A 419 629-2311
New Bremen *(G-10358)*

Dragon Products LLC............................. E 330 345-3968
Wooster *(G-14635)*

Eagle Industrial Truck Mfg LLC.............. E 419 866-6301
Swanton *(G-12683)*

Enviri Corporation.................................. F 740 387-1150
Marion *(G-8969)*

Forte Industrial Equipment Systems Inc E 513 398-2800
Mason *(G-9100)*

G & T Manufacturing Co......................... F 440 639-7777
Mentor *(G-9522)*

General Electric Company....................... E 513 977-1500
Cincinnati *(G-2662)*

Gradall Industries LLC........................... D 330 339-2211
New Philadelphia *(G-10448)*

Grand Harbor Yacht Sales & Svc........... G 440 442-2919
Cleveland *(G-3784)*

Hobart Brothers LLC............................... A 937 332-5439
Troy *(G-13222)*

Jh Industries Inc.................................... E 330 963-4105
Twinsburg *(G-13321)*

Lane Field Materials Inc......................... E 330 526-8082
Canton *(G-1930)*

Lange Precision Inc................................ F 513 530-9500
Lebanon *(G-8273)*

Macton Corporation................................ D 330 259-8555
Youngstown *(G-14892)*

Miller Products Inc................................. E 330 308-5934
New Philadelphia *(G-10458)*

Miners Tractor Sales Inc......................... F 330 325-9914
Rootstown *(G-11649)*

Mitchs Welding & Hitches....................... G 419 893-3117
Maumee *(G-9311)*

Parobek Trucking Co.............................. G 419 869-7500
West Salem *(G-14189)*

Perfecto Industries Inc........................... E 937 778-1900
Piqua *(G-11372)*

Pollock Research & Design Inc............... E 330 332-3300
Salem *(G-11805)*

Pucel Enterprises Inc............................. D 216 881-4604
Cleveland *(G-4206)*

Saf-Holland Inc...................................... G 513 874-7888
Fairfield *(G-6773)*

Stock Fairfield Corporation..................... C 440 543-6000
Solon *(G-12185)*

Sweet Manufacturing Company.............. E 937 325-1511
Springfield *(G-12381)*

Tarpco Inc.. F 330 677-8277
Kent *(G-8086)*

Trailer Component Mfg Inc..................... E 440 255-2888
Mentor *(G-9640)*

Uhrden Inc.. E 330 456-0031
Canton *(G-2030)*

Volens LLC.. G 216 544-1200
Macedonia *(G-8721)*

Waltco Lift Corp...................................... C 330 633-9191
Streetsboro *(G-12530)*

Youngstown-Kenworth Inc...................... F 330 534-9761
Hubbard *(G-7819)*

TRUCKS: Forklift

Forklift Solutions LLC............................ G 419 717-9496
Napoleon *(G-10279)*

Hyster-Yale Inc...................................... C 440 449-9600
Cleveland *(G-3847)*

Marlow-2000 Inc..................................... F 216 362-8500
Cleveland *(G-3991)*

TRUCKS: Indl

ADSr Ent LLC... F 773 280-2129
Columbus *(G-4674)*

All Around Primo Logistics LLC............. G 513 725-7888
Cincinnati *(G-2347)*

Elliott Machine Works Inc.................. E 419 468-4709
Galion *(G-7189)*

Express Ground Services Inc................ G 216 870-9374
Cleveland *(G-3700)*

Grand Aire Inc.................................... E 419 861-6700
Swanton *(G-12684)*

Load32 LLC... F 614 984-6648
Columbus *(G-5072)*

Op Dawg Logistics LLC..................... E ... 937 844-3135
Dayton *(G-5928)*

Ready Rigs LLC.................................. F 740 963-9203
Reynoldsburg *(G-11579)*

S&M Trucking LLC............................. F 661 310-2585
Mason *(G-9146)*

Sb Trans LLC...................................... F 407 477-2545
Cincinnati *(G-3066)*

Sher International Inc........................ F 800 895-9581
Middletown *(G-9893)*

Surplus Freight Inc............................ G 614 235-7660
Gahanna *(G-7171)*

Tbt Hauling LLC................................. G 904 635-7631
Bowling Green *(G-1441)*

Triumphant Enterprises Inc.............. G 513 617-1668
Goshen *(G-7298)*

Truckcorp LLC.................................... D 234 666-5702
Canton *(G-2029)*

TRUSSES & FRAMING: Prefabricated Metal

C Green & Sons Incorporated............... F 740 745-2998
Saint Louisville *(G-11728)*

Jentgen Steel Services LLC.................. F 614 268-6340
Columbus *(G-5037)*

Shrock Prefab LLC............................. E 419 994-1900
Loudonville *(G-8594)*

TRUSSES: Wood, Floor

Khempco Bldg Sup Co Ltd Partnr.......... D 740 549-0465
Delaware *(G-6159)*

TUBES: Paper

Ohio Paper Tube Co............................ E 330 478-5171
Canton *(G-1967)*

Precision Products Group Inc............. G 330 698-4711
Apple Creek *(G-475)*

Sonoco Products Company.................. E 937 429-0040
Beavercreek Township *(G-1006)*

TUBES: Steel & Iron

Crest Bending Inc............................... E 419 492-2108
New Washington *(G-10478)*

Kirtland Capital Partners LP............... E 216 593-0100
Beachwood *(G-924)*

Nanogate North America LLC.............. B 419 747-1096
Mansfield *(G-8835)*

Phillips Mfg and Tower Co................. D 419 347-1720
Shelby *(G-11972)*

Universal Metals Cutting Inc.............. G 330 580-5192
Canton *(G-2038)*

TUBES: Wrought, Welded Or Lock Joint

Lsp Tubes Inc..................................... D 216 378-2092
Orwell *(G-11024)*

Tubetech Inc....................................... E 330 426-9476
East Palestine *(G-6409)*

United Tube Corporation.................... D 330 725-4196
Medina *(G-9461)*

TUBING: Copper

Arem Co.. G 440 974-6740
Willoughby *(G-14426)*

TUBING: Flexible, Metallic

Lincoln Electric Automtn Inc................. B 937 295-2120
Fort Loramie *(G-6950)*

Tubular Techniques Inc..................... G 614 529-4130
Hilliard *(G-7708)*

TUBING: Glass

Glasstech Inc..................................... C 419 661-9500
Perrysburg *(G-11226)*

Techneglas Inc................................... E 419 873-2000
Perrysburg *(G-11267)*

TUBING: Rubber

Eagle Elastomer Inc........................... E 330 923-7070
Peninsula *(G-11182)*

First Brnds Group Holdings LLC........... E 216 589-0198
Cleveland *(G-3719)*

First Brnds Group Intrmdate LL........... F 216 589-0198
Cleveland *(G-3720)*

Meridian Industries Inc....................... D 330 673-1011
Kent *(G-8051)*

Meridian Industries Inc....................... D 330 359-5447
Winesburg *(G-14607)*

Meteor Sealing Systems LLC.............. C 330 343-9595
Dover *(G-6253)*

Trico Products Corporation................. C 800 388-7428
Cleveland *(G-4425)*

TUGBOAT SVCS

Shelly Materials Inc............................ F 740 247-2311
Racine *(G-11506)*

Shelly Materials Inc............................ D 740 246-6315
Thornville *(G-12770)*

The Great Lakes Towing Company........ D 216 621-4854
Cleveland *(G-4383)*

TURBINES & TURBINE GENERATOR SETS

Alin Machining Company Inc................. D 740 223-0200
Marion *(G-8964)*

Babcock & Wilcox Company................. E 740 687-6500
Lancaster *(G-8178)*

Babcock & Wilcox Entps Inc................ E 740 687-4370
Lancaster *(G-8179)*

Babcock & Wilcox Holdings LLC........... A 330 453-4511
Akron *(G-69)*

Bwx Technologies Inc......................... D 740 687-4180
Lancaster *(G-8183)*

Canvus Inc.. E 216 340-7500
Rocky River *(G-11632)*

Diamond Power Intl Inc....................... D 740 687-6500
Lancaster *(G-8198)*

Eaton Leasing Corporation.................. B 216 382-2292
Beachwood *(G-916)*

Fluidpower Assembly Inc..................... G 419 394-7486
Saint Marys *(G-11737)*

Great Lakes Turbines Inc................... G 419 705-0490
Holland *(G-7765)*

Mendenhall Technical Services Inc........ E 513 860-1280
Fairfield *(G-6754)*

Metalex Manufacturing Inc.................. C 513 489-0507
Blue Ash *(G-1310)*

Miba Bearings US LLC......................... B 740 962-4242
Mcconnelsville *(G-9364)*

Pfpc Enterprises Inc........................... G 513 941-6200
Cincinnati *(G-2960)*

Powder Alloy Corporation.................... E 513 984-4016
Loveland *(G-8646)*

Precision Castparts Corp.................... F 440 350-6150
Painesville *(G-11106)*

R H Industries Inc.............................. E 216 281-5210
Cleveland *(G-4221)*

Rolls-Royce Energy Systems Inc........... A 703 834-1700
Mount Vernon *(G-10263)*

TURBINES: Gas, Mechanical Drive

Onpower Inc.. E 513 228-2100
Lebanon *(G-8280)*

TURBINES: Hydraulic, Complete

Fluid System Service Inc..................... G 216 651-2450
Cleveland *(G-3728)*

TURBINES: Steam

Siemens Energy Inc............................ G 740 504-1947
Mount Vernon *(G-10265)*

Steam Trbine Altrntive Rsrces............. E 740 387-5535
Marion *(G-9001)*

TYPESETTING SVC

A-A Blueprint Co Inc.......................... E 330 794-8803
Akron *(G-10)*

Activities Press Inc............................ E 440 953-1200
Mentor *(G-9469)*

AGS Custom Graphics Inc................... D 330 963-7770
Macedonia *(G-8676)*

American Printing & Lithog Co............. F 513 867-0602
Hamilton *(G-7463)*

Anderson Graphics Inc....................... E 330 745-2165
Barberton *(G-793)*

Andrin Enterprises Inc....................... F 937 276-7794
Moraine *(G-10146)*

Asist Translation Services................... F 614 451-6744
Columbus *(G-4729)*

Baesman Group Inc............................. D 614 771-2300
Hilliard *(G-7674)*

Bindery & Spc Pressworks Inc............. D 614 873-4623
Plain City *(G-11398)*

Black River Group Inc......................... E 419 524-6699
Mansfield *(G-8765)*

Blt Inc.. F 513 631-5050
Norwood *(G-10866)*

Bookmasters Inc.................................. C 419 281-1802
Ashland *(G-522)*

Brass Bull 1 LLC................................. G 740 335-8030
Wshngtn Ct Hs *(G-14735)*

Carlisle Prtg Walnut Creek Ltd............. E 330 852-9922
Sugarcreek *(G-12635)*

Characters Inc.................................... G 937 335-1976
Troy *(G-13204)*

Clints Printing Inc.............................. G 937 426-2771
Dayton *(G-5703)*

Colortech Graphics & Printing.............. F 614 766-2400
Columbus *(G-4816)*

Consoldated Graphics Group Inc.......... C 216 881-9191
Cleveland *(G-3559)*

Copley Ohio Newspapers Inc................ C 330 364-5577
New Philadelphia *(G-10439)*

COS Blueprint Inc............................... E 330 376-0022
Akron *(G-107)*

Crossbridge Mktg & Media Inc.............. G 330 682-5066
Orrville *(G-10979)*

Daubenmires Printing Co LLC.............. G 513 425-7223
Middletown *(G-9853)*

Davis Printing Company...................... E 330 745-3113
Barberton *(G-803)*

Dayton Legal Blank Inc...................... G 937 435-4405
Dayton *(G-5729)*

Earl D Arnold Printing Company............ E 513 533-6900
Cincinnati *(G-2574)*

Eugene Stewart.................................. G 937 898-1117
Dayton *(G-5770)*

Franklin Printing Company.................. F 740 452-6375
Zanesville *(G-15016)*

Employee Codes: A=Over 500 employees, B=251-500
C=101-250, D=51-100, E=20-50, F=10-19, G=1-9

2025 Harris Ohio
Industrial Directory

1401

PRODUCT

Gazette Publishing Company.................. E 419 483-4190
Oberlin (G-10917)

Greg Blume.. G 740 574-2308
Wheelersburg (G-14353)

Harlan Graphic Arts Svcs Inc.............. E 513 251-5700
Cincinnati (G-2706)

Hecks Direct Mail Prtg Svc Inc.......... F 419 697-3505
Toledo (G-12990)

Hkm Drect Mkt Cmmnications Inc......... C 800 860-4456
Cleveland (G-3832)

HP Industries Inc................................... E 419 478-0695
Toledo (G-12997)

Hubbard Publishing Co........................ G 937 592-3060
Bellefontaine (G-1110)

Imprints.. F 330 650-0467
Hudson (G-7846)

Jack Walker Printing Co........................ F 440 352-4222
Mentor (G-9540)

Keener Printing Inc............................... G 216 531-7595
Cleveland (G-3911)

Kehl-Kolor Inc.. E 419 281-3107
Ashland (G-545)

Kevin K Tidd.. G 419 885-5603
Sylvania (G-12714)

Keystone Press Inc............................... G 419 243-7326
Toledo (G-13018)

Laurenee Ltd... G 513 662-2225
Cincinnati (G-2814)

Lee Corporation..................................... G 513 771-3602
Cincinnati (G-2817)

Legal News Publishing Co.................... E 216 696-3322
Cleveland (G-3949)

Liming Printing Inc................................ F 937 374-2646
Xenia (G-14769)

Middleton Printing Co Inc.................... G 614 294-7277
Gahanna (G-7166)

Mmp Printing Inc.................................... F 513 381-0990
Cincinnati (G-2883)

Multi-Craft Litho Inc............................. E 859 581-2754
Blue Ash (G-1312)

Network Printing & Graphics................. F 614 230-2084
Columbus (G-5124)

Old Trail Printing Company................. C 614 443-4852
Columbus (G-5159)

Onetouchpoint East Corp.................... D 513 421-1600
Cincinnati (G-2933)

Orange Blossom Press Inc.................. G 216 781-8655
Willoughby (G-14502)

Painesville Publishing Inc.................... G 440 354-4142
Austinburg (G-701)

Penguin Enterprises Inc....................... E 440 899-5112
Westlake (G-14322)

Preisser Inc... G 614 345-0199
Columbus (G-5203)

Prime Printing Inc................................. E 937 438-3707
Dayton (G-5956)

Printed Image... F 614 221-1412
Columbus (G-5207)

Printing Arts Press Inc........................ F 740 397-6106
Mount Vernon (G-10260)

Progrssive Communications Corp........ F 740 397-5333
Mount Vernon (G-10261)

Quick Tab II Inc.................................... D 419 448-6622
Tiffin (G-12796)

Quick Tech Graphics Inc..................... F 937 743-5952
Springboro (G-12266)

Robin Enterprises Company................ C 614 891-0250
Westerville (G-14274)

Royal Acme Corporation....................... E 216 241-1477
Cleveland (G-4256)

RR Donnelley & Sons Company........... G 614 221-8385
Columbus (G-5237)

Ryans Newark Leader Ex Prtg Co........... F 740 522-2149
Newark (G-10532)

St Media Group Intl Inc........................ D 513 421-2050
Blue Ash (G-1332)

Standard Printing Co of Canton........... D 330 453-8247
Canton (G-2012)

Suburban Press Incorporated............... F 216 961-0766
Cleveland (G-4340)

The Photo-Type Engraving Company.... D 513 281-0999
Cincinnati (G-3149)

Watkins Printing Company.................... E 614 297-8270
Columbus (G-5358)

West-Camp Press Inc.......................... D 614 882-2378
Westerville (G-14281)

Western Roto Engravers Inc................. E 330 336-7636
Wadsworth (G-13677)

Wfsr Holdings LLC................................ A 877 735-4966
Dayton (G-6081)

Winkler Co Inc....................................... G 937 294-2662
Dayton (G-6082)

Workflowone LLC.................................. A 877 735-4966
Dayton (G-6087)

TYPESETTING SVC: Computer

Heritage Press Inc................................ E 419 289-9209
Ashland (G-539)

Wolters Kluwer Clinical Dru.................. D 330 650-6506
Hudson (G-7862)

UNIFORM SPLY SVCS: Indl

Cintas Corporation................................ D 513 631-5750
Cincinnati (G-2494)

Cintas Corporation................................ A 513 459-1200
Mason (G-9086)

Cintas Sales Corporation..................... B 513 459-1200
Cincinnati (G-2495)

UNIFORM STORES

K Ventures Inc....................................... F 419 678-2308
Coldwater (G-4579)

Kip-Craft Incorporated.......................... D 216 898-5500
Cleveland (G-3924)

The Fechheimer Brothers Co................ C 513 793-5400
Blue Ash (G-1342)

UNSUPPORTED PLASTICS: Floor Or Wall Covering

Rjf International Corporation................. A 330 668-2069
Fairlawn (G-6809)

UPHOLSTERY WORK SVCS

Casco Mfg Solutions Inc...................... D 513 681-0003
Cincinnati (G-2441)

URANIUM ORE MINING, NEC

Centrus Energy Corp............................ D 740 897-2217
Piketon (G-11306)

USED CAR DEALERS

Cars and Parts Magazine...................... D 937 498-0803
Sidney (G-12001)

Dawn Enterprises Inc........................... E 216 642-5506
Cleveland (G-3601)

Knippen Chrysler Ddge Jeep Inc........... F 419 695-4976
Delphos (G-6188)

Suburbanite Inc.................................... G 419 756-4390
Mansfield (G-8856)

United Ignition Wire Corp...................... G 216 898-1112
Cleveland (G-4443)

UTENSILS: Cast Aluminum, Cooking Or Kitchen

Range Kleen Mfg Inc............................. B 419 331-8000
Elida (G-6487)

UTILITY TRAILER DEALERS

M R Trailer Sales Inc............................ G 330 339-7701
New Philadelphia (G-10456)

OReilly Equipment LLC........................ G 440 564-1234
Newbury (G-10559)

VACUUM CLEANERS: Indl Type

HI-Vac Corporation................................ C 740 374-2306
Marietta (G-8923)

VALUE-ADDED RESELLERS: Computer Systems

Sutter Llc.. F 513 891-2261
Blue Ash (G-1339)

VALVES

Aswpengg LLC....................................... F 216 292-4620
Bedford Heights (G-1069)

Brooks Manufacturing............................ G 419 244-1777
Toledo (G-12905)

Buckeye BOP LLC.................................. F 740 498-9898
Newcomerstown (G-10569)

Valv-Trol LLC... F 330 686-2800
Stow (G-12469)

VALVES & PARTS: Gas, Indl

Honeywell International Inc................... A 937 484-2000
Urbana (G-13466)

VALVES & PIPE FITTINGS

Alloy Precision Tech Inc....................... D 440 266-7700
Mentor (G-9477)

Anchor Flange Company....................... D 513 527-3512
Cincinnati (G-2369)

Bay Corporation.................................... E 440 835-2212
Westlake (G-14290)

Bowden Manufacturing Corp................. E 440 946-1770
Willoughby (G-14432)

Bowes Manufacturing Inc..................... F 216 378-2110
Solon (G-12087)

Calvin J Magsig.................................... G 419 862-3311
Elmore (G-6488)

Crane Pumps & Systems Inc................ F 937 773-2442
Piqua (G-11340)

Cylinders and Valves Inc...................... G 440 238-7343
Strongsville (G-12552)

Eaton Corporation................................. E 330 274-0743
Aurora (G-667)

Edward W Daniel LLC........................... F 440 647-1960
Wellington (G-13885)

Fcx Performance Inc............................. E 614 253-1996
Columbus (G-4922)

H P E Inc... G 330 833-3161
Massillon (G-9199)

H-P Products Inc................................... C 330 875-5556
Louisville (G-8602)

Kirtland Capital Partners LP................. E 216 593-0100
Beachwood (G-924)

Knappco Corporation............................ C 513 870-3100
Hamilton (G-7509)

Lsq Manufacturing Inc.......................... F 330 725-4905
Medina (G-9421)

Mack Iron Works Company.................... E 419 626-3712
Sandusky (G-11855)

Northcoast Valve and Gate Inc.............. G 440 392-9910
   Mentor *(G-9573)*

Nupro Company.................................. E 440 951-9729
   Willoughby *(G-14498)*

Opw Engineered Systems Inc.............. E 888 771-9438
   West Chester *(G-14039)*

Pima Valve LLC................................ D 330 337-9535
   Salem *(G-11804)*

Precision McHning Cnnction LLC........ F 440 943-3300
   Wickliffe *(G-14392)*

Pressure Connections Corp.............. D 614 863-6930
   Columbus *(G-5204)*

Robeck Fluid Power Co..................... D 330 562-1140
   Aurora *(G-687)*

Ruthman Pump and Engineering.......... G 937 783-2411
   Blanchester *(G-1238)*

Spirex Corporation........................... C 330 726-1166
   Youngstown *(G-14938)*

Stelter and Brinck Inc...................... E 513 367-9300
   Harrison *(G-7569)*

Stephens Pipe & Steel LLC................ C 740 869-2257
   Mount Sterling *(G-10229)*

Superior Holding LLC....................... G 216 651-9400
   Cleveland *(G-4344)*

Superior Products LLC..................... D 216 651-9400
   Cleveland *(G-4347)*

Swagelok Company........................... F 440 442-6611
   Cleveland *(G-4355)*

Swagelok Company........................... D 440 349-5934
   Solon *(G-12191)*

The Sheffer Corporation.................... D 513 489-9770
   Cincinnati *(G-3150)*

Thogus Products Company................ D 440 933-8850
   Avon Lake *(G-771)*

Tylok International Inc...................... D 216 261-7310
   Cleveland *(G-4436)*

Waxman Industries Inc..................... C 440 439-1830
   Bedford *(G-1065)*

William Powell Company................... D 513 852-2000
   Cincinnati *(G-3224)*

Xomox Pft Corp............................... B 936 271-6500
   Cincinnati *(G-3238)*

VALVES & REGULATORS: Pressure, Indl

Rogers Industrial Products Inc.............. E 330 535-3331
   Akron *(G-290)*

Swagelok Company........................... G 440 248-4600
   Solon *(G-12187)*

Swagelok Company........................... E 440 349-5652
   Solon *(G-12189)*

Swagelok Company........................... E 440 349-5836
   Solon *(G-12190)*

Swagelok Company........................... E 440 248-4600
   Willoughby Hills *(G-14564)*

Swagelok Company........................... A 440 248-4600
   Solon *(G-12188)*

Tylok International Inc...................... D 216 261-7310
   Cleveland *(G-4436)*

William Powell Company................... D 513 852-2000
   Cincinnati *(G-3224)*

VALVES: Aerosol, Metal

Accurate Mechanical Inc.................... D 740 681-1332
   Lancaster *(G-8174)*

Jfdb Ltd... C 513 870-0601
   Cincinnati *(G-2766)*

VALVES: Aircraft, Control, Hydraulic & Pneumatic

Eaton Corporation............................ B 440 523-5000
   Cleveland *(G-3652)*

VALVES: Aircraft, Fluid Power

Malabar... E 419 866-6301
   Swanton *(G-12687)*

Taiyo America Inc.............................. F 419 300-8811
   Saint Marys *(G-11753)*

VALVES: Aircraft, Hydraulic

Aerocontrolex Group Inc................... D 216 291-6025
   South Euclid *(G-12216)*

Hydraulic Manifolds USA LLC............. E 973 728-1214
   Stow *(G-12436)*

Parker-Hannifin Corporation.............. D 419 542-6611
   Hicksville *(G-7650)*

VALVES: Control, Automatic

Flow Technology Inc........................ G 513 745-6000
   Cincinnati *(G-2629)*

Superb Industries Inc....................... D 330 852-0500
   Sugarcreek *(G-12652)*

VALVES: Electrohydraulic Servo, Metal

Pioneer Solutions LLC...................... E 216 383-3400
   Euclid *(G-6669)*

VALVES: Fluid Power, Control, Hydraulic & pneumatic

Dana Limited................................... B 419 887-3000
   Maumee *(G-9282)*

DNC Hydraulics LLC......................... F 419 963-2800
   Rawson *(G-11551)*

Hunt Valve Company Inc................... D 330 337-9535
   Salem *(G-11788)*

Hy-Production LLC............................ C 330 273-2400
   Valley City *(G-13499)*

Hydrotech Inc.................................. D 888 651-5712
   West Chester *(G-14126)*

National Aviation Products Inc............. G 330 688-6494
   Stow *(G-12444)*

National Machine Company................ C 330 688-6494
   Stow *(G-12446)*

Parker-Hannifin Corporation.............. A 216 896-3000
   Cleveland *(G-4143)*

SMC Corporation of America............. F 330 659-2006
   Richfield *(G-11601)*

The Sheffer Corporation.................... D 513 489-9770
   Cincinnati *(G-3150)*

Valv-Trol LLC................................... F 330 686-2800
   Stow *(G-12469)*

VALVES: Gas Cylinder, Compressed

Kaplan Industries Inc....................... D 856 779-8181
   Harrison *(G-7558)*

VALVES: Indl

4matic Valve Automtn Ohio LLC........... F 614 806-1221
   Columbus *(G-4653)*

Alkon Corporation........................... F 614 799-6650
   Dublin *(G-6274)*

Bosch Rexroth Corporation............... C 330 263-3300
   Wooster *(G-14627)*

Curtiss-Wright Flow Ctrl Corp............. E 440 838-7690
   Brecksville *(G-1461)*

Maass Midwest Mfg Inc..................... G 419 894-6424
   Arcadia *(G-482)*

Meador Supply Company Inc............. F 330 405-4403
   Walton Hills *(G-13700)*

Nupro Company.............................. E 440 951-9729
   Willoughby *(G-14498)*

Parker-Hannifin Corporation.............. D 419 542-6611
   Hicksville *(G-7650)*

Parker-Hannifin Corporation.............. E 937 644-3915
   Marysville *(G-9041)*

Pima Valve LLC................................ D 330 337-9535
   Salem *(G-11804)*

Richards Industrials Inc.................... D 513 533-5600
   Cincinnati *(G-3044)*

Ruthman Pump and Engineering.......... G 937 783-2411
   Blanchester *(G-1238)*

Seawin Inc...................................... D 419 355-9111
   Fremont *(G-7132)*

Sherwood Valve LLC........................ E 216 264-5023
   Cleveland *(G-4296)*

Valv-Trol LLC................................... F 330 686-2800
   Stow *(G-12469)*

Vickers International Inc.................... G 419 867-2200
   Maumee *(G-9329)*

Watts Water..................................... F 614 491-5143
   Groveport *(G-7457)*

Waxman Industries Inc..................... C 440 439-1830
   Bedford *(G-1065)*

VALVES: Plumbing & Heating

Xomox Corporation........................... E 936 271-6500
   Cincinnati *(G-3237)*

VALVES: Regulating, Process Control

Akron Steel Fabricators Co................ E 330 644-0616
   Akron *(G-42)*

Clark-Reliance LLC........................... C 440 572-1500
   Strongsville *(G-12550)*

Hearth Products Controls Co............. F 937 436-9800
   Miamisburg *(G-9697)*

Xomox Corporation........................... G 513 745-6000
   Blue Ash *(G-1355)*

Xomox Pft Corp............................... B 936 271-6500
   Cincinnati *(G-3238)*

VAN CONVERSIONS

Mobile Conversions Inc.................... F 513 797-1991
   Amelia *(G-434)*

National Fleet Svcs Ohio LLC............. F 440 930-5177
   Avon *(G-766)*

Steves Vans ACC Unlimited LLC.......... G 740 374-3154
   Marietta *(G-8950)*

VARNISHES, NEC

David E Easterday and Co Inc............. F 330 359-0700
   Wilmot *(G-14594)*

Superior Printing Ink Co Inc.............. G 216 328-1720
   Cleveland *(G-4346)*

VAULTS & SAFES WHOLESALERS

McIntosh Safe Corp.......................... F 937 222-7008
   Dayton *(G-5871)*

VEHICLES: Recreational

Bulk Carriers Service Inc.................. G 330 339-3333
   New Philadelphia *(G-10435)*

L & R Racing Inc.............................. E 330 220-3102
   Brunswick *(G-1601)*

Rv Xpress Inc.................................. G 937 418-0127
   Piqua *(G-11383)*

VENDING MACHINE REPAIR SVCS

Superior Soda Service LLC................ G 937 657-9700
   Beavercreek *(G-996)*

VENDING MACHINES & PARTS

Best Result Marketing Inc................. G 234 212-1194
   Bedford *(G-1017)*

Five Star Healthy Vending LLC............. F 330 549-6011
   Akron *(G-149)*

Employee Codes: A=Over 500 employees, B=251-500
C=101-250, D=51-100, E=20-50, F=10-19, G=1-9

2025 Harris Ohio
Industrial Directory

1403

PRODUCT

Giant Industries Inc.................................E 419 531-4600
Toledo *(G-12975)*

Gold Medal Products Co............................B 513 769-7676
Cincinnati *(G-2680)*

Innovative Vend Solutions LLC..............F 866 931-9413
Dayton *(G-5822)*

Securastock LLC.......................................E 844 732-8727
Cleveland *(G-4284)*

Ve Global Vending Inc...........................G 216 785-2611
Cleveland *(G-4459)*

VENTILATING EQPT: Metal

Famous Industries Inc.............................E 330 535-1811
Akron *(G-145)*

VENTILATING EQPT: Sheet Metal

Venti-Now...F 513 334-3375
Montgomery *(G-10125)*

VENTURE CAPITAL COMPANIES

Brain Brew Ventures 30 Inc...................F 513 310-6374
Newtown *(G-10583)*

Linsalata Cpitl Prtners Fund I...............G 440 684-1400
Cleveland *(G-3962)*

VETERINARY PHARMACEUTICAL PREPARATIONS

Berlin Industries Inc...............................F 330 549-2100
Youngstown *(G-14819)*

VIDEO & AUDIO EQPT, WHOLESALE

Technical Artistry Inc.............................G 614 299-7777
Columbus *(G-5316)*

VIDEO TAPE PRODUCTION SVCS

Master Communications Inc...................G 208 821-3473
Cincinnati *(G-2849)*

World Harvest Church Inc.......................C 614 837-1990
Canal Winchester *(G-1800)*

VIDEO TAPE WHOLESALERS, RECORDED

Allied Shipping and Packagi...................F 937 222-7422
Moraine *(G-10144)*

VIDEO TRIGGERS: Remote Control TV Devices

Universal Electronics Inc........................G 330 487-1110
Twinsburg *(G-13389)*

VINYL RESINS, NEC

BCi and V Investments Inc......................G 330 538-0660
North Jackson *(G-10683)*

Morbern USA..F 937 298-2176
Dayton *(G-5893)*

VISUAL COMMUNICATIONS SYSTEMS

Findaway World LLC.................................E 440 893-0808
Solon *(G-12111)*

VITAMINS: Natural Or Synthetic, Uncompounded, Bulk

Nufacturing Inc.......................................E 330 814-5259
Brunswick *(G-1603)*

Vitamin Shoppe Florida LLC..................F
Delaware *(G-6178)*

Vitamin Shoppe Industries LLC.............A
Delaware *(G-6179)*

VOCATIONAL REHABILITATION AGENCY

Quadco Rehabilitation Ctr Inc................C 419 682-1011
Stryker *(G-12626)*

VOCATIONAL TRAINING AGENCY

Jeffco Sheltered Workshop.....................G 740 264-4608
Steubenville *(G-12404)*

WALL COVERINGS WHOLESALERS

The Blonder Company..............................C 216 431-3560
Cleveland *(G-4379)*

WALL COVERINGS: Rubber

Rjf International Corporation..................A 330 668-2069
Fairlawn *(G-6809)*

WALLPAPER & WALL COVERINGS

4wallscom LLC...F 216 432-1400
Cleveland *(G-3277)*

WALLPAPER: Made From Purchased Paper

The Blonder Company..............................C 216 431-3560
Cleveland *(G-4379)*

WALLS: Curtain, Metal

Midwest Curtainwalls Inc........................D 216 641-7900
Cleveland *(G-4036)*

Wt Acquisition Company Ltd....................E 513 577-7980
Cincinnati *(G-3234)*

YKK AP America Inc..................................E 513 942-7200
West Chester *(G-14094)*

WAREHOUSING & STORAGE FACILITIES, NEC

Abbott Laboratories.................................D 847 937-6100
Columbus *(G-4662)*

Ballreich Bros Inc....................................C 419 447-1814
Tiffin *(G-12777)*

Kuhlman Corporation...............................E 419 897-6000
Maumee *(G-9303)*

Lalac One LLC..E 216 432-4422
Cleveland *(G-3937)*

Littlern Corporation................................G 330 848-8847
Fairlawn *(G-6807)*

Multi Fittings Corporation.......................C 513 942-9910
West Chester *(G-14032)*

SH Bell Company......................................E 412 963-9910
East Liverpool *(G-6396)*

Vista Industrial Packaging LLC..............E 800 454-6117
Columbus *(G-5351)*

WAREHOUSING & STORAGE, REFRIGERATED: Cold Storage Or Refrig

Youngs Locker Service Inc.....................F 740 599-6833
Danville *(G-5601)*

WAREHOUSING & STORAGE, REFRIGERATED: Frozen Or Refrig Goods

Pettisville Meats Incorporated...............F 419 445-0921
Pettisville *(G-11286)*

WAREHOUSING & STORAGE: General

Atotech Usa LLC.......................................F 216 398-0550
Cleveland *(G-3385)*

Cooper Tire Vhcl Test Ctr Inc..................F 419 423-1321
Findlay *(G-6857)*

Dayton Bag & Burlap Co..........................F 937 253-1722
Dayton *(G-5721)*

Fuchs Lubricants Co................................F 330 963-0400
Twinsburg *(G-13306)*

P-Americas LLC.......................................E 330 746-7652
Youngstown *(G-14910)*

Performance Packaging Inc....................F 419 478-8805
Toledo *(G-13094)*

Precision Strip Inc...................................D 419 674-4186
Kenton *(G-8112)*

Precision Strip Inc...................................D 937 667-6255
Tipp City *(G-12836)*

SH Bell Company......................................E 412 963-9910
East Liverpool *(G-6396)*

Taylor Communications Inc....................F 614 351-6868
Columbus *(G-5312)*

Trane Technologies Company LLC..........E 419 633-6800
Bryan *(G-1665)*

Vectra Inc...C 614 351-6868
Columbus *(G-5345)*

Victory White Metal Company.................F 216 271-1400
Cleveland *(G-4474)*

Workflowone LLC.....................................A 877 735-4966
Dayton *(G-6087)*

WAREHOUSING & STORAGE: Refrigerated

Produce Packaging Inc............................C 216 391-6129
Willoughby Hills *(G-14562)*

WAREHOUSING & STORAGE: Self Storage

John D Oil and Gas Company..................G 440 255-6325
Mentor *(G-9543)*

McCrary Metal Polishing Co Inc.............F 937 492-1979
Port Jefferson *(G-11454)*

WARM AIR HEATING/AC EQPT/SPLYS, WHOL Warm Air Htg Eqpt/Splys

Air-Rite Inc...E 216 228-8200
Cleveland *(G-3316)*

Shape Supply Inc.....................................G 513 863-6695
Hamilton *(G-7525)*

WASHERS

Die-Cut Products Co.................................F 216 771-6994
Cleveland *(G-3615)*

WASHERS: Metal

Andre Corporation....................................E 574 293-0207
Mason *(G-9061)*

Atlas Bolt & Screw Company LLC............C 419 289-6171
Ashland *(G-519)*

Master Products Company.......................D 216 341-1740
Cleveland *(G-3998)*

Peterson American Corporation..............E 419 867-8711
Holland *(G-7777)*

WATCH & CLOCK STORES

Quality Gold Inc.......................................B 513 942-7659
Fairfield *(G-6769)*

WATCH REPAIR SVCS

White Jewelers Inc...................................G 330 264-3324
Wooster *(G-14697)*

WATER HEATERS

RAD Technologies Incorporated.............F 513 641-0523
Cincinnati *(G-3030)*

Rv Mobile Power LLC................................E 855 427-7978
Columbus *(G-5239)*

WATER PURIFICATION EQPT: Household

De Nora Holdings Us Inc.........................B 440 710-5300
Concord Township *(G-5389)*

Evoqua Water Technologies LLC.............F 614 491-5917
Groveport *(G-7431)*

R D Baker Enterprises Inc.................. G 937 461-5225
Dayton (G-5971)

WATER SOFTENING WHOLESALERS

R D Baker Enterprises Inc.................. G 937 461-5225
Dayton (G-5971)

WATER SUPPLY

American Water Services Inc.................. G 440 243-9840
Strongsville (G-12536)

Aqua Pennsylvania Inc.................. G 440 257-6190
Mentor On The Lake (G-9656)

City of Athens.................. F 740 592-3344
Athens (G-636)

City of Middletown.................. D 513 425-7781
Middletown (G-9844)

City of Troy.................. F 937 339-4826
Troy (G-13205)

Greene County.................. G 937 429-0127
Dayton (G-5613)

Victory White Metal Company.................. F 216 271-1400
Cleveland (G-4474)

WATER TREATMENT EQPT: Indl

Advanced Green Tech Inc.................. G 614 397-8130
Plain City (G-11392)

Ameriwater LLC.................. E 937 461-8833
Dayton (G-5657)

Aqua Pennsylvania Inc.................. G 440 257-6190
Mentor On The Lake (G-9656)

Chemtreat.................. G 937 644-2525
East Liberty (G-6384)

City of Athens.................. F 740 592-3344
Athens (G-636)

City of Middletown.................. D 513 425-7781
Middletown (G-9844)

City of Xenia.................. E 937 376-7269
Xenia (G-14758)

County of Lake.................. F 440 428-1794
Madison (G-8728)

Crown Solutions Co LLC.................. C 937 890-4075
Vandalia (G-13553)

De Nora North America Inc.................. G 440 357-4000
Painesville (G-11076)

De Nora Tech LLC.................. G 440 285-0368
Painesville (G-11077)

Imet Corporation.................. G 440 799-3135
Cleveland (G-3852)

Industrial Fluid MGT Inc.................. F 419 748-7460
Mc Clure (G-9351)

Kinetico Incorporated.................. B 440 564-9111
Newbury (G-10556)

McNish Corporation.................. G 614 899-2282
Westerville (G-14222)

N-Viro International Corp.................. F 419 535-6374
Toledo (G-13061)

Norwalk Wastewater Eqp Co.................. D 419 668-4471
Norwalk (G-10857)

Or-Tec Inc.................. G 216 475-5225
Maple Heights (G-8889)

Samsco Corp.................. F 216 400-8207
Cleveland (G-4271)

Tipton Environmental Intl Inc.................. F 513 735-2777
Batavia (G-891)

Trinity Water Solutions LLC.................. E 740 318-0585
Caldwell (G-1730)

Trionetics Inc.................. F 216 812-3570
Brooklyn Heights (G-1542)

Trumbull Manufacturing Inc.................. E 330 270-7888
Youngstown (G-14953)

Under Pressure Systems Inc.................. G 330 602-4466
New Philadelphia (G-10469)

Veolia Wts Systems Usa Inc.................. G 513 794-1010
Cincinnati (G-3201)

Veolia Wts Systems Usa Inc.................. F 330 929-1639
Stow (G-12470)

Water & Waste Water Eqp Co.................. G 440 542-0972
Solon (G-12207)

WATER: Distilled

Rambasek Realty Inc.................. F 937 228-1189
Dayton (G-5974)

WATER: Pasteurized, Canned & Bottled, Etc

On US LLC.................. E 330 286-3436
Kent (G-8057)

WATERPROOFING COMPOUNDS

Mar-Flex Systems LLC.................. E 513 422-7285
Carlisle (G-2068)

Republic Powdered Metals Inc.................. D 330 225-3192
Medina (G-9441)

RP Hoskins Inc.................. G 216 631-1000
Cleveland (G-4261)

RPM International Inc.................. D 330 273-5090
Medina (G-9442)

Urethane Polymers Intl.................. F 216 430-3655
Cleveland (G-4450)

WAXES: Petroleum, Not Produced In Petroleum Refineries

The Kindt-Collins Company LLC.................. D 216 252-4122
Cleveland (G-4387)

WEATHER STRIP: Sponge Rubber

Canton OH Rubber Speclty Prods.................. G 330 454-3847
Canton (G-1857)

WEATHER STRIPS: Metal

M-D Building Products Inc.................. D 513 539-2255
Middletown (G-9873)

WEIGHING MACHINERY & APPARATUS

Hobart LLC.................. D 937 332-2797
Piqua (G-11355)

Hobart LLC.................. E 937 332-3000
Troy (G-13225)

Hobart LLC.................. D 937 332-3000
Troy (G-13226)

WELDING & CUTTING APPARATUS & ACCESS, NEC

Kaliburn Inc.................. F 843 695-4073
Cleveland (G-3905)

Lincoln Electric Holdings Inc.................. B 216 481-8100
Cleveland (G-3956)

Luvata Ohio Inc.................. D 740 363-1981
Delaware (G-6161)

Miller Weldmaster Corporation.................. D 330 833-6739
Navarre (G-10307)

O E Meyer Co.................. G 419 332-6931
Fremont (G-7124)

Otto Konigslow Mfg Co.................. F 216 851-7900
Cleveland (G-4128)

Postle Industries Inc.................. E 216 265-9000
Cleveland (G-4177)

Quality Components Inc.................. F 440 255-0606
Mentor (G-9601)

Weld-Action Company Inc.................. G 330 372-1063
Warren (G-13813)

WELDING EQPT

Accurate Manufacturing Company.................. F 614 878-6510
Dublin (G-6272)

Aerowave Inc.................. G 440 731-8464
Elyria (G-6492)

AK Fabrication Inc.................. F 330 458-1037
Canton (G-1827)

Ch Transition Company LLC.................. C 800 543-6400
Cincinnati (G-2457)

Hobart Brothers LLC.................. C 937 332-5953
Piqua (G-11354)

Hobart Brothers LLC.................. C 937 332-5023
Troy (G-13223)

Hobart Brothers LLC.................. A 937 332-5439
Troy (G-13222)

Imax Industries Inc.................. F 440 639-0242
Painesville (G-11095)

Mansfield Welding Service LLC.................. G 419 594-2738
Oakwood (G-10898)

Nelson Stud Welding Inc.................. D 440 329-0400
Elyria (G-6568)

O E Meyer Co.................. E 614 428-5656
Columbus (G-5135)

Peco Holdings Corp.................. D 937 667-5705
Tipp City (G-12835)

Polymet Corporation.................. E 513 874-3586
West Chester (G-14051)

Process Equipment Co Tipp City.................. E 937 667-5705
Tipp City (G-12838)

Select-Arc Inc.................. C 937 295-5215
Fort Loramie (G-6955)

Semtorq Inc.................. F 330 487-0600
Twinsburg (G-13377)

Sherbrooke Corporation.................. E 440 942-3520
Willoughby (G-14525)

Sherbrooke Metals.................. G 440 542-3066
Willoughby (G-14526)

Spiegelberg Manufacturing Inc.................. D 440 324-3042
Strongsville (G-12604)

Stryver Mfg Inc.................. E 937 854-3048
Dayton (G-6028)

Summit Machine Solutions LLC.................. G 330 785-0781
Akron (G-321)

Taylor - Winfield Corporation.................. C 330 259-8500
Hubbard (G-7817)

Taylor-Winfield Tech Inc.................. D 330 259-8500
Youngstown (G-14943)

Worker Automation Inc.................. G 937 473-2111
Dayton (O-0000)

WELDING EQPT & SPLYS WHOLESALERS

Addup Inc.................. E 513 745-4510
Blue Ash (G-1242)

Airgas Usa LLC.................. G 740 353-5710
Portsmouth (G-11463)

Airgas Usa LLC.................. G 440 232-6397
Twinsburg (G-13270)

ARC Solutions LLC.................. E 419 542-9272
Hicksville (G-7646)

Delille Oxygen Company.................. G 937 325-9595
Springfield (G-12300)

Lefeld Welding & Stl Sups Inc.................. E 419 678-2397
Coldwater (G-4580)

Linde Gas & Equipment Inc.................. G 513 821-2192
Cincinnati (G-2823)

Matheson Tri-Gas Inc.................. F 419 865-8881
Holland (G-7772)

Matheson Tri-Gas Inc.................. E 330 425-4407
Twinsburg (G-13335)

Modern Machine Development.................. F 937 253-4576
Dayton (G-5891)

Salem Welding & Supply Company.................. G 330 332-4517
Salem (G-11811)

Sausser Steel Company Inc................... G 419 422-9632
Findlay (G-6916)

T & D Fabricating Inc........................... E 440 951-5646
Eastlake (G-6445)

Weld-Action Company Inc.................... G 330 372-1063
Warren (G-13813)

Weldco Inc.. E 513 744-9353
Cincinnati (G-3218)

Welders Supply Inc............................... F 216 241-1696
Cleveland (G-4500)

Wright Brothers Inc.............................. F 513 731-2222
Cincinnati (G-3232)

WELDING EQPT & SPLYS: Gas

Rexarc International Inc........................ E 937 839-4604
West Alexandria (G-13921)

WELDING EQPT & SPLYS: Generators, Arc Welding, AC & DC

Lincoln Electric Company....................... A 216 481-8100
Cleveland (G-3955)

WELDING EQPT REPAIR SVCS

ARS Recycling Systems LLC................. F 330 536-8210
Lowellville (G-8658)

Hannon Company................................ F 330 343-7758
Dover (G-6246)

Hannon Company................................ F 740 453-0527
Zanesville (G-15019)

Lyco Corporation................................. G 412 973-9176
Lowellville (G-8663)

Quality Components Inc........................ F 440 255-0606
Mentor (G-9601)

Unified Scrning Crshing - OH I............. G 937 836-3201
Englewood (G-6627)

WELDING EQPT: Electric

Ivostud LLC... G 440 925-4227
Brookpark (G-1553)

Production Products Inc....................... D 734 241-7242
Columbus Grove (G-5384)

Tech-Sonic Inc..................................... G 614 792-3117
Dublin (G-6354)

WELDING EQPT: Electrical

Pacific Highway Products LLC.............. G 740 914-5217
Marion (G-8988)

WELDING MACHINES & EQPT: Ultrasonic

Cecil C Peck Co.................................... F 330 785-0781
Akron (G-93)

WELDING REPAIR SVC

3-B Welding Ltd................................... G 740 819-4329
New Concord (G-10384)

A & C Welding Inc............................... E 330 762-4777
Peninsula (G-11179)

A & G Manufacturing Co Inc................ E 419 468-7433
Galion (G-7176)

Abbott Tool Inc................................... E 419 476-6742
Toledo (G-12861)

Active Metal and Molds Inc................. F 419 281-9623
Ashland (G-514)

Advanced Wldg Fabrication Inc............ F 440 724-9165
Sheffield Lake (G-11953)

Albright Radiator Inc........................... G 330 264-8886
Wooster (G-14622)

All - Do Weld & Fab LLC...................... G 740 477-2133
Circleville (G-3246)

All Ohio Welding Inc............................ G 937 663-7116
Saint Paris (G-11755)

All-Type Welding & Fabrication............. E 440 439-3990
Cleveland (G-3329)

Allied Fabricating & Wldg Co............... E 614 868-8680
Columbus (G-4687)

Amptech Machining & Welding............. G 419 652-3444
Nova (G-10875)

Apollo Welding & Fabg Inc.................. E 440 942-0227
Willoughby (G-14423)

ARC Solutions LLC............................... E 419 542-9272
Hicksville (G-7646)

Arctech Fabricating Inc....................... E 937 525-9353
Springfield (G-12282)

Athens Mold and Machine Inc............. D 740 593-6613
Athens (G-633)

B & R Fabricators & Maint Inc............. F 513 641-2222
Cincinnati (G-2395)

Bamf Welding & Fabrication LLC.......... G 440 862-8286
Novelty (G-10880)

Baughman Machine & Weld Sp Inc....... G 330 866-9243
Waynesburg (G-13875)

Bayloff Stmped Pdts Knsman Inc......... D 330 876-4511
Kinsman (G-8140)

Bear Welding Services LLC.................. F 740 630-7538
Caldwell (G-1723)

Blackwood Sheet Metal Inc.................. G 614 291-3115
Columbus (G-4764)

Blevins Metal Fabrication Inc............... E 419 522-6082
Mansfield (G-8766)

Bob Lanes Welding Inc........................ G 740 373-3567
Marietta (G-8904)

Breitinger Company............................. C 419 526-4255
Mansfield (G-8767)

Buckeye State Wldg & Fabg Inc........... G 440 322-0344
Elyria (G-6507)

Byron Products Inc.............................. D 513 870-9111
Fairfield (G-6715)

C & R Inc... E 614 497-1130
Groveport (G-7427)

C-N-D Industries Inc............................ F 330 478-8811
Massillon (G-9176)

Camelot Manufacturing Inc.................. G 419 678-2603
Coldwater (G-4569)

Cardinal Welding Inc........................... G 330 426-2404
East Palestine (G-6400)

Carter Manufacturing Co Inc................ F 513 398-7303
Mason (G-9077)

Case-Maul Manufacturing Co............... F 419 524-1061
Mansfield (G-8771)

Ceramic Holdings Inc.......................... C 216 362-3900
Brook Park (G-1511)

City Machine Technologies Inc............. F 330 747-2639
Youngstown (G-14836)

Clemens Mobile Welding LLC............... E 419 782-4220
Defiance (G-6103)

Clipsons Metal Working Inc.................. G 513 772-6393
Cincinnati (G-2499)

Cmt Machining & Fabg LLC................. F 937 652-3740
Urbana (G-13459)

Columbus Pipe and Equipment Co....... F 614 444-7871
Columbus (G-4831)

Combs Manufacturing Inc.................... D 330 784-3151
Akron (G-104)

Complete Metal Services...................... G 740 694-0000
Fredericktown (G-7074)

Comptons Precision Machine............... F 937 325-9139
Springfield (G-12293)

Connaughton Wldg & Fence LLC.......... G 513 867-0230
Hamilton (G-7480)

Crazeweld LLC..................................... G 419 210-3668
Norwalk (G-10833)

Creative Fab & Welding LLC................. E 937 780-5000
Leesburg (G-8298)

Creative Fabrication Ltd....................... G 740 262-5789
Richwood (G-11614)

Creative Mold and Machine Inc............ E 440 338-5146
Newbury (G-10548)

Crest Bending Inc................................ E 419 492-2108
New Washington (G-10478)

Custom Machine Inc............................ E 419 986-5122
Tiffin (G-12781)

Custom Weld & Machine Corp............. G 330 452-3935
Canton (G-1875)

D & G Welding Inc.............................. G 419 445-5751
Archbold (G-492)

Dana White Machining Wldg Inc.......... G 419 652-3444
Nova (G-10876)

Dayton Brick Company Inc................... F 937 293-4189
Moraine (G-10156)

Dbcr Inc.. E 330 920-1900
Cuyahoga Falls (G-5537)

Dover Fabrication and Burn Inc............ G 330 339-1057
Dover (G-6239)

Dover Machine Co............................... G 330 343-4123
Dover (G-6241)

Drabik Manufacturing Inc.................... F 216 267-1616
Cleveland (G-3629)

Drj Welding Services LLC..................... G 740 229-7428
New Philadelphia (G-10443)

Duco Tool & Die Inc............................ F 419 628-2031
Minster (G-10056)

Dynamic Weld Corporation.................. E 419 582-2900
Osgood (G-11026)

E & M Liberty Welding Inc................... G 330 866-2338
Waynesburg (G-13876)

Eagle Welding & Fabg Inc................... E 440 946-0692
Willoughby (G-14453)

East End Welding LLC.......................... C 330 677-6000
Kent (G-8028)

Fabrication Shop Inc........................... F 419 435-7934
Fostoria (G-6978)

Falls Stamping & Welding Co............... C 330 928-1191
Cuyahoga Falls (G-5541)

Fredrick Welding & Machining............. G 614 866-9650
Reynoldsburg (G-11571)

Friess Welding Inc............................... G 330 644-8160
Coventry Township (G-5482)

Garland Welding Co Inc....................... F 330 536-6506
Lowellville (G-8662)

Gaspar Inc... D 330 477-2222
Canton (G-1898)

Gdn Welding LLC................................. E 740 398-6109
Danville (G-5599)

General Technologies Inc..................... E 419 747-1800
Mansfield (G-8791)

General Tool Company.......................... C 513 733-5500
Cincinnati (G-2666)

George Steel Fabricating Inc................ E 513 932-2887
Lebanon (G-8259)

Gilson Machine & Tool Co Inc.............. E 419 592-2911
Napoleon (G-10282)

Glenridge Machine Co.......................... E 440 975-1055
Solon (G-12116)

Gmp Welding & Fabrication Inc............ G 513 825-7861
Cincinnati (G-2679)

Greber Machine Tool Inc..................... G 440 322-3685
Elyria (G-6541)

Greggs Specialty Services.................... F 419 478-0803
Toledo (G-12977)

H & H Machine Shop Akron Inc........... E 330 773-3327
Akron (G-167)

Habco Tool and Dev Co Inc................. F 440 946-5546
Mentor (G-9525)

Harris Welding and Machine Co........... F 419 281-8351
Ashland (G-537)

HI Tecmetal Group Inc	E	216 881-8100
Wickliffe (G-14378)		
Hi-Tek Manufacturing Inc	C	513 459-1094
Mason (G-9108)		
Highs Welding Inc	G	937 464-3029
Belle Center (G-1096)		
Holdren Brothers Inc	F	937 465-7050
West Liberty (G-14175)		
Holdsworth Industrial Fabg LLC	G	330 874-3945
Bolivar (G-1384)		
Holmview Welding LLC	F	330 359-5315
Fredericksburg (G-7064)		
Independent Machine & Wldg Inc	G	937 339-7330
Troy (G-13228)		
J & S Industrial Mch Pdts Inc	E	419 691-1380
Toledo (G-13012)		
J A B Welding Service Inc	E	740 453-5868
Zanesville (G-15023)		
J&J Precision Fabricators Ltd	F	330 482-4964
Columbiana (G-4621)		
Jerl Machine Inc	D	419 873-0270
Perrysburg (G-11232)		
JMw Welding and Mfg Inc	E	330 484-2428
Canton (G-1922)		
Johns Welding & Towing Inc	G	419 447-8937
Tiffin (G-12785)		
K & J Machine Inc	G	740 425-3282
Barnesville (G-845)		
K-M-S Industries Inc	G	440 243-6680
Brookpark (G-1554)		
Kann Custom Welding LLC	G	330 231-2719
Dundee (G-6366)		
Kda Manufacturing LLC	F	330 590-7431
Norton (G-10825)		
Kel-Par Co Inc	F	740 344-2627
Newark (G-10513)		
Kellys Wldg & Fabrication Ltd	G	440 593-6040
Conneaut (G-5406)		
Kendel Wldg & Fabrication Inc	G	330 834-2429
Massillon (G-9210)		
Kings Welding and Fabg Inc	G	330 738-3592
Mechanicstown (G-9368)		
Kinninger Prod Wldg Co Inc	D	419 629-3491
New Bremen (G-10361)		
Kirbys Auto and Truck Repr Inc	G	513 934-3999
Lebanon (G-8272)		
Kottler Metal Products Co Inc	E	440 946-7473
Willoughby (G-14478)		
Kramer Power Equipment Co	G	937 456-2232
Eaton (G-6457)		
Lakecraft Inc	G	419 734-2828
Port Clinton (G-11444)		
Lima Sheet Metal Mch & Mfg Inc	F	419 229-1161
Lima (G-8426)		
Lincoln Electric Automtn Inc	B	937 295-2120
Fort Loramie (G-6950)		
Logan Welding Inc	G	740 385-9651
Logan (G-8520)		
Long-Stanton Mfg Company	E	513 874-8020
West Chester (G-14024)		
Lunar Tool & Mold Inc	E	440 237-2141
North Royalton (G-10771)		
M & M Certified Welding Inc	F	330 467-1729
Macedonia (G-8703)		
M & M Concepts Inc	G	937 355-1115
West Mansfield (G-14179)		
Majestic Tool and Machine Inc	G	440 248-5058
Solon (G-12144)		
Marengo Fabricated Steel Ltd	F	800 919-2652
Cardington (G-2055)		
Marsam Metalfab Inc	E	330 405-1520
Twinsburg (G-13334)		

Martin Welding LLC	F	937 687-3602
New Lebanon (G-10400)		
Mc Elwain Industries Inc	F	419 532-3126
Ottawa (G-11038)		
Mc Machine Llc	E	216 398-3666
Cleveland (G-4007)		
Meta Manufacturing Corporation	E	513 793-6382
Blue Ash (G-1308)		
Mike Loppe	F	937 969-8102
Tremont City (G-13189)		
Mk Welding & Fabrication Inc	G	937 603-4430
Waynesville (G-13880)		
Modern Machine Development	F	937 253-4576
Dayton (G-5891)		
Montgomery & Montgomery LLC	G	330 858-9533
Akron (G-236)		
Ms Welding LLC	G	419 925-4141
Maria Stein (G-8900)		
Mt Vernon Mold Works Inc	E	618 242-6040
Akron (G-238)		
National Wldg Tanker Repr LLC	G	614 875-3399
Grove City (G-7404)		
Northwind Industries Inc	G	216 433-0666
Cleveland (G-4099)		
Oaks Welding Inc	G	330 482-4216
Columbiana (G-4624)		
Ohio Hydraulics Inc	E	513 771-2590
Cincinnati (G-2924)		
Ohio Trailer Inc	G	330 392-4444
Warren (G-13787)		
Ohio Trailer Supply Inc	G	614 471-9121
Columbus (G-5155)		
Ottawa Defense Logistics LLC	F	419 596-3202
Ottawa (G-11040)		
Patriot Stainless Welding	G	740 297-6040
Zanesville (G-15038)		
Paul Wilke & Son Inc	F	513 921-3163
Cincinnati (G-2947)		
Pentaflex Inc	C	937 325-5551
Springfield (G-12360)		
Perry Welding Service Inc	F	330 425-2211
Twinsburg (G-13355)		
Phillips Mfg and Tower Co	D	419 347-1720
Shelby (G-11972)		
Phoenix Inds & Apparatus Inc	F	513 722-1085
Loveland (G-8645)		
PMRservices LLC	F	937 219-0062
Spring Valley (G-12242)		
Pr-Weld & Manufacturing Ltd	F	419 633-9204
West Unity (G-14197)		
Precision Assemblies Inc	F	330 549-2630
North Lima (G-10710)		
Precision Mtal Fabrication Inc	D	937 235-9261
Dayton (G-5950)		
Precision Reflex Inc	G	419 629-2603
New Bremen (G-10365)		
Precision Welding & Mfg Inc	F	937 444-6925
Mount Orab (G-10221)		
Precision Welding Corporation	E	216 524-6110
Cleveland (G-4187)		
Prout Boiler Htg & Wldg Inc	E	330 744-0293
Youngstown (G-14921)		
Quality Welding Inc	G	419 483-6067
Bellevue (G-1128)		
Quick Service Welding & Mch Co	F	330 673-3818
Kent (G-8066)		
Rbm Environmental & Cnstr Inc	G	419 693-5840
Oregon (G-10967)		
Rex Welding Inc	F	740 387-1650
Marion (G-8992)		
RI Alto Mfg Inc	F	740 914-4230
Marion (G-8993)		

Ridge Engineering Inc	G	513 681-5500
Cincinnati (G-3045)		
Ridge Machine & Welding Co	G	740 537-2821
Toronto (G-13186)		
Rodney Wells	G	740 425-2266
Barnesville (G-846)		
Roetmans Welding LLC	G	216 385-5938
Akron (G-289)		
Romar Metal Fabricating Inc	G	740 682-7731
Oak Hill (G-10894)		
Rose Metal Industries LLC	F	216 881-3355
Cleveland (G-4250)		
Rsv Wlding Fbrction McHning In	F	419 592-0993
Napoleon (G-10298)		
Salem Welding & Supply Company	G	330 332-4517
Salem (G-11811)		
Sauerwein Welding	G	513 563-2979
Cincinnati (G-3065)		
Schmidt Machine Company	F	419 294-3814
Upper Sandusky (G-13455)		
Semtorq Inc	F	330 487-0600
Twinsburg (G-13377)		
Simpson & Sons Inc	G	513 367-0152
Harrison (G-7568)		
Sky Climber Fabricating LLC	G	740 990-9430
Delaware (G-6173)		
Smp Welding LLC	F	440 205-9353
Mentor (G-9616)		
Somerville Manufacturing Inc	E	740 336-7847
Marietta (G-8949)		
Spradlin Bros Welding Co	F	800 219-2182
Springfield (G-12375)		
Stan-Kell LLC	F	440 998-1116
Ashtabula (G-617)		
State Metal Hose Inc	G	614 527-4700
Hilliard (G-7703)		
Steve Vore Welding and Steel	F	419 375-4087
Fort Recovery (G-6971)		
Stud Welding Associates	F	216 392-7808
Elyria (G-6593)		
Suburban Metal Products Inc	F	740 474-4237
Circleville (G-3263)		
Superior Weld and Fabg Co Inc	G	216 249-5122
Cleveland (G-4349)		
Systech Handling Inc	F	419 445-8226
Archbold (G-512)		
T & R Welding Systems Inc	F	937 228-7517
Dayton (G-6037)		
Tbone Sales LLC	G	330 897-0131
Baltic (G-781)		
Temperature Controls Co Inc	F	330 773-6633
New Franklin (G-10395)		
Tendon Manufacturing Inc	E	216 663-3200
Cleveland (G-4374)		
Toney Tool Manufacturing Inc	G	937 890-8535
Dayton (G-6057)		
Tonys Wldg & Fabrication LLC	F	740 333-4000
Wshngtn Ct Hs (G-14748)		
Tri-State Plating & Polishing	G	304 529-2579
Proctorville (G-11500)		
Triangle Precision Inds Inc	D	937 299-6776
Dayton (G-6062)		
Tru-Fab Technology Inc	F	440 954-9760
Willoughby (G-14543)		
Two M Precision Co Inc	F	440 946-2120
Willoughby (G-14546)		
US Welding Training LLC	G	440 669-9380
Fairport Harbor (G-6822)		
Valley Machine Tool Inc	E	513 899-2737
Morrow (G-10204)		
Viking Fabricators Inc	G	740 374-5246
Marietta (G-8960)		

PRODUCT

Webers Body & Frame Inc.................. G 937 839-5946
West Alexandria *(G-13923)*

Welders Supply Inc.................................. E 216 267-4470
Brookpark *(G-1560)*

Welding Consultants Inc..................... G 614 258-7018
Columbus *(G-5360)*

Welding Consultants LLC.................... G 614 258-7018
Columbus *(G-5361)*

Weldments Inc....................................... F 937 235-9261
Dayton *(G-6077)*

Wenrick Machine and Tool Corp........... F 937 667-7307
Tipp City *(G-12854)*

Whitt Machine Inc................................ F 513 423-7624
Middletown *(G-9904)*

Witts Services LLC.............................. G 740 543-8526
Bergholz *(G-1197)*

Wpc Successor Inc.............................. F 937 233-6141
Tipp City *(G-12855)*

WELDING SPLYS, EXC GASES: *Wholesalers*

Airgas Usa LLC.................................... G 440 232-6397
Twinsburg *(G-13270)*

Delille Oxygen Company...................... E 614 444-1177
Columbus *(G-4876)*

WELDING TIPS: *Heat Resistant, Metal*

Forgeo LLC... E 614 873-7030
Plain City *(G-11408)*

WELDMENTS

A H Marty Co Ltd................................. F 216 641-8950
Cleveland *(G-3282)*

A-1 Welding & Fabrication.................... F 440 233-8474
Lorain *(G-8544)*

American Tank & Fabricating Co........... D 216 252-1500
Cleveland *(G-3348)*

Loveman Steel Corporation.................. D 440 232-6200
Bedford *(G-1044)*

Northeast Fabricators LLC..................... E 330 747-3484
Youngstown *(G-14905)*

Universal Dsign Fbrication LLC............ F 419 202-5269
Sandusky *(G-11880)*

WET CORN MILLING

Fluid Quip Ks LLC............................... D 937 324-0352
Springfield *(G-12313)*

Primary Pdts Ingrdnts Amrcas L........... F 937 235-4074
Dayton *(G-5954)*

WHEELCHAIR LIFTS

Plumb Builders Inc............................... F 937 293-1111
Dayton *(G-5942)*

Serving Veterans Mobility Inc.............. G 937 746-4788
Franklin *(G-7048)*

Steves Vans ACC Unlimited LLC........... G 740 374-3154
Marietta *(G-8950)*

WHEELCHAIRS

Columbus Prescr Rehabilitation............ G 614 294-1600
Westerville *(G-14250)*

Healthwares Manufacturing.................. F 513 353-3691
Cleves *(G-4539)*

Invacare Corporation............................ F 440 329-6000
Elyria *(G-6550)*

Invacare Corporation............................ G 800 333-6900
Elyria *(G-6551)*

Invacare Holdings Corporation.............. B 440 329-6000
Elyria *(G-6554)*

Npl Homecare LLC............................... E 440 365-8581
Strongsville *(G-12579)*

Reliable Wheelchair Trans.................... G 216 390-3999
Beachwood *(G-944)*

WHEELS & PARTS

Americana Development Inc................. D 330 633-3278
Tallmadge *(G-12730)*

Ernie Green Industries Inc................... E 614 219-1423
New Madison *(G-10420)*

Marion Industries LLC.......................... A 740 223-0075
Marion *(G-8977)*

Pacific Industries USA Inc.................... E 513 860-3900
Fairfield *(G-6761)*

Piston Automotive LLC......................... A 740 223-0075
Marion *(G-8989)*

WHEELS, GRINDING: *Artificial*

Action Super Abrasive Pdts Inc............ E 330 673-7333
Kent *(G-8014)*

Carborundum Grinding Wheel .... E 740 385-2171
Logan *(G-8510)*

Performance Superabrasives LLC......... G 440 946-7171
Mentor *(G-9586)*

WHEELS: *Abrasive*

Buckeye Abrasive Inc........................... F 330 753-1041
Barberton *(G-799)*

Research Abrasive Products Inc............ E 440 944-3200
Wickliffe *(G-14394)*

WHEELS: *Disc, Wheelbarrow, Stroller, Etc, Stamped Metal*

IBI Brake Products Inc......................... G 440 543-7962
Chagrin Falls *(G-2166)*

WHEELS: *Iron & Steel, Locomotive & Car*

Xtek Inc.. B 513 733-7800
Cincinnati *(G-3240)*

WHEELS: *Railroad Car, Cast Steel*

Engines Inc of Ohio.............................. E 740 377-9874
South Point *(G-12223)*

WHITING MINING: *Crushed & Broken*

Ayers Limestone Quarry Inc................. F 740 633-2958
Martins Ferry *(G-9009)*

WINCHES

American Power Pull Corp..................... G 419 335-7050
Archbold *(G-485)*

Drc Acquisition Inc............................... E 330 656-1600
Streetsboro *(G-12498)*

Malta Dynamics LLC............................ F 740 749-3512
Waterford *(G-13828)*

WINDMILLS: *Electric Power Generation*

Cleveland Wind Company LLC............... G 216 269-7667
Cleveland *(G-3530)*

WINDOW & DOOR FRAMES

Creative Millwork Ohio Inc................... D 440 992-3566
Ashtabula *(G-588)*

Desco Corporation................................ G 614 888-8855
New Albany *(G-10339)*

Midwest Curtainwalls Inc..................... D 216 641-7900
Cleveland *(G-4036)*

Rosatis Window Co LLC........................ D 614 777-4806
Columbus *(G-5235)*

WINDOW FRAMES & SASHES: *Plastic*

Champion Opco LLC............................. B 513 327-7338
Cincinnati *(G-2458)*

Creative Millwork Ohio Inc................... D 440 992-3566
Ashtabula *(G-588)*

Vinylume Products Inc.......................... F 330 799-2000
Youngstown *(G-14964)*

WINDOW FRAMES, MOLDING & TRIM: *Vinyl*

Builder Tech Wholesale LLC................. G 419 535-7606
Toledo *(G-12908)*

Comfort Line Ltd.................................. D 419 729-8520
Toledo *(G-12928)*

Duo-Corp.. F 330 549-2149
North Lima *(G-10707)*

Great Lakes Window Inc....................... A 419 666-5555
Walbridge *(G-13684)*

Larmco Windows Inc............................ E 216 502-2832
Cleveland *(G-3942)*

Modern Builders Supply Inc.................. C 419 241-3961
Toledo *(G-13058)*

Owens Corning Sales LLC.................... A 419 248-8000
Toledo *(G-13088)*

Plastics Family Holdings Inc................. F 614 272-0777
Columbus *(G-5196)*

Solutions In Polycarbonate LLC............ G 330 572-2860
Medina *(G-9449)*

Stanek E F and Assoc Inc.................... C 216 341-7700
Macedonia *(G-8717)*

Tsp Inc.. F 513 732-8900
Batavia *(G-892)*

Vinyl Design Corporation...................... E 419 283-4009
Holland *(G-7790)*

WINDOW SCREENING: *Plastic*

Gateway Industrial Pdts Inc.................. E 440 324-4112
Elyria *(G-6539)*

WINDOWS: *Wood*

M21 Industries LLC.............................. G 937 781-1377
Dayton *(G-5859)*

Yoder Window & Siding Ltd.................. F 330 695-6960
Fredericksburg *(G-7072)*

WINDSHIELD WIPER SYSTEMS

First Brands Group LLC........................ E 888 565-9632
Cleveland *(G-3718)*

Trico Products Corporation................... C 800 388-7428
Cleveland *(G-4425)*

WINDSHIELDS: *Plastic*

Few Atmtive GL Applcations Inc............ D 234 249-1880
Wooster *(G-14637)*

WIRE

Advance Industries Group LLC............. E 216 741-1800
Cleveland *(G-3301)*

AJD Holding Co.................................... D 330 405-4477
Twinsburg *(G-13271)*

Bekaert Corporation............................. E 330 683-5060
Orrville *(G-10975)*

D C Controls LLC................................. G 513 225-0813
West Chester *(G-14113)*

Hawthorne Wire Ltd............................. G 216 712-4747
Lakewood *(G-8167)*

Injection Alloys Incorporated................ F 513 422-8819
Middletown *(G-9865)*

Radix Wire & Cable LLC....................... D 216 731-9191
Solon *(G-12172)*

Reinforcement Systems of Ohio LLC..... G 330 469-6958
Warren *(G-13793)*

Scovil Hanna LLC................................ E 216 581-1500
Cleveland *(G-4281)*

WIRE & CABLE: *Aluminum*

Mac Its LLC... G 937 454-0722
Vandalia *(G-13565)*

WIRE & CABLE: Nonferrous, Building

Ribbon Technology Corporation............ F 614 864-5444
 Gahanna (G-7168)

WIRE & WIRE PRDTS

Adcura Mfg.................................. G 937 222-3800
 Dayton (G-5635)

Advance Wire Forming Inc................ F 216 432-3250
 Cleveland (G-3304)

Alabama Sling Center Inc................ F 440 239-7000
 Cleveland (G-3318)

Alcan Corporation........................ E
 Cleveland (G-3320)

Amanda Bent Bolt Company.............. C 740 385-6893
 Logan (G-8508)

Ametco Manufacturing Corp.............. D 440 951-4300
 Willoughby (G-14418)

Bekaert Corporation..................... F 330 683-5060
 Orrville (G-10974)

Bloomngburg Spring Wire Form I........ E 740 437-7614
 Bloomingburg (G-1239)

Brushes Inc.............................. F 216 267-8084
 Cleveland (G-3447)

Busch & Thiem Inc....................... E 419 625-7515
 Sandusky (G-11825)

C & F Fabrications Inc................... G 937 666-3234
 East Liberty (G-6383)

C C M Wire Inc........................... F 330 425-3421
 Twinsburg (G-13283)

Canron Manufacturing Inc................ F 330 497-1131
 Greentown (G-7332)

Clamps Inc............................... E 419 729-2141
 Toledo (G-12921)

Dayton Wire Products Inc................ E 937 236-8000
 Dayton (G-5741)

Die Co Inc............................... E 440 942-8856
 Eastlake (G-6423)

Dysinger Incorporated.................... E 937 297-7761
 Dayton (G-5757)

Engineered Wire Products Inc............ E 330 469-6958
 Warren (G-13762)

Engineered Wire Products Inc............ C 419 294-3817
 Upper Sandusky (G-13440)

Ever Roll Specialties Co................. E 937 964-1302
 Springfield (G-12309)

Fence One Inc............................ F 216 441-2600
 Cleveland (G-3712)

G & S Titanium Inc....................... E 330 263-0564
 Wooster (G-14641)

Gateway Con Forming Svcs Inc........... D 513 353-2000
 Miamitown (G-9758)

General Chain & Mfg Corp................ E 513 541-6005
 Cincinnati (G-2659)

Helical Line Products Co................. E 440 933-9263
 Avon Lake (G-759)

Illinois Tool Works Inc.................. E 216 292-7161
 Bedford (G-1039)

Malin Co................................. E 216 267-9080
 Cleveland (G-3982)

Marik Spring Inc......................... E 330 564-0617
 Tallmadge (G-12740)

Mazzella Jhh Company Inc................ D 440 239-7000
 Cleveland (G-4004)

Mazzella Lifting Tech Inc................ D 440 239-7000
 Cleveland (G-4005)

McM Ind Co Inc.......................... F 216 641-6300
 Cleveland (G-4013)

McM Ind Co Inc.......................... F 216 292-4506
 Cleveland (G-4012)

Meese Inc............................... F 440 998-1202
 Ashtabula (G-604)

Merchants Metals LLC.................... E 513 942-0268
 West Chester (G-14028)

Mid-West Fabricating Co................. C 740 969-4411
 Amanda (G-424)

Mueller Electric Company Inc............ D 216 771-5225
 Akron (G-239)

Ohio Wire Form & Spring Co............. F 614 444-3676
 Columbus (G-5156)

Options Plus Incorporated............... F 740 694-9811
 Fredericktown (G-7083)

Panacea Products Corporation........... E 614 429-6320
 Columbus (G-5170)

Panacea Products Corporation........... E 614 850-7000
 Columbus (G-5171)

Parker-Hannifin Corporation............. G 330 336-3511
 Wadsworth (G-13658)

Peterson American Corporation.......... E 419 867-8711
 Holland (G-7777)

Polymet Corporation..................... E 513 874-3586
 West Chester (G-14051)

Premier Manufacturing Corp............. C 216 941-9700
 Cleveland (G-4190)

Production Plus Corp.................... F 740 983-5178
 Ashville (G-630)

Pwp Inc................................. E 216 251-2181
 Ashland (G-567)

Qualtek Electronics Corp................ C 440 951-3300
 Mentor (G-9603)

R G Smith Company....................... D 330 456-3415
 Canton (G-1988)

Rjs Corporation......................... E 330 896-2387
 Akron (G-287)

Saxon Products Inc...................... G 419 241-6771
 Toledo (G-13122)

Schweizer Dipple Inc.................... D 440 786-8090
 Cleveland (G-4277)

Sheffield Metals Intl Inc............... E 440 934-8500
 Sheffield Village (G-11965)

Spring Team Inc......................... D 440 275-5981
 Austinburg (G-703)

Starr Fabricating Inc................... D 330 394-9891
 Vienna (G-13618)

Stephens Pipe & Steel LLC............... C 740 869-2257
 Mount Sterling (G-10229)

Stolle Machinery Company LLC........... C 937 497-5400
 Dayton (G-6027)

T & R Welding Systems Inc............... F 937 228-7517
 Dayton (G-6037)

Therm-O-Link Inc........................ D 330 527-2124
 Garrettsville (G-7228)

Top Knotch Products Inc................. G 419 543-2266
 Cleveland (G-4402)

Tyler Haver Inc......................... E 440 974-1047
 Mentor (G-9645)

Ver-Mac Industries Inc.................. E 740 397-6511
 Mount Vernon (G-10268)

W J Egli Company Inc.................... F 330 823-3666
 Alliance (G-414)

Wire Products Company LLC............... D 216 267-0777
 Cleveland (G-4510)

Wrwp LLC................................ D 330 425-3421
 Twinsburg (G-13399)

Yost Superior Co........................ E 937 323-7591
 Springfield (G-12397)

WIRE CLOTH & WOVEN WIRE PRDTS, MADE FROM PURCHASED

Ofco Inc................................ D 740 622-5922
 Coshocton (G-5466)

Unified Scrning Crshing - OH I.......... G 937 836-3201
 Englewood (G-6627)

WIRE MATERIALS: Aluminum

Alcan Corporation....................... E
 Cleveland (G-3320)

WIRE MATERIALS: Copper

Alcan Corporation....................... E
 Cleveland (G-3320)

American Wire & Cable Company.......... E 440 235-1140
 Olmsted Twp (G-10944)

Core Optix Inc.......................... F 855 267-3678
 Cincinnati (G-2517)

Republic Wire Inc....................... D 513 860-1800
 West Chester (G-14063)

WIRE MATERIALS: Steel

American Wire & Cable Company.......... E 440 235-1140
 Olmsted Twp (G-10944)

Armco Inc............................... G 740 829-3000
 Coshocton (G-5450)

Bayloff Stmped Pdts Knsman Inc......... D 330 876-4511
 Kinsman (G-8140)

Contour Forming Inc..................... F 740 345-9777
 Newark (G-10499)

Custom Cltch Jint Hydrlics Inc.......... F 216 431-1630
 Cleveland (G-3584)

Dayton Superior Corporation............. C 937 866-0711
 Miamisburg (G-9687)

Engineered Wire Products Inc............ C 419 294-3817
 Upper Sandusky (G-13440)

Enterprise Machine Inc.................. G 513 681-4409
 Cincinnati (G-2592)

Flextur Corp............................ D 877 435-3988
 Dalton (G-5585)

G & S Bar and Wire LLC.................. E 260 747-4154
 Wooster (G-14640)

JR Manufacturing Inc.................... C 419 375-8021
 Fort Recovery (G-6968)

McHenry Industries Inc.................. D 330 799-8930
 Youngstown (G-14896)

Midwestern Industries Inc............... D 330 837-4203
 Massillon (G-9223)

Polymet Corporation..................... E 513 874-3586
 West Chester (G-14051)

Republic Steel Wire Proc LLC............ E 440 996-0740
 Solon (G-12175)

Republic Wire Inc....................... D 513 860-1800
 West Chester (O-14063)

Save Edge Inc........................... E 937 376-8268
 Xenia (G-14774)

Summit Engineered Products Inc.......... F 330 854-5388
 Canal Fulton (G-1779)

Tru-Form Steel & Wire Inc............... E 765 348-5001
 Toledo (G-13166)

Unison Industries LLC................... F 937 426-0621
 Alpha (G-419)

WIRE PRDTS: Ferrous Or Iron, Made In Wiredrawing Plants

American Spring Wire Corp............... C 216 292-4620
 Bedford Heights (G-1068)

Fenix LLC............................... F 419 739-3400
 Wapakoneta (G-13710)

Seneca Wire & Manufacturing Co Inc..... F 419 435-9261
 Fostoria (G-7002)

WIRE PRDTS: Steel & Iron

North Shore Strapping Company.......... E 216 661-5200
 Brooklyn Heights (G-1536)

Radix Wire & Cable LLC.................. D 216 731-9191
 Solon (G-12172)

Trupoint Products LLC........................ F 330 204-3302
  Sugarcreek *(G-12654)*

WIRE WINDING OF PURCHASED WIRE

Providence REES Inc........................... G 614 833-6231
  Columbus *(G-5212)*

WIRE, FLAT: Strip, Cold-Rolled, Exc From Hot-Rolled Mills

American Spring Wire Corp.................. C 216 292-4620
  Bedford Heights *(G-1068)*

Hynes Industries Inc............................ D 800 321-9257
  Youngstown *(G-14874)*

WIRE: Communication

Astro Industries Inc............................. E 937 429-5900
  Beavercreek *(G-966)*

AT&T Enterprises LLC......................... G 513 792-9300
  Cincinnati *(G-2384)*

Ohio Associated Entps LLC.................. F 440 354-3148
  Painesville *(G-11101)*

Xponet Inc... G 440 354-6617
  Painesville *(G-11123)*

WIRE: Magnet

Sam Dong America Inc......................... F 740 363-1985
  Delaware *(G-6170)*

WIRE: Mesh

Midwestern Industries Inc.................... D 330 837-4203
  Massillon *(G-9223)*

WIRE: Nonferrous

Alcan Corporation................................ E
  Cleveland *(G-3320)*

American Wire & Cable Company......... E 440 235-1140
  Olmsted Twp *(G-10944)*

Arnco Corporation............................... F 800 847-7661
  Elyria *(G-6498)*

Calvert Wire & Cable Corp................... E 330 494-3248
  North Canton *(G-10631)*

Connectors Unlimited Inc..................... E 440 357-1161
  Painesville *(G-11074)*

Electrovations Inc................................ G 330 274-3558
  Solon *(G-12103)*

Flex Technologies Inc.......................... E 740 922-5992
  Midvale *(G-9910)*

Legrand North America LLC................. B 937 224-0639
  Dayton *(G-5843)*

Mueller Electric Company Inc.............. D 216 771-5225
  Akron *(G-239)*

Projects Unlimited Inc......................... C 937 918-2200
  Dayton *(G-5968)*

Radix Wire Co...................................... F 330 995-3677
  Aurora *(G-686)*

Radix Wire Co...................................... F 216 731-9191
  Solon *(G-12174)*

Radix Wire Co...................................... D 216 731-9191
  Solon *(G-12173)*

Rah Investment Holding Inc................. D 330 832-8124
  Massillon *(G-9237)*

Schneider Electric Usa Inc.................. B 513 523-4171
  Oxford *(G-11064)*

Scott Fetzer Company.......................... C 216 267-9000
  Cleveland *(G-4278)*

Therm-O-Link Inc................................. G 330 393-7600
  Warren *(G-13801)*

Therm-O-Link Inc................................. D 330 527-2124
  Garrettsville *(G-7228)*

Vulkor Incorporated............................ E 330 393-7600
  Warren *(G-13809)*

Wiremax Ltd... G 419 531-9500
  Toledo *(G-13179)*

WIRE: Steel, Insulated Or Armored

Euclid Steel & Wire Inc........................ G 216 731-6744
  Lakewood *(G-8166)*

Marlin Thermocouple Wire Inc.............. E 440 835-1950
  Westlake *(G-14314)*

Ram Sensors Inc.................................. E 440 835-3540
  Cleveland *(G-4222)*

WIRE: Wire, Ferrous Or Iron

Solon Specialty Wire Co...................... E 440 248-7600
  Solon *(G-12183)*

WIRING DEVICES WHOLESALERS

Astro Industries Inc............................. E 937 429-5900
  Beavercreek *(G-966)*

WOMEN'S & CHILDREN'S CLOTHING WHOLESALERS, NEC

Fluff Boutique..................................... G 513 227-6614
  Cincinnati *(G-2630)*

McCc Sportswear Inc........................... G 513 583-9210
  Milford *(G-9942)*

West Chester Holdings LLC.................. C 513 705-2100
  Cincinnati *(G-3220)*

Zimmer Enterprises Inc........................ E 937 428-1057
  Dayton *(G-6090)*

WOMEN'S & GIRLS' SPORTSWEAR WHOLESALERS

Barbs Graffiti Inc................................ E 216 881-5550
  Cleveland *(G-3405)*

Design Original Inc.............................. F 937 596-5121
  Jackson Center *(G-7961)*

Precision Imprint................................. G 740 592-5916
  Athens *(G-646)*

R & A Sports Inc.................................. E 216 289-2254
  Euclid *(G-6674)*

Unisport Inc... F 419 529-4727
  Ontario *(G-10953)*

WOMEN'S CLOTHING STORES

City Apparel Inc................................... F 419 434-1155
  Findlay *(G-6852)*

Fluff Boutique..................................... G 513 227-6614
  Cincinnati *(G-2630)*

WOOD & WOOD BY-PRDTS, WHOLESALE

Cindoco Wood Products Co................... G 937 444-2504
  Mount Orab *(G-10216)*

Gross Lumber Inc................................. G 330 683-2055
  Apple Creek *(G-469)*

WOOD CHIPS, PRODUCED AT THE MILL

Calvin W Lafferty................................ G 740 498-6566
  Kimbolton *(G-8136)*

Miller Logging Inc................................ G 330 279-4721
  Holmesville *(G-7802)*

WOOD FENCING WHOLESALERS

Df Supply Inc....................................... E 330 650-9226
  Twinsburg *(G-13294)*

Double D D Mtls Instlltion Inc............... G 937 898-2534
  Dayton *(G-5750)*

WOOD PRDTS: Laundry

Adroit Thinking Inc.............................. F 419 542-9363
  Hicksville *(G-7645)*

P Graham Dunn Inc.............................. B 330 828-2105
  Dalton *(G-5591)*

WOOD PRDTS: Moldings, Unfinished & Prefinished

Clark Wood Specialties Inc.................. G 330 499-8711
  Clinton *(G-4553)*

Cox Interior Inc.................................... F 270 789-3129
  Norwood *(G-10867)*

J McCoy Lumber Co Ltd....................... F 937 587-3423
  Peebles *(G-11170)*

Laborie Enterprises LLC...................... G 419 686-6245
  Portage *(G-11458)*

Midwest Wood Trim Inc........................ E 419 592-3389
  Napoleon *(G-10291)*

Quality Woodproducts LLC.................. G 330 279-2217
  Fredericksburg *(G-7069)*

Seneca Millwork Inc............................ E 419 435-6671
  Fostoria *(G-7001)*

WOOD PRDTS: Mulch Or Sawdust

American Wood Fibers Inc.................... E 740 420-3233
  Circleville *(G-3247)*

Garick LLC.. E 216 581-0100
  Cleveland *(G-3755)*

Hope Timber & Marketing Group........... F 740 344-1788
  Newark *(G-10507)*

Hope Timber Mulch LLC....................... G 740 344-1788
  Newark *(G-10508)*

Ohio Mulch Supply Inc......................... G 740 548-6242
  Lewis Center *(G-8347)*

Roe Transportation Entps Inc............... G 937 497-7161
  Sidney *(G-12045)*

WOOD PRDTS: Mulch, Wood & Bark

Gayston Corporation............................ C 937 743-6050
  Miamisburg *(G-9693)*

H Hafner & Sons Inc............................ E 513 321-1895
  Cincinnati *(G-2698)*

Hauser Services Llc............................ E 440 632-5126
  Middlefield *(G-9798)*

Irvine Wood Recovery Inc..................... E 513 831-0060
  Miamiville *(G-9762)*

Mulch Manufacturing Inc..................... E 614 864-4004
  Reynoldsburg *(G-11575)*

Scotts Company LLC............................ C 937 644-0011
  Marysville *(G-9045)*

Yoder Lumber Co Inc............................ D 330 893-3121
  Millersburg *(G-10020)*

WOOD PRDTS: Plugs

Sealco Inc... G 740 922-4122
  Uhrichsville *(G-13405)*

WOOD PRDTS: Signboards

Blang Acquisition LLC......................... G 937 223-2155
  Dayton *(G-5679)*

Signature Sign Co Inc.......................... G 216 426-1234
  Cleveland *(G-4301)*

WOOD PRDTS: Trophy Bases

Hit Trophy Inc...................................... G 419 445-5356
  Archbold *(G-498)*

J & D Wood Ltd.................................... G 937 778-9663
  Piqua *(G-11359)*

WOOD TREATING: Millwork

Couch Business Development Inc......... G 937 253-1099
  Dayton *(G-5711)*

Joseph Sabatino................................. G 330 332-5879
  Salem *(G-11791)*

WOOD TREATING: Structural Lumber & Timber

Clark Rm Inc..................................... F 419 425-9889
  Findlay *(G-6853)*

Flagship Trading Corporation................ E
  Cleveland *(G-3722)*

Luxus Products LLC............................. G 937 444-6500
  Mount Orab *(G-10218)*

Urbn Timber LLC............................... G 614 981-3043
  Columbus *(G-5341)*

WOODWORK & TRIM: Exterior & Ornamental

Robura Inc...................................... G 330 857-7404
  Orrville *(G-11004)*

WOODWORK & TRIM: Interior & Ornamental

Lckbm Company................................ D 419 636-4555
  Bryan *(G-1648)*

Richardson Woodworking.................... G 614 893-8850
  Blacklick *(G-1229)*

WOODWORK: Interior & Ornamental, NEC

Saw Dust Ltd................................... G 740 862-0612
  Baltimore *(G-787)*

Stull Woodworks Inc........................... E 937 698-8181
  Troy *(G-13259)*

WORK EXPERIENCE CENTER

TAC Industries Inc............................. B 937 328-5200
  Springfield *(G-12382)*

WOVEN WIRE PRDTS, NEC

Roy I Kaufman Inc............................. G 740 382-0643
  Marion *(G-8994)*

Utility Wire Products Inc...................... G 216 441-2180
  Cleveland *(G-4455)*

WRENCHES

Norbar Torque Tools Inc...................... F 440 953-1175
  Willoughby *(G-14495)*

Wright Tool Company.......................... C 330 848-0600
  Barberton *(G-842)*

X-RAY EQPT & TUBES

Control-X Inc................................... G 614 777-9729
  Columbus *(G-4845)*

Dentsply Sirona Inc............................ E 419 865-9497
  Maumee *(G-9291)*

Leisure Time Pdts Design Corp............. G 440 934-1032
  Avon *(G-731)*

Metro Design Inc.............................. F 440 458-4200
  Elyria *(G-6563)*

North Coast Medical Eqp Inc................. F 440 243-6189
  Berea *(G-1183)*

Philips Med Systems Clvland In............. C 617 245-5510
  Beachwood *(G-940)*

Philips Med Systems Clvland In............. B 440 483-3000
  Cleveland *(G-4159)*

X-RAY EQPT REPAIR SVCS

Metro Design Inc.............................. F 440 458-4200
  Elyria *(G-6563)*

PRODUCT